HARRAP'S ESSENTIAL ENGLISH DICTIONARY

HARRAP'S ESSENTIAL ENGLISH DICTIONARY

Managing Editor
Elaine Higgleton

Senior Editor
Anne Seaton

HARRAP

Published by Chambers Harrap Publishers Ltd
43–45 Annandale Street, Edinburgh EH7 4AZ

A CIP catalogue record for this book is available from the British Library.

ISBN 0 245 60566 5 Hardback
ISBN 0 245 60561 4 Paperback

The British National Corpus is a collaborative initiative carried out by Oxford University Press, Longman, Chambers Harrap, Oxford University Computing Services, Lancaster University's Unit for Computer research in the English Language, and the British Library. The project received funding from the UK Department of Trade and Industry and the Science and Engineering Research Council and was supported by additional research grants from the British Academy and the British Library.

Typeset in Great Britain at the University Press, Cambridge
Printed in Great Britain by Clays Ltd, St Ives plc

Contents

Contributors

Publishing Director	Robert Allen
Managing Editor	Elaine Higgleton
Senior Editor	Anne Seaton
Compilers	Kay Cullen Howard Sargeant
Illustrations	John Martin
Keyboarders	Louise Blair Shona Sutherland
Computer Officer	Ilona Morison
Computer Software	Compulexis Ltd Charlton-on-Otmoor Oxford

Preface

Harrap's Essential English Dictionary is a new dictionary for intermediate and advanced learners that focuses on those words that are most frequently used in everyday speech and writing. It is these often highly idiomatic words that learners find most difficult to use correctly, and yet they are the very words that are essential to successful communication. It has been our aim in this dictionary to give the most complete information about these essential or 'core' words. We have drawn throughout on the authoritative British National Corpus for evidence of how words are used, and for examples of real English. The exceptionally clear layout enables users to find the information they need quickly and easily. Full-sentence definitions show the word in the right grammatical context; sense and usage are readily understood, and the learner is immediately able to use the word correctly. In short, this dictionary gives information about everyday English that no learner should be without.

Every dictionary is the work of a dedicated team of people, and the editors would like to thank everyone involved, especially Kay Cullen and Howard Sargeant for their unfailing energy and commitment to the project, Ilona Morison for keeping the computer systems running, John-Paul Young for help with the appendices, and Stephanie Pickering for help with proof-reading. We would also like to thank Penny Hands, whose work in the final stages of the project has been invaluable.

Elaine Higgleton
Anne Seaton
May 1995

Organization of entries

Grammatical forms or 'parts of speech': the grammatical forms in which the word can be used are shown at the beginning of the entry; each is repeated as a heading to the section where its meanings are given. The plurals of nouns, the comparative and superlative forms of adjectives, and the third person singular, present participle, past tense and past participle of verbs, are also shown. The parts of speech are explained in their own separate entries within the dictionary text.

Examples supported by the British National Corpus show the range of ways in which the word can be used, and the grammatical constructions it can take.

Essential or 'core' vocabulary is dealt with in detail; long entries are divided into paragraphs containing related groups of meanings.

Definitions are numbered and written as whole sentences, showing the word being used in a natural and grammatically correct way. No abbreviations except *AmE* (American English), *BrE* (British English), and *eg* (meaning 'for example'), are used in the dictionary

Phrases and idioms using the word are grouped alphabetically in one paragraph, usually at the end of the entry, before the phrasal verbs, if there are any. Phrases in most cases have been placed at the noun, if they contain one; otherwise, you will find them at their most significant word.

part /pɑːt/ *noun; verb*

▻ ***noun*: parts**

1 a (*count or uncount*) A **part** of a thing is a piece, bit or portion of it: *I passed the early part of my life in Ireland.* □ *They spend part of the year abroad.* □ *An earth tremor had caused parts of the building to collapse.* □ *I'll leave the complicated part of the work to you.* □ *The film was OK in parts.* **b** (*count or uncount*) One of the **parts** of something is one of the pieces of which it consists; one thing is **part** of another if it belongs to it: *the various organs and parts of the body* □ *The shop sold spare parts for motor bikes.* □ *Sports and games form part of the school curriculum.* □ *The disabled need to feel part of the community.* **c** (*used in the singular*) The best or worst **part** of a situation is the best or worst circumstance in it: *The worst part of being unemployed is never having any money.*

2 a A **part** of a town, country or the world is an area or region in it: *people from the wealthy part of town.* □ *I know that part of Germany well.* □ *The promise of gold drew men from all parts of the world.* **b** (*used in the plural*) You can refer to the area you are in as 'these **parts**': *I don't come from these parts myself.*

3 a A **part** is one of the sections that something may be divided into: *The subject can be split into two parts.* **b** A book, programme or course of study may be divided into several **parts**: *You will study the anatomy of the insect in Part 4 of your course.* **c** The proportions in which things are present in a mixture can be described as so many **parts** of one to so many **parts** of the other: *Dilute the bleach in the proportion one part bleach to ten parts water.*

4 a A **part** in a play or film is one of the roles in it: *One of the boy actors played the part of Juliet.* **b** A singer's or instrumental player's **part** is the music that he or she has to perform in a musical composition *eg* for choir or orchestra: *The altos and tenors are still unsure of their parts.* □ *He practised the trumpet part.* **c** (*used in the singular*) Your **part** in an event is the extent to which you are involved in it: *He was feeling guilty about the part he'd had in the deception.*

▻ ***verb*: parts, parting, parted**

1 People **part** when they leave one another: *Maggie gave Jean a hug as they parted at the street door.* □ *He couldn't bear to part from her.* □ *Who will have the children if you and your husband decide to part?* **2** Something **parts** people, or they **are parted**, if they are separated and cannot be together: *She had never been parted for long from her family.* □ *Death parted them at last.* **3 a** Crowds or clouds **part** when they separate and a gap opens in them. **b** You **part** your lips or **part** the curtains when you open them. **4** You **part** your hair by dividing it and combing the two sections away from the dividing line or 'parting': *I usually part my hair on the left.*

▻ ***phrases*** **1** The **best** or **better part of** a year or other period is most of it: *She had been waiting for the best part of three years for an operation.* **2** Someone **does their part** when they help or co-operate in the way that they ought to: *Nowadays fathers are expected to do their part in looking after the children.* **3** You say that **for your part** you think something when you are stating your personal opinion: *I, for my part, have difficulty accepting that view.* [*same as* **personally**]

fork /fɔːk/ *noun*; *verb*

▻ ***noun***: **forks**

1 A **fork** is a tool for eating with, with three or four points, called prongs, for piercing and lifting food. [see picture at **tableware**] **2** A **fork** is also a long-handled garden tool with prongs, used for digging. [see picture at **tool**] **3** A **fork** in a road is the point where it divides into two branches; each of these branches can also be called a **fork**: *Take the left fork for Didsbury.*

▻ ***verb***: **forks, forking, forked**

1 A road **forks** when it divides into two branches; you **fork** left or right when you follow the left or right branch: *At the next junction you fork right for Bramhall.* **2** You **fork** food somewhere when you lift it there on a fork: *He forked some spaghetti on to his plate.*

> ***phrasal verb***
> (*informal*) You **fork out** for something when you pay for it: *I had to fork out £50 for the meal.*

Picture references and note references: if an item is included in one of the illustrations or usage notes in the dictionary, a reference is given to the picture or usage note it appears in, introduced by the words 'see' or 'see also'.

Phrasal verbs are put in boxes, usually at the end of the entry, after the phrases. Boxes are also used for the auxiliary verbs (*be, have* and *do*), and the modal verbs (such as *can* and *would*).

sadism /ˈseɪdɪzm/ *noun* (*uncount*)

1 **Sadism** is the practice of getting sexual pleasure by inflicting pain on another person. **2** Used more generally, **sadism** also means the practice of getting pleasure or satisfaction from being cruel to, or hurting, other people. [compare **masochism**]

flying /ˈflaɪɪŋ/ *adjective*

1 A **flying** creature can fly, or is able to make long gliding leaps: *flying insects.* **2** A **flying** squad is a body of police trained for fast action, or available for duty wherever they are required. **3** A **flying** visit is a very quick one: *I paid a flying visit to my family last weekend.* **4** You take a **flying** leap at something when you run towards it and jump: *He took a flying leap at the wall and managed to grasp the top of it.*

▻ ***phrase*** For **get off to a flying start** see **start**.

Cross references: references are made to other entries in the dictionary if they are useful for comparison, or give you extra information; they are introduced by the words 'see', 'see also' or 'compare'. If a phrase that includes the word is to be found elsewhere in the dictionary, a cross reference is often made to the entry in which it is included.

damned /damnd/ *adverb*; *adjective*; *noun*

▻ ***adverb*** (*intensifying; swearword*)

Damned is used before adjectives and adverbs as an expression of annoyance, anger, or to give emphasis: *I'll make damned certain she doesn't get that job.*

Usage information: labels telling you the grammatical use of a word, or giving you other useful information, eg whether it is formal or informal, are provided in brackets at the beginning of the entry, or at the beginning of individual definitions. The words used in these labels have their own entries in the dictionary, where the exact significance of the label is explained.

frank /fraŋk/ *adjective*: **franker, frankest**

People are **frank** when they are open and honest in stating what they think or want: *Our discussions were frank and fruitful.* ▫ *Do you want my frank opinion?* ▫ *To be frank, I think you're making a mistake.* [*same as* **candid, outspoken, truthful**; *opposite* **evasive, insincere**] — *adverb* **frankly:** *Tell us frankly what you think.* ▫ (*sentence adverb*) *Frankly, I think you're talking nonsense.* — *noun* (*uncount*) **frankness:** *We appreciate your frankness.*

Synonyms and antonyms are supplied at the end of the definitions, wherever appropriate; the words '*same as*' introduce a synonym, and the word '*opposite*' introduces an antonym.

Derivative words are included in the entry in some cases; they are always followed by examples of usage.

frugal /ˈfruːgəl/ *adjective*

1 A **frugal** person is careful with money and spends very little on themselves: *She had a simple, frugal lifestyle.* [*opposite* **wasteful**] **2** A **frugal** meal is a small one that does not cost much. — *noun* (*uncount*) **frugality** /fruːˈgalɪtɪ/: *We quite enjoyed the frugality of the backpacking life.* — *adverb* **frugally:** *He eats frugally and doesn't smoke.*

Pronunciation is shown for every entry, and is supplied for derivative words if their stress is different from that of the main word. An explanation of the phonetic symbols is given on page *xiii*.

fruit /fruːt/ *noun*; *verb*

▻ ***noun***: **fruit** or **fruits**

1 (*count or uncount*) A **fruit** is the seed-carrying part of a plant, especially if it has edible flesh: *The fruit of the tree looks like a cross between a tomato and a pepper.* ▫ *We grow our own fruit and vegetables.* ▫ *Breakfast consisted of cereal and a glass of fruit juice.* ▫ *apples, pears and other fruits*

> You use 'a fruit' to mean a kind of fruit: *mangoes and other exotic fruits.* A single apple, pear, banana or orange is referred to as 'a piece of fruit': *Eat a couple of pieces of fruit each day.*

Usage notes give extra information on grammar and usage.

Pronunciation guide

Key to the phonetic symbols used in the dictionary

CONSONANTS		
p	/piː/	**p**ea
t	/tiː/	**t**ea
k	/kiː/	**k**ey
b	/biː/	**b**ee
d	/daɪ/	**d**ye
g	/gaɪ/	**g**uy
m	/miː/	**m**e
n	/njuː/	**n**ew
ŋ	/sɒŋ/	so**ng**
θ	/θɪn/	**th**in
ð	/ðɛn/	**th**en
f	/fan/	**f**an
v	/van/	**v**an
s	/siː/	**s**ea
z	/zuːm/	**z**oom
ʃ	/ʃiː/	**sh**e
ʒ	/beɪʒ/	bei**g**e
tʃ	/iːtʃ/	ea**ch**
dʒ	/ɛdʒ/	e**dge**
h	/hat/	**h**at
l	/leɪ/	**l**ay
r	/reɪ/	**r**ay
j	/jɛs/	**y**es
w	/weɪ/	**w**ay

VOWELS		
Short vowels		
ɪ	/bɪd/	b**i**d
ɛ	/bɛd/	b**e**d
a	/bad/	b**a**d
ʌ	/bʌd/	b**u**d
ɒ	/pɒt/	p**o**t
ʊ	/pʊt/	p**u**t
ə	/əˈbaʊt/	**a**bout
Long vowels		
iː	/biːd/	b**ea**d
ɑː	/hɑːm/	h**ar**m
ɔː	/ɔːl/	**a**ll
uː	/buːt/	b**oo**t
ɜː	/bɜːd/	b**ir**d
Diphthongs		
eɪ	/beɪ/	b**ay**
aɪ	/baɪ/	b**uy**
ɔɪ	/bɔɪ/	b**oy**
aʊ	/haʊ/	h**ow**
oʊ	/goʊ/	g**o**
ɪə	/bɪə(r)/	b**eer**
ɛə	/bɛə(r)/	b**are**
ʊə	/pʊə(r)/	p**oor**

Notes

(1) The stress mark (ˈ) is placed before the stressed syllable (*eg* **invent** /ɪnˈvɛnt/).

(2) The symbol '(r)' is used to represent *r* when it comes at the end of a word, to indicate that it is pronounced when followed by a vowel (as it is in 'four' in the phrase *four or five* /fɔːr ɔː ˈfaɪv/).

A or **a** /eɪ/: **As** or **a's**
1 A is the first letter of the English alphabet. **2** The letter **A** is used as a mark for grading quality, indicating the highest grade: *She got As in all her exams.* **3 A** is a musical note: *in the key of A minor.*
▻ ***phrases*** **1** You get **from A to B** when find your way from one place to another. **2 From A to Z** means from the beginning to the end: *She went through the whole explanation again from A to Z.*

a /eɪ/ or /ə/ or **an** /an/ or /ən/ *determiner* (*indefinite article*)

> You use **a** before words beginning with a consonant or consonant sound: *a hotel; a yacht; a unit; a European.*
> You use **an** before words beginning with a vowel or vowel sound: *an adult; an honour; an hourly rate; an MP.*
> The pronunciations /eɪ/ (for **a**) and /an/ (for **an**) are used for emphasis: *I haven't seen your pen, but here's a pen for you. I've thought of an answer, even if it's not the right one.*

You use **a** and **an** before nouns or noun groups:
1 to refer to actual people or things without saying which you mean: *I'm going to a concert tonight.* □ *She's having lunch with an old friend.*
2 to refer to classes of people or things, meaning no particular one: *A concert is a musical performance.* □ *Why not discuss it with a friend?* □ *She's an expert in computer graphics.* □ *He wants to be a psychiatrist.* □ *She was a kind person.*

> You use **a** and **an** mostly with singular count nouns: *Can you recommend a good electrician? Do make an effort to understand.*
> You can omit **a** or **an** before the second and following count nouns in a pair or list: *He handed me a knife and fork. She packed a swimsuit, swimming hat and towel.*
> With plural nouns and uncount nouns you show indefinite meaning by using no article: *He's crazy about trains. Coping with illness takes courage and patience. Will you have tea or coffee?*
> But you can treat an uncount noun like a count noun, using **a** or **an**, (i) when you are referring to a type, kind or class: *She chose a red wine to drink with the meal. Brie is a soft cheese.*
> (ii) when you mean a serving of something, *eg* in a cup or glass: *She ordered me a coffee.*
> (iii) when you are referring to an example or occurrence of a particular quality: *She had a natural love of language.*

3 to mean 'one' in expressing number or quantity: *a year* □ *a week* □ *a hundred pounds* □ *a thousand francs* □ *a million dollars* □ *a dozen (12) eggs.*

> **One** is used instead of **a** or **an** for emphasis or contrast: *She wrote all five books in one year. How many copies shall we print? One thousand or two?*

4 in certain other expressions of quantity: *a few books* □ *a lot of paper* □ *a little milk.*
5 to turn a proper name into a count noun: *There's a Mr Green* [= someone called Mr Green] *on the telephone for you.* □ *You'll never be a Marilyn Monroe* [= a woman like Marilyn Monroe].
6 in expressing frequency, rate or cost: *I clean the house once a week.* □ *They get paid $6.50 an hour.* □ *Petrol is 54p a litre here.* [see also **per**]
7 with count nouns formed from verbs, meaning an act of doing something: *Let me have a think.* □ *Have a try.*

aback /əˈbak/ *adverb*
▻ ***phrase*** You are **taken aback** when you are surprised, usually unpleasantly: *She blinked, taken aback by his accusation.*

abacus /ˈabəkəs/ *noun*: **abacuses**
An **abacus** is a frame fitted with bars, each one with a certain number of beads on it, which is used for counting and calculation.

abandon /əˈbandən/ *verb*; *noun*
▻ ***verb***: **abandons, abandoning, abandoned**
1 To **abandon** someone or something that you are responsible for is to leave them for a long time or for ever: *We have seen a few cases of unmarried mothers abandoning their newborn babies.* □ *My car broke down and I had to abandon it on the main road.* **2** You **abandon** an activity or an attempt to do something when you stop it: *They abandoned the search at midnight and resumed in the morning.* □ *He abandoned all pretence at politeness.* [*same as* **give up**] **3** You **abandon** yourself to sorrow or a similar feeling when you let yourself be overcome by it: *She refused to abandon herself to despair.* — *adjective* **abandoned:** *After the snowstorm the roads were full of abandoned vehicles.* — *noun* (*uncount*) **abandonment:** *The abandonment of the project will mean a lot of unemployment.*
▻ ***noun*** (*uncount*)
People do something with **abandon** when they do it with enthusiasm or with apparent lack of embarrassment or caution: *I saw you at the party, dancing with abandon.*

abase /əˈbeɪs/ *verb*: **abases, abasing, abased**
You **abase** yourself when you abandon your pride and behave in a humble manner, *eg* when you are forced to beg for something or apologize. [*same as* **humble**]

abashed /əˈbaʃt/ *adjective*
You are **abashed** when you feel embarrassed or shy: *Both men looked slightly abashed, like a pair of guilty schoolboys.*

abate /əˈbeɪt/ *verb*: **abates, abating, abated**
Something such as a storm or someone's anger **abates** when it becomes less fierce and calms down. [*same as* **let up, subside**]

abattoir /ˈabətwɑː(r)/ *noun*: **abattoirs**
An **abattoir** is a place where animals, *eg* cattle or pigs, are killed to provide food. [*same as* **slaughterhouse**]

abbess /ˈabɛs/ *noun*: **abbesses**
An **abbess** is the female principal of an abbey or convent.

abbey /ˈabɪ/ *noun*: **abbeys**
An **abbey** is a church that has or once had a group of buildings attached to it for a religious community of monks or nuns to live in.

abbot /ˈabət/ *noun*: **abbots**
An **abbot** is the male principal of an abbey or monastery.

abbreviate /əˈbriːvɪeɪt/ *verb*: **abbreviates, abbreviating, abbreviated**
A word or phrase **is abbreviated** when it is shortened by omitting some letters or using only first letters: *Katharine didn't like her name being abbreviated to Kate.*

abbreviation /əbriːvɪˈeɪʃən/ *noun*: **abbreviations**
An **abbreviation** of a word or phrase is a short form of it, either with some letters omitted, or with each word represented by its first letter: *The abbreviation VDU stands for 'visual-display unit'.*

ABC *noun*: **ABCs**
1 (*used in the singular*) Children learn their **ABC** when they learn the alphabet. **2** The **ABC** of a subject is the basic facts or skills you need to learn, or a book explaining them.

abdicate /ˈabdɪkeɪt/ *verb*: **abdicates, abdicating, abdicated**
1 You **abdicate** your responsibility for something if you refuse to go on being responsible for it. **2** A king or queen **abdicates** when they resign from the throne. — *noun* (*uncount*) **abdication** /abdɪˈkeɪʃən/: *the abdication of Edward VIII.*

abdomen /ˈabdəmən/ *noun*: **abdomens**
Your **abdomen** is the front part of your body between your waist and thighs, containing organs such as your liver, kidneys, stomach and bowels. — *adjective* **abdominal** /abˈdɒmɪnəl/: *She was taken to hospital with severe abdominal pain.*

abduct /əbˈdʌkt/ *verb*: **abducts, abducting, abducted**
Someone **abducts** another person when they take them away by force: *She was abducted on her way home from school.* [see also **kidnap**] — *noun* (*uncount or count*) **abduction** /abˈdʌkʃən/: *The abduction of her husband.*

aberration /abəˈreɪʃən/ *noun*: **aberrations**
An **aberration** is a departure from what is normal, *eg* an unusual or untypical piece of behaviour.

abeyance /əˈbeɪəns/ *noun* (*uncount*)
▻ ***phrase*** A law, rule or arrangement is **in abeyance** if it has been cancelled temporarily or is no longer in use.

abhor /əbˈhɔː(r)/ *verb*: **abhors, abhorring, abhorred**
You **abhor** something if you hate it or disapprove of it strongly. [*same as* **detest, loathe**]

abhorrence /əbˈhɒrəns/ *noun* (*uncount*)
Abhorrence is strong disapproval or disgust: *Ordinary citizens have demonstrated again and again their abhorrence of terrorism.* [*same as* **repugnance**]

abhorrent /əbˈhɒrənt/ *adjective*
Something is **abhorrent** to you if you strongly disapprove of it or are disgusted or shocked by it. [*same as* **repugnant**]

abide /əˈbaɪd/ *verb*: **abides, abiding, abided**
You say you cannot **abide** someone or something if you dislike them strongly. [*same as* **bear, stand**]

> ***phrasal verb***
> You **abide by** a rule, law or decision if you obey it or act according to it: *These are the terms of her will, and we must abide by them.* [*same as* **adhere to**]

abiding /əˈbaɪdɪŋ/ *adjective*
An **abiding** joy, love, dislike or fear lasts for a long time: *A childhood accident had left him with an abiding fear of water.* [*same as* **lasting**]

ability /əˈbɪlɪtɪ/ *noun* (*uncount or count*): **abilities**
Someone's **ability** to do something is their state of being able to do it, or the skill they possess to do it: *I used to doubt my ability to cope with a crisis like this.* □ *He's now lost the ability to walk.* □ *You're certainly a person of unusual abilities.* □ *She has this extraordinary ability to foresee difficulties.* □ *She showed remarkable ability as an organizer.* □ *a scholar of great linguistic ability.* [compare **capacity, power, talent, skill, competence, capability**]
▻ ***phrase*** You do something **to the best of your abilities** or **ability** when you do it as well as you can.

-ability /əˈbɪlɪtɪ/ *suffix*
Nouns formed from adjectives ending with the suffix **-able** have the suffix **-ability**. [see also **-ibility**]

abject /ˈabdʒɛkt/ *adjective*
1 Someone who is in an **abject** condition is in so desperate a state of misery or poverty that they have no pride left. [*same as* **wretched**] **2 Abject** behaviour shows a shameful lack of courage and pride: *an abject coward* □ *abject obedience.* — *adverb* **abjectly:** *He apologized abjectly.*

ablaze /əˈbleɪz/ *adjective*
1 Something that is **ablaze** is on fire or burning strongly: *Within seconds the room was ablaze.* **2** A place that is full of bright lights or colours is said to be **ablaze** with light or colour. **3** Someone's face or eyes can be **ablaze** with a passion such as anger or love.

able /ˈeɪbəl/ *adjective*: **abler, ablest**
1 You are **able** to do something if you have the knowledge, skill, strength, power, time, opportunity or money to do it: *I was able to answer the first three questions.* □ *He was able to walk again within a week.* □ *A monkey is able to hang by its tail.* □ *She was able to retire at the age of 50.* [*opposite* **unable**]

> **Be able to** is used like **can** and **could**: *I'm still able to* (or *can still*) *read without glasses. She was able to* (or *could*) *read music by the age of three.*
> When you are talking about a single occasion in the past, use **was able to** rather than **could**: *She was able to* (*not could*) *climb through a window and escape.* [see note at **could**]
> **Be able to** is used where **can** and **could** are not possible: *I'll be able to get to work more quickly when I move house. The ape seemed to be able to reason like a human. I might be able to come on Thursday. He's been able to visit us more often recently. It's lovely being able to see you every day.*

2 An **able** person is sensible, intelligent and efficient, or is good at their particular job: *She's an able leader in every way.* □ *You can rely on him; he's very able.* □ *He's one of the ablest teachers I know.* □ *The abler children are encouraged to help the less able.* [*same as* **capable**; *opposite* **incompetent**]

-able /əbəl/ *suffix*
-able is added to verbs to form adjectives meaning 'able to be ...', *eg eat +-able = eatable*, meaning 'able to be eaten' or 'safe or pleasant to eat'.

able-bodied /eɪbəlˈbɒdɪd/ *adjective*
An **able-bodied** person is someone who is fit, strong and healthy.

ably /ˈeɪblɪ/ *adverb*
Someone does something **ably** if they do it well: *The choir was ably conducted by Idris Evans.*

abnormal /abˈnɔːməl/ *adjective*
An **abnormal** person or thing is different from what is usual, especially in a way that worries you: *Don't worry; your baby isn't abnormal.* □ *an abnormal desire for attention* □ *abnormal behaviour.* [*opposite* **normal**]

abnormality /abnɔːˈmalɪtɪ/ or /abnəˈmalɪtɪ/ *noun*: **abnormalities**
1 (*uncount*) **Abnormality** is the state or condition of being abnormal: The X-rays showed no evidence of abnormality. **2** An **abnormality** is something abnormal: *a heart abnormality.*

abnormally /əbˈnɔːməlɪ/ *adverb*
1 Abnormally means in a strange or unusual manner: *He was acting abnormally.* [*opposite* **normally**] **2 Abnormally** also means unusually, or more than usually: *She's abnormally thin.*

aboard /əˈbɔːd/ *preposition*; *adverb*
▻ ***preposition***
You go, or are, **aboard** a ship or plane when you get on it or are on it.
▻ ***adverb:*** *All 21 aboard are feared drowned.* [*same as* **on board**]

abode /əˈboʊd/ *noun* (*uncount*)
▻ ***phrase*** (*BrE*; *legal*) Someone who is **of no fixed abode** has no regular home or address.

abolish /əˈbɒlɪʃ/ *verb*: **abolishes, abolishing, abolished**
A law, system, custom or activity **is abolished** when it is ended, cancelled or stopped. — *noun* (*uncount*) **abolition** /abəˈlɪʃən/: *the abolition of capital punishment.*

abominable /əˈbɒmɪnəbəl/ *adjective*
You call something **abominable** if you think it is very bad, wicked or unpleasant: *the abominable practice of torturing prisoners.* — *adverb* **abominably:** *You behaved abominably this evening.*

Aboriginal /abəˈrɪdʒɪnəl/ *noun*: **Aboriginals**
An **Aboriginal** is a member of the race of people that were already living in Australia when European settlers arrived.

abort /əˈbɔːt/ *verb*: **aborts, aborting, aborted**
1 A pregnancy **is aborted** when it is ended deliberately. [*same as* **terminate**] **2** A plan, project or process **is aborted** when it is stopped before it has been fully developed or carried out, *eg* because of difficulties or dangers: *The launch of the satellite had to be aborted.* [*same as* **call off, axe**]

abortion /əˈbɔːʃən/ *noun* (*count or uncount*): **abortions**
An **abortion** is an operation to end an unwanted or dangerous pregnancy: *She decided to have an abortion.*

abortive /əˈbɔːtɪv/ *adjective*
An **abortive** scheme or attempt is one that fails: *There was an abortive attempt at a coup during the President's absence.* [*same as* **failed**]

abound /əˈbaʊnd/ *verb*: **abounds, abounding, abounded**
A place **abounds** with, or in, certain things, or they **abound**, where there are a lot of them: *Stories abound on the subject of his numerous marriages.* □ *woods abounding with wildlife.*

about /əˈbaʊt/ *preposition*; *adverb*
▻ ***preposition***
1 You think, talk or write **about** a subject: *Tell me about your holiday.* □ *Did you watch that programme about AIDS?* □ *I've heard all about your work.*

> You use **on** instead of **about** in referring to the subject of more serious or scholarly books and articles: *an article on the poet Dante*; *a novel about Cyprus.*

2 You do something **about** a matter when you deal with it: *I'll see what can be done about it.* **3** Something *eg* good or bad **about** something or someone is a good or bad point, feature or quality that they have: *The nice thing about moving house is the chance to make new friends.* □ *There's something very strange about her.* **4** People or things are, or move, **about** a place if they are, or move, here and there in it: *I've been walking about the town, exploring.* □ *Clothes were scattered about the room.* [*same as* **around**]
▻ ***adverb***
1 About means 'approximately' when used before a number, measurement or period of time: *I'll stay in Oxford for about a week.* □ *She's about 25.* □ *We live about three miles from here.* **2** Someone or something is **about** when they are nearby or easily available: *Hallo; is there anyone about?* □ *There's plenty of fresh fruit about just now.* **3** You move **about**, or move something **about**, when you go, or move something, in different directions: *The children were running about happily.* □ *Stop waving that knife about.* **4 About** is used with some verbs to indicate a lack of sensible purpose: *I wish we could do something instead of just fiddling about.* [*same as* **around**]
▻ ***phrases*** **1** You **are about to** do something when you are just going to do it, or will be doing it soon: *I was just about to serve dinner.* □ *My son is about to leave school.* **2** (*informal*) You say you **are not about to** do something when you are determined not to do it: *I wasn't about to take orders from a nobody like him.* **3** You say to someone **how about** something when you are suggesting doing it or having it: *How about going for a walk?* □ *How about a drink?* **4** You say **that's about it** when you have finished doing something, *eg* telling someone something. **5** You say to someone **what about** something when you are reminding them of it or asking them to consider it: *We've got enough food for today, but what about tomorrow?*

about-turn /əbaʊtˈtɜːn/ *noun*: **about-turns**
An **about-turn** or **about-face** is also a complete change, or reversing of policy, *eg* by a government. [*same as* **U-turn**]

above /əˈbʌv/ *preposition*; *adverb*; *adjective*; *noun*
▻ ***preposition***
1 Something is **above** something else if it is higher than it: *We flew above the clouds most of the way.* □ *The sun shone fiercely above us.* [*opposite* **below**]

> **Above** and **over** are both possible where there is a clear vertical relationship: *Can you read the sign above* (or *over*) *the door? They live in the flat above* (or *over*) *ours.*

2 You use **above** in relation to a standard point on a scale of measurement: *The mountain summit is 2556 metres above sea level.* □ *We've been having above-average temperatures for the time of year.* [*opposite* **below**]

> **Over** is used more often than **above** where the comparison is with a specified measurement or amount: *people over* (or *above*) *the age of sixty*; *The tickets cost over £30.*

3 Someone's rank or position is **above** another person's if it is senior to it: *There are so many people above me that I can never hope to reach a senior post myself.* [*opposite* **below**]

> Use **over** where the meaning is 'in charge of' or 'supervising': *We have someone called a 'project manager' over us.*

4 People are said to be **above** some activity if they disapprove of it and refuse to take part in it: *He allowed his wife to gamble, though apparently he was above it himself.* **5** You are **above** something such as suspicion or criticism if you are so well respected that no-one could suspect you or criticize you. [*same as* **beyond**] **6** Something is **above** you if it is too difficult for you to understand: *I'm afraid all this computer language is above me.*
▻ ***adverb***
1 Above means higher in position, amount, level or

rank: *The apartment above is empty.* □ *The noise seemed to be coming from above.* □ *James and his bride are pictured above left, leaving for their honeymoon.* □ *temperatures of 80° and above.* □ *She made friends with a student in the year above.* [*opposite* **below**] **2** In a written work or paper, reference is sometimes made to a passage **above**, meaning a piece of text before the bit you are reading. [*opposite* **below**]

▷ ***adjective:*** *Read the above statement and make sure it is accurate before signing your name.* □ *Please contact us at the above address.*

▷ ***noun:*** *If you have read the above and agree with it, sign here.*

▷ ***phrases*** **1** You use **above all** to emphasize your most important point: *It's too far, too late, and above all, too dangerous.* **2** People say you are **above yourself** if they think you are too pleased with yourself, or rather conceited.

above-board /əbʌv'bɔːd/ *adjective*
Something such as a deal or arrangement is said to be **above-board** if it has been explained or made known to everyone who has a right to know about it, and accepted as fair and honest. [*opposite* **underhand**, **shady**]

abrasion /ə'breɪʒən/ *noun*: **abrasions**
An **abrasion** is an injury to the skin caused by scraping or rubbing. [*same as* **graze**]

abrasive /ə'breɪsɪv/ *adjective*
1 An **abrasive** material is any rough material such as sandpaper, that is used for smoothing and polishing surfaces. **2** You call someone, or their manner, **abrasive** if they behave or speak in a way that seems rude, or that hurts people. [*same as* **caustic**, **brusque**]

abreast /ə'brɛst/ *adverb*
1 Someone walks **abreast** with another person, or two people walk **abreast**, when they walk one beside the other. [*same as* **side by side**] **2** You are, or keep, **abreast** of the news or other subject if you are always checking up on the most recent facts. [*same as* **up to date**, **in touch**]

abridge /ə'brɪdʒ/ *verb*: **abridges, abridging, abridged**
A book **is abridged** when sections of its text are removed to make it shorter. — *noun* (*count or uncount*) **abridgement** or **abridgment:** *They've been reading an abridgement of her novel on the radio.*

abroad /ə'brɔːd/ *adverb*
You go **abroad** when you travel to a foreign country: *Are you going abroad this year?* □ *He'll contact you when he returns from abroad.*

abrupt /ə'brʌpt/ *adjective*
1 Something such as a stop or change is **abrupt** if it comes suddenly and unexpectedly: *Our holiday came to an abrupt end when we lost all our money.* **2** Someone is **abrupt** in the way they speak if they sound rude and unfriendly: *You were a bit abrupt with your father just now.* [*same as* **curt**] — *adverb* **abruptly:** *He said goodbye abruptly and walked away.*

abscess /'absɛs/ or /'absəs/ *noun*: **abscesses**
An **abscess** is a painful, infected swelling, *eg* one in the gum caused by a bad tooth.

abscond /əb'skɒnd/ *verb*: **absconds, absconding, absconded**
1 Someone **absconds** from a place such as a prison when they run away from it. **2** A member of a business firm or other body **absconds** with something such as the firm's money when they steal it and run away with it.

absence /'absəns/ *noun*: **absences**
1 (*uncount or count*) **Absence** is a period or occasion of being away: *The new manager had arrived during her absence.* □ *After so long an absence from school he may find the work difficult.* **2** (*used in the singular*) An **absence** of something is a lack of it: *In the absence of any encouragment or support, he was forced to drop his plan.*
[see also **presence**]

absent /'absənt/ *adjective*
1 Someone or something is **absent** from a place or occasion if they are not there: *She was absent from the meeting* □ *How many pupils are absent today?* □ *Let's drink to absent friends.* [*opposite* **present**] **2** An **absent** expression on someone's face shows that they are not paying attention or concentrating. [*same as* **preoccupied**; *opposite* **attentive**] — *adverb* **absently:** *She was staring absently out of the window*

absentee /absən'tiː/ *noun*: **absentees**
An **absentee** is someone who is not present where or when they ought to be.

absent-minded /absənt'maɪndɪd/ *adjective*
An **absent-minded** person is forgetful and also tends not to notice what is happening around them. — *adverb* **absent-mindedly:** *He absent-mindedly picked up someone else's briefcase.*

absolute /'absəluːt/ or /'absəljuːt/ *adjective*
1 **Absolute** means complete, total or entire: *I'm telling you this in absolute confidence*; *no-one else must know.* **2** (*informal*) You call a person or thing an **absolute** something for emphasis: *I've been an absolute idiot.* □ *He's an absolute darling.* □ *It'll be an absolute disaster if I fail my exams.* **3** Someone who has **absolute** power, authority or control *eg* over a country or organization can decide how it should be run without consulting anyone else: *an absolute ruler* □ *Her power is absolute.* [*same as* **supreme**] **4** You discuss a thing in **absolute** terms, when you are thinking of it as independent of any of the things it might be related to or compared with; an **absolute** truth, rule or principle is one that is always right or valid.

absolutely /absə'luːtlɪ/ or /absə'ljuːtlɪ/ *adverb*
1 **Absolutely** means completely or totally: *I agree with you absolutely.* □ *I'm absolutely convinced.* □ *Funding is absolutely essential if research is to continue.* □ *Was your journey absolutely necessary?* **2** (*with a negative*) **Absolutely** is used to mean 'at all': *This map is absolutely no help.* **3** (*intensifying*; *informal*) **Absolutely** is used for emphasis: *The weather is absolutely awful.* **4** (*used as an answer*) **Absolutely** means 'I completely agree with you': *'He really ought to take more rest at his age.' 'Absolutely.'*

absolution /absə'luːʃən/ *noun* (*uncount*)
In the Christian Church, **absolution** is the forgiving of a person's sin or wrongdoing by a priest, as God's representative.

absolve /əb'zɒlv/ *verb*: **absolves, absolving, absolved**
Someone **is absolved** from responsibility or blame for something that has gone wrong when it is officially stated that they are not responsible or guilty. [*same as* **clear, exonerate**]

absorb /əb'zɔːb/ *verb*: **absorbs, absorbing, absorbed**
1 Something **absorbs** *eg* heat, light or a liquid when it takes it in or soaks it up: *Plants absorb light from the sun and moisture from the soil.* □ *You wear this patch on your arm and the drug is absorbed through the skin.* **2** A smaller organization or business **is absorbed** into a larger one when it becomes part of it. **3** A person, thing or system **absorbs** something such as a shock or change when they deal with it without being badly affected or damaged by it. **4** You **absorb** facts when you learn them. [*same as* **take in**] **5** You **are absorbed**

in something such as a book or task when you are concentrating completely on it, and paying attention to nothing else. [*same as* **engross**, **preoccupy**] — *adjective* **absorbing:** *an absorbing play.* [*same as* **interesting**, **fascinating**]

absorbent /əb'zɔ:bənt/ *adjective*
An **absorbent** substance or material soaks up liquid or moisture. — *noun* (*uncount*) **absorbency:** *the absorbency of the material.*

absorption /əb'zɔ:pʃən/ *noun* (*uncount*)
1 **Absorption** is the process of absorbing liquid, light, heat or gas. **2** Someone's absorption in something such as a book or task is their state of being completely absorbed by it and concentrating on it wholly.

abstain /əb'steɪn/ *verb*: **abstains, abstaining, abstained**
1 You **abstain** from something that you enjoy, such as food or alcohol, when you choose not to have it. **2** You **abstain** during an election or vote when you decide not to vote yourself.

abstemious /əb'sti:mɪəs/ *adjective* (*formal*)
An **abstemious** person is careful not to eat or drink too much.

abstention /əb'stɛnʃən/ *noun*: **abstentions**
1 A decision not to vote, or a person who decides not to vote, is an **abstention.** **2** (*uncount*) **Abstention** is the refusal or avoiding of food or drink.

abstinence /'abstɪnəns/ *noun* (*uncount*)
Abstinence is the practice of going without something you enjoy, *eg* food or drink.

abstract *adjective*; *noun*; *verb*
▻ ***adjective*** /'abstrakt/
1 (*grammar*) An **abstract** noun is one that represents an idea or quality rather than an actual physical object: *abstract nouns such as truth and beauty.* [*opposite* **concrete**] **2** **Abstract** reasoning and argument deal with ideas and principles in a general and theoretical way rather than with particular things or happenings. **3** (*art*) An **abstract** painting or sculpture uses shapes and patterns to represent ideas and objects in a symbolic rather than realistic manner.
▻ ***noun*** /'abstrakt/: **abstracts**
An **abstract** of a book, article, report, lecture or speech is a brief statement of its subject matter and arguments. [*same as* **summary**]
▻ ***verb*** /əb'strakt/: **abstracts, abstracting, abstracted**
You **abstract** a book or article when you reduce its subject matter and arguments to a brief statement. [*same as* **summarize**]
▻ ***phrase*** You discuss something **in the abstract** when you talk about it in a purely theoretical way, without reference to actual examples or instances.

abstracted /əb'straktɪd/ *adjective*
An **abstracted** expression on someone's face shows that they are thinking about something not connected with what is happening around them. [*same as* **preoccupied**]

abstraction /əb'strakʃən/ *noun*: **abstractions**
An **abstraction** is an idea or principle considered or discussed in a purely theoretical way without reference to actual examples and instances: *philosophical abstractions.*

abstruse /ab'stru:s/ *adjective*
An **abstruse** subject or argument is difficult to understand, usually because it is unfamilar, or uses terms that are unfamiliar, to most people. [*same as* **obscure**, **cryptic**]

absurd /əb'sɜ:d/ *adjective*
You call something **absurd** if you think it is stupid or ridiculous: *That's the most absurd idea I ever heard.* □ *It is absurd that the law should deny women this privilege.* — *noun* (*uncount or count*) **absurdity:** *the absurdities of English spelling.* — *adverb* **absurdly:** *absurdly optimistic sales forecasts.*

abundance /ə'bʌndəns/ *noun* (*uncount, or used in the singular*)
An **abundance** of something is a plentiful supply of it: *The visitor to Oxford has an abundance of sights to see.* [*same as* **wealth**; *opposite* **shortage**, **dearth**]
▻ ***phrase*** Something exists **in abundance** if there is plenty of it: *There was food and drink in abundance.*

abundant /ə'bʌndənt/ *adjective*
Something is **abundant** if there is plenty of it: *We have abundant evidence of the dangers of smoking.* [*same as* **plentiful**, **ample**]

abundantly /ə'bʌndəntlɪ/ *adverb*
1 (*intensifying*) Something is **abundantly** clear or obvious if there is more than enough evidence for it or proof of it. **2** Something occurs **abundantly** if it is found in large quantities: *Mushrooms are found most abundantly in the early autumn.*

abuse *verb*; *noun*
▻ ***verb*** /ə'bju:z/: **abuses, abusing, abused**
1 You **abuse** something such as your power or authority when you make use of it to do something wrong. **2** Someone **abuses** another person **a** when they insult them or speak rudely to them or about them. **b** if they treat them cruelly or harm them sexually: *Some of the children had been sexually abused.* **3** People **abuse** drugs, especially dangerous drugs that lead to addiction, if they take them unnecessarily and habitually.
▻ ***noun*** /ə'bju:s/: **abuses**
1 (*uncount or count*) **Abuse**, or an **abuse**, of something such as one's power or authority, is the practice, or an example, of using it to do something wrong. **2** (*uncount*) **Abuse** of a person is cruel or sexually harmful treatment of them: *child abuse* □ *Some wives suffer years of abuse and never report it.* **3** **Abuse** is rude or insulting words said to or about someone: *Most immigrants say they're used to having abuse shouted after them.* **4** Drug **abuse** is the unnecessary and habitual taking of drugs, especially those that lead to addiction.

abusive /ə'bju:sɪv/ *adjective*
You are being **abusive** when you say something rude or insulting to or about another person: *abusive language.*

abysmal /ə'bɪzməl/ *adjective* (*informal*)
Abysmal means bad, shocking or disgraceful: *He has an abysmal ignorance of grammar.* — *adverb* **abysmally:** *She treated him abysmally.*

abyss /ə'bɪs/ *noun*: **abysses**
1 An **abyss** is a large and dangerous hole, pit or opening in the ground, so deep that you cannot see the bottom. **2** (*literary*) An **abyss** is also a dangerous situation that could involve you or others in disaster if you do not avoid it: *We must draw back from the abyss of war.* **3** (*literary*) Someone who is in an **abyss** of despair, grief or misery is deeply unhappy. [*same as* **the depths**]

academic /akə'dɛmɪk/ *adjective*
▻ ***adjective***
1 **Academic** means relating to places of education such as schools or universities, or to the teaching and studying done in them: *Britain's academic system* □ *the start of the academic year.* **2** An **academic** subject is a non-technical or non-practical one for which you have to use your mind and memory: *He enjoyed drawing and painting more than the academic subjects.* **3** An **academic** person is someone who is good at

study and research, and enjoys them. [*same as* **studious**] **4** You call a remark or question **academic** if it has no practical relevance: *I can't go out tonight, so the question of where to go and eat is academic.* — *adverb* **academically:** *Even as a child she was academically inclined.*

academy /ə'kadəmɪ/ *noun*: **academies**
1 An **academy** is a school or college, especially one that provides training in a particular subject or skill: *The Royal Academy of Music.* **2** An **academy** is also a society or institution founded to encourage the arts or sciences, or the building it uses: *The Royal Academy of Arts, Piccadilly.*

accede /ək'siːd/ *verb* (*formal*): **accedes, acceding, acceded**
You **accede** to a request when you agree to it.

accelerate /ək'sɛləreɪt/ *verb*: **accelerates, accelerating, accelerated**
1 Drivers or vehicles **accelerate** when they go faster: *Some drivers accelerate deliberately when you're trying to overtake them.* [*same as* **speed up**] **2** The rate at which something happens **accelerates** when it increases: *Plant growth accelerates in the spring.* [*same as* **speed up**]

acceleration /əksɛlə'reɪʃən/ *noun* (*uncount*)
1 Acceleration is the process of going faster or of increasing the speed of something. **2** The **acceleration** of a vehicle is its capacity to increase speed and the rate at which it does so: *The De Luxe model has even better acceleration.*

accelerator /ək'sɛləreɪtə(r)/ *noun*: **accelerators**
The **accelerator** in a vehicle is the foot pedal that you press to go faster. [see picture at **car**]

accent *noun*; *verb*
▻ ***noun*** /'aksənt/: **accents**
1 The **accent** you speak with is your individual way of pronouncing the words of a language, especially as an indication of your social class or the area or country you come from: *The caller had a strong Irish accent.* **2** An **accent** is also a mark placed over or under a letter or syllable to show how it is pronounced: *'Elite' is sometimes spelt 'élite', with an acute accent on the 'e'.* **3** In speaking words or playing music, you put the **accent** on the syllable or note that you speak or play with a heavier stress, or more loudly, than the others: *The accent comes on the second syllable.* [*same as* **stress**] **4** You put the **accent** on a particular feature of something when you emphasize it or give it special importance: *In this dictionary the accent is on ease of use.* [*same as* **emphasis**]
▻ ***verb*** /ak'sɛnt/: **accents, accenting, accented**
In speaking words or playing music, you **accent** a syllable or note when you make it louder, or stress it more heavily, than the others.

accentuate /ək'sɛntjʊeɪt/ *verb*: **accentuates, accentuating, accentuated**
A feature or quality **is accentuated** when it is emphasized or made more noticeable by some circumstance: *The style of her dress accentuated her small waist.* [*same as* **emphasize, highlight**]

accept /ək'sɛpt/ *verb*: **accepts, accepting, accepted**
1 a You **accept** something that is being offered to you when you agree to take it: *I've decided to accept the job in America.* □ *Miraculously, her novel was accepted by the first publisher she approached.* □ *We regret that we cannot accept cheques without a banker's card.* **b** You **accept** an offer or an invitation when you say 'yes' to it: *I thankfully accepted her offer of a bed for the night.* □ *They didn't invite me to the wedding, but I wouldn't have accepted anyway.* **c** You **accept** advice or a proposal from someone when you are willing to do as they suggest. **d** You **accept** a story, theory or explanation if you are willing to believe it. **e** (*formal*) When offering someone something such as sympathy or an apology, you can say, *eg* 'please **accept** my apology'.
2 A machine **accepts** cash in a particular form if it operates as it should when the cash is inserted: *This machine accepts the old 10-penny piece.* [*same as* **take**]
3 a You **accept** the blame for something when you admit you are responsible for it. **b** You **accept** a fact, situation or argument when you admit its existence or truth: *I still can't accept the fact that he's dead.* □ *I accept that we must teach children more grammar.* **c** You **accept** something unpleasant or unsatisfactory, such as illness or ill-treatment, if you are willing to tolerate it without complaining or protesting. **d** You **accept** something such as a risk, danger, challenge or responsibility if you are willing to face it, *eg* as part of your job.
4 a You **are accepted** by a college or university, or by a firm or other organization, if they give you a place or a job there: *I've been accepted for the training course.* **b** People **accept** you when they get used to you and begin to treat you as if you belong to their group: *His children never really accepted his second wife.*

acceptable /ək'sɛptəbəl/ *adjective*
1 Something is **acceptable** if it is generally tolerated or allowed to happen: *You must make it clear to her that her behaviour is not acceptable.* [*same as* **admissible**]
2 Something is **acceptable** if it is considered satisfactory or pleasing: *I think we've at last found a solution that is acceptable to everyone.* [*opposite* **unacceptable**] — *adverb* **acceptably:** *For once he looked acceptably tidy.*

acceptance /ək'sɛptəns/ *noun* (*usually uncount*): **acceptances**
1 Acceptance of an offer, invitation, proposal, suggestion or challenge is the act of accepting it: *He was flattered by her acceptance of his advice.* □ *She immediately wrote a letter of acceptance.* **2** (*count*) An **acceptance** is a letter or other communication announcing the acceptance *eg* of an invitation, of a student for a university place, or of a book for publication. **3** An idea gains **acceptance** as more people start believing it. [*same as* **credence**] **4** A person gains **acceptance** in a group when he or she begins to be treated by its members as one of themselves. **5** Your **acceptance** of a situation is your willingness to tolerate it, or your acknowledgement that it cannot be changed.

accepted /ək'sɛptɪd/ *adjective*
An **accepted** practice, fact or theory is one that people have learnt to acknowledge as permitted or correct. [*same as* **recognized, established**]

access /'aksɛs/ *noun*; *verb*
▻ ***noun*** (*uncount*)
1 Access to a place is a means of approaching or entering it: *We still don't know how the thieves gained access.* **2 Access** to someone or something is the right to see them: *No-one except the librarian has access to these manuscripts.* □ *She tried to see her husband in prison but was denied access.* □ *The divorce court granted him access to his children.*
▻ ***verb***: **accesses, accessing, accessed**
You **access** facts or files in a computer when you locate and use them.

accessible /ək'sɛsəbəl/ *adjective*
1 A place is **accessible** if it is possible to reach it: *The village is accessible from the motorway.* □ *The cave is only accessible at low tide.* **2** A book, subject, work of art or piece of music is **accessible** if people find it easy to understand, appreciate or enjoy. **3** Things that are

accessible to people are easily available: *The voters' lists are accessible to everyone at the local library.*

accession /ək'sɛʃən/ *noun*: **accessions**
1 (*uncount*) The **accession** of a king or queen to the throne is the official start of their rule. **2** An **accession** is a newly obtained item, *eg* a new book added to a library. [*same as* **addition, acquisition**]

accessory /ək'sɛsərɪ/ *noun*: **accessories**
1 Accessories are extra parts or items you can add to *eg* a computer or a car that enable it to do more jobs for you: *With the printer and other accessories the computer cost her £2000.* **2** In women's clothing, **accessories** are items such as gloves, hats, belts, shoes and handbags, especially when they are specially chosen to match, or contrast with, the main outfit. **3** (*legal*) An **accessory** to a crime is a person who helps the criminal in some way, or who knows about the crime but does not tell the police. [compare **accomplice**]

accident /'aksɪdənt/ *noun*: **accidents**
An **accident** is an unexpected or unplanned happening, especially one that causes damage or injury: *Her husband was killed in a car accident.* □ *She's had an accident with the kettle and burnt herself.* □ *I didn't mean to break it; it was an accident.*
▻ ***phrase*** Something, whether good or bad, happens **by accident** if it happens unexpectedly, without planning: *I discovered by accident that the programme was on when I was changing channels.* [*same as* **by chance, accidentally**]

accidental /aksɪ'dɛntəl/ *adjective*
Something that is **accidental** occurs by chance: *The jury brought in a verdict of accidental death.* — *adverb* **accidentally:** *He kicked her accidentally.* □ *We accidentally discovered the right answer.*

acclaim /ə'kleɪm/ *verb*; *noun*
▻ ***verb***: **acclaims, acclaiming, acclaimed**
Someone or something **is acclaimed** when they are enthusiastically praised or seen as being something new or important: *Their work is being acclaimed as the greatest breakthrough of the decade in cancer research.* [*same as* **hail**]
▻ ***noun*** (*uncount*)
Something such as a new book or show meets with great **acclaim** if people praise it enthusiastically.

acclimatize or **acclimatise** /ə'klaɪmətaɪz/ *verb*: **acclimatizes, acclimatizing, acclimatized**
You **acclimatize, get acclimatized**, or **acclimatize** yourself, to something when you become used to it: *It didn't take him long to acclimatize to Singapore's humidity.* [*same as* **adjust**]

accommodate /ə'kɒmədeɪt/ *verb*: **accommodates, accommodating, accommodated**
1 You **accommodate** someone somewhere when you provide them with a place to stay, live or work: *Some of the homeless families are being temporarily accommodated in hotels.* [*same as* **put up**] **2** A place can **accommodate** a certain number of people or things if it has enough room for them: *The new conference centre can accommodate up to 400 delegates.* [*same as* **take, hold**] **3** (*formal*) You **accommodate** a person when you give them what they need or help them in the way they ask you to. [*same as* **oblige**]

accommodating /ə'kɒmədeɪtɪŋ/ *adjective*
Someone who is **accommodating** is willing to help you, *eg* by altering arrangements to suit you: *My boss is always very accommodating when any of my children are ill.* [*same as* **obliging**]

accommodation /əkɒmə'deɪʃən/ *noun* (*usually uncount*)
Accommodation is a room, apartment, house, hotel or other building to stay, live or work in: *The tourist information office may be able to find you accommodation.*

accompaniment /ə'kʌmpənɪmənt/ *noun*: **accompaniments**
1 (*uncount or count*) The **accompaniment** to a song, or to a tune played on a solo instrument, is the music played, *eg* on a piano, to give it backing and support: *Some of her songs are sung to a cello accompaniment.* **2** Something that is an **accompaniment** to something else is found with it or goes with it: *Serve the white wine as an accompaniment to fish.*

accompanist /ə'kʌmpənɪst/ *noun*: **accompanists**
An **accompanist** is a person who plays a musical accompaniment, especially on the piano, for a song or instrumental solo.

accompany /ə'kʌmpənɪ/ *verb*: **accompanies, accompanying, accompanied**
1 You **accompany** someone somewhere when you go with them: *In the doorway stood her son, accompanied by a policeman.* **2** One thing **accompanies** another if it is found with it or goes with it: *The new edition of the dictionary is accompanied by a pronunciation cassette.* **3** You **accompany** someone who is singing or playing a solo instrument when you play music that gives them backing and support.

accomplice /ə'kʌmplɪs/ or /ə'kɒmplɪs/ *noun*: **accomplices**
A criminal's **accomplice** is a person who helps them to commit the crime. [compare **accessory**]

accomplish /ə'kʌmplɪʃ/ or /ə'kɒmplɪʃ/ *verb*: **accomplishes, accomplishing, accomplished**
You **accomplish** something when you manage to do it: *The task was accomplished in less than the time allowed.* □ *Unless you practise you'll accomplish nothing.* [*same as* **achieve**]

accomplished /ə'kʌmplɪʃt/ or /ə'kɒmplɪʃt/ *adjective*
Someone who is **accomplished** at something is skilful at it: *She was an accomplished pianist as well as singer.*

accomplishment /ə'kʌmplɪʃmənt/ or /ə'kɒmplɪʃmənt/ *noun*: **accomplishments**
1 (*uncount*) The **accomplishment** of a task is the completing of it; the **accomplishment** of an object or goal is the achieving of it. **2** Your **accomplishments** are your skills and talents: *One of his less-well-known accomplishments was his ability to draw cartoons.* **3** Something impressive that has been achieved is sometimes referred to as 'no mean **accomplishment**'. [*same as* **feat, achievement**]

accord /ə'kɔːd/ *verb*; *noun*
▻ ***verb*** (*formal*): **accords, according, accorded**
1 One thing **accords** with another if it fits with, agrees with, or corresponds to, it: *The newspaper review of the play didn't in the least accord with my opinion of it.* **2** You **accord** a person or their achievements something such as approval when you give it to them: *In time, her work will be accorded the recognition it deserves.* [*same as* **grant**]
▻ ***noun*** (*uncount*; *formal*)
People are in **accord** when they agree with each other: *I'd say my wife and I were in accord over most things.*
▻ ***phrase*** You do something **of your own accord** if you do it without anyone asking you to: *He'll soon get bored of screaming and stop of his own accord.*

accordance /ə'kɔːdəns/ *noun* (*uncount*)
▻ ***phrase*** Something is done or happens **in accordance with** a rule, law or principle, if it obeys it: *Nowadays you are encouraged to look after yourself first, which is not in accordance with Christian principles.*

according /ə'kɔːdɪŋ/
▻ ***phrase***
1 You say that something is so **according to** a person or other source when you are quoting that person or source: *According to this book we ought to be educating our children at home.*

> You use **according to** when you are quoting another person or something they have written. When you are quoting your own opinion you use a phrase such as 'in my opinion': *In my view* (not *according to me*) *he's making a mistake.*

2 Things happen **according to** a system or a plan if they go as it says they should: *The wedding arrangements all went according to plan.* **3** Something is organized **according to** a particular system if it is organized on the basis of this system: *The books are arranged according to subject.*

accordingly /ə'kɔːdɪŋlɪ/ *adverb*
1 You use **accordingly** to mean 'as a result of that', or 'for that reason': *He tended to be dishonest and was distrusted accordingly.* **2 Accordingly** also means 'to suit the occasion' or 'appropriately': *The forecast said it would be hot and I dressed accordingly.*

accordion /ə'kɔːdɪən/ *noun*: **accordions**
An **accordion** is a box-like musical instrument, with an expandable middle section, that you hold between both hands and play by pressing keys or buttons with your fingers.

accost /ə'kɒst/ *verb*: **accosts, accosting, accosted**
Someone, usually a stranger, **accosts** you when they approach you face to face and speak to you boldly, or even threateningly: *You often get accosted by beggars in the street nowadays.*

account /ə'kaʊnt/ *noun; verb*
▻ ***noun***: **accounts**
1 An **account** of an event or happening is a description or report of it: *You can read his own personal account of the expedition in his journal.* **2** You give an **account** of your behaviour or movements when you explain them or give details of them: *The police asked everyone for an account of their movements the previous Saturday.* **3** Your **account** with a bank is your arrangement to keep money there and take it out when you need it; your **account** is also the amount of money you have in the bank at any time: *He withdrew £200 from his account on 15 July.* □ *My account is already overdrawn.* □ *I'd like to open a bank account.* **4** Your **account** with a shop or business is your arrangement to obtain goods or services there on credit, and pay for them later, usually at the end of the month: *I've got an account at the grocer's.* **5** (*used in the plural*) The **accounts** of a business or organization are the day-to-day records it keeps of the money it receives and spends: *The auditors discovered irregularities in the accounts.*
▻ ***phrases*** **1** You say something is true **by all accounts** if it is the general opinion of the people you are inclined to believe: *It'll be a match worth watching, by all accounts.* **2** You say something is **of no account** if it is not important, or does not matter: *Whether or not you see him again is of no account to me.* **3** You do something **on account of** a thing or person if you do it because of them: *He walked slowly on account of his heart.* □ *Don't stay at home on my account.* **4** You say that something should **on no account**, or **not on any account**, be done, if it must never be done: *Don't on any account switch off the computer.* [*same as* **in no circumstances**] **5** You **take** something **into account** or **take account of** something if it is one of the things you think about it or consider when making a decision, judgement or statement: *Remember to take your travelling expenses into account when you submit your bill.* [*same as* **take into consideration**]
▻ ***verb***: **accounts, accounting, accounted**

> ***phrasal verb***
> **account for 1** You **account for** something that has happened when you explain it: *I couldn't account for the mistake.* □ *How do you account for the missing money?* □ *Ah, that accounts for her strange behaviour this morning.* **2** Something **accounts for** a proportion of something if it amounts to or constitutes that proportion: *Exports to the Far East account for at least a third of our sales abroad.* [*same as* **make up**]

accountable /ə'kaʊntəbəl/ *adjective*
1 You are **accountable** for something if you are responsible for it: *With a mental age of seven, the man was not accountable for his actions.* [*same as* **responsible**] **2** You are **accountable** to someone for something if it is your duty to explain to them any action or incident concerning it: *You will be accountable to me for office discipline.* [*same as* **responsible**]

accountancy /ə'kaʊntənsɪ/ *noun* (*uncount*)
Accountancy is the work or profession of preparing and keeping financial records or accounts, *eg* those of a business or organization: *she was taking a course in accountancy.*

accountant /ə'kaʊntənt/ *noun*: **accountants**
An **accountant** is a person who prepares and keeps financial accounts, *eg* in a business or organization.

accounting /ə'kaʊntɪŋ/ *noun* (*uncount*)
Accounting is the work of preparing or keeping financial accounts and records: *Our firm has recently installed a new accounting system.*

accredited /ə'krɛdɪtɪd/ *adjective*
A business of a specified type or a person in a specified job is **accredited** if they have official recognition for the work they do: *an accredited agent.*

accumulate /ə'kjuːmjʊleɪt/ *verb*: **accumulates, accumulating, accumulated**
You **accumulate** things, or they **accumulate**, when you collect them, or they collect, in an increasing quantity: *I've accumulated far too many books over the last few years.* — *noun* (*uncount or count*) **accumulation** /əkjuːmjʊ'leɪʃən/: *Pain increases with the gradual accumulation of blood in the joints.* □ *He promised to deal with any small accumulations of mail after the holiday.*

accuracy /'akjʊrəsɪ/ *noun* (*uncount*)
1 Accuracy is the quality of being truthful or correct: *You can't rely on the accuracy of the reporting in a lot of these newspapers.* **2** The **accuracy** of a person or machine in performing a task is their ability to do it with precision, or without any errors: *Weather-forecasters now achieve something like 90% accuracy.* [*opposite* **inaccuracy**]

accurate /'akjʊrət/ *adjective*
1 A report or description that is **accurate** is a true representation of what it reports or describes: *On the whole the programme provided an accurate picture of the effects of AIDS.* **2** A machine, or a person, that is **accurate** does a task with precision, without making mistakes: *The test is only 75% accurate.* □ *You were pretty accurate in your calculations.* [*opposite* **inaccurate**] — *adverb* **accurately:** *The incident was not accurately reported.*

accusation /akjʊ'zeɪʃən/ *noun*: **accusations**
1 An **accusation** is a statement charging someone with having done something wrong, *eg* with having com-

mitted a crime: *An accusation of fraud was brought against her.* **2** (*uncount*) Your voice, expression or eyes are full of **accusation** when they indicate to someone that you think they have done something wrong.

accuse /ə'kju:z/ *verb*: **accuses, accusing, accused**
1 Someone **accuses** you of something when they charge you with having done something wrong: *Are you accusing me of cheating?* **2** Someone who is on trial for a crime **is accused** of that crime: *He stands accused of murder.*

accused /ə'kju:zd/ *noun* (*singular or plural*)
The **accused** is or are the person or people on trial for a crime: *The accused have decided to plead guilty.*

accuser /ə'kju:zə(r)/ *noun*: **accusers**
Your **accuser** is the person who accuses you of a crime or of doing wrong.

accusing /ə'kju:ziŋ/ *adjective*
Someone gives you an **accusing** look, or says something in an **accusing** voice, when their look or voice suggest that you have done something wrong. — *adverb* **accusingly:** *'Look at that scratch on the door,' she said accusingly.*

accustom /ə'kʌstəm/ *verb*: **accustoms, accustoming, accustomed**
You **accustom** yourself to something new when you manage to get used to it or familiarize yourself with it: *I'm gradually accustoming myself to the new software.*

accustomed /ə'kʌstəmd/ *adjective*
1 You are **accustomed**, or become **accustomed**, to something when you are, or get, used to it: *Don't move till your eyes become accustomed to the dark.* **2 Accustomed** also means usual: *She was sitting in her accustomed chair.* [*same as* **customary**]

ace /eɪs/ *noun*: **aces**
1 (*cards*) The **ace** is the card with a single symbol: *She was holding the ace of hearts.* **2** (*often adjectival*) An **ace** is also a person who is excellent at something: *the flying aces of World War I* ▫ *She's an ace shot with a rifle.* **3** (*tennis*) An **ace** is a serve that is so fast and cleverly placed that the opposing player cannot hit the ball back.

ache /eɪk/ *verb; noun*
▻ ***verb***: **aches, aching, ached**
1 You, or a part of you, **aches** when you have a continuous, dull rather than sharp, pain: *I'm aching all over.* ▫ *My legs ache after that walk.* **2** You say you **are aching** for something, or to do something, if you want it, or want to do it, very much: *I was aching to tell her about my promotion.* [*same as* **long**]
▻ ***noun***: **aches**
An **ache** is a continuous dull pain: *He began to tell me all about his aches and pains.*

-ache /eɪk/: **-aches**
You use **-ache** with *head* and *stomach* to form countable nouns, and with *back*, *ear* and *tooth* to form usually uncountable nouns, that mean pain in those parts of the body: *He gets terrible headaches.* ▫ *Have you got toothache again?*

achieve /ə'tʃi:v/ *verb*: **achieves, achieving, achieved**
1 You **achieve** something when you succeed in doing it or getting it done, usually with some effort: *You won't achieve much sitting around looking miserable.* ▫ *It's a relief to have achieved agreement on a few points at least.* **2** You **achieve** an aim or ambition when you succeed in fulfilling it: *I've achieved a few of the goals I set myself.*

achievement /ə'tʃi:vmənt/ *noun*: **achievements**
1 An **achievement** is something you have succeeded in doing or getting done, especially with some effort: *Getting the whole family together for the weekend was quite an achievement.* ▫ *It's a small step in the right direction but hardly a major achievement.* **2** (*uncount*) The **achievement** of something is the process or fact of achieving it: *It's nice to finish the day's work with a sense of achievement.*

acid /'asɪd/ *noun; adjective*
▻ ***noun*** (*chemistry*): **acids**
1 (*count or uncount*) **Acid**, or an **acid**, is a substance, usually in liquid form, that contains hydrogen, is able to dissolve metals and form salts, and is likely to burn holes in clothing and damage skin: *a bottle of sulphuric acid* ▫ *Use one of the weaker acids.* [*opposite* **alkali**] **2** (*uncount; informal*) **Acid** is the drug LSD.
▻ ***adjective***
1 An **acid** substance contains acid: *What grows well in an acid soil?* [*opposite* **alkaline**] **2 Acid** fruits are those such as lemons, which have a sour taste: *The juice tasted acid.* **3** An **acid** remark is bitter or unkind. [*same as* **sarcastic**] — *adverb* **acidly:** *'It's a woman driver,' he observed acidly.*

acidic /ə'sɪdɪk/ *adjective*
Acidic substances contain acid or taste acid.

acidity /ə'sɪdɪtɪ/ *noun* (*uncount*)
Acidity is the quality, in a substance, of being acid in taste or content, or, in a remark, of being bitter or unkind.

acid rain /asɪd 'reɪn/ *noun* (*uncount*)
Acid rain is rain that contains harmful acids formed from waste gases released into the atmosphere *eg* from factories.

acknowledge /ək'nɒlidʒ/ *verb*: **acknowledges, acknowledging, acknowledged**
1 You **acknowledge** something, or that something is so, when you admit it or recognize it as a fact: *Most people would acknowledge her as one of the greatest philosophers of this century.* **2** You **acknowledge** someone as what they claim, or are claimed, to be, when you officially recognize them as that thing: *He never acknowledged the boy as his son.* **3** You **acknowledge** a letter or parcel, or **acknowledge** receipt of it, by telling the sender it has arrived, and thanking them: *I still haven't acknowledged that book from Erik.* **4** When you meet someone you know, you **acknowledge** them by nodding, smiling or waving, to show that you have seen and recognized them. **5** The writer of a book or article **acknowledges** the contribution of people who helped with it by mentioning and thanking them, *eg* in the introduction. **6** A performer or speaker **acknowledges** the audience's applause by *eg* bowing to show they appreciate it; you **acknowledge** praise or a compliment by thanking the person who gives it.

acknowledgement or **acknowledgment** /ək'nɒlɪdʒmənt/ *noun*: **acknowledgements**
1 (*uncount or count*) **Acknowledgement** is the act of acknowledging something: *His gesture was an acknowledgement of defeat.* ▫ *She recognized him and waved a hand in acknowledgement.* **2** An **acknowledgement** of a letter or parcel is a message to the sender saying it has arrived, and thanking them: *I sent in my application last week and have already had an acknowledgement.* **3** The **acknowledgements** in a book or article are a section in the introduction or at the end in which the writer lists and thanks those who have helped with it.

acne /'aknɪ/ *noun* (*uncount*)
Acne is an unhealthy condition of the skin, especially of greasy skin, in which the pores become infected and inflamed, so that red spots appear on the face, neck and back.

acorn /ˈeɪkɔːn/ *noun*: **acorns**
An **acorn** is the nut-like fruit of the oak tree, which has a cup-shaped outer case.

acoustic /əˈkuːstɪk/ *adjective*
1 Acoustic means concerned with sound, or with the sense of hearing, or with acoustics. **2** An **acoustic** guitar or piano is the normal traditional kind, not an electric one. — *adverb* **acoustically:** *The smaller hall is better acoustically.*

acoustics /əˈkuːstɪks/ *noun*
1 (*plural*) The **acoustics** of a hall, room or theatre are the qualities of it that determine how well or clearly sound, especially music or speech, can be heard in it: *The acoustics are poor in here.* **2** (*uncount*) **Acoustics** is the science of sound.

acquaint /əˈkweɪnt/ *verb* (*formal*): **acquaints, acquainting, acquainted**
You **acquaint** someone with something when you inform them of it: *Let me acquaint you with the facts of the case.*

acquaintance /əˈkweɪntəns/ *noun*: **acquaintances**
1 An **acquaintance** is someone you know: *It's a long job informing your friends and acquaintances of your change of address.* **2** (*used in the singular*) Your **acquaintance** with a person is your friendship with them or the circumstance of your knowing them: *How did your acquaintance with her begin?* **3** (*used in the singular*) Your **acquaintance** with something is your knowledge of it or familiarity with it: *She has some acquaintance with the Czech language.*
▻ ***phrases*** **1** You **make the acquaintance of** someone when you meet them and get to know them: *I made his acquaintance at University.* **2** A person **of your acquaintance** is someone you know. **3** You have **a passing acquaintance** with someone if you know them slightly.

acquainted /əˈkweɪntɪd/ *adjective*
1 You are **acquainted** with a person if you know them or have met them: *I'm acquainted with her but don't know her well.* □ *How did you two become acquainted?* □ *It's time we got better acquainted.* **2** (*formal*) You are **acquainted** with something if you have some knowledge of it or are familiar with it: *I'm not acquainted with the book you mean.* [*opposite* **unfamiliar**]

acquiesce /akwɪˈɛs/ *verb* (*formal*): **acquiesces, acquiescing, acquiesced**
You **acquiesce** in a plan, or **acquiesce** to a demand, when you agree to it, especially unwillingly. [*same as* **consent**] — *noun* (*uncount*) **acquiescence:** *She took his silence for acquiescence.*

acquire /əˈkwaɪə(r)/ *verb*: **acquires, acquiring, acquired**
1 You **acquire** something when you get it or obtain it: *I've managed to acquire a copy of the report.* **2** You **acquire** a skill, ability, habit or liking by developing it or establishing it gradually: *You should go to bed before midnight; it's a good habit to acquire.* □ *It was in the Far East that I acquired a liking for shellfish.*

acquired /əˈkwaɪəd/ *adjective*
1 Acquired characteristics are those that you develop, in contrast to those you are born with. **2** An **acquired** taste is something that people develop a liking for only gradually, rather than immediately: *Oysters are an acquired taste.*

acquisition /akwɪˈzɪʃən/ *noun*: **acquisitions**
1 An **acquisition** is something you have obtained: *Her latest acquisition is a car phone.* **2** (*uncount*) The **acquisition** of something, *eg* a possession or skill, is the process of gaining it.

acquit /əˈkwɪt/ *verb*: **acquits, acquitting, acquitted**
1 Someone who is on trial **is acquitted** of the crime they are accused of when the judge declares them innocent of it: *Only one of the accused was convicted of murder; the rest were acquitted.* [*same as* **clear**; *opposite* **convict**] **2** You **acquit** yourself well or badly when you behave or perform well or badly: *She acquitted herself satisfactorily at the interview.* [*same as* **conduct**]

acquittal /əˈkwɪtəl/ *noun* (*uncount or count*): **acquittals**
Acquittal, or an **acquittal**, is the act by a judge of declaring someone innocent of the crime of which they have been accused. [*opposite* **conviction**]

acre /ˈeɪkə(r)/ *noun*: **acres**
An **acre** is a measurement of land area, equal to 4840 square yards or 4047 square metres.

acreage /ˈeɪkərɪdʒ/ *noun* (*uncount*)
The **acreage** of a piece of land is its measurement in acres.

acrid /ˈakrɪd/ *adjective*
1 An **acrid** taste or smell is a strong and unpleasantly bitter one: *The room began to fill with acrid smoke.* **2** An **acrid** comment is a bitterly worded one expressing disgust or scorn. [*same as* **caustic**]

acrimonious /akrɪˈmoʊnɪəs/ *adjective*
An **acrimonious** discussion or quarrel is one that is full of bitter anger and ill feeling.

acrimony /ˈakrɪmənɪ/ *noun* (*uncount*)
Acrimony is bitter ill feeling and quarrelling between people: *Their money discussions usually ended in acrimony.*

acrobat /ˈakrəbat/ *noun*: **acrobats**
An **acrobat** is an entertainer, *eg* in a circus, who performs skilful balancing acts and other athletic tricks.

acrobatic /akrəˈbatɪk/ *adjective*
1 Acrobatic means concerned with or involving acrobatics: *an acrobatic display.* **2** An **acrobatic** feat or movement is an athletically skilful one. — *adverb* **acrobatically:** *He stood acrobatically poised on one leg for an instant.*

acrobatics /akrəˈbatɪks/ *noun* (*plural*)
Acrobatics are athletic movements such as jumping, balancing, swinging, somersaulting, bending, standing on the head or walking on the hands: *The monkeys' acrobatics always attract a crowd.*

acronym /ˈakrənɪm/ *noun*: **acronyms**
An **acronym** is a word that is made from the first letters of words composing a title or phrase, and is used as a short form of it: *The acronym ROM stands for 'read-only memory'.*

across /əˈkrɒs/ *preposition*; *adverb*
▻ ***preposition***
1 To go **across** somewhere or something is to move from one side of it to the other: *We've somehow got to get across the river.* □ *The stream's too wide to jump across.* □ *Rain will spread right across the country.* □ *Their eyes met across the table.* □ *His shadow fell across her book.*[*same as* **over**] **2** Something extends **across** something else if it extends from one side of it to the other: *He had long scar across his back.* □ *He stood with his arms folded across his chest.* □ *There was a temporary barrier across the road.* **3** Something is **across** a road or river if it is on the opposite side of it: *My car's parked across the street.* □ *They live across the road.*
▻ ***adverb***
1 Across means from one side to the other, or on the other side: *There was no traffic coming, so she ran across.* □ *We flew across to the island.* □ *She glanced across at me.* □ *He lives across on the other side of town.* [see also **over**] **2** You use **across** in giving a mea-

surement of width: *The bullet had left a hole about two centimetres across.*

acrylic /ə'krɪlɪk/ *noun* (*often adjectival*)
Acrylic is a manmade material produced by a chemical process, used similarly to wool: *an acrylic pullover.*

act /akt/ *verb; noun*
▻ ***verb*: acts, acting, acted**
1 You **act** in a certain way when you behave in that way: *Stop acting like a coward, and face facts.* ▫ *He was acting very strangely this evening.* **2** You **act** when you do something for a purpose: *I had to act fast to prevent an accident.* ▫ *I would have acted differently if I'd had time to think.* **3** A lawyer or agent **acts** for or on behalf of someone when he or she represents their interests in dealings or discussions: *I rang the lawyer who was acting for my mother.* **4** One thing **acts** as another when it works like that thing: *Your third gear acts as a brake if you use it going downhill.* [*same as* **serve, function**] **5** You **act** if you are a professional or amateur actor or actress: *She used to act a bit.* **6** You **act**, or **act** a part, in a play or film if you perform a part in it; people say you **are acting** or **acting** a part, if you behave insincerely or unnaturally, or as if you were performing to an audience. **7** A medicine, drug or poison **acts** when it works or takes effect: *These pills will take an hour or so to act.* [see also **act on**]
▻ ***noun*: acts**
1 An **act** is a deed or the doing of something: *You never know what acts of bravery you may be capable of.* [see note at **action**] ▫ *It was an act of kindness to shoot the animal.* ▫ *The act of telling someone your problems is usually a relief.* **2** (*used in the singular*) An **act** is an insincere piece of behaviour intended to impress people: *All that sympathy of hers was just an act.* ▫ *He's putting on an act as usual.* **3** An **act** is a short entertainment, *eg* as part of a show; the people performing it are also an **act**: *The jugglers were the best act.* **4** The **acts** of a play, opera or ballet are its main sections, usually divided into scenes: *You'll find the quotation about spectacles in Act II, Scene 7, of 'As You Like It'.* **5** An **Act** is a law passed by a law-making body such as Parliament: *the Social Security Act of 1989.*
▻ ***phrases*** **1** An **act of God** is an event beyond human control, *eg* a natural disaster such as an earthquake. **2** (*informal*) You **get in on the act** when you get yourself involved in some profitable deal or activity in order to share the benefits. **3** (*informal*) You **get your act together** when you organize yourself, your time and your work efficiently. **4** You are **in the act** of doing something when you are just doing it, or are in the process of doing it: *I was in the act of looking up your phone number when you called.* ▫ *She insisted that she hadn't been cheating, even though she'd been caught in the act.*

phrasal verbs
act on or **act upon** **1** You **act on** or **upon** advice, suggestions or ideas when you obey or follow them. **2** Something such as a drug, or an influence present in your surroundings, **acts on** you when it has an effect on you: *The music acted on her senses and made her feel relaxed and sleepy.*
act out You **act out** your feelings, emotions or fears when you express them in your behaviour, usually unconsciously.
act up (*informal*) **1** You say a machine **is acting up** when it won't work properly. **2** You say a person, especially a child, **is acting up** when they behave badly or unco-operatively and cause trouble. [*same as* **play up**]

acting /'aktɪŋ/ *noun; adjective*
▻ ***noun*** (*uncount*)
Acting is the profession or art of an actor or actress.
▻ ***adjective***
Someone who is, *eg*, the **acting** headmaster of a school or the **acting** manager of a department, is doing that job temporarily.

action /'akʃən/ *noun*: **actions**
1 (*uncount*) **Action** is the doing of something, usually for a purpose: *Action must be taken to prevent such an accident happening again.* ▫ *Shaw's plays are all talk and no action.* **2** People's **actions** are the things that they do: *But for your prompt action he might have drowned.*

You can use both **act** and **action** to mean a deed or something done: *a foolish act* (or *action*). Note however: *an act* (not *action*) *of foolishness.*

3 (*count or uncount*) An **action** is a movement or gesture: *a song with actions as well as words* ▫ *Golf requires good wrist action.* **4** (*used in the singular*) People say they want to be where the **action** is if they want to be involved in the most important area of activity in any project or situation. **5** (*uncount*) **Action** is the fighting that goes on in war: *So many young men were killed in action.* ▫ *He saw action in Vietnam.* **6** (*used in the singular*) The **action** of a play or novel is the series of events that form its plot: *The action is set partly in Venice and partly at Belmont.*
▻ ***phrases*** **1 a** You go **into action** when you do what you have been preparing or training to do: *Firemen must always be ready to go into action.* **b** You put something such as an idea or plan **into action** when you carry it out or start it working. [*same as* **into practice**] **2** A machine or vehicle is **out of action** if it is broken or not working.

activate /'aktɪveɪt/ *verb*: **activates, activating, activated**
You **activate** something such as a device when you start it working: *The braking mechanism is activated when you pull the emergency cord.*

active /'aktɪv/ *adjective*
1 An **active** person is someone who is lively and energetic and keeps themselves busy: *She's very active for her age.* [*opposite* **inactive**] **2** An **active** member of a club takes part in its organization and affairs; someone who is **active**, or takes an **active** part, in a movement or cause works hard for it: *She was active in the campaign for spelling reform.* ▫ *As a student he had been quite active politically.* **3** The **active** ingredients in a medicine are the ones that have the effect. **4** An **active** volcano is one that has recently erupted and may erupt soon again. [*opposite* **extinct, dormant**] **5** (*grammar*) The **active** form of a verb is the form used when the subject performs the action, as in 'He drove the car into a wall'. [*see also* **passive**]

actively /'aktɪvlɪ/ *adverb*
1 You are **actively** involved in something if you take an active part in it. **2** You do something such as encourage or discourage someone **actively** when you do so in a definite and deliberate way: *My parents actively discouraged me from taking up rock-climbing.*

activist /'aktɪvɪst/ *noun*: **activists**
An **activist** is a person who takes a leading part in a political or social movement.

activity /ak'tɪvɪtɪ/ *noun*: **activities**
1 (*uncount*) **Activity** is the busy or continuous doing of things: *There's always plenty of activity in the office, but no-one seems to get much done.* [*opposite* **inactivity**] **2** An **activity** is something such as a sport, pastime or project, that you take part in for pleasure,

interest or exercise: *The old people can join in various organized activities, such as sight-seeing tours and theatre visits.* □ *We're sending the children on one of those activity holidays.* **3** A person's or organization's **activities** are things that they typically or regularly do: *They were involved in various criminal activities.* **4** (*used in the singular*) The **activity** of doing something is the physical and mental process of doing it: *the activity of walking.*

actor /'aktə(r)/ *noun*: **actors**
An **actor** is a man or woman who acts in plays or films, or whose profession is acting.

actress /'aktrɪs/ *noun*: **actresses**
An **actress** is a woman who acts in plays or films, or whose profession is acting.

actual /'aktʃʊəl/ *adjective*
1 An **actual** person or thing is one that exists in fact or reality, not an imaginary or theoretical one: *You wouldn't get actual people behaving like the characters in his plays.* □ *People don't know that Timbuctoo is an actual place.* [*same as* **real**] **2** You refer to a thing or person as the **actual** one involved in some event when you mean that one and no other: *Is this the actual pistol that killed Lincoln?* □ *Did you happen to hear her actual words?* [*same as* **very**] **3 Actual** is used to mean true or real as distinct from supposed or guessed at: *The estimate was £500 but the actual bill came to £650.* **4 Actual** also identifies something as the main or essential item, as distinct from associated ones: *We were disappointed not to get into the actual palace, but we walked round the grounds.* □ *What time does the actual film start?*

actuality /aktʃʊ'alɪtɪ/ *noun* (*uncount*)
Actuality is reality or fact.
▻ ***phrase*** **In actuality** is used in the same way as **actually** to mean 'in fact' or 'in reality': *There are fewer cases of real poverty than you'd expect, in actuality.*

actually /'aktʃʊəlɪ/ *adverb*
1 Something **actually** happens if it does happen: *Did you actually see him fall?* □ *Did she actually mention this?* □ *Could you actually hear what they were saying?* **2 Actually** is used to mean 'in fact', as distinct from what people may think: *He used to say he was born in 1910, though he was actually older, wasn't he?* **3** You use **actually** to emphasize the surprising part of what you are saying: *She took her degree eventually and actually got a first class.* □ *He actually apologized to me.* **4 Actually** also means 'in the true sense of the word': *I was never actually dishonest.* **5** (*sentence adverb*) You use **actually**, often as a way of sounding polite **a** when you are disagreeing with or correcting someone, or simply stating something surprising or unexpected: *Actually, you've slightly misunderstood me.* □ *The problem is not quite that, actually.* □ *Actually, I did the journey in under three hours.* **b** when you are making a request or suggestion, or giving instructions: *Actually, if you're going shopping, could you get me a newspaper?* **c** with various other types of comment or statement: *Actually, I'll have to go now. Sorry.* □ *You won't get a better bargain than this, actually.* □ *Actually, that reminds me; the tutorial has been cancelled.*

acumen /'akjʊmən/ *noun* (*uncount*)
Someone's **acumen** is their ability to judge circumstances quickly and correctly and make the right decision about how to act: *I could do with some of your business acumen when it comes to investing money.*

acupuncture /'akjʊpʌŋktʃə(r)/ *noun* (*uncount*)
Acupuncture is a method of treating pain and disease by inserting small needles into the skin at specific points so as to stimulate connections in the nervous system.

acute /ə'kjuːt/ *adjective*
1 A serious situation such as a crisis or a shortage, or a troubled state of mind such as depression or anxiety, is described as **acute** if it is severe or needs urgent attention: *The water shortage is becoming acute.* □ *He was suffering from acute depression.* **2** An **acute** illness is one that has developed quickly and soon become severe or dangerous: *acute appendicitis.* [*opposite* **mild, chronic**] **3** Your hearing, sense of smell, powers of observation or understanding are **acute** if they are very good: *He'd always had acute hearing.* □ *Her paper contained some acute observations on international banking practices.* [*same as* **sharp, shrewd**] **4** In geometry, an **acute** angle is an angle of less than 90%. [*opposite* **obtuse**]

acute accent /əkjuːt 'aksənt/ *noun*
An **acute accent** is a mark (′) put over a vowel in certain languages, *eg* French, showing pronunciation, as in 'début' and 'élite'.

acutely /ə'kjuːtlɪ/ *adverb*
1 You feel something **acutely** if you feel it strongly or intensely: *He was acutely aware of her presence.* **2** (*intensifying*) **Acutely** is used to mean very, intensely, gravely or painfully: *He was acutely ill.*

ad /ad/ *noun* (*informal*): **ads**
An **ad** is an advertisement: *television ads* □ *Put an ad in the local paper.*

adamant /'adəmənt/ *adjective*
You are **adamant** about something such as a decision you have made if you are absolutely determined on it and refuse to change your mind: *His parents were adamant that he should finish his studies before marrying.* — *adverb* **adamantly:** *She adamantly refused to lend him the money.*

adam's apple /adəmz 'apəl/ *noun*: **adam's apples**
A man's **adam's apple** is the slight lump, part of the thyroid gland, that projects from the front of his neck.

adapt /ə'dapt/ *verb*: **adapts, adapting, adapted**
1 You **adapt** to a new environment or situation when you alter your behaviour and expectations to fit in with it: *The children adapted quickly to camp life.* [*same as* **adjust**] **2** You **adapt** something when you alter it so as to make it suitable for a use different from the one it was designed for: *The council are adapting the building for use as a pre-school nursery.* **3** You **adapt** *eg* a novel for television, radio or the stage when you re-arrange its text for performance as a television, radio or stage play.

adaptable /ə'daptəbəl/ *adjective*
Someone who is **adaptable** is good at fitting into new circumstances and changing their behaviour and attitude as necessary. [*same as* **flexible**]

adaptation /adəp'teɪʃən/ *noun*: **adaptations**
1 An **adaptation** is a re-arrangement or alteration of *eg* a novel for performance as a play on the stage, television or radio. **2** (*uncount*) **Adaptation** is the process of adapting to fit a changed environment or situation: *The evolutionary process provides us with many examples of animal adaptation to climatic and environmental change.*

adaptor /ə'daptə(r)/ *noun*: **adaptors**
An **adaptor** is an electrical plug for connecting a plug of one type to a socket of another type, or for connecting several plugs to the same socket.

add /ad/ *verb*: **adds, adding, added**
1 You **add** one thing to another when you include or attach something extra to it: *I've added an introduction to the book.* □ *If the mixture is too stiff, add some milk.* **2** You **add** numbers or amounts together to get their

total: *You learn to add and subtract as soon as you go to school.* □ *Add the figures in the left-hand column together.* **3** You **add** something when you say something extra: *'Thanks all the same,' she added.* □ *I've nothing further to add.*

phrasal verbs
add in You **add** something **in** when you include it in the total: *Have you added in the cost of the taxi?*
add on You **add** something **on** when you include it or attach it as an extra: *Add on £2.50 for packing and postage.* □ *When did you add the garage on to the house?*
add to One thing **adds to** another, or **adds** something **to** it, if it increases it: *The rain added to her misery.* □ *Tips can add £100 or more to your holiday bill.*
add up **1** You **add up** numbers or amounts when you work out their total: *Add up your score.* **2** You say that figures or numbers don't **add up** if their total has been wrongly calculated. **3** (*informal*) Things **add up** if they make sense: *I can't think why she left so suddenly; it doesn't add up.*
add up to **1** Numbers **add up to** a certain amount if that is their total. **2** Circumstances **add up to** something if, taken together, they have a meaning or significance: *This all adds up to the possibility that they're going to award us the contract.*

added /ˈadɪd/ *adjective*
Added means extra or additional: *Far from spoiling his looks, his crooked mouth gave him an added attraction.*

adder /ˈadə(r)/ *noun*: **adders**
An **adder** is a small poisonous snake, also called a viper, with a black zig-zag pattern on its back, found in northern parts of Europe and Asia.

addict /ˈadɪkt/ *noun*: **addicts**
1 An **addict** is someone who has a harmful habit, especially drug-taking, and is unable to stop it: *heroin addicts.* [*same as* **junkie**] **2** (*informal*) Someone who is so keen on a particular pastime or activity that they spend all their available time on it, is also called an **addict**: *a chess addict.* [*same as* **freak**]

addicted /əˈdɪktɪd/ *adjective*
Someone who **is addicted** to *eg* alcohol or a drug cannot stop taking it: *Children as young as eight are becoming addicted to cigarettes.*

addiction /əˈdɪkʃən/ *noun* (*usually uncount*): **addictions**
1 Addiction is the state of being unable to stop taking something such as alcohol or a drug: *a victim of alcohol addiction.* **2** (*usually in the singular*) An **addiction** to something is a constant need for it, developed as an initial liking that leads to habitual use: *My addiction to chocolate began when I was pregnant.*

addictive /əˈdɪktɪv/ *adjective*
A drug or other substance is **addictive** if people who take it find they cannot stop taking it: *nicotine and other addictive substances.*

addition /əˈdɪʃən/ *noun*: **additions**
1 (*uncount*) **Addition** is the process or operation of adding numbers together to find their total. **2** (*uncount*) The **addition** of something is the adding, attaching or including of it: *The usefulness of the book would be increased by the addition of an index.* **3** An **addition** is something added, attached or included: *The index is a welcome addition to the work.*
▻ ***phrase*** You use **in addition** to mean 'also' or 'as well', and **in addition to** to mean 'as well as': *The department can spare some funds, but we should apply for a grant in addition.* □ *She's looking after her sister's children in addition to her own.*

additional /əˈdɪʃənəl/ *adjective*
Additional things are things that are added or extra: *There's an additional charge for insurance.*

additionally /əˈdɪʃənəlɪ/ *adverb*
Additionally means 'also' or 'as an extra consideration': *She was the the most intelligent applicant, and happened additionally to have keyboarding skills.*

additive /ˈadɪtɪv/ *noun*: **additives**
An **additive** is a substance that is added to food to keep it fresh longer or improve its taste or colour.

address /əˈdrɛs/ *noun*; *verb*
▻ ***noun***: **addresses**
1 (*AmE* /ˈadrɛs/) Your **address** is the number or name of the house or building, the name of the street, and the town, where you live or work: *I took down her name, address and telephone number.* **2** (*formal*) An **address** is a speech or lecture: *We arrived too late for the President's opening address.*
▻ ***verb***: **addresses, addressing, addressed**
1 You **address** an envelope when you write the name and address on it; you **address** a letter or note to someone when you put their name and address on it, or if you use their name when you write 'Dear ...': *The postcard was addressed to me but I let the others read it.* **2** (*formal*) You **address** an audience when you give a speech or lecture: *She addressed us entertainingly on the subject of 18th-century footwear.* **3** (*formal*) You **address** someone, or **address** a remark to them, when you speak or say something to them: *Always look at the person you're addressing.* **4** You **address**, or **address** yourself to, a problem or other matter, when you give your attention to it.

address book /əˈdrɛs bʊk/ *noun*: **address books**
An **address book** is a note book in which you write names and addresses.

adept /ˈadɛpt/ or /əˈdɛpt/ *adjective*
Someone who is **adept** at something is expert at it: *The Tories are normally adept at explaining away bad local-election results.* □ *Unlike her sister, she was not adept with words.* □ *These were powerful and adept warriors.* [*same as* **skilful, proficient**]

adequate /ˈadəkwət/ *adjective*
1 Something is **adequate** if there is enough of it: *The amount of food they're being given isn't adequate for growing children.* [*same as* **sufficient**] **2** Something that is satisfactory, or good enough, is **adequate**: *The teaching standard at the school is adequate, but could be improved.* [*opposite* **inadequate**] — *noun* (*uncount*) **adequacy:** *The adequacy of his training and qualifications was not in doubt.* [*opposite* **inadequacy**] — *adverb* **adequately:** *I hope you're getting adequately paid for your trouble.*

adhere /ədˈhɪə(r)/ *verb*: **adheres, adhering, adhered**
1 One thing **adheres** to another when it sticks firmly to it: *She pulled the stamp off before it had time to adhere to the envelope.* **2** You **adhere** to a belief, opinion or principle if you continue to support it: *It's amazing what oldfashioned notions some people adhere to.* **3** You **adhere** to a plan, arrangement, agreement or rule when you do as it instructs: *The provisions of his will must be adhered to.* [*same as* **stick, abide by**] — *noun* **adherence:** *He could not be sure of the continued adherence of his supporters.* □ *Strict adherence to the official procedure is essential.* [compare **loyalty, obedience**]

adherent /ədˈhɪərənt/ *noun* (*usually in the plural*): **adherents**
The **adherents** of a political party, leader or cause are its loyal supporters.

adhesive /ədˈhiːzɪv/ *adjective*; *noun*
▻ ***adjective***
Something that is **adhesive** sticks to other surfaces: *adhesive labels.* [*same as* **sticky**]

▻ ***noun*** *(count or uncount)*
Any kind of glue is an **adhesive**: *You can get special adhesives for sticking leather.* □ *A tube of adhesive.*

ad hoc /ad hɒk/ *adjective*
An arrangement that is **ad hoc** is set up for a present need only, and is not permanent: *An ad hoc committee has been appointed to find accommodation for those made homeless by the floods.*

adjacent /ə'dʒeɪʃənt/ *adjective*
One thing is **adjacent** to another, or things are **adjacent**, when they are next to each other, or side by side: *The bookshop is in the street adjacent to this one.* □ *The three of us had adjacent bedrooms in the college.*

adjectival /adʒək'taɪvəl/ *adjective*
Adjectival means relating to adjectives, or acting like an adjective; nouns that are frequently used like adjectives before another noun are labelled (*often adjectival*) in this dictionary: *The noun 'school' is found in adjectival use in 'school uniform' and 'school desks'.* — *adverb* **adjectivally:** *Lots of nouns are used adjectivally.*

adjective /'adʒəktɪv/ *noun*
1 An **adjective** is one of the 'parts of speech' and is used to describe a noun or pronoun, telling you such things as its size (*eg large, small*), its colour (*eg red, blue*), or its quality. **2** Most adjectives can be used both before a noun (*eg a tall man, fine weather*) and after a verb like *be, become, seem, look* (*eg He grew tall, the weather's fine*). **3** Many adjectives can be used in a comparative and superlative form, either formed with *-er* and *-est* (*eg taller, tallest*) or with *more* and *most* (*eg more beautiful, most efficient*). **4** You can adjust the degree of an adjective using an intensifying adverb (*eg very nice, extremely hot*) or a moderating adverb (*eg quite nice, fairly warm*).

> You can use two or more adjectives before a noun. When the adjectives are of different classes (*eg* size, colour, kind), commas should not be used between them (*eg a long red cotton skirt*), but where they are of the same class (usually quality), commas should be used (*eg a cold, dark, wet night*).

adjoin /ə'dʒɔɪn/ *verb*: **adjoins, adjoining, adjoined**
One thing **adjoins** another if it is next to it: *The bathroom adjoins the main bedroom.* — *adjective* **adjoining:** *We had adjoining bedrooms on the top landing.*

adjourn /ə'dʒɜːn/ *verb*: **adjourns, adjourning, adjourned**
A meeting or a court trial **adjourns** or **is adjourned** when it is stopped temporarily, so as to continue later: *The trial was adjourned till after lunch.* — *noun* (*uncount or count*) **adjournment:** *The judge called for an adjournment of the trial till Monday morning.*

adjudge /ə'dʒʌdʒ/ *verb* (*usually in the passive; formal*): **adjudges, adjudging, adjudged**
Someone or something **is adjudged** to be something if they are estimated or judged to be that thing after careful consideration: *She had been interviewed and adjudged a suitable leader for the project.*

adjudicate /ə'dʒuːdɪkeɪt/ *verb*: **adjudicates, adjudicating, adjudicated**
1 To **adjudicate** at a competition, or **adjudicate** it, is to serve officially as a judge of it: *She was invited to adjudicate at the dancing championships.* **2** To **adjudicate** on a disagreement, or **adjudicate** it, is to decide officially how it is to be solved or dealt with. — *noun* **adjudicator:** *She was asked to serve on the panel of adjudicators.*

adjunct /'adʒʌŋkt/ *noun* (*grammar*): **adjuncts**
An **adjunct** is a part of a sentence or clause that tells you about the manner, time or place of the action. In the following sentences, the adjuncts are underlined: *She writes <u>neatly</u>. He arrived <u>the next morning</u>. I took my coat <u>off the peg</u>.*

adjust /ə'dʒʌst/ *verb*: **adjusts, adjusting, adjusted**
1 You **adjust** something when you alter it to your satisfaction, or correct it: *The left-hand knob adjusts the brightness of the picture and the right-hand one the contrast.* □ *He adjusted his watch.* **2** You **adjust** to new circumstances when you become accustomed to them, or alter your attitude and behaviour to suit them: *You need time to adjust to the arrival of a baby.* [*same as* **adapt**] — *noun* (*count or uncount*) **adjustment:** *The engine still needs some minor adjustments.* □ *Adjustment to married life took her a surprisingly long time.*

adjustable /ə'dʒʌstəbəl/ *adjective*
Something that is **adjustable** can be altered to a variety of settings, levels or positions: *The back of the seat is adjustable.*

adjusted /ə'dʒʌstɪd/ *adjective* (*psychology*)
Adjusted is used in combinations such as *well-adjusted* and *badly adjusted* in reference to people's ability to deal with their emotions and control their social behaviour: *She was a cheerful, well-adjusted child and coped happily with school life.*

ad lib /ad 'lɪb/ *adverb*; *verb*
▻ ***adverb***
You do something such as give a speech or lecture **ad lib** when you do it without preparation: *I admire people who can just get up and speak ad lib in public.* [*compare* **impromptu, off the cuff**]
▻ ***verb***: **ad-libs, ad-libbing, ad-libbed**
You **ad-lib** in a play or speech when you make up what to say as you are speaking, *eg* because you have forgotten your words: *I completely forgot my lines and had to ad-lib for a bit.*

administer /əd'mɪnɪstə(r)/ *verb*: **administers, administering, administered**
1 To **administer** something such as a country, institution, project or organization is to be in charge of running or governing it: *How are the universities administered in this country?* **2** To **administer** something such as the law or justice is to discharge it or deal it out: *Punishment had been duly administered.* **3** You **administer** medicine or a drug to someone when you give them a dose: *Who actually administered the injection?*

administration /ədmɪnɪ'streɪʃən/ *noun*: **administrations**
1 (*uncount*) **Administration** is the directing, managing or governing of the affairs of a country, company or institution: *Steps must be taken to reduce administration costs.* **2** (*with a singular or plural verb*) In an organization, business, or institution, the **administration** is the department responsible for running it: *The administration are planning more staff cuts.* **3** (*count*) An **administration** is a particular government or its period of being in power: *the Clinton administration.* **4** (*uncount*) The **administration** of something is also the act or process of administering it: *The sister-in-charge supervises the administration of drugs on each ward.*

administrative /əd'mɪnɪstrətɪv/ *adjective*
Administrative means relating to management or administration: *She has an administrative job in the University.*

administrator /əd'mɪnɪstreɪtə(r)/ *noun*: **administrators**
An **administrator** is a person who manages, governs or directs the affairs of an institution, country, or estate:

It is to be hoped that the country has an able administrator at last in the new prime minister.

admirable /'admərəbəl/ *adjective*
An **admirable** person or thing deserves praise and admiration: *His self-control in such difficult circumstances was admirable.* — *adverb* **admirably:** *He was admirably suited for the job.*

admiral /'admɪrəl/ *noun*: **admirals**
An **admiral** is the most senior naval officer, commanding the whole navy or a fleet of ships.

admiration /admɪ'reɪʃən/ *noun* (*uncount*)
Admiration is what you feel for someone or something you respect or admire: *He expressed his admiration openly and spontaneously.*

admire /əd'maɪə(r)/ *verb*: **admires, admiring, admired**
1 You **admire** someone or something if you have a strong liking or respect for them: *She admired him for his perseverance.* □ *I admire her honesty.* **2** You **admire** something when you look at it with enjoyment, or express your pleasure on seeing it: *Everyone came out and admired her new car.*

admirer /əd'maɪərə(r)/ *noun*: **admirers**
1 An **admirer** of a particular person is someone who greatly respects them or their achievements: *I'm a great admirer of Virginia Woolf.* **2** A woman's **admirers** are the men who are in love with her or attracted to her: *She was never short of admirers.*

admiring /əd'maɪərɪŋ/ *adjective*
Someone gives you an **admiring** glance when they look at you with an expression that shows their liking or admiration for you: *She was used to drawing admiring glances.* — *adverb* **admiringly:** *Critics commented admiringly on her acting.*

admissible /əd'mɪsɪbəl/ *adjective* (*especially legal*)
Something that is **admissible** can be accepted or allowed: *evidence that is admissible in a court of law.*

admission /əd'mɪʃən/ *noun*: **admissions**
1 (*uncount or count*) **Admission** is permission to enter a place, or acceptance into an institution: *The notice on the door read 'No admission except on business'.* □ *He was refused admission to the club.* □ *Medical schools have all reduced numbers of admissions this year.* **2** (*uncount*) **Admission** is also the price you pay for permission to enter a place: *The art gallery was charging £3 admission.* [*same as* **entrance fee**] **3** (*count*) An **admission** is a statement you make that something, especially something bad that causes you shame or embarrassment, is true: *an admission of guilt.*

admit /əd'mɪt/ *verb*: **admits, admitting, admitted**
1 You **admit** something, or **admit to** something, especially something bad that causes you shame or embarrassment, when you agree that it is true: *He admitted lying to the police.* □ *I admit that I misjudged her.* □ *'I behaved stupidly,' she admitted.* □ *She admitted to the theft of two wristwatches.* □ *I must admit to feeling a certain pleasure at his failure.* **2** You **are admitted** to a place or an institution when you are allowed to enter, or are accepted as a member; you **are admitted** to hospital when you are accepted as a patient into one of the wards: *A small fee of £2 admits you to the special-collection room.* □ *The notice read 'Dogs not admitted except on a lead'.*

admittance /əd'mɪtəns/ *noun* (*uncount*)
1 Admittance is the right to enter, or permission to enter, a place: *He had been refused admittance to the courtroom.* □ *We can't go in; it says 'No admittance to non-members'.* **2 Admittance** is also entry, or the means of getting in: *Crowds of photographers were straining to gain admittance to the church.*

> **Admission** and **admittance** can both mean permission to enter, but only **admission** can mean the act of admitting a fault or crime.

admittedly /əd'mɪtɪdlɪ/ *adverb* (*sentence adverb*)
You use **admittedly** when you are admitting, or agreeing to the truth of, something: *Admittedly we don't yet know all the facts.*

admonish /əd'mɒnɪʃ/ *verb* (*formal*): **admonishes, admonishing, admonished**
You **admonish** someone when you scold or rebuke them for doing something wrong: *He was officially admonished for wasting the club's money.* [*same as* **reprimand**]

ado /ə'duː/ *noun* (*uncount*)
▷ ***phrase*** You announce that you are about to do something, especially perform some official ceremony, **without more ado**, or **without further ado**, when you intend to do it immediately, without any more delay: *You must all be getting impatient to know the results, so without further ado I shall ask Mrs Rennie to read out the names of the winners.*

adolescence /adə'lɛsəns/ *noun* (*uncount*)
Your **adolescence** is the stage in your growth and development at which you are passing from childhood to adulthood: *the problems of adolescence.*

adolescent /adə'lɛsənt/ *noun*; *adjective*
▷ ***noun***: **adolescents**
An **adolescent** is a young person, especially between the ages of 13 and 16, who is passing from childhood to adulthood: *The trouble with many adolescents is that they're too shy to discuss their problems.*
▷ ***adjective***
1 Someone who is **adolescent** is at the stage between childhood and adulthood: *She has two adolescent sons.* **2** (*derogatory*) People sometimes refer to silly or immature conduct as **adolescent** behaviour.

adopt /ə'dɒpt/ *verb*: **adopts, adopting, adopted**
1 You **adopt** children of other parents when you take them into your own family, becoming their legal parent yourself: *They've adopted a four-month-old boy.* □ *We've decided to adopt.* [see also **foster**] **2** You **adopt** a policy, attitude, behaviour or a habit when you develop it or start using it: *We've adopted a new procedure for testing reading skills.* **3** You **adopt** someone's idea or suggestion when you use it or follow it: *The committee voted to adopt her suggestion for money-raising.* **4** You **adopt** a position when you put your body into it: *Conscious of the camera, she tried to adopt an elegant pose.* — *adjective* **adopted:** *They have two adopted children and two of their own.*

adoption /ə'dɒpʃən/ *noun*: **adoptions**
1 (*uncount or count*) **Adoption** is the act of adopting a child or the process of being adopted: *Single mothers are being persuaded to give their babies up for adoption.* □ *The number of adoptions has decreased as a result of widespread contraception.* **2** (*uncount*) The **adoption** of a policy or suggestion is the act of accepting and following it: *the adoption of new measures to fight the spread of AIDS.*

adoptive /ə'dɒptɪv/ *adjective*
People who adopt a child are its **adoptive** parents.

adorable /ə'dɔːrəbəl/ *adjective* (*informal*)
You call something such as a baby or young animal **adorable** if you think they are very sweet and pretty.

adoration /adə'reɪʃən/ *noun* (*uncount*)
Adoration is great love and admiration for someone: *The adoration she felt for her professor was only too obvious to him.*

adore /ə'dɔː(r)/ *verb*: **adores, adoring, adored**
1 You **adore** someone whom you love or admire deeply: *He secretly adored his music teacher.* **2** (*informal*) You say you **adore** something if you like it a lot: *I adore apricots.* **3** (*religion*) People **adore** God when they worship him. — *adjective* **adoring:** *He gave her an adoring glance.* — *adverb* **adoringly:** *She leant adoringly over the baby's cot.*

adorn /ə'dɔːn/ *verb*: **adorns, adorning, adorned**
To **adorn** something is to make decorative additions to it: *Adorning a tree with coloured lights and hanging ornaments seems a strange custom.* — *noun* (*uncount or count*) **adornment:** *Of all the animals, only man goes in for bodily adornment.* □ *Her only adornment was a narrow gold chain round her neck.*

adrenalin or **adrenaline** /ə'drɛnəlɪn/ *noun* (*uncount*)
Adrenalin is a hormone that is produced in your body when you are angry, excited or frightened, which makes your heart beat faster, so as to build up a store of energy in case you need to act quickly.

adrift /ə'drɪft/ *adjective*
A boat is **adrift** if it is not tied up or is floating about without being steered: *The boat had been cut adrift.*

adroit /ə'drɔɪt/ *adjective*
Someone who is **adroit** at something does it skilfully: *He was adroit at defending himself and the interests of his family.* □ *We called in one of our most adroit negotiators.* [*same as* **expert**] — *adverb* **adroitly:** *She steered the car adroitly through the rush-hour traffic.*

adulation /adjʊ'leɪʃən/ *noun* (*uncount*)
Adulation is praise of an extreme, excessive or uncritical kind: *Most groups realize that the adulation they get from teenagers is not going to last for ever.*

adult /'adʌlt/ or /ə'dʌlt/ *noun*; *adjective*
▷ ***noun***: **adults**
An **adult** is a fully grown and mature person: *This game should appeal to adults and children alike.* [*same as* **grown-up**]
▷ ***adjective***
1 An **adult** person or animal is one that is fully grown and mature in development and behaviour: *The adult butterfly emerges fully formed from the chrysalis.* **2** **Adult** concerns and interests are those that are typical of, or suitable for, mature people: *She felt she wasn't yet ready for adult responsibilities.* [*same as* **grown-up**]

adulterate /ə'dʌltəreɪt/ *verb*
To **adulterate** something such as food or drink is to add some inferior substance to it: *The cooking oil had been adulterated with a dangerous petrol-based chemical.*

adultery /ə'dʌltərɪ/ *noun* (*uncount*)
A married man or woman commits **adultery** when they have sexual relations with a person who is not their wife or husband: *He divorced her on the grounds of adultery.*

adulthood /'adʌlthʊd/ *noun* (*uncount*)
Adulthood is the state of being fully grown, developed and mature, or the period of your life after you reach this state: *Her children had all reached adulthood and left home.*

advance /əd'vɑːns/ *verb*; *noun*; *adjective*
▷ ***verb***: **advances, advancing, advanced**
1 To **advance** is to move forward or progress: *She advanced towards him, holding out her hand.* **2** Troops **advance**, or their commander **advances** them, when they move forward, *eg* to capture some objective, or in preparation for attack: *Enemy troops were advancing towards the capital.* **3** Someone **advances** on you when they come towards you threateningly: *He advanced on her, holding a knife.* **4** People or things **advance** when they develop further or make progress: *Computer technology advances further every day.* **5** You **advance** something such as an appointment, or its date, when you schedule it for a time earlier than the time originally planned: *They had to advance the wedding by a fortnight.* [*same as* **bring forward**] **6** You **advance** a sum of money to someone when you lend it to them, or pay it to them before it is due for payment: *Could you advance me £150?* — *adjective* **advancing:** *They fled before the advancing troops.* □ *an advancing storm.*
▷ ***noun***: **advances**
1 (*count or uncount*) The **advance** of something is its development or progress forward; an **advance** is a move or step forward: *The army were preparing for the next day's advance.* □ *recent advances in medicine.* **2** An **advance** is a sum of money lent to someone, or paid before it is due: *I've already given you an advance this month.* **3** (*used in the plural*; *old*) Someone makes **advances** to you if they indicate that they would like to make friends, or have a sexual relationship, with you: *She rejected his advances.*
▷ ***adjective***
Advance warning or notice is warning or notice of some event given before it occurs: *They gave us advance warning that the electricity would be cut off for two hours.* [*same as* **prior**]
▷ ***phrases*** **1** You do something such as book a theatre seat, or pay the rent, **in advance**, if you do so before the event or date concerned: *The rent is £50 a week and payable in advance.* **2** A person or thing is **in advance of** others if they have progressed further than others: *Their research is far in advance of ours.*

advanced /əd'vɑːnst/ *adjective*
1 Countries that are described as **advanced** have a high standard of living and of medical and social services, education, technology and industry: *the industrially advanced democracies of the West.* **2** An **advanced** course of study is suitable for **advanced** students, or those who have already learnt the basic principles, facts or skills and are ready for more complicated or difficult work: *She's taking her advanced driver's test.* **3** **Advanced** ideas are new or modern ones: *advanced methods of teaching number.*

advancement /əd'vɑːnsmənt/ *noun* (*uncount*)
1 **Advancement** is progress and development: *The Royal Society for the Advancement of Science.* **2** A person's **advancement** is their promotion at work or their improvement in status: *Her chief concern in life was her personal advancement.*

advantage /əd'vɑːntɪdʒ/ *noun* (*count or uncount*): **advantages**
1 An **advantage** that a person or thing has over others is a circumstance that may help them to do better than others, or succeed where others fail: *Your knowledge of computers gives you an advantage over the other candidates.* [*same as* **edge**] **2** The **advantage** of something is the benefit it brings: *the advantages of electric light.* **3** (*tennis*) The score is announced as '**Advantage** so-and-so' when so-and-so has won the point after deuce.
▷ ***phrases*** **1** You **take advantage of** an opportunity or situation when you make the best use of it: *Why don't you take advantage of his offer while it lasts?* **2** You **take advantage of** a person when you treat them unfairly or make selfish use of their kindness or good nature: *The children tend to take advantage of their grandparents.* **3 a** Something that is **to your advantage** is useful to you: *It would be to your advantage to get experience in English-teaching abroad.* **b** You use a cir-

cumstance **to your advantage** if you use it to benefit yourself: *She had very early on learnt to use her good looks to her advantage.*

advantageous /advən'teɪdʒəs/ *adjective*
Something that is **advantageous** helps you or benefits you in some way: *It would not be advantageous for you to go abroad at this stage in your career.* [*same as* **beneficial**]

advent /'advɛnt/ *noun* (*used in the singular*)
The **advent** of something is its first appearance in the world, or its invention: *Life has changed so much since the advent of electric light.*

adventure /əd'vɛntʃə(r)/ *noun*: **adventures**
1 An **adventure** is an exciting or dangerous experience, such as a daring or eventful journey: *They had had some exciting adventures in Africa, including an encounter with a crocodile.* **2** (*uncount*) **Adventure** is the excitement of risk or danger: *This is the holiday for young people in search of adventure.*

adventurer /əd'vɛntʃərə(r)/ *noun*: **adventurers**
An **adventurer** is someone eager for adventure, who enjoys dangerous experiences and daring activities: *She had gone off to Antarctica with some fellow adventurers.*

adventurous /əd'vɛntʃərəs/ *adjective*
1 An **adventurous** person enjoys dangerous experiences and daring activities, and likes to take risks. [*same as* **intrepid**] **2** An **adventurous** experience is full of excitement, danger, or daring activities: *They spent an adventurous three weeks crossing the Sahara.*

adverb /'advɜːb/ *noun*: **adverbs**
1 An **adverb** is one of the 'parts of speech', and usually describes or modifies the action of a verb, and may come before or after it (*She stopped immediately. He suddenly sat up. They proceeded cautiously.*). **2** Some **adverbs** can modify adjectives or other adverbs (*I'm particularly grateful. You've done particularly well.*). The commonest adverbs of this kind are those labelled *intensifying* in this dictionary, which have a meaning like 'very', and those labelled *moderating*, which have a meaning like 'fairly'. **3** The **adverbs** of direction, such as *down, up, in, out, back, forward, across*, which are commonly used to form phrasal verbs, cannot come before the verb (*He threw the envelope away. They ran off.*). **4** Some **adverbs** are used to comment on a whole sentence (*Unfortunately he couldn't come. I have no serious objections however. Apparently I should have asked his permission.* Such adverbs are labelled *sentence adverbs* in this dictionary. **5** A small group of **adverbs** have a meaning similar to 'not' (*I had hardly arrived when the telephone rang. You seldom see them nowadays. I'd scarcely call him an expert. Rarely have I experienced such rudeness.*). Such adverbs are labelled '*used like a negative*' in this dictionary.

adverbial /əd'vɜːbɪəl/ *adjective*
Adverbial means relating to, or like, an adverb: *the adverbial ending -ly.* — *adverb* **adverbially:** *'Hard' is used adverbially in 'He hit her hard'.*

adversary /'advəsərɪ/ *noun*: **adversaries**
An **adversary** is an opponent or an enemy: *He had a formidable adversary in Becker.*

adverse /'advɜːs/ *adjective*
Adverse circumstances, comments, results or effects are those that are unfavourable to you: *It's amazing how the schoolchildren learn anything in such adverse conditions.* □ *All this worry is likely to have an adverse effect on her health.* — *adverb* **adversely:** *I'm afraid their advertising campaign has affected our sales adversely.*

adversity /əd'vɜːsɪtɪ/ *noun* (*uncount*)
Adversity is circumstances that cause trouble, difficulty or sorrow: *She struggled on bravely in the face of adversity.*

advert /'advɜːt/ *noun* (*informal*): **adverts**
An **advert** is an advertisement.

advertise /'advətaɪz/ *verb*: **advertises**, **advertising**, **advertised**
1 You **advertise** a product or something for sale, or services you are offering, when you tell the public about them, *eg* by means of a short television film, or a notice or article in a newspaper or magazine: *The shampoo was currently being advertised on television.* □ *They're advertising a management job in this Sunday's Observer, which I thought I might apply for.* **2** You **advertise** something such as the time of a performance or meeting when you announce it publicly, *eg* in a newspaper: *The time of the funeral had been wrongly advertised.* **3** You **advertise** for a person or thing when you tell people publicly that you are wanting them or looking for them, *eg* by putting a notice in a newspaper or shop window: *We advertised for a nanny and got over 60 applications.*

advertisement /əd'vɜːtɪsmənt/ *noun*: **advertisements**
An **advertisement** is a public notice or announcement, or a picture or poster, *eg* in a magazine or on a wall in the street, or a short television film, that advertises or tells people about something such as a product, services or something else for sale, or a vacant job that can be applied for: *She was studying the advertisement page of the Evening News.*

advertiser /'advətaɪzə(r)/ *noun*: **advertisers**
The **advertiser** is the person or business that pays for a product, services or goods for sale to be advertised in a newspaper or on television.

advertising /'advətaɪzɪŋ/ *noun* (*uncount*)
Advertising is the business of designing and showing advertisements for products and services: *He went into advertising after leaving university.*

advice /əd'vaɪs/ *noun* (*uncount*)
You give someone **advice** when you suggest what they should do in a certain situation; you take or follow someone's **advice** when you do as they suggest: *I asked her advice about the most suitable schools for the children.* □ *My advice on that would be just to wait and see.*

advisable /əd'vaɪzəbl/ *adjective*
Something that is **advisable** is a wise or sensible thing to do: *It's advisable to insure your jewellery and valuables separately from your house contents.* □ *What's the most advisable course in the circumstances?*

advise /əd'vaɪz/ *verb*: **advises**, **advising**, **advised**
1 You **advise** someone when you give them advice or suggest what they should do in a particular situation: *I would advise you to tell the police immediately.* □ *She advised me not to say anything.* □ *I wouldn't advise flying in the circumstances.* □ *I advised him that he should apply for a grant.* **2** You **advise** something when you recommend or prescribe it: *The doctor had advised a week's bed rest.* **3** You **advise** someone on something when you give them advice or guidance on it: *Our staff can advise you on the type of career you could consider.* **4** (*formal or legal*) You **advise** someone of something when you inform them about it: *Please advise us of your intentions in this matter.* □ *I was advised that the fee would be £150.* [*same as* **notify**]

adviser (*also AmE* **advisor**) /əd'vaɪzə(r)/ *noun*: **advisers**
An **adviser** is someone who gives advice, information or guidance, *eg* to a person in government or administration: *He had been her personal adviser on press relations.*

advocate *noun; verb*
▷ ***noun*** /ˈadvəkət/: **advocates**
1 An **advocate** is a lawyer who defends an accused person in a court trial, or, *eg* in Scotland, is similar to an English barrister and speaks for or against the accused. **2** An **advocate** of an idea, policy or course of action is a person who supports or recommends it: *She was one of the earliest advocates of contraception.*
▷ ***verb*** /ˈadvəkeɪt/: **advocates, advocating, advocated**
You **advocate** a policy, idea or proposal when you recommend or support it, usually publicly: *There's now quite a strong pressure group advocating spelling reform in English.* [*same as* **promote**]

aerial /ˈɛərɪəl/ *noun; adjective*
▷ ***noun***: **aerials**
An **aerial** is a wire or rod on a radio or television set, or on a building or vehicle, that sends or receives signals. [*same as* **antenna**; see picture at **car**]
▷ ***adjective***
1 Aerial describes things that are positioned, or happen, above the ground or in the air: *aerial combat* □ *an aerial railway.* **2 Aerial** photographs are taken from the air of things on the ground.

aerobics /ɛəˈroʊbɪks/ *noun* (*uncount*)
Aerobics is a system of physical exercise consisting of rapidly repeated, energetic movements, intended to increase the supply of oxygen in the blood and strengthen the heart and lungs: *an aerobics class.*

aerodrome /ˈɛərədroʊm/ *noun* (*BrE*): **aerodromes**
An **aerodrome** is an airfield for private or military aircraft.

aerodynamic /ɛərədaɪˈnamɪk/ *adjective*
Aerodynamic means relating to the movement of objects through the air; an **aerodynamic** design for a vehicle or aircraft is one that aims at speed with minimum use of energy. — *adverb* **aerodynamically:** *Aerodynamically, the bee is badly designed.*

aeroplane /ˈɛərəpleɪn/ *noun*: **aeroplanes**
An **aeroplane** is a vehicle with wings and one or more engines, designed for flying through the air.

aerosol /ˈɛərəsɒl/ *noun*: **aerosols**
An **aerosol** is a container in which a mixture of liquid or solid particles, and gas, is packed under pressure, to be released in a fine spray or foam at the press of a button.

aesthetic (*AmE* **esthetic**) /ɪsˈθɛtɪk/ *adjective*
Aesthetic means relating to beauty and art and to people's perception, understanding, appreciation and enjoyment of them. — *adverb* **aesthetically:** *an aesthetically satisfactory design.*

afar /əˈfɑː(r)/ *adverb* (*literary*)
▷ ***phrase*** **From afar** means from a long distance away: *He had admired her from afar but never dared speak to her.*

affable /ˈafəbəl/ *adjective*
An **affable** person is someone who has a pleasant, friendly manner, and is easy to talk to: *She was being very affable to all the guests.* [*same as* **genial**] — *adverb* **affably:** *He smiled affably.*

affair /əˈfɛə(r)/ *noun*: **affairs**
1 An **affair** is a particular matter, situation or connected series of incidents: *A report will be submitted to directors outlining the whole disgraceful affair.* **2** An event can be called an **affair**: *The party was rather a noisy affair.* **3** You say that something is your own **affair** when you think it is a private and personal matter and that other people shouldn't interfere in it: *What I do in my free time is my own affair.* **4** If you tell someone that something is their **affair**, you mean that you are taking no responsibility for it: *If you want to risk losing your job, that's your affair.* **5** Two people, one at least of whom is married to someone else, are said to be having an **affair** if they are having a sexual relationship: *She had a shortlived affair with him some years ago.* **6** (*used in the plural*) **Affairs** are matters relating to a particular subject or situation: *The Foreign Minster is the member of the cabinet responsible for foreign affairs.* [see also **current affairs, state of affairs**] **7** (*used in the plural*) Your **affairs** are personal matters relating to such things as finance, tax and citizenship: *It's time you organized your affairs properly.*

affect /əˈfɛkt/ *verb*: **affects, affecting, affected**
1 A person or thing **is affected** by something if it has an effect on them and influences or alters them in some way: *All these interruptions have seriously affected the schedule.* □ *How will the new tax arrangements affect you?* □ *The century has been full of inventions that have affected the way we live.* **2** You **are affected** by something if it moves or touches you and causes strong emotions in you, such as sorrow or pity: *She was deeply affected by the poverty and starvation she had witnessed* **3** A disease **affects** the body or part of it when it infects or attacks it: *Multiple sclerosis affects the protective sheaths that cover the nerves.* □ *His lungs were already badly affected.* **4** Someone **affects** an attitude or way of behaving when they adopt it and pretend that it is genuine and natural for them: *Sometimes she affected an annoying childish tone.* □ *He affects helplessness when it comes to computers.* □ *She affected to enjoy modern music.* [*same as* **put on, feign**]

affectation /afɛkˈteɪʃən/ *noun* (*count or uncount*): **affectations**
An **affectation** is an unnatural way of behaving adopted or put on to impress or interest other people: *I think his stammer is just an affectation.*

affected /əˈfɛktɪd/ *adjective* (*derogatory*)
Someone who is **affected** tends to behave unnaturally, apparently to impress other people with their good taste, breeding and intelligence: *He had an affected voice.* — *adverb* **affectedly:** *He dressed rather affectedly.*

affection /əˈfɛkʃən/ *noun* (*uncount*)
Affection is strong liking, close to love, that you feel for another person, or for a pet, or for something such as your home: *She had a special affection for the place.*

affectionate /əˈfɛkʃənət/ *adjective*
Someone who is **affectionate** towards you shows their love or liking for you in the special way they treat you: *She gave him an affectionate hug.* □ *They were an affectionate pair, always supporting and helping each other.* — *adverb* **affectionately:** *She used to tease him affectionately.*

affiliate /əˈfɪlɪeɪt/ *verb*: **affiliates, affiliating, affiliated**
A smaller organization **is affiliated** to another, larger, organization when it is joined to it as its associate or branch: *Some of the industrial research centres are affiliated to the university.*

affiliation /əfɪlɪˈeɪʃən/ *noun*: **affiliations**
1 (*uncount*) **Affiliation** is the process of affiliating a smaller body or organization to a larger one, or of being affiliated. **2** (*count*) Your **affiliations** are your connections and loyalties, especially political ones.

affinity /əˈfɪnɪtɪ/ *noun* (*count, often in the singular, or uncount*): **affinities**
1 You have an **affinity** for or with something or someone if you have a strong natural liking for them or attraction towards them: *She had a natural affinity for languages.* □ *She felt a strange affinity with him, as*

though they had been friends in another life. **2** Something that has an **affinity** with something else has a similarity to it in such things as appearance or structure: *The computer does have some affinities with the human brain.* [*same as* **resemblance**]

affirm /ə'fɜːm/ *verb*: **affirms, affirming, affirmed**
1 You **affirm** something when you state it positively as the truth: *She again affirmed that she had seen him just before the accident.* [*same as* **assert**] **2** You **affirm** something such as a belief or religious faith when you state or confirm your support for it: *He affirmed his continued support of the government's economic strategy.* — *noun* **affirmation** /afə'meɪʃən/ (*uncount*): *She signalled her affirmation with a nod.*

affirmative /ə'fɜːmətɪv/ *adjective*; *noun*
▻ ***adjective***
An **affirmative** reply, word or gesture is one that says 'yes' or expresses agreement.
▻ ***noun***: **affirmatives**
The word 'yes', or any word or gesture meaning 'yes' is an **affirmative**.
▻ ***phrase*** You answer someone **in the affirmative** when you say 'yes', or indicate your agreement *eg* with a nod.

affix *verb*; *noun*
▻ ***verb*** /ə'fɪks/: **affixes, affixing, affixed**
You **affix** something such as a stamp or label to something when you stick it on or attach it.
▻ ***noun*** /'afɪks/ (*grammar*): **affixes**
An **affix** is a word-forming element that is added to a word to form another word with a related meaning; affixes such as *un-*, which are added to the beginning of a word, are **prefixes**; affixes such as *-ness*, which are added to the end of a word, are **suffixes**.

afflict /ə'flɪkt/ *verb*: **afflicts, afflicting, afflicted**
Something that is wrong with you and causes you suffering, such as a physical or mental illness or disability, **afflicts** you, or you **are afflicted** with it: *He has been afflicted with severe headaches since his accident.*

affliction /ə'flɪkʃən/ *noun* (*count or uncount*)
1 An **affliction** is something that is wrong with you and causes you suffering, such as a physical or mental illness or disability: *She has never regarded her blindness as an affliction.* **2** (*uncount*) **Affliction** is pain, suffering or distress.

affluent /'afluənt/ *adjective*
Affluent people have a lot of money and usually live expensively: *She had been used to an affluent lifestyle.* [*same as* **wealthy**] — *noun* (*uncount*) **affluence:** *The affluence of some of these young executives is extraordinary.* [*same as* **wealth**]

afford /ə'fɔːd/ *verb*: **affords, affording, afforded**
1 You can **afford** something, or can **afford** to do something, if you have enough money for it: *They couldn't possibly afford the music-school fees.* **2** You can **afford** to do something, or can **afford** something, if you can do it, or allow it to happen, without risk: *We can't afford any more mistakes of that kind.* **3** (*formal*) A circumstance **affords** you something if it provides you with it: *Not many of the students took full advantage of the library privileges afforded by their membership of the college.*

affordable /ə'fɔːdəbəl/ *adjective*
You call something **affordable** if you think you, or most people, could afford it. [*opposite* **unaffordable**]

affront /ə'frʌnt/ *noun*; *verb*
▻ ***noun***: **affronts**
An **affront** is an insult: *His wife's superiority as an athlete was an affront to his masculinity.*
▻ ***verb***: **affronts, affronting, affronted**
You **are affronted** by something if you feel hurt or insulted by it: *She was affronted by the way the men on the committee ignored her opinions.*

afield /ə'fiːld/ *adverb*
▻ ***phrase*** People come from **far afield** if they come from somewhere far away.

afloat /ə'floʊt/ *adjective*
1 You are **afloat** when you are floating: *She kicked gently to keep herself afloat.* **2** A business company is able to stay, or be kept, **afloat** if it can keep paying its debts.

afoot /ə'fʊt/ *adjective*
You say that there is a plan or scheme **afoot** when something particular is being planned: *There's a proposal afoot to change the accounting system.*

aforementioned /ə'fɔːmɛnʃənd/ *adjective*; *noun*
▻ ***adjective*** (*legal*)
Aforementioned means mentioned already in the same document or paper: *the aforementioned property.*
▻ ***noun*** (*singular or plural*)
The **aforementioned** is the person or people already mentioned in the same document or paper: *All the aforementioned have right of access.*

aforesaid /ə'fɔːsɛd/ *adjective*
Aforesaid means the same as **aforementioned**: *the aforesaid contract.*

afraid /ə'freɪd/ *adjective*
1 You are **afraid** of someone or something if you are frightened of them because of the harm they may do you: *She's always been afraid of thunder.* □ *Don't be afraid.* □ *Tell me what you're afraid of.* [*same as* **frightened**] **2** You are **afraid** to do something, or **afraid** of doing something, if you don't want to do it, or dare not do it, because of a possible danger: *Women are more and more afraid to go out alone in the dark these days.* □ *Never be afraid of telling the truth.* [*same as* **frightened**] **3** You are **afraid** of doing something you don't want to do, such as failing, or hurting someone, if you don't want to take the risk of doing it: *You're far too afraid of making mistakes.* □ *He was afraid of upsetting his mother.* □ *She was afraid of not being able to finish the exam in the time allowed.* [*same as* **frightened**] **4** You are **afraid** of something happening, or **afraid** that something may happen, or may have happened, when you realize there is a worrying possibility of it: *She was afraid he might be offended if she refused to have lunch with him.* □ *He was afraid he was going to be late and began to run.* □ *I was afraid you'd be angry.* □ *When I couldn't find you I was afraid you might have left without me.* □ *They were afraid I'd got lost.* □ *He was afraid of her dying and leaving him all alone.* [*same as* **frightened**] **5** You say you are **afraid** that something is so to show that you are sorry or concerned that it is, sometimes just as a polite way of expressing regret or disagreement, or apologizing: *I'm afraid she's quite badly hurt.* □ *I'm afraid we must expect more deaths before a cure is found.* □ *This has come as a shock to you, I'm afraid.* □ *I'm afraid Mr Thomas is engaged at the moment.* □ *I'm afraid I've spilt coffee on your magazine.* □ *You've missed the point, I'm afraid.* □ *'Am I too late to get a ticket?' 'I'm afraid so.'* □ *'Are you coming with me?' 'I'm afraid not; I'm busy.'*

afresh /ə'frɛʃ/ *adverb*
You start **afresh** when you start doing something all over again from the beginning, usually in a different way: *She deleted everything she'd written and started afresh.* [*same as* **anew**]

African /'afrɪkən/ *adjective*; *noun*
▻ ***adjective***
African means belonging to the continent of Africa, its countries, peoples or languages.

▻ ***noun***: **Africans**
An **African** is a person, usually black, who lives in Africa or comes from Africa.

Afro- /ˈafroʊ/ *prefix*
Afro- is combined with geographical adjectives to mean belonging or relating both to Africa and to somewhere else, so **Afro-Caribbean** means belonging or relating both to Africa and the Caribbean area, and **Afro-American** both to Africa and America.

after /ˈɑːftə(r)/ *preposition; adverb; conjunction*
▻ ***preposition***
1 a Something happens **after** an event, time or date when it happens later than it, or in the time following it: *Are you free after lunch?* □ *I don't like going out alone after dark.* □ *After leaving university she worked abroad for a year.* □ *I must wash the dishes and make the beds; after that there's the shopping.* □ *He died on or sometime after 10 August.* □ *I won't be back till after 11.30.* [*opposite* **before**] **b** (*AmE*) In stating the time, **after** means the same as 'past': *It's already ten after two.* **c** Something that happens time **after** time keeps happening, or happens often; something that happens day **after** day, week **after** week, or year **after** year, happens every day, week or year: *He was making the same mistake time after time.* **d** Events of a certain kind happen, or people do a certain thing, one **after** another, or one **after** the other, when they follow one another quickly: *Disasters came one after the other.* □ *One after another, her friends deserted her.*
2 a Something is or comes **after** another thing if it follows it in position, order or arrangement: *She has a string of degrees and qualifications after her name.* □ *Take the first turning left after the church.* [*opposite* **before**] **b** You go **after** someone when you follow them: *I ran after him with his umbrella.* **c** You call or gaze **after** someone when you shout to them, or watch them, as they move away: *'Good luck!' she shouted after them.* **d** You close the door **after** you when you close it behind you as you come through it. **e** You clear up **after** someone when you tidy up the mess they have made.
3 You call a child **after** a person, or call a place **after** *eg* a person or event when you give them the name of the person or event: *We're going to call him Michael after his uncle.* □ *The village was named Waterloo after the battle.*
4 a Someone who is **after** you is looking for you or chasing you, in order *eg* to kill, arrest or punish you: *The police will be after you if you park there.* **b** You are **after** something when you want it or are trying to get it: *She's after a managerial job.* **c** You ask or enquire **after** a person when you ask a friend or relation of theirs how they are.
5 You use **after** to mean as a result of, or because of: *I never want to see him again after the mean way he treated me.*
▻ ***adverb***
After is sometimes used, usually with *soon*, to mean later: *She agreed to take the job, but regretted her decision soon after.*

> **Afterwards** is more idiomatic than **after**: *She's having lunch with me, and afterwards* (not *after*) *we're going for a walk.*

▻ ***conjunction:*** *After she left university she worked in publishing.* □ *You can peel the potatoes after you've done the washing-up.*
▻ ***phrases***
1 a You use **after all** with the meaning 'in spite of what was expected' when stating something surprising: *She didn't get the job after all.* **b After all** also means 'because it must be remembered that': *You can't expect to master English in a few days; after all, it's a difficult language.*

> **After all** is never used to mean 'finally' or 'at last'.

2 You say '**after you**' politely to someone to ask them to go in front of you, *eg* through a door.

after-effect /ˈɑːftərɪfɛkt/ *noun* (*usually in the plural*): **after-effects**
The **after-effects** of a happening are circumstances or conditions, especially unpleasant ones, that follow as a result of it: *She died from the after-effects of smoke-inhalation.*

afterlife /ˈɑːftəlaɪf/ *noun* (*used in the singular*)
The **afterlife** is the continued existence of your spirit or soul after your death.

aftermath /ˈɑftəmaθ/ *noun* (*used in the singular*)
The **aftermath** of an event, especially a great or terrible one such as a war, is the situation or conditions that result from it: *There was panic and confusion in the aftermath of the earthquake.*

afternoon /ɑːftəˈnuːn/ *noun* (*count or uncount*): **afternoons**
The **afternoon** is the part of the day that starts at lunchtime or midday and finishes when evening begins, at about 6.00 pm: *Could we meet this afternoon?* □ *Tomorrow afternoon would be more convenient.* □ *He telephoned me on Tuesday afternoon.* □ *The meeting went on till 3 o'clock in the afternoon.* □ *The accident happened on the afternoon of 31 August.*

aftershave /ˈɑːftəʃeɪv/ *noun* (*uncount*)
Aftershave, or **aftershave lotion**, is a scented liquid men put on their faces after shaving.

afterthought /ˈɑːftəθɔːt/ *noun*: **afterthoughts**
You do, say or suggest something as an **afterthought** when you do it casually at a late stage, *eg* when plans are almost complete, or an activity almost over: *'You could come too,' he suggested as an afterthought.*

afterwards /ˈɑːftəwədz/ (*AmE also* **afterward**) *adverb*
Something happens **afterwards** when it happens later than the event already mentioned: *I was a bit rude to her at the meeting, and afterwards I apologized.* □ *I've got some shopping to do, but I can join you afterwards.*

> **Afterwards** comes at the end of the sentence, or just before the subject.

again /əˈgɛn/ or /əˈgeɪn/ *adverb*
1 Something happens **again** if it happens another time, or for the second time: *I'll ring you again tonight to confirm the arrangement.* □ *It was lovely to meet you again.*

> At the beginning of a sentence, **again** is often used with 'once': *Once again, rain spoilt the outing.*

2 Something or someone is in a certain state or position **again** when they return to their previous or normal state or place: *I had flu last week but I'm better again.* □ *Would you switch the light on again?* □ *It's good to be home again.* **3** Twice as much **again** means twice the quantity already mentioned. **4** (*sentence adverb*) You use **again** when you are asking someone to repeat information they have already given you: *What's the name of your hotel again?* **5** (*sentence adverb*) You use **again** to indicate that the present case being discussed is like one considered previously: *Again, it's a question of willpower.*
▻ ***phrases*** **1** Something happens **again and again**, or **over and over again**, or **time and time again**, or **time and again** if it happens often or repeatedly: *I've told her*

time and again to switch off the computer at night. **2** You use **then again** or **there again** when making a comment that conflicts with something that has just been said: *I know the children shouldn't eat so many chips; there again, there isn't much else they actually like.* □ *He says he'll come, but then again he may not manage to.*

against /ə'gɛnst/ or /ə'geɪnst/ *preposition; adverb*

▷ ***preposition***

1 a Something is, or leans, or presses, **against** something else when it is touching it or pressing on it: *She stood the ladder against the wall.* □ *He leant against the railings to get his breath back.* □ *We were all pushing against one another, trying to get into the lift.* **b** You knock **against** something when you bump into it: *I knocked against her and spilt her coffee.* **c** Heavy rain beats **against** the window when it strikes it.

2 a You compete or fight **against** someone or something when you try to beat them: *You vary your strategy according to whom you're playing against.* □ *The match against Rangers has been cancelled.* □ *We're losing the fight against pollution.* **b** You use force, a weapon, or other means **against** someone or something in fighting or combating them: *The police used tear gas against the demonstrators.* **c** You guard **against**, take precautions **against**, or protect yourself **against**, possible harm, when you do something to prevent it or lessen its effects: *Are you properly insured against fire?* □ *I'm protected against most tropical diseases.* **d** Something is **against** the law if there is a law forbidding it: *It's against the law to park on a double yellow line.* **e** You are **against** someone or something if you oppose them or disagree with them: *Everyone seems to be against me.* □ *Are you for or against corporal punishment for children?* □ *I was against borrowing the money.* **f** A personal circumstance or quality is **against** you if it is a disadvantage to you: *His youth is against him.*

3 a You move, sail or swim **against** the tide or current when you move in the opposite direction to it. **b** The odds or chances **against** a certain thing happening are the odds or chances that it won't happen.

4 a Currencies move up or down **against** one another when their relative values alter: *The pound lost two cents against the dollar.* **b** Something is seen **against** a certain background when it is seen in contrast to it, or in relation to it.

▷ ***adverb:*** *There were five in favour of the idea and two against.* □ *The English team might just win, but the odds against are high.*

▷ ***phrases*** **1** You use **as against** when making comparisons: *Our sales total this year was $5504000, as against last year's $4600000.* **2** You **have** something **against** someone or something if you have a reason for disliking or disapproving of them: *She's constantly rude to me; I don't know what she's got against me.*

age /eɪdʒ/ *noun; verb*

▷ ***noun*** (*uncount or count*): **ages**

1 Your **age** is the number of years you have been alive: *What age were you in 1981?* □ *What ages are your sons?* □ *She finally learnt to drive at the age of eighty.* □ *He died at a great age.* □ *She's only three years of age.* □ *I think she's my age.* □ *At your age I wasn't allowed to stay up late.* **2** (*uncount*) You use **age** in combinations such as *old age* or *middle age* to mean a particular period of life: *the troubles of old age* □ *school-age children* □ *She reaches retirement age next year.* **3** (*uncount*) **Age** is also the state or circumstance of being old: *Age has its compensations.* □ *The pages were yellow with age.* **4** An **age** is a period in the development or history of the world: *the succession of ice ages* □ *pottery of the Bronze Age* □ *the Middle Ages* □ *the Jazz Age* □ *the age of the motor car* □ *the fascinating study of fashion through the ages.* **5** (*informal*) You use **ages** or, more rarely, an **age**, to mean a long time: *We waited ages for a bus.* □ *It took him ages to get changed.*

▷ ***verb***: **ages, ageing** or **aging, aged**

1 People **age** as they look and feel older: *He's aged a lot since he lost his wife.* **2** Something **ages** you when it causes you to look or feel older: *All this worry has aged her.* □ *Sunlight ages the skin.*

▷ ***phrases*** **1** If you tell someone to **act their age** or **be their age** you are telling them to stop being childish or silly. **2** You **come of age** when you become legally old enough to have an adult's rights and duties. **3** You **feel** or **look your age** if you feel or look as old as you are. **4** Someone who does something when they are **under age** is too young to be legally allowed to do it: *the problem of under-age drinking.*

aged *adjective; noun*

▷ ***adjective***

1 /eɪdʒd/ You use **aged** in stating someone's age: *We have two sons, aged 14 and 12.* □ *middle-aged and elderly people.* **2** /'eɪdʒɪd/ An **aged** person is someone very old: *We both have aged parents to take care of.*

▷ ***noun*** /'eɪdʒɪd/ (*plural*)

The **aged** are old people as a class.

age group /'eɪdʒ gru:p/ *noun*

An **age group** is the people of a certain age, or between two particualr ages: *the 35-45 age group.*

ageing or **aging** /'eɪdʒɪŋ/ *adjective*

An **ageing** person is growing, and usually looking, older: *an ageing actor.*

ageless /'eɪdʒləs/ *adjective*

Ageless means never growing old, or never looking any older.

agency /'eɪdʒənsɪ/ *noun*: **agencies**

1 An **agency** is an office or business providing a particular service: *advertising agencies.* **2** (*AmE*) A government department can be called an **agency**: *the Central Intelligence Agency.*

agenda /ə'dʒɛndə/ *noun*: **agendas**

An **agenda** is the list of matters to be discussed at a meeting, or a list of things to be done or dealt with: *Shall we go on to item 4 on the agenda?*

agent /'eɪdʒənt/ *noun*: **agents**

1 An **agent** is a person who represents an organization and acts on its behalf: *travel agents* □ *house agents* □ *insurance agents* □ *our company's agent in Cairo.* **2** An actor's or musician's **agent** is a person who seeks suitable work for them, and arranges interviews, auditions and fees; a person's business **agent** attends to his or her financial affairs. **3** (*now old*) An **agent** or **secret agent** is a spy. **4** (*technical*) A substance that has a particular effect, especially one that is used for the purpose of producing this effect, is an **agent**: *water-purifying agents* □ *detergents and other cleansing agents.*

age-old /eɪdʒ'oʊld/ *adjective*

An **age-old** custom or tradition is one that has existed for centuries, or longer than people can remember.

aggravate /'agrəveɪt/ *verb*: **aggravates, aggravating, aggravated**

1 Something **aggravates** a bad situation, problem or illness if it makes it worse: *He was suffering from an unpleasant infection aggravated by malnutrition and exhaustion.* [*same as* **exacerbate**; *opposite* **alleviate**] **2** Someone or something that **aggravates** you makes you annoyed: *His constant questions aggravated her.* [*same as* **annoy**, **irritate**; *opposite* **soothe**] — *adjective* **aggravating:** *She had an aggravating habit of finishing* *off your sentences for you.* — *noun* (*uncount or count*) **aggravation** /agrə'veɪʃən/: *minor daily aggravations* □ *aggravation in the workplace.*

aggression /ə'grɛʃən/ *noun* (*uncount*)
1 Aggression is violent or hostile behaviour towards others, or the attacking of others, without reasonable cause: *The invasion was condemned as an act of aggression.* **2** Your **aggression** is the emotional force in you that makes you behave in a competitive, dominant or hostile manner towards others.

aggressive /ə'grɛsɪv/ *adjective*
1 (*derogatory*) An **aggressive** person is someone who is too ready to attack others or behave in a rude or hostile manner towards them: *aggressive behaviour* □ *Don't be so aggressive.* **2** An **aggressive** salesperson or business person deals with others in a determined and assertive way in trying to achieve his or her goals and ambitions. [*same as* **pushy**] — *adjective* **aggressively:** *He started to behave aggressively so she called the police.*

aggressor /ə'grɛsə(r)/ *noun*: **aggressors**
An **aggressor** is someone who attacks someone else without reasonable cause: *There were accusations that the US had been the blatant aggressor in the conflict.* [*same as* **attacker, assailant**]

aggrieved /ə'gri:vd/ *adjective*
1 You feel **aggrieved** when you think you have been treated badly or unfairly and are angry and upset about it. **2** (*legal*) The **aggrieved** party in a legal case is the person against whom an illegal act has been committed.

aggro /'agroʊ/ *noun* (*uncount*; *BrE*; *informal*)
1 Aggro is violent or threatening behaviour. **2** Something causes **aggro** if it causes ill feeling and quarrelling between people.

aghast /ə'gɑ:st/ *adjective*
You are **aghast** when you are filled with horror and astonishment: *I was aghast at her rudeness.* [*same as* **horrified, appalled**]

agile /'adʒaɪl/ (*AmE* /'adʒəl/) *adjective*
1 An **agile** person or animal is quick, lively and athletic in movement: *The more agile members of the party climbed to the top of the rock.* [*same as* **nimble, athletic**] **2** Someone who has an **agile** mind or wits thinks quickly and argues cleverly. [*same as* **astute**] — *noun* (*uncount*) **agility** /ə'dʒɪlɪtɪ/: *That child has the agility of a monkey.* □ *agility of thought.*

agitate /'adʒɪteɪt/ *verb*: **agitates, agitating, agitated**
1 Something **agitates** you if it makes you nervous and anxious: *This news is bound to agitate him.* [*same as* **worry, trouble, unsettle**] **2** People **agitate** for or against something when they try to stir up public opinion in favour of it or against it: *We should start agitating for spelling reforms in English.* — *adjective* **agitated:** *His face wore an agitated expression.* — *noun* (*uncount*) **agitation** /adʒɪ'teɪʃən/: *He was in a state of visible agitation.* □ *periods of political agitation.*

agitator /'adʒɪteɪtə(r)/ *noun* (*often derogatory*): **agitators**
An **agitator** is a person who tries to bring about social or political change by stirring up public feeling and causing discontent.

agnostic /ag'nɒstɪk/ *noun*; *adjective*
▻ ***noun***: **agnostics**
An **agnostic** is a person who believes that it is impossible to know whether there is a God or not.
▻ ***adjective:*** *He takes an agnostic view.*

ago /ə'goʊ/ *adverb*
Something happened a certain length of time **ago** if it is that amount of time since it happened: *I was speaking to her only a week ago.* □ *It all happened a long time ago.* □ *How long ago did you buy this house?* □ *We must have moved in twenty-three years ago.*

> **Ago** means back in time from now. When you want to refer to a time before a particular time in the past, use *before*, *earlier*, or *previously*: *He lost his job three months ago.* But: *We eventually found the restaurant we'd eaten at many years before, on our honeymoon.*

agog /ə'gɒg/ *adjective*
People are **agog** when they are full of excitement, expectation and curiosity about something: *The children were all agog to know who had won.* □ *They crowded round the window, agog with curiosity.*

agonize or **agonise** /'agənaɪz/ *verb*: **agonizes, agonizing, agonized**
You **agonize** over something such as a difficult decision when you keep worrying about it and can't stop thinking about it.

agonized or **agonised** /'agənaɪzd/ *adjective*
An **agonized** voice, face, expression or cry indicates severe distress or suffering: *He knew from her agonized tone that something had gone badly wrong.*

agonizing or **agonising** /'agənaɪzɪŋ/ *adjective*
An **agonizing** pain or an **agonizing** decision causes you severe suffering or anxiety. — *adverb* **agonizingly:** *agonizingly uncomfortable.*

agony /'agənɪ/ *noun* (*uncount or count*): **agonies**
Agony is severe physical pain or mental suffering: *He died in agony.* □ *In an agony of despair he watched her leave.*

agree /ə'gri:/ *verb*: **agrees, agreeing, agreed**
1 You **agree** with someone when you have, or indicate that you have, the same opinion about something as they have: *'I believe he was wrongly punished.' 'I quite agree.'* □ *He agreed with me that we needed more time.* □ *She and I agree on most major issues, but I didn't agree with her over* (or *about*) *these new education plans.* **2** (*informal*) You **agree** with something such as a system or policy if you approve of it: *I don't agree with forcing children to eat things they don't like.* **3** You **agree** to something such as a proposal, suggestion or request when you say yes, or accept it: *He wants me to give up my job when we're married, but I could never agree to that.* [*same as* **consent, assent**] **4** People **agree** on, or **agree**, something such as a schedule, a date, or a policy, when they decide on it after discussion. **5** You **agree** to do something when you undertake or promise to do it after discussion or persuasion; it **is agreed**, or people **agree**, that something should be done when a common decision is made that it should be: *She reluctantly agreed to move her mother into the nursing home.* □ *It was agreed that money should be made available for the project.* □ *He agreed not to mention it again.* **6** (*often with a negative*) A food or climate **agrees** with you if it does you good: *Milk doesn't agree with me.* **7** Two reports of something such as an event, or two calculations of an amount, **agree** if they are the same: *His wife's description by no means agreed with his.* [*same as* **tally, accord, match**]
▻ ***phrases*** **1** For **agree to differ** see **differ**. **2** People **are agreed** when they have made a decision and all know what they have decided: *Are we all agreed on the plan for the day?*

agreeable /ə'gri:əbəl/ *adjective*
1 Something is **agreeable** if it is pleasant: *The hotel was good and the weather agreeable.* **2** An **agreeable**

person is someone who is friendly, and pleasant to know. **3** You are **agreeable** to a proposal or suggestion if you are happy to say yes to it or agree to it: *We could visit that exhibition, if you're agreeable.*

agreement /ə'gri:mənt/ *noun*: **agreements**
1 An **agreement** is a joint decision reached after discussion, or a contract or document stating what has been agreed: *a trade agreement* □ *An agreement was drawn up and signed by all five parties.* **2** (*uncount*) **Agreement** is the reaching of a joint decision after discussion, or the state of agreeing or holding the same opinion: *The discussion on wage increases eventually ended in agreement.*
▷ ***phrase*** You **are in agreement** with someone if you have the same opinion as they do.

agriculture /'agrɪkʌltʃə(r)/ *noun* (*uncount*)
Agriculture is the science of cultivating the land, especially for growing crops or rearing animals. — *adjective* **agricultural** /agrɪ'kʌltʃərəl/: *agricultural machinery.*

aground /ə'graʊnd/ *adjective or adverb*
A ship goes or runs **aground** when it gets stuck on rocks or sand, usually in shallow water.

ahead /ə'hɛd/ *adverb*
1 Someone or something is **ahead** of you, or **ahead**, if they are in front of you: *Look at those dark clouds ahead of us.* □ *He glanced ahead.* □ *Keep straight ahead and you can't miss the school.* □ *She was about 100 yards ahead, walking quickly.* **2 Ahead** also means in front of you in the future: *Many difficulties lie ahead.* □ *Always plan ahead.* □ *I can't think that far ahead.* **3** You are **ahead** of other people, or **ahead**, if you have progressed further in your work or studies than they have, or if you are beating them in a race or competition: *She finished well ahead.* **4** You go on **ahead** when you start off for somewhere before others: *He was sent on ahead of the others to find a good place to camp.* [*same as* **in advance**] **5** You are **ahead** of schedule in your work or journey if you are taking less time to complete it than that allowed in the plans or timetable: *The work was completed ahead of time.* [*same as* **in advance of**]
[see also **get ahead, go ahead**]

aid /eɪd/ *noun*; *verb*
▷ ***noun***: **aids**
1 (*uncount*) **Aid** is help in the form of food, money, medical supplies or treatment, equipment or services, given to people who need it: *Not enough aid is getting through to the refugees.* [see also **first aid**] **2** An **aid** is something, especially a piece of equipment, that helps you do something: *video recordings and other teaching aids* □ *a hearing aid.*
▷ ***verb***: **aids, aiding, aided**
You **aid** someone when you help them: *He managed to walk to the ambulance, aided by a passer-by.*
▷ ***phrases*** **1** (*legal*) Someone **aids and abets** another person to do something wrong or criminal when they help or encourage them to do it. **2 a** An event is held **in aid of** something such as a charity if the the money made by the event is to be given to it. **b** (*informal*) You ask what something is **in aid of** when you want to know the reason for it: *What's all this noise in aid of?* **3** (*formal*) You go **to the aid of** someone when you go and help them: *Thanks for coming to my aid.* **4** You do something **with the aid of** a person or thing when they help you to do it or support you: *He walks with the aid of a stick.*

aide /eɪd/ *noun*: **aides**
An **aide** is an assistant or adviser, especially to the head of a government.

AIDS or **Aids** /eɪdz/ *noun* (*uncount*)
AIDS or **acquired immune deficiency syndrome** is a condition caused by a virus that attacks the body's system of defence against disease, so that the patient easily catches infections, which may be severe and cause death.

ailing /'eɪlɪŋ/ *adjective*
1 A person is **ailing** if they are ill or weak: *He knew he should visit his ailing mother.* **2** An **ailing** business is one that is losing money and failing.

ailment /'eɪlmənt/ *noun*: **ailments**
An **ailment** is an illness, especially a mild or unimportant one.

aim /eɪm/ *verb*; *noun*
▷ ***verb***: **aims, aiming, aimed**
1 You **aim** something, especially a weapon, at, or **aim** at, a person or thing, when you point something in their direction, ready to throw or shoot at them: *She aimed a snowball at me, but I ducked in time.* **2** You **aim** at or for something when you try to achieve it: *We must aim at a success rate of 95%.* **3** You **aim** at doing something, or **aim** to do it, when you are intending, or trying, to do it: *We're aiming at completing the job by August '94.* □ (*AmE*) *I aim to arrive about 9.30.* **4** You **aim** something at someone when you intend it for them, or intend them to notice and react to it: *We're aiming this safety-in-the-home campaign at parents.* **5** A procedure **is aimed** at doing something when it is intended to do it: *The reforms are aimed at improving school-attendance levels.*
▷ ***noun***: **aims**
1 Your **aims** are your ambitions, or the things you want to achieve: *One of my aims is to learn Japanese.* **2** Your **aim** in doing something is your purpose, or what you intend to achieve; the **aim** of something such as a project is its purpose: *The main aim of this dictionary is to present English in a friendly way for the intermediate learner.* **3** (*uncount*) Your **aim** is also your ability to aim accurately at something so that you hit it when you shoot or throw: *He had been taking lessons to improve his aim.*
▷ ***phrase*** You **take aim** when you point a weapon or missile at someone or something, so as to hit them when you throw or shoot.

aimless /'eɪmləs/ *adjective*
People or pursuits are **aimless** if they have no particular purpose or aim: *aimless and time-wasting discussion.* — *adverb* **aimlessly:** *He sat aimlessly turning the pages of a magazine.*

ain't /eɪnt/ *auxiliary verb*
Ain't is used in non-standard or dialect English, or sometimes humorously, as a short form of **am not, are not, is not, have not** and **has not**: *Ain't he clever?* □ *You ain't lived yet.*

air /ɛə(r)/ *noun*; *verb*
▷ ***noun***: **airs**
1 (*uncount*) **Air** is the mixture of gases, mainly oxygen, nitrogen and carbon dioxide, that is breathed by living things and makes up the earth's atmosphere: *I'm going out for some fresh air.* □ *air pollution.* **2** (*used in the singular*) The **air** is the space above the ground: *Hundreds of birds suddenly rose into the air.* **3** (*uncount*) **Air** is used in talking about travel by aircraft: *The air fare is about $400 return.* □ *air travel* □ *Why don't you go by air?* **4** (*used in the singular*) You say that a person or place has an **air** of something, such as a quality, if they give you an impression of it: *She had an air of determination about her that morning.*
▷ ***verb***: **airs, airing, aired**

1 You **air** clothes or bedclothes, or let them **air**, by hanging them in a warm place to make sure they are quite dry. **2** You **air** a bed, especially one that has not been used recently, by warming it up. **3** You **air** a room by opening the windows and letting cool air circulate through it. **4** You **air** your opinions or thoughts when you express them to other people, or in public.

▻ ***phrases*** **1** Something such as a quarrel or argument **clears the air** if it gives people the opportunity to express their opinions frankly and so reduces tension. **2 a** A possibility is **in the air** if you hear people discussing it a lot. **b** A project is still a bit **in the air** if its future is doubtful or undecided. **3** Someone or something disappears **into thin air** if they disappear suddenly and completely; they appear **out of thin air** if they appear suddenly and unexpectedly. **4** Someone is **on the air** when they are being broadcast on radio or television, and **off the air** when the broadcasting equipment is switched off. **5** (*derogatory*) You **put on airs** or **give yourself airs** if you behave in a way that you think will show other people how important you are, or what good taste you have.

airborne /ˈɛəbɔːn/ *adjective*
An aircraft or bird is **airborne** when it is in the air, especially just after leaving the ground.

air-conditioning /ˈɛəkəndɪʃənɪŋ/ *noun* (*uncount*)
Air-conditioning is the machinery for, or the process of, controlling the temperature and moisture level of the air inside a building, usually to cool and dry it. — *adjective* **air-conditioned:** *fully air-conditioned bedrooms.*

aircraft /ˈɛəkrɑːft/ *noun*: **aircraft**
An **aircraft** is any vehicle that can fly, such as an aeroplane or helicopter: *military aircraft.*

aircraft-carrier /ˈɛəkrɑːftkarɪə(r)/ *noun*: **aircraft-carriers**
An **aircraft-carrier** is a large naval warship with a flat deck which aircraft can take off from and land on.

airfield /ˈɛəfiːld/ *noun*: **airfields**
An **airfield** is a piece of ground used by private or military aircraft for taking off and landing.

air force /ˈɛəfɔːs/ *noun*
A country's **air force** is the branch of its fighting forces trained in air warfare.

air hostess /ˈɛəhoʊstɛs/ *noun*: **air hostesses**
An **air hostess** is a woman member of an airliner's crew, responsible for the comfort of passengers.

airing /ˈɛərɪŋ/ *noun* (*used in the singular*)
1 You give a room an **airing** by opening the windows to let in fresh air; you give clothes and bedclothes an **airing** by hanging them somewhere warm to let them dry thoroughly. **2** You give your opinions an **airing** when you express them publicly.

airing cupboard /ˈɛərɪŋ kʌbəd/ *noun*: **airing cupboards**
An **airing cupboard** is a heated cupboard for putting clean laundry in, to dry it thoroughly.

airless /ˈɛələs/ *adjective*
A room that is **airless** lacks fresh air. [*same as* **stuffy**; *opposite* **airy**]

air letter /ˈɛə lɛtə(r)/ *noun*: **air letters**
An **air letter** is a form for writing a letter on, designed to be folded over, sealed, and sent by air without an envelope.

airlift /ˈɛəlɪft/ *noun*; *verb*
▻ ***noun***: **airlifts**
An **airlift** is an operation to take people or supplies by air into or out of an area that is difficult to reach by other means.
▻ ***verb***: **airlifts, airlifting, airlifted:** *Most of the children were airlifted to safety.*

airline /ˈɛəlaɪn/ *noun*: **airlines**
An **airline** is a company or organization providing a regular transport service for passengers or cargo by aircraft: *There are five airlines operating on this route.*

airmail /ˈɛəmeɪl/ *noun* (*uncount*)
Airmail is the system of carrying mail by air: *airmail envelopes* □ *I'll send you the book by airmail.*

airman /ˈɛəmən/ *noun*: **airmen**
An **airman** is a member of the air force below officer rank.

airplane /ˈɛəpleɪn/ *noun* (*AmE*): **airplanes**
An **airplane** is an aeroplane.

airport /ˈɛəpɔːt/ *noun*: **airports**
An **airport** is a place where aircraft arrive and depart, with buildings for administration and facilities such as toilets, restaurants and shops for passengers.

air raid /ˈɛə reɪd/ *noun*: **air raids**
An **air raid** is a bombing attack made on a place by military aircraft.

airship /ˈɛəʃɪp/ *noun*: **airships**
An **airship** is an aircraft, nowadays rare, consisting of a long gas-filled balloon with the engines and cabin compartment hanging from it.

airsick /ˈɛəsɪk/ *adjective*
Passengers in an aircraft are **airsick** when the motion of the aircraft makes them feel sick or be sick. — *noun* (*uncount*) **airsickness:** *I don't usually suffer from airsickness.*

airspace /ˈɛəspeɪs/ *noun* (*uncount*)
A country's **airspace** is the part of the sky extending over it and regarded as belonging to it: *They needed a permit to pass through Libyan airspace.*

airstrip /ˈɛəstrɪp/ *noun*: **airstrips**
An **airstrip** is a piece of ground prepared for aircraft to land on and take off from.

air terminal /ˈɛə tɜːmɪnəl/ *noun*: **air terminals**
An **air terminal** is **1** a building in a town centre from which passengers can be transported to an airport out of town. **2** a building at an airport where passengers wait to board their aircraft.

airtight /ˈɛətaɪt/ *adjective*
An **airtight** container has a tight-fitting lid that prevents air from getting into it or escaping from it.

air-traffic control /ˈɛətrafɪk kənˈtroʊl/ *noun* (*uncount*)
Air-traffic control is the airport staff who give pilots instructions by radio about when and where to land or take off, and information about their routes.

airwaves /ˈɛəweɪvz/ *noun* (*plural*)
The **airwaves** are the radio waves used by radio and television stations for their broadcasts.

airy /ˈɛərɪ/ *adjective*: **airier, airiest**
1 An **airy** room or building has plenty of fresh air in it, usually because it has large windows and high ceilings. **2** Someone does or says something in an **airy** manner if they do it in a casual, light-hearted way, usually inappropriate to the serious matter that is being dealt with. — *adverb* **airily:** *'I've decided to leave school and get a job,' he told her airily.*

aisle /aɪl/ *noun*: **aisles**
An **aisle** is a gap forming a passageway between rows of seats *eg* in a church or theatre, or between the rows of shelves in a supermarket.

ajar /əˈdʒɑː(r)/ *adjective*
A door is **ajar** when it is partly open: *She left the door ajar as she went out.*

akin /əˈkɪn/ *adjective*
One thing is **akin** to another if it is like it: *He seemed to regard his children with something akin to disgust.*

alacrity /ə'lakrɪtɪ/ *noun* (*uncount*)
You do something with **alacrity** if you do it eagerly and enthusiastically: *He agreed to the suggestion with alacrity.*

alarm /ə'lɑːm/ *noun*; *verb*
▻ ***noun***: **alarms**
1 (*uncount*) **Alarm** is a feeling of anxiety and fear: *Darkness fell and he began to feel some alarm for her safety.* ▫ *She swung round in alarm.* **2** An **alarm** is a device such as a bell or light, that is set to operate automatically, *eg* as a warning of trouble or danger, or as a reminder; the sound or signal produced by the device is also an **alarm**: *You ought to fit a burglar alarm.* ▫ *The alarm must have gone off without me hearing it.*
▻ ***verb***: **alarms, alarming, alarmed**
1 Something **alarms** you if it frightens you or makes you anxious: *The slightest noise or movement seemed to alarm him.* **2** To **alarm** a building or vehicle is to fit it with an alarm, which operates if anyone tries to break into it. — *adjective* **alarmed:** *Don't be alarmed!* ▫ *He glanced round with an alarmed expression.* — *adjective* **alarming:** *I heard some rather alarming news today.* — *adverb* **alarmingly:** *She looked alarmingly thin.*
▻ ***phrase*** You **raise** or **sound the alarm** when you warn people of trouble or danger or report an alarming circumstance *eg* to the police.

alarm clock /ə'lɑːm klɒk/ *noun*: **alarm clocks**
An **alarm clock** is a clock fitted with an alarm that makes a noise, which you can set to go off at a particular time to wake you up.

alas /ə'las/ *adverb* (*sentence adverb*) *or interjection* (*literary*)
You use **alas** to indicate your own feeling of regret about what you are saying: *She died before she completed the book, alas.*

albatross /'albətrɒs/ *noun*: **albatrosses**
An **albatross** is a long-winged sea bird like a large seagull, found in the southern oceans.

albeit /ɔːl'biːɪt/ *conjunction* (*formal*)
You use **albeit** to mean 'even if', when making a comment that takes some of the force out of what you are saying: *I did give him the correct instructions, albeit rather hurriedly.*

albino /al'biːnoʊ/ (*AmE*) /al'baɪnoʊ/ *noun*: **albinos**
An **albino** is a person or animal that lacks natural colouring and so has white hair, pale pink skin, and pink eyes.

album /'albəm/ *noun*: **albums**
1 An **album** is a record with about 20 minutes' music on each side, all performed by the same musician or group: *I've got their latest album.* **2** An **album** is also a book in which to keep your photographs, your collection of stamps, or written contributions from your friends.

alcohol /'alkəhɒl/ *noun* (*uncount*)
1 Alcohol is drink that is capable of making people drunk, such as wine, beer and spirits: *I'm trying to cut down on alcohol.* **2 Alcohol** is also the colourless liquid produced by the fermentation or distillation of sugar, that is contained in drinks such as beer and wine, and is also used as a solvent: *low-alcohol beer.*

alcoholic /alkə'hɒlɪk/ *adjective*; *noun*
▻ ***adjective***
1 Alcoholic drinks contain alcohol. **2 Alcoholic** also means relating to, or caused by, alcohol: *alcoholic poisoning.*
▻ ***noun***: **alcoholics**
An **alcoholic** is a person who is addicted to alcohol, and so cannot stop taking it.

alcoholism /'alkəhɒlizm/ *noun* (*uncount*)
Alcoholism is a name for the set of harmful effects that drinking too much alcohol too often has on the body.

alcove /'alkoʊv/ *noun*: **alcoves**
An **alcove** is a partially enclosed area extending back from the main wall of a room: *The ground floor consisted of a sitting room, and a kitchen with a dining alcove.* [*same as* **recess**]

ale /eɪl/ *noun*: **ales**
1 (*uncount*) **Ale** is a name for beer, as distinct from beer-like drinks such as lager and stout: *a glass of ale.* **2** An **ale** is a type of ale, or a serving of it: *light ales.*

alert /ə'lɜːt/ *adjective*; *noun*; *verb*
▻ ***adjective***
1 Someone who is **alert** is good at noticing what is happening round them and reacts quickly and intelligently. [*same as* **sharp**] **2** You are **alert** to something, such as a problem or danger, if you are well aware of it. — *adverb* **alertly:** *The dog had its ears alertly pricked.*
▻ ***noun***: **alerts**
An **alert** is a warning of danger, or a population's state of readiness for it, or the period this lasts for: *There had been a bomb alert earlier in the day, but the shops were now open again.*
▻ ***verb***: **alerts, alerting, alerted**
You **alert** someone to something such as a danger when you warn them of it.
▻ ***phrase*** You are **on the alert** when you are watching for trouble or danger or for developments of other kinds: *Teachers have to be constantly on the alert for signs of confusion and misunderstanding in their pupils.*

A level /'eɪ lɛvəl/ *noun*: **A levels**
1 (*uncount*) **A level** or **Advanced level** is the set of examinations held in England, Wales and Northern Ireland which school pupils take at about the age of 17 or 18: *She's taking three subjects at A level.* **2** An **A level** or **Advanced level** is any of the examinations, or a pass in any of them: *He took five A levels.* ▫ *I've got A levels in English, French and History.*

algebra /'aldʒəbrə/ *noun* (*uncount*)
Algebra is a form of mathematics that uses letters and symbols to represent quantities in calculations and equations. — *adjective* **algebraic** /aldʒə'breɪɪk/: *the algebraic formula 2ax – 2ay.*

alias /'eɪlɪəs/ *noun*; *adverb*
▻ ***noun***: **aliases**
An **alias** is a false name and identity, used *eg* by a criminal or spy: *She had used several aliases.*
▻ ***adverb***
You use **alias** to mean 'otherwise known as', when supplying the other name, whether the real or false one, of someone who uses a false name: *The new arrival at the advertising agency was Mr Death Bredon, alias Lord Peter Wimsey.*

alibi /'alɪbaɪ/ *noun*: **alibis**
You have an **alibi** for the time during which a crime was committed if you can prove you were somewhere else at that time: *The police had been interviewing possible suspects and checking their alibis.*

alien /'eɪlɪən/ *adjective*; *noun*
▻ ***adjective***
1 Something that is **alien** belongs to a country or race different from your own: *Happy as they are to find homes here, the refugees will have difficulty adapting to an alien culture.* [*same as* **foreign**] **2** You find yourself in an **alien** environment, or **alien** surroundings, when you are somewhere unfamiliar and rather frightening. [*same as* **strange**] **3** A way of behaving is **alien** to you if

it would be unnatural and uncharacteristic for you to behave in that way: *She found she had to discipline the children with a brutality that was alien to her nature.*

▻ ***noun***: **aliens**

1 An **alien** is a foreign-born resident of a country who has not adopted that country's nationality. **2** In science-fiction stories, an **alien** is an inhabitant of another planet.

alienate /ˈeɪlɪəneɪt/ *verb*: **alienates, alienating, alienated**

1 You **alienate** people when you do or say things that make them grow to dislike you: *She had alienated most of her former friends.* [*same as* **distance, estrange**] **2** People **are alienated** from their own culture or environment when circumstances remove them so far from it that they no longer belong there: *Her lifestyle as a media personality had alienated her from her working-class background.* [*same as* **separate, cut off**] — *noun* (*uncount*) **alienation** /eɪlɪəˈneɪʃən/: *She watched her friends concentrating on their careers with a growing sense of isolation and alienation.*

alight[1] /əˈlaɪt/ *adjective*

1 Something is **alight** if it is burning: *He poured petrol over the rubbish and set it alight.* [*same as* **on fire**] **2** Someone's face or eyes are **alight** when they are bright, *eg* with happiness or excitement.

alight[2] /əˈlaɪt/ *verb*: **alights, alighting, alighted**

1 (*formal*) You **alight** from a train or other public vehicle, or from an aircraft, when you get off it: *Will passengers alighting at the next station please ensure that they have all their baggage with them?* **2** A bird or insect **alights** on something when it lands on it: *A ladybird alighted momentarily on his trouser leg.*

align /əˈlaɪn/ *verb*: **aligns, aligning, aligned**

1 You **align** yourself with a particular political party or group when you give your loyalty and support to it: *Suddenly he broke with the Liberals and aligned himself with the Greens.* [*same as* **ally**] **2** You **align** things when you place them in a symmetrical relationship, especially parallel, to one another: *Ensure that the panels are aligned squarely to each other.* [*same as* **arrange**] — *noun* (*uncount or count*) **alignment:** *What's her political alignment?* ▫ *The riders advanced in perfect alignment.*

alike /əˈlaɪk/ *adjective; adverb*

▻ ***adjective***

People or things are **alike** if they are, or look, similar: *She and her cousin look very alike.* ▫ *The two situations are far from alike.* ▫ *a row of houses, all completely alike.* [see also **like**]

> **Alike** is not used before a noun: *They had similar* (not *alike*) *hairstyles.*

▻ ***adverb***

1 Alike means in the same way or similarly: *Boys and girls should be treated alike as far as possible.* ▫ *The twins dressed alike until they were at least 18.* **2** You can use **alike** to mean equally: *His retirement from politics amazed his friends and enemies alike.*

alimony /ˈalɪmənɪ/ *noun* (*uncount; legal*)

Alimony is money that someone who is divorced or separated has to pay regularly to their former wife or husband. [see also **maintenance**]

alive /əˈlaɪv/ *adjective*

1 People, animals and plants are **alive** if they are living, not dead: *Are your parents alive still?* ▫ *Michael, aged 5, missing from home since Tuesday, has been found alive and well.* ▫ *Bring the plant indoors if you want it to stay alive throughout the winter.* **2** An issue is said to be **alive** if people are continuing to discuss it; an activity or institution is **alive** if people are continuing to take part in it or support it: *The debate about correct spelling was kept alive for some weeks in the correspondence columns of the newspaper.* ▫ *The Esperanto Society is still very much alive.* **3** You describe a person or place as **alive** if they seem lively and full of activity: *I liked her because she was so alive.* [*same as* **animated, vivacious**] **4** A place is **alive** with people or other living things if it is full of them: *They found the island alive with tourists.* ▫ *The air was alive with insects.* [*compare* **crawl, swarm, teem**] **5** You are **alive** to something such as a danger or other possibility if you are aware of it: *Young people are not always fully alive to their opportunities.* [*same as* **alert** to]

> **Alive** is not used before a noun: *It's a shame to keep live* (not *alive*) *animals caged like this.*

alkali /ˈalkəlaɪ/ *noun* (*chemistry*): **alkalis**

An **alkali** is a substance that reacts with an acid to form a salt. [see also **acid**] — *adjective* **alkaline:** *alkaline substances such as chalk.*

all /ɔːl/ *determiner; pronoun; adverb*

▻ ***determiner***

1 (*with another determiner and a plural or uncount noun, or with a demonstrative or possessive pronoun*) **All** the people or things, or **all** the thing, is the full known group of people or things, or the full known amount of a thing: *All the senior staff have been told about the pay freeze.* ▫ *All the rest have gone home.* ▫ *I've carried out all your instructions.* ▫ *Statements have been taken from all five witnesses.* ▫ *Are all these children staying with you?* ▫ *All mine are grown up now.* ▫ *All those who have borrowed books are asked to return them.* ▫ *Who's eaten all the ice cream?* ▫ *He complained all the way home.* [= during the whole journey] ▫ *She invests all the money she earns.* ▫ *I've put all her private correspondence in this drawer.* ▫ (with the sense 'this enormous amount of') *All this publicity is upsetting him.* ▫ *You know all that already.* **2** (*followed immediately by a plural or uncount noun*) **All** people or things, or **all** something, means every one, or any, in existence: *All men are the same.* ▫ *Not all cities are as beautiful as this one.* ▫ *All paper yellows with time.* ▫ *The new immunization programme will affect all babies born after January 1995.*

> **Every** can be used with count nouns in the same way as **all**, but is followed by a singular noun and verb: *All possible precautions are being taken.* But: *Every possible precaution is being taken.*

3 Followed by a word such as 'day', 'week' or 'year', **all** means 'for the whole of': *I had to stay up all night to finish the work.*

▻ ***pronoun***

1 (*especially AmE*) The form '**all** of' is used in the same way as **all** (sense 1): *All of these rules are important.* ▫ *I'll give you some of my chocolate if you've eaten all of yours.*

> '**All** of' is the form that must be used with personal pronouns: *I've told all of them* (not *all them*). *Do you want all of it* (not *all it*)? *'How many are coming?' 'All of us* (not *all we*)'.

2 (*after a plural noun or pronoun, or after an uncount noun or pronoun representing it*) You use **all** to indicate that you mean the whole group, whole amount, or situation as a whole: *Our relations were all delighted at the news.* ▫ *You all helped to make the evening a success.* ▫ *We've all of us met this problem before.* ▫ *These all need to be sorted out.* ▫ *She receives lots of invitations but refuses them all.* ▫ *'Who wants to join in?' 'We* *all do.'* □ *You can't all get into the car.* □ *The snow has all disappeared.* □ *The sun has melted it all.* □ *This is all so new and exciting.* □ *It all goes to show how useful friends are.*

3 (*used independently*) **All** can be used to mean **a** everything concerning some situation: *All seems to be well again.* □ *That's all for the time being.* □ *Have you told me all you know?* □ *I've heard all about his troubles already.* **b** the only thing or things: *All I want is a bit of peace.* □ *All he ever cared about was money.* □ *All I know is that she was meeting a friend tonight.* □ *Is that all you can remember?*

> Otherwise, in reference to things, **everything**, not **all**, is more common: *Make sure you take everything* (not *all*) *with you. I've thought of everything* (not *all*). In reference to people, **everybody** and **everyone** tend to be used in preference to **all**: *She charmed everyone* (or *all*) *who met her. I think you've met everyone* (not *all*) *in this office before.*

▷ ***adverb***

1 You use **all** to mean 'completely', or to emphasize the great extent to which something is so: *You've got jam all over your face.* □ *He spilt wine all down his trousers.* □ (*informal*) *He goes all shy when people speak to him.* □ (*informal*) *My research is going all wrong.* □ *He was all alone* (or *all by himself*, or *all on his own*). □ *She did it all by herself* (or *all on her own*). **2** Someone is *eg* **all** politeness, or **all** smiles, when they are being very polite, or smiling a lot. **3** In games or competitions, **all** is used to indicate an equal score for both sides or teams: *The score is five all.*

▷ ***phrases*** **1** You **all but** do something when you almost do it: *We all but succeeded.* □ *The news all but killed her.* **2 a** (*informal*) Someone is **all in** when they are exhausted: *You look all in.* **b** Something such as a holiday costs a certain amount **all in** if all the major expenses are included in the price: *an all-in price.* **3** You use **all in all** to sum up what you think, or give your conclusion: *All in all, we did pretty well.* **4** You say that someone or something must be **all of** a certain size, amount or measurement if you think they are at least that size, amount or measurement: *She must have been all of six feet.* **5** You go **all out** to achieve something when you try as hard as you can to do so: *an all-out effort* **6 a** An event is **all over** when it is finished: *We'll discuss it again when the excitement is all over.* **b** (*informal*) You say that something is someone **all over** if you think it is typical of them: *That kind of generosity is her all over.* **7 a All right** means satisfactory or satisfactorily: *Was your meal all right?* □ *You seem to be managing all right.* **b** Someone is **all right** if they are safe or unhurt: *Are you sure you're all right?* **c** You answer **'all right'** when you agree to something: *'Don't tell him.' 'All right.'* **d** You use **all right** when asking or giving permission: *Is it all right if I leave early today?* □ *'May I borrow your typewriter?' 'All right.'* **e** You sometimes finish giving an instruction with **'all right'**, to make sure you have been understood: *The black ones go in this box, and the white ones in this, all right?* **f** You use **all right** when you are trying to organize people: *All right, children, stop talking now.* [*same as* **OK**] **8** You say that something is not **all that** good or bad, or not as good or bad as **all that**, when you think it isn't particularly good or bad: *The timing isn't all that important.* **9 All the** better, or **all the** more, mean even better or even more because of some circumstance: *It will be all the better if you can create the index automatically.* □ *If he doesn't want his share that'll mean all the more for us.* □ *She's looking all the healthier for her holiday.* **10** (*informal*) Someone is **all there** if they are intelligent and alert; if you say someone is not **all there**, you mean they are not completely sane. **11** You use **all told** after giving a total, to emphasize that everyone or everything has been included: *There were only three of us all told to look after the ward.* **12** You use **all too** to mean 'very, even painfully': *I'm all too aware of the problem.* □ *Her visit was all too brief.* [*same as* **only too**] **13** You say what someone does is **all very well** when you think it is wrong or unsuitable: *It's all very well for her to joke, but we have a serious problem.* **14** You **are all for** something if you are enthusiastically in favour of it: *I'm all for co-education.* **15** You use **at all** to give emphasis, especially to a negative: *I haven't seen her at all this week.* □ *'Haven't we got any milk?' 'No, none at all.'* □ *If there's anything at all I can do to help, let me know.* □ *Will you be using your computer at all today?* **16 a For all** means in spite of, or despite: *He's a nice person, for all his silly ways.* □ *Our holiday didn't go the way we planned it, but we enjoyed it, for all that.* **b** You say that something could be so **for all** someone knows or cares, to emphasize how little they know, or care: *I could be dying for all you care.* □ *For all I know, she may be dead by now.* **17 a** You use **in all** when stating a total: *We were twelve in all at the table.* □ *The bill came to $75 in all.* **b** You refer to someone or something **in all their** *eg* beauty or glory to emphasize a typical and abundant quality that they have: *jealousy in all its destructiveness.* **18a Of all** gives emphasis after a superlative: *the most extraordinary circumstance of all* □ *First of all let me welcome the new members.* **b** You also use 'of **all**' in expressing a strong reaction to something: **Well, of all the cheek!** [= I never heard such cheek before] **19** Someone or something that fails in some way **with all their** *eg* wealth, fails in spite of having so much wealth: *With all her possessions, she's never been a happy person.*

allay /ə'leɪ/ *verb*: **allays, allaying, allayed**
Something **allays** a feeling such as pain, fear, or suspicion when it lessens it: *The latest news had done nothing to allay his anxiety.*

all clear /ɔːl 'klɪə(r)/ *noun* (*used in the singular*)
An **all clear** is a signal that danger is past: *Have they sounded the all clear?*

allegation /alə'geɪʃən/ *noun*: **allegations**
Someone makes an **allegation** against you when they claim that you have done something wrong or dishonest: *He resigned amid allegations of fraud.*

allege /ə'lɛdʒ/ *verb*: **alleges, alleging, alleged**
You **allege** that something is so when you say it is, but without giving evidence or proof: *It was alleged by some of his acquaintances that he had a child from a previous relationship.* [*same as* **claim**]

alleged /ə'lɛdʒd/ *adjective*
An **alleged** circumstance is one that has been reported but is not a proved fact: *her alleged neglect of her child.* — *adverb* **allegedly** /ə'lɛdʒɪdlɪ/: *She had allegedly left her two-year-old daughter alone in the house for two days.*

allegiance /ə'liːdʒəns/ *noun* (*uncount*)
Your **allegiance** to a cause, a party, or your country, is your loyalty towards it: *I don't owe allegiance to any political party.* □ *They were made to swear allegiance to their leader.*

allegorical /alə'gɒrɪkəl/ *adjective*
An **allegorical** picture, poem, story or play is one in the form of an allegory, or that uses allegory.

allegory /'aləgərɪ/ *noun*: **allegories**
1 An **allegory** is a story, play, poem or picture in which the characters represent or symbolize moral,

political or spiritual ideas or themes. **2** (*uncount*) **Allegory** is this kind of symbolism.

alleluia /alɪ'lu:jɑ:/ or /aleɪ'lu:jɑ:/ or **halleluiah**, **hallelujah** *interjection*
'**Alleluia!**' is a shout expressing God's praise, used in Christian services and hymns.

allergic /ə'lɜ:dʒɪk/ *adjective*
You are **allergic** to something such as a food or material if it makes you ill or gives you a skin rash when you eat it or come in contact with it: *an allergic reaction* □ *Lots of babies are allergic to wool.*

allergy /'alədʒɪ/ *noun* (*count or uncount*): **allergies**
You have an **allergy** to something such as a food, plant, substance, material or domestic creature if your body is sensitive to it, so that you become ill or develop a skin rash when you eat it or come in contact with it: *Have you any food allergies?* □ *the science of allergy.*

alleviate /ə'li:vɪeɪt/ *verb*: **alleviates, alleviating, alleviated**
Something **alleviates** a problem if it makes it less serious: *Food parcels would go some way towards alleviating the distress of the refugees.* [*same as* **ease, relieve**]

alley /'alɪ/ *noun*: **alleys**
1 An **alley** or **alleyway** is a passage or narrow street between buildings. **2** A bowling **alley** or skittle **alley** is a place where forms of the game skittles are played; the long narrow wooden strips that you bowl the balls along are also **alleys**.

alliance /ə'laɪəns/ *noun* (*count or uncount*): **alliances**
An **alliance** between two or more countries, bodies of people, or individuals, is an agreement to work together for a joint purpose, or for their common benefit: *In 1758 they entered into an alliance with Spain.* □ *Many more university departments could work in alliance with industry.*

allied /'alaɪd/ or /ə'laɪd/ *adjective*
1 Things are **allied** if they are related or connected: *They do say genius is closely allied to madness.* **2** People use **allied** or **Allied** to mean 'of the allies', especially in reference to Britain and her allies in World Wars 1 and 2: *the Allied invasion.*

alligator /'alɪgeɪtə(r)/ *noun*: **alligators**
An **alligator** is a large reptile closely related to the crocodile but with a broader and shorter head, that liver in America and China.

alliteration /əlɪtə'reɪʃən/ *noun* (*uncount*)
Alliteration is the effect produced by using a series of words that begin with the same letter or sound, as in *Sing a song of sixpence.* — *adjective* **alliterative** /ə'lɪtərətɪv/: *alliterative poetry.*

allocate /'aləkeɪt/ *verb*: **allocates, allocating, allocated**
You **are allocated** something when you are given it for some purpose; something **is allocated** for a special use when a decision is made that it should be used that way: *They've allocated me the beginners' class to teach this year.* — *noun* (*uncount*) **allocation** /alə'keɪʃən/: *allocation of available funds.*

allot /ə'lɒt/ *verb*: **allots, allotting, allotted**
Something **is allotted** to you when it is given to you as your share of something: *Shares in the new company will be allotted on a first-come-first-serve basis, so apply early.* — *adjective* **allotted:** *We laid our sleeping bags down in our allotted spaces.*

allotment /ə'lɒtmənt/ *noun* (*BrE*): **allotments**
An **allotment** is a piece of ground rented to someone to grow vegetables on, usually one of several such pieces that an area of land, *eg* in a town, is divided into.

allow /ə'laʊ/ *verb*: **allows, allowing, allowed**
1 You **are allowed** to do something if you are permitted, or not forbidden, to do it, or if it is all right to do it: *You're not allowed to park here.* □ *My mother always allowed me to sleep late on Saturday mornings.* □ *He was allowed to drop maths from his course in the second year.* [see note at **could**]

> **Permit** can be used like **allow**, but belongs to formal, especially written, English: *College members are permitted to borrow up to five books from the library.*
> **Let** is slightly less formal than **allow**; it takes the infinitive without 'to', and cannot be used in the passive: *They let me go* (not *to go*) *home early.* But: *I was allowed to go home early.*

2 You **are allowed** somewhere if someone lets you go there: *We weren't allowed into her hospital room.* □ *They allowed us in later.* □ *The children aren't allowed out alone after dark.* **3** You **are allowed** something, or something **is allowed**, if it is permitted: *We were allowed one visit to the cinema each term.* □ *The landlady didn't allow pets.* □ *You know fighting isn't allowed in the playground.* **4** You **are allowed** something such as money or time for something when it is provided: *We're allowed £50 for expenses.* □ *Suppose I allow you a day to think about it?* **5** You **allow** something to happen, or it **is allowed** to happen, when you don't prevent it happening: *He allowed himself to be led away.* □ *This should never have been allowed to go on for so long.* **6** One thing **allows** another to happen if it makes it possible: *We have little holes in our skin called pores, which allow us to perspire.* [*same as* **enable**] **7** You **allow** that something is so, when you admit it: *I'll allow that he is under a lot of pressure.* [*same as* **admit, concede**] **8** You **allow** a certain amount of time for something when you leave time for it in your schedule, plan or calculation: *In the written exam, allow 25 minutes per question.*

> ***phrasal verb***
> You **allow for** something such as a possible delay or difficulty, or extra expense, when you take it into consideration in your planning: *We're allowing for price increases of 5%.* □ *We should be home by 7.30, allowing for possible delays.*

allowable /ə'laʊəbəl/ *adjective*
Something is **allowable** if it can be allowed, or if it is not unacceptable: *A variation here and there in the school uniform is allowable.* [*same as* **permissible**]

allowance /ə'laʊəns/ *noun*: **allowances**
1 An **allowance** is a sum of money given regularly to someone to help them with daily expenses, or with expenses of a special kind: *My mother gave me an allowance of £60 a month.* □ *a clothing allowance.* **2** An **allowance** is also a permitted amount of something: *Your baggage allowance for all flights is 20kg.*
▻ ***phrase*** You **make allowances** for something or someone when you take someone's special circumstances into consideration before making a judgement: *I'm tired of making allowances for her lack of experience.*

alloy /'alɔɪ/ *noun*: **alloys**
An **alloy** is a metal such as brass or steel, that is a mixture of two or more metals, or of a metal and non-metallic elements.

all-powerful /ɔ:l'paʊəfəl/ *adjective*
Someone is **all-powerful** if they are in absolute control and their authority cannot be challenged.

all-purpose /'ɔ:lpɜ:pəs/ *adjective*
An **all-purpose** tool or other device is one that is

designed, or used, for a variety of purposes: *Aspirin became an all-purpose remedy.*

all-round /ˈɔːlraʊnd/ *adjective*
1 An **all-round** athlete or **all-round** expert is good at a wide range of things. **2 All-round** experience, or an **all-round** education, includes a full range of useful elements or subjects. **3** A vehicle that gives the driver **all-round** vision gives a clear view to the front, left and right.

all-rounder /ɔːlˈraʊndə(r)/ *noun*: **all-rounders**
An **all-rounder** is a person with a wide range of skills and talents.

allude /əˈluːd/ or /əˈljuːd/ *verb*: **alludes, alluding, alluded**
You **allude** to something when you refer to it in an indirect way, or mention it while talking of something else: *I was alluding to his well-known fondness for jelly beans.* [*same as* **refer**]

allure /əˈlʊə(r)/ or /əˈljʊə(r)/ *noun* (*uncount*)
The **allure** of something is its power to attract you: *She could not resist the allure of riches.*

alluring /əˈlʊərɪŋ/ or /əˈljʊərɪŋ/ *adjective*
You call someone or something **alluring** if you find them attractive: *the alluring prospect of a free holiday.*

allusion /əˈluːʒən/ or /əˈljuːʒən/ *noun* (*count or uncount*): **allusions**
An **allusion** to something is an indirect reference to it or a brief mention of it: *Milton makes frequent allusions to Greek and Roman myths.*

ally /ˈalaɪ/ *noun*; *verb*
▻ ***noun*: allies**
1 A country's **allies** are the countries that have formally agreed to help and support it against its enemies, *eg* in war: *America was our ally in two world wars.* **2** Someone is your **ally** if they support you against others who disapprove of you or oppose you: *She found herself an ally in George.* [*same as* **supporter**]
▻ ***verb*** /əˈlaɪ/ or /ˈalaɪ/: **allies, allying, allied**
People, or countries, **ally** themselves with others when they promise them support and help.

almighty /ɔːlˈmaɪtɪ/ *adjective*; *noun*
▻ ***adjective*** (*informal*)
An **almighty** noise, row or fuss is a great or terrible one: *They've had an almighty quarrel.*
▻ ***noun***
The **Almighty** is God: *the power of the Almighty.*

almond /ˈɑːmənd/ *noun*: **almonds**
An **almond** is an oval nut with pointed ends.

almost /ˈɔːlmoʊst/ *adverb*
Almost means 'nearly' or 'not quite': *It's almost one o'clock.* □ *I'll be away almost three weeks.* □ *We've almost finished.* □ *I almost missed the turning off the motorway.* □ *I almost forgot; there's a message for you.* □ *I got there almost in time to catch the earlier train.* □ *I think you already know almost everyone here.* □ *Almost anything could happen in the next few weeks.* □ *He seems to have learnt almost nothing at school.*

aloft /əˈlɒft/ *adverb* (*literary*)
Something or someone is **aloft** when they are high above the ground or in the air: *She held the trophy proudly aloft.*

alone /əˈloʊn/ *adjective or adverb*
1 You are **alone** if you are without the company of other people: *He preferred to go for walks alone.* □ *May I talk to you? Are you alone?* **2** You are **alone** with another person, or the two of you are **alone** together, if no-one else is present: *Don't you dare leave me alone with him!* **3** You are **alone** if you are surrounded by people you don't know, or if you have no friends or relations: *He was all alone in New York.* □ *Her parents died and left her alone in the world.* **4** You do something **alone** when you do it without help from others: *I was left to cope alone with the children and the bills.* [*same as* **by yourself, on your own**] **5** You **alone** can do something if you are the only person who can: *She alone could put things right.* □ *Sam alone knew how to do it.* **6** One thing **alone** is responsible for something if it is the only thing involved: *She survived through willpower alone.*
▻ ***phrases*** **1** (*informal*) You **go it alone** when you take the step to act or work independently of other people. **2 a** You ask someone to **leave** you **alone** when you want them to stop bothering you. **b** You tell someone to **leave** something **alone** when you want them to stop interfering with it.

along /əˈlɒŋ/ *preposition*; *adverb*
▻ ***preposition***
1 You move **along** something such as a road when you move in the same direction as its length: *I was just walking along the street when I saw Annabel.* □ *We sat watching the barges sailing along the canal.* □ *She looked back along the track and saw someone following her.* □ *He slid the book along the table to me.* **2** Things are **along** something such as a road, or **along** the side of it, if they form a line or row beside it: *Willow trees grew along the river bank.* **3** Buildings or other objects positioned at the side of, or on, something such as a road are also **along** it: *There's a pedestrian crossing further along the street.* □ *I know I parked the car somewhere along this road.* □ *Her room is along this corridor on the right.*
▻ ***adverb***
1 Along is used with verbs of movement to indicate continuous progress in the direction taken: *I was just driving along when a wheel came off.* □ *Hurry along, please.* **2** Something is coming **along** well if it is progressing or proceeding well: *My research is coming along slowly.* □ *Things were drifting along as usual.* **3** You take someone or something **along**, or someone comes **along**, when you take them or they come, with you: *Why don't you come along too?* □ *Bring a friend along.* □ *I took my photos along to the meeting.*
▻ ***phrases*** **1** Something has been so **all along** if it has been so without people realizing it: *The truth was staring us in the face all along and we couldn't see it.* □ *To think I was right all along!* [*same as* **all the time**] **2 a** You do something **along with** others if you are one of a number doing it: *Along with hundreds of others he had invested money in the venture.* **b** You deal with something **along with** something else when you deal with the two things together, or at the same time: *I returned his book along with his file of notes.*

alongside /əlɒŋˈsaɪd/ *preposition*; *adverb*
▻ ***preposition***
1 One thing is **alongside** another if it is beside it: *There was a police car drawn up alongside the kerb.* [*same as* **beside**] **2** Systems or peoples of different types exist **alongside** each other when they exist or live together, usually in harmony and co-operation: *Suddenly there was racial hatred between people who had been living alongside one another for centuries.* [*same as* **side by side** with] **3** You work **alongside** someone else when you work with them or in their company: *You'll have the chance to work alongside some of the best scientists in the country.*
▻ ***adverb:*** *They lived in a neat brick house with a garage built alongside.*

aloof /əˈluːf/ *adjective*
1 You describe someone as **aloof** if they prefer to be on their own rather than with others, and don't want

to talk or make friends: *He seemed distant and aloof.* [*same as* **standoffish**] **2** You keep yourself **aloof** from something if you avoid getting involved with it: *She tended to keep herself aloof from office politics.*

aloud /əˈlaʊd/ *adverb*
You read or say something **aloud** when you speak loudly enough for people to hear you, not in a whisper, or to yourself: *All the children practise reading aloud from their favourite books.* [*same as* **out loud**]

alp /alp/ *noun* (*usually in the plural*): **alps**
Alps are high mountains; the **Alps** are a mountain range forming a barrier between France, Switzerland and Italy.

alphabet /ˈalfəbɛt/ *noun*: **alphabets**
The **alphabet** is the set of letters, arranged in a fixed order, that are used in writing a language.

alphabetical /alfəˈbɛtɪkəl/ *adjective*
Words or names are arranged in **alphabetical** order if they are arranged according to the order of the letters of the alphabet: *an alphabetical list of titles.* — *adverb* **alphabetically:** *names listed alphabetically.*

alpine /ˈalpaɪn/ *adjective*
Alpine plants and vegetation grow in mountainous regions.

already /ɔːlˈrɛdɪ/ or /ɒlˈrɛdɪ/ *adverb*
1 Something has happened **already** if it has happened before the present time, or before the time being considered: *She may have read the book already.* □ *He had already had his breakfast when I came downstairs.* □ *I already knew him by sight by the time we were introduced.*

> For happenings or events, BrE uses the perfect form, *eg I've already told you,* but in AmE the simple past form, *eg I already told you,* is possible.

2 Already is used to mean 'even now' or 'even then', emphasizing the earliness of some development: *He's only two and he can already count to ten.* □ *As a schoolgirl she was already showing remarkable literary ability.* **3** You use **already** to mean 'so soon', indicating surprise: *You can't be hungry again already!* □ *Surely they haven't left already?*

> Compare **still** and **yet** with **already**. You use **already** when something has happened; you use **still** when something is continuing to happen; you use **yet** when something has not happened, or is not known to have happened, up to the present time: *She's already done the shopping. She's still doing the shopping. Has she done the shopping yet?* [see note at **yet**]
> Notice the difference between *already* and *all ready*: *Are those parcels all ready for posting? They've been posted already.*

alright /ɔːlˈraɪt/
Alright is another spelling of **all right**.

also /ˈɔːlsoʊ/ *adverb*
1 You use **also** to add another statement about a person or thing: *She plays the piano and is also a violinist of some skill.* □ *He could sometimes be bad-tempered but he was also kind and affectionate.* □ *The condition is also common in horses.* **2** You use **also** when adding another person or thing that a statement applies to: *Her other son is also a doctor.* **3** (*sentence adverb*) You can introduce another statement you consider relevant with **also**: *We haven't got room for a visitor; also, the house is far too untidy.* □ *There's also the matter of payment.*

> **Also** can be used in AmE at the the end of a sentence, but in BrE **as well** or **too** are used: *She's written a few novels; she writes poetry as well* (or *too*).
> Note the difference between **also** and **even**: *Even* (not *also*) *in old age she was beautiful.*
> With **not**, use **either**, not **also**: *I don't eat meat and I'm not fond of fish either* (not *also not fond of fish*).

altar /ˈɔːltə(r)/ *noun*: **altars**
An **altar** is a sacred table used in religious ceremonies, *eg* one at the east end of a Christian church, or one in a temple for making sacrifices on.

alter /ˈɔːltə(r)/ *verb*: **alters, altering, altered**
You **alter** something when you change it; someone or something **alters** when they change: *They've altered the starting time of the race to 3.30.* □ *She seems not to have altered at all in 10 years.* □ *He may be sorry now, but that doesn't alter the fact that he cheated.* — *noun* (*count or uncount*) **alteration** /ɔːltəˈreɪʃən/: *We want to add a bathroom to the house and make a few other alterations.* □ *The timetable is subject to alteration.*

alternate *adjective*; *verb*
▷ ***adjective*** /ɔːlˈtɜːnət/
1 Alternate processes or happenings keep being repeated one after the other: *He experienced alternate bouts of depression and cheerfulness.* **2** Something happens on **alternate** days if it happens every other day, that is, one day, not the day after, but again the day after that, and so on repeatedly: *We used to spend alternate Sundays with my husband's parents.* □ *The festival is held in alternate years.* — *adverb* **alternately:** *The days passed by, alternately wet and fine.*
▷ ***verb*** /ˈɔːltəneɪt/: **alternates, alternating, alternated**
1 One thing **alternates** with another when each keeps following the other in turn; you **alternate** one thing with another when you make one thing follow the other repeatedly: *Blazing hot days alternated with freezing cold nights.* □ *You should alternate days of travelling with days of rest.* **2** You **alternate** between two states or activities when you keep changing from one to the other: *She alternated between dieting and overeating.* — *noun* (*uncount or count*) **alternation** /ɔːltəˈneɪʃən/: *the constant alternation of summer and winter.*

alternative /ɔːlˈtɜːnətɪv/ *adjective*; *noun*
▷ ***adjective***
1 An **alternative** possibility is one that is available instead of the one being considered: *You could take the alternative route avoiding the bridge.* **2 Alternative** also describes kinds of *eg* medical treatment, ways of living, methods of manufacture, that people consider more natural or less damaging to the environment than the usual kind: *alternative medicine* □ *alternative fuels.* — *adverb* (*sentence adverb*) **alternatively:** *There's a train at 11.00 pm on Sunday; alternatively, you could catch the 7.45 on Monday morning.*
▷ ***noun*: alternatives**
An **alternative** to something is a possibility that is available instead of it: *Try grilling as an alternative to frying.* □ *Let's see what the available alternatives are.*

although /ɔːlˈðoʊ/ *conjunction*
1 Although means 'in spite of the fact that', or 'in spite of being', and you use it when mentioning circumstances that contrast surprisingly with your main statement: *She never complained, although she was in constant pain.* □ *Although exhausted, he insisted on coming with us.*

> **Even though** can be used like **although**, but 'even although' is not possible: *She got top marks even though* (or *although*, but not *even although*) *she was ill at the time.*

2 You can also use **although** to modify the impression you have given in your main statement: *I'm not much of a gardner, although I do grow a few vegetables.*

> You can use **though** like **although**: *She still enjoys walking, though* (or *although*) *she doesn't get out as much as she used to.*

altitude /ˈæltɪtjuːd/ or /ˈɔːltɪtjuːd/ *noun* (*count or uncount*): **altitudes**
Something is at a certain **altitude** if it is at that height above sea level: *We were flying at an altitude of 12000 metres.* □ *At high altitude, oxygen becomes scarce.*

alto /ˈæltoʊ/ *noun*: **altos**
1 An **alto** is a woman or boy with a low singing voice, or a man who sings in a high voice of the same range. **2** (*uncount*) People who have or use this voice sing **alto**. [see also **contralto**]

altogether /ɔːltəˈgɛðə(r)/ *adverb*
1 Something stops **altogether** if it stops entirely or completely: *I don't want to stop seeing her altogether.* □ *Some species have disappeared altogether in the last decade.* **2** Something is *eg* **altogether** different or **altogether** better if it is entirely different, or obviously much better: *The new checking procedure is altogether more efficient.* **3** (*with a negative*) You say, *eg*, that you do not **altogether** believe something, or that something is not **altogether** fair, when you don't believe it, or think it is unfair. **4** You use **altogether** to mean in total: *The meal came to £30.60 altogether.* **5** (*sentence adverb*) You use **altogether** when summing up what you think: *Altogether, the meal was good value for money.*

> Note that **all together** is used in examples like the following: *The children sat all together* (not *altogether*) *in one corner.*

altruism /ˈæltrʊɪzm/ *noun* (*uncount*)
Altruism is a generous concern for the welfare of other people. — *adjective* **altruistic:** *His offer of help is not entirely altruistic.* — *adverb* **altruistically:** *act altruistically.*

aluminium /æljəˈmɪnɪəm/ (*AmE* **aluminum** /əˈluːmɪnəm/) *noun* (*uncount*)
Aluminium is a light, silver-coloured metal used in the construction of aircraft and, especially formerly, for making pans and other cooking equipment.

always /ˈɔːlweɪz/ *adverb*
1 Always is used with the simple present, past and future tenses in talking about habits and permanent states or situations, and means 'regularly', 'every time', or 'all the time': *I always thought there was something odd about him.* □ *Do you always go home at weekends?* □ *We always follow up our customers' complaints.* □ *She had always waited for him before.* □ *I'll always remember that remark of yours.*

> In instructions, **always** comes before the main verb: *Always make sure the road is clear before overtaking.* □ *Don't always assume that deaf people are stupid.*

2 Always is used with the progressive tenses to mean 'again and again' or 'continually', sometimes suggesting annoyance: *He'll never gain any confidence if you're always criticizing him.* □ *She was a studious girl, always borrowing books from the public library.* □ *You're always getting in my way.* [*same as* **constantly**, **forever**] **3** You use **always** after **can** and **could** to suggest a possible alternative course of action: *If the bridge is closed you can always go via Kincardine.* □ *I could always take a temporary typing job, I suppose.*

Alzheimer's Disease /ˈæltshaɪməz dɪziːz/ *noun* (*uncount*)
Alzheimer's Disease is an illness affecting the brain, which attacks elderly and middle-aged people, causing loss of memory and mental confusion.

am /æm/ *verb*
Am is the form of the present tense of **be** that is used with *I*.

> The negative form is *I am not* or *I'm not*. In BrE the negative question form is *aren't I?*, which AmE tends to avoid using.

amalgamate /əˈmælgəmeɪt/ *verb*: **amalgamate, amalgamating, amalgamated**
Two or more organizations or businesses **amalgamate** when they join together to form a single large organization. [*same as* **merge**] — *noun* (*uncount*) **amalgamation** /əmælgəˈmeɪʃən/: *the amalgamation of two factories on a single site.*

amass /əˈmæs/ *verb*: **amasses, amassing, amassed**
You **amass** such things as possessions or facts when you gradually collect a lot of them: *She had amassed a fortune by the time she was thirty.* [*same as* **accumulate**]

amateur /ˈæmətə(r)/ or /æməˈtɜː(r)/ *noun*; *adjective*
▻ ***noun***: **amateurs**
1 An **amateur** is someone who takes part in a sport or other activity as a hobby, not as a job: *The golf tournament is open to both amateurs and professionals.* [*opposite* **professional**] **2** (*derogatory*) An **amateur** is also someone who does a job clumsily or unskilfully: *I refuse to have the electric wiring done by a bunch of amateurs.* [*opposite* **expert**]
▻ ***adjective:*** *the Amateur Athletics Association* □ *His violin-playing sounds pretty amateur to me.*

amateurish /ˈæmətərɪʃ/ *adjective* (*derogatory*)
If you call a piece of work or a performance **amateurish**, you mean it is clumsy or unskilful.

amaze /əˈmeɪz/ *verb*: **amazes, amazing, amazed**
Something **amazes** you if it greatly surprises you: *It amazed me to discover how long the dinosaur age lasted.* [*same as* **astonish**] — *adjective* **amazed:** *I was amazed by the view.* □ *She looked at him with an amazed expression.* [*same as* **astonished**]

amazement /əˈmeɪzmənt/ *noun* (*uncount*)
Amazement is a feeling of great surprise: *She gazed at the picture in amazement.* □ *I found to my amazement that it was already midday.* [*same as* **astonishment**]

amazing /əˈmeɪzɪŋ/ *adjective*
You call something **amazing** if it greatly surprises or impresses you: *He has an amazing memory.* □ *The amazing thing about Prague is its architecture.* — *adverb* (*intensifying*) **amazingly:** *They got here amazingly quickly.*

ambassador /æmˈbæsədə(r)/ *noun*: **ambassadors**
A country's **ambassador** to another country is his or her own government's most senior official representative in that country, and acts on its behalf: *Britain's ambassador to Austria.* [see also **embassy**]

amber /ˈæmbə(r)/ *noun* (*uncount, often adjectival*)
1 Amber is a hard golden-brown transparent substance, scientifically a fossil resin, that is used in jewellery: *an amber bracelet.* **2 Amber** is also the colour of this substance, often used instead of 'orange' in references to traffic lights: *Red and amber come on together just before green.* □ *You would call her eyes amber rather than brown.*

ambidextrous /æmbɪˈdɛkstrəs/ *adjective*
An **ambidextrous** person uses both hands equally well, being neither particularly right-handed nor left-handed.

ambience or **ambiance** /ˈambɪəns/ *noun* (*used in the singular*)
The **ambience** of a place is its feeling, atmosphere and setting.

ambiguity /ambɪˈgjuːɪtɪ/ *noun*: **ambiguities**
1 (*uncount*) **Ambiguity** is uncertainness of meaning where two or more different interpretations are possible. **2** An **ambiguity** is a word or expression that can be understood in two or more different ways: *a statement full of ambiguities.*

ambiguous /amˈbɪgjʊəs/ *adjective*
An **ambiguous** statement, question or remark is unclear because it can be understood in two or more ways: *Her reply was deliberately ambiguous.* — *adverb* **ambiguously:** *an ambiguously expressed message.*

ambition /amˈbɪʃən/ *noun*: **ambitions**
1 (*uncount*) **Ambition** is the desire for, and the determination to achieve, such things as success, power, wealth and fame: *I started out full of ambition.* □ *He lacks ambition.* □ *We're looking for people with plenty of ambition, drive and initiative.* **2** Your **ambitions** are the things you want to achieve: *It's one of my ambitions to get a novel published.* [*same as* **aim, goal**]

ambitious /amˈbɪʃəs/ *adjective*
1 An **ambitious** person wants such things as success, power, wealth and fame, and works hard to achieve them: *You need to be ambitious to succeed in this world.* **2** An **ambitious** project is one that requires a lot of effort and skill and often large-scale expenditure of money, to be successful: *My next book will be more ambitious.*

ambivalent /amˈbɪvələnt/ *adjective*
You are **ambivalent** about something, or have an **ambivalent** attitude towards it, if you have opposing, conflicting or mixed feelings about it: *She had ambivalent feelings about marriage.* — *noun* (*uncount*) **ambivalence:** *the Church's well-known ambivalence on sexual matters.*

amble /ˈambəl/ *verb*: **ambles, ambling, ambled**
You **amble** when you walk at a slow, easy, pace: *We ambled along the street looking in shop windows.* [*same as* **stroll, saunter**]

ambulance /ˈambjʊləns/ *noun*: **ambulances**
An **ambulance** is a specially equipped vehicle for transporting ill or injured people, especially to hospital.

ambush /ˈambʊʃ/ *verb*; *noun*
▻ ***verb***: **ambushes, ambushing, ambushed**
A band of *eg* soldiers **ambushes** a group of *eg* enemy soldiers when they wait in hiding for them to come past and then make a surprise attack on them.
▻ ***noun***: **ambushes**
An **ambush** is a surprise attack of this kind: *We were caught in an ambush in the pass.*

amen /ɑːˈmɛn/ or /eɪˈmɛn/ *interjection*
Christians say **Amen**, meaning 'may it be so', at the end of their prayers.

amenable /əˈmiːnəbəl/ *adjective*
You are **amenable** to something such as advice if you are willing to accept it or follow it.

amend /əˈmɛnd/ *verb*: **amends, amending, amended**
To **amend** *eg* a document or a parliamentary bill is to alter it or improve it: *The Society's constitution has been amended to allow women to become president.* — *noun* (*count or uncount*) **amendment:** *Several amendments to the bill were recommended.*
▻ ***phrase*** You **make amends** for harm you have done by doing something to help or please the person you have hurt or upset.

amenity /əˈmiːnɪtɪ/ or /əˈmɛnɪtɪ/ *noun*: **amenities**
The **amenities** of a place are things such as a sports centre, park or library that are provided for the use and enjoyment of the public. [*same as* **facility**]

American /əˈmɛrɪkən/ *adjective*; *noun*
▻ ***adjective***
American means concerned with or belonging to the United States of America or the continent of America, especially North America: *the American constitution* □ *an American accent.*
▻ ***noun***: **Americans**
An **American** is a person who is born in, or is a citizen of, the United States of America.

amethyst /ˈaməθɪst/ *noun* (*count or uncount*): **amethysts**
An **amethyst** is a purple stone used in jewellery: *an amethyst brooch.*

amiable /ˈeɪmɪəbəl/ *adjective*
An **amiable** person is friendly and good-tempered, with a pleasant manner: *Her face had an amiable expression.* [*same as* **genial**] — *adverb* **amiably:** *He smiled amiably.*

amicable /ˈamɪkəbəl/ *adjective*
Dealings between people are described as **amicable** if they are conducted in a friendly, fair and polite way, without anger or quarrelling: *They remained on amicable terms after the divorce.* □ *I'm sure we can come to some amicable arrangement about book-borrowing.* [*opposite* **hostile**] — *adverb* **amicably:** *The dispute was eventually settled amicably.*

amid /əˈmɪd/ or **amidst** /əˈmɪdst/ *preposition* (*literary*)
Something is, or happens, **amid** or **amidst** a lot of other things, when they are, or are happening, all around it: *Amidst the trees stood a statue of the goddess Diana.*

amiss /əˈmɪs/ *adjective or adverb* (*old*)
You say that something is **amiss** when there is something wrong: *Something's gone amiss with these calculations.*
▻ ***phrases*** **1** You **take** something such as a remark **amiss** if you are offended or upset by it. **2** You say that something **would not come amiss** when you want it or would welcome it: *A little patience wouldn't come amiss.*

ammunition /amjʊˈnɪʃən/ *noun* (*uncount*)
1 Ammunition is missiles such as bullets, shells and rockets, for firing from guns. **2** In an argument, your **ammunition** is all the pieces of information and evidence you have ready to use against your opponents.

amnesia /amˈniːzɪə/ or /amˈniːʒə/ *noun* (*uncount*)
People who are suffering from **amnesia** have lost their memory.

amnesty /ˈamnəstɪ/ *noun*: **amnesties**
1 An **amnesty** is a pardon officially granted by the state to prisoners guilty of political crimes. **2** A period during which criminals may admit to crimes or hand in weapons without being punished, is also called an **amnesty**.

amok /əˈmɒk/ or /əˈmʌk/ or **amuck** /əˈmʌk/ *adverb*
▻ ***phrase*** Someone **runs amok** or **amuck** when they run crazily about trying to kill people.

among /əˈmʌŋ/ or **amongst** /əˈmʌŋst/ *preposition*
1 A person or thing is **among** others when they are surrounded by them: *I spotted David amongst the guests.* □ *His birthplace was a tiny village set amongst snowy peaks.* **2** You are **among** friends or enemies when you are in the company of friends or enemies. **3** You divide something **among** a number of people when you give each of them a share of it: *We divided*

the left-over food amongst us. **4** People do something **among** themselves if they do it with each other: *We were just chatting amongst ouselves.* **5** You say that something is **among** the best or worst of a class of things if it is one of the best or worst: *Cancer is now amongst the commonest causes of death.* **6** You deal with one thing **among** other things when it is one of several things you deal with; you say that one person, **among** others, does something, when they are one of several who do it: *We discussed, amongst other things, the problem of parking.* □ *Amongst others, I protested loudly at the changes.* **7** A certain phenomenon or circumstance exists **among** a group of people if it affects some or all of them: *Breast cancer is far rarer among the Oriental races than among Europeans* □ *The feeling among the employees is extremely bitter.*
[compare **between**]

amoral /eɪ'mɒrəl/ or /a'mɒrəl/ *adjective*
You call someone or their behaviour **amoral** if they have no moral principles, and so act without caring whether what they do is right or wrong.

amorous /'amərəs/ *adjective*
People feel **amorous** when they are filled with sexual desire: *amorous behaviour.* — *adverb* **amorously:** *He clasped her hand amorously.*

amount /ə'maʊnt/ *noun; verb*
▻ ***noun*: amounts**
1 An **amount** of something is a quantity of it, or how much there is of it: *I was impressed by the amount of work she'd done.* □ *Add a small amount of milk to the mixture.* □ *You shouldn't carry such large amounts of money around with you.* □ *A computer virus can cause any amount* [= a lot] *of damage in the system.* **2** An **amount** can refer to a sum of money: *Unless you appeal you will be liable for the full amount.*

> You normally use **amount** with uncount nouns, **quantity** with count nouns or uncount mass nouns such as *water* or *money*, and **number** with count nouns: *a large amount* (or *quantity*) *of water; a minimal amount* (not *quantity*) *of damage; a small number* (or *quantity*) *of items.*

▻ ***verb*: amounts, amounting, amounted**

> ***phrasal verb***
> **amount to 1** Something **amounts to** a certain total if all the items in it make that total when added together: *The repair bill amounted to $750.* [*same as* **come to**, **run to**] **2** You say that something **amounts to** little or a lot according to how important or significant it is: *They gave me the latest news, but it doesn't amount to much.* **3** One thing **amounts to** another, usually greater, thing, if it seems to be almost the same thing: *Giving presents to potential customers amounts to bribery.* □ *Her feelings for her teacher amounted to adoration.*

amp /amp/ *noun*: **amps**
An **amp** is a unit of measurement for electric current: *a 13-amp plug.*

amphibian /am'fɪbɪən/ *noun*: **amphibians**
An **amphibian** is an animal, such as a frog or toad, that can live both on land and in water. — *adjective* **amphibious:** *amphibious creatures.*

amphitheatre (*AmE* **amphitheater**) /'amfɪθɪətə(r)/ *noun*: **amphitheatres**
An **amphitheatre** is a round building without a roof, with rows of seats rising from a central open area, used as a theatre.

ample /'ampəl/ *adjective* (*old, or formal*)
1 You have **ample** time or room for something, or an **ample** quantity of something, when you have plenty, or more than enough: *Customers will be given ample warning before the electricity is cut off.* **2** **Ample** also means large: *a sitting room of ample proportions.* [*same as* **generous**] — *adverb* **amply:** *He was amply rewarded for his trouble.*

amplifier /'amplɪfaɪə(r)/ *noun*: **amplifiers**
An **amplifier** is an electronic device for increasing signals or sounds in radio or stereo equipment.

amplify /'amplɪfaɪ/ *verb*: **amplifies, amplifying, amplified**
1 You **amplify** a sound or signal when you make it stronger by electronic means. **2** You **amplify** something you have said when you add more facts and details: *Would you like me to amplify that statement?* [*same as* **expand, enlarge on**] — *noun* (*uncount*) **amplification** /amplɪfɪ'keɪʃən/: *sound amplification* □ *a list of points requiring amplification.*

amputate /'ampjʊteɪt/ *verb*: **amputates, amputating, amputated**
To **amputate** a limb is to cut it off by surgery. — *noun* (*uncount*) **amputation** /ampjʊ'teɪʃən/: *Amputation of the whole leg won't be necessary.*

amuck see **amok**.

amuse /ə'mju:z/ *verb*: **amuses, amusing, amused**
1 Something funny **amuses** you and makes you want to laugh or smile: *The thought amused her.* **2** You **amuse** yourself or others, when you find things to do to stop yourself, or them, getting bored: *He thought of various activities that might amuse the children till bedtime.* □ *Even as a child she was good at amusing herself.* [*same as* **occupy**] — *adjective* **amused:** *I couldn't help being amused by his holiday stories.* □ *She glanced up with an amused smile.* □ *Can you keep yourself amused while I make some telephone calls?*

amusement /ə'mju:zmənt/ *noun*: **amusements**
1 (*uncount*) **Amusement** is what you feel when you find something funny: *A look of amusement came into her eyes.* □ *There was a lot of amusement at his comment.* □ *He pretended to cry, much to their amusement.* **2** (*uncount*) Activities and entertainments that are provided for your **amusement** are intended to occupy you and keep you happy. **3** **Amusements** are activities, facilities *eg* for sports, or such things as fairground rides or gambling machines, available *eg* at holiday resorts to stop people getting bored.

amusing /ə'mju:zɪŋ/ *adjective*
A person or thing that is **amusing** makes you want to laugh or smile: *I suppose the film was mildly amusing.* [*same as* **funny, entertaining**] — *adverb* **amusingly:** *It was an amusingly written article.*

an /ən/ or /an/ *determiner*
An is the form of the indefinite article used before a vowel. See **a**.

anachronism /ə'nakrənɪzm/ *noun*: **anachronisms**
People refer to something they consider oldfashioned or out of date as an **anachronism**: *He upset his audience by calling the monarchy an anachronism.* — *adjective* **anachronistic** /ənakrə'nɪstɪk/: *Shakespeare's anachronistic reference to a clock striking in 'Julius Caesar'* □ *His political views are anachronistic.*

anaemia (*AmE* **anemia**) /ə'ni:mɪə/ *noun* (*uncount*)
You are suffering from **anaemia** if you haven't enough red cells in your blood, and are tired and pale as a result. — *adjective* **anaemic** (*AmE* **anemic**) /ə'ni:mɪk/: *a pale, anaemic-looking girl.*

anaesthesia (*AmE* **anesthesia**) /anəs'θi:zɪə/ *noun* (*uncount*)
The use of pain-killing drugs in surgery or medicine is called **anaesthesia**.

anaesthetic (*AmE* **anesthetic**) /anəs'θɛtɪk/ *noun*: **anaesthetics**
An **anaesthetic** is a substance, such as a drug or gas, used for pain-killing during surgical operations, a **general anaesthetic** causing complete unconsciousness, and a **local anaesthetic** causing loss of sensation in a particular part of the body.

anaesthetist (*AmE* **anesthetist**) /ə'niːsθətɪst/ *noun*: **anaesthetists**
An **anaesthetist** is a doctor who gives anaesthetics to patients.

anaesthetize or **anaesthetise** (*AmE* **anesthetize**) /ə'niːsθətaɪz/ *verb*: **anaesthetizes, anaesthetizing, anaesthetized**
Doctors **anaesthetize** patients when they make them unconscious by giving them an anaesthetic.

anagram /'anəgram/ *noun*: **anagrams**
An **anagram** is a word or phrase consisting of the rearranged letters of another word: *'Glean' is an anagram of 'angle'.*

anal /'eɪnəl/ *adjective*
Anal means relating to the anus.

analogous /ə'naləgəs/ *adjective*
One thing is **analogous** to another if it matches it in some way: *The two situations are analogous.* [*same as* **similar**]

analogy /ə'nalədʒɪ/ *noun*: **analogies**
1 You make an **analogy** between two things when you show that they match each other or are parallel in some way: *People sometimes draw an analogy between the human brain and a computer.* [*same as* **parallel**] **2** (*uncount*) You use **analogy**, or illustrate something by **analogy**, when you explain a difficult notion in terms of a simple illustration that provides a model or parallel.

analyse (*AmE* **analyze**) /'anəlaɪz/ *verb*: **analyses, analysing, analysed**
1 You **analyse** something when you examine it in detail in order to understand it, especially by considering separately all the elements it consists of: *We're analysing the results of the poll and will report on our findings tomorrow.* **2** (*AmE*) To **analyze** a person is to psychoanalyze them.

analysis /ə'nalɪsɪs/ *noun*: **analyses** /ə'naləsiːz/
1 (*uncount or count*) **Analysis** of something is the process of identifying and examining each element or feature of it in detail in order to understand it: *textual analysis* □ *chemical analyses.* **2** An **analysis** is a statement of the results of this kind of detailed examination: *a recent analysis of the Aids situation.* **3** (*AmE*) **Analysis** is the same as psychoanalysis.
▻ ***phrase*** You say that something is so **in the final analysis** when you are stating what you believe to be the key fact in a situation.

analyst /'anəlɪst/ *noun*: **analysts**
1 An **analyst**'s job is to examine and report on such things as political or economic situations, or to analyse chemicals. **2** (*AmE*) An **analyst** is a psychoanalyst.

analytic /anə'lɪtɪk/ or **analytical** /anə'lɪtɪkəl/ *adjective*
Analytic and **analytical** mean relating to analysis, or to the use of logical argument and reasoning: *She had a sharp analytical mind.* — *adverb* **analytically:** *Always tackle any problem calmly and analytically.*

anarchism /'anəkɪzm/ *noun* (*uncount*)
Anarchism is the political theory or belief that governments and laws are unnecessary, and should be abolished in favour of a free society in which people live in willing co-operation with one another.

anarchist /'anəkɪst/ *noun*: **anarchists**
An **anarchist** is a person who believes in anarchism.

anarchy /'anəkɪ/ *noun* (*uncount*)
Anarchy is the confusion and disorder that result from the absence of, or disregard for, rules, laws or government: *The old headmaster retired and anarchy took over.* [*same as* **chaos, mayhem**] — *adjective* **anarchic** /ə'nɑːkɪk/: *Their filing system is anarchic.*

anathema /ə'naθəmə/ *noun* (*uncount*)
Something that is **anathema** to you is something you hate: *Nosiness was anathema to him.*

anatomy /ə'natəmɪ/ *noun*: **anatomies**
1 (*uncount*) **Anatomy** is the science of the structure of the human body or the bodies of animals. **2** (*usually in the singular*) The **anatomy** of any animal is the structure of its body: *the anatomy of the bee.* — *adjective* **anatomical** /anə'tɒmɪkəl/: *anatomical drawings* □ *anatomical structure.* — *adverb* **anatomically:** *anatomically accurate models.*

ancestor /'ansɛstə(r)/ *noun*: **ancestors**
1 Your **ancestors** are the former members of your family from whom you are descended. [*same as* **antecedent**] **2** In terms of evolution or historical development, the **ancestor** of something existing now is the thing from which it can be said to have come: *It is the lizard-hipped rather than the bird-hipped dinosaurs that are the true ancestors of birds.*

ancestral /an'sɛstrəl/ *adjective*
Ancestral means relating to, or belonging to, former generations of your family: *Blair Castle, the ancestral home of the Dukes of Atholl.*

ancestry /'ansɛstrɪ/ *noun* (*count or uncount*): **ancestries**
Your **ancestry** is the series of people of previous generations from whom you are descended: *He claimed Scottish ancestry.* [*same as* **origin, descent, extraction**]

anchor /'aŋkə(r)/ *noun*; *verb*
▻ ***noun***: **anchors**
An **anchor** is a heavy metal object, typically a shaft with a curved crosspiece ending in points, attached by a chain or cable to a ship's side, and dropped so that it fixes itself in the sea bed and holds the ship in that position.
▻ ***verb***: **anchors, anchoring, anchored**
1 You **anchor** a ship somewhere, or it **anchors**, when the anchor is dropped into the water at a particular place to hold it in that position: *We anchored off the coast of Jamaica.* □ *Several fishing boats were anchored in the bay.* **2** You **anchor** something that might move or be blown away when you attach it to, or weight it down with, something heavy or immovable: *She tried to anchor the newspaper with a large stone.*

ancient /'eɪnʃənt/ *adjective*
1 Ancient civilizations are those of the far distant past, especially of the time before the fall of the Roman empire: *ancient history* □ *Malta's ancient monuments.* **2** Something that is **ancient** is very old: *She wore an ancient straw hat.*

ancillary /an'sɪlərɪ/ *adjective*
1 The **ancillary** staff in a place such as a hospital are the people who work as cooks, cleaners and porters, assisting, rather than involved in, the main work of the institution. [*same as* **auxiliary**] **2** One thing is **ancillary** to another if it is secondary to it: *mathematics and ancillary subjects.* [*same as* **subsidiary**]

and /ənd/ or /and/ *conjunction*
1 You use **and** to link words or word groups of the same grammatical class, *eg* nouns, adjectives, verbs, adverbs: *dogs and cats* □ *truth and beauty* □ *a pencil and a pair of scissors* □ *you and I* □ *looking well and*

happy □ *She slipped and fell* □ *quickly and accurately done.*

When linking pairs of count nouns, you can usually omit the determiner before the second one: *a knife and fork; my hat and coat.*
A comma usually replaces **and** before all but the last item in a list of more than two things: *a knife, fork and spoon; tall, dark, handsome and intelligent.*

2 a You use **and** to express addition: *Two and three are five.* **b** You can use **and** with a repeated verb or noun for emphasis, or with a repeated comparative to express continuing increase; a repeated noun after **and** can also express contrast: *It snowed and snowed.* □ *She got iller and iller.* □ *less and less enthusiastically* □ *There are books and books.* [= all sorts of books, or bad books as well as good ones].
3 You link clauses with **and** to express a variety of meanings: *He put the children to bed and* [= while] *I made supper.* □ *She was crying and* [= so] *I comforted her.* □ *I washed the clothes and* [= then] *ironed them.* □ *Tell me the truth and* [= because if you do] *I'll give you a sweet.* □ *Deprive someone of air and* [= if you deprive someone of air] *they'll die in a few minutes*
4 a And is often used instead of 'to' after verbs like 'come', 'go' and 'try': *Do come and stay sometime.* □ *Go and see who's at the door.* □ *I'll try and finish by lunchtime.* **b** (*informal*) **And** is used with 'nice' and 'lovely' before another adjective, for emphasis: *It's nice and quiet in here.* □ *The weather's lovely and warm.*

anecdote /'anəkdoʊt/ *noun*: **anecdotes**
An **anecdote** is a usually amusing account of an incident: *I'd heard all his office anecdotes before.*

anemia (*AmE*)
Anemia and **anemic** are variant spellings of **anaemia** and **anaemic**.

anesthesia (*AmE*)
Anesthesia, **anesthetic**, **anesthetist** and **anesthetize** are variant spellings of **anaesthesia**, **anaesthetic**, **anaesthetist** and **anaesthetize**.

anew /ə'nju:/ *adverb*
You start **anew** when you start doing something again from the beginning, usually in a different way. [*same as* **afresh**]

angel /'eɪndʒəl/ *noun*: **angels**
1 Angels are beings believed to inhabit heaven and serve God as attendants and messengers, often represented in human form, dressed in white, with wings.
2 (*informal*) You call someone an **angel** if they're kind and helpful to you, or you think them beautiful, good or adorable: *Be an angel and polish my shoes for me.* [*same as* **gem**, **darling**, **dear**] — *adjective* **angelic** /an'dʒɛlɪk/ (*often informal*): *angelic-looking children.* — *adverb* **angelically** (*often informal*): *The children behaved angelically.*

anger /'aŋgə(r)/ *noun*; *verb*
▻ ***noun*** (*uncount*)
Anger is the strong emotion you feel *eg* when someone insults you or treats you cruelly or unfairly, or when you see cruelty or injustice, so that you may want to fight or quarrel: *She tried to keep her anger under control.* □ *His face was white with anger.*
▻ ***verb***: **angers, angering, angered**
Something **angers** you when it makes you angry: *His lack of interest in the children used to anger her.*

angle[1] /'aŋgəl/ *noun*; *verb*
▻ ***noun***: **angles**
1 An **angle** is the space, or difference in direction, between two straight lines or surfaces that meet, measured in degrees: *All three angles of an equilateral triangle measure 60 degrees.* □ *The bookcase formed a right angle with the wall.* **2** The particular viewpoint from which something is looked at, or the way in which a subject is presented *eg* by a writer, film-maker or television producer, is also an **angle**: *She photographed the building from several different angles.* □ *The feminist angle of the magazine used to annoy a lot of people.*
▻ ***verb***: **angled, angling, angled**
1 You **angle** something when you adjust its position so as to aim, face or slant it in a particular direction: *He angled the camera so as to take in the whole statue.*
2 You **angle** a report or story when you present it so as to express a certain point of view.
▻ ***phrase*** Something is **at an angle** when it is sloping or slanting, not vertical or horizontal: *It was the fashion at school to wear your hat at an angle.*

angle[2] /'aŋgəl/ *verb*: **angles, angling, angled**

phrasal verb
You **angle for** something when you try to get it in an indirect way, without actually asking: *I think she's angling for an invitation to our wedding.* [*same as* **fish**]

angler /'aŋglə(r)/ *noun*: **anglers**
An **angler** is a person who goes fishing with a rod and line.

angling /'aŋglɪŋ/ *noun* (*uncount*)
Angling is the pastime of fishing with a rod and line.

Anglo- /'aŋgloʊ/ *prefix*
Anglo- is combined with adjectives or nouns relating to geographical areas to mean belonging or relating both to England, or sometimes Britain, and somewhere else: *the Anglo-French trade agreement* □ *She calls herself an Anglo-American.*

angry /'aŋgrɪ/ *adjective*: **angrier, angriest**
1 You are **angry** when you are filled with anger, a strong emotion that may make you want to quarrel or fight, *eg* when you are insulted or treated unfairly, or meet with injustice, cruelty or carelessness: *I was angry with her for losing my book.* □ *My father gets angry if I stay out late.* □ *What's he so angry about?* □ *He's angry at having to queue so long.* □ *angry words.*
2 An **angry** wound is one that looks red, sore and infected. **3** The sky looks **angry** when it is full of dark, stormy clouds. — *adverb* **angrily**: *She angrily rejected his suggestion.*

anguish /'aŋgwɪʃ/ *noun* (*uncount*)
Anguish is very severe distress or pain, usually of a mental or emotional kind: *a widow's anguish.* — *adjective* **anguished**: *They could hear the anguished cries of people trapped under the rubble.*

angular /'aŋgjʊlə(r)/ *adjective*
1 Something that is **angular** has sharp corners, points or angles: *He recognized her angular handwriting on the envelope.* **2** An **angular** person is thin and bony: *a thin, angular face.*

animal /'anɪməl/ *noun*; *adjective*
▻ ***noun***: **animals**
1 Animals are living creatures other than human beings, birds, fish, reptiles such as crocodiles or snakes, and insects: *deer and other wild animals* □ *cats and other domestic animals.* **2** All living things other than plants can be referred to as **animals**: *Man is the most intellectually advanced of the animals.* **3** (*derogatory*) If you call a person an **animal** you mean that their behaviour is savage, uncivilized or disgusting. [*same as* **beast**]
▻ ***adjective***
Animal describes
1 things that come from animals: *animal fats* □ *animal*

skins. **2** qualities associated with people's physical needs and nature as opposed to their minds: *animal desires* □ *animal instincts.*

animate /'anɪmət/ *adjective*
An **animate** thing has life, or is alive, as distinct from things that do not have life, such as stone and metal. [*opposite* **inanimate**]

animated /'anɪmeɪtɪd/ *adjective*
1 A lively person, face, expression or conversation can be described as **animated**: *The lecture was followed by an animated discussion.* **2** An **animated** film consists of a series of drawings altering slightly frame by frame, so that figures appear to move when the film is run: *animated cartoons.* — *adverb* **animatedly:** *They were talking animatedly to each other.*

animation /anɪ'meɪʃən/ *noun* (*uncount*)
1 Animation is liveliness, in facial expression, speech or gesture: *She was beautiful, certainly, but her eyes lacked animation.* [*same as* **life, vitality**] **2 Animation** is also the name of the process used to record a series of drawings on film so that when the film is run the drawn figures appear to move.

animosity /anɪ'mɒsɪtɪ/ *noun* (*uncount or count*): **animosities**
Animosity is strong hatred or dislike: *She felt no animosity towards the driver who had injured her.* □ *political animosities.* [*same as* **antagonism**]

aniseed /'anɪsiːd/ *noun* (*uncount*)
Aniseed is the liquorice-flavoured seed of a certain Mediterranean plant, used in making sweets, drinks and some medicines.

ankle /'aŋkəl/ *noun*: **ankles**
Your **ankle** is the joint that links your foot to your leg, or the part of the leg just above the joint: *I sprained my ankle falling downstairs.* [see picture at **body**]

annals /'anəlz/ *noun* (*plural*)
A person or event has a place in the **annals** if they are noted in recorded history: *the annals of the nation.*

annex /ə'nɛks/ or /'anɛks/ *verb*: **annexes, annexing, annexed**
One country **annexes** the territory of another country when it takes possession of it, *eg* by invasion, conquest and occupation: *Britain was annexed by Rome in 55 BC.* — *noun* (*uncount*) **annexation** /anɛk'seɪʃən/: *the annexation of parts of Africa by Britain, France, Germany and Portugal.*

annexe or **annex** /'anɛks/ *noun*: **annexes**
An **annexe** is a building added to or standing close to a larger building, used *eg* to provide additional space: *He was lying in a ward in the hospital annexe.*

annihilate /ə'naɪəleɪt/ *verb*: **annihilates, annihilating, annihilated**
1 Something **is annihilated** when it is completely destroyed or wiped out: *Indiscriminate hunting of wild animals has annihilated many species.* **2** (*informal*) You **annihilate** an opponent in an argument or contest when you defeat them completely. — *noun* (*uncount*) **annihilation** /ənaɪə'leɪʃən/: *Nuclear war would lead inevitably to the annihilation of the human race.*

anniversary /anɪ'vɜːsərɪ/ *noun*: **anniversaries**
The **anniversary** of an event, especially an important one, is its date in any following year, on which it may be commemorated or celebrated in some way: *the 45th anniversary of the outbreak of World War 2.* □ *a wedding anniversary.*

annotated /'anəteɪtɪd/ *adjective*
An **annotated** text includes notes to help the reader.

announce /ə'naʊns/ *verb*: **announces, announcing, announced**
You **announce** something when you inform people publicly or officially about it: *The government will have to announce the date of the election soon.* □ *His death was announced in today's paper.* □ *When are you two going to announce your engagement?*

announcement /ə'naʊnsmənt/ *noun*: **announcements**
1 An **announcement** is an official or public statement informing people about something that has happened or is to happen: *There was an official announcement of his resignation on the news today.* **2** (*uncount*) The **announcement** of something is the act of making it officially or publicly known.

announcer /ə'naʊnsə(r)/ *noun*: **announcers**
An **announcer** is a person who introduces programmes on radio or television.

annoy /ə'nɔɪ/ *verb*: **annoys, annoying, annoyed**
1 Something or someone **annoys** you if they make you rather angry, impatient or bad-tempered: *It used to annoy me when she whistled to herself.* [*same as* **irritate**] **2** Someone **annoys** you when they keep bothering you or disturbing you. [*same as* **pester**]

annoyance /ə'nɔɪəns/ *noun*: **annoyances**
1 (*uncount*) **Annoyance** is the impatient feeling you have when something annoys and upsets you: *She couldn't hide her annoyance at his stupidity.* **2** An **annoyance** is something that upsets or annoys you: *The loud background music was an added annoyance.*

annoyed /ə'nɔɪd/ *adjective*
You are **annoyed** when you feel rather angry and impatient: *I get annoyed when I'm interrupted unnecessarily.* □ *We felt annoyed at the unhelpfulness of the staff.* □ *I was annoyed that he forgot to come.* □ *I'm so annoyed with myself for making that mistake.*

annoying /ə'nɔɪɪŋ/ *adjective*
Something that is **annoying** makes you rather angry or impatient: *She had an annoying habit of finishing your sentences for you.* □ *It was annoying to have to wait so long.* — *adverb* **annoyingly:** *He was annoyingly calm about the whole affair.*

annual /'anjʊəl/ *adjective; noun*
▻ ***adjective***
1 An **annual** event happens once every year: *The annual general meeting of the society will precede the lecture.* □ *The plans are outlined in the annual report.* **2** An **annual** amount is the total for a whole year: *She has an annual budget of £2000 to buy books for the school library.* □ *annual profits.*
[*same as* **yearly**]
▻ ***noun***: **annuals**
An **annual** is a book that is published once a year under the same title, usually containing material relating to the year of publication: *a copy of 'The Cricket Annual'.* — *adverb* **annually:** *The shareholders met annually, usually in March.* □ *We make only about £1200 annually.* [*same as* **yearly**]

annul /ə'nʌl/ *verb*: **annuls, annulling, annulled**
Something such as a marriage or other contract **is annulled** when it is publicly declared no longer valid, so that legally it does not exist. — *noun* (*uncount or count*) **annulment:** *Their marriage ended in annulment.*

annum see **per annum**.

anoint /ə'nɔɪnt/ *verb*: **anoints, anointing, anointed**
Someone **is anointed** when oil, ointment or water is put on their head as part of a religious ceremony such as baptism.

anomalous /ə'nɒmələs/ *adjective*
Something that is **anomalous** is exceptional or different from what is normal or expected: *The computer*

has come up with some rather anomalous statistics. [*same as* **unusual, unexpected, abnormal, irregular**]

anomaly /əˈnɒməlɪ/ *noun*: **anomalies**
An **anomaly** is an irregular, abnormal or inconsistent feature of something: *There are still a number of legal anomalies relating to the rights of married women.*

anonymity /anəˈnɪmɪtɪ/ *noun* (*uncount*)
1 Anonymity is the state of not being known, recognized or identified by name: *They were interviewed with their backs to the camera, so as to preserve their anonymity.* □ *The police informant insisted on anonymity.* **2** The **anonymity** of something such as an environment is **a** the way it hides who you are: *They spent the weekend in peaceful anonymity, away from the press and the television studios.* **b** its lack of distinctive characteristics or features: *the anonymity of the long grey parallel streets.*

anonymous /əˈnɒnɪməs/ *adjective*
1 Anonymous means 'having no name'; a written work or a letter is **anonymous** if the writer's name is not known, or not shown: *an anonymous poem* □ *The note was anonymous, signed only 'A well-wisher'.* □ *the anonymous heroine of 'Rebecca'.* **2** You remain **anonymous** if you do something, *eg* give money to a charity, without letting your name be known: *They received $4000 from an anonymous donor.* **3** Something is **anonymous** if it hides your identity: *The handwritten letter is being replaced by these anonymous word-processed communications.* **4** Something or someone that lacks distinctive characteristics can be called **anonymous**: *a row of anonymous-looking houses.* — *adverb* **anonymously:** *The money was donated anonymously.*

anorak /ˈanərak/ *noun*: **anoraks**
An **anorak** is a waterproof jacket, usually with a hood. [see picture at **clothing**]

another /əˈnʌðə(r)/ *determiner; pronoun*
▷ ***determiner***
1 Another thing or person is an additional one: *I can get you another copy of the book.* □ *The bus has gone but there'll be another one along in four minutes.* □ *It's been yet another wet day in most areas.* □ *Another woman was attacked last night.* □ *She'll end up as another Mrs Thatcher.* **2 Another** thing or person also means a different one: *We had to find another school for him as he wasn't happy where he was.* □ *This is another man I'm talking about, not Edward.* □ *Jill disappeared in another direction.*

> **Another** is used with singular count nouns, but can be used with 'few' or a particular number, followed by a plural count noun: *We'd better wait another five minutes. I need another few volunteers.*

▷ ***pronoun:*** *You solve one problem and along comes another.* □ *Our manager has resigned so we're looking for another.* □ *It's one thing to make a promise but quite another to keep it.*
▷ ***phrases***
1 You refer to things occurring **one after another** to indicate that they happen repeatedly or continuously: *We've had one problem after another.* □ *One after another her friends deserted her.* **2** You use **one another** in describing situations where each member of a group does the same to, or has the same relationship with, each of the others: *We must support one another.* □ *They all got on well with one another.* □ *They respected one another's privacy.* [compare **each other**]

> Notice the difference between: *The leaders blamed one another* [= each one blamed the others] and *The leaders blamed themselves* [= they all accepted the blame].

answer /ˈɑːnsə(r)/ *verb; noun*
▷ ***verb***: **answers, answering, answered**
1 You **answer** someone who has spoken to you or asked you a question, when you reply or say something back to them: *Why don't you answer me?* □ *It's an impossible question to answer.* □ *She asked what had happened, but he didn't answer.* □ *'That's all OK, then.' 'Yes', she answered.* □ *I answered that I was busy on Monday.* **2** You **answer** a letter when you write back to the writer: *Sorry to take so long to answer your last letter.* **3** You **answer** an advertisement when you write to the advertiser as instructed. **4** You **answer** the telephone when you lift the handset and speak to the person who is calling; you **answer** the door when you open it in response to someone knocking on it or ringing the doorbell: *She rang the doorbell but no-one answered.* **5** You **answer** a question on a particular subject in an examination when you write something to show what you know about it: *I didn't answer Question 6.*
▷ ***noun***: **answers**
1 An **answer** is a reply or something said or done in response to a question, request or letter: *Have you had any answers to your advertisement yet?* □ *She shrugged by way of an answer.* **2** The solution to a problem is its **answer**; something written on a particular examination question is an **answer**: *The answers are at the back of the book.* □ *The answer to number 4 was 327.6.* □ *I don't know the answer to that.* □ *You wrote an excellent answer on the Reform Bill.* **3** Certain adverbs, such as *exactly*, *absolutely*, *quite* and *hardly*, can be used on their own in conversation as a response. In this dictionary these adverbs are labelled (*used as an answer*).
▷ ***phrase*** You do or say something **in answer to** someone when you respond to them in some way: *She nodded in answer to his question.* □ *He glared at her in answer.*

> ***phrasal verbs***
> **answer back** Someone **answers** you **back**, or **answers back**, when they reply rudely.
> **answer for 1** You say that you can **answer for** someone, or for some quality such as their loyalty, when you are sure that they can be relied on or trusted. [*same as* **vouch for**] **2** Someone has a lot to **answer** for if something they have done has caused problems and difficulties.
> **answer to 1** You **answer to** someone for something if they hold you responsible for whatever goes wrong with it: *You'll have to answer to me if you break it.* **2** Something or someone **answers to** a description if it matches or identifies them.

answerable /ˈɑːnsərəbəl/ *adjective*
You are **answerable** to someone for something if they hold you responsible for it, and for whatever goes wrong with it: *I'm answerable to the directors for office discipline.* [*same as* **accountable**]

ant /ant/ *noun*: **ants**
An **ant** is a small crawling insect, some types of which are wingless, that lives in organized colonies and is thought of as very hard-working: *swarms of ants* □ *an enormous ant hill.*

antagonism /anˈtagənɪzm/ *noun* (*uncount or count*)
Antagonism is a feeling of dislike or hostility towards someone: *I don't remember feeling any antagonism towards my brother.* □ *It's good to get away from the office antagonisms.* [*same as* **animosity**]

antagonist /anˈtagənɪst/ *noun*: **antagonists**
Your **antagonist** is your enemy or your opponent.

antagonistic /antagəˈnɪstɪk/ *adjective*
Someone who is **antagonistic** towards you is hostile,

and typically shows their dislike in the way they treat you: *antagonistic behaviour.*

antagonize or **antagonise** /an'tagənaɪz/ *verb*: **antagonizes, antagonizing, antagonized**
You **antagonize** someone when you behave in a way that makes them feel dislike for you: *Her aggressiveness antagonizes nearly everyone she has contact with.*

Antarctic /ant'ɑːktɪk/ *noun*; *adjective*
▻ ***noun*** (*used in the singular*)
The **Antarctic** is the area of the world round the South Pole.
▻ ***adjective:*** *Antarctic exploration* □ *the Antarctic winter.*

ante- /'antɪ/ *prefix*
Ante- means before something in time or place, as in *antenatal*, before birth.

antecedent /antɪ'siːdənt/ *noun*: **antecedents**
1 An **antecedent** of something is a thing or circumstance in the past from which it has developed or been derived: *We're looking here at some of the flying machines that were the antecedents of the aeroplane.* **2** (*used in the plural*) Your **antecedents** are your ancestors, the people from whom you are descended.

antelope /'antɪloʊp/ *noun*: **antelopes** or **antelope**
An **antelope** is a graceful, deer-like animal related to the goat, found especially in Africa: *herds of antelope.*

antenatal /antɪ'neɪtəl/ *adjective*
Antenatal means before birth, and refers especially to the later stages of pregnancy: *an antenatal clinic.*

antenna /an'tɛnə/ *noun*: **antennae** /an'tɛniː/ or **antennas**
1 An insect's **antennae** are the pair of long thin projections that extend from its head, used for feeling and touching. [*same as* **feeler**] **2** An **antenna** is also a rod or wire fixed to a television or radio set, or to the roof of a building or vehicle, that receives and sends signals. [*same as* **aerial**; see picture at **car**]

anthem /'anθəm/ *noun*: **anthems**
An **anthem** is a hymn or song, especially one composed to celebrate something, or one sung or played on special occasions: *the national anthem.*

anthology /an'θɒlədʒɪ/ *noun*: **anthologies**
An **anthology** is a book containing a collection of pieces of poetry or other writing by a variety of authors.

anthropologist /anθrə'pɒlədʒɪst/ *noun*: **anthropologists**
An **anthropologist** is someone who studies, or is an expert in, anthropology.

anthropology /anθrə'pɒlədʒɪ/ *noun* (*uncount*)
Anthropology is the study of human beings, especially in relation to the kind of societies they live in, and their customs and beliefs. — *adjective* **anthropological** /anθrəpə'lɒdʒɪkəl/: *anthropological investigations.*

anti- /'antɪ/ (*AmE* /'antaɪ/) *prefix*
Anti- means against, and forms words that mean
1 opposed to or disliking something, as in *anti-apartheid*, disapproving of the apartheid system. **2** preventing or fighting something, as in *antiseptic*, preventing infection, and *anti-tank missiles*.

antibiotic /antɪbaɪ'ɒtɪk/ *noun* (*usually in the plural*): **antibiotics**
Antibiotics are medicines or drugs used to kill the bacteria that cause disease: *The doctor has put her on a course of antibiotics.*

anticipate /an'tɪsɪpeɪt/ *verb*: **anticipates, anticipating, anticipated**
1 You **anticipate** something when you think it may happen and prepare yourself for it: *The police had anticipated trouble from the soccer fans and were at the ground in large numbers.* □ *They anticipate that deaths from AIDS will have doubled by 1998.* [*same as* **foresee, reckon on**] **2** You **anticipate** someone's needs when you give them what they want without their having to ask for it. **3** You **anticipate** a future event or situation when you look ahead to it, *eg* with pleasure or anxiety: *He anticipated the hazardous car journey across Europe with some alarm.*

anticipation /antɪsɪ'peɪʃən/ *noun* (*uncount*)
1 Anticipation of something is the state of expecting it or the circumstance of preparing for it: *Customers were buying more groceries than they needed, in anticipation of a shortage.* **2 Anticipation** is also a state of excited expectation: *She contemplated the plans for the evening with eager anticipation.*

anticlimax /antɪ'klaɪmaks/ *noun* (*count or uncount*): **anticlimaxes**
You call something such as an event an **anticlimax** if it is not as exciting or remarkable as you thought it would be, or if it follows something that was particularly exciting: *His performance was a bit of an anticlimax after all that publicity.* □ *There was inevitably a feeling of anticlimax about the journey home.* [*same as* **letdown**]

anticlockwise /antɪ'klɒkwaɪz/ *adjective or adverb*
Something moves **anticlockwise**, or in an **anticlockwise** direction, when it moves in a circle or curve in the opposite direction to that of the hands of a clock: *You unscrew a normal lid by twisting it anticlockwise.*

antics /'antɪks/ *noun* (*plural*)
You refer to an animal's or person's behaviour or activities, when they are amusing or silly, as their **antics**: *I could have spent another hour watching the monkeys' antics.*

anticyclone /antɪ'saɪkloʊn/ *noun*: **anticyclones**
An **anticyclone** is a system of winds circling outwards from an area of high air pressure, usually producing good weather.

antidote /'antɪdoʊt/ *noun*: **antidotes**
1 An **antidote** is a medicine or treatment given to stop the harmful effects of a poison: *A wasp sting is alkaline, so use vinegar as an antidote.* **2** Something that prevents or gets rid of something bad can be called an **antidote** to it: *Buying some new clothes is the best antidote to depression that I know.*
[*same as* **remedy, cure**]

antifreeze /'antɪfriːz/ *noun* (*uncount*)
Antifreeze is a substance you put in water, especially the water in a car engine, to stop it freezing.

antipathy /an'tɪpəθɪ/ *noun* (*uncount or count*): **antipathies**
Antipathy is a feeling of dislike or hostility: *The deep antipathy between the two men was only too evident.* □ *His antipathy to modernization might make him unpopular.* □ *one's personal antipathies.*

antiquated /'antɪkweɪtɪd/ *adjective* (*derogatory*)
You call something **antiquated** if it is old, worn out, out of date or oldfashioned: *She rode an antiquated bicycle.* □ *antiquated education policies.*

antique /an'tiːk/ *noun*; *adjective*
▻ ***noun***: **antiques**
Antiques are such things as pieces of furniture, china, or jewellery, that are old and valuable: *They collect antiques.*
▻ ***adjective***
1 An **antique** object is an old and valuable one: *antique clocks.* **2** (*informal, or humorous*) If you call someone or something **antique**, you mean they are

very old: *To a child, someone aged 50 is absolutely antique.*

antiquity /an'tɪkwɪtɪ/ *noun*: **antiquities**
1 (*uncount*) **Antiquity** is the ancient past, especially the time before the end of the Roman Empire in AD 476: *the great civilizations of antiquity.* **2** (*uncount*) The **antiquity** of something is its age, especially great age: *The vase was elegant, certainly, but of no very great antiquity.* **3** (*usually in the plural*) **Antiquities** are buildings, works of art and other objects surviving from past times, especially those of archaeological interest: *The Department of Egyptian Antiquities.*

anti-Semitism /antɪ'sɛmətɪzm/ *noun* (*uncount*)
Anti-Semitism is prejudice against, or dislike of, the Jewish race. — *adjective* **anti-Semitic** /antɪsə'mɪtɪk/: *She insisted that she wasn't anti-Semitic.*

antiseptic /antɪ'sɛptɪk/ *noun*; *adjective*
▻ ***noun*** (*count or uncount*): **antiseptics**
An **antiseptic** is a substance that kills germs and so prevents infection or disease: *antiseptics such as Dettol* □ *She cleaned the cut with antiseptic.*
▻ ***adjective:*** *a tube of antiseptic ointment.*

antisocial /antɪ'soʊʃəl/ *adjective*
1 An **antisocial** person dislikes mixing with or being friendly to other people. [*same as* **unsociable**] **2 Antisocial** behaviour is behaviour that upsets or annoys other people, such as making a noise or playing loud music at night. — *adverb* **antisocially:** *Stop behaving so antisocially.*

antithesis /an'tɪθəsɪs/ *noun*: **antitheses**
The **antithesis** of something is its absolute opposite: *Her study of moral philosophy had developed in her political opinions that were pretty well the antithesis of those she had started with.* [*same as* **reverse**, **converse**]

antler /'antlə(r)/ *noun*: **antlers**
A deer's **antlers** are the pair of branching horns on its head.

antonym /'antənɪm/ *noun*: **antonyms**
The **antonym** of a word is a word opposite to it in meaning: *'Cowardice' is an antonym of 'courage'.*

> In this dictionary, antonyms are shown in bold type preceded by the word *opposite*, and are placed at the end of the definition, or the entry, to which they apply.

anus /'eɪnəs/ *noun*: **anuses**
The **anus** is the opening between the buttocks, through which the faeces leave the body.

anvil /'anvɪl/ *noun*: **anvils**
An **anvil** is a heavy iron block on which metal objects are hammered into shape after being heated in a fire.

anxiety /aŋ'zaɪətɪ/ or /aŋ'zaɪtɪ/ *noun*: **anxieties**
1 (*uncount*) **Anxiety** is a feeling of fear, worry or nervousness, resulting from uncertainty: *She listened to the news with increasing anxiety.* □ *Anxiety is growing for the children's safety.* □ *There's no cause for anxiety yet.* □ *You need feel no anxiety on that issue.* □ *She never seemed to suffer a moment's anxiety about money.* **2** An **anxiety** is something that causes you worry or fear: *One's life is rarely free of anxieties.* □ *The school fees were another anxiety.* **3** Your **anxiety** to do something is your eagerness to do it: *The waiters almost fell over themselves in their anxiety to please.*

anxious /'aŋkʃəs/ or /'aŋʃəs/ *adjective*
1 You are **anxious** when you are worried, nervous or fearful about something: *You can't help being anxious about your children's future.* □ *She works so hard that I sometimes get anxious for her health.* □ *Don't look so anxious.* [*same as* **apprehensive**] **2** An **anxious** time is a period during which you are worried or uncertain about something: *We spent an anxious three days waiting for news.* [*same as* **tense**, **uneasy**] **3** You are **anxious** for something, or to do something, if you want it, or want to do it: *He was anxious to contact his wife.* □ *We're all anxious for the project to succeed.* □ *I'm anxious that we should all understand one another.* [*same as* **eager**, **keen**] — *adverb* **anxiously:** *He enquired anxiously after the children.*

any /'ɛnɪ/ *determiner*; *pronoun*; *adverb*
▻ ***determiner***
1 Any, like **some**, represents an indefinite amount, quantity or number; it is used in place of **some** in negative sentences and questions, after *if*, and after words that behave like negatives: *I haven't bought any milk.* □ *I don't think there are any tickets left.* □ *Do you need any extra help?* □ *Are you taking any pills for the pain?* □ *Are there any others you'd like to invite?* □ *We enquired whether there were any more vacancies.* □ *If you have any financial problems, please tell the staff.* □ *She has scarcely any friends.* □ *I've done hardly any piano practice today, and I won't be able to do any more till Monday.* □ *The plant will die without any water.* **2 Any** can also have a range of meanings in which it is said with emphasis and can be used in positive statements as well as with negatives, in questions, after *if*, and after words like *hardly*; and it can be used with singular count nouns as well as with uncount nouns and plural nouns: *She can solve any problem for you.* [= every problem, no matter what it is] □ *Any passer-by will tell you the way.* [= every passer-by, no matter which you ask] □ *Any literature contains some instruction.* [= all literature, no matter how good or bad] □ *Any fat in her diet may be harmful.* [= the least amount, even a tiny amount] □ *Isn't there any solution?* [= at least one, no matter what] □ *Haven't you got any common sense?* [= at least some, no matter how little] □ *Absolutely any accommodation would do.* [= whatever accommodation is available, no matter what kind it is] □ *We don't watch just any programmes.* [= whatever programmes are on, no matter what they are] □ *Any grammar book would be better than none.* [= whatever grammar book exists, no matter how bad] □ *I'd like you to report any incident of this kind to me.* [= every such incident that you notice] □ *Choose any three questions.* [= whichever three you like]
▻ ***pronoun:*** *I didn't see any of the other students today.* □ *Do you want to go to any of these lectures?* □ *Is any of that honey left?* □ *If any of you see her, please give her the message.* □ *She's a good teacher; ask any of her students.* □ *All this clothing is spare; you can have any of it.* □ *There were plenty of neighbours about, any of whom could have seen her leaving.* □ *He wanted to borrow some money, but I told him I didn't have any.* □ *Tell your pupils about the job, in case there are any who'd like an application form.* □ *Few people, if any* [= or perhaps none] *could have achieved as much as she did.* □ *Complaints, if any,* [= if you have any] *should be made to the office.* □ *We specialize in antique furniture but we'll buy any that's in good condition.* □ *'Which of these computers can I use?' 'Any.'*

> Notice that you use **any** when you are referring to a possible group of three or more; when you are referring to two only, use **either**: *Any child can tell you that.* But: *You can look through a telescope with either eye. The disease can affect any of the muscles of the body.* But: *He didn't remember either of his parents very clearly.*

▻ ***adverb***
1 Before comparative adjectives and adverbs, and the word *different*, **any** can be used for emphasis to mean

'at all', 'in the least' or 'the least bit': *He isn't any better.* □ *Can't you work any more quickly than that?* □ *His case isn't any different from the previous ones.* □ *I won't be seeing her any less than before.* **2** (*AmE*; *informal*) **Any** can be used after a verb to mean 'at all': *This hasn't changed my opinion any.*

▻ ***phrases*** **1 Any amount**, **quantity** or **number** can mean 'a huge amount, quantity or number': *She has any number of dresses.* **2** You use **any longer** and **any more** with negatives to mean 'at all now' or 'ever again', where something that happened or was so before is not going to happen again, or is not so now: *She isn't teaching any longer.* □ *I don't want to go there any more.* **3** You say that something is going to happen **any minute now**, or **any time now**, if you expect it to happen very soon: *We're expecting a call from him any minute now.* **4** (*informal*) **Any old** is used like sense 2 of **any** as a determiner, and means 'any, no matter what': *You can tell him any old rubbish and he'll believe it.* □ *I want a good novel to read, not any old one.*

anybody /'ɛnɪbɒdɪ/ or **anyone** *pronoun*

1 Anybody and **anyone**, like **somebody** and **someone**, represent an indefinite person; they are used instead of **somebody** and **someone** in negative sentences, in questions, after *if*, and after words like *hardly*: *I never told anybody.* □ *I don't think anyone else knows yet.* □ *Is anyone at home?* □ *Can't anyone help?* □ *Did you meet anyone nice there?* □ *If anyone calls, take a message.* □ *She knew scarcely anybody there.*

Anybody and **Anyone** are never used as the subject of a negative sentence: *Nobody saw me* (not *Anyone didn't see me*).

2 Anybody and **anyone** can also mean 'any or every person, no matter who', and can be used in positive statements in this sense: *It could happen to anyone.* □ *Anybody might make a mistake like that.* □ *Anyone who reads so much is sure to know a lot.* □ *She knows as well as anybody what the dangers are.* □ *He seems to have more problems than anybody else.* □ *She said she wouldn't go out with just anyone.*

Notice that although **anybody** and **anyone** are singular, both are often followed by the pronoun *they*, which takes a plural verb: *If anybody asks, they have* (or in very formal English, *he or she has*) *a right to know. Anybody's allowed in, aren't they? If anyone else arrives, tell them we're closed. Has anyone got room in their car for an extra passenger?*.
Notice that adjectives describing **anybody** and **anyone** come after them: *Did you want to speak to anyone particular? Was there anybody interesting at the conference?*.

3 Anybody and **anyone** can also mean 'an important person': *I'll never be anybody.* □ *You needn't think you're anyone.*

Notice the difference between **anyone** and **any one** (which can refer to things, and means 'one, no matter which one'): *Any one of you could be the murderer. The helmets are all the same size; wear any one.*

anyhow /'ɛnɪhaʊ/ *adverb*

1 (*sentence adverb*) **Anyhow** can mean the same as **anyway**, usually in sense 1: *It's too late to go now, and anyhow, we haven't got enough petrol.* **2 Anyhow** also means 'not in any order' or 'in a disorganized, unplanned or untidy manner': *The books are arranged anyhow; we haven't had time to sort them out.*

anyone /'ɛnɪwʌn/

The uses of **anyone** are shown in the entry for **anybody**.

anything /'ɛnɪθɪŋ/ *pronoun; adverb*

▻ ***pronoun***

1 Anything, like **something**, represents an indefinite thing; it is used instead of **something** in negative statements, in questions, after *if*, and after words like *hardly*: *I don't have anything to wear.* □ *Is anything wrong?* □ *There isn't anything the matter, is there?* □ *Is there anything you haven't told us?* □ *Let me know if you're worried about anything.* □ *If anything new turns up, call us.* □ *There was hardly anything left.*

You never use **anything** as the subject of a negative sentence: *Nothing is wrong* (not *Anything isn't wrong*, or *Not anything is wrong*).

2 Anything can also mean 'any or every thing, no matter what'; in this sense it can be used in positive statements: *Absolutely anything could happen now.* □ *Anything in the way of food would be better than nothing.* □ *We were prepared for almost anything.* □ *I'll do anything you want.* □ *I want decent furniture, not just anything.*

Notice that adjectives describing **anything** come after it: *I didn't notice anything unusual.*

3 Anything can also mean 'something important or serious': *One of the children was sick, but it turned out not to be anything.*

▻ ***adverb***

Anything is used before *like* to mean 'at all': *Does she look anything like her mother?* □ *It isn't anything like the traditional kind of school.* □ *The work isn't anything like complete* [= is very incomplete].

▻ ***phrases*** **1** You describe something as **anything but** something to indicate that the opposite would be truer: *This is anything but easy.* □ *'Was the weather nice?' 'Anything but.'* **2** Someone or something does something **like anything**, or, *eg* **as** hard **as anything**, if they do it a lot, very much, or very hard: *It's raining like anything.* □ *They've been working as hard as anything to finish the job.* **3 Or anything** means 'or anything else of that kind': *Can I get you a drink or anything?* □ *You're not ill or anything, are you?*

anyway /'ɛnɪweɪ/ *adverb* (*sentence adverb*)

1 You use **anyway** to mean 'in any case', when making a comment that supports something already said: *She didn't want the job; anyway, she's pregnant now.* [see also **anyhow**] **2** You use **anyway** to mean 'in spite of that', when making a comment that contrasts with something already said: *The book was rather expensive, but I bought it anyway.* **3** You use **anyway** to mean 'at least', when correcting or adjusting something already said: *Hundreds of people have offered to help; a dozen or so, anyway.* **4** You use **anyway** to refer back to something already said or agreed, or to refer to a circumstance on which a present point or question depends: *Anyway, I'll see you on 17 October at the meeting.* □ *Anyway, why do you want to know?*

Notice the difference between **anyway** and **any way** (which means 'any means or manner, no matter what'): *Can we help in any way? I'll dress any way I want.*

anywhere /'ɛnɪwɛə(r)/ *adverb*

1 Anywhere, like **somewhere**, represents an indefinite place; it is used instead of **somewhere** in negative statements, in questions, after *if*, and after words like *hardly*; it can mean in or to any place: *I'm not going anywhere tonight.* □ *She couldn't find him anywhere.* □ *Isn't there anywhere we can talk privately?* □ *She'll be in the library, if anywhere.* [= she's likely to be there] □ *She seldom goes anywhere nowadays.* **2 Anywhere**

also means 'any or every place, no matter where'; in this sense it can be used in positive statements: *Pick a word from anywhere in the dictionary.* □ *This is the friendliest hotel anywhere in town.* □ *I'll work anywhere within reason.* □ *I'm happier here than anywhere else.* □ *We're not going just anywhere for our holidays.*

> Notice that **anywhere** can be followed by an adjective: *Are you going anywhere exciting?*

3 You use **anywhere** to mean at any point within a range, *eg* of time: *I could have dropped it anywhere between here and Princes Street.* □ *She might be aged anywhere between 50 and 65.* □ *It happened anywhere between 20 and 40 million years ago.* **4** You use **anywhere** with *near* to mean 'nearly': *We aren't anywhere near ready.*

apart /ə'pɑːt/ *adverb*
1 Two things are **apart**, or one thing is **apart** from another, when there is space between them, or they are separate: *He was standing apart from the others.* □ *Keep these two sets of application forms apart.* **2** Things are a certain distance **apart** when there is that distance between them: *Plant the seeds 20 centimetres apart.* □ *Their faces got closer and closer till their noses were barely an inch apart.* □ *Our opinions on grammar-teaching are pretty far apart.* **3** Two people are **apart** when they are not together: *They had never been apart for long.* □ *She's now living apart from her husband.* **4** You pull two things **apart** when you separate them from each other; things come **apart** when they separate into parts: *She got bitten when she tried to pull the two dogs apart.* □ *The two halves come apart quite easily.* **5** You take, pull or tear something **apart**, or it comes or falls **apart**, when it is separated into parts or pieces, breaks, or is destroyed: *He took the clock apart to mend it, and never put it together again.* □ *The glass just came apart in my hand.* □ *Their marriage has been falling apart for some years.*
▻ ***phrases*** **1** You use **apart from** as a preposition, meaning **a** 'except for', or 'not counting', when giving an exception: *There was no-one in the building apart from the watchman.* □ *I was in Plymouth last weekend, but apart from that I've been at home all summer.* **b** 'not considering or counting', when dismissing one consideration and mentioning another: *They were going to have other expenses, apart from the school fees.* □ *Quite apart from the cost of the repair, there's the inconvenience of being without a car.* **2** You say you **can't tell** two things **apart** if they are very alike and look the same to you: *He could never tell the twins apart.*

apartheid /a'pɑːtheɪt/ or /a'pɑːthaɪt/ *noun* (*uncount*)
Apartheid was the former official policy in South Africa of keeping people of different races apart by law.

apartment /ə'pɑːtmənt/ *noun*: **apartments**
1 (*especially AmE*) An **apartment** is a set of rooms, usually on one floor, suitable for living in, usually in a large building containing several sets of rooms: *They're wanting to rent a two-bedroomed apartment for July and August.* [*same as* **flat**] **2** An **apartment** can also be a large room used for formal occasions in an important residence such as a palace: *The state apartments are open to the public on a Thursday.*

apathetic /apə'θɛtɪk/ *adjective*
An **apathetic** person is uninterested in everything, or lacks enthusiasm and energy; you feel **apathetic** about something if you are not interested in it: *Perhaps it's the teacher's fault if the students are apathetic.* — *adverb* **apathetically:** *She glanced through the book apathetically.*

apathy /'apəθɪ/ *noun* (*uncount*)
Apathy is the state of lacking interest, enthusiasm or energy to take part in activities: *His friends tried everything to shake him out of his apathy.*

ape /eɪp/ *noun*; *verb*
▻ ***noun***: **apes**
An **ape** is one of the group of tailless animals, related to human beings and monkeys, that includes gorillas and chimpanzees.
▻ ***verb*** (*usually derogatory*): **apes, aping, aped**
One person **apes** the actions, behaviour, manners or speech of another when they imitate them: *He's like a child, aping the conventional responses of an adult.*

aperitif /əpɛrə'tiːf/ *noun*: **aperitifs**
An **aperitif** is an alcoholic drink taken before a meal to sharpen or stimulate the appetite.

aperture /'apətʃə(r)/ *noun*: **apertures**
An **aperture** is a small hole or opening, *eg* one in a camera that can be adjusted to control the amount of light entering it.

apex /'eɪpɛks/ *noun*: **apexes**
The **apex** of something such as a pyramid or triangle is its highest point or its tip. [see picture at **shape**]

aphorism /'afərɪzm/ *noun*: **aphorisms**
An **aphorism** is a short, clever or humorous saying expressing some well-known truth. [*same as* **maxim**; compare **axiom**]

aphrodisiac /afrə'dɪzɪak/ *noun*: **aphrodisiacs**
An **aphrodisiac** is a drink, food or drug that increases people's sexual desire.

apiece /ə'piːs/ *adverb*
You give people so many or so much **apiece** when you give them each the same quantity: *The porters were supplied with a blanket apiece.*

aplomb /ə'plɒm/ *noun* (*uncount*)
You do something, especially something difficult, with **aplomb** when you do it with calmness and confidence: *She delivered her speech with aplomb.* [*same as* **self-assurance, composure**]

apocryphal /ə'pɒkrəfəl/ *adjective*
You call a story **apocryphal** if it is untrue, or unlikely to be true.

apolitical /eɪpə'lɪtɪkəl/ *adjective*
You call someone **apolitical** if they have no interest in politics, or do not sympathize with any particular political viewpoint or party.

apologetic /əpɒlə'dʒɛtɪk/ *adjective*
You are **apologetic** when you say or show you are sorry about something you have done, or are responsible for, that hurts or upsets someone, or causes them trouble: *The shop was very apologetic about the mistake.* — *adverb* **apologetically:** *She smiled apologetically.*

apologize or **apologise** /ə'pɒlədʒaɪz/ *verb*: **apologizes, apologizing, apologized**
You **apologize** to someone for something when you say you are sorry for hurting or upsetting them, or causing them trouble: *I apologize for not having written earlier.* □ *I apologize for my late reply.* □ *She knocked his elbow and apologized.*

apology /ə'pɒlədʒɪ/ *noun* (*count or uncount*): **apologies**
You make or write someone an **apology** when you say or write that you are sorry for hurting or upsetting them, or causing them trouble or difficulty: *He accepted our apology.* □ *We had a letter of apology from the manufacturers.* □ *She returned the book with many apologies for keeping it so long.*

apostle /ə'pɒsəl/ *noun*: **apostles**
1 (*religion*) The **Apostles** or **apostles** were the people

sent out to preach the message of Christ in the early Christian church, especially his twelve original disciples. **2** An **apostle** of a cause or belief is someone who supports and recommends it enthusiastically: *the apostles of a united Europe.*

apostrophe /ə'pɒstrəfɪ/ *noun*: **apostrophes**
An **apostrophe** is the punctuation mark ('), used
1 to show the omission of a letter or letters, as in *I'm* (for *I am*), *we'd* (for *we had* or *we would*) or *can't* (for *cannot*). **2** before or after *s*, at the end of a name or other word, to show possession, as in *Hazel's desk, Hannibal's defeat, the girls' changing room.* **3** to make the plural of a letter clearer to read, as in *a row of a's.*

appal /ə'pɔːl/ *verb*: **appals, appalling, appalled**
Something bad **appals** you when it shocks, horrifies or disgusts you: *His ignorance appalled her.* □ *They were appalled by the news of the crash.* —*adjective* **appalled:** *Don't look so appalled.* □ *I'm appalled at your attitude.*

appalling /ə'pɔːlɪŋ/ *adjective*
1 You call something **appalling** if you are shocked or disgusted by it: *Your behaviour was appalling.* □ *They work in appalling conditions.* [*same as* **dreadful**] **2** (*informal*) You use **appalling** to emphasize the severity of something bad: *I've got an appalling headache.* [*same as* **terrible**] —*adverb* **appallingly:** *It was appallingly careless of them.*

apparatus /apə'reɪtəs/ or /apə'rɑːtəs/ *noun* (*uncount or count*): **apparatuses**
1 The **apparatus** for a job or activity is the equipment you need for it: *The gym was equipped with various pieces of weight-training apparatus.* **2** The **apparatus** of something is its organization, parts, structure and system of working: *the apparatus of government.*

apparent /ə'parənt/ *adjective*
1 Something that is **apparent** is clear and obvious to you: *Her distrust of him was all too apparent.* □ *It was becoming quite apparent to me that they weren't going to finish the job in time.* □ *For no apparent reason he felt himself getting nervous.* **2** An **apparent** quality or circumstance is one that looks real enough, but may not actually exist: *Her apparent calmness didn't deceive them.* □ *The improvement in his health was only apparent.*

apparently /ə'parəntlɪ/ *adverb*
1 (*sentence adverb*) You use **apparently** to mean 'it seems that', when mentioning something that you have heard or been told, which may possibly not be true: *Apparently they're divorced now.* □ *He didn't like the job, apparently.* □ *'Were there any witnesses?' 'Apparently not.'* **2 Apparently** also means 'in appearance, at least': *She sat there calmly, apparently unaware of the chaos around her.*

apparition /apə'rɪʃən/ *noun*: **apparitions**
An **apparition** is a strange vision or appearance, especially the ghost of a dead person.

appeal /ə'piːl/ *verb; noun*
▷ ***verb***: **appeals, appealing, appealed**
1 You **appeal** for something such as money or help for a cause when you request it urgently: *They're appealing on television for medical volunteers to treat the earthquake victims.* **2** Something **appeals** to you if you like it or think it is attractive or interesting: *They suggested a visit to the museum, but the idea didn't appeal.* **3** You **appeal** to someone's good qualities when you ask them to prove they have them, by doing what you want: *I'm appealing to your common sense.* **4** (*especially legal*) You **appeal** against an official or legal decision or judgement when you ask a higher authority or court to reconsider the case, in the hope that they will declare the first decision wrong: *He decided to appeal to the High Court against his prison sentence.*
▷ ***noun***: **appeals**
1 You make an **appeal** for something when you ask urgently for it: *Over a million pounds was donated to the cause in response to the television appeal.* □ *Her appeal for silence was ignored.* **2** (*uncount*) The **appeal** of something is its power to attract and interest you: *Dieting soon lost its appeal for her.* □ *Where is the appeal in a game like cricket?* □ *The second holiday plan held more appeal.* **3** (*especially legal*) An **appeal** against an offical or legal decision is a formal request to a higher authority or court to reconsider the case and if possible declare the decision wrong.

appealing /ə'piːlɪŋ/ *adjective*
Something that is **appealing** is attractive, delightful, charming or touching: *The boy had an appealing grin.* □ *The thought of a wet walk home was not appealing.*

appear /ə'pɪə(r)/ *verb*: **appears, appearing, appeared**
1 Something or someone **appears** when they become visible, come into sight, or arrive: *A bus appeared in the distance.* □ *You can't expect the money to appear from nowhere.* □ *Her appointment was for 10.00 am, but she didn't appear till 10.30.* [*opposite* **disappear**] **2** You say that something **appears** to be so if it seems to be so, or if you believe it is so from what you have noticed or heard: *Our new secretary appeared to be quite efficient.* □ *A second man arrived, who appeared to be some sort of official.* □ *The situation is less worrying than it appears.* □ *He appeared perfectly normal to me.* □ *It appears that she failed to follow our instructions.* □ *'Was his appeal successful?' 'It appears so.'* □ *'Did she win?' 'It appears not.'* [*same as* **seem**] **3** A new thing **appears** when it starts to exist, is invented or becomes available to people; a book **appears** when it is published: *Nylon stockings appeared on the market just after World War 2.* **4** A performer, actor or other personality **appears** *eg* in a play, show or programme when they take part in it: *She last appeared on stage in 1988.* **5** (*legal*) You **appear** in a court of law when you present yourself to answer a charge or accusation, or to give evidence as a witness, or as a lawyer to speak on behalf of, or against, the accused person.

appearance /ə'pɪərəns/ *noun*: **appearances**
1(*used in the singular*) The **appearance** of someone or something is their arrival: *The appearance of the ambulance came as a relief.* □ *He was a bit embarrassed by her sudden appearance at his door.* [*opposite* **disappearance**] **2** (*used in the singular*) The **appearance** of something new is the start of its existence or availability to the public: *It's now five years since the appearance of her first novel.* **3** (*uncount*) A person's or thing's **appearance** is the way they look: *He took great care of his personal appearance.* □ *The boys were alike in appearance if not in personality.* **4** An actor, performer or personality makes an **appearance** when they appear in public, *eg* in a play, show or programme: *his innumerable television appearances.*
▷ ***phrases*** **1** You **keep up appearances a** when you pretend to be cheerful, or in good health, or financially well off, while suffering private misfortunes and worries. **b** when you maintain a respectable standard of dress and behaviour. **2** You **put in an appearance** at something such as a meeting or party when you attend it briefly. **3** You say that something is so **to** or **by all appearances** if you believe it is so from what you have observed: *It was an expensive wedding by all appearances.*

appease /ə'piːz/ *verb*: **appeases, appeasing, appeased**
1 You **appease** someone or their anger when you do something to calm or satisfy them: *Just saying sorry is*

not going to appease her. [*same as* **pacify**] **2** Something **appeases** your hunger or appetite when it satisfies it: *Some sort of statement will be necessary to appease public curiosity.* [*same as* **quench**]

appendicitis /əpendɪ'saɪtɪs/ *noun* (*uncount*)
Appendicitis is an illness in which the appendix becomes infected and inflamed, causing severe abdominal pain.

appendix /ə'pɛndɪks/ *noun*: **appendixes** or **appendices** /ə'pɛndɪsiːz/
1 (**appendices**) An **appendix** is a section containing extra information or notes at the end of a book or document. **2** (**appendixes**) Your **appendix** is a small piece of intestine shaped like a closed tube, attached to the lower end of the large bowel.

appetite /'apətaɪt/ *noun* (*uncount or count, usually in the singular*)
1 Your **appetite** is your desire for food: *The walk had given me a good appetite.* □ *a small appetite* □ *I don't seem to have much appetite today.* **2** Your **appetite** for a particular thing is your desire for it: *All the tabloid newspapers do is feed the public appetite for sensation.* [*same as* **hunger**, **thirst**, **taste**]

appetizing or **appetising** /'apətaɪzɪŋ/ *adjective*
Food that is **appetizing** tastes good; it smells or looks **appetizing** if it has an attractive appearance or smell that gives you a good appetite. [*opposite* **unappetizing**]

applaud /ə'plɔːd/ *verb*: **applauds, applauding, applauded**
1 An audience **applauds** a performer or speaker when they clap their hands in approval: *Her speech was enthusiastically applauded.* **2** You **applaud** something when you express approval of it: *On the whole the press had applauded the government's efforts at negotiation.*

applause /ə'plɔːz/ *noun* (*uncount*)
Applause is praise or approval expressed by clapping: *The audience burst into applause.*

apple /'apəl/ *noun* (*count or uncount*): **apples**
An **apple** is a firm, round, edible fruit with a green, red or yellow skin and sweet white flesh: *apple tart* □ *apple trees* □ *a piece of apple.*[see picture at **fruit**]

appliance /ə'plaɪəns/ *noun*: **appliances**
A machine, instrument or tool for doing a job can be called an **appliance**: *hairdryers and other electrical appliances.*

applicable /ə'plɪkəbəl/ or /'aplɪkəbəl/ *adjective*
Something that is **applicable** to a certain situation or person is relevant to them or relates to them: *Questions 2 and 3 are applicable only to people living alone.* □ *The rule on wives' earnings is not applicable in your case.* [*same as* **appropriate**, **relevant**; *opposite* **inapplicable**, **inappropriate**]

applicant /'aplɪkənt/ *noun*: **applicants**
An **applicant** for something such as a job, a university place or a grant is a person who applies for it, making a formal request for it to be given or offered to them: *There were 400 applicants for only 50 places.* [*same as* **candidate**]

application /aplɪ'keɪʃən/ *noun*: **applications**
1 (*count or uncount*) An **application** is a formal request for something such as a job, a place at a university or on a course, or a grant: *They had received at least 200 applications for the advertised post.* □ *Further details will be sent to you on application.* □ *An application form is enclosed.* **2** (*count or uncount*) The **application** of a skill or of knowledge is the use made of it, or that can be made of it, in certain situations: *What applications can philosophy have in the practical world?* □ *The production of reference books has been speeded up with the application of computer technology to the task.* **3** (*uncount*) **Application** is concentration, conscientiousness, and hard work: *He showed a lot more application than the other students.* [*same as* **dedication**, **diligence**]

applied /ə'plaɪd/ *adjective*
A subject with a name such as **applied** science, **applied** mathematics or **applied** psychology is studied for the practical uses that can be made of it.

apply /ə'plaɪ/ *verb*: **applies, applying, applied**
1 You **apply** for something when you write a formal request for it, or to be considered for it: *Are you applying for the lectureship?* □ *I've applied to join a skiing course.* **2** Something **applies** to you if it concerns you or relates to you: *The new pension arrangements won't apply to people born before 1960.* **3** A law or rule **is applied** when it is enforced: *They still apply the death penalty for murder.* **4** You **apply** a skill or piece of knowledge when you use it in a practical way: *Nowadays computing skills can be applied to a large variety of academic tasks.* **5** You **apply** paint when you brush it on to a surface; you **apply** ointment when you rub it into your skin: *Apply the moisturizer thinly over the face and neck.* **6** You **apply** a word or name to something or someone when you use it for or about them: *You might understandably, if inaccurately, apply the term 'insect' to a spider.*
▻ ***phrase*** You **apply yourself** to a task when you concentrate on doing it with all your attention and energy.

appoint /ə'pɔɪnt/ *verb*: **appoints, appointing, appointed**
1 Someone **is appointed** to a post or position when they are officially chosen for it: *She is likely to appoint him Foreign Minister.* **2** (*formal*) You **appoint** a time or place for an event such as a meeting when you arrange where and when it will take place. — *adjective* **appointed:** *the newly appointed Secretary of State for Education* □ *She duly arrived at the appointed place and time.*

appointment /ə'pɔɪntmənt/ *noun*: **appointments**
1 You make an **appointment** to meet someone or to see a professional person when you arrange a time for the meeting or consultation: *She had a doctor's appointment for 10.30.* □ *I was given an appointment to meet the project manager.* **2** (*uncount or count*) The **appointment** of a person to a job or post is the official choice of that person for it: *He was largely responsible for her appointment as headteacher.* □ *There have been several new appointments recently.* **3** An **appointment** is a job or post: *She was offered and accepted a teaching appointment in Bradford.*
▻ ***phrase*** You see someone or do something **by appointment** when you arrange in advance when to do it: *Visits to the cathedral library are by appointment only.*

appraise /ə'preɪz/ *verb*: **appraises, appraising, appraised**
You **appraise** something when you consider or examine it and form an opinion or estimate of it: *She took a moment to appraise the situation before deciding how to act.* [*same as* **assess**] — *noun* (*uncount or count*) **appraisal:** *There was a short appraisal of her life and writings in the book section of the paper.*

appreciable /ə'priːʃɪəbəl/ or /ə'priːsɪəbəl/ *adjective*
An **appreciable** change, effect or amount is one that is great enough to be noticeable or significant: *The next day there was an appreciable drop in temperature.* [*same as* **noticeable**, **significant**; *opposite* **insignificant**, **negligible**] — *adverb* **appreciably:** *His health has improved appreciably with the new treatment.*

appreciate /ə'pri:ʃɪeɪt/ or /ə'pri:sɪeɪt/ *verb*: **appreciates, appreciating, appreciated**
1 You **appreciate** something good if you realize its worth, or value its quality: *In countries where it's difficult to get an education, people appreciate it more when they do get it.* **2** You say that you **appreciate** something someone has done for you or given you when you want to express your gratitude: *I very much appreciated your help.* **3** You **appreciate** a fact, possibility or circumstance if you are aware of it, or understand it: *We appreciate that you will want to consult your family before making a decision.* [*same as* **realize, recognize**]

appreciation /əpri:ʃɪ'eɪʃən/ or /əpri:sɪ'eɪʃən/ *noun* (*usually uncount*): **appreciations**
1 (*uncount, or used in the singular*) **Appreciation** of something good is the realization or recognition of its worth, or the valuing of its fine qualities: *As quite a small child she showed a marked appreciation of good music.* **2** Your **appreciation** of or for something someone has done for you or given you is your gratitude for it: *We should send them a present to show our appreciation of their kindness.* **3** **Appreciation** of a fact, situation, circumstance or difficulty is an awareness or understanding of it: *You can have no appreciation of the problems of divorce till you are involved in the situation yourself.* **4** (*count, usually in the singular*) An **appreciation** of a person or their achievements is an account of them, usually giving some praise: *Next day most of the papers carried an appreciation of his life and work as a composer.*

appreciative /ə'pri:ʃɪətɪv/ or /ə'pri:sɪətɪv/ *adjective*
1 People are **appreciative** of something when they are grateful for it: *We're all most appreciative of the work you've done for the club.* **2** An **appreciative** response is one that expresses gratitude or approval: *She accepted his help with an appreciative 'Thanks a lot.'* — *adverb* **appreciatively:** *They clapped appreciatively.*

apprehension /aprɪ'hɛnʃən/ *noun* (*uncount, or used in the plural*)
Apprehension is a feeling of fear and anxiety: *As yet he felt no apprehension for her safety.* □ *He was filled with vague apprehensions about the future.*

apprehensive /aprɪ'hɛnsɪv/ *adjective*
You are **apprehensive** when you are anxious or fearful about something: *Most children feel a bit apprehensive on their first day at school.* □ *He was always apprehensive about any new project.* [*same as* **uneasy**] — *adverb* **apprehensively:** *He glanced apprehensively behind him.*

apprentice /ə'prɛntɪs/ *noun:* **apprentices**
An **apprentice** is a young person who works for someone who is skilled in their craft, for an agreed period and on low pay, in order to learn the skill or craft: *an apprentice plumber.*

apprenticeship /ə'prɛntɪsʃɪp/ *noun*: **apprenticeships**
A young person who has an **apprenticeship** with someone experienced in a skill or craft works for them on low pay for an agreed period in order to learn the skill.

approach /ə'proʊtʃ/ *verb*; *noun*
▷ ***verb***: **approaches, approaching, approached**
1 You **approach** a person or place as you get nearer to them: *The accident happened as the train was approaching Winchester.* **2** You **approach** someone when you come to them with a suggestion, request or offer you want to make to them: *A music publisher had approached her with a suggestion for a biography of Shostakovitch.* **3** You **approach** a situation or problem in a certain way when you take a certain attitude to it in dealing with it: *She approached the matter of discipline with her usual determination.* **4** An event or its date **approaches**, or you **approach** it, as it gets nearer in time: *He's approaching his final exams.* **5** One thing **approaches** another if it almost matches it in standard or quality; something **approaches** a certain standard, level or condition when it almost nearly reaches it: *Their speed on the bends approached 150 kmh.*
▷ ***noun***: **approaches**
1 (*uncount*) The **approach** of someone or something is the process or manner of their getting nearer: *He went on reading, unaware of her approach.* **2** (*uncount or count*) Your **approach** to a situation or problem is the attitude you take to it or the way you deal with it: *Let's try a new approach.* **3** You make an **approach** to someone when you come to them with an offer, request or suggestion: *She had had several approaches from publishers offering substantial sums for her memoirs.* **4** An **approach** to a place is a road or track leading to it.

approachable /ə'proʊtʃəbəl/ *adjective*
1 You call a person **approachable** if they are friendly and ready to listen and help. **2** A place is **approachable** by a certain route if you can get to it that way.

approbation /aprə'beɪʃən/ *noun* (*uncount*)
Approbation is approval: *The committee had given its approbation to the plan.*

appropriate *adjective*; *verb*
▷ ***adjective*** /ə'proʊprɪət/
Something is **appropriate** for or to a certain situation if it is suitable: *The children were all given tasks appropriate to their abilities.* — *adverb* **appropriately:** *Make sure you dress appropriately for the occasion.*
▷ ***verb*** /ə'proʊprɪeɪt/: **appropriates, appropriating, appropriated**
To **appropriate** something that does not belong to you is to take it for your own use: *It was suspected that a large proportion of the emergency food packages were being appropriated by officials and never reached those in need.* — *noun* (*uncount*) **appropriation** /əproʊprɪ'eɪʃən/: *the secret appropriation of company funds.*

approval /ə'pru:vəl/ *noun* (*uncount*)
1 **Approval** is consent or agreement given to a proposal, plan or request: *The planning department had given its approval to the proposed extension.* □ *You must get your parents' approval for your choice of subjects.* □ *We are withholding our approval of the plans till we have a second opinion on them.* □ *I'm glad to have had an idea that meets with your approval at last.* □ *The school-building programme was going ahead with the council's approval.* **2** You show **approval** of someone or something when you show or express pleased satisfaction with them.

approve /ə'pru:v/ *verb*: **approves, approving, approved**
1 You **approve** of something if you regard it as acceptable or satisfactory, or admire it; you **approve** of someone if you admire or like them: *I just don't approve of killing animals.* [*opposite* **disapprove**] **2** Something such as a plan **is approved** when someone in authority agrees to it or accepts it. [*opposite* **reject**]

approved /ə'pru:vd/ *adjective*
1 The **approved** procedure for doing something is the one accepted by people as correct: *He didn't seem to teach reading by any of the approved methods.* [*same as* **orthodox**; *opposite* **unorthodox**] **2** **Approved** also means passed or accepted by someone in authority: *the list of approved reading books.*

approving /ə'pru:vɪŋ/ *adjective*
An **approving** response is one that expresses satisfaction or admiration: *an approving nod.* — *adverb* **approvingly:** *He glanced approvingly at the results.*

approximate *adjective; verb*
▻ ***adjective*** /ə'prɒksɪmət/
1 An **approximate** amount, number, measurement or time is not exact or accurate but is close to being so: *These figures are only approximate.* [*same as* **rough**] **2** An **approximate** description or idea of something is a vague rather than precisely accurate one: *an approximate picture of the situation.* [*same as* **rough**] — *adverb* **approximately:** *It happened at approximately 8.45.* □ *a room measuring approximately 5 by 7 metres.*
▻ ***verb*** /ə'prɒksɪmeɪt/: **approximates, approximating, approximated**
1 Something **approximates** to a certain number or measurement if it is not exactly that, but is a close estimate or an average: *We had to produce work at a rate approximating to 25 pages per week.* **2** One thing **approximates** to another if it is similar to it or imitates it: *At high altitudes you can get weather approximating to the severest winter conditions.*

approximation /əprɒksɪ'meɪʃən/ *noun* (*count or uncount*)
1 An **approximation** is a guessed or estimated number, amount or measurement, rather than an accurately calculated one: *The number quoted was only an approximation.* **2** One thing is an **approximation** to another if it is similar to it, or imitates it: *The bath towel she seemed to be wearing was evidently intended as an approximation to a dress.*

apricot /'eɪprɪkɒt/ *noun*: **apricots**
1 An **apricot** is a fruit like a small peach, with a stone and pale orange skin and flesh. **2** (*uncount, often adjectival*) **Apricot** is also the pale orange colour of the fruit.

April /'eɪprəl/ *noun* (*uncount*)
April is the fourth month of the year, coming after March and before May: *Her baby isn't due till next April.* □ *The meeting is on Thursday the twenty-third of April* (written *Thursday 23 April*). □ *April the ninth,* or (*AmE*) *April nine* (written *April 9*) □ *It can be pretty cold in April.* □ *showery April weather.*

apron /'eɪprən/ *noun*: **aprons**
An **apron** is a piece of clothing that covers the front part of you, which you tie round your waist over your clothes, to stop them getting dirty *eg* when you are cooking or doing housework: *He was wearing a plastic apron.*

apt /apt/ *adjective*
1 You call a word, description or consequence **apt** if it fits a person, thing or situation in a satisfactory or suitable way: *an apt punishment for cheating.* [*same as* **fitting, appropriate**] **2** A person is **apt** to do something if they tend to do it, or can't help doing it: *Nowadays she's apt to forget appointments unless she writes them down.* [*same as* **inclined**] — *adverb* **aptly:** *The smaller of the two islands was aptly named The Calf.*

aptitude /'aptɪtjuːd/ *noun*: **aptitudes**
You have an **aptitude** for a particular skill or activity if you are naturally good at it or learn it easily: *Her aptitude for story-writing was soon noticed by her teacher.* [*same as* **flair**]

aquarium /ə'kwɛərɪəm/ *noun*: **aquariums** or **aquaria**
1 An **aquarium** is a glass tank filled with water, in which to keep live fish. **2** A building, *eg* at a zoo, where fish and other water creatures are kept in tanks is also called an **aquarium**.

aquatic /ə'kwatɪk/ *adjective*
1 Aquatic creatures and plants live or grow in water. **2 Aquatic** sports and activities take place in the water.

aqueduct /'akwɪdʌkt/ *noun*: **aqueducts**
An **aqueduct** is a bridge constructed to carry a canal or water supply across a valley.

Arab /'arəb/ *noun* (*often adjectival*): **Arabs**
An **Arab** is one of a race of people inhabiting the Middle East and North Africa: *Arab dress* □ *the Arab nations.*

Arabian /ə'reɪbɪən/ *adjective*
1 Arabian means relating to Arabia, the peninsula between the Red Sea and the Persian Gulf, or to Saudi Arabia, one of the countries within it. **2 Arabian** can also mean relating to the Arab peoples.

Arabic /'arəbɪk/ *noun; adjective*
▻ ***noun*** (*uncount*)
Arabic is the language of the Arab peoples of the Middle East and North Africa and is used in the Islamic religion.
▻ ***adjective***
Arabic means relating to this language and to the people who speak it: *written in Arabic script.*

Arabic numeral /arəbɪk 'njuːmərəl/: **Arabic numerals** *noun*
The **Arabic numerals** are the figures 0, 1, 2, 3, 4, 5, 6, 7, 8 or 9, as distinct from the Roman numerals, which are made up of letters.

arable /'arəbəl/ *adjective*
Arable land is farm land used for crop-growing rather than animal-rearing: *arable farming.*

arbiter /'ɑːbɪtə(r)/ *noun*: **arbiters**
An **arbiter** is a person or an authority that acts as judge, *eg* in a quarrel or disagreement between people, groups or countries.

arbitrary /'ɑːbɪtrərɪ/ or /'ɑːbɪtrɪ/ *adjective*
An **arbitrary** decision or conclusion is one reached without proper reasoning, or without consideration for other people's opinions or the likely results. — *adverb* **arbitrarily** /'ɑːbɪtrərɪlɪ/: *He was arbitrarily dismissed from his job.*

arbitrate /'ɑːbɪtreɪt/ *verb*: **arbitrates, arbitrating, arbitrated**
To **arbitrate** between people or groups is to act as judge in a disagreement between them, after discussing the issue with both sides and looking at all the facts. — *noun* (*uncount*) **arbitration** /ɑːbɪ'treɪʃən/: *The dispute was resolved by arbitration.* □ *The union decided to go to arbitration over the wages issue.* — *noun* **arbitrator:** *She acted as arbitrator in the rail dispute.*

arc /ɑːk/ *noun*: **arcs**
An **arc** is a curved line or, in geometry, part of the line that forms the edge or circumference of a circle. [see picture at **shape**]

arcade /ɑː'keɪd/ *noun*: **arcades**
An **arcade** is a roofed street with shops or stalls along it: *the new shopping arcade.*

arch /ɑːtʃ/ *noun; verb*
▻ ***noun*: arches**
1 An **arch** is a curved structure forming an entrance or doorway, or forming one of the openings between the supporting pillars of a roof or bridge: *We went through an arch that led us out of the quadrangle and into a small garden.* **2** A curved shape can be called an **arch**: *the arch of the foot.* [see picture at **body**]
▻ ***verb*: arches, arching, arched**
Animals **arch** their backs, or people **arch** their eyebrows, when they form them into a curve or arched shape.

archaeology (*especially AmE* **archeology**) /ɑːkɪ'ɒlədʒɪ/ *noun* (*uncount*)
Archaeology is the study of the history and society of earlier peoples through the examination of objects or

buildings that they have left behind them or that have been discovered by digging, such as tools, jewellery and. — *adjective* **archaeological** /ɑːkɪəˈlɒdʒɪkəl/: *The Spartans left few archaeological remains.* — *noun* **archaeologist:** *The archaeologists working on the site report exciting new finds.*

archaic /ɑːˈkeɪɪk/ *adjective*
1 An **archaic** form of something is an older or more ancient form that has gone out of use or belongs to an earlier time: *the archaic form of the language* □ *an archaic style of pottery decoration.* **2** (*informal*) You call something **archaic** if you consider it very oldfashioned or out-of-date: *Their computer system is archaic.*

archbishop /ɑːtʃˈbɪʃəp/ *noun*: **archbishops**
An **archbishop** is a senior bishop, in charge of all the other bishops, clergy and churches in a country or a large part of it.

arched /ɑːtʃt/ *adjective*
A shape or structure that is **arched** curves upwards towards the middle, or has an upward-curving top, frame or roof: *arched windows.*

archeology see **archaeology**.

archery /ˈɑːtʃərɪ/ *noun* (*uncount*)
Archery is the art or sport of shooting with a bow and arrows.

archetype /ˈɑːkɪtaɪp/ *noun*: **archetypes**
You call a person or thing the **archetype** of something if you think they are a perfect example of it, with all the essential qualities and features: *With his moustache and abrupt manner he was the archetype of an army colonel.* — *adjective* **archetypal** /ɑːkɪˈtaɪpəl/: *an archetypal 1930s cinema.*

archipelago /ɑːkɪˈpɛləgoʊ/ *noun*: **archipelagos** or **archipelagoes**
An **archipelago** is a group of small islands.

architect /ˈɑːkɪtɛkt/ *noun*: **achitects**
1 An **architect** is a person who designs buildings. **2** Sometimes a person responsible for a movement, system or idea is referred to as its **architect**: *Keynes, the architect of modern economic theory.*

architecture /ɑːkɪˈtɛktʃə(r)/ *noun* (*uncount*)
1 Architecture is the art of planning, designing and constructing buildings: *She's studying architecture.* **2** The **architecture** of an age, period, culture or part of the world is the building style belonging to it or typical of it: *Victorian architecture.* — *adjective* **architectural** /ɑːkɪˈtɛktʃərəl/: *a bold architectural style.* — *adverb* **architecturally:** *an architecturally satisfying building.*

archive /ˈɑːkaɪv/ *noun* (*usually in the plural*): **archives**
The **archives** of a community, society, organization or family are a store or collection of documents relating to its history.

archway /ˈɑːtʃweɪ/ *noun*: **archways**
An **archway** is an entrance or passageway with an arch over it: *Go through that archway and turn left.*

Arctic /ˈɑːktɪk/ *noun*; *adjective*
▷ ***noun*** (*used in the singular*)
The **Arctic** is the area of the world around the North Pole.
▷ ***adjective***
1 Arctic means relating to the area around the North Pole: *the Arctic Ocean.* **2** (*informal*) Very cold conditions are described as **arctic**: *arctic weather.* [*same as* **freezing, frozen**]

ardent /ˈɑːdənt/ *adjective*
You are **ardent** about something if you are intensely enthusiastic, eager or passionate about it: *an ardent social reformer.* — *adverb* **ardently:** *He declared himself ardently in love with her.*

ardour /ˈɑːdə(r)/ *noun* (*uncount*)
Ardour is passionate enthusiasm, eagerness or love: *He remained devoted to liberalism, though his ardour cooled over the years.*

arduous /ˈɑːdjʊəs/ *adjective*
Something that is **arduous** is difficult and tiring: *the arduous business of moving house.*

are /ɑː(r)/ *verb, auxiliary verb*
(*negative forms* **are not** *or* **aren't**, *short form* **'re**)
Are is the form of the present tense of **be** that is used with *you* (singular and plural), *we* and *they*: *They're here now.* □ *Are you ready?* □ *'You are coming, aren't you?' 'Yes, we are.'* [see also **be, aren't**]

area /ˈɛərɪə/ *noun*: **areas**
1 An **area** is a part of the world, or part of a country or town: *the Muslim areas of the city.* **2** An **area** of something such as the body is a part of its surface or a place on or in it: *The rash extended over a wide area of the body.* **3** A locality, or part of a building or room that is set aside or designed for a particular purpose, is an **area** of a particular kind: *a kitchen with dining area.* **4** An **area** of activity is a certain kind or range of activities; an **area** of knowledge or interest is a particular subject or a related range of subjects: *Dancing is your area of activity, isn't it?* □ *I'm afraid the question is outside my subject area.* [*same as* **field**] **5** The measurement of a space or piece of land, *eg* in square metres or kilometres, is its **area**: *a yard about 170 square metres in area.*
▷ ***phrase* In the area of** is used to mean near or around and can refer to a place or amount: *There was bruising in the area of the left shoulder blade.* □ *The total cost will be in the area of £550.*

arena /əˈriːnə/ *noun*: **arenas**
1 An **arena** is a place for sports competitions or other events, with seats for spectators. **2** An **arena** is also an area of activity, especially public life, in which there is competition and conflict: *the political arena.*

aren't /ɑːnt/ *verb, auxiliary verb*
1 Aren't is the spoken, and informal written, form of **are not**: *You aren't a doctor yet.* □ *We're going to be late, aren't we?* **2** (*BrE*) **Aren't** is also short for **am not** in negative questions: *I'm too fat, aren't I?* □ *Aren't I getting fat?*

arguable /ˈɑːgjʊəbəl/ *adjective*
1 You say that it is **arguable** that something is so if you think it could be proved from the available evidence: *It's arguable that he wrote this review without even opening the book.* **2** Something that is **arguable** can be doubted or questioned: *It's arguable whether grants should be supplied for recreational purposes.* [*same as* **debatable**] — *adverb* **arguably:** *She's arguably Britain's finest living philosopher.*

argue /ˈɑːgjuː/ *verb*: **argues, arguing, argued**
1 You **argue** with someone about or over something when you express strong disagreement with each other about it, especially if you do so angrily or impatiently: *They were arguing about who should wash the dishes.* □ *We're always arguing over money.* □ *Stop arguing and do as I ask.* **2** You **argue** for or against something such as a plan when you give reasons for supporting it or reasons for rejecting it; you **argue** a case or point when you give reasons in support of it. **3** You **argue** that something is so when you offer it as your opinion during a discussion, or try to prove it by giving reasons or evidence. **4** You **argue** someone out

of doing something when you persuade them not to do it.

argument /ˈɑːgjʊmənt/ *noun* (*count or uncount*): **arguments**
1 You have an **argument** with someone when you express your disagreement with each other, especially angrily or impatiently: *They were having one of their endless arguments about politics.* □ *Let's have no more argument; just do it.* [*same as* **dispute**] **2** An **argument** is a piece or sequence of reasoning: *There are convincing arguments both for and against giving addicts drugs on prescription.* □ *She won't be persuaded even by logical argument.*

argumentative /ɑːgjʊˈmɛntətɪv/ *adjective*
An **argumentative** person tends to disagree with you or question your instructions: *He was in an argumentative mood.* [*same as* **quarrelsome**] — *adverb* **argumentatively:** *'It isn't my turn,' he said argumentatively.*

aria /ˈɑːrɪə/ *noun*: **arias**
An **aria** is a song for one of the soloists in an opera or choral work.

arid /ˈarɪd/ *adjective*
1 An **arid** region is a dry area with low rainfall, where few plants will grow. **2** You call a book, subject or discussion **arid** if it is dull, boring and unproductive.

arise /əˈraɪz/ *verb*: **arises, arising, arose, arisen**
1 Something such as a situation, possibility or difficulty **arises** when it comes into being or begins to exist: *Should the need arise, we can lend you the money.* [*same as* **emerge, occur**] **2** One thing **arises** from or out of another when it is caused by it: *There are one or two points to deal with, arising from the report.* [*same as* **result**]

aristocracy /arɪˈstɒkrəsɪ/ *noun* (*count, with a singular or plural verb*): **aristocracies**
The **aristocracy** is the highest social class in certain countries, consisting especially of land-owning families with noble titles: *the European aristocracies.*

aristocrat /ˈarɪstəkrat/ or /əˈrɪstəkrat/ *noun*: **aristocrats**
An **aristocrat** is someone whose family belongs to the aristocracy.

aristocratic /arɪstəˈkratɪk/ or /ərɪstəˈkratɪk/ *adjective*
1 An **aristocratic** family belongs to the aristocracy: *She was of aristocratic birth.* **2** Someone whose face, features or bearing are described as **aristocratic** has the kind of proud or noble-looking appearance that people think is typical of the aristocracy.

arithmetic /əˈrɪθmətɪk/ *noun; adjective*
▻ ***noun*** (*uncount*)
Arithmetic is the area of mathematics concerned with the simple calculation of numbers by addition, subtraction, multiplication and division. — *adjective* **arithmetical** /arɪθˈmɛtɪkəl/: *arithmetical skills.*

arm¹ /ɑːm/ *noun*: **arms**
1 Your **arms** are your two upper limbs, attached to your body at the shoulder and ending in your hands: *She sat with her arms folded.* [see picture at **body**] **2** The **arms** of a piece of clothing are its sleeves, the parts that cover your arms. **3** The **arms** of a chair are two projecting supports at each side, for resting your arms on when you are sitting in it. **4** A branch or section of an organization can also be called an **arm**: *the air arm of the fighting forces.*
▻ ***phrases*** **1** You walk **arm in arm** with someone when you walk with one arm linked through one of theirs. **2 a** You hold something that you are reading or looking at **at arm's length** when you hold it away from your body. **b** You keep someone **at arm's length** when you behave in a cool or unfriendly manner towards them, to avoid becoming involved. **3** (*informal*) You **chance your arm** when you take a risk. **4** You **fold your arms** when you cross them over your chest and tuck your hands, one into, and the other under, your elbows. **5** You **twist someone's arm** when you try hard to persuade them to do something. **6** You welcome someone or something **with open arms** if you are delighted or relieved at their arrival.

arm² /ɑːm/ *verb*: **arms, arming, armed**
1 To **arm** someone is to equip them with weapons: *The big question is whether to arm the whole police force.* **2** You **arm** yourself with a weapon, or something that can be used as a weapon, when you take hold of it so as to be ready to defend yourself or fight someone; you **arm** yourself with facts or information when you get them ready to use in support of your argument: *She armed herself with a hammer and tiptoed downstairs.* [see also **armed**]

armament /ˈɑːməmənt/ *noun* (*usually in the plural*): **armaments**
Armaments are a country's military equipment and weapons.

armchair /ˈɑːmtʃɛə(r)/ *noun*: **armchairs**
An **armchair** is a chair, especially a large comfortable one, with supports for your arms: *Do sit in the armchair.* [see picture at **living room**]

armed /ɑːmd/ *adjective*
1 Someone who is **armed** is carrying a weapon: *Could you see if your attacker was armed?* □ *an armed assailant.* **2** An **armed** attack or **armed** robbery is carried out by people carrying weapons. **3** An **armed** struggle or conflict is one in which people use weapons against each other. **4** A country's **armed** forces are its army, navy and air force. **5** You are **armed** with something if you have it ready to use as a weapon: *Armed with a kitchen knife she went to investigate the noise.* **6** You are **armed** with something such as a qualification, or a piece of information, if you have it ready to prove your ability, or to use in argument or discussion: *Now armed with all the facts, he was ready for his battle with the authorities.*

armful /ˈɑːmfʊl/ *noun*: **armfuls**
An **armful** of something is an amount carried, or that can be carried, in both arms, or in or under one arm: *He returned with an armful of files.*

armhole /ˈɑːmhoʊl/ *noun*: **armholes**
The **armholes** of a piece of clothing are the openings at the shoulders through which you put your arms.

armistice /ˈɑːmɪstɪs/ *noun*: **armistices**
An **armistice** is an agreement between countries or parties that are at war to stop fighting, while ways of making peace are discussed. [*same as* **ceasefire, truce**]

armour (*AmE* **armor**) /ˈɑːmə(r)/ *noun* (*uncount*)
1 In earlier times, a soldier's **armour**, or suit of **armour**, was the protective metal suit he wore in battle: *a knight in shining armour.* **2 Armour** is also the metal covering that protects warships and tanks from missiles. **3** The hard protective casing or scaly covering of certain animals can also be referred to as their **armour**.

armoured /ˈɑːməd/ *adjective*
An **armoured** vehicle is protected from missiles by a covering of strong metal plating.

armpit /ˈɑːmpɪt/ *noun*: **armpits**
Your **armpits** are the hollow areas under your arms at the shoulders. [see picture at **body**]

arms /ɑːmz/ *noun* (*plural*)
1 Arms are weapons: *a secret supply of arms and ammunition* □ *The police don't carry arms as a regular*

thing. **2** The **arms** of a family or nation are its coat of arms, its own distinctive heraldic design. [see **coat of arms**]

▻ ***phrase*** You are **up in arms** if you are angry about something and are threatening action or protesting indignantly.

army /ˈɑːmɪ/ *noun* (*with a singular or plural verb*): **armies**

1 An **army** is a fighting force equipped for warfare on land, especially as a part of a country's armed forces distinguished from its navy and air force: *a captain in the army* □ *He applied to join the army.* □ *army officers.* **2** An **army** of people or animals is a large number regarded as a force of some kind: *An army of workmen are presently engaged in clearing the rubble.*

aroma /əˈroʊmə/ *noun*: **aromas**

An **aroma** is a pleasant, strong rather than sweet, smell: *The aroma of cooking greeted her as she opened the door.* [compare **smell, odour, whiff**]

aromatic /arəˈmatɪk/ *adjective*

An **aromatic** plant or food has a pleasant, strong rather than sweet, smell: *aromatic herbs and spices* □ *an aromatic smell.*

arose /əˈroʊz/ *verb*

Arose is the past tense of **arise**.

around /əˈraʊnd/ *adverb; preposition*

▻ ***adverb***

1 Someone or something is **around** if they are nearby or easily available: *I called at your house but there was no-one around.* □ *There are a lot of new travel books around.* [*same as* **about**] **2** You move **around**, or move something **around**, when you go, or move something, in different directions: *People were walking around looking at the exhibits.* □ *Stop waving your fork around.* □ *I've just been looking around for you.* [*same as* **about**] **3 Around** is used with some verbs to indicate the lack of a sensible purpose: *They were messing around instead of working.* □ *Don't stand around doing nothing.* [*same as* **about**] **4** (*especially AmE*) **Around** means 'approximately' when used before a number, measurement, time or period: *I'll be in your neighbourhood for around a week.* □ *I'll call you around 5.30.* □ *He's around 45.* □ *I guess she weighs around 140 pounds.* [*same as* **about**] **5** People gather **around** when they group together in a rough circle round something. [*same as* **round**] **6** Something passes, or is passed, **around**, when it goes from person to person: *The photos were passed around for everyone to see.* [*same as* **round**] **7** (*especially AmE*) You turn **around** when you turn to face the opposite way. [*same as* **round**] **8** (*especially AmE*) Something moves **around** when it moves in a circle, especially repeatedly: *The wheel keeps going around.* [*same as* **round**]

▻ ***preposition***

1 People or things are, or move, **around** a place when they are, or move, here and there in it: *Her belongings were lying around the room.* □ *We've been driving around the country visiting cathedrals.* [*same as* **about**] **2** People or things are, or move, **around** something when they are on all sides of it, or move in a circle round it: *We all sat around the kitchen table.* □ *She wore a gold chain around her neck.* □ *They danced around the fire.* [*same as* **round**] **3** A thing or place is **around** something such as a bend or corner when it is reached by a change of direction: *The newsagent's is just around the next bend.* [*same as* **round**]

arouse /əˈraʊz/ *verb*: **arouses, arousing, aroused**

1 Something **arouses** a feeling in you when it causes it: *The man's behaviour aroused her suspicions.* □ *It wasn't until money was mentioned that his interest was aroused.* **2** Something **arouses** you if it makes you angry: *It isn't often that he's so aroused.* **3** (*literary*) Something **arouses** you when it wakes you up: *He woke early, aroused by the birds.* [*same as* **rouse**] — *noun* (*uncount*) **arousal:** *the arousal of sexual interest.*

arrange /əˈreɪndʒ/ *verb*: **arranges, arranging, arranged**

1 You **arrange** a future event when you make the plans for it and settle details concerning it: *What time is the meeting arranged for?* **2** You **arrange** to do something, *eg* with another person, when you make, or agree on, plans for doing it: *I arranged with her that whoever arrived first should buy the tickets.* □ *We arranged to meet on the platform.* □ *I've arranged for a taxi to pick us up at 7.15.* **3** Someone **arranges** something for you when they make it possible for you, *eg* as a favour: *I believe a bank loan could be arranged.* **4** You **arrange** such things as books, furniture or flowers, when you put them in an order, position or grouping satisfactory to you: *They've asked me to arrange the flowers for the wedding.*

arrangement /əˈreɪndʒmənt/ *noun*: **arrangements**

1 (*used in the plural*) You make **arrangements** for a future event when you plan all the details in advance. [*same as* **preparations, plans**] **2** (*count or uncount*) An **arrangement** is an agreement with someone to do something, or a plan for doing something: *I made an arrangement with her to meet for lunch.* □ *What are the arrangements for collecting the entrance money?* □ *the seating arangements.* **3** (*count or uncount*) An **arrangement** of such things as flowers is a particular grouping or display of them: *artistic flower arrangements.*

array /əˈreɪ/ *noun* (*usually in the singular*): **arrays**

An **array** of things is a collection of them, on show or display: *an impressive array of captured arms.*

arrears /əˈrɪəz/ *noun* (*plural*)

Arrears are the amount of money you still owe when you have failed to pay a bill, especially one that becomes due for payment regularly: *Unless the arrears are paid immediately the telephone will be disconnected.*

▻ ***phrase***

1 You are **in arrears** with a regular payment, or it is **in arrears**, if you failed to pay an instalment of it when it became due for payment and you still owe it: *The rent is already three months in arrears.* **2** To pay an employee **in arrears** is to pay them at the end of the period for which they have earned their wages.

arrest /əˈrɛst/ *verb; noun*

▻ ***verb***: **arrests, arresting, arrested**

1 The police **arrest** someone they suspect of a crime or offence when they catch them and take them to a secure place before charging them formally: *She was arrested for shoplifting.* □ *A second man has been arrested in connection with the murder.* □ *They've arrested her on suspicion of drug-dealing.* **2** To **arrest** something such as a disease is to prevent its progress: *Ways must be found of arresting the spread of AIDS.* [*same as* **halt, check**] **3** Your attention may **be arrested** by something interesting, surprising or impressive: *His strange outfit arrested her attention.* — *adjective* **arresting:** *The most arresting feature of this church is its amazing spire.* □ *She had combed her hair off her face, and looked eye-catching, even arresting.* [*same as* **striking**]

▻ ***noun*** (*uncount or count*): **arrests**

Arrest is the act of arresting or the circumstance of being arrested: *She faced arrest for fraud.* □ *Dutch police made 75 arrests during football riots in Amsterdam.* [see also **cardiac** arrest, **house arrest**]

▻ ***phrase*** Someone who is **under arrest** has been caught by the police and is being kept in a secure place.

arrival /ə'raɪvəl/ *noun* (*uncount or count*): **arrivals**
1 The **arrival** somewhere of a person or thing is the circumstance of their arriving there: *We await the arrival of fresh medical supplies.* ▫ *His unexpected arrival was rather an embarrassment.* ▫ *She apologized for her late arrival.* **2** The **arrival** of a baby is its birth. **3** The **arrival** of something new is its invention or the beginning of its existence: *The arrival of the credit card simplified shopping for the housewife.* **4** Someone who has just arrived is an **arrival**: *A party will be held to welcome the new arrivals on the staff.*

arrive /ə'raɪv/ *verb*: **arrives, arriving, arrived**
1 You **arrive** somewhere when you get there after, or at the end of, a journey: *We were late arriving at our destination.* ▫ *What time did you arrive?* [*opposite* **leave, depart**]

> You **arrive** *in* a country or city, but you **arrive** *at* a place such as an airport or station: *We arrive at Schiphol airport at 8.30. She arrived at the theatre rather early. What time does your train arrive in Glasgow?*

2 You **arrive** somewhere when you come there for the first time, to live or work: *She's made a few changes since arriving at the office.* ▫ *He arrived in Britain in 1978 and settled in Manchester.* **3** A baby **arrives** when it is born. **4** Something such as news or mail **arrives** when you receive it or it is given to you: *News of the air crash took two days to arrive.* **5** Something new **arrives** when it starts to exist or be available: *Women's tights didn't arrive on the market as everyday wear till the '60s.* **6** A moment or day you have been waiting for **arrives** when it occurs or you reach it: *The day of the exam arrived.* **7** You **arrive** at a decision, conclusion or solution when you make it or reach it: *We eventually arrived at a satisfactory compromise.* **8** (*informal*) You say someone such as an actor or musician **has arrived** when they have their first important public success.

arrogance /'arəgəns/ *noun* (*uncount*)
Arrogance is the belief or assumption that you are superior to other people and can behave rudely towards them if you want to.

arrogant /'arəgənt/ *adjective*
Someone who is **arrogant** thinks they are superior to other people and can behave rudely and inconsiderately towards them when they want to: *arrogant remarks* ▫ *I think he's wrong but it would be thought arrogant of me if I said so.* — *adverb* **arrogantly:** *She arrogantly believed she could tell us all how to do our work.*

arrow /'aroʊ/: **arrows** *noun*
1 An **arrow** is a long narrow weapon with a sharp point, and is shot from a bow. **2** An **arrow** is also a sign for telling people where to go, in the shape of a straight line with a bent line at its end, forming a point: *Passengers should follow the green arrows if they have nothing to declare.*

arsenic /'ɑːsənɪk/ *noun* (*uncount*)
Arsenic is a strong poison that can cause death.

arson /'ɑːsən/ *noun* (*uncount*)
The crime of **arson** is the act of deliberately setting fire to a building.

art /ɑːt/ *noun*: **arts**
1 (*uncount*) **Art** is the creation of works of beauty such as drawings, paintings and sculptures: *She's studying history of art in Florence.* **2** (*uncount*) **Art** is also the works created: *the art and artists of the Italian Renaissance* ▫ *Islamic art* ▫ *London art galleries.* **3** An activity that involves creation, or the creative interpretation and expression of ideas, such as painting, sculpture, poetry, drama, or music, can be called an **art**: *visual arts such as photography.* **4** (*used in the plural*) The **arts** are these activities collectively, regarded as part of any country's culture: *In real terms, Government spending on the arts has diminished.* **5** (*used in the plural*) **Arts**, or the **arts**, are subjects of study such as history, literature, languages and philosophy, that involve appreciation, imagination and personal interpretation, as distinct from sciences such as mathematics or physics: *an arts degree.* **6** Any activity that requires physical, practical, mental, artistic or social skill may be called an **art**: *the art of public speaking.*
▻ ***phrase*** You say you have **got** something **down to a fine art** if after much practice you have discovered the best way of doing it.

artefact or **artifact** /'ɑːtɪfakt/ *noun*: **artefacts**
An **artefact** is an object made by a human being, such as a tool or piece of jewellery, especially if it is of archaeological interest.

artery /'ɑːtərɪ/ *noun*: **arteries**
Your **arteries** are the tubes that carry oxygen-containing blood from your heart to all parts of your body. [compare **vein**] — *adjective* **arterial** /ɑː'tiːrɪəl/: *arterial blood.*

artful /'ɑːtfʊl/ *adjective*
You describe someone, or something they do, as **artful** if it seems clever in a cunning or crafty way: *His apparent generosity was just an artful move to avoid paying tax.* — *adverb* **artfully:** *She wore a dress with a loose top that artfully disguised her pregnancy.*

arthritis /ɑː'θraɪtɪs/ *noun* (*uncount*)
Someone who suffers from **arthritis** has swollen and painful joints, and so finds movement difficult. — *adjective* **arthritic** /ɑː'θrɪtɪk/: *arthritic joints.*

artichoke /'ɑːtɪtʃoʊk/ *noun*: **artichokes**
An **artichoke** is one of two sharp-tasting vegetables, either the **globe artichoke**, round in shape and closely covered with thick green leaves, or the **Jerusalem artichoke**, a root vegetable like a long, irregularly shaped potato. [see picture at **vegetable**]

article /'ɑːtɪkəl/ *noun*: **articles**
1 An **article** is an object, or an item of something: *Could you describe the missing articles?* ▫ *The floor was littered with books, papers, and articles of clothing.* **2** A piece of writing dealing with a particular subject, in a newspaper, journal or magazine, is an **article**: *Did you read her article on marriage in The Spectator?* **3** (*legal*) An **article** is also a paragraph dealing with a particular point in a formal document or agreement: *I refer to Article 25 of the contract.* **4** (*grammar*) An **article** is one of two types of determiner, the **definite article** (in English the determiner *the*) and the **indefinite article** (in English the determiner *a* or *an*).

articulate *adjective*; *verb*
▻ ***adjective*** /ɑː'tɪkjʊlət/
Someone who is **articulate** can express themselves and their ideas clearly and well: *The most articulate interviewees aren't necessarily the best people for the job.* [*same as* **eloquent, fluent**]
▻ ***verb*** /ɑː'tɪkjʊleɪt/: **articulates, articulating, articulated**
1 You **articulate** your thoughts or feelings when you express them in words: *She was so excited that she had difficulty in articulating her ideas.* **2** You **articulate** words when you pronounce them: *Don't rush; articulate each word carefully.*

articulated /ɑː'tɪkjʊleɪtɪd/ *adjective*
In an **articulated** truck or lorry, the driver's cab and

trailer are separately constructed, and connected by a jointed bar, making it easier to turn corners.

artifact see **artefact**.

artificial /ɑːtɪˈfɪʃəl/ *adjective*
1 Artificial materials or objects are produced by a chemical or manufacturing process rather than a natural one, often in deliberate imitation of a natural material or object: *artificial silk* □ *I didn't even notice that the flowers were artifical.* [*same as* **synthetic**] **2** An **artificial** limb is an arm or leg fitted to someone's body to replace one that has been removed or amputated. [*same as* **false**] **3** You describe a person, or their behaviour or manner, as **artificial** if they behave in a manner, or pretend to have opinions or feelings, that you know are not natural to them: *Politicians tend to develop an artifical smile.* [*same as* **false**, **affected**, **assumed**] **4** Conditions are described as **artificial** if they have been created or established through human agency rather than occurred naturally: *Learners tend to pick up English idiom more quickly away from the artificial environment of the classroom.* — *noun* (*uncount*) **artificiality** /ɑːtɪfɪʃɪˈalɪtɪ/: *There was inevitably a degree of artificiality about the experiment.* — *adverb* **artificially:** *He was being artificially kept alive.*

artificial insemination /ɑːtɪfɪʃəl ɪnsɛmɪˈneɪʃən/ *noun* (*uncount*)
Artificial insemination is the inserting of male semen into a woman's womb using an instrument, as an alternative to the natural means of insertion, in an attempt to achieve pregnancy.

artificial intelligence /ɑːtɪfɪʃəl ɪnˈtɛlɪdʒəns/ *noun* (*uncount*)
Artificial intelligence is the branch of computer science that deals with methods of getting computers to perform tasks associated with human intelligence, such as learning, judging and deciding.

artificial respiration /ɑːtɪfɪʃəl rɛspɪˈreɪʃən/ *noun* (*uncount*)
Artificial respiration is the process of forcing air into and out of the lungs of someone who has stopped breathing, to try to make them start breathing naturally again.

artillery /ɑːˈtɪlərɪ/ *noun* (*uncount*)
An army's **artillery** is the part of its firing equipment consisting of large fixed guns and guns transported on wheels.

artisan /ɑːtɪˈzan/ *noun* (*formal*): **artisans**
An **artisan** is a skilled worker in a trade or industry, especially someone who works with their hands.

artist /ˈɑːtɪst/ *noun*: **artists**
1 An **artist** is someone who produces drawings and paintings or other works of art, for their living or as a hobby: *abstract artists.* **2** Someone who is highly skilled at doing something can be referred to as an **artist**: *This chair was evidently made by an artist.* **3** A performer such as an actor, musician or dancer is also an **artist**: *He learnt a lot from acting with artists of Gielgud's standing.*

artistic /ɑːˈtɪstɪk/ *adjective*
1 An **artistic** person is someone who draws or paints well or produces other successful works of art, has a feeling for colour and design, or has taste and ability in music or dance. [*same as* **creative**] **2** People call a creation, design or arrangement **artistic** if they consider it tasteful and attractive, or think it shows talent. **3 Artistic** means relating to artists or art: *artistic expression and interpretation.* — *adverb* **artistically:** *She was musically and artistically talented.*

artistry /ˈɑːtɪstrɪ/ *noun* (*uncount*)
The **artistry** of someone such as a musician, dancer, actor, writer, poet, painter or craftworker is their imaginative, creative and executive skill.

arty /ˈɑːtɪ/ *adjective* (*informal, often derogatory*): **artier**, **artiest**
If you call someone **arty** you mean that they are inclined to demonstrate their feeling for art in too obvious or deliberate a way, *eg* in their style of dress or their choice of furniture and decoration.

as /az/ or /əz/ *conjunction; preposition*
▷ ***conjunction***
1 As is a conjunction of time, meaning 'at the moment that' (often used with *just*), 'during the time that' or 'when': *The telephone rang just as I was leaving the apartment.* □ *Her asthma improved as she grew older.* □ *As a teenager* [= when he was a teenager], *he learnt to enjoy classical music.* **2 As** is a conjunction of reason, meaning 'seeing that': *As she was the oldest, she was put in charge of the others.* □ *We'd better go by the most direct route, as it's getting so late.* [*same as* **since**, **because**] **3 As** is also a conjunction of manner, meaning 'in the way that', and is often used to add comments of various kinds and constructions: *He won't do as he's told.* □ *She was buried at Aeschi, as she had requested.* □ *Let's leave things as they are for the moment.* □ *We'll be away for the weekend as usual.* [= as we usually are] □ *You're welcome, as always.* □ *As expected, he had come without his key.* □ *The weather was chilly, as it can be sometimes, even in July.* □ *The electricity went off, as frequently happens in a thunderstorm.* □ *He's sorry about the mistake, as we all are.* □ *He loves opera, as do I.* [= and I do, too] □ *The message read as follows.* □ *The story was as follows.* □ *As you see, we're in a bit of a mess.* □ *As it happens, I've got a spare light bulb.* [= I happen to have one] □ *I can't lend you the money; I've only got two pounds as it is.* [= even without giving any away] **4 As** is a conjunction of concession, meaning 'though': *Improbable as it seems, I enjoy housework.* □ *Angry as he was, he managed to speak calmly.* □ *We couldn't persuade her, try as we might.* [= although we tried our best] □ *Much as I'd like to, I can't join you for lunch.*
▷ ***preposition***
1 You use **as** in describing or referring to the roles, jobs or functions of people and things: *She worked as a taxi-driver for four months.* □ *They were offering their services as financial advisers.* □ *He will be greatly missed both as a teacher and as an inspired musician.* □ *Most doctors aren't really interested in their patients as people.* □ *Her resignation came as an utter surprise.* □ *As her sister, I was closer to her than anyone.* □ *Speaking as your tutor, I think you should pass the exam all right.* □ *She quite often dressed as* (or *like*) *a man.* □ *I wish you wouldn't use my saucers as ashtrays.* □ *I only need a computer as a word-processor.*

> Notice the difference between **as** and **like**: **like** is used in comparisons and similes, but **as** is not: *As his mother, she couldn't help loving him. She loved him like a mother* [although she wasn't his mother]. *She works as a librarian. She works like a horse.* [= she works very hard].

2 Some verbs of regarding and describing take **as** in a variety of constructions after their object: *Fortunately she viewed the whole incident as a joke.* □ *She was recognized as being a possible leader.* □ *He sees everyone as a potential customer.* □ *He never thought of himself as especially hardworking.* □ *The situation was later described as calm.*

But not all verbs of this kind need **as**: *She found teaching a rewarding job. He considered himself intelligent.*

▻ ***phrases***
1 You use the construction '**as** something **as** something else' to express equality in comparisons; the first **as** is an adverb, but the second **as** can be either a conjunction or a preposition: *He tries as hard as I do to save money.* □ *She's not as tall as me.* □ *I love you just as much as your mother.* [= either 'just as much as I love your mother', or 'just as much as your mother loves you']

Notice that with a negative, the first **as** can be replaced by **so**: *He isn't quite so patient as he used to be. This apartment isn't so spacious as our previous one.*

2 You use **as for** and **as to** to mean 'regarding' in dealing with the subject of a certain thing or person: *Some people have complained, but as for me* (not *as to me*), *I'm perfectly satisfied.* □ *As to her work, she seems very thorough.* □ *As for finding a job, still no luck.* □ *He reassured us as to* (not *as for*) *the reliability of the company.* □ *As for your request for a free meal, you can forget it.* **3** Something is so **as from** or **as of** a certain date, if it starts being so on that date: *As of* (or *as from*) *1 October, you will be able to pay your account through any post office.* □ *First-class letters will cost 25 pence as from today.* **4** You use **as if** and **as though** to express probability and possibility in terms of comparison; the past tense of the verb can be used with a present sense where the possibility is not a real one: *I feel as if I'm* (or *I was*, or *I were*) *going mad.* □ *It sounds as though he'll be late.* □ *It doesn't look as if we'll be able to meet you after all.* □ *Why ask? It's not as if you didn't know.* □ *It was as if I'd been transported somewhere by magic.* □ *He lent forward as if about to say something.* □ *She shrieked as though in agony.* **5** You use **as it were** to mean 'in a sense', or to indicate that you are speaking metaphorically: *She was releasing me from the nest, as it were.* **6** For **as far as** see **far**. **7** For **as well, as well as**, and **just as well**, see **well**. **8** For **as yet** see **yet**. **9** For **so as** see **so**.

asbestos /az'bɛstɒs/ *noun* (*uncount, often adjectival*)
Asbestos is a soft grey mineral that is used to make fireproof materials: *asbestos ceiling tiles.*

ascend /ə'sɛnd/ *verb*: **ascends, ascending, ascended**
1 (*literary*) You **ascend** something such as a stair or mountain when you go up it: *They were the first climbers to ascend the Eiger by the north face.* **2** (*literary*) Something **ascends** when it rises: *We were relieved to see smoke ascending from the chimney.*
▻ ***phrase*** A person **ascends the throne** when they begin to reign as king or queen: *Princess Elizabeth ascended the throne on her father's death in February 1952.*

ascendancy /ə'sɛndənsɪ/ *noun* (*uncount*)
One person or party has the **ascendancy** over others if they are stronger, more powerful and more influential than the others: *In terms of support, the Big Bang theory has the ascendancy over other explanations of the universe.*

ascendant /ə'sɛndənt/ *noun* (*used in the singular*)
▻ ***phrase*** A person or party is **in the ascendant** if they are growing in importance or power: *By 1945 Labour was already in the ascendant.*

ascending /ə'sɛndɪŋ/ *adjective*
You arrange things such as numbers in **ascending** order when you start with the lowest and continue with the second-lowest and so on until you reach the highest.

ascent /ə'sɛnt/ *noun*: **ascents**
1 (*uncount*) Someone's **ascent** is their rise to an important or powerful position: *her rapid ascent to power.* **2** (*uncount or count*) The **ascent** of a mountain is the act or process of climbing it: *Bonington's ascent of the east face.* **3** An **ascent** is an upward slope: *The path led up a steep rocky ascent.*

ascertain /asə'teɪn/ *verb*: **ascertains, ascertaining, ascertained**
You **ascertain** that something is so when you find out, or make sure, that it is: *It should be possible to ascertain where he was born.* □ *At this stage it is almost impossible to ascertain the truth.* [*same as* **establish**]

ascetic /ə'sɛtɪk/ *adjective*; *noun*
▻ ***adjective***
An **ascetic** person lives in a simple manner, severely restricting their physical comforts and the amount they eat and drink: *She led an ascetic life.* — *adverb* **ascetically:** *He lived ascetically.*
▻ ***noun*: ascetics**
An **ascetic** is a religious person who leads a simple life with a minimum of physical comfort so as to be able to concentrate on matters concerning the soul.

ascribe /ə'skraɪb/ *verb*: **ascribes, ascribing, ascribed**
1 You **ascribe** an event to some circumstance or factor if you believe the event was caused by it: *We can't ascribe all our economic ills to Tory mismanagement.* [*same as* **attribute, put down to**] **2** A work of literature or art **is ascribed** to someone if it is thought to have been written or produced by them: *The painting is known as 'The Forest Fire' and is generally ascribed to Piero di Cosimo.* [*same as* **attribute**] **3** You **ascribe** a quality to someone if you think they have it: *Generosity is not a virtue I would have ascribed to her.* [*same as* **attribute**]

asexual /eɪ'sɛkʃʊəl/ *adjective*
An **asexual** reproduction process involves no sexual activity; a plant or creature that is **asexual** has no sexual parts or organs.

ash[1] /aʃ/ *noun*: **ashes**
1 (*uncount, or used in the plural*) **Ash** is the powdery greyish dust that remains after something has been burnt: *He kept dropping cigarette ash on the carpet.* □ *Nothing remained of the letters but a pile of ashes in the grate.* **2** (*used in the plural*) A person's **ashes** are the remains of their body after cremation.

ash[2] /aʃ/ *noun* (*count or uncount*): **ashes**
1 (*count or uncount*) An **ash**, or **ash tree**, is a forest tree with silvery-grey bark: *an ash wood.* **2** (*uncount*) **Ash** is the wood of this tree: *A table made of ash.*

ashamed /ə'ʃeɪmd/ *adjective*
1 You are **ashamed** of something you have done when you feel bad, guilty or embarrassed about it: *I felt ashamed of myself for swearing.* □ *You should be ashamed of yourself, telling lies at your age.* □ *I'm ashamed that I've taken so long to reply to your letter.* **2** You are **ashamed** of another person when they do something that makes you feel embarrassed at your connection with them: *She was ashamed of her son's rudeness.* **3** You are **ashamed** to do something when guilt, pride or shame make you reluctant to do it: *I was too ashamed to tell you I'd lost it.*

Notice that **shameful** is not a synonym of **ashamed**; it means 'disgraceful'.

ashore /ə'ʃɔ:(r)/ *adverb*
You come **ashore** when you come out of the water, or get out of a ship, on to land: *The passengers were allowed ashore for half an hour at Corfu.*

ashtray /ˈaʃtreɪ/ *noun*: **ashtrays**
An **ashtray** is a dish used by people smoking cigarettes and cigars as a receptacle for their ash.

Asian /ˈeɪʃən/ or /ˈeɪʒən/ *adjective*; *noun*
▻ ***adjective***
Asian means relating to the continent of Asia, its countries or its peoples: *The Asian influence on Africa's east coast is evident in the place names.*
▻ ***noun***: **Asians**
An **Asian** is someone who belongs to or comes from any of the countries of Asia: *Asians as well as West Indians were the targets in a fresh wave of racism.*

aside /əˈsaɪd/ *adverb*; *noun*
▻ ***adverb***
1 You move or shift something **aside** when you put it on one side of you: *She put her mending aside to answer the telephone.* **2** You move or step **aside** when you get out of someone's way: *I stood aside to let him pass.* **3** You take someone **aside** when you lead them away from a group to talk privately to them: *She drew me aside and whispered a warning.* **4** You sweep something such as an objection **aside** when you refuse to consider it seriously: *He brushed all our fears aside.* **5** You use **aside** after a noun to indicate that you are not considering that thing for the present, or have finished considering it and want to discuss something else: *Repair costs aside, there's the matter of who was responsible for the accident.*
▻ ***noun***: **asides**
1 An **aside** is a remark made by a character in a play which the audience is intended to hear, supposedly without the other characters hearing it. **2** An **aside** is also a remark you make that is not directly related to what you are saying: *Here and there she threw in vicious asides about her colleagues' wives.*
▻ ***phrase*** (*AmE*) **Aside from** means the same as **apart from**: *There was nothing I could do, aside from comforting him.* ▫ *Aside from from tutors' fees, there's the travel cost.*

ask /ɑːsk/ *verb*: **asks, asking, asked**
1 You **ask** someone something when you address a question to them: *Don't ask me such difficult questions.* ▫ *I've been asked that many times.* ▫ *I asked him his name.* ▫ *I notice you didn't bother to ask my opinion.* ▫ *Excuse me, but could I ask you the time?* ▫ *He stopped some children and asked the way to Curzon Street.* ▫ *She asked if the train had left.* ▫ *I'll go and ask whether there's a later bus.* ▫ *He asked me where the stationery was kept.* ▫ *If you can't find the right platform, ask at the ticket office.* ▫ *What are you up to, may I ask?* ▫ *There's someone here asking about vacancies.* ▫ *'Are you absolutely certain?' she asked.* **2** You make requests by **asking** someone to do something, or **asking** to do something, or **asking** someone for something, or **asking** for something to be done: *I asked her to help me.* ▫ *Nowadays a woman can ask a man to marry her, can't she?* ▫ *Passengers were asked to take all their baggage with them.* ▫ *I asked her if she would look after the children for an hour.* ▫ *He asked to use the telephone.* ▫ *She asked to speak to Mrs Lee.* ▫ *They asked to be allowed into the ward.* ▫ *Could I ask you for a lift?* ▫ *He asked for an application form.* ▫ *I asked for their essays to be handed in by Friday.* ▫ *If you need anything else, just ask.* ▫ *All I ask is a bit of peace and quiet.* ▫ *She asked permission to leave early.* ▫ *I must ask your forgiveness for my unintentional rudeness.* **3** You **ask** someone somewhere when you invite them there: *Why don't you ask her round?* ▫ *He was too shy to ask me in.* ▫ *Over a hundred have been asked to the wedding.*
▻ ***phrase*** You use **if you ask me** when offering your own opinion: *She was just pretending, if you ask me.*

phrasal verbs
ask after You **ask after** someone when you ask how they are: *She's always asking after you.* ▫ *He remembered to ask after my mother.*
ask for 1 You **ask for** someone when you say you want to speak to them: *A Mr Davies rang a few minutes ago, asking for you.* [see also **ask** sense 2 above] **2** You say someone **is asking for** it, or **asking for** trouble, if the way they are behaving is bound to get them into trouble or difficulties: *It was asking for it to drive after four whiskies.*

askew /əˈskjuː/ *adjective or adverb*
Something is **askew** when it is not straight: *The picture was hanging askew.*

asleep /əˈsliːp/ *adjective*
You are **asleep** when you are sleeping: *Aren't the childen asleep yet?*
▻ ***phrases*** **1** You **fall** or **drop asleep** when you begin to sleep: *She had dropped asleep over her newspaper.* **2** You are **fast** or **sound asleep** when you are sleeping deeply: *The dog was sound asleep in front of the fire.*

asparagus /əˈsparəgəs/ *noun* (*uncount*)
The vegetable **asparagus** is the thick juicy stems of a plant related to the lily, eaten as a vegetable. [see picture at **vegetable**]

aspect /ˈaspɛkt/ *noun*: **aspects**
1 An **aspect** of a subject or thing is an area or element of it, especially as a matter for consideration: *The computer has altered so many aspects of life.* [*same as* **side**] **2** Something takes on a different **aspect** when it changes appearance or character: *With the offer of financial support, the project acquired an altogether more promising aspect.* **3** A building's **aspect** is the direction in which it faces: *The house had a northerly aspect, and was rather cold and dark.*

aspersions /əˈspɜːʃənz/ *noun* (*plural*)
▻ ***phrase*** (*literary, or humorous*) You **cast aspersions** on something when you make critical or derogatory remarks about it: *Are you casting aspersions on my singing ability?*

asphalt /ˈasfalt/ *noun* (*uncount*)
Asphalt is a thick black sticky substance that is mixed with pieces of stone to make a surfacing material for roads and playgrounds.

asphyxiate /əsˈfɪksɪeɪt/ *verb*: **asphyxiates, asphyxiating, asphyxiated**
Someone **asphyxiates** or **is asphyxiated** when air is prevented from getting into their lungs, *eg* when they breathe in smoke or a poisonous gas, or when they are strangled, so that they die from lack of oxygen. [*same as* **choke, suffocate**] — *noun* (*uncount*) **asphyxiation** /əsfɪksɪˈeɪʃən/: *Most of the victims had died of asphyxiation.*

aspirant /ˈaspɪrənt/ or /əˈspaɪərənt/ *noun* (*formal*): **aspirants**
An **aspirant** to a high or important office or position is someone whose ambition is to obtain it.

aspiration /aspɪˈreɪʃən/ *noun* (*count, usually in the plural, or uncount*)
Your **aspirations** are your aims and ambitions, the things you want to achieve in life.

aspire /əˈspaɪə(r)/ *verb*: **aspires, aspiring, aspired**
You **aspire** to an important office or position if you have an ambition to achieve it: *Many aspire to greatness but few achieve it.* — *adjective* **aspiring:** *aspiring young politicians.*

aspirin /ˈasprɪn/ *noun* (*count or uncount*): **aspirins** or **aspirin**
Aspirin is a mild pain-killing drug supplied in the form of pills or tablets: *I took a couple of aspirin for my headache.*

ass /as/ *noun*: **asses**
1 An **ass** is a long-eared animal of the horse family, often used for carrying loads. [*same as* **donkey**] **2** (*informal*) If you call someone an **ass**, you mean they are being stupid or behaving foolishly.

assail /ə'seɪl/ *verb*: **assails, assailing, assailed**
1 To **assail** someone is to attack or criticize them vigorously: *Her newly published memoirs had been assailed by the newspaper critics.* **2** You **are assailed** by such things as doubts or worries when they keep coming into your mind and disturbing you.

assailant /ə'seɪlənt/ *noun*: **assailants**
A person's **assailant** is someone who attacks them: *It was dark and she didn't recognize her assailant until he struck.* [*same as* **attacker**]

assassin /ə'sasɪn/ *noun*: **assassins**
An **assassin** is a person who murders someone, especially someone important, usually from a political motive.

assassinate /ə'sasɪneit/ *verb*: **assassinates, assassinating, assassinated**
Someone, especially someone politically important, **is assassinated** when they are murdered: *We were shown the spot outside the theatre where the Swedish prime minster was assassinated.* — *noun* (*uncount*) **assassination** /əsasɪ'neɪʃən/: *There has been an assassination attempt on the President.*

assault /ə'sɔːlt/ *verb*; *noun*
▻ ***verb*** (*formal*): **assaults, assaulting, assaulted**
To **assault** someone is to attack them: *She was arrested for assaulting a member of the police force.*
▻ ***noun***: **assaults**
1 An **assault** is an attack: *She felt that his criticisms were an assault on her dignity and integrity.* **2** (*uncount; legal*) **Assault** is the offence of making a physical attack on someone: *He was found guilty of assault.*

assemble /ə'sɛmbəl/ *verb*: **assembles, assembling, assembled**
1 People **assemble** or **are assembled** when they gather or are brought together in a group for some purpose: *Delegates were assembling in Geneva for the conference.* **2** You **assemble** facts when you collect them and have them ready to use, *eg* as evidence in an argument. **3** You **assemble** a product, machine or other item when you fit its parts together as a final stage of manufacture or production: *It took me less than an hour to assemble the bookcase.* [*same as* **put together**] — *adjective* **assembled:** *He addressed the assembled company.*

assembly /ə'sɛmblɪ/ *noun*: **assemblies**
1 (*count or uncount*) An **assembly** of people is a gathering of them for a purpose such as a meeting or conference: *She addressed the assembly of delegates on the first evening.* **2** An **assembly** can also be an officially elected or summoned body of people responsible for law-making in a country or any division of it: *The Athenian legislative assembly was known as the Boule, and every citizen was required to attend it.* **3** (*uncount*) The **assembly** of a product, machine or other item, or of its parts, is the fitting together of its parts as a final stage in its production or manufacture: *The kit comes with full instructions for assembly.*

assembly line /ə'sɛmblɪ laɪn/ *noun*: **assembly lines**
An **assembly line** is a line, row or series of workers and machines along which an article or product passes in the process of going through its various stages of manufacture.

assent /ə'sɛnt/ *noun*; *verb*
▻ ***verb***: **assents, assenting, assented**
You **assent** to something such as a proposal, or a proposed scheme, when you agree to it or give permission for it: *The Board had assented to the plans.*
▻ ***noun*** (*uncount*)
You give your **assent** to a proposal or scheme when you agree to it or give your permission for it: *The Queen has given her assent to the Bill.*

assert /ə'sɜːt/ *verb*: **asserts, asserting, asserted**
1 You **assert** a fact or belief, or **assert** that something is so, when you state it firmly and positively: *He had always asserted his innocence in spite of his conviction.* **2** You **assert** something such as a right when you insist on it: *She asserted her right to speak in her own defence.* **3** You **assert** something such as your authority or independence when you show by the way you behave that you are in control, or can act on your own. **4** You **assert** yourself when you speak and behave firmly and confidently in company or in your relations with others, so that people listen to you and take notice of you as an individual. — *noun* (*count or uncount*) **assertion** /ə'sɜːʃən/: *I would challenge most of the assertions she makes in her book about her political colleagues.* ▫ *the firm assertion of authority.*

assertive /ə'sɜːtɪv/ *adjective*
An **assertive** person speaks and acts firmly and confidently in company, or in their relations with others, so that people listen to them and take notice of them: *You must try and be more assertive.* — *adverb* **assertively:** *Behave assertively and you'll get what you want in life.*

assess /ə'sɛs/ *verb*: **assesses, assessing, assessed**
1 You **assess** a situation, or a person's abilities and achievements, by considering them in some detail and making a judgement about them: *He looked round at the other competitors and assessed his chances of winning.* ▫ *As a writer, she is difficult to assess.* [*same as* **appraise**] **2** You **assess** the value, worth or cost of something when you estimate it or calculate it: *The value of the stolen jewellery was assessed at $20000.* — *noun* (*count or uncount*) **assessment:** *The BBC correspondent was giving us his assessment of the situation in Teheran.* ▫ *Full assessment of the damage will take time.*

asset /'asɛt/ *noun*: **assests**
1 A person, quality or skill that is an **asset** helps towards the success of an organization or towards personal success: *Conscientious and responsible pupils are always an asset to the school.* [*same as* **boon**]: *One of her assets was an ability to concentrate under any circumstances.* [*same as* **strength, strong** point] **2** (*usually in the plural*) A company's or individual person's **assets** are their total possessions and property.

assiduous /ə'sɪdjʊəs/ *adjective*
An **assiduous** worker is someone who works hard and conscientiously: *After months of painstaking and assiduous investigation, he was at last getting results.* [*same as* **diligent, hardworking**] — *adverb* **assiduously:** *She worked her way assiduously through the reading list.*

assign /ə'saɪn/ *verb*: **assigns, assigning, assigned**
1 You **are assigned** something when it is given to you individually to have, use, do or perform: *I was assigned a desk by the window.* ▫ *The children obediently performed the tasks assigned to them.* [*same as* **allot**] **2** Someone **is assigned** to a particular job, department or case when they are given responsibility for it or within it: *A social worker is assigned to each family.*

assignation /asɪg'neɪʃən/ *noun* (*literary*): **assignations**
An **assignation** is a secret meeting with someone, especially a lover.

assignment /ə'saɪnmənt/ *noun*: **assignments**
1 An **assignment** is a piece of work or a task you are

given to do, *eg* as part of your academic studies or your job: *His most terrifying assignment as a foreign correspondent was to report the war in Serbia.* **2** (*uncount*) **Assignment**, *eg* of a thing to a person, or of a person to a job, is the act of assigning: *There was some disbelief at the assignment of Inspector Clouzot to the case.*

assimilate /ə'sɪmɪleɪt/ *verb*: **assimilates, assimilating, assimilated**
1 You **assimilate** such things as facts, information, ideas, skills and customs when you learn them, or they become part of your working methods or your way of life: *We need people who can assimilate new techniques quickly.* [*same as* **pick up, take in**] **2** Immigrants into a country, or newcomers into an area, **assimilate** or **are assimilated** into their local community when they behave, or are treated, as though they belonged to it: *It's chiefly the parents that have difficulty assimilating.* — *noun* (*uncount*) **assimilation** /əsɪmɪ'leɪʃən/: *the rapid assimilation of computer technology by the workforce.*

assist /ə'sɪst/ *verb*: **assists, assisting, assisted**
1 You **assist** someone in or with something when you help them: *She assisted me with my research work.* **2** You **assist** someone when you supply them with something they need, such as money, advice or facts: *She offered to assist him with his education expenses.* **3** You **are assisted** by some factor or circumstance when it makes your task easier: *We shall find him now that we have your description to assist us.*

assistance /ə'sɪstəns/ *noun* (*uncount*)
You give someone **assistance** when you help them, physically support them, or give them the money, information or advice they need: *I could not have succeeded without the assistance of my colleagues.* □ *She could only stand with her husband's assistance.*

assistant /ə'sɪstənt/ *noun*: **assistants**
1 In job titles, the word **assistant** indicates junior or lower rank, so that an **assistant** manager, or **assistant** lecturer, is a rank lower than a manager or lecturer. **2** An **assistant** or **shop assistant** serves customers in a shop. **3** A person's **assistant** is someone who helps them with their job or the work they are doing: *She employed a personal assistant to do her paperwork and answer letters.*

associate *verb*; *noun*; *adjective*
▻ ***verb*** /ə'soʊʃɪeɪt/ or /ə'soʊsɪeɪt/: **associates, associating, associated**
1 You **associate** one thing with another if you connect them in your mind: *I'd never have associated you with athletic activities.* **2** Things **are associated** if they are linked or connected: *dangers associated with pregnancy.* **3** You **associate** yourself with a cause or organization, or **are associated** with it, if you support it openly: *He associated himself with the Liberal cause at one time.* [*same as* **align**] **4** You **associate** with certain people if you are often in their company: *At school she tended to associate with the older girls.* □ *I hope he's not associating with drug addicts.* [*same as* **mix**]
▻ ***noun*** /ə'soʊʃɪət/ or /ə'soʊsɪət/: **associates**
Your **associates** are your colleagues, or the people you have contact with, especially through your work: *He's a business associate of mine.*
▻ ***adjective*** /ə'soʊʃɪət/ or /ə'soʊsɪət/
1 In job titles, **associate** indicates joint responsibility: *his associate directors.* **2** An **associate** member of a society has some of the privileges, but not the full status, of membership.

association /əsoʊʃɪ'eɪʃən/ or /əsoʊsɪ'eɪʃən/ *noun*: **associations**
1 An **association** is a group or organization of people with a common profession, interest or purpose: *The Amateur Athletics Association.* [*same as* **society, club**] **2** (*uncount or count*) Your **association** with a person or organization is your connection with them: *He was requested to drop his association with the National Front.* **3** Something has an **association** for you if it reminds you of something, or is connected with something in your past: *For me that smell has an association with hospitals.*
▻ ***phrase*** Someone does something **in association with** someone else when they co-operate or collaborate in doing it: *The book is published by the University Press in association with the Council for Archaeology.*

assorted /ə'sɔːtɪd/ *adjective*
A number of **assorted** things is a mixture of things all of the same kind but in a variety of *eg* colours, sizes, shapes or flavours: *a tin of assorted biscuits.*

assortment /ə'sɔːtmənt/ *noun*: **assortments**
An **assortment** is a mixture of things of the same kind but in a variety of *eg* shapes, sizes, colours or flavours: *Try our new milk-chocolate assortment.*

assume /ə'sjuːm/ or /ə'suːm/ *verb*: **assumes, assuming, assumed**
1 You **assume** that something is so when you imagine it is so, or decide to regard it as so in order to consider the consequences: *People wrongly assume that he's a Tory.* □ *Let's assume that she'll catch the 5.30 and be here by 7.00.*

> You **assume** that something is so without knowing whether or not it is. You **presume** that something is so when you have some evidence for thinking it is: *Your coat had gone, so I presumed you'd left.*

2 You **assume** a way of behaving, or an expression, when you begin to have it, or adopt it deliberately: *She tried to assume an air of indifference.* **3** Something **assumes** a quality when it takes it on or begins to have it: *Don't let the matter assume too much importance for you.* **4** Someone **assumes** power, control, authority or responsibility when they are officially given it or start to have it: *Labour assumed control in 1945.*

assumed /ə'sjuːmd/ or /ə'suːmd/ *adjective*
An **assumed** name or identity is a false one: *She had applied for membership under an assumed name.*

assuming /ə'sjuːmɪŋ/ or /ə'suːmɪŋ/ *conjunction*
You say **assuming**, or **assuming that**, something is so when you are regarding it as so in order to consider the consequences: *Assuming that we all work at the same rate, we should be finished by January.*

assumption /ə'sʌmʃən/ or /ə'sʌmpʃən/ *noun*: **assumptions**
1 You make an **assumption** when you imagine that something is so, or decide to regard it as so: *I think we should plan ahead on the assumption that the money will be available.* **2** (*uncount*) A person's **assumption** of power or control is the circumstance of their taking it: *It was now five years since his assumption of office.*

assurance /ə'ʃʊərəns/ or /ə'ʃɔːrəns/ *noun*: **assurances**
1 (*count or uncount*) You give someone an **assurance** that something is going to happen, or is so, when you promise that it will happen, or say there is no doubt that it is so, in order to calm their worries: *I wasn't satisfied with their assurances that money could be found.* □ *The doctors could offer us little assurance as to his full recovery.* [*same as* **guarantee**] **2** (*uncount*) You do something with **assurance** if you do it with confidence and certainty: *Young musicians seem to perform in public with remarkable assurance these days.* [compare **self-assurance**] **3** (*BrE*) **Assurance** is another word for insurance, especially of a person's life.

assure /ə'ʃuə(r)/ or /ə'ʃɔː(r)/ *verb*: **assures, assuring, assured**
1 You **assure** someone that something is so, or will happen, or **assure** them of something, when you tell them that there is no doubt about it, in order to calm their worries: *They assured me that no harm would come to me if I kept quiet.* **2** Something **is assured** if it is secured or guaranteed: *Her survival until the next election could not be assured.*
▻ *phrase* You say **'rest assured'** to someone when trying to reassure them or calm their worries about something: *Rest assured that everything possible is being done.*

assured /ə'ʃuəd/ or /ə'ʃɔːd/ *adjective*
1 A person who is **assured** is confident: *She found herself in the company of a lot of smartly dressed, assured young women.* [*same as* **self-assured**] **2** An **assured** performance is a skilful as well as confident one.

assuredly /ə'ʃuərədlɪ/ or /ə'ʃɔːrədlɪ/ *adverb* (*sentence adverb*)
Assuredly means 'you can be sure that': *The bombers will assuredly strike again.*

asterisk /'astərɪsk/ *noun*: **asterisks**
An **asterisk** is a star-shaped mark (*) used in printing and writing, *eg* to draw the reader's attention to a note or omitted material included at the bottom or side of the page.

asthma /'asmə/ *noun* (*uncount*)
Asthma is an illness, in many cases associated with an allergy, which causes breathing difficulties.

asthmatic /a'smatɪk/ *adjective and noun*: **asthmatics**
Someone who is **asthmatic** suffers from asthma; an **asthmatic** is an asthmatic person.

astonish /ə'stɒnɪʃ/ *verb*: **astonishes, astonishing, astonished**
Something **astonishes** you if it amazes or surprises you: *His memory for names never fails to astonish me.*

astonished /ə'stɒniʃt/ *adjective*
You are **astonished** at something if it amazes or surprises you: *I couldn't help feeling astonished when she won.* ▫ *They seemed astonished that I could program a computer.*

astonishing /ə'stɒnɪʃɪŋ/ *adjective*
Something that is **astonishing** amazes or surprises you: *You got here with astonishing speed.* — *adverb* **astonishingly** (*intensifying or sentence adverb*): *You sounded astonishingly knowledgeable.* ▫ *Astonishingly, everything worked out as planned.*

astonishment /ə'stɒnɪʃmənt/ *noun* (*uncount*)
Astonishment is a feeling of great surprise or amazement: *They stared in astonishment.* ▫ *To my astonishment, he agreed.*

astound /ə'staʊnd/ *verb*: **astounds, astounding, astounded**
Something **astounds** you if it amazes or shocks you: *We were astounded by the report of his death.* — *adjective* **astounded:** *I'm astounded at your ignorance.* ▫ *We were astounded to hear that she'd resigned.* — *adjective* **astounding:** *It's astounding that half of all crime in Britain is committed by people under the age of 21.* ▫ *They can measure the land with astounding accuracy.*

astray /ə'streɪ/ *adverb*
▻ *phrases* **1** You **lead** someone **astray** when you teach them bad habits or are responsible for making them do something wrong. **2** Something **goes astray** when it gets lost, *eg* when it is being sent or taken somewhere: *I think my last letter may have gone astray.*

astride /ə'straɪd/ *preposition*
You sit **astride** something such as a horse or motor bike when you sit with one leg on each side of it.

astrologer /ə'strɒlədʒə(r)/ *noun*: **astrologers**
An **astrologer** is a person who, with the help of astrology, tells people about their character or predicts their future.

astrology /ə'strɒlədʒɪ/ *noun* (*uncount*)
Astrology is the study of the movements of the stars and planets and the influence that these are believed to have on people's lives. — *adjective* **astrological** /astrə'lɒdʒikəl/: *astrological forecasts.*

astronaut /'astrənɔːt/ *noun*: **astronauts**
An **astronaut** is a person trained for space travel.

astronomer /ə'strɒnəmə(r)/ *noun*: **astronomers**
An **astronomer** is someone who studies the stars and the planets.

astronomy /ə'strɒnəmɪ/ *noun* (*uncount*)
Astronomy is the scientific study of the stars and planets.

astute /ə'stjuːt/ *adjective*
An **astute** person is clever and quick at understanding the deeper meaning of situations and knows how to take advantage of them: *That was one of her more astute political moves.* [*same as* **shrewd**] — *adverb* **astutely:** *an astutely worded statement.*

asylum /ə'saɪləm/ *noun*: **asylums**
1 (*uncount*) The government of a country gives or grants **asylum** to someone who has left their own country for political reasons, when they give them protection and permission to stay: *She sought political asylum in Britain.* **2** (*old*) A hospital for mentally ill patients was formerly called an **asylum**.

asymmetric /eɪsɪ'mɛtrɪk/ or **asymmetrical** /eɪsɪ'mɛtrɪkəl/ *adjective*
A shape, form, pattern or design is **asymmetrical** or **asymmetric** if its two sides or halves do not match. [*opposite* **symmetric, symmetrical**] — *adverb* **asymmetrically:** *asymmetrically placed eyes.* [*opposite* **symmetrically**]

at /ət or at/ *preposition*
1 At is a preposition of place: *She waited at the bus stop.* ▫ *We stayed at the Beach Motel.* ▫ *I'll meet you at the station.* ▫ *She wasn't at the office today.* ▫ *Is he at home?* ▫ *Which university were you at?*

> Notice that you use **at** with such things as towns or buildings when you are thinking of them as points or locations on a map or journey: *The train stops at Perth.* But: *We decided to stay in Perth. Let's meet at the theatre.* But: *It's always rather cold in the theatre. She lives at 17 Hopetoun Street.* But: *She lives in* (or AmE *on*) *Hopetoun Street.*

2 At is a preposition of time: *They're due to arrive at 8.55.* ▫ *He returned at midnight.* ▫ *The money is always counted at the end of the day.* ▫ *We'll be away at the weekend.* ▫ *They start school at the age of 5 and leave at about 16 or 17.* ▫ *She's coming home at Christmas.* ▫ *He doesn't have a job at present.* ▫ *She can't come at the moment.* ▫ *I'll call at a more convenient time.* ▫ *We left at that point in the conversation.*

> Notice that if a determiner is used before certain expressions of time, **at** is not used: *He was here at Easter.* But: *He was here last Easter. We let the cat out at night.* But: *We let the cat out every night.*

3 At can indicate position in front of something: *She was seated at the computer as usual.* ▫ *There were seven of us at the table.* ▫ *A man was standing at the door.*
4 At expresses direction towards something: *Look at this.* ▫ *What are you staring at?* ▫ *She smiled at me.* ▫ *She aimed the snowball at his departing figure.*

Notice that **at**, in contrast to **to**, can express attack or hostility: *He was throwing stones at the ducks.* But: *Could you throw that pencil to me? Mum was always shouting at us for not doing this or that.* But: *He shouted to me from upstairs. He's inclined to talk at you rather than to you.*

5 At can express reaction or response: *He kept laughing at the she way spoke.* ▫ *I'm shocked at your extravagance.* ▫ *I'm surprised at you.* ▫ *At that I got very angry.* **6 At** is used in expressions of physical relationship and of manner: *The track joins the main road at a sharp angle.* ▫ *We were flying at a height of 30000 feet.* ▫ *He remained at a distance, watching the dancing.* ▫ *Choose a number at random.* ▫ *He forced her into the car at gun point.* **7** You are **at** certain activities when you are engaged in them: *He's out at work.* ▫ *It's fascinating watching kids at play.* ▫ *She's at lunch right now.* ▫ *You won't pass Chemistry unless you work at it.* **8 At** can express certain states: *when Britain was at war with Spain* ▫ *The murderer is still at large.* ▫ *You're at liberty to choose what you want.* **9** You are good or bad **at** something if you do it well or badly: *She's quick at making decisions.* ▫ *He's very clever at getting his own way.* ▫ *I'm not very good at maths.* **10** Some verbs can be followed by **at** to indicate activity at the edge or on the surface of something: *Someone's knocking at the door.* ▫ *Something's been gnawing at the woodwork.* ▫ *That cat's been scratching at the chair again.* ▫ *She sipped at her coffee.* **11** You buy or sell something **at** a certain price: *These are on sale at £1.99 in the supermarket.* ▫ *The paperback edition is published at $6.50.* **12** Things move or happen **at** a certain rate, speed or frequency: *I was only driving at 25 miles per hour.* ▫ *They're making progress at a remarkable rate.* ▫ *Take care when you're travelling at speed.* ▫ *Deal with your problems one at a time.* ▫ *He calls at fortnightly intervals.* **13** You do something **at** someone's command when you obey them: *We had arrived early, at his own request.* ▫ *At the signal we rushed forward to attack.*

ate /ɛt/ or /eɪt/ *verb*
Ate is the past tense of **eat**.

atheism /ˈeɪθiːɪzm/ *noun* (*uncount*)
Atheism is the belief that there is no god. — *noun* **atheist:** *Not all philosophers are atheists.*

athlete /ˈaθliːt/ *noun*: **athletes**
An **athlete** is someone who can run and jump well, especially if they train seriously and enter competitions.

athletic /aθˈlɛtɪk/ *adjective*
1 An **athletic** person is someone fit, strong and energetic, especially someone who takes part in sports and trains seriously for them. **2 Athletic** also means relating to athletics: *athletic ability* ▫ *The Amateur Athletic Association.* — *adverb* **athletically:** *She was tall and athletically built.*

athletics /aθˈlɛtɪks/ *noun* (*uncount*)
Athletics is the area of sport consisting of track and field events involving running, jumping and throwing.

atlas /ˈatləs/ *noun*: **atlases**
An **atlas** is a book of maps: *a road atlas.*

atmosphere /ˈatməsfɪə(r)/ *noun*: **atmospheres**
1 The **atmosphere** of a planet is the layer of gases surrounding it. **2** A place's **atmosphere** is **a** the air you breathe in it: *People developed chest complaints in the smoky atmosphere of the big city.* **b** its general feel, or the impression it makes on you: *She liked the relaxed and welcoming atmosphere of the college.* [*same as* **ambience**] **3** A place that has **atmosphere** has a distinctive character: *The new office lacked atmosphere.* — *adjective* **atmospheric** /atməˈsfɛrɪk/: *atmospheric pressure.*

atom /ˈatəm/ *noun*: **atoms**
1 An **atom** is the smallest particle of an element that can take part in a chemical reaction. **2** (*informal*) An **atom** can mean 'the least bit' when used with a negative, after *if*, or with words like *hardly*: *Don't you feel an atom of sympathy for him?* [*same as* **jot**, **scrap**, **shred**]

atom bomb /ˈatəm bɒm/ *noun*: **atom bombs**
An **atom bomb** or **atomic bomb** is a bomb whose explosion is the result of atoms being split with a massive release of nuclear energy.

atomic /əˈtɒmɪk/ *adjective*
1 Atomic energy and **atomic** weapons use the explosive force produced by the splitting of atoms. [*same as* **nuclear**] **2 Atomic** also means relating to an atom as the smallest particle of an element capable of chemical reaction.

atone /aˈtoʊn/ *verb* (*formal*): **atones, atoning, atoned**
You **atone** for something wrong that you have done when you do something to show that you are sorry: *She tried to atone for her rudeness by being extra helpful in the house.* [*same as* **make amends**] — *noun* (*uncount*) **atonement:** *He tried to think of some means of atonement.*

atrocious /əˈtroʊʃəs/ *adjective* (*often informal*)
Atrocious means shocking or wicked, and can be used to emphasize the gravity or severity of something bad: *an atrocious crime* ▫ *The acting was atrocious.*
▻ ***adverb*** (*often informal or intensifying*) **atrociously:** *You behaved atrociously.* ▫ *He's atrociously lazy.* — *noun* (*uncount*) **atrociousness:** *the atrociousness of the weather.*

atrocity /əˈtrɒsɪtɪ/ *noun* (*count or uncount, often in the plural*): **atrocities**
An **atrocity** is an act of shocking wickedness or cruelty: *the atrocities of war.*

attach /əˈtatʃ/ *verb*: **attaches, attaching, attached**
1 One thing **is attached** to another if it is stuck, fastened, sewn or joined to the other: *I attached name tapes to all their school clothes.* ▫ *See attached note.* ▫ *a large house with a certain amount of land attached.* **2** You are **attached** to an organization or institution if you are working as a member of it, especially temporarily: *She was one of the research students attached to the college.* **3** A smaller institution controlled by a larger one **is attached** to it: *a centre for industrial research attached to the University of Reading.* **4** You **attach** a quality such as importance to something if you think it has it; something such as blame **attaches** to someone if they are thought to deserve it: *Don't attach any significance to what happened today.* ▫ *Please don't think that any suspicion attaches to you.* [see also **attached**]

attaché /əˈtaʃeɪ/ *noun*: **attachés**
An **attaché** is a junior official in an embassy.

attaché case /əˈtaʃeɪ keɪs/ *noun*: **attaché cases**
An **attaché case** is a small case for documents and papers. [*same as* **briefcase**]

attached /əˈtatʃt/ *adjective*
You are **attached** to someone or something if you like them or are fond of them: *He would never get rid of his books; he's too attached to them.*

attachment /əˈtatʃmənt/ *noun*: **attachments**
1 You have an **attachment** to or for someone or something if you are fond of them: *Since their schooldays he had felt a strong attachment for her.* **2** An **attach-**

ment is an extra device that can be fitted to a machine or a tool to add a function to it: *It has an attachment for loosening screws.* **3** You have an **attachment** to an institution if you are working as a member of it for a limited period.

attack /ə'tak/ *verb; noun*
▻ ***verb*: attacks, attacking, attacked**
1 To **attack** a person or place is to make a violent attempt to injure, damage, defeat or capture them: *The wounds suggested that he had been attacked by a leopard.* **2** You **attack** a person or their ideas when you criticize them severely or strongly: *He bitterly attacked the government's education policy.* **3** Something such as a disease, chemical or insect **attacks** something when it destroys it: *Multiple sclerosis attacks the protective covering of the nerves.* **4** You **attack** a task or problem when you start dealing with it with determination, energy and enthusiasm: *I'd better go and attack that pile of dishes.* [*same as* **tackle**] **5** In a game such as football, one side or team **attacks** when they take control of the ball and try to score; you can also **attack** a weak point in your opponent's play: *Try to attack her backhand.* □ *I decided to attack his bishop.*
▻ ***noun*** (*count or uncount*): **attacks**
1 An **attack** is a violent attempt to injure or overcome a person, or damage or capture a place: *The police launched a second attack against the demonstrators.* □ *defences against air attack.* **2** An **attack** is a strong or hostile criticism: *Her research methods had come under attack from academics.* □ *The leader page of the Independent carried an attack on government health cuts.* **3** (*count*) An **attack** of an illness is an instance or period of suffering from it: *a heart attack* □ *an attack of dysentery.* **4** In games, an **attack** is an attempt to score or to take control: *You've left your queen open to attack.*
▻ ***phrase*** You are **on the attack** when you are making an attack: *The away team were on the attack throughout the second half.*

attacker /ə'takə(r)/ *noun*: **attackers**
A person's **attacker** is someone who attacks them: *She was asked if she would recognize her attacker again.* [*same as* **assailant**]

attain /ə'teɪn/ *verb*: **attains, attaining, attained**
You **attain** something such as an ambition or aim when you achieve it: *By sheer hard practice she had attained an extraordinary level of skill as a pianist.* [*same as* **achieve**]

attainable /ə'teɪnəbəl/ *adjective*
Something is **attainable** if it can be achieved: *With today's technology a high degree of accuracy is attainable in long-range weather-forecasting.* [*same as* **achievable**; *opposite* **unattainable**]

attainment /ə'teɪnmənt/ *noun*: **attainments**
1 (*often in the plural*) Your **attainments** are your skills, achievements or talents: *Her list of artistic attainments was impressive.* [*same as* **accomplishment**] **2** (*uncount*) The **attainment** of something is the circumstance of achieving it: *The publication of his book represented the attainment of his life's ambition.* [*same as* **achievement**]

attempt /ə'tɛmpt/ *verb; noun*
▻ ***verb*: attempts, attempting, attempted**
You **attempt** something, or **attempt** to do something, when you try to do it, sometimes without much expectation of success: *She attempted to push the car to the side of the road.* [compare **try, endeavour**]
▻ ***noun*: attempts**
1 You make an **attempt** to do something when you try to do it: *She passed her driving test at the second attempt.* □ *She made no attempt to conceal her dislike.* [*same as* **endeavour, effort**; compare **try**] **2** To make an **attempt** on someone's life is to try to kill them.

attempted /ə'tɛmptɪd/ *adjective*
An **attempted** action, especially a crime, is an unsuccessful attempt at it: *Reports are coming in of an attempted coup in Iraq.* □ *Attempted suicide used to be treated as a crime.*

attend /ə'tɛnd/ *verb*: **attends, attending, attended**
1 You **attend** an event such as a meeting or performance when you are present at it: *Much as he loves music, he hasn't time to attend concerts.* **2** You **attend** an institution such as school when you go there regularly: *He was asked to attend the out-patient clinic for a weekly check-up.* **3** A doctor or nurse **attends** a patient when they treat him or her: *I'm afraid Dr Allan is out attending a case.* **4** You **attend** to something when you deal with it: *We still have one or two problems that need attending to.* [*same as* **see to, handle**] **5** (*formal*) You **attend** to something that is being said or done when you listen or watch carefully: *She wasn't really attending to the lecture.* **6** (*formal*) One person **is attended** by another when they are accompanied or escorted by them: *The bride was attended by three bridesmaids.*

attendance /ə'tɛndəns/ *noun*: **attendances**
1 (*count or uncount*) The **attendance** at an event is the number of people attending it: *the steady decline in church attendances.* **2** (*uncount*) **Attendance** at an institution or an event is the circumstance of attending it: *Regular attendance at school is not essential once your exams are over.*
▻ ***phrases*** **1** (*literary*) One person **dances attendance on** another when they follow them about and attend to all their needs and wishes. **2** (*formal*) One person is **in attendance** on another if they are looking after them: *Four bridesmaids were in attendance.*

attendant /ə'tɛndənt/ *noun; adjective*
▻ ***noun*: attendants**
1 An **attendant** in a public insitution such as a library or museum is a person employed to help people visiting it and using it; an **attendant** at a petrol station serves customers. **2** A bride's **attendants** are her bridemaids and pages.
▻ ***adjective*** (*formal*)
Attendant means resulting or accompanying: *late pregnancy and its attendant dangers.*

attention /ə'tɛnʃən/ *noun*: **attentions**
1 (*uncount*) You give your **attention** to something when you concentrate on it, or listen or watch carefully: *I've a few announcements to make, if I may have your attention for a moment.* □ *I had been letting my attention wander.* **2** (*uncount*) A person or thing receives **attention** when they are dealt with, looked after, or treated as important: *Unconscious casualties need immediate attention.* □ *Trouble-makers like him deserve no attention.* **3** (*usually in the plural*; *formal*) **Attentions** are polite or affectionate acts you perform for someone to show your regard for them: *Flattered as she was by his attentions, she did not want to encourage him.*
▻ ***phrases*** **1** Something **attracts** or **catches** your **attention** when it makes you notice it; you **attract** or **catch** someone's **attention** when you do something to make them look at you: *Could you try and attract the waiter's attention?* **2** You **draw** someone's **attention** to something, or **bring** something to someone's **attention** when you mention it to them or point it out: *Thank you for bringing the error to our attention.* **3 a** You **pay attention** to something when you concentrate on it, or listen or watch carefully: *You won't learn anything*

unless you pay attention to your teacher. **b** People **pay** something **attention** when they treat it as important, or take notice of it: *We pay far too much attention to economists.* **4** Soldiers are told to **stand to attention**, or given the command '**Attention!**', when they are required to stand tall and straight with their arms at their sides.

attentive /ə'tɛntɪv/ *adjective*
1 An **attentive** listener or audience listens or watches carefully or with concentration: *I've never before taught such an attentive and appreciative set of students.* **2** Someone who is **attentive** looks after you in a polite or affectionate way: *She noticed that Geoffrey had become rather more attentive recently.* — *adverb* **attentively:** *They listened attentively and took notes.*

attest /ə'tɛst/ *verb*: **attests, attesting, attested**
One thing **attests**, or **attests to**, another if it serves to prove its truth or validity: *The enormous sales of her children's books attest to their popularity and appeal, if not to their worth.* [*same as* **demonstrate, show**]

attic /'atɪk/ *noun*: **attics**
An **attic** is a room or space at the top of a house under the roof.

attire /ə'taɪə(r)/ *noun* (*uncount literary, sometimes humorous*)
Someone's **attire** is the clothing or outfit they are wearing, especially if it is formal or elegant: *He was looking very splendid in his formal evening attire.* [*same as* **dress**]

attired /ə'taɪəd/ *adjective* (*literary, sometimes humorous*)
You are **attired** in particular clothes when you are wearing them: *She arrived already attired for the occasion in a T-shirt and shorts.*

attitude /'atɪtju:d/ *noun*: **attitudes**
1 Your **attitude** to something is the way you feel about it or regard it: *They took the attitude that quantity of work was more important than quality.* [*same as* **view, opinion**] **2** Your **attitude** to a person is the way you regard them, as shown in your manner or behaviour towards them: *She clearly has a very patronizing attitude towards the local population.* **3** You sit or stand in a certain **attitude** when you put your body into a particular position, especially one that expresses or indicates something: *He was leaning against the wall in an attitude of unconcern.* [*same as* **posture**]
▻ ***phrase*** You **strike an attitude** when you adopt a physical or conversational pose for dramatic effect.

attorney /ə'tɜ:nɪ/ *noun* (*AmE*): **attorneys**
An **attorney** is a lawyer.
▻ ***phrase*** **Power of attorney** is the right to act for another person in legal and business matters.

attract /ə'trakt/ *verb*: **attracts, attracting, attracted**
1 Something **attracts** people or creatures if it has qualities that bring them to it: *The brightly lit window had attracted a quantity of moths.* **2** Someone or something **attracts** you if they have qualities and features that make you like them; a quality of a person or thing **attracts** you to them if it is the cause of your liking them: *He certainly attracted her physically, though she would hardly have called him good-looking.* □ *It was the very loneliness and bleakness of the mountains that attracted her to them.* **3** Something **attracts** your attention or notice if it makes you notice it: *He waved to attract my attention.* **4** A magnet or something magnetic **attracts** metallic objects when it makes them move towards it. **5** Something such as a cause **attracts** support or publicity when it is widely supported or publicized: *Any potential cure for AIDS is bound to attract publicity.*

attracted /ə'traktɪd/ *adjective*
You are **attracted** to someone or something if they interest you and make you like them: *I found myself becoming attracted to him.*

attraction /ə'trakʃən/ *noun*: **attractions**
1 (*uncount or used in the singular*) **Attraction** is the power or circumstance of attracting, especially sexually, or the feeling of being attracted, or the quality of desirability: *She liked him as a friend though she felt no physical attraction towards him.* □ *I can't see the attraction of a subject like history.* **2** (*often in the plural*) The **attractions** of something are the features or qualities about it that make you like it or want it: *The generous pension scheme was an added attraction.* **3** An **attraction** is a place, building or show that people like visiting or going to: *The travel literature included a list of local tourist attractions.*

attractive /ə'traktɪv/ *adjective*
1 Someone who is **attractive** is good-looking or physically desirable: *Despite myself I found him attractive.* **2** Something that is **attractive** looks or sounds nice, or is desirable: *The city centre didn't look very attractive.* — *adverb* **attractively:** *He had decorated the room attractively in dark strong colours.* — *noun* (*uncount*) **attractiveness:** *Her eccentric clothes were part of her attractiveness.*

attribute *verb*; *noun*
▻ ***verb*** /ə'trɪbju:t/: **attributes, attributing, attributed**
1 You **attribute** something to a particular circumstance if you think the circumstance caused it: *She was inclined to attribute all her troubles to a lack of understanding on the part of other people.* [*same as* **put down to, ascribe**] **2** A comment, joke, work of art, poem or other piece of writing, **is attributed** to someone if they are thought to have made it or written it: *The statue had been wrongly attributed to Bernini.* [*same as* **ascribe**] **3** You **attribute** qualities or properties to people or things if you think of them as having them: *People tend to attribute human characteristics such as obstinacy to their computers.* [*same as* **ascribe**] — *noun* (*uncount or count*) **attribution** /atrɪ'bju:ʃən/: *Several formerly mistaken attributions have been corrected in the new museum catalogue.*
▻ ***noun*** /'atrɪbju:t/: **attributes**
The **attributes** of something are its qualities, properties, characteristics or features: *It was a democracy in name but had all the attributes of a dictatorship.*

attributive /ə'trɪbjətɪv/ *adjective* (*grammar*)
An adjective is **attributive** if it is used before the noun that it qualifies, as in *a distant object, his apparent reluctance.* — *adverb* **attributively:** *The noun 'buffet' is being used attributively in 'buffet car'.* [compare **predicative**]

attuned /ə'tju:nd/ *adjective*
1 You are **attuned** to something if you can appreciate it: *Oriental people seem better attuned to Western music than Westerners are to Oriental music.* **2** Your ears are **attuned** to a certain sound if you hear and recognize it immediately: *She seemed to have her ear attuned to the grammatical and logical sequence of every sentence I uttered.*

atypical /eɪ'tɪpɪkəl/ *adjective*
Something that is **atypical** is not typical: *These results are atypical.* [*opposite* **typical**]

aubergine /'oʊbəʒi:n/ *noun*: **aubergines**
An **aubergine** is a tropical oval-shaped fruit with a purple skin and white flesh, which is cooked and eaten as a vegetable. [*same as* **egg plant**; see picture at **vegetable**]

auburn /'ɔ:bən/ *adjective*
Auburn hair is a reddish-brown colour.

auction /ɔːkʃən/ *noun; verb*
▻ ***noun*** *(count or uncount)*: **auctions**
An **auction** is a public sale in which items are sold to the person who offers most money for them: *She buys most of her jewellery at auction sales.* ▫ *goods sold at* (or *by*) *auction.*
▻ ***verb***: **auctions, auctioning, auctioned**
Something **is auctioned** when it is sold at an auction.

> ***phrasal verb***
> A collection of things are **auctioned off** when they are got rid of by being sold at an auction.

auctioneer /ɔːkʃəˈnɪə(r)/ *noun*: **auctioneers**
An **auctioneer** is the person who conducts an auction.

audacious /ɔːˈdeɪʃəs/ *adjective*
Audacious conduct or behaviour is bold or daring, often so much so as to seem rude, impudent or cheeky: *Her report was outspoken, even audacious, in its criticism of the management.* — *adverb* **audaciously:** *She was wearing a dress with an audaciously low neck.*

audacity /ɔːˈdasɪtɪ/ *noun (uncount)*
Audacity is boldness or daring, especially if seen as rudeness or impudence: *He had the audacity to suggest that my attitude was out of date.*

audible /ˈɔːdɪbəl/ *adjective*
A sound that is **audible** is loud enough to be heard: *Her once-powerful voice had dwindled to a barely audible whisper.* — *adverb* **audibly:** *The audience were becoming audibly impatient.*

audience /ˈɔːdɪəns/ *noun (with a singular or plural verb)*: **audiences**
1 An **audience** is a group of people watching and listening to a performance such as a play, show, film, concert or talk: *He called for a member of the audience to join him on stage.* **2** A radio or television **audience** is the people who listen to or watch any particular programme: *a programme that appeals to a wide audience.* **3** The people who read a writer's books can also be referred to as his or her **audience**: *Her ideas were known to reach an audience of academics the world over.* [*same as* **readership**]
▻ ***phrase*** You **have an audience with** someone important when you have an interview with them.

audio /ˈɔːdɪoʊ/ *adjective*
Audio equipment is used for the recording and reproduction of sound.

audio-visual /ɔːdɪoʊ ˈvɪʒʊəl/ *adjective*
Audio-visual equipment is involved with the recording and reproduction of both sound and images: *audio-visual teaching aids.*

audit /ˈɔːdɪt/ *noun; verb*
▻ ***noun***: **audits**
An **audit** is an official inspection of an organization's accounts by an accountant.
▻ ***verb***: **audits, auditing, audited**
An accountant **audits** the accounts of an organization when he or she examines them officially.

audition /ɔːˈdɪʃən/ *noun; verb*
▻ ***noun***: **auditions**
An **audition** is a short performance you give in front of someone who is looking for people to perform in a play, film, show or orchestra, so that they can decide whether you are good enough to take part.
▻ ***verb***: **auditions, auditioning, auditioned**
You **audition** or **are auditioned** for a part in a play, show or film, or for a choir or orchestra, when you do an audition.

auditor /ˈɔːdɪtə(r)/ *noun*: **auditors**
An **auditor** is an accountant who officially examines the accounts of an organization or business.

auditorium /ɔːdɪˈtɔːrɪəm/ *noun*: **auditoriums**
An **auditorium** is the part of a theatre or concert hall where the audience sit, or a building used for events attended by a large audience, such as concerts or meetings.

augment /ɔːgˈmɛnt/ *verb*: **augments, augmenting, augmented**
To **augment** something such as your income is to increase it by adding something extra to it: *She was forced to try and augment her earnings by taking on a cleaning job in the evenings.*

augur /ˈɔːgə(r)/ or /ˈɔːgjə(r)/ *verb*: **augurs, auguring, augured**
▻ ***phrase*** A circumstance that **augurs well** or **badly** for the future is a good or bad sign for the future. [*same as* **bode**]

August /ˈɔːgəst/ *noun (uncount)*
August is the eighth month of the year, coming after July and before September: *He stayed with us last August.* ▫ *The meeting is on Friday the twenty-first of August* (written *Friday 21 August*). ▫ *August the eleventh,* or (*AmE*) *August eleven* (written *August 11*) ▫ *We usually travel during August.* ▫ *hot August weather.*

august /ɔːˈgʌst/ *adjective*
Something or someone that is **august** is dignified, grand, solemn, noble or impressive: *the opening of Parliament and other august state occasions.*

aunt /ɑːnt/ *noun*: **aunts**
Your **aunt** is the sister of your father or mother, or the wife of your uncle: *I ought to visit Aunt Margaret.*

auntie or **aunty** /ˈɑːntɪ/ *noun (informal)*: **aunties**
Auntie is an informal name you use, especially as a child, for an aunt, or for a close friend of your parents: *Have you written to thank Auntie Hazel yet?*

au pair /oʊ pɛə(r)/ *noun*: **au pairs**
An **au pair** is a young person from abroad, especially a woman, who lives with a family in order to learn the language, and helps with the housework and care of the children in return for accommodation and food.

aura /ˈɔːrə/ *noun*: **auras**
An **aura** surrounding a person or place is a distinctive impression or quality that seems to be associated with them or to come from them: *She had about her this aura of mystery.* [*same as* **air**]

aural /ˈɔːrəl/ *adjective*
Aural means relating to the ears or the sense of hearing: *aural comprehension.* [see note at **oral**]

auspices /ˈɔːspɪsɪz/ *noun (plural)*
▻ ***phrase*** Something is done **under the auspices** of an organization if it has been arranged by them, or is done with their official support, encouragement and approval: *The 'Enjoy Reading' scheme was being run under the auspices of the British Council.*

auspicious /ɔːˈspɪʃəs/ *adjective*
Something **auspicious** is lucky, or is a good sign for the future: *Their 5-nil win last weekend was an auspicious start to the season.* — *adverb* **auspiciously:** *The season did not start auspiciously for his team.*

austere /ɒˈstɪə(r)/ *adjective*
1 Something that is **austere** in appearance is severely simple and plain: *an austere black dress.* **2** **Austere** also means strict and severe: *A smile briefly illuminated her austere features.* **3** **Austere** times are times when there is no money available for luxuries or comforts: *the austere post-war years.* — *adverb* **austerely:** *an austerely furnished room.* — *noun (uncount)* **austerity** /ɒˈstɛrɪtɪ/: *The Chancellor will hardly offer us an austerity budget so close to an election.*

Australian /ɒˈstreɪlɪən/ *adjective; noun*

▻ *adjective*
Australian means concerned with or belonging to the country or continent of Australia, its people, or their form of English: *I didn't realize you were Australian.* □ *Australian words.*
▻ *noun*: **Australians**
A person who is born in or is a citizen of Australia is an **Australian**.

authentic /ɔːˈθɛntɪk/ *adjective*
1 Something that is **authentic** is genuine, not fake or artificial or an imitation: *The signature appeared to be authentic.* □ *Join our safari and see wild animals in their authentic surroundings.* **2** An **authentic** account of something is a true and accurate representation of it: *We're told that his book gives an authentic picture of life in the prison camps.* — *adverb* **authentically:** *an authentically prepared medieval banquet.* — *noun* (*uncount*) **authenticity** or /ɔːθɛnˈtɪsɪtɪ/: *There are doubts as to the letter's authenticity.*

authenticate /ɔːˈθɛntɪkeɪt/ *verb*: **authenticates, authenticating, authenticated**
To **authenticate** something such as a signature or work of art is to prove it genuine or declare it so after examination; an account or description **is authenticated** when it is confirmed as accurate or supported by independent witness: *There are well-authenticated reports of atrocities committed by our own troops.* [*same as* **verify**]

author /ˈɔːθə(r)/ *noun*: **authors**
1 The **author** of *eg* a play, book or poem is the person who wrote it: *the anonymous author of the work.* **2** An **author** is someone who writes books for a living: *We shall be talking to the well-known author PD James.*

authorise see **authorize**.

authoritarian /ɔːθɒrɪˈtɛərɪən/ *adjective*; *noun* (*derogatory*)
▻ *adjective* You call a person or government **authoritarian** if they try to control people instead of allowing them the independence to make their own choices and decisions: *dictatorships and other authoritarian regimes.*
▻ *noun*: **authoritarians:** *Headteachers are not the authoritarians they once were.*

authoritative /ɔːˈθɒrətətɪv/ *adjective*
1 An **authoritative** account of something can be taken as a reliable source of information: *He sounded very authoritative but I don't actually think he's right.* **2** A person, their manner or voice are described as **authoritative** if they have a quality likely to command attention and obedience from other people: *She deepened her tone and spoke more slowly, so as to sound more authoritative.* — *adverb* **authoritatively:** *'You have five minutes left,' she announced authoritatively.*

authority /ɔːˈθɒrətɪ/ *noun*: **authorities**
1 (*uncount*) **Authority** is the right to command other people, or the position of control this gives you: *You must assert your authority if you want to get things done.* **2** (*uncount*) Your **authority** to do something is official permission or power given to you to do it: *He had apparently been using the company's official cheques without authority.* **3** (*uncount*) **Authority** is the ability to command obedience or attention from other people: *She had an unmistakable air of authority.* **4** An **authority** on a particular subject is someone who is an expert on it or knows a lot about it: *He was an authority on the Indian Mutiny, among other things.* **5** (*used in the plural*) The **authorities** are a body of people such as the national or local government, with official power to make political or administrative decisions: *The authorities must act now to prevent further abuses of the benefit system.* **6** (*with a singular or plural verb*) An official controlling body such as a department of government is an **authority**: *The local authority are responsible for road repairs.*
▻ *phrase* You **have it on good authority** that something is so if you have been told about it by someone whose word you trust.

authorize /ˈɔːθəraɪz/ or **authorise** *verb*: **authorizes, authorizing, authorized**
Someone in authority **authorizes** something such as a proposed activity or scheme when they give official permission for it; you **are authorized** to do something if you have official permission to do it: *Who authorized the police raid?* □ *I'm not authorized to lend the club's money to individual members.* — *noun* (*uncount*) **authorization** /ɔːθəraɪˈzeɪʃən/: *We shall have to call headquarters for authorization.* — *adjective* **authorized:** *an authorized biography of the Princess.* [*opposite* **unauthorized**]

authorship /ˈɔːθəʃɪp/ *noun* (*uncount*)
Someone's **authorship** of a book is the circumstance of their having written it: *Scott's authorship of the Waverley novels was kept secret for some time.*

autistic /ɔːˈtɪstɪk/ *adjective* (*psychology*)
Autistic children have no understanding of themselves or others as individuals with separate personalities and thought processes, and therefore cannot relate to people in a normal way.

auto /ɔːtoʊ/ *noun*: **autos** (*AmE*; *informal*)
An **auto** is an automobile or motor car.

autobiography /ɔːtəbaɪˈɒgrəfɪ/ *noun* (*count or uncount*): **autobiographies**
Your **autobiography** is the story of your life written by yourself: *Publishers are only interested in the autobiographies of famous people.* □ *The important thing with autobiography is to give it general appeal.*

autocracy /ɔːˈtɒkrəsɪ/ *noun*: **autocracies**
Autocracy is dictatorship or government by a single person with absolute power.

autocrat /ˈɔːtəkrat/ *noun*: **autocrats**
1 An **autocrat** is a ruler or controller with absolute or unlimited power. **2** You call a person an **autocrat** if they give orders without asking anyone's advice or considering what other people may want or think. — *adjective* **autocratic:** *an autocratic regime.*

autograph /ˈɔːtəgrɑːf/ *noun*; *verb*
▻ *noun*: **autographs**
An **autograph** is someone's signature, especially the signature of someone famous obtained by request and kept as a souvenir: *I wrote to her for her autograph.*
▻ *verb*: **autographs, autographing, autographed**
Someone famous **autographs** something such as a photograph of themselves when they write their signature on it: *I had an autographed copy of her first novel,' A Case of Knives'.*

automate /ˈɔːtəmeɪt/ *verb*: **automates, automating, automated**
A manufacturing process **is automated** when the human workers previously involved in it are replaced by machines that perform its various stages automatically.

automatic /ɔːtəˈmatɪk/ *adjective*
1 An **automatic** machine does work by itself with little or no operation by people: *It wasn't till the '50s that you could get fully automatic washing machines.* **2** An **automatic** action is something you do without thinking, from habit or instinct: *Closing your eyes is an automatic response to bright light.* [*same as* **instinctive**] **3** An **automatic** consequence or penalty is one that always or normally follows: *Non-return of library*

books carries an automatic fine. **4** An **automatic** firearm reloads itself and so can fire continuously. **5** An **automatic** motor vehicle has gears that change by themselves according to the speed of the vehicle. — *adverb* **automatically:** *The air-conditioning comes on and goes off automatically.* □ *automatically processed data* □ *He automatically lit a cigarette.* □ *Drink-drivers are automatically disqualified in some countries.*

automation /ɔːtəˈmeɪʃən/ *noun* (*uncount*)
Automation is the replacement of the manpower formerly needed in manufacturing and other processes with machines, equipment or electronic devices that perform the processes automatically.

automaton /ɔːˈtɒmətən/ *noun*: **automatons** or **automata**
1 An **automaton** is a machine operated by a concealed mechanism, that imitates the movement, and to some extent the appearance, of a living creature. **2** Someone is described as an **automaton** if they seem to be acting by routine, without intelligence, interest or feeling.

automobile /ˈɔːtəməbiːl/ *noun* (*AmE*): **automobiles**
An **automobile** is a motor car.

autonomous /ɔːˈtɒnəməs/ *adjective*
A state or organization that is **autonomous** is self-governing, or is independent of control by any other power or authority. — *noun* (*uncount*) **autonomy:** *Many of the administrative regions are seeking more autonomy.*

autopsy /ˈɔːtɒpsɪ/ *noun*: **autopsies**
A doctor carries out an **autopsy** on a dead person when he or she examines the body, or cuts it open, to discover the cause of death. [*same as* **post mortem**]

autumn /ˈɔːtəm/ *noun* (*uncount or count*)
Autumn is the season of the year that comes between summer and winter, when the weather cools and trees drop their leaves, lasting from September to late November in northern regions: *The trees here are always spectacular in autumn.* □ *autumn weather* □ *in the autumn of 1990.* [see also **fall**]

> Notice that you say *'an autumn day'*, never *'an autumn's day'*. [compare **summer, winter**]

autumnal /ɔːˈtʌmnəl/ *adjective*
Autumnal means belonging to, or like, autumn: *autumnal shades such as brown, gold, yellow and orange* □ *The weather's already beginning to feel autumnal.*

auxiliary /ɔːgˈzɪlɪərɪ/ *adjective*; *noun*
▻ ***adjective***
Auxiliary staff or personnel are people attached *eg* to a medical establishment or military force, to support or maintain work that is going on: *auxiliary nurses.* [*same as* **ancillary**]
▻ ***noun***: **auxiliaries**
1 Auxiliaries are auxiliary staff, personnel or troops: *medical and nursing auxiliaries.* **2** (*grammar*) An **auxiliary** is an auxiliary verb.

auxiliary verb /ɔːgˈzɪlɪərɪ ˈvɜːb/ *noun*: **auxiliary verbs**
The verbs *be*, *have* and *do* are used as **auxiliary verbs**, helping other verbs to do certain things.

> Auxiliary verbs are used by themselves in short replies, in question tags, and after *so*, *neither* and *nor*, where the verb they support is understood without being said: *'Are you going?' 'No, I'm not.' 'Hasn't she finished?' 'Yes, she has.' You don't want it, do you? She was getting angry and so were we. He doesn't need your advice and neither* (or *nor*) *do I.*

[see also **modal verb**]

avail /əˈveɪl/ *verb*; *noun*
▻ ***verb*** (*formal*): **avails, availing, availed**
You **avail** yourself of something such as an opportunity when you make use of it: *I'll avail myself of your kind offer of a bed for the night, if I may.*
▻ ***noun*** (*uncount*)
Something is done to no **avail** if it does not help you to achieve what you want: *They pushed against the door, but to little avail.*

available /əˈveɪləbəl/ *adjective*
1 Something is **available** if it can be obtained, or if it is ready for the purpose you need it for: *Have you any rooms available for next weekend?* **2** A person is **available** if they are not engaged or busy, and are therefore free to talk to you: *Mrs Morison will be available in a minute.* [*opposite* **unavailable**] — *noun* (*uncount*) **availability** /əveɪləˈbɪlɪtɪ/: *The availability of certain foods varies with the seasons.*

avalanche /ˈavəlɑːnʃ/ *noun*: **avalanches**
1 An **avalanche** is the fall of a large mass of snow down the side of a mountain: *A party of skiers was today buried under an avalanche in the French Alps.* **2** The sudden arrival of people or things in large numbers can be called an **avalanche**: *The advertisement produced an avalanche of applications.* [*same as* **flood, deluge**]

avant-garde /avɒŋˈgɑːd/ *adjective*
An idea, work of art, musical composition, or literary or dramatic work that is described as **avant-garde** is very modern and original, especially in an experimental way: *avant-garde educational theories.*

avarice /ˈavərɪs/ *noun* (*uncount*)
Avarice is greed for such things as money and possessions.

avaricious /avəˈrɪʃəs/ *adjective*
An **avaricious** person is greedy for money and possessions.

avenge /əˈvɛndʒ/ *verb*: **avenges, avenging, avenged**
You **avenge** a wrong that has been done when you punish the person who did it, or harm them in return; you **avenge** yourself on someone who has harmed you when you punish or harm them in return: *Her sole desire was to avenge the murder of her comrades.* □ *He feels he must avenge himself on society for the injustices he has suffered.* [compare **revenge, vengeance**]

avenue /ˈavənjuː/ *noun*: **avenues**
1 An **avenue** is a broad road with trees along the sides *eg* in the shopping area of a big city, or leading the way up to a great house. **2 Avenue** is a common name for a street: *She lives at 18 Marathon Avenue.* **3** A possible way of achieving something can be called an **avenue**: *We've been exploring various avenues but have not yet decided on the best method.*

average /ˈavərɪdʒ/ *noun*; *adjective*; *verb*
▻ ***noun***: **averages**
1 An **average** is the result you get by adding together a set of numbers and dividing the total by the number of numbers you added together: *The total rainfall for November was 21 inches, an average of 0.7 inches per day.* **2** A quantity or level that is referred to as the **average** is the usual or typical quantity or level: *We have been enjoying above-average temperatures for the time of year.*
▻ ***adjective***
1 You find what the **average** number is amongst a set of numbers by adding together all the numbers and dividing the total by the number of numbers you added together: *The average failure rate nationally is 15%.* **2** (*used in the singular*) □ *Their reading ability is well below the average.* □ *They can take upto ten*

subjects, seven is about the average. An **average** person or thing is a typical or normal one: *The average native speaker rarely uses a dictionary except to look up spellings.* **3** You call something **average** if its quality is not particularly good, nor very bad: *It was an average performance, not very exciting.* [*same as* **mediocre**] — *adverb* **averagely:** *It was an averagely warm summer day.*

▻ *verb*: **averages, averaging, averaged**
To **average** a certain amount is to come to, or achieve, that amount as an average: *Our takings averaged $950 a month over the first year.*

▻ *phrase* **On average** or **on an average** means as the average of a range of numbers or quantities: *They publish 40 books a year on average.*

phrasal verb
A range of numbers **averages out** at a certain number if that number is the average of the whole range; you **average out** a range of numbers when you work out their average.

averse /ə'vɜːs/ *adjective*
You say you are not **averse** to something if you quite like it, or don't object to it: *We're not averse to lending the children money if it's for a worthwhile purpose.*

aversion /ə'vɜːʃən/ *noun*: **aversions**
1 You have an **aversion** to something if you dislike it strongly: *She had an aversion to dogs of any sort.* **2** An **aversion** is also the thing you dislike: *His special aversion was wire coathangers.*

avert /ə'vɜːt/ *verb*: **averts, averting, averted**
1 You **avert** your eyes from something when you look away from it: *He could no longer bear to watch and averted his gaze from the screen.* **2** You **avert** something such as a disaster when you prevent it happening: *Thanks to her timely intervention catastrophe was averted.*

aviary /'eɪvɪərɪ/ *noun*: **aviaries**
An **aviary** is a large enclosed area in which birds are kept.

aviation /eɪvɪ'eɪʃən/ *noun* (*uncount*)
Aviation is either the flying and operating of aircraft, or their design and production.

avid /'avɪd/ *adjective*
1 Avid means keen or enthusiastic: *She used to be an avid reader of detective stories.* **2** You are **avid** for something if you are eagerly wanting it or waiting for it: *They were avid for the latest gossip.* — *noun* (*uncount*) **avidity** /ə'vɪdətɪ/: *He seized upon the newspaper with avidity.* — *adverb* **avidly:** *We listened avidly to the reports from Berlin.*

avocado /avə'kɑːdoʊ/ *noun*: **avocados**
An **avocado**, or **avocado pear**, is a pear-shaped tropical fruit with leathery green skin, pale yellow flesh and a large smooth stone.

avoid /ə'vɔɪd/ *verb*: **avoids, avoiding, avoided**
1 You **avoid** something if you act so as to prevent it happening: *Book now to avoid disappointment.* □ *Whatever we say to her, we can't avoid hurting her feelings.* **2** You **avoid** something or someone when you keep away from them: *We like to set off early to avoid the rush hour.* □ *She was getting tired of him and tried to avoid him whenever possible.* **3** You **avoid** doing something, especially something you ought to do, when you find ways of not doing it: *He had somehow avoided paying any income tax for three years.* □ *She used to try and avoid her share of the washing-up.* — *adjective* **avoidable:** *Certain risks are avoidable.* — *noun* (*uncount*) **avoidance:** *'Tax avoidance' refers to legitimate ways of saving yourself tax.*

avowal /ə'vaʊəl/ *noun* (*formal or literary*): **avowals**
You make an **avowal** of something when you make a declaration or confession of it: *She was unprepared for his avowal of love.*

avowed /ə'vaʊd/ *adjective*
1 An **avowed** aim or principle is one that is openly declared and firmly kept to: *It was their avowed intention to oust her from power.* **2** An **avowed** enemy or ally of someone or something is a person who has openly declared their opposition or support: *She was an avowed enemy of European monetary unity.*

await /ə'weɪt/ *verb*: **awaits, awaiting, awaited**
1 To **await** someone or something is to wait for them: *There's a pile of letters here awaiting your return.* **2** Something that **awaits** you is going to happen to you: *It's a good thing we don't know what troubles await us, or we'd never do anything or go anywhere.*

awake /ə'weɪk/ *adjective*; *verb*
▻ ***adjective***
1 You are **awake** when you are not sleeping: *I can't stay awake any longer.* **2** (*literary*) You are **awake** to something such as a danger or possibility if you know about it or are aware of it.

▻ *verb* (*literary*): **awakes, awaking, awoke, awoken**
You **awake** when you wake up; someone or something **awakes** you when they wake you up: *I was awoken by the birds at about 4.00 am.* [compare **wake, waken, awaken**]

▻ *phrase* You are **wide awake** when you are fully awake.

awaken /ə'weɪkən/ *verb* (*literary*): **awaken, awakening, awakened**
1 Something **awakens** a feeling in you if it is the cause of that feeling: *The story awakened her sympathy.* [*same as* **stir, arouse**] **2** Something or someone **awakens** you to a fact or circumstance when they makes you realize it; you **awaken** to something when you realize it: *It's time they were awakened to their obligations.* **3** You **awaken** when you wake up; someone or something **awakens** you when they wake you up: *She was awakened by the alarm.*

awakening /ə'weɪkənɪŋ/ *noun* (*used in the singular*)
The **awakening** of a feeling in you is the start or arousal of it: *the awakening of desire.*

▻ *phrase* You get **a rude awakening** when you realize an unpleasant fact: *It was a rude awakening for her, to discover that she had no supporters left.*

award /ə'wɔːd/ *noun*; *verb*
▻ *noun*: **awards**
1 An **award** is a prize someone is given for good work or a good performance: *The award went to a British director.* **2** (*legal*) An **award** of money to someone is a sum that a court of law decides should be given to them: *He won his libel case and received an award of £10 000 in settlement.*

▻ *verb*: **awards, awarding, awarded**
1 Someone **is awarded** a prize or a certain mark when they are given it: *Teachers are careful to award marks for effort as well as for achievement.* **2** (*legal*) A judge or court of law **awards** a sum of money to someone when they decide that the person should be given it: *He was awarded a record £50 000 damages.*

aware /ə'wɛə(r)/ *adjective*
1 You are **aware** of a fact or circumstance if you know about it: *We're well aware of the problem.* □ *As far as I'm aware, she has no objections.* **2** You become **aware** of things around you when you notice or sense them: *He was suddenly aware of the smell of burning.* □ *I was aware that I was being watched.* [*same as* **conscious**] **3** You describe people as **aware** if they are good at

noticing developments in a situation: *Reading the newspapers would make you more politically aware.* — *noun* (*uncount*) **awareness:** *Until the '70s there was little general awareness of environmental pollution.*

awash /əˈwɒʃ/ *adjective*
1 The ground is **awash** when it is flooded: *The streets of Perth are awash tonight after heavy rain.* **2** A place is **awash** with something if it is full of it: *The village was suddenly awash with reporters.* [*same as* **crawling, teeming**]

away /əˈweɪ/ *adverb; adjective*
▻ ***adverb***
1 You move **away** from a place or person when you leave them and increase your distance from them as you move: *He said goodbye and hurried away.* ▫ *A man was being led away from the spot by two policemen.* ▫ *We've sent the specimen away for analysis.* **2** You look or turn **away** from something when you turn yourself or your head so that you are no longer facing in that direction: *He turned his eyes away from her.* ▫ *She looked away to hide her embarrassment.* ▫ *The chair was facing away from the fire.* **3** Something is **away** from a place if is at a distance from it: *They live well away from the town.* ▫ *We're only five minutes away from the school.* ▫ *How far away is the petrol station from the main road?* **4** A future event is a certain length of time **away** when it is due to happen at the end of that time: *The exams were a bare ten days away.* **5** You are **away** when you are not at home, or not at your place of work: *They're away on holiday.* ▫ *He's gone away for the weekend.* ▫ *I've been away in France for the last week.* ▫ *She'll be away from the office for a day or two.* **6** You put something **away** when you put it where it is usually kept, or put it out of sight, or put it in a safe place: *He dried the dishes and put them away in the cupboard.* ▫ *She tidied away her painting things.* ▫ *I've hidden the presents away till Christmas.* **7** You no longer have something that you have given **away**, or that someone has taken **away** from you: *I must have given away that red coat.* ▫ *She threatened to take his water pistol away from him.* **8** Something dies or fades **away** when it gradually disappears: *Their voices grew louder and then faded away.* ▫ *His savings had dwindled away to nothing.* **9** **Away** is used with some verbs to express the energy, thoroughness or continuousness of the action: *She was digging away in her garden all afternoon.* ▫ *I left them chattering away in the kitchen.* ▫ *'May I ask you a question?' 'Ask away!'* **10** A football or hockey team plays **away** when they play a match on their opponents' own home ground.
▻ ***adjective***
A team plays an **away** match when they play on their opponent's own home ground.
▻ ***phrase*** You do something **straight away** or **right away** when you do it immediately: *I'll phone him straight away.*

awe /ɔː/ *noun; verb*
▻ ***noun*** (*uncount*)
Awe is a feeling of wonder and respect, sometimes combined with fear: *His first sight of the mountains filled him with awe.*
▻ ***verb*** (*usually in the passive*): **awes, awed**
You **are awed** by something if it amazes and overwhelms you: *We were awed by his brilliance as a pianist.* — *adjective* **awed:** *They watched in awed silence.*
▻ ***phrase*** You **are in awe of** someone or something, or **stand in awe of** them, if you feel deep respect for them, to the point of being rather afraid of them.

awe-inspiring /ˈɔːɪnspaɪərɪŋ/ *adjective*
Something **awe-inspiring** fills you with wonder, amazement or deep respect: *Her memory for detail was awe-inspiring.*

awesome /ˈɔːsəm/ *adjective*
Something **awesome** is very impressive or overwhelming: *The Oxford English Dictionary was an awesome achievement by any standard.*

awestruck /ˈɔːstrʌk/ *adjective*
You are **awestruck** when you are amazed or deeply impressed: *He spoke in an awestruck whisper.*

awful /ˈɔːfʊl/ *adjective* (*rather informal*)
1 **Awful** means **a** shocking or terrible: *What an awful way to die!* **b** poor or unsatisfactory: *The weather's been pretty awful recently.* **2** **Awful** can be used to emphasize the severity or gravity of something bad: *I've got an awful migraine.* ▫ *It's an awful shame you can't come.* **3** **Awful** is used with the expression *a lot* for emphasis: *I've got an awful lot of work to do.* **4** Someone looks or feels **awful** if they look or feel ill. — *adverb* (*intensifying*) **awfully:** *She's awfully good at drawing.* ▫ *The weather forecast isn't awfully good.* [= is bad]

awhile /əˈwaɪl/ *adverb* (*literary*)
Awhile means for a short time: *He stood awhile in thought.*

awkward /ˈɔːkwəd/ *adjective*
1 An **awkward** movement or position looks clumsy and ungraceful or feels uncomfortable: *Her legs felt stiff and awkward.* **2** You feel **awkward** when you feel embarrassed or shy: *He always felt awkward at parties.* **3** An **awkward** situation is an embarrassing or difficult one: *You're putting me in an awkward position.* **4** An **awkward** task is a difficult or tricky one, requiring skill and concentration: *The software is quite awkward to install.* **5** An **awkward** person is someone who is difficult to please or persuade: *I hope he's not going to be awkward about the money.* — *adverb* **awkwardly:** *She fell awkwardly, with one leg bent under her.* ▫ *He smiled rather awkwardly.*

awning /ˈɔːnɪŋ/ *noun*: **awnings**
An **awning** is a length of canvas or plastic fitted over a shop front or hotel entrance, that can be extended to form a shelter from the sun or rain.

awoke /əˈwoʊk/ *verb*
Awoke is the past tense of **awake**.

awoken /əˈwoʊkən/ *verb*
Awoken is the past participle of **awake**.

awry /əˈraɪ/ *adjective or adverb*
1 Something that is **awry** is crooked or untidily twisted out of place: *Your skirt is a bit awry.* **2** Plans go **awry** when they go wrong: *We don't want the schedule to go awry again.*

axe (*AmE* **ax**) /aks/ *noun; verb*
▻ ***noun*****: axes**
1 An **axe** is a tool with a long handle and a heavy metal blade, used for chopping wood. [see picture at **tool**] **2** (*used in the singular; informal*) A project or job gets the **axe** when it is cancelled or got rid of.
▻ ***verb*****: axes, axing, axed**
1 A project or job **is axed** when it is cancelled or got rid of. **2** A government **axes** funds or services when it greatly reduces them.

axiom /ˈaksɪəm/ *noun*: **axioms**
An **axiom** is a well-known or obvious truth, or a principle that people accept as true.

axiomatic /aksɪəˈmatɪk/ *adjective*
Something that is **axiomatic** is obviously true, or is accepted as true: *It's axiomatic that people would rather be employed than unemployed.*

axis /ˈaksɪs/ *noun*: **axes**
1 The **axis** of a body such as the earth is the imagined line or pole round which it spins. **2** (*geometry*) The **axis** of a flat geometrical shape is a real or imagined line that divides it into two identical halves. **3** The two **axes** of a graph are the fixed horizontal and vertical lines along which the measurements or grades are marked.

axle /ˈaksəl/ *noun*: **axles**
A vehicle's front or back **axle** is the rod on which its front or back pair of wheels turn.

aye /aɪ/ *interjection*; *noun*
▷ ***interjection*** (*especially Scottish*)
Aye means yes.
▷ ***noun***: **ayes**
In a parliamentary ballot, the **ayes** are the votes saying 'yes' to the proposal.

azure /ˈaʒə(r)/ or /ˈeɪʒʊə(r)/ *noun* (*uncount*, *often adjectival*)
Azure is a deep blue colour, like that of a clear sky.

B /biː/ or **b** *noun*: **Bs** or **b's**

1 **B** is the second letter of the English alphabet. **2** The letter **B** is used as a mark for grading quality, representing the second-highest grade: *He got a B for his essay.* **3** **B** is also a musical note: *in the key of B minor.*

babble /'babəl/ *verb*; *noun*

▻ ***verb***: **babbles, babbling, babbled**

1 People **babble** when they talk so quickly that it is difficult to hear what they are saying: *He babbled an apology.* **2** (*formal, literary*) A stream **babbles** when it makes a low murmuring sound as it flows: *a babbling brook.*

▻ ***noun*** (*used in the singular*): *There was a sudden excited babble of voices in the corridor outside.*

babe /beɪb/ *noun*: **babes**

1 (*old*) A **babe** is a baby. **2** (*informal*: *especially AmE*) Some people use **'babe'** as a familiar or affectionate form of address for a person, especially a woman: *Hi there, babe!*

baboon /bə'buːn/ *noun*: **baboons**

A **baboon** is a large African monkey with a dog-like face.

baby /'beɪbɪ/ *noun*: **babies**

1 A **baby** is a newly born child, or one still in its mother's womb, or a very young child, usually not able to walk or talk yet: *She's expecting a baby at the end of April.* **2** (*often adjectival*) The young of an animal are often referred to as its **babies**: *baby birds.* **3** (*informal*) The **baby** of a family or other group is the youngest member of it: *You can go first, since you're the baby round here.* **4** (*informal*) People sometimes refer to someone's own special project or responsibility as their **baby**: *We'd better not alter the temperature readings; that's Jo's baby.* **5** (*informal*; *especially AmE*) Some people use **'baby'** as an affectionate form of address for a person, especially a woman: *Take it easy, baby.*

babyhood /'beɪbɪhʊd/ *noun* (*uncount*)

Your **babyhood** is the period of your life when you are a baby.

babyish /'beɪbɪɪʃ/ *adjective* (*derogatory*)

Adults or older children who do **babyish** things, or like **babyish** things, behave in a silly or immature way, or choose things suitable for someone much younger: *You're being selfish and babyish.* ▫ *She wore a babyish frock with little pink flowers embroidered on it.*

babysit /'beɪbɪsɪt/ *verb*: **babysits, babysitting, babysat**

You **babysit** for someone when you look after their child in their own home while they are out: *My sister's babysitting for me this evening.* — *noun* **babysitter:** *It's difficult finding babysitters.* — *noun* (*uncount*) **babysitting:** *I do a lot of babysitting for my daughter.*

bachelor /'batʃələ(r)/ *noun*: **bachelors**

1 A **bachelor** is a man who has never been married. **2** Someone who has taken a first degree in the arts or sciences has the title **'Bachelor** of Arts' or **'Bachelor** of Science'. [compare **master, doctor**]

back /bak/ *adverb*; *noun*; *adjective*; *verb*

▻ ***adverb***

1 a You move **back** when you move in the opposite direction to the one you are facing in: *I stepped back in surprise.* ▫ *She pushed back her chair and stood up.* ▫ *Take two steps forward and two steps back.* [*same as* **backwards**; *opposite* **forwards**] **b** Something that is **back** from something else is positioned away from it, as distinct from being beside it or touching it: *She usually wore her long hair tied back from her face.* ▫ *Stand back and let the ambulance pass.* ▫ *Keep back, please.* ▫ *One house was set back from the rest.* [*opposite* **forwards**] **c** You think **back**, or talk about something **back** in a certain period, when you are referring to the past: *They would sometimes look back to happier days.* ▫ *Think back to 1989.* ▫ *if we could only travel back in time* ▫ *back in the 70s, before everyone sat behind their individual PC* ▫ *unpaid bills dating back to last year.* [*opposite* **forwards**] **d** You put a clock **back** when you adjust it so that it shows an earlier time. [*opposite* **forwards**] **e** You keep **back** laughter or tears when you control yourself and manage not to laugh or cry: *She was obviously fighting back the tears.*

2 a You go **back** somewhere when you go to the place where you were before, or return there: *She went back inside the house.* ▫ *I want to go back to the States soon.* ▫ *We seem to be back where we started.* ▫ *When are you coming back home?* **b** You put something **back** when you put it where it was before or where it belongs: *Shall I put the book back on the shelf?* ▫ *I'd better put it back where I got it.* **c** Something or someone is **back** in a certain state or situation when they are in it again: *Go back to sleep.* ▫ *He was back at work within two days.* ▫ *The situation is gradually getting back to normal.* **d** A condition or feeling comes **back** when it starts again: *Take another pill if the pain comes back.* ▫ *Long-forgotten anxieties came flooding back.* **e** You give something **back** when you give it, or return it, to the person you got it from; you get **back** something that belongs to you when it is returned to you: *Remind me to give you back that money I owe you.* ▫ *Could I have my book back sometime?* ▫ *We want our baby back.* **f** You do something **back** to someone when you respond to their action by doing the same to them: *He hit me and I hit him back.* ▫ *She glanced at him and he glanced back.* ▫ *I've written to him several times but he's never written back.* ▫ *She called earlier and asked if you would call her back.* **g** In reference to telephoning or calling, **back** can mean 'again': *I said you weren't in, and he said he'd ring back in the morning.*

▻ ***noun***: **backs**

1 Your **back** is the part of your body extending from your neck to your bottom or the base of your spine: *I lay on my back looking up at the sky.* ▫ *Keep your back straight.* ▫ *She stroked the dog's back.* [*opposite* **front, stomach**; see picture at **body**] **2** The **back** of something is **a** the side or surface furthest from the front, or opposite to it: *We walked round to the back of the house.* ▫ *A nice bungalow with a big garden at the back*

□ *The backs of his legs got badly sunburnt on the walk.* □ *She has trouble getting into clothes that zip up the back.* □ *The disease affected the backs of his hands as well as the palms.* **b** the surface that faces away from you: *Sign your name on the back of the cheque.* **c** the area towards the rear: *Put the bags in the back of the car.* □ *We were at the back of the queue.* **d** the part furthest from the front: *Our seats were right at the back of the stalls and we could hardly see.* □ *I found these gloves at the back of a drawer.* [*opposite* **front**] **3** The **back** of a chair is the upright part that you lean against when sitting on it. **4** The **back** of a book is the end of it, or the cover next to the end of it: *He looked up the notes at the back.* [*opposite* **front**] **5** (*sport*) In football or hockey, a **back** is a player whose task is to defend the goal rather than score. [*opposite* **forward**]

▻ ***adjective***

1 **Back** describes anything positioned at the back: *My back tyre's got a puncture.* □ *I put my bag on the back seat.* □ *We sat in the back row.* □ *Did you remember to lock the back door?* □ *The back page was very torn.* □ *There was a map printed inside the back cover.* [*opposite* **front**; compare **rear**] **2** A **back** street or road is usually a narrow one, less used by traffic than the main street or main road. [*opposite* **main**]

▻ ***verb***: **backs, backing, backed**

1 You **back** a vehicle, or it **backs**, when you drive it, or it is driven, backwards: *She backed the car out of the garage.* □ *You shouldn't back out of a side road.* □ *A lorry was backing down the lane.* **2** You **back** a person or company when you give them support or money: *Thanks for backing me.* □ *Local businesses have promised to back the project.* [see also **backing**] **3** You **back** *eg* a horse or team when you bet money on their success: *He always seems to back a winner.* **4** You **back** one thing with another if you fix the second behind the first, *eg* for strength or support: *photos backed with card.* [see also **backing**]

▻ ***phrases*** **1** People or things move **back and forth** when they move first in one direction, and then in the opposite one, or when they pass each other in opposite directions, or move about in various directions: *driving back and forth between the hospital and home.* □ *People were going back and forth along the corridor.* [*same as* **to and fro**] **2** You have clothing on **back to front** if you are wearing it the wrong way round, with the back on the front of your body. **3** You do something **behind** someone's **back** if you do it without telling them or without asking their permission. **4** (*informal*) If you tell someone to **get off your back** you mean you want them to leave you in peace instead of criticizing you and pressurizing you. **5** (*informal*) You **put your back into** something if you try to do it well. **6** (*informal*) You **put** someone's **back up** if you annoy them. **7** (*informal*) You are glad to **see the back of** someone or something unpleasant and annoying if you are pleased to have finished with them. **8** You **turn your back on** someone or something when you ignore them, leave them or refuse to help them.

phrasal verbs

back away You **back away** when you move away or backwards, especially in fear: *She backed away from the dog.*

back down You **back down** when you give up your claim to something or stop demanding it: *The unions refused to back down over pay and conditions.* [*same as* **give in**]

back off You **back off** when you move off or away, usually to avoid difficulties or a fight: *We decided to back off before someone got hurt.* [*same as* **retreat**]

back on to One thing **backs on to** another if its back is next to or facing it: *The house backs on to fields.*

back out You **back out** when you decide not to do something you had previously agreed or promised to do: *They want to back out of the arrangement.* □ *You can't back out at this stage!*

back up **1** You **back** someone **up** **a** when you support or help them: *If you want to make the proposal officially I promise to back you up.* [see also **backup**] **b** when you confirm that they are telling the truth: *My sister will back me up.* □ *No-one would back up her story.* **2** You **back up** a statement when you supply evidence that confirms it: *She had plenty of arguments and evidence to back up her claim.* **3** (*computers*) You **back up** information or files stored on your computer when you copy them on to a separate system, or on to a floppy disk. [see also **backup**]

backache /ˈbakeɪk/ *noun* (*uncount*)
Backache is pain in the back: *She suffers from backache.*

backbiting /ˈbakbaɪtɪŋ/ *noun* (*uncount*)
Backbiting is the activity of speaking unkindly or unpleasantly about someone who is absent.

backbone /ˈbakboʊn/ *noun*: **backbones**
1 Your **backbone** is the row of bones down the centre of your back. [*same as* **spine**] **2** (*usually in the singular*) People or things that have a key role in some organization, or provide its main strength, are sometimes referred to as its **backbone**: *Infantry were the backbone of most armies.* **3** (*uncount*) People who lack **backbone** have a weak character, or not enough will power or determination.

backbreaking /ˈbakbreɪkɪŋ/ *adjective*
A **backbreaking** job or task is very hard or tiring.

back crawl /bak ˈkrɔːl/ see **backstroke**.

backdate /bakˈdeɪt/ *verb*: **backdates, backdating, backdated**
You **backdate** something such as a cheque or written settlement when you write an earlier date on it than the date on which you are signing it, which makes it valid from the earlier date: *The pay rise has been backdated to January.*

backdoor /ˈbakdɔː(r)/ *adjective*
Backdoor activities or moves are carried out in a secret, unofficial manner instead of publicly and officially: *backdoor negotiations.*

backer /ˈbakə(r)/ *noun*: **backers**
The **backers** of some enterprise are the people who provide money to help it succeed: *Business was booming and she thanked her backers for their generous support in the early months.* [compare **sponsor**]

backfire /bakˈfaɪə(r)/ *verb*: **backfires, backfiring, backfired**
1 Something you do or plan **backfires** when it has the opposite effect from the one you intended: *His gamble of calling a referendum totally backfired.* **2** An engine or vehicle **backfires** when gases explode in the exhaust pipe with a loud bang.

backgammon /ˈbakgamən/ *noun* (*uncount*)
Backgammon is a game for two people, played on a board with pieces that are moved according to the throws of a dice.

background /ˈbakgraʊnd/ *noun* (*usually in the singular*): **backgrounds**
1 The **background** in a scene, view or picture is the part of it that is behind, or partly hidden by, the main

figures or objects in it: *Tell me if you recognize the girl in the background of this shot.* [*opposite* **foreground**] **2** People who remain in the **background** are in jobs or positions where they do not attract public notice: *Later, as owner of the paper, he preferred to stay in the background and let his editor run it.* **3** Sounds that are in the **background** are sounds that you can hear but are not listening to: *one of those restaurants with classical numbers playing softly in the background* □ *background music.* **4** The **background** to an event or situation is everything that explains why it occurred: *I'm collecting a few background facts.* □ *A pattern of strikes and riots emerged against the background of increasing poverty and unemployment.* **5** Your **background** is the sort of family you are from, and the kind of education you have had: *She came from a working-class background.*

backhand /'bakhand/ *noun*: **backhands**
(*tennis, squash*) A **backhand** is a shot made with your arm across your body and the back of your hand towards the ball. [compare **forehand**]

backhanded /'bakhandɪd/ *adjective*
You describe something such as a compliment as **backhanded** if it is intended unkindly, or could be interpreted that way.

backing /'bakɪŋ/ *noun*: **backings**
1 (*uncount*) Something or someone has the **backing** of a person or organization if they receive support, money or encouragement from them to help them succeed: *Research of this type is enabled to continue with the powerful backing of industry.* **2** (*count or uncount*) The **backing** of something such as a sticky label is the layer of paper or other material that is attached to its back for protection, strength or support: *Pull away the plastic backing.* **3** (*usually in the singular*) The **backing** of a pop song is the music or singing that accompanies the main singer.

backlash /'baklaʃ/ *noun* (*usually in the singular*): **backlashes**
A **backlash** is a sudden violent reaction to an action, event or situation: *a Communist backlash against the reform movement.*

backlog /'baklɒg/ *noun* (*usually in the singular*): **backlogs**
A **backlog** of tasks is a number of tasks that are still waiting to be done but have not yet been done, *eg* because of lack of time or resources: *hospitals with a large backlog of operations.*

backpack /'bakpak/ *noun*; *verb*
▻ ***noun*** (*especially AmE*): **backpacks**
A **backpack** is a rucksack, especially a large one.
▻ ***verb***: **backpacks, backpacking, backpacked**
People go **backpacking** when they spend time walking from place to place carrying rucksacks and camping equipment.

back-seat driver /'baksiːt 'draɪvə(r)/ *noun*: **back-seat drivers**
A **back-seat driver** is a passenger in a car who keeps giving the driver unwanted advice.

backside /bak'saɪd/ *noun* (*informal*): **backsides**
Your **backside** is your bottom or buttocks. [*same as* **behind**]

backslide /'bakslaid/ *verb*: **backslides, backsliding, backslid**
You **backslide** when you return to your old bad habits after a period of improved or reformed behaviour.

backstage /bak'steɪdʒ/ *adjective or adverb* (*theatre*)
Things that take place **backstage** happen in the areas behind the stage and out of sight of the audience, such as the dressing rooms: *The start was delayed because of some crisis backstage.* □ *backstage quarrels and tensions.*

backstreet /'bakstriːt/ *adjective*
Backstreet activities are usually illegal activities carried on secretly and unofficially: *a backstreet abortion.*

backstroke /'bakstroʊk/ *noun* (*uncount or used in the singular*)
Backstroke or **back crawl** is a swimming stroke that you perform on your back, extending your arms one at a time behind your head and bringing them down to your sides through the water, using a leg kick in which you keep your legs side by side: *She won the 100 metres backstroke by half a second.* □ *I do ten lengths of backstroke and ten of breaststroke.*

backup /'bakʌp/ *noun*: **backups**
1 You make a **backup** of a computer file or disk when you make a copy of it, in case the original is lost or deleted. [see also **back up**] **2** (*uncount*) **Backup** is the additional technical or other support that you need for achieving some goal: *We can't hope to reach our target without backup from the computing department.* [see also **back up**] **3** (*used in the singular*) A piece of equipment or plan that is available as a **backup** is an extra one for use if the original one fails: *Fortunately we have an immersion heater as a backup in case the gas water-heater isn't working.*

backward /'bakwəd/ *adverb*; *adjective*
▻ ***adverb*** (also **backwards**; the form **backward** is used especially in AmE)
1 To move or look **backward** or **backwards** is to move or look in the direction opposite to the one you are facing in: *He fell backwards against the bookcase.* □ *She looked backwards over her shoulder.* □ *The car began to roll backwards down the hill.* □ *Some old cars had a backward-facing rear seat.* [*opposite* **forwards**] **2** You do something **backwards** or **backward** when you start at the end and move towards the beginning: *He ran the film backwards to make us laugh.* [*opposite* **forwards**] **3** To travel **backward** or **backwards** in time is to return to an earlier period; you describe people's attitudes as **backward**-looking if they seem old-fashioned and conservative. [*opposite* **forwards**]
▻ ***adjective***
1 Backward describes a movement in the direction opposite to the one you are facing in: *She marched out of the restaurant without a backward glance.* [*opposite* **forward**] **2** (*old, now derogatory*) A **backward** child has difficulty in understanding and learning: *He'd been put in a class for backward kids.* [*opposite* **advanced**] **3** A **backward** country or society does not have a modern way of life or modern industries. [*opposite* **advanced**]
▻ ***phrases*** **1** You move **backwards and forwards** when you move first in one direction and then in the opposite direction: *She paced backwards and forwards outside the cinema.* □ *swinging his legs backwards and forwards.* [*same as* **back and forth, to and fro**] **2** (*informal*) You **bend, fall** or **lean over backwards** when you try very hard to do something, especially please someone: *They're obviously falling over backwards to offer us what we want.* **3** You **know** something **backwards** when you know it very well: *We'd studied the novel till we knew it backwards.*

backwater /'bakwɔːtə(r)/ *noun* (*usually derogatory*): **backwaters**
If you call a place a **backwater** you mean that it is isolated from the world outside and is not affected or noticed by it: *The place remained an economic backwater for more than a generation.*

backwoods /ˈbakwʊdz/ *noun* (*plural*)
People who live in the **backwoods** live a long way from large cities and their modern way of life: *his childhood in the Canadian backwoods.* □ *isolated backwoods communities.*

back yard /bak ˈjɑːd/ *noun*: **back yards**
Someone's **back yard** is **1** the area of ground behind their house, sometimes walled or fenced usually with a stone or concrete surface. **2** (*AmE*) a lawn or garden behind their house.

bacon /ˈbeɪkən/ *noun* (*uncount*)
Bacon is salted or smoked meat from the back and sides of a pig, usually cut in thin slices and fried.

bacteria /bakˈtɪərɪə/ *noun* (*plural*)
Bacteria are a very small organisms, some of which cause disease. — *adjective* **bacterial:** *a bacterial infection of the throat.*

bad /bad/ *adjective*: **worse, worst**
1 Something that is **bad** is **a** unpleasant or troublesome: *I'm afraid it's really bad news.* □ *We've been having such bad weather recently.* □ *There's a bad smell in here.* **b** of a poor or unsatisfactory standard: *The building's in a bad state.* □ *The game continued till 7.15, when bad light stopped play.* □ *bad driving* □ *It was purely the result of bad organization.* **c** grave, serious, severe or intense in degree: *I've had a bad cold.* □ *a bad headache* □ *Is the pain very bad?* □ *That was a bad error of judgement.* □ *a bad accident* □ *The traffic's always bad at this time of day.* **d** wrong or unsuitable: *It was a bad choice.* □ *Is this a bad moment to call?* □ *I'm a bad person to ask; I really wouldn't know.* **e** morally wrong or socially unacceptable: *I've rarely witnessed such bad behaviour.* □ *You mustn't set a bad example to the children.* **2** You describe a person as **bad** if you think them evil, wicked or immoral; a **bad** child is a naughty one: *He got into bad company.* □ *These are bad men; they'll stop at nothing.* □ *You've been a very bad little girl.* **3** Someone who is **bad** at doing something does it unsatisfactorily, or doesn't do it at all: *I'm a bad organizer.* □ *I'm awfully bad at remembering people's names.* □ *She's bad at sticking to a schedule.*

> Notice that the less strong **'not very good'** is generally preferred to **'bad'**: *He's not a very good dentist. She isn't very good at organizing her time. I'm afraid I'm not a very good dancer.*

4 Something that is **bad** for you is harmful to your health: *Smoking is bad for you.* □ *Sugar is bad for your teeth.* **5** Food that is **bad** has started to rot and is not fit to eat: *That fish smells bad.* □ *We should eat these peaches before they go bad.* **6** You have *eg* a **bad** leg or a **bad** back if it is giving you a lot of pain; someone who has a **bad** heart has heart disease. **7** You are in a **bad** mood or a **bad** temper when you are cross and inclined to be rude and impatient.
▻ ***phrases*** **1** A situation **goes from bad to worse** when it gets even worse. **2** You **feel bad** about something when you are sorry about it or regret it: *I felt so bad about letting you down.* **3** (*informal*) You describe something as **not bad** if you think it is quite good, and as **not too bad** if it is satisfactory: *That's not a bad drawing.* □ *'How's your sore throat?' 'Not too bad.'* **4** (*informal*) You say **'Too bad'** to comment rather rudely that nothing can be done to alter the situation: *'I don't want to go to the concert tonight.' 'Well too bad, I've already bought the tickets.'*

bad debt /bad ˈdɛt/ *noun*: **bad debts**
A **bad debt** is a debt that will never be paid.

bade /bad/ or /beɪd/ *verb*
Bade is the past tense of **bid**[2].

badge /badʒ/ *noun*: **badges**
1 A **badge** is a small button-like object, or a small piece of cloth with a design on it, that you wear attached to your cap or jacket, indicating *eg* your membership of a society, or your rank: *She was last seen wearing a blazer with a school badge on the pocket.* **2** Something is referred to as the **badge** of some quality if it is a sign of it: *The rifle was as much his badge of power as the captain's insignia on his cap.*

badger /ˈbadʒə(r)/ *noun*; *verb*
▻ ***noun***: **badgers**
A **badger** is a grey furry animal with black and white stripes on its head, which lives underground and is active at night.
▻ ***verb***: **badgers, badgering, badgered**
You **badger** someone when you keep bothering them about something, or begging them to do something: *Tom finally badgered her into going.* □ *She badgered him to let her come along.* □ *The kids continued to badger him about it.*

bad language /bad ˈlaŋgwɪdʒ/ *noun* (*uncount*)
People use **bad language** when they use offensive words, obscene words, or swearwords.

badly /ˈbadlɪ/ *adverb*: **worse, worst**
1 a Something is **badly** done if it is done in an unsatisfactory or incompetent way: *The play was badly directed.* □ *badly built houses.* [*same as* **poorly**; *opposite* **well**] **b** You do **badly**, or things go **badly** for you, if you are unsuccessful: *I did very badly in the exams.* [*opposite* **well**] **c** People behave **badly** when they are rude or uncooperative: *She had behaved badly and was ashamed of herself.* [*opposite* **well**]

> Notice that the less strong **'not very well'** is often preferred to **'badly'**: *He didn't do very well in the election. I do play tennis but not very well.*

2 You want or need something **badly** when you want or need it very much: *I'm badly in need of a hair cut.* □ *He wanted the job badly.* □ *The school badly needs money to buy books.* **3 Badly** emphasizes the degree to which something unpleasant or unfortunate is the case: *She hurt herself badly when she fell.* □ *The whole area has been badly affected by snow.* □ *Her plan had gone badly wrong.* [*same as* **seriously, severely, gravely**; *opposite* **slightly, mildly**]

badly off /badlɪ ˈɒf/ *adjective*: **worse off, worst off**
1 People who are **badly off** are poor. **2** You are **badly off** for something when you need more of it: *She is badly off for school clothes.*

badminton /ˈbadmɪntən/ *noun* (*uncount*)
Badminton is a game played by two or four players with light rackets and a small light feathered object called a **shuttlecock**, which they hit over a high net.

bad-tempered /badˈtɛmpəd/ *adjective*
A **bad-tempered** person is inclined to be impatient and rude to other people: *He grew more bad-tempered with age.*

baffle /ˈbafəl/ *verb*: **baffles, baffling, baffled**
You **are baffled** by something if you cannot explain or understand it: *The police are evidently still baffled.* □ *Her attitude baffles me.* — *adjective* **baffling:** *He disappeared in baffling circumstances.*

bag /bag/ *noun*; *verb*
▻ ***noun***: **bags**
1 A **bag** is a container made of *eg* cloth, leather, plastic or paper, often with handles or straps, for carrying things in: *She arrived with her swimming things in a plastic bag.* □ *She packed her bags and caught a taxi to the station.* □ *I need a new shopping bag.* **2** A woman's

bag is her handbag: *She put her purse back in her bag.* [compare **purse**] **3** A **bag** of something is the bag and its contents, or just the contents: *Get one of those 2-kilo bags of potatoes.* □ *I ate a whole bag of chocolate raisins this morning.* **4** People have **bags** under their eyes if they have dark circles, or folds of skin, under them, *eg* when they have not had enough sleep.

▻ ***verb***: **bags, bagging, bagged**

1 (*informal*) You **bag** something such as a seat when you reserve it: *I've bagged us a couple of seats at the front.* **2** Clothes **bag** when they stretch and lose their shape, *eg* over the elbow or knee: *Trousers tend to bag at the knee.* [see also **baggy**]

▻ ***phrases*** **1** (*informal*) You have **bags of** something if you have a lot of it: *We needn't hurry; there's bags of time yet.* □ *There are bags of odd jobs to do still.* **2** (*informal*) Something is **in the bag** if it is certain to be achieved or obtained: *I believe the contract's in the bag.*

baggage /ˈbagɪdʒ/ *noun* (*uncount*)

Your **baggage** consists of all the bags and cases you take with you when you travel anywhere: *How many pieces of baggage do you have between you?* [*same as* **luggage**]

baggy /ˈbagɪ/ *adjective*: **baggier, baggiest**

Baggy clothes are either clothes that are large and loose, or clothes that have stretched and lost their shape in places: *a baggy jumper* □ *trousers that are baggy at the knee.* [see also **bag**]

bagpipes /ˈbagpaɪps/ *noun* (*plural*)

Bagpipes are a musical instrument played by blowing air into a bag through a pipe and forcing the air out through other pipes: *He bought a second-hand set of bagpipes.* □ *We could hear bagpipes in the distance.* □ *bagpipe music* □ *I used to play the bagpipes.*

bail[1] /beɪl/ *noun*; *verb*

▻ ***noun*** (*uncount*)

Someone who has been arrested is granted **bail** when they are released on payment of sum of money to the law court in charge of the case; **bail** is also the money paid, given as a guarantee that they will return to the court for trial: *She was released on bail.*

▻ ***verb***: **bails, bailing, bailed**

> ***phrasal verb***
> **bail out** **1** You **bail** a prisoner **out** when you pay bail so that they can be released: *He agreed to bail his brother out.* **2** You **bail** someone **out** when you help them out of a difficult situation.

bail[2] or **bale** /beɪl/ *verb*: **bails, bailing, bailed**

> ***phrasal verb***
> **bail out** or **bale out** **1** You **bail out** when you remove water from a boat with a container such as a bucket. **2** You **bail out** of an aircraft when jump out of it wearing a parachute.

bailiff /ˈbeɪlɪf/ *noun*: **bailiffs**

A **bailiff** is **1** (*BrE*) an officer of a law court, especially one who takes possession of the contents of people's houses when they have not paid money that they owe the court. **2** a person who looks after property or an estate for its owner.

bait /beɪt/ *noun*; *verb*

▻ ***noun*** (*uncount or used in the singular*)

1 **Bait** is food that you put on a hook or in a trap to attract fish or animals, so that you can catch them. **2** Someone or something is used as a **bait** when they are used to tempt or persuade people to do something: *The promise of freedom was held out as a bait to trap prisoners into talking.* □ *He realized he'd fallen for the bait like a fool.*

▻ ***verb***: **baits, baiting, baited**

1 You **bait** a hook or trap when you put food on or in it to attract fish or animals. **2** You **bait** someone when you tease them, deliberately to upset them and make them angry: *She does nothing but bait you.*

▻ ***phrase*** You **rise to the bait** or **take the bait** if you let yourself get annoyed when someone is teasing you and trying to upset you: *Hubert pretended to rise to the bait.*

baize /beɪz/ *noun* (*uncount*)

Baize is the green woollen cloth that is used to cover tables designed for games, *eg* snooker tables and card tables.

bake /beɪk/ *verb*: **bakes, baking, baked**

1 You **bake** food such as cakes, bread and potatoes when you cook it in the oven without additional fat or water: *My sister's going to bake the wedding cake, and ice it.* □ *Can you wait? I've got some bread baking in the oven.* **2** Earth, mud or clay **bakes** or **is baked** when it dries and hardens in the heat of the sun or a fire. — *adjective* **baked:** *baked potatoes filled with cheese.* [see also **baking**]

baked beans /beɪkt ˈbiːnz/ *noun* (*plural*)

Baked beans are small white beans that have been boiled and baked, usually sold in tins in tomato sauce.

baker /ˈbeɪkə(r)/ *noun*: **bakers**

1 A **baker** is a person who bakes bread and cakes, especially as their job. **2** A **baker** or a **baker's** is a baker's shop: *She bought some rolls at the baker's.* □ *There isn't a baker in the village any longer.*

bakery /ˈbeɪkərɪ/ *noun*: **bakeries**

A **bakery** is a place where bread and cakes are baked.

baking /ˈbeɪkɪŋ/ *noun*; *adjective*

▻ ***noun*** (*uncount*)

Baking is the activity or skill of making bread and cakes: *I got a lot of baking done this afternoon.*

▻ ***adjective or adverb*** (*informal*)

Baking, and **baking** hot, are used to mean very hot: *It was a baking-hot day.* □ *It's baking in this office.* □ *You must be baking in that jacket.*

balance /ˈbaləns/ *verb*; *noun*

▻ ***verb***: **balances, balancing, balanced**

1 People or things **balance**, or **are balanced**, somewhere, when they are in, or get into, or are put into, a steady enough position not to fall: *The waiters scurried to and fro, balancing enormous piles of crockery on their trays.* □ *She balanced the glass of whisky on the arm of her chair.* □ *Try balancing on one leg for a whole minute.* □ *He balanced himself on the branch.* **2** You **balance** one thing against another when you consider their relative importance: *The need for new roads must be balanced against the inevitable damage to the environment.* **3** You **balance** one element with another in any situation when you ensure that each gets the attention it deserves: *It's difficult to balance the needs of your family with the demands of a full-time job.* **4** One thing **is balanced** by another if the effect of the first is reduced by the opposite effect that the second has: *Poor home sales are satisfactorily balanced by successes abroad.* **5** (*accounting*) You **balance** the books, or get the books to **balance**, when you ensure that the amount of money that is spent does not exceed the amount that is received.

▻ ***noun***: **balances**

1 (*uncount*) **Balance** is the state of being in a steady enough position not to fall: *She slipped, lost her balance, and regained it just in time to prevent herself from falling.* □ *He somehow managed to keep his balance on* *the ice.* [compare **footing**] **2** (*uncount*) **Balance** is also a state in which the various factors involved in something have their proper size, strength or importance, and so are in a satisfactory relationship with one another: *Any kind of pollution upsets the ecological balance of the environment.* **3** The **balance** is what is left of an amount after some of it has been subtracted or removed: *If you pay the deposit now, you can pay the balance next month.* **4** The **balance** in your bank account is the amount of money in it. **5** A **balance** is any of several kinds of weighing instrument. [*same as* **scales**]

▻ ***phrases*** **1** Something is **in the balance** if it is uncertain or in doubt: *The future of the school hangs in the balance till the governors reach a decison.* **2** You are **off balance** when you are in an unsteady position and about to fall: *The wind blew me off balance.* **3** You use '**on balance**' when stating a conclusion after considering all the evidence and possibilities: *On balance, it's probably not advisable to change the company's name.*

> ***phrasal verb***
> **balance out** **1** The various factors in a situation **balance out** when a satisfactory relationship is achieved between them: *I expect everything will balance out in the end.* **2** One thing **balances** another **out** when it reduces its effect by having the opposite effect: *Higher rents in the centre of town are balanced out by the saving on commuting costs.*

balanced /'balənst/ *adjective*
1 A **balanced** account, report or judgement of something represents or assesses the facts involved in a fair and reasonable way: *Read his column in the 'Independent' for a balanced view of the subject.* **2** **Balanced** describes something in which all the important elements are included, in the right proportions: *a balanced diet.* **3** A **balanced** person is someone who is perfectly sane and able to make sensible decisions and judgements: *someone with a well-balanced mind.*

balance of payments /baləns əv 'peɪmənts/ *noun* (*used in the singular*)
A country's **balance of payments** is the difference between the amount of money coming into it and the amount going out of it.

balance of power /baləns əv 'pɑʊə(r)/ *noun* (*used in the singular*)
The **balance of power**, *eg* in an international situation, is the even distribution of political or military power between states or groups, so that none of them has too much power for the safety of the others.
▻ ***phrase*** A group or person that **holds the balance of power** is in a position to make one or the other of two parties more powerful by giving it their support.

balcony /'balkənɪ/ *noun*: **balconies**
1 A **balcony** is a platform projecting from the outside of a building, surrounded by a wall or railing: *They had breakfast on the balcony.* **2** The **balcony** in a theatre or cinema is an upper-floor area of seating.

bald /bɔːld/ *adjective*: **balder, baldest**
1 Someone who is **bald** has no hair, or very little hair, on top of their head: *He went bald in his twenties.* ▫ *You're getting a bald patch.* **2** A vehicle tyre is **bald** when it has worn smooth. **3** A **bald** statement is simple and direct, with no unnecessary words: *The bald truth is that you have wasted your money.* — *adverb* **baldly:** *He told her baldly that he didn't love her any more.* — *noun* (*uncount*) **baldness:** *I don't think men should be embarrassed about their baldness; I like bald men.*

balding /'bɔːldɪŋ/ *adjective*
A person who is **balding** is becoming bald.

bale¹ /beɪl/ *noun*: **bales**
A **bale** of something such as cloth, paper or hay is a bundle of it, usually oblong in shape and tightly tied with wire or string: *trucks loaded with hay bales.*

bale² /beɪl/ *verb*: **bales, baling, baled**
see **bail²**.

baleful /'beɪlfəl/ *adjective*
Someone gives you a **baleful** look when they look at you in a hostile or threatening way. — *adverb* **balefully:** *The child eyed her balefully.*

balk or **baulk** /bɔːlk/ *verb*: **balks, balking, balked**
You **balk** at doing something when you feel or express unwillingness to do it: *Employees balked at working on a Sunday.*

ball¹ /bɔːl/ *noun*: **balls**
1 A **ball** is the round object used in sports such as football, tennis and golf: *She'd been hit in the eye by a squash ball.* **2** Anything round in shape can be referred to as a ball: *She rolled the dough into a ball.* ▫ *a ball of knitting wool* ▫ *Someone threw a snowball at the window.* **3** The **ball** of your foot is the fleshy part of your sole, where your toes join your foot; the **ball** of your thumb is its fleshy base. [see picture at **body**]
▻ ***phrases*** **1** (*informal*) Someone who is **on the ball** about something has all the latest information about it, and is alert to developments. **2** (*informal*) You agree to **play ball** with someone if you are willing to co-operate with them. **3** You **set**, or **start**, **the ball rolling**, or **keep the ball rolling**, when you cause some activity to begin, or make sure it continues: *Our lecturer has agreed to answer questions, so I'll set the ball rolling by picking him up on one point.*

ball² /bɔːl/ *noun*: **balls**
A **ball** is a large and usually formal social event at which people dance. [*same as* **dance**]
▻ ***phrase*** (*informal*) Someone who is **having a ball** is having an enjoyable time, usually socially.

ballad /'baləd/ *noun*: **ballads**
A **ballad** is a long poem or song telling a story, especially a popular or traditional one.

ballast /'baləst/ *noun* (*uncount*)
Ballast is any heavy substance such as sand or water used in *eg* ships or balloons to keep them steady.

ball bearing /bɔːl 'bɛərɪŋ/ *noun*: **ball bearings**
Ball bearings are small steel balls placed between the moving parts of a machine to help them move smoothly.

ballerina /balə'riːnə/ *noun*: **ballerinas**
A **ballerina** is a female ballet dancer.

ballet /'baleɪ/ *noun*: **ballets**
1 (*uncount*) **Ballet** is a skilled style of dancing requiring training in strength and mobility, and consisting of set steps and movements: *ballet dancers* ▫ *I was sent to ballet school.* **2** A **ballet** is a musical work composed for this kind of dancing, or the series of dances arranged to it: *a ballet by Petipa.*

ball game /'bɔːl geɪm/ *noun*: **ball games**
(*AmE*) A **ball game** is a baseball game.
▻ ***phrase*** (*informal*) You can describe a situation as **a whole new ball game** when it is completely new to you.

ballistics /bə'lɪstɪks/ *noun* (*uncount*)
Ballistics is the scientific study of the movement of objects through the air, especially missiles such as bullets.

balloon /bə'luːn/ *noun*; *verb*
▻ ***noun***: **balloons**
1 A **balloon** is a small rubber or plastic bag that

expands when filled with air, and is used as a toy or for decoration. **2** A **balloon** or **hot-air balloon** is a large bag, made of light material and filled with hot air or a light gas, that floats in the air and can carry passengers in a basket hung beneath it.
▻ ***verb***: **balloons, ballooning, ballooned**
Something **balloons** when it swells quickly or suddenly becomes large and round in shape: *He blew into the mouthpiece, his cheeks ballooning.*

ballot /'balət/ *noun; verb*
▻ ***noun*** *(count or uncount)*: **ballots**
A **ballot** is a vote taken secretly, *eg* by the method used at an election, with each voter putting a piece of paper marked with his or her choice into a sealed box, to be counted later: *A ballot was held every three years to elect a new club president.* □ *School prefects are elected by ballot.*
▻ ***verb***: **ballots, balloting, balloted**
You **ballot** people when you ask them to vote in a ballot to express their preference on some issue: *The union balloted its members on strike action.* — *noun (uncount)* **balloting:** *Balloting takes place today in the Newham by-election.*

ballot box /'balət bɒks/ *noun*: **ballot boxes**
1 A **ballot box** is the box into which voters put their ballot papers after voting. **2** *(used in the singular)* 'The **ballot box**' is also a symbolic way of referring to the democratic system of voting by ballot: *The best way to obtain political change is through the ballot box.*

ballot paper /'balət peɪpə(r)/ *noun*: **ballot papers**
A **ballot paper** is the piece of paper on which you mark your choice when voting in a ballot, *eg* in an election.

ballpoint /'bɔːlpɔɪnt/ *noun*: **ballpoints**
A **ballpoint**, or **ballpoint pen**, is a pen that has a small metal ball as its writing point. [see picture at **office**]

ballroom /'bɔːlruːm/ *noun*: **ballrooms**
A **ballroom** is a large hall where formal dances or balls are held.

ballroom dancing /'bɔːlruːm dɑːnsɪŋ/ *noun (uncount)*
Ballroom dancing is the kind of dancing you do facing a partner, usually holding them by the hand and round the waist, and performing a set pattern of steps.

balm /bɑːm/ *noun*
1 *(uncount or used in the singular)* **Balm** is a term used for substances, especially ointments, that heal or soothe: *Make a healing balm by infusing the flowers in boiling water* **2** *(literary; uncount)* Something that is **balm** to you brings you calm or contentment: *The peace of the hills was balm to his troubled spirit.*

balmy /'bɑːmɪ/ *adjective*: **balmier, balmiest**
The weather is **balmy** when it is pleasantly warm or mild.

balustrade /balə'streɪd/ *noun*: **balustrades**
A **balustrade** is a row of shaped posts joined along the top by a parapet or rail, built *eg* along the outside edge of a balcony. [see also **banister**]

bamboo /bam'buː/ *noun (uncount, often adjectival)*
Bamboo is a tropical plant with hollow jointed woody stems that are used to make furniture; the young shoots of the plant are eaten as a vegetable: *bamboo shoots* □ *a bamboo chair.*

bamboozle /bam'buːzəl/ *verb (informal)*: **bamboozles, bamboozling, bamboozled**
Someone **bamboozles** you when they confuse or trick you: *Prisoners could bamboozle prison chaplains with ease into believing that their characters had been reformed.*

ban /ban/ *noun; verb*
▻ ***noun***: **bans**
A **ban** is an official order forbidding some activity, or forbidding someone to do something: *There is a ban on smoking in this office.* □ *He has served a three-match ban already this season.* [compare **prohibition**]
▻ ***verb***: **bans, banning, banned**
An activity **is banned** when it is forbidden; a person **is banned** from doing something when they are forbidden to do it: *She was banned from driving for a year.* □ *A proposal to ban fishing for cod for ten days each month was supported by Britain.* [*same as* **forbid, prohibit**]

banal /bə'nɑːl/ *adjective*
Something that is **banal** is dull and unoriginal: *It had not struck her before how terribly banal his conversation was.* [*opposite* **original, interesting, stimulating**] — *noun (uncount)* **banality** /bə'nalɪtɪ/: *Her writing never rises above the level of utter banality.*

banana /bə'nɑːnə/ *noun*: **bananas**
A **banana** is a long curved fruit with a yellow skin and pale pinkish-yellow flesh, that grows in bunches. [see picture at **fruit**]
▻ ***phrase*** *(informal, usually humorous)* If you say you must be **going bananas** you mean you must be going crazy.

band[1] /band/ *noun*: **bands**
1 A **band** is a flat strip of something such as cloth, paper or metal: *She kept her hair in place with a velvet band.* □ *a red hatband.* [compare **ribbon**, see also **elastic band, rubber band**] **2** Any contrasting strip, *eg* of colour or light, can be referred to as a **band**: *the closely packed band of stars known as the Milky Way.* **3** Things such as people's ages or incomes are divided into **bands** when they are divided into ranges between an upper and lower limit: *ratepayers in Band G.* **4** *(radio)* A **band** or **waveband** is a range of wavelengths between two limits.

band[2] /band/ *noun; verb*
▻ ***noun*** *(with a singular or plural verb)*: **bands**
1 A **band** is a group of musicians, especially one that plays jazz, or performs on brass or percussion instruments: *a military band.* □ *The band meets* (or *meet*) *for practice every Friday.* **2** A **band** of people of a certain kind is a group of them with a common purpose or interest: *Bands of looters and marauders roamed the city.* □ *her ever-growing band of disciples.*
▻ ***verb***: **bands, banding, banded**

> ***phrasal verb***
> People **band together** when they join together in a group for a common purpose: *Objectors banded together to form a pressure group.*

bandage /'bandɪdʒ/ *noun; verb*
▻ ***noun***: **bandages**
A **bandage** is a strip of cloth for putting on or round an injured part of the body, for protection or support.
▻ ***verb***: **bandages, bandaging, bandaged**
You **bandage** a wound, or an injured part of the body, when you tie a bandage round it: *He bandaged the chlld's head.* — *adjective* **bandaged:** *She wore her bandaged hand in a sling.*

bandit /'bandɪt/ *noun*: **bandits**
A **bandit** is an armed robber, especially one of a gang that attacks and steals from travellers.

bandstand /ˈbandstand/ *noun*: **bandstands**
A **bandstand** is a platform protected by a roof, in an area such as a city park, where bands can play for the entertainment of the public.

bandwagon /ˈbandwagən/ *noun*
▻ ***phrase*** Someone **jumps on the bandwagon** when they involve themselves in some activity or cause simply because it has become fashionable or popular, and they think it will bring them public notice and approval: *shops and supermarkets that are jumping on the green bandwagon.*

bandy¹ /ˈbandɪ/ *verb*: **bandies, bandying, bandied**

> ***phrasal verb***
> Things such as names or ideas get **bandied about** or **around** when they get mentioned a lot by people in general conversation, especially in a careless or ignorant way: *They don't like the way the term 'fundamentalist' is bandied about.*

bandy² /ˈbandɪ/ *adjective*: **bandier, bandiest**
Bandy legs curve apart at the knee and calf. — *adjective* **bandy-legged** /bandɪ-ˈlɛgɪd/: *He told me it was horse-riding that had made him bandy-legged.*

bang /baŋ/ *noun*; *verb*; *adverb*
▻ ***noun***: **bangs**
1 A **bang** is a sudden loud noise like an explosion: *There was a horrible bang as the cars collided.* □ *She shut the register with a bang.* **2** You get a **bang** when something hits you, or you hit part of yourself on something: *He's a bit shaky; he's had a nasty bang on the head.* [*same as* **knock**, **bump**]
▻ ***verb***: **bangs, banging, banged**
1 You **bang** a door when you shut it violently and noisily; it **bangs** when it closes noisily: *I could hear a door banging in the wind.* □ *He went out, banging the door.* **2** You **bang** on a door when you knock on it loudly; you **bang** a surface, or **bang** on it, when you hit it violently: *He banged the table angrily with his fist.* **3** You **bang** part of you against something when you bump into it accidentally and hurt yourself: *She banged her head on the edge of the table as she fell.* [*same as* **hit**, **bump**, **knock**]
▻ ***adverb*** (*informal*)
Bang in a certain place, or at a certain point, means exactly there or then: *He landed bang in the middle of the lawn.* □ *Fortunately his train was bang on time.* [compare **dead**]
▻ ***phrases*** **1** (*informal*) An event **goes with a bang** if it is successful. **2** (*informal*) If you say '**bang goes** something', you mean that there's now no chance of its happening or succeeding: *Bang goes my skiing trip!*

banger /ˈbaŋə(r)/ *noun* (*informal*): **bangers**
A **banger** is **1** a sausage: *We'll have to have bangers and mash again.* **2** an old car in poor condition, especially one with a noisy engine. **3** a small firework that explodes with a loud bang.

bangle /ˈbaŋgəl/ *noun*: **bangles**
A **bangle** is a piece of jewellery in the form of a solid band, *eg* of gold, silver or another metal, for wearing round your wrist, arm or ankle. [compare **bracelet**]

banish /ˈbanɪʃ/ *verb*: **banishes, banishing, banished**
1 A person **is banished** from their own country when they are sent away from it as a punishment. [*same as* **exile**] **2** Someone or something **is banished** from somewhere when they are sent away, excluded, or got rid of from it: *I was banished to the kitchen while the grown-ups conversed in the lounge.* □ *Simply avoiding any mention of race is one way of banishing racial prejudice from society.* **3** You **banish** something from your thoughts when you force yourself to stop worrying about it: *She could not banish the image from her mind.* — *noun* (*uncount*) **banishment:** *The first act of the new régime was to order the banishment of the generals.* [compare **exile**]

banister or **bannister** /ˈbanɪstə(r)/ *noun* (*often used in the plural*): **banisters**
The **banister**, or the **banisters**, is the row of posts joined along the top by a rail, constructed up the outer edge of a staircase: *She usually slid down the banisters if her parents weren't around.*

banjo /ˈbandʒoʊ/ *noun*: **banjos** or **banjoes**
A **banjo** is a stringed musical instrument with a long neck and a round body, played like a guitar.

bank¹ /baŋk/ *noun*; *verb*
▻ ***noun***: **banks**
1 A **bank** is an organization, usually with local offices, that keeps people's money for them in accounts, and from which people can borrow money: *I'm sure the bank would give you a loan.* □ *In 1986 they started paying our salaries directly into our bank accounts.* **2** A **bank** of something is a store of it, ready for use when required: *a blood bank* □ *a data bank.*
▻ ***verb***: **banks, banking, banked**
You **bank** money when you put it into your bank account.

> ***phrasal verb***
> You **bank on** something happening when you rely on it happening: *There may be enough snow for skiing, but I wouldn't bank on it.* □ *We can't bank on their support.*

bank² /baŋk/ *noun*: **banks**
1 The **bank** of a river or lake is the raised ground forming its side: *He swam to the bank and pulled himself up on to it.* **2** A turf-covered wall along the edge of a road or field can be called a **bank**. **3** A **bank** of something is a mass or pile of it: *a bank of cloud was thickening to the west.*

bank account /ˈbaŋk əkaʊnt/ *noun*: **bank accounts**
Your **bank account** is your arrangement with a bank for keeping money there, and for taking it out when you need it: *Children as young as ten are opening bank accounts.* □ *I had £33 left in my bank account.*

banker /ˈbaŋkə(r)/ *noun*: **bankers**
A **banker** is a person who works in the banking profession at a senior level: *international bankers.*

bank holiday /baŋk ˈhɒlɪdeɪ/ *noun* (*BrE*): **bank holidays**
A **bank holiday** is a day, usually a public holiday, on which the banks are closed.

banking /ˈbankɪŋ/ *noun* (*uncount*)
Banking is the business done by banks and bankers: *a career in international banking.* □ *the banking profession.*

banknote /ˈbaŋknoʊt/ *noun*: **banknotes**
A **banknote** is a piece of paper money printed by a bank: *He took a wad of banknotes from his pocket.* [*same as* **note**]

bankrupt /ˈbaŋkrʌpt/ *adjective*; *verb*; *noun*
▻ ***adjective***
People or organizations that are **bankrupt** do not have enough money to pay their debts: *The company almost went bankrupt about a year ago.*
▻ ***verb***: **bankrupts, bankrupting, bankrupted**
Something **bankrupts** a person or company when it makes them bankrupt: *These loss-making products will ultimately bankrupt the company.*

▻ ***noun*: bankrupts**
A **bankrupt** is a person who has legally been declared unable to pay his or her debts.

bankruptcy /ˈbaŋkrʌpsɪ/ *noun* (*count or uncount*): **bankruptcies**
Bankruptcy is the condition of not having enough money to pay your debts, or the process of being declared bankrupt: *The club was plunged into bankruptcy.* □ *an increasing number of bankruptcies among small shopkeepers.*

bank statement /ˈbaŋk steɪtmənt/ *noun*: **bank statements**
Your **bank statement** is a list, sent to you by your bank, of all the sums of money you have added to and withdrawn from your bank account over a particular period: *my monthly bank statement.*

banner /ˈbanə(r)/ *noun*: **banners**
A **banner** is **1** a piece of cloth supported on a pole, or a pair of poles, with a design or slogan on it, carried at public meetings and parades. **2** a strip of cloth with a slogan or message on it, stretched across the street.

bannister see **banister**.

banquet /ˈbaŋkwɪt/ *noun*: **banquets**
A **banquet** is a formal dinner for a large number of people, especially one held for a special occasion, at which speeches are made: *They attended a sumptuous banquet aboard the royal yacht Britannia.*

banter /ˈbantə(r)/ *noun* (*uncount*)
Banter is friendly, joking talk: *They exchanged banter and gossip about old friends and past scandals.*

baptism /ˈbaptɪzm/ *noun* (*count or uncount*)
Baptism is the Christian ceremony of baptizing someone. [*same as* **christening**]

baptize or **baptise** /bapˈtaɪz/ *verb*: **baptizes, baptizing, baptized**
Someone **is baptized** when they are dipped in water or sprinkled with it as a sign that they have become a member of the Christian church; when babies **are baptized**, they are usually officially given a name: *We had the baby baptized at Easter.* □ *He was baptized Robert John.* [*same as* **christen**]

bar /bɑː(r)/ *noun*; *verb*; *preposition*
▻ ***noun*: bars**
1 A **bar** is a long narrow rigid piece of metal, *eg* one of a number forming an animal's cage, or placed vertically or horizontally over a window to prevent people getting in or out: *He had hanged himself from the bars of his cell window.* **2** A **bar** of something is a rectangular block of it: *bars of soap* □ *We packed a couple of chocolate bars each.* **3** Something that is a **bar** to doing something prevents you from doing it: *The costs were the biggest bar to people setting up their own business.* **4** A **bar** is **a** (*especially BrE*) a room *eg* in a hotel, theatre or public house, where alcoholic drinks are served: *Enjoy a drink in the bar before the show.* **b** the counter where you buy alcoholic drinks: *He was standing at the bar waiting to be served.* **c** (*especially AmE*) a place where alcoholic drinks are sold and drunk: *I met her in a bar in Boston.* **5** (*music*) A **bar** is one of the sections into which a piece of music is divided, each having in it the same number of beats: *on the first beat of each bar* □ *How many beats to the bar are there?* **6** (*legal; used in the singular, with a singular or plural verb*) The **Bar** is **a** in Britain and Australia, the lawyers qualified to argue cases in the higher courts. **b** in the US, all lawyers, regarded as a group or profession.
▻ ***verb*: bars, barring, barred**
1 You **bar** doors or windows when you fasten them securely by fixing metal bars or strips of wood across them: *The door was bolted and barred.* **2** Someone **is barred** from a place or event when they are officially forbidden to enter it or take part in it; they **are barred** from doing something when they are officially forbidden to do it: *He has been barred from the Club.* □ *The national team would be barred from the 1994 World Cup final.* **3** Someone or something **bars** your way when they prevent you from progressing further: *His escape was barred by the shop's automatically locking door.*
▻ ***preposition***
Bar is used to mean 'except': *Every match, bar one which we won, has ended in a 2-2 draw.*
▻ ***phrases*** **1** Someone who is **behind bars** is in prison. **2** (*BrE, Australia*) Lawyers **are called to the Bar** when they qualify to argue cases in the higher courts.

barb /bɑːb/ *noun*: **barbs**
1 A **barb** is a backward-facing point on a fish hook. **2** An unkind or sarcastic remark is also referred to as a **barb**.

barbarian /bɑːˈbeərɪən/ *noun*; *adjective*
▻ ***noun*: barbarians**
In ancient times, the **barbarians** were tribes that had not come under the civilizing influence of Greece and Rome.
▻ ***adjective:*** *when Rome fell to the barbarian tribes during the fourth and fifth centuries.*

barbaric /bɑːˈbarɪk/ *adjective*
Barbaric behaviour or treatment is brutal, cruel, or uncivilized: *a barbaric form of punishment* □ *foxhunting and other barbaric sports.* — *adverb* **barbarically:** *We treated the native peoples barbarically, plundering their land and resources.*

barbarism /ˈbɑːbərɪzm/ *noun* (*uncount*)
Barbarism is brutal, cruel or uncivilized behaviour: *He had devoted his life to the struggle against fascist barbarism.*

barbarity /bɑːˈbarɪtɪ/ *noun*: **barbarities**
1 (*uncount*) **Barbarity** is cruel or uncivilized behaviour: *the barbarity of terrorism.* **2 Barbarities** are acts of cruelty: *barbarities committed by the invading forces.*

barbarous /ˈbɑːbərəs/ *adjective*
1 Barbarous treatment or behaviour is brutally cruel: *They were subjected to the most barbarous forms of torture.* **2 Barbarous** also describes things that are rough, primitive or uncivilized: *Early child-rearing practices were barbarous by modern standards.* — *adverb* **barbarously:** *In 1679 hundreds of his followers were barbarously imprisoned.*

barbecue /ˈbɑːbɪkjuː/ *noun*; *verb*
▻ ***noun*: barbecues**
A **barbecue** is **a** a metal grid on which food is grilled over an open fire. **b** an open-air party at which food is cooked on a barbecue.
▻ ***verb*: barbecues, barbecuing, barbecued**
You **barbecue** food when you cook it on a barbecue: *barbecued chicken.*

barbed wire /bɑːbd ˈwaɪə(r)/ *noun* (*uncount*)
Barbed wire is wire with short sharp points projecting from it, used for making fences.

barber /ˈbɑːbə(r)/ *noun*: **barbers**
1 A **barber** is a man who cuts men's hair and shaves their beards. **2** A **barber** or a **barber's** is a barber's shop or premises: *There isn't a barber in the village any more.* □ *I see you've been to the barber's.*

barbiturate /bɑːˈbɪtjʊərət/ *noun*: **barbiturates**

A **barbiturate** is a drug that calms people's nerves or helps them to sleep.

bar code /ˈbɑː koʊd/ *noun*: **bar codes**
A **bar code** is a set of thick and thin lines on the packaging of a product, that represents coded information on its price and size and can be read by a computer.

bare /bɛə(r)/ *adjective*; *verb*
▻ ***adjective***: **barer, barest**
1 a A part of your body that is **bare** is not covered by clothing: *summer clothes that leave your arms and legs bare* □ *walking about with bare feet.* **b** A tree or branch that is **bare** has no leaves on it. **c** A **bare** floor has no carpet or rugs on it; **bare** walls have no pictures on them; a room is **bare** when it has no furniture in it: *The room was bare except for a single table and chair.* **d** Shelves and cupboards are **bare** when they are empty: *The supermarket shelves became barer and barer.* **2 a** You refer to the main facts of something as the **bare** facts: *The bare facts of the matter are apparently these.* **b** The **bare** essentials, the **bare** necessities, or the **bare** minimum of something, are the very least that you need: *He allowed himself only hand luggage, packed with the barest essentials.* □ *She had brought the bare minimum of clothing.*
▻ ***verb***: **bares, baring, bared**
You **bare** a part of your body, such as your breast, when you uncover it, especially as a symbolic gesture; A dog **bares** its teeth when it draws back its lips in an angry snarl.
▻ ***phrases*** **1** A place or surface that is **bare of** something has none of it in it or on it: *The walls were bare of pictures or posters.* □ *shelves bare of food.* **2** For **with your bare hands** see **hand**.

bareback /ˈbɛəbak/ *adverb*
You ride **bareback** when you ride a horse without a saddle.

barefaced /ˈbɛəfeɪst/ *adjective*
You tell a **barefaced** lie when you lie without shame.

barefoot /ˈbɛəfʊt/ *adjective or adverb*
Someone who is, or goes about, **barefoot** or **barefooted**, is not wearing any shoes or socks: *barefooted children* □ *running about barefoot on the beach.*

bareheaded /bɛəˈhɛdɪd/ *adjective or adverb*
Someone who is, or goes about, **bareheaded** is not wearing a hat.

barely /ˈbɛəlɪ/ *adverb* (*used like a negative*)
1 Something that is **barely** so is almost not so, or only just so: *They have barely enough to eat.* □ *I could barely hear her, the line was so bad.* □ *What are you doing up so early? It's barely six o'clock.* □ *It's barely a month since his last car accident.* [*same as* **hardly**, **scarcely**; compare '**only just**'] **2** You say that **barely** had one thing happened when another did to emphasize how quickly the second event followed the first: *He'd barely said hallo before he was called away urgently to look at another patient.* [*same as* **hardly**, **scarcely**; compare '**only just**']

bargain /ˈbɑːgɪn/ *noun*; *verb*
▻ ***noun***: **bargains**
1 You make a **bargain** with someone from whom you want something when you reach an agreement with them about what each of you is to pay, receive or do: *I watched the two men concluding some sort of bargain and shaking hands on it.* □ *You didn't keep your side of he bargain.* **2** Something that is being offered for sale is a **bargain** if it is being sold cheaply and is good value: *You may get some bargains in the sales.* □ *I can never resist a bargain.* □ *furniture available at bargain prices.*
▻ ***verb***: **bargains, bargaining, bargained**
You **bargain** with someone when you discuss the terms of an agreement about what you each want and are prepared to give or do in exchange: *The trade union's purpose in life is to bargain on behalf of its members for better pay and conditions.* □ *I left them bargaining over the price.* — *noun* (*uncount*) **bargaining:** *Pay-bargaining continued over the next few days.*
▻ ***phrases*** **1** Someone who **drives a hard bargain** insists on terms that are difficult to satisfy. **2** You use **into the bargain** to emphasize the striking aspect of some additional comment you have just made about something: *She was incompetent at her job, and was unpleasantly bossy into the bargain.*

> ***phrasal verbs***
> Something that you hadn't **bargained for**, or hadn't **bargained on**, is a difficulty that you weren't prepared for: *I don't think any of us had bargained for such terrible weather.* □ *I hadn't bargained on her refusing to help.*

barge /bɑːdʒ/ *noun*; *verb*
▻ ***noun***: **barges**
A **barge** is a long boat with a flat bottom, used *eg* for transporting heavy loads by river or canal.
▻ ***verb***: **barges, barging, barged**
1 You **barge** somewhere when you push your way there in a rough, inconsiderate manner: *He barged past her through the doorway.* □ *The house was full of policemen barging about.* **2** You **barge** into someone when you bump into them rudely.

> ***phrasal verb***
> You **barge in** when you enter a place rudely or unexpectedly, or push your way into company, or interrupt a conversation: *Sorry to barge in on your cosy evening.*

bargepole /ˈbɑːdʒpoʊl/ *noun*
▻ ***phrase*** (*BrE*; *informal*) If you say you **wouldn't touch** a certain thing **with a bargepole**, you mean that you want nothing to do with it, *eg* because you do not consider it safe or reliable: *I warned investors not to touch the company with a bargepole.*

baritone /ˈbarɪtoʊn/ *noun*: **baritones**
1 A **baritone** is a man with a singing voice between bass and tenor. **2** (*uncount*) Men with this singing voice sing **baritone**.

bark[1] /bɑːk/ *verb*; *noun*
▻ ***verb***: **barks, barking, barked**
1 A dog or fox **barks** when it gives its typical short sharp cry: *He shouldn't bark at me; I'm one of the family.* **2** Someone **barks** at you when they shout at you, or say something to you in a sharp impatient voice: *The sergeant continued to bark orders at us.* □ *'Quiet, please!' he barked.*
▻ ***noun***: **barks:** *The dog backed a few steps, giving a bark of alarm.*
▻ ***phrases*** **1** (*informal*) If you say about someone that **their bark is worse than their bite** you mean that they are not as bad-tempered and critical as they seem to be from the way they shout and complain. **2** For **bark up the wrong tree** see **tree**.

bark[2] /bɑːk/ *noun* (*uncount*)
Bark is the tough material covering the trunk and branches of a tree.

barley /ˈbɑːlɪ/ *noun* (*uncount*)
Barley is **1** a tall grass-like plant, grown for its grain. **2** the grain from this plant, used as food and for making beer and whisky.

barmaid /ˈbɑːmeɪd/ *noun*: **barmaids**
A **barmaid** is a woman who serves drinks in a pub or bar.

barman /ˈbɑːmən/ *noun*: **barmen**
A **barman** is a man who serves drinks in a pub or bar.

barmy /ˈbɑːmɪ/ *adjective* (*informal*): **barmier, barmiest**
Someone or something that is **barmy** is crazy: *The endless loud pop music was driving me barmy.* □ *It's just another of his barmy ideas.* □ *He's absolutely barmy about her.* [*same as* **crazy, daft, mad**]

barn /bɑːn/ *noun*: **barns**
A **barn** is a large farm building for keeping *eg* grain, animals or equipment in.

barnacle /ˈbɑːnəkəl/ *noun*: **barnacles**
A **barnacle** is a small shellfish that sticks to rocks and to the bottoms of ships.

barometer /bəˈrɒmɪtə(r)/ *noun*: **barometers**
1 A **barometer** is an instrument that measures air pressure and shows when the weather is changing for better or worse. **2** Something that is referred to as a **barometer** of a mood or situation is considered an indication of changes taking place in it: *Local-election results generally serve as a barometer of current public feeling about the government.*

baron /ˈbarən/ *noun*: **barons**
1 In Britain and elsewhere, a **baron** is a man of the lowest rank of nobility. **2** Powerful business people who control large areas of industry are referred to as **barons**: *oil barons* □ *the press barons.*

baroness /ˈbarənɪs/ *noun*: **baronesses**
A **baroness** is a woman who is a baron's wife or who has the same rank as a baron.

baronet /ˈbarənɛt/ *noun*: **baronets**
Baronet is an honorary British title that can be given to a man by the king or queen; a **baronet** can pass the title on to his son.

baroque /bəˈrɒk/ *adjective*
Baroque describes the elaborate and graceful style of art, architecture and music used in Europe in the 17th and 18th centuries: *baroque churches.*

barrack /ˈbarək/ *verb*: **barracks, barracking, barracked**
To **barrack** a speaker is to interrupt him or her with shouts and loud objections [*same as* **heckle**]. — *noun* (*uncount*) **barracking:** *There was a lot of barracking from the back of the hall.*

barracks /ˈbarəks/ *noun*: *plural* **barracks**
A **barracks** is a building or group of buildings where soldiers live: *during the attack on the military barracks at Tadjoura.* □ *He had been given a reprimand and confined to barracks.*

barrage /ˈbarɑːʒ/ *noun*: **barrages**
1 A **barrage** of fire is a long burst of continuous firing from heavy guns. **2** You face a **barrage** of questions or complaints when you have a great number of them to deal with, usually coming all at the same time from a lot of different people.

barred /bɑːd/ *verb*; *adjective*
▻ ***verb***
Barred is the past tense and past participle of **bar**.
▻ ***adjective***
Barred windows have bars fitted over them, to prevent people getting in or out.

barrel /ˈbarəl/ *noun*: **barrels**
1 A **barrel** is a round container *eg* for beer, wine or oil, usually made of curved strips of wood held together at top and bottom with iron hoops. **2** A **barrel** is also the beer, wine or oil, or the quantity of it, contained in a barrel: *Before 1985 the price of oil was an average $18 a barrel.* **3** The **barrel** of a gun is the metal tube-shaped part through which the ammunition is fired.
▻ ***phrases*** **1** You **have** someone **over a barrel** when you are in a position to get whatever you want from them. **2** For **lock, stock and barrel** see **lock**. **3** You say you **are scraping the barrel** when you are having to choose things of poor quality, because the best ones have already been taken.

barren /ˈbarən/ *adjective*
1 (*old*) A woman is **barren** if she is not able to have children. [*same as* **infertile**; *opposite* **fertile**] **2 Barren** land or soil is of such poor quality that nothing grows in it. [*same as* **infertile**; *opposite* **fertile**]

barricade /ˈbarɪkeɪd/ *noun*; *verb*
▻ ***noun***: **barricades**
A **barricade** is a barrier that people construct quickly from vehicles and other objects, to block a street, passage or entrance, during times of civil disturbance.
▻ ***verb***: **barricades, barricading, barricaded**
1 To **barricade** a street, passage or entrance is to construct a barrier across it. **2** You **barricade** yourself inside a place when you put heavy objects against the doors to prevent people from getting in: *He had barricaded himself into an upstairs bedroom with his three hostages.*

barrier /ˈbarɪə(r)/ *noun*: **barriers**
1 A **barrier** is anything such as a fence or wall that separates one area from another, or stops movement from one area to another: *The crowds broke through police barriers and burst on to the pitch.* □ *He waved his press pass at the official on duty at the barrier.* □ *the flood barriers on the Thames.* **2** A difficulty that stops people agreeing, or communicating satisfactorily with each other, can be called a **barrier**: *After a couple of months the language barrier begins to fade at a rapid rate.* **3** Something that is a **barrier** to or against something prevents it happening: *Administered regularly at the start of winter, the injections are an effective barrier against infection.* □ *Law was the one career in which blindness presented no barrier to success.*

barring /ˈbɑːrɪŋ/ *preposition*
Barring introduces an exception to what you are saying, and can mean **1** 'except' or 'except for': *Nobody barring a complete idiot would go by that route.* **2** except in the event of: *His income can be expected to reach a peak in early manhood, barring disasters like unemployment.*

barrister /ˈbarɪstə(r)/ *noun*: **barristers**
In *eg* England, Wales and Australia, a **barrister** is a lawyer qualified to argue a case in a court of law. [compare **advocate, solicitor**]

barrow /ˈbaroʊ/ *noun*: **barrows**
A **barrow** is **1** a wheelbarrow. **2** a cart used for selling fruit and vegetables in the street.

bartender /ˈbɑːtɛndə(r)/ *noun* (*AmE*): **bartenders**
A **bartender** is a person who serves drinks in a bar. [see also **barmaid, barman**]

barter /ˈbɑːtə(r)/ *verb*; *noun*
▻ ***verb***: **barters, bartering, bartered**
People **barter** goods when they exchange them for other goods, as distinct from selling them for money: *The farmers hoarded grain to barter for machinery and goods.*
▻ ***noun*** (*uncount*): *The beads and gems were used for barter.* □ *As the currency dropped in value people resorted to barter.*

base /beɪs/ *noun*; *verb*
▻ ***noun***: **bases**

1 The **base** of soemthing is **a** its lowest part or point: *tangled briars growing round the base of the tree.* □ *There was a funny ache at the base of her spine.* **b** the part on which it stands: *Trim the base off a washing-up-liquid bottle.* □ *He signed most of his pots on the base.* **c** the point at which it is attached to something: *a bird with a patch of white at the base of each wing.* **d** (*geometry*) The **base** of a triangle is the side opposite to its apex. [see picture at **shape**] **2** Your **base** is the place where you stay or work most of the year time; a company's or organization's **base** is the place that is the centre of their activities: *The couple organize special-interest cruises from their base in Argyll.* □ *The Isle of Dogs was their main base of operations.* **3** A military **base** is a place from which armed forces operate: *an extensive American naval base in Bahrain* □ *the airbase in Eastern Libya.* **4** A **base** is also **a** something regarded as a framework, core or foundation that can be developed or used in various ways: *The findings will be used primarily as an information base for formulating policy.* □ *their failure to mobilize a broad base of political support* □ *a structured database.* [compare **basis**] **b** a main ingredient with which various others can be mixed: *dishes that use whipped cream as their base.*

▻ ***verb***: **bases, basing, based**

1 One thing **is based** on or upon another if it is dependent on it or uses it extensively, or has it as its foundation: *the growth of computer-based research* □ *recognizing the special nature of EC farming as family-based, rather than corporate-based, as in the USA.* □ *Current government policy is based on choice, market forces and competition.* □ *a numbering system based on tens and tenths* □ *They had nothing at all to base a charge on.* □ *the film based on his life.* **2** You **are based** somewhere if you live there and do most of your work there: *The new company will be based at Culham in Oxfordshire.* □ *The recession in the Gulf of Mexico hit our US-based business.* □ *They joined the French forces based in Chad.*

baseball /ˈbeɪsbɔːl/ *noun* (*uncount*)
Baseball is a game played with a bat and ball by two teams of nine people, in which the person batting scores by running round all four corners of the pitch, called bases, before the other team recovers the ball.

baseless /ˈbeɪsləs/ *adjective*
Stories or fears are **baseless** if there is no good reason for them, because they are not based on fact or reality: *baseless suspicions* □ *A spokesman denied the reports as baseless.* [*same as* **groundless**]

basement /ˈbeɪsmənt/ *noun*: **basements**
The **basement** is the lowest floor of a building, usually below ground level: *There's a drying room in the basement.* □ *We rented a basement flat for six months.*

bases *noun* (*plural*)
Bases is **1** (/ˈbeɪsɪz/) the plural of **base**. **2** (/ˈbeɪsiːz/) the plural of **basis**.

bash /baʃ/ *verb*; *noun*

▻ ***verb*** (*informal*): **bashes, bashing, bashed**

1 You **bash** someone when you hit them hard deliberately: *We used to bash each other over the head with coat-hangers.* **2** You **bash** into or against something when you bump into it hard, usually by accident: *I swerved and bashed into a lamp post.* □ *He bashed his head against the fender when he fell.* □ *The boat bashed against the jetty.*

▻ ***noun*** (*informal*): **bashes:** *I must have got a bash on the head as I slid down the bank.*

▻ ***phrase*** (*informal*) You **have a bash at** something, or **give it a bash** when you try it: *I thought I might have a bash at the Marathon this year.* □ *You don't know you can't do it unless you give it a bash.*

bashful /ˈbaʃfʊl/ *adjective*
A **bashful** person is shy and gets embarrassed easily: *I was then a bashful young lady of sixteen.* □ *Lily, suddenly bashful, could think of nothing to say.* — *adverb* **bashfully:** *She smiled bashfully.* — *noun* (*uncount*) **bashfulness:** *the bashfulness of youth.*

basic /ˈbeɪsɪk/ *adjective*
1 Basic describes things **a** that have to be learnt, understood, recognized or dealt with before progress can be made: *The course had taught me basic computing skills.* □ *the basic techniques of child care* □ *A young child quickly learns the language and basic behaviour patterns of its society.* □ *understanding such basic concepts as space and time* □ *This is the basic reason for Britain's poor investment record.* □ *our basic rights as citizens of a free country* □ *the basic necessities of life* □ *basic needs such as housing, health care and employment.* [*same as* **fundamental**] **b** that represent a standard or minimum level, to which additions may be made: *A supplement to the basic rate of pay may be allowed in certain cases.* □ *the plight of old people trying to survive on the basic state pension.* [*same as* **standard, minimum**] **c** that are simple or rough, or consist only of what is absolutely necessary: *the accommodation in the huts is pretty basic; no electric light or running water, for instance.* □ *They lack even quite basic facilities such as a bath or a shower.* [*same as* **primitive, elementary**] **2** Something that is **basic** to something else **a** is an essential part of it: *The love of nature that was basic to his character.* [*same as* **essential, inherent** in] **b** is essential for obtaining or achieving it: *organizational skills that are basic to good management.* [*same as* **essential, necessary**]

basically /ˈbeɪsɪkəlɪ/ or /ˈbeɪsɪklɪ/ *adverb*
1 Something that is **basically** so is so as far as it matters, or in all important aspects: *He found himself basically in agreement with them on most issues.* □ *theories that are basically incompatible* □ *Native Fijians were basically Melanesian.* [*same as* **essentially, fundamentally**] **2** (*sentence adverb*) You use **basically** to introduce a simple statement about something detailed or complicated, or to introduce the main or essential fact about something: *Basically, there are two schools of thought.* □ *Basically, the fear of crime is out of proportion to the probability of being a victim of it.* [*same as* **essentially**]

basics /ˈbeɪsɪks/ *noun* (*plural*)
The **basics** of something such as a subject or a skill are the simple and most important things about it that you learn first: *a chance to learn the basics of sailing* □ *They introduce the concepts of rhyme and wordplay, as well as covering basics like alphabet and spelling.* □ *The basics of toilet training are usually mastered quickly.* □ *trying to grasp the basics of Swedish* □ *if you want to go back to basics and assess the kind of person you are.*

basin /ˈbeɪsən/ *noun*: **basins**
1 A **basin** is a deep bowl for mixing or storing food in, or a larger, shallower one for holding water: *Turn the mixture into a pudding basin.* □ *She brought in a basin of hot water and a towel.* [*same as* **bowl**] **2** The **basin** in a bathroom is the washbasin. **3** The **basin** of a large river or lake is the valley or area of land from which water runs down into it: *the Irrawaddy basin.*

basis /ˈbeɪsɪs/ *noun*: **bases** /ˈbeɪsiːz/
1 The **basis** of something is the structure, framework or material from which it is developed, or on which it rests or depends: *This research will form the basis of a*

book. ▫ *an experience that formed the basis for a collection of short stories* ▫ *There's some basis of fact in the legend.* ▫ *an artist whose vision mocks the moral and spiritual basis on which society is founded* ▫ *The percussion provides the necessary rhythmic basis and no more.* ▫ *a model that could provide the basis for a general theory.* **2** The **basis** for some action or opinion is the circumstance that provides a reason for it: *There was no factual basis for the view that the child would be placed in an intolerable situation.* ▫ *if there were any serious basis on which it could be argued that there was party-political disagreement on the issue of smoking.*
▻ ***phrases*** **1** You make a decision or form an opinion **on the basis of** something if it is the reason for your decision or opinion: *Students are able, on the basis of experience, to choose which subjects to specialize in.* ▫ *He could consider himself a gentleman on the basis of having attended a university.* ▫ *It is on this basis alone that they support the change.* **2** You do something **on a** certain **basis** if that is the system, arrangement or limit you are applying: *Other staff were hired on a seasonal basis.* ▫ *The kit had been issued to some army units on a trial basis.* ▫ *three- and four-year-olds who receive education on a part-time basis* ▫ *The treatment would continue on a daily basis.* ▫ *the interpretation of archaeology on a world-wide basis.*

bask /bɑːsk/ *verb*: **basks, basking, basked**
1 You **bask** in the sun when you lie enjoying its warmth: *I was looking forward to two weeks of basking in the sunshine.* **2** You **bask** in someone's approval, favour or admiration when you get pleasure from having it. [compare **wallow**]

basket /ˈbɑːskɪt/ *noun*: **baskets**
A **basket** is a container made of woven strips of cane or wood: *a shopping basket* ▫ *a wastepaper basket* ▫ *a laundry basket* ▫ *a basket of laundry.*

basketball /ˈbɑːskɪtbɔːl/ *noun*: **basketballs**
1 (*uncount*) **Basketball** is a game in which two teams of five players score points by throwing a ball into a net on a high post at each end of the court. **2** A **basketball** is the ball used in this game.

bass /beɪs/ *noun*; *adjective*
▻ ***noun***: **basses**
1 (*uncount*) The **bass** in a piece of written music is the lower range of notes in it, especially those played with the left hand on a piano. [see also **clef**] **2** A **bass** is a man with the lowest singing voice. **3** (*uncount*) People who have this singing voice sing **bass**. **4** (*informal*; *count or uncount*) A bass guitar or a double bass may be referred to as a **bass**: *He plays lead guitar and his brother plays bass.*
▻ ***adjective***
A **bass** instrument is the one with the deepest sound, or lowest range of notes, in its group: *a bass trombone* ▫ *the bass drum.*

bassoon /bəˈsuːn/ *noun*: **bassoons**
A **bassoon** is a large woodwind instrument with a deep sound. [see picture at **orchestra**]

bastard /ˈbastəd/ or /ˈbɑːstəd/ *noun*: **bastards**
1 (*very offensive*) If you call someone a **bastard** you are insulting them or expressing disgust at their behaviour. **2** (*old*) A **bastard** is a child born of parents who are not married to each other: *the father of her bastard child.*

bastion /ˈbastɪən/ *noun*: **bastions**
Something that is described as a **bastion** of a particular thing preserves, protects or promotes it: *All three women were elected, breaching the all-male bastion.* ▫ *The unions are the last bastion of Labour power.* [compare **stronghold**]

bat[1] /bat/ *noun*; *verb*
▻ ***noun***: **bats**
A **bat** is a piece of wood suitably shaped in various ways for hitting the ball in cricket, baseball, rounders and table tennis.
▻ ***verb***: **bats, batting, batted**
You **bat** when it is your turn to hit the ball in cricket, basball or rounders.
▻ ***phrase***
1 For **not bat an eyelid** see **eyelid**. **2** (*informal*) You do something **off your own bat** when you do it without being asked to.

bat[2] /bat/ *noun*: **bats**
A **bat** is a mouse-like flying animal with leathery wings, that is active at night.

batch /batʃ/ *noun*: **batches**
A **batch** of things or people is a set or group of them dealt with at the same time, or in one operation: *The second batch of bread would soon be ready to take out of the oven.* ▫ *We interviewed the candidates in two separate batches.*

bath /bɑːθ/ *noun*; *verb*
▻ ***noun***: **baths**
1 A **bath** is a long container that you fill with water and sit or lie in to wash your whole body. **2** (*usually in the singular*) You have a **bath** or take a **bath** when you sit or lie in a bath and wash your body: *Do have a bath if you want.* **3** (*used in the plural*) A public swimming pool is referred to as the **baths**: *The baths are open from 8 am to 8 pm.*
▻ ***verb*** /bɑːθ/: **baths, bathing, bathed**
You **bath** *eg* a baby or small child when you wash them in a bath: *I'd bathed the baby and put her to bed.*

bathe /beɪð/ *verb*; *noun*
▻ ***verb***: **bathes, bathing, bathed**
1 You **bathe** when you swim for pleasure in the sea, or in a lake or river: *We often went bathing in the cold North Sea.* **2** You **bathe** a wound, injury, or an injured part of your body, when you wash it gently: *He bathed the cut with antiseptic.* **3** (*AmE*) You **bathe** when you have a bath: *He returned home to bathe and sleep.* **4** A place that **is bathed** in light has light pouring over it: *The fields and woods were bathed in a golden light.*
▻ ***noun***: **bathes**
You have a **bathe** when you go swimming in the sea, or in a lake or river: *She'd gone down to the river for a bathe.* — *noun* **bather**: *He watched the early-morning bathers racing each other down to the water's edge.*

bathing costume /ˈbeɪðɪŋ kɒstjuːm/ *noun*: **bathing costumes**
A **bathing costume** is a swimming costume or swimsuit.

bathmat /ˈbɑːθmat/ *noun*: **bathmats**
A **bathmat** is a thick mat beside a bath, for you to stand on when you are drying yourself.

bathrobe /ˈbɑːθroʊb/ *noun*: **bathrobes**
1 A **bathrobe** is a loose coat-shaped garment made of towelling, that you wear before or after having a bath. **2** (*AmE*) A **bathrobe** is a dressing gown. [*same as* **robe**]

bathroom /ˈbɑːθruːm/ *noun*: **bathrooms**
1 A **bathroom** is a room in a house which contains a bath, a washbasin and usually a toilet. **2** (*especially AmE*) People refer to the toilet or lavatory as the **bathroom**: *Could I go to the bathroom, please?* [see picture on page 78]

bathtub /bɑːθtʌb/ *noun* (*old*): **bathtubs**
A **bathtub** is a bath.

baton /ˈbatɒn/ (*AmE* /bəˈtɒn/) *noun*: **batons**
1 A conductor's **baton** is the light thin stick that he or

bathroom

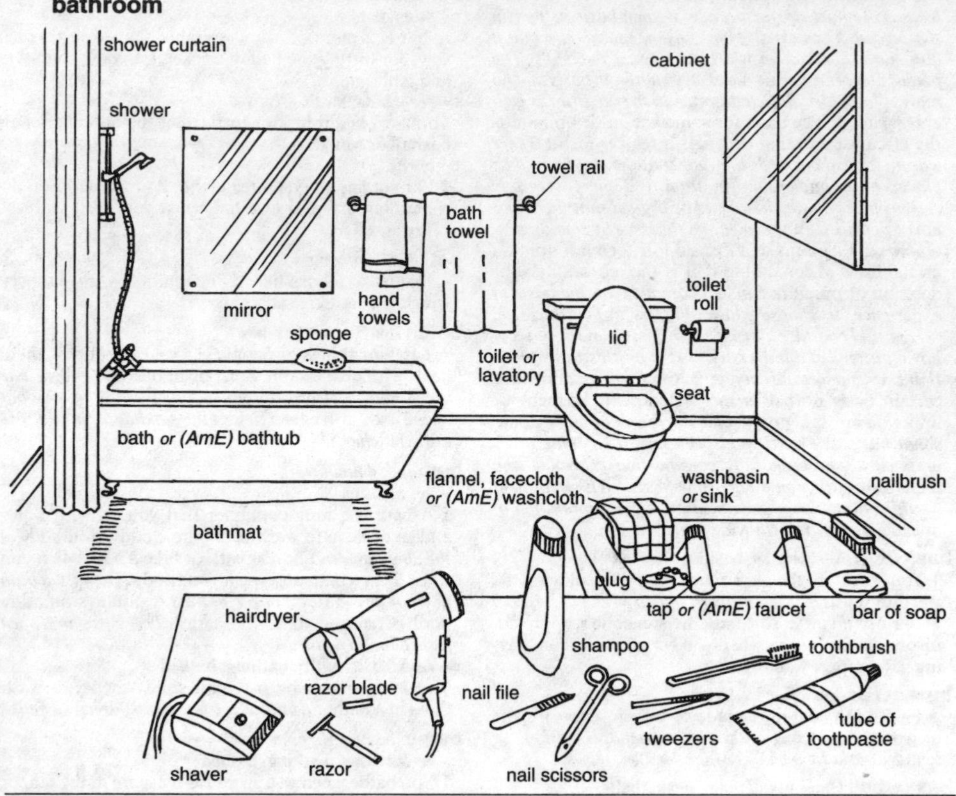

she uses for directing an orchestra or choir. [see picture at **orchestra**] **2** A policeman's **baton** is a short heavy stick designed as a weapon. [*same as* **truncheon**] **3** In a relay race a **baton** is a short stick passed by one runner to the next one.

battalion /bəˈtalıən/ *noun*: **battalions**
A **battalion** is an army unit consisting of three or more companies.

batter[1] /ˈbatə(r)/ *verb*: **batters, battering, battered**
1 To **batter** something, or **batter** on or against it, is to keep striking it violently: *We watched the waves battering the end of the pier.* □ *She battered frantically on the door with her fists.* **2** One person **batters** another when they hit them repeatedly and cause injury: *the crime of child-battering.* □ *refuges for battered wives.*

> ***phrasal verb***
> You **batter** a door **down** when you break it or knock it off its hinges by hitting it hard.

batter[2] /ˈbatə(r)/ *noun (uncount)*
Batter is a mixture of eggs, flour and milk, beaten together and used *eg* to make pancakes or cover food before frying it.

battered /ˈbatəd/ *adjective*
Something that is **battered** has had a lot of rough handling and is damaged as a result: *A small battered truck was being loaded with fruit.* [see also **batter**[1]]

battering /ˈbatərıŋ/ *noun (usually in the singular)*: **batterings**
Someone or something takes a **battering**, or takes a lot of **battering**, when they are roughly treated: *He was still black and blue from the battering he'd received in the boxing ring.* □ *The ship took a severe battering in the storm.* [see also **batter**[1]]

battery /ˈbatərı/ *noun*; *adjective*
▷ ***noun***: **batteries**
1 A **battery** is a device that produces electricity for making something such as a radio or torch work: *The car battery was flat.* [see picture at **car**] **2** A **battery** of things is a lot of them, either forming an array or collection, or following quickly one after the other: *She could move nowhere without being confronted by a battery of cameras.* □ *He was to be subjected to a battery of health checks.*
▷ ***adjective***
Battery hens are kept in small cages and are forced to keep producing eggs.

battle /ˈbatəl/ *noun*; *verb*
▷ ***noun***: **battles**
A **battle** is **a** (*count or uncount*) a fight between enemies or opposing forces, especially one of many during a war: *great sea battles of the past.* □ *new warships vital for the Battle of the Atlantic.* □ *King James IV was killed in battle.* **b** a struggle between two people or groups for power or control: *There had been a boardroom battle, and Eliot had emerged triumphant.* □ *in the battle of wills between child and parent.* □ *The situation had turned into a battle of wits between him and his pursuers.* **c** a long or difficult struggle against something, or to achieve something: *He helped her in her two-year battle against cancer.*

▻ *verb*: **battles, battling, battled**
You **battle** when you fight or struggle: *Firemen are still battling to put the fire out.* ▫ *when you're battling with tent poles in a high wind* ▫ *Recently she's been battling with the local authorities over the provision of pedestrian crossings.* ▫ *He was battling for his life in St Mary's Hospital.*
▻ ***phrases*** **1** You are **fighting a losing battle** if you are trying to achieve something but are certain to fail. **2** You say that something is **half the battle** if it is the most important step towards success.

battlefield /ˈbatəlfiːld/ *noun*: **battlefields**
A **battlefield** is a place where a battle is fought: *a tour of Napoleonic battlefields.*

battleground /ˈbatəlgraʊnd/ *noun*: **battlegrounds**
1 A **battleground** is a battlefield. **2** A matter over which people disagree, or compete with each other, can be referred to as a **battleground**: *Education was becoming a battleground of personalities, while objectivity was being pushed aside.*

battlements /ˈbatəlmənts/ *noun* (*plural*)
The low wall or parapet round the top of castles or fortresses, with regularly placed gaps in it for shooting through, is known as the **battlements**.

battleship /ˈbatəlʃɪp/ *noun*: **battleships**
A **battleship** is a large armoured warship.

batty /ˈbatɪ/ *adjective* (*informal*): **battier, battiest**
If you describe someone or something as **batty**, you mean they are crazy: *I must be going batty.* ▫ *His constant whining drives me batty.* ▫ *I don't know what gave you that batty idea.*

bauble /ˈbɔːbəl/ *noun*: **baubles**
A **bauble** is a small, cheap ornament or piece of jewellery: *The diamond on her third finger made Liz Taylor's look like a bauble.*

baulk /bɔːlk/ see **balk**.

bawdy /ˈbɔːdɪ/ *adjective*: **bawdier, bawdiest**
Language that is **bawdy** contains humorous and rather coarse references to sex: *bawdy jokes* ▫ *singing bawdy songs.*

bawl /bɔːl/ *verb* (*informal*): **bawls, bawling, bawled**
1 Children **bawl** when they cry loudly: *Taking a deep breath, the baby began to bawl his head off.* **2** Someone **bawls** something when they shout it or yell it: *Rugby fans were still bawling songs in the street at 3 am.* ▫ *'Can't you watch where you're going?' he bawled.* ▫ *I'll hang up if you keep bawling down the phone like that.*

> ***phrasal verb***
> **bawl out 1** You **bawl** something **out** when you shout it or yell it: *Someone was bawling out the words of 'I belong to Glasgow'.* **2** Someone **bawls** you **out** when they scold you angrily: *I was always being bawled out for driving too fast.* [compare **scold, rebuke, reprimand**]

bay[1] /beɪ/ *noun*: **bays**
A **bay** is **a** an inward curve in a coastline: *Dublin Bay* ▫ *We landed in a little bay a mile or so from Tintagel.* **b** an area or space enclosed or partly enclosed *eg* by a painted line or partition of some kind, used or reserved for a special purpose: *A certain number of parking bays are reserved for the sole use of medical staff.* ▫ *Leave the loading bay clear.*

bay[2] /beɪ/ *noun*
▻ ***phrase*** You **keep** something frightening or unwanted **at bay** when you prevent it from reaching you or affecting you: *His weekly visits were just enough to keep loneliness at bay.*

bay[3] /beɪ/ *verb*: **bays, baying, bayed**
A dog or wolf **bays** when it makes a howling sound.

bayonet /ˈbeɪənɪt/ *noun*: **bayonets**
A **bayonet** is a steel blade that can be fixed to the end of a soldier's rifle, for use as a weapon.

bay window /beɪ ˈwɪndoʊ/ *noun*: **bay windows**
A **bay window** is a three-sided or rounded window that projects from the outside wall of a house: *In the dining room, a bay window overlooks the front lawn.*

bazaar /bəˈzɑː(r)/ *noun*: **bazaars**
1 A **bazaar** is a sale of goods to raise money for a particular organization, purpose or charity. **2** In the Middle East, a **bazaar** is a market place, or an area of shops.

be[1] /biː/ *verb* (*present tense:* **I am** (or **I'm**), you **are** (or you**'re**), she, he or it **is** (or she**'s**, he**'s**, it**'s**) we **are** (or we**'re**), they **are** (or they**'re**); *present participle* **being**, *past participle* **been**, *infinitive, imperative and subjunctive* **be**; *past tense:* **I was**, you **were**, he, she or it **was**, we **were**, they **were**; *negative forms:* **aren't**, **isn't**, **wasn't**, **weren't**; you can also use 'you**'re not**, 'it**'s not**' and so on)

> Notice that in BrE the negative question form of **'I'm not'** is **'aren't** I?'.

You use **be 1** to link a subject with what you want to say about it: *He's a doctor.* ▫ *Jennifer's ill.* ▫ *That book wasn't mine.* ▫ *The time is now 5.25.* ▫ *Is he Hungarian?* ▫ *How old are you?* ▫ *I'm sixteen.* ▫ *I'm glad to have been useful.* ▫ *Being already half asleep she merely grunted.* **2** to talk about the position, place, time, situation or movements of someone or something: *She's still in hospital.* ▫ *Where's my purse?* ▫ *Here are your gloves.* ▫ *The meeting is at 2.15 in the conference room.* ▫ *Lunch will be early today.* ▫ *I'll be home this evening about six.* ▫ *We'll be there by 7.30.* ▫ *We weren't back till very late.* ▫ *Could you wait for me? I'll only be another five minutes.* ▫ *She's off to Boston on Sunday.* ▫ *'Where are you from?' 'I'm from Peru.'* ▫ *I've never been to Peru.* ▫ *The children had all been to the museum before.* ▫ *Having been in that situation herself, she could sympathize.* [see also **been**] **3** before names or proper nouns, to identify a person, place or thing: *I'm Dr Wilson.* ▫ *Is that the Tower of London?* ▫ *This is France, remember.* **4** to talk about choosing jobs: *She's decided to be a nurse.* ▫ *What do you want to be when you grow up?* **5** to talk about people's behaviour: *I'm being as patient as I can be.* ▫ *Stop being silly.* ▫ *Do be quiet!* ▫ *Don't be so unhelpful.* ▫ *Be brave!* ▫ *Just be yourself.* **6** with *it* **a** to talk about such things as the time, weather, environment, or a particular situation: *It was a bright sunny day.* ▫ *It's lovely and warm in here.* ▫ *Isn't it quiet?* ▫ *It's a shame you can't come.* ▫ *It's quicker to take the underground.* **b** to re-arrange a sentence so as to put emphasis on a particular part of it, *eg*, instead of '*You should contact the Department of Employment*' you can say: *'It's the Department of Employment you should contact.'* **7** with *there*, to refer to the existence or presence of things, people or circumstances: *Is there such a person as Santa Claus?* ▫ *There's food in the fridge for you.* ▫ *There was a crowd of photographers at the gate.* ▫ *Are there any paper clips?* ▫ *I don't want there to be any problems.* **8** by itself, to avoid repetition **a** in referring to something already mentioned: *Phyllis is in agreement with us but Peter isn't.* ▫ *I'm not a smoker myself. Are you?* **b** in answers: *'Are they ready?' 'No, they aren't* (or *they're not*).*'* ▫ *'He's really nice.' 'So he is* (not *he's*).*'* **c** in question tags: *You're OK, aren't you?* ▫ *They weren't very friendly, were they?* ▫ *'Phil's in Nepal.' 'He's not, is he?'*

be² /biː/ *auxiliary verb* (see **be**[1] for the parts, short forms and negative forms)
You use **be**
1 with the present participle of another verb **a** to form its continuous tenses: *The children are playing in the garden.* □ *while I was peeling the potatoes* □ *I've been waiting half an hour already.* □ *We've been seeing a lot of each other recently.* □ *I heard they'd been making enquiries.* **b** to refer to future plans or intentions: *I'm meeting him for lunch tomorrow.* □ *We're leaving at 7.00 in the morning.* □ *We were setting off very early so we packed the night before.* **c** with *will, would, shall, should* and expressions such as *likely to*, to refer to plans and intentions for activities sometime in the future, whether continuous or not: *I wonder what we'll be doing this time tomorrow?* □ *I thought I'd be seeing her the following week.* □ *Are you likely to be passing a chemist's on your way home?* □ *When will you be collecting it?*
2 with the past participle of another verb **a** to form its passive: *I'm forced to agree.* □ *The film was shown last night.* □ *He's been injured.* □ *They had been warned not to mention it.* □ *When will it be collected?* □ *Surely it will have been repaired by then?* □ *I suggest that David be* (or *should be*) *asked to take the chair.* □ *Having been disappointed before I was cautious about agreeing.* **b** combined with *being* to express the continuous passive: *She's being trained as a dancer.* □ *We were being given a special demonstration.*
3 before *to* and an infinitive to say what is expected to happen, what you intend to happen, what might happen, what fate decides, to wonder what to do, and to give orders: *He is to arrive in Britain today.* □ *She was to have arrived at 5.00 but her train was late.* □ *He was to have been speaking today, but he couldn't get here in time.* □ *This food is to last over the weekend.* □ *If they were to increase my salary I might stay.* □ *The expedition was to end in disaster.* □ *What on earth am I to tell her parents?* □ *You're to do as I say!* □ *Hospital Property. Not to be Removed.*

beach /biːtʃ/ *noun*: **beaches**
A **beach** is a flat sandy or stony area beside a sea or lake: *She'd gone down to the beach for a swim.* [*same as* **shore**]

beacon /ˈbiːkən/ *noun*: **beacons**
A **beacon** is a fire or light on a hill or tower, that can be seen from a long distance away and gives a signal or warning.

bead /biːd/ *noun* (*often in the plural*): **beads**
1 Beads are little balls of glass, wood or some other material, with a hole through the middle, that are threaded on to a piece of string or wire to form necklaces and bracelets: *a string of beads* □ *She was wearing her red wooden beads.* **2** A **bead** of liquid is a small drop: *Beads of sweat broke out on his forehead.*

beady /ˈbiːdɪ/ *noun*: **beadier, beadiest**
Beady eyes are small, round and bright: *a little sparrow with darting beady eyes* □ *She fixed me suddenly with a beady stare.*

beak /biːk/ *noun*: **beaks**
A bird's **beak** is the hard projecting part of its mouth, with a pointed or rounded end: *It was carrying a worm in its beak.*

beaker /ˈbiːkə(r)/ *noun*: **beakers**
A **beaker** is a plastic cup without a handle.

beam /biːm/ *noun*; *verb*
▷ ***noun***: **beams**
1 A **beam** is a long thick straight piece of wood, used *eg* in a building to support a roof or ceiling. **2** A **beam** of light is a line, ray or shaft of it, coming from a source such as the sun, the moon or a torch: *The fox was caught momentarily in the beam of her headlights.* □ *laser beams.* [*same as* **ray, shaft**] **3** Someone gives you a **beam** when they smile brightly at you: *He gave me a beam of approval.*
▷ ***verb***: **beams, beaming, beamed**
1 People **beam** when they smile brightly: *She beamed at me from behind her huge spectacles.* **2** Signals **are beamed** somewhere when they are sent there by radio waves: *now that satellite TV is being beamed into homes all across Europe.*

bean /biːn/ *noun* (*often in the plural*): **beans**
Beans are **a** the pods of various climbing plants, or the fleshy seeds contained in them, eaten as a vegetable: *french beans* □ *broad beans* □ *soya beans.* [see picture at **vegetable**, see also **baked beans**] **b** the seeds of other plants, used for various purposes, *eg* for making drinks: *Get me a pound of coffee beans.*
▷ ***phrases*** **1** (*informal*) People are **full of beans** when they are feeling cheerful and lively. **2** (*informal*) You **spill the beans** when you tell someone something that has been kept a secret: *If he spills the beans about you, you'll never get another job in banking.*

beansprout /ˈbiːnspraʊt/ *noun* (*usually in the plural*): **beansprouts**
Beansprouts are small shoots that grow from beans and are served as a vegetable, especially in Chinese cookery.

bear¹ /bɛə(r)/ *noun*: **bears**
A **bear** is a large, heavily built, four-legged animal with thick fur. [see also **polar bear, teddy**]

bear² /bɛə(r)/ *verb*: **bears, bearing, bore, borne**
1 You say you can't **bear** something if you hate or dislike it: *I can't bear cockroaches.* □ *I don't think I could bear a husband who snored.* □ *I never could bear waiting in a queue.* □ *I can't bear you being so unhappy.* □ *How can you bear to leave such a lovely place?* □ *I couldn't bear her to discover the truth.* [compare **stand**] **2** You **bear** something difficult or unpleasant when you manage to accept it and cope with it: *She bore the pain bravely.* □ *These financial burdens are more than our pockets can bear.* [compare **put up with, stand, tolerate**] **3** (*formal*) You **bear** something somewhere when you carry or take it there: *He arrived at the hospital bearing a large bunch of flowers.* **4** One thing **bears** the weight of another when it supports it: *That chair is too fragile to bear your weight.* **5** (*formal*) Trees or plants **bear** fruit or flowers when they produce them; something you have done **bears** fruit if it has useful results. **6** (*formal*) Women **bear** children when they give birth to them: *My grandmother had borne five children by the age of 26.*

> Notice that you use the form **born** when referring to someone's birth: *I was born* (not *borne*) *in 1940.*

7 (*formal*) You **bear** something such as responsibility if you have it: *Parents bear a heavy responsibility.* **8** (*literary*) A surface **bears** such things as writing or designs if they are on it: *The cover of the book bore a picture of the prince in a kilt.* □ *a card bearing the signatures of all her colleagues.* **9** (*literary*) One thing **bears** the marks, signs or traces of another if it shows evidence of them: *The room bore the signs of a struggle.* □ *His work bears all the marks of haste.* □ *Her cheeks bore traces of tears.* **10** You **bear** someone something such as malice, love or affection if you feel it towards them: *I bore him no ill will in spite of his dislike of me.* □ *She continued to bear him a grudge for not including her in the discussions.* **11** You **bear** left or right when you turn slightly to travel in that direction: *The road bore round to the left.* **12** One thing **bears** a relation or resemblance to another if they are noticeably similar: *The final draft of the constitution bore no relation to the original.* □ *She bore a striking resemblance to her great-grandmother.*

▻ ***phrase*** You **bring** *eg* pressure or influence **to bear** when you use it to try and get what you want: *Pressure was brought to bear on us to join the union.*

phrasal verbs

bear down on Someone or something **bears down on** you if they move towards you in a threatening way: *He saw her figure bearing down on him from the other end of the corridor.*

bear out One thing **bears out** another when it supports or confirms it: *Her allegations are not borne out by the facts.*

bear up You **bear up** when you remain strong and brave in a difficult or upsetting situation: *She's borne up wonderfully under the strain.*

bear with You **bear with** someone if you are patient with them: *Please bear with me while I get a few last-minute jobs done.*

bearable /ˈbɛərəbəl/ *adjective*

Something is **bearable** if you feel you can accept it and cope with it: *The pain subsided to a just-bearable ache.* □ *The separation was made more bearable by his frequent phone calls and letters.* [*opposite* **unbearable**]

beard /bɪəd/ *noun*: **beards**

A man's **beard** is the hair that grows on his chin and cheeks: *When did you grow your beard?* □ *a man with a pointed white beard.* — *adjective* **bearded:** *He was a tall bearded man.*

bearer /ˈbɛərə(r)/ *noun*: **bearers**

1 The **bearers** of a coffin or stretcher are the people carrying it: *The bearers raised the coffin between them.* **2** The **bearer** of something such as a letter or invitation is the person who brings it: *For once I'm the bearer of good news.* **3** (*formal*) The **bearer** of a document is the person who has it in their possession and has a right to it: *The bearer of the warrant is entitled to the shares specified.* **4** Someone who is the **bearer** of a name or title has that name: *He was looking for other bearers of the surname Garrideb.*

bearing /ˈbɛərɪŋ/ *noun*: **bearings**

(*uncount or used in the singular*) Your **bearing** is the way you stand and move: *an elderly gentleman of military bearing.*

▻ ***phrases*** **1** (*informal*) You **find**, or **get, your bearings** when you discover where you are, where you need to go, or what you need to do; you **lose your bearings** when you don't know where you are any more, and don't know what to do next: *the young child's attempts to find his or her bearings in a world of hidden meanings.* □ *It's only too easy to lose your bearings in the mist.* **2** One thing **has a bearing on** another if it affects it or is relevant to it: *That may be true, but it has no bearing on the issue we're discussing.*

beast /biːst/ *noun*: **beasts**

1 A **beast** is an animal, especially a large wild one. **2** (*rather old, informal*) If you call someone a **beast**, you are complaining about their cruel, mean or selfish behaviour.

beastly /ˈbiːstlɪ/ *adjective* (*rather old, informal*): **beastlier, beastliest**

1 Beastly describes anything unpleasant: *What a beastly day it is!* □ *I hated boarding school; it was beastly.* **2** Someone is **beastly** to you when they treat you meanly or unkindly: *She was beastly to her younger sister.*

beat /biːt/ *verb; noun*

▻ ***verb***: **beats, beating, beat, beaten** (notice that the past tense is **beat**)

1 a To **beat** someone is to hit them hard and repeatedly: *Riot police had beaten a student protester to death.* □ *He used to beat my mother black and blue.* □ *She would beat me with a bamboo stick for the slightest misdemeanour.* **b** Something **beats** on or against a surface when it hits it hard and continuously; you **beat** *eg* your fists on or against something when you keep hitting it with them: *He groaned and beat his fist against his forehead.* □ *A moth was beating itself against the hot glass of the electric bulb.* □ *The wind blustered and beat against the window.* □ *I woke to the sound of torrential rain beating down on the tin roof.* □ *He continued climbing, the hot sun beating down on his back.* **c** You **beat** a drum when you hit it rhythmically: *He led the marching column, beating a bass drum.* □ *Each morning the temple drummers beat a tattoo.* □ *They paraded the streets, drums beating and colours flying.* **d** You **beat** time when you move your hand or something you are holding up and down to mark the rhythm of the music you are listening to: *She beat time with her pencil.* **e** A bird or insect **beats** its wings when it moves them up and down: *The locust reduces speed by beating its wings less strongly.* **f** Your heart **beats** when it makes its regular movement: *His heart beat faster and a sudden sweat drenched him.* **g** You **beat** *eg* eggs or cream when you stir them fast and hard, *eg* with a fork or whisk: *Beat the eggs and cream together.* □ *Beat the mixture till smooth.* [*same as* **whip**]

2 a You **beat** someone in a game, competition or race when you defeat them: *He beat Jack Dempsey in the third round to win the world middleweight title.* □ *Surrey beat Lancashire by an innings and 25 runs.* □ *He used to let me beat him at chess.* □ *Kennedy was 43 when he beat Nixon to the White House.* [compare **defeat, win**] **b** You **beat** a record or score when you do better than it: *Our target is to beat last year's total.* [*same as* **surpass, exceed**] **c** You **beat** the clock when you complete a task in less than the time allowed. **d** If you say about something that you can't **beat** it, you mean that it's the best thing: *There's nothing to beat the sense of victory achieved through your own efforts.* □ *In my opinion you can't beat fresh strawberries and cream.* **e** You **beat** a disease or problem when you overcome it: *how to beat depression* □ *I gradually beat my craving for the drug.* [*same as* **overcome**]

▻ ***noun***: **beats**

A **beat** is **1** one of the regular movements of the heart or pulse: *Adam checked his pulse: 150 beats a minute.* □ *My heart missed a beat or two.* **2** one of the regular up-and-down movements of a bird's or insect's wing: *each beat of a butterfly's wing.* **3** the rhythm of a piece of music, or one of the sounds or notes that mark it: *the monotonous beat of pop music* □ *The drums took up a slower beat* □ *There are four beats in the bar.* □ *on the first beat of the next bar.* **4** the noise made by something striking a surface: *I heard hoof beats behind me.*

▻ ***phrases*** **1** For **beat about the bush** see **bush**. **2** For **beat a retreat** see **retreat**. **3** (*informal*) People **beat it** when they rush away, usually to avoid trouble: *Let's beat it, quick!* □ *Now beat it, you two, before I call the* *police.* **4** Someone **beats you to it** when they get to where you want to go, or do the thing you want to do, before you do: *There was only one girl I thought of asking to the dance, and someone beat me to it.* **5** (*informal*) If you say **'It beats me'** in reference to some question or circumstance, you mean you can't understand it: *What beats me is how he got into the hospital without anyone stopping him.* **6** A police officer is **on the beat** when he or she is on duty and is walking round, or patrolling, the area he or she is responsible for.

> ***phrasal verbs***
> **beat down** You **beat** someone **down** when you make them reduce the price of something you are buying from them: *He wanted £500 for the car but I beat him down to £450.* □ *I beat him down by £50.*
> **beat off** You **beat off** an attacker or rival when you get rid of them by fighting them in a determined way: *But they will have to beat off a challenge from the French.* □ *He could hardly have beaten off an armed attacker without suffering some sort of injury.* [*same as* **fight off**]
> **beat up** To **beat** someone **up** is to hit or kick them violently and repeatedly: *They threatened to beat me up if I went to the police.*

beating /ˈbiːtɪŋ/ *noun*: **beatings**
1 Someone gives you a **beating** when they hit you hard and repeatedly, with a stick or other object, usually as a punishment. **2** (*usually in the singular*) A team gets or takes a **beating** when it is soundly defeated.
▻ ***phrase*** If you say that something **takes a lot of beating**, or will **take some beating**, you mean that it is excellent, and you don't think there is likely to be anything better.

beautician /bjuːˈtɪʃən/ *noun*: **beauticians**
A **beautician** is a person who styles people's hair, treats their skin, polishes their nails and applies their make-up.

beautiful /ˈbjuːtɪfʊl/ *adjective*
1 A **beautiful** person is very attractive in appearance: *Flavia was beautiful, and I danced with her again and again* [*opposite* **plain, ugly**; compare **pretty, handsome**] **2** You describe something as **beautiful** if you find it very attractive, pleasant or delightful: *The view was amazingly beautiful.* □ *beautiful poetry* □ *the beautiful first movement of the symphony.* [*opposite* **ugly**] **3** You describe what someone does as **beautiful** if it is very clever or skilful: *She responded with a beautiful backhand return low over the net.* — *adverb* **beautifully:** *a beautifully designed kitchen* □ *He dances beautifully.*

beautify /ˈbjuːtɪfaɪ/ *verb*: **beautifies, beautifying, beautified**
You **beautify** something when you make its appearance more attractive: *The Council had been attempting to beautify the area by planting trees everywhere.*

beauty /ˈbjuːtɪ/ *noun*: **beauties**
1 (*uncount*) **Beauty** is the quality of being beautiful: *the summer landscape in all its beauty* □ *It was only when I re-read his poems recently that I began to appreciate their beauty.* **2** (*used in the plural*) The **beauties** of something are its delightful qualities or features: *I love Moscow, and think its beauties are many.* **3** A beautiful woman or girl is referred to as a **beauty**: *Dorothy had thick auburn hair and was considered a beauty.* **4** (*informal*) You call something a **beauty** if you think it is a splendid specimen: *He's bought himself a motor bike; it's a beauty.* **5** (*used in the singular*) You say that a certain feature is the **beauty** of some plan or device if you think that this feature is what makes it so good: *The beauty of it is that he'll never know who betrayed him.* **6** (*uncount, often adjectival*) **Beauty** describes products, publications and activities concerned with making people look attractive: *A lot of stores employ a beauty consultant.* □ *the beauty industry.*

beauty spot /ˈbjuːtɪ spɒt/ *noun*: **beauty spots**
A **beauty spot** is a place that is popular because of its natural beauty: *The family had been picnicking at a local beaty spot.*

became /bɪˈkeɪm/ *verb*
Became is the past tense of **become**.

because /bɪˈkɒz/ or /bɪˈkəz/ *conjunction*
You use **because** to give the reason for saying something, or for something happening or being so: *'Why can't I have one?''Because it's too expensive.'* □ *I hope you've got your own car; because if you haven't we may have to hire one.* □ *Because she was very young for her age we decided not to send her to school till she was six.* □ *I don't need to tell you your work is appreciated, because you know that.* □ *I objected not because I disapproved but because not everyone had been consulted.*
▻ ***phrase*** **Because of** is used as a preposition: *I won't be able to get to work on Monday because of the rail strike.* □ *He left his job because of the way he was being treated.* □ *Because of the holiday most of the shops were closed.* □ *We're in this mess purely because of your impatience.*

beck /bɛk/ *noun*
▻ ***phrase*** You are **at** someone's **beck and call** when you are always ready to carry out their orders or wishes: *He has several assistants at his beck and call.*

beckon /ˈbɛkən/ *verb*: **beckons, beckoning, beckoned**
1 You **beckon** someone, or **beckon** to them, when you signal to them to come to you, by gesturing with your hand or forefinger: *He beckoned the waitress over to his table.* □ *I suddenly realized he was beckoning to me urgently.* **2** A place or prospect **beckons** if you feel drawn towards it: *He preferred to make feature films, and Hollywood beckoned.*

become /bɪˈkʌm/ *verb*: **becomes, becoming, became**
You **become** something when you begin to be that thing: *We became friends at university.* □ *He became king in 1830, on the death of his brother.* □ *I was becoming more and more depressed.* □ *It was becoming increasingly clear that we would not meet the deadline.* □ *He'd become a cantankerous old man.* [*compare* **get**]
▻ ***phrase*** You wonder **what has become of** someone or something if you haven't heard of them for a long time, and wonder what has happened to them; you wonder **what will become** of someone if you are worried that something bad is going to happen to them: *By the way, what became of that book you were planning to write?* □ *I haven't a clue what became of him after he went off to Australia.* □ *The situation worsens by the hour and we have no idea what will become of us.*

becoming /bɪkʌmɪŋ/ *adjective* (*informal*)
Something such as a garment, hairstyle or colour that is **becoming** makes you look attractive: *When I met her again she was wearing her hair in a much more becoming style.*

bed /bɛd/ *noun*; *verb*
▻ ***noun*: beds**
1 (*count or uncount*) A **bed** is a piece of furniture for lying on when you sleep: *He sat down on the edge of my bed.* □ *I went to bed early that evening.* □ *It's time I put the children to bed.* □ *She was fast asleep in bed.* □ *I got out of bed to check on the baby.* [see picture at **bedroom**] **2** (*usually in the singular*) The **bed** of the sea, or of a lake or river, is the solid ground at the bottom of it: *the river bed* □ *the numerous wrecks littering the sea*

bed. [*same as* **bottom**] **3** A flower **bed** is an area of earth or soil in which you grow flowering plants: *rose beds.*

▻ ***phrases*** **1** You **go to bed with** someone when you have sexual intercourse with them. **2** You **make** a **bed** when you tidy it and pull up the sheets and covers after it has been slept in: *The children make their own beds.*

▻ ***verb***: **beds, bedding, bedded**

> ***phrasal verb***
> You **bed down** somewhere when you make yourself comfortable there and go to sleep: *He had to bed down on the sofa.*

bed and breakfast /bɛd ənd ˈbrɛkfəst/ *noun*: **bed and breakfasts**
1 (*uncount*) **Bed and breakfast** is overnight accommodation in a private house or guest house that includes breakfast: *Bed and breakfast is £15 per night.* **2** A **bed and breakfast** is a private house or guest house where people can stay overnight: *We stayed in a bed and breakfast near Thirsk.*

bedclothes /ˈbɛdkloʊðz/ *noun* (*plural*)
Bedclothes are the sheets, blankets and covers that you put on a bed: *She pushed back the bedclothes and got out.*

bedding /ˈbɛdɪŋ/ *noun* (*uncount*)
Bedding refers to the sheets, blankets, covers, pillow, and sometimes also the mattress, that you use on a bed: *She fetched bedding from the cupboard.*

bedevil /bɪˈdɛvəl/ *verb*: **bedevils, bedevilling** (*AmE* **bedeviling**), **bedevilled** (*AmE* **bedeviled**)
You **are bedevilled** by something if it continually causes you difficulties, problems or trouble: *He has been bedevilled by injury this season.*

bedfellow /ˈbɛdfɛloʊ/ *noun*: **bedfellows**
Two people or things that are referred to as **bedfellows** have become associated with each other in some way: *They make unlikely bedfellows.*

bedlam /ˈbɛdləm/ *noun* (*uncount; informal*)
If you describe place or situation as **bedlam** you mean that it is noisy, confused and disorderly. [*same as* **pandemonium**]

bedraggled /bɪˈdragəld/ *adjective*
People or animals that are **bedraggled** are in an untidy, wet or dirty state: *crowds of bedraggled refugees fleeing eastward.*

bedridden /ˈbɛdrɪdən/ *adjective*
Someone who is **bedridden** is so old, ill or disabled that they cannot get out of bed.

bedrock /ˈbɛdrɒk/ *noun* (*uncount*)
The **bedrock** of something is the basic principle, idea or theory on which it rests or depends: *For many, still, marriage and children are the bedrock of existence.*

bedroom /ˈbɛdru:m/ *noun*: **bedrooms**
A **bedroom** is a room for sleeping in: *a house with four bedrooms.*

bedside /ˈbɛdsaɪd/ *noun* (*used in the singular*)
The **bedside** is the area beside a bed: *She sat in a chair at his bedside.* □ *a bedside lamp.*□ bedside table.

bedsitter /ˈbɛdsɪtə(r)/ *noun* (*BrE*): **bedsitters**
A **bedsitter** or **bedsit** is a furnished room that you rent, for living, sleeping and eating in: *I had a bedsit not far from college.*

bedspread /ˈbɛdsprɛd/ *noun*: **bedspreads**
A **bedspread** is a decorative top cover for a bed.

bedtime /ˈbɛdtaɪm/ *noun* (*uncount or count*): **bedtimes**
Your **bedtime** is the time at which you usually go to bed: *It's long past my bedtime.* □ *Mealtimes and bedtimes were becoming irregular.*

bee /bi:/ *noun*: **bees**
A **bee** is a black-and-yellow-striped insect that buzzes as it flies, lives in large groups, and makes honey.

▻ ***phrase*** If you say that someone has **a bee in their bonnet** about something, you mean that they are particularly, or too, concerned about it.

beech /bi:tʃ/ *noun* (*often adjectival*): **beeches**
1 (*count or uncount*) A **beech**, or **beech tree**, is a tree with smooth silver-grey bark: *The path took us through a beech wood.* □ *a row of beeches.* □ *forests of beech.* **2** (*uncount*) **Beech** is the wood of the beech tree: *beech furniture.*

beef /bi:f/ *noun* (*uncount*)
Beef is the meat of a bull, cow or ox: *roast beef* □ *beef stock.*

beefburger /ˈbi:fbɜ:gə(r)/ *noun*: **beefburgers**
A **beefburger** is a flat round cake of minced beef, usually fried or grilled and served in a bread roll.

beefy /ˈbi:fɪ/ *adjective* (*informal*): **beefier, beefiest**
A **beefy** person is large and muscular: *a couple of beefy rugby players.*

beehive /ˈbi:haɪv/ *noun*: **beehives**
A **beehive** is a box-like hut that bees are kept in, where they make and store their honey, and from which it can be collected.

beekeeper /ˈbi:ki:pə(r)/ *noun*: **beekeepers**
A **beekeeper** is a person who keeps bees for their honey.

beeline /ˈbi:laɪn/ *noun*
▻ ***phrase*** (*usually humorous*) You **make a beeline for** a particular place when you go towards it by the quickest and most direct route: *She made a beeline for an unoccupied chair in the corner.*

been /bi:n/ or /bɪn/ *verb*
1 Been is the past participle of **be**. [see **be**[1] and **be**[2]] **2** You use **been** with *have*, *has* and *had* to refer to people's movements, *eg* **a** you **have been** to a place if you have visited it: *I haven't been to Portugal.* □ *They'd been to France before.* **b** you **have been** somewhere such as to school or church if you have been attending it: *We've already been to church once today.* □ *He hasn't been to work for eight weeks.*

> Notice the difference between **been** and **gone**: *They've been to Spain on holiday* [and have come back now]. But: *They've gone to Spain on holiday* [and are still there]. *She hasn't been to school today.* But: *She's gone to school* [and is still there].

c Someone such as the postman, milkman or dustman **has been** when they have called at your house: *Has the postman been yet?*

beer /ˈbɪə(r)/ *noun*: **beers**
1 (*uncount*) **Beer** is a bitter alcoholic drink made from grain, sugar and water. **2** A **beer** is a glass, can or bottle of beer: *He had a couple of beers with his lunch.*

beet /bi:t/ *noun*: **beets**
1 (*uncount*) **Beet** is a root vegetable that is given to animals as food, and used as a source of sugar. **2** (*AmE*) A **beet** is a beetroot.

beetle /ˈbi:təl/ *noun*: **beetles**
A **beetle** is an insect whose front wings have developed into a hard shell-like covering for its back wings.

beetroot /ˈbi:tru:t/ *noun* (*count or uncount*): **beetroots**

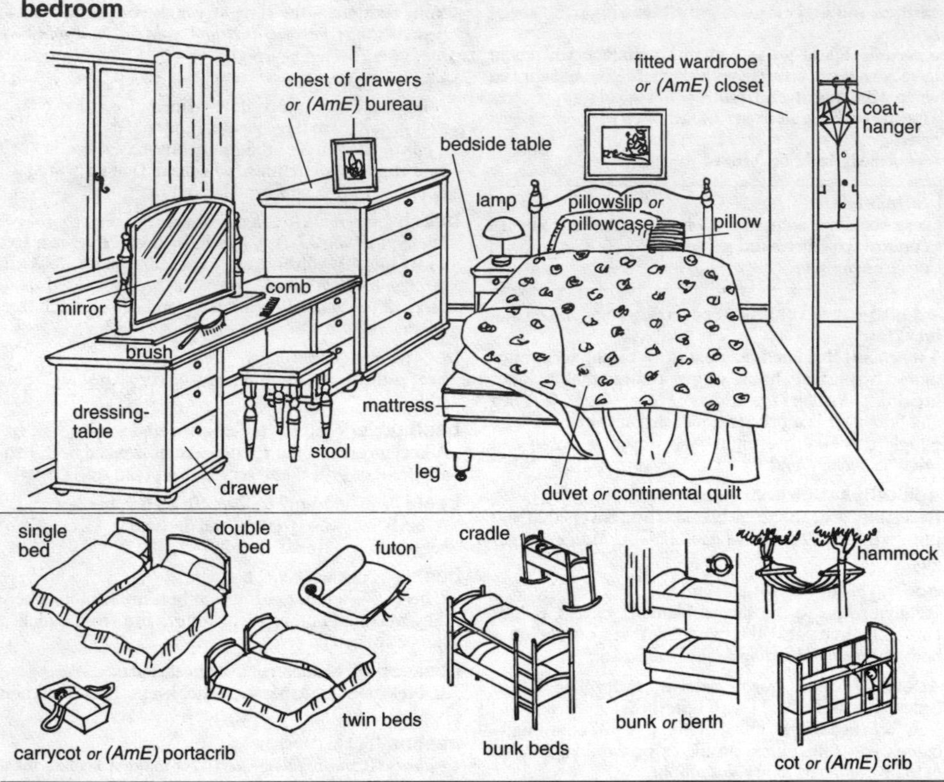

A **beetroot** is a round, juicy, dark red root vegetable that is cooked or pickled before eating, and often used in salads.

befall /bɪˈfɔːl/ *verb* (*literary*): **befalls, befalling, befell, befallen**
Something unlucky or unfortunate **befalls** you when it happens to you: *Whenever the children were late home she would imagine that some harm had befallen them.*

befit /bɪˈfɪt/ *verb* (*formal*): **befits, befitting, befitted**
Behaviour or treatment that **befits** you, is appropriate for you, or suitable to your rank or position: *She led the procession of mourners, as befitted the man's closest relative.* ▫ *The place had the air of a royal residence, befitting a Renaissance prince.*

before /bɪˈfɔː(r)/ *preposition or conjunction; preposition; adverb*
▻ ***preposition or conjunction***
1 You do one thing **before** you do another if you do it first or earlier, or if you do it as a preparation or precaution: *She had been an actress before becoming a model.* ▫ *Come and see me before you leave.* ▫ *Warm the pot before you put the tea bags in.* ▫ *You should think carefully before giving up your job.* [= don't give it up unless you're certain it's the right thing to do] **2** You do something **before** someone else if you beat them by doing it first: *Amundsen got to the South Pole before Scott.* ▫ *I finished before him.* ▫ *The Chinese were grinding lenses long before Europeans started using glass to improve vision.* **3** You do one thing **before** another happens if you do it to stop the other thing happening: *I'll write it down in my diary before I forget.* ▫ *We'd better eat that fruit before it goes bad.* **4** One thing happens **before** another can happen if it happens too quickly or too soon for the other to happen: *The car disappeared into the distance before I could take down its number.* ▫ *He rang off before I'd finished speaking.* **5** Something happens **before** very much time has passed if it happens soon: *Before many weeks had passed* [= after only a few weeks] *she found she was becoming quite proficient on the keyboard.*
▻ ***preposition***
1 Something happens **before** a certain time or a certain event if it happens earlier than it: *I'll try to arrive before noon.* ▫ *We must get home before dark.* ▫ *I'm bound to see you sometime before your departure.* ▫ *I ought to have contacted you before now.* **2** One thing is **before** another in time or in order if it comes first: *the day before yesterday* ▫ *in 'gauge', 'a' comes before 'u'.* ▫ *I think you were before me in the queue.* **3** (*formal or literary*) Something is **before** you if it faces you: *Before them was a solid wall of rock.* [*same as* **in front of**] **4** (*formal*) You do something **before** someone when you do it in their presence: *performing before Her Majesty the Queen* ▫ *summoned to give evidence before a court of law.* [*same as* **in front of**] **5** A task or experience that is **before** you is one that you still have to deal with or have: *I've got weeks of hard work before me.* ▫ *with the prospect of a long holiday before me.* [*same as* **ahead of, in front of**] **6** You put one thing **before** another if you treat it as more important than the other: *Should you put your career before your family?*
▻ ***adverb***
1 Something has happened **before**, or you have done it **before**, if it already has happened, or you have already

done it, at an earlier time, or on a previous occasion: *Haven't we met before?* □ *I've never been skiing before.* □ *Having been let down by her before, I was rather cautious about agreeing.* □ *I ought to have written before, but I've been so busy.* [*same as* **previously**, **earlier**] **2** You use **before** instead of *ago* when looking further back into the past from a point in the past: *I'd last heard from him about two years before.* [*same as* **earlier**] **3** The day, week, month, or year **before** is the one earlier than the one just mentioned: *I had been to Poland the year before.* □ *It had rained the night before.* [*same as* **previous**]

▻ ***phrase*** For **before long** see **long**.

beforehand /bɪˈfɔːhand/ *adverb*
You do something **beforehand** when you do it before, especially in preparation for, a certain event: *Mum had done most of the cooking beforehand, so we weren't tied to the kitchen.* □ *She'd left suddenly, without telling anyone beforehand of her plans.* [*same as* **in advance**]

befriend /bɪˈfrɛnd/ *verb*: **befriends, befriending, befriended**
You **befriend** someone when you make friends with them and treat them kindly: *When they arrived in Paris they were befriended by various members of the intellectual set.*

befuddle /bɪˈfʌdəl/ *verb*: **befuddles, befuddling, befuddled**
You **are befuddled** when you are confused and can't think clearly.

beg /bɛg/ *verb*: **begs, begging, begged**
1 You **beg** someone to do something, or **beg** them for something, when you ask them eagerly or anxiously: *They begged her to stay for a meal.* □ *I begged to be allowed to go with them.* □ *I might try begging the college for financial assistance.* □ *'Please tell me what's wrong,' she begged.* **2** Poor people **beg** when they ask others for *eg* money or food: *Crippled children sat begging at the supermarket entrances.* □ *They begged for small change from the shoppers.* □ *We used to beg bread from the baker.* [see also **beggar**]

▻ ***phrase*** For **I beg your pardon** see **pardon**.

began /bɪˈgan/ *verb*
Began is the past tense of **begin**.

beget /bɪˈgɛt/ *verb* (*literary*): **begets, begetting, begot, begotten**
One thing **begets** another when it causes it: *War begets poverty and disease.*

beggar /ˈbɛgə(r)/ *noun*: **beggars**
A **beggar** is a person who lives by asking other people for money and food.

begin /bɪˈgɪn/ *verb*: **begins, beginning, began, begun**
1 You **begin** to do something when you do something that you were not doing before, and continue doing it: *I'm beginning to wonder if I was wrong.* □ *It was just beginning to rain.* □ *Personal contacts begin to be built up.* □ *She went upstairs to begin packing.* □ *The eggs all begin developing at the same time.* [*same as* **start**; *opposite* **stop**, **finish**; compare **commence**] **2** Something **begins a** when it happens or takes place from a certain time: *We sat waiting for the ceremonial to begin.* □ *The entertainment was due to begin at 8.30.* □ *The fun was only just beginning.* □ *Work was about to begin on a new hotel.* [*same as* **commence**] **b** when it comes into existence: *The universe actually did begin with a Big Bang.* **c** if it has its edge or boundary somewhere: *The Highlands begin at Dunkeld.* □ *This is where the Pyrenees really begin.* [*same as* **start**; *opposite* **finish**, **end**] **3** You **begin** something when you start doing or dealing with it, or set it going: *I begin work at 8.30am.* □ *getting out of bed to begin the day* □ *We sat down to begin our meal.* □ *Begin each question at the top of a page.* □ *Most specialists begin their analysis in the same basic way.* □ *I didn't want to begin another chapter.* □ *We begin rehearsals in a week's time.* □ *They were threatening to begin legal proceedings.* [*same as* **start**; *opposite* **finish**, **end**] **4** You **begin** when you start doing something, *eg* speaking, or explaining or discussing something: *It's difficult to know where to begin.* □ *It's time we began.* □ *Begin again.* □ *Begin by carefully analysing the question.* □ *'But you can't -' began Lesley.* [*same as* **start**; *opposite* **end, finish**]

▻ ***phrases*** (*informal*) Something that you **do not**, or **cannot**, **begin to** do is something that you do not or cannot do at all: *for reasons I can't begin to understand* □ *You don't even begin to see the point, do you?*

phrasal verb
begin with 1 Something **begins with** a certain thing, or you **begin** it **with**, or **begin with**, that thing **a** if it acts as an introduction: *Let me begin with a quotation.* □ *Each chapter began with a little verse.* □ *We begin each section with a brief summary of its contents.* **b** if it is the first item to be dealt with: *We begin with the minutes of the last meeting.* **c** if it forms its first element: *'Pneumonia' begins with a 'p'.* □ *I'd been taught never to begin a sentence with 'And'.* **2** Something is the case 'to **begin with**' if it is the case at first, or in the early stages of something: *I quite enjoyed her company, at least to begin with.* [*same as* **at first, to start with**] **3** You use 'to **begin with**' to introduce the first of several reasons or arguments: *To begin with, it would have meant putting the dog in quarantine.* [*same as* **to start with**]

beginner /bɪˈgɪnə(r)/ *noun*: **beginners**
A **beginner** is someone who has just started to learn how to do something: *She's in the beginners' class.*

beginning /bɪˈgɪnɪŋ/ *noun*: **beginnings**
1 The **beginning** of something is **a** (*usually in the singular*) the first part or first stage of it: *The beginning of term is always a bit disorganized.* □ *Do see the film, and don't be put off by the beginning.* [*opposite* **end**] **b** (*usually in the singular*) its process of starting: *Perhaps we're witnessing the beginning of a new era.* [*opposite* **end**] **c** (*uncount or used in the singular*) the point at which it starts: *You'll have to start from the beginning again, I'm afraid.* □ *We're off to the States at the beginning of July.* □ *Her story was a pack of lies from beginning to end.* [*opposite* **end**] **2** (*used in the plural*) The **beginnings** of something are its early stages of development: *I was having the beginnings of an idea.*

▻ ***phrase*** You use **in** or **at the beginning** to refer to the early stages of a situation: *But surely you knew that at the beginning?* [*same as* **at the start**; compare **to start with, to begin with**]

begot /bɪˈgɒt/ *verb*
Begot is the past tense of **beget**.

begotten /bɪˈgɒtən/ *verb*
Begotten is the past participle of **beget**.

begrudge /bɪˈgrʌdʒ/ *verb*: **begrudges, begrudging, begrudged**
You say that you do not **begrudge** someone something if you are not jealous of them of them for having it, or think they don't deserve it: *Why begrudge him his success?*

beguiling /bɪˈgaɪlɪŋ/ *adjective*
Something that is **beguiling** seems delightful but may have dangers or disadvantages: *the beguiling prospect*

of a free cruise round the Greek islands [*same as* **tempting, seductive**]

begun /bɪ'gʌn/ *verb*
Begun is the past participle of **begin**.

behalf /bɪ'hɑːf/ *noun*
▻ ***phrase*** You do something **on behalf of** someone, or **on** someone's **behalf**, when you do it for them and as their representative: *I'm speaking now on behalf of the whole society.* □ *His wife accepted the prize on his behalf.*

behave /bɪ'heɪv/ *verb*: **behaves, behaving, behaved**
1 You **behave**, **behave** yourself, or **behave** well, when you act in a way that people approve of, and are *eg*, kind, considerate, polite or obedient; children who behave well are described as well-**behaved** and those who behave badly as badly-**behaved**: *Children who behave badly are rejecting adult values.* □ *I've really tried to behave better.* □ *Most people behave worst in their own homes.* □ *Now behave yourself and don't get your frock grubby.* □ *I'll behave myself in future.* □ *I promise I'll behave.* □ *They were polite, well-behaved boys.* **2** People **behave** in a certain way when they act in that way: *Most landowners don't behave aggressively.* □ *Try to behave as normally as possible.* □ *He had behaved improperly in failing to inform Parliament.* □ *How you behave to people affects the way they behave back.* □ *He returned to the lab and behaved as if nothing had happened* □ *They treat us like adults and expect us to behave as such.* □ *People can't just behave as they want to.* □ *I can't bear to see you behave like this towards each other.* □ *Gods always behave like the people who make them.* **3** Things **behave** in a certain way under certain circumstances if they react or respond in that way: *understanding why chemical compounds behave as they do* □ *Electrons behave as if they were miniature spinning tops.*

behaviour (*AmE* **behavior**) /bɪ'heɪvjə(r)/ *noun* (*uncount*)
1 A person's **behaviour** is the way they behave: *Had you noticed anything strange about his behaviour recently?* □ *Her behaviour is intolerable.* □ *the typical behaviour of a rejected child.* **2** The **behaviour** of a thing in certain circumstances is the way it responds or reacts: *I've been studying the behaviour of certain elements at high temperatures.*
▻ ***phrase*** People are **on their best behaviour** when they are behaving as well, helpfully, or politely as they can.

behead /bɪ'hɛd/ *verb*: **beheads, beheading, beheaded**
Someone **is beheaded** when they are executed by having their head cut off: *King Henry had two of his wives beheaded.*

beheld /bɪ'hɛld/ *verb*
Beheld is the past tense and past participle of **behold**.

behind /bɪ'haɪnd/ *preposition or adverb*; *preposition*; *adverb*; *noun*
▻ ***preposition or adverb***
1 One thing is **behind** another if it faces the back of the other, or is at the back of it: *I was sitting behind a woman in a large hat.* □ *There is a small shed behind the garage.* □ *She hid behind a bush.* □ *She heard footsteps behind her.* □ *It's a nice house with a big garden behind.* □ *I walked along the ledge with Jim following a few steps behind.* [*opposite* **in front of, in front, ahead of, ahead**] **2** You leave a place or thing in a particular state **behind** you if that is the state it is in when you have been there or passed through: *Remember to lock the door behind you.* □ *The workmen always leave such a mess behind them.* □ *clearing up the muddle left behind by the previous government.* **3** You put something **behind** you when you try to forget it, or leave it in the past: *I'm glad to say those problems are all behind me now.* □ *He's put his accident behind him.* □ *years later, when we had all left our schooldays behind.* **4** One place is a particular number of hours **behind** another when the time is that many hours earlier there: *We're eight hours behind Singapore.* □ *Don't forget New York is about seven hours behind.* [*opposite* **ahead of, ahead**] **5** You are **behind** schedule, or **behind** other people, if you have not progressed as fast as you should have done, or as fast or well as other people: *The train is thirty minutes behind schedule.* □ *I've been falling behind with my work this week.* □ *He finished several seconds behind the leaders.* [*opposite* **ahead of, ahead**]
▻ ***preposition***
1 You are **behind** someone if you support them: *We're all behind you in your decision.* **2** One thing is **behind** another if it is the cause of it or is responsible for it: *What were the reasons behind the change of policy?* □ *Who's behind all this?* □ *the lady behind London's new telephone codes.* **3** Something lies **behind** a surface if it is concealed by it: *There's a passionate personality behind that calm exterior of hers.*
▻ ***adverb***
1 You leave something **behind** when you forget to take it with you, or decide not to take it: *It's amazing the things people leave behind on the bus.* □ *I'm afraid we'll have to leave the dog behind.* **2** You stay **behind** when you stay after everyone else has left: *Could you stay behind for a few minutes after the meeting? I'd like a word with you.*
▻ ***noun***: **behinds**
Your **behind** is the part of your body that you sit on. [*same as* **bottom, buttocks**]
▻ ***phrase*** For **behind someone's back** see **back**.

behold /bɪ'hoʊld/ *verb* (*literary*): **beholds, beholding, beheld**
You **behold** someone or something when you see them or look at them: *Never before had I beheld anyone so wretched.* □ *The ruins of the opera house were a melancholy sight to behold.*

beholden /bɪ'hoʊldən/ *adjective* (*formal*)
You are **beholden** to someone when you are in their debt for something they have done for you: *I don't like to be beholden to anyone; I like to be my own boss* [*same as* **indebted**]

beige /beɪʒ/ *noun*; *adjective*
▻ ***noun*** (*uncount or count*)
Beige is a very pale brown colour: *You shouldn't wear so much beige.* □ *a mixture of creams and beiges.*
▻ ***adjective:*** *a beige cotton jacket.*

being /'biːɪŋ/ *noun*; *verb*
▻ ***noun***: **beings**
A **being** is any creature, especially a person of some kind: *human beings* □ *imaginary beings* □ *Is there such a being as the Devil?* □ *strange beings from other worlds.*
▻ ***verb***
Being is the present participle of **be**. [see **be**[1] *and* **be**[2]]
▻ ***phrase*** Something is **in being** when it exists; something comes **into being** when it begins to exist: *The company came into being in 1897.*

belated /bɪ'leɪtɪd/ *adjective*
A **belated** action happens later than it ought to have done: *Please accept my belated congratulations on your new job.* □ *He made a belated attempt to placate her.* — *adverb* **belatedly**: *He swore loudly, and apologized somewhat belatedly.*

belch /bɛltʃ/ *verb*; *noun*
▻ ***verb***: **belches, belching, belched**

1 To **belch** is to give out air noisily from the stomach through the mouth: *The baby belched.* [*same as* **burp**] **2** A chimney or volcano **belches** *eg* smoke or flames when they pour out of it.

▻ ***noun***: **belches:** *He gave a belch and apologized.* [*same as* **burp**]

beleaguered /bɪ'li:gəd/ *adjective*

1 A **beleaguered** person faces so much difficulty, opposition and criticism that they seem to be under attack from all directions. **2** A **beleaguered** place is surrounded, or being beseiged, by enemies: *in the beleaguered city of Bihac.*

belfry /'bɛlfrɪ/ *noun*: **belfries**

A church **belfry** is a tower in which the bells are hung.

belie /bɪ'laɪ/ *verb*: **belies, belying, belied**

One thing **belies** another **1** when it shows it to be untrue or false: *Such statistics belie the myth of an enormously popular President.* **2** when it makes it seem surprising: *Her obvious energy belies her age.*

belief /bɪ'li:f/ *noun* (*count or uncount*): **beliefs**

Belief is a feeling of certainty that something exists, is so, or is right and good: *our belief in God* ▫ *It's my belief that the original design was faulty.* ▫ *people who have died for their religious beliefs* ▫ *His belief in himself helped him to achieve the impossible.* [compare **faith**]

▻ ***phrases*** **1** You do something **in the belief that** something is so when your action depends on its being so: *I locked up the building and set the alarm, in the belief that everyone was out.* **2** Something that is **beyond belief** is extraordinary: *Her arrogance is beyond belief.* ▫ *She was patient beyond belief with his moods.* [*same as* **incredible, incredibly**]

believable /bɪ'li:vəbəl/ *adjective*

Something that is **believable** could exist or be true: *That's the first believable explanation I've heard.* ▫ *There wasn't a single believable character in that play.* [*same as* **plausible, likely**; *opposite* **unlikely**]

believe /bɪ'li:v/ *verb*: **believes, believing, believed**

1 You **believe** that something is so **a** if you know or remember that it is, or have information that it is: *I believe he's an inspector of mines.* ▫ *She's in hospital at present, I believe.* ▫ *I don't believe you've met my mother, Peter?* ▫ *'Did you tell her?' 'I don't believe I did, no.'* ▫ *'Is he applying?' 'I believe so.'* ▫ *'Has she any experience?' 'I don't believe so* (or *I believe not*).*'* [*same as* **think**; see note at **think**] **b** if you have formed the opinion that it is: *We believe higher standards of care are required.* ▫ *It is believed that an electrical appliance may have started the fire,* ▫ *Incidents like this are commoner than most people believe.* ▫ *I believed him to be an evil person.* [*same as* **think, consider**] **c** (*usually with a negative*) if you accept it as the truth: *You can't believe how badly he drives.* ▫ *You won't believe what's happened.* ▫ *I would never have believed him capable of such kindness.* ▫ *How can she believe herself in love with a man like that?* ▫ *I don't believe it was a coincidence.* **2** You **believe** a story, or something you are told, if you accept it as the truth: *We believed everything the grown-ups told us.* ▫ *That's what she said, but I didn't believe a word of it.* ▫ *You may find it hard to believe, but he used to be very thin.* ▫ *'You've won!' 'I don't believe it!'* **3** You **believe** a person if you accept what they say as the truth: *Why was I fool enough to believe him?* ▫ *If you don't believe me go and see for yourself.* **4** You say you couldn't **believe** your eyes or ears when you are reporting something astonishing: *I could hardly believe my eyes when I looked out of the window.* ▫ *I listened to his story, scarcely able to believe my ears.*

▻ ***phrases*** **1** You say '**believe it or not**' when you are telling someone something you think will surprise them: *Believe it or not, I ended his life because I loved him.* **2** You use '**believe me**' to emphasize what you are saying: *You expect it to get easier, but believe me, it doesn't.* **3** People sometimes use '**would you believe**' when telling you something surprising: *He's 92, would you believe, and just as bright as ever.*

> ***phrasal verb***
>
> **believe in** You **believe in** people or things **1** if you believe that they exist or are a fact: *I believe in the effectiveness of prayer, but not in God.* ▫ *Do you believe in heaven and hell?* ▫ *those who believe in the immortality of the soul.* ▫ *I don't believe in miracles.* **2** if you are in favour of them or approve of them: *I didn't think pacifists believed in hurting people.* ▫ *We believe in hard work, plain food, simple clothes, and no luxury of any kind.* [*same as* **approve** of, **favour, encourage, recommend**] **3** if you put your faith and trust in them or their capabilities: *This proves that we were quite right to believe in her.* ▫ *I couldn't quite believe in this big idea of his.* [*same as* **trust**]

believer /bɪ'li:və(r)/ *noun*: **believers**

1 A **believer** in something is someone who thinks that it is good or worthwhile: *I'm a great believer in learning poetry by heart.* **2** A **believer** is someone who is religious, or believes in God. [*opposite* **atheist**]

belittle /bɪ'lɪtəl/ *verb*: **belittles, belittling, belittled**

You **belittle** someone or something if you make them seem unimportant or worthless: *I have never intended to belittle or humiliate her in public.*

bell /bɛl/ *noun*: **bells**

A **bell** is **a** a deep hollow metal object open at one end, with a piece of metal hanging inside it, that makes a ringing sound as it strikes the sides: *the sound of church bells.* **b** any other device that makes a ringing sound and is used *eg* to attract people's attention: *He rang the door bell.* ▫ *a bicycle bell.* [see picture at **bicycle**]

▻ ***phrase*** (*BrE informal*) You say that something **rings a bell** if it is familiar, or reminds you of something that you can't quite identify: *His name rings a bell.*

belligerent /bə'lɪdʒərənt/ *adjective*

A **belligerent** person is eager to fight or argue when other people oppose them or disagree with them: *The Scots were more audacious and belligerent than ever.* [*same as* **aggressive**] — *noun* (*uncount*) **belligerence:** *There was an unusual belligerence in her tone.* — *adverb* **belligerently:** *He glared belligerently at us.*

bellow /'bɛloʊ/ *verb*; *noun*

▻ ***verb***: **bellows, bellowing, bellowed**

1 To **bellow** is to shout loudly, or produce a shout of laughter: *The audience bellowed with laughter.* ▫ *Someone bellowed out his name.* ▫ *'Watch out!' he bellowed.* **2** A bull **bellows** when it makes its typical deep loud roar.

▻ ***noun***: **bellows:** *There was a bellow of mirth from next door.* ▫ *the distant bellow of a bull.*

bellows /'bɛloʊz/ *noun*: *plural* **bellows**

A **bellows** is a device for creating a current of air, *eg* for making a fire burn more strongly.

belly /'bɛlɪ/ *noun*: **bellies**

1 (*BrE*; *informal*) Your **belly** is your stomach: *a group of men with large bellies and hearty laughs.* **2** The **belly** of an animal is the downward-facing part of its body: *The cat crept along on its belly.*

belong /bɪ'lɒŋ/ *verb*: **belongs, belonging, belonged**

1 Something **belongs** to you if you own it: *Who* (or *whom*) *does the house belong to?* ▫ *Melanie thought* *that the gloves must belong to Uncle Philip.* □ *Would you take what doesn't belong to you?* □ *His lips were pretty enough to belong to a girl.* **2** People **belong** to each other when there is a loving and loyal relationship between them, or each has a need for the other: *You don't seem to belong to me any more.* □ *You two belong together, I can see that.* **3** One thing **belongs** to another if it is part of it: *This lid obviously belongs to another pan.* □ *Our past and present belong together, like two sides of the same coin.* **4** A person or thing **belongs** to a group if they are a member of it: *You get a feeling of belonging to a community.* □ *the right to belong to a trade union* □ *The rattlesnakes belong to the viper family.* □ *words belonging to a particular grammatical category.* **5** A person or thing **belongs** in a place if that is where they should be, or where they are known, accepted, or feel at home: *I don't really belong anywhere.* □ *No, I don't belong here; I'm only visiting.* □ *I didn't belong in her world of small talk and recipes.* □ *It's good to feel I belong again.* □ *Coffee cups belong in the top cupboard.* **6** Something or someone **belongs** to a certain period if that is when they lived, were made, or date from: *He was only a year older than me but seemed to belong to a different generation.* □ *Most of the tunes belong to the twenties.* — *noun* (*uncount*) **belonging:** *Their need for affection and a sense of belonging can be fulfilled.*

belongings /bɪ'lɒŋɪŋz/ *noun* (*plural*)
Your **belongings** are your personal possessions: *He packed his belongings and left.*

beloved *adjective*
1 /bɪ'lʌvɪd/ A **beloved** person or thing is one that you love very much: *her beloved Scotland* **2** /bɪ'lʌvd/ Someone or something that is **beloved** of or by people is greatly loved by them: *the Queen Mother, beloved of the Brtish public.*

below /bɪ'loʊ/ *preposition or adverb*; *adverb*
▻ ***preposition or adverb***
1 One thing is **below** another if it is in a lower position: *in the village below the castle* □ *many feet below the surface* □ *His office is three floors below mine.* □ *They live in the flat below.* □ *Sounds of life rose from the valley below.* □ *He grabbed her foot from below.* [*same as* **beneath**; *opposite* **above**]

The prepositions **below** and **under** are both possible where there is a clear vertical relationship: *I signed my name below* (or *under*) *hers. She has the apartment below* (or *under*) *mine.*

2 You use **below** in relation to a standard point on a scale of measurement: *The reclaimed land is below sea level.* □ *when the temperature is freezing or just below* □ *below-zero temperatures* □ *below-average marks.* [*opposite* **above**]

Under is used more often than **below** where the comparison is with a specified measurement or amount: *people with incomes of £5000 and under; people under* (or *below*) *the age of 45.*

3 One person's rank or position is **below** another's if it is lower than, or junior to, the other's: *He was below her in rank.* □ *A general is below a field marshal.* □ *She made friends with a girl in the class below.* [*opposite* **above**]

Use **under** where the meaning is 'in your charge' or 'being supervised by you': *She had three assistants under her.*

▻ ***adverb***
In a written work, reference is sometimes made to a passage **below**, meaning a piece of text lower down on the same page, or on a later page: *See below.*

belt /bɛlt/ *noun*; *verb*
▻ ***noun***: **belts**
1 A **belt** is **a** a long strip of *eg* leather or cloth worn around the waist to keep clothes in place, or for decoration. [see picture at **clothing**, see also **safety belt**, **seat belt**] **b** a continuously moving band of material used for various purposes in machinery or industry, *eg* for conveying goods along for checking, or operating machinery parts: *a conveyor belt.* **2** A **belt** of something is a narrow area of it: *A belt of rain is approaching from the south west.* □ *America's cotton belt.*
▻ ***verb*** (*informal*): **belts**, **belting**, **belted**
1 To **belt** someone is to hit them hard. **2** You **belt** somewhere when you move or travel there fast: *From my window I could see vehicles belting along the motorway.*
▻ ***phrases*** **1** A remark or comment that is **below the belt** is unkind and unfair. **2** You **tighten your belt** when you try to save money by living more cheaply and not buying unnecessary things. **3** You have something **under your belt** when you have achieved it: *It would be a good idea to get a degree under your belt first.*

phrasal verb
(*informal*, *offensive*) If you tell someone to **belt up** you are rudely asking them to be quiet.

bemoan /bɪ'moʊn/ *verb* (*formal*): **bemoans, bemoaning, bemoaned**
You **bemoan** something when you express your sadness over it: *People wept at her funeral, bemoaning her husband's treatment of her.*

bemused /bɪ'mju:zd/ *adjective*
You are **bemused** when you are puzzled or confused.

bench /bɛntʃ/ *noun*: **benches**
1 A **bench** is a long wooden or stone seat: *We sat and chatted on the garden bench.* **2** A **bench** is also a work table in *eg* a factory or laboratory. **3** In the British Parliament, the government **benches** are the seats where members of the party in power sit, and the opposition **benches** those where members of the party in opposition sit: *the government front bench.*

bend /bɛnd/ *verb*; *noun*
▻ ***verb***: **bends, bending, bent**
1 You **bend** *eg* over or down when you move the top part of your body forwards and downwards towards the floor: *She bent down to pick up a sweet paper.* **2** You **bend** part of your body such as your arm or leg when you move it so as to make an angle at the elbow or knee: *I found I couldn't bend my arm.* □ *Bend your knees.* □ *She bent her head to look at the text.* [see also **bent**] **3** You **bend** something that is straight or flat when you use force to make a curve or angle in it: *Bend the wire into an S shape.* □ *The metal bends easily.* [compare **twist**, see also **bent**] **4** Something such as a road **bends** in a certain direction if it curves that way: *The road bends round to the right.*
▻ ***noun***: **bends**
A **bend** in *eg* a road or river is a place where it forms a curve: *a series of sharp bends in the road.*
▻ ***phrases*** **1** For **bend over backwards** see **backwards**. **2** (*informal*) Someone who is **round the bend** is mad or crazy: *The noise of drilling was driving me round the bend.*

beneath /bɪ'ni:θ/ *preposition or adverb*; *preposition*
▻ ***preposition or adverb***
One thing is **beneath** another if it is under or below it:

the wet grass beneath her feet □ *She quickly concealed her book beneath the cushions.* □ *We stood on the clifftop and watched the waves breaking on the rocks beneath.* [*same as* **below**; *opposite* **above**]

▻ ***preposition***

1 Something lies **beneath** a surface if it is concealed by it: *Beneath that calm appearance of hers is a lot of suppressed anger.* [*same as* **behind**] **2** You regard some action or activity as **beneath** you if you think it would damage your dignity: *I fear that most party games would be beneath her.* □ *It's beneath her dignity to admit she's wrong.*

benefactor /ˈbɛnɪfaktə(r)/ *noun*: **benefactors**

A **benefactor** is someone who gives money, or assistance in some other form, to a person, or to a charity or other cause: *I never learnt the name of my secret benefactor.*

beneficial /bɛnɪˈfɪʃəl/ *adjective*

Something that is **beneficial** brings benefits, or has a good effect: *There were reports of the drug's beneficial effects in some patients.* [*same as* **advantageous, favourable**; *opposite* **detrimental, harmful**]

beneficiary /bɛnɪˈfɪʃərɪ/ *noun*: **beneficiaries**

1 The **beneficiaries** of something are the people who are helped by it: *Schools in southern Africa will be the main beneficiaries of the charity.* **2** (*legal*) The **beneficiaries** of a dead person's will are the people who receive money and property through it.

benefit /ˈbɛnɪfɪt/ *noun*; *verb*

▻ ***noun***: **benefits**

1 A **benefit** is something good that improves your life: *the benefits of exercise.* **2** (*uncount*) Something that brings **benefit**, or is of **benefit**, or is to your **benefit**, is helpful: *This kind of approach may be of some benefit to dyslexic children.* **3** (*uncount*) Money provided by the government for people such as the poor, ill or unemployed to live on is referred to as **benefit**: *social security benefit* □ *You would be entitled to receive child benefit.*

▻ ***verb***: **benefits, benefiting, benefited**

Something **benefits** you, or you **benefit** from it or by it, if it gives you some advantage, or improves your life: *You'd benefit from the additional exercise.* □ *These tax changes will benefit only those in the upper-income bracket.*

▻ ***phrases*** **1** You do something **for the benefit of** someone if you do it specially for them: *She repeated the instructions for the benefit of those who had arrived late.* □ *She arranged her face in a smile for the benefit of the photographers.* **2** You **give** someone **the benefit of the doubt** if you accept what they say as true even though there is no evidence to support it.

benevolent /bəˈnɛvələnt/ *adjective*

A **benevolent** person is kind and helpful: *He was a marvellously benevolent headmaster.* □ *Her expression was benevolent behind the large glasses.* — *adverb* **benevolently:** *He smiled benevolently.* — *noun* (*uncount*) **benevolence:** *Children should be taught through benevolence and sympathy, not harshness and cruelty.*

benign /bɪˈnaɪn/ *adjective*

1 A **benign** person is kind and gentle: *a benign and peaceable race of people.* □ *Her expression was benign, even humorous.* **2** A tumour that is **benign** will not spread or grow again after treatment. [*opposite* **malignant**] — *adverb* **benignly:** *She smiled benignly over her spectacles.*

bent /bɛnt/ *verb*; *adjective*; *noun*

▻ ***verb***

Bent is the past tense and past participle of **bend**: *She was bent over her books.* □ *I was bent double with pain.* □ *Keep your knees bent at a right angle.*

▻ ***adjective***

1 Something that is **bent** has been forced into a curve or angle: *My front wheel was horribly bent and twisted.* **2** (*BrE slang*) Someone who is **bent** is dishonest: *bent policemen.* **3** You are **bent** on something if you are determined to have it or achieve it: *He's bent on a career in medicine.*

▻ ***noun*** (*used in the singular*)

You have a **bent** for some activity if you are naturally good at it: *She had a bent for sport of all kinds.*

bequeath /bɪˈkwiːð/ *verb*: **bequeaths, bequeathing, bequeathed**

1 You **bequeath** something to someone when you arrange for it to be given to them when you die, by leaving it to them in your will: *My grandmother bequeathed most of her jewellery to me.* □ *great museum collections that were bequeathed to the nation.* **2** Situations and systems **are bequeathed** by one person or group to their successors when their successors have the task of developing or dealing with them: *the social problems bequeathed by the previous government.*

bequest /bɪˈkwɛst/ *noun* (*formal*): **bequests**

A **bequest** is a sum of money, or a piece of property, that someone leaves you in their will, which you inherit when they die: *an anonymous bequest.* □ *The collection owes its origin to a major bequest of drawings and sculpture made in the 1840s.*

berate /bɪˈreɪt/ *verb* (*literary*): **berates, berating, berated**

You **berate** someone when you scold them severely.

bereaved /bɪˈriːvd/ *adjective*

You are **bereaved** when someone close to you, especially a close relation, has died: *Bereaved relatives were gathering for the funeral.*

bereavement /bɪˈriːvmənt/ *noun* (*formal*): **bereavements**

1 (*uncount*) **Bereavement** is the experience, especially the grief, of being bereaved: *coping with bereavement.* **2** A **bereavement** is the death of a close relation or friend: *We've had several bereavements this past year.*

bereft /bɪˈrɛft/ *adjective* (*formal*)

You are **bereft** of something if it has been taken away from you: *refugees bereft of the least hope or comfort.*

beret /ˈbɛreɪ/ (*AmE* /bəˈreɪ/) *noun*: **berets**

A **beret** is a round flat hat made of soft material.

berry /ˈbɛrɪ/ *noun* (*usually in the plural*): **berries**

Berries are small round juicy fruits with seeds and no stone, usually growing on a bush or tree: *a holly tree laden with berries.* □ *gooseberry bushes.* [see picture at **fruit**, compare **currant**]

berserk /bəˈzɛːk/ *adjective*

Someone goes **beserk** when they go wild and behave with uncontrollable violence: *The Italian crowd went berserk when they realized their team had lost.*

berth /bɜːθ/ *noun*: **berths**

1 A **berth** is a bed or other sleeping place provided for one person, *eg* in a ship or train. [see picture at **bedroom**] **2** A **berth** for a ship is a place in port where it can be tied up.

▻ ***phrase*** You **give** someone or something **a wide berth** if you keep away from them, usually because you consider them unpleasant or dangerous.

beseech /bɪˈsiːtʃ/ *verb* (*old or literary*): **beseeches, beseeching, besought** or **beseeched**

You **beseech** someone to do something if you beg them desperately to do it: *They besought him to intercede for them.* [*same as* **implore, plead** with] — *adjec-*

tive **beseeching:** *Flora turned a beseeching face to Anna.* — *adverb* **beseechingly:** *The dog looked beseechingly at us.*

beset /bɪ'sɛt/ *verb* (*literary or formal*): **besets, besetting, beset**

A person, or a project, **is beset** by worries or difficulties when there are a lot of them to deal with: *The expedition was beset by difficulties from the start.* □ *She began to be beset by fears about her future.*

beside /bɪ'saɪd/ *preposition*

One thing is **beside** another if it is next to it or at its side: *She sat down beside her son.* □ *He was sitting at the desk with the dictionary beside him.* □ *My wife has been right beside me during this difficult time.* [*same as* **next to**]

▻ ***phrase*** You are **beside yourself** with *eg* worry or anger if you are so worried or angry that you lose your self-control: *He was beside himself with anxiety.*

besides /bɪ'saɪdz/ *preposition or adverb*; *adverb*

▻ ***preposition or adverb***

Besides means 'in addition to' or 'as well as' something else: *Besides supervising the candidates you will be responsible for distributing and collecting the question papers.* □ *Who else is coming besides me?* □ *What other subjects are you studying besides English?* □ *I've got the house to clean, the shopping to do, and masses of other things besides.*

▻ ***adverb*** (*sentence adverb*)

Besides introduces a point that supports, or gives another reason, for what you say: *I'm afraid I'm too busy to come; and besides, I've seen the film before.* [compare **anyway**]

besiege /bɪ'siːdʒ/ *verb*: **besieges, besieging, besieged**

1 You **are besieged** by things that cause you annoyance when they surround you and you can't get away from them: *She was besieged by the world's press.* **2** Enemy troops **besiege** a town or city when they surround it in order to force the inhabitants to surrender. [*same as* **blockade**]

besought /bɪ'sɔːt/ *verb*

Besought is the past tense and past participle of **beseech.**

best /bɛst/ *adjective*; *adverb*; *pronoun*; *noun*

▻ ***adjective***

1 Best is the superlative form of **good**: *It's one of the best articles I've read on the subject.* □ *Parents may not be the best communicators of these facts.* □ *It's probably best not to* [= I advise you not to] *feed your fish for the first day or two.* □ *We have to make the best use of our resources.* □ *My job is to obtain the best possible price for my client.* □ *whichever method had the best chance of succeeding.* □ *English was my best subject; what were you best at?* □ *Best wishes for your future.* **2** Your **best** friend is your closest friend, or the friend you are fondest of.

▻ ***adverb***

1 Best is the superlative form of **well**: *I can illustrate this best by a recent example.* □ *The results are best expressed as a graph.* □ *She's best known for her novels.* □ *Consult the people who are best trained to help you.* □ *the best-educated classes* □ *An afternoon appointment would suit me best.* □ *The individual must discover how best to manage.* □ *They enjoy showing off; that's what actors do best.* [*opposite* **worst**] **2** You like something **best**, or the **best**, if you like it more than others, or prefer it: *I like the red best.* □ *She liked Lesley the best of all.* [*opposite* **least**]

▻ ***pronoun:*** *standards of care at the best of these local hospitals.* □ *He was the best of husbands and fathers.*

▻ ***noun*** (*used in the singular*)

1 You try or do your **best** to do something when you try as hard as you can to do it: *The government was trying its best to play down the crisis of confidence.* □ *doing my best to remember what I'd been taught.* □ *Stop criticizing; I'm doing my best.* **2** The **best** is **a** the highest possible standard in anything: *If you want the best you must expect to pay for it.* □ *Parents want the best for their children.* □ *Praise your staff if you want to get the best out of them.* **b** the limited amount or level that can be achieved, obtained or expected: *We don't expect to win; the best we can hope for is a draw.* □ *Is that the best you can manage?* **3** People are in the **best** of health when they are very well; people are the **best** of friends when they have a very friendly relationship with each other: *He hadn't been in the best of spirits recently.* **4** Your **best** is your smartest or prettiest outfit, kept for special occasions: *little kids, all dressed in their best for the party.*

▻ ***phrases*** **1** (*informal*) People say '**All the best**' to express good wishes to someone, *eg* at the end of a letter. **2** You do something **as best you can** if you try to do it in difficult circumstances: *crowds of refugees surviving as best they can on the bare hillside.* **3** You describe something unsatisfactory as a certain thing **at best** if that is the most optimistic or favourable way you can regard it: *It would be a setback at best if we were denied use of their software.* [compare **at the worst**] **4** Someone or something is **at their best** when they are performing at, or achieving, the highest standard they are capable of: *Shakespeare on the subject of jealousy is Shakespeare at his best.* □ *I'm not at my best late at night.* **5** Something that is **for the best** or **all for the best** may seem unsatisfactory when it happens but is really to your advantage: *It seems hard to accept now, but it's probably all for the best in the long run.* **6** For **hope for the best** see **hope. 7** For **know best** see **know. 8** You **look your best** when you look as smart and attractive as you are capable of looking: *The garden always looks its best in July.* **9** People **make the best of** unsatisfactory circumstances when they try to accept them as cheerfully as possible: *We were allowed one blanket apiece and had to make the best of it.* **10** Something is seen **to best effect** or **to best advantage** when its good qualities are evident: *The city was seen to best effect at night.*

bestial /'bɛstɪəl/ *adjective*

If you describe people or their behaviour as **bestial**, you mean that they are disgustingly unpleasant or cruel.

best man /bɛst 'man/ *noun*

A bridegroom's **best man** is a male companion that he chooses to assist him during the wedding, and to perform certain ceremonial duties.

bestow /bɪ'stoʊ/ *verb* (*formal*): **bestows, bestowing, bestowed**

A title or award **is bestowed** on you when it is formally or ceremonially given to you: *Her Majesty the Queen bestowed a knighthood on him.*

best-seller /bɛst'sɛlə(r)/ *noun*: **best-sellers**

A book or other product that is a **best-seller** sells in very large numbers.

bet /bɛt/ *verb*; *noun*

▻ ***verb***: **bets, betting, bet**

You **bet** on a future event, or **bet** money on it, when you guess what the outcome or result will be, winning more money if your guess is correct and losing your money if your guess is wrong: *I bet her a pound that she'd pass her driving test.* □ *I wouldn't bet on that horse if I were you.* [compare **gamble, wager**]

▻ ***noun***: **bets**

1 A **bet** is an act of betting, or the sum you bet: *I like to have a bet now and then on a race.* ▫ *I put a small bet on him.* **2** (*informal*) You can introduce a likely guess with 'My **bet** is' or 'It's my **bet**': *It's my bet that he'll make for the continent.*

▻ ***phrases*** **1** (*informal*) If you say '**I bet** something is so, or will happen', you mean that you are almost certain of it: *I bet she did it on purpose.* ▫ *I bet he'll change his mind again.* **2** (*informal*) You use '**you bet**' as emphatic form of 'yes', or to emphasize what you are saying: *'Are you going to complain officially?' 'You bet I am.'* [*same as* **certainly**, **definitely**, **of course**] **3** If you tell someone that their **best bet** is to do a certain thing, when there is a choice of several, you are advising them to do that thing: *Your best bet would be to change the money into dollars at a bank.*

betray /bɪ'treɪ/ *verb*: **betrays, betraying, betrayed**

1 You **betray** your country, or **betray** someone who depends on your love and loyalty, when you are disloyal to them, or deliberately help their enemies or opponents. **2** You **betray** a secret when you tell it to people who should not be allowed to know it. **3** You **betray** someone's trust when you behave towards them in a way that shows you did not deserve to be trusted: *What was so disgusting was that the valet had betrayed the Prince's trust in his discretion.* **4** You **betray** your principles when you do something that is forbidden by them. **5** You **betray** a feeling or emotion when your face or expression show evidence of it: *For a brief moment her face betrayed irritation, and then she was all smiles again.* ▫ *'What have I got, doctor?' she whispered, trying not to betray any anxiety.*

betrayal /bɪ'treɪəl/ *noun* (*count or uncount*): **betrayals**

A **betrayal** is the act of betraying someone or something: *It would be a betrayal of my principles to punish children for disobedience.* ▫ *I realized she had been quoting my words to her husband, and felt hurt by her betrayal.*

betrothed /bɪ'troʊðd/ *adjective* (*formal or old*)

You are **betrothed** to someone if you are engaged to marry them.

better /'betə(r)/ *adjective; adverb; pronoun; verb*

▻ ***adjective***

1 Better is the comparative form of **good**: *The Indians tended to get the teaching jobs because of their better knowledge of English.* ▫ *The wider tape gives better-quality reproduction.* ▫ *getting a better, clearer picture of the way forward* ▫ *Better and better telescopes are being constructed.* ▫ *whichever product gives better value for money* ▫ *Better luck next time!* ▫ *Some systems are obviously better than others.* ▫ *Maybe it would be better if we sat facing each other.* ▫ *You'd be better waiting* [= I advise you to wait] *till tomorrow.* ▫ *if wholemeal bread is really better for you than white bread.* ▫ *This was as good as, if not better than, a holiday.* ▫ *It's not marvellous, but it's better than nothing.* ▫ *I was much better at driving than he was.* ▫ *The more you practise, the better you get at sifting historical evidence.* ▫ *She got better-looking as she grew up.* [*opposite* **worse**] **2** You are **better** after being ill **a** if you are less ill than you were: *I'm feeling much better today.* ▫ *She's getting better.* [*opposite* **worse**] **b** if you have fully recovered: *I'm quite better, thanks.* ▫ *I do hope your cold's better again.*

▻ ***adverb***

1 Better is the comparative form of **well**: *I'm looking for a better-paid job.* ▫ *He could hardly have expressed it better.* ▫ *GPs need to be better informed.* ▫ *I'd done well, probably much better than I deserved to.* ▫ *He's better known in his native land.* ▫ *Naturally some children settle down better than others.* [*opposite* **worse**] **2** You like one thing or person **better** than another if you prefer them: *We liked the first flat better than all the others.* ▫ *I liked him better before he became a successful businessman.* [*opposite* **less**]

▻ ***pronoun:*** *trying to decide which was the better of the two plans.*

▻ ***verb***: **betters, bettering, bettered**

1 You **better** your previous performance, or someone else's performance, when you beat it: *bettering his previous best time by several seconds.* ▫ *Let's hope we can better their score.* [*same as* **beat**] **2** (*old*) People from a poor background **better** themselves when they do well in life, *eg* by acquiring a good education and a good job. [*same as* **improve**]

▻ ***phrases*** **1** You are **better off** **a** if you have more money: *a situation where those who do not work are better off than those who do.* **b** if they are in more satisfactory circumstances: *There are disturbed people in prison who'd be better off in hospital.* **2** Something that is the case **for better or worse** is the case whatever you may think of it: *For better or worse, the computer has taken control of our lives.* **3** Things change **for the better** when they improve: *On the whole the alterations are a change for the better.* **4 a** Someone **gets the better of you** when they defeat or outwit you: *He usually got the better of his brother in any argument.* **b** An emotion **gets the better** of you when you fail to control it: *Curiosity eventually got the better of him, and he approached to see what was happening.* **5** If you say you **had better** do something you mean you will have to: *We'd better hurry.* ▫ *We'd better not disturb her yet.* ▫ *You'd better assume that I won't arrive before nine.* ▫ *I'd better warn you she's in a poor state.* ▫ *She'd better turn up soon or it'll be too late.* ▫ *'Should I go and tell her it was my fault?' 'You'd better, or I will!'* **6** For **know better** see **know**. **7** You **are the better for** an experience if it has benefited you: *I was feeling somewhat the better for a proper night's rest.*

between /bɪ'twiːn/ *preposition*

1 a A thing is **between** two other things when it separates them, or is in the space that separates them: *I was sitting between Lorna and her husband.* ▫ *He was holding the object between his thumb and forefinger.* ▫ *Slough is halfway between London and Reading.* ▫ *the wall between our garden and the next one.* ▫ *As we approached adulthood a barrier grew up between us.* **b** You travel **between** two places when you regularly go from one to the other and back again: *a regular bus service between Leeds and Bradford* ▫ *commuting between home and work.* **c** Something happens **between** two times or events if it happens after the first and before the second: *The town hall must have been built between 1900 and 1910.* ▫ *She spent the time between lunch and dinner studying.*

> **Between** can link more than two places or things when it means 'in the space or interval from one to the next': *You should use the loo between stations, not when the train is standing at a platform. There was often time for a coffee between lectures.*

d An amount or measurement is **between** two others if it is greater than the first and smaller than the second: *an average daytime temperature of between 25°C and 30°C.* ▫ *children aged between 7 and 9.* ▫ *She's between 30 and 35.*

2 a Two or more people do something **between** them when they each contribute something: *They bought the car between them.* ▫ *Between them they had a total* *of six children.* **b** You divide something **between** people when you give each of them some of it: *Her property was divided between her sons.*

You can usually use **between** even when the group consists of more than two: *We divided the sweets equally between* (or *among*) *the four of us.*

c Something that happens **between** two or more people or groups involves them both or all: *There had been some sort of quarrel between the two sisters.* □ *the love between parents and their children.*

You use **between** even in reference to groups of more than two if you are thinking of their individual relations with one another; **among** is used where the group is being referred to as a whole: *relationships between the various members of the family*; *the general opinion among members of the union*; *during the discussions we had between* (or *among*) *ourselves.*

d You say that something is **between** you and one or more others if you are both or all going to keep it a secret: *This is just between you and me.* [= it's our secret] □ *This is between ourselves.*
3 You often use **between** to refer to choices and differences: *They should know the difference between right and wrong.* □ *the choice between raising a family and* (or *or*) *pursuing a career.*
▻ ***phrase*** **In between** is used as an adverb: *There's a pub four miles away, and there's the local one, but there's nothing in between.* □ *two armchairs arranged side by side with a low table in between.*

beverage /ˈbɛvərɪdʒ/ *noun* (*formal*): **beverages**
A **beverage** is any liquid for drinking except water, especially tea or coffee.

bevy /ˈbɛvɪ/ *noun*: **bevies**
A **bevy** of people, especially women or girls, is a group or crowd of them: *He turned the corner and bumped into a bevy of schoolgirls on their way home.*

beware /bɪˈwɛə(r)/ *verb* (only used in the imperative or infinitive form)
If someone tells you to **beware** of someone or something, they mean that you could be harmed by them: *There was a big notice on the gate saying 'Beware of the dog.'*

bewildered /bɪˈwɪldəd/ *adjective*
You are **bewildered** when you are confused or puzzled: *I was completely bewildered by the new traffic arrangements.* □ *His eyes held a hurt and bewildered expression.*

bewildering /bɪˈwɪldərɪŋ/ *adjective*
Something that is **bewildering** puzzles or confuses you: *There was a bewildering array of books to choose from.* □ *The range of options is bewildering.*

bewilderment /bɪˈwɪldəmənt/ *noun* (*uncount*)
Bewilderment is a feeling of confusion: *She woke up suddenly and looked round her in bewilderment.*

bewitch /bɪˈwɪtʃ/ *verb*: **bewitches, bewitching, bewitched**
Someone or something **bewitches** you if you are so charmed or enchanted by them that you can think of nothing else: *I was used to seeing men bewitched by Judith.* — *adjective* **bewitching:** *bewitching music* □ *the bewitching Miss Peabody.*

beyond /bɪˈjɒnd/ *preposition or adverb*; *preposition*
▻ ***preposition or adverb***
1 One thing is **beyond** another if it is on the far side of it: *the fields beyond the house* □ *The post office is just beyond the bank on this side.* □ *I could see as far as the fence but not beyond.* □ *From the bedroom window there was a view of the fields and the mountains beyond.*
2 Something extends or progresses **beyond** a certain point if it extends or progresses further than that point, or exceeds it: *The sale can't last beyond Friday.* □ *pupils staying on at school beyond the age of 16* □ *The deadline may be extended up to the end of April or beyond.* □ *We had succeeded beyond expectation.* □ *She had been learning to swim for four years but had not yet progressed beyond the beginners' stage.* □ *His behaviour went beyond mere rudeness.*
▻ ***preposition***
1 Something is **beyond** you if you cannot understand it: *How they could have made such a mistake is quite beyond me.* **2** Someone or something that is **beyond** *eg* help or recognition can no longer be helped or recognized: *This job is far beyond his capacity.* □ *She had changed beyond recognition.* □ *The situation was getting beyond his control.* **3** (*with a negative*) **Beyond** is also used like 'except for' or 'apart from': *Beyond offering sympathy there was little any of us could do to help.* [compare **other than**]

bias /ˈbaɪəs/ *noun* (*uncount or used in the singular*)
Someone who shows **bias** makes unfair decisions because they allow their own feelings and opinions to influence them, instead of considering the facts: *Coloured candidates became more and more aware that they were up against a racial bias.* □ *The examiners were accused of bias.* [*same as* **prejudice**]

biased /ˈbaɪəst/ *adjective*
1 Someone who is **biased** shows prejudice or bias in their attitudes or judgments: *Granny thinks you're lovely, but then she's biased.* □ *He gives a somewhat biased account of the incident in his autobiogrpahy.* [*same as* **prejudiced**] **2** Something **is biased** towards a particular thing if it caters for it more than for other things: *The school curriculum was heavily biased towards athletic and outdoor activities.*

bib /bɪb/ *noun*: **bibs**
A **bib** is a piece of cloth or plastic that you fasten under a baby's chin to protect its clothes while it is eating.

Bible /ˈbaɪbəl/ *noun*: **Bibles**
1 The **Bible** is the book that contains the sacred writings of the Christian religion. **2** A **bible** is a copy of this book. **3** A book full of useful information on a particular subject can be referred to as someone's **bible**: *You need a copy of this; it's the computer-user's bible.* — *adjective* **biblical** /ˈbɪblɪkəl/: *in the biblical version of the Flood.*

bibliography /bɪblɪˈɒgrəfɪ/ *noun*: **bibliographies**
A **bibliography** is **1** a list of books by one author or on one subject. **2** a list of books used as sources by the author of a book or article.

bicentenary /baɪsɛnˈtiːnərɪ/ or **bicentennial** (*especially AmE*) /baɪsɛnˈtɛnɪəl/ *noun*: **bicentenaries** or **bicentennials**
The **bicentenary** of some event is a day or year exactly two hundred years after it: *Ex-pupils were asked to submit ideas about how to celebrate the bicentenary of the school's foundation.*

biceps /ˈbaɪsɛps/ *noun*: *plural* **biceps**
Your **biceps** is the muscle in your upper arm that bends your elbow.

bicker /ˈbɪkə(r)/ *verb* (*informal*): **bickers, bickering, bickered**
People **bicker** when they argue or quarrel, usually about unimportant things: *I believe they had an enormous affection for each other, but they bickered con-*

bicycle

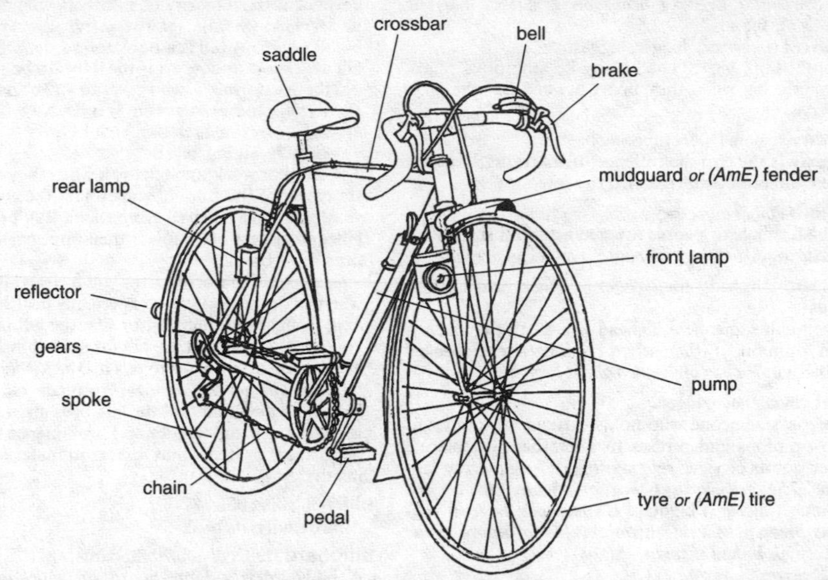

stantly. [*same as* **squabble**] — *noun* (*uncount*) **bickering:** *I was exhausted by the children's bickering.*

bicycle /'baɪsɪkəl/ *noun*: **bicycles**
A **bicycle** is a vehicle consisting of a metal frame with a seat, and two wheels one behind the other, which you ride by turning pedals with your feet.

bid[1] /bɪd/ *verb*; *noun*
▻ ***verb***: **bids, bidding, bid**
You **bid** for something at an auction sale, or **bid** money for it, when you offer to buy it for a particular amount of money: *She bid over half a million dollars for the painting.* □ *He was planning to bid for the little Corot.* — *noun* **bidder:** *The property will be sold to the highest bidder.* [= the person who offers most money for it] □ *There were few bidders for the drawing.* — *noun* (*uncount*) **bidding:** *Who would care to start the bidding?* □ *Reluctantly she dropped out of the bidding.*
▻ ***noun***: **bids**
1 A **bid** is an offer of a particular amount of money to buy something: *We have received a bid by telephone of £20 000 for this piece.* **2** (*usually in the singular*) You make a **bid** for something, or to do something, when you try to reach it or achieve it: *The next day we were going to make a bid for the summit.* □ *His bid for power had failed.* □ *a bid to win over the floating voters.*

bid[2] /bɪd/ *verb* (*old or formal*): **bids, bidding, bade, bidden**
1 You **bid** someone do something when you ask or tell them to do it: *She bade me tell her all the news from England.* □ *He did as he was bidden, and held the door open.* **2** You **bid** someone *eg* good morning, good day, goodbye or farewell when you say hallo or goodbye to them: *Gentlemen, I bid you goodnight.* □ *He bade us good day and left.*

bide /baɪd/ *verb*: **bides, biding, bided**
▻ ***phrase*** You **bide** your **time** when you wait patiently for a good opportunity to do or say something.

biennial /baɪ'ɛnɪəl/ *adjective*
A **biennial** event happens every two years: *Venice's great biennial art event.* [compare **annual, perennial**]

big /bɪg/ *adjective*; *adverb*
▻ ***adjective***: **bigger, biggest**
1 a Big things are large in size; **big** people are usually tall and rather heavy: *The housing problems in the big cities would not go away.* □ *She had big blue eyes.* □ *a big dark bearded man.* □ *I didn't get very big with my last pregnancy.* [*same as* **large**; *opposite* **little, small**] **b** You use **big** in questions and comparisons relating to size: *spiders as big as a man's hand* □ *How big is the smallest angle?* □ *He was wearing a jacket several sizes too big for him.* □ *Human brains may be big, but they're not the biggest.* □ *Their whole house was no bigger than this bathroom.* □ *producing bigger and better eggs.* [*same as* **large**] **c** Your **big** brother or sister is a brother or sister older than you are; the **big** children in any group are the older ones: *Sometimes the big girls bullied the little ones.* □ *The new baby loves her big brother.* □ *Gerry was put in the big boys' class.* [*same as* **older**]
2 a Big movements or gestures are strong, powerful or emphatic: *She gave me a great big hug.* □ *A big smile for the camera, please.* □ *There was a big explosion.* **b Big** can be used with the meaning 'great' or 'considerable' to intensify certain nouns: *He's a bigger fool than I thought he was.* □ *You're making a big mistake.* □ *The baby's going to make a big change.* □ *There's been a big improvement.* □ *It's too big a responsibility for us.* □ *big challenges.* □ *Electronic mail was proving a big success in the UK.* [*same as* **great, considerable**] **c** (*used with some uncount nouns*) **Big** business is business done on a large scale; if you make **big** money you make large profits; **big** talk is ambitious talk: *Canals soon became big business.* □ *There's still big money to be had in software.* **d** You are **big**, or make a **big** name for yourself, in a certain area of activity, if you have a lot of influence in it, or are recognized as being important: *She'd never expected to become a big name in the fashion world.* □ *directors like Oliver Stone who are are big in the American film industry at the*

moment. [*same as* **important**] **e** A **big** event is an important and significant one: *Their big celebration is on Christmas Eve.* □ *I hear you're getting married; when's the big day?*

▻ ***adverb*** (*informal*): **bigger, biggest**

People think **big** when they make ambitious plans; they talk **big** when they boast about what they can achieve.

bigamy /ˈbɪgəmɪ/ *noun* (*uncount*)

Bigamy is the criminal offence of marrying someone when you are already married to someone else.

biggish /ˈbɪgɪʃ/ *adjective*

Biggish things or people are a substantial size: *What I'd like would be a biggish house, Victorian, perhaps.*

bighead /ˈbɪghɛd/ *noun* (*informal, derogatory*): **bigheads**

If you call someone a **bighead** you mean they have a high opinion of themselves. — *adjective* **bigheaded** /bɪgˈhɛdɪd/: *He's so bigheaded about his job.*

bigot /ˈbɪgət/ *noun*: **bigots**

A **bigot** is someone who holds extreme or unreasonable opinions and refuses to alter them or tolerate other points of view: *religious bigots.* — *adjective* **bigoted**: *They're just a bunch of bigoted hypocrites.* — *noun* (*uncount*) **bigotry**: *He intended to fight religious bigotry, believing it responsible for many of the social evils he had encountered.*

big toe /ˈbɪgˈtoʊ/ *noun*: **big toes**

Your **big toe** is the largest toe on your foot. [see picture at **body**]

bigwig /ˈbɪgwɪg/ *noun* (*informal, often derogatory*): **bigwigs**

People refer to someone important as a **bigwig**: *All the local bigwigs were invited to the opening.*

bike /baɪk/ *noun* (*informal*): **bikes**

A **bike** is a bicycle or motorcycle: *He fell off his bike and cut his knee.*

bikini /bɪˈkiːnɪ/ *noun*: **bikinis**

A **bikini** is a brief two-piece swimming costume for women.

bilateral /baɪˈlatərəl/ *adjective*

Bilateral agreements, discussions, declarations or negotiations are participated in by both the groups or sides involved in some issue or debate: *Bilateral negotiations for a peace plan begin next week.* [compare **unilateral, multilateral**]

bile /baɪl/ *noun* (*uncount*)

Bile is a thick bitter liquid produced by the liver that helps you to digest food.

bilingual /baɪˈlɪŋgwəl/ *adjective*

1 Bilingual describes things written or spoken in two languages: *bilingual road signs.* **2** A **bilingual** dictionary has the list of words in one language and their explanations in another. **3** A person is **bilingual** if they speak two languages, especially if they speak both fluently: *He married a Hungarian and his children are completely bilingual.* □ *I grabbed a bilingual passer-by to act as interpreter.*

bilious /ˈbɪlɪəs/ *adjective*

1 You feel **bilious** when you feel sick. **2** (*derogatory*) **Bilious** colours are disgusting, or are combined unpleasantly.

bill¹ /bɪl/ *noun; verb*

▻ ***noun***: **bills**

1 A **bill** is a written statement of the amount of money you owe for goods or services you have received: *I've just been sent a huge telephone bill.* □ *He got up from his table, paid his bill, and left.* **2** In parliament, a **bill** is a written proposal that will become a new law if the majority of members vote in favour of it: *Members on both sides of the House supported the bill.* **3** (*AmE*) A **bill** is a banknote: *a dollar bill.* **4** The **bill** of a show or concert is the items to be performed, or the performers who are to take part: *Opera Camerata's autumn offering is a double bill consisting of 'Suor Angelica' and 'Gianni Schicchi'.*

▻ ***verb***: **bills, billing, billed**

1 A shop or workman **bills** you when they send you a statement of the amount you owe for the goods or services you have received from them. **2** A performer **is billed** to appear in a show if their appearance in it has been advertised.

▻ ***phrases*** **1** The doctor gives you **a clean bill of health** when he or she declares you perfectly healthy. **2** (*informal*) Something that **fills,** or **fits, the bill** is just what you need. **3** You **foot the bill** for something when you are the person who has to pay it: *The landlord is left to foot the bill for the damage.* [compare **tab**] **4** A performer or item that **tops the bill,** or **is given top billing,** is given more importance and prominence than other performers or items that appear in material advertising the show.

bill² /bɪl/ *noun*: **bills**

A bird's **bill** is its beak.

billboard /ˈbɪlbɔːd/ *noun*: **billboards**

A **billboard** is a large board on which advertising posters are displayed.

billiards /ˈbɪlɪədz/ *noun* (*uncount*)

Billiards is a game played on a cloth-covered table with pockets at the sides and corners, into which you strike balls, using long thin sticks called **cues**.

billion /ˈbɪljən/ *noun; determiner; pronoun*

▻ ***noun***: **billion** or **billions**

In Britain and Europe, a **billion** is a million millions; in the US, and increasingly in Britain and Europe, a **billion** is a thousand millions: *a total of five billion* □ *They were reckoning the cost in billions.*

▻ ***determiner:*** *He had gambled several billion pounds of investors' money.*

▻ ***pronoun*** (*used in the plural, informal*): *She owns billions of pairs of shoes.* [compare **trillion**]

billow /ˈbɪloʊ/ *verb; noun*

▻ ***verb***: **billows, billowing, billowed**

1 Smoke or cloud **billows** somewhere when it rises or is carried along by the wind: *White clouds billowed across the sky.* **2** Cloth **billows** when it swells and flaps like a sail in the wind: *Her full skirt billowed out.*

▻ ***noun***: **billows**

A **billow** of smoke is a rising mass of it.

bimbo /ˈbɪmboʊ/ *noun* (*slang, usually derogatory*): **bimbos**

A **bimbo** is an attractive but not very intelligent young woman: *She was furious at being treated like a brainless bimbo.*

bin /bɪn/ *noun*: **bins**

1 A **bin** is a large container for rubbish: *a litter bin.* **2** A **bin** is also any container for storing things, especially some kinds of food: *a bread bin.*

binary system /ˈbaɪnərɪ sɪstəm/ *noun* (*uncount*)

The **binary system** is a system of calculating, used *eg* in computers, which uses 2 as its base number instead of 10, and which uses only the numbers 0 and 1.

bind /baɪnd/ *verb; noun*

▻ ***verb***: **binds, binding, bound**

1 You **bind** something when you tie it or fasten it tightly: *They bound his hands together behind his back.*

2 To **bind** someone to a particular course or action is to oblige or force them to do it: *You are legally bound to reply.* **3** To **bind** a book is to fasten all the pages together and put a cover on it: *She sent her thesis away to be bound.* **4** Something **binds** people if it unites them: *We are bound together today by a common grief.*
▻ ***noun*** (*used in the singular; informal*)
People refer to something that is a nuisance as a **bind**: *It's an absolute bind not having a car of my own.*

binder /'baındə(r)/ *noun*: **binders**
A **binder** is a hard cover with metal rings inside, that is used to keep loose pieces of paper in order.

binding /'baındıŋ/ *noun; adjective*
▻ ***noun***: **bindings**
1 The **binding** of a book is its cover: *books with leather bindings.* **2** (*uncount*) **Binding** is a strip of cloth used *eg* to bind or decorate something.
▻ ***adjective***
An agreement or promise is **binding** if it formally or legally makes you do what you've agreed or promised to do.

binge /bındʒ/ *noun; verb*
▻ ***noun*** (*informal*): **binges**
Someone goes on a **binge** when they have a period of excessive drinking or money-spending.
▻ ***verb*** (*informal*): **binges, binging, binged**
People **binge** when they have a period of eating too much.

bingo /'bıŋgoʊ/ *noun* (*uncount*)
Bingo is a game of chance in which each player has a card with different numbers on, which they cross off as someone calls out numbers that have been selected at random, the winner being the first person to cross off all the numbers on their card.

binoculars /bı'nɒkjələz/ *noun* (*plural*)
A pair of **binoculars** is an instrument like two small telescopes joined together, for making distant objects look nearer.

biochemistry /baıə'kɛmıstrı/ *noun* (*uncount*)
Biochemistry is the branch of chemistry that studies the chemicals and chemical changes in living things. — *adjective* **biochemical** /baıə'kɛmikəl/: *biochemical changes in the body.*

biodegradable /baıoʊdı'greıdəbəl/ *adjective*
Biodegradable substances are able to be broken down by bacteria, and so decay naturally.

biographer /baı'ɒgrəfə(r)/ *noun*: **biographers**
A **biographer** is an author who writes about another person's life: *Johnson's biographer Boswell.*

biographical /baıə'grafıkəl/ *adjective*
Biographical material is material about someone's life: *The directors' photographs, with brief biographical details, are to be found on page 10.*

biography /baı'ɒgrəfı/ *noun*: **biographies**
1 A **biography** is an account of someone's life written by someone else. **2** (*uncount*) **Biography** is the art of writing accounts of other people's lives, or such accounts in general. [compare **autobiography**]

biological /baıə'lɒdʒıkəl/ *adjective*
1 Biological means **a** relating to the way living things grow and behave: *the biological activity in ponds and streams.* **b** relating to biology: *the biological section in the library.* **2 Biological** warfare and **biological** weapons use bacteria to cause disease amongst the enemy troops or population.

biology /baı'ɒlədʒı/ *noun* (*uncount*)
Biology is the science and study of living things. — *noun* **biologist:** *a team of university biologists*

biopsy /'baıɒpsı/ *noun* (*medicine*): **biopsies**
A **biopsy** is carried out on a sample of cells or liquid from a sick person's body when it is examined in a laboratory to find out if the person is suffering from a particular disease.

birch /bɜːtʃ/ *noun*: **birches**
1 (*count or uncount*) A **birch**, or **birch tree**, is a slender tree with small leaves and smooth bark: *forests of birch.* **2** (*used in the singular*) The **birch** is a bundle of branches or a cane, formerly used to beat people as a punishment.

bird /bɜːd/ *noun*: **birds**
1 A **bird** is a two-legged, egg-laying creature with feathers, a beak and two wings. **2** (*BrE; slang, rather offensive*) Some people refer to girls and women as **birds**.
▻ ***phrase*** (*informal*) You **kill two birds with one stone** if you manage to achieve two things in a single operation.

bird of prey /bɜːd əv 'preı/ *noun*: **birds of prey**
A **bird of prey** is any bird that kills animals or other birds for food, such as the owl, hawk or eagle.

bird's-eye view /bɜːdʒaı 'vjuː/ *noun* (*used in the singular*)
You get a **bird's-eye view** of a place when you are looking down on it from a great height: *We got a fascinating bird's-eye view of London from the helicopter.*

Biro /'baıroʊ/ *noun* (*trademark*): **Biros**
A **Biro** is a pen whose writing tip is in the form of a small ball. [*same as* **ballpoint pen**; see picture at **office**]

birth /bɜːθ/ *noun*: **births**
1 (*count or uncount*) The **birth** of a baby is process by which it is born: *She had gone into hospital for the birth of her baby* □ *the Register of Births, Marriages and Deaths* □ *He'd been blind from birth.* **2** (*used in the singular*) The **birth** of something is its beginning or origin: *the birth of socialism.*
▻ ***phrases*** A woman **gives birth** when the baby she has been carrying inside her is born: *She gave birth to her son in the back of a taxi.*

birth certificate /'bɜːθ sətıfıkət/ *noun*: **birth certificates**
A **birth certificate** is an official form stating the time and place of a person's birth and his or her parents' names and address.

birth control /'bɜːθ kəntroʊl/ *noun* (*uncount*)
Birth control is the prevention of pregnancy by any of the various methods of contraception, or by the limitation of sexual intercourse to the beginning and end of the menstrual cycle.

birthday /'bɜːθdeı/ *noun*: **birthdays**
Your **birthday** is the anniversary of the day on which you were born: *Happy Birthday!* □ *a birthday party.*

birthmark /'bɜːθmɑːk/ *noun*: **birthmarks**
A **birthmark** is a permanent mark on your skin, especially a noticeable one, that you were born with.

birthplace /'bɜːθpleıs/ *noun*: **birthplaces**
The **birthplace** of a person or thing is the place where they were born or came into existence: *The Middle East was the birthplace of Islam.*

birthrate /'bɜːθreıt/ *noun*: **birthrates**
The **birthrate** in a place or country is the number of babies born there over some standard period such as a year.

biscuit /'bıskıt/ *noun*: **biscuits**
A **biscuit** is any of several types of sweet or savoury crisp flat cakes: *a packet of chocolate biscuits.* [*same as* **cookie**]

bisect /baɪˈsɛkt/ *verb*: **bisects, bisecting, bisected**
One thing **bisects** another when it divides it into two equal parts: *the busy main street that bisects the town of Pitlochry.*

bisexual /baɪˈsɛkʃʊəl/ *adjective*
Someone who is **bisexual** is sexually attracted to both men and women. [compare **heterosexual, homosexual**]

bishop /ˈbɪʃəp/ *noun*: **bishops**
1 A **bishop** is a senior Christian priest or minister in the Roman Catholic, Anglican and Orthodox churches, who is in charge of the churches within a certain area: *the Bishop of Durham.* **2** In chess, a **bishop** is a piece that can only move diagonally across the board.

bison /ˈbaɪsən/ *noun*: **bison**
A **bison** is a large bull-like animal with a heavy, shaggy head and shoulders, and short horns.

bistro /ˈbiːstroʊ/ *noun*: **bistros**
A **bistro** is a small bar or informal restaurant. [compare **café**]

bit[1] /bɪt/ *noun*: **bits**
A **bit** of something is a piece or item of it, or an amount of it, especially a small amount: *Have a bit of cake.* □ *today's interesting bit of news* □ *one or two bits of shopping still to do* □ *We shall have to put our few bits of furniture into store.* □ *I managed to do a bit of reading in the vacation.* □ *A big bit of plaster fell down from the ceiling.* □ *Bits of the wreckage were washed up on shore.* □ *torn bits of paper.* □ *Read the next chapter thoroughly, especially the bit about comets.*
▻ ***phrases*** **1** (*informal*) **a** You use **a bit** with adjectives and adverbs, and **a bit of** with 'a' and a noun, as a kind of moderating adverb meaning 'to some extent', or 'rather': *She's finding the job a bit boring.* □ *I'm afraid I'm a bit late.* □ *It's a bit late* [= rather too late] *to change your mind now.* □ *The brain is a bit like a computer.* □ *It's a bit warmer today.* □ *It's a bit too early to judge.* □ *'Aren't you fed up?' 'Yes, a bit.'* □ *I expected, perhaps a bit foolishly, that they'd agree.* □ *I felt a bit of a fool.* □ *We've got a bit of a problem here.* □ *It's come as a bit of a shock.* □ *I'm in a bit of a muddle.* □ *It's a bit of a nuisance having to start again.* **b** You wait **a bit**, or do something **for a bit**, if you do it for a short time, or for a while: *Hang on a bit; isn't this the list we were shown before?* □ *Wear new walking boots round the house for a bit, so that your feet get used to them.* □ *I worked as a waitress for a bit.* **2** (*informal*) Something that is **a bit much** is unacceptable, unreasonable, or unfair: *It's a bit much, expecting me to wait for her and give her a lift home.* **3** Something that happens **bit by bit** happens gradually, or in stages: *She tidied the garden up bit by bit.* □ *Bit by bit the truth emerged.* **4 Bits and pieces** are small things of various kinds: *a few interesting bits and pieces she'd brought back from Africa.* **5** You **do your bit** if you do your fair share of *eg* work: *You've certainly done your bit for the company.* **6** Something that is **every bit as** *eg* good or useful as something else is equally good or useful: *Prague is every bit as handsome as Vienna.* **7** (*informal*) **Not a bit** is used as a strong negative, meaning 'not at all': *I don't mind a bit if you want to change your mind.* □ *Things were relaxed and casual, not a bit like the old days.* □ *She hasn't altered a bit.* **8** If you say **'not a bit of it'** in reference to something you expected to be so, you mean that it is not so at all: *I expected her to be apologetic, but not a bit of it.* **9 Quite a bit** of something is quite a lot of it: *have quite a bit of money saved up.* **10** (*informal*) For **take a bit of doing** see **do**[2]. **11** Something falls or comes **to bits** if it is breaks, or separates, into several pieces: *The car's falling to bits.* [= wearing out] □ *He took the keyboard to bits in order to clean it.* [*same as* **to pieces**]

bit[2] /bɪt/ *verb*
Bit is the past tense of **bite**.

bit[3] /bɪt/ *noun* (*computers*): **bits**
A **bit** is a unit of information stored in a computer, expressed as either 0 and 1.

bitch /bɪtʃ/ *noun*; *verb*
▻ ***noun***: **bitches**
1 A **bitch** is a female dog. **2** (*informal, very offensive*) If someone refers to a woman as a **bitch**, they mean that she is spiteful and unpleasant.
▻ ***verb*** (*informal*): **bitches, bitching, bitched**
To **bitch** about someone or something is to complain about them crossly or rudely.

bite /bait/ *verb*; *noun*
▻ ***verb***: **bites, biting, bit, bitten**
1 A person or animal **bites** something when they use their teeth to cut through it or into it: *The dog bit his leg.* □ *She bit into the peach.* □ *I bit a big piece out of my apple.* □ *He bit off the end of his cigar.* □ *She still bites her fingernails.* **2** An insect or snake **bites** you when it pierces your skin and causes that area of it to become red, painful or itchy. **3** Measures taken by those in authority begin to **bite** when they start having a noticeable effect, especially one that people find unpleasant or difficult to cope with: *The rise in fuel costs was beginning to bite.*
▻ ***noun***: **bites**
1 A **bite** is the action of biting something: *She took a bite of her sandwich.* □ *The cat gave him a bite on his ankle.* □ *Very few snake bites prove fatal.* **2** A **bite** is also a wound, a red spot, or an inflamed area on your skin, made by a creature that has bitten you: *Always wash and disinfect a dog bite.* □ *He was covered with flea bites.* **3** (*used in the singular*) You have a **bite** to eat when you have a small snack.

> ***phrasal verb***
> (*informal*) You **bite back** a remark when you just manage to stop yourself making it.

biting /ˈbaɪtɪŋ/ *adjective*
1 A **biting** wind is a very cold strong wind that seems to pierce through you: *On the summit they were exposed to a biting north-easterly gale.* [*same as* **bitter**] **2** A **biting** remark, or **biting** criticism, is deliberately unkind, hurtful or sarcastic. [*same as* **scathing**]

bitten /ˈbɪtən/ *verb*
Bitten is the past participle of **bite**: *ragged, bitten fingernails.*

bitter /ˈbɪtə(r)/ *adjective*; *noun*
▻ ***adjective***
1 You are **bitter** about something if it makes you sad, angry and resentful: *She was bitter about the way she had been treated.* □ *That period held a lot of bitter memories for her.* □ *He spoke in a bitter tone.* **2 Bitter** describes intense conflict or opposition: *bitter criticism* □ *bitter fighting* □ *They have always been bitter enemies.* **3** A **bitter** disappointment is a severe one that is difficult to accept: *His failure to get into an Oxford college came as a bitter disappointment.* □ *Her career had ended in bitter failure.* **4** Something tastes **bitter** if it has a sharp, acid taste, often an unpleasant one: *The fruit tasted bitter, like a lemon.* [*same as* **sour**; *opposite* **sweet**] **5 Bitter** weather or winds are very cold: *a bitter east wind.* — *noun* (*uncount*) **bitterness:** *She harboured no feelings of bitterness towards him.* □ *the extreme bitterness of the fruit.*

▻ ***noun*** (*uncount*; *BrE*)
Bitter is a type of beer strongly flavoured with hops, which gives it a bitter taste.
▻ ***phrase*** You continue with something **to the bitter end** if you continue doing it to the very end, however unpleasant it is, and in spite of any problems or difficulties.

bitterly /ˈbɪtəlɪ/ *adverb*
1 You speak **bitterly** when you say something in a resentful or sarcastic manner: *'I'm glad someone's pleased,' she said bitterly.* **2** You are **bitterly** angry, upset, or disappointed when you are intensely so: *He's bitterly resentful about it.* □ *No-one could have hated him more bitterly than she did.* □ *She wept bitterly.* **3 Bitterly** cold winds or weather are intensely cold: *It was a bitterly cold day.*

bizarre /bɪˈzɑː(r)/ *adjective*
Something is **bizarre** if it is odd or very strange: *The situation was becoming more bizarre by the minute.* □ *He admitted it was the most bizarre case he'd ever come across.*

black /blak/ *adjective*; *noun*; *verb*
▻ ***adjective***
1 Black things are the colour of coal or the night sky: *a black dress* □ *They're black, not blue.* □ *We've painted the door black.* □ (*with the noun omitted*) *The green dress is pretty but the black is more elegant.* **2** A **black** person belongs to one of the dark-skinned, especially African, races: *talented black athletes.* **3 Black** tea or coffee have no milk in them. **4** A situation looks **black** if its outcome is likely to be bad: *Things look black for the men still trapped down the mine.* [*same as* **bleak**, **gloomy**, **hopeless**] **5 Black** comedy and **black** humour contain bitter jokes about unpleasant things.
▻ ***noun***: **blacks**
1 (*uncount*) **Black** is the colour of coal or the night sky: *Conventionally, people wear black to a funeral.* **2** A **black** is a black person: *one of the first blacks to be made a judge.*
▻ ***verb***: **blacks, blacking, blacked**
1 You **black** something such as your face when you colour it black: *The paratroopers had blacked their faces so they couldn't be seen in the dark.* **2** A group such as a union **blacks** certain goods or people when it refuses to deal with them.
▻ ***phrase*** (*informal*) You are **black and blue** when you are covered with bruises.

> ***phrasal verb***
> **black out 1** A place or building **is blacked out** when it is completely unlit, *eg* because the electricity has failed. **2** A person **blacks out** when they faint or lose consciousness.
> [see also **blackout**]

blackberry /ˈblakbərɪ/ *noun*: **blackberries**
A **blackberry** is a small dark purple fruit that grows on prickly bushes called brambles. [see picture at **fruit**]

blackbird /ˈblakbɜːd/ *noun*: **blackbirds**
A **blackbird** is a small European bird, the male of which is black with a yellow beak.

blackboard /ˈblakbɔːd/ *noun*: **balckboards**
A **blackboard** is black or dark-coloured board in a classroom, on which the teacher or lecturer writes things with chalk.

blackcurrant /blakˈkʌrənt/ *noun*: **blackcurrants**
A **blackcurrant** is a small round black or dark-coloured fruit that grows in bunches on a bush. [see picture at **fruit**]

blacken /ˈblakən/ *verb*: **blackens, blackening, blackened**
1 You **blacken** something if you make it black or very dark in colour: *walls blackened by smoke.* **2** You **blacken** someone's name or reputation if you say things that make other people have a low opinion of them.

black eye /blak ˈaɪ/ *noun*: **black eyes**
You have a **black eye** when the skin round one of your eyes is bruised and swollen, because you have been hit on or near the eye.

blackhead /ˈblakhɛd/ *noun*: **blackheads**
A **blackhead** is a small black spot in your skin caused by sweat or grease blocking a pore, and dirt collecting on top.

black magic /blak ˈmadʒɪk/ *noun* (*uncount*)
Black magic is magic that involves communication with the devil or evil spirits.

blackmail /ˈblakmeɪl/ *verb*; *noun*
▻ ***verb***: **blackmails, blackmailing, blackmailed**
To **blackmail** someone is to force them to give you money, or do what you want, by threatening to reveal a secret about them: *I found out that some woman was blackmailing my husband.* — *noun* **blackmailer:** *Police arrested his blackmailers.*
▻ ***noun*** (*uncount*): *threats that amount to blackmail.*

black market /blak ˈmɑːkɪt/ *noun* (*usually in the singular*): **black markets**
The **black market** is the illegal buying and selling, at high prices, of goods which a lot of people want to buy and that are scarce or rationed: *Mothers used to get extra sugar on the black market.*

blackout /ˈblakaʊt/ *noun*: **blackouts**
1 There is a **blackout** when all the lights are switched off or go off and it becomes completely dark. **2** A person has a **blackout** if they lose consciousness.
[see also **black out** at **black**]

black sheep /blak ˈʃiːp/ *noun*: **black sheep**
A **black sheep** is a member of a family or group who is disapproved of in some way: *the black sheep of the family.*

blacksmith /blaksmɪθ/ *noun*: **blacksmiths**
A **blacksmith** is a person who makes and repairs iron goods, such as horseshoes and gates, by hand.

bladder /ˈbladə(r)/ *noun*: **bladders**
The **bladder** is the bag-like organ in the body which collects and stores urine until it leaves the body.

blade /bleɪd/ *noun*: **blades**
1 The **blade** of *eg* a knife or sword is the sharp part that cuts. **2** A **blade** of grass is a single leaf of it. **3** The **blade** of an oar or bat is the wide flat part of it. **4** The **blades** of a helicopter or a propeller are the parts that spin round. [compare **rotor**]

blame /bleɪm/ *verb*; *noun*
▻ ***verb***: **blames, blaming, blamed**
1 You **blame** a person or thing for something bad or wrong if you think, or say, that they are responsible for it: *The poor sales figures can be blamed on the recession.* □ *Don't try and blame it on me.* □ *Untidy as he was himself, he usually blamed me for the mess the house was in.* **2** (*usually with a negative*) You say that you do not **blame** someone for doing something if you think it was reasonable behaviour in the circumstances: *She went straight to one of the directors and complained, and I can't say I blame her.* □ *'I'm thinking of resigning in protest.' 'I don't blame you.'*
▻ ***noun*** (*uncount*)
The **blame** for something bad that has happened is the responsibility for letting it happen, or causing it: *I refuse to take the blame for this.* [compare **fault**, **responsibility**]

▻ ***phrase*** You **are to blame** for something bad that has happened if you caused it, or let it happen. [*same as* be **responsible**]

blameless /ˈbleɪmləs/ *adjective*
You are **blameless** if you have not done anything bad or wrong. [*same as* **innocent**; *opposite* **guilty**]

blanch /blɑːntʃ/ *verb*: **blanches, blanching, blanched**
1 You **blanch** if your face suddenly becomes white with fear or shock. **2** (*cookery*) You **blanch** vegetables when you put them into boiling water briefly, *eg* to loosen their skins.

bland /bland/ *adjective*: **blander, blandest**
1 Bland food has almost no taste or flavour. [*same as* **tasteless**; *opposite* **piquant, tasty**] **2** A **bland** person has a calm, uniformly pleasant manner, but does not show much genuine warmth or feeling: *He smiled his bland smile.* **3** A **bland** artistic or musical style is quite pleasant but not interesting or stimulating: *bland architecture.* [*opposite* **exciting**] — *adverb* **blandly:** *'Well, thank you Miss Staines,' he said blandly, concluding the interview.*

blandishments /ˈblandɪʃmənts/ *noun* (*plural; formal*)
Blandishments are flattering things you say to someone to try to persuade them to do something, especially something wrong.

blank /blaŋk/ *adjective; noun*
▻ ***adjective***: **blanker, blankest**
1 A **blank** piece of paper has nothing written or printed on it: *Blank pages are supplied at the back of the diary for your personal memoranda.* **2** A **blank** audio or video tape has no sound or pictures recorded on it. **3** A **blank** form is a printed form with spaces on it for writing in details, which has not yet been filled in: *I left the spaces in Section C blank.* **4** Someone's face or expression is **blank** if it shows that they don't understand what you are saying to them, or don't know the answer to your question, or are not aware of what is going on around them: *I mentioned your name but he looked blank.* □ *She looked up at us with a blank expression, not the least recognition in her eyes.* — *adverb* **blankly:** *I stopped a passer-by and tried asking him the way in French, but he just looked at me blankly.* □ *She sat staring blankly into space.*
▻ ***noun***: **blanks**
1 The **blanks** in a form are the spaces left for details, information or your signature. **2** (*used in the singular*) You can say that your mind is a **blank** when you can remember nothing: *My mind went a complete blank.*
▻ ***phrase*** You **draw a blank** when you get no results, especially when you cannot find someone or something you are looking for: *The police have so far drawn a blank in their search for the man last seen with her.*

blank cheque /blaŋk ˈtʃɛk/ *noun*: **blank cheques**
A **blank cheque** is a cheque that has been signed but on which the amount to be paid has been left out, to be filled in later.

blanket /ˈblaŋkɪt/ *noun; adjective; verb*
▻ ***noun***: **blankets**
1 A **blanket** is a thick warm covering for a bed, usually made of wool. **2** A **blanket** of *eg* fog, cloud or snow covers an area thickly.
▻ ***adjective***
Blanket means general or applying to or covering all cases: *a blanket rule that will effect all employees.*
▻ ***verb***: **blankets, blanketing, blanketed**
Something such as fog, cloud or snow **blankets** an area when it covers it thickly.

blare /blɛə(r)/ *verb, noun*
▻ ***verb***: **blares, blaring, blared**
Something such as a radio or television **blares** when it is turned on loud and is producing a harsh noise: *Drivers sat impatiently at their wheels, horns blaring.*
▻ ***noun*** (*used in the singular*): *the blare of the loudspeakers.*

> ***phrasal verb***
> Something such as a radio **blares out** sound, or sound **blares out** of it, when it makes a loud harsh sound: *disco music blaring out from one of the shops along the street.*

blasé /blɑːˈzeɪ/ or /ˈblɑːzeɪ/ *adjective*
You are **blasé** about something that other people would consider exciting if you have had plenty of experience of it before, and so are not excited or impressed by it: *By the age of ten she was quite blasé about appearing on television.* [*same as* **nonchalant, unconcerned**; *opposite* **excited, enthusiastic**]

blaspheme /blasˈfiːm/ *verb*: **blasphemes, blaspheming, blasphemed**
People **blaspheme** when they speak disrespectfully about God or holy things, or use the name of God as a swearword.

blasphemous /ˈblasfəməs/ *adjective*
Blasphemous words or actions are disrespectful to God or holy things: *blasphemous writings* □ *I don't like you being blasphemous like that.*

blasphemy /ˈblasfəmɪ/ *noun* (*uncount*)
Blasphemy is the use of language that is rude or disrespectful to God or holy things, or the use of God's name as a swearword: *He was accused of blasphemy.* [compare **sacrilege**]

blast /blɑːst/ *noun; verb; interjection*
▻ ***noun***: **blasts**
1 A **blast** is an explosion: *windows shattered by the blast* □ *a bomb blast.* **2** A **blast** of *eg* wind or air is a strong, sudden stream or gust of it. **3** A **blast** is a sudden loud sound of *eg* a trumpet or car horn: *The driver gave a blast on his horn.*
▻ ***verb***: **blasts, blasting, blasted**
A hole **is blasted** in something when it is made by means of explosives: *A tunnel had been blasted through the solid rock.*
▻ ***interjection*** (*swearword*)
People use **'blast!'** to express extreme annoyance: *Blast! I've forgotten my keys.*
▻ ***phrase*** A machine is on **at full blast** if it is producing as much power, heat or sound as it can: *Do you really need the heater on at full blast?*

> ***phrasal verb***
> A spacecraft **blasts off** when it is launched by means of rocket power. [see also **blast-off**]

blasted /ˈblɑːstɪd/ *adjective* (*swearword*)
People use **blasted** to refer to something that they are annoyed by: *The blasted train is going to be late again.*

blast-off /ˈblɑːstɒf/ *noun* (*uncount*)
Blast-off is the moment when a spacecraft is launched. [see also **blast off** at **blast**]

blatant /ˈbleɪtənt/ *adjective*
Someone whose bad or wrong behaviour is **blatant** does not bother to disguise it or conceal it: *a blatant lie* □ *blatant disobedience* □ *People were quite blatant about helping themselves to the office stationery.* [*same as* **flagrant**] — *adverb* **blatantly:** *She blatantly ignored the instructions she was given.*

blaze /bleɪz/ *noun; verb*

▻ ***noun***: **blazes**

1 A **blaze** is a bright strong fire or flame: *Several people were injured in the blaze.* **2** (*used in the singular*) You do something in a **blaze** of publicity if you are the centre of media attention when you do it: *They married in a blaze of publicity.* **3** (*used in the singular*) A **blaze** of *eg* colour or light is a brilliant display of it: *The flower beds were a blaze of colour.*

▻ ***verb***: **blazes, blazing, blazed**

1 A fire **blazes** when it burns brightly; light **blazes** when it shines brightly: *A log fire was blazing in the grate.* □ *The sun blazed down on them.* **2** A place that **is blazing** with *eg* light or colour is full of it: *The streets were blazing with light.* **3** Someone's eyes **blaze** when they flash with anger.

▻ ***phrase*** (*informal*) You do something **like blazes** when you do it as fast and vigorously as you can: *I've been working like blazes the get the spare room painted in time for Mum's visit.*

blazer /ˈbleɪzə(r)/ *noun*: **blazers**

A **blazer** is a light jacket, often in the colours of a school or club, sometimes worn as part of a uniform: *a school blazer.*

blazing /ˈbleɪzɪŋ/ *adjective or adverb*; *adjective*

▻ ***adjective or adverb***

Weather that is **blazing**, or **blazing** hot, is very hot: *a blazing hot day.* □ *It was absolutely blazing here yesterday.* □ *blazing June weather.*

▻ ***adjective***

1 People have a **blazing** row when they quarrel angrily. **2** You are **blazing** when you are very angry: *I could see he was blazing.*

bleach /bliːtʃ/ *noun*; *verb*

▻ ***noun*** (*uncount*)

Bleach is a liquid chemical used to make fabric white or to lighten the colour of hair.

▻ ***verb***: **bleaches, bleaching, bleached**

You **bleach** fabric when you use bleach to make it white; you **bleach** your hair when you use bleach to lighten its colour; fabrics or hair **bleach** in the sun when they become paler in colour; the sun **bleaches** things when it makes them paler in colour: *sun-tanned children, their hair bleached by the sun.* □ *The cotton is spread out in the sun to bleach.*

bleak /bliːk/ *adjective*

1 A place that is **bleak** is bare and desolate: *a farm set in bleak countryside.* [*same as* **bare, desolate**] **2** You say that the situation is **bleak** when it is bad, and unlikely to get better: *The company's future looks bleak.* [*same as* **hopeless**] **3** You feel **bleak** when you feel depressed: *You look a bit bleak. What's the matter?* □ *She gave him a bleak little smile.* [*same as* **depressed**; *opposite* **cheerful, bright**] **4 Bleak** weather is cold and dull. [*same as* **dreary**; *opposite* **bright, pleasant**] — *adverb* **bleakly:** *He was gazing bleakly out of the window.* — *noun* (*uncount*) **bleakness:** *the bleakness of the countryside around Haworth.*

bleary /ˈblɪərɪ/ *adjective*: **blearier, bleariest**

Your eyes are **bleary** when they are red and dim, *eg* from sleepiness: *He stirred slightly and opened one bleary eye.* — *adverb* **blearily:** *She glanced blearily round the room.*

bleat /bliːt/ *verb*; *noun*

▻ ***verb***: **bleats, bleating, bleated**

1 Sheep or goats **bleat** when they make their typical cry. **2** People **bleat** when they speak in a whining, complaining voice: *'But I don't want to go without my Mum,' bleated the child.*

▻ ***noun***: **bleats:** *The fields were alive with bleats as lambs and their mothers communicated.*

bleed /bliːd/ *verb*: **bleeds, bleeding, bled**

A person, part of their body, or a wound, **bleeds** when blood comes from them: *His nose was bleeding.* □ *Oh, look; I'm bleeding.* □ *The cut bled for ages.* — *noun* (*uncount*) **bleeding:** *The priority is always to stop the bleeding.*

bleep /bliːp/ *verb*; *noun*

▻ ***verb***: **bleeps, bleeping, bleeped**

A machine **bleeps** when it gives out a short high sound.

▻ ***noun***: **bleeps:** *Please leave your message after the bleep.* □ *The smoke alarm was emitting a piercing repetitive bleep.*

bleeper /ˈbliːpə(r)/ *noun*: **bleepers**

A **bleeper** is a small radio receiver that you carry in your pocket and that makes a bleeping sound when it picks up a signal, used *eg* to call a doctor in a hospital.

blemish /ˈblemɪʃ/ *noun, verb*

▻ ***noun***: **blemishes**

A **blemish** is a stain or mark that spoils the appearance of someone or something: *She had clear white skin with hardly a blemish upon it.*

▻ ***verb***: **blemishes, blemishing, blemished**

One thing **blemishes** another if it spoils its perfection: *There were tales of a scandal that had blemished his reputation in his youth.* [*same as* **damage, compromise**]

blend /blɛnd/ *verb*; *noun*

▻ ***verb***: **blends, blending, blended**

1 You **blend** two or more things when you mix them together: *Blend the cream with the melted chocolate.* **2** Two things **blend** when they go well together: *A choir needs people whose voices blend well.* □ *I like the colours you've chosen; they blend nicely.* **3** One thing **blends** into another when it merges into it: *At the horizon the sea blended into the sky.*

▻ ***noun***: **blends**

A **blend** is anything produced by mixing two or more substances together: *The finest coffee beans have been used in this blend.*

blender /ˈblɛndə(r)/ *noun*: **blenders**

A **blender** is a machine for mixing or liquidizing food.

bless /blɛs/ *verb*: **blesses, blessing, blessed** or **blest**

1 A priest **blesses** people or things when he asks God to protect them or look favourably on them: *The minister raised his hands to bless to congregation.* **2** You **are blessed** with something that is considered an advantage if you have it: *She has always been blessed with good health.* **3** If you say you **bless** someone or something you mean you are grateful for them: *I bless the day I bought this washing-up machine.*

▻ ***phrase*** (*informal*) **1** You use *eg* **'bless you!'** or **'bless her!'** as an expression of affection or sympathy: *The baby's fallen fast asleep, bless him!* □ *You needn't have done all that washing-up, bless you!* **2** You traditionally say **'bless you!'** to someone who has just sneezed.

blessed /ˈblɛsɪd/ *adjective*

You use **blessed** in reference to things you are very grateful for: *a few moments of blessed silence.* — *adverb* **blessedly:** *This week has been blessedly warm after last week's storms.*

blessing /ˈblɛsɪŋ/ *noun*: **blessings**

1 Something that is a **blessing** is something good that you are grateful for: *What a blessing it is that the winter has been so mild.* [compare **a good thing**] **2** You have someone's **blessing**, or do something with their **blessing**, if they approve of what you are doing and hope you will be successful: *Her parents deeply disapproved of him, and she married him without their blessing.* □ *The board of directors have given their blessing to*

the idea. **3** A priest says the **blessing** at the end of a religious service when he says a prayer asking God to look after the congregation.
▻ ***phrases*** **1** Something that is **a blessing in disguise** seems unfortunate or inconvenient when it happens but turns out to have been the best thing that could have happened. **2** You **count your blessings** if you remember what is good in your life instead of complaining. **3** A situation that is **a mixed blessing** has disadvantages as well as advantages.

blew /bluː/ *verb*
Blew is the past tense of **blow**[1].

blight /blaɪt/ *noun; verb*
▻ ***noun*: blights**
1 (*usually in the singular*) People refer to something that causes a lot of difficulty, or spoils things, as a **blight**: *Hilary got flu, which rather cast a blight over our half-term holiday.* **2** (*count or uncount*) A **blight** is a disease that spreads through plants and destroys them: *an outbreak of potato blight.*
▻ ***verb*: blights, blighting, blighted**
Something that **is blighted** by something else is damaged or destroyed by it: *Constant trouble with his knee this season has blighted his chances of a place in the Olympic team.* ▫ *people who go through life blighted by a stammer* ▫ *blighted hopes.*

blind /blaɪnd/ *adjective; adverb; verb*
▻ ***adjective***
1 A person or animal that is **blind** cannot see, usually because there is something wrong with their eyes: *Hundreds of children go blind every year.* ▫ *He's blind in his right eye.* ▫ *She's been blind since birth.* ▫ *The cubs are born blind and helpless.* **2** You describe someone as **blind** if they do not notice, or refuse to acknowledge, what is happening; you are **blind** to a fact or circumstance if you are unaware of it: *She could only blame herself for being so blind and trusting.* ▫ *Most people are blind to their own faults.* ▫ *We tend to be blind to the sufferings of others.* **3** Your attitude to something, or your feelings about it, are **blind** if they prevent you from judging it impartially: *their blind belief in the righteousness of their cause* ▫ *It's true that love is blind.* ▫ *the old automatic responses that result from blind prejudice.* [*same as* **unreasoning**] **4** A **blind** corner is one that you can't see round: *The driver had parked on a blind bend.* ▫ *He had tried to overtake on a blind summit.* — *noun* (*uncount*) **blindness:** *blindness caused by disease.*
▻ ***adverb***
You perform a task **blind** when for the sake of impartiality, or for some other reason, relevant facts or data, such as details of identification, are not supplied to you: *Samples will be analysed blind by an independent pathologist.*
▻ ***noun*: blinds**
1 A **blind** is a fitted covering for a window made *eg* of cloth or of metal sections, that can be pulled down over the window, or pulled up to let in light: *Emily lowered the blind again.* [see also **Venetian blind**] **2** (*plural*) The **blind** are people who cannot see: *training more guide dogs for the blind* ▫ *I went to a special school for the blind.* ▫ *workshops for the blind and disabled.*
▻ ***verb*: blinds, blinding, blinded**
1 Something **blinds** you when it makes you blind, or temporarily unable to see: *A piece of metal flew out of the machine and blinded him.* ▫ *The flash temporarily blinded me.* ▫ *He looked away, blinded by tears.* **2** Something **blinds** you to a fact or situation if it prevents you from noticing it or acknowledging it: *It's certainly not the case that tolerance blinds you to people's imperfections.* ▫ *Excitement could blind her to the dangers.* **3** You **are blinded** by an emotion if it makes you behave unreasonably: *Blinded by rage, he refused to listen to their pleas.*
▻ ***phrases*** **1** (*informal*) Someone who does not take a **blind bit** of notice of something, or does not pay it a **blind bit** of attention, ignores it: *When a valued ally of the West attacks a defenceless people no-one pays a blind bit of attention.* **2** For **turn a blind eye to** see **eye**.

blind alley /blaɪnd ˈalɪ/ *noun*: **blind alleys**
1 A **blind alley** is a narrow road with an opening at one end only. **2** You can describe a course of action as a **blind alley** if it does not lead anywhere, or produce useful results: *The police were led up a blind alley owing to the false information they had received*

blind date /blaɪnd ˈdeɪt/ *noun*: **blind dates**
Someone arranges a **blind date** for you when they arrange for you to go out with a person that you have not met before.

blindfold /ˈblaɪndfoʊld/ *noun; verb*
▻ ***noun*: blindfolds**
A **blindfold** is a strip of cloth that is tied over someone's eyes to prevent them from seeing.
▻ ***verb*: blindfolds, blindfolding, blindfolded**
To **blindfold** someone is to tie a strip of cloth over their eyes so that they cannot see: *He was tied to a chair and then gagged and blindfolded.*

blinding /ˈblaɪndɪŋ/ *adjective*
1 Blinding light is very bright: *There was a sudden blinding flash.* **2** You use **blinding** to emphasize how obvious something is: *It amazed me that they could not see what to me was the blinding truth.* — *adverb* **blindingly:** *Look, it's blindingly obvious she's not interested in you.*

blindly /ˈblaɪndlɪ/ *adverb*
You do something **blindly** if you do it **1** without being able to see properly or without looking properly: *She stared blindly at the ground as a feeling of utter panic swept over her.* **2** without knowing all the facts, or without considering them: *We should not blindly make easy moralistic assumptions.* ▫ *It's ridiculous to go blindly on taking no account of the difficulties.*

blind spot /ˈblaɪnd spɒt/ *noun*: **blind spots**
1 A **blind spot** is a part that you cannot see properly or clearly, usually because something is in the way: *a motorist's blind spot.* **2** You have a **blind spot** about a subject if you cannot understand it: *Gerald had a blind spot as far as languages were concerned.* **3** (*technical*) Your **blind spot** is a small area at the back of the eye which is not sensitive to light and has no vision.

blink /blɪŋk/ *verb; noun*
▻ ***verb*: blinks, blinking, blinked**
1 You **blink** when you open and shut your eyes very quickly: *The bright light made her blink.* **2** A light **blinks** when it flashes on and off or shines unsteadily: *We could see lights blinking on the ships out in the bay.* [*same as* **flicker, twinkle**]
▻ ***noun*** (*usually in the singular*): *a blink of light.*
▻ ***phrases*** **1** Something happens **in the blink of an eye** if it happens very quickly. **2** (*informal*) A machine is **on the blink** if it is not working properly.

blinkered /ˈblɪŋkəd/ *adjective* (*BrE; derogatory*)
Someone who is **blinkered**, or has a **blinkered** attitude, cannot, or will not even try to, understand the opinions of others.

blinkers /ˈblɪŋkəz/ *noun* (*plural*)
1 Blinkers are the two small, flat pieces of leather attached to a horse's bridle to stop it from seeing side-

ways. **2** You say someone is wearing **blinkers** if they cannot understand other people's attitudes, or will not try to do so.

bliss /blɪs/ *noun* (*uncount*)
1 Bliss is a state of carefree happiness: *living a life of bliss.* **2** Something that is **bliss** is delightful: *It was bliss not having to get up and go to work.*

blissful /ˈblɪsfʊl/ *adjective*
1 Something that is **blissful** makes you feel happy: *We had a blissful holiday in Crete.* **2** You are in **blissful** ignorance of some important or unpleasant fact if you are unaware of it. — *adverb* **blissfully:** *They continued to converse in loud voices, blissfully unaware that the lecture had begun.*

blister /ˈblɪstə(r)/ *noun*; *verb*
▻ ***noun*: blisters**
1 A **blister** is a painful swelling on the skin containing liquid, caused by a burn, or by something rubbing the skin: *These shoes have given me blisters.* **2** A **blister** on a painted or plastic surface is bubble-like projection: *The heat had raised blisters in the paintwork.*
▻ ***verb*: blisters, blistering, blistered**
Skin or other surfaces **blister** or **are blistered** when blisters appear on them: *Fair-skinned people can blister easily in the hot sun.* □ *blistered heels* □ *The doors were all blackened and blistered after the fire.*

blistering /ˈblɪstərɪŋ/ *adjective*
1 The weather is **blistering** when it is very hot. **2** A **blistering** remark is full of anger and is meant to hurt someone: *He faced blistering criticism from the Opposition benches.*

blithe /blaɪð/ *adjective*
Blithe describes things people do or say thoughtlessly, usually in cheerful ignorance of some serious reality: *He came in with some blithe remark about the fine day.* □ *She chattered on, in blithe unawareness of his presence.* [*same as* **cheerful**, **unthinking**] — *adverb* **blithely:** *I don't know what you're so worried about,' she continued blithely.*

blizzard /ˈblɪzəd/ *noun*: **blizzards**
There is a **blizzard** when snow is falling thickly and being blown by the wind: *The rescuers are faced with blizzard conditions on the mountain.*

bloated /ˈbloʊtɪd/ *adjective*
1 Something that is **bloated** is swollen with gas or liquid that has built up inside it: *bloated corpses.* **2** *You feel* **bloated** *after a big meal when you feel uncomfortably full.*

blob /blɒb/ *noun*: **blobs**
1 A **blob** of some thick, sticky liquid is a small, soft, round mass of it: *a blob of jam.* **2** Something is a **blob** when you cannot see it clearly, *eg* because it is a long way away: *By now the cottage was a scarcely distinguishable blob on the horizon.*

bloc /blɒk/ *noun*: **blocs**
A **bloc** of countries is a group of them with common interests, that act together: *the former Soviet bloc.* [see also **en bloc**]

block /blɒk/ *noun*; *verb*
▻ ***noun*: blocks**
1 A **block** of *eg* stone, wood or ice is a solid mass of it, usually rectangular in shape. **2** A **block** is a large building containing *eg* offices or flats: *office blocks near the centre of town.* **3** (*especially AmE*) A **block** is a group of buildings with roads on all four sides: *The cinema is six blocks away.* **4** A **block** in *eg* a pipe or road is something that prevents things passing through it or along it: *The police set up road blocks on all the roads leading out of town.* [*same as* **obstruction**] **5** You have a mental **block** when you can't remember something, or how to do it or deal with it.
▻ ***verb*: blocks, blocking, blocked**
1 Something **blocks** *eg* a road, channel, tunnel or pipe if it prevents things passing through or along it: *There's a piece of bread blocking his windpipe.* [*same as* **obstruct**] **2** Someone or something **blocks** your way if they are in front of you and stop you from moving forwards. [*same as* **obstruct**] **3** Something **blocks** your view if it is between you and the object you are looking at and so stops you from seeing it properly. **4** You **block** something that is being proposed if you stop it from happening: *The council blocked his plans to build a new supermarket.* [*same as* **obstruct, veto**] — *adjective* **blocked:** *Could you give me a hand? Our kitchen sink is blocked.* □ *He awoke next morning with a headache, a sore throat and a blocked nose.* □ *An accident has left both lanes completely blocked.*

phrasal verbs
block in Someone or something **blocks** you **in** if they stop you from moving or from getting out: *I returned to my car to find it blocked in by a parked van.*
block off To **block off** *eg* a street or passageway is to place something across it so that people cannot go along it.
block out 1 Something **blocks out** light if it stops light from getting in: *A large cupboard stood in front of the window, completely blocking out the light.* [*same as* **shut out**] **2** You **block out** *eg* memories or bad experiences when you stop yourself thinking about them: *She had tried to block out the accident, but it kept returning to haunt her.* [*same as* **shut out**]
block up An opening or passage **is blocked up** when there is something across it that stops movement through it: *The old entrance had been blocked up.* □ *Something is blocking up the sink.*

blockade /blɒˈkeɪd/ *noun*; *verb*
▻ ***noun*: blockades**
The **blockade** of a place is the action of surrounding it with troops or ships, to stop supplies from reaching it. [*same as* **siege**]
▻ ***verb*: blockades, blockading, blockaded**
To **blockade** a place is to put a blockade round it or besiege it: *Rebel troops were blockading the town.* [*same as* **besiege**]

blockage /ˈblɒkɪdʒ/ *noun*: **blockages**
A **blockage** is anything that blocks *eg* a road, channel, tunnel or pipe: *He had a blockage in one of his arteries, but it's cleared now.* [*same as* **obstruction**]

block capital /blɒk ˈkapɪtəl/ *noun*: **block capitals**
Block capitals or **block letters** are capital letters: *Please write your address clearly in block capitals.*

bloke /bloʊk/ *noun* (*informal*): **blokes**
People sometimes refer to a man as a **bloke**: *I like Bill; he's a good bloke.* □ *A bloke from the Gas Board called while you were out.* [*same as* **guy**, **fellow**]

blonde or **blond** /blɒnd/ *adjective*; *noun*
(the form **blond** is used especially in reference to men and their hair)
▻ ***adjective***
1 Blonde hair is pale yellow or golden: *Kathy had beautiful thick blonde wavy hair.* **2** A **blonde** person has pale yellow or golden hair: *a tall blond Frenchman.* □ *Their children were all blonde and blue-eyed.*
▻ ***noun*: blondes**
A **blonde** is a person with pale yellow or golden hair: *Hal was a blond and his hair flopped attractively over*

his forehead. □ *He was accompanied by a nice-looking blonde.* [compare **brunette**]

blood /blʌd/ *noun* (*uncount*)
1 Blood is the red liquid pumped through your body by your heart: *She'd lost a lot of blood as a result of the accident.* **2** Someone's **blood** can also be a reference to their racial or family origins: *There was certainly some royal blood on his mother's side.* □ *She was always hot-tempered; I suppose that was her Celtic blood.* [*same as* **ancestry**]
▷ ***phrases*** **1** There is **bad blood** between people if they have quarrelled, and hate each other. **2** For **flesh and blood** see **flesh**. **3** Someone commits a crime **in cold blood** when they do it in a planned, deliberate way, as distinct from being emotionally out of control at the time: *The victims had been murdered in cold blood.* **4** Something such as a talent **is in your blood** if it is natural to you, and is shared by other members of your family: *Acting was in their blood.* **5** Someone or something **makes your blood boil** if they make you very angry: *The rude way she treats her mother makes my blood boil.* **6** Something that **makes your blood run cold** makes you feel very frightened: *There came a noise that made our blood run cold.* **7** Someone who is **out for your blood** is angry with you and determined to punish you. **8** You **sweat blood** if you work very hard: *I sweated blood getting my thesis written in time for the deadline.* **9** New people in a profession, business or job are sometimes referred to as **new blood**, **fresh blood** or **young blood**.

bloodbath /ˈblʌdbɑːθ/ *noun*: **bloodbaths**
A fight or battle in which a lot of people get killed or badly injured is described as a **bloodbath**. [*same as* **massacre, carnage**]

bloodcurdling /ˈblʌdkɜːdlɪŋ/ *adjective*
A **bloodcurdling** noise or scene is a very frightening one: *Out of the darkness came a bloodcurdling scream.*

blood donor /ˈblʌd doʊnə(r)/ *noun*: **blood donors**
A **blood donor** is a person who gives some of their blood so that it can be injected into people who have lost blood through injury or illness.

blood group /ˈblʌd gruːp/ *noun*: **blood groups**
A **blood group** is any one of the four types of human blood, A, B, AB and O.

bloodless /ˈblʌdləs/ *adjective*
1 A **bloodless** victory is one achieved without violence or anybody being killed: *a bloodless military coup.* **2** A person's face or lips are **bloodless** when they are very pale.

blood poisoning /ˈblʌd pɔɪzənɪŋ/ *noun* (*uncount*)
Blood poisoning is a serious infection of the blood.

blood pressure /ˈblʌd prɛʃə(r)/ *noun* (*uncount*)
Your **blood pressure** is the force with which your blood flows through your body, or the amount that this force measures: *Lisbeth was having problems with high blood pressure.*

bloodshed /ˈblʌdʃɛd/ *noun* (*uncount*)
Bloodshed is fighting that results in people getting killed or badly injured: *Now that a precarious peace has been established we certainly don't want there to be any bloodshed over this comparatively minor issue.*

bloodshot /ˈblʌdʃɒt/ *adjective*
Your eyes are **bloodshot** when the whites of them are covered with a network of red veins.

blood sports /ˈblʌd spɔːts/ *noun* (*plural*)
Blood sports are those sports that involve the killing of animals.

bloodstained /ˈblʌdsteɪnd/ *adjective*
Something that is **bloodstained** is stained with blood: *bloodstained clothing.*

bloodstream /ˈblʌdstriːm/ *noun*: **bloodstreams**
Your **bloodstream** is the blood flowing through your body.

bloodthirsty /ˈblʌdθɜːstɪ/ *adjective*
1 Someone who is **bloodthirsty** enjoys watching violence or killing, or enjoys taking part in it. **2 Bloodthirsty** films or books have a lot of violence and killing in them.

blood transfusion /ˈblʌd trɑːnsfjuːʒən/ *noun*: **blood transfusions**
A **blood transfusion** is the procedure or process of giving an ill or injured person blood taken from someone healthy.

blood vessel /ˈblʌd vɛsəl/ *noun*: **blood vessels**
Your **blood vessels** are the tubes, arteries and veins in your body, which your blood flows through.

bloody /ˈblʌdɪ/ *adjective or adverb*; *adjective*
▷ ***adjective or adverb*** (*swearword*)
People use **bloody** for emphasis in referring to things that annoy them: *The bloody car won't start.* □ *I think you're being a bloody fool.* □ *The bus service here is bloody awful.*
▷ ***adjective***: **bloodier, bloodiest**
1 Something that is **bloody** is covered with blood; a **bloody** mark is one made with blood: *There was a trail of bloody footprints leading down the path.* □ *His fingers were torn and bloody.* **2** A **bloody** fight or battle involves a lot of people getting killed or badly injured.

bloody-minded /blʌdɪˈmaɪndɪd/ *adjective*
Someone who is being **bloody-minded** is being unreasonable and refusing to co-operate. [*same as* **stubborn, obstinate**] — *noun* (*uncount*) **bloody-mindedness:** *It's just bloody-mindedness on her part.*

bloom /bluːm/ *noun*; *verb*
▷ ***noun***: **blooms**
1 A **bloom** is a flower: *She selected several blooms from the rose bush.* **2** (*used in the singular*) The **bloom** on something such as a peach or someone's skin is its soft smooth surface or delicate colour: *The light breeze had given her cheeks a delicate pink bloom.*
▷ ***verb***: **blooms, blooming, bloomed**
1 a A flower **blooms** when the bud opens fully. **b** A tree or plant **blooms** when its flowers develop and open. **2** Someone or something that **is blooming** is healthy or growing and developing well: *I expect your children are all blooming as usual.* [*same as* **flourish**]
▷ ***phrases*** Trees or plants **come into bloom** when they produce flowers, and are **in bloom** when their flowers have developed: *It was early May, and the lilacs were in full bloom in the gardens of north Oxford.*

blossom /ˈblɒsəm/ *noun*; *verb*
▷ ***noun***: **blossoms**
1 (*uncount*) **Blossom** is a mass of flowers, especially on a fruit tree: *apple blossom.* **2** A **blossom** is a flower, or one of the flowers forming a mass of flowers on *eg* a fruit tree: *pink blossoms on the cherry trees.*
▷ ***verb***: **blossoms, blossoming, blossomed**
1 A tree **blossoms** when it develops flowers or blossom. **2** A person **blossoms** when they develop in a healthy, pleasing or attractive way: *Dorothy had blossomed into a beautiful young woman.* □ *He really blossomed out when he went to university.*
▷ ***phrase*** A tree is **in blossom** when it has blossom on it.

blot /blɒt/ *noun, verb*

▻ ***noun*: blots**
1 A **blot** is a drop of liquid, usually ink, that has been spilt on a surface and has dried: *The essay she handed in was the usual mass of blots and crossings-out.* **2** Something that is a **blot** on the landscape spoils its beauty: *There was an ugly quarry in the side of the hill, but the locals seemed not to regard it as a blot on the landscape.* **3** Something that is a **blot** on someone's reputation is a scandal or other incident that damages it.
▻ ***verb*: blots, blotting, blotted**
You **blot** a wet surface when you dry it by pressing cloth or paper over it.

phrasal verb
blot out 1 One thing **blots out** another if it covers it and stops it from being seen: *A big cloud had blotted out the sun.* **2** You **blot out** a painful or unpleasant memory if you try not to think about it or remember it: *I could not blot out the image of the injured man.*

blotch /blɒtʃ/ *noun*: **blotches**
A **blotch** on a surface, especially skin, is a round patch of colour: *I woke to find my face covered with ugly red blotches.*

blotchy /ˈblɒtʃɪ/ *adjective*: **blotchier, blotchiest**
Something that is **blotchy** has blotches on it: *blotchy skin.*

blotting paper /ˈblɒtɪŋ peɪpə(r)/ *noun* (*uncount*)
Blotting paper is soft thick paper that you use for drying writing done in ink.

blouse /blaʊz/ *noun*: **blouses**
A **blouse** is a woman's shirt-like garment. [see picture at **clothing**]

blow /bloʊ/ *verb*; *noun*; *interjection*
▻ ***verb*: blows, blowing, blew, blown**
1 a A wind or breeze **is blowing** when the air is moving strongly enough for you to feel it doing so: *A bitter wind was blowing from the north.* □ *High winds blew constantly across the moors.* **b** A wind, breeze or draught **blows** something somewhere when it carries it there; something **blows** somewhere when the wind carries it there: *The wind was strong enough to blow us through the Bristol Channel.* □ *The gale threatened to blow her into the water.* □ *The wind blew the leaves into little heaps.* □ *My tent got blown away and some of my stuff with it.* □ *Our old oak tree was blown down in a storm.* □ *Litter was blowing about the streets.* □ *She had fair fluffy hair that blew across her face.* **c** You **blow** when you shape your mouth into an 'O' and force air out through it: *She blew again on the hot cocoa.* □ *It was a sound like someone blowing through a piece of pipe.* □ *He was smoking a cigarette, blowing out streams of smoke.* □ *I blew the dust off the book cover.* **d** You **blow** bubbles by forcing air from your mouth either through liquid, creating a lot of bubbles, or into individual soap bubbles, making them expand: *I gave her a straw to blow bubbles with.* **e** You **blow** a whistle, or an instrument such as a trumpet or horn, when you make it sound by forcing air through it from your mouth; drivers can be said to **blow** their horns when they operate the mechanism that makes their horn sound: *I got back to my compartment just as the guard was blowing his whistle.* □ *A whistle blew and the match ended.* □ *Bus-drivers never blow their horns at other buses.* [compare **sound**] **f** You **blow** your nose when you breath sharply through it, usually into a handkerchief, to clear it: *To avoid nose bleeds, try not to blow your nose too hard.* **g** You **blow** someone a kiss by kissing the tips of your fingers and pretending to blow the kiss in their direction: *He blew a kiss to one of the women.*
2 a Part of something **is blown** off or away when it is removed by the force of a blast or explosion: *I nearly got my head blown off.* □ *The device hit a curtain, fell to the ground, and blew a hole in the floor.* □ *The vehicle had been blown to pieces by remote control.* □ *A bomb exploded in the city, blowing out thousands of windows.* **b** A fuse **blows** or **is blown** when it burns, because too much electricity has been sent through it. **c** (*informal*) You **blow** a chance or opportunity when you waste it, or fail to use it properly: *You had a real chance of winning, and you blew it.* **d** (*informal*) You **blow** a lot of money when you spend it quickly, especially on something risky or unimportant: *Don't be tempted to blow all your redundancy money on a cruise.*
▻ ***noun*: blows**
1 You give someone a **blow** when you hit them: *The facial bruising is typical of an injury caused by a blow from a human fist.* □ *He had been struck a blow on the back of the head.* □ *She had died as a result of a blow to the head.* □ *She hit him hard, a stinging blow across the cheek.* □ *She tried to protect her head from the blows raining down on it.* **2** A **blow** is a happening that disappoints you, upsets you, or ruins you: *The loss of any animal is a severe blow to a small farmer with 10 cows and a few pigs.* □ *His death was a bitter blow to her.* □ *His failure to get a place on the course was a painful blow to his pride.* □ *The Second World War dealt a devastating blow to the country's thriving economy, from which it never recovered.* **3** You strike a **blow** for, or against, a cause or policy when you do something that helps to persuade people to support it, or reject it: *Yorkshire's Indian cricketing hero had struck a mighty blow against racism in cricket.* □ *We are striking a blow for common sense and ordinary human decency.* **4** (*used in the singular*) A **blow** is an act of blowing: *He gave his nose a good blow.*
▻ ***interjection*** (*informal*)
1 'Blow!' expresses mild annoyance: *Oh, blow! I've forgotten my keys.* **2** (*informal*) If you say **'blow** something!', you usually mean that you are not going to worry about it: *I want that machine, and I'm going to have it; blow the expense!* [*same as* **hang**]
▻ ***phrases* 1** (*informal*) **a** (*old*) People sometimes say 'Well, **I'll be blowed**' or 'Well, **I'm blowed**' to express astonishment. **b** If you say you **are blowed if** you're going to do something, you mean you are determined not to do it: *I'm blowed if I'm going to let her have her own way all the time.* **2** You relate a series of events **blow by blow** when you tell people every detail of how they happened: *I didn't feel like hearing a blow-by-blow account of his courtship of Yvonne.* **3** For **blow hot and cold** see **hot**. **4** Something moving **catches you a blow** somewhere when it hits you there; you **catch** part of you **a blow** on something when you hit yourself on it: *The stone caught her a blow on the forehead.* □ *She caught her head a blow on the edge of the table as she fell.* **5** People **come to blows** when they start fighting: *The geologists often came to blows with the Indians over the possession of the richest sites.* **6** A circumstance that **softens** or **cushions the blow** makes something bad that happens to you feel slightly less bad: *To cushion the blow, wages and pensions were increased.*

phrasal verbs
blow out You **blow** a flame **out** when you blow hard at it, so that it stops burning or goes out; it **blows out** when it goes out in this way: *It's like watching your baby blow her birthday candles out.* □ *The wind had blown the lamp out.* □ *The night light blew out.* [*same as* **extinguish**, **go out**]

blow over 1 Trouble **blows over** when people forget about it, or no longer feel its effects: *Fortunately the quarrel blew over as suddenly as it had begun.* □ *It'll all blow over; you'll see.* **2** A storm **blows over** when the weather becomes calm again.

blow up 1 To **blow** something **up** is to destroy it by means of an explosion; something **blows up** when it is destroyed by an explosion: *They were threatening to blow up the embassy if their demands were not met.* □ *We were afraid the reserve fuel tank might blow up.* [*same as* **explode**] **2** You **blow up** *eg* a tyre or balloon when you fill it with air or gas: *As we blow the balloon up, its surface expands.* **3** You **blow** a photograph **up** when you increase its size, or enlarge it: *He pointed to a large X-ray photograph blown up on the screen in front of them.* [*same as* **enlarge**] **4** A storm, or trouble, **blows up** when it quickly becomes severe: *the crisis that had blown up between Israel and Egypt* □ *Concern over her dismissal was likely to blow up into a first-class row.* **5** Something gets **blown up** too much when too much fuss is made about it: *The incident had been blown up out of all proportion.*

blow-dry /ˈbloʊdraɪ/ *verb; noun*
▻ ***verb*: blow-dries, blow-drying, blow-dried**
You **blow-dry** your hair when you dry it in the style you want using a brush and a hairdryer.
▻ ***noun*** (*used in the singular*): *I made an appointment for a cut and blow-dry.*

blower /ˈbloʊə(r)/ *noun* (*old, informal; used in the singular*)
The **blower** is the telephone: *I'll get on the blower to him straight away.*

blown /bloʊn/ *verb*
Blown is the past participle of **blow**[1].

blowy /ˈbloʊɪ/ *adjective* (*informal*): **blowier, blowiest**
The weather is **blowy** when it is windy: *It was one of those bright, blowy days.*

bludgeon /ˈblʌdʒən/ *verb*: **bludgeons, bludgeoning, bludgeoned**
1 To **bludgeon** someone is to hit them repeatedly with a heavy weapon: *He had been bludgeoned to death.* **2** You **bludgeon** someone into doing something when you bully or threaten them till they do it: *I won't be bludgeoned into submission.*

blue /bluː/ *noun; adjective*
▻ ***noun*** (*count or uncount*): **blues**
Blue is the colour of the sky on a clear, cloudless day: *They painted the ceiling a bright blue.* □ *I suppose I do wear a lot of blue.* □ *She was dressed all in blue.* □ *the blues and greens of the sea.*
▻ ***adjective*: bluer, bluest**
1 Blue things are the colour of the sky on a clear, cloudless day: *They're blue, not green.* □ (*with the noun omitted*) *In the end I chose the pink flowers rather than the blue.* **2** (*rather old*) You feel **blue** when you feel sad or depressed. [see also **blues**] **3** Your skin is **blue** when it is pale blue or purple because you are cold. **4 Blue** films or stories are mainly about sex. [*same as* **indecent, obscene, pornographic**]
▻ ***phrases*** **1** Something that happens **out of the blue** happens without warning: *My cousin rang up out of the blue and asked to come and stay.* [*same as* **unexpectedly**] **2** For **till you are blue in the face** see **face**.

bluebell /ˈbluːbɛl/ *noun*: **bluebells**
A **bluebell** is a small wild plant with blue bell-shaped flowers.

blueberry /ˈbluːbərɪ/ *noun*: **blueberries**
Blueberries are dark blue berries that grow on low bushes in North America. [see picture at **fruit**]

bluebottle /ˈbluːbɒtəl/ *noun*: **bluebottles**
A **bluebottle** is a large fly with a shiny dark-blue body.

blueprint /ˈbluːprɪnt/ *noun*: **blueprints**
A **blueprint** is a detailed plan of work to be done or a description of how it is expected to proceed.

blues /bluːz/ *noun* (*with a singular or plural verb*)
The **blues** is slow, sad jazz music of Black American origin: *a blues singer.*
▻ ***phrase*** (*rather old, informal*) You've **got the blues** when you are feeling sad or depressed. [see also **blue**]

bluff /blʌf/ *verb; noun*
▻ ***verb*: bluffs, bluffing, bluffed**
Someone **bluffs** you when they deceive or trick you; someone who **is bluffing** is pretending: *He bluffed us into believing he had all the right academic qualifications.* □ *I still had no idea how she had managed to bluff her way into their favour.* □ *She was lying on the floor with her eyes closed, and at first I thought she was bluffing.* □ *Children begin to realize that their parents are only bluffing when they threaten them.*
▻ ***noun*** (*count or uncount*)
A **bluff** is an attempt to trick or deceive people, especially about your intentions: *We thought all those threats about suicide were just bluff.* □ *It was all an elaborate bluff.*
▻ ***phrase*** You **call** someone's **bluff** when you challenge them to carry out what they are threatening to do, or claiming to be able to do, because you don't think they will do it.

bluish /ˈbluːɪʃ/ *adjective*
Bluish things are slightly blue.

blunder /ˈblʌndə(r)/ *verb; noun*
▻ ***verb*: blunders, blundering, blundered**
1 You **blunder** when you make a stupid and usually serious mistake: *I realized I had blundered.* **2** People **blunder** somewhere when they move clumsily: *He got out of bed and blundered towards the window.*
▻ ***noun*: blunders**
A **blunder** is a stupid, clumsy and usually serious mistake: *A blunder by goalkeeper Peter Schmeichel cost Manchester United the game yesterday.*

blunt /blʌnt/ *adjective; verb*
▻ ***adjective*: blunter, bluntest**
1 A **blunt** knife or blade has a thick, worn-down edge, so does not cut very well. [*opposite* **sharp**] **2** A **blunt** pencil has a thick, worn-down point instead of a sharp one. [*opposite* **sharp**] **3** A **blunt** object has a smooth or rounded end as distinct from a sharp pointed one: *He had been hit on the head with a blunt instrument of some sort.* [*opposite* **pointed**] **4** You are **blunt** when you say what you think without trying to be polite or avoid hurting people's feelings: *I'm afraid I was a bit blunt about her cooking.* [*same as* **candid, frank**; *opposite* **subtle, tactful**] — *adverb* **bluntly:** *She was, to put it bluntly, not a born actress.* — *noun* (*uncount*) **bluntness:** *'We don't want your company,' he added, with his ususal bluntness*
▻ ***verb*: blunts, blunting, blunted**
1 Something **blunts** *eg* a knife or blade when it thickens its edge and reduces its sharpness. **2** One thing **blunts** another if it weakens it, or reduces its effectiveness: *People will insist that watching TV blunts children's imaginations.*

blur /blɜː(r)/ *noun; verb*
▻ ***noun*** (*usually in the singular*): **blurs**
Something is a **blur** if you cannot see it or remember it

clearly: *Everything in the room was a blur, like an out-of-focus photograph.* □ *My early childhood is no more than a blur.* □ *His memory of the accident was a blur.*

▻ ***verb***: **blurs, blurring, blurred**

1 Something **blurs** when it becomes rough and indistinct: *Shapes blurred and were lost in the gathering darkness.* **2** Something **blurs** or **is blurred** when it becomes dim or indistinct: *My memories of that time have blurred over the years.* □ *This cult of screen violence inevitably blurs the distinction between acceptable and unacceptable behaviour.* — *adjective* **blurred:** *an old blurred snapshot.* □ *the blurred boundaries between the public sector and the private sector.*

blurt /blɜːt/ *verb*: **blurts, blurting, blurted**

> ***phrasal verb***
> You **blurt** something **out** if you say it suddenly or without thinking what effect or result it will have: *He blurted out our secret before I had time to stop him.*

blush /blʌʃ/ *verb; noun*

▻ ***verb***: **blushes, blushing, blushed**

You **blush** when your face becomes red or pink because of *eg* shame or embarrassment: *She could feel herself blushing.*

▻ ***noun***: **blushes**: *She could feel a blush spreading over her cheeks.*

bluster /ˈblʌstə(r)/ *verb, noun*

▻ ***verb***: **blusters, blustering, blustered**

People **bluster** when they speak in an angry, defensive way, because they feel uneasy or unsure of themselves: *'You had no right to do this!' he blustered.*

▻ ***noun*** (*uncount*): *After a lot of ineffectual bluster he admitted he had been wrong.*

blustery /ˈblʌstərɪ/ *adjective*

The weather is **blustery** when it is windy. [*same as* **blowy**; *opposite* **calm**]

boa /ˈboʊə/ *noun*: **boas**

A **boa**, or **boa constrictor**, is a large South American snake that kills animals by winding itself round them and crushing them.

boar /bɔː(r)/ *noun*: **boar** or **boars**

1 A **boar** is a male pig kept for breeding. **2** A **boar** is also a wild pig.

board /bɔːd/ *noun; verb*

▻ ***noun***: **boards**

1 A **board** is **a** (*count or uncount*) a flat piece of wood, normally rectangular in shape, used *eg* in building or construction, or for a particular household purpose: *A board creaked beneath her feet as she crossed the floor.* □ *The window behind the altar had been replaced by a piece of board.* □ *a large polished-wood board inscribed with the names of all the past presidents* □ *one of those cheese boards with a knife attached* □ *Every cook needs a chopping board.* **b** a square piece of cardboard or wood designed for playing a particular game on: *a chess board with up to eight pieces on it.* **c** any of a number of flat pieces of wood or other hard material designed for a special use, usually referred to simply as a **board**, such as a diving board, blackboard or notice board: *He was drawing a diagram of a feather on the board, with some difficulty and much rubbing out.* □ *I pinned the announcement up on the board.* **2** (*with a singular or plural verb*) The **board** of a company or other organization is the group of directors who control it: *She was offered a directorship and a seat on the board.* □ *Only members of the board may sign cheques.* □ *He was on the board of a number of organizations.* □ *The board of directors of a limited company is itself a committee appointed by the shareholders.* □ *The Board are considering your application.* □ *at the next Board meeting* □ *I'm entitled to know the reason for the Board's decision.* **3** (*with a singular or plural verb*) A department of local or national government may be called a **board**: *Her husband works for the Gas Board.* □ *when the Parole Board decides that a prisoner's continued detention is necessary.* **4** (*uncount*) Your **board** at *eg* a guest house, hostel, or the place where you both live and work, is the food or meals that are provided for you in return for your work, or for the money or fees you pay: *Students get a board-and-lodging allowance.*

▻ ***verb***: **boards, boarding, boarded**

1 You **board** a ship, aircraft, bus or train when you get on to it: *You've obviously never tried to board a bus while folding a pushchair and holding on to a toddler.* **2** It is announced at an airport that a certain flight **is boarding** when it is time for the passengers to get on the aircraft: *Flight JE 602 for Madrid is now boarding from Gate 12.*

▻ ***phrases*** **1** Something such as a deal is **above board** if it is legal, honest, and is known about by everyone whom it concerns or affects: *It's OK; it's all above board.* **2** An arrangement that applies **across the board** applies to everyone: *There were to be across-the-board salary increases.* **3** (*informal*) An arrangement **goes by the board** if it is ignored or abandoned: *We used to have to sign a borrowing register, but I think that's gone by the board now.* **4** You are **on board** a ship, train or aeroplane when you are on it or in it: *Visitors were welcomed on board the liner whenever it docked.* [*same as* **aboard**] **5** Someone who **sweeps the board** in a series of competitions wins all the prizes. **6** You **take** something **on board** when you make yourself responsible for it: *Try not to take too much on board this year.* **7** You **take** an idea **on board** when you take it into consideration or accept it: *The younger members were much readier to take new ideas on board.*

> ***phrasal verb***
> You **board up** *eg* a hole, window or door when you cover it by fixing boards across it: *In anticipation of trouble, Asian citizens were boarding up their property and staying indoors.*

boarding house /ˈbɔːdɪŋ haʊs/ *noun*: **boarding houses**

A **boarding house** is a house where people live and take meals as paying guests.

boarding pass /ˈbɔːdɪŋ pɑːs/ *noun*: **boarding passes**

Your **boarding pass** or **boarding card** is a card you need before being allowed to board an aeroplane or ship.

boarding school /ˈbɔːdɪŋ skuːl/ *noun*: **boarding schools**

A **boarding school** is a school where pupils live during term time.

boardroom /ˈbɔːdruːm/ *noun*: **boardrooms**

1 A **boardroom** is a room in which the directors of a company meet. **2** (*used in the singular*) The **boardroom** of a company is its group of directors.

boast /boʊst/ *verb; noun*

▻ ***verb***: **boasts, boasting, boasted**

1 You **boast** about your experiences, achievements or possessions when you talk about them in a way that shows you are proud of them: *He likes to boast that he has never been drunk in his life.* □ *She was boasting about her kids again, I could hear.* □ *Lying is scarcely something to boast about.* □ *He boasted tediously of his familiarity with computers.* **2** (*formal*) A place **boasts** something if it has it: *The hotel boasts a swimming pool and a sauna.*

▻ *noun*: **boasts:** *Despite his frequent boasts about the progress made under his rule he was turning the country into an undeveloped nation.*

boastful /ˈboustful/ *adjective* (*derogatory*)
A **boastful** person boasts about their achievements, experiences and possessions: *He thought too well of himself; he was like a boastful child.* — *adverb* **boastfully:** *He boastfully claimed that three women had already asked him to marry them.*

boat /bout/ *noun*: **boats**
1 A **boat** is a small vessel used for travelling on water: *We borrowed a boat and rowed a little way up the river.* ▫ *The bay was full of yachts and fishing boats.* [compare **ship**] **2** Larger vessels are also frequently referred to as **boats**: *Once the car was safely installed on the boat we began to relax and enjoy the trip.* [compare **ship, ferry**]
▻ ***phrases*** **1** Two or more people are **in the same boat** if they are in the same difficult circumstances: *The aim of the help group is for people to meet others who are in the same boat.* **2** (*informal*) Someone **rocks the boat** if they disturb the balance or calmness of a situation or cause trouble.

boating /ˈboutɪŋ/ *noun* (*uncount*)
Boating is the sailing of boats for pleasure: *go boating on the river.*

bob¹ /bɒb/ *verb*: **bobs, bobbing, bobbed**
1 Something that is floating **bobs** up and down when it rises and falls with the movement of the water; people or things **bob** up and down, or **bob** about, when they keep jumping about: *Her plastic duck was still bobbing up and down in the bath* ▫ *Oh, do stop bobbing about and sit still.* **2** You **bob** somewhere when you move there quickly: *She bobbed back into the house.*

bob² /bɒb/ *noun*: **bobs**
You have your hair in a **bob** when it is short and straight, and cut the same length, usually about chin level, all round your head. — *adjective* **bobbed:** *I like your new bobbed style.*

bob³ /bɒb/ *noun* (*old, informal*): *plural* **bob**
A **bob** is a shilling: *It cost me 10 bob.*

bobbed /bɒbd/ see **bob²**.

bobble /ˈbɒbəl/ *noun*: **bobbles**
A **bobble** is a little ball made of cut wool, used to decorate clothes, especially knitted hats.

bode /boud/ *verb* (*formal*): **bodes, boding, boded**
▻ ***phrases*** Something **bodes ill** or **does not bode well** if it is a bad sign for the future; something **bodes well** if it is a good sign for the future.

bodice /ˈbɒdɪs/ *noun*: **bodices**
The **bodice** of a dress is the part of it that covers the upper part of the body.

-bodied /ˈbɒdɪd/ *suffix*
-bodied is used to form adjectives describing the shape of bodies: *a wide-bodied passenger jet.* [see also **body**]

bodily /ˈbɒdɪlɪ/ *adjective*; *adverb*
▻ ***adjective***
Your **bodily** needs are your physical needs: *bodily functions* ▫ *bodily comforts.*
▻ ***adverb***
Bodily describes actions that involve the whole body; *eg*, if you lift someone up **bodily**, you lift them off the ground: *He lifted her bodily and threw her on to the bed.* ▫ *She braced herself and then flung herself bodily at her attacker.*

body /ˈbɒdɪ/ *noun*: **bodies**
1 A person's or animal's **body** is all their physical parts, or all these excluding the head, arms and legs: *Her whole body was aching.* ▫ *He had a bruise on his left arm and three on his body.* [compare **trunk**; see picture on next page] **2** A **body** is also a person's dead body. [*same as* **corpse**] **3** (*formal*) solid objects are sometimes referred to as **bodies**: *the sun, moon, stars and other heavenly bodies.* ▫ *Do not attempt to remove foreign bodies from the eye with your fingers.* **4** (*usually in the singular*) The **body** of something is the main or central part of it: *We found a seat in the body of the hall.* **5** (*uncount*) Fabric that has **body** is fairly heavy and stiff; your hair has **body** when it feels thick and healthy. **6** (*with a singular or plural verb*) A **body** is also a group of people with some official function: *the governing body of the university* ▫ *the Arts Council and similar bodies.*
▻ ***phrase*** (*informal*) You respond to some suggested future event with the words '**over my dead body**' to indicate that you are completely opposed to it and will try every means of preventing it: *The takeover will go ahead over my dead body!*

body-building /ˈbɒdɪbɪldɪŋ/ *noun* (*uncount*)
Body-building is physical exercise that makes your muscles bigger and stronger.

bodyguard /ˈbɒdɪgɑːd/ *noun*: **bodyguards**
Someone's **bodyguard** is a person, or a group of people, that protect him or her against attack: *one of the Queen's bodyguards* ▫ *a member of the royal bodyguard.*

bodywork /ˈbɒdɪwɜːk/ *noun* (*uncount*)
The **bodywork** of a motor vehicle is its outer structure, made up of panels of painted metal.

bog /bɒg/ *noun*: **bogs**
A **bog** is an area of very wet, muddy ground.

bogged down /bɒgd ˈdaun/ *adjective*
You get **bogged down** in something when it prevents you from making progress: *Her plans for working overseas have got bogged down in red tape.* ▫ *Our car got bogged down in the mud.*

boggle /ˈbɒgəl/ *verb* (*informal*): **boggles, boggling, boggled**
If you say the mind **boggles** at something, or that something **boggles** the mind, you mean that it is hard to believe or understand: *The imagination boggles at the mere mention of such sums.*

boggy /ˈbɒgɪ/ *adjective*: **boggier, boggiest**
Boggy ground is very wet and muddy.

bogus /ˈbougəs/ *adjective*
Someone or something that is **bogus** is not real or genuine: *He was using a bogus identity.* ▫ *Her manner struck me as bogus and patronizing.* [*same as* **false**; *opposite* **genuine, spontaneous**]

bohemian /bouˈhiːmɪən/ *noun*; *adjective*
▻ ***noun***: **bohemians**
Someone, typically an artist, who is described as a **bohemian**, behaves and dresses in a casual and unconventional way that other people find unacceptable.
▻ ***adjective:*** *He himself reacted against his parents' bohemian lifestyle.*

boil¹ /bɔɪl/ *verb*: **boils, boiling, boiled**
1 Liquids **boil** when they get hot and start to bubble and turn into steam; you **boil** liquids when you heat them until they start to bubble and turn into steam: *When the milk boils, add the cocoa.* ▫ *He boiled the water for tea.* **2** You **boil** the kettle when you heat it till the water inside it boils; a kettle **boils** when the water inside it gets hot and starts to bubble and turn into steam. **3** You **boil** food when you cook it by boiling it in water: *Shall I boil you an egg?*

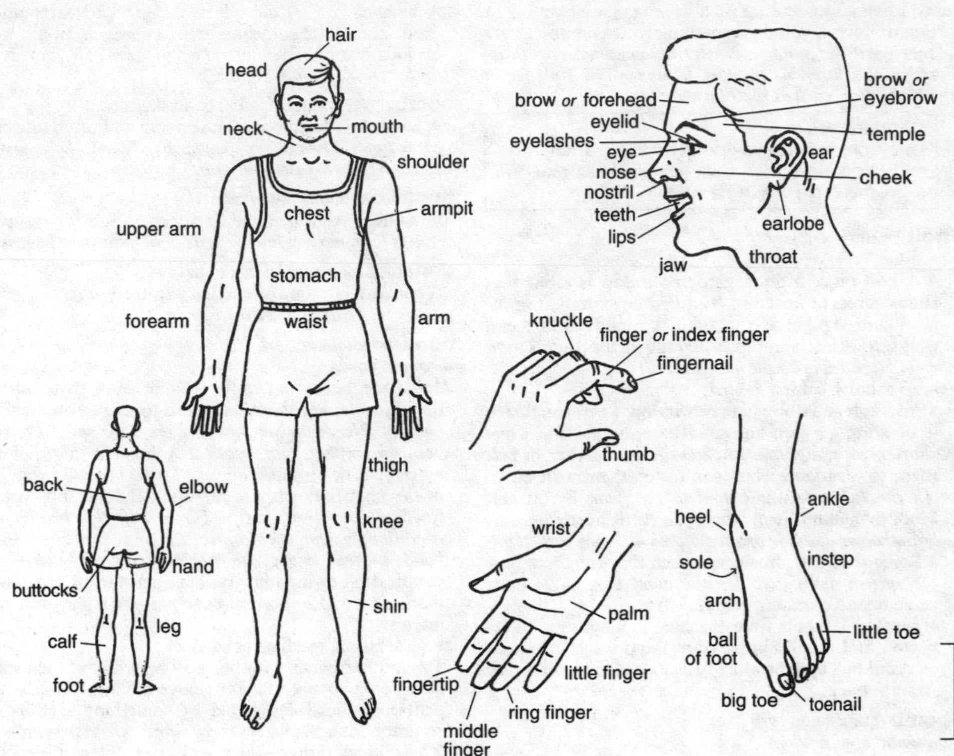

▻ ***phrases*** **1** You **bring** a liquid **to the boil** when you heat it until it starts to boil. **2** A liquid **comes to the boil** when it begins to boil. **3** A liquid is **on the boil** when it just beginning to boil.

phrasal verbs
boil away Liquid **boils away** when it all turns to steam.
boil down to (*informal*) A situation **boils down to** a particular thing if that is the most important point about it: *It all boils down to this.*
boil over 1 A liquid such as milk **boils over** when it boils, rises in the pan, and flows over the edge. **2** A person **boils over** when they lose control of their temper.

boil² /bɔɪl/ *noun*: **boils**
A **boil** is a painful red swelling on the skin, containing pus.

boiler /ˈbɔɪlə(r)/ *noun*: **boilers**
A **boiler** is an apparatus for heating a building's hot water supply.

boiling /ˈbɔɪlɪŋ/ *adjective or adverb*; *adjective*
▻ ***adjective or adverb***
Something that is **boiling**, or **boiling** hot, is very hot: *I'm boiling in this jacket.* □ *It was a boiling hot day yesterday.* □ *Feel his forehead; it's boiling hot.*
▻ ***adjective***
You are **boiling** with anger or rage when you are very angry.

boiling point /ˈbɔɪlɪŋ pɔɪnt/ *noun*: **boiling points**
1 (*count or uncount*) **Boiling point** is the temperature at which a liquid, especially water, boils: *The boiling point of water is 100°C.* **2** (*uncount*) A situation reaches **boiling point** when it gets to the point where people start losing their tempers or becoming violent.

boisterous /ˈbɔɪstərəs/ *adjective*
A **boisterous** person or animal is lively, noisy and playful: *Their house always seemed to be full of boisterous children*

bold /boʊld/ *adjective*: **bolder, boldest**
1 Someone who is **bold** is not afraid to take risks or do dangerous things: *Even as a small child she had shown herself bold and adventurous.* □ *It was a bold and imaginative step to take, and it succeeded.* [*same as* **adventurous, courageous, intrepid**; *opposite* **cowardly, nervous**] **2** A **bold** person is also someone who is confident, as distinct from being shy and easily embarrassed: *She had a bold, confident manner.* □ *After my second glass of wine I felt bold enough to ask 'So you're not married?'* [*same as* **assured**; *opposite* **diffident**] **3 Bold** designs, colours, patterns or outlines are strong and clear: *a portrait painted with big bold strokes.* [*same as* **definite**] **4** Letters that are in **bold** type are especially thick and black, **like these**. — *adverb* **boldly:** *those early explorers who boldly ventured across uncharted oceans* □ *One little girl came boldly up to me and held out her hand.*

bollard /ˈbɒlɑːd/ *noun*: **bollards**

Bollards are small posts used to keep traffic away from a certain area.

bolster /ˈboʊlstə(r)/ *verb*: **bolsters, bolstering, bolstered**
You **bolster** something such as someone's courage or position when you do something to strengthen it: *We said what we could to bolster his confidence.* □ *In an effort to bolster his support, he demanded a pledge of loyalty from each of his ministers.*

> ***phrasal verb***
> One thing **bolsters up** another when it strengthens and supports it: *We have new evidence that will undoubtedly bolster up our case.*

bolt /boʊlt/ *noun*; *verb*
▷ ***noun***: **bolts**
1 A **bolt** on *eg* a door, gate or window is a bar that slides across to fasten it: *We fitted an extra bolt to the back door.* **2** A **bolt** is a small thick round bar of metal that screws into a nut to fasten things together: *I went round tightening all the nuts and bolts.*
▷ ***verb***: **bolts, bolting, bolted**
1 You **bolt** *eg* a door, gate or window when you fasten it by sliding a bolt across: *We bolted the doors and shutters every night.* **2** You **bolt** things together, or **bolt** them to a surface, when you fasten them with bolts: *All the furniture was bolted to the floor.* **3** You **bolt** food, or **bolt** it down, when you eat it hurriedly: *She bolted down a couple of sandwiches and then rushed off.* **4** Someone **bolts** somewhere when they run there fast: *He turned and bolted for the door.* **5** A horse **bolts** when it starts running very fast, from fright.
▷ ***phrases*** **1 A bolt from the blue** is a sudden, unexpected and usually unpleasant happening. **2** You sit or stand **bolt upright** when you sit or stand with a very straight back.

bomb /bɒm/ *noun*; *verb*
▷ ***noun***: **bombs**
1 A **bomb** is a weapon consisting of a hollow case packed with chemicals, that explodes and causes death and destruction over a wide area. **2** (*used in the singular*) Nuclear weapons in general are sometimes referred to as the **bomb**: *the Ban-the-Bomb marches of the 1950s.* **3** (*BrE*; *informal*) If you say that something costs a **bomb**, you mean it is very expensive: *The air tickets alone will cost you a bomb.* **4** (*AmE*; *informal*) Something that is a **bomb** is a failure: *The film was a bomb.*
▷ ***verb***: **bombs, bombing, bombed**
1 To **bomb** a place is to attack it with bombs: *the towns and cities bombed during the war.* **2** (*informal*) You **bomb** somewhere when you move or drive quickly: *I was bombing along the M90 in my Micra.* **3** (*AmE*; *informal*) A show or project **bombs** if it fails badly. — *noun* **bombing** (*count or uncount*) *a wave of bombings* □ *a bombing raid.*
▷ ***phrase*** (*BrE*; *informal*)
1 Something such as a party **goes like a bomb** if it is very successful. **2** A vehicle **goes like a bomb** if it goes fast and is reliable.

bombard /bɒmˈbɑːd/ *verb*: **bombards, bombarding, bombarded**
1 Troops **bombard** a place when they attack it with heavy guns. **2** People **bombard** you with questions or criticisms when they ask you a lot of questions, or keep criticizing you. — *noun* **bombardment** (*count or uncount*): *the buildings destroyed in the nightly bombardments* □ *The town was coming under increasingly heavy bombardment from Serb forces.*

bombastic /bɒmˈbastɪk/ *adjective*
Bombastic language contains a lot of impressive-sounding or boastful words but has little real significance: *bombastic threats.* [*same as* **pompous**; *opposite* **moderate**]

bomber /ˈbɒmə(r)/ *noun*: **bombers**
A **bomber** is **1** an aeroplane designed to carry and drop bombs. **2** someone who causes a bomb to explode in a public place: *The police are still searching for last Friday's pub-bombers.*

bombshell /ˈbɒmʃɛl/ *noun*: **bombshells**
A **bombshell** is a piece of surprising and often unwelcome news: *Then he dropped his bombshell. 'Of course, we shall have to lose some staff.'*

bona fide /boʊnə ˈfaɪdɪ/ *adjective*
Bona fide means genuine or sincere: *The hotel restaurant is for bona fide hotel guests only.* [compare **bogus**]

bonanza /bəˈnanzə/ *noun*: **bonanzas**
A **bonanza** is a time of sudden wealth: *Profits rose and rose, and we all enjoyed a bonanza.*

bond /bɒnd/ *noun*; *verb*
▷ ***noun***: **bonds**
1 A **bond** between people is something that unites them and makes them feel close to one another: *the bond of friendship that linked them* □ *the special bond between mother and baby.* **2** A **bond** is a binding agreement or promise: *His word is his bond.* **3** (*usually in the plural*) **Bonds** are anything that restrict your freedom or your spirit: *Throw off the bonds of conditioning and take control of your own life.* □ *the bonds of fear and guilt.* **4** A government **bond** is a certificate showing that you have lent the government money, on which it promises to pay you a fixed rate of interest.
▷ ***verb***: **bonds, bonding, bonded**
1 A mother **bonds** with her new-born baby when she develops a loving and protective feeling towards it; people **are bonded** together by something such as a common danger when they unite to deal with it. **2** You **bond** things when you stick them together: *Special glue is needed to bond the two surfaces.*

bondage /ˈbɒndɪdʒ/ *noun* (*uncount*; *literary*)
Someone who is in **bondage** is in captivity or working as a slave. [*same as* **slavery**; *opposite* **freedom**]

bone /boʊn/ *noun*; *verb*
▷ ***noun***: **bones**
1 Your **bones** are the pieces of hard material that fit together to form your skeleton: *She broke a bone in her foot.* **2** (*uncount*) **Bone** is the hard material of which your skeleton is composed: *bone cancer* □ *the bone tools used by early man.*
▷ ***verb***: **bones, boning, boned**
You **bone** a piece of meat when you take the bones out of it.
▷ ***phrases*** **1** (*informal*) Someone who is a **bag of bones** or **all skin and bone** is very thin. **2** The **bare bones** of something are the basic or essential parts of it: *I believe I've understood the bare bones, but I'm not too sure about the interpretation of the details.* **3** (*informal*) You can say that you **feel** something **in your bones** if you are certain about it even though you have no definite proof: *It's going to rain; I can feel it in my bones.* **4** You **make no bones about** doing something that might be considered awkward for you if you do it without hesitation: *He made no bones about stating his own opinions and criticizing theirs.*

> ***phrasal verb***
> (*informal*) You **bone up on** a subject when you improve your knowledge of it: *I see you've been boning up on your anatomy.*

bone-dry /boʊnˈdraɪ/ *adjective*

Something that has been damp or wet, and is now **bone-dry** is completely dry: *You can put on your socks again; they're bone-dry.*

bonfire /'bɒnfaɪə(r)/ *noun*: **bonfires**
A **bonfire** is a large fire built out of doors, *eg* for burning garden rubbish, or to celebrate some special event.

bonhomie /'bɒnəmiː/ *noun* (*uncount; literary*)
Bonhomie is the quality of relaxed and jolly friendliness: *The best time for a driving test is early afternoon, when the examiner has just had lunch and is full of bonhomie.*

bonnet /'bɒnɪt/ *noun*: **bonnets**
1 (*BrE*) A motor vehicle's **bonnet** is the hinged cover over its engine. [*same as* **hood**; see picture at **car**] **2** A **bonnet** is a type of hat with a forward-facing brim framing the face, that is fastened under the chin with ribbon, now worn especially by baby girls.

bonny or **bonnie** /'bɒnɪ/ *adjective* (*especially Scots*): **bonnier, bonniest**
A **bonny** person or child looks very healthy, attractive or pretty.

bonus /'boʊnəs/ *noun*: **bonuses**
1 A **bonus** is an extra sum of money given on top of what is due as interest or wages: *He was paid a bonus for finishing the job early.* **2** A **bonus** is also any unexpected extra benefit: *the good weather is a bonus.*

bony /'boʊnɪ/ *adjective*: **bonier, boniest**
A **bony** person is thin.

boo /buː/ *interjection; verb; noun*
▻ ***interjection***
Members of an audience sometimes shout '**boo!**' to express dissatisfaction or contempt for a speech or performance.
▻ ***verb***: **boos, booing, booed**
People **boo** a speaker or performer when they shout '**boo**' at them to express contempt or dissatisfaction at their performance: *She was hissed and booed.*
▻ ***noun***: **boos:** *There were loud boos from the audience.*

boob /buːb/ *noun* (*informal*): **boobs**
1 A **boob** is a stupid or foolish mistake: *Sorry; I seem to have made a bit of a boob.* **2** (*used in the plural*) A woman's **boobs** are her breasts.

booby prize /'buːbɪ praɪz/ *noun*: **booby prizes**
A **booby prize** is a prize given for the lowest score or to the person who comes last in a competition.

booby-trap /'buːbɪtrap/ *noun; verb*
▻ ***noun***: **booby-traps**
A **booby-trap** is a bomb or mine which is hidden so that it is set off by the victim.
▻ ***verb***: **booby-traps, booby-trapping, booby-trapped**
A place or thing **is booby-trapped** if a booby-trap has been placed in or on it.

book /bʊk/ *noun; verb*
▻ ***noun***: **books**
1 A **book** is **a** a number of printed pages bound together along one edge and protected by covers: *children's picture books* □ *a small book called 'Baby and You'* □ *He'd written one of those popular books about the universe.* □ *Look up a good book on grammar.* □ *the Carlton Book of Puzzles* □ *'The Hip and Thigh Diet', a recent book by Rosemary Conley.* □ *The first edition of the book appeared in 1948.* □ *Oxford are publishing my book.* □ *The book's no longer in print.* □ *A slip of paper dropped out from between the pages of the book.* □ *Have you returned your library books?* **b** a number of pages for writing on, bound or fixed together, usually between covers: *on the right-hand page of the examination book* □ *Please sign the Visitors' Book.* **2** A **book** of *eg* stamps, matches or tickets is a number of them fixed together between covers, so that they can be torn out for use. **3** (*used in the plural*) A company's or society's **books** are its records of the money it has earned and spent: *Our books were regularly examined by an independent auditor.*
▻ ***verb***: **books, booking, booked**
1 You **book** *eg* a ticket, seat or hotel room when you arrange for it to be available for you at a certain time: *Airline seats should be booked at least a fortnight before you want to travel.* □ *Have you booked your flight to the States yet?* □ *Steven had booked a table at their favourite restaurant.* □ *The whole ballroom suite had been booked for the occasion.* □ *Would you book me a taxi for five-thirty?* □ *Calls abroad can be booked in advance.* □ *His dance band had been booked to play for four hours nightly.* □ *She's booked us on an escorted tour of the Holy Land.* **2** (*especially football*) Someone in authority **books** you when they write your name down, officially recording that you have committed a serious foul or other offence: *A number of Arsenal players were booked during the match.*
▻ ***phrases*** **1** Something such as a restaurant or a theatre performance that **is fully booked** has no places left: *I'm afraid we're fully booked for both nights.* **2** You are **in** someone's **good books** if they are pleased with you; you are **in** their **bad books** if they are annoyed with you.

phrasal verbs
book in or **book into 1** You **book into** a hotel, or **book in**, when you arrive there and sign your name in the guests' register: *He booked into a cheap little hotel near the railway station.* **2** To **book** someone **into** *eg* a hotel is to arrange for them to stay there: *I eventually admitted that I had a problem, and booked myself into a clinic.*
book up Something such as a hotel, performance, tour or course **is booked up** when there are no places left: *Both safari buses were booked up solid for the following month.*

bookcase /'bʊkkeɪs/ *noun*: **bookcases**
A **bookcase** is a piece of furniture fitted with shelves for books. [see picture at **living room**]

booking /'bʊkɪŋ/ *noun*: **bookings**
You make a **booking**, *eg* for a travel ticket, theatre seat or hotel room when you arrange in advance for it to be reserved for you.

bookish /'bʊkɪʃ/ *adjective*
A **bookish** person reads alot.

bookkeeping /'bʊkkiːpɪŋ/ *noun* (*uncount*)
Bookkeeping is the job of keeping a record of the money a company or society earns and spends.

booklet /'bʊklət/ *noun*: **booklets**
A **booklet** is a small, thin book with a paper cover, especially one that gives you information about something.

bookmaker /'bʊkmeɪkə(r)/ *noun*: **bookmakers**
A **bookmaker** is a person who takes people's bets on races and pays money to the people who bet successfully.

bookmark /'bʊkmɑːk/ *noun*: **bookmarks**
A **bookmark** is a strip of *eg* leather or card that you put between the pages of a book to mark the place you have reached.

bookshelf /'bʊkʃɛlf/ *noun*: **bookshelves**
A **bookshelf** is
1 a shelf for keeping books on. **2** a bookcase.

bookshop /'bʊkʃɒp/ *noun* (*especially BrE*): **bookshops**
A **bookshop** is a shop that sells books.

bookstall /ˈbʊkstɔːl/ *noun*: **bookstalls**
A **bookstall** is a small shop in *eg* a station, where books, newspapers and magazines are sold.

bookstore /ˈbʊkstɔː(r)/ *noun* (*especially AmE*): **bookstores**
A **bookstore** is a bookshop.

book token /ˈbʊk toʊkən/ *noun*: **book tokens**
A **book token** is a paper token worth a certain amount of money which can be used to buy books.

bookworm /ˈbʊkwɔːm/ *noun* (*informal*): **bookworms**
A **bookworm** is a person who reads a lot.

boom¹ /buːm/ *verb*; *noun*
▻ ***verb***: **booms, booming, boomed**
Something such as a person's voice or a drum **booms** when it makes a loud deep resounding noise: *Thunder boomed in the sky overhead.* □ *'And how's the world been treating you?' he boomed genially.* — *adjective* **booming:** *She had one of those booming voices that can be heard for miles around.*
▻ ***noun*** (*usually in the singular*): **booms:** *We could hear the distant boom of guns.*

> ***phrasal verb***
> Someone **booms** something **out**, or their voice **booms out**, when they speak in a loud deep resounding voice: *She boomed out her orders from her office.* □ *A familiar voice boomed out of the receiver.*

boom² /buːm/ *noun*; *verb*
▻ ***noun***: **booms**
A **boom** is a sudden increase or growth, *eg* in business or wealth: *People with houses to sell are benefiting from the boom in property prices.* □ *the population boom.* [*opposite* **fall**]
▻ ***verb***: **booms, booming, boomed**
Business **is booming** if a lot of money is being made.

boomerang /ˈbuːməraŋ/ *noun*: **boomerangs**
A **boomerang** is a flat, curved piece of wood that returns to you if you throw it correctly, used originally by native Australians for hunting.

boon /buːn/ *noun* (*usually in the singular*)
You can say that something is a **boon** if it is a great help or makes life easier: *The free bus service to the supermarket is a great boon to the elderly.* [*same as* **advantage, benefit, blessing**]

boor /bʊə(r)/ *noun* (*derogatory*): **boors**
A **boor** is a person, usually a man, who behaves in a rude, rough, ill-mannered way. — *adjective* **boorish** *boorish behaviour* □ *boorish manners.*

boost /buːst/ *verb*; *noun*
▻ ***verb***: **boosts, boosting, boosted**
1 Something that **boosts** your confidence or morale makes you more cheerful and confident: *Finding a new job had boosted her spirits a lot.* **2** One thing **boosts** another if it causes it to increase: *Adverse as the reviews were, the effect of them has been to boost ticket sales.* **3** To **boost** a product is to advertise it by giving it a lot of publicity: *She had a couple of radio interviews lined up, and hoped to use them to boost her book.*
▻ ***noun*** (*usually in the singular*): *Saturday's victory has given a boost to our morale.* □ *Christmas usually gives the sales a good boost.*

boot¹ /buːt/ *noun*; *verb*
▻ ***noun***: **boots**
1 A **boot** is a kind of shoe that covers your foot and the lower part of your leg: *She was wearing long black leather boots.* □ *I'm going to need a new pair of walking boots soon.* □ *football boots.* [see picture at **clothing**] **2** (*BrE*) The **boot** of a car is the covered area, usually at the rear end, for holding *eg* luggage and shopping: *I put all the shopping in the boot* [*same as* **trunk**; see picture at **car**]
▻ ***verb*** (*informal*): **boots, booting, booted**
You **boot** *eg* a ball when you kick it: *Graham boots it to Keir.*
▻ ***phrases*** **1** (*informal*) You **get the boot** or **are given the boot** when you are dismissed from your job. [*same as* **get the sack**] **2** (*informal*) If you say that someone **is getting too big for their boots** you mean they are getting too pleased with themselves. **3** (*informal*) Someone **puts the boot in a** if they repeatedly kick a person who is already lying on the ground. **b** if they say cruel or hurtful things to a person who is already feeling sad and upset.

> ***phrasal verbs***
> **boot out** (*informal*) Someone **is booted out** if they are forced to leave: *She said she left of her own accord, but Geoff's theory is that she was booted out.* [*same as* **kick out**]
> **boot up** (*computers*) You **boot up** when you start a computer by loading the programs which control its basic functions.

boot² /buːt/
▻ ***phrase*** (*literary*) **To boot** means 'as well' or 'in addition': *He had long curly hair, and a long curly beard to boot.* [*same as* **into the bargain**]

booth /buːð/ *noun*: **booths**
1 A **booth** is a small building for a particular purpose: *a polling booth* [= where people cast votes in an election] □ *a telephone booth.* [compare **kiosk**] **2** A **booth** is a small tent or stall, especially at a fair.

bootlace /ˈbuːtleɪs/ *noun*: **bootlaces**
A **bootlace** is a a long strong shoelace used to fasten boots: *She bent down to do up her bootlaces.*

booty /ˈbuːtɪ/ *noun* (*uncount*)
Booty is valuable property that has been seized by force, *eg* from an enemy population by invading troops: *The museum collection displayed ancient everyday items and war booty.*

booze /buːz/ *noun*; *verb*
▻ ***noun*** (*uncount; slang*)
Booze is alcoholic drink: *He smells of booze.*
▻ ***verb*** (*slang*): **boozes, boozing, boozed**
Someone who **boozes** drinks a lot of alcohol: *He'd been out boozing all evening.*

boozer /ˈbuːzə(r)/ *noun* (*informal*): **boozers**
A **boozer** is **1** a person who drinks a lot of alcohol: *I think her husband's a bit of a boozer.* **2** a public house: *He's always in the boozer.*

bop /bɒp/ *noun*; *verb*
▻ ***noun*** (*informal*): **bops**
A **bop** is a dance.
▻ ***verb*** (*informal*): **bops, bopping, bopped:** *She bopped the night away at the local disco.*

border /ˈbɔːdə(r)/ *noun*; *verb*
▻ ***noun***: **borders**
1 The **border** between two countries or areas is the line dividing them: *She lives in France, near the border with Germany.* □ *the Italian border* □ *He crossed the border into Mexico.* [see note at **frontier**] **2** A **border** is also **a** a narrow strip of ground planted with flowers, surrounding a small area of grass. [see picture at **house**] **b** a decorated edge, *eg* round a tablecloth or handkerchief: *silk sheets with a lace border.*
▻ ***verb***: **borders, bordering, bordered**
1 One country **borders** another if it lies next to it.

2 One thing **borders** another if it forms a border along its edge: *streets bordered with trees.*

> ***phrasal verb***
> One thing **borders on** another when it could almost be called the other thing: *Her actions bordered on lunacy.*

borderline /ˈbɔːdəlaɪn/ *noun; adjective*
▻ ***noun*: borderlines**
The **borderline** between two opposing or extreme conditions is the line dividing them: *You were just on the borderline between passing and failing.*
▻ ***adjective***
Something that is **borderline** does not belong clearly to either of two opposing categories: *We can think about including him; but he's a borderline case.*

bore[1] /bɔː(r)/ *verb; noun*
▻ ***verb*: bores, boring, bored**
Someone or something **bores** you if you find them dull and uninteresting: *He bores everyone to death with his stories about all his wonderful achievements.*
▻ ***noun*: bores**
1 A **bore** is a person that you find dull and uninteresting. **2** (*used in the singular*) A situation is a **bore** if it annoys you or is a nuisance: *I know it's a bore, but all this work will have to be done again.*

bore[2] /bɔː(r)/ *verb*: **bores, boring, bored**
1 You **bore** a hole in something when you drill a hole in it. **2** You **bore** *eg* a well or tunnel when you make one by drilling. **3** Someone's eyes **bore** into you if they stare at you so intently that you feel uncomfortable.

bore[3] /bɔː(r)/ *verb*
Bore is the past tense of **bear**[2].

bored /bɔːd/ *adjective*
You are **bored** if you feel tired because you have been doing something dull and uninteresting, or because you have nothing interesting or exciting to do: *I'm bored with this book.*

boredom /ˈbɔːdəm/ *noun* (*uncount*)
Boredom is the state of being bored: *To avoid boredom, vary the activities, and don't let any one activity go on for too long.*

boring /ˈbɔːrɪŋ/ *adjective*
Something that is **boring** is dull and uninteresting: *a long boring journey* ▫ *I thought the museum was a bit boring.* [*same as* **dreary**; *opposite* **exciting**]

born /bɔːn/ *adjective*
1 A baby is **born** when it comes out of its mother's body at birth: *She was born in Dublin.* ▫ *He was born in 1967.* ▫ *a child born of an English father and Indian mother.* **2** A thing or idea is **born** when it is thought of or comes into being. **3** You call someone *eg* a **born** teacher, or a **born** leader, if you think their personality and talents make them naturally a good teacher or leader.
[see also **bear**[2]]

-born /bɔːn/
-born is used to form adjectives relating to birth or to nationality; *his Irish-born wife* ▫ *newborn babies.*

borne /bɔːn/ *verb*
Borne is the past participle of **bear**[2].

borough /ˈbʌrə/ *noun*: **boroughs**
A **borough** is a division of a large town, especially of London or New York: *the London borough of Hillingdon.*

borrow /ˈbɒroʊ/ *verb*: **borrows, borrowing, borrowed**
You **borrow** something that belongs to someone else if you have their permission to take it and use it, usually for a short period of time: *She let me borrow her car to go to the shops.* ▫ *I had to borrow the money from the bank.*

borrower /ˈbɒroʊə(r)/ *noun*: **borrowers**
A **borrower** is a person who borrows money from a bank or building society.

borrowing /ˈbɒroʊɪŋ/ *noun* (*uncount*)
Borrowing is the act of borrowing money *eg* from a bank: *High bank charges and interest rates make borrowing expensive.*

bosom /ˈbʊzəm/ *noun*: **bosoms**
1 (*old, literary*) A woman's **bosom** is her chest or breasts: *She hugged the child to her bosom.* **2** (*used in the singular*) You are in the **bosom** of *eg* your family if you are surrounded by members of your family who love, protect and support you. **3** (*literary*) Your **bosom** is the part of you associated with your feelings and emotions: *the anger and hatred seething in her bosom.* [*same as* **breast**]
▻ ***phrase*** You **take** someone **to your bosom** when you treat them with kindness and affection.

bosom friend /ˈbʊzəm ˈfrɛnd/ *noun*: **bosom friends**
A **bosom friend** or **pal** is a very close friend: *Yes, I knew her, but we'd never been bosom pals.* [*same as* **buddy**]

boss /bɒs/ *noun; verb*
▻ ***noun*** (*informal*): **bosses**
Your **boss** is the person who employs you or who supervises you in your job: *I'm my own boss.* [= I work for myself] ▫ *Who's the boss around here?*
▻ ***verb*** (*informal*): **bosses, bossing, bossed**
Someone who **bosses** you, or **bosses** you about or around, keeps telling you what to do, especially unnecessarily, in a manner that suggests they have some authority over you: *Stop bossing me around.* ▫ *Some people don't seem to mind being bossed.*

bossy /ˈbɒsɪ/ *adjective* (*informal, derogatory*): **bossier, bossiest**
A **bossy** person enjoys telling other people what to do: *her bossy older sister.*

botany /ˈbɒtənɪ/ *noun* (*uncount*)
Botany is the scientific study of plants. — *adjective* **botanic** /bəˈtanɪk/ or **botanical** /bəˈtanɪkəl/: *the local botanic gardens* ▫ *the botanical section of the museum.* — *noun* **botanist** /ˈbɒtənɪst/: *He and his wife are keen amateur botanists.*

botch /bɒtʃ/ *verb; noun*
▻ ***verb*** (*informal*): **botches, botching, botched**
You **botch** something you do, or **botch** it up, if you do it badly: *I botched up my interview.* [*same as* **make a mess of**]
▻ ***noun*** (*informal*): **botches**
You make a **botch** of a piece of work, or make a **botch-up** of it, if you do it badly or carelessly: *He made a botch of repairing the television.*

both /boʊθ/ *determiner; pronoun; conjunction*
▻ ***determiner*** (*with a plural noun, often with another determiner, and sometimes with a pronoun*)
Both refers to each one of two people or things: *Both sons are doing well in their individual careers.* ▫ *Both the boys chose to study medicine.* ▫ *She broke both her legs in a skiing accident.* ▫ *Both these tables will be required.* ▫ *My husband's parents are alive, but I've lost both mine.* [compare **either, neither, each, all**]
▻ ***pronoun***
1 The form '**both** of' frequently replaces the determiner, and it must be used before personal pronouns: *Both of my parents have brown eyes.* ▫ *I've checked both of the machines.* ▫ *You can't do both of those jobs at once.* ▫ *My own parents are alive but both of hers are dead.* ▫ *She wants to see both of them after school today.* ▫ *with lots of love to both of you from both of us.*

2 Both is often used after a plural noun or pronoun: *My parents were both thrilled at the news.* □ *Their twins are a boy and a girl but ours are both girls.* □ *You both contributed such a lot to the project.* □ *We're both hoping to come.* □ *They're both of them going to Hull University.* □ *We can't both refuse.* □ *How are you both?* □ *with best wishes from us both.* **3 Both** can be used independently: *I'll buy you one of these dresses, but not both.* □ *We have interviewed the two candidates and we consider that both are suitable.*

▻ ***conjunction***

Both is used before the first of two alternatives or possibilities that you are saying the same thing about, with the second introduced by **and**: *Both my mother and my aunt have red hair.* □ *Both my husband and I send you our sincere congratulations.* □ *Both he and my son are applying to read engineering.* □ *Both you and she stand a good chance of the job.* □ *Please sign both Section I and Section II.* □ *This book should appeal both to children and to adults.* □ *It's wonderful news, both from my point of view and from his.* □ *if she both works and has a family to care for.*

bother /ˈbɒðə(r)/ *verb, noun, interjection*

▻ ***verb*: bothers, bothering, bothered**

1 (*usually with a negative*) You do not **bother** to do something if you do not do it because it would take too much effort, or because it is unnecessary: *She didn't bother to reply.* □ *How are you going to learn if you don't bother to listen?* □ *Some days he didn't even bother getting dressed.* □ *They should sign when they borrow the key, but they often don't bother to.* □ *It was good of him to write, but he needn't have bothered.* □ *Maybe I should learn French properly, but then again, why bother?* □ *'Would you like tea?' 'No, it's OK, don't bother.'* □ *He offered to send me a list, but I told him not to bother.* □ *Thanks for coming; it was good of you to bother.* **2** (*usually with a negative*) You **bother** with or about something, or **bother** yourself with it, when you concern yourself with it, or make an effort to deal with it: *Rachaela never usually bothered with Christmas.* □ *He was too wrapped up in his career to bother about his wife.* □ *We viewed the incident as too small to bother about.* □ *He refused to bother himself with day-to-day things like the washing-up.* **3** (*often with a negative*) You **bother** someone when you disturb them, interrupt them, or require them to attend to something: *One more question and we won't bother you any more.* □ *I won't bother you with the details now.* □ *Sorry to bother you at this time of night.* [*same as* **trouble**, **disturb**] **4** (*often with a negative*) Something **bothers** you, or you **bother** about it, if it concerns, worries, annoys or upsets you: *This fact need not bother us.* □ *The heat seemed not to bother her.* □ *Smoke if you like. It doesn't bother me.* □ *Treading on graves had never bothered me all that much.* □ *Georges was untidy; he never seemed to bother how he looked.* □ *His absence bothered me.* □ *It bothered me that he'd left no message.* [*same as* **concern**, **worry**, **upset**]

▻ ***noun***

1 (*uncount*) **Bother** is trouble, fuss or a disturbance of some sort: *Apparently there'd been a spot of bother in the public bar.* □ *I couldn't afford to get into any bother with the police.* [*same as* **trouble**] **2** (*uncount*) **Bother** is effort or difficulty: *Making proper meals is hardly worth the bother when you live by yourself.* □ *Sorry to cause all this extra bother.* □ *We managed to load the software without any bother.* [*same as* **trouble**] **3** (*used in the singular or uncount*) A person or thing that is a **bother** is a nuisance: *Sorry to be a bother, but could you help me?* □ *She liked looking after Mr Phipps. He was no bother really.* □ *On the whole girls were less bother to bring up.* □ *I'd love a cup if you're sure it's no bother.* [*same as* **nuisance, trouble**]

▻ ***interjection*** (*BrE*)

People sometimes use '**bother**' as a mild exclamation of annoyance: *Bother! We should have turned left there.* □ *Bother him; he's not answering his telephone.*

▻ ***phrase*** You say that you **can't be bothered** to do something, or **can't be bothered** with it, if you intend not to do it, or concern yourself with it, because it takes too much effort or because it is unnecessary: *She couldn't be bothered with the niceties of drawing-room conversation.* □ *I can hardly be bothered to move.* □ *if we could actually be bothered to work it out.*

bottle /ˈbɒtəl/ *noun*; *verb*

▻ ***noun*: bottles**

1 A **bottle** is a hollow glass or plastic container with a narrow neck, for holding liquids. **2** A **bottle** of something is the bottle and its contents, or just the contents: *There were two bottles of milk on the front step.* □ *That's the second bottle of beer you've drunk tonight.* **3** A **bottle** is also a baby's feeding bottle, with a piece of shaped rubber at the top for sucking the liquid through: *He gave the baby her bottle.* **4** (*uncount*; *informal*) **Bottle** is courage, nerve or confidence: *He hasn't got the bottle to say it to her face.*

▻ ***verb*: bottles, bottling, bottled**

To **bottle** *eg* beer or wine is to put it into bottles after it has been made. — *adjective* **bottled:** *bottled beer.*

> ***phrasal verb***
> You **bottle up** strong feelings such as anger, sadness and fear if you hide them from other people: *She kept her anger bottled up inside her.*

bottom /ˈbɒtəm/ *noun*; *adjective*; *adjective or adverb*; *verb*

▻ ***noun*** (*usually in the singular*): **bottoms**

1 The **bottom** of something is the lowest part of it: *Write the total at the bottom of each page.* □ *Dad steadied the bottom of the ladder.* □ *The letter was hidden at the bottom of a drawer.* □ *She was standing at the bottom of the stairs looking up.* □ *Porridge tends to stick to the bottom of the pan.* **2** The **bottom** of something such as a jug or mug is its base, or the part on which it stands: *a round-bottom flask for chemical experiments* □ *The potter's signature can usually be found on the bottom.* [*same as* **base**] **3** The **bottom** of *eg* a garden is the end of it: *He worked in a shed down at the bottom of the garden.* □ *She woke to find a policeman sitting at the bottom of the bed.* [*same as* **end**, far **end**] **4** The **bottom** of *eg* the sea or a river is the solid ground under the water: *I could just reach the bottom with my toes.* □ *A sandy bottom indicates slow currents.* [*same as* sea **bed**, river **bed**] **5** The people or things at the **bottom** of a scale or system of ranks are the ones at the lowest level: *people at the bottom of the income scale* □ *children at the bottom of the class* □ *At the bottom of any organization are the people who do the actual work.* **6** Your **bottom** is the part of your body that you sit on: *Balance on your bottom, knees together, feet off the ground.* □ *people with nice small firm bottoms.* [*same as* **buttocks**] **7** (*used in the plural*) The **bottoms** of a set of clothes are the trousers: *She was dressed in an old shirt and a pair of tracksuit bottoms.* □ *Where are my pyjama bottoms?*

▻ ***adjective***

The **bottom** thing is **a** the lowest of several: *He tripped on the bottom step.* □ *The kitchen is on the bottom floor.* □ *The bottom note of the chord.* □ *driving along in bottom gear.* [*same as* **lowest**] **b** the lower of two: *He bit his bottom lip in consternation.* □ *The bottom jaw was missing.* □ *wearing the bottom half of a pair of pyjamas*

□ *Machine along the bottom edge of the tape.* [*same as* **lower**]

▻ ***adjective or adverb***

A student who is **bottom** or comes **bottom** in the class is the one who gets the lowest marks: *He was always bottom in physical education, and hated baseball.* □ *I keep coming bottom in all the tests.* [*opposite* **top**]

▻ ***phrases*** **1** A person or thing that is **at the bottom of** something is the cause of it, or explanation for it: *What's at the bottom of all this extra security, she wondered.* **2** You **get to the bottom of** *eg* a mystery when you find out its cause: *I'll talk to Natalie and get to the bottom of this glue-sniffing business.* **3** For **from top to bottom** see **top**. **4** People use **'the bottom line is'** to introduce the point that really matters in a situation, and will influence what is decided or done: *The bottom line is that it's simply not profitable.*

▻ ***verb***: **bottoms, bottoming, bottomed**

> ***phrasal verb***
> Something such as a recession **bottoms out** when things get no worse, but remain at the same level, ready to start improving: *The decline in sales is beginning to bottom out.*

bottomless /'bɒtəmləs/ *adjective*

Bottomless means

1 very deep: *a bottomless pit.* **2** so great that it will never run out: *a bottomless supply of funds.* [*same as* **inexhaustible**]

bough /baʊ/ *noun*: **boughs**

A **bough** is a branch of a tree.

bought /bɔːt/ *verb*

Bought is the past tense and past participle of **buy**.

boulder /'boʊldə(r)/ *noun*: **boulders**

A **boulder** is a large rock or stone, rounded and worn smooth by the weather.

boulevard /'buːləvɑːd/ *noun*: **boulevards**

A **boulevard** is a broad, tree-lined street.

bounce /baʊns/ *verb*; *noun*

▻ ***verb***: **bounces, bouncing, bounced**

1 Something such as a ball **bounces** when it springs back from a solid surface: *The ball bounced back off the wall.* **2** You **bounce** something such as a ball when you throw it against a hard surface so that it springs back from it: *She bounced the ball against the wall.* **3** Light or sound **bounces** when it is reflected back from a surface. **4** You **bounce** if you jump up and down: *Her little daughter bounced up and down on the bed.* **5** A person **bounces** somewhere when they move there noisily and energetically: *She bounced out of the room in a temper.* □ *Willy bounced about filling up everyone's glasses.* **6** (*informal*) You can say that a cheque **bounces** if the bank refuses to pay it because the person who wrote it does not have enough money in their account.

▻ ***noun***: **bounces**

1 A **bounce** is the action a ball when it springs back from a solid surface: *Her racquet just failed to get to the ball before its second bounce.* **2** (*uncount*) Your hair has **bounce** when it is thick and healthy. [*same as* **body**]

> ***phrasal verb***
> Someone **bounces back** if they recover *eg* their health or a former good position after a period of bad health or bad luck: *Boris Becker bounced back after a poor spell with an easy victory over Courier in the Paris Open.*

bouncer /'baʊnsə(r)/ *noun* (*informal*): **bouncers**

A **bouncer** is a strong person employed by *eg* clubs and restaurants to stop unwanted guests entering, and to throw out people who cause trouble.

bouncy /'baʊnsɪ/ *adjective*: **bouncier, bounciest**

1 A **bouncy** person is lively and energetic: *She's one of those talkative, jolly, busy women; I suppose you'd describe her as bouncy.* **2** A **bouncy** ball is able to bounce well.

bound[1] /baʊnd/ *adjective*

1 Something that is **bound** to happen is certain to happen, or is to be expected: *The plan was almost bound to go wrong.* □ *I'd be bound to be found out.* □ *Troubles at home are bound to affect their schoolwork.* □ *The paint was bound to fade within a decade.* □ *Anything that flourishes in our garden is bound to be a weed.* **2** You are **bound** by a law or rule if you must do as it says; you are **bound** to do something when you are morally or legally obliged to do it: *The Court of Appeal is bound by its previous decisions.* □ *All employees are bound by these regulations.* □ *The fire and ambulance services are bound to respond to 999 calls.* □ *I am not bound to answer your questions.* □ *I felt bound to ask if the expenditure was justified.* [see also **duty-bound, honour-bound**] **3** You say you are **bound** to say or admit something, or agree about something, when recognizing or acknowledging a fact: *They've made much better progress than I'd expected, I'm bound to admit.* **4** **Bound** is the past tense and the past participle of **bind**, and means 'tied' in the literal or metaphorical sense: *He was found gagged and bound in the cellar of his house.* □ *Our two countries are bound together in friendship.* [see also **bind**]

▻ ***phrase*** One thing is **bound up with** another if it is closely connected with it, or if the two things are dependent on each other: *their political system, with which their religion is inextricably bound up.*

bound[2] /baʊnd/ *adjective*; *adverb*

▻ ***adjective***

1 A person or vehicle is **bound** for a place when they are going there: *trucks bound for the slaughterhouse* □ *a Norwegian ship bound from Stavanger to Hull* □ *London-bound flights are subject to delay owing to fog at Heathrow.* □ *Bristol? That's where I'm bound myself.* **2** A traveller or vehicle that is *eg north***bound**, is going north; the *north***bound** carriageway or platform is the one used by travellers going north: *Cross over to the southbound platform.* □ *a multiple crash on the westbound carriageway of the M62.* □ *the eastbound train* □ *Westbound travellers have a choice of routes.*

▻ ***adverb*** (*sentence adverb*): *Southbound, there are tailbacks for miles.*

bound[3] /baʊnd/ *noun*; *verb*

▻ ***noun*** (*usually in the plural*): **bounds**

The **bounds** of something are the limits that restrict it: *It is not beyond the bounds of possibility that this agreement will lead to peace.*

▻ ***verb***: **bounds, bounding, bounded**

One thing **is bounded** by another if that thing lies next to it and forms its boundary: *The park is bounded on two sides by the river.*

▻ ***phrase*** Something is **out of bounds** if people are not allowed to go there: *The playing fields are out of bounds to pupils during the lunch break.*

bound[4] /baʊnd/ *verb*; *noun*

▻ ***verb***: **bounds, bounding, bounded**

People or animals **bound** somewhere when they move with leaps: *She bounded down the stairs.*

▻ ***noun***: **bounds:** *The horse galloped towards the stream and was over in a single bound.*

boundary /'baʊndərɪ/ *noun*: **boundaries**

1 The **boundary** of an area is a line that represents its limit, or separates it from other areas: *a small lane which once formed the boundary between the two villages* □ *a disputed boundary.* **2** The **boundaries** of a subject or an activity are the limits it is understood to have: *people who in their time have pushed back the boundaries of human knowledge.* [*same as* **limit**]

boundless /ˈbaʊndləs/ *adjective*
Boundless means very great: *the child's boundless energy.* [*same as* **limitless**]

bountiful /ˈbaʊntɪfʊl/ *adjective*
Something that is **bountiful** is given or provided in large amounts: *a bountiful supply of fine wines.* [*same as* **abundant**, **plentiful**]

bounty /ˈbaʊntɪ/ *noun* (*usually in the singular; old, formal*)
Bounty is the giving of things generously: *The charity could not survive without the bounty of its supporters.* [*same as* **generosity**]

bouquet /buːˈkeɪ/ or /boʊˈkeɪ/ *noun*: **bouquets**
A **bouquet** is a bunch of flowers arranged in an artistic way, *eg* to be given as a gift or carried by a bride: *She carried a bouquet of roses and lilies.*

bourbon /ˈbɜːbən/ *noun* (*uncount*)
Bourbon is a type of whisky made from maize and rye, popular in the US.

bourgeois /ˈbʊəʒwɑː/ *adjective* (*derogatory*)
Bourgeois describes people or things that are typically middle class, or belong to, and are typical of, a capitalist system.

bourgeoisie /bʊəʒwɑːˈziː/ *noun* (*with a singular or plural verb; derogatory*)
The **bourgeoisie** is the middle classes, especially seen as politically conservative and interested only in social position and money.

bout /baʊt/ *noun*: **bouts**
1 A **bout** of some activity is a period of it: *a bout of hard work* □ *a drinking bout.* **2** You have a **bout** of some illness if you suffer from it for a short period of time: *a bout of flu.* **3** A **bout** is also a boxing or wrestling match.

boutique /buˈtiːk/ *noun*: **boutiques**
A **boutique** is a small shop, especially one selling fashionable clothes.

bow[1] /baʊ/ *verb; noun*
▻ ***verb***: **bows, bowing, bowed**
1 You **bow** when you bend your head or the upper part of your body forwards and downwards, usually as a sign of greeting or respect, or to acknowledge applause: *The singer came to the front of the stage and bowed.* **2** You **bow** your head when you bend it forwards and downwards. **3** (*formal*) You **bow** to something when you accept it or agree to it, usually unwillingly: *I bowed to his wishes and did as I was asked.* □ *He had to bow to the inevitable and accept defeat.*
▻ ***noun***: **bows**
A **bow** is an act of bowing: *He welcomed her with a bow.*

> ***phrasal verbs***
> **bow down** You **bow down** to someone if you agree to obey them: *He vowed never to bow down to his enemies.*
> **bow out** You **bow out** of something if you stop taking part in it: *She had to bow out of the competition through injury.* [*same as* **withdraw**]

bow[2] /boʊ/ *noun*: **bows**
1 A **bow** is a knot with a double loop and two loose ends, used *eg* for tying shoes or ribbons: *a young girl with a bow in her hair.* **2** A **bow** is also a weapon made of a piece of curved wood with a string attached to each end, used for shooting arrows. **3** (*music*) A **bow** is a long thin piece of wood with hair stretched along its length, used for playing *eg* the violin and cello.[see picture at orchestra]

bow[3] /baʊ/ *noun*: **bows**
The **bow** of a ship is the front part of it.

bowel /baʊəl/ *noun* (*usually in the plural*): **bowels**
1 Your **bowels** are your intestines, the long coiled tubes in your body that digest food; food passes through your bowels when it leaves the stomach. [*same as* **intestines**] **2** The **bowels** of something are the deep hidden or mysterious inner parts of it: *deep in the bowels of the earth.*

bowl[1] /boʊl/ *noun*: **bowls**
1 A **bowl** is a deep, usually rounded dish or container for various purposes, *eg* holding, mixing or storing food, serving food, holding liquids, or holding flowers: *Help yourself to a cereal bowl and have some muesli.* □ *Where's the washing-up bowl?* [see pictures at **kitchen; tableware**] **2** A **bowl** of something is the bowl and its contents, or just its contents: *a bowl of fruit* □ *I wouldn't mind another bowl of soup.* **3** The **bowl** of an object such as a spoon, a tobacco pipe, or a toilet is the rounded hollow part of it.

bowl[2] /boʊl/ *verb*: **bowls, bowling, bowled**
(*cricket*) A player from one team **bowls** by throwing the ball towards the player who is batting and trying to score runs for the opposing team. [compare **pitch[1]**]

> ***phrasal verbs***
> **bowl along** A vehicle **bowls along** when it moves along in smooth but lively way: *The motor bike was bowling along the coastal road, the police car still a mile behind it.*
> **bowl over 1** You **bowl** someone **over** if you knock them over, usually by accident. **2** (*informal*) You **are bowled over** when you are very impressed: *He was bowled over by the beauty of Venice.*

bow-legged /ˈboʊlɛgɪd/ *adjective*
A person is **bow-legged** if their legs curve outwards at the knees.

bowler /ˈboʊlə(r)/ *noun*: **bowlers**
1 The **bowler** is the person who is bowling the ball in cricket. **2** A **bowler**, or **bowler hat**, is a man's hard round narrow-brimmed felt hat.

bowling /boʊlɪŋ/ *noun* (*uncount*)
1 (*cricket*) **Bowling** is the act or skill of throwing the ball to the person with the bat. **2 Bowling** is a game played indoors in which you try to knock down a group of skittles by rolling a heavy wooden ball along the ground towards them.

bowls /boʊlz/ *noun* (*uncount*)
Bowls is a game played on smooth grass with heavy wooden balls, the object of the game being to roll your balls as close as possible to a smaller white ball.

bow tie /boʊ ˈtaɪ/ *noun*: **bow ties**
A **bow tie** is a tie which is tied in a double loop, worn especially on formal occasions.

box[1] /bɒks/ *noun; verb*
▻ ***noun***: **boxes**
1 A **box** is a container for holding things, made *eg* of cardboard or wood, sometimes with a lid, and usually square or rectangular in shape: *We spent the morning packing books into boxes.* **2** A **box** of something is the

box and its contents, or just the contents: *We carried the boxes of rubbish outside.* □ *I sat and ate my way through a whole box of chocolates* **3** A **box** is a separate compartment for a particular purpose, *eg* for a group of people in a theatre, for a horse in a stable or vehicle, or for a witness in a lawcourt. **4** A **box** is also a small enclosed area for a particular purpose: *a telephone box.* **5** A **box** is a section on *eg* a piece of paper, field or road, marked out by straight lines: *Write your name in the box at the top of the page.* □ *a penalty box.* **6** (*used in the singular; BrE; informal*) The **box** is the television: *Is there anything good on the box tonight?*
▻ ***verb*: boxes, boxing, boxed**

phrasal verb
You **are boxed in** if you cannot move from a place because you are surrounded by *eg* other people or vehicles. [*same as* **confine, enclose, block in**]

box² /bɒks/ *verb*: **boxes, boxing, boxed**
Two people **box** when they fight with their hands formed into fists and protected by thick leather gloves, according to the rules of boxing.

boxer /ˈbɒksə(r)/ *noun*: **boxers**
1 A **boxer** is a person who takes part in the sport of boxing. **2** A **boxer** is also a medium-sized dog with a short, smooth coat.

boxing /ˈbɒksɪŋ/ *noun* (*uncount*)
In the sport of **boxing**, two people, each wearing thick padded gloves on their hands, fight each other by punching.

Boxing Day /ˈbɒksɪŋ deɪ/ *noun* (*BrE; uncount*)
Boxing Day is 26 December, the day after Christmas Day.

box office /ˈbɒks ɒfɪs/ *noun*: **box offices**
A **box office** is an office which sells theatre, cinema and concert tickets.

boy /bɔɪ/ *noun; interjection*
▻ ***noun*: boys**
1 A **boy** is a male child: *They've got two children, a boy and a girl.* **2** You can also call a young man a **boy**: *the boy she's going to marry.* **3** (*used in the plural; informal*) A man may refer to his group of male friends, or to a group of his colleagues as 'the **boys**': *He always goes out with the boys on Friday nights.* □ *the technical boys.*
▻ ***interjection*** (*especially AmE*)
You can say **'boy'** or **'oh boy'** to express excitement, surprise or pleasure.

boycott /ˈbɔɪkɒt/ *verb; noun*
▻ ***verb*: boycotts, boycotting, boycotted**
To **boycott** a company or country is to refuse to have any business or social links with them because you disapprove of something they are doing: *We were urged to boycott goods from South Africa until black people were allowed to vote in elections.*
▻ ***noun*: boycotts**
A **boycott** is a refusal to have business or social links with a country or company, or a refusal to take part in some event: *a boycott of Cuban goods* □ *an Olympic boycott.*

boyfriend /ˈbɔɪfrɛnd/ *noun*: **boyfriends**
A girl's or young woman's **boyfriend** is the man or boy with whom she has a romantic friendship or sexual relationship: *She married her first boyfriend.* [compare **girlfriend**]

boyhood /ˈbɔɪhʊd/ *noun* (*uncount*)
A man's **boyhood** is the period of life during which he is a boy: *He spent his boyhood in Orkney.*

boyish /ˈbɔɪɪʃ/ *adjective*
1 A man is described as **boyish** if he looks younger than he is: *his boyish good looks.* **2** A girl or woman is **boyish** if she looks or behaves like a boy. — *adverb* **boyishly:** *He laughed boyishly.*

bra /brɑː/ *noun*: **bras**
A **bra** is an undergarment worn by a woman to support her breasts.

brace /breɪs/ *verb*: **braces, bracing, braced**
1 You brace yourself for something such as a shock or an unpleasant task when you prepare yourself for it: *They took their coats from the cloakroom and braced themselves against the snowy winter's night.* **2** You **brace** yourself or your body when you get yourself into a firmer position by pressing part of your body against something solid, for support: *I braced my leg against the side of the vehicle as we swung violently off the main road.* **3** You **brace** your shoulders when you hold them stiffly back: *Back straight! Shoulders braced!*
▻ ***noun*: braces**
1 A **brace** is any of various devices, usually made of metal, for supporting or strengthening things or holding them together. **2** (*used in the plural; BrE*) **Braces** are a pair of straps worn over the shoulders, for holding trousers up: *a pair of yellow braces.* **3** A **brace** for teeth is a piece of wire worn over them to straighten them. **4** (*plural* **brace**) A **brace** of *eg* birds is a pair of them: *two brace of pheasant.*

bracelet /ˈbreɪslət/ *noun*: **bracelets**
A **bracelet** is a band or chain worn as a piece of jewellery round the arm or wrist: *a gold bracelet.*

bracing /ˈbreɪsɪŋ/ *adjective*
The wind or air is **bracing** when it is cold and fresh and makes you feel full of energy: *bracing sea air.*

bracken /ˈbrakən/ *noun* (*uncount*)
Bracken is a type of fern that grows on hills and in woods.

bracket /ˈbrakɪt/ *noun; verb*
▻ ***noun*: brackets**
1 **Brackets** are a pair of symbols, such as () or [], used to group words, letters or numbers together. **2** A **bracket** is also a group or category that has a particular range: *children in the 5-8 age bracket* □ *This new car is out of my price bracket.* **3** A **bracket** is an L-shaped piece metal or wood that is attached to a wall to support a shelf.
▻ ***verb*: brackets, bracketing, bracketed**
1 You **bracket** a word or group of words if you put brackets round them. **2** You **bracket** people together if you treat them as being related or similar in some way: *You can't bracket boys with grown men in this way.*

brag /brag/ *verb*: **brags, bragging, bragged**
You **brag** if you talk proudly about yourself, what you have done and things you own: *She kept on bragging about her new car.* □ *He bragged to me that he'd easily win the race.* [*same as* **boast**]

braid /breɪd/ *noun, verb*
▻ ***noun*: braids**
1 (*uncount*) **Braid** is a band or tape, often made from threads of gold and silver twisted together, used as a decoration *eg* on uniforms. **2** (*especially AmE*) A **braid** is a length of hair woven into a plait.
▻ ***verb*** (*especially AmE*): **braids, braiding, braided**
You **braid** *eg* hair or thread when you twist lengths of it into plaits.

brain /breɪn/ *noun*: **brains**
1 Your **brain** is the soft grey organ inside your head which controls *eg* thought, sight and hearing. **2** Your

brain is also your mind. **3** (*used in the plural*; *informal*) You can refer to cleverness or intelligence as **brains**: *She's got brains but doesn't bother to use them.* **4** (*used in the plural, with a singular verb*; *informal*) The **brains** behind a plan or scheme is the person who thinks of it and controls it: *He's the brains behind the idea.*

▻ ***phrases*** **1** (*informal*) You **pick** someone's **brains** when you ask them for information about a subject that they have a lot of knowledge and experience of. **2** (*informal*) You have something **on the brain** if you cannot stop thinking about it. **3** (*informal*) You **rack your brains** if you think very hard, *eg* when trying to remember something: *I racked my brains to remember where I'd seen him before.*

brainchild /breɪntʃaɪld/ *noun* (*used in the singular*)
A person's **brainchild** is the particular theory, idea or plan that they have thought up or had.

brain-dead /ˈbreɪndɛd/ *adjective*
A person is **brain-dead** if their brain has stopped working, especially if it has stopped controlling the breathing and the heart.

brainless /ˈbreɪnləs/ *adjective* (*informal*)
A person is **brainless** if they are stupid or silly.

brainstorm /ˈbreɪnstɔːm/ *noun*: **brainstorms**
1 (*BrE*) You have a **brainstorm** if you are suddenly unable to think clearly and act properly. **2** (*AmE*; *informal*) A **brainstorm** is a brainwave.

brainwash /ˈbreɪnwɒʃ/ *verb*: **brainwashes, brainwashing, brainwashed**
To **brainwash** someone is to force them to accept new beliefs or ideas by continually telling them that their original beliefs and ideas are wrong.

brainwave /ˈbreɪnweɪv/ *noun* (*informal*): **brainwaves**
A **brainwave** is a bright or clever idea that you suddenly have: *I've had a brainwave.*

brainy /ˈbreɪnɪ/ *adjective* (*informal*): **brainier, brainiest**
A **brainy** person is clever. [*same as* **intelligent**; *opposite* **stupid**]

brake /breɪk/ *noun*; *verb*
▻ ***noun***: **brakes**
1 A **brake** is a device on a vehicle for making it slow down or stop: *She brought the car to a halt and pulled on the brake.* [see pictures at **bicycle, car**] **2** (*formal*) You put a **brake** on something, or put the **brakes** on it, when you try to control it: *It is too late now for governments to put the brake on reform in ex-communist countries.*
▻ ***verb***: **brakes, braking, braked**
A driver **brakes** when he or she applies the brake to slow down or stop: *the car in front braked suddenly.*

brake light /ˈbreɪk laɪt/ *noun*: **brake lights**
A vehicle's **brake lights** are the red lights at the back of the vehicle that light up when the driver uses the brakes.

brambles /ˈbrambəlz/ *noun* (*plural*)
Brambles are wild prickly bushes which produce blackberries.

bran /bran/ *noun* (*uncount*)
Bran is the outer covering of grain separated from flour.

branch /brɑːntʃ/ *noun*; *verb*
▻ ***noun***: **branches**
1 A **branch** is a shoot or stem growing out like an arm from the main body of a tree. **2** A **branch** is a main division of a railway line, river, road or mountain range: *a branch line on the railway.* **3** A **branch** of *eg* a subject or group of languages is one of several divisions that it can be separated into: *Anatomy is a branch of medicine.* **4** A **branch** is a local office of a large company or organization: *the bank's Scottish branches.*
▻ ***verb***: **branches, branching, branched**

> ***phrasal verbs***
> **branch off** A road or path **branches off** when it divides from the main part by going off to one side: *a road branching off to the left.*
> **branch out** You **branch out** when you develop different interests and projects: *Do you see yourself branching out into other kinds of music, or will you always be a jazz musician?*

brand /brand/ *noun*; *verb*
▻ ***noun***: **brands**
A **brand** of something such as a product is a particular variety or type of it: *The company is hoping to develop a new brand of dog food.* □ *her own brand of humour* □ *a new brand of politics.*
▻ ***verb***: **brands, branding, branded**
1 Someone **is branded** as something bad if people decide that is what they are: *He has been branded a liar.* **2** Cattle **are branded** when they have a mark made on their skin with a piece of hot metal, *eg* to show who owns them.

brandish /ˈbrandɪʃ/ *verb*: **brandishes, brandishing, brandished**
Someone **brandishes** *eg* a weapon when they wave it, usually as a threat: *He brandished the walking stick as if it were a sword.*

brand name /brand neɪm/ *noun*: **brand names**
The **brand name** of a product from a certain manufacturer is the name displayed on it: *The drug was being marketed under several different brand names.*

brand-new /brand ˈnjuː/ *adjective*
Something is **brand-new** when it is completely new.

brandy /ˈbrandɪ/ *noun* (*count or uncount*): **brandies**
Brandy is a strong alcoholic drink made from wine or fruit juice: *He drank two brandies.*

brash /braʃ/ *adjective*
Someone whose behaviour is **brash** acts in a noisy, over-confident way: *The politician's brash personal style had provoked many dangerous moments in world affairs.*

brass /brɑːs/ *noun*: **brasses**
1 (*uncount, often adjectival*) **Brass** is a hard yellowish metal, a mixture of copper and zinc: *a brass button.* **2** (*used in the plural*) **Brasses** are objects, especially ornaments, made of brass. **3** (*with a singular or plural verb*) The **brass** are wind instruments made of brass, such as trumpets and horns. [see picture at **orchestra**]
▻ ***phrase*** (*informal*) You **get down to brass tacks** if you begin to discuss the most important details of something.

brat /brat/ *noun* (*informal*): **brats**
A **brat** is a child, especially one that is rude or that behaves badly.

bravado /brəˈvɑːdoʊ/ *noun* (*uncount*)
Bravado is an appearance or display of courage or confidence, especially when put on to impress other people: *acts of bravado.*

brave /breɪv/ *adjective*; *verb*
▻ ***adjective***
A person is **brave** if they have no fear of *eg* danger or pain, or do not show their fear: *She was a brave child who never cried when she hurt herself.* — *adverb* **bravely:** *He bravely held back the tears as the nurse cleaned the wound.*
▻ ***verb***: **braves, braving, braved**

You **brave** *eg* danger or pain if you face it without fear, or without showing your fear: *men who would brave the storm to rescue sailors in trouble at sea.*
▻ ***phrase*** For **put on a brave face** see **face**.

bravery /ˈbreɪvəri/ *noun* (*uncount*)
Bravery is the quality of being brave or behaving bravely: *soldiers decorated for bravery.*

bravo /brɑːˈvoʊ/ *interjection*
People shout '**bravo!**' to express their appreciation and approval of someone's performance: *There were shouts of 'bravo' from the audience.*

brawl /brɔːl/ *noun*; *verb*
▻ ***noun***: **brawls**
A **brawl** is a noisy quarrel or fight, especially one in a public place.
▻ ***verb***: **brawls, brawling, brawled**
People **brawl** when they quarrel or fight noisily, especially in a public place: *They were arrested for brawling in the street.*

brawn /brɔːn/ *noun* (*uncount*)
Brawn is physical strength: *Success in sport requires brain as well as brawn.*

bray /breɪ/ *noun*; *verb*
▻ ***noun***: **brays**
A **bray** is the loud, harsh sound made by an ass or donkey.
▻ ***verb***: **brays, braying, brayed**
1 An ass or donkey **brays** when it makes its typical loud, harsh sound. **2** (*literary*) People **bray** when they speak or laugh with a loud, harsh sound: *Bertrand's braying laugh.*

brazen /ˈbreɪzən/ *adjective*; *verb*
▻ ***adjective***
Someone who is **brazen** is not ashamed of their bad behaviour, and does not care what people think of them: *He hadn't been at all prepared for her brazen admission that she had been cheating him.* [*same as* **bold, impudent, shameless**; *opposite* **ashamed, shamefaced**]
▻ ***verb***: **brazens, brazening, brazened**

phrasal verb
You **brazen** an embarrassing or difficult situation **out** if you face it boldly and confidently, and without being ashamed.

brazier /ˈbreɪzɪə(r)/ *noun*: **braziers**
A **brazier** is a metal frame or container for holding burning coal, used to provide warmth for people who have to work outside in cold weather.

breach /briːtʃ/ *noun*; *verb*
▻ ***noun***: **breaches**
1 (*count or uncount*) A **breach** of a law, promise or agreement is a failure to do what it says you must do: *This constitutes a breach of contract.* □ *You can be sacked for breach of contract.* **2** A **breach** is a serious disagreement between people: *The argument led to a serious breach in their friendship.* **3** (*formal*) A **breach** in *eg* a wall or barrier is a gap, break or hole.
▻ ***verb***: **breaches, breaching, breached**
1 To **breach** *eg* a law, promise or agreement is to break it or to fail to do what it says you must do: *They were held to have breached the law on copyright.* **2** (*formal*) You **breach** *eg* a wall or barrier if you make an opening or hole in it.
▻ ***phrases*** **1** You are **in breach of** *eg* a law if you do not follow it or do not do what it says you must do. **2** You **step into the breach** if you take responsibility, or an absent person's place, in a crisis.

bread /brɛd/ *noun* (*uncount*)
Bread is a food made from flour, water and yeast, baked in an oven: *a loaf of bread* □ *cut six slices of bread* □ *Would you like some bread and butter with your soup?* □ *buy some more wholemeal bread.*

breadboard /ˈbrɛdbɔːd/ *noun*: **breadboards**
A **breadboard** is a wooden board that you put bread on when you cut it. [see picture at **kitchen**]

breadcrumbs /ˈbrɛdkrʌmz/ *noun* (*plural*)
Breadcrumbs are very tiny pieces of bread.

bread knife /ˈbrɛd naɪf/ *noun*: **bread knives**
A **bread knife** is a long knife with a serrated edge, for cutting bread. [see picture at **tableware**]

breadline /ˈbrɛdlaɪn/ *noun*
▻ ***phrase*** Someone who is **on the breadline** is very poor and hardly able to buy the necessities of life.

breadth /brɛdθ/ *noun*: **breadths**
1 (*uncount or count*) The **breadth** of something is the measurement from one side of it to the other: *The garden is ten yards in breadth.* □ *She swam a breadth of the pool.* [see picture at **shape**] **2** (*uncount*) The **breadth** of something is also its range, or its quality of covering or including a wide variety of things: *The university's breadth of interest is represented by the twenty-one departments that make up the Faculty of Arts.* □ *Tribute was paid to her breadth of vision.*

breadwinner /brɛdwinə(r)/ *noun*: **breadwinners**
The **breadwinner** in a family is the person who earns money to support it.

break /breɪk/ *verb*; *noun*
▻ ***verb***: **breaks, breaking, broke, broken**
1 a You **break** something when you damage or spoil it, or cause it to divide or fall into pieces; something **breaks** when it falls to pieces, or is damaged or spoilt, *eg* by being dropped: *The glass dropped to the floor with a tinkle and broke in two.* □ *The cat had broken a saucer.* □ *The stick had broken in the middle.* □ *That was the time I broke one of my violin strings.* □ *The bullet just grazed his cheek, scarcely even breaking the skin.* □ *I broke the chocolate into three large sections.* **b** A machine or instrument **breaks** or **is broken** when it is damaged and no longer works properly: *I think I've broken the photocopier.* □ *Unfortunately the television's broken.* **c** You **break** a bone, or **break** *eg* an arm or leg, when the bone is cracked, and separates into two or more pieces: *He'd had the misfortune to break a bone in his wrist.* □ *Andrew suffered a broken leg, broken arm, and internal injuries.* □ *a disease that causes broken bones and humped backs in one in four elderly women* □ *She lost her footing on the stair and fell and broke her neck.* □ *He broke his arm playing for Great Britain.* [*same as* **fracture**] **d** Something **breaks** someone, or **breaks** their heart or their spirit, when it makes them so unhappy or depressed that their life or prospects of success are ruined, permanently or temporarily: *The loss could have broken him, particularly with the other hardships he had suffered.* □ *The French army's spirit was broken.* □ *It was losing you that really broke her heart.* □ *Her nerves were reaching breaking point.*
2 a You **break** a law or rule when you disobey it: *In conversation we frequently break the grammar rules that are appropriate to written language.* □ *drivers who break the speed limit.* [*same as* **disobey**] **b** You **break** an agreement, contract or promise if you do not keep it, or if you do something that it does not allow you to do: *What if she had decided to break her promise and didn't come?* [*same as* **dishonour**]
3 a Someone who is working **breaks** when they stop working for a short time: *At mid-morning they broke for coffee.* [*same as* **stop, pause**] **b** You **break** a journey

if you stop somewhere for a rest or for some other purpose on the way to your destination. [*same as* **interrupt**]

4 a You **break** something such as a spell, silence, connection or deadlock when you do something that brings it to an end: *To say anything might break the spell and spoil the magic.* □ *She felt she must say something to break the silence.* □ *Ruth was the first to break the contact, lowering her eyes to her coffee cup.* □ *The deadlock was broken when a government-appointed conciliator persuaded the chairman to agree to talks.* **b** You **break** a habit, or **break** yourself of a habit, when you stop yourself having it: *A period in hospital is an opportunity for the patient to try and break the smoking habit.* □ *The habit of giving in to him was still hard to break.* □ *Now's your chance to break yourself of the addiction.*

5 a Someone such as an athlete **breaks** a record when they do better than the best performance up to the present: *She set off on her first solo long-distance flight and broke the record for England to Australia.* [*same as* **beat**] **b** Something **breaks** the force of a fall or blow when it reduces it, and so limits damage or injury: *I saw her put out a hand to break her fall.* **c** You **break** someone's hold or control over something when you destroy their power or control over it: *China's grip on the sport was broken in the women's singles.* □ *Their ascendancy on the high seas had been broken.* **d** You **break** a code when you work out how to understand messages written in it. [*same as* **crack**] **e** (*tennis*) You **break** your opponent's serve when you win a game for which he or she is serving.

6 a You **break** news to someone when you tell them it; news **breaks** when people hear it: *Efforts were being made to contact them and break the dreadful news to them.* □ *Journalists and photographers hurried to the scene as the news broke.* **b** Day **breaks** when it gets light in the morning: *It was not until daylight broke that the full scale of the devastation could be seen.* [see also **daybreak**] **c** A wave **breaks** when its edge turns white and it collapses: *A wave is at its height just before it breaks.* **d** The weather **breaks** when it becomes bad after being continuously fine for several days or weeks; an expected storm **breaks** when it starts, *eg* with heavy rain, thunder and lightning. **e** A boy's voice **breaks** when it gets lower at about the age of 13, as he begins to mature sexually: *People don't realize that girls' voices break too.*

▻ ***noun*: breaks**

1 A **break** in a bone is a crack in it that separates it into two parts: *The X-ray revealed a break in both lower-leg bones.* [*same as* **fracture**] **2** A **break** in something is an interruption: *during a break in the conversation* □ *To him Christmas was no more than an inconvenient break in his routine.* □ *We apologize for a break in transmission affecting viewers in the Manchester area.* **3** You take a **break** when you stop work and have a short rest: *They would work for up to eight hours without a break.* □ *We could all do with a break.* □ *Take regular breaks for fresh air.* **4** (*count or uncount*) The lunch **break**, tea **break** or coffee **break** at an office, factory or institution is a period during which people stop work and have lunch, or a cup of tea or coffee; at a school, **break** is a period of about 15 minutes' rest, especially in the morning timetable: *Have you had your tea break yet?* □ *How long is your lunch break?* □ *They were friends now, sitting on the schoolyard wall together at break.* □ *He'd had a disagreement with a colleague during morning break.* **5** A **break** is also a holiday, especially a short one: *A lot of hotels offer weekend breaks at reduced prices.* □ *golfing breaks in France, Belgium and Holland* □ *She planned to get some reading done during the long Christmas break.* [*same as* **holiday**, **vacation**] **6** (*informal*) You get your big **break** when you have an opportunity to show how good you are at something and advance your career: *His big break came when English Opera were looking for a boy soprano for 'Turn of the Screw'.* **7** (*informal*) A lucky **break**, or a bad **break**, is piece of good, or bad, luck, usually something that affects your career.

▻ ***phrases*** **1** A business **breaks even** when it makes as much money as it spends, but does not make a profit: *Although we had broken even we were unable to go on paying wages.* **2** Someone or something **breaks free** or **breaks loose** when they escape from the person or thing that is controlling or restricting them: *He broke free from his guards and escaped into the crowd.* □ *Several sailing ships had broken loose from their moorings in the storm.* **3** You **break** a locked container or door **open** if you use force to open it: *He'd broken open his daughter's money box and borrowed a few pounds.* **4** You **make a break**, or **make a clean break**, when you escape from a place or situation, or separate yourself completely from it: *Men may suffer as much as women when a relationship fails, but they seem better able to make a clean break.*

phrasal verbs

break away You **break away** from a group when you leave it or stop associating with it: *I've broken away from that whole junkie crowd.* [see also **breakaway**]

break down 1 You **break** a locked door **down** if you force it off its hinges, in order to get in or out: *I called the police and they broke down the door.* **2** A machine or vehicle **breaks down** when it stops working: *The van broke down on the way to Stranraer.* [see also **breakdown**] **3** A relationship, system, or any form of communication **breaks down** when it fails: *if you consider that your marriage has broken down irretrievably* □ *Normal hospital procedure had broken down under sheer pressure of work.* □ *Negotiations had again broken down over this question.* [*same as* **fail**; see also **breakdown**] **4** Your health **breaks down** when you become ill. **5** People **break down** when they become emotionally upset and start to weep: *Her father broke down and wept during a television interview yesterday.* **6** Something **breaks down** or **is broken down** when it is separated into several parts: *Large molecules are rapidly broken down in the gut into their component parts.* □ *Words themselves can be broken down into minimal grammatical units.* [*same as* **divide**; *opposite* **build up**]

break in 1 People **break in** when they enter a building by force, usually to steal something: *Thieves broke in while she was at the funeral, hoping to find money and jewellery.* [compare **break into**, see also **break-in**] **2** Someone or something **breaks in** on *eg* a conversation when they interrupt it: *The ringing of the telephone broke in on her thoughts.* **3** To **break in** an animal such as a horse is to accustom it to having a saddle and rider, or to doing a certain kind of work: *He used to break in horses for the brewery.*

break into 1 People **break into** *eg* a locked place or container when they enter it or open it by force: *How dare you break into my house and assault me like this?* □ *A pharmaceutical laboratory on the outskirts of town had been broken into.* □ *Someone had broken into my filing cabinet.* [compare **break in**] **2** You **break into** a supply of something when you start using it: *We'd have to break into the stores we'd bought for the voyage.* **3** You **break into** a run, or

into laughter or song, when you suddenly begin to run, laugh or sing: *Only when she was out of sight did she allow herself to break into a swift trot.* □ *Overcome by his own joke he broke into a fit of choking laughter.* □ *His face finally broke into a grin.*
break off 1 A piece of something **breaks off** or **is broken off** when it falls, or is removed, from the main part: *Turner broke off some more bread.* □ *The road was littered with branches that had broken off in the wind.* □ *The handle just broke off in my hand.* **2** You **break off** a relationship with someone, especially an engagement to marry them, when you end it: *Without warning she broke off her engagement.* **3** You **break off** some activity when you interrupt it: *The Prime Minister broke off his holiday in Spain to try and save his Yugoslav peace initiative.* □ *He broke off his conversation with his assistant and approached us respectfully.* **4** You **break off** when you stop speaking in the middle of saying something: *She broke off as the doorbell rang.*
break out 1 Someone in captivity **breaks out** when they escape, sometimes by using force: *A convicted murderer is reported to have broken out of prison.* **2** War, fighting or conflict **break out** when they start: *If the war had not broken out they would have married.* □ *In May 1937 street fighting broke out in Barcelona.* [see also **outbreak**] **3** Fire **breaks out** when it starts somewhere: *A mystery blaze broke out at Madame Tussaud's earlier today.* [see also **outbreak**] **4** A disease **breaks out** when cases of it begin to appear and it spreads quickly among people: *the cholera epidemic which first broke out in Peru in late January 1991.* [see also **outbreak**] **5** You **break out** in sweat or a rash, or it **breaks out** over your body, when you become covered with it: *Sweat broke out all over his body.* □ *My whole body broke out in a sweat.* □ *Next day he broke out in a severe rash.*
break through 1 Someone or something **breaks through** a barrier when they manage to get past it: *Demonstrators had broken through the police cordon.* □ *The light hardly breaks through the dense greenery even at midday.* [see also **breakthrough**] **2** Something hidden **breaks through** when it suddenly shows itself: *It started dull but eventually the sun broke through.* □ *Her sense of humour kept breaking through in spite of her sadness.*
break up 1 Something **breaks up** or **is broken up** when it is destroyed and reduced to pieces: *The vessel broke up on the rocks.* □ *He broke the box up with an axe.* **2** Something **breaks up** or **is broken up** when it is divided into parts: *We argued that Marxism could be broken up into three elements.* **3** A meeting or other gathering **breaks up** or **is broken up** when it finishes and people leave: *The conference broke up at 4.30.* □ *The police broke the party up.* **4** You **break up** with your partner when you end your relationship with him or her: *He may have broken up with Pat, but he's always talking about her.* [see also **break-up**] **5** A school **breaks up** when the term ends and the holidays begin: *Now that school had broken up, Christine could devote six whole weeks to Anna.* □ *We had broken up for the summer.*
break with You **break with** people when you stop being friendly with them or spending time with them: *He had broken with his family long ago.*

breakable /ˈbreɪkəbəl/ *adjective*
Breakable things can be broken easily: *I put all my breakable objects away when my grandchildren come to visit me.* [*same as* **delicate**, **fragile**]

breakage /ˈbreɪkɪdʒ/ *noun*: **breakages**
1 (*uncount*) **Breakage** is the act of breaking something: *This insurance policy covers accidental breakage.* **2** A **breakage** is a broken thing: *The cost of any breakages will be deducted from the advance deposit.*

breakaway /ˈbreɪkəweɪ/ *adjective*
A **breakaway** group is a group of people that have decided to end their connection with the main group: *breakaway factions within the Conservative party.* [see also **break away** at **break**]

breakdown /ˈbreɪkdaʊn/ *noun*: **breakdowns**
1 You have a **breakdown** if the vehicle you are travelling in stops working: *We had a breakdown on the motorway.* **2** There is a **breakdown** in *eg* a relationship, agreement or discussion if it comes to an end because the people involved have an argument or disagreement: *the breakdown in talks between the union and management.* **3** Someone suffers or has a **breakdown** if they become depressed and anxious, and cannot cope with everyday life.
[see also **break down** at **break**]

breaker /ˈbreɪkə(r)/ *noun* (*usually in the plural*): **breakers**
Breakers are large waves that crash on to rocks or the beach.

breakfast /ˈbrɛkfəst/ *noun*; *verb*
▻ ***noun*** (*count or uncount*): **breakfasts**
Breakfast is the first meal of the day, usually eaten early in the morning: *He was late getting up and missed his breakfast.* □ *The hotel serves breakfast at 8am.* □ *children who eat their breakfasts on the way to school.*
▻ ***verb***: **breakfasts, breakfasting, breakfasted**
You **breakfast** when you have breakfast: *I usually breakfast late on Sundays.*

break-in /ˈbreɪkɪn/ *noun*: **break-ins**
There is a **break-in** at a house or business premises if someone gets in by force: *There was a break-in at the office over the weekend and a lot of computer equipment was stolen.* [see also **break in** at **break**]

breakneck /ˈbreɪknɛk/
▻ ***phrase*** Something that moves or happens **at breakneck speed** happens very fast: *He ran down the street at breakneck speed.*

breakthrough /ˈbreɪkθruː/ *noun*: **breakthroughs**
There is a **breakthrough** when someone manages to do something successfully, or discovers something, after a period of hard work and failure: *The development of the new drug has been hailed as a breakthrough in the treatment of cancer.* [see also **break through** at **break**]

break-up /ˈbreɪkʌp/ *noun*: **break-ups**
A **break-up** occurs when something ends, *eg* when a relationship or marriage fails, or when people decide not to work together any more: *He blamed the break-up of his marriage on stress.* □ *the break-up of the peace talks.* [see also **break up** at **break**]

breakwater /ˈbreɪkwɔːtə(r)/ *noun*: **breakwaters**
A **breakwater** is a wall built on a beach to break the force of the waves.

breast /brɛst/ *noun*: **breasts**
1 A woman's **breasts** are the two fleshy parts on the front of her body which produce milk. **2** A person's, animal's or bird's **breast** is the front part of their body between the neck and stomach. **3** (*literary*) Your **breast** is the part of you associated with your feelings and emotions: *Anger and hatred seethed in her breast.* [*same as* **bosom**]
▻ ***phrase*** You **make a clean breast of it** if you tell the truth about something wrong that you have done, thought or felt.

breastbone /'brɛstboun/ *noun*: **breastbones**
Your **breastbone** is the thin, flat bone running down the front of your chest.

breastfeed /'brɛstfi:d/ *verb*: **breastfeeds, breastfeeding, breastfed**
A mother **breastfeeds** her baby when she feeds it with milk from her breasts.

breaststroke /'brɛststrouk/ *noun* (*uncount*)
Breaststroke is a swimming stroke performed on your front in which you push your arms out in front of you and pull them back through the water, using a leg kick in which you separate your legs.

breath /brɛθ/ *noun*: **breaths**
1 (*uncount or count*) **Breath** is the air that you take into and send out of your lungs: *You breath smells of chocolate.* ▫ *Some swimmers come up for a breath after every three strokes, and some after every four.* **2** You take a **breath** when you breathe air in. **3** A **breath** of something is a slight trace, hint or suggestion of it: *a breath of scandal.*
▻ ***phrases*** **1** You **catch your breath** if you stop breathing for a moment, *eg* because of fear, amazement or pain: *The sight made her catch her breath.* **2** You **get your breath back** when you begin to start breathing normally again, *eg* after exercise. **3** You **hold your breath** if you stop breathing for a short period of time, *eg* because you are worried, or to avoid being heard. **4** You are **out of breath** or **short of breath** if you are breathing quickly or with difficulty, especially after taking exercise. **5** Something **takes** your **breath away** if you find it very beautiful, pleasing, surprising, shocking or exciting. [see also **breathtaking**] **6** You say something **under** your **breath** if you say it quietly or in a whisper. **7** (*informal*) You can say that someone **is wasting their breath** if no-one is listening to, or taking any notice of, what they are saying.

breathalyze or **breathalyse** /'brɛθəlaɪz/ *verb*: **breathalyzes, breathalyzing, breathalyzed**
The police **breathalyze** drivers when they ask them to breathe into a bag-like device that shows whether they have been drinking alcohol.

breathe /bri:ð/ *verb*: **breathes, breathing, breathed**
1 You **breathe** when you take air into your lungs and send it out again: *Mammals cannot breathe under water.* ▫ *He breathed deeply.* ▫ *It was pleasant to breathe the cool air again after being in the stuffy office.* **2** You **breathe** *eg* air or smoke when you take it into your lungs: *It felt wonderful to breathe the fresh mountain air and feel the breeze on our faces* ▫ *Protect children; don't let them breathe your smoke.* **3** You **breathe** *eg* something unpleasant such as smoke over someone if you send it out from your mouth towards them: *Don't breathe garlic over me.* **4** You **breathe** something when you whisper it: *'Ssh! They're coming!' she breathed.* **5** You **breathe** *eg* life or enthusiasm into other people when you encourage them to be energetic, lively and enthusiastic.
▻ ***phrases*** **1** You **breathe again**, **breathe easily** or **breathe freely** if you feel safe or relaxed after a period of worry or fear: *She felt she could breathe freely now the exams were over.* **2** For **breathe down someone's neck** see **neck**.

> ***phrasal verbs***
> **breathe in** You **breathe in** when you take air into your lungs.
> **breathe out** You **breathe out** when you send air out of your lungs.

breather /'bri:ðə(r)/ *noun* (*informal*): **breathers**
A **breather** is a short rest or break from work: *She took a breather for a cup of coffee.* ▫ *Let's have a bit of a breather now.*

breathing space /'bri:ðɪŋ speɪs/ *noun* (*usually in the singular*)
A **breathing space** is a short time allowed for rest between two activities.

breathless /'brɛθləs/ *adjective*
1 People are **breathless** when they are having difficulty in breathing normally, either because they are ill, or because they have been taking energetic exercise: *She was breathless by the time she got to the top of the hill.* **2** You are **breathless** when you are very eager or excited: *He was breathless with excitement. — adverb* **breathlessly:** *He ran home and breathlessly told his mother what had happened.* ▫ *She waited breathlessly for his phone call.*

breathtaking /'brɛθteɪkɪŋ/ *adjective*
Something is **breathtaking** if it is very surprising, exciting or impressive: *The view from the top of the castle was breathtaking. — adverb* **breathtakingly:** *She is breathtakingly beautiful.*

bred /brɛd/ *verb*
Bred is the past tense and past participle of **breed**.

breeches /brɪtʃɪz/ *noun* (*plural*)
Breeches are short trousers fastened below the knee: *a pair of riding breeches.*

breed /bri:d/ *verb*; *noun*
▻ ***verb*: breeds, breeding, bred**
1 Animals **breed** when they produce young. **2** A person **breeds** animals or plants if they keep them for the purpose of producing more, or developing new types: *My aunt breeds dogs.* **3** Someone **is bred** to do something or to behave in a certain way if they are educated so that they behave in that way: *children bred to be polite* ▫ *well-bred children.* **4** One thing **breeds** another when it causes it to happen or produces it: *Dirt breeds disease.* ▫ *Success breeds success.*
▻ ***noun*: breeds**
1 A **breed** of domestic or farm animal is a particular type: *Spaniels were originally a Spanish breed of dog.* **2** A **breed** of person or thing is a particular type of person or thing: *one of the new breed of computers.*

breeding /'bri:dɪŋ/ *noun* (*uncount*)
1 Breeding is **a** the activity of keeping animals or growing plants in order to produce more: *She keeps a flock of ewes and a couple of rams for breeding.* **b** the process of mating and producing young: *the breeding season.* **2** Someone who has **breeding** has been well brought up, is polite and considerate, and generally behaves in a manner that people associate with the upper classes: *She was a rather pretty woman, not very young, with an air of good breeding that he found attractive.*

breeding ground /'bri:dɪŋ graʊnd/ *noun*: **breeding grounds**
1 A **breeding ground** is a place where animals, birds or fish go to produce their young: *the breeding ground of the herring in the North Sea.* **2** A place or situation is a **breeding ground** for something if it develops or is encouraged there: *The university was a breeding ground for communism.*

breeze /bri:z/ *noun*; *verb*
▻ ***noun*: breezes**
1 A **breeze** is a gentle wind. **2** (*informal*) A **breeze** is also any job or task that you find easy to do: *It'll be a breeze.*
▻ ***verb*** (*informal*): **breezes, breezing, breezed**
1 You **breeze** along if you move quite quickly in a cheerful, casual, confident manner: *She breezed into*

the room. □ *He breezed out, slamming the door behind him.* **2** You **breeze** through something if you do it easily and without any difficulty: *She expects to breeze through the exam.*

breezy /'bri:zɪ/ *adjective*: **breezier**, **breeziest**
1 The weather is **breezy** when it is a bit windy: *a breezy day.* **2** A person is **breezy** if they are lively, confident and casual: *his brisk, breezy way of dealing with problems.*

brethren /'brɛðrən/ *noun*
Brethren is a plural of **brother**. [see note at **brother**]

brevity /'brɛvɪtɪ/ *noun* (*uncount; formal*)
1 Brevity, in something written or spoken, is the quality of being short or concise: *When making a speech in public, aim for brevity; people will be left wanting more, and so will ask questions.* **2** The **brevity** of something is the circumstance of its lasting only for a short time: *the pitiful brevity of our life on this earth.*

brew /bru:/ *verb; noun*
▻ ***verb*: brews, brewing, brewed**
1 You **brew** *eg* tea or coffee when you pour boiling water over the leaves or grains to make it. **2** Someone **brews** beer when they mix and boil the liquid, and leave it to ferment. **3** An unpleasant situation **is brewing** if it is beginning to develop or get stronger: *There's a storm brewing.*
▻ ***noun*: brews**
A **brew** is a drink produced by mixing something with boiling water, especially tea or coffee: *I'll make us all a brew.*

brewer /'bru:ə(r)/ *noun*: **brewers**
A **brewer** is a person or company that brews and sells beer.

brewery /'bru:ərɪ/ *noun*: **breweries**
A **brewery** is a place where beer is brewed.

briar /'braɪə(r)/ *noun*: **briars**
A **briar** is any prickly bush, especially a wild rose bush.

bribe /braɪb/ *noun; verb*
▻ ***noun*: bribes**
A **bribe** is a gift, usually money, that one person offers to another to persuade them to do something: *You shouldn't accept bribes.*
▻ ***verb*: bribes, bribing, bribed**
One person **bribes** another if they give, offer or promise them money to persuade them to do something: *She tried to bribe the judge, but failed.* — *noun* (*uncount*) **bribery** /'braɪbərɪ/: *The President has been accused of bribery and corruption.*

bric-à-brac /'brɪkəbrak/ *noun* (*uncount*)
Bric-à-brac is small objects that are not valuable but which are kept as decorations or ornaments.

brick /brɪk/ *noun; verb*
▻ ***noun*: bricks**
1 (*count or uncount, often adjectival*) A **brick** is a rectangular block of baked clay used for building: *After the explosion, all that was left of the building was a pile of bricks.* □ *Duke's Road, with its extraordinary terrace of chequered houses built in red and yellow brick.* □ *Do you see that red brick building?* **2** A **brick** is also a piece of wood or plastic, especially cube-shaped, used by children as a building toy.
▻ ***verb*: bricks, bricking, bricked**

phrasal verbs
You **brick** a hole or gap **in**, or **brick** it **up**, if you close it or fill it in with bricks: *We're going to have this door bricked in.* □ *The window has been bricked up.*

bricklayer /'brɪkleɪə(r)/ *noun*: **bricklayers**
A **bricklayer** is someone whose job is to build *eg* walls for houses with bricks.

brickwork /'brɪkwɜ:k/ *noun* (*uncount*)
A building's **brickwork** is the part of it that is made of brick.

bridal /'braɪdəl/ *adjective*
Bridal things are for a wedding or for a bride: *Have the bridal cars been ordered?*

bride /braɪd/ *noun*: **brides**
A **bride** is a woman who has just been, or is about to be, married.

bridegroom /'braɪdgru:m/ *noun*: **bridegrooms**
A **bridegroom** is a man who has just been, or is about to be, married.

bridesmaid /'braɪdzmeɪd/ *noun*: **bridesmaids**
A **bridesmaid** is a girl or young woman who accompanies the bride on her wedding day and has special duties to perform during the ceremony.

bridge[1] /brɪdʒ/ *noun; verb*
▻ ***noun*: bridges**
1 A **bridge** is a structure that joins the two sides of a road, railway or river, allowing people or vehicles to cross from one side to the other: *a road bridge joining the island to the mainland* □ *a railway bridge* □ *You cross a bridge and then immediately turn left.* **2** A **bridge** is also anything that joins or connects two separate things: *a bridge between the rich and poor in society.* **3** A ship's **bridge** is the narrow raised platform from which the captain directs its course. **4** The **bridge** of your nose is the hard bony upper part of it.
▻ ***verb*: bridges, bridging, bridged**
Something **bridges** *eg* a gap between two groups if it brings them closer together: *Measures must be taken to bridge the gap between rich and poor.*
▻ ***phrase*** If you say, in reference to some possible future problem, that you will **cross that bridge when you come to it**, you mean that you are going to deal with it when it arises and not before.

bridge[2] /brɪdʒ/ *noun* (*uncount*)
Bridge is a card game for four people playing in pairs.

bridle /'braɪdəl/ *noun; verb*
▻ ***noun*: bridles**
A horse's **bridle** is the set of leather straps that are fitted over its head, by means of which the rider controls it.
▻ ***verb*: bridles, bridling, bridled**
1 You **bridle** a horse when you put a bridle on it. **2** Someone **bridles** when they react impatiently, typically with a toss of the head, in response to something that makes them feel angry or insulted: *She bridled at his tone, irritated by his assumption that she would stop what she was doing and go with him.*

brief /bri:f/ *adjective; noun; verb*
▻ ***adjective*: briefer, briefest**
1 Something **brief** lasts for only a short time; a **brief** description or account is a concise one, using few words: *He gave a brief speech to open the proceedings.* □ *I had a delightful, if very brief, holiday in Malta.* □ *Parkin gave a brief summary of the previous night's events.* [*same as* **short**, **concise**, **succinct**; *opposite* **long**, **extensive**, **wordy**] **2** You are **brief** when you say what you need to say in as few words as you can: *Time is short, so I must be very brief.* **3 Brief** clothing does not cover much of your body; a **brief** skirt or pair of shorts is very short.
▻ ***noun*: briefs**
1 (*used in the singular*) You are given a **brief** if you are given official or formal instructions for a job or task: *He's been given a brief to prepare the illustrations for*

the book. **2** (*legal*) A **brief** is a case taken by a barrister.
[see also **briefs**]
▻ ***verb***: **briefs, briefing, briefed**
You **brief** someone when you prepare them by giving them the instructions or information they will need in advance: *I must brief him on the procedure before the meeting.* [*same as* **inform, instruct**]

briefcase /ˈbriːfkeɪs/ *noun*: **briefcases**
A **briefcase** is a light, usually flat case for carrying *eg* papers, documents and books.

briefing /ˈbriːfɪŋ/ *noun*: **briefings**
1 (*count or uncount*) A **briefing** is a meeting at which instructions and information are given: *The government will hold a press briefing.* [= a briefing for journalists] **2** A **briefing** is also the instructions or information given at a meeting.

briefly /ˈbriːflɪ/ *adverb*
1 Something happens or exists **briefly** if it happens or exists for only a short period of time: *She was briefly married to my brother.* **2** You say or write something **briefly** if you talk or write about it using very few words or giving very little information: *The President spoke only briefly to the journalists.* [compare **concisely**] **3** (*sentence adverb*) You can use **briefly** to indicate that what follows is a short or concise account of something: *Briefly, my opinion is that the company should abandon the project.*

briefs /briːfs/ *noun* (*plural*)
Briefs are a woman's pants or a man's underpants. [*same as* **knickers, pants**]

brigade /brɪˈgeɪd/ *noun*: **brigades**
A **brigade** is one of the divisions in the army. [see also **fire brigade**]

brigadier /brɪgəˈdɪə(r)/ *noun*: **brigadiers**
A **brigadier** is a senior army officer, above a colonel but below a major-general.

bright /braɪt/ *adjective*: **brighter, brightest**
1 A **bright** light or object is giving out a lot of light; a **bright** place is shining with a lot of light: *the bright sun* □ *The bedrooms that face south are brighter than those facing east.* [*opposite* **dark**] **2** A **bright** colour is strong, light and clear: *a bright red flower* □ *bright blue eyes.* [*opposite* **dark, dull**] **3 a** A **bright** person is clever and quick at learning: *My daughter is not very bright at maths.* **b** A **bright** idea is clever or ingenious. [*same as* **smart**; *opposite* **stupid**] **4** You look, sound or are **bright** if you are lively and cheerful: *You look much brighter now you've had a rest.* **5** The future is **bright** if it seems likely everything will go well. — *adverb* **brightly:** *The lamp was shining brightly.* □ *a brightly lit room* □ *a brightly coloured dress* □ *'All right', she said brightly.* — *noun* (*uncount*) **brightness:** *the brightness of the sun.*
▻ ***phrase*** You do something **bright and early** if you do it very early in the morning.

brighten /ˈbraɪtən/ *verb*: **brightens, brightening, brightened**
1 You **brighten**, or **brighten** up, when you become happier and livelier: *She brightened up when she heard the news.* □ *His eyes brightened when he saw his baby daughter.* **2** You **brighten** a place, or **brighten** it up, if you make it brighter, lighter or more colourful: *A fresh coat of paint will brighten the room.* □ *New curtains and pictures on the walls will help brighten the place up a bit.* **3** Someone or something **brightens**, or **brightens** up, a situation if they make it more fun and easier to bear: *A good film really brightens up a dull Sunday afternoon.* □ *You brighten my day.*

brilliant /ˈbrɪljənt/ *adjective*
1 (*informal*) You can describe something as **brilliant** when you think it is excellent or are very pleased with it: *The holiday was brilliant.* □ *That's a brilliant idea.* **2** A **brilliant** person is very intelligent or talented: *a brilliant young scientist.* **3** A **brilliant** colour is bright and vivid: *brilliant orange and red flowers.* **4** Light is **brilliant** when it is very bright and sparkling: *The brilliant sunshine made her blink.* **5** Someone who has a **brilliant** career is very successful in their work or profession; someone who is said to have a **brilliant** future is likely to be very successful. — *noun* (*uncount*) **brilliance:** *a scientist of great brilliance* □ *They are working hard to restore the palace to its former brilliance.* □ *the brilliance of the sunshine.* — *adverb* **brilliantly:** *The party went brilliantly.* □ *She sings brilliantly.* □ *a garden full of brilliantly coloured flowers* □ *The stars shone brilliantly in the night sky.*

brim /brɪm/ *noun*; *verb*
▻ ***noun***: **brims**
1 The **brim** of a cup, glass or bowl is the top edge of it. **2** The **brim** of a hat is the wide, flat part that sticks out.
▻ ***verb***: **brims, brimming, brimmed**
One thing **is brimming** with another if it is full of it: *His eyes were brimming with tears.*

> ***phrasal verb***
> **brim over 1** A container **brims over** when it has more liquid in it than it can hold: *She poured so much tea into the cup that it brimmed over.* [*same as* **overflow**] **2** You **are brimming over** with a good feeling when you look very pleased and excited about it: *She was brimming over with happiness.* □ *He's brimming over with enthusiasm for his new job.* [*same as* **bubble over**]

brine /braɪn/ *noun* (*uncount*)
Brine is very salty water, used for preserving food: *a tin of olives in brine.*

bring /brɪŋ/ *verb*: **brings, bringing, brought**
1 a You **bring** someone or something with you if you have them with you when you come: *Applicants were asked to bring their references with them.* □ *I've forgotten to bring my camera.* □ *I'll bring a bottle of wine.* □ *All members are cordially invited and are welcome to bring a guest.* □ *May I bring a friend to stay?* □ *Sorry to bring the baby but I had no-one I could leave him with.* **b** Someone **brings** a person or thing towards you, or into your range of vision, or to the place where you are, or you **bring** a person or thing to the place where your listener is, when you move, carry or lead them there: *He was brought to school in a taxi every day.* □ *the day she was able to bring her baby home from the hospital* □ *Get to bed and I'll bring you a hot drink.* □ *when the accused man was brought into court* □ *He put his hand in his pocket and brought out a bar of chocolate.* □ *Bring your arms down to your sides again.* [see note at **take**, sense 1b]
2 a You **bring** a quality or skill that you have to some activity if that quality or skill is seen as an advantage or a useful contribution: *new recruits who bring a high level of expertise to the project.* **b** People or things **are brought** somewhere when they are attracted there: *The idea is to bring people into the bookshops.* □ *how to bring people back to God* □ *measures that will bring new jobs to areas of coal and steel closures.* [*same as* **attract**]
3 a To **bring** someone or something into a certain state or situation is to put them into it: *Teachers try desperately to think of exercises that will bring grammar alive.* □ *the story about the statue that was brought*

to life □ *I couldn't bring him to his senses.* □ *Bring a large pan of salted water to the boil.* □ *bringing conflicting elements into harmony with one another* □ *It's best to bring these issues out into the open.* □ *before you bring yet another child into the world.* **b** One thing **brings** another if it produces it or causes it: *Never expect virtue to bring a reward.* □ *TV programmes that bring pleasure to millions* □ *The memory never failed to bring a smile to her face.* □ *1991 will bring a whole range of new challenges.* □ *Intervention by the UN is unlikely to bring a quicker end to the war.* □ *Promotion would bring a seat on the board.* [*same as* **produce**, **result** in] **c** You say you cannot **bring** yourself to do something if you find it too unpleasant or upsetting to do it: *subjects that many married couples can't bring themselves to discuss* □ *How can you bring yourself to tell a small child that his pet is going to die?* **d** (*legal*) One person **brings** *eg* a case, action, charge or claim against another when they formally accuse them of having done something illegal: *We decided to bring an action claiming damages against the tour operators.* □ *They can't bring a criminal prosecution against you.* [compare **sue**, **prosecute**]

phrasal verbs

bring about To **bring** something **about** is to make it happen: *Refrigeration brought about a complete change in people's lifestyles.* □ *The army worked with the civil authority to bring about an end to the chaos.* □ *high interest rates that could bring about a recession.* [*same as* **produce**, **effect**, **result** in]

bring along You **bring** someone or something **along** if you bring them with you when you come: *Teachers are asked to bring along tapes and records they have used in their classes.* □ *Don't forget our Christmas party on 12 December; bring your friends and colleagues along.*

bring back 1 You **bring** something **back** when you return it to the person or place you got it from: *Bring the basket back, won't you?* [*same as* **return**] **2** You **bring** something **back** from somewhere, *eg* a present for someone, when you return with it: *He brought me back one of those thick Icelandic jackets.* **3** If you say that a dead person cannot **be brought back** you mean they cannot be made to live again: *Well, wishing he was still alive isn't going to bring him back.* **4** Something **brings back** memories if it reminds you of past times: *The place brought back memories of happier times.* [*same as* **evoke**] **5** To **bring back** a particular practice is to introduce it again: *Some banks were planning to bring back charges for customers.* □ *There were calls to bring back hanging.* [*same as* **reintroduce**]

bring down 1 A government, or someone in a powerful position, **is brought down** when they are defeated or overthrown: *Depression, inflation or other economic distress can bring a government down.* □ *It's not the American way to bring a good man down by rumour and insinuation.* [*same as* **topple**, **defeat**, **overthrow**, **destroy**] **2** You **bring** something **down** when you reduce its level: *She was given tablets to bring her blood pressure down.* □ *It's vital to bring a high fever down immediately.* [*same as* **reduce**]

bring forward 1 You **bring** a planned event **forward** when you change it to an earlier date or time than it was previously scheduled for: *They were planning to bring the wedding forward to the first Saturday in October.* [*same as* **advance**; *opposite* **postpone**] **2** You **bring forward** a suggestion or proposal when you offer it for consideration: *when private developers bring forward proposals for new housing.* [*same as* **advance**, **produce**]

bring in 1 You **bring** someone **in** when you ask them to work with you or take part in what you are doing: *We may bring in an outside specialist to manage this part of the communications exercise.* [*same as* **invite** in, **co-opt**] **2** A body such as a government **brings in** a new law or system when they introduce it: *In 1912 legislation to bring in accident and sickness insurance was passed.* [*same as* **introduce**] **3** Someone or something **brings in** a certain amount of money when they earn that amount: *Their sons are working too and they bring in 300 rupees a month.* □ *Her investments brought in a reasonable income.* [*same as* **earn**] **4** (*legal*) A jury **brings in** a verdict of guilty or not guilty when they announce it before the court.

bring off (*informal*) You **bring** something difficult **off** if you manage to do it: *Both goalkeepers managed to bring off vital saves.* □ *He could bring off the most brilliant and surprising business coups.* [*same as* **pull off**, **achieve**]

bring on A particular thing **brings on** something such as a headache if it makes you have one: *Stress may bring on asthma attacks.* [*same as* **cause**]

bring out 1 Companies **bring out** new products when they introduce them into the market; publishers **bring out** books when they publish them: *In future it may be possible to bring out a first novel in paperback.* [*same as* **produce**, **publish**] **2** Something **brings** you **out** in *eg* a rash or spots when it causes you to have a rash or spots: *The sun always brings him out in a rash.* **3** You **bring out** some aspect or point when you emphasize it: *That was what I was trying to bring out in my story.* [*same as* **highlight**, **emphasize**] **4** A circumstance **brings out** certain, especially unusual, behaviour in people when it makes them behave that way; something that **brings out** the best or worst in someone or something shows their best or worst qualities: *I'd hoped the baby would bring out all the good things Alan had the potential to be.* □ *There's nothing like the Sunday trading issue to bring out the worst in retailers.* □ *To bring out the best in your cooking make sure you use the purest soy sauce.*

bring round or **bring to 1** An unconscious person **is brought round**, or **brought to**, when something makes them become conscious again: *tugging his hair in an effort to bring him round.* [*same as* **revive**, **resuscitate**] **2** You **bring** someone who disagrees with you **round** when you persuade them to accept your ideas or suggestions. [*same as* **persuade**, **win over**]

bring together A circumstance **brings** people **together 1** when it makes them friendly and co-operative towards one another: *Incidents such as this bring a community together.* [*same as* **unite**] **2** when it collects or assembles them in one place, usually for a special purpose: *an exhibition that brings together a stunning collection of maps, charts and aerial photographs* □ *how to bring together the most active British researchers.* [*same as* **assemble** together]

bring up 1 You **bring up** children when you care for them and educate them until they are grown up: *women who choose to bring up children alone without a male partner* □ *I imagined I'd brought my sons up to be polite.* □ *I was rather strictly brought up myself.* □ *The children were all brought up as Catholics.* [*same as* **rear**, **raise**] **2** You **bring** a subject **up** when you introduce it for discussion: *Someone brought up the subject of marital fidelity.* [*same as* **introduce**, **mention**] **3** You **bring up** food when you vomit: *He brought up most of his lunch.* [*same as* **vomit**]

brink /brɪŋk/ *noun*
▻ ***phrase*** You are **on the brink** of something frightening, terrible or exciting when you are just about to do it or experience it: *two countries on the brink of war* □ *scientists on the brink of new discoveries.*

brisk /brɪsk/ *adjective*
1 A **brisk** person behaves and moves in a bright confident way, giving the impression that they are getting things done quickly and efficiently: *She tried to remain brisk and businesslike, while inside she was shocked and embarrassed.* **2** Trade or business is **brisk** when a lot of buying and selling is going on, and people are making lots of money: *The shop does a brisk lunchtime trade in sandwiches and snacks.* **3 Brisk** movement is swift and lively: *They went for a brisk walk along the cliffs.* **4** The weather is described as **brisk** when it is cold and fresh. — *adverb* **briskly:** *She moved around briskly tidying things away.* □ *They walked briskly along the road.* □ *The wind was blowing briskly.* — *noun* (*uncount*) **briskness:** *'Good morning!' she called with her usual annoying briskness.*

bristle /'brɪsəl/ *noun; verb*
▻ ***noun*: bristles**
1 Bristles are **a** the short hairs that grow again on a man's chin after he has shaved. **b** the short, stiff hairs that grow on an animal's back, used to make some kinds of brush: *I prefer the old-fashioned bristle hairbrushes.* **2** (*used in the plural*) The **bristles** of a brush are its tufts of hair, or its hair-like plastic or nylon projections: *toothbrushes with nylon bristles.*
▻ ***verb*: bristles, bristling, bristled**
1 The hairs on your skin **bristle** when they rise in reaction to cold, or to emotions such as fear or anger: *The hairs on the back of my neck bristled at the sound.* **2** You **bristle** when you react angrily to something that you feel annoyed or insulted by: *She bristled at being referred to as 'one of the mums'.* □ *He was obviously bristling with fury.*

> ***phrasal verb***
> **bristle with** Something **bristles with** with things or people if it is full of them: *The conference centre was bristling with uniformed policemen.* □ *The room bristled with instruments and equipment of all shapes and sizes.* □ *Next morning the papers bristled with tributes to 'a man who stood for tradition and dignity'.*

bristly /'brɪslɪ/ *adjective*: **bristlier, bristliest**
Bristly hair is rough; a man's chin is **bristly** if it feels rough because there are bristles growing on it.

Brit /brɪt/ *noun* (*informal*): **Brits**
A **Brit** is a British person.

British /'brɪtɪʃ/ *adjective; noun*
▻ ***adjective***
British people or things belong to or are from Great Britain: *British industry.*
▻ ***noun*** (*plural*)
The **British** are the people from Great Britain: *The British complain a lot about the weather.*

Briton /brɪtən/ *noun*: **Britons**
1 A **Briton** is a person from Great Britain: *Several Britons were killed in the plane crash in America.* **2** (*history*) A **Briton** was a member of the people who lived in Britain before the Roman invasion.

brittle /'brɪtəl/ *adjective*: **brittler, brittlest**
1 A substance or object is **brittle** if it is hard but easily broken or likely to break: *a child with brittle bones.* **2** A **brittle** sound is short, hard and sharp: *a brittle laugh.*

broach /broʊtʃ/ *verb*: **broaches, broaching, broached**
You **broach** a subject, especially one that is likely to cause arguments or problems, when you start discussing it: *I didn't like to broach the subject of a pay rise when I spoke to my boss.*

broad /brɔːd/ *adjective*: **broader, broadest**
1 Something that is **broad** is large in extent from one side to the other: *a broad tree-lined avenue* □ *He has very broad shoulders.* [*same as* **wide**; *opposite* **narrow**]

> **Broad** and **wide** have a similar meaning and can both be used in most contexts, *eg a broad* (or *wide*) *smile; a wide* (or *broad*) *grin*; however in talking about the measurement of something from side to side, you usually use **wide**: *How wide is the bedroom? It's twelve feet wide.*

2 Broad also means general and without a lot of detail: *Give me a broad description of the place.* **3** A **broad** variety, selection or range includes lots of different things: *The college has a broad syllabus that allows students to study several different subjects at the same time.* □ *She has broad experience of teaching English to foreign learners.* [*same as* **wide**; *opposite* **limited, restricted**] **4 Broad** also describes something that affects, is felt or is believed by a lot of people: *There is broad support for the Government's policies on law and order.* [*same as* **widespread**; *opposite* **limited**] **5 Broad** describes remarks or hints that have a very clear or obvious meaning: *He gave me a broad hint that I should resign before I was sacked.* **6** An accent is **broad** if it is strongly marked by local features: *broad Scots* □ *My daughter speaks with a broad Glasgow accent.*
▻ ***phrase*** A crime is committed **in broad daylight** if it is committed during the day and not at night: *He was attacked in broad daylight.*

broad bean /brɔːd 'biːn/ *noun*: **broad beans**
Broad beans are large flat green pods containing large flat white seeds which are eaten as a vegetable. [see picture at **vegetable**]

broadcast /'brɔːdkɑːst/ *verb; noun*
▻ ***verb*: broadcasts, broadcasting, broadcast**
1 An organization **broadcasts** radio or television programmes when it sends them out using radio waves: *The BBC broadcasts the news every hour on the radio.* □ *The film was broadcast on television last night.* **2** You **broadcast** something if you tell it to a lot of people: *Please don't broadcast the news round the whole company.*
▻ ***noun*: broadcasts**
A **broadcast** is a television or radio programme.

broadcaster /'brɔːdkɑːstə(r)/ *noun*: **broadcasters**
A **broadcaster** is a person who gives talks on serious subjects on the television or radio.

broadcasting /'brɔːdkɑːstɪŋ/ *noun* (*uncount*)
Broadcasting is the process of making and sending out radio and television programmes using radio waves: *She works in broadcasting.*

broaden /'brɔːdən/ *verb*: **broadens, broadening, broadened**
1 Something **broadens**, or **broadens**, out when it becomes broader: *The road broadens out once it has passed through the village.* **2** You **broaden** something, or **broaden** it out, when you make it include or affect more people or things; something **broadens** when it begins to include or affect more people or things: *The government want to broaden the scope of the enquiry to include dentists as well as doctors and nurses.*

broadly /ˈbrɔːdlɪ/ *adverb*
1 (*sentence adverb*) You use **broadly**, or '**broadly** speaking' to say what you think is true in most cases, or in a very general way: *Broadly speaking, the children here are from deprived backgrounds.* □ *Broadly, one can identify two main trends.* **2** Something that is **broadly** so is so to a substantial extent: *Delegates expressed themselves broadly in support of the proposed measures.* **3** People smile **broadly** when they have a wide smile of genuine pleasure on their faces.

broadminded /brɔːdˈmaɪndɪd/ *adjective*
A **broadminded** person is tolerant of other people's behaviour, opinions and beliefs: *She's got a very broadminded attitude to sex.*

broadsheet /ˈbrɔːdʃiːt/ *noun*: **broadsheets**
A **broadsheet** is a newspaper printed on large sheets of paper. [compare **tabloid**]

brocade /brəˈkeɪd/ *noun* (*uncount*)
Brocade is a heavy silk material with a raised design on it: *gold brocade curtains.*

broccoli /ˈbrɒkəlɪ/ *noun* (*uncount*)
Broccoli is a type of vegetable with green or purple flower-like heads growing on thick stems. [see picture are **vegetable**]

brochure /ˈbroʊʃə(r)/ *noun*: **brochures**
A **brochure** is a short book or pamphlet giving information about *eg* holidays or products: *holiday brochures.*

broil /brɔɪl/ *verb* (*AmE*): **broils, broiling, broiled**
You **broil** food when you grill it.

broke /broʊk/ *verb*; *adjective*
▻ ***verb***
Broke is the past tense of **break**.
▻ ***adjective*** (*informal*)
You are **broke** when you have no money at all: *I'm afraid I'm broke till the weekend.*
▻ ***phrase*** (*informal*) A person or company **goes broke** if they lose all their money and cannot continue to work or trade properly.

broken /ˈbroʊkən/ *verb*; *adjective*
▻ ***verb***
Broken is the past participle of **break**.
▻ ***adjective***
1 An object is **broken** when it is cracked or has been smashed to pieces, usually by being hit or dropped: *broken glass.* □ *He has a fractured skull and a broken leg.* **2** A piece of equipment or machinery is **broken** when it is damaged and not working properly: *The video recorder is broken.* **3** A **broken** promise or agreement is one that has not been kept. **4** A **broken** marriage is one that has ended in divorce. **5** (*old*) A foreigner speaks in *eg* **broken** English or French when they speak it hesitantly, with a lot of grammatical errors, because they don't know the language very well: *her broken English.*

broken-down /ˈbroʊkəndaʊn/ *adjective*
A **broken-down** vehicle or machine is not working: *There was a broken-down car parked at the side of the road.* [see also **break down** at **break**]

broken-hearted /broʊkən ˈhɑːtɪd/ *adjective*
You are **broken-hearted** if you are extremely sad. [*same as* **heartbroken**]

broken home /broʊkən ˈhoʊm/ *noun*: **broken homes**
A child who comes from a **broken home** has parents who are divorced or separated.

broker /ˈbroʊkə(r)/ *noun*: **brokers**
A **broker** is a person employed to buy and sell shares, currency, or goods and services, on behalf of other people: *an insurance broker.* [see also **stockbroker**]

brolly /ˈbrɒlɪ/ *noun* (*BrE*; *informal*): **brollies**
A **brolly** is an umbrella.

bronchial tubes /brɒŋkɪəl ˈtjuːbz/ *noun* (*plural*)
Your **bronchial tubes** are the two large tubes leading from your windpipe to your lungs, through which you breathe air into your lungs.

bronchitis /brɒŋˈkaɪtɪs/ *noun* (*uncount*)
Bronchitis is an infection of the two large air tubes in the lungs, that causes coughing and difficulty in breathing.

bronze /brɒnz/ *noun*; *adjective*
▻ ***noun*: bronzes**
1 (*uncount*) **Bronze** is a metal made from a mixture of copper and tin: *During Roman times, bronze and marble were the materials most commonly used for sculpture.* **2** A **bronze** is a sculpture, especially a statue, made of bronze: *Renaissance bronzes.* **3** (*usually in the singular*) A competitor who wins the **bronze** wins the bronze medal.
▻ ***adjective***
Bronze describes things that are made of bronze, or are the red-brown colour of bronze: *a row of bronze busts* □ *the animal's shiny bronze coat.*

bronzed /brɒnzd/ *adjective*
Someone who is **bronzed** is deeply sun-tanned: *a bronzed, athletic man with a steady gaze and narrow hips.*

bronze medal /brɒnz ˈmɛdəl/ *noun*: **bronze medals**
A **bronze medal** is a medal given to the person who comes third in a race or competition.

brooch /broʊtʃ/ *noun*: **brooches**
A **brooch** is a piece of jewellery that you fasten to clothes with a pin.

brood /bruːd/ *noun*; *verb*
▻ ***noun*: broods**
1 A **brood** is a number of young animals, especially birds, that are born or hatch at the same time. **2** (*humorous*) A person's **brood** is their children: *her lively brood.*
▻ ***verb*: broods, brooding, brooded**
You **brood** about something if you worry about it for a period of time: *Some of the students are brooding about their exam results.* □ *He tends to brood over his problems.* [*same as* **fret**]

brooding /ˈbruːdɪŋ/ *adjective*
Brooding describes something threatening or sinister: *his brooding presence.*

broody /ˈbruːdɪ/ *adjective*: **broodier, broodiest**
1 A bird is **broody** when it wants to sit on eggs to make them hatch. **2** A person is **broody** if they are thinking deeply and anxiously about something.

brook /brʊk/ *noun*: **brooks**
A **brook** is a small stream.

broom /bruːm/ *noun*: **brooms**
A **broom** is a brush with a long handle, for sweeping the floor.

broomstick /ˈbruːmstɪk/ *noun*: **broomsticks**
A **broomstick** is the long handle of a broom.

broth /brɒθ/ *noun* (*uncount*)
Broth is clear soup made by boiling meat, fish or vegetables.

brothel /ˈbrɒθəl/ *noun*: **brothels**
A **brothel** is a house where men pay money for sexual intercourse with women.

brother /ˈbrʌðə(r)/ *noun*: **brothers** or **brethren** (this old plural form is still sometimes used in sense 3)
1 Your **brother** is a boy or man who has the same par-

ents as you do: *My brother is two years older than me.* **2** People may refer to fellow members of the same trade union, church or society as their brothers. **3** The members of a religious group such as a monastery are sometimes referred to as **brothers**: *Brother Michael looks after the vegetable garden.* □ *This is the brothers' reading room.*
[compare **sister**]

brotherhood /'brʌðəhʊd/ *noun*: **brotherhoods**
1 (*uncount*) **Brotherhood** is a feeling of friendliness felt towards people that you have something in common with. **2** A **brotherhood** is an organization whose members, usually men, share a common religious belief or common aims.

brother-in-law /'brʌðəɪnlɔː/ *noun*: **brothers-in-law**
Your **brother-in-law** is **1** your husband's or your wife's brother. **2** your sister's husband. **3** the husband of your husband's or your wife's sister.

brotherly /'brʌðəlɪ/ *adjective*
Brotherly feelings are the feelings such as love and loyalty that brothers have for each other.

brought /brɔːt/ *verb*
Brought is the past tense and past participle of **bring**.

brow /braʊ/ *noun*: **brows**
1 (*usually in the plural*) Your **brows** are your eyebrows. **2** Your **brow** is your forehead: *She mopped the sweat from her brow.* [see picture of **body**] **3** The **brow** of *eg* a hill or the road is the top of it: *You can see the village from the brow of the hill.*

browbeat /'braʊbiːt/ *verb*: **browbeats**, **browbeating**, **browbeaten**
You **browbeat** people such as your relations or employees when you bully them and make them frightened of you: *Don't let yourself be browbeaten by him.* [*same as* **bully**] — *adjective* **browbeaten:** *The team left the pitch browbeaten, after their ninth defeat of the season.*

brown /braʊn/ *noun*; *adjective*; *verb*
▻ ***noun*** (*uncount or count*): **browns**
Brown is the colour of coffee, earth, bark or tanned skin, or any shade of this colour: *a nice shade of brown* □ *the browns and golds of autumn* □ *I don't wear a lot of brown.* □ *He painted the floorboards a dark brown.*
▻ ***adjective***: **browner**, **brownest**
1 Brown things are the same colour as coffee, earth, bark or tanned skin: *brown hair and eyes* □ *They're dark brown, not black.* □ (*with the noun omitted*) *I prefer the black shoes to the brown.* **2 Brown** bread is brown in colour, usually because it has been made with wholemeal flour. **3** A person can be described as **brown** if they have a dark skin or complexion. **4** You are **brown** if your skin is tanned from being in the sun.
▻ ***verb***: **browns**, **browning**, **browned**
You **brown** something, or it **browns**, if it becomes browner by being cooked or burned in the sun: *Cook the onions until they begin to brown.*

brownish /'braʊnɪʃ/ *adjective*
Something is **brownish** if it is slightly brown in colour: *There were brownish patches on the wallpaper.*

browse /braʊz/ *verb*; *noun*
▻ ***verb***: **browses**, **browsing**, **browsed**
1 You **browse** through a book, magazine or group of books or magazines when you look through it casually, reading only bits and pieces: *She browsed through the magazines before choosing one to buy.* **2** You **browse** in *eg* a shop if you look casually at the things there: *He spent the afternoon browsing in the museum.*
▻ ***noun*** (*usually in the singular*)
You have a **browse** when you look casually at or through something: *I always enjoy a good browse round the shops.*

bruise /bruːz/ *noun*; *verb*
▻ ***noun***: **bruises**
A **bruise** is an injury caused by a blow that turns the skin a dark colour without breaking it: *She had a nasty bruise on her leg where she'd banged it against the table.* □ *cuts and bruises.*
▻ ***verb***: **bruises**, **bruising**, **bruised:** *I've bruised myself countless times on the corner of that table.* — *adjective* **bruised:** *He touched his bruised cheek very gently.*

brunette /bruː'nɛt/ *noun*: **brunettes**
A **brunette** is a white-skinned woman with dark brown hair: *A tall pale brunette sat behind the desk.* [compare **blonde**]

brunt /brʌnt/ *noun*
▻ ***phrase*** You **bear the brunt** of something such as a blow or attack if you receive the main force or shock of it: *His wife had to bear the brunt of his anger.*

brush /brʌʃ/ *noun*; *verb*
▻ ***noun***: **brushes**
1 A **brush** is a tool fitted with bristles or tufts of material, for tidying your hair, or for other jobs, such as sweeping the floor, or painting. [see picture at **bedroom**] **2** (*usually in the singular*) You give something a **brush** when you use a brush to clean or tidy it: *Your hair needs a good brush.* **3** You have a **brush** with someone if you have an argument or disagreement with them: *He's had several brushes with the police, though he's never actually been in prison.*
▻ ***verb***: **brushes**, **brushing**, **brushed**
1 You **brush** something when you make it tidy or clean it with a brush or some other object: *She brushed her hair.* **2** You **brush** something *eg* away, or on to a surface when you remove it or apply it with a brush or brushing movement: *She brushed the crumbs away with the side of her hand.* **3** You **brush** against someone or something when you touch them lightly as you move past.

phrasal verbs
brush aside You **brush** something **aside** if you do not consider it: *She brushed aside his comments.*
brush up You **brush up** something when you refresh or improve your knowledge of it: *I'll need to brush up my Shakespeare before the course starts.* □ *You could do with brushing up on your French vocabulary.*

brushwood /'brʌʃwʊd/ *noun* (*uncount*)
Brushwood is a collection of small dead and broken branches from trees and bushes.

brusque /bruːsk/ *adjective*
A person who is **brusque** does not bother to be polite when dealing with other people: *You shouldn't be so brusque with people.* [*same as* **curt**] — *adverb* **brusquely:** *'I'm sorry, I can't wait,' he said brusquely.*

brussels sprout /brʌsəls 'spraʊt/ *noun*: **brussels sprouts**
Brussels sprouts are small, round, cabbage-like buds, eaten as a vegetable. [see picture at **vegetable**]

brutal /'bruːtəl/ *adjective*
1 A **brutal** person or thing is very cruel or violent: *a brutal man* □ *the government's brutal treatment of its opponents.* **2** You say something with **brutal** honesty if you say it openly and plainly and do not care if you upset or offend the person you are talking to: *She described her feelings for him with brutal frankness.* — *adverb* **brutally:** *He was brutally attacked by a gang of young men.* □ *She was brutally honest and told him she didn't love him any more.*

brutality /bruːˈtalɪtɪ/ *noun*: **brutalities**
1 (*uncount*) **Brutality** is cruel or violent behaviour towards other people: *There is too much brutality in the film.* **2 Brutalities** are cruel or violent acts: *brutalities committed in war.*

brutalize or **brutalise** /ˈbruːtəlaɪz/ *verb*: **brutalizes, brutalizing, brutalized**
An unpleasant experience **brutalizes** a person if it makes them cruel and violent: *children brutalized by years of abuse and neglect.*

brute /bruːt/ *noun*; *adjective*
▷ ***noun***: **brutes**
1 You can describe a cruel, violent man as a **brute**. **2** A **brute** is also any animal, especially a large one: *I like elephants but I always feel sorry for the poor brutes when I see them in circuses.*
▷ ***adjective***
You use **brute** force or strength when you use physical strength alone to achieve something: *Explanations and persuasion are much more likely to produce results than brute force.*

bubble /ˈbʌbəl/ *noun*: **bubbles**
1 A **bubble** is a thin film of liquid forming a ball round air or gas, especially one that floats in liquid: *soap bubbles.* **2** A **bubble** is also a ball of air or gas which has formed in a solid: *an air bubble in glass.*
▷ ***verb***: **bubbles, bubbling, bubbled**
1 Liquid **bubbles** when bubbles form in it or rise to its surface: *Grill the cheese until it starts to bubble.* **2** Liquid **bubbles**, or **bubbles** away, when it makes a sound like water boiling: *The stew was bubbling away in the pan.*

> ***phrasal verb***
> **bubble over 1** Liquid **bubbles over** when it boils violently and flows over the edge of the container. [*same as* **boil over**] **2** You **are bubbling over** with *eg* happiness, excitement, enthusiasm or good ideas when you are full of them. [*same as* **brim over**]

bubble gum /ˈbʌbəl gʌm/ *noun* (*uncount*)
Bubble gum is chewing gum which can be blown into bubbles.

bubbly /ˈbʌblɪ/ *adjective*; *noun*
▷ ***adjective***: **bubblier, bubbliest**
1 Bubbly liquid is full of bubbles: *bubbly lemonade.* **2** A **bubbly** person is very lively and cheerful and full of high spirits: *A bubbly young woman.*
▷ ***noun*** (*uncount*; *informal*)
Bubbly is champagne.

buck[1] /bʌk/ *noun* (*AmE*; *informal*): **bucks**
A **buck** is a dollar: *It cost a couple of bucks.*
▷ ***phrase*** (*informal*) Someone **makes a fast buck** or **makes a quick buck** if they make money quickly and easily, and often dishonestly.

buck[2] /bʌk/ *noun*
▷ ***phrase*** (*informal*) You **pass the buck** when you refuse to accept responsibility for dealing with something, and pass it on to someone else.

buck[3] /bʌk/ *noun*; *verb*
▷ ***noun***: **bucks**
A **buck** is the male of some animals, especially the rabbit, hare or deer.
▷ ***verb***: **bucks, bucking, bucked**
A horse **bucks** when it jumps into the air several times in quick succession, with its back arched and legs held stiff: *The horse bucked and the rider fell off.*

> ***phrasal verb***
> **buck up 1** You **buck** someone **up** if you make them more cheerful; someone **bucks up** if they become more cheerful: *An evening out will buck you up a bit.* **2** (*informal*) If you tell someone to **buck up** you are telling them to hurry: *Buck up or we'll be late.*

bucket /ˈbʌkɪt/ *noun*: **buckets**
1 A **bucket** is a round, open-topped container for holding or carrying *eg* liquids or sand. **2** A **bucket** of something is the bucket and its contents, or just the contents: *She was coming up the stairs carrying a heavy bucket of water.* □ *She threw a bucket of water over him.* **3** (*used in the plural*; *informal*) **Buckets** of a liquid is a large quantity of it: *She wept buckets.* □ *It rained buckets all day.*

buckle /ˈbʌkəl/ *noun*; *verb*
▷ ***noun***: **buckles**
A **buckle** is a flat piece of metal attached to one end of a strap or belt, with a pin in the middle which goes through a hole in the other end of the strap or belt to fasten it: *These shoes fasten with buckles.* [see picture at **clothing**]
▷ ***verb***: **buckles, buckling, buckled**
1 You **buckle** *eg* your shoes, a belt, a piece of clothing or a strap when you fasten them with a buckle: *She buckled her coat tightly about her.* **2** Metal **buckles** when it bends or becomes bent out of shape, usually as a result of great heat or force. **3** Your legs or knees **buckle** when they bend and can't support you properly because they are tired or weak.

> ***phrasal verb***
> (*informal*) You **buckle down** when you begin to work seriously or hard: *It's time you buckled down to some work if you're going to pass that exam.*

bud /bʌd/ *noun*; *verb*
▷ ***noun***: **buds**
A **bud** is a small swelling on the stem of a tree or plant that will develop into leaves or a flower: *As spring approaches the flower buds begin to appear.*
▷ ***verb***: **buds, budding, budded**
A tree or plant **buds** when buds appear on it.
▷ ***phrases*** **1** A tree or plant is **in bud** when it has buds on it. **2** (*informal*) You **nip** something **in the bud** when you put an end to it at an early stage: *The new policy means that bad decisions can be nipped in the bud before any damage is done.*

Buddhism /ˈbʊdɪzm/ *noun* (*uncount*)
Buddhism is the religion that teaches its followers to be spiritually pure and how to be free from the usual human or worldly concerns.

Buddhist /ˈbʊdɪst/ *noun*; *adjective*
▷ ***noun***: **Buddhists**
A **Buddhist** is a follower of Buddhism.
▷ ***adjective:*** *Buddhist texts.*

budding /ˈbʌdɪŋ/ *adjective*
Budding describes people who are beginning to show talent and develop skill at something: *Budding tennis-players as young as five can start gaining skills at the new school for young players in California.* [*same as* **promising**]

buddy /ˈbʌdɪ/ *noun* (*AmE*; *informal*): **buddies**
Your **buddy** is your friend or companion: *They've been buddies since high school.*

budge /bʌdʒ/ *verb* (*usually with a negative*): **budges, budging, budged**
1 Something will not **budge** if it will not move, or if you cannot move it: *The window's stuck; it just won't budge.* **2** Someone will not **budge** if they refuse to change their mind or their opinions: *She is determined to resign; nothing you say will make her budge.*

budgerigar /ˈbʌdʒərɪgɑː(r)/ *noun*: **budgerigars**
A **budgerigar** is a type of small parrot found in Australia, often kept as a pet.

budget /ˈbʌdʒɪt/ *noun*; *adjective*; *verb*
▻ ***noun***: **budgets**
A **budget** is any plan that a person, organization or government has that shows how they will raise money and how they will spend the money they have.
▻ ***adjective*** (*informal*)
Budget means cheap: *a budget holiday* □ *budget prices.*
▻ ***verb***: **budgets, budgeting, budgeted**
You **budget** when you calculate how much money you are earning and how much you are spending, so that you do not spend more than you have: *The school has to budget carefully if it is to afford extra computer equipment.* — *noun* (*uncount*) **budgeting:** *Careful budgeting will allow you to pay your debts within two years.*

> ***phrasal verb***
> You **budget for** something if you allow for it in a budget, especially when you save money regularly to be able to afford something: *She had budgeted carefully for her Icelandic trip, and was not going to miss it.*

budgetary /ˈbʌdʒɪtərɪ/ *adjective* (*formal*)
Budgetary matters are concerned with the money that governments, organizations or private individuals have available for spending, and the things on which they are going to spend it.

budgie /ˈbʌdʒɪ/ *noun* (*informal*): **budgies**
A **budgie** is a budgerigar.

buff /bʌf/ *noun*: **buffs**
1 (*informal*) A **buff** is a person who is enthusiastic and knowledgeable about a certain subject: *She's an opera buff.* **2** (*uncount, often adjectival*) **Buff** is a dull yellow colour: *buff-coloured envelopes.*

buffalo /ˈbʌfəloʊ/ *noun*: **buffalo** or **buffaloes**
A **buffalo** is a an animal of the cattle family, with long curved horns.

buffer /ˈbʌfə(r)/ *noun*: **buffers**
1 The **buffers** on a train are the two round pieces of metal on springs that take the shock when the carriage hits something. **2** A thing that acts as a **buffer** shields something against serious harm: *Temporary workers often act as a buffer against market fluctuations.* **3** (*computers*) A **buffer** is a temporary memory in a computer where information is stored until it can be printed or transferred to another computer system.

buffet[1] /ˈbʊfeɪ/ *noun*: **buffets**
1 A **buffet** is a place where light meals and drinks may be bought and eaten, especially at a station or on a train. [see also **buffet car**] **2** A **buffet** is also a cold meal set out on tables where people may serve themselves: *We invited some friends round for a buffet supper.*

buffet[2] /ˈbʌfɪt/ *verb*: **buffets, buffeting, buffeted**
To **buffet** means to strike or knock about roughly: *The ship was buffeted by the waves.*

buffet car /ˈbʊfeɪ kɑː(r)/ *noun*: **buffet cars**
A **buffet car** is a carriage in a train where light meals and drinks may be bought.

buffoon /bəˈfuːn/ *noun*: **buffoons**
A **buffoon** is a person who does amusing or silly things. [*same as* **clown**]

bug /bʌg/ *noun*; *verb*
▻ ***noun***: **bugs**
1 A **bug** is any tiny insect, especially one with a flat body and a mouth which can suck blood. **2** (*informal*) A **bug** is any germ or virus causing infection or illness: *a stomach bug.* **3** (*informal*) A **bug** is also a small hidden microphone. **4** (*informal; computers*) A **bug** is a fault in a machine or computer program which stops it from working properly. **5** (*informal*) You are bitten by a **bug** when you become very enthusiastic about something: *She got bitten by the climbing bug while she was on holiday in the Alps.*
▻ ***verb***: **bugs, bugging, bugged**
1 (*informal*) A place that **is bugged** has a tiny microphone hidden in it so that private conversations can be recorded without the speakers knowing. **2** (*informal*) Something **bugs** you if it annoys or worries you: *It's been bugging me for a while, but I think I've got it all worked out now.*

bugle /ˈbjuːgəl/ *noun*: **bugles**
A **bugle** is a brass instrument like a small trumpet, used mainly for military signals.

build /bɪld/ *verb*; *noun*
▻ ***verb***: **builds, building, built**
1 You **build** something when you make it by joining its separate parts together: *workmen building a new hospital* □ *I built the car from a kit.* □ *The company is planning to build on derelict land near the river.* **2** You **build** something if you develop it gradually: *The government is trying to build a fairer society.* □ *These magazines will build into a complete cookery course.*
▻ ***noun*** (*uncount or count*)
Your **build** is the shape and size of your body: *a young man of slim build* □ *her athletic build.* □ *people of difficult builds*

> ***phrasal verbs***
> **build in** or **build into 1** You **build** furniture **in**, or **into** a room, when you have it constructed against the wall, and fixed to it: *He's having some bathroom cupboards built in.* **2** You **build** something **into** a system or construction when you include it in its design: *They've built a large number of safety checks into the system.*
> [see also **built-in**]
> **build on 1** You **build** a new room or part of a building **on** to an existing building when you add it: *We're hoping to build a new conservatory on to the house next summer.* **2** You **build on** *eg* a previous success when you use it as a basis from which to develop further: *We must build on previous experience and not make the same mistakes again.* **3** One thing is **built on** another if it is based on it: *Her success as a lawyer was built on her ability to argue and discuss well.*
> **build up 1** Something **builds up** when it gradually increases in size, strength or amount; you **build** something **up** when you make it increase gradually in size, strength or amount: *Traffic has been building up in the area all day.* □ *She won't discuss her problems with you until you've built up her confidence.* **2** You **build** someone or something **up** if you make them seem more important than they really are: *Her reputation has been built up by the media.*
> [see also **build-up**]

builder /ˈbɪldə(r)/ *noun*: **builders**
A **builder** is a person whose job is to build, or organize the building of, *eg* houses.

building /ˈbɪldɪŋ/ *noun*: **buildings**
1 A **building** is a structure with walls and a roof, such as a house: *derelict factory buildings.* **2** (*uncount*) **Building** is the business or process of constructing *eg* houses: *He works in the building industry.*

building society /'bɪldɪŋ səsaɪətɪ/ *noun*: **building societies**
A **building society** is a business firm that lends people money for buying or improving houses, and where you can save money to earn interest on it.

build-up /'bɪldʌp/ *noun* (*usually in the singular*): **build-ups**
1 A **build-up** of something is a gradual increase: *a build-up of traffic on the motorway during the day.* **2** The **build-up** to an event is the preparation or increasing excitement before it: *the build-up to the football World Cup.*
[see also **build up** at **build**]

built /bɪlt/ *verb*
Built is the past tense and past participle of **build**.

built-in /bɪlt'ɪn/ *adjective*
1 Built-in cupboards and wardrobes are constructed against the walls of a room, and fixed to them. **2** A **built-in** feature of a system is something included in its design or construction.

built-up /bɪlt'ʌp/ *adjective*
Land, or an area of land, that is **built-up** is covered with buildings, especially houses: *a built-up area.* [see also **build up** at **build**]

bulb /bʌlb/ *noun*: **bulbs**
1 A plant's **bulb** is the onion-shaped part of the stem that the roots grow from. **2** A **bulb** is also a flower grown from a bulb, such as a daffodil or hyacinth. **3** A **bulb**, or **light bulb**, is a piece of pear-shaped glass that gives out light: *The bulb needs replacing.* [see picture at **living room**]. **4** A **bulb** is also anything shaped like a pear: *the bulb of a thermometer.*

bulbous /'bʌlbəs/ *adjective*
A **bulbous** object is fat and bulging.

bulge /bʌldʒ/ *noun*; *verb*
▷ ***noun***: **bulges**
A **bulge** is a swelling, especially where you would expect to see something flat: *There was a bulge under his coat where he was trying to hide the book.*
▷ ***verb***: **bulges, bulging, bulged**
1 Something **bulges** when it swells or sticks outwards: *She was five months pregnant and beginning to bulge noticeably.* **2** Something **is bulging** with things when it is full of them: *Her bag was bulging with presents for the children.* — *adjective* **bulging:** *a bulging suitcase.*

bulk /bʌlk/ *noun* (*used in the singular*)
1 The **bulk** of something is the greater or main part of it: *The bulk of the applicants are women.* **2** A **bulk** is a large body, shape or person: *The dark bulk of the ship loomed up out of the fog.*
▷ ***phrase*** You buy or sell something **in bulk** when you buy or sell very large quantities of it: *Flour and rice are cheaper if you buy them in bulk.*

bulky /'bʌlkɪ/ *adjective*: **bulkier, bulkiest**
Something that is **bulky** is large in size and awkward to carry or move: *a bulky package.*

bull /bʊl/ *noun*: **bulls**
1 A **bull** is the male of animals in the cattle family. **2** A **bull** is also the male elephant, whale and other large animals.

bulldog /'bʊldɒg/ *noun*: **bulldogs**
A **bulldog** is a small, fierce, heavily built dog with a large head.

bulldoze /'bʊldoʊz/ *verb*: **bulldozes, bulldozing, bulldozed**
1 To **bulldoze** *eg* a building is to demolish it using a bulldozer. **2** You **bulldoze** someone into doing something they don't want to do if you force them to do it: *She bulldozed him into taking part in the school play.*

bulldozer /'bʊldoʊzə(r)/ *noun*: **bulldozers**
A **bulldozer** is a large, powerful tractor with a vertical blade at the front, for pushing heavy objects, clearing the ground or making it level.

bullet /'bʊlɪt/ *noun*: **bullets**
A **bullet** is a small metal cylinder with a pointed end, that is fired from small guns and rifles: *He died from a bullet wound.* □ *bullet holes.*

bulletin /'bʊlətɪn/ *noun*: **bulletins**
1 A **bulletin** is a short news report, *eg* on television or radio. **2** A **bulletin** is also a short printed newspaper or leaflet, especially one produced regularly by a group or organization: *The company publishes an annual staff bulletin.*

bullet-proof /'bʊlɪtpruːf/ *adjective*
Something that is **bullet-proof** is made of material strong enough to prevent bullets passing through it: *a bullet-proof vest* □ *the Pope's bullet-proof car.*

bullfight /'bʊlfaɪt/ *noun*: **bullfights**
A **bullfight** is a public show popular in Spain, in which men on horseback and on foot torment and then kill a bull.

bullfighter /'bʊlfaɪtə(r)/ *noun*: **bullfighters**
A **bullfighter** is the person who tries to kill the bull during a bullfight.

bullion /'bʊljən/ *noun* (*uncount*)
Bullion is gold or silver in large bars.

bullock /'bʊlək/ *noun*: **bullocks**
A **bullock** is a young castrated bull.

bull's-eye /'bʊlzaɪ/ *noun*: **bull's-eyes**
1 (*used in the singular*) The **bull's-eye** is the small circle at the centre of a target used in shooting and darts. **2** A **bull's-eye** is a shot with *eg* an arrow or dart that hits this.

bullshit /'bʊlʃɪt/ *noun* (*swearword*)
People say something is **bullshit** if they think it is nonsense, rubbish or a lie.

bully /'bʊlɪ/ *noun*; *verb*
▷ ***noun***: **bullies**
A **bully** is a person who uses their strength or power to hurt or frighten weaker, smaller or less powerful people: *school bullies* □ *His boss is a bully.*
▷ ***verb***: **bullies, bullying, bullied**
1 One person **bullies** another when they use their strength or power to hurt or frighten then: *My son was badly bullied at school.* **2** Someone **bullies** you into doing something you don't want to do if they force you to do it: *I managed to bully him into helping us with the cleaning.* — *noun* (*uncount*) **bullying:** *The school will punish all cases of bullying.*

bulrush /'bʊlrʌʃ/ *noun* (*usually in the plural*): **bulrushes**
Bulrushes are tall strong grass-like plants that grow in water.

bulwark /'bʊlwək/ *noun*: **bulwarks**
A **bulwark** is any person or thing that protects another person or thing from harm or danger.

bum[1] /bʌm/ *noun* (*BrE*; *informal*): **bums**
A person's **bum** is the part of the body they sit on. [*same as* **behind, bottom, buttocks**]

bum[2] /bʌm/ *noun* (*AmE*; *informal*): **bums**
1 A **bum** is a tramp. **2** A **bum** is a lazy person who will not take responsibility for anything: *He's a lazy bum.*

bumble /'bʌmbəl/ *verb*: **bumbles, bumbling, bumbled**
To **bumble** is to speak or behave in a confused, awk-

ward or clumsy way, making a lot of mistakes: *She managed to bumble through her speech.* — *adjective* **bumbling:** *a foolish, bumbling person.*

bumblebee /ˈbʌmbəlbiː/ *noun*: **bumblebees**
A **bumblebee** is a large, hairy bee which makes a loud hum.

bump /bʌmp/ *verb*; *noun*
▻ ***verb***: **bumps, bumping, bumped**
1 You **bump** into a person or thing if you accidentally knock or hit them, sometimes damaging or hurting them as a result: *She bumped against the table and hurt her leg.* ▫ *I bumped the wall with my car.* **2** A vehicle **bumps** along if it moves or travels with rough, bouncy movements: *The bicycle bumped along the road.* ▫ *The jeep bumped over the stony ground.*
▻ ***noun***: **bumps**
1 A **bump** is a knock or minor accident: *He had a bump in his car at the weekend.* **2** A **bump** on the body is a lump or swelling, usually caused by a blow: *He's got a nasty bump on his head.* **3** A **bump** is also the dull sound caused by one thing hitting or knocking another: *The passengers breathed a sigh of relief as they heard the soft bump of the wheels touching down on the runway.* **4** A **bump** in a surface is a lump in it: *She fell off when the bike went over a bump.*

phrasal verb
bump into (*informal*) You **bump into** someone if you meet them by chance: *I bumped into him at the supermarket.*
bump off (*slang*) To **bump** someone **off** is to kill them.

bumper /ˈbʌmpə(r)/ *noun*; *adjective*
▻ ***noun*** (*BrE*): **bumpers**
A **bumper** is a bar on the front or back of a motor vehicle that protects it if it hits anything. [see picture at **car**]
▻ ***adjective***
Bumper means exceptionally good or large: *a bumper crop.*

bumpy /ˈbʌmpɪ/ *adjective*: **bumpier, bumpiest**
1 A **bumpy** road, path or track is very uneven. **2** A **bumpy** ride is uncomfortable because the surface the vehicle is travelling over is rough and uneven, or, if the vehicle is an aircraft, because it is very windy: *I don't like bumpy landings.*

bun /bʌn/ *noun*: **buns**
1 A **bun** is a small round sweetened roll, often containing currants. **2** A woman has her hair in a **bun** if it is drawn back and arranged in a round shape at the back of her head.

bunch /bʌntʃ/ *noun*; *verb*
▻ ***noun***: **bunches**
1 A **bunch** of *eg* bananas or grapes is a number of them growing together. **2** (*informal*) A **bunch** of things is a group or collection of them, fastened together: *a bunch of flowers* ▫ *a bunch of keys.* **3** (*informal*) A **bunch** of people is a group of them: *She went to the park with a bunch of friends.* **4** (*usually in the plural*) A woman or girl has her long hair in **bunches** when she has divided it into two pieces and tied each section separately at each side or the back of her head.
▻ ***verb***: **bunches, bunching, bunched**
1 People or things **bunch** together, or **are bunched** together, when they are in a tight group: *The runners were still bunched together on the track.* **2** You **bunch** something up if you gather it up in folds: *They went paddling, their long skirts bunched up round their knees.*

bundle /ˈbʌndəl/ *noun*; *verb*
▻ ***noun***: **bundles**
A **bundle** of things is a number of them tied or wrapped up together loosely: *She gathered the sticks into a bundle.* ▫ *a bundle of old clothes.*
▻ ***verb***: **bundles, bundling, bundled**
1 You **bundle** things up or together if you make them into a bundle, especially quickly or untidily: *She bundled all the papers together and put a rubber band round them.* **2** You **bundle** someone or something somewhere if you put them or send them there quickly, and often roughly or untidily: *The police bundled him into the taxi.* ▫ *I bundled the papers into the drawer.* ▫ *She was bundled off to school to avoid the scandal.* ▫ *He bundled the clothes away in the cupboard.*

bung /bʌŋ/ *verb* (*informal*): **bungs, bunging, bunged**
You **bung** something somewhere if you throw or put it there carelessly, roughly or untidily: *Just bung the forks in the drawer with the knives.* [see also **bunged up**]

bungalow /ˈbʌŋgəloʊ/ *noun*: **bungalows**
A **bungalow** is a house with only one storey. [see picture at **house**]

bunged up /bʌŋd ʌp/ *adjective* (*informal*)
Something is **bunged up** when it is blocked: *The sink is bunged up.* ▫ *a bunged-up nose.*

bungle /ˈbʌŋgəl/ *verb*: **bungles, bungling, bungled**
You **bungle** something if you do it carelessly, badly or clumsily: *I bungled the whole thing.* — *adjective* **bungled:** *a bungled affair.* — *adjective* **bungling:** *an incompetent, bungling policeman.*

bunion /ˈbʌnjən/ *noun*: **bunions**
A **bunion** is a painful swelling on the first joint of a person's big toe.

bunk[1] /bʌŋk/ *noun*: **bunks**
A **bunk** is a narrow bed attached to the wall, *eg* in a cabin in a ship, or in a caravan. [see picture at **bedroom**]

bunk[2] /bʌŋk/ *noun* (*BrE*; *slang*)
▻ ***phrase*** Someone **does a bunk** when they run away from a place: *Several of the pupils did a bunk during the morning break.*

bunk bed /ˈbʌŋk bɛd/ *noun*: **bunk beds**
Bunk beds are two narrow beds fixed one on top of the other. [see picture at **bedroom**]

bunker /ˈbʌŋkə(r)/ *noun*: **bunkers**
1 A **bunker** is a large container or cupboard for storing coal. **2** A **bunker** is also an underground shelter where people go to be protected from gunfire and bombs.

bunny /ˈbʌnɪ/ *noun*: **bunnies**
A **bunny**, or **bunny rabbit**, is a rabbit; this word is used by small children: *Ask the little girl if she likes bunny rabbits.*

bunting /ˈbʌntɪŋ/ *noun* (*uncount*)
Bunting is rows of small cloth or paper flags and other decorations, hung across streets and on buildings on special occasions.

buoy /bɔɪ/ *noun*; *verb*
▻ ***noun***: **buoys**
A **buoy** is a brightly coloured floating object fastened to the bottom of the sea by an anchor, that warns ships of rocks and marks where they should sail.
▻ ***verb***: **buoys, buoying, buoyed**

phrasal verb
You **buoy** someone **up**, or **buoy up** their spirits, if you make them happier or more cheerful: *She was buoyed up by the news.*

buoyant /ˈbɔɪənt/ *adjective*
1 An object that is **buoyant** is able to float in a liquid: *These air tanks will help make the submarine more buoyant in the water.* **2** You are **buoyant** if you are cheerful and lively: *He was beginning to feel confident and buoyant.* **3** The economy is **buoyant** if trade is increasing and companies are making good profits; trade is **buoyant** if a lot of goods are being bought and sold and a lot of money is being made. — *noun* (*uncount*) **buoyancy:** *We're working on ways to increase the craft's buoyancy.* □ *his buoyancy of mood.* — *adverb* **buoyantly:** *I awoke feeling well rested, buoyantly happy, and ready for the day ahead.*

burble /ˈbɜːbəl/ *verb*: **burbles, burbling, burbled**
Something such as a stream **burbles** when it makes a bubbling, murmuring sound: *The baby was burbling to himself in his cot.*

burden /ˈbɜːdən/ *noun*: **burdens**
1 Something is a **burden** to you if it causes you a lot of hard work or worry, or is time-consuming or expensive: *Many pupils find homework a burden.* □ *the increased burden of work on teaching staff.* **2** A **burden** is a heavy load that is difficult to carry.

burdened /ˈbɜːdənd/ *adjective*
You are **burdened** with something if it causes you a lot of work or worry: *women burdened with an endless routine of housework and child care.*

bureau /ˈbjʊəroʊ/ *noun*: **bureaus** or **bureaux**
1 (*BrE*) A **bureau** is a desk for writing at, with drawers and usually a front flap which opens downwards to provide the writing surface. **2** (*AmE*) A **bureau** is a chest of drawers. **3** (*AmE*) A **bureau** is an office, department or organization that collects and supplies information. **4** (*AmE*) A **bureau** is a branch office of an organization such as a newspaper that has its central office or headquarters elsewhere: *The newspaper is based in New York and has bureaux in Washington and Boston.*

bureaucracy /bjʊəˈrɒkrəsɪ/ *noun*: **bureaucracies**
1 A **bureaucracy** is any system of administration run by officials at a lot of different levels, all following complicated rules of procedure. **2** (*uncount*; *derogatory*) **Bureaucracy** refers to the unnecessarily complicated rules of procedure followed by officials in government and elsewhere, and to the delays these cause: *the irritating bureaucracy of local government*

bureaucrat /ˈbjʊərəkrat/ *noun*: **bureaucrats**
A **bureaucrat** is an official in government or any organization who follows rules so rigidly as to create delays and problems.

bureaucratic /bjʊərəˈkratɪk/ *adjective*
Bureaucratic is used to describe procedures that are too long and complicated, and that result in unnecessary delays and problems.

bureaux /ˈbjʊəroʊz/ *noun*
Bureaux is the plural of **bureau**.

burglar /ˈbɜːglə(r)/ *noun*: **burglars**
A **burglar** is a person who enters a building illegally to steal things.

burglar alarm /ˈbɜːglə(r) əlɑːm/ *noun*: **burglar alarms**
A **burglar alarm** is an alarm fitted in a building that can be set so that it rings loudly if someone tries to enter the building illegally.

burglary /ˈbɜːglərɪ/ *noun* (*count or uncount*): **burglaries**
Someone carries out a **burglary** if they enter a building illegally and steal things: *He was found guilty of burglary.*

burgle /ˈbɜːgəl/ *verb*: **burgles, burgling, burgled**
To **burgle** a building is to enter it illegally and steal things from it; to **burgle** a person is to enter their home illegally and steal things from them: *I was burgled at the weekend.* □ *His house was burgled twice last year.*

burial /ˈbɛrɪəl/ *noun* (*count or uncount*): **burials**
A **burial** is the ceremony of burying of a dead body in a grave: *the burial service.*

burly /ˈbɜːlɪ/ *adjective*: **burlier, burliest**
A **burly** man is big, strong and heavy in build: *a burly farm worker.*

burn¹ /bɜːn/ *verb*; *noun*
▻ ***verb***: **burns, burning, burned** or **burnt**
1 A fire **is burning** when it is alight; something such as a building **is burning** when it is on fire: *The warehouse was burning fiercely by the time the fire brigade arrived.* **2** You **burn** something if you destroy it using fire: *The hospital burns its rubbish in its incinerator.* [see also **burn down, burn up**] **3** You **burn** yourself or part of your body when you are injured by coming into contact with fire or something hot; something **burns** you if it is too hot and injures you: *I burned my arm on the oven door.* □ *She could feel the sun burning her face.* □ *My skin burns easily in the sun.* **4** You **burn** a hole in something when you cause a hole to form in it by letting it come into contact with fire or something hot; a chemical or something hot, **burns** a hole in something when it causes a hole to form in it: *Acid can burn holes in material.* □ *He burnt a hole in his cardigan with a cigarette.* **5** You **burn** food if you damage it by cooking it at too high a temperature: *I've burnt the porridge again.* **6** Something **is burning**, or **burning** hot, if it is very hot: *The rock surface was burning hot, too hot to walk on.* **7** Something that you eat or drink **burns** you if it makes you feel a stinging pain: *Vodka burns my throat.* **8** You **are burning** with a strong emotion when that is what you are feeling: *I was burning with anger and resentment after the meeting.* **9** Your face **is burning** if it is red with *eg* embarrassment: *She could feel her face burning with shame.* **10** (*informal*) You **are burning** to do something or **burning** for something when you want it very much: *She was burning for revenge.* — *noun* (*uncount*) **burning:** *There are local laws against the burning of rubbish in gardens.*
▻ ***noun***: **burns**
A **burn** is an injury or mark caused by *eg* fire, heat or acid: *She's in hospital with serious burns to her legs and arms.*

phrasal verbs
burn down Something such as a building **burns down** if it is destroyed by fire; you **burn** a building **down** if you use fire to destroy it: *The phone box was burnt down by vandals.*
burn out 1 A fire **burns** itself **out** when it stops burning because there is nothing left to burn. [see also **burnt-out**] **2** (*informal*) You **burn** yourself **out** if you become extremely tired or ill by working too hard or doing too much exercise.
burn up 1 Something **burns up** if it is completely destroyed by *eg* fire, heat or acid: *The space craft is in danger of burning up as it enters the earth's atmosphere.* **2** A vehicle **burns up** fuel when it uses a lot of it.

burn² /bɜːn/ *noun*: **burns**
In Scotland, a **burn** is a small stream.

burner /ˈbɜːnə(r)/ *noun*: **burners**
The **burner** is the part of a gas lamp or store that produces the flame.

▻ ***phrase*** (*informal*) You **put** something **on the back burner** if you delay doing it until later.

burnish /ˈbɜːnɪʃ/ *verb*: **burnishes, burnishing, burnished**
You **burnish** metal when you make it shine by polishing it. — *adjective* **burnished:** *burnished gold.*

burnt /bɜːnt/ *verb*
Burnt is the past tense and past participle of **burn**.

burnt-out /ˈbɜːntaʊt/ or **burned-out** /ˈbɜːndaʊt/ *adjective*
Burnt-out buildings or vehicles have been badly damaged or destroyed by fire.

burp /bɜːp/ *verb*; *noun*
▻ ***verb*** (*informal*): **burps, burping, burped**
Someone **burps** if they let air escape noisily from their stomach through their mouth. [*same as* **belch**]
▻ ***noun*** (*informal*): **burps:** *a loud burp.*
[*same as* **belch**]

burrow /ˈbʌroʊ/ *noun*; *verb*
▻ ***noun***: **burrows**
A **burrow** is a hole or tunnel dug by rabbits and other small animals for shelter.
▻ ***verb***: **burrows, burrowing, burrowed**
1 An animal **burrows** when it digs a hole or tunnel in the ground for shelter: *The crab burrowed into the sand.* **2** You **burrow** in something when you use your hands to search through it to see what is in it or to find something: *She burrowed in her pocket for her keys.*

bursary /ˈbɜːsərɪ/ *noun*: **bursaries**
A **bursary** is an award or grant of money made to a student. [*same as* **scholarship**]

burst /bɜːst/ *verb*; *noun*
▻ ***verb***: **bursts, bursting, burst**
1 You **burst** something when you suddenly or violently break it open or into pieces; something **bursts** when it suddenly or violently breaks open or into pieces: *The police burst the door down.* ▫ *The balloon burst.* ▫ *I carry a spare tyre in the boot of the car in case one bursts.* **2** You **burst** into a place if you enter it suddenly or violently: *She burst into the room.* ▫ *A group of children burst through the door.* **3** Something **bursts** open if it opens suddenly and violently: *The door burst open and he came running in.* **4** Something **is bursting** with things if it is full of them: *She is always bursting with good ideas.* **5** You **are bursting** with a strong emotion when you are full of it: *He was bursting with anger.* ▫ *I could have burst with pride at my son's graduation ceremony.* — *adjective* **bursting:** *a bag bursting with shopping* ▫ *gardens bursting with flowers.*
▻ ***noun*** (*used in the singular*)
A **burst** of something is a sudden brief period of it: *a burst of speed* ▫ *a burst of gunfire.*

phrasal verbs
burst in on You **burst in on** someone when you enter the room they are in suddenly or violently: *I was sitting reading when the children burst in on me.*
burst into 1 You **burst into** *eg* tears or laughter when you suddenly or noisily begin to cry or laugh. **2** Something **bursts** into flames when it suddenly starts burning.
burst out You **burst out** *eg* crying or laughing when you begin to cry or laugh, usually noisily.

bury /ˈberɪ/ *verb*: **buries, buring, buried**
1 A dead person **is buried** when their body is placed in a grave: *Sailors are often buried at sea.* **2** To **bury** something is to hide it in the ground: *The dog trotted off into the garden to bury its bone.* ▫ *buried treasure* ▫ *My passport was buried at the bottom of the drawer.* **3** You **bury** your face *eg* in your hands if you cover it with your hands so that it cannot be seen: *She buried her face in the pillow.* **4** You **bury** yourself in something if you concentrate on it or occupy yourself with it: *He buried himself in his work.*

bus /bʌs/ *noun*: **buses**
A **bus** is a usually large road vehicle which carries passengers to and from fixed stopping points for payment: *I take the bus to work every morning.* ▫ *You could go by bus or train.* ▫ *This is where we wait for the bus.* ▫ *a bus driver.* [compare **coach**, see picture at **vehicle**]

bus conductor /ˈbʌs kəndʌktə(r)/ *noun*: **bus conductors**
A **bus conductor** is a person on a bus who collects the fares from passengers and gives out tickets.

bush /bʊʃ/ *noun*: **bushes**
1 A **bush** is a thick plant with a lot of branches, that is smaller than a tree: *a rose bush* ▫ *children hiding in the bushes.* **2** (*used in the singular*) The **bush** is wild, uncultivated country in *eg* Australia, New Zealand and Africa: *We went camping in the bush.* ▫ *a bush fire.*
▻ ***phrase*** If you tell someone not to **beat about the bush**, you are telling them to speak openly and directly without hiding anything.

bushy /ˈbʊʃɪ/ *adjective*: **bushier, bushiest**
Hair or fur is **bushy** when it is thick.

busily /ˈbɪzɪlɪ/ *adverb*
You do something **busily** when you do it in an active or busy way: *The children were busily building a castle with their bricks.*

business /ˈbɪznɪs/ *noun*: **businesses**
1 (*uncount or used in the singular*) **Business** is the work of producing goods and trading in them, and of buying and selling services: *He took no interest in business or economic affairs.* ▫ *You can't mix business with friendship.* ▫ *Hollywood became big business as cinema audiences grew.* ▫ *I went into business with the two brothers, developing and producing a new type of sunbed.* ▫ *What line of business is she in?* ▫ *She's abroad on business.* ▫ *Home sales have been poor, but we're doing good business abroad.* ▫ *Here's my business address.* ▫ *She refused to get involved in his business activities.* ▫ *He's a business associate of my husband's.* ▫ *He's fair in all his business dealings.* ▫ *I opted for economics, maths and business studies as A-level courses.* ▫ *decisions based on sound business sense* ▫ *The book business has changed.* ▫ *They're in the hotel business in America.* **2** A **business** is any commercial organization, such as a company or shop, that produces or sells goods, or provides a service: *He's just set up his own business selling computers.* ▫ *His father's tailoring business collapsed.* ▫ *She ran a hairdressing business.* ▫ *The local grocery was one of those old-established family businesses.* **3** (*uncount*) You have some **business** to attend to when you have certain matters to deal with, especially important ones: *The handling of current diplomatic business will be taken over by Freda.* ▫ *He had some pressing business to attend to.* ▫ *If there is no other business I declare this meeting closed.* **4** (*used in the singular*) Something that is your **business** is a private matter that concerns or affects you personally, and should not concern anybody else: *What you do in your spare time is your own business.* ▫ *This is Arthur's business, not yours.* ▫ *It's not their business to make such enquiries.* ▫ *It was a place where everyone knew everyone else's business.* **5** Something that is *eg* a woman's **business** is a job or duty suitable to, or expected of, a woman: *It isn't a woman's business to fly into space.* ▫ *Discipline should be the parents' business,*

not the teacher's. **6** (*usually in the singular*) Any situation, incident or series of events can be referred to as a **business**: *That business about the dancer in the Thames sounds a bit incredible.* □ *Did you hear about the dreadful business at the tech?* □ *This accident is a rotten business.* □ *Let's forget the whole unhappy business.* □ *Life's a funny business anyway.* □ *I'm not sure I approve of this marriage business.* [*same as* **affair**] **7** The **business** of doing something is the process or procedure of doing it: *Winding up Elise's affairs after her death had been a painful business.* □ *I set about the difficult business of picking a winner.* □ *the time-consuming business of interviewing witnesses.*

▻ ***phrases*** **1** You **do business** with someone when you transact it, *eg* when you sell them something: *It's a pleasure doing business with someone so appreciative.* **2** People **get down to business** when they start dealing with, or discussing, something in a serious and practical way. **3** People **go about their business** when they attend to their normal everyday tasks and duties: *We watched the small boats going about their business in the harbour.* **4** If you say that someone **has no business to** do something, you mean that they have no right to do it, or that they ought not to do it: *He had absolutely no business to use the tapes without my permission.* **5** You are **in business** when you have something to sell and people are willing to buy it: *We want to demonstrate to the local community that the church is back in business again.* **6** You **make it your business** to do something when you deliberately try to do it: *She did not know the answer, but was going to make it her business to find out.* □ *We make it our business to learn all we can about our client's product.* **7** (*informal*) People **mean business** when they are seriously determined to do what they suggest or propose: *This time they were not just threatening; they clearly meant business.* **8** (*informal, offensive*) If you tell someone to **mind their own business**, you mean that you think they are being too curious and inquisitive about your private affairs: *I asked if he'd returned home and she told me to mind my own business.* **9** (*informal*) If you tell someone that something they are being curious about is **none of their business**, or **no business of theirs**, you mean that it is a private matter and does not concern them: *It's no business of mine how she gets the money for her foreign trips.* □ *I don't see that this is any business of yours.* □ *I know it's none of my business, but I don't want you to get hurt again.* **10** A company goes **out of business** when it stops trading, usually because it is losing money, or failing to make a profit: *Smaller firms are being forced out of business.*

businesslike /ˈbɪznɪslaɪk/ *adjective*
Someone who is **businesslike** is practical and efficient and doesn't waste time: *She adopted a brisk, businesslike tone: 'Would you leave immediately, please?'*

businessman /ˈbɪznɪsmən/ *noun*: **businessmen**
A **businessman** is a man who works in trade or commerce at quite a senior level.

businesswoman /ˈbɪznɪswʊmən/ *noun*: **businesswomen**
A **businesswoman** is a woman who works in trade or commerce at quite a senior level.

busker /ˈbʌskə(r)/ *noun*: **buskers**
A **busker** is someone who sings or plays a musical instrument in the streets for money.

bus stop /ˈbʌs stɒp/ *noun*: **bus stops**
A **bus stop** is one of several fixed places where a bus can stop along a route: *I usually catch the bus at the bus stop outside the station.* [see picture at **street**]

bust¹ /bʌst/ *noun*: **busts**
1 A woman's **bust** is the part of her chest where her breasts are, or the measurement round this part: *What bust size are you?* **2** A **bust** of someome is a sculpture of their head and shoulders.

bust² /bʌst/ *verb; adjective*
▻ ***verb*** (*informal*): **busts, busting, busted** or **bust**
You **bust** something if you break it or damage it badly: *Someone's bust the television.*
▻ ***adjective*** (*informal*)
Something is **bust** when it is broken or badly damaged: *The radio's bust.*
▻ ***phrase*** (*informal*) A company **goes bust** if it loses so much money that it has to close down.

bustle /ˈbʌsəl/ *verb; noun*
▻ ***verb***: **bustles, bustling, bustled**
1 You **bustle** about if you are busy in a noisy and active way: *She bustled about getting the supper ready.* **2** You **bustle** somewhere if you go there quickly; you **bustle** someone somewhere if you make them go there quickly: *They bustled her out of the room.* [*same as* **hurry**]
▻ ***noun*** (*uncount*)
Bustle is hurried, noisy and excited activity: *the usual bustle in the shops on Friday and Saturday.*

bustling /ˈbʌslɪŋ/ *adjective*
Bustling means very lively, energetic and busy: *The airport was bustling with activity.* □ *a bustling provincial city.*

busy /ˈbɪzɪ/ *adjective; verb*
▻ ***adjective***: **busier, busiest**
1 You are **busy** when you are working hard on something and have no time for anything else: □ *She's going to be busy for the next couple of weeks.* □ *I can't come; I'm far too busy.* **2** You are **busy** doing something when you are engaged in doing it: We were busy looking at the holiday photos when you rang. [*same as* **in the middle of**] **3** A **busy** time is time that you spend working hard: *I've had a busy day.* **4** A place is **busy** when it is full of people who are working hard or moving a lot: *a busy office* □ *The shop is usually busiest in the afternoons.* □ *a busy street in the town centre.* **5** (*especially AmE*) A telephone line is **busy** when it is engaged.
▻ ***verb***: **busies, busying, busied**
You **busy** yourself with something when you occupy yourself doing it: *She busied herself with her knitting.*

busybody /ˈbɪzɪbɒdɪ/ *noun* (*informal*): **busybodies**
A **busybody** is a person who is always interfering in other people's affairs.

but /bʌt/ *conjunction; preposition or conjunction; adverb*
▻ ***conjunction***
1 But introduces clauses, phrases or single words that contrast with something that has just been said, or express an objection: *I was glad to meet her again, but I didn't want to spend all day with her.* □ *'We could copy their results.' 'But that would be cheating!'* □ *I would be interested in freelance work, but not in an in-house position.* □ *She would make an imaginative head teacher, but hardly an efficient one.* □ *Our technicians have discovered a simple but effective solution to the problem.* [compare **yet**] **2** You use **but** to change the direction of a conversation or discussion: *I'll tell you all about that in a minute, but first let's hear about your French trip.* **3** You sometimes use **but** after apologizing for what you are about to say: *I'm sorry, but I just can't agree with you.* □ *Excuse the interruption, but aren't we forgetting something?* **4** (*informal*) **But** can also express surprise and pleasure: *'My wife's expecting a baby in the new year.' 'But that's wonderful news!'*
▻ ***preposition or conjunction***
1 But is used after *no, nothing, all, every* and *any*, and

words formed from them, to mean 'except': *It has to be a test tough enough to eliminate all but the most skilled candidates.* □ *They do nothing but quarrel, those two.* □ *You've mentioned everything but the one vital point.* □ *I have no option but to resign.* □ *No-one but a fool* [= only a fool] *would believe that nonsense.* □ *The dog's anything but obedient.* [= it's very disobedient] **2** The last thing **but** one is the one just before the one that is last; the next thing **but** one is the one just after the one that is next: *It was our last day but one at the old office.* □ *My mother lives next door but two to us.*

▻ ***adverb*** (*literary*)

If you say you can **but** do something, you mean that it is worth doing it, even though you don't expect much success: *I doubt if she'll be willing; however, we can but ask.* [*same as* **only**]

▻ ***phrases*** **1** You use **but also** after 'not only' to add a statement that supports your point of view: *Adding synonyms and antonyms not only helps learners to build up their vocabulary, but also helps them to understand the exact meaning of the defined word.* **2** Something that might have happened **but for** another thing, would have happened if the other thing had not prevented it: *But for your timely help I'd have been dead by now.* [*same as* **without, if it had not been for**] **3 But then** is used to introduce a remark that slightly contradicts or modifies what you have just said: *She performed better than the others in the written test; but then, she spent much longer on it that they did.*

butch /bʊtʃ/ *adjective* (*offensive, slang*)

You can describe a woman as **butch** if she is aggressive, tough and strong-looking.

butcher /ˈbʊtʃə(r)/ *noun; verb*

▻ ***noun*: butchers**

1 A **butcher** is a person who sells meat. **2** A **butcher** or **butcher's** is a butcher's shop: *I bought some sausages at the butcher's.*

▻ ***verb*: butchers, butchering, butchered**

To **butcher** people is to kill them cruelly: *Hundreds of people were butchered in the war.*

butler /ˈbʌtlə(r)/ *noun*: **butlers**

A **butler** is the head male servant in a house.

butt[1] /bʌt/ *verb*: **butts, butting, butted**

To **butt** something is to push or hit it hard or roughly with your head.

> **phrasal verb**
> (*informal*) You **butt in** if you interrupt someone while they are speaking.

butt[2] /bʌt/ *noun*: **butts**

A **butt** is a large barrel for collecting and storing *eg* beer or rain.

butt[3] /bʌt/ *noun* (*usually in the singular*)

Someone is the **butt** of *eg* jokes or criticism when other people laugh at them or criticize them. [*same as* **target**]

butt[4] /bʌt/ *noun*: **butts**

1 The **butt** of a weapon is the thick, heavy end of its handle. **2** The **butt** of a cigarette is the end that is not smoked. **3** (*AmE; informal*) A person's **butt** is their buttocks.

butter /ˈbʌtə(r)/ *noun; verb*

▻ ***noun*** (*uncount*)

1 Butter is a pale yellow solid fat made from cream or milk, that is spread on bread and used in cooking: *a slice of bread and butter.* **2 Butter** is also any thick, creamy substance: *peanut butter.*

▻ ***verb*: butters, buttering, buttered**

You **butter** *eg* bread when you spread butter on it.

> **phrasal verb**
> (*informal*) You **butter** someone **up** if you flatter or praise them to try to persuade them to do something for you.

buttercup /ˈbʌtəkʌp/ *noun*: **buttercups**

A **buttercup** is a plant with small yellow cup-shaped flowers.

butterfly /ˈbʌtəflaɪ/ *noun*: **butterflies**

1 A **butterfly** is a type of insect with large, delicate, and usually brightly coloured, wings. **2** (*uncount*) **Butterfly** is a swimming stroke performed on your front, in which you throw both arms forward through the air and pull them back through the water, using a leg kick in which you keep your legs side by side.

▻ ***phrase*** You **have butterflies**, or **have butterflies in your stomach**, if you have a nervous feeling in your stomach: *She's got butterflies about the exam.*

buttock /ˈbʌtəks/ *noun* (*used in the plural*)

Your **buttocks** are the fleshy parts of the body that you sit on. [*same as* **behind, bottom**; see picture at **body**]

button /ˈbʌtən/ *noun, verb*

▻ ***noun*: buttons**

1 A **button** is a small piece of *eg* metal or plastic, usually round in shape, that is sewn on to clothes. **Buttons** are passed through holes called **buttonholes** to fasten the clothes. [see picture at **clothing**] **2** A **button** is also a small round disc pressed to operate a machine or device: *Press the button to call the lift.*

▻ ***verb*: buttons, buttoning, buttoned**

You **button** a piece of clothing when you fasten it using buttons.

> **phrasal verb**
> **button up 1** You **button up** a piece of clothing when you fasten it using buttons: *Don't go out without buttoning your coat up.* **2** (*slang*) If you tell someone to **button up**, you are telling them rudely to stop talking.

buttonhole /ˈbʌtənhoʊl/ *noun; verb*

▻ ***noun*: buttonholes**

1 A **buttonhole** is a small hole through which a button is passed to fasten a piece of clothing. [see picture at **clothing**] **2** A **buttonhole** is also a flower worn pinned to a jacket lapel.

▻ ***verb*: buttonholes, buttonholing, buttonholed**

You **buttonhole** someone if you stop them and force them to listen or speak to you.

buttress /ˈbʌtrəs/ *noun; verb*

▻ ***noun*: buttresses**

A **buttress** is a support built on to the outside of a wall.

▻ ***verb*: buttresses, buttressing, buttressed**

1 To **buttress** a wall is to support it with buttresses. **2** To **buttress** *eg* an argument or system is to support it, encourage it or make it stronger.

buxom /ˈbʌksəm/ *adjective*

A woman can be described as **buxom** if she is plump and healthy-looking in an attractive way.

buy /baɪ/ *verb; noun*

▻ ***verb*: buys, buying, bought**

1 You **buy** something when you get it by paying a sum of money for it: *the business of buying and selling property* □ *We were saving up to buy a cooker and a fridge.* □ *You can buy Saturday's bread cheap on a Monday.* □ *I bought the car second-hand from a friend.* □ *He stopped to buy a few essentials at the supermarket.* □ *All paint is cheaper when bought in quantity.* □ *We could not buy tickets in advance.* □ *A good camera* *can be bought for as little as £50.* ▫ *She bought a long T-shirt for sleeping in.* ▫ *the big dictionary my father had bought for me by mail order* ▫ *What did he buy you for your birthday?* ▫ *I bought myself a new raincoat today.* [*same as* **purchase**] **2** You **buy** something such as support or privileges when you give people money or presents to persuade them to support or favour you: *It's a mistake to think you can buy a child's love.* ▫ *Nowadays no-one can buy their way into Parliament.* ▫ *Extra money won't necessarily buy better health.*

▻ ***noun*****: buys**

You can refer to something you buy as a **buy** of some sort; a **good** buy is something that is worth the money you spend on it: *A classic blazer is always a good buy.* ▫ *The curtains faded in the sun; they were a terribly bad buy.* ▫ *Our white garden furniture had been an impulse buy.* [*same as* **purchase**]

> ***phrasal verbs***
>
> **buy in** You **buy in** supplies of something when you buy large quantities of it for a special purpose: *We bought in several sacks of sugar in case there was a shortage.*
>
> **buy off** (*informal*) You **buy off** someone who is threatening you when you give them money to leave you alone: *Just find out what the blackmailer wants and we'll buy him off.*
>
> **buy out** You **buy** someone **out** if you buy all the shares they have in a company: *Suppose one partner leaves the business, and the other hasn't enough money to buy him out?*
>
> **buy up** You **buy up** something when you buy large quantities of it, or buy all that is available: *Merchants buy up corn and move it from the district where it was grown.* ▫ *They buy up empty houses and rent them to homeless families.*

buyer /ˈbaɪə(r)/ *noun*: **buyers**

1 A **buyer** is a person who buys something: *I think I've found find a buyer for the old car.* **2** A **buyer** is also a person employed by a large shop or firm to buy goods on its behalf.

buzz /bʌz/ *verb; noun*

▻ ***verb*****: buzzes, buzzing, buzzed**

1 Insects, especially bees, **buzz** when they make a continuous humming sound: *The bees buzzed round the flowers.* **2** A place **buzzes** with *eg* activity, excitement or conversation if it is filled with active, excited or noisy people: *The airport was buzzing with activity.* **3** Your head **is buzzing**, or thoughts **are buzzing** round your head, if your mind is full of confused thoughts: *I left the conference with my head buzzing*

▻ ***noun*** (*used in the singular*)

1 A **buzz** is a continuous humming sound: *the buzz of bees and other insects.* **2** The **buzz** of *eg* voices or conversation is a low murmuring sound made by people talking.

▻ ***phrase*** (*informal*) You **give** someone **a buzz** when you call them on the telephone.

> ***phrasal verb***
>
> (*informal*) If you tell someone to **buzz off** you are telling them rudely them to go away.

buzzard /ˈbʌzəd/ *noun*: **buzzards**

A **buzzard** is a large bird that hunts small animals for food.

buzzer /ˈbʌzə(r)/ *noun*: **buzzers**

A **buzzer** is an electrical device which makes a buzzing sound: *Press the buzzer to open the door.*

by /baɪ/ *preposition; adverb*

▻ ***preposition***

1 a Something is done **by** a person or thing if they do it or cause it: *The building was designed by Lutyens.* ▫ *She had been taught by Dalcroze himself.* ▫ *The letter was evidently written by a foreigner.* ▫ *He didn't seem in the least upset by his failure.* ▫ *The report discussed the use of public transport by the elderly.* **b** Your child **by** a particular person was conceived when that person was your sexual partner: *He had two children by his first wife, and another by Sylvia.* ▫ *That's Hermann; he was my child by Otto.* **c** You achieve something **by** doing a certain thing if that action is the means of your achieving it: *She made a bit of money by selling her paintings.* ▫ *I arrived just in time, but only by running all the way.* ▫ *You poach an egg by breaking it into boiling water.* **d** You do something **by** a certain means if that is the means you use to do it: *May I pay by credit card?* ▫ *The invitation had been sent by first-class mail.* ▫ *The message came by fax.* ▫ *She's arriving in London by air this afternoon.* ▫ *Apparently the thieves had entered by the kitchen window.* **e** You go somewhere **by** a certain place or route if you pass through the place, or along the route, on your way there: *Let's go by Chichester and see the cathedral.* ▫ *We went back to Douglas by the old road.* [*same as* **via**] **f** You hold someone or something **by** a certain part of them if you grasp that part: *Grandfather took Peter firmly by the hand.* ▫ *She lifted her kittens by the scruff of the neck.* ▫ *He took hold of the knife by its blade.* **g** Something happens **by** accident or chance if it happens without being planned, arranged or intended: *Purely by chance I encountered him again that weekend, in the wine shop.* **h** You do something **by** mistake when you say or do the wrong thing through carelessness or forgetfulness: *I called John David by mistake.* **i** What you mean **by** a particular word, name or expression is the thing you intend it to refer to: *By 'the Island' I presumed he meant the Isle of Wight.* **j** A book, play, work of art or musical composition that is **by** someone is their own work or creation: *In which picture by which artist do you find this detail?* ▫ *'Unclaimed Territory', the most recent novel by this remarkable young writer* ▫ *They will perform early works by Mozart.*

2 a One thing is **by** another if it is beside it: *There was a low table by her chair.* ▫ *They were standing by the gate chatting.* ▫ *That's Josephine, over by the window.* ▫ *He had his gun by his side.* [*same as* **beside**] **b** A person or thing goes **by** another when they go past them: *She passed by us without a sign of recognition.* [*same as* **past**] **c** Something that happens **by** a certain time happens at that time or before it: *By 5.30 she was feeling pretty hungry.* ▫ *Try and be home by 8.00.* ▫ *Library books must be returned by Friday at the latest.* ▫ *Possibly by the end of the century doctors will have a cure for AIDS.* **d** You do something **by** day, or **by** night, if you do it during the day, or during the night: *Owls sleep by day and hunt by night.* **e** You are a certain kind of person **by** nature if that is your character; you are *eg* a weaver **by** trade, or a teacher **by** profession, if that is your job: *He was shy and diffident by nature.* ▫ *Her next boyfriend was Jack, who was a psychologist by profession.* **f** Something that happens **by** law happens according to the law: *Employers must by law appoint candidates from certain minority groups.* **g** Something that is so **by** a certain standard is so according to that standard: *We'd had quite a good summer by Scottish standards.* ▫ *Mona was a beautiful girl by any standard.* ▫ *It's five past three by my watch.* [*same as* **according to**]

3 a You use **by** in referring to the processes of multiplying or dividing: *Divide twenty-seven by three.*

□ *Four multiplied by three is twelve.* **b** You use **by** in specifying measurements, *eg* of a room: *The bedroom was about 10 metres by 6.* [= 10 metres long and 6 metres wide] **c** You are paid **by** the hour, day or week if you are paid a certain amount of money for each hour's, day's or week's work. **d** Things are produced or sold **by** *eg* the thousand or million when they are produced or sold in those quantities: *Prints like that were made by the thousand in the twenties.* □ *They are packed and despatched by the gross.* **4 By** is used in phrases such as *little by little* or *day by day* to express gradual but regular progress: *Add the flour spoonful by spoonful.* □ *Month by month his strength returned.* □ *One by one the musicians get up and leave the stage.* **a** Something changes *eg* **by** the hour, or **by** the minute when it changes surprisingly quickly: *The situation was worsening by the minute.* **b By** is used in expressing the extent of an increase or decrease, excess or shortage: *Prices have risen by an average of 4% this year.* □ *Grants are to be cut by 15%.* □ *Her sister was the taller by at least two inches.* □ *I only missed my train by a couple of minutes.*

▻ ***adverb***

1 Things that are close **by** are near: *The shops are quite close by, so she hasn't far to walk.* [*same as* **near, nearby**] **2** Someone or something goes **by** when they go past the place where you are: *We waited till the two policemen had gone by.*

▻ ***phrases*** **1** For **by and large** see **large**. **2 a** You are **by yourself** when you are alone: *She lives by herself.* □ *He was all by himself in the playground.* □ *You shouldn't be walking through the streets by yourself at this time of night.* [*same as* **alone, on your own**] **b** You do something **by yourself** when you do it without anyone else's help, participation or interference: *I can manage by myself, thanks.* □ *Did you build the extension all by yourselves?* [*same as* **on your own**]

bye /baɪ/ or **bye-bye** *interjection* (*informal*)
Bye and **bye-bye** mean goodbye.

bye-law see **by-law**.

by-election /ˈbaɪɪlɛkʃən/ *noun*: **by-elections**
A **by-election** is an election held while parliament is meeting, to fill a seat which has become empty because the member has died or resigned.

bygone /ˈbaɪgɒn/ *adjective*
Bygone means happening or occurring in the past: *bygone customs* □ *customs from bygone centuries.*

▻ ***phrase*** You say **let bygones be bygones** to someone when you agree that you should both forget quarrels or problems of the past.

by-law or **bye-law** /ˈbaɪlɔː/ *noun*: **by-laws**
A **by-law** is a law or rule made by a local authority: *The local by-laws forbid parking on this road on Saturday mornings.*

bypass /ˈbaɪpɑːs/ *noun*; *verb*

▻ ***noun***: **bypasses**

1 A **bypass** is a road which avoids a busy area or town: *the Hayes bypass.* **2** A **bypass** is also an operation to insert a tube into the body to carry blood so that the blood does not need to flow through a blood vessel that is blocked.

▻ ***verb***: **bypasses, bypassing, bypassed**

1 You **bypass** a place if you take a road that goes around it instead of through it. **2** You **bypass** someone in authority if you discuss something with their superior and not with them: *He decided to bypass the personnel manager and speak directly to the company director.*

by-product /ˈbaɪprɒdʌkt/ *noun*: **by-products**
1 A **by-product** is a substance or product that is obtained or formed while something else is being made: *Cattle feed is a by-product of whisky.* **2** A **by-product** of an event is something that happens or occurs unexpectedly as result of it.

bystander /ˈbaɪstandə(r)/ *noun*: **bystanders**
A **bystander** is a person who watches what is happening but does not take part in it.

byte /baɪt/ *noun* (*computers*): **bytes**
A **byte** is a group of eight binary digits forming a unit of memory in a computer.

byword /ˈbaɪwɜːd/ *noun*: **bywords**
1 Someone or something is a **byword** for a particular quality if they are a well-known example of it: *Their name is a byword for luxury.* **2** A **byword** is a word or phrase that everyone is using.

C

C or **c** /siː/ *noun*: **Cs** or **c's**
1 C is the third letter of the English alphabet: *'Chauffeur' begins with a C.* **2 C** is also an abbreviation for **a** century: *a famous 17th c writer.* **b** Centigrade or Celsius: *temperatures below 8°C.*

cab /kab/ *noun*: **cabs**
1 A **cab** is a taxi: *We took a cab.* **2** The **cab** in a lorry or railway engine is the driver's compartment.

cabaret /'kabəreɪ/ *noun* (*uncount or count*): **cabarets**
Cabaret is entertainment in clubs and restaurants: *She's a dancer working in cabaret.* □ *the hotel cabaret.*

cabbage /'kabɪdʒ/ *noun* (*count or uncount*)
A **cabbage** is a large round vegetable with thick firm green or red leaves: *a plate of cabbage and bacon.* [see picture at **vegetable**]

cabin /'kabɪn/ *noun*: **cabins**
1 A **cabin** is a small wooden house: *a log cabin.* **2** A **cabin** in a ship is a small room for living, sleeping or working in. **3** A **cabin** in a passenger aeroplane is either the section where the pilot and crew sit, or the section where the passengers sit.

cabinet /'kabɪnət/ *noun*: **cabinets**
1 A **cabinet** is a piece of furniture with shelves and doors, for storing or displaying things: *a medicine cabinet.* [see picture at **bathroom**] **2** (*with a singular or plural verb, often adjectival*) The **Cabinet** is the group of senior government ministers who meet regularly with the Prime Minister to discuss policies: *several Cabinet ministers.*

cable /'keɪbəl/ *noun*; *verb*
▻ ***noun*** (*count or uncount*)
1 A **cable** is a very strong thick rope, especially one made from strands of metal. **2** A **cable** is also a set of wires carrying telephone signals or electricity, encased in plastic. **3** (*AmE*) A **cable** is a telegram: *a message sent by cable.*
▻ ***verb*** (*AmE*): **cables, cabling, cabled**
To **cable** someone is to send them a telegram.

cable car /'keɪbəl kɑː(r)/ *noun*: **cable cars**
A **cable car** is a small box-shaped vehicle that hangs from a cable, used for carrying passengers up and down mountains.

cable television /keɪbəl 'telɪvɪʒən/ *noun* (*uncount*)
Cable television is a system of sending television signals along wires to viewers who pay directly for the service, rather than broadcasting the signals using radio waves.

cackle /'kakəl/ *noun*; *verb*
▻ ***noun***: **cackles**
1 A **cackle** is the sound that a hen or goose makes. **2** A **cackle** is also a high-pitched laugh, especially one that suggests evil or mischievous thoughts.
▻ ***verb***: **cackles, cackling, cackled**
A person **cackles** when they laugh in this way: *'You will never see him again,' she cackled.*

cactus /'kaktəs/ *noun*: **cactuses** or **cacti** /'kaktaɪ/
A **cactus** is a prickly desert plant that stores water inside its thick stem.

cadence /'keɪdəns/ *noun* (*formal*): **cadences**
Cadences in speech or music are the rising and falling patterns in it.

cadet /kə'det/ *noun*: **cadets**
A **cadet** is a person training to be a member of the armed forces or of the police force.

cadge /kadʒ/ *verb* (*informal*): **cadges, cadging, cadged**
You **cadge** something from someone when you ask them to give it to you, especially when you make no effort to get it for yourself: *There's a limit to how long you can cadge off your friends.*

caesarean (*AmE* **cesarean**) /sɪ'zeərɪən/ *noun*: **caesareans**
A **caesarean**, or **caesarean section**, is an operation to remove a baby through an opening made in the pregnant woman's abdomen, when an ordinary birth would be dangerous: *My first baby was a caesarean.*

café /'kafeɪ/ or /'kafɪ/ *noun*: **cafés**
A **café** is an informal restaurant serving drinks, snacks and simple meals.

cafeteria /kafə'tɪərɪə/ *noun*: **cafeterias**
A **cafeteria** is an informal restaurant selling simple food which you get for yourself from a counter.

caffeine /'kafiːn/ *noun* (*uncount*)
Caffeine is a substance contained in coffee and tea, that makes the brain and heart more active.

caftan /'kaftan/ *noun*: **caftans**
A **caftan** is a long loose garment with wide sleeves worn by men in Africa and the Middle East, copied as casual female wear in the West. [see picture at **clothing**]

cage /keɪdʒ/ *noun*: **cages**
A **cage** is a container of any size in which birds or other animals are kept, made from wire or metal bars. — *adjective* **caged:** *Luke prowled the room, like a caged and angry tiger.*

cagey /'keɪdʒɪ/ *adjective* (*informal*): **cagier, cagiest**
Someone who is **cagey** speaks cautiously or secretively, rather than frankly and openly: *She was rather cagey about her relationship with Brian.* — *adverb* **cagily**: *He answered pretty cagily.*

cagoule /kə'guːl/ *noun*: **cagoules**
A **cagoule** is a lightweight waterproof jacket with a hood.

cahoots /kə'huːts/ (*informal*)
▻ ***phrase*** Two or more people are **in cahoots** when they secretly plan to do something unpleasant or dishonest together: *The shop manager had been in cahoots with the thieves.*

cajole /kə'dʒoʊl/ *verb*: **cajoles, cajoling, cajoled**
You **cajole** someone into doing something when you persuade them to do it, especially by flattery or with promises: *He would cajole, flatter and persuade congressmen to support him.*

cake /keɪk/ *noun*: **cakes**
1 (*uncount or count*) **Cake**, or a **cake**, is a sweet solid

food made by baking a mixture of flour, fat, eggs and sugar: *I thought I'd bake a cake.* □ *a piece of ginger cake.* **2** A portion of food pressed into a particular, usually rounded, shape is also a **cake**: *fish cakes.* **3** A **cake** of something solid, such as soap or wax, is a small block of it.

▻ ***phrases*** (*informal*)

1 Something that is very easy to do can be described as **a piece of cake**: *She imagined that housekeeping would be a piece of cake.* **2** When you tell someone that they **can't have their cake and eat it** you mean that they cannot enjoy the advantages of both alternatives, but must choose one or the other.

caked /ˈkeɪkt/ *adjective*

A surface is **caked** with a substance such as mud when it is covered with a thick mass of the substance: *a wound caked with dried blood.*

calamitous /kəˈlamɪtəs/ *adjective* (*formal*)

A **calamitous** event is a very unfortunate one that brings destruction and suffering: *His decision to invest in such as risky venture proved calamitous for the family's financial security.*

calamity /kəˈlamɪtɪ/ *noun*: **calamities**

A **calamity** is an event that causes great disappointment, sadness or suffering: *No other calamity has quite the shattering effects on personality and behaviour as the experience of acute hunger.* [*same as* **disaster**]

calcium /ˈkalsɪəm/ *noun* (*uncount*)

Calcium is a substance found in chalk and marble, and is necessary for the health of your bones and teeth: *calcium deficiency.*

calculate /ˈkalkjʊleɪt/ *verb*: **calculates, calculating, calculated**

1 You **calculate** something when you work it out using mathematics: *She has calculated that it would take five workers eight months to complete the job.* **2** When something **is calculated** to have a particular effect, it is done deliberately to achieve that result: *My response was calculated to make him feel even more jealous.*

calculated /ˈkalkjʊleɪtɪd/ *adjective*

1 A **calculated** insult is intentional or deliberate. **2** You take a **calculated** risk when you consider its possible consequences before taking it.

calculating /ˈkalkjʊleɪtɪŋ/ *adjective*

A **calculating** person carefully plans how best to use people and situations for their own benefit.

calculation /kalkjʊˈleɪʃən/ *noun*: **calculations**

You do a **calculation** when you work something out using mathematics: *Some of her earlier calculations must have been wrong.*

calculator /ˈkalkjʊleɪtə(r)/ *noun*: **calculators**

A **calculator** is a small electronic machine for doing mathematical calculations: *a pocket calculator.* [see picture at **office**]

calendar /ˈkalɪndə(r)/ *noun*: **calendars**

1 A **calendar** is a chart that shows the months and days of the year: *a calendar on the wall.* **2** A particular **calendar** is a system for dividing up the year and for fixing its beginning and end: *the Jewish calendar.* **3** A **calendar** is also any timetable or list of important dates or events: *the sporting calendar.*

calendar month /ˈkalɪndə mʌnθ/ *noun*: **calendar months**

A **calendar month** is the period from a date in one month to the same date in the following month, rather than simply a period of four weeks or thirty days.

calf[1] /kɑːf/ *noun*: **calves**

A **calf** is a young cow, or the young of any of several other animals, such as the elephant and the whale.

calf[2] /kɑːf/ *noun*: **calves**

Your **calf**, or **calf** muscle, is the thick fleshy back part of your leg below the knee. [see picture at **body**]

calibre (*AmE* **caliber**) /ˈkalɪbə(r)/ *noun*: **calibres**

1 (*uncount*) A person's **calibre** is the standard of their ability or character: *We need a manager of the highest calibre.* **2** The **calibre** of a gun is the width of the inside of its barrel: *a small calibre air rifle.*

call /kɔːl/ *verb*; *noun*

▻ ***verb***: **calls, calling, called**

1 Someone or something **is called** a name or title if they have, or are given, that name or title, or are described as that thing, by others: *A man called Corbett is waiting to see you.* □ *She didn't like the way his friends called him 'Tiny'.* □ *At the office we all call each other by our first names.* □ *Do call me David; 'Dr Vernon' sounds so formal.* □ *Her latest book is called 'Footsteps in the Sand'.* □ *What is this kind of carving called?* □ *Don't you dare call me lazy!* □ *I don't think she should have called him a cheat.* □ *You call it development; I call it destruction of the countryside.* □ *'How did the party go?' 'Well, I wouldn't have called it a success.'* **2** You **call**, or **call** something, when you shout or speak loudly, *eg* to attract attention: *He could hear her calling 'Jonathan! Where are you?'* □ *She stopped when she heard someone call her name.* □ *The person in the boat was calling to them for help.* [*same as* **shout**] **3** You **call** someone when you telephone them: *I call my parents at least once a week.* □ *Your sister called; she'll meet you at one o'clock.* □ *Who's calling?* [*same as* **ring, telephone**] **4** You also **call** someone when you ask them to come: *The boss called me into his office.* □ *She called me across to her desk.* □ *We'd better call a doctor straight away.* [*same as* **summon**] **5** You ask someone to **call** you at a certain time the next morning when you ask them to wake you up then. **6** You **call** something such as a meeting when you tell people when it will happen, and ask them to attend: *The minister was quick to call a press conference.* **7** The government **calls** an election when it announces that it will be held on a particular date: *I don't think they will call an election before the spring.* **8** When you **call** somewhere you make a short visit there, or stop there during a journey: *We called at the baker's to collect the wedding cake.* □ *I'll call at the hospital and see how Peter is.*

▻ ***noun***: **calls**

1 A **call** for something is an appeal or demand for it: *There have been several calls for his resignation.* □ *He repeated his call for tighter immigration controls.* **2** A **call** is an act of telephoning someone: *We've had numerous calls from worried parents.* □ *Were there any calls for me this morning?* **3** You ask someone to give you a **call** at a certain time the next morning when you ask them to wake you up then. **4** A bird's **call** is the typical sound that it makes.

▻ ***phrases*** **1** You **make**, or **pay**, **a call on** someone when you visit them for a short time. **2** If there is **no call for** something there is no need for it: *There was no call for her to be so rude.* □ *There isn't much call for Latin teachers in today's schools.* **3** Someone such as a doctor is **on call** during a particular period if they are officially on duty then and may be contacted to deal with emergencies or any cases that need attention.

phrasal verbs

call back You **call back** when **1** you visit someone again: *I'll call back in a week to see how you're feeling.* **2** you return someone's telephone call, or you telephone them again: *Can I call you back? I'm busy at the moment.* □ *I'm just calling back to confirm the date of that meeting.*

call for 1 You **call for** someone or something when you go to collect or fetch them: *He said he would call for me at seven o'clock.* ▫ *You can call for the results of your test any time this afternoon.* [*same as* **pick up**, **collect**] **2** A situation, problem or crisis **calls for** something if that is what is needed to deal with it: *It was an embarrassing situation that called for tact and diplomacy.* ▫ *Congratulations! This calls for a celebration!* [*same as* **require**] **3** You **call for** something when you ask or demand that it should happen: *Faced with the threat of a civil war, the President has called for self-control and calm.* [*same as* **request**, **appeal** for]
call in 1 You **call in** at a place when you visit it: *She decided to call in at Ruth's on the way home.* **2** You **call** someone **in** when you ask them to come and help: *We had no hesitation in calling the police in.* ▫ *They've called in scientific experts to comment on the case.*
call off You **call off** a event that has already been planned or scheduled when you cancel it: *They've decided it would be best to call the wedding off.* [*same as* **cancel**]
call on 1 You **call on** someone when you pay them a short visit: *We called on the Jessops on the way north.* **2** When you **call on** or **upon** someone to do something you ask or demand that they should do it: *MPs are calling on the Prime Minister to make her position clear.* ▫ *The Council have been called upon to stop the new road being built.*
call out 1 You **call out**, or **call** something **out**, when you shout something, or say it loudly: *She was calling out for help.* ▫ *Wait till your names are called out.* **2** You **call** someone **out** when you ask them to come and help: *We had to call the fire brigade out when the cooker blew up.* [*same as* **summon**]
call up 1 You **call** someone **up** when you telephone them. **2** A person **is called up** when they are ordered to join the armed forces: *I was called up in 1939 and served abroad for four years.* [*same as* **draft**]

call box /ˈkɔːl bɒks/ *noun*: **call boxes**
A **call box** is a public telephone box.

caller /ˈkɔːlə(r)/ *noun*: **callers**
1 A **caller** is a person visiting: *There have been several callers at the house today.* **2** A **caller** is also a person making a telephone call.

calling /ˈkɔːlɪŋ/ *noun*: **callings**
A person's **calling** is the job they believe they have been specially chosen, or are specially able, to do, especially one that involves caring for others: *a calling to the priesthood.*

callous /ˈkaləs/ *adjective*
A **callous** person is deliberately cruel and shows no concern for the suffering of others: *callous behaviour.* ▫ *His cruel and callous comments about the murder made me shiver.*

calm /kɑːm/ *adjective*; *noun*; *verb*
▻ ***adjective***
1 You are **calm** when you do not feel anxious, upset or angry or when you do not show any of these feelings: *She remained calm throughout the whole ordeal.* ▫ *He's normally a very calm person.* **2 Calm** weather is not at all windy or stormy; a **calm** sea or lake is still and not made rough by wind. — *adverb* **calmly:** *She calmly told her attacker to put down the knife.*
▻ ***noun*** (*uncount*)
1 Calm is a state of peacefulness in your mind, or of quiet in your surroundings: *A feeling of calm had replaced the usual panic.* **2 Calm** is also a state of stillness of weather: *the calm before the storm.*
▻ ***verb***: **calms, calming, calmed**
You **calm** someone, or **calm** them down, when you help them to stop feeling anxious, upset or angry; you **calm** something when you make it less strong or forceful: *Try to calm her fears.*

calorie /ˈkalərɪ/ *noun*: **calories**
A **calorie** is a measure of the energy for your body contained in a particular kind of food: *low-calorie drinks* ▫ *You need to count the calories to lose weight.*

calve /kɑːv/ *verb*: **calves, calving, calved**
A cow **calves** when it gives birth to a calf.

calves /kɑːvz/ (*noun*)
Calves is the plural of **calf**.

came /keɪm/ *verb*
Came is the past tense of **come**.

camel /ˈkaməl/ *noun*: **camels**
A **camel** is a large desert animal with a long neck and either one or two humps on its back, that people ride on, or use for carrying baggage.

cameo /ˈkamɪoʊ/ *noun*: **cameos**
1 A **cameo**, or **cameo** role, is a small part in a play or film played by a well-known actor. **2** A **cameo**, or **cameo** brooch, is a piece of jewellery, usually oval-shaped, with a stone or design set on top of a flat surface of a different colour.

camera /ˈkamərə/ *noun*: **cameras**
A **camera** is a piece of equipment for taking photographs, making films or creating television pictures: *How does the camera work?*

cameraman /ˈkamərəmən/ *noun*: **cameramen**
A **cameraman** is a person who operates a film or television camera.

camouflage /ˈkaməflɑːʒ/ *noun*; *verb*
▻ ***noun*** (*uncount*)
1 Camouflage is anything such as branches, leaves or paint used to make soldiers and military equipment difficult for an enemy to see: *special camouflage used in night-time operations* ▫ *a man in camouflage uniform.* **2 Camouflage** is also the colour or texture of an animal's skin that makes it difficult to see in its natural surroundings.
▻ ***verb***: **camouflages, camouflaging, camouflaged**
To **camouflage** something is to make it difficult to see using camouflage.

camp /kamp/ *noun*; *verb*
▻ ***noun***: **camps**
1 A **camp** is an area in which people have put up tents. **2** A **camp** is also a group of huts or other light buildings used as temporary accommodation, or for short stays for a particular purpose: *a holiday camp.* **3** In a dispute or a contest, a **camp** is a group of people who have the same opinions or beliefs, or who belong to the same team: *the Welsh camp.*
▻ ***verb***: **camps, camping, camped**
You **camp** when you live in a tent. — *noun* (*uncount, often adjectival*) **camping:** *We went camping last summer.* ▫ *a camping holiday.*

phrasal verb
camp out When you **camp out** you sleep outdoors, with or without a tent.

campaign /kamˈpeɪn/ *noun*; *verb*
▻ ***noun***: **campaigns**
A **campaign** is an organized series of actions carried out by a group of people in order to achieve a particular aim: *a campaign against the new motorway.* ▫ *an election campaign.*

▻ *verb*: **campaigns**, **campaigning**, **campaigned**
You **campaign** for something when you take part in a campaign in support of it: *We've been campaigning for equal pay for women.*

camp bed /kamp 'bɛd/ *noun*: **camp beds**
A **camp bed** is a lightweight folding bed that is easily carried.

camper /'kampə(r)/ *noun*: **campers**
A **camper** is a person who goes camping.

campsite /'kampsaɪt/ *noun*: **campsites**
A **campsite** is a piece of land for camping on, often a fixed area with pathways and some facilities, such as a shop and showers.

campus /'kampəs/ *noun* (*count or uncount*): **campuses**
A **campus** is an area in which the buildings of a college or university are grouped together: *Most first-year students live on campus.*

can[1] /kan/ or /kən/ *modal verb* (*negative form* **cannot** or **can't**, *past tense* **could** (see separate entry))
1 You **can** do something:
a if you are able to do it or have the skill to do it, or if it is possible to do it: *I don't like the seaside because I can't swim.* □ *Of course I can ride a bike!* □ *She says she cannot remember his name.* □ *I can't understand this clue. Can you?* □ *I can speak a few words of Japanese.* □ *Don't worry; anyone can make mistakes.* □ *It can get very cold here in winter.* □ *I can see someone in the boat; I think he's waving to us.* □ *Speak up, please; I can't hear you.* [see also **able**]

Notice that **can** is idiomatic with verbs of sensing, such as *see*, *hear* and *feel*: *I can hear* (rather than *I hear*) *someone shouting. Can you* (rather than *do you*) *feel the difference?*
Notice also that when you talk about people being able to do things, or things being possible, in a future situation but not yet, you use **will be able to**, not **can**: *The baby will be able to* (not *can*) *walk soon. We'll be able to* (not *can*) *get there in half the time when the bridge is built.*

b if you may do it, or are allowed to do it: *Can I borrow your pen, please?* □ *Can she just have a quick word with you?* □ *You can go to the party if you promise to be home by 11 o'clock.* □ *I'm afraid you can't smoke in here.* [see also **may**]
2 You use **can**:
a to talk about possibilities and plans and make offers and suggestions: *I can't meet you on Monday; I'm going on holiday.* □ *The tables can be set out the day before the party.* □ *You don't have to decide now; you can call me with your decision next week.* □ *I can give you a lift to the airport if you like.* □ *Good morning! Can I help you?* □ *We can look up the hotel in the AA booklet, can't we?* □ *You can* [= please will you] *all write me an essay on the character of Angelo.*
b to ask or invite people to do something: *Can you help me move this table?* □ *Can you come to the theatre with me on Friday?* □ *Can we meet for lunch sometime?*
c in questions in the negative, to make impatient complaints, requests or suggestions: *Can't they play that music somewhere else?* □ *Can't he wait till the morning?* □ *Can't we discuss this somewhere private?* □ *Can't you do anything right?*
d in questions or in the negative, to wonder about possibilities, and express doubt about something being possible (note that '**can have**' is used if the possibility is in the past): *Who can be wanting to speak to him at this late hour?* □ *How can you say such a stupid thing?* □ *What can have happened to Phil? He said he would be here at eight.* □ *She can't have got lost, can she?* □ *I don't believe she can have got lost; she knows the roads very well.* □ *The weather's been so beautiful; surely it can't last much longer.* □ *Can he really be her father? He doesn't look old enough.* □ *She can't seriously be thinking of resigning at this stage!*
e in the negative, to say that something should not happen: *We can't abandon the campaign now! We might still win.* □ *But you can't leave her standing there waiting all day!*
[see also **could**]

can[2] /kan/ *noun*; *verb*
▻ *noun*: **cans**
A **can** is a sealed metal container in which food, drink and other substances are sold: *a can of baked beans* □ *beer cans* □ *an old paint can.* [*same as* **tin**]
▻ *verb*: **cans**, **canning**, **canned**
To **can** something is to put it into a can or cans ready for selling.

canal /kə'nal/ *noun*: **canals**
A **canal** is a narrow channel of water made for boats to travel on, or made for directing water on to dry land: *an irrigation canal.*

canary /kə'nɛərɪ/ *noun*: **canaries**
A **canary** is a small yellow singing bird often kept in a cage as a pet.

cancel /'kansəl/ *verb*: **cancels**, **cancelling** (*AmE* **canceling**), **cancelled** (*AmE* **canceled**)
1 You **cancel** something arranged when you decide or announce that it will not take place: *The singer has had to cancel next week's concert because of illness.* [*same as* **call off**] **2** You **cancel** something you have booked or reserved when you say that you no longer want it: *I shall have to cancel my reservation.*

phrasal verb
cancel out Two things **cancel** each other **out** when each thing has the opposite effect of the other so that, when they occur together, no effect is produced: *Savings made because of lower rents have been cancelled out by higher fuel bills.*

cancellation /kansə'leɪʃən/ *noun*: **cancellations**
A **cancellation** is an act of cancelling something booked or reserved, or an opportunity to have something now that someone else has said they no longer want: *I phoned the doctor for an appointment for tomorrow and managed to get a cancellation for today.*

cancer /'kansə(r)/ *noun*: **cancers**
1 (*uncount*) **Cancer** is a serious disease in which cells in the body grow rapidly into lumps which can spread and may cause death: *We heard that he had died of cancer* □ *throat cancer.* □ *cancer of the bowel.* **2** A **cancer** is a lump caused by this disease. — *adjective* **cancerous:** *a unique protein produced by all cancerous cells* □ *We do not yet know what causes a cell to become cancerous.*

candid /'kandɪd/ *adjective*
You are **candid** when you speak honestly and openly, without hiding anything: *a candid interview.* — *adverb* **candidly:** *She spoke candidly about her years as Prime Minister.* [see also **candour**]

candidacy /'kandɪdəsɪ/ *noun* (*uncount*)
Someone's **candidacy** is their state of being a candidate for something: *She has announced her candidacy.*

candidate /'kandɪdeɪt/ *noun*: **candidates**
1 A **candidate** is someone competing with others, *eg*

in an election: *We have interviewed over fifty candidates for this job.* **2** A **candidate** is a person taking an examination: *Candidates are required to answer three questions.* **3** A person or thing is a **candidate** for something when they are considered suitable for something or likely to suffer from something: *He's not experienced enough to be a candidate for promotion.* □ *The multi-storey car park is a likely candidate for demolition.*

candle /'kandəl/ *noun*: **candles**
A **candle** is a stick of wax with a piece of string running lengthwise through it, designed to give light as the string burns slowly: *The candle has gone out; I'll light it again.*

candlelight /'kandəllaɪt/ *noun (uncount)*
Candlelight is the light given off by a candle or candles: *They had to read by candlelight.*

candlestick /'kandəlstɪk/ *noun*: **candlesticks**
A **candlestick** is a base in which a candle can be fitted and set on a table or carried.

candour /'kandə(r)/ (*AmE* **candor**) *noun (uncount)*
Candour is the quality of speaking honestly and openly, without hiding anything: *She impressed me very forcibly with her candour and her excellent memory.* [see also **candid**]

candy /'kandɪ/ *noun (AmE; count or uncount, often adjectival)*: **candies**
A **candy** is a sweet: *kids wasting their money on candy.* □ *a candy bar* □ *a box of candy.*

cane /keɪn/ *noun; verb*
▷ ***noun***: **canes**
1 (*uncount, often adjectival*) **Cane** is the long hard hollow stems of various tropical plants such as bamboo, often woven together to make baskets and furniture: *cane tables and chairs.* **2** A **cane** is a walking-stick. **3** In some schools, a **cane** is a stick used to hit pupils as a punishment: *He was given the cane for being cheeky.*
▷ ***verb***: **canes, caning, caned**
Pupils are **caned** when they are hit with a cane as a punishment.

canine /'keɪnaɪn/ *adjective*
Canine means relating to or like a dog: *canine behaviour.*

canister /'kanɪstə(r)/ *noun*: **canisters**
A **canister** is a small metal container, especially one used in industry: *The gas is stored in these canisters.*

cannabis /'kanəbɪs/ *noun (uncount)*
Cannabis is a kind of drug smoked for pleasure. It is illegal in many countries: *He was arrested for selling cannabis.*

canned /'kand/ *adjective*
1 Canned foods are preserved in cans. **2 Canned** laughter is the recorded sound of laughter added to a television programme to give the effect of a live audience.

cannibal /'kanɪbəl/ *noun*: **cannibals**
A **cannibal** is a person who eats human flesh.

cannibalism /'kanɪbəlɪsm/ *noun (uncount)*
People who practise **cannibalism** eat human flesh.

cannibalize or **cannibalise** /'kanɪbəlaɪz/ *verb*: **cannibalizes, cannibalizing, cannibalized**
You **cannibalize** something such as a vehicle when you take parts from it in order to make or repair another one or something else: *He had cannibalized old washing machines and cars to make the controversial racing bike.*

cannon /'kanən/ *noun*: **cannons**
1 A **cannon** is a large old-fashioned gun mounted on wheels: *They needed horses to pull the cannons.* **2** A **cannon** is also a rapid-firing gun fitted to an aircraft or ship.

cannonball /'kanənbɔːl/ *noun*: **cannonballs**
A **cannonball** is a large heavy metal ball fired from an old-fashioned cannon.

cannot /'kanət/ or /'kanɒt/ *verb*
Cannot is the negative form of the verb **can**[1]: *The management cannot be held responsible for the loss of personal property.*

canny /'kanɪ/ *adjective*: **cannier, canniest**
A **canny** person is wise, alert and not easily fooled: *a canny businessman.*

canoe /kə'nuː/ *noun*: **canoes**
A **canoe** is a small narrow boat, that you usually sit or kneel in facing forwards, and that you row using a paddle.

canoeing /kə'nuːɪŋ/ *noun (uncount)*
Canoeing is the sport or pastime of paddling a canoe: *We went canoeing on the river.*

canon /'kanən/ *noun*: **canons**
1 A **canon** is a Christian priest who helps to run the affairs of a cathedral. **2** A **canon** is also a general rule, principle or belief: *the canons of literary taste.*

canonize or **canonise** /'kanənaɪz/ *verb*: **canonizes, canonizing, canonized**
When the Church **canonizes** a dead person, it declares them officially to be a saint: *Pope Alexander III was preparing to canonize Thomas Becket.*

canopy /'kanəpɪ/ *noun*: **canopies**
1 A **canopy** is a sheet of fabric hung up above something for shelter or decoration: *a garden seat with a canvas canopy.* **2** (*literary*) Something that forms a wide covering above something else can be referred to as a **canopy**: *The branches intertwined, creating a leafycanopy.*

can't /kɑːnt/ *verb*
Can't is the spoken, and informal written, form of **cannot**.

cantankerous /kan'taŋkərəs/ *adjective*
A **cantankerous** person is bad-tempered and ready to argue or complain: *Her father is a cantankerous old devil.*

canteen /kan'tiːn/ *noun*: **canteens**
A **canteen** is a simple restaurant for workers in a factory, office or other large building: *The staff canteen doesn't serve hot meals.*

canter /'kantə(r)/ *noun; verb*
▷ ***noun***: (*used in the singular*)
A horse runs at a **canter** when it runs at a medium pace, faster than a trot and slower than a gallop.
▷ ***verb***: **canters, cantering, cantered**
A horse **canters** when it runs at this pace.

canvas /'kanvəs/ *noun*: **canvases**
1 (*uncount, often adjectival*) **Canvas** is thick heavy coarse cloth used for making tents, sails and other outdoor items: *a canvas bag.* **2** A **canvas** is a piece of this cloth prepared for painting a picture on, or the picture painted on it: *I bought a few of his earlier canvases.*
▷ ***phrase*** You live **under canvas** when you live in a tent.

canvass /'kanvəs/ *verb*: **canvasses, canvassing, canvassed**
1 To **canvass** for a political party is to go around asking people to give their support to it: *She has canvassed tirelessly for the local candidate.* **2** To **canvass** opinion is to find out what people in general think about a particular matter: *They should have canvassed opinion before putting the scheme into practice.*

canyon /ˈkanjən/ *noun*: **canyons**
A **canyon** is a long narrow deep valley with steep sides: *the Grand Canyon.*

cap /kap/ *noun; verb*
▷ ***noun***: **caps**
1 A **cap** is any flat hat with a curved shade at the front, especially when worn by men or as part of a uniform: *a cloth cap* □ *a baseball cap* □ *an officer's cap.* **2** A **cap** on a bottle or pen is a small tight-fitting lid: *I unscrewed the cap.*
▷ ***verb***: **caps, capping, capped**
1 You **cap** something when you do something else that is better or more impressive than it is: *She was able to cap every story that was told.* **2** To **cap** something is to be, form or cover the top of it: *mountains capped with snow.* **3** To **cap** an organization is to limit, by law, the amount of money it may spend or charge: *Several local councils will be rate-capped under the government's new proposal.*
▷ ***phrases*** **1** You go to someone **cap in hand** when you go to ask them humbly if they will give you something or do something: *We were forced to go cap in hand to the bank manager to ask for a loan.* **2** You say **to cap it all** before telling someone about the last, and perhaps the worst, in a series of unpleasant events: *Then, to cap it all, our house was burgled!*

capability /keɪpəˈbɪlɪtɪ/ *noun*: **capabilities**
You have the **capability** to do something when you have the ability, power or opportunity to do it: *I think the task is beyond his capabilities.* □ *a country with an impressive nuclear capability.*

capable /ˈkeɪpəbəl/ *adjective*
1 You are **capable** of doing something when you have the ability or the necessary personal qualities to do it: *I don't believe he is capable of murder.* □ *The aircraft is capable of some incredible manoeuvres.* **2** A **capable** person is talented and efficient: *She's a very capable surgeon.* □ *He was a capable but not outstanding artist.* — *adverb* **capably:** *She coped capably with the crisis.* □ *a capably executed manoeuvre.*

capacity /kəˈpasɪtɪ/ *noun*: **capacities**
1 (*uncount*) **a** The **capacity** of something is the amount that it can contain or produce: *barrels with a fifty-litre capacity* □ *The stadium has a capacity of over 100,000.* □ *The amplifier has a capacity of 35 watts per channel.* [compare **volume**] **b** A **capacity** crowd completely fills *eg* a theatre or stadium: *They were expecting a capacity crowd for the match.* **2** You have the **capacity** to do something when you are able to do it, or able to learn how to do it: *Not everyone has a capacity for languages.* **3** (*uncount*) Your **capacity** for something is the amount of it you can eat, drink, use or absorb: *He had a seemingly limitless capacity for beer.* □ *The public's capacity for newspaper scandal seems limitless.* **4** A person's **capacity** is also their position or function, *eg* within an organization: *He was speaking in his capacity as Leader of the Council.* □ *I was asked along in a purely advisory capacity.*
▷ ***phrase*** Something is filled **to capacity** when there is no room left for any more.

cape /keɪp/ *noun*: **capes**
1 A **cape** is a short cloak: *She wrapped the cape around her shoulders.* **2** A **cape** is also a large area of land that sticks out into the sea: *the seas around the Cape of Good Hope.*

caper /ˈkeɪpə(r)/ *noun* (*informal*): **capers**
A **caper** is an adventure, or a dishonest or illegal activity: *The chapter is entitled 'The Times Newspaper Caper'.*

capital /ˈkapɪtəl/ *noun; adjective*
▷ ***noun***: **capitals**
1 The **capital**, or **capital** city, of a country is the city where the government is based: *New York is not the capital of the United States.* **2** A **capital**, or **capital** letter, is the form of a letter used, in English and many other languages, at the beginning of a sentence or a name. **3** A place can be referred to as the **capital** of a particular activity if it is the place where that activity happens the most: *London is no longer regarded as the financial capital of Europe.* **4** (*uncount*) **Capital** is money, especially money used to start a business, or money invested in order to make more money: *You'll need capital if you want to open a restaurant.*
▷ ***adjective***
1 Capital expenditure or investment is money used to buy property or equipment for business. **2** A **capital** offence is a serious crime for which the punishment may be death: *Murder in the first degree is still a capital crime in many American states.*
▷ ***phrase*** You **make capital out of** a situation when you use that situation to win or gain something for yourself: *His opponents were quick to make capital out of his problems.*

capitalism /ˈkapɪtəlɪzm/ *noun* (*uncount*)
Capitalism is an economic system in which people themselves are allowed to own and control property and businesses, rather than one in which everything is owned and controlled by the government: *the rejection of Socialism in favour of capitalism.*

capitalist /ˈkapɪtəlɪst/ *noun; adjective*
▷ ***noun***: **capitalists**
1 A **capitalist** is a person who believes that capitalism is the best kind of economic system. **2** A **capitalist** is also a person who owns a business, especially someone who makes a lot of money for themselves through business.
▷ ***adjective***
A **capitalist** country or economy is one organized according to the principles of capitalism: *modern capitalist society.*

capitalize or **capitalise** /ˈkapɪtəlaɪz/ *verb*: **capitalizes, capitalizing, capitalized**
You **capitalize** on something when you use it to gain a personal advantage: *We must capitalize on our opponents' weaknesses.*

capital punishment /kapɪtəl ˈpʌnɪʃmənt/ *noun* (*uncount*)
Capital punishment is the legal killing of a person who has committed a very serious crime such as murder.

capitulate /kəˈpɪtjʊleɪt/ *verb* (*formal*): **capitulates, capitulating, capitulated**
You **capitulate** when you stop opposing or resisting someone and agree to do what they ask: *It seems clear that the unions will have to capitulate to the government's demands.* [*same as* **give in**, **submit**; *opposite* **resist**]

caprice /kəˈpriːs/ *noun* (*count or uncount; formal*)
A **caprice** is a sudden change of mood, or a sudden and usually unreasonable decision to change something: *We are at the mercy of the whims and caprices of the owners.* □ *It all seems to have more to do with mood, caprice and atmosphere than carefully thought-out argument.* [*same as* **whim**]

capricious /kəˈprɪʃəs/ *adjective* (*formal*)
A **capricious** person often changes their mind for no good reason or has sudden changes of mood: *He rewrote the whole scene in his typically capricious way.*

capsize /kapˈsaɪz/ *verb*: **capsizes, capsizing, capsized**
When a boat **capsizes** it turns over completely, so that

it is upside down in the water: *She leaned out too far and the boat capsized.*

capsule /ˈkapsjuːl/ *noun*: **capsules**
A **capsule** is **1** a very small rounded case containing a powdered medicine, that you swallow whole. **2** any small container in which something can be safely stored. **3** the part of a spacecraft in which the astronauts travel, which separates from the main rocket for the return to earth.

captain /ˈkaptɪn/ *noun*; *verb*
▻ ***noun***: **captains**
1 In the armed forces, a **captain** is an officer of middle rank. **2** The **captain** of a ship is the officer in charge of it. **3** The **captain** of an aircraft is its senior pilot. **4** The **captain** of a team is its leader.
▻ ***verb***: **captains, captaining, captained**
You **captain** a team when you are its leader: *She first captained Scotland at the age of 23.*

caption /ˈkapʃən/ *noun*: **captions**
A **caption** is the words printed underneath a photograph or cartoon, that explains what it shows: *The caption read, 'Winter on the Isle of Mull'.*

captivate /ˈkaptəveɪt/ *verb*: **captivates, captivating, captivated**
Something **captivates** you when it is so interesting or impressive that it holds all your attention: *She has captivated audiences all over the world.* — *adjective* **captivating:** *a captivating performance.*

captive /ˈkaptɪv/ *noun*; *adjective*
▻ ***noun***: **captives**
A **captive** is a person or animal that has been caught or taken prisoner: *She was to remain Henry's captive for as long as he chose.*
▻ ***adjective***
1 You are held **captive** when you are kept as a prisoner: *captive birds.* **2** A **captive** audience is one that is so interested or impressed by what they are watching that they do not want to leave, or, they are unable to leave: *Children would ignore the policeman on the street, but if he visits the classroom he has a captive audience.*

captivity /kapˈtɪvɪtɪ/ *noun* (*uncount*)
Captivity is the state of being held as a captive: *Most zoo animals, after years in captivity, would not know how to survive in the wild.*

captor /ˈkaptə(r)/ *noun*: **captors**
Someone's **captor** is the person holding them prisoner: *With her servants' help, Mary Queen of Scots escaped from her captors.*

capture /ˈkaptʃə(r)/ *verb*; *noun*
▻ ***verb***: **captures, capturing, captured**
1 You **capture** someone when you take them prisoner: *He was captured by the enemy and spent the remainder of the war in a prisoner-of-war camp.* **2** Troops **capture** *eg* a town when they take possession or control of it after a fight or battle: *A small division of troops had captured the hill.* **3** You **capture** an animal when you catch it, usually with the intention of keeping it. **4** You **capture** *eg* a feeling or mood when you represent or record it perfectly in the form of pictures, words or music: *His writing manages to capture the villagers' sense of despair.* □ *The artist has succeeded in capturing her expression exactly.*
▻ ***noun*** (*used in the singular*)
The **capture** of someone or something is the act of capturing them or it: *We left shortly before the capture of the city by enemy troops.*

car /kɑː(r)/ *noun*: **cars**
1 A **car** is a motor vehicle that carries a small number of people: *We couldn't all fit into the family car.* □ *We're not travelling by air; we're going to take the car.* □ *We'll go by car.* [see picture on the next page] **2** In America, ordinary railway carriages are called **cars**. In Britain, they are only called **cars** when they are used for a particular purpose: *sleeping cars.* **3** The passenger compartment in an airship or cable railway is also called a **car**.

carafe /kəˈraf/ or /kəˈrɑːf/ *noun*: **carafes**
A **carafe** is a wide-necked bottle or flask in which *eg* wine or water is served at a table: *a carafe of red wine.*

caramel /ˈkarəmɛl/ *noun* (*count or uncount*): **caramels**
1 A **caramel** is a soft sweet made with sugar and butter: *a box of caramels.* □ *a chocolate bar containing caramel and hazelnuts.* **2** (*uncount*) **Caramel** is sugar boiled until it is slightly burnt, used for flavouring food.

carat /ˈkarət/ *noun*: **carats**
1 A **carat** is a measure of the weight of diamonds and other precious stones, equal to 0.2 grams. **2** A **carat** is also a measure of how pure gold is, the purest gold being 24 carats.

caravan /ˈkarəvan/ *noun*: **caravans**
1 A **caravan** is a large vehicle equipped for living in, either designed to be pulled by a motor vehicle or kept in one place as a holiday home. [see picture at **vehicle**] **2** A **caravan** is also a large group of people, often traders, travelling together in desert countries.

caravanning /ˈkarəvanɪŋ/ *noun* (*uncount*)
You go **caravanning** when you take a holiday in a caravan.

caravan site /ˈkarəvan saɪt/ *noun*: **caravan sites**
A **caravan site** is a place where caravans may be parked, permanently or temporarily, usually with some facilities such as showers, toilets and a shop.

carbohydrate /kɑːrbouˈhaɪdreɪt/ *noun* (*count or uncount*)
Carbohydrates are substances contained in some kinds of food, that give you energy: *His diet is too high in carbohydrate.*

carbon /ˈkɑːbən/ *noun* (*uncount*)
Carbon is a substance that all living things contain, and the substance that coal is made of: *Diamonds are just a form of carbon.*

carbonated /ˈkɑːbəneɪtɪd/ *adjective*
Carbonated water has had the gas carbon dioxide added to it to make it fizzy.

carbon dioxide /ˈkɑːbən daɪˈɒksaɪd/ *noun* (*uncount*)
Carbon dioxide is a gas present in the air. Plants take in carbon dioxide through their leaves and give out oxygen; animals, including humans, take in oxygen and breathe out carbon dioxide.

carbon monoxide *noun* (*uncount*)
Carbon monoxide is the harmful gas produced *eg* by vehicle engines burning petrol: *They had died from carbon monoxide poisoning.*

carcass or **carcase** /ˈkɑːkəs/ *noun*: **carcasses**
A **carcass** is the dead body of an animal.

card /kɑːd/ *noun*: **cards**
1 (*uncount*) **Card** is very thick stiff paper: *The photos were first mounted on card.* □ *pieces of card.* **2** A **card** is **a** a rectangular piece of card with a picture or design printed on it, for sending a message or greeting on: *Christmas cards* □ *a birthday card* □ *a postcard* **b** a rectangular piece of card or plastic with your name and often your photograph on, that you show as proof of your identity: *Can I see your membership card, please?* **3** A playing **card** is one of a set of rectangular pieces of card with numbers and symbols

car

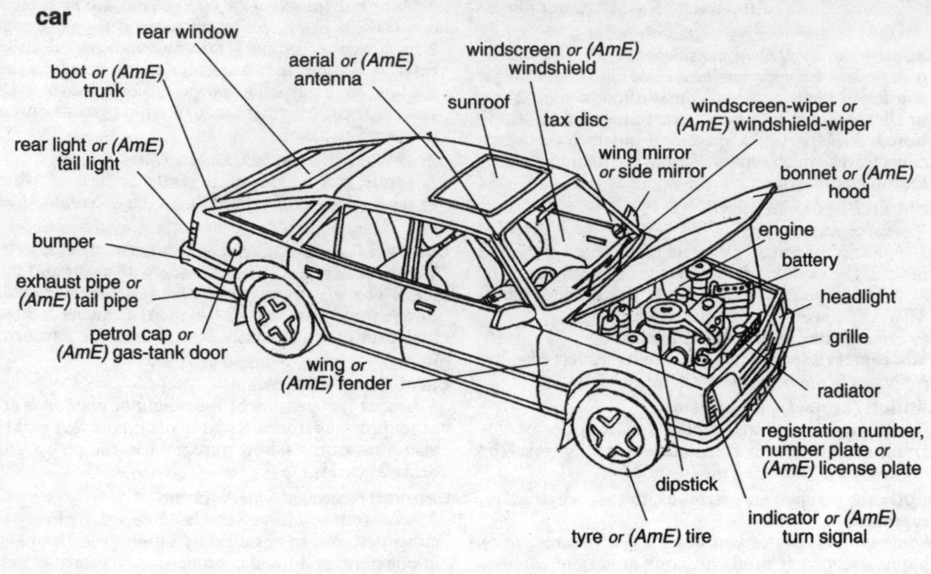

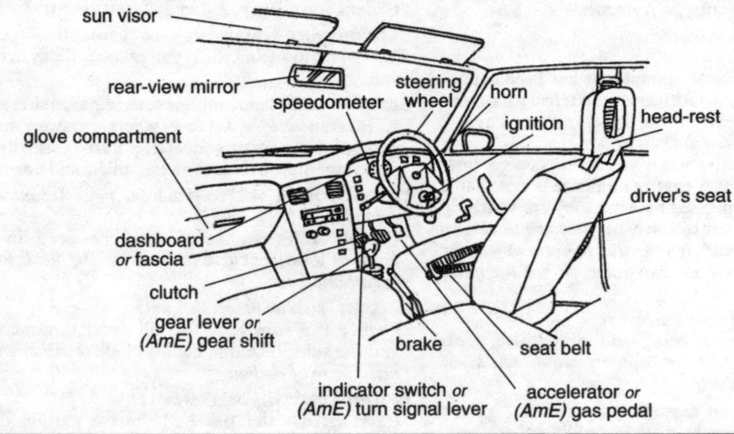

on, used for playing numerous games: *a pack of cards* □ *Would you like a game of cards?* **4** A **card** is also a credit card: *I've had all my cards stolen.* **5** An advantage that you can make use of at a chosen time can also be referred to as a **card**: *The unions still have one or two cards they haven't played yet.*

▷ ***phrases*** **1** You **lay** or **put your cards on the table** when you reveal your thoughts, ideas or intentions. **2** Something is **on the cards** when it is likely to happen. **3** You **play your cards right** when you make good use of your opportunities and advantages: *Play your cards right and you could be running this company in a few years.*

cardboard /ˈkɑːdbɔːd/ *noun* (*uncount*, *often adjectival*)
Cardboard is a very thick stiff material made from waste paper, used for making boxes and packets: *a pile of cardboard boxes.*

cardiac /ˈkɑːdɪak/ *adjective*
Cardiac means relating to the heart: *cardiac massage.* □ *'Cardiac arrest' is the technical term for heart failure.*

cardigan /ˈkɑːdɪgən/ *noun*: **cardigans**
A **cardigan** is a long-sleeved knitted jacket that has buttons down the front. [see picture at **clothing**]

cardinal /ˈkɑːdɪnəl/ *noun*; *adjective*
▷ ***noun*: cardinals**
A **cardinal** is a very senior priest in the Roman Catholic Church: *Cardinal Hume.*
▷ ***adjective***
1 Cardinal means of the highest importance: *This is the cardinal principle in his whole philosophy.* **2** A **cardinal** number is a number that represents quantity, such as the numbers 1, 2 and 3, as opposed to numbers such as 1st, 2nd and 3rd that represent a sequence or order. [see also **ordinal**]

cardinal sin /ˈkɑːdɪnəl sɪn/ *noun*: **cardinal sins**
A **cardinal sin** is a humorous way of referring to something bad or wrong, or something that someone strongly disapproves of: *She had committed the cardinal sin of interrupting him while he was talking.*

care /kɛə(r)/ *noun*; *verb*
▷ ***noun*: cares**
1 (*uncount*) You do something with **care** when you

make an effort to do it properly and thoroughly, avoiding mistakes, accidents or damage: *Handle these glasses with care.* **2** (*uncount*) **Care** is also the activity of looking after someone or something, or the state of being looked after: *We maintain a very high standard of care in all our hospitals.* □ *She was happy to entrust the animals to my care for a few days.* **3** (*uncount*) Children in **care** are looked after by the state, because their parents are either dead or not able to look after them properly themselves: *The children were hastily taken into care till the allegations against their parents could be investigated.* **4** (*often used in the plural*) **Cares** are worries or responsibilities: *a happy child without a care in the world* □ *ground down by financial cares.*

▷ ***verb***: **cares, caring, cared**

1 You **care** about something if you think it is important or you are interested in it: *Most people don't seem to care what they eat.* □ *I don't care what you think.* □ *He doesn't care how he dresses.* □ *She couldn't care less about her exams.* □ *I don't care if I fail.* **2** You **care** for someone when you look after them: *Children as young as ten are expected to cope with the task of caring for a sick relative.* □ *elderly patients who cannot be cared for in their own homes.* **3** (*formal*) You **care** for someone if you like or love them: *You don't much care for Tony, do you?* □ *I don't think he cares for me at all any more.* **4** (*old or humorous*) Something that you do not **care** for is something you dislike, or do not enjoy: *What they don't care for is to be reminded where the money comes from.* □ *I didn't care for the way he was staring at me.* □ *I don't care for his taste in ties.* **5** (*formal*) You ask someone if they would **care** to do something, or would **care** for something, when you invite them to do it, or offer it to them: *Would you care to join me for dinner?* □ *Would you care for a drink?*

▷ ***phrases***

1 You **take care** of someone or something when you look after them: *They should take better care of their children.* **2** You also **take care** of something when you deal with it or organize it: *Leave your suitcase here; the truck-driver will take care of it.* □ *You prepare the main course and I'll take care of dessert.* **3** When you **take care** to do something you make sure that you do it: *Take care to lock the door when you leave.* □ *I took the greatest care not to crease the dress.* **4** People often say '**Take care!**' as a friendly and informal way of saying goodbye.

career /kə'rɪə(r)/ *noun*; *verb*

▷ ***noun***: **careers**

1 A **career** is a job, usually a profession, that someone works in for a large part of their life: *a career in law.* **2** Your **career** is the part of your life during which you work: *The latter half of my career was spent in Africa.*

▷ ***verb***: **careers, careering, careered**

A person or vehicle **careers** somewhere when they rush there in an uncontrolled way: *The car came careering round the corner and hit a lamp post.*

carefree /'kɛəfriː/ *adjective*

A **carefree** person is happy because they do not worry about anything: *a carefree approach to finding a job.*

careful /'kɛəfəl/ *adjective*

You are **careful** when you make an effort to do something properly and thoroughly, avoiding mistakes, accidents or damage: *Please be careful with that painting; it's very valuable.* □ *She was careful not to show her real feelings.* □ *a careful worker.* □ *After careful consideration, we have decided to let you stay.* — *adverb* **carefully:** *They listened carefully to every detail of the plan.* □ *a carefully made copy.*

careless /'kɛələs/ *adjective*

1 You are **careless** when you make a mistake or have an accident through not paying enough attention or not being concerned enough: *She was a bit careless with the ink and spilled some on the carpet.* □ *a careless piece of work.* **2** You do something in a **careless** way when you do it easily and without effort: *careless charm.* — *adverb* **carelessly:** *He had carelessly left the door open.* — *noun* (*uncount*) **carelessness:** *It happened because of his carelessness.*

carer /'kɛərə(r)/ *noun*: **carers**

A **carer** is a person who looks after someone else, often a member of their own family who is not able to look after themselves *eg* because they are elderly, seriously ill or disabled: *People who act as voluntary carers for their elderly relatives save the state millions of pounds each year.*

caress /kə'rɛs/ *verb*; *noun*

▷ ***verb***: **caresses, caressing, caressed**

You **caress** someone when you touch or stroke them gently and lovingly: *She caressed his face.*

▷ ***noun***: **caresses**

A **caress** is a gentle, loving touch or stroke.

caretaker /'kɛəteɪkə(r)/ *noun*: **caretakers**

A **caretaker** is a person employed to look after a public building such as a school and carry out minor repairs.

cargo /'kɑːgoʊ/ *noun* (*uncount or count*): **cargoes**

A ship's or aircraft's **cargo** is the goods that it is transporting: *a cargo of medical supplies.*

caricature /'karɪkətjʊə(r)/ *noun*; *verb*

▷ ***noun*** (*count or uncount*): **caricatures**

1 A **caricature** of someone is a humorous drawing of them with their most noticeable features exaggerated: *There's an excellent caricature of the President in today's 'Time' magazine.* **2** One thing is a **caricature** of another when it is an exaggerated and bad copy or account of it: *This book is a caricature of the truth.*

▷ ***verb***: **caricatures, caricaturing, caricatured**

To **caricature** someone is to draw a caricature of them, or to describe them in an exaggerated way that may, or may not be, humorous: *His friends were dismayed to find themselves caricatured in his novels.*

caring /'kɛərɪŋ/ *adjective*

1 You are **caring** when you show concern for others: *a caring father* □ *We have tried to encourage a more caring society.* **2** The **caring** professions are jobs that involve looking after people, *eg* nursing or social work.

carnage /'kɑːnɪdʒ/ *noun* (*uncount*; *literary*)

Carnage is the violent killing of great numbers of people: *We were horrified to witness such terrible carnage.*

carnal /'kɑːnəl/ *adjective* (*literary*)

Carnal means relating to sex or sexual feelings: *carnal desires.*

carnation /kɑː'neɪʃən/ *noun*: **carnations**

A **carnation** is a sweet-smelling red, white or pink flower: *The men will wear white carnations in their buttonholes.*

carnival /'kɑːnɪvəl/ *noun*: **carnivals**

A **carnival** is a period of public celebration, usually with parades and singing and dancing in the streets by people dressed in colourful costumes: *Rio's Mardi Gras is the world's most famous carnival.*

carnivore /'kɑːnɪvɔː(r)/ *noun*: **carnivores**

A **carnivore** is any animal that eats meat rather than plants. — *adjective* **carnivorous** /kɑː'nɪvərəs/: *All the big cats are carnivorous.*

carol /'karəl/ *noun*: **carols**

A **carol** is a Christian religious song sung at

Christmas: *We went round the streets singing Christmas carols.*

carousel /karə'sɛl/ *noun*: **carousels**
1 (*AmE*) A **carousel** is a merry-go-round. 2 A **carousel** is also a moving platform from which passengers collect their luggage before leaving an airport.

carp /kɑːp/ *noun*: **carp**
A **carp** is a large fish found in lakes and rivers whose flesh is used as food.

car park /kɑː pɑːk/ *noun*: **car parks**
A **car park** is a building or piece of land where cars can be parked.

carpenter /'kɑːpɪntə(r)/ *noun*: **carpenters**
The job of a **carpenter** is to make and repair wooden things and the wooden parts of buildings and ships.

carpentry /kɑːpɪntrɪ/ *noun* (*uncount*)
Carpentry is the work or skill of a carpenter.

carpet /'kɑːpɪt/ *noun*; *verb*
▻ ***noun***: **carpets**
1 (*uncount or count*) **Carpet** is a covering for floors and stairs, made of thick heavy woven wool or other fabric; a **carpet** is a large piece of this material: *Cover it with an old piece of carpet.* □ *How much did your new carpet cost?* 2 (*literary*) A **carpet** of something such as snow is a covering of it over a wide area: *the lawn with its autumn carpet of leaves.*
▻ ***verb***: **carpets, carpeting, carpeted**
To **carpet** a floor is to cover it with carpet: *It would cost thousands of pounds to carpet the whole house.*

carriage /'karɪdʒ/ *noun*: **carriages**
1 A **carriage** is a four-wheeled horse-drawn passenger vehicle: *We watched the Queen pass in the royal carriage.* 2 A railway coach for passengers is also a **carriage**: *We're in the carriage next to the dining-car.* 3 (*uncount*) **Carriage** is the process or cost of transporting goods: *The company will pay carriage.*

carriageway /'karɪdʒweɪ/ *noun*: **carriageways**
A major road is divided into two **carriageways**, each carrying traffic travelling in one direction: *There's a build-up of traffic on the northbound carriageway.*

carrier /'karɪə(r)/ *noun*: **carriers**
1 A **carrier** is a vehicle designed to carry goods of a particular kind: a *troop-carrier*. 2 A **carrier** is also a person or animal infected by a disease in such a way as to be able to pass it on to others without actually suffering from it.

carrier bag /'karɪə bag/ *noun*: **carrier bags**
A **carrier bag** is a plastic or paper bag with handles, given to shop customers for carrying the things they have bought.

carrot /'karət/ *noun*: **carrots**
1 A **carrot** is a long tapering orange-coloured vegetable: *boiled carrots* □ *carrot cake.* [see picture at **vegetable**] 2 A **carrot** is also something offered to someone to try to persuade them to do something: *He was considering accepting the job, seeing they were holding out the carrot of free medical care.*

carry /'karɪ/ *verb*: **carries, carrying, carried**
1 a You **carry** something when you take it somewhere, holding it off the ground, especially in your hands: *We carried the desk into the hall.* □ *The women walk for miles carrying their children on their backs.* **b** You **are carrying** a piece of equipment when you are wearing it on your body or have it with you, *eg* in your pocket: *Our police officers don't carry guns.* □ *I wasn't carrying a camera at the time, unfortunately.* **c** A vehicle **carries** people when they travel in it from one place to another: *The coach was only designed to carry 52 passengers.* **d** Something such as the wind or a river **carries** something somewhere when it takes it there by the force of its movement: *The seeds are carried in all directions by the wind.* □ *The current had carried us off course.* **e** Sound **carries** if it can easily be heard a long distance away: *She had the kind of voice that carries.*
2 a A woman who **is carrying** a child is pregnant. **b** Someone who **carries** themselves well or badly stands and walks gracefully or ungracefully.
3 a A proposal **is carried** at a meeting when people vote in favour of it: *The motion was carried by six votes to four.* **b** You **carry** an idea or principle to a particular point when you develop it to that point: *This scheme carries the notion of equality to ridiculous extremes.* □ *We can actually carry the comparison a stage further.*
4 a A person or thing that **carries** a disease is infected by it and can pass it on to other people or animals: *We were concerned to know what diseases these animals might be carrying.* **b** Newspapers **carry** reports or photographs if they include them: *This month's edition carries an interview with the Prime Minister.* **c** Actions **carry** something such as a risk or penalty if they involve it: *Drug-smuggling carries the death penalty in some countries.* **d** Your opinion **carries** weight or authority if people trust or believe you.
▻ ***phrase*** You **get carried away** with something if you let your enthusiasm for it get out of proportion or out of control: *We got so carried away with the plan that we didn't stop to consider the problems.*

phrasal verbs
carry off You **carry** something **off** when you manage to do it successfully: *We were going to have to give them the impression that there was nothing we didn't know about gardening, and I didn't think I could carry it off.*
carry on 1 You **carry on** doing something when you continue to do it: *Don't let me interrupt you; just carry on with what you were doing.* □ *She carried on talking even though the film had started.* 2 You **carry on** a particular kind of activity when you do it or take part in it: *We couldn't carry on a conversation with all that noise.* □ *Last year's teaching was carried on against a background of drastic cuts in education funding.* 3 (*informal*) To **carry on** is to behave in a silly way: *The two of them spent the whole lesson carrying on at the back of the class.* [see also **carry-on**]
carry out You **carry out** something such as a task, duty, procedure or order when you do it, perform it, or put it into operation or practice: *She appears to carry out her duties efficiently.* □ *An investigation will be carried out by the Police Complaints Commission.* □ *He has failed to carry out my instructions on a number of occasions.* [*same as* **perform, undertake, fulfil**]
carry through 1 You **carry** something **through** when you put it into practice or complete it: *We hope that the plan can be carried through in its entirety.* 2 Something **carries** you **through** a difficult experience if it helps you to survive it: *It was my religious faith that carried me through those years in captivity.*

carrycot /'karɪkɒt/ *noun*: **carrycots**
A **carrycot** is a lightweight box-like cot for a baby, with handles for carrying it. [see picture at **bedroom**]

carry-on /'karɪɒn/ *noun* (*informal*): **carry-ons**
A **carry-on** is an incident involving silly or annoying behaviour: *I had a bit of a carry-on with a cashier at the bank who refused to cash my cheque.* [see also **carry on** at **carry**]

cart /kɑːt/ *noun*; *verb*

▷ ***noun***: **carts**

1 A **cart** is a two- or four-wheeled, horse-drawn vehicle for carrying goods or passengers: *a horse and cart.* **2** A **cart** is also a lightweight vehicle for carrying goods, pushed or pulled by hand.

▷ ***verb*** (*informal*): **carts, carting, carted**

You **cart** something somewhere when you carry it there, especially with difficulty: *I'm not carting that box around with me all day.*

carte blanche /kɑːt'blɑːnʃ/ *noun* (*uncount; formal*)

If you are given **carte blanche** to do something, you are given the freedom to do it in whichever way you think is best without restrictions or conditions: *The board has given the new sales manager carte blanche to reorganize the sales team countrywide.*

carton /'kɑːtən/ *noun*: **cartons**

A **carton** is a cardboard or plastic container in which some kinds of food and drink are sold: *two cartons of milk.*

cartilage /'kɑːtɪlədʒ/ *noun*: (*uncount*)

Cartilage is the strong flexible substance that protects the joints in your body.

cartoon /kɑː'tuːn/ *noun*: **cartoons**

1 A **cartoon** is a humorous drawing or group of drawings in a newspaper or magazine. **2** A **cartoon** is also a film in which the characters are drawings.

cartoonist /kɑː'tuːnɪst/ *noun*: **cartoonists**

A **cartoonist** is an artist who draws cartoons for newspapers or magazines.

cartridge /'kɑːtrɪdʒ/ *noun*: **cartridges**

1 A **cartridge** is a small cylindrical case containing the explosive charge and bullet for a gun: *spent cartridges.* [= cartridges that have been used] **2** A **cartridge** is also a plastic case of various kinds, *eg* one containing photographic film or sound-recording tape.

carve /kɑːv/ *verb*: **carves, carving, carved**

1 You **carve** a piece of cooked meat when you cut slices from it: *carve the Sunday joint.* **2** You **carve** an object when you make it out of a block of wood or stone that you cut pieces off: *the figure of an elephant carved from a solid piece of marble.* **3** You **carve** a design on a surface when you cut pieces off that surface to form the design: *The children carved their names on the old tree.*

phrasal verbs

carve out You **carve** something **out** for yourself when you establish or create it for yourself through hard work: *She has managed to carve out a nice little career for herself in publishing.*

carve up A group of people **carve** something **up** when they divide it up or share it out between them, especially roughly or greedily: *It seemed as though the United States and the Soviet Union were carving up the world between them.*

carving /kɑːvɪŋ/ *noun*: **carvings**

A **carving** is an object carved out of wood, stone or some other material.

carving knife /kɑːvɪŋ naɪf/ *noun*: **carvingknives**

A **carving knife** is a long sharp knife for cutting meat. [see picture at **tableware**]

cascade /ka'skeɪd/ *noun; verb*

▷ ***noun***: **cascades**

1 A **cascade** is a waterfall or series of waterfalls. **2** (*literary*) A **cascade** is also anything that flows or seems to flow like a waterfall: *Lavender forms a cascade of colour on either side of the steps.*

▷ ***verb*** (*literary*): **cascades, cascading, cascaded**

Something **cascades** when it moves or falls like a waterfall: *Crowds of protesters cascaded down the parliament steps.*

case[1] /keɪs/ *noun*: **cases**

1 A **case** is a particular occasion or situation, or a particular occurrence or example of something: *Children are not normally allowed into the reading room, but I'm prepared to make an exception in this case.* □ *In some cases the whole paragraph will need to be rewritten.* □ *The disease can be very severe; in his case, it happened to prove fatal.* □ *Several new cases of the infection have been reported.* □ *The symptoms did not recur in cases where patients took the drug regularly.* □ *This was a particularly bad case of parental neglect.* □ *It was one of those cases you sometimes get of ambiguous instructions leading to disaster.* **2** Doctors often refer to their patients as **cases**: *How's that appendicitis case this morning?* **3** A crime, mystery or the investigation into it is referred to as a **case**: *We spoke to the detective in charge of the murder case.* **4** A legal **case** is a matter that is tried or examined in a court of law: *The case is to be brought to trial next month.* □ *We're fully expecting to win this case.* **5** The **case** for or against a proposal or theory is the evidence and reasoning that is used to support it or oppose it: *We have more than once argued the case against building another school.* □ *the case for bringing back the death penalty* □ *They can now make out a good case for the extinction of the dinosaurs being due to the impact of a meteorite.*

▷ ***phrases*** **1** Something that is **a case in point** is a good example of what you are talking about: *There has been rapid change in recent years; education is a case in point.* **2** You use **as the case may be** and **whichever the case may be** to indicate that what you say applies whichever of two or more possible situations is the actual one: *Once goods have been paid for by the purchaser they are legally his (or hers, as the case may be).* **3** You use **in any case a** to indicate that what you say remains true whichever of two or more possible situations turns out to be the actual one: *She may leave at Christmas or wait until Easter; in any case, we should start looking for a new manager.* **b** to add something that supports what you have just said: *It would have been embarrassing to ask her and, in any case, she'd have refused to tell me.* **4** You do one thing **in case** of another when you prepare for the possibility of the other happening or being so: *I'll say goodbye now, in case I don't get time to come to the airport to see you off.* □ *I don't think he's at home but I'll phone him just in case.* □ *We keep the doctor's number by the phone, in case of emergencies.* □ *In case of fire* [= if there is a fire] *break the glass.* **5** You use **in that case** and **in which case** to announce what will follow next in the actual or possible situation just mentioned: *'I'm afraid the job has already been taken.' 'In that case, I won't bother sending in my application.'* □ *The company could collapse, in which case we'd lose a lot of money.* **6** Something **is the case** if it is so, or if it is true: *She could be away on holiday, but if that were the case she'd have cancelled the milk and newspapers.* □ *Is it really the case that men can't tolerate as much pain as women can?* □ *The seats are usually sold out by this stage, but if this turns out not to be the case, could you book two?* □ *If, as is sometimes the case, the child really is lying, the problem is a different one.*

case[2] /keɪs/ *noun*: **cases**

1 A **case** is a box, container or cover for storing, protecting or carrying something: *She slid the camera back into its case.* □ *Each pen comes with a leather presentation case.* **2** A **case** is also a suitcase or briefcase: *I had to sit with my case on my knee.*

case history /keɪs 'hɪstərɪ/ *noun*: **case histories**

A person's **case history** is the record of details from their past, *eg* as kept by a doctor.

cash /kaʃ/ *noun; verb*
▻ ***noun*** (*uncount*)
1 Cash is money in the form of notes or coins, as distinct from, *eg*, cheques: *I didn't have my cheque book so I paid in cash.* **2** (*informal*) Money in any form is also often referred to as **cash**: *We can't afford a holiday; cash is pretty short at the moment.*
▻ ***verb*: cashes, cashing, cashed**
When you **cash** a cheque you obtain notes and coins in return for it, usually at a bank: *We were able to cash our traveller's cheques at the hotel.*

> ***phrasal verb***
> You **cash in on** something when you take advantage of it, especially unfairly or dishonestly: *The company was accused of cashing in on employees' fears of redundancy.*

cashier /ka'ʃɪə(r)/ *noun*: **cashiers**
A **cashier** is a person in a bank, shop or business who receives, pays out or generally deals with money.

cashmere /'kaʃmɪə(r)/ *noun* (*uncount, often adjectival*)
Cashmere is a very fine soft kind of wool: *a cashmere sweater.*

casino /kə'siːnoʊ/ *noun*: **casinos**
A **casino** is a private club, or a room within a hotel or club, where people can gamble.

cask /kɑːsk/ *noun*: **casks**
A **cask** is a kind of barrel for holding liquids, especially alcoholic drinks: *The wine is stored in oak casks before bottling.*

casket /'kɑːskɪt/ *noun*: **caskets**
1 A **casket** is a small case for storing valuables such as jewels. **2** (*AmE*) A **casket** is a coffin.

casserole /'kasəroʊl/ *noun*: **casseroles**
1 A **casserole** is a large heavy cooking pot with a lid. **2** (*count or uncount*) A **casserole** is also a meal cooked in such a pot, especially meat and vegetables cooked slowly in a liquid: *We had beef casserole for dinner.*

cassette /kə'sɛt/ *noun*: **cassettes**
1 A **cassette** is **a** a small sealed plastic case containing sound-recording tape. **b** any similar case, such as one containing video tape or photographic film. **2** (*informal*) A cassette recorder is also often referred to as a **cassette.**

cassette recorder /kə'sɛt rɪkɔːdə(r)/ *noun*: **cassette recorders**
A **cassette recorder** is a machine that records or plays music and other sounds on cassette.

cast /kɑːst/ *verb; noun*
▻ ***verb*: casts, casting, cast**
1 (*old, literary*) You **cast** something somewhere when you throw it there: *He cast the sword into the lake.* **2 a** Something such as light **is cast** on to something when it falls or is directed on to it: *His hand cast a large shadow on the wall.* **b** Light **is cast** on a mystery when something happens that helps people to understand it: *No light has been cast on this puzzle as yet.* **3** You **cast** your eyes, or a glance, at or over something when you look at it briefly: *I had already cast an eye over his designs and selected a couple of possible ones.* ▫ *She cast a hurried glance at the clock.* **4** You **cast** your mind back to some period or incident when you remember it. **5** You **cast** doubt on a particular thing when you say something that makes people unsure or doubtful about it: *The report casts suspicion on the chairman's motives.* **6** You **cast** your vote when you vote in an election: *The last vote had been cast and the work of counting had begun.* **7** A director or producer **casts** a play or film when he or she chooses actors to play the various parts or roles in it; an actor **is cast** in a certain part when he or she is chosen to play it: *She has been cast in the role of the mother.* ▫ *It's fun to be cast as the villain for a change.* **8** A metal object such as a scuplture **is cast** by pouring hot liquid metal into a container formed into the desired shape, and letting it harden: *The original statue was cast in bronze.*
▻ ***noun*: casts**
1 The **cast** of a play or film consists of all the actors in it: *an epic film with a cast of thousands.* **2** A **cast** is a covering of plaster hardened around a broken limb to support it while it heals: *He had his leg in a plaster cast for two months.*

> ***phrasal verbs***
> **cast about** or **cast around** (*formal*) You **cast about** or **around** for something when you try to find it or think of it: *She cast about for the appropriate word.*
> **cast aside** (*formal*) You **cast** someone or something **aside** when you get rid of them because you don't want them any longer: *Many old people feel unwanted and cast aside.*
> **cast off 1** (*formal*) You **cast** something **off** when you get rid of it because it is no longer useful: *Both sides have agreed to cast off the ideological narrowness of the past.* [see also **cast-off**] **2** You **cast off** when you untie your boat and move out into the water.

caste /kɑːst/ *noun*: **castes**
A **caste** is any of the social classes into which people in some societies are strictly divided: *the Hindu caste system.*

caster see **castor.**

castigate /'kastɪgeɪt/ *verb* (*formal*): **castigates, castigating, castigated**
You **castigate** someone when you criticize them severely: *Several of the ministers involved were castigated by the prime minister.*

cast-iron /kɑːst 'aɪən/ *adjective*
1 Cast-iron objects are made by pouring liquid iron containing carbon into a shaped container and letting it harden. **2 Cast-iron** is also used to describe things that are very strong, firm or reliable: *She has a cast-iron will.* ▫ *a cast-iron guarantee.*

castle /'kɑːsəl/ *noun*: **castles**
1 A **castle** is a large, often very old building with thick high walls and towers, originally built to protect important people such as kings and queens in times of war: *the castles of Wales* ▫ *Edinburgh Castle.* **2** (*chess*) A **castle** is a piece that can move forwards, backwards or sideways.

cast-off /'kɑːstɒf/ *noun* (*often in the plural*): **cast-offs**
Cast-offs are things, especially clothes, that are given away because they are no longer wanted or useful: *The younger children had to wear the older ones' cast-offs.*

castor or **caster** /'kɑːstə(r)/ *noun*: **castors**
Castors are small wheels fitted to furniture so that it can be moved easily.

castrate /ka'streɪt/ *verb*: **castrates, castrating, castrated**
A male animal **is castrated** when its testicles are removed so that it can no longer produce young. — *noun* (*uncount*) **castration** /ka'streɪʃən/: *the castration of male lambs.*

casual /'kaʒuəl/ *adjective*
1 Someone behaves in a **casual** way when they seem not to be interested, concerned or worried: *She was very casual about being sacked.* **2 Casual** clothes are comfortable and informal: *a casual jacket.* **3 Casual**

work is temporary, usually for short periods only. **4 Casual** is also used to describe events that are not planned or intended, and things that are not done seriously or thoroughly: *a casual meeting in the street* □ *I just had a casual glance at the newspaper.* — *adverb* **casually:** *She strolled casually across the road, ignoring the traffic.* □ *The Czechs dress casually.*

casualty /ˈkaʒʊəltɪ/ *noun*: **casualties**
1 A **casualty** is a person killed or injured in an accident or war: *The precise number of casualties is not known.* **2** (*uncount*, *often adjectival*) In a hospital, **casualty** is the department that treats people injured in accidents: *She was immediately rushed to casualty.* □ *a casualty department.* **3** One thing is a **casualty** of another when it is lost, destroyed or sacrificed as a result of it: *Car manufacturers were an early casualty of the economic crisis.*

cat /kat/ *noun*: **cats**
1 A **cat** is a small four-legged furry animal with claws and whiskers, kept as a pet. **2** A **cat** is also any of numerous larger related animals, such as the lion and tiger: *You should see the big cats in their natural surroundings.*

cataclysm /ˈkatəklɪzm/ *noun* (*formal*): **cataclysms**
A **cataclysm** is an event such as an earthquake that brings sudden and violent change: *the upheaval in Russia as it underwent the cataclysm of revolution.*

cataclysmic /katəˈklɪzmɪk/ *adjective* (*literary*)
A sudden event might be described as **cataclysmic** if it causes great harm or destruction: *a cataclysmic earthquake.*

catalogue (*AmE* **catalog**) /ˈkatəlɒg/ *noun*; *verb*
▻ ***noun***: **catalogues**
1 A **catalogue** is a book or booklet with details and often pictures of items for sale, *eg* in a shop or at an auction. **2** A **catalogue** in *eg* a library is an ordered list or record of all the books kept there. **3** A **catalogue** of things is series of them listed one by one: *She reeled off a catalogue of her husband's faults.*
▻ ***verb***: **catalogues, cataloguing, catalogued**
To **catalogue** things is to make an ordered list or record of them.

catalyst /ˈkatəlɪst/ *noun*: **catalysts**
One thing is a **catalyst** for another when it causes or encourages the other to happen: *The takeover, with its attendant uncertainties, served as a catalyst for the formation of a staff council.*

catapult /ˈkatəpʌlt/ *noun*; *verb*
▻ ***noun***: **catapults**
A **catapult** is a weapon for firing stones, used especially by children, consisting of a forked stick with a rubber band attached to it.
▻ ***verb*** (*informal*): **catapults, catapulting, catapulted**
Someone **is catapulted** somewhere when they are sent or taken there very quickly: *Yesterday's brilliant speech has catapulted him to the top of the popularity polls.*

cataract /ˈkatərakt/ *noun*: **cataracts**
A **cataract** is a harmful growth on a person's eyeball which can eventually make them blind: *an operation to have a cataract removed.*

catastrophe /kəˈtastrəfɪ/ *noun*: **catastrophes**
A **catastrophe** is an unexpected event that causes great suffering, destruction or loss of life: *It would be a catastrophe for our country if its national team didn't win.* [**disaster, tragedy**] — *adjective* **catastrophic** /katəˈstrɒfɪk/: *There was a catastrophic fall in the value of our shares.*

catcall /ˈkatkɔːl/ *noun*: **catcalls**
A **catcall** is a loud whistle made by a member of an audience to show disapproval of a performer or speaker: *The minister's speech was met by jeers and catcalls from a hostile crowd of protestors against the bill.*

catch /katʃ/ *verb*; *noun*
▻ ***verb***: **catches, catching, caught**
1 a You **catch** a person or animal when you manage to capture them after a hunt or chase, or when you trap them with some device: *He always seems to move so silently, like a cat hoping to catch a mouse.* □ *He promised that the terrorists would be caught.* □ *He'd been fishing in the stream and had caught a few trout for supper.* **b** You **catch** someone doing something wrong or embarrassing when you discover them doing it: *Two boys had been caught smoking in the toilets.* □ *Don't let me catch you at it again!*
2 a You **catch** an object that is moving through the air when you grab it or let it fall into your hands: *She caught the ball with one hand.* **b** You **catch** falling liquid when you collect it in a container: *I put a bucket under the leak to catch the drips.* **c** You **catch** a cold or other disease when you get it and become ill: *Unfortunately I caught flu and had to spend a week in bed.* **d** (*often with a negative*) You **catch** something that someone says when you hear it: *I'm sorry, I didn't quite catch your name.* **e** You **catch** sight or a glimpse of something when you see it briefly: *I caught a glimpse of her just as she turned the corner and disappeared.* **f** You **catch** something when you succeed in recording or representing it: *The artist had caught her expression perfectly.* □ *His poem catches the mood of despair felt by the soldiers in the trenches.* [*same as* **capture**]
3 a You **catch** a bus or train when you get on it to make a journey: *We arrived in time to catch the 3.30 from Doncaster.* **b** You **catch** something when you succeed in seeing, doing or using it while it is available: *You might just catch the post; the last collection is at 6.30.* □ *We arrived home in time to catch the late film on TV.*
4 a You **are caught** in the rain or a storm, or something else unpleasant, when you cannot escape from it: *I got caught in a heavy shower and arrived home soaked.* **b** One thing **catches** on another, or **is caught** on it or in it, when it accidentally becomes attached to it or held by it: *My dress caught on a nail as I was climbing over the fence.* □ *I caught my little finger in the door.* □ *His jacket got caught in the machinery.* **c** Something moving **catches** you somewhere when it hits you there; you **catch** part of you of you on something when you hit yourself on it: *The blow caught him on the chin.* □ *She caught her head on the edge of the desk as she fell.* **d** Something **catches** your eye or your interest when you notice it: *The Scottish accent caught my ear, and I looked around to see Bob standing there.* □ *I picked up the newspaper and my attention was immediately caught by a headline.* **e** The light **catches** something, or something **catches** the light, when it reflects the light and looks bright: *The sunlight was catching the dew and making the grass sparkle.* □ *Her hair caught the light.*
▻ ***noun***: **catches**
1 A **catch** is **a** an act of catching a ball, *eg* in a sport such as cricket: *Gower is out after an amazing catch by Johnson.* **b** a device for keeping something such as a lid or door closed: *I couldn't move the catch on the window.* **2** A **catch** is also a hidden problem or disadvantage: *They're giving away free holidays! What's the catch?* **3** Your **catch** when you have been fishing is the number of fish you have caught: *Regulations are being drawn up to limit the size of herring catches.*
▻ ***phrase*** You **get caught up in** something unpleasant when you become involved in it, often unintention-

ally: *Her government was determined not to get caught up in another country's civil war.*

phrasal verbs

catch at Someone or something **catches at** something when they try to grab or hold it: *He caught at my sleeve and tried to stop me.* □ *The thorns caught at my clothes.*

catch on (*informal*) **1** Something **catches on** when it becomes popular: *The new rock and roll music caught on quickly with youngsters.* **2** You **catch on** when you understand what is happening or being said; you **catch on** to something when you become aware that it is happening: *It doesn't take him long to catch on.* □ *Then the teachers caught on to our little scheme and we were all punished.*

catch out You **catch** someone **out** when you trick them into making a mistake, *eg* one that shows they have been lying.

catch up 1 You **catch up** with someone moving ahead of you when you manage to reach them by moving faster: *You'll have to run faster if you want to catch him up.* □ *Slow down and let the others catch up.* **2** You also **catch up** with someone when you reach the same standard or level as they are at: *She's a bit behind the other children, but if she works hard she should soon catch up.* **3** People in authority **catch up** with someone who has done something wrong when they manage to find them: *The police eventually caught up with her as she was about to board the ferry in the stolen car.* **4** An unpleasant task or situation that you have been avoiding **catches up** with you when you are forced to deal with it. **5** When you **catch up** on something that you normally do regularly but have not done for a while, you spend a lot of time doing it when you have the chance: *Now that my thesis is finished, I mean to catch up on my social life.*

catch-22 /katʃtwɛntɪ'tuː/ *noun* (*used in the singular*)
If you are in a **catch-22** situation, you are unable to make progress or get what you want because every possible course of action depends on something that is impossible: *Actors can't get work without having a union card, and they can't get a union card unless they're working; it's a catch-22 situation.*

catching /'katʃɪŋ/ *adjective* (*informal*)
A disease or other condition that is **catching** can be passed easily from one person to another: *People often think, wrongly, that all skin diseases are catching.* □ *His enthusiasm was catching.* [same as **contagious**, **infectious**]

catchment area /'katʃmənt ɛərɪə/ *noun*: **catchment areas**
The **catchment area** of an institution such as a school or hospital is the area it serves, in that people from that area are allowed to or must use it.

catchphrase /'katʃfreɪz/ *noun*: **catchphrases**
A **catchphrase** is a phrase that is currently very popular, usually something that was first said by someone famous: *The finance minister's expression 'the green shoots of economic recovery' has become something of a catchphrase.*

catchword /'katʃwɜːd/ *noun*: **catchwords**
A **catchword** is a popular word or phrase, associated *eg* with some current trend: *After World War II the catchword for a newly health-conscious society was 'protein'.* [compare **byword**]

catchy /'katʃɪ/ *adjective*: **catchier, catchiest**
A **catchy** tune is immediately appealing and stays in your mind after you have heard it.

categorical /katə'gɒrɪkəl/ *adjective*
A **categorical** statement is firm and clear, making no exceptions and not allowing any misunderstanding: *She gave a categorical assurance that this would not happen.* — *adverb* **categorically:** *He has categorically denied that his firm was in any way responsible.*

category /'katəgərɪ/ *noun*: **categories**
A **category** is a set of people or things grouped together because they are similar in some way and different from the members of other sets: *These poems fall into the category of 'romantic verse'.*

cater /'keɪtə(r)/ *verb*: **caters, catering, catered**
1 You **cater** for someone, or for someone's needs, when you provide what they want or require: *The restaurant caters mainly for people who want simple food served quickly.* **2** You **cater** to someone when you satisfy their desire for something bad or something that is generally disapproved of: *The popular newspapers cater to the public's taste for scandal and sensation.*

caterer /'keɪtərə(r)/ *noun*: **caterers**
A **caterer** is a person whose job is to provide food and drinks for people at parties and other social occasions: *We've hired a local firm of caterers for our daughter's wedding.*

caterpillar /'katəpɪlə(r)/ *noun*: **caterpillars**
A **caterpillar** is a small worm-like creature with many legs, that later turns into a butterfly or a moth.

cathedral /kə'θiːdrəl/ *noun*: **cathedrals**
A **cathedral** is the main church in an area that a bishop has responsibility for: *Durham Cathedral.*

Catholic /'kaθəlɪk/ *noun*: **Catholics**
A **Catholic** is a member of the Roman Catholic Church, the branch of the Christian Church that has the Pope as its head.

Catholicism /kə'θɒlɪsɪzm/ (*uncount*)
Catholicism is the set of beliefs held by Catholics.

cattle /'katəl/ *noun* (*plural*)
Cattle are cows and bulls: *a herd of cattle.*

caught /kɔːt/ *verb*
Caught is the past tense and past participle of **catch**.

cauldron (*AmE* **caldron**) /'kɔːldrən/ *noun*: **cauldrons**
A **cauldron** is a very large round metal pot for heating liquids over a fire.

cauliflower /'kɒlɪflaʊə(r)/ *noun* (*count or uncount*): **cauliflowers**
A **cauliflower** is a large round vegetable with a firm white edible centre surrounded by thick green leaves: *cauliflower soup.* [see picture at **vegetable**]

cause /kɔːz/ *noun*; *verb*
▻ ***noun*: causes**
1 (*count or uncount*) The **cause** of something is what makes it happen: *Experts are investigating the cause of the crash.* □ *It was established that he had died of natural causes and had not been poisoned.* □ *Unemployment is still a major cause of urban unrest.* □ *the need to distinguish cause and effect.* **2** (*uncount*) You have **cause** for a certain feeling, or a certain kind of behaviour if you have a good reason or excuse for it; there is **cause** for something if there is a good reason for it: *There was no cause for such rudeness.* □ *You had plenty of cause for complaint.* □ *We have every cause to be satisfied.* □ *We were told there was no cause for alarm.* **3** A **cause** is an ideal or principle that people support and work to achieve; a charity working to achieve something with the help of public support can also be referred to as a **cause**: *It is hoped that the talks will further the cause of world peace.* □ *She does*

voluntary work for a number of good causes. □ *I don't mind giving money to a worthy cause.*

▻ ***verb*: causes, causing, caused**

One thing **causes** another if it makes it happen: *What is causing the delay?* □ *I can think of nothing that might have caused him to want to kill himself.* □ *I do apologize for causing you so much trouble.*

causeway /ˈkɔːzweɪ/ *noun*: **causeways**

A **causeway** is a raised road or track crossing marshy ground or shallow water.

caustic /ˈkɔːstɪk/ *adjective*

1 Caustic chemicals can burn or dissolve substances: *caustic soda.* **2** (*formal*) A **caustic** remark is cruel or sharply critical: *Her teacher's sarcastic smiles and caustic comments led to her lifelong dislike of mathematics* [*same as* **sarcastic, scathing**]

caution /ˈkɔːʃən/ *noun*; *verb*

▻ ***noun*: cautions**

1 (*uncount*) **Caution** is care taken to avoid possible danger or difficulty: *We must act with caution.* □ *A word of caution; don't take Scottish notes, because they only accept Bank of England ones.* **2** A **caution** is a warning not to do something again, especially from a police officer or someone in authority.

▻ ***verb*: cautions, cautioning, cautioned**

1 You **caution** someone when you warn them about possible danger: *They cautioned her against speaking to strangers.* **2** A police officer **cautions** someone who has been arrested when they tell them that anything they say can be used later as evidence in court.

cautionary /ˈkɔːʃənərɪ/ *adjective*

Cautionary remarks or stories give a warning about possible danger or problems: *a cautionary tale about a man who tried to fool the tax office.*

cautious /ˈkɔːʃəs/ *adjective*

You are **cautious** when you take care to avoid danger or problems: *She's a very cautious driver.* □ *We should try a more cautious approach.* — *adverb* **cautiously:** *They were warned to proceed cautiously.* [*same as* **careful, prudent**; *opposite* **careless, imprudent**]

cavalier /kavəˈlɪə(r)/ *adjective*

Someone has a **cavalier** attitude to something when they think it is not important enough to be serious about: *It was an indication of his cavalier attitude that he had not even bothered to sign the contract.* [*same as* **off-hand, scornful**]

cavalry /ˈkavəlrɪ/ *noun* (*with a singular or plural verb*)

1 The **cavalry** is the part of an army in which soldiers ride horses, *eg* on ceremonial occasions. **2** The **cavalry** is also the part of an army in which soldiers fight in armoured vehicles: *The cavalry were ordered to move south.*

cave /keɪv/ *noun*; *verb*

▻ ***noun*: caves**

A **cave** is a large natural hollow in a cliff or hillside, or underground.

▻ ***verb*: caves, caving, caved**

phrasal verb

cave in 1 When something such as a roof **caves in**, it collapses inwards: *The ceiling had caved in and there was plaster all over the floor.* **2** You **cave in** when you stop opposing someone or arguing against them, and agree to do what they ask: *The council finally caved in and approved the residents' proposals.*

caveman /ˈkeɪvmən/ *noun*: **cavemen**

Cavemen were primitive people that lived in caves in prehistoric times.

cavern /ˈkavən/ *noun*: **caverns**

A **cavern** is a large cave.

cavernous /ˈkavənəs/ *adjective* (*literary*)

A building, space or hole that is **cavernous** has a large, hollow interior like a cave: *the whale's cavernous mouth.*

caviar or **caviare** /ˈkavɪɑː(r)/ *noun* (*uncount*)

Caviar is the salted eggs of a fish called a sturgeon, used as food: *A small jar of caviar might cost you over ten pounds.*

cavity /ˈkavɪtɪ/ *noun*: **cavities**

1 A **cavity** is a hole or hollow area: *The insulating foam is sprayed into the cavity between the two walls.* **2** A **cavity** in a tooth is a hole caused by decay.

cavort /kəˈvɔːt/ *verb*: **cavorts, cavorting, cavorted**

People **cavort** when they jump or dance about in a noisy or excited way: *Later in the film, we are shown the two lovers cavorting on a sofa.*

CD /siː ˈdiː/ *noun*: **CDs**

1 A **CD** is a compact disc, a small circular piece of hard plastic that high-quality sound is recorded on, or large amounts of information are stored on, electronically: *Many of the old Beatles records are now available on CD.* **2** A **CD**, or **CD player**, is a compact disc player, a machine that plays compact discs.

cease /siːs/ *verb* (*formal*): **ceases, ceasing, ceased**

Something **ceases** when it stops or comes to an end; you **cease** to do something when you stop doing it: *This issue has ceased to be important.* □ *The company has ceased trading.*

ceasefire /ˈsiːsfaɪə(r)/ *noun*: **ceasefires**

A **ceasefire** is an agreement not to fight, agreed by the sides involved in a war.

ceaseless /ˈsiːslɪs/ *adjective* (*formal*)

Ceaseless is used to describe things that continue for a long time without a pause or break: *The public is fed up with this ceaseless squabbling between the political parties.* [*same as* **incessant**] — *adverb* **ceaselessly:** *It had been raining ceaselessly for a week.*

cedar /ˈsiːdə(r)/ *noun*: **cedars**

A **cedar** is a tall evergreen tree with needle-like leaves.

cede /siːd/ *verb* (*formal*): **cedes, ceding, ceded**

One person or country **cedes** something to another person or country when they give it to them formally and usually unwillingly: *Tudjman remained adamant that Croatia would not cede Krajina to Serbia.*

ceiling /ˈsiːlɪŋ/ *noun*: **ceilings**

1 The **ceiling** in a room is its inner roof: *a grand old building with a beautifully decorated ceiling.* [see picture at **living room**] **2** A **ceiling** is also an upper limit on things such as prices: *The government has refused to impose a ceiling on rents charged by private landlords.*

celebrate /ˈsɛləbreɪt/ *verb*: **celebrates, celebrating, celebrated**

1 You **celebrate** when you have a party or do something else enjoyable to mark a special occasion such as a birthday: *The whole family went out to a restaurant to celebrate my exam results.* **2** A priest **celebrates** a religious ceremony when they conduct or perform it: *Holy Communion is celebrated at 8.00 am.*

celebrated /ˈsɛləbreɪtɪd/ *adjective* (*formal*)

Celebrated means famous: *Scotland is celebrated for its beautiful scenery.*

celebration /sɛləˈbreɪʃən/ *noun* (*count or uncount*): **celebrations**

A **celebration** is a party or other enjoyable event that marks a special occasion: *New Year celebrations* □ *a party in celebration of the success of her first book.*

celebrity /sə'lɛbrɪtɪ/ *noun*: **celebrities**
A **celebrity** is a famous person: *She's one of our most popular television celebrities.*

celery /'sɛlərɪ/ *noun* (*uncount*)
Celery is a vegetable whose thick firm stalks are often eaten raw in salads: *a stick of celery.* [see picture at **vegetable**]

celestial /sɪ'lɛstɪəl/ *adjective* (*formal*)
Celestial describes things relating to the sky or to heaven: *stars and other celestial bodies.*

celibacy /'sɛlɪbəsɪ/ *noun* (*uncount*)
Celibacy is the state of being celibate: *priests who take a vow of celibacy.* [compare **chastity**]

celibate /'sɛlɪbət/ *adjective*
1 A person who is **celibate** for a certain period has no sexual intercourse during that time. **2 Celibate** also describes someone who does not get married or have sexual intercourse because of their religious beliefs.

cell /sɛl/ *noun*: **cells**
1 All living things are made up of **cells**, tiny units of living matter: *skin cells.* **2** A prison **cell** is a small room that a prisoner lives in: *three prisoners to a cell.* **3** A **cell** is also the room in a monastery or convent that a monk or nun lives in. **4** A **cell** is also a secret group of people existing within a larger group: *a Fascist cell within the Conservative Party.*

cellar /'sɛlə(r)/ *noun*: **cellars**
1 A **cellar** is an underground room in a house or other building, used for storing things, especially wine: *a beer cellar.* **2** A stock of wines is also referred to as a **cellar**: *The hotel's cuisine is excellent and they have a first-class cellar.*

cellist /'tʃɛlɪst/ *noun*: **cellists**
A **cellist** is someone who plays the cello.

cello /'tʃɛloʊ/ *noun*: **cellos**
A **cello** is a stringed musical instrument similar to a violin but much larger, that you play sitting down, with the instrument's neck against your shoulder: *As a child I had been taught to play the cello.* [see picture at **orchestra**]

cellophane /'sɛləfeɪn/ *noun* (*uncount, often adjectival; trademark*)
Cellophane is a thin transparent wrapping material: *a cellophane bag.*

cellular /'sɛljʊlə(r)/ *adjective*
1 Things with a **cellular** structure are made up of cells or many small separate compartments that are joined to form the whole: *Honey is stored in the cellular structure inside the hive known as the honeycomb.* **2 Cellular** is also used to describe a network of radio stations that pass signals from one to the other, such as is used to send signals to mobile telephones.

celluloid /'sɛljʊlɔɪd/ *noun* (*uncount; trademark*)
1 Celluloid is a kind of plastic that cinema film used to be made of. **2 Celluloid** is also used to refer to modern cinema film, and to cinema films in general.

Celsius /'sɛlsɪəs/ *noun* (*uncount*)
Celsius is the scale used on a centigrade thermometer, in which the freezing-point of water is 0° and its boiling-point 100°: *eighteen degrees Celsius.*

cement /sɪ'mɛnt/ *noun; verb*
▻ ***noun*** (*uncount*)
1 Cement is a grey powder that hardens to form concrete when water and sand are mixed with it. **2** Various types of glue are also referred to as **cement**.
▻ ***verb***: **cements, cementing, cemented**
1 You **cement** two things together when you stick them together. **2** Two people **cement** something such as a friendship when they make it firm or strong: *The President's visit has helped to cement Britain's relationship with America.*

cemetery /'sɛmətrɪ/ *noun*: **cemeteries**
A **cemetery** is an area of ground where dead people are buried, especially one that is not attached to a church. [*same as* **graveyard**; compare **churchyard**]

censor /'sɛnsə(r)/ *noun; verb*
▻ ***noun***: **censors**
A **censor** is a government offical who examines books, films, newspapers and broadcasts, and has the power to cut out any parts they consider offensive or undesirable in some way.
▻ ***verb***: **censors, censoring, censored**
To **censor** something such as a book or film is to officially remove parts of it before it is published or shown in public; to **censor** parts of something such as a book or film is to remove them: *Prisoners-of-war had their letters censored before they were sent.* □ *His reply was censored because of bad language.*

censorship /'sɛnsəʃɪp/ *noun* (*uncount*)
Censorship is the censoring of things such as books and films: *None of us are in favour of censorship.*

censure /'sɛnʃə(r)/ *noun; verb*
▻ ***noun*** (*uncount; formal*)
Censure is severe criticism or disapproval: *When the truth about the famous sportsman was revealed, the public's adoration soon turned to censure and contempt.*
▻ ***verb*** (*formal*): **censures, censuring, censured**
To **censure** someone is to criticize them severely or show strong disapproval of them, especially formally: *The minister was censured for negligence.*

census /'sɛnsəs/ *noun*: **censuses**
A **census** is an official survey of a country's population, finding out *eg* how old the population is and what people do for a living.

cent /sɛnt/ *noun*: **cents**
A **cent** is a hundredth part of the standard currency unit of several countries, *eg* the American dollar.

centenary /sɛn'tiːnərɪ/ or /sɛn'tɛnərɪ/ *noun*: **centenaries**
The **centenary** of some event is the 100th anniversary of it: *an exhibition to mark the centenary of the painter's death.*

center see **centre**.

centigrade /'sɛntɪgreɪd/ *noun* (*uncount*)
The **centigrade** scale of temperature is based on 100 degrees, with the freezing point of water at 0 and its boiling point at 100: *a centigrade thermometer.* [see also **Celsius**]

centimetre (*AmE* **centimeter**) /'sɛntɪmiːtə(r)/ *noun*: **centimetres**
A **centimetre** is a hundredth part of a metre.

centipede /'sɛntɪpiːd/ *noun*: **centipedes**
A **centipede** is a small creature whose long body is divided into many sections, each section having a pair of legs.

central /'sɛntrəl/ *adjective*
1 Something that is **central** is in the middle: *The roof is supported by a central pillar.* □ *central Glasgow.* **2** A place that is **central** is near the centre of a city and easy to reach: *Our flat is quite central; only minutes from the train station.* **3 Central** also means principal or most important: *the central character in the book* □ *This point is central to his whole argument.* **4 Central** is also used to describe groups which have control over a whole organization or area: *more power to local government, with central government having less influence.*

central heating /sɛntrəl 'hiːtɪŋ/ *noun* (*uncount*)
Central heating is a system in which heat from a

single boiler is carried by pipes to radiators throughout a whole building: *We're having central heating installed.*

centralize or **centralise** /ˈsɛntrəlaɪz/ *verb*: **centralizes, centralizing, centralized**
To **centralize** the administration of something is to bring all its regional branches or offices under the authority and guidance of a single head office or central office. [*opposite* **decentralise**] — *noun* (*uncount*) **centralization** /sɛntrəlaɪˈzeɪʃən/: *centralization of power in Brussels and Strasbourg.*

centre (*AmE* **center**) /ˈsɛntə(r)/ *noun*; *adjective*; *verb*
▻ ***noun***: **centres**
1 The **centre** of something is the middle of it, or the area or part at the middle: *She placed the vase at the centre of the table.* ▫ *These chocolates have soft centres.* ▫ *a journey to the centre of the Earth.* **2** A **centre** is a building or group of buildings where a particular activity takes place, or where facilities or services of a particular kind are available: *a sports centre* ▫ *the medical centre.* **3** In politics, the **centre** refers to those parties or groups whose ideas are moderate, neither left-wing nor right-wing. **4** Somewhere is a **centre** for an activity if it is the main place where that activity takes place within an area: *Frankfurt will become the financial centre of Europe.* **5** Someone or something is the **centre** of attention when everyone else is interested in them: *Her recently published memoirs are very much the centre of interest.*
▻ ***adjective:*** *The centre section of the table is removable.* ▫ *discussions between the left-wing and centre parties.*
▻ ***verb***: **centres, centring, centred**
You **centre** something when you place it in or at the middle: *The painting should be centred over the fireplace.*

> ***phrasal verb***
> Things **centre on** or **around** a person or thing when they are the chief subject of attention: *Discussions centred around plans for the general election.*

century /ˈsɛntʃəri/ *noun*: **centuries**
1 A **century** is any of the 100-year periods used in giving a date: *the 19th century.* **2** A **century** is also any period of 100 years: *Thousands of centuries passed before man's first appearance on Earth.*

ceramic /sɪˈramɪk/ *adjective*
Ceramic means made of clay that has been heated in a very hot oven, or kiln: *ceramic tiles.*

cereal /ˈsɪərɪəl/ *noun* (*count or uncount*): **cereals**
1 A **cereal** is any plant from which edible grain is obtained, such as wheat or rice: *farmers who grow cereals.* **2** **Cereal** is also breakfast food made from grain: *Try a different cereal.*

cerebral /ˈsɛrəbrəl/ *adjective* (*medical*)
Cerebral means relating to the brain: *She suffered a cerebral haemorrhage.*

ceremonial /sɛrəˈmoʊnɪəl/ *adjective*
Ceremonial means relating to, involving or used for ceremonies: *the ceremonial opening of Parliament.* — *adverb* **ceremonially:** *Converts have their heads ceremonially dipped in the river.*

ceremonious /sɛrəˈmoʊnɪəs/ *adjective*
Ceremonious means very formal and polite: *a ceremonious greeting.* ▫ *He opened the door for her and ushered her through with a ceremonious bow.* [compare **unceremonious**] — *adverb* **ceremoniously:** *He ceremoniously removed his hat and bowed his head in recognition.*

ceremony /ˈsɛrəməni/ *noun*: **ceremonies**
1 A **ceremony** is a formal or traditional event or set of actions carried out to mark a special occasion: *a wedding ceremony.* **2** (*uncount*) **Ceremony** is formality, or formal politeness: *She wanted to get married with proper ceremony.* ▫ *He was taken away in a police van and dumped, without ceremony, in a cell for the night.*
▻ ***phrase*** To **stand on ceremony** is to insist on behaving formally: *We don't stand on ceremony in this house.*

certain /ˈsɜːtən/ *adjective*; *determiner*; *pronoun*
▻ ***adjective***
1 You are **certain** about something or **certain** that it is so when you have no doubts about it: *I feel certain that I told him the correct address.* ▫ *He appeared to be so certain of his facts.* ▫ *'Can you be certain about the exact time you left?' 'Yes, I'm quite certain.'* ▫ *She could never be certain that he wasn't telling a lie.* [*same as* **sure, positive**; *opposite* **unsure, uncertain**] **2** You say you are not **certain** about something if you do not know about it: *I wasn't certain which train they were arriving on.* ▫ *I'm not certain how to get there.* ▫ *We weren't certain whether you'd want a ticket.* [*same as* **sure**] **3** Something is **certain** to happen if it is probably or definitely going to happen: *You're certain to get a reply from them tomorrow.* ▫ *She seems certain to get the job.* ▫ *It's certain to rain if we plan a walk.* ▫ *There are certain to be objections.* [*same as* **sure, bound**] **4** You act in some way so as to be **certain** of achieving something when you act so as not to risk failing to achieve it: *We'll have to apply now to be certain of getting good seats.* [*same as* **sure**] **5** Something that is **certain** is known to be true: *One thing is certain: she doesn't like him.* ▫ *It's more or less certain that they'll cancel the flight.* ▫ *It's not certain yet if she'll be fit to travel.* [*same as* **definite**; *opposite* **uncertain**] **6** You act in the **certain** knowledge that something will be so if you act knowing that you can expect it: *I asked him the question in the certain knowledge that he would tell me the truth.*
▻ ***determiner***
1 **Certain** is used to refer to a particular person or thing, or to particular people or things, without stating which, and to refer to particular amounts, without saying how much: *I met a certain friend of yours today.* ▫ *There's a certain matter I need to discuss with you.* ▫ *Certain householders will not be affected.* ▫ *In certain cases, we might ignore the rules.* ▫ *He can only be contacted at certain times of day.* ▫ *They tell you to do a certain thing and then they object when you do it.* ▫ *people below a certain income* ▫ *These trees don't grow beyond a certain height.* ▫ *A certain amount of progress has been made* [compare **particular**]. **2** **Certain** describes a quality that is noticeable but difficult to analyse: *The beard gave his appearance a certain authority.*
▻ ***pronoun:*** *Certain of the children continued to board during the holidays.* ▫ *Viewers may be distressed by certain of these pictures.*
▻ ***phrases*** **1** You know something **for certain** when you have no doubt about it: *We knew for certain that the documents were not in the house.* ▫ *I don't yet know for certain if they're coming.* **2** You **make certain** that something happens when you act so that there is no risk of it not happening; you **make certain** that something is the case when you investigate and see for yourself that it is: *We must make certain that everyone knows exactly what to do.* ▫ *Have you made certain that the trains are running tomorrow?* [*same as* **make sure, ensure**] **3** Something that is so **to a certain degree** or **to a certain extent** is partly so: *You're right to a certain extent.* ▫ *To a certain degree it's their own fault.*

certainly /ˈsɜːtənlɪ/ *adverb*
1 (*sentence adverb*) You use **certainly** with the mean-

ing 'definitely' or 'without doubt' to emphasize what you are saying: *It's certainly cheaper to go by bus.* □ *You certainly look better for your holiday.* □ *I'll certainly do my best to finish the work in time.* □ *She's better, certainly, but still very weak.* [*same as* **definitely**] **2** (*used as an answer*) **Certainly** expresses agreement with something said, or agreement to a request, proposal or suggestion; '**Certainly** not' is an emphatic way of saying 'no': *'Do you accept that this is the more efficient system?' 'Oh, certainly.'* □ *'I take it you're in favour?' 'Certainly I am.'* □ *'Would you mind moving your chair a little?' 'Certainly.'* □ *'Could I borrow your bike? 'Certainly.'* □ *'You'll give my regards to your parents, won't you?' 'Certainly I will'.* □ *'You won't tell anyone, will you?' 'Certainly not!'* [*same as* **definitely**, **of course**]

certainty /'sɜːtəntɪ/ *noun*: **certainties**
1 Something that is a **certainty** will definitely happen: *It's an absolute certainty that she'll get the job.* **2** (*uncount*) **Certainty** is the state of being sure about something: *I can say with certainty that you will not succeed.* □ *She can't identify the driver with any certainty.*

certificate /sə'tɪfɪkət/ *noun*: **certificates**
A **certificate** is an official document formally stating that certain facts are true or that something has been achieved: *a marriage certificate.* □ *a degree certificate.*

certify /'sɜːtɪfaɪ/ *verb*: **certifies, certifying, certified**
1 To **certify** something is to officially state that it is true: *She had no papers certifying that she was an American citizen.* **2** To **certify** someone is to officially declare that they are mad: *If she is certified, the court will commit her to a mental hospital.*

cesarean see **caesarean**.

cessation /sɛ'seɪʃən/ *noun* (*used in the singular; formal*)
There is a **cessation** of something when it stops or comes to an end: *The government has again called for a total cessation of terrorist activity.*

chafe /tʃeɪf/ *verb*: **chafes, chafing, chafed**
Something that **chafes** your skin rubs it and makes it sore: *The new shoes chafed her heels.*

chaff /tʃɑːf/ *noun* (*uncount*)
Chaff is the outer covering of wheat, or other grains used as food, that is separated from the grain during the process of threshing.

chagrin /'ʃagrɪn/ *noun* (*uncount; formal*)
Chagrin is a feeling of disappointment or irritation you have when you have failed or made a mistake: *Much to his chagrin, he found that he had posted his application too late.*

chain /tʃeɪn/ *noun*; *verb*
▷ ***noun***: **chains**
1 (*count or uncount*) A **chain** is a series of rings, especially of metal, connected together in a line: *He wore a gold chain.* □ *a bicycle chain.* [see picture at **bicycle**] □ *We need a longer piece of chain.* **2** A **chain** of things such as shops is a group of them that is owned by the same person or company: *a hotel chain.* **3** A **chain** of events is a series of things that happen one after another and are connected in some way.
▷ ***verb***: **chains, chaining, chained**
To **chain** something somewhere is to fasten it with a chain or chains: *Pens had to be chained to the counter so they wouldn't be stolen.* □ *The protestors had chained themselves to the factory gates.*

chain store /'tʃeɪn stɔː(r)/ *noun*: **chain stores**
A **chain store** is one of a series of shops, usually department stores, owned by the same company and each selling the same goods.

chair /tʃɛə(r)/ *noun*; *verb*
▷ ***noun***: **chairs**
1 A **chair** is a seat for one person, with legs and a support for the person's back: *dining-chairs* □ *The baby has her meals in a high-chair.* **2** At a formal meeting, the **chair** is the person officially in charge: *Members must make their comments to the chair.* **3** Someone who has the **Chair** in a certain subject at a university is the professor of that subject: *He had the Chair of English Language at Gothenberg University.*
▷ ***verb***: **chairs, chairing, chaired**
To **chair** a meeting is to be officially in charge of it: *She's been asked to chair the new committee.*

chairman /'tʃɛəmən/ *noun*: **chairmen**
The **chairman** of a formal meeting is the person, usually but not always a man, who is formally in charge: *She's chairman of the Public Accounts Committee.* — *noun* (*usually in the singular*) **chairmanship:** *The company returned to profitability under his chairmanship.*

chairperson /'tʃɛəpɜːsən/ *noun*: **chairpersons**
At a formal meeting, the **chairperson** is the person in formal charge of it: *She's been elected chairperson for this year.*

chairwoman /'tʃɛəwʊman/ *noun*: **chairwomen**
The **chairwoman** of a formal meeting is the woman formally in charge of it.

chalet /'ʃaleɪ/ *noun*: **chalets**
A **chalet** is a small simple house, especially made of wood and with a tall sloping roof: *a chalet in the Swiss mountains.*

chalk /tʃɔːk/ *noun*: **chalks**
1 (*uncount*) **Chalk** is a soft white rock, widely used in the form of small sticks, for writing with: *a piece of chalk.* **2** **Chalks** are pieces of chalk for writing and drawing with on a blackboard.

> ***phrasal verb***
> You **chalk up** a success when you achieve it: *Our basketball team has chalked up another victory.*

chalkboard /'tʃɔːkbɔːd/ (*AmE*) *noun*: **chalkboards**
A **chalkboard** is a blackboard.

chalky /'tʃɔːkɪ/ *adjective*: **chalkier, chalkiest**
Something **chalky** looks, feels, or tastes like chalk: *her chalky-white face.*

challenge /'tʃalɪndʒ/ *verb*; *noun*
▷ ***verb***: **challenges, challenging, challenged**
1 You **challenge** someone when you invite them to compete with you, often as a way of settling an argument: *I challenged him to a chess match.* **2** You also **challenge** someone when you demand that they justify their behaviour, or when you question their right to do something: *She challenged his decision to sack the women.* **3** Something that **challenges** you is an exciting test of your ability: *The ascent by the north face will challenge all but the most experienced climbers.*
▷ ***noun***: **challenges**
1 A **challenge** is something that represents an exciting or exacting test of your ability: *Bringing up a child is the toughest challenge most people will face.* **2** A **challenge** is also an invitation to compete against someone: *She refused to take up the challenge that was offered.* **3** Someone makes a **challenge** to something when they oppose it or question whether it is right or justified: *How would you deal with a challenge to your authority as manager?*

challenger /'tʃalɪndʒə(r)/ *noun*: **challengers**
In a contest, the **challenger** is the person trying to win the title held by his or her opponent: *The champion is a little taller than the challenger.*

challenging /ˈtʃalɪndʒɪŋ/ *adjective*
Something that is **challenging** is an exciting or exacting test of your ability: *a challenging profession.*

chamber /ˈtʃeɪmbə(r)/ *noun*: **chambers**
1 A **chamber** is a hall for formal meetings, *eg* of a parliament or or a local council: *Several councillors were absent from the chamber.* **2** A **chamber** is also a compartment with a particular function: *a glass-walled inspection chamber.* **3** (*used in the plural*) Lawyers' offices or consultation rooms are referred to as their **chambers**.

chambermaid /ˈtʃeɪmbəmeɪd/ *noun*: **chambermaids**
A **chambermaid** is a woman who cleans bedrooms in a hotel.

chamber music /ˈtʃeɪmbə mjuːzɪk/ *noun* (*uncount*)
Chamber music is classical music for a small group of players to perform in a room, rather than in a concert hall.

chamber of commerce /ˈtʃeɪmbər əvˈkɒmɜːs/ *noun*: **chambers of commerce**
A town's **chamber of commerce** is a group of local business people working together to improve local trade.

chameleon /kəˈmiːlɪən/ *noun*: **chameleons**
A **chameleon** is a kind of lizard that changes its skin colour to blend with its surroundings.

chamois /ˈʃamwɑː/ or /ˈʃamɪ/ *noun* (*uncount or count*)
Chamois, or **chamois leather**, is a type of very soft leather made from the skin of sheep or goats; a **chamois**, or **chamois leather**, is a piece of this used for polishing and cleaning *eg* metal or glass.

champ[1] /tʃamp/ *verb*: **champs, champing, champed**
To **champ** is to chew noisily: *horses champing away at straw.* [*same as* **chomp**]
▷ ***phrase*** (*informal*) You are **champing at the bit** when you are very impatient and eager to act.

champ[2] /tʃamp/ *noun* (*informal*): **champs**
A **champ** is a champion.

champagne /ʃamˈpeɪn/ *noun* (*uncount*)
Champagne is an expensive fizzy white wine made in the Champagne region of France and traditionally drunk at celebrations: *a bottle of champagne.*

champion /ˈtʃampɪən/ *noun*; *verb*
▷ ***noun***: **champions**
1 In a contest, competition or tournament, the **champion** is the person who defeats all others: *He's the school chess champion.* **2** A **champion** of a particular cause or principle is someone who has worked hard in support of that cause: *The minister is one of the champions of freedom of speech.*
▷ ***verb***: **champions, championing, championed**
To **champion** something is to support and promote it: *As a soloist and composer Bach did much to champion the pianoforte*

championship /ˈtʃampɪənʃɪp/ *noun*: **championships**
1 A **championship** is a contest held to find the best player or team: *the Wimbledon tennis championships.* **2** The **championship** is the title or position of champion: *competing for the middleweight championship of the world.*

chance /tʃɑːns/ *noun*; *verb*
▷ ***noun***: **chances**
1 There is a **chance** that something will happen when it is possible that it will happen: *There's still a chance she'll agree.* □ *We've got no chance of getting in without a ticket.* □ *What are his chances of being accepted?* **2** A **chance** is also an opportunity: *I didn't have the chance to talk to him before he left.* **3** (*uncount*) Something happens by **chance** when it was not planned or expected: *It was quite by chance that I met his brother at the supermarket.* □ *It was someone's chance remark that gave her the first big clue.*
▷ ***verb*** (*formal*): **chances, chancing, chanced**
You **chance** to do something when it happens by chance, without being planned or intended: *I chanced to catch a glimpse of the letter.*
▷ ***phrases*** **1** You **are in with a chance** when you have some hope of success. **2** (*informal*) You say **chances are** that something will happen when you think it may, or is quite likely to, happen: *He might arrive on time, but chances are he'll be late again.* **3** When someone doesn't **stand a chance** of succeeding, there is no possibility that they will succeed: *It's pointless applying; I don't stand a chance of even getting an interview.* [see also **off-chance**]

> ***phrasal verb***
> (*formal*) You **chance on** or **upon** something when you find it by chance: *Rummaging through the wardrobe, she chanced upon her old school uniform.*

chancellor /ˈtʃɑːnsələ(r)/ *noun*: **chancellors**
1 In certain European countries, the **chancellor** is the head of the government: *Chancellor Kohl.* **2** In Britain, the **Chancellor**, or **Chancellor of the Exchequer**, is the government minister responsible for finance.

chandelier /ʃandəˈlɪə(r)/ *noun*: **chandeliers**
A **chandelier** is a decorative frame with several candles or light-bulbs fitted on it, for hanging from a ceiling.

change /tʃeɪndʒ/ *verb*; *noun*
▷ ***verb***: **changes, changing, changed**
1 To **change** something is to make it different; something **changes** when it becomes different: *the processes that change ice into water and water into steam.* □ *The aircraft changed direction towards Mexico.* □ *I watched the expression on his face change from horror to relief.* □ *Halifax changed from a quiet provincial town into a bustling industrial centre.* □ *The film shows how a caterpillar changes into a butterfly.* □ *Wait for the traffic lights to change.* □ *You haven't changed at all.* [compare **alter**] **2** You **change** a particular thing when you replace it with a new or different one: *Could I change my appointment from Monday to Tuesday?* □ *We got a flat tyre and had to change the wheel.* □ *He was up a ladder changing a light bulb.* □ *She's been wanting to change her job for a while.* □ *The talk of babies was evidently boring him, so I tried to change the subject.* □ *He seems to have changed his plans yet again.* **3** You **change** trains or buses when you get off one train or bus and on to another in order to continue your journey towards your destination: *You'll have to change trains at Doncaster; there's no direct train to Nottingham.* □ *Change at Perth for Edinburgh.* **4** You **change**, get **changed**, or **change** your clothes, when you put on different ones: *I must go and change my shoes.* □ *Hadn't you better change out of those wet things?* □ *We were evidently expected to change into evening dress for dinner.* □ *It'll only take me a minute or two to change.* □ *She's gone to get changed.* **5** You **change** money when you exchange it for different notes or coins of the same total value: *Could you change this ten-pound note for two fives?* □ *They'll change money for you at the hotel, but the bank will give you a better exchange rate.* **6** You **change** a baby, or **change** its nappy or diaper, when you put a fresh one on it. **7** You **change** a bed, or **change** the sheets, when you put fresh sheets on it. — *adjective* **changing:** *the changing landscape* □ *changing attitudes to women.*
▷ ***noun***: **changes**
1 (*count or uncount*) There is a **change** in something

when it becomes different: *There's been a marked change in the weather; it's much colder today.* □ *We've had a few changes in the office; there's a new managing director, for a start.* □ *I've made a few changes to the original list.* □ *The doctors reported no change in his condition.* □ *I don't do much decorating, the excuse being that my husband doesn't like change.* **2** There is a **change** of a particular thing when it is replaced with a new or different one: *What this country needs is a change of government.* □ *We were to have gone to Corsica, but there's been a change of plan.* □ *The car's due for an oil change.* **3** A **change** of clothes is a fresh set of clothes for changing into later: *I packed my toothbrush and a change of underwear.* **4** (*uncount*) Your **change** is the money you get back when you pay for something with more than the exact amount that it costs: *I handed over a pound and got 38 pence change.* **5** (*uncount*) You have **change** for a note or a large coin when you have money of the same value in smaller notes or coins: *'That'll be £8.75, please.' 'I've only got a £20 note; do you have change?'* **6** (*uncount*) **Change** is coins as distinct from notes: *Could you give me some change for the phone?*

▻ ***phrases*** **1** For **change your mind** see **mind**. **2** Something happens **for a change** if it is different from what usually happens, especially pleasantly so: *I'm tired of visiting your parents every weekend; can't we have a weekend by ourselves for a change?* □ *It's nice to see you not working for a change.* **3** Something **makes a change** when it is pleasantly different from what usually happens: *This hot weather makes a refreshing change from the dreary British winter.* □ *It makes a pleasant change to see her smiling.*

phrasal verbs

change over You **change over** from one thing to another when you replace one thing with another: *The building trade, like every other line of business, has had to change over from feet and inches to the metric system.* [see also **changeover**]

change up or **change down** When you are driving, you **change up** when you put the car into a higher gear, and **change down** when you put it into a lower gear.

changeable /ˈtʃeɪndʒəbəl/ *adjective*
Something that is **changeable** often changes or is likely to change soon: *a period of changeable weather.*

changeover /ˈtʃeɪndʒoʊvə(r)/ *noun*: **changeovers**
A **changeover** is a complete change from one thing to another: *the changeover from one accounting system to another* [see also **change over** at **change**]

channel /ˈtʃanəl/ *noun; verb*
▻ ***noun***: **channels**
1 A **channel** is a passage that water flows along, whether natural, like a river, or man-made, like a canal: *a network of irrigation channels in the desert.* **2** A **channel** is also a fixed frequency on which television or radio programmes are broadcast: *There's sport on all the other channels.* □ *Remember to change channels at 10 o'clock; I want to watch the film.* **3** When you speak of something being done through certain **channels**, you are referring to the processes involved in getting it done, or the people you have to deal with: *We applied for a grant through the usual channels.* **4** The **Channel** or English **Channel** is the stretch of water separating Britain and France, and linking the North Sea to the Atlantic Ocean.
▻ ***verb***: **channels, channelling** (*AmE* **channeling**), **channelled** (*AmE* **channeled**)
You **channel** money, energy or another resource into something when you use it for that thing: *All profits from our existing business will be channelled into the new project.*

chant /tʃɑːnt/ *verb; noun*
▻ ***verb***: **chants, chanting, chanted**
To **chant** something is to keep repeating it, especially loudly and rhythmically: *football crowds chanting the name of their favourite player.*
▻ ***noun***: **chants**
A **chant** is a **1** word or phrase repeated loudly and rhythmically. **2** a prayer or religious song sung on only a few notes.

chaos /ˈkeɪɒs/ *noun* (*uncount*)
Chaos is a state of complete confusion or disorder: *There was chaos in the office when the central computer broke down.*

chaotic /keɪˈɒtɪk/ *adjective*
A situation is **chaotic** when there is complete confusion or disorder: *She leads a very chaotic life, always running around doing several things at once.* □ *There were chaotic scenes in shops as people found out that food stocks would soon run out.*

chap /tʃap/ *noun* (*informal*): **chaps**
A **chap** is a man or boy: *He's rather a handsome chap.*

chapel /ˈtʃapəl/ *noun*: **chapels**
1 A **chapel** inside a church is a separate area with its own altar, for private worship. **2** A **chapel** is also a small church attached to a house, school or other institution.

chaperone or **chaperon** /ˈʃapəroʊn/ *noun; verb*
▻ ***noun***: **chaperones**
A **chaperone** is an older woman who accompanies young unmarried women on social occasions.
▻ ***verb***: **chaperones, chaperoning, chaperoned**
To **chaperone** a young woman is to act as her chaperone.

chaplain /ˈtʃaplɪn/ *noun*: **chaplains**
A **chaplain** is a priest attached to a school, hospital or other institution, or to the armed forces.

chapped /ˈtʃapt/ *adjective*
Your skin is **chapped** when it sore or cracked because it is too dry.

chapter /ˈtʃaptə(r)/ *noun*: **chapters**
1 A **chapter** is one of the numbered or titled sections that a book is divided into: *She dies at the end of the fourth chapter.* **2** A period of time, especially one in someone's life characterized by certain experiences, can be referred to as a **chapter**: *That was an unfortunate chapter in my life.* [*same as* **episode**]

character /ˈkarəktə(r)/ *noun*: **characters**
1 A person's **character** consists of the combination of qualities that make up their personality: *I've never seen that cruel side of his character.* □ *The film manages to capture the character of the city.* **2** The **characters** in a book, film or play are people who feature in it. **3** (*uncount*) When you say that someone has **character**, you mean that they have admirable qualities such as determination, courage and honesty. **4** (*uncount*) A place that has **character** has interesting qualities that make it unusual or individual: *a house with great character.* **5** (*informal*) A **character** is also a person of a particular kind: *She's an odd character.* **6** When you describe someone as a **character**, you mean that they are known by others for being amusing or eccentric. **7** (*formal*) A **character** is also a letter, number or other written or printed symbol: *Chinese characters.*
▻ ***phrase*** When someone behaves **in character** their behaviour is typical of them; when they behave **out of character** they behave in way that is untypical of

them: *I've never seen him get so angry; it's quite out of character.*

characteristic /karəktə'rıstık/ *noun; adjective*
▻ ***noun***: **characteristics**
A **characteristic** of someone or something is one of their typical features or qualities: *Is a desire to show off a characteristic of all actors?*
▻ ***adjective***
Characteristic features or qualities are typical of a particular person or thing: *the gently sloping hills so characteristic of northern Germany.* — *adverb* **characteristically:** *He gave a characteristically determined performance.*

characterize or **characterise** /'karəktəraız/ *verb*: **characterizes, characterizing, characterized**
1 One thing **characterizes** another if it is a typical feature of it: *the materialism and greed that characterized the Britain of the late '80s.* **2** You **characterize** someone or something by describing what their typical features or qualities are: *He was characterized by his teachers as lazy and dull.* [*same as* **portray**, **represent**]

charade /ʃə'rɑːd/ (*AmE* /ʃə'reıd/) *noun*: **charades**
You refer to someone's actions as a **charade** when they have no serious intentions and only want to give the appearance of taking action: *The council then went through the charade of consulting local residents.*

charcoal /'tʃɑːkoʊl/ *noun* (*uncount*)
Charcoal is a black substance produced by partially burning wood, used in the form of sticks for drawing, or burnt as a fuel: *a charcoal sketch.*

charge /tʃɑːdʒ/ *verb; noun*
▻ ***verb***: **charges, charging, charged**
1 You **charge** someone a certain amount of money for something you are selling to them, or for something you are doing for them, when you ask them to pay that amount: *They're charging £100 less at the other shop for exactly the same computer.* □ *How much does your window-cleaner charge?* □ *What would you charge to wash this car?* □ *They charged us only £15 each for bed and breakfast.* **2** You **charge** something to someone when you send them the bill for it: *If you buy any books for use on the job, charge them to the firm.* □ *Handle the glass on display with care. Breakages will be charged to the customer.* **3** Someone **is charged** by the police with a crime or other offence when they are officially accused of it: *They have charged her with driving without due care and attention.* **4** Animals or troops **charge** when they rush forward to attack something: *There was a worrying moment when I thought the bull was going to charge at us.* □ *The colonel gave the order to charge.* **5** You **charge** a battery when you pass an electric current through it to increase its power or lengthen its life.
▻ ***noun***: **charges**
1 You pay a **charge** for a service or for something you buy when you pay the price that is asked for it: *We make no charge for repairs while the machine is under guarantee.* □ *There will be an increase in postal charges in the new year.* [see note at **cost**] **2** (*uncount or used in the singular*) You have **charge** of something when you are responsible for looking after, managing or controlling it: *The police arrived and took charge of the situation.* □ *The five children had been left in the charge of a teenage girl.* □ *The department is in your charge while I'm away.* [see also **in charge of** below] **3** A **charge** is an official accusation made against someone that they have committed a crime or offence: *Lack of evidence forced the police to drop the charges against him.* □ *The prosecution have changed the charge of murder to one of manslaughter.*
▻ ***phrases*** **1** Something that is **free of charge** costs nothing: *The solicitor kindly gave his advice free of charge.* **2** You are **in charge of** something or someone if you are the person who is responsible for looking after them or controlling them: *Who was supposed to be in charge of the group?* □ *I was put in charge of the wedding arrangements.* □ *I want to speak to the person in charge, please.* **3** You **prefer charges** against someone when you make an official accusation against them, which has to be dealt with in a court of law.

charged /tʃɑːdʒd/ *adjective*
You might describe a situation as **charged** if there is a lot of excitement, anger or other strong emotion: *the charged atmosphere in the meeting-room.*

charisma /kə'rızmə/ *noun* (*uncount*)
When someone has **charisma** they have a special ability to attract, influence and inspire people: *Do modern political leaders lack charisma?*

charismatic /karız'matık/ *adjective*
A **charismatic** person has charisma: *the Liberal Party and their charismatic leader.*

charitable /'tʃarıtəbəl/ *adjective*
1 Someone who is **charitable** is kind and understanding in their attitude to others: *That's not a very charitable description of her.* **2** **Charitable** organizations do work to help and support people in need: *The money was raised by a number of charitable institutions.*

charity /'tʃarıtı/ *noun*: **charities**
1 (*count or uncount*) A **charity** is an organization that raises money to help people in need: *She does voluntary work for a number of local charities.* □ *Some people give large portions of their income to charity.* □ *Oxfam, Save the Children, and other charities* **2** (*uncount*) **Charity** is kindness and understanding in your attitude towards other people: *You should try to show a little more charity.* **3** (*uncount*) **Charity** is also money given to people who need it: *She was far too proud to accept charity from her friends.*

charlatan /'ʃɑːlətən/ *noun*: **charlatans**
A **charlatan** is someone who deceives people by pretending to have knowledge or special skill, especially in medicine: *He has been exposed as a charlatan; none of his 'miracle cures' were genuine.*

charm /tʃɑːm/ *noun; verb*
▻ ***noun***: **charms**
1 (*uncount*) Someone who has **charm** has an attractive personality, and the ability to make people like them. **2** (*uncount*) A place that has **charm** is pleasant, attractive and interesting. **3** A **charm** is an object believed to have magical powers. **4** A **charm** is also one of several small ornaments worn on a bracelet.
▻ ***verb***: **charms, charming, charmed:** *I was charmed by her quiet manner and soft voice.* — *adjective* **charming:** *I found her a very charming woman.* □ *They have a charming little cottage by the river.*

charmer /'tʃɑːmə(r)/ *noun*: **charmers**
When you refer to someone as a **charmer** you mean that they have a very attractive personality which makes people like them immediately: *Janey's such a little charmer everyone finds her irresistible.*

charred /'tʃɑːd/ *adjective*
Something that is **charred** is black through being burnt: *the charred remains of the hat.*

chart /tʃɑːt/ *noun; verb*
▻ ***noun***: **charts**
1 A **chart** is a sheet of information presented in the form of a table, diagram or graph: *a chart showing the patient's temperature and blood pressure* **2** A map of

an area of sea, used by sailors, is a **chart**. **3** (*used in the plural*) The **charts** are the official lists of the best-selling pop records in a particular week: *Their new single shot to the top of the charts.*

▻ ***verb***: **charts, charting, charted**

To **chart** something is to observe and record its progress: *We charted the growth of all four animals over a six-month period.*

charter /'tʃɑːtə(r)/ *noun; verb; adjective*

▻ ***noun***: **charters**

A **charter** is an official document stating that a certain group of people have particular rights and privileges: *The introduction of a passengers' charter has done little to improve the service on our railways.*

▻ ***verb***: **charters, chartering, chartered**

To **charter** an aircraft or other vehicle is to hire it for private use: *The company has chartered a jet for the trip.*

▻ ***adjective***

A **charter** plane is one hired privately, usually by a holiday company: *charter flights to and from Glasgow.*

chartered /'tʃɑːtəd/ *adjective*

A **chartered** accountant, surveyor or librarian has a professional qualification in their field.

chase /tʃeɪs/ *verb; noun*

▻ ***verb***: **chases, chasing, chased**

1 You **chase** someone when you go after them in order to catch them: *I chased him for about a mile and then gave up.* **2** You **chase** someone, or **chase** them away, when you force them to leave: *She chased the thieves from the shop.* **3** To **chase** something is to try to obtain it: *too many applicants chasing too few jobs.*

▻ ***noun***: **chases:** *The robbers' car was too fast and the police gave up the chase.*

chasm /'kazm/ *noun*: **chasms**

1 A **chasm** is a very deep crack in the ground: *One of the climbers slipped and nearly fell into a chasm.* **2** When there is a **chasm** between two people or things they are very different in some way, *eg* in their opinions or feelings: *In spite of the intellectual chasm between them, they are happy in their partnership.*

chaste /tʃeɪst/ *adjective* (*old*)

A person who is **chaste** does not have sex at all, or only with their husband or wife: *She's lived a completely chaste life.* [see also **chastity**]

chasten /'tʃeɪsən/ *verb* (*formal*): **chastens, chastening, chastened**

You **are chastened** by something when it makes you feel guilty about your bad behaviour and keen to behave better in future: *She was chastened by the sight of the little boy's tears.*

chastise /tʃa'staɪz/ *verb* (*formal*): **chastises, chastising, chastised**

To **chastise** someone is to scold or punish them: *The boys were chastised for failing to complete their homework.*

chastity /'tʃastɪtɪ/ *noun* (*uncount*)

Chastity is the state or quality of being chaste: *All the nuns are required to take a vow of chastity.*

chat /tʃat/ *verb; noun*

▻ ***verb***: **chats, chatting, chatted**

People **chat** when they talk in a friendly, informal way, usually about unimportant things: *The two of them chatted away for hours.* ▫ *What were you chatting about?*

▻ ***noun*** (*count or uncount*): **chats**

A **chat** is a friendly, informal conversation: *We had a nice chat about the children.*

phrasal verb

(*informal*) To **chat** someone **up** is to try to attract them sexually by talking to them in a friendly or amusing way: *When I got back, some young lad was chatting up my wife.*

chatter /'tʃatə(r)/ *verb; noun*

▻ ***verb***: **chatters, chattering, chattered**

1 To **chatter** is to talk, especially fast or noisily and usually about unimportant matters: *I couldn't hear the film with her chattering away all the time.* **2** You teeth **chatter** when they keep knocking together because you are cold or frightened. **3** Animals such as monkeys and some birds **chatter** when they make their typical high-pitched cry.

▻ ***noun*** (*uncount*): *schoolgirl chatter.*

chatterbox /'tʃatəbɒks/ *noun*: **chatterboxes** (*informal*)

A **chatterbox** is a person who likes to talk a lot, especially about unimportant things.

chatty /'tʃatɪ/ *adjective*: **chattier, chattiest** (*informal*)

Someone who is **chatty** likes to talk to people in a friendly way: *She's a lively, chatty young woman.*

chauffeur /'ʃoʊfə(r)/ *noun*: **chauffeurs**

A **chauffeur** is a person employed to drive someone around in a car.

chauvinist /'ʃoʊvənɪst/ *noun*: **chauvinists**

1 A man who is a 'male **chauvinist**' behaves in a way that shows he thinks men are superior to women. **2** A **chauvinist** is also someone who regards people from other countries as inferior. — *noun* (*uncount*) **chauvinism:** *Male chauvinism at last appears to be in retreat.*

chauvinistic /ʃoʊvə'nɪstɪk/ *adjective*

You describe a person or their behaviour as **chauvinistic** if they regard their own country and its people as superior in every way to all others: *There is a thin line between national pride and a chauvinistic disdain for other nations.*

cheap /tʃiːp/ *adjective*: **cheaper, cheapest**

1 Something is **cheap** when it is low in price, or less than the usual price: *This jewellery is actually quite cheap.* ▫ *Electric heaters are not cheap to run.* ▫ *They are selling some of last year's stock cheap.* **2** You also describe something as **cheap** when it is low in price but of poor quality: *a cheap paperback edition.* **3** Something is also **cheap** when people think it is worth very little: *War makes human life seem cheap.* **4** **Cheap** jokes or comments make fun of other people in a cruel way.

▻ ***phrase*** You get something **on the cheap** when you spend less than the usual amount of money on it, often because it is of inferior quality: *They had their house decorated on the cheap.*

cheat /tʃiːt/ *verb; noun*

▻ ***verb***: **cheats, cheating, cheated**

1 Someone **cheats** when they behave dishonestly, especially when they deceive others: *It wasn't the first time he'd cheated in an exam.* ▫ *He'd been caught cheating at cards.* **2** To **cheat** someone out of something is to get it from them by deceiving them, or prevent them from having it by behaving dishonestly: *She believes she was cheated out of her inheritance.* ▫ *He feels cheated by the judicial system.*

▻ ***noun***: **cheats**

A **cheat** is a person who cheats.

check /tʃɛk/ *verb; noun*

▻ ***verb***: **checks, checking, checked**

1 You **check** something when you make sure that it is true, satisfactory, safe or properly done: *Check your work for mistakes* ▫ *I think he is free; I'll just check* *with his secretary.* □ *Check that all doors and windows are firmly shut.* □ *I'll check if the dinner's ready* □ *When she checked on the children they were both fast asleep.* **2** You **check** something when you find it out: *He looked for a clock to check the time.* **3** To **check** something is to stop or prevent it: *He nearly swore, but checked himself.* □ *Measures are being taken to check the spread of the infection.*

▻ ***noun***: **checks**

1 A **check** is an act of checking: *We make frequent checks on his progress.* □ *regular security checks.* **2** (*count or uncount, often adjectival*) A **check** is a pattern of squares: *a check shirt.* □ *a suit in a bold black and white check.* **3** (*AmE*) A **check** is **a** a cheque. **b** a restaurant bill: *Could we have the check, please?* **c** a tick.

> ***phrasal verbs***
> **check in** You **check in**, *eg* at a hotel or airport, when you go to an official desk and show your tickets or announce your arrival: *Passengers are asked to check in half an hour before their flight leaves.* □ *We checked into a small hotel just off the main road.* [see also **check-in**]
> **check out 1** You **check out** of a hotel when you pay the bill and leave: *We checked out at around 12 o'clock.* [see also **checkout**] **2** You **check** something **out** when you examine it or find out about it: *She phoned the council to check out the procedure for applying for an education grant.*
> **check up** You **check** information **up** when you find out if it is true or accurate by consulting a reliable source: *I wasn't sure if what he told me was true, so I checked up.* [see also **check-up**]
> **check up on** You **check up on** someone when you obtain information about them, usually in order to find out if they are doing or not doing something, or to decide if they are suitable for something.

checked /tʃɛkt/ *adjective*
Something that is **checked** has a pattern of squares on it: *checked curtains.*

checkered see **chequered**.

check-in /'tʃɛkɪn/ *noun*: **check-ins**
A **check-in**, or **check-in** desk, is a desk at an airport where passengers' tickets are checked and luggage weighed and accepted for loading. [see also **check in** at **check**]

checkout /'tʃɛkaʊt/ *noun*: **checkouts**
The **checkout** in a shop or supermarket is the desk where you pay. [see also **check out** at **check**]

check-up /'tʃɛkʌp/ *noun*: **check-ups**
A **check-up** is a general examination carried out by a doctor or dentist.

cheek /tʃiːk/ *noun*; *verb*

▻ ***noun***: **cheeks**

1 Your **cheeks** are the fleshy sides of your face below the eyes: *She slapped him across the cheek.* **2** (*uncount, used in the singular*; *informal*) **Cheek** is rude or disrespectful behaviour: *a child with a lot of cheek* □ *You've got a cheek, talking to my wife like that!* [see picture at **body**]

▻ ***verb***: **cheeks**, **cheeking**, **cheeked** (*informal*)

To **cheek** someone is to behave in a rude or disrespectful way towards them: *You mustn't cheek the teacher.*

cheekbone /'tʃiːkboʊn/ *noun*: **cheekbones**
Your **cheekbones** are the bones at the top of the cheeks, that stick out below the eye.

cheeky /'tʃiːkɪ/ *adjective*: **cheekier**, **cheekiest**
You are **cheeky** to someone when you behave in a rude or disrespectful way towards them: *She's a really cheeky little girl.* [*same as* **impudent**] — *adverb* **cheekily:** *The little boy smiled cheekily.*

cheer /tʃɪə(r)/ *verb*; *noun*

▻ ***verb***: **cheers**, **cheering**, **cheered**

1 To **cheer** is to shout encouragement or approval, *eg* as a spectator may do to someone playing a sport: *When he volunteered to go up on stage his friends cheered and whistled.* □ *We stood on the terrace laughing, joking and cheering our team.* **2** When you **are cheered** by something, it makes you feel happier or more hopeful: *They were cheered by the news that there had been some survivors.*

▻ ***noun***: **cheers**

1 A **cheer** is a shout of approval or encouragement: *She was spurred on by the cheers of the crowd.* **2** (*used in the plural*) People say **'cheers'** to each other as a toast when they start to drink an alcoholic drink. **3** (*used in the plural*) Some people also say **'cheers'** as an informal way of saying goodbye or thank you.

> ***phrasal verbs***
> **cheer on** You **cheer** someone **on** when you shout encouragement to them: *We all jumped about cheering on our horse.*
> **cheer up** You **cheer** someone **up** when you make them feel happier or more hopeful; they **cheer up** when they become happier or more hopeful.

cheerful /'tʃɪəfʊl/ *adjective*
1 A **cheerful** person is happy in a lively, energetic way: *Somehow, she was able to remain cheerful throughout the crisis.* [*same as* **jolly**] **2** Something that is **cheerful** makes you feel happy: *a cheerful tune.* □ *The walls were painted a cheerful yellow.* — *noun* (*uncount*) **cheerfulness**: *her natural cheerfulness.*

cheerfully /'tʃɪəfʊlɪ/ *adverb*
1 You do something **cheerfully** when you do it in a happy, lively way: *The children sat at the back, singing away cheerfully.* **2** If you say you could **cheerfully** do something, especially something that others might think was wrong or cruel, you mean you would get pleasure from doing it: *He's such an arrogant man*; *I could cheerfully slap him sometimes.*

cheerio /tʃɪərɪ'oʊ/ *interjection* (*informal*)
Cheerio means goodbye.

cheerless /'tʃɪəlɪs/ *adjective*
Something **cheerless** makes you feel gloomy or depressed: *The lounge was a drab, cheerless room.*

cheers see **cheer**.

cheery /'tʃɪərɪ/ *adjective*: **cheerier**, **cheeriest**
Someone is **cheery** when they are happy in a lively, energetic way: *I was a little surprised by such a cheery welcome from people I had not met before.*

cheese /tʃiːz/ *noun* (*uncount or count*): **cheeses**
1 Cheese is a solid food made from milk: *The French produce over two hundred types of cheese.* □ *This is one of the nicest cheeses I've ever tasted.* **2** Some other foods not made from milk, especially ones for spreading on bread, are called **cheese**: *a jar of lemon cheese.*

▻ ***phrase*** (*informal*) If you are annoyed or angry, you can say you are **cheesed off**: *I was a bit cheesed off about having to pay extra.*

cheesecake /'tʃiːzkeɪk/ *noun* (*count or uncount*): **cheesecakes**
A **cheesecake** is a cake consisting of a base of biscuit topped with a creamy mixture flavoured with cheese and often decorated with fruit: *a slice of strawberry cheesecake.*

cheetah /'tʃiːtə/ *noun*: **cheetahs**

A **cheetah** is a large long-legged spotted wild animal of the cat family that can run very fast.

chef /ʃɛf/ *noun*: **chefs**
A **chef** is a cook in a restaurant or hotel, often the chief cook.

chemical /'kɛmɪkəl/ *adjective*; *noun*
▻ ***adjective***
Chemical means relating to chemistry or made by the processes of chemistry: *a course in chemical engineering* □ *chemical substances.*
▻ ***noun***: **chemicals**
A **chemical** is a substance made by the processes of chemistry: *the industrial use of hazardous chemicals.*

chemist /'kɛmɪst/ *noun*: **chemists**
1 A **chemist** is someone who prepares and sells medicines. **2** A **chemist** or **chemist's** is a shop selling medicines and usually also toiletries and cosmetics: *She got them from the chemist's in the high street.* **3** A **chemist** is also a scientist specializing in chemistry.

chemistry /'kɛmɪstrɪ/ *noun* (*uncount*)
Chemistry is the scientific study of the physical nature of solids, liquids and gases, and of what happens to them when they are mixed: *an A-level in chemistry* □ *a chemistry degree.*

cheque (*AmE* **check**) /tʃɛk/ *noun*: **cheques**
A **cheque** is a printed form from your bank used as money. You write the amount of money that you're spending and the name of the person you are paying on it and sign it, so that the money can be taken out of your account: *I'll write a cheque* □ *You can pay by cheque.*

chequebook (*AmE* **checkbook**) /'tʃɛkbʊk/ *noun*: **chequebooks**
A **chequebook** is a book of cheques ready for use, with your name printed on them.

cheque card /'tʃɛk kɑːd/ *noun*: **cheque cards**
A **cheque card** is a small plastic card issued by a bank which guarantees that cheques written by the person named on the card will be honoured by the bank up to a stated limit, *eg* £100: *We regret that cheques cannot be accepted without a cheque card.* [compare **credit card**]

chequered (*AmE* **checkered**) /'tʃɛkəd/ *adjective*
1 Chequered means patterned with squares of alternating colour: *a chequered flag.* **2** A person's life or career is described as **chequered** when there have been periods of both sadness and happiness or good and bad luck.

cherish /'tʃɛrɪʃ/ *verb*: **cherishes, cherishing, cherished**
1 You **cherish** someone when you care for them lovingly: *a sweet woman, who asked for nothing but to love and cherish her husband* **2** When you **cherish** something such as a tradition or privilege you want very much to keep or preserve it. **3** You **cherish** hopes and memories when you keep them in your mind because they make you feel happy: *For the rest of her life Beth would cherish the time they had spent together.* □ *He had long cherished a a secret fantasy, in which he led an effortlessly successful life.*

cherry /'tʃɛrɪ/ *noun*: **cherries**
A **cherry** is a small round red or dark purple fruit with a stone at the centre: *rows of cherry trees.* [see picture at **fruit**]

chess /tʃɛs/ *noun* (*uncount*)
Chess is a board game for two players who have 16 playing-pieces each. The pieces are moved in different ways, and the object of the game is to trap your opponent's king: *a game of chess.*

chest /tʃɛst/ *noun*: **chests**
1 Your **chest** is the part of your body between the neck and the stomach, where the heart and lungs are: *men with hairy chests.* [see picture at **body**] **2** A **chest** is a big strong box used for storage or transport: *an old tea chest.*
▻ ***phrase*** (*informal*) When you **get something off your chest** you tell someone about something that has been annoying or worrying you.

chestnut /'tʃɛsnʌt/ *noun*: **chestnuts**
A **chestnut** is a shiny reddish-brown nut that exists in two varieties, one of which can be eaten: *roast chestnuts.*

chest of drawers /tʃɛst əv 'drɔːəz/ *noun*: **chests of drawers**
A **chest of drawers** is a large piece of furniture fitted with drawers, usually for holding clothes. [see picture at **bedroom**]

chew /tʃuː/ *verb*: **chews, chewing, chewed**
1 You **chew** food when you use your teeth to break it up before swallowing it: *I wish he didn't chew so loudly.* **2** To **chew** something is also to bite it, or damage or destroy it by biting: *The dog chewed a hole in my curtains.*
▻ ***phrase*** (*informal*) When you say that someone **has bitten off more than they can chew**, you mean that they have chosen to do something that is too difficult for them.

> ***phrasal verb***
> (*informal*) You **chew** something **over** when you spend time considering or discussing it: *We had a few problems to chew over.* □ *They meet regularly to chew over the problems which arise at workd.*

chewing gum /'tʃuːɪŋ gʌm/ *noun* (*uncount*)
Chewing gum is a sweet, usually mint-flavoured substance that you chew for long periods but do not swallow.

chick /tʃɪk/ *noun*: **chicks**
A **chick** is a baby bird.

chicken /'tʃɪkɪn/ *noun*: **chickens**
1 A **chicken** is a kind of bird kept for its eggs and meat. **2** (*count or uncount*) A **chicken** is also this bird used as food: *Would anyone like another piece of chicken?* **3** (*informal*) People call someone who is afraid or lacks courage **chicken**, or a **chicken**.

> ***phrasal verb***
> (*informal*) Someone **chickens out** of something when they decide not to do it because they are afraid: *I could tell she was going to chicken out.*

chickenpox /'tʃɪkɪnpɒks/ *noun* (*uncount*)
Chickenpox is an infectious disease, especially of childhood, which produces a fever and a rash of raised itchy spots.

chide /tʃaɪd/ *verb* (*formal*): **chides, chiding, chided**
To **chide** someone is to scold them: *Our parents were always quick to chide us when it came to bad table manners.* □ *'Aren't the children asleep yet?' she chided gently.*

chief /tʃiːf/ *noun*; *adjective*
▻ ***noun***: **chiefs**
1 The **chief** of a tribe of people is their leader. **2** The leader of any group or organization is also often referred to as the **chief**: *a meeting of NATO defence chiefs.*
▻ ***adjective***
1 The **chief** officer or official of any kind is the most senior in rank: *the chief accountant.* **2 Chief** means main, principal or most important: *Keeping taxes down is our chief concern.*

chiefly /'tʃiːflɪ/ *adverb*
Chiefly means mainly: *That's chiefly why we are here.*

chieftain /'tʃiːftən/ *noun*: **chieftains**
A **chieftain** is the leader of a tribe or clan: *great Scottish chieftains like the Campbells of Argyll and Breadalbane.*

chiffon /'ʃɪfɒn/ *noun* (*uncount*)
Chiffon is a thin, almost transparent, fabric made of silk or nylon: *a chiffon scarf.*

chilblain /'tʃɪlbleɪn/ *noun*: **chilblains**
Chilblains are painful red swellings on the toes or fingers, caused by cold or poor blood supply.

child /tʃaɪld/ *noun*: **children**
1 A **child** is a young person who is not yet an adult: *a game for children between the ages of 5 and 11.* **2** Your son or daughter of any age is also your **child**: *My children are all married now, and some have children of their own.*

childbearing /'tʃaɪldbeərɪŋ/ *noun* (*uncount, often adjectival*)
Childbearing is the process of giving birth to babies: *a condition affecting women of childbearing age.*

childbirth /'tʃaɪldbɜːθ/ *noun* (*uncount*)
Childbirth is the act or process of giving birth to a child: *the pain of childbirth* □ *She died in childbirth.*

childhood /'tʃaɪldhʊd/ *noun* (*uncount*)
Your **childhood** is the first part of your life, during which you are a child: *Very few of us remember the early part of our childhood.*

childish /'tʃaɪldɪʃ/ *adjective* (*derogatory*)
You describe someone as **childish** if you think they behave in a silly way more typical of a child than an adult: *She has a childish need to impress other people.* — *adverb* **childishly:** *You're behaving childishly.*

childless /'tʃaɪldləs/ *adjective*
People, especially married couples, are **childless** if they have no children or cannot have any children.

childlike /'tʃaɪldlaɪk/ *adjective*
You might describe someone as **childlike** when they are like a child in some way: *childlike innocence* □ *a frank, childlike smile.*

childminder /'tʃaɪldmaɪndə(r)/ *noun*: **childminders**
A **childminder** is someone who looks after children while their parents go out to work, usually in the childminder's home. [compare **nanny**]

children /'tʃɪldrən/ *noun*
Children is the plural of **child**: *children's books* □ *children's games* □ *They have no children.*

chili see **chilli**.

chill /tʃɪl/ *noun; verb*
▻ ***noun***: **chills**
1 A **chill** is a feeling of coldness: *a wintry chill in the air.* **2** When you catch a **chill** you catch a cold which also produces a fever. **3** A **chill** is also a sudden feeling of fear or anxiety: *When I heard the wolves howling, a chill ran down my spine.*
▻ ***verb***: **chills, chilling, chilled**
1 You **chill** food or drink when you make it very cold: *a light wine that can be served chilled or at room temperature.* **2** You **are chilled** by something when it frightens you: *The thought that he might be in the same building chilled me to the heart.*

chilli or **chili** /tʃɪlɪ/ *noun*: **chillies** or **chillis**
1 Chillies are the hot-tasting seed-cases of a type of pepper plant, used to flavour food. **2** (*uncount*) **Chilli**, or **chilli con carne**, is a meal of minced meat and beans flavoured with chillies: *a bowl of chilli.*

chilling /'tʃɪlɪŋ/ *adjective*
Chilling means frightening: *a chilling story.*

chilly /'tʃɪlɪ/ *adjective*: **chillier, chilliest**
1 Chilly weather is rather cold: *It was a chilly autumnal day.* **2** (*informal*) **Chilly** also means unfriendly: *They gave us rather a chilly reception.*

chime /tʃaɪm/ *verb; noun*
▻ ***verb***: **chimes, chiming, chimed**
When bells **chime** they ring: *As we entered, the hall clock chimed.*
▻ ***noun***: **chimes:** *the chimes of the grandfather clock.*

> ***phrasal verb***
> Someone **chimes in** when they interrupt a conversation: *'Yes, that's true', Peter chimed in, eagerly.*

chimney /'tʃɪmnɪ/ *noun*: **chimneys**
A **chimney** is a narrow vertical shaft that smoke from a fire or furnace can escape through, or just the top part of this that sticks out above a roof; the short pipe on top of the chimney is the **chimney pot**. [see picture at **house**].

chimp /tʃɪmp/ *noun* (*informal*): **chimps**
A **chimp** is a chimpanzee.

chimpanzee /tʃɪmpan'ziː/ *noun*: **chimpanzees**
A **chimpanzee** is a small intelligent African ape.

chin /tʃɪn/ *noun*: **chins**
Your **chin** is the part of your face below the mouth. [see picture at **body**]

china /'tʃaɪnə/ *noun* (*uncount, often adjectival*)
China is articles made from a fine kind of clay: *Tea was served in the best china.* □ *a china vase.*

chink /tʃɪŋk/ *noun*: **chinks**
1 A **chink** in a wall is a small narrow crack: *She could see daylight through a chink in the ceiling.* **2** A **chink** of light is a narrow beam of light shining through a narrow crack.

chip /tʃɪp/ *noun; verb*
▻ ***noun***: **chips**
1 Chips are long thin pieces of fried potato: *fish and chips from a chip shop.* **2** A **chip** is a small piece broken off something, or the hole it has left: *This teacup has a chip in it.* **3** (*AmE*) **Chips**, or potato **chips**, are crisps. **4** A **chip**, or silicon **chip**, is one of numerous tiny squares of metal that form electrical connections inside a computer.
▻ ***verb***: **chips, chipping, chipped**
To **chip** something is to knock a small piece off it: *One of the glasses has been chipped* □ *a very brittle clay that chips easily.*
▻ ***phrase*** (*informal*) Someone who **has a chip on their shoulder** behaves unpleasantly or angrily because they feel they have not had the same advantages or good luck as others: *She's got a chip on her shoulder about coming from a poor family.*

> ***phrasal verb***
> **chip in** (*informal*) **1** To **chip in** during a conversation is to interrupt in order to say something: *Yvonne chipped in with a suggestion.* **2** When a number of people **chip in** they each give some money to pay for something.

chiropodist /kɪ'rɒpədɪst/ *noun*: **chiropodists**
A **chiropodist** is a person whose job is to treat minor complaints of the feet.

chirp /tʃɜːp/ *verb*: **chirps, chirping, chirped**
Birds and insects **chirp** when they make a short high-pitched sound.

chisel /'tʃɪzəl/ *noun; verb*
▻ ***noun***: **chisels**
A **chisel** is a tool with a thick metal blade sharp at one

end that is used for cutting and shaping wood or stone. [see picture at **tool**]

▻ ***verb***: **chisels**, **chiselling** (*AmE* **chiseling**), **chiselled** (*AmE* **chiseled**)

To **chisel** wood or stone is to cut or shape it with a chisel: *The design was chiselled out by hand.*

chivalrous /ˈʃɪvəlrəs/ *adjective*

You describe a man as **chivalrous** if he behaves in a formally polite and respectful way towards women: *He made the rather chivalrous gesture of standing up whenever his wife entered the room.*

chivalry /ˈʃɪvəlrɪ/ *noun* (*uncount*)

A man behaves with **chivalry** when he is polite, respectful and considerate, especially towards women: *I was touched by his old-fashioned chivalry.*

chlorine /ˈklɔːriːn/ *noun* (*uncount*)

Chlorine is a poisonous strong-smelling gas used in industry and often added to public swimming pools to keep the water clean.

chock-a-bloc /tʃɒkəˈblɒk/ *adjective* (*informal*)

A place or area is **chock-a-block** when it is filled with a great number of people or things and there is no space for more: *Don't take the motorway; it's always chock-a-bloc at this time of the day.* □ *The hallway was chock-a-bloc with reporters and photographers.*

chock-full /tʃɒkˈfʌl/ *adjective* (*informal*)

When something is **chock-full** it is completely full, with no room or space left at all.

chocolate /ˈtʃɒklɪt/ *noun*: **chocolates**

1 (*uncount, often adjectival*) **Chocolate** is a sweet, hard, usually brown food made from the roasted seeds of a tropical tree, often with milk added: *We bought one bar of milk chocolate and one bar of dark.* **2** A **chocolate** is a sweet made of or coated with chocolate: *a box of chocolates.*

choice /tʃɔɪs/ *noun*; *adjective*

▻ ***noun***: **choices**

1 (*uncount or used in the singular*) There is a **choice** when there are several things available and you have the chance to choose any of them: *For lunch, we had the choice of fish or chicken, with a wide choice of desserts.* □ *There wasn't much choice on the menu.* □ *New customers have a choice of over twenty methods of payment.* [compare **selection**] **2** The **choice** between one thing and another is the act or task of choosing one or the other, or of deciding which to have or do; the thing you choose is your **choice**: *They're at the stage of facing the choice between getting a job and going to university.* □ *They've got so many choices and decisions to make.* □ *I think you've made just the right choice.* □ *I like your choice of wallpaper.* □ *She made an excellent choice of husband in Kevin.* □ *White wouldn't have been my choice for a carpet.*

▻ ***adjective*** (*formal or literary*): **choicer**, **choicest**

Choice describes things of especially good quality: *Use only the choicest cuts of meat for this recipe.*

▻ ***phrases*** **1** You **have no choice** but to do something when you are forced or obliged to do it: *I had to go with her; I had no choice.* **2** When you are allowed to have the thing **of your choice** you can choose whichever thing you prefer: *We give all newly-married couples the room of their choice.* **3** You do something **out of choice** or **from choice** when you do it because you want to: *I'd never go by this route from choice.*

choir /kwaɪə(r)/ *noun* (*with a singular or plural verb*): **choirs**

A **choir** is an organized group of singers, especially one that sings in a church: *He's in the school choir.* □ *The choir meet on Fridays.*

choke /tʃoʊk/ *verb*; *noun*

▻ ***verb***: **chokes**, **choking**, **choked**

1 When someone **chokes** they are unable to breathe properly or cannot breathe at all: *She choked to death on a fish bone.* □ *He was choked by the fumes from the engine.* **2** To **choke** someone is to grip their throat tightly so that they cannot breathe: *He had been choked to death.* **3** To be **choked** with things is to be so full of them that nothing can move: *The roundabout was choked with traffic.* □ *plants choked by weeds.*

▻ ***noun***: **chokes**

In a car or other vehicle, the **choke** is a device that helps the engine to start in cold weather, by reducing the amount of air that mixes with the petrol: *These modern cars all have automatic chokes.*

phrasal verb

You **choke back** an emotion, such as anger, when you try hard not to show it: *I could tell he was choking back his tears.*

cholera /ˈkɒlərə/ *noun* (*uncount*)

Cholera is a very infectious disease that causes severe vomiting and diarrhoea and can kill people: *We need a supply of clean water if cholera is to be avoided.*

cholesterol /kəˈlestərɒl/ *noun* (*uncount*)

Cholesterol is a fatty substance found in some foods and in the blood.

chomp /tʃɒmp/ *verb*: **chomps**, **chomping**, **chomped**

To **chomp** is to chew noisily: *The children were on the sofa, chomping junk food and watching television.*

choose /tʃuːz/ *verb*: **chooses**, **choosing**, **chose**, **chosen**

1 You **choose** something when you decide to have it rather than any of the other things available; you **choose** between things when you decide which to have: *In the end we chose the red carpet in preference to the purple one.* □ *There's a huge range of colours to choose from.* □ *We've now got the job of choosing between curtains or blinds for the bathroom.* □ *I had to choose between getting married and taking up a career in ballet.* □ *She was one of five girls chosen for special training.* □ *I've chosen Paul a teddy bear for his birthday.* [compare **select**] **2** You **choose** to do something when you decide to do it: *When all her sisters were moving to the city, she chose to go on living with her parents.* □ *If you choose to ignore my warning, I'm afraid I can't be responsible for the consequences.* [*same as* **decide**, **elect**] — *adjective* **chosen:** *We wish them all the best in their chosen careers.*

▻ ***phrase*** When you say that there is **nothing to choose between** two or more things you mean that it is difficult to decide which is better because they are about the same: *Frank and Juliet are both highly suitable candidates; in fact, there's not much to choose between them.*

choosy or **choosey** /ˈtʃuːzɪ/ *adjective* (*informal*): **choosier**, **choosiest**

Someone who is **choosy** cares very much or too much about being given exactly what they want: *In a climate of high unemployment, you can't afford to be too choosy about jobs.*

chop /tʃɒp/ *verb*; *noun*

▻ ***verb***: **chops**, **chopping**, **chopped**

You **chop** something, or **chop** it up, when you cut it into pieces by slicing it several times: *Chop the onion finely.* □ *chopping up logs for firewood.*

▻ ***noun***: **chops**

1 A **chop** is a thick slice of pork or lamb containing a bone, especially a rib: *Lightly grill the lamb chops on both sides.* **2** (*used in the plural*; *informal*) Your **chops**

are your mouth: *I smacked him across the chops.* □ *The dog sat licking its chops.*

▻ ***phrases*** **1** People keep **chopping and changing** when they keep changing their minds about something. **2** (*informal*) Someone is **for the chop** when they are going to be punished; something is **for the chop** when it is going to be stopped or closed: *Old Henry's for the chop if the boss catches him smoking.* □ *The council has had its arts budget reduced and our project is for the chop.* **3** (*informal*) Someone **gets the chop** when they are dismissed from their job; something **gets the chop** when it is stopped or closed: *Our Croydon branch was the first to get the chop.*

> ***phrasal verb***
> Trees **are chopped down** when they are cut down or felled.

chopper /ˈtʃɒpə(r)/ *noun* (*informal*): **choppers**
A **chopper** is a helicopter.

choppy /ˈtʃɒpɪ/ *adjective*: **choppier**, **choppiest**
When a lake or the sea is **choppy**, the surface of the water is rather rough, with small irregular waves.

chopping board /ˈtʃɒpɪŋ bɔːd/ *noun*: **chopping boards**
A **chopping board** is a board on which to chop up vegetables or fruit. [see picture at **kitchen**]

chopstick /ˈtʃɒpstɪk/ *noun*: **chopsticks**
Chopsticks are a pair of long thin sticks, usually of wood or plastic, used for eating with, especially in China and Japan. [see picture at **tableware**]

choral /ˈkɔːrəl/ *adjective*
Choral means relating to, or sung by, a choir: *choral music.*

chord /kɔːd/ *noun*: **chords**
A **chord** is a combination of musical notes played together: *I can play a few basic chords on the guitar.*

chore /tʃɔː(r)/ *noun*: **chores**
A **chore** is a piece of housework, or any task that you find boring or difficult: *My husband is happy to do some of the household chores.* □ *I find writing Christmas cards a bit of a chore.*

choreography /kɒrɪˈɒgrəfɪ/ *noun* (*uncount*)
Choreography is the arrangement of the sequence and pattern of movements in dancing, especially in ballet.

chortle /ˈtʃɔːtəl/ *verb*: **chortles, chortling, chortled**
You **chortle** when you laugh with pleasure or satisfaction: *Jarvis chortled triumphantly.*

chorus /ˈkɔːrəs/ *noun*: **choruses**
1 In a song, the **chorus** is the set of lines repeated after each verse: *We all joined in with the chorus.* **2** (*with a singular or plural verb*) A **chorus** is a large choir. **3** A **chorus** is also a piece of music for a large choir. **4** (*with a singular or plural verb*) In an opera or musical show, the **chorus** is the group of singers and dancers supporting the main performers. **5** When people react to something with similar comments, you can call their reaction a **chorus** of something: *His suggestion met with a chorus of disapproval.*

chose /tʃoʊz/ *verb*
Chose is the past tense of **choose**.

chosen /ˈtʃoʊzən/ *verb*
Chosen is the past participle of **choose**.

Christ /kraɪst/ *noun*
Christ, or Jesus **Christ**, is Jesus of Nazareth, whom Christians believe to be the Son of God.

christen /ˈkrɪsən/ *verb*: **christens, christening, christened**
1 To **christen** someone, usually a baby, is to give them a name as part of the religious ceremony in which they are accepted formally as a member of the Christian church: *She was christened 'Albertine' but prefers to use the name 'Tina'.* [*same as* **baptize**] **2** To **christen** something is to give it a name: *They christened it 'the emerald forest' because it was so green.* **3** To **christen** an object is to use it for the first time: *Help us to christen these new wine glasses.*

christening /ˈkrɪsənɪŋ/ *noun*: **christenings**
A **christening** is a Christian ceremony in which a baby is accepted into the church and given its name or names. [*same as* **baptism**]

Christian /ˈkrɪstʃən/ *noun*; *adjective*
▻ ***noun*: Christians**
1 A **Christian** is a person who believes that Jesus Christ is the Son of God, especially someone who tries to live according to Christ's teaching: *Only half the pupils in this school are Christians.* **2** (*informal*) A kind or sympathetic person might also be referred to as a **Christian.**
▻ ***adjective:*** *followers of the Christian religion* □ *That's not a very Christian attitude!*

Christianity /krɪstɪˈanɪtɪ/ *noun* (*uncount*)
Christianity is the religion based on the teachings of Jesus Christ: *Relations between Christianity and Science have always been complex.*

Christian name /krɪstɪˈən neɪm/ *noun*: **Christian names**
A person's **Christian name** is the name given to them when they are born or christened, as opposed to their family name: *His Christian names are Charles Robert.* □ *I only know her as Mrs Smith; I don't know her Christian name.*

Christmas /ˈkrɪsməs/ *noun* (*usually uncount, often adjectival*)
Christmas is the annual Christian festival that occurs on 25 December and commemorates the birth of Christ, or the period of celebration surrounding this date: *This year we are going to my parents' house for Christmas.* □ *They're spending Christmas with friends.* □ *Christmas dinner* □ *My wife gave me this book as a Christmas present.*

Christmas Day /krɪsməs ˈdeɪ/ *noun* (*uncount*)
Christmas Day is 25 December, the day on which Christmas is celebrated.

Christmas Eve /krɪsməs ˈiːv/ *noun* (*uncount*)
Christmas Eve is 24 December, the day before Christmas Day: *In some European countries, children open their presents on Christmas Eve.*

Christmas tree /krɪsməs ˈtriː/ *noun*: **Christmas trees**
A **Christmas tree** is a fir tree, either real or artificial, hung with decorations and lights and displayed *eg* in people's homes during the Christmas period.

chrome /kroʊm/ *noun* (*uncount, often adjectival; informal*)
Chrome is chromium: *old-fashioned cars with their chrome bumper bars.*

chromium /ˈkroʊmɪəm/ *noun* (*uncount, often adjectival*)
Chromium is a hard shiny metal used to coat other metal surfaces to prevent rust: *chromium-plated taps.*

chronic /ˈkrɒnɪk/ *adjective*
1 A **chronic** illness lasts a very long time or is always present: *She suffers from chronic bronchitis.* **2 Chronic** is also used to describe someone who has for a long time suffered from some illness or condition: *a chronic alcoholic.* **3** (*informal*) **Chronic** also describes a situation or condition that is very bad or severe: *'The bus service isn't too good, is it?' 'Not too good! It's chronic!'* □ *a chronic lack of books in our schools.* — *adverb* **chronically:** *chronically ill patients.* □ *The country is chronically short of resources.*

chronicle /ˈkrɒnɪkəl/ *noun; verb*
▻ ***noun*** (*formal*): **chronicles**
A **chronicle** is a record of historical events in the order in which they happened: *Her autobiography is not the faithful chronicle we had expected.*
▻ ***verb*** (*formal*): **chronicles, chronicling, chronicled**
To **chronicle** events is to write an account of them: *The whole period is interestingly chronicled in his memoirs.*

chronological /krɒnəˈlɒdʒɪkəl/ *adjective*
When events are presented in **chronological** order they are shown in the sequence in which they actually occurred: *a strictly chronological account of the war.* — *adverb* **chronologically:** *The photographs are arranged chronologically.*

chrysalis /ˈkrɪsəlɪs/ *noun*: **chrysalises**
A **chrysalis** is a developing insect still inside its protective case, before it has grown wings and can fly: *What they had found was a butterfly chrysalis.*

chrysanthemum /krɪˈsanθɪməm/ *noun*: **chrysanthemums**
A **chrysanthemum** is a large yellow or pink garden flower with many narrow petals growing closely together.

chubby /ˈtʃʌbɪ/ *adjective*: **chubbier, chubbiest**
You might describe someone, especially a child, as **chubby** if they are rather fat: *the baby's chubby little cheeks.*

chuck /tʃʌk/ *verb* (*informal*): **chucks, chucking, chucked**
1 You **chuck** something somewhere when you throw it there, especially in a rough or casual way: *Chuck me that newspaper, will you?* □ *I chucked it away a few days ago, but it might still be in the bin.* **2** Someone **is chucked** out of a place when they are ordered to leave: *They got chucked out of the pub for fighting.* **3** You **chuck** something when you give it up, abandon it or reject it: *I don't smoke any more; I chucked the habit months ago.* □ *She chucked her boyfriend because he was seeing another woman.*

chuckle /ˈtʃʌkəl/ *verb; noun*
▻ ***verb***: **chuckles, chuckling, chuckled**
You **chuckle** when you laugh quietly, especially in a private or secret way: *He sat reading the comic, chuckling to himself.*
▻ ***noun***: **chuckles:** *A gentle chuckle made itself heard from behind his newspaper.*

chuffed /tʃʌft/ *adjective* (*informal*)
You are **chuffed** when you are very pleased: *She's really chuffed about her exam results.*

chug /tʃʌg/ *verb*: **chugs, chugging, chugged**
An old vehicle **chugs** when its engine makes a repeated dull beating noise: *The little van came chugging up the street.*

chum /tʃʌm/ *noun* (*old, informal*): **chums**
A **chum** is a friend: *one of her old school chums.*

chunk /tʃʌŋk/ *noun*: **chunks**
1 A **chunk** of something solid is a large thick piece of it: *Chop the meat into chunks.* **2** (*informal*) A **chunk** of something is also a large part or amount of it: *A substantial chunk of our budget goes on employees' wages.*

chunky /ˈtʃʌŋkɪ/ *adjective*: **chunkier, chunkiest**
1 You might describe someone as **chunky** if they are big and strong, or if they are rather fat: *She was pretty chunky as a teenager.* **2 Chunky** objects are thick and solid-looking: *a chunky sweater* □ *a chunky chocolate bar.*

church /tʃɜːtʃ/ *noun*: **churches**
1 A **church** is a building where Christians worship in public: *There had been some damage to the church roof.* □ *visitors to the Church of St Francis Xavier.* **2** People go to **church** when they attend a religious service held in a church, or do this regularly: *My husband doesn't go to church.* **3** The different branches of the Christian religion are referred to as **Churches**: *the Church of England* □ *the Methodist Church* □ *the Church of Rome.*

churchyard /ˈtʃɜːtʃjɑːd/ *noun*: **churchyards**
A **churchyard** is the enclosed area round a church, in which dead people are buried. [compare **cemetery**]

churlish /ˈtʃɜːlɪʃ/ *adjective* (*formal*)
Churlish behaviour is rude or unfriendly: *It would be churlish of you to refuse such a generous invitation.*

churn /tʃɜːn/ *noun; verb*
▻ ***noun***: **churns**
1 A **churn** is a machine which stirs milk constantly until it turns into butter. **2** A **churn** is also a large barrel-like can in which milk is stored or transported.
▻ ***verb***: **churns, churning, churned**
1 Milk **is churned** to make butter when it is stirred forcefully and repeatedly. **2** When your stomach **is churning** you feel sick: *My stomach churned at the thought of having to go through that again.* **3** To **churn** something such as water or mud, or to **churn** it up, is to cause it to splash about violently: *The truck wasn't making any progress; its wheels were simply churning up the muddy track.*

> ***phrasal verb***
> To **churn** things **out** is to produce them in great quantities and at great speed: *A lot of writers seem to make their money by churning out the same old novel again and again in a slightly different form.*

chute /ʃuːt/ *noun*: **chutes**
1 A **chute** is a sloping channel that something such as water or rubbish can be sent down from one level to another: *She had fallen down the hotel's laundry chute.* **2** A **chute** is also a slide in a children's playground or swimming-pool.

chutney /ˈtʃʌtnɪ/ *noun* (*uncount*)
Chutney is a spicy kind of pickle, often made from fruit.

cider /ˈsaɪdə(r)/ *noun* (*uncount*)
Cider is an alcoholic drink similar to beer, made from apples: *He'd already drunk three pints of cider.*

cigar /sɪˈgɑː(r)/ *noun*: **cigars**
A **cigar** is a roll of dried tobacco leaves for smoking: *packets of cigars and cigarettes.*

cigarette /sɪgəˈrɛt/ *noun*: **cigarettes**
A **cigarette** is a narrow tube of thin paper filled with small pieces of dried tobacco leaves, for smoking: *She lit another cigarette, then put it out immediately.*

cigarette lighter /sɪgəˈrɛtlaɪtə(r)/ *noun*: **cigarette lighters**
A **cigarette lighter** is a small device that produces a small flame, used for lighting cigarettes and cigars.

cinch /sɪntʃ/ *noun* (*informal*)
You say that something is a **cinch** when it is very easy to do or achieve: *This week's homework was a cinch.*

cinder /ˈsɪndə(r)/ *noun* (*usually in the plural*): **cinders**
Cinders are ashes left over after wood or coal has been burned.
▻ ***phrase*** When something is **burnt to a cinder** it is very severely burnt, so that there is almost nothing left of it.

cinema /ˈsɪnɪmə/ *noun*: **cinemas**
1 A **cinema** is a theatre in which films are shown on a big screen: *Many cinemas have been converted to bingo*

halls. **2** The **cinema** refers to these theatres in general, or to the business of making films: *We don't go to the cinema much now that we have a video.* □ *The government has reduced its funding of the arts, and of the cinema in particular.*

cinematic /sɪnɪ'matɪk/ *adjective*
Cinematic means relating to the cinema or to films: *She's one of the most inventive exponents of the cinematic art.*

cinematography /sɪnɪmə'tɒgrəfɪ/ *noun* (*uncount*)
Cinematography is the technique or art of making films: *The film won an award for its cinematography.*

cinnamon /'sɪnəmən/ *noun* (*uncount*)
Cinnamon is a spice obtained from the bark of a tropical tree, used *eg* for flavouring cakes and biscuits and in curries.

cipher or **cypher** /'saɪfə(r)/ *noun*: **ciphers**
A **cipher** is a code used for writing secret messages.

circa /'sɜːkə/ *preposition*
Used before a date, **circa** means 'approximately' or 'about': *This kind of pottery was first produced in Staffordshire circa 1760.*

circle /'sɜːkəl/ *noun; verb*
▷ ***noun*: circles**
1 A **circle** is a line that curves evenly and continuously to form a perfectly round figure, with every point on it an equal distance from the centre: *squares, circles and other geometric shapes.* [see picture at **shape**] **2** Anything that is round can also be referred to as a **circle**: *little circles of paint on the floor where the tin had been set down.* **3** A **circle** is also a group of people associated in some way: *She's not part of his circle of friends.* □ *He's never been comfortable moving in aristocratic circles.* **4** In a theatre or cinema, the **circle** is the balcony or upper floor.
▷ ***verb*: circles, circling, circled**
1 To **circle** something is to move round it repeatedly: *The pilot circled the airfield a few times before making his landing.* **2** You **circle** something when you draw a circle round it: *Here's the paper; I've circled one or two articles you might be interested in.*
▷ ***phrase*** You say you are **going round in circles** when your discussions or actions make no progress at all and simply lead you back to the point you started from.

circuit /'sɜːkɪt/ *noun*: **circuits**
1 An electrical **circuit** is a circle of connections that an electric current passes round to bring power to a number of points. **2** A race track or running-track is often referred to as a **circuit**. **3** A **circuit** is also a set of places regularly visited by a professional performer, or tournaments regularly entered by a professional sportsperson: *She's been on the international tennis circuit for two years now.*

circuitous /sə'kjuːɪtəs/ *adjective* (*formal*)
A **circuitous** route is one that does not lead you directly to the place you are travelling to.

circular /'sɜːkjʊlə(r)/ *adjective; noun*
▷ ***adjective***
1 Something **circular** has the shape or form of a circle: *a circular arrangement of chairs* □ *We took a fairly circular route around the continent, ending where we had started.* **2** A **circular** theory is not valid because the truth of the conclusion depends on a point that itself depends on the conclusion being true: *These are very circular arguments which get us nowhere.*
▷ ***noun*: circulars**
A **circular** is a message or letter copies of which are sent to many different people at the same time.

circulate /'sɜːkjʊleɪt/ *verb*: **circulates, circulating, circulated**
1 When something **is circulated** among a group of people it is passed from one person to another until all have seen it: *A copy of the letter has been circulated round the office.* □ *A rumour has been circulating that she's been offered the chief's job.* **2** Something **circulates** when it moves around freely: *With the opening of the new junction, traffic is once again circulating smoothly.* **3** At a party or other social occasion, you **circulate** when you move around talking to different people.

circulation /sɜːkjʊ'leɪʃən/ *noun* (*uncount*)
1 Your **circulation** is the healthy flow of blood around your body: *Garlic is supposed to thin the blood and improve circulation.* **2** A newspaper's **circulation** is the number of copies of each issue of it that are sold: *The magazine now has a circulation of over half a million.* **3 Circulation** also refers to the free movement of something, such as air: *Improving the circulation of air will make for a fresher, healthier environment.* **4** The **circulation** of something, such as a rumour or a piece of writing, is the way it is passed on from one person to another: *The circulation of rumours fed an atmosphere of crisis and fear*

circumcise /'sɜːkəmsaɪz/ *verb*: **circumcises, circumcising, circumcised**
To **circumcise** a boy or man is to cut away the loose skin at the end of his penis, usually for religious but sometimes for medical reasons; to **circumcise** a girl or woman is to cut off the most sensitive part of her outer sexual organs. — *noun* (*uncount or count*) **circumcision** /sɜːkəm'sɪʒən/: *Some of the mothers in the tribe were opposed to female circumcision.*

circumference /sə'kʌmfərəns/ *noun*: **circumference**
1 The **circumference** of a circle or circular area is its outer edge. [see picture at **shape**] **2 Circumference** also refers to the distance around this outer edge: *attempts to accurately measure the circumference of the Moon.*

circumscribe /'sɜːkəmskraɪb/ *verb* (*formal*): **circumscribes, circumscribing, circumscribed**
Your freedom or power **is circumscribed** if it is limited in some way: *The government has introduced laws that severely circumscribe religious freedom.*

circumspect /'sɜːkəmspekt/ *adjective* (*formal*)
You are **circumspect** if you are wary and do not take risks: *Be more circumspect in choosing your close friends.*

circumstance /'sɜːkəmstəns/ *noun* (*usually in the plural*): **circumstances**
1 The **circumstances** of something are the facts and events involving or surrounding it: *She died in rather mysterious circumstances.* **2** Your personal **circumstances** are your present situation, especially with regard to how much money you have: *Her husband died a few years ago, leaving her in impoverished circumstances.* **3** A **circumstance** is a particular detail or aspect of a situation: *Then there was the strange circumstance of the unclaimed glove.* [compare **matter**, **fact**] **4** (*uncount; literary*) **Circumstance** is fate, the force that controls events: *She has just been an unfortunate victim of circumstance.*
▷ ***phrases*** **1** When you say that **in** or **under no circumstances** would you do something, you mean that you would never do it, not for any reason at all: *She would not under any circumstances betray my secret.* **2 In** or **under the circumstances** means 'considering all aspects of the situation': *Ordinarily I would advise you to rest but, under the current circumstances, you should perhaps take advantage of what energy you have.* □ *I thought I behaved quite politely in the circumstances.*

circumstantial /sɜːkəmˈstanʃəl/ *adjective*
Circumstantial evidence suggests that something probably happened, but does not prove that it happened: *We have collected plenty of evidence, though it is all circumstantial.*

circumvent /sɜːkəmˈvɛnt/ *verb* (*formal*): **circumvents, circumventing, circumvented**
You **circumvent** a law when you alter your circumstances so that the law does not apply to you; you **circumvent** a difficulty when you find a way of avoiding it: *Various devices were employed by traders to circumvent the import restrictions.*

circus /ˈsɜːkəs/ *noun*: **circuses**
1 A **circus** is a travelling company of performers, traditionally including acrobats, clowns and trained animals and performing in a large circular tent: *The circus is in town.* **2** You go to the **circus** when you attend a performance by such a company: *She took the children to the circus as a birthday treat.*

cirrhosis /səˈroʊsɪs/ *noun* (*uncount*)
Cirrhosis, or **cirrhosis** of the liver, is a serious liver disease often caused by drinking too much alcohol.

cissy see **sissy**.

cistern /ˈsɪstən/ *noun*: **cisterns**
A **cistern** is a small tank containing water used for flushing a toilet.

citation /saɪˈteɪʃən/ *noun*: **citations**
1 When someone receives a **citation** they are officially and publicly thanked for their bravery or other good work, and often given a certificate: *A number of firefighters received citations.* **2** (*formal*) A **citation** is a quotation or short passage taken from a piece of writing or speech.

cite /saɪt/ *verb*: **cites, citing, cited**
To **cite** something, usually some fact from a book or other writing, is to mention it as an example or as proof of something: *This is a rare but frequently cited example of ministerial incompetence.*

citizen /ˈsɪtɪzən/ *noun*: **citizens**
1 The **citizens** of a city or town are the people who live there: *an attack on innocent citizens.* **2** A person who is a **citizen** of a country is officially accepted as belonging to it: *She has applied to become an American citizen.*

citizenship /ˈsɪtɪzənʃɪp/ *noun* (*uncount*)
You have **citizenship** of a country if you are legally recognized as belonging to it: *Originally from Africa, he obtained French citizenship over a year ago.*

citrus fruit /ˈsɪtrəs fruːt/ *noun*: **citrus fruits**
Citrus fruits are thick-skinned, sharp-tasting fruits such as oranges and lemons.

city /ˈsɪtɪ/ *noun*: **cities**
1 A **city** is a large town: *the residents of the City of Nottingham.* **2** (*used in the singular*) The **City** is the part of London where many banks and other financial organizations have their main offices: *News from the City is that the pound has lost heavily against the dollar.*

civic /ˈsɪvɪk/ *adjective*
1 Civic is used to describe things connected with the government of a town or city: *visitors to the Civic Centre.* **2 Civic** also refers to a person's connection with a particular town because they are a citizen of it: *People no longer seem to have a sense of civic pride.*

civil /ˈsɪvɪl/ *adjective*
1 Civil means relating to or involving ordinary citizens: *The situation will soon become a full-scale civil war.* □ *They stop short of advocating violence, but have called for a campaign of civil disobedience.* □ *This represents a violation of civil liberties.* **2** You are **civil** when you are polite without being too friendly: *Try to be at least civil to our guests.* — *noun* (*uncount*) **civility** /sɪˈvɪlɪtɪ/: *The discussions were conducted in an atmosphere of civility.* — *adverb* **civilly:** *She answered civilly, if not with enthusiasm.*

civil engineering /sɪvɪl ɛndʒɪˈnɪərɪŋ/ *noun* (*uncount*)
Civil engineering is the planning, design and building of *eg* roads, public buildings, bridges and tunnels: *She studied civil engineering at university.*

civilian /sɪˈvɪljən/ *adjective*; *noun*
▻ ***adjective***
Civilian refers to people and things not connected with the armed forces or the police force: *They don't like the idea of a civilian agency doing police work.*
▻ ***noun***: **civilians:** *How is he adjusting to life as a civilian?*

civilised see **civilized**.

civilization or **civilisation** /sɪvəlaɪˈzeɪʃən/ *noun*: **civilizations**
1 A **civilization** is a people regarded as an individual social group with their own identifiable customs and practices: *As human civilization grows and develops, it does not lead to an increase in human happiness.* □ *the great civilizations of biblical times.* **2** (*uncount*) **Civilization** is the state of being advanced as a society, in terms of politics, culture and technology: *These people don't want civilization; they want to be left alone.*

civilized or **civilised** /ˈsɪvəlaɪzd/ *adjective*
1 A **civilized** society is one regarded as advanced in terms of politics and technology: *How can we, in our so-called civilized society, accept such cruelty to animals?* **2 Civilized** also means pleasant and without harshness or coarseness: *We moved from the barn to the more civilized surroundings of the drawing-room.* □ *She had a polite, civilized manner.*

civil liberties /sɪvɪl ˈlɪbətɪz/ *noun* (*plural*)
Your **civil liberties** are the rights you have to speak and act freely, without interference from the state or from other people.

civil rights /sɪvɪl ˈraɪts/ *noun* (*plural*)
Your **civil rights** are the rights you have to be treated fairly and equally by the society you live in, no matter whether you are a man or a woman, no matter which religion you follow, and no matter what colour your skin.

civil servant /sɪvɪl ˈsɜːvənt/ *noun*: **civil servants**
A **civil servant** is a person employed in the Civil Service.

Civil Service /sɪvɪl ˈsɜːvɪs/ *noun* (*with a singular or plural verb*)
The **Civil Service** consists of all the officials who work in all the government departments in a country: *The Civil Service are to be given pay rises averaging 5%.*

clad /klad/ *adjective* (*literary*)
You are **clad** in the clothes that you are wearing: *He arrived on time, clad in cloak and hat.* □ *She was an elegant woman, richly clad.* □ *mountains clad in a dense covering of forest.*

claim /kleɪm/ *verb*; *noun*
▻ ***verb***: **claims, claiming, claimed**
1 To **claim** that something is true is to insist that it is true when it cannot be proved: *He claims he was at home alone at the time of the murder.* □ *She claims to have been the first person to see it.* □ *He claimed that he was her long-lost brother from America.* [*same as* **maintain**] **2** You **claim** something when you ask for or demand it because you believe you have a right to have it: *She has claimed over £1000 of business*

expenses this month. □ *People on a state pension can claim a reduction on their council tax.* □ *This is the first time we've claimed on our car insurance.* **3** You **claim** responsibility or credit for something when you say that you did it: *A separatist terrorist organization has claimed responsibility for the bombing.* □ *It was she who wrote the report but her manager will claim the credit for it.* **4** An incident **claims** someone's life when they are killed by being involved in it: *A serious road accident claimed the lives of three people.* [*same as* **take**]
▻ ***noun***: **claims**
1 A **claim** is a statement insisting that something is true when it is difficult to prove: *These latest trade figures don't support the Chancellor's claim that the economic crisis is over.* **2** A **claim** is also a request for something that you believe you have a right to; you have a **claim** to something if you have a right to it: *The company has accepted his claim for compensation.* □ *Lady Macbeth actually had a better claim to the throne than Macbeth,* **3** You have a **claim** on someone when you have the right to expect them to do what you ask: *She ceased to have any claims on me when she took up with another man.* □ *I can't agree to do it; there are already too many claims on my time.*
▻ ***phrases*** **1** A person's **claim to fame** is the reason why they are famous: *His only claim to fame is that he was the first journalist to speak to Mrs Thatcher after her resignation.* **2** You **lay claim to** something when you insist that it belongs to you.

claimant /ˈkleɪmənt/ *noun*: **claimants**
A **claimant** is a person who makes a claim for something, especially money, that they believe they should receive: *Most claimants find that insurance companies treat them suspiciously.*

clairvoyant /kleəˈvɔɪənt/ *adjective*; *noun*
▻ ***adjective***
Someone who is **clairvoyant** claims to be able to know what will happen in the future.
▻ ***noun***: **clairvoyants:** *The clairvoyant she consulted told her that her son was alive and well and living in London.*

clam /klam/ *noun*; *verb*
▻ ***noun***: **clams**
A **clam** is a kind of shellfish: *a pizza topped with anchovies and baby clams.*
▻ ***verb*** (*informal*): **clams, clamming, clammed**

phrasal verb
Someone **clams up** when they stop talking suddenly, especially refusing to answer any more questions: *After giving the police his name, he just clammed up.*

clamber /ˈklambə(r)/ *verb*: **clambers, clambering, clambered**
You **clamber** somewhere when you climb there with difficulty using your hands as well as your feet: *We had to clamber up the rocky slope.*

clammy /ˈklamɪ/ *adjective*: **clammier, clammiest**
Something that is **clammy** is unpleasantly damp or moist: *There were signs of dampness on the ceiling and the walls were clammy to the touch.*

clamour (*AmE* **clamor**) /ˈklamə(r)/ *verb*; *noun*
▻ ***verb***: **clamours, clamouring, clamoured**
When people **are clamouring** for something they are demanding it, especially noisily and angrily: *Huge crowds had gathered outside the Town Hall, clamouring for his resignation.*
▻ ***noun*** (*uncount*)
Clamour is loud noise caused by a lot of people talking at the same time: *We had to shout above the clamour of children's voices in the street.*

clamp /klamp/ *noun*; *verb*
▻ ***noun***: **clamps**
A **clamp** is any device used to hold something still or firm, or press something into place: *The wooden staves are glued and held together with a clamp until dry.* □ *the police's widespread use of wheel clamps to immobilize illegally parked vehicles.* [see picture at **tool**]
▻ ***verb***: **clamps, clamping, clamped**
To **clamp** something is to grip or fasten it firmly, with or without a clamp: *The posts are clamped into position until the concrete sets.* □ *The animal clamped its jaws round my ankle.*

phrasal verb
People in authority **clamp down on** something when they bring it under very strict control or stop it altogether: *They're clamping down on illegal parking in the city centre.*

clampdown /ˈklampdaʊn/ *noun*: **clampdowns**
When there is a **clampdown** on something it is brought under very strict control or stopped altogether: *another government clampdown on local council spending.*

clan /klan/ *noun*: **clans**
1 A **clan** is a large group of families all related to each other, generally with the same surname: *representatives of the Macgregors and one or two other old Scottish clans.* **2** (*humorous*) You might refer to your family or relations as your **clan**, especially when there are many members: *The Johnson clan will take up at least two tables.*

clandestine /klanˈdestɪn/ *adjective*
Something **clandestine** is secret or done secretly, often because it is illegal: *a clandestine meeting of members of an outlawed political organization.*

clang /klaŋ/ *verb*; *noun*
▻ ***verb***: **clangs, clanging, clanged**
When metal objects **clang** they make a loud deep ringing sound as they strike each other or a hard surface.
▻ ***noun***: **clangs:** *The shelf collapsed and the saucepans fell to the floor with a clang.*

clanger /ˈklaŋə(r)/ *noun* (*informal*): **clangers**
▻ ***phrase*** Someone **drops a clanger** when they make an embarrassing mistake in public.

clank /klaŋk/ *verb*; *noun*
▻ ***verb***: **clanks, clanking, clanked**
Metal objects **clank** when they make a short sharp noise as they strike each other or a hard surface: *I could hear the chains clank as they were dragged across the floor.*
▻ ***noun***: **clanks:** *The engine was producing an alarming clank every so often.*

clap /klap/ *verb*; *noun*
▻ ***verb***: **claps, clapping, clapped**
1 You **clap**, or **clap** your hands, when you strike the palms of your hands together to produce a noise, *eg* to get people's attention, to mark a rhythm, or to give applause: *The noise of conversation rose again, and again she clapped her hands for silence.* □ *They clapped along in time to the music.* □ *The audience clapped politely rather than enthusiastically, uncertain whether the piece had come to an end.* □ *She was clapped and cheered as she stepped up on to the platform.* **2** You **clap** something or someone somewhere you put them there quickly: *She clapped her hand to her forehead in a gesture of exasperation.* □ *I don't suppose they'd clap me into jail for this, but I'd rather no-one found out, all the same.*
▻ ***noun***: **claps**
A **clap** of thunder is a sudden loud explosion of noise produced by thunder.
▻ ***phrase*** For **clap eyes on** see **eye**.

clapped-out /klapt'aʊt/ *adjective* (*informal*)
A **clapped-out** vehicle or machine is an old one that is not working properly: *a clapped-out old typewriter.*

claptrap /'klaptrap/ *noun* (*uncount*; *informal*)
If you describe what someone says as **claptrap** you think it is nonsense: *The minister gave us another load of claptrap about 'traditional values'.*

claret /'klarət/ *noun* (*uncount*)
1 Claret is French red wine from the Bordeaux district: *a mediocre bottle of claret.* **2** (*often adjectival*) **Claret** is also a deep reddish-purple colour: *a claret-and-blue football strip.*

clarify /'klarɪfaɪ/ *verb*: **clarifies, clarifying, clarified**
You **clarify** something when you explain it again in a different way that makes it easier to understand: *Could the minister clarify the government's policy on South Africa?* [*same as* make **clear**] — *noun* (*uncount*) **clarification** /klarɪfɪ'keɪʃən/: *As the document was impossible to understand, we have sent them a letter asking for clarification.* □ *We are waiting for clarification of their position.*

clarinet /klarɪ'nɛt/ *noun*: **clarinets**
A **clarinet** is a woodwind instrument with keys that is held out in front of the player. [see picture at **orchestra**]

clarity /'klarɪtɪ/ *noun* (*uncount*)
1 Clarity is the quality of being clear, or of being easy to see, hear or understand: *She played the piece with remarkable fluency and clarity of tone.* □ *There seemed to be a lack of clarity about what the job involved.* **2 Clarity** is also the quality of thinking or expressing yourself clearly: *In her days as a schoolteacher she'd been known for the quickness of her wit and her clarity of thought.*

clash /klaʃ/ *verb*; *noun*
▻ ***verb***: **clashes, clashing, clashed**
1 When one person or group **clashes** with another, or when the two of them **clash**, they have an argument, contest or fight: *The party leaders clashed in parliament today over the issue of cuts in the health service.* □ *There were violent scenes as crowds of protesters clashed with police.* **2** Two events **clash** when they both happen at the same time, so that you can only attend one of them: *We won't see them because their visit to Scotland clashes with our weekend in Berlin.* **3** Two theories or opinions **clash** when they are so different that you cannot accept both and must decide which to support: *At this point, his family responsibilities and his career plans clashed and a choice had to be made.* **4** When two different colours or styles **clash** they look unpleasant together: *Don't you think the pink carpet clashes a bit with the orange wallpaper?* **5** Metal objects **clash** when they strike each other with a loud noise.
▻ ***noun***: **clashes:** *an exciting clash between the two former champions* □ *the clash of the cymbals.*

clasp /klɑːsp/ *verb*; *noun*
▻ ***verb***: **clasps, clasping, clasped**
You **clasp** something when you hold it tightly: *He sat nervously clasping the briefcase to his chest.*
▻ ***noun***: **clasps**
A **clasp** is small device for fastening things: *The purse had a delicate gold clasp.*

class /klɑːs/ *noun*; *verb*
▻ ***noun***: **classes**
1 A **class** is a lesson or lecture: *I'll be late for my history class.* **2** A **class** is also a group of pupils or students taught together: *She's not in my class this year.* **3** (*count or uncount*) **Classes** are groups that people in society are divided into, formally or informally, according to their job, wealth or other social status: *various members of the upper classes* □ *It is intended really for the educated classes.* □ *problems of class and race.* [see also **middle class, upper class, working class**] **4** A **class** is also a grade or standard: *We could only afford to fly economy class.* □ *A first-class ticket would be too expensive.* **5** A **class** of things is a group whose members are similar in some identifiable way: *Insurance companies recognize two main classes of claim; genuine and fraudulent.* **6** (*uncount*) When you say that someone has **class** you are impressed by their expensive tastes and by how confidently and stylishly they behave.
▻ ***verb***: **classes, classing, classed**
You **class** a person or thing as something when you regard them as being that thing: *She was classed as a 'high-achiever' by her teachers.* □ *The film has been classed as suitable for adults only.*
▻ ***phrase*** Something is **in a class of its own** when it is much better than all the others: *As an athlete, she is in a class of her own.*

classic /'klasɪk/ *adjective*; *noun*
▻ ***adjective***
1 Classic is used to describe things still regarded as the best of their kind, which new ones are always compared with: *It's one of the classic suspense films of American cinema.* **2 Classic** also means absolutely typical: *This is a classic example of a working-class inferiority complex.*
▻ ***noun***: **classics**
A **classic** is something regarded as one of the best of its kind: *It has become one of the classics of post-war literature.* [see also **Classics**]

classical /'klasɪkəl/ *adjective*
1 Classical is used to describe things that have a traditional form or style: *The whole building is a masterpiece of classical architecture.* □ *classical poetic styles.* **2 Classical** music is generally accepted as being serious and of lasting value, and is played on the traditional instruments of the orchestra: *They argued that the study of jazz music was as valid as that of classical.* **3 Classical** also refers to the art and literature of ancient Greece and Rome: *a revival of the classical style.*

Classics /'klasɪks/ *noun* (*uncount*)
You study **Classics** if you study the literature, languages and philosophy of ancient Greece and Rome.

classified /'klasɪfaɪd/ *adjective*
Classified information is officially kept secret, usually because it relates to the government.

classify /'klasɪfaɪ/ *verb*: **classifies, classifying, classified**
To **classify** things is to divide them into groups on the basis of how alike they are in some way, or to identify them as belonging to a particular group: *She's classified her record collection according to musical styles.* □ *These criminals have been classified as a danger to the public.* — *noun* (*uncount*) **classification** /klasɪfɪ'keɪʃən/: *She pioneered the classification of Australasian flowering plants.*

classmate /'klɑːsmeɪt/ *noun*: **classmates**
Your **classmates** are the people who are in your class at school or college.

classroom /'klɑːsruːm/ *noun*: **classrooms**
A **classroom** is a room in a school or college where classes are taught.

classy /'klɑːsɪ/ *adjective* (*informal*): **classier, classiest**
Classy is used to describe people or things that are expensive and stylish: *They're staying in some classy hotel on the sea front.*

clatter /'klatə(r)/ *noun*; *verb*

▻ ***noun*** (*used in the singular*)
A **clatter** is a loud noise made by a number of hard objects striking each other, or falling on to a hard surface: *We heard the clatter of pots and pans being washed.*
▻ ***verb***: **clatters, clattering, clattered:** *She dropped the bucket and it went clattering down the stairs.*

clause /klɔːz/ *noun*: **clauses**
1 In grammar, a **clause** is a part of a sentence that contains a verb and its subject: *Students were asked to identify the main clause and the subordinate clause.* **2** A **clause** is also a section of a legal document, such as a contract or will.

claustrophobia /klɔːstrəˈfoʊbɪə/ *noun* (*uncount*)
Someone who suffers from **claustrophobia** feels uneasy or frightened whenever they are in a small enclosed space. — *adjective* **claustrophobic** /klɔːstrəˈfoʊbɪk/: *She gets a bit claustrophobic if you close the door.* □ *It was rather a claustrophobic little room with too much furniture in it*

claw /klɔː/ *noun*; *verb*
▻ ***noun***: **claws**
1 The **claws** of a bird or animal are its sharply-pointed hooked nails. **2** The **claws** of a crab, lobster or other shellfish are its large front feet with pointed parts for gripping on the end.
▻ ***verb***: **claws, clawing, clawed**
When an animal **claws** something it scratches or tears it with its claws: *The cat was clawing at the door.*

clay /kleɪ/ *noun* (*uncount, often adjectival*)
Clay is soft sticky earth that is shaped and baked hard to form pottery and bricks: *a mixture of red and brown clay* □ *a beautifully decorated clay pot.*

clean /kliːn/ *adjective*; *verb*; *adverb*
▻ ***adjective***: **cleaner, cleanest**
1 Something that is **clean** is free from dirt or stains: *Do put on a clean shirt.* □ *All working surfaces must be kept clean.* □ *She moistened her hanky and wiped his face clean.* [*opposite* **dirty**] **2** People are described as **clean** if they wash themselves and their clothes regularly and keep their surroundings clean: *His friends struck me as not very clean.* □ *I'd prefer a nice clean animal, like a cat.* □ *It's important to teach children clean habits.* [*opposite* **dirty**] **3 Clean** also means new, fresh, or not marked or used in any way: *Take a clean sheet of paper.* □ *There was no trace of the recorded interview; the tape had been wiped clean.* **4 Clean** lines and edges are straight and even: *Make a clean straight cut.* □ *a nice clean design.* **5** Your record is **clean** if you are not known ever to have behaved wrongly or illegally: *Applicants must possess a clean driving licence.* **6 Clean** jokes are not offensive or obscene: *His humour is usually clean, which is more than you can say for that of most comedians.* [*opposite* **dirty**]
▻ ***verb***: **cleans, cleaning, cleaned**
1 You **clean** something when you make it free from dirt or stains, by *eg* washing, wiping, brushing or polishing it: *It's about time I cleaned these windows.* □ *We cleaned the house from top to bottom.* □ *The wound should be thoroughly cleaned and then dressed.* □ *Have you cleaned your teeth?* □ *Your shoes need cleaning.* **2** You **clean** when you do such jobs as dusting and polishing furniture, sweeping floors and vacuuming carpets: *The council will find someone to clean for you if you apply to them.* — noun (*uncount*) **cleaning:** *My husband does most of the cooking and cleaning.* □ *You could easily find a cleaning job.*
▻ ***adverb*** (*informal*)
Clean means **1** smoothly and directly, without meeting any obstructions: *The brick went clean through the windscreen.* **2** completely: *I'd clean forgotten that it was his birthday.* □ *Her attacker got clean away.*
▻ ***phrase*** You **come clean** about something that you have been keeping secret when you admit it or tell people about it.
1 For **make a clean break** see **break**. **2** For **make a clean sweep of** see **sweep**. □ *I'm sorry; I'd better come clean.*

phrasal verbs
clean out You **clean out** something such as a cupboard or room when you empty it completely and clean it thoroughly: *I'll clean the wardrobe out and make some space in it.*
clean up 1 You **clean up** something that has got dirty when you make it clean: *We'll have to clean you up before your mum comes to collect you.* □ *I'll clean the place up tomorrow.* □ *I hate cleaning up after a party.* **2** You **clean up** a mess when you get rid of it from somewhere: *She was on her knees cleaning up the spilt food.* **3** You **clean up** after someone when you clean a place that they have made dirty: *I'm tired of cleaning up after you.*

clean-cut /kliːnˈkʌt/ *adjective*
Someone who is **clean-cut** has a neat appearance: *a pleasant, clean-cut young man.*

cleaner /kliːnə(r)/ *noun*: **cleaners**
1 A **cleaner** is a person employed to clean inside buildings. **2** A **cleaner** is also a machine or usually liquid substance used for cleaning: *a bottle of lemon-scented cream cleaner for the bathroom.* [see also **vacuum cleaner**] **3** The **cleaner** or the **cleaner's** is a shop where clothes are dry-cleaned: *take a coat to the cleaner's.*

cleanliness /ˈklɛnlɪnəs/ *noun* (*uncount*)
Cleanliness is the habit of keeping yourself clean and tidy by regular washing.

cleanly /ˈkliːnlɪ/ *adverb*
Something is done **cleanly** if it is done smoothly, well and completely: *She broke the top cleanly off.*

cleanse /klɛnz/ *verb*: **cleanses, cleansing, cleansed**
To **cleanse** your skin is to make it thoroughly clean, usually with a special cream or other substance: *The wound should be cleansed before bandaging.*

clean-shaven /kliːnˈʃeɪvən/ *adjective*
A **clean-shaven** man does not have a beard or moustache.

clear /ˈklɪə(r)/ *adjective*; *adjective or adverb*; *verb*
▻ ***adjective***: **clearer, clearest**
1 a Something that is **clear** is easy to see, hear or understand: *The outline of his face was sharp and clear against the light.* □ *She spoke in a clear, musical voice.* □ *His explanation was not very clear.* □ *clear, logical reasoning.* **b** Something is **clear** if it is obvious and you cannot be in any doubt about it: *It was clear from her behaviour that she disliked Johnson intensely.* □ *Her choice was clear: either stay and suffer, or complain and be sacked.* □ *You will have to make it clear to him* [= make him realize] *that you will tolerate his rudeness no longer.* □ *If you don't make your wishes clear you can't expect people to do what you want.* **c** You are **clear** about something if you understand it fully, or have made a definite decision about it: *You should be clear in your own mind about what you expect from this relationship.* □ *I'm not clear whether we should accept their terms or not.* **d** You make yourself **clear** when you express yourself in such a way that no-one can doubt what you mean: *There will be trouble if this occurs again. Do I make myself clear?* **e Clear** ideas or inten-

tions are definite ones: *He still has no clear idea what he'll do when he leaves university.* [*same as* **definite**]
2 a Something such as a surface, road or path is **clear** if there is nothing covering, blocking or obstructing it in any way: *Snowploughs have been operating on the bypass and it is now clear.* □ *Make sure both surfaces are clear of dust and grease before applying the adhesive.* □ *Fortunately there has been no further house-building and we still have a clear view of the mountains from the front window.* **b** A period of time is **clear** if it is free from appointments or planned activities: *Remember to keep the weekend clear; my parents are coming to stay.* □ *I've got a clear day on Friday.* [*same as* **free**] **c** You have a **clear** conscience when you know you have done nothing wrong and have nothing to feel guilty about: *I shall tell the truth, however painful, and will be able look back on the whole episode with a clear conscience.* [*opposite* **guilty**]
3 a Clear liquids and substances can be seen through easily: *The clear liquid in her glass was probably gin rather than water.* [*same as* **transparent**; *opposite* **opaque**, **cloudy**] **b** The sky is **clear** when there are no clouds; a **clear** day is one on which there is no mist: *On a clear day you can see the Eiffel Tower from here.* **c** Your skin is **clear** if it has no spots or blemishes. **d** Someone's eyes are **clear** if they are attractively bright and healthy-looking: *clear grey eyes.* **e** Your mind, thoughts or head are **clear** if you are able to think sensibly and reasonably.

▻ ***adjective or adverb***
One thing is, or is standing, **clear** of another if it is not touching it or obstructing it: *Always make sure you keep the electric flex clear of the mower's blades.* □ *The spectators were asked to stand clear of the line of play.* □ *The car was coming straight at him and he managed to jump clear only just in time.*

▻ ***verb***: **clears, clearing, cleared**
1 You **clear** a place when you remove unwanted things that are covering, blocking or obstructing it: *Waiters were clearing the floor ready for the dancing.* □ *I cleared a space on my desk to put the printer down on.* □ *He cleared the table and started the washing-up.* □ *Did you manage to clear the drain?* **2** You **clear** your throat when you cough slightly to remove mucus from your throat, or when you make a slight coughing noise merely to get people's attention, *eg* when you are about to make a public announcement. **3** You **clear** something unwanted from a place when you remove it: *There'll be more room if we clear these chairs to one side.* □ *Once the guests have finished eating, clear the plates quickly.* **4** People **clear** a room or building when they leave it: *The bomb-disposal people insisted that the building should be cleared.* [*same as* **evacuate**] **5** A person or animal **clears** something such as a fence when they jump over it without touching it; you clear your name or reputation when you prove yourself innocent of some wrong doing that people suspect you of: *He's the only athlete ever to have cleared 2.65 metres.* **6** A plan or proposal **is cleared** when official permission is given for it to be put into practice: *We must clear it first with head office.* **7** Someone **is cleared** of a crime when they are declared to be innocent of it: *She was cleared of all charges.* **8** Something **clears** your mind or head when it makes your thoughts less confused; your mind, head, thoughts or vision **clear** when they become less confused: *Perhaps a walk by the sea would clear your head.* □ *Slowly my vision cleared and I was aware of someone standing over me.* **9** Fog **clears** when it disappears: *We waited for the mist to clear before climbing any further.*

▻ ***phrases*** **1** You are **in the clear** with regard to some offence when you cannot be blamed or held responsible for it. **2** You **steer clear** or **stay clear** of someone or something when you keep away from them, or avoid them: *I always steer clear of her when she's in this mood.*

phrasal verbs
clear away You **clear away**, or **clear** things **away**, when you remove or put away the things you have been using, *eg* for a meal: *We cleared away and washed up.* □ *I cleared away the dishes and piled them beside the sink.*
clear off (*informal*) If you say **'clear off!'** to someone, you are asking them rudely to go away.
clear out 1 You **clear** something such as a room or cupboard **out** when you make it tidy by taking out all rubbish or unwanted things. [*same as* **tidy** out] **2** (*informal*) To **clear out** is also to leave: *We've been told to clear out of the house unless we pay the rent today.* [*same as* **leave**]
clear up 1 You **clear up**, or **clear** a place **up**, when you make it tidy and put things away in their proper place: *She realized she'd been left to clear up as usual.* □ *I've told the kids to clear up their room.* [*same as* **tidy**] **2** You **clear up** after someone when you tidy a place that they have made untidy. [*same as* **tidy up** after] **3** You **clear up** a disagreement, problem or mystery when you settle or solve it. [*same as* **solve**] **4** The weather **clears up** when it stops raining or becomes brighter and sunnier. [*same as* **brighten**] **5** Something such as a cold or headache **clears up** when it gets better.

clearance /'klɪərəns/ *noun* (*uncount*)
1 Clearance is the distance between one object and another passing beside or under it: *The lorry passed under the bridge with a good six inches' clearance.* **2** You get **clearance** for something when you are given official permission to do it: *The captain has to wait for clearance from the control tower before he can take off.*

clear-cut /'klɪəkʌt/ *adjective*
Something is **clear-cut** when there is no doubt or misunderstanding about it: *This was a clear-cut case of sexual harassment.*

clear-headed /klɪə'hɛdɪd/ *adjective*
A person is **clear-headed** if they are able to think clearly and sensibly, especially in difficult situations.

clearing /'klɪərɪŋ/ *noun*: **clearings**
A **clearing** is an area in a wood or forest where there are no trees.

clearly /'klɪəlɪ/ *adverb*
1 Clearly means in a clear way: *I couldn't see clearly for the mud on my glasses.* □ *You'll have to speak clearly; she's a little deaf.* **2** (*sentence adverb*) **Clearly** also means 'obviously' or 'without doubt': *Clearly, he wouldn't want to do anything that put the business at risk.* □ *This has clearly been a great shock to all of you.*

clear-sighted /klɪə'saɪtɪd/ *adjective*
Someone is **clear-sighted** when they are able to judge situations clearly and decide sensibly how to act.

cleavage /'kliːvɪdʒ/ *noun*: **cleavages**
A woman's **cleavage** is the narrow line or space between her breasts.

clef /klɛf/ *noun* (*music*): **clefs**
A **clef** is a symbol placed at the beginning of a piece of music to show which range of notes it uses; the **treble clef** indicates the upper range of notes, played on the piano by the right hand; the **bass clef** indicates the lower range, played on the piano the left hand.

cleft /klɛft/ *noun*: **clefts**

A **cleft** is a narrow opening in *eg* rocks, a cliff or the ground.

clemency /ˈklɛmənsɪ/ *noun* (*uncount; formal*)
Someone in authority shows **clemency** when they decide to be kind and give a less severe punishment than is possible: *Defence counsel appealed to the judge for clemency.*

clementine /ˈklɛmənti:n/ *noun*: **clementines**
A **clementine** is a fruit like a small orange.

clench /klɛntʃ/ *verb*: **clenches, clenching, clenched**
1 You **clench** your fist when you make a tight fist, usually because you are angry. **2** You **clench** your teeth when you press them together firmly, *eg* in anger or pain. **3** You **clench** something when you hold it tightly: *With the bottle top clenched between his teeth, he pulled hard.*

clergy /ˈklɜ:dʒɪ/ *noun* (*plural*)
The **clergy** are priests or religious ministers in general: *a member of the clergy.*

clergyman /ˈklɜ:dʒɪmən/ *noun*: **clergymen**
A **clergyman** is a male priest.

cleric /ˈklɛrɪk/ *noun*: **clerics**
A **cleric** is a member of the clergy.

clerical /ˈklɛrɪkəl/ *adjective*
1 Clerical means relating to general office work: *clerical tasks* □ *a clerical worker.* **2 Clerical** also means relating to the clergy: *a woman priest in full clerical dress.*

clerk /klɑ:k/ *noun*: **clerks**
A **clerk** is a person who deals with things such as papers, accounts, records and files in an office, bank or law court.

clever /ˈklɛvə(r)/ *adjective*: **cleverer, cleverest**
1 Someone who is **clever** is good or quick at learning and understanding: *one of our cleverest pupils* □ *It was clever of you to think of that.* □ *She's the cleverest criminal we've ever encountered.* [*same as* **bright, intelligent**] **2** A **clever** plan or scheme has been carefully thought out by talented people: *an extremely clever bank robbery.* — *adverb* **cleverly:** *She had very cleverly planted the letter where they were sure to look for it.* □ *a cleverly executed scheme.*

cliché /ˈkli:ʃeɪ/ *noun*: **clichés**
A **cliché** is a familiar phrase or expression that people use when they cannot think of an original way to express their ideas, or perhaps when their ideas are not very clear: *We're fed up with hearing the same tired old clichés.*

click /klɪk/ *noun*; *verb*
▻ ***noun***: **clicks**
A **click** is a short sharp sound, such as the sound made by two parts of a mechanism locking into place: *I heard a faint click as he released the safety catch.*
▻ ***verb***: **clicks, clicking, clicked:** *The machine whirred and clicked.*

client /ˈklaɪənt/ *noun*: **clients**
A **client** is a customer, especially one paying for the services of a professional person, *eg* a lawyer: *Their company is this bank's most valued client.*

clientele /kli:ənˈtɛl/ or /klaɪənˈtɛl/ *noun* (*with a singular or plural verb*)
The **clientele** of a hotel, restaurant or other establishment consists of the people who go there: *a club with an almost exclusively male clientele* □ *Our clientele is very discerning.*

cliff /klɪf/ *noun*: **cliffs**
A **cliff** is a high steep rock face, especially on the coast.

climactic /klaɪˈmaktɪk/ *adjective*
Climactic means of or involving a climax: *the climactic scene in the film when Rett Butler finally leaves Scarlet o'Hara forever.*

climate /ˈklaɪmət/ *noun*: **climates**
1 The **climate** of an area is the typical weather conditions there: *She wouldn't enjoy living in such a cold climate.* **2** You can talk about the **climate** when you are referring to people's opinions or attitudes in general, or to a particular situation: *the fairly hostile climate that exists in parliament at the moment* □ *Tax increases are not what is needed in the current economic climate.* — *adjective* **climatic** /klaɪˈmatɪk/: *climatic changes caused by the greenhouse effect.*

climax /ˈklaɪmaks/ *noun*: **climaxes**
The **climax** of something such as a story or an event is the most exciting or important point in it, often near the end: *The film fails because the audience anticipates the climax.*

climb /klaɪm/ *verb*; *noun*
▻ ***verb***: **climbs, climbing, climbed**
1 You **climb** something such as a ladder or a mountain, or you **climb** up it, when you move towards or reach the top of it: *She climbed the stairs quietly, taking care not to wake the children.* □ *It took seven days to reach the summit, climbing by the west face.* □ *She has climbed all the mountains of Canada.* □ *I can see him climbing to the top of the management ladder.* **2** You also **climb** somewhere when you move there, usually awkwardly or with great effort: *She climbed down from the horse.* □ *Only the thinnest of us could climb through the hole in the fence.* **3** Something **climbs** when it rises or increases: *The number of people unemployed has climbed to over 3 million.*
▻ ***noun***: **climbs:** *After such an exhausting climb, we rested at the top for over an hour.* □ *Getting to the top position in any company is a hard climb.*

climber /ˈklaɪmə(r)/ *noun*: **climbers**
1 A **climber** is someone who climbs mountains as a sport or hobby: *Another climber is reported missing on Ben Nevis.* **2** An animal is a good **climber** if it can climb well: *Bears are usually accomplished climbers.* **3** A **climber** is also a climbing plant.

climbing /ˈklaɪmɪŋ/ *noun* (*uncount*)
Climbing is the activity or sport of climbing mountains or rocks: *They're going climbing this weekend.*

climbing plant /ˈklaɪmɪŋ/ *noun*: **climbing plants**
A **climbing plant** is a plant that sends out shoots and branches that cling to supports such as walls, and can grow up or down: *Ivy is a common climbing plant.*

clinch /klɪntʃ/ *verb* (*informal*): **clinches, clinching, clinched**
To **clinch** something such as an argument or decision is to settle it finally and firmly: *top business men clinching deals over dinner* □ *It was a difficult choice between the two; what clinched it for us was the size of the garden in this house.*

cling /klɪŋ/ *verb*: **clings, clinging, clung**
1 You **cling** to something when you hold it firmly or tightly by wrapping your arms round it: *The child was clinging to its mother's legs.* □ *He clung on to the branch and hoped it would support his weight.* **2** You **cling** to ideas or methods when you continue to insist that they are the best or most valid: *an old family firm clinging rather bravely to traditional techniques* □ *Her supporters still cling to the belief that she is the Messiah, the new Christ.* **3** Clothes that **cling** fit very tightly or closely.

clinging /ˈklɪŋɪŋ/ *adjective*
1 Clinging clothes fit very tightly or closely: *The*

blouse was a bit too clinging to wear for work. **2** You describe someone as **clinging** if you think they depend too much on someone else, usually emotionally: *He was rather a clinging husband.*

clinic /ˈklɪnɪk/ *noun*: **clinics**
A **clinic** is a department of a hospital, or a separate building, where people receive medical treatment or advice of a particular kind: *the family planning clinic* □ *She suggested I go to the ear, nose and throat clinic.*

clinical /ˈklɪnɪkəl/ *adjective*
1 Clinical is used to refer to practical aspects of medicine, rather than to theory: *Clinical trials of the drug have been very promising.* **2** You describe a place as **clinical** if it is severely plain and simple, with little or no decoration: *Light-heartedness was unthinkable in the rather clinical atmosphere of the lecture hall.* **3** Someone's behaviour or attitude might be described as **clinical** if it is only concerned with what is practical, rather cruelly ignoring people's feelings: *Governments inevitably adopt a rather clinical approach to unemployment.*

clink /klɪŋk/ *noun*; *verb*
▻ ***noun***: **clinks**
A **clink** is a short sharp ringing sound, like the sound glasses make when they knock against one another.
▻ ***verb***: **clinks, clinking, clinked:** *The sound of laughter and of clinking glasses floated across the lawn.*

clip /klɪp/ *noun*; *verb*
▻ ***noun***: **clips**
1 A **clip** is a small device for holding or fastening things together, usually made of metal or plastic: *a box of hair clips* □ *The pages were held together with a paper clip.* **2** A **clip** is also a short piece of a film or television programme, shown on its own: *Identify the actors in this film clip.*
▻ ***verb***: **clips, clipping, clipped**
1 You **clip** something when you fasten it with a clip: *She clipped the pen to her top pocket.* **2** You also **clip** something when you shape it or make it neat by cutting small pieces off it: *She spent the afternoon clipping rose bushes.*

clipboard /ˈklɪpbɔːd/ *noun*: **clipboards**
A **clipboard** is a board with a strong clip at the top, used for holding papers together, and to give you a firm surface to write on.

clipped /ˈklɪpt/ *adjective*
1 Clipped hair or fur has been trimmed neatly, using scissors or clippers: *a clipped moustache* □ *poodles with closely clipped coats.* **2** A person's voice or accent is **clipped** if they pronounce words quickly in a series of short rather sharp sounds, often shortening or changing the sound of words as they speak.

clippers /ˈklɪpəz/ *noun* (*plural*)
Clippers are a tool with two sharp blades used to cut things such as fingernails or toenails, hair, or hedges.

clipping /ˈklɪpɪŋ/ *noun*: **clippings**
A **clipping** is a piece cut out of a newspaper or magazine, such as an article or advertisement.

clique /kliːk/ *noun*: **cliques**
You call a small group of people a **clique** if they tend not to mix with other people and do not willingly accept others into their group.

cloak /kloʊk/ *noun*; *verb*
▻ ***noun***: **cloaks**
1 A **cloak** is a loose sleeveless kind of coat fastened at the neck. **2** Something used to hide something else might be referred to as a **cloak**: *The secretarial work had been a cloak for her spying activities.*
▻ ***verb***: **cloaks, cloaking, cloaked**
To **cloak** something is to cover or conceal it: *The moor was cloaked in mist.* □ *strange goings-on cloaked in mystery.*

cloakroom /ˈkloʊkrʊm/ *noun*: **cloakrooms**
1 In a place such as a theatre or restaurant, the **cloakroom** is a room where customers' coats and hats may be left. **2** Some people refer to the toilets in a public building as the **cloakroom**.

clobber /ˈklɒbə(r)/ *verb* (*informal*): **clobbers, clobbering, clobbered**
1 To **clobber** someone is to hit or beat them with your fists: *I said I would clobber him if he ever spoke to my wife again.* **2** To **clobber** someone is to defeat them easily: *They've been clobbered in their first three games this season.*

clock /klɒk/ *noun*; *verb*
▻ ***noun***: **clocks**
1 A **clock** is an instrument for measuring and showing time: *an electronic clock with a digital display* □ *She heard the clock strike four o'clock.* **2** A **clock**, or time **clock**, is a part of a machine that a person can adjust to make the machine switch itself on at a desired time. **3** In a vehicle, the **clock** is an instrument that shows the total distance it has travelled: *It's an old car but it only has 40 000 miles on the clock.*
▻ ***verb***: **clocks, clocking, clocked**
To **clock** something is to measure or record how much time it takes: *We clocked the runners for the first half mile.*
▻ ***phrases*** **1** You work **round the clock** when you work constantly, during the night as well as during the day: *Volunteers have worked round the clock to get it finished.* **2** When you tell someone that they cannot **put** or **turn clock back** you mean that they cannot return to the past or to a time before some regrettable event happened: *Forget all about it and look to the future; you can't turn the clock back.*

phrasal verb
You **clock up** a particular speed, distance or score when you reach or achieve it: *The truck has just clocked up 100 000 kilometres.* □ *That's the fifteenth win they've clocked up this season.*

clockwise /ˈklɒkwaɪz/ *adjective and adverb*
A **clockwise** direction is the direction that the hands on a clock turn in: *Turn the screwdriver clockwise.* [*opposite* **anticlockwise**]

clockwork /ˈklɒkwɜːk/ *adjective*
A **clockwork** device operates by means of a mechanism like an old-fashioned clock, with springs that must be tightened periodically by winding: *a child's clockwork bear that beats a drum.*
▻ ***phrase*** Something works **like clockwork** when it works very smoothly or successfully: *The whole plan went like clockwork.*

clod /klɒd/ *noun*: **clods**
A **clod** is a lump of earth or soil.

clog /klɒg/ *noun*; *verb*
▻ ***noun***: **clogs**
A **clog** is a heavy shoe carved from a piece of wood, or a leather shoe with a thick wooden sole.
▻ ***verb***: **clog, clogging, clogged**
When a passage is **clogged** with something, or **clogged** up with it, it is completely blocked or obstructed by it: *The drain was clogged with leaves.* □ *My nose was so clogged up that I could hardly breathe.*

cloister /ˈklɔɪstə(r)/ *noun*: **cloisters**
A **cloister** is a paved covered walkway around a square in *eg* a monastery or church.

cloistered /'klɔɪstəd/ *adjective*
A person leads a **cloistered** life if they live a quiet life away from the noise and activity of everyday life. [*same as* **secluded**, **sheltered**]

clone /kloʊn/ *noun*; *verb*
▻ ***noun***: **clones**
A **clone** is a person, animal or thing that has been produced artificially *eg* in a laboratory, and is an exact copy of another person, animal or thing.
▻ ***verb***: **clones, cloning, cloned**
To **clone** a person, animal or thing means to make another or several others that are an exact copy of them.

close¹ /kloʊs/ *adjective*; *adverb*
▻ ***adjective***: **closer, closest**
1 One thing is **close** to another when it is only a short distance away from it: *Her flat is close to the centre of town.* □ *Their house is quite close; we usually walk there.* □ *I'm looking for a flat closer to the centre of town.* □ *He put the cup down on a table close by.* □ *We found her sitting with her face close up to the window, listening to the rain.* □ *The gun was fired at close range.* [compare **near**] **2** A **close** friend is someone you feel strongly attached to; a **close** relative is someone directly related to you: *She was distraught when her friend died; they were very close.* **3 Close** also means thorough, with great attention paid to details: *A closer examination of the facts revealed that she had to be innocent.* □ *They kept him under close observation.* **4** One thing is **close** to another, or there is a **close** link between them, if they are very similar or directly connected: *They have expressed extreme right-wing views that are close to Fascism.* □ *Arrogance is psychologically very close to insecurity.* □ *a close resemblance between the two.* **5** Events or happenings are **close** when they are about to occur: *They feel that a solution to the problem is quite close.* □ *I was very moved, and close to tears more than once.* **6** A contest or competition is **close** when it is difficult to judge who will win or who should win: *The vote was so close that a recount was inevitable.* **7 Close** is also used in stating approximate values, amounts or distances: *He was paid close on £1 million for singing at the concert.* □ *We must have walked close to three miles without seeing another soul.* **8** You say it is **close** when the atmosphere is unpleasantly warm with no breeze, or a lack of fresh air. — *adverb* **closely:** *They're closely related.* □ *The two firms have worked closely together.* □ *She has closely observed their behaviour in the wild.* — *noun* (*uncount*) **closeness:** *I sensed the closeness of another person in the room.* □ *She has always envied the closeness of her brothers' relationship.*
▻ ***adverb***: **closer**, **closest:** *Mills was leading, with Jackson following close behind.* □ *Move closer, so I can see your eyes.* □ *He held her very close.*

close² /kloʊz/ *verb*; *noun*
▻ ***verb***: **closes, closing, closed**
1 You **close** something when you shut it or move it into a position in which it covers an opening, or in which its opening is covered; it **closes** when it shuts or moves so as to cover an opening: *He closed the gate behind him.* □ *The door closed softly.* □ *She lay back and closed her eyes.* □ *He put the documents back into the box and closed the lid.* □ *I saw him close the drawer hastily.* □ *Would you mind closing the window a bit?* □ *To stop the flow of gas, close this valve.* [*same as* **shut**; *opposite* **open**] **2** A gap **closes** or **is closed** when the two sides of it join or move closer together: *The gap between the two runners was gradually closing.* □ *We shall put in a couple of stitches to close that wound.* **3** A person or animal that is chasing you **closes** on you when they get nearer to you: *He could hear his pursuer closing on him.* □ *The police car was still some distance behind but closing every second.* **4** A shop or place of business **closes** or **is closed** when it stops being open to the public, or when the people in it stop working and go home: *This store closes at 6.00 pm Monday to Friday.* □ *What time does the library close?* □ *They close the store at 5.30 on Saturdays.* [*same as* **shut**; *opposite* **open**] **5** Something such as a factory or business **closes** when it stops operating for ever. [see also **close down** below] **6** A meeting or discussion **closes** or **is closed** when it comes to an end: *Before proceedings close, I should like to thank the organizers.* □ *He closed the interview rather abruptly and walked out.* [*opposite* **open**]
▻ ***noun*** (*uncount or used in the singular*)
The **close** of something is the end or conclusion of it: *At close of trading today, the value of the pound had fallen by two points.* □ *The cricket score was 250 for 6 at close of play.* □ *Discussions drew to a close around midnight.* [*opposite* **start**]

phrasal verbs
close down A factory or business **closes down** or **is closed down** when it stops operating for ever: *The paper would be taken over or closed down.* □ *The works closed down with a loss of 1500 jobs.*
close in 1 Darkness or night **closes in** when it gets dark. **2** People or troops **close in** on a person or place when they surround them from different directions: *The Allies were closing in on Paris.* [see also **close** sense 3]

close³ /kloʊs/ *noun*
Close is used as a name for a small quiet street finishing in a dead end.

closed /kloʊzd/ *adjective*
1 Something such as a door is **closed** when it is shut, or placed so that it covers an opening: *She was sitting bolt upright with tightly closed eyes, evidently thinking hard.* □ *It isn't healthy to sleep with the window closed.* [*same as* **shut**; *opposite* **open**] **2** A shop, office or public building is **closed** when it is not open for the public to go into or use: *Most of the stores will be closed by now.* □ *The museum is closed on Mondays.* [*same as* **shut**; *opposite* **open**] **3** A **closed** group or circle of people restricts its membership to a select few, and does not allow others to join it. **4** A factory or business that is described as a '**closed** shop' is one in which all employees must belong to a particular trade union. **5** A television system that is used within a building, *eg* in a shop to guard against stealing, is referred to as '**closed**-circuit television'.

close-knit /kloʊs'nɪt/ *adjective*
People are **close-knit** if they are closely linked and share common beliefs and background.

close-set /kloʊs'sɛt/ *adjective*
Two or more things are **close-set** when they are very close to each other, or closer to each other than is usual: *He has close-set, heavy-lidded eyes.* □ *a ring with small, close-set diamonds.*

closet /'klɒzɪt/ *noun*; *adjective*
▻ ***noun***: **closets**
A **closet** is **1** a large cupboard. **2** (*AmE*) a fitted or built-in wardrobe [see picture at **bedroom**]
▻ ***adjective***
Closet is used to describe a person who has a particular habit that they keep secret: *Many so-called 'Christians' are closet atheists.*

close-up /kloʊs'ʌp/ *noun*: **close-ups**
A **close-up** is a photograph, or a film or television shot, taken near the subject to show a lot of detail.

closing /ˈkloʊzɪŋ/ *adjective*
The **closing** part of an event is the final part of it: *They scored in the closing moments of the game.*

closure /ˈkloʊʒə(r)/ *noun (uncount or count)*: **closures**
1 The **closure** of something such as a factory is the act of closing it down permanently: *Three of the firms are facing closure.* **2** The **closure** of a road is the act of blocking it so traffic cannot use it: *lane closures on the motorway.*

clot /klɒt/ *noun*; *verb*
▻ ***noun***: **clots**
1 A blood **clot** is a soft mass of half-solid blood that forms either on the skin as a wound heals, or inside the body when blood is not flowing properly. **2** (*informal*) If you call someone a **clot** you think they are stupid or foolish.
▻ ***verb***: **clots, clotting, clotted**
Blood **clots** when it forms soft half-solid lumps.

cloth /klɒθ/ *noun*: **cloths**
1 (*uncount*) **Cloth** is fabric of any kind, especially before it is made into clothes or other things: *four metres of cloth.* **2** A **cloth** is a piece of fabric used for something in particular, *eg* washing or cleaning: *a linen tablecloth* □ *a clean dishcloth.*

clothe /kloʊð/ *verb*: **clothes, clothing, clothed**
1 To **clothe** someone is to provide them with clothes: *They can hardly afford to clothe their children.* **2** (*literary*) You **are clothed** in what you are wearing: *She arrived early, clothed in the usual tweed suit.*

clothes /kloʊðz/ *noun* (*plural*)
Clothes are shirts, trousers, dresses and other things that people wear: *I didn't want to take my clothes off in front of my aunt.*

clothes line *noun*: **clothes lines**
A **clothes line** is a rope that you hang washing on to dry, *eg* in your garden.

clothes peg *noun*: **clothes pegs**
Clothes pegs are pegs.

clothing /ˈkloʊðɪŋ/ *noun* (*uncount*)
Clothing is clothes: *one or two items of clothing.*

cloud /klaʊd/ *noun*; *verb*
▻ ***noun***: **clouds**
1 Clouds are grey or white masses of water vapour that float in the sky: *Huge black rainclouds had gathered over the hills.* **2** A **cloud** of something such as dust or smoke is a moving mass of it in the air.
▻ ***verb***: **clouds, clouding, clouded**
1 Something that **clouds** your judgement prevents you from judging fairly or reasonably: *Passion must not be allowed to cloud our thinking.* **2** You say that something **clouds** the issue when it makes a subject or situation more confusing or difficult to understand.
▻ ***phrase*** Someone is **under a cloud** if other people have a poor opinion of them or are cross with them for some reason.

> ***phrasal verb***
> When it **clouds over** the sky fills up with clouds that hide the sun: *We abandoned the picnic when it began to cloud over.*

cloudless /ˈklaʊdləs/ *adjective*
A **cloudless** sky is clear and has no clouds in it.

cloudy /ˈklaʊdɪ/ *adjective*: **cloudier, cloudiest**
1 A **cloudy** sky is full of clouds: *In the South, it will be cold and cloudy.* **2** A **cloudy** liquid is not clear, especially when it should be: *The beer was a bit cloudy.*

clout /klaʊt/ *verb*; *noun*
▻ ***verb*** (*informal*): **clouts, clouting, clouted**
To **clout** someone is to hit them with your hand or fist.
▻ ***noun*** (*informal*): **clouts**
1 A **clout** is a blow with the hand: *She gave him a clout round the ear.* **2** (*uncount*) Someone who has **clout** is able to influence or control other people: *an organization with a lot of political clout.*

clove /kloʊv/ *noun*: **cloves**
A **clove** of *eg* garlic is one of the small sections that together form the bulb.

clover /ˈkloʊvə(r)/ *noun* (*uncount*)
Clover is a small plant, with flat rounded leaves and pink, purple or white flowers, that often grows wild in grass.

clown /klaʊn/ *noun*; *verb*
▻ ***noun***: **clowns**
1 A **clown** is a comic performer who wears ridiculous clothes and make-up, especially one performing in a circus. **2** (*informal*) People refer to a foolish or stupid person as a **clown**: *Some clown had parked in front of the gates.*
▻ ***verb***: **clowns, clowning, clowned**
To **clown**, or **clown** about or around, is to behave in a silly way: *Concentrate on your homework and spend less time clowning about.*

cloying /ˈklɔɪɪŋ/ *adjective*
A taste that is **cloying** is so sweet that it lingers unpleasantly in your mouth; **cloying** sentiment is too sweet and intense.

club /klʌb/ *noun*; *verb*
▻ ***noun***: **clubs**
1 A **club** is an organized group of people who meet regularly to take part in a particular activity that they are all interested in; a **club** is also the building that they meet in: *She's just joined our chess club.* □ *They've started a swimming club at the local pool.* □ *We'll meet outside the club.* **2** A **club** is also a stick with a specially shaped head, for playing golf with: *He wasn't swinging the club properly.* **3** Any stick used as a weapon is also a **club**, especially when it is heavy and thicker at one end than at the other. **4** A **club** is also a nightclub. **5 Clubs** are one of the four suits (♣) of cards in a pack of playing cards: *the six of clubs*
▻ ***verb***: **clubs, clubbing, clubbed**
A person **is clubbed** when they are beaten severely with a stick or other heavy object: *It was clear that he had been clubbed to death.*

> ***phrasal verb***
> Several people **club together** to buy something when they each give money towards the cost.

cluck /klʌk/ *verb*: **clucks, clucking, clucked**
A hen **clucks** when it makes its typical sound.

clue /kluː/ *noun*: **clues**
1 A **clue** is a piece of discovered information that helps you to solve a mystery: *The police found several important clues in the dead man's bedroom.* **2** In a crossword puzzle, the **clues** are the sets of words or phrases that lead you to the answers to the different parts of the puzzle.
▻ ***phrase*** (*informal*) You can say that you **haven't a clue** when you mean you do not know at all: *I haven't a clue where your tie is.* □ *She hasn't got a clue why he left so suddenly.*

clump /klʌmp/ *noun*; *verb*
▻ ***noun***: **clumps**
A **clump** of things, such plants, small trees or buildings, is a small group of them growing or standing close together: *a clump of heather.*
▻ ***verb***: **clumps, clumping, clumped**
To **clump** about is to walk with loud, heavy footsteps: *Dad clumped around the kitchen in his old boots.*

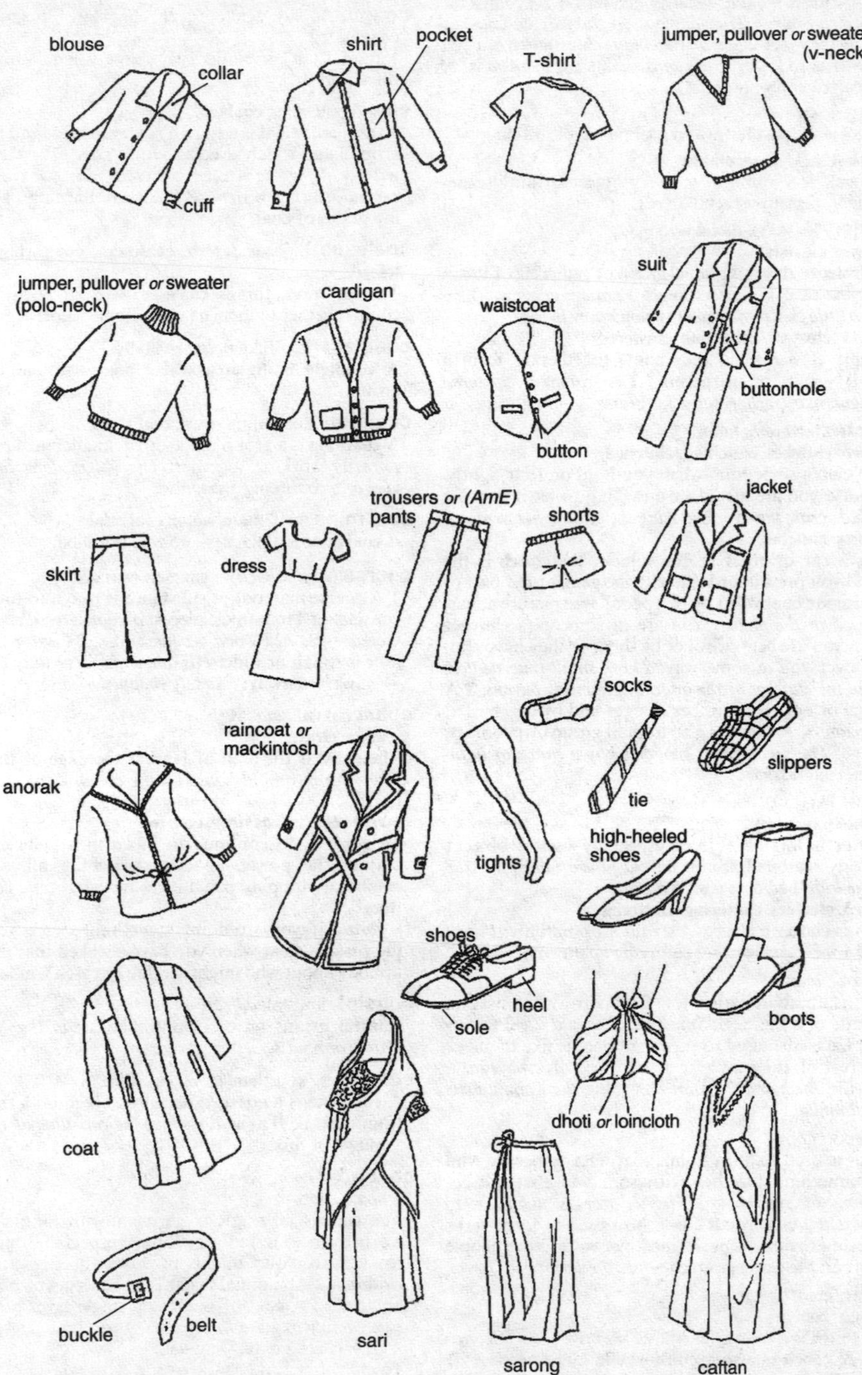

clumsy /ˈklʌmzɪ/ *adjective*: **clumsier, clumsiest**
1 A **clumsy** person is careless or unskilful with their hands, or awkward in the way they walk or move: *The clumsy oaf has broken my desk lamp.* □ *He always managed to look clumsy on the dance floor.* **2** Your behaviour is **clumsy** when you upset or embarrass someone because you have not understood their feelings properly: *He made a clumsy attempt to comfort*

her. **3** Objects are described as **clumsy** if they are awkward to use: *The cabinet had been fitted with a rather clumsy metal handle.* — *adverb* **clumsily:** *She folded the paper clumsily.* □ *They apologized clumsily and dashed out of the room.* — *noun* (*uncount*) **clumsiness:** *She felt embarrassed by her own clumsiness.* □ *the clumsiness of his marriage proposal.*

clung /klʌŋ/ *verb*
Clung is the past tense and past participle of **cling**.

clunk /klʌŋk/ *noun*: **clunks**
A **clunk** is a sound of a heavy object striking something, especially a metal object.

cluster /ˈklʌstə(r)/ *noun; verb*
▷ ***noun***: **clusters**
A **cluster** of things is a small group or gathering of them: *Sow the seeds in clusters to get a natural effect.* □ *There was a little cluster of regular customers by the bar.*
▷ ***verb***: **clusters, clustering, clustered**
People **cluster** when they come together to form a small group or gathering: *The children clustered around their teacher, eager for praise.*

clutch /klʌtʃ/ *verb; noun*
▷ ***verb***: **clutches, clutching, clutched**
You **clutch** something when you hold on to it tightly, because you are afraid or unwilling to let it go: *She waded across the river clutching the baby in her arms.*
▷ ***noun***: **clutches**
1 In a car or other motor vehicle, the **clutch** is the pedal you press in order to change gear, or the part of the engine controlled by this pedal. [see picture at **car**] **2** (*used in the plural*) You are in someone's **clutches** when you are held prisoner by them or they have control over you in some way: *These small-time dealers are in the clutches of the international drug barons.* **3** A **clutch** of eggs is a number of eggs laid by one bird at one time. **4** A **clutch** is also a small group of people or things: *The senator was supported by a clutch of influential congressmen.*

clutter /ˈklʌtə(r)/ *noun; verb*
▷ ***noun*** (*uncount*)
Clutter is lots of objects, especially useless objects, untidily scattered about: *an old house full of clutter.* □ *The kids' bedroom is such a clutter.*
▷ ***verb***: **clutters, cluttering, cluttered**
Things **clutter** a place if they fill it up untidily: *I don't want your old magazines cluttering up my front room.*

Co /koʊ/ *noun*
1 Co is an abbreviation for 'Company' when used in the title of a business: *Smith, Jenkins and Co.* **2** (*informal*) **Co** is also used to mean 'all people like them' or 'the rest of the people in the group': *We should ask Reagan, Bush and Co what they think the Communists are planning.*

co- /koʊ-/ *prefix*
1 Co- is used to form nouns that refer to people who do something together with someone else: *the co-authors of the book* □ *Her co-star is unknown to American audiences.* **2 Co-** is also used to form verbs referring to actions performed by two or more people together: *the women who co-wrote the script.*

coach /koʊtʃ/ *noun; verb*
▷ ***noun***: **coaches**
1 A **coach** is a railway carriage: *We have seats in coach F.* **2** A **coach** is also a comfortable bus designed for long-distance travel. **3** A person who trains a sportsperson or team is often called their **coach**. **4** A **coach** is also a four-wheeled vehicle pulled by horses, especially one with a roof.
▷ ***verb***: **coaches, coaching, coached**
To **coach** someone, *eg* in a sport or in a subject, is to train or instruct them: *We could tell by his answers that he had been coached by someone*

coagulate /koʊˈagjʊleɪt/ *verb*: **coagulates, coagulating, coagulated**
Liquid such as blood **coagulates** when it becomes thick and sticky.

coal /koʊl/ *noun*: **coals**
1 (*uncount*) **Coal** is a hard black mineral found underground and widely used as a fuel: *They filled the cellar with coal for the winter.* □ *a coal mine* □ *a coal-fired central-heating system.* **2 Coals** are burning or glowing pieces of coal.

coalesce /koʊəˈlɛs/ *verb*: **coalesces, coalescing, coalesced**
Two or more things **coalesce** when they merge or come together to form a larger, single whole.

coalfield /ˈkoʊlfiːld/ *noun*: **coalfields**
A **coalfield** is an area where coal is found underground.

coalition /koʊəˈlɪʃən/ *noun*: **coalitions**
A **coalition** is a group made up of smaller groups temporarily working together: *The voters don't like the idea of a coalition government.*

coal mine /koʊl maɪn/ *noun*: **coal mines**
A **coal mine** is a place where coal is mined.

coarse /kɔːs/ *adjective*: **coarser, coarsest**
1 A **coarse** material or substance is rough to touch or consists of large thick pieces: *a coarse woollen fabric* □ *coarse-grained wood* □ *coarse salt.* **2 Coarse** behaviour is rough or rude: *His language was rather coarse.* — *adverb* **coarsely:** *coarsely chopped meat.*

coast /koʊst/ *noun; verb*
▷ ***noun***: **coasts**
The **coast** is the area of land at the edge of the sea: *They live in an old house on the coast.* □ *the Adriatic coast.*
▷ ***verb***: **coasts, coasting, coasted**
To **coast** is to continue to move in a vehicle after cutting the power, *eg* after switching off a car's engine or stopping pedalling a bicycle. [*same as* **freewheel**]
▷ ***phrase*** If you are doing something secret, you say **the coast is clear** when you have checked that there is nobody about who might see you or catch you.

coastal /ˈkoʊstəl/ *adjective*
Coastal means on or near the coast: *in the coastal waters around Jersey.*

coastline /ˈkoʊstlaɪn/ *noun*: **coastline**
A **coastline** is a coast, especially as seen on a map or from the sea: *We could just see the coastline of France through the fog.*

coat /koʊt/ *noun; verb*
▷ ***noun***: **coats**
1 A **coat** is an outdoor garment with long sleeves, worn over your indoor clothes, especially one that reaches to your thighs or lower. [see picture at **clothing**] **2** An animal's **coat** is its covering of hair, fur or wool. **3** A **coat** of paint is a single layer of it *eg*: *Each door was given three coats of varnish.*
▷ ***verb***: **coats, coating, coated**
To **coat** something is to cover it with a layer of some substance: *toffees coated with chocolate.*

coat-hanger /ˈkoʊthaŋə(r)/ *noun*: **coat-hangers**
A **coat-hanger** is a shaped piece of wood, plastic or metal with a hook at the top, on which you hang clothes. [see picture at **bedroom**]

coating /ˈkoʊtɪŋ/ *noun*: **coatings**
A **coating** of a substance is a layer of it covering something: *There was a thin coating of snow on the ground.*

coat of arms /koʊt əv ˈɑːmz/ *noun*: **coats of arms**
A family's or town's **coat of arms** is a design on a shield that it uses as a symbol or emblem.

coax /koʊks/ *verb*: **coaxes, coaxing, coaxed**
You **coax** someone to do something when you persuade them to do it using kind or gentle words, or by insincere flattery: *They managed to coax the fox out of the garden hut.* □ *She was able to coax him into agreeing to lend them the money.*

cobble /ˈkɒbəl/ *noun; verb*
▻ ***noun***: **cobbles**
Cobbles are cobblestones.
▻ ***verb*** (*informal*): **cobbles, cobbling, cobbled**

> ***phrasal verb***
> You **cobble** something **together** when you make it quickly and without enough care: *They just cobbled together a report from old bits of research.*

cobbled /ˈkɒbəld/ *adjective*
A **cobbled** street is one with a road surface made of cobblestones.

cobbler /ˈkɒblə(r)/ *noun* (*old*): **cobblers**
A **cobbler** is a person who makes or repairs shoes.

cobblestone /ˈkɒbəlstoʊn/ *noun*: **cobblestones**
Cobblestones are small square blocks of stone with a rounded surface, laid in rows to form the surface of a road: *They're replacing the old cobblestones with tarmac.*

cobra /ˈkoʊbrə/ *noun*: **cobras**
A **cobra** is a poisonous snake that expands the skin at the back of its head as a warning.

cobweb /ˈkɒbwɛb/ *noun*: **cobwebs**
A **cobweb** is a network of threads made by a spider, in which it catches insects and other prey.

cocaine /koʊˈkeɪn/ *noun* (*uncount*)
Cocaine is a drug used in medicine to prevent pain, also taken illegally for pleasure.

cock /kɒk/ *noun; verb*
▻ ***noun***: **cocks**
A **cock** is a male bird, especially an adult male chicken: *She could hear the cocks crowing in the farmyard.*
▻ ***verb***: **cocks, cocking, cocked**
To **cock** a part of your body is to lift it into a certain position or in a certain direction: *She cocked an ear towards the door but could hear nothing of their conversation.* □ *She stepped back to admire the painting, her head cocked to one side.*

> ***phrasal verb***
> (*slang*) You **cock** something **up** when you do it wrongly or very badly and ruin it: *She cocked up the whole experiment.* □ *That's cocked up my chances of getting accepted.* [see also **cock-up**]

cockerel /ˈkɒkərəl/ *noun*: **cockerels**
A **cockerel** is a young cock.

cock-eyed /kɒkˈaɪd/ *adjective* (*informal*)
1 Something is **cock-eyed** if if is not straight: *That shelf looks a bit cock-eyed to me.* **2** An idea or plan is **cock-eyed** if it not sensible and is likely to be unsuccessful: *another of his cock-eyed schemes for making money.*

cockney /ˈkɒknɪ/ *noun; adjective*
▻ ***noun***: **cockneys**
1 A **cockney** is a person who was born in East London. **2** (*uncount*) **Cockney** is the dialect of East London.
▻ ***adjective:*** *Would you call that a cockney accent?*

cockpit /kɒkpɪt/ *noun*: **cockpits**
In a small aeroplane, the **cockpit** is the compartment where the pilot sits; in a racing car, the small compartment in which the driver sits is also called the **cockpit**.

cockroach /ˈkɒkroʊtʃ/ *noun*: **cockroaches**
A **cockroach** is a large black or brown insect found in damp and dirty rooms.

cocksure /kɒkˈʃʊə(r)/ *adjective*
When you describe someone as **cocksure** you think they are too confident: *He's rather a cocksure young lad.*

cocktail /ˈkɒkteɪl/ *noun*: **cocktails**
1 A **cocktail** is an alcoholic drink consisting of several ingredients. **2** Some mixed dishes of food are referred to as **cocktails**: *a seafood cocktail.*

cock-up /ˈkɒkʌp/ *noun* (*slang*): **cock-ups**
A **cock-up** is a mistake that ruins or spoils something, or the disordered situation that results from it: *He's made a real cock-up of the travel arrangements; we've been given the wrong tickets.* [see also **cock up** at **cock**]

cocky /ˈkɒkɪ/ *adjective* (*informal*): **cockier, cockiest**
If you describe someone as **cocky** you think they are too confident: *That cocky little madam will get her face slapped one of these days.* [*same as* **arrogant**]

cocoa /ˈkoʊkoʊ/ *noun* (*uncount*)
1 Cocoa is a powder made from the roasted crushed seeds of a tropical tree, used to make chocolate. **2 Cocoa** is also a hot drink made from cocoa powder mixed with milk and sugar: *a cup of cocoa.*

coconut /ˈkoʊkənʌt/ *noun*: **coconuts**
A **coconut** is a large tropical nut with a hard hairy brown shell filled with solid edible white flesh and a clear, sweet-tasting liquid. [see picture at **fruit**]

cocoon /kəˈkuːn/ *noun; verb*
▻ ***noun***: **cocoons**
A **cocoon** is a case that a young insect makes round itself before it turns into its adult form.
▻ ***verb***: **cocoons, cocooning, cocooned**
Someone **is cocooned** when they are protected from the problems of everyday life: *academics sitting cocooned in their libraries.*

cod /kɒd/ *noun* (*count or uncount*): **cod**
A **cod** is a large sea fish whose flesh is used as food: *a plate of cod and chips.*

code /koʊd/ *noun; verb*
▻ ***noun***: **codes**
1 (*count or uncount*) A **code** is a system of words, letters, symbols or signals used to replace the real words or letters when sending messages, especially secret messages: *They have managed to crack the code the enemy was using.* □ *It was written in code.* □ *Morse code.* **2** A **code** is also a set of letters and numbers that identify something: *Remember to put the post code at the end of the address.* □ *Every published book has its own code number.* **3** A **code** is also an organized set of rules or principles: *All drivers should learn the Highway Code thoroughly.* □ *Does your club have a dress code?*
▻ ***verb***: **codes, coding, coded**
1 To **code** a message is to change the words and letters according to a secret code, so that others cannot understand it. **2** Something such as a threat **is coded** if it is expressed in an indirect way.

code name /ˈkoʊd neɪm/ *noun*: **code names**

A **code name** is a secret name given to a person, organization or operation, known and used by the people directly involved with it. — *adjective* **code-named:** *The invasion was code-named 'Operation Fearless'.*

codify /ˈkoudɪfaɪ/ *verb*: **codifies, codifying, codified**
You **codify** *eg* rules or a system when you list or present them in a clear and properly ordered way.

co-educational /kouɛdjʊˈkeɪʃənəl/ *adjective*
A **co-educational** school is attended by both boys and girls. [*same as* **mixed**]

coerce /kouˈɜːs/ *verb*: **coerces, coercing, coerced**
Someone **is coerced** into doing something when they are forced into doing it: *None of our employees will be coerced into retiring.* — *noun* (*uncount*) **coercion** /kouˈɜːʃən/: *There were claims that they had used coercion.*

coexist /kouɪgˈzɪst/ *verb*: **coexists, coexisting, coexisted**
Two or more things **coexist** when they exist next to each other, in the same place at the same time: *You wouldn't think that such different animals could coexist in such a confined area.* — *noun* (*uncount*) **coexistence** /kouɪgˈzɪstəns/: *Here, there has been peaceful coexistence between Christians and Muslims for years.*

coffee /ˈkɒfɪ/ *noun*: **coffees**
1 (*uncount*) **Coffee** consists of the roasted and crushed seeds of a tropical plant, used to make a hot drink; the hot drink is also called **coffee**: *eight ounces of coffee* □ *Make yourself a cup of coffee.* □ *She buys the coffee beans and grinds them herself.* **2** A **coffee** is a cup of coffee: *I've ordered three coffees and a tea.* □ *Can I get you a coffee?*

coffee bar *noun*: **coffee bars**
A **coffee bar** is a café where coffee and snacks are sold.

coffee table *noun*: **coffee tables**
A **coffee table** is a small low table: *The coffee table was covered with newspapers.* [see picture at **living room**]

coffers /ˈkɒfəz/ *noun* (*plural*; *sometimes humorous*)
The **coffers** of a government or an organization are its supplies of money: *Donations to party coffers are drying up as businesses cut back on unnecessary expense.*

coffin /ˈkɒfɪn/ *noun*: **coffins**
A **coffin** is a large box that a dead person is buried or cremated in. [*same as* **casket**]

cog /kɒg/ *noun*: **cogs**
A **cog** is one of a series of metal wheels whose edges are shaped to fit into each other, so that all the wheels turn together: *Inside the clock was an intricate system of cogs and springs.*

cogent /ˈkoudʒənt/ *adjective* (*formal*)
A **cogent** argument is one that convinces or persuades other people. [*same as* **convincing**]

cognac /ˈkɒnjak/ *noun* (*uncount*)
Cognac is fine brandy.

cohabit /kouˈhabɪt/ *verb*: **cohabits, cohabiting, cohabited**
Two unmarried people **cohabit** when they live together and carry on a sexual relationship. — *noun* (*uncount*) **cohabitation** /kouhabɪˈteɪʃən/: *Many young couples choose cohabitation in preference to marriage.*

coherent /kouˈhɪərənt/ *adjective*
1 An argument or theory that is **coherent** has been well thought out and it makes sense. **2** Someone is **coherent** when they are calm enough or well enough to speak clearly so that others can understand them: *He could hardly have been coherent after drinking all that whisky.* [*opposite* **incoherent**]

cohesion /kouˈhiːʒən/ *noun* (*uncount*)
Cohesion is the condition or state in which several things fit together well and form a whole: *The team is suffering from a lack of cohesion*

cohesive /kouˈhiːsɪv/ *adjective*
A **cohesive** group is made of separate parts that fit together well to form a whole: *Family life is often considered a cohesive force required for the well-being of society as a whole.*

coil /kɔɪl/ *noun*; *verb*
▷ ***noun***: **coils**
A **coil** of something such as wire or rope is a length of it formed into a continuous series of rings or loops, each laid on top of the other.
▷ ***verb***: **coils, coiling, coiled:** *A spring is just a coiled piece of wire.* □ *The snake had coiled itself round the rabbit.*

coin /kɔɪn/ *noun*; *verb*
▷ ***noun***: **coins**
A **coin** is a small metal disc used as money: *the new pound coins.* [*compare* **note**]
▷ ***verb***: **coins, coining, coined**
You **coin** a word or phrase when you invent it: *Was it Marx who coined the word 'capitalism'?*
▷ ***phrase*** You say **to coin a phrase** before or after using a much-used expression when you cannot think of an original phrase: *If the company doesn't find the money by tomorrow it will be, to coin a phrase, the end of the road.*

coinage /ˈkɔɪnɪdʒ/ *noun* (*uncount*)
Coinage is coins in general: *before Britain switched to decimal coinage.*

coincide /kouɪnˈsaɪd/ *verb*: **coincides, coinciding, coincided**
1 Two or more events **coincide** when they happen at the same time: *His arrival in Africa coincided with the beginning of a period of civil war.* **2** The opinions of different people or groups **coincide** when they are the same and the people agree: *the only area in which the views of Parliament and the European Court coincided.*

coincidence /kouˈɪnsədəns/ *noun* (*count or uncount*): **coincidences**
When two unconnected things unexpectedly happen at the same time it is a **coincidence**: *What a coincidence that we should end up living in the same street!* □ *They arrived at the same time purely by coincidence.*

coincidental /kouɪnsɪˈdɛntəl/ *adjective*
Something is **coincidental** if it happens by coincidence: *It was merely coincidental that the letter arrived just as I was leaving.* — *adverb* **coincidentally:** *All of these climbers have, coincidentally, climbed Nanga Parbat.*

coke /kouk/ *noun*: **cokes**
1 (*uncount*) **Coke** is a dark brown, fizzy drink: *a bottle of coke.* **2** A **coke** is a serving of this drink: *Two cokes and a packet of crisps, please.* **3** (*uncount*) **Coke** is fuel produced by removing the gases from coal.

colander /ˈkɒləndə(r)/ or /ˈkʌləndə(r)/ *noun*: **colanders**
A **colander** is a metal or plastic bowl with holes in, used for separating food from the liquid it was soaked, washed or cooked in.

cold /kould/ *adjective*; *adverb*; *noun*
▷ ***adjective***: **colder, coldest**
1 Something that is **cold** is low in temperature, or lower than it usually is or than you would like it to be: *The washing machine mixes hot and cold water.* □ *Eat your food before it gets cold.* □ *We are to expect cold weather this weekend.* □ *It feels colder today than yesterday.* □ *Make sure the baby doesn't get too cold.*

2 Cold is also used to describe food that is cooked but not eaten hot: *a selection of cold meats.* **3** A person's behaviour is **cold** when it is shows no friendliness: *We were given a polite but rather cold welcome.* ▫ *She's quite a cold person.* [*same as* **frigid**] — *adverb* **coldly:** *I hadn't expected to be greeted so coldly.*

▻ ***adverb***

You do something **cold** when you do it without first preparing or practising it: *Coming to the job cold, you may think of ways in which our working methods could be improved.*

▻ ***noun*: colds**

1 (*uncount*) The **cold** is lack of heat or warmth, especially in the weather: *You're bound to feel the cold without a coat on.* **2** A **cold** is a common illness that causes a running nose, sneezing, coughing and sometimes headaches: *It's so easy for children at school to catch colds from each other.*

cold-blooded /kould'blʌdɪd/ *adjective*

1 Cold-blooded animals have a body temperature that varies according to their surroundings. [compare **warm-blooded**] **2** A **cold-blooded** person is able to act cruelly without having any feelings of pity or guilt: *The newspapers described her as a cold-blooded killer.*

cold sweat /kould 'swet/ *noun* (*used in the singular*)

If you in a **cold sweat** your skin feels cold and damp because you are very nervous or frightened: *He came out in a cold sweat every time he thought about the exam.*

cold war /kould 'wɔ:(r)/ *noun* (*uncount or used in the singular*)

Cold war is unfriendly political relations between countries who are not actually at war with each other: *We in Britain could not have imagined there would be an end to the cold war, and that Russia would become an ally.*

coleslaw /'koulslɔ:/ *noun* (*uncount*)

Coleslaw is a mixture of thin strips of raw cabbage, carrot and onion, in mayonnaise or another salad dressing.

colic /'kɒlɪk/ *noun* (*uncount*)

A baby has **colic** when it has pains in its stomach.

collaborate /kə'labəreɪt/ *verb*: **collaborates, collaborating, collaborated**

1 Two or more people **collaborate** when they work together to produce or create something: *The Art School has collaborated with the local council to put on this exhibition.* **2** Someone who **collaborates** with an enemy occupying their country gives them support or helps them. — *adjective* **collaborative** /kə'labərətɪv/: *a collaborative venture by British Aerospace and Air France.* — *noun* (*uncount*) **collaboration** /kəlabə'reɪʃən/: *They publish a weekly poetry magazine in collaboration with the Arts Council.* — *noun* **collaborator**: *They were accused of having been traitors and collaborators.*

collage /kɒ'lɑ:ʒ/ *noun*: **collages**

A **collage** is a picture that you make by sticking pieces of *eg* coloured paper and fabric on to stiff paper or cardboard.

collapse /kə'laps/ *verb*; *noun*

▻ ***verb*: collapses, collapsing, collapsed**

1 When a structure such as a building or a piece of furniture **collapses** it falls to pieces: *In these high winds, many of the huts are in danger of collapsing.* ▫ *The bed collapsed as soon as we got in.* **2** An organization or institution **collapses** when violent or dramatic events suddenly bring it to an end and it ceases to exist: *The dictator died and his military government collapsed.* ▫ *Their relationship has all but collapsed as a result of the affair.* **3** You **collapse** when you fall down or faint because you are ill or extremely tired: *Several of the prisoners collapsed in the heat.* ▫ *He dropped his bags of shopping and collapsed into a chair.* **4** Someone **collapses** when their strong emotions cause them to lose control of themselves: *She collapsed in tears at the news.* **5** An object such as a chair **collapses** when you can fold it flat so that it can be stored easily.

▻ ***noun*** (*uncount*): *Our whole economic system was on the verge of collapse.* ▫ *the collapse of Communism in former Eastern Europe.*

collapsible /kə'lapsəbəl/ *adjective*

A **collapsible** object, such as a chair or table, is one that you can fold flat so that it can be stored easily: *We have a small collapsible bed for unexpected guests.* [*same as* **folding**]

collar /'kɒlə(r)/ *noun*; *verb*

▻ ***noun*: collars**

1 The **collar** of a shirt, coat, dress or other garment is the band or flap of material round the neck, that is often folded over. [see picture at **clothing**] **2** A pet animal's **collar** is the band of leather or other material round its neck, that a lead can be attached to.

▻ ***verb*** (*informal*): **collars, collaring, collared**

To **collar** someone is to catch or capture them: *She collared me in the corridor and forced me to apologize.* ▫ *It wasn't long before the police had collared her.*

collarbone /'kɒləboun/ *noun*: **collarbones**

Your **collarbones** are the two long bones that run from your shoulders to the base of your neck.

collate /kə'leɪt/ *verb*: **collates, collating, collated**

You **collate** information that you have gathered from various sources when you organize it and examine it: *The doctors are still collating the results of the tests.*

collateral /kə'latərəl/ *noun* (*uncount*)

Collateral is property that you guarantee to give to a lender if you fail to pay back money that you have borrowed: *We had to offer the house as collateral.* [*same as* **security**]

colleague /'kɒli:g/ *noun*: **colleagues**

A **colleague** is a person that you work with: *One of her university colleagues wrote the book.*

collect /kə'lɛkt/ *verb*: **collects, collecting, collected**

1 You **collect** several things, or **collect** them up, when you gather them together: *The room would look a lot tidier if you collected up those newspapers.* ▫ *Three of them went off to collect firewood.* ▫ *There simply isn't a more efficient way of collecting this tax.* ▫ *A few people had collected round the man's body.* **2** You **collect** objects of a particular kind when you acquire more and more of them because you are interested in them: *His daughter collects stamps.* **3** You **collect** something when you fetch it from a place where it is being kept for you; you **collect** someone when you go to take them away from somewhere at an arranged time: *We'll phone you when it arrives in the shop, and you can come and collect it.* ▫ *I normally collect the children from school at 3.30.* **4** To **collect** for a charity or other organization is publicly to ask people to give you money for that organization: *We're collecting door to door and in the high street.* **5** You **collect** yourself when you make an effort to become calm after being angry or upset; you **collect** your thoughts when you prepare yourself mentally for some task.

collected /kə'lɛktɪd/ *adjective*

1 An author's or poet's **collected** works are all their most important writings gathered together and published in one book. **2** A person is described as **collected** when they have their emotions or thoughts under control so that they are able to behave in a calm and rational way: *I don't understand how she can stay so calm and collected before big competitions.*

collecting /kə'lɛktɪŋ/ *noun* (*uncount*)
Collecting is the hobby of acquiring or buying particular things because you are interested in them: *stamp collecting.*

collection /kə'lɛkʃən/ *noun*: **collections**
1 (*uncount*) **Collection** is the process of collecting something: *Your order should be ready for collection next week.* □ *They argued that the collection of taxes could be streamlined.* **2** A **collection** of objects is a number of them acquired gradually, out of interest or enthusiasm: *one of the world's finest collections of impressionist paintings.* **3** A **collection** is a public request for money, *eg* in the street on behalf of a charity, or during a church service.

collective /kə'lɛktɪv/ *adjective*
1 Collective refers to actions or events that involve all the members of a group: *We all share a collective responsibility for the work produced by our department.* **2** (*grammar*) A **collective** noun is a noun such as *furniture* or *staff* which refers to a number of individual things or people.

collectively /kə'lɛktɪvlɪ/ *adverb*
1 People do something **collectively** if they do it together. **2** You can use **collectively** when referring to a group of things as a single unit.

collector /kə'lɛktə(r)/ *noun*: **collectors**
A **collector** is a person who collects, as a job or hobby: *Her Majesty's tax-collectors* □ *a local association of stamp-collectors.*

college /'kɒlɪdʒ/ *noun*: **colleges**
1 (*count or uncount*) A **college** is one of the places where education continues for students beyond the age of leaving school, usually in practical or technical subjects and often in training for a job: *She had to make the choice between drama college and university.* □ *He goes to college three days a week.* **2** Some older British universities are divided into separate **colleges**, institutions which govern themselves: *My friend was at New College, Oxford.* **3** Some schools call themselves **colleges**: *She was a pupil at Cheltenham Ladies' College.*

collide /kə'laɪd/ *verb*: **collides, colliding, collided**
Two objects **collide** when they crash into each other: *The car swerved to avoid the dog and collided with a lamp post.*

colliery /'kɒljərɪ/ *noun*: **collieries**
A **colliery** is a coalmine.

collision /kə'lɪʒən/ *noun* (*count or uncount*): **collisions**
A **collision** occurs when two or more objects crash into each other: *Few drivers survive high-speed collisions on motorways.* □ *A lorry was in collision with two cars.*

colloquial /kə'loʊkwɪəl/ *adjective*
Colloquial language is informal language that people use in conversation, rather than in formal speech or writing.

collude /kə'lu:d/ *verb* (*formal*): **colludes, colluding, colluded**
One person **colludes** with another when they cooperate or act together in secret to deceive others or to do something illegal: *It was discovered that the alleged victim had colluded with the thieves to defraud the insurance company.*

collusion /kə'lu:ʒən/ *noun* (*uncount*)
Two or more people are in **collusion** with each other when they are acting together secretly in some crime or other wrongdoing: *There has been a suggestion that the bank manager was in collusion with the thieves.*

colon[1] /'koʊlən/ *noun*: **colons**
A **colon** is the punctuation mark (:), used to introduce a list, an example, or an explanation. [see **Punctuation** in Appendices]

colon[2] /'koʊlən/ *noun* (*used in the singular*)
In your body, the **colon** is the main part of your intestine.

colonel /'kɜ:nəl/ *noun*: **colonels**
A **colonel** is a senior army officer.

colonial /kə'loʊnɪəl/ *adjective*
Colonial refers to countries that are colonies, or to the practice of powerful countries ruling less powerful countries as colonies: *British colonial rule in India.* — *noun* (*uncount*) **colonialism** /kə'loʊnɪəlɪzm/: *Many of the leaders were opposed to colonialism.*

colonize or **colonise** /'kɒlənaɪz/ *verb*: **colonizes, colonizing, colonized**
To **colonize** a foreign country is to take control of it and rule it by setting up a branch of your government there: *Many parts of Africa have been colonized by Europeans.*

colony /'kɒlənɪ/ *noun*: **colonies**
1 A **colony** is a country ruled by a more powerful country which sets up a branch of its government there. **2** A **colony** is also a large group of animals or birds of one type living together.

color see **colour**.

coloration /kʌlə'reɪʃən/ *noun* (*uncount*)
A creature's **coloration** is its arrangement of colours: *This species of moth has evolved with darker coloration on the wings so that it blends in with the sooty industrial environment.*

colossal /kə'lɒsəl/ *adjective*
Colossal means extremely large: *It is a colossal stadium.* □ *additions to an already colossal debt.*

colour (*AmE* **color**) /'kʌlə(r)/ *noun*; *adjective*; *verb*
▻ ***noun***: **colours**
1 (*count or uncount*) The **colour** of something is the appearance it has, created by the way it reflects light. **Colour** is one of the features that can identify an object, along with shape, size and texture: *They painted it two different colours; green on the top and blue on the bottom.* □ *They're slightly different shades of the same colour.* □ *What colour is the bear's fur?* □ *The fruit is yellowish in colour.* **2** (*uncount*) Something, such as a newspaper photograph, appears in **colour** when there are different colours in it, not simply black, white and grey. **3** (*uncount*) A person's **colour** is the shade of their skin: *She's perfectly healthy, as you can see from her good colour.* **4** (*uncount*) Something has **colour** when it contains interesting or convincing details: *The book fails mainly because many of the characters lack colour.*
▻ ***adjective***
A **colour** picture or illustration is one that contains different colours, not simply black, white and grey; a **colour** television shows pictures in all colours, and not simply black, white and grey.
▻ ***verb***: **colours, colouring, coloured**
1 To **colour** something such as a drawing, or to **colour** it in, is to put colours on it, *eg* by painting: *Aren't you going to colour his face in?* **2** Something **colours** your judgement when it influences the way you think or the opinions you have.
▻ ***phrases***
1 You see someone **in their true colours** when their behaviour, *eg* in a crisis, reveals unworthy motives that you had not suspected in them before. **2** (*informal*) Someone who is **off colour** is feeling unwell. **3** You do

something **with flying colours** when you do it very well or very successfully: *She passed all her exams with flying colours.*

colour-blind (*AmE* **color-blind**) /'kʌləblaɪnd/ *adjective*
Someone who is **colour-blind** is unable to distinguish certain colours.

coloured (*AmE* **colored**) /'kʌləd/ *adjective*
1 Coloured means having a particular colour or colours: *lemon-coloured cupboard doors* □ *brightly coloured tropical birds.* **2** (now offensive) People who do not belong to a pale-skinned race are sometimes described as **coloured**.

colourful (*AmE* **colorful**) /'kʌləfəl/ *adjective*
1 Something is **colourful** if it has a lot of different, usually bright colours: *They've used a very colourful wallpaper.* **2** Something, such as a story or description, can be described as **colourful** when it is full of interesting details: *International journalists can lead a very colourful life.* **3** A person can be described as **colourful** if they are interesting and amusing: *He's one of the village's more colourful characters.*

colouring (*AmE* **coloring**) /'kʌlərɪŋ/ *noun* (*uncount*)
1 Colouring is a substance added to processed food to give it a more attractive colour. **2** The **colouring** of something is its colour, or its pattern of different colours: *a classic motorbike with its distinctive gold colouring.* **3** A person's **colouring** is the normal colour of their skin, often also including the colour of their hair and eyes: *This will suit her very fair colouring.*

colourless (*AmE* **colorless**) /'kʌləlǝs/ *adjective*
1 Something such as a liquid is **colourless** if it has no colour: *It is a colourless, odourless gas.* **2** You describe something dull and uninteresting as **colourless**: *He's rather a colourless character.*

colour supplement /'kʌlə sʌplɪmənt/ *noun*: **colour supplements**
A **colour supplement** is a magazine that is given away free with a newspaper, especially at the weekend.

colt /koʊlt/ *noun*: **colts**
A **colt** is a young male horse.

column /'kɒləm/ *noun*: **columns**
1 In a building, a **column** is a cylindrical pillar used to support a roof. **2** A **column** is also a row or line of things or people: *She added up the first column of figures and entered the total at the bottom.* □ *The children arranged themselves into four columns.* **3** In a newspaper, a **column** is one of the vertical strips of print that each page is divided into; a **column** is also an article that regularly appears in a newspaper: *Read out the advertisement in the second column.* □ *She writes a column in the 'Daily Express'.*

columnist /'kɒləmnɪst/ *noun*: **columnists**
A **columnist** is a person who writes a regular article in a newspaper.

coma /'koʊmə/ *noun*: **comas**
Someone who is in a **coma** remains deeply unconscious for a very long time, *eg* after an injury or because of illness.

comatose /'koʊmətoʊs/ *adjective* (*technical or humorous*)
Someone who is **comatose** is in a coma, or is very soundly asleep: *Caroline was still comatose on the sofa.*

comb /koʊm/ *noun*; *verb*
▷ ***noun***: **combs**
A **comb** is a flat metal or plastic device with a series of teeth, that you pull through your hair to tidy or arrange it. [see picture at **bedroom**]
▷ ***verb***: **combs, combing, combed**
1 You **comb** your hair when you tidy or arrange it with a comb. **2** To **comb** a place is to search it thoroughly in an attempt to find a person or thing: *Police combed the woods near where the body was found.*

combat *noun*; *verb*
▷ ***noun*** /'kɒmbat/ (*uncount*)
Combat is fighting, especially between armies or trained fighters: *He was wounded in combat.* □ *She's taking classes in unarmed combat.*
▷ ***verb*** /'kɒmbat/ or /kəm'bat/: **combats, combating, combated**
To **combat** something is to oppose it or try to prevent it from happening: *The government has pledged to spend more resources on combating homelessness.*

combative /'kɒmbətɪv/ *adjective*
A **combative** person is always willing to argue or fight: *This latest interview shows the minister in a rather combative mood.* [*same as* **aggressive, argumentative**]

combination /kɒmbɪ'neɪʃən/ *noun*: **combinations**
1 A **combination** of people or things is two or more of them brought together, or the resulting mixture: *a rather bizarre combination of circumstances* □ *an interesting combination of colours.* **2** A **combination** is also a set of numbers or letters that opens a combination lock: *She had forgotten the combination to her briefcase.*
▷ ***phrase*** One thing occurs, or is used, **in combination with** another, if it occurs or is used together with it: *You use '-legged' in combination with a number, as in 'four-legged animals'.*

combination lock /kəmbɪneɪʃən'lɒk/ *noun*: **combination locks**
A **combination lock** is a lock operated by one or more numbered dials that release the lock when they are turned according to a fixed sequence of numbers.

combine /kəm'baɪn/ *verb*: **combines, combining, combined**
You **combine** two or more things when you bring them together or join them, or when you have both or all of them at the same time: *The two political parties were combined to form the Liberal Democrats.* □ *The four teams have decided to combine to form a single British team.* □ *The white aluminium frames combine durability with good looks.* — *adjective* **combined:** *The union and management made a combined effort to settle the dispute.*

combustion /kəm'bʌstʃən/ *noun* (*uncount*; *formal*)
Combustion is the process of catching fire and burning: *Charcoal is produced by the incomplete combustion of wood.*

come /kʌm/ *verb*: **comes, coming, came, come**
1 a Someone **comes** somewhere, especially towards you, or with you in any direction, when they move there: *She came over to my desk.* □ *Come and have a look at this.* □ *Jeff came straight into her room without knocking.* □ *The train came steaming round the bend at full speed.* □ *Have you come a long way today?* □ *The man's come to mend the television.* □ *Why don't you come and stay with us?* □ *We'll come and see you on Friday.* □ *Would you like to come on holiday with us?* □ *Could I come shopping with you?* **b** You **come** to a place when you reach it or arrive there: *After walking for about an hour they came to the river.* **c** In a discussion, the point that you **come** to next is the one you are going to discuss next: *Now we come to the matter of parking.* □ *We'll come to that later.* **d** A particular date, time, period or event **comes** when it arrives or happens: *The moment has come for action.* □ *The time will come when there'll be no money left.* □ *The summer holidays are coming soon.* **e** A thought or idea **comes** to you when you think of it, usually after some time: *The answer suddenly came to me.* **f** A person or thing **comes** from somewhere if that is their home, place of

origin, source or starting point: *She comes from some little village in South Wales.* □ *The cutlery comes from Sweden.* □ *According to the postmark, the parcel had come from Nottingham.* □ *A funny smell was coming from the kitchen.* **g** One thing **comes** from another when the first is a result of the second; if you say 'that's what **comes** of' certain behaviour, you mean that such behaviour was bound to have bad results: *Her arrogance comes from a deep sense of insecurity.* □ *Disappointment is what always comes of expectations that are too high.* □ *That's what comes of trusting people!*

2 a To **come** to a certain state is to pass into it or enter it: *The situation is bad; it may come to war.* □ *It happened the year before this government came to power.* □ *Just as the train came into view, its whistle sounded.* □ *My dream actually came true.* □ *We must hope that things come right in the end.* **b** You use **come** with various adverbs and adjectives in expressions that describe things breaking or getting separated: *The box came apart* (or *came to pieces*) *in my hands.* □ *The handle's come off.* □ *One of the screws has come loose.* □ *Some of the tiles are coming away from the wall.* □ *Your button's come undone.* □ *Several trees came down* [= fell down] *in the storm.* **c** Something **comes** to a point or level if it reaches it: *Her jacket came to just below her waist.* □ *The snow came up to our knees.* □ *Did the holiday come up to expectations?* **d** Items or quantities **come** to an amount if that is the total when they are added together: *Last week's shopping came to over £50.* **e** You **come** to feel a certain way if you develop the feeling gradually: *I disliked him at first but I came to respect and admire him after working with him.* **f** If you ask how someone **came** to do something, you are asking how it happened: *How did he come to hurt himself so badly?* □ *How did you come to be working in China?*

3 a Someone or something **comes** at a certain place in an order or sequence if that is where they are, or where they finish: *Mike came second in the cycle race.* □ *In 'ceiling', 'e' comes before 'i'.* □ *The solution to the mystery will no doubt come at the end of the play.* □ *What comes next on the agenda?* **b** An object **comes** in certain sizes or colours if it is available in those sizes and colours: *This pattern of wallpaper comes in blue or green.* □ *Some dresses come only in sizes 10 to 14.*

▻ ***phrases*** **1** An expression such as '**come** the spring' means 'when the spring comes': *Come the summer, the garden should be a blaze of colour.* □ *Come 5 o'clock I'll be finished with this job for good.* **2** An event or fact **comes as a** shock or surprise if it shocks or surprises you when you hear about it: *It came as no surprise when they got divorced.* **3** You say '**Come to think of it**' when you have suddenly realized something, especially something obvious that you should have thought of before: *Come to think of it, why don't we travel in one car instead of two?* **4** You say you do **not know whether you are coming or going** when you are in a state of confusion. **5** When you refer to a time or an event **to come** you are referring to a future time or event: *We hope that the factory won't close for some time to come.* □ *You'll regret it in time to come.* □ *I consoled myself with the thought of the holiday to come.* **6** If you say '**when it comes to** a certain thing', you mean 'in cases of a certain thing', or 'in cases where a certain thing is needed': *When it came to bad table manners, our parents were quick to scold us.* □ *When it comes to hard work, you can rely on Jim.*

phrasal verbs

come about When you ask how something **came about** you are asking how it happened: *How did the discovery come about?*

come across 1 You **come across** something when you discover or encounter it: *Searching through his briefcase, he came across a letter.* □ *We came across one or two nasty problems.* **2** Something or someone **comes across** in a certain way if that is the impression they make on people: *His speech came across well.* □ *She came across as a very competent manager.* [*same as* **come over**]

come along 1 If you ask how someone or something is **coming along** you want to know about their progress: *How's our young trainee coming along?* **2** You say '**come along**' when you want someone to hurry up, or do something they do not want to do: *Come along now, ladies and gentleman; it's closing time.* □ *Come along, eat up your vegetables.* **3** Something such as an opportunity or a new idea **comes along** when it occurs or arrives: *I haven't got another job to go to yet; I'll wait till something comes along.* [*same as* **crop up**]

come at A person **comes at** you when they attack you: *The man came at him with a knife.* [see also **come for** sense 1]

come back 1 Something **comes back** to you when you remember it: *Scenes of his childhood came back to him.* **2** You say you will **come back** to something when you do not want to discuss it further until later. **3** Something **is coming back** when it is becoming fashionable again: *I see flared trousers are coming back.* [see also **comeback**]

come by You **come by** something when you acquire it: *How did you come by such a good job?* □ *Reliable staff are hard to come by.*

come down Levels and amounts **come down** when they decrease, are reduced, or get lower: *We want to see the unemployment figures coming down.* □ *Her temperature has come down a bit since yesterday.*

come down on You **come down on** someone or something when you criticize or punish them severely: *The new headmaster has come down heavily on bullying.*

come down to A problem **comes down to** a certain thing if that is the most important issue or factor: *It all comes down to what can be managed in the time available.*

come down with You **come down with** an illness when you get it: *Jane's come down with flu.*

come for 1 Someone **comes for** you when they approach you threatening to attack you: *She was coming for me with a big stick.* **2** Someone **comes for** a person or thing when they call to collect them: *I'll come for you at seven.* □ *I've come for my mother's hearing aid.*

come forward You **come forward** when you offer to help or offer to give information: *Several witnesses came forward.*

come in 1 Something such as news **comes in** when you receive it: *Reports are coming in of a bad accident on the M4 motorway.* **2** Someone or something **comes in** if they have a role, function or use: *That's the stage of the plan where you come in.* □ *This pan comes in very useful for making soup.* □ *The money will come in useful when the baby's born.* **3** Someone **comes in** on a discussion when they join it. **4** The money you have **coming in** is your income.

come in for You **come in for** praise, blame or criticism when you are praised, blamed or criticized.

come into 1 You **come into** money when you inherit it. **2** You say that someone '**comes into** their own' when they have the opportunity, in particular circumstances, to display their talents: *Sport is where she really comes into her own.* **3** Something

comes into a situation if it is one of the factors or issues involved in it: *Pride doesn't come into it; I just want to try my best.*

come off 1 Something **comes off** if it is successful: *Let's try your idea; it might come off.* **2** You **come off** well or badly when you end in a good or bad position or condition after an event: *It was a hard fight for Bruno, but he came off the better of the two.* **3** (*informal*) If you say '**come off** it!' to someone you are telling them rather rudely that what they are saying is not true.

come on 1 When you ask how something **is coming on** you want to know about its progress: *The new project is coming on fine.* **2** You say **'come on!'** to someone as a way of encouraging them to hurry up, or to do something, or to be more reasonable: *Oh, come on, Bill! Things aren't that bad.* □ *Come on; we'll be late.*

come out 1 When the sun or moon **come out** they appear in the sky. **2** Facts **come out** when they become known: *During the interview, it came out that she had never liked Astaire.* □ *What came out of the statistical analysis was how infrequently people actually use these idioms.* [*same as* **emerge**] **3** Marks or stains **come out** when they disappear as a result of washing. **4** The colour **comes out** of a fabric if it fades, *eg* as a result of washing. **5** You **come out** in favour of or against something when you openly declare your support for or opposition to it. **6** You **come out** of an event or process in a certain position if that is the position you are in at the end of it: *The minister came out of the affair very much on top.* [*same as* **emerge**] **7** A photograph **comes out** if it is successful and its subject can be clearly seen: *The picture has come out a bit blurred.* **8** A new product **comes out** when it becomes available to the public; a book **comes out** when it is published.

come out in You **come out in** spots when they appear on your skin. [*same as* **develop**]

come out with (*informal*) Someone **comes out with** a remark, especially a funny one, when they make it: *What will the child come out with next?*

come over 1 Something such as a feeling **comes over** you when it affects you: *I apologize for losing my temper; I don't know what came over me.* **2** (*informal*) You **come over** faint or dizzy when you feel as if you are going to faint. **3** Someone or something **comes over** in a certain way if they make that impression on people: *She came over as very enthusiastic at the interview.* [*same as* **come across**]

come round 1 Someone who is unconscious **comes round** when they regain consciousness. [*same as* **come to**] **2** You **come round** to an idea when you change your mind and accept it: *I knew she would eventually come round to our way of thinking.* □ *I expect he'll come round.* **3** A particular period or event **comes round** when it occurs at its regular time: *Spring came round, bringing with it new plant and animal life.*

come through 1 You **come through** a difficult or dangerous event when you survive it: *You can't expect to come through a scandal like that with your reputation undamaged.* **2** A particular quality or meaning **comes through** to you when you notice or observe it in what is happening: *The conductor's sensitivity to the changes of mood came through in her handling of the orchestra.* **3** Something such as a document that you are waiting for **comes through** when it arrives: *Your passport has come through at last.*

come to Someone who is unconscious **comes to** when they regain consciousness: *When he came to he found himself in a hospital bed.* [*same as* **come round**]

come under 1 Something **comes under** a heading if it is in the category that has that heading: *Mystery novels come under 'crime'.* **2** Something **comes under** a certain body or authority if that authority controls it or has responsibility for it: *Swimming pools come under the local council.*

come up 1 Something **is coming up** when it is about to happen or appear: *Coming up after the break, Robert de Niro in his first-ever television interview.* **2** A message or display **comes up** on a computer screen when it appears there: *The same error message kept coming up.* **3** Something **comes up** when it happens suddenly and unexpectedly: *I'm afraid something has come up and I won't be able to go after all.* **4** Something **comes up** in a conversation or discussion when it is mentioned: *The question of the trade deficit is sure to come up at this morning's Cabinet meeting.* **5** Someone or something **is coming up** for a particular process when they are due to be dealt with by it: *Three members of the committee come up for re-election this time.* □ *The car's coming up for its road test soon.*

come up against You **come up against** a problem when you are faced with it: *Many black recruits still come up against prejudice within the police force.*

come upon You **come upon** something when you find it by chance: *I came upon this bundle of letters when I was sorting out her correspondence.*

come up to 1 To **come up to** a time is to approach it: *She must be coming up to retirement soon.* □ *It was coming up to 9.30 when I left.* **2** Someone **comes up** to you when they approach you, *eg* to speak to you: *An officer came up to him and saluted.*

come up with You **come up with** an idea when you think of it: *That's what we'll do, unless anyone can come up with a better suggestion.*

comeback /'kʌmbak/ *noun*: **comebacks**

A performer makes a **comeback** when they start to appear in public again after a period of not working; something makes a **comeback** when it becomes fashionable again.

comedian /kə'mi:dıən/ *noun*: **comedians**

A **comedian** is an entertainer who tells jokes or funny stories.

comedienne /kəmi:dı'en/ *noun*: **comediennes**

A **comedienne** is a female comedian.

comedy /'kɒmədı/ *noun*: **comedies**

1 A **comedy** is an amusing play, film or television programme. **2** (*uncount, often adjectival*) **Comedy** is amusing drama, or the art of making people laugh: *one of his finest comedy roles* □ *She has a talent for comedy.*

comely /'kʌmlı/ *adjective* (*old*)

A woman is **comely** if she is attractive.

comet /'kɒmıt/ *noun*: **comets**

A **comet** is a star-like object that moves round the sun and leaves a bright trail of gases behind it.

come-uppance /kʌm'ʌpəns/ *noun*

▻ ***phrase*** Someone **gets their come-uppance** if they get what they deserve, especially if they are punished for doing something wrong.

comfort /'kʌmfət/ *noun*; *verb*

▻ ***noun*** (*uncount or count*)

1 Comfort is the state of being contented, not worried

or anxious: *She got tremendous comfort from sharing her problems with others.* **2 Comfort** is also the state of having all that you need for a pleasant life: *Compared with some people, they live in relative comfort.* □ *A warm house is one of the comforts of life.* **3** A person or thing is a **comfort** if they help you stop worrying: *It's a comfort to know that you're here if I need you.* □ *My daughter is a great comfort to me.*

▻ ***verb***: **comforts, comforting, comforted**

You **comfort** someone when you try to make them feel less upset or worried, *eg* by saying kind things. — *adjective* **comforting:** *It's comforting to know that you're here if I need you.*

comfortable /ˈkʌmfətəbəl/ *adjective*

1 You are **comfortable** when your body is in a relaxed position: *You don't look very comfortable on that stool.* □ *Come in and make yourself comfortable.* **2** Something such as a chair is **comfortable** if you can easily relax on or in it: *It's not a very comfortable bed.* **3** You have a **comfortable** life when you have things, such as a nice house and sufficient money, that make life pleasant. **4** You feel **comfortable** about something when you are not embarrassed or offended by it: *She doesn't feel comfortable talking to her father about it.* **5** A sick or injured person is described as **comfortable** if they are in a stable condition and not likely to die suddenly. — *adverb* **comfortably:** *Are you sitting comfortably?* □ *They live quite comfortably.*

comic /ˈkɒmɪk/ *adjective; noun*

▻ ***adjective***

Comic means relating to comedy: *an actor with a wealth of comic devices.*

▻ ***noun***: **comics**

1 A **comic** is a magazine containing stories told through a series of pictures: *children's comics.* **2** A **comic** is also a comedian.

comical /ˈkɒmɪkəl/ *adjective*

Something **comical** is funny or amusing: *a comical expression.*

coming /ˈkʌmɪŋ/ *adjective*

Coming refers to things that will happen soon: *in the coming months.*

comma /ˈkɒmə/ *noun*: **commas**

A **comma** is the punctuation mark (,) that separates parts of a sentence or items in a list.

command /kəˈmɑːnd/ *verb; noun*

▻ ***verb***: **commands, commanding, commanded**

1 Someone in authority **commands** you to do something when they order you formally to do it: *The soldier commanded us to stop and show our papers.* □ *The Queen commands your presence at the Royal Garden Party.* **2** An officer in the armed forces **commands** the part of the force that they are in charge of or have responsibility for: *He's not fit to command this regiment.* **3** A person **commands** respect when other people feel that they ought to respect him or her. **4** A room or building **commands** a view if there is an impressive view from it: *The window commands a view of the bay.*

▻ ***noun***: **commands**

1 A **command** is an order, especially a formal one. **2** (*uncount*) **Command** is a position of control or responsibility: *He is second in command.* **3** (*uncount*) Your **command** of something is your knowledge of it and your ability to use it: *She's acquired a good command of the language.*

▻ ***phrase***

1 You have skills or talents **at your command** when you possess them: *a politician with both tenacity and diplomacy at his command.* **2** You are **in command** of yourself when you can control your feelings and behave as you want to behave.

commandeer /kɒmənˈdɪə(r)/ *verb*: **commandeers, commandeering, commandeered**

Someone **commandeers** something when they take possession of it officially or unfairly: *The soldiers commandeered his truck.*

commander /kəˈmɑːndə(r)/ *noun*: **commanders**

A **commander** is a person who commands, especially a senior officer in the armed forces or the police force.

commanding /kəˈmɑːndɪŋ/ *adjective*

1 You are in a **commanding** position if you are able to control the people around you and the events you are involved in: *The British runner now has a commanding lead in the race.* **2** A **commanding** voice or manner is confident and forceful. **3** A building is in a **commanding** position if it is situated so as to give a good, clear view of the surrounding land and buildings.

commandment /kəˈmɑːndmənt/ *noun*: **commandments**

The Ten **Commandments** are the ten rules for righteous living that God gave to Moses, listed in the Old Testament.

commando /kəˈmɑːndoʊ/ *noun*: **commandos**

A **commando** is a soldier specially trained to carry out dangerous and difficult attacks.

commemorate /kəˈmɛməreɪt/ *verb*: **commemorates, commemorating, commemorated**

To **commemorate** an important historical person or event is to make people remember them, *eg* by building a monument or by holding an official celebration. — *adjective* **commemorative** /kəˈmɛmərətɪv/: *a commemorative stamp showing Lord Nelson and HMS Victory.* — *noun* (*uncount*) **commemoration** /kəmɛməˈreɪʃən/: *events held in commemoration of the end of the war.*

commence /kəˈmɛns/ *verb* (*formal*): **commences, commencing, commenced**

Something **commences** when it begins: *Let battle commence!* — *noun* (*uncount*) **commencement** /kəˈmɛnsmənt/: *after the commencement of hostilities between the two nations.*

commend /kəˈmɛnd/ *verb*: **commends, commending, commended**

1 To **commend** something is to give it special praise or recognition: *Her roses won two second prizes and a 'highly commended'.* **2** (*formal*) You **commend** something to someone when you tell them it is worth their attention: *May I commend this passage to you for further study?* **3** (*literary*) You **commend** someone or something to someone when you entrust them to them: *Into God's hands I commend my spirit.* — *noun* (*count or uncount*) **commendation** /kɒmənˈdeɪʃən/: *He had several commendations for bravery during his army career.* □ *a performance worthy of commendation.*

commendable /kəˈmɛndəbəl/ *adjective*

Something **commendable** deserves to be praised or admired by others: *She managed the whole affair with commendable tact.* [*same as* **admirable, praiseworthy**]

comment /ˈkɒmɛnt/ *noun; verb*

▻ ***noun*** (*count or uncount*): **comments**

You make a **comment** about something when you give an opinion on it or make a judgement about it: *Do you have any comments on what has been planned?* □ *We approached the councillor concerned but were told that he was unavailable for comment.*

▻ ***verb***: **comments, commenting, commented:** *She commented on the fact that he was looking tired.* □ *'He's rather an aggressive man,' Julia commented.*

▻ ***phrase*** People often say **no comment** as a way of refusing to answer a question.

commentary /kɒˈməntərɪ/ *noun* (*count or uncount*): **commentaries**
1 A **commentary** is a continuous broadcast report on an event, such as a sporting contest, as it is taking place: *And now, with live commentary from Wembley Stadium, here's Brian Moore.* **2** A **commentary** is also a book or article that explains events, or explains the meaning of another book: *13th-century Bible commentaries.*

commentate /kɒˈməntaɪt/ *verb*: **commentates, commentating, commentated**
To **commentate** on an event is to give a commentary on it.

commentator /ˈkɒmənteɪtə(r)/ *noun*: **commentators**
A **commentator** is a person who gives commentaries: *a sports commentator.*

commerce /ˈkɒmɜːs/ *noun* (*uncount*)
Commerce is the buying and selling of goods and services of all kinds.

commercial /kəˈmɜːʃəl/ *adjective; noun*
▻ ***adjective***
1 Commercial means relating to or involved in commerce or business: *the building of units for commercial use.* **2 Commercial** is also used to describe activities carried out in order to make a profit: *The whole enterprise was a commercial disaster.* **3 Commercial** radio and television companies get the money to make their programmes by broadcasting advertisements for businesses who pay them. — *adverb* **commercially:** *a commercially viable product.*
▻ ***noun***: **commercials**
A **commercial** is a radio or television advertisement.

commercialized or **commercialised** /kəˈmɜːʃəlaɪzd/ *adjective* (*derogatory*)
A place or event has become **commercialized** if making money has become its main function: *Christmas has become commercialized in Europe and America.*

commiserate /kəˈmɪzəreɪt/ *verb*: **commiserate, commiserating, commiserated**
You **commiserate** with someone when you express sympathy for their sadness or disappointment. — *noun* (*uncount or count*) **commiseration** /kəmɪzəˈreɪʃən/: *expressions of commiseration* □ *Congratulations to the winners and commiserations to the gallant losers.*

commission /kəˈmɪʃən/ *noun; verb*
▻ ***noun***: **commission, commissions**
1 A **commission** is a formal or official request to someone to carry out a duty or a piece of work, usually a work of art, or the duty or work that they carry out: *This painting of the town hall has been my only commission as an artist this year.* **2** A **commission** is also an organization or group of people officially appointed to carry out a task or duty: *The government set up the Equal Opportunities Commission.* **3** (*uncount*) **Commission** is money paid by a company to a person who sells their products or services, usually a percentage of the cost of the product or service: *She gets 15% commission on every photocopier she leases.*
▻ ***verb***: **commissions, commissioning, commissioned**
To **commission** someone to do something is officially to request them to do it; to **commission** something is officially to request someone to do it: *The palace was commissioned in 1683, but not completed until 1711.*

commissionaire /kəmɪʃəˈneə(r)/ *noun* (*especially BrE*): **commissionaires**
A **commissionaire** is a man in uniform who stands outside the entrance to a cinema, hotel or restaurant and whose job includes opening the door for customers, and ordering taxis for them.

commissioner /kəˈmɪʃənə(r)/ *noun*: **commissioners**
A **commissioner** is an official of high rank in an organization.

commit /kəˈmɪt/ *verb*: **commits, committing, committed**
1 To **commit** something such as a crime or a sin is to do it or carry it out: *She had committed several offences before.* □ *The jury must decide if there was an intention to commit murder.* **2** You **commit** yourself when you promise to do something: *We don't want to commit ourselves to buying something we haven't seen.* **3** You **are committed** to a cause when you give a lot of your time and energy to it because you think it is important: *This government is committed to reducing industrial pollution.* □ *a committed Christian.* **4** You **commit** something to memory when you make an effort to keep it in your mind; you **commit** something to paper when you write it down. **5** Someone **is committed** to a place, especially a mental hospital or a prison, when they are officially sent there.

commitment /kəˈmɪtmənt/ *noun*: **commitments**
1 (*uncount*) You show your **commitment** to something by giving it the strong support that you promised: *We question this government's commitment to reducing unemployment.* **2** A **commitment** is a duty or responsibility: *I have commitments at home as well as in the workplace.*

committee /kəˈmɪtɪ/ *noun* (*with a singular or plural verb*): **committees**
A **committee** is a group of members of an organization chosen by the other members to run it: *She's chairman of the cricket club's catering committee.* □ *The relevant parliamentary committee have given their ruling.*

commodious /kəˈmoʊdɪəs/ *adjective* (*formal*)
A room or building is **commodious** if it has a lot of space in it: *a commodious hotel bedroom.* [*same as* **roomy, spacious**]

commodity /kəˈmɒdɪtɪ/ *noun*: **commodities**
1 A **commodity** is something that is bought and sold, especially a manufactured product or a raw material: *Spices are an important commodity in the East.* **2** Other things regarded as valuable, such as personal qualities, are often referred to as **commodities**: *Courtesy has become a scarce commodity.*

common /ˈkɒmən/ *adjective; noun*
▻ ***adjective***
1 Something is **common** if many people have it, have experience of it or know about it: *They still can't find a cure for the common cold.* □ *Jealousy is a common response in fathers when the first baby is born.* □ *It's quite common for the woman to look after the household money.* □ *It's common knowledge that apples grow on trees.* **2** Something is **common** to two or more people when each or all of them have it or share it: *These characteristics are common to both animals.* □ *Both parties share a common belief in the need for a firm law-and-order policy.* **3 Common** land is publicly owned and ordinary people have the right to walk on it. **4** (*derogatory, old*) If you describe a person or their behaviour as **common** you mean they lack good manners or good taste: *The way she speaks is so common!* **5 Common** also describes the ordinary variety of something: *the common British toad.* — *adverb* **commonly:** *Stomach upset is the reason most commonly given for absence from work.* □ *Spinach is commonly believed to give you strength.*
▻ ***noun***: **commons**
A **common** is an area of land that is publicly owned

and that ordinary people have the right to walk on: *You can't stop them camping on the common.*

▻ ***phrase*** You have something **in common** with someone when you both have similar interests, or when you have both had similar experiences in life: *We hardly knew what to talk about, we had so little in common.*

commoner /ˈkɒmənə(r)/ *noun*: **commoners**
A **commoner** is someone who is not a member of the nobility: *He was the first heir to the throne to marry a commoner.*

common ground /ˈkɒmən graʊnd/ *noun* (*uncount*)
Two or more people are on **common ground** when they agree about something: *There seems to be no common ground at all between the two sides.*

common-law /ˈkɒmən lɔː/ *adjective*
Someone's **common-law** husband or wife is the man or woman that they have lived with in a sexual relationship for a long time, without having married.

Common Market /kɒmən ˈmɑːkɪt/ *noun* (*used in the singular*)
The **Common Market** is an organization of Western European countries who have close political and economic contacts with each other, now officially known as the European Union.

commonplace /ˈkɒmənpleɪs/ *adjective*
Something is **commonplace** when it often happens or is widely available and is therefore not particularly interesting or exciting: *Foreign holidays have long been commonplace for the average British citizen.*

common room /ˈkɒmən ruːm/ *noun*: **common rooms**
A **common room** is a room in a university, college or school where students can sit together when they are not working.

common sense /ˈkɒmən ˈsɛns/ *noun* (*uncount, often adjectival*)
Common sense is practical good sense: *If only he'd used his common sense a little.* □ *It's common sense to wear warm clothes in winter.* □ *a common-sense solution to the problem.*

commotion /kəˈmoʊʃən/ *noun* (*used in the singular*)
A **commotion** is a scene of noisy confusion or excitement: *There was a bit of a commotion when he was asked to leave.*

communal /ˈkɒmjʊnəl/ *adjective*
Communal describes things that are shared by several people: *three guest rooms with a communal bathroom* □ *communal ownership of the land.* — *adverb* **communally:** *The land is communally owned.*

commune *noun*; *verb*
▻ ***noun*** /ˈkɒmjuːn/: **communes**
A **commune** is a group of people who, though not members of the same family, live together and share everything they have: *They set up a hippy commune on a remote Scottish island.*
▻ ***verb*** /kəˈmjuːn/ (*literary*): **communes, communing, communed**
You **commune** with nature or some higher power such as God when you get very close to them and seem to be exchanging thoughts or feelings with them: *He's gone off alone into the mountains to commune with nature.*

communicate /kəˈmjuːnɪkeɪt/ *verb*: **communicates, communicating, communicated**
1 You **communicate** with someone when you contact them in any way, *eg* by speaking to them, writing to them or telephoning them: *They have been divorced for years and never communicate.* **2** You **communicate** something such as information to someone when you pass it on to them: *He has communicated his opinion to me in a letter.* **3** Two people **communicate** when they understand each other's feelings very well: *We talk about lots of things but we never really communicate.* — *noun* (*uncount or count*) **communication** /kəmjuːnɪkeɪʃən/: *His only means of communication with the mainland was an old short wave radio.* □ *modern communications systems* □ *We have received several communications from the Minister detailing his proposals.*

communicating /kəˈmjuːnɪkeɪtɪŋ/ *adjective*
A **communicating** door is one linking two rooms.

communicative /kəˈmjuːnɪkətɪv/ *adjective*
Someone who is **communicative** enjoys talking to other people: *Carol was a confident, communicative pupil.* □ *The prisoner has not been very communicative so far.* [*opposite* **uncommunicative**]

communion /kəˈmjuːnjən/ *noun* (*uncount*)
1 Communion, or **Holy Communion**, is the Christian ceremony at which people take bread and wine symbolizing Christ's body and blood as a way of remembering him. **2** (*literary*) **Communion** is the sharing of feelings.

communiqué /kəˈmjuːnɪkeɪ/ *noun*: **communiqués**
A **communiqué** is an official announcement.

communism /ˈkɒmjʊnɪzm/ *noun* (*uncount*)
Communism is a political theory or system in which all land, property and industry is owned by the state and all people are allowed to have equal shares of it: *the collapse of communism in former Eastern Europe* — *noun, adjective* **communist**: *He was accused of having once been a Communist.* □ *We can understand the appeal of the communist system.*

community /kəˈmjuːnɪtɪ/ *noun*: **communities**
1 A **community** consists of all the people living in a particular area: *prominent members of the local community* □ *These plans were opposed by the whole community.* **2** A **community** is also a group of people within a society who share a common feature, such as a religion, nationality or occupation: *the Bangladeshi community.* □ *I'm speaking as a representative of the black community.*

commute /kəˈmjuːt/ *verb*: **commutes, commuting, commuted**
People **commute** when they travel quite a long distance between their home and their place of work: *Rail strikes have affected nearly 200 000 people who commute from towns all round the region.* — *noun* **commuter:** *cheaper rail fares for commuters.*

compact *adjective*; *verb*; *noun*
▻ ***adjective*** /kəmˈpakt/ or /ˈkɒmpakt/
Something is **compact** when it is conveniently small, or has its parts neatly arranged within a small space: *Mobile telephones have become increasingly compact.* □ *a very compact bathroom.*
▻ ***verb*** /kəmˈpakt/: **compacts, compacting, compacted**
To **compact** something such as mud is to press it down so that it becomes firmer or harder: *If the soil becomes compacted you might get drainage problems.*
▻ ***noun*** /ˈkɒmpakt/: **compacts**
A **compact** is a small flat case containing women's face powder, and a small mirror.

compact disc /kɒmpakt ˈdɪsk/ *noun*: **compact discs**
A **compact disc** is a CD (sense 1).

companion /kəmˈpanjən/ *noun*: **companions**
A **companion** is a friend that you spend a lot of time with, or someone you are travelling with: *We invited the American lady and her young companion.*

companionable /kəmˈpanjənəbəl/ *adjective*
A person who is **companionable** is friendly and sociable.

companionship /kəm'panjənʃɪp/ *noun (uncount)*
Companionship is the fact of being with someone you like: *I think he misses the companionship of his school friends.*

company /'kʌmpənɪ/ *noun*: **companies**
1 (*uncount*) **Company** is the presence of another person or other people: *If you'd like to come, I'd be glad of your company.* □ *She enjoys the company of others.* **2** (*uncount*) **Company** is also guests or visitors: *I can't come tonight; my wife and I are expecting company.* **3** A **company** is a business organization: *She works for the local bus company.* □ *My company is willing to donate £1000.* □ *a letter from Jenkins and Company.* **4** A **company** is also a group of actors or entertainers: *a travelling theatre company.* **5** (*military*) A **company** is a large body of soldiers forming part of a regiment or battalion.
▻ ***phrases*** **1** You **keep** someone **company** when you spend time with them so they will not be alone: *I could come over and keep you company while your husband's away.* **2** Two or more people **part company** when they separate: *We travelled together as far as Athens, where we parted company.*

comparable /'kɒmpərəbəl/ *adjective*
Two things are **comparable** if they are similar, especially similar enough to make it fair to compare one to the other: *It was much cheaper than any comparable hotel in the area.* □ *The film was comparable in suspense to anything that Hitchcock produced.*

comparative /kəm'parətɪv/ *adjective*
1 Comparative describes things judged by ordinary or average standards: *They live in comparative comfort.* **2 Comparative** also means 'making a comparison between things': *They made a comparative study of North and South American cultures.* □ *What are the comparative strengths of the two teams?* **3** In grammar, the **comparative** form of an adjective or adverb ends in '-er', or uses the word 'more', to indicate a greater degree of the quality in question: *The comparative form of 'ugly' is 'uglier', but the comparative form of 'beautiful' it is 'more beautiful'.* — *adverb* **comparatively:** *In France, there are comparatively* [=fairly] *large numbers of teenagers who smoke.*

compare /kəm'pɛə(r)/ *verb*: **compares, comparing, compared**
1 You **compare** one person or thing with another when you consider in what ways they are similar or different: *The reviewer had evidently spent some time comparing the new edition of the dictionary with the old one.* □ *We compared prices of vegetables at a number of supermarkets.* **2** You **compare** one person or thing to another when you say that the one is like the other, *eg* in expressions called similes: *The poet compares his lover to a summer's day.* □ *Thomas has often been compared to Yeats, who I feel was a much more sensitive poet.* **3** You say that one thing does not **compare** with another if you think it is not nearly as good as the other: *He doesn't compare with his predecessor in academic ability.* □ *How do house prices in the States compare with British prices?*
▻ ***phrase*** You use **compared with** to mean 'in comparison with' or 'considered in relation to': *Compared with most of the children in her class, she's a slow learner.* □ *The work is pretty easy, compared with my old job.*

comparison /kəm'parɪsən/ *noun* (*count or uncount*): **comparisons**
You make a **comparison** between two or more things when you consider in what ways they are similar or different: *We need a lot more data before we can do a proper comparison* **4** In this dictionary notes such as '[compare **convex**]' are used to draw your attention to another word in the dictionary that provides a useful contrast to the word you are looking up. □ *I'll give you both sets of figures for comparison.*
▻ ***phrase*** **By comparison** and **in comparison** are ways of indicating a difference between two people or things: *She's a very career-orientated person. Her sister, by comparison, prefers the role of housewife and mother.* □ *Her behaviour made me feel calm and relaxed in comparison.* □ *They are quite wealthy in comparison to most people.*

compartment /kəm'pɑːtmənt/ *noun*: **compartments**
1 A **compartment** is a separate section within something: *I remembered placing the letter in the outside compartment of my briefcase.* **2** A **compartment** is also one of the enclosed sections that a railway carriage is divided into: *He followed me along the platform and got into the same compartment.* □ *We had the compartment to ourselves.*

compass /'kʌmpəs/ *noun*: **compasses**
1 A **compass** is a direction-finding instrument consisting of a dial with a magnetic needle that always points north. **2** A pair or set of **compasses** is an instrument consisting of two movable legs joined together at the top, used for drawing circles and measuring distances on maps. **3** (*formal*) The **compass** of something is its range or scope.

compassion /kəm'paʃən/ *noun (uncount)*
Compassion is a feeling of sympathy for someone in difficulty and a desire to help or show mercy: *She felt little compassion for this drunken misfit.* — *adjective* **compassionate** /kəm'paʃənɪt/: *She had not received the compassionate treatment she had hoped for.* — *adverb* **compassionately:** *He looked at her compassionately.*

compatible /kəm'patɪbəl/ *adjective*
1 People or things are **compatible** if they are similar enough to live or exist together without problems or conflicts: *In the eyes of many, religion and politics are simply not compatible.* □ *She feels that a job in advertising would not be compatible with her Christian beliefs.* **2** Two pieces of electronic or other equipment are **compatible** if they can be connected to each other and used together.

compel /kəm'pɛl/ *verb*: **compels, compelling, compelled**
You **are compelled** to do something when you are forced to do it: *She felt compelled to accept his invitation.*

compelling /kəm'pɛlɪŋ/ *adjective*
1 Something that is **compelling** holds your interest or attention completely: *It is a compelling story.* **2** An argument or theory is **compelling** when you are convinced that it is right or true: *She had presented a compelling case for ending the subsidy.*

compensate /'kɒmpənseɪt/ *verb*: **compensates, compensating, compensated**
1 Someone **is compensated** when they are given money or other payment to make up for some loss, injury or other wrong they have suffered: *The company will compensate you for any inconvenience caused.* **2** To **compensate** for the effect of something is to take action that cancels that effect: *They've developed a new braking system that compensates for changes in the road surface.* — *noun (uncount or count)* **compensation** /kɒmpən'seɪʃən/: *The firm is considering his claim for compensation.* □ *We may be far away from the centre of things but life in the country has its compensations.*

compere /'kɒmpɛə(r)/ *noun; verb*
▻ ***noun***: **comperes**
The **compere** on a stage, television or radio show is the person who introduces the various acts.

▻ *verb*: **comperes, compering, compered:** *Bruce Forsyth is compering this year's Royal Command Performance from the London Palladium.*

compete /kəm'pi:t/ *verb*: **competes, competing, competed**
1 You **compete** in a contest when you take part in it: *She's never competed at international level before.* **2** People or groups **compete** with each other when each tries to get what only one can have: *We are having to compete with three other departments for the money.* □ *Several companies are competing for the contract.* **3** Firms **compete** with each other when each tries to get the public to buy its product in preference to those of other firms.

competent /'kɒmpətənt/ *adjective*
1 You are **competent** to do something if you have the necessary knowledge, skill or training to do it: *It has been argued that the selectors are not competent to select.* [*opposite* **incompetent**] **2 Competent** is also used to describe something that is of a satisfactory or acceptable standard, but not excellent or outstanding: *She is a competent storyteller, not a great writer.* — *adverb* **competently:** *She managed to carry out the work competently.* — *noun* (*uncount*) **competence**: *I don't question his competence, but he has no flair.*

competition /kɒmpə'tɪʃən/ *noun*: **competitions**
1 A **competition** is an event in which people compete to establish who is best: *She's entered the 'Young Musician of the Year' competition.* **2** (*uncount*) **Competition** is the desire to win or to prove yourself to be the best: *The world's best players are here and competition is fiercer than ever.* **3** (*uncount*) Your **competition** is also your rivals, *eg* in business: *They've introduced several new products in order to keep up with the competition.*

competitive /kəm'petɪtɪv/ *adjective*
1 You are **competitive** if you are keen to win or to prove that you are the best: *She has been forced to adopt a very competitive attitude to her work.* **2** Business or industry is **competitive** when a lot of companies are competing for the work available: *Television has become an extremely competitive industry.* **3** A company's prices are **competitive** when they are as low as the prices charged by all or most other companies: *This makes our product very competitive indeed.* — *adverb* **competitively:** *It is very competitively priced at £3.75.*

competitor /kəm'petɪtə(r)/ *noun*: **competitors**
A **competitor** is a person or group who competes with others, *eg* in a sporting contest or in business.

compilation /kɒmpɪ'leɪʃən/ *noun*: **compilations**
1 A **compilation** is a collection of several things made available as a single unit: *Her latest album is a compilation of her best-known songs.* **2** (*uncount*) **Compilation** is the process of compiling: *The price of the dictionary had still not been fixed by the time compilation had started.*

compile /kəm'paɪl/ *verb*: **compiles, compiling, compiled**
You **compile** *eg* a book or list when you collect and organize all the information needed for it: *This report has been compiled by two of the secretaries.*

complacent /kəm'pleɪsənt/ *adjective*
You say that someone is **complacent** when you think they are wrong to be satisfied with what they have done and should want to do more: *This government has made remarkable progress on bringing unemployment down, but it must not be complacent.* [*same as* **smug, self-satisfied**] — *noun* (*uncount*) **complacency:** *Business is showing some signs of improvement, but there is still no room for complacency.* — *adverb* **complacently:** *She couldn't help smiling complacently to herself.*

complain /kəm'pleɪn/ *verb*: **complains, complaining, complained**
1 You **complain** when you say you are not satisfied with something: *They complained to the restaurant manager about the service they'd received.* □ *Women workers complain that they do not get equal treatment.* **2** You **complain** of something when you say you are suffering from it: *They took him to the doctor when he complained of violent headaches.* □ *She complained of being forced to work overtime.*

complaint /kəm'pleɪnt/ *noun*: **complaints**
1 (*count or uncount*) You make a **complaint** when you say that you are not satisfied with something: *I have registered a complaint with the local council.* □ *I have received many complaints about the pollution from my constituents.* □ *a letter of complaint.* **2** A **complaint** is also an illness, especially a minor one: *skin complaints.*

complement /'kɒmplɪmənt/ *noun*; *verb*
▻ ***noun***: **complements**
1 One thing is a **complement** to another when it creates a pleasant contrast to it or makes the combination of the two things pleasantly balanced: *Yoghurt can be used as a complement to spicy dishes.* □ *His quiet determination was the perfect complement to the inspector's rather abrasive flair.* **2** In grammar, a **complement** is a word or phrase that must be added to a verb such as *be*, *become*, *grow*, for it to make sense: (*She's a biologist*; *He got very angry*).
▻ ***verb***: **complements, complementing, complemented**
One thing **complements** another when it acts as a complement to it: *The garden layout complements the classical lines of the house perfectly.* [compare **compliment**]
▻ ***phrase*** The **full complement** of a group is every person or thing that is part of it: *an adult with a full complement of teeth.*

complementary /kɒmplɪ'mentərɪ/ *adjective*
Two things are **complementary** when they complement each other: *using complementary colours in all her furnishings.* [compare **complimentary**]

complete /kəm'pli:t/ *adjective*; *verb*
▻ ***adjective***
1 Something is **complete** when it is whole or finished, with no parts missing: *With this latest acquisition, her collection is now complete.* □ *The French half of the tunnel will be complete by early 1994.* **2 Complete** also means absolute or total: *She made me feel a complete fool.* □ *The news came as a complete surprise.* — *adverb* **completely:** *The place is completely different now.* □ *I was completely unaware that he was standing beside me.* □ *I was completely taken by surprise.* □ *I must be going completely mad.* [*same as* **totally, utterly, absolutely**]
▻ ***verb***: **completes, completing, completed**
1 You **complete** something when you finish it or make it whole: *This last programme completes our series on household repairs.* □ *The palace was not completed until 1864.* **2** You **complete** a form when you write in answers to the questions on it. **3** Something **completes** a group when it is the last thing added to it and makes it whole: *Sheer silk stockings completed Harriet's outfit.*
▻ ***phrase*** One thing comes **complete with** another when it has the other as an additional part or feature: *He bought the farmhouse complete with stables and other outbuildings.*

completion /kəm'pli:ʃən/ *noun* (*uncount*)
Completion is the state of being complete: *The new bridge is due for completion next January.*

complex /'kɒmplɛks/ or /kəm'plɛks/ *adjective*; *noun*
▻ ***adjective***
Something that is **complex** is made up of many different parts, which may make it difficult to understand

or deal with: *We got lost in the rather complex network of roads linking the two towns.* ▫ *It is a complex problem for which there is no easy solution.*

▻ ***noun***: **complexes**

1 A **complex** is something made of up of several parts: *The new sports complex comprises a main hall, a swimming pool, and cricket and football pitches.* **2** Someone who has a **complex** has very strong emotions that they always feel in a particular situation or when they think about a particular subject: *She still has a complex about her weight, and won't accept that she's not fat.*

complexion /kəm'plɛkʃən/ *noun* (*uncount*)

Your **complexion** is the colour or appearance of the skin on your face: *She has fair hair and a pale complexion.*

complexity /kəm'plɛksɪtɪ/ *noun*: **complexities**

1 (*uncount*) **Complexity** is the quality of being complex: *He hadn't appreciated the complexity of the situation.* **2** The **complexities** of something are the many different parts that it is made up of, that make it difficult to understand or deal with.

compliance /kəm'plaɪəns/ *noun* (*uncount*; *formal*)

Compliance is the act of doing something you have been asked to do or agreeing with something decided by someone else: *He was surprised at the union's compliance.*

complicate /'kɒmplɪkeɪt/ *verb*: **complicates, complicating, complicated**

To **complicate** something is to add other things that make it difficult to understand or deal with: *My mother's refusal to help just complicated the situation even further.*

complicated /'kɒmplɪkeɪtɪd/ *adjective*

Something **complicated** has many different parts or features that make it difficult to understand or deal with: *Taking someone to court can be a very complicated procedure.*

complication /kɒmplɪ'keɪʃən/ *noun*: **complications**

A **complication** is something that makes a situation more difficult to deal with: *There is the added complication that the children are on holiday from school at the same time.*

complicity /kəm'plɪsɪtɪ/ *noun* (*uncount*; *formal*)

Complicity is the fact of being involved with other people in something, especially in something illegal: *The police have charged her with complicity.*

compliment /'kɒmplɪmənt/ *noun*; *verb*

▻ ***noun***: **compliments**

1 You pay someone a **compliment** when you say something good about them that shows you admire them in some way: *She described him as an inspired writer, which is indeed a compliment coming from such a great poet.* **2** (used in the *plural*) **Compliments** is a word used in formal greetings sent in a letter: *We received a rather formal Christmas card in which he had simply written 'compliments of the season'.* ▫ *The Prince sends his compliments and hopes you will accept this humble gift.*

▻ ***verb***: **compliments, complimenting, complimented**

You **compliment** someone when you pay them a compliment: *I complimented him on his choice of partner.* ▫ *She has often been complimented for her powerful verse.* [compare **complement**]

complimentary /kɒmplɪ'mɛntərɪ/ *adjective*

1 You say something **complimentary** to someone when what you say shows that you admire them in some way: *That was not a very complimentary remark.* **2** Something that is **complimentary** is given free of charge: *She presented us with two complimentary tickets for the concert.* [compare **complementary**]

comply /kəm'plaɪ/ *verb*: **complies, complying, complied**

You **comply** with an order or rule when you do what it requires: *All child car seats must comply with EC safety regulations.*

component /kəm'poʊnənt/ *noun* (*often adjectival*): **components**

The **components** of something such as a machine are the parts that it is made of: *a fault in one of the electrical components* ▫ *They learned to identify all its component parts.*

compose /kəm'poʊz/ *verb*: **composes, composing, composed**

1 Something **is composed** of the different parts that make it up: *The management board is composed of three directors and two outside consultants.* **2** To **compose** music is to invent or write it; to **compose** a poem or other work is to write it. **3** You **compose** yourself when you become calm after being angry, upset or nervous. — *adjective* **composed:** *I don't know how she managed to look so calm and composed.*

composer /kəm'poʊzə(r)/ *noun*: **composers**

A **composer** is someone who writes music: *music by a number of composers, including Bach and Beethoven.*

composite /'kɒmpəzɪt/ *adjective*; *noun*

▻ ***adjective***

Composite things are made up of several different parts or materials: *a composite resolution at the Trades Union Conference.*

▻ ***noun***: **composites:** *The picture was a composite of several old photographs.*

composition /kɒmpə'zɪʃən/ *noun*: **compositions**

1 A **composition** is something composed, usually a piece of music or writing. **2** (*uncount*) The **composition** of something is the arrangement of the parts it is made up of: *They haven't yet established the chemical composition of the mystery substance.* ▫ *She is a master of cinematographic composition.* **3** (*uncount*) **Composition** is the act of composing *eg* music or a poem: *study composition as part of the music course.*

compost /'kɒmpɒst/ *noun* (*uncount*)

Compost is a soil-like mixture of rotted plants and vegetables, added to soil to feed the plants that grow there.

composure /kəm'poʊʒə(r)/ *noun* (*uncount*)

Composure is the state of being calm: *He managed to recover his composure.*

compound *noun*; *verb*

▻ ***noun*** /'kɒmpaʊnd/: **compounds**

1 A **compound** is an enclosed area of land: *a prison compound.* **2** A **compound** is also a substance made up of two or more chemical elements.

▻ ***verb*** /kəm'paʊnd/: **compounds, compounding, compounded**

A problem or difficulty **is compounded** by some additional circumstance when it adds to it and makes it worse: *Her misery was compounded by the discovery of a leak in the roof.*

comprehend /kɒmprɪ'hɛnd/ *verb* (*formal*): **comprehends, comprehending, comprehended**

When you cannot **comprehend** something you do not understand it or you are unable to imagine it: *She simply could not comprehend how upset this news made him.*

comprehensible /kɒmprɪ'hɛnsɪbəl/ *adjective*

Something that is **comprehensible** can be understood: *The statistics were not presented in a comprehensible way.* [*opposite* **incomprehensible**]

comprehension /kɒmprɪ'hɛnʃən/ *noun*: **comprehensions**

1 (*uncount*) Something is beyond your **comprehension** when you cannot understand it or imagine it: *The distances involved in space travel are beyond the comprehension of the ordinary person.* **2** A **comprehension** is an exercise that tests how well you understand written or spoken language.

comprehensive /kɒmprɪ'hɛnsɪv/ *adjective*; *noun*
▷ ***adjective***
Something is **comprehensive** when it includes or deals with everything that is necessary or relevant: *We carried out a comprehensive survey of plant life in the area.* □ *Of course, a comprehensive insurance policy would cost you more.*
▷ ***noun*** (*BrE*): **comprehensives**
A **comprehensive** is a school which teaches children of all abilities.

compress /kəm'prɛs/ *verb*: **compresses, compressing, compressed**
1 To **compress** something is to press or squeeze it so that it becomes smaller or takes up less space: *The petrol and air mixture is compressed in the cylinder and then exploded.* **2** You **compress** something such as a piece of writing when you take parts of it out to make it shorter: *The article had been compressed into afew lines, inserted at the bottom of the page.* [*same as* **condense**] — *noun* (*uncount*) **compression** /kəm'prɛʃən/: *the compression of air in the engine* □ *the compression of data in the report.*

comprise /kəm'praɪz/ *verb* (*formal*): **comprises, comprising, comprised**
Something **comprises** the things that it contains, includes or consists of: *The flat comprises hall, living-room, kitchen, two bedrooms and a bathroom.* □ *Single mothers comprise less than 1% of people claiming income support.* □ *The committee is comprised of three sub-committees with different areas of responsibility.*

compromise /'kɒmprəmaɪz/ *noun*; *verb*
▷ ***noun*** (*count or uncount*): **compromises**
A **compromise** is an agreement between two opposing people or groups, achieved when each of them offers to give up some of their earlier claims or demands: *We are hoping to reach some kind of compromise.*
▷ ***verb***: **compromises, compromising, compromised**
1 Two people or groups **compromise** when they achieve a compromise: *Neither party seems willing to compromise.* **2** You **compromise** yourself when you act in a way that leads other people to doubt your honesty or sincerity: *She refused to compromise her principles and took the decision to resign.* — *adjective* **compromising:** *compromising photographs taken of the princess on holiday with a male friend.*

compulsion /kəm'pʌlʃən/ *noun*: **compulsions**
1 (*uncount*) Someone uses **compulsion** when they force someone else to do something: *Money paid under compulsion is recoverable by law.* **2** You have a **compulsion** to do something when you have a strong and irresistible desire to do it: *She felt a compulsion to give up the job and start a new life.*

compulsive /kɒm'pʌlsɪv/ *adjective*
1 Compulsive is used to describe a person with a bad habit that they find impossible to give up: *It's not easy living with a compulsive gambler.* **2** Something such as a book or film is **compulsive** if it is so interesting that you feel you must read or watch it to the end: *This programme makes compulsive viewing.* — *adverb* **compulsively:** *She gambles compulsively.*

compulsory /kəm'pʌlsərɪ/ *adjective*
Something is **compulsory** when certain rules or laws oblige you to do it: *new laws which will make the wearing of seatbelts compulsory* □ *compulsory military service.*

computation /kɒmpjʊ'teɪʃən/ *noun* (*uncount or count*)
Computation is the process of mathematical calculation or computing; **computations** are mathematical calculations or results obtained by mathematical calculation: *finding distance by computation* □ *a powerful machine capable of millions of computations per minute.*

compute /kəm'pjuːt/ *verb* (*formal*): **computes, computing, computed**
To **compute** a number means to calculate it: *It will take several days to compute all the price changes.*

computer /kəm'pjuːtə(r)/ *noun* (*count or uncount*): **computers**
A **computer** is an electronic machine that stores large amounts of information, or a similar machine that can be made to control some mechanical operation: *manufacturers of portable computers* □ *Our criminal records are kept on computer.* □ *the latest computer-controlled security system.* □ *a process done entirely by computer.*

computerized or **computerised** /kəm'pjuːtəraɪzd/ *adjective*
1 A system or operation is **computerized** when it is controlled by a computer or computers: *a computerized accounting system.* **2** Information is **computerized** when it is stored on a computer: *computerized medical records.*

computing /kəm'pjuːtɪŋ/ *noun* (*uncount*)
Computing is the act of using a computer or computers and writing programs for them to use: *study computing at school.*

comrade /'kɒmrɪd/ or /'kɒmreɪd/ *noun*: **comrades**
A **comrade** is a friend or fellow worker.

con /kɒn/ *verb*; *noun*
▷ ***verb*** (*informal*): **cons, conning, conned**
You **con** someone into doing something when you persuade them to do it by telling lies: *Old people are being conned into parting with their life savings.*
▷ ***noun*** (*informal*): **cons:** *The entire scheme was just a con.*

concave /kɒŋ'keɪv/ *adjective*
A **concave** surface curves inwards, like the inside of a bowl. [*opposite* **convex**]

conceal /kən'siːl/ *verb*: **conceals, concealing, concealed**
1 You **conceal** something when you hide it or cover it up so that it cannot be seen: *A little make-up will easily conceal the scar.* **2** You also **conceal** something when you keep it secret: *But how would he conceal the fact from his wife?* — *noun* (*uncount*) **concealment:** *Who had authorized the concealment of the information from Parliament?*

concede /kən'siːd/ *verb*: **concedes, conceding, conceded**
1 You **concede** that something is true when you admit it: *I insisted it was her responsibility and she finally conceded the point.* **2** You **concede** defeat when you declare that you have lost: *The Conservatives conceded defeat while the votes were still being counted.*

conceit /kən'siːt/ *noun* (*uncount*)
Conceit is too much pride in yourself or your own abilities: *It is her conceit that makes her so unlikeable.* — *adjective* **conceited** (*derogatory*): *He's so conceited!* □ *such a conceited thing to say.*

conceivable /'kənsiːvəbəl/ *adjective*
Conceivable describes things that you can imagine or think of: *We tried every conceivable tool, but the screw wouldn't budge.* □ *It is just conceivable that the country will go to war over this.* [*opposite* **inconceivable**]

conceive /kən'siːv/ *verb*: **conceives, conceiving, conceived**
1 You can **conceive** of something when you can imag-

ine it or believe that it might happen: *We could not conceive of a situation in which that would be necessary.* □ *I can't conceive how anyone could be so stupid.* **2** You **conceive** something such as a plan when you form it or think of it: *The system was conceived by a team of agricultural experts.* **3** A woman **conceives** when she becomes pregnant; a child **is conceived** at the time when its mother becomes pregnant with it: *Our first girl was conceived just a few weeks after our wedding.* **4** (*formal*) You **conceive** of something as a particular thing when you consider that it is that thing: *Some religious people conceive of the world as the battleground between good and evil.*

concentrate /'kɒnsəntreɪt/ *verb*: **concentrates, concentrating, concentrated**

1 You **concentrate** on something when you give all your attention, time or energy to dealing with it: *Don't talk; just concentrate on your driving.* □ *She's concentrating on getting a good grade for her French.* **2** You **concentrate** *eg* your energies or attention on something when you spend most or all of your time dealing with it: *We should concentrate our efforts on making the system more efficient.* **3** Something **is concentrated** somewhere when a lot of it or most of it is there: *Sheep farming was concentrated in the western half of the island.*

concentrated /'kɒnsəntreɪtɪd/ *adjective*

1 A **concentrated** substance has been made stronger by removing some of the water in it: *two teaspoons of concentrated tomato purée.* **2** A **concentrated** attack is one using all the forces available to attack a single target.

concentration /kɒnsən'treɪʃən/ *noun*: **concentrations**

1 (*uncount*) **Concentration** is mental effort, or attention paid to something: *This task requires all your powers of concentration.* □ *A split-second break in your concentration could lead to disastrous mistakes being made.* **2** (*count or uncount*) A **concentration** of something is a large amount of it in a small area: *Critics of the nuclear plant are demanding an explanation for the high concentration of cancer cases in the region.* □ *rock containing low concentrations of salt.*

concentration camp /kɒnsən'treɪʃən kamp/ *noun*: **concentration camps**

A **concentration camp** is a prison camp holding citizens of a certain race, religion or other group disliked by a government: *There were not only Jews in the Nazi concentration camps.*

concentric /kən'sɛntrɪk/ *adjective*

Concentric circles fit each inside the next one in a set, and all have the same centre.

concept /'kɒnsɛpt/ *noun*: **concepts**

A **concept** is an idea or notion: *They discussed the concepts of good and evil.* □ *The concept of equality has dominated twentieth-century political thought.*

conception /kən'sɛpʃən/ *noun*: **conceptions**

1 Your **conception** of something is what you think it is or consists of, or how you imagine it will be: *Their conception of love seems to be very different from our own.* □ *I had no conception of the finished product.* **2** (*uncount*) **Conception** is the fact of becoming pregnant: *the time from conception to birth.* **3** (*uncount*) **Conception** also refers to the process of thinking of or inventing something: *The scheme took four months from conception to execution.*

concern /kən'sɜːn/ *verb*; *noun*

▻ ***verb***: **concerns, concerning, concerned**

1 Something **concerns** you, or you **are concerned** in it, if you are affected by it or involved in it: *This is a private matter that doesn't concern the company.* □ *This need not concern you.* □ *I shall speak individually to all the people concerned in this project.* □ *The arrangements worked perfectly; many thanks to all concerned.* **2** A person or body **is concerned** with a particular thing if that is what they deal with or are interested in: *Police investigations are concerned only with the crime, not with its punishment.* □ *I'm chiefly concerned with proving my case.* **3** A book, passage, article, piece of information, suggestion or question **concerns** a particular thing, or **is concerned** with it, if it is about it: *My question concerns bank charges.* □ *The second half of the book is concerned with methods of recording information.* **4** You **concern** yourself with something when you become involved with it or spend time thinking about it: *You shouldn't concern yourself with other people's problems.* **5** Something **concerns** you, or you **are concerned** about it, if you are worried about it: *Business people were concerned at the increase in imports.* □ *What concerns me most is that he wasn't even aware that he'd driven the car home.* □ *We were concerned for her safety.* — *adjective* **concerned:** *She looked up from the patient with a concerned expression.* — *preposition* **concerning:** *The head teacher wanted to speak to her about an incident concerning her son.* □ *a newspaper article concerning nutrition.*

▻ ***noun***: **concerns**

1 (*uncount or count*) **Concern** is worry about something: *There is no cause for concern so far.* □ *There was growing concern over the rise in unemployment.* □ *The lack of medical supplies is our most urgent concern.* □ *Just now, the state of the garden is the least of my concerns.* **2** (*uncount*) **Concern** for someone or something is regard or consideration for them: *business enterprises that have no concern for the environment* □ *These teenagers show genuine concern for the happiness and comfort of old people.* □ *His concern for his little sister was quite touching.* **3** (*usually used in the singular*) Something is your **concern** if you have a duty to attend to it or to be involved in it: *My private affairs are no concern of yours.* □ *Safety in the workplace is the management's concern.* [*same as* **business**] **4** A **concern** is a business, company or firm: *A lot of new business concerns have sprung up locally in recent years.*

▻ ***phrase***

1 As far as I am concerned is a way of introducing your own opinion or reaction: *As far as I'm concerned, they're making an unnecessary fuss.* □ *He can stay out all night, as far as I'm concerned.* **2 As far as,** or **where**, a certain thing **is concerned** means with regard to a certain thing: *They seem to be very casual where school discipline is concerned.* □ *We had few worries as far as their safety was concerned.*

concert /'kɒnsət/ *noun*: **concerts**

A **concert** is a musical performance by singers or musicians: *i bought tickets for the school concert.*

concerted /kən'sɜːtɪd/ *adjective*

People make a **concerted** effort to do something when they work together to do it.

concerto /kən'tʃɛətoʊ/ *noun*: **concertos**

A **concerto** is a piece of music for one or more solo instruments and orchestra: *a piano concerto.*

concession /kən'sɛʃən/ *noun*: **concessions**

1 You make a **concession** when you admit something, or agree to give or allow something that you originally refused: *The dispute will not end unless concessions are made by both sides.* **2** A **concession** is also a reduction in the price of something, allowed to certain groups of people, *eg* students or the unemployed.

concessionary /kən'ʃɛʃənərɪ/ *adjective*

Concessionary fares or tickets are fares or tickets that are given free or at a reduced price to certain groups of people as a right: *Will private bus companies continue to offer concessionary fares for old aged pensioners?*

conciliation /kənsılı'eıʃən/ *noun* (*uncount; formal*)
Conciliation is the fact or process of reaching an agreement: *Has there been any progress towards conciliation?*

concise /kən'saıs/ *adjective*
Something **concise** is brief while covering the essential points: *a concise statement of the organization's policy.* — *adverb* **concisely:** *Students need to write concisely in the exam.* □ *Try to make your points clearly and concisely.*

conclude /kəŋ'klu:d/ *verb*: **concludes, concluding, concluded**
1 (*formal*) You **conclude** something when you bring it to an end or finally settle it: *Monday's lecture concludes the course on psychoanalysis.* □ *He was hoping to conclude a business deal in Tokyo that day.* **2** To **conclude** also means to reach an opinion or decision: *They concluded that this was not a safe drug for young children.* **3** (*formal*) You **conclude** when you make your last comment or remark: *'Well', he concluded, 'we have enjoyed doing business with you'.* — *adjective* **concluding:** *her concluding remarks at the end of her speech.*

conclusion /kəŋ'klu:ʒən/ *noun*: **conclusions**
1 (*usually used in the singular*) The **conclusion** of something is the end of it: *We hope to bring the investigation to a successful conclusion.* **2** You reach a **conclusion** about something when you form an opinion about it after considering it: *We came to the conclusion that the murderer must have left by the window.* □ *What conclusions does he draw from these facts?*
▻ ***phrases*** **1** Something is a **foregone conclusion** if it is certain to happen or be the case: *His promotion is a foregone conclusion.* **2** You **jump to conclusions** if you make up your mind about something without knowing all the facts: *I don't want people jumping to conclusions about why I'm divorcing my wife.*

conclusive /kəŋ'klu:sıv/ *adjective*
Conclusive evidence or proof of something shows that it is definitely true. [*opposite* **inconclusive**] — *adverb* **conclusively:** *This proves conclusively that the thief was a woman.*

concoct /kəŋ'kɒkt/ *verb*: **concocts, concocting, concocted**
1 You **concoct** something strange or impressive when you make it from a variety of unlikely ingredients: *He managed to concoct a delicious meal for four from what was left in the cupboard.* [*same as* **put together**] **2** You **concoct** an excuse when you invent one: *I can't wait to hear the fabulous story he'll concoct to explain this!* [*same as* **make up**]

concoction /kəŋ'kɒkʃən/ *noun*: **concoctions**
A **concoction** is a meal or drink made from a variety of ingredients: *a splendid concoction of cream, egg whites and rum*

concomitant /kəŋ'kɒmıtənt/ *adjective* (*formal*)
One thing is **concomitant** with another when it occurs at the same time, and sometimes as a result, of it: *poverty and concomitant social problems.* [*same as* **attendant**]

concord /'kɒŋkɔ:d/ *noun* (*uncount; formal*)
Concord is the state of friendly agreement that exists between people who live together in peace: *an incident that shattered the centuries-old concord between their two peoples.* [*opposite* **discord**]

concrete /'kɒŋkri:t/ *noun; adjective; verb*
▻ ***noun*** (*uncount, often adjectival*)
Concrete is a building material consisting of cement, sand and gravel mixed with water, that becomes hard like stone when dry: *We poured in concrete for the foundations.* □ *The walls were made of concrete blocks.*
▻ ***adjective***
1 Concrete is used to describe things that have a physical existence, as opposed to things that exist only in the mind: *We've listened enough to theories; we want to see concrete action.* **2 Concrete** also describes things that are definite or positive, not vague or general: *concrete evidence.*
▻ ***verb***: **concretes, concreting, concreted**
To **concrete** something is to cover it with concrete.

concur /kəŋ'kɜ:(r)/ *verb* (*formal*): **concurs, concurring, concurred**
You **concur** with someone when you agree with them: *The members concurred that a change of plan was needed.*

concurrently /kəŋ'kʌrəntlı/ *adverb*
Two or more things happen **concurrently** when they happen at the same time: *It was decided that the two races couldn't be run concurrently.* [compare **consecutively**]

concussed /kəŋ'kʌst/ *adjective*
Someone is **concussed** if they fully or partially lose consciousness for a while after being hit on the head. — *noun* (*uncount*) **concussion** /kəŋ'kʌʃən/: *She's suffering from concussion.*

condemn /kən'dɛm/ *verb*: **condemns, condemning, condemned**
1 You **condemn** something when you say that you strongly disapprove of it: *They had once condemned it as an evil régime.* □ *Opposition parties condemned her for her callousness.* **2** To **condemn** someone is to say that they are guilty and state what their punishment will be: *Previously, offenders had been condemned to death for less.* **3** You **are condemned** to do something unpleasant when you are forced to do it: *We seemed condemned to spend the morning in traffic queues.* **4** A building is **condemned** if it is not safe and a decision has been taken officially to destroy it. — *noun* (*uncount*) **condemnation** /kɒndɛm'neıʃən/: *All the newspapers reported her condemnation of Major's policy on Europe.*

condensation /kɒndɛn'seıʃən/ *noun* (*uncount*)
Condensation is tiny drops of water on a surface, formed when steam hits the surface and cools quickly.

condense /kən'dɛns/ *verb*: **condenses, condensing, condensed**
1 You **condense** something such as a piece of writing when you take parts of it out to make it shorter: *The report will have to be condensed to a few paragraphs.* **2** Steam **condenses** when it cools to form tiny drops of water.

condescend /kɒndı'sɛnd/ *verb*: **condescends, condescending, condescended**
1 Someone **condescends** to you when they behave in a way that shows they think they are better or more important than you: *He was one of those teachers who rather condescended to you and addressed you as if you were a different species.* [*same as* **patronize**] **2** Someone **condescends** to do something when, in agreeing to do it, they behave as if they were doing you a great favour: *Has she condescended to join us?* □ *When he did condescend to talk to his children, he spoke with the loud authority of a sergerant major.* — *adjective* **condescending**: *I felt constantly irritated by his condescending manner.* — *noun* (*uncount*) **condescension** /kɒndı'sɛnʃən/: *a manager who treats his workers with condescension.*

condition /kən'dıʃən/ *noun; verb*
▻ ***noun***: **conditions**
1 (*uncount or used in the singular*) The **condition** of

someone or something is the state they are in, especially their state of health or repair: *Her condition was causing the doctors concern.* □ *He's in no condition to travel.* □ *His liver is in a very diseased condition.* □ *I'm looking for a second-hand car in good condition.* **2** (*used in the plural*) The **conditions** in which people live or work are the circumstances, situation and environment in which they do so: *The strikers want better working conditions.* □ *They have to bring up their children in the most dreadful living conditions.* **3** An illness or disease is often referred to as a **condition**: *a patient with a heart condition.* **4** A **condition** is a circumstance that must exist for something else to be possible or permitted: *Applicants for membership must satisfy certain conditions.* □ *It was a condition of the job that she should live at the hospital.*

▻ ***verb***: **conditions, conditioning, conditioned**

1 To **condition** something is to get it into good condition: *a shampoo that cleans and conditions.* **2** Someone **is conditioned** to think or behave in a certain way when they are gradually influenced by the people or groups they spend time with: *The boarding-school environment conditioned boys to feel embarrassed by their feelings.* — *noun* (*uncount*) **conditioning:** *prejudices that are the product of early conditioning.*

▻ ***phrases*** **1** If you agree to do one thing **on condition that** another thing happens, you mean that you will not do the first thing unless the second happens or is promised: *The protesters agreed to go home on condition that the management considered new proposals for keeping the hospital open.* □ *I'll have dinner with you on one condition: that you let me buy the wine.* □ *I'll lend you £20 on the condition that I can have it back by Friday.* **2 On no condition** means absolutely not: *On no condition must she be allowed to hear of this.* **3** Someone who is **out of condition** is not fit and healthy.

conditional /kɒn'dɪʃənəl/ *adjective*

Conditional describes something that you will only allow, accept or agree to if what you ask for is given or done: *Glasgow University has made her a conditional offer of a place provided she passes all five exams.* — *adverb* **conditionally:** *She has accepted his offer conditionally.*

conditioner /kən'dɪʃənə(r)/ *noun* (*count or uncount*): **conditioners**

A **conditioner** is a substance that makes *eg* your hair or clothes softer: *a fabric conditioner* □ *conditioners for different types of hair.*

condolences /kən'doʊlənsɪz/ *noun* (*plural; formal*)

You offer someone your **condolences** when you formally express your sympathy for them, usually because a relation or friend of theirs has died.

condom /'kɒndɒm/ *noun*: **condoms**

A **condom** is a cover of thin rubber that a man wears over his penis during sex, as a way of preventing pregnancy.

condone /kən'doʊn/ *verb*: **condones, condoning, condoned**

You **condone** something wrong or bad when you ignore or accept it: *It is a simple fact that this government is condoning cruelty to animals.*

conducive /kən'dju:sɪv/ *adjective*

One thing is **conducive** to another if it encourages it or makes it likely: *The noisy atmosphere was not conducive to a romantic evening.*

conduct *verb; noun*

▻ ***verb*** /kən'dʌkt/: **conducts, conducting, conducted**

1 You **conduct** something such as an investigation when you carry it out: *results from surveys conducted in a number of areas.* [see picture at **orchestra**] **2** You also **conduct** something when you manage or control it: *She's conducted the firm's financial affairs for years.* **3** You **conduct** someone on a tour of a place when you show them all the interesting things there: *We were conducted round the castle and told something of its history.* **4** A substance **conducts** heat or electricity when heat or electricity can travel through it. **5** The way you **conduct** yourself is the way you behave: *She had conducted herself badly in front of the children.* **6** To **conduct** an orchestra is to direct its performance.

▻ ***noun*** /'kɒndʌkt/ (*uncount*)

Your **conduct** is your behaviour: *The boy's conduct in class has improved enormously.*

conductor /kən'dʌktə(r)/ *noun*: **conductors**

1 A **conductor** is someone who directs the performance of an orchestra. **2** On some buses, the **conductor** is the person who collects the fares from passengers.

cone /koʊn/ *noun*: **cones**

1 A **cone** is a solid geometrical figure with a circular base and a pointed top. [see picture at **shape**] **2** A **cone** is also anything similar to this in shape, such as a wafer containing ice cream, or a plastic marker placed in the road to direct traffic. **3** The large woody seed-cases of some evergreen trees are also called **cones**: *the smell of pine cones.*

confectionery /kən'fɛkʃənərɪ/ *noun* (*uncount*)

Confectionery is sweets, biscuits and cakes.

confederation /kənfɛdə'reɪʃən/ *noun*: **confederations**

A **confederation** is a group or organization formed by individual groups of people, usually for business or political purposes: *a confederation of southern European states.* [*same as* **league**]

confer /kən'fɜ:(r)/ *verb*: **confers, conferring, conferred**

1 You **confer** with someone when you discuss something with them: *Councillors will have to confer on this matter before action can be taken.* **2** (*formal*) To **confer** something such as an award on someone is to give it to them: *She felt that the title of 'Doctor' conferred a certain authority on her husband.*

conference /'kɒnfərəns/ *noun*: **conferences**

1 A **conference** is an organized meeting where formal discussions take place and decisions are often taken: *The vote was different at last year's party conference.* **2** (*uncount; formal*) You are in **conference** with someone when you are busy discussing something with them: *She'll be in conference with the Prime Minister all morning.*

confess /kən'fɛs/ *verb*: **confesses, confessing, confessed**

You **confess** to a crime, offence or other wrongdoing, or to something you are ashamed of, when you admit that you did it: *She has confessed to the murder of the old man.* □ *I don't expect him to confess that he wrote the letter.* □ *I confess that I disliked him originally because of the way he dressed.*

▻ ***phrase*** You can say **I must confess** when you admit something honestly: *I must confess I didn't like her when I first met her.*

confession /kən'fɛʃən/ *noun* (*count or uncount*): **confessions**

A **confession** is a formal statement admitting that you are guilty of a crime or other offence: *We'd obtained a signed confession from the prisoner within minutes.* □ *She's made a full confession.*

confetti /kən'fɛtɪ/ *noun* (*uncount*)

Confetti is small pieces of coloured paper that people throw over the bride and groom after a wedding ceremony.

confidant or **confidante** /kɒnfɪ'dant/ *noun* (*formal*): **confidants** or **confidantes**
A **confidant** is a male friend that you discuss personal things with; a **confidante** is a female friend that you discuss these things with.

confide /kən'faɪd/ *verb*: **confides, confiding, confided**
You **confide** in someone when you tell them something secret or private: *He was a friend I knew I could confide in.* □ *She confided to me that she was intending to leave her husband.*

confidence /'kɒnfɪdəns/ *noun*: **confidences**
1 (*uncount*) You have **confidence** in someone or something when you trust them, or believe that they will succeed: *It was clear she had little confidence in my ability.* **2** (*uncount*) You have **confidence** in yourself when you have a good opinion of yourself or your abilities: *She's obviously capable of it; she just needs a little confidence.* **3** A **confidence** is something secret or private that you tell someone.
▻ ***phrases*** **1** You tell someone something **in confidence** when you want them to keep it secret. **2** You **take** someone **into your confidence** when you tell them something secret or private.

confident /kɒnfɪ'dɛnt/ *adjective*
1 You are **confident** of something when you believe that it will happen: *They seem confident that MacSween will agree.* □ *She was confident of winning a prize.* **2** A **confident** person is sure of their own ability or personality: *She answered with a confident smile.* — *adverb* **confidently:** *He can confidently be expected to arrive on time.* □ *She smiled confidently at the examiners.*

confidential /kɒnfɪ'dɛnʃəl/ *adjective*
1 Confidential information is intended to be kept secret: *The precise date of the proposed attack remains confidential.* **2** You speak to someone in a **confidential** way when you want them to keep what you are saying a secret. — *noun* (*uncount*) **confidentiality** /kɒnfɪdɛnʃɪ'alɪtɪ/: *Doctors are expected to respect their patients confidentiality.* — *adverb* **confidentially:** *You can write to your doctor confidentially if necessary.* □ *whispers confidentially.*

confine /kən'faɪn/ *verb*: **confines, confining, confined**
1 To **confine** something is to limit or restrict it: *It was first thought that the disease was confined to the homosexual community.* □ *Please confine yourself to answering the questions and refrain from passing comment.* **2** To **confine** someone is to keep them prisoner: *She was confined to a small cell which she shared with two other women.*

confined /kən'faɪnd/ *adjective*
A **confined** space is a small, enclosed space.

confinement /kən'faɪnmənt/ *noun* (*uncount*)
Confinement is the state of being a prisoner.

confines /'kɒnfaɪnz/ *noun* (*plural; formal*)
The **confines** of a place are its boundaries or limits: *Prisoners are not allowed beyond the confines of the prison.*

confirm /kən'fɜːm/ *verb*: **confirms, confirming, confirmed**
1 Something **confirms** what you think or suspect when it proves that it is true: *His silence confirmed his guilt.* □ *Further investigations confirmed that he had not left alone.* □ *The minister refused to confirm reports that he had been sacked.* **2** You **confirm** something reserved or arranged earlier when you say that you definitely want it or will definitely do it: *She telephoned to confirm the booking.* □ *I sent a note confirming that I would arrive on the 8 o'clock train.* — *noun* (*uncount*) **confirmation** /kɒnfə'meɪʃən/: *We are still waiting for official confirmation of the arrests.* □ *They have already sent a letter of confirmation.*

confirmed /kən'fɜːmd/ *adjective*
Confirmed describes people who are settled into a particular habit or way of life and are unlikely to change: *Her brother is a confirmed bachelor.*

confiscate /'kɒnfɪskeɪt/ *verb*: **confiscates, confiscating, confiscated**
A person in authority **confiscates** something when they take it away from someone: *The teacher had confiscated their knives.* — *noun* (*uncount*) **confiscation** /kɒnfɪs'keɪʃən/: *the confiscation of knives and other weapons.*

conflict *noun; verb*
▻ ***noun*** /'kɒnflɪkt/: **conflicts**
1 (*count or uncount*) A **conflict** is a disagreement or quarrel: *There had obviously been a conflict of some sort.* □ *It may bring the two sides into conflict.* **2** A war is often referred to as a **conflict**. **3** (*count or uncount*) **Conflict** also refers to opposition between two things such as beliefs or sets of principles: *She had jobs with both companies and there was clearly a conflict of interest there.*
▻ ***verb*** /kən'flɪkt/: **conflicts, conflicting, conflicted**
1 Two or more things **conflict** with each other when they cannot be done or had at the same time: *The demands of a career often conflict with those of family life.* **2** One thing **conflicts** with another when they are very different from or opposed to each other, and they cannot both be true: *Our findings conflict with the results of the government's survey.* — *adjective* **conflicting:** *She finds she has to juggle conflicting interests.* □ *They reach two rather conflicting conclusions.*

conform /kən'fɔːm/ *verb*: **conforms, conforming, conformed**
1 Something **conforms** to a rule, law or standard when it satisfies it or reaches it: *All our toys conform to EC safety regulations.* **2** You **conform** when you behave like everyone else, in a way that a society or other group expects or demands: *She was unwilling to conform, and finished up being expelled from school.*

conformist /kən'fɔːmɪst/ *noun* (*often adjectival*): **conformists**
A **conformist** is a person who conforms: *She had very conformist attitudes as a youngster.* [*opposite* **nonconformist**]

conformity /kɒn'fɔːmɪtɪ/ *noun* (*uncount; formal*)
Conformity is the condition of conforming to or agreeing with established rules, customs or patterns of behaviour: *He wasn't interested in any political party that demanded strict conformity to the party line.*

confound /kən'faʊnd/ *verb* (*formal*): **confounds, confounding, confounded**
Something **confounds** you when it puzzles or confuses you: *I was confounded by his sudden willingness to speak openly.*

confront /kən'frʌnt/ *verb*: **confronts, confronting, confronted**
1 You **are confronted** with problems or difficulties when you have to deal with them: *We were confronted with the task of explaining it to Wilkins.* □ *In next week's lecture, we will confront the question of human morality.* **2** You **confront** someone when you prepare to argue or fight with them: *Silence fell as the two ministers confronted each other across the table.* **3** You **confront** someone with an accusation or criticism when you force them to respond to it: *We confronted her with the charge of bullying made against her.* — *noun* (*count or uncount*) **confrontation** /kɒnfrən'teɪʃən/: *Further confrontations are expected.*

□ *We hope to avoid any confrontation between strikers and replacement staff.*

confuse /kən'fju:z/ *verb*: **confuses, confusing, confused**
1 Something **confuses** you when you do not understand it or cannot decide what to do or what to believe: *We were confused by his silence; did it mean he was guilty?* □ *She spoke in riddles to try to confuse me.* **2** You **confuse** two things when you mistake one for the other: *It is a common mistake to confuse 'compliment' with 'complement'.* **3** To **confuse** a situation is to complicate it: *Matters were further confused by my sister's refusal to come out of the bathroom.* — *adjective* **confused:** *I had listened carefully, but was still confused.* — *adjective* **confusing:** *I must confess to finding the whole situation thoroughly confusing.*

confusion /kən'fju:ʒən/ *noun (uncount)*
1 Confusion is the cirumstance of mistaking one person or thing for another. **2 Confusion** is the state or situation of being unclear, complicated or muddled: *shots were fired, and the prisoners managed to escape in the confusion that followed.* **3 Confusion** is the state of not understanding something clearly, or not knowing clearly what you should do: *a look of confusion on his face.*

congeal /kən'dʒi:l/ *verb*: **congeals, congealing, congealed**
A liquid **congeals** when it becomes thick and sticky as it dries or cools: *a patch of congealed blood on his cheek.*

congenial /kən'dʒi:nɪəl/ *adjective (formal)*
A place is **congenial** when it is pleasant to be in, especially because it has a friendly atmosphere: *We had lunch at a most congenial inn.*

congenital /kən'dʒɛnɪtəl/ *adjective (medical)*
Congenital describes illnesses that a person was born with, and has suffered from ever since: *congenital blindness.*

congested /kən'dʒɛstɪd/ *adjective*
An area is **congested** when it is so busy with people or traffic that you only make progress very slowly.

congestion /kən'dʒɛstʃən/ *noun (uncount)*
1 There is **congestion** in a place if it so crowded with traffic and people that people find it difficult to move, or can only move very slowly: *congestion on the motorway caused by road works.* **2** There is **congestion** in part of the body if that part is blocked: *nasal congestion.*

conglomerate /kəŋ'glɒmərət/ *noun*: **conglomerates**
A **conglomerate** is a large business company formed from a number of smaller ones.

congratulate /kən'gratʃʊleɪt/ *verb*: **congratulates, congratulating, congratulated**
1 You **congratulate** someone when you say you are pleased about their happiness or success: *We all lined up to congratulate the newly-weds.* □ *I'd like you congratulate you on a brilliant performance.* **2** You **congratulate** yourself when you feel pleased about something you have done: *She congratulated herself on her narrow escape.* — *noun (uncount)* **congratulation** /kəngratʃʊ'leɪʃən/: *I sent him a congratulation card when he passed his driving test.*

congratulations /kəngratʃʊ'leɪʃənz/ *interjection*
You say **congratulations** to someone as a way of congratulating them: *Congratulations on your marriage, from Ted and Jean.* □ *Let me offer you my sincere congratulations.*

congregate /'kɒŋgrɪgeɪt/ *verb*: **congregates, congregating, congregated**
People **congregate** somewhere when they gather together to form a crowd: *Dozens of fans had congregated around his dressing-room door.*

congregation /kɒŋgrɪ'geɪʃən/ *noun*: **congregations**
The people present at a church service are referred to as the **congregation**: *Will the congregation please stand.*

congress /'kɒŋgrɛs/ *noun (with a singular or plural verb)*: **congresses**
A **congress** is a large meeting held to discuss policies: *the annual trades union congress.*

conical /'kɒnɪkəl/ *adjective*
Something **conical** is shaped like a cone: *a witch's black conical hat.*

conifer /'kɒnɪfə(r)/ *noun*: **conifers**
A **conifer** is a tree with needle-shaped leaves and seedcases that are cones.

conjecture /kən'dʒɛktʃə(r)/ *noun (uncount; formal)*
Conjecture is the process of forming opinions or judgements without having all the facts: *The precise course of events remains a matter for conjecture.*

conjugal /'kɒndʒʊgəl/ *adjective*
Conjugal refers to marriage and the relationship, especially the sexual relationship, between a husband and wife: *over thirty-five years of conjugal bliss.*

conjunction /kən'dʒʌŋkʃən/ *noun*: **conjunctions**
In grammar, a **conjunction** is a word such as **1** *and, but, or,* which can link words (*bacon <u>and</u> egg*), phrases (*a strange, <u>but</u> not unattractive, face*), or two main clauses (*She didn't wait to go herself, <u>nor</u> did she want him to go without her*. **2** *if, unless, until, because,* which link a subordinate clause to a main one (*He took great care of his mother <u>although</u> he was only three*).
▻ ***phrase*** **In conjunction with** means together with: *The fraud squad, in conjunction with the customs officials, had tracked him to southern Spain.*

conjure /'kʌndʒə(r)/ *verb*: **conjures, conjuring, conjured**
To **conjure** is to practise conjuring, or to make something appear by conjuring: *She conjured three coins from behind the boy's ear.*

> ***phrasal verb***
> Something **conjures up** a memory or image when it puts it into your mind: *The smell of olive oil conjures up the warmth and beauty of Tuscany.*

conjurer or **conjuror** /'kʌndʒərə(r)/ *noun*: **conjurers**
A **conjurer** is an entertainer who performs conjuring tricks.

conjuring /'kʌndʒərɪŋ/ *noun (uncount)*
Conjuring is the performing of tricks that deceive the eye or seem to defy nature, with quick and skilful use of the hands.

connect /kə'nɛkt/ *verb*: **connects, connecting, connected**
1 You **connect** two objects when you join one to the other: *Then connect the wheel to the frame by means of this bolt.* **2** You **are connected** with something that you are associated with or involved in: *This will affect dozens of other companies connected with the tourist industry.* **3** An electrical appliance **is connected** when it is linked to a supply of electricity. **4** You **connect** two or more people or things when you realize or prove that they are linked in some way: *The police have not managed to connect him with the murder.* **5** One aeroplane, train or bus **connects** with another when it arrives in a place in time for passengers to transfer to the other one before it leaves, and so continue their journey. — *adjective* **connected:** *The increase in poverty is connected with the disintegration of the welfare state.*

connection /kə'nɛkʃən/ *noun*: **connections**
1 (*count or uncount*) A **connection** is a link or direct relationship between things or people: *There seems to be a connection between the arrival of the letter and Bill's sudden departure shortly afterwards.* □ *The police are questioning her in connection with the Bishopsgate bomb attack.* **2** The **connection** between pipes or electrical wires is the place where they are joined to each other: *The radio wasn't broken; the problem turned out to be a loose connection.* **3** A **connection** is also an aeroplane, train or bus that connects with the one you are currently travelling on: *If we are more than half an hour late I'll miss my connection.* **4** (*usually in the plural*) **Connections** are people you know, especially important or influential people: *We can always get tickets; my wife has connections in the theatre.*

connive /kə'naɪv/ *verb*: **connives, conniving, connived**
1 You **connive** at some offence or wrongdoing when you ignore it and allow it to continue: *There were those who said he had known of the crime and had connived at it.* □ *It is the government's responsibility to explain why they connived at arms exports, instead of controlling them.* **2** You **connive** with someone to commit an offence or other wrongdoing when together you plan to do it.

connoisseur /kɒnə'sɜː(r)/ *noun*: **connoisseurs**
A **connoisseur** of something such as food or art is a person who knows a lot about it: *When it comes to wine, she's something of a connoisseur.*

connotation /kɒnə'teɪʃən/ *noun*: **connotations**
The **connotation** of a word or phrase is what it makes you think of or the impression it makes, in addition to its straightforward meaning: *The poet has clearly chosen the word because of its sexual connotation.*

conquer /'kɒŋkə(r)/ *verb*: **conquers, conquering, conquered**
1 To **conquer** an enemy in war is to defeat them and gain possession of their territory: *in the centuries before the Spanish had conquered most of South America.* **2** You **conquer** a difficult problem when you solve it or overcome it: *He had finally conquered his fear of flying.* □ *scientists working to conquer AIDS.*

conquest /'kɒŋkwɛst/ *noun*: **conquests**
1 (*count or uncount*) The **conquest** of something is the process or achievement of conquering it: *Then they added China to their list of conquests.* □ *We are all working for the eventual conquest of these diseases.* **2** (*informal*) A person's **conquests** are the people they have had sexual relationships with, especially when these relationships are short and casual: *Diana is his latest conquest.*

conscience /'kɒnʃəns/ *noun* (*count or uncount*): **consciences**
Your **conscience** is the sense of right and wrong that guides your behaviour: *I can go to work with a clear conscience, knowing that I followed my principles.* □ *She felt no twinge of conscience; she knew she had done what was right.*
▻ ***phrase*** You have a **guilty conscience** if you feel guilty because you know you have done something wrong: *I didn't visit her while she was dying and I'll have to live with a guilty conscience for the rest of my life.*

conscientious /kɒnʃɪ'ɛnʃəs/ *adjective*
A **conscientious** person thinks it is important that they should do their work properly and with care: *She's a fair and conscientious manager.* — *adverb* **conscientiously:** *He always does his work conscientiously.*

conscious /'kɒnʃəs/ *adjective*
1 You are **conscious** when you are awake and aware of your surroundings: *He lay in the road in a half-conscious state.* [*opposite* **unconscious**] **2** You are **conscious** of something when you are aware of it: *She became conscious that someone was standing behind her.* [*opposite* **unaware**] **3** You make a **conscious** attempt or effort to do something when you try hard to do it: *She was having to make a conscious effort to be polite to the scoundrel.* **4** **Conscious** can be used after *eg* adverbs and nouns when you think that they describe something that is important: *She wasn't very politically conscious as a student.* □ *She's very class-conscious, and generally a bit of a snob.*

consciousness /'kɒnʃəsnɪs/ *noun* (*uncount*)
1 **Consciousness** is the state of being awake and aware of your surroundings: *The patient has now regained consciousness.* **2** **Consciousness** is also awareness of or belief in the importance of something: *Women's rights have unfortunately not grown at the same pace as their political consciousness.* □ *I must have lost consciousness.* **3** Your **consciousness** is your mind: *Fear was beginning to enter his consciousness.*

conscript *verb; noun*
▻ ***verb*** /kən'skrɪpt/: **conscripts, conscripting, conscripted**
Someone **is conscripted** when they are officially required to join the armed forces. [compare **volunteer**]
▻ ***noun*** /'kɒnskrɪpt/: **conscripts**
A **conscript** is a person who has been conscripted. [compare **volunteer**] — *noun* (*uncount*) **conscription** /kən'skrɪpʃən/: *They ended the conscription of women shortly afterwards.*

consecrated /'kɒnsəkreɪtɪd/ *adjective*
A **consecrated** place has been officially declared to be holy and is used only for religious purposes: *He was buried in consecrated ground.*

consecutive /kən'sɛkjʊtɪv/ *adjective*
Consecutive is used to describe things that follow one after the other, without a break or interruption: *They spent three consecutive summers in Tuscany.* — *adverb* **consecutively:** *It rained for twenty-two days consecutively.* [compare **concurrently**]

consensus /kən'sɛnsəs/ *noun* (*uncount*)
Consensus is general agreement amongst people: *There is a major lack of consensus among politicians over the basic role of the government in the economy.*

consent /kən'sɛnt/ *verb; noun*
▻ ***verb***: **consents, consenting, consented**
You **consent** to something when you agree that it should be done, or when you give your permission: *My parents would never consent to such an unsuitable marriage.*
▻ ***noun*** (*uncount*)
Consent is agreement or permission: *The Queen has given her consent.* □ *The scheme went ahead by common consent.*

consequence /'kɒnsɪkwəns/ *noun*: **consequences**
1 One thing is a **consequence** of another when it happens as a result of it: *It's impossible to know what the consequences of such a decision would be.* □ *There may be grave consequences for our country if the peace talks fail.* **2** (*uncount; formal*) **Consequence** is importance: *His opinions are of no consequence.*
▻ ***phrase*** One thing happens **in consequence** of another if it happens as the result of it: *He was rude to his boss, and lost his job in consequence.*

consequently /'kɒnsɪkwəntlɪ/ *adverb* (*sentence adverb*)
Consequently means 'therefore' or 'as a result': *Briggs has refused to join; consequently, we need one more member.*

conservation /kɒnsə'veɪʃən/ *noun* (*uncount*)
1 **Conservation** is the practice of protecting the natural environment of plants and animals: *Her job is connected with nature conservation.* **2** The **conserva-**

tion of something is the careful use of it, making sure that as little as possible is wasted: *energy conservation in the home.*

conservatism /kən'sɜːvətɪzm/ *noun (uncount)*
Conservatism is dislike of change and the wish that things should stay as they are: *They feel, quite rightly, that the management's conservatism is stifling progress.*

conservative /kən'sɜːvətɪv/ *adjective; noun*
▻ ***adjective***
1 Someone who is **conservative a** dislikes new ideas, styles or methods and wants to keep things as they are: *She argues from a rather conservative standpoint.* ▫ *dressed in a very conservative grey suit.* **b** has right-wing opinions: *conservative politicians.* **2** A **conservative** estimate is cautiously low: *They expect to earn, at a conservative estimate, around £3 million in the first year.* — *adverb* **conservatively:** *She always dresses conservatively for work.*
▻ ***noun***: **conservatives:** *How will we get the conservatives on the committee to accept such a radical proposal?*

conservatory /kən'sɜːvətrɪ/ *noun*: **conservatories**
A **conservatory** is a room with glass walls and ceiling, attached to the outside of a house: *On summer evenings they like to take their dinner in the conservatory.* [see picture at **house**]

conserve /kən'sɜːv/ *verb*: **conserves, conserving, conserved**
You **conserve** something when you prevent it from being wasted, damaged or changed: *All households should try to conserve as much electricity as possible.* ▫ *The building has been thoroughly renovated and its style respected and conserved* [compare **preserve**]

consider /kən'sɪdə(r)/ *verb*: **considers, considering, considered**
1 You **consider** something when you think about it carefully, usually in order to reach an opinion or make a decision: *The management will consider all serious suggestions.* ▫ *They are currently considering whether to withdraw the product.* ▫ *Has she considered the damaging effect this might have on the children?* ▫ *You could consider the possibility of working abroad.* ▫ *Three candidates are being considered for the job.* **2** You **consider** someone or something to be something if you think that is what they are; you **consider** that something is so if you think it is: *We consider ourselves very privileged to have been included.* ▫ *She was considered the most suitable applicant of the three.* ▫ *Whom do you consider the leading authority on this?* ▫ *It was considered to be unnecessary to educate girls.* ▫ *I considered that I had done enough already.* **3** You **consider** someone when you pay attention to their needs or wishes: *I can't just please myself; there are the children to consider.* **4** You use 'when you **consider**' to draw attention to a surprising circumstance: *When you consider that she's only fourteen, it's a remarkable achievement.* ▫ *When you consider her age, she's an amazing phenomenon.* [*same as* **considering**]
▻ ***phrase*** You say **all things considered** when you give a general opinion after taking all the circumstances into account: *I think it was a success, all things considered.*

considerable /kən'sɪdərəbəl/ *adjective*
Considerable means large or great: *We've given considerable thought to your suggestion.* ▫ *a considerable increase in the cost of raw materials.* — *adverb* **considerably:** *His performance at work has deteriorated considerably as a result.* ▫ *The second house was considerably larger.*

considerate /kən'sɪdərət/ *adjective*
A **considerate** person is careful not to offend others or cause trouble for them.

consideration /kənsɪdə'reɪʃən/ *noun*: **considerations**
1 (*uncount*) **Consideration** is attention paid to the wishes or feelings of others: *You could have shown us a little more consideration.* **2** (*uncount*) **Consideration** is careful thought about something: *After careful consideration, we have decided to go ahead with it.* **3** A **consideration** is a fact or circumstance to be taken into account, *eg* when you are planning something: *The cost of insuring the car was an important consideration.*
▻ ***phrases*** **1** You **take** something **into consideration** when you consider how it will affect your final decision about something: *The magistrate will take into consideration the fact that this is your first offence.* **2** Something is **under consideration** when someone is still considering it and they have not yet made a decision about it.

considered /kən'sɪdəd/ *adjective*
A **considered** opinion or act is one that you have thought very hard and carefully about: *a carefully considered change of plan.*

considering /kən'sɪdərɪŋ/ *conjunction or preposition*
Considering introduces a circumstance that explains why you think something: *She's still very active, considering that she's over 80.* ▫ *Considering his previous bad experiences, I'm surprised he's trying it again.*

consign /kən'saɪn/ *verb (formal)*: **consigns, consigning, consigned**
You **consign** something somewhere when you put it there, often as a way of getting rid of it: *She had consigned the file to the care of her secretary.* ▫ *That old jumper should be consigned to the dustbin!*

consignment /kən'saɪnmənt/ *noun (formal)*: **consignments**
A **consignment** of things is a load of them sent or delivered: *We received another consignment of wine from Provence.*

consist /kən'sɪst/ *verb*: **consists, consisting, consisted**
1 Something **consists** of the things that form it or make it up: *The jury consisted of eight men and four women.* **2** Something **consists** in the thing that is its essential or most important feature: *The pleasure of holidaying in Greece consists for me in briefly being part of a relaxed and casual culture.*

consistency /kən'sɪstənsɪ/ *noun (uncount)*
1 The **consistency** of a substance is how much it is like a solid or a liquid: *Mix it into a thin paste about the consistency of yogurt.* **2 Consistency** is also the quality of being consistent. [*opposite* **inconsistency**]

consistent /kən'sɪstənt/ *adjective*
1 One thing is **consistent** with another when it matches it, or when it fits in with it: *Your version of what happened is not consistent with what your colleague has told us.* ▫ *Her injuries are consistent with a fall from a height.* **2** You are **consistent** when your opinions or principles do not change or vary; things are **consistent** when they keep happening according to a certain pattern: *There has been a consistent improvement in sales performance.* ▫ *My attitude, I believe, has been consistent throughout.* [*opposite* **inconsistent**] — *adverb* **consistently:** *She has been consistently late for work this week.*

consolation /kɒnsə'leɪʃən/ *noun*: **consolations**
1 A **consolation** is a circumstance that makes a bad situation seem not quite so bad: *Her only consolation is that people still admire her early work.* **2** (*uncount*) **Consolation** is the act of trying to make someone who is unhappy or disappointed feel better: *He mumbled a few words of consolation.*

console[1] /kən'soʊl/ *verb*: **consoles, consoling, consoled**
You **console** a sad or disappointed person when you try to make them feel better: *I was consoled by the fact that my marriage, at least, was intact.*

console[2] /'kɒnsoʊl/ *noun*: **consoles**
A **console** is a panel of instruments or controls, *eg* the keys and stops on an organ or the dials and switches in the cockpit of an aeroplane.

consolidate /kən'sɒlɪdeɪt/ *verb*: **consolidates, consolidating, consolidated**
1 You **consolidate** something such as power or support when you strengthen it to make your situation more secure: *The Conservatives are looking to consolidate their following in the southeast.* **2** Business companies **consolidate** when they combine to form a larger single company. — *noun* (*uncount*) **consolidation** or /kənsɒlɪ'deɪʃən/: *the consolidation of their following in the area.*

consonant /'kɒnsənənt/ *noun*: **consonants**
A **consonant** is a speech sound such as 'f' or 'n', that you make by stopping the breath in some way, or the letter that represents such a sound. [compare **vowel**]

consortium /kən'sɔːtɪəm/ *noun*: **consortiums** or **consortia**
A **consortium** is a group of people or companies that agree to work together: *A business consortium formed to take over control of the bank.*

conspicuous /kən'spɪkjʊəs/ *adjective*
Something is **conspicuous** when people notice it immediately: *There was a very conspicuous bruise on her cheek.* □ *I was dismayed by the conspicuous absence of eligible bachelors.* [*opposite* **inconspicuous**]

conspiracy /kən'spɪrəsɪ/ *noun* (*count or uncount*): **conspiracies**
A **conspiracy** is a plan made in secret by a number of people to do something illegal or wrong: *Police had uncovered evidence of a conspiracy to defraud the tax office.* □ *They were charged with conspiracy to murder Mrs Bentley's husband.*

conspirator /kən'spɪrətə(r)/ *noun*: **conspirators**
A **conspirator** is a person who is a member of a conspiracy.

conspire /kən'spaɪə(r)/ *verb*: **conspires, conspiring, conspired**
1 People **conspire** when they plan secretly together to do something, usually something illegal or wrong: *They had conspired to defraud the company of money.* **2** (*formal*) You can say that events or circumstances **conspire** against you when bad luck prevents you from doing something: *Everything conspired to make me miss my train.*

constable /'kʌnstəbəl/ *noun*: **constables**
A **constable** is a police officer of the lowest rank in the British police force.

constabulary /kən'stabjʊlərɪ/ *noun* (*BrE*): **constabularies**
A **constabulary** is the police force of a particular district or region: *officers from the Staffordshire Constabulary.*

constant /'kɒnstənt/ *adjective*
1 Something that is **constant** continues without stopping or failing: *We faced a constant barrage of questions.* □ *I've had a constant headache for three days now.* **2** Something such as a standard or level remains **constant** when it does not change: *Air pressure must be kept constant.* **3** (*old*) You are **constant** if you are faithful, *eg* to the person you love. — *adverb* **constantly:** *It has rained constantly for several days.*

consternation /kɒnstə'neɪʃən/ *noun* (*uncount*)
Consternation is a feeling of worry or fear: *She approached the room with a growing feeling of consternation.*

constipated /'kɒnstɪpeɪtɪd/ *adjective*
Someone who is **constipated** is unable to pass solid waste matter from their body through their anus. — *noun* (*uncount*) **constipation** /kɒnstɪ'peɪʃən/: *suffering from constipation.*

constituency /kən'stɪtjʊənsɪ/ *noun*: **constituencies**
A **constituency** is the area whose citizens are represented by a particular member of parliament: *letters from several people in my constituency.*

constituent /kən'stɪtjʊənt/ *noun*: **constituents**
1 A **constituent** is person living in a parliamentary constituency: *Several of her constituents were worried about the new road.* **2** (*often adjectival*) The **constituents** of something are the parts that it is made up of: *the constituent elements of the mixture.*

constitute /'kɒnstɪtjuːt/ *verb*: **constitutes, constituting, constituted**
1 To **constitute** something is to be that thing, or represent it: *His remarks constitute a serious challenge to Major's leadership.* **2** To **constitute** something is to be the parts that form it or make it up: *the six counties that constitute the province.*

constitution /kɒnstɪ'tjuːʃən/ *noun*: **constitutions**
1 A country's **constitution** is the set of rules or principles that its government must follow, guaranteeing the rights of its people: *The problem arises out of the fact that the UK has no written constitution.* **2** (*formal*) Your **constitution** is your health: *He has a particularly fragile constitution.*

constitutional /kɒnstɪ'tjuːʃənəl/ *adjective*
Constitutional describes things that relate to or form part of a country's constitution: *It is a constitutional right.*

constrain /kən'streɪn/ *verb* (*formal*): **constrains, constraining, constrained**
1 You feel **constrained** to do something when you feel forced or obliged to do it: *She felt constrained to tell the truth, however unpleasant.* **2** To **constrain** something is to limit it, or prevent it from spreading or developing: *Their passion was constrained by the social codes of the time.*

constraint /kən'streɪnt/ *noun* (*count or uncount; formal*)
A **constraint** is something that limits or restricts freedom or development: *The major constraint on hospitals is lack of funding.* □ *Small businesses cannot be expected to flourish in a climate of economic constraint.*

constrict /kən'strɪkt/ *verb*: **constricts, constricting, constricted**
1 You **constrict** something when you squeeze it tightly: *The python kills its prey by constricting it.* **2** Something **constricts** you when it prevents you from acting freely: *Most educational establishments are constricted by the limits of their budget.* — *noun* (*uncount*) **constriction** /kən'strɪkʃən/: *snakes that kill their prey by constriction.*

construct /kən'strʌkt/ *verb*: **constructs, constructing, constructed**
1 To **construct** something large, such as a road or building, is to build it: *The bridge is constructed largely of concrete.* **2** You **construct** something such as a theory when you form it, usually after much effort and time: *a carefully constructed plan.*

construction /kən'strʌkʃən/ *noun*: **constructions**
1 (*uncount*) The **construction** of something is the

process of constructing it: *The tower will cost £30 million, and construction will take 20 months.* □ *The bridge is still in the process of construction.* **2** A building or other large structure is often referred to as a **construction**: *The cathedral is a magnificent construction.*

constructive /kən'strʌktɪv/ *adjective*
Constructive advice or comments help towards useful progress or development: *Criticism is welcome only when it is constructive criticism.* — *adverb* **constructively:** *She asked for people to criticize his plan constructively.*

construe /kən'stru:/ *verb* (*formal*): **construes, construing, construed**
Your words or actions **are construed** as some quality, such as cowardice, when they are regarded by others as displaying that quality: *His failure to attend would be construed as weakness, or at best indecision.*

consul /'kɒnsəl/ *noun*: **consuls**
A **consul** is an official representing your government in a foreign city, to whom you can go for legal protection or other help when you are in that city. — *adjective* **consular** /'kɒnsjʊlə(r)/: *the consular building in Marseille.*

consulate /'kɒnsjʊlət/ *noun*: **consulates**
A **consulate** is the building where a consul works and sometimes lives as well.

consult /kən'sʌlt/ *verb*: **consults, consulting, consulted**
1 You **consult** someone when you ask their advice or opinion: *They've decided to consult a lawyer.* **2** Two people **consult** each other when they discuss ideas, plans and opinions: *I must first consult with my business partner.* **3** You **consult** something such as a map or reference book when you look at it in order to find information: *I'm not sure if I'm free; I'll have to consult my diary.*

consultancy /kən'sʌltənsɪ/ *noun* (*uncount or count*): **consultancies**
Consultancy is the job or service of giving professional advice on a particular subject to people who need it; a **consultancy** is a group of people whose business is to give such advice: *He's in management consultancy.* □ *She's going to stand down at the next election and set up a consultancy with her husband.*

consultant /kən'sʌltənt/ *noun*: **consultants**
1 A **consultant** is a person whose job is to give expert advice on something: *a firm of financial consultants.* **2** In a hospital, a **consultant** is a senior doctor specializing in a particular branch of medicine.

consultation /kɒnsəl'teɪʃən/ *noun*: **consultations**
1 A **consultation** is a meeting to exchange ideas or opinions. **2** (*uncount*) **Consultation** is discussion: *They couldn't proceed without prior consultation with the Minister.* **3** (*uncount*) **Consultation** is also the act of looking for information in a book or other reference source: *Encyclopaedias are available for consultation in the reading room.*

consulting room /kən'sʌltɪŋ ru:m/ *noun*: **consulting rooms**
A doctor's **consulting room** is the room that he or she sees patients in.

consume /kən'sju:m/ *verb*: **consumes, consuming, consumed**
1 (*formal*) You **consume** things when you eat and drink them: *They had consumed most of the potatoes by Wednesday.* **2** You **consume** something such as energy when you use it up: *These modern machines consume far less electricity.* **3** You **are consumed** with an emotion when it dominates your mind: *Her husband is consumed with jealousy.*

consumer /kən'sju:mə(r)/ *noun*: **consumers**
People who buy goods or make use of services are **consumers**: *It's clear that the modern consumer prefers to do all their shopping in supermarkets.*

consummate *verb*; *adjective*
▻ ***verb*** /kən'səmeɪt/ (*formal*): **consummates, consummating, consummated**
Two people **consummate** their marriage or relationship when they have sexual intercourse for the first time. — *noun* (*uncount*) **consummation** /kən'səmeɪʃən/: *the consummation of their marriage.*
▻ ***adjective*** /kən'sʌmət/
Consummate describes a person or thing that is a perfect or excellent example of something: *She's a consummate liar.* □ *a dancer of consummate skill.*

consumption /kən'sʌmpʃən/ *noun* (*uncount*)
1 Your **consumption** of something such as food or energy is the amount that you use up: *Older cars tend to have higher fuel consumption.* **2** **Consumption** is also the act of eating or drinking something: *water that is not fit for human consumption.*

contact /'kɒntakt/ *noun*; *verb*
▻ ***noun***: **contacts**
1 (*uncount*) One thing is in **contact** with another when it is touching it: *The glue hardens as soon as it comes into contact with another surface.* **2** (*uncount*) You are in **contact** with someone when you are communicating with them, regularly or at the moment: *He hasn't been in contact with the office for several days.* □ *The radio was her only means of contact with the shore.* □ *She's broken off all contact with her family.* **3** A **contact** is someone you know, especially someone whose knowledge or influence are useful to you: *You could ask some of your criminal contacts.*
▻ ***verb***: **contacts, contacting, contacted**
You **contact** someone when you communicate with them: *I should contact Jameson and let him know.*

contact lens /kɒntakt 'lenz/ *noun*: **contact lenses**
Contact lenses are two small, round pieces of plastic that you put on to your eyes to help you see, instead of wearing glasses.

contagious /kən'teɪdʒəs/ *adjective*
1 A **contagious** disease is spread when a person suffering from it is in contact with other people: *The condition does not appear to be contagious.* **2** Something such as laughter or a mood is **contagious** when it affects everyone present: *The gloomy atmosphere of the hotel was contagious.*

contain /kən'teɪn/ *verb*: **contains, containing, contained**
1 Something such as a place, building, room, cupboard or drawer **contains** things if they are inside it: *The room contained nothing but piles of old furniture.* □ *The guards lost count of the number of prisoners contained in the camps.* **2** A substance **contains** something if that thing is part of it, or is one of its ingredients: *The water was found to contain large quantities of lead.* □ *Avoid foods containing acid.* **3** You say a place **contains** certain things when you are describing its contents and features: *The National Library contains some of the world's rarest books.* □ *This area contains some amazing wildlife.* **4** A book, play or film **contains** certain ideas, images or other material if they are included in it, or are a feature of it: *The speech contained nothing new.* □ *His last film contained several scenes of violence.* □ *Her novels contain some of the best writing in the English language.* **5** Something said or written **contains** a quality or attitude if it expresses it: *Her words contained an unmistakable threat.* **6** You **contain** something when you control it, limit it or stop it from spreading: *Our priority is to contain the fire.* □ *measures to contain the spread of this destructive*

plant. **7** You **contain** yourself when you control your excitement and behave calmly.

container /kən'teɪnə(r)/ *noun*: **containers**
1 A **container** is any object such as a box designed for holding or storing things. **2** (*often adjectival*) A **container** is also a huge sealed metal box of standard size and design for carrying goods by lorry or ship: *The container trucks were easily unloaded.*

contaminate /kən'tamɪneɪt/ *verb*: **contaminates, contaminating, contaminated**
To **contaminate** something is to pollute it or make it harmful or unhealthy: *The priority is to clean up the contaminated rivers in the south.* □ *The wound might become contaminated.* — *adjective* **contaminated:** *contaminated water* — *noun* (*uncount*) **contamination** /kəntamɪ'neɪʃən/: *high levels of radioactive contamination.*

contemplate /'kɒntəmpleɪt/ *verb*: **contemplates, contemplating, contemplated**
1 You **contemplate** doing something when you think that you might do it: *She was at one time contemplating leaving the convent altogether.* **2** You **contemplate** something when you spend a lot of time thinking seriously about it: *the image of the great philosopher contemplating the huge questions of human existence.* **3** You also **contemplate** something when you spend time looking at it: *She sat contemplating the shape of her legs.* — *noun* (*uncount*) **contemplation** /kɒntəm'pleɪʃən/: *They spend two hours a day in religious contemplation.*

contemporary /kən'tempərərɪ/ *adjective; noun*
▻ ***adjective***
1 Contemporary describes modern things, as opposed to things from past periods of history: *Contemporary theologians regard God as a force, not a being.* □ *She has worked in both classical and contemporary dance.* **2 Contemporary** also describes things from the same period in history as the thing being discussed: *another poetic movement contemporary with French symbolism.*
▻ ***noun***: **contemporaries**
One person is a **contemporary** of another if he or she lived at the same time in the past as the other: *a contemporary of Mozart.* □ *Several of the greatest Austrian composers were contemporaries.* □ *She was a contemporary of mine at university.*

contempt /kən'tempt/ *noun* (*uncount*)
You have **contempt** for someone when you have no respect for them: *She looked at him with contempt.*
▻ ***phrase*** You **hold** someone **in contempt** if you feel contempt for them.

contemptible /kən'temptɪbəl/ *adjective*
You describe something as **contemptible** when you have no respect for it and are offended or disgusted by it: *this government's contemptible treatment of the most vulnerable in our society.*

contemptuous /kən'temptʃʊəs/ *adjective*
You are **contemptuous** of something when you show contempt for it: *He fixed me with a contemptuous stare.*

contend /kən'tend/ *verb*: **contends, contending, contended**
1 You have to **contend** with a problem when you are faced with it and must deal with it: *She had troubles of her own to contend with.* [*same as* **cope** with, **grapple** with] **2** (*formal*) You **contend** that something is true when you insist that it is true: *She contended that her actions were sanctioned by the minister himself.* **3** People **contend** for something when they compete with each other for it: *We have an ex-Chancellor and a Home Secretary both contending for the party leadership.* [*same as* **compete, vie for**]

contender /kən'tendə(r)/ *noun*: **contenders**
If someone is a **contender** in a competition, especially a sporting competition, they are one of the people taking part: *Bruno was regarded by many as a serious contender for the heavyweight championship of world.* [= was thought to have a very good chance of becoming world champion]

content¹ /kən'tent/ *adjective; verb*
▻ ***adjective***
You are **content** with something when you are satisfied with it or you accept it: *We were quite content with the new arrangements.* □ *I was content to sit and watch.*
▻ ***verb***: **contents, contenting, contented**
You **content** yourself with what you have or are given when you accept that you cannot have or do more: *We had no time for lunch, so I had to content myself with a cup of coffee and a biscuit.*

content² /'kɒntent/ *noun*: **contents**
1 (*used in the plural*) The **contents** of something such as a box are things contained in it: *We examined the contents of his pockets.* □ *It seemed wrong that the contents of the report should remain confidential.* **2** (*uncount*) **Content** is used to refer to the amount of a substance that something contains: *a diet with a high starch content.*

contented /kən'tentɪd/ *adjective*
You are **contented** when you are peacefully happy or satisfied: *a contented smile.*

contention /kən'tenʃən/ *noun*: **contentions**
1 (*formal*) You say 'It is my **contention**' as a way of introducing an opinion or belief: *It is the inspector's contention that the murderer is a woman.* **2** (*uncount*) **Contention** is argument or competition: *This has been a matter of some contention which may destroy the Party itself.*
▻ ***phrase*** You are **in contention** if you stand a good chance of winning some contest or competition: *two football teams in contention for the cup.*

contentious /kən'tenʃəs/ *adjective* (*formal*)
A **contentious** issue is something that people strongly disagree about. [*same as* **controversial**]

contentment /kən'tentmənt/ *noun* (*uncount*)
Contentment is a state of peaceful satisfaction or happiness: *He sat quiet with a look of utter contentment on his face.*

contest *noun; verb*
▻ ***noun*** /'kɒntest/: **contests**
A **contest** is a competition or a struggle: *The teacher organized a spelling contest.* □ *the contest for the control of the sales areas in the north.*
▻ ***verb*** /kən'test/ (*formal*): **contests, contesting, contested**
1 You **contest** something when you argue that it is wrong, unfair or untrue: *Her late husband's family are contesting the will.* **2** You **contest** *eg* an election if you take part in it and try to win it: *Three candidates will be contesting this seat at the next election.*

contestant /kən'testənt/ *noun*: **contestants**
A **contestant** is someone who takes part in a contest or competition.

context /'kɒntekst/ *noun*: **contexts**
1 (*count or uncount*) A **context** is the passage in a text or speech that a particular word or statement occurs in: *But 'love' in a Biblical context has nothing to do with sex.* □ *She claims that her comments were quoted out of context.* **2** The **context** of something is the background or set of circumstances that it happens

in: *The Church's attitude has to be viewed in its proper historical context.* ▫ *These words were spoken in a context of civil war.*

continent /ˈkɒntɪnənt/ *noun*: **continents**
1 A **continent** is a large mass of land divided into different countries: *within the continent of Asia.* **2** People in Britain often say 'on the **Continent**' to refer to those parts of Europe other than the United Kingdom: *They have different attitudes to animals on the Continent.* — *adjective* **continental:** *the prospect of inter-continental wars* ▫ *How would this policy be received in Continental Europe?*

continental quilt /kɒntɪnɛntal ˈkwɪlt/ *noun*: **continental quilts**
A **continental quilt** is a duvet. [see picture at **bedroom**]

contingency /kənˈtɪndʒənsɪ/ *noun* (*formal*): **contingencies**
A **contingency** is something that may happen: *The government is making contingency plans for war.*

contingent /kənˈtɪndʒənt/ *noun*; *adjective*
▻ ***noun***: **contingents**
A **contingent** is a group of people with a particular job, especially a group of policemen or soldiers: *the British and French contingents in Bosnia.*
▻ ***adjective*** (*formal*)
One thing is **contingent** on a second thing if it is only true or able to exist if the second thing is true or exists, or if it depends on it: *Your promotion is contingent on your performance over the next six months.*

continual /kənˈtɪnjuəl/ *adjective*
Continual describes something that continues for a long time without stopping, or something that happens frequently or repeatedly: *the continual drumming of rain on the roof* ▫ *The noise continued despite continual complaints from local residents.* [compare **continuous**] — *adverb* **continually:** *She is continually making complaints.* ▫ *It rained continually all day.*

continuation /kəntɪnjuːˈeɪʃən/ *noun*: **continuations**
1 (*uncount*) The **continuation** of something is the fact that it continues, often after a break or pause: *This is a good scheme, and we support its continuation.* ▫ *Join us after the commercial break for the continuation of this discussion.* **2** Something is a **continuation** of something else when it is joined to it in such a way that no gap occurs: *At first, I thought the lane was a continuation of the road.*

continue /kənˈtɪnjuː/ *verb*: **continues, continuing, continued**
1 You **continue** to do something, or **continue** doing it, when you keep doing it and do not stop: *If he continues to disrupt classes we shall have consider moving him to a special school.* ▫ *She continued talking for over ten minutes, and none of us could interrupt her.* **2** Something **continues** when it does not stop; you **continue** something when you keep it going: *If the storm continues we may not get over to the island at all.* ▫ *I'd like to continue my training if possible.* ▫ *The discussion continued for two hours or more.* **3** Something **continues**, or you **continue** it, when it starts again after stopping for a period: *The course continues in the spring semester with the study of medieval poetry.* ▫ *In 1891 she arrived in Paris and continued her studies at the Sorbonne.* **4** You **continue** with something when you keep doing it: *He encouraged me to continue with my music.* **5** You **continue** when you start talking again after a pause: *'And then there's the problem of where she'll sleep,' my father continued.* ▫ *Please let me continue.* **6** You **continue** somewhere when you keep going in that direction: *We stopped for a short rest and then continued on our way.* ▫ *He continued up the hill without looking back.*

continuity /kɒntɪˈnjuːɪtɪ/ *noun* (*uncount*)
Continuity is the state of continuing without a break, or without change: *It was thought that a change of leader might upset the continuity of the whole campaign.*

continuous /kənˈtɪnjuːəs/ *adjective*
Something is **continuous** when there is no gap, break or change in it: *His eyebrows formed a continuous line above his eyes.* ▫ *There is a continuous theme in all your books.* ▫ *One doctor collapsed after 42 hours' continuous work.* [compare **continual**]

contorted /kənˈtɔːtɪd/ *adjective*
Something that is **contorted** is twisted out of its usual shape: *among the wreckage of the vehicles and the contorted bodies.*

contour /ˈkɒntʊə(r)/ *noun*: **contours**
1 The **contour** of something is the outline of it: *Moonlight marked out the contour of her face.* **2** The **contours** on a map are the lines joining points of land at the same height.

contraband /ˈkɒntrəband/ *noun* (*uncount*)
Contraband is goods that are taken into and out of a country or prison illegally: *smuggling contraband cigarettes across the border* ▫ *The prison officers found drugs, knifes and other contraband hidden in prisoners' cells.*

contraception /kɒntrəˈsɛpʃən/ *noun* (*uncount*)
Contraception is the various methods used to prevent pregnancy practised before or during sex.

contraceptive /kɒntrəˈsɛptɪv/ *noun*: **contraceptives**
A **contraceptive** is a drug or device that prevents pregnancy.

contract *noun*; *verb*
▻ ***noun*** /ˈkɒntrakt/: **contracts**
A **contract** is an agreement, especially one that is legally enforceable, or the document on which it is recorded: *They've won the contract to supply the council's stationery.* ▫ *He's just signed a contract with another football club.*
▻ ***verb*** /kənˈtrakt/: **contracts, contracting, contracted**
1 Something **contracts** when it becomes smaller, thinner or shorter: *The metal then contracts when it cools.* **2** You **contract** a disease when you catch it: *There was a danger that she would contract pneumonia.* — *noun* (*uncount*) **contraction** /kənˈtrakʃən/: *the contraction of metal as it cools* ▫ *'Don't' is a contraction of 'do not'.* ▫ *muscle contractions.*

contradict /kɒntrəˈdɪkt/ *verb*: **contradicts, contradicting, contradicted**
1 You **contradict** someone when you argue that what they say is incorrect or untrue: *We all knew that was rubbish but nobody dared to contradict her.* **2** One statement **contradicts** another when it suggests that the other is incorrect or untrue: *The results of our clinical trials contradict the claims made about the drug.* — *noun* (*count or uncount*) **contradiction** /kɒntraˈdɪkʃən/: *I can say, without fear of contradiction, that we are all pleased with the results.* ▫ *We don't feel that there's a contradiction between our socialist principles and our involvement in advertising.* ▫ *a book that claims to resolve the apparent contradictions in the Bible.*
▻ ***phrase*** Something that is described by a quality it cannot have is called **a contradiction in terms**: *Maybe 'a righteous war' is just a contradiction in terms.*

contradictory /kɒntrəˈdɪktərɪ/ *adjective*
Contradictory ideas or statements unreasonably suggest that two opposite things are both true: *The claims of both parties are contradictory; clearly they cannot both be right.*

contralto /kən'traltoʊ/ *noun*: **contraltos**
1 A **contralto** is a woman with the lowest type of female singing voice. **2** (*uncount*) Women who have this singing voice sing **contralto**.

contraption /kən'trapʃən/ *noun* (*informal*): **contraptions**
You call a machine or other apparatus a **contraption** when it has a strange appearance or when you are not sure how it works or what it is for: *an odd contraption that looked like a medieval sewing-machine.*

contrary /'kɒntrərı/ *adjective*
Contrary means opposite or opposing: *It would be impossible to reconcile such contrary viewpoints.*
▷ ***phrases*** **1** You use **contrary to** when making a statement that contradicts someone's opinion or belief: *Contrary to what his parents think, he's a very hard-working boy in school.* □ *It turned out to be a bright day, contrary to what the weatherman had predicted.* **2** You use **on the contrary** to introduce a statement that contradicts what has just been said: *'It's a hopeless case, isn't it?' 'On the contrary; I have just found the solution we were searching for'.* **3 To the contrary** means 'stating or suggesting that the opposite is true': *In spite of all the evidence to the contrary, Holmes was convinced the woman was innocent.*

contrast *noun*; *verb*
▷ ***noun*** /'kɒntrɑːst/: **contrasts**
1 There is a **contrast** between things or people being compared when they are different, especially when they have opposing qualities: *It snowed yesterday — today is warm by contrast.* □ *These figures look pretty good in contrast to last year's.* □ *His mood in the evening was a complete contrast to the gloom that had enveloped him all afternoon.* **2** (*uncount*) In a photograph or television picture, **contrast** is the degree of difference in tone between the colours, or the light and dark areas.
▷ ***verb*** /kən'trɑːst/: **contrasts, contrasting, contrasted**
1 You **contrast** people or things when you compare them to see in what ways they are different. **2** One things **contrasts** with another when it is very different from it: *Her cheerless expression contrasted sharply with the summery dress.* — *adjective* **contrasting:** *A dark blue suit would look better with a contrasting shirt.*

contravene /kɒntrə'viːn/ *verb* (*formal*): **contravenes, contravening, contravened**
To **contravene** a law or rule is to break or disobey it: *The absence of a blade guard on this machine contravenes the 'safety at work' regulations.* — *noun* (*uncount or count*) **contravention** /kɒntrə'vɛnʃən/: *Breeding conditions were in contravention of several of the rules governing animal welfare.*

contribute /kən'trıbjuːt/ *verb*: **contributes, contributing, contributed**
1 You **contribute** when, together with others, you give something such as money or effort to a cause or aim: *The youngest children had the most energy and imagination to contribute to the project.* **2** To **contribute** to something is also to be one of the causes of it or one of the reasons for it: *The evidence suggests that our high unemployment level contributes to the uneasiness felt by foreign investors.* — *noun* (*count or uncount*) **contribution** /kɒntrı'bjuːʃən/: *His poetry has made an invaluable contribution to the literature of the 20th century.* □ *Some people gave contributions of £10 and over.* — *noun* **contributor:** *generous contributors to charity.*

contributory /kən'trıbjʊtərı/ *adjective* (*formal*)
A **contributory** factor or reason is one of several factors or reasons that cause something to happen: *The bad weather was a contributory factor to the crash.*

contrite /'kɒntraıt/ *adjective* (*formal*)
You are **contrite** if you feel ashamed of something you have done wrong: *I could tell she had done something wrong because she looked so contrite.* [*same as* **penitent, repentant**]

contrive /kən'traıv/ *verb*: **contrives, contriving, contrived**
1 You **contrive** to do something when you manage to do it: *He had somehow contrived to put the blame on me.* □ *She contrived a little smile.* **2** You **contrive** something when you manage to make it happen, using you cunning: *It struck her that that Iain might be just the man for Mary, and she decided to contrive a meeting between them.* [*same as* **engineer**]

contrived /kən'traivd/ *adjective*
Something **contrived** seems unnatural or artificial: *It was an entertaining film, slightly spoiled by a rather contrived ending.*

control /kən'troʊl/ *noun*; *verb*
▷ ***noun***: **controls**
1 (*uncount*) **Control** is authority, or the power to influence or guide something: *The police were in control of the situation.* □ *Serb armies have taken control of the hills overlooking the city.* □ *The fire is now under control.* □ *Mounted police will be called in if the angry crowds get out of control.* **2 Controls** are the levers, switches and other instruments for operating a vehicle, machine or other device.
▷ ***verb***: **controls, controlling, controlled**
1 You **control** a vehicle or other device when you operate it or guide its operation: *Some of the larger motorbikes are difficult to control.* **2** To **control** something such as a country or a commercial company is to be in complete charge of it: *Enemy forces controlled all main roads and water supplies.* **3** To **control** something is to prevent it from growing or spreading, or to stop it going beyond certain limits: *The illness can be efficiently controlled using drugs.* □ *Central government ultimately controls the level of the council tax.* **4** You **control** yourself when you make an effort not to become angry, upset or excited.

controller /kən'troʊlə(r)/ *noun*: **controllers**
A **controller** is a person who is responsible for directing or controlling something such as traffic or a particular operation within a company: *a strike by air traffic controllers* □ *a production controller.*

controversial /kɒntrə'vɜːʃəl/ *adjective*
Something is **controversial** if many people disagree with it or disapprove of it, or if they are offended by it: *the Chancellor's controversial policy of imposing VAT on domestic fuel bills* □ *It is purely because of its sex scenes that the film is so controversial.*

controversy /'kɒntrəvɜːsı/ *noun* (*uncount or count*): **controversies**
There is **controversy** about something when many people disagree about it, disapprove of it, or are offended by it: *There followed a long-running controversy over the publishing of his third book.*

convalescence /kɒnvə'lɛsəns/ *noun* (*uncount*)
Convalescence is time spent getting better after an illness.

convene /kən'viːn/ *verb* (*formal*): **convenes, convening, convened**
1 You **convene** a meeting if you arrange for it to happen. **2** People **convene** when they come together, *eg* for a meeting: *The court will convene at 10am.*

convenience /kən'viːnıəns/ *noun*: **conveniences**
1 (*uncount*; *often adjectival*) **Convenience** is the quality of being quick and easy to do: *For the sake of convenience, I had prepared the meal in advance.* □ *She*

bought ready-prepared vegetables for convenience. □ *convenience food.* **2** (*uncount*) When you do something at your **convenience** you do it when and how you choose. **3** A **convenience** is something that makes your everyday life easier: *modern flats with every conceivable convenience.*

convenient /kən'viːnɪənt/ *adjective*
Something **convenient** makes life easier by saving time or effort: *The flat has a central position, convenient for the railway and bus stations.* □ *It would be more convenient for me if the meeting could be arranged for Tuesday.* — *adverb* **conveniently:** *The supermarket is conveniently situated near the bus stop.*

convent /'kɒnvənt/ *noun*: **convents**
A **convent** is a community of nuns, or the building they live in; a **convent** is also a school they run.

convention /kən'vɛnʃən/ *noun*: **conventions**
1 A **convention** is a large and formal meeting: *She was a speaker at the Railway Workers' convention in 1956.* **2** A **convention** is also a treaty or formal agreement, for example between nations. **3** (*count or uncount*) A **convention** is a custom, especially in social behaviour: *She was a free spirit who rejected convention in all its forms.*

conventional /kən'vɛnʃənəl/ *adjective*
Conventional describes people and things that follow traditional styles or methods, and sometimes suggests that this makes them uninteresting: *It would be cheaper to continue with the conventional coal-fired system.* □ *dressed in a conventional three-piece suit.* □ *conventional, as opposed to nuclear weapons.* — *adverb* **conventionally:** *She always dresses conventionally for work.* [*opposite* **unconventional**]

converge /kən'vɜːdʒ/ *verb*: **converges, converging, converged**
1 Several people **converge** on something when they move towards it from different directions: *Angry crowds converged on the minister's car before it pulled away.* **2** Roads and paths **converge** when they meet.

conversant /kən'vɜːsənt/ *adjective* (*formal*)
You are **conversant** with something when you have knowledge or experience of it: *They receive thorough training until they are fully conversant with all aspects of police work.*

conversation /kɒnvə'seɪʃən/ *noun* (*count or uncount*)
You have a **conversation** with someone when you talk to them, usually informally: *We had a rather serious conversation.* □ *We would spend hours in idle conversation.*

converse[1] /kən'vɜːs/ *verb* (*formal*): **converses, conversing, conversed**
You **converse** with someone when you talk to them.

converse[2] /kən'vɜːs/ *noun* (*used in the singular; formal*)
The **converse** of something is the opposite of it.

conversely /kən'vɜːslɪ/ *adverb* (*sentence adverb*)
Conversely is used to introduce a statement that is the opposite of what has just been said: *Summer pruning encourages growth; conversely, you prune in winter to inhibit growth.*

conversion /kən'vɜːʃən/ *noun* (*count or uncount*): **conversions**
1 A **conversion** is something changed so that it can have another use: *We could create another bedroom by having a loft conversion done.* **2** Someone's **conversion** is a change in the beliefs they have, especially when they discover that they have religious beliefs: *his conversion to Judaism.*

convert *verb; noun*
▻ ***verb*** /kən'vɜːt/: **converts, converting, converted**
1 You **convert** something when you change it so that it has a different use: *They converted the old barn into a holiday home.* □ *The high chair converts into a table and chair for the older child.* **2** To **convert** something is to change its form: *Plant cells convert sunlight into food.* □ *This table converts inches into centimetres.* **3** You **convert** to a particular set of beliefs, especially religious beliefs, when you adopt them: *Many of the former Soviet states have converted to capitalism.*
▻ ***noun*** /'kɒnvɜːt/: **converts**
A **convert** is someone who has changed their beliefs: *She is the latest convert to the government's new scheme for schools.*

convertible /kən'vɜːtɪbəl/ *adjective*
1 A **convertible** is a car with a roof that can be folded down or taken off. **2** (*technical*) Money is **convertible** if it can be easily changed into money of a different currency: *Dollars are convertible.*

convex /'kɒnvɛks/ *adjective*
A **convex** surface curves outwards, like the surface of the eye. [compare **concave**]

convey /kən'veɪ/ *verb*: **conveys, conveying, conveyed**
1 You **convey** your feelings or opinions to others when you make others aware of them: *His comments conveyed the impression that he had actually visited the place.* □ *the excitement conveyed by their bright eyes and smiling faces.* **2** (*formal*) To **convey** something somewhere is also to carry or transport it there: *They are then conveyed to the other end of the tunnel on rollers.*

conveyor belt /kən'veɪə bɛlt/ *noun*: **conveyor belts**
A **conveyor belt** is a strip of *eg* rubber or metal that moves continuously, used *eg* in factories to move goods being produced and packed.

convict *verb; noun*
▻ ***verb*** /kən'vɪkt/: **convicts, convicting, convicted**
Someone **is convicted** of a crime when they are officially declared to be guilty.
▻ ***noun*** /'kɒnvɪkt/: **convicts**
A **convict** is a person in prison: *The police are hunting the escaped convicts.*

conviction /kən'vɪkʃən/ *noun*: **convictions**
1 A **conviction** is a firm belief or opinion: *Nothing would sway him from his conviction that Julia was innocent.* **2** (*uncount*) You speak with **conviction** when you are confident that what you say or believe is true: *'Yes, of course I'm thrilled,' replied Douglas, without obvious conviction.*

convince /kən'vɪns/ *verb*: **convinces, convincing, convinced**
You **convince** someone when you make them believe that something is true: *There is convincing evidence from clinical trials that these patches are an effective aid to stopping smoking.* □ *We managed to convince the children that nothing was wrong.* □ *She is convinced that it will harm our chances of winning the election.*

convinced /kən'vɪnst/ *adjective*
You are **convinced** of something when you are sure that it is true: *'Look, here's the proof.' 'I'm sorry, I'm still not convinced.'*

convincing /kən'vɪnsɪŋ/ *adjective*
Something that is **convincing** gives the impression of being real or genuine: *We would have to think of a convincing reason for being late.* □ *Her performance was very convincing.*

convoluted /'kɒnvəluːtɪd/ *adjective* (*formal*)
A **convoluted** sentence or idea is complicated and difficult to understand. [*same as* **complex**]

convoy /kɒn'vɔɪ/ *noun*: **convoys**
A **convoy** is a group of vehicles travelling together: *The first convoy of relief supplies is expected tomorrow.*

convulsion /kən'vʌlʃən/ *noun*: **convulsions**
Someone has **convulsions** when they suffer violent uncontrollable movements of their limbs because of an illness.

cook /kʊk/ *verb*; *noun*
▻ ***verb***: **cooks, cooking, cooked**
You **cook** food when you heat it ready for eating; you **cook** a meal of hot food when you prepare the ingredients and heat them: *Cook the mixture over a medium flame.* ▫ *Who's cooking dinner tonight?* — *noun* (*uncount*) **cooking:** *I really enjoy cooking.*
▻ ***noun***: **cooks**
A **cook** is a person who cooks or prepares food: *He's an excellent cook.* ▫ *She's a well-known pastry cook.*

> ***phrasal verb***
> **cook up** (*informal*) **1** You **cook up** an excuse when you invent it: *She cooked up an incredible story about having to go fishing for the weekend.* **2** People **cook up** a plan when they form it together: *His colleagues had cooked up a scheme to get him transferred out of the office.*

cooker /'kʊkə(r)/ *noun*: **cookers**
A **cooker** is a device for cooking food on, especially a large apparatus that cooks food in different ways: *They have a lovely range of new gas cookers.* [see picture at **kitchen**]

cookery /'kʊkərɪ/ *noun* (*uncount*)
Cookery is the skill or practice of cooking food: *He goes to cookery classes.*

cookie /'kʊkɪ/ *noun* (*AmE*): **cookies**
A **cookie** is a biscuit.

cool /ku:l/ *adjective*; *verb*
▻ ***adjective***: **cooler, coolest**
1 Something is **cool** when it is fairly cold, pleasantly cold or too cold: *The dough should be cool to the touch.* ▫ *The evening brought a cool breeze that refreshed us.* ▫ *This soup's a bit cool.* **2 Cool** also means calm, not angry or upset: *Just try and stay cool.* **3 Cool** behaviour is unfriendly or unenthusiastic: *We were given rather a cool reception.* ▫ *Most of her suggestions were met with a cool response.* — *adverb* **coolly** /'ku:llɪ/: *'No, it's not,' she answered, coolly.* — *noun* (*uncount*) **coolness:** *the coolness of the water.* ▫ *Did I detect a certain coolness in her voice?*
▻ ***verb***: **cools, cooling, cooled**
Something **cools, cools** down or **cools** off when it becomes cooler: *Wait until the meat cools slightly before carving it.* ▫ *It should have cooled down enough to be drinkable by now.* ▫ *We sat in the shade of a tree to cool off.*

> ***phrasal verb***
> Someone **cools down** when they become calm after being angry: *We tried to cool him down.*

coop /ku:p/ *verb*: **coops, cooping, cooped**
▻ ***phrase*** You feel **cooped up** when you are in a place that is so small, or a place that you have not been out of for such a long time, that you feel like a prisoner: *I couldn't stay cooped up in that little flat for a moment longer.*

co-operate /koʊ'ɒpəreɪt/ *verb*: **co-operates, co-operating, co-operated**
1 People **co-operate** when they work together: *A number of local companies are co-operating with the council in their latest anti-litter initiative.* **2** You **co-operate** with someone when you do what they ask: *They threatened me with violence if I didn't co-operate.* — *noun* (*uncount*) **co-operation** /koʊɒpə'reɪʃən/: *close co-operation between management and workers* ▫ *We expect the full co-operation of all members.*

co-operative /koʊ'ɒpərətɪv/ *adjective*; *noun*
▻ ***adjective***
1 You are **co-operative** when you are willing to do what others ask: *The bank manager was not very co-operative.* **2 Co-operative** describes projects or businesses managed or owned jointly by a number of people who each get an equal share of the benefits or profits produced.
▻ ***noun***: **co-operatives:** *They've formed a workers' co-operative.*

co-opt /koʊ'ɒpt/ *verb* **co-opts, co-opting, co-opted**
Bodies such as committees **co-opt** extra individuals as members when they invite them to join them for some purpose.

co-ordinate /koʊ'ɔ:dɪneɪt/ *verb*; *noun*
▻ ***verb***: **co-ordinates, co-ordinating, co-ordinated**
1 To **co-ordinate** people or things is to organize them in such a way that they combine efficiently or attractively: *With so many different bands involved, co-ordinating the concert will be a mammoth task.* ▫ *The effect will be spoiled if the colours of your decorations and furnishings aren't properly co-ordinated.* **2** You **co-ordinate** the parts of your body when you move them together in a smooth and controlled way.
▻ ***noun***: **co-ordinates**
The **co-ordinates** of a point on a map are the two sets of numbers or letters that lead you to find that point. — *noun* (*uncount*) **co-ordination** /koʊɔ:dɪ'neɪʃən/: *You will be responsible for the co-ordination of the whole enterprise.* ▫ *I'm a very poor dancer; I have no co-ordination at all.*

cop /kɒp/ *noun* (*slang*): **cops**
A **cop** is a policeman.

cope /koʊp/ *verb*: **copes, coping, coped**
1 You **cope** with a problem when you deal with it successfully: *It was a difficult thing to do, but she coped remarkably well.* **2** You have things to **cope** with when you are faced with them and have to deal with them: *She doesn't want to listen to your moaning; she already has enough to cope with.*

co-pilot /'koʊ paɪlət/ *noun*: **co-pilots**
A **co-pilot** is the person who assists the chief pilot of an aeroplane.

copious /'koʊpɪəs/ *adjective* (*formal*)
There are **copious** amounts of something when there is a lot of it: *Copious references guide the reader to other important works on the subject.*

copper¹ /'kɒpə(r)/ *noun*: **coppers**
1 (*uncount, often adjectival*) **Copper** is a soft reddish-brown metal: *a piece of copper piping.* **2 Coppers** are coins of low value.

copper² /'kɒpə(r)/ *noun* (*slang*): **coppers**
A **copper** is a policeman.

copy /'kɒpɪ/ *noun*; *verb*
▻ ***noun***: **copies**
1 A **copy** of something is a version of it that is identical to the original one: *Copies of the letter were sent to all members.* ▫ *The vase is a modern copy of a 17th-century Japanese design.* **2** A **copy** of a book, newspaper or magazine is a single specimen of all those identical ones published or printed: *I stopped to pick up a copy of today's 'Times'.*
▻ ***verb***: **copies, copying, copied**
1 You **copy** someone when you do the same as they do: *Our management structure has been copied by a number or companies worldwide.* **2** You **copy** some-

thing such as a piece of writing when you make another version of it that is identical to it: *I copied Steve's notes.* □ *She looked up his number and copied it into her address book.*

> ***phrasal verbs***
> **copy down** You **copy down** what someone has said or written when you write it down exactly: *I copied down the figures from the blackboard.*
> **copy out** You **copy out** something that has been written when you write it out in full: *She copied out the whole letter for me.*

copyright /'kɒpɪraɪt/ *noun* (*uncount*)
The **copyright** on something such as a book or song is the legal right of the author or songwriter to be paid by others who want to copy it or perform it.

coral /'kɒrəl/ *noun* (*uncount*)
Coral is a hard pink, red or white rock-like material under the sea, made up of the skeletons of tiny sea creatures: *coral earrings.*

cord /kɔ:d/ *noun*: **cords**
1 (*count or uncount*) A **cord** is a piece of thin rope or thick string: *a length of cord.* **2** (*informal*) **Cords** are corduroy trousers.

cordial /'kɔ:dɪəl/ *adjective*; *noun*
▻ ***adjective***
Cordial behaviour is warm and friendly: *They gave me the very cordial welcome.* □ *Relations between them had been far from cordial.* — *adverb* **cordially:** *They embraced cordially.*
▻ ***noun*** (*uncount*)
Cordial is a sweet drink of fruit juice and water.

cordon /'kɔ:dən/ *noun*; *verb*
▻ ***noun***: **cordons**
There is a **cordon** around an area when ordinary members of the public are prevented from entering it, *eg* by police officers or by official barriers: *Police have thrown a cordon round the streets affected by the bomb blast.*
▻ ***verb***: **cordons, cordoning, cordoned**

> ***phrasal verb***
> An area **is cordoned off** when a cordon is put around it.

corduroy /'kɔ:dərɔɪ/ *noun*: **corduroys**
1 (*uncount, often adjectival*) **Corduroy** is a thick cotton fabric woven to have a pattern of raised lines: *a corduroy skirt.* **2** (*used in the plural*) **Corduroys** are trousers made of corduroy.

core /kɔ:(r)/ *noun*: **cores**
1 The **core** of fruits such as apples and pears is the hard part at the centre, containing the seeds: *an apple core.* [see picture at **fruit**] **2** The most important part, person or group is often referred to as the **core**: *There is a core group of about ten, with a few others who attend from time to time.* □ *This is really the core of the problem.*

cork /kɔ:k/ *noun*: **corks**
1 (*uncount*) **Cork** is the bark of a kind of tree. **Cork** is very light, floats easily and is used for making stoppers for bottles, flooring and the soles of shoes. **2** A **cork** is a piece of this bark used as a stopper for a bottle: *You can tell nothing about the wine by smelling the cork.*

corkscrew /'kɔ:kskru:/ *noun*: **corkscrews**
A **corkscrew** is a tool for removing corks from bottles.

corn[1] /kɔ:n/ *noun* (*uncount*)
1 Corn is any cereal plant, especially wheat, or its seeds: *stacks of corn* □ *scattering corn for the hens.* **2 Corn** is also maize: *corn on the cob.* [see picture at **vegetable**]

corn[2] /kɔ:n/ *noun*: **corns**
A **corn** is a small area of hardened skin on a person's toe.

corned beef *noun* (*uncount*)
Corned beef is beef that has been cooked in salt water as a way of preserving it.

corner /'kɔ:nə(r)/ *noun*; *verb*
▻ ***noun***: **corners**
1 A **corner** is an angle made by two lines or edges that join each other: *I bumped my head on the corner of the table.* □ *She put it on the chair in the corner of the room.* **2** A **corner** is also a place where two roads meet: *There's a shop on the next corner.* **3** A sharp bend in a road is also a **corner**: *The driver took the corner at over 70 miles per hour.* **4** You are in a **corner** when you are in a difficult or embarrassing situation: *A letter from Evans might help him get out of this tight corner.*
▻ ***verb***: **corners, cornering, cornered**
1 You **corner** someone when you force them into a place or situation that they cannot easily escape from: *They knew the tiger would turn nasty if cornered.* □ *A couple of tricky questions and they had him cornered.* **2** A business firm **corners** a market when they become the only company selling goods of a particular kind, allowing them to control prices.
▻ ***phrase*** You **cut corners** when you spend less time or money on something than you should, producing a poor result: *After spending so much money on building the house, it seems ridiculous to cut corners on the decorating.*

cornerstone /'kɔ:nəstoun/ *noun*: **cornerstones**
The **cornerstone** of something is the most important part of it, that everything else depends on: *Liberal citizenship regulations are the cornerstone of our immigration policy.*

cornet /'kɔ:nɪt/ *noun*: **cornets**
1 An ice-cream **cornet** is a cone-shaped wafer with ice cream in it. **2** A **cornet** is also a small trumpet.

cornflakes /'kɔnfleɪks/ *noun* (*plural*)
Cornflakes are a breakfast food eaten cold with milk: *a bowl of cornflakes.*

corny /'kɔ:nɪ/ *adjective* (*informal*): **cornier, corniest**
You describe something such as a joke or a story as **corny** if it is ridiculously simple or unoriginal: *Most of the old black-and-white films seemed pretty corny.*

coronary /'kɒrənərɪ/ *noun*: **coronaries**
A **coronary** is a heart attack.

coronation /kɒrə'neɪʃən/ *noun*: **coronations**
A **coronation** is the ceremony of crowning a king or queen: *shortly after the Queen's coronation in 1953.*

coroner /'kɒrənə(r)/ *noun*: **coroners**
A **coroner** is an official who investigates the deaths of people who die suddenly or as a result of accidents.

corporal /'kɔ:pərəl/ *noun*: **corporals**
A **corporal** is an army officer of low rank.

corporal punishment /kɔ:pərəl 'pʌnɪʃmənt/ *noun* (*uncount*)
Corporal punishment is physical punishment such as beating or caning.

corporate /'kɔ:pərɪt/ *adjective*
Corporate refers to a business firm as a whole, rather than to departments within it: *developing a new corporate strategy.*

corporation /kɔ:pə'reɪʃən/ *noun*: **corporations**
A **corporation** is a large business firm.

corps /kɔː(r)/ *noun*: *plural* **corps**
1 In the armed forces, a **corps** is a specially trained group of people with responsibility for a particular task: *the signal corps.* **2** A **corps** is also a group of people involved in the same activity: *the diplomatic corps.*

corpse /kɔːps/ *noun*: **corpses**
A **corpse** is the dead body of a human being.

corpulent /ˈkɔːpjʊlənt/ *adjective* (*formal, humorous*)
Someone who is **corpulent** is fat: *He has squashed his corpulent little frame into a suit two sizes too small.*

correct /kəˈrɛkt/ *adjective; verb*
▻ ***adjective***
1 Something is **correct** if it is accurate and free from mistakes: *She gave the correct answer.* □ *'She's responsible for overseas trade, isn't she?' 'That's correct.'* **2** The **correct** thing is the proper or appropriate one, the one required: *Make sure you connect it to the correct wire.* **3** **Correct** behaviour is considered by others to be proper or appropriate: *They insisted that their standpoint in the whole affair had been morally correct.*
▻ ***verb***: **corrects, correcting, corrected**
1 You **correct** a mistake when you take action to make it right: *The letter was perfect, apart from one or two spelling errors, which I have corrected.* **2** You **correct** someone when you state that they have said something inaccurate, and you give the accurate information yourself: *I must correct you there; it was in 1979, not 1980, that the two leaders met.*

correction /kəˈrɛkʃən/ *noun* (*count or uncount*): **corrections**
A **correction** is an act of correcting a mistake: *There were few corrections to be made; the bulk of the writing was fine.* □ *one or two errors in need of correction.*

correlate /ˈkɒrəleɪt/ *verb* (*formal*): **correlates, correlating, correlated**
Two or more things **correlate** when they are linked or related: *A mother's smoking in pregnancy correlates with low birth weight in her baby.* — ***noun*** (*uncount*) **correlation** /kɒrəˈleɪʃən/: *It is difficult to prove a correlation between exposure to low-level radiation and the incidence of leukaemia.*

correspond /kɒrɪˈspɒnd/ *verb*: **corresponds, corresponding, corresponded**
1 One thing **corresponds** to another if it is similar or equivalent to it: *The American position of 'professor' corresponds with simple 'lecturer' in this country.* **2** Two sets of things **correspond** if they match: *The goods delivered don't correspond with what was on the order form.* **3** People **correspond** when they write letters to each other: *She regularly corresponds with her friends in New England.*

correspondence /kɒrɪˈspɒndəns/ *noun* (*uncount; formal*)
Correspondence is communication by letter, or a letter or letters received or sent: *There has been much correspondence on the subject.*

correspondent /kɒrɪˈspɒndənt/ *noun*: **correspondents**
A **correspondent** is a newspaper, television or radio reporter working in a particular part of the world, or on a particular topic: *Here's our economics correspondent, Dominic Harrod.*

corresponding /kɒrɪˈspɒndɪŋ/ *adjective*
Corresponding describes something of the same kind, size or extent as the thing just mentioned: *After the Bank's announcement of interest rate cuts of 1%, we expected a corresponding announcement from the building societies.*

corridor /ˈkɒrɪdɔː(r)/ *noun*: **corridors**
A **corridor** is a long passageway with rooms on one or both sides: *The train was so full that some passengers had to stand in the corridor.*

corroborate /kəˈrɒbəreɪt/ *verb* (*formal*): **corroborates, corroborating, corroborated**
You **corroborate** what someone has said when you make a statement or give other evidence that supports it or proves that it is true: *Several witnesses corroborated her version of events.* — *noun* (*uncount*) **corroboration** /kərɒbəˈreɪʃən/: *We'll need the corroboration of at least one independent witness before we can take the case to court.*

corrode /kəˈroʊd/ *verb*: **corrodes, corroding, corroded**
Metals **corrode** when they gradually become damaged or destroyed by chemicals or by rust: *The car's underside had corroded through prolonged exposure to salt water.* — *noun* (*uncount*) **corrosion** /kəˈroʊʒən/: *the corrosion of some metals by the weaker acids.*

corrosive /kəˈroʊsɪv/ *adjective*
1 A **corrosive** substance can wear away or destroy materials such as metal by reacting chemically with them. **2** Something has a **corrosive** effect or influence on something else when it wears away or destroys that other thing gradually over time: *He argued that the consumer society had a corrosive effect on public morals.*

corrugated /ˈkɒrəgeɪtɪd/ *adjective*
A surface or material that is **corrugated** is formed into a series of rounded folds: *a hut with a corrugated iron roof.*

corrupt /kəˈrʌpt/ *verb; adjective*
▻ ***verb***: **corrupts, corrupting, corrupted**
1 To **corrupt** someone is to make them become wicked or evil, or to persuade them that being evil is normal or acceptable: *The judge argued that such films might corrupt young people.* **2** To **corrupt** something is to spoil it by making it less pure: *The Academy ruled that such foreign expressions were not permitted, as they corrupted the language.*
▻ ***adjective***
A **corrupt** person is dishonest: *a corrupt system in which the boss's favourites get promotion.* — *noun* (*uncount*) **corruption** /kəˈrʌpʃən/: *stories of bribery and corruption amongst senior police officers.*

corset /ˈkɔːsɪt/ *noun*: **corsets**
A **corset** is a tightly fitting undergarment worn, especially by women, to give the upper body a more attractive shape.

cosmetic /kɒzˈmɛtɪk/ *noun; adjective*
▻ ***noun***: **cosmetics**
Cosmetics are substances such as lipstick that people, usually women, put on their face to make them look more attractive.
▻ ***adjective***
Cosmetic describes something that improves only the appearance of something, not its true nature: *one or two cosmetic changes to the wording of the policy.*

cosmic /ˈkɒzmɪk/ *adjective*
1 **Cosmic** describes things relating to the whole universe: *Modern theologians see God as more of a cosmic force.* **2** (*informal*) **Cosmic** also means very large or important: *an improvement of cosmic proportion.*

cosmopolitan /kɒzməˈpɒlɪtən/ *adjective*
1 **Cosmopolitan** describes things that display the traditions and cultures of many different countries: *a very cosmopolitan city.* **2** A **cosmopolitan** person has experience and knowledge of the traditions and cultures of many different countries: *The new Minister for the Arts has a very cosmopolitan outlook.*

cosmos /ˈkɒzmɒs/ *noun* (*singular*)

The **cosmos** is the universe seen an ordered whole: *working to unlock the secrets of the cosmos.*

cosset /ˈkɒsɪt/ *verb*: **cossets, cosseting, cosseted**
You **cosset** someone or something when you spend a lot of time and effort making sure that they are happy, comfortable and protected from harm: *Of course he will find life in the city a little hard to begin with, having been cosseted in a cosy little village up until now.* [*same as* **pamper**]

cost /kɒst/ *noun*; *verb*
▷ ***noun***: **costs**
1 The **cost** of something is the total amount of money needed to do or have it: *the cost of sending the kids to a private nursery* □ *the cost of a foreign holiday for four* □ *£200 should be enough to cover your costs.*

> **Cost, price, charge,** and **fee** have their own distinct uses. You talk about the **price** of goods in a shop: *She asked the price of the ring.* You use **cost** for the amount you pay for a process, *eg* a repair, to be carried out: *the cost of redecorating the house.* You pay a **charge** for a service: *postal charges.* When you enter a museum or gallery you may have to pay an entrance *fee* or *charge* for admission. Professional people, *eg* lawyers, charge **fees** for their services, and students pay **fees** for their courses.

2 (*used in the singular*) The **cost** of something is the damage or loss it involves: *It's impossible to calculate the cost in lost working time.*
▷ ***verb***: **costs, costing, cost**
1 A thing **costs** the amount of money you need to spend to have or do it: *A solicitor's advice can cost hundreds of pounds.* □ *It cost me over £10 to get these shoes repaired.* **2** Something **costs** you what you lose as a result of having or doing it: *I tended to put my job before the family, and it cost me my marriage.*
▷ ***phrase*** You say that something must be done **at all costs** when every necessary effort or sacrifice should be made in order to achieve it: *A war must be avoided at all costs.*

costly /ˈkɒstlɪ/ *adjective*: **costlier, costliest**
1 Something is **costly** when it is costs a lot of money: *Isn't that rather a costly way of doing it?* **2** Something is also **costly** when it involves big losses or sacrifices: *Let's hope that victory will not be so costly this time.*

costume /ˈkɒstjuːm/ *noun*: **costumes**
1 A **costume** is a set of clothes worn by an actor when playing a part: *We've had to borrow costumes from a neighbouring theatre.* **2** A **costume** is also a garment or outfit for a special activity: *a swimming costume.* **3** (*uncount*) The clothes that people wore in a certain period of history are often referred to as **costume**: *dressed in authentic 16th-century costume.*

cosy (*AmE* **cozy**) /ˈkoʊzɪ/ *adjective*: **cosier, cosiest**
1 A **cosy** room is warm and comfortable; you are **cosy** when you feel warm and comfortable: *The flat was small but cosy.* **2** A **cosy** relationship between people is friendly or private: *We had quite a cosy little chat.*

cot /kɒt/ *noun*: **cots**
1 A **cot** is a small bed with high sides, for a young child. **2** (*AmE*) A **cot** is also a camp bed.

cottage /ˈkɒtɪdʒ/ *noun*: **cottages**
A **cottage** is a small house, especially an old one in a village or in the countryside.

cottage cheese /kɒtɪdʒ ˈtʃiːz/ *noun* (*uncount*)
Cottage cheese is a type of soft white cheese made from sour milk: *a tub of cottage cheese.*

cotton /ˈkɒtən/ *noun*; *verb*
▷ ***noun*** (*uncount*)
1 (*often adjectival*) **Cotton** is a common fabric made from the soft fibres of a plant that grows in hot countries: *He prefers cotton shirts to nylon.* **2 Cotton** is also thread made from these fibres, used for sewing: *Have you got a needle and cotton I could borrow?* **3** The plant itself is also called **cotton**: *fields of cotton.*
▷ ***verb*** (*informal*): **cottons, cottoning, cottoned**

> ***phrasal verb***
> You **cotton on** to something when you realize it or understand it, especially after a time: *I kept hinting that he should leave but he didn't cotton on.*

cotton wool *noun* (*uncount*)
Cotton wool is cotton in the form of a soft fluffy mass, with many household uses such as dressing wounds and applying cosmetics.

couch /kaʊtʃ/ *noun*; *verb*
▷ ***noun***: **couches**
1 A **couch** is a sofa. [see picture at **living room**] **2** A **couch** is also a bed in a doctor's surgery, for patients to lie on when being examined.
▷ ***verb***: **couches, couching, couched**
You say that a statement **is couched** in words of a certain kind when it is expressed in such words: *I received a threat from their solicitors, couched in the most graciously formal language.*

cough /kɒf/ *verb*; *noun*
▷ ***verb***: **coughs, coughing, coughed**
You **cough** when you force air or mucus out of your throat or lungs with a sharp rough noise: *I could hear him coughing through the wall.* □ *She knew it was serious when she started coughing blood.*
▷ ***noun***: **coughs**
A **cough** is an illness of the throat or lungs that causes you to cough: *I've had this cough for weeks.*

> ***phrasal verb***
> **cough up 1** You **cough up** mucus when you bring it from your throat or lungs into your mouth by coughing: *He started coughing up blood.* **2** (*informal*) You might tell someone to **cough up** when you want them to give you the money that they owe you.

could /kʊd/ or /kəd/ *modal verb*
(*negative forms* **could not** or **couldn't**)
Could is used:
1 as the past tense of **can**
a in the sense 'be able to': *She could speak four languages by the age of eight.* □ *She tried to lift it but she couldn't.* □ *He said he could finish it by Tuesday.* □ *He could be very charming when he wanted to be.* □ *She could hear someone shouting in the distance.*
b in the sense 'be allowed to': *She could stay out late provided her parents knew where she was.* □ *She said I could invite you.*

> Notice that where a single occasion in the past is referred to, **could** is used only with a negative, or in reported speech (*He said he could finish..., She said I could invite...*), or with verbs of sensing, such as **see, hear** and **feel**: *She managed to* (not *could*) *contact him last night. He was allowed to* (not *could*) *stay up late that evening.* But: *I couldn't find my purse anywhere. She could see he was disappointed.*

2 to ask permission politely: *Could I borrow your bicycle?*
3 to make polite requests: *Could you carry this for*

me? □ You couldn't lend me a pound, could you? □ Please could I speak to Janet?
4 to make suggestions: *You could enquire at the lost-property office.* □ *Could I suggest that we wait till tomorrow?*
5 to make offers and issue invitations: *I could run you to the station, if you like.* □ *Could you have lunch with me on Wednesday?* □ *Could we meet for a coffee?*
6 to talk about possibilities (note that **could have** is usually used if the possibility is in the past): *It could snow tomorrow* [= might].. □ *You could have drowned.* [= might have] □ *She couldn't fail a second time.* [= surely she won't] □ *Surely he couldn't have said that.* [= it's unlikely that he did] □ *If you moved over I could sit down.* [= would be able to] □ *I could have finished if I'd had more time.* [= would have been able to finish] □ *I could come next Friday.* [= would be able to] □ *I couldn't have come last Friday.* [= wouldn't have been able to] □ *You could help.* [= why don't you?] □ *You could have telephoned to say you would be late.* [= why didn't you?] □ *Couldn't this wait till later?* [= it ought to be possible for it to] □ *Couldn't you have warned me?* [= you should have] □ *I'm so happy I could shout.* [= I want to shout] □ *I was so furious I could have hit him.* [= I wanted to hit him] □ *I couldn't leave the dog behind!* [= it wouldn't have been fair to] □ *How could you insult her like that?* [= it's incredible that you did] □ *How could you have been so careless?* [= it's incredible that you were] □ *I couldn't agree more.* [= I absolutely agree] □ *The sky is so dark it could be midnight.* [= might be, though of course it isn't] □ *It was so hot it could have been summer.* [= might have been, though of course it wasn't]
[see also **can**]

couldn't /'kʊdənt/ *verb*
Couldn't is the spoken, and informal written, form of **could not**. See **could**.

council /'kaʊnsəl/ *noun*: **councils**
1 The **council** is the organization that runs the affairs of a town or region: *Road repairs are the responsibility of the regional council.* **2 Council** is a title used by some other organizations, usually those established by the government: *chairman of the Arts Council.*

council house /'kaʊnsɪl haʊs/ *noun*: **council houses**
A **council house** is owned by a local council and rented out to a person or family.

councillor /'kɒʊnsələr/ *noun*: **councillors**
A **councillor** is a person elected to take decisions about the running of a local council.

counsel /'kaʊnsəl/ *verb*; *noun*
▷ ***verb***: **counsels, counselling** (*AmE* **counseling**), **counselled** (*AmE* **counseled**)
To **counsel** someone is to give them advice about problems they have: *Our role is to counsel couples considering divorce.*
▷ ***noun***: **counsels**
A lawyer representing someone in court is usually referred to in court as **counsel**: *the opinions of my learned friend, the counsel for the prosecution.*

counsellor (*AmE* **counselor**) /'kaʊnsələ(r)/ *noun*: **counsellors**
A **counsellor** is someone trained to give people advice about problems of a particular kind: *a marriage-guidance counsellor.*

count[1] /kaʊnt/ *verb*; *noun*
▷ ***verb***: **counts, counting, counted**
1 You **count** when you say the numbers in order: *Let's hear you count from one to ten.* □ *I can count up to a hundred.* **2** You **count** things when you find how many of them there are by adding them up one by one: *The result isn't known yet; the votes are still being counted.* **3** You **count** something when you include it in your calculation: *Over thirty people attended the meeting, not counting members of the committee.* □ *Remember to count the people in the sanatorium.* **4** The thing that **counts** in any situation is the most important thing: *It's speed that counts, not accuracy.* □ *You've been honest with yourself, and that's what counts.* **5** Something that **counts** for nothing is not valued or respected: *Attention to detail counts for very little these days.* **6** Something **counts** as a particular thing if it can rightly be regarded as being or representing that thing: *Record-breaking times achieved in practice do not normally count officially as records.*
▷ ***noun***: **counts**
1 A **count** is an act of counting a set of things, or the number you get when you count them: *At the last count, there were over 3000 businesses in this region alone.* □ *The official count is now over 250.* **2** A statement that is right or wrong on several **counts** is right or wrong on several points, or for several reasons: *The statistics are considered suspect on two counts.*
▷ ***phrases*** **1** You **keep count** of things when you keep a record of how many there are or have been: *She's asked me to keep count of all the complaints we receive.* **2** You **lose count** of things when you forget how many of them there are or have been: *I've lost count of the number of times he's told that story.*

phrasal verbs
count against Something **counts against** you if people reject you or penalize you because of it: *Your lack of teaching experience need not count against you.*
count in You **count** someone **in** when you include them in an activity: *If you're looking for volunteers, count me in.*
count on 1 You can **count on** someone if you can rely on them: *We can count on Lizzie to keep her promise.* **2** You **count on** something when you are so sure that it will happen that you take account of it in your plans: *We should count on taking at least three days to get there.* □ *If you're self-employed you can't count on a regular income.*
count out 1 You **count out** an amount of money when you count the notes and coins one by one to find their total value. **2** You ask people to **count** you **out** if you are not willing to be included in a scheme or activity: *If you're looking for people to contribute money, you can count me out.*
count up You **count up** all the things in a set when you add them all together to find the total.

count[2] /kaʊnt/ *noun*: **counts**
A **count** is a European nobleman equal in rank to a British earl: *It is time we visited Count von Schlieffen.*

count[3] /kaʊnt/ *adjective*
In this dictionary, **count** describes nouns (also called **countable** nouns) that have both a singular and a plural form, and are used with a determiner when in the singular (*a jacket, my nose, houses*), as distinct from nouns that have only one form, such as *courage* and *shame*. [see also **uncount**]

countenance /'kaʊntənəns/ *noun* (*uncount*; *literary*)
A person's **countenance** is the appearance of their face: *It was a pleasure to gaze upon his youthful countenance.*

counter[1] /'kɒʊntə(r)/ *noun*: **counters**
1 In shops and other places, a **counter** is a long table-like surface where goods are displayed, or where you pay for them: *I walked over to the perfume counter.* □ *I leaned across the counter and handed him the money.*

2 A **counter** is also a small flat disc used as a playing-piece in various board games.

counter² /ˈkaʊntə(r)/ *verb*: **counters, countering, countered**
1 You **counter** something when you say or do something that opposes it: *Her complaints were countered by threats to withdraw the service completely.* **2** You **counter** when you return a criticism or other attack that someone has made: *She accused him of being a careless worker, and he countered with the charge that she had unattainable standards.*
▻ ***phrase*** Something **runs counter to** something else when it is the opposite of it: *Results ran counter to expectations.*

counter- /ˈkaʊntə(r)-/ *prefix*
Counter- is used before nouns and verbs to mean 'opposite' or 'against': *Turn it counterclockwise.* ▫ *The enemy then launched a counter-attack.* ▫ *His lack of sensitivity to staff problems is very counter-productive.*

counteract /kaʊntərˈact/ *verb*: **counteracts, counteracting, counteracted**
One thing **counteracts** another when it reduces or cancels its effect: *Adding sugar helps to counteract the bitterness of the lemons.*

counterfeit /ˈkaʊntəfɪt/ *adjective; verb*
▻ ***adjective***
Something is **counterfeit** when it a close imitation of something, made with the purpose of deceiving: *counterfeit banknotes.*
▻ ***verb***: **counterfeits, counterfeiting, counterfeited:** *the warehouse where the coins had been counterfeited.*

counterpart /ˈkaʊntəpɑːt/ *noun*: **counterparts**
The **counterpart** of something is a person or thing that has a corresponding position or function to theirs elsewhere: *The Dutch foreign minister has had discussions with his Belgian counterpart.* ▫ *The valve is smaller than its counterpart in the diesel engine.*

countess /ˈkaʊntɪs/ *noun*: **countesses**
A **countess** is a noblewoman of the same rank as an earl or count, or a woman married to an earl or count: *an invitation from the Countess de Rosemonde.*

countless /ˈkaʊntləs/ *adjective*
Countless means very many: *I had warned him on countless occasions.*

country /ˈkʌntrɪ/ *noun*: **countries**
1 A **country** is a division of the world ruled by a particular government or monarch, often with its own distinct language and culture: *Living standards in this country are lower than in many European countries.* **2** (*used in the singular*) The people of a particular country are often referred to as the **country**: *The whole country was talking about it.* **3** (*used in the singular*) The **country** is also open land away from towns and cities: *going for long walks in the country.* **4** (*uncount*) **Country** is also used to refer to an area associated with a particular person or activity: *visits to Shakespeare country.*

countryman /ˈkʌntrɪmən/ *noun* (*usually used in the plural*): **countrymen**
Your **countrymen** are the people who come from the same country as you do: *He was pleased to find several of his countrymen were also living in Paris.*

countryside /ˈkʌntrɪsaɪd/ *noun* (*uncount*)
Countryside is open land away from towns and cities: *breathing the fresh air of the countryside.*

county /ˈkaʊntɪ/ *noun*: **counties**
A **county** is a large area containing several towns, often with its own local government, smaller than a region in Britain, and smaller than a state in the United States: *You should apply to the county council planning department before beginning any building work.*

coup /kuː/ *noun*: **coups**
1 A **coup**, or **coup d'état** /kuːdeɪˈtɑː/, is the act of using force to remove a government and take political control of a country: *There has been a military coup in the islands before.* **2** A **coup** is also something achieved by acting quickly and cleverly: *She's pulled off a remarkable publishing coup.*

couple /ˈkʌpəl/ *noun; verb*
▻ ***noun***: **couples**
1 (*with a singular or plural verb*) A **couple** is **a** a husband and wife, boyfriend and girlfriend, or other pair of people in a sexual or romantic relationship: *The couple next door are very nice.* ▫ *young couples kissing on park benches.* **b** any two people who happen to be together on a particular occasion: *Two or three couples were left on the dance floor.* **2** A **couple** of people or things is two of them, or a few of them: *a couple of tickets for the theatre* ▫ *I saw him a couple of days ago.* [compare **pair**]
▻ ***verb***: **couples, coupling, coupled**
Two or more things **are coupled** when they are linked or connected to each other: *The heat, coupled with poor sanitation, has accelerated the spread of the disease.*

coupon /ˈkuːpɒn/ *noun*: **coupons**
A **coupon** is a small printed piece of paper of various kinds, such as one entitling you to a reduced price for certain goods: *For more information on our range of gas fires, fill in the coupon and send it to the address below.*

courage /ˈkʌrɪdʒ/ *noun* (*uncount*)
You have **courage** when you are willing to do something difficult or dangerous: *She showed great courage throughout the ordeal.* ▫ *He doesn't have the courage to say what he really thinks.*

courageous /kəˈreɪdʒəs/ *adjective*
A **courageous** person has courage: *We all agreed that it was a courageous effort.*

courgette /kʊəˈʒet/ *noun*: **courgettes**
A **courgette** is a long green vegetable similar in shape and appearance to a cucumber, usually eaten cooked. [*same as* **zucchini**; see picture at **vegetable**]

courier /ˈkʊərɪə(r)/ *noun*: **couriers**
1 A **courier** is a person paid to deliver letters or parcels: *We've arranged for a motorcycle courier to deliver the parcel.* **2** A **courier** is a representative of a holiday company who looks after tourists abroad: *We told the courier that the shower didn't work.*

course /kɔːs/ *noun*: **courses**
1 A **course** is a series of lessons and study assignments on a particular subject: *I've enrolled on the poetry course this term.* ▫ *She failed to complete her typing course.* **2** (*count or uncount*) The **course** of a ship or aircraft is the direction it moves in, or the planned route it follows: *Our captain set a southerly course.* ▫ *We changed course and began to head west.* ▫ *They found they had drifted slightly off course.* ▫ *The aircraft was now back on course.* **3** The **courses** of a meal are the parts or stages it is divided into: *The first course was soup, and we both chose vegetable curry for the main course and ice cream for dessert.* ▫ *a three-course lunch.* **4** (*used in the singular*) Something that happens in the **course** of a period of time happens during it: *Could you tell him I'd like to speak to him some time in the course of the next hour?* ▫ *He lost his temper twice during the course of the meeting.* **5** (*used in the singular*) You can refer to the way things develop as *eg*

the **course** of events, or the **course** of history: *He'll recover his spirits in the course of time.* □ *Sometimes we should let nature take its course instead of swallowing pills for the slightest ailment.* **6** A **course** of action is one of the ways you can act in a particular situation: *Your best course is to wait.* **7** A **course** of treatment is a number of doses or units of medicine that you have to take over a certain period, or a series of treatment sessions or injections that a doctor gives you: *It's important that you finish this course of tablets.* **8** A **course** is also a golf course or a racecourse: *I was just approaching the last hole on the course.*

▻ ***phrases*** **1** Something happens **as a matter of course** if it happens as part of a normal routine or pattern of events: *If you're promoted, your salary will be increased as a matter of course.* **2** Something that is going to happen **in due course** is going to happen at some suitable time in the future rather than immediately: *You will be hearing from us in due course.* **3** (*often used as an answer*) You use **of course a** as a polite way of giving permission or agreeing: *'May I borrow your pen?' 'Of course.'* □ *'John will help you with your bags, won't you, John?' 'Of course I will.'* **b** when you think the person you are speaking to probably knows what you are telling them already: *She's much younger than he is, of course.* **c** when stating something that is not surprising: *She never wrote to say thank you, of course.* **d** for emphasis: *'Do you still love me?' 'Of course I do!'* **e** in '**of course** not' as an emphatic way of saying 'no': *'You're not angry, are you?' 'Of course not!'* [compare **certainly**] **4** An illness **runs its course** when it develops, gets worse, and gets better again in the normal way.

court /kɔːt/ *noun*; *verb*

▻ ***noun***: **courts**

1 A **court** is a room or building in which legal matters are examined and the results or punishments decided: *the county court* □ *the High Court* □ *Do you really want your wife dragged through the courts?* **2** (*uncount*) The people in the room or building are also often referred to as the **court**: *Please tell the court what happened on the night in question.* **3** In some sports, the area marked out for playing on is called the **court**: *the tennis courts in the public park.* **4** **Court** is used in the names of some streets where buildings are arranged around an open area in the middle, and in the names of some blocks of flats arranged in the same way.

▻ ***verb*** (*old*): **courts, courting, courted**

A couple who **are courting** regularly go out together with the intention of eventually getting married: *We were still courting when the war started; we got married six months after it ended.*

courteous /ˈkɜːtɪəs/ *adjective*

Someone who is **courteous** is polite and respectful.

courtesy /ˈkɜːtəsɪ/ *noun*: **courtesies**

1 (*uncount*) **Courtesy** is polite and respectful behaviour: *They greeted us with courtesy.* **2** A **courtesy** is something polite that you say or do: *after the usual exchange of courtesies.*

court-martial /cɔːt ˈmɑːʃəl/ *noun*; *verb*

▻ ***noun***: **court-martials** or **courts-martial**

A **court-martial** is a court made up of military officers which tries servicemen who have broken military law; a **court-martial** is also a trial held before such a court.

▻ ***verb***: **court-martials, court-martialling** (*AmE* **court-martialing**), **court-martialled** (*AmE* **court-martialed**) (*usually in the passive*)

A member of the armed forces **is court-martialled** when they are tried by a military court: *He's to be court-martialled for being absent without leave.*

courtroom /ˈkɔːtruːm/ *noun*: **courtrooms**

A **courtroom** is a room where a legal court sits: *The trial is being held in courtroom number three.*

courtship /ˈkɔːtʃɪp/ *noun* (*uncount*; *formal*)

Courtship is the process of, or the length of time spent courting: *observing the birds' complicated courtship ritual* □ *They married in 1875 after a long courtship.*

court shoe /ˈkɔːt ʃuː/ *noun*: **court shoes**

Court shoes are shoes for women with plain fronts and heels of medium height.

courtyard /kɔːtjɑːd/ *noun*: **courtyards**

A **courtyard** is an open space surrounded by buildings or walls.

cousin /ˈkʌzən/ *noun*: **cousins**

Your **cousin,** or **first cousin**, is the son or daughter of your uncle or aunt. [see also **second cousin**]

cove /koʊv/ *noun*: **coves**

A **cove** is a small sheltered bay in a coastline: *The boys moored the boat is a sandy cove.*

covenant /ˈkʌvənənt/ *noun*: **covenants**

A **covenant** is

1 a formal agreement between two or more people or groups of people: *They made a solemn covenant to help each other in times of trouble.* **2** a formal written agreement or pledge made by an individual to pay a fixed amount of money at regular intervals to *eg* a charity.

cover /ˈkʌvə(r)/ *verb*; *noun*

▻ ***verb***: **covers, covering, covered**

1 One thing **covers** another when it forms a layer over it: *My hands were covered with flour.* □ *snow-covered roofs.* **2** You **cover** something when you protect or hide it by putting something over it: *She covered her eyes with her hands.* □ *The gunman had covered his face with a mask.* □ *They were advised to cover the furniture with dust sheets.* [see also **cover up** below] **3** Something that **covers** an area extends over it: *The estate covers some 400 acres.* **4** You **cover** a distance when you travel that distance: *We covered more than a thousand miles in four days.* **5** Something that **is covered** is included; you **cover** a subject or topic when you deal with it; journalists **cover** an event when they report on it: *The English course covers poetry and drama, as well as the novel.* □ *Let's end the meeting there; I think we've covered everything of importance.* □ *A report now from Dave Dickson, who is at Wembley covering the match for BBC1.* **6** Things such as laws and insurance policies **cover** the people and situations that they apply to: *The new regulations have been extended to cover imported goods as well.* □ *It appears that we are not covered for damage caused by flooding.* **7** An amount of money **covers** something if it is enough to pay for it: *£50 should cover my travel expenses.*

▻ ***noun***: **covers**

1 A **cover** is something that is put or fitted over an object to protect it: *The seat covers are machine-washable.* **2** (*used in the plural*) The **covers** on a bed are the sheets and blankets that you have over you: *She slept with her head right under the covers.* **3** The **cover** of a magazine is the outside of it; the **cover** of a book is its outside or its loose paper jacket: *The front cover carried a photo of Diana.* **4** (*uncount*) **Cover** is shelter or protection; you take **cover** when you shelter from the weather or from gunfire: *We heard gunshots and took cover behind a wall.* □ *It began to pour and we looked round for cover.* □ *I prefer to keep the car under cover at night.* □ *The thieves escaped under cover of darkness.* **5** You have insurance **cover** for something if your insurance company guarantees to pay expenses in connection with it: *Your travel insurance gives you full cover for* *medical treatment abroad.* **6** A person uses something such as a job as a **cover** for some secret or illegal activity when they use it to conceal or disguise that activity; their **cover** is 'blown' when their secret is discovered.

> ***phrasal verb***
> **cover up 1** You **cover** something **up** when you put something over it to protect or hide it: *She lay down on the sofa and covered herself up with a rug.* **2** You **cover up** something dishonest or embarrassing when you try to prevent people from finding out about it: *It was clear that the minister's staff had been ordered to cover up the whole affair.* **3** You **cover up** for someone else who has done something wrong when you try to prevent other people from finding them out.

coverage /ˈkʌvərɪdʒ/ *noun (uncount)*
Coverage of something is the reporting of it in the media: *criticisms of the BBC's coverage of royal affairs.*

covering /ˈkʌvərɪŋ/ *noun*: **coverings**
A **covering** is a layer of something that covers or hides something else: *There were no floor coverings in the flat; only bare boards.* □ *hills with a light covering of snow.*

covert /ˈkʌvət/ *adjective (formal)*
Something **covert** is done secretly or so that others do not notice it: *investigations into covert military operations* □ *with a covert glance at her watch.*

cow /kaʊ/ *noun*: **cows**
1 A **cow** is the female of a large animal kept on farms for its milk and meat. **2** The female of many other large animals, such the elephant, is also called a **cow**. **3** (*offensive*) Some people refer to a woman they dislike as a **cow**.

coward /kaʊəd/ *noun*: **cowards**
You might call someone a **coward** if they are easily frightened or not willing to deal with difficult or dangerous situations. — *adjective* **cowardly:** *That would be a cowardly course of action.*

cowardice /ˈkaʊədɪs/ *noun (uncount)*
Cowardice is cowardly behaviour: *She accused him of cowardice.*

cowboy /ˈkaʊbɔɪ/ *noun*: **cowboys**
1 In some parts of America, a **cowboy** is a man in charge of cattle, often seen as a character in films set in past times: *cowboys and indians.* **2** You refer to someone who does work on people's houses as a **cowboy** if they are not properly trained or equipped and their work is poor: *The firm who did our roof were a bunch of cowboys*

cower /kaʊə(r)/ *verb*: **cowers, cowering, cowered**
Someone **cowers** when they move back because they are frightened: *The dog cowered away into a corner.*

coy /kɔɪ/ *adjective*
1 Someone who is being **coy** is pretending to be shy or embarrassed: *She nodded her head and gave a coy little smile.* **2** When someone behaves in a secretive way about something that seems unimportant to you, you might describe them as **coy**: *There's no need to be coy about it; just tell us if you intend to accept the job.*

cozy see **cosy**

crab /krab/ *noun*: **crabs**
A **crab** is an edible sea creature with a wide flat shell and five pairs of legs, the front pair of which are large pincers.

crack /krak/ *verb; noun*
▻ ***verb***: **cracks, cracking, cracked**
1 Something such as glass **cracks** when a thin break occurs in it but no pieces fall off: *Some of these teacups cracked in the dishwasher.* **2** Something such as a whip **cracks** when it make a sudden sharp loud noise. **3** You **crack** something against a surface when you hit it hard against that surface, usually accidentally: *She cracked her head on the door.* **4** (*informal*) Someone **cracks** when they are no longer able to tolerate pressure, or resist persuasion or temptation: *I thought I was going to crack under such a barrage of questions.* □ *I haven't had a cigarette for 15 days, although I nearly cracked once or twice last week.* **5** (*informal*) You **crack** a problem or difficulty when you solve it: *I think we've cracked it! We should screw the bracket to the wall first.* **6** To **crack** a joke is to tell it.
▻ ***noun***: **cracks**
1 A **crack** in something is a thin break in it, without any pieces falling off: *one or two cracks in the ceiling.* **2** (*informal*) A **crack** is also an unpleasant comment or a criticism, especially one intended to be amusing: *He made a couple of cracks about the weight she'd put on.*
▻ ***phrases* 1** (*informal*) You get up **at the crack of dawn** when you get up very early. **2** (*informal*) You **have a crack at** something when you attempt to do it: *They're hoping for another crack at the doubles championship.* **3** (*informal*) You say that something is **not what it's cracked up to be** when you think it is not as good as people say it is.

> ***phrasal verbs***
> **crack down on** A government or other authority **cracks down on** something when they take firm action to prevent or control it: *The police have cracked down on the carrying of knives.* [see also **crackdown**]
> **crack up** Someone **cracks up** when they lose control of their emotions and become extremely frightened, nervous, upset or angry.

crackdown /krakˈdaʊn/ *noun*: **crackdowns**
A **crackdown** on something is official action taken to prevent or control it: *the recent government crackdown on social security fraud.* [see also **crack down at crack**]

cracked /ˈkrakt/ *adjective*
1 Something such as glass is **cracked** when it has a crack in it. **2** (*informal*) You might say that someone is **cracked** when you think they are mad or foolish.

cracker /krakə(r)/ *noun*: **crackers**
1 A **cracker** is a thin crisp unsweetened biscuit for eating with cheese and other savoury foods. **2** A **cracker** is also a party toy consisting of a brightly decorated paper tube containing small gifts, that explodes when two people pull it at the ends.

crackle /ˈkrakəl/ *verb; noun*
▻ ***verb***: **crackles, crackling, crackled**
Something such as a fire **crackles** when it makes a continuous series of low cracking or popping sounds.
▻ ***noun***: **crackles:** *the crackle of the old radio set.*

crackpot /ˈkrakpɒt/ *noun; adjective*
▻ ***noun*** (*informal, derogatory*): **crackpots**
If you call someone a **crackpot** you think that they are mad or their behaviour is very strange: *He's a complete crackpot.*
▻ ***adjective:*** *He's always coming up with crackpot ideas.*

cradle /ˈkreɪdəl/ *noun; verb*
▻ ***noun***: **cradles**
A **cradle** is a box-like cot for a small baby, especially one that can be rocked from side to side.
▻ ***verb***: **cradles, cradling (cradled)**
You **cradle** something when you hold it gently or with

tenderness: *the first time she cradled the baby in her arms.*

craft /krɑ:ft/ *noun*: **crafts** or **craft**
1 A **craft** is the job or activity of making something such as pottery with the skilful use of your hands: *the disappearance of many of the traditional crafts like weaving.* **2** Other jobs or activities requiring skill are often referred to as **crafts**: *a poet with a fine command of his craft.* **3** (*plural* **craft**) A **craft** is also a boat or ship, or an air or space vehicle: *venturing outside the spacecraft.* □ *A number of aircraft have been delayed by fog.*

craftsman /'krɑ:ftsmən/ *noun*: **craftsmen**
A **craftsman** is a man who is skilled at making things with his hands: *The pews were carved by local craftsmen.*

crafty /'krɑ:ftɪ/ *adjective*: **craftier**, **craftiest**
A **crafty** person is clever at getting or achieving things, often by deceiving people: *He thought up rather a crafty ploy to get Fisher to change his vote.* [*same as* **cunning**, **wily**]

cram /kram/ *verb*: **crams**, **cramming**, **crammed**
To **cram** people or things somewhere is to force them into a space that is not big enough: *She sat there cramming chocolates into her mouth.* □ *The four of us crammed into the back of Andy's car.* □ *Her office was crammed with people complaining about the delay.*

cramp /kramp/ *noun*; *verb*
▻ ***noun*** (*uncount or count*): **cramps**
You have **cramp** in a part of your body when the muscles in that part suddenly tighten, causing pain: *She's got cramp in her leg.* □ *stomach cramps.*
▻ ***verb***: **cramps**, **cramping**, **cramped**
To **cramp** something is to prevent it from developing or being expressed: *Criticizing children for spelling errors may cramp their creative talents.*
▻ ***phrase*** For **cramp** someone's **style** see **style**.

cramped /'krampt/ *adjective*
A **cramped** room is unpleasantly small, or it is made too small by being so crowded.

crane /kreɪn/ *noun*; *verb*
▻ ***noun***: **cranes**
1 A **crane** is a machine with a long arm for lifting heavy weights, fixed to the ground or to a lorry. **2** A **crane** is also a large, long-legged, long-necked bird.
▻ ***verb***: **cranes**, **craning**, **craned**
You **crane** your neck when you stretch out your head in a particular direction in order to see something.

crank /krank/ *noun*; *verb*
▻ ***noun***: **cranks**
1 A **crank** is an apparatus consisting of an L-shaped bar that you turn to make something move. **2** (*informal*) When you refer to someone as a **crank** you mean that they have strange or unusual ideas or behave in s strange way: *Of course, you always get the cranks who think any new technological development will mean the end of the world as we know it.* [*same as* **eccentric**]
▻ ***verb***: **cranks**, **cranking**, **cranked**
You **crank** a mechanism or engine, or you **crank** it up, when you use a crank to make it move: *It was one of these old movie cameras that you had to crank.*

cranky /'krankɪ/ *adjective* (*informal*): **crankier**, **crankiest**
1 A person who is **cranky** has strange ideas or behaves in a strange or unusual way: *He had some cranky idea about eating lots of tomatoes to prevent lung cancer.* [*same as* **eccentric**] **2** (*especially AmE*) A **cranky** person is bad-tempered: *You're a bit cranky this morning, aren't you?*

cranny /'kranɪ/ *noun*: **crannies**
A **cranny** is a very narrow opening, especially in rock: *Even in the Antartic, some lichens manage to survive in crannies in the rock where they are protected from the wind.*
▻ ***phrase*** For **every nook and cranny** see **nook**.

crap /krap/ *noun* (*vulgar*; *slang*)
Some people refer to a thing as **crap** if they think it is of a very poor standard or quality; some people say that what someone says is **crap** if they think it is nonsense: *This paint's crap.* □ *Don't talk such crap.*

crash /kraʃ/ *verb*; *noun*; *adjective*
▻ ***verb***: **crashes**, **crashing**, **crashed**
1 A vehicle **crashes** when it is damaged by hitting another vehicle or object: *The bus skidded and crashed into a lamp post.* □ *the impact of the two cars crashing.*
2 Something **crashes** when it hits something with force and makes a loud noise: *She heard the dinner tray crash to the floor.* □ *waves crashing against the rocks.*
▻ ***noun***: **crashes:** *He was injured in a serious car crash.*
▻ ***adjective***
Crash describes things done in a very short time in order to achieve results quickly: *She took a crash course in Spanish before her holiday.* □ *a crash diet.*

crash helmet /'kraʃ hɛlmət/ *noun*: **crash helmets**
A **crash helmet** is a protective helmet worn by motorcyclists and racing drivers.

crass /kras/ *adjective*
Crass behaviour is stupid and shows a lack of respect for other people's feelings: *How could you be so crass as to suggest that she was too old to look after the children?*

crate /kreɪt/ *noun*: **crates**
A **crate** is a strong wooden, plastic or metal box for carrying breakable things such as bottles: *Bring up a few crates of beer from the cellar.*

crater /'kreɪtə(r)/ *noun*: **craters**
1 A **crater** is the bowl-shaped mouth of a volcano.
2 A **crater** is also a bowl-shaped hole in the ground where a bomb has exploded.

cravat /krə'vat/ *noun*: **cravats**
A **cravat** is a piece of clothing for men consisting of a wide piece of fabric folded loosely and tied around the neck: *a silk cravat.*

crave /kreɪv/ *verb*: **craves**, **craving**, **craved**
You **crave** something, or you **crave** for it, when you have a very strong desire to have it: *a man who craved wealth and power* □ *the excitement and adventure for which he craved.*

craving /'kreɪvɪŋ/ *noun*: **cravings**
A **craving** for something is a very strong desire to have it: *I had a craving for mayonnaise throughout my pregnancy.*

crawl /krɔ:l/ *verb*; *noun*
▻ ***verb***: **crawls**, **crawling**, **crawled**
1 Animals that **crawl** move along or close to the ground and other surfaces: *There was a beetle crawling up his leg.* **2** You **crawl** somewhere when you move there on your hands and knees, close to the ground; a baby **crawls** when it moves about in this way before learning to walk. **3** Something **crawls** when it moves very slowly: *Traffic crawled along past the roadworks.*
4 To **crawl** to someone is to behave very politely or humbly towards them because you think they are more important than you, or because you want something from them: *I hate to see my father crawling to the landlord.* **5** A place **is crawling** with people or things if it is full of them: *The town centre seemed to be crawling with police.*

▻ ***noun*** (*uncount*)
Crawl is a swimming stroke performed on your front in which you take your arms forward alternately through the air, and pull them back through the water, using a leg kick in which you keep your legs side by side.

crayon /kreɪən/ *noun*: **crayons**
A **crayon** is a coloured pencil, or a stick of coloured wax or chalk for drawing with.

craze /kreɪz/ *noun*: **crazes**
A **craze** is something that is extremely popular or fashionable for a short time only: *the latest teenage craze.*

crazed /'kreɪzd/ *adjective*
A **crazed** person or animal has been driven mad or behaves in a wild, uncontrolled way as if they are mad: *He was half-crazed with hunger and thirst.*

crazy /'kreɪzɪ/ *adjective* (*informal*): **crazier, craziest**
1 You call someone **crazy** if they behave in a foolish way: *It would be crazy to go hillwalking in this weather.* □ *another crazy idea.* **2 Crazy** also means very strange or unusual: *He turned up in another of his crazy outfits.* **3** You are **crazy** about something if you are extremely enthusiastic about it: *Martin and Craig are crazy about football.* □ *He was crazy about Kevin's sister.* □ *The audience went crazy when Bowie appeared.*
▻ ***phrase*** (*informal*) You do something **like crazy** when you do it at the fastest possible speed: *He drove like crazy, but we still missed the train.*

creak /kri:k/ *verb*; *noun*
▻ ***verb***: **creaks, creaking, creaked**
Something **creaks** when it makes a long high-pitched noise like an opening door whose hinges need oiling: *Outside, the gate creaked in the wind.*
▻ ***noun***: **creaks:** *They heard the creak of a loose floorboard.* — *adjective* **creaky:** *a creaky door.*

cream /kri:m/ *noun*; *verb*
▻ ***noun*** (*uncount*)
1 Cream is the yellowish-white fatty substance that forms on the top of milk, from which butter and cheese are made: *Pour the cream slowly into the soup.* **2** A cosmetic product in the form of a thick liquid is often referred to as **cream**: *a jar of cleansing cream.* **3** (*often adjectival*) **Cream** is also a yellowish-white colour: *He chose a cream shirt with a brown tie.* **4** The **cream** of something is the best part of it: *These three are definitely the cream of the group.*
▻ ***verb***: **creams, creaming, creamed**

> ***phrasal verb***
> You **cream off** something good or desirable when you select or take it from among others: *The Civil Service was unrivalled in creaming off the best graduates.* □ *They cream off 80% of the profits, and the rest is invested.*

creamy /'kri:mɪ/ *adjective*: **creamier, creamiest**
Something **creamy** has the thick liquid consistency of cream: *Add in the cornflour and stir until the mixture is creamy.*

crease /kri:s/ *noun*; *verb*
▻ ***noun***: **creases**
A **crease** is a line made by folding, pressing or crushing something, especially fabric: *I asked her not to iron a crease in my jeans.* □ *I'll never get the creases out of this dress.*
▻ ***verb***: **creases, creasing, creased**
Something such as fabric **creases** when it develops creases easily when you crush it: *The skirt creases too much to wear for travelling.* — *adjective* **creased:** *My dress was all creased.*

create /kri:'eɪt/ *verb*: **creates, creating, created**
You **create** something when you make or invent it, or when you cause it to happen or exist: *They were asked to create a whole new accounting system.* □ *She managed to create a marvellous meal out of a few leftovers.* □ *Light-coloured walls and furnishings create an impression of space.* □ *Soft violin music helped to create a romantic atmosphere.* □ *They believe that God created the universe literally in six of our days.*

creation /kri:'eɪʃən/ *noun*: **creations**
1 (*uncount*) The **creation** of something is the act of creating it: *The money has been set aside for the creation of a new regional transport network.* **2** A **creation** is something that someone has made: *Mandy was wearing one of Gaultier's latest creations.*

creative /kri:'eɪtɪv/ *adjective*
A **creative** person has the talent and imagination to create new things, especially works of art; something **creative** displays someone's talent and imagination: *The programme implies that the best chefs are those considered to be the most creative.* — *noun* **creativity** /kri:eɪ'tɪvɪtɪ/: *The early films were simply an outlet for his artistic creativity.*

creator /kri:'eɪtə(r)/ *noun*: **creators**
The **creator** of something is the person who invents or makes it: *critical acclaim for both the character of Poirot and its creator, Agatha Christie.*

creature /'kri:tʃə(r)/ *noun*: **creatures**
1 Animals are often referred to as **creatures**: *the creatures of the sea.* **2** A person described in a particular way might be referred to as a **creature**: *She was the most beautiful creature I ever saw.*

crèche /krɛʃ/ *noun*: **crèches**
A **crèche** is a nursery, especially one that is part of some larger building such as an office or shopping centre: *I take my children to work and leave them at the crèche.*

credence /'kri:dəns/ *noun* (*uncount; formal*)
You give **credence** to something when you say or show that you believe it is true or genuine: *Serious commentators are giving little credence to rumours of an early election.*

credentials /krə'dɛnʃəlz/ *noun* (*plural*)
1 Your **credentials** consist of your past experience and achievements, that make you suitable for a particular job or position: *The new minister's Socialist credentials are very impressive.* **2 Credentials** are also official papers proving that a person is who they say they are: *Did you ask to see his credentials?*

credibility /krɛdɪ'bɪlɪtɪ/ *noun* (*uncount*)
Something has **credibility** when people have respect for it and believe that it is sincere or genuine: *the government's loss of credibility over the issue.*

credible /'krɛdɪbəl/ *adjective*
You regard something as **credible** when you can believe that it might be true or possible, or when you feel that you should trust or respect it: *He had committed suicide; no alternative theory was credible.* □ *The minister needs to come up with a credible solution to the problem of homelessness.*

credit /'krɛdɪt/ *noun*; *verb*
▻ ***noun***: **credits**
1 (*uncount*) Shops and businesses allow you **credit** if they allow you to pay at a later date for goods or services that you receive now: *Most of the electrical stores are offering interest-free credit.* □ *We bought most of our furniture on credit.* **2** (*uncount*) People give you **credit** for something good or successful when they acknowledge that you are the person responsible for it, or praise you for it: *She doesn't really get the credit she deserves.* □ *Hugh should be given full credit for the*

success of the occasion. □ *Much of the credit goes to my colleagues.* □ *Why work so hard when someone else takes all the credit for what you do?* **3** (*used in the plural*) The **credits** at the end of a film or programme are the list of names of people who helped to make it.

▻ ***verb***: **credits, crediting, credited**

1 You **are credited** with some achievement, or it **is credited** to you, when people acknowledge or believe that you are responsible for it: *It's usually Freud rather than Jung who is credited with the invention of psychoanalysis.* □ *one of the many reforms wrongly credited to her.* **2** (*formal*) If you cannot **credit** something you do not believe it is true: *These reports of miracle cures are difficult to credit.*

▻ ***phrases*** **1** Something that **does you credit** is something you deserve respect and admiration for: *Your loyalty does you credit.* **2 a** Something that is **to your credit** is something you deserve respect and admiration for: *To her credit, she never criticized her colleague publicly.* **b** You have a certain number of things **to your credit** if you have achieved them: *By the age of 24 she already had three published novels to her credit.* **3** You **are given credit for** a particular quality if people believe you have it: *She has a great deal more intelligence than people usually give her credit for.*

creditable /ˈkrɛdɪtəbəl/ *adjective*

A performance, or someone's behaviour, is **creditable** if it is good enough to deserve praise or respect: *He scored a very creditable 89% in the maths test.* □ *Arthur's self-control was creditable in the circumstances.* [*opposite* **discreditable**]

credit card /ˈkrɛdɪt kɑːd/ *noun*: **credit cards**

A **credit card** is a card allowing you to buy goods or services on credit, supplied by a company who agrees to pay the shop on your behalf and claim the money from you later.

creditor /ˈkrɛdɪtər/ *noun*: **creditors**

A business company's **creditors** are the people or companies that it owes money to.

credulity /krəˈdjuːlɪtɪ/ *noun* (*uncount*)

Credulity is readiness to believe that something is true: *His story stretches credulity just a little too far.* [= it is impossible to believe it is true]

credulous /ˈkrɛdjuːləs/ *adjective*

A **credulous** person is easily deceived because they are too ready to believe things that they are told: *Only the most credulous of voters would believe all the promises made before a general election.* [*same as* **gullible**]

creed /kriːd/ *noun*: **creeds**

A **creed** is a set of principles or beliefs, especially religious beliefs.

creep /kriːp/ *verb*; *noun*

▻ ***verb***: **creeps, creeping, crept**

You **creep** somewhere when you move there slowly and quietly, usually because you do not want others to hear you: *She crept down the stairs and into the kitchen.*

▻ ***noun*** (*informal*): **creeps**

A woman might refer to a man she does not like as a **creep**, especially if the man shows, in an unpleasant or offensive way, that he is sexually attracted to her.

▻ ***phrase*** (*informal*) Something strange **gives you the creeps** when it frightens you or makes you feel nervous: *The old abandoned house gave him the creeps.*

creeper /ˈkriːpə(r)/ *noun*: **creepers**

A **creeper** is a plant that grows over the ground or up trees and walls by putting out long winding shoots.

creepy /ˈkriːpɪ/ *adjective* (*informal*): **creepier, creepiest**

You describe something strange as **creepy** if you are frightened by it or it makes you nervous: *a creepy little man with an evil smile.*

cremate /krɪˈmeɪt/ *verb*: **cremates, cremating, cremated**

To **cremate** a dead person's body is to burn it: *She doesn't like the idea of being cremated.* — *noun* (*uncount*) **cremation** /krɪˈmeɪʃən/: *I would prefer burial to cremation.*

crematorium /krɛməˈtɔːrɪəm/ *noun*: **crematoriums** or **crematoria**

A **crematorium** is a place where dead bodies are cremated as part of a funeral service.

crepe or **crêpe** /kreɪp/ *noun* (*uncount*)

1 Crepe is a thin fabric with a wrinkled surface: *a crepe bandage.* **2 Crepe**, or **crepe paper**, is thin, often brightly coloured paper with a wrinkled surface that is used to make decorations.

crept /krɛpt/ *verb*

Crept is the past tense and past participle of **creep**.

crescent /ˈkrɛsənt/ or /ˈkrɛzənt/ *noun*: **crescent**

1 A **crescent** is a curved shape wider in the middle than at the ends, like the shape that the moon has in its early and late stages. [see picture at **shape**] **2 Crescent** is also a word used in street-names, for streets that curve: *They used to live in Witchford Crescent.*

crest /krɛst/ *noun*: **crests**

1 The **crest** of a hill or wave is the top of it. **2** A bird's **crest** is a set of feathers that stick up on top of its head.

crestfallen /ˈkrɛstfɔːlən/ *adjective*

Someone who looks **crestfallen** looks disappointed, usually because their hopes or ambitions have failed: *A slightly crestfallen look passed across his features as she excused herself and left hurriedly.*

cretin /ˈkrɛtɪn/ *noun* (*informal*, *offensive*): **cretins**

If you call someone a **cretin**, you think they are very stupid.

crevice /ˈkrɛvɪs/ *noun*: **crevices**

A **crevice** is a thin crack in rock.

crew /kruː/ *noun*: **crews**

1 The **crew** of a ship, aircraft or other vehicle is the group of people who operate it or work on it: *for the safety of passengers and crew.* **2** Other groups of people working together are also referred to as **crews**: *a film crew.*

crib /krɪb/ *noun* (*especially AmE*): **cribs**

A **crib** is a cot for a small baby, especially a simple wooden one. [see picture at **bedroom**]

crick /krɪk/ *verb*; *noun*

▻ ***verb***: **cricks, cricking, cricked**

You **crick** your neck when the muscles in your neck tighten as you move it suddenly, causing pain that lasts for some time.

▻ ***noun***: **cricks:** *I've got a crick in my neck.*

cricket[1] /ˈkrɪkɪt/ *noun* (*uncount*)

Cricket is an outdoor game between two sides of eleven players, in which points are scored by hitting a ball with a heavy wooden bat: *The boys played cricket all afternoon.* □ *the world of professional cricket.*

cricket[2] /ˈkrɪkɪt/ *noun*: **crickets**

A **cricket** is a small insect of warm countries that lives in grass and makes a high-pitched noise by rubbing its wings together.

cricketer /ˈkrɪkɪtə(r)/ *noun*: **cricketers**

A **cricketer** is a person who plays cricket, especially professionally.

crime /kraɪm/ *noun*: **crimes**

1 Someone commits a **crime** when they do something illegal, that they can be punished for by law: *The crime of murder carries the most serious penalties.* □ *It is a crime in most countries to smoke marijuana.*

2 (*uncount*) Illegal actions in general are referred to as **crime**: *How can they be expected to change after a life of crime?* **3** Something considered morally wrong might also be referred to as a **crime**: *It is a crime to withhold love from a child in this way.*

criminal /ˈkrɪmɪnəl/ *noun; adjective*
▻ ***noun*: criminals**
A **criminal** is a person guilty of committing a crime: *a high-security prison for hardened criminals.*
▻ ***adjective***
1 A **criminal** offence is an illegal action: *She refused to get involved in Colclough's criminal activities.* **2 Criminal** also means relating to crime or its punishment: *the criminal justice system.* **3** (*informal*) You describe something as **criminal** if it is morally wrong: *a criminal waste of good food.*

crimson /ˈkrɪmzən/ *noun (uncount, often adjectival)*
Crimson is a deep purplish-red colour: *a crimson dress.*

cringe /krɪndʒ/ *verb*: **cringes, cringing, cringed**
1 You **cringe** when you experience an uncomfortable feeling of shame or embarrassment: *Thinking about how stupid I must have sounded made me cringe.* **2** You also **cringe** when you move back from someone or something because you are afraid. [*same as* **cower**]

crinkle /ˈkrɪŋkəl/ *noun; verb*
▻ ***noun*: crinkles**
A **crinkle** is a narrow fold or thin crease in fabric, paper or skin: *When she laughs she gets these crinkles around her eyes.*
▻ ***verb*: crinkles, crinkling, crinkled**
You **crinkle** something when you cause crinkles to form in it: *'What's that horrid smell?' he asked, crinkling his nose up in disgust.* — *adjective* **crinkly:** *His face was all lined and crinkly.*

crinkled /ˈkrɪŋkəld/ *adjective*
Something is **crinkled** when there are lots of small creases in it: *His shirt was all crinkled at the back.*

cripple /ˈkrɪpəl/ *verb*: **cripples, crippling, crippled**
1 Someone **is crippled** when they suffer a serious injury, or suffer from a serious disease, that makes them no longer able to walk or move properly: *She is crippled with arthritis.* **2** To **cripple** something is to damage it or make it weak or ineffective: *The new tax increases have crippled small businesses.*

crippled /ˈkrɪpəld/ *adjective*
A **crippled** person or animal has been so badly hurt or injured that they cannot move their body properly: *Tiny Tim, the crippled boy in Dickens's 'Christmas Carol'* □ *The crippled warship limped slowly into port.*

crippling /ˈkrɪplɪŋ/ *adjective*
1 Pain is **crippling** when it is so severe you are unable to move. **2** If you are dealt a **crippling** blow it disables you temporarily or permanently. **3** (*informal*) You can also say that the charge made for something is **crippling** when it is very high and people find it difficult to pay: *the crippling cost of electricity* □ *the top rate of income tax at a crippling 98%.*

crisis /ˈkraɪsɪs/ *noun (count or uncount)*: **crises** /ˈkraɪsiːz/
A **crisis** is a situation or event that causes serious problems or difficulties for many people: *before the economic crisis that wiped so much off the value of their currency* □ *We hope we can survive this time of crisis.*

crisp /krɪsp/ *adjective; noun*
▻ ***adjective***
1 Something **crisp** is pleasantly firm or stiff: *These biscuits are very crisp.* □ *a couple of crisp apples* □ *She pulled back the crisp clean sheets and got into bed.* **2 Crisp** weather is refreshingly cold.
▻ ***noun*: crisps**
Crisps are very thin slices of potato fried until very hard, sold in packets as a snack.

criss-cross /ˈkrɪskrɒs/ *verb; adjective*
▻ ***verb*: criss-crosses, criss-crossing, criss-crossed**
Things **criss-cross** when they cross and recross each other to form a pattern of crossed lines: *The trails left by herds of migrating animals criss-crossed the grasslands.*
▻ ***adjective:*** *The roads and lanes formed a criss-cross pattern on the landscape.*

criterion /kraɪˈtɪərɪən/ *noun*: **criteria**
A **criterion** is a standard or principle that guides your judgement or decision: *What are a lawyer's criteria for accepting a case?*

critic /ˈkrɪtɪk/ *noun*: **critics**
1 A **critic** is a person whose job is to comment on things such as books, films and musical performances: *If the newspaper critics like the play, your future is assured.* **2** The **critics** of something are people who are opposed to it or disapprove of it: *She is an outspoken critic of the government's transport policy.*

critical /ˈkrɪtɪkəl/ *adjective*
1 You are **critical** of something when you are opposed to it or you disapprove of it: *My mother was very critical of my decision to go back to work.* **2 Critical** means relating to the work of professional critics: *The new book has received widespread critical acclaim.* **3 Critical** also means extremely important: *This is a critical period in the holiday season, when the future of many small hotels is decided.* **4** A **critical** illness is extremely serious. — *adverb* **critically:** *His wife is critically ill in hospital.*

criticism /ˈkrɪtɪsɪzm/ *noun*: **criticisms**
1 (*count or uncount*) You make **criticisms** of something when you say that it has faults: *His main criticism of the scheme was that it was unfair to single parents.* □ *Nobody is above criticism.* **2** (*uncount*) **Criticism** is the work of professional critics: *one of the pioneers of literary criticism.*

criticize or **criticise** /ˈkrɪtɪsaɪz/ *verb*: **criticizes, criticizing, criticized**
You **criticize** something when you say that it has faults, or when you say that you disapprove of it: *The decision was sharply criticized by businessmen nationwide.* □ *Mr Major was criticized for not consulting with the opposition parties.*

critique /krɪˈtiːk/ *noun*: **critiques**
A **critique** is a piece of writing that critically examines or analyses a particular situation or someone's work: *His first published article was a critique of Dylan Thomas's early poetry.*

croak /kroʊk/ *verb; noun*
▻ ***verb*: croaks, croaking, croaked**
An animal such as a frog **croaks** when it makes its typical deep harsh sound; a person **croaks** when they speak with a deep harsh voice, *eg* because they have a sore throat.
▻ ***noun*: croaks:** *They heard the croak of a toad.*

crochet /ˈkroʊʃeɪ/ *noun; verb*
▻ ***noun*** (*uncount*)
Crochet is a technique for making things from thread or wool by forming stitches using a single needle with a small hook on the end: *This isn't knitting; it's crochet.*
▻ ***verb*: crochets, crocheting, crocheted:** *She crocheted a christening shawl for her grandson.*

crock /krɒk/ *noun*: **crocks**
A **crock** is a jar or pot made from earthenware.

crockery /ˈkrɒkərɪ/ *noun (uncount)*

Crockery is plates, cups and other pottery items used for eating and drinking.

crocodile /ˈkrɒkədaɪl/ *noun*: **crocodiles**
A **crocodile** is a large reptile of warm countries, with thick rough skin, huge pointed jaws and a long thick tail.

crocus /ˈkroʊkəs/ *noun*: **crocuses**
Crocuses are low-growing plants with purple, white or yellow flowers that open in the spring.

croissant /ˈkrwɑːsɒŋ/ *noun*: **croissants**
Croissants are pieces of rich bread dough baked in the shape of crescents and eaten for breakfast.

crony /ˈkroʊnɪ/ *noun* (*informal*): **cronies**
You can refer to someone's friends as their **cronies**, especially if you do not like them: *He'll be out playing golf with some of his cronies.*

crook /krʊk/ *noun*: **crooks**
1 (*informal*) You call someone a **crook** if they are a criminal, or if you think they are behaving dishonestly or illegally: *a bunch of crooks.* **2** The **crook** of your arm is the part inside your elbow; the **crook** of your leg is the part behind your knee.

crooked /ˈkrʊkɪd/ *adjective*
1 Something is **crooked** when it is bent or twisted, or when it is not level or straight: *He smiled, revealing a row of crooked yellow teeth.* **2** (*informal*) **Crooked** also means dishonest: *crooked businessmen.*

crop /krɒp/ *noun*; *verb*
▷ ***noun***: **crops**
1 Crops are plants grown on farms in large quantities for use as food. **2** The number of such plants grown in a particular year or season is referred to as a **crop**: *We had a particularly good crop of plums this year.* **3** (*informal*) A number of people or things grouped together at a particular time are often referred to as a **crop**: *this year's crop of graduates.*
▷ ***verb*** (*informal*): **crops, cropping, cropped**

> ***phrasal verb***
> Something **crops up** when it occurs or appears, especially unexpectedly: *One or two problems have cropped up since our last meeting.*

cropped /ˈkrɒpt/ *adjective*
Cropped hair is cut very short.

cropper /ˈkrɒpə(r)/ *noun* (*informal*)
▷ ***phrase*** When someone **comes a cropper** they have an accident or they suffer a serious failure: *If he goes on driving like a maniac, he's going to come a cropper one of these days.*

croquet /ˈkroʊkeɪ/ *noun* (*uncount*)
Croquet is an outdoor game in which long-handled wooden sticks are used to hit wooden balls through metal hoops.

cross /ˈkrɒs/ *noun*; *verb*; *adjective*
▷ ***noun***: **crosses**
1 A **cross** is a written symbol like the letter X, that you use *eg* to mark the answer to a question wrong, or to mark a position on a map: *pages of sums marked with ticks and just the occasional cross.* **2** A **cross** is also **a** a figure consisting of a vertical bar or line with a horizontal bar or line across it. [see picture at **shape**] **b** the symbol of the Christian religion, an upright stone or wooden pillar with a shorter horizontal bar across it, or a vertical line with a shorter horizontal line across it, or an ornament or piece of jewellery in this shape; the **Cross** is the cross on which Christ was crucified: *I hadn't noticed that she was wearing a cross.* □ *He died on the Cross to save us.* **3** Something that is a **cross** between two things is a mixture of both: *It isn't exactly a dictionary; it's a cross between a dictionary and an encyclopedia.* □ *A mule is actually a cross between a donkey and a horse.*
▷ ***verb***: **crosses, crossing, crossed**
1 You **cross** something such as a road or river when you move or travel from one side of it to the other: *We crossed the stream on stepping stones.* **2** You **cross** to somewhere when you move from one side of something to the other side of it: *She crossed to the other side of the room.* □ *We crossed over to the other bank.* **3** When you are sitting in a chair, you **cross** your legs by placing one thigh on top of the other; you **cross** your arms when you fold them. [see also **fold, cross-legged**] **4** Roads or lines **cross** when they meet at a point and continue past each other. **5** An expression **crosses** someone's face when it appears there briefly: *A look of despair crossed her features.*
▷ ***adjective***
You are **cross** when you are rather angry or in a bad temper: *I was cross with her for being late.* □ *The children were getting tired and cross.* □ *She looked round with a cross expression.* — *adverb* **crossly:** *'How should I know?' she asked crossly.*
▷ ***phrase*** Something **crosses** your **mind** when you suddenly think of it: *It never crossed my mind that I might have offended her.*

> ***phrasal verbs***
> **cross off** You **cross** a word or name **off** a list when you draw a line through it to indicate that it is no longer on the list: *I had to cross most of the schools off because they were too far away.*
> **cross out** You **cross out** a word or letter in a text when you draw a line through it to get rid of it or replace it with another: *I went through my essay again crossing out all the unnecessary adjectives.*

crossbar /ˈkrɒsbɑː(r)/ *noun*: **crossbars**
The **crossbar** on a man's bicycle is the horizontal bar joining the saddle to the handlebars.

cross-country /krɒsˈkʌntrɪ/ *adjective*
A **cross-country** race takes place on open ground, across fields rather than on roads or a track.

cross-examine /krɒsɪgˈzamɪn/ *verb*: **cross-examines, cross-examining, cross-examined**
If someone **cross-examines** you about something, they ask you a lot of questions about it, often to compare your answers with the answers you have given before: *When the witness has given his evidence for the prosecution, the defence will have an opportunity to cross-examine.* □ *Why are you always asking me questions about my school work? I don't like being cross-examined about it, you know.* — *noun* (*count or uncount*) **cross-examination** /krɒsɪgzamɪˈneɪʃən/: *I'm fed up with all these cross-examinations about what I'm doing and who I'm seeing.* □ *During cross-examination, the witness admitted that he had not told the court everything he knew.*

cross-eyed /krɒsˈaɪd/ *adjective*
1 A **cross-eyed** person has eyes that look towards their nose. **2** (*informal*) If you say that something is making you **cross-eyed**, you mean that your eyes are being strained by trying to focus on it: *The print in this book is so small it's making me cross-eyed.*

crossing /ˈkrɒsɪŋ/ *noun*: **crossings**
1 A **crossing** is a place where you can cross a road on foot: *a pedestrian crossing.* **2** A **crossing** is also a journey across water: *We had rather a rough crossing.*

cross-legged /krɒsˈlɛgd/ *adjective or adverb*
You are **cross-legged**, or are sitting **cross-legged**, when you are sitting on the floor with your legs bent so that

your knees are wide apart and your ankles are crossed in front of you.

cross-purposes /krɒs'pɜːpəs/ *noun*
▻ *phrase* If two people are **at cross-purposes** they are talking about different things though they think they are talking about the same thing: *He was talking about the meeting last week and I was talking about the one yesterday, and it was several minutes before we realized we were talking at cross-purposes.*

cross reference /krɒs'rɛfərəns/ *noun*: **cross references**
A **cross reference** in a book is an instruction to the reader to look at some other place in the book for the information they want.

crossroads /'krɒsroʊdz/ *noun*: **crossroads**
1 A **crossroads** is a place where two or more roads meet. **2** A **crossroads** is also a point in time at which an important choice or decision has to be made: *The peace talks are now at a crossroads.*

cross section /'krɒs sekʃən/ *noun* (*usually used in the singular*): **cross sections**
1 A **cross section** of a solid object is a drawing of the inside of it, as if you had sliced through the object and taken part of it away: *looking at a cross section of the human eye.* **2** A **cross section** of a group of people or things is a sample of them containing examples of every kind within the group: *a survey of a cross section of supermarket shoppers.*

crosswalk /'krɒswɔːk/ *noun*: (*AmE*): **crosswalks**
A **crosswalk** is a pedestrian crossing.

crossword /'krɒswɜːd/ *noun*: **crosswords**
A **crossword** is a puzzle in the form of sets of squares connected to each other horizontally and vertically, in which you write the answers to a set of questions, producing a pattern of connected words.

crotch /krɒtʃ/ *noun*: **crotches**
Your **crotch** is the area of your body where your legs join at the top; the **crotch** of a pair of trousers is the part that covers this area.

crouch /kraʊtʃ/ *verb*: **crouches, crouching, crouched**
You **crouch**, or **crouch** down, when you bend your legs and back so that your bottom is close to the ground: *He crouched down behind the desk so nobody would see him.*

crow /kroʊ/ *noun*; *verb*
▻ *noun*: **crows**
A **crow** is a large black bird with a loud harsh cry.
▻ *verb*: **crows, crowing, crowed**
1 A cock **crows** when it makes its typical loud cry. **2** (*informal*) Someone **crows** about something when they talk about it in a very proud or boastful way that irritates others: *We had to listen to him crowing over his latest business triumph.*

crowd /kraʊd/ *noun*; *verb*
▻ *noun*: **crowds**
1 A **crowd** is a large number of people gathered together: *Yelstin addressed a crowd of over a hundred thousand people in Red Square.* □ *Crowds of people had gathered around the entrance to his hotel.* **2** The spectators at an event such as a football match are often referred to as the **crowd**. **3** A **crowd** is also any set or group of people: *She's not part of the usual university crowd.*
▻ *verb*: **crowds, crowding, crowded**
People **crowd** when they gather or move in a large tightly-packed group: *Teenage fans crowded round the pop stars.* □ *We all crowded into the little café.* — *adjective* **crowded:** *The city centre is crowded with tourists.* □ *crowded bars and restaurants.*

crown /kraʊn/ *noun*; *verb*
▻ *noun*: **crowns**
1 A king's or queen's **crown** is the circular ornament they wear on their head on formal occasions, as a symbol of monarchy. **2** People often refer to the king or queen of a country as the **Crown**: *land rented by the Crown.* **3** The **crown** of your head is the top part: *His hair isn't receding, but he's balding a little at the crown.*
▻ *verb*: **crowns, crowning, crowned**
1 A king or queen **is crowned** when they are officially declared to be king or queen in a formal ceremony. **2** To **crown** something is to make it perfect or complete by adding something very special: *His brilliant political career was crowned by his appointment in 1976 as Prime Minister.* — *adjective* **crowning:** *Her crowning achievement was a Royal Command Performance in 1969.*

crucial /'kruːʃəl/ *adjective*
Something **crucial** is essential or extremely important: *It's absolutely crucial that you remember to switch it off.* □ *Fine weather is crucial to the success of this expedition.*

crucifix /'kruːsɪfɪks/ *noun*: **crucifixes**
A **crucifix** is a cross with the figure of Christ on it, used as a symbol of the Christian religion.

crucify /'kruːsɪfaɪ/ *verb*: **crucifies, crucifying, crucified**
1 Christ **was crucified** when he was killed by having his hands and feet nailed to a wooden cross. **2** (*informal*) To **crucify** someone is to defeat them completely: *They crucified Rangers in the last game between the two teams.*

crude /kruːd/ *adjective*: **cruder, crudest**
1 A **crude** substance such as oil is in its natural state, before it has been prepared for use. **2** Something that is **crude** is very simple, rough or undeveloped: *using rather crude surgical methods.* **3** **Crude** behaviour is vulgar: *I wish he weren't so crude.*

cruel /krʊəl/ *adjective*: **crueller, cruellest**
A **cruel** person causes pain or suffering to others deliberately and without pity: *That does not excuse such cruel treatment of children.* □ *Don't you think that remark was rather cruel?*

cruelty /'krʊəltɪ/ *noun* (*uncount*)
Cruelty is cruel behaviour: *How did they survive such mental cruelty?*

cruise /kruːz/ *noun*; *verb*
▻ *noun*: **cruises**
A **cruise** is a holiday spent on a ship, travelling from place to place: *They went on a Caribbean cruise.*
▻ *verb*: **cruises, cruising, cruised**
1 To **cruise** is to travel by ship to various places, for pleasure: *They spent the summer cruising round the Mediterranean.* **2** A vehicle **cruises** when it travels at a steady, unhurried speed: *We are now cruising at a comfortable 20 knots.*

crumb /krʌm/ *noun*: **crumbs**
1 **Crumbs** are tiny pieces of dry food, especially bread, cakes or biscuits. **2** A **crumb** of something is a small amount of it: *looking for a crumb of comfort in this desperate situation.*

crumble /'krʌmbəl/ *verb*: **crumbles, crumbling, crumbled**
1 Something dry or hard **crumbles** when it breaks into crumbs or tiny powdery pieces: *Some of the plaster had begun to crumble.* □ *Crumble the bread and add it to the mixture.* **2** Something such as an organization **crumbles** when it fails or collapses: *The Communist system began to crumble.*

crumbly /'krʌmblɪ/ *adjective*: **crumblier, crumbliest**
Something **crumbly** crumbles easily: *These crackers are rather crumbly.*

crumple /ˈkrʌmpəl/ *verb*: **crumples, crumpling, crumpled**
Something **crumples** when it is crushed or squeezed and lots of wrinkles or folds appear in it: *The front of the car crumpled under the impact.* □ *She crumpled up the drawing and threw it into the basket.* □ *Her face crumpled with displeasure.*

crunch /krʌntʃ/ *verb*; *noun*
▷ ***verb***: **crunches, crunching, crunched**
1 You **crunch** hard food when you crush or grind it noisily between your teeth: *We all sat crunching Christmas nuts.* **2** Something **crunches** when it makes a grinding noise: *The snow crunched underfoot.*
▷ ***noun*** (*used in the singular*; *informal*)
A moment when an important decision has to be made is sometimes referred to as the **crunch**: *When the crunch comes, we live or die together.*

crusade /kruːˈseɪd/ *noun*: **crusades**
A **crusade** is a set of activities that support or oppose some cause, organized over a long period by people who feel strongly about that cause: *They feel they've won another battle in their crusade against nuclear power.*

crusader /kruːˈseɪdə(r)/ *noun*: **crusaders**
A **crusader** is someone who takes part in a crusade: *a tireless crusader for women's rights.*

crush /krʌʃ/ *verb*; *noun*
▷ ***verb***: **crushes, crushing, crushed**
1 Something **is crushed** when it is broken, damaged or injured by being pressed or squeezed violently: *The car was crushed by a falling tree.* □ *Jackson's leg was crushed in a pneumatic press.* **2** You **crush** something when you make it into a powder or pulp by grinding or pressing it: *Crush three cloves of garlic.* **3** To **crush** something such as an attack is to defeat it completely: *Government forces have crushed the military coup.* **4** You **are crushed** by something when you are extremely disappointed or upset by it. — *adjective* **crushing:** *a crushing defeat* □ *the crushing news of her death.*
▷ ***noun***: **crushes**
1 A **crush** is a crowd of people packed tightly together, or an act of their moving all at once: *A number of children were injured in the crush.* **2** (*informal*) A young person has a **crush** on someone older when they feel love or great admiration for them, usually for a short time only: *It seems that a number of the boys have a crush on Miss Foster.*

crust /krʌst/ *noun*: **crusts**
1 The **crust** on a loaf of bread is the hard-baked outer surface of it; the **crust** of a pie is its pastry cover. **2** A **crust** is also any other hardened outer or upper surface: *snow with a crust of ice on top.* — *adjective* **crusty:** *crusty bread.*

crutch /krʌtʃ/ *noun*: **crutches**
1 A **crutch** is a long stick, usually one of a pair, used as a support for walking by someone with an injured leg or foot. **2** Anything that gives you support or help might be referred to as a **crutch**: *His wife has long been his emotional crutch.* **3** Your **crutch** is your crotch.

crux /krʌks/ *noun* (*used in the singular*)
The **crux** of a problem or other matter is the most important element of it: *The crux of the issue is Stephenson's reluctance to make staff redundant.*

cry /kraɪ/ *verb*; *noun*
▷ ***verb***: **cries, crying, cried**
1 You **cry** when tears appear in your eyes, *eg* because you are sad or in pain: *I cried for days after my husband died.* **2** You **cry**, or **cry out**, when you shout or make a loud noise, *eg* because you are afraid or in pain, or in order to get someone's attention. **3** You also **cry** when you say something in a loud voice: *'That's wonderful!,' she cried.*
▷ ***noun***: **cries**
1 You let out a **cry** when you shout or make a loud noise: *They could heard his cries of pain through the thin walls.* □ *Could anyone hear her cries for help?* **2** The **cry** of a bird or other animal is its typical sound. **3** A **cry** is a period of crying: *You'll feel better after a good cry.*

phrasal verbs
cry off You **cry off** when you decide not to do something that you had previously arranged or agreed to do.
cry out for You say that one thing **is crying out for** another when it urgently needs or greatly deserves it: *human rights abuses crying out for justice* □ *This occasion is crying out for a bottle of champagne.*

cryptic /ˈkrɪptɪk/ *adjective*
Comments and remarks are **cryptic** when they seem to contain a hidden meaning that you do not understand: *She made a rather cryptic comment about a woman's sense of family duty.*

crystal /ˈkrɪstəl/ *noun*: **crystal**
1 A **crystal** is a regular-shaped piece of a mineral, naturally formed: *quartz crystals.* **2** (*uncount, often adjectival*) **Crystal** is high quality glass that is particularly clear and shining: *a crystal vase.*

cub /kʌb/ *noun*: **cubs**
A **cub** is the young of certain animals, such as the fox, bear, lion and wolf: *a tiny tiger cub.*

cube /kjuːb/ *noun*; *verb*
▷ ***noun***: **cubes**
1 A **cube** is a solid geometrical shape with six square sides of equal size. [see picture at **shape**] **2** A **cube** is also a solid square piece of anything: *sugar cubes.* **3** The **cube** of a number is the product of multiplying the number by itself twice, so that the **cube** of the number 4 is 64 (4 x 4 x 4).
▷ ***verb***: **cubes, cubing, cubed**
1 A number **is cubed** when it is multiplied by itself twice: *3 cubed is 27.* **2** You **cube** something such as a piece of meat when you cut it into cubes.

cubic /ˈkjuːbɪk/ *adjective*
Cubic describes units of measurement of volume, indicating size in terms of length, width and height, so that a **cubic** centimetre is a space one centimetre long, one centimetre wide and one centimetre high.

cubicle /ˈkjuːbɪkəl/ *noun*: **cubicles**
A **cubicle** is a small enclosed private area with enough room for one person only, *eg* where you can undress at a public swimming baths.

cuckoo /ˈkʊkuː/ *noun*: **cuckoos**
A **cuckoo** is a bird with an easily recognized two-note call, that lays its eggs in other birds' nests.

cucumber /ˈkjuːkʌmbə(r)/ *noun*: **cucumbers**
A **cucumber** is a long green vegetable with juicy white flesh, usually eaten raw in salads. [see picture at **vegetable**]

cuddle /ˈkʌdəl/ *verb*; *noun*
▷ ***verb***: **cuddles, cuddling, cuddled**
You **cuddle** someone when you show love or affection for them by putting your arms round them: *She sat cuddling her little brother.* □ *young couples cuddling on park benches.*
▷ ***noun***: **cuddles:** *Give me a cuddle.*

> ***phrasal verb***
> You **cuddle up** to someone, or **cuddle in**, when you sit or lie close to them and hold them close: *The girls cuddled up to each other in bed.*

cuddly /ˈkʌdlɪ/ *adjective*: **cuddlier, cuddliest**
Cuddly people or animals are ones you like to cuddle, usually because they are soft and round: *cuddly teddy bears.*

cue[1] /kjuː/ *noun*: **cues**
1 A **cue** is a signal for a performer to do something, *eg* the last word spoken by another actor before an actor is due to speak: *Jane says 'My God!' and falls into a chair; that's your cue, Bill.* **2** A **cue** is also anything that leads you to act in a particular way: *Mother got out the old photo album: that was my cue to disappear for a couple of hours.*
▻ ***phrase*** Something happens **on cue** when it happens at precisely the arranged or expected moment: *Dixon entered and the phone rang dead on cue.*

cue[2] /kjuː/ *noun*: **cues**
A **cue** is a stick with a soft fabric tip, used to strike the ball in games such as snooker and pool.

cuff /kʌf/ *noun*: **cuffs**
A **cuff** is the lower end of a sleeve, at the wrist, where the material is usually a double thickness. [see picture at **clothing**]
▻ ***phrase*** (*informal*) You are speaking **off the cuff** when you have not prepared in advance what you are saying: *I would say, off the cuff, that the number of jobs affected is around two thousand.*

cufflink /ˈkʌflɪnk/ *noun*: **cufflinks**
A **cufflink** is one of a pair of small buttonlike objects used to fasten the cuffs of a shirt at the wrists: *a pair of gold cufflinks.*

cuisine /kwɪˈziːn/ *noun* (*uncount*)
The **cuisine** of a country or region is the typical style of cooking of the people who live there: *Tomatoes are the quintessential ingredient in Mediterranean cuisine.*

cul-de-sac /ˈkʌldəsak/ *noun*: **cul-de-sacs**
A **cul-de-sac** is a short street closed at one end: *We'll have to turn the car round; this is a cul-de-sac.*

culinary /ˈkʌlɪnərɪ/ *adjective*
Culinary means relating to cookery: *different chefs displaying their culinary talents.*

cull /kʌl/ *verb*: **culls, culling, culled**
1 Wild animals **are culled** when the oldest or weakest ones are killed to reduce their numbers: *We have to cull the deer to control their numbers or the herds would starve in winter.* **2** (*formal*) You **cull** *eg* information when you choose and collect the pieces of information you want from various sources: *I was able to cull a good deal of evidence from old manuscripts.*

culminate /ˈkʌlmɪneɪt/ *verb*: **culminates, culminating, culminated**
A situation **culminates** in the event that finally happens as a result or as the outcome: *a series of disagreements and disputes culminating in the resignation of five board members.* — *noun* (*uncount*) **culmination** /kʌlmɪˈneɪʃən/: *Her appointment as Professor was the culmination of a brilliant career.*

culpable /ˈkʌlpəbəl/ *adjective* (*formal*)
You are **culpable** when you are responsible for something bad or unpleasant.

culprit /ˈkʌlprɪt/ *noun*: **culprits**
The **culprit** is the person responsible for something bad or unpleasant, or the person guilty of a crime: *The culprits, when found, will be severely punished.* □ *Bad weather is the main culprit in train cancellations.*

cult /kʌlt/ *noun*: **cults**
1 A **cult** is a secret religious group led by a person claiming to be holy, whose beliefs and practices are regarded as strange. **2** (*often adjectival*) A **cult** is also a person or thing that has become extremely popular or fashionable: *a comedy programme with something of a cult following.*

cultivate /ˈkʌltɪveɪt/ *verb*: **cultivates, cultivating, cultivated**
1 To **cultivate** land or soil is to grow crops on it; to **cultivate** a particular crop is to grow it, usually on a large scale: *We cultivate over 500 acres in the Scottish Lowlands.* □ *Barley has been cultivated here for centuries.* **2** You **cultivate** something such as a friendship or a hobby when you develop it: *She has cultivated a taste for fine wines.* — *noun* (*uncount*) **cultivation** /kʌltɪˈveɪʃən/: *land under cultivation* □ *the cultivation of artistic interests.*

cultivated /ˈkʌltɪveɪtɪd/ *adjective*
1 Cultivated plants are grown for a specific purpose, as opposed to wild plants. **2** A **cultivated** person is polite and has good manners.

culture /ˈkʌltʃə(r)/ *noun*: **cultures**
1 A **culture** is a particular society, identifiable by their customs, beliefs and especially their art: *comparative studies of the culture of Africa and South America* □ *people of different cultures.* **2** (*uncount*) **Culture** consists of arts of all kinds, such as music, painting and literature: *We could do with more culture on television.* — *adjective* **cultural:** *disregarding any cultural differences* □ *a programme of cultural events.*

cultured /ˈkʌltʃəd/ *adjective*
A **cultured** person is well educated and has a good knowledge of the arts.

-cum- /kʌm/ *preposition*
-cum- is used between two words to describe something that has two uses or functions: *a kitchen-cum-dining room.*

cumbersome /ˈkʌmbəsəm/ *adjective*
1 Something **cumbersome** is large or heavy and awkward to carry or handle: *I hadn't realized how cumbersome a wedding-dress could be.* **2** A process or system is **cumbersome** if it is slow, complicated and inefficient: *The corporation is a huge, cumbersome and bureaucratic body, reminiscent of a nationalized industry.*

cumulative /ˈkjuːmjʊlətɪv/ *adjective*
Cumulative refers to the total number or amount of things, or to the combination of all of them: *The cumulative effect of these delays could be commercially disastrous.*

cunning /ˈkʌnɪŋ/ *adjective*; *noun*
▻ ***adjective***
A **cunning** person is clever at achieving things using secret or indirect methods.
▻ ***noun*** (*uncount*) *She would have to use all her charm and cunning.*

cup /kʌp/ *noun*; *verb*
▻ ***noun*: cups**
1 A **cup** is a small round container with a handle, from which you drink hot liquids such as tea or coffee: *a coffee cup.* **2** A **cup** of something is the cup and its contents, or just the contents: *He reappeared, carrying two cups of coffee.* □ *Add two cups of flour.* **3** A **cup** is also a container or something else shaped like a cup: *egg cups* □ *bra cups.* **4** A large decorated metal container given as a prize is usually called a **cup**; a competition or tournament in which such a container is the prize is also often referred to as a **cup**: *The cap-*

tain lifted the cup, to deafening cheers from the crowd. □ *one of the horses running in this year's Cheltenham Gold Cup.*

▻ ***verb*: cups, cupping, cupped**

You **cup** your hands when you form them into a cup shape: *It's easier to catch the ball if you cup your hands first.*

cupboard /ˈkʌbəd/ *noun*: **cupboards**

A **cupboard** is a piece of furniture for storing things in, fitted with doors and often having shelves inside: *the kitchen cupboards* □ *a broom cupboard.* [see picture at **kitchen**]

curable /ˈkjʊərəbl/ *adjective*

A disease is **curable** if it can be cured: *Arthritis may not be curable but we can now relieve many of the more acute symptoms.* [*opposite* **incurable**]

curate /ˈkjʊərət/ *noun*: **curates**

In the Church of England, a **curate** is a priest who is appointed to help a parish priest.

curator /kjʊˈreɪtə(r)/ *noun*: **curators**

The person who is in charge of the objects in a museum, art gallery or library is the **curator** of that collection.

curb /kɜːb/ *verb*; *noun*

▻ ***verb*: curbs, curbing, curbed**

You **curb** something when you control or restrict it: *new laws which curb the powers of local councils.*

▻ ***noun*: curbs 1** (*used in the singular*) You keep a **curb** on something when you keep it under control: *We have to keep a club on inflation.* **2** (*AmE*) A **curb** is a kerb.

curdle /ˈkɜːdəl/ *verb*: **curdles, curdling, curdled**

Milk, cream or yoghurt **curdles** when it thickens and forms lumps *eg* when it goes bad or when acid is added to it: *Before you add the cream, take the pan off the heat so that the sauce doesn't curdle.*

▻ ***phrase*** If something **makes your blood curdle** it makes you very frightened and nervous. [see also **bloodcurdling**]

cure /kjʊə(r)/ *verb*; *noun*

▻ ***verb*: cures, curing, cured**

1 To **cure** a disease is to get rid of it; to **cure** someone of a disease is to make them well again: *Doctors have little confidence that the brain disorder can be cured.* □ *You could be completely cured within days.* **2** Something **cures** a problem or other difficulty when it solves it or gets rid of it: *Better public transport would go some way to curing our inner-city pollution problems.* **3** To **cure** someone of a habit is to make them give up the habit: *Visiting lung cancer patients in hospital cured her of smoking.* **4** To **cure** foods such as ham and materials such as leather is to dry them so that they will last longer.

▻ ***noun*: cures:** *scientists searching for a cure for cancer.*

curiosity /kjʊərɪˈɒsɪtɪ/ *noun*: **curiosities**

1 (*uncount*) **Curiosity** is eagerness to know or find out something: *He had to look inside the box, just to satisfy his curiosity.* **2** A **curiosity** is something strange, odd or rare: *White women were still regarded as something of a curiosity in that part of Africa.*

curious /ˈkjʊərɪəs/ *adjective*

1 Something that is **curious** is strange or odd: *wearing a rather curious-looking hat* □ *It is curious that you didn't receive any of my letters.* **2** You are **curious** when you are eager or interested to find out something: *I'm curious to see what she says when he tells her the news.* — *adverb* **curiously:** *a rather curiously decorated room* □ *They all stared at him curiously.* □ (*sentence adverb*) *Curiously enough, not one of them replied to my invitation.*

curl /kɜːl/ *verb*; *noun*

▻ ***verb*: curls, curling, curled**

1 To **curl** hair is to twist or wind it into coils or rings; hair that **curls** grows naturally this way. **2** Something **curls** when it moves along a curving course: *Smoke from the chimneys curled upwards into the evening sky.*

▻ ***noun*: curls**

Curls are small coils or rings of hair: *The baby had a beautiful head of blonde curls.*

> ***phrasal verb***
> You **curl up** when you sit or lie with your body in a rounded position, with your legs folded underneath you: *She curled up in the armchair by the fire.*

curly /ˈkɜːlɪ/ *adjective*: **curlier, curliest**

Curly hair is full of curls, whether naturally or artificially.

currant /ˈkʌrənt/ *noun*: **currants**

1 (*often adjectival*) **Currants** are a small dried grapes: *a slice of currant cake.* **2 Currant** is a word used in the name of several small soft berries: *a handful of blackcurrants.*

currency /ˈkʌrənsɪ/ *noun*: **currencies**

1 A country's **currency** consists of the coins and notes that its people use as money: *The French franc is one of the stronger European currencies.* **2** (*uncount*; *formal*) Something such as a theory or idea has **currency** when it is popular, or when people accept it as valid: *Concepts of people with learning difficulties as objects of pity still have some currency today.*

current /ˈkʌrənt/ *adjective*; *noun*

▻ ***adjective***

1 Current describes things that exist or are happening now, in the present: *in the current economic climate* □ *Profits for the current year are showing an increase.*

> Notice that when you are referring to the past, 'current' is a useful substitute for 'present': *The current Foreign Secretary was James Callaghan.*

2 Theories and ideas are **current** when they are popular, or accepted by people as valid: *Such attitudes are no longer current.* — *adverb* **currently:** *She is currently touring America promoting her new book.*

▻ ***noun*: currents**

1 A **current** is a continuous flow of water or air in a particular direction: *swimming against the current.* **2** An electric **current** is a flow of electricity through a circuit or wire. **3 Current** also refers to the attitudes and ideas of people in general: *currents of opinion.*

current account /kʌrənt əˈkaʊnt/ *noun*: **current accounts**

A **current account** is a bank account that allows you to take money out at any time, but which pays no interest on the money held in it.

current affairs /kʌrənt əˈfɛəz/ *noun* (*plural*)

Current affairs are important or interesting events of the kind reported in newspapers.

curriculum /kəˈrɪkjʊləm/ *noun*: **curriculums** or **curricula**

A **curriculum** consists of the things that form a course of study at a school, college or university: *20th-century poetry is now a part of the English curriculum.* □ *It's a shame that there isn't more Flaubert on the curriculum.*

curriculum vitae /kəˈrɪkjʊləm ˈviːtaɪ/ *noun*: **curricula vitae**

Your **curriculum vitae** is your CV.

curry /ˈkʌrɪ/ *noun* (*count or uncount*): **curries**

A **curry** is an Indian dish of meat, fish or vegetables cooked with spices: *We had beef curry for dinner.*

curse /kɜːs/ *verb; noun*
▻ ***verb*: curses, cursing, cursed**
1 You **curse** when you swear: *I didn't want the children to hear him cursing.* **2** You **curse** someone when you say insulting or offensive things about them because you are angry; you **curse** something when you complain angrily about it: *She cursed her mother for interfering.* □ *He was too busy cursing the rain to see that I didn't care what the weather was like.* **3** You **are cursed** with something unpleasant that you have to tolerate: *He was cursed with a violent father who was insanely protective of his peace and quiet.*
▻ ***noun*: curses**
1 A **curse** is an act of swearing: *He sat holding his sore thumb, uttering mild curses.* **2** When you say that there is a **curse** on someone, you mean that lots of unpleasant things happen to them, as if some unseen force was making them happen: *He was afraid she might be a witch and would put a curse on him.*

cursory /ˈkɜːsərɪ/ *adjective*
If you give something, especially a document, a **cursory** glance you look at it very briefly without paying attention to the details: *The border guards didn't give our passports even the most cursory of glances, but simply waved us through.*

curt /kɜːt/ *adjective*
A **curt** remark is brief and made in an unfriendly or impolite way: *She was rather curt with them; has there been an argument?*

curtail /kɜːˈteɪl/ *verb* (*formal*): **curtails, curtailing, curtailed**
You **curtail** something when you limit it or make it shorter, for example by ending it earlier than arranged: *The lecture had to be curtailed when the fire alarm sounded.*

curtain /ˈkɜːtən/ *noun*: **curtains**
1 A **curtain** is a hanging cloth over a window, often one of a pair, to give privacy or to keep out light: *It was beginning to get dark, so Gran drew the curtains.* [see picture at **living room**] **2** Any piece of cloth hanging round or in front of something, to prevent it from being seen, is a **curtain**: *The curtain rose again and the actors stepped forward to receive applause once more.* **3** Something that forms a vertical barrier, that prevents you from seeing something else, might be referred to as a **curtain**: *The house was masked by a curtain of thick fog.*

curtsy or **curtsey** /ˈkɜːtsɪ/ *verb; noun*
▻ ***verb*: curtsies, curtsying, curtsied**
A woman **curtsies** when she bends her knees with one leg behind the other, as a formal gesture of respect when meeting an important person.
▻ ***noun*: curtsies:** *We all practised our curtsies, ready for when the Princess arrived.*

curve /kɜːv/ *noun; verb*
▻ ***noun*: curves**
A **curve** is a rounded line or surface, with no straight or flat part: *The houses had been built to follow the curve of the street.* □ *The dress emphasises the curves of her body.*
▻ ***verb*: curves, curving, curved**
Something **curves** when it has the shape of a curve, or when it travels on a course of this shape: *The bay curved round to the cliffs.* □ *Hopkins' glider curved away into the sun.*

cushion /ˈkʊʃən/ *noun; verb*
▻ ***noun*: cushions**
1 A **cushion** is a fabric case stuffed with soft material, that forms or covers the part of a chair that you sit on, or is placed loosely to make sitting or kneeling more comfortable. [see picture at **living room**] **2** A **cushion** is also anything that gives protection from shock or impact, or reduces unpleasant effects: *The hovercraft moves on a cushion of air.* □ *We need a few thousand in the bank as a cushion against rises in company tax.*
▻ ***verb*: cushions, cushioning, cushioned**
To **cushion** something is to reduce the violent or unpleasant effect of it: *In the event of a crash with another vehicle, the impact is cushioned by bumpers on the front of the car.* □ *I couldn't think of anything to say that might cushion the blow.*

cushy /ˈkʊʃɪ/ *adjective* (*informal*): **cushier, cushiest**
A **cushy** job or situation is easy or pleasant because it involves very little work or effort: *Working in the storeroom was pretty cushy.*

custard /ˈkʌstəd/ *noun* (*uncount*)
Custard is a sweet sauce for a dessert, made with milk, eggs and flour: *apple pie and custard.*

custodial /kʌˈstoʊdɪəl/ *adjective*
Custodial means of or relating to prison or custody; when a person found guilty of a crime is given a **custodial** sentence, they are sent to prison.

custodian /kʌˈstoʊdɪən/ *noun*: **custodians**
A **custodian** is a person who looks after something such as an important monument or art collection: *a self-appointed custodian of public morals.*

custody /ˈkʌstədɪ/ *noun* (*uncount*)
1 Custody is the right to look after and bring up a child, given to one or both parents by a court of law when they separate or divorce: *Custody was given to the mother.* **2 Custody** is also the condition of being held by the police or kept in prison because of being suspected of committing a crime: *She was taken into custody around midday.*

custom /ˈkʌstəm/ *noun*: **customs**
1 A **custom** is something that people traditionally do, especially on specific occasions: *It is no longer the custom for a man to stand up when a woman enters the room.* □ *She finds the customs of the French most charming.* **2** (*used in the plural, often with a singular verb, often adjectival*) **Customs** is the place where you take your luggage to be inspected when you arrive in a foreign country: *a customs officer at the airport.* **3** (*uncount*) **Custom** is what you give to a shop when you buy things there, especially regularly: *If you won't serve me, I'll take my custom elsewhere.*

customary /ˈkʌstəmərɪ/ *adjective*
Something is **customary** if people usually do it, or if they are expected to do it, on certain occasions: *In most European countries, it is customary to shake hands when you first meet someone.* □ *after we had exchanged the customary greetings.*

customer /ˈkʌstəmə(r)/ *noun*: **customers**
1 A shop's **customers** are the people who buy things from it: *She's a valued customer that we wouldn't want to lose.* **2** (*informal*) **Customer** is also used to refer to a particular kind of person that you have to deal with: *Corbett was an awkward customer.*

cut /kʌt/ *verb; noun*
▻ ***verb*: cuts, cutting, cut**
1 a You **cut** something when you divide it, separate it or shape it using a knife, scissors, or other instrument with a blade: *Cut the paper in half.* □ *We cut the pizza into three pieces.* □ *Could you cut me a piece of cheese?* □ *The meat should be cut into small cubes.* □ *When are we going to cut the cake?* □ *Cut a hole for your head in the centre of the blanket.* □ *Cut along the dotted line.* □ *thick-cut slices of brown bread.* □ *Cut flowers won't last as long as a pot plant will.* **b** You **cut** hair when you shorten it with scissors and make it neat and tidy; you

cut grass when you shorten it with a mower: *I must get my hair cut.* □ *The grass needs cutting every few days in the summer.* [compare **trim**] **c** You **cut** something when you damage or injure it, usually with a blade: *He tried to kill himself by cutting his wrists.* **d** You **cut** yourself when you accidentally hurt yourself on a sharp object and make yourself bleed: *He cut himself shaving.* □ *She ran into a glass door and cut her head open.* □ *I seem to have cut my finger.* □ *He cut his foot on some broken glass.* **e** Clothes that **are** well or badly **cut** are well or badly designed and made: *an elegantly cut suit.* **f** You **cut** a pack of cards when you divide it in two.

2 a You **cut** something when you reduce it in amount: *Our arts budget has been cut by 10%.* □ *He's repeating all the usual promises about cutting taxes.* □ *We must cut costs by at least a third.* [*same as* **reduce**] **b** You **cut** a text or film when you reduce its length: *The producer insisted that we cut the film to under two hours.* □ *The text of the play had to be heavily cut for use as a film script.* [compare **edit**] **c** You **cut** parts of a text if you remove them so that they are not broadcast or published: *Several scenes have been cut.* □ *You can cut the three final paragraphs.* □ *His reply contained offensive language and was cut.* [*same as* **omit**; compare **delete**]

▻ ***noun*: cuts**

1 A **cut** is **a** a mark, hole or injury made by cutting: *Make a cut along this line.* □ *She suffered a few minor cuts and bruises but was otherwise uninjured.* □ *Let me put a plaster on that cut for you.* **b** a reduction in the amount of something: *local-council spending cuts* □ *massive cuts in government funding* □ *some minor tax cuts.* **c** a part removed from a text in preparing and editing it for publishing or broadcasting: *They had to make cuts, especially in the sex scenes, before the film could be shown on television.* **2** A power **cut** is the failure of an electricity supply: *We keep candles in the cupboard in case of an electricity cut.* **3** (*informal*) Someone gets their **cut** of a sum of money, especially stolen money, when they get their share of it. [*same as* **share**] **4** A particular **cut** of meat is meat from a particular part of an animal: *Choose a lean cut of pork for this recipe.* **5** The **cut** of a garment is the shape and style of it.

▻ ***phrases*** **1** (*informal*) One thing is **a cut above** others if it is superior to them: *Our hotel was certainly a cut above the rest.* **2** For **cut it fine** see **fine**.

phrasal verbs

cut across 1 You **cut across** an area when you make your route shorter by crossing it: *We could get ahead of them if we cut across this field.* **2** An issue that **cuts across** the divisions between opposing groups affects all groups: *Grief over his death cut across party divisions.*

cut back You **cut back**, or **cut back** spending, when you spend less money; you **cut back** on something when you spend less money, or no money, on it: *When my husband lost his job, we had to cut back on all sorts of things, including holidays and clothes for the kids.* [see also **cutback**]

cut down 1 You **cut** a tree **down** when you cut or saw through its trunk so that it falls to the ground. [*same as* **fell**] **2** You **cut** something **down** when you reduce it in amount: *ways of cutting down expenses.* □ *We shall have to cut the text down.* [*same as* **reduce**] **3** You **cut down** on food or an activity when you eat less of it, or do it less: *The doctor told her she was drinking too much and advised her to cut down* □ *Cut down on fatty foods.*

cut in Someone **cuts in**, or **cuts in** on a conversation, when they interrupt: *'But that's ridiculous,' cut in Jack.* [*same as* **interrupt**]

cut into 1 You **cut into** something when you make a cut in it with a blade: *I found a knife and cut into the fruitcake.* **2** One thing **cuts into** another when it invades it: *All these interruptions are cutting into the time left for checking and revising.*

cut off 1 You **cut** something **off** when you remove it by cutting: *Cut the fat off the meat before cooking.* □ *He cut his own ear off.* **2** One thing or person **is cut off** from others that they are normally linked to when they are separated or isolated from them: *Many of the smaller villages have been completely cut off by snow.* □ *She deliberately cut herself off from her family.* [*same as* **separate**, **isolate**] **3** A supply of something **is cut off** when it is stopped: *The electricity will be cut off during the repair work.* □ *If you don't pay your bill the gas company will cut you off.* [*same as* **disconnect**] **4** You **are cut off** while talking on the telephone to someone if you lose contact with them. [*same as* **disconnect**]

cut out 1 You **cut** something **out** when you cut round its edge to remove it from the object or material that it is part of: *I cut this article out of the newspaper for you.* □ *She was kneeling on the floor cutting out a dress.* □ *The peaches will taste perfectly OK if you cut out the mouldy bits.* **2** You **cut** something **out** of a text when you remove or delete it: *We cut out some of the weaker poems and added some unpublished material.* [*same as* **omit**] **3** (*informal*) You **cut out** something when you stop doing it: *You'd feel a lot better if you cut out the smoking.* [*same as* **give up**, **stop**] **4** An engine **cuts out** when it suddenly stops working. **5** (*informal*) You **are cut out** for a job or activity if you are suited to it: *She wasn't really cut out for the outdoor life.*

cut through You **cut through** something **a** when you make a cut in it, or divide it by cutting: *The meat was so tough we couldn't cut through it.* **b** when you move through it easily: *We watched its prow cutting rapidly through the waves.* **c** when you shorten your journey by going through it: *At this time of night it's quicker to cut through the city centre than go round by the bypass*

cut up 1 You **cut** something **up** when you divide it into pieces: *Shall I cut up your meat for you?* **2** (*informal*) You **are cut up** about something if you are upset about it: *She was very cut up about failing her driving test.*

cut-and-dried /kʌtən'draɪd/ *adjective*

Something that is **cut-and-dried** is definite or has been settled or decided beforehand: *There is no cut-and-dried method for learning a language.* □ *The result of the ballot was cut-and-dried before the vote took place.*

cutback /'kʌtbak/ *noun*: **cutbacks**

A **cutback** is a reduction in something, *eg* in the amount of money an organization spends: *government cutbacks in the health service.* [see also **cut back** at **cut**]

cute /kjuːt/ *adjective*: **cuter**, **cutest**

Someone or something that is **cute** when they are pretty or attractive: *a bunch of cute little girls.*

cutlery /'kʌtlərɪ/ *noun* (*uncount*)

Cutlery consists of knives, forks and spoons for eating with.

cutlet /'kʌtlət/ *noun*: **cutlets**

A **cutlet** is **1** a small piece of meat, often with a piece of bone attached: *We had a couple of grilled lamb cutlets each.* **2** a small cake for frying or grilling made from a mixture of chopped vegetables, nuts or fish.

cut-price /kʌt'praɪs/ *adjective*
1 Cut-price goods are offered for sale at a reduced price: *Book your holiday early to take advantage of some of our great cut-price deals.* **2** A **cut-price** shop or store is one selling goods at reduced prices: *I started buying petrol at that cut-price garage in the high street.*

cut-throat /'kʌtθroʊt/ *adjective*
Competition is **cut-throat** when the various competitors will use any means that they can to keep what they already have or to get what they want: *When you get to the top in ballroom dancing, the competition is cut-throat.*

cutting /'kʌtɪŋ/ *noun*; *adjective*
▻ ***noun***: **cuttings**
A **cutting** is an article or picture cut from a newspaper or magazine.
▻ ***adjective***
Cutting remarks offend someone or hurt their feelings.

CV /siː'viː/ *noun*: **CVs**
Your **CV** is a written account of personal details such as the schools or universities you have attended and the academic qualifications you have gained, which you send to people when you are applying for a job. [*same as* **résumé**]

cycle /'saɪkəl/ *noun*; *verb*
▻ ***noun***: **cycles**
1 A **cycle** is a bicycle or motorcycle. **2** A **cycle** is also a series of events that happen or are repeated again and again: *How can we stop the unending cycle of violence?*
▻ ***verb***: **cycles, cycling, cycled**
To **cycle** is to ride a bicycle or to travel by bicycle: *We cycled into town.*

cyclical /'sɪklɪkəl/ *adjective*
Something that is **cyclical** is repeated regularly in a set order or pattern: *the tendency of economic activity to be cyclical.*

cyclist /'saɪklɪst/ *noun*: **cyclists**
A **cyclist** is a person riding a bicycle: *The car swerved and hit a cyclist.*

cyclone /'saɪkloʊn/ *noun*: **cyclones**
A **cyclone** is a violent tropical storm with high winds circling around a calm area of low atmospheric pressure at the centre of the storm. [compare **hurricane, typhoon**]

cygnet /'sɪgnət/ *noun*: **cygnets**
A **cygnet** is a young swan.

cylinder /'sɪlɪndə(r)/ *noun*: **cylinders**
1 A **cylinder** is a solid geometrical shape with a circular top and base and straight sides. [see picture at **shape**] **2** A **cylinder** is any container or object of this shape, especially those parts of an engine where fuel is burned.

cylindrical /sɪ'lɪndrɪkəl/ *adjective*
Something **cylindrical** is shaped like a cylinder.

cymbal /'sɪmbəl/ *noun*: **cymbals**
A **cymbal** is a plate-like brass instrument, either beaten with a drumstick or used as one of a pair struck together to produce a loud crashing sound. [see picture at **orchestra**]

cynic /'sɪnɪk/ *noun*: **cynics**
A **cynic** is a cynical person. — *noun* (*uncount*) **cynicism** /'sɪnɪsɪzm/: *his cynicism about the real motives of local councillors.*

cynical /'sɪnɪkəl/ *adjective*
A **cynical** person **1** believes that people are all selfish, even the apparently unselfish ones: *She has a rather cynical view of human relationships.* **2** uses people and exploits their weaknesses for his or her own profit or gain: *cynical politicians.*

cypher see **cipher**.

cyst /sɪst/ *noun*: **cysts**
A **cyst** is a hollow liquid-filled growth that forms in or on one of your internal organs or your skin.

D or **d** /diː/ *noun*: **Ds** or **d's**
1 D is the fourth letter of the English alphabet. **2 D** is a musical note: *the key of D.* **3 3-D** stands for **three-dimensional**. **4** Before decimal coinage was introduced into Britain in 1971, **d** was used as written form of 'penny'.

d' *verb*
d' is an informal spoken and written short form of **do**: *How d'you know?*

'd *verb*
1 'd is a short form of **would** in spoken English and in informal written English: *I'd like that.* **2** You also use **'d** as a spoken or informal written form of **had**, especially when it is acting as an auxiliary verb: *She said she'd told me before.*

dab /dab/ *verb*; *noun*
▻ ***verb***: **dabs, dabbing, dabbed**
You **dab** at something such as a wound, or **dab** it, when you touch it gently and lightly with soft material; you **dab** a substance on to a surface when you apply it gently and lightly; you **dab** something off a surface when you remove it with light gentle touches: *He dabbed at his eyes with a handkerchief.* □ *She dabbed some powder on her nose.* □ *She tried to dab the ink off her blouse with a paper hanky.*
▻ ***noun***: **dabs**
1 You give something a **dab** when you touch it gently with soft material: *paint with little dabs of the brush.* **2** A **dab** of a substance is a small amount applied to a surface: *The doors need a dab of paint.* [*same as* **touch**]
▻ ***phrase*** (*informal*) Someone who **is a dab hand at** doing something is very good at it: *You're certainly a dab hand at onion soup.*

dabble /ˈdabəl/ *verb*: **dabbles, dabbling, dabbled**
1 You **dabble** your toes or fingers in the water, *eg* when you are in a boat, when you move or trail them about in it for fun. **2** People **dabble** in an activity or pursuit when they take part in it, or take an interest in it, without getting seriously or deeply involved in it: *He had dabbled in local politics.*

dad /dad/ *noun* (*informal*): **dads**
Dad is an informal name people use for their father: *Thanks, Dad.* □ *Her dad's a doctor.*

daddy /ˈdadɪ/ *noun* (*informal*): **daddies**
Daddy is a name that people, especially children, call their father: *Where are you, Daddy?* □ *His daddy's in hospital.*

daffodil /ˈdafədɪl/ *noun*: **daffodils**
A **daffodil** is a yellow trumpet-shaped spring flower with a tall straight thick stem.

daft /daft/ *adjective* (*informal, derogatory*): **dafter, daftest**
If you call someone **daft** you mean they are foolish, stupid, mad or crazy: *It's daft to go on smoking when you know the dangers.*

dagger /ˈdagə(r)/ *noun*: **daggers**
A **dagger** is a weapon like a pointed knife or short sword, sharp along both edges.
▻ ***phrases*** **1** Two people are **at daggers drawn** when they hate each other or are very angry with each other about something. **2** Someone **looks daggers at** you when they look at you with an expression of anger or dislike.

daily /ˈdeɪlɪ/ *adverb*; *adjective*; *noun*
▻ ***adverb***
Something that happens **daily** happens every day: *Milk and newspapers can be delivered daily.*
▻ ***adjective***
1 A **daily** happening is one that takes place every day: *daily newspapers* □ *a twice-daily mail delivery.* **2** A **daily** wage, rate or timetable relates to each single day: *We engaged porters at a daily rate of $2.*
▻ ***noun***: **dailies**
1 A **daily** is a newspaper published every day except Sunday. **2** (*BrE old, informal*) A **daily** is a person, especially a woman, that someone employs to come to their house every day, or regularly, to do the housework.

dainty /ˈdeɪntɪ/ *adjective*: **daintier, daintiest**
A **dainty** person, thing or movement is small, neat and pretty or graceful: *She had small dainty feet.* □ *She took dainty little steps.* [*same as* **delicate**] — *adverb* **daintily:** *She was nibbling daintily from the plate she was holding.* □ *daintily cut sandwiches.* — *noun* (*uncount*) **daintiness:** *dolls'-house furniture of an exquisite daintiness.*

dairy /ˈdeərɪ/ *noun*: **dairies**
1 A **dairy** is a shop that sells milk, butter, cheese and other milk products, or a company or factory that processes and supplies them. **2** A **dairy** on a farm is a building where milk is stored and butter and cheese are made. **3 Dairy** products are such things as milk, cheese, cream and butter; **dairy** cattle are cattle kept for milking rather than for slaughtering as meat: *dairy foods* □ *a dairy herd.*

dais /ˈdeɪɪs/ *noun* (*usually in the singular*): **daises**
A **dais** is a raised area of floor at one end of a hall, *eg* for speakers at a meeting. [*same as* **platform, podium**]

daisy /ˈdeɪzɪ/ *noun*: **daisies**
A **daisy** is a small common wild flower with a yellow centre and narrow white petals.

dale /deɪl/ *noun*: **dales**
A **dale** is a name for a valley, especially in the North of England: *the Yorkshire Dales.*

dally /ˈdalɪ/ *verb*: **dallies, dallying, dallied**
1 You **dally** when you waste time by going slowly or stopping to do something unnecessary: *Don't let's dally over lunch.* [*same as* **dawdle, linger**] **2** You **dally** with an idea when you consider it in a casual rather than serious way: *I dallied with the possibility of going abroad to teach.* [*same as* **toy, flirt**]

dam /dam/ *noun*; *verb*
▻ ***noun***: **dams**
A **dam** is a wall built across a river to hold back the water, so that a lake or reservoir is formed behind it; the lake or reservoir so formed is also called a **dam**.

▻ ***verb***: **dams, damming, dammed**
To **dam** a river is to build a barrier across it so as to hold back the water and create a lake or reservoir.

> ***phrasal verb***
> To **dam up** a river or stream is to block it so that the water is held up, or to build a dam across it: *The stream was all dammed up with rubbish.*

damage /'dæmɪdʒ/ *verb; noun*
▻ ***verb***: **damages, damaging, damaged**
1 To **damage** something is to cause physical harm to it, spoiling or breaking it in some way: *The bomb damaged several classrooms.* □ *Our environment is being damaged by pollution.* **2** Something **damages** a person, their reputation, or something else that has been built up or achieved, if it is has a harmful effect on them: *All this gossip is bound to damage his career.* □ *If it became publicly known it would damage his chances of success.*
▻ ***noun*** (*usually uncount*): **damages**
1 Damage is physical harm done to something: *The insurance company will pay for the damage to the roof.* □ *Damage caused by the fire has been estimated at £12500.* **2** Something does **damage** to someone or something if it has a harmful effect on them: *Unthinking criticism can do a child a lot of emotional damage.* **3** (*used in the plural, legal*) A court awards **damages** to someone when it orders money to be paid to them by someone who has injured them physically or done harm to their reputation or property: *She was awarded £40000 damages.* □ *pay £10000 in damages.* — *adjective* **damaging:** *the failure was damaging to his self-confidence.* □ *damaging criticism.*

dame /deɪm/ *noun*: **dames**
1 (*AmE; informal*) A **dame** is a woman. **2** In Britain **Dame** is a title of honour awarded to a woman for exceptional achievements or services to the country: *Dame Janet Baker.* [see also **knight, sir**]

damn /dæm/ *interjection; adverb; adjective; verb*
▻ ***interjection*** (*swearword*)
Damn is an expression of anger, annoyance or disappointment: *Oh damn, I've forgotten my purse.* □ *Damn that car! Now I'll have to walk.*
▻ ***adverb*** (*intensifying, swearword*)
Damn is used before adjectives and adverbs as an expression of annoyance, or just for emphasis: *You know damn well what the rules say.*
▻ ***adjective*** (*swearword*)
Damn is used before nouns to express annoyance or just for emphasis: *Keep that damn dog under control!*
▻ ***verb***: **damns, damning, damned**
1 You **damn** something when you declare it bad or worthless, or are severely critical of it: *The film was universally damned by the reviewers.* [*same as* **condemn**] **2** A circumstance or piece of evidence **damns** someone if it proves their guilt. **3** (*religion*) God **damns** people when he sends them to hell.
▻ ***phrase*** (*informal*) You **don't give** or **care a damn** about something if you don't care at all about it.

damnation /dæm'neɪʃən/ *noun; interjection*
▻ ***noun*** (*religion, uncount*)
Damnation is the state of being damned and sent to hell, or the everlasting punishment suffered in hell.
▻ ***interjection*** (*swearword*)
Damnation is an expression of annoyance or anger.

damned /dæmd/ *adverb; adjective; noun*
▻ ***adverb*** (*intensifying; swearword*)
Damned is used before adjectives and adverbs as an expression of annoyance, anger, or to give emphasis: *I'll make damned certain she doesn't get that job.*
▻ ***adjective*** (*intensifying; swearword*): *It's a damned disgrace, the way she's been treated.*
▻ ***noun*** (*plural; religion*)
The **damned** are people condemned to endless punishment in hell.
▻ ***phrases* 1** (*informal*) You say **'I'm damned if I'll** do something' when you have no intention of doing it, implying that you could not reasonably be expected to do it: *I'm damned if I'm going to do her work for her.* **2** (*informal*) You say **'Well, I'm damned'** or **'I'll be damned'** to express amazement.

damning /'dæmɪŋ/ *adjective*
1 Damning words are words that are severely critical of something or someone, or condemn them decisively: *a damning remark.* **2 Damning** evidence against someone indicates or proves their guilt.

damp /dæmp/ *adjective; noun; verb*
▻ ***adjective***: **damper, dampest**
Something is **damp** when it is slightly wet: *damp, misty weather* □ *The house felt damp.* □ *a damp cloth.*
▻ ***noun*** (*uncount*)
1 Damp is moisture or slight wetness in the atmosphere: *Some days the damp just seems to get into your bones.* **2 Damp** in a building is wetness on the interior surfaces: *a patch of damp on the ceiling.* — *noun* (*uncount*) **dampness:** *I can't stand the dampness of the British climate.*
▻ ***verb***: **damps, damping, damped**

> ***phrasal verb***
> You **damp down** something such as a fire or people's anger when you do something to reduce its fierceness or strength.

dampen /'dæmpən/ *verb*: **dampens, dampening, dampened**
1 You **dampen** something when you make it slightly wet: *Cotton always irons better if you dampen it first.* **2** Enthusiasm or high spirits **are dampened** when something happens to reduce them: *The walkers refused to let the rain dampen their spirits.*

damper /'dæmpə(r)/ *noun* (*used in the singular*)
▻ ***phrase*** Something **puts a damper on** cheerful spirits or a cheerful occasion when it makes people feel discouraged or depressed: *The bad news put a damper on the celebrations.*

damsel /'dæmzəl/ *noun* (*old, literary*): **damsels**
A **damsel** is a girl or young woman.

damson /'dæmzən/ *noun*: **damsons**
A **damson** is a purple-skinned fruit like a small plum: *a damson tart.*

dance /dɑːns/ *verb; noun*
▻ ***verb***: **dances, dancing, danced**
1 You **dance** when you move about or step in time to music: *At school they tried to teach us to dance things like waltzes and quicksteps.* **2** You **dance** somewhere when you go along with a skipping or jumping step, from happiness or excitement: *They danced along the beach with shrieks of delight.* **3** Things such as trees or flames **dance** when they sway or leap about: *He watched the daffodils fluttering and dancing in the breeze.*
▻ ***noun***: **dances**
1 A **dance** is a series of movements and steps you do in time to music: *We learnt a new dance at this evening's class.* **2** A piece of music composed for dancing to is also a **dance**: *Dvorak's 'Slavonic Dances'.* **3** A **dance** is a social gathering at which people dance: *Are you going to the graduation dance?* **4** (*uncount*) **Dance** is the activity of dancing or of performing

dances, especially professionally or as public entertainment: *She included modern dance high among her list of interests.*
▻ ***phrases*** **1** For **dance attendance on** see **attendance**. **2** Someone **leads** you **a dance** when they create unnecessary problems and difficulties for you. **3** For **make a song and dance** see **song**.

dancer /ˈdansə(r)/ *noun*: **dancers**
A **dancer** is someone who is dancing, or who dances for their living or for enjoyment: *be quite a good dancer.*

dancing /ˈdansɪŋ/ *noun* (*uncount*)
Dancing is the activity, skill or profession of performing dances: *The dancing went on till 4.00 am.* □ *He considered dancing as a career before taking up acting.*

dandelion /ˈdandɪlaɪən/ *noun*: **dandelions**
A **dandelion** is a common wild flower with narrow, bright yellow petals, which drop off to leave round fluffy heads containing the seeds.

dandruff /ˈdandrʌf/ *noun* (*uncount*)
Dandruff is dead skin cells from the scalp, appearing as small white flakes or scales in the hair; you say someone has **dandruff** if their hair is full of it or it falls on to their shoulders in large amounts.

Dane /deɪn/ *noun*: **Danes**
A **Dane** is a person who was born in, or is a citizen of, Denmark.

danger /ˈdeɪndʒə(r)/ *noun*: **dangers**
1 (*uncount, or used in the singular*) **Danger** is the possibility of something bad happening to a person or thing, such as being hurt, killed, destroyed or harmed: *She never seemed to be put off by danger.* □ *The hospital assured her that his life was in no danger.* □ *The notice said 'Danger! Keep out'.* □ *We were warned that the buildings were in danger of collapse.* □ *She realized she was in danger of falling in love.* □ *The danger to the environment should not be underestimated.* □ *a danger of fire on the hills* □ *There's no danger of her resigning, is there?* **2** Something or someone that can harm or hurt you is a **danger**: *People like that are a danger to society.*

dangerous /ˈdeɪndʒərəs/ *adjective*
Something **dangerous** can hurt or harm you: *dangerous rocks* □ *dangerous driving.* — *adverb* **dangerously:** *She was walking dangerously close to the cliff edge.*

dangle /ˈdaŋgəl/ *verb*: **dangles, dangling, dangled**
1 Something **dangles** when it hangs loosely; you **dangle** something when you hold it so that it hangs loosely: *Her spectacles were dangling from her neck on a ribbon.* □ *He was dangling a bunch of keys from his finger.* **2** You **dangle** something tempting or attractive in front of someone when you offer it to them, in order to persuade them to do something.

Danish /ˈdeɪnɪʃ/ *adjective*; *noun*
▻ ***adjective***
Danish means concerned with or belonging to Denmark, its people or their language: *I'm Danish, not Swedish.* □ *Danish butter.*
▻ ***noun*** (*uncount*)
Danish is the language of Denmark: *We were used to hearing Danish spoken on the radio.*

dank /daŋk/ *adjective*
A place that is **dank** is unpleasantly cold and damp: *Prisoners were kept chained up in small dank cells.*

dapper /ˈdapə(r)/ *adjective*
A man who is described as **dapper** is usually rather small and slim, and is smart and neat in appearance and lively in movement.

dappled /ˈdapəld/ *adjective*
A **dappled** animal has a coat with patches of contrasting colour on it; an area of ground can be **dappled** with patches of colour, or with patches of sunlight: *dappled horses* □ *The hillside was dappled with autumn colours.*

dare¹ /dɛə(r)/ *modal verb*: **dare** or **dares, daring, dared** (*negative forms* **dare not** or **daren't**)
You **dare** do, or **dare** to do, something dangerous, frightening, upsetting or shocking if you are brave, bold, or rude, enough to do it: *I daren't ask her for any more money.* □ *She knows she should leave him but she says she wouldn't dare to.* □ *He didn't dare tell her the truth.* □ *I dared not even let myself hope.* □ *He got angry whenever we dared to mention the subject of retirement.* □ *Dare I suggest an alternative?* □ *Fancy you telling him that! I don't know how you dared!* □ *I was so frightened of making a noise that I scarcely dared breathe.* □ *I'll be surprised if he actually dares to telephone her.* □ *She can do no wrong in their eyes; criticize her if you dare!*

Notice that **dare** is used mostly with negatives, in questions, after *if*, and with words like *hardly*.
Notice also that **dare not**, **dared not**, and **daren't** never take '*to*' before a following infinitive: *I daren't go* (not *to go*).

▻ ***phrases***
1 You say **'how dare you!'** when you are angry with someone for doing or saying something: *How dare you suggest I'm lying!* **2** The expression **I daresay** means 'perhaps', 'I suppose' or 'I expect': *I daresay you're right.* □ *I could get into Oxford, I daresay, if I worked hard.* **3** You use **you dare** or **don't you dare** to warn someone, especially angrily, not to do something: *Here's your ticket and don't you dare lose it.* □ *You dare give up now!*

dare² /dɛə(r)/ *verb*; *noun*
▻ ***verb***: **dares, daring, dared**
You **dare** someone to do something dangerous or shocking when you challenge them to do it: *They dared me to dive off the highest diving board.* □ *'I think she's an absolute idiot!' 'OK, I dare you to tell her that to her face.'*
▻ ***noun***: **dares**
A **dare** is a challenge to someone to do something dangerous or shocking: *'Why did she climb on to the roof in the first place?' 'She did it for a dare.'*

daren't /dɛənt/ *verb*
Daren't is the spoken, and informal written, form of **dare not**. [see **dare**]

daresay /dɛəˈseɪ/ see dare¹.

daring /ˈdɛərɪŋ/ *adjective*; *noun*
▻ ***adjective***
A **daring** person is someone who likes adventure and has the courage to do new and dangerous things, or things that may shock people: *She was a daring little girl, quite unafraid of danger.* □ *daring designs* □ *a daring dress* □ *It was daring of you to suggest a change.* [*same as* **bold**] — *adverb* **daringly:** *He daringly chose snails from the menu.*
▻ ***noun*** (*uncount*)
Daring is courage and boldness in attempting new and dangerous activities, or in doing things that may shock people: *This job calls for initiative and a bit of daring.*

dark /dɑːk/ *adjective*; *noun*
▻ ***adjective***: **darker, darkest**
1 It is **dark** when there isn't enough light for you to see: *It gets dark so early these days.* □ *The car might*

have been red, but it was too dark to see. □ *long dark winter evenings* □ *dark streets* □ *His bedroom was small and rather dark.* [*opposite* **light**, **bright**] **2 Dark** colours, or **dark** shades of a colour are nearer to black than to white: *He was wearing a light-coloured jacket and dark trousers.* □ *a dark blue skirt* [*opposite* **light**, **pale**] **3** Someone who is **dark** has black or brown hair and may also have brown skin; **dark** hair is brown or black hair: *a small dark man* □ *Her hair was dark and cut very short.* □ *Do you remember whether he was dark or fair?* [*opposite* **fair**] **4** A **dark** time is a period of sadness, depression or worry: *during the dark days of the war.* **5 Dark** thoughts are sad, depressing thoughts. **6 Dark** can also mean mysterious or sinister, with a suggestion of possible trouble or evil: *The events of that night were still a dark secret.* □ *There were dark rumours about redundancies.* □ *Dark powers were supposed to have been at work.* — *adverb* **darkly:** *'There could be trouble,' she hinted darkly.* — *noun* (*uncount*) **darkness:** *He returned home just as darkness fell.* □ *The house was in complete darkness; not a light anywhere.*

▻ ***noun*** (*used in the singular*)

1 The **dark** is the lack or absence of light: *I couldn't see his face in the dark.* □ *She was lying awake in the dark.* [*opposite* the **light**, the **daylight**] **2** Before **dark** or after **dark** means before or after the time of day when light disappears and night begins: *Please be home before dark.* □ *He won't be arriving till after dark.* [*opposite* **daybreak**, **dawn**]

▻ ***phrases*** **1** You are **in the dark** about something if you don't know about it: *We'd tell you if we knew, but we're still in the dark ourselves.* **2** You **keep** something **dark** when you keep it secret, or tell no-one about it: *I'm pregnant, but please keep it dark for the time being.*

darken /'dɑːkən/ *verb*: **darkens, darkening, darkened**

1 The sky **darkens** as night falls; you **darken** a room by shutting out the light from it: *The patient should be put to bed in a darkened room.* **2** You **darken** a surface by making it a darker colour; a surface **darkens** when it becomes a darker colour: *Wood darkens over the years.* **3** A person's face **darkens** when they frown or look angry.

dark glasses /dɑːk 'glɑːsɪz/ *noun* (*plural*)

Dark glasses have dark-coloured lenses that hide your eyes and protect them from bright light. [same as **sunglasses**]

darkroom /'dɑːkruːm/ *noun*: **darkrooms**

A **darkroom** is a room used for developing photographs, from which all daylight and ordinary artificial light are excluded.

darling /'dɑːlɪŋ/ *noun*; *adjective*

▻ ***noun***: **darlings**

1 You call someone **darling** as an indication of your love or affection for them; in some circles people address many of their friends and acquaintances as **darling**: *Are you free tonight, darling?* **2** (*informal*) A kind or lovable person is sometimes described as a **darling**; people sometimes refer to someone as a **darling** when they feel affectionate or sympathetic towards them: *Be a darling and fetch my spectacles.* □ *They had to walk, the poor darlings.* [*same as* **angel**] **3** Someone is the **darling** of a certain class or group if they are its particular favourite: *With her looks, position and striking taste, she became the darling of the fashion world.*

▻ ***adjective***

1 You use **darling** to mean 'very dear' or 'dearly loved' *eg* when writing to someone: *She began her letter 'My darling Jim'.* **2 Darling** also means 'sweet': *What a darling baby!*

darn[1] /dɑːn/ *verb*: **darns, darning, darned**

You **darn** a piece of clothing that has a hole in it by filling the hole with stitching, *eg* by making long stitches across the hole, and weaving thread under and over the stitches: *They wore woollen socks, which needed constant darning.*

▻ ***noun***: **darns**

A **darn** is a darned hole in a piece of clothing: *His favourite sweater was full of darns.*

darn[2] /dɑːn/ or **darned** *adjective or adverb*

Darn and **darned** are used as less offensive forms of **damn** and **damned**, to express annoyance or just for emphasis: *She's darned difficult to please.*

dart /dɑːt/ *verb*; *noun*

▻ ***verb***: **darts, darting, darted**

1 A person or animal **darts** somewhere when they suddenly move there quickly and lightly: *He darted out of the room.* [*same as* **dash**, **shoot**] **2** You **dart** a look or glance at someone or something when you look quickly at them. [*same as* **flash**]

▻ ***noun***: **darts**

1 A **dart** is a narrow pointed missile for throwing or shooting. **2** (*used in the plural, uncount*) **Darts** is a game played by throwing darts at a circular **dartboard**, marked out so that each throw gets a particular score: *a darts match.* **3** (*used in the singular*) Someone makes a **dart** towards something when they make a sudden movement towards it. **4** A **dart** is also a narrow triangular fold sewn into a piece of clothing to make it fit the shape of the body.

dash /daʃ/ *verb*; *noun*

▻ ***verb***: **dashes, dashing, dashed**

1 You **dash** somewhere when you hurry there or move there fast; you say you must **dash** when you have to leave because are in a hurry to get somewhere: *He dashed across the street.* □ *I'll just dash upstairs and fetch my purse.* □ *Sorry, I have to dash now. See you tomorrow.* [*same as* **rush**] **2** Waves **dash** against rocks when they crash on to them; a boat **is dashed** to pieces on rocks when it is smashed against them by the waves. [*same as* **smash**] **3** (*literary*) You **dash** something somewhere when you throw or knock it violently: *He dashed the book out of her hand.* **4** Your hopes or spirits **are dashed** when something happens to disappoint you. [*same as* **crush**]

▻ ***noun***: **dashes**

1 (*used in the singular*) You make a **dash** for something when you rush towards it: *Everyone made a dash for the nearest exit.* **2** (*usually in the singular*) A **dash** of something is a small quantity of it: *Add a dash of lemon juice.* **3** (*uncount*) **Dash** is a quality that is a mixture of energy, talent, confidence and enthusiasm: *Everything she did showed dash and determination.* [*same as* same as **flair**] **4** A **dash** is a short horizontal line used in writing (–), *eg* as an informal punctuation mark **a** in the same way as a colon or semicolon, as in *I know what she needs – a new bathrobe.* **b** in the same way as brackets, as in *Her husband – a doctor, I think – is retiring soon.* **c** to link the first and last items in a sequence, as in *the years 1950-55.* **5** A **dash** is the longer of the two Morse-code signals, dot or dash, written as a short horizontal line.

> ***phrasal verb***
> You **dash off** an essay or a letter when you write it quickly without thinking.

dashboard /'daʃbɔːd/ *noun* (*BrE*): **dashboards**

The **dashboard** in a motor vehicle is the panel of switches and dials facing the driver, that control the ignition, lights, heating and ventilation. [see picture at **car**]

dashing /'daʃɪŋ/ *adjective*

A **dashing** person is smart and attractive and behaves with style: *You look very dashing in that hat.* [*same as* **chic, debonair**]

data /ˈdeɪtə/ or /ˈdɑːtə/ *noun* (*uncount, or plural*)
Data is, or are, facts, statistics and other information relating to something, especially as material for processing in a computer: *This data is stored on the network and can be accessed by anybody.*

database /ˈdeɪtəbeɪs/ *noun*: **databases**
A **database** is a range or block of material stored in analyzed or organized form in a computer, in such a way that individual items of information can easily and quickly be obtained from it.

data-processing /deɪtəˈprousɛsɪŋ/ *noun* (*uncount*)
Data-processing is the series of operations by which a computer analyzes, organizes and stores material that is fed into it.

date¹ /deit/ *noun; verb*
▻ ***noun***: **dates**
1 A **date** is either the year (*eg 1989*) or the day (*eg 22 November 1990*) when something happened or is going to happen: *Which date would suit you better, Thursday 27 September or Tuesday 2 October?* □ *What date was the Battle of Trafalgar?*

You can write a date in several different ways: *30 March* (or *30th March*) *1993* or *30/3/93* (said as '*the thirtieth of March, nineteen ninety-three*'); also: *March 30* (or *March 30th*) *1993* or *3/30/93* (said as '*March the thirtieth* (or in *AmE* '*March thirty*'), *nineteen ninety-three*').

2 A certain **date** is also a point or period in the past or future: *This black vase belongs to a much earlier date.* □ *We can discuss this at some future date.* **3** (*informal*) You make a **date** with someone you are attracted to when you arrange to meet them socially or go out with them: *I've got a date with Jim this evening.* **4** (*AmE; informal*) A person that you are attracted to, with whom you have a social appointment is your **date**: *I'm meeting my date at 7.30.*
▻ ***verb***: **dates, dating, dated**
1 You **date** a letter, cheque or report when you write the day's date on it: *The cheque was dated 28/11/93.* **2** You **date** an object when you state or guess what period it belongs to, or when it was made or produced: *We can date the skeleton to approximately 2500BC.* **3** (*AmE; informal*) You say you **are dating** someone if you regularly go out with them: *We've been dating since last year.* **4** Something **dates** if it goes out of fashion too soon: *I like to buy classical styles that won't date.*
▻ ***phrases*** **1** Something or someone is **out of date** if they **a** are oldfashioned: *Your opinions are out of date.* □ *out-of-date styles.* **b** lack the most recent information: *an out-of-date timetable.* □ *Tell me the latest; I'm terribly out of date.* **2** The news **to date** is all the information about something up to the present moment. **3** Something or someone is **up to date** if they **a** are modern or fashionable: *up-to-date teaching methods* □ *If you're not using this software, you're not up to date.* **b** have the latest information: *Is this the most up-to-date telephone directory we've got?* □ *Bring me up to date with the news.*

phrasal verbs
date back Something **dates back** to a certain time if that was when it began or was made: *The central part of the castle dates back to the 13th century.*
date from Something **dates from** a particular time if it began then or was made then: *a custom dating from the 11th century.*

date² /deɪt/ *noun*: **dates**
A **date** is a small oval sticky brown fruit with a long narrow stone, that grows on a palm tree or **date palm**. [see picture at **fruit**]

dated /ˈdeɪtɪd/ *adjective* (*derogatory*)
Something that has been fashionable is **dated** when it looks or seems oldfashioned: *Some of their earlier models are beginning to look dated.*

date of birth /deɪtəvˈbɜːθ/ *noun*: **dates of birth**
Your **date of birth** is the date you were born: *He gave his date of birth as 19 June 1958.*

daub /dɔːb/ *verb*: **daubs, daubing, daubed**
You **daub** something wet and sticky on to or over a surface when you smear it on; something **is daubed** with a wet, sticky substance when it is smeared or covered with it: *Someone had daubed the words 'Jackson OK' across the wall.*

daughter /ˈdɔːtə(r)/ *noun*: **daughters**
Someone's **daughter** is their female child: *She was the daughter of a missionary.*

daughter-in-law /ˈdɔːtərɪnlɔː/ *noun*: **daughters-in-law**
Someone's daughter-in-law is their son's wife: *She was on good terms with both her daughters-in-law.*

daunt /dɔːnt/ *verb*: **daunts, daunting, daunted**
Something **daunts** you if it discourages you or makes you rather afraid: *Always teach one step at a time; children are daunted by being given too much information all at once.* [*same as* **intimidate**] — *adjective* **daunting:** *a daunting task* □ *It was a bit daunting to be told I was the wrong shape for a dancer.*
▻ ***phrase*** You go on doing something **nothing daunted** when you continue to do it in spite of difficulties or objections.

dawdle /ˈdɔːdəl/ *verb*: **dawdles, dawdling, dawdled**
You **dawdle** when you spend an unnecessarily long time going somewhere or doing something: *I hate dawdling over meals.* [*same as* **dally, linger**]

dawn /dɔːn/ *noun*: **dawns**
1 (*uncount or count*) **Dawn** is the time of day when the light begins to appear as the sun rises: *We had to get up before dawn.* [*same as* **daybreak, sunrise**; *opposite* **dusk, nightfall, sunset**] **2** The **dawn** of something is the start of it: *the dawn of civilization.*
▻ ***verb***: **dawns, dawning, dawned**
1 Light, or the day, **dawns**, when the sky begins to get light and the darkness disappears: *The day dawned bright and clear.* **2** Something such as hope or realization **is dawning** when it is beginning to be felt: *Hopes were dawning for a peace settlement.*
▻ ***phrases*** **1** (*informal*) You wake up or get up **at the crack of dawn** when you get up very early. **2** You do something **from dawn to dusk** if you do it all day long.

phrasal verb
Something such truth or a fact **dawns on** or **upon** you when you realize it: *It dawned on me that she was deaf.*

day /deɪ/ *noun*: **days**
1 A **day** is one of the twenty-four-hour periods between one midnight and the next: *It's my birthday in three days' time.* □ *She visits her mother every day of the week.* □ *He's arriving the day after tomorrow.* □ *We were in Florence the day before yesterday.* □ *One day he simply disappeared.* **2** (*uncount or count*) A **day** is also the period between dawn and nightfall, when it is light, or the period during which you are awake and active, or working: *What time of day would suit you best?* □ *I'll be at home all day tomorrow.* □ *You'll find me at this number during the day.* □ *As soon as it was*

day they continued their journey. ▫ *Nocturnal animals sleep by day.* ▫ *The job is going to take several days' work.* ▫ *Good Friday is a normal working day in Scotland.* **3** 'A good or bad **day**' may refer to the weather, or to your experiences during it: *What a horrible day!* ▫ *It was a lovely day yesterday.* ▫ *I've had a frantic day.* **4** A particular period in the past can be referred to as this or that **day**, or the **days** of something: *I wasn't so fat in those days.* ▫ *The days of cheap labour are over.* ▫ *He must have been good-looking in his day.* [= in his youth or prime] ▫ *It was a much-admired book in its day.* [= There was a time when people admired it] ▫ *In our day* [= when we were that age] *we were made to work at school.*

▻ ***phrases*** **1** Something happens **all day long** if it continues for the whole day. **2** Something is **all in a day's work** if it causes no extra difficulty. **3** You expect something to happen **any day now** when you expect it very soon. **4** You **call it a day** when you decide to stop work or whatever you are doing, till another time. **5** Something goes on **day and night** or **night and day** if it continues all the time. **6** Something, especially something annoying, happens **day in, day out** if it happens every day. **7** A situation changes **day by day** or **by the day** when it alters with each day that passes: *He grew stronger day by day.* **8** You live **from day to day** or **from one day to the next** when you concentrate on each day's activities without worrying about the future. **9** If you say that someone or something **has had their day**, you mean that their time of popularity or usefulness is past. **10** (*AmE*; *informal*) You tell someone to **have a nice day** as a way of saying goodbye to them. **11** Something **has seen better days** if it is old and worn out. **12 In this day and age** means at this advanced stage of civilization: *It's a disgrace that there are still beggars on the streets in this day and age.* **13** When you say **it's early days yet**, you mean that it is too soon to judge whether something is going to be successful or unsuccessful. **14** You **make** someone's **day** when you do something, or tell them something, that makes them happy. **15** You say that something will happen **one day**, or **some day**, or **one of these days**, when you expect it to happen at some indefinite time in the future. **16** You **pass the time of day** with someone when you greet them or have a casual conversation with them. **17** (*informal*) You say **that'll be the day** in response to a suggestion you consider very unlikely: *'You may get married again.' 'That'll be the day!'* **18 The other day** means a few days ago: *I met her only the other day.* **19 The present day** is now, or the time we are living in: *present-day attitudes.* **20 These days** means now, nowadays, or in our present time: *Nobody reads his books these days.* **21** You say **those were the days** in reference to a time in the past that was particularly good in some way: *Those were the days, when you could get a bag of fish and chips for 20 pence.* **22** You say it's a year **to the day** since some event if it is exactly a year since it happened. **23** Someone or something **wins** or **carries the day** when they win a struggle against rivals.

daybreak /ˈdeɪbreɪk/ *noun* (*uncount*)
Daybreak is the time of the morning when light first appears in the sky: *He left before daybreak.* [*same as* **dawn, sunrise**; *opposite* **nightfall, sunset**]

daydream /ˈdeɪdriːm/ *noun*; *verb*
▻ ***noun***: **daydreams**
A **daydream** is a sequence of thoughts in which you imagine pleasant things happening to you, which takes your mind away from the present.
▻ ***verb***: **daydreams, daydreaming, daydreamed**
You **are daydreaming** when you are having a daydream: *Don't sit there daydreaming when there's work to do.*

daylight /ˈdeɪlaɪt/ *noun* (*uncount*)
1 Daylight is the natural light supplied by the sun during the day, sometimes as distinct from artificial light: *The colours look different by daylight.* ▫ *during daylight hours.* **2 Daylight** is the time in the morning when light first appears in the sky: *It was scarcely daylight when we set off.*
▻ ***phrase*** Someone who commits a crime **in broad daylight** is bold enough to commit it during the day, when there is a greater risk of being noticed and caught.

day off /deɪ ˈɒf/ *noun*: **days off**
A **day off** is a day when you don't have to go to work yourself, in spite of its being a normal working day: *How many days off have you had this month?* ▫ *Thursday is Bob's day off.*

day return /deɪ rɪˈtɜːn/ *noun* (*BrE*): **day returns**
A **day return** is a bus ticket or rail ticket with which you can travel somewhere and back on the same day, for less than the price of an ordinary return ticket.

daytime /ˈdeɪtaɪm/ *noun* (*uncount*)
Daytime is the time between sunrise and sunset, when there is daylight, or the morning and afternoon, as distinct from the evening and night: *It's a waste of electricity, having the lights on in the daytime.*

day-to-day /deɪtəˈdeɪ/ *adjective*
Day-to-day duties and tasks are those that are part of the routine of every day: *During my absence Dianne will see to the day-to-day running of the department.*

daze /deɪz/ *verb* (*usually in the passive*): **dazes, dazing, dazed**
You **are dazed** by a blow on the head or a shock if it makes you feel confused and unable to think clearly. [*same as* **stun, stagger**] — *adjective* **dazed:** *He was too dazed by the news to answer straight away.*
▻ ***phrase*** You are **in a daze** when you feel confused and unable to think clearly, *eg* as the result of a shock: *I found her walking around in a daze.*

dazzle /ˈdazəl/ *verb*; *noun*
▻ ***verb***: **dazzles, dazzling, dazzled**
1 A bright light **dazzles** you when it makes you unable to see properly: *He rounded a bend and was suddenly dazzled by the low sun.* [*same as* **blind**] **2** You **are dazzled** by someone or something when you are so impressed by them as to be quite overwhelmed: *He was dazzled by her beauty and talents.* [*same as* **bewitch, hypnotize**] — *adjective* **dazzling:** *a dazzling smile* ▫ *dazzling white sheets* ▫ *a dazzling performance.* — *adverb* **dazzlingly:** *She was attractive, without being dazzlingly beautiful.*
▻ ***noun*** (*uncount or used in the singular*): *the glamour and dazzle of the theatre world.*

de- /diː/ or /dɪ/ *prefix*
de- is used to form words, and has the meaning 'off', as in *decapitate*, 'down', as in *devalue*, or 'reversing a process' as in *defrost*.

dead /dɛd/ *adjective*; *adverb*; *noun*
▻ ***adjective***
1 A **dead** person, animal or plant is no longer living: *The stage is covered with dead bodies at the end of 'Hamlet'.* ▫ *These flowers look a bit dead.* ▫ *He shot dead one policeman and wounded another.* **2** A **dead** language is a language such as Latin, that is no longer spoken for everyday communication. [*opposite* **living**] **3** A subject, issue or topic that is **dead** is no longer important enough to be being discussed. [*opposite* **live**] **4** Parts of your body, such as your fingers, go **dead** when when the flow of blood to

them is interrupted and you lose the feeling in them. [*same as* **numb**] **5** A telephone or radio goes **dead** when it stops functioning and you can get no sound from it. **6 Dead** is used with some nouns for emphasis, with the meaning 'absolute' or 'complete': *Why does the light fitting always have to be in the dead centre of the ceiling?* □ *They listened to him in dead silence.* □ *The train came to a dead stop outside Halifax.*

▷ ***adverb***

1 (*informal*) In describing positions or directions, **dead** is used for emphasis with the meaning 'directly', 'straight' or 'immediately': *The post office is dead opposite the library.* □ *There was this lady with an enormous hairdo sitting dead in front of me.* □ *Keep looking dead ahead and you'll spot it.* **2** (*intensifying, informal*) **Dead** can be used for emphasis with the meaning 'absolutely' or 'completely': *Try it; it's dead easy.* □ *You were dead right about the play.* □ *I'm dead certain she said 8.30.* □ *We're dead against physical punishment for kids.* □ *I arrived dead on time for once.* □ *He's dead set on teaching.* □ *Go dead slow on this bend.* **3** Something stops **dead** when it stops suddenly and completely: *The train jerked forward and then stopped dead.*

▷ ***noun***

1 (*plural*) The **dead** are the people who are dead: *The women wept as they buried their dead.* **2** The **dead** of night is the darkest and quietest part of the night; the **dead** of winter is the coldest and darkest part of the winter: *She stole out of the house at the dead of night.* □ *It goes on flowering even in the dead of winter.*

▷ ***phrases*** **1** Someone is **dead to the world** when they are fast asleep. **2** For **over my dead body** see **body**. **3** (*informal*) You say you **wouldn't be seen dead** wearing something or doing something if you consider it unfashionable or dreadful in some other way: *I wouldn't be seen dead in a knitted hat.*

dead beat /dɛd 'bi:t/ *adjective* (*informal*)

You are **dead beat** when you are exhausted or very tired: *You look dead beat.* [*same as* **shattered**, **whacked**]

deaden /'dɛdən/ *verb*: **deadens, deadening, deadened**

1 Something **deadens** pain or hunger when it makes you feel it less; a sound **is deadened** when something makes it less loud: *He took an aspirin to deaden the pain.* [*same as* **dull**] **2** Something such as boring or repetitive work **deadens** your imagination and enthusiasm.

dead end /dɛd 'ɛnd/ *noun*: **dead ends**

1 A **dead end** is a road closed off at one end. [*same as* **cul-de-sac**] **2** A situation or activity in which there is no scope for development or progress is also a **dead end**: *You don't want, at the age of 40, to find yourself in a dead-end, underpaid job.*

dead heat /dɛd 'hi:t/ *noun*: **dead heats**

A race finishes in a **dead heat** when two or more competitors reach the finishing line at the same moment. [compare **draw**]

deadline /'dɛdlaɪn/ *noun*: **deadlines**

A **deadline** is the time by which something must be done, or a task completed: *It's going to be impossible to meet the deadline.*

deadlock /'dɛdlɒk/ *noun* (*uncount, or used in the singular*)

Deadlock is a stage in the course of a dispute where neither side is willing to give in or compromise in any way, so that no further progress can be made towards agreement: *They are still in a state of deadlock on the pay issue.* □ *reach a deadlock* □ *break the deadlock.* [*same as* **stalemate**]

deadly /'dɛdlɪ/ *adjective*; *adverb*

▷ ***adjective***

1 Something **deadly** is likely to cause death: *deadly poisons* □ *deadly weapons.* [*same as* **lethal**] **2** A **deadly** insult is a wickedly effective one, likely to cause maximum hurt: *She mimicked his voice with deadly accuracy.* **3** People who are **deadly** enemies hate each other to an extreme degree. [*same as* **mortal**] **4** You are in **deadly** earnest when you mean what you say absolutely seriously. **5** (*informal*) A **deadly** book or lecture is a dull one.

▷ ***adverb*** (*intensifying*)

Deadly is used for emphasis with certain adjectives: *His talk was deadly dull.* □ *She's deadly serious about resigning.*

deadpan /'dɛdpan/ *adjective or adverb*

You remain **deadpan** when saying something funny or startling when you sound serious and keep a serious expression on your face: *He looked at me deadpan.* □ *a deadpan expression.*

dead weight /dɛd 'weɪt/ *noun*: **dead weights**

Something is a **dead weight** if it is very heavy to lift and carry: *Someone who is unconscious is a dead weight when it comes to carrying them.*

deaf /dɛf/ *adjective*; *noun*

▷ ***adjective***

1 Someone who is **deaf** is unable to hear at all, or cannot hear well: *She became increasingly deaf.* □ *deaf students.* **2** Someone is **deaf** to what is being said if they refuse to listen to it: *She was deaf to criticism.* — *noun* (*uncount*) **deafness:** *Deafness tends to cut you off from other people.*

▷ ***noun*** (*plural*)

The **deaf** are deaf people: *Nowadays most theatres cater for the deaf.*

▷ ***phrase*** You **turn a deaf ear** to what people are telling you if you refuse to pay any attention to it.

deafen /'dɛfən/ *verb* (*usually in the passive*): **deafens, deafening, deafened**

You **are deafened** by a noise if it is so loud that you can hear nothing else: *All the office workers complained of being deafened by the road drill.* — *adjective* **deafening:** *There was a deafening clap of thunder overhead.* — *adverb* **deafeningly:** *The radio was turned up deafeningly loud.*

deal[1] /di:l/ *noun* (*used in the singular*)

▷ ***phrases*** **A great deal** and **a good deal** are used *eg* before uncountable nouns and comparatives to mean 'a lot': *There's a good deal of truth in what she says.* □ *I do a great deal of reading on holiday.* □ *Things might have been a good deal worse than they are.*

deal[2] /di:l/ *noun*; *verb*

▷ ***noun*: deals**

1 You make a **deal** with someone, *eg* in business or politics when you make an agreement, bargain or arrangement with them: *They're willing to make a deal with us.* □ *She made a lot of money from the deal.* □ *It was a profitable deal for everyone.* **2** Someone gets a certain sort of **deal** out of life if they receive that sort of treatment: *Handicapped people get a rotten deal.* □ *We want a new deal for working wives.* **3** In card games the **deal** is the act of sharing out the cards to the players, or the result of it, or a player's turn to perform it: *It's your deal.*

▷ ***verb*: deals, dealing, dealt**

1 You **deal** someone a blow when you hit them: *She dealt him a blow on the side of the head.* □ *Desk-top publishing has dealt a damaging blow to the printing* *industry.* **2** You **deal** cards when you share them out among the players: *It's my turn to deal.* □ *I was dealt three aces.*

▻ ***phrases*** (*informal*) You say **big deal** to indicate that you are not impressed by something that has just been said to you: *'He says he likes you.' 'Big deal.'*

phrasal verbs

deal in Someone **deals in** particular goods if they buy and sell them: *They deal in new and second-hand jewellery.* [*same as* **trade** in]

deal out You **deal out** things when you give a share of them to each of a number of people; you **deal out** cards when you divide them among the players. [compare **distribute, dole out**]

deal with 1 You **deal with** situations, problems, people, or other matters when you attend to them or do whatever is necessary about them: *Would you deal with these bills, please?* □ *She's good at dealing with difficult people.* □ *It's an impossible issue to deal with satisfactorily.* [*same as* **attend to, cope with**; compare **tackle, address**] **2** A book, article, speech or film **deals with** a subject if it is about it: *His novel deals with the emotions of a small boy whose parents' marriage is breaking down.* **3** You **deal with** a particular shop or firm when you do business with them: *We've always dealt with Brodies in the past.*

dealer /ˈdiːlə(r)/ *noun*: **dealers**
A **dealer** is someone who buys and sells goods of a particular kind: *a dealer in second-hand cars* □ *an antique dealer.*

dealing /ˈdiːlɪŋ/ *noun*: **dealings**
1 (*uncount*) **Dealing** is the activity of trading in something: *drug-dealing.* **2** (*used in the plural*) Your **dealings** with someone are the relations or contact you have with them, or the business you do with them: *I've been absolutely fair in all my dealings with her.*

dealt /dɛlt/ *verb*
Dealt is the past tense and past participle of **deal**.

dean /diːn/ *noun*: **deans**
A **dean** is **1** in the Church of England, a senior clergyman in a cathedral. **2** in the Roman Catholic Church, the cardinal who is head of the college of cardinals. **3** a senior official in a university or college, sometimes with responsibility for student discipline. **4** the head of a subject faculty at a university or college: *the Dean of the Faculty of Law.*

dear /dɪə(r)/ *adjective*; *noun*
▻ ***adjective***: **dearer, dearest**
1 You write **dear** as a polite form of address before the name of the person you are addressing, at the beginning of a letter: *Dear Dad, I hope you had a good journey.* **2** You use **dear** as a term of affection in referring to, or addressing, someone you are fond of or friendly with: *as my dear old granny used to say.* **3** Someone or something is **dear** to you if you care about them a lot: *His native island always remained dear to his heart.* **4** Your **dearest** wish is the thing that you most want to do or to happen: *Her dearest wish was to win a scholarship to Cambridge.* **5** Something that is **dear** is expensive: *If petrol gets any dearer we'll have to sell the car.* **6** People use **dear** with 'little' to mean sweet or charming: *They live in a dear little cottage.*
▻ ***noun***: **dears**
1 (*rather old*) You call someone **dear** as an expression of your affection for them: *Thank you, dear.* □ *Goodbye, my dears.* **2** Someone who is kind and lovable is sometimes referred to as a **dear**: *She's an absolute dear.*
▻ ***phrases*** You use **Oh dear** and **Dear me** as expressions of regret or concern: *Dear me, it's raining.*

dearly /ˈdɪəlɪ/ *adverb*
1 You love someone or something **dearly** if you love them very much. **2** You say you would **dearly** like to do something if you want to very much: *She would dearly have liked to stay on as prime minister.* **3** You pay **dearly** for something wrong or foolish you have done if you suffer as a result of it: *She paid dearly for ignoring her colleagues' warnings.*

dearth /dɜːθ/ *noun* (*uncount or used in the singular*)
A **dearth** of something is a lack or scarceness of it: *There's no dearth of entertainment locally.* □ *in times of dearth.*

death /dɛθ/ *noun* (*uncount or count*): **deaths**
1 Death is the end of a person's or animal's life: *He was stabbed to death in a street fight.* □ *This flu virus has already been responsible for 13 deaths.* **2** The **death** of an institution or system is its end or destruction: *We are witnessing the death of the welfare state.* [*same as* **demise**]
▻ ***phrases* 1** Someone is **at death's door** when they are so ill that they may die. **2** Someone **is put to death** when they are executed: *He was put to death for trying to blow up the House of Commons.* **3 a** You are frightened or worried **to death** by something if you are desperately frightened or worried by it: *He worries me to death, driving at that speed.* **b** You are sick **to death** of something that has been annoying you for a long time when you can't bear it any longer: *I'm sick to death of her complaints.*

deathbed /ˈdɛθbɛd/ *noun*: **deathbeds**
Someone's **deathbed** is the bed they lie dying in.

deathly /ˈdɛθlɪ/ *adjective or adverb* (*intensifying*)
Deathly is used to give emphasis to words that are associated with death: *His face was deathly pale.* □ *a deathly silence.*

death penalty /ˈdɛθ pɛnəltɪ/ *noun* (*used in the singular*)
The **death penalty** is the use of death as a punishment for the most serious crimes. [compare **capital punishment**]

debacle or **débâcle** /deɪˈbɑːkəl/ *noun*: **debacles**
A **debacle** is something that fails publicly and disastrously: *The government managed to survive the debacle of the poll tax.* [*same as* **fiasco**]

debar /dɪˈbɑː(r)/ *verb*: **debars, debarring, debarred**
You **are debarred** from doing something if a law or rule prevents you from doing it: *His age debarred him from joining the army.*

debase /dɪˈbeɪs/ *verb*: **debases, debasing, debased**
To **debase** something is to reduce its quality or value; to **debase** coinage is to add cheap metal to it. — *adjective* **debased:** *You find plenty of debased imitations of this pottery.*

debatable /dɪˈbeɪtəbəl/ *adjective*
Something that is **debatable** is not certainly true, and so can be argued about: *It's debatable whether animal fats are really bad for you.* [*same as* **arguable**]

debate /dɪˈbeɪt/ *noun*; *verb*
▻ ***noun*** (*count or uncount*): **debates**
A **debate** is a discussion in which people express their different opinions, especially a formal one with speakers in favour and against a motion, at which a vote is taken: *There has been much debate about the real effectiveness of flu remedies.*
▻ ***verb***: **debates, debating, debated**
1 People **debate** something when they discuss it, espe-

cially in a formal way, by putting forward different opinions and arguments: *The future of the coal industry will be debated in Parliament tomorrow.* **2** You **debate** what to do or how to do it when you consider possible courses of action, or ways of doing something: *She debated how best to break the news to them.*

▻ ***phrase*** Something is **open to debate** if it is not certainly true, and so can be argued about: *Whether jogging is good for you is open to debate.* [*same as* **debatable**]

debauched /dɪ'bɔːtʃt/ *adjective* (*derogatory*)
If you call someone **debauched** you mean that they indulge too much in drinking or casual sex.

debauchery /dɪ'bɔːtʃərɪ/ *noun* (*uncount*)
Debauchery is habitual over-indugence in drinking or casual sex.

debilitated /dɪ'bɪlɪteɪtɪd/ *adjective*
A person, country or institution that is **debilitated** is in a weakened state: *a nation debilitated by war and disease.*

debilitating /dɪ'bɪlɪteɪtɪŋ/ *adjective*
Something has a **debilitating** effect on someone or something if it weakens them: *Overwork and lack of exercise are bound to have a debilitating effect on your health.*

debility /dɪ'bɪlɪtɪ/ *noun* (*uncount*)
Debility is bodily weakness: *The virus is known to cause long-term debility.*

debit /'dɛbɪt/ *noun*; *verb*

▻ ***noun***: **debits**
A **debit** is a record kept by your bank of the amount taken out of your bank account when you write a cheque or use your bank card to get money or pay for something; the **debit** side of your account or bank statement is the side or column recording the debits.

▻ ***verb***: **debits, debiting, debited**
Your bank **debits** your account when it deducts from it the amount that you have taken out by writing a cheque or using your bank card: *My bank statement showed that my account had been debited with £100 on 22 October.*
[*opposite* **credit**]

debonair /dɛbə'nɛə(r)/ *adjective*
A **debonair** person (formerly especially a man) dresses smartly and has a lot of charm and confidence.

debris /'dɛbrɪ/ or /'deɪbrɪ/ or **débris** *noun* (*uncount*)
Debris is the remains of something that has been destroyed or broken, or rubbish left lying about: *They searched for survivors amongst the debris.*

debt /dɛt/ *noun*: **debts**
1 A **debt** is an amount of money that you owe somebody: *Her debts amounted to $14000.* **2** (*uncount*) **Debt** is the state of owing money: *Don't get into debt.* **3** You owe someone a **debt** of gratitude when their kindness to you makes you feel that you can never thank them enough. **4** (*uncount*) You say you are in someone's **debt** when you are grateful to them for doing something for you, and feel you must find a way of repaying their kindness. [see also **indebted**]

debtor /'dɛtə(r)/ *noun*: **debtors**
A **debtor** is a person who owes someone else money. [see also **creditor**]

debug /diː'bʌg/ *verb*: **debugs, debugging, debugged**
To **debug** a computer program is to search for and correct faults in it.

debunk /diː'bʌŋk/ *verb* (*informal*): **debunks, debunking, debunked**
To **debunk** a claim, theory or idea is to prove or show that it is false, or deserves no attention or respect. [*same as* **discredit**]

début or **debut** /'deɪbjuː/ or /'dɛbjuː/ *noun*: **debuts**
Someone such as an actor, singer, musician or other performer makes their **début** when they first appear and perform in public.

decade /'dɛkeɪd/ *noun*: **decades**
A **decade** is a period of ten years, especially from a year ending in 0 to the next one ending in 9, *eg* 1970-1979.

decadent /'dɛkədənt/ *adjective*
1 (*derogatory*) A **decadent** person is someone who adopts low standards of personal discipline and morality, especially in a deliberate, self-conscious way. **2** A **decadent** style in art or architecture develops from an existing style, but shows a drop in standards, especially of taste. — *noun* (*uncount*) **decadence:** *aesthetic and moral decadence.*

decaffeinated /diː'kafɪneɪtɪd/ *adjective*
Decaffeinated coffee has had its caffeine extracted from it.

decant /dɪ'kant/ *verb*: **decants, decanting, decanted**
You **decant** alcoholic drinks such as sherry, port or wine when you pour them from the bottle into another container.

decanter /dɪ'kantə(r)/ *noun*: **decanters**
A **decanter** is a glass container, often with a glass stopper, into which alcoholic drinks such as sherry, port or wine are poured for serving.

decapitate /dɪ'kapɪteɪt/ *verb*: **decapitates, decapitating, decapitated**
To **decapitate** a person is to cut off their head.

decathlon /dɪ'kaθlən/ *noun*: **decathlons**
A **decathlon** is a sporting contest in which athletes compete in ten different events.

decay /dɪ'keɪ/ *verb*; *noun*

▻ ***verb***: **decays, decaying, decayed**
1 Living matter **decays** when it rots: *the smell of decaying meat.* **2** A building **decays** when necessary repairs are not carried out on it, and its condition worsens. **3** A culture, society or institution **decays** when it becomes weak and disorganized and gradually collapses. — *adjective* **decayed:** *decayed teeth.*

▻ ***noun*** (*uncount*)
1 Decay is the process of rotting: *Fluoride prevents tooth decay.* **2** A rotten area in a tooth is also referred to as **decay**: *The dentist drilled away the decay.* **3** Buildings fall into **decay** when necessary repairs are not carried out on them and their condition worsens. **4** The **decay** of social or political institutions is their gradual collapse through weakness and disorganization.

deceased /dɪ'siːst/ *adjective*; *noun*

▻ ***adjective*** (*formal or legal*)
A **deceased** person is someone who has just died: *He was a personal friend of the deceased couple.*

▻ ***noun*** (*used in the singular*)
A person who has just died is referred to as the **deceased**: *relatives of the deceased.*

deceit /dɪ'siːt/ *noun* (*uncount or count*)
Deceit is dishonest behaviour such as lying, that is intended to make people believe something that is not true: *I could no longer stand his lies and deceit.* □ *Some little deceits and pretences are to be expected in any marriage.*

deceitful /dɪ'siːtfəl/ *adjective*
A **deceitful** person tells lies or uses other dishonest behaviour to try and make people believe things that

are not true: *deceitful behaviour.* — *adverb* **deceitfully:** *You acted deceitfully.* — *noun* (*uncount*) **deceitfulness:** *I've come across instances of her deceitfulness before.*

deceive /dɪˈsiːv/ *verb*: **deceives, deceiving, deceived**
1 You **deceive** someone when you intentionally make them believe something that is not true: *He deceived us into believing he was academically qualified for the job.* **2** You **deceive** yourself when you won't admit something, though you really know it's true: *She tried to deceive herself that she was not putting on weight.* **3** Something **deceives** you if it misleads you: *An illusion is something that deceives the eye.* **4** You **are deceived** in someone when you believe they are better in some way than they really are: *I was deceived in her; she seemed so capable at the interview.*

December /dɪˈsɛmbə(r)/ *noun* (*uncount*)
December is the twelfth and last month of the year, coming after November and before January: *The party is on Saturday the twenty-seventh of December* (written *Saturday 27 December*). ▫ *December the tenth,* or (*AmE*) *December ten* (written *December 10*). ▫ *freezing December weather.*

decency /ˈdiːsənsɪ/ *noun* (*uncount*)
1 Decency is the standard in dress, behaviour and language that we take care to maintain in public to avoid offending or disgusting people: *We see so much on television nowadays that offends against decency.* **2 Decency** is also moral and social behaviour of a standard that people normally expect of each other: *At least he had the decency to apologize.*

decent /ˈdiːsənt/ *adjective*
1 Behaviour, dress or language that is **decent** is respectable, or acceptable in public, and does not offend or disgust people: *She wore a dress so short as to be barely decent.* [*opposite* **indecent**] **2 Decent** treatment is fair, humane treatment: *These are examples of prison as a decent, constructive place.* **3** Something can be described as **decent** if it is satisfactory or acceptable: *It's not hard to find a decent bed and breakfast in the area.* **4 Decent** people are respectable, honest people. **5** (*old, informal*) **Decent** can mean kind and considerate: *I say, that's very decent of you.* **6** (*informal*) **Decent** can mean rather good or competent: *She'll make a decent tennis-player one day.* — *adverb* **decently:** *He evidently doesn't know how to behave decently in public.*

decentralize or **decentralise** /diːˈsɛntrəlaɪz/ *verb*: **decentralizes, decentralizing, decentralized**
To **decentralize** government or an organization is to move departments or responsibilities from the central administrative office to the control of local offices or branches. [*opposite* **centralise**] — *noun* (*uncount*) **decentralization** /diːsɛntrəlaɪˈzeɪʃən/: *the decentralization of the health service.*

deception /dɪˈsɛpʃən/ *noun*: **deceptions**
1 (*uncount*) **Deception** is the act of deceiving someone, or the state of being deceived: *Don't be taken in by the hypnotism act; it's a blatant piece of deception.* **2** A **deception** is a lie or other piece of behaviour intended to deceive people: *She had to resort to a variety of deceptions to keep him from guessing the true state of things.*

deceptive /dɪˈsɛptɪv/ *adjective*
Something that is **deceptive** has the power to deceive or mislead you: *People's voices tend to convey an impression of their physical appearance, but can be very deceptive.* — *adverb* **deceptively:** *She demonstrated the procedure in a way that made it look deceptively easy.*

decibel /ˈdɛsɪbɛl/ *noun*: **decibels**
A **decibel** is the unit used in measuring the loudness of sounds: *The television was turned up several decibels louder than it need have been.*

decide /dɪˈsaɪd/ *verb*: **decides, deciding, decided**
1 You **decide** to do something when you choose to do it, especially after carefully considering a variety of possibilities: *I've decided to go by air.* ▫ *Did you decide not to attend the conference after all?* ▫ *He's decided at last that it's time for him to retire.* ▫ *She hasn't decided what to do after leaving university.* ▫ *Have you decided where to go for your elective year?* ▫ *She decided against a church wedding.* ▫ *Naturally we hope that you will decide in favour of our proposal.* ▫ *I haven't decided about that yet.* ▫ *He's thinking of going but he hasn't decided definitely.* **2** A factor or circumstance **decides** something when it makes a particular result or outcome definite or inevitable: *It was her superior stamina and staying power that decided the race today.* **3** A matter or case **is decided** when a person or people in authority judge what is to be done about it: *The case will go to a higher court to be decided.* ▫ *It is now up to the Home Secretary to decide the convicted man's fate.* [*same as* **settle, determine**] **4** You **decide** that something is so when that is what you conclude after considering the evidence: *I couldn't decide whether they really agreed with me or were just being polite.* ▫ *I decided that there was no-one in, and came away.* — *adjective* **deciding:** *The proposal is certainly an attractive one, but the deciding factor must be cost.* ▫ *the deciding goal.*

> ***phrasal verb***
> You **decide on** or **upon** something when you choose it: *She decided on a fried egg and chips.*

decided /diˈsaɪdɪd/ *adjective*
A **decided** difference, improvement, preference or advantage is a clear and definite one: *She enjoyed all her Shakespearean roles, but Rosalind in 'As You Like It' was a decided favourite.*

decidedly /dɪˈsaɪdɪdlɪ/ *adverb*
1 (*intensifying*) **Decidedly** is used to mean 'very' or 'very obviously': *They looked decidedly relieved.* **2** You say something **decidedly** when you state it in a manner that shows you have made up your mind about it: *'This government must be got rid of,' she announced decidedly.*

deciduous /dɪˈsidjuːəs/ *adjective*
A **deciduous** tree drops its leaves yearly in the autumn. [*opposite* **evergreen**]

decimal /ˈdɛsɪməl/ *adjective*; *noun*
▻ ***adjective***
1 A **decimal** currency or a **decimal** system of measurement uses the number ten as its basis of calculation. **2** A **decimal** point is the dot that is written at the beginning of a fraction shown in the form of a decimal.
▻ ***noun***: **decimals**
A **decimal** is a fraction written as a dot or comma followed by numbers representing tenths, hundredths and thousandths, in that order, as in *5.7*; *4,67*.

decimalize or **decimalise** /ˈdɛsɪməlaɪz/ *verb*: **decimalizes, decimalizing, decimalized**
A currency or system of measurement **is decimalized** when it is converted to a decimal system, using the number ten as its basis of calculation. — *noun* (*uncount*) **decimalization** /dɛsɪməlaɪˈzeɪʃən/: *the pre-decimalization complications of calculating in pounds, shillings and pence.*

decimate /'dɛsɪmeɪt/ *verb*: **decimates, decimating, decimated**
A population or other group **is decimated** when a large proportion of it is killed or put out of action: *Wildlife in the area has been decimated by recent forest fires.*

decipher /dɪ'saɪfə(r)/ *verb*: **deciphers, deciphering, deciphered**
You **decipher** something such as a piece of writing or a coded message when you work out what it says; you **decipher** a code or a form of script when you work out what its symbols represent: *His handwriting was tiny and difficult to decipher.* — *adjective* **decipherable:** *Parts of the manuscript are easily decipherable.*

decision /dɪ'sɪʒən/ *noun*: **decisions**
1 You make a **decision** when you make a choice about what to do, or which possibility or alternative is the best one: *We haven't yet reached a decision on where to meet.* □ *We must make the right decision.* □ *What was your decision in the end?* **2** (*uncount*) **Decision** is the act of deciding or choosing: *She could not put off the moment of decision any longer.* **3** (*uncount*) **Decision** is the ability to decide quickly and firmly: *a woman of decision* □ *'What we all need now is a good long walk,' he said with decision.*

decisive /dɪ'saɪsɪv/ *adjective*
1 A circumstance, factor or event is **decisive** if it leads to a certain result, or is itself a clear and definite result: *Of the various battles in the North African campaign, this could be regarded as the decisive one.* [*same as* **crucial**, **critical**] **2** A **decisive** person is someone able to make quick firm decisions: *I'm sorry not to be more decisive, but there are so many aspects to consider.* — *adverb* **decisively:** *Our team had never been quite so decisively beaten.* □ *We need people who can act quickly and decisively.* — *noun* (*uncount*) **decisiveness:** *Her voice lacked its customary decisiveness.*

deck¹ /dɛk/ *noun*: **decks**
1 A **deck** on a ship is one of its levels or floors: *Your cabin is on Deck 3.* **2** (*used in the singular*) The **deck** of a ship is its top level, forming both a covering for its interior and a floor open to the sky: *We went out on deck.* **3** The **decks** of a bus are the downstairs and upstairs levels of seating: *Let's sit on the top deck.* **4** (*especially AmE*) A **deck** of playing cards is a pack of them. **5** The **deck** of a record-player is the platform which supports and includes the turntable; the **deck** or **tape deck** of a tape-recorder is the part on or in which the cassette or tape is supported for playing.

deck² /dɛk/ *verb* (*literary*): **decks, decking, decked**
You **deck** something with flowers or other pretty objects when you decorate it with them.

> ***phrasal verb***
> You **deck** someone or something **out** when you dress or decorate them attractively: *The ship was decked out with flags.*

deckchair /'dɛktʃɛə(r)/ *noun*: **deckchairs**
A **deckchair** is a folding chair for use out of doors, consisting of a wooden frame with a strip of canvas forming the seat.

-decker /'dɛkə(r)/ *suffix*
-decker is used to form adjectives and nouns and has the meaning 'having the specified number of decks or levels': *a single-decker bus.*

declaim /dɪ'kleɪm/ *verb*: **declaims, declaiming, declaimed**
You **declaim** a speech, *eg* in parliament or in a play, when you deliver it in an impressive and dramatic voice.

declaration /dɛklə'reɪʃən/ *noun*: **declarations**
1 You make a **declaration** when you make a firm, strongly-expressed statement: *Mr Darcy's declaration of love took Elizabeth entirely by surprise.* **2** An official and formal statement, especially of intention, is called a **declaration**: *They have issued a declaration of war.*

declare /dɪ'klɛə(r)/ *verb*: **declares, declaring, declared**
1 You **declare** that something is so when you state it firmly and strongly: *She declared that the whole project was a waste of time and money.* **2** You **declare** your own position or intention with regard to something when you state it formally and publicly; you **declare** for or against something or someone when you state your intention of supporting or opposing them: *He declared himself a loyal supporter of the Prime Minister.* □ *She declared her intention to stand for election.* □ *A large number were already declaring for Mr Major.* **3** Someone **is declared** innocent or guilty when they are officially or formally announced to be so. **4** The result of a ballot **is declared** when it is announced in public after the votes are counted. **5** Countries **declare** war on each other when they announce officially that a state of war exists between them. **6** You **declare** goods you have bought abroad, or income you have received, when you inform customs or tax officials about them, to show your willingness to pay tax on them. — *adjective* **declared:** *It was her openly declared intention to oppose the deal.*

decline /dɪ'klaɪn/ *verb*; *noun*
▻ ***verb***: **declines, declining, declined**
1 Something **declines** when it grows smaller or less, becomes weaker, or worsens: *Membership of the club has declined from 500 to 350 over the last two years.* □ *His health was declining rapidly.* [*same as* **wane**; *opposite* **grow**] **2** You **decline** an invitation or offer, or **decline** to do something, when you politely refuse: *She declined a place on the committee.* [*same as* **refuse**; *opposite* **accept**] — *adjective* **declining:** *his declining power and influence.* [*same as* **waning**]
▻ ***noun*** (*uncount, or count used in the singular*)
There is a **decline** in something when it grows smaller or less, weaker, or worse: *Church attendance is sadly in decline.* □ *There's a noticeable decline in the borrowing figures.*
▻ ***phrase*** Something is **on the decline** when it is declining: *Her mental powers were by now on the decline.*

decode /diː'koʊd/ *verb*: **decodes, decoding, decoded**
You **decode** a message that has been written or spoken in code when you put it into ordinary language.

decompose /diːkəm'poʊz/ *verb*: **decomposes, decomposing, decomposed**
Living matter **decomposes** when it decays or rots. — *adjective* **decomposed:** *a badly decomposed body.* — *noun* (*uncount*) **decomposition** /diːkɒmpə'zɪʃən/: *All living organisms are subject to decomposition after death.*

decor or **décor** /'dɛkɔː(r)/ or /'deɪkɔː(r)/ *noun* (*uncount*)
The **decor** of a house or room is the style and colour scheme of the decoration and furnishings.

decorate /'dɛkəreɪt/ *verb*: **decorates, decorating, decorated**
1 You **decorate** something when you add things to it to make it pleasing to look at: *She had brought some pictures and posters with her to decorate the walls of her room.* **2** You **decorate** a room when you paint or paper the walls and ceiling, and paint the doors and window frames: *The sitting room had been decorated in deep blue and bright orange.* **3** A person **is decorated** when they are awarded a medal for brave conduct, distinguished service, or a remarkable achievement.

— *noun* (*uncount*) **decorating:** *He promised to do the decorating for his mother when she moved house.*

decoration /dɛkə'reɪʃən/ *noun*: **decorations**
1 (*count or uncount*) A **decoration** is something you add to a thing or place to make it pleasing to look at: *the Christmas decorations* □ *I stuck a piece of holly in the pudding for decoration.* **2** (*uncount*) The **decoration** of a room or building is the process of painting, papering, fitting and furnishing it, or the style in which this is done. **3** A **decoration** is a medal awarded for bravery, distinguished service or valuable work.

decorative /'dɛkrətɪv/ *adjective*
A **decorative** thing has the purpose of adding to the attractiveness of something, and usually has no practical function: *She had filled the sitting room with china ornaments and other decorative objects.* [*same as* **ornamental**]

decorator /'dɛkəreɪtə(r)/ *noun*: **decorators**
A **decorator** is a person whose job is to paint and paper rooms or buildings.

decorous /'dɛkərəs/ *adjective* (*sometimes humorous*)
Decorous behaviour is polite, modest and socially correct behaviour that does not offend people: *a decorous kiss on the cheek.* — *adverb* **decorously:** *She decorously waited outside while he changed.*

decorum /dɪ'kɔːrəm/ *noun* (*uncount*)
Decorum is polite, modest and socially correct behaviour.

decoy *verb*; *noun*
▻ ***noun*** /'diːkɔɪ/: **decoys**
A **decoy** is someone or something used to lead a person or animal away from their intended direction and into a trap.
▻ ***verb***: **decoys, decoying, decoyed:** *He was decoyed into the side street where the murderers were waiting.*

decrease /diː'kriːs/ *verb*; *noun*
▻ ***verb***: **decreases, decreasing, decreased**
Something **decreases**, or **is decreased** when it becomes smaller or less: *She decreased her speed to 40 kmh as she approached the bend.* [*opposite* **increase**] — *adjective* **decreasing:** *decreasing profits.*
▻ ***noun*** /'diːkriːs/ (*count, usually in the singular, or uncount*): **decreases**
A **decrease** is a reduction or lessening of something, or the amount of this: *Numbers of girls taking scientific subjects is on the decrease.* □ *At night the decrease in temperature could be as much as 30 degrees.* [*opposite* **increase**]

decree /dɪ'kriː/ *noun*; *verb*
▻ ***noun***: **decrees**
1 A **decree** is an official order or ruling issued by someone in supreme authority, such as a monarch or parliament. **2** (*legal*) A ruling made by a divorce court is also a **decree**, a **decree absolute** granting immediate divorce, and a **decree nisi** divorce at the end of a certain period.
▻ ***verb***: **decrees, decreeing, decreed**
Someone in a position of supreme authority **decrees** that something shall be done when they officially order it to be done.

decrepit /dɪ'krɛpɪt/ *adjective*
1 Something described as **decrepit** is old and in poor condition, *eg* from long use: *That decrepit old car of yours is a danger to the public.* [*same as* **run-down, broken-down**] **2** (*derogatory*) A person who is **decrepit** is elderly and in poor health: *a decrepit old man.*

decry /dɪ'kraɪ/ *verb*: **decries, decrying, decried**
You **decry** something when you express disapproval or scorn for it: *Far from decrying her artistic efforts, I always praised and encouraged them.* [*same as* **belittle, disparage**]

dedicate /'dɛdɪkeɪt/ *verb*: **dedicates, dedicating, dedicated**
1 You **dedicate** yourself, your energy or your time to something if you work long and hard at it, because you believe in its worth: *She dedicated all her energies to the campaign for women's rights.* [*same as* **devote, commit**] **2** You **dedicate** a work such as a book to someone when you add a short statement at the beginning saying it is for them, as an expression of your love or respect for them.

dedicated /'dɛdɪkeɪtɪd/ *adjective*
You are **dedicated** to something if you give a lot of time and effort to it, because you believe in its worth: *It takes a dedicated teacher to try and educate some of today's kids.* [*same as* **devoted, committed**] — *adverb* **dedicatedly:** *He gave himself dedicatedly to the job for over 30 years.*

dedication /dɛdɪ'keɪʃən/ *noun*: **dedications**
1 A **dedication** at the beginning of a book or other work is a statement by the author that it is for a certain person, as an expression of love or respect for them: *The dedication read 'For Bill, for being so understanding'.* [*same as* **inscription**] **2** (*uncount*) Someone shows **dedication** when they give a lot of their time and energy to something: *He survived, thanks largely to the dedication of the nurses and doctors who attended him.* [*same as* **commitment**]

deduce /dɪdjuːs/ *verb*: **deduces, deducing, deduced**
You **deduce** something from known facts or circumstances, or from your own observations, when you draw a certain conclusion from them: *I deduced from his tone that he was not pleased.* [*same as* **infer**]

deduct /dɪ'dʌkt/ *verb*: **deducts, deducting, deducted**
You **deduct** a certain sum from a total amount when you subtract it, or reduce the total by that amount: *The examiners may deduct marks for spelling mistakes.* [compare **subtract**]

deduction /dɪ'dʌkʃən/ *noun* (*count or uncount*): **deductions**
1 A **deduction** is a sum subtracted from a total amount: *He earns about £800 a month after tax and insurance deductions.* **2 Deduction** is the reasoning process by which you conclude something from known facts or circumstances, or from your own observations: *I was led by a process of deduction to a certain apartment in Montmartre.*

deed /diːd/ *noun* (*old, or literary*): **deeds**
1 A **deed** is an act performed by someone, especially a notable one: *Who could have done such a wicked deed?* **2** A **deed** is also a legal document recording an agreement, *eg* one relating to the change in ownership of a house or other property: *the house deeds.*

deem /diːm/ *verb* (*formal*): **deems, deeming, deemed**
You **deem** something to be so when you judge that it is so: *I leave you to take whatever action you deem suitable.* [*same as* **consider**]

deep /diːp/ *adjective or adverb*; *adjective*
▻ ***adjective or adverb***: **deeper, deepest**
1 Something that is **deep** extends downwards a long way from the surface, or measures a lot from top to bottom: *We went swimming in the river where the water was deepest.* □ *I got hold of a deep cardboard box to put the kittens in.* □ *We dug the trench deep and wide.* □ *He had already climbed down as deep as he dared into the shaft.* □ *Venice sinks deeper into the mud every year.* □ *Don't get any deeper into debt.* [= don't let your debts increase further] □ *a deep wound* □ *The knife had pene-*

trated deep into the flesh. ▫ *We found ourselves knee-deep in rubbish.* [= with rubbish up to our knees] ▫ *The river looked at least waist-deep.*
2 Something is **deep** inside an area when it is a long way inside it: *They came upon a tiny dwelling deep in the woods.* ▫ *We were now deep inside the enemy lines.* **3** Something is so many metres or centimetres **deep** if that is what it measures from top to bottom or from front to back: *The cake tin needs to be at least 20 cm wide and 10 cm deep.* ▫ *These shelves are barely six inches deep.* ▫ *I got the children to line up four deep.* [= in four rows one behind the other]
▻ ***adjective***: **deeper, deepest**
1 Deep feelings are strong ones: *His death is the cause of deep sorrow.* ▫ *May we express our deep regret.* ▫ *You have our deepest sympathy.* ▫ *I have a deep distrust of all ambitious people.* [*same as* **profound**] **2** You take a **deep** breath when you fill your lungs full of air and empty them completely: *He gave a deep sigh.* **3** You are in a **deep** sleep when you are sleeping soundly and are difficult to wake. [*opposite* **light**] **4 Deep** sounds are low ones: *deep male voices* ▫ *He gave a deep groan.* [*opposite* **high-pitched**] **5 Deep** colours or shades are strong and dark: *The curtains were a deep shade of purple.* ▫ *She had large deep-blue eyes.* [*opposite* **pale, light**] **6 Deep** matters or thoughts are serious and complex ones; a person who is described as **deep** has a mysterious or complex personality. [*opposite* **frivolous, superficial**]
▻ ***phrases*** **1** You feel something **deep down** or **deep inside** when you feel it strongly but do not show it: *Deep down he had a child's need for praise.* **2** You are **deep in thought** when you are thinking hard about something and giving it all your attention. [*same as* **preoccupied**] **3** You say something **runs** or **goes deep** if it has established itself firmly and is difficult to change: *Racial prejudice runs deep here.* **4** You get **thrown in at the deep end** when you have to do something difficult for the first time, with little warning and no help.
[see also **depth**]

deepen /ˈdiːpən/ *verb*: **deepens, deepening, deepened**
1 To **deepen** something is to increase its depth, or its measurement from surface to bottom: *The harbour was deepened to allow larger ships to enter it.* **2** The sea, a lake or a river **deepens** as its bed slopes downwards: *The pool deepens towards the middle.* **3** A crisis **deepens** when it becomes graver. **4** A feeling or emotion **deepens** or **is deepened** as it becomes stronger: *Their respect for each other deepened over the years.* [*same as* **intensify**] **5** Your understanding or knowledge of something **deepens** or **is deepened** as you learn more about it: *Her investigations had deepened her awareness of the problems.* **6** A sound **deepens** or **is deepened** when it becomes lower in tone: *She deliberately deepened her voice so as to sound more commanding.* — *adjective* **deepening:** *the deepening crisis.*

deep freeze /diːp ˈfriːz/ *noun*; *verb*
▻ ***noun***: **deep freezes**
A **deep freeze** is a container for storing food at temperatures below freezing point. [*same as* **freezer**]
▻ ***verb*** **(deep-freeze)**: **deep-freezes, deep-freezing, deep-froze, deep-frozen**
You **deep-freeze** food when you store it at a temperature below freezing point.

deep-fry /diːp ˈfraɪ/ *verb*: **deep-fries, deep-frying, deep-fried**
You **deep-fry** food when you fry it in a deep pan, in oil or fat that completely covers it.

deeply /ˈdiːplɪ/ *adverb*
1 Deeply means down to a deep level: *The road was deeply rutted.* **2** (*intensifying*) **Deeply** is used like 'very', or 'very much', especially in descriptions of people's feelings or emotional states: *We were never deeply in love.* ▫ *Emma was deeply humiliated by Mr Knightley's rebuke.* ▫ *Her book impressed me deeply.* ▫ *I'm deeply grateful.* ▫ *a deeply touching story* ▫ *a deeply personal matter.* **3** You sigh or breathe **deeply** when you fill your lungs with air and empty them completely. **4** You think **deeply** about something when you consider it thoroughly.

deep-rooted /diːp ˈruːtɪd/ *adjective*
Deep-rooted or **deeply rooted** notions and prejudices are so firmly established in a person or group of people that it is difficult to alter them.

deep-sea /diːp ˈsiː/ *adjective*
Deep-sea fishing and **deep-sea** diving are carried on at a long distance from the coast.

deep-seated /diːp ˈsiːtɪd/ *adjective*
Deep-seated feelings, emotions and fears are firmly fixed ones that influence the personality and are difficult to alter.

deer /dɪə(r)/ *noun*: **deer**
A **deer** is any member of a family of generally large, four-footed, swift-running, hoofed animals, many of the males of which have horns that divide into branches, called antlers.

deface /dɪˈfeɪs/ *verb*: **defaces, defacing, defaced**
To **deface** something such as a notice, wall or statue is to spoil its appearance deliberately by writing or drawing on it, or cutting into its surface: *Even the trees had been defaced with graffiti.*

defamation /dɛfəˈmeɪʃən/ *noun* (*uncount*)
Defamation of character is the criminal offence of damaging someone's reputation by saying things about them that are both harmful and untrue. — *adjective* **defamatory** /dɪˈfamətrɪ/: *defamatory allegations.*

default /dɪˈfɔːlt/ *verb*; *noun*
▻ ***verb***: **defaults, defaulting, defaulted**
1 You **default** on the rent or other regular payment when you fail to pay the agreed amount at the arranged time; you **default** on a bargain or promise when you fail to fulfil it. **2** (*computing*) A computer **defaults** to a certain programmed procedure when it is given no other instruction.
▻ ***noun*** (*uncount*)
1 Default is the failure to do or pay what you have promised or agreed. **2** (*computing*) **Default** is the procedure that a computer is programmed to follow when it is given no other instruction.
▻ ***phrase*** Something happens **by default** if it happens only because the thing that might have prevented it has not happened: *The job became hers by default when no other candidates offered themselves for it.*

defeat /dɪˈfiːt/ *verb*; *noun*
▻ ***verb***: **defeats, defeating, defeated**
1 You **defeat** someone when you beat them or win a victory over them in a fight, game, election or competition: *Napoleon was finally defeated in 1815 at the Battle of Waterloo.* ▫ *We were defeated by 3 goals to 2.* **2** Something such as a problem or a task **defeats** you when it is too difficult for you to solve or perform: *I'm afraid the puzzle has defeated the lot of us.* **3** Your hopes or ambitions **are defeated** when something happens to stop you fulfilling them; a plot or conspiracy **is defeated** when it is discovered and stopped; a strike **is defeated** when the strikers return to work with their

demands unfulfilled. [*same as* **thwart**] **4** The motion or proposal in a debate **is defeated** when there are more votes against it than for it: *The motion was defeated by 301 votes to 256.*

▻ ***noun*** (*uncount or count*): **defeats**

1 Defeat is the state of being beaten or defeated in a fight, war, game, election or competition: *His invasion ended in defeat and surrender.* □ *The recent run of defeats had been bad for the team's morale.* □ *Labour suffered their worst defeat in 1959.* **2 Defeat** is failure to achieve what you want to: *A few reached the summit but the rest of us gave up in defeat.* □ *I'll never admit defeat.*

defeatism /dɪˈfiːtɪzm/ *noun* (*uncount*)
Defeatism is the attitude of someone who expects to be defeated. — *noun* (*often adjectival*) **defeatist:** *You're all such defeatists.* □ *Stop talking that defeatist nonsense.*

defecate /ˈdɛfəkeɪt/ *verb*: **defecates, defecating, defecated**
You **defecate** when you pass faeces, or get rid of your body's waste matter, through your anus. — *noun* (*uncount*) **defecation** /dɛfəˈkeɪʃən/: *The process of defecation rids our bodies of solid waste.*

defect *noun*; *verb*

▻ ***noun*** /ˈdiːfɛkt/: **defects**
A **defect** is an imperfection or fault in a thing or person: *a heart defect.* □ *The system still has major defects.*

▻ ***verb*** /dɪˈfɛkt/: **defects, defecting, defected**
You **defect** from your country or your political party when you leave it for another: *Nureyev defected from the Soviet Union in 1961.* — *noun* (*uncount or count*) **defection:** *an increasing number of defections.* — *noun* **defector:** *defectors from the Soviet Union.*

defective /dɪˈfɛktɪv/ *adjective*
Something such as a machine or a bodily organ is **defective** if it does not work properly: *He was born with a defective liver.* □ *Send us the defective part and we will replace it free of charge.* [*same as* **faulty**]

defence (*AmE* **defense**) /dɪˈfɛns/ *noun*: **defences**
1 (*uncount*) **Defence** is the means you take to protect yourself or others from attack: *She explained that she always carried a knife in her handbag for defence.* **2 Defence** is **a** (*uncount*) the resources a country has for its own protection against attack, such as its armed forces and weapons, seen as the responsibility of the government: *The government is to cut spending on defence.* □ *rising defence costs.* **b** (*used in the plural*) a country's armed forces, its stock of weapons and its fortifications. **3** A **defence** is a means of protection: *The Romans built the wall as a defence against raids from the north.* **4** (*uncount*) You speak in **defence** of someone or something that has been criticized when you say something to support or protect them: *In his defence it should be mentioned that he has had a blameless driving record till now.* □ *We must speak out in defence of our principles.* **5** A **defence** is a statement or argument explaining and supporting something that has been criticized: *They listened to his defence of government policy.* **6** In a law court, the **defence** is **a** (*uncount or used in the singular*) the case opposing the charge, prepared by lawyers on behalf of the accused person: *She was one of the witnesses for the defence in the bribery case.* **b** (*with a singular or plural verb*) the lawyers speaking and acting for the accused person: *The defence has* (or *have*) *tried to give us the opposite impression.* **7** (*with a singular or plural verb*) In a football team, or a team for similar games, the **defence** are the players who defend the goal and prevent the opposing team from scoring: *The Welsh defence was* (or *were*) *too strong for us.*

defenceless (*AmE* **defenseless**) /dɪˈfɛnsləs/ *adjective*
Someone or something that is **defenceless** hasn't the means or ability to defend themselves against attack: *The bombers have again targeted defenceless civilians.*

defend /dɪˈfɛnd/ *verb*: **defends, defending, defended**
1 You **defend** someone or something against attack when you take action to protect them: *Singapore was defended only from the sea.* □ *We must defend our right to privacy.* **2** You **defend** someone or something that has been criticized when you say something to support them: *She fiercely defended her opinions.* **3** In a law court, a lawyer **defends** an accused person by trying to prove that they did not commit the crime, or that they had some excuse for committing it. **4** (*games*) Players in a football team **defend** when they try to prevent the opposing team from scoring. **5** Someone who is a champion in a game or sport **defends** their title when they play against a challenger for the championship. — *noun* **defender:** *The few remaining defenders were rounded up and shot.*

defendant /dɪˈfɛndənt/ *noun*: **defendants**
The **defendant** in a trial in a court of law is the person accused of a crime.

defense see **defence**.

defensible /dɪˈfɛnsəbəl/ *adjective*
Something such as an action, opinion or procedure is **defensible** if it can be justified or supported as being right: *a defensible reaction.* [*same as* **justifiable**; *opposite* **indefensible**]

defensive /dɪˈfɛnsɪv/ *adjective*
1 Defensive describes equipment, devices and means relating to defence: *defensive weapons.* **2** Someone who is **defensive** speaks or behaves as if they think they are being criticized: *a defensive reply* □ *She became quite defensive about her plans.* — *adverb* **defensively:** *'It was a bargain,' he said defensively.*

▻ ***phrase*** You are **on the defensive** when you say or do something to protect or justify yourself, because you think you are being criticized or attacked: *'What do you mean by 'over-detailed'?' she asked, immediately on the defensive.*

defer[1] /dɪˈfɜː(r)/ *verb*: **defers, deferring, deferred**
You **defer** to someone, or to their experience, when you accept their opinion, or do as they want, out of respect for them: *He seemed to defer to his wife in everything.* [see also **deference**]

defer[2] /dɪˈfɜː(r)/ *verb*: **defers, deferring, deferred**
You **defer** something when you postpone it or put it off till a later time: *Could we defer our discussions till tomorrow?* □ *I can't defer my departure any longer.*

deference /ˈdɛfərəns/ *noun* (*uncount*)
You show **deference** to someone when you treat them respectfully and politely: *In my day teachers were always treated with deference.*

▻ ***phrases*** You do something **in deference to** or **out of deference to** someone when you act towards them in a particular way from motives of respect: *He used to dress respectably when staying at home, out of deference to his parents.* □ *In deference to her professor she refused to discuss the department's affairs with the press.*

deferential /dɛfəˈrɛnʃəl/ *adjective*
Deferential behaviour is respectful and polite: *He had been instructed to behave in a deferential manner towards customers.* — *adverb* **deferentially:** *He took their coats deferentially and led them to a table.*

defiance /dɪ'faɪəns/ *noun* (*uncount*)
Defiance is disobedient or uncooperative behaviour combined with a lack of concern about whether people disapprove of you or not: *She walked out, banging the door in a final gesture of defiance.*
▻ ***phrase*** You do something **in defiance of** a person, order or rule, when you do something that is forbidden by them: *They went on wearing make-up in defiance of school rules.*

defiant /dɪ'faɪənt/ *adjective*
You are **defiant** when you refuse to obey or co-operate with someone, and show that you don't mind their disapproval: *I've tried to get him to apologize, but he remains defiant.* □ *a defiant glance.* [*opposite* **submissive, cowed**] — *adverb* **defiantly:** *She used to remain defiantly sitting during the National Anthem.*

deficient /dɪ'fɪʃənt/ *adjective*
1 Something is **deficient** if it is not enough, or not good enough: *Teachers have to put up with rebellious pupils and deficient equipment.* [*same as* **inadequate**] **2** Someone or something is **deficient** in something when they do not have enough of it: *Old people's bones are generally deficient in calcium.* [*same as* **lacking**] — *noun* (*uncount or count*) **deficiency:** *vitamin deficiency* □ *She was perfectly aware of her deficiencies as an organizer.*

deficit /'dɛfəsɪt/ *noun*: **deficits**
A **deficit** is the amount by which a quantity, especially of money, is less than what is required, *eg* the amount by which a person's or organization's expenditure is greater than their income: *The deficit for the year amounted to £9,050.* □ *the trade deficit.* [*same as* **shortfall**; *opposite* **surplus**]

defile /dɪ'faɪl/ *verb*: **defiles, defiling, defiled**
To **defile** something pure, precious or holy is to spoil, dirty or pollute it: *Our rivers and lakes are being defiled by factory waste.*

define /dɪ'faɪn/ *verb*: **defines, defining, defined**
1 You **define** something such as a purpose or duty when you explain what it is: *The aims of the project must be clearly defined before we start.* [*same as* **set out**] **2** You **define** a word when you explain what it means: *Older dictionaries define a hobby as 'a small horse'.* **3** Something that **is** clearly **defined** against a contrasting background has a strong clear outline or form: *mountains clearly defined against the setting sun.*

definite /'dɛfɪnət/ *adjective*
1 A **definite** arrangement, or date for something, has been settled and is unlikely to be altered: *Can we arrange a definite time for the meeting?* [*opposite* **provisional**] **2** A **definite** plan or purpose has been clearly thought out: *I was wandering round the shops with no very definite aim.* [*opposite* **vague**] **3 Definite** news is news that is certain, or known to be true: *I'll call you as soon as I have any definite facts to report.*

definite article /dɛfɪnət 'ɑːtɪkəl/ *noun* (*grammar*): **definite articles**
The **definite article** is the determiner *the*. [see also **article, indefinite article**]

definitely /'dɛfɪnətlɪ/ *adverb*
1 (*sentence adverb*) You say that something is **definitely** so if it is certain, or known to be so: *You were definitely told about this before.* □ *He's definitely leaving at the end of the month.* **2** (*sentence adverb*) You say you **definitely** think something if that is your firm opinion: *I definitely agree that we should wait.* **3** Something is decided **definitely** when it is settled and unlikely to be altered: *We won't decide definitely about tomorrow's walk till we see what the weather is like.*

definition /dɛfɪ'nɪʃən/ *noun*: **definitions**
1 A **definition** of a thing or a word is an explanation of what it is or what it means: *One of the definitions of 'nice' is 'hard to please'.* **2** (*uncount*) **Definition** is clearness of outline or form: *Some of the photos lack definition.*
▻ ***phrase*** You say that something is a certain kind of thing, or has a certain quality, **by definition**, if that is the way it is because of what it is: *An essay is by definition experimental or exploratory.*

definitive /dɪ'fɪnɪtɪv/ *adjective*
1 The **definitive** book on a particular subject, or production of a particular play, or performance of a piece of music, is the best or most satisfactory that has been done, or that could ever, in your opinion, be done. **2** A **definitive** judgement or ruling on something is a clear one, about which there can be no doubt. — *adverb* **definitively:** *Sherwin has written definitively on this subject in a recently published article.*

deflate /diː'fleɪt/ *verb*: **deflates, deflating, deflated**
1 You **deflate** a tyre by letting air out of it; a balloon or tyre **deflates** when it collapses or shrinks as air comes out of it. **2** To **deflate** someone's reputation or opinion of themselves is to lower it or reduce it considerably: *It was merely an attempt to deflate his confidence.* **3** You **are deflated** when something happens to disappoint you or destroy your confidence or expectations: *The news deflated us a bit.* **4** (*economics*) To **deflate** a country's economy is to reduce the amount of money in circulation, and therefore also the amount of economic activity. — *adjective* **deflated:** *He didn't get the job, and seemed very deflated when I last saw him.*

deflation /diː'fleɪʃən/ *noun* (*uncount*; *economics*)
Deflation of a country's economy is the reduction of the amount of money in circulation, resulting in a lower level of industrial activity, industrial output and employment, and a lower rate of increase in wages and prices. [see also **inflation**] — *adjective* **deflationary:** *The Chancellor must take deflationary measures.*

deflect /dɪ'flɛkt/ *verb*: **deflects, deflecting, deflected**
1 Something that is moving **is deflected** when it is caused to change direction: *He demonstrated that a compass needle could be deflected by an electric current.* **2** You **deflect** someone from their purpose when you persuade them to change their mind, *eg* by suggesting a more attractive course of action: *She refused to be deflected.* [*same as* **sidetrack**] **3** You **deflect** something such as attention or criticism from something or someone by directing it towards something else, or reducing its effect: *They emphasized the drop in inflation and the closing of the trade gap, in an attempt to deflect attention from unemployment.* [*same as* **divert**]

deform /dɪ'fɔːm/ *verb*: **deforms, deforming, deformed**
Something **deforms** a person's body or an object when it alters its shape from what is normal and natural: *Arthritis can severely deform the hands and fingers.* — *adjective* **deformed:** *deformed limbs.*

deformity /dɪ'fɔːmɪtɪ/ *noun*: **deformities**
1 A **deformity** is a wrongly shaped part of a person's body, or of an object: *The drug had long been suspected of causing deformities in the unborn child.* **2** (*uncount*) **Deformity** is the condition of having a deformed part: *What types of deformity can the drug cause?*

defraud /dɪ'frɔːd/ *verb*: **defrauds, defrauding, defrauded**
To **defraud** a person or organization is to cheat them by preventing them from getting something they have a right to, or stealing something that belongs to them:

She had already defrauded the company of $40000 when she was discovered. [*same as* **cheat**; see also **fraud**]

defray /dɪˈfreɪ/ *verb*: **defrays, defraying, defrayed**
(*formal*) You **defray** someone's costs or expenses when you give money that equals what they have spent. [*same as* **reimburse**]

defrost /diːˈfrɒst/ *verb*: **defrosts, defrosting, defrosted**
1 You **defrost** frozen food by removing it from the freezer and letting it reach a temperature at which it is suitable for eating or cooking; frozen food **defrosts** when its temperature rises above freezing point. **2** You **defrost** a freezer or refrigerator by switching it off to allow the ice formed inside it to melt; a fridge or freezer **defrosts** when the ice formed inside it melts.

deft /dɛft/ *adjective*
A **deft** movement is skilful, neat and quick: *She wound the bandage round his arm and tied it in a deft bow.* — *adverb* **deftly:** *She deftly steered him away from the computer-games counter.*

defunct /dɪˈfʌŋkt/ *adjective* (*sometimes humorous*)
Something that is **defunct** no longer exists, no longer works, is no longer usable, or has already served its function: *I used to serve on the entertainments committee, now defunct.*

defuse /diˈfjuːz/ *verb*: **defuse, defusing, defused**
1 To **defuse** a bomb is to remove the fuse from it so that it cannot explode. **2** You **defuse** a dangerous or tense situation when you succeed in calming it down by sorting out the trouble that is causing it.

defy /diˈfaɪ/ *verb*: **defies, defying, defied**
1 You **defy** people, laws, or an authority, when you refuse to obey them: *You are defying the law if you keep a dog without a licence.* [*same as* **flout**] **2** You **defy** someone to do something you consider impossible when you challenge them to do it: *I defy you to think of any good reason why school blazers should not be abolished.* **3** Something **defies** explanation, understanding, analysis or description if it is so strange that it cannot be explained, understood, analysed or described: *Her enthusiasm for cold wet walks defies comprehension.*

degenerate *verb*; *adjective*; *noun*
▻ ***verb*** /dɪˈdʒɛnəreɪt/: **degenerates, degenerating, degenerated**
Someone or something **degenerates** when they pass into a worse state: *As soon as money was mentioned the conversation degenerated into an argument.* [compare **deteriorate**] — *noun* (*uncount*) **degeneration** /dɪdʒɛnəˈreɪʃən/: *The speed of mental degeneration in Alzheimer's Disease varies from patient to patient.*
▻ ***adjective*** /dɪˈdʒɛnərət/
You call a person **degenerate** if morally and spiritually they fall below the standard that you consider right.
▻ ***noun***: **degenerates**
You call someone a **degenerate** if they behave in a way that you consider disgracefully self-indulgent or morally shocking.

degradation /dɛgrəˈdeɪʃən/ *noun* (*uncount*)
Someone who lives in, or is reduced to, **degradation** lives in conditions of extreme poverty and dirt: *the degradation of life in the refugee camp.*

degrade /dɪˈgreɪd/ *verb*: **degrades, degrading, degraded**
1 Something **degrades** people if it reduces others' respect for them: *Pornographic films and magazines tend to degrade women.* **2** (*chemistry*) Materials **degrade** when they decompose. — *adjective* **degrading:** *It's degrading for charities to have to beg the public for money when funding could be organized through the government.*

degree /dɪˈgriː/ *noun*: **degrees**
1 The **degree** to which something is so is the extent to which it is so; the **degree** of something is the amount of it: *Her mental faculties had deteriorated to a worrying degree.* □ *By the end of the course they could all juggle with three balls, with varying degrees of skill.* **2** You take a **degree** when you take a course at a university, with a set of exams at the end of your studies; you obtain a **degree** when you pass the exams: *She has a Cambridge degree.* □ *He got a first-class degree in chemistry from Manchester University.* **3** A **degree** is **a** a unit of measurement of temperature, expressed by the symbol (°): *18° centigrade.* **b** a unit of measurement of angles, latitude or longitude, expressed by the symbol (°): *Singapore is 1.75° north of the equator.*

dehydrate /diːhaɪˈdreɪt/ *verb*: **dehydrates, dehydrating, dehydrated**
1 Food **is dehydrated** by removing all the water from it. **2** People **are dehydrated** when they are weak and exhausted as a result of losing too much water from their bodies. — *adjective* **dehydrated:** *We keep packets of dehydrated soup in stock for campers.* — *noun* (*uncount*) **dehydration** /diːhaɪˈdreɪʃən/: *Dysentery can cause severe dehydration in a young baby.*

deign /deɪn/ *verb*: **deigns, deigning, deigned**
You **deign** to do something that you consider too unimportant for you when you unwillingly do it: *He occasionally deigned to attend school plays and concerts.* [*same as* **condescend**]

deity /ˈdeɪətɪ/ *noun* (*formal*): **deities**
A **deity** is a god or goddess: *the Greek and Roman deities.*

dejected /dɪˈdʒɛktɪd/ *adjective*
Someone who is **dejected** is miserable, depressed or disappointed: *She wore a dejected expression.* □ *The team returned home thoroughly dejected.* — *adverb* **dejectedly:** *She gazed dejectedly out at the rain.* — *noun* (*uncount*) **dejection** /dɪˈdʒɛkʃən/: *He was in a state of utter dejection about his exam results.*

delay /dɪˈleɪ/ *verb*; *noun*
▻ ***verb***: **delays, delaying, delayed**
1 Something **delays** you when it slows you down or makes you late: *The train was delayed for 25 minutes outside Newcastle.* □ *The 10.50 flight has been delayed by fog.* □ *What delayed you?* [*same as* **hold up**] **2** You **delay** doing something when you put it off or postpone it to a later time: *The start of the meeting was delayed by five minutes.* □ *I delayed writing till I had more information.* □ *We've got a bare week to get this job done, so we mustn't delay.* **3** Something **delays** a process if it causes it to take longer than expected: *Even a slight degree of deafness can delay a child's development.* [*same as* **hold up**]
▻ ***noun*** (*count or uncount*): **delays**
There is a **delay** when something takes longer, or happens later, than expected: *After a series of delays and difficulties the building work is now complete.* □ *We'll send an ambulance without delay.* □ *All flights to Europe are subject to delay.*

delectable /dɪˈlɛktəbəl/ *adjective* (*literary, or informal*)
1 You call food **delectable** if it is delicious. **2** If you call a person **delectable**, you mean that they are attractive: *These clothes may look OK on delectable young models, but they'd do nothing for me.*

delegate *noun*; *verb*
▻ ***noun*** /ˈdɛlɪgət/: **delegates**
A **delegate** at a meeting or conference is someone chosen by a group of people to be their representative at it and act and speak for them: *Each local branch was invited to send two delegates to the annual conference.*

▷ ***verb*** /ˈdɛlɪgeɪt/: **delegates, delegating, delegated**
1 You **delegate** someone to do something when you ask them officially or formally to do it for you: *A spokesman was delegated by the Palace to make an announcement to the press.* **2** You **delegate** a responsibility or duty when you ask someone else to carry it out for you: *It's time you delegated some of these tasks to junior colleagues.*

delegation /dɛlɪˈgeɪʃən/ *noun*: **delegations**
1 A **delegation** is a group of people sent to a meeting or conference by a large body of people to be their representatives, and act or speak for them: *The British delegation arrived late.* **2** (*uncount*) **Delegation** is the act of asking someone, especially a junior colleague, to carry out, or take over, a duty or responsibility of yours.

delete /dɪˈliːt/ *verb*: **deletes, deleting, deleted**
You **delete** something written down when you cross it out or rub it out; you **delete** material from a computer disk, file or screen when you get rid of it: *Highlight the passage to be deleted.* [*same as* **rub out, erase**] — *noun* (*count or uncount*) **deletion** /dɪˈliːʃən/: *The essay was untidily written and full of deletions.*

deliberate *adjective*; *verb*
▷ ***adjective*** /dɪˈlɪbərət/
1 Something you do is **deliberate** if you intended or planned to do it, as distinct from doing it by accident: *You made a deliberate attempt to mislead us.* □ *deliberate lies* □ *That didn't look like an accident to me; it looked deliberate.* [*same as* **intentional**] **2** A movement or action is slow and **deliberate** if it is slow and careful: *slow deliberate steps.*
▷ ***verb*** /dɪˈlɪbəreɪt/: **deliberates, deliberating, deliberated**
You **deliberate** about something when you think about it carefully before taking a decision: *I'm still deliberating over the job offer.* □ *The jury were out deliberating for six hours before reaching a verdict.*

deliberately /dɪˈlɪbərətlɪ/ *adverb*
1 You **deliberately** do something, or do it **deliberately**, if you do it having planned or intended to do it: *You deliberately disobeyed me.* □ *Don't be angry with him; he didn't break it deliberately.* [*same as* **intentionally, purposely, on purpose**] **2** You do something slowly and **deliberately** when you do it in a slow and careful manner: *She spoke slowly and deliberately, as if slightly stunned.*

deliberation /dɪlɪbəˈreɪʃən/ *noun*: **deliberations**
1 (*uncount*) **Deliberation** is careful thought about something: *I decided after an hour or so's deliberation to accept her offer.* **2** (*used in the plural*) **Deliberations** are discussions, especially of a formal kind: *The committee carried on its deliberations in secret.* **3** (*uncount*) You do something with **deliberation** when you do it in a slow and careful manner: *She worked through the evidence with deliberation, making sure she missed nothing.*

delicacy /ˈdɛlɪkəsɪ/ *noun*: **delicacies**
1 (*uncount*) **Delicacy** of shape or form is a quality that combines neatness, prettiness and gracefulness: *His face and features had an almost feminine delicacy.* [*same as* **daintiness**] **2** You act or speak with **delicacy** when you do so with care for people's feelings: *With admirable delicacy she changed the subject.* [*same as* **tact**] **3** The **delicacy** of a situation or issue is its ability to become embarrassing, awkward or dangerous if not handled carefully: *She wished to consult my friend Holmes on a matter of the utmost delicacy.* **4** A **delicacy** is a rare, expensive and delicious food: *The table was laden with delicacies such as smoked salmon, caviare and truffles.*

delicate /ˈdɛlɪkət/ *adjective*
1 Something that is **delicate** is neat, pretty and graceful: *The frost had created delicate patterns on the window.* □ *narrow, delicate fingers.* [*same as* **dainty**; *opposite* **coarse**] **2** A **delicate** object is easily broken, so must be handled gently: *delicate china dishes.* [*same as* **fragile**] **3** A **delicate** situation or issue may become embarrassing, awkward or dangerous unless it is dealt with carefully: *the delicate subject of money.* [*same as* **sensitive**] **4** You are **delicate** in your handling of a person when you try to avoid offending or embarrassing them; a situation or issue requires **delicate** handling if it is likely to become embarrassing, awkward or dangerous: *She passed over his blunder in delicate silence.* [*same as* **tactful**] **5** A person who is **delicate** is frequently ill: *As a boy he was delicate and missed a lot of schooling.* [*opposite* **robust**] **6** A **delicate** colour, taste or smell is pleasantly subtle rather than strong: *a delicate shade of blue.* **7** A **delicate** movement is light and graceful: *Their dancing consists chiefly of delicate arm and hand gestures.* [*opposite* **clumsy**] **8** A **delicate** scientific instrument or device is one that is sensitive to small variations. [*same as* **precision**] — *adverb* **delicately:** *delicately carved figures* □ *He delicately avoided the topic of punctuality.* □ *The whole matter is too delicately poised to leave in the hands of amateurs.*

delicatessen /dɛlɪkəˈtɛsən/ *noun*: **delicatessens**
A **delicatessen** is a shop selling foods prepared ready for the table, especially cooked meats, cheeses and unusual or imported foods.

delicious /dɪˈlɪʃəs/ *adjective*
1 Food that is **delicious** has a very pleasant taste: *That dessert was simply delicious.* [*same as* **tasty, palatable**] **2** (*informal*) Something pleasing or delightful may be described as **delicious**: *She had a delicious sense of humour.* [*same as* **delightful, exquisite**] — *adverb* (*usually intensifying*) **deliciously:** *The whole situation was deliciously funny.*

delight /dɪˈlaɪt/ *noun*; *verb*
▷ ***noun***: **delights**
1 (*uncount*) **Delight** is a feeling of great pleasure or satisfaction: *To her delight she realized that she was well in the lead.* **2** (*uncount or count*) You take **delight** or a **delight** in something if you enjoy it or get pleasure from it: *He evidently took a delight in hurting people's feelings.* [*same as* take **pleasure** in] **3** Something that gives you pleasure or joy can be referred to as a **delight**: *The delights of camping are not for me.*
▷ ***verb***: **delights, delighting, delighted**
1 Something **delights** you if it fills you with pleasure: *The prospect of a grandchild delighted them both.* **2** You **delight** in something if you enjoy it or get pleasure from it: *He used to delight in grammatical problems of all sorts.*

delighted /dɪˈlaɪtɪd/ *adjective*
1 You are **delighted** when you are very pleased about something: *We're delighted at the response to the appeal.* □ *I'm delighted to meet your wife at last.* **2** You say you are **delighted** to do something if you are glad or willing to do it: *I'm delighted to have been of assistance.* — *adverb* **delightedly:** *The children laughed and clapped delightedly.*

delightful /dɪˈlaɪtfʊl/ *adjective*
Someone or something that is **delightful** gives a lot of joy or pleasure: *a delightful performance*
▷ ***adverb***: **delightfully:** *The evening passed delightfully.*

delinquent /dɪˈlɪŋkwənt/ *adjective*; *noun*
▷ ***adjective*** (*old*)
Delinquent describes young people who frequently

break the law, or the behaviour young people like these: *delinquent conduct.*

▻ ***noun***: **delinquents:** *juvenile delinquents.*

delirious /dɪˈlɪrɪəs/ *adjective*

1 A person with a high fever is **delirious** when they are so ill that their thoughts and speech become muddled and confused. **2** (*informal*) People are **delirious** about something if they are thrilled or excited about it: *They toured Europe, performing to delirious audiences of teenagers.*

▻ ***adverb*** (*often intensifying; informal*) **deliriously:** *He lay talking deliriously.* □ *They seem deliriously happy.*

delirium /dɪˈlɪrɪəm/ *noun* (*uncount*)

1 Delirium is a state of mental confusion in a person who is very ill with a high fever. **2** (*literary*) Wild excitement or delight can also be called **delirium**: *the delirium of first love.*

deliver /dɪˈlɪvə(r)/ *verb*: **delivers, delivering, delivered**

1 Something **is delivered** to you when it is brought to you, especially at your home address or office: *The mail usually gets delivered at about 8.30 am.* □ *Your order will be delivered on Friday.* **2** You **deliver** a speech or lecture when you give it: *He had to deliver his series of lectures in a disused cinema.* **3** A doctor or nurse **delivers** a baby when they attend to the mother during its birth: *As a medical student he had had plenty of practice at delivering babies.* **4** (*formal*) You **deliver** a blow to someone when you hit them: *She delivered a sharp blow to the side of his head.* **5** (*old, or literary*) To **deliver** someone from harm or captivity is to rescue them from it: *Deliver us from evil.* **6** (*literary*) Fate or chance **delivers** something or someone into your hands when you suddenly have them in your power. **7** A business **delivers** something that it has been asked to make or produce when it completes and hands over the finished product to the purchaser: *They have a bad reputation for taking orders and failing to deliver.*

▻ ***phrase*** (*informal*) People **deliver the goods** when they do what they have promised or undertaken to do.

deliverance /dɪˈlɪvrəns/ *noun* (*uncount; literary*)

Deliverance from harm, evil or captivity is rescue from it: *We thank God for our deliverance from this dreadful disease.*

delivery /dɪˈlivərɪ/ *noun*: **deliveries**

1 (*uncount*) **Delivery** of letters and parcels is the act or process of bringing them to you at your home address or office: *Allow 21 days for delivery.* **2** A **delivery** is an individual act of delivering mail or goods, or the goods or mail delivered: *We have two deliveries of mail a day.* □ *They're sending over an extra delivery of groceries this afternoon.* **3** (*count or uncount*) **Delivery** is the process of giving birth to a baby: *It was a straightforward delivery.* **4** (*uncount*) A person's **delivery** is the way they speak when talking to an audience: *His delivery was too fast and not loud enough.*

delta /ˈdɛltə/ *noun*: **deltas**

A **delta** is a flat, triangular area of land at the mouth of a river, where it splits into several small rivers that spread out towards the coast: *the Nile Delta.*

delude /dɪˈluːd/ *verb*: **deludes, deluding, deluded**

You **are deluded** when you are persuaded to believe something that is not true: *We were deluded into thinking that our jobs were safe.* □ *She was deluded by their flattering talk.* □ *I could no longer delude myself that there was any future for me in the firm.*

deluge /ˈdɛljuːdʒ/ *noun; verb*

▻ ***noun***: **deluges**

1 A **deluge** is a heavy fall of rain or a flood: *They arrived home soaked, having been caught in a deluge on the way.* **2** A **deluge** of things is an overwhelming number of them all arriving at the same time: *There was another deluge of fan mail by today's post.*

▻ ***verb***: **deluges, deluging, deluged**

You **are deluged** with things when an overwhelming number of them arrive at the same time: *We advertised a baldness cure on television and were immediately deluged with queries.*

delusion /dɪˈluːʒən/ *noun*: **delusions**

A **delusion** is a false or mistaken belief, especially one that may be a symptom of mental disturbance: *She's under the delusion that she can do any job better than anyone else.*

de luxe /dɪˈlʌks/ *adjective*

A **de luxe** model or version of something is one that is better equipped or more luxurious than the standard model or version: *de luxe bathroom fittings.*

delve /dɛlv/ *verb*: **delves, delving, delved**

1 You **delve** inside or into something such as a bag, box or cupboard when you search inside it: *She delved into her shopping bag and brought out her library book.* **2** You **delve** into a subject when you investigate it: *There isn't space in this book to delve deeper into their history.*

demagogue /ˈdɛməgɒg/ *noun* (*derogatory*): **demagogues**

A **demagogue** is a political leader and public speaker who tries to win people's support by appealing to their feelings, emotions and prejudices, rather than by using reason and logical argument.

demand /dɪˈmɑːnd/ *verb; noun*

▻ ***verb***: **demands, demanding, demanded**

1 You **demand** something that you think you have a right to when you ask for it in a determined manner: *They are demanding higher pay and better conditions of work.* □ *I demand to see my lawyer.* □ *She said the file was confidential and demanded that I should return it* (or *that I return it*) *immediately.* **2** You **demand** something when you ask a question in an impatient manner: *'Where do you think you're going?' he demanded.* **3** A job or task **demands** certain qualities if they are needed for it: *Teaching demands patience and dedication.* [*same as* **require**]

▻ ***noun***: **demands**

1 A **demand** is a strongly expressed request for something: *We must not give in to the hijackers' demands.* □ *The police agreed to his demand for a secret interview.* **2** (*uncount, or used in the singular*) There is a **demand** for something when people want it: *We're having 50000 extra copies printed to cope with the demand.* **3** (*usually in the plural*) The **demands** of something are the things it needs or requires: *Mothers somehow manage to cope with the demands of a job and family.*

▻ ***phrases*** **1** Something is **in demand** if people want it: *ELT textbooks are always in demand.* **2** Something is available **on demand** if you can get it when you ask for it: *You can have an HIV test on demand.* [*same as* **on request**]

demanding /dɪˈmɑːndɪŋ/ *adjective*

1 A **demanding** job or task needs a lot of attention, energy and skill: *The work is demanding but I enjoy it.* [compare **challenging**] **2** A **demanding** person is someone who is difficult to deal with or to please: *The children were always at their most troublesome and demanding on holiday.*

demarcation /diːmɑːˈkeɪʃən/ *noun* (*uncount*)

Demarcation is the establishment of limits, *eg* between territories, or indicating which workers do what types of work in a factory or other workplace.

demean /dɪˈmiːn/ *verb*: **demeans, demeaning, demeaned**

You **demean** yourself when you act in an undignified

or unworthy way; you **demean** something such as your position or office when you do something that is unworthy of it: *I would not demean myself by arguing about such a trivial sum.*

demeaning /dɪ'miːnɪŋ/ *adjective*
1 A **demeaning** job or task is undignified or humiliating. **2 Demeaning** behaviour is unworthy of you, and reduces people's respect for you.

demeanour (*AmE* **demeanor**) /dɪ'miːnə(r)/ *noun* (*uncount*)
Your **demeanour** is the way you move and behave, seen as an indication of your personality or of your present mood: *a woman of calm and dignified demeanour* □ *Did you observe any change in his demeanour?* [compare **bearing**]

demented /dɪ'mɛntɪd/ *adjective* (*sometimes informal*)
Someone who is **demented** is mad or crazy: *He was nearly demented with the pain.* □ *demented behaviour.* — *adverb* **dementedly:** *Everyone was rushing round dementedly.*

dementia /dɪ'mɛnʃə/ *noun* (*uncount*; *psychology*)
Dementia is a loss or severe lessening of normal mental ability and functioning, occurring especially in the elderly.

demise /dɪ'maɪz/ *noun* (*used in the singular, formal*)
The **demise** of someone or something is their death or end: *his tragically early demise* □ *Are we seeing the demise of the health service?*

demo /'dɛmoʊ/ *noun* (*informal*): **demos**
A **demo** is a demonstration (senses 1 and 2).

democracy /dɪ'mɒkrəsɪ/ *noun*: **democracies**
1 (*uncount*) **Democracy** is a system of government or management in which people choose their leaders and take decisions by voting. **2** A **democracy** is a country in which the citizens choose their government by voting.

democrat /'dɛməkrat/ *noun*: **democrats**
Someone who is a **democrat** supports the principles of democracy and is in favour of personal liberty and equality between people.

democratic /dɛmə'kratɪk/ *adjective*
1 In a **democratic** country or organization, people choose their leaders and take decisions by voting: *a democratic form of government.* **2** A **democratic** person is someone who supports the principles of democracy, is in favour of personal liberty and equal rights, and of taking decisions by voting: *Our boss is fairly democratic.* □ *a democratic decision.* — *adverb* **democratically:** *democratically elected leaders.*

demolish /dɪ'mɒlɪʃ/ *verb*: **demolishes, demolishing, demolished**
1 A building is **demolished** when it is pulled down, *eg* because it is dangerous, old, or not needed any more: *The old city centre was almost completely demolished to make way for the new civic buildings.* **2** You **demolish** a theory or argument when you destroy it by proving it wrong. — *noun* (*uncount*) **demolition** /dɛmə'lɪʃən/: *A large crowd had gathered to watch the demolition of the tower block.*

demon /'diːmən/ *noun*: **demons**
A **demon** is an evil spirit or a devil: *He fled in terror as though pursued by demons from hell.*

demonic /dɪ'mɒnɪk/ *adjective*
Something **demonic** is evil, or associated with the Devil: *demonic powers.*

demonstrable /dɪ'mɒnstrəbəl/ *adjective*
Something that is **demonstrable** can be proved or shown: *Sadly, children show a demonstrable variation in performance in relation to social background.* — *adverb* **demonstrably:** *The old method is demonstrably better.*

demonstrate /'dɛmənstreɪt/ *verb*: **demonstrates, demonstrating, demonstrated**
1 You **demonstrate** something to someone when you show them how it works or how to do it: *They demonstrated how to do the dance.* **2** Something **demonstrates** a particular fact or circumstance when it is, or provides, an example of it: *This demonstrates the need for even tighter surveillance at shopping centres.* **3** You **demonstrate** a particular quality when you show that you have it: *No-one demonstrated any enthusiasm for an office party this year.* **4** People **demonstrate** when they join in a meeting or a march to show their support of, or opposition to, something: *Crowds demonstrating against the poll tax poured into Trafalgar Square.* [*same as* **display, exhibit**]

demonstration /dɛmən'streɪʃən/ *noun*: **demonstrations**
1 A **demonstration** is a public march or meeting that people take part in to express their support of, or opposition to, something: *Demonstrations were held in many cities today to protest against the coal-pit closures.* **2** Someone gives a **demonstration** of something when they show people how to do it, or how it works, sometimes with a formal talk or explanation: *Flower-arranging demonstrations have always proved very popular.* **3** (*used in the singular*) Something is a **demonstration** of a fact or circumstance if it is, or provides, an example of it: *I think the size of tonight's audience is an impressive demonstration of how much public support there is for the cause.* **4** (*count or uncount*) A **demonstration** of a feeling or quality is an expression or indication of it: *We greatly appreciated the many demonstrations of sympathy from the public.*

demonstrative /dɪ'mɒnstrətɪv/ *adjective*
1 A **demonstrative** person shows their affection openly and easily through physical gestures such as kisses and hugs. **2** (*grammar*) The **demonstrative** pronouns and determiners are *this, that, these* and *those*, which indicate or point out people or things.

demonstrator /'dɛmənstreɪtə(r)/ *noun*: **demonstrators**
A **demonstrator** is **1** someone taking part in a public protest, meeting or march, in support of, or in opposition to, something: *A crowd of demonstrators had surrounded the embassy.* **2** a person who explains how something works, or shows you how to do something: *Our demonstrator will shortly show you how to fit the parts of the vacuum cleaner.*

demoralize /dɪ'mɒrəlaɪz/ or **demoralise** *verb*: **demoralizes, demoralizing, demoralized**
Something **demoralizes** you when it depresses you and reduces your confidence in what you are doing: *Naturally we were demoralized by our lack of success.* [*same as* **discourage**] — *adjective* **demoralized:** *The streets are full of homeless, jobless, demoralized teenagers.* — *noun* (*uncount*) **demoralization:** *Her demoralization increased as she realized how few allies she had left.*

demote /diː'moʊt/ *verb*: **demotes, demoting, demoted**
You **are demoted** when you are reduced to a lower rank, *eg* in the armed forces, as a punishment: *He was demoted to the ranks.*

demur /dɪ'mɜː(r)/ *verb* (*formal*): **demurs, demurring, demurred**
You **demur** when you politely refuse an offer or an invitation to do something: *I invited him to join us for a drink, but he demurred.*

demure /dɪ'mjʊə(r)/ *adjective*
Someone, especially a girl or a young woman, who is

demure, has a shy, quiet manner, and behaves and dresses modestly and correctly: *Her manner was demure and ladylike.* □ *demure-looking schoolgirls.* — *adverb* **demurely:** *She sat with her hands demurely folded in her lap.*

den /dɛn/ *noun*: **dens**
1 The **den** of a wild animal such as a wolf, fox, bear or lion is its home. **2** The secret meeting place or headquarters of a group of criminals may be referred to as a **den**: *a den of forgers.*

denial /dɪˈnaɪəl/ *noun*: **denials**
1 (*count or uncount*) You issue a **denial** of a charge or accusation made against you when you state that it is false: *She made a complete denial of all charges.* **2** (*uncount, or used in the singular*) The **denial** of a right to someone is a refusal to let them have it: *the denial of justice to political prisoners.*

denigrate /ˈdɛnɪgreɪt/ *verb*: **denigrates, denigrating, denigrated**
You **denigrate** someone or something when you criticize them unjustly: *The very newspapers that had idolized the princess now denigrated her.* [*same as* **disparage, malign, revile**]

denim /ˈdɛnɪm/ *noun*: **denims**
1 (*uncount*) **Denim** is the strong thick cotton cloth from which clothes, especially jeans, are made: *a denim jacket.* **2** **Denims** are denim trousers, or jeans: *You can pay the earth for a new pair of denims these days.*

denomination /dɪnɒmɪˈneɪʃən/ *noun*: **denominations**
A **denomination** is one of the groups or divisions within a particular religion.

denominator /dɪˈnɒmɪneɪtə(r)/ *noun* (*mathematics*): **denominators**
The **denominator** in a fraction is the number below the line, like 13 in $\frac{2}{13}$.

denote /dɪˈnoʊt/ *verb*: **denotes, denoting, denoted**
1 A sign or symbol that **denotes** something represents or stands for it: *The number of stripes on an officer's sleeve denotes his or her rank.* **2** One thing **denotes** another if it is an indication or sign of it: *I take it that your silence denotes agreement?* **3** A word or name **denotes** something if that is what it means or indicates: *The placename element 'knock' denotes a hill.*

denounce /dɪˈnaʊns/ *verb*: **denounces, denouncing, denounced**
You **denounce** someone or something when you publicly accuse or condemn them: *Some historians have denounced them as unscrupulous.*

dense /dɛns/ *adjective*: **denser, densest**
1 Something such as a crowd or forest, that is **dense**, contains people or things closely packed together: *The body was discovered in dense bushes at the edge of the park.* **2** **Dense** smoke, fog or mist is very thick and difficult to see through. **3** (*informal, derogatory*) If you call someone dense you mean that they are too stupid to understand even simple things. [*same as* **thick**] — *adverb* **densely:** *in the densely populated London area.*

density /ˈdɛnsɪtɪ/ *noun*: **densities**
1 The **density** of something within an area is its distribution within it, or the extent to which it fills it: *The density of population is high at the coast, low in the mountainous interior.* **2** (*technical*) The **density** of a substance is the relation of its mass to its volume: *the comparative densities of air and water.*

dent /dɛnt/ *verb*; *noun*
▷ ***verb***: **dents, denting, dented**
You **dent** something when you hit it hard enough to make a hollow in its surface: *I dented the door backing into the garage.* — *adjective* **dented:** *a dented old tin trunk.*
▷ ***noun***: **dents**
1 A **dent** is a hollow in a surface caused by a blow or by pressure: *There was still a dent in the pillow where his head had been.* **2** (*informal*) You say that something has made a **dent** in your income or savings if it cost a lot. [*same as* **hole**]

dental /ˈdɛntəl/ *adjective*
Dental means relating to the teeth, to dentists or to dentistry: *I've got a dental appointment at 11.30.* □ *dental treatment.*

dental surgeon /ˈdɛntəl sɜːdʒən/ *noun*: **dental surgeons**
A **dental surgeon** is a dentist.

dentist /ˈdɛntɪst/ *noun*: **dentists**
1 A **dentist** is a person who looks after and treats people's teeth. **2** A dentist's surgery or place of work is referred to as the **dentist's** or the **dentist**: *an appointment at the dentist's* □ *I need to go to the dentist.*

dentistry /ˈdɛntɪstrɪ/ *noun* (*uncount*)
Dentistry is the study of dental care, or the work or profession of a dentist.

denture /ˈdɛntʃə(r)/ *noun* (*usually in the plural*): **dentures**
Dentures are artificial teeth.

denude /dɪˈnjuːd/ *verb*: **denudes, denuding, denuded**
Something **is denuded** when it is stripped of its covering and made bare: *The November storms arrived, denuding the trees of their last remaining leaves.*

denunciation /dɪnʌnsɪˈeɪʃən/ *noun* (*count or uncount*)
A **denunciation** of someone or something is a strongly expressed public criticism or condemnation of them: *Her speech was a denunciation of the government's financial policy.*

deny /dɪˈnaɪ/ *verb*: **denies, denying, denied**
1 You **deny** something when you say it is not true; you **deny** a charge or accusation when you claim it is false: *He denied the allegations.* □ *He denies taking money from the safe.* □ *She denied that she was responsible for the error.* **2** You **deny** someone something that they want or have a right to when you refuse to let them have it: *He was denied access to his children.*

deodorant /dɪˈoʊdərənt/ *noun* (*uncount or count*): **deodorants**
A **deodorant** is a scented liquid that you apply to your body to get rid of the smell of perspiration: *a bottle of deodorant.*

depart /dɪˈpɑːt/ *verb*: **departs, departing, departed**
1 To **depart** from a place is to leave it: *The bus departs from Victoria Coach Station at 2.25.* **2** You **depart** from the usual or expected way of doing something when you do something different: *Parliament departed from tradition in electing a woman speaker.*

departed /dɪˈpɑːtɪd/ *adjective*
Departed friends and relations are those that have died.

department /dɪˈpɑːtmənt/ *noun*: **departments**
A **department** is a section or division of something, *eg* a part of a store where a particular type of product is sold, or a university faculty teaching a certain subject, or an area of administration within the government: *the men's shoe department.* □ *the English Language department.* □ *the Department of Health and Social Security.* — *adjective* **departmental** /diːpɑːtˈmɛntəl/: *All the teaching staff are required to attend the monthly departmental meeting.*

department store /dɪˈpɑːtmənt stɔː(r)/ *noun*: **department stores**
A **department store** is a large shop, often one of a

chain or series, that contains a number of departments each selling a certain type of product.

departure /dɪˈpɑːtʃə(r)/ *noun*: **departures**
1 (*uncount or count*) **Departure** is the act of leaving a place: *Our departure was delayed while the train was checked.* □ *You have to confirm your flight three days before departure.* **2** A **departure** from a normal or expected procedure is a new or different way of doing things: *This year's office party represents a departure from the usual Christmas Eve drink.*

depend /dɪˈpɛnd/ *verb*: **depends, depending, depended**
1 One person or thing **depends** on another if they cannot live, or survive economically, without them: *The island depends almost entirely on tourism.* □ *She couldn't afford to be ill, with three children depending on her for support.* [*same as* **rely**] **2** You say you can **depend** on someone or something if you know that they will help you or do what is needed: *Can they be depended on to keep to the schedule?* □ *He depended on his wife to correct his English and spelling.* □ *That's the bad thing about Scotland; you can't depend on the weather.* [*same as* **rely**] **3** One circumstance **depends** on another if it cannot come into being without the other: *My acceptance for the course depends on whether I pass all my exams.* □ *'Do you want to go swimming tomorrow?' 'I don't know; it depends on the weather.'*
▻ ***phrases*** **1** You use **depending on** when expressing variation according to circumstances: *We expect a certain level of ability in children applying to the dance school, depending on their age.* **2** You say **it depends** when you are uncertain what answer to make, because of the variety of considerations: *'Am I right or am I wrong?' 'It depends.'*

dependable /dɪˈpɛndəbəl/ *adjective*
You call someone or something **dependable** if you know they will do what you expect or want them to do: *He was one of the most dependable secretaries the club has ever had.* [*same as* **reliable**]

dependant /dɪˈpɛndənt/ *noun*: **dependants**
Your **dependants** are your children and anyone else whom you support financially: *In the event of your death your dependants will be adequately looked after.*

dependence /dɪˈpɛndəns/ *noun* (*uncount*)
Dependence is the state of needing something constantly in order to survive or function properly: *drug dependence.*

dependent /dɪˈpɛndənt/ *adjective*
One person or thing is **dependent** on another if they cannot survive or function without them: *She was crippled with arthritis and physically dependent on her husband.* □ *We are increasingly dependent on television for entertainment.* [see also **dependant**]

depict /dɪˈpɪkt/ *verb*: **depicts, depicting, depicted**
1 An artist or photographer **depicts** someone or something in a certain way when he or she paints, draws or photographs them like that: *Italian life as depicted in films by Fellini.* **2** Writers and others **depict** someone or something in a certain way when they describe or present them like that: *Her novels depict the restricted world of an upper-class country society.* [*same as* **portray**] — *noun* (*count or uncount*) **depiction:** *depictions of the Greek gods* □ *Chaucer's depiction of life in medieval England.*

deplete /dɪˈpliːt/ *verb*: **depletes, depleting, depleted**
A resource, stock or supply **is depleted** when it is reduced: *The office staff has been sadly depleted by redundancies.* — *noun* (*uncount*) **depletion:** *The figures show a serious depletion in stocks.*

deplorable /dɪˈplɔːrəbəl/ *adjective* (*sometimes informal or intensifying*)
If you call something **deplorable** you mean that it is bad, unpleasant or shocking: *The refugees are living in deplorable conditions.* □ *a deplorable waste.* [*same as* **disgraceful**, **scandalous**] — *adverb* **deplorably:** *I think they've treated you deplorably.*

deplore /dɪˈplɔː(r)/ *verb*: **deplores, deploring, deplored**
You say you **deplore** something if you greatly disapprove of it, or consider it wrong, shocking or immoral: *We can only deplore the waste of human life.*

deploy /dɪˈplɔɪ/ *verb*: **deploys, deploying, deployed**
1 To **deploy** troops, resources or equipment is to position or distribute them where they will be most effective. **2** You **deploy** arguments when you prepare them and put them to effective use in a discussion or dispute. — *noun* (*uncount*) **deployment:** *Hospital managers see to the effective deployment of staff.*

depopulate /diːˈpɒpjəleɪt/ *verb*: **depopulates, depopulating, depopulated**
An area **is depopulated** when the number of people living in it is greatly reduced. — *noun* (*uncount*) **depopulation** /diːpɒpjəˈleɪʃən/: *the depopulation of the countryside.*

deport /dɪˈpɔːt/ *verb*: **deports, deporting, deported**
Foreigners **are deported** from a country when its government makes them leave because they have no legal right to be living there, or if they have committed a crime. — *noun* (*uncount or count*) **deportation** /dɪpɔːˈteɪʃən/: *an increase in deportations* □ *She may have to face deportation.*

deportment /dɪˈpɔːtmənt/ *noun* (*uncount, rather old*)
Your **deportment** is the way you hold yourself as you stand or walk. [*same as* **posture, carriage, bearing**]

depose /dɪˈpoʊz/ *verb*: **deposes, deposing, deposed**
Rulers or leaders **are deposed** when they are removed from power by force.

deposit /dɪˈpɒzɪt/ *verb*; *noun*
▻ ***verb***: **deposits, depositing, deposited**
1 (*especially geology or chemistry*) A substance **is deposited** somewhere when it is dropped there and remains lying or collecting: *A layer of volcanic ash several feet thick was deposited over most of the city.* **2** You **deposit** something somewhere when you place it safely there and leave it till you need it again: *We found a left-luggage locker to deposit our bags in for the day.*
▻ ***noun***: **deposits**
1 (*especially geology or chemistry*) A **deposit** is a layer of some substance that has dropped and collected, *eg* over a surface: *deposits of iron ore* **2** You make a **deposit** at the bank when you pay a sum into an account. **3** You pay a **deposit** on something that you have agreed to buy when you pay part of its price: *We've paid the deposit on our new house.* **4** You are charged a **deposit** on equipment that you hire, in addition to the hiring fee, to guarantee the owners against loss or damage, and it is repaid to you when you return the equipment undamaged: *We had to pay a deposit of 20 pence on the locker key.*

depot /ˈdɛpoʊ/ (AmE /ˈdiːpoʊ/ *noun*: **depots**
A **depot** is **1** a storehouse or warehouse. **2** a place where vehicles such as buses or railway locomotives are kept when not in use. **3** (*AmE*) a bus station or railway station.

depraved /dɪˈpreɪvd/ *adjective*
If you call someone **depraved** you mean that they are morally bad or wicked: *depraved minds.* — *noun* (*uncount*) **depravity** /dɪˈpravɪtɪ/: *The story of slavery is a story of depravity and cruelty.*

deprecating /ˈdɛprɪkeɪtɪŋ/ *adjective*

You make a **deprecating** comment or gesture when acknowledging that something is not as good as it could be.

depreciate /dɪ'pri:ʃɪeɪt/ *verb*: **depreciates, depreciating, depreciated**
Something **depreciates** when it loses value: *Property shares have depreciated rapidly.* [*opposite* **appreciate**] — *noun* (*uncount*) **depreciation** /dɪ'pri:ʃɪ'eɪʃən/: *Precious metals are not normally subject to depreciation.*

depress /dɪ'prɛs/ *verb*: **depresses, depressing, depressed**
1 Something **depresses** you when it makes you feel disappointed and hopeless: *It depresses me terribly that I can no longer get about as energetically as I used to.* **2** Business, prices or wages **are depressed** when they are reduced: *The recession has depressed house prices disastrously.* **3** (*formal*) You **depress** something such as a lever or handle when you press it down: *As you depress the key, a hammer strikes the string.*

depressed /dɪ'prɛst/ *adjective*
You are **depressed** when you feel disappointed and hopeless, or when you are suffering from a mental illness that makes you doubt your own worth and abilities: *She's very depressed about not winning.*

depressing /dɪ'prɛsɪŋ/ *adjective*
Something that is **depressing** causes disappointment and a feeling of hopelessness: *It's depressing to fail after trying so hard.* □ *another depressing piece of news.* — *adverb* **depressingly:** *The weather was depressingly cold.*

depression /dɪ'prɛʃən/ *noun*: **depressions**
1 (*uncount*) **Depression** is a feeling of disappointment and hopelessness, or a mental illness that makes you doubt your own worth and abilities: *He suffers from periodic bouts of depression.* **2** A **depression** is a period of economic and industrial inactivity, with high unemployment: *Successive depressions had left their mark on the car industry.* **3** A **depression** in a surface is a hollow: *The archaeologists call these little circular depressions 'cup marks'.*

deprive /dɪ'praɪv/ *verb*: **deprives, depriving, deprived**
To **deprive** someone of something that they need or want is to take it away from them or prevent them from having it: *Deprive someone of air and they can only live a few minutes.* — *noun* (*uncount or count*) **deprivation** /dɛprɪ'veɪʃən/: *They're used to hardship and deprivation.*

deprived /dɪ'praɪvd/ *adjective*
Someone who is **deprived** does not have enough of the things that are considered essential in life: *a deprived childhood.*

depth /dɛpθ/ *noun*: **depths**
1 (*uncount or count*) **Depth** is the distance from the top to bottom of something, or from front to back, or from the surface inwards: *Plant the seeds at a depth of about 4 cm.* □ *The children's pool is less than a metre in depth.* □ *What's the depth of the bookcase?* [see picture at **shape**] **2** (*uncount*) The **depth** of a feeling or emotion is its strength; the **depth** of someone's knowledge is its thoroughness. **3** (*used in the plural*) The **depths** of something are its deepest places or its deepest point: *in the depths of the sea* □ *in the depths of winter* [= in the coldest part of the winter] □ *They were in the depths of despair.* [= they were very unhappy]
▻ ***phrases*** **1** You examine a subject or question **in depth** when you do so thoroughly: *an in-depth report.* **2** You are **out of your depth a** when you are in water too deep to stand up in: *Don't swim out of your depth.* **b** when you are in a situation that is too difficult for you to understand or deal with: *I'm out of my depth in mathematical discussions.*

deputation /dɛpjə'teɪʃən/ *noun*: **deputations**
A **deputation** is a group of people chosen out of a larger body to represent them and speak on their behalf to someone, *eg* to make a protest or complaint.

deputize or **deputise** /'dɛpjətaɪz/ *verb*: **deputizes, deputizing, deputized**
You **deputize** for someone when you temporarily fill their post for them, or act on their behalf: *Mrs Henderson was deputizing for the Principal that week.* [*same as* **stand in**]

deputy /'dɛpjətɪ/ *noun* (*often adjectival*): **deputies**
A **deputy** is second in importance to the boss or head of an organization or department, and is sometimes required to act for them: *the deputy head of the school.*

derail /di:'reɪl/ *verb*: **derails, derailing, derailed**
A train **is derailed** when it comes off the railway lines.

deranged /dɪ'reɪndʒd/ *adjective*
Someone who has become **deranged** has gone mad, especially with grief or worry. [*same as* **unbalanced, insane**]

derelict /'dɛrəlɪkt/ *adjective*
A **derelict** building is an empty, abandoned and neglected one that is becoming a ruin.

deride /dɪ'raɪd/ *verb*: **derides, deriding, derided**
You **deride** someone or something when you laugh scornfully at them: *He used to deride her efforts at drawing.*

derision /dɪ'rɪʒən/ *noun* (*uncount*)
Derision is scornful laughter: *Her suggestion was greeted with derision.*

derisive /dɪ'raɪsɪv/ *adjective*
Derisive expressions, noises or comments are scornful ones: *derisive whistles and catcalls.* — *adverb* **derisively:** *She cackled derisively at the suggestion.*

derisory /dɪ'raɪzərɪ/ *adjective*
Something such as an offer of money is **derisory** if it is so small and inadequate as to be ridiculous: *She works for a derisory salary.*

derivation /dɛrɪ'veɪʃən/ *noun* (*uncount or count*)
The **derivation** of a word is the history of its development, or its origin: *a word of Greek derivation such as 'criticize'.*

derivative /dɪ'rɪvətɪv/ *noun*; *adjective*
▻ ***noun***: **derivatives**
1 A word that is a **derivative** of another has been formed from it: *'Teaching' and 'teacher' are derivatives of 'teach'.* **2** One thing is a **derivative** of another if it has developed from it: *The pantomime of today is a derivative of 16th-century Italian comedy.*
▻ ***adjective*** (*derogatory*)
If you call someone's work or performance **derivative**, you mean that they have copied ideas that people have used before. [*same as* **unoriginal**; *opposite* **original, inventive, innovative**]

derive /dɪ'raɪv/ *verb*: **derives, deriving, derived**
1 You **derive** a feeling such as pleasure or satisfaction from something if it gives you that feeling: *He derives a lot of pleasure from his research.* **2** A word **derives** from, or **is derived** from, another if it has developed from it: *The word 'Latin' derives from the place name Latium, a district of ancient Italy.* **3** One thing **derives** or **is derived** from another if it arises out of it; you **derive** something such as power from something if that is its source: *Kings were believed to derive their authority from God.*

derogatory /dɪ'rɒgətrɪ/ *adjective*
1 A **derogatory** word or phrase is one that expresses disapproval or scorn: *In Shakespeare's day 'ambitious' was derogatory.* **2** In this dictionary, a lot of words, such as **bossy**, have the label (*derogatory*) to show that they are used in a critical or disapproving way.

descend /dɪ'sɛnd/ *verb*: **descends, descending, descended**

1 You **descend** when you move down from a higher to a lower level; you **descend** something such as a flight of stairs or a hill when you come down it: *The track got steeper as they descended into the gorge.* [*opposite* **ascend**] **2** People **descend** on a place when they arrive there in a threatening or overwhelming way: *I hope your parents are not thinking of descending on us next weekend.* **3** An unhappy feeling **descends** on a place or people when they begin to be affected by it: *Depression descended on the walkers as the rain got heavier.* **4** You **descend** to a certain kind of behaviour or activity when you do something that you would normally be ashamed of: *She had never before descended to betraying a colleague.* [*same as* **stoop**] **5** Darkness, dusk or night **descends** when it gets dark.

descendant /dɪ'sɛndənt/ *noun*: **descendants**

Your **descendants** are people such as your children, grandchildren, great-grandchildren, and so on, who descend from you.

descended /dɪ'sɛndɪd/ *adjective*

1 You are **descended** from someone if you are their child, grandchild, great-grandchild, or of any later generation of their family: *She claims to be descended from Dante.* **2** One type of animal or thing is **descended** from another if it developed from it: *Gorillas and humans descend from a common ancestor.*

descending /dɪ'sɛndɪŋ/ *adjective*

You arrange things such as numbers in **descending** order when you start with the highest, continue with the second-highest, and so on until you reach the lowest. [*opposite* **ascending**]

descent /dɪ'sɛnt/ *noun*: **descents**

1 (*usually in the singular*) A **descent** is an act of moving from a higher to a lower level: *He fell just as they were making their descent from the summit.* [*opposite* **ascent**] **2** A **descent** is a downward slope: *a steep descent.* **3** (*uncount*) Your **descent** is the line of people from whom you come; your parents, grandparents, great-grandparents and so on back through the generations, often from the point of view of their nationality or social class: *Many Canadians are of Scottish descent.*

describe /dɪ'skraɪb/ *verb*: **describes, describing, described**

You **describe** someone or something when you give an account of them or say something about their appearance or qualities: *He described the events of that evening.* □ *Would you describe yourself as a good listener?* □ *She described how she had been beaten by her husband.*

description /dɪ'skrɪpʃən/ *noun*: **descriptions**

1 A **description** is an account of a person or thing, or something said about their appearance or qualities: *I recognized her from your description.* □ *She gave us a detailed description of the wedding.* **2** (*uncount*) **Description** is the act of describing or giving an account: *The scene was beyond description.* [= was too terrible or too beautiful to describe] **3** Things of a particular **description** are things of a particular kind: *They stock tools of every description.*

descriptive /dɪ'skrɪptɪv/ *adjective*

Descriptive writing gives an account of the appearance and qualities of something: *She earned her living writing descriptive travel articles for the newspapers.*

desecrate /'dɛsɪkreɪt/ *verb*: **desecrates, descrating, desecrated**

People **desecrate** something holy, precious or special when they damage it deliberately or use it in a wrong or unworthy way: *The tomb had been desecrated by robbers.* — *noun* (*uncount*) **desecration** /dɛsɪ'kreɪʃən/: *the desecration of the cathedral and other holy places.*

desert[1] /dɪ'zɜːt/ *verb*: **deserts, deserting, deserted**

1 You **desert** someone when you leave them, and stop helping or supporting them: *He suddenly deserted his wife and family and went off with one of his students.* [*same as* **abandon**] **2** People **desert** a place when they all go away from it, leaving it empty. [*same as* **abandon**] **3** You **desert** a political party or other group to whom you have been loyal when you stop supporting them: *She deserted to the Greens.* **4** You **desert** your post or place of duty when you leave it without permission; a soldier or other member of the armed forces **deserts** when they leave their position, or the service, without permission: *He deserted from the army.* — *adjective* **deserted:** *deserted farms and villages.* — *noun* **deserter:** *Any army deserters who were caught were shot.* — *noun* (*uncount or count*) **desertion:** *a disturbing increase in the number of desertions from the armed forces* □ *She divorced her husband on the grounds of desertion.*

desert[2] /'dɛzət/ *noun* (*count or uncount*): **deserts**

1 A **desert** is an area of land with little rainfall and few plants, often covered by sand: *The Gobi Desert.* **2** People refer to a place as a **desert** if it has nothing of cultural or architectural interest, or no social life.

deserve /dɪ'zɜːv/ *verb*: **deserves, deserving, deserved**

You **deserve** a certain treatment such as a punishment or a reward if you ought to get it because of your qualities, or because of what you have done: *They deserve a better salary for the work they do.* □ *She deserves all the criticism she gets.* [*same as* **merit, warrant**] — *adjective* **deserved:** *He's having a well-deserved rest.* — *adverb* **deservedly** /dɪ'zɜːvɪdlɪ/: *She was expelled from the school, deservedly in my opinion.*

deserving /dɪ'zɜːvɪŋ/ *adjective*

1 You call a person or cause **deserving** if you think they should be rewarded or helped: *If no-one claims the money we'll give it to some deserving charity.* **2** (*formal*) You are **deserving** of a certain treatment if you ought to get it, because of your qualities or because of what you have done: *Some of these offenders are hardly deserving of imprisonment.* [*same as* **worthy**]

design /dɪ'zaɪn/ *verb*; *noun*

▻ ***verb***: **designs, designing, designed**

1 You **design** an object or building when you plan how it should look and how it should be constructed, and do accurate and detailed drawings for the builders or manufacturers to follow: *The school and church were designed by the same architect.* □ *She designs for a jewellery manufacturer.* **2** You **design** something such as a project or system when you plan it and arrange its details so as to make sure that it fulfils its purpose: *The system is designed to prevent abuses.*

▻ ***noun***: **designs**

1 (*uncount*) **Design** is the art or process of planning, and making drawings for, such things as buildings, clothes and household objects: *fashion design.* **2** (*uncount*) The **design** of an object is the way in which it has been planned and constructed: *A jug that can't pour obviously has a serious design fault.* **3** A **design** is a drawing or model showing how something is to look and be constructed: *a design for the new museum.* **4** The **design** on *eg* wallpaper or fabric is the pattern of lines, shapes and colours on it: *Her delicate floral designs were to be seen everywhere on furnishing materials.* **5** Your **design** in doing something is your aim or intention: *His design in retiring early had been to give himself time to write.*

▻ ***phrases*** **1** You do something **by design** when you do it intentionally: *Had he got into the same compartment* *by accident or by design?* [*same as* **deliberately**] **2** You **have designs on** something, especially something that belongs to someone else, when you want it and are trying hard to get it: *She realized that Philip had designs on her job.*

designate *verb; adjective*
▻ ***verb*** /ˈdɛzɪgneɪt/: **designates, designating, designated**
1 A sign or symbol **designates** something when it represents or indicates it: *The number of stars on his tunic designates his rank.* [*same as* **denote**] **2** Something **is designated** something when it is officially classified as that thing: *The street had been designated a children's play area.* **3** You **are designated** to do something when you are formally chosen to do it: *I've been designated to hand round the drinks.*
▻ ***adjective*** /ˈdɛzɪgnət/
Someone who is described as *eg* chairman **designate**, or manager **designate** has been appointed to that job but has not started doing it.

designation /dɛzɪgˈneɪʃən/ *noun*: **designations**
A **designation** is a name, title or description: *She's entitled to the designation 'Professor' but rarely uses it.*

designer /dɪˈzaɪnə(r)/ *noun*: **designers**
A **designer** is a person who designs things such as clothes, furniture, machinery, vehicles or books by producing drawings and models for them.

desirable /dɪˈzaɪərəbəl/ *adjective*
1 Something is **desirable** if it is useful or necessary and therefore worth doing or having: *A degree in economics is desirable but not essential for this job.* **2** A **desirable** house or job is one with a lot of advantages or good features: *desirable residences in a quiet area of the city.* [*same as* **sought-after**] **3** Someone who is described as **desirable** is sexually attractive. — *noun* **desirability** /dɪzaɪərəˈbɪlɪtɪ/: *I question the desirability of a merger between our two companies at this stage.*

desire /dɪˈzaɪə(r)/ *verb; noun*
▻ ***verb***: **desires, desiring, desired**
1 You **desire** something if you want it: *The interview can be conducted in private if you so desire.* [*same as* **wish**] **2** You **desire** someone if you are strongly attracted to them physically and want to have sex with them.
▻ ***noun***: **desires**
1 A **desire** is a feeling of wanting something, or wanting to do something: *His desires were very simple.* □ *I've not the least desire to live abroad.* **2** (*uncount*) **Desire** for a person is a strong feeling of physical attraction towards them and of wanting to have sex with them: *There was no trace of the desire she had once felt for him.*
▻ ***phrases*** You say something **leaves a lot**, or **much, to be desired** if it is not as good as it ought to be: *His spelling leaves much to be desired.*

desist /dɪˈsɪst/ *verb* (*formal*): **desists, desisting, desisted**
You **desist** from some activity when you stop it: *I must beg you to desist from harassing my client.*

desk /dɛsk/ *noun*: **desks**
1 A **desk** is a table, often with drawers, for sitting at while writing, word-processing or reading. [see picture at **office**] **2** A **desk** is also a counter, *eg* in a public building where some service is provided: *the information desk* □ *the enquiry desk.*

desk-top /ˈdɛsktɒp/ *adjective*
Desk-top describes computing tasks that can be accomplished by someone sitting at a desk or work station using a personal computer: *desk-top publishing.*

desolate /ˈdɛsələt/ *adjective*
1 A **desolate** place is empty, neglected and depressing: *The rooms were empty and desolate.* **2** You are **desolate** when you are feeling lonely, friendless and hopeless.

desolation /dɛsəˈleɪʃən/ *noun* (*uncount*)
Desolation is
1 a feeling of loneliness and despair: *She had experienced the desolation of bereavement.* **2** a quality of frightening emptiness, *eg* after destruction: *The streets presented a scene of desolation.*

despair /dɪˈspɛə(r)/ *noun; verb*
▻ ***noun*** (*uncount*)
Despair is the state of having lost all hope: *She was in the depths of despair over the exams.* □ *They eventually gave up in despair.*
▻ ***verb***: **despairs, despairing, despaired**
1 You **despair** when you give up hope: *We'll manage somehow; don't despair yet.* **2** You **despair** of something when you lose hope of achieving it, or of its happening or improving: *She despaired of finding her ring again.* — *adjective* **despairing:** *She gave me a despairing look.* — *adverb* **despairingly:** *'It's no good,' he said despairingly.*

despatch see **dispatch.**

desperate /ˈdɛspərət/ *adjective*
1 You are **desperate**, or your situation is **desperate**, when you are as worried or frightened as you can possibly be, and will try anything: *I'd had no news for a month and was desperate with anxiety.* □ *She made a last desperate attempt to escape.* **2** You are **desperate** for something, or to do something when you very much want to have it or do it: *By that age they're all desperate to leave school.* — *adverb* **desperately:** *She desperately wanted a child.* □ *He struggled desperately to free himself.* — *noun* (*uncount*) **desperation** /dɛspəˈreɪʃən/: *We could hear the trapped occupants screaming in panic and desperation.*

despicable /dɪˈspɪkəbəl/ *adjective*
A person or action that is **despicable** is disgraceful, shameful or evil: *a despicable act of betrayal.* [*same as* **contemptible**] — *adverb* **despicably:** *You acted despicably.*

despise /dɪˈspaɪz/ *verb*: **despises, despising, despised**
You **despise** someone or something if you regard them with scorn or disgust: *She despised him for his ignorance and prejudice.*

despite /dɪˈspaɪt/ *preposition*
1 You use **despite** like 'in spite of', to introduce a circumstance that makes a surprising contrast with the rest of your statement: *Despite her lack of training, she managed to convince them that she could do the job.* □ *They greeted me as warmly as ever, despite the fact that I was 15 minutes late.* [*same as* **in spite of**] **2** You do something **despite** yourself when you do it although you don't want to, intend to, or expect to: *He always said he didn't want a television set, but he enjoys it despite himself.* [*same as* **in spite of**]

despondent /dɪˈspɒndənt/ *adjective*
You are **despondent** when you feel that you can never succeed or that things will never improve: *She was becoming despondent about getting another job.* — *noun* (*uncount*) **despondency:** *He returned from the interview filled with despondency.* — *adverb* **despondently:** *They gazed despondently out at the rain.*

despot /ˈdɛspɒt/ *noun*: **despots**
A **despot** is a ruler who keeps all power to himself or herself; a person who behaves in a tyrannical way can also be called a **despot**. [*same as* **tyrant**]

despotic /dɛˈspɒtɪk/ *adjective*
Despotic describes behaviour or a system of government that is tyrannical or unfair. — *adverb* **despoti-**

cally: *She had ruled the company despotically for thirty years.*

dessert /dɪ'zɜːt/ *noun* (*uncount or count*): **desserts**
Dessert is a sweet course served after the main course of a meal: *There was chocolate ice cream or apple tart for dessert.* [*same as* **sweet, pudding**]

dessertspoon /dɪ'zɜːtspuːn/ *noun*: **dessertspoons**
1 A **dessertspoon** is a medium-sized spoon, about half the size of a tablespoon and twice the size of a teaspoon, used to eat *eg* a sweet course or a breakfast cereal. [see picture at **tableware**] **2** A **dessertspoon** or **dessertspoonful** of something is the amount that a dessertspoon will hold: *Add three dessertspoons* (or *dessertspoonfuls*) *of sugar.*

destination /dɛstɪ'neɪʃən/ *noun*: **destinations**
The **destination** of a person or thing is the place to which they are going or being sent: *The letter never reached its destination.*

destined /'dɛstɪnd/ *adjective*
1 Something or someone is **destined** for something, or **destined** to do something, if that is the fate or future that has been planned for them: *They felt that they were destined to meet again one day.* □ *animals destined for the slaughterhouse.* **2** A person or thing is **destined** for a certain place if that is where they are travelling: *Passengers destined for Glasgow must change at Perth.* [*same as* **bound**]

destiny /'dɛstɪnɪ/ *noun*: **destinies**
1 Your **destiny** is what fate has planned will happen to you in the future: *I believe she has an exciting destiny in store for her.* **2** (*uncount*) **Destiny** is the power or force that people think of as controlling future events: *She wanted to be an artist, but destiny had decreed otherwise.* [*same as* **fate**]

destitute /'dɛstɪtjuːt/ *adjective*
People who are **destitute** have no money, possessions or home: *Destitute children begged in the streets.* [*same as* **poverty-stricken**] — *noun* (*uncount*) **destitution** /dɛstɪ'tjuːʃən/: *His gambling and extravagance had brought the family to the brink of desitution.*

destroy /dɪ'strɔɪ/ *verb*: **destroys, destroying, destroyed**
1 To **destroy** something is to damage it so badly as to ruin it completely: *Bombing destroyed the centre of Valletta in 1941.* **2** To **destroy** a feeling or quality is to stop it existing: *His selfishness finally destroyed our relationship.* **3** A misfortune **destroys** a person if they cannot recover from it. **4** An animal **is destroyed** if it is killed, *eg* because it is badly injured, incurably ill, or dangerous. [*same as* **put down, put to sleep**]

destroyer /dɪ'strɔɪə(r)/ *noun*: **destroyers**
1 A **destroyer** is a small fast warship. **2** A thing or person that destroys something is its **destroyer**: *Alcohol is a terrible destroyer of the complexion.*

destruction /dɪ'strʌkʃən/ *noun* (*uncount*)
Destruction is the act of destroying or the process of being destroyed: *We have witnessed in our lifetime both the establishment and the destruction of the welfare state.*

destructive /dɪ'strʌktɪv/ *adjective*
1 Someone or something that is **destructive** damages or ruins things: *the destructive power of gossip.* **2 Destructive** criticism points out faults without suggesting improvements. [*opposite* **constructive**] — *noun* (*uncount*) **destructiveness:** *jealousy in all its destructiveness.*

desultory /'dɛsəltrɪ/ *adjective*
A **desultory** activity is carried on in a disorganized and unsystematic manner: *There was some desultory discussion but nothing was decided.*

detach /dɪ'tatʃ/ *verb*: **detaches, detaching, detached**
1 You **detach** a part of something when you remove it: *Please detach the reply form and return it to us.* □ *The doll's head had been detached from its body.* **2** You **detach** yourself from a situation when you withdraw from it or involve yourself less: *Doctors must learn to detach themselves from their patients' problems.* [*same as* **distance**]

detachable /dɪ'tatʃəbəl/ *adjective*
A part of something that is **detachable** is designed to be removed from it: *Men's shirts used to have detachable collars.*

detached /dɪ'tatʃt/ *adjective*
1 A **detached** house stands on its own, as distinct from being joined to another house on one or both sides. [see picture at **house**, see also **semi-detached**] **2** Someone who is **detached** from a situation is not personally involved in it, and is not affected by emotion or prejudice: *He was feeling calm and detached.*

detachment /dɪ'tatʃmənt/ *noun*: **detachments**
1 (*uncount*) **Detachment** is a state of not being personally or emotionally involved in a situation: *A marriage counsellor could look at your problems with detachment.* **2** A **detachment** of soldiers is a group selected from the main force to perform some special duty.

detail /'diːteɪl/ *noun*; *verb*
▻ ***noun*: details**
1 A **detail** is any of the particular points, items or features of which something consists, that can be noticed when it is observed or examined closely: *She could remember certain events down to the smallest detail.* **2** You call something a **detail** if it is unimportant and doesn't affect the main issue: *The salary is a detail; the main thing is to find a job.* **3 Details** about a person or thing are facts and information about them: *your name, address, date of birth and other personal details.* **4** (*uncount*) **Detail** is the mass of individual features, points and items of which something consists, that can be noticed when it is observed or examined closely: *She always paid close attention to detail.* □ *He has an eye for detail.* **5** A **detail** is a small section of a painting reproduced separately and usually enlarged.
▻ ***verb*: details, detailing, detailed**
You **detail** things when you list and describe them: *If you care to detail your requirements, we shall see to them for you.*
▻ ***phrases*** **1** You **go into detail** or **into details** when you explain something thoroughly: *Can you give me a rough idea of what happened, without going into detail?* **2** You discuss or explain something **in detail** when you do so fully or thoroughly: *She told them in detail what they would be expected to know for the exam.*

detailed /'diːteɪld/ *adjective*
Something that is **detailed** is full of details or is very thorough: *a detailed report* □ *I need a more detailed map.*

detain /dɪ'teɪn/ *verb*: **detain, detaining, detained**
1 Someone **is detained** by the police or other authority when they are prevented from leaving a place: *She was detained for four hours at the police station for questioning.* [*same as* **hold**] **2** Someone **detains** you when they stop you and delay you, usually by talking to you. [*same as* **hold up**]

detect /dɪ'tɛkt/ *verb*: **detects, detecting, detected**
You **detect** something that is difficult to discover when you notice or find it: *She thought she detected a smell of gas.* — *adjective* **detectable:** *The scar is barely detectable now.*

detection /dɪ'tɛkʃən/ *noun* (*uncount*)
1 The **detection** of something is the process of discov-

ering it, especially if it is difficult to find out about: *There are probably a lot of computer frauds that escape detection altogether.* **2 Detection** is also the investigation of crimes and the capture of those responsible for them, seen as the work of a detective.

detective /dɪ'tɛktɪv/ *noun*: **detectives**
A police **detective** is a police officer whose job is to investigate and solve crimes by collecting and examining evidence; a private **detective** is a person employed by someone to investigate a matter of concern to themselves.

detective story /dɪ'tɛktɪv stɔːrɪ/ *noun*: **detective stories**
A **detective story** is a story or novel about the solving of a crime.

detector /dɪ'tɛktə(r)/ *noun*: **detectors**
A **detector** is an instrument or device used to discover or detect the presence of something: *You should get a smoke-detector fitted in the kitchen.*

détente /deɪ'tɒnt/ *noun* (*uncount*)
Détente is the return to relaxed and friendly relations between countries that have been on unfriendly and uncooperative terms: *We look at the growing détente between the US and its former foes.*

detention /dɪ'tɛnʃən/ *noun* (*uncount*)
Detention is the act of arresting or imprisoning someone, or the condition of being under arrest or in prison, especially for political reasons: *People are being kept in detention without trial.*

deter /dɪ'tɜː(r)/ *verb*: **deters, deterring, deterred**
To **deter** someone from doing something is to discourage them from doing it, or persuade them not to do it: *I was not going to be deterred by his threats.* [*same as* **put off, dissuade**]

detergent /dɪ'tɜːdʒənt/ *noun* (*count or uncount*): **detergents**
A **detergent** is a chemical substance, as distinct from soap, used in the form of a liquid or powder for washing, *eg* dishes or clothes: *We've run out of detergent.*

deteriorate /dɪ'tiːrɪəreɪt/ *verb*: **deteriorate, deteriorating, deteriorated**
1 Something **deteriorates** when it gets worse: *The patient's condition deteriorated in the night.* [*same as* **worsen**] **2** A situation or relationship **deteriorates** when it becomes difficult, unpleasant or quarrelsome. [*same as* **degenerate**]: *The discussion deteriorated into a shouting match.* — *noun* (*uncount, or in the singular*) **deterioration** /dɪtiːrɪə'reɪʃən/: *The deterioration in her health was noticeable.*

determination /dɪtɜːmɪ'neɪʃən/ *noun* (*uncount*)
1 Determination is will power or the quality of being and staying firm in your intentions and aims: *I couldn't help admiring her courage and determination.* [*same as* **resolve, tenacity**] **2** The **determination** of what happened or what is to happen is the process of reaching a conclusion about it after proper consideration: *Determination of the exact time of death is the pathologist's job.*

determine /dɪ'tɜːmɪn/ *verb*: **determines, determining, determined**
1 A result or outcome **is determined** by some factor if that factor is what controls it: *Your state of fitness determines the speed at which the heart rate returns to normal after exercise.* **2** You **determine** what has happened when you consider the facts and reach a conclusion: *Can we determine how long he has been dead?* [*same as* **establish, ascertain**] **3** You **determine** what is to happen when you consider all the circumstances and reach a decision: *The committee will meet to determine a suitable venue for the event.* [*same as* **fix, settle**] **4** You **determine** to do something when you decide to do it: *She determined to get up early and do the housework before leaving.* [*same as* **resolve**]

determined /dɪ'tɜːmɪnd/ *adjective*
1 You are **determined** to do something when you firmly intend to do it: *I'm determined to clear up this mess today.* [*same as* **intent on, set on**] **2** A **determined** person is someone with strong will power: *She was always very determined as a child, not to say obstinate.* [*same as* **resolute, single-minded**] — *adverb* **determinedly:** *He kept going determinedly.*

determiner /dɪ'tɜːmɪnə(r)/ *noun* (*grammar*): **determiners**
1 A **determiner** is one of the 'parts of speech' and is used before nouns for people or things to indicate which ones you mean. **2** Some determiners are used to identify particular people or things. They are: the definite article *the*, the demonstrative determiners *this*, *that*, *these* and *those*, and the possessive determiners *my*, *your*, *his*, *her*, *its*, *our*, *their*. When you use these determiners you expect your hearer to know which things or people you mean. When you use the interrogative determiners *what*, *which* and *whose* you are asking for particular people or things to be identified: *Hand me that fork.* □ *Post these letters for me.* □ *Where's my coat?* □ *Which road did you come by?* **3** Other determiners do not refer to particular people or things. They are: the indefinite article *a*, and words such as *all*, *any*, *some*, *other*, *each*, *every*, *both*, *either*, *neither*, *another*, *such*. When you use these determiners you do not expect your hearer to identify any particular person or thing: *Any date will be OK.* □ *I need another copy.* □ *We shall be writing to every candidate.* □ *Other people may think differently.* **4** In this dictionary, words indicating quantity, such as *many*, *several*, *few*, *five*, *hundred*, are also called determiners. **5** Determiners can be used together in a variety of combinations: *I've told all the children about it.* □ *the first three rows.* □ *I need another five copies.* □ *I've got such a headache!* □ *Both those letters are for you.* □ *my other son.* **6** As noted above, you use the indefinite article *a* as a determiner with a singular countable noun when you are not referring to a particular person or thing; when you refer to uncountable nouns or plural nouns in a similarly general way, you use them without a determiner: *A dog has four legs.* □ *I admire courage.* □ *People are changeable.*

deterrent /dɪ'tɛrənt/ *noun*; *adjective*
▷ ***noun*: deterrents**
1 A **deterrent** is something such as a fixed punishment for some offence, the threat of which prevents people from committing the offence: *It's difficult to assess how far the prospect of imprisonment acts as a deterrent.* **2** A nuclear **deterrent** is a nuclear weapon, the possession of which by a country makes other countries afraid to attack it. **3** Anything that discourages you from doing something can be called a **deterrent**: *I thought of taking a walk, but the rain was a bit of a deterrent.*
▷ ***adjective:*** *The police presence will, we hope, have a deterrent effect on any intending shoplifters.*

detest /dɪ'tɛst/ *verb*: **detests, detesting, detested**
You **detest** someone or something if you dislike or hate them: *I detest having to repeat myself.* [*same as* **hate, loathe, abhor**]

detestable /dɪ'tɛstəbəl/ *adjective*
If you call someone or something **detestable** you dislike or hate them: *What a detestable man!* [*same as* **hateful**] — *adverb* **detestably:** *He's so detestably smug.*

detonate /'dɛtəneɪt/ *verb*: **detonates, detonating, detonated**

A bomb **detonates** when it explodes; you **detonate** a bomb when you cause it to explode. — *noun* (*uncount*) **detonation** /dɛtə'neɪʃən/: *at the moment of detonation.*

detour /'di:tʊə(r)/ *noun*: **detours**
A **detour** is a route different from and longer than the direct route, which you take for interest or to avoid traffic problems on the direct road: *We made a detour to visit Old Sarum.*

detract /dɪ'trakt/ *verb*: **detracts, detracting, detracted**
A factor **detracts** from something if it makes it less good or worthy than it would normally be: *Any cracks or chips will certainly detract from the value of the plates.*

detriment /'dɛtrɪmənt/ *noun* (*uncount*)
▻ ***phrase*** Something that happens **to the detriment** of someone or something harms or damages them: *He took up acting in his second year, to the detriment of his academic progress.*

detrimental /dɛtrɪ'mɛntəl/ *adjective*
Something that is **detrimental** to something else has a harmful or damaging effect on it: *Tension over money is detrimental to any relationship.*

deuce /dju:s/ *noun* (*uncount*; *tennis*)
Deuce is the score in a tennis game when both players or sides have forty points.

devalue /di:valju/ *verb*: **devalues, devaluing, devalued**
1 You **devalue** something or someone if you regard them as less good or valuable than they are: *She tended to devalue the work done by her staff.* **2** A country's currency **is devalued** when its value is reduced in relation to other currencies. — *noun* (*uncount*) **devaluation** /di:valju:'eɪʃən/: *the devaluation of the French franc.*

devastate /'dɛvasteɪt/ *verb*: **devastates, devastating, devastated**
1 Something **devastates** an area when it damages it badly or ruins it: *The floods devastated acres of farmland.* **2** You **are devastated** by something if you are badly shocked or upset by it: *We were devastated by the announcement.*
▻ ***adjective*** (*sometimes informal*) **devastating:** *Her failure was a devastating blow to her pride.* [*same as* **shattering**] — *adverb* (*intensifying*) **devastatingly:** *It was devastatingly funny.* — *noun* (*uncount*) **devastation** /dɛvə'steɪʃən/: *The forest fires caused devastation over hundreds of square miles.*

develop /dɪ'vɛləp/ *verb*: **develops, developing, developed**
1 Something or someone develops when they grow, change and progress; you **develop** something when you put your efforts and energy into making it progress: *We couldn't believe that the little black blobs would develop into frogs.* □ *He had developed the business almost entirely on his own.* **2** Something such as a crisis or problem **develops** when it begins to exist and gets worse: *Tensions were developing between the Christian and Muslim elements of the population.* **3** To **develop** a feature, characteristic, fault or illness is to begin to have it: *The tadpoles first develop a tail, then legs.* **4** You **develop** something new when you produce something that is an improvement on previous designs, models and techniques: *the team who developed the new model.* **5** You **develop** a theory, argument or idea when you work on it and find more ways of supporting it. **6** A photographic film **is developed** when slides, negatives and prints are made from it.

developer /dɪ'vɛləpə(r)/ *noun*: **developers**
1 A **developer** is a person who buys land in order to build houses on it, or buys buildings in order to convert them and increase their value. **2** (*uncount*) **Developer** is a chemical used to develop photographic film. **3** You say a child is a late or early **developer** according to whether they develop physically or mentally later or earlier than the average for children of their age.

developing /dɪ'vɛləpɪŋ/ *adjective*
A **developing** country is one that has traditionally had a rural economy based on agriculture, but is developing its industry and technology so as to become more powerful economically.

development /dɪ'vɛləpmənt/ *noun*: **developments**
1 (*uncount*) **Development** is the process of growing, changing and progressing: *the industrial development of Britain in the 19th century.* **2** (*uncount or count*) **Development** is work done on studying and improving on previous or basic models, designs or techniques: *They receive an annual grant for development.* □ *recent developments in genetic engineering.* **3** (*uncount*) The **development** of an area of land is the improvement of it so as to make it more fertile, useful or profitable. **4** A housing **development** is an area of housing built by a developer. **5** A **development** in a situation is an occurrence that affects or influences it: *a new development in the war.*

deviant /'di:vɪənt/ *noun*; *adjective*
▻ ***noun*: deviants**
A **deviant** is someone whose beliefs, behaviour or sexual preferences are not what are generally considered normal and acceptable.
▻ ***adjective:*** *deviant behaviour.*

deviate /'di:vɪeɪt/ *verb*: **deviates, deviating, deviated**
1 To **deviate** from what is normal is to behave in an unusual way: *The statistics for September seem to deviate from the norm.* **2** You **deviate** from your previous opinions or normal habits when you think or do something different: *He was a man who deviated not once from the path of duty.* — *noun* (*uncount or count*) **deviation** /di:vɪ'eɪʃən/: *No deviations were allowed from the school uniform.*

device /dɪ'vaɪs/ *noun*: **devices**
1 A **device** is a tool or instrument for doing some job: *You can get a device for taking the stones out of cherries.* **2** A **device** is a means of achieving what you want, sometimes involving slight dishonesty: *The tax changes are just a device to win support before the election.* [*same as* **ruse**]
▻ ***phrase*** You **leave** someone **to their own devices** when you leave them to occupy or amuse themselves: *The afternoon's lecture finished at 3.00 pm, and we were left to our own devices till dinner time.*

devil /'dɛvəl/ *noun*: **devils**
1 In the Christian religion the **Devil** is Satan, thought of as the ruler of Hell, the personification of evil, and God's chief opponent. **2** A **devil** is any evil spirit or demon. **3** (*informal*) Anyone you are making a remark about can be referred to as a **devil**: *The poor devil's got to have another operation.* □ *They've won a holiday in the Bahamas, lucky devils.*
▻ ***phrase*** You start a question with a phrase such as **what the devil, why the devil, how the devil**, or **who the devil** when you want to express annoyance or surprise: *How the devil did you know that?* □ *What the devil are you doing here?*

devilish /'dɛvəlɪʃ/ *adjective*
A **devilish** plan or scheme is a cruel and evil one: *He had his own devilish reasons for making the suggestion.* [*same as* **wicked**]

devious /'di:vɪəs/ *adjective*
1 A **devious** person behaves in a secretive and unstraightforward way for reasons that they don't

want people to know about: *You can't trust these devious politicians.* **2** A **devious** route is an indirect and complicated one: *a devious tour through the back streets.* [*same as* **roundabout**, **rambling**]

devise /dɪ'vaɪz/ *verb*: **devises, devising, devised**
You **devise** something such as a method, plan or system for something when you work it out: *We'll have to devise some means of getting the piano up the stairs.* [*same as* **invent**, **contrive**]

devoid /dɪ'vɔɪd/ *adjective*
Someone or something is **devoid** of a quality if they do not have it at all: *He's quite devoid of humour.*

devolution /diːvə'luːʃən/ *noun* (*uncount*)
Devolution is the process of transferring power from a central department or administration to regional departments or minor branches.

devolve /dɪ'vɒlv/ *verb*: **devolves, devolving, devolved**
A duty or responsibility **devolves** on you if it is transferred to you, usually from someone senior to you: *One of the pleasanter duties that has devolved on me during the headteacher's absence is the presentation of the end-of-term prizes.*

devote /dɪ'voʊt/ *verb*: **devotes, devoting, devoted**
You **devote** yourself, your life, or your time and energy to something when you give your efforts, time and energy to it: *He devoted his whole life to fighting slavery.*

devoted /dɪ'voʊtɪd/ *adjective*
1 You are **devoted** to someone if you love them very much: *She was a devoted mother and wife.* **2** Work that is described as **devoted** takes all someone's time and energy: *The embroidery has taken months of devoted labour.* [*same as* **dedicated**] — *adverb* **devotedly:** *The doctors and nurses worked devotedly to save her life.*

devotee /dɛvə'tiː/ *noun*: **devotees**
A **devotee** of some subject or activity is someone who takes an enthusiastic interest or part in it: *devotees of camping.* [*same as* **fan**, **enthusiast**]

devotion /dɪ'voʊʃən/ *noun* (*uncount*)
1 Devotion is strong deep love for someone: *His devotion to his wife was obvious and touching.* **2 Devotion** to your work or duty is the giving of yourself, your time and energy to it: *Her years of devotion to her research were rewarded with success.* **3** Religious **devotion** is sincere reverence for and worship of God: *They bent their heads in devotion.*

devour /dɪ'vaʊə(r)/ *verb* (*slightly humorous*): **devours, devouring, devoured**
1 You **devour** something when you eat it greedily: *I watched her devour a mound of tiny pink shrimps.* [*same as* **guzzle**, **consume**] **2** You **devour** a book when you read it eagerly and finish it quickly.

devout /dɪ'vaʊt/ *adjective*
A **devout** believer in something is a loyal, enthusiastic and sincere one: *She had been a devout socialist since her student days.* □ *devout Muslims.* — *adverb* **devoutly:** *his devoutly religious parents.*

dew /djuː/ *noun* (*uncount*)
Dew is little drops of water that form on grass and plants during the night: *A heavy dew had fallen.*

dexterity /dɛk'stɛrɪtɪ/ *noun* (*uncount*)
Dexterity is skill or cleverness, especially with the hands: *I admired her dexterity with a needle.*

dexterous or **dextrous** /'dɛkstrəs/ *adjective*
A **dexterous** person is someone skilful, especially with their hands: *With dexterous strokes she carved a particularly exquisite figure.* □ *He had achieved notoriety for his dexterous accounting ability.* — *adverb* **dexterously:** *He dexterously side-stepped to avoid the blow.*

dhoti /'doʊtɪ/ *noun*: **dhotis**
A **dhoti** is a strip of cloth worn by men in India, wrapped round the hips, passed between the legs, and fastened at the waist. [see picture at **clothing**]

diabetes /daɪə'biːtiːz/ *noun* (*uncount*)
Diabetes is an illness that causes an inability in the patient to control the level of sugar in their blood.

diabetic /daɪə'bɛtɪk/ *noun*; *adjective*
▻ ***noun***: **diabetics**
A **diabetic** is someone who suffers from diabetes.
▻ ***adjective***
Diabetic means relating to diabetes or suitable for people suffering from it: *a diabetic coma* □ *a bar of diabetic chocolate.*

diabolical /daɪə'bɒlɪkəl/ *adjective* (*sometimes informal*)
Something that is **diabolical** is wicked or evil: *I've got the most diabolical toothache.*

diagnose /daɪəg'noʊz/ *verb*: **diagnoses, diagnosing, diagnosed**
A doctor **diagnoses** an illness in a patient when he or she identifies it: *She diagnosed his pain immediately as appendicitis.*

diagnosis /daɪəg'noʊsɪs/ *noun* (*uncount or count*): **diagnoses** /daɪəg'noʊsiːz/
The **diagnosis** of an illness is the identification of it in a patient: *a mistaken diagnosis* □ *What is your diagnosis?*

diagnostic /daɪəg'nɒstɪk/ *adjective*
Diagnostic methods and devices are used for identifying illness in a patient: *new diagnostic equipment.*

diagonal /daɪ'agənəl/ *adjective*; *noun*
▻ ***adjective***
A **diagonal** line is a slanting or sloping one, as distinct from a vertical or horizontal one: *Draw a diagonal line from the top left to the bottom right* — *adverb* **diagonally:** *He kicked the ball diagonally across the field.*
▻ ***noun***: **diagonals**
A **diagonal** is a diagonal line: *The two diagonals intersect at the centre of the square.*

diagram /'daɪəgram/ *noun*: **diagrams**
A **diagram** is a simple drawing done to show the structure of something, or how it works: *Look at the diagram of the heart on page 14.* — *adjective* **diagrammatic** /daɪəgrə'matɪk/: *The circulation of the blood can be simply represented in diagrammatic form.* — *adverb* **diagrammatically:** *It's easiest to show you diagrammatically how muscles work.*

dial /daɪl/ *noun*; *verb*
▻ ***noun***: **dials**
1 A **dial** on a piece of electrical or radio equipment is a disc or panel with a circularly arranged set of figures or letters and a pointing hand or indicator, which shows such things as speed, temperature or frequency, or can be adjusted to control the equipment. **2** The **dial** on a clock or watch is its face, especially one with circularly arranged figures or symbols, and two hands. **3** Older telephones have a **dial** in the form of a disc with finger holes, that you turn to select a number.
▻ ***verb***: **dials, dialling, dialled**
You **dial** a telephone number when you select it by turning a dial, or by pressing keys: *I dialled the office number.*

dialect /'daɪəlɛkt/ *noun*: **dialects**
A **dialect** is a form of a language spoken in a particular region, differing from other forms in pronunciation, grammar and vocabulary: *one of the dialects of German.*

dialogue (*AmE* **dialog**) /ˈdaɪəlɒg/ *noun* (*uncount or count*): **dialogues**
1 Dialogue is conversation, especially between two people, *eg* in a book, play or film. **2 Dialogue** is also formal discussion between people or groups held for the purpose of negotiation or to solve difficulties: *We shall continue to seek dialogue with the management.* □ *The matter was discussed in one of the recent dialogues between the two presidents.*

diameter /daɪˈamitə(r)/ *noun*: **diameters**
The **diameter** of a round object, whether a sphere or a circle, is the length of a real or imaginary line drawn through its centre: *The earth is about 15 000 kilometres in diameter.* [see picture at **shape**]

diametrically /daɪəˈmɛtrɪklɪ/ *adverb*
You say that two things are **diametrically** opposed or opposite when you think they are completely different from each other: *She and I have diametrically opposed opinions on education.*

diamond /ˈdaɪəmənd/ *noun*: **diamonds**
1 A **diamond** is a shining, colourless and transparent precious stone used in jewellery and for industrial purposes: *a diamond ring* □ *diamond mines.* **2** A diamond is also a flat shape with four equal sides and angles that are not right angles. [see picture at **shape**] **3** (*used in the plural*) **Diamonds** are one of the four suits (◆) in a pack of playing cards: *the queen of diamonds.* **4** A **diamond** is one of the 13 cards in the suit of diamonds.

diaper /ˈdaɪpə(r)/ *noun* (*AmE*): **diapers**
A **diaper** is a baby's nappy.

diaphragm /ˈdaɪəfram/ *noun*: **diaphragms**
1 Your **diaphragm** is the layer of muscle that separates your lungs from your stomach, which you use when you breathe. **2** A **diaphragm** is also a contraceptive device consisting of a thin rubber cap, that a woman fits over the entrance to her uterus before she has sex.

diarrhoea (*AmE* **diarrhea**) /daɪəˈrɪə/ *noun* (*uncount*)
Diarrhoea is an illness of the bowels that causes the frequent passing of soft, liquid faeces.

diary /ˈdaɪərɪ/ *noun*: **diaries**
A **diary** is a book with a space for each day, in which you write your appointments, or keep a record of what happens to you day by day: *I used to keep a diary as a teenager.* [*same as* **journal**]

dice /daɪs/ *noun*; *verb*
▻ ***noun***: **dice**
A **dice** is a small plastic or wooden cube, with from one to six spots on each of its six sides, that you throw in games of chance to decide such things as who makes the first move, or how many moves they can make: *We use two dice for this game.*
▻ ***verb***: **dices, dicing, diced**
You **dice** vegetables or meat by cutting them into small cubes. — *adjective* **diced:** *diced carrots.*

dicey /ˈdaɪsɪ/ *adjective* (*informal*): **dicier**, **diciest**
Something that is **dicey** involves risk or danger, or is unsettled and uncertain: *It's too dicey for women to walk about alone at night round here.* [*same as* **risky**]

dichotomy /daɪˈkɒtəmɪ/ *noun* (*formal*): **dichotomies**
You say there is a **dichotomy** between things if there is a strong difference or contrast between them: *the dichotomy between rich and poor in our society.*

dictate *verb*; *noun*
verb or /dɪkˈteɪt/: **dictates, dictating, dictated**
1 You **dictate** something to someone when you read it or say it aloud for them to write down: *She rang her secretary and dictated a letter over the phone.* **2** You **dictate** to someone when you tell them what they must do: *I refuse to be dictated to by them.* [*same as* **boss**]
▻ ***noun*** /ˈdɪkteɪt/: **dictates**
A **dictate** is an order, instruction or guiding principle: *We had no choice but to obey the dictates of the management.*

dictation /dɪkˈteɪʃən/: **dictations** *noun*
1 (*uncount*) **Dictation** is the giving of orders or instructions in a commanding or impatient manner: *The system is liable to change at the dictation of the government.* **2 Dictation** is the process of saying or reading something aloud for someone else to write down; a **dictation** is a test of your understanding, *eg* of a foreign language, in which you write down a passage of text that is read aloud to you: *She took down the message at her boss's dictation.* □ *a French dictation.*

dictator /dɪkˈteɪtə(r)/ *noun*: **dictators**
A **dictator** is a ruler who has total power over a country, especially after gaining it by force. [*same as* **tyrant, autocrat**]

dictatorial /dɪktəˈtɔːrɪəl/ *adjective*
1 Dictatorial means relating to a dictator or to a ruler with total power: *dictatorial powers.* **2** Someone who has a **dictatorial** manner or way of behaving tells other people what to do in a commanding or impatient way, allowing no-one to oppose him or her. [*same as* **domineering, overbearing**]

dictatorship /dɪkˈteɪtəʃɪp/ *noun*: **dictatorships**
1 (*uncount*) **Dictatorship** is government by a dictator: *It may be called government by consent but it's dictatorship in effect.* **2** A **dictatorship** is a country that is ruled by a dictator: *the military dictatorships of the world.*

diction /ˈdɪkʃən/ *noun* (*uncount*)
Your **diction** is your style of speaking and the clarity of your pronunciation: *Her diction was clear and precise.*

dictionary /ˈdɪkʃənərɪ/ *noun*: **dictionaries**
1 A **dictionary** is a book containing the words of a language arranged alphabetically with their meanings, or the words of one language followed by their meanings in another language: *an English-Dutch, Dutch-English dictionary.* **2** An alphabetically arranged book of information can also have the title **dictionary**: *Chambers Dictionary of Science and Technology.*

did /dɪd/ *verb*; *auxiliary verb*
▻ ***verb***
Did is the past tense of the verb **do**[2]: *I did the dishes before going to bed.*
▻ ***auxiliary verb*** (*negative forms* **did not** or **didn't**)
Did is the past tense of **do**[1]: *Did you see her?* □ *He did not impress me.* □ *They did tell you, didn't they?* [see also **do**[1], [2], **didn't**]

didactic /daɪˈdaktɪk/ *adjective*
Writing or speech that is **didactic** is intended to teach or instruct, especially in a moral way: *We resented his constantly didactic tone.* — *adverb* **didactically:** *a didactically phrased speech.*

didn't /ˈdɪdənt/ *auxiliary verb*
Didn't is the spoken, and informal written, form of **did not**: *She didn't know what to do next.* □ *They went to the same school, didn't they?* [see also **do**[1]]

die /daɪ/ *verb*: **dies, dying, died**
1 People, animals or plants **die** when they stop living: *She died of cancer.* □ *The cat eventually died of old age.* □ *All the plants were dying from lack of rain.* □ *She couldn't bring herself to tell him he was dying.* □ *He*

died in terrible pain. □ *The inquest will establish whether or not he died of natural causes.* □ *She was destined to die a violent death at the hands of an armed intruder.* □ *No-one should be afraid of dying.* **2** Something **dies** when it fades and disappears: *Don't let the fire die.* □ *The daylight was dying fast.* □ *The more intense the passion, the quicker it dies.* □ *They gave their lives for us, but their names will never die.* [see also **dead**, **dying**]

▻ ***phrases*** **1** For **die hard** see **hard**. **2** You say you **are dying for** something, or **dying to** do something if you want something, or want to do it, very much: *I'm dying for a cup of tea.* □ *She was dying to tell them her news.*

phrasal verbs

die away A sound **dies away** when it becomes fainter and stops, or can no longer be heard: *The applause died away.* □ *The sound of conversation got louder and died away as people came and went.* [*same as* **fade**]

die down Something **dies down** when it decreases in level and disappears: *The excitement took a long time to die down.* □ *They waited for the storm to die down.*

die off People or things **die off** when they die one by one: *Our pot plants died off in the winter frost.* □ *My parents' friends have all died off now.*

die out Something **dies out** when it gets rarer and rarer and finally disappears: *Many species of fish are in danger of dying out.* □ *The tradition has died out in most parts of the country.*

diesel /ˈdiːzəl/ *noun*: **diesels**

1 (*uncount*) **Diesel**, or **diesel oil**, is a heavy type of fuel oil used in motor vehicles, that burns by being compressed, as distinct from being set on fire by a spark. **2** A **diesel**, or **diesel engine**, is a vehicle engine fuelled by diesel oil. **3** A **diesel** is also a train or other vehicle with a diesel engine.

diet /ˈdaɪət/ *noun*; *verb*

▻ ***noun***: **diets**

1 (*count or uncount*) Your **diet** is the food you normally eat: *Most people do not have enough fibre in their diet.* □ *A balanced diet is essential.* **2** You are on a **diet** when you are avoiding certain kinds of food so as to try to lose weight, or eating special foods as part of the treatment for an illness: *a fat-free diet* □ *I'm going on a diet tomorrow.* □ *There are diet versions of most of the popular drinks.*

▻ ***verb***: **diets, dieting, dieted**

You **diet** when you avoid certain foods in order to try to lose weight: *I don't allow myself any chocolate when I'm dieting.*

dietary /ˈdaɪətərɪ/ *adjective*

Dietary means relating to the food you eat, or to diets: *The causes of illness are largely dietary.*

dietician or **dietitian** /daɪəˈtɪʃən/ *noun*: **dieticians**

A **dietician** is a person who gives people advice about what to eat to be healthy and plans their diet for them.

differ /ˈdɪfə(r)/ *verb*: **differs, differing, differed**

1 Things or people **differ** if they are unlike each other: *rows of houses differing one from another only in the colour of their front door.* **2** People **differ** about something when they disagree: *We differ over issues like physical punishment.*

▻ ***phrase*** Two people **agree to differ** when they acknowledge that they have different opinions about something, but agree to stop arguing.

difference /ˈdɪfrəns/ *noun*: **differences**

1 (*count or uncount*) The **difference** between things or people is the way in which they are unlike each other: *What are the essential differences between the actions of walking and running?* □ *There's very little difference in quality between the two computers.* **2** (*used in the singular*) The **difference** between two amounts is what remains when you subtract the smaller from the larger: *The difference between 12 and 20 is 8.* **3** Two people have a **difference** or have their **differences** when they disagree or quarrel about things.

▻ ***phrases*** **1** You say something **makes a difference** if it alters the situation in some way; something **makes all the difference** if it is a significant advantage: *It makes a big difference whether you learn a language in babyhood or as an adult.* □ *It makes no difference which road you take.* □ *Does it make any difference if you're over 60?* □ *It made all the difference winning that scholarship.* **2** You **split the difference** between two amounts when you settle for an amount halfway between them. **3** You say you can't **tell the difference** between two things or people if they seem the same to you: *These days it's difficult to tell the difference between artificial flowers and the real thing.* [*same as* **differentiate**]

different /ˈdɪfrənt/ *adjective*

1 One thing or person is **different** from another if they are unlike them in some way, or not the same: *She looks quite different from her sister.* □ *The new style of management is very different to the old.* □ (*AmE*) *Concealing the truth is no different than lying.* □ *He said he'd lost weight but I didn't think he looked any different.* □ *We have very different opinions about this.* □ *He gives a different explanation every time he's asked.*

BrE uses both *different from* and *different to*, but some people disapprove of *different to*. *Different than* is used in AmE.

2 You use **different** to mean separate or individual in referring to a series of items in the same class: *We've looked at about 12 different appartments this week and still haven't found one to suit us.* □ *There are several different ways of treating the disease.* — *adverb* **differently:** *He was treated differently from the other children.* □ *We each regarded the issue differently.*

differentiate /dɪfəˈrɛnʃɪeɪt/ *verb*: **differentiates, differentiating, differentiated**

1 You **differentiate** one thing from another, or **differentiate** between them, when you see or show the difference between them: *Children must be taught early to differentiate right from wrong.* [*same as* **distinguish**] **2** A quality or feature of something that **differentiates** it from something else makes it different: *What differentiates determination from intention?* [*same as* **distinguish**] **3** You **differentiate** between people if you treat them differently: *We never differentiated between the boys and girls.* [*same as* **discriminate**] — *noun* (*uncount*) **differentiation** /dɪfərɛnʃɪˈeɪʃən/: *There was never any question of differentiation between their own and their adopted child.*

difficult /ˈdɪfɪkəlt/ *adjective*

1 Something that is **difficult** is not easy to do, understand or solve, but requires skill or effort: *a difficult exam question* □ *The journey was long and difficult.* □ *It's a difficult question to answer.* □ *He's difficult to hear sometimes.* □ *She has found it difficult to adjust to retirement.* [*same as* **hard**; *opposite* **easy**, **simple**] **2** A **difficult** person behaves in an unhelpful, unreasonable or uncooperative way: *He was very difficult as a child.* □ *How do you deal with difficult clients?* □ *Do stop being difficult.*

difficulty /'dɪfɪkəltɪ/ *noun*: **difficulties**
1 (*uncount*) You have **difficulty** doing something if you cannot do it easily, but have to make an effort: *I had difficulty in understanding what she was saying.* □ *He had no difficulty deciding who to vote for.* □ *Germans have difficulty with the English sound 'th'.* □ *He was 93 and could still walk, though with difficulty.* **2** (*uncount*) The **difficulty** of something such as a task is its quality of being hard to do, or the amount of effort it requires: *jobs of varying degrees of difficulty.* **3** (*uncount*) Something causes **difficulty** if it causes problems: *There's been a lot of difficulty over his application.* **4** A **difficulty** is a problem or an objection: *She's good at foreseeing difficulties.* □ *I don't think there would be any difficulty if you wanted to use the library.*
▻ ***phrases*** **1** You are **in difficulty** or **in difficulties** if you are in trouble, danger, or a situation that is hard or impossible to deal with: *Several swimmers got into difficulties in the rough sea.* **2** You **make difficulties** when you object to something or refuse to co-operate: *My boss never makes difficulties if I need extra leave to cope with a family crisis.*

diffident /'dɪfɪdənt/ *adjective*
Someone who is **diffident** is shy or nervous, and lacks confidence: *He's diffident about his abilities.* [*opposite* **confident**] — *adverb* **diffidently:** *She answered diffidently.* — *noun* (*uncount*) **diffidence:** *He was overcome with diffidence at the interview.* [*same as* **shyness, timidity**; *opposite* **confidence**]

diffuse *verb*; *adjective*
▻ ***verb*** /dɪ'fju:z/: **diffuses, diffusing, diffused**
1 Something such as light or heat **diffuses** or **is diffused** when it is spread throughout an area in all directions: *I stopped shivering as the warmth gradually diffused itself through my body.* **2** Something such as knowledge **diffuses** or **is diffused** when it is communicated to an increasing number of people: *The Christian message was diffused rapidly throughout the civilized world.* — *noun* (*uncount*) **diffusion** /dɪ'fju:ʒən/: *the diffusion of information.*
▻ ***adjective*** /dɪ'fju:s/
1 Something that is **diffuse** is spread or scattered over a wide area: *The area was mountainous and its population necessarily diffuse.* **2** You call someone's style of writing or speaking **diffuse** if it is vague and expressed in too many words, rather than methodical and concentrated. [*same as* **wordy, long-winded**; *opposite* **concise, succinct**]

dig /dɪg/ *verb*; *noun*
▻ ***verb***: **digs, digging, dug**
1 You **dig** when you make a hole in the ground, *eg* with a spade: *He hurt his back digging in the garden.* □ *Dig the flower bed thoroughly before planting.* □ *The dog has been digging holes again.* **2** One thing **digs** into another when it is pressed into it; you **dig** one thing into another when you press the one into the other: *She dug her elbow sharply into my side.* **3** You **dig** into something such as a bag when you search inside it: *He dug into his pockets and brought out some change.* **4** (*old, informal*) You **dig** something if you like it: *I don't like the style but I dig the colour.*
▻ ***noun***: **digs**
1 (*usually in the singular*) A **dig** is the activity or action of digging: *The garden needs a good dig.* □ *He gave me a dig in the ribs.* **2** You make a **dig** at someone when you say something to hurt or embarrass them: *I've had enough of his sarcastic digs.* **3** A **dig** is also an archaeological site that is being dug or excavated. [*same as* **excavation**] **4** (*used in the plural*; *old*) Someone's **digs** are rooms or a room that they rent to live in, in someone else's house: *Where are your digs?*

phrasal verbs
dig out 1 You **dig** something or someone **out** of somewhere when you get them out by digging or by other means: *We had to dig our car out of the snow.* **2** (*informal*) You **dig out** something that has been stored away when you search for it and find it: *We should be able to dig the information out of the records.*
dig up 1 You **dig** ground **up** when you dig it thoroughly, breaking up the top surface: *The police have been digging up his back garden.* **2** You **dig** something **up** when you remove it from the earth by digging: *They've dug up a 3000-year-old skeleton.* [*same as* **unearth**] **3** (*informal*) You **dig up** facts that are not generally known when you find them out: *Local-history researchers have been digging up some amazing statistics.* [*same as* **unearth, discover**]

digest *verb*; *noun*
▻ ***verb*** /daɪ'dʒɛst/: **digests, digesting, digested**
1 You **digest** food when it is broken up and processed in the stomach and bowels into a form that the body can use: *She can't digest any wheat products.* **2** You **digest** facts and information when you become aware of them, understand them and remember them: *I'll let you have time to digest the report fully.* — *adjective* **digestible:** *Fresh vegetables are not as digestible as cooked ones.*
▻ ***noun*** /'daɪdʒɛst/: **digests**
A **digest** of something is a short version or summary of it: *a weekly digest of parliamentary business.*

digestion /daɪ'dʒɛstʃən/ or /dɪ'dʒɛstʃən/ *noun*: **digestions**
1 (*uncount*) **Digestion** is the process of digesting food: *Exercise speeds up digestion.* **2** Your **digestion** is your ability to digest the food that you eat, or your body's system of processing it.

digestive /daɪ'dʒɛstɪv/ *adjective*
Digestive relates to the digestion of food: *digestive problems* □ *your digestive system.*

digit /'dɪdʒɪt/ *noun*: **digits**
1 The ten figures from 0 to 9 are **digits**: *six-digit telephone numbers.* **2** (*technical*) A finger or toe is also a **digit**.

digital /'dɪdʒɪtəl/ *adjective*
A **digital** watch or clock displays the time in figures, as distinct from having a dial with two hands.

dignified /'dɪgnɪfaɪd/ *adjective*
Someone who is **dignified** behaves in the kind of calm, serious and sensible way that gains others' respect: *She decided it would not be dignified to run for the bus.* □ *She tried to think of a dignified reply.*

dignify /'dɪgnɪfaɪ/ *verb*: **dignifies, dignifying, dignified**
To **dignify** something is to make it seem impressive: *I would hardly dignify my verses with the name poetry.*

dignitary /'dɪgnətrɪ/ *noun*: **dignitaries**
A **dignitary** is a person of high rank or position, especially in public life: *the dignitaries of the church.*

dignity /'dɪgnɪtɪ/ *noun* (*uncount*)
1 Dignity is the quality of being calm, sensible and serious in the way you look and behave: *She held her head high and retreated with calm dignity.* **2** Your **dignity** is the respect you feel for yourself and that you deserve from others: *You mustn't lose your dignity by getting angry in public.* [*same as* **pride, self-respect**] **3** The **dignity** of an occasion is its importance and seriousness. [*same as* **solemnity**]
▻ ***phrases*** You consider a task or a way of behaving

beneath your dignity if you think yourself too important or respectable for it: *It was beneath her dignity to tell lies.*

digress /daɪ'grɛs/ *verb*: **digresses, digressing, digressed**
You **digress** from the subject you are talking about when you deal briefly with something else: *I should like to insert a warning here, if you don't mind my digressing for a minute.* — *noun* (*count or uncount*) **digression** /daɪ'grɛʃən/: *His hearers tended to get bored by his constant anecdotes and digressions.*

dike see **dyke**.

dilapidated /dɪ'lapɪdeɪtɪd/ *adjective*
A building or piece of furniture that is **dilapidated** is old and in a bad state: *a dilapidated armchair.* [*same as* **broken-down, ramshackle**] — *noun* (*uncount*) **dilapidation** /dɪlapɪ'deɪʃən/: *The palace was now in an advanced state of dilapidation.*

dilate /daɪ'leɪt/ *verb*: **dilates, dilating, dilated**
Openings in the body, especially the eyes or pupils, **dilate** when they get wider: *Your pupils dilate when you move from a brightly lit environment to a dark one.* — *adjective* **dilated:** *Unevenly dilated pupils is one of the signs of a brain haemorrhage.*

dilatory /'dɪlətərɪ/ *adjective*
Someone who is **dilatory** is too slow in performing tasks.

dilemma /daɪ'lɛmə/ *noun*: **dilemmas**
You are in a **dilemma** if you have a difficult choice to make between two unsatisfactory alternatives: *His mother's deteriorating mental state put him in a dilemma, as he was reluctant to hand her over to the care of others, but knew he couldn't look after her properly himself.*

diligent /'dɪlɪdʒənt/ *adjective*
A **diligent** person works hard, seriously and conscientiously: *It was a change to teach such a diligent class of students.* □ *a diligent piece of work.* [*opposite* **lax, negligent, careless**] — *noun* (*uncount*) **diligence:** *She was impressed by the diligence of the new office-cleaner.* — *adverb* **diligently:** *You can all pass the exam if you work diligently from now on.*

dilute /daɪ'luːt/ *verb*: **dilutes, diluting, diluted**
You **dilute** a liquid by adding water to it to make it weaker: *The contents should be diluted by adding two parts water.*

dim /dɪm/ *adjective; verb*
▻ ***adjective*: dimmer, dimmest**
1 A place that is **dim** does not have enough light in it for you to see clearly: *They peered into the dim interior of the cave.* **2** Something that is **dim** is difficult to see: *We could see the dim outline of the ship through the fog.* **3** Someone's eyes are **dim** if their eyesight is poor. **4** Your memory of something is **dim** if you can hardly remember it: *He retained only dim recollections of his childhood in India.* [*same as* **vague, faint**] **5** (*derogatory*) If you call someone **dim**, you mean they are stupid. [*opposite* **bright**] — *adverb* **dimly:** *in the dimly lit church* □ *She dimly recalled the occasion.* □ *Her figure was dimly outlined in the moonlight.* — *noun* (*uncount*) **dimness:** *The eye condition causes increasing dimness of vision.*
▻ ***verb*: dims, dimming, dimmed**
A light **dims** when it becomes less bright; you **dim** a light when you make it less bright: *This switch dims the lights.*

dime /daɪm/ *noun*: **dimes**
A **dime** is a coin of the United States and Canada worth ten cents or one tenth of a dollar.

dimension /daɪ'mɛnʃən/ *noun*: **dimensions**
1 (*often in the plural*) The **dimensions** of something are such measurements as its height, width, breadth, length or depth: *There was a suitable-looking table in the second-hand shop, and I took a note of its dimensions.* **2** (*used in the plural*) The **dimensions** of something are its size: *the full dimensions of the problem* □ *These creatures can grow to huge dimensions.* **3** A **dimension** is a factor that affects a situation and the way you regard it: *The increase in tuberculosis amongst those sleeping rough adds a new dimension to the homelessness problem.*

diminish /dɪ'mɪnɪʃ/ *verb*: **diminishes, diminishing, diminished**
Something **diminishes** or **is diminished** when it lessens or decreases: *Her patience with the children diminished as the hours went by.* — *adjective* **diminished:** *Where the offender is mentally unstable the court may treat the case as one of diminished responsibility.* — *adjective* **diminishing:** *She was taking an ever-diminishing part in the running of the household.*

diminution /dɪmɪ'njuːʃən/ *noun* (*uncount, or used in the singular, formal*)
A **diminution** in something is a lessening or decrease in it: *Over the years there had been little diminution in her popularity as a novelist.*

diminutive /dɪ'mɪnjʊtɪv/ *adjective; noun*
▻ ***adjective***
Someone or something that is **diminutive** is very small: *He caught sight of a diminutive figure on the horizon.*
▻ ***noun*** (*grammar*): **diminutives**
A **diminutive** is a word formed with a **diminutive suffix** such as *-let* (*eg booklet*) or *-ette* (*eg statuette*), used to indicate a small kind or version of something.

dimmer, dimmest see **dim**.

dimple /'dɪmpəl/ *noun*: **dimples**
A **dimple** is a small hollow in the cheek or chin or, in babies, in the hands and feet and at the knees and elbows: *Dimples appeared in both cheeks when she smiled.* — *adjective* **dimpled:** *The baby grasped her finger in his dimpled fist.*

din /dɪn/ *noun* (*informal, used in the singular*)
A **din** is a loud noise: *the din of the radio.*

dine /daɪn/ *verb* (*formal*): **dines, dining, dined**
1 You **dine** when you have dinner: *We dined that evening at a little vegetarian restaurant.* **2** You **dine** on or off something when you eat it for dinner: *They dined on turkey as usual.*

> ***phrasal verb***
> You **dine out** when you have dinner at a restaurant, or at someone else's house, instead of at home.

diner /'daɪnə(r)/ *noun*: **diners**
A **diner** is **1** a person who dines. **2** a dining compartment on a train. **3** (*especially AmE*) a small, cheap restaurant.

dinghy /'dɪŋgɪ/ *noun*: **dinghies**
A **dinghy** is **1** a small open boat that you sail or row. **2** a small rubber boat that you inflate with air for use, kept especially for emergencies.

dingy /'dɪndʒɪ/ *adjective*: **dingier, dingiest**
1 Dingy clothes or fabrics are dirty or faded in colour: *dingy curtains.* **2** A **dingy** room, building or street is dark, depressing, unattractive and neglected.

dining room /'daɪnɪŋ ruːm/ *noun*: **dining rooms**
A **dining room** is the room in a house or hotel where you have your meals.

dinner /'dɪnə(r)/ *noun*: **dinners**
1 (*uncount or count*) **Dinner** is the main meal of the

day, eaten in the evening or in the middle of the day: *They have an early dinner as soon as they get in from work.* □ *I've bought fish for dinner.* **2** A **dinner** is a formal meal given in the evening, *eg* to honour a person or celebrate an event: *The club's annual dinner is on 20 December.* [compare **tea**]

dinner jacket /ˈdɪnə dʒakɪt/ *noun*: **dinner jackets**
A **dinner jacket** is a black jacket worn by men at formal social gatherings in the evening, normally with a bow tie.

dinner party /ˈdɪnə pɑːtɪ/ *noun*: **dinner parties**
A **dinner party** is a small social gathering at someone's house in the evening, for a meal and conversation.

dinosaur /ˈdaɪnəsɔː(r)/ *noun*: **dinosaurs**
The **dinosaurs** were the reptiles that inhabited the earth many millions of years ago and died out.

diocese /ˈdaɪəsɪs/ *noun*: **dioceses** /ˈdaɪəsiːz/
A **diocese** is the district over which a bishop has authority.

dip /dɪp/ *verb, noun*
▷ ***verb*: dips, dipping, dipped**
1 You **dip** things into a liquid or powder when you put them into it briefly and lift them out again: *Dip the meat into flour before frying.* **2** Something **dips** when it makes a downward movement: *The ship's bow dipped and lifted.* **3** A road or other surface **dips** when it drops down to a lower level: *The track dips suddenly as you come to the river.* **4** Drivers **dip** their lights when they operate the control that directs them on to the road surface instead of straight ahead. **5** Animals **are dipped** when they are put briefly into a disinfectant bath.
▷ ***noun*: dips**
1 (*used in the singular*) A **dip** is an act of dipping: *A quick dip in boiling water will loosen the skins of the tomatoes.* **2** A **dip** in a road or other surface is a downward slope or hollow: *A dip in the road may hide an approaching vehicle.* **3** You have or take a **dip** when you go for a swim. **4** A **dip** is a thick creamy sauce that you eat with biscuits or vegetables, by dipping them into it: *a selection of savoury dips.* **5** (*uncount or count*) A **dip** is also a disinfectant bath in which animals are dipped: *sheep dip.*

phrasal verb
dip into 1 You **dip into** a book when you open it occasionally and read a passage here or there. **2** You **dip into** your savings, your pocket or your purse when you spend money: *Many people resent being asked to dip into their pockets for every little charity.*

diphtheria /dɪpˈθiːrɪə/ or /dɪfˈθiːrɪə/ *noun* (*uncount*)
Diphtheria is a serious infectious disease of the throat which makes breathing and swallowing difficult.

diphthong /ˈdɪpθɒŋ/ or /ˈdifθɒŋ/ *noun*: **diphthongs**
A **diphthong** is a sound consisting of two vowel sounds pronounced as one syllable, like the sound represented by the *ou* in *sound*, the *i* in *line* or the *a* in *plate*.

diploma /dɪˈploʊmə/ *noun*: **diplomas**
A **diploma** is a qualification gained at a college or university after passing an examination or completing a course of study; the document certifying that you have done so is also a **diploma**: *She's doing a teaching diploma.* □ *a diploma in fashion design.*

diplomacy /dɪˈploʊməsɪ/ *noun* (*uncount*)
1 Diplomacy is the management of relations between countries, especially by their various ambassadors and official representatives: *The incident turned into a matter for international diplomacy.* **2 Diplomacy** is also skill in dealing with, or persuading, people in such a way that you do not offend them: *It took a certain amount of diplomacy to get him to agree.* [*same as* **tact**]

diplomat /ˈdɪpləmat/ *noun*: **diplomats**
1 A **diplomat** is someone such as an ambassador, who represents his or her country in international relations and negotiations. **2** People sometimes call a person who is considerate, polite, understanding and yet persuasive in dealing with others a **diplomat**.

diplomatic /dɪpləˈmatɪk/ *adjective*
1 Diplomatic means relating to the management of relations between countries, or to diplomats and diplomacy: *diplomatic links between the two countries* □ *the diplomatic service.* **2** A **diplomatic** person is someone who is considerate, polite, understanding and yet persuasive in dealing with others. [*same as* **tactful**] — *adverb* **diplomatically:** *You dealt with her objections most diplomatically.*

dipstick /ˈdɪpstɪk/ *noun*: **dipsticks**
The **dipstick** in a car engine is a removable metal rod that shows you how much oil you have in the engine. [see picture at **car**]

dire /ˈdaɪə(r)/ *adjective* (*often intensifying or informal*)
Dire means bad or terrible: *They were living in dire poverty and distress.*

direct /daɪˈrɛkt/ or /dɪˈrɛkt/ *adjective or adverb*; *adjective*; *verb*
▷ ***adjective or adverb***
1 A journey or movement that is **direct** takes the shortest route: *There are no longer any direct flights from Edinburgh to the Isle of Man but you can fly there direct from Glasgow.* □ *Is there a train direct to Inverness, or do we have to change at Perth?* □ *Passengers not yet checked in are requested to go direct to the departure lounge.* **2 Direct** communication between people is from one to the other without any other person being involved: *She had a direct telephone link with the manager's office.* □ *You can call me direct using this number.* **3** A **direct** challenge or attack is one that is clearly intentional: *Her reply was a direct insult.* □ *I had dared at last to challenge him direct to his face.*
▷ ***adjective***
1 A **direct** cause or result of something, or a **direct** link between situations, involves no other factors: *The direct cause of the accident seems to have been a misleading road sign.* **2** A **direct** descendant of someone belongs to the unbroken line of descent through that person's children, grandchildren, great-grandchildren and so on. **3** Someone who is **direct** is frank, open and honest in expressing their opinions, especially too much so: *She could be embarrassingly direct in saying what she thought.* □ *I liked his direct manner.* [*same as* **straight**, **forthright**; *opposite* **sly**, **devious**] — *noun* (*uncount*) **directness:** *He was inclined to tell you what he thought of you with startling directness.*
▷ ***verb*: directs, directing, directed**
1 You **direct** something to or towards something or someone when you aim it at them: *He directed our attention to the archaeological exhibits.* □ *I knew her comment was directed at Jack.* **2** You **direct** a person somewhere when you tell them how to get there: *We asked a passer-by to direct us to the museum.* **3** You **direct** a letter somewhere when you put a name and address on it: *The parcel had been directed to our old address.* **4** You **direct** a scheme or project when you supervise its progress: *Frank was asked to direct operations.* **5** Police officers **direct** traffic at crossings when they signal to drivers when to stop or move on.

6 Someone **directs** a film, programme or play when they supervise its production. **7** You **direct** someone to do something when you ask, instruct or order them to do it: *We were directed to sit down and wait.*

direct current /ˈdaɪrɛkt kʌrənt/ *noun* (*uncount or count*): **direct currents**
Direct current is an electric current which flows in one direction. [see also **alternating current**]

direct debit /daɪrɛkt ˈdɛbɪt/ *noun* (*uncount*)
You arrange with your bank to have your regular bills paid by **direct debit** when you sign an order for the money to be drawn straight from your bank account by the person you owe it to.

direction /daɪˈrɛkʃən/ or /dɪˈrɛkʃən/ *noun*: **directions**
1 The **direction** someone or something is going in is the line they are moving along, or the point they are moving towards: *I'll give you a lift, since we're going in the same direction.* □ *He ran off in the direction of the swimming pool* □ *Does this road go in the Manchester direction?* **2** The **direction** something is taking is the way in which it is progessing or developing: *I was pleased with the direction my career was moving in.* **3** (*usually in the plural*) Someone gives you **directions** when they tell you what to do, or how to get somewhere: *I followed your directions for deleting the file, but I still couldn't get the computer to do it.* [*same as* **instructions**] **4** (*uncount*) **Direction** is the activity of supervising and controlling others in some task; **direction** is also the work of the director of a film, programme or play: *Under her direction we rearranged the library books according to subject.*

directive /daɪˈrɛktɪv/ or /dɪˈrɛktɪv/ *noun*: **directives**
A **directive** is an official instruction issued by someone in authority: *A directive came from the management that we were to increase our work rate.*

directly /daɪˈrɛktlɪ/ or /dɪˈrɛktlɪ/ *adverb*; *conjunction*
▻ ***adverb***
1 Directly means straight, with nothing coming in between, or with no extra person or consideration being involved; something that is **directly** behind, in front of, above, below, or opposite something else, is exactly in that position: *He was gazing directly at her.* □ *I'd prefer to talk directly to the manager.* □ *He was standing directly behind her.* □ *The library is directly opposite the post office.* □ *The North Star is always directly overhead.* **2** You do something **directly** when you do it immediately, without doing anything in between: *He went directly from the station to the hospital.* □ *We'll proceed directly to the matter of wages.* **3** You say something will happen **directly** when it is going to happen very soon: *Tell them I'll be there directly.*
▻ ***conjunction***
Directly means as soon as: *Please call me directly you get any news.* □ *Directly I'd said it I realized my mistake.*

direct object /daɪrɛkt ˈɒbdʒɛkt/ *noun* (*grammar*): **direct objects**
The **direct object** of a verb is the noun, noun phrase or pronoun that is affected by the action of the verb: *In 'He gave the boy a pound' the direct object is 'a pound' and the indirect object is 'the boy'.* [see also **indirect object**]

director /daɪˈrɛktə(r)/ or /dɪˈrɛktə(r)/ *noun*: **directors**
A **director** is **1** one of the people on the board of a business firm, who take decisions about how it is to be run: *She has been made a director of the company.* **2** the person in charge of an organization, institution, or project: *the director of the opera company.* **3** the person who supervises the production of a film, programmme or play: *She won the award for best director.*

directory /daɪˈrɛktərɪ/ or /dɪˈrɛktərɪ/ *noun*: **directories**
1 A **directory** is a book containing alphabetically arranged information, *eg* a list of people's names, addresses and telephone numbers: *a telephone directory.* **2** (*computers*) A **directory** is a location in the memory of a computer where a particular group of files are stored.

direct speech /daɪrɛkt ˈspiːtʃ/ *noun* (*uncount*; *grammar*)
Direct seech is speech reported in the actual words of the speaker: *'She said "I'm just leaving" 'is the direct-speech version of 'She said she was just leaving'.* [see also **indirect speech, reported speech**]

dirge /dɜːdʒ/ *noun*: **dirges**
A **dirge** is a slow sad song, hymn, or musical composition, used especially at a funeral.

dirt /dɜːt/ *noun* (*uncount*)
1 Dirt is any unclean substance, such as dust or mud, on a usually clean surface: *How did you get that dirt on your blouse?* **2 Dirt** is also loose earth covering the ground: *We drove for miles on dirt roads.* **3 Dirt** is another name for faeces, usually a dog's: *The pavements were covered with dog dirt.*
▻ ***phrase*** (*informal*) One person **treats** another **like dirt** if they treat them very rudely, as if they were worthless.

dirt-cheap /dɜːt ˈtʃiːp/ *adjective or adverb* (*informal*)
You buy something **dirt-cheap** if you buy it cheaply: *They supply much of Ukraine's oil dirt-cheap.* □ *living in dirt-cheap accommodation.*

dirty /ˈdɜːtɪ/ *adjective*; *verb*
▻ ***adjective***: **dirtier, dirtiest**
1 Something that is **dirty** has dirt such as mud, dust or stains on it and needs to be washed or cleaned: *Don't get your uniform dirty.* □ *My hands are dirty.* □ *There were dirty marks all over the wallpaper.* **2** A baby's nappy is **dirty** when the baby has passed faeces in it. **3** A **dirty** job is one that you get dirty doing: *She hated dirty jobs like gardening.* **4** You do something **dirty** if you act dishonestly or unfairly: *That was a dirty trick.* **5 Dirty** films, pictures, stories or jokes deal with sex in a deliberately shocking way. [*same as* **smutty**, **bawdy**, **lewd**] **6** A **dirty** word is **a** a word referring offensively to sex or the excretory functions. **b** (*humorous*) a concept that people no longer approve of: *The emphasis is on quantity; quality is a dirty word these days.*
▻ ***verb***: **dirties, dirtying, dirtied**
1 You **dirty** something when you get dirt on it or make it dirty: *Don't dirty your clean dress.* **2** Babies **dirty** their nappies when they pass faeces in them.

dis- /dɪs/ *prefix*
Dis- is used
1 before nouns, verbs, adjectives and adverbs to mean the opposite of something, or the lack of it, as in *discomfort*, *disapprove*, *disobedient* and *disagreeably*. **2** before verbs to indicate the undoing or reversal of something, as in *dislocate*. **3** before verbs to indicate the removal of something, as in *disarm*.

disability /dɪsəˈbɪlɪtɪ/ *noun* (*count or uncount*): **disabilities**
A **disability** is an injury or a physical or mental illness or handicap that seriously affects or restricts your way of life; **disability** is the condition of being restricted in what you can do by an injury or handicap: *She doesn't regard her blindness as a disability.*

disable /dɪsˈeɪbəl/ *verb*: **disables, disabling, disabled**
Something **disables** a person if it injures or affects them so severly physically or mentally that their way

of life is seriously restricted: *He had been disabled in the Vietnam war.*

disabled /dɪs'eɪbəld/ *adjective*; *noun*

▻ ***adjective***

A **disabled** person has an injury, or a physical or mental illness or handicap, that seriously restricts their way of life: *disabled by arthritis.*

▻ ***noun*** (*plural*)

The **disabled** are disabled people: *The disabled are encouraged to seek work that they can do in the home.*

disablement /dɪs'eɪbəlmənt/ *noun* (*uncount*)

Disablement is the state of being, or the process of becoming, disabled: *He claimed that his disablement had been caused by management negligence.*

disadvantage /dɪsəd'vɑːntɪdʒ/ *noun*: **disadvantages**

A **disadvantage** is a circumstance that causes a problem or difficulty: *The plan has a number of disadvantages.* [*same as* **drawback**]

▻ ***phrases*** **1** You are **at a disadvantage** if you are affected by some circumstance that does not affect other people, which may prevent your success: *Your inexperience with computers will put you at a disadvantage in the race for jobs.* **2** A circumstance is, or works, **to your disadvantage**, if it gives you problems that do not affect others.

disadvantaged /dɪsəd'vɑːntɪdʒd/ *adjective*

Someone who is **disadvantaged** is from a poor background and lacks the benefit of a good education and cultured environment.

disadvantageous /dɪsadvən'teɪdʒəs/ *adjective*

Something is **disadvantageous** if it causes you difficulties, or puts you in a bad position in relation to others: *The new tax arrangments will be disadvantageous to people on low incomes.*

disaffected /dɪsə'fɛktɪd/ *adjective*

A supporter of a cause, idea or party is **disaffected** when they become dissatisfied with it and are no longer loyal.

disaffection /dɪsə'fɛkʃən/ *noun* (*uncount*)

Disaffection is the dissatisfaction and disloyalty of former supporters of an idea, cause or party: *There was growing disaffection among the troops.*

disagree /dɪsə'griː/ *verb*: **disagrees**, **disagreeing**, **disagreed**

1 You **disagree** with someone about something when you have a different opinion from theirs about it: *We disagreed about which method to use.* □ *I disagree with her on most political issues.* □ *I'm sorry, but I absolutely disagree.* **2** You **disagree** with an idea if you think it is wrong: *I disagree with the theory that people are naturally lazy.* **3** (*informal*) You **disagree** with an action, policy or decision if you disapprove of it: *I still disagree with capital punishment.* **4** A type of food **disagrees** with you if it makes you ill: *Fish tended to disagree with him.*

[*opposite* **agree**]

disagreeable /dɪsə'griːəbəl/ *adjective*

1 Something **disagreeable** is annoying or unpleasant: *The smell was strong but not disagreeable.* □ *a disagreeable task.* [*opposite* **pleasant**, **agreeable**] **2** A **disagreeable** person is bad-tempered or unfriendly: *disagreeable neighbours.* — *adverb* **disagreeably:** *disagreeably loud music* □ *'Do it yourself,' he said disagreeably.*

disagreement /dɪsə'griːmənt/ *noun*: **disagreements**

1 A **disagreement** is an argument or quarrel: *We had another disagreement over money today.* □ *disagreements between husband and wife.* **2** (*uncount*) **Disagreement** is a state of things in which people have different opinions about something: *They were in total disagreement on the important matter of grants.* □ *There was some disagreement between us about how to deal with the crisis.*

disallow /dɪsə'laʊ/ *verb*: **disallows**, **disallowing**, **disallowed**

Something such as a claim, appeal or move **is disallowed** by an authority when they do not permit it, accept it or approve it: *Certain kinds of football tackle are disallowed by the rules of the game.* □ *Her objection was disallowed, and the court case proceeded.*

disappear /dɪsə'pɪə(r)/ *verb*: **disappears**, **disappearing**, **disappeared**

1 Someone or something **disappears** when they go out of sight: *We waved to them till they disappeared into the distance.* **2** People or things **disappear** when they go, or are put, where they cannot be found: *My pen has disappeared again.* **3** Something such as an institution, activity, movement or species **disappears** when it stops existing: *By the mid-80s the hippies had quite disappeared.* — *noun* (*count or uncount*) **disappearance:** *Things go missing from here every day and the number of disappearances is on the increase.* □ *Frequent prolonged droughts led to the disappearance of several of the smaller mammals.*

disappoint /dɪsə'pɔɪnt/ *verb*: **disappoints**, **disappointing**, **disappointed**

Someone or something **disappoints** you when they fail to satisfy you, because they are not what you want, or do not do what you want, or are not good enough: *She didn't want to disappoint her parents' expectations by giving up her degree course.* □ *Unfortunately we have to disappoint a large number of capable candidates.* □ *Venice disappointed them.*

disappointed /dɪsə'pɔɪntɪd/ *adjective*

You are **disappointed** when something that you hoped for does not happen, or turns out not to be good enough, or not what you wanted: *I was disappointed in my performance; I could have done much better.* □ *She realized that her parents were disappointed in her.* □ *Of course we're disappointed by the decision.* □ *I was so disappointed not to see you.* □ *I'm disappointed that the weather isn't better than it is.*

disappointing /dɪsə'pɔɪntɪŋ/ *adjective*

Something is **disappointing** if it is not as good as you hoped, or not what you wanted: *The response to the television appeal was disappointing.* □ *disappointing results.* — *adverb* **disappointingly:** *a disappoiningly low number of volunteers.*

disappointment /dɪsə'pɔɪntmənt/ *noun*: **disappointments**

1 (*uncount*) **Disappointment** is the condition of feeling disappointed: *He tried to hide his disappointment at her answer.* □ *To my disappointment the shop was closed.* **2** A **disappointment** is something that makes you disappointed: *It must have been a great disappointment to him not to get the job.* □ *The concert turned out to be a big disappointment.*

disapprobation /dɪsaprə'beɪʃən/ *noun* (*uncount*)

Disapprobation is disapproval, especially on a moral issue. [*opposite* **approbation**]

disapproval /dɪsə'pruːvəl/ *noun* (*uncount*)

You show or express **disapproval** of something or someone when you show or say that you are not pleased or satisfied with them: *He frequently voiced his disapproval of the way she dressed.* [opposite **approval**]

disapprove /dɪsə'pruːv/ *verb*: **disapproves**, **disapproving**, **disapproved**

You **disapprove** of someone or something if you are not pleased or satisfied with them, or do not consider them acceptable: *Her parents disapproved of her fiancé.* [opposite **approve**]

disapproving /dɪsə'pruːvɪŋ/ *adjective*
A **disapproving** comment or expression indicates dislike of, displeasure at, or dissatisfaction with, someone or something: *She cast a disapproving look at my dog.* — *adverb* **disapprovingly:** *She wagged her finger at him disapprovingly.*

disarm /dɪs'ɑːm/ *verb*: **disarms, disarming, disarmed**
1 To **disarm** someone is to take away their weapons: *Two police officers cornered the gunman and disarmed him.* **2** A country **disarms** when it reduces, or gets rid of, its stock of weapons, especially its nuclear weapons. **3** Someone **disarms** you when they charm you, or make you feel less hostile towards them: *They had quite made up their minds to dislike his girlfriend, but were disarmed by her naturalness and friendliness.* [*same as* **win over**]

disarmament /dɪs'ɑːməmənt/ *noun* (*uncount*)
Disarmament by a country is its act of reducing or getting rid of its stock of weapons, especially its nuclear weapons: *nuclear disarmament.*

disarming /dɪs'ɑːmɪŋ/ *adjective*
Someone's manner, behaviour or expression is **disarming** if it charms you, or makes you less hostile towards them: *She gave them a disarming smile.* [*same as* **winning**] — *adverb* **disarmingly:** *The boy grinned disarmingly.*

disarrange /dɪsə'reɪndʒ/ *verb*: **disarranges, disarranging, disarranged**
To **disarrange** something is to make it untidy: *The wind had disarranged her hairstyle.*

disarray /dɪsə'reɪ/ *noun* (*uncount*)
1 Things are in **disarray** if they are untidy: *Clothes lay in disarray all over the floor.* □ *The kitchen was in complete disarray.* **2** A party or armed force is in **disarray** when they are in a state of disorganization, confusion or demoralization: *The troops were thrown into disarray by the death of their leader.*

disassociate /dɪs'soʊʃɪeɪt/ or /dɪsə'soʊsɪeɪt/ *verb*: **disassociates, disassociating, disassociated**
You **disassociate** yourself from people or activities when you make it clear that you are not involved or connected with them, especially if you disapprove of them: *I disassociate myself entirely from my brother's political activities.* [*same as* **dissociate**]

disaster /dɪ'zɑːstə(r)/ *noun*: **disasters**
1 A **disaster** is a great and terrible event that happens unexpectedly and causes damage, destruction, suffering or deaths: *Over 1200 people died in the disaster.* [*same as* **catastrophe**] **2** You call something a **disaster** if it fails badly, or is very unsatisfactory or unpleasant: *This exam is going to be a disaster.* □ *The journey was a disaster.* [*same as* **fiasco**] **3** (*uncount*) **Disaster** is serious trouble, failure or ruin: *Disaster struck as their expedition neared its end.*

disastrous /dɪ'zɑːstrəs/ *adjective*
1 A **disastrous** happening is one that causes damage, destruction, suffering or deaths: *a disastrous famine.* **2** You call something **disastrous** if it fails badly, or is very unsatisfactory or unpleasant: *One disastrous appearance on television and you're finished* — *adverb* **disastrously:** *We failed disastrously.*

disband /dɪs'band/ *verb*: **disbands, disbanding, disbanded**
A military unit or other organized body **disbands** or **is disbanded** when it officially stops existing: *Some of the trade unions were disbanded during the '70s.*

disbelief /dɪsbɪ'liːf/ *noun* (*uncount*)
Disbelief is the state of not believing that something is true or exists: *She listened to him with evident disbelief.* □ *I can see you all shaking your heads in disbelief.* [*opposite* **belief**]

disbelieve /dɪsbɪ'liːv/ *verb*: **disbelieves, disbelieving, disbelieved**
You **disbelieve** a person or something they tell you when you refuse to believe them: *I've never known her to be dishonest, so I saw no reason to disbelieve her explanation.* [*opposite* **believe**]

disc /dɪsk/ *noun*: **discs**
A **disc** is **1** any flat thin circular object: *From the earth the moon looks like a silver disc.* □ *There was a metal disc on the dog's collar, with its owner's name on.* **2** a gramophone record. [see also **compact disc**] **3** (*anatomy*) a circular piece of cartilage between the vertebrae of your spine. **4** (*computers*) another spelling of **disk**.

discard /dɪs'kɑːd/ *verb*: **discards, discarding, discarded**
You **discard** something unwanted or useless when you get rid of it or throw it away: *Discard the lemon pips before chopping up the peel.* — *adjective* **discarded:** *plastic bags full of discarded clothing.*

discern /dɪ'sɜːn/ *verb*: **discerns, discerning, discerned**
1 You **discern** a person or thing when you see them by looking carefully: *I could just discern his familiar figure at the end of the passage.* [*same as* **make out**] **2** You **discern** something when you notice it or realize it through careful observation or reasoning: *I discerned a note of fear in his voice.* [*same as* **detect**]

discernible /dɪ'sɜːnəbəl/ *adjective*
Something is **discernible** if it can be seen, observed, noticed or realized: *A faint scar was discernible on her left cheek.*

discerning /dɪ'sɜːnɪŋ/ *adjective*
A **discerning** person is good at judging the quality of things and people: *She was a discerning judge of character.* [*same as* **shrewd, astute**]

discharge /dɪs'tʃɑːdʒ/ *verb*; *noun*
▻ *verb*: **discharges, discharging, discharged**
1 A person **is discharged** from the armed forces, or from hospital or prison, when they are given official permission to leave: *Patients were having to be discharged before they had fully recovered.* **2** You **discharge** your duties when you perform them: *He is now too ill to discharge the tasks expected of him.* **3** You **discharge** a debt when you pay it. **4** A substance **is discharged** from something when it flows out from it: *Clouds of yellow smoke were being discharged into the atmosphere from the chimneys.* **5** A ship **discharges** its cargo when it is unloaded.
▻ *noun* /'dɪstʃɑːdʒ/: **discharges**
1 (*uncount*) **Discharge** from hospital, prison or the army is the circumstance of being officially permitted to leave: *He was counting the days till his discharge.* **2** (*uncount*) Your **discharge** of your duties is your performance of them. **3** (*uncount or count*) The **discharge** of a substance by or from something is the process of sending it flowing out; a **discharge** is a substance flowing out of something: *a sticky discharge from the ear.*

disciple /dɪ'saɪpəl/ *noun*: **disciples**
The **disciples** of a great teacher or religious leader are the people who believe in, support and follow his or her teaching; the Twelve **Disciples** were the original followers of Christ.

disciplinarian /dɪsəplɪ'neərɪən/ *noun*: **disciplinarians**
A **disciplinarian** is someone in authority who is very strict with the people in his or her charge, and makes them behave well and obey the rules.

disciplinary /dɪsə'plɪnərɪ/ *adjective*
Disciplinary relates to the enforcement of rules and discipline, and the punishment of disobedience and other offences: *Disciplinary action will be taken against the children who started the fight.*

discipline /'dɪsəplɪn/ *noun; verb*
▷ ***noun***: **disciplines**
1 (*uncount*) **Discipline** is the training of people in orderly and controlled behaviour by insisting that they obey rules, and punishing them when they disobey: *Teachers must maintain good classroom discipline in order to teach effectively.* **2** (*uncount*) **Discipline** is the self-control, orderly behaviour and conscientious attitude to work and duty that results from this kind of training: *To train as a gymnast takes enormous discipline.* **3** A **discipline** is a subject of study at a university or college: *Opinions were invited from teachers and students of all disciplines.*
▷ ***verb***: **disciplines, disciplining, disciplined**
1 You **discipline** people when you train them to obey rules and behave or work in a controlled, orderly and conscientious manner: *She had disciplined herself over the years not to waste time.* **2** You **discipline** someone who has broken a rule or done something wrong when you punish them.

disciplined /'dɪsəplɪnd/ *adjective*
A **disciplined** person behaves and works in an orderly, controlled and methodical way: *She used to be so disciplined and hardworking.*

disc jockey /'dɪsk dʒɒkɪ/ *noun*: **disc jockeys**
A **disc jockey** is a person who presents a programme of recorded popular music on the radio or at a disco.

disclaim /dɪs'kleɪm/ *verb*: **disclaims, disclaiming, disclaimed**
You **disclaim** responsibility for, or knowledge of, something, when you say you are not responsible for it, or that you do not know about it: *She disclaimed all responsibility for the mistake.* [compare **deny**]

disclose /dɪs'kloʊz/ *verb*: **discloses, disclosing, disclosed**
You **disclose** something that others do not know when you tell it to them: *The caller refused to disclose his identity.* ▫ *She disclosed that her husband had been depressed for some months.* [*same as* **reveal**] — *noun* (*uncount or count*) **disclosure** /dɪs'kloʊʒə(r)/: *Disclosure of the plans at this stage would mean disaster.* ▫ *Every day the press issue fresh disclosures about his private life.* [*same as* **revelation**]

disco /'dɪskoʊ/ *noun*: **discos**
A **disco** is a party or occasion at which people dance to recorded pop music, or a place where this is done: *We're off to Paddy's Disco tonight.*

discolour /dɪs'kʌlə(r)/ *verb*: **discolours, discolouring, discoloured**
Something **discolours**, or **is discoloured**, when it loses its original colour and becomes faded, stained or dirty-looking: *Cigarette-smoking tends to discolour the teeth.* — *adjective* **discoloured:** *curtains discoloured with age and exposure to light.*

discomfort /dɪs'kʌmfət/ *noun*: **discomforts**
1 (*uncount*) **Discomfort** is pain or an uncomfortable feeling in a part of the body: *She's been in a lot of discomfort since her operation.* **2** (*used in the plural*) The **discomforts** of something are its inconvenient and uncomfortable features: *the discomforts of long-distance air travel.* **3** (*uncount*) **Discomfort** is embarrassment: *Her discomfort grew as more and more people turned and stared at her.*

disconcert /dɪskən'sɜːt/ *verb*: **disconcerts, disconcerting, disconcerted**
Something **disconcerts** you if it embarrasses, upsets or worries you: *Her remark disconcerted him.* ▫ *She was disconcerted by his long silence.* — *adjective* **disconcerting:** *The child gave her a disconcerting stare.* — *adverb* **disconcertingly:** *There was a disconcertingly small audience.*

disconnect /dɪskə'nɛkt/ *verb*: **disconnects, disconnecting, disconnected**
1 You **disconnect** an electrical device when you break its connection with the power supply, usually by removing its plug from a wall socket: *You should disconnect the television set every night as well as switching it off.* [*same as* **unplug**] **2** You **disconnect** things that are joined or fitted together when you take or pull them apart: *Disconnect these two wires.* **3** Your telephone, gas or electricity **are disconnected** when the connection or supply to your house is cut off or turned off by the authority in charge, *eg* when you have failed to pay your bill. — *noun* (*uncount or count*) **disconnection** /dɪskə'nɛkʃen/: *There should be no more disconnections for non-payment of bills.*

disconnected /dɪskə'nɛktɪd/ *adjective*
Thought, speech or writing that is **disconnected** is confused and does not flow logically: *All he had written was a few disconnected sentences.* [*same as* **disjointed, incoherent, rambling**]

disconsolate /dɪs'kɒnsələt/ *adjective*
Someone who is **disconsolate** is unhappy or depressed at something, and refuses to be comforted or to cheer up: *She was quite disconsolate at the death of her cat.* — *adverb* **disconsolately:** *Golfers and spectators waited disconsolately as the rain poured down.*

discontent /dɪskən'tɛnt/ *noun* (*uncount*)
Discontent is the feeling of not being contented or satisfied with your situation or circumstances: *Discontent with wage levels and conditions of work was growing among the employees.*

discontented /dɪskən'tɛntɪd/ *adjective*
You are **discontented** if you are not satisfied with your circumstances or situation: *He was getting increasingly discontented with his life.* ▫ *Her face had a discontented expression.*

discontinue /dɪskən'tɪnjuː/ *verb*: **discontinues, discontinuing, discontinued**
An activity **is discontinued** when it is stopped: *The practice of beating or caning children has been discontinued at most schools.*

discord /'dɪskɔːd/ *noun*: **discords**
1 (*uncount; formal*) **Discord** between people is disagreement, conflict or quarrelling: *The pay system in this office has always been a cause of discord.* **2** In music, a **discord** is a combination of notes played together as a cord, that lacks harmony.

discordant /dɪs'kɔːdənt/ *adjective*
1 A **discordant** sound lacks harmony or is an unpleasant mixture of noises: *The radio was playing some discordant modern music.* **2** Things are **discordant** if they produce an unpleasant, disagreeable impression: *His outburst of temper introduced a discordant note into the meeting.*

discotheque /'dɪskətɛk/ *noun* (*formal*): **discotheques**
A **discotheque** is a disco.

discount *noun; verb*
▷ ***noun*** /'dɪskaʊnt/: **discounts**
A **discount** is a reduction in price, or an amount taken off the normal price: *Employees can purchase the firm's products at a discount of 40%.*
▷ ***verb*** /dɪs'kaʊnt/: **discounts, discounting, discounted**
You **discount** something when you ignore it because

you think it is probably untrue or unimportant: *She discounted the dangers of the journey in her enthusiasm for adventure.* [*same as* **disregard**, **brush aside**]

discourage /dɪsˈkʌrɪdʒ/ *verb*: **discourages**, **discouraging**, **discouraged**
1 Something or someone **discourages** you when they make you lose hope or confidence, or take away your will to do something: *The sight of the rain discouraged her from going out that evening.* **2** You **discourage** someone from doing something when you try to persuade them not to: *Her parents actively discouraged her from taking up music professionally.* — *noun* (*uncount or count*) **discouragement:** *When she tried to introduce the scheme into the area, she met with a lot of disapproval and discouragement.* □ *a feeling of discouragement* □ *life's little setbacks and discouragements.* — *adjective* **discouraged:** *He was feeling depressed and discouraged about his future.* — *adjective* **discouraging:** *discouraging news.* — *adverb* **discouragingly:** *He spoke discouragingly about the prospects of peace.*

discourse /ˈdɪskɔːs/ *noun*; *verb*
▻ ***noun*** (*rather old, or formal*): **discourses**
1 A **discourse** is a talk, lecture or essay: *He was preparing a discourse on recent developments in American speech.* **2** **Discourse** is conversation, speech or communication between people: *We rarely entered into discourse about anything more interesting than the weather.*
▻ ***verb*** /dɪsˈkɔːs/ (*formal*): **discourses**, **discoursing**, **discoursed**
Someone **discourses** on something when they talk or lecture about it: *She'll discourse for hours on the stupidity of the older generation, if you give her a chance.*

discourteous /dɪsˈkɜːtɪəs/ *adjective*
Discourteous means impolite or rude: *a discourteous reply* □ *She'll think it most discourteous of you if you don't write and thank her.* — *adverb* **discourteously:** *We mustn't treat her discourteously by keeping her waiting.*

discourtesy /dɪsˈkɜːtəsɪ/ *noun* (*uncount*)
Discourtesy is impoliteness or rudeness towards someone: *I apologize for my discourtesy in not returning your call.*

discover /dɪsˈkʌvə(r)/ *verb*: **discovers**, **discovering**, **discovered**
1 You **discover** a fact or means of doing something when you find out about it: *I discovered that she was related to me by marriage.* □ *The cat has discovered how to open the door.* **2** You **discover** something when you find it by chance: *The 3000-year-old corpse was discovered in the mountains by two walkers.* **3** Someone **discovers** a thing or place that has not been known about before when they are the first person to find it: *The planets Pluto and Neptune were not discovered till this century.* **4** An athlete, performer or artist **is discovered** when someone recognizes their ability or talent, and helps them to become well known. **5** You **discover** an experience when you have it for the first time: *This summer I discovered the joys of climbing.* — *noun* **discoverer:** *Marie Curie, the discoverer of radium.*

discovery /dɪsˈkʌvərɪ/ *noun*: **discoveries**
1 (*uncount or count*) The **discovery** of something that no-one has known about before is the finding of it for the first time: *Fleming is usually credited with the discovery of penicillin.* □ *one of the most important scientific discoveries this century.* **2** (*uncount or count*) Your **discovery** of a fact you did not know is your realization of it; the **discovery** of an object is the finding of it by chance: *his discovery that his wife was being unfaithful to him* □ *After the discovery of the body events moved fast.* **3** (*count*) Someone such as an athlete, artist or performer who is a **discovery** has become famous with the help of people who recognized their talents or ability: *the fashion model Twiggy, a discovery of the '60s.*

discredit /dɪsˈkrɛdɪt/ *verb*; *noun*
▻ ***verb***: **discredits**, **discrediting**, **discredited**
1 An idea or theory **is discredited** when it is proved wrong or shown to be doubtful: *As each slimming formula is discredited a new one comes along.* [*same as* **debunk**] **2** To **discredit** someone is to give them a bad reputation, and destroy people's respect for them: *the present campaign to discredit members of the Cabinet.*
▻ ***noun*** (*uncount*)
Discredit is shame, disgrace or disapproval: *Some pupils have brought discredit on the school by misbehaving on the buses.*
▻ ***phrase*** Something that is **to** your **discredit** is something for which you deserve blame: *To my discredit I've never read her poetry.*

discreditable /dɪsˈkrɛdɪtəbəl/ *adjective*
Behaviour that is **discreditable** is disgraceful or shameful.

discreet /dɪsˈkriːt/ *adjective*
1 Someone who is **discreet** is careful to avoid causing embarrassment or trouble for others, and does not talk about secret, private or personal matters: *He's exceptionally discreet about his private life.* [*opposite* **indiscreet**] **2** A **discreet** notice or advertisement is designed to attract as little attention as possible. [see also **discretion**] — *adverb* **discreetly:** *He coughed discreetly to announce his presence in the room.*

discrepancy /dɪsˈkrɛpənsɪ/ *noun* (*count or uncount*): **discrepancies**
A **discrepancy** is a difference between things that ought to match or be the same: *The auditors discovered discrepancies in the accounts.* □ *A small degree of discrepancy is allowable.*

discrete /dɪsˈkriːt/ *adjective* (*formal*)
Things that are **discrete** are separate: *The office is now run as three discrete units.*

discretion /dɪsˈkrɛʃən/ *noun* (*uncount*)
1 **Discretion** is the quality of being careful not to cause embarrassment or trouble for others, and not to talk about secret, private or personal matters: *Please behave with discretion in all matters concerning his financial affairs.* [*opposite* **indiscretion**] **2** **Discretion** is also good sense and wisdom in making judgements and decisions: *I leave the arrangements to your discretion.*
▻ ***phrase*** Something is done **at** someone's **discretion** if it depends on their decision rather than on a fixed arrangement or rule: *Increases in salary are at the discretion of the Board.*

discretionary /dɪsˈkrɛʃənrɪ/ *adjective*
Matters that are **discretionary** are decided by a person in authority, rather than according to a fixed rule or arrangement: *The Board may award a discretionary grant in cases of need.*

discriminate /dɪsˈkrɪmɪneɪt/ *verb*: **discriminates**, **discriminating**, **discriminated**
1 You are able to **discriminate** between things if you can see and understand the difference between them: *Parents must teach their children to discriminate between right and wrong.* [*same as* **differentiate**, **distinguish**] **2** You **discriminate** against or in favour of someone when you unfairly treat them worse or better than others in the same situation: *He was accused of discriminating against female employees.*

discriminating /dɪsˈkrɪmɪneɪtɪŋ/ *adjective*
A **discriminating** person notices and chooses things of

good quality: *a discriminating judge of furniture.* □ *The design earned respect from discriminating critics.* [*opposite* **indiscriminate**]

discrimination /dɪskrɪmɪ'neɪʃən/ *noun* (*uncount*)
1 Discrimination against or in favour of a person or people is the practice of unfairly treating them worse or better than others in the same situation: *discrimination against people on the grounds of sex or race.* **2 Discrimination** is the ability to identify and select whatever is of good or worthy quality: *He lacks discrimination in his choice of friends.* [*same as* **judgement**] **3 Discrimination** between things is the act or skill of distinguishing between them: *Discrimination between fact and rumour isn't always easy.*

discursive /dɪs'kɜːsɪv/ *adjective* (*formal*)
People who write or speak in a **discursive** style take a long time to say what they want to, and add unnecessary material. [*same as* **diffuse, rambling**; *opposite* **concise, succinct**]

discus /'dɪskəs/ *noun* (*athletics*): **discuses**
A **discus** is a heavy metal disc, thicker towards the centre, which is thrown from the shoulder.

discuss /dɪs'kʌs/ *verb*: **dicusses, discussing, discussed**
1 You **discuss** something when you talk about it with other people: *They discussed ways of ending the industrial trouble.* **2** A speaker or writer **discusses** a subject when they deal with it or examine it in a talk, book or article.

discussion /dɪs'kʌʃən/ *noun*: **discussions**
1 (*uncount or count*) **Discussion** is talk or argument between people about a certain subject: *There has been a lot of discussion recently about how to deal with young criminals.* □ *Discussions between heads of state will take place in strict security.* **2** A **discussion** of a subject in a book, article or speech is an examination of it: *You'll find a discussion of the results on page 21.*
▷ ***phrase*** A matter is **under discussion** when it is being discussed: *The future of the company is still under discussion.*

disdain /dɪs'deɪn/ *noun*; *verb*
▷ ***noun*** (*uncount*)
Disdain is scorn you feel for something you consider worthless, or not good enough or important enough for you: *He regarded any kind of housework with disdain.* — *adjective* **disdainful:** *He was disdainful of his wife's writing activities.* — *adverb* **disdainfully:** *She looked at the painting and turned away disdainfully.*
▷ ***verb*: disdains, disdaining, disdained**
1 You **disdain** something when you reject it, from scorn or a feeling of your own superiority: *She disdained our company and sat down at another table.* **2** You **disdain** to do something when you you refuse to do it, because you are too proud or too rude to: *She disdained to save herself by lying.* □ *He disdained to answer my question.*

disease /dɪ'ziːz/ *noun*: **diseases**
1 (*count or uncount*) A **disease** is an illness caused by infection or by something that goes wrong with your body: *Disease is spread by flies.* □ *plant diseases.* **2** A harmful trend in society is sometimes called a **disease**: *Selfishness was a disease that people caught in the '80s.*

diseased /dɪ'ziːzd/ *adjective*
Something that is **diseased** is affected by disease: *Her liver was too diseased to function properly.*

disembark /dɪsɪm'bɑːk/ *verb*: **disembarks, disembarking, disembarked**
You **disembark** from a ship or aircraft when you get off it: *The passengers were permitted to disembark for an hour at Dar-es-Salaam.*

disenchanted /dɪsɪn'tʃɑːntɪd/ *adjective*
You are **disenchanted** with something that you once liked, enjoyed or approved of, when you become dissatisfied with it: *She was disenchanted with her job.* — *noun* (*uncount*) **disenchantment:** *There was growing disenchantment with the government.*

disengage /dɪsɪn'geɪdʒ/ *verb*: **disengages, disengaging, disengaged**
You **disengage** things that are linked or joined when you separate them: *He tried to give her a hug, but she disengaged herself from his arms.*

disentangle /dɪsɪn'taŋgəl/ *verb*: **disentangles, disentangling, disentangled**
You **disentangle** things that have become mixed up together or attached when you separate them: *She disentangled the dog's lead from the lamp post.*

disfavour (*AmE* **disfavor**) /dɪs'feɪvə(r)/ *noun* (*uncount*)
Disfavour is disapproval; you are in **disfavour** with someone when they dislike or disapprove of you: *He regarded all women drivers with disfavour.* □ *She had fallen into disfavour with her head of department.*

disfigure /dɪs'fɪgə(r)/ *verb*: **disfigures, disfiguring, disfigured**
Something **disfigures** a person, place or thing if it spoils their appearance: *Her face had been badly disfigured in a fire when she was a child.*

disgrace /dɪs'greɪs/ *noun*; *verb*
▷ ***noun***
1 (*uncount*) **Disgrace** is shame and disapproval; you are in **disgrace** when you have done something to make people angry with you and ashamed of you: *Your behaviour has brought disgrace on the whole household.* □ *He was sent home from school in disgrace.* **2** (*used in the singular*) You say that someone is a **disgrace** to those with whom they are connected if they bring shame on them by behaving in a shocking way: *You're a disgrace to the university.* **3** (*used in the singular*) You call something a **disgrace** if you are shocked or disgusted by it: *It's a disgrace that people in our own day should have to beg in the streets.* [*same as* **scandal**]
▷ ***verb*: disgraces, disgracing, disgraced**
1 You **disgrace** someone with whom you are connected when you bring shame on them by your bad behaviour: *He has disgraced his parents.* **2** You **disgrace** yourself when you do something that shocks people and makes them lose respect for you: *She disgraced herself by getting drunk.*

disgraceful /dɪs'greɪsfəl/ *adjective*
You call something **disgraceful** if it shocks or disgusts you: *Their selfish attitude is disgraceful.* [*same as* **scandalous, outrageous**] — *adverb* **disgracefully:** *I apologized for behaving so disgracefully.*

disgruntled /dɪs'grʌntəld/ *adjective*
You are **disgruntled** when you are disappointed, dissatisfied or angry about something: *Members continued to be disgruntled at the unequal distribution of funds.*

disguise /dɪs'gaɪz/ *noun*; *verb*
▷ ***noun*** (*count or uncount*): **disguises**
A **disguise** is make-up and clothing that you wear to alter your appearance, so that people will not recognize you; you are in **disguise** when you have altered your appearance in this way: *He was wearing a clever disguise.* □ *He arrived in disguise.*
▷ ***verb*: disguises, disguising, disguised**
1 You **disguise** yourself, or **are disguised**, as another person, when you dress and behave as they would: *She disguised herself as an ordinary tourist.* **2** You **disguise** something such as your voice or handwriting when you alter it so that people will not recognize it. **3** You

disguise your true feelings when you behave in a way that prevents people from knowing what they are: *She couldn't disguise her disappointment.* [*same as* **hide, conceal**]

disgust /dɪsˈgʌst/ *noun; verb*
▻ ***noun*** (*uncount*)
Disgust is strong disapproval and dislike for something that shocks or offends you: *He switched off the television in disgust.* □ *She expressed disgust at their cowardice.*
▻ ***verb***: **disgusts, disgusting, disgusted**
Something **disgusts** you if it shocks or offends you: *His selfish concern with his own career disgusted me.* — *adjective* **disgusted:** *I was disgusted with myself for doing so badly in the exam.* — *adjective* **disgusting:** *What disgusting behaviour!* □ *That fish smells disgusting.* — *adverb* **disgustingly:** *They were disgustingly greedy.*

dish /dɪʃ/ *noun; verb*
▻ ***noun***: **dishes**
1 A **dish** is a container, typically a round shallow one, for serving or cooking food in: *Serve the dessert in individual glass dishes.* **2** Food prepared and served as part, or one of the courses, of a meal is also a **dish**: *We'll have lemon chicken as the main dish, with some vegetable side dishes.* **3** (*used in the plural*) The **dishes** are the plates, containers and cutlery used for cooking, serving and eating a meal; you do the **dishes** when you wash and dry them: *We'll leave the dishes till the morning.* **4** A **dish** or **satellite dish** is a dish-like receiver for television programmes broadcast by means of artificial satellite, which people attach to the side of their houses.
▻ ***verb***: **dishes, dishing, dished**

> ***phrasal verbs***
> **dish out** (*informal*) You **dish out** something to people when you give it out or distribute it to them, especially in generous amounts: *He dished out the rice.*
> **dish up** (*informal*) **1** You **dish up** food when you serve it to people: *I'll dish up the first course.* **2** You **dish up** such things as facts, statistics or arguments, especially ones that have been heard before, when you present them to people.

dishcloth /ˈdɪʃklɒθ/ *noun*: **dishcloths**
A **dishcloth** is a cloth you use for wiping dishes when you wash them. [see picture at **kitchen**]

disheartened /dɪsˈhɑːtənd/ *adjective*
You are **disheartened** when you have lost hope or confidence, or feel depressed or disappointed about something: *He's failed his driving test again, but he doesn't seem very disheartened about it.* [*same as* **discouraged, downhearted**]

disheartening /dɪsˈhɑːtənɪŋ/ *adjective*
A circumstance that is **disheartening** depresses and disappoints you: *It's very disheartening when your hard work goes unnoticed.*

dishevelled /dɪˈʃɛvəld/ *adjective*
You are **dishevelled** when your clothes and hair are in an untidy state: *She came in from the garden looking hot and dishevelled.* [*same as* **bedraggled, unkempt**]

dishonest /dɪsˈɒnɪst/ *adjective*
Someone who is **dishonest** cheats or lies, or commits illegal acts such as stealing, and is unable to be trusted: *It would be dishonest of me to claim sickness benefit when I can still work.* □ *dishonest workmen.* — *adverb* **dishonestly:** *She acted dishonestly in not declaring her full income.* — *noun* (*uncount*) **dishonesty:** *I suspect them of slight dishonesty in the way they've presented the figures.*

dishonour /dɪsˈɒnə(r)/ *noun; verb*
▻ ***noun*** (*uncount*)
Dishonour is shame or disgrace: *The newspaper stories about her private life had brought dishonour on her family.*
▻ ***verb***: **dishonours, dishonouring, dishonoured**
1 You **dishonour** someone when you do something publicly to show your disapproval of them. **2** A bank **dishonours** a customer's cheque when it refuses to pay the stated amount of money, because the customer hasn't enough in his or her account.

dishonourable /dɪsˈɒnərəbəl/ *adjective*
Behaviour that is **dishonourable** is unworthy, dishonest, or not morally acceptable: *He would do nothing dishonourable, even to save himself.* — *adverb* **dishonourably:** *You acted dishonourably.*

dish rack /ˈdɪʃ rak/ *noun*: **dish racks**
A **dish rack** is a rack on which to drain dishes after they have been washed. [*same as* **drainer**; see picture at **kitchen**]

dish towel /ˈdiʃ taʊəl/ *noun*: **dish towels**
A **dish towel** is a cloth for drying dishes with. [*same as* **tea towel**; see picture at **kitchen**]

dishwasher /ˈdɪʃwɒʃə(r)/ *noun*: **dishwashers**
A **dishwasher** is a machine that washes dishes and cutlery used for cooking and eating a meal. [see picture at **kitchen**]

disillusion /dɪsɪˈluːʒən/ or /dɪsɪˈljuːʒən/ *verb; noun*
▻ ***verb***: **disillusions, disillusioning, disillusioned**
Something **disillusions** you if it makes you disappointed in something that you approved of or that you expected to be better: *She had always admired the medical profession, but her experience of working in a hospital had disillusioned her.* — *adjective* **disillusioned:** *I was feeling disillusioned with university and wondering whether to leave.*
▻ ***noun*** (*uncount*): *His disillusion with teaching grew as the months passed.* — *noun* (*uncount*) **disillusionment:** *He shared my disillusionment with the present government.*

disinclination /dɪsɪnklɪˈneɪʃən/ *noun* (*uncount, or used in the singular*)
You feel a **disinclination** to do something when you do not want to do it: *I had a profound disinclination to settle down to work.*

disinclined /dɪsɪnˈkleɪnd/ *adjective*
You are **disinclined** to do something when you do not want to do it, or are unwilling to do it: *You feel disinclined to get up on cold mornings like this.*

disinfect /dɪsɪnˈfɛkt/ *verb*: **disinfects, disinfecting, disinfected**
You **disinfect** something when you wash or clean it with a substance that kills germs: *I cleaned and disinfected the wound before bandaging it.*

disinfectant /dɪsɪnˈfɛktənt/ *noun* (*uncount or count*): **disinfectants**
A **disinfectant** is a chemical substance, usually in liquid form, that kills germs: *He poured some disinfectant down the lavatory.*

disinherit /dɪsɪnˈhɛrɪt/ *verb*: **disinherits, disinheriting, disinherited**
A parent **disinherits** a son or daughter when they arrange with their lawyer that the son or daughter will not inherit any property or money from them when they die.

disintegrate /dɪsˈɪntɪgreɪt/ *verb*: **disintegrates, disintegrating, disintegrated**

1 Something **disintegrates** when it breaks into a lot of small pieces: *The windscreen is designed to disintegrate in the event of a crash.* **2** Something such as society or a relationship **disintegrates** when it becomes less and less stable and collapses: *He watched his parents' marriage disintegrate.* [*same as* **fall apart**, **collapse**] — *noun* (*uncount*) **disintegration** /dɪsɪntɪ'greɪʃən/: *The defeat had caused a general disintegration of confidence and morale.*

disinterested /dɪs'ɪntrəstɪd/ *adjective*
1 A **disinterested** person is someone who is not involved personally in a certain situation and can be expected to judge it fairly: *Tell us what you think, as a disinterested observer.* [*same as* **impartial**] **2** Some people use **disinterested** to mean uninterested or unenthusiastic; others consider this an incorrect use: *a classful of disinterested students.*

disjointed /dɪs'dʒɔɪntɪd/ *adjective*
What someone says or writes is **disjointed** if it is confused and does not develop logically or make sense: *The woman was in a state of shock and could only give a very disjointed account of what had happened.* [*same as* **disconnected**; *opposite* **coherent**]

disk or **disc** /dɪsk/ *noun* (*computers*): **disks**
1 A **disk** or **floppy disk** is a flat plastic disc, coated with a magnetic substance, on to which data can be copied. [see picture at **office**] **2** A **disk** or **hard disk** is a stack of flat metal disks on which data is stored inside a computer.

disk drive /'dɪsk draɪv/ *noun* (*computers*): **disk drives**
A **disk drive** is the device that controls the transfer of information on to a floppy disk.

dislike /dɪs'laɪk/ *verb*; *noun*
▻ ***verb***: **dislikes**, **disliking**, **disliked**
You **dislike** someone or something if you disapprove of them or hate them: *You can't help disliking certain pupils.* ▫ *I dislike noisy children.* ▫ *He disliked having to get up early.* ▫ *What did you dislike most about school?*
▻ ***noun***: **dislikes**
1 (*uncount*) **Dislike** is the feeling of hating or not liking something or someone: *He made his dislike of her very obvious.* **2** (*used in the plural*) Your **dislikes** are the things you don't like: *On the subject of food, have you any particular dislikes?* [*opposite* **likes**]
▻ ***phrase*** You **take a dislike to** someone or something when you start hating or disliking them: *She took an immediate dislike to her new music teacher.*

dislocate /'dɪsləkeɪt/ *verb*: **dislocates**, **dislocating**, **dislocated**
You **dislocate** a part of your body when it is pulled out of its joint: *He dislocated his knee.* — *noun* (*uncount or count*) **dislocation** /dɪslə'keɪʃən/: *dislocation of the jaw* ▫ *fractures and dislocations.*

dislodge /dɪs'lɒdʒ/ *verb*: **dislodges**, **dislodging**, **dislodged**
1 You **dislodge** something when you knock it out of its fixed position: *She dislodged a few stones from the wall as she was climbing over it.* **2** To **dislodge** a person from a hiding place or a position of defence is to force them out of it.

disloyal /dɪs'lɔɪəl/ *adjective*
You are **disloyal** to a person or organization that expects your loyalty when you betray them or fail to support them, or when you are unfaithful to them: *She didn't want to be disloyal to her husband by criticizing him in public.* — *noun* (*uncount*) **disloyalty:** *She was accused of disloyalty to her friends and her country.*

dismal /'dɪzməl/ *adjective*
1 You describe something as **dismal** if it is depressing or gloomy: *dismal news* ▫ *Her face wore a dismal expression.* **2** Your performance at something is **dismal** if it is unsuccessful: *I was a dismal failure at most sports.* — *adverb* **dismally:** *It's dismally cold.*

dismantle /dɪs'mantəl/ *verb*: **dismantles**, **dismantling**, **dismantled**
1 You **dismantle** a machine or piece of equipment when you reduce it to the parts that it is made up of: *He completely dismantled the bicycle and rebuilt it.* [*same as* **take apart**; *opposite* **put together**] **2** You **dismantle** a structure or system when you get rid of it bit by bit: *The government seems intent on dismantling the welfare state.*

dismay /dɪs'meɪ/ *noun*; *verb*
▻ ***noun*** (*uncount*)
Dismay is a feeling of horrified realization: *I found to my dismay that I'd locked myself out of the house.* ▫ *We stared at one another in dismay.*
▻ ***verb***: **dismays**, **dismaying**, **dismayed**
Something **dismays** you if it shocks or upsets you: *There were no further unexpected happenings to dismay the guests.* — *adjective* **dismayed:** *I could see from her dismayed expression that I'd said something unforgivable.*

dismember /dɪs'mɛmbə(r)/ *verb*: **dismembers**, **dismembering**, **dismembered**
To **dismember** a body is to cut or tear it to pieces: *We watched a couple of lionesses dismembering a zebra.*

dismiss /dɪs'mɪs/ *verb*: **dismisses**, **dismissing**, **dismissed**
1 A person in authority **dismisses** you when they give you permission to leave: *She usually dismissed her class early on a Friday afternoon.* **2** You **dismiss** an idea or a theory when you reject it: *Nowadays most experts dismiss the strange phenomenon as the work of practical jokers.* [*same as* **reject**] **3** You **dismiss** something or someone from your mind when you decide not to think about them any more: *I dismissed the whole incident from my mind.* [*same as* **banish**] **4** You **are dismissed** from your job when your employer gives you the sack or gets rid of you: *She was dismissed for careless work.*

dismissal /dɪs'mɪsəl/ *noun*: **dismissals**
1 (*uncount or count*) **Dismissal** is the act of dismissing someone from their job, or the circumstance of being dismissed: *She knew she faced dismissal if she failed to meet work targets.* ▫ *It had been a year of dismissals and redundancies.* **2** (*uncount*) Your **dismissal** of an idea, theory or suggestion is your rejection of it.

dismissive /dɪs'mɪsɪv/ *adjective*
You are **dismissive** of something such as an idea or possibility if you reject it or refuse to consider it; you are **dismissive** of or about people's work or achievements if you indicate that you don't think they are of a very high standard. — *adverb* **dismissively:** *She spoke dismissively of her rival's work.*

dismount /dɪs'maʊnt/ *verb*: **dismounts**, **dismounting**, **dismounted**
You **dismount** from a horse or bicycle when you get off it: *She dismounted and wheeled her bicycle through the gate.*

disobedient /dɪsə'biːdɪənt/ *adjective*
Someone who is **disobedient** deliberately disobeys a rule or order from a person in authority: *disobedient children.* — *noun* (*uncount*) **disobedience:** *Disobedience will be severely punished.*

disobey /dɪsə'beɪ/ *verb*: **disobeys**, **disobeying**, **disobeyed**
You **disobey** a rule, or an order from someone in authority, when you deliberately do not do what they tell you: *She disobeyed orders.* ▫ *You'll be punished if you disobey.*

disorder /dɪs'ɔːdə(r)/ *noun*: **disorders**
1 (*uncount*) **Disorder** is a state of untidiness, confusion or disorganization: *The tenants had left the apartment in terrible disorder.* **2** (*uncount*) **Disorder** is violent, noisy and uncontrolled behaviour, such as rioting: *scenes of public disorder.* **3** (*count*) A **disorder** is an illness or disease: *skin disorders.*

disordered /dɪs'ɔːdəd/ *adjective*
Someone who has a **disordered** mind or imagination is mentally ill.

disorderly /dɪs'ɔːdəlɪ/ *adjective*
1 Disorderly behaviour is noisy, uncontrolled or violent: *He was arrested for being drunk and disorderly.* **2 Disorderly** also means untidy and disorganized: *I hate this disorderly way of working.* [*same as* **chaotic**]

disorganized /dɪs'ɔːgənaɪzd/ or **disorganised** *adjective*
1 Things are **disorganized** if they are in a state of confusion: *The timetable is always a bit disorganized at the beginning of term.* [*same as* **chaotic**] **2** You call a person **disorganized** if they are bad at making plans and decisions or doing things methodically: *I found him very disorganized to work with.*

disorientated /dɪs'ɔːrɪənteɪtɪd/ or **disoriented** /dɪs'ɔːrɪentɪd/ *adjective*
You are **disorientated** or **disoriented** when you are confused about where you are, or what day or time it is: *She woke up, at first disorientated and unaware of where she was.* — *noun* (*uncount*) **disorientation** /dɪsɔːrɪən'teɪʃən/: *Feelings of panic and disorientation seized her.*

disown /dɪs'oʊn/ *verb*: **disowns, disowning, disowned**
You **disown** someone or something that belongs to you or is connected with you when you refuse to acknowledge the connection, or formally end it: *I feel you should support your children when they get into trouble with the police, not disown them.* [*same as* **abandon, forsake**]

disparage /dɪs'parɪdʒ/ *verb*: **disparages, disparaging, disparaged**
You **disparage** someone or their achievements when you express scorn for them or indicate that you do not admire them: *We shouldn't disparage the pioneering work done by these early astronomers.* — *noun* (*uncount*) **disparagement:** *There's so much disparagement of charitable work these days.* — *adjective* **disparaging:** *We can do without your disparaging comments.* — *adverb* **disparagingly:** *He wrote disparagingly about modern poetry.*

disparate /'dɪspərət/ *adjective*
Things that are **disparate** are different, separate and distinct: *Reading and comprehending are two quite disparate skills.* [*same as* **discrete**]

disparity /dɪs'parətɪ/ *noun* (*count or uncount*): **disparities**
A **disparity** between things is a difference or inequality: *There was a disparity of 21 years in the ages of husband and wife.* [*same as* **impartial, detached**]

dispassionate /dɪs'paʃənət/ *adjective*
Someone who is **dispassionate** is able to judge a situation calmly and fairly, and is not influenced by personal feelings: *a dispassionate opinion.* — *adverb* **dispassionately:** *Try to view the problem dispassionately.*

dispatch or **despatch** /dɪs'paʃ/ *verb*; *noun*
▻ ***verb***: **dispatches, dispatching, dispatched**
1 You **dispatch** someone or something somewhere when you send them there: *The books will be dispatched from our warehouse tomorrow to your address.* **2** The business of a meeting **is dispatched** when it is dealt with, especially quickly and efficiently.
▻ ***noun***: **dispatches**
A **dispatch** is an official military or diplomatic report or communication, sent to headquarters from abroad by a representative.

dispel /dɪ'spɛl/ *verb*: **dispels, dispelling, dispelled**
Things such as doubts, worries or fears **are dispelled** when they are got rid of, or dismissed from people's minds: *Her cheerful presence was enough to dispel the gloom.*

dispensable /dɪ'spɛnsəbəl/ *adjective*
Something or someone that is **dispensable** is unnecessary, and can be got rid of: *Some of these items can be regarded as dispensable extras.* [*opposite* **indispensable**]

dispensary /dɪ'pɛnsərɪ/ *noun*: **dispensaries**
A **dispensary** is a place where medicines are issued, *eg* in a hospital.

dispensation /dɪspɛn'seɪʃən/ *noun* (*count or uncount*): **dispensations**
A **dispensation** is permission from someone in authority to do something that is not normally allowed, *eg* in a matter of religion: *Because of his health he was granted a dispensation from attending mass.*

dispense /dɪ'spɛns/ *verb*: **dispenses, dispensing, dispensed**
1 A person who **dispenses** medicine prepares it and gives it out to people. **2** To **dispense** something such as justice or advice is to administer it or give it out.

phrasal verb
You **dispense with** something you do not need when you get rid of it: *We can dispense with our old typewriter now that we have the word-processor.*

dispenser /dɪ'spɛnsə(r)/ *noun*: **dispensers**
A **dispenser** is **1** a machine that issues something to you: *a cash-dispenser.* **2** a holder or container from which you can get something: *a serviette-dispenser.*

disperse /dɪ'spɜːs/ *verb*: **disperses, dispersing, dispersed**
1 A crowd or mass **disperses** or **is dispersed** when it breaks up and goes away: *The police used tear gas to disperse the crowd.* **2** Something **is dispersed** when it is spread in all directions: *The seed is dispersed by the wind.* — *noun* (*uncount*) **dispersal:** *the dispersal of information.*

dispirited /dɪ'spɪrɪtɪd/ *adjective*
You feel **dispirited** when something has happened to take away your enthusiasm and confidence and make you depressed.

displace /dɪs'pleɪs/ *verb*: **displaces, displacing, displaced**
1 One thing **displaces** another when it forces it out and takes its place: *Word-processors long ago displaced typewriters as the one indispensable piece of office equipment.* [compare **replace, supersede**] **2** Something such as a bone **is displaced** when it is forced out of position: *I had a fall and displaced a couple of vertebrae.* — *noun* (*uncount*) **displacement:** *There is a certain amount of displacement in the upper part of the spine.*

displaced /dɪs'pleɪst/ *adjective*
A **displaced** person is someone forced to leave their own country, *eg* because of war or political, religious or racial intolerance.

display /dɪ'spleɪ/ *verb*; *noun*
▻ ***verb***: **displays, displaying, displayed**
1 You **display** something when you put it somewhere for people to see: *Some of the library's rarest books were displayed in glass cases in a special exhibition room.* **2** You **display** feelings when you behave in a

way that shows you have them: *She displayed no concern over her husband's illness.*
[*same as* **exhibit**]
▻ ***noun*: displays**
1 (*used in the singular*) A **display** of something such as a feeling is the act of showing it: *That was a disgraceful display of bad temper.* **2** A **display** of things is an arrangement of them laid out for people to see: *She walked along the street admiring the shop-window displays.* **3** A **display** of something is also a performance or event featuring a particular thing: *a gymnastics display.* **4** The **display** on a piece of electronic equipment is the part of it where information is presented visually: *Keep pressing the button till the display shows the right time.*
▻ ***phrase*** Something is **on display** when it is laid out for people to see: *On parents' evenings the children's work is on display in the classrooms.*

displease /dɪs'pliːz/ *verb*: **displeases, displeasing, displeased**
Something or someone **displeases** you when you are offended or annoyed by them, or not satisfied with them: *She had to admit that his appearance did not displease her.* [= she liked his appearance] — *adjective* **displeased:** *She made it clear that she was displeased with us for interfering.*

displeasure /dɪs'plɛʒə(r)/ *noun* (*uncount*)
Displeasure is what you feel when you are annoyed or offended at something, or not satisfied with it: *She expressed her displeasure by leaving before the end of the play.*

disposable /dɪ'spoʊzəbəl/ *adjective*
1 Something that is **disposable** is designed to be thrown away or destroyed after you have used it, usually after you have used it once: *disposable nappies.* **2** Your **disposable** income is the amount of your income that you have left for your own use when you have paid your taxes and bills.

disposal /dɪ'spoʊzəl/ *noun* (*uncount*)
The **disposal** of something is the act or process of getting rid of it: *the disposal of nuclear waste.*
▻ ***phrase*** You have something **at** your **disposal** if you can use it when and as you want to: *They put a car at her disposal during her stay.*

dispose /dɪ'spoʊz/ *verb*: **disposes, disposing, disposed**

> ***phrasal verb***
> You **dispose of** something that you do not want or need when you get rid of it, *eg* by selling it or throwing it away: *She decided to dispose of some of her books and pictures.* ▫ *This rubbish is a fire hazard and must be disposed of straight away.* ▫ *He quickly disposed of their objections.*

disposed /dɪs'poʊzd/ *adjective* (*formal*)
1 Someone who is well **disposed** to you likes you. **2** You are **disposed** to do something when you are willing or inclined to do it: *If you won't talk clearly it's not surprising that people don't feel disposed to listen.*

disposition /dɪspə'zɪʃən/ *noun*: **dispositions**
1 You **disposition** is your personality or character: *He had a naturally friendly and helpful disposition.* **2** (*used in the singular*) You have a **disposition** to do something if you are inclined to do it: *She showed no disposition to follow our advice.*

dispossess /dɪspə'zɛs/ *verb*: **dispossesses, dispossessing, dispossessed**
You **are dispossessed** of property or land when it is taken away from you: *After the civil war he was dispossessed of his house and estate.*

disproportionate /dɪsprə'pɔːʃənət/ *adjective*
Something that is **disproportionate** is surprisingly or unreasonably large or small in relation to other things: *Apparently we spend a disproportionate amount of our incomes on food.* — *adverb* **disproportionately:** *His ears seemed disproportionately small.*

disprove /dɪs'pruːv/ *verb*: **disproves, disproving, disproved**
You **disprove** something such as a theory when you show that it cannot be true: *The existence of God can be neither proved nor disproved.*

dispute /dɪs'pjuːt/ *verb*; *noun*
▻ ***noun*** (*count or uncount*): **disputes**
A **dispute** is an argument, disagreement or quarrel between people: *There has been a lot of dispute recently about whether sugar is really bad for you.*
▻ ***verb*: disputes, disputing, disputed**
1 People **dispute** something such as territory when they fight for control or ownership of it: *the disputed borderland.* **2** You **dispute** something such as a statement when you question it or deny it: *I wouldn't dispute that many old people are neglected.*
▻ ***phrase***
1 People are **in dispute** when they are arguing or disagreeing about something: *Management and employees were in constant dispute about pay.* **2** A matter is **in dispute** when people are arguing and disagreeing about it: *The ownership of the property is still in dispute.*

disqualify /dɪs'kwɒlɪfaɪ/ *verb*: **disqualifies, disqualifying, disqualified**
1 You **are disqualified** from doing something when you are forbidden to do it, *eg* because you have broken the law: *She was disqualified from driving for a year.* **2** You **are disqualified** from a competition if you are not allowed to enter, or are made to withdraw during the event, *eg* because you have broken a rule: *They were disqualified from the race for taking drugs.* **3** Something such as a personal circumstance **disqualifies** you for something if it stops you being suitable or eligible for it: *His poor eyesight disqualified him for a career in the navy.* — *noun* (*uncount or count*) **disqualification** /dɪskwɒlɪfɪ'keɪʃən/: *Anyone found cheating is liable to immediate disqualification.*

disquiet /dɪs'kwaɪət/ *noun* (*uncount*)
Disquiet is a feeling of anxiety, worry or concern: *Did you feel no disquiet at leaving the children alone in the house?*

disregard /dɪsrɪ'gɑːd/ *verb*; *noun*
▻ ***verb*: disregards, disregarding, disregarded**
You **disregard** something when you ignore it, or refuse to consider it: *Please disregard this reminder if you have already paid the bill.*
▻ ***noun*** (*uncount*): *She showed complete disregard for her own safety and that of others.*

disrepair /dɪsrɪ'pɛə(r)/ *noun* (*uncount*)
Something is in **disrepair** if it is in a bad condition and needs to be repaired: *When the last tenants left the building was neglected and fell into disrepair.*

disreputable /dɪs'rɛpjʊtəbəl/ *adjective*
1 You call someone or something **disreputable** if you disapprove of them because they are not respectable, or not honourable, or have a bad reputation: *I had heard of his disreputable business activities.* [*same as* **discreditable, shady**] **2** Something that looks dirty, untidy or worn-out may be called **disreputable**: *The caller was a young man of rather disreputable appearance.* [*same as* **shabby**]

disrepute /dɪsrɪ'pjuːt/ *noun* (*uncount*)

A thing falls, or is brought, into **disrepute** when something happens to spoil its good reputation and make people disapprove of it: *Their advertising methods had brought the firm into disrepute.*

disrespect /dɪsrɪ'spɛkt/ *noun* (*uncount*)
You show **disrespect** for someone or something when you fail to show them proper respect, or treat them rudely or impolitely: *Her disrespect for authority got her into a lot of trouble.* — *adjective* **disrespectful:** *Children are amazingly disrespectful to their teachers these days.* — *adverb* **disrespectfully:** *I apologize for speaking so disrespectfully.*

disrupt /dɪs'rʌpt/ *verb*: **disrupts, disrupting, disrupted**
A process or system **is disrupted** when something prevents or interferes with its smooth running: *Demonstrators tried to disrupt the meeting but were arrested by the police.* — *noun* (*uncount or count*) **disruption** /dɪs'rʌpʃən/: *Any further disruption to the schedule could mean cancellation of the whole project.* □ *The repair work is a major disruption for the whole museum.* — *adjective* **disruptive:** *Teachers in these schools are more likely to encounter disruptive behaviour* □ *children who get labelled disruptive.*

dissatisfaction /dɪssatɪs'fakʃən/ *noun* (*uncount*)
Dissatisfaction is a feeling of not being pleased or contented with something: *She expressed strong dissatisfaction at the way she had been treated.*

dissatisfied /dɪs'satɪsfaɪd/ *adjective*
You are **dissatisfied** with something when you are not pleased or contented with it: *She had become dissatisfied with her career.*

dissect /daɪ'sɛkt/ or /dɪ'sɛkt/ *verb*: **dissects, dissecting, dissected**
1 To **dissect** a plant, or the dead body of a person or animal, is to cut it up carefully little by little, in order to examine its structure. **2** You **dissect** something such as a problem when you examine it or discuss it in great detail. — *noun* (*uncount or count*) **dissection:** *Tomorrow we shall continue with the dissection of the upper arm.*

disseminate /dɪ'sɛmɪneɪt/ *verb*: **disseminates, disseminating, disseminated**
To **disseminate** something such as information is to spread it widely among a lot of people: *The more widely the facts about AIDS are disseminated, the better our chances of halting the epidemic.* — *noun* (*uncount*) **dissemination** /dɪssɛmɪ'neɪʃən/: *the dissemination of information.*

dissension /dɪ'sɛnʃən/ *noun* (*uncount or count*): **dissensions**
Dissension is quarrelling and disagreement: *causes of dissension with in the church* □ *quarrels and dissensions.*

dissent /dɪ'sɛnt/ *noun*; *verb*
▻ ***noun*** (*uncount*)
Dissent is disagreement, especially open and hostile, with an established idea or policy: *Within the party itself there was dissent on some key issues.*
▻ ***verb***: **dissents, dissenting, dissented**
You **dissent** from an established opinion or policy when you disagree with it: *I dissent from the common view that human beings are naturally lazy.* — *adjective* **dissenting:** *The policy was agreed on with only a few dissenting voices.* — *noun* **dissenter:** *Political dissenters were imprisoned.*

dissertation /dɪsə'teɪʃən/ *noun*: **dissertations**
A **dissertation** is a long formal piece of writing or essay on a particular theme, composed as part of a degree course at a university: *She's writing her dissertation on the growth of the slave trade in the 18th century.*

disservice /dɪ'sɜːvɪs/ *noun* (*used in the singular*)
You do someone a **disservice** when you do something that is harmful to them: *You are doing your children a disservice by doing their homework for them.*

dissident /'dɪsɪdənt/ *noun*: **dissidents**
A **dissident** is someone who expresses disagreement with the policies of the government or other organization that they belong to: *Known dissidents were rounded up and imprisoned.*

dissimilar /dɪ'sɪmɪlə(r)/ *adjective*
Things that are **dissimilar** are different from each other: *Fashions today are not dissimilar* [= are quite like] *to those of the '30s.*

dissipate /'dɪsɪpeɪt/ *verb*: **dissipates, dissipating, dissipated**
1 Something **dissipates** or **is dissipated** when it disappears: *The fog dissipated as the sun rose.* **2** You **dissipate** a resource such as money or energy when you waste it or use it carelessly: *Let's not dissipate our efforts on pointless and time-wasting schemes.*

dissociate /dɪ'soʊʃɪeɪt/ or /dɪ'soʊsɪeɪt/ *verb*: **dissociates, dissociating, dissociated**
1 You **dissociate** yourself from something when you deny that you have any involvement in it: *I should like to dissociate myself from the decision taken by my colleagues.* [*same as* **disassociate**] **2** You **dissociate** one thing from another when you separate them in your mind: *She began as a children's writer, and it's difficult to dissociate her from that role.*

dissolution /dɪsə'luːʃən/ *noun* (*uncount*)
The **dissolution** of an organization or assembly, or of a relationship such as a marriage, is the breaking-up or ending of it: *King Henry VIII ordered the dissolution of the monasteries.*

dissolve /dɪ'zɒlv/ *verb*: **dissolves, dissolving, dissolved**
1 A substance **dissolves**, or **is dissolved**, in a liquid, when it breaks up in the the liquid and disappears: *Dissolve 100 grams of sugar in one-eighth of a litre of water.* **2** A marriage or partnership **is dissolved** when it is ended: *Their marriage was dissolved in 1989.* **3** You **dissolve** into tears or laughter when you lose control of yourself and begin to weep or laugh helplessly. [*same as* **collapse**]

dissuade /dɪ'sweɪd/ *verb*: **dissuades, dissuading, dissuaded**
You **dissuade** someone from doing something when you persuade them not to do it: *We could not dissuade her from resigning.*

distance /'dɪstəns/ *noun*; *verb*
▻ ***noun***: **distances**
1 (*count or uncount*) The **distance** between places is the length of the space between them: *What's the distance from Blantyre to Zomba?* □ *Some of the children walk long distances to school.* □ *This picture is best viewed from a distance of about 2 metres.* □ *It's quite a distance* [= a long way] *to the next village.* □ *It's difficult to judge distance when driving at night.* **2** (*used in the singular*) You are at a **distance** from something when you are far away from it; you look at something from a **distance** when you look at it from far away; you see or hear something in the **distance** if you see or hear it when it is far away: *We live at some distance from the main road.* □ *From a distance, the hill looked like an elephant's head.* □ *She saw another ship in the distance.* □ *I could hear a train in the distance.* **3** (*uncount*) **Distance** is the circumstance of being far away from something or someone: *They say distance increases your affection for people.*
▻ ***phrase*** You are **within striking distance** of a place when you are close to it: *We were almost within striking distance of the shore.*

▷ ***verb***: **distances, distancing, distanced**
1 You **distance** yourself from a situation when you avoid becoming too involved in it: *Social workers must learn to distance themselves from the cases they are dealing with.* **2** A circumstance **distances** you from someone or something if it makes you feel less close to or involved with them: *She refused to let her career distance her from her family and background.*

distant /ˈdɪstənt/ *adjective*
1 Something that is **distant** is far away in space or time: *There was a distant rumble of thunder.* □ *I hope we shall meet again in the not-too-distant future* [= soon]. **2** A **distant** relative is one that is not closely related to you: *I've got some distant cousins in Canada.* **3** A person is **distant** when they are cool and unfriendly in their manner towards you: *She was courteous but distant as she opened the door to us.* **4** Someone's eyes or expression are **distant** when they look as if they are not concentrating, but thinking about something else: *Her eyes had a distant expression.* — *adverb* **distantly:** *He's distantly related to the Royal Family.*

distaste /dɪsˈteɪst/ *noun* (*uncount, or used in the singular*)
Distaste is a feeling of disapproval, disgust or dislike: *She looked round the room with an expession of distaste.* □ *He had a distaste for any kind of gossip.*

distasteful /dɪsˈteɪstfəl/ *adjective*
You find something **distasteful** if you disapprove of it or are disgusted by it: *The press's tireless investigation of the private lives of celebrities is distasteful to most of us.*

distended /dɪsˈtendɪd/ *adjective*
A part of the body is **distended** if it is swollen and unnaturally enlarged: *A distended belly is one of the signs of malnutrition.*

distil (*AmE* **distill**) /dɪˈstɪl/ *verb*: **distills, distilling, distilled**
1 You **distil** a liquid when you produce it in purified or concentrated form by boiling it till it evaporates as steam, then cooling it so that it becomes liquid again. **2** You **distil** facts from a mass of information when you find and record them after careful study and analysis. — *noun* (*uncount*) **distillation** /dɪstəˈleɪʃən/: *Whisky is produced from grain by distillation.*

distinct /dɪˈstɪŋkt/ *adjective*
1 One thing is **distinct** from another if it is different and separate from it: *The word has two distinct meanings.* [*same as* **different**] **2** Something that you see or hear is **distinct** if you can see it or hear it clearly: *The image of her face is still distinct in my mind.* [*same as* **clear**; *opposite* **vague**] **3** Something is **distinct** if it is definite or certain: *There is a distinct probability that I'll be sent abroad next year.* □ *a distinct likeness between mother and daughter.* [*same as* **definite**; *opposite* **vague**] — *adverb* **distinctly:** *I couldn't see the ship very distinctly.* □ *I distinctly told you to wait.*
▷ ***phrase*** You say you mean one thing **as distinct from** another when you mention something different or contrasting in order to make the thing that you mean clearer: *games such as football or hockey, as distinct from athletic activities such as running.*

distinction /dɪˈstɪŋkʃən/ *noun*: **distinctions**
1 (*count or uncount*) A **distinction** is a difference between things regarded as similar: *What is the distinction between turnips and swedes?* □ *There's little distinction between bravery and courage.* **2** (*used in the singular*) You make or draw a **distinction** between similar things if you regard them as different in some way: *We all make a distinction between hearing and listening.* **3** (*uncount*) **Distinction** is excellence in quality or achievement: *Her children all became people of distinction in one field or another.* **4** (*uncount or count*) You pass an exam with **distinction** if you achieve marks within the highest range: *I got four distinctions in my exams.* **5** (*used in the singular*) You have the **distinction** of being or doing something if that is a reason for you to be admired or respected: *I have the distinction of being descended from the founder of the college.*

distinctive /dɪˈstɪŋktɪv/ *adjective*
Something that is **distinctive** has particular individual qualities by which you can easily recognize it: *I caught sight of her distinctive handwriting on the envelope.* — *adverb* **distinctively:** *The distinctively shaped windows suggested a 16th-century date for the building.*

distinguish /dɪˈstɪŋgwɪʃ/ *verb*: **distinguishes, distinguishing, distinguished**
1 You are able to **distinguish** between things, or **distinguish** one thing from another, if you can see the difference between them: *The fake banknotes can easily be distinguished from genuine ones.* [*same as* **differentiate**] **2** You are able to **distinguish** something when you can just see it or detect it with one sense or another: *Two sails could be distinguished on the horizon.* [*same as* **make out**] **3** A feature or characteristic **distinguishes** one thing from another if it is one of the reasons why they are recognized as different: *The ability to use language distinguishes human beings from animals.* **4** You **distinguish** yourself when you do something that makes people praise, respect or admire you: *At school she distinguished herself both academically and athletically.* — *adjective* **distinguishing:** *One of this crow's distinguishing marks is a white ring round the neck.* [*same as* **identifying**]

distinguishable /dɪˈstɪŋgwɪʃəbəl/ *adjective*
Two things are **distinguishable** if you can see the difference between them: *As small children the twins were scarcely distinguishable.*

distinguished /dɪˈstɪŋgwɪʃt/ *adjective*
Someone who is **distinguished** is important and respected: *a distinguished surgeon* □ *He was tall and distinguished-looking.*

distort /dɪˈstɔːt/ *verb*: **distorts, distorting, distorted**
1 Something **is distorted** when it is twisted or pushed out of its normal shape: *The swelling round the tooth had distorted his jaw.* [*same as* **deform**] **2** You **distort** things such as facts, or someone's words, when you alter them by reporting or representing them inaccurately, usually to suit your own purposes: *She distorts and misreports everything I tell her.* [*same as* **pervert**] — *adjective* **distorted:** *Her finger joints were swollen and distorted with rheumatism.* — *noun* (*uncount or count*) **distortion:** *The disease is likely to cause severe distortion of the spine.* □ *The newspapers print nothing but lies and distortions.*

distract /dɪˈstrakt/ *verb*: **distracts, distracting, distracted**
1 Something **distracts** you or your attention when it stops you concentrating: *Passengers are requested not to distract the driver's attention while the bus is moving.* **2** You try to **distract** someone when you try to occupy their attention with something that will stop them being anxious or restless: *Fortunately a television cartoon distracted the children long enough for him to cook the supper.* [compare **amuse, divert**] — *adjective* **distracting:** *She needed to get away somewhere where there would no distracting telephone calls.*

distracted /dɪˈstraktɪd/ *adjective*
1 You are **distracted** when you are so anxious or wor-

ried that you cannot think clearly: *Distracted mothers were searching for their children in the ruins of the school.* [*same as* **distraught**] **2** Your attention is **distracted** when you are not concentrating on what you are doing: *He escaped while the guards' attention was distracted.* — *adverb* **distractedly:** *She rushed distractedly from room to room looking for the child.*

distraction /dɪ'strakʃən/ *noun*: **distractions**
1 (*count or uncount*) A **distraction** is something that stops you concentrating: *He wanted to get on with his research, and resented the distractions of family life.* □ *She worked mostly at the library as she found there was too much distraction at home.* **2** A **distraction** is also something such as an activity that entertains or amuses you: *The hotel provides a games room, swimming pool, organized sports and other distractions to keep the children busy.* [*same as* **amusement**, **diversion**]
▻ ***phrase*** Someone or something **drives** you **to distraction** when they upset or annoy you continually: *That noise is driving me to distraction.*

distraught /dɪ'strɔːt/ *adjective*
You are **distraught** when you are so worried or anxious that you cannot think properly: *Telephone lines were jammed with calls from distraught relatives.*

distress /dɪ'strɛs/ *noun*; *verb*
▻ ***noun*** (*uncount*)
1 Distress is mental or physical pain caused by grief, anxiety, injury or illness: *We did what we could to comfort the bereaved families in their distress.* **2** People in **distress** are in great danger or trouble and need urgent aid: *Food and warm clothing are needed to relieve the immediate distress of the flood victims.*
▻ ***verb***: **distresses, distressing, distressed**
Something **distresses** you when it upsets or worries you: *This news is bound to distress her.* □ *I don't want to distress him unnecessarily, but he must be told the truth.* — *adjective* **distressed:** *His family were too distressed at his death to talk to the press.* — *adjective* **distressing:** *I'm afraid I have some rather distressing facts to report.*

distribute /dɪ'strɪbjuːt/ or /'dɪstrɪbjuːt/ *verb*: **distributes, distributing, distributed**
1 You **distribute** things when you give, pass or hand them to a number of people: *The teacher began to distribute the test papers, one to each desk.* [*same as* **hand out**] **2** You **distribute** something when you share it between people: *You should learn to distribute tasks instead of undertaking them all yourself.* [*same as* **share out**] **3** (*commerce*) To **distribute** goods is to supply them to the shops that are going to sell them: *We distribute for a number of different publishers.* — *noun* (*uncount*) **distribution** /dɪstrɪ'bjuːʃən/: *You can't hope to sell your product without an efficient means of distribution.*

distributor /dɪ'strɪbjuːtə(r)/ *noun*: **distributors**
A **distributor** is a company or agent that receives products from manufacturers and supplies them to the shops that are going to sell them.

district /'dɪstrɪkt/ *noun*: **districts**
A **district** is an area of a town or country, sometimes as an administrative or geographical unit: *We were planning to spend a weekend in the Lake District.*

distrust /dɪs'trʌst/ *verb*; *noun*
▻ ***verb***: **distrusts, distrusting, distrusted**
1 You **distrust** someone if you do not believe them, because you think they are dishonest: *I distrust all politicians.* [*same as* **mistrust**] **2** You **distrust** someone or something that you consider unreliable or unsafe: *I saw no reason to distrust her judgement.* [*same as* **doubt**]
▻ ***noun*** (*uncount*): *The problems she had experienced had given her a strong distrust of anything electronic.*

distrustful /dɪs'trʌstfəl/ *adjective*
You are **distrustful** of someone or something if you do not believe them or think them unreliable: *I'm inclined to be distrustful of any reports I read in that paper.* [*same as* **suspicious**, **sceptical**]

disturb /dɪ'stɜːb/ *verb*: **disturbs, disturbing, disturbed**
1 You **disturb** someone when you interrupt what they are doing: *Sorry to disturb you when you're working, but I need your help.* [*same as* **bother**] **2** You **disturb** someone when you wake them up: *He asked not to be disturbed before 9.00 am.* [*same as* **rouse**] **3** Something **disturbs** you if it worries you: *The change in her appearance disturbed me.* **4** You **disturb** something when you move it or disarrange it: *Someone had disturbed the pile of papers she had left on her desk.* **5** Something **disturbs** a peaceful situation when it upsets its calm: *There was not even a breeze to disturb the stillness of the afternoon.* — *adjective* **disturbing:** *There have been disturbing overnight developments in the Middle East.* — *adverb* **disturbingly:** *The ozone layer is now disturbingly thin.*

disturbance /dɪ'stɜːbəns/ *noun*: **disturbances**
1 A **disturbance** is an outbreak of violent behaviour, especially in public: *The building had been damaged during a public disturbance.* **2** (*uncount or count*) **Disturbance** to or of someone or something is the act of disturbing or disorganizing them: *We shall ensure that the building work will cause minimum disturbance to readers using the library.* □ *The day had been full of interruptions and disturbances.* **3** (*uncount*) Mental or emotional **disturbance** is psychological damage or illness: *Most of the abused children show signs of emotional disturbance.*

disturbed /dɪ'stɜːbd/ *adjective*
1 (*psychology*) Someone who is **disturbed** is mentally or emotionally ill or damaged: *Teachers should not be expected to cope with mentally disturbed pupils.* **2** You are **disturbed** about something when you are very anxious about it: *He didn't appear in the least disturbed at having caused so much inconvenience.* **3** A **disturbed** time is a period full of trouble and anxiety: *She had had a disturbed and unhappy adolescence.*

disuse /dɪs'juːs/ *noun* (*uncount*)
Something such as a practice or tradition falls in to **disuse** when it is no longer followed: *Some Christmas customs are kept up, others have fallen into disuse.*

disused /dɪs'juːzd/ *adjective*
A **disused** building or other structure is no longer being used: *long-disused mines.*

ditch /dɪtʃ/ *noun*; *verb*
▻ ***noun***: **ditches**
A **ditch** is a drainage channel cut alongside a road or field: *He got the car stuck in a ditch as he was trying to turn it.*
▻ ***verb*** (*informal*): **ditches, ditching, ditched**
1 You **ditch** something that you no longer want when you get rid of it: *I've ditched my old typewriter and bought a word-processor.* [*same as* **scrap**] **2** You **ditch** a person with whom you have been having a relationship when you end it: *Marguérite tells Armand that she is ditching him for a rich old baron.*

dither /'dɪðə(r)/ *verb*: **dithers, dithering, dithered**
You **dither** when you hesitate and cannot decide about something: *She's still dithering about whether to sell her house.* [*same as* **waver**]

ditto /'dɪtoʊ/
Ditto is used to indicate the repetition of a word, and is often represented by the sign ("), placed beneath the repeated word.

divan /dɪˈvan/ *noun*: **divans**
1 A **divan** or **divan bed** is a bed consisting of a mattress on top of a thick base, usually without a board at the head or foot. **2** A **divan** is also a long low couch for sitting on, without a back or arms.

dive /daɪv/ *verb; noun*
▻ ***verb***: **dives, diving, dived** (*AmE* **dove**)
1 You **dive** into water when you leap into it headfirst with your hands stretched forward. **2** A diver **dives** when he or she goes down under the water wearing a special suit and breathing equipment. **3** A bird or aircraft **dives** when it descends steeply headfirst through the air; a fish **dives** when it goes down headfirst through the water. **4** You **dive** in a certain direction when you make a swift movement in that direction: *I saw her disappearing down a street and dived after her.* **5** You **dive** into something such as a bag or cupboard when you suddenly start looking or searching inside it: *She dived into her handbag and brought out the letter.*
▻ ***noun*** (*count*): **dives:** *He executed a rather wobbly dive from the side of the pool.*

diver /ˈdaɪvə(r)/ *noun*: **divers**
A **diver** is someone who works or explores under water, especially in the sea, wearing a special suit and breathing equipment.

diverge /daɪˈvɜːdʒ/ *verb*: **diverges, diverging, diverged**
1 Things such as lines or routes **diverge** when they separate and lead in different directions: *We walked along together to the point where our paths diverged.* [*same as* **part, split, fork**] **2** Things **diverge** when they are, or become, different from each other: *The situation here diverges too widely from that in the States to be compared with it.* [*same as* **differ, conflict**] — *noun* (*uncount, or used in the singular*) **divergence:** *The correspondence columns revealed a divergence of public opinion on the issue.* — *adjective* **divergent:** *Delegates expressed widely divergent views on sex education for teenagers.*

diverse /daɪˈvɜːs/ *adjective*
1 Things that are **diverse** are different from each other: *Activities as diverse as housework and dancing have a common movement element.* [*same as* **dissimilar**] **2** You can use **diverse** to mean 'various': *She decided to tell no-one she was pregnant, for diverse reasons.*

diversify /daɪˈvɜːsɪfaɪ/ *verb*: **diversifies, diversifying, diversified**
A manufacturer or other business company **diversifies** when it starts producing or doing a greater variety of things: *We shall have to expand and diversify if we are to keep our place in the market.* [*same as* **branch out**] — *noun* (*uncount*) **diversification** /daɪvɜːsɪfɪˈkeɪʃən/: *Should we opt for the safety of specialization or go for the risks of diversification?*

diversion /daɪˈvɜːʃən/ *noun*: **diversions**
1 (*uncount or count*) The **diversion** of something is the changing of its direction or purpose; a traffic **diversion** is an altered route to be followed by vehicles, *eg* because of roadworks or an accident: *There were a lot of roadworks and diversions on the motorway today.* □ *We have an arrangement for the diversion of funds to finance emergency measures.* **2** You create or cause a **diversion** when you draw people's attention away from something: *Her reappearance with a tray of coffee came as a welcome diversion.* **3** A **diversion** is something such as an activity that amuses or entertains you: *You don't have to spend your time sunbathing; there are organized beach games and other diversions.* [*same as* **amusement, distraction**]

diversity /daɪˈvɜːsɪtɪ/ *noun* (*uncount*)
Diversity is variety or range: *The project will bring together a great diversity of talent, from computing expertise to building skills.*

divert /daɪˈvɜːt/ *verb*: **diverts, diverting, diverted**
1 You **divert** something when you change its direction or purpose: *There had been an accident and traffic was being diverted by the police.* □ *Money set aside for development was being diverted to finance the famine-relief operation.* [*same as* **redirect**] **2** You **divert** someone's attention when you draw it away from something: *She managed to divert her mother's attention so that I could slip out of the house unnoticed.* [*same as* **distract**] **3** (*old*) To **divert** people is to amuse them: *We were greatly diverted by your account of the school expedition.*

divest /daɪˈvɛst/ *verb* (*formal*): **divests, divesting, divested**
1 You **divest** yourself of something you are wearing or carrying when you take it off or put it down: *I was relieved to be able to divest myself of the heavy rucksack.* **2** To **divest** a person or thing of a quality or function is to take it away from them, or deprive them of it: *Intense media coverage has divested the Royal Family of its special glamour and mystery.*

divide /dɪˈvaɪd/ *verb; noun*
▻ ***verb***: **divides, dividing, divided**
1 Something **divides** or **is divided** when it is separated into parts: *The search party divided into three at the foot of the mountain.* □ *Those who answered the questionnaire can be divided into two main groups.* [*same as* **split**] **2** Something that consists of a number of sections **is divided** into these sections: *The country is divided into regions, and each region is divided into districts.* [*same as* **split**] **3** You **divide** something between or among *eg* people when you share it out between them: *The money was to be equally divided between* (or *among*) *her three children.* **4** Something **divides** an area in or into two, or **divides** two areas, if it acts as a boundary or barrier: *The Ural Mountains are regarded as dividing Europe and Asia.* □ *The room was divided into two by a large bookcase.* **5** An issue **divides** people when they disagree over it: *The contraception debate is dividing the Catholic church.* **6** (*mathematics*) You **divide** a larger number by a smaller one when you calculate how many times the smaller one is contained by, or goes into, the larger one: *100 divided by 20 is 5* (written *100 ÷ 20 = 5*).
▻ ***noun***: **divides**
A **divide** is a split or division, especially between two attitudes or points of view: *Increasingly they found themselves on different sides of the great political divide.* — *adjective* **divided:** *The public are divided on this issue.*

> ***phrasal verb***
> You **divide** something **up** between or among people when you share it out: *We divided up the remaining food between us.*

dividend /ˈdɪvɪdɛnd/ *noun*: **dividends**
A **dividend** is a proportion of a company's profits that is paid to each shareholder.
▻ ***phrase*** Something you do **pays dividends** if it brings you benefits or advantages later on: *Learning poetry and literature by heart when your memory is young pays dividends in later life.*

dividers /dɪˈvaɪdəz/ *noun* (*plural*)
Dividers are, or a pair of **dividers** is, a two-legged geometrical instrument used for measuring angles.

divine /dɪˈvaɪn/ *adjective; verb*

▻ ***adjective***

1 A **divine** being is a god or goddess; something that is **divine** belongs to, or comes from, God, a god or goddess: *divine wisdom.* **2** You call something **divine** if you think it is lovely or delightful: *What divine weather!* — *adverb* **divinely:** *divinely inspired poetry* ▫ *(informal) a divinely beautiful girl.*

▻ ***verb*** *(formal; literary)*: **divines, divining, divined**

You **divine** something when you guess it correctly: *I think she may already have divined the truth.*

diving /ˈdaɪvɪŋ/ *noun (uncount)*

1 Diving is the sport or profession of going down under the water, wearing a special suit and breathing equipment, for the purpose of exploring or carrying out various types of work. **2 Diving** is also the activity or sport of leaping headfirst into water with the arms stretched forward.

diving board /ˈdaɪvɪŋ bɔːd/ *noun*: **diving boards**

A **diving board** is a narrow platform from which swimmers can dive into a swimming pool.

divinity /dɪˈvɪnɪtɪ/ *noun*: **divinities**

1 *(uncount)* **Divinity** is the study of religion or theology. **2** *(uncount)* **Divinity** is the quality of being divine: *Many hereditary rulers through the ages have laid claim to divinity.* **3** A **divinity** is a god or goddess.

divisible /dɪˈvɪzəbəl/ *adjective*

Something that is **divisible** can be divided; a number that is **divisible** by a smaller number can be divided by that number: *256 is divisible by 8.* [opposite **indivisible**]

division /dɪˈvɪʒən/ *noun*: **divisions**

1 *(uncount or count)* The **division** of something is the separation of it into individual parts: *rapid cell-division* ▫ *the division of society into classes.* **2** *(uncount, or used in the singular)* The **division** of something between or among people is the sharing of it: *We must work out a fair division of labour.* **3** A **division** is a disagreement or difference of opinion between people or groups: *There are deep divisions within the party.* **4** A **division** is a section or department of an organization: *She works in the administrative division.* **5** In sports or other activities, people may be put into graded **divisions** according to ability: *the first-division football teams.* **6** A **division** can be a boundary or barrier between areas: *To the north, a mountain ridge forms the division between Perthshire and Inverness-shire.* **7** *(uncount; mathematics)* **Division** is the process of calculating how many times a smaller number is contained by, or goes into, a larger number, and is represented by the **division** sign (÷): *multiplication and division.*

divisive /dɪˈvaɪsɪv/ *adjective*

Things that are **divisive** tend to cause disagreement and hostility between people: *His policy of creating a hierarchy in a department of formally equal colleagues was unpopular and divisive.*

divorce /dɪˈvɔːs/ *noun; verb*

▻ ***noun*** *(uncount or count)*: **divorces**

Divorce is the formal and legal ending of a marriage, leaving the former husband and wife free to marry again: *His first two marriages had ended in divorce.* ▫ *Her husband refused to give her a divorce.*

▻ ***verb***: **divorces, divorcing, divorced**

1 A married couple **divorces**, or one member of it **divorces** their husband or wife, when their marriage is legally and formally ended: *She divorced him on the grounds of adultery.* **2** To **divorce** one thing from another is to regard and treat the two things as different and separate: *Politics is a product of economics; you can't divorce the two.* — *adjective* **divorced:** *a divorced mother of three* ▫ *We decided to get divorced.*

divorcee /dɪvɔːˈsiː/ *noun*: **divorcees**

A **divorcee** is a divorced person: *He's engaged to a divorcee with four children.*

divulge /daɪˈvʌldʒ/ *verb*: **divulges, divulging, divulged**

You **divulge** something that is secret when you tell people about it: *He refused to divulge details of his income to the press.* [*same as* **disclose**]

DIY /diːaɪˈwaɪ/ *noun (uncount)*

DIY stands for 'do-it-yourself' and is the activity of making and repairing articles in your own home, without employing professional experts: *They built the boat from a DIY kit.*

dizzy /ˈdɪzɪ/ *adjective*: **dizzier, dizziest**

1 You are **dizzy** when you feel unsteady and unbalanced, as if you might fall, and things seem to be going round and round: *The dancing made her feel dizzy and she had to sit down.* [*same as* **giddy**] **2** A **dizzy** height is somewhere very high: *She had reached the dizzy heights of fame and success.* — *noun (uncount)* **dizziness:** *He complained of dizziness and a headache.*

do[1] /duː/ *auxiliary verb; noun*

▻ ***auxiliary verb*** *(negative forms* **do not** *or* **don't**): **does** *(negative forms* **does not** *or* **doesn't**): **did** /dɪd/ *(negative forms* **did not** *or* **didn't**)

1 Do is used with *not* or *-n't* before the infinitive form of a verb to form its negative in the simple present and past: *I don't know her.* ▫ *She did not want to see him ever again.* ▫ *It doesn't feel very warm.*

2 Do is used with the infinitive form of a verb to form questions in the simple present and past, and is placed before the subject: *Does the committee make all the decisions?* ▫ *Doesn't she care?* ▫ *Do you take a lot of exercise?* ▫ *Don't they realize that yet?* ▫ *Did you tell her?* ▫ *Where did you put it?* ▫ *Why didn't you do as I asked?*

> Note that **do** is not used with the verb *be*, or with the verb *have* when used as an auxiliary verb, or with modal verbs: *Can you* (not *do you can*) *see her?* But notice *have* meaning 'own' or 'possess': *Do you have* (or *have you got*, or *have you*) *a match?*;
> Note also that in questions **do** can be used with the words *who*, *what* and *which* only where they are the object, not where they are the subject: *What did you do?* But *Who told you?* (not *Who did tell you?*)

3 Do is used to form negative commands: *Don't cross the road yet.* ▫ *Don't talk to your mother like that.*

> Note that in this use, **do** can occur with *be*: *Don't be silly!*

4 Do is used to refer back to a verb already used, so as to avoid repeating it: *Even Esther knew her English Literature better than I did.* ▫ *'Do you have the time on you?' 'No, sorry, I don't.'* ▫ *He loves walking and so does she.* ▫ *If you haven't yet collected your mail, please do so now.*

5 Do is used in question tags: *They call on Fridays, don't they?* ▫ *He works too hard, doesn't he?* ▫ *You didn't like her, did you?*

6 Do is used for emphasis, with a strong stress on it: *I did tell you about it.* ▫ *Do come in.*

> Note that in this use **do** can occur in questions with *who*, *what* and *which* as subject: *Well, who does care about the homeless nowadays?*

▻ ***noun*** *(used in the plural)*

Dos and **don'ts** are things you must do or must not do, in certain circumstances: *the dos and don'ts of first aid.*

do² /duː/ *verb; noun*

▻ ***verb*: does, doing, did, done**

1 a You **do** something when you perform an action, task or activity: *I haven't done the washing or ironing yet.* □ *I stayed at home and did some work.* □ *Did you do these drawings yourself?* □ *What are you doing?* □ *Are you doing anything special tomorrow?* □ *You get bored when you've nothing to do.* **b** You **do** something when you act or take action: *Can we do anything to help?* □ *We must do something.* **c** You **do** something about or with a thing or person when you deal with them: *Is the government doing anything about unemployment?* □ *What are you going to do with the children when you go abroad?* □ *My hair's such a mess; I can't do a thing with it.* **d** You ask someone what they **did** with something when you want to know where they put it: *What did you do with my pen?*

2 a You **do** something such as your hair, or your teeth, when you do what usually needs to be done to them, that is, comb your hair, or brush your teeth: *Have you done* [= made] *the beds?* □ *I'll go and do* [= wash and dry] *the dishes.* **b** You **do** a room or a piece of furniture or equipment when you clean it: *I'll do the sitting room next.* □ *I haven't done the silver for weeks.* **c** You **do** something such as the flowers or your hair when you arrange them: *You've done your hair a new way.* **d** (*informal*) People **do** drugs when they use them or inject them.

3 a You ask someone what they **do** when you want to know what their job is: *'What does she do?' 'She's a dentist.'* □ *'What would you like to do?' 'I'd like to be an archaeologist.'* **b** You **do** a subject when it is one of the things you study at school or university: *I'm doing French, English and History at Advanced Level.* **c** A business or company **does** a service when it provides it: *The large hotels usually do theatre bookings for you.* □ *We do deliveries every weekday.*

4 a A person **does** well or badly when they are successful or unsuccessful: *She did well in her exams.* **b** You **do** someone something such as harm or good when your actions have that effect on them: *You did me a good turn when you made me go for a walk.* □ *The government's new measures will do nothing but damage.* □ *We don't yet know what the delay will do to the schedule.*

5 A vehicle or its driver **is doing** a certain speed when they are moving at that speed: *He was doing 110 mph on the motorway.* □ *These trains can do 150 mph.*

6 You say that something will **do**, or will **do** you, if you think it is satisfactory or sufficient: *I can't find the knife you wanted, but will this one do?* □ *Would £20 do you till I get to the bank?* □ *Your spelling and grammar simply will not do.*

▻ ***noun*: dos or do's**

1 (*informal*) A **do** is a party, celebration or other social event: *I'm going to have a big do for my 21st birthday.* **2** For **dos** and **don'ts** see **do**¹.

▻ ***phrases*** (*informal*) **1** You say you **can't be doing with** something or someone if you don't approve of them: *I can't be doing with people who don't finish a job properly.* **2** You say you **could do with** something when you need it; if you say you **could do without** something, you mean it is a nuisance and you would rather not have to deal with it: *We could do with some help.* **3** You **do your best** to achieve something when you try as hard as you can to achieve it: *It doesn't matter if you fail, as long as you do your best.* □ *The weather was doing its best to spoil the picnic.* **4 a** You **do it** when you achieve what you want to: *Congratulations! I knew you'd do it.* □ *I've done it!* **b** (*informal*) Someone or something **does it** when they spoil or ruin something: *You've done it now!* □ *That does it!* **5 a** One thing **has**, or **is**, **to do with** another if it is connected or involved with it: *Hasn't the binary system got something to do with computers?* □ *Is your question to do with the assignment you've been given?* □ *He took an arts degree and now he's something to do with the theatre.* □ *This has nothing to do with what we were discussing.* **b** When you tell people that a matter **has** or **is** nothing **to do with** them, you mean that it does not concern them and you don't want them to interfere in it. **6** (*formal*) People use the greeting **'how do you do?'** when they are introduced to each other. **7** (*informal*) You say that something does **not do much for**, or **does nothing for**, someone if you think it gives others a bad impression of them: *This scandal won't do much for his reputation.* □ *Those jeans do nothing for you.* **8** For **nothing doing** see **nothing**. **9** (*informal*) If you say that a certain task will **take some doing**, or **take a bit of doing**, you mean it will be difficult. **10** You ask **what** someone or something **is doing** in a certain place when you want to know why they are there: *Fancy meeting you! What are you doing in Prague?* □ *What is my file doing on your desk?* **11** For **well done** see **well**.

phrasal verbs

do away with You **do away with** something when you get rid of it: *We've done away with many of the traditional teaching methods.*

do down (*informal*) You **do** someone or something **down** when you describe them in a critical or derogatory way to other people.

do for (*informal*) Something **does for** you, or you **are done for** when you are ruined or destroyed: *Drink did for him in the end.* □ *I'm done for unless I pass this exam.*

do in (*slang*) To **do** someone **in** is to kill or murder them: *In the end she gets done in by a jealous lover.*

do out of (*informal*) Someone **does** you **out of** something if they do something unfair or dishonest to stop you getting it: *We were done out of £1000.*

do up 1 You **do up** something such as a piece of clothing when you fasten it: *He did his coat up and put on his hat.* [*opposite* **undo**] **2** You **do up** something in a parcel when you wrap it: *prettily done-up gifts.* **3** You **do up** a building when you repair and decorate it: *She buys properties and does them up for letting.*

do without You **do without** something when you manage in spite of not having it: *We did without a television for several months.* □ *If we can't get the right flour, we'll just have to do without.*

docile /ˈdoʊsaɪl/ (*AmE*/ˈdɒsəl/) *adjective*

A person or animal that is **docile** is quiet, obedient and easy to control. — *noun* (*uncount*) **docility** /doʊˈsɪlətɪ/: *These ponies are noted for their docility.*

dock¹ /dɒk/ *noun; verb*

▻ ***noun*: docks**

A **dock** is a part of a harbour where ships are loaded, unloaded, and repaired; the **docks** are the harbour area: *Liverpool Docks.*

▻ ***verb*: docks, docking, docked**

1 A ship **docks** or **is docked** when it comes into a dock after a voyage: *We're due to dock at Hull in 50 minutes.* **2** Space craft **dock** or **are docked** when they link up in space.

dock² /dɒk/ *verb*: **docks, docking, docked**

You **dock** someone's wages when you reduce them: *They dock your wages if you damage the equipment.*

dock³ /dɒk/ *noun*: **docks**

In a court of law, the **dock** is the enclosure in which the accused person sits or stands.

docker /'dɒkə(r)/ *noun*: **dockers**
A **docker** is a labourer who works in the docks, mainly loading and unloading ships.

doctor /'dɒktə(r)/ *noun*; *verb*
▻ ***noun*: doctors**
1 A **doctor** is a person trained and qualified in medical science, who treats people when they are ill or injured: *We had to call the doctor in the middle of the night* □ *Dr Robinson.* **2** You go to the **doctor's** when you attend a doctor's surgery or clinic. **3** Someone who holds a postgraduate degree called a doctorate also has the title **doctor**. [compare **bachelor, master**]
▻ ***verb*: doctors, doctoring, doctored**
1 To **doctor** accounts, reports or results is to alter them dishonestly to suit one's own purpose and to deceive others: *He was later proved to have doctored the statistics to fit his theory.* [*same as* **falsify**] **2** To **doctor** food or drink is to put poison or a drug in it.

doctorate /'dɒktərət/ *noun*: **doctorates**
A **doctorate** is a high academic degree, awarded to someone by a university, usually for research.

doctrinaire /dɒktrɪ'nɛə(r)/ *adjective* (*derogatory*)
Someone who is **doctrinaire** depends too much on the correctness of theories, and takes no notice of practical objections.

doctrine /'dɒktrɪn/ *noun* (*count or uncount*): **doctrines**
A **doctrine** is a teaching or set of teachings, especially relating to religious belief and principle: *the doctrine of redemption.* — *adjective* **doctrinal** /dɒk'traɪnəl/: *doctrinal dificulties.*

document /'dɒkjəmənt/ *noun*; *verb*
▻ ***noun*: documents**
A **document** is a formal paper bearing important or official information: *They asked to see my passport and driving licence, and other personal documents.*
▻ ***verb*** /'dɒkjəmɛnt/: **documents, documenting, documented**
You **document** something when you produce a written or filmed account of it, supporting your statements with evidence and proof: *a well-documented report on the spread of leprosy in the 19th century.* — *noun* (*uncount*) **documentation** /dɒkjəmɛn'teɪʃən/: *I can supply documentation for these stories.*

documentary /dɒkjə'mɛntərɪ/ *noun*; *adjective*
▻ ***noun*: documentaries**
A **documentary** is a television or radio programme presenting the facts about something: *Did you watch the documentary on cancer?*
▻ ***adjective***
Documentary evidence or proof consists of documents or certificates that support your claims: *Will they require documentary proof of my degree and other qualifications?*

doddle /'dɒdəl/ *noun* (*informal*; *used in the singular*)
You call something you do, such as a task, a **doddle**, if it is very easy: *The exam was a doddle.* [*same as* **cinch, piece of cake**]

dodge /dɒdʒ/ *verb*; *noun*
▻ ***verb*: dodges, dodging, dodged**
1 You **dodge** something, or **dodge**, when you move swiftly to avoid being hit, or noticed: *We tried to dodge the falling rocks.* □ *I dodged down a side street when I saw her coming.* **2** You **dodge** something that you ought to face or deal with when you avoid doing so: *We cannot continue to dodge the issue of unemployment.* [*same as* **avoid, evade**]
▻ ***noun*: dodges**
1 A **dodge** is a quick movement to avoid being hit or noticed: *He avoided the blow with a dodge to the left.* **2** A deception or trick by which you avoid something is also a **dodge**: *She knows all the tax dodges.*

dodgy /'dɒdʒɪ/ *adjective* (*informal*): **dodgier, dodgiest**
Something that is **dodgy** is risky, unreliable or slightly dishonest: *Some of the climbs are a bit dodgy in wet weather.* □ *one of those dodgy business arrangements.*

doe /doʊ/ *noun*: **does**
A **doe** is the female of any of the small deer, or of a hare or rabbit.

does /dʌz/ *verb*; *auxiliary verb*
▻ ***verb***
Does is the third person singular of the present tense of the verb **do**[2]: *She does the football pools every week.*
▻ ***auxiliary verb*** (*negative forms* **does not** or **doesn't**)
Does is the third person singular of the present tense of the verb **do**[1]: *Does she do the football pools?* □ *It does not make any difference.* □ *She does want to come, doesn't she?* [see also **do**[1], [2]]

doesn't /'dʌzənt/ *auxiliary verb*
Doesn't is the spoken, and informal written, form of **does not**: *She doesn't do much walking now.* □ *He looks thinner, doesn't he?* [see also **do**[1]]

dog /dɒg/ *noun*; *verb*
▻ ***noun*: dogs**
1 A **dog** is an animal that people keep as a pet, or for hunting, or for work on farms, *eg* with sheep: *The dog barks whenever the doorbell rings.* **2** A **dog** is also the male of the dog and of other animals of the dog family, such as the fox. [compare **bitch**]
▻ ***verb*: dogs, dogging, dogged**
1 You **dog** someone when you follow them closely: *A glance in the rear-view mirror told him that the police van was still dogging him.* [*same as* **track, tail**] **2** Something such as bad luck **dogs** you when you are affected by it continually: *She has been dogged by ill health and injury throughout the season.* [*same as* **plague, haunt**]
▻ ***phrase*** If you say that some form of existence or occupation **is a dog's life**, you mean that it is wretched: *It's a dog's life being a cleaner.*

dog collar /'dɒg kɒlə(r)/ *noun*: **dog collars**
A **dog collar** is a round white collar worn by priests and ministers in the Christian church.

dog-eared /'dɒgɪed/ *adjective*
A book that is **dog-eared** has been read or fingered so much that the corners of the pages are bent over and dirty.

dogged /'dɒgɪd/ *adjective*
A **dogged** person continues or perseveres with what they are doing in a determined way, in spite of difficulties: *With dogged perseverence, she gradually taught herself to walk again.* [*same as* **determined, obstinate, resolute, persistent**] — *adverb* **doggedly:** *He doggedly refused to give up the work, despite his failing health.* — *noun* (*uncount*) **doggedness:** *She was well known on the research project for her determination and doggedness of spirit.*

doggerel /'dɒgərəl/ *noun* (*uncount*)
Doggerel is clumsy or silly poetry, or quickly composed verse with a comic purpose.

dogma /'dɒgmə/ *noun*: **dogmas** (*count or uncount*)
A **dogma** is a religious or political teaching or belief: *dogmas of the early Christian church* □ *Communist dogma.*

dogmatic /dɒg'matɪk/ *adjective*
Someone who is **dogmatic** about something insists that they are right about it and won't consider other opinions: *You can't possibly know for certain, so how can you be so dogmatic?* □ *She was full of dogmatic*

pronouncements about how food should or should not be cooked. — *adverb* **dogmatically:** *He dogmatically insisted that children must be punished whatever their offence.*

dogsbody /ˈdɒgsbɒdɪ/ *noun* (*informal*): **dogsbodies**
A **dogsbody** is a person who is given the unpleasant and boring jobs that no-one else wants: *The club secretary tends to turn into the poor dogsbody who does all the work.*

doings /ˈduːɪŋz/ *noun* (*plural*)
A person's **doings** are their activities: *I was bored of hearing about her child's amazing doings.*

do-it-yourself /duː ɪt yəˈsɛlf/ *noun* (*uncount*)
Do-it-yourself or **DIY** is the activity of making and repairing things yourself instead of employing professional experts: *You can get all the materials you need at a do-it-yourself store.*

doldrums /ˈdɒldrəmz/ *noun* (*plural*)
▻ ***phrases*** **1** You are **in the doldrums** when you are depressed or miserable. **2** A type of activity is **in the doldrums** when it failing to progress and develop: *Business remained in the doldrums for several months before sales began to pick up.*

dole /doʊl/ *noun*; *verb*
▻ ***noun*** (*used in the singular*; *informal*)
The **dole** is the money that is paid regularly by the government to people who are unemployed: *More jobless graduates join the dole queue every summer.*
▻ ***phrase*** People who are **on the dole** are unemployed and receiving money regularly from the government: *I spent three years on the dole before getting this job.*
▻ ***verb***: **doles, doling, doled**

> ***phrasal verb***
> You **dole out** something such as food when you share it out or serve it, giving some to each person: *She doled a ladleful of porridge out into each bowl.*

doleful /ˈdoʊlfəl/ *adjective*
You are **doleful** when you are miserable or depressed: *He had a thin face with a permanently doleful expression.*
▻ **adverb:** *Dolefully she recounted the sad affair of the broken teapot.*

doll /dɒl/ *noun*; *verb*
▻ ***noun***: **dolls**
A **doll** is a toy in the shape of a small human being, especially a baby or a little girl: *She was playing with her baby doll on the living-room floor.*
▻ ***verb***: **dolls, dolling, dolled**

> ***phrasal verb***
> **doll up** (*usually in the passive*) A woman gets **dolled up** when she dresses herself smartly: *There's no point in getting dolled up just to go to the pub.*

dollar /ˈdɒlə(r)/ *noun*: **dollars**
A **dollar** is the unit of currency in several countries, *eg* the US, Canada and Australia; it is represented by the symbol ($) and usually divided into 100 cents: *What is the exchange rate between the pound and the Singapore dollar?*

dollop /ˈdɒləp/ *noun* (*informal*): **dollops**
A **dollop** of soft semi-liquid food is a large spoonful of it: *He decorated each plateful of dessert with a dollop of cream.*

dolphin /ˈdɒlfɪn/ *noun*: **dolphins**
A **dolphin** is a sea animal with a long nose and smooth shiny skin, related to the whale and similar to the porpoise, and noted for its intelligence and friendliness.

dolt /doʊlt/ *noun* (*derogatory*): **dolts**
If you call someone a **dolt** you mean that they are stupid: *I'm an absolute dolt when it comes to mathematics.*

domain /dəˈmeɪn/ *noun*: **domains**
1 Someone's **domain** is the area over which they have control: *Each charity seemed to have its own domain within the Third World, and resented intrusion by the others.* **2** The **domain** of a particular subject is the range of material or topics it covers or includes: *Social psychology comes to a certain extent within the domain of philosophy.* [*same as* **realm, field**]

dome /doʊm/ *noun*: **domes**
A **dome** is a rounded, hemispherical shape, especially as a roof or part of a roof, *eg* on a church or mosque: *The inside of the dome was decorated with scenes from the life of Christ.* — *adjective* **domed:** *a domed roof.*

domestic /dəˈmɛstɪk/ *adjective*
1 Your **domestic** responsibilities are those relating to your home and family: *He was accused of putting his career before his domestic duties.* [*same as* **household**] **2 Domestic** equipment or supplies are for use in your home: *washing machines and other domestic appliances* □ *water for domestic use.* [*same as* **household**] **3** You describe a person as **domestic** if they enjoy home life and household tasks. [*same as* **homely**] **4 Domestic** animals are animals such as dogs and cats, that are kept as pets, or animals such as cattle, pigs, sheep and horses, that are kept on a farm for work or as a source of food or other need. **5** A government's **domestic** policy concerns affairs within the country as distinct from affairs abroad. [*same as* **home, internal**; *opposite* **foreign**]

domesticated /dəˈmɛstɪkeɪtɪd/ *adjective*
1 Animals that are **domesticated** are used to living near people and being controlled by them, and may be trained to work for them: *domesticated breeds of cattle.* [*same as* **tame**; *opposite* **wild**] **2** A **domesticated** person enjoys household tasks and duties and does them efficiently: *I don't know how they'll cope with married life; they're neither of them very domesticated.*

domesticity /doʊmɛˈstɪsɪtɪ/ *noun* (*uncount*)
Domesticity is home life with its household and family responsibilities, or a liking for it: *He was enjoying the quiet domesticity of married life.*

dominant /ˈdɒmɪnənt/ *adjective*
1 A **dominant** person or thing has a lot of power, control or influence over people: *The household arrangements and furnishings reflected his mother's dominant taste and personality.* **2** A building has a **dominant** position if it is in a high place and easily seen above other buildings. [*same as* **commanding**] **3** (*technical*) In genetics, a **dominant** gene is a gene for a physical characteristic, *eg* dark eyes, that is more likely than other genes to be passed down through the generations of a family. — *noun* (*uncount*) **dominance:** *The Japanese were maintaining their dominance of the small-car market.* □ *the dominance of the gene for brown eyes.*

dominate /ˈdɒmɪneɪt/ *verb*: **dominates, dominating, dominated**
1 Someone or something **dominates** a situation if they strongly influence or control it: *The issue of racial discrimination dominated the discussion.* □ *American products were tending to dominate the market in the developing countries.* **2** A building or other physical feature **dominates** a landscape or scene if it is the most noticeable element in it: *The castle on its rocky height dominates the city of Edinburgh.* — *adjective* **dominating:** *The dominating fashion colour this spring will be green.* □ *a woman with a dominating personality.* — *noun* (*uncount*) **domination** /dɒmɪˈneɪʃən/: *the*

domination of world culture by western values and concepts.

domineering /dɒmɪˈnɪərɪŋ/ *adjective* (*derogatory*)
A **domineering** person tries to force their own will on other people and to control them: *She had a domineering older sister.* [*same as* **overbearing, bossy**]

dominion /dəˈmɪnjən/ *noun*: **dominions**
1 (*uncount*) A state or ruler has **dominion** over a territory if they have control and authority over it: *in the days when Britain held dominion over a large part of the world.* **2** A ruler's **dominions** are the territories under his or her control: *throughout her wide dominions.* **3** A **Dominion** is a self-governing territory with the British Commonwealth.

domino /ˈdɒmɪnoʊ/ *noun*: **dominoes**
1 A **domino** is a small flat rectangular piece of *eg* wood or plastic with a white surface divided in two, each half bearing a set of spots, from one to five in number, used for playing dominoes and other games. **2** (*uncount*) **Dominoes** is a game played with 28 dominoes, in which players attempt to match pieces according to numbers of spots, laying them end to end on a flat surface.

don¹ /dɒn/ *noun*: **dons**
A **don** is a university teacher, especially at Oxford or Cambridge.

don² /dɒn/ *verb* (*literary*): **dons, donning, donned**
You **don** a piece of clothing when you put it on: *They had to don protective gear before descending into the mine.*

donate /doʊˈneɪt/ *verb*: **donates, donating, donated**
You **donate** something, *eg* money to a charity, when you give it: *How much does the average person donate to charity per year?* — *noun* (*count or uncount*) **donation:** *All donations, however small, are gratefully received.* □ *The following books were acquired by donation.*

done /dʌn/ *verb*; *adjective*; *interjection*
▻ ***verb***
Done is the past participle of the verb **do²**: *I haven't done my teeth yet.* □ *Much work remains to be done.*
▻ ***adjective***
1 A job that is **done** is finished: *Thank goodness that's done!* **2** Food is **done** when it is fully cooked: *The meat doesn't look done.* **3** A piece of behaviour is **done** if it is socially acceptable: *It isn't done to dip your bread in your soup.* □ *The done thing is to lay your knife and fork side by side when you have finished eating.*
▻ ***interjection***
You say **'done!'** when you agree to a bargain or bet with someone: *'£250?' 'Done!'*
▻ ***phrases*** **1** (*informal*) You say you **are** or **have done with** something or someone when you no longer want to be involved or associated with them; you **have done with** something when you get rid of it; an affair that is **over and done with** is finished and should be forgotten: *I'm done with waitressing.* □ *I've done with you for good.* □ *Let's have done with all pretence and hypocrisy, and speak the truth for once.* □ *That episode of my life is over and done with.* **2** (*informal*) Something or someone that is **done for** is about to be destroyed or to die: *We're done for unless we find a way out.* [see also **do²**]

donkey /ˈdɒŋkɪ/ *noun*: **donkeys**
1 A **donkey** is an animal like a small horse, with long ears, used traditionally for carrying baggage. **2** (*derogatory*) If you call someone a **donkey** you mean they are stupid.
▻ ***phrase*** Something that has been so **for donkey's years** has been so for a long time: *I've had this coat for donkey's years.*

donor /ˈdoʊnə(r)/ *noun*: **donors**
1 A **donor** to a charity or other organization is someone who gives money or a gift to it: *the anonymous donor of a kidney machine* □ *We depend entirely on the generosity of donors.* **2** A **donor** is someone who gives blood or an organ for use in the medical treatment of someone else: *Are you a blood donor?* □ *a kidney donor.*

don't /doʊnt/ *auxiliary verb*; *noun*
▻ ***auxiliary verb***
Don't is the spoken, and informal written, form of **do not**: *I don't want to go.* □ *Don't cross yet!* □ *Don't be so certain!* □ *You do know them, don't you?* [see also **do¹**]
▻ ***noun*** (*used in the plural*)
For **dos** and **don'ts** see **do¹**.

doodle /ˈduːdəl/ *noun*; *verb*
▻ ***noun*: doodles**
A **doodle** is a drawing or scribble that you do in an unintentional or purposeless way when you are concentrating on something else: *The telephone pad was covered with doodles.*
▻ ***verb*: doodles, doodling, doodled:** *Someone had been doodling in the margin of the text.*

doom /duːm/ *noun*; *verb*
▻ ***noun*** (*uncount*)
Your **doom** is your inescapable fate, especially a terrible one: *This particular rock face had sent many climbers to their doom.*
▻ ***verb*: dooms, dooming, doomed**
Some circumstance **dooms** you to a particular fate or way of life when it makes it unavoidable for you: *The violent circumstances of his death doomed him to walk the earth as a ghost.* □ *I thought I was doomed to spend the rest of my life in a wheelchair.* [*same as* **condemn**]

doomed /duːmd/ *adjective*
Someone or something that is **doomed** is certain to be destroyed, to die or to fail: *The project was doomed from the beginning, it was so badly planned.* [*same as* **ill-fated**]

doomsday /ˈduːmzdeɪ/ *noun* (*used in the singular*)
Doomsday is the day when the world will come to an end and, according to Christian theology, God will judge everybody.
▻ ***phrase*** To do something **till doomsday** is to do it for an indefinitely long time: *We could wait till doomsday for an answer.*

door /dɔː(r)/ *noun*: **doors**
1 A **door** is the piece of wood or other heavy solid material, usually supported on hinges, that swings to close or open the entrance to a building, room, cupboard or vehicle: *The fridge door wouldn't close.* □ *I unlocked the door to the cellar.* □ *Somebody's knocking at the door.* **2** A **door** is also the entrance itself: *People go in and out of that door all day.* □ *I looked through the door into the sitting room.*
▻ ***phrases*** **1** A person is **at death's door** when they are so ill that they are about to die. **2** You **lay** the blame or responsibility for something **at** someone's **door** when you blame them for it: *I won't have the responsibility for the failure laid at my door.* **3** Someone who is or lives **next door** to you is in the house next to yours: *I haven't met the new next-door neighbours yet.* **4** Something that **opens the door to** new possibilities makes them available to you: *Her success in the competition opened the door to a musical career.* **5** You are **out of doors** when you are outside in the open air, rather than inside a building: *Tutorials are held out of doors in fine weather.*

doorbell /ˈdɔːbel/ *noun*: **doorbells**
A **doorbell** is a bell on the outside of the front door of

a house, which you ring to ask those inside to open the door: *She rang the doorbell and waited.*

doorknob /ˈdɔːnɒb/ *noun*: **doorknobs**
A **doorknob** is a ball-shaped handle on a door: *The doorknob appeared to be slowly turning.*

doormat /ˈdɔːmat/ *noun*: **doormats**
A **doormat** is a mat, usually of rough material, kept inside or outside a door for people to wipe their shoes on as they come in.

doorstep /ˈdɔːstɛp/ *noun*: **doorsteps**
A **doorstep** is a step leading up to the front door of a house: *The children were sitting on the doorstep playing.*
▷ ***phrase*** A place is **on your doorstep** if it is very close by: *The cathedral is on our doorstep.*

door-to-door /dɔːtəˈdɔː(r)/ *adjective*
Door-to-door operations involve calling at each house in turn in a neighbourhood: *The police were making door-to-door enquiries.* □ *door-to-door salesmen.*

doorway /ˈdɔːweɪ/ *noun*: **doorways**
The **doorway** of a room, house or other building is its entrance: *A policeman stood in the doorway.*

dope /doʊp/ *noun*; *verb*
▷ ***noun*** (*informal*): **dopes**
1 (*uncount*) **Dope** is an illegal drug, especially cannabis: *They were arrested for selling dope.* **2** (*uncount*) The **dope** on something is the essential information about it: *I called at the office and collected all the dope on unemployment benefit.* **3** (*derogatory*) If you call someone a **dope** you mean they are stupid: *Don't be such a dope!*
▷ ***verb***: **dopes, doping, doped**
To **dope** a person or animal is to add a drug to their food or drink: *The racehorse was found to have been doped.*

dopey /ˈdoʊpɪ/ *adjective* (*informal*): **dopier, dopiest**
1 You are **dopey** when you are sleepy or half-conscious, *eg* after being given a drug: *I began to feel dopey as the anaesthetic took effect.* **2** (*derogatory*) If you call someone **dopey** you mean they are stupid: *another of her dopey ideas.*

dormant /ˈdɔːmənt/ *adjective*
Something that is **dormant** is quiet or inactive, but has been active in the past and may become so again: *He felt the stirring of an emotion that had been dormant for a long time.* □ *dormant volcanoes.*

dormitory /ˈdɔːmətrɪ/ *noun*: **dormitories**
1 A **dormitory** is a large bedroom shared by a number of people, especially in a boarding school. **2** (*AmE*) A **dormitory** is a student residence at an American college or university.

dormouse /ˈdɔːmaʊs/ *noun*: **dormice**
A **dormouse** is a small forest animal, like a mouse with a squirrel's tail, that sleeps during the winter.

DOS /dɒs/ *noun* (*uncount*; *computers*)
DOS stands for disk-operating system, a program for handling information on a disk.

dosage /ˈdoʊsɪdʒ/ *noun* (*uncount or count*): **dosages**
The recommended **dosage** of a drug or medicine is the amount that should be taken at stated times for it to be effective: *It is dangerous to exceed the stated dosage.*

dose /doʊs/ *noun*; *verb*
▷ ***noun***: **doses**
1 A **dose** of medicine or a drug is an amount of it given at one time to someone: *You should take your next dose at 11 o'clock.* **2** You get a **dose** of something, usually unpleasant, when you experience or suffer it: *He had had a nasty dose of flu.* [*same as* **bout**]
▷ ***verb***: **doses, dosing, dosed**
You **dose** someone when you give them medicine: *She dosed herself with aspirin and went to bed.*
▷ ***phrases*** You give someone **a dose of their own medicine** when you treat them as badly as they treat others.

doss *verb*: **dosses, dossing, dossed**

> ***phrasal verb***
> (*informal*) You **doss down** somewhere unusual or uncomfortable when you sleep there for convenience: *By that time I'd missed the last bus home, so he let me doss down on his sofa for the night.*

dossier /ˈdɒsɪeɪ/ *noun*: **dossiers**
The **dossier** of a certain person or matter is a detailed record or file of information on them: *We've kept a dossier on the affair.*

dot /dɒt/ *noun*; *verb*
▷ ***noun***: **dots**
1 A **dot** is a small round mark or spot: *a white dress with little pink dots* □ *He marked the position with a dot.* **2** A **dot** is the shorter of the two Morse-code signals, dot or dash, and is written as a point.
▷ ***verb***: **dots, dotted, dotting**
A surface **is dotted** with things when they are scattered about on it; things **are dotted** about on a surface when they are scattered over it: *The rolling hills were dotted with grazing sheep.* [see also **dotted**]
▷ ***phrases*** **1** Something happens **on the dot** when it happens at exactly the scheduled time: *Our guests arrived on the dot.* **2** (*informal*) Something that happened in **the year dot** happened a long time ago.

dote /doʊt/ *verb*: **dotes, doting, doted**
You **dote** on someone if you love them very much, especially so much that you cannot see their faults: *She had no family except one nephew, whom she doted on. — adjective* **doting:** *My doting grandparents paid for me to go to a private school.* [*same as* **adoring**]

dotted /ˈdɒtɪd/ *adjective*
A **dotted** line is a line consisting of dots, *eg* on a printed form: *Cut along the dotted line.* □ *Sign on the dotted line.* [see also **dot**]

dotty /ˈdɒtɪ/ *adjective* (*informal*): **dottier, dottiest**
Someone who is **dotty** is slightly crazy. [*same as* **barmy, batty, daft, loony**]

double /ˈdʌbəl/ *determiner*; *adjective*; *adjective or adverb*; *adverb*; *noun*; *verb*
▷ ***determiner***
Double the amount of something is twice as much of it: *The material had taken double the amount of disk space it was expected to take.* □ *Children over 12 should be given double that quantity.* □ *They offered me double what I had been earning in publishing.*
▷ ***adjective***
1 A **double** serving is twice the normal amount: *She ordered a double whisky.* **2** Things that are **double** consist of two of those things: *'You're always late for your funeral' plays on the double meaning of 'late'.* □ *an egg with a double yolk* □ *Double doors led into the dining room.* □ *You must never park on a double yellow line.* □ *Her surname is Swann, with a double n.* **3** **Double** figures are the numbers from 10 upwards: *The number of food-poisoning cases in the class is already in double figures.* [*opposite* **single**] **4** **Double** accommodation is for two people: *I booked a double room.* □ *A double ticket for the dance costs £40.* [*opposite* **single**] **5** You can use **double** to indicate a repeated figure when you say a telephone number, or a repeated letter when you spell a word: *Five double four oh two.* [= 54402]
▷ ***adjective or adverb***
You bend **double**, or are bent **double** when you bend or

are bent over completely; you fold something **double** when you fold it over once: *He was bent double with the pain.*

▻ ***adverb***

You say you are seeing **double** when you are seeing two images of everything.

▻ ***noun*: doubles**

1 A person's **double** is someone who looks very like them: *He's his brother's double.* **2** (*uncount*) **Doubles** is the form of tennis or badminton in which two players play two others: *I enjoy mixed doubles most.*

▻ ***verb*: doubles, doubling, doubled**

1 An amount **doubles** when it becomes twice as much; you **double** an amount when you increase it to twice as much: *I doubled my income within three years.* □ *The number of AIDS deaths will have doubled by the year 2000.* **2** One person or thing **doubles** as another when they have a second job or function: *Some of the kitchen staff have to double as waiters.* □ *The kitchen table doubles as a work station.* **3** You **double** for someone when you substitute for them in their job: *I have to double for the college principal when she's away.*

phrasal verbs

double back You **double back** when you turn and go back the way you came: *I had to double back to get on to the motorway again.*

double over You **double** something **over** when you fold it.

double up 1 You **double up** or **are doubled up** when you bend or are bent completely over: *She makes me double up with laughter.* **2** People **double up** when they get into pairs in order to share something: *Some of us may have to double up if there aren't enough bedrooms.*

double bass /dʌbəl 'beɪs/ *noun*: **double basses**

A **double bass** is the largest stringed instrument in the violin family, and is supported upright by the player, who sits on a high stool, or stands: *a double-bass player.* [see picture at **orchestra**]

double bed /'dʌbəl bɛd/ *noun*: **double beds**

A **double bed** is a wide bed for two people. [see picture at **bedroom**]

double-breasted /dʌbəl'brɛstɪd/ *adjective*

A **double-breasted** coat or jacket has wide front flaps that fasten with one lying over the other, usually with two sets of buttons.

double-check /dʌbəl'tʃɛk/ *verb*: **double-checks, double-checking, double-checked**

You **double-check** something when you check it again to make sure it is correct or reliable: *The examination results are double-checked before being sent to the candidates.*

double chin /dʌbəl 'tʃɪn/ *noun*: **double chins**

A **double chin** is a fold of flesh under your chin: *You're getting a double chin; you'll have to lose weight.*

double cream /dʌbəl 'kriːm/ *noun* (*uncount*)

Double cream is thick cream suitable for whipping.

double-cross /dʌbəl'krɒs/ *verb*: **double-cross, double-crossing, double-crossed**

Someone whom you trust **double-crosses** you when they cheat you or betray you.

double-dealing /dʌbəl'diːlɪŋ/ *noun* (*uncount*)

Double-dealing is dishonest behaviour such as deceit or cheating.

double-decker /dʌbəl'dɛkə(r)/ *noun*: **double-deckers**

A **double-decker** is a bus with two floors.

double glazing /dʌbəl 'gleɪzɪŋ/ *noun* (*uncount*)

Double glazing is windows consisting of a double thickness of glass, or the process of fitting windows of this sort.

doubly /'dʌblɪ/ *adverb*

1 (*intensifying*) **Doubly** is used to mean 'especially' or 'extra': *Politicians have to be doubly careful to avoid any sort of scandal about their private lives.* **2** Something is **doubly** so if it is so in two ways: *He was doubly responsible for the failure of the company.*

doubt /dɑʊt/ *noun; verb*

▻ ***noun*** (*uncount or count*): **doubts**

Doubt is a feeling of uncertainty or hesitation about something: *I was full of doubt and suspicion.* □ *We had our doubts at the time of the takeover.* □ *She never had a moment's doubt about making acting her career.* □ *There's some doubt about where the castle actually stood.* □ *There was serious doubt whether they could pay.* □ *I had no doubt* [= I was certain] *that we were doing the right thing.*

▻ ***verb*: doubts, doubting, doubted**

1 You **doubt** whether or if something is so, or will happen, when you think it is unlikely: *I doubt if he ever really intended to pay the money back.* □ *I doubt whether we shall succeed.* **2** You say you do not **doubt** that something is so or will happen if you think it is likely or certain: *No-one doubted that she was guilty.* **3** You **doubt** a thing when you do not believe in it: *I never doubted his ability.* □ *Many people seriously doubt the existence of a deity.* **4** You **doubt** a person or their word when you disbelieve or distrust them: *You know I would never doubt you.* [*same as* **distrust**]

Note that in positive constructions **doubt**, as a verb or noun, is normally followed by *whether* or *if*; in negative constructions it is usually followed by *that*, or by a noun clause with *that* omitted: *I doubt if she suffered much* [= I don't think she suffered], but *I've no doubt* (*that*) *you're right* [= I'm sure you're right].

▻ ***phrases***

1 Something that is certain **beyond doubt** is known definitely: *The identity of the dead woman has been proved beyond all doubt.* **2** To **cast doubt on** something is to suggest that it is not true or reliable: *New facts were emerging that cast doubt on the theory.* **3** You are **in doubt** about something when you are uncertain about it: *If in doubt, consult your nearest chemist.* □ *We were still in some doubt as to who was responsible.* **4** Something is **in doubt** or **open to doubt** if it is not certain or reliable: *Recent police confessions had left the reliability of certain past convictions open to doubt.* **5 No doubt** means probably: *You've all no doubt heard the news.* **6** Something that is so **without doubt** or **without a doubt** is definitely so: *He is without doubt the most selfish person I know.*

doubtful /'dɑʊtfəl/ *adjective*

1 You are **doubtful** about something if you are unsure about it: *I was doubtful about going abroad.* □ *He's doubtful whether it's a good idea.* □ *I'm a bit doubtful of the statistics he's given us.* **2** Something that is **doubtful** is unlikely, uncertain or unreliable: *It's doubtful whether there'll be any flights today.* □ *The survival of the firm is doubtful.* □ *The project has a doubtful future.* □ *Surgeons do operate on these children, but with doubtful success.* **3 Doubtful** can also mean suspicious: *He died in doubtful circumstances.* □ *He looks a doubtful character.* [*same as* **dubious**]

doubtless /'dɑʊtləs/ *adverb* (*sentence adverb*)

Doubtless means probably: *Doubtless you all saw the televised documentary on the future of the planet.* [*same as* **no doubt**]

dough /doʊ/ *noun* (*uncount*)
1 Dough is a mixture of flour, water and fat from which bread or pastry is made. **2** (*informal*) People refer to money as **dough**: *The guy's got enough dough to pay for a hotel room.*

doughnut /ˈdoʊnʌt/ *noun*: **doughnuts**
A **doughnut** is a sweet cake made of fried dough, sometimes in the shape of a ring.

dour /dʊə(r)/ *adjective*
A **dour** person has a rather stern and unfriendly manner: *It's time you got rid of that dour receptionist.* — *adverb* **dourly:** *She eyed the party decorations dourly.*

douse or **dowse** /daʊs/ *verb*: **douses, dousing, doused**
1 You **douse** something or someone with a liquid when you soak them in it, or throw it over them: *I doused myself with cologne.* **2** You **douse** a fire when you stop it burning, *eg* by pouring water over it.

dove[1] /dʌv/ *noun*: **doves**
A **dove** is a bird of the pigeon family, typically smaller than a pigeon, and often used as a symbol of peace.

dove[2] /doʊv/ *verb* (*AmE*)
Dove is the past tense of **dive**.

dovetail /ˈdʌvteɪl/ *verb*: **dovetails, dovetailing, dovetailed**
Plans or events **dovetail** with one another when they fit neatly together in a general scheme.

dowdy /ˈdaʊdɪ/ *adjective* (*derogatory*): **dowdier, dowdiest**
Someone who is described as **dowdy** wears dull unfashionable clothes: *I think I look dowdy in this skirt.* □ *a dowdy old coat.*

down[1] /daʊn/ *preposition*; *adverb*; *adjective or adverb*; *adjective*; *verb*
▻ ***preposition***
1 You go **down** something when you move to a lower position or level on it, or go to its bottom: *She was carrying a tray down the stairs.* □ *I freewheeled down the hill.* □ *He fell down a cliff.* [*opposite* **up**] **2** You go **down** a road when you go along it; something that is **down** a road is somewhere along it; to go **down** a river is go along it in the direction of its mouth: *Turn down Finch Road and you'll come to the hospital.* □ *The cinema is down Strand Street.* □ *Enormous trees were being washed down the river.* [compare **up**] **3** Something is **down** a surface if it covers or marks it from the top towards the bottom: *She spilt wine all down her dress.* □ *He had a long scar down one cheek.*
▻ ***adverb***
1 a Down means towards or at a lower level or position, or towards or on the ground: *I'm upstairs; I'll be down shortly.* □ *the people down in the basement* □ *Do sit down.* □ *I lay down for a minute.* □ *The sun was going down.* □ *The piano had to be let down through a window.* □ *She was down on her knees cleaning the floor.* □ *We're moving Jane down to the lower set for mathematics.* □ *He was paralysed from the waist down.* [*opposite* **up**] **b** You put something that you are carrying **down** when you put it on a surface: *Put your bags down and rest.* □ *I've put my spectacles down somewhere and can't find them.* **c** You put money **down** on something when you pay a deposit on it: *We've put down £2000 on the house.*
2 a Down is used after verbs like *fall* to indicate collapse, destruction or failure: *The tower fell down in 1413.* □ *They're going to pull the church down.* □ *One night the whole house burnt down.* □ *The talks seem to have broken down again.* **b** A dangerous or disorderly situation settles or calms **down** when it becomes calmer. **c** Things are reduced **down** to a finer, thinner or more concentrated form: *Metal objects were melted down to make bullets.* □ *They grind the stones down to a powder.* □ *The liquid must be boiled down.*
3 a You fasten or stick something **down** when you fix it to a surface: *She licked the label and stuck it down firmly.* **b** You write something **down** when you write it on paper: *I noted down her address.* □ *Take down these numbers.*
4 a You go **down** somewhere when you go south: *I'm coming down to Birmingham next week.* **b** Things go **down** through time when they exist through the ages or pass from one generation to the next: *traditional crafts handed down from father to son.* **c** You plan something **down** to its details when you include everything possible in your plan: *The wedding was all arranged, down to the colour of the bridesmaids' shoes.* □ *It was planned down to the last detail.* **d** Everyone in an organization, from the most senior person **down**, is every member of it.
▻ ***adjective or adverb***
1 Things are **down**, or go **down**, when they decrease in size, quantity or force: *I managed to get my weight down to 140 pounds.* □ *Houses prices are down on* [= less than] *last month's.* □ *The storm died down in a day or two.* □ *Somebody let my tyres down.* **2** A team or side is **down** by a certain score when they are losing by that amount: *We were down by two goals at half time.* **3** You are **down** when you are miserable or depressed: *I was feeling down.* **4** You are **down** with an illness when you are suffering from it: *He's down with flu again.* **5** A computer system is **down** when it is not working and cannot be used.
▻ ***adjective***
1 A **down** pipe is a vertical one, *eg* leading from a roof; a **down** train travels away from a city centre to the country. **2** A **down** payment is a deposit.
▻ ***verb*** (*informal*): **downs, downing, downed**
You **down** a drink when you swallow it: *She downed it in one gulp.* [see also **down tools** at **tool**]
▻ ***phrases*** **1** Someone who is **down and out** has no home and no money. **2** A person, or their name, is **down for** something when their name has been put on a list for something: *Your name is down for the 200-metre race.* □ *The family is down for rehousing.* **3** (*especially AmE*) You say that something is **down to** a certain person if it is their achievement or responsibility: *The firm's recovery was entirely down to the new managing director* □ *It's down to you to decide on the next move.* **4** (*informal*) **Down under** means in Australia or New Zealand. **5** People shout **'down with'** something when they want it to be got rid of: *Down with landowners!* **6** You **have a down on** someone or something if you feel and show dislike for them.

down[2] /daʊn/ *noun* (*uncount*)
Down is fine soft hair or feathers: *quilts filled with duck down.*

downcast /ˈdaʊnkɑːst/ *adjective*
1 You are **downcast** when you are miserable and depressed: *He was looking very downcast.* [*same as* **dejected**] **2** Someone's eyes are **downcast** if they are looking down at the ground instead of at anyone, *eg* through shyness or sadness.

downfall /ˈdaʊnfɔːl/ *noun* (*uncount*)
1 Someone's **downfall** is their fall from a powerful and successful position to ruin or failure: *He had plenty of enemies working to bring about his downfall.* **2** Something such as a personal fault, that causes someone's ruin or failure can also be called their **downfall**: *Drink was her downfall.*

downgrade /daʊnˈgreɪd/ *verb*: **downgrades, downgrading, downgraded**
To **downgrade** something is to reduce it to a level or

rank of less importance: *Her job was going to be downgraded.* [*opposite* **upgrade**]

downhearted /daʊn'hɑːtɪd/ *adjective*
You are **downhearted** when you are feeling discouraged and depressed: *We refuse to be downhearted.*

downhill /daʊn'hɪl/ *adverb*; *adjective*
▻ ***adverb***
1 You move **downhill** when you go down a slope: *No-one minds cycling downhill.* [*opposite* **uphill**] **2** Something that is going **downhill** is getting worse or failing: *The business was going downhill.* □ *Her health went quickly downhill after her fall.*
▻ ***adjective*** /'daʊnhɪl/
1 Downhill means going down a slope: *I prefer cross-country skiing to the downhill kind.* □ *The walking is all downhill from here.* **2** The process of completing a task may be described as **downhill** once all the hard work has been done and the difficulties have been dealt with. [*opposite* **uphill**]

download /daʊn'loʊd/ *verb*: **downloads, downloading, downloaded**
You **download** data when you transfer it from one computer to another, usually smaller, one.

downpour /'daʊnpɔː(r)/ *noun*: **downpours**
A **downpour** is a heavy fall of rain.

downright /'daʊnraɪt/ *adjective or adverb* (*intensifying*)
Downright is used like 'positive' and 'positively' for emphasis, usually of something bad: *It's a downright disgrace.* □ *Her remark was downright insulting.*

downs /daʊnz/ *noun* (*plural*)
The **downs** are an area of low hills, especially those of Southern England: *the Sussex downs.*

downspout /'daʊnspaʊt/ *noun*: **downspouts**
A **downspout** is a downpipe. [see picture at **house**]

Down's Syndrome /'daʊnz sɪndroʊm/ *noun* (*uncount*)
A baby born with **Down's syndrome** has an abnormality in its chromosomes, and typically has a face with rather flattened features, and is of lower-than-average intelligence.

downstairs /daʊn'stɛəz/ *adverb*; *adjective*
▻ ***adverb***
You go **downstairs** when you go down a staircase to a lower floor; something that is **downstairs** is on a lower floor or the ground floor: *She ran downstairs to the kitchen.* □ *I've left my book downstairs.* [*opposite* **upstairs**]
▻ ***adjective*** /'daʊnstɛəz/: *We live in the downstairs flat and let the upstairs one to tenants.*

downstream /daʊnstriːm/ *adverb*
Something that is moving **downstream** is floating towards the mouth of a stream or river: *The logs drift downstream.* [*opposite* **upstream**]

down-to-earth /daʊn tuː 'ɜːθ/ *adjective*
Someone who is **down-to-earth** is practical and sensible. [*same as* **matter-of-fact**]

downtown *adverb*; *adjective*
▻ ***adverb*** /daʊn'taʊn/
You go **downtown** when you go into the centre of a city or town, where the large shops are: *I'm taking a bus downtown this morning.*
▻ ***adjective*** /'daʊntaʊn/ (*especially AmE*)
The **downtown** area of a city is its centre: *in downtown New York.*

downtrodden /'daʊntrɒdən/ *adjective*
People who are **downtrodden** are ill-treated and completely controlled by the people with power, and haven't the strength or means to resist or rebel.

downturn /'daʊntɜːn/ *noun*: **downturns**
There is a **downturn** in a situation when it gets worse: *The country's economy has taken a downturn.*

downward /'daʊnwəd/ *adverb*; *adjective*
▻ ***adverb*** (also **downwards**)
1 You go or look **downward** or **downwards** when you go or look towards a lower level, or towards the ground: *The path led downwards to the village.* □ *I was scared to look downwards.* □ *She was lying face downwards on the ground.* [*opposite* **upward, upwards**] **2** An amount goes **downward** or **downwards** when it decreases: *Prices are spiralling downwards.* [*opposite* **upward, upwards**] **3** Everyone in an organization from the most senior **downward** or **downwards** is every member of it.
▻ ***adjective*** (**downward**): *a downward trend in the market.* □ *the downward track.* [*opposite* **upward**]

downwind /daʊn'wɪnd/ *adverb*
Downwind means in the direction in which the wind is blowing: *The fire was spreading downwind.* □ *If you keep downwind of the deer they won't scent you.*

downy /'daʊnɪ/ *adjective*: **downier, downiest**
1 Downy skin is covered with fine soft hair: *downy-headed babies.* **2 Downy** chicks are covered with small soft feathers; a **downy** bed, mattress or quilt is filled with soft feathers.

dowry /'daʊrɪ/ *noun*: **dowries**
A woman's **dowry** is the money and property that her family give to the man she marries, in certain societies.

dowse see **douse**.

doze /doʊz/ *verb*; *noun*
▻ ***verb***: **dozes, dozing, dozed**
You **doze** when you sleep lightly: *She was dozing in a chair by the fire.*
▻ ***noun***: **dozes:** *He settled back in his armchair for an after-dinner doze.*

> ***phrasal verb***
> **doze off** You **doze off** when you fall into a light sleep: *I never heard you come in; I must have dozed off.* [*same as* **drop off**]

dozen /'dʌzən/ *noun*: **dozens**
1 A **dozen** things of a certain kind is twelve of them: *I bought a dozen eggs this morning.* **2 Dozens** of things means a lot of them: *We've had dozens of requests for application forms.*

dozy /'doʊzɪ/ *adjective*: **dozier, doziest**
1 You are **dozy** when you are feeling sleepy. [*same as* **drowsy**] **2** (*informal*) A **dozy** person is not as attentive and alert as they should be: *That dozy secretary has sent me the wrong letter.*

Dr /'dɒktə(r)/: **Drs**
Dr is the written abbreviation of the title 'Doctor': *Dr Fischer* □ *Drs Brown and Macdonald did the research.*

drab /drab/ *adjective*
Something that is **drab** is dull and boring: *She changed from her drab weekday clothes into her best dress.* □ *There was something drab and uninspiring about the place.* [*same as* **dreary**]

draconian /drə'koʊnɪən/ *adjective*
Laws or penalties that are described as **draconian** are harsh, severe or cruel.

draft /drɑːft/ *noun*; *verb*
▻ ***noun***: **drafts**
1 A **draft** of a book, article or speech is a roughly prepared first version of it. **2** A bank **draft** is an order for the payment of money from one bank to another. **3** (*uncount*) In the US, the **draft** is the ordering of

young men into one of the armed forces for a period of national service. [*same as* **conscription**] **4** (*AmE*) A **draft** is the same as a **draught**.

▻ ***verb***: **drafts, drafting, drafted**

1 You **draft** a speech or article when you prepare a rough first version of it: *He was asked to draft a chapter on punctuation for the new book on English usage.* **2** A person **is drafted** into one of the armed forces when they are ordered to serve in it; people **are drafted** into an organization when they are taken into it for a special job: *He was drafted into the navy in 1978.* □ *We drafted in extra staff to help us run the project.*

draftsman see **draughtsman**.

drafty see **draughty**.

drag /drag/ *verb; noun*

▻ ***verb***: **drags, dragging, dragged**

1 You **drag** something heavy somewhere when you pull it: *There's a trail of blood where they dragged the body across the floor.* [*same as* **haul**] **2** If something **drags** along the ground, or you **drag** it, it scrapes or touches the ground as it moves along: *Her hem was dragging on the ground.* □ *He dragged his feet as he walked.* **3** You **drag** a person somewhere when you pull them roughly: *He dragged her screaming out of the car.* **4** You **drag** someone somewhere when you make them come: *She wants to drag me off to some party.* **5** You **drag** yourself somewhere when you get there with difficulty, because you are weak or ill, or when you go there unwillingly: *She managed to drag herself to the phone and ring for help.* □ *Come round for a drink, if you can drag yourself away from your work.* **6** The police **drag** a river or lake when they search its bed with a net or hook, *eg* when looking for someone's body. **7** Something **drags** if it is boring: *The second half of the concert dragged.*

▻ ***noun*** (*usually in the singular*)

1 (*informal*) You call something or someone a **drag** if they are boring or disagreeable: *Washing up is such a drag.* [*same as* **pain**] **2** Someone takes a **drag** at a cigarette when they suck in air through it. **3** A circumstance is a **drag** on your progress if it slows you down: *He felt that his poor English was a drag on his career.* **4** (*uncount*) **Drag** is women's clothing worn by men: *We were entertained by a singer in drag.*

phrasal verbs

drag down Something **drags** you **down** if it slows you down or depresses you: *Her constant ill health dragged her down.*

drag in You **drag** a subject **in**, or **drag** it **into** something, when you mention it or involve it unnecessarily: *There's no need to drag her name into this.*

drag on An event or procedure **drags on** if it lasts a long time, especially unnecessarily: *These compensation cases tend to drag on.*

drag out 1 You **drag** information **out** of someone when you make them tell you it: *I managed to drag the truth out of her.* **2** To **drag out** an event or proceeding is to make it last longer than necessary: *They'll try and drag out the discussion to play for time.* [*same as* **spin out, stretch out**]

dragon /'dragən/ *noun*: **dragons**

A **dragon** is a fire-breathing dinosaur-like creature, usually with wings, that is found in stories, myths and legends.

dragonfly /'dragənflaɪ/ *noun*: **dragonflies**

A **dragonfly** is an insect with a long brightly coloured body and two sets of transparent wings.

drain /dreɪn/ *verb; noun*

▻ ***verb***: **drains, draining, drained**

1 Something **drains**, or you **drain** it, when you let liquid flow off it: *Let the dishes drain for a moment before drying them.* **2** To **drain** land is to remove water from it, *eg* by cutting ditches for the water to flow away through: *The marsh was drained in the 18th century.* **3** Liquid **drains** somewhere when flows away somewhere: *They found that liquid waste from the factory was draining into the stream.* **4** You **drain** a glass when you drink all its contents. **5** Something **drains** out of you or away when it disappears: *The blood drained from his face at the sight.* □ *Her anxieties and tensions drained away.* **6** Something **drains** you or your strength when it gradually weakens you: *The experience left her emotionally drained.* □ *Defence expenditure is draining the country's resources.* [*same as* **sap**]

▻ ***noun***: **drains**

1 A **drain** is a pipe taking water or liquid waste away from somewhere: *The drain's blocked.* **2** A metal grid in a roadway, through which rainwater flows away, is also a **drain**: *He dropped his keys down a drain.* [see picture at **street**] **3** Something that is a **drain** on your strength or resources gradually uses them up: *The fees for the special school were a drain on their savings.*

▻ ***phrase*** (*informal*) Something such as money goes **down the drain** when it is wasted.

drainage /'dreɪnɪdʒ/ *noun* (*uncount*)

1 Drainage is the system of pipes, channels and ditches through which water is drained from an area: *Roman houses had efficient drainage systems.* **2** Soil with good **drainage** is loose coarse soil that does not easily become soaked or saturated with water.

drainer /'dreɪnə(r)/ *noun*: **drainers**

A **drainer** is a rack on which to drain dishes after they have been washed. [*same as* **dish rack**; see picture at **kitchen**]

draining board /'dreɪnɪŋ bɔːd/ *noun*: **draining boards**

A **draining board** is a ridged surface fitted beside a kitchen sink, and sloping down towards it, on which you put dishes to drain after washing them. [see picture at **kitchen**]

drainpipe /'dreɪnpaɪp/ *noun*: **drainpipes**

A **drainpipe** is a vertical pipe fitted to the outside wall of a building, through which rainwater from the roof and waste water from baths and basins flows down to the ground. [see picture at **house**]

drake /dreɪk/ *noun*: **drakes**

A **drake** is a male duck.

dram /dram/ *noun*: **drams**

A **dram** of an alcoholic drink such as whisky is a small serving of it.

drama /'drɑːmə/ *noun*: **dramas**

1 A **drama** is a serious play for the theatre, television or radio: *a drama set in medieval Provence.* **2** (*uncount*) **Drama** is acting, plays, and the work of theatre in general: *She studied music and drama.* **3** You can refer to an exciting, upsetting or frightening experience as a **drama**: *She turns every small problem into a drama.* □ *the little dramas of school life.* **4** (*uncount*) Excitement, danger and adventure can be referred to as **drama**: *She felt that her life lacked drama.*

dramatic /drə'matɪk/ *adjective*

1 Dramatic means relating to the theatre, plays or acting: *the Royal Academt of Dramatic Art.* **2** A **dramatic** event is an exciting and impressive one: *There have been dramatic developments in the Middle- East situation.* □ *a dramatic breakthrough in the treatment of cancer.* **3** A **dramatic** change is a sudden, great and noticeable one: *Doctors report a dramatic improvement* *in patients using this drug.* **4 Dramatic** behaviour, actions or gestures are the kind you see in plays, used deliberately to impress or startle people: *She flung out her arms in a dramatic gesture.* — *adverb* **dramatically:** *In the mountains the weather can change dramatically.* □ *'Be warned!' he said dramatically.*

dramatics /drəˈmatɪks/ *noun*
1 (*uncount*) **Dramatics** is the activity of performing plays: *amateur dramatics.* **2** (*plural*) Someone indulges in **dramatics** when they behave over-emotionally in order to gain people's sympathy: *I've had enough of her dramatics.*

dramatist /ˈdramətɪst/ *noun*: **dramatists**
A **dramatist** is a writer of plays.

dramatize or **dramatise** /ˈdramətaɪz/ *verb*: **dramatizes, dramatizing, dramatized**
1 To **dramatize** a story or novel is to rewrite and rearrange it for performance as a play: *She's dramatizing Louisa M Alcott's 'Little Women' for television.* **2** People **dramatize** events or other situations when they describe or report them in a way that makes them seem graver or more exciting than they are: *The press have dramatized what was essentially a trivial incident.* — *noun* (*uncount*) **dramatization** /dramətaɪˈseɪʃən/: *the televized dramatization of George Eliot's 'Middlemarch'.*

drank /draŋk/ *verb*
Drank is the past tense of **drink**.

drape /dreɪp/ *verb*: **drapes, draping, draped**
You **drape** something such as a cloth over or round someone or something when you hang it loosely round them; you **drape** someone or something with something such as a cloth when you cover them loosely with it: *She had draped a long orange scarf round her neck.* □ *The furniture was all draped in white sheets.*
▻ ***noun***: **drapes**
(*used in the plural*) **Drapes** are curtains.

drapery /ˈdreɪpərɪ/ *noun*: **draperies**
1 (*uncount*) **Drapery** is the term used in shops for cloth or fabric: *The drapery department is on the first floor.* **2** (*uncount, or used in the plural*) **Drapery** or **draperies** are terms used for hanging folds of clothing, especially in drawing or sculpture: *the treatment of drapery in early Greek scuplture.*

drastic /ˈdrastɪk/ *adjective*
1 People take **drastic** action when they act in an extreme and decisive manner to deal with some problem or crisis: *We shall have to make drastic cuts in expenditure.* **2 Drastic** results or effects are extreme, especially in a bad way: *He tried mending the electric toaster himself, with drastic results.* **3** A **drastic** change is a sudden and noticeable one: *We have witnessed a drastic deterioration in people's sense of social reponsibility.* — *adverb* **drastically:** *You can drastically alter your appearance by dyeing your hair.*

draught (*AmE* **draft**) /drɑːft/ *noun; adjective*
▻ ***noun***: **draughts**
1 A **draught** is a current of cold air coming into a room, *eg* from an open door or window: *He found he was sitting in a draught.* **2** A **draught** of air or liquid is an amount breathed in or swallowed: *She filled her cup from the river and took a long satisfying draught.* **3** A ship's **draught** is the depth of water it needs to be able to float. **4** (*uncount*) **Draughts** is a game for two people played with 24 pieces on a checked board.
▻ ***adjective***
Draught beer is beer sold from a barrel as distinct from a bottle or can.

draughtsman (*AmE* **draftsman**) /ˈdrɑːftsmən/ *noun*: **draughtsmen**
A **draughtsman** is a person employed, *eg* in industry, to do technical drawings.

draughty /ˈdrɑːftɪ/ (*AmE* **drafty**) *adjective*: **draughtier, draughtiest**
A **draughty** room or building is one with currents of cold air blowing into it, *eg* from open doors or windows.

draw /drɔː/ *verb; noun*
▻ ***verb***: **draws, drawing, drew, drawn**
1 You **draw** a person or thing when you do a picture of them using a pencil or pen; you **draw** a picture or diagram when you do it with a pencil or pen: *He drew his sister sewing in the armchair.* □ *The children were drawing patterns with coloured crayons.* □ *Draw a straight line.* □ *I'll draw you a little map.* □ *I didn't know you could draw.*
2 Someone or something **draws** somewhere when they move in that direction: *The procession drew nearer.* □ *Winter was drawing near.* □ *The train was just drawing out of the station.* □ *I managed to jump on a bus as it was drawing away from the kerb.* □ *Simon was rapidly drawing ahead of the other runners.* □ *We drew back in horror at the sight.* □ *They had been standing close together but drew apart as I came into the room.*
3 a You **draw** something somewhere when you move it with a pulling action: *Why don't you draw your chair up to the fire?* □ *She drew the letter from its envelope.* □ *She got into bed and drew the blankets up to her chin.* □ *The snail drew in its horns.* **b** You **draw** the curtains when you open or close them. **c** Someone **draws** a weapon when they get it out of their pocket or belt and hold it ready for use. **d** An animal **draws** a vehicle when it pulls it along behind it: *a carriage drawn by four horses.*
4 a You **draw** a breath when you breathe in. **b** People **draw** water from somewhere, *eg* a well, when they get it from there. **c** You **draw** money from a bank when you take it out of your account for use. **d** Something **is drawn** from somewhere if it is obtained from there: *The contributors to the survey were drawn from all classes of society.* **e** Someone who is writing or composing something **draws** their material from somewhere if that is their source: *George Eliot's characters are believable; she surely drew them from real life.* □ *the Finnish landscape from which Sibelius drew his inspiration.* **f** You allow yourself, or you refuse, to **be drawn** on something, if you are willing, or unwilling, to talk about it: *She refused to be drawn on her marriage plans.*
5 In a game or lottery, you **draw** something such as a card, ticket, number or name when you select one at random from a supply of them: *Draw any card from the pack.* □ *She drew the winning number.* □ *I'll ask Mrs Henderson here to draw a name from the hat.*
6 a You **draw** someone's attention to something when you show it to them or make them aware of it: *Thank you for drawing our attention to this error.* **b** You **draw** praise or criticism for something you do if that is people's reaction to it: *Her novel 'Possession' drew warm praise from the critics.* **c** You **are drawn** to someone or something if you like them or are attracted to them: *It was his cheerful frankness that first drew me to him.*
7 a You **draw** a conclusion when you reach it after an analysis of the available facts: *It's difficult to draw any conclusion from so little evidence.* **b** You **draw** something such as a distinction, comparison or parallel between things when you make it: *Should we draw a distinction between courage and bravery?*
8 Two teams, sides or competitors in a match or contest **draw** when they finish with the same score: *We drew with Cambridge in the semifinals.* □ *He and I drew for second place.*

▻ ***noun***: **draws**
1 The result of a match is a **draw** when both sides or competitors finish equal. **2** Something such as a show or exhibition is a **draw** if a lot of people go to see it. [*same as* **attraction**] **3** In a game of chance or a lottery, the **draw** is the selection of a card, ticket, number or name at random: *The prize draw will take place on 2 March.* **4** Someone who is quick on the **draw** is quick at getting out their gun and aiming it.

phrasal verbs
draw into You **draw** someone **into** something when you involve them in it: *I refused to be drawn into their argument.*
draw on 1 You **draw on** something when you use it as a resource: *A concern as big as the BBC has a great amount of expertise to draw on.* **2** Someone who is smoking **draws on** their pipe or cigarette when they suck air in through it.
draw out 1 A vehicle **draws out** when it moves out into the road from the side. **2** You **draw** money **out** when you take it out of your bank account: *I drew out £50.* [*same as* **withdraw**] **3** You **draw** a shy person **out** when you encourage them to talk to you and express themselves freely.
draw up 1 A vehicle **draws up** somewhere when it stops there: *She drew up outside his house.* **2** You **draw up** a plan, schedule or document when you prepare and write it: *We're drawing up the new timetable.* **3** You **draw** yourself **up** when you stand upright, as tall and straight as you can: *He drew himself up to his full height.*
draw upon You **draw upon** a resource when you use it: *She draws heavily upon her medical knowledge in many of her stories.*

drawback /ˈdrɔːbak/ *noun*: **drawbacks**
A **drawback** is a disadvantage that something, especially something otherwise attractive, has: *One of the drawbacks of living in the tropics is that it gets dark so early.*

drawer /drɔː(r)/ *noun*: **drawers**
A **drawer** is a box-like container forming part of a chest or desk, that you pull out or push in with a sliding action: *He keeps his socks in the top righthand drawer of the chest of drawers.* [see picture at **bedroom**, **kitchen**]

drawing /ˈdrɔːɪŋ/ *noun*: **drawings**
1 (*uncount*) **Drawing** is the activity or skill of doing pictures with a pencil or pen: *drawing and painting.* **2** A **drawing** is a picture done with a pencil or pen: *He's done some good drawings of the children.*

drawing pin /ˈdrɔːɪŋ pɪn/ *noun*: **drawing pins**
A **drawing pin** is a strong short pin with a round flat head, used for pinning papers to a notice board or wall.

drawing room /ˈdrɔːɪŋ ruːm/ *noun*: **drawing rooms**
A **drawing room** is a sitting room or living room.

drawl /drɔːl/ *verb*; *noun*
▻ ***verb***: **drawls, drawling, drawled**
Someone **drawls** when they speak in a slow, lazy-sounding way, with lengthened vowels: *'Yeah,' he drawled.*
▻ ***noun*** (*used in the singular*) *She spoke with a slight southern drawl.*

drawn /drɔːn/ *verb*; *adjective*
▻ ***verb***
Drawn is the past participle of **draw**.
▻ ***adjective***
1 A **drawn** match or game is one in which the teams or competitors finish with an equal score. **2** **Drawn** curtains are pulled across a window so as to cover it. **3** A person, or their face, looks **drawn** when they look tired or ill. **4** **Drawn** means 'pulled by': *horse-drawn carriages.*

drawstring /ˈdrɔːstrɪŋ/ *noun*: **drawstrings**
A **drawstring** is a cord threaded *eg* through the top of a bag or the waistband of a piece of clothing, which is pulled tight to close or secure it.

dread /drɛd/ *verb*; *noun*
▻ ***verb***: **dreads, dreading, dreaded**
You **dread** something that is going to happen, or may do so, when you are afraid of it: *I was dreading the exams.* □ *I've got to make a speech and I'm dreading it.* □ *I always dread going to hospital to visit him.* □ *She dreaded that the child would be born handicapped.* — *adjective* **dreaded** (*often humorous*): *I'm off to visit the dreaded dentist.*
▻ ***noun*** (*uncount or used in the singular*): *She had a terrible dread of old age and disability.* □ *the common dread that the world will run out of resources.*
▻ ***phrase*** You say you **dread to think** what may be the case if you suspect it is something bad: *I dread to think what the standard of teaching is in that school.*

dreadful /ˈdrɛdfəl/ *adjective*
1 **Dreadful** means terrible or unpleasant: *I've had a dreadful day.* □ *The journey was dreadful.* [*same as* **awful**] **2** (*sometimes informal*) **Dreadful** is used to emphasize the severity of something bad: *It's been a dreadful shock for her.* □ *It's a dreadful shame you can't come.* [*same as* **frightful**] **3** **Dreadful** also means of a poor standard or quality: *The food was fine but the service was dreadful.* [*same as* **appalling**] — *adverb* (*often intensifying*) **dreadfully:** *I've been dreadfully silly.*

dream /driːm/ *noun*; *verb*; *adjective*
▻ ***noun***: **dreams**
1 A **dream** is a series of happenings that you experience in your mind when you are asleep: *I had a funny dream about him last night.* □ *In my dream I was flying around the kitchen ceiling.* **2** People say you are in a **dream** when you are occupied with your own thoughts and not concentrating on what is happening round you. [*same as* **daydream**] **3** You have a **dream** of doing or achieving something, or of something happening, if you very much want it to come about: *Her dream of competing in the Olympics was suddenly close to becoming a reality.* **4** (*informal*) People call something a **dream** if they think it is marvellous or beautiful: *Their new house is a dream.*
▻ ***verb***: **dreams, dreaming, dreamed** or **dreamt**
1 You **dream** when you experience imaginary happenings while you are asleep: *I dreamt about the exam last night.* □ *He dreamt that I'd won a million pounds.* **2** You **dream** of doing something, or of something happening, when you very much want it to come about: *He dreamt of one day winning the world championship.*
▻ ***adjective*** (*informal*)
Something such as a **dream** kitchen or **dream** husband is the ideal one that you wish or long for.
▻ ***phrases*** **1** You say you **never dreamt** that something would happen when you are surprised that it has happened: *I never dreamed that I would see him again.* **2** You say you **would not dream of** doing something when you want to stress that you have no intention of doing it: *I wouldn't dream of telling your mother.*

phrasal verb
You **dream up** something such as a scheme or plan when you invent it: *It's just another idiotic idea dreamt up by the council.* [*same as* **cook up**]

dreamer /ˈdriːmə(r)/ *noun*: **dreamers**
A **dreamer** is an impractical or unrealistic person whose mind is filled with impossible schemes and ambitions.

dreamt /drɛmt/ *verb*
Dreamt is the past tense of **dream**.

dreamy /ˈdriːmɪ/ *adjective*: **dreamier, dreamiest**
A **dreamy** person lets their mind and imagination wander, and does not concentrate on what they should be doing.

dreary /ˈdrɪərɪ/ *adjective*: **drearier, dreariest**
Dreary people or things are dull or depressing: *dreary weather* □ *Nothing could be drearier than a seaside resort in winter.* [*same as* **dismal**] — *adverb* **drearily:** *'More bills,' he commented drearily.*

dredge /drɛdʒ/ *verb*: **dredges, dredging, dredged**
A river, harbour or channel **is dredged** when its bed is cleared of mud.

> ***phrasal verb***
> You **dredge up** something that people have forgotten when you rediscover it and mention it again: *The press had been dredging up some old scandals from his past.* [*same as* **dig up**]

dregs /drɛgz/ *noun* (*plural*)
1 The **dregs** of something such as coffee or wine are the solid bits left when you have finished drinking it. **2** The **dregs** of society are the people in it who are considered most worthless and useless.

drenched /drɛntʃt/ *adjective*
You are **drenched** when your clothes are very wet: *rain-drenched spectators.* [*same as* **soaked**]

dress /drɛs/ *noun*; *verb*
▻ ***noun***: **dresses**
1 A **dress** is a piece of clothing for a woman or girl that covers the body from the shoulders down, with the lower part in the form of a skirt: *She was wearing a short-sleeved cotton dress with a full skirt.* [see picture at **clothing**] **2** (*uncount*) Both men's and women's clothing can be referred to as **dress**: *The men were in evening dress.* □ *They wear national dress for ceremonial occasions.*
▻ ***verb***: **dresses, dressing, dressed**
1 You **dress** or **dress yourself** when you put your clothes on; you **dress** someone such as a baby when you put clothes on them: *The children are old enough to dress themselves.* □ *She dressed and went down to breakfast.* □ *She was dressing her dolls.* **2** You **are dressed** when you are wearing clothes, as distinct from being naked, or are wearing normal clothes as distinct from night clothes: *Don't come in; I'm not dressed yet.* **3** You **are dressed** in a certain way, style or colour if you are wearing clothes of a certain kind, style or colour: *She was dressed in black.* □ *He was casually dressed in a sweater and jeans.* □ *You're not suitably dressed for church.* **4** You **dress** in a certain style if you wear clothes of that style: *She always dressed in a youthful style.* □ *Should we dress formally for this concert?* **5** People **dress** when they put on formal evening clothes: *We never bothered to dress for dinner.* **6** You **dress** a wound when you clean and bandage it. **7** You **dress** a shop window when you arrange goods in it for passers-by to look at. **8** To **dress** stone is to smooth and shape it for use in building. **9** You **dress** food when you prepare it for serving.
▻ ***phrase*** You **get dressed** when you put your clothes on; you **get** someone such as a child **dressed** when you put clothes on them: *I hate getting dressed or undressed in a cold room.* □ *She got breakfast while her husband got the children dressed.*

> ***phrasal verb***
> **dress up 1** People **dress up** when they put on smart clothes: *I like to dress up when I'm going out in the evening.* **2** You **dress up** as something or someone when you put on clothes and make-up that make you look like that person: *Every Christmas he dressed up as Santa Claus.* **3** You **dress up** something when you make additions to it to make it more impressive or attractive: *You should consider dressing up your PhD thesis for publication.* **4** You **dress up** unpleasant facts when you try to make them sound more acceptable: *The plain fact is that they're giving me the sack, however they try to dress it up.*

dresser /ˈdrɛsə(r)/ *noun*: **dressers**
1 A **dresser** is a piece of kitchen furniture in two sections, the top section fitted with shelves and the bottom section with drawers or cupboards. **2** (*AmE*) A **dresser** is a chest of drawers, usually with a mirror on top.

dressing /ˈdrɛsɪŋ/ *noun*: **dressings**
1 A **dressing** is a covering or bandage for protecting a cut or wound while it heals: *The patient's dressing must be changed every day.* **2** (*uncount or count*) A **dressing** is a sauce, especially for salad: *oil and vinegar dressing* □ *a choice of salad dressings.*

dressing-down /drɛsɪŋ ˈdaʊn/ *noun* (*old, informal*): **dressing-downs**
Someone in authority gives you a **dressing-down** when they scold you.

dressing-gown /ˈdrɛsɪŋ gaʊn/ *noun*: **dressing gowns**
A **dressing gown** is loose-fitting coat-like piece of clothing for wearing over your nightclothes or when you are not fully dressed. [*same as* **robe**]

dressing room /ˈdrɛsɪŋ ruːm/ *noun*: **dressing rooms**
An actor's or performer's **dressing room** in a theatre is the room where they put on or take off the make-up and clothes they wear on stage.

dressing table /ˈdrɛsɪŋ teɪbəl/ *noun*: **dressing tables**
A **dressing table** is a piece of bedroom furniture that you can sit at, with drawers and a large mirror. [see picture at **bedroom**]

dressmaker /ˈdrɛsmeɪkə(r)/ *noun*: **dressmakers**
A **dressmaker** is someone who makes clothes, especially a woman who makes clothes professionally for women and children. [compare **tailor**] — *noun* (*uncount*) **dressmaking:** *the art of dressmaking.*

drew /druː/ *verb*
Drew is the past tense of **draw**.

dribble /ˈdrɪbəl/ *verb*; *noun*
▻ ***verb***: **dribbles, dribbling, dribbled**
1 A person, especially a baby, **dribbles**, when saliva or liquid food drips or trickles out of their mouth: *The baby has dribbled down my blouse.* [*same as* **drool, slobber**] **2** Liquid **dribbles** from somewhere when it drips or trickles in a thin stream from there; something such as a tap **dribbles** when a thin stream of liquid drips or trickles from it. **3** A footballer or hockey-player **dribbles** the ball, or **dribbles**, when they move the ball smoothly along with short kicks or hits.
▻ ***noun***: **dribbles**
A **dribble** of liquid is a small quantity or a thin stream: *There was a dribble of blood at the corner of his mouth.*

dried *verb*; *adjective*
▻ ***verb***
Dried is the past tense and past participle of **dry**.

▻ *adjective*
Dried food is food from which the water has been removed to preserve it: *packets of dried soup.*

drier see **dryer**.

drift /drɪft/ *noun; verb*
▻ *verb*: **drifts, drifting, drifted**
1 Something **drifts** somewhere when it floats along, carried by water or wind: *Bits of wreckage drifted past.* ▫ *Our boat drifted helplessly with the tide.* ▫ *The cloud of poisonous gas was expected to drift towards the town.* **2** People **drift** somewhere when they move there gradually in little groups: *The guests began to drift towards the food.* **3** People **drift** towards a dangerous situation when they are carried helplessly towards it: *Before we know where we are we'll be drifting towards war.* **4** You **drift** about when you wander from place to place with no particular aim or plan: *He drifted from town to town in search of casual work.* [*same as* **roam**]
▻ *noun*: **drifts**
1 A **drift** is a snowdrift: *The car got stuck in a drift.* ▫ *six-foot drifts.* **2** (*used in the singular*) The **drift** somewhere is the general movement of people there: *the drift away from traditional values towards a more profit-based culture.* **3** (*used in the singular*) The **drift** of what a speaker or writer is saying is their general meaning: *I couldn't hear every word she said but I got her general drift.* [*same as* **gist**]

> ***phrasal verb***
> You **drift off** when you slowly fall asleep. [*same as* **drop off, doze off**]

drifter /'drɪftə(r)/ *noun*: **drifters**
A **drifter** is a person who wanders from place to place or from job to job without any particular aim or plan.

driftwood /'drɪftwʊd/ *noun* (*uncount*)
Driftwood is pieces of wood floating on the sea or washed up on the shore by the tide.

drill /drɪl/ *noun; verb*
▻ *noun*: **drills**
1 A **drill** is a tool for making holes: *a dentist's drill* ▫ *an electric drill.* [see picture at **tool**] **2** (*uncount*) In the armed forces, **drill** is training in marching and manoeuvres, and in the use of weapons, by means of routine exercises: *We did two hours' drill every day.* **3** (*count or uncount*) A **drill** is any routine exercise that gives people practice in some skill or subject: *She gave the children daily drills in spelling and mental arithmetic.* **4** A **drill** is also a routine to be followed in an emergency: *All staff are requested to read the fire-drill instructions.*
▻ *verb*: **drills, drilling, drilled**
1 You **drill** into something, or **drill** a hole in it, when you make a hole in it with a drill: *Drill four holes to take the screws.* **2** People **drill** for oil or water when they drill deep holes into the ground or the sea bed in order to search for it. **3** You **drill** people in something when you train them by means of repeated exercises: *Before the appearance of calculators children had to be thoroughly drilled in their multiplication tables.* **4** Soldiers **drill** or **are drilled** when they do routine exercises in marching and using weapons.

drily see **dry**.

drink /drɪŋk/ *verb; noun*
▻ *verb*: **drinks, drinking, drank, drunk**
1 You **drink** a liquid when you swallow it: *They used to tell us to drink a pint of milk a day.* ▫ *Drink up your fruit juice.* **2** People **drink** when they drink alcohol, especially too much and too often: *Don't drink and drive.*
▻ *noun*: **drinks**
1 (*count or uncount*) A **drink** is an alcoholic or non-alcoholic liquid for drinking, or an amount of it that you drink: *sweet drinks* ▫ *food and drink.* **2** (*uncount*) **Drink** is alcohol: *Drink ruins your health.* ▫ *He has a drink problem.*

> ***phrasal verb***
> **drink to** You **drink to** someone or something when you raise your glass and say their name as a way of wishing them success. [*same as* **drink a toast to**]

drinkable /'drɪŋkəbəl/ *adjective*
A liquid that is **drinkable** is fit for drinking. [*opposite* **undrinkable**]

drinker /'drɪŋkə(r)/ *noun*: **drinkers**
1 You call yourself a tea-**drinker** or a coffee-**drinker** if that is the drink you normally prefer. **2** A **drinker** is a person who drinks a lot of alcohol.

drinking /'drɪŋkɪŋ/ *noun* (*uncount*)
Drinking is the activity of drinking alcohol: *the dangers of drinking and driving.*

drip /drɪp/ *verb; noun*
▻ *verb*: **drips, dripping, dripped**
1 Liquid **drips** when it falls in drops: *Rain was dripping from the roof.* **2** Something or someone **drips**, or **drips** a liquid, when liquid falls in drops from them: *Don't leave taps dripping.* ▫ *Her finger was dripping blood.*
▻ *noun*: **drips**
1 A **drip** is a falling drop of liquid: *I've put a bucket under the leak to catch the drips.* **2** (*uncount*) The **drip** of water is the sound of it dripping: *We awoke to the steady drip of rain.* **3** (*medicine*) A **drip** is an apparatus for passing a liquid slowly and continuously into a patient's vein.
▻ *phrase*
1 Someone or something is **dripping with** a liquid when it is dripping from them: *He arrived dripping with sweat.* **2** Someone or something that is **dripping wet** is very wet: *dripping-wet clothes.* [*same as* **soaking wet**]

drive /draɪv/ *verb; noun*
▻ *verb*: **drives, driving, drove, driven**
1 a You **drive** a car or other vehicle when you operate its controls and steer it: *Can you drive a tractor?* ▫ *Do you want to drive or shall I?* ▫ *We'd already driven 150 kilometres.* ▫ *You were driving at over 100 miles an hour.* ▫ *I drove into Chichester to get petrol.* ▫ *She drove the car into the garage.* ▫ *She drives* [= she has] *an ancient Mini car.*

> You **drive** a four-wheeled vehicle, but **ride** a bicycle or motor bike: *He rode his motor bike into a wall.*

b You **drive** someone somewhere when you take them in a car: *Let me drive you home.* **c** Machinery **is driven** by a type of power such as electricity or steam if that is what makes it work: *water-driven mills.* **d** You say a person **is driven** by some need or emotion if that is what makes them behave the way they do: *She was driven by a desire to impress people.*
2 a You **drive** animals somewhere when you guide them there: *He was driving a herd of cows across the road into a field.* **b** People or animals **are driven** somewhere or from somewhere when they are forced to go there or from there: *Thousands of people were driven from their homes by the invaders.* ▫ *We kept the fire going to drive away the bears.* ▫ *I'll try to drive off the reporters.* **c** People **are driven** to do something, or into a certain state, when they are forced into that situa-

tion: *What could have driven him to take his own life?* □ *She was driven to despair by her increasing debts.* □ *That noise is driving me crazy.*

3 a You **drive** a nail or post into a surface when you hit or hammer it firmly into it. **b** A golfer or cricketer **drives** the ball somewhere when they hit it hard.

▻ ***noun***: **drives**

1 A **drive** is a journey in a car or other vehicle: *Shall we go out for a drive?* □ *It's a 20-mile drive to the airport from here.* **2** A **drive** or **driveway** is a private road leading to a house from its gate: *I've parked my car in your drive.* [see picture at **house**] **3** (*count or uncount*) The **drive** of a piece of machinery is the part or system that makes it operate: *cars with front-wheel drive.* **4** The **drives** in a computer are the slots into which you put disks of various sizes, or the mechanisms inside that turn them: *Put the 3.5-inch disk in drive A.* **5** (*uncount*) Someone who has **drive** has the energy, enthusiasm and determination necessary for getting things done.

6 People have a **drive** to do something when they launch a campaign or make a special effort to do it: *We're having a big drive to save fuel.* **7** A **drive** by a golfer or cricketer is a stroke or hit played by them.

▻ ***phrase*** You realize **what** someone **is driving at** when you understand what they mean: *I've no idea what you're driving at.*

drivel /ˈdrɪvəl/ *noun* (*uncount*)

If you say that someone is talking **drivel** you mean that they are talking nonsense.

driven /ˈdrɪvən/ *verb*

Driven is the past participle of **drive**.

driver /ˈdraɪvə(r)/ *noun*: **drivers**

1 A **driver** is a person who drives, is qualified to drive, or is driving, a motor vehicle: *The car stopped and the driver got out.* **2** A taxi-**driver**, bus-**driver** or ambulance-**driver** is a person who drives a taxi, bus or ambulance as their job.

driveway *noun*: **driveways**

A **driveway** is a drive (sense 2).

driving /ˈdraɪvɪŋ/ *noun*; *adjective*

▻ ***noun*** (*uncount*)

Driving is the activity or skill of driving a motor vehicle, or the manner in which you drive: *He was charged with dangerous driving.*

▻ ***adjective***

1 Someone or something that is described as the **driving** force behind something is the person or thing that makes it progress and develop: *His wife was the driving force behind his political career.* **2 Driving** rain is heavy rain that is being blown by the wind.

driving licence /ˈdraɪvɪŋ laɪsəns/ *noun*: **driving licences**

Your **driving licence** is a card or certificate showing that you are qualified to drive.

drizzle /ˈdrɪzəl/ *noun*; *verb*

▻ ***noun*** (*uncount*)

Drizzle is thin light rain: *The rain turned to drizzle and eventually stopped altogether.*

▻ ***verb***: **drizzles, drizzling, drizzled**

You say **it is drizzling** when it is raining slightly.

drone /droʊn/ *verb*; *noun*

▻ ***verb***: **drones, droning, droned**

Something **drones** when it makes a low humming noise: *An aircraft droned overhead.*

▻ ***noun*** (*used in the singular*): *The only sound was the distant drone of traffic.*

> ***phrasal verb***
> Someone **drones on** when they go on speaking for a long time in a boring manner: *The lecturer droned on and on.*

drool /druːl/ *verb*: **drools, drooling, drooled**

1 A person or animal **drools** when saliva drips from their mouth. [*same as* **dribble, slobber**] **2** People **drool** over something when they admire it in a silly or over-enthusiatic way: *We were all drooling over the new baby.*

droop /druːp/ *verb*; *noun*

▻ ***verb***: **droops, drooping, drooped**

1 Something **droops** when it hangs downward: *It was late and the children's heads were beginning to droop.*

2 Plants **droop**, or **droop** their heads, when they are weak from lack of water. — *adjective* **drooping:** *a drooping moustache* □ *a plant with a drooping bell-shaped flower.*

drop /drɒp/ *verb*; *noun*

▻ ***verb***: **drops, dropping, dropped**

1 You **drop** something when you let it fall by accident or intentionally: *She dropped the plate with a clatter.* □ *I must have dropped my keys as I got out of the car.* □ *UN pilots have begun dropping emergency supplies into the refugee camps.* □ *Atomic bombs were dropped on Hiroshima and Nagasaki in 1945.* **2** Something **drops** when it falls: *It was so quiet you could have heard a pin drop.* □ *Something dropped to the ground and she bent to pick it up.* □ *I was ready to drop with exhaustion.* □ *The cat dropped on its paws and ran off.* **3** An amount **drops** in level when it decreases: *Prices have dropped considerably.* □ *The temperature drops to minus 20° at night.* [*same as* **fall**] **4** You **drop** your voice, or your voice **drops**, when you speak more quietly: *They dropped their voices as they entered the church.* [*same as* **lower**] **5** The driver of a vehicle **drops** a passenger somewhere when he or she lets them get out there: *Could you drop me at the corner of Byres Road?* **6** You **drop** something that you are doing when you leave it in order to do something else: *I can't just drop everything to look after casual visitors.* **7** The police **drop** a charge, or someone **drops** a legal case, when they decide not to continue with it: *The charges against her were dropped.* **8** You **drop** an idea or plan when you decide not to use it. **9** You **drop** a habit when you stop it or give it up.

10 You **drop** a friend when you stop communicating with them.

11 You **drop** a hint when you give someone one casually: *He kept dropping hints about marriage.*

12 You **drop** someone a note or line when you write a short note to them and post it: *I'll drop you a postcard from Vienna.*

▻ ***noun***: **drops**

1 A **drop** of liquid is a little tear-shaped mass of it that falls from somewhere: *I think I felt a drop of rain.* □ *There were drops of blood all the way along the pavement.* **2** A **drop** of liquid is also a small quantity of it: *Is there a drop of tea left in the pot?* □ *She gave the patient a drop of brandy.* □ *The plants could do with a drop of water.* **3** (*used in the plural*) **Drops** are a medical treatment for your eyes, ears or nose in the form of a liquid that you put into them in small drops. **4** A **drop** is a vertical descent, or distance from the top to the bottom of something such as a cliff or wall: *There was a thirty-foot drop on the other side of the wall.* **5** A **drop** in the level of something is a decrease or reduction: *a sudden drop in temperature* □ *a drop in wages.* [*same as* **fall**] **6** An air **drop** is the dropping of supplies into an area by an aircraft. **7** A **drop** is a small round flat sweet: *chocolate drops* □ *peppermint drops.*

> ***phrasal verbs***
> **drop away** Your friends or supporters **drop away** when they abandon you.

drop back or **drop behind** You **drop back**, or **drop behind** others when you move more slowly than them, and they gradually move ahead of you.
drop by Someone **drops by** when they visit you informally and unexpectedly: *I'll drop by for a chat one day soon.*
drop in Someone **drops in**, or **drops in** on you, when they visit you unexpectedly and informally: *Do drop in sometime.*
drop off **1** You **drop off** when you fall asleep: *I must have dropped off for a few minutes.* **2** An amount or rate **drops off** when it decreases: *Sales usually drop off in January.* **3** You **drop** a passenger off somewhere when you let them get out of your car there: *Could you drop me off at the supermarket?*
drop out **1** You **drop out** of a competition, or some planned activity, when you take no further part in it. **2** Students **drops out** of school or university when they leave it without finishing their course of study: *A lot of medical students drop out after the first year.*

drop-out /ˈdrɒpaʊt/ *noun*: **drop-outs**
1 A **drop-out** is a student who leaves school or university without finishing his or her course of study. **2** A **drop-out** from society is a person who rejects normal social standards, *eg* by refusing to take a regular job, or dress and behave in the accepted way.

droppings /ˈdrɒpɪŋz/ *noun* (*plural*)
Droppings are the faeces of birds and animals: *sheep droppings.*

drought /draʊt/ *noun* (*count or uncount*): **droughts**
A **drought** is a long period without rain: *All the rivers dried up during the months of drought.* □ *There were frequent droughts during the early '80s.*

drove[1] /droʊv/ *verb*
Drove is the past tense of **drive**.

drove[2] /droʊv/ *noun*: **droves**
People move somewhere in **droves** when they go there in enormous crowds: *Sightseers were arriving in droves.*

drown /draʊn/ *verb*: **drowns, drowning, drowned**
1 A person or animal **drowns** or **is drowned** when they die as a result of sinking under water and being unable to breathe: *He fell into the river and drowned.* □ *He drowned all but two of the kittens.* **2** One sound **drowns** another when the one is so loud that you can't hear the other: *The end of her speech was drowned in applause.*

drowse /draʊz/ *verb*: **drowses, drowsing, drowsed**
You **drowse** when you are nearly asleep or just asleep: *He was drowsing in an armchair.*

drowsy /ˈdraʊzɪ/ *adjective*: **drowsier, drowsiest**
You are **drowsy** when you are sleepy: *drowsy children.* — *adverb* **drowsily:** *She sat up drowsily, rubbing her eyes.* — *noun* (*uncount*) **drowsiness:** *Warning: these pills may cause drowsiness.*

drudge /drʌdʒ/ *noun*: **drudges**
Someone who is called a **drudge** has to do a lot of hard, unpleasant and boring work, usually for very little pay.

drudgery /ˈdrʌdʒərɪ/ *noun* (*uncount*)
Drudgery is hard, unpleasant, boring but necessary work: *the drudgery of washing up.*

drug /drʌg/ *noun*; *verb*
▻ ***noun*: drugs**
1 A **drug** is a chemical substance used as a medicine: *I was injected with a pain-killing drug.* **2** (*usually in the plural*) **Drugs** are substances, often addictive and sold illegally, that people smoke or inject into themselves for the sake of the feelings of pleasure and happiness they produce: *She's on drugs.* □ *He takes drugs.* □ *drug-addicts.*
▻ ***verb*: drugs, drugging, drugged**
1 You **drug** a person or animal when you give them, or inject them with, a chemical substance that makes them fall asleep or become unconscious. **2** To **drug** someone's food or drink is to add a substance to it that makes them fall asleep or become unconscious.

drugstore /ˈdrʌgstɔː(r)/ *noun* (*especially AmE*): **drugstores**
A **drugstore** is a shop selling medicines and other products, including drinks and snacks.

drum /drʌm/ *noun*; *verb*
▻ ***noun*: drums**
1 A **drum** is a round hollow musical instrument of the percussion family, covered with a tightly stretched skin, which the player beats with the fingers, or with a stick or pair of sticks. [see picture at **orchestra**] **2** Something that is cylindrical in shape may be called a **drum**, especially a fuel-container of that shape: *steel oil drums*
▻ ***verb*: drums, drumming, drummed**
1 Rain or hail **drums** on a surface such as a metal roof when it hits it with a rapid beating sound. **2** You **drum** your fingers when you make a rhythmical beating noise with your finger tips on a surface such as a table: *He drummed his fingers impatiently.*

phrasal verbs
drum into You **drum** a fact **into** someone when you keep repeating it to them until they learn it: *We had our multiplication tables drummed into us at school.*
drum up You **drum up** something such as help or support when you persuade a number of people to give it: *We expect to drum up a good audience of friends and relations for the concert.*

drummer /drʌmə(r)/ *noun*: **drummers**
A **drummer** is someone who plays the drum, or the drums, in a band or pop group.

drunk /drʌŋk/ *verb*; *adjective*; *noun*
▻ ***verb***
Drunk is the past participle of **drink**.
▻ ***adjective***
Someone who is **drunk** has drunk so much alcohol that they cannot speak or think properly, or control their behaviour and movements: *He fell downstairs after getting drunk one night.*
▻ ***noun*: drunks**
A **drunk** is someone who is drunk, or who frequently gets drunk.

drunkard /ˈdrʌŋkəd/ *noun*: **drunkards**
A **drunkard** is someone who frequently gets drunk.

drunken /ˈdrʌŋkən/ *adjective*
1 A **drunken** person is drunk: *a crowd of drunken sailors.* **2** **Drunken** behaviour is the kind of silly, noisy and uncontrolled behaviour that is typical of someone who is drunk: *There were roars of drunken laughter.* — *adverb* **drunkenly:** *She was leaning drunkenly against the wall.* — *noun* (*uncount*) **drunkenness:** *He had occasional spells of drunkenness.*

dry /draɪ/ *adjective*; *verb*
▻ ***adjective*: drier, driest**
1 Something that is **dry** has little or no liquid on it or in it: *Put the dishes away if they're dry.* □ *She grabbed a towel and rubbed herself dry.* □ *Make sure both surfaces are dry before applying glue.* □ *The ground was dry and hard.* □ *The dry wood quickly caught fire.* [*opposite* **wet**] **2** A river or lake that is **dry** has no water in it. **3** You talk about being on **dry** land as distinct from being in

a boat: *It's nice to be back on dry land.* **4** The weather is **dry** when it doesn't rain: *It will remain dry tomorrow over the whole country.* ▫ *a spell of dry weather.* [*opposite* **wet**] **5** A piece of **dry** bread has no butter, jam or other form of spread on it. **6** You say you are **dry** if you are thirsty. **7 Dry** wine is not sweet-tasting. **8** If you call something such as a lecture or a book **dry** you mean that it is dull. **9** A **dry** remark, or **dry** humour, is funny in a quiet, subtle way: *She made some dry observations about people's use of English.* — *adverb* **drily** or **dryly:** *He drily commented that the book was a good one for going to sleep with.* — *noun* (*uncount*) **dryness:** *She preferred the dryness of the South African climate to the humidity of Singapore.*

▻ ***verb***: **dries, drying, dried**

You **dry** something when you make it dry; something **dries** when it becomes dry: *Do you dry the dishes or do you leave them to dry?* ▫ *She dried her hands on the towel.*

> ***phrasal verbs***
>
> **dry out** Something **dries out** when all the moisture disappears from it: *After picking the bay leaves, allow them to dry out for a week or so before using them in your cooking.*
>
> **dry up 1** A river or lake **dries up** when the water in it becomes shallower and eventually disappears: *Some of the streams dry up in summer.* **2** A supply of something **dries up** when it decreases and comes to an end. **3** (*informal*) A speaker or actor **dries up** when they stop speaking because they can't remember what they were going to say next. **4** (*informal*) If you tell someone to **dry up** you are rudely telling them that they are talking nonsense and should be quiet. **5** You **dry up** when you dry the dishes after they have been washed.

dry-clean /draɪ 'kli:n/ *verb*: **dry-cleans, dry-cleaning, dry-cleaned**

Clothes **are dry-cleaned** when they are cleaned with a liquid chemical rather than with water.

dryer or **drier** /'draɪə(r)/ *noun*; *adjective*

noun: **dryers**

A **dryer** is a machine or device for drying something: *Clothes take no time to dry in a tumble-dryer.* ▫ *a hair-drier.*

▻ ***adjective***

Dryer or **drier** is the comparative form of **dry**.

drying-up cloth /draɪɪŋʌp klɒθ/ *noun*: **drying-up cloths**

A **drying-up cloth** is a cloth you use for drying dishes on. [*same as* **tea towel**, **dish towel**; see picture at **kitchen**]

dual /'dju:əl/ *adjective*

1 Dual describes things that consist of two of those things: *the dual role of mother and housekeeper* ▫ *a dual-purpose tool* ▫ *The instructor's car has dual controls.* **2** Two people have **dual** ownership, *eg* of a property, if they own it jointly.

dual carriageway /dju:əl 'kærɪdʒweɪ/ *noun*: **dual carriageways**

A **dual carriageway** is a road with a strip of grass or a barrier down the middle, to separate vehicles travelling in opposite directions.

dub /dʌb/ *verb*: **dubs, dubbing, dubbed**

1 Something or someone **is dubbed** a certain name or nickname if they are given it: *Edinburgh was dubbed by some 'the drugs capital of Europe'.* **2** To **dub** a film is to replace the actors' voices on the soundtrack with the voices of actors speaking another language: *The best-known Italian films have been dubbed into English.*

dubious /'dju:bɪəs/ *adjective*

1 You are **dubious** about something if you are uncertain or suspicious about it: *I was dubious about his claims to have cured people of the disease.* **2** You call something **dubious** if you are suspicious about it, or think it is unreliable or dishonest: *dubious business dealings* [*same as* **shady**] — *adverb* **dubiously:** *She eyed the caller dubiously.*

duchess /'dʌtʃɪs/ *noun*: **duchesses**

A **duchess** is a woman who is the wife or widow of a duke, or has the same rank as a duke.

duck[1] /dʌk/ *noun*: **ducks** or **duck**

1 (*count or uncount*) A **duck** is a water bird with short legs, webbed feet and a broad flat beak, whose typical cry is a quack; **duck** is its flesh used as food: *She chose duck from the menu.* **2** A **duck** is also a female duck. [*opposite* **drake**]

▻ ***phrases* 1** You **take to** an activity **like a duck to water** when you find that you are good at it and enjoy it. **2** A scolding or criticism is **like water off a duck's back** if it has no effect on the person for whom it is intended.

duck[2] /dʌk/ *verb*: **ducks, ducking, ducked**

1 You **duck** your head, or **duck**, when you suddenly lower your head to avoid something: *They had to duck as they came through the door.* ▫ *She ducked her head to avoid his fist.* ▫ *He ducked down out of sight.* **2** To **duck** someone is to push their head under the water: *The children were splashing about and ducking one another* **3** You **duck** a responsibility or a duty when you avoid it. [*same as* **shirk, evade**]

> ***phrasal verb***
>
> You **duck out** of something you don't want to do when you avoid doing it: *I'm afraid I ducked out of helping at the children's party.*

duckling /'dʌklɪŋ/ *noun*: **ducklings**

A **duckling** is a baby duck.

duct /dʌkt/ *noun*: **ducts**

1 A **duct** is a tube in your body through which a bodily fluid passes: *The baby had a blocked tear duct.* **2** A **duct** is a pipe or channel carrying liquid or gas: *air ducts.*

dud /dʌd/ *noun, or adjective* (*informal*): **duds**

You call something **dud** or a **dud** if it is useless or does not work: *a dud battery* ▫ *dud cheques* ▫ *These bulbs seem to be duds.*

due /dju:/ *adjective*; *noun*; *adverb*

▻ ***adjective***

1 You say that one thing is **due** to another if the one is caused by the other: *Our survival as a firm was due entirely to his leadership.* ▫ *There are considerable delays, due to major roadworks.* [compare **owing to**] **2** Something is **due**, or **due** to happen, at a certain time, if it is expected then according to the timetable or to previously made arrangements: *What time are the guests due?* ▫ *The train was due in at 11.45.* ▫ *Another bus is due in ten minutes.* ▫ *The windows are due to be cleaned again next week.* ▫ *When is the baby due for her next feed?* **3** Something, especially a sum of money, is **due** to you if it is owed to you, or you have a right to it: *The remainder of the sum due to you will be paid next month.* ▫ *Thanks are also due to the organizers of the event.* **4** You give **due** attention or consideration to something when you think about it as thoroughly as you ought to: *After due consideration the board have decided against appointing a new managing director for the time being.* ▫ *With all due respect for your authority, I believe you are making a mistake.*

▻ ***noun***: **dues**

1 (*used in the singular*) Something that is your **due** is

something that you deserve or have a right to: *She never quite achieved the recognition that was her due.* **2** (*used in the plural*) **Dues** are sums of money that you pay regularly to an organization that you belong to.
▻ ***adverb***
You use **due** with the directions of the compass, meaning 'exactly': *Carlisle is due south of Edinburgh.*
▻ ***phrases*** **1** For **in due course** see **course**. **2** You say '**to give them their due**' to introduce something good about people who are being blamed or criticized: *To give the girl her due, she was only trying to help.*

duel /'dju:əl/ *noun*: **duels**
1 A **duel** is a fight arranged between two people as a means of settling a quarrel, traditionally fought with pistols or swords. **2** Any struggle between two people or groups can be called a **duel**: *The two teams are locked in a duel for first place.*

duet /dju:'ɛt/ *noun*: **duets**
A **duet** is a piece of music for two singers or musicians: *a piano duet.*

duffel coat /'dʌfəl koʊt/ *noun*: **duffel coats**
A **duffel coat** is a heavy coat of coarse woollen fabric, usually with a hood and little rod-like fastenings called toggles.

duffer /'dʌfə(r)/ *noun* (*informal*): **duffers**
If you call someone a **duffer** you mean that they are stupid.

dug /dʌg/ *verb*
Dug is the past tense and past participle of **dig**.

duke /dju:k/ *noun*: **dukes**
A **duke** is a nobleman of the highest rank after a prince: *He was created Duke of Wellington in 1814.*

dull /dʌl/ *adjective*; *verb*
▻ ***adjective***: **duller**, **dullest**
1 You call something or someone **dull** if they are boring or uninteresting: *He's given us yet another long dull book to read before next week.* □ *Life is pretty dull here at home.* □ *They were dull but well-meaning people.* [*opposite* **lively**] **2** You appear **dull** when you look bored and lifeless: *She stared round her with a dull, blank expression.* **3** The weather is **dull** when the sky is grey and cloudy: *It was a dull day.* [*opposite* **bright**, **sunny**] **4 Dull** colours are colours such as grey and brown, as distinct from bright colours like red and yellow. [*opposite* **bright**] **5** You describe a pain as **dull** if it is troublesome and uncomfortable without being intense or acute: *He had had a dull ache in his side for some weeks.* [*opposite* **sharp**, **acute**] **6** You describe the noise of something such as a fall or impact as **dull** if it is heavy-sounding but indistinct: *We heard a dull thud next door.* — *adverb* **dully:** *He stared dully out of the window.* □ *Her head ached dully.* — *noun* (*uncount*) **dullness:** *I lead a life of depressing dullness.*
▻ ***verb*** (*literary*): **dulls**, **dulling**, **dulled**
1 Something such as a drug **dulls** a pain if it makes it less acute: *She drank secretly to dull the pain of losing him.* [*same as* **deaden**] **2** Something **dulls** when it becomes dull: *Her head sank back and her eyes dulled as we watched.*

duly /'dju:lɪ/ *adverb*
1 Something is **duly** done when it is done properly: *I declare that Mr James Edwards has been duly elected.* **2** Something is **duly** carried out if it is the right and appropriate procedure in the circumstances: *He has done wrong and will be duly punished.* **3** Something **duly** happens if it happens as expected or arranged: *I duly arrived for my interview to find no-one there.*

dumb /dʌm/ *adjective*: **dumber, dumbest**
1 Someone who is **dumb** is unable to speak: *Children born deaf and dumb can nowadays be taught to speak and lip-read.* **2** You are **dumb**, or struck **dumb**, with a feeling such as amazement, when it temporarily makes you unable to say anything: *She sat dumb with dismay at the news.* **3** (*offensive*) If you call someone **dumb** you mean they are stupid: *Don't be so dumb!* □ *another of your dumb ideas.* **4** A person accused of **dumb** insolence is thought to show a contempt for authority in the way they look or behave, even though they don't express it in words.

dumbfounded /dʌm'faʊndɪd/ *adjective*
You are **dumbfounded** when you are too astonished to speak: *She listened dumbfounded to his accusation.*

dumbly /'dʌmlɪ/ *adverb*
You do something **dumbly** when you do it without saying anything, *eg* because you are too astonished or miserable to speak: *She nodded dumbly.*

dummy /'dʌmɪ/ *noun*; *adjective*
▻ ***noun***: **dummies**
1 A **dummy** is a teat-shaped rubber object that people give babies to suck, to comfort them and stop them crying. **2** A **dummy** is a human-shaped figure used for various purposes: *They use dummies in road-safety experiments, to find out what happens to real people in traffic accidents.* □ *a tailor's dummy.*
▻ ***adjective***
Dummy describes things that are not real: *Builders often incorporated dummy doors and windows into their design, for the sake of symmetry.*

dump /dʌmp/ *verb*; *noun*
▻ ***verb***: **dumps, dumping, dumped**
1 (*informal*) You **dump** something, usually something heavy, somewhere when you put it down somewhere, especially carelessly or temporarily: *Dump your bags in the hall and come straight into tea.* **2** People **dump** waste materials when they get rid of them by leaving them somewhere, especially improperly: *The factory had been dumping its waste in the river.* **3** (*computers*) You **dump** data from a computer's memory on to a disk when you transfer it there.
▻ ***noun***: **dumps**
1 A **dump** or **rubbish dump** is a place, especially outside a town, where people throw rubbish that they can't dispose of at home. **2** (*informal*) If you call a place a **dump** you mean that is dirty, untidy, and uncomfortable to live in. [*same as* **tip**]
▻ ***phrase*** You are **in**, or **down in**, **the dumps** when you are feeling miserable and depressed.

dumpling /'dʌmplɪŋ/ *noun*: **dumplings**
1 Dumplings are balls of dough, usually boiled in a meat dish such as in stew or mince. **2** A **dumpling** is also a baked pudding made of dough, containing fruit.

dumpy /'dʌmpɪ/ *adjective* (*derogatory*)
A **dumpy** person is short and fat.

dunce /dʌns/ *noun*: **dunces**
If you call a person a **dunce** you mean they are stupid or slow to learn: *I was such a dunce at mathematics at school.*

dune /dju:n/ *noun*: **dunes**
A **dune** is a ridge or mound of sand built up by wind on the sea shore or in a desert.

dung /dʌŋ/ *noun* (*uncount*)
Dung is the faeces of large animals such as cows and horses: *cattle dung*

dungarees /dʌŋgə'ri:z/ *noun* (*plural*)
Dungarees are loose cotton trousers with an upper flap that covers the chest, and straps that go over the shoulders, worn *eg* for doing rough or dirty work in: *a pair of denim dungarees.*

dungeon /ˈdʌndʒən/ *noun*: **dungeons**
A **dungeon** is an underground prison in a castle.

dupe /djuːp/ *verb*; *noun*
▻ ***verb***: **dupes, duping, duped**
Someone **dupes** you when they trick you: *He had duped several old ladies into giving him large sums of money.*
▻ ***noun***: **dupes**
You are the **dupe** of someone if you have been tricked by them: *Yet again we have been made the dupes of the management.*

duplex /ˈdjuːplɛks/ *noun* (*AmE*): **duplexes**
1 A **duplex** is a pair of houses joined together at the side, so that they share one wall. [*same as* **semidetached house**; see picture at **house**] **2** A **duplex** is also an apartment on two floors.

duplicate *verb*; *noun*; *adjective*
▻ ***verb*** /ˈdjuːplɪkeɪt/: **duplicates, duplicating, duplicated**
1 You **duplicate** a document, article or drawing when you make a copy of it on a copying machine: *She had taken the precaution of duplicating her birth certificate.* **2** Two people or groups that are co-operating **duplicate** their efforts when one unnecessarily does work that the other is already doing.
▻ ***noun*** /ˈdjuːplɪkət/: **duplicates**
A **duplicate** of something is an identical copy of it: *She kept duplicates of her diplomas and certificates in case the originals went missing.*
▻ ***adjective*** /ˈdjuːplɪkət/: *Duplicate keys are kept in the manager's office.*
▻ ***phrase*** You supply documents or forms to someone **in duplicate** when you give them two copies.

duplicity /djuːˈplɪsɪtɪ/ *noun* (*uncount*; *formal*)
Duplicity is dishonest behaviour such as lying or deceit.

durable /ˈdjʊərəbəl/ *adjective*
Something that is **durable** is strong and lasts well: *This is a durable fabric highly suitable for children's clothes.* — *noun* (*uncount*) **durability** /djʊərəˈbɪlɪtɪ/: *materials of proved durability.*

duration /djʊˈreɪʃən/ *noun* (*used in the singular*)
The **duration** of something is the length of time it lasts or takes: *For the duration of the pedestrianization experiment traffic will be diverted via Duke Street.*

duress /djʊˈrɛs/ *noun* (*uncount*)
▻ ***phrase*** You do something **under duress** when you are forced to do it, or do it unwillingly at the order of someone else: *He had resigned under duress.*

during /ˈdjʊərɪŋ/ *preposition*
Something that happens **during** a period of time happens either **1** continuously or repeatedly in that period: *We lived in Sidney during my childhood.* □ *I play tennis a lot during the summer.* **2** at some point in that period: *He had a bad car accident during the vacation.*

dusk /dʌsk/ *noun* (*uncount*)
Dusk is the time of day when the daylight fades and darkness begins to fall: *It was dusk by the time they returned from their walk.* □ *The park gates are closed at dusk.*

dusky /ˈdʌskɪ/ *adjective*: **duskier, duskiest**
1 Dusky means dark or full of shadow: *He was certain that monsters were lurking in the dusky corners of the room.* **2** A **dusky** colour is a dark colour: *a dusky shade of red.*

dust /dʌst/ *noun*; *verb*
▻ ***noun*** (*uncount*)
1 Dust is very fine particles of earth or dirt: *The truck approached in a cloud of red dust.* □ *A thick layer of dust lay on the furniture.* **2 Dust** of a specified kind is a material in the form of very fine particles: *gold dust* □ *sawdust* □ *chalk dust.*
▻ ***verb***: **dusts, dusting, dusted**
1 You **dust** a room or its contents when you clear dust off surfaces using a duster: *He swept the floor and dusted the furniture.* **2** You **dust** the surface of something with a powder when you sprinkle or apply it lightly over the surface: *Dust the top of the cake with icing sugar.*

dustbin /ˈdʌstbɪn/ *noun*: **dustbins**
A **dustbin** is a large container for rubbish, usually kept outside your house or the building you work in. [*same as* **trashcan**]

dustcover /ˈdʌstkʌvə(r)/ *noun*: **dustcovers**
A **dustcover** or **dustjacket** is a loose paper cover for a hardback book. [*same as* **cover, jacket**]

duster /ˈdʌstə(r)/ *noun*: **dusters**
A **duster** is a small soft cloth for removing dust from furniture and surfaces.

dustjacket /ˈdʌstdʒakɪt/ see **dustcover**.

dustman /ˈdʌstmən/ *noun*: **dustmen**
A **dustman** is a person employed to take away household rubbish from people's dustbins.

dustpan /ˈdʌstpən/ *noun*: **dustpans**
A **dustpan** is an open-sided container with a handle, into which you sweep dust and dirt from the floor.

dust-up /ˈdʌstʌp/ *noun* (*informal*): **dust-ups**
A **dust-up** is a violent quarrel or a fight: *There was a dust-up outside the pub.*

dusty /ˈdʌstɪ/ *adjective*: **dustier, dustiest**
Something that is **dusty** is covered with dust: *dusty furniture* □ *The house is terribly dusty.* □ *a hot dusty track.*

Dutch /dʌtʃ/ *adjective*; *noun*
▻ ***adjective***
Dutch means concerned with the Netherlands or belonging to it, its people or their language: *He's Dutch, not Belgian.* □ *Dutch cheeses* □ *Dutch national costume.*
▻ ***noun*** (*uncount*)
Dutch is the language of the Netherlands: *I can speak some Dutch.*

dutiful /ˈdjuːtɪfəl/ *adjective*
Someone who is **dutiful** does what they ought to do and what people expect them to do: *I helped my mother with the shopping and housework like a dutiful daughter.* — *adverb* **dutifully:** *She dutifully laughed at his joke.*

duty /ˈdjuːtɪ/ *noun*: **duties**
1 (*used in the singular*) Something that is your **duty** is something that is your reponsibility, and that you ought to do: *It's your duty as parents to ensure the safety of your children.* □ *I've never failed in my duty.* **2** (*usually in the plural*) Your **duties** in your job are the tasks you do as part of it: *She had officially retired but continued with some of her regular duties.* **3** (*uncount*) You are on **duty** when you are officially working at your job, and off **duty** when you are not: *The next shift reports for duty at 8.00 pm.* □ *Sister McLean comes on duty at 7.45 pm and goes off at 8.00 am.* **4** (*uncount or count*) You pay **duty** or **duties** on imported or exported goods, or on the transfer of property, when you pay a tax to the government: *I had to pay duty on the watch I bought in Japan.*

duty-bound /djuːtɪ ˈbaʊnd/ *adjective*
You say you are **duty-bound** to do something if you think it is your duty and you must do it: *As a citizen I felt duty-bound to inform the police about the incident.*

duty-free /djuːtɪ 'friː/ *adjective or adverb*
Duty-free goods are goods that you can buy cheaper than usual, *eg* in international airports and on board ships on international routes, because you do not have to pay tax on them: *You're entitled to buy a certain amount of alcohol duty-free.* □ *duty-free perfume* □ *I had a look round the duty-free shop.*

duvet /'duːveɪ/ *noun*: **duvets**
A **duvet** is a thick bed cover filled with feathers or other light material, usually covered with a washable case, and used instead of a sheet and blankets. [*same as* **continental quilt**; see picture at **bedroom**]

dwarf /dwɔːf/ *noun*; *adjective*; *verb*
▻ ***noun***: **dwarfs** or **dwarves**
1 (*offensive*) A **dwarf** is someone who is abnormally small because their arms and legs have failed to grow to adult size. **2** In fairy stories, a **dwarf** is a small being in human shape with magical powers.
▻ ***adjective***
Dwarf plants are deliberately cultivated small varieties.
▻ ***verb***: **dwarfs, dwarfing, dwarfed**
One thing **dwarfs** another if the first is much larger, and makes the other look even smaller than usual: *He was looking old and bent, and was completely dwarfed by his two tall sons.*

dwell /dwɛl/ *verb* (*literary*): **dwells, dwelling, dwelt** or **dwelled**
You **dwell** somewhere if you live there: *in the days when people dwelt in caves.*

> ***phrasal verb***
> You **dwell on** a subject if you keep thinking or talking about it: *There's nothing you can do about it now, so stop dwelling on it.* □ *She dwells on the past a good deal.*

dweller /'dwɛlə(r)/ *noun*: **dwellers**
Dweller is used in combinations such as 'city-**dweller**' and 'town-**dweller**' to indicate a person's typical home environment: *the cave-dwellers of the Stone Age*

dwelling /'dwɛlɪŋ/ *noun* (*formal*): **dwellings**
A **dwelling** is a house, apartment, or other place where people live: *slum dwellings.*

dwelt /dwɛlt/ *verb*
Dwelt is the past tense of **dwell**.

dwindle /'dwɪndəl/ *verb*: **dwindles, dwindling, dwindled**
Something **dwindles** when it decreases in size or quantity: *Our supplies of food were rapidly dwindling away.* □ *Her supporters gradually dwindled to two or three loyal friends.* [*same as* **shrink**] — *adjective* **dwindling:** *the dwindling population of the Highland glens* □ *They discussed how to boost the newspaper's dwindling circulation.*

dye /daɪ/ *verb*; *noun*
▻ ***verb***: **dyes, dyeing, dyed**
You **dye** something such as cloth or your hair when you change its colour by dipping it into coloured liquid: *I dyed my jacket green.* □ *I'm going to dye my hair red.* □ *I think she dyes her hair.* — *adjective* **dyed:** *His hair was obviously dyed.* □ *boys with dyed blonde hair.*
▻ ***noun*** (*uncount*)
Dye is a colouring substance mixed with liquid, that you can use for changing the colour of your clothes or your hair: *a bottle of hair dye.*

dyed-in-the-wool /daɪd ɪn ðə 'wʊl/ *adjective*
Dyed-in-the-wool describes people with strong opinions who cannot be persuaded to change them: *dyed-in-the-wool Tories.* [*same as* **confirmed**]

dying /'daɪɪŋ/ *verb*; *adjective*; *noun*
▻ ***verb***
Dying is the present participle of **die**.
▻ ***adjective***
A **dying** art, skill or tradition is one that is neglected and will soon disappear.
▻ ***noun*** (*plural*)
The **dying** are people who are so ill or badly hurt that they will very soon die: *the cries of the dying.*

dyke or **dike** /daɪk/ *noun*: **dykes**
A **dyke** is a strong thick wall built to prevent a river or the sea from overflowing on to the land.

dynamic /daɪ'namɪk/ *adjective*
1 A **dynamic** person is full of energy, enthusiasm, and new ideas, and is good at getting things done. **2** (*technical*) **Dynamic** means relating to movement, forces and the science of dynamics. — *adverb* **dynamically:** *The campaign must be run as dynamically as possible.*

dynamics /daɪ'namɪks/ *noun*
1 (*uncount*) **Dynamics** is the branch of physics that deals with movement and force. **2** (*plural*) The **dynamics** of something such as a social movement are the forces and influences behind it.

dynamism /'daɪnəmɪzm/ *noun* (*uncount*)
Dynamism is energy, enthusiasm and the ability to get things done: *The success of the venture so far is entirely due to one man's dynamism.*

dynamite /'daɪnəmaɪt/ *noun*; *verb*
▻ ***noun*** (*uncount*)
Dynamite is an explosive used *eg* in quarrying and mining.
▻ ***verb***: **dynamites, dynamiting, dynamited**
To **dynamite** something is to blow it up with dynamite.

dynamo /'daɪnəmoʊ/ *noun*: **dynamos**
A **dynamo** is a device that converts a machine's movement into electrical energy.

dynasty /'dɪnəstɪ/ (*AmE*) /'daɪnəstɪ/ *noun*: **dynasties**
A **dynasty** is a series of rulers that come from one particular family: *The Plantagenet dynasty came to an end with the death of Richard III and the accession of Henry Tudor.*

dysentery /'dɪsəntrɪ/ *noun* (*uncount*)
Dysentery is an infection that causes severe diarrhoea.

dyslexia /dɪs'lɛksɪə/ *noun* (*uncount*)
Dyslexia is difficulty with reading and spelling caused by a defect of perception or vision that prevents the sufferer from seeing words as meaningful shapes. — *adjective* **dyslexic:** *Extra coaching was provided for dyslexic children.* □ *Both my children are dyslexic.*

E or **e** /iː/ *noun*: **Es** or **e's**
E is the fifth letter of the English alphabet: *There are only two e's in 'freest'.*

each /iːtʃ/ *determiner; pronoun*
▻ ***determiner***
Each person, animal or thing in a group is every single one individually: *Each school has been invited to send two pupils to take part.* □ *With only twenty competitors, surely we can afford some sort of prize for each one?*
▻ ***pronoun***
1 Each of a group of people, animals or things is every member of it: *You may answer two questions from each of the three sections.* □ *I didn't know if you wanted red or white wine, so I bought a bottle of each.* □ *Both plans are possible, and each has its own attractions.* **2** You use **each** after a plural noun or pronoun, with a plural verb if it is the subject of the clause, to show that you mean every member of the group individually: *We're each allowed to take a guest.* □ *You each of you know what your duties are.* □ *I'll give them each some money for the journey.* □ *He gave us £6 each.*

> **Each** and **every**: **each** is a determiner or a pronoun; **every** is a determiner only: *Each* (or *every*) *copy has been signed by the artist. The artist's signature appears on each.*
> **Each** can be used where the group consists of two or more; **every** is used only where there are more than two: *Try to get a ball into each* (or *every*) *hole. Take a ball in each hand.*
> **Each** is often used rather than **every** where there is a known group: *Every car is now fitted with rear seat belts. Each seatbelt has been personally checked by our supervisor.*

▻ ***phrase*** You use **each other** in describing situations where each member of a group does the same to, or has the same relationship with, each of the others: *They're divorced now, but they still say they love each other.* □ *The twins refuse to speak to each other any more.* □ *We're all familiar with each other's prejudices by now.*

> **One another** is used like **each other**, though some people prefer **one another** where the group consists of more than two: *They've always been fond of each other* (or *one another*).
> Notice the difference between: *The two doctors blamed each other* [= each doctor blamed the other one] and *The two doctors blamed themselves* [= they both accepted the blame].

eager /ˈiːgə(r)/ *adjective*
You are **eager** for something, or **eager** to do something, when you want it, or want to do it, very much: *Several were eager for a chance to give their opinions.* □ *She was eager to explain that she too had done the work.* □ *Crowds of eager fans flocked around his dressing-room door.* [*same as* **keen**, **enthusiastic**; *opposite* **reluctant**, **unenthusiastic**] — *adverb* **eagerly:** *We are all eagerly awaiting the result of the vote.* — *noun* (*uncount*) **eagerness:** *In her eagerness to get away, she left the list lying on the table.*

eagle /ˈiːgəl/ *noun*: **eagles**
An **eagle** is a large bird that catches small animals for food.

ear /ɪə(r)/ *noun*: **ears**
1 Your **ears** are the parts of your body, one on each side of your head, by means of which you hear sounds. [see picture at **body**] **2** (*used in the singular; formal*) When you have someone's **ear**, or they give or lend you an **ear**, you have their attention, or they listen to what you have to say: *Would you just lend an ear to my last suggestion?* □ *It seemed he was quite incapable of giving a sympathetic ear to anyone.* □ *He has the ear of the Prime Minister.* **3** The **ears** of a cereal plant are the thicker top parts that contain the seeds.
▻ ***phrases* 1** You say that you **are all ears** when you are listening with close attention and great interest: *Well, go on, tell me what he said; I'm all ears.* **2** (*informal*) When someone tells you something, and it **goes in one ear and out the other**, you listen to it then immediately disregard it. **3** (*informal*) Someone **has their ear to the ground** when they make sure they are well informed about what is happening around them: *As a policeman, you have to have your ear to the ground.* **4** You can **play** a tune **by ear** when you are able to play it after simply listening to it, without the help of printed music. **5** (*informal*) You say you will **play it by ear** when you intend to act according to how a situation develops, rather than according to a plan worked out in advance. **6** You **turn a deaf ear** to something you hear when you disregard or ignore it: *I've made a habit of turning a deaf ear to her little pieces of advice.*

earache /ˈɪəreɪk/ *noun* (*uncount or used in the singular*)
You have **earache** when you have a constant pain inside your ear.

eardrum /ˈɪədrʌm/ *noun*: **eardrums**
The **eardrum** is the membrane, or thin piece of skin, inside each of your ears that carries sound into the ear by vibrating.

earl /ɜːl/ *noun*: **earls**
An **earl** is a British nobleman of quite high rank: *the 8th Earl Spencer.*

earlier /ˈɜːlɪə(r)/ *adjective or adverb*
1 Earlier is the comparative of **early**: *We get up an hour earlier in the summer.* □ *I looked at my watch; it was earlier than I thought.* □ *I finished earlier than I'd expected to.* [compare **sooner**] **2** One thing happens **earlier** than another if it happens before it; **'earlier'** and **'earlier** on' mean before the present time, or before the time you are referring to: *He began work here earlier than I did, in about 1977.* □ *The weather had been quite bad earlier in the summer but had improved by August.* □ *She arrived earlier this week.* □ *Attitudes were very different earlier this century.* □ *In the earlier lectures we discussed Shakespeare's characterization of women.* □ *one of his earlier poems* □ *I was told he had left two hours earlier.* □ *It was, as I men-*

tioned earlier, a great mistake. □ *They had rung earlier on to warn us that the water was going to be turned off.* [*opposite* **later**]

earliest /ˈɜːlɪəst/ *adjective or adverb*
Earliest is the superlative of **early**: *my earliest memories* □ *the earliest-known use of the word* □ *He always arrives the earliest.*
▻ ***phrase*** **At the earliest** means not before, and probably later than, the time stated: *She wouldn't be able to see you until three o'clock at the earliest.* [compare **latest**]

earlobe /ˈɪələʊb/ *noun*: **earlobes**
Your **earlobes** are the soft, loosely hanging pieces of skin that form the lower part of each ear. [see picture at **body**]

early /ˈɜːlɪ/ *adjective or adverb*: **earlier, earliest**
1 Something or someone that is **early** comes, arrives or happens before others, or before the usual, expected or intended time: *Let's go early and get a good seat.* □ *I was a few minutes early, and had to wait for the others to turn up.* □ *Don't get there too early or you'll have to wait outside.* □ *He gave no reason for his early departure.* □ *She went to bed early, too tired to watch the film.* □ *She had an early beakfast and caught the 7.15 train.* □ *I'm going to have an early night* [= go to bed early]. □ *They were forced to end the game early because of the rain.* [*opposite* **late**] **2 Early** also means not far on in the day, or near the beginning of something: *It's too early to wake her.* □ *It's best to water plants early in the morning or late at night.* □ *She loved to go for walks in the early-morning mist.* □ *I guessed quite early in the book who the murderer was.* □ *She showed musical talent very early in life.* □ *Mozart's early compositions* □ *It was written in the early part of the century.* □ *We're going abroad in early February.* [*opposite* **late**]
▻ ***phrases*** **1 As early as** draws attention to a date or time that is surprisingly early or soon: *The Nazis emerged as the most popular party as early as 1932.* **2** Something happens **early on** if it happens at or near the beginning of something: *She realized early on in their relationship that he was the man she wanted.* **3** (*informal*) If you say **it's early days** you mean that it is too soon to know how a situation will develop: *It's early days yet; things will improve as we get used to the work.*
[see also **earlier, earliest**]

earmark /ˈɪəmɑːk/ *verb*: **earmarks, earmarking, earmarked**
Something **is earmarked** for a special purpose when it is set aside or reserved for that purpose: *This land has been earmarked for the construction of a new shopping centre.*

earn /ɜːn/ *verb*: **earns, earning, earned**
1 You **earn** money or a wage when you work in return for it: *He earns a living as a car mechanic.* **2** You **earn** something, such as admiration or praise, when you rightly receive it because of your actions or behaviour: *She's earned her promotion through years of hard work.* □ *Her latest book has earned her worldwide acclaim.*

earnest /ˈɜːnɪst/ *adjective*
You describe someone as **earnest** if you think they always behave very seriously, perhaps too seriously: *She's a very earnest young woman who regards joking as inappropriate in the workplace.* — *adverb* **earnestly:** *groups of students earnestly discussing the world's problems.*
▻ ***phrase*** **1** You do something **in earnest** when you do it properly, with concentration and determination: *We'd been on the job for a few days before work really began in earnest.* **2** You are **in earnest** about something that you sincerely mean or seriously intend to do: *I feared that he was in earnest about leaving his wife.*

earnings /ˈɜːnɪŋz/ *noun* (*plural*)
Your **earnings** are the money that you earn from your work: *This sum is added to your total earnings for the year.* [*same as* **income**]

earphones /ˈɪəfoʊnz/ *noun* (*plural*)
A pair of **earphones** is a piece of equipment that you wear over your ears to allow you to listen in private to recorded music or to the radio: *These earphones are the most expensive in the shop.*

earpiece /ˈɪəpiːs/ *noun*: **earpiece**
The **earpieces** on a telephone is the part you hold up to your ear. [see picture at **office**]

earplugs /ˈɪəplʌgz/ *noun* (*plural*)
Earplugs are small pieces of rubber or other material that you put in your ears to protect them from loud noise, or to keep out water or cold air.

earring /ˈɪərɪŋ/ *noun*: **earrings**
An **earring** is a piece of jewellery worn on the ear, usually attached to the earlobe. They are often worn in pairs, one in each ear.

earshot /ˈɪəʃɒt/ *noun* (*uncount*)
You are within **earshot** of a sound when you are close enough to hear it, and out of **earshot** when you are too far away to hear it. [*same as* **hearing**]

ear-splitting /ˈɪəsplɪtɪŋ/ *adjective*
An **ear-splitting** noise is extremely and unpleasantly loud.

earth /ɜːθ/ *noun*: **earths**
1 (*uncount or used in the singular*) The **Earth** is the planet that we live on, the third planet in order of distance from the Sun: *It will be several weeks before the astronauts return to Earth.* □ *the discovery that the Earth revolves around the Sun.* **2** (*uncount*) **Earth** is soil, the substance that lies on the surface of the land: *They carried bucketfuls of earth to fill in the hole.* **3** (*BrE*) The **earth** in a system of electrical wires is the wire connected to the ground to make the system safe: *They wrapped the cable around a water pipe to form an earth.*
▻ ***phrases*** **1** (*informal*) You say that something **costs the earth** when it is extremely expensive. **2** You use **on earth a** in questions as a way of emphasizing how puzzled, surprised, shocked or angry you are: *How on earth did you come to break your leg so badly?* □ *Why on earth didn't you keep your mouth shut?* **b** in statements as a way of emphasizing how strongly you feel about the thing you are talking about: *This must be the loveliest place on earth!* □ *He felt like the most hated man on earth.*

earthenware /ˈɜːθənwɛə(r)/ *noun* (*uncount, often adjectival*)
Earthenware is pottery made of ordinary baked clay: *a collection of china and earthenware from Spain* □ *a large earthenware flowerpot.*

earthly /ˈɜːθlɪ/ *adjective*
1 Earthly means belonging to our physical world as opposed to heaven or the spirit world: *The Bible tells us not to cherish earthly rewards.* **2** (*informal*) **Earthly** is also used in negative statements for emphasis: *She's got no earthly chance of passing the exam.* □ *There's no earthly reason why we should help him.*

earthquake /ˈɜːθkweɪk/ *noun*: **earthquakes**
An **earthquake** is a violent shaking of the ground caused by rock movements below the earth's surface.

earthworm /ˈɜːθwɜːm/ *noun*: **earthworms**
An **earthworm** is a kind of worm that lives in and feeds on soil.

earthy /ˈɜːθɪ/ *adjective*: **earthier, earthiest**
1 Something **earthy** is like soil in some way: *The vegetables still had that fresh earthy smell.* **2** Someone who often uses coarse language, or who speaks frankly about sex and similar subjects, might be described as **earthy**: *She was slightly embarrassed by his earthy humour.*

ease /iːz/ *noun*; *verb*
▻ ***noun*** *(uncount)*
1 Ease is the quality of being easy or simple: *He lifted the trunk with ease.* □ *The chair folds flat for ease of storage.* **2** You live a life of **ease** when you live very comfortably with no worries or troubles: *Family life rolled on with its customary ease.*
▻ ***verb***: **eases, easing, eased**
1 Something **eases** pain, trouble or other unpleasantness when it makes it less severe: *The speech was intended to ease tensions between hostile racial groups.* [*same as* **relieve**] **2** Something **eases** when it becomes less strong, severe or intense: *The pain had eased a little.* □ *This latest economic recession shows no sign of easing.* [*same as* **abate**] **3** You **ease** something somewhere when you move it there slowly or gently: *He managed to ease the injured hand out of the glove.* □ *I eased the door shut so as not to wake her.*
▻ ***phrases*** **1** You feel **at ease** when you are completely relaxed and free from worry or embarrassment: *You know you've told the truth; you can be at ease with yourself.* □ *She had a gift for putting even the most nervous students at their ease.* **2** You are **ill at ease** when you feel nervous, anxious or embarrassed: *She felt very ill at ease in such unfamiliar surroundings.* [*same as* **uneasy**]

phrasal verb
Something **eases off** when it becomes less strong, severe, or intense: *I think the rain's eased off a little.* [*same as* **abate, diminish**]

easel /ˈiːzəl/ *noun*: **easels**
An **easel** is a wooden stand for supporting a blackboard or a picture that an artist is painting.

easily /ˈiːzɪlɪ/ *adverb*
Easily means **1** without difficulty: *I could easily have it finished by tomorrow.* □ *I can easily run you to the airport.* **2** obviously, clearly, beyond doubt or by a long way: *We won easily.* □ *He is easily the best of the candidates.* **3** more quickly or more readily than most people: *He cries very easily.* □ *She's one of those people who communicates easily with others.* **4** very possibly: *She could easily be somewhere in the neighbourhood.*

east /iːst/ *noun*; *adverb*; *adverb*
▻ ***noun*** *(used in the singular)*
1 The **east** is the direction from which the sun rises: *The city lay ahead of us, with the sea to the east.* □ *The wind had shifted round from north to east.* **2** The **east** is the part of a country or other area that lies towards the east: *They decided on farming, and bought a few hundred acres in the rural east.* **3** The **East** is also used to refer to the countries of eastern Asia, such as India, China and Japan, and sometimes to the countries of eastern Europe, especially those that have or used to have Communist governments: *These spices give the dish an authentic taste of the East.* □ *That was the period of deepest hostility between East and West.* [see also **Far East, Middle East**]
▻ ***adverb***
East means to the east: *I decided to take any train travelling east.* □ *The lake lay east of the mountain range.* □ *Plants on the east-facing wall will get the morning sun.*
▻ ***adjective***
1 A part of a place referred to as **east** is in or towards the east: *Large sections of the east wall were crumbling.* □ *We lived for a while in East Sussex.* **2** An **east** wind blows from the east.

eastbound /ˈiːstbaʊnd/ *adjective*
1 Eastbound traffic is travelling east. **2** The **eastbound** carriageway of a motorway is the one used by traffic travelling east.

Easter /ˈiːstə(r)/ *noun (uncount)*
Easter is a Christian festival that occurs in March or April and commemorates the death and resurrection of Christ: *I'm expecting my daughter home for Easter.* □ *She's going abroad in the Easter holidays.*

Easter egg /ˈiːstəɛg/ *noun*: **Easter eggs**
An **Easter egg** is an egg, traditionally a painted hard-boiled egg, but now more commonly a chocolate egg, given as a present at Easter.

easterly /ˈiːstəlɪ/ *adjective*
1 An **easterly** direction or region lies towards the east: *We walked in an easterly direction for two miles.* □ *the most easterly tip of the island.* **2** An **easterly** wind blows from the east.

eastern /ˈiːstən/ *adjective*
Eastern means **1** in or belonging to the east of a country or other area: *the temperate eastern climate* □ *Eastern districts will see the best of the sunshine.* **2** relating to or concerned with the countries of **eastern** Asia: *She developed an interest in Eastern religion and philosophy.* **3** relating to or concerned with the countries of **eastern** Europe, especially those that have or used to have Communist governments: *many of the former Eastern bloc countries.*

eastward /ˈiːstwəd/ or **eastwards** /ˈiːstwədz/ *adverb*
You are travelling towards the east when you are travelling **eastward**: *We sailed eastwards for four days.* □ *(used as an adjective) in an eastward direction.*

easy /ˈiːzɪ/ *adjective*: **easier, easiest**
1 Something is **easy** if it is not difficult to do: *It's not an easy task.* □ *I think this is an easier tune to sing.* □ *These laptops are quite easy to operate.* □ *The exercises looked easy.* □ *How easy would it be for you to get away for a holiday?* □ *It's so easy to make a mistake.* [*same as* **simple**; *opposite* **difficult**] **2 Easy** also means relaxed, without anxiety, effort or formality: *I shall retire to an easy life in the country.* □ *He continued at an easy pace.* □ *They have a casual, easy relationship.* □ *the easy atmosphere typical of Mediterranean countries.*
▻ ***phrases*** **1** You say **easier said than done** when someone suggests something that is difficult to do: *'Cheer up.' 'Easier said than done.'* **2** (*informal*) You **go easy on** someone when you treat them less harshly than you could: *Don't expect the judge to go easy on you.* **3** (*informal*) You **go easy with** something when you use as moderate a quantity of it as possible: *Go easy with that milk; it's the last pint we have.* **4** (*informal*) You **take it easy**, or **take things easy**, when you spend time relaxing.

easy chair /iːzɪ ˈtʃɛə(r)/ *noun*: **easy chairs**
An **easy chair** is any large, soft, comfortable chair, usually one with arms.

easy-going /iːzɪˈgoʊɪŋ/ *adjective*
An **easy-going** person is always relaxed, cheerful and tolerant: *You're lucky to have such easy-going parents.*

eat /iːt/ *verb*: **eats, eating, ate, eaten**
1 You **eat** food when you bite, chew and swallow it: *She only had time to eat one sandwich.* □ *Eat up your dinner, then you can have some chocolate.* □ *He said if I*

won he would eat his hat. □ *He ate all his rice pudding.* **2** You **eat** when you have a meal: *What time would you like to eat?* □ *I haven't eaten since breakfast.*

phrasal verbs
eat in You **eat in** when you eat at home, rather than in a restaurant.
eat into 1 A substance, such as an acid, **eats into** a material when it destroys part of it: *Rust had eaten into a large part of the machine.* **2** Something **eats into** a supply of something else when it uses up a lot of it: *A string of unplanned expenses have really eaten into our savings.*
eat out You **eat out** when you eat at a restaurant, rather than at home.

eater /ˈiːtə(r)/ *noun*: **eaters**
Eater is used to refer to a person who eats in a particular way, or who eats a particular kind of food: *Granny was an annoyingly noisy eater.* □ *We also cooked some sausages for the meat-eaters.*

eau-de-cologne /oʊ də kəˈloʊn/ *noun* (*uncount*)
Eau-de-cologne is a mild type of perfume, usually with quite a sweet smell: *several bottles of eau-de-cologne.*

eaves /iːvz/ *noun* (*plural*)
The **eaves** of a house are the parts of a roof that stick out beyond the walls. [see picture at **house**]

eavesdrop /ˈiːvzdrɒp/ *verb*: **eavesdrops, eavesdropping, eavesdropped**
Someone **eavesdrops** when they listen secretly to a private conversation between others: *He was caught eavesdropping outside the door.* □ *They lowered their voices in case anyone was eavesdropping on their conversation.* [*same as* **listen in**] — *noun* **eavesdropper:** *Come in and close the door to guard against eavesdroppers.*

ebb /ɛb/ *verb*: **ebbs, ebbing, ebbed**
1 Something such as a person's confidence **ebbs**, or **ebbs away**, when it slowly becomes weaker or disappears: *What little courage she had was slowly ebbing away.* [*same as* **dwindle, diminish**] **2** The sea **is ebbing** during that period when the tide is getting lower.
▻ ***phrases*** **1** Someone is **at a low ebb** when they are feeling physically weak or ill, or lacking in hope or enthusiasm; something, such as trade or business activity, is **at a low ebb** when there is very little of it. **2** You refer to **the ebb and flow** of something when you want to show that it frequently changes, especially when it alternates between good and bad or positive and negative: *Governments soon become familiar with the ebb and flow of public opinion.*

ebony /ˈɛbənɪ/ *noun* (*uncount, often adjectival*)
Ebony is a type of very hard, almost black, wood: *The cabinet is in oak with ebony drawer handles.*

ebullient /ɪˈbʌlɪənt/ *adjective* (*formal*)
An **ebullient** person is full of cheerfulness or enthusiasm: *I've never seen him in such an ebullient mood.* — *noun* (*uncount*) **ebullience:** *He was attracted by her youthful ebullience.*

eccentric /ɪkˈsɛntrɪk/ *adjective*; *noun*
▻ ***adjective***
An **eccentric** person behaves in a way that other people find amusingly odd or unusual: *This was another crazy scheme dreamt up by my eccentric old aunt.* □ *His political opinions are now dismissed as rather eccentric.*
▻ ***noun***: **eccentrics**
An **eccentric** is a person who behaves in an eccentric way: *He was little more than a harmless old eccentric.* — *adverb* **eccentrically** — *noun* (*count or uncount*) **eccentricity** /ɛksɛnˈtrɪsɪtɪ/: *a family whose eccentricity has shocked many a neighbour* □ *I have learned to tolerate her little eccentricities.*

ecclesiastical /ɪkliːzɪˈastɪkəl/ *adjective*
Ecclesiastical means relating to the Christian church or its ministers.

echelon /ˈɛʃəlɒn/ *noun* (*formal*): **echelons**
The **echelons** within an organization are the different ranks or levels of power within it: *members of the aristocracy and others on the higher echelons of society.*

echo /ˈɛkoʊ/ *noun*; *verb*
▻ ***noun***: **echoes**
1 An **echo** is what you hear when a sound you have just heard hits a surface, such as a wall, and comes back to be heard a second time: *What they could hear was, in fact, the echo of their own footsteps.* **2** Something that reminds you of a past event or experience might be referred to as an **echo** of the past: *There were too many echoes of the life he had tried to leave behind.*
▻ ***verb***: **echoes, echoing, echoed**
1 A sound **echoes** when it hits a surface and comes back to be heard a second time: *their voices echoing off the high ceiling.* **2** A place, such as a cave, **echoes** when it reflects sounds so that they can be heard a second time: *The cavernous dining-hall echoed with the sounds of the boys' laughter and clinking cutlery.* **3** You **echo** something when you repeat it or imitate it: *I can only echo what has already been said.* □ *This latest work echoes an earlier painting by a less well-known artist.*

éclair /ɪˈklɛə(r)/ *noun*: **éclairs**
An **eclair** is a long thin cake of light pastry, with a cream filling and usually with chocolate on the top: *I've bought some chocolate éclairs to have with coffee.*

eclectic /ɪˈklɛktɪk/ *adjective* (*formal*)
Something, such as a style of writing or painting, might be described as **eclectic** if it seems to be a mixture of elements of other things: *The cuisine of at least three continents was in evidence in this rather eclectic buffet.*

eclipse /ɪˈklɪps/ *noun*; *verb*
▻ ***noun***: **eclipses**
1 An **eclipse** of the sun occurs when the moon comes between the sun and the earth, partly or totally blocking out the sun's light for a while. **2** An **eclipse** of the moon occurs when the earth comes between the sun and the moon, with the earth's shadow partly or totally covering the moon for a while. **3** (*used in the singular*) The **eclipse** of something is its complete loss of popularity, influence or importance: *The discovery of the drug led to the eclipse of all conventional medical theory about the disease.*
▻ ***verb***: **eclipses, eclipsing, eclipsed**
To **eclipse** something is to make it seem insignificant by being far more impressive than it is: *She's a champion who's eclipsed even the most talented of the post-war players.* [*same as* **outshine**]

ecologist /ɪˈkɒlədʒɪst/ *noun*: **ecologists**
An **ecologist** is **1** someone who studies, or is an expert in, ecology: *an eminent ecologist and broadcaster.* **2** someone who believes that our world will not survive if all its plants and animals are not properly cared for and preserved.

ecology /ɪˈkɒlədʒɪ/ *noun* (*uncount*)
1 Ecology is the study of the relationships between plants and animals and their surroundings. **2** The **ecology** of a particular area is all its plants and animals, and the relationships between them, considered as a whole: *Experts say the development would cause irreparable harm to the region's ecology.* — *adjective*

ecological /iːkəˈlɒdʒɪkəl/: *This oil spill is without doubt the worst ecological disaster this century.*

economic /iːkəˈnɒmɪk/ or /ɛkəˈnɒmɪk/ *adjective*
1 Economic means concerned with the finances and trade of a nation or other area: *changes in government economic policy* □ *a depressed economic climate.* **2** An **economic** business is one that makes a profit: *It wouldn't be economic for us to cut prices any further.* [*same as* **viable**]

economical /iːkəˈnɒmɪkəl/ or /ɛkəˈnɒmɪkəl/ *adjective*
1 Something is **economical** if it does not cost a lot of money to use or operate: *Gas is thought to be a more economical household fuel than electricity.* **2** Something is also **economical** if it makes good use of resources, without any waste: *Printing on both sides would be a more economical use of paper.* □ *The shot was achieved with one swift and economical movement of the wrist.* **3** People are **economical** when they spend money carefully and wisely: *I had become quite an economical housewife.* [*same as* **thrifty**, **careful**] — *adverb* **economically:** *The heating system can be operated quite economically.* □ *We were forced to live very economically.*

economics /iːkəˈnɒmɪks/ or /ɛkəˈnɒmɪks/ *noun* (*uncount*)
1 Economics is the study of how a nation's trade is organized and its money managed: *a professor of economics* □ *an economics textbook.* **2** The **economics** of a situation is that part of it concerned with money: *He's been hired to look after the economics of the project.*

economist /ɪˈkɒnəmɪst/ *noun*: **economists**
An **economist** is an expert in economics.

economize or **economise** /iːˈkɒnəmaɪz/ *verb*: **economizes, economizing, economized**
1 You **economize** when you spend less money or use your resources more efficiently: *Times were hard, and the whole nation was forced to economize.* **2** You **economize** on something when you use less of it or spend less money on it: *She refused to economize on food for the children.*

economy /ɪˈkɒnəmɪ/ *noun*; *adjective*
▻ ***noun*** (*count and uncount*): **economies**
1 (*uncount or count*) A nation's **economy** is the system it has for creating wealth through trade and industry: *The economy of the region depends largely on manufacturing industries.* □ *a country with a socialist economy.* **2** (*uncount*) **Economy** is the careful use of money or other resources in order to make savings or cut down waste: *We've cut out business lunches for reasons of economy.* **3** (*usually in the plural*) You make **economies** when you make efforts to spend less money or use fewer resources.
▻ ***adjective***
Economy is used to refer to **1** the cheapest kind of service available: *I could only afford an economy-class ticket.* **2** a size of packet that is larger than the standard size, and proportionally cheaper: *She buys the economy packs to save money in the long run.*

ecstasy /ˈɛkstəsɪ/ *noun* (*uncount*)
Ecstasy is a feeling of great joy, happiness or pleasure: *I was in ecstasy when she kissed me.*
▻ ***phrase*** You **go into ecstasies** about something when you talk about how wonderful you think it is: *He went into ecstasies about the present.* [*same as* **go into raptures**]

ecstatic /ɪkˈstatɪk/ *adjective*
You are **ecstatic** when you are extremely happy or enthusiastic. [*same as* **overjoyed**] — *adverb* **ecstatically:** *They shouted and waved their arms ecstatically.*

ecumenical /ɛkjʊˈmɛnɪkəl/ *adjective*
Ecumenical organizations and activities are designed to bring together the different branches of the Christian church: *He's one of the leading forces within the ecumenical movement.*

eczema /ˈɛksɪmə/ or /ɪgˈziːmə/ *noun* (*uncount*)
Someone who suffers from **eczema** has patches of dry, rough and itchy skin on their body.

eddy /ˈɛdɪ/ *noun*: **eddies**
An **eddy** is a circular current of water, or a circular flow of air, smoke, fog or anything similar.

edge /ɛdʒ/ *noun*; *verb*
▻ ***noun***: **edges**
1 The **edge** of something is the line where it ends, or the area around this line: *a little house on the southern edge of the forest* □ *He swam quickly to the edge of the pool.* □ *a plain white tablecloth with blue embroidery round the edge* □ *The pages were torn and yellowed at the edges.* □ *A family of ducks swam lazily at the water's edge.* **2** The **edges** of a flat object are its thin sides: *the cutting edge of a knife* □ *the edge of a ruler.* **3** You come to the **edge** of something when you arrive at the point where you must stop to avoid it or prevent it happening: *These policies had brought the nation to the edge of war.* □ *She had never before felt herself so close to the edge of madness.* [*same as* **brink**] **4** There is an **edge** to someone's voice or to what they say when you can tell from it that they feel angry or bitter: *There was an edge to his comments that made me think he was resentful.*
▻ ***verb***: **edges, edging, edged**
1 Something **is edged** with something different that it has all along its edges: *The lawn was edged with flowering herbs.* □ *an old book whose pages were edged with gold.* [*same as* **border**, **trim**] **2** You **edge** somewhere when you move there slowly or carefully: *We edged our way along the narrow path.* □ *I edged away from him and towards the door.* [*same as* **inch**]
▻ ***phrases*** **1** You **have the edge on** or **over** someone when you have an advantage over them: *With their strong defensive play, they seem to have the edge on most teams.* □ *Her superior fitness has given her the edge over her opponent.* **2** You are **on edge** when you are feeling nervous or anxious: *He's been a bit on edge all day.*

edgeways /ˈɛdʒweɪz/ *adverb*
You say you cannot get a word in **edgeways** when you do not have the chance to speak because others are talking too much.

edging /ˈɛdʒɪŋ/ *noun*: **edgings**
An **edging** is a decorative border: *a white cotton dress with a pink edging.*

edgy /ˈɛdʒɪ/ *adjective* (*informal*): **edgier**, **edgiest**
You are **edgy** when you feel so nervous or anxious that you are likely to get angry or upset very easily.

edible /ˈɛdɪbəl/ *adjective*
Something **edible** is fit to be eaten because it is still fresh, or safe to eat because it is not poisonous: *some mouldy cheese and a piece of bread that was barely edible* □ *It's hard to tell which are the edible berries.* □ *edible mushrooms.* [*opposite* **inedible**]

edict /ˈiːdɪkt/ *noun*: **edicts**
An **edict** is a formal public order made by someone in a position of power, *eg* a king. [*same as* **decree**]

edifice /ˈɛdɪfɪs/ *noun* (*formal*): **edifices**
1 An **edifice** is a building, especially a large impressive one. **2** People sometimes refer to a large and complex organization as an **edifice**: *They feared that the whole edifice of parliamentary democracy would crumble.*

edify /ˈɛdɪfaɪ/ *verb* (*formal*): **edifies, edifying, edified**
Something **edifies** you when it improves your mind by teaching you what is right, good or beautiful: *The film's aim is not to edify, but simply to entertain.* — *noun* (*uncount*) **edification** /ɛdɪfɪˈkeɪʃən/: *The book was clearly written for the edification of its readers.* — *adjective* **edifying:** *It was a most edifying lecture.* [*same as* **elevating**]

edit /ˈɛdɪt/ *verb*: **edits, editing, edited**
1 Someone **edits** a text when they check it and make corrections or alterations before it is published. **2** The person who **edits** a newspaper or magazine is in overall charge of the process of producing it. **3** The person who **edits** a book containing writings from different authors is responsible for choosing what to include. **4** A television or radio programme **is edited** by the person who decides what will be included in it.

edition /ɪˈdɪʃən/ *noun*: **editions**
1 An **edition** of a book is one of the versions it has been published in at a particular time or by a particular publishing company: *The third edition of the dictionary contains 3000 more words than the second edition.* ▫ *We only have the Dickens book in the Oxford University Press edition.* **2** An **edition** of a book is also one of the forms it has been published in: *They only have the paperback edition.* **3** An **edition** of a newspaper, or of a radio or television programme, is the one printed or broadcast on a particular day: *an article in Friday's edition of 'The Times'.*

editor /ˈɛdɪtə(r)/ *noun*: **editors**
An **editor** is **1** a person who checks and corrects written texts before they are published. **2** the person in overall charge of a newspaper or magazine. **3** the person who decides what to include in a collection of writings by different authors. **4** the person who decides what to include in a television or radio programme.

editorial /ɛdɪˈtɔːrɪəl/ *adjective*; *noun*
▻ ***adjective***
Editorial means relating to or concerned with the process of editing: *She questioned my editorial judgement.* ▫ *the editorial staff.*
▻ ***noun***: **editorials**
An **editorial** is a newspaper or magazine article that expresses the opinion of the editor or publisher on a current topic.

educate /ˈɛdjʊkeɪt/ *verb*: **educates, educating, educated**
1 Someone **is educated** at the school, college or university that they attend: *She lives in America but was educated in the UK.* **2** To **educate** someone means to teach them to behave in a certain way: *a campaign to educate the public about the benefits of healthy eating.*

educated /ˈɛdjʊkeɪtɪd/ *adjective*
1 An **educated** person has acquired a high standard of knowledge in various subjects, usually at college or university: *She has educated tastes in art and music.* **2** An **educated** guess is based on experience or knowledge: *I'm not sure, but I could make an educated guess.*

education /ɛdjʊˈkeɪʃən/ *noun*
1 (*uncount*) **Education** is the process or system of teaching in schools and other establishments: *The government has reduced the funds available for education.* ▫ *encouraging pupils to stay in full-time education beyond the age of 16.* **2** (*uncount or used in the singular*) **Education** is also the development of a person's knowledge, especially the development of a child's knowledge at school: *He took little interest in his daughter's education.* ▫ *Three of the candidates had a university education.* **3** (*used in the singular*) You describe an experience as an **education** if you think you have learnt something from it: *Working in the factory was a real education.*

educational /ɛdjʊˈkeɪʃənəl/ *adjective*
1 Educational means concerned with formal teaching: *schools and other educational establishments.* **2** Something **educational** is concerned with giving information, rather than simply entertaining or amusing: *an educational film.* — *adverb* **educationally:** *educationally subnormal children.*

-ee /iː/ *suffix*
-ee is used **1** to form nouns meaning a person who has the action of the verb done to them, such as *payee* and *employee*. **2** to form nouns meaning a person in a stated condition, such as *absentee* and *escapee*.

eel /iːl/ *noun*: **eels**
An **eel** is a fish with a long thin snake-like body.

-eer /ˈɪə(r)/ *suffix*
-eer is used **1** to form nouns meaning a person performing activities of a particular kind, such as *auctioneer* and *mountaineer*. **2** to form verbs meaning to carry out tasks relating to a particular activity, as in *electioneer*.

eerie /ˈɪərɪ/ *adjective*: **eerier, eeriest**
Something that is **eerie** is strange and disturbing or frightening: *She stared through the windscreen into the eerie darkness of the winding lane.* [*same as* **spooky, creepy**] — *adverb* **eerily:** *At the end of the garden, the statue shone eerily in the moonlight.*

efface /ɪˈfeɪs/ *verb* (*formal*): **effaces, effacing, effaced**
You **efface** something when you rub it out or remove it: *The rain had not effaced the greasy fingermarks on the window.* ▫ *She could only hope that time would efface the memory of this awful experience.* [*same as* **erase**]

effect /ɪˈfɛkt/ *noun*; *verb*
▻ ***noun***: **effects**
1 (*count or uncount*) The **effect** of something is what happens because of it: *the damaging effects of smoking on the human lung* ▫ *She wondered what effect her decision would have on him.* ▫ *His speech had the effect of turning the party against the Prime Minister.* ▫ *'Will this have any effect on the outcome?' 'No effect whatsoever.'* ▫ *I don't think complaining will have much effect.*

> **Effect** is the noun that matches the verb **affect**; one thing has an **effect** on another if it **affects** it.

2 An **effect** is also an impression, produced by chance or created deliberately: *Can you see how the artist creates the effect of light playing on water?* ▫ *She ruined the whole effect by giggling.* [*same as* **impression**] **3** (*used in the plural*; *theatre*) **Effects** are devices used in the theatre for producing sounds and lighting that make the play more realistic or dramatic: *lighting effects.* **4** (*used in the plural*; *formal*) Your **effects** are your personal possessions.
▻ ***verb*** (*formal*): **effects, effecting, effected**
You **effect** something when you make it happen or carry it out: *The required adjustments will be effected without delay.*
▻ ***phrases*** **1** Something **comes into effect**, **takes effect** or **is put into effect** when it starts to work or apply, starts to be used or comes into operation: *The new charges will come into effect next April.* ▫ *It will be a few hours before the medicine begins to take effect.* ▫ *Drawing up a plan is easy; putting it into effect is another matter.* **2** You do something **for effect** when you do it for the sake of impressing people or making them look at you: *You could say that his hat serves a purpose, but the cloak is worn for effect.* ▫ *She lowered*

her voice for dramatic effect. **3** You use **in effect** to introduce what you regard as the truth or reality of a situation: *It sounds as if I'm getting a pay rise, but in effect I'm losing money.* [*same as* **effectively**] **4** (*formal*) You use **to this effect**, **to that effect** or **to the effect that** when reporting the general content of what is said or written: *He said, 'Get out and don't come back!' or words to that effect.* □ *I've heard rumours to the effect that she's thinking of resigning.*

effective /ɪ'fɛktɪv/ *adjective*
1 Something is **effective** if it does very well what it is intended to do: *Painting metal is a simple but effective way of preventing rust.* □ *a disinfectant that is really effective against household germs.* [*opposite* **ineffective**] **2** Something that looks good or creates a pleasing impression is also **effective**: *A red scarf would look very effective with that blouse.* **3** When something becomes **effective** it comes into operation or is put into force: *They agreed on an oil embargo, effective from next month.* **4 Effective** also means actual or practical, although probably not formal or official: *The king is the nominal head of state, although the effective ruler is his son, the prince.* — *noun* (*uncount*) **effectiveness:** *It's too early to assess the political effectiveness of this latest move.*

effectively /ɪ'fɛktɪvlɪ/ *adverb*
1 Something works **effectively** when it does very well what it is supposed to do: *This new detergent removes greasy stains very effectively.* **2** You use **effectively** to indicate that a condition or fact is the real or actual consequence of some action though it may not appear so or have been intended: *They put her in a separate office, effectively isolating her from the rest of the team.*

effeminate /ɪ'fɛmɪnət/ *adjective*
If you describe a man as **effeminate**, you mean that his appearance or behaviour is more typical of a woman: *She found herself feeling irritated by his effeminate little hand gestures.*

effervescent /ɛfə'vɛsənt/ *adjective*
1 An **effervescent** drink bubbles because it is full of gas. [*same as* **fizzy**, **sparkling**] **2** (*literary*) An **effervescent** person is full of energy and enthusiasm: *She has a cheery, effervescent personality.* [*same as* **bubbly**]

efficacious /ɛfɪ'keɪʃəs/ *adjective* (*formal*)
Something **efficacious** has the desired or intended effect or result: *I have always found it a particularly efficacious remedy for headaches.* [*same as* **effective**] — *noun* (*uncount*) **efficacy** /'ɛfɪkəsɪ/: *Doctors now have doubts about the drug's efficacy.*

efficient /ɪ'fɪʃənt/ *adjective*
1 An **efficient** process works quickly and without wasting energy or materials: *The new diesel engine is more efficient than ever.* □ *There must be a more efficient way of working.* [*opposite* **inefficient**] **2** Someone is **efficient** when they are capable of fast accurate work. — *noun* (*uncount*) **efficiency:** *the environmental benefits of energy efficiency* □ *the speed and efficiency of the investigation.* — *adverb* **efficiently:** *The scheme could have been more efficiently managed.*

effigy /'ɛfɪdʒɪ/ *noun*: **effigies**
An **effigy** is a roughly made doll or model representing a real person, that is destroyed in some way, *eg* by burning, as a way of showing hatred or contempt for the person.

effluent /'ɛflʊənt/ *noun* (*uncount*)
Effluent is waste from factories or sewage released into a river or the sea.

effort /'ɛfət/ *noun*: **efforts**
1 (*uncount or count*) **Effort** is hard mental or physical work: *We've all put a lot of effort into developing this project.* □ *They made no effort to give us a proper explanation.* □ *I have the time to do it; it's just a question of making the effort.* □ *She promised to make every effort to finish the work on time.* □ *We lost the contract, in spite of all our efforts.* □ *It didn't seem worth the effort, so I didn't bother.* **2** (*uncount or used in the singular*) You do something with **effort** when it takes a lot of energy or determination for you to do it: *The old man lifted himself up with an effort.* **3** (*used in the singular*) You say that something is an **effort** when it is difficult for you to do: *The conversation had become so dull that it was an effort simply to stay awake.* **4** (*usually in the singular*) If you say that something is a poor **effort**, you mean that it has been badly done or badly made: *That last shot was a rather feeble effort.*

effortless /'ɛfətləs/ *adjective*
Something is **effortless** when it is, or seems to be, achieved extremely easily, with little or no effort: *She plays a variety of musical instruments with effortless competence.* □ *He has an effortless humour and charm that makes him the perfect dinner guest.* — *adverb* **effortlessly:** *seabirds gliding effortlessly along the coastline.*

effrontery /ɪ'frʌntərɪ/ *noun* (*uncount*)
Effrontery is bold behaviour regarded as rude or offensive: *She had the effrontery to criticize my taste in music.* [*same as* **cheek**, **gall**]

effusive /ɪ'fjuːsɪv/ *adjective* (*formal*)
Someone is **effusive** when they show their pleasure, excitement or enthusiasm very energetically, in a way that some people find embarrassing or insincere: *I was not prepared for such an effusive display of gratitude.*

egalitarian /ɪgalɪ'tɛərɪən/ *adjective*
An **egalitarian** society is one in which all members are treated the same and all have the same rights: *his egalitarian principles* □ *not a very egalitarian system.*

egg[1] /ɛg/ *noun*: **eggs**
1 An **egg** is a hard oval shell with a developing baby bird or other animal inside, released by the mother: *Most reptiles lay eggs.* **2** The contents of a hen's **egg**, when used as food, is referred to simply as an **egg**: *a fried egg.*

▷ ***phrase*** You **put all your eggs in one basket** when your success depends entirely on a single plan, and you have no alternative if it fails.

egg[2] /ɛg/ *verb*: **eggs, egging, egged**

> ***phrasal verb***
> You **egg** someone **on** when you urge or encourage them to take a risk or to do something foolish: *Egged on by his friends, he threw stones at the police car.*

eggcup /'ɛgkʌp/ *noun*: **eggcups**
An **eggcup** is a small cup-shaped container for holding a boiled egg steady while you eat it. [see picture at **tableware**]

egghead /'ɛghɛd/ *noun* (*informal*): **eggheads**
If you call someone an **egghead** you mean they are academically very intelligent, but perhaps not very good at doing practical things.

eggplant /'ɛgplɑːnt/ *noun*: **eggplants** (*AmE*)
An **eggplant** is an aubergine. [see picture at **vegetable**]

eggshell /'ɛgʃɛl/ *noun*: **eggshells**
An **eggshell** is the hard thin oval shell covering an egg.

ego /'iːgoʊ/ *noun*: **egos**
A person's **ego** is the combination of feelings they have about the kind of person they are, especially

when the main feelings are confidence and pride: *Another failure would be a severe blow to his ego.* □ *I'm in no mood to indulge his ego.*

egocentric /iːgoʊˈsɛntrɪk/ or /ɛgoʊˈsɛntrɪk/ *adjective*
If you describe someone as **egocentric**, you mean that they are interested only in their own needs and wishes and show no concern for other people.

egotism /ˈiːgətɪzm/ or /ˈɛgətɪzm/ *noun* (*uncount*)
Egotism is selfish behaviour that shows you have no concern for other people, and that you think you are more important than anyone else.

egotist /ˈiːgətɪst/ or /ˈɛgətɪst/ *noun*: **egotists**
An **egotist** is someone who behaves selfishly and as if they were more important than anyone else. — *adjective* **egotistical** /iːgəˈtɪstɪkəl/: *I thought her vain and egotistical.*

eh /eɪ/ *interjection* (*informal*)
You say **'eh' 1** as a way of prompting someone to answer you or agree with you: *What do you think, eh?* □ *It looks better over here, eh?* **2** as a way of asking someone to repeat what they just said, because you did not hear it: *'Did you manage to fix it?' 'Eh?' 'I said, did you manage to fix it?'*

eiderdown /ˈaɪdədaʊn/ *noun* (*old*): **eiderdowns**
An **eiderdown** is a top cover for a bed, filled with duck feathers or any other light soft material. [*same as* **quilt**, **duvet**]

eight /eɪt/ *noun*; *adjective*; *determiner*; *pronoun*
▻ ***noun***: **eights**
1 (*uncount or count*) **Eight** is **a** the number or figure 8: *Six and two are eight.* □ *Three plus five makes eight.* □ *Five eights are forty.* □ *That's a zero, not an eight.* **b** a garment whose size is represented by the number 8, or a person who wears clothes this size: *These shoes are eights.* □ *He takes eight in shoes.* □ *Do you have an eight in this dress?* □ *I was an eight before I was pregnant.* **2** (*uncount*) **Eight** is **a** the age of 8: *They start learning English at eight.* **b** the time of 8 o'clock: *We left at eight in the morning.* **3** An **eight** is **a** a set of 8 people or things, *eg* the crew of an eight-oared boat: *She rows in the first eight.* **b** a playing card with 8 symbols: *She played the eight of diamonds.*
▻ ***adjective***
Someone who is **eight** is 8 years old: *My son will be eight next week.* □ *children aged eight and over.*
▻ ***determiner:*** *The ticket cost eight pounds.* □ *The front eight rows of seats are reserved.* □ *Eight weeks is a long time to be off school.* □ *I've done eight days' work without a break.* □ *An octagon is an eight-sided figure.* □ *an eight-hour operation* □ *an eight-year-old child* □ *books for eight-year-olds.*
▻ ***pronoun:*** *There are eight of us in the one office.* □ *I've a few copies left, perhaps as many as eight.* □ *All eight had been sold by lunchtime.*

eighteen /eɪˈtiːn/ *noun*; *adjective*; *determiner*; *pronoun*
▻ ***noun***: **eighteens**
1 (*uncount or count*) **Eighteen** is the number or figure 18: *Twelve and six are eighteen.* □ *Nine plus nine makes eighteen.* □ *Two eighteens are thirty-six.* **2** (*uncount*) **Eighteen** is the age of 18: *They leave school at eighteen.* **3** (*count or uncount*) An **eighteen** is a garment whose size is represented by the number 18, or a person who wears clothes this size: *I'll try on an eighteen.* □ *I was an eighteen when I got married.* □ *He takes eighteen in hats.* **4** An **eighteen** is also a film officially classified as suitable to be seen by people aged 18 and over.
▻ ***adjective***
Someone who is **eighteen** is 18 years old: *As soon as I'm eighteen I'm getting a job.*
▻ ***determiner:*** *I worked abroad for eighteen months.* □ *eighteen-year-old students.*
▻ ***pronoun:*** *We had thirty students at the start of the course, but now there are only eighteen.*

eighteenth /eɪˈtiːnθ/ *determiner*; *pronoun*; *adjective or adverb*; *noun*: **eighteenths**
1 (often written **18th**) The **eighteenth** person or thing is the one numbered eighteen in a series. **2** (often written $\frac{1}{18}$) An **eighteenth** of something is one of eighteen equal parts of it.

eighth (often written **8th**) /eɪtθ/ *determiner*; *pronoun*; *adjective or adverb*; *noun*
▻ ***determiner***
The **eighth** person or thing is the one that is numbered eight in a series: *The exams are being held in the eighth week of term.* □ *the 8th Duke of Atholl.*
▻ ***pronoun:*** *Tonight she delivers the eighth of her lectures.* □ *He's the eighth from the left in the second row.* □ *She's arriving on the eighth of August.* [see also note at **date**] □ *in the reign of Henry the Eighth (*written *Henry VIII).*
▻ ***adjective or adverb:*** *I was (*or *came) eighth in the maths exam.* □ *Her horse came in eighth.*
▻ ***noun*** (often written $\frac{1}{8}$): **eighths**
An **eighth** of something is one of eight equal parts of it: *A kilometre is equal to about five eighths (*written $\frac{5}{8}$*) of a mile.* □ *One eighth of the world's population is starving.* □ *Only an eighth of the voters are white.*

eighties see **eighty**.

eightieth /ˈɛɪtɪɪθ/ *determiner*; *pronoun*; *adjective or adverb*; *noun*: **eighteenths**
1 (often written **80th**) The **eightieth** person or thing is the one numbered eighty in a series. **2** (often written $\frac{1}{80}$) An **eightieth** of something is one of eighty equal parts of it.

eighty /ˈeɪtɪ/ *noun*; *adjective*; *determiner*; *pronoun*
▻ ***noun***: **eighties**
1 (*uncount or count*) **Eighty** is the number or figure 80: *Forty times two is eighty.* □ *Three eighties are two hundred and forty.* **2** (*uncount*) **Eighty** is the age of 80: *She was still hill-walking at eighty.* **3** (*used in the plural*) Someone who is in their **eighties** is aged between 80 and 89. **4** (*used in the plural*) The temperature is in the **eighties** when it is between 80° Fahrenheit and 89° Fahrenheit. **5** (*used in the plural*) The **eighties** are the period between the eightieth and ninetieth years of a century: *born in the eighties* □ *the nineteen-eighties.*
▻ ***adjective***
Someone who is **eighty** is 80 years old.
▻ ***determiner:*** *An octogenarian is an eighty-year-old.*
▻ ***pronoun:*** *Five people were killed and a further eighty injured.*

either /ˈaɪðə(r)/ or /ˈiːðə(r)/ *determiner*; *pronoun*; *adverb*; *conjunction*
▻ ***determiner***
1 Either person, animal or thing means **a** one or the other of two possible ones, it doesn't matter which: *Either solution is possible.* □ *Either way, you get a big reduction in the fare.* **b** one or the other of two, but not both: *I can let you have either copy.* **c** (*especially with a negative*) the one or the other, where you are including both in your statement: *I could get no reply from either number.* □ *I doubted if either man was quite trustworthy.* □ *In either emergency, please contact us.* **2** When you are referring to things such as sides or hands, where there are known to be two, **either** can mean both or each: *On either side of the river lie long fields of barley and rye.* □ *She emerged holding an egg in either hand.*

▻ ***pronoun***
Either matches senses 1a and 1b of the determiner: *'Wine or beer for you?' 'Oh, either.'* □ *Either of those men stands a chance; she's in love with both.* □ *I went out for milk and bread and came back without either.* □ *I don't think either of them knows what they're doing.*

> **'Either** of' is used before plural nouns and pronouns, usually with a singular verb, but it may take a plural verb, especially after a negative, or in questions: *I don't believe either of them works as hard as he should* (or *work as hard as they should*, or *works as hard as they should*). *Has* (or *have*) *either of your parents ever had a heart attack?*.

▻ ***adverb***
1 Either is used at the end of a sentence when negative statements are being made about two similar or related people or things: *I thought he was rather unpleasant, and I didn't like his wife either.* □ *She refused to play tennis, and didn't want to go for a walk either.* □ *He didn't look very enthusiastic about it, and she didn't seem keen either.* □ *'I've not read any of her novels.' 'I haven't either.'* **2 Either** is also used at the end of a sentence when a second statement about a person or thing is added, and this statement is in the negative form: *She plays golf, and she's not bad, either.* [compare **too**]

▻ ***conjunction***
Either is used **1** before the first of two alternatives, only one of which is possible or true, with the second alternative introduced by **or**: *Either you apologize, or you leave immediately.* □ *You either leave now, or I phone the police.* □ *People either love hot weather or hate it.* □ *Either she's missed the train and is waiting for the next one, or she's decided to stay the night there.* [compare **or else** at **else**] **2** more generally, to present alternatives and possibilities: *There's either porridge or cornflakes for breakfast.* □ *You should either type these letters or do some filing.* □ *Either Philip of I are always here to help.* **3** before the first of two things that a negative statement, question or *if*-clause refers to, with the second thing introduced by **or**: *I'm not aware that either my wife or my daughter know* (or *knows*) *about this.* □ *She knew she was not behaving either fairly or sensibly.* □ *If either the Brodies or the Petries want to come, could you ask them to let me know?* □ *Is either Tuesday or Thursday possible for you?*

> Notice that even where **either ... or** is used with singular nouns or pronouns it commonly occurs with a plural verb, except in formal English: *Do* (or, in formal English, *does*) *either your mother or your father smoke?*

[see also **neither, both**]

ejaculate /ɪ'dʒakjʊleɪt/ *verb*: **ejaculates, ejaculated, ejaculating**
1 A man **ejaculates** when semen is released through his penis when he is having sex. **2** (*literary*) When words **are ejaculated** they are spoken suddenly and with force, *eg* in anger or with surprise: *'Excellent news!', ejaculated Mr Saunders.* [*same as* **exclaim**]

eject /ɪ'dʒɛkt/ *verb*: **ejects, ejecting, ejected**
1 Something **is ejected** when it is sent out with force: *She pressed the button and the canister ejected a fine spray of oil.* **2** You **eject** someone from somewhere when you force them to leave: *Security staff have instructions to eject any troublemakers.* [*same as* **throw out**]

eke /iːk/ *verb*: **ekes, eking**

> ***phrasal verb***
> **eke out 1** You **eke** something **out**, such as food or money, when you make it last as long as possible: *We must eke out our supplies till we can get to a shop.* **2** You **eke out** a living when you survive on very small earnings.

elaborate *adjective*; *verb*
▻ ***adjective*** /ɪ'labərət/
1 Something, such as a design, is **elaborate** when it consists of many different parts or details: *The cathedral doors are noted for their elaborate carvings.* [*same as* **complex, intricate**] **2** An **elaborate** plan or scheme is very complicated and has been carefully worked out. — *adverb* **elaborately:** *an elaborately embroidered bedspread.*
▻ ***verb*** /ɪ'labəreɪt/: **elaborates, elaborating, elaborated**
1 You **elaborate** on something, such as a story or account, when you give more details about it: *The minister declined to elaborate on his statement.* □ *I'm not sure what you mean - would you care to elaborate?* **2** You **elaborate** something, such as a manufacturing process, by adding features which make it more advanced or efficient. [*same as* **expand, develop**]

elapse /ɪ'laps/ *verb* (*formal*): **elapses, elapsing, elapsed**
When time **elapses**, it passes: *Three years elapsed before I saw her again.*

elastic /ɪ'lastɪk/ *noun*; *adjective*
▻ ***noun*** (*uncount*)
Elastic is cord or fabric that contains rubber and is able to return to its original shape or size after being pulled or pressed out of shape.
▻ ***adjective***
1 An **elastic** material is one that is made of elastic. **2** Policies, rules or demands are **elastic** when they change, or can be changed, according to changing circumstances: *Consumer demand for such goods is traditionally fairly elastic.* [*same as* **flexible**; *opposite* **rigid**] — *noun* (*uncount*) **elasticity** /iːla'stɪsɪtɪ/: *the skin's natural elasticity.*

elasticated /ɪ'lastɪkeɪtɪd/ *adjective*
An **elasticated** fabric has elastic sewn into it: *Are these trousers available with an elasticated waistband?*

elastic band /ɪlastɪk 'band/ *noun*: **elastic bands**
An **elastic band** is a small thin loop of rubber for holding things together or in place. [*same as* **rubber band**]

elated /ɪ'leɪtɪd/ *adjective*
You are **elated** when you are happy and excited, *eg* as a result of success: *She was feeling elated at her progress.* [*same as* **overjoyed, ecstatic**]

elation /ɪ'leɪʃən/ *noun* (*uncount*)
Elation is the feeling of being extremely happy and excited: *We shared the general mood of elation at the overall success of the conference.*

elbow /'ɛlboʊ/ *noun*; *verb*
▻ ***noun***: **elbows**
1 Your **elbow** is the joint where your arm bends in the middle: *He dug his right elbow into his attacker's chest.* [see picture at **body**] **2** The **elbow** of your coat, jacket or other garment is the part of the sleeve that covers your elbow: *elbows worn thin through years of leaning on his desk.* **3** An **elbow** is also a sharp turn or bend, such as in a road or pipe.
▻ ***verb***: **elbows, elbowing, elbowed**
1 You **elbow** someone when you push or strike them with one of your elbows: *He elbowed me in the ribs.* **2** You **elbow** your way through a crowd by pushing other people aside with your elbows.

▻ ***phrase*** (*slang*) You **give** someone **the elbow** when you end a relationship or partnership with them: *No wonder his girlfriend gave him the elbow!*

elbow grease /ˈɛlbou griːs/ *noun* (*uncount*; *informal*)
Elbow grease is the effort you put into doing hard physical work with your arms, such as scrubbing or polishing: *You'll need lots of elbow grease to shift those stains.*

elbow room /ˈɛlbou ruːm/ *noun* (*uncount*; *informal*)
1 Elbow room is space to move in, especially the minimum amount of space needed to be comfortable: *I could make a bit more elbow room by putting these books on the floor.* **2 Elbow room** is also the freedom to do what you want, without interference from others: *She had a boss who never gave her much elbow room.*

elder[1] /ˈɛldə(r)/ *adjective*; *noun*
▻ ***adjective***
Your **elder** brother or sister is a brother or sister who is older than you: *My elder brother is a surgeon.*

> **Elder** only occurs before a noun, is never used with *than*, and is used only about people in the same family; use **older** for other comparisons relating to age: *It was the older lady who spoke first. I'm four months older than Inga. Should I use the carton of milk or the bottle? Which is older?*

▻ ***noun***: **elders**
1 (*used in the plural*) Your **elders** are people who are older than you, especially those as old as, or older than, your parents: *Today's youngsters have no respect for their elders.* **2** A person who is your **elder** is older than you: *I found myself being taught by a young woman who was my elder by only six years.* □ *His sister was three years his elder.* **3** The **elder** of two people is the older one: *'Which of you is the elder?' 'Neither; we're twins.'* □ *when William Pitt the Elder was a Government minister.* **4** In some branches of the Christian Church, the **elders** are the officials who help the minister to run the Church's affairs: *I didn't know he was a Church elder.* **5** The **elders** of a tribe are the older members, whose wisdom and authority is respected by the others.
[see also **eldest**]

elder[2] /ˈɛldə(r)/ *noun*: **elders**
An **elder** is a kind of bush or small tree with white flowers and purple-black or red berries called **elderberries**.

elderly /ˈɛldəlɪ/ *adjective*; *noun*
▻ ***adjective*** (*euphemistic*)
An **elderly** person is rather old: *an elderly gentleman with grey hair.*
▻ ***noun*** (*plural*)
Old people in general are sometimes referred to as the **elderly**: *New taxes on heating will cause grave problems for the elderly in winter.*

elder statesman /ɛldə(r) ˈsteɪtsmən/ *noun*: **elder statesmen**
An **elder statesman** is an elderly politician respected for his authority, experience and past achievements.

eldest /ˈɛldɪst/ *adjective*
The **eldest** family member in a group of three or more is the oldest: *the husband of my eldest sister* □ *Her eldest son is in the army.* □ *She has four sons, three at school and the eldest at university.* [see also **elder**]

elect /ɪˈlɛkt/ *verb*; *adjective*
▻ ***verb***: **elects, electing, elected**
1 Someone **is elected** to an official post or position when they are chosen by others in a vote: *the year I was first elected Prime Minister* □ *She was quickly elected as club secretary.* □ *members of a democratically elected council* □ *The committee will meet to elect a new treasurer.* **2** (*formal*) You **elect** to do something when you choose to do it: *She elected to stay at home instead.*
▻ ***adjective***
Elect is used to refer to a person who has been elected to a position, but who is not yet formally occupying it: *not yet spoken to the President elect.*

election /ɪˈlɛkʃən/ *noun*: **elections**
1 An **election** is a formal vote to choose the person or people who will hold an official position or positions: *We held an election to choose a new committee* □ *The Prime Minister has no intention of calling a general election before next year.* [see also **by-election**, **general election**] **2** (*uncount*) **Election** is the process of electing or being elected: *the election of a new councillor* □ *his election as Member of Parliament.*

elector /ɪˈlɛktə(r)/ *noun*: **electors**
Electors are the people who have the right to vote in an election: *a policy which won't find favour with the electors.* [*same as* **voter**]

electoral /ɪˈlɛktərəl/ *adjective*
Electoral means relating to an election or elections: *You can't vote if your name's not on the electoral roll.* □ *Voters no longer have faith in the electoral process.*
— *adverb* **electorally:** *a policy that proved electorally disastrous.*

electorate /ɪˈlɛktərət/ *noun*: **electorates**
The **electorate** is all the people who have the right to vote in a particular election, considered as a whole: *The Scottish electorate is more sophisticated than we care to admit.*

electric /ɪˈlɛktrɪk/ *adjective*
1 Electric devices, such as cookers and irons, work by means of electricity: *old gas lamps replaced by electric lights.* **2 Electric** also means relating to electricity in some way: *electric plugs and sockets* □ *It is the magnetic force that creates the electric current.* **3** You describe a situation or an atmosphere as **electric** when it is filled with great excitement, tension or expectation. [*same as* **charged**]

electrical /ɪˈlɛktrɪkəl/ *adjective*
1 Electrical appliances work by means of electricity: *selling fridges, washing machines and other electrical goods.* **2 Electrical** also means concerned with or relating to the use of such appliances: *an electrical engineer* □ *breakdowns caused by electrical faults.*
— *adverb* **electrically:** *electrically operated gates.*

electric chair /ɪlɛktrɪk ˈtʃɛə(r)/ *noun* (*used in the singular*)
The **electric chair** is a means of execution in which a powerful electric current is sent through the body of the person sitting in it.

electrician /ɪlɛkˈtrɪʃən/ *noun*: **electricians**
An **electrician** is a person whose job is to install and repair electrical equipment.

electricity /ɪlɛkˈtrɪsɪtɪ/ *noun* (*uncount*)
1 Electricity is a form of energy used to power many modern machines and other appliances, such as household lights and heating systems. **2** A supply of this energy, *eg* to houses and factories, is also referred to as **electricity**: *The cottage had no running water and no electricity.*

electric shock /ɪlɛktrɪk ˈʃɒk/ *noun*: **electric shocks**
An **electric shock** is the sudden sharp pain you feel when electricity passes through your body, *eg* when you touch a live electric wire: *You shouldn't get an electric shock if the appliance is wired correctly.*

electrify /ɪ'lɛktrɪfaɪ/ *verb*: **electrifies, electrifying, electrified**
1 To **electrify** a railway line is to supply it with electric cables overhead or electric lines alongside, from which trains can take power. **2** Something, such as a fence, **is electrified** when an electric current is caused to flow through it. **3** Something that **electrifies** you excites and impresses you: *a performer who has been electrifying West-End audiences this week.* — *noun* (*uncount*) **electrification** /ɪlɛktrɪfɪ'keɪʃən/: *electrification of the railways.* — *adjective* **electrifying:** *an electrifying performance.*

electrocute /ɪ'lɛktrəkjuːt/ *verb*: **electrocutes, electrocuting, electrocuted**
Someone **is electrocuted** when they are badly injured or killed by coming into contact with electricity. — *noun* (*uncount*) **electrocution** /ɪlɛktrə'kjuːʃən/: *death by electrocution.*

electrode /ɪ'lɛktroʊd/ *noun*: **electrodes**
Electrodes are the small metal connectors through which electric current passes from a battery or other source to a piece of equipment.

electron /ɪ'lɛktrɒn/ *noun*: **electrons**
Electrons are particles contained within atoms and are the means by which electricity travels.

electronic /ɪlɛk'trɒnɪk/ *adjective*
1 A piece of **electronic** equipment, such as a computer, is operated by means of very small electrical circuits which use very low levels of electric current. **2 Electronic** also means involving the use of such equipment: *electronic music.* — *adverb* **electronically:** *information stored electronically.*

electronics /ɪlɛk'trɒnɪks/ *noun*
1 (*uncount*) **Electronics** is the science or industry of building electronic equipment: *an electronics company* □ *His wife works in electronics.* **2** (*plural*) The **electronics** of a machine or other device are its electronic parts: *The equipment looks sophisticated but its electronics are really very basic.*

elegant /'ɛlɪgənt/ *adjective*
1 An **elegant** person is someone whose appearance is graceful and dignified: *A tall elegant lady glided across the room.* **2** Something, such as an item of clothing, that is **elegant** has a pleasingly simple shape or design: *an elegant black evening dress* □ *In the middle sits the cathedral, with its elegant spire.* **3** An **elegant** scheme or plan is simple and ingenious. — *adverb* **elegantly**: *She was elegantly dressed in a Dior suit.* — *noun* (*uncount*) **elegance**: *She was impressed by the sheer elegance of the design.*

elegy /'ɛlədʒɪ/ *noun*: **elegies**
An **elegy** is a sad or sorrowful poem, especially one dealing with death.

element /'ɛləmənt/ *noun*: **elements**
1 The **elements** of something are the features of it or the parts it is made up of: *Cost and timescale were the two most important elements of our discussion.* □ *The single most important element in my life is my family.* **2** There is an **element** of some quality in something when that quality is present in some small degree: *There must have been an element of truth in what he said.* **3** An **element**, or a chemical **element**, are any of a group of substances, such as oxygen and iron, that cannot be split by chemical means into simpler substances: *Refer to the table of elements at the back of the book.* **4** An identifiable group of people within a larger group is sometimes referred to as an **element** of a particular kind: *how to deal with the criminal element in society* □ *There were clearly many hostile elements outside the organization.* **5** The **element** in an electric fire or other appliance is the wire coil that electricity passes through to produce heat. **6** (*plural*) The weather, especially stormy weather, is often referred to as the **elements**: *I donned my coat and prepared to brave the elements.* **7** The **elements** of a subject are the basic facts or skills you need to learn. [*same as* **basics**, **rudiments**]
▻ ***phrase*** You are **in your element** if you are in the situation that you find most natural and enjoyable: *He's in his element in a roomful of people.*

elemental /ɛlə'mɛntəl/ *adjective* (*literary*)
Elemental feelings or actions are expressed or performed with basic, intense, uncontrolled force: *She spat the words out with elemental hatred.*

elementary /ɛlə'mɛntərɪ/ *adjective*
1 Elementary means dealing with or relating to the most basic facts or skills: *a course in elementary biology.* **2** (*formal*) **Elementary** also means very easy to do or understand: *'How?' 'It's elementary. We simply pretend not to know.'*

elephant /'ɛləfənt/ *noun*: **elephants**
An **elephant** is a large land animal with thick grey skin, a nose in the form of a long hanging trunk, and two long curved tusks. [see also **white elephant**]

elephantine /'ɛləfantaɪn/ *adjective* (*literary*)
Someone or something that is **elephantine** is clumsy and not at all graceful, often because of being very big: *He plodded round the dance floor with elephantine strides.*

elevate /'ɛləveɪt/ *verb*: **elevates, elevating, elevated**
1 Someone **is elevated** to a new position or job when they are promoted or given a higher rank: *She is to be elevated to the chairman's position.* **2** When you speak of something as if it was something else more important, you **are elevating** it to the status of that more important thing: *The programme elevated television producers to guardians of public taste, which they are clearly not.* **3** You **elevate** something when you lift it up to a higher level: *We discussed with the engineers ways of elevating the whole bridge.*

elevated /'ɛləveɪtɪd/ *adjective*
1 An **elevated** rank or position is very high or important. **2 Elevated** thoughts or ideas are intellectually advanced or very moral. **3 Elevated** land or property is higher up than its surroundings: *The house enjoys an elevated position overlooking the valley.*

elevating /'ɛləveɪtɪŋ/ *adjective*
Something, such as a work of art or literature, is **elevating** when it educates you or improves your mind in some way. [*same as* **edifying**]

elevation /ɛlə'veɪʃən/ *noun*: **elevations**
1 (*uncount*) **Elevation** is the act of elevating a person to a higher rank, or of regarding someone or something as having a higher-than-usual status: *his elevation to the post of Home Secretary* □ *His book argues for the elevation of cricket to an Olympic sport.* **2** The **elevation** of an area of land is its height above sea level: *The town lies to the north of the lake, at an elevation of 500 metres.* **3** (*technical*) An **elevation** is a drawing or diagram of one side of something, such as a building or a machine: *We studied both the side and front elevations.*

elevator /'ɛləveɪtə(r)/ *noun* (*AmE*): **elevators**
An **elevator** is a lift.

eleven /ɪ'lɛvən/ *noun*; *determiner*; *adjective*
▻ ***noun***: **elevens**
1 Eleven is **a** the number or figure 11. **b** something, such as a garment, whose size is denoted by the number 11: *Do you have an eleven in this sandal?* **c** a set of 11 people or things, especially a team of eleven play-

ers: *He's playing in the first eleven on Saturday.* **2 Eleven** is **a** the age of 11: *By eleven, he had already mastered the guitar.* **b** 11 o'clock: *I arrived just after eleven.*
▷ ***determiner***
Eleven means 11 in number: *Eleven Conservative MPs voted against the government.* ▫ *Eleven of us voted against the motion.*
▷ ***adjective***
Someone who is **eleven** is 11 years old: *I took up the piano when I was eleven.*
[for more examples of how numerals are used, see **eight**]

eleventh /ɪ'lɛvənθ/ *determiner; adjective; adverb; noun*
▷ ***determiner***
The **eleventh** person or thing comes after the tenth: *She's the eleventh person to phone in sick this week.* ▫ *Ten people have been bullied into resigning and I'm determined not to become the eleventh.*
▷ ***adjective***
A person or thing that is **eleventh** is next in order after 10th: *She's eleventh in order of company seniority.*
▷ ***adverb***
A person or thing that comes after 10th comes **eleventh**: *She finished eleventh in a field of over a hundred runners.*
▷ ***noun*: elevenths**
An **eleventh** is one of 11 parts that something is divided into: *The council spends an eleventh of its budget on telephone calls.*
▷ ***phrase*** You do something **at the eleventh hour** when you do it at the last possible moment: *A major dispute was avoided when the Prime Minister intervened at the eleventh hour.*

elf /ɛlf/ *noun*: **elves**
An **elf** is a tiny mischievous character in fairy stories who uses magical powers to play tricks on people.

elicit /ɪ'lɪsɪt/ *verb (formal)*: **elicits, eliciting, elicited**
1 You **elicit** something, such as information, from someone when you get it after a lot of effort: *The promise was finally elicited from them after hours of careful negotiation.* [*same as* **extract**] **2** You **elicit** a reaction or a response from someone when your behaviour provokes it: *His comments only succeeded in eliciting howls of laughter from the others.*

eligible /'ɛlɪdʒɪbəl/ *adjective*
1 You are **eligible** for something when you have a right to receive it: *It's for the court to decide whether you are eligible for compensation.* **2** You are **eligible** for a job or other post if you are suitable for it, because you have good experience or qualifications: *We interviewed a number of eligible candidates.* **3** An **eligible** man or woman is regarded as a suitable partner for marriage: *There were a number of eligible males at the party.* — *noun (uncount)* **eligibility** /ɛlɪdʒɪ'bɪlɪtɪ/: *Check with our secretary if you are in doubt about your eligibility to participate in the scheme.*

eliminate /ɪ'lɪmɪneɪt/ *verb*: **eliminates, eliminating, eliminated**
1 You **eliminate** something when you get rid of or remove it because it is not wanted or needed: *The police are committed to eliminating racism.* **2** A competitor **is eliminated** when they are defeated in an early part of a competition and so excluded from the later part. [*same as* **knock out**] **3** (*slang*) To **eliminate** someone also means to murder them. — *noun (uncount)* **elimination** /ɪlɪmɪ'neɪʃən/: *the elimination of unsuitable applicants.*

elite or **élite** /ɪ'li:t/ or /eɪ'li:t/ *noun; adjective*
▷ ***noun*: elites**
An **elite** is a small group of people regarded as superior in some way to others within the larger group: *Teachers are no longer regarded as part of the intellectual elite.*
▷ ***adjective***
An **elite** person or group is regarded as superior to others: *a student at one of the elite universities.*

elitism or **élitism** /ɪ'li:tɪzm/ or /eɪ'li:tɪzm/ *noun (uncount)*
Elitism is **1** the belief in the need for elites within society: *Many felt that the Tories were simply promoting elitism.* **2** the belief that some people are naturally superior to others: *Such policies derive from the worst kind of elitism.* **3** feeling superior because you know you belong to an elite: *It would seem that the aristocracy creates institutions guaranteed to engender such elitism.* — *noun* **elitist:** *This is likely to find favour with the elitists within society.* ▫ (*used as an adjective*) *an elitist viewpoint.*

elixir /ɪ'lɪksɪə(r)/ *noun*: **elixirs**
In folklore, an **elixir** was a liquid with magical powers, such as the power to give people everlasting life or turn ordinary metals into gold.

elk /ɛlk/ *noun*: **elks** or **elk**
An **elk** is a very large kind of deer with flat rounded antlers.

ellipse /ɪ'lɪps/ *noun (technical)*: **ellipses**
An **ellipse** is an oval shape.

elm /ɛlm/ *noun*: **elms**
1 An **elm** is a tall tree with broad leaves and clusters of small flowers: *She sat reading in the shade of a huge elm tree.* **2** (*uncount*) **Elm** is the hard heavy wood of this tree.

elocution /ɛlə'kju:ʃən/ *noun (uncount)*
Elocution is the art of speaking clearly and without a regional accent: *She has the kind of featureless accent you can only acquire through elocution lessons.*

elongated /'i:lɒŋgeɪtɪd/ *adjective*
Something is **elongated** when it is long and narrow: *Printed on it was a strange symbol like an elongated f.*

elope /ɪ'loʊp/ *verb*: **elopes, eloping, eloped**
Someone **elopes** with a lover, or the two of them **elope**, when they run away secretly in order to be together, especially to get married. — *noun (uncount or count)* **elopement:** *the scandal caused by their elopement.*

eloquent /'ɛləkwənt/ *adjective*
An **eloquent** person speaks clearly and confidently choosing the right words: *She's a most eloquent speaker.* ▫ *It was just the kind of eloquent speech needed to get them on his side.* [*same as* **fluent**, **articulate**] — *noun (uncount)* **eloquence:** *I'm constantly amazed the eloquence he's capable of, even under pressure.* — *adverb* **eloquently:** *I think the Minister made his point very eloquently.*

else /ɛls/ *adverb*
Else is used after words beginning *any-*, *every-*, *no-*, *some-*, after the question words *who*, *what*, *where*, *how*, *why*, and after *little* and *much*, to mean other than what is already known or has already been mentioned: *Do we need anything else?* ▫ *I was the only one sitting on the floor; everyone else had a seat.* ▫ *It's not mine; it must be someone else's.* ▫ *Sorry about the pile of books, but I've nowhere else to put them.* ▫ *What else did he say?* ▫ *Where else can you buy it?* ▫ *Why else would she have wanted to know?* ▫ *How else do you think I found out?* ▫ *There's little else left to say.* ▫ *There wasn't much else to do apart from watch the ships.*
▷ ***phrase***
1 You use **or else** to introduce **a** the consequence of not doing what you suggest: *Hurry up or else you'll*

miss the bus. [*same as* **otherwise**, **or**] **b** the second of two possibilities: *He was drunk, or else he'd been taking those pills again.* □ *We can take the motorway as far as Wolverhampton, or else take the A53 to Shrewsbury.* [compare the conjunctions **either ... or** at **either**] **2** (*informal*) If you say **or else** after telling someone to do something you are threatening them with harm or punishment if they don't do it: *Leave her alone, or else!*

elsewhere /ɛls'wɛə(r)/ *adverb*
Elsewhere means in or to another place or other places: *They carried out searches in Yorkshire and elsewhere.* □ *If the shop closes, I shall have to go elsewhere.*

elucidate /ɪ'lu:sɪdeɪt/ *verb*: **elucidates, elucidating, elucidated**
You **elucidate** something when you make it easier to understand by giving a clearer explanation: *It was a complex issue, in no way elucidated by Alan's little speech.* [*same as* **illuminate, clarify**] — *noun* (*uncount*) **elucidation** /ɪlu:sɪ'deɪʃən/: *The reader seeking further elucidation of these points is referred to the appendix.*

elude /ɪ'lu:d/ *verb*: **eludes, eluding, eluded**
1 Something **eludes** you when you cannot remember it, understand it or work it out: *I knew I'd seen him before, but his name eluded me.* □ *The problem did not seem complex in theory, but the answer still eluded him.* [*same as* **escape**] **2** You **elude** something when you avoid it or escape from it: *The gunman has so far eluded capture.*

elusive /ɪ'lu:sɪv/ *adjective*
Something **elusive** is difficult to find, achieve or remember: *Contentment was an elusive quality.* □ *Again we tried to coax him out, but the animal remained as elusive as ever.*

elves /ɛlvz/ *noun*
Elves is the plural of **elf**.

'em /əm/ *pronoun* (*informal*)
'Em is sometimes used in writing to represent the way some people say 'them'.

emaciated /ɪ'meɪsɪeɪtɪd/ *adjective*
Someone who is **emaciated** is unhealthily thin, because of illness or lack of food.

emanate /'ɛməneɪt/ *verb*: **emanates, emanating, emanated**
1 Something, such as an idea or a rumour, **emanates** from someone when it is first thought of or talked about by them: *The latest gossip emanating from the palace suggests the Prince is keen to remarry.* **2** Something, such as a liquid or a smell, **emanates** from somewhere when it flows out from there: *Foul odours emanated from the kitchen.*

emancipate /ɪ'mansɪpeɪt/ *verb*: **emancipates, emancipating, emancipated**
Groups of people **are emancipated** when they are given the same social or political freedom enjoyed by the others in a society: *Emancipating the working classes no longer seems to be the party's principal aim.* — *noun* (*uncount*) **emancipation** /ɪmansɪ'peɪʃən/: *the emancipation of women.*

embalm /ɪm'bɑ:m/ *verb*: **embalms, embalming, embalmed**
A dead person's body **is embalmed** when it is preserved, in the past with oils and spices, but now with chemicals or drugs.

embankment /ɪm'baŋkmənt/ *noun*: **embankments**
1 An **embankment** is a wall of earth made to prevent a river or lake from overflowing. **2** An **embankment** is also a long thin mound of earth built to carry a road or railway. **3** The slope of earth or grass that rises from either side of a road or railway is also called an **embankment**.

embargo /ɪm'bɑ:goʊ/ *noun*: **embargoes**
An **embargo** is an official order forbidding something, usually trade of some kind with another country: *The government will consider imposing an arms embargo on all Middle Eastern countries.* □ *There are no signs that the oil embargo will be lifted.*

embark /ɪm'bɑ:k/ *verb*: **embarks, embarking, embarked**
1 When you start something new and uncertain, such as a new career, you **embark** on it: *As new students, you are embarking on a journey of self-discovery.* **2** When you **embark**, you get on a ship at the start of a voyage: *Embarking at Athens, I had the feeling of leaving a whole different world behind.* [*opposite* **disembark**] — *noun* (*uncount*) **embarkation** /ɛmbɑ:'keɪʃən/: *We learned that Bari was to be our new port of embarkation.*

embarrass /ɪm'barəs/ *verb*: **embarrasses, embarrassing, embarrassed**
You **embarrass** someone when you make them feel nervous or self-conscious, or ashamed or guilty, in the presence of others: *All this talk of sex was clearly embarrassing him.* □ *The Chancellor's remarks have embarrassed the government before.* — *adjective* **embarrassed:** *His comments were greeted with an embarrassed silence.* — *adjective* **embarrassing:** *a thoroughly embarrassing incident.*

embarrassment /ɪm'barəsmənt/ *noun*: **embarrassments**
1 Embarrassment is the feeling of being embarrassed: *She tried hard not to show her embarrassment at the remark.* **2** A person or thing that embarrasses you is an **embarrassment**: *He couldn't admit that she was an embarrassment to him.*

embassy /'ɛmbəsɪ/ *noun*: **embassies**
1 An **embassy** is a group of diplomats, led by an ambassador, who represent their government in a foreign country: *The embassy will have to be informed.* **2** The building occupied by an ambassador and his or her staff is also an **embassy**.

embattled /ɪm'batəld/ *adjective*
An **embattled** person is having to deal with many difficult problems all at once: *Still further troubles beset the embattled minister.* [*same as* **beleaguered**]

embedded /ɪm'bɛdɪd/ *adjective*
1 A thing is **embedded** in something when it is fixed or set in it firmly and deeply: *The hull of the boat had become embedded in the mud.* **2** Something, such as a custom or an attitude, is **embedded** in a society, or in a person's mind, when it is extremely difficult to change or get rid of because it has come to be accepted as normal. [*same as* **entrenched**]

embellish /ɪm'bɛlɪʃ/ *verb*: **embellishes, embellishing, embellished**
1 You **embellish** a report, account or story when you try to make it more interesting by adding details which may not be true: *One suspects that his version of events has been more than a little embellished.* [*same as* **embroider**] **2** An object is **embellished** with something when it is decorated or made more beautiful: *An essentially simple dress had been embellished with embroidered roses in pink and white.* — *noun* **embellishment:** *It is built in a simple, severe style, without embellishment.* □ *They didn't like the modern embellishments of traditional tunes.*

ember /'ɛmbə(r)/ *noun*: **embers**
Embers are pieces of glowing coal or wood in a dying fire.

embezzle /ɪm'bɛzəl/ *verb*: **embezzles, embezzling, embezzled**

Someone **embezzles** money that they have been entrusted with when they take it secretly and dishonestly. — *noun* (*uncount*) **embezzlement:** *She will appear in court next week on charges of embezzlement.*

embittered /ɪm'bɪtəd/ *adjective*
An **embittered** person feels very bitter: *I had a vision of her dying a lonely and embittered woman.*

emblazon /ɪm'bleɪzən/ *verb*: **emblazons, emblazoning, emblazoned**
A design that **is emblazoned** on an object is very big, bright or otherwise striking: *The back of the jacket is emblazoned with an eagle's head and the words 'God bless America'.*

emblem /'ɛmbləm/ *noun*: **emblems**
An **emblem** is an object chosen to represent something, such as a country, a political aim or a personal quality. [*same as* **symbol**]

embody /ɪm'bɒdɪ/ *verb*: **embodies, embodying, embodied**
1 Someone **embodies** something such as an idea or a quality when their whole appearance, personality or behaviour seems to reflect or express it: *His wife embodied every man's dream of the perfect marriage partner.* □ *It has long been an organization that embodied equality and social justice.* [*same as* **represent, personify, epitomize, stand for**] **2** To **embody** also means to include or incorporate: *This draft embodies policy changes decided on at the last meeting.* — *noun* **embodiment:** *Officers are no longer the embodiment of fair play.*

embossed /ɪm'bɒst/ *adjective*
An **embossed** surface, or a surface with an **embossed** design, is decorated in such a way that the design sticks out above the rest of the surface: *a leather-bound cover with embossed lettering.*

embrace /ɪm'breɪs/ *verb*; *noun*
▻ ***verb***: **embraces, embracing, embraced**
1 You **embrace** someone when you wrap your arms around them as a greeting or a sign of affection: *She smiled warmly, then embraced me.* □ *The picture was called 'Lovers embracing'.* [*same as* **hug**] **2** You **embrace** something when you adopt or accept it eagerly and wholeheartedly: *She spoke to foreigners who had embraced the native religion.* [*same as* **espouse**] **3** To **embrace** also means to include: *Not all literature courses embrace the eighteenth-century classics.* [*same as* **take in**]
▻ ***noun***: **embraces**
An **embrace** is an act of embracing someone: *He felt embarrassed witnessing such a passionate embrace.*

embroider /ɪm'brɔɪdə(r)/ *verb*: **embroiders, embroidering, embroidered**
1 You **embroider** fabric when you sew designs on it. **2** You **embroider** an account, report or story when you try to make it more interesting by adding untrue details or by exaggerating. [*same as* **embellish**] — *adjective* **embroidered:** *a pink cotton embroidered dress.*

embroidery /ɪm'brɔɪdərɪ/ *noun* (*uncount*)
Embroidery is **1** the art or practice of sewing designs on to cloth: *She teaches classes in embroidery.* **2** the designs sewn on to cloth: *The collar was edged with fine embroidery.* **3** articles decorated in this way: *a sale of embroidery.*

embroiled /ɪm'brɔɪld/ *adjective*
You become **embroiled** in a difficult situation when you become deeply involved in it: *You wouldn't want to become embroiled in some big family dispute.*

embryo /'ɛmbrɪoʊ/ *noun*: **embryos**
1 An **embryo** is a baby in the earliest stages of its development before birth: *Many were opposed to medical experiments on embryos.* □ *Some research has been carried out on ape embryos.* [see also **foetus**] **2** Something in its early stages of development can be described as being at or in the **embryo** stage: *Research is still in the embryo stage.*
▻ ***phrase*** Something that exists **in embryo** is in its early stages of development: *Plans for the dictionary had been around, in embryo at least, for one or two years.*

embryonic /ɛmbrɪ'ɒnɪk/ *adjective*
Embryonic means in an early stage of development: *Nothing planned, just one or two embryonic ideas.*

emend /ɪ'mɛnd/ *verb*: **emends, emending, emended**
You **emend** a text when you remove errors from it and make improvements to it. — *noun* (*uncount or count*) **emendation** /iːmɛn'deɪʃən/: *his own methods of text-editing and emendation.* □ *A few emendations to the text had been necessary.*

emerald /'ɛmərəld/ *noun*: **emeralds**
1 An **emerald** is a bright-green precious stone used in jewellery. **2** (*uncount*) **Emerald** or **emerald green** is the bright-green colour of emeralds: *window boxes painted emerald green* □ *a white dress with an emerald collar.*

emerge /ɪ'mɜːdʒ/ *verb*: **emerges, emerging, emerged**
1 Someone **emerges** from somewhere when they come out and into view. [*same as* **appear**] **2** Something, such as a fact, **emerges** when it becomes known: *It emerged from their conversation that he had never been to the house.* □ *The fact emerged that she was older than she claimed.* [*same as* **come out**] **3** You **emerge** from a situation when it is over or finished: *This was a severe attack from which no Prime Minister could have emerged completely unscathed.* **4** Someone **emerges** as something, such as a hero, when they come to be regarded as it by others: *They have emerged as one of the UK's most successful companies.* — *noun* (*uncount*) **emergence:** *his emergence as a statesman on the world stage* □ *They witnessed the emergence of Thatcher as one of the great political manipulators.*

emergency /ɪ'mɜːdʒənsɪ/ *noun*; *adjective*
▻ ***noun***: **emergencies**
An **emergency** is an unexpected and serious happening which needs to be dealt with immediately: *She had been taught how to react in an emergency.* □ *In case of emergency, phone the hospital immediately.*
▻ ***adjective***
Emergency action is what needs to be taken in an emergency: *Emergency measures were taken to evacuate the whole town.* □ *We decided to break into the emergency supplies.*

emigrant /'ɛmɪgrənt/ *noun*: **emigrants**
An **emigrant** is a person who emigrates or who has emigrated. [see also **immigrant**]

emigrate /'ɛmɪgreɪt/ *verb*: **emigrates, emigrating, emigrated**
Someone **emigrates** when they leave their native country and settle in another: *Have you ever regretted emigrating when you did?* □ *We once had plans to emigrate to Australia.* — *noun* (*uncount*) **emigration** /ɛmɪ'greɪʃən/: *They have failed to halt the flow of youth emigration.*

émigré /'ɛmɪgreɪ/ *noun*: **émigrés**
An **émigré** is a person who has left their country for political reasons and settled in another country.

eminent /'ɛmɪnənt/ *adjective*
An **eminent** person is widely regarded as one of the most talented people in a particular profession:

Simpson is a broadcaster and eminent modern historian. [*same as* **distinguished**] — *noun* (*uncount*) **eminence:** *a mathematician of some eminence.*

eminently /ˈɛmɪnəntlɪ/ *adverb* (*formal; intensifying*)
Eminently means 'very' or 'very much': *It was an eminently appropriate gesture.* □ *It is a reward to which you are eminently entitled.*

emissary /ˈɛmɪsərɪ/ *noun* (*formal*): **emissaries**
An **emissary** is an official sent by one country's government to talk to another country's government.

emission /ɪˈmɪʃən/ *noun* (*formal*): **emissions**
An **emission** of something, such as gas, is an amount of it released into the air: *reducing carbon monoxide emissions from car exhausts.*

emit /ɪˈmɪt/ *verb*: **emits, emitting, emitted**
Something, such as light, heat or a sound, **is emitted** when it is given off or sent out: *The fumes it emits are enough to turn your stomach.*

emotion /ɪˈmoʊʃən/ *noun* (*count or uncount*): **emotions**
An **emotion** is a strong feeling, such as anger or love: *Jealousy is a most destructive emotion.* □ *The lack of emotion in her voice struck him as odd.*

emotional /ɪˈmoʊʃənəl/ *adjective*
1 Emotional means relating to, provoking or expressing an emotion, especially love, affection or sympathy: *She had never satisfied his emotional needs.* □ *The meeting was an emotional moment for both of them.* **2** An **emotional** person expresses their feelings easily and openly. **3** An **emotional** reaction is one based on feelings rather than on clear thinking: *Isn't that rather an emotional response?* [*opposite* **rational**] — *adverb* **emotionally:** *It's a film that leaves you emotionally drained.*

emotive /ɪˈmoʊtɪv/ *adjective*
An **emotive** issue arouses very strong feelings in people: *Is child abuse too emotive a topic for a television debate?*

empathy /ˈɛmpəθɪ/ *noun* (*uncount*)
You have **empathy** with someone when you understand their feelings so well that you feel the same yourself. [see also **sympathy**]

emperor /ˈɛmpərə(r)/ *noun*: **emperors**
An **emperor** is the male ruler of an empire or of a country which was once the centre of an empire: *the last Emperor of China.*

emphasis /ˈɛmfəsɪs/ *noun* (*uncount or count*): **emphases** /ˈɛmfəsiːz/
Emphasis is **1** particular importance or attention that you give something: *In countries where they lay great emphasis on management-worker co-operation.* □ *There was undoubtedly an emphasis on parental involvement.* [*same as* **stress**] **2** greater force or loudness with which you speak a word or part of a word to show its importance: *'It's your responsibility,' she said, with emphasis on the 'your'.* [*same as* **stress, accent**]

emphasize or **emphasise** /ˈɛmfəsaɪz/ *verb*: **emphasizes, emphasizing, emphasized**
1 You **emphasize** something when you give it special importance: *She emphasized the need for continued government support.* [*same as* **stress**] **2** You **emphasize** a word or part of a word when you speak it more loudly to show that it is especially important. [*same as* **stress**]

emphatic /ɪmˈfatɪk/ *adjective*
1 An **emphatic** statement or gesture is expressed clearly and with force: *There was an emphatic refusal to take the matter further.* **2** You are **emphatic** when you state your opinions or intentions firmly and forcefully: *She would not go; about that she was quite emphatic.*

emphatically /ɪmˈfatɪklɪ/ *adverb*
1 You say something **emphatically** when you say it firmly and forcefully: *He denied most emphatically any involvement in such dealings.* **2** (*intensifying*) **Emphatically** also means definitely or absolutely: *I am emphatically not willing to speak on his behalf.*

empire /ˈɛmpaɪə(r)/ *noun*: **empires**
An **empire** is **1** a group of nations ruled by a single country or a single ruler: *after the collapse of the Roman Empire.* **2** a large group of companies controlled by a single person or organization: *This gave her the opportunity to expand her cosmetics empire.*

empirical /ɪmˈpɪrɪkəl/ *adjective*
Empirical means resulting from or involving practical experience rather than theory: *This, more than any other discipline, demands empirical study.* — *adverb* **empirically:** *The validity of such unquestioned assumptions can actually be demonstrated empirically.* — *noun* (*uncount*) **empiricism** /ɪmˈpɪrɪsɪzm/: *The school of thought known as empiricism insisted that experience was the basis of human knowledge.*

employ /ɪmˈplɔɪ/ *verb*: **employ, employing, employs**
1 You **employ** someone when you pay them to work for you: *He's employed on a part-time basis.* □ *I was employed as a postman for a while.* **2** (*formal*) To **employ** something means to use it: *She needed to employ all her powers of persuasion.*

employee /ɪmˈplɔɪiː/ or /ɛmplɔɪˈiː/ *noun*: **employees**
A company's **employees** are its workers: *He's a former employee of ours.*

employer /ɪmˈplɔɪə(r)/ *noun*: **employers**
Your **employer** is the person or company that you are paid to work for.

employment /ɪmˈplɔɪmənt/ *noun* (*uncount*)
1 You are in **employment** when you have a job from which you earn money: *It's regarded as a privilege simply to be in employment these days.* **2 Employment** is also used to refer to the availability of paid work in general: *But can full employment ever be achieved in a market economy?* [see also **unemployment**]

empower /ɪmˈpaʊə(r)/ *verb*: **empowers, empowering, empowered**
Someone **is empowered** to do something when they are given the power or authority to do it: *The police are not empowered to break up peaceful demonstrations.*

empress /ˈɛmprɪs/ *noun*: **empresses**
An **empress** is **1** the female ruler of an empire or of a country which was once the centre of an empire. **2** the wife of an emperor.

empty /ˈɛmptɪ/ *adjective; verb*
▷ ***adjective***: **emptier, emptiest**
1 Something is **empty** when it has nothing or nobody inside it: *Your glass is empty; would you like more wine?* □ *A row of empty houses greets you at the edge of the village.* **2 Empty** gestures and **empty** statements have no value because the people making them lack sincerity or determination: *We've heard enough of the minister's empty promises.* □ *Those are the empty threats of the classic coward.* [*same as* **hollow**] **3** Something, such as a person's life, is **empty** when nothing interesting happens in it: *That was a particularly empty period of my life.* — *noun* (*uncount*) **emptiness:** *The room had a disconcerting emptiness.* □ *After years of emotional emptiness she was, she felt, truly happy.*
▷ ***verb***: **empties, emptying, emptied**
1 You **empty** a container when you take out its con-

tents: *We'd better empty the chest before we try and lift it.* □ *He emptied the toybox all over the floor.* [*opposite* **fill, fill up**] **2** You **empty** something out of a container when you tip or pour it out: *You could empty the paint into another bucket.* **3** A room **empties** when all the people in it leave: *Most students go home at the weekends; the halls empty on a Friday evening.* [*opposite* **fill, fill up**]

empty-handed /ɛmptɪ'handɪd/ *adjective*
You return from somewhere **empty-handed** when you fail to get what you went for: *After nine hours of intense negotiations, the union leaders emerged empty-handed.*

empty-headed /ɛmptɪ'hɛdɪd/ *adjective*
If you say that someone is **empty-headed**, you think they are foolish and not capable of thinking sensibly: *It was the kind of mindless drivel that would fail to entertain even the most empty-headed schoolgirl.*

emu /'iːmjuː/ *noun*: **emus**
An **emu** is a large grey or brown Australian bird that cannot fly.

emulate /'ɛmjʊleɪt/ *verb*: **emulates, emulating, emulated**
You **emulate** someone or something you like or admire when you copy them or it: *It's obvious, particularly in the camerawork, that he's trying to emulate Hitchcock.*

enable /ɪ'neɪbəl/ *verb*: **enables, enabling, enabled**
To **enable** someone to do something is to make it possible for them to do it: *The rear-view mirror enables the driver to see what's behind him at all times.* [*same as* **allow**]

enact /ɪ'nakt/ *verb*: **enacts, enacting, enacted**
1 People **enact** a story when they perform it or act it out: *Children from the Sunday school enacted Jesus's life.* □ *I hate it when they enact the 'happily married couple' routine.* **2** A government or other body **enacts** a policy or proposal when they officially establish it as a law: *They have little chance of enacting this bill.* — *noun* (*uncount*) **enactment:** *the eventual enactment of the bill* □ *in my own interpretation and enactment of the role.*

enamel /ɪ'naməl/ *noun* (*uncount*)
Enamel is **1** a hard glass-like substance that metal and pottery can be coated with for decoration or protection. **2** the hard white substance covering the teeth. — *adjective* **enamelled:** *a set of red enamelled saucepans.*

enamoured (*AmE* **enamored**) /ɪ'naməd/ *adjective*
1 (*formal*) You are **enamoured** of something, or **enamoured** with it, when you like it very much: *Generally speaking, I wasn't too enamoured with his choice of restaurant.* **2** (*literary*) You are **enamoured** of someone when you are in love with them: *She spent her adolescence enamoured of the local vicar.*

en bloc /ɒn 'blɒk/ *adverb* (*formal*)
Several people do something **en bloc** when they do it together, as a group: *The companies resisted en bloc all government proposals to restrict imports.* [see also **bloc**]

encampment /ɪn'kampmənt/ *noun*: **encampments**
An **encampment** is a group of tents or other temporary shelters, such as those put up by soldiers.

encapsulate /ɪŋ'kapsjʊleɪt/ *verb* (*formal*): **encapsulates, encapsulating, encapsulated**
Something small or brief **encapsulates** something much larger when it expresses or reflects it perfectly: *That single shrug of her shoulders encapsulated their whole miserable, pointless relationship.* [*same as* **sum up**]

encase /ɪŋ'keɪs/ *verb*: **encases, encasing, encased**
Something **is encased** in something that surrounds or covers it completely: *The glass tubes are then encased in steel to protect them from the intense heat.*

enchanted /ɪn'tʃɑːntɪd/ *adjective*
1 You are **enchanted** by someone or something if you think them exceptionally lovely or charming: *Enchanted by her smile, I found myself quite speechless.* [*same as* **bewitch, hypnotize, captivate**] **2** An **enchanted** place is so beautiful and mysterious that it seems almost unreal: *At the bottom of this enchanted garden stood an old summerhouse.*

enchanting /ɪn'tʃɑːntɪŋ/ *adjective*
An **enchanting** person or thing is exceptionally charming or delightful: *Their little cottage is enchanting.*

encircle /ɪn'sɜːkəl/ *verb*: **encircles, encircling, encircled**
One thing **encircles** another if it goes all the way round it like a circle: *The roads have been extended so that they now fully encircle the town.*

enclave /'ɛŋkleɪv/ *noun*: **enclaves**
An **enclave** is any place that is in some way different from the areas that surround it, *eg* because it is inhabited by people of a different nationality: *Once at the heart of the superpower's empire, this land is now reduced to a communist enclave.*

enclose /ɪŋ'kloʊz/ *verb*: **encloses, enclosing, enclosed**
1 Something **is enclosed** by something else that surrounds, contains or separates it completely: *The grounds were enclosed by high walls.* □ *The metal bin is enclosed in a rubber case for waterproofing.* **2** You **enclose** something that you send with a letter or parcel, in the same envelope or package: *I enclose a copy of the book for you to study at your leisure.*

enclosure /ɪŋ'kloʊʒə(r)/ *noun*: **enclosures**
1 An **enclosure** is a small piece of land surrounded by a fence or wall: *The sheep were herded into an enclosure near the barn.* **2** (*formal*) An **enclosure** is also something sent in an envelope along with a letter.

encode /ɪŋ'koʊd/ *verb*: **encodes, encoding, encoded**
A message **is encoded** when it is expressed in the form of a code, usually so that strangers cannot understand it.

encompass /ɪŋ'kʌmpəs/ *verb*: **encompasses, encompassing, encompassed**
Something **encompasses** things that it includes, contains or covers, especially when these things are large, numerous, far apart or different from each other: *The modern art course encompasses not only painting and sculpture, but also photography, design and architecture.* □ *The region's farmland encompasses nearly five hundred square miles.*

encore /'ɒŋkɔː(r)/ *interjection*; *noun*
▻ ***interjection***
People in an audience shout **"Encore!"** at the end of a concert when they want the performer to sing an extra song or play an extra piece of music.
▻ ***noun***: **encores**
An **encore** is an extra item performed at the end of a concert, because the audience has asked for it: *Then he sang "My Way" as an encore.* □ *She played for two hours and did three encores.*

encounter /ɪŋ'kaʊntə(r)/ *verb*; *noun*
▻ ***verb***: **encounters, encountering, encountered**
1 (*formal*) You **encounter** someone when you meet them unexpectedly or for the first time: *On the train, I encountered an old man who told thrilling stories about the war.* **2** You **encounter** problems or difficulties when you experience them and have to deal with them: *I had never encountered such old-fashioned attitudes before.* [*same as* **meet with**]

▷ ***noun*: encounters**
An **encounter** is **1** an unplanned meeting, or a meeting with someone you have not met before: *Encounters with the local people confirmed that Greece was a friendly country.* **2** any meeting that involves danger or difficulty: *We had rather a frightening encounter with an angry bull.* **3** a contest between rivals or opponents: *their first encounter in a major tournament.*

encourage /ɪŋˈkʌrɪdʒ/ *verb*: **encourages, encouraging, encouraged**
1 You **encourage** someone when you make them feel confident about what they are doing or planning to do: *My parents always encouraged me in my drawing and painting.* **2** When you **encourage** someone to do something, you tell them that they should do it: *Her English teacher encouraged her to write short stories.* □ *parents who encouraged their children to smoke.* **3** An activity or practice **is encouraged** when people show that they want it to happen, or when they create a situation in which it is likely to happen: *Some teachers thought that corporal punishment encouraged violence amongst the children.* [opposite **discourage**] — *noun* (*uncount*) **encouragement:** *The pupils were not given any encouragement to read.* □ *She whispered a few words of encouragement.*

encouraging /ɪŋˈkʌrɪdʒɪŋ/ *adjective*
Something that is **encouraging** gives you confidence or hope: *We expect business to improve this year; January's sales figures were very encouraging.*

encroach /ɪŋˈkroʊtʃ/ *verb*: **encroaches, encroaching, encroached**
To **encroach** on something is gradually to grow or spread so as to take away or use up more and more of it: *The job began to encroach on my family life.* □ *Urban development has continued to encroach upon local farmland.* [*same as* **impinge**]

encumber /ɪŋˈkʌmbə(r)/ *verb* (*formal*): **encumbers, encumbering, encumbered**
Something that **encumbers** you is heavy or difficult to carry and slows your progress, or restricts you and prevents you doing what you want to do: *The children struggled through the snow, each encumbered with heavy boots and an overcoat.* □ *Holidays were impossible, the family was so encumbered by debt.* [*same as* **burden**] — *noun* **encumbrance** /ɪŋˈkʌmbrəns/: *These extra responsibilities may turn out to be more of an encumbrance than a challenge.* □ *Most of the possessions we accumulate are no more than useless encumbrances.*

encyclopaedia or **encyclopedia** /ɪnsaɪkləˈpiːdɪə/ *noun*: **encyclopaedias**
An **encyclopaedia** is a book or set of books containing information on all areas of knowledge, usually arranged in alphabetical order.

end /ɛnd/ *noun*; *verb*
▷ ***noun*: ends**
1 (*used in the singular*) The **end** of something is the point where it stops, or the part, area or period near this point: *The hero dies at the end of the film.* □ *I read the book from beginning to end without putting it down.* □ *The weather began to improve towards the end of July.* **2** The two **ends** of something long and narrow are the extreme points that are furthest away from the middle; the **end** of something long and narrow is the point furthest away from the attached point: *They sat at opposite ends of the table.* □ *with one hand clinging to the end of the rope.* **3** One or the other **end** of a scale are its extremes: *The brightest children go on to university, while at the other end of the scale some leave school unable to read.* **4** A cigarette **end** is the bit left over when the cigarette has been smoked. **5** You can refer to two people who are communicating by telephone or post as the person at one or the other **end**: *I couldn't make the woman at the other end understand.* □ *How are things at your end?* □ *It's most impolite to keep someone hanging on the end of the line.* **6** (*often in the plural*) An **end** is also a purpose or object: *She was using her influence as a committee member to gain her own private ends.* □ *Should we kill for the sake of political freedom? Does the end justify the means?* **7** (*used in the singular*) The **end** of someone or something is their downfall, destruction or death: *This latest scandal could mean the end of the government.* □ *Holmes was believed to have met a violent end at the Reichenbach Falls.*
▷ ***verb*: ends, ending, ended**
1 Something **ends**, or **is ended**, when it stops or finishes: *The play ends with everyone on stage.* □ *Term ended early because of the flu epidemic.* □ *Family gatherings tended to end with everyone quarrelling and taking sides.* □ *Even our best efforts ended in failure.* □ *The road ended half a mile from the house.* □ *We hope to find a solution that will end the bloodshed.* **2** You **end** when you finish speaking: *He ended by wishing her a happy retirement.* **3** An object **ends** in something when it has that thing as its end or tip: *The animal's scaly tail ended in a sharp point.*
▷ ***phrases*** **1** You call some activity **an end in itself** if you think it is worth doing whether or not you gain anything by it: *Language-learning is an end in itself, quite apart from the social advantages it gives you.* **2** (*informal*) You are **at a loose end** when you have nothing to do: *Join us this afternoon if you're at a loose end.* **3** Something is **at an end** when it is finished: *Our holiday was nearly at an end.* **4** Something **comes to an end** when it stops or finishes: *Several years passed before the fighting finally came to an end.* **5 In the end** means finally, after much time, activity or consideration: *In the end she decided to go to university after all.* **6** You are able to **make ends meet** if you have just enough money to buy what you need to survive. **7** (*informal*) You can use **no end** to mean 'a lot': *These changes have confused me no end.* □ *No end of people have complained about the noise.* **8** Something continues for days, weeks or months **on end** when it continues for several days, weeks or months without a pause or break: *There were periods when she didn't leave the house for days on end.* **9** To **put an end to** something is to stop it: *It's time they put an end to these abuses.*

> ***phrasal verb***
> You **end up** in a particular place or doing a particular thing when you find yourself in that place or doing that thing, especially when it was not your intention: *We took the first train that came, and ended up in Florence.* □ *The car wouldn't start, so I ended up having to walk.* □ *He ended up in a secondary school teaching computing.* [compare **land up**]

endanger /ɪnˈdeɪndʒə(r)/ *verb*: **endangers, endangering, endangered**
You **endanger** someone or something when you put them in a situation in which they might be harmed, damaged or lost: *Is the pregnant woman who smokes endangering the health of her unborn baby?* [*same as* **jeopardize**]

endangered species /ɪndeɪndʒəd ˈspiːʃɪz/ *noun*: **endangered species**
When a certain kind of animal is becoming gradually rarer, so that soon there will be none left in the world,

it is called an **endangered species**: *The whale is no longer considered an endangered species.* □ *My grandmother says that polite young men are an endangered species.*

endear /ɪn'dɪə(r)/ *verb*: **endears, endearing, endeared**
Your behaviour **endears** you to someone when it causes them to like you or feel affection for you: *His speech will not have endeared him to the voters.* — *adjective* **endearing:** *She had a very endearing way of greeting you.* — *noun* (*uncount or count*) **endearment** /ɪn'dɪəmənt/: *She smiled shyly at his whispered endearments.*

endeavour (*AmE* **endeavor**) /ɪn'dɛvə(r)/ *verb; noun*
▻ ***verb*** (*formal*): **endeavours, endeavouring, endeavoured**
You **endeavour** to do something when you try to do it, usually seriously and with effort: *The company endeavours to deal with clients' complaints as promptly as possible.* [*same as* **strive**]
▻ ***noun*** (*formal*): **endeavours**
1 (*count*) An **endeavour** is a determined attempt or effort: *In spite of their best endeavours, the whole scheme was a complete failure.* □ *They make every endeavour to treat employees fairly.* **2** (*uncount*) **Endeavour** is the energy and effort that people put into doing things: *in every field of human endeavour.*

endemic /ɛn'dɛmɪk/ *adjective* (*formal*)
A disease or other condition is **endemic** in a particular place when it regularly occurs or is found there: *Tuberculosis was once endemic in Britain.* □ *Appalling poverty is endemic in Western society.*

ending /'ɛndɪŋ/ *noun*: **endings**
An **ending** is the way a story ends: *I enjoyed the film as a whole, but would have preferred a happy ending.*

endless /'ɛndləs/ *adjective*
If you describe something as **endless** you mean that it seems to go on for ever: *The task seemed endless.* □ *Her life appeared to be an endless round of parties.* — *adverb* **endlessly:** *They argued endlessly about it.* □ *The sand stretched endlessly in all directions.*

endorse /ɪn'dɔːs/ *verb*: **endorses, endorsing, endorsed**
You **endorse** someone or something when you say openly that you support or approve of them: *The scheme was endorsed by the Prime Minister himself.* — *noun* (*uncount or count*) **endorsement:** *He gave the proposal his official endorsement.*

endow /ɪn'daʊ/ *verb*: **endows, endowing, endowed**
1 Someone or something **is endowed** with a certain quality or ability when they have it: *She was endowed with a beauty that most women dream of.* **2** Someone **endows** a school, hospital or other organization when they give a large amount of money to be spent on it. — *noun* **endowment:** *The college receives several substantial endowments from private individuals.*

endurance /ɪn'djʊərəns/ *noun* (*uncount*)
Endurance is a person's ability to survive long periods of hard physical or mental strain: *This race is a severe test of any runner's endurance.* [*same as* **stamina**]

endure /ɪn'djʊə(r)/ *verb* (*formal*): **endures, enduring, endured**
1 You **endure** something difficult or unpleasant when you tolerate it or bear it patiently: *How did they manage to endure such extreme poverty and hardship?* □ *The pain was more than I could endure.* [*same as* **put up with**] **2** Something **endures** when it lasts or continues to exist: *We all hope that peace between our nations will endure.* — *adjective* **enduring:** *his enduring youthful looks.*

enemy /'ɛnəmɪ/ *noun*: **enemies**
1 A person or thing that opposes you or acts against you in some way can be referred to as your **enemy**: *a long career during which he made many friends and more than a few enemies* □ *They view criminals as enemies of society.* **2** (*often adjectival*) In a war, the **enemy** is the nation or force that you are fighting against: *The enemy has been forced to retreat.* □ *Are the enemy clever enough to think of that?* □ *the shooting down of enemy aircraft.*

energetic /ɛnə'dʒɛtɪk/ *adjective*
1 An **energetic** person **a** is very active physically: *For an old man, he's surprisingly energetic.* **b** puts a lot of effort into what they are doing: *She's an energetic supporter of the peace movement.* **2** An **energetic** activity involves a lot of physical effort: *a less energetic pastime like chess.* [*same as* **strenuous**]

energy /'ɛnədʒɪ/ *noun* (*uncount*)
1 Someone who has a lot of **energy** can be active physically for long periods without becoming tired: *She didn't have the energy to play for much longer.* □ *Dad wouldn't have enough energy for football.* [*same as* **stamina**] **2 Energy** is also the mental effort that you put into doing something: *You would do better to direct your energy towards something more useful.* **3** The power produced by burning fuels such as coal and gas is also **energy**: *nuclear energy.*

enforce /ɪn'fɔːs/ *verb*: **enforces, enforcing, enforced**
1 A law **is enforced** when people are made to obey it: *The new regulations will be difficult to enforce.* **2** You **enforce** something when you cause it to happen by force or by making threats: *an unpleasant atmosphere of enforced silence inside the school.* — *noun* (*uncount*) **enforcement:** *Law enforcement in many areas was weak or non-existent.*

engage /ɪŋ'geɪdʒ/ *verb* (*formal*): **engages, engaging, engaged**
1 You **engage** in some activity, or you **are engaged** in it, when you do it: *He was engaged in the task of mending a fuse.* **2** You **engage** someone when you hire them to work for you: *He was engaged as stage-manager.* □ *We should perhaps engage the services of a professional accountant.* [*same as* **take on, employ, hire**] **3** You **engage** someone in conversation when you have a long talk with them, so that you take all their attention. **4** When two parts of a machine **engage** they come together to make a firm connection: *The gear was not properly engaged.* **5** Something **engages** you when it takes all your attention, concentration or interest: *You have to engage the audience's interest within the first five minutes.* [*same as* **grip**]

engaged /ɪŋ'geɪdʒd/ *adjective*
1 Two people are **engaged** when they have made a formal decision and promise to marry each other: *That was the day that we got engaged.* □ *Have you heard that they are engaged to be married?* □ *I was engaged to another man when I met your father.* **2** When a telephone line or number is **engaged**, the person you are phoning is already speaking to someone else and you cannot contact them. [*same as* **busy**] **3** A public toilet is **engaged** when it is being used by someone else.

engagement /ɪŋ'geɪdʒmənt/ *noun*: **engagements**
An **engagement** is
1 the period of time during which two people are engaged to be married: *Ours was a long engagement.* **2** a firm agreement between two people to marry each other: *We will announce our engagement at the party.* **3** (*formal*) an arrangement to do something at a particular time, made in advance: *I've cancelled all my engagements for the week.* [*same as* **appointment**]

engaging /ɪŋ'geɪdʒɪŋ/ *adjective*

Something is **engaging** when it is charming or attractive: *an engaging smile.* [*same as* **attractive, charming**]

engender /ɪn'dʒendə(r)/ *verb* (*formal*): **engenders, engendering, engendered**
Someone or something **engenders** a particular feeling, state or condition when they produce it or cause it to happen: *It is impossible to prove that watching violent films engenders violence among children.* [*same as* **generate**]

engine /'endʒɪn/ *noun*: **engines**
An **engine** is
1 a machine that turns the energy produced by burning fuel into movement, especially one that powers a vehicle: *The engine wouldn't start, which was surprising because the car was new.* [see picture at **car**] **2** the vehicle that pulls a train: *The train sat at York for half an hour while they changed engines.*

engineer /endʒɪ'nɪə(r)/ *noun*; *verb*
▷ ***noun***: **engineers**
An **engineer** is **1** a person who repairs machines or appliances of a particular kind: *a telephone engineer.* **2** (often **civil engineer**) a person who designs large structures such as roads and bridges, and supervises their construction. **3** an officer in charge of a ship's engines.
▷ ***verb***: **engineers, engineering, engineered**
You **engineer** something when you cause it to happen after careful and usually secret planning: *They discovered that he had engineered the whole affair.* [*same as* **contrive, orchestrate**]

engineering /endʒɪ'nɪərɪŋ/ *noun* (*uncount*)
Engineering is the profession or work of any kind of engineer: *a career in electrical engineering.*

English /'ɪŋglɪʃ/ *adjective*; *noun*
▷ ***adjective***
English means concerned with or belonging to England, or to its people or their language: *the English countryside* □ *This is typical of English behaviour.* □ *the grammar of the English language.*
▷ ***noun***
1 (*uncount*) **English** is the main language of Britain, North America and Australia, and an official language in some other countries: *She speaks English very well.* □ *He tried to translate it into English.* **2** (*plural*) The **English** are the people of England.

Englishman /'ɪŋglɪʃmən/ *noun*: **Englishmen**
An **Englishman** is a man who comes from England, or who has English parents.

engrave /ɪŋ'greɪv/ *verb*: **engraves, engraving, engraved**
1 Someone **engraves** a design on a surface when they cut away pieces of the surface to form the design: *The tombstone was simply engraved with his name.* **2** You say that something **is engraved** on your mind when it is firmly fixed in your mind and will never be forgotten: *The look of hatred on his face is engraved on my memory for ever.* [*same as* **etch**]

engraving /ɪŋ'greɪvɪŋ/ *noun*: **engravings**
An **engraving** is a design cut into a surface, or a picture printed from a metal plate with a design cut into it.

engrossed /ɪŋ'groʊst/ *adjective*
You are **engrossed** in something when it holds your attention and interest completely: *He was engrossed in the film.* [*same as* **absorbed, riveted**]

engulf /ɪŋ'gʌlf/ *verb* (*literary*): **engulfs, engulfing, engulfed**
1 One thing **engulfs** another when it surrounds and covers it completely, so that it can no longer be seen: *The whole street was engulfed in thick fog.* □ *Each wave seemed to about to engulf the ship.* **2** Something such as an emotion **engulfs** you when it occupies your mind or senses completely: *Despair engulfed him.*

enhance /ɪn'hɑːns/ *verb*: **enhances, enhancing, enhanced**
To **enhance** something is to improve it: *This will certainly enhance your promotion prospects.* □ *The design would be enhanced by the addition of a decorative border.* [*same as* **improve, increase**]

enigma /ɪ'nɪgmə/ *noun*: **enigmas**
A person, thing or event that is mysterious or difficult to understand is sometimes referred to as an **enigma**: *Her death remains an enigma.* [*same as* **mystery**]

enigmatic /enɪg'matɪk/ *adjective*
Someone or something described as **enigmatic** is mysterious or difficult to understand: *As usual, the enigmatic Mr Jones revealed nothing.* [*same as* **mysterious**] *— adverb* **enigmatically:** *He smiled enigmatically.*

enjoy /ɪn'dʒɔɪ/ *verb*: **enjoys, enjoying, enjoyed**
1 You **enjoy** something when you get pleasure from doing it or experiencing it: *I'd always enjoyed dancing.* □ *I really didn't enjoy that film.* □ *Sketching portraits is something she very much enjoys doing.* **2** You **enjoy** yourself when you have fun, or do things that give you pleasure: *We all thoroughly enjoyed ourselves at the beach.* **3** (*formal*) You **enjoy** a benefit or advantage if you are lucky enough to have it: *Until his final few years he had enjoyed continual good health.* □ *We still enjoy the benefit of a free education.* □ *The Scillies enjoy a mild climate throughout the year. — noun* (*uncount or count*) **enjoyment:** *She got great enjoyment out of watching television.* □ *I hope the poor recording didn't spoil your enjoyment of the music.* □ *They have so few enjoyments left in life.*

enjoyable /ɪn'dʒɔɪəbəl/ *adjective*
Something is **enjoyable** when you enjoy doing it or experiencing it: *I find reading very enjoyable.* □ *That was a very enjoyable concert.*

enlarge /ɪn'lɑːdʒ/ *verb*: **enlarges, enlarging, enlarged**
1 You **enlarge** something when you make it bigger: *The car park will have to be enlarged.* **2** When a photograph **is enlarged** a second print of it is made, bigger than the original. [*same as* **blow up**] **3** When something **enlarges** it becomes bigger: *The hole had enlarged, and water was now running through.*

> ***phrasal verb***
> (*formal*) You **enlarge on** or **upon** something when you say or write more about it, giving further details: *He was asked to enlarge on his plans.* [*same as* **expand on**]

enlargement /ɪn'lɑːdʒmənt/ *noun*: **enlargements**
1 An **enlargement** is a photograph that is bigger than the original. **2** (*uncount*) **Enlargement** is the process of enlarging something or the increase in its size after it has been enlarged.

enlighten /ɪn'laɪtən/ *verb* (*formal*): **enlightens, enlightening, enlightened**
You **enlighten** someone when you explain something that they do not know or understand, or when you correct their false beliefs: *Perhaps you will allow me to enlighten you. — adjective* **enlightening:** *a most enlightening lecture. — noun* (*uncount*) **enlightenment:** *He looked up the word in his father's dictionary, but found little enlightenment there.*

enlightened /ɪn'laɪtənd/ *adjective* (*formal*)
An **enlightened** person has attitudes that are regarded by people in modern society as sensible, right and fair: *a company with very enlightened working practices.*

enlist /ɪn'lɪst/ *verb*: **enlists, enlisting, enlisted**
1 People **enlist**, or they **are enlisted**, when they join one of the armed forces: *Most of my friends have enlisted in the air force.* [*same as* **join up**] **2** You **enlist** someone, or **enlist** their help, when you get them to help you: *We managed to enlist the support of some very influential people.*

enliven /ɪn'laɪvən/ *verb* (*formal*): **enlivens, enlivening, enlivened**
Something that **enlivens** an occasion makes it more lively or cheerful: *A little music might enliven the evening.* [*same as* **liven up**]

en masse /ɒn 'mas/ *adverb*
When several people do something **en masse**, they do it together, as a group: *The directors resigned en masse.*

enmity /'ɛnmɪtɪ/ *noun* (*uncount*)
Enmity is a feeling of strong dislike or hatred towards someone: *There was distrust and enmity between the two communities.* □ *the open expression of hostility and enmity towards the Jews.*

enormity /ɪ'nɔːmɪtɪ/ *noun* (*uncount*)
1 (*formal*) **Enormity** is the quality of being evil or wicked: *It was clear that he could not appreciate the enormity of his crime.* **2** Some people use **enormity** to mean the quality of being enormous or great in size: *I felt more and oppressed by the enormity of the task I'd undertaken.*

enormous /ɪ'nɔːməs/ *adjective*
Something is **enormous** when it is extremely large in size, amount or extent: *an enormous house in the country* □ *She inherited an enormous fortune.* □ *The play was an enormous success.* [*same as* **huge, immense**] — *adverb* **enormously**: *We are enormously grateful.* □ *The amount of work has increased enormously.* □ (*intensifying*) *She's become enormously fat.*

enough /ɪ'nʌf/ *determiner; pronoun; adverb*
▻ ***determiner***
1 Enough is as much or as many as you need or want: *We had only enough food for four people.* □ *Do you have enough knives and forks?* □ *We haven't been given enough data.* □ *Were there enough pencils to go round?* □ *The guilty look on her face was evidence enough.* [*same as* **sufficient**] **2 Enough** can mean as much or as many as can be borne or tolerated, so that any more will make the situation worse: *I've got enough troubles of my own without having to listen to yours.*
▻ ***pronoun:*** *Here are the plates; tell me if there aren't enough.* □ *Has everyone got enough to eat?* □ *There weren't enough of them to form a team.* □ *Can't you attend to that yourself? I've got enough on my mind.* □ *This is enough of a problem without you making it worse.* □ *That's enough of your cheek!*
▻ ***adverb***
1 Enough is used after adjectives, verbs and other adverbs to mean to the extent needed or wanted: *Are you sure those shoes are wide enough?* □ *Would this be a big enough hall for your classes?* □ *She's old enough to realize what's happening.* □ *I obviously didn't impress the selectors enough to be picked.* □ *Some work too hard, some don't work hard enough.* □ *We don't go far enough in trying to stop young people smoking.* **2 Enough** can mean to an extent that is as much as can be borne or tolerated: *Things are bad enough already.* □ *He was conceited enough before he got promoted.* **3 Enough** used after adjectives and adverbs also means 'quite' or 'fairly': *She's pretty enough, I suppose.* □ *He's a nice enough fellow.* **4** You often use **enough** after sentence adverbs such as *funnily* or *strangely*, which gives them slight emphasis: *Oddly enough, I can't remember his name now.* □ *Interestingly enough, her birthday is the same day as mine.*
▻ ***phrases*** **1** You say '**enough is enough**', or '**that's enough**' if you don't want something that is happening to continue: *That's enough now! Be quiet!* **2** For **fair enough** see **fair**. **3** When you say that you **have had enough**, you mean that you cannot bear the situation you are in any longer: *I've had enough of this; I'm going home.* □ *I've had enough of her complaints.* **4** For **sure enough** see **sure**.

enquire see **inquire**.

enquiry see **inquiry**.

enrage /ɪn'reɪdʒ/ *verb*: **enrages, enraging, enraged**
Something **enrages** you when it makes you very angry: *She was enraged by his irresponsible attitude.* [*same as* **incense**] — *adjective* **enraged:** *They received letters of complaint from enraged customers.*

enrich /ɪn'rɪtʃ/ *verb*: **enriches, enriching, enriched**
1 Something **is enriched** when it is improved by having things added to it: *The discovery that she enjoys reading has enriched her life.* **2** (*formal*) To **enrich** someone is to make them richer or wealthier: *trade that would enrich the nation.* — *adjective* **enriched:** *a vitamin-enriched breakfast drink.* — *noun* (*uncount*) **enrichment:** *After five years of marriage baby Calum arrived, to the great enrichment of both their lives.*

en route /ɒn 'ruːt/ *adverb*
When you are **en route** to somewhere you are travelling there, and when something happens **en route** it happens during the journey: *We had something to eat en route.* [*same as* **on the way, in transit**]

ensemble /ɒn'sɒmbəl/ *noun*: **ensembles**
An **ensemble** is **1** (*formal*) a number of things considered as a group or as a single item: *You couldn't add anything else without spoiling the look of the whole ensemble.* **2** a small group of musicians who regularly perform together: *They are one of the world's most talented ensembles.*

enshrined /ɪn'ʃraɪnd/ *adjective* (*formal*)
Something, such as a person's right to do something, is **enshrined** in law when it forms an official part of the law and cannot be ignored: *The freedom of the press is enshrined in our nation's constitution.*

ensue /ɪn'sjuː/ *verb* (*formal*): **ensues, ensuing, ensued**
Something **ensues** when it happens immediately after something else, often as a result of it: *I wished I had not stayed to witness the argument that ensued.* [*same as* **follow, result**] — *adjective* **ensuing:** *Several people were injured in the ensuing riots.*

ensure /ɪn'ʃʊə(r)/ *verb*: **ensures, ensuring, ensured**
You **ensure** something, or **ensure** that it happens, when you make it certain to be achieved or obtained, or certain to happen: *This new treaty will ensure peace between the nations.* □ *No amount of locks and alarms can ensure that your house will not be burgled.* [*same as* **guarantee**]

entail /ɪn'teɪl/ *verb*: **entails, entailing, entailed**
When doing something **entails** something else, it makes something else necessary; when you want to know what something **entails**, you want to know what is involved in doing or having it: *Accepting the new job would entail moving house.* □ *He took on the new post without having the faintest idea of what it entailed.* [*same as* **involve**]

entangled /ɪn'taŋgəld/ *adjective*
1 Something becomes **entangled** in something else, such as a net, when it becomes tied up and cannot easily get free: *Her foot got entangled in the rope.* **2** You are **entangled** in problems or difficulties when you cannot easily solve them or escape from them: *The company was entangled in a serious financial crisis.* **3** When you are **entangled** with someone, the relation-

ship that you have with them causes you difficulties that you cannot easily escape from: *I don't know how he managed to get himself entangled with criminals.* [*same as* **tangle up**]

enter /'ɛntə(r)/ *verb*: **enters, entering, entered**
1 You **enter** a place when you come or go into it: *She had just entered the building.* □ *No sooner had I knocked than a loud voice shouted, 'Enter!'* □ *The door opened and Phil entered.* **2** You **enter** a contest, or you **enter** for it, when you state formally that you want to take part: *She has entered for the cycle race.* □ *I entered two of my photographs in the competition.* **3** You **enter** something when you write it in a book, or key it into a computer, as a record: *She entered the day's figures into the cash book.* **4** When you **enter** an organization you join it as a member; you **enter** a profession or area of activity when you become involved in it: *I entered university just before my eighteenth birthday.* □ *That was before she entered the shallow world of show business.* **5** When a particular quality **enters** something, it becomes noticeable within it: *An atmosphere of hostility has entered the discussions.* □ *Bitterness had suddenly entered his voice.* **6** Something **enters** a new period when its situation changes and different circumstances begin to affect it: *The whole nation entered a period of social and political chaos.* **7** It **enters** your head to do something when you think of doing it: *It never entered her head to invite her parents.* □ *'Do you think he will be offended?' 'The thought never entered my head'.*

phrasal verb
enter into 1 You **enter into** something, such as discussions or an agreement, when you begin it or start being involved in it: *We have no intention of entering into negotiations with the management.* **2** When something **enters into** a situation, it affects the situation or has an influence on it: *I hired her because she's good; our friendship never entered into it.*

enterprise /'ɛntəpraɪz/ *noun*: **enterprises**
1 An **enterprise** is **a** a company or business firm: *the owners of several industrial enterprises* □ *a letter from Shawlands Steel Enterprises.* **b** a new and uncertain project or activity: *Have you heard about their latest money-making enterprise?* [*same as* **venture**] **2** (*uncount*) **Enterprise** is **a** the ability to think of new ideas and the willingness to use new methods: *a young woman full of enterprise.* [*same as* **initiative**] **b** the way that business and industry is organized within a country or a society: *a combination of state ownership and private enterprise.*

enterprising /'ɛntəpraɪzɪŋ/ *adjective*
An **enterprising** person has the ability to think of new ideas and is willing to try new methods.

entertain /ɛntə'teɪn/ *verb*: **entertains, entertaining, entertained**
1 You **entertain** someone when you do things that amuse or interest them, whether as a professional performer or simply for fun: *Several well-known singers were sent to entertain the troops.* □ *He entertained his friends with stories from his childhood.* **2** To **entertain**, or **entertain** someone, is to invite someone to your house for a meal or a drink, or to pay for their evening out at a restaurant, theatre, *etc*: *They are a couple who never entertain.* □ *My husband is in the kitchen; we are entertaining the Smiths this evening.* □ *My wife is entertaining some important clients at the opera.* **3** (*formal*) Someone refuses to **entertain** an idea or suggestion when they are not willing even to consider it or think about it: *Why had I entertained the thought of taking a holiday; it was a stupid idea!* [compare **contemplate**]

entertainer /ɛntə'teɪnə(r)/ *noun*: **entertainers**
An **entertainer** is a person who entertains people professionally, *eg* by singing or telling jokes.

entertaining /ɛntə'teɪnɪŋ/ *adjective*
Someone or something that is **entertaining** gives people pleasure or amusement: *His stories were richly entertaining.* □ *We had a most entertaining evening.*

entertainment /ɛntə'teɪnmənt/ *noun*: **entertainments**
1 (*uncount, often adjectival*) **Entertainment** is performances and activities that amuse and interest people: *She works in the entertainment business.* □ *What entertainment have you got planned for this evening?* **2** An **entertainment** is a performance or activity organized for the public: *The library has a list of local entertainments.*

enthral (*AmE* **enthrall**) /ɪn'θrɔ:l/ *verb*: **enthrals** (*AmE* **enthralls**), **enthralling, enthralled**
You **enthral** someone when you hold their interest, attention or imagination completely: *an actor who is enthralling audiences all over the country* □ *They listened enthralled to his wartime stories.* [*same as* **captivate**] — *adjective* **enthralling:** *an enthralling performance.*

enthuse /ɪn'θju:z/ *verb*: **enthuses, enthusing, enthused**
You **enthuse** over something, or **enthuse** about it, when you speak or write excitedly about how much you like or enjoy it: *'Great dance!' she enthused, smiling at him.*

enthusiasm /ɪn'θju:zɪazm/ *noun* (*uncount*)
Enthusiasm is lively or passionate interest in something or eagerness to do or have something: *Her enthusiasm for the job was not diminished.* □ *They reacted with enthusiasm when I mentioned ice cream.*

enthusiast /ɪn'θju:zɪast/ *noun*: **enthusiasts**
An **enthusiast** is a person who is passionately interested in a particular activity or subject: *Dad is a great cricket enthusiast.* [*same as* **fan**]

enthusiastic /ɪnθju:zɪ'astɪk/ *adjective*
You are **enthusiastic** about something when you are eager to do or have it, or when you show that you like it very much: *He didn't sound very enthusiastic when I told him about the trip.* □ *There was an enthusiastic response from most of the members.* [*same as* **keen**] — *adverb* **enthusiastically:** *They reacted enthusiastically when she told them her news.*

entice /ɪn'taɪs/ *verb*: **entices, enticed, enticing**
You **entice** someone into doing something or going somewhere when you tempt or persuade them by showing or promising something desirable: *She was enticed into the shop by the lovely window display.* □ *It is hoped that the new maternity arrangements will entice young mothers back to work.* [*same as* **lure**]

enticing /ɪn'taɪsɪŋ/ *adjective*
Something **enticing** is very appealing or attractive and difficult to resist or refuse: *an enticing proposal.* [*same as* **attractive, beguiling**]

entire /ɪn'taɪə(r)/ *adjective*
Entire is used before a noun to mean whole, complete or absolute: *You have the trust of the entire management team.* □ *The entire factory was destroyed.* □ *There is entire agreement between the two sides.* [compare **whole, complete, absolute, total**]

entirely /ɪn'taɪəlɪ/ *adverb*
Entirely means wholly, fully or absolutely: *I entirely agree with you.* □ *It was not entirely true.* □ *It's his responsibility entirely.* [compare **completely, totally, utterly, absolutely**]

entirety /ɪn'taɪərətɪ/ *noun (uncount)*
When you refer to something in its **entirety**, you are considering it as a single item rather than a set of separate parts: *We must examine the plan in its entirety.* □ *The art collection is to be sold in its entirety.*

entitle /ɪn'taɪtəl/ *verb*: **entitles, entitling, entitled**
1 You **are entitled** to do or receive something when you have the right to do or receive it: *Junior members of staff are only entitled to 22 days holiday a year.* □ *Special membership entitles you to play without booking in advance.* [*same as* **allow**] **2** The title of something such as a book or film is what it **is entitled**: *His latest exhibition of photographs is entitled 'American Life'.* [*same as* **call**]

entitlement /ɪn'taɪtəlmənt/ *noun (uncount)*
1 Your **entitlement** to do or receive something is your right to do or receive it: *This will not affect their entitlement to welfare benefit.* **2** Your **entitlement** is also what you have the right to do or receive: *A day taken off due to illness will not count as part of your holiday entitlement.*

entity /'ɛntɪtɪ/ *noun (formal)*: **entities**
An **entity** is something that has its own separate identity and is not simply part of another thing: *The companies share the same building but they are separate commercial entities.*

entomology /ɛntə'mɒlədʒɪ/ *noun (uncount)*
Entomology is the scientific study of insects: *a biologist specializing in entomology.*

entourage /'ɒntʊrɑːʒ/ *noun*: **entourages**
The **entourage** of a famous or important person is the group of followers or assistants that usually accompany them: *a party attended by the film star and his entourage.*

entrails /'ɛntreɪlz/ *noun (plural)*
The **entrails** of a person or animal are their intestines.

entrance[1] /'ɛntrəns/ *noun*: **entrances**
1 An **entrance** is a way in, such as a door or gate: *We met at the main entrance to the stadium.* **2** *(formal)* Someone's **entrance** is the way they arrive, or the fact that they have arrived: *She made her usual grand entrance down the spiral stair.* □ *A man in a suit announced my entrance to the rest of the guests.* [*same as* **entry**] **3** *(uncount)* You gain **entrance** to a place when you go in or you are allowed in: *They refused me entrance to the restaurant because I wasn't wearing a tie.* □ *She claims she was denied entrance to the medical profession because of her criminal record.* [*same as* **entry**]

entrance[2] /ɪn'trɑːns/ *verb (usually in the passive)*: **entrances, entrancing, entranced**
You **are entranced** by something that you find charming or delightful: *The audience was entranced by her beautiful singing.* [*same as* **enchant, bewitch**]

entrant /'ɛntrənt/ *noun*: **entrants**
An **entrant** is a person who enters a competition or contest, or someone who becomes a member of a profession or an institution, such as a college or university.

entreat /ɪn'triːt/ *verb (formal)*: **entreats, entreating, entreated**
You **entreat** someone to do something important or essential when you ask them to do it with urgency and desperation in your voice: *She entreated him to leave the gun behind.* [*same as* **beg, implore**] — *noun* **entreaty:** *He left that day, despite Anna's passionate entreaties.*

entrenched /ɪn'trɛntʃt/ *adjective (formal)*
When something, such as an idea or custom, is **entrenched** it is fixed or established firmly and would be very difficult to change or get rid of: *deeply entrenched racist attitudes.* [*same as* **embedded**]

entrepreneur /ɒntrəprə'nɜː(r)/ *noun*: **entrepreneurs**
An **entrepreneur** is a person who starts a business or businesses using their own ideas and usually their own money.

entrust /ɪn'trʌst/ *verb*: **entrusts, entrusting, entrusted**
You **entrust** someone with something important or valuable, or you **entrust** it to them, when you give them the responsibility of dealing with it or taking care of it: *I wouldn't entrust my child's education to such incompetent teachers.* □ *She was entrusted with the task of finding partners for everyone.*

entry /'ɛntrɪ/ *noun*: **entries**
1 An **entry** is **a** a piece of work, such as a painting or a photograph, that you enter in a competition: *The winning entries will be displayed in the local museum.* **b** a single item of recorded information, such as in a diary, a computer or a dictionary: *She read again the entry for 25 November.* **2** *(uncount)* You are allowed **entry** to a place when you are allowed to go in or to join as a member: *She was refused entry to the country because she didn't have a visa.* [*same as* **entrance**] **3** *(uncount)* **Entry** is also the act of going in or becoming a member: *Everyone in court stood up at the entry of the judge.* [*same as* **entrance**]

entwine /ɪn'twaɪn/ *verb*: **entwines, entwining, entwined**
Two or more things **are entwined** when they are curled round each other like pieces of rope: *They sat quietly on the bench with their arms entwined.*

enumerate /ɪ'njuːməreɪt/ *verb (formal)*: **enumerates, enumerating, enumerated**
You **enumerate** several things when you list them one by one: *She began to enumerate all the things she disliked about him.* [*same as* **list**]

enunciate /ɪ'nʌnsɪeɪt/ *verb*: **enunciates, enunciating, enunciated**
1 You **enunciate** a word when you pronounce it clearly: *Not all actors enunciate well.* **2** *(formal)* When you **enunciate** an idea you express it clearly: *an interview during which the minister enunciated government policy on the issue.* [same as **articulate**]

envelop /ɪn'vɛləp/ *verb*: **envelops, enveloping, enveloped**
Something **envelops** something else when it surrounds or covers it completely like a blanket: *The lake was enveloped in mist.* [*same as* **engulf**]

envelope /'ɛnvəloʊp/ *noun*: **envelopes**
An **envelope** is a thin flat rectangular paper packet in which a letter or card is sent by post: *The envelope is still sealed; nobody has opened it.* [see picture at **office**]

envious /'ɛnvɪəs/ *adjective*
You are **envious** of someone who has something that you would like for yourself: *It was hard not to be envious of such a beautiful woman.* □ *I'm not the least bit envious of his fame and wealth.* [compare **jealous**] — *adverb* **enviously:** *Enviously he watched the walkers depart, and returned to his studies.*

environment /ɪn'vaɪərənmənt/ *noun*: **environments**
1 Someone's **environment** is a combination of the surroundings and the conditions that they live or work in: *The hotel provides a quiet, restful environment for our guests to relax in.* **2** *(used in the singular)* The **environment** is the combination of elements, such as the air, plants, animals and rivers, that make up the natural world around us: *the release of chemicals that damage and destroy the environment.*

environmental /ɪnvaɪərən'mɛntəl/ *adjective*
Environmental means relating to or concerned with the environment: *an unacceptable level of environmen-*

tal damage □ *She's an expert on environmental issues.* — *adverb* **environmentally:** *environmentally friendly consumer products.*

environmentalist /ɪnvaɪərən'mɛntəlɪst/ *noun*: **environmentalists**
An **environmentalist** is a person who works to protect or preserve the natural world, or a person who supports such work.

environs /ɪn'vaɪərənz/ *noun* (*plural; formal*)
The **environs** of a town or city are the areas that surround it: *Manchester and its environs.*

envisage /ɪn'vɪzɪdʒ/ *verb*: **envisages, envisaging, envisages**
You **envisage** something when you imagine it, or when you think it is likely to happen in the future: *I tried to envisage a life without Lily.* □ *We don't envisage being able to borrow more money.*

envoy /'ɛnvɔɪ/ *noun*: **envoys**
An **envoy** is a government official sent abroad to meet with a foreign government: *the United Nations envoy to Bosnia.*

envy /'ɛnvɪ/ *noun; verb*
▻ ***noun*** (*uncount*)
1 Envy is the feeling of wanting what someone else has: *She kissed him warmly on the lips, while the other men looked on with envy.* **2** Something you have is the **envy** of other people when they want to have it; you are the **envy** of other people when you have something that they would like: *Her large, airy office was the envy of all the other managers.*
▻ ***verb***: **envies, envying, envied**
You **envy** someone when you want for yourself something that they have: *Many people said they envied him, but few would enjoy his lifestyle.* □ *I think she envies us our success.*

ephemeral /ɪ'fɛmərəl/ *adjective* (*literary*)
Something is **ephemeral** when it lasts for a very short time only: *the ephemeral nature of life's pleasures* □ *But his success as a pop singer was ephemeral.* [*same as* **fleeting, transient, short-lived**]

epic /'ɛpɪk/ *noun; adjective*
▻ ***noun***: **epics**
An **epic** is a long book, poem or film that describes great events such as wars.
▻ ***adjective***
An **epic** story deals with great events or exciting adventures: *the family's epic journey across an entire continent.*

epidemic /ɛpɪ'dɛmɪk/ *noun*: **epidemics**
An **epidemic** is a sudden and widespread outbreak of a disease: *The whole country was in the grip of a flu epidemic.* □ *an epidemic of meningitis.*

epilepsy /'ɛpɪlɛpsɪ/ *noun* (*uncount*)
Epilepsy is a medical condition that attacks the sufferer only occasionally, causing him or her to lose consciousness and make violent uncontrolled body movements: *She suffers from epilepsy.*

epileptic /ɛpɪ'lɛptɪk/ *adjective; noun*
▻ ***adjective***
1 Someone who is **epileptic** suffers from epilepsy. **2 Epileptic** also means caused by epilepsy: *an epileptic fit.*
▻ ***noun***: **epileptics**
An **epileptic** is a person who suffers from epilepsy.

epilogue (*AmE* **epilog**) /'ɛpɪlɒg/ *noun*: **epilogues**
An **epilogue** is a short concluding passage or scene at the end of a book, play or film.

episode /'ɛpɪsoʊd/ *noun*: **episodes**
An **episode** is **1** an important or memorable event or period of time: *an embarrassing episode from his past.* **2** one of the individual programmes that make up a series on radio or television: *Tonight's episode is called 'Kiss of the Enemy'.*

epistle /ɪ'pɪsəl/ *noun* (*literary or humorous*): **epistles**
An **epistle** is a letter, especially a long one dealing with important matters.

epitaph /'ɛpɪtɑːf/ *noun*: **epitaphs**
An **epitaph** is the short description of a dead person written on their gravestone, or a short speech or poem about them.

epitome /ɪ'pɪtəmɪ/ *noun* (*used in the singular*)
You say that someone or something is the **epitome** of a thing when you think they are a perfect example of that thing: *His mother was the epitome of kindness.* □ *The new cathedral is the epitome of '90s architecture.* [*same as* **embodiment**]

epitomize or **epitomise** /ɪ'pɪtəmaɪz/ *verb*: **epitomizes, epitomizing, epitomized**
Someone or something that **epitomizes** a thing is a perfect or typical example of that thing: *Her designs epitomize elegance and good taste.*

epoch /'iːpɒk/ *noun* (*formal*): **epochs**
An **epoch** is one of the periods that history can be divided into, whose beginning or end represented an important change: *Our nation stands at the dawn of a new epoch.*

equal /'iːkwəl/ *adjective; noun; verb*
▻ ***adjective***
1 Several things are **equal**, or one thing is **equal** to another, if they are the same in size, amount or value: *Each partner will receive an equal share of the profits.* □ *The cars are equal in price.* □ *All three issues are of equal importance.* □ *The women say they do the same work as the men and are demanding equal pay.* **2** Different groups of people are **equal** when they have the same rights or the same status within society as each other: *God created all men equal.* **3** (*formal*) You are **equal** to a task when you have the ability, strength or courage to deal with it successfully: *This is a difficult problem, but I'm confident that she's equal to it.* [*same as* **up to**]
▻ ***noun***: **equals**
Someone who is your **equal** is the same as you, especially if they have the same rights or abilities as you, or if they deserve the same respect: *Management and workers are treated as equals.*
▻ ***verb***: **equals, equalling** (*AmE* **equaling**), **equalled** (*AmE* **equaled**)
1 When two sets of numbers or mathematical symbols **equal** each other they have the same value: *If 3y equals 6, what does y equal?* □ *Five times five equals twenty five.* **2** To **equal** someone or something is to match them or be as good as them: *No other dancer equals her for sheer passion.*

equality /ɪ'kwɒlɪtɪ/ *noun* (*uncount*)
Equality within a group or society is equal treatment for all the people in it: *a political party campaigning for racial equality* □ *We want equality of opportunity for children from all social backgrounds.* [*opposite* **inequality**]

equally /'iːkwəlɪ/ *adverb*
1 Equally means **a** in parts or amounts of the same size or value as each other: *Profits will be divided equally between the partners.* □ *They shared the responsibility equally.* **b** to the same degree or extent as each other: *Both women are equally capable of doing the job.* □ *I agree that he's an excellent painter, but his father was equally talented.* **2** (*sentence adverb*) **Equally** is used to introduce a second comment which is of equal

importance to the first: *Surgery is an important way of preserving life, but equally, many people still feel uneasy about the idea of surgeons playing God.*

equate /ɪ'kweɪt/ *verb*: **equates, equating, equated**
You **equate** one thing with another when you regard both things as being the same: *Most people make the mistake of equating fame and wealth with happiness.*

equation /ɪ'kweɪʒən/ *noun*: **equations**
An **equation** is a mathematical expression stating that two quantities or groups of symbols have the same value as each other: *He wrote on the board the equation $3x = 2y$.*

equator /ɪ'kweɪtə(r)/ *noun* (*used in the singular*)
The **equator** is an imaginary line, or a line drawn on a map, that passes round the middle of the Earth at an equal distance from the North and South poles: *The ship sailed across the equator into the southern hemisphere.*

equatorial /ɛkwə'tɔːrɪəl/ *adjective*
Equatorial refers to areas of land, and weather conditions, around the equator: *my first visit to equatorial Africa.*

equestrian /ɪ'kwɛstrɪən/ *adjective* (*technical*)
Equestrian means connected with horse-riding: *He's a great fan of equestrian sports.*

equi- /ɛkwɪ/ *prefix*
Equi- is used before adjectives and adverbs to mean 'equal' or 'equally': *The two houses are roughly equidistant from the town centre.*

equilibrium /ɛkwɪ'lɪbrɪəm/ *noun* (*uncount; formal*)
Equilibrium is a state of balance between weights, forces or influences, so that there is no movement or change: *A long period of strikes and civil unrest was followed by a kind of political equilibrium.*

equinox /'ɛkwɪnɒks/ *noun*: **equinoxes**
The **equinoxes** are the two occasions in the year when night and day are the same length: *The spring equinox occurs around 21 March.*

equip /ɪ'kwɪp/ *verb*: **equips, equipping, equipped**
1 You **are equipped** with something you need to do a particular job when you are provided with it: *They had equipped themselves with maps and compasses.* □ *Most new cars are equipped with a security alarm.* [*same as* **kit out, fit**] **2** Your past experiences **equip** you for a particular situation when they make you capable of dealing with it: *His years as a boxer have equipped him well for the aggressive world of big business.* □ *Her loving but over-protective parents had left her ill equipped to face life on her own.* [*same as* **prepare**]

equipment /ɪ'kwɪpmənt/ *noun* (*uncount*)
Equipment consists of the things you need to carry out a particular kind of work or activity: *She sells office equipment.* □ *The amplifier is an expensive piece of equipment.*

equivalent /ɪ'kwɪvələnt/ *adjective; noun*
▷ ***adjective***
Two or more things are **equivalent** when they are the same, *eg* in value, quality or meaning: *The equivalent house in Scotland would cost you £20000 less.* □ *The French expression 'Santé!' is equivalent to the English 'Good health!'.*
▷ ***noun***: **equivalents**
Something that is the **equivalent** of something else is the same as it: *an Arabic term for which there is no English equivalent.*

equivocal /ɪ'kwɪvəkəl/ *adjective* (*formal*)
You are **equivocal** when you give a vague or unclear answer or comment because you do not want to tell the truth: *The minister was frustratingly equivocal on the issue.* □ *She made some fairly equivocal remarks.* [*same as* **ambiguous, vague;** opposite **unequivocal**]

era /'ɪərə/ *noun*: **eras**
An **era** is one of the periods that history can be divided into, whose beginning or end represented an important change: *The break-up of the Soviet Union marks a new era in world politics.*

eradicate /ɪ'radɪkeɪt/ *verb* (*formal*): **eradicates, eradicating, eradicated**
You **eradicate** something when you get rid of it completely: *Poverty is proving hard to eradicate.* □ *They introduced the scheme in an attempt to eradicate underage drinking.* — *noun* (*uncount*) **eradication** /ɪradɪ'keɪʃən/: *We are working towards the eradication of all such illnesses.*

erase /ɪ'reɪz/ *verb*: **erases, erasing, erased**
1 You **erase** writing or a mark when you make it disappear by rubbing it with a rubber or some other device. [*same as* **rub out**] **2** You **erase** something such as a memory or a problem when you destroy or remove it: *She would never be able to erase the memory of that horrific event.*

eraser /ɪ'reɪzə(r)/ *noun* (*especially AmE*)
An **eraser** is a piece of rubber for removing writing from a page. [*same as* **rubber**; see picture at **office**]

erect /ɪ'rɛkt/ *adjective; verb*
▷ ***adjective***
1 You are **erect**, or you stand **erect**, when you stand up straight, rather than bending or leaning. **2** A part of the body, such as a dog's ears or a man's penis, is **erect** when it is stiff and sticking up.
▷ ***verb*** (*formal*): **erects, erecting, erected**
1 A building or other structure **is erected** when it is built or put up: *There are plans to erect a new monument in the school.* □ *We will erect the tent over there.* **2** Something such as an organization **is erected** when it is set up or established: *Our plan was to erect a worldwide network of healthcare institutions.*

erection /ɪ'rɛkʃən/ *noun*: **erections**
1 (*uncount*) The **erection** of a building or other structure is the act of building it or putting it up: *Fire destroyed the temple shortly after its erection.* **2** A man has an **erection** when his penis is erect through sexual excitement **3** (*formal*) People sometimes refer to a building or other structure as an **erection**: *It is, after all, a most hideous erection.*

erode /ɪ'roʊd/ *verb*: **erodes, eroding, eroded**
1 Something such as soil or rock **erodes** or **is eroded** when it is worn away gradually by the force of the sea, wind or rain: *The clifftops are slowly eroding.* **2** (*formal*) When something such as your confidence **erodes** or **is eroded** it becomes gradually weaker until it disappears completely: *Support for the proposal has significantly eroded.* [*same as* **dwindle**]

erosion /ɪ'roʊʒən/ *noun* (*uncount*)
1 Erosion is the gradual wearing away of soil or rock by the force of the sea, wind or rain. **2** The **erosion** of something such as your confidence, or your freedom, is its gradual reduction until it disappears completely: *the erosion of the citizen's right to freedom of speech.*

erotic /ɪ'rɒtɪk/ *adjective*
Something that is **erotic** involves or describes sexual pleasure, or causes you to feel sexual desire: *a collection of erotic poems* □ *a profoundly erotic experience.* — *adverb* **erotically**: *In the film, she dances erotically in front of a crowd of soldiers.*

err /ɜː(r)/ *verb* (*formal*): **errs, erring, erred**
You **err** when you make a mistake or do something

wrong: *I realised that I had erred in thinking him an arrogant man.*

▻ ***phrase*** When someone **errs on the side of** caution, they choose to act too cautiously rather than make mistakes by not being cautious enough: *I would prefer to err on the side of generosity than have other people think I'm mean.*

errand /ˈɛrənd/ *noun*: **errands**
You go on an **errand**, or run an **errand**, when you make a short journey in order to get or do something for someone else; when you have **errands** to do, you are usually doing them for yourself: *My mum gave me a few errands to do in the town.*

erratic /ɪˈratɪk/ *adjective*
Something that is **erratic** is not regular or predictable and changes unexpectedly: *The ship has been forced to steer a rather erratic course.* □ *She's a little too erratic to be a championship player.* — *adverb* **erratically:** *She was inclined to behave erratically.*

erroneous /ɪˈroʊnɪəs/ *adjective* (*formal*)
Something such as a belief or an impression is **erroneous** when it is wrong, false or mistaken: *Several eminent cosmologists consider that the theory is erroneous.* — *adverb* **erroneously:** *They believed erroneously that they were in some way superior to us.*

error /ˈɛrə(r)/ *noun*: **errors**
An **error** is a mistake: *I was guilty of making an error of judgement.* □ *The amount shown is incorrect, the result of an accounting error.*

▻ ***phrase*** When something is done **in error** it is the result of a mistake and should not have happened: *The letter was sent in error to his son.*

erupt /ɪˈrʌpt/ *verb*: **erupts, erupting, erupted**
1 A situation or incident **erupts** when it happens suddenly and without warning: *Then a major financial crisis erupted.* □ *Within minutes fierce fighting had erupted.* [*same as* **flare up, break out**] **2** When a volcano **erupts** it throws out melted rock, smoke and gases in violent bursts. **3** A person **erupts** when they suddenly lose their temper and start shouting. [*same as* **blow up**] — *noun* (*uncount or count*) **eruption** /ɪˈrʌpʃən/: *Extra police have been deployed, to guard against the eruption of violence.* □ *This is the volcano's third eruption in 24 hours.*

escalate /ˈɛskəleɪt/ *verb*: **escalates, escalating, escalated**
A bad situation or circumstance **escalates** when it becomes worse, more serious or more intense: *Fighting in the hills has escalated to all-out war.* □ *If the government does not act now, the problem will escalate to a full-blown crisis.* [*same as* **intensify**] — *noun* (*uncount*) **escalation** /ɛskəˈleɪʃən/: *take measures to prevent the escalation of violence.*

escalator /ˈɛskəleɪtə(r)/ *noun*: **escalators**
An **escalator** is a moving staircase that carries people between the floors of a shop or other building: *We looked for the up escalator, but could only find one going down.*

escapade /ˈɛskəpeɪd/ *noun*: **escapades**
An **escapade** is a daring or adventurous act, often one that breaks rules or laws: *This latest escapade might get him thrown out of school.* [*same as* **stunt, exploit**]

escape /ɪˈskeɪp/ *verb; noun*

▻ ***verb***: **escapes, escaping, escaped**
1 Someone **escapes** from somewhere, such as a prison, when they manage to get away from it: *She escaped from her captors in the middle of the night.* □ *They escaped over the border to Switzerland.* **2** You **escape** something unpleasant, such as a punishment, or you **escape** from it, when you manage to avoid it: *He should not be allowed to escape his duties.* [*same as* **evade, shirk**] **3** You **escape** when you survive a dangerous experience without being harmed: *The scandal seemed set to destroy the Prime Minister, but he's escaped largely unscathed.* **4** Something **escapes** you when you cannot remember it; something **escapes** your notice when you fail to notice it: *I recognize her face, but her name escapes me for the moment.* □ *There is one possibility that's escaped your notice.* [*same as* **elude**] **5** When water or gas **escapes** from a pipe or container, it accidentally flows out of a crack or hole caused by damage. [*same as* **leak**]

▻ ***noun*** (*uncount or count*): **escapes**
Escape, or an **escape**, is the act of escaping or a way of escaping: *They looked for a means of escape.* □ *a high-security prison from which there has never been an escape* □ *It was the narrowest of escapes, with the tree falling only inches from the car.* □ *Prayer was her only escape from a hostile world.*

escapism /ɪˈskeɪpɪzm/ *noun* (*uncount*)
Escapism is anything that takes your thoughts or your mind away from the dullness or unpleasantness of everyday life: *The film doesn't pretend to be anything other than pure escapism.* — *adjective* **escapist:** *Her stories are unashamedly escapist.*

escort *noun; verb*

▻ ***noun*** /ˈɛskɔːt/: **escorts**
An **escort** is **1** a person or vehicle, or a group of them, accompanying another as protection from attack or in order to show the way: *The President was given a full military escort.* **2** a person of the opposite sex asked or hired to accompany another at a social event such as a formal party: *He phoned the agency to arrange for an escort.*

▻ ***verb*** /ɪˈskɔːt/: **escorts, escorting, escorted**
You **escort** someone somewhere when you accompany them there, usually to show them the way or to make sure that they leave: *The waiter escorted the drunken man to the door.* [*same as* **show, conduct, lead**]

▻ ***phrase*** Someone goes somewhere **under escort** when they are accompanied there by guards, either for protection or to prevent them escaping.

especial /ɪˈspɛʃəl/ *adjective* (*literary*)
Especial is used before nouns to mean special: *We must take especial care not to cause offence.* [compare **particular**]

especially /ɪˈspɛʃəlɪ/ *adverb*
1 Especially is used to mean particularly, referring to one person or thing among several: *It's a very dangerous disease, especially in children.* □ *She loves Greece, the islands especially.* [*same as* **particularly**] **2** (*intensifying*) **Especially** is used before adjectives and adverbs for emphasis, meaning 'very' or 'more than usually': *The weather was especially hot today.* □ *The job isn't especially difficult.* [*same as* **particularly**]

> Notice that when a comment applies to one particular person or thing among several, **especially** is normally used; **specially** is only used in this sense in informal English: *The children enjoyed it very much, especially the younger ones.* You use **specially** to mean 'for a specific purpose': *The music was written specially for the play. Please have some wine; I bought it specially.*

espionage /ˈɛspɪənɑːʒ/ *noun* (*uncount*)
Espionage is the activity of spying, or the use of spies to gather information: *The three men were charged with espionage.* □ *She got a job with a rival company for the purpose of industrial espionage.*

espouse /ɪ'spaʊz/ *verb* (*formal*): **espouses, espousing, espoused**
You **espouse** something, such as a political system or set of beliefs, when it becomes a major influence in your life: *We knew him in the days before he espoused socialism.* [*same as* **embrace**]

essay /'ɛseɪ/ *noun*: **essays**
An **essay** is a short formal piece of writing on a particular subject, written by **1** a student as part of a course of education: *The professor refused to mark my essay because it was handed in late.* **2** an author who intends it to be published: *I've just bought a copy of her latest collection of political essays.*

essence /'ɛsəns/ *noun*
1 (*used in the singular*) The **essence** of something is the true nature or character of it, or its most important part or quality: *The essence of her lecture was the assertion that the justice system is unfair.* **2** (*uncount or count*) **Essence** is a liquid containing all the qualities of a particular plant, such as its flavour for use in cooking, or its healing powers for use in medicine: *a small bottle of vanilla essence* □ *herbal essences.*
▻ ***phrase*** (*formal*) You refer to something **in essence** when you are commenting on its true or basic quality or nature: *This is in essence a religious war, not a political one.* [*same as* **essentially**]

essential /ɪ'sɛnʃəl/ *adjective*; *noun*
▻ ***adjective***
1 Something is **essential** when it is absolutely necessary: *The ability to make quick decisions is essential in this job.* □ *It is essential that you arrive on time.* □ *Patience is an essential quality for a nursery nurse.* [*same as* **crucial, vital**] **2 Essential** is also used to refer to the true or basic nature or quality of something: *They may not appear to be similar, but there is in fact no essential difference between them.*
▻ ***noun*: essentials**
Essentials are **1** things that you need in order to live, or in order to do something: *We were given no special tools; just the bare essentials.* **2** the most important elements or aspects of a situation or a particular subject: *We should really discuss essentials and leave the refinements of the system for later.*
[*same as* **basics**]

essentially /ɪ'sɛnʃəlɪ/ *adverb*
Essentially is used when you want to refer to the true or general nature of something, rather than to its appearance or to individual parts or details of it: *He's essentially a very sad character.* □ *It's not essentially different from our own system.* □ *Essentially, he was making the point that we all need someone to talk to.* [*same as* **in essence**]

establish /ɪ'stablɪʃ/ *verb*: **establishes, establishing, established**
1 You **establish** something, such as a business company, when you create it or set it up: *The firm was established in 1878.* **2** You **establish** something, or **establish** that it is true, when you find it out or prove it: *The pathologist was unable to establish the exact time of death.* □ *Further investigations established that she had indeed visited the area several times.* [*same as* **demonstrate, prove**] **3** You **establish** yourself as something when you become widely known and accepted as being it: *He had established a reputation for himself as a fair man.* — *adjective* **established:** *established truths* □ *Celebrating the harvest is a well-established custom in many cultures.*

establishment /ɪ'stablɪʃmənt/ *noun*: **establishments**
1 (*uncount*) The **establishment** of something is the act of creating it or setting it up: *We discussed the establishment of a new maternity policy for female workers.* **2** A shop or business is sometimes referred to as an **establishment**: *Such practices would never be allowed in this establishment.* **3** (*with a singular or plural verb*) The group of people in a country or a society who are considered to control or influence what happens are often referred to as the **establishment**: *The students dismissed the Minister as a remote and indifferent member of the Establishment.*

estate /ɪ'steɪt/ *noun*: **estates**
1 A housing **estate** is an area of land on which a lot of houses are built, quite close to each other. **2** An industrial or trading **estate** is an area of land with several factories, offices or other commercial buildings on it. **3** An **estate** is also a large area of rural land owned by one person or group of people: *the Duke of Devonshire's estate.* **4** (*legal*) A person's **estate** is the total amount of their wealth and possessions that they leave to other people when they die.

estate agent /ɪ'steɪt eɪdʒənt/ *noun*: **estate agents**
An **estate agent** is a person who arranges the buying and selling of other people's houses or other property: *I saw an advertisement in the estate agent's window.*

estate car /ɪ'steɪt kɑː(r)/ *noun*: **estate cars**
An **estate car** has an extended area at the back for luggage, and a back door rather than a boot.

esteem /ɪ'stiːm/ *noun* (*uncount; formal*)
You have or feel **esteem** for someone when you respect and admire them.
▻ ***phrase*** You **hold** someone **in high esteem** when you respect and admire them very much.

esthetic see **aesthetic**.

estimate *verb*; *noun*
▻ ***verb*** /'ɛstɪmeɪt/: **estimates, estimating, estimated**
You **estimate** something when you try to judge it without measuring, or with only a little knowledge or information: *It was difficult to estimate the cost of building a new one.* □ *We estimated that it would take a week to finish the job.* □ *The cost of equipping the new hospital has been estimated at £2 million.*
▻ ***noun*** /'ɛstɪmət/: **estimates**
An **estimate** is **1** a judgement made without measuring, or with only a little knowledge or information: *According to their estimates, the company will go bankrupt within two years.* □ *His estimate of the potential market was very wide of the mark.* **2** a calculation of the probable cost of work to be done, prepared by a person or company willing to carry it out: *We've had estimates from a few companies.* [compare **quotation**]

estimation /ɛstɪ'meɪʃən/ *noun* (*uncount*)
Your **estimation** of someone or something is your opinion or judgement of them: *He was, in my estimation, not capable of doing the job.*

estranged /ɪ'streɪnʒd/ *adjective*
1 You are **estranged** from your husband or wife when you no longer live with him or her: *a letter from his estranged wife.* **2** You are **estranged** from your family when you no longer see them or have contact with them.

estuary /'ɛstjʊərɪ/ *noun*: **estuaries**
An **estuary** is the wide part of a river where it flows into the sea.

etc. /ɛt'sɛtərə/ *adverb*
Etc. is an abbreviation of the Latin phrase 'et cetera' meaning 'and other similar things or people'. It is used at the end of a list: *a shop selling paper, pens, typewriters, etc.*

etch /ɛtʃ/ *verb*: **etches, etching, etched**

1 A design that **is etched** on to a hard surface, such as metal, is made by cutting away pieces of the surface, or by burning them off using acid. **2** Something **is etched** on your mind or memory when you still think about it or remember it very clearly a long time after: *The dreadful scene is etched on my memory forever.* [*same as* **engrave**]

etching /'ɛtʃɪŋ/ *noun*: **etchings**
An **etching** is a picture printed from a piece of metal with a design etched on it.

eternal /ɪ'tɜːnəl/ *adjective*
1 Something that is **eternal** lasts for ever or never changes: *As a child, I dreamt of eternal school holidays.* □ *Many medieval physicians believed it was possible to discover the secret of eternal life.* [*same as* **everlasting**] **2** You use **eternal** to describe boring and annoying situations and circumstances that you never seem to be free of or get away from: *I wish the children would stop their eternal squabbling.* [*same as* **endless**] — *adverb* **eternally:** *We are eternally grateful to you.*

eternity /ɪ'tɜːnɪtɪ/ *noun* (*uncount or count*): **eternities**
1 (*uncount*) **Eternity** is the state of going on for ever, or time regarded as having no end: *They promised their love would last throughout eternity.* **2** (*usually in the singular*) Something boring, annoying or unpleasant lasts for an **eternity** when it continues for a very long time: *After what seemed like an eternity, the pain went away.*

ethic /'ɛθɪk/ *noun*: **ethics**
1 A particular **ethic** is a principle that a person or society follows in their daily life: *The idea that hard work is more virtuous than enjoyment became known as 'the Protestant work ethic'.* **2** (*used in the plural*) **Ethics** are moral principles or rules about what is right and wrong: *This is a matter of medical ethics.* **3** (*used in the plural, with a singular verb*) **Ethics** is philosophical study of morals.

ethical /'ɛθɪkəl/ *adjective*
1 **Ethical** means relating to or concerning morals, justice or duty: *This is essentially an ethical issue.* **2** A person's actions are **ethical** when they are morally right: *They argued that it was simply not ethical to tax poor people at the same rate as the rich.* [*opposite* **unethical**] — *adverb* **ethically:** *There was nothing ethically questionable about the scheme.*

ethnic /'ɛθnɪk/ *adjective*
Ethnic is used to refer to a person's race, rather than to their nationality or religion, and to groups of people of different races: *people from ethnic minorities* □ *outbreaks of ethnic violence* □ *What are her ethnic origins?*

ethos /'iːθɒs/ *noun* (*used in the singular*)
The **ethos** of a particular community of people consists of its typical attitudes, ideas and customs: *Hard work and pure, spiritually ordered living combined to produce the ethos of Victorian Britain.*

etiquette /'ɛtɪkɛt/ *noun* (*uncount*)
The rules and customs for polite behaviour on formal occasions, or for correct behaviour within a particular profession, are referred to as **etiquette**: *We're not bothered about conforming to social etiquette.* □ *It was a question of parliamentary etiquette.* [*same as* **protocol**]

euphemism /'juːfəmɪzm/ *noun*: **euphemisms**
A **euphemism** is a mild or polite term used in place of one that some people might find offensive or embarrassing: *'Departed' and 'passed on' are euphemisms for 'dead'.*

euphemistic /juːfə'mɪstɪk/ *adjective*
Euphemistic words or expressions are mild or polite terms people use in place of embarrassing or offensive ones; certain words that are used in this way, *eg* intimacy, are labelled (*euphemistic*) in this dictionary: *I find the euphemistic language more embarrassing than the real words!* — *adverb* **euphemistically:** *The toilet is what the Americans euphemistically refer to as 'the bathroom'.*

euphoria /juː'fɔːrɪə/ *noun* (*uncount*)
Euphoria is a feeling of excited happiness: *She had never seen such a display of euphoria.*

euphoric /juː'fɒrɪk/ *adjective*
You are **euphoric** when you are wildly or excitedly happy: *I remember feeling simply euphoric when our daughter was born.*

European /jʊərə'pɪən/ *adjective*; *noun*
▷ ***adjective***
European means coming from or relating to the continent of Europe, or to the people or countries within Europe: *the European Union* □ *European languages.*
▷ ***noun***: **Europeans**
A **European** is a person who comes from a country in Europe.

euthanasia /juːθə'neɪzɪə/ *noun* (*uncount*)
Euthanasia is the practice of painlessly killing people who have illnesses that cause them great pain and cannot be cured: *Several eminent doctors are in favour of euthanasia.*

evacuate /ɪ'vakjʊeɪt/ *verb*: **evacuates, evacuating, evacuated**
People **evacuate** a place, or they **are evacuated** from it, when they leave it for a time because it has become dangerous: *Several thousand children were evacuated from their homes in the cities to areas which weren't being bombed.* □ *We were told to evacuate the building when it was discovered that poisonous gas had been accidentally released.* — *noun* (*used in the singular*) **evacuation** /ɪvakjʊ'eɪʃən/: *Plans were made for the swift evacuation of the city.*

evade /ɪ'veɪd/ *verb*: **evades, evading, evaded**
1 You **evade** something when you manage to avoid dealing with it or accepting it: *He was never a person who evaded responsibility or duty.* □ *As usual, the Minister evaded the question.* **2** You **evade** someone or something moving towards you when you move so that they do not hit or catch you: *She managed to evade the attacker's grasp.* [*same as* **avoid, dodge**] **3** Something **evades** you when you do not manage to obtain it or achieve it: *Success has so far evaded her.* [*same as* **elude, escape**]

evaluate /ɪ'valjʊeɪt/ *verb*: **evaluates, evaluating, evaluated**
You **evaluate** something when you form a judgement about how important or valuable it is, after examining it carefully: *Artistic talent is extremely difficult to evaluate.* — *noun* (*uncount or count*) **evaluation** /ɪvaljʊ'eɪʃən/: *The evaluation of a student's work takes time.* □ *Was it a fair evaluation of festival as a whole?*

evaporate /ɪ'vapəreɪt/ *verb*: **evaporates, evaporating, evaporated**
1 A liquid such as water **evaporates** when it changes into steam and disappears. **2** Something, such as a feeling or desire, **evaporates** when it weakens then disappears completely: *Support for the scheme had largely evaporated.* [*same as* **fade, melt away**] — *noun* (*uncount*) **evaporation** /ɪvapə'reɪʃən/: *A lot of water is lost through evaporation.*

evasion /ɪ'veɪʒən/ *noun* (*uncount or count*): **evasions**
1 **Evasion** is the act of avoiding something, or not dealing with or accepting something. **2** An **evasion** is an instance of avoiding something, especially talking

about it: *We cannot forgive this evasion of your responsibilities.* □ *She's been accused of tax evasion.* □ *You will never get him to give a straight answer; only evasions and meaningless waffle.*

evasive /ɪˈveɪsɪv/ *adjective*
You are **evasive** when you avoid speaking directly, honestly or openly: *She became evasive when I asked her why she had left the job.* □ *a rather evasive answer.* [*same as* **cagey**, **vague**] — *adverb* **evasively:** *'I can't remember,' said Phil evasively.*

eve /iːv/ *noun* (*used in the singular*)
1 Christmas **Eve** is the day or evening before Christmas Day; New Year's **Eve** is the day or evening before New Year's Day. **2** The **eve** of an event or occasion is the day or period before it: *the eve of war.*

even /ˈiːvən/ *adjective; adverb*
▻ ***adjective***
1 An **even** surface is smooth and flat: *a nice even putting green* □ *The pavement is far from even.* [*same as* **smooth**, **flat**; *opposite* **uneven**; compare **level**] **2** Someone who has an **even** temper is always calm. [*same as* **calm**] **3** An **even** temperature, rate or measurement stays at the same level: *quiet, even breathing* □ *an even noise level* □ *maintaining an even body temperature.* [*same as* **steady**] **4** An **even** distribution or division of something is one in which every person, place or thing involved receives an equal share: *Luckily there was an even spread of musical talent throughout the family.* [*same as* **equal**] **5** There is an **even** chance of something happening if it is as likely not to happen as to happen: *I realized that my chances of success were no more than even.* [*same as* **equal**] **6** A competition is **even** if all the competitors are equally strong or skilled. [*same as* **equal**; *opposite* **uneven**; compare **level**] **7** An **even** number is a number such as 2, 4 or 6, that can be divided by 2 with nothing left over: *The even-numbered houses are on the right-hand side of the street.* [*opposite* **odd**] — *adverb* **evenly:** *He was breathing quietly and evenly.* □ *The parties are evenly matched as the election approaches.* □ *Loyalties are evenly divided.* [*opposite* **unevenly**]
▻ ***adverb***
Even is used **1** before a comparative, for emphasis: *Things were even worse than I feared.* □ *That sounds even more promising.* □ *an even more acceptable offer* □ *She didn't seem to care, and I cared even less.* □ *He has even fewer reasons to be satisfied than most of us.* □ *She had even more to report when she returned.* **2** to draw attention to something odd or surprising: *She didn't even know the man's name.* □ *I can't read it even with my glasses on.* □ *Your brain is busy even when you're asleep.* □ *No-one agreed with me, not even Mother.* □ *I'd take any job, voluntary work even.* □ *Those are things even a child could do.* □ *Even Beethoven himself might have approved.*
▻ ***phrases*** **1** You use **even if** or **even though** to introduce a clause that does not change the truth of what you say in the main clause: *Even if you fail, you will have the satisfaction of knowing that you tried.* □ *Even though this house was not my first choice, I'm very happy here.*

> Notice that **even though** means roughly the same as **although**, so 'even although' sounds wrong, and should be avoided.

2 Even so is used to introduce a statement that might seem surprising after what has just been said: *We were both ill for several days; even so, we enjoyed the holiday.* **3** You **get even with** someone who has harmed you when you harm them in return.

phrasal verbs
even out Things **even out** or **are evened out** when they become, or are made, more level or equal: *The path climbed steeply and then evened out.* □ *A rationing system was introduced to even out the grain supply over the whole year.*
even up Things **even up** or **are evened up** when they become, or are made, more equal: *That's two points to Ian and Neil, which evens up the scores a bit.*

evening /ˈiːvnɪŋ/ *noun* (*count or uncount*): **evenings**
The **evening** is the last part of the day, from late afternoon until bedtime: *It was a cool evening.* □ *She spent the whole evening reading.* □ *He works three evenings a week.* □ *I saw her last Friday evening.* □ *(used as an adjective) We arrived just in time for the evening meal.*

event /ɪˈvɛnt/ *noun*: **events**
1 An **event** is something that happens, especially something important or notable: *The book examines the events leading up to the outbreak of war.* **2** People often refer to all that is happening within a particular situation as **events**: *We shall have to make sure that events move quite quickly now, if we are to publish on time.* **3** An **event** is also one of the individual races or other contests that make up a sporting tournament: *The high jump will be the next event.*
▻ ***phrases*** **1** You say **in any event** or **at all events** as a way of introducing a statement that remains true in spite of other things already said: *She may well refuse to come; in any event, the evening will be a success.* [*same as* **at any rate**, **in any case**] **2** (*formal*) You say **in the event of** something, or **in the event that** something happens, as a way of introducing a possibility: *In the event of rain, the match will have to be cancelled.* □ *In the event that only half the members turn up, the meeting will be deferred to a later date.*

eventful /ɪˈvɛntfʊl/ *adjective*
An **eventful** period of time is full of important or exciting events or happenings: *The children are exhausted; we've had rather an eventful day.*

eventual /ɪˈvɛntʃʊəl/ *adjective*
Eventual is used to refer to what happens at the end of a period of time, or to what happens as a result of some process: *A series of disagreements with the management led to his eventual dismissal from employment.* — *adverb* (*sometimes sentence adverb*) **eventually:** *We waited for over two hours before eventually realizing he wasn't going to come.* □ *Eventually she decided she didn't want the job at all.* □ *I think eventually we should supply every member of staff with their own PC.*

eventuality /ɪvɛntʃʊˈalɪtɪ/ *noun* (*formal*): **eventualities**
An **eventuality** is a possible happening or result: *We have planned for every eventuality.*

ever /ˈɛvə(r)/ *adverb*
1 Ever is used in negative sentences, in questions, after *if*, and after words such as *hardly* and *scarcely* to mean 'at any time': *Have you ever been to Spain?* □ *I can't remember ever discussing it with him.* □ *We hardly ever go to the cinema these days.* □ *If ever you need a bed for the night, just call me.* □ *I have seldom, if ever* [= in fact probably never], *experienced such rudeness.* **2** You can emphasize *never* by following it with **ever**: *She's never ever thanked me for all that extra work I did.* □ *I've never seen her look so happy, ever!* **3 Ever**, meaning 'at any time', is also used for emphasis with comparatives and superlatives, in comparisons formed with *as ... as*, and with *first* and *only*: *Their welcome was warmer than ever* [= they were even more welcoming than usual]. □ *That must have been my worst-ever performance.* □ *The island was looking as lovely as ever.*

□ *That incident was as close as I've ever come to death.* □ *I've only ever seen him wearing a suit, never casual clothes.* □ *This is my first-ever plane journey.* **4 Ever** is used before words such as *present* or *increasing* to mean 'all the time' or 'constantly': *the ever-growing possibility of war in the Middle East* □ *The threat of redundancy was ever present.* **5** You use **ever** before an adjective or a noun phrase to comment that someone is behaving typically: *Ever the perfect gentleman, Fritz helped the ladies one by one over the stile.* [*same as* **always**] **6 Ever** is used after question words for emphasis and to express surprise: *Why ever didn't you tell me you were in trouble?* □ *How ever did she find out?* □ *What ever will you tell her?* □ *Who ever told you such rubbish?* [see also **however, whatever, whoever**]

▻ ***phrases*** **1 Ever since** emphasizes that something that is so now has always been so from the time mentioned: *She's been confident and outspoken ever since she was a small child.* □ *He joined the firm in '73, and has been one of our top salesmen ever since.* **2 As ever** is used to mean 'as always happens': *As ever, the women were expected to do the cooking.* **3** (*informal*) You use **ever so** and **ever such** to emphasize the degree of a quality: *It was ever so kind of you to lend me your car.* □ *She's ever such a lovely person.* □ *It was ever such a long way.* **4** For **for ever** see **forever**. **5** People sometimes use **'Yours ever'** as an ending to a letter to someone that they write to often.

[see also **never**]

evergreen /ˈɛvəgriːn/ *noun*: **evergreens**

An **evergreen** is a tree or bush that does not lose its leaves in winter, but keeps them all year round: *We've planted the front garden with evergreens.* □ *(used as an adjective) evergreen plants.*

everlasting /ɛvəˈlɑːstɪŋ/ *adjective*

Something is **everlasting** when it continues to happen or exist for ever, or when it goes on for so long that you think it will never end: *their everlasting love for each other* □ *across the everlasting plains of southern Africa.* [*same as* **eternal, endless**]

every /ˈɛvrɪ/ *determiner*

Every is used **1** with singular countable nouns; **every** person or thing is all the people or things in the group or class referred to: *She had approached every member of staff for their opinion.* □ *They've opened a shop in every major city in the country.* □ *I've had bad dreams every night since she died.* □ *The first hotel was superior in every way.* □ *I answered all the questions and got every single one right.* [*opposite* **no**; see note on the differences between **each** and **every** at **each**] **2** with certain singular count nouns to mean 'all possible': *We're making every effort to avoid war.* □ *There is every chance* [= it is very likely] *that the President will agree.* □ *The economy is showing every sign of recovery.* [= is obviously recovering] □ *After his past unreliability, you have every reason to doubt* [= you are quite justified in doubting] *his promises.* □ *At the time I had every intention of keeping my promise.* □ *My every move* [= whatever I tried] *seemed to end in frustration.* **3** with uncountable nouns that refer to feelings or states, with the meaning 'complete' or 'total': *I have every confidence in her abilities.* □ *We have every sympathy for your situation.* **4** with expressions of time to indicate that something happens or is done regularly, or at regular intervals: *We visit my grandmother every Sunday.* □ *The doctor gives me a medical examination every six months.* □ *Check the water level every few days.* □ *I do a washing every other* (or *every second*) *day* [= on alternate days]. □ *They hold a big celebration every tenth year.* **5** with numbers in expressing the proportion of people or things affected: *The company is cutting jobs; one worker in every hundred will be sacked.* □ *One person in every 40 is a twin.*

▻ ***phrases*** Something that happens **every now and then**, or **every so often**, happens only occasionally: *Every now and then she would feel an overwhelming urge to abandon her husband, home and family entirely.*

[compare **each, all, no**]

everybody /ˈɛvrɪbɒdɪ/ see **everyone**.

everyday /ˈɛvrɪdeɪ/ *adjective*

An **everyday** happening or occurrence is common, usual or part of ordinary life: *Arguments between her parents were an everyday occurrence.*

everyone /ˈɛvrɪwʌn/ *pronoun*

Everyone or **everybody** refers to **1** all the people in a group: *Everyone I asked said they were satisfied with the new parking arrangements.* □ *Mairi sang the verses and everybody else joined in the chorus.* □ *Everyone on the staff sends you their best wishes.* □ *Has everyone got a copy?* □ *Not everyone was pleased, but most were.* **2** all the people in the world, or all people in general: *Everyone knows that elephants can't fly.* □ *Tennyson isn't everybody's favourite poet.* □ *We'd get along better if everyone minded their own business.* [*opposite* **no-one, nobody**]

> Notice that although **everyone** and **everybody** are singular, and take a singular verb, both are commonly followed by *they*, which takes a plural verb: *Everybody's invited, aren't they? Everyone has a right to their* (or in formal English, *his or her*) *own opinion.*
>
> **Everyone** and **every one**: **everyone** can refer only to people, and means every person; **every one** can refer to people or things, and means all the people or things just mentioned: *I interviewed at least 80 passers-by, and every one was in favour of a period of community service for school-leavers.* □ *We viewed dozens of houses but every one of them had some major disadvantage.*

[compare **all, anybody** and **anyone, somebody** and **someone**]

everything /ˈɛvrɪθɪŋ/ *pronoun*

1 Everything refers to **a** all the things that are concerned in a particular situation: *We examined everything in the room.* □ *'Here's a pair of scissors for you; have you got everything else you need?' 'Everything but* (or *except*) *a wastebin.'* □ *Are you sure you've told me everything?* □ *I lost my wife, my job, everything important to me.* □ *I don't approve of everything he does.* **b** all possible or likely situations: *Thanks for warning me; you think of everything.* □ *Physical punishment is not the answer to everything.* **c** life in general, or all the experiences and situations in which you are involved: *Fortunately not everything is as depressing as that.* □ *Is everything all right? You look a bit upset.* □ *Everything went on as though the incident had never occurred.* [*opposite* **nothing**] **2** Something that is, or means, **everything** is the thing that matters most: *Fitness is everything in sport.* □ *Winning means everything to her.*

▻ ***phrase*** People use **'and everything'** to mean 'and so on': *What with the excitement and everything I completely forgot my dental appointment.* [compare **anything, something, nothing**]

everywhere /ˈɛvrɪwɛə(r)/ *adverb*

Everywhere means the whole of an area, all places within an area or all places in general, or in or to all places: *Everywhere was covered in snow.* □ *We decided to stay in Siena; everywhere else was too crowded.* □ *Visitors were arriving from everywhere.* □ *These gangs are operating everywhere in the world.*

□ *Environmentalists everywhere are deeply concerned.* □ *I've never had a car; I walk everywhere locally and take the bus for longer journeys.* □ *Everywhere you go you see piles of litter in the streets.*

evict /ɪ'vɪkt/ *verb*: **evicts, evicting, evicted**
Someone **is evicted** when they are legally forced to leave their house or the land they are living on: *They've been evicted for not paying their rent.* □ *I was evicted from my flat earlier in the year.* — *noun* (*uncount or count*) **eviction** /ɪ'vɪkʃən/: *Failure to pay your rent could end in eviction.* □ *This court has authorized over a hundred evictions this year.*

evidence /'ɛvɪdəns/ *noun* (*uncount*)
1 Evidence consists of anything that suggests or proves that something is true or has happened: *There was no evidence of a struggle; the victim must have been hit from behind.* □ *Do you have any evidence that her husband was planning to leave her?* [*same as* **indication**] **2** Someone gives **evidence** in a court of law when they tell formally what they know about a particular matter.

evident /'ɛvɪdənt/ *adjective*
Something is **evident** when it is clearly true or when it obviously exists: *It is evident that you are not fond of each other.* □ *She received the news with evident displeasure.*

evidently /ɛvɪdəntlɪ/ *adverb* (*sentence adverb*)
Evidently is used **1** in reference to what you conclude from the available facts: *She said she'd definitely be here; evidently she changed her mind about coming.* [*same as* **apparently, seemingly**] **2** to mean 'clearly' or 'obviously': *She was very evidently upset.*

evil /'iːvɪl/ *adjective; noun*
▻ ***adjective***
1 An **evil** person enjoys causing harm or destruction: *It would be wrong to call the child evil; he is simply mischievous.* **2** Something is **evil** when it causes great harm: *the evil influence of racist propaganda.* **3** (*informal*) People often use **evil** to describe things that are very bad or unpleasant: *an evil smell.*
▻ ***noun***: **evils**
1 (*uncount*) **Evil** consists of harmful or destructive actions or feelings in general: *She must struggle against the evil inside her.* **2** You can describe something that is very wicked or harmful as an **evil**: *Child abuse is another of our modern social evils.*
▻ ***phrase***: For **the lesser of two evils** see **lesser**.

evoke /ɪ'voʊk/ *verb*: **evokes, evoking, evoked**
Something **evokes** a feeling, memory or reaction when it causes or produces it: *The smell of cinnamon always evokes vivid memories of childhood Christmases.* [*same as* **arouse**]

evolution /iːvə'ljuːʃən/ *noun* (*uncount*)
1 Evolution refers to the natural way that primitive plants and animals have developed throughout history to become the modern plants and animals that we know today: *Many scientists do not accept the traditional theories of evolution.* **2** The **evolution** of something is its gradual development: *Today's programme looks at the evolution of modern transport systems.*

evolve /ɪ'vɒlv/ *verb*: **evolves, evolving, evolved**
1 Plants and animals **evolve** when they develop from primitive forms into more advanced forms: *It is simply not possible to prove that people evolved from early apes.* **2** Something **evolves** when it develops gradually: *The story evolves into a violent tragedy.*

ewe /juː/ *noun*: **ewes**
A **ewe** is an adult female sheep.

ex- /ɛks/ *prefix*
Ex- is used before nouns to mean 'former': *She's my ex-wife.* □ *an ex-policeman who is now a security guard.*

exacerbate /ɪg'sasəbeɪt/ *verb*: **exacerbates. exacerbating, exacerbated**
A circumstance that **exacerbates** a bad situation makes it worse.

exact /ɪg'zakt/ *adjective; verb*
▻ ***adjective***
1 Something that is **exact** is absolutely accurate or correct: *It was around ten o'clock; I don't remember the exact time.* □ *We've made an exact replica of the machine.* **2 Exact** can be used for emphasis, *eg* with *opposite*: *She's the exact opposite of her sister.* **3** Someone who is **exact** takes care to make sure that things are completely accurate and precise: *You have to adopt a very exact approach.*
▻ ***verb*** (*formal*): **exacts, exacting, exacted**
You **exact** something from someone when you demand and obtain it: *We were not in a position to exact any guarantees from them.*

exacting /ɪg'zaktɪŋ/ *adjective*
1 Something that is **exacting** requires a lot of hard work: *We impose very exacting standards on our employees.* **2** Someone who is **exacting** expects others to work very hard: *She's suffered under a succession of very exacting managers.* [*same as* **demanding**]

exactly /ɪg'zaktlɪ/ *adverb*
1 Exactly means precisely or absolutely: *It's in here somewhere; I don't remember exactly where.* □ *Tell me exactly what he said.* □ *That's exactly what we need.* **2** (*sentence adverb, used as an answer*) You say **'exactly'** to indicate that you agree completely with what someone has said, and that what they have said is absolutely true: *'I think she needs to find herself a new job.' 'Exactly.'* □ *'Are you saying that the system itself is wrong?' 'Exactly!'*
▻ ***phrase*** People use **not exactly** to say **1** that something is not quite true, but is almost true: *She's not exactly an expert, but she is very good.* **2** that the opposite is true: *'So, did the meeting go well?' 'Not exactly; only three out of fifty members turned up!'*

exaggerate /ɪg'zadʒəreɪt/ *verb*: **exaggerates, exaggerating, exaggerated**
1 You **exaggerate** something when you regard or describe it as being greater, better or worse than it really is: *I think you're exaggerating the importance of this issue.* □ *In her letter, she has clearly exaggerated her talents a little.* [*same as* **overstate**] **2** To **exaggerate** something is also to make it more obvious or noticeable: *The tight skirt exaggerated her thick waist.* [*same as* **emphasize**] — *noun* (*count or uncount*) **exaggeration** /ɪgzadʒə'reɪʃən/: *It wouldn't be an exaggeration to say that the house is dilapidated.* □ *Please tell us, in your own words and without exaggeration, exactly what happened.*

exam /ɪg'zam/ *noun* (*informal*): **exams**
An **exam** is an examination (sense 1a).

examination /ɪgzamɪ'neɪʃən/ *noun*: **examinations**
1 An **examination** is **a** a formal test of someone's ability or knowledge: *Before we can offer you a university place, you must sit and pass our entrance examination.* **b** an inspection of a person's state of health, carried out by a doctor. **2** (*count or uncount*) You make an **examination** of something when you consider it or look at it carefully: *We will carry out a thorough examination of all the evidence.* □ *The company's accounts are still under examination.*

examine /ɪg'zamɪn/ *verb*: **examines, examining, examined**
1 You **examine** something when you carefully look at it or consider it: *Let's examine the facts.* □ *I examined the gun closely and was sure that it had not been fired.*

2 When a doctor **examines** you, he or she tests various parts of your body to check how healthy you are.

example /ɪɡ'zɑːmpəl/ *noun*: **examples**
1 An **example** of a certain thing is a thing of that kind, or an instance of it: *His refusal to help us is just another typical example of his selfishness* □ *This is an excellent example of a really fine-quality Persian carpet.* □ *You keep telling me he's naughty; are there any specific examples of his naughtiness you can tell me about?* [*same as* **specimen**, **instance**] **2** A person whose good behaviour deserves to be copied by others, or whose bad behaviour should not be copied, is sometimes referred to as an **example**: *You're not setting a very good example for your little brother.* □ *His bravery is an example to us all.* □ *We just hope she won't follow her friend's bad example.*
▷ ***phrases*** **1** You use '**for example**' when presenting an example of what you are talking about: *Some of these off-shore islands enjoy quite a degree of independence; what about the Isle of Man, for example?* □ *You should do something less energetic; reading, for example.* [*same as* **for instance**] **2** You **make an example of** someone when you punish them as a warning that others should not copy their behaviour.

exasperate /ɪɡ'zɑːspəreɪt/ *verb*: **exasperates, exasperating, exasperated**
You **are exasperated** by something or someone that makes you very annoyed and frustrated. — *adjective* **exasperating:** *an exasperating series of delays.* — *noun* (*uncount*) **exasperation** /ɪɡzɑːspə'reɪʃən/: *a look of exasperation on his face.*

excavate /'ɛkskəveɪt/ *verb*: **excavates, excavating, excavated**
1 To **excavate** ancient objects is to dig away the soil that, through time, has gradually covered them, so that they can be studied: *The team has excavated part of an old Roman road.* □ *We've been excavating in an area north of the town.* **2** To **excavate** also means to dig a hole in the ground, *eg* as preparation for building a house.

exceed /ɪk'siːd/ *verb*: **exceeds, exceeding, exceeded**
1 Something **exceeds** an amount or quantity when it is greater than it: *Several areas have had rainfall levels exceeding two centimetres.* **2** You **exceed** a limit when you go beyond it, especially when this breaks a rule or restriction: *Most motorists regularly exceed the speed limit.*

exceedingly /ɪk'siːdɪŋlɪ/ *adverb* (*intensifying*)
Exceedingly means extremely: *He's an exceedingly charming fellow.*

excel /ɪk'sɛl/ *verb*: **excels, excelling, excelled**
You **excel** at something, or **excel** in it, when you are exceptionally good at it: *It was in the field of biological research that she really excelled.*

excellence /'ɛksələns/ *noun* (*uncount*)
Excellence is very high quality or exceptional ability: *a hotel proud of its excellence of service* □ *moments of sporting excellence.*

excellent /'ɛksələnt/ *adjective*
1 Something that is **excellent** is very good: *He's done some excellent work.* □ *The standard of care at this hospital is excellent.* **2 Excellent** is often used as a response to something said, to show that you are pleased: *'All the guests have now arrived, my lord.' 'Excellent! Show them to their tables.'* — *adverb* **excellently:** *Our investments are performing excellently.*

except /ɪk'sɛpt/ *preposition or conjunction*
'**Except**' and '**except** for' introduce the only person or thing that a statement does not apply to, or the only circumstance that prevents it from being absolutely true: *By now we had interviewed all the candidates except Miss Roberts.* □ *The street was empty, except for the occasional huddled figure sleeping in a doorway.* □ *There's little we can do except hope for the best.* □ *Nothing new emerged from the meeting, except that the two sides appear to be more bitterly opposed than ever.* □ *I see a lot of her except when she's abroad.* □ *I knew nothing about first aid except what I'd learnt at school.* [*same as* **other than**, **apart from**; *opposite* **including**]

exception /ɪk'sɛpʃən/ *noun*: **exceptions**
An **exception** is a person or thing that a comment or statement does not apply to: *We feel that the residents of this area, with one or two exceptions, support the council's policy.* □ *Normally, parents aren't allowed to attend the classes, but in your case we can make an exception.* □ *With the exception of the Northern team, all groups handed in their results on time.*
▷ ***phrases*** **1** You **take exception to** something when you are offended or annoyed by it, and refuse to accept it: *I take exception to being spoken to like a naughty child.* **2** Something happens **without exception** when it happens in all cases: *All sectors of the economy are, without exception, in decline.*

exceptional /ɪk'sɛpʃənəl/ *adjective*
1 An **exceptional** person is unusual or outstanding in some way, especially in being very talented: *She was a most exceptional musician.* **2 Exceptional** events happen only very rarely and cannot be predicted or prepared for: *The application would only be refused in exceptional circumstances.*

exceptionally /ɪk'sɛpʃənəlɪ/ *adverb*
1 (*intensifying*) **Exceptionally** means very: *She was an exceptionally gifted pupil.* □ *a run of exceptionally fine weather.* **2** (*sentence adverb*) **Exceptionally** is used to indicate that the situation spoken of is very unusual and rare: *We might agree, exceptionally, to allow the widow to claim the husband's full pension.*

excerpt /'ɛksɜːpt/ *noun*: **excerpts**
An **excerpt** is a short piece of writing, music or film taken from the whole work: *He illustrated the point by showing an excerpt from one of his earlier films.*

excess *noun*; *adjective*
▷ ***noun*** /ɪk'sɛs/ or /'ɛksɛs/: **excesses**
1 An **excess** of something is more than is needed, wanted or allowed: *Nowadays people don't have quite such an excess of cholesterol in their diet.* **2** (*used in the plural; literary*) **Excesses** are unacceptable or wicked actions: *He described some of what he referred to as the excesses of the Communist regime.*
▷ ***adjective*** /'ɛksɛs/
An **excess** amount or level of something is too much: *The doctor said that excess weight was her main health problem.*
▷ ***phrases*** **1 In excess of** means greater than: *The debts total a sum of money in excess of £3 million.* **2** You do something **to excess** when you do it too much: *Drinking alcohol to excess can cause serious health problems.*

excessive /ɪk'sɛsɪv/ *adjective*
When something is **excessive** it is too great or too extreme: *We must take care not to make excessive demands on our workforce.* — *adverb* (*intensifying*) **excessively:** *a teacher who applies excessively strict standards to his pupils.*

exchange /ɪks'tʃeɪndʒ/ *verb*; *noun*
▷ ***verb***: **exchanges, exchanging, exchanged**
1 You **exchange** something when you give it back and take something else instead: *I'd like to exchange this red sweater for a green one.* **2** Two or more people

exchange things when each person gives something to the other or others and receives something from them in return: *The political leaders exchanged gifts.* □ *From the moment we exchanged glances, I knew I was in love.* [*same as* **swap**]

▻ ***noun***: **exchanges**

1 An **exchange** is **a** the act of giving one thing in return for another, or the thing given: *There was a frank exchange of opinions between both sides.* **b** the act of temporarily changing places with another person, usually either living with each other's family or doing each other's job: *My daughter is going to live with a French family on an exchange.* **c** (*formal*) a short conversation: *a few angry exchanges outside the meeting room.* **2** (*uncount*) **Exchange** is the practice of giving the currency of one country in return for the currency of another: *a small bank that doesn't handle foreign exchange* □ *The rate of exchange used to be four deutschmarks to one pound sterling; it's a much lower exchange rate now.*

▻ ***phrase*** You give something **in exchange for** something else when you give one thing and receive another in return.

excitable /ɪk'saɪtəbəl/ *adjective*

An **excitable** person is easily made excited or nervous.

excite /ɪk'saɪt/ *verb*: **excites, exciting, excited**

1 Something **excites** you when it fills you with lively enthusiasm or expectation, or when it gives you a pleasing sense of danger: *The children are very excited at the prospect of going to the zoo.* □ *Driving at high speed excites me beyond description.* **2** Something **excites** feelings or reactions when it causes or provokes them: *His sudden promotion has excited a lot of jealousy within the office.* [*same as* **arouse**] — *adjective* **excited:** *She was so excited that she couldn't think about anything else.* □ *the excited cheers of the children.* — *adverb* **excitedly:** *We spent the whole week excitedly preparing the party.* □ *He giggled excitedly.* — *adjective* **exciting:** *She leads a very exciting life.*

excitement /ɪk'saɪtmənt/ *noun* (*uncount*)

Excitement is the state of being excited: *the look of excitement on the child's face* □ *This has been a tournament full of excitement.*

exclaim /ɪk'skleɪm/ *verb*: **exclaims, exclaiming, exclaimed**

You **exclaim** when you speak suddenly and loudly, *eg* in surprise or anger: *'What intolerable rudeness!' exclaimed Mr Jenkins.*

exclamation /ɛksklə'meɪʃən/ *noun*: **exclamations**

An **exclamation** is a word or expression spoken suddenly and loudly: *They greeted her with exclamations of welcome.*

exclamation mark /ekskla'meɪʃən mɑːk/ *noun*: **exclamation marks**

An **exclamation mark** is the punctuation mark (!), used to indicate an exclamation, or a remark intended to be humorous.

exclude /ɪk'skluːd/ *verb*: **excludes, excluding, excluded**

1 You **exclude** someone when you prevent them from sharing or taking part: *Why was I excluded from the discussions?* **2** You **exclude** something when you do not include it or consider it: *All church officials, excluding the clergy, will be expected to attend.* □ *We have not excluded the possibility that he may have started the fire himself.*

excluding /ɪk'skluːdɪŋ/ *preposition*

Excluding means not including or counting: *There are forty-six seats in all, excluding the two drivers' seats.*

exclusion /ɪk'skluːʒən/ *noun* (*uncount*)

The **exclusion** of someone or something is the act of not including them or allowing them in: *They were not prepared to give a reason for my exclusion from the members' bar.* □ *With the exclusion of one or two troublemakers, the pupils in this school are exemplary in their behaviour.*

exclusive /ɪk'skluːsɪv/ *adjective*

1 An **exclusive** place, such as a restaurant or hotel, is intended only for very wealthy people: *a rather exclusive sports club.* [*same as* **select**] **2** Something is **exclusive** when it is limited to only one place, person or group: *This offer is exclusive to readers of the 'Daily Star'.* □ *Managers have exclusive use of the showers.* □ *These birds are exclusive to this part of southern Africa.* **3** **Exclusive** of something means not including it: *The menu at 80 francs is exclusive of a 10% service charge.* **4** Two things are mutually **exclusive** when they cannot exist together at the same time: *I don't believe that Good and Evil are mutually exclusive; they both exist in all of us to varying degrees.* — *adverb* **exclusively:** *He devotes his spare time exclusively to church work.* □ *This car park is intended exclusively for customers of Brown & Sons.*

excrement /'ɛkskrəmənt/ *noun* (*uncount; formal*)

Excrement is solid waste matter passed out of the body through the anus.

excruciating /ɪk'skruːʃɪeɪtɪŋ/ *adjective*

Something is **excruciating** when it causes extreme pain: *It must have been an excruciating injury.* □ *The pain was excruciating.*

excursion /ɪk'skɜːʃən/ *noun*: **excursions**

1 An **excursion** is a short trip, usually made for pleasure: *a charity organizing excursions for disabled children.* **2** An **excursion** into something new is a brief change from your usual routine or occupation: *a novelist making an excursion into journalism.*

excusable /ɪk'skjuːzəbəl/ *adjective*

Someone's mistake or other wrongdoing is **excusable** if you can excuse it, *eg* because it is not serious, or was not deliberate: *It was an excusable error.* [*opposite* **inexcusable**]

excuse *verb; noun*

▻ ***verb*** /ɪk'skjuːz/: **excuses, excusing, excused**

1 You **excuse** someone for something bad they have done when you forgive them: *Such rudeness cannot easily be excused.* □ *We will excuse you this once, but don't be late again.* □ *Please excuse my brother's manners; he's not used to the company of ladies.* **2** To **excuse** something is to justify it or make it acceptable: *The Home Secretary argued that poverty does not excuse crime.* **3** You **excuse** someone from a duty or obligation when you allow them to ignore it or not carry it out: *You may be excused from school only if you have a note from your parents or your doctor.* **4** You ask someone to **excuse** you as a polite way of saying that you are leaving the room for a moment: *Please excuse me; I have an urgent telephone call to make.*

▻ ***noun*** /ɪk'skjuːs/: **excuses**

An **excuse** is an explanation of why you did something, especially when it is not believed or accepted as reasonable by others: *What was his excuse for arriving late?* □ *She said she wouldn't be able to come, with the excuse that she would have to look after the children.* □ *It's no use making excuses; you shouldn't have spoken to him like that.*

▻ ***phrase*** **Excuse me** is a polite expression used **1** to attract someone's attention: *Excuse me, could we have our bill please?* **2** to indicate that you are going to leave: *Excuse me, gentlemen, but I have a lunch appointment in ten minutes.* **3** to apologize for disturbing or interrupting someone: *Excuse me for barging in, but there's a man in reception who demands to see you now.* **4** to correct someone: *Excuse me, but I think you'll find that Saskatchewan is in Canada, not America.* **5** (*AmE*) to apologize for a mistake you have made: *Where do you live back in England, excuse me, Scotland?*

execute /ˈɛksəkjuːt/ *verb*: **executes, executing, executed**
1 To **execute** someone is to kill them as a punishment, usually by order of the law: *They were found to have unlawfully executed several prisoners of war.* **2** (*formal*) You **execute** something, such as a plan or a movement, when you carry it out or perform it: *Who could have executed such a masterly crime?* □ *The dancers executed a series of complex twists.* — *noun* (*count or uncount*) **execution** /ɛksɪˈkjuːʃən/: *He carried out executions at the order of the king.* □ *The pilot throttles back just prior to the execution of the spin.*

executive /ɪgˈzɛkjʊtɪv/ *noun*; *adjective*
▻ ***noun***: **executives**
1 An **executive** is an employee concerned with management or administration, usually at a senior level. **2** The **executive** of an organization, such as a political party, is the group of people who decide what action to take.
▻ ***adjective***
1 **Executive** is often used to describe expensive or luxurious things: *a small block of executive apartments.* **2** **Executive** also means responsible for taking action or making important decisions: *a committee which has no executive powers.*

exemplary /ɪgˈzɛmplərɪ/ *adjective* (*formal*)
Someone or something that is **exemplary** is excellent or admirable: *He was an exemplary teacher.* □ *She handled the situation with exemplary diplomacy.*

exemplify /ɪgˈzɛmplɪfaɪ/ *verb*: **exemplifies, exemplifying, exemplified**
1 When something **exemplifies** a stated quality, it is a typical example or illustration of that quality: *Her unwillingness to vote exemplifies her lack of understanding of this issue.* **2** If you **exemplify** something, you provide an example or examples of it to show what you mean.

exempt /ɪgˈzɛmpt/ *adjective*; *verb*
▻ ***adjective***
You are **exempt** from something that applies to others, such as duty or responsibility, when it does not apply to you: *People receiving a state pension are exempt from this tax.*
▻ ***verb***: **exempts, exempting, exempted**
To **exempt** someone from an obligation or responsibility is to free them from it: *My status as a university teacher exempts me from compulsory service in the armed forces.*

exercise /ˈɛksəsaɪz/ *noun*; *verb*
▻ ***noun***: **exercises**
1 (*uncount*) **Exercise** consists of physical movements or games performed in order to stay healthy, or just for pleasure: *The doctor says I don't get enough exercise.* □ *I haven't taken any exercise for months.* **2** An **exercise** is a task designed to test or practise your ability: *The teacher gave us a few spelling exercises to do.* □ *I've done my piano exercises for the day.* **3** (*uncount*; *formal*) The **exercise** of rights or powers is the act of using or applying them: *Our approach encourages the exercise of the pupils' creative abilities.*
▻ ***verb***: **exercises, exercising, exercised**
1 You **exercise** when you perform physical movements or play sports in order to stay healthy, or just for pleasure: *You should exercise more.* □ *She must exercise the injured leg if it is to regain its original strength.* **2** You **exercise** something, such as a right, when you bring it into use: *The unions can no longer claim to exercise an influence on government policy.*

exert /ɪgˈzɜːt/ *verb*: **exerts, exerting, exerted**
1 You **exert** influence or pressure when you apply it forcefully: *She exerts considerable authority over several government ministers.* **2** You **exert** yourself when you make a great physical effort or perform tiring physical movements: *The doctor has warned me that if I exert myself too much I may be ill for a long time.* — *noun* (*uncount or count*) **exertion** /ɪgˈzɜʃən/: *My body ached with exertion.* □ *You must be exhausted after all your exertions.*

exhale /ɛksˈheɪl/ *verb* (*formal*): **exhales, exhaling, exhaled**
You **exhale** when you breathe out. [opposite **inhale**]

exhaust /ɪgˈzɔːst/ *verb*; *noun*
▻ ***verb***: **exhausts, exhausting, exhausted**
1 Something **exhausts** you when it makes you thoroughly tired: *All this talk of exercise is exhausting me.* [*same as* **wear out, tire out**] **2** You **exhaust** a supply when you use it up completely: *What will we do, now that we've exhausted our reserves of oil?* **3** When you have said all that can be said about something, you **have exhausted** the subject. — *adjective* **exhausted:** *I was absolutely exhausted.* — *adjective* **exhausting:** *Looking after children can be an exhausting job.*
▻ ***noun***: **exhausts**
1 The **exhaust**, or **exhaust pipe**, on a car is the part that waste gases from the engine are released from. **2** (*uncount*) **Exhaust** consists of the waste gases themselves: *exhaust fumes.* [see picture at **car**]

exhaustion /ɪgˈzɔːstʃən/ *noun* (*uncount*)
Exhaustion is the state of being thoroughly tired: *It emerged that he had died of exhaustion on the way up the mountain.*

exhaustive /ɪgˈzɔːstɪv/ *adjective*
Something, such as a search or investigation, is **exhaustive** if it is extremely thorough, so that nothing is ignored: *An exhaustive examination of the remains revealed that the dead man had had both ears pierced.* — *adverb* **exhaustively:** *The evidence has been exhaustively prepared.*

exhibit /ɪgˈzɪbɪt/ *verb*; *noun*
▻ ***verb***: **exhibits, exhibiting, exhibited**
1 Objects **are exhibited** when they are displayed in public, *eg* in a museum: *Her photographs have been exhibited in numerous New York galleries.* **2** (*formal*) You **exhibit** a feeling or quality when your behaviour displays or reveals it: *The native people exhibited a deep mistrust of all visitors.*
▻ ***noun***: **exhibits**
An **exhibit** is **1** an object displayed publicly, *eg* in a museum: *Some of our finest exhibits are now in storage.* **2** an object displayed in a court of law as part of the evidence presented: *The knife will be referred to as exhibit A.*

exhibition /ɛksɪˈbɪʃən/ *noun*: **exhibitions**
1 An **exhibition** is a collection of objects on public display, *eg* in a museum: *The college is putting on a Dickens exhibition.* **2** (*uncount*) **Exhibition** is the fact of being displayed in public: *Some of her work is on exhibition at the local art gallery.*
▻ ***phrase*** You **make an exhibition of yourself** when you behave foolishly in public.

exhilarate /ɪgˈzɪləreɪt/ *verb*: **exhilarates, exhilarating, exhilarated**
Something **exhilarates** you when it makes you feel excitedly happy or full of energy: *We were exhilarated*

by our walk in the snow. — *adjective* **exhilarating:** *an exhilarating ride on horseback.* — *noun* (*uncount*) **exhilaration** /ɪgzɪlə'reɪʃən/: *a feeling of exhilaration.*

exhort /ɪg'zɔːt/ *verb* (*formal*): **exhorts, exhorting, exhorted**
You **exhort** someone to do something when you urge them to do it. — *noun* **exhortation** /ɛksɔː'teɪʃən/: *In spite of all his exhortations, not one of the dancers managed to smile.*

exile /'ɛksaɪl/ or /'ɛgzaɪl/ *noun*; *verb*
▻ ***noun***: **exiles**
1 (*uncount*) Someone lives in **exile** when they live in another country because they have been forced to leave their own, or because they want to avoid something in their own: *She will never get used to a life of exile.* **2** An **exile** is a person who lives in another country for these reasons: *a political exile* □ *tax exiles.*
▻ ***verb***: **exiles, exiling, exiled**
Someone **is exiled** when they are forced to go and live in another country: *She was exiled from Spain in 1963, only allowed to return twelve years later.*

exist /ɪg'zɪst/ *verb*: **exists, existing, existed**
1 Something **exists** when it is present and can be found in the real world, rather than in story or imagination: *A strong feeling of dislike exists between them.* □ *I don't believe such a word exists; I think you made it up.* □ *There exists an atmosphere of gloom throughout the whole organization.* **2** To **exist** is also to live or manage to stay alive: *I don't know how she can exist on only £25 a week.* □ *Many wild animals cannot exist in captivity.* [*same as* **survive**]

existence /ɪg'zɪstəns/ *noun*: **existences**
1 (*uncount*) **Existence** is the state of existing: *Most young children believe in the existence of Santa Claus.* **2** People sometimes refer to someone's life or way of living as their **existence**: *Living with such an uncaring man must be a pretty miserable existence.*

exit /'ɛksɪt/ or /'ɛgzɪt/ *noun*; *verb*
▻ ***noun***: **exits**
1 An **exit** is a way out of somewhere, especially a public building: *Please leave the cinema by the rear exit.* □ *We should have come off the motorway at the last exit.* **2** (*used in the singular*) Someone makes an **exit** when they leave: *They made a swift exit when they saw there was no food.*
▻ ***verb*** (*formal*): **exits, exiting, exited**
You **exit** from somewhere when you leave: *In the event of fire, you should exit from the building quickly but calmly.*

exodus /'ɛksədəs/ *noun*: **exoduses**
An **exodus** is the departure of a lot of people from a place at the same time: *How will police cope with the mass exodus of 200 000 people at the end of the tournament?* □ *the exodus of the Israelites from Egypt.*

exonerate /ɪg'zɒnəreɪt/ *verb* (*formal*): **exonerates, exonerating, exonerated**
To **exonerate** someone is to prove or declare that they are not guilty or not to blame: *His mental state at the time exonerates him from all responsibility.* [*same as* **clear**]

exorbitant /ɪg'zɔːbɪtənt/ *adjective*
Something that is **exorbitant** is unfairly or unreasonably expensive: *They charge exorbitant rates for their work.* [*same as* **extortionate**]

exotic /ɪg'zɒtɪk/ *adjective*
Something **exotic** is interestingly unusual or strange because it comes from another very different country: *exotic plants.*

expand /ɪk'spand/ *verb*: **expands, expanding, expanded**
Something **expands** when it becomes greater in size, extent or importance: *In hot weather, the door expands so much that it is impossible to open.* □ *We hope our new advertising campaign will help the business to expand.* □ *The bank is aiming to expand its share of the mortgage market.*

> ***phrasal verb***
> You **expand on** something when you say more about it or give more information: *The essay would have been better if you had expanded on your first point more.* [*same as* **enlarge on**]

expanse /ɪk'spans/ *noun*: **expanses**
An **expanse** of something, such as sky or land, is a wide area of it: *Beyond the hill was an expanse of yellow cornfield stretching as far as the eye could see.* [*same as* **stretch**]

expansion /ɪk'spanʃən/ *noun* (*uncount*)
Expansion is the process of becoming greater in size, extent or importance: *Under heat, the metal undergoes considerable expansion.* □ *This will help to finance the expansion of the business.*

expatriate /ɛks'patrɪət/ *noun*: **expatriates**
An **expatriate** is someone living or working abroad.

expect /ɪk'spɛkt/ *verb*: **expects, expecting, expected**
1 You **expect** something to happen if you believe it is going to happen: *I was expecting you to telephone last night.* □ *We weren't expecting to meet you here.* □ *No-one expected the book to be such a success.* □ *What time do you expect to finish tonight?* □ *I don't expect I'll be very late.* □ *'Will your father be pleased?' 'I don't expect so.'* **2** You **are expecting** something when you are waiting for it to arrive or occur: *I can't talk now; I'm expecting guests at any minute.* □ *She was expecting a letter from her boyfriend.* □ *I'm afraid we must expect trouble.* **3** You **expect** someone to do something if you are relying on them to do it: *We expect you to behave responsibly while we're away.* □ *Staff are expected to work overtime as required.* □ *No-one expects you to achieve the impossible.* **4** You **expect** a certain kind of attitude or treatment from people if you think you have a right to it: *We expect loyalty from our staff.* □ *She evidently expected to be treated like royalty.* **5** If you say you **expect** that something is so you are guessing that it is so: *He said he would be here by 7 o'clock; I expect he's forgotten.* □ *I don't expect you've got the key for this cupboard, have you?* [*same as* **suppose**; compare **imagine**] **6** A woman who **is expecting** is pregnant: *She's expecting her first baby in June.* — *adjective* **expected:** *The expected storm never came.*

expectancy /ɪk'spɛktənsɪ/ *noun* (*uncount*)
Expectancy is the feeling of excitement that you get when you know something good is about to happen: *There was a look of expectancy on her face.* [see also **life expectancy**]

expectation /ɛkspɛk'teɪʃən/ *noun*: **expectations**
1 (*uncount*) **Expectation** is a firm belief that something will happen: *Contrary to expectation, several people survived the crash.* □ *I came in the expectation that I would see some good football.* **2** An **expectation** is a hope that something will happen: *Our children have prospered beyond all our expectations.*

expedition /ɛkspə'dɪʃən/ *noun*: **expeditions**
An **expedition** is **1** a journey made for a purpose, especially a long and carefully planned journey involving many people: *Our second expedition to the South Pole was to be more successful.* □ *The four of us went on a little shopping expedition.* **2** the people making such a

journey: *Three of our expedition were suffering from frostbite.*

expel /ɪk'spɛl/ *verb*: **expels, expelling, expelled**
1 You **are expelled** from a place when you are ordered to leave, especially when your right to return is taken away, often as a punishment: *His repeatedly drunken behaviour got him expelled from the club.* □ *She was expelled from school for cheating in an exam.* **2** (*formal*) A substance, such as a gas, **is expelled** when it is forced out: *The liquid is then expelled from the tube at the other end.* [see also **expulsion**]

expend /ɪk'spɛnd/ *verb* (*formal*): **expends, expending, expended**
You **expend** something, such as time or energy, when you spend it or use it up: *We would not want to expend any more of our resources on this project.*

expendable /ɪk'spɛndəbəl/ *adjective*
Someone or something is **expendable** when they are not absolutely necessary and could be dismissed or disposed of if required: *The secret is to work so hard that they'll not get the chance to claim that you're expendable.*

expenditure /ɪk'spɛndɪtʃə(r)/ *noun* (*uncount*)
Expenditure is money spent: *Is this scheme important enough to justify such huge amounts of public expenditure?*

expense /ɪk'spɛns/ *noun*: **expenses**
1 (*uncount*) **Expense** is cost in terms of money: *The government has pushed ahead with this campaign, at great expense to the taxpayer.* □ *We were not prepared for the expense involved in renovating the house.* **2** An **expense** is something that costs a lot of money: *Travelling by train is quite an expense these days.* **3** (*used in the plural*) Someone's **expenses** consist of the money they spend in the course of doing their job, which their company pays them back: *I'll have to make a claim for travelling expenses.*
▻ ***phrase***
1 You do something **at** someone's **expense** when **a** they pay for it: *He took his family to restaurants at the company's expense.* **b** they are harmed or disadvantaged by it: *But you can only devote more time and energy to your career at the expense of your family life.* **2** When you make a joke **at** someone's **expense**, they are the subject of the joke and are made to look foolish or ridiculous.

expensive /ɪk'spɛnsɪv/ *adjective*
Something is **expensive** when it costs a lot of money: *Her hobbies include eating in expensive restaurants and wearing expensive clothes.* □ *You can hire me, but my time is very expensive.* [*opposite* **inexpensive, cheap**] — *adverb* **expensively:** *The hotel was very expensively furnished.*

experience /ɪk'spɪərɪəns/ *noun*; *verb*
▻ ***noun***
1 (*uncount*) **Experience** is knowledge or skill gained through practice, or through having seen or done something before: *She has a lot of experience in this field.* □ *This will be a chance for you to gain some valuable experience.* □ *I have had no experience of this kind of racial hatred before.* □ *Speaking from my own experience, I think such people are in a small minority.* **2** An **experience** is an event that affects or involves you: *Speaking in front of an audience can be a frightening experience.* □ *I hadn't enjoyed the experience of hearing enemy bombers overhead.*
▻ ***verb***: **experiences, experiencing, experienced**
You **experience** something when it happens to you, or when you feel it or are affected by it: *She had never experienced war.* □ *I'm experiencing a spinning sensation in my head.*

experienced /ɪk'spɪərɪənst/ *adjective*
Someone is **experienced** when they have a lot of knowledge or skill gained from experience: *She's an experienced player on the international circuit.* [*same as* **seasoned, practised**]

experiment /ɪk'spɛrɪmənt/ *noun*; *verb*
▻ ***noun*** (*count or uncount*): **experiments**
An **experiment** is **1** a scientific test carried out in order to discover something unknown or to check a theory: *Clinical experiments with the drugs have had very positive results.* □ *It is only by experiment that we can really be sure.* **2** an attempt to do something new or original: *His experiments in political verse were not very successful.*
▻ ***verb***: **experiments, experimenting, experimented**
1 To **experiment** on or with something is to carry out a scientific test on it or using it: *She has refused to experiment on live animals.* □ *We experimented with different levels of heat to see how the metal would respond.* **2** To **experiment** with something is also to attempt to do something new or original: *They were the first in Britain to experiment with regular management-worker consultation.*

experimental /ɪkspɛrɪ'mɛntəl/ *adjective*
Something that is **experimental** is being done for the first time, to see if it will be successful: *This is an experimental type of library layout; we're just trying it for a term.* — *adverb* **experimentally:** *He tried a little of the powder experimentally on his tongue.*

expert /'ɛkspɜːt/ *noun*; *adjective*
▻ ***noun***: **experts**
Someone who has great skill or knowledge in a particular subject is an **expert** in it: *She's an expert on all sea birds.*
▻ ***adjective***
Someone who is **expert** is highly skilled or knowledgeable: *She removed the splinter with expert precision.* □ *We got some expert advice.* — *adverb* **expertly:** *She handled the situation expertly.*

expertise /ɛkspɜː'tiːz/ *noun* (*uncount*)
Expertise is special skill or knowledge: *an apparently simple painting which is in fact the product of considerable artistic expertise.*

expire /ɪk'spaɪə(r)/ *verb*: **expires, expiring, expired**
1 (*formal*) Something such as a ticket **expires** when it ceases to be valid: *I'm sorry, sir, but this bus pass expired yesterday.* [*same as* **run out**] **2** (*literary*) When someone dies you might say that they **have expired**. — *noun* (*uncount*) **expiry** /ɪk'spaɪərɪ/: *What is the expiry date on your credit card?*

explain /ɪk'spleɪn/ *verb*: **explains, explaining, explained**
You **explain** something **1** when you supply information or details that make it clear or easy to understand: *I tried to explain the legal complications to her.* □ *Could somebody explain to me what is meant by the term 'structuralism'?* □ *She explained that she was doing research on audience response.* **2** when you tell people the reason for it: *The board called a meeting to explain their decision.* □ *I think I can explain his strange behaviour.* □ *She has so far not explained why she left.* □ *'Where's Sheila?' 'She's ill in bed.' 'Oh, that explains why she wasn't at the meeting.'* □ *You must think I'm mad; let me explain.* □ *I explained to her about the possible delay.*

phrasal verb
You **explain away** something bad or wrong, such as a mistake, when you try to show that it was not important or was not your fault: *They can't hope to explain away an error as disastrous as this.*

explanation /ɛkspləˈneɪʃən/ *noun* (*count or uncount*): **explanations**
An **explanation** is **1** a statement or fact that provides a reason for something: *She has given me no explanation for her decision to resign.* ▫ *His recent hostility is quite without explanation.* **2** a detailed description of what something is or of how it works: *There is still no satisfactory scientific explanation of the creation of the universe.* ▫ *These are intended as aids to classroom explanation.*

explanatory /ɪkˈsplanətərɪ/ *adjective*
Something is **explanatory** when it aims to explain something: *a brief explanatory statement.*

explicit /ɪkˈsplɪsɪt/ *adjective*
1 Something **explicit** is clearly stated or explained and impossible to be mistaken about: *She gave explicit instructions as to what the children were to be allowed to eat.* [*same as* **clear**, **precise**; *opposite* **vague**] **2** You are **explicit** when you speak plainly and openly: *He was surprisingly explicit about his relationship with Thomas.* [*opposite* **cagey**] **3 Explicit** scenes of sex, *eg* in films or books, are scenes in which sex is openly shown or described, rather than just suggested or implied.

explode /ɪkˈsploʊd/ *verb*: **explodes, exploding, exploded**
1 A bomb or other device **explodes** when it bursts open with great force, damaging or destroying the things around it. [*same as* **blow up**] **2** When something increases suddenly and rapidly, you might say that it **explodes**: *After the war, the population in these areas exploded.* [*same as* **mushroom**] **3** When someone suddenly becomes very angry you might also say that they **explode**: *My father exploded with rage at the news.* [*same as* **blow up**] **4** You **explode** a theory or belief when you prove that it is wrong: *His book explodes the myth of playboy actors with sumptuous lifestyles.*

exploit *noun*; *verb*
▻ ***noun*** /ˈɛksplɔɪt/: **exploits**
Exploits are bold or exciting things that someone does: *He entertained the children with stories of his wartime exploits.*
▻ ***verb*** /ɪkˈsplɔɪt/: **exploits, exploiting, exploited**
1 You **exploit** something or someone when you take unfair advantage of them in order to achieve your own aims: *Political parties should not exploit the sick or elderly in their campaign literature.* **2** To **exploit** something, such as a supply of fuel, means to make good use of it: *We should be exploiting wind and wave power, not messing around with nuclear energy.* ▫ *It would be a crime not to exploit such a perfect opportunity.* — *noun* (*uncount*) **exploitation** /ɛksplɔɪˈtəɪʃən/: *The exploitation of children is part of their culture.* ▫ *Technology can enhance our exploitation of fossil fuels.*

explore /ɪkˈsplɔː(r)/ *verb*: **explores, exploring, explored**
1 You **explore** a place when you travel through it to find out about it: *We explored large stretches of the Spanish coastline.* **2** You **explore** something such as an idea when you think about it very carefully: *They had already explored the possibility of taking her to a psychiatrist.* — *noun* (*uncount*) **exploration** /ɛkspləˈreɪʃən/: *a journey of exploration.*

explosion /ɪkˈsploʊʒən/ *noun*: **explosions**
An **explosion** is **1** the sudden and violent bursting open of a bomb or other device, or the noise this makes: *Three officers were killed in the explosions.* ▫ *The explosion could be heard several miles away.* **2** a sudden great increase in something: *a population explosion.* **3** an outburst of anger.

explosive /ɪkˈsploʊzɪv/ *adjective*; *noun*
▻ ***adjective***
1 An **explosive** substance can be made to explode. **2** An **explosive** situation is one in which outbursts of anger or of violence seem likely to occur.
▻ ***noun***: **explosives**
Explosives are substances that can be made to explode.

export *verb*; *noun*
▻ ***verb*** /ɪkˈspɔːt/: **exports, exporting, exported**
To **export** goods is to send them to another country to be sold: *They have not only exported their tea and coffee to Europe, but their system of fairer trading as well.*
▻ ***noun*** /ˈɛkspɔːt/: **exports**
1 Exports are goods exported: *You cannot boost the economy simply by increasing exports.* **2** (*uncount*) **Export** is the process of being exported: *None of these ever reach the home market; they are produced purely for export.*

expose /ɪkˈspoʊz/ *verb*: **exposes, exposing, exposed**
1 To **expose** something is to remove what covers, protects or shelters it so that it can be seen or touched: *The plaster has fallen off, exposing the bare brick behind.* ▫ *Without the trees, the north side of the house would be exposed to severe winds.* **2** You **expose** someone to something when you cause or allow them to experience or suffer it: *This latest blunder has exposed the government to severe criticism.* ▫ *They were keen to expose their children to all forms of art.* **3** To **expose** a person or organization is to reveal something about them, usually something unpleasant, that has been kept secret: *The three police officers were exposed as having sold official information to several major drug dealers.*

exposure /ɪkˈspoʊʒə(r)/ *noun* (*usually uncount*): **exposures**
Exposure is **1** the state of being forced or allowed to experience something or be affected by something: *We should be worried about our children's exposure to violence on television.* ▫ *It is only through exposure to the disease that your body can build up a resistance to it.* **2** appearance or mention in public, *eg* on television or in newspapers: *Any health campaign should be given the widest possible exposure.* **3** the extremely harmful effects of severe cold on a person's body: *One of the climbers has already died of exposure.* **4** the fact of revealing something about someone, usually something unpleasant, that has been kept secret: *He was threatened with the exposure of his love affair if he did not co-operate.* **5** (*count*; *photography*) An **exposure** is single photograph or frame on a film: *I had six exposures left on my film.*

express /ɪkˈsprɛs/ *verb*; *adjective*; *adverb*; *noun*
▻ ***verb***: **expresses, expressing, expressed**
1 You **express** something such as a feeling, idea or opinion when you do or say something to show how you feel or what you think: *The audience were already expressing impatience at the delay by performing a slow hand-clap.* ▫ *I cannot find words adequate to express our gratitude.* ▫ *I'm just writing to express my deep sympathy.* ▫ *She expressed some doubt about the expected result.* ▫ *He expressed the hope that we should meet again soon.* ▫ *She had expressed the intention of meeting me at the airport.* ▫ *The view was expressed by several members of the audience that a fund could be started.* ▫ *I was tired of hearing her express her opinions on the existence of God.* **2** You **express** yourself well when you say what you mean in a clear manner, so that everyone understands you; you **express** yourself badly when you fail to make people understand what you mean. **3** A quality or feeling **is expressed** or

expresses itself in someone's behaviour or actions if it is demonstrated by them: *His grief at last expressed itself in uncontrollable tears.* □ *Her creativeness is also expressed in the way she has furnished the house.* **4** (*technical*) You **express** a quantity in a certain form when you write it in that form: *The result is expressed as a ratio.*

▻ ***adjective***

1 An **express** train or bus travels long distances at high speed and makes few stops. **2** An **express** letter or parcel is sent by a fast delivery service. **3 Express** wishes are wishes that are clearly stated: *It is the express order of the headmaster that pupils should wear uniform at all times.* **4** An **express** purpose is a clear and definite one: *She refused to come, apparently with the express intention of irritating her ex-husband.* — *adverb* **expressly:** *She had expressly requested him not to mention it.* □ *We had chosen that holiday expressly so that Mother could join us.* [compare **purposely**]

▻ ***adverb:*** *The letter has been sent express.*

▻ ***noun***: **expresses**

1 An **express** is an express train or bus: *We caught the 4.00 pm express to Prague.* **2** (*uncount*) You send something, or travel, by **express** when you send it, or travel, by a fast service.

expression /ɪk'sprɛʃən/ *noun*: **expressions**

1 An **expression** is a word or phrase used in a particular situation: *There is no equivalent expression in French.* **2** Your **expression** is the look on your face, showing how you are feeling: *He looked at her with an expression of disappointment.* □ *There was such a guilty expression on her face!* **3** (*uncount*) The **expression** of something, such as an idea, is the way it is communicated to others, whether in words or some other way: *The leaflet contains the precise expression of our party's financial policy.* □ *We will study the expression of sadness in music and dance.* **4** (*uncount*) **Expression** is the extent to which someone shows their feelings, *eg* in their performance of music: *The acting was immature and devoid of expression.*

expressive /ɪk'sprɛsɪv/ *adjective*

1 Something **expressive** shows feelings or intentions clearly or in a lively way: *a very expressive performance* □ *A single raised finger can be quite expressive.* **2** To be **expressive** of something is to express it: *words expressive of anger.* — *adverb* **expressively:** *She shrugged her shoulders expressively.*

expulsion /ɪk'spʌlʃən/ *noun* (*uncount*)

Expulsion is the act of expelling someone or something: *A series of violent episodes led to his expulsion from boarding school.* □ *the expulsion of waste gases.*

exquisite /ɪk'skwɪzɪt/ *adjective*

Something **exquisite** is extremely beautiful: *the baby's exquisite little nose* □ *tapestries of an exquisite 18th century design.* — *adverb* **exquisitely:** *exquisitely carved picture frames.*

extend /ɪk'stɛnd/ *verb*: **extends, extending, extended**

1 You **extend** something when you make it bigger or longer: *We've extended the kitchen to give us room for a dining area.* □ *They decided to extend the holiday another week.* **2** Something **extends** for a certain distance or time when it reaches or goes on that far or that long: *Our farmland extends well beyond that hill.* □ *Discussions extended into the night.* **3** Something **extends**, or you **extend** it, when it includes or is made to include other things not stated or not originally included: *The law should be extended to cover all cases of industrial injury.* □ *Our authority extends beyond the limits you mention.* **4** You **extend** a part of your body when you stretch it out: *Extend your arms fully as you breathe out.* **5** (*formal*) You **extend** something friendly, such as an invitation, to someone when you offer it to them: *We hope to show you the same kindness you have extended to us.*

extension /ɪk'stɛnʃən/ *noun*: **extensions**

1 An **extension** is **a** an added part that makes the original thing bigger or longer: *We had an extension built on to our kitchen.* □ *She asked for an extension to the original time limit.* **b** an extra telephone in a house, or one of a series of telephones connected to a main switchboard in an office: *She was listening to our conversation on the extension in the bedroom.* □ *Mrs Donaldson can be reached on extension 214.* **2** (*uncount*) The **extension** of something is the process of making it bigger or longer, or of making it include or apply to extra things: *They demand the extension of the rights of women members, to bring them in line with the men's rights and privileges.*

extensive /ɪk'stɛnsɪv/ *adjective*

Something **extensive** covers a large area or range: *Extensive damage was caused to shops when the first bomb went off.* □ *The minister is engaged in extensive discussions with his French counterpart.* — *adverb* **extensively:** *These issues have been extensively dealt with in our policy document.*

extent /ɪk'stɛnt/ *noun* (*uncount*)

The **extent** of something is the area or range that it covers or affects: *We had not been told of the full extent of the planned demolition.* □ *We have not been able to assess the full extent of the crisis.* □ *I agree with him to some extent, but there are still some areas of sharp disagreement between us.* □ *To what extent has the pollution affected local residents?* □ *Their relationship had deteriorated to the extent that they were simply not talking to each other.*

exterior /ɪk'stɪərɪə(r)/ *adjective*; *noun*

▻ ***adjective***

Exterior describes things that are outside: *We'll need masonry paint for the exterior walls.* □ *With the exception of a few exterior scenes, the film was shot in a studio.* [*opposite* **interior**]

▻ ***noun***: **exteriors**

1 The **exterior** of something is its outside part or surface: *The satellite's exterior is coated with a reflective substance.* [*opposite* **interior**] **2** Your **exterior** is the expression on your face or the way you behave, especially when this hides the way you really feel: *Beneath that confident exterior she's a very insecure person.*

exterminate /ɪk'stɜːmɪneɪt/ *verb*: **exterminates, exterminating, exterminated**

To **exterminate** a group of animals or people is to kill all of them: *The rats need to be exterminated before they breed further.* — *noun* (*uncount*) **extermination** /ɪkstɜːmɪ'neɪʃən/: *We must prevent the extermination of these rare species.*

external /ɪk'stɜːnəl/ *adjective*

External is used to describe **1** things that happen or exist on the outside: *Within the company, we all feel that we should act now, but there has been external opposition to this.* □ *'For external use only' means you must rub the oil on your skin, not drink it.* **2** matters involving foreign nations: *external affairs.* **3** affairs that take place outside an organization or institution, or that are conducted by people that do not belong to the organization: *I was questioned by my professor and two external examiners.* □ *an external examination.* [*opposite* **internal**] — *adverb* **externally:** *Apply the cream externally.*

extinct /ɪk'stɪŋkt/ *adjective*

1 When all animals of a particular kind are dead, that animal is said to be **extinct**: *Exactly when did* *dinosaurs become extinct?* **2** An **extinct** volcano has not erupted for many years. [*opposite* **active**]

extinction /ɪk'stɪŋkʃən/ *noun* (*uncount*)
The **extinction** of an animal is its state of no longer existing, because all the animals of its kind are dead: *Scientists still fear that some species of whale will be hunted to extinction.*

extinguish /ɪk'stɪŋgwɪʃ/ *verb*: **extinguishes, extinguishing, extinguished**
1 You **extinguish** a fire or a cigarette when you stop it burning. [*same as* **put out**; see also **fire-extinguisher**] **2** (*literary*) Things such as hopes or memories **are extinguished** when they are destroyed: *All his hope and confidence had been extinguished.*

extort /ɪk'stɔ:t/ *verb*: **extorts, extorting, extorted**
To **extort** something, such as money, from someone is to get it by force or by threatening them: *They were found to have extorted information from junior officers.* — *noun* (*uncount*) **extortion** /ɪk'stɔ:ʃən/: *She has been accused of extortion.*

extortionate /ɪk'stɔ:ʃənət/ *adjective*
Something, such as a price, is **extortionate** when it is unreasonably high: *They make extortionate demands on their workforce.* [*same as* **exorbitant**]

extra /'ɛkstrə/ *adjective*; *noun*; *adverb*
▻ ***adjective***
1 An **extra** person or thing is added to the usual, necessary or expected number or amount: *We could do with an extra waitress at weekends.* **2** Something is **extra** when you have to pay an additional charge for it: *The price includes breakfast and dinner; lunch is extra.*
▻ ***noun***: **extras**
An **extra** is **1** something for which there is an additional charge: *With extras like drinks at the bar and telephone calls, the bill came to over £200.* ▫ *That's the full price; there are no hidden extras.* **2** an actor appearing briefly in a film, usually in a non-speaking role, and employed for a short time only.
▻ ***adverb*** (*intensifying*)
Extra means very: *Be extra careful with those crystal glasses.*

extra- /ɛkstrə/ *prefix*
Extra- is used to form adjectives that mean 'not directly concerned with something' or 'coming from outside or beyond something': *Members of Parliament do spend some time engaged in extra-parliamentary matters.* ▫ *Some people believe that our world has already been visited by extra-terrestrial creatures.*

extract *verb*; *noun*
▻ ***verb*** /ɪk'strakt/: **extracts, extracting, extracted**
1 (*formal*) You **extract** something when you pull or draw it out, especially by force or with effort: *She extracted a pen from her handbag.* ▫ *She had to have all her teeth extracted.* **2** To **extract** a substance is to take it out physically or chemically: *Would it be economically viable to extract the iron ore?* ▫ *Dyes of all colours can be extracted from plants.* **3** You **extract** something from someone when you get it with difficulty, or by using force or threats: *She did not manage to extract an apology from him.* ▫ *He's extracted considerable sums of money from his grandmother.*
▻ ***noun*** /'ɛkstrakt/: **extracts**
1 An **extract** is a short passage selected from a book or piece of music: *We read a few extracts from 19th-century novels.* **2** (*uncount*) **Extract** is used to refer to a substance produced in a concentrated form: *a spoonful of yeast extract.*

extraction /ɪk'strakʃən/ *noun* (*uncount*)
1 The **extraction** of something is the process of drawing it out, whether with force or difficulty, or chemically: *I think the extraction of the whole tooth is the only answer.* ▫ *the extraction of certain valuable minerals.* **2** Your **extraction** is the country or racial group that your family comes from: *She is of Dutch extraction.*

extraneous /ɪk'streɪnɪəs/ *adjective* (*formal*)
Something **extraneous** happens or exists outside, or is not directly concerned or related: *There is a lot of extraneous noise on the recording.* ▫ *We do not have the time to address extraneous problems.*

extraordinary /ɪk'strɔ:dənərɪ/ *adjective*
1 An **extraordinary** person or thing has very rare and special qualities that you like or admire. **2** Something very strange or unusual might also be described as **extraordinary**. [*same as* **exceptional**]

extravagant /ɪk'stravəgənt/ *adjective*
1 Someone who is **extravagant** **a** spends large amounts of money unwisely, especially on luxuries: *Real cream! That was extravagant of you!* ▫ *No-one minds being extravagant with someone else's money.* ▫ *They used to go on these extravagant cruises.* **b** uses too much of a resource, or wastes it: *There's only a limited supply of water, so we mustn't be extravagant with it.* **2** **Extravagant** claims or ideas are not realistic or based on fact: *Manufacturers in the beauty industry make such extravagant claims for their products.* [*same as* **exaggerated, unrealistic**] **3** **Extravagant** language or behaviour is extreme and often merely intended for effect: *He spread his hands in an extravagant gesture of bewilderment.* ▫ *praising her in extravagant terms.* [*same as* **exaggerated**] — *adverb* **extravagantly:** *He lived extravagantly, eating out a good deal, and entertaining on a lavish scale.* ▫ *an extravagantly furnished house* ▫ *He was one of those extravagantly demonstrative people.*

extreme /ɪk'stri:m/ *adjective*; *noun*
▻ ***adjective***
1 **Extreme** means very high, or highest, in degree or intensity: *You should take extreme care over your child's education.* ▫ *They live in extreme poverty.* **2** **Extreme** also means very far, or furthest, in any direction, especially out from the centre: *at the extreme southern tip of the island.* **3** **Extreme** action is taken in very difficult or dangerous circumstances: *Extreme measures are what is required.*
▻ ***noun***: **extremes**
Unusually or unacceptably intense behaviour of a particular kind is often described as an **extreme**: *They have gone from one extreme to the other; after threatening to execute him, they are now proposing to make him President!*
▻ ***phrases*** **1** When you describe behaviour as **going to extremes** you think that it is unreasonable or unacceptable. **2** **In the extreme** means extremely or as much as is possible: *The scheme was ridiculous in the extreme.* — *adverb* (*intensifying*) **extremely:** *She was extremely beautiful.* ▫ *They understand each other extremely well.*

extremity /ɪk'strɛmɪtɪ/ *noun*: **extremities**
1 (*used in the singular*)The **extremity** of something is the part furthest away from the middle in any direction: *at the northern extremity of the field.* **2** Your **extremities** are those parts of your body that are furthest away from your heart, especially your hands and feet: *One on the main symptoms to look out for is loss of sensation in the extremities.* **3** (*uncount*) **Extremity** is the state of being extreme: *She seemed such a mild person; the extremity of her political views took me by surprise.*

extricate /ˈɛkstrɪkeɪt/ *verb* (*formal*): **extricates, extricating, extricated**
You **extricate** someone from a place they are trapped in, or from a difficult situation, when you get them out of it: *He was finding it difficult to extricate himself from this embarrassing situation.*

extrovert /ˈɛkstrəvɜːt/ *noun* (*often adjectival*): **extroverts**
A lively cheerful person who enjoys being with other people is an **extrovert**: *an extrovert personality.* [compare **introvert**]

exuberant /ɪgˈzjuːbərənt/ *adjective*
An **exuberant** person is cheerful, enthusiastic and energetic. **hem16.ps** *noun* (*uncount*) **exuberance:** *a very creative woman who radiates exuberance.*

eye /aɪ/ *noun; verb*
▻ ***noun*: eyes**
1 Your **eyes** are the pair of features in your face that you see with: *She's got brown eyes.* □ *Close your eyes and imagine you're somewhere else.* □ *It was broad daylight when she opened her eyes again.* □ *He had lost the sight in his right eye in a childhood accident.* □ *Wait till your eyes get accustomed to the dark.* [see picture at **body**] **2** The **eye** of a needle is the hole through which you put the thread. **3** An **eye** is also a metal loop through which a hook fits, forming a fastening on a piece of clothing.
▻ ***verb*: eyes, eyeing or eying, eyed**
You **eye** something when you look at it very hard or watch it carefully: *Michael was eyeing the cream cakes, wondering if he might be allowed two.*
▻ ***phrases*** **1** (*informal*) Someone is **all eyes** when they are watching something with great interest and concentration. **2** Something happens **before your eyes** if you actually see it happen: *He took some money out of her purse before my very eyes.* **3** You **cast** or **run an eye over** something when you look at it quickly or briefly: *She cast an eye over the letter to check the spelling.* **4** Something **catches your eye** when you notice it: *An advertisement caught my eye.* **5** You try to **catch** someone's **eye** when you try to attract their attention: *Brian was trying to catch the waiter's eye.* **6** You **close** or **shut your eyes** to something if you ignore it: *They just close their eyes to the problems.* **7** You **have an eye for** something if you are good at noticing it and judging it: *It's an advantage to have an eye for detail in this job.* **8** You **have your eye on** something when you intend to get it or have it; you **have your eye on** someone when you are watching them closely to check what they do or how they behave. **9** (*informal*) You **keep an eye out for** something or someone when you are watching for them or waiting to see them arrive. **10** You **keep an eye on** someone or something when you look after them and keep them safe: *It's impossible for me to keep an eye on the children while I'm cooking.* **11** You **lay**, **set** or (*informal*) **clap eyes on** someone or something when you see them: *He was the oddest creature I'd ever set eyes on.* **12** You **look** someone **in the eye** when you look directly at their face while you are talking to them, as an indication that you are being honest, or mean what you say; someone refuses **to look you in the eye**, or **meet your eye**, when they avoid looking at your face. **13** When you say that there is **more to** something **than meets the eye**, you mean that it is more complicated or difficult than it appears. **14** A happening **opens your eyes** if it makes you realize that you have been mistaken about something. **15** When you do not **see eye to eye with** someone you disagree with them. **16** You **turn a blind eye to** something, *eg* someone's misbehaviour, if you pretend not to notice it: *She turned a blind eye to his drug-taking.* **17** You are **up to your eyes in** something when you are deeply involved in it or very busy with it: *They're up to their eyes in wedding preparations.*

eyeball /ˈaɪbɔːl/ *noun*: **eyeballs**
Your **eyeballs** are the white ball-shaped parts of the eye.

eyebrow /ˈaɪbraʊ/ *noun*: **eyebrows**
Your **eyebrows** are the arches of hair above each eye.
▻ ***phrase*** Something **raises eyebrows** when it surprises or interests people: *A few eyebrows were raised when he walked in with a different woman.*

eye-catching /ˈaɪkatʃɪŋ/ *adjective*
Something **eye-catching** attracts your attention very quickly: *a number of eye-catching designs.*

eyelash /ˈaɪlaʃ/ *noun*: **eyelashes**
Your **eyelashes** are the short hairs that grow on the edge of your eyelids. [see picture at **body**]

eyelid /ˈaɪlɪd/ *noun*: **eyelids**
Your **eyelids** are the two folds of skin that you lower or raise to cover or uncover your eyes. [see picture at **body**]
▻ ***phrase*** Someone who **does not bat an eyelid** when something surprising, shocking or insulting is said or done shows no sign of surprise or dismay.

eye-opener /ˈaɪ-oʊpənə(r)/ *noun* (*informal*): **eye-openers**
A very surprising or shocking piece of information that changes your opinion of someone or something can be described as an **eye-opener**: *The film of his life is quite an eye-opener.*

eyesight /ˈaɪsaɪt/ *noun* (*uncount*)
Your **eyesight** is your ability to see: *She has very good eyesight.* □ *As he gets older, his eyesight is beginning to fail.*

eyesore /ˈaɪsɔː(r)/ *noun*: **eyesores**
Something very ugly can be referred to as an **eyesore**: *The new office block is a real eyesore.*

eyewitness /ˈaɪwɪtnəs/ *noun*: **eyewitnesses**
An **eyewitness** is a person who actually sees something happen: *An eyewitness was able to give a good description of the thief.*

F

F or **f** /ef/: **Fs** or **f's**

1 F is the sixth letter of the English alphabet: *'Photo' begins with P, not F.* **2 F** is a musical note: *in the key of F major.* **3** In stating temperature, **F** is short for **Fahrenheit**.

fable /'feɪbəl/ *noun*: **fables**

1 A **fable** is a traditional story with a moral message, often with animals as characters. [*same as* **legend**] **2** (*uncount*) Myths and legends generally may be referred to as **fable**: *Some creatures are met with only in fable.*

fabric /'fabrɪk/ *noun*: **fabrics**

1 (*count or uncount*) A **fabric** is any kind of cloth: *nylon and other synthetic fabrics* □ *a small scrap of fabric.* **2** (*used in the singular*) The **fabric** of a building is its walls, floors and roof: *The fabric of the church will deteriorate if it is not properly maintained.* **3** The **fabric** of society is its orderly structure: *The break-up of the family is destroying the fabric of society.* [*same as* **foundations**]

fabricate /'fabrɪkeɪt/ *verb*: **fabricates, fabricating, fabricated**

1 To **fabricate** information is to invent it with the intention of deceiving people: *It was later proved that the police had fabricated evidence to obtain a conviction.* [*same as* **fake**] **2** You **fabricate** a structure or a device when you construct it from available materials: *She had fabricated a bookcase of sorts from a couple of wooden planks and some odd bricks.* — *noun* (*count or uncount*) **fabrication** /fabrɪ'keɪʃən/: *The police report was a fabrication.* □ *Was it the truth or pure fabrication?*

fabulous /'fabjʊləs/ *adjective*

1 (*informal*) You call something **fabulous** if you are greatly impressed or delighted with it: *We had a fabulous evening.* [*same as* **marvellous, splendid**] **2** A quality of someone or something that is described as **fabulous** is famous for its greatness: *a city of fabulous wealth and beauty.* **3 Fabulous** creatures are found only in stories: *dragons and other fabulous beasts.* — *adverb* (*often intensifying*) **fabulously:** *They're fabulously well off.*

facade or **façade** /fə'sɑːd/ *noun*: **facades**

1 The **facade** of a building is its front: *This type of decoration is found typically on 18th-century facades.* **2** (*used in the singular*) A **facade** is also a false appearance deliberately maintained to hide the reality: *They managed to keep up a facade of matrimonial harmony, which deceived their friends and neighbours.* [*same as* **front, semblance**]

face /feɪs/ *noun*; *verb*

▻ ***noun***: **faces**

1 Your **face** is the front part of your head, from forehead to chin: *He cut his face while shaving.* □ *She has a lovely face.* **2** The **faces** of something such as a mountain, a solid geometrical figure, or a precious stone, are its sides: *A cube has six faces.* □ *the west face of Chambe Peak.* **3** In a mine, the **face** is the exposed surface from which coal or other material is being cut: *working at the coalface.* **4** The **face** of a clock or watch is the part bearing the numbers and showing the time: *a watch with a luminous face.* [*same as* **dial**] **5** The **face** of a place or area is its appearance: *Skyscrapers sprang up, changing the face of America's cities.*

▻ ***verb***: **faces, facing, faced**

1 One person or thing **faces** another, or **faces** in a certain direction, when they have their fronts towards them, or are opposite them: *She turned to face me.* □ *We sat facing each other.* □ *The library is on Broad Street, facing the bank.* □ *She found a backward-facing seat in the first carriage.* □ *The house faces west.* **2** You **are faced** with or **face** something unpleasant or difficult when you are about to suffer it, or you have to deal with it: *He faced financial ruin.* □ *They face the death penalty.* □ *We were faced with the huge task of listing all the books.* □ *I hate being faced with decisions.* **3** You **face** facts or the truth when you acknowledge or accept them: *He knew he must face the possibility of defeat.* □ *We're none of us perfect, let's face it.* **4** You say you cannot **face** something or someone when you feel unable to deal with them: *I couldn't face him after the terrible things I'd said to him.* □ *I can't face clearing out all those cupboards.*

▻ ***phrases*** **1** You do something till you are **blue in the face** if you do it energetically and continually, but without achieving the result you want: *You can cry till you're blue in the face; you're not coming with me, and that's that.* **2** Someone or something is **face down** or **downwards** when their front is towards the ground; they are **face up** or **upwards** when their front is turned upwards: *Place the cards face upwards.* □ *She was lying face downwards on the carpet.* **3 a** Two people are **face to face** when they are positioned so as to look straight at each other: *We came face to face in the corridor.* □ *The two men stood face to face.* **b** You see someone **face to face** when you meet them physically, as distinct from seeing or hearing them on the media, or being told about them: *I once met Gielgud face to face in Oxford, while he was working on a production at the Playhouse.* **c** You come, or are brought, **face to face** with a fact, possibility or problem when you have to acknowledge it, accept it or deal with it: *The incident brought her face to face with reality.* **4** You **fly in the face of** something such as tradition when you act in a way that is contrary to it: *They use methods that fly in the face of accepted academic procedure.* **5** You manage to do something **in the face of** difficulties when you do it in spite of them: *She kept cheerful in the face of terrible hardship.* **6** You **look** someone **in the face** when you look straight into their eyes without shame or embarrassment: *I could hardly look her in the face after calling her by the wrong name.* **7** You **lose face** when you lose other people's respect for you: *She had lost face by failing to get the job.* **8** You **make** or **pull a face** when you put on a very obvious and usually ugly expression, *eg* of dislike or disgust: *He tasted the wine and pulled a face.* □ *What were you making faces at me* *for?* **9** For **off** or **from the face of the earth** see **earth**. **10** Something that looks as if it is so **on the face of it** seems to be so, though on further consideration it may not be: *On the face of it, her decision seemed to be the right one.* **11** You **put a good**, or **brave, face on** something when you hide your disappointment over it by appearing cheerful: *She was deeply hurt by his rejection, but tried to put a brave face on it.* **12** You **save face** or **save your face** when you avoid losing other people's respect: *The team managed to save their faces by scoring at the last minute to avoid a 3-0 defeat.* **13** You **set your face against** something when you oppose it strongly: *They had set their faces against reform.* **14** You **show your face** somewhere when you dare to appear there openly: *I don't know how he dares show his face here after his disgraceful behaviour.* **15** Something such as the answer to a problem **is staring you in the face** if it is quite obvious: *The solution was staring me in the face.* **16** You say something **to** someone's **face** when you dare to say it to them openly: *I told him to his face he was a liar.*

phrasal verb
You **face up to** something difficult or unpleasant when you accept it and deal with it: *We've got to face up to reality.*

facecloth /ˈfeɪsklɒθ/ *noun*: **facecloths**
A **facecloth** is a small square cloth for washing yourself with. [*same as* **flannel**; see picture at **bathroom**]

faceless /ˈfeɪsləs/ *adjective*
You call people **faceless** if they seem to have no personality, individuality or interesting qualities; a **faceless** organization is one that seems to take no interest in people as individuals: *My query was dealt with by a series of faceless civil servants.*

facet /ˈfasɪt/ *noun*: **facets**
1 The **facets** of a precious stone are its several flat surfaces or faces. **2** A **facet** of something such as a person's character is a side or feature of it: *I had not known about this facet of her personality before.* [*same as* **side, aspect**]

facetious /fəˈsiːʃəs/ *adjective*
You are being **facetious** when you make remarks that are intended to be funny, especially in rather unsuitable circumstances: *Let's have no more facetious suggestions.* □ *I was only being facetious.* — *adverb* **facetiously:** *Someone facetiously described the place as a cemetery with lights on.*

facial /ˈfeɪʃəl/ *adjective*
Facial means relating to the face: *the complex facial nerves* □ *smiling, frowning and other facial expressions.*

facile /ˈfasaɪl/ *adjective* (*derogatory*)
Facile opinions, arguments or conclusions are over-simple ones that have not been carefully thought out: *His reasoning struck me as facile.*

facilitate /fəˈsɪlɪteɪt/ *verb*: **facilitates, facilitating, facilitated**
To **facilitate** a process or task is to make it easier to carry out: *Nowadays students have access to all sorts of visual aids that facilitate the learning process.*

facility /fəˈsɪlətɪ/ *noun*: **facilities**
1 (*uncount*) Someone does something with **facility** if they do it easily: *She had mastered Swahili with remarkable facility.* [*same as* **ease**; *opposite* **difficulty**] **2** (*used in the singular*) You have a **facility** for something if you are good at it: *She had a facility for grasping problems and knowing how to deal with them.* [*same as* **talent**] **3** (*usually in the plural*) **Facilities** are places or equipment provided for particular activities: *It has one of the best golf courses anywhere and also provides facilities for tennis and squash.* **4** A **facility** is an additional feature or attachment for something such as a machine, that allows it to perform extra tasks: *Most modern cassette-players have a high-speed tape-copying facility.*

facsimile /fakˈsɪmɪlɪ/ *noun*: **facsimiles**
A **facsimile** of something such as a manuscript or picture is an exact copy, *eg* produced by a photographic process: *She included a facsimile of the titlepage in her article on the book.*

fact /fakt/ *noun*: **facts**
1 A **fact** is something that is known to be true, or to exist, or to have happened: *We can't usefully discuss the incident till we know all the facts.* □ *The fact of my mother's being a university graduate impressed Miss Brooks, who was a great snob.* **2** A **fact** is also a statement of the truth, or a piece of information: *Tell me some facts about yourself and your background.* □ *Study these facts and figures and let me have your conclusions.* **3** (*uncount*) **Fact** is truth or reality, as distinct from someone's belief or statement: *His story seemed to be a mixture of fact and fantasy.*
▻ ***phrases*** **1** You say that you know something **for a fact** when you are insisting that it is true: *I know for a fact that she's looking for a new tenant.* **2** You introduce an unpleasant or unwelcome truth with '**the fact is**': *The fact is, I'm too old to change jobs now.* **3** You can use **the fact that** to introduce a clause after verbs or constructions that do not take a simple *that*-clause: *I'm interested in the fact that you speak Hungarian.* □ *The fact that the candidate is a woman should make no difference to your decision.* **4** You use the phrases **in fact, in actual fact, as a matter of fact** and **in point of fact** to emphasize the truth or accuracy of what you are reporting, or to correct a wrong impression that may have been made: *They never in fact read the report.* □ *In point of fact temperatures are higher than usual for August.* □ *He's older than he looks; over 60, in fact.* □ *As a matter of fact, we also received a letter from him.* **5** You say **the fact remains that** to emphasize the relevance of some circumstance to what you are discussing: *Whatever the results, the fact remains that he lied.* **6** For **the facts of life** see **life**.

faction /ˈfakʃən/ *noun*: **factions**
A **faction** is an active group within a larger group or organization, that opposes some of the group or organization's policies: *The party seemed in danger of splitting into a number of opposing factions.*

factor /ˈfaktə(r)/ *noun*: **factors**
1 A **factor** is a circumstance that affects a particular situation, or that contributes to a result: *Parental attitude is still one of the main factors affecting a child's progress at school.* **2** (*mathematics*) The **factors** in a multiplication sum are the numbers that are multiplied together.

factory /ˈfaktərɪ/ *noun*: **factories**
A **factory** is a building or set of buildings with machinery and equipment for the large-scale manufacture of goods: *She has a job in a toy factory.* □ *a factory employee.*

factual /ˈfaktjʊəl/ *adjective*
Something such as a report, that is described as **factual**, contains or consists of facts, or is concerned with them: *The story he tells is largely factual, based on his own experiences in Somalia.* □ *plenty of factual information.* [*opposite* **fictional**] — *adverb* **factually:** *The statement is factually correct, so far as it goes.*

faculty /ˈfakəltɪ/ *noun*: **faculties**
1 (*used in the plural*) Your **faculties** are your mental and physical powers: *He's still in full possession of all his faculties at the age of 93.* □ *the faculty of reasoning.* **2** (*used in the singular; sometimes humorous*) You have a faculty for something if you have a talent for it: *She had a faculty for annoying people.* **3** (*BrE*) A **faculty** at a university is a group of departments teaching related subjects: *the Arts Faculty* □ *The Faculty of Medicine.* **4** (*AmE; with a singular or plural verb*) The **faculty** of a school, college or university are the staff.

fad /fad/ *noun*: **fads**
1 A **fad** is a fashion or trend that is popular for a short time: *Taking cold baths is one of those health fads that come and go.* **2** Someone's **fads** are their dislikes, or unreasonable prejudices, especially with regard to food.

fade /feɪd/ *verb*: **fades, fading, faded**
1 Colours or coloured objects **fade** when they become paler; something such as sunlight **fades** things when it makes them paler in colour: *The curtains had faded in the sun.* □ *Constant washing had faded the fabric.* **2** An image or something you are looking at **fades** when it becomes less clear and distinct: *The features of the landscape were fading fast as night approached.* **3** The light **fades** as the sun sinks: *In the tropics the light doesn't so much fade as go out suddenly.* **4** Sounds **fade** as they get quieter and can no longer be heard: *Their voices faded away as they moved off.* [*same as* **die away**] **5** Feelings and memories **fade** as they get less strong and disappear: *Her enthusiasm for early-morning exercises rapidly faded.* □ *The image of her face faded from his memory.* **6** Someone's smile **fades** when they gradually stop smiling. — *adjective* **faded:** *faded flowers* □ *She was pretty in a faded sort of way.*

> ***phrasal verbs***
> (*radio, television, films*) To **fade in** a sound or image is to make it gradually appear or become more distinct; to **fade out** a sound or image is to make it gradually become fainter and disappear.

faeces (*AmE* **feces**) /ˈfiːsiːz/ *noun* (*plural*)
Faeces are the solid pieces of bodily waste that you get rid of through the anus.

fag /fag/ *noun* (*informal*): **fags**
1 A **fag** is a cigarette: *a packet of fags.* **2** (*used in the singular*) A boring or tiring task can be called a **fag**: *Analysing the data is going to be a fag, but it's got to be done.* [*same as* **drag**]

fagged /fagd/ *adjective*
▻ ***phrase*** You are **fagged out** when you are completely exhausted: *You look fagged out.*

Fahrenheit /ˈfarənhaɪt/ *noun* (*uncount*)
Fahrenheit is a scale for measuring temperature, according to which water boils at 212° and freezes at 32°.

fail /feɪl/ *verb; noun*
▻ ***verb***: **fails, failing, failed**
1 a You **fail** when you do not succeed in doing what you are trying to do: *They failed in their attempt to find the source of the Nile.* □ *He failed to get all the qualifications he needed for university entrance.* □ *We failed to reach the trapped men in time to save them.* □ *The military coup failed.* [*opposite* **succeed**] **b** You **fail** to do something, especially something you ought to do, when you do not do it: *She was fined for failing to bring back a library book.* □ *When they failed to return by sunset he sent out a search party.* **c** You **fail** an exam or test when you do not reach the required standard for passing it; an examiner **fails** you when he or she judges that you have not reached the required standard for passing: *I've failed my driving test for the second time.* [*opposite* **pass**]
2 a Something such as a machine or a bodily organ or faculty **fails** when it stops functioning or working properly: *Suddenly the engine failed.* □ *My memory is failing.* **b** A business **fails** when it loses money instead of making a profit, and has to stop operating. [*same as* **collapse**] **c** A crop **fails** when it doesn't grow as it should: *The potato crop failed several years running, bringing famine to many parts of Ireland.*
3 a A person **fails** you when they do not do what they promised to do, or were expected to do: *Have I ever failed you when you needed my help?* [*same as* **let down**] **b** A quality or talent that you have **fails** you if you lose it just when you need it most: *It's a dreadful thing for poets when their inspiration fails them.* □ *My nerve failed me when it came to telling her the truth.*
▻ ***noun***: **fails**
You get a **fail** in a exam if you do not pass it: *six passes and two fails.* [*opposite* **pass**]
▻ ***phrases*** **1** You say you **fail to see** something when you don't understand it: *I fail to see why the women workers should be paid less than the men.* **2 a** Something that you are told to do **without fail** is something you must do: *Be here at 9.00 without fail.* **b** Something that happens regularly **without fail** happens every time: *He visited her in hospital every day without fail.*

failed /feɪld/ *adjective*
1 Someone who is described as a **failed** poet, **failed** artist, or **failed** writer is a poet, artist or writer who has never achieved success or fame. [*opposite* **successful**] **2** A **failed** attempt is one that is unsuccessful. [same as **abortive**]

failing /ˈfeɪlɪŋ/ *noun; adjective*
▻ ***noun***: **failings**
A person's or thing's **failings** are their faults or weaknesses: *The new design proved to have several failings.* □ *One of his failings was an inability to plan ahead.* [*same as* **weakness**; *opposite* **strength, virtue**]
▻ ***adjective***
People suffer from **failing** health or **failing** eyesight when their health or eyesight is worsening.
▻ ***phrase*** You use **'failing that'** if what you have arranged may not be possible, and you are suggesting an alternative: *Could you get me a copy of the Times, or failing that, the Guardian?*

failure /ˈfeɪljə(r)/ *noun*: **failures**
1 (*uncount*) **Failure** is the circumstance of being unsuccessful: *Our efforts to obtain financial help ended in failure.* □ *His failure to gain a university place was a great blow to him.* [*opposite* **success**] **2** (*uncount*) A person's or thing's **failure** to do something is the circumstance of their not doing it: *She was alarmed at his failure to return home after school.* **3** Something that is unsuccessful is a **failure**: *The scheme was a complete failure.* [*same as* **flop**; *opposite* **success**] **4** Someone who is described as a **failure** keeps failing in the things they try to achieve: *I feel such a failure.* **5** (*uncount or count*) The **failure** of a machine or a bodily organ is the circumstance of its ceasing to function, or not functioning properly: *engine failure* □ *heart failure.* **6** (*uncount or count*) The **failure** of a business is its financial collapse. **7** (*uncount or count*) You experience a **failure** of one of your abilities or qualities when you lose it suddenly: *I suffered a sudden failure of memory.* [compare **lapse**]

faint /feɪnt/ *adjective; verb; noun*
▻ ***adjective***
1 A sound, feeling or image that is **faint** is dim, weak

or indistinct rather than strong and clear: *They heard a faint scratching.* □ *The signature is very faint.* □ *He detected a faint smell of glue.* **2** A **faint** possibility is a slight one: *There's a faint possibility that he'll phone.* [*same as* **slight**; *opposite* **strong**] **3** A **faint** response is one that lacks strength, enthusiasm or warmth: *She reacted to his joke with a faint smile.* **4** The superlative **faintest** is used with a negative to deny any suggestion of something: *I haven't the faintest intention of telling her.* [*same as* **least**, **slightest**] **5** You feel **faint** when you feel dizzy and ill, *eg* after an injury or shock. — *adverb* **faintly:** *A light shone faintly through the trees.* □ *She was led to the ambulance, protesting faintly.* — *noun* **faintness:** *A feeling of faintness came over him and he had to sit down.* □ *the faintness of the signature.*

▻ ***verb***: **faints, fainting, fainted**

You **faint** when you lose consciousness: *He used to faint at the sight of blood.* [*same as* **black out, pass out**]

▻ ***noun*** (*used in the singular*): *She had fallen to the ground in a faint.*

fair[1] /fɛə(r)/ *adjective; adverb*

▻ ***adjective***

1 A person or thing that is **fair** is just or reasonable: *The headmaster had a reputation for being very fair.* □ *I'm trying to be fair to everyone.* □ *It isn't fair to her not to tell her the truth.* □ *Socialism aims at a fairer distribution of wealth.* □ *All suggestions will get a fair hearing.* □ *'Obstinate' would be a fair description of her attitude.* [*opposite* **unfair**] **2 Fair** means quite large: *There have been a fair number of complaints.* [*opposite* **small**] **3 Fair** also means quite good, or not very good: *He has a fair chance of winning.* □ *Her health is fair.* [= rather poor] **4** A **fair** guess or idea is likely to be right: *I don't know the answer, but I can make a fair guess.* **5** Someone who is **fair** has blonde or gold-coloured hair: *She was very fair as a child.* [*opposite* **dark**] **6 Fair** skin is pale: *The sun can easily damage fair skin.* [*opposite* **dark**] **7** (*old*) Someone described as **fair** is beautiful. [*opposite* **plain**] **8** The weather is **fair** when it is calm and settled and there is no rain: *Sunday will remain fair.*

▻ ***adverb***

Someone who does not play **fair** in a game or argument uses dishonest, unlawful or improper methods to win.

▻ ***phrases*** **1** You use **fair enough** to express agreement or understanding: *'I won't know definitely till Friday.' 'Fair enough.'* **2** You use **to be fair** to add a comment that corrects a false or unfair impression: *To be fair, he wasn't at the last meeting, so he wasn't told.*

fair[2] /fɛə(r)/ *noun*: **fairs**

1 A **fair** or **funfair** is an outdoor event consisting of amusements such as machines to ride on, food stalls, and sideshows such as shooting galleries where people compete for prizes: *We won a goldfish at the fair.* **2** (*old*) In earlier times a **fair** was a market for the sale of farm produce and animals. **3** A **fair** or **trade fair** is an indoor exhibition of goods from various countries and firms, held to encourage trade: *The Frankfurt Book Fair.* **4** A charity event at which goods are sold to raise money for a cause may also be called a **fair**: *the annual Christmas fair.* [*same as* **fête**]

fairground /ˈfɛəgraʊnd/ *noun*: **fairgrounds**

A **fairground** is the piece of land on which the stalls, sideshows, rides and other amusements are set up for a fair (sense 1).

fairly /ˈfɛəlɪ/ *adverb*

1 You deal with people or matters **fairly** when you do so in a just and reasonable way: *You're not treating me fairly.* □ *This system could fairly be described as a mess.* [*opposite* **unfairly**] **2** (*moderating*) **Fairly** means 'rather' or 'to a noticeable extent' when unstressed: *I'm glad to say we're making fairly good progress.* [*same as* **rather**, **pretty**, **quite**] **3 Fairly** means 'only moderately' or 'to a limited extent' when stressed: *His work is fairly satisfactory but he must learn to concentrate.* [see also **quite**, see note at **rather**] **4 Fairly** can be used with some verbs to mean 'absolutely, in the real sense of the word': *She fairly flew along the corridor.* [= she ran very fast]

fairness /ˈfɛənəs/ *noun* (*uncount*)

Fairness is the quality of being reasonable or just in your treatment of people: *As a competition judge she had a reputation for fairness.* [*same as* **impartiality**]

▻ ***phrase*** You use '**in all fairness**' when you are about to add a comment that corrects a false or unfair impression: *In all fairness to Jack, he was just trying to be helpful.*

fair play /fɛəˈpleɪ/ *noun* (*uncount*)

Fair play is the principle or practice of treating everybody equally, or of dealing with people in a just, reasonable and honourable manner: *Where's your sense of fair play?*

fairy /ˈfɛərɪ/ *noun*: **fairies**

A **fairy** is a being with magical powers, found in stories, typically in the form of a very small and beautiful girl or woman, with wings.

fairy tale /ˈfɛərɪ teɪl/ *noun*: **fairy tales**

A **fairy tale** or **fairy story** is a children's story about magical happenings, involving creatures such as fairies.

fait accompli /feɪtəkɒmˈpliː/ *noun* (*used in the singular*)

Something that is described as a **fait accompli** has already been decided and settled, and cannot be changed: *If it's a fait accompli, why are we bothering to discuss it?*

faith /feɪθ/ *noun*: **faiths**

1 (*uncount*) You have or put **faith** in someone or something when you trust them or believe in their ability, goodness or effectiveness: *Have faith in God.* □ *I don't put much faith in these remedies.* □ *I have no faith in his judgement.* [*opposite* **mistrust**, **distrust**] **2** A **faith** is any religion such as Christianity, Islam or Buddhism: *people of other faiths.* **3** (*uncount*) **Faith** is religious belief: *His strong faith helped him to cope with the tragedy.*

▻ ***phrases*** **1** (*literary*) You **break faith** with someone when you do not do what you promised them; you **keep faith** with them when you do what you promised: *The management have broken faith with us in declaring further redundancies.* **2** You do something **in good faith** when you do it genuinely believing that you are doing the right thing: *The nurse had administered the drug in good faith, not realizing that the bottle was wrongly labelled.*

faithful /ˈfeɪθfəl/ *adjective; noun*

▻ ***adjective***

1 You are **faithful** to an idea, a person or an organization if you are loyal to them and keep supporting them: *He always remained faithful to his principles.* □ *the Labour Party and its faithful supporters.* [*opposite* **disloyal**] **2** Someone who is **faithful** to their wife, husband or sexual partner does not have a sexual relationship with anyone else. [*opposite* **unfaithful**] **3** A **faithful** description, representation or translation of something is an accurate one: *The television adaptation has remained pretty faithful to the original novel.*

▻ ***noun*** (*plural*)
People who firmly believe in and practise their religion, or firmly support a certain political party are referred to as the **faithful**: *It happened on Sunday morning, when the faithful were at church.* ▫ *a meeting of the party faithful.*

faithfully /ˈfeɪθfəlɪ/ *adverb*
1 Faithfully means loyally: *She stood by him faithfully.* **2 Faithfully** also means accurately and consistently: *The film stuck faithfully to the book.*
▻ ***phrase*** You end a formal letter, especially to someone you have addressed as 'Dear Sir' or 'Dear Madam', by putting '**yours faithfully**' before your signature.

fake /feɪk/ *noun*; *adjective*; *verb*
▻ ***noun***: **fakes**
1 A **fake** is anything that has been deliberately created to look like something real or valuable, so as to deceive people: *The jewels are fakes.* ▫ *Some of the fakes are good enough to deceive even the art experts.* **2** Someone who is a **fake** is not what they present themselves as or pretend to be: *I feel a fake, lying in bed when I'm not ill.* [*same as* **fraud**]
▻ ***adjective:*** *fake diamonds* ▫ *a fake Picasso.* [*opposite* **genuine**]
▻ ***verb***: **fakes, faking, faked**
1 You **fake** something when you create it deliberately to look like something real or valuable, in order to deceive people: *He actually gave lessons in how to fake old-master paintings.* **2** You **fake** an emotion or a reaction when you pretend to have it: *She faked a fainting attack.*

falcon /ˈfɔːlkən/ *noun*: **falcons**
A **falcon** is a bird of prey that can be trained to hunt small birds and animals.

fall /fɔːl/ *verb*; *noun*
▻ ***verb***: **falls, falling, fell, fallen**
1 a Someone or something **falls** when they drop or move suddenly towards the ground, usually in an uncontrolled manner or by accident: *One of the chicks had fallen out of the nest.* ▫ *She fell 30 feet on to a rock ledge.* ▫ *He fell downstairs.* ▫ *The book fell to the floor with a bang.* ▫ *Bombs were falling on the city all night.* ▫ *This postcard must have fallen off the mantelpiece.* ▫ *He was hit by falling rocks.* **b** Someone or something that is standing or moving in an upright position **falls** when they lose their balance, are knocked off balance, or collapse, and finish lying on the ground: *She tripped and fell as she was running for a bus.* ▫ *He fell and scraped his knee.* ▫ *A tree had fallen across the road.* ▫ *The tower fell down in 1326.* ▫ *London Bridge is falling down.* **c** Rain or snow **falls** when it comes down from out of the sky: *Rain had been falling steadily all morning.* **d** Your tears **fall** when they drop from your eyes.
2 a People **fall** in a battle, war or fight when they are killed: *the soldiers who fell in two world wars.* **b** A ruler, leader, regime or government **falls**, or **falls** from power, when they are defeated: *The Conservatives fell in 1974.* ▫ *Soviet leaders rose and fell one after the other in the decades following Stalin's death.* **c** A country **falls** when it is defeated in war; a place **falls** when it is captured during a war; a parliamentary seat **falls** to a political party when it is gained by them in an election: *France fell in 1940.* ▫ *Quebec fell to General Wolfe in 1759.* ▫ *Edinburgh North fell to Labour in the recent by-election.*
3 A rate, amount, standard or value **falls** when it decreases: *Temperatures will fall overnight to about 4° Celsius.* ▫ *House prices have fallen considerably.* ▫ *The pound has again fallen against the dollar.* ▫ *The rate of inflation has fallen for the second month running.* ▫ *Standards of health care are falling.*
4 a Your hair **falls** in a certain way when it hangs like that: *Her hair fell thickly round her shoulders.* **b** Land **falls** gently or steeply when it slopes down gradually or suddenly: *The ground fell steeply towards the cliff edge.*
5 a Silence **falls** when people become silent: *An awkward silence fell.* **b** Darkness or night **falls** when the sun sinks and the light disappears: *Night fell and they called off the search.* **c** Light or a shadow **falls** on something when it reaches it or covers it: *A shaft of sunlight fell across the bed.* ▫ *His shadow fell across the page as he passed behind her desk.* **d** Your eye **falls** on something when you notice it: *Her eye fell on the pile of library books on his desk.*
6 People **fall** into a certain state when they pass into it: *He realized he had fallen in love with her.* ▫ *The audience fell silent.* ▫ *It wasn't long before he fell asleep.* ▫ *She fell ill and died.* ▫ *His methods have fallen into disrepute.* **7** Someone's face **falls** when they suddenly look disappointed: *His face fell when I refused.*
8 a Things **fall** into classes or categories if they are readily grouped or classified like that: *Our correspondents fall into three main groups.* **b** Things **fall** into place when they re-organize themselves, especially in your mind, in an order or arrangement that makes sense or works well: *Leave the problem alone for a while and when you come back to it everything will have fallen into place.* **c** A book **falls** open at a certain page if that is where it opens naturally, without you turning any pages. **9 a** You say that an anniversary or festival such as Easter or Christmas or your birthday **falls** on a certain day of the week, or date, if that is when it occurs: *My birthday falls on a Saturday this year.* **b** The stress or accent in a word **falls** on a certain syllable if that is the syllable that is stressed: *The accent in the noun 'convert' falls on the first syllable.*
▻ ***noun***: **falls**
1 (*especially in the singular*) Someone has a **fall** when they fall from an upright position, or from a higher position towards the ground: *She had a bad fall on the icy pavement.* ▫ *She had survived a 50-foot fall in the Alps.* **2** A **fall** of snow or rain is an amount that falls at one time; a **fall** of rock is a pile of rocks that have fallen from somewhere: *The road was blocked by a fall of rock.* ▫ *There had been a heavy fall of snow in the night.* **3** (*used in the plural*) **Falls** are a waterfall: *Niagara Falls.* ▫ *the Falls of Shin.* **4** (*usually in the singular*) A **fall** in a rate, value, amount or standard is a decrease: *a rapid fall in temperature* ▫ *a fall in educational standards.* **5** (*used in the singular*) The **fall** of a regime, government, leader or ruler is their defeat: *the fall of Kruschev.* **6** (*used in the singular*) The **fall** of a city or country is its capture or defeat in a war: *the fall of Paris.* **7** (*AmE; uncount or count*) **Fall**, or the **fall**, is the season between summer and winter, when the trees lose their leaves and the weather cools: *I hope to start a new job this fall.* [*same as* **autumn**]
▻ ***phrases*** **1** For **fall flat** see **flat**. **2** Something **falls to pieces** or **falls to bits** when it breaks up into separate pieces or disintegrates: *I used the dictionary such a lot that it eventually fell to pieces.*

phrasal verbs
fall about (*informal*) People **fall about** when they laugh uncontrollably or helplessly: *They fell about at the mere suggestion.*
fall apart 1 Things **fall apart** when they break up into separate pieces or disintegrate: *The books are so badly bound that they fall apart as soon as you start using them.* **2** Something such as a system,

organization or partnership **falls apart** when it collapses or fails: *Their marriage was showing signs of falling apart.*
fall away 1 The land **falls away** where it slopes downward. **2** Something **falls away** from somewhere when it becomes loose or detached, and breaks off: *A large slab of rock had fallen away from the cliff face.* **3** Your friends and supporters **fall away** when they become fewer.
fall back You **fall back** when you retreat or move back: *The troops fell back to the frontier line.*
fall back on You **fall back on** a previously prepared plan or supply when you use it, *eg* in an emergency.
fall behind 1 You **fall behind** when you progress more slowly than other people and they get ahead of you: *We mustn't let Britain fall behind in technology.* [*same as* **drop** behind] **2** You **fall behind** with something such as the rent when you fail to pay it when it is due.
fall for
1 You **fall for** a person when you fall in love with them: *It was evident that Rosamund had fallen for Dr Lydgate.* **2** You **fall for** a trick or a lie when you are deceived by it: *You didn't fall for that old story, did you?*
fall in 1 A ceiling or roof **falls in** when it collapses. **2** When soldiers are ordered to **fall in** they take their place in military formation.
fall in with You **fall in with** a suggestion when you agree to it.
fall off An amount, number, rate or standard **falls off** when it decreases: *The number of competitors has fallen off in recent years.* [*same as* **drop off**; see also **falling-off**]
fall on 1 To **fall on** enemies or on an enemy position is to attack them: *We fell on them as they lay asleep.* [*same as* **attack**] **2** People **fall on** food when they eat it eagerly.
fall out 1 Hair, fur or teeth **fall out** when they become loose and get detached from the body: *My hair fell out in handfuls.* **2** One person **falls out** with another when they quarrel: *They frequently fell out but always made friends again.* [*same as* **quarrel**]
fall over 1 Someone or something that is upright **falls over** when they lose their balance or are knocked off balance, and finish lying on the ground: *Several gravestones had fallen over.* □ *She fell over on the pavement.* **2** You **are falling over** yourself to do something when you are very eager to do it: *They were falling over themselves to please us.* **3** For **fall over backwards** see **backwards**.
fall through A plan **falls through** when it fails or cannot be achieved: *My holiday arrangements have fallen through.* [*same as* **collapse**]
fall to 1 People **fall to** when they start eating: *We sat down and immediately fell to.* **2** It **falls to** you to do something if it is your responsibility or duty: *It falls to me to propose the health of the bridesmaids.*

fallacious /fəˈleɪʃəs/ *adjective*
A **fallacious** argument or notion is one that is wrong because it is based on false information, or on faulty reasoning: *The conclusion she comes to is clearly fallacious.* [*same as* **mistaken**; *opposite* **correct**, **valid**] — *adverb* **fallaciously:** *He argues, fallaciously in my judgement, that communist regimes must necessarily become tyrannical.*

fallacy /ˈfaləsɪ/ *noun*: **fallacies**
A **fallacy** is a mistake in reasoning that spoils a whole argument, or a mistaken idea based on false information or faulty reasoning: *It's a fallacy that women have less stamina than men.* [*same as* **misconception**]

fallen /ˈfɔːlən/ *verb*; *adjective*
▷ ***verb***
Fallen is the past participle of **fall**.
▷ ***adjective***
1 Fallen means having dropped or fallen: *fallen trees.* **2 Fallen** means killed in battle: *fallen heroes.*

fallible /ˈfalɪbəl/ *adjective*
1 You describe people as **fallible** if they are likely to make mistakes, because their knowledge is incomplete, or their judgement faulty: *We are all fallible.* **2** Something such as a system or method is **fallible** if it has faults and is therefore unreliable: *The pregnancy test they use has been shown to be fallible.*
[*opposite* **infallible**]

falling-off /fɔːlɪŋˈɒf/ *noun* (*used in the singular*)
A **falling-off** in an amount or rate is a decrease: *There has been a worrying falling-off in theatre attendances.* [*opposite* **rise, increase**]

fallout /ˈfɔːlaʊt/ *noun* (*uncount*)
Fallout is the cloud of radioactive dust that results from a nuclear explosion.

fallow /ˈfaloʊ/ *adjective*
Fallow land or land that is lying **fallow** has been ploughed and left to recover its natural fertility, instead of being planted with a crop.

false /fɔːls/ *adjective*
1 A statement that is **false** is not true: *a false accusation* □ *We must decide for ourselves whether his story is true or false.* [*same as* **untrue**, **incorrect**; *opposite* **true, correct**] **2** A **false** idea is a mistaken one, based on wrong information, faulty observation, or illogical reasoning: *I got a completely false impression of you when I first met you.* [*same as* **wrong**] **3** An action that is described as **false** is a mistake; a **false** step or move is something you do that spoils your chance of succeeding, or puts you in danger; **false** imprisonment is wrongful or unlawful imprisonment. **4 False** describes objects that are artificial: *false teeth.* [*opposite* **real**] **5 False** describes things that are intended to deceive people: *a false passport* □ *She was using a false name and identity.* [*same as* **fake**] **6 False** expressions or emotions are insincere: *She gave him one of her false smiles.* [*opposite* **sincere**, **genuine**] **7 False** means disloyal or treacherous: *false friends.* — *adverb* **falsely:** *He was falsely accused of rape.* □ *He smiled falsely.* — *noun* (*uncount*) **falsity** /ˈfɔːlsɪtɪ/: *the falsity of first impressions.*

false alarm /fɔːls əˈlɑːm/ *noun*: **false alarms**
A **false alarm** is a warning or fuss that turns out to have been unnecessary, because there was no real danger or cause for worry: *She was worried that she might be pregnant, but it was a false alarm.*

falsehood /ˈfɔːlshʊd/ *noun*: **falsehoods**
1 (*count or uncount*) A **falsehood** is a lie; **falsehood** is lying: *That's a complete falsehood.* □ *She's incapable of falsehood.* **2** (*uncount*) **Falsehood** is the circumstance or quality of being untrue: *The truth or falsehood of the rumour will no doubt emerge before long.*

false start /fɔːls stɑːt/ *noun*: **false starts**
1 A **false start** is the beginning of a race that is spoilt because one or more of the competitors move before the signal to do so is given. **2** You make a **false start** on some activity when you make an unsatisfactory beginning, and have to abandon it and start again: *After several false starts the project went ahead smoothly.*

falsetto /fɔːlˈsɛtoʊ/ *noun* (*uncount or count, usually in the singular*): **falsettos**
A man sings or speaks in a **falsetto** when he uses an artificially high voice: *Can you sing falsetto?* □ *a falsetto voice.*

falsify /ˈfɔːlsɪfaɪ/ *verb*: **falsifies, falsifying, falsified**
To **falsify** information is to alter it dishonestly: *He had falsified the firm's accounts.* □ *As usual the Government is falsifying the facts.* — *noun* (*uncount or count*) **falsification** /fɔːlsɪfɪˈkeɪʃən/: *the usual rumour and falsification.* [*same as* **misrepresentation**]

falsity see **false**.

falter /ˈfɔːltə(r)/ *verb*: **falters, faltering, faltered**
1 You **falter** when you slow down or move unsteadily or with difficulty: *He walked steadily beside me and only faltered occasionally.* **2** Something **falters** when it starts functioning unreliably, wrongly or irregularly: *His pulse faltered and became increasingly faint.* **3** You **falter** in what you are doing when you lose confidence and hesitate from uncertainty: *Once we were sure of what we were doing we never faltered.* □ *He faltered once or twice in his speech.* **4** People **falter** when they speak hesitantly or nervously: *'Please don't ...,' he faltered.*

fame /feɪm/ *noun* (*uncount*)
Fame is the condition of being well known or widely admired: *She achieved fame early.* □ *Her novels brought her world-wide fame.*

famed /feɪmd/ *adjective*
A person, place or thing that is **famed** for something, is well-known because of it: *He was famed throughout the university for his unusual lectures.* □ *Knutsford in Cheshire, famed as the model for Mrs Gaskell's Cranford.* [*same as* **renowned**]

familial /fəˈmɪlɪəl/ *adjective* (*formal*)
Familial means belonging to families, or relating to them: *This eye defect tends to be familial.* □ *familial influences.*

familiar /fəˈmɪlɪə(r)/ *adjective*
1 Someone or something is **familiar** to you if you recognize them easily, or know them well: *His face was familiar to us from television.* □ *He was glad to be back in his own familiar bedroom.* □ *She heard a familiar voice on the stair.* [*opposite* **unfamiliar**] **2** You are **familiar** with something if you know it thoroughly: *I'm not very familiar with Trollope's novels.* **3** Someone who behaves in a **familiar** manner towards you treats you like a close friend, especially unsuitably, so as to seem over-friendly and offensively informal: *She was offended at the familiar way he put his arm round her.* [*ame as* **forward**] — *noun* (*uncount*) **familiarity** /fəmɪlɪˈarɪtɪ/: *Her face had a puzzling familiarity.* □ *A familiarity with standard computer software is essential.* □ *He addressed her with cheeky familiarity by her first name.* — *adverb* **familiarly:** *He patted my shoulder familiarly.*

familiarize or **familiarise** /fəˈmɪlɪəraɪz/ *verb*: **familiarizes, familiarizing, familiarized**
You **familiarize** yourself with something when you learn about it and accustom yourself to it: *It'll take me a week or so to familiarize myself with the new software.*

family /ˈfamɪlɪ/ *noun*: **families**
1 (*with a singular or plural verb*) A **family** is a set of people related to one another, especially a household consisting of parents and children: *The Muir family live at No.11.* □ *I won't be going on the annual family holiday this year.* **2** (*count or uncount, or with a plural verb*) You refer to your children as your **family**: *Have you any family?* □ *The family usually come home in the holidays.* □ *Most career women are waiting till their 30s to raise a family.* □ *parents of large families.* **3** (*with a singular or plural verb*) Your **family** is also the line of ancestors that you come from: *My mother's family come from Ayrshire.* □ *a long-established family firm.* **4** (*count*) A **family** of plants, animals, or things such as languages, is a related group of them: *a plant of the pea family.*

family name /famɪlɪ ˈneɪm/ *noun*: **family names**
Your **family name** is your surname or the name you share with the rest of your family.

family planning /famɪlɪ ˈplanɪŋ/ *noun* (*uncount*)
Family planning is the principle or practice of controlling the number of children born in a family, especially through the use of contraceptives: *the family-planning clinic.*

family tree /famɪlɪ ˈtriː/ *noun*: **family trees**
Your **family tree** is the series of generations and relationships within your family, or a diagram showing these.

famine /ˈfamɪn/ *noun* (*uncount or count*): **famines**
Famine is a shortage of food in a country, often so severe that people die of starvation: *The drought led to famine and death.* □ *The country suffered frequent famines throughout the 70s.*

famished /ˈfamɪʃt/ *adjective* (*informal*)
You say you are **famished** when you are very hungry: *I'm famished; what's for tea?* [*same as* **starving**]

famous /ˈfeɪməs/ *adjective*
Someone or something that is famous is well known: *in the famous poem by Burns* □ *You're getting quite famous.* □ *The Isle of Man is famous chiefly for its tail-less cats.* [*same as* **well known**] — *adverb* **famously:** *Nelson famously put the telescope to his blind eye.*

fan[1] /fan/ *noun; verb*
▻ ***noun*: fans**
1 A **fan** is an instrument that you wave in front of your face to cool yourself, traditionally in the form of a semicircle of pleated paper or fine fabric, that folds into a narrow shape when not in use. **2** Something with parts extending outwards from a central point may be called a **fan**: *She arranged her cards into a fan.* **3** A **fan** is also a machine with revolving blades, for producing a current of air in a room or building, or for getting rid of smells.
▻ ***verb*: fans, fanning, fanned**
1 You **fan** yourself when you wave a fan or other thin flat object in front of your face to cool it: *He picked up a folder and fanned himself with it.* **2** You **fan** a fire when you create a current of air to make it burn more strongly: *The wind fanned the flames.* **3** To **fan** feelings or emotions, especially public ill-feeling, is to encourage or increase them: *The death of two children from the effects of the drug fanned public fury.* [*same as* **arouse, provoke**]

> ***phrasal verb***
> People or things **fan out** when they move forwards and outwards from a central point: *The six planes flew in parallel formation and then fanned out.*

fan[2] /fan/ *noun*: **fans**
A **fan** of someone or something is an enthusiastic supporter or admirer of them: *We all become tennis fans during Wimbledon fortnight.* □ *fan mail.*

fanatic /fəˈnatɪk/ *noun; adjective*
▻ ***noun*: fanatics**
1 A **fanatic** is someone with an extreme enthusiasm

for something: *a video-game fanatic.* **2** A religious or political **fanatic** is someone with dangerously extreme religious or political beliefs.
▻ ***adjective*** (also **fanatical**): *The heretics were pursued and put to death with fanatic zeal.* □ *fanatical enthusiasm.* — *adverb* **fanatically:** *He was fanatically devoted to the cause of independence.*

fanaticism /fəˈnatɪsɪzm/ *noun* (*uncount*)
Fanaticism is extreme or fanatical behaviour or opinions: *religious fanaticism.*

fanciful /ˈfansɪfəl/ *adjective*
1 A **fanciful** person is someone whose imagination is stronger than their sense of reality; **fanciful** ideas come from the imagination as distinct from the real world of facts; **fanciful** creatures are imaginary: *dragons and other fanciful beasts.* **2** A **fanciful** creation is elaborate and odd-looking, rather than simple and ordinary: *Gaudi's fanciful spires.*

fancy /ˈfansɪ/ *verb*; *noun*; *adjective*; *interjection*
▻ ***verb***: **fancies, fancying, fancied**
1 You **fancy** something if you would like it, or want to do it: *What do you fancy for lunch today?* □ *What do you fancy doing tonight?* **2** (*informal*) You **fancy** yourself if you are pleased with yourself and your abilities, or sure of your chances of success in some activity: *He fancies himself as a ladies' man.* **3** (*informal*) You **fancy** a person if you feel sexually attracted to them: *I think he fancies you.* **4** You **fancy** that something is so if you think or suppose it is: *She'll be at the library, I fancy.* **5** You **fancy** you see or hear something if you think you do: *I fancied I heard a noise downstairs.*
▻ ***noun***: **fancies**
1 A **fancy** is an improbable idea or notion: *facts and fancies* □ *She gets the strangest fancies sometimes.* **2** (*uncount*) **Fancy** is the power of the mind to imagine things, or the improbable ideas and notions that come from the imagination: *This looks like another of his flights of fancy.*
▻ ***adjective***
Something that is **fancy** is heavily decorated, complex, unusual, special or of superior quality: *fancy cakes* □ *The carpet's a bit too fancy for a bedroom.* □ *The hotel serves plain wholesome food; nothing fancy.* [*opposite* **plain, simple, ordinary**]
▻ ***interjection***
You use **fancy** to express surprise: *Fancy him getting married at last!* □ *I've won a prize; fancy that!*
▻ ***phrases*** **1** You **take a fancy to** someone or something when you find that you particularly like them, especially if there is no obvious reason for it: *She took a fancy to the house as soon as she saw it.* **2** Something **takes your fancy** if, when you see it, you find that you like it and want it: *I sent for a dress that had taken my fancy in the catalogue.*

fancy dress /fansɪ ˈdrɛs/ *noun* (*uncount*)
Fancy dress is clothing or make-up you put on for a special occasion, to make yourself look like *eg* a character from a book, or a historical figure, or someone of a particular nationality, trade or historical period: *a fancy-dress party* □ *The guests were asked to arrive in fancy dress.*

fanfare /ˈfanfɛə(r)/ *noun*: **fanfares**
A **fanfare** is a short piece of music played on trumpets to announce an important event or the arrival of someone important.

fang /faŋ/ *noun*: **fangs**
An animal's **fangs** are its long sharp teeth; a snake's **fangs** are its poisonous teeth.

fanlight /ˈfanlaɪt/ *noun*: **fanlights**
A **fanlight** is a semicircular window over a door or window.

fantasize or **fantasize** /ˈfantəsaɪz/ *verb*: **fantasizes, fantasizing, fantasized**
You **fantasize** about something pleasant and improbable happening to you when you imagine it happening: *He used to fantasize about impressing her with his extraordinary achievements.*

fantastic /fanˈtastɪk/ *adjective*
1 (*informal*) You call something or someone **fantastic** if you are very impressed by them and admire them: *She gave us a fantastic meal.* □ *The weather's been fantastic.* □ *She's fantastic at skiing.* **2** (*informal*) A size, amount or extent that is **fantastic** is very great: *She gets a fantastic increase in salary in this new post.* **3** A **fantastic** story is an unlikely or unbelievable one. **4** **Fantastic** shapes, images or creatures are strange or wonderful-looking. — *adverb* (*often intensifying*) **fantastically:** *He's fantastically good at cooking* □ *They're fantastically rich.*

fantasy /ˈfantəsɪ/ *noun*: **fantasies**
1 A **fantasy** is a situation you imagine, often one in which something pleasant but improbable happens to you: *A first novel must surely contain many of its author's favourite fantasies.* **2** (*uncount*) **Fantasy** is the activity of imagining things, or the stories, events and situations that people create in their imaginations: *As a child she lived in her own fantasy world.* □ *It's good to be able to indulge in fantasy now and then.* [*opposite* **reality**] **3** A strange or unusual creation or composition by a writer, artist or musician is sometimes called a **fantasy**.

far /fɑː(r)/ *adverb*; *adjective*: **farther** or **further**, **farthest** or **furthest**

> Note that both **farther, farthest** and **further, furthest** can be used in expressions about distance, but only **further, furthest** can be used in expressions of degree or extent. [see separate entries for **farther, farthest, further, furthest**]

▻ ***adverb***

> Note that **far** is usually used with negatives, or in questions (especially with *how*), or in combination with *as*, *so* and *too*. In simple affirmative statements an expression such as *a long way* sounds more idiomatic than **far**: *We'd travelled a long way from home* (rather than *we'd travelled far from home*).

1 a A place that is **far**, or **far** away, from another is a long distance from it: *Zomba was not far from Blantyre.* □ *We can walk to the supermarket if it isn't too far away.* □ *Is the post office far from here?* □ *The book shop was further along the street than I'd realized.* **b** You go or progress **far** in some direction when you go a long way in that direction: *We hadn't gone far when we met a flock of sheep.* □ *They were so far ahead that we lost sight of them.* □ *I didn't get as far as I wanted to that day.* □ *Gävle in Sweden was the furthest north I'd ever been.* **c** You ask questions about the distance between places, or the distance already travelled, using 'how **far**': *How far away is Portsmouth?* □ *How far is the library from here?* □ *How far is it from Edinburgh to Glasgow?* □ *I don't know how far it is.* □ *How far did you cycle today?* □ *How much further have we got to walk?* **d** You use **far** in expressing the length of time from the present to some event in the past or future: *The exams are not far off.* □ *You don't*

have to go very far back to discover instances of the wrong person being hanged.
2 a Far is used in expressing extent, degree and state of progress: *I never trust statistics very far.* ▫ *We must follow her instructions as far as possible.* ▫ *How far have you got with those letters?* ▫ *We can't progress any further without funding.* ▫ *Temperatures are unlikely to rise very far.* ▫ *£20, that's as far as I'll go.* **b Far** is used for emphasis with comparative adjectives and adverbs, and in other expressions of comparison (see **by far** in the phrases below for its use with the superlative): *I did far better than I was expecting to.* ▫ *The sun is far further away than the moon.* ▫ *It's far worse than that.* ▫ *Sales have far exceeded expectation.* ▫ *I'd far rather tell her now than wait till tomorrow.*
▻ ***adjective***
1 The **far** or **farther** side or end of something is the one that is the longer distance away: *A figure appeared in the doorway at the far end of the hall.* ▫ *She was sitting fishing on the farther bank of the river.* **2** You use **far** with words of direction to indicate the part that is the greatest possible distance in that direction: *in the far west of Ireland* ▫ *the figure on the far left of the photograph.*
▻ ***phrases*** **1 a** You use **as far as** in various expressions that indicate or limit the circumstances in which something is so: *As far as work is concerned, I'm making good progress.* ▫ *The play was OK as far as the acting went.* ▫ *As far as I'm concerned* [= if you need my opinion or permission] *she can move into the flat tomorrow.* **b** You use expressions like '**as far as**, or **so far as** I know' when you are not certain that the information you are giving is correct: *As far as I remember we started this project in November '91.* ▫ *He hasn't mentioned it, so far as I'm aware.* **2** You use **by far** and **far and away** for emphasis with superlatives: *The film was by far the best I'd seen all year.* ▫ *She's far and away the nicest of the three.* **3 Far and wide** means over a wide area, covering many places: *I searched far and wide for the kind of shoelaces you wanted.* **4** A situation that is **far from** what you expect or require is very different from it, or is the opposite of it: *Far from being pleased with us, she seemed annoyed.* ▫ *I'm not dissatisfied. Far from it.* ▫ *Her bedroom was far from tidy.* **5** For **few and far between** see **few**. **6** You **go so far as to** do something when you behave in a surprisingly extreme manner: *She even went so far as to call me a liar.* **7** Someone **goes too far** when they behave in an unsuitably extreme way: *The police go too far sometimes.* ▫ *I can't possibly agree with you; that's going too far.* **8** You use **in so far as** or **insofar as** to give the limited circumstances in which something is so: *She enjoyed having her husband at home, in so far as he could help her with the housework and shopping.* **9** Something such as a guess, or the person making it, is **not far out**, **not far off**, or **not far wrong**, if they are almost right: *I guessed that he'd died in 1917, which wasn't far out.* ▫ *Your estimate wasn't far off.* ▫ *I wasn't far wrong in my first impression of him.* **10 So far** means up to the present stage or moment: *What do you think of the course so far?* ▫ *So far the weather has been fairly reasonable.* ▫ *I've only read the introduction so far.* [compare *as yet*] **11** You say **so far so good** to express satisfaction with what has happened or been achieved up to the present moment: *So far so good. What do we do next?*

faraway /ˈfɑːrəweɪ/ *adjective*
1 A **faraway** place or sound is a long distance away: *faraway countries.* **2** Someone who has a **faraway** look or expression looks as if they are thinking hard about something, and not concentrating on what is happening around them.
[*same as* **far-off**]

farce /fɑːs/ *noun* (*count or uncount*): **farces**
1 A **farce** is a comedy in which people get involved in an unlikely series of amusingly silly situations; comedies of this type generally are referred to as **farce**: *Feydeau, the most famous writer of farce.* **2** A **farce** can be a funny or silly situation in everyday life: *What a farce!* ▫ *The incident ended in farce.* **3** Something unsatisfactory or badly organized is often called a **farce**: *His lectures were a farce.* — *adjective* **farcical:** *a farcical situation* ▫ *Their security system is farcical.* [*same as* **ridiculous**] — *adverb* **farcically:** *Most vehicles are farcically easy to break into.*

fare /fɛə(r)/ *noun*; *verb*
▻ ***noun***: **fares**
1 Your **fare** on a bus, train, ship or aircraft is the price you pay to travel on it as a passenger: *What is the fare to Haymarket?* ▫ *I've already paid my fare.* ▫ *An increase in fares is likely.* **2** (*uncount old, formal*) **Fare** is food: *The food on board the ferry was adequate, but nothing like the delicious fare they used to serve on the transatlantic liners.*
▻ ***verb*** (*literary*): **fares, faring, fared**
You **fare** well or badly when you are successful or unsuccessful in some activity or situation, or are treated well or badly: *We fared better once we got into calmer waters.* ▫ *How do you think you fared in the exam?*

Far East *noun* (*uncount*)
The **Far East** is the countries of East and Southeast Asia, including Japan and China.

farewell /fɛəˈwɛl/ *interjection*; *noun*
▻ ***interjection*** (*old*)
Farewell means goodbye: *Farewell, my son.* ▫ *He bade his father farewell.*
▻ ***noun***: **farewells:** *She made her farewells and left.* ▫ *We joined them for a farewell drink.* [*same as* **goodbye**]

far-fetched /fɑːˈfetʃt/ *adjective*
You call a story, idea or theory **far-fetched** if it seems improbable or incredible: *He had some far-fetched idea about the history of the word.* ▫ *far-fetched crossword clues.*

far-flung /fɑːˈflʌŋ/ *adjective*
1 A **far-flung** territory or kingdom covers a wide area and extends to distant places: *throughout her far-flung dominions.* **2 Far-flung** places are distant places: *in some far-flung corner of the British Isles.*

farm /fɑːm/ *noun*; *verb*
▻ ***noun***: **farms**
1 A **farm** is a piece of land containing buildings and fields, used for growing crops or breeding and keeping animals such as cows, horses, sheep and pigs: *I was brought up on a farm.* ▫ *farm animals.* **2** A **farm** is also the farmer's house and the buildings round it. **3** A place specializing in the rearing of particular animals may be called a **farm**: *a fish farm.*
▻ ***verb***: **farms, farming, farmed**
To **farm** a piece of land is to prepare and use it for crop-growing or animal-rearing: *She farms an area of 30 000 acres in Perthshire.*

phrasal verb
farm out 1 A business firm **farms out** its work when it distributes what it can't manage itself to other businesses or individuals to complete. **2** Parents **farm out** their children when they hand them over temporarily into someone else's care.

farmer /ˈfɑːmə(r)/ *noun*: **farmers**
A **farmer** is a person who owns or runs a farm.

farmhand /ˈfɑːmhand/ *noun*: **farmhands**
A **farmhand** is a person employed to work on a farm.

farmhouse /ˈfɑːmhaʊs/ *noun*: **farmhouses**
A **farmhouse** is the farmer's house on a farm.

farming /ˈfɑːmɪŋ/ *noun (uncount)*
Farming is the business of running a farm, growing crops and rearing animals such as cows, horses, sheep and pigs.

farmland /ˈfɑːmland/ *noun (uncount)*
Farmland is land that is being farmed, or is suitable for farming: *The fire has destroyed acres of farmland.*

farmyard /ˈfɑːmjɑːd/ *noun*: **farmyards**
A **farmyard** is the central yard at a farm, surrounded by farm buildings.

far-off /fɑːrˈɒf/ *adjective*
1 A **far-off** place is a long distance away: *in a remote, far-off region.* **2** A **far-off** time is a long way off in the past or the future: *She might, at some far-off date, decide to get married.* [*same as* **distant**, **remote**]

far-reaching /fɑːˈriːtʃɪŋ/ *adjective*
Something that is **far-reaching** has great, important or extensive effects: *If it's passed the bill is bound to have far-reaching consequences for secondary schools.*

far-sighted /fɑːˈsaɪtɪd/ *adjective*
Someone who is described as **far-sighted** is good at judging what is going to happen in the future, and taking the right decisions. — *noun (uncount)* **far-sightedness:** *She has a reputation for far-sightedness*

farther /ˈfɑːðə(r)/ *adverb; adjective*
▻ ***adverb***
Farther is the comparative of **far** and is used in expressions about distance: *Jupiter is farther away from the sun than Earth is.* ▫ *It was farther to the summit than it looked.* ▫ *The chemist's is a bit farther along the street.* ▫ *Have we much farther to go?* [see also **far**, **further**]
▻ ***adjective***
The **farther** side or end of something is the more distant one: *He was standing on the pavement on the farther side of the street.*

farthest /ˈfɑːðɛst/ *adjective or adverb*
Farthest is the superlative of **far** and is used in expressions about distance: *Which is farthest from the sun, Jupiter, Saturn or Uranus?* ▫ *In the farthest corners of the world.* ▫ *Jeremy walked the farthest.* [see also **furthest**]

farthing /ˈfɑːðɪŋ/ *noun (history)*: **farthings**
A **farthing** is an old coin, worth one quarter of an old British penny.

fascia /ˈfeɪʃɪə/ *noun*: **fascias**
The **fascia** in a motor vehicle is the board in front of the driver where the controls are. [*same as* **dashboard**; see picture at **car**]

fascinate /ˈfasɪneɪt/ *verb*: **fascinates, fascinating, fascinated**
Something or someone **fascinates** you if they interest you a lot: *Physics had always fascinated her.* ▫ *I was fascinated by the stories she told of her early life.* — *adjective* **fascinated:** *I'm fascinated at the way children learn language.* — *adjective* **fascinating:** *I thought the film was fascinating.* ▫ *fascinating shapes.* [*opposite* **boring**, **uninteresting**] — *adverb* **fascinatingly:** *He writes fascinatingly about changes in word use.* — *noun (uncount or count)* **fascination** /fasɪˈneɪʃən/: *There was a look of fascination on the children's faces as they watched.* ▫ *the fascination of crossword puzzles* ▫ *One of the fascinations of Venice is the Marcian Library.* ▫ *Part of the fascination of movies is that they trigger off so many memories.*

fascism /ˈfaʃɪzm/ *noun (uncount)*
Fascism is a political system in which there is, typically, state control over all areas of society, a strong dictator, and emphasis on nationalism and military strength.

fascist /ˈfaʃɪst/ *noun; adjective*
▻ ***noun***: **fascists**
1 A **fascist** is someone who supports fascism. **2** If you call someone in authority a **fascist** you mean they believe in strong control, and that they tend to ignore or suppress opposition, criticism and individual opinion.
▻ ***adjective:*** *a fascist regime* ▫ *She was suspected of having fascist sympathies.*

fashion /ˈfaʃən/ *noun; verb*
▻ ***noun***: **fashions**
1 (*used in the singular*) You do something in a particular **fashion** when you do it in that way: *He moved in a strangely clumsy fashion.* ▫ *She addressed the meeting in her usual relaxed fashion.* ▫ *I manage perfectly well in my own fashion.* [*same as* **manner**, **way**] **2** (*uncount*) **Fashion** is style, especially in clothing and personal appearance; **fashion** is also this particular area of interest and the business relating to it: *She became a fashion correspondent with one of the national newspapers.* ▫ *fashion magazines.* **3** A **fashion** is a style of clothing, or an activity, or a way of behaving, that is popular for a time: *There were pictures of the latest fashions from the Paris show.* ▫ *The '70s generation set a fashion for jogging and healthy living.* [*same as* **trend**]
▻ ***phrases*** **1** You say that you can do something **after a fashion** if you are able to do it, but not very well: *I speak German after a fashion.* **2** Something that is **in fashion** is popular at the present moment; something that is **out of fashion** is no longer popular: *Tweed jackets are in fashion again.* ▫ *When did the mini skirt first come into fashion?* ▫ *Wearing a lot of make-up is out of fashion.*
▻ ***verb*** (*literary*): **fashions, fashioning, fashioned**
You **fashion** something when you make or create it with your hands: *Stone-Age people fashioned clothes for themselves from animal skins.*

fashionable /ˈfaʃənəbəl/ *adjective*
1 Clothes or behaviour that are **fashionable** are popular at the present moment: *Long skirts became very fashionable in the late '60s.* ▫ *It has become fashionable in recent years to buy environmentally friendly products.* **2** **Fashionable** also describes an area of a city where there are expensive shops, or where wealthy people have houses: *They lived in a fashionable district of Vienna.* [*opposite* **unfashionable**] — *adverb* **fashionably:** *fashionably dressed young women.*

fast[1] /fɑːst/ *adjective or adverb; adjective*
▻ ***adjective or adverb***: **faster, fastest**
1 Someone or something that is, or moves, **fast**, acts, goes or happens at great speed: *She's our fastest swimmer.* ▫ *They were talking too fast for me to understand.* ▫ *He likes driving fast cars.* ▫ *The beat was getting faster and faster.* ▫ *She was fast realizing that her marriage was a mistake.* ▫ *new faster-acting pain-relievers.* [*opposite* **slow**, **slowly**] **2** You ask questions about speed using 'how **fast**?': *How fast can you type?* ▫ *I glanced at the speedometer to see how fast we were going.* **3** Something that happens **fast** happens very soon or without delay: *We must get him into hospital fast.* ▫ *I came as fast as I could.* **4** A clock or watch that is, or is going, **fast** is showing a time that is later

than the right time: *My watch is three minutes fast.* **5** Something that is fixed **fast** is firmly fixed and cannot be moved: *The car was stuck fast in the mud.* ▫ *I made the rope fast* [= I tied the rope] *to a tree.*

▻ ***adjective***

1 The **fast** lane on a motorway is the one for the use of the fastest traffic. [*opposite* **slow**] **2** A **fast** photographic film needs to be exposed only for a very short time. **3** Fabric colours that are **fast** do not fade or run out of the fabric when it is washed: *colour-fast cottons.*

▻ ***phrases*** **1** You are **fast asleep** when you are sleeping deeply. **2** (*informal*) Someone **pulls a fast one** on you when they cheat you. **3** For **thick and fast** see **thick**.

fast² /fɑːst/ *verb*; *noun*

▻ ***verb***: **fasts, fasting, fasted**

You **fast** when you don't eat any food for a certain period, *eg* for religious or medical reasons: *They fast during the day, for a whole month.*

▻ ***noun:*** *Imogen was on one of her periodic fasts.*

fasten /ˈfɑːsən/ *verb*: **fastens, fastening, fastened**

1 You **fasten** something when you secure it in its closed position: *Could you fasten my necklace for me?* ▫ *Fasten your seat belts.* ▫ *My skirt fastens at the side.* [*same as* **do up**] **2** You **fasten** one thing to another when you attach the one to the other: *The bicycle was fastened to the railings with a chain.* **3** Something **fastens** round or on to something else when it grips it firmly: *She felt the dog fasten its teeth round her ankle.*

phrasal verb

fasten on to 1 You **fasten on to** an idea when you concentrate eagerly on it, and refuse to drop it. **2** Someone **fastens on to** you when they follow you about, keep talking to you, and won't let you go.

fastener /ˈfɑːsnə(r)/ *noun*: **fasteners**

A **fastener** is a device that fastens something: *The dress had a zip fastener.*

fastening /ˈfɑːsnɪŋ/ *noun*: **fastenings**

A **fastening** is a fastener: *a silk purse with silver fastenings.*

fast food /fɑːst ˈfuːd/ *noun* (*uncount*)

Fast food is food that is prepared and served quickly: *a fast-food restaurant* ▫ *fast food such as hamburgers and meat pies.*

fastidious /faˈstɪdɪəs/ *adjective*

1 Someone who is **fastidious** is difficult to please, and likes things properly done in every detail: *We can't afford to be fastidious about every little comma.* **2** A **fastidious** person is easily disgusted: *The bathroom would have satisfied the most fastidious guest.* — *adverb* **fastidiously:** *He took out a handkerchief and fastidiously wiped the chair seat.*

fat /fat/ *noun*; *adjective*

▻ ***noun***: **fats**

1 (*uncount*) **Fat** is the solid greasy substance contained in cells just below the skin in animals, that stores energy and generates warmth; **fat** is also the layer of excess flesh formed by this: *I must get rid of some of this fat.* ▫ *He's too thin; we're trying to build him up and get a little fat on him.* **2** A **fat** is a greasy or oily substance obtained from animals or plants and used in liquid or solid form as food or in cooking: *cheese, cream, butter and other fats.*

▻ ***adjective***: **fatter, fattest**

1 A **fat** person has a lot, especially too much, flesh on their body: *I'm getting too fat.* ▫ *She had grown a lot fatter.* [*same as* **plump**; *opposite* **thin**] **2** A **fat** object is a thick one: *He handed me a fat envelope.* [*same as* **plump**] **3** (*informal*) A **fat** fee or profit is a large one: *These cosmetics are cheaply produced and bring the manufacturers a fat profit.* [*same as* **substantial**] — *noun* (*uncount*) **fatness:** *A person's relative fatness was considered an indicaton of their wealth.*

▻ ***phrases*** (*informal*) **A fat lot** means none at all, not any, or nothing: *Well, it's a fat lot of use sitting here doing nothing!* ▫ *Those pills will do you a fat lot of good!* ▫ *A fat lot you'll achieve by saying that!*

fatal /ˈfeɪtəl/ *adjective*

1 You describe an action as **fatal** if it brings unpleasant or unfortunate results; **fatal** results are what come from such actions: *She made the fatal mistake of giving him her telephone number.* ▫ *I tried repairing the vacuum cleaner myself, with fatal consequences.* **2** A **fatal** disease or accident is one that causes death: *Some patients don't want to be told that they have a fatal illness.* ▫ *I last saw her about a month before her fatal motorway crash.* — *adverb* **fatally:** *The doctor warned us that she was fatally ill.*

fatalism /ˈfeɪtəlɪzm/ *noun* (*uncount*)

Fatalism is the belief that fate controls everything that happens, and that humans cannot prevent or alter anything: *'It's no good trying,' she said with typical fatalism.* — *noun* **fatalist:** *The fatalists among us were unwilling to fight back.* — *adjective* **fatalistic** /feɪtəˈlɪstɪk/: *She took the fatalistic view that we would all be made redundant sooner or later.*

fatality /fəˈtalɪtɪ/ *noun*: **fatalities**

1 A **fatality** is the accidental or violent death of someone: *With the increased use of seat belts the number of fatalities from road accidents dropped.* **2** (*uncount*) **Fatality** is also the condition of being controlled by fate: *We had a feeling of fatality about events at the time.*

fate /feɪt/ *noun*: **fates**

1 **Fate** is the apparent power that decides the course of events, over which humans have no control: *I wanted to be a musician, but Fate decreed that I should become a doctor.* **2** Someone's or something's **fate** is what happens to them, or their individual destiny: *Her paper on future development ended in the managing director's wastepaper basket, and I think mine on funding must have met with the same fate.* [*same as* **doom**] **3** A person's or thing's **fate** is also their death or destruction: *After three days we were forced to give up the search and leave the missing men to their fate.* [*same as* **doom**]

fated /ˈfeɪtɪd/ *adjective*

1 You are **fated** to do something, or something is **fated** to happen, when it has already been decided by fate: *We were fated not to meet again for eighteen years.* **2** A scheme or project is **fated** if it is bound to end in failure or disaster: *The expedition was fated from the start.* [*same as* **doomed**]

fateful /ˈfeɪtfəl/ *adjective*

1 You describe something that happens, or is decided or done, as **fateful** if it turns out to have an important, especially bad, effect on future events: *his fateful decision to return to his home town.* **2** A **fateful** day is one that brings trouble or disaster. **3** A **fateful** remark is a casual comment that turns out to have been a prediction of some future event.

father /ˈfɑːðə(r)/ *noun*; *verb*

▻ ***noun***: **fathers**

1 Your **father** is your male parent: *I never knew my father.* ▫ *Fathers are expected to do their share of looking after the children.* **2** (*literary*) A man who has invented something, or been an early leader in its development, may be referred to as its **father**: *He is widely regarded as the father of the trade-union movement.* **3** Christians often refer to, or address, God as their **father**: *Father in heaven, listen to our prayers.* **4 Father** is used as a title or form of address for a priest, in some Christian churches: *Thank you for calling, Father.* □ *Ask Father Dillon.*

▻ ***verb***: **fathers, fathering, fathered**

A man **fathers** a child when he makes a woman pregnant and their baby is born: *He had fathered at least six children by different mothers.*

Father Christmas /fɑːðə ˈkrɪsməs/ *noun*

Father Christmas is a white-bearded old man in a red coat, traditionally supposed to deliver presents on Christmas Eve. [*same as* **Santa Claus**]

fatherhood /ˈfɑːðəhʊd/ *noun* (*uncount*)

Fatherhood is the condition or circumstance of being a father: *He took the duties of fatherhood very seriously.*

father-in-law /ˈfɑːðər-ɪn-lɔː/ *noun*: **fathers-in-law**

Your **father-in-law** is the father of your wife or husband.

fatherland /ˈfɑːðəland/ *noun* (*literary*; *usually in the singular*): **fatherlands**

Your **fatherland** is your native country.

fatherless /fɑːðələs/ *adjective*

Fatherless children are children whose father is dead or unknown.

fatherly /ˈfɑːðəlɪ/ *adjective*

You describe a person, or their attitude to you, as **fatherly** if they behave towards you like a kind, caring, or protective father: *I hope you won't mind my giving you some fatherly advice.*

fathom /ˈfaðəm/ *noun*; *verb*

▻ ***noun***: **fathoms**

A **fathom** is a unit of measurement of the depth of water, equal to 6 feet or 1.8 metres: *The lake was many fathoms deep.*

▻ ***verb***: **fathoms, fathoming, fathomed**

You **fathom** something mysterious or puzzling, or **fathom** it out, when you manage to understand it after some thought: *I couldn't fathom why she was so anxious.* □ *We'll fathom it out together somehow.*

fatigue /fəˈtiːg/ *noun*; *verb*

▻ ***noun*** (*uncount*)

1 Fatigue is tiredness after work or effort: *She was dropping with fatigue.* **2** (*technical*) **Fatigue** is weakness in metals or other hard materials caused by variations in stress.

▻ ***verb***: **fatigues, fatiguing, fatigued**

Something **fatigues** you if it makes you tired or exhausted: *The slightest effort seems to fatigue him.* — *adjective* **fatigued:** *She arrived home utterly fatigued every evening.* — *adjective* **fatiguing:** *I've had a fatiguing day.*

fatten /ˈfatən/ *verb*: **fattens, fattening, fattened**

You **fatten**, or **fatten**, up an animal when you give it a lot of food, so that it gets fat; an animal **fattens** when it gets fat from eating more: *Geese were being fattened ready for the feast.* □ *Let me get you an ice cream; you look as if you need fattening up.* — *adjective* **fattening:** *cheese, butter and other fattening foods* □ *Is bread fattening?*

fatty /ˈfatɪ/ *adjective*; *noun*

▻ ***adjective***: **fattier, fattiest**

1 Fatty foods are greasy or oily, or contain a lot of fat. **2** (*technical*) **Fatty** acids are found in, obtained from, or chemically related to, animal or vegetable fats.

▻ ***noun***: **fatties** (*informal*, *derogatory*)

If you call a person a **fatty** you mean they are too fat.

fatuous /ˈfatjʊəs/ *adjective*

You call a remark or idea **fatuous** if you think it is stupid: *another of his fatuous notions.* — *adverb* **fatuously:** *'It would be a nice day if the clouds went away and the sun came out,' she remarked fatuously.*

faucet /ˈfɔːsɪt/ *noun* (*AmE*): **faucets**

A **faucet** is a tap. [see **tap**[2]]

fault /fɔːlt/ *noun*; *verb*

▻ ***noun***: **faults**

1 Your **faults** are the bad things in your personality, or your weaknesses: *Her main fault was assuming that she could do everything better than other people.* **2** A **fault** in a system, structure, or machine is a defect in the way it is designed, or one that develops during use: *a major fault in the design of the bridge* □ *structural faults.* **3** (*used in the singular*) You say that something that has gone wrong is someone's **fault** if you think they are responsible for it or should be blamed for it: *The accident was the cyclist's fault.* □ *I'm sorry, it was all my fault.* □ *It isn't my fault if the weather's bad.* □ *It's your own fault that you're tired.* **4** (*geology*) A **fault** in the earth's surface is a long crack where a section of the rock layer has slipped. **5** In tennis, a **fault** is a service that breaks the rules, *eg* when the server steps over the base line or the ball touches the net as it goes over it: *He served a double fault.*

▻ ***verb***: **faults, faulting, faulted**

You say you cannot **fault** someone if they are quite right in their opinion, or so good at something that you cannot find anything to criticize: *I couldn't fault his logic.*

▻ ***phrases*** **1** You are **at fault** when you deserve the blame for something, or when you are mistaken: *The Government is at fault in the present crisis.* **2** You **find fault with** someone or something when you complain about them, or criticize them, especially unfairly: *Of course your children will rebel if you find fault with them unnecessarily.* **3** You say someone is generous or modest **to a fault** if you think they are too generous, or too modest.

faultless /ˈfɔːltləs/ *adjective*

Something that you do is **faultless** if it is perfect: *Her technique is faultless.* □ *The letter was written in faultless English.* — *adverb* **faultlessly:** *He spoke French faultlessly.*

faulty /ˈfɔːltɪ/ *adjective*: **faultier, faultiest**

Something that is **faulty** has a fault or defect in it, or is not working properly: *The cause of the fire was a faulty electrical socket.* □ *I think your reasoning is a bit faulty.* [*same as* **defective**]

fauna /ˈfɔːnə/ *noun* (*plural*)

The **fauna** of an area are the animals, birds, fish and insects that inhabit it. [see also **flora**]

faux pas /foʊ ˈpɑː/ *noun*: **faux pas** /foʊ ˈpɑːz/

You make a **faux pas** when you say or do something stupid, or make an embarrassing mistake: *I committed the terrible faux pas of calling her by her first husband's surname.* [*same as* **gaffe**]

favour (*AmE* **favor**) /ˈfeɪvə(r)/ *noun*; *verb*

▻ ***noun***: **favours**

1 Someone's **favour** is their approval: *She had succeeded in winning the favour of the management for her proposal.* □ *He was accused of showing unfair favour to his own relations.* **2** You do someone a **favour** when you do something helpful for them, from kindness rather than duty: *Could I ask you a favour? Would you look after the baby this afternoon?*

▻ ***verb***: **favours, favouring, favoured**
1 You **favour** one thing among a number of possibilities if you prefer it, or support it: *teachers who favour the traditional methods.* **2** You **favour** someone when you treat them better or more kindly than you treat others: *My mother tended to favour me, as the baby of the family.* **3** A circumstance **favours** someone or something if it helps them to succeed: *The state of the pitch favoured the spin bowlers.* **4** (*formal*) You **favour** someone with something such as your opinion when you give it to them; you **favour** a meeting or other gathering with your presence when you attend it: *He favoured us with his views.*
▻ ***phrases*** **1 a** You are **in favour** of something if you support it or approve of it: *I had never been in favour of imprisonment as a form of punishment.* [*opposite* **against**] **b** You make a decision **in** someone's **favour** when you decide or state officially that they are right: *The referee ruled in favour of the home side.* [*opposite* **against**] **c** The way a system is organized is biased, loaded or weighted **in favour of** someone if it gives them an advantage: *The entrance requirements are weighted in favour of native applicants.* [*opposite* **against**] **d** You reject one thing **in favour** of another when you choose the second rather than the first: *We discarded the old show-of-hands voting system in favour of a secret ballot.* **2** Something is **out of favour** when it is no longer popular or approved of; something that is **in favour** is generally approved of: *The language-teaching methods of the '60s and '70s have now fallen out of favour.* □ *Grammar-teaching is in favour again.*

favourable (*AmE* **favorable**) /ˈfeɪvərəbəl/ *adjective*
1 You are **favourable** to something when you give it your approval or agreement: *Her new novel had met with a favourable reaction from the critics.* **2** Something makes a **favourable** impression on people if they approve of it: *You seem to have made a favourable impression on my parents.* **3** You try to present something in a **favourable** light when you try to make it seem attractive, so that people will like it or approve of it: *Recent television productions have succeeded in presenting Shakespeare to schoolchildren in a more favourable light.* **4** Conditions that are **favourable** to something are helpful to it: *The noisy environment of the office is scarcely favourable to the kind of concentration that is expected of us.* **5** A **favourable** comparison between one thing and another makes the first thing seem just as good as the second, if not better. [*opposite* **unfavourable**] — *adverb* **favourably:** *Television audiences had responded favourably to the series.* □ *The hospitals there compare favourably with British ones.* [*opposite* **unfavourably**]

favourite (*AmE* **favorite**) /ˈfeɪvərɪt/ *adjective; noun*
▻ ***adjective***
Your **favourite** thing of a particular kind is the one you like most: *I promised to read the children their favourite story.*
▻ ***noun***: **favourites**
1 Your **favourite** among a variety of things of a particular kind is the one you like most: *Chocolate ice cream is my favourite; which is yours?* **2** Someone who is the **favourite** of a person in authority is treated particularly kindly by them, especially unfairly so: *Teachers shouldn't have favourites.* **3** In horse-racing and other competitive sports the **favourite** is the horse or competitor that is expected to win: *I bet £5 on the favourite.*

favouritism /ˈfeɪvərɪtɪzm/ (*AmE* **favoritism**) *noun* (*uncount*)
Favouritism is the unfair practice, by someone in authority, of treating one person or group more kindly, or helping and supporting them more, than others: *Some of the teachers were certainly guilty of favouritism.*

fawn[1] /fɔːn/ *noun*: **fawns**
1 A **fawn** is the baby of one of the smaller types of deer. **2** (*uncount, often adjectival*) **Fawn** is the pale brown colour of a fawn: *She was wearing a fawn coat.* [*same as* **beige**]

fawn[2] /fɔːn/ *verb*: **fawns, fawning, fawned**
1 A dog **fawns** on you when it shows affection for you by licking you and rubbing its nose against you. **2** To **fawn** on a person is to flatter them and behave over-humbly towards them, in order to gain their approval or friendship.

fax /faks/ *noun; verb*
▻ ***noun*** (*count or uncount*): **faxes**
1 A **fax** or **fax machine** is a machine that reads documents electronically and transmits a photographic image of the contents to a receiving machine by telephone line: *I sent her a copy of the diagram on the office fax.* □ *I received this message by fax this morning.* **2** A **fax** is also the copy transmitted by fax machine: *He keeps sending me faxes making alterations to the original plan.* [see picture at **office**]
▻ ***verb***: **faxes, faxing, faxed**
You **fax** a document when you transmit a photographic image of it by fax machine; you **fax** a person when you send them a communication by fax machine: *I'll fax you the plans later this morning.* □ *Could you fax me at my London office?*

fear /fɪə(r)/ *noun; verb*
▻ ***noun***: **fears**
1 (*uncount, or used in the singular*) **Fear** is an unpleasant feeling of anxiety caused by the awareness of danger or expectation of pain: *He turned white with fear.* □ *She seemed to have no fear of danger.* □ *He never overcame his fear of flying.* □ *Fear of the dark is common among small children.* **2** A **fear** is a worry about something: *We all have our hopes and fears.* □ *Her fear that the children might have got lost turned out to have been groundless.* □ *Fears of redundancy affected us all.*
▻ ***verb***: **fears, fearing, feared**
1 You **fear** someone or something when you are afraid of them: *She apparently feared no-one.* **2** You **fear** something bad when you think that it may happen or may have happened: *We feared a repeat of last year's poor sales performance.* □ *Two climbers are feared dead in the Alps tonight.* □ *Teachers fear that funds for equipment will again be cut.* **3** You **fear** for someone or something when you are anxious because you think they are at risk or in danger: *I couldn't help fearing for his safety.* □ *I fear for her health if she goes on working like this.* **4** (*formal*) You say you **fear** that something is so if you are sorry that it is so: *He's unlikely to succeed, I fear.* □ *'Will he disapprove?' 'I fear so.'*
▻ ***phrases*** **1** You do not do one thing **for fear** of another thing when you avoid doing the first so as to prevent the second: *I didn't give her all the details for fear of confusing her.* □ *We didn't tell him, for fear that he'd pass it on to the wrong people.* **2** You **have fears for** someone or something when you are anxious about them because you think they may be at risk or in danger: *I began to have fears for my own sanity.* **3** People are **in fear of** someone or something if they are frightened of them: *It's shocking that people should have to go about in fear of their lives.* [= go about feeling afraid they might be killed]

fearful /ˈfɪəfəl/ *adjective*
1 People are **fearful** of something, or of doing something, when they are afraid of it: *Mothers are now*

fearful of letting their children out alone in the streets. **2** Something described as **fearful** is frightening, bad or unpleasant: *Doctors can make mistakes, sometimes with fearful consequences.* **3** (*informal*) **Fearful** can be used to emphasize the severity of something bad: *I've got a fearful headache.* — *adverb* **fearfully:** *She glanced fearfully at his stern face.* □ (*intensifying, informal*) *He's fearfully upset.*

fearless /'fɪələs/ *adjective*
Someone who is **fearless** is not afraid: *fearless explorers* □ *her fearless defence of the right of free speech.* [*same as* **brave**, **courageous**; *opposite* **fearful**, **timid**] — *adverb* **fearlessly:** *They marched fearlessly on into the gunfire.* [*opposite* **fearfully**]

fearsome /'fɪəsəm/ *adjective*
Something described as **fearsome** is horrible or frightening: *'We're going up there,' he said, pointing to some fearsome-looking cliffs.*

feasible /'fi:zɪbəl/ *adjective*
Something that is **feasible** is capable of being done or achieved: *Make sure that the task is feasible before asking someone to do it.* — *noun* (*uncount*) **feasibility** /fi:zɪ'bɪlɪtɪ/: *Any plan should involve a feasibility study.*

feast /fi:st/ *noun*; *verb*
▻ ***noun***: **feasts**
1 (*rather literary*) A **feast** is a large and especially fine meal, *eg* held to celebrate something: *Hundreds of guests attended the prince's wedding feast.* [*same as* **banquet**] **2** (*religion*) In the Christian calendar, a **feast** is a festival such as Christmas Day.
▻ ***verb***: **feasts, feasting, feasted**
You **feast** when you eat a splendid meal, *eg* one held to celebrate something: *We went on feasting all night.* □ *They feasted on roast goose and plum pudding.* — *noun* (*uncount*) **feasting:** *The feasting and celebrations continued for several days.*
▻ ***phrase*** For **feast your eyes on** see **eye**.

feat /fi:t/ *noun*: **feats**
A **feat** is a deed or achievement, especially a remarkable one: *She could perform amazing feats of memory.* □ *Those early railway builders managed some extraordinary feats of engineering.*

feather /'fɛðə(r)/ *noun*: **feathers**
A **feather** is one of the fine soft objects that grow from a bird's skin and cover its body: *We cleaned the oil from the gull's feathers.* — *adjective* **feathered:** *all feathered creatures* □ *a large feathered hat.*

feathery /'fɛðəɪ/ *adjective*
Something **feathery** is either made of feathers or covered with them, or has a light, soft, delicately uneven appearance or texture: *feathery clouds* □ *She stroked the baby's feathery curls.*

feature /'fi:tʃə(r)/ *noun*; *verb*
noun: **features**
1 (*often in the plural*) Your **features** are your eyes, nose, mouth and other parts of your face: *He had small neat features.* **2** A **feature** of something is an important part or quality of it: *The dictionary has many useful features, including grammar notes and illustrations.* **3** A geographical **feature**, or a **feature** of the landscape, is something such as a river, lake, hill or valley. **4** A **feature** in a newspaper or magazine is a special article dealing with something; a television **feature** is a special programme on something: *a feature on third-world poverty* □ *Did you watch that feature about dieting?* **5** A full-length cinema film is a **feature** or a **feature film**.
▻ ***verb***: **features, featuring, featured**
1 A film or exhibition **features** someone or something if they take part in it, or are a part of it: *'The Godfather', featuring Marlon Brando in one of his most famous roles* □ *The current exhibition features the work of several young artists.* **2** You **feature** in some story, event or happening if you take part in it, or are part of it: *You featured in our discussion but I can't remember what we said about you.* □ *Someone I know featured in an article in the Sunday Times Magazine last month.* □ *Hercule Poirot features in many of Agatha Christie's books, but certainly not all of them*

February /'fɛbrʊərɪ/ *noun* (*uncount*)
February is the second month of the year, coming after January and before March, and usually consisting of only 28 days: *Last February we had a lot of snow.* □ *There's no twenty-ninth of February* (written *29 February*) *except in a leap year.* □ *February the fourteenth* (written *14 February*) □ *The coldest winter weather comes in February.* □ *chilly February nights.*

feces see **faeces**.

feckless /'fɛkləs/ *adjective* (*derogatory*)
Someone who is **feckless** has no sense of purpose or responsibility, and lives their life in a careless, disorganized way: *His feckless mother would sometimes forget to collect him from school.* — *adverb* **fecklessly:** *She flitted fecklessly from job to job.*

fed /fɛd/ *verb*
Fed is the past tense and past participle of **feed**.

federal /'fɛdərəl/ *adjective*
1 Federal describes a group of states independent in local matters but united under a central government for other purposes, *eg* defence: *a federal organization like that of the US.* **2** A **federal** government is the central government of a federal union.

federation /fɛdə'reɪʃən/ *noun*: **federations**
1 A **federation** is a group of states independent in local matters but united under a central government for other purposes, *eg* defence. **2** A union of business organizations or of associations is also a **federation**: *The International Federation of Booksellers.* **3** (*uncount*) **Federation** is the act of uniting in a league: *The smaller countries were in favour of federation.*

fed up /fɛd 'ʌp/ *adjective* (*informal*)
You say you are **fed up** when you are bored or annoyed, or tired of something that has been continuing for a long time: *You look a bit fed up.* □ *I'm fed up with this awful weather.* □ *I was fed up of correcting his mistakes.*

fee /fi:/ *noun*: **fees**
1 A **fee** is a charge made for professional services, *eg* by a doctor or lawyer: *He charged a fee of £19.50 per consultation.* **2** A **fee** is also a charge for something such as membership of a society, sitting an examination, or entrance to a museum: *The entrance fee for the gallery was £1.50.* **3** (*used in the plural*) Your **fees** at a school or college are the regular payments you make for your course of instruction: *My parents couldn't afford the fees for me to study music.* [see note at **cost**]

feeble /'fi:bəl/ *adjective*
1 Someone or something that is **feeble** is weak: *Some of us are getting old and feeble.* □ *He spoke her name in a feeble whisper.* **2** A person or authority that is **feeble** lacks power, influence, or effectiveness: *The government was too feeble to deal effectively with the drug barons.* **3** You call something that someone says **feeble** if it is not very effective: *feeble jokes* □ *You always seem to have some feeble excuse for not finishing your work.* — *noun* (*uncount*) **feebleness:** *advancing age and feebleness.* — *adverb* **feebly:** *He was still breathing feebly when I reached him.* □ *She scolded him feebly and he continued to misbehave.*

feed /fiːd/ *verb; noun*

▻ ***verb***: **feeds, feeding, fed**

1 You **feed** a baby or an animal when you give it food: *The baby was crying and wanted to be fed.* ▫ *Can she feed herself yet?* ▫ *We usually feed the sheep on turnips during the winter.* ▫ *We fed the remains of the fish to the cat.* **2** You say that a mother **is feeding** her baby herself if she breastfeeds it. **3** An animal or baby **feeds** when they eat or drink: *The baby was refusing to feed.* **4** You **feed** your family when you pay for, provide or prepare food for them: *Some single mothers can hardly afford to feed their families.* **5** To **feed** something such as a fire is to supply it with fuel; one thing **feeds** on another, or **is fed** by it, if it increases in strength as a consequence: *The flames leapt higher, fed by the sudden draught.* ▫ *Prejudice feeds on ignorance.* ▫ *Her continual flattery fed his vanity.* **6** You **feed** something into a machine or device when you supply it with whatever it needs for continued operation: *We fed the data into the computer.* ▫ *I fed two twenty-pence pieces into the parking meter.*

▻ ***noun***: **feeds**

1 You give a baby or animal a **feed** when you feed them: *He's getting four feeds a day at present.* ▫ *When is her next feed due?* **2** (*uncount*) **Feed** is food prepared for animals: *We need some more cattle feed.* **3** The **feed** in a machine or other device is the channel or opening through which it is supplied with whatever it needs for continued operation: *The automatic feed on the printer isn't working.*

> ***phrasal verb***
> You **feed** a person or animal **up** by giving them plenty of good food to make them fatter: *You're too thin; you need feeding up.*

feedback /ˈfiːdbak/ *noun* (*uncount*)

You get **feedback** on something you have made, done or designed when people tell you whether or not they like it, and you learn from their comments how you can improve it: *Has there been any feedback from teachers on the new school dictionary?*

feel /fiːl/ *verb; noun*

▻ ***verb***: **feels, feeling, felt**

1 a You **feel** a sensation or emotion when you experience it: *I was feeling tired and hungry.* ▫ *Are you feeling cold?* ▫ *I feel ill.* ▫ *She felt no bitterness over the way she had been treated.* ▫ *She felt an urge to kiss him.* ▫ *You feel so helpless sometimes.* ▫ *I do feel an idiot!* ▫ *You're making me feel like a traitor.* ▫ *I felt as if I was going to be sick.* ▫ *My leg feels sore.* ▫ *My head felt as if it was going to burst.* ▫ *These shoes feel too tight.* **b** You **feel** that something is so if you think it is so: *She feels you may be hiding the truth.* ▫ *I feel sure you're right.* ▫ *I feel I ought to explain.* ▫ *We mustn't feel bound to do everything they suggest.* ▫ *We can discuss this further if you feel it necessary to do so.* ▫ *It was felt to be the right decision.* ▫ *It was felt that the project should be terminated.* **c** The way you **feel** about something is your opinion about it, or your attitude to it: *You know how I feel about killing animals.* **d** You **feel** like something, or like doing something, when you want to have it or do it: *I feel like a coffee.* ▫ *Do you feel like a walk?* ▫ *I just felt like bursting into tears.* ▫ *Don't you ever feel like hitting him?*

2 a You describe something you are touching or holding by saying it **feels** a certain way: *The parcel felt quite light.* ▫ *a new face cream that will make your skin feel soft and smooth* ▫ *His forehead felt hot.* ▫ *Your hands feel like ice.* ▫ *synthetics that look and feel like wool* ▫ *This feels like* [= it has the texture of] *plastic, not wood.* ▫ *That felt like a drop of rain.* **b** You use 'it **feels**' to describe the weather or the atmosphere: *It feels much warmer today.* ▫ *It feels like rain* [= I think it may rain]. ▫ *It felt as if it was going to snow.* ▫ *It feels chilly in here.* **c** You use 'it **feels**' to describe experiences and sensations: *It felt strange coming home after so many years away.* ▫ *What did it feel like to win all that money?*

3 a You **feel** things that are touching you, happening to you or happening near you, when you are aware of them through your senses: *She loved feeling the wind in her hair.* ▫ *He felt her hand on his shoulder.* ▫ *He could feel her presence nearby, though he could not see her.* ▫ *I felt my face going red.* ▫ *Didn't you feel the wasp sting you?* ▫ *She felt herself getting sleepier.* **b** You **feel** the effect of something when you experience it: *Old people feel the cold more than the young.* ▫ *It's just a small injection; you won't feel a thing.* ▫ *Many firms are feeling the effects of the recession.*

4 a You **feel** an object when you touch it intentionally to find out about its qualities: *Feel this lump on my head.* ▫ *She felt his forehead.* **b** You **feel** for something when you try to find it with your hands: *She felt about for the light switch.* ▫ *He felt in his pocket for his wallet.* ▫ *I felt my way along the passage.* [*same as* **grope**]

▻ ***noun***

1 (*used in the singular*) The **feel** of something is the way it feels to you, the sensation it gives you, or the impression it makes on you: *I like the feel of this material.* ▫ *The place had a genuinely medieval feel.* **2** (*used in the singular*) You have a **feel** for an activity if you are naturally good at it: *She seemed to have a feel for computer-programming.* **3** (*uncount*) **Feel** is the sense of touch: *Doctors learn to diagnose by feel.*

▻ ***phrases*** **1** (*informal*) You **feel up to** some activity if you feel well or energetic enough for it: *Do you feel up to a game of tennis?* **2** You **feel yourself** when you are feeling as well as normal: *He hasn't been feeling himself recently.* ▫ *I'm sure you'll feel yourself again in a few days.* **3** You **get the feel of** a job when you gradually learn how to do it.

> ***phrasal verb***
> You **feel for** someone when you are sympathetic towards them: *We all feel for you in your sorrow.*

feeler /ˈfiːlə(r)/ *noun*: **feelers**

A **feeler** is an organ of touch found in certain creatures, especially one of two thread-like projections on an insect's head. [*same as* **antenna**]

feeling /ˈfiːlɪŋ/ *noun*: **feelings**

1 A **feeling** is an emotion: *She was overwhelmed by a feeling of despair.* ▫ *He dared not show his real feelings.* **2** A **feeling** is a physical sensation: *I had a prickly feeling down my back.* ▫ *He experienced a brief feeling of nausea.* **3** (*uncount*) You have no **feeling** in a part of your body if there is no sensation in it, and you cannot tell when it is being touched: *The feeling gradually came back into my fingers.* **4** (*often in the plural*) Your **feelings** about something are your attitude to it or your opinion about it: *She had strong feelings about people smoking in the house.* **5** (*uncount*) **Feeling** is strong emotion, sincerity or enthusiasm, or a display of it: *He spoke with feeling about the plight of African students.* **6** You say you have a **feeling** that something is so if that is your impression or opinion: *I've a horrible feeling we've no milk left.* ▫ *My feeling is that we should wait.* **7** You have a **feeling** for some subject or activity if you have a natural ability for it or understanding of it: *She has a feeling for finance.* **8** (*uncount or count*) **Feeling** for someone or something is affection or sympathy: *Don't be influenced by feeling for your former colleagues.* □ *Her feelings for him grew.* **9** (*used in the plural*) You hurt someone's **feelings** when you upset them. — *adverb* **feelingly:** *She spoke feelingly* [= with sincerity or strong emotion] *about the terrible conditions of the refugees.*

▻ ***phrases*** **1** There is **bad feeling** between people if they dislike each other. **2** You say **'no hard feelings'** to someone when you have had an argument, disagreement or quarrel with them, and hope that you can still be friends with each other.

feet /fi:t/ *noun*
Feet is the plural of **foot**.

feign /feɪn/ *verb*: **feigns, feigning, feigned**
You **feign** a feeling or emotion when you pretend to be experiencing it: *She feigned an optimism she was far from feeling.* — *adjective* **feigned:** *He raised his eyebrows in feigned astonishment.*

feint /feɪnt/ *noun*: **feints**
In boxing, fencing, football and other sports, a **feint** is a movement intended to deceive or mislead your opponent.

feline /'fi:laɪn/ *adjective*
1 Feline means relating to or belonging to cats: *feline habits.* **2** You describe a person as **feline** if they remind you of a cat in the way they look, behave or move: *moving with feline grace.*

fell[1] /fɛl/ *verb*
Fell is the past tense of **fall**.

fell[2] /fɛl/ *verb*: **fells, felling, felled**
1 You **fell** a tree when you cut it down: *The diseased trees will have to be felled.* **2** (*literary*) You **fell** a person when you knock them down: *She felled her attacker with some sort of karate movement.*

fellow /'fɛloʊ/ *noun; adjective*
▻ ***noun***: **fellows**
1 (*informal*) A **fellow** is a man or boy: *She's going out with such a nice fellow just now.* **2** (*used in the plural; formal*) Your **fellows** are your companions, equals or colleagues: *Disabled students are looked after by their able-bodied fellows.* **3** A **fellow** of an academic institution such as a college or university is a senior member of it, or a postgraduate student awarded research funding by the institution; a **fellow** of a society is a member of it: *She's a Fellow of Royal Academy.*
▻ ***adjective***
Fellow describes a person who has the same status, or is in the same situation, as you: *Learn to love your fellow men.* □ *I'll discuss it with my fellow editors.*

fellowship /'fɛloʊʃɪp/ *noun*: **fellowships**
1 (*uncount*) **Fellowship** is friendship amongst people who are involved in doing something together: *There was a strong bond of fellowship amongst the aid workers.* **2** A society or association may be called a **fellowship**: *the University Bible Fellowship.* **3** The post or position of a fellow of a college or university is also a **fellowship**: *She had a research fellowship at St Hugh's.*

felony /'fɛlənɪ/ *noun* (*legal*): **felonies**
A **felony** is a serious crime such as murder.

felt[1] /fɛlt/ *verb*
Felt is the past tense and past participle of **feel**.

felt[2] /fɛlt/ *noun* (*uncount*)
Felt is a fabric formed by pressing together short fibres of wool or other material: *brightly coloured felt rugs.*

felt tip /fɛlt 'tɪp/ *noun*: **felt tips**
A **felt tip** or **felt-tip pen** or **felt pen** is a pen whose nib or writing point is made of stiffened fibres.

female /'fi:meɪl/ *adjective; noun*
▻ ***adjective***
1 Female describes the sex, or any creature belonging to it, that gives birth to babies or lays eggs: *a female giraffe* □ *members of the female sex.* **2** A **female** plant bears seeds or fruit. **3 Female** means being a woman, as distinct from a man: *female employees.* **4 Female** means relating to, concerning, or belonging to women: *The female skeleton differs considerably from the male one.* □ *articles of female clothing.*
[*opposite* **male**]
▻ ***noun***: **females**
1 A **female** is a female animal: *Most of the hunting is left to the female.* **2** (*rather offensive*) A **female** is a woman.
[*opposite* **male**]

feminine /'fɛmɪnɪn/ *adjective*
1 Feminine describes qualities, characteristics, clothing, concerns and interests that typically belong to or relate to women, or are considered suitable for them: *He told her her clothes weren't feminine enough.* □ *Sewing and knitting were considered suitably feminine occupations in those days.* [*opposite* **unfeminine**] **2** A woman is described as **feminine** if, in appearance and character, she has the qualities traditionally considered essential for women: *She was dainty and feminine.* [*opposite* **unfeminine**] **3** (*grammar*) In some languages, **feminine** nouns are nouns that belong to the gender that contains words referring to females: *'Waitress' and 'lioness' are feminine nouns.*
[*opposite* **masculine**]

femininity /'fɛmɪnɪnɪtɪ/ *noun* (*uncount*)
1 Femininity is the circumstance of being a woman. **2 Femininity** is also the quality of being feminine, or of having physical and mental characteristics traditionally thought suitable and essential for women: *Femininity is emphasized in the latest styles emerging from the fashion industry.*
[*opposite* **masculinity**]

feminism /'fɛmɪnɪzm/ *noun* (*uncount*)
Feminism is a movement, or the attitude of those who support it, insisting that women's rights and opportunities should be equal to those of men. — *noun* **feminist:** *Lots of husbands consider themselves feminists.* □ *The play is clearly written from a feminist angle.*

fence[1] /fɛns/ *noun; verb*
▻ ***noun***: **fences**
A **fence** is a barrier, *eg* of wood or wire supported by posts, for enclosing or protecting land: *Some of the fences need repairing.* [see picture at **house**]
▻ ***verb***: **fences, fencing, fenced**
You **fence** land when you build a fence round it. — *adjective* **fenced:** *The monument stood in a fenced enclosure.*
▻ ***phrase*** You **sit on the fence** when you avoid supporting either side in an argument.

> ***phrasal verbs***
> **fence in** You **fence in** something when you enclose or confine it within a fence: *The dogs are safely fenced in and can't escape.*
> **fence off** You **fence off** a piece of land when you build a fence round it, or separate it with a fence: *They've fenced off part of the park as a children's play area.*

fence[2] /fɛns/ *verb*: **fences, fencing, fenced**
You **fence** when you take part in the sport of **fencing**.

fencing[1] /'fɛnsɪŋ/ *noun* (*uncount*)
Fencing is the sport of fighting with narrow, blunt-ended swords: *He'd first taken up fencing as a schoolboy.*

fencing[2] /ˈfɛnsɪŋ/ *noun* (*uncount*)
Fencing is material such as wire netting, for constructing fences.

fend /fɛnd/ *verb*: **fends, fending, fended**
▻ ***phrase*** You **fend for yourself** when you look after yourself, and find everything you need, without relying on other people: *He had had to fend for himself from the age of twelve.*

> ***phrasal verb***
> **fend off 1** You **fend off** an attacker, or blows, when you defend yourself against them: *He put up his hands to fend off the birds.* **2** You **fend off** questions when you avoid answering them: *She successfully fended off inquiries from dozens of reporters.*

fender /fɛndə(r)/ *noun*: **fenders**
1 (*AmE*) The **fender** of a car or bicycle is its wing or mudguard. [see pictures at **bicycle, car**] **2** (*BrE*) A **fender** is a low frame fitted round a fireplace to keep ash and coal within the hearth. [compare **fireguard**]

ferment *noun*; *verb*
▻ ***noun*** /ˈfɜːmɛnt/ (*uncount*)
A place is in **ferment** when it is in a state of excitement or disorder: *Parliament was in ferment today over the new education bill.*
▻ ***verb*** /fəˈmɛnt/: **ferments, fermenting, fermented**
Drinks such as beer or wine **ferment** when they go through a chemical change during their production that makes them alcoholic. — *noun* (*uncount*) **fermentation** /fɜːmɛnˈteɪʃən/: *the fermentation process.*

fern /fɜːn/ *noun*: **ferns**
A **fern** is a long-stemmed plant with feathery leaves and no flowers.

ferocious /fəˈroʊʃəs/ *adjective*
People or animals that are described as **ferocious** are fierce or savage; **ferocious** fighting is violent and cruel: *The beasts could be ferocious once they smelt danger.* ▫ *hordes of ferocious invaders from the northeast.* [*opposite* **tame, gentle**] — *adverb* **ferociously:** *The dog bared its teeth ferociously.* — *noun* (*uncount*) **ferocity:** *The zebra had been attacked with horrible ferocity by three lionesses.*

ferret /ˈfɛrɪt/ *noun*; *verb*
▻ ***noun***: **ferrets**
A **ferret** is a small animal related to the weasel, used for driving rabbits and rats from their holes.
▻ ***verb***: **ferrets, ferreting, ferreted**

> ***phrasal verb***
> You **ferret out** information when you discover it after a determined search.

ferry /ˈfɛrɪ/ *noun*; *verb*
▻ ***noun***: **ferries**
A **ferry** is a boat that carries people, vehicles and goods across a river or a narrow strip of water, usually as a regular service: *We caught the night ferry from Dover to Ostend.*
▻ ***verb***: **ferries, ferrying, ferried**
To **ferry** people or goods anywhere is to take them there by boat or any other form of transport: *Thousands of passengers are ferried across to Zeebrugge every week.* ▫ *I spend my time ferrying the children to and from school.*

fertile /ˈfɜːtaɪl/ *adjective*
1 You describe land or soil as **fertile** if crops grow well on it: *a fertile valley.* [*opposite* **infertile, barren**] **2** People or animals that are **fertile** are capable of producing babies. [*opposite* **infertile, sterile, barren**] **3** Someone who has a **fertile** mind is quick at producing interesting, useful or original ideas: *We welcome another fine novel from the fertile imagination of Muriel Spark.* **4** A situation or place that is described as **fertile** ground for something provides good possibilities for it to grow and increase: *The northern working-class towns proved fertile ground for the spread of trade-unionism.* — *noun* (*uncount*) **fertility** /fɜːˈtɪlɪtɪ/: *Intensive cultivation reduces the fertility of the soil.* ▫ *It is suspected that the proximity of the nuclear power station has affected male fertility in the area.*

fertilize or **fertilise** /ˈfɜːtɪlaɪz/ *verb*: **fertilizes, fertilizing, fertilized**
1 An egg or a plant **is fertilized** when sperm or pollen enter them, to start the process of reproduction. **2** To **fertilize** soil is to add manure or chemical substances to it to make crops grow well on it. — *noun* (*uncount*) **fertilization** /fɜːtɪlaɪˈzeɪʃən/: *Fertilization doesn't actually take place inside the womb.*

fertilizer or **fertiliser** /ˈfɜːtɪlaɪzə(r)/ *noun* (*count or uncount*): **fertilizers**
A **fertilizer** is a natural or chemical substance that is dug into soil to make it more fertile: *There are some new organic fertilizers on the market.* ▫ *a bag of fertilizer.*

fervent /ˈfɜːvənt/ *adjective*
Fervent describes the attitude of someone who has strong, sincere or enthusiastic feelings about something: *a fervent believer in democracy* ▫ *I'm a fervent admirer of your books.* [*same as* **ardent**] — *adverb* **fervently:** *They prayed fervently for peace.*

fervour (*AmE* **fervor**) /ˈfɛːvə(r)/ *noun* (*uncount*)
Fervour is strong enthusiasm for something: *A wave of religious fervour swept the US in the '50s.* ▫ *He spoke with fervour about the need for reform.* [*opposite* **apathy**]

fester /ˈfɛstə(r)/ *verb*: **festers, festering, festered**
1 A wound **festers** when it becomes infected and inflamed: *a deep, festering cut on her leg.* **2** Something such as hatred or ill feeling **festers** when it goes on growing or getting worse.

festival /ˈfɛstɪvəl/ *noun*: **festivals**
1 A **festival** is a day or period of celebration in honour of some event, especially a religious one: *Christian festivals such as Christmas and Easter.* [*same as* **feast**] **2** A **festival** is a programme of musical, theatrical or other cultural events such as art exhibitions and filmshows: *the three-week-long Edinburgh Festival* ▫ *a drama festival.*

festive /ˈfɛstɪv/ *adjective*
Things that are **festive** are bright, colourful and joyful, in honour of some celebration; a **festive** occasion is a time for celebration; the **festive** season is the period round Christmas: *At my age I don't regard my birthday as a festive occasion.* ▫ *It was nearly Christmas and the shops were looking very festive.*

festivity /fɛˈstɪvɪtɪ/ *noun*: **festivities**
1 (*uncount*) **Festivity** is the celebration of some event, with eating, drinking and parties: *After a week of idle festivity I was glad to get back to work.* **2** (*used in the plural*) **Festivities** are activities such as eating, drinking and dancing, in celebration of some event: *He returned home in time for the wedding festivities.*

festooned /fɛˈstuːnd/ *adjective*
An object that is **festooned** with something is covered with hanging decorations, *eg* consisting of flowers

and ribbons: *The walls were festooned with balloons and streamers.*

fetal see **foetal**.

fetch /fɛtʃ/ *verb*: **fetches, fetching, fetched**
1 You **fetch** something from somewhere when you go and get it, and bring it back: *Could you fetch me my spectacles from the bedroom?* □ *It's time to fetch the children from school.* □ *Every day they have to fetch water from the river.* **2** Something that you sell **fetches** a certain amount of money if you sell it for that amount: *His picture fetched an amazing £2000.*

> ***phrasal verb***
> (*informal*) You **fetch up** somewhere when you arrive there, especially unexpectedly or unintentionally: *I broke my leg and fetched up in hospital.* [*same as* **end up**]

fetching /ˈfɛtʃɪŋ/ *adjective* (*informal, slightly humorous*)
You say that a woman looks **fetching** if you think she looks attractive: *Susan was looking fetching in a pink dress.* □ *She wore a fetching green hat.*

fête or **fete** /feɪt/ *noun; verb*
▻ ***noun***: **fêtes**
A **fête** is an outdoor event with competitions, stalls selling food, and various entertainments, held to raise money for some cause, *eg* a charity.
▻ ***verb***: **fêtes, fêting, fêted**
A famous or important person **is fêted** when they are honoured with a public welcome and generously entertained: *After her Olympic victory she was fêted wherever she went.*

fetid or **foetid** /ˈfiːtɪd/ or /ˈfɛtɪd/ *adjective*
Something that is **fetid** has a nasty smell because it is stale or rotting: *a fetid atmosphere.* [***same as*** **foul**]

fetter /ˈfɛtə(r)/ *noun; verb*
▻ ***noun*** (*usually in the plural*): **fetters**
1 Fetters are chains that are put round prisoners' ankles to reduce their range of movement. **2** (*literary*) **Fetters** are also circumstances or rules that limit what you can do, or prevent you from acting as freely as you want to: *One country after another tore off the fetters of communism and embraced capitalism.*
▻ ***verb***: **fetters, fettering, fettered**
To **fetter** someone is to prevent them behaving as freely as they want: *fettered to the endless routine of feeding and nappy-changing* □ *the bourgeois preconceptions that fetter our imaginations.* [*same as* **restrict, shackle**]

fetus see **foetus**.

feud /fjuːd/ *noun; verb*
▻ ***noun***: **feuds**
A **feud** is a long-lasting bitter quarrel, *eg* between families, or between members of the same family: *There was some feud over money between the two branches of the family.*
▻ ***verb***: **feuds, feuding, feuded:** *One tribe always seemed to be feuding with another.*

feudal /ˈfjuːdəl/ *adjective* (*history*)
A **feudal** society is one in which powerful nobles and landowners make weaker people work and fight for them, and in return give them land and protection. — *noun* (*uncount*) **feudalism:** *the medieval system of feudalism.*

fever /ˈfiːvə(r)/ *noun*: **fevers**
1 (*uncount, or used in the singular*) You have a **fever** when you are ill if you have an abnormally high body temperature and a fast pulse: *She has a high fever.* □ *Most pain-killing drugs also reduce fever.* **2** (*count or uncount*) A **fever** is an illness in which you have a high temperature; **fever** is also used in the name of some diseases: *tropical fevers* □ *yellow fever* □ *hay fever.* **3** (*uncount, or used in the singular*) People are in a **fever** of excitement or anxiety when they are very excited, anxious or nervous: *The tension had reached fever pitch.*

feverish /ˈfiːvərɪʃ/ *adjective*
1 You are **feverish** when you have a fever: *Her cold had reached the feverish stage.* **2** People are in a **feverish** state, or behave in a **feverish** manner, when they are very excited, anxious or nervous: *feverish activity* — *adverb* **feverishly:** *I stayed up all night feverishly trying to finish the work.*

few /fjuː/ *determiner; pronoun*
▻ ***determiner***: **fewer, fewest**
1 'A **few**' means 'some', or 'a small number', and is used with plural count nouns: *There are a few copies left.* □ *I've only a few more letters to write.* □ *He was handing round drinks to the first few guests.* □ *The weather is supposed to remain fine for the next few days.* □ *I visit my mother every few months.* [= with a gap of a few months between visits]
2 (*used like a negative*) **Few** means 'hardly any' or 'not many': *Very few people read Scott nowadays, do they?* □ *The class had to be cancelled because too few people attended it.* □ *He has few interests outside his work.* □ *There are so few job opportunities for today's young people.* □ *It's amazing how few books there are on this subject.* □ *Far fewer people turned up than we'd catered for.* □ *There were fewer than 20 applications.* □ *This year we had the fewest runners since the race began.*
▻ ***pronoun:*** *'Have you any matches?' 'Yes, a few.'* □ *I haven't quite finished these forms; I'll leave the last few till tomorrow.* □ *A few of us objected; too few to make them change their minds.* □ *Very few of the candidates managed all the questions.* □ *'Did you sell as many as 200?' 'No, fewer than that.'*
▻ ***phrases*** **1 As few as** means 'no more than': *There could have been as few as 25 people at the meeting.* **2** Things that are **few and far between** are scarce: *Opportunities like this are few and far between.* **3** You use **a good few** and **quite a few** to mean quite a lot: *There have been quite a few letters to the newspapers about this.* □ *I don't know how many, but certainly a good few.* **4** You use **no fewer than** to mean 'as many as', when you want to emphasize the largeness of the number: *We had no fewer than 60 complaints about the product.* **5 Precious few** means hardly any: *He had precious few supporters left.*

fiancé or **fiancée** /fɪˈɑ̃seɪ/ or /fɪˈɒnseɪ/ *noun*: **fiancés** or **fiancées**
A woman's **fiancé** is the man to whom she is engaged to be married; a man's **fiancée** is the woman to whom he is engaged to be married.

fiasco /fɪˈaskoʊ/ *noun*: **fiascos** or **fiascoes**
You call an event a **fiasco** if it fails very obviously and disastrously: *The election campaign was a complete fiasco.*

fib /fɪb/ *noun; verb*
▻ ***noun*** (*informal*): **fibs**
You tell a **fib** when you tell a small unimportant lie: *I don't believe you! That's a fib!*
▻ ***verb*** (*informal*): **fibs, fibbing, fibbed**
You **fib** when you tell small unimportant lies: *He fibbed about how much computing experience he'd had.* □ *You're fibbing!*

fibre /ˈfaɪbə(r)/ *noun*: **fibres**
1 A **fibre** is a fine thread, or a thread-like cell, of a natural or artificial substance: *wool fibres* □ *nylon fibres* □ *muscle and nerve fibres.* **2** (*count or uncount*) A **fibre** is a material composed of fibres or threads of some substance: *cotton, wool and other natural fibres* □ *synthetic fibres such as nylon.* **3** (*uncount*) **Fibre** is the parts of edible plants and seeds that the body is unable to digest, which help to move food quickly through the body: *There's too little fibre in some breakfast cereals.* **4** (*uncount*) **Fibre** is strength of character: *He seems to lack moral fibre.*

fibreglass /ˈfaɪbəglɑːs/ *noun* (*uncount*)
1 Fibreglass is a strong light plastic strengthened with glass fibres, used as a construction material, especially for making boats. **2 Fibreglass** is also a fluffy-looking material consisting of fine, tangled fibres of glass, that is laid in lofts or round water pipes, to stop them from getting too cold in winter.

fibrous /ˈfaɪbrəs/ *adjective*
Fibrous substances consist of, or contain, fibre: *fibrous vegetables such as celery.*

fickle /ˈfɪkəl/ *adjective* (*derogatory*)
People who are **fickle** are easily persuaded to change their opinion, and do not remain loyal to one person or idea for long: *The tabloid newspapers are so fickle in their loyalties.* [*same as* **capricious**; *opposite* **constant**] — *noun* **fickleness:** *the fickleness of the public.*

fiction /ˈfɪkʃən/ *noun*: **fictions**
1 (*uncount*) **Fiction** is literature or stories about imaginary people or events: *She writes children's fiction.* **2** (*count or uncount*) A **fiction** is something untrue that you tell people is so: *The report in the press was utter fiction.* □ *Some people don't seem to know the difference between fact and fiction.*

fictional /ˈfɪkʃenəl/ *adjective*
Fictional people, places and events are those found in stories as distinct from real life: *Mr Casaubon is a fictional clergyman from George Eliot's 'Middlemarch'.* □ *Jules Verne's fictional journey to the centre of the earth.*

fictitious /fɪkˈtɪʃəs/ *adjective*
Fictitious means invented or imaginary: *In our report we have used fictitious names for the people concerned in the incident, in order to protect them.* □ *The events shown in this series are entirely fictitious.*

fiddle /ˈfɪdəl/ *verb*; *noun*
▻ ***verb*: fiddles, fiddling, fiddled**
1 You **fiddle** with something. or **fiddle** about or around with it, when you keep touching it, moving it about, or adjusting it: *She fiddled with her earrings as she talked.* □ *Do stop fiddling about with the television!* □ *Don't fiddle!* **2** You **fiddle** about or around when you waste time, or do unimportant things when there is something more important you ought to be doing. **3** You **fiddle** things such as accounts, figures or statistics when you alter them dishonestly for your own purpose, benefit or advantage: *He had to fiddle the figures to hide the evidence of his unauthorized borrowing from the firm's account.* **4** (*informal*) You **fiddle** if you play the violin: *I could hear him fiddling away in the next room, practising for his next concert.*
▻ ***noun*** (*informal*): **fiddles**
1 A **fiddle** is a dishonest arrangement or scheme by which someone gets money or privileges that they have no right to get: *She had managed to work some fiddle that gave her the occasional free weekend in a luxury hotel.* **2** A **fiddle** is a violin, especially when used to play folk music or jazz: *a fiddle band* □ *She plays the fiddle with the Meadows Orchestra.*
▻ ***phrases*** **1** Someone who is **fit as a fiddle** is very healthy. **2** (*informal*) You say someone is **on the fiddle** if they are making money dishonestly. **3** You **play second fiddle to** someone with whom you are working jointly if your position or rank is less important than theirs.

fiddler /ˈfɪdlə(r)/ *noun* (*informal*): **fiddlers**
A **fiddler** is someone who plays the violin, especially with a folk group or jazz band.

fiddly /ˈfɪdlɪ/ *adjective* (*informal*): **fiddlier, fiddliest**
You describe a small device or piece of equipment as **fiddly** if it is awkward to handle; a **fiddly** job is one involving awkward little movements or adjustments.

fidelity /fɪˈdelɪtɪ/ *noun* (*uncount*)
1 Fidelity is the quality of being loyal or faithful to someone or something: *'Greyfriars Bobby' is the true story of a dog's fidelity to its dead master.* **2** The **fidelity** of something such as a description, translation or dramatization is the degree of accuracy with which it represents the facts, or the original form: *The television series is quite remarkable for its fidelity to the original novel.* **3 Fidelity** also means accuracy in sound reproduction: *high-fidelity recordings.*

fidget /ˈfɪdʒɪt/ *verb*: **fidgets, fidgeting, fidgeted**
People **fidget** when they can't keep still, and keep changing their position and moving their hands and feet around: *You can't expect children to sit for a long time without fidgeting.*

fidgety /ˈfɪdʒɪtɪ/ *adjective*
People get **fidgety** when they start fidgeting, or when they get nervous.

field /fiːld/ *noun*; *verb*
▻ ***noun*: fields**
1 A **field** is a piece of land, usually enclosed by a wall or fence, used for growing crops or keeping animals such as cattle, sheep or horses. **2** (*often in the plural*) A **field** is also a piece of open grassland: *Green fields stretched away to the hills on all sides.* [*same as* **meadow**] **3** A sports **field** is an area of short grass suitably marked with lines for the playing of a particular game: *a football field.* [compare **pitch**] **4 Field** is used in combinations such as *coalfield* and *oilfield* to mean an area rich in a particular mineral. **5** An area of knowledge, interest or study is called a **field**: *She's an expert in the field of military history.* □ *What is your own particular field?* **6** Your **field** of vision is the range of what you can see without changing your position or turning your head. **7** A gravitational or magnetic **field** is the area over which a magnetic or gravitational force extends. **8** Work in the **field** is practical work or investigation as distinct from theoretical work; a **field** trip or **field** study involves practical work or research in a real-life situation or environment. **9** (*used in the singular*) The competitors in a race or competition are sometimes referred to collectively as the **field. 10** A **field** of battle is an area of fighting in a war: *the soldiers who fell in the field.*
▻ ***verb*: fields, fielding, fielded**
1 In cricket and similar games, the team that **is fielding** is fetching the ball back, or trying to catch it, as it is hit by members of the batting team. **2** You **field** a number of questions or enquiries when you answer them as they come.
▻ ***phrases*** **1** You **have a field day** when you have especially good opportunities for your activities: *On occasions like this the reporters have a field day.* **2** Someone or something **leads the field** if they are the best or most advanced: *Edinburgh University leads the field in this research.*

field marshal /fiːld ˈmɑːʃəl/ *noun*: **field marshals**
A **field marshal** is an army officer of the highest rank: *Field Marshal Haig.*

fieldmouse /ˈfiːldmaʊs/ *noun*: **fieldmice**
A **fieldmouse** is a small long-tailed mouse that lives in the fields and woods.

fieldwork /ˈfiːldwɜːk/ *noun* (*uncount*)
Fieldwork is practical work or investigation as distinct from theoretical work: *Students are required to do at least a month's fieldwork.*

fiend /fiːnd/ *noun*: **fiends**
1 You call someone a **fiend** if you think they are evil, wicked or cruel: *her jealous fiend of a husband.* [*same as* **beast**] **2** (*informal*) Someone who is very enthusiastic about something can be called a **fiend**: *health fiends* □ *She's one of those fresh-air fiends that keep opening windows.* [*same as* **fanatic**]

fiendish /ˈfiːndɪʃ/ *adjective*
1 Something or someone that is **fiendish** is evil or wicked: *a fiendish plot.* **2 Fiendish** is used to emphasize the extreme quality of something bad: *He had a fiendish temper.* **3 Fiendish** can mean very clever or complicated: *fiendish crossword clues.* — *adverb* (*intensifying*) **fiendishly:** *a fiendishly clever plan.*

fierce /fɪəs/ *adjective*: **fiercer, fiercest**
1 A **fierce** animal is likely to attack you: *Wild cats are much fiercer than domestic ones.* [*same as* **aggressive**] **2 Fierce** weather is wild and stormy: *fierce winds* □ *fierce storms.* [*same as* **severe**; *opposite* **calm**] **3** Something such as competition or rivalry between people is **fierce** if it is strong, keen and lively: *fierce competition* □ *fierce opposition.* [*same as* **aggressive**] **4** Emotions described as **fierce** are deep and strong: *fierce devotion to duty.* [*same as* **keen, intense**] — *adverb* **fiercely:** *The storm raged fiercely for several days.* □ *They were fiercely loyal to their leader.*

fiery /ˈfaɪərɪ/ *adjective*: **fierier, fieriest**
1 Fiery means like fire, or consisting of it: *The sun was now sinking, a fiery ball of light in the west.* □ *a fiery sunset.* **2** A part of the body is **fiery**, or **fiery** red, when it is hot and red: *His tonsils looked fiery and swollen.* [*same as* **inflamed**] **3** A person is said to have a **fiery** temper if they get angry easily. [*same as* **hot-tempered**] **4** A **fiery** speech is a passionate one that is likely to stir people's feelings: *fiery oratory.* [*same as* **impassioned**]

fifteen /fɪfˈtiːn/ *noun*; *adjective*; *determiner*; *pronoun*
▷ ***noun***: **fifteens**
1 (*uncount or count*) **Fifteen** is the number or figure 15: *Six and nine are fifteen.* □ *Two fifteens are thirty.* **2** (*uncount*) **Fifteen** is the age of 15: *He had to start earning his living at fifteen.* **3** (*count or uncount*) A **fifteen** is a piece of clothing whose size is represented by the number 15, or a person who wears clothes of this size. **4** (*count*) A rugby team is sometimes referred to as a **fifteen**: *He's been selected for the first fifteen.* **5** (*count*) A film classified as suitable for people aged 15 and over is a **fifteen**.
▷ ***adjective***
Someone who is **fifteen** is fifteen years old: *My mother died when I was fifteen.*
▷ ***determiner:*** *I ordered fifteen copies.* □ *a fifteen-year-old drug addict.*
▷ ***pronoun:*** *I can supply more leaflets, but here are fifteen to start with.*

fifteenth /fɪfˈtiːnθ/ *determiner*; *pronoun*; *adjective or adverb*; *noun*: **fifteenths**
1 (often written **15th**) The **fifteenth** person or thing is the one numbered fifteen in a series. **2** (often written $\frac{1}{15}$) A **fifteenth** of something is one of fifteen equal parts of it.

fifth (often written **5th**) /fɪfθ/ *determiner*; *pronoun*; *adjective or adverb*; *noun*
▷ ***determiner***
The **fifth** person or thing is the one that is numbered five in a series: *This is the fifth class of the term.* □ *the 5th Earl of Bute.*
▷ ***pronoun:*** *Diana was the fifth and youngest of their children.* □ *Our house is the fifth on the left.* □ *The 5th of July was then known as Midsummer's Day.* [see note at **date**] □ *in the reign of Henry the Fifth* (written *Henry V*)
▷ ***adjective or adverb:*** *He was* (or *came*) *fifth in the French paper.* □ *He had engine trouble and came in fifth.*
▷ ***noun*** (often written $\frac{1}{5}$): **fifths**
A **fifth** of something is one of five equal parts of it: *Eighty is three fifths* (written $\frac{3}{5}$) *of a hundred.* □ *One fifth of the total police force is located in the London area.* □ *A fifth of our students are from abroad.*

fiftieth /ˈfɪftɪεθ/ *determiner*; *pronoun*; *adjective or adverb*; *noun*: **fiftieths**
1 (often written **50th**) The **fiftieth** person or thing is the one numbered fifty in a series. **2** (often written $\frac{1}{50}$) A **fiftieth** of something is one of fifty equal parts of it.

fifty /ˈfɪftɪ/ *noun*; *adjective*; *determiner*; *pronoun*
▷ ***noun***: **fifties**
1 (*uncount or count*) **Fifty** is the number or figure 50: *Twenty-five times two is fifty.* □ *Three fifties are 150.* **2** (*uncount*) **Fifty** is the age of 50: *By fifty you are probably showing some signs of aging.* **3** (*used in the plural*) Someone who is in their **fifties** is aged between 50 and 59. **4** (*used in the plural*) The temperature is in the **fifties** when it between 50° and 59° Fahrenheit. **5** (*used in the plural*) The **fifties** are the period between the fiftieth and sixtieth years of a century: *The house was built in the early fifties.* □ *during the nineteen-fifties.*
▷ ***adjective***
Someone who is **fifty** is 50 years old.
▷ ***determiner:*** *Many fifty-year-olds are healthier than the average twenty-five-year-old.*
▷ ***pronoun:*** *Seventy cases of food poisoning were reported yesterday, and another fifty today.*

fifty-fifty /fɪftɪ ˈfɪftɪ/ *adjective*; *adjective or adverb*
▷ ***adjective***
The chances of something happening are **fifty-fifty** if it just as likely to happen as not to happen: *The chances of finding her alive are less than fifty-fifty.*
▷ ***adjective or adverb***
Something is divided or split **fifty-fifty** between two people if they get half each: *We agreed on a fifty-fifty share of the bill.*

fig /fɪg/ *noun*: **figs**
A **fig** is a soft sweet juicy fruit full of tiny seeds: *fig trees* □ *a packet of dried figs.* [see picture at **fruit**]

fight /faɪt/ *verb*; *noun*
▷ ***verb***: **fights, fighting, fought**
1 People **fight** when they struggle together and try to hurt each other, or attack each other with weapons: *He was always fighting with the other children.* □ *Why don't you fight someone your own size?* □ *People were fighting in the streets.* □ *He fought in the desert campaign.* □ *We fought two world wars within 30 years.* □ *Frazier fought and defeated world champion Muhammad Ali in 1971.* **2** People **fight** about or over something when they quarrel about it, or go to war over it: *We were fighting about money as usual.* □ *They fought bitterly over possession of the coastal strip.* **3** You **fight** something, or **fight** against it, when you try to resist it, stop it or prevent it: *He fought social injustice wherever he met it.* □ *It is up to us to fight the*

proposed takeover. □ *We should fight against further government interference in our lives.* **4** You **fight** for something when you struggle to obtain it: *What the disabled are fighting for is independence.* □ *We must fight to keep our countryside unspoilt.* **5** Politicians **fight** an election or a seat when they try to persuade people to vote for them and elect them. **6** You **fight** an urge or a feeling when you try not to yield to it: *She fought the temptation to say something cruel.* **7** You **fight** your way somewhere when you get there with difficulty: *He fought his way to the front of the crowd.* — *noun* (*uncount*) **fighting:** *They didn't want to get mixed up in the fighting so they ran away.*

▻ ***noun*: fights**

1 A **fight** is a battle or an occasion of fighting: *He was injured in a street fight* □ *a gunfight* □ *Our dog was always getting into fights with bigger dogs.* **2** A boxing match is a **fight**: *the fight between Bruno and Lewis.* **3** A **fight** is a quarrel: *We had a fight about housework.* **4** (*used in the singular*) A **fight** for or against something is a struggle for or against it: *the fight against prejudice and intolerance* □ *the fight for equal rights.*

▻ ***phrases*** **1** You describe someone as **fighting fit** if they are strong and healthy, especially after having been ill. **2** For **fight a losing battle** see **battle**. **3** For **fight shy of** see **shy**. **4** You say someone **has a fighting chance** of doing something, *eg* recovering from an illness, if they may manage it with strength and determination. **5** You **put up a fight** when you fight against someone or something that is too strong for you: *She put up a brave fight against cancer.*

phrasal verbs

fight back 1 You **fight back** against someone who has attacked you when you defend yourself and attack them in turn: *Fight back! Don't accept defeat!* **2** You **fight back** tears when you make a great effort to stop yourself crying.

fight off 1 You **fight off** an illness when you get rid of it and recover from it: *She managed to fight off her cold in time for the party.* **2** You **fight off** people who are attacking you or bothering you when you manage to drive them away: *We had to fight off the reporters as we went into the house.*

fight out People **fight** something **out** when they keep arguing or fighting about it until one person or group wins: *I don't know whose turn it is to wash the dishes; you'll have to fight it out between you.*

fighter /ˈfaɪtə(r)/ *noun*: **fighters**

1 A **fighter** is a person who fights, *eg* a professional boxer. **2** A person with the determination to overcome difficulties or adversity is called a **fighter**: *He may recover; he was always a fighter.* **3** A **fighter** is also an aircraft equipped to attack other aircraft.

figment /ˈfɪgmənt/ *noun*: **figments**

You say that something is a **figment** of someone's imagination if you think they are imagining or inventing it, and it doesn't really exist: *Are you sure your neighbour's hostility to you isn't just a figment of your imagination?*

figurative /ˈfɪgərətɪv/ *adjective*

The **figurative** use of a word is the use of it in an imaginative or metaphorical sense, as distinct from its real or literal sense, *eg* the use of 'glued' in the sentence *Her eyes were glued to the television screen.* [*opposite* **literal**] — *adverb* **figuratively:** *I was using the word 'fatal' figuratively.* [*opposite* **literally**]

figure /ˈfɪgə(r)/ *noun*; *verb*

▻ ***noun*: figures**

1 a A **figure** is a symbol representing a number; single **figures** are the numbers from 0 to 9; double **figures** are the numbers from 10 to 99: *They practised writing figure 2s and figure 3s.* [*same as* **numeral**] **b** You suggest or name a **figure** when you state a number representing an amount, cost or price: *It's difficult to put a figure on the damage.* **c** (*used in the plural*) **Figures** are arithmetical calculations or statistics: *The government manipulate the unemployment figures so as to give a better impression of the situation.*

2 a A **figure** is an indistinctly seen or unidentified person: *A figure appeared walking quickly towards her, and she recognized it as Philip.* **b** Your **figure** is the shape of your body, with regard to your height, proportions, and your slimness or fatness: *I had a good figure once.* □ *a woman with a lovely figure.* **c** A well-known **figure** is someone who is familiar from being frequently seen and recognized; a public **figure** is someone who is important, especially politically: *By then she had become a well-known figure on television.* □ *public figures such as the prime minister.* **d** In art or drawing, a **figure** is a representation of a person: *Some of the greatest artists were not very good at drawing figures.* □ *Lowry's matchstick figures.*

3 a A **figure** in a book or article is a diagram or illustration: *Look at Figure 5 on page 32.* **b** A design, pattern or geometrical shape is a **figure**: *a three-dimensional figure.* **c** In skating or dancing, a **figure** is a pattern of steps or movements: *They had completed the compulsory figures.* **d** A **figure** is also a figure of speech.

▻ ***verb*: figures, figuring, figured**

1 A person or thing **figures** in an event if they take part in it: *She had figured recently in one or two parliamentary debates on child abuse.* **2** A person or thing **figures** in a story or conversation if they are mentioned a lot: *Her recently dead husband figured all the time in her conversation.* **3** (*informal*) You **figure** something when you think it: *I figure I'd better catch the 4 o'clock train.* □ *I figured she'd missed the train.* **4** (*informal*) You say something **figures** if you think it is typical or predictable from what you know of the situation: *'The accounts department have lost my invoice.' 'That figures.'*

▻ ***phrases*** **1** Someone **cuts a poor figure** if they act or behave in a way that does not impress people. **2** Someone or something **figures large** in some event if they take an important part in it. **3** You **keep** or **lose your figure** when you remain slim or get fat.

phrasal verbs

figure on 1 You **figure on** doing something when you intend to do it: *I figure on finishing the book by the end of the year.* [*same as* **plan** on] **2** You **figure on** something happening when you make plans that depend on it happening: *I'd figured on seeing her at the library, but she wasn't there.*

figure out You **figure out** a problem when you think hard about it and solve it: *I can't figure out why she left home so suddenly* [*same as* **work out**]

figurehead /ˈfɪgəhɛd/ *noun*: **figureheads**

1 (*history*) A ship's **figurehead** is a carved wooden figure fixed to its prow. **2** A leader of a country or organization who is referred to as a **figurehead** is a leader without real power: *In most of these countries the president is merely a figurehead.*

figure of speech /fɪgə əv ˈspiːtʃ/ *noun*: **figures of speech**

A **figure of speech** is an imaginative device such as a metaphor or simile that you use in speech or writing to make your style more lively.

filament /ˈfɪləmənt/ *noun*: **filaments**
1 A **filament** is a fine thread or fibre. **2** (*elecricity*) The **filament** in an electric light bulb is the loop of fine wire in it that lights up when the light is switched on.

filch /fɪltʃ/ *verb* (*informal*): **filches, filching, filched**
Someone **filches** something when they steal it: *He occasionally filched small sums from his mother's purse.*

file[1] /faɪl/ *noun*; *verb*
▻ ***noun***: **files**
1 A **file** is a box or a folder in which to keep loose papers, usually fitted with ring-shaped fasteners or other devices for securing them. [see picture at **office**] **2** A **file** is also the collection of papers kept in a box or folder, especially dealing with a particular subject or person: *The police had kept a file on her for some years.* **3** (*computing*) A **file** is a collection of data stored in a computer under one reference number or name: *You save what you've written as a file and give it a file name, which you select from the list of files when you want to open that particular file again.* **4** A **file** of people or vehicles is a moving line or queue of them: *The long file of mourners reached the cemetery.*
▻ ***verb***: **files, filing, filed**
1 You **file** papers when you put them into a file: *I've filed the report on playgrounds under P in the top drawer of the cabinet.* **2** You **file** a complaint, application, request or accusation when you make it officially; you **file** for divorce when you apply to a law court for it: *She filed a complaint against the manufacturers of the product.* **3** People **file** somewhere when they walk along one behind the other: *The mourners filed slowly past his coffin.*
▻ ***phrases*** **1** People move **in single file** when they walk one behind the other. **2** You keep information **on file** or **on the files** when you keep it in a file for reference: *We shall retain your suggestions on file for future use.*

file[2] /faɪl/ *noun*: **files**
A **file** is a tool with a rough surface for smoothing surfaces or edges: *a nail file.* [see picture at **tool**]
▻ ***verb***: **files, filing, filed**
You **file** a surface or edge when you smooth it and shape it with a file: *He was filing his fingernails.*

filial /ˈfɪlɪəl/ *adjective*
Filial means relating to a son or daughter, especially with reference to their duties, loyalty or affection towards their parents: *She gave him a filial kiss on the cheek.*

filing cabinet /ˈfaɪlɪŋ kabɪnət/ *noun*: **filing cabinets**
A **filing cabinet** is a piece of office furniture with drawers, for keeping files in. [see picture at **office**]

fill /fɪl/ *verb*; *noun*
▻ ***verb***: **fills, filling, filled**
1 You **fill** a container or a place when you put enough of something into it to make it full: *He filled the pan with water.* ▫ *We filled two photo albums with our holiday pictures.* **2** Something **fills** a place or thing when it occupies all the space in it: *Protesters filled the square.* ▫ *The hallway was filled with luggage.* ▫ *Tears filled her eyes.* **3** A space or thing **fills** with something when it becomes full of it: *The hall was filling quickly with people.* ▫ *His eyes filled with tears and he turned away.* **4** You **are filled** with a feeling or with ideas when you are strongly affected by them; something **fills** you with a feeling when it causes you to experience it strongly: *The thought of the exams filled me with dread.* ▫ *He was filled with a desire to get away into the country for a while.* ▫ *The conference had filled her head with new ideas.* **5** Something **fills** a need when it satisfies it: *There was a time when reading and conversation filled the need for entertainment.* ▫ *This portable printer should fill your requirements adequately.* ▫ *Eat fresh fruit when you need to fill that hunger gap between meals.* **6** Something **fills** a role when it performs it satisfactorily: *I was an only child and my toys filled the role of friends.* **7** You **fill** time when you do something to pass or occupy it: *When it rained we filled the time reading and chatting.* **8** A job, vacancy or post **is filled** when someone is appointed for it: *I regret to inform you that the position has already been filled.* **9** You **fill** a hole when you put material into it to level the surface; a dentist **fills** a cavity in your tooth when he or she removes the decayed part and replaces it with artificial material. **10** A sail **fills** when it expands in the wind.
▻ ***noun*** (*used in the singular*)
1 (*old*) You say you have eaten your **fill** when you have had enough to eat. **2** You say you have had your **fill** of something when you cannot bear any more of it: *I'd had my fill of computers for one day.*

phrasal verbs
fill in 1 You **fill in** a form when you write information in the spaces as required: *Please fill in this form; fill in your name and age at the top.* **2** You **fill** someone **in** on something when you inform them fully about it: *Could you fill me in on the latest developments?* **3** You **fill in** for someone who is unable to do their usual job when you do their job temporarily for them: *Could you fill in for me for a few days?* **4** You **fill in** time when you do something to occupy or pass the time while waiting for something to happen: *We filled in the four hours between flights by taking a bus into town and exploring.*
fill out 1 You **fill out** a form when you write information in the spaces as required: *He was getting tired of filling out application forms.* **2** A thin person **fills out** when they get fatter: *Her cheeks had filled out and acquired a healthy colour.*
fill up 1 You **fill up** a container when you put enough of something into it to make it full; a place fills up with something when it becomes full of it: *I've filled up the petrol tank.* ▫ *The shop filled up with customers as soon as the doors opened.* **2** You **fill up** a form when you write information in the spaces as required: *You have to fill up so many forms when you take your car abroad.*

fillet (*AmE* **filet**) /ˈfɪlɪt/ *noun* (*count or uncount*): **fillets**
A **fillet** is a piece of meat or fish without any bones in it.

filling /ˈfɪlɪŋ/ *noun*; *adjective*
▻ ***noun***: **fillings**
1 A **filling** is a small quantity of artificial material that a dentist puts into a hole in a decayed tooth: *I had to have four fillings last time I went to the dentist.* **2** The **filling** in a pie, sandwich, cake or chocolate is the food or mixture put inside it: *sandwiches with a choice of fillings.*
▻ ***adjective***
You describe food as **filling** if it satisfies you or makes you feel full: *A filling meal of fish and chips.*

filling station /ˈfɪlɪŋ steɪʃən/ *noun*: **filling stations**
A **filling station** is a place where you can get your petrol tank filled: *Stop at the next filling station.*

filly /ˈfɪlɪ/ *noun*: **fillies**
A **filly** is a young female horse.

film /fɪlm/ *noun*; *verb*
▻ ***noun***: **films**
1 (*count or uncount*) A photographic **film** is a rolled strip of thin plastic or other material, specially coated so as to be sensitive to light, on which still or

moving pictures are recorded when it is exposed to light inside a camera: *six rolls of film* □ *I loaded a fresh film into the camera.* **2** A **film** is a motion picture for showing in the cinema, or on television or video: *I saw a good film on television yesterday; did you watch it too?* □ *The film was made on location in India.* [*same as* **movie**] **3** A **film** of something such as oil, powder or liquid is a fine layer of it: *Everything in the kitchen seemed to be covered with a film of grease.*

▻ ***verb*: films, filming, filmed**

You **film** something when you take moving pictures of it, *eg* with a video camera: *We filmed the children a lot when they were growing up.*

> ***phrasal verb***
> A transparent surface **films over** when a dull or cloudy layer forms over it: *His eyes filmed over with tears at the memory.*

filmy /ˈfɪlmɪ/ *adjective*: **filmier, filmiest**

A **filmy** fabric is light, thin and transparent.

filter /ˈfɪltə(r)/ *noun*; *verb*

▻ ***noun*: filters**

1 A **filter** is a device that allows such substances as liquid, gas, or smoke through it but traps solid particles and impurities: *Have you checked the vehicle's oil filter?* □ *filter-tipped cigarettes.* **2** (*photograhy*) A **filter** is a disc that is fitted over a camera lens to reduce the strength of certain types of light entering the camera. **3** At traffic lights, a **filter** is a signal that allows left-turning or right-turning vehicles to proceed while the main queue is halted.

▻ ***verb*: filters, filtering, filtered**

1 You **filter** a substance when you pass it through a filter to trap, or get rid of, solid particles or impurities: *Water in swimming pools is filtered constantly to keep it clean.* **2** Light or sound **filters** somewhere when it reaches there faintly; news **filters** somewhere when it gets there eventually, or gradually: *Sunlight filtered in through a crack in the door.* □ *Reports of the coup filtered through to us.* **3** Vehicles **filter** left or right at traffic lights when they turn left or right while the main queue is halted.

> ***phrasal verb***
> To **filter out** something is to remove it using a filter or filter-like process: *You can filter dirt out of the oil quite easily.* □ *Start by filtering out the applicants who have no computing experience.*

filth /fɪlθ/ *noun* (*uncount*)

1 Filth is disgusting dirt or rubbish: *streets full of filth.* **2** (*informal*) Disgusting or vulgar writing and pictures are sometimes described as **filth**; someone who writes **filth** about you is telling disgusting lies about you.

filthy /ˈfɪlθɪ/ *adjective*: **filthier, filthiest**

1 Things that are **filthy** are disgustingly dirty: *Who's been walking over the carpet in their filthy boots?* **2** (*informal*) **Filthy** books, magazines, pictures or films contain vulgar or offensive sexual material. [*same as* **pornographic**]

fin /fɪn/ *noun*: **fins**

1 A **fin** is a thin wing-like projection on a fish's body, with which it balances and steers itself. **2** The tail **fin** of an aircraft is the vertical projection in its tail.

final /ˈfaɪnəl/ *adjective*; *noun*

▻ ***adjective***

1 The **final** thing in a series is the last: *the third and final day of the horse trials* □ *They made one final attempt to reach the trapped miners.* [*same as* **last**] **2 Final** also describes something that concludes an occasion or a series of happenings: *He scored the winning goal with the final kick of the match.* [*same as* **concluding**] **3** The **final** result is the situation at the end of a series of happenings: *What was the final score?* □ *the final collapse of the Roman Empire.* [*same as* **eventual, ultimate**] **4** The **final** possibility is the most extreme: *soldiers who made the final sacrifice.* [*same as* **ultimate, supreme**] **5** A decision that is **final** concludes all argument and discussion, and is not to be altered: *The judges' decision is final.* □ *You may not borrow the car, and that's final.* **6 Final** arrangements are procedures that have been agreed on and will not be altered. [*same as* **definite**]

▻ ***noun*: finals**

1 The **final** of a competition or sports event is the last and concluding game or round, which decides the winner: *Becker went on to meet Lendl in the final.* **2** (*used in the plural*) Your **finals** are the last and most important set of examinations in your university degree course: *I take my finals this June.*

finale /fɪˈnɑːlɪ/ *noun*: **finales**

A **finale** or **grand finale** is a final act or section that forms the impressive conclusion to a show, performance or musical composition: *The whole cast took part in the grand finale.*

finalist /ˈfaɪnəlɪst/ *noun*: **finalists**

A **finalist** in a competition is someone who takes part in its final round, game or contest.

finality /faɪˈnalɪtɪ/ *noun* (*uncount*)

You say something, or act, with **finality**, when you speak or act in a manner that shows you will not change your mind: *'We can take no further action on the matter,' she said with finality.*

finalize or **finalise** /ˈfaɪnəlaɪz/ *verb*: **finalizes, finalizing, finalized**

You **finalize** plans or arrangements for something when you complete them and decide definitely on them: *Have you finalized your holiday dates yet?*

finally /ˈfaɪnəlɪ/ *adverb*

1 Something happens **finally** if it happens after a long time, or after a delay or period of uncertainty: *So you've finally got your book published!* □ *I finally chose the blue material.* □ *Our car broke down, but finally we did get there.* [*same as* **eventually, in the end, at last**] **2** Something that happens **finally** happens as the last in a series of happenings: *We spent a few years in Bangor, then moved to Manchester, and finally settled in Glasgow.* [*same as* **eventually, in the end**] **3** (*sentence adverb*) You use **finally** to introduce your last point or conclusion: *Finally, I should like to thank you all for coming and to wish you a pleasant journey home.* [*same as* **lastly**]

finance /faɪˈnans/ or /ˈfaɪnans/ *noun*; *verb*

▻ ***noun*: finances**

1 (*uncount*) **Finance** is the management of money and related matters such as loans and investment: *She's an expert in corporate finance.* **2** (*uncount*) **Finance** for something is the money needed or used to pay for it: *We shall have no difficulty getting hold of finance for the expedition.* [*same as* **funding**] **3** (*used in the plural*) Your **finances** are the amount of money that you have at any particular time: *The company's finances were not in a healthy state.*

▻ ***verb*: finances, financing, financed**

To **finance** a scheme or project is to provide money for it: *They financed the play scheme out of their own pockets.*

financial /faɪ'nanʃəl/ or /fɪ'nanʃəl/ *adjective*
Financial means relating to money or finance: *The college has been in financial difficulties for some time.* □ *Financial arrangements have been made for the children's education.* — *adverb* **financially:** *He practised as a lawyer and did well financially.*

financier /fɪ'nansɪə(r)/ or /faɪ'nansɪə(r)/ *noun*: **financiers**
A **financier** is a someone who manages or lends large sums of money, or is engaged in important financial deals.

finch /fɪnʃ/ *noun*: **finches**
A **finch** is a small singing bird with a short beak adapted for seed-crushing.

find /faɪnd/ *verb; noun*
▻ ***verb***: **finds, finding, found**
1 You **find** something when you discover it by searching, notice it by chance, or become aware of it: *You'll find the key in the kitchen drawer.* □ *I did find that missing cheque again, by the way.* □ *I found a hole in my tights.* □ *I think we've found a solution to the problem.* □ *She woke to find the doctor by her bed.* □ *I found her waiting in the hall.* **2** You **find** something you are trying to obtain when you manage to get it: *He found work as a hospital porter.* □ *I'll find you a copy of the book.* **3** You **find** that something is so when you realize or discover that it is: *She found that she knew most of the people there.* □ *I find I work better in the mornings.* □ *We found the door locked.* □ *I didn't find it easy to get a job.* **4** You use **find** to describe your feelings about someone or something, or your reaction to them: *We found the journey very tiring.* □ *I don't find that amusing.* □ *I found him a great help whenever I asked his advice.* □ *Did you find the book of any interest?* □ *How are you finding your new job?* **5** You **find** yourself somewhere when you get there, especially unexpectedly; you **find** yourself doing something when you do it without having expected or intended to: *We found ourselves back where we had started.* □ *She started on the book reluctantly, and found herself actually enjoying it.* **6** You **find** something such as the time or the courage to do something when you manage to do it in spite of difficulties: *She somehow found time to make clothes for the children.* □ *It was weeks before I found the courage to tell her the truth.* **7** (*usually in the passive*) Something that **is found** in a particular place exists or is present there: *a bird found only in Madagascar* □ *Vitamin A is found in carrots and dairy products.* **8** (*legal*) In a court of law, a jury **finds** against an accused person, or **finds** them guilty, when it decides that they did do what they are accused of; a jury **finds** for an accused person, or **finds** against them: *She was found guilty of manslaughter.* **9** (*literary*) Something such as a missile or bullet **finds** its mark or target when it hits the thing it was aimed at.
▻ ***noun***: **finds**
1 You call someone or something that has been discovered a **find** if you think they are important, valuable or interesting: *This restaurant is quite a find.* □ *The little girl who plays the pianist's daughter is a great find.* **2** (*used in the plural*) The **finds** in an archaeological excavation are the objects that are dug up: *The finds included coins and pottery of the fourth century AD.*
▻ ***phrase***
1 You **find your way** somewhere when you get there by deciding on the right direction to go: *I found my way to her house without difficulty.* **2** Something **finds its way** somewhere when it ends up there: *How did the cat's dish find its way into the sitting room?* □ *Some of the charity's money found its way into his private bank account.*

> ***phrasal verb***
> **find out 1** You **find out** something you did not know when you discover it or learn about it, by chance or through investigation: *Could you find out when the bus leaves?* □ *I found out that she had left home three days earlier.* □ *Find something out about Columbus before tomorrow's lesson.* □ *He found out about her criminal activities quite by chance.* **2** You **find** someone **out** when you discover that they have done something wrong or dishonest: *Aren't you afraid of being found out?*

finder /'faɪndə(r)/ *noun*: **finders**
The **finder** of something is the person who finds it: *Would the finder of the ring please bring it straight to the office?*

finding /'faɪndɪŋ/ *noun* (*usually in the plural*): **findings**
Your **findings** are the conclusions you come to, or the facts you collect, as a result of your researches or investigations: *A committee of enquiry has been appointed and will report its findings next month.*

fine[1] /faɪn/ *adjective; adverb*
▻ ***adjective***: **finer, finest**
1 You describe something as **fine** if you think it is splendid or excellent: *There's always a fine show of flowers in the garden at this time of year.* □ *That's a fine-looking bike you've got there.* □ *You get a fine view of the hills from here.* **2 Fine** articles are of high-quality: *fine china.* **3** The weather is **fine** when it is not raining, especially if it is also clear and sunny. **4** You say you are **fine** when you are well: *'How's your family?' 'They're fine, thanks.'* □ *Sit down and you'll feel fine again in a minute.* **5** You say something is **fine** if it is OK, satisfactory, or acceptable: *'Do you want more sugar in your coffee?' 'No, thanks, it's fine the way it is.'* □ *'Come and sit by the fire.' 'No, thanks, I'm fine here.'* □ *If your husband would like to accompany you, that's fine.'* **6** Threads that are **fine** are thin or narrow: *fine strands of silk* □ *Her hair was blond and very fine.* **7 Fine** particles are very small: *fine grains of sand* □ *Porcelain is produced from particularly fine clay.* **8 Fine** means very precise, exact, slight or subtle: *fine workmanship* □ *the fine distinction between self-confidence and conceit* □ *The engine still needs some fine adjustments.* — *adverb* **finely:** *Add some finely chopped pieces of apple.* □ *finely embroidered details.* — *noun* (*uncount*) **fineness:** *fineness of detail.*
▻ ***adverb***
You get on **fine** when you are successful or make good progress; you get on, or get along, **fine** with someone if you have a friendly relationship with them.
▻ ***phrases*** **1** (*informal*) You **cut it fine** or **run it fine** when you leave scarcely enough time for doing something. **2** For **get** something **down to a fine art** see **art**.

> ***phrasal verb***
> You **fine** something such as a process **down** when you make it more effective, efficient or economical by cutting out whatever is unnecessary.

fine[2] /faɪn/ *noun; verb*
▻ ***noun***: **fines**
A **fine** is an amount of money that you are ordered to pay as a punishment for breaking a rule or law: *They've increased the fines for late return of library books.*
▻ ***verb***: **fines, fining, fined**
You **are fined** when you are ordered to pay a sum of money as a punishment for breaking a rule or law: *I was fined for speeding in a built-up area.*

fine arts /faɪn 'ɑːts/ *noun* (*plural*)
The **fine arts** are the types of art that appeal to your sense of beauty, such as painting, drawing, sculpture and architecture.

finery /'faɪnərɪ/ *noun* (*uncount*)
Finery is splendid clothes and jewellery: *She appeared at the door in all her finery, ready for the dance.*

finesse /fɪ'nɛs/ *noun* (*uncount*)
You do something with **finesse** when you do it with obvious skill, ease and style.

finger /'fɪŋgə(r)/ *noun; verb*
▻ ***noun*: fingers**
1 Your **fingers** are the five separate jointed parts at the end of your hands, including the thumb, or four if the thumb is excluded: *He ran his fingers through his hair.* □ *She examined the object closely, holding it between her thumb and forefinger.* [see picture at **body**] **2** A **finger** is also the part of a glove that fits over a finger. **3** Narrow rectangular portions of food are sometimes called **fingers**: *fish fingers.*
▻ ***verb*: fingers, fingering, fingered**
You **finger** something when you touch it or feel it with your fingers: *She fingered the bruise on her forehead.*
▻ ***phrases*** **1** You say superstitiously that you **are crossing your fingers** or **keeping your fingers crossed** to try and make something happen, come true, or go well. **2** Someone who **has green fingers** is good at growing plants. **3** You say that you **have not laid a finger on** someone if you have not touched or harmed them. **4** You say that someone **does not lift a finger** to do something if they do not make the slightest effort to do it: *He never lifts a finger to help with the housework.* **5** You **point the finger**, or **point a finger at** someone, when you blame someone for something, or accuse them of it. **6** You **put your finger on** something when you identify a particular point or difficulty: *The doctors don't seem able to put their finger on what's wrong with her.* **7** Someone or something **slips through your fingers** if you lose them or let them escape: *You mustn't let this opportunity slip through your fingers.* **8** You are able to **twist** someone **round your little finger** if you can usually persuade them easily to do what you want.

fingermark /'fɪŋgəmɑːk/ *noun*: **fingermarks**
A **fingermark** is a dirty mark left on a surface by a finger: *The window was covered with greasy fingermarks.*

fingernail /'fɪŋgəneɪl/ *noun*: **fingernails**
Your **fingernails** or **nails** are the small areas of hard material at the tips of your fingers: *She got out her nail scissors and began trimming her fingernails.* □ *He bites his fingernails.* [see picture at **body**; see also **toenail**]

fingerprint /'fɪŋgəprɪnt/ *noun; verb*
▻ ***noun*: fingerprints**
1 A **fingerprint** is a mark you leave with your finger when you touch a surface, showing the lines on your skin: *The police have identified the fingerprints.* **2** The police take your **fingerprints** when they record them by making you press your fingers on to an ink-covered surface, then on to paper.
▻ ***verb*: fingerprints, fingerprinting, fingerprinted**
The police **fingerprint** you when they record, or take, your fingerprints.

fingertip /'fɪŋgətɪp/ *noun*: **fingertips**
Your **fingertips** are the ends of your fingers.
▻ ***phrases*** **1** You **have** a subject or facts **at your fingertips** if you know them thoroughly. **2** You say that someone is something **to their fingertips** if they seem to fulfil that role or function perfectly, or in every possible detail: *She's an actress to her fingertips.* [see picture at **body**]

finicky /'fɪnɪkɪ/ *adjective*
1 Someone who is **finicky** is too concerned with details; **finicky** details are little unimportant ones. **2** A **finicky** eater is someone who refuses to eat certain things and is difficult to please. [*same as* **fussy**]

finish /'fɪnɪʃ/ *verb; noun*
▻ ***verb*: finishes, finishing, finished**
1 You **finish** a task, or **finish** doing or making something, when you have done everything that needs to done: *When do they hope to finish this section of the motorway?* □ *Have you finished typing that report?* □ *I'll call you back when we've finished eating.* □ *If everyone's finished, I'll serve coffee.* □ *Haven't you finished in the bathroom yet?* □ *I'll return your book as soon as I've finished it.* □ *Don't interrupt; let me finish.* □ *Try and finish your speech with a joke.* [*same as* **complete**] **2** Something **finishes** when it continues no longer, or comes to an end: *Term finishes on 17 December.* [*same as* **end**] **3** You **finish** school or work when you stop lessons or work and go home: *We start work at 8.30 and finish at 5.00.* [*same as* **stop**] **4** You **finish** something you have been eating or drinking when you eat or drink the last bit of it; someone **finishes** a cigarette when they have smoked as much as they can of it, and extinguish it: *I finished my apple and put the core in the bin.* □ *Have you finished your meal?* □ *We haven't finished dinner yet.* **5** The place or position you **finish** in, in a race or competition, is the position you are in at the end of it: *She finished fourth in the compulsory figure-skating section.*
▻ ***noun***
1 (*used in the singular*) The **finish** of something is the end of it, or its last stage: *The crowds cheered and yelled as they watched the exciting finish to the race.* **2** (*uncount*) The **finish** of a manufactured product is its appearance of having been made well or badly: *Their furniture always has such a professonal finish.* **3** (*uncount or count*) The **finish** on a material such as cloth or wood is its surface texture: *Cotton can be treated to give it a shiny finish.*
▻ ***phrase*** Two people **fight to the finish** when they go on fighting till one of them is dead or too severely injured to continue.

phrasal verbs
finish off **1** You **finish off** a task when you do everything that needs to be done: *I'm just finishing off this essay.* [*same as* **complete**] **2** You **finish off** food or drink when you eat or drink the last bit of it: *Finish off your pudding quickly.* **3** (*informal*) To **finish** someone **off** is to kill them.
finish up You **finish up** somewhere, or in some situation, if that is what happens to you in the end: *He'll finish up in jail.* □ *I finished up as a waitress in Birmingham.* □ *She finished up stage-managing for the local theatre.* [*same as* **end up**]
finish with **1** You **finish with** a person when you end a relationship with them, or when you let them go after telling them something important, or scolding them: *I finished with Jane last week.* □ *Wait; I haven't finished with you yet.* **2** You **finish with** something you have been using when you do not need it any more, and stop using it: *Have you finished with the French dictionary yet?*

finished /'fɪnɪʃt/ *adjective*
1 You say you are **finished** when you have completed a task, or stopped doing something: *I'll be finished in about an hour.* **2** You say you are **finished** with something when you no longer need it, or when you don't want ever to be involved with it again: *I'm finished with the stapler if you want it.* □ *I'm finished with teach-*

ing. **3** You describe a person as **finished** if they are no longer considered important, creative or effective.

finite /ˈfaɪnaɪt/ *adjective*
1 Something that is **finite** has limits or boundaries, as distinct from lasting, continuing or extending for ever: *As you know, world resources are finite.* [*same as* **limited**; *opposite* **infinite**] **2** (*grammar*) A **finite** verb is in a form that shows person (first, second or third person), number (singular or plural), and tense (past, present or future), as distinct from being a participle or an infinitive.

Finnish /ˈfɪnɪʃ/ *adjective*; *noun*
▷ ***adjective***
Finnish means relating or belonging to Finland, its people, or their language: *She told us she was Finnish.* □ *the Finnish epic 'Kalevala'.*
▷ ***noun*** (*uncount*)
Finnish is the language of Finland: *I realized they were speaking in Finnish.*

fiord see **fjord**.

fir /fɜː(r)/ *noun*: **firs**
A **fir**, or **fir tree**, is a tall evergreen tree of the pine family, with cones and thin needle-like leaves: *a fir plantation.*

fire /faɪə(r)/ *noun*; *verb*
▷ ***noun***: **fires**
1 (*uncount*) **Fire** is flames coming from something that is burning: *He was met by a wall of fire as he opened the door.* **2** (*count or uncount*) A **fire** is an occurrence of destructive, uncontrolled burning: *Three people are reported to have lost their lives in a warehouse fire.* □ *There was a shout of 'Fire!'* **3** A **fire** is a pile of burning wood, coal or other fuel, that you have prepared and lit, for warmth or cooking: *I put another log on the fire.* **4** A **fire** is also a gas or electric room-heater: *Do turn on the fire if you're cold.* **5** (*uncount*) Shots from guns are referred to as **fire**: *We heard a burst of fire.* □ *the sound of gunfire.*
▷ ***verb***: **fires, firing, fired**
1 To **fire** a gun is to shoot a bullet or other missile from it; to **fire** a bullet is to shoot it from a gun; to **fire** an arrow is to shoot it from a bow; to **fire** a rocket is to launch it or send it: *Snipers were firing from the rooftops.* □ *They fired a distress rocket.* **2** Someone **fires** questions at you when they ask you a lot of questions one after the other, hardly giving you time to reply. **3** To **fire** someone is to dismiss them from your employment: *He was fired for incompetence.* [*same as* **sack**] **4** A vehicle engine **fires** when a spark lights the fuel, and the engine starts working. **5** You say someone **is fired** by something if that is what inspires or stimulates them: *Fired by his love of all things Celtic he began to teach himself Welsh.* — *noun* (*uncount*) **firing:** *We could hear firing in one of the nearby streets*
▷ ***phrases*** **1** Something **catches fire** when it begins to burn: *The curtains caught fire.* **2** Armies that are attacking each other **cease fire** when they stop shooting at each other. **3** You are **in the line of fire** when you are between the guns and the target. [see also **firing line**] **4** Something is **on fire** when it is burning: *Her clothes were on fire.* **5** To **open fire** is to start shooting with a gun; to **open fire** on someone is to start shooting at them. **6** You say that someone **is playing with fire** if you think they are taking stupid risks: *It's playing with fire to lend your credit cards to other people.* **7** You **set fire to** something, or **set** something **on fire**, when you start it burning: *Careful with those matches; you'll set the house on fire.* □ *Someone had deliberately set fire to the wastepaper basket.* **8** You are **under fire** **a** when you are being shot at. **b** when people are criticizing you or blaming you.

phrasal verb
You tell someone to **fire away** when you invite them to say or ask whatever it is they want to: *'May I ask you something?' 'Fire away!'*

fire alarm /ˈfaɪə əlɑːm/ *noun*: **fire alarms**
A **fire alarm** is a bell installed in a building that is rung to warn people when there is a fire.

firearm /ˈfaɪərɑːm/ *noun*: **firearms**
Firearms are such weapons as guns, pistols, revolvers or rifles.

fire brigade /ˈfaɪə brɪgeɪd/ *noun*: **fire brigades**
A **fire brigade** is a team of people who are professionally trained to prevent and extinguish fires.

fire engine /ˈfaɪər ɛndʒɪn/ *noun*: **fire engines**
A **fire engine** is a vehicle carrying firemen and equipment for extinguishing fires.

fire escape /ˈfaɪər ɪskeɪp/ *noun*: **fire escapes**
A **fire escape** is a metal staircase or ladder fixed to the outside wall of a building, or some other device, by which people can escape if the building is burning.

fire-extinguisher /ˈfaɪərɪkstɪŋgwɪʃə(r)/ *noun*: **fire-extinguishers**
A **fire-extinguisher** is a cylinder containing water or chemicals for directing at fires to extinguish them.

fire-fighting /ˈfaɪəfaɪtɪŋ/ *noun* (*uncount*)
Fire-fighting is the work of extinguishing fires.

fireguard /ˈfaɪəgɑːd/ *noun*: **fireguards**
A **fireguard** is a protective metal or wire screen for putting round an open fire. [compare **fender**]

fire hydrant see **hydrant**.

firelight /ˈfaɪəlaɪt/ *noun* (*uncount*)
Firelight is the light that is produced by fire: *The room looked cosy in the firelight.*

fireman /ˈfaɪəmən/ *noun*: **firemen**
A **fireman** is a member of a fire brigade, a person professionally trained to extinguish fires and to rescue people and animals trapped in dangerous places.

fireplace /ˈfaɪəpleɪs/ *noun*: **fireplaces**
A **fireplace** is an opening in the wall of a room for lighting a fire in, with a chimney above it. [see picture at **living room**]

firepower /ˈfaɪəpaʊə(r)/ *noun* (*uncount*)
The **firepower** of a military force, or of something such as a tank or aircraft is its destructive power, as represented by the amount of ammunition it can fire.

fireproof /ˈfaɪəpruːf/ *adjective*
Things that are **fireproof** cannot be damaged by fire or by intense heat: *fireproof suits.*

fireside /ˈfaɪəsaɪd/ *noun* (*singular*)
The **fireside** is the area round a fireplace, especially as a symbol of home: *He loved it when the whole family was gathered round the fireside.*

fire station /ˈfaɪə steɪʃən/ *noun*: **fire stations**
A **fire station** is the headquarters of a fire brigade, where its fire engines and fire-fighting equipment are kept and where firemen are always on duty.

firewood /ˈfaɪəwʊd/ *noun* (*uncount*)
Firewood is wood for burning as fuel.

firework /ˈfaɪəwɜːk/ *noun*: **fireworks**
Fireworks are devices containing explosive chemicals that produce bangs and flashes when you light them, used especially to entertain people: *a firework display* □ *People were setting off fireworks.*

firing line /ˈfaɪərɪŋ laɪn/ *noun* (*used in the singular*)
You are in the **firing line** when you are in the front row

of battle and therefore likely to be shot at, or when you are the person whom other people are most likely to attack or criticize.

firing squad /'faɪərɪŋ skwɒd/ *noun*: **firing squads**
A **firing squad** is a small troop of soldiers with the job of shooting someone who has been found guilty of a crime: *He will be executed by a firing squad at dawn.*

firm[1] /fɜːm/ *adjective*
1 Something that is **firm** is strong and steady, and does not shake when you put weight on it: *You need a nice firm table to work at.* □ *This step ladder doesn't feel very firm.* **2** A **firm** surface does not yield much or change shape when you press it: *firm muscles* □ *It's much better for you to sleep on a firm bed.* **3 a** You have a **firm** hold or grip of or on something when you are holding it tightly and strongly: *Keep a firm grasp on your end of the rope.* **b** You have a **firm** grasp of a subject when you know a lot about it or are very familiar with it. **4** You give something a **firm** push or pull when you push or pull it in a strong, steadily controlled manner: *Constant firm pressure will eventually stop the bleeding.* **5** Someone who has a **firm** mouth or chin looks strong and determined. **6** If you have made a **firm** decision, or have a **firm** opinion or preference, you are unlikely to change your mind: *She had very firm views about people smoking in the office.* □ *He was quite firm that he did not want to come with us.* **7** Someone who is **firm** shows that they are in control and quite determined about what they want done: *Be firm with them and don't listen to any excuses.* □ *a strong firm leader.* **8 Firm** news or information is definite or confirmed as fact: *We have no firm evidence that this is so.* □ *At last we had received a firm offer for the house.* **9** Prices remain **firm** when they stay the same, not increasing or decreasing. — *adverb* **firmly:** *Make sure your weight is firmly supported.* □ *You have to shut the door firmly or it will open again.* □ *I'm firmly of the opinion that we should accept the offer.* □ *'Do your homework first,' said Mother firmly.* — *noun* (*uncount*) **firmness:** *She refused with surprising firmness.*
▷ ***phrase*** You **hold firm** to your decisions or your principles, or **stand firm** on or by them, when you are determined not to change them: *We must stand firm against further interference in our private lives.*

firm[2] /fɜːm/ *noun* (*with a singular or plural verb*): **firms**
A **firm** is a business company or organization that manufactures or sells something, or provides a service: *a firm of accountants* □ *Our firm has recently moved into larger premises.*

first /fɜːst/ (sometimes written **1st**) *determiner; pronoun; adjective or adverb; adverb; noun*
▷ ***determiner***
1 The **first** person or thing is the earliest in time or order, coming before all others: *the first king of Rome* □ *My first school was a convent.* □ *We lived in Timor during the first five years of my life.* □ *Robert was always the first person to arrive in the morning.* □ *Our first lesson was French.* □ *Their first task was to collect up the rubbish.* □ *I liked him the first time I saw him.* **2** The **first** person or thing in position or order is the one nearest to you or nearest to the front: *The first two rows of seats were reserved for the important guests.* **3 First** also means most important or basic: *Our first aim was to save lives.* □ *My first duty is to my parents.* □ *Let's get back to first principles.* **4** You win **first** prize in a competition when you get the award for the best work or performance. **5** (*music*) **First** describes an instrument or a singing or instrumental part in a musical composition that is the most important or prominent: *She plays with the first violins.* **6** The **first** gear of a motor vehicle or bicycle is its lowest forward gear: *Are you in first gear?* □ *Engage first gear.*
▷ ***pronoun:*** *The first of six episodes will be shown on television tonight.* □ *She's the first on the left in the back row.* □ *I'm arriving on the 1st of September.* [see note at **date**] □ *in the reign of Richard the First* (written *Richard I*) □ *Hilary was the first to break the silence.* □ *We want you to be the first to know about our engagement.* □ *As far as we're aware this scheme is the first of its kind in the country.*
▷ ***adjective or adverb***
You are, or come, **first** in a competition or exam when you get the highest marks or score: *I was first in English this term.* □ *She came first in the soprano solo.*
▷ ***adverb***
1 You do something **first** if you do it before anyone else does it: *Judy arrived first.* **2** You do something **first** when you do it before you do anything else: *We must first make sure that she's able to come.* **3** (*sentence adverb*) You use '**first**' to introduce the first of a list of things: *There are several reasons: first, it's too late; second, we haven't enough money; third ...* **4** When you **first** do something, you have never done it before: *I first took an interest in archaeology at the age of ten.* □ *When I first read her letter I could hardly believe what she wrote.* [compare **for the first time** in phrases below] **5** You put something **first** if you regard it as the most important thing: *Nowadays young people seem to put their careers first.* □ *His family always came first with him.* **6** You move somewhere feet **first** or head**first** when your feet or head are the leading part of you: *He went feet first down the chute.*
▷ ***noun*: firsts**
1 You call something a **first** if it has never happened before: *This kind of holiday is a first for us.* **2** People refer to a first-class degree as a **first**: *She got a first in law at Birmingham.* **3** (*uncount*) The driver of a motor vehicle is in **first** when he or she is driving in first gear: *I had to change down into first.*
▷ ***phrases*** **1** You do something **first of all** when you do it before you do anything else: *First of all, make sure you've got enough petrol.* **2** You do something **first thing** when you do it early in the morning before you do anything else: *I'll call you first thing.* **3** You say '**first things first**' to emphasize that the most important matters must be dealt with before others. **4** Someone who is doing something **for the first time** has never done it before: *I visited Venice for the first time in 1965.* **5** For **in the first place** see **place**. **6** You say you **do not know the first thing** about something if you know nothing about it: *I don't know the first thing about golf.* **7 The first you know** or **hear** about something is the time when you first become aware of it: *'Is Joan getting married?' 'If so, it's the first I've heard.'* □ *The first I knew of his death was when I read the announcement in the paper.*

first aid /fɜːst 'eɪd/ *noun* (*uncount*)
First aid is simple and immediate emergency treatment that you give to an injured or ill person: *We went on a first-aid course.*

firstborn /'fɜːstbɔːn/ *adjective; noun*
▷ ***adjective***
Your **firstborn** child is your first, or oldest, child.
▷ ***noun*** (*used in the singular*): *Jimmie, her firstborn, was her favourite.*

first-class /fɜːst'klɑːs/ *adjective; adverb*
▷ ***adjective***
1 A person or thing that is **first-class** is excellent: *Some of his essays are first-class.* **2** A **first-class** degree is a degree awarded for the highest class of academic

performance. **3** A **first-class** ticket permits you to travel in the best class of accommodation on board a train, ship or aircraft: *Is this the first-class compartment?* **4** **First-class** postage is the more expensive postage that allows your mail to travel at a faster rate. [see also **second-class**]
▻ ***adverb:*** *He decided to travel first-class on the train.* □ *We'd better send these letters first-class.*

first cousin see **cousin**.

first floor /fɜːst ˈflɔː(r)/ *noun* (*used in the singular*)
1 (*BrE*) The **first floor** of a building is the floor above the ground floor: *The enquiry office is on the first floor* □ *a first-floor flat.* **2** (*AmE*) The **first floor** is the ground floor.

firsthand /fɜːstˈhand/ *adjective*; *adverb*
▻ ***adjective***
Firsthand knowledge or experience of something is gained through personal involvement in it, rather than through what you read, or are told by others: *He had had firsthand experience of jungle warfare.*
▻ ***adverb***: *You can only acquire that sort of skill firsthand.*
▻ ***phrase*** You gain knowledge or experience **at first hand** when you get it through personal involvement: *She knew at first hand about the problems of teaching English to foreign students.*

firstly /ˈfɜːstlɪ/ *adverb* (*sentence adverb*)
You use **firstly** to introduce the first of a list of things: *I must remind you firstly that we have very little time, secondly that money is short, and thirdly ....*

first name /ˈfɜːst neɪm/ *noun*: **first names**
Your **first name** is your personal name as distinct from your family name or surname: *His first name is John.* □ *We're all on first-name terms here.* [same as **forename, given name, Christian name**]

first night /fɜːst ˈnaɪt/ *noun*: **first nights**
The **first night** of a play or show is its first public performance: *He was a drama critic and frequently attended first nights.*

first person /fɜːst ˈpɜːsən/ *noun* (*used in the singular*; *grammar*)
In speech analysis, the **first person** is the term used to refer to the speaker or speakers, represented by the pronouns *I* or *we*; writers tell a story **in the first person** when they tell it as one of the characters in the story. [see also **second person, third person**]

first-rate /fɜːstˈreɪt/ *adjective*
Something or someone that is **first-rate** is excellent: *She'll make a first-rate expedition leader.*

fiscal /ˈfɪskəl/ *adjective*
Fiscal relates to government money, especially income from taxation.

fish /fɪʃ/ *noun*; *verb*
▻ ***noun***: **fish** or **fishes**

> The plural **fish** is always correct, but you can also use **fishes**, *eg* when referring to different types of fish: *the fishes of the Indian Ocean.*

1 A **fish** is a creature with a tail and fins, with or without a spine, that lives in the water and takes in oxygen through gills; various other water-inhabiting creatures are also called **fish**: *shellfish* □ *jellyfish.* **2** (*uncount*) **Fish** is the flesh of fish used as a food: *We had fish and chips for tea.*
▻ ***verb***: **fishes, fishing, fished**
1 You **fish** when you to try to catch fish, as a sport or for food: *He goes fishing on Saturdays and usually catches a salmon for supper.* **2** You **fish** a river, or an area of water or sea, when you try to catch fish in it: *The waters round the sea coast have all been overfished, and stocks are low.* **3** (*informal*) You **fish** in a container for something when you search for it with your hands: *She fished in her bag for a pen.* **4** (*informal*) You **fish** something out of water or somewhere else when you get it out: *He fished a fly out of his soup.* □ *She fished out a notebook and pencil.* **5** (*informal*) You **fish** for something such as information or praise when you try to get it by indirect means: *'Am I suitably dressed for the evening?' she asked, fishing for compliments.*
▻ ***phrase*** (*informal*) You say someone is **like a fish out of water** if they are in unfamiliar surroundings that they do not enjoy.

fisherman /ˈfɪʃəmən/ *noun*: **fishermen**
A **fisherman** is a person who fishes as a job or for sport.

fishery /ˈfɪʃərɪ/ *noun*: **fisheries**
A **fishery** is an area of sea where fishing is carried on: *the North-Sea fisheries.*

fish finger /fɪʃ ˈfɪŋgə(r)/ *noun*: **fish fingers**
Fish fingers are narrow rectangular breadcrumb-covered portions of fish.

fishing /ˈfɪʃɪŋ/ *noun* (*uncount*)
Fishing is the sport or business of catching fish.

fishing line /ˈfɪʃɪŋ laɪn/ *noun*: **fishing lines**
A **fishing line** is a line, usually made of strong nylon, with a hook attached, for catching fish.

fishing rod /ˈfɪʃɪŋ rɒd/ *noun*: **fishing rods**
A **fishing rod** is a long flexible rod to which a line with a hook is attached, for catching fish.

fishmonger /ˈfɪʃʊŋgə(r)/ *noun*: **fishmongers**
1 A **fishmonger** is shopkeeper who sells fish. **2** A **fishmonger** or **fishmonger's** is a fish shop: *I'll get a couple of haddock on my way past the fishmonger's.*

fish slice /ˈfɪʃ slaɪs/ *noun*: **fish slices**
A **fish slice** is a cooking tool for lifting and turning food that is being fried or grilled. [see picture at **kitchen**]

fishy /ˈfɪʃɪ/ *noun*: **fishier, fishiest**
1 Something that smells or tastes **fishy** smells or tastes of fish, or like it. **2** You call something **fishy** if it makes you feel suspicious: *Her story sounded a bit fishy to me.* [*same as* **dubious, implausible**]

fission /ˈfɪʃən/ *noun* (*uncount*)
Nuclear **fission** is the splitting of the nucleus of an atom, with a release of energy.

fissure /ˈfɪʃə(r)/ *noun*: **fissures**
A **fissure** is a crack, especially in rock, or in the earth.

fist /fɪst/ *noun*: **fists**
Your **fist** is the shape you put your hand into when you bend your fingers tightly into your palm, *eg* in order to hit someone.
▻ ***phrases*** **1** Someone spends money **hand over fist** when they spend a lot. **2** Someone **shakes their fist** at you when they wave their fist towards you to express anger or threats.

fistful /ˈfɪstfəl/ *noun*: **fistfuls**
A **fistful** is an amount that can be gripped in a closed hand: *They were fighting, and pulling each other's hair out in fistfuls*

fit¹ /fɪt/ *verb*; *noun*; *adjective*
▻ ***verb***: **fits, fitting, fitted**
1 a Something **fits** a person or thing if it is the right size to go over them or on to them: *Do the shoes fit you?* □ *It's difficult getting any clothes to fit when you're as tall as I am.* □ *This skirt doesn't fit properly over the hips.* □ *Which lid fits which jar?* □ *His cycling*

cape was big enough to fit over him and his rucksack. **b** A garment or cover **fits** a person or thing tightly or loosely if it is tight or loose when it is on them: *The dress fitted her figure closely.* **c** You **are fitted** for clothes that are being made for you when you are measured for them, or they are tried on you so that adjustments can be made. **d** Things **fit** into, or **fit**, a space if they are small enough or few enough to go into it: *Will all these books fit into that bookcase?* □ *Everything I need fits into my rucksack.* □ *The dining-room table exactly fitted the recess.* **e** You **fit** something into its correct position when you put it there: *I fitted the key into the keyhole.* □ *These two parts fit together.*

2 a One thing **fits** another if it is suitable or right for it: *a punishment that fits the crime* □ *Her name fitted her perfectly.* **b** One thing **fits** another if it is consistent with it: *Her story doesn't fit the facts.* **c** You **fit** one activity round, or in with, another when you arrange the first to suit, or allow for, the second: *We shall have to fit rehearsals round normal school lessons.* □ *I can fit my plans in with your schedule.* **d** (*formal*) Personal qualities **fit** you for a certain type of work if they make you suitable for it: *Her patience fitted her particularly for work with children.*

3 To **fit** a bath or a washing machine, or other piece of equipment, is to instal it: *We're getting the dishwasher fitted on Friday.* □ *He fitted a new lock to the front door.* **4** To **fit** something with an extra part is to attach an extra part to it: *My suitcase was fitted with wheels so that I could pull it along.*

▻ ***noun*** (*used in the singular*)

Something that is a good or bad **fit** fits well or badly: *The jacket's a good fit.* □ *a loose fit.*

▻ ***adjective***: **fitter**, **fittest**

1 Someone or something that is **fit** for a certain purpose is suitable, or good enough, for it: *The debris has been cleared and the classrooms will be fit for use again tomorrow.* □ *There's no fitter person for the job than Hazel.* □ *Any woman who neglects her children like that isn't fit to be a mother.* □ *I can't go out in these clothes; I'm not fit to be seen!* **2** You are **fit** when you are healthy, especially as a result of exercise; you are **fit** to do something when you are well enough to do it: *He kept himself fit by taking long walks.* □ *How do you keep fit?* □ *I should be fit to go back to work again in a couple of weeks.* — *noun* (*uncount*) **fitness:** *Do these exercises daily to maintain a high level of physical fitness.* □ *I've started going to fitness classes.*

▻ ***phrases*** **1** Someone **sees fit** or **thinks fit** to do something when they decide that it is the right thing to do, and do it: *I suppose you didn't think fit to tell anyone you would be taking a day's holiday?* □ *If he sees fit to treat staff so rudely he must expect resignations.* □ *You must act as you see fit.* **2** For **in a fit state** see **state**.

phrasal verbs

fit in or **fit into** **1** You **fit in**, or **fit into** a group, if you behave in a way that people accept, so that they feel comfortable with you, and you feel comfortable with them: *They leave hospital unable to fit into normal society.* □ *He's enthusiastic in class and fits in well with the other children.* **2** You **fit in** with someone else's plans when you adjust your own to suit theirs: *I'll fit in with whatever's convenient for you.* **3** You **fit** something **in**, or **fit** something **into** your schedule, when to find time to do it or deal with it: *You seem to fit so much into your week!* □ *Could we fit in a meeting this afternoon?* □ *Come back at 11.30 and we'll fit you in somehow.*

fit out To **fit out** a ship or expedition is to equip it with all it needs.

fit up To **fit up** an office or hotel is to instal all the equipment it needs.

fit² /fɪt/ *noun*: **fits**

1 Someone has a **fit** when they suddenly lose consciousness and their body moves in a violent, uncontrolled way: *She had an epileptic fit at school today.* **2** You have a **fit** of something such as laughing when you start doing it in an uncontrolled way: *We were in fits of laughter.* □ *a fit of coughing* □ *She had a fit of the giggles.* **3** You do something in a **fit** of rage or frustration when your rage or frustration makes you do it: *In a fit of jealousy she had torn up her sister's drawing.*

▻ ***phrases*** **1** You do something **in**, or **by**, **fits and starts** when you keep starting and then stopping again: *I'd been carrying on my research in fits and starts for several years.* **2** (*informal*) You say that someone will **have a fit** when they see or hear something if you think they will be shocked or made angry by it: *She'll have a fit when she sees the designs for the front cover.* **3** (*informal*) You are **in fits** when you are laughing uncontrollably: *He had us in fits with his stories of the holiday.*

fitful /ˈfɪtfəl/ *adjective*

Something that is **fitful** goes on in an irregular, interrupted way: *She fell at last into a fitful sleep.* [*same as* **disturbed**] — *adverb* **fitfully:** *She dozed fitfully.* □ *The sun shone fitfully.* [*same as* **erratically**]

fitment /ˈfɪtmənt/ *noun*: **fitments**

A **fitment** is a fixed piece of equipment or furniture: *bathroom fitments.* [*same as* **fitting**]

fitness see **fit**¹.

fitted /ˈfɪtɪd/ *adjective*

1 Fitted covers or clothes are made the same shape and size as what they are designed to go over, so as to fit closely: *fitted sheets.* **2** A **fitted** carpet is cut the same shape as the room, so that it covers the floor completely. **3 Fitted** cupboards or wardrobes are designed so as to fill a certain space, and are fixed in that position. [*same as* **built-in**] [see picture at **bedroom**] **4** The design of a **fitted** kitchen includes shelves, cupboards, working surfaces, and sink, with spaces for other equipment such as the cooker and washing machine. **5** You are **fitted** for or to something, or to do something, if you have the right qualities for it: *She was well fitted to cope with the frustrations of scientific research.*

fitter /ˈfɪtə(r)/ *noun*: **fitters**

A **fitter** is a person who instals, adjusts or repairs machinery and equipment: *a gas fitter.*

fitting /ˈfɪtɪŋ/ *adjective*; *noun*

▻ ***adjective***

1 You say that something is **fitting** if it is right and suitable: *It seemed fitting to say a few words in praise of the dead man.* **2** You use **-fitting** in describing the way in which things fit: *a loose-fitting jacket* □ *a close-fitting hat* □ *a tight-fitting knitted dress* □ *ill-fitting shoes.*

▻ ***noun***: **fittings**

1 A **fitting** is something installed in a house, such as a cooker or washing machine, that you can take with you if you move to another house. **2 Fittings** are also such things as door handles and electric lights and switches: *We're waiting for the builders to put in the light fittings.* **3** You have a **fitting** for a piece of clothing that is being made for you when you try it on to see where adjustment is necessary. — *adverb* **fittingly:** *He was fittingly dressed for the interview in a neat black suit.*

five /faɪv/ *noun; adjective; determiner; pronoun*
▻ ***noun*: fives**
1 (*uncount or count*) **Five** is **a** the number or figure 5: *Seven minus two is five.* □ *Six fives are thirty.* **b** A shoe or piece of clothing whose size is represented by the number 5, or a person who wears a piece of clothing of this: *These shoes are fives.* □ *Have you got a five in this kind of boot?* **2** (*uncount*) **Five** is **a** the age of 5: *Children in the UK start school at five.* **b** the time of 5 o'clock: *We finish work at five.* **3** (*count*) A **five** is **a** a set of 5 people or things. **b** a playing card with 5 symbols: *She was holding the five of hearts.*
▻ ***adjective***
Someone who is **five** is five years old: *When is he going to be five?*
▻ ***determiner:*** *The dictionary cost five pounds.* □ *The back five rows of seats are the cheapest.* □ *Five years is a long time in a child's life.* □ *After five hours' work you need a rest.* □ *a five-day working week* □ *a five-year-old horse* □ *books for five-year-olds.*
▻ ***pronoun:*** *Five of us have been invited.* □ *We didn't have enough copies, so I bought another five.*
[for more examples of how numerals are used, see **eight**]

fiver /'faɪvə(r)/ *noun* (*informal*): **fivers**
A **fiver** is five pounds or a five-pound note: *I can lend you a fiver.*

fix /fɪks/ *verb; noun*
▻ ***verb*: fixes, fixing, fixed**
1 You **fix** something somewhere when you place it or attach it firmly there: *They fixed the flagpole into the ground.* □ *He'd already fixed his nameplate to the front door.* □ *The dreadful sight fixed itself for ever in her memory.* **2** You **fix** your eyes or attention on something when you look at it or consider it with great concentration: *Her gaze was fixed on the figure in the doorway.* □ *He fixed his attention for a moment on the statue.* **3** You **fix** the date of some future event when you decide on it: *We fixed a date for our next meeting.* **4** You **fix** something when you arrange for it to happen: *Could you fix it for us to get to Paris the day before the conference starts?* **5** You **fix** something that is broken, or not working, when you repair it: *A man came to fix the telephone.* [*same as* **mend**] **6** (*especially AmE*) You **fix** food or a drink for someone when you prepare it: *Can I fix you a sandwich or something?* **7** (*especially AmE*) A woman **fixes** her face or makeup when she puts makeup on.
▻ ***noun*: fixes** (*informal*)
1 (*usually in the singular*) You are in a **fix** when you are in difficulty or trouble: *I'm in a terrible fix; could me lend me some money?* □ *He would always help a friend out of a fix.* **2** People give themselves a **fix** when they take, or inject themselves with, a drug, especially an addictive one.

phrasal verbs
fix on You **fix on** something when you choose it or decide on it: *We haven't yet fixed on the kind of wedding we'd like.*
fix up 1 You **fix** something **up** when you arrange it: *We've fixed up a holiday in Switzerland.* **2** You **fix** someone **up** with something when you provide them with it: *I can easily fix you up with a bed for the night.*

fixation /fɪk'seɪʃən/ *noun*: **fixations**
1 You have a **fixation** about something if you are concerned about it to an abnormal degree: *He had a fixation about hygiene.* [*same as* **obsession**] **2** (*psychology*) You have a **fixation** on a person if your mind and actions are constantly influenced by the thought of them: *girls with a father fixation.*

fixative /'fɪksətiv/ *noun* (*count or uncount*): **fixatives**
1 A **fixative** is a substance such as glue, for holding something in place: *a jar of fixative.* **2** A **fixative** is also a chemical that makes things such as dye or colour permanent.

fixed /fɪkst/ *adjective*
1 A **fixed** amount, rate or period is one that does not alter: *The foghorns sounds at fixed intervals of 30 seconds.* □ *There's a fixed charge for late return of videos.* **2** People with **fixed** ideas or opinions are unwilling to change their minds. **3** Something is **fixed** in your mind or memory if you know it or remember it well: *all those history dates that are permanently fixed in our memories.* **4** A **fixed** point is one that is stationary: *the fixed stars.* **5** An expression on someone's face is **fixed** if it doesn't vary: *Models walked to and fro with fixed, unnatural smiles.* — *adverb* **fixedly** /fɪksɪdlɪ/: *She was staring fixedly at the wall.*

fixity /'fɪksɪtɪ/ *noun* (*uncount*)
Fixity is the quality of remaining steady and never changing: *She continued to work for social reform with admirable fixity of purpose.*

fixture /'fɪkstʃə(r)/ *noun*: **fixtures**
1 The **fixtures** in your house are the permanently fixed pieces of furniture or equipment, such as the bath and toilet, which you leave in place when you move house. **2** A **fixture** is a match or other event in a sports calendar: *She consulted the fixture list.* **3** You call something or someone a **fixture** in a certain place if they seem always to be there: *Senator Breer was becoming quite a fixture in that corner of the library.*

fizz /fɪz/ *verb*: **fizzes, fizzing, fizzed**
A liquid **fizzes** when it produces and gives off bubbles, usually with a hissing noise.

fizzle /'fɪzəl/ *verb*: **fizzles, fizzling, fizzled**

phrasal verb
An activity or project **fizzles out** when it comes to an unexpectedly early and rather feeble end: *The play scheme eventually fizzled out because of lack of support.*

fizzy /'fɪzɪ/ *adjective*: **fizzier, fizziest**
A **fizzy** drink is full of little bubbles, which it gives off with a hissing noise.

fjord or **fiord** /'fiːɔːd/ or /fjɔːd/ *noun*: **fjords**
A **fjord** is a long narrow inlet in a high rocky coast, especially in Norway.

flabbergasted /'flabəgɑːstɪd/ *adjective* (*informal*)
You are **flabbergasted** when you are astonished: *We were flabbergasted at the news of her resignation.* [*same as* **amazed, astonished, dumbfounded**]

flabby /'flabɪ/ *adjective* (*informal, derogatory*): **flabbier, flabbiest**
Flesh that is **flabby** hangs loosely on the body: *You tend to get flabby as you get older.*

flaccid /'flasɪd/ *adjective*
A part of the body that is **flaccid** is soft and limp, not firm: *He gave me his rather flaccid hand to shake.*

flag[1] /flag/ *noun; verb*
▻ ***noun*: flags**
1 A **flag** is a piece of cloth, usually rectangular, with a distinctive and brightly coloured design, that is used as a symbol to represent a country, group or associa-

tion, or is used for signalling: *The ship was flying a Japanese flag from its mast.* **2** A **flag** is any object similar to this, such as a small paper badge with a pin that you are given to wear when you support a charity, or a similar device for sticking into a map as a marker, or a larger device for marking the extent of an area of land, the start or end point of a race, or a distance from a given point. **3** A **flag** is also a symbol with which you mark items in a set of data, *eg* in a computer file, so that you are able to find them again easily.

▻ ***verb*: flags, flagging, flagged**
You **flag** items in a set of data, *eg* in a computer file, when you mark them with some symbol by which they can be quickly identified.

> ***phrasal verb***
> You **flag down** a vehicle when you wave at it to get the driver to stop: *We flagged a taxi down in the Strand.*

flag² /flag/ *verb*: **flags, flagging, flagged**
You or your spirits **flag** when you get tired and lose your energy and enthusiasm: *After two hours' walking the younger children began to flag.* — *adjective* **flagging:** *his flagging strength.*

flagon /ˈflagən/ *noun*: **flagons**
A **flagon** is a large bottle or jug with a narrow neck, usually with a spout and handle: *a flagon of wine.*

flagpole or **flagstaff** /ˈflagpoʊl/ *noun*: **flagpoles**
A **flagpole** is a pole for attaching a flag to.

flagrant /ˈfleɪgrənt/ *adjective*
Flagrant describes wrong behaviour that is all the more shocking because it is not concealed or disguised: *She told a flagrant lie.* — *adverb* **flagrantly:** *It's flagrantly unfair.*

flail /fleɪl/ *verb*: **flails, flailing, flailed**
Your arms or legs **flail** if they move about in a violent, uncontrolled way; you **flail** your arms or legs about if you move or wave them about violently: *The man was flailing about in the river, gasping, coughing and protesting.* □ *From above the angry crowd was a sea of flailing fists.*

flair /flɛə(r)/ *noun*
1 (*uncount, or used in the singular*) You have a **flair** for something if you have a natural ability or talent for it: *I was amazed by her business flair.* **2** (*uncount*) Someone who has **flair** does things in a stylish and original way: *We need a designer with plenty of flair.*

flak /flak/ *noun* (*uncount*)
1 Flak is fire directed from the ground at enemy aircraft flying overhead. **2** Unfriendly criticism is described as **flak**: *We shall have to take a lot of flak from the press.*

flake /fleɪk/ *noun*; *verb*
▻ ***noun*: flakes**
1 A **flake** is a small thin flat particle of something: *The old paint was peeling off the wall in large flakes.* **2** A **flake** is a snowflake: *Soft white flakes were beginning to float past the window.*
▻ ***verb*: flakes, flaking, flaked**
1 Something such as plaster or paint **flakes** when it drops off a surface in thin curling pieces: *The paint was flaking away in patches.* **2** (*cooking*) You **flake** cooked fish when you break it up into small pieces.

> ***phrasal verb***
> (*informal*) You **flake out** when you faint or drop asleep from exhaustion.

flaky /ˈfleɪkɪ/ *adjective*: **flakier, flakiest**
A **flaky** substance or surface breaks up easily into small thin flat particles: *flaky pastry.*

flamboyant /flamˈbɔɪənt/ *adjective*
1 You describe a person or their behaviour as **flamboyant** if they are daring and stylish. **2 Flamboyant** clothes or designs are bold, bright and unusual: *Today she was dressed in a flamboyant yellow and green outfit.* [*opposite* **modest**, **restrained**] — *adverb* **flamboyantly:** *He was wearing a flamboyantly checked tweed jacket.* — *noun* (*uncount*) **flamboyance:** *Her handwriting reflected the flamboyance of her character.*

flame /fleɪm/ *noun* (*count or uncount*): **flames**
Flame is the bright mass of burning gases coming from something that is on fire; a **flame** is a single point of this: *The candle burnt with a soft flickering flame.* □ *Flames leapt into the air from the burning vehicle.* □ *He opened the door and was met by a wall of flame.*
▻ ***phrases*** **1** Something **bursts into flames** when it suddenly starts burning strongly: *The can of petrol immediately burst into flames.* **2** Something **goes up in flames** when it is destroyed by fire: *The whole factory went up in flames last year.* **3** Something is **in flames** when it is on fire: *She got back to find the house in flames.* **4** (*old*) You can refer to a former lover or admirer as an **old flame**.

flaming /ˈfleɪmɪŋ/ *adjective*
1 Flaming describes something that is burning: *The driver was dragged from his flaming vehicle.* **2 Flaming** also describes very bright shades of red, orange or yellow: *She had flaming red curls.* **3** Your cheeks are **flaming** if they are red from anger or embarrassment: *She glanced across at me, her cheeks flaming.* **4** (*informal*) Someone who is **flaming** is very angry: *He was absolutely flaming when he heard about it.* **5** (*swearword*) People use **flaming** to express annoyance: *Keep your flaming dog under control!*

flamingo /fləˈmɪŋgoʊ/ *noun*: **flamingos** or **flamingoes**
A **flamingo** is a large long-legged water bird with a curved beak and pink feathers.

flammable /ˈflaməbəl/ *adjective*
A material that is **flammable** catches fire and burns easily. [*same as* **inflammable**; *opposite* **non-flammable**]

flan /flan/ *noun* (*count or uncount*): **flans**
A **flan** is a dish consisting of a pastry or sponge base with a filling of fruit or a savoury mixture: *a slice of cheese flan.*

flank /flaŋk/ *noun*; *verb*
▻ ***noun*: flanks**
1 The **flanks** of an animal are its sides: *She patted the horse's flank affectionately.* **2** The **flanks** of something such as a body of troops or a fleet are its sides when it is arranged in formation: *We decided to attack the enemy's exposed right flank.*
▻ ***verb*: flanks, flanking, flanked**
One thing **is flanked** by two others if it has them on either side of it: *We could see him taking a walk in the prison grounds sometimes, flanked by two guards.*

flannel /ˈflanəl/ *noun*: **flannels**
1 Flannel is a soft light woollen cloth used to make clothes: *He wore a light grey flannel suit.* **2** (*used in the plural*) **Flannels** are men's trousers made of flannel: *dressed in a pair of grey flannels and a tweed jacket.* **3** (*BrE*) A **flannel** or **face flannel** is a small square cloth for washing yourself with. [*same as* **facecloth**; see picture at **bathroom**]

flap /flap/ *verb*; *noun*
▻ ***verb*: flaps, flapping, flapped**
1 You **flap** a piece of cloth or paper when you wave it

up and down or from side to side, producing a noise; a piece of cloth or paper **flaps** when it moves up and down or from side to side, making a noise as it does so: *Her raincoat flapped against her legs as she ran.* **2** You **flap** your hands when you wave them about with loose wrists. **3** A bird **flaps** its wings when it moves them up and down: *I could hear the bats as they flapped about in the dark.* **4** (*informal*) You **flap** when you let yourself get into a state of anxiety: *Don't flap; I'm sure she'll be back soon.* [*same as* **panic**]

▷ ***noun***: **flaps**

1 A **flap** is a broad flat piece or part of something attached along one edge and hanging loosely: *She stuck down the flap of the envelope.* **2** The wing **flaps** on an aircraft are hinged sections along the edge of each wing, that are adjusted to control direction. **3** (*used in the singular*) The **flap** of wings is the action of flapping them, and the sound this makes. **4** (*informal; used in the singular*) You are in a **flap** when you are in a state of extreme anxiety: *Now don't get in a flap.*

flare /flɛə(r)/ *verb*; *noun*

▷ ***noun***: **flares**

1 A **flare** is a sudden blaze of bright light: *The flare of white light seemed to illuminate the whole countryside for an instant.* **2** A **flare** is a device for producing a blaze of light, used as a signal or for emergency lighting; a **flare** is also a device for burning unneeded gas or oil. **3** (*used in the plural*) **Flares** are flared trousers.

▷ ***verb***: **flares, flaring, flared**

1 A fire or flame **flares**, or **flares** up, when it burns with sudden brightness: *The fire flared up as she threw the letter on it.* **2** Anger or conflict **flares**, or **flares** up, when it starts, or when it gets suddenly worse; you **flare** up when you get angry: *Violence soon flared up again in the townships.* **3** Skirts or trousers that **flare** out get wider towards the hem: *Their skirts and petticoats flared out as they danced.*

flared /flɛəd/ *adjective*

Flared trousers or skirts get wider towards the hem.

flare-up /ˈflɛərʌp/ *noun*: **flare-ups**

A **flare-up** is an occurrence of violence or conflict: *another flare-up in the Middle East.*

flash /flaʃ/ *noun*; *verb*

▷ ***noun***: **flashes**

1 A **flash** is a sudden quick blaze of light: *A flash of lightning briefly lit up their faces.* **2** A **flash** of something such as a feeling or expression is a sudden brief occurrence of it: *He had a flash of inspiration.* **3** On a camera, the **flash** is a device for producing a flash of light for indoor photography: *The flash isn't working.* [see also **flashbulb**] **4** A news **flash** is a brief but important news announcement on radio or television.

▷ ***verb***: **flashes, flashing, flashed**

1 A light **flashes** when it shines briefly, once or repeatedly; you **flash** a light when you shine it briefly, once or repeatedly: *The driver signalled to me by flashing his headlights.* **2** Something **flashes** by if it moves or passes quickly: *A figure flashed past the window.* □ *The weeks flashed by.* **3** Your eyes **flash** when they brighten with anger or some other strong feeling. **4** You **flash** a smile or a look at someone when you glance at them with that expression on your face: *She flashed a look of warning in my direction.* **5** You **flash** a bright object when you wave it about so that people notice it: *She kept flashing her engagement ring at us.* **6** You **flash** a message or news somewhere when you send it there instantly, *eg* by radio, television or satellite: *News of the air crash was flashed around the world.*

▷ ***phrases*** **1** For **a flash in the pan** see **pan**. **2** Something happens **in a flash** if it happens quickly: *It was all over in a flash.* **3** You do something **quick as a flash** when you do it instantly: *She answered quick as a flash.*

flashback /ˈflaʃbak/ *noun*: **flashbacks**

A **flashback** is a return to the past, especially as a scene in a film or a passage in a novel.

flashbulb /ˈflaʃbʌlb/ *noun*: **flashbulbs**

A **flashbulb** is a small light bulb used to produce a brief bright flash of light for indoor photography.

flashlight /ˈflaʃlaɪt/ (*AmE*) *noun*: **flashlights**

A **flashlight** is a torch.

flashy /ˈflaʃɪ/ *adjective* (*derogatory*): **flashier, flashiest**

You describe something smart and new as **flashy** if you consider it rather too obviously expensive: *He came to work in a flashy new car.* [*same as* **ostentatious**] — *adverb* **flashily:** *She was rather flashily dressed.* [*same as* **loudly**]

flask /flɑːsk/ *noun*: **flasks**

A **flask** is **1** a small flat bottle for alcoholic drink, designed for carrying in the pocket. **2** a vacuum flask: *She took a flask of tea to drink on the journey.* **3** a narrow-necked bottle used in laboratory work.

flat /flat/ *adjective*; *adverb*; *noun*

▷ ***adjective***: **flatter, flattest**

1 A **flat** surface is a horizontal one, as distinct from a vertical or sloping one: *She took out her notebook and looked round for a flat surface to write on.* **2** A **flat** surface is an even, level or smooth one, without raised or hollow areas: *He opened the newspaper and spread it out flat.* **3** Something **flat** does not project as much as usual, or have much, or the usual, mass or bulk: *She had a wide face, with a broad flat nose.* □ *I want chairs that fold flat for storage.* **4** **Flat** shoes are shoes that do not have a raised heel; **flat** heels are low heels: *flat-heeled shoes.* [*opposite* **high-heeled**] **5** You say that someone has **flat** feet if their legs are shaped so that their knees are close together, their ankles apart, and their toes turned outwards. **6** You get a **flat** tyre when the air goes out of it, *eg* because it has a hole in it. **7** A battery is **flat** when it has little or no electrical charge remaining in it. **8** You feel **flat** when you feel bored, depressed and dull. [*opposite* **cheerful, lively**] **9** Someone says something in a **flat** voice when they speak without expression or liveliness. [*opposite* **lively, animated**] **10** A **flat** fee, price or charge is one that does not vary according to circumstances: *They charge a flat rate for a week's car hire.* [*same as* **standard, fixed**] **11** (*music*) A note that is sung or played **flat** is sung or played slightly lower than it should be. [*opposite* **sharp**] **12** A **flat** refusal or denial is a definite or emphatic one. — *adverb* **flatly:** *She flatly refused to lend me the money.* [*same as* **categorically, point-blank**]

▷ ***adverb***

1 Something is lying **flat** if it is in a horizontal as distinct from vertical position: *Some of the gravestones were still standing upright; others were lying flat.* **2** Something is **flat** against a surface if the whole of it is touching the surface: *Stand with both feet flat on the floor.* **3** You do something in a certain time **flat** when you take no longer than that: *She drove from Inverness to Edinburgh in two hours flat.* **4** (*music*) You sing **flat** when you sing notes slightly lower than they should be sung. [*opposite* **sharp**]

▷ ***noun***: **flats**

1 A **flat** is a set of rooms for living in, especially all on one floor. [*same as* **apartment**] **2** (*music*) A **flat** is a note lowered by half a note, indicated by the sign (♭).

▷ ***phrases*** **1** Something **falls flat** if it fails to achieve the effect that was hoped for: *My joke fell a bit flat.* **2** (*informal*) You do something **flat out** when you do it as hard, fast or energetically as you can: *We all worked* *flat out to get the project finished.* **3** (*informal*) You say **'that's flat'** to emphasize that your decision is definite, and you will not change your mind: *You may not go, and that's flat.*

flatmate /ˈflatmeɪt/ *noun*: **flatmates**
Your **flatmate** is someone who shares a flat with you.

flatten /ˈflatən/ *verb*: **flattens, flattening, flattened**
1 You **flatten** something, or **flatten** it out, when you make it flat or flatter; something **flattens**, or **flattens** out, when it becomes flat or flatter: *She unfolded the map and flattened it out.* □ *The landscape flattened out as they drove south.* **2** You **flatten** an object when you squash it flat: *He flattened his nose against the shop window.* **3** You **flatten** yourself against a surface when you press your body flat against it, usually so as not to be seen: *I flattened myself against the wall as he passed.* **4** To **flatten** buildings is to knock them down: *The whole of Valletta's main street was flattened in the air raid.* **5** Crops **are flattened** when storms or heavy rain force them to lie flat. **6** (*informal*) You **flatten** someone when you hit them so hard that they fall over: *The blow flattened him.*

flatter /ˈflatə(r)/ *verb*: **flatters, flattering, flattered**
1 You **flatter** someone when you praise them insincerely, or too much, implying that they are cleverer, more important, or more attractive than they really are, so as to please them, or persuade them to do something for you: *I don't believe you; you're just flattering me.* **2** A picture or description **flatters** a person or thing if it makes them look or seem more attractive than they really are: *The portrait flattered her.* **3** Something such as a piece of clothing, or a particular kind of lighting, **flatters** you if it makes you look attractive: *Candlelight flatters the complexion.* **4** You **are flattered** by someone's behaviour towards you if it shows that they like you or think you important: *I was greatly flattered to be invited.* **5** You **flatter** yourself that something is so when you believe something good about yourself, sometimes wrongly: *He flattered himself that he looked younger than he was.*

flattering /ˈflatərɪŋ/ *adjective*
Something that is **flattering** makes you look attractive, or seem important: *a flattering style of dress* □ *a flattering photo* □ *It was flattering to be asked to join the committee.* [*opposite* **unflattering**]

flattery /ˈflatərɪ/ *noun* (*uncount*)
Flattery is language or behaviour that flatters you: *He was not in the least influenced by her flattery.*

flaunt /flɔːnt/ *verb*: **flaunts, flaunting, flaunted**
You **flaunt** some possession, quality, power or influence that you have when you display it to people in a deliberate and obvious way, so that they will respect or admire you: *He liked to flaunt his wealth.* [*same as* **show off**]

flavour (*AmE* **flavor**) /ˈfleɪvə(r)/ *noun*; *verb*
▻ ***noun*** (*count or uncount*): **flavours**
1 The **flavour** of a food or drink is its taste: *Extra salt would certainly improve the soup's flavour.* □ *wine with a fruity flavour.* **2** The **flavour** of something such as a place is its characteristic quality or atmosphere: *Come to Tahiti and experience the full flavour of the South Pacific.*
▻ ***verb***: **flavours, flavouring, flavoured**
You **flavour** food or drink by adding something to it that gives it a particular taste: *They tend to flavour everything with garlic.* □ *chocolate-flavoured soya dessert.*

flavouring (*AmE* **flavoring**) /ˈfleɪvərɪŋ/ *noun*: **flavourings**
Flavouring is a substance that you add to food to give it a particular taste: *vanilla and other flavourings.*

flavourless (*AmE* **flavorless**) /ˈfleɪvələs/ *adjective*
Food that is **flavourless** has no taste. [*same as* **tasteless**; *opposite* **tasty**]

flaw /flɔː/ *noun*: **flaws**
1 A **flaw** in something such as fabric, glass or pottery is a mark or a small damaged area: *The ruby had a slight flaw in it.* **2** A **flaw** in the design of a product is something that makes it unsatisfactory. [*same as* **defect**] **3** A **flaw** in someone's character is a fault: *If she had one flaw in her personality it was impatience.* [*same as* **defect, failing, weakness**] **4** A **flaw** in an argument or policy is a mistake that makes it unsatisfactory: *Your theory has one basic flaw.*

flawed /ˈflɔːd/ *adjective*
Something that is **flawed** has a flaw in it: *Their policy is fundamentally flawed.* □ *a flawed and discredited argument.*

flawless /ˈflɔːləs/ *adjective*
Something that is **flawless** has no defects, faults or flaws: *Her complexion was pale and flawless.* [*same as* **perfect**] — *adverb* **flawlessly:** *She executed her solo flawlessly.* [*same as* **perfectly**]

flax /flaks/ *noun* (*uncount*)
Flax is a plant whose stem contains a fibre that is used for making linen, and whose seeds are used to make linseed oil.

flaxen /ˈflaksən/ *adjective* (*literary*)
Flaxen hair is very pale yellow, or very fair: *flaxen-haired children.*

flay /fleɪ/ *verb*: **flays, flaying, flayed**
To **flay** a dead animal is to remove its skin.

flea /fliː/ *noun*: **fleas**
A **flea** is a tiny wingless jumping insect that sucks blood: *a flea-bitten dog* □ *He was covered with flea bites.*
▻ ***phrase*** You send someone away **with a flea in their ear** when you dismiss them after scolding them severely.

fleck /flɛk/ *noun*: **flecks**
A **fleck** is a small mark or spot, especially of some contrasting colour: *Her eyes were grey with flecks of brown.*

flecked /ˈflɛkt/ *adjective*
Something that is **flecked** with marks or spots of another colour is covered with them: *His eyes were deep brown, flecked with gold.*

fled /flɛd/ *verb*
Fled is the past tense and past participle of **flee**.

fledgling or **fledgeling** /ˈflɛdʒlɪŋ/ *noun*; *adjective*
▻ ***noun***: **fledglings**
A **fledgling** is a young bird that is learning to fly.
▻ ***adjective***
Fledgling describes a person just starting on their career, or an industry in its early stages: *a fledgling journalist* □ *fledgling electronics companies.*

flee /fliː/ *verb*: **flees, fleeing, fled**
1 You **flee** when you run away from someone or something: *People were fleeing across the border into Malawi.* **2** You **flee** a place where you are in danger when you escape from it: *He was forced to flee the country.* **3** (*literary*) Something such as happiness **flees** when it disappears.

fleece /fliːs/ *noun*; *verb*
▻ ***noun***: **fleeces**
1 A sheep's **fleece** is its woolly coat. **2** A **fleece** is also a

sheep's wool cut from it in a single piece. **3** (*uncount*) **Fleece** is sheepskin or a fluffy fabric, *eg* for lining coats: *fleece-lined jackets.*
▻ ***verb*** (*informal*): **fleeces, fleecing, fleeced**
Someone **fleeces** you when they get a lot of money from you by cheating you or charging you too much for something.

fleecy /ˈfliːsɪ/ *adjective*: **fleecier, fleeciest**
Something **fleecy** is either made of sheep's fleece, or is fluffy or furry like it: *A coat with a fleecy lining.*

fleet /fliːt/ *noun*: **fleets**
1 A **fleet** is a number of ships or boats under the management, control or command of a single business or state: *a fishing fleet.* **2** A country's **fleet** is its navy. **3** A number of vehicles such as buses or taxis, under the same ownership or management, may be called a **fleet**: *By this time Stagecoach had increased their fleet to 200.*

fleeting /ˈfliːtɪŋ/ *adjective*
Fleeting describes something that lasts for only a short time: *We had a fleeting glimpse of the Queen as she got into the car.* [*same as* **brief**] — *adverb* **fleetingly:** *She smiled fleetingly.*

flesh /fleʃ/ *noun* (*uncount*)
1 Your **flesh** is the substance covering your bones, consisting mainly of muscle, usually thought of as enclosed by skin: *The animal's teeth had deeply penetrated the flesh of his thigh.* **2** The **flesh** of a fruit or vegetable is its soft inside part that you eat. [*same as* **pulp**]
▻ ***phrases*** **1** If you say that someone is **flesh and blood**, you mean they are human, or that they have the usual human weaknesses. **2** A person who is your own **flesh and blood** is a member of your own family. **3** You see someone **in the flesh** when you see them in solid bodily form, as distinct from in a photograph, or on television: *I've never actually met her in the flesh.* [*same as* **in person**]

phrasal verb
You **flesh out** something such as a report when you add descriptive detail to it.

fleshy /ˈfleʃɪ/ *adjective*: **fleshier, fleshiest**
1 A **fleshy** person has a lot of flesh on their body: *His shoulders were broad and fleshy.* [*same as* **plump**] **2 Fleshy** stems and leaves are thick.

flew /fluː/ *verb*
Flew is the past tense of **fly**.

flex /fleks/ *verb*; *noun*
▻ ***verb***: **flexes, flexing, flexed**
You **flex** a limb or joint by bending it; you **flex** a muscle by tightening or contracting it so as to bend a joint. [*opposite* **extend, straighten**]
▻ ***noun*** (*count or uncount*): **flexes**
The **flex** of an electrical machine or device is the plastic-covered electric cable through which electricity is transferred to the machine from the plug: *Don't trip over the flex.* [*same as* **wire**]

flexible /ˈfleksəbəl/ *adjective*
1 A **flexible** material or product bends easily without breaking: *tough flexible plastic dishes.* [*opposite* **rigid, stiff**] **2** A **flexible** arrangement or system is one that can be easily altered to suit changing circumstances; you are **flexible** if you are willing to change your plans or policies to suit other people or a new situation: *The staff would prefer flexible working hours to fixed ones.* — *noun* (*uncount*) **flexibility** /fleksəˈbɪlɪtɪ/: *She liked the flexibility of the new computer system.* — *adverb* **flexibly:** *I think we should view the matter flexibly.*

flexitime /ˈfleksɪtaɪm/ *noun* (*uncount*)
Flexitime is a system of flexible working hours operated in some organizations, by which employees may choose their time of arrival and departure, provided they work the agreed number of hours.

flick /flɪk/ *verb*; *noun*
▻ ***verb***: **flicks, flicking, flicked**
1 To **flick** is to move quickly and lightly: *The creature's tail was flicking to and fro.* **2** You **flick** something somewhere when you throw it there lightly; you **flick** something off a surface when you knock it away lightly, usually with the back of your fingertips: *He flicked a crumb off his jacket.* **3** You **flick** a whip, or something you are using like a whip, when you raise it and pull it sharply down again: *She kept flicking the horse's neck with her whip.* **4** You **flick** pages over, or **flick** through a book, when you turn the pages quickly: *He was flicking idly through a magazine.* **5** You **flick** an object by holding your middle finger pressed against the inside of your thumb, and then releasing it sharply against the object: *He kept flicking the back of her newspaper as she sat reading.* **6** You **flick** a switch, or the catch of a case, when you operate it with a quick movement of the fingers: *She flicked a couple of switches and the screen sprang into life.* □ *He flicked the light on.*
▻ ***noun***: **flicks**
1 A **flick** is a flicking action: *With two flicks of its tail the lizard disappeared.* □ *He gave his jacket a quick flick with the clothes brush.* **2** (*used in the plural*; *old*) The **flicks** is the cinema, or the films shown there.

flicker /ˈflɪkə(r)/ *verb*; *noun*
▻ ***verb***: **flickers, flickering, flickered**
1 A light or flame **flickers** when it burns or shines unsteadily; a smile **flickers** across someone's face when they smile briefly: *I could see the street lights flickering through the trees.* **2** Something **flickers** when it moves quickly up and down or to and fro: *flickering shadows* □ *His eyelids flickered slightly when I shouted his name.*
▻ ***noun*** (*usually in the singular*): **flickers**: *There was no movement in the room except for the flicker of the fire in the grate.* □ *a faint flicker of hope.*

flier see **flyer**.

flight /flaɪt/ *noun*: **flights**
1 (*uncount*) **Flight** is the power or action of flying: *creatures with the power of flight* □ *Have you ever watched a seagull in flight?* **2** (*used in the singular*) The **flight** of something flying or moving through the air is the path or direction it takes: *The flight of the condor takes it the length of the Andes.* **3** A **flight** is a journey made in or by an aircraft: *Did you have a good flight?* □ *Drinks will be served during the flight.* **4** An aeroplane that takes passengers on a particular route at a scheduled time is also a **flight**: *Manx Airlines announce the arrival of Flight JE 607 from Glasgow.* **5** A **flight** of aircraft, or of birds of a particular type, is a group flying together: *A flight of geese passed high overhead.* **6** A **flight** of steps or stairs is a set of them leading straight up, without turning any corners: *She climbed the four flights of steps to her apartment.* **7** An idea that is original or imaginitive but not very sensible or practical can be described as a **flight** of fancy or of the imagination. **8** (*uncount*) **Flight** is the action of running away, escaping or fleeing: *During his flight from the police he had taken refuge in a disused warehouse.*
▻ ***phrases*** **1** (*formal*) You **take flight** when you run away or flee. **2** (*old*) To **put** someone **to flight** is to make them flee or run away.

flightless /ˈflaɪtləs/ *adjective*
Flightless birds or insects are those that cannot fly.

flighty /ˈflaɪtɪ/ *adjective* (*old, derogatory*): **flightier, flightiest**
A **flighty** person is someone who is not sensible or reliable.

flimsy /ˈflɪmzɪ/ *adjective*: **flimsier, flimsiest**
1 Flimsy clothing or fabric is light and thin: *The wind pierced through our flimsy bridesmaids' dresses.* **2** A **flimsy** building or structure is not strongly made, and collapses easily: *Their flimsy homes could hardly be expected to withstand even the mildest earthquake.* **3** A **flimsy** excuse or explanation is a feeble one that no-one believes.

flinch /flɪntʃ/ *verb*: **flinches, flinching, flinched**
1 You **flinch** when you give a quick little jump or jerk, from pain or fright: *She flinched as the doctor touched her wound.* **2** You **flinch** from an unpleasant task, duty or subject when you are unwilling to do it or consider doing it: *He flinched from telling her the truth.* □ *She flinched from the thought that this might be her last chance.*

fling /flɪŋ/ *verb*; *noun*
▻ ***verb***: **flings, flinging, flung**
1 You **fling** something somewhere when you throw it there carelessly or violently: *He flung his coat over the back of a chair.* □ *I'll just fling a few clothes into my suitcase.* □ *She ran up to him and flung her arms round his neck.* **2** You **fling** yourself somewhere when you get there in one violent movement: *They flung themselves face downwards on the floor.* **3** You **fling** yourself into some activity when you put all your energy into it: *She flung herself into her research.*
▻ ***noun*** (*used in the singular; informal*)
You have a **fling** when you have a short period of enjoying yourself in a very free or lively way: *Of course we had quite a fling when we won all that money.* □ *We never had a serious relationship; just a brief fling over the summer.*

flint /flɪnt/ *noun*: **flints**
1 (*uncount*) **Flint** is a hard stone found in areas of limestone and chalk: *Most of Norwich's churches are built of local flint.* **2** (*archaeology*) A **flint** is a piece of this stone shaped for use as a tool. **3** A **flint** is a piece of hard metal from which a spark can be struck for lighting a fire, used also in cigarette-lighters.

flip /flɪp/ *verb*; *noun*
▻ ***verb***: **flips, flipping, flipped**
1 You **flip** something somewhere when you throw it there quickly or lightly: *From time to time he flipped his cigarette ash into a saucer lying in front of him.* [*same as* **flick**] **2** You **flip** a coin when you throw it up so that it turns over in mid air. [*same as* **toss**] **3** You **flip** pages over, or **flip** through a book, when you turn the pages quickly: *He was flipping through his notebook.* [*same as* **flick**] **4** You **flip** something such as a switch or a catch when you operate it with a quick light movement of the fingers: *He flipped open the lid of his briefcase.* [*same as* **flick**] **5** (*informal*) You say someone has **flipped** if you think they have gone crazy, or if they are suddenly very angry.
▻ ***noun***: **flips**
1 A **flip** is a quick light throw: *We can't make these decisions at the flip of a coin.* **2** (*gymnastics*) A **flip** is a somersault performed in mid air: *a back flip.* **3** An alcoholic drink made with beaten egg is a **flip**.

flippant /ˈflɪpənt/ *adjective*
A **flippant** person is not serious enough about grave and important matters: *Some students had a rather flippant attitude to their work.* □ *Don't be flippant.* [*same as* **frivolous, disrespectful**; *opposite* **serious, respectful**] — *noun* (*uncount*) **flippancy:** *This isn't the moment for flippancy.* — *adverb* **flippantly:** *Someone flippantly suggested holding a party in the graveyard.*

flipper /ˈflɪpə(r)/ *noun*: **flippers**
1 The **flippers** of a whale, dolphin, seal or penguin are the flat limbs that it uses for swimming. **2 Flippers** are also rubber foot-coverings imitating an animal flipper, that people wear for diving or underwater swimming: *a pair of rubber flippers.*

flirt /flɜːt/ *verb*; *noun*
▻ ***verb***: **flirts, flirting, flirted**
1 You **flirt** with someone when you behave towards them in a sexually affectionate way, but without serious intentions: *He would flirt with other women just to annoy her.* **2** You **flirt** with something such as an idea or a religion when you take an interest in it without committing yourself seriously to it: *He had flirted with Buddhism when he was in his twenties.* **3** You **flirt** with danger when you take unnecessary risks. — *noun* (*count or uncount*) **flirtation** /flɜːˈteɪʃən/: *She was well aware of his periodic flirtations with female students.*
▻ ***noun***: **flirts**
A **flirt** is someone who flirts a lot with other people.

flirtatious /flɜːˈteɪʃəs/ *adjective*
A **flirtatious** person often behaves towards others in a sexually affectionate way, without very serious intentions: *She gave him a flirtatious wink when her husband wasn't looking.* — *adverb* **flirtatiously:** *She patted him flirtatiously on the knee.*

flit /flɪt/ *verb*: **flits, flitting, flitted**
1 To **flit** is to fly lightly from place to place: *Butterflies flitted about in the sunshine.* [*same as* **flutter**] **2** People **flit**, *eg* from job to job, when they keep moving from one thing to another, never staying anywhere long. **3** A look or expression **flits** across someone's face when it appears there briefly and disappears: *A look of amusement flitted across his usually stern features.*

float /floʊt/ *verb*; *noun*
▻ ***verb***: **floats, floating, floated**
1 A substance or object that **floats** is light enough to stay on the surface of a liquid without sinking; someone or something that **is floating** is staying on the surface of a liquid without sinking: *She taught the children how to float.* **2** Something **floats** when it moves on the surface of a liquid; you **float** something when you set it moving on the surface of a liquid: *The children were quite happy floating their plastic ducks in the bath.* **3** Something light **floats** through the air when it moves about above ground: *The balloon floated away into the heavens.* **4** A sound **floats** somewhere when it travels there: *The sound of their voices floated up from the valley.* **5** To **float** a financial venture such as a business company is to start it by selling shares in it. **6** (*economics*) The government **floats** the national currency when it allows it to vary in value in relation to other currencies.
▻ ***noun***: **floats**
1 A **float** is a floating device fixed to a fishing line or fishing net to stop it sinking. **2** A low-powered delivery vehicle may be called a **float**: *a milk float.* **3** A truck decorated as an exhibit in a street parade is a **float**. **4** A **float** is also an amount of money given *eg* to salespeople in a shop at the start of business, from which they can give customers change.

floating /ˈfloʊtɪŋ/ *adjective*
1 A **floating** population is one that moves around and changes. **2** A **floating** voter is someone who is not committed to supporting any particular party.

flock /flɒk/ *noun*; *verb*
▻ ***noun***: **flocks**
1 A **flock** of sheep or birds is a group of them. **2** A **flock** of people is a crowd of them: *He was pursued by flocks of schoolgirls wherever he went.* **3** (*with a singular or plural verb*) A priest's or church minister's **flock** are the people that belong to his or her congregation.
▻ ***verb***: **flocks, flocking, flocked**
People **flock** somewhere when they go there in large numbers or in a large crowd: *Everyone flocked to see the new musical.*

flog /flɒg/ *verb*: **flogs, flogging, flogged**
1 (*informal*) You **flog** something when you sell it: *I'm going to flog my computer and get a better one.* **2** To **flog** someone is beat them or whip them. — *noun* (*count or uncount*) **flogging:** *He was given a public flogging.* ▫ *Flogging was to be banned in all schools.*
▻ ***phrases*** **1** For **flog a dead horse** see **horse**. **2** An idea or an expression **is flogged to death** when it is used too often, and so loses its effect and becomes boring.

flood /flʌd/ *noun*; *verb*
▻ ***noun***: **floods**
1 There is a **flood** when water covers an area of dry land, or any dry place, *eg* when a river overflows: *Hundreds of homes in central Perth were damaged in last year's floods when the River Tay burst its banks.* ▫ *millions of pounds' worth of flood damage.* **2** A **flood** of things is an overwhelming quantity arriving or occurring: *There's been a flood of complaints about this particular product.* **3** Someone is in **floods** of tears when they are crying a lot: *The child was in floods of tears when the hamster died.*
▻ ***verb***: **floods, flooding, flooded**
1 Water **floods** a dry place or an area of dry land when it flows over or into it; a place **floods** when it gets covered with water; a river **floods** when it overflows, *eg* after continuous heavy rain: *Water poured in from the street and flooded the basement.* **2** To **flood** a place with things is to fill it so full of them that there is no room for anything else: *Their idea is to flood the market with their own cheap products.* [*same as* **inundate**] **3** You **flood** a vehicle engine when you let too much petrol into it, so that it cannot start. **4** People **flood** somewhere when they move there in large crowds: *Crowds of supporters were flooding out of the football ground.* **5** Things such as memories or feelings **flood** back when they fill your mind or you experience them strongly again: *All her old worries came flooding back.* **6** Colour **floods** into someone's face when it becomes pink or red: *I was relieved to see the colour flooding back into her cheeks.* **7** Light **floods** a place, or **floods** into it, when it fills it: *Sunlight flooded the bedroom as she opened the shutters.* — *adjective* **flooded:** *flooded fields.* — *noun* (*uncount*) **flooding:** *The River Severn has overflowed at several points, causing widespread flooding.*

floodgates /ˈflʌdgeɪts/ *noun* (*plural*)
▻ ***phrase*** To **open the floodgates** to something is suddenly to let it happen on a large scale: *If we give one person permission we'll open the floodgates to hundreds of similar requests.*

floodlight /ˈflʌdlaɪt/ *noun*; *verb*
▻ ***noun***: **floodlights**
Floodlights are powerful lamps used at night to light football pitches or the outside of buildings.
▻ ***verb***: **floodlights, floodlighting, floodlit**
A place or building **is floodlit** when it is lit by floodlights: *The castle is floodlit at night.*

floor /flɔː(r)/ *noun*; *verb*
▻ ***noun***: **floors**
1 The **floor** of a room is the surface you stand on and walk on: *A pile of papers had fallen off his desk on to the floor.* **2** A **floor** of a building is all the rooms on one particular level: *Men's shoes are on the third floor.* **3** The **floor** of a valley, forest, cave or the sea is the ground at its bottom: *creatures of the ocean floor.* **4** The **floor** at a public meeting is the part of the hall or auditorium where the audience are sitting, as distinct from the platform or stage: *The speaker will be happy to answer questions from the floor at the end of the lecture.*
▻ ***verb*** (*informal*): **floors, flooring, floored**
You **are floored** by a problem or a question if you are quite unable to deal with it, often from surprise or confusion: *Her query floored me.*
▻ ***phrases*** **1** You **hold the floor** when you are the person who is talking while others listen. **2** You **take the floor** when you rise to speak in public, *eg* in a debate. **3** (*informal*) You **wipe the floor** with someone when you defeat them very thoroughly and publicly, in a competition or in an argument.

floorboard /ˈflɔːbɔːd/ *noun* (*usually in the plural*): **floorboards**
Floorboards are the long narrow boards of which a wooden floor is made: *There was a creaking floorboard somewhere near the door.* ▫ *Police found a cache of drugs hidden under the floorboards.*

flop /flɒp/ *verb*; *noun*
▻ ***verb***: **flops, flopping, flopped**
1 You **flop** somewhere when you sit or lie down suddenly and heavily: *He flopped down beside me on the sofa.* **2** Something soft and heavy **flops** somewhere when it falls, hangs, moves or sways in a loose, uncontrolled way: *Her hair kept flopping over her face.* **3** (*informal*) A play, show or project **flops** if it is a failure: *The musical flopped on Broadway.*
▻ ***noun*** (*informal*): **flops**
Something that is a **flop** is a failure: *Most of his plays were flops.* [*same as* **failure**; *opposite* **success, hit**]

floppy /ˈflɒpɪ/ *adjective*: **floppier, floppiest**
Something **floppy** is soft and loose rather than firm, so that it sways about or hangs down: *hats with floppy brims.* [*opposite* **stiff, rigid**]

floppy disk /flɒpɪ ˈdɪsk/ *noun*: **floppy disks**
A **floppy disk** is a flexible magnetic disk for storing data for use in a computer. [see picture at **office**]

flora /ˈflɔːrə/ *noun* (*plural*)
The **flora** of an area are the trees and plants that grow there. [see also **fauna**]

floral /ˈflɔːrəl/ *adjective*
1 Floral describes things that are made of, or relate to, flowers: *a magnificent floral display.* **2** A **floral** fabric is patterned with flowers: *floral wallpaper.* [*same as* **flowered, flowery**]

florid /ˈflɒrɪd/ *adjective*
1 Someone who has a **florid** complexion has a pink or red face: *florid cheeks.* **2** A **florid** writing style is unsuitably literary.

florist /ˈflɒrɪst/ *noun*: **florists**
1 A **florist** is someone who sells bunches of cut flowers, or indoor plants. **2** A **florist** or **florist's** is a shop selling flowers or indoor plants: *She ordered a bouquet from the local florist's.*

floss /flɒs/ *noun* (*uncount*)
Dental **floss** is fine thread that you use for cleaning between the teeth.

flounce /flaʊns/ *verb*: **flounces, flouncing, flounced**
Someone **flounces** somewhere when they move there in a deliberately noisy, bad-tempered manner, as a way of expressing their anger or impatience: *She flounced out of the room, banging the door.*

flounder /ˈflaʊndə(r)/ *verb*: **flounders**, **floundering**, **floundered**
1 People **flounder** in deep water when they kick and move their arms wildly, to try and stop themselves drowning. **2** You say someone **is floundering** when they are expected to say something but cannot think what to say: *Her question had me floundering for a moment.*

flour /flaʊə(r)/ *noun* (*uncount*)
Flour is fine white or brown powder produced by grinding grain, especially wheat, used for making bread, pastry and cakes.

flourish /ˈflʌrɪʃ/ *verb*; *noun*
▻ ***verb***: **flourishes**, **flourishing**, **flourished**
1 People **are flourishing** when they are in good health, and making good progress: *Best wishes to your family; I hope they are all flourishing.* [*same as* **thrive**] **2** A plant or animal **flourishes** when it grows strong and healthy in conditions that suit it. [*same as* **thrive**] **3** Something **flourishes** when it develops and increases in circumstances that suit it: *drug-ridden districts in which crime flourishes.* [*same as* **thrive**] **4** You **flourish** an object when you wave it about for people to see: *She flourished the letter triumphantly.* [*same as* **brandish**]
▻ ***noun***: **flourishes**
1 A **flourish** is a grand sweeping gesture with the arm or hand: *He removed his hat with a flourish.* **2** A **flourish** in handwriting is a decorative curl or twist.

flout /flaʊt/ *verb*: **flouts**, **flouting**, **flouted**
You **flout** a law or rule when you disobey it deliberately.

flow /floʊ/ *verb*; *noun*
▻ ***verb***: **flows**, **flowing**, **flowed**
1 Water and other liquids **flow** when they move or pour steadily somewhere, or from somewhere: *Water was flowing across the road from the burst pipe.* ▫ *Arteries and veins are the vessels through which our blood flows.* **2** A river or stream **flows** somewhere when it goes in that direction: *The Danube rises in south Germany, and flows east to the Black Sea.* **3** Gas and electricity **flow** somewhere when they pass there through pipes or cables. **4** People or things **flow** when they move steadily along: *The traffic began to flow normally again.* **5** A person's long hair or long clothes **flow** about them if they hang or swing loosely round them. **6** Words or ideas **flow** when they come quickly and easily to you as you speak, write or think: *Once we settled down to a serious discussion, ideas began to flow.* **7** Talk or conversation **flows** freely when people are talking in a lively manner. **8** Something **flows** from a certain situation or circumstance if it results naturally from it: *Certain consequences inevitably flow from this conclusion.* [*same as* **proceed**] — *adjective* **flowing:** *flowing hair* ▫ *a flowing skirt.*
▻ ***noun*** (*uncount, or used in the singular*)
The **flow** of something is its action of flowing or moving along steadily: *Pressure applied to an artery will cut off the flow of blood.* ▫ *the steady flow of traffic.*
▻ ***phrase*** Someone is **in full flow** when they are talking fluently and energetically: *Her question interrupted him in full flow.*

flower /flaʊə(r)/ *noun*; *verb*
▻ ***noun***: **flowers**
1 The **flowers** on a plant or tree are the parts from which the fruit or seeds are produced. Many plants have brightly coloured flowers so as to attract insects for pollination. [*same as* **bloom**, **blossom**] **2** A **flower** is a small plant bearing flowers, as distinct from a tree or a vegetable: *Spring flowers such as daffodils and tulips must be planted in the autumn.* ▫ *a bunch of flowers.* **3** (*literary*) The **flower** of something is its best or most splendid part: *They died in the flower of their youth.*
▻ ***verb***: **flowers**, **flowering**, **flowered**
1 A tree or plant **flowers** when it produces flowers. **2** Something such as a skill, an artistic style, or a political movement **flowers** when it develops fully and successfully: *It wasn't until her teens that her musical talent really began to flower.*
▻ ***phrase*** A tree or plant is **in flower** when it has flowers on it.

flower bed /ˈflaʊəbɛd/ *noun*: **flower beds**
A **flower bed** is a piece of earth prepared and used for growing plants in.

flowered /flaʊəd/ *adjective*
Something **flowered** is decorated or patterned with flowers. [*same as* **floral**, **flowery**]

flowerpot /ˈflaʊəpɒt/ *noun*: **flowerpots**
A **flowerpot** is a clay or plastic container for growing plants in.

flowery /ˈflaʊərɪ/ *adjective*
1 Something **flowery** is covered, decorated or patterned with flowers: *flowery cotton dresses.* [*same as* **flowered**, **floral**] **2** (*derogatory*) Speech or writing that is described as **flowery** is too fancy or literary.

flown /floʊn/ *verb*
Flown is the past participle of **fly**.

flu /fluː/ *noun* (*uncount*)
Flu is an illness like a bad cold, usually with a fever, headache and aching muscles: *I feel as if I'm getting flu.* [*same as* **influenza**]

fluctuate /ˈflʌktjʊeɪt/ *verb*: **fluctuates**, **fluctuating**, **fluctuated**
Something **fluctuates** if it keeps altering in amount, level or character: *House prices fluctuated wildly over the next few months.* — *adjective* **fluctuating:** *fluctuating temperatures.* — *noun* (*uncount or count*) **fluctuation** /flʌktjʊˈeɪʃən/: *periodic fluctuations in voltage.*

flue /fluː/ *noun*: **flues**
A **flue** is a chimney or pipe for the passage or escape of heat, smoke or gas.

fluent /fluːənt/ *adjective*
1 You are **fluent** in a language if you speak and write it easily and well: *She speaks fluent Italian.* ▫ *He's fluent in Czech.* **2** You are a **fluent** speaker, reader or writer if you can speak, read or write fast, easily and well: *Most childen are fluent readers by the age of 10.* — *noun* (*uncount*) **fluency:** *She spoke Polish with impressive fluency.* — *adverb* **fluently:** *They can read English fluently, but can they understand what they're reading?*

fluff /flʌf/ *noun*; *verb*
▻ ***noun*** (*uncount*)
1 Fluff is soft masses of dust or woolly material. **2** The soft fur or feathers on a young creature are referred to as **fluff**: *The chicks were little balls of yellow fluff.*
▻ ***verb***: **fluffs**, **fluffing**, **fluffed**
1 You **fluff** something up or out when you shake it or arrange it into a soft mass: *Birds keep warm by fluffing out their feathers.* **2** You **fluff** something you are doing when you spoil it by doing it badly; actors **fluff** their lines when make mistakes in saying them.

fluffy /ˈflʌfɪ/ *adjective*: **fluffier**, **fluffiest**
Something **fluffy** is soft and furry: *fluffy kittens* ▫ *The clouds looked fluffy, like cotton wool.*

fluid /ˈfluːɪd/ *noun*; *adjective*
▻ ***noun*** (*count or uncount*): **fluids**
A **fluid** is a liquid or other substance that can flow

freely: *a bottle of cleaning fluid.* □ *Stay in bed and drink plenty of fluids.*
▻ ***adjective***
1 Something **fluid** is able to flow like a liquid: *The windscreen wash remains fluid at temperatures well below freezing.* **2 Fluid** movements are smooth and graceful: *the fluid elegance of a tiger.* **3** Arrangements and plans that are **fluid** are easily altered to suit different circumstances; opinions or ideas that are **fluid** are not yet definite. — *noun (uncount)* **fluidity** /fluːˈɪdətɪ/: *Our plans are still in a state of fluidity.*

fluid ounce /fluːɪd ˈaʊns/ *noun*: **fluid ounces**
A **fluid ounce** is a unit of liquid measurement, equal to a twentieth of a British pint or a sixteenth of a US pint.

fluke /fluːk/ *noun*: **flukes**
A **fluke** is a success achieved through good luck rather than through skill or effort: *It'll be a fluke if I pass this exam.*

flung /flʌŋ/ *verb*
Flung is the past tense and past participle of **fling**.

fluorescent /flʊəˈrɛsənt/ *adjective*
Fluorescent describes materials that absorb radiation and give out electromagnetic radiation in the form of light; **fluorescent** colours shine brightly when light is directed on to them; a **fluorescent** light is one in which light is produced by passing an electric current through a tube covered with fluorescent material.

fluoride /ˈflʊəraɪd/ *noun (uncount)*
Fluoride is a chemical that stops teeth decaying, and is added to some toothpastes, and to the drinking water in some areas.

flurry /ˈflʌrɪ/ *noun; verb*
▻ ***noun***: **flurries**
1 A **flurry** of rain or snow is a sudden brief shower of it accompanying a strong wind. **2** A **flurry** of activity is a sudden rush or burst of it: *The wedding preparations went ahead in a flurry of excitement.* [*same as* **commotion**]
▻ ***verb***: **flurries, flurrying, flurried**
You **are flurried** when you are confused and upset, especially when you are having to do something in a hurry. [*same as* **fluster**]

flush[1] /flʌʃ/ *verb; noun*
▻ ***verb***: **flushes, flushing, flushed**
1 You **flush** when your face goes red, *eg* when you are hot or embarrassed: *He flushed crimson at the compliment.* **2** You **flush** a toilet when you operate the handle that makes water rush into into the bowl to clean it; you **flush** something down the toilet when you put it into the bowl and wash it away by operating the handle; a toilet **flushes** when water rushes into the bowl: *The toilet won't flush.* **3** To **flush** people or animals out of a place is to force them to come out of it: *The remaining rebels were being flushed out of the woods where they had taken refuge.*
▻ ***noun***: **flushes**
1 (*usually in the singular*) A **flush** spreads over your face, cheeks or neck when they become red. **2** The **flush** of a toilet is the device you operate to make water rush into the bowl to clean it.
▻ ***phrase*** You are **in the first flush** of something such as youth or freedom when you are in the early stages of it and are feeling especially fresh or enthusiastic.

flush[2] /flʌʃ/ *adjective or adverb; adjective*
▻ ***adjective or adverb***
Something that is **flush** with a surrounding or adjoining surface is level with it and does not project above it or drop below it.
▻ ***adjective*** (*informal*)
You say you are **flush** when you have plenty of money: *I'll pay; I'm pretty flush at present.*

flushed /flʌʃt/ *adjective*
1 You are **flushed** when your face is hot and red: *He had a fever and looked very flushed.* **2** You are **flushed** with something such as success or victory when you are still in a state of excitement about having achieved it.

fluster /ˈflʌstə(r)/ *verb; noun*
▻ ***verb***: **flusters, flustering, flustered**
Something **flusters** you if it makes you confused and nervous. [*same as* **flurry**] — *adjective* **flustered:** *Try and look calm even if you feel flustered inside.*
▻ ***noun*** (*used in the singular*): *Anyone can get into a fluster when they're made to do things in a hurry.*

flute /fluːt/ *noun*: **flutes**
A **flute** is a musical instrument of the woodwind family; you hold it in a horizontal position when you are playing it. [see picture at **orchestra**]

fluted /ˈfluːtɪd/ *adjective*
A **fluted** surface has long parallel grooves or channels cut into it for decoration: *fluted columns.*

flutter /ˈflʌtə(r)/ *verb; noun*
▻ ***verb***: **flutters, fluttering, fluttered**
1 Something light and thin **flutters** when it waves up and down or from side to side rapidly: *The washing fluttered on the line.* **2** Something such as a small bird or an insect **flutters** somewhere when it flies there with rapid wing movements: *Bats were fluttering about in the twilight.* **3** Something small and light such as a leaf **flutters** somewhere when it falls slowly with a rapid twisting motion: *A bit of paper fluttered to the ground.* **4** You **flutter** your eyelashes or eyelids at someone when you move your eyelids up and down rapidly at them, usually as a flirtatious gesture. **5** Your heart or stomach **flutters** when you feel excited, nervous or anxious.
▻ ***noun*** (*used in the singular*): *She glanced across at him with a slight flutter of the eyelids.* □ *He felt a flutter of nervousness at the thought of the interview.*

flux /flʌks/ *noun (uncount)*
Something that is in a state of **flux** is in a constantly changing state: *Our plans are in a state of flux.*

fly /flaɪ/ *verb; noun*
▻ ***verb***: **flies, flying, flew, flown**
1 a A bird, insect or bat **flies** somewhere when it moves through the air on wings: *A wasp had flown in through the open window.* **b** An aircraft or spacecraft **flies** somewhere when it travels through the air or through space: *Our planes fly regularly to Singapore.* **c** You **fly** somewhere when you travel there in an aircraft: *I'm flying to Amsterdam tomorrow.* **d** To **fly** people somewhere is to convey them there in an aircraft: *We can fly you to the Far East for half that price.* **e** You **fly** an aircraft when you are the pilot of it, and control it in the air; you **fly** something such as a kite when you operate it from the ground, controlling its movements in the air: *People used to fly their model planes in the park on a Sunday afternoon.* **f** You **fly** an area of water when you cross it in an aircraft: *Lindbergh flew the Atlantic nonstop in 1927.*
2 a You **fly** a flag when you raise and display it on a flagpole; a flag **flies** when it is attached to a flagpole and is blown by the wind: *The ship was flying a Taiwanese flag.* **b** Clothing **flies** about when it rises into the air, *eg* when you move rapidly: *She raced along, hair and skirt flying.*
3 a Something or someone **flies** somewhere when they move with great speed or force: *She was hit by a piece*

of flying glass. □ *She flew upstairs.* **b** News, reports or rumours **fly** around when one person quickly passes them on to another and you hear them everywhere. **c** A period of time **flies** past if it seem to pass quickly: *The weeks flew by.* □ *Time flies, as they say.* **d** (*informal*) You say you must **fly** when you have to leave immediately: *Cheerio; I must fly.*
4 a You **fly** into a rage or temper when you suddenly get very angry. **b** You **fly** at someone when you attack them, either by hitting them or shouting angrily at them.
5 To **fly** a country is to escape from it. — *noun* (*uncount*) **flying:** *She took up flying when she was a student and got her pilot's licence at the age of 22.*
▻ ***noun*: flies**
1 A **fly** is a two-winged insect, as distinct from four-winged ones such as wasps and bees: *He waved his stick to keep the flies away.* **2** You also find **fly** used in the names of various kinds of insects: *dragonflies* □ *butterfly.* **3** (*usually in the plural*) The zip or set of buttons that fasten the front of a pair of trousers are called the **flies** or the **fly**: *Your flies are undone.*
▻ ***phrases*** **1** People **drop like flies** when they fall ill or die in large numbers. **2** For **fly in the face of** see **face**. **3 A fly in the ointment** is something that spoils an otherwise pleasant or satisfactory situation. **4 A fly on the wall** is the invisible observer you would like to be on interesting occasions that as a human being you would not be entitled to witness. **5** You **let fly** at someone when you attack them physically or shout angrily at them: *The boy suddenly let fly with his fists.* □ *She let fly at me with a stream of insults.* **6** A blow that **sends you flying** is so hard that you fall over.

flyer or **flier** /flaɪə(r)/ *noun*: **flyers**
1 A bird or insect that is a strong **flyer** can fly far and fast: *the swallows and other long-distance flyers.* **2** Someone who flies an aircraft can be called a **flyer**. [*same as* **pilot, aviator**]

flying /ˈflaɪɪŋ/ *adjective*
1 A **flying** creature can fly, or is able to make long gliding leaps: *flying insects.* **2** A **flying** squad is a body of police trained for fast action, or available for duty wherever they are required. **3** A **flying** visit is a very quick one: *I paid a flying visit to my family last weekend.* **4** You take a **flying** leap at something when you run towards it and jump: *He took a flying leap at the wall and managed to grasp the top of it.*
▻ ***phrase*** For **get off to a flying start** see **start**.

flying saucer /flaɪɪŋ ˈsɔːsə(r)/ *noun*: **flying saucers**
A **flying saucer** is any of various circular flying objects in the sky, occasionally reported by people, and thought by some to be spacecraft from other planets.

flyover /ˈflaɪoʊvə(r)/ *noun*: **flyovers**
A **flyover** is a bridge taking one road over another.

flysheet /ˈflaɪʃiːt/ *noun*: **flysheets**
A **flysheet** is a protective outer covering for a tent.

foal /foʊl/ *noun*: **foals**
A **foal** is a baby horse.

foam /foʊm/ *noun* (*uncount*)
1 Foam is a mass of tiny bubbles that form in or on a liquid when air is mixed with it: *They peered down the cliff at the swirling white foam.* **2 Foam**, or **foam plastic** or **foam rubber**, is a light material full of tiny holes, produced by passing gas through plastic or rubber when it is liquid, then solidifying it: *foam mattresses.*
▻ ***verb*: foams, foaming, foamed:** *Below them the waves crashed and foamed.* — *adjective* **foaming:** *a tankard of foaming beer* □ *the foaming waters of the straits.*
▻ ***phrase*** For **foam at the mouth** see **mouth**.

fob /fɒb/ *verb*: **fobs, fobbing, fobbed**

phrasal verb
Someone **fobs** you **off** with something when they give you something that is not what you asked for, or not as good as you expected: *Don't be fobbed off with promises; insist on compensation here and now.*

focal point /ˈfoʊkəl pɔɪnt/ *noun*: **focal points**
The **focal point** of something is its area of greatest interest or activity: *For the children the model space ship was the focal point of the exhibition.*

focus /ˈfoʊkəs/ *noun; verb*
▻ ***verb*: focuses** or **focusses**, **focusing** or **focussing**, **focused** or **focussed**
1 You **focus** your eyes on something when you concentrate on it till it becomes clear; you **focus** a camera, telescope or binoculars on something when you go on adjusting them till they give you a clear image of it: *She focused her binoculars on the zebra.* □ *Try and focus on something in the foreground.* **2** (*physics*) Light rays **are focused** at a certain point if they meet there. **3** You **focus** a beam of light when you direct it at something, or when you make it narrower: *They kept the spotlight focused on her as she moved from one side of the stage to the other.* **4** You **focus** your attention on something when you concentrate on it: *The disaster focused public attention on the problem of chemical waste.*
▻ ***noun*: focuses**
1 (*physics*) A **focus** is the point at which rays of light meet, *eg* after passing through a lens or being reflected by a mirror. **2** (*uncount or count, usually in the singular*) The **focus** of an instrument such as a camera or telescope is the device you adjust to get a clear image of something, or the adjustment that provides a satisfactory image; an image is in **focus** if it is clear and sharp-edged: *Most of the people in the photo were recognizable, though it was very out of focus.* **3** (*used in the singular*) Something is the **focus** of attention or interest if people are showing particular interest in it: *As a result of the television documentary the island became for some time the focus of international concern.* **4** (*uncount*) The **focus** on a particular thing is the circumstance that particular attention is being paid to it: *The focus on competition means that too little attention is paid to non-competitive sports.*

fodder /ˈfɒdə(r)/ *noun* (*uncount*)
Fodder is food, especially hay and straw, for cattle and other farm animals.

foe /foʊ/ *noun* (*literary*): **foes**
Your **foe** is your enemy.

foetal or **fetal** /ˈfiːtəl/ *adjective*
Foetal means relating to a foetus: *They were able to listen to the foetal heart beating.*

foetid see **fetid**.

foetus /ˈfiːtəs/ *noun*: **foetuses**
A **foetus** is an unborn creature growing in an egg or womb, especially an unborn human baby of two or more months' development.

fog /fɒg/ *noun* (*uncount or count*): **fogs**
There is a **fog** when the air close to the earth's surface is filled with a thick cloud of water vapour that makes it difficult for you to see your surroundings: *The fog is expected to lift during the morning.* [see note at **mist**]

foggy /ˈfɒgɪ/ *adjective*: **foggier, foggiest**
It is **foggy** when there is a fog: *It was a foggy November day.*
▻ ***phrase*** (*informal*) You say you **haven't the foggiest idea**, or you **haven't the foggiest**, as an emphatic way

of saying you do not know: *I haven't the foggiest what time it is.*

foghorn /ˈfɒghɔːn/ *noun*: **foghorns**
A **foghorn** is a horn, on a ship or on the coast, that is sounded at regular intervals when it is foggy to indicate to ships in the area the position of land or other ships.

foible /ˈfɔɪbəl/ *noun*: **foibles**
A **foible** is a rather strange or silly personal habit or preference: *After so many years of marriage you tolerate each other's foibles.*

foil[1] /fɔɪl/ *verb*: **foils, foiling, foiled**
You **foil** a person or their attempt to do something when you prevent them from succeeding: *Guards on duty at the gallery last night foiled an attempt to carry off its prize exhibit.* [*same as* **thwart, frustrate**]

foil[2] /fɔɪl/ *noun*
1 (*uncount*) **Foil** is metal beaten or rolled out into sheets as thin as paper, used for packaging food: *foil-wrapped chocolates.* **2** (*used in the singular*) One thing or person is a **foil** for another if the first contrasts with, and emphasizes the impressive qualities of, the second: *The heavy dark hair was the perfect foil for her small pale face with its flawless skin.*

foist /fɔɪst/ *verb*: **foists, foisting, foisted**
1 You **foist** something unwanted on someone when you force them to receive it: *It isn't the job of lecturers to foist their political views on students.* [*same as* **impose, thrust**] **2** You **foist** something inferior on someone when you sell it to them pretending it is better than it is: *The librarian had allowed a series of useless academic theses to be foisted on him by a dealer.*

fold[1] /foʊld/ *verb*; *noun*
▻ ***verb***: **folds, folding, folded**
1 You **fold** paper or cloth by bending it so that one part lies on top of another; you **fold** it double, or in two, or in half, by bending it over once so that one part lies exactly over the other; you **fold** it in: *Fold your sheet of paper in two and tear along the crease.* □ *The corners of the pages had been folded back.* [*opposite* **unfold**] **2** You **fold** things such as clothes, blankets or sheets, or **fold** them up, when you fold them several times to make them into a smaller, neater shape: *He folded the clean towels and put them away.* [*opposite* **unfold**] **3** A piece of furniture or equipment **folds** if it is designed to collapse into a flat shape for convenient storage; you **fold** it when you make it collapse: *The deck chairs had been folded and stacked against the wall.* [*opposite* **unfold**] **4** You **fold** your arms when you cross them over your chest and tuck your hands, one into, and the other under, your elbows; a bird **folds** its wings when it brings them in close to its body. [*opposite* **unfold**] **5** (*cooking*) You **fold** an ingredient into a mixture when you mix it in gently with an action like folding. **6** A business, organization or scheme **folds**, or **folds** up, if it fails and has to close or stop: *I was surprised to find that the firm had folded.*
▻ ***noun***: **folds**
1 A **fold** is the action of folding, or a bend or crease made in paper or cloth by folding it: *She spread the silk out on the table and smoothed out the folds.* **2** A **fold** is also a rounded or hollow shape in cloth that is hanging or lying loosely, not stretched flat: *The skirt hung in soft folds.*

fold[2] /foʊld/ *noun*: **folds**
1 A **fold** is a walled or fenced enclosure for sheep or cattle. **2** A church or religion, or a political party, is sometimes called the **fold** with reference to members leaving it or returning to it: *The Liberal Democrats will no doubt be glad to welcome him back into the fold.*

-fold /foʊld/ *suffix*
Adjectives or adverbs that start with a number and end with **-fold** mean **1** multiplied by that number: *a threefold increase in cases of computer fraud.* **2** having that number of parts: *The benefit of your donation will be twofold: we receive a steady input of cash, and we recover the tax on it.*

folder /ˈfoʊldə(r)/ *noun*: **folders**
A **folder** is a folded cardboard or plastic cover in which to keep loose papers. [see picture at **office**]

folding /ˈfoʊldɪŋ/ *adjective*
A **folding** chair, table or bed can be folded into a flat shape for storage: *a folding kitchen stool.*

foliage /ˈfoʊliːɪdʒ/ *noun* (*uncount*)
The leaves on a tree or plant are its **foliage**.

folk /foʊk/ *noun*; *adjective*
▻ ***noun***: **folks**
1 (*plural*) **Folk** are people: *Some folk never stop complaining.* □ *old folk's club.* **2** (*informal*) You can address a group of people as '**folks**': *Goodnight, folks.* **3** (*especially AmE*; *informal*) Your **folks** are your family: *I'll be going home to celebrate Christmas with my folks.* **4** A **folk** is a people or tribe: *They are a nomadic folk.* **5** (*uncount*; *informal*) **Folk** is folk music: *We listen to folk mostly.*
▻ ***adjective***
The **folk** music, dancing or art of a particular people or country is that which is regarded as traditional amongst them: *Irish folk songs.*

folklore /ˈfoʊklɔː(r)/ *noun* (*uncount*)
Folklore is the customs, beliefs, stories and traditions of particular countries, peoples or communities, or the study and investigation of these: *Manx folklore* □ *a folklore museum.*

follow /ˈfɒloʊ/ *verb*: **follows, following, followed**
1 a You **follow** someone when you go along behind them: *He followed me into the kitchen.* □ *Follow that taxi!* □ *In came Robert followed by the others.* **b** You **follow** someone somewhere when you join them in the place they have gone to: *He eventually followed her to England.* □ *She arrived at the party about 8.30, followed a little later by her husband.* **c** You **follow** someone into a certain profession if you choose it as your profession too: *She wanted to follow her father into medicine.* **d** You **follow** someone everywhere if you go with them wherever they go: *His faithful servant followed him throughout his travels.* **e** You **are being followed** if someone is secretly pursuing you and watching your movements: *He realized he was being followed.* **f** You **follow** something or someone with your eyes, or your eyes **follow** something or someone, when you watch them moving from place to place: *Her eyes followed him up the street.* **g** You **follow** a person when you accept them as leader and respect their authority: *the disciples who followed Jesus Christ.*
2 a An event or period that **follows** another comes after it, or comes next: *A discussion will follow the lecture.* □ *During the months that followed, the police intensified their search.* □ *We had a short holiday in the Lake District, followed by a visit to my parents.* **b** Something that **follows** in a speech or text comes next: *What follows is not necessarily my own opinion.* **c** Something **follows** if it is a result or consequence: *I may be old but it doesn't follow that I've lost my wits.*
3 a You **follow** a road when you go along it; you **follow** a river when you go alongside it; you **follow** the signs to somewhere when you take the route or path indicated by them: *They followed a winding track up the mountain.* □ *Follow the signs for Inverness as far as Aviemore.* **b** You **follow** a particular way of life, course

of action, or profession, when you practise it: *He had decided to follow a legal career.* □ *She followed a life of service to others.* [*same as* **pursue**] **c** A set of data or circumstances **follow** a pattern if they match or repeat it: *The events in each case follow a familiar pattern.* **d** You **follow** advice or instructions, or **follow** them out, when you obey them. [*same as* **carry out**] **e** You **follow** someone's example when you try to do what they have done, or copy them: *I followed my sister's example and spent a year abroad before university.* **f** You say you can **follow** something such as an explanation, or the plot of a play or story, if you can understand it: *The first time I saw the film I couldn't follow it at all.* □ *I'm sorry; I don't follow you.* **g** You **follow** something such as a sport, or a series of events, or a television serial, when you take an interest in it and keep yourself informed about the latest developments: *Have you been following the rape case?* **h** You **follow** the text of a play when you read it while listening to a performance of it.

▻ ***phrases*** **1** You use **as follows** to introduce something such as a list, a quotation, a description or a set of instructions: *Saturday's team is as follows...* □ *She addressed the meeting as follows...* □ *The boy was dressed as follows...* □ *Add the ingredients as follows...* **2** For **follow suit** see **suit**.

phrasal verb
follow up 1 You **follow** something **up** when you investigate it further: *I'm tempted to follow up her theory.* **2** You **follow** one thing **up** with another when you do the second as the next step after the first: *She followed up her magnificent success with a world tour.*

follower /'fɒloʊə(r)/ *noun*: **followers**
The **followers** of a person or of a religious, scientific or political philosophy are the people who support them or believe in them: *Nazism still has its followers.*

following /'fɒloʊɪŋ/ *adjective; preposition; noun*
▻ ***adjective***
1 The **following** day, week, month or year is the one after the one you have just mentioned: *On the following day he telephoned me again.* □ *She was due to leave for Hong Kong the following week.* □ *The following few hours were a nightmare.*

In referring to the immediate future, use *next*, or *the coming*, not *the following*: *I'm going to the theatre next* (or *this coming*) *Thursday evening and on the following Thursday.*

2 You refer to things you are about to mention as the **following** things, or the **following**: *We must deal with the following points...* □ *Would the following three delegates please contact me: Mrs Surtees, Dr Klein and Mr Leow.* □ *Prepare the dish in the following way...* □ *You will need the following: paper, scissors and glue.*
▻ ***preposition***
Following is used to mean 'after': *There was complete silence immediately following his announcement.* □ *Following her resignation a temporary headteacher was appointed.*
▻ ***noun*** (*used in the singular*)
A person, party or organization has a **following** if there are people who support them: *The Greens have always attracted a large following in the North West.*

folly /'fɒlɪ/ *noun* (*uncount or count*): **follies**
You call a course of action or a way of behaving **folly**, or a **folly**, if you think it is foolish or dangerous: *It's absolute folly to drive as fast as that in the fog.*

foment /fə'mɛnt/ *verb*: **foments, fomenting, fomented**
To **foment** discontent or ill feeling among people is to encourage it or make it increase. [*same as* **stir up**]

fond /fɒnd/ *adjective*: **fonder, fondest**
1 You are **fond** of someone if you like them or feel affection for them: *You know how fond I am of you.* □ *He was fondest of his second daughter Elizabeth.* **2** You are **fond** of something if you like it, or like doing it: *I had never been fond of shellfish.* □ *She was fond of criticizing people.* **3 Fond** means 'affectionate' or 'loving'; a **fond** look or word expresses affection: *Fond uncles and aunts used to send him money occasionally.* **4 Fond** expectations, wishes or dreams are foolish or impractical, and unlikely to be fulfilled: *It had been her parents' fond hope that she would win a scholarship to Cambridge.* — *adverb* **fondly:** *He glanced fondly out of the train window at the familiar countryside.* □ *I fondly imagined that the money would be easy to obtain.* — *noun* (*uncount*) **fondness:** *her well-known fondness for the odd glass of wine.*

fondle /'fɒndəl/ *verb*: **fondles, fondling, fondled**
To **fondle** a person or animal is to touch or stroke them affectionately: *He fondled the dog's ears lovingly.* [*same as* **caress**]

font /fɒnt/ *noun*: **fonts**
The **font** in a church is the bowl that holds the water for baptisms.

food /fu:d/ *noun* (*uncount or count*): **foods**
1 Food is anything that people or animals eat: *They're short of food and clothing.* □ *Have we got enough food and drink for the weekend?* □ *We specialize in vegetarian foods.* **2** (*uncount*) Something that is **food** for thought or argument is something that encourages you to think or argue: *Today's lecture has provided us with plenty of food for discussion.*

food poisoning /'fu:d pɔɪzənɪŋ/ *noun* (*uncount*)
Food poisoning is illness caused by eating food that has gone bad or contains bacteria.

food-processor /'fu:dproʊsɛsə(r)/ *noun*: **food-processors**
A food-processor is an electric machine for chopping or mixing food. [see picture at **kitchen**]

foodstuff /'fu:dstʌf/ *noun*: **foodstuffs**
A **foodstuff** is any substance used as food: *basic foodstuffs such as bread and cheese.*

fool /fu:l/ *noun; verb*
▻ ***noun*: fools**
If you call someone a **fool** you mean they are stupid or that what they have done is stupid: *We're not fools; we know what the real reason is.* □ *Who would be fool enough to believe that?* □ *I stood there quite unable to remember her name, looking a complete fool.* □ *I feel such a fool.*
▻ ***verb*: fools, fooling, fooled**
1 You **fool** someone when you trick them or deceive them: *Don't let them fool you into thinking you owe them money.* **2** Someone who **is fooling** is pretending something for fun, or behaving in a deliberately silly way: *Stop fooling, Dad!*
▻ ***phrases*** **1 a** You **make a fool of** someone when you trick them, or when you make them seem silly by doing something, or saying something about them, that makes people laugh at them: *No kid wants to be made a fool of in front of their classmates.* **b** You **make a fool of** yourself when you do or say something silly that makes people laugh at you: *She had never skied before and was afraid of making a fool of herself.* **2** You say that someone is **no fool** or **nobody's fool** if

you think they are too clever and cautious to be tricked or deceived. **3** You **play the fool** when you behave in a deliberately silly way, sometimes to amuse people.

> ***phrasal verb***
> **fool about** or **fool around** **1** You **fool about** or **fool around** when you behave in a deliberately silly way, sometimes to amuse people. **2** To **fool about** or **around** with something or someone is to interfere with them in an irresponsible manner: *I think he may be fooling about* [= having a sexual relationship] *with my wife.*

foolhardy /ˈfuːlhɑːdɪ/ *adjective*
A **foolhardy** person takes foolish and unnecessary risks: *It would be foolhardy to sell now.* [*same as* **irresponsible**; *opposite* **cautious**]

foolish /ˈfuːlɪʃ/ *adjective*
1 You describe behaviour as **foolish** if it is not sensible or wise: *It's so foolish to get yourself involved with drugs.* □ *foolish suggestions.* [*same as* **stupid**, **silly**; *opposite* **sensible**, **wise**] **2** Things or people that are so silly or funny that they make you laugh can be described as **foolish**: *He was wearing his usual foolish expression.* [*same as* **idiotic**]
▻ ***adverb:*** *I've behaved foolishly; I'm sorry.* □ (*sentence adverb*) *Foolishly, I forgot to ask for her phone number.* — *noun* (*uncount*) **foolishness:** *It's the height of foolishness to leave your child alone in a parked vehicle.*

foolproof /ˈfuːlpruːf/ *adjective*
1 You describe a plan or method as **foolproof** if you think it cannot go wrong: *a foolproof recipe for bread.* **2** A **foolproof** device or machine is one that is very simple to use, or has features that prevent you from using it wrongly.

foot /fʊt/ *noun*: **feet**
1 Your **feet** are the parts of your body at the end of your legs, on which you stand and walk: *The dog lay curled up on the floor at her feet.* □ *He had his left foot in plaster.* [see picture at **body**] **2** (*used in the singular*) The **foot** of something is its bottom or lower end: *Their house is at the foot of the hill.* □ *They found her lying at the foot of the stairs.* □ *She came and stood at the foot of my bed.* **3** (*plural* **feet** or **foot**) A **foot** is a measurement of length equal to twelve inches (30.48 centimetres): *a trench about 20 feet long and 4 feet deep* □ *a wall 2 feet thick and 40 feet high* □ *a terrifying 70-foot drop* □ *a 20-foot-high wall* □ *He was standing a few feet away.* □ *She was a little over five feet* (or *foot*) *tall.* □ *He was about six foot two inches.*

> Notice that you use **foot** as the plural especially when giving a person's height. [see note at **tall**]

▻ ***phrases***
1 You **fall on your feet** when something turns out unexpectedly well for you, or you are luckier than you deserve to be. **2** (**foots, footing, footed**) For **foot the bill** see **bill**. **3** You **get**, or **have**, **cold feet** about something you were intending to do when you become nervous about doing it. **4** You **get off on the wrong foot** with someone when you make a bad start in your relationship with them. **5** You **get**, or **rise**, **to your feet** when you stand up; you **jump to your feet** when you stand up quickly. **6** Someone who **has their feet on the ground** has plenty of common sense. **7** (*informal*) You use **'my foot!'** to express strong disbelief in what you have just been told. **8** Someone who **never puts a foot wrong** knows how to make a good impression and never does or says anything foolish. **9** You go somewhere **on foot** when you walk there rather than using any kind of transport: *You need to see Prague on foot.* **10** You **put your feet up** when you rest, especially lying on a bed or sofa. **11** Someone in authority **puts their foot down** about something when they forbid it, or refuse to let it continue. **12** (*informal*) You **put your foot in it** when you say or do something embarrassing and stupid, *eg* that hurts someone's feelings. **13** You **set foot in** a place when you go there: *I've never yet set foot in Austria.* □ *I refuse to set foot in that house again.* **14** You have to **stand on your own feet**, or **your own two feet**, when you must look after yourself and not depend on anyone to help you.

football /ˈfʊtbɔːl/ *noun*: **footballs**
1 (*uncount*) **Football** is a game between two teams of eleven, played with a large ball that players try to kick into the opposing team's goal. **2** A **football** is the ball used in the game.

footbridge /ˈfʊtbrɪdʒ/ *noun*: **footbridges**
A **footbridge** is a narrow bridge for pedestrians, *eg* over a motorway.

-footed /ˈfʊtɪd/ *adjective*
You use **-footed** in combination with a number or other word to describe something or someone in terms of their feet: *four-footed beasts* □ *web footed birds.*

foothill /ˈfʊthɪl/ *noun*: **foothills**
The **foothills** of a range of high mountains are the smaller hills surrounding them.

foothold /ˈfʊthoʊld/ *noun*: **footholds**
1 **Footholds** are holes or ledges in a rock face where you can put your feet when climbing. **2** You get a **foothold** when you establish yourself firmly in a position from which you can advance: *They seized this opportunity to gain a foothold in the health-food market.*

footing /ˈfʊtɪŋ/ *noun*
1 (*uncount*) You lose your **footing** when you slip and fall: *She lost her footing on the icy pavement and fell heavily.* **2** (*used in the singular*) Something is on a certain kind of **footing** if that is the kind of basis or foundation it has: *The business is now on a secure footing.* **3** (*used in the singular*) You are on a certain kind of **footing** with someone if you have that kind of relationship with them: *Students were expected to put forward their views on an equal footing with members of staff.*

footlights /ˈfʊtlaɪts/ *noun* (*plural*)
The **footlights** in a theatre are the row of lights set along the front edge of the stage.

footman /ˈfʊtmən/ *noun*: **footmen**
A **footman** is a male servant wearing a uniform, *eg* in a grand house or hotel, who does jobs such as opening doors for people and carrying their luggage.

footmark /ˈfʊtmɑːk/ *noun*: **footmarks**
Footmarks are footprints.

footnote /ˈfʊtnoʊt/ *noun*: **footnotes**
A **footnote** is a note at the bottom of a page, which adds information about something in the text above. [*same as* **annotation**]

footpath /ˈfʊtpɑːθ/ *noun*: **footpaths**
1 A **footpath** is a path or track for walkers: *Follow the footpath through the trees.* **2** A pavement or sidewalk can also be called a **footpath**: *Stay on the footpath.*

footprint /ˈfʊtprɪnt/ *noun*: **footprints**
Footprints are the marks that your feet leave, *eg* in

mud or snow or, when they are wet, on other surfaces: *We followed the two sets of footprints through the snow.* □ *The children left muddy footprints all over the clean kitchen floor.*

footstep /ˈfʊtstɛp/ *noun*: **footsteps**
Your **footsteps** are the the sounds you make with your feet when you walk or run: *He heard running footsteps behind him.*
▻ ***phrase*** You **follow in** someone's **footsteps** when you do the same thing as they did earlier: *He decided to follow in his grandfather's footsteps and become a doctor.*

footwear /ˈfʊtwɛə(r)/ *noun* (*uncount*)
Footwear refers to anything you wear on your feet, such as shoes, boots, sandals or slippers, and sometimes also socks.

footwork /ˈfʊtwɜːk/ *noun* (*uncount*)
Footwork is the movement of the feet in dancing or sport: *agile footwork.*

for /fɔː(r)/ *preposition*; *conjunction*
▻ ***preposition***
1 a Something that is **for** someone is to be given to them or used by them; you do something **for** someone when you do something to help or benefit them: *This letter's for you.* □ *A parcel has arrived for him.* □ *She writes books for children.* □ *What can I do for you today?* □ *We're holding a party for the new members of staff.* □ *There are plenty of things for the children to do.* **b** You work **for** someone if you are employed by them: *She works for British Telecom.* **c** You act **for** someone when you represent them or act on their behalf: *She's the MP for Greenfield.* □ *Speaking for myself, I'd rather wait.* **d** You feel a certain emotion **for** someone or something if that is how you feel towards them: *I'm so sorry for them.* □ *She had a passion for 17th-century music.* □ *I've no sympathy for him.* □ *You can only feel scorn for that sort of behaviour.* **e** You feel **for**, or feel a certain way **for**, someone when you sympathize with them, or feel that way on their behalf: *We feel for you in your sorrow.* □ *Congratulations on your success! I'm so pleased for you.* **f** You say something is good, bad, difficult, easy, or unpleasant **for** someone if that is how it affects them: *Exercise is good for you.* □ *It can't be enjoyable for them to spend so much time underground.* □ *What was it like for you both, meeting after so long?* □ *It isn't an agreeable job for anyone to do.* □ *Tasks like these are too complicated for an untrained person to tackle.* □ *Do you think the course is too difficult for you?* □ *Which date would be most convenient for you?* □ *It's normal for children to rebel at this age.* **g** You say that it is **for** someone to decide or deal with a certain matter if it is their responsibility to do so: *It's for her to decide what kind of wedding she wants.* □ *If you think he's wrong, it's for you to tell him.* [*same as* **up to**]
2 a A person or vehicle is bound or heading **for** a place when they are going there: *I was just leaving for the office.* □ *Is this the train for Ipswich?*

> Note the difference between *I caught the train for Norwich* [= the train that was going to Norwich) and *I caught the train to Norwich* [= I travelled all the way to Norwich].

b You use **for** to express purpose and preparation: *We must fight for freedom.* □ *We're aiming for completion by August.* □ *She's gone to Oxford for a conference.* □ *Let's meet sometime for a chat.* □ *She's been training for the big race.* □ *I haven't revised for my exam yet.* □ *We were not prepared for such a shock.* □ *I feel ready for anything.* **c** You use **for** in expressing needs, wants, desires and requests: *We waited an hour for the train.* □ *We'll have to queue for tickets.* □ *I've been hunting for that book.* □ *the desire for revenge.* □ *I was longing for her to make a mistake.* □ *I'm keen for you to win.* □ *There's no need for you to swear.* □ *They appealed to the president for mercy.* □ *I've decided to apply for the job.* **d** You have something such as time, money, space or ability **for** something, if you have enough of it: *There's no time for chatting.* □ *Have you enough money for the taxi?* □ *We've got room for one more person.* □ *I haven't the patience for a job like that.* □ *He spoke too fast for me to understand.* [see also **too**] **e** Something such as a device that is **for** something has that as its function or purpose: *Have you got any scissors for cutting hair?* □ *What's this lever for?* □ *It's a gadget for undoing staples.* □ *Here's a holder for your pencils and pens.* **f** You have permission **for** something when you have permission to do it: *You need a special licence for exporting these goods.* **g** A proposal or design **for** something is intended to be followed in obtaining or producing it: *Plans for a peace settlement are being drafted.* □ *Here's a nice pattern for a maternity dress.* □ *Any suggestions for a title?* **h** You have something **for** a meal if that is what you eat at it: *I like toast for breakfast.* □ *What's for dinner?* **i** You use **for** to indicate the future placing, use or treatment decided for someone or something: *I've chosen some curtains for the bedroom* □ *I'm afraid we've already selected someone for that job.* □ *Some of these pictures aren't for sale.* □ *That pile of clothes is for sending to Oxfam.*
3 You are **for**, or argue **for**, something or someone when you support them or are in favour of them: *I'm all for teaching children grammar.* □ *Are you for or against the proposal?* □ *I've always argued for a fairer tax system.* □ *Which candidate are you going to vote for?*
4 a You use **for** when giving reasons and explanations: *Her parents gave her a computer for passing her exams.* □ *I was fined for speeding.* □ *Have you a good excuse for being late?* □ *That's my main reason for asking.* □ *What are you doing that for?* □ *I can't account for the missing money.* □ *I got this book for my birthday.* □ *A man renowned throughout the world for his wisdom and humanity.* □ *the city of Lichfield, famous for its connections with Dr Johnson.* **b** You are unable to do something **for** some circumstance if the circumstance prevents you from doing it: *I couldn't see for tears.* □ *We couldn't speak for laughing.*
5 a You use **for** in giving thanks and apologizing: *Thank you so much for your letter.* □ *I was grateful for your help.* □ *I apologize for causing all this trouble.* **b** You use **for** in referring to payment and exchange: *I got the violin for only £50.* □ *They sold the house for some vast sum.* □ *Have you paid for the milk?* □ *She is paid far too little for the work she does.* □ *Guests are expected to pay for breakages.* □ *You must charge for your services.* □ *I gave them a cheque for £25.* □ *They promised to withdraw from the frontier in exchange for their prisoners of war.* **c** You use **for** to mean 'in proportion to': *They employ one woman for every five men.* **d** You use **for** in expressing scores and marks: *I got full marks for maths today.* **e** You take or mistake one thing or person **for** another when you wrongly think the first is the second: *Never mistake lust for love.*
6 a For can mean 'with regard to': *You can't beat our furniture for quality.* **b For** can mean 'in spite of': *She's quite nice for all her faults.* □ *He's rather serious for his age.* [= considering how young he is] □ *It's very warm for* [= considering that it is] *winter.*
7 A word **for** a particular thing is a word meaning it: *What's the term for telling lies in a court of law?* □ *What's the word for 'lazy' in German?*

8 a Something happens **for** a particular period if it happens or continues throughout it: *I lived in Leicester for 16 years.* □ *He's going to be here for a fortnight in June.* □ *We haven't heard from her for ages.* □ *I've finished with exams for ever.*

For and **ago** are used with phrases meaning a period of time; **since** is used with a specific date or time: *I've been waiting for two hours. I arrived here two hours ago. I've been waiting since 10 o'clock.*

b Something that extends or continues **for** a certain distance extends or continues that far: *roadworks for the next six miles.* **c** An appointment **for** a particular time or day is at that time or on that day: *I've got a dental appointment for 12.00 on 28 May.* □ *The next meeting is scheduled for Tuesday morning.* **d** You are invited somewhere at 7.30 **for** 8.0 o'clock if you are expected to arrive any time after 7.30 so as to be ready to start at 8 o'clock.

▷ ***conjunction*** *(old)*

For means the same as 'because': *He remained silent, for there was nothing he could say.*

▷ ***phrases*** **1** (*informal*) You say someone is **for it** when you expect them to be punished for something. **2** You say that something might, or might not, be so **if it had not been for**, or **was not for**, some person or circumstance if that person or circumstance is responsible for it being so: *We'd never have got home alive if it hadn't been for you.* □ *I could be away skiing for the weekend if it wasn't for this stupid exam on Monday.*

forage /ˈfɒrɪdʒ/ *verb*: **forages, foraging, foraged**

1 Animals or soldiers **forage** when they search for food. **2** You **forage** for something when you hunt for it: *She foraged about in the cupboard for some clean bed linen.*

foray /ˈfɒreɪ/ *noun*: **forays**

1 Soldiers make a **foray** into enemy territory when they enter it briefly to steal supplies. [*same as* **raid**] **2** You make a **foray** somewhere when you go out of doors for some purpose: *I rarely go out, apart from the odd foray to collect milk and newspapers.* **3** Someone makes a **foray** into a new activity when they try it: *That was the year he made a foray into local politics.*

forbade /fɔːˈbad/ or /fəˈbeɪd/ *verb*

Forbade is the past tense of **forbid**.

forbear /fɔːˈbɛə(r)/ *verb*: **forbears, forbearing, forbore, forborne**

You **forbear** to do something that might upset someone when you do not do it: *I forbore to tell her the real reason for the company's decision.*

forbearing /ˈfɔːbɛərɪŋ/ *adjective*

A **forbearing** person is someone who is patient, kind and understanding with people whom they might be justified in getting angry with. [*same as* **tolerant, patient, indulgent**] — *noun* (*uncount*) **forbearance:** *We wish to thank members of the public for the forbearance they have shown during this period of disruption.* [*same as* **patience, understanding, indulgence, tolerance**]

forbid /fəˈbɪd/ *verb*: **forbids, forbidding, forbade, forbidden**

1 You **forbid** someone to do something when you order them not to do it: *I forbade them to disturb her.* □ *We were forbidden to take calculators into the exam.* □ *There's no law forbidding activities of this sort.* **2** Circumstances **forbid** something if they prevent it or do not allow it: *Shortness of time forbids me to speak longer.* □ *The state of his heart forbids anything more strenuous than a short daily walk.*

▷ ***phrase*** You say **God forbid**, or **Heaven forbid**, that something should happen if you don't want it to happen: *Heaven forbid that I should do anything to hurt her feelings.*

forbidden /fəˈbɪdən/ *adjective*

1 Something is **forbidden** if it is not allowed: *Running in the corridors is forbidden.* **2 Forbidden** ground is an area where you are not allowed to go: *The vegetable garden was forbidden territory for the children.* **3** A **forbidden** subject is one that you are not allowed to mention: *Sex was a forbidden topic in our family.* [*same as* **taboo**]

forbidding /fəˈbɪdɪŋ/ *adjective*

You describe something as **forbidding** if you think it is frightening or threatening: *forbidding-looking mountains.* [*same as* **menacing, sinister**]

forbore /fɔːˈbɔː(r)/ and **forborne** /fɔːˈbɔːn/ *verb*

Forbore and **forborne** are the past tense and the past participle of **forbear**.

force /fɔːs/ *verb*; *noun*

▷ ***verb***: **forces, forcing, forced**

1 You **force** someone to do something they do not want to do when you make them do it: *They forced her to sign the agreement.* □ *I forced myself to look grateful.* □ *She managed to force a weak smile.* □ *Apparently the police had forced the confession from him.* **2** You **are forced** to do something you do not want to do when circumstances give you no alternative: *We were forced to sell the house and move to a cheaper area.* □ *I find myself forced to ask for your resignation.* **3** You **force** your ideas or opinions on people when you make them hear them or accept them. **4** You **force** people or things into a certain position if you make them go into it, especially by using physical strength: *The invading troops had been forced back to the frontier.* □ *You shouldn't be forcing your feet into shoes that are too small for you.* □ *I forced his arm behind his back.* **5** You **force** your way somewhere when you get there by physical strength or violence, or by determination, especially if it involves hurting other people: *They forced their way into the house by breaking down the door.* □ *We forced our way through the crowd.* □ *He forced his way to the senior management post.* **6** To **force** a lock on a door or lid, or **force** a door or lid open, is to open it by breaking the lock. **7** To **force** plants or fruit is to treat them in a special way that makes them grow or ripen unnaturally quickly.

▷ ***noun***: **forces**

1 (*uncount*) Things are achieved by **force** when military power or violent physical means are used to achieve them: *The government had no right to use force in dealing with the strike.* □ *NATO has threatened the aggressors with force if they refuse to stop bombarding the city.* **2** (*uncount*) The **force** with which you push, pull or hit something is the amount of strength, energy, effort or power you use: *My fist caught his chin with tremendous force.* [*same as* **impetus, momentum**] **3** (*uncount*) You express yourself with **force** when you speak or write in strong and sincere language. **4** (*used in the singular*) The **force** of a word in a particular context is its meaning. **5** A person, organization or country that is considered to have important influence is called a **force**: *By the 1960s we were no longer a force in international politics.* **6** A person or thing that is described as a **force** for good or evil is a good or bad influence in society: *On the whole organizations such as the Scouts are a force for good.* **7** (*physics*) A power that has a pulling or pushing effect is a **force**: *the force of gravity.* **8** Other unseen powers are also called **forces**: *the forces of nature.* **9** (*uncount*) **Force** is used in specifying wind speed: *a force-10 gale.*

10 A military body is a **force; the forces** or **the** armed **forces** are a nation's armed services: *He advanced into the mountains with a small, highly trained force of men.* **11** Any body of people organized to do a particular job may be called a **force**: *We have an extremely high-powered workforce engaged on this project.*

▻ ***phrases*** **1 a** You achieve something by **force of** will if you achieve it because of your determination to do so. **b** You do something from **force of** habit if you do it automatically, because you are so used to doing it: *Sometimes she set two places at the table from force of habit.* **2** For **force someone's hand** see **hand**. **3 a** A rule, law or arrangement is **in force** when it is in use and must be obeyed: *The parking restrictions are in force between 8.30 am and 5.30 pm.* ▫ *The new pay arrangements come into force on 1 January.* **b** People or things arrive **in force** when they come in large numbers: *The police were out in force on the morning of the President's visit.* **4** You **join** forces with someone when you start working together with them for a common purpose: *The fifth- and sixth-year students joined forces to put on an end-of-term show.*

forced /'fɔːst/ *adjective*
1 A **forced** smile or laugh is an unnatural one that you produce with an effort: *The laughter sounded forced.* **2 Forced** labour is compulsory hard labour carried out as a punishment for crime. **3** A pilot performs a **forced** landing when he or she lands an aircraft somewhere in an emergency.

forceful /'fɔːsfəl/ *adjective*
1 A **forceful** person expresses their opinions and wishes strongly and confidently, and is good at convincing and persuading other people: *her forceful personality.* **2** A **forceful** argument is a strong and believable one. [*same as* **convincing**, **powerful**; *opposite* **weak**, **feeble**] **3** Something is a **forceful** warning or reminder of something if it forces you to be aware of or remember it. [*same as* **forcible**, **powerful**] — *adverb* **forcefully:** *Today's two deaths forcefully remind us of the dangers of winter hill-walking.* ▫ *She put her point of view forcefully.*

forceps /'fɔːseps/ *noun* (*plural*)
A pair of **forceps** is a medical instrument with two narrow arms, used for gripping things firmly.

forcible /'fɔːsɪbəl/ *adjective*
1 Forcible means carried out using physical force or compulsion: *the forcible removal of the children from their families.* **2** The **forcible** expression of a view is strong and effective. **3** Something is a **forcible** reminder of something if it forces you to be aware of or remember it. [*same as* **forceful**, **powerful**] — *adverb* **forcibly:** *I was forcibly detained for three hours at the police station.*

ford /fɔːd/ *noun*; *verb*
▻ ***noun***: **fords**
A **ford** is a shallow part of a river where you can cross it on foot, or drive across it.
▻ ***verb***: **fords, fording, forded:** *We found a good place to ford the stream.*

fore /fɔː(r)/ *noun* (*used in the singular*)
▻ ***phrase*** Someone or something comes **to the fore** when they become important and well known: *She came to the fore in local politics during the 70s.*

forearm /'fɔːrɑːm/ *noun*: **forearms**
Your **forearms** are the lower parts of your arms between your wrist and elbow. [see picture at **body**]

forebear /'fɔːbeə(r)/ *noun*: **forebears**
Your **forebears** are your ancestors: *Her forebears had come from Ireland.*

foreboding /fɔː'boʊdɪŋ/ *noun* (*uncount or count*): **forebodings**
Foreboding is a feeling of approaching trouble or disaster: *When they had still not returned by 7 o'clock he began to be filled with foreboding.* ▫ *I had the usual forebodings about going abroad.*

forecast /'fɔːkɑːst/ *noun*; *verb*
▻ ***noun***: **forecasts**
A **forecast** is a statement about what is expected to happen: *The weather forecast is promising.* [*same as* **prediction**]
▻ ***verb***: **forecasts, forecasting, forecast** or **forecasted**
You **forecast** future happenings or developments when you say what you expect to happen: *Even at that early stage her teachers forecast a brilliant future for her.* ▫ *Snow has been forecast for tomorrow.* [*same as* **predict**]

forecourt /'fɔːkɔːt/ *noun*: **forecourts**
A **forecourt** is an open, usually paved, area in front of a building such as a petrol station.

forefather /'fɔːfɑːðə(r)/ *noun* (*literary*): **forefathers**
Your **forefathers** are your ancestors, especially your male ones. [*same as* **forebears**]

forefinger /'fɔːfɪŋgə(r)/ *noun*: **forefingers**
Your **forefinger** is the finger next to your thumb, which you use for pointing at things. [*same as* **index finger**]

forefront /'fɔːfrʌnt/ *noun* (*used in the singular*)
Someone or something that is at the **forefront** of some activity is important in it, or is leading the way forward in it: *His team of scientists were at the forefront of research into breast cancer.*

forego or **forgo** /fɔː'goʊ/ *verb*: **foregoes, forewent, foregone**
You **forego** something when you give it up, or are willing not to have it: *We had to forego our summer holiday this year.* [*same as* **go without**]

foregoing /'fɔːgoʊɪŋ/ *adjective* (*formal*)
You can refer to a statement you have just made, or material you have just mentioned, as the **foregoing** statement or material, or the **foregoing**: *the foregoing announcement.* [*same as* **aforementioned**]

foregone /'fɔːgɒn/ *adjective*
▻ ***phrase*** You say that the result of something is a **foregone conclusion** if you think it is obvious what the result will be: *It was a foregone conclusion who would win.*

foreground /'fɔːgraʊnd/ *noun* (*used in the singular*)
The **foreground** of a view, photograph or picture is the part that is nearest to the person looking at it: *That's our old house, with my sister in the foreground.* [*opposite* **background**]

forehand /'fɔːhand/ *noun* (*tennis*, *squash*): **forehands**
A **forehand** is a stroke performed with your arm out to the side and the palm of your hand facing forward. [see also **backhand**]

forehead /'fɔːhɛd/ *noun*: **foreheads**
Your **forehead** is the part of your face above your eyebrows and below the line where your hair begins. [see picture at **body**]

foreign /'fɒrɪn/ *adjective*
1 Someone or something **foreign** belongs to a country that is not your own: *foreign languages* ▫ *The caller sounded foreign.* **2** The **foreign office** is the department of a government that is concerned with **foreign** affairs, or relations with other countries; the **foreign** minister or **foreign** secretary is the government minister in charge of foreign affairs. **3** (*formal*) A **foreign** object, substance or body is something that has got into a

place where it does not belong. **4** Something is **foreign** to you if you have not experienced it before: *The technique was foreign to her.* **5** A mood, emotion or way of behaving is **foreign** to you if it is not at all typical of you: *He acted without hesitating; caution was foreign to him.*

foreigner /ˈfɒrɪnə(r)/ *noun*: **foreigners**
A **foreigner** is a person who belongs to a country that is not your own: *No wonder foreigners have difficulty with English pronunciation.*

foreleg /ˈfɔːlɛg/ *noun*: **forelegs**
A four-legged animal's **forelegs** are its two front legs. [*opposite* **hind legs**]

foreman or **forewoman** /ˈfɔːmən/ *noun*: **foremen** or **forewomen**
1 A **foreman** or **forewoman** is a man or woman in charge of a group of fellow workers. **2** In a court of law, the **foreman** or **forewoman** of the jury is the man or woman who speaks on behalf of the jury and announces its decision.

foremost /ˈfɔːmoʊst/ *adjective*; *adverb*
▻ ***adjective***
The **foremost** person or thing in any class is the most important or best: *Picasso, the foremost painter of the 20th century.*
▻ ***adverb*** You move somewhere head or feet **foremost** when it is your head or feet that lead or go first: *He felt safer sliding down the chute feet foremost.* [*same as* **first**]
▻ ***phrase*** **First and foremost** means before, or more than, anything else: *This dictionary is first and foremost a learning tool.* [*same as* **above all, primarily**]

forename /ˈfɔːneɪm/ *noun*: **forenames**
Your **forename** is your personal name, as distinct from your family name or surname. [*same as* **first name, given name, Christian name**]

forensic /fəˈrɛnsɪk/ *adjective*
Forensic describes scientific and medical work that is concerned with criminal investigations: *The objects found in the vehicle have been sent for forensic analysis.*

forerunner /ˈfɔːrʌnə(r)/ *noun*: **forerunners**
A **forerunner** of something is a person or thing that is an early example of it, or is a sign of its future coming or development: *The abacus is the forerunner of the modern computer.*

foresee /fɔːˈsiː/ *verb*: **foresees, foreseeing, foresaw, foreseen**
You **foresee** some future event when you realize it is going to happen: *This was a problem I had not foreseen.* [*same as* **anticipate**]

foreseeable /fɔːˈsiːəbəl/ *adjective*
1 You say that something is **foreseeable** if you expect it to happen: *A disaster like this was foreseeable and could have been prevented.* **2** The **foreseeable** future is the period during which you can predict what is going to happen: *The situation will remain as it is for the foreseeable future.*

foreshadow /fɔːˈʃadoʊ/ *verb*: **foreshadows, foreshadowing, foreshadowed**
One thing **foreshadows** another if it is a sign or warning of it, or if it is an earlier instance of it: *The recession was foreshadowed by the usual familiar run of events.*

foresight /ˈfɔːsaɪt/ *noun* (*uncount*)
Foresight is the ability to realize how things are likely to develop, and to take the right action: *They had shown extraordinary foresight in deciding which products to specialize in.*

foreskin /ˈfɔːskɪn/ *noun* (*count, rarely used in the plural*)
A man's or boy's **foreskin** is the loose skin covering the end of his penis.

forest /ˈfɒrəst/ *noun* (*count or uncount*): **forests**
A **forest** is a large area of land covered by trees growing closely together: *pine forests* □ *Acres of forest have been destroyed.*

forestall /fɔːˈstɔːl/ *verb*: **forestalls, forestalling, forestalled**
1 You **forestall** someone when you do something that they were about to do themselves, and so stop them doing it: *I was going to mention that when you forestalled me.* **2** You **forestall** someone when you realize what they are going to do, and do something to prevent them: *We guessed what they were planning and decided to forestall them.*

forestry /ˈfɒrəstrɪ/ *noun* (*uncount*)
Forestry is the management of forests, or the science of growing and caring for trees.

foretaste /ˈfɔːteɪst/ *noun* (*used in the singular*)
Something that is a **foretaste** of an expected future event is a brief experience that shows you what it will be like: *Her talk this evening has given us a foretaste of the kind of life we shall lead on safari.*

foretell /fɔːˈtɛl/ *verb*: **foretells, foretelling, foretold**
To **foretell** the future is to say correctly what is going to happen: *The prophets foretold how he would be betrayed.*

forethought /ˈfɔːθɔːt/ *noun* (*uncount*)
Forethought is the consideration you give to what may happen in the future, and the plans you make as a result: *With a little forethought you can save yourself a lot of money.*

foretold /fɔːˈtoʊld/ *verb*
Foretold is the past tense and past participle of **foretell**.

forever or **for ever** /fəˈrɛvə(r)/ *adverb*
1 Something that is going to continue **forever** or **for ever** will go on happening always: *We shall love each other for ever.* **2** You leave a place or person **for ever** if you intend never to return to them; you stop something **for ever** if you intend never to start it again; something is gone or lost **for ever** or **forever** if it will never be found again: *I've given up smoking for ever.* □ *Sometimes I feel that my inspiration has disappeared forever.* [*same as* **for good**] **3** (*informal*) Someone who is **forever** doing something does it a lot, especially too much: *He was forever criticizing his wife.* [compare **always**] **4** (*informal*) Something that takes or lasts **for ever** takes or lasts a long time: *The lecture seemed to last for ever.*

forewarn /fɔːˈwɔːn/ *verb*: **forewarns, forewarning, forewarned**
You **forewarn** someone when you warn them about something that is going to, or may, happen, or prepare them for it: *We were forewarned that she might not recognize us any more.*

forewent /fɔːˈwɛnt/ *verb*
Forewent is the rarely used past tense of **forego**.

forewoman /ˈfɔːwʊmən/ see **foreman**.

foreword /ˈfɔːwɜːd/ *noun*: **forewords**
A **foreword** is an introduction to a book, often by a writer other than the author.

forfeit /ˈfɔːfɪt/ *verb*: **forfeits, forfeiting, forfeited**
1 You **forfeit** something when you lose it as a penalty or punishment for breaking a rule: *He had to forfeit his driving licence.* **2** You say that someone **has for-**

feited their right to do something if their behaviour has shown that they do not deserve it: *She has forfeited her right to lead the country.* **3** You **forfeit** something when you give it up for the sake of something else: *They were forced to forfeit benefits during the period of the strike.*

forgave /fəˈgeɪv/ *verb*
Forgave is the past tense of **forgive**.

forge[1] /fɔːdʒ/ *verb*; *noun*
▻ ***verb***: **forges**, **forging**, **forged**
1 To **forge** metal or a metal object is to shape it by heating and hammering. **2** You **forge** a friendship, alliance or link when you succeed in establishing it: *I believe strong links have now been forged between our two countries.* **3** Someone who **forges** banknotes, documents, signatures or paintings copies them dishonestly or makes false ones that are intended to deceive people.
▻ ***noun***: **forges**
A **forge** is a workshop where metal is shaped into such objects as horseshoes, by heating and hammering.

forge[2] /fɔːdʒ/ *verb*: **forges**, **forging**, **forged**

> ***phrasal verb***
> **forge ahead 1** You **forge ahead** when you progress fast: *The building work is forging ahead.* **2** You **forge ahead** of other people when you take the lead in a race or competition.

forger /ˈfɔːdʒə(r)/ *noun*: **forgers**
A **forger** is someone who forges such things as banknotes, documents or paintings.

forgery /ˈfɔːdʒərɪ/ *noun*: **forgeries**
1 (*uncount*) **Forgery** is the crime of forging banknotes, documents, signatures or paintings. **2** A forged banknote, document, signature or painting is a **forgery**: *Her passport was a forgery.*

forget /fəˈgɛt/ *verb*: **forgets**, **forgetting**, **forgot**, **forgotten**
1 You **forget** something that you previously knew if you cannot think of it, or have not kept it in your memory; you **forget** how to do something that you could previously do when you can no longer think how to do it: *You never forget how to swim once you've learnt.* □ *I'd forgotten that you played the violin.* □ *He never forgets a name.* □ *I've forgotten all those poems I could once recite.* □ *They soon forgot about the incident.* □ *I forget when she last visited us, it's so long ago.* □ *I'll never forget watching the Pope's helicopter landing in the park.* [*opposite* **remember**, **recall**, **recollect**] **2** You **forget** something or **forget** to do something when you do not remember to deal with it or to do it: *I'm so sorry I forgot your birthday.* □ *Don't forget to ring me on Tuesday.* □ *I meant to watch that programme but I quite forgot to.* □ *I forgot all about collecting the dry cleaning.* □ *'Did you write to her?' 'No, sorry, I forgot.'* [*opposite* **remember**] **3** You **forget** something that you had intended to bring when you leave it behind accidentally: *I've forgotten my key again.* [*opposite* **remember**] **4** You **forget**, or **forget** about, a pain or worry if you stop being aware of it: *He forgot his headache in his excitement.* **5** If you tell someone to **forget** a person or thing you are advising them stop thinking about them: *You can forget your proposed skiing trip.* □ *I'd forget him if I were you.* **6** (*formal*) You **forget** yourself when you behave badly, or lose control of your emotions: *He forgot himself so far as to swear at the attendant.*
▻ ***phrases*** **1** (*informal*) You use '**forget it**' to mean 'it doesn't matter': *'I still owe you 5p.' 'Oh, forget it.'* **2 Not forgetting** can be used to mean 'and also': *There's the meal and the theatre tickets, not forgetting the taxi fare.*

forgetful /fəˈgɛtfəl/ *adjective*
Someone who is **forgetful** tends to forget things: *Please remind me nearer the date; I'm getting so forgetful.* — *noun* (*uncount*) **forgetfulness:** *She worried about her increasing forgetfulness.*

forgivable /fəˈgɪvəbəl/ *adjective*
You say that something is **forgivable** if you can understand it and therefore forgive it: *It was a forgivable error.* [*opposite* **unforgivable**]

forgive /fəˈgɪv/ *verb*: **forgives**, **forgiving**, **forgave**, **forgiven**
1 You **forgive** someone who has done something wrong when you stop being angry with them: *He never forgave me for what I said about him.* □ *I'll forgive him if he apologizes.* **2** You ask people to **forgive** you when you want to apologize politely: *Please forgive the intrusion, but there's a telephone call for you.* [*same as* **excuse**] **3** You say that people could **be forgiven** for making some mistake if you would expect them to make it in the circumstances: *She seemed so pleased with herself that you could be forgiven for assuming that she'd actually won.*

forgiveness /fəˈgɪvnəs/ *noun* (*uncount*)
You ask someone for their **forgiveness** when you ask them to forgive you for something: *I must beg your forgiveness for keeping you waiting so long.*

forgiving /fəˈgɪvɪŋ/ *adjective*
A **forgiving** person is willing to forgive other people for their faults: *She was a very forgiving wife; she had to be.*

forgo see **forego**.

forgot /fəˈgɒt/ *verb*
Forgot is the past tense of **forget**.

forgotten /fəˈgɒtən/ *verb*; *adjective*
▻ ***verb***
Forgotten is the past participle of **forget**.
▻ ***adjective***: *forgotten heroes.* □ *A long-forgotten poem.*

fork /fɔːk/ *noun*; *verb*
▻ ***noun***: **forks**
1 A **fork** is a tool for eating with, with three or four points, called prongs, for piercing and lifting food. [see picture at **tableware**] **2** A **fork** is also a long-handled garden tool with prongs, used for digging. [see picture at **tool**] **3** A **fork** in a road is the point where it divides into two branches; each of these branches can also be called a **fork**: *Take the left fork for Didsbury.*
▻ ***verb***: **forks**, **forking**, **forked**
1 A road **forks** when it divides into two branches; you **fork** left or right when you follow the left or right branch: *At the next junction you fork right for Bramhall.* **2** You **fork** food somewhere when you lift it there on a fork: *He forked some spaghetti on to his plate.*

> ***phrasal verb***
> (*informal*) You **fork out** for something when you pay for it: *I had to fork out £50 for the meal.*

forked /ˈfɔːkt/ *adjective*
1 Something that is **forked** divides into two branches or parts: *a snake with a forked tongue.* **2 Forked** lightning is a zigzag streak of lightning, or a streak with sharp bends in it.

forlorn /fəˈlɔːn/ *adjective*

1 A **forlorn** person is unhappy and all alone: *She looked a bit forlorn, standing there waving goodbye.* **2** A **forlorn** place is one that is deserted or neglected: *The old playground was a forlorn sight.* **3** A **forlorn** attempt is a desperate one that has no chance of succeeding; a **forlorn** hope is a vain one: *They made a last forlorn effort to rescue the trapped men.* — *adverb* **forlornly:** *The foghorn sounded forlornly across the bay.* □ *The door hung forlornly on broken hinges.*

form /fɔːm/ *noun; verb*

▻ ***noun*: forms**

1 (*count or uncount*) A thing's **form** is its shape: *The room was in the form of a letter L.* □ *In form, the creature looked like a dinosaur.* **2** A person or thing seen as a figure or object of a particular shape is a **form**: *Two familiar forms approached us through the mist.* □ *On the bed lay a form covered by a white sheet.* **3** (*count or uncount*) A particular **form** of something is a kind, type or variety of it, or any of the shapes or appearances it can occur in: *The exercise system turned out to be a form of Yoga.* □ *I dislike whisky in any form.* □ *Plato presents his arguments in the form of dialogues.* □ *property in the form of buildings or land* □ *The novel took the form of a series of love letters.* **4** (*count or uncount*) A **form** of a word is a way of spelling it, or one of the ways it appears according to its grammatical use: *You sometimes find the form 'gaol' instead of 'jail'.* □ *'Better' is the comparative form of both 'good' and 'well'.* □ *The word 'scissors' is plural in form.* **5** A **form** is a printed document asking you for particular pieces of information, and providing spaces for you write them in. **6** (*uncount*) **Form** is structure and organization, *eg* in a piece of writing or work of art: *Her lecture lacked form.* **7** (*uncount*) An athlete's **form** is his or her best possible level of performance: *It was a long time before she found her form again after her illness.* **8** In a school, a **form** is a class, or a set of classes containing children of the same age: *fourth-form pupils.* **9** (*old*) A **form** is a long seat or bench.

▻ ***verb*: forms, forming, formed**

1 People **form** a society or organization when they start or establish it: *The association was formed in 1922.* **2** Things **form** or **are formed** when they begin to exist or start developing: *Gradually an idea formed in her mind.* □ *A plan was forming itself.* □ *A friendship began to form between the two boys.* □ *These mountains were formed millions of years before the Himalayas.* □ *Lakes form as soon as the rains come.* **3** You **form** material into something, or **form** something from material, when you shape it: *Form the clay into a ball.* □ *He took three matches and formed a triangle on the tablecloth.* **4** People **form**, or **form** themselves, into a shape when they group themselves together in that shape: *We formed a ring round the demonstrator.* □ *The dancers formed themselves into two parallel lines.* **5** Things or people **form** a particular thing if they have the shape, role or function of that thing, or if they are what it consists of: *The rock ledge widened to form a kind of platform.* □ *The bookcase formed a right angle with the wall.* □ *This morning's lectures will form the basis of our discussions this afternoon.* □ *The story of their relationship forms the central theme of the novel.* □ *University students formed the core of the audience.* **6** You **form** words, or such things as tenses or plurals when you construct them: *With verbs such as 'burn' and 'learn' the past tense is formed by adding either '-t' or '-ed'.*

▻ ***phrases*** **1** You say that someone is **in good form** if they seem cheerful and in good health. **2** You are **on form** when you are performing your usual work or activity well; you are **off form** when you are performing badly. **3** Someone or something behaves **true to form** when they behave in their usual, typical, or characteristic way: *True to form, he made an excuse at the last minute and didn't come.*

formal /ˈfɔːməl/ *adjective*

1 Formal behaviour or speech is polite and serious rather than relaxed and friendly, and is used in official communications and situations; words used in this sort of situation are marked '(*formal*)' in this dictionary: *'Forthwith' is a rather formal word for 'immediately'.* [*opposite* **informal**] **2 Formal** occasions are events at which people have to behave politely and correctly and wear smart clothes: *a formal occasion such as a funeral.* [*same as* **informal**] **3 Formal** clothes are smart clothes that you wear on important, official or ceremonial occasions: *Formal evening dress will be worn.* [*same as* **informal**] **4** A **formal** statement, agreement or arrangement is an official one. **5** You work in a **formal** way if what you do is organized and methodical: *formal teaching methods.* **6 Formal** education is education that is officially provided at a school, college or university: *He had had no formal medical training.* **7** A **formal** design or arrangement is balanced or symmetrical, and sometimes rather complex: *a formal garden.* —*adverb* **formally:** *The letter was rather formally expressed.* □ *She usually dressed formally for the office.* □ *He has formally announced his resignation.*

formality /fɔːˈmalɪtɪ/ *noun*: **formalities**

1 (*uncount*) **Formality** is correct regard for the rules of social behaviour or official procedure: *They behaved towards each other with strict formality.* **2** (*used in the plural*) **Formalities** are certain official procedures or ceremonies that must be performed on particular occasions: *Once the formalities of the wedding ceremony and speeches were over everyone relaxed and enjoyed themselves.* **3** You say that some procedure is just a **formality** if it must be officially carried out for the sake of correctness or legality, but has no other importance or significance: *The interviews were a mere formality.*

formalize or **formalise** /ˈfɔːməlaɪz/ *verb*: **formalizes, formalizing, formalized**

You **formalize** something such as an arrangement or agreement when you make it official by putting it in writing and give it a definite or legal form.

format /ˈfɔːmat/ *noun; verb*

▻ ***noun*: formats**

1 The **format** of a book is its size and shape. **2** The way something such as a television programme is structured or presented is its **format**: *All the interviews followed a pre-arranged format.* **3** (*computing*) A **format** is a system of a particular type by means of which data are entered into a computer: *a word-processing format.*

▻ ***verb*: formats, formatting, formatted**

1 You **format** material or data when you organize them according to a plan, structure or design. **2** (*computing*) You **format** a disk when you prepare it for receiving and distributing data.

formation /fɔːˈmeɪʃən/ *noun*: **formations**

1 (*uncount*) The **formation** of something is the process of forming, making, developing or establishing it: *Since its formation, the society has been active in the cause of world peace.* **2** (*count or uncount*) Things that are in a particular **formation** are in a particular arrangement, pattern or order: *The girls were practising swimming in formation.* **3** A shape or structure in *eg* rocks or clouds is called a **formation:** *a spectacular rock formation.*

formative /ˈfɔːmətɪv/ *adjective*

You use **formative** to describe something such as an

early period of your life, which has had an important effect on your development: *I spent my formative years in East Africa.*

former /ˈfɔːmə(r)/ *adjective*
1 **Former** describes **a** the previous holder of a post: *former Prime Minister Edward Heath.* **b** something you once had: *in my former job.* **c** what someone or something used to be: *His wife is a former concert pianist.* **2** You refer to the first-named of two things or people that have just been mentioned as the **former** thing or person, or the **former**: *We approached both Bill and Jack and the former has agreed to stand for election.* [*opposite* **latter**]

formerly /ˈfɔːməlɪ/ *adverb*
Something that was **formerly** so was so in the past: *He was formerly in the oil business.* □ *The school was formerly a hotel.* □ *in Malawi (formerly Nyasaland).*

formidable /ˈfɔːmɪdəbəl/ *adjective*
1 A **formidable** problem, task, enemy or opponent is difficult to deal with or overcome and so is alarming or frightening: *a formidable enemy* □ *The difficulties proved more formidable than we had expected.* [*same as* **intimidating, daunting**] **2** Something that is **formidable** is great and impressive: *a formidable array of weapons.* — *adverb* **formidably:** *She was formidably well-qualified.*

formless /ˈfɔːmləs/ *adjective*
Something that is **formless** lacks shape or structure.

form of address /fɔːməv əˈdrɛs/ *noun*: **forms of address**
A **form of address** is a title that you use before a person's name, or a respectful name that you use in talking to them: *You use 'Father' as a form of address for a Catholic priest.*

formula /ˈfɔːmjʊlə/ *noun*: **formulas** or **formulae**
1 (*chemistry*) A chemical **formula** is the composition of a chemical compound expressed in symbols. **2** (*mathematics*) A mathematical **formula** is a rule expressed in figures and letters. **3** A **formula** is a method or plan for dealing with particular situation or difficulty: *They must sit down together and devise a formula for making peace.*

formulate /ˈfɔːmjʊleɪt/ *verb*: **formulates, formulating, formulated**
1 You **formulate** your ideas when you express or explain them in words. **2** You **formulate** a plan when you invent it and develop it in detail. — *noun* (*uncount*) **formulation** /fɔːmjʊˈleɪʃən/: *the formulation of a strategy.*

forsake /fɔːˈseɪk/ *verb* (*literary*): **forsakes, forsaking, forsook, forsaken**
1 You **forsake** a person when you leave them, or stop looking after them: *He was forsaken by his friends in the very hour of need.* **2** You **forsake** your principles when you break them or act against them: *She forsook her principles and begged money from a friend.* [*same as* **abandon**] — *adjective* **forsaken:** *a forsaken wife.* [*same as* **abandoned**]

fort /fɔːt/ *noun*: **forts**
A **fort** is a strong building or enclosure used as a military base or position.
▻ ***phrase*** You **hold the fort** when you supervise or run things in the absence of the person normally in charge.

forte /ˈfɔːteɪ/ *noun*: **fortes**
You say that something is your **forte** if you believe it is something you excel at: *Making speeches is not one of my fortes.*

forth /fɔːθ/ *adverb* (*literary or formal*)
1 You go **forth** from a place when you leave it; you bring something **forth** from somewhere when you take it out: *She reached inside her cloak and brought forth a small package.* **2** You set **forth** on a journey when you start on it: *They set forth very early.* [*same as* **out**] **3** A woman brings **forth** a baby when she has it. **4** To move back and **forth** is to go backwards and forwards, to and fro, or in all directions: *Students were going back and forth to lectures as usual.* [*same as* to and **fro**] **5** From this day **forth** means 'ever again' or 'always, after today': *She never spoke again, from that day forth.* [*same as* **on**]
▻ ***phrases*** **1** **And so forth** means the same as **and so on**: *a box full of paper clips, safety pins and so forth.* **2** Someone **holds forth** when they speak, especially for a long time: *He was holding forth about bad grammar as usual.*

forthcoming /fɔːθˈkʌmɪŋ/ *adjective*
1 **Forthcoming** events are due to happen soon: *our forthcoming spring publications.* [*same as* **impending**] **2** Something such as help is **forthcoming** when it is provided: *I rang the Post Office but no information was forthcoming.* [*same as* **available**] **3** A person who is **forthcoming** is willing to tell you what you want to know: *He was not very forthcoming about what he earned.* [*same as* **communicative**, **frank**; *opposite* **reticent**]

forthright /ˈfɔːθraɪt/ *adjective*
A **forthright** person has strong opinions and expresses them in a firm, frank and decisive manner: *Her forthright condemnation of the invasion.* — *noun* (*uncount*) **forthrightness:** *his reputation for forthrightness*

forthwith /fɔːθˈwɪθ/ or /fɔːθˈwɪð/ *adverb* (*formal*)
Something happens **forthwith** when it happens immediately: *She will assume the role of managing director forthwith.*

fortieth /ˈfɔːtɪəθ/ *determiner*; *pronoun*; *adjective or adverb*; *noun*: **fortieths**
1 (often written **40th**) The **fortieth** person or thing is the one numbered forty in a series. **2** (often written $\frac{1}{40}$) A **fortieth** of something is one of forty equal parts of it.

fortification /fɔːtɪfɪˈkeɪʃən/ *noun*: **fortifications**
1 (*usually in the plural*) **Fortifications** are walls and other defensive structures built around a place to protect it from attack: *The cruise took them on a tour of Malta's fortifications.* **2** (*uncount*) **Fortification** is the process of fortifying or being fortified: *I can give you a drink if you're in need of fortification.*

fortify /ˈfɔːtɪfaɪ/ *verb*: **fortifies, fortifying, fortified**
1 To **fortify** a place is to strengthen it by building walls and other defensive structures round it, to protect it from attack: *The town was fortified at the time of the Crusades.* **2** Such things as food and drink **fortify** you if they make you feel stronger and more energetic.

fortitude /ˈfɔːtɪtjuːd/ *noun* (*uncount*)
People show **fortitude** when they bear pain or misfortune bravely, without complaining: *She bore her disappointment with admirable fortitude.* [*same as* **strength, courage**]

fortnight /ˈfɔːtnaɪt/ *noun*: **fortnights**
A **fortnight** is a period of 14 days, or two weeks: *I'll be in Leeds during the second fortnight of April.*

fortnightly /ˈfɔːtnaɪtlɪ/ *adjective*; *adverb*
▻ ***adjective***
A **fortnightly** publication appears once every fortnight; a **fortnightly** event happens once every fortnight: *She mentioned it on one of her fortnightly visits.*
▻ ***adverb***: *The magazine used to appear fortnightly.* □ *We arranged to see each other fortnightly.*

fortress /ˈfɔːtrəs/ *noun*: **fortresses**
A **fortress** is a large fortified building such as a castle or fort, or a town surrounded by high walls or other defensive structures.

fortuitous /fɔːˈtjuːɪtəs/ *adjective*
Something that is **fortuitous** happens by chance and is usually helpful to you: *It was someone's quite fortuitous mention of the advertisement that found me in my present job.* [*same as* **chance**] — *adverb* **fortuitously:** *I learnt fortuitously that an expedition was already being planned.*

fortunate /ˈfɔːtʃənət/ *adjective*
1 People who are **fortunate** are lucky, *eg* in having what they need or want: *We must help those less fortunate than ourselves.* [*same as* **unfortunate, unlucky**] **2** A **fortunate** circumstance is one that is lucky for you: *It was fortunate for him that he had decided to take the later plane.* [*same as* **unfortunate, unlucky**] — *adverb* (*sentence adverb*) **fortunately:** *Fortunately, I've kept a copy.* □ *Fortunately for me, the train was late leaving.* [*opposite* **unfortunately, unluckily**]

fortune /ˈfɔːtʃən/ *noun*: **fortunes**
1 (*uncount especially old*) **Fortune** is chance, seen as a force in human affairs: *Fortune favours the brave.* [*same as* **fate**] **2 Fortune**, or good **fortune**, is good luck, and ill **fortune** is bad luck: *By an amazing stroke of fortune he found exactly what he wanted.* **3** (*used in the plural*) The **fortunes** of something such as war are unpredictable happenings that swing affairs this way or that. **4** (*used in the plural*) Your **fortunes** are the changes you experience in life, with regard to how well or badly things go for you: *She found a job and her fortunes improved.* **5** Someone who owns a **fortune** has a lot of money: *He was left a fortune by an uncle.* **6** (*informal*) You can call any large sum of money a **fortune**: *The cruise must have cost them a fortune.*
▻ ***phrases*** **1** Someone **makes their fortune** when they become rich. **2** Someone **tells your fortune** when they tell you what is going to happen to you in the future, after looking at something such as the lines on the palm of your hand.

fortune-teller /ˈfɔːtʃən-tɛlə(r)/ *noun*: **fortune-tellers**
A **fortune-teller** is a person who claims to be able to tell people what is going to happen to them in the future.

forty /ˈfɔːtɪ/ *noun*; *adjective*; *determiner*; *pronoun*
▻ ***noun***: **forties**
1 (*uncount or count*) **Forty** is the number or figure 40: *Two times twenty is forty.* □ *Four forties are 160.* **2** (*uncount*) **Forty** is the age of 40: *She got married at forty.* **3** (*used in the plural*) Someone who is in their **forties** is aged between 40 and 49. **4** (*used in the plural*) The temperature is in the **forties** when it is between 40° and 49° Celsius or Fahrenheit. **5** (*used in the plural*) The **forties** or **'40s** are the period between the fortieth and fiftieth years of a century: *died in the forties* □ *the eighteen-forties.*
▻ ***adjective***
Someone who is **forty** is 40 years old.
▻ ***determiner:*** *I've got at least forty cousins.* □ *a forty-year-old divorcee.*
▻ ***pronoun:*** *I gave up counting the errors after the first forty or so.*

forum /ˈfɔːrəm/ *noun*: **forums**
A **forum** is a place, or something such as a television programme or a journal, in which people can discuss things and express their opinions: *The producers of Question Time intended it to be a forum for public debate.*

forward /ˈfɔːwəd/ *adverb*; *adjective*; *noun*; *verb*
▻ ***adverb***
1 To move or face **forward** or **forwards** is to move or face in the direction in front of you or ahead of you: *He leant forwards and tapped me on the knee.* □ *He looked along the compartment for a forward-facing seat.* **2 Forward** and **forwards** also indicate progress towards something better or more modern: *We're not very far forward yet.* □ *As far as social responsibility goes, we are moving backwards, not forwards.* □ *This discovery represents a major step forward.* **3 Forward** is used for referring to the future: *We must look forward.* **4** You put a clock **forward** when you adjust it so that it shows a later time. **5** You put or bring an event **forward** when you reschedule it for an earlier time: *We shall have to bring the wedding forward a month.* **6** You put **forward** an idea when you suggest it to people. [see also **backwards and forwards**]
▻ ***adjective***
1 A **forward** movement is towards the direction in front of you: *The boat gave a forward lurch.* **2** A **forward** position, *eg* on a sportsfield, is a position at the front. **3 Forward** planning concerns the future. **4** A child that is **forward** for his or her age is advanced educationally. **5** (*derogatory*) A **forward** person is too bold in expressing their own opinions or in trying to advance themselves in front of others. [*same as* **pushy, presumptuous, assertive**]
▻ ***noun*** (*sport*): **forwards**
In football and hockey a **forward** is a player whose task is to score rather than defend the goal.
▻ ***verb***: **forwards, forwarding, forwarded**
1 You **forward** mail to someone who has moved house or is on holiday when you send it to the address they are at. [*same as* **send on**] **2** A circumstance **forwards** something if it helps it to progress: *Publishing articles is a sure way of forwarding your career.* [*same as* **advance**]

forwarding address /ˈfɔːwədɪŋ ədrɛs/ *noun*: **forwarding addresses**
Your **forwarding address** is the address you give someone such as a neighbour when you move house, so that they can send your mail on to you.

forward-looking /ˈfɔːwədlʊkɪŋ/ *adjective*
A person or scheme that is **forward-looking** is progressive and takes probable future developments into account. [*same as* **enterprising, go-ahead**; *opposite* **conservative**]

forwent *verb*
Forwent is the same as **forewent.**

fossil /ˈfɒsɪl/ *noun*: **fossils**
A **fossil** is the hardened remains of, or the impression left by, a prehistoric animal or vegetable in rock.

fossil fuel /ˈfɒsɪl fjuːəl/ *noun*: **fossil fuels**
Fossil fuels are fuels such as coal, oil and peat that have been formed naturally in the earth from the remains of plants.

fossilize or **fossilise** /ˈfɒsɪlaɪz/ *verb*: **fossilizes, fossilizing, fossilized**
The remains of an animal or plant **fossilize** or **are fossilized** when they harden and form a fossil.

foster /ˈfɒstə(r)/ *verb*; *adjective*
▻ ***verb***: **fosters, fostering, fostered**
1 You **foster** a child that is not your own when you take it into your family for a period of time, without becoming its legal parent: *He had been fostered from the age of four.* **2** To **foster** ideas, feelings or activities is to encourage them and help their development: *We must foster local talent in all its forms.*

▻ ***adjective***
Foster parents are people who foster a child; the child is their **foster** child, and they are its **foster** father and **foster** mother; their other children are its **foster** brothers and sisters.

fought /fɔːt/ *verb*
Fought is the past tense and past participle of **fight**.

foul /faʊl/ *adjective; noun; verb*
▻ ***adjective***
1 Something that is **foul** is dirty or disgusting: *a foul smell.* **2 Foul** air or water is polluted. **3** (*informal*) **Foul** means bad or awful, or emphasizes the severity of something bad: *He was in a foul mood.* **4** (*informal*) Someone is **foul** to you when they are rude or unkind to you. **5 Foul** language is rude, offensive or full of swearwords. **6 Foul** weather is stormy weather.
▻ ***noun*: fouls** (*sport*)
A **foul** is a move or action that breaks the rules; you commit a **foul** when you make a move that breaks the rules.
▻ ***verb*: fouls, fouling, fouled**
To **foul** something is to dirty it or pollute it: *We suspected that cattle had fouled the stream.*
▻ ***phrases*** **1** You **fall foul of** someone when you unintentionally do something that upsets them and makes them dislike you: *She fell foul of the headmistress soon after her arrival.* **2** You say you will achieve or obtain something **by fair means or foul** if you are absolutely determined to do so.

phrasal verb
(*informal*) To **foul up** something such as an arrangement or plan is to spoil it: *My holiday plans have been fouled up.*

foul play /faʊl ˈpleɪ/ *noun* (*uncount*)
Foul play is treachery or criminal violence, especially where someone is killed: *His death appears to have been from natural causes; foul play is not suspected.*

found¹ /faʊnd/ *verb*
Found is the past tense and past participle of **find**.

found² /faʊnd/ *verb*: **founds, founding, founded**
1 To **found** something such as an organization or institution is to start or establish it, often providing funds for its establishment and for its future: *King's College was founded by Henry VI.* **2** To **found** a town or city is to be responsible for its being built. **3** One thing **is founded** on another if it is based on it, or depends on it: *Their regime was founded on fear.*

foundation /faʊnˈdeɪʃən/ *noun*: **foundations**
1 (*uncount*) The **foundation** of an organization, institution or city is the event of its being started or established: *since the foundation of the college in 1879.* **2** A **foundation** is an organization providing funds for a charitable cause or a purpose such as research: *charitable foundations.* **3** (*used in the plural*) The **foundations** of a building are the underground structures of brick or stone on which it is supported. **4** (*usually in the singular*) Something that is the **foundation** of a social system, belief or theory is the principle on which it is based: *Respect for one another's freedom must form the foundation of life together in a community.* [*same as* **basis**] **5** (*uncount*) A story or theory that is without **foundation** is not supported by facts: *It's an argument with no foundation in fact.*

founder¹ /ˈfaʊndə(r)/ *noun*: **founders**
1 The **founder** of an organization, institution or city is the person who starts or establishes it, or is responsible for its being built: *Romulus, the founder of Rome.* **2** A **founder** member of a society is one of the original members of it.

founder² /ˈfaʊndə(r)/ *verb*: **founders, foundering, foundered**
1 A ship **founders** when it fills with water and sinks. **2** A business, plan or scheme **founders** when it fails.

foundry /ˈfaʊndrɪ/ *noun*: **foundries**
A **foundry** is a place where metal or glass is melted and poured into moulds to form various objects.

fount /faʊnt/ *noun*: **founts**
1 (*literary*) A **fount** is a spring of water. **2** You call a person or thing a **fount** of something if you regard them as a plentiful source of it: *She seemed to be a fount of information.*

fountain /ˈfaʊntɪn/ *noun*: **fountains**
1 A **fountain** is a decorative structure in a pool, producing jets or sprays of water. **2** A **fountain** or **drinking fountain** is a structure producing a jet of water for drinking.

fountain pen /ˈfaʊntɪn pɛn/ *noun*: **fountain pens**
A **fountain pen** is a pen fitted with a container that you fill with a supply of ink. [see picture at **office**]

four /fɔː(r)/ *noun; adjective; determiner; pronoun*
▻ ***noun*: fours**
1 (*uncount or count*) **Four** is **a** the number or figure 4: *Three and one make four.* □ *Three fours are twelve.* **b** a piece of clothing whose size is represented by the number 4, or a person who wears clothes of this size: *Are these shoes fours?* □ *Can I try on a four in this shoe?* □ *I take four in shoes.* **2** (*uncount*) **Four** is **a** the age of 4: *They start in the kindergarten at four.* **b** the time of 4 o'clock: *It gets dark by four in the afternoon.* **3** (*count*) A **four** is **a** a set of 4 things or people, *eg* the crew of a four-oared boat. **b** a playing card with four symbols: *Who's got the four of clubs?*
▻ ***adjective***
Someone who is **four** is four years old: *She's going to be four on Sunday.*
▻ ***determiner:*** *There are four reasons.* □ *We're waiting for the last four competitors to finish.* □ *It took four hours' work.* □ *Four minutes is all we need.* □ *a four-page booklet* □ *four-footed animals* □ *four-year-old children* □ *The mare is a four-year-old.*
▻ ***pronoun:*** *I can give four of you a lift.* □ *We four were the first to arrive.*
[For more examples of how numerals are used, see **eight**]
▻ ***phrase*** You are **on all fours** when you are supporting yourself, or moving along, on your hands and knees: *The tunnel was so low we had to crawl along it on all fours.*

four-letter word /fɔːlɛtə ˈwɜːd/ *noun*: **four-letter words**
Four-letter words are short words referring to sex or the excreting processes, that people consider offensive.

foursome /ˈfɔːsəm/ *noun*: **foursomes**
A **foursome** is a set or group of four people.

fourteen /fɔːˈtiːn/ *noun; adjective; determiner; pronoun*
▻ ***noun*: fourteens**
1 (*uncount or count*) **Fourteen** is the number or figure 14: *Twenty minus six is fourteen.* □ *Two fourteens are twenty-eight.* **2** (*uncount*) **Fourteen** is the age of 14: *They start specializing as early as fourteen.* **3** (*count or uncount*) A **fourteen** is a piece of clothing whose size is represented by the number 14, or a person who wears clothes of this size: *I usually need a fourteen in swimsuits.*
▻ ***adjective***
Someone who is **fourteen** is fourteen years old: *When he was fourteen he became seriously ill.*
▻ ***determiner***: *The expedition took fourteen weeks.* □ *a fourteen-year-old cat.*
▻ ***pronoun***: *I worked in England for three years and spent the next fourteen in Italy.*

fourteenth /fɔːˈtiːnθ/ *determiner; pronoun; adjective or adverb; noun*: **fourteenths**
1 (often written **14th**) The **fourteenth** person or thing is the one numbered fourteen in a series. **2** (often written $\frac{1}{14}$) A **fourteenth** of something is one of fourteen equal parts of it.

fourth /fɔːθ/ (often written **4th**) *determiner; pronoun; adjective or adverb; noun*
▻ ***determiner***
The **fourth** person or thing is the one numbered four in a series: *This is the fourth time you've been late.* □ *the 4th Duke of Bedford.*
▻ ***pronoun:*** *Our house is the fourth on the right.* □ *I get home on the 4th of October.* [see note at **date**] □ *when William the Fourth* (written *William IV*) *was on the throne.*
▻ ***adjective or adverb:*** *I was* (or *came*) *fourth in English.* □ *She came in fourth in the marathon run.*
▻ ***noun*** (often written $\frac{1}{4}$): **fourths**
1 A **fourth** of something is a quarter of it, or one of four equal parts: *Three fourths* (written $\frac{3}{4}$) *of the island's population suffer from diabetes.* □ *burns covering one fourth of the skin area.* [*same as* **quarter**] **2** (*uncount*) The driver of a motor vehicle is in **fourth** when he or she is driving in fourth gear, the gear above third gear.

fowl /faʊl/ *noun*: **fowls** or **fowl**
A **fowl** is a bird, especially a farmyard bird such as a chicken or turkey, that can be eaten.

fox /fɒks/ *noun; verb*
▻ ***noun***: **foxes**
A **fox** is a dog-like wild animal with a thick tail, especially the reddish-brown variety found in Europe and North America.
▻ ***verb***: **foxes, foxing, foxed**
Something or someone **foxes** you if they puzzle or confuse you: *Now you've completely foxed me.*

foxhunting /ˈfɒkshʌntɪŋ/ *noun* (*uncount*)
Foxhunting is the sport of hunting foxes on horseback, with a pack of dogs.

foyer /ˈfɔɪeɪ/ or /fɔɪə(r)/ *noun*: **foyers**
The **foyer** of a theatre or hotel is the entrance hall where people wait or meet each other.

fracas /ˈfrakɑː/ *noun* (*used in the singular*)
A **fracas** is a noisy quarrel or fight.

fraction /ˈfrakʃən/ *noun*: **fractions**
1 A **fraction** is a numerical quantity that is not a whole number, *eg* 0.25 or $\frac{1}{4}$ or $\frac{22}{7}$. **2** (*used in the singular*) A **fraction** of something is a small amount or proportion of it: *You can fly for a fraction of the normal cost.* □ *For a fraction of a minute I thought I was going to faint.*

fractionally /ˈfrakʃənəlɪ/ *adverb*
Fractionally means very slightly: *This brand is fractionally superior.*

fractious /ˈfrakʃəs/ *adjective*
You say that someone is getting **fractious** when they get impatient and bad-tempered: *The children were getting bored and fractious.* [*same as* **fretful**] — *adverb* **fractiously:** *The baby was crying fractiously.* [*same as* **fretfully**]

fracture /ˈfraktʃə(r)/ *noun; verb*
▻ ***noun***: **fractures**
A **fracture** is a break in something hard, especially a bone.
▻ ***verb***: **fractures, fracturing, fractured**
Something hard such as a bone **fractures** or **is fractured** when it breaks: *He fell off a swing and fractured his arm.* [*same as* **break**]

fragile /ˈfradʒaɪl/ (*AmE*/ˈfradʒəl/) *adjective*
1 Fragile things are easily broken or damaged: *fragile materials such as glass.* **2** Something that is **fragile** is easily spoilt or destroyed: *For a few months a fragile peace was maintained.* **3 Fragile** can also mean delicate: *the fragile beauty of her features.* **4** People look or feel **fragile** when they are in a weak state of health. — *noun* (*uncount*) **fragility** /frəˈdʒɪlɪtɪ/: *Bone increases in fragility as you get older.*

fragment *noun; verb*
▻ ***noun*** /ˈfragmənt/: **fragments**
1 A **fragment** of something that is broken is a small piece of it: *The road was covered with fragments of glass.* **2** A **fragment** of something is a bit of it: *I caught only fragments of their conversation.* □ *Only fragments of his poetry remain.*
▻ ***verb*** /fragˈmɛnt/: **fragments, fragmenting, fragmented**
Something **fragments** or **is fragmented** when it breaks or separates into small bits: *The glass will fragment on impact.* — *noun* (*uncount*) **fragmentation** /fragmɛnˈteɪʃən/: *the fragmentation of the party.*

fragmentary /ˈfragməntərɪ/ *adjective*
Something that is **fragmentary** consists of small pieces, not amounting to a connected whole: *Such accounts as we have are fragmentary and inconclusive.* [*same as* **incoherent, disjointed**; *opposite* **coherent, complete**]

fragrance /ˈfreɪgrəns/ *noun* (*count or uncount*): **fragrances**
Fragrance is a sweet or pleasant smell: *They enjoy the fragrance of flowers even if they can't see them.* [*same as* **scent, perfume**]

fragrant /ˈfreɪgrənt/ *adjective*
Something **fragrant** has a sweet or pleasant smell: *The air was fragrant with summer scents.*

frail /freɪl/ *adjective*: **frailer, frailest**
1 Something that is **frail** is easily broken or destroyed: *The frail boat was dashed to pieces against the rocks.* **2** Someone who is **frail** is in a weak state of health: *She looks older and frailer every time I visit her.* [*opposite* **robust, strong**] — *noun* (*uncount*) **frailness:** *his physical frailness.* [*opposite* **strength**]

frailty /ˈfreɪltɪ/ *noun*: **frailties**
1 Frailty is physical or moral weakness: *human frailty.* **2** A person's **frailties** are their moral weaknesses: *She loved him with all his frailties.*

frame /freɪm/ *noun; verb*
▻ ***noun***: **frames**
1 A **frame** is a hard main structure round which something is built or to which other parts are added: *We found an old bicycle frame and put wheels on it.* **2** A **frame** is a structure designed to surround and support something: *an ornate picture frame.* **3** Spectacle **frames** are the plastic or wire parts that support the lenses and go over your ears: *I needed new frames for my reading glasses.* **4** Your **frame** is your body, especially with regard to its size and shape: *He eased his tall frame into the chair.* **5** Any of the pictures that make up a strip of film is a **frame**. **6** A garden **frame** is a glass structure for protecting young plants growing out of doors. **7** A **frame** can be an arrangement of bars for some purpose: *The kids spent most of their time on the climbing frame.*
▻ ***verb***: **frames, framing, framed**
1 You **frame** a picture when you put it in a frame: *I must get this photograph framed.* **2** One thing **is framed** by another if the second surrounds the first like a frame: *Her small face was framed by a cloud of dark hair.* **3** You **frame** something you want to say in a

certain way if you express it that way: *She framed her reply as politely as she could.* **4** (*informal*) To **frame** an innocent person is to arrange things deliberately and dishonestly so as to direct suspicion for a crime at them.

frame of mind /freɪm əv 'maɪnd/ *noun* (*used in the singular*)
Your **frame of mind** at any particular time is the mood you are in: *I wasn't in the right frame of mind for concentrating on my essay.*

framework /'freɪmwɜːk/ *noun*: **frameworks**
1 A **framework** is a basic supporting structure for something, or a structure composed of horizontal and vertical bars or shafts: *The building will be made of concrete on a steel framework.* **2** A basic plan or system may be called a **framework**: *Now that we have a framework for the project we can start planning the details.*

franc /fraŋk/ *noun*: **francs**
A **franc** is the standard unit of money in France, Belgium, Switzerland and several other French-speaking countries: *a two-hundred-franc note.*

franchise /'frantʃaɪz/ *noun*; *verb*
▷ ***noun***: **franchises**
1 (*used in the singular*) The **franchise** is the right to vote, especially in a parliamentary election. **2** A **franchise** is also a right, privilege, or release from a duty, granted to a person or organization. **3** A business **franchise** is an agreement by which a business company gives someone the right to market its products in a certain area; the area concerned is that person's **franchise**.
▷ ***verb***: **franchises, franchising, franchised**
To **franchise** someone is to grant them a franchise.

frank /fraŋk/ *adjective*: **franker, frankest**
People are **frank** when they are open and honest in stating what they think or want: *Our discussions were frank and fruitful.* □ *Do you want my frank opinion?* □ *To be frank, I think you're making a mistake.* [*same as* **candid, outspoken, truthful**; *opposite* **evasive, insincere**] — *adverb* **frankly:** *Tell us frankly what you think.* □ (*sentence adverb*) *Frankly, I think you're talking nonsense.* — *noun* (*uncount*) **frankness:** *We appreciate your frankness.*

frantic /'frantɪk/ *adjective*
1 You are **frantic** when you are desperate, *eg* with fear or anxiety: *I had a frantic search for that cheque.* **2 Frantic** activity is hurried and often disorganized: *The last few days have been frantic.* [*same as* **hectic**] — *adverb* **frantically:** *She pulled frantically at the door handle.* □ *I rushed round frantically doing last-minute shopping.*

fraternal /frə'tɜːnəl/ *adjective*
1 Fraternal means relating to, or suitable to, a brother: *He gave her a fraternal kiss.* [*same as* **brotherly**] **2 Fraternal** also describes the relationship between groups of people who share the same aims or principles: *The other unions sent fraternal messages of support.* [*same as* **comradely**]

fraternity /frə'tɜːnɪtɪ/ *noun*: **fraternities**
1 (*uncount*) **Fraternity** is the relationship between brothers, or the friendship and affection that exists between people who are comrades and equals. **2** A **fraternity** is a group of people who belong to the same profession or have common interests: *the banking fraternity.*

fraternize or **fraternise** /'fratənaɪz/ *verb*: **fraternizes, fraternizing, fraternized**
You **fraternize** with people from another group when you meet or associate with them as friends: *Muslims and Christians fraternized with each other without apparent tension.* — *noun* (*uncount*) **fraternization** or **fraternisation** /fratənaɪ'zeɪʃən/: *Our parents frowned on any attempts at fraternization with the Catholic girls.*

fraud /frɔːd/ *noun*: **frauds**
1 (*uncount*) **Fraud** is the crime of obtaining money by dishonest means, deceit or trickery: *He was convicted of fraud.* **2** Something that is deliberately arranged to deceive people in an unfair or illegal manner is a **fraud**: *The trial was a fraud.* **3** A person who pretends to be something they are not is a **fraud**: *People who claim to cure baldness are just frauds.*

fraudulent /'frɔːdjʊlənt/ *adjective*
Something that is **fraudulent** is deliberately dishonest or intended to deceive or mislead people: *Her claims were fraudulent.* [*same as* **dishonest**; *opposite* **genuine, honest**] — *adverb* **fraudulently:** *He obtained the money fraudulently and must return it.*

fraught /frɔːt/ *adjective*
1 A situation is **fraught** with such things as danger, difficulties or problems if it is full of them: *Every step we take is fraught with risk.* **2** (*informal*) You say you are feeling **fraught** when you are anxious, worried or under stress.

fray[1] /freɪ/ *verb*: **frays, fraying, frayed**
1 Cloth or rope **frays** when the threads or strands along its edge or end, or at a place where it gets rubbed, become worn and loose: *The rope had frayed where it had been rubbing against the rock.* **2** Your nerves **fray** or your temper **frays** when you are under stress and you start getting angry and impatient. — *adjective* **frayed:** *frayed cuffs* □ *frayed nerves.*

fray[2] /freɪ/ *noun* (*often humorous*): **frays**
A **fray** is a fight, quarrel or argument, or any exciting and stressful activity: *I wasn't looking forward to joining the fray again on Monday morning.*

freak /friːk/ *noun*; *adjective*; *verb*
▷ ***noun***: **freaks**
1 If you call someone a **freak** you mean they are odd or unusual: *Hardworking students were treated as freaks.* **2** (*offensive if used about people*) A physically abnormal animal or human being is a **freak**. **3** (*informal*) A **freak** is also someone who is very enthusiastic about something: *fitness freaks.* **4** A **freak** can be an extraordinary occurrence: *freaks of nature.*
▷ ***adjective***
A **freak** occurrence is an extraordinary one: *She was injured in a freak accident.*
▷ ***verb*** (*informal*): **freaks, freaking, freaked**
People **freak**, or **freak** out, when they get very angry or abnormally excited.

freakish /'friːkɪʃ/ *adjective*
Something that is **freakish** is very odd or unusual: *He had some freakish habits.*

freckle /'frɛkəl/ *noun* (*usually in the plural*)
Freckles are small light-brown marks on the skin, especially of fair-skinned people. — *adjective* **freckled:** *His face used to get very freckled in the summer.*

free /friː/ *adjective or adverb*; *adjective*; *verb*
▷ ***adjective or adverb***: **freer, freest**
1 A person who is **free** is not a prisoner or a slave: *After 12 years' imprisonment he was again a free man.* □ *Under the new regime all political prisoners were set free.* □ *The wrong man was hanged, while the real murderer walked free.* **2** You are **free** when you are not restricted or controlled, but allowed to speak, act or move as you want: *You are free to draw what conclusions you please about his motives.* □ *You needn't go if you don't want to; it's a free country.* □ *a free press* □ *The countryside was a comparatively safe environment, in which children could be allowed to run free.*

□ *The animals are free to roam over the hills.* □ *They're not kept in cages but able to wander free.* **3** Something that is **free** is not tied, fastened, caught or trapped: *She pulled off the scarf and her long heavy hair swung free.* □ *Grab the free end of the rope.* □ *He caught hold of her arm but she pulled it free.* **4** Something is **free** if you can get it or do it without paying: *Children used to get free milk daily at school.* □ *Disabled people can park free in the city centre.* □ *Children under two travel free.* □ *I've been given two free seats for tonight.* □ *I got these tickets free.* □ *Information booklets are available free from the office.* □ *They replaced the defective tyre free of charge.*

▻ ***adjective***

1 A person or thing is **free** of, or **free** from, something unwanted if they are without it, or no longer have it or suffer it: *She was rarely free from pain.* □ *Keep the wound free of dirt.* □ *The river is never free of ice till April.* □ *Ideally all small villages should be free of heavy traffic.* □ *I'll deal with it when I'm free of my other commitments.* **2** You are **free** when you are not working, busy, engaged or having another appointment: *Friday's a free day for me.* □ *What do you do in your free time?* □ *Are you free to come for a drink?* □ *I'm free for lunch today if you are.* **3** Something such as a seat or table that is **free** is not not being used by someone else: *Is this chair free?* □ *The bathroom's free now.* [*same as* **vacant**, **empty**; *opposite* **occupied**, **engaged**] **4** Someone is **free** with something such as money, help or advice if they give it generously: *She was always free with her hospitality.* **5** A **free** translation expresses the sense of the original words without being absolutely exact. **6** **Free** progress, movement or communication is not hindered by obstructions or restrictions: *We must encourage the free flow of ideas.* □ *frank and free discussions.* **7** **Free** trade between countries is the importing or exporting of goods from one to another without customs duties: *Groups of the old Soviet-block countries set up their own free-trade areas.* **8** Your **free** hand is the one you are not already using for some task: *She was trying to wave away the flies with her free hand.* **9** **Free** movement is easy and relaxed: *Keep your arms loose and free as you walk.*

▻ ***verb***: **frees**, **freeing**, **freed**

1 You **free** a slave or a prisoner when you release them: *He was arrested by the police but later freed again.* **2** You **free** something when you remove it, or let it get away, from where it has been held or fixed: *She freed the bird from the net.* □ *I tried to free my hand from his grasp.* **3** To **free** someone of or from something unwanted is to remove it from them: *He had freed himself from debt at last.* □ *They longed to free their country of its foreign rulers.* **4** To **free** someone or something for some purpose, or **free** them up, is to make them available for it: *It may be possible to free some of our funds for training purposes.* □ *The children's departure for school freed her up to get on with her writing.*

▻ ***phrases*** **1** (*informal*) You say **feel free** to someone when you give them permission to do something: *'Could I use your computer?' 'Feel free.'* **2** (*informal*) You get something **for free** when you get it without paying; you do something **for free** when you do it without being paid: *He repaired her car for free.* **3** People or arrangements that are **free and easy** are informal and casual: *The librarian was rather free and easy about borrowing.* □ *a free-and-easy attitude to discipline.* **4** For **a free hand** see **hand**. **5** For **free of charge** see **charge**. **6** You **make free with** something that is not your own when you use it without permission, or make too much, or wrong, use of it: *My tenant was inclined to make free with the contents of my fridge.*

-free /friː /

-free is added to nouns to make **1** adjectives and adverbs meaning without payment of the charge mentioned: *He lived with them rent-free for several months.* □ *duty-free goods.* **2** adjectives meaning not having or not affected by the thing mentioned: *He was put on a fat-free diet.* □ *a trouble-free journey.*

freebie /ˈfriːbiː/ *noun* (*informal*): **freebies**

A **freebie** is something that you are given without having to pay for it, *eg* by some commercial organization: *We were issued with a tourist map and some other freebies.*

freedom /ˈfriːdəm/ *noun*; **freedoms**

1 (*uncount*) **Freedom** is the condition of being allowed to do or say what you want to, or go where you want to: *We are all entitled to freedom under the law.* **2** (*uncount or count*) A right or liberty is referred to as the **freedom** of something: *freedom of speech* □ *the freedom of the press.* **3** (*uncount*) Prisoners or slaves gain their **freedom** when they escape or are released: *After three years' incarceration he was finding it difficult to adjust to freedom.* [*opposite* **confinement**] **4** (*uncount*) **Freedom** from something unwanted is the condition of being without it: *The drug gave her complete freedom from pain.* **5** (*uncount*) **Freedom** of movement is the ability to move in different directions. [*same as* **mobility**]

freedom fighter /ˈfriːdəm faɪtə(r)/ *noun*: **freedom fighters**

A **freedom fighter** is someone who fights to free their country from a government they believe to be bad.

free enterprise /friː ˈɛntəpraɪz/ *noun* (*uncount*)

Free enterprise is competition between businesses without government interference or control.

free-for-all / ˈfriːfərɔːl/ *noun*: **free-for-alls**

A **free-for-all** is a fight, argument, discussion or rush for something, in which everybody joins: *What started as a gentle dialogue turned into a angry free-for-all.*

freehand /ˈfriːhand/ *adjective or adverb*

A **freehand** drawing is done without the help of things such as a ruler or compasses: *I could draw a pretty good circle freehand.*

free kick /friː ˈkɪk/ *noun*: **free kicks**

(*football*) A **free kick** is a kick allowed to a member of one side without tackling from the other side, as a penalty to the second side for breaking a rule.

freelance /ˈfriːlans/ *adjective or adverb*; *noun*; *verb*

▻ ***adjective or adverb***

Someone who is, or works, **freelance**, is self-employed, offering their services wherever they are needed, rather than having a contract with any one employer: *freelance reporters and photographers.*

▻ ***noun***: **freelances:** *She started as a freelance with an Edinburgh publisher.*

▻ ***verb***: **freelances**, **freelancing**, **freelanced**

You **freelance** when you work freelance. — *noun* **freelancer:** *Most of our editorial workers are freelancers.*

freely /ˈfriːlɪ/ *adverb*

1 You can talk **freely** when you can talk openly without being careful about what you say: *You're amongst friends; you may talk freely.* **2** You move or act **freely** when nothing stops, restricts, limits or controls you: *People may now travel freely between East and West Europe.* **3** Things that are **freely** available can be obtained easily: *Contraceptive devices should be freely available.* **4** You do something **freely** if you do it willingly, or with generosity: *He freely supplied us with the information we needed.* **5** You spend money **freely** when you spend a lot. **6** You perspire **freely** when you perspire a lot. **7** Parts of your body move **freely** if they have the full possible range of movement; you move them **freely** when you move them in a loose relaxed manner.

freer /frɪə(r)/ *adjective*
Freer is the comparative of **free**.

free-range /ˈfriːreɪndʒ/ *adjective*
Free-range eggs or other animal products come from hens and animals that are allowed to move about freely out of doors, as distinct from being kept in cages.

freest /ˈfriːɪst/ *adjective*
Freest is the superlative of **free**.

free-standing /ˈfriːstandɪŋ/ *adjective*
A **free-standing** cupboard or other piece of furniture stands by itself, as distinct from being attached to a wall or fitted into another structure.

freestyle /ˈfriːstaɪl/ *noun* (*uncount*)
In swimming, wrestling or skiing, a **freestyle** event is one that allows competitors freedom to choose their own style or programme.

freeway /ˈfriːweɪ/ *noun* (*AmE*): **freeways**
A **freeway** is a wide road built for fast-moving, long-distance traffic, with several lanes. [*same as* **expressway, motorway**]

freewheel /friːˈwiːl/ *verb*: **freewheels, freewheeling, freewheeled**
You **freewheel** in a vehicle or on a bicycle when you travel, usually downhill, without using the engine or the pedals.

free will /friː ˈwɪl/ *noun* (*uncount*)
Free will is the power of making choices that human beings are generally believed to have.
▻ ***phrase*** You do something **of your own free will** when you do it because you have chosen to, and not because you were forced to. [*same as* **of your own accord, voluntarily**]

freeze /friːz/ *verb*; *noun*
▻ ***verb***: **freezes, freezing, froze, frozen**
1 A liquid **freezes** or **is frozen** when it turns into ice or becomes solid as a result of cold: *The water has frozen in the pipes.* **2** A river or lake **freezes**, **freezes** over, or **is frozen** when it becomes covered with ice. **3** Pipes **freeze**, **freeze** up, or **are frozen** when the water inside them freezes and they become blocked. **4** You say it **is freezing** if the temperature has fallen below freezing point: *The weather forecast says it's going to freeze tonight.* **5** (*informal*) You **freeze** if you get very cold: *Don't stand and freeze out there; come inside.* **6** You **freeze** food when you preserve it by storing it at a temperature below freezing point; food **freezes** well or badly if it is suitable or unsuitable for preserving at below freezing point. **7** You **freeze** when you suddenly stop moving, or become unable to move, *eg* from fear: *He froze at the sound.* [*same as* **stiffen**] **8** To **freeze** prices, wages or salaries is to fix them officially at a certain level for a certain period, during which they must not be increased. **9** To **freeze** assets such as money or shares is to prevent them officially from being used. [see also **freezing, frozen**]
▻ ***noun***: **freezes**
1 A **freeze** or **freeze-up** is a period of very cold weather with temperatures below freezing point. **2** A **freeze** is a period during which wages and prices are officially fixed at a certain level and prevented from increasing.

> ***phrasal verb***
> You **freeze** someone **out** of an activity or a conversation when you discourage them from taking part in it by ignoring them or being unfriendly to them.

freezer /ˈfriːzə(r)/ *noun*: **freezers**
A **freezer** is a refrigerated container, or a compartment of a fridge, in which to preserve food at below freezing point.

freezing /ˈfriːzɪŋ/ *adjective*; *noun*
▻ ***adjective***
1 If you say it is **freezing** you mean the weather is very cold, or the temperature is very low: *It's freezing in here with that window open.* **2** Something is **freezing** if it is very cold: *The water was freezing so we didn't swim for very long.* [*same as* **icy**]
▻ ***noun*** (*uncount*)
Freezing is freezing point: *The temperature is not expected to rise above freezing at all today.*

freezing point /ˈfriːzɪŋ pɔɪnt/ *noun*: **freezing points**
1 The **freezing point** of any liquid is the temperature at which it freezes. **2** (*uncount*) **Freezing point** is the freezing point of water, 0° Celsius or 32° Fahrenheit: *For three weeks the temperature stayed below freezing point.*

freight /freɪt/ *noun* (*uncount*)
1 Freight is the transport of goods by rail, road, sea or air: *We paid an enormous sum in freight charges.* **2 Freight** is also goods transported by rail, road, sea or air: *a freight train.*

freighter /ˈfreɪtə(r)/ *noun*: **freighters**
A **freighter** is a ship or aircraft that carries cargo rather than passengers.

French /frɛntʃ/ *adjective*; *noun*
▻ ***adjective***
French means concerned with or belonging to France, its people or their language: *He's Belgian, not French.* □ *French wines.*
▻ ***noun***
1 (*uncount*) **French** is the language spoken in France, and in parts of Belgium, Switzerland, Canada and Africa: *We started French at primary school.* **2** (*plural*) The **French** are the people of France.

French beans /frɛntʃ ˈbiːnz/ *noun* (*plural*)
French beans are narrow, dark green bean pods that are eaten as a vegetable. [see picture at **vegetable**]

French fries /ˈfrɛntʃ fraɪz/ *noun* (*plural*)
French fries are narrow pieces of potato fried in oil or fat. [*same as* **chips**]

French horn see **horn**.

Frenchman /ˈfrɛntʃmən/ or **Frenchwoman** *noun*: **Frenchmen** or **Frenchwomen**
A **Frenchman** or **Frenchwoman** is a man or woman of French nationality.

French windows /frɛntʃ ˈwɪndoʊz/ *noun* (*plural*)
French windows are a pair of glass doors that open on to a garden or balcony.

frenetic /frəˈnɛtɪk/ *adjective*
Frenetic activity or behaviour is wildly energetic and rather disorganized. [*same as* **frenzied**, **frantic**; *opposite* **calm**] — *adverb* **frenetically:** *We rushed round frenetically buying stuff for the party.* [*same as* **frenziedly**, **frantically**; *opposite* **calmly**]

frenzied /ˈfrɛnzɪd/ *adjective*
Frenzied activity or behaviour is wildly excited and uncontrolled: *They sang to the accompaniment of frenzied shrieks from the teenage audience.* — *adverb* **frenziedly:** *She searched frenziedly through the collapsed remains of her home.*

frenzy /ˈfrɛnzɪ/ *noun* (*count or uncount*): **frenzies**
1 A **frenzy** is a state of violent excitement or mental disturbance: *She waited for news in a frenzy of anxiety.* **2** A **frenzy** of activity is a period of being very busy and energetic in a rather disorganized way.

frequency /ˈfriːkwənsɪ/ *noun*: **frequencies**
1 (*uncount*) **Frequency** is the condition of happening often: *I'm amazed at the frequency of this kind of coincidence.* [*opposite* **infrequency**] **2** (*uncount*) **Frequency**

is the number of times something happens: *Cases of criminal neglect are occurring with increasing frequency.* □ *Her visits increased in frequency.* **3** (*radio, electricity*) The number of times a function such as a vibration, alternation or wave repeats itself in a given time is its **frequency**; a high-**frequency** sound wave produces a high-pitched sound. **4** (*radio*) A radio **frequency** is the particular rate of waves per second at which the signal from a particular radio station is sent out.

frequent *adjective; verb*
▻ ***adjective*** /ˈfriːkwənt/
Something that is **frequent** happens often: *Her headaches became more frequent.* □ *He has frequent bouts of malaria.* [*opposite* **infrequent**] — *adverb* **frequently:** *I'm frequently asked that question.* □ *How frequently does this happen?* [*opposite* **infrequently**]
▻ ***verb*** /frɪˈkwɛnt/: **frequents, frequenting, frequented**
You **frequent** a place if you visit it often: *She hunted in vain for him in the pubs he normally frequented.*

fresco /ˈfrɛskoʊ/ *noun*: **frescoes** or **frescos**
A **fresco** is a picture painted on a wall, usually while the plaster is still damp.

fresh /frɛʃ/ *adjective*: **fresher, freshest**
1 Food that is **fresh a** has just been made: *fresh bread.* **b** is not old and stale: *Bread keeps fresh in the fridge for at least a week.* **2 Fresh** fruit and vegetables are not canned or frozen. **3 Fresh** flowers have just been gathered or cut. **4** Something that is **fresh** has been recently done or made: *a smell of fresh paint.* **5** A memory or experience that is **fresh** is a recent one: *I didn't know how he could go on rock-climbing, with the experience of his friend's death so fresh in his memory.* **6** Someone who is **fresh** from some place, activity or experience has just arrived from the place, just finished doing something or just had some experience: *Get students fresh from university and you can train them to do anything.* **7** A **fresh** amount or item is an addition to, or replacement for, a previous one: *He took a fresh sheet of paper.* □ *They'll issue a fresh report in the morning.* □ *a fresh cup of coffee* □ *After my divorce I wanted to make a completely fresh start.* □ *There had been a fresh fall of snow in the night.* **8** You describe something as **fresh** if it seems new and different: *Her writing was fresh and original.* **9** You feel **fresh** if you are feeling bright and energetic. **10** Things that are **fresh** feel, look, taste or smell pleasantly refreshing: *a cool fresh breeze* □ *a breath of fresh air.* **11 Fresh** water is water that comes from lakes, rivers or streams, and is not salty. [*opposite* **salt**] **12** The weather is **fresh** when it is rather cold or windy. — *noun* (*uncount*) **freshness:** *His style had a charming freshness.*

freshen /ˈfrɛʃən/ *verb*: **freshens, freshening, freshened**
1 You **freshen** something when you to make it cleaner, brighter, clearer or pleasanter: *We opened all the windows to freshen the air in the room.* **2** Wind **freshens** when it gets stronger: *The breeze freshened from the north.*

> ***phrasal verb***
> You **freshen up** when you get washed and tidy: *I'll just go and freshen up before dinner.*

fresher /ˈfrɛʃə(r)/ *noun*: **freshers**
A **fresher** is a first-year college or university student, especially at the beginning of their first term.

freshly /ˈfrɛʃlɪ/ *adverb*
Something that has been **freshly** made or dealt with in some way has recently been made or dealt with: *freshly baked bread.*

freshwater /frɛʃˈwɔːtə(r)/ *adjective*
1 Freshwater lakes contain fresh, not salt, water. **2 Freshwater** fish live in rivers or lakes, not in the sea.

fret /frɛt/ *verb*: **frets, fretting, fretted**
People **fret** about something when they worry or fuss about it, especially unnecessarily: *She was forever fretting about things like the shopping or cleaning.*

fretful /ˈfrɛtfəl/ *adjective*
People get **fretful** when they start behaving in a manner that shows they are feeling anxious, unhappy or discontented: *tired, fretful children.* [*same as* **fractious**]

friar /fraɪə(r)/ *noun*: **friars**
A **friar** is a member of a religious order that, especially formerly, worked as teachers of the Christian religion and lived by begging.

friction /ˈfrɪkʃən/ *noun*: **frictions**
Friction is **1** (*uncount*) the rubbing of one thing against another: *It's the friction that makes the match head burst into flame.* **2** (*uncount*) the resistance met with by an object that is moving against another or moving through liquid or gas. **3** (*uncount, or used in the plural*) quarrelling, disagreement or conflict between people: *The friction between mother and daughter was obvious.* □ *the usual staff-room frictions.*

Friday /ˈfraɪdɪ/ *noun* (*uncount or count*): **Fridays**
Friday is the sixth day of the week, coming after Thursday and before Saturday: *I'm leaving on Friday.* □ *She often works at home on a Friday* (or *on Fridays*). □ (*AmE*) *He doesn't work Fridays.* □ *Last Friday's meeting was postponed; we'll hold it next Friday instead.* □ *Goodbye! I'll see you on Friday evening.*

fridge /frɪdʒ/ *noun*: **fridges**
A **fridge** is a metal container kept cool by electricity, in which to store food to keep it fresh: *You'll find milk and eggs in the fridge.* [*same as* **refrigerator**]

fridge-freezer /frɪdʒ ˈfriːzə(r)/ *noun*: **fridge-freezers**
A **fridge-freezer** is a piece of kitchen apparatus consisting of a fridge and freezer as two separate compartments. [see picture at **kitchen**]

friend /frɛnd/ *noun*: **friends**
1 Your **friends** are the people that you know and like, and that you enjoy spending your time with: *He's a friend of yours, isn't he?* □ *She's my best friend.* □ *close friends* □ *an old family friend.* [compare **acquaintance**] **2** Someone who is a **friend** of or to a group, country or cause helps and supports them: *She was always a friend to those in need.* [*same as* **supporter, ally**] **3** Something that has often been mentioned or met with can be referred to as a **friend**: *The trouble is caused by our old friend the cold virus.*
▻ ***phrases*** **1** You **are friends** with someone if you like them and enjoy spending time with them: *I was friends with her at school.* **2** You **make friends** with someone when you start a friendship with each other: *We made friends with another couple on the boat.*

friendless /ˈfrɛndləs/ *adjective*
A **friendless** person has no friends: *She found herself alone and friendless in a foreign city.*

friendly /ˈfrɛndlɪ/ *adjective; noun*
▻ ***adjective***: **friendlier, friendliest**
1 You are **friendly** to someone when you behave in a kind, pleasant manner towards them: *I was only trying to be friendly to her.* □ *a friendly wave* □ *He remained on friendly terms with his former colleagues.* [*opposite* **unfriendly**] **2** You are **friendly** with someone if they are a friend of yours and you enjoy spending time with them: *My family had always been friendly with the Hamptons.* **3 Friendly** nations or organizations are those that support rather than oppose your own.

[*opposite* **hostile**] **4** You have a **friendly** argument with someone when you argue without trying to upset, offend or hurt each other. **5** A **friendly** environment makes you feel welcome, relaxed and comfortable: *a hotel with a friendly atmosphere.* **6** (*sport*) A **friendly** match is played for enjoyment or practice rather than as a serious contest.

▻ ***noun*** (*sport*): **friendlies**
A **friendly** is a friendly match.

-friendly /ˈfrɛndlɪ/
1 -friendly is used with nouns such as *user* or *customer* to make adjectives, usually relating to a product or service, that mean 'made easy for the person for whom it is intended': *reader-friendly dictionaries.* **2** 'environment-**friendly**' goods have been manufactured by a process that does not damage the environment or harm wildlife.

friendship /ˈfrɛndʃɪp/ *noun*: **friendships**
1 (*uncount*) **Friendship** is the having and keeping of friends: *the joys of friendship.* **2** (*count or uncount*) **Friendship** is the state of being friends with someone, or the relationship between two friends: *Our friendship has developed through the years.* □ *lose her friendship* □ *Many of my most valued friendships date from my university days.* **3** (*uncount*) **Friendship** between countries is the relationship of allies who support and help each other: *Britain's special friendship with the United States.*

frieze /friːz/ *noun*: **friezes**
A **frieze** is a decorated or carved strip running round the top of the walls of a room, or round the outside wall of a building.

frigate /ˈfrɪgət/ *noun*: **frigates**
A **frigate** is a naval vessel that accompanies and protects other ships.

fright /fraɪt/ *noun*: **frights**
1 (*uncount*) **Fright** is a sudden feeling of fear: *He was shaking with fright.* □ *Her eyes were wide with fright.* [*same as* **fear**] **2** A **fright** is a shock, or an experience that fills you with sudden fear: *You gave me a terrible fright coming into the room so quietly.* [*same as* **shock**]
▻ ***phrase*** People **take fright** when they get nervous or are suddenly filled with fear: *The deer smelt us, took fright, and ran off.*

frighten /ˈfraɪtən/ *verb*: **frightens, frightening, frightened**
Something **frightens** you when it makes you nervous or afraid: *The noise frightened us.* [*same as* **scare, terrify**]

> ***phrasal verbs***
> **frighten away** You **frighten away** a person or animal that might harm you when you make them afraid, so that they run away: *They kept the camp fire burning to frighten the bears away.*
> **frighten into** You **frighten** someone **into** doing something when you use threats to persuade them, so that they are afraid of not doing it: *They frightened him into confessing.*
> **frighten off** You **frighten** someone **off** when you make them afraid to continue with, or get involved in, something: *She wanted to join the expedition but I frightened her off.*

frightened /ˈfraɪtənd/ *adjective*
1 You are **frightened** when you are afraid or full of fear: *I'm still frightened of spiders.* [*same as* **scared, afraid**] **2** You are **frightened** when you are nervous or anxious about something: *He was frightened of seeming ignorant.* □ *I'm frightened that he'll have an accident one day.* □ *She was frightened to move in case she slipped again.* [*same as* **scared, afraid**]

frightening /ˈfraɪtənɪŋ/ *adjective*
Something that is **frightening** makes you afraid or anxious: *It all happened with frightening speed.* □ *The wind can be frightening at that height.* [*same as* **alarming, scary**] — *adverb* **frighteningly:** *We came frighteningly close to death.*

frightful /ˈfraɪtfəl/ *adjective*
1 Something **frightful** is frightening or terrible: *I'll never forget the frightful scene.* **2** (*informal*) If you describe something as **frightful** you mean it is very bad: *What frightful handwriting she's got.* **3** (*old, informal*) People use **frightful** to emphasize the severity of something bad, or for emphasis generally: *I've got a frightful headache.* — *adverb* **frightfully:** *I'm sorry; I've behaved frightfully.* □ (*intensifying, informal*) *That's frightfully kind of you.*

frigid /ˈfrɪdʒɪd/ *adjective*
A woman who is **frigid** does not respond easily to sexual stimulation.

frill /frɪl/ *noun*: **frills**
1 A **frill** is a gathered strip of cloth attached along one edge *eg* to a piece of clothing for decoration: *She wore a white blouse with frills at the wrists.* **2** (*used in the plural*) **Frills** are extra features or additions that are not very useful: *We just want the basic model without all the frills.* [*same as* **trimmings**] — *adjective* **frilled:** *a frilled tablecloth.*

frilly /ˈfrɪlɪ/ *adjective*: **frillier, frilliest**
Frilly clothes or furnishings are decorated with frills.

fringe /frɪndʒ/ *noun*: **fringes**
1 A **fringe** is a border of loose threads on a carpet, tablecloth, or piece of clothing: *He was wearing a white silk evening scarf with a fringe at each end.* **2** A **fringe** is hair that is cut so as to hang down over your forehead: *Who's the girl with short black hair and a fringe?* **3** (*usually in the plural*) The **fringes** of a place are the outer edges of it, or the part farthest from the centre: *on the northern fringes of the desert.* **4** (*usually in the plural*) Someone who is on the **fringes** of an activity is not very seriously involved in it: *He remained on the fringes of the controversy.* **5** The **fringe** of a profession is the area of activity of people who have moved away from its standard practices: *fringe medicine.* — *adjective* **fringed:** *She wore a fringed silk shawl.* □ *His eyes were deep blue, and fringed with thick dark lashes.*

frisk /frɪsk/ *verb*: **frisks, frisking, frisked**
1 Animals **frisk** when they jump or run about happily: *lambs frisking in the fields.* **2** (*informal*) The police or someone else with authority **frisks** you when they search your body with their hands to see if you are carrying weapons or drugs: *We got frisked at the airport.*

frisky /ˈfrɪskɪ/ *adjective*: **friskier, friskiest**
A **frisky** animal or person is lively and active and enjoys having fun: *a frisky puppy.* [*same as* **playful**]

fritter[1] /ˈfrɪtə(r)/ *noun*: **fritters**
A **fritter** is a piece of meat or fruit that has been covered with batter and fried: *banana fritters.*

fritter[2] /ˈfrɪtə(r)/ *verb*: **fritters, frittering, frittered**

> ***phrasal verb***
> You **fritter away** your time or money when you waste it or gradually use it up on unimportant or unnecessary things. [*same as* **squander**]

frivolous /ˈfrɪvələs/ *adjective*
1 A **frivolous** person has a cheerfully irresponsible attitude to life: *On first acquaintance she seemed silly and frivolous.* [*opposite* **sensible, serious**] **2** You are **frivolous** about something grave, serious or important when you treat it without respect: *I don't want to*

sound frivolous about so worrying an issue. [*opposite* **serious**] **3 Frivolous** things or activities are rather silly and unimportant, not useful and sensible: *I feel like doing something frivolous and amusing.* □ *a frivolous play.*

frizzy /'frɪzɪ/ *adjective*: **frizzier, frizziest**
Frizzy hair is full of very small wiry curls.

fro /froʊ/ *adverb*
▻ ***phrase*** To move **to and fro** is to move forwards and backwards or from side to side, or in all directions: *The gate was swinging to and fro.* □ *People were going to and fro about their business as usual.* [*same as* **back and forth**]

frock /frɒk/ *noun* (*rather old*): **frocks**
A **frock** is a woman's or girl's dress.

frog /frɒg/ *noun*: **frogs**
A **frog** is a small smooth-skinned animal with large eyes that lives near water and has long powerful back legs adapted for jumping.
▻ ***phrase*** You say you **have a frog in your throat** when your voice does not sound clear when you speak, because you have some phlegm on your vocal cords.

frogman /'frɒgmən/ *noun*: **frogmen**
A **frogman** is an underwater swimmer wearing a protective rubber suit and using breathing equipment. [*same as* **diver**]

frogmarch /'frɒgmɑːtʃ/ *verb*: **frogmarches, frogmarching, frogmarched**
You **are frogmarched** somewhere when you are forced to walk there by two people holding you firmly by each arm: *Shouting and protesting, he was frogmarched away to the cells.*

frolic /'frɒlɪk/ *verb; noun*
▻ ***verb***: **frolics, frolicking, frolicked**
Animals or children **frolic** when they run, play and jump about enjoying themselves.
▻ ***noun***: **frolics**
1 (*used in the singular*) A **frolic** is a period of running, playing and jumping about happily: *The cubs were enjoying a frolic in the sun.* **2** A **frolic** is also something silly done as a joke: *It all started as a harmless undergraduate frolic.*

from /frɒm/ or /frəm/ *preposition*
1 a From indicates the place that someone or something leaves when they move or are moved somewhere else: *She arrived from Paris last night.* □ *Where have you come from today?* □ *We drove away from the farm.* □ *He picked up a book from the table.* □ *The invaders came from across the sea.* □ *She'll be back from lunch soon.* □ *When will you be back from shopping?* □ *What time do they come home from school?* □ *I listen to the radio as I drive to and from work.* □ *Water was dripping from the tap.* □ *We fetched water from the stream.* □ *There's a funny smell coming from the kitchen.* □ *Someone's moved the keys from where I left them.*

> **From** can be used like **out of** to indicate the movement of something that was in something to a position outside it: *She drew the letter from* (or *out of*) *its envelope.* □ *He took a key from* (or *out of*) *the drawer.*

b From is often used with *to* or *into*: *He took the plane from Paris to New York.* □ *She drove from Inverness to Edinburgh in two hours.* □ *We moved the television from the sitting room into the bedroom.* **c From** is used with *to* in constructions with pairs of words to indicate continued or progressive movement: *We'll be travelling from town to town visiting museums.* □ *We went from shop to shop in search of pink ballet shoes.* □ *I went from one bookshop to another asking for a copy.* □ *His mind keeps jumping from one thing to another.* □ *Tolerance of change varies from person to person.*
2 a From is used, sometimes with *to*, in expressing distance, extent or direction between two points, rather than movement between them: *Our village is about seven miles from York.* □ *We're only a few yards from where the body was found.* □ *How far is London from York?* □ *We're not very far from home now.* □ *Snow covered the country from coast to coast.* □ *A narrow lane leads from the house to the beach.* **b From** is used to indicate a point or position at which you do something that involves a person or thing somewhere else: *You can see the beach from here.* □ *He rang me from his hotel room.* □ *I wish you would try and see things from my point of view.*
3 a From is used, sometimes with *away*, in expressing removal or separation: *Take that knife away from him.* □ *I'm trying to remove the stains from this jersey.* □ *Take three from seven and you get four.* □ *Two from five leaves three.* □ *She's away from home just now.* □ *He stayed away from work.* □ *She used to steal sweets from the supermarket.* **b From** is also used in expressing exclusion: *I omitted her from my list by mistake.* □ *They were banned from the club.* □ *He was expelled from school.* □ *They tried to exclude her from the discussion.*
4 a From is used, often with *to*, *till* or *until*, in expressions of time to indicate when a period or situation begins: *I'll be on holiday from 20 December onwards.* □ *He's been blind from birth.* □ *They knew from the moment they met that they'd be friends.* □ *Her neck problems dated from when she started using a desktop computer.* □ *From then on everything started going wrong.* □ *Start the story again from the beginning.* □ *The Museum is open from Monday to Friday.* □ (*AmE*) *Guides are available from April through September.* □ *I'm in my office from 9.00 till 5.00 every day.* □ *She lived in Malawi from 1957 till 1967.* □ *I've heard nothing of her from that day to this.* **b From** is used in constructions with pairs of words to express repeated occurrence or a continuing situation: *Problems like this do arise from time to time.* □ *Our life changed very little from one day to the next.* □ *We just lived from day to day hoping to go on surviving.*
5 From introduces the starting point in a range of amounts or other things: *Prices range from £10 upwards.* □ *They stock every sort of book from cheap romance to Plato.* □ *The job could take anything from two to four months.*
6 a From indicates a source or origin: *He got a letter from his mother this morning.* □ *Who did you buy your car from?* □ *He comes from a wealthy family.* □ *She's from Ireland.* □ *Where are you from?* □ *I'm not from round here.* □ *She painted the scene from memory.* □ *Water from streams isn't always pure.* □ *Here's the book I got the recipe from.* □ *a quotation from Shakespeare* □ *We need more information from them.* □ *There's a man from the Electricity Board at the door.* **b** One thing is made **from** another if the second is used to make the first: *He made a toy sword from two pieces of wood.* □ *a curtain made from an old blanket.* □ *Paper is made from rags or wood.* [see note at **make**]
7 From is used in expressing a change of state, such as the process of translation: *Nowadays students are not expected to translate from English into Latin.* □ *This next poem has been translated from Italian.* □ *She'd changed a lot from the girl I'd known at university.*
8 From is used in expressing ways in which one thing is attached or connected to another, or relates to it: *There was a mirror hanging from a nail on the wall.* □ *The shelves projected about 14 inches from the wall.*

9 From is used to express a cause or reason, or the basis for an opinion: *He's ill from overwork.* □ *Should any damage result from our activities, our company will pay.* □ *From the way she was screaming you'd have thought she was being attacked.* □ *I kept quiet from a feeling of shame.* □ *You could see from her face she was angry.* □ *I know from experience how difficult it is.*

10 From is used also **a** in expressing such things as protecting, saving, remaining, hiding, preventing and freeing: *We looked for somewhere to shelter from the rain.* □ *You must have a woollen hat to protect your head from the cold.* □ *Please keep them safe from harm.* □ *He needs a rest from his work.* □ *Is any food left over from last night's meal?* □ *I couldn't hide the truth from her for long.* □ *Can we prevent them from coming?* □ *May I be excused from attending this class?* **b** in comparing: *I can't tell one twin from the other.* □ *Is bravery any different from courage?* □ *bravery as distinct from daring.* [see note at **different**] **c** in talking about choice: *There's a great range of styles to choose from.* □ *She was picked for the job from a large number of applicants.*

frond /frɒnd/ *noun*: **fronds**
A **frond** is a long feathery leaf, *eg* of a fern, a palm tree, or seaweed.

front /frʌnt/ *noun*; *adjective*
▻ ***noun***: **fronts**
1 (*usually in the singular*) The **front** of something is **a** the part of it that is furthest forward: *She pushed her way to the front of the crowd.* [*opposite* **back**] **b** the part of it that is facing you, or is the important part that people usually see: *He spilt wine down his shirt front.* □ *Her dress buttoned down the front.* □ *Doctors now say you shouldn't put babies to sleep on their fronts.* □ *We can only afford to paint the front of the house.* [*opposite* **back**] **2** A **front** of a large or historic building is any side of it: *carvings on the west front of the cathedral.* **3** (*used in the singular*) The **front** of a vehicle or vessel is the part that faces forward, in the direction in which it moves: *The front of the truck was slightly damaged.* □ *She got into the front beside the driver.* [*opposite* **back**, **rear**] **4** (*used in the singular*) The **front** in a theatre or cinema is the area of seating closest to the stage or screen: *I booked a seat at the front.* [*opposite* **back**] **5** (*used in the singular*) The **front** of a book is its cover or its first few pages: *There's a key to the abbreviations at the front of the dictionary.* [*opposite* **back**] **6** In war, the area where soldiers are actually fighting the enemy is the **front**: *They were recalled to the front.* **7** You refer to a matter of concern or interest as a **front** of a certain kind: *I've had no luck on the job front.* **8** (*meteorology*) A **front** is the leading edge of a mass of warm or cold air: *A cold front is approaching from the Atlantic.* **9** (*used in the singular*) You put on a **front** when you behave differently from the way you feel: *She put on a brave front.* **10** A political movement may have the title **Front**: *the National Liberation Front.*
▻ ***adjective:*** *I sat down in the front row.* □ *There was the photo, on the front page of the newspaper.* □ *Have you locked the front door?* [*opposite* **back**]
▻ ***phrases*** **1 a** A thing that is **in front** is on the forward-facing side of something: *houses with gardens in front.* [*opposite* **behind**] **b** A person or thing that is **in front** is further forward than, or ahead of, others: *We talked to the couple sitting in the seat in front.* □ *Let's try and catch up the people in front.* □ *He stayed in front throughout the race.* **2 In front of** is used as a preposition. One person or thing is **in front of** another when they are facing them, or ahead of them, or beside the front part of them: *I hope I'll never have to stand up in front of an audience and give a speech.* □ *I was sitting a few rows in front of the others.* □ *Two men pushed in front of us.* □ *He ran straight across the road in front of a bus.* □ *The taxi-driver pulled up in front of the hotel.* [opposite **behind**] **3** You do something **in front of** someone when you do it while they are present: *I wouldn't dare say that in front of my mother.* **4** (*informal*) From an actor's or performer's point of view, the people **out front** are the audience. **5** (*informal*) People ask for money **up front** if they want to be paid for goods or services before they supply them.

frontage /ˈfrʌntɪdʒ/ *noun*: **frontages**
The **frontage** of a building is the wall facing the street.

frontal /ˈfrʌntəl/ *adjective*
1 Frontal means relating to the front: *Some portraits were frontal views and some were profiles.* □ *His troops were not prepared for a frontal attack.* **2** A **frontal** attack is also one that is direct and deliberate: *This campaign must be seen as a frontal assault on the government.*

frontier /ˈfrʌntɪə(r)/ *noun*: **frontiers**
1 A **frontier** is the border or boundary between two countries: *Our passports were inspected when we came to the Czech frontier.*

> **Frontier** and **border** are both used to refer to an international boundary: *the French-Spanish border* (or *frontier*). **Border**, but not **frontier**, is used for a boundary between the divisions of a country, or between countries united under one government: *the border between Scotland and England*; *the Welsh border*; *the Yorkshire-Lancashire border*.

2 (*used in the plural*) The **frontiers** of a subject, or of an area of activity, are its limits: *people who have advanced the frontiers of science.*

frontispiece /ˈfrʌntɪspiːs/ *noun*: **frontispieces**
A **frontispiece** is a picture at the beginning of a book, facing the title page.

front line /frʌnt ˈlaɪn/ *noun*: **front lines**
In war, the **front line** is the area where soldiers are actually fighting the enemy.

front-page /ˈfrʌntpeɪdʒ/ *adjective*
Front-page stories and pictures are printed on the front page of a newspaper because of their importance: *Most papers carried front-page articles on the discovery.*

frost /frɒst/ *noun*: **frosts**
1 Frost is frozen water vapour forming patterns on glass and a white powdery deposit on other surfaces: *The ground was white with frost.* **2** (*count or uncount*) There is a **frost** when the air temperature is below freezing point: *The young shoots may be damaged by a late frost.* □ *There were 12 degrees of frost in the night.*

frostbite /ˈfrɒstbaɪt/ *noun* (*uncount*)
Frostbite is injury to parts of the body, such as the fingers, toes and ears, caused by extreme cold.

frosted /ˈfrɒstɪd/ *adjective*
Frosted glass has a patterned or roughened surface that is difficult to see through: *The front door had two frosted glass panels.*

frosty /ˈfrɒstɪ/ *adjective*: **frostier**, **frostiest**
1 A **frosty** landscape is covered with frost. **2 Frosty** weather is cold enough for frost to form. **3** You describe someone's behaviour or attitude towards you as **frosty** if they are cold, unfriendly or disapproving: *She gave me a frosty stare.* [*same as* **cold**, **icy**; *opposite* **warm**] — *adverb* **frostily:** *He nodded frostily at me by way of acknowledgement.* [*same as* **coldly**; *opposite* **warmly**]

froth /frɒθ/ *noun*; *verb*
▻ ***noun*** (*uncount*)
Froth is a mass of tiny bubbles forming *eg* on the sur-

face of a liquid, or round the mouth in certain diseases. [*same as* **foam**]

▻ ***verb***: **froths**, **frothing**, **frothed:** *The sea frothed and foamed.* □ *The creature was frothing at the mouth.*

frothy /ˈfrɒθɪ/ *adjective*: **frothier**, **frothiest**
A liquid that is **frothy** has a lot of bubbles on its surface: *mugs of frothy coffee* □ *white frothy waves.*

frown /fraʊn/ *verb*; *noun*

▻ ***verb***: **frowns, frowning, frowned**
You **frown** when you draw your eyebrows together in worry, disapproval or deep thought: *She was frowning with concentration.* □ *He frowned angrily at me.*

▻ ***noun***: **frowns:** *He glanced at me with a frown of disapproval.*

> ***phrasal verb***
> People **frown on** or **upon** something if they disapprove of it: *Smoking is frowned on at most public gatherings.*

froze /froʊz/ *verb*
Froze is the past tense of **freeze**.

frozen /ˈfroʊzən/ *verb*; *adjective*

▻ ***verb***
Frozen is the past participle of **freeze**.

▻ ***adjective***
1 **Frozen** food has been preserved by freezing: *packets of frozen vegetables.* **2** A lake or river is **frozen**, or **frozen** over, when its surface has turned to ice: *All the ponds were frozen over in the London parks.* **3** You say you are **frozen** when you are very cold. [*same as* **freezing**] **4** You are **frozen** with something such as fear when you are too frightened to move: *I stood frozen with horror at the sound.*

frugal /ˈfruːgəl/ *adjective*
1 A **frugal** person is careful with money and spends very little on themselves: *She had a simple, frugal lifestyle.* [*opposite* **wasteful**] **2** A **frugal** meal is a small one that does not cost much. — *noun* (*uncount*) **frugality** /fruːˈgalɪtɪ/: *We quite enjoyed the frugality of the backpacking life.* — *adverb* **frugally:** *He eats frugally and doesn't smoke.*

fruit /fruːt/ *noun*; *verb*

▻ ***noun***: **fruit** or **fruits**
1 (*count or uncount*) A **fruit** is the seed-carrying part of a plant, especially if it has edible flesh: *The fruit of the tree looks like a cross between a tomato and a pepper.* □ *We grow our own fruit and vegetables.* □ *Breakfast consisted of cereal and a glass of fruit juice.* □ *apples, pears and other fruits*

> You use 'a fruit' to mean a kind of fruit: *mangoes and other exotic fruits*. A single apple, pear, banana or orange is referred to as 'a piece of fruit': *Eat a couple of pieces of fruit each day*.

2 (*uncount or used in the plural*) The **fruit** or **fruits** of something you have done are its results: *The present book is the fruit of twenty years' research.* **3** Dried **fruits** are fruits such as currants, raisins and sultanas, preserved by being dried in the sun. **4** Soft **fruits** are small fruits and berries such as blackcurrants, blackberries, raspberries and strawberries whose many small seeds are enclosed in soft flesh.

▻ ***verb***: **fruits, fruiting, fruited**
A tree or bush **fruits** when it produces fruit.

▻ ***phrase*** Something you do **bears fruit** when it has successful results: *The months of painstaking investigation and analysis were at last bearing fruit.*

fruitcake /ˈfruːtkeɪk/ *noun* (*count or uncount*): **fruitcakes**
A **fruitcake** is a cake containing dried fruits.

fruitful /ˈfruːtfəl/ *adjective*
Something that is **fruitful** produces good or useful results: *I hope the discussions proved fruitful?* [*same as* **productive**; *opposite* **fruitless**]

fruition /frʊˈɪʃən/ *noun* (*uncount*)
Your efforts come to **fruition** when you achieve what you have been aiming for.

fruitless /ˈfruːtləs/ *adjective*
Something that is **fruitless** does not produce useful

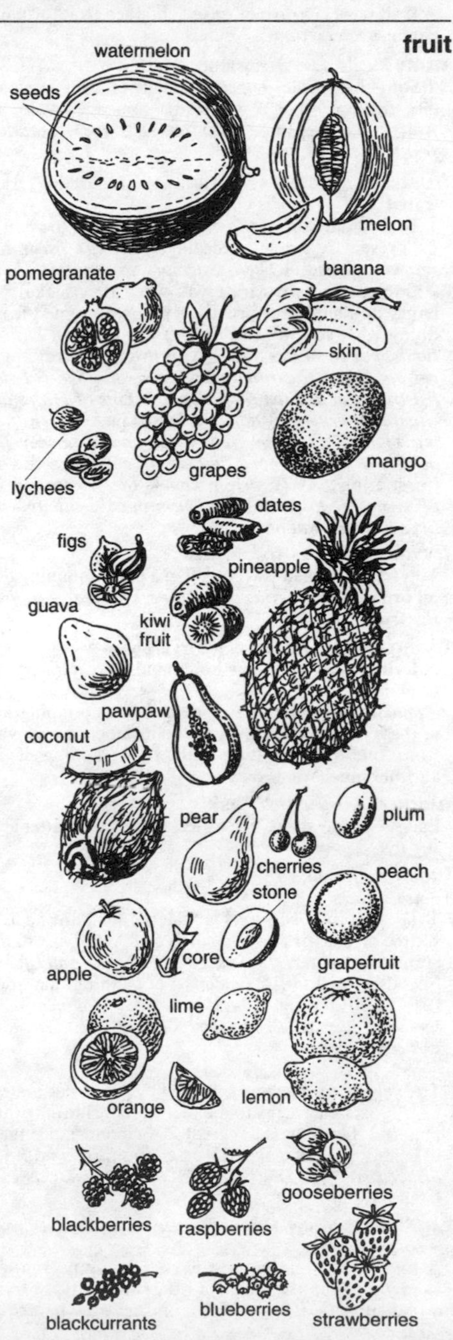

results: *a fruitless search* □ *hours of fruitless discussion.* [*same as* **unproductives**; *opposite* **productive, fruitful**]

fruit machine /ˈfruːt məʃiːn/ *noun*: **fruit machines**
A **fruit machine** is a machine used for gambling that you operate by inserting a coin and pulling a handle, which makes pictures of fruits appear in a variety of combinations, some of which win a prize.

fruit salad /fruːt ˈsaləd/ *noun* (*uncount or count*): **fruit salads**
A **fruit salad** is a dish of mixed chopped fruits, usually eaten as a dessert.

fruity /ˈfruːtɪ/ *adjective*: **fruitier, fruitiest**
1 Something **fruity** tastes or smells of fruit: *a pleasant, fruity wine.* **2** You describe someone's voice as **fruity** if it is deep and rich in tone: *His voice was rather fruity, like an actor's.*

frustrate /frʌˈstreɪt/ *verb*: **frustrates, frustrating, frustrated**
1 To **frustrate** someone's plan or attempt is to spoil it or prevent it from succeeding: *She was frustrated several times in her attempt to contact him.* **2** Circumstances **frustrate** you when they make you angry and impatient because you are prevented from doing what you want to do: *It's this constant lack of funds that frustrates me.* — *adjective* **frustrated:** *You'd get bored and frustrated working in an office.* □ *I was frustrated to find the shop closed.* □ *Lots of critics are frustrated writers.* — *adjective* **frustrating:** *It's frustrating to have all these great plans and no money for achieving them.* — *noun* (*uncount or count*) **frustration** /frʌˈstreɪʃən/: *Every driver knows the frustration of being unable to overtake.* □ *Learn to cope calmly with life's little frustrations.*

fry /fraɪ/ *verb*: **fries, frying, fried**
You **fry** food when you cook it in a pan containing hot oil or fat: *Shall I fry a couple of eggs for tea?* — *adjective* **fried:** *fried bread.*

frying pan /ˈfraɪɪŋ pan/ *noun*: **frying pans**
A **frying pan** is a shallow long-handled pan for frying food in.
▻ ***phrase*** Something that is described as jumping **out of the frying pan into the fire** is an instance of escaping from one bad situation only to find yourself in another much worse one.

fudge /fʌdʒ/ *noun* (*uncount*)
Fudge is a soft sweet, like toffee, made from butter and sugar.

fuel /fjuːəl/ *noun*; *verb*
▻ ***noun*: fuels**
1 (*uncount or count*) **Fuel** is material for burning as a source of heat or power, such as coal, oil or wood: *the rising cost of fuel* □ *wood, coal and other solid fuels.* [see also **fossil fuel**] **2** (*uncount*) Something that adds **fuel** to ill feeling makes it worse: *The enormous increases in managerial salaries added fuel to employees' resentment.*
▻ ***verb*: fuels, fuelling, fuelled**
1 A vehicle or machine **is fuelled** by particular material if it gets the energy to make it work by burning that material. [*same as* **is powered**] **2** A circumstance **fuels** ill feeling when it makes it worse: *This further evidence of her sister's popularity fuelled her jealousy.* [*same as* **inflame**]

fugitive /ˈfjuːdʒɪtɪv/ *noun*; *adjective*
▻ ***noun*: fugitives**
A **fugitive** is someone who is running away from an enemy, or from the police or other authority, or from a bad situation: *Fugitives from justice used to hide in these caves.*
▻ ***adjective***
1 Fugitive describes a person who is running away from someone or something: *The picture shows a British family of about* AD *200 sheltering a fugitive Christian missionary from pagan persecutors.* **2** (*literary*) **Fugitive** also describes something that lasts a very short time: *She paid us the occasional fugitive visit.* □ *a fugitive smile.* [*same as* **fleeting**]

-ful /fəl/ or /fʊl/ *suffix*
1 (**-fuls**) **-ful** is added to words for containers, or objects thought of as containers, to form nouns that mean the amount held by the container: *three teaspoonfuls of sugar* □ *two sackfuls of potatoes* □ *an armful of books.*

> Note that the plural of something such as *spoonful* is usually *spoonfuls*, not *spoonsful*.

2 You will also find **-ful** added to nouns to form adjectives, with the meaning 'full of' (*meaningful, graceful, beautiful, merciful, colourful*), 'having the qualities of' (*youthful*), 'in obedience to' (*lawful*); it is also added to some verbs to form adjectives (*forgetful, mournful, watchful*).

fulcrum /ˈfʊlkrəm/ *noun* (*usually in the singular physics*): **fulcrums**
The **fulcrum** of something such as a lever, or of something that is balancing, is the point at which it is fixed or supported.

fulfil (*AmE* **fulfill**) /fʊlˈfɪl/ *verb*: **fulfils** (*AmE* **fulfills**), **fulfilling, fulfilled**
1 You **fulfil** a task or promise when you perform it or carry it out: *You can trust him to fulfil his promises.* □ *She had a number of duties to fulfil.* **2** Something or someone **fulfils** a need, role or function if they perform whatever is required by it: *For people living alone the television set fulfils the function of a companion.* **3** Something **fulfils** requirements if it satisfies them: *We may consider applications even where applicants' particulars do not strictly fulfil requirements.* **4** You **fulfil** aims and ambitions when you achieve them: *I should be satisfied, having fulfilled so many of my childhood dreams.* **5** Something you do **fulfils** you if it makes you satisfied with the way you are living your life; you **fulfil** yourself when you are able to make full use of your talents and abilities. — *adjective* **fulfilled:** *With her family and career, she's a very fulfilled person.* — *adjective* **fulfilling:** *Most people want a job that is fulfilling as well as profitable.* — *noun* (*uncount*) **fulfilment** (*AmE* **fulfillment**): *On fulfilment of each task, pupils record their own score.* □ *The realization of her ambition brought with it a sense of fulfilment.*

full /fʊl/ *adjective*; *adverb*
▻ ***adjective*: fuller, fullest**
1 Something that is **full**, or **full** up, holds or contains as much as it can: *The bus was already full up.* □ *The tank isn't quite full.* □ *My hands are full; I can't carry anything more.* [see also **hand**] **2** Something that is **full** of things contains a lot of them: *gardens full of flowers* □ *The shops were full of people.* □ *His work is full of errors.* **3** A person or thing is **full** of a quality if they have a lot of it: *They returned full of hope.* □ *Her eyes were full of hate.* **4** People are **full** of something such as complaints when they make a lot of them: *He was full of apologies for keeping us waiting.* □ *I thought they'd be pleased, but they were full of objections.* **5** People are **full** of their experiences when they can't stop talking about them: *She was full of her trip to Africa.* **6 Full** is used to mean 'as great as is possible': *It will be a while before you get the full range of movement back in your shoulder.* □ *I regret now that I didn't take full advantage of my opportunities.* [*same as* **maximum**] **7 Full** also means whole or com-

plete: *She returned to a full day's work only a few weeks after having her baby.* □ *Could you give me your full name, please?* **8** A **full** report is detailed, thorough, and includes everything that it should: *A full account of the incident will be submitted to the authorities.* **9** A **full** life is an enjoyably varied and eventful one. **10** A **full** day, week or schedule is a busy one: *I've had a very full week.* **11** You see the **full** horror of a situation when you realize just how horrible it really is: *By daylight they realized the full grimness of their position.* **12** You say you are **full** when you have eaten till you don't want any more. **13 Full** lips are thick lips. **14** A woman who is described as having a **full** figure is rather plump. **15** A **full** skirt is made with a lot of material, which is gathered in to the waist in folds or pleats. **16** A **full** flavour is rich and strong: *full-flavoured wines.* **17** A **full** brother or sister has the same parents as you have, and a **full** cousin the same grandparents as you have. [compare **half-brother**, **half-sister**] **18** A **full** member of an organization pays the complete membership fee and has all a member's rights. **19** The moon is **full** when it is at the stage of being a complete disc: *It's a full moon tonight.*

▻ ***adverb***

1 An apparatus such as a heater is **full** on when it being used at maximum power: *The room was empty but the gas fire was full on.* **2** Something that strikes you **full** in the face, or on the nose, hits you directly on it, or exactly in the middle of it: *the blow caught him full on the chest.*

▻ ***phrases*** **1** For **come full circle** see **circle**. **2** For **full of beans** see **bean**. **3** People are **full of themselves** if they are pleased with themselves and rather too sure of their own importance. **4** You know a fact or circumstance **full well** if you are very aware of it: *I knew full well that she was lying.* **5** For **have your hands full** see **hand**. **6 a** A matter is dealt with **in full** when everything that should be done about it is done: *British Rail will compensate you in full for the serious delay to your journey.* **b** You report something **in full** when you give all the facts: *We shall be reporting in full on that accident later in the programme.* **7** You do something **to the full** when you do it to the greatest possible extent: *Book with us and we guarantee that you will enjoy your holiday to the full.*

full-blooded /fʊl'blʌdɪd/ *adjective*

Full-blooded support or encouragement is enthusiastic.

full-blown /fʊl'bloʊn/ *adjective*

A **full-blown** thing has all the features or characteristics you could expect it to have in order to be that thing: *This conflict must not be allowed to turn into a full-blown war.*

full board /fʊl 'bɔːd/ *noun* (*uncount*)

A hotel that provides **full board** serves breakfast, lunch and an evening meal.

full-grown /fʊl'groʊn/ *adjective*

Full-grown animals and plants have stopped growing, having reached their natural size: *a full-grown elephant* □ *The trees stand 60 feet high when full grown.* [*same as* **mature**; *opposite* **undeveloped**]

full-length /fʊl'lɛŋθ/ *adjective*; *adverb*

▻ ***adjective***

1 A **full-length** film, play or novel is of the usual or standard length, as distinct from shorter than normal. **2** A **full-length** mirror is a tall one reflecting your whole body. **3** A **full-length** portrait of someone shows their whole body, especially standing, as distinct from just their head and shoulders. **4** A **full-length** skirt is one that comes down to the ankles.

▻ ***adverb***

Someone who is lying **full-length** is lying flat with legs straight.

full marks /fʊl 'mɑːks/ *noun* (*plural*)

1 You get **full marks** in a test or exam paper when you answer every question correctly: *I got full marks for English.* **2** You say you give someone **full marks** for something if you think they deserve praise for it: *Full marks to the design team for inspiration.*

fullness /'fʊlnəs/ *noun* (*uncount*)

The **fullness** of something is **1** the quality of being strong or intense: *the fullness of my gratitude.* **2** the condition of being full of things, or of being rich and varied: *married life in all its fullness.*

▻ ***phrase*** Something that you say will happen **in the fullness of time** will happen eventually: *No doubt we shall learn the truth in the fullness of time.*

full-page /fʊl'peɪdʒ/ *adjective*

A **full-page** picture, advertisement or article covers a whole page of a newspaper or magazine.

full-scale /fʊl'skeɪl/ *adjective*

1 A **full-scale** drawing is the same size as the subject. [*same as* **full-size**] **2** A **full-scale** procedure uses all available means and resources: *A full-scale search has been mounted for the missing climbers.* [*same as* **thorough**, **intensive**] **3** A **full-scale** thing has all the features and characteristics you would expect it to have in order to be that thing: *a full-scale rebellion.* [*same as* **out-and-out**]

full-size /fʊl'saɪz/ *adjective*

1 A **full-size** model or drawing is the same size as what it represents: *a full-size model of the space capsule.* [*same as* **full-scale**] **2** Trees that are **full-size** or **full-sized** have finished growing.

full stop /fʊl 'stɒp/ *noun*: **full stops**

A **full stop** is the punctuation mark (.) showing the end of a sentence. [*same as* **period**; see **Punctuation** in Appendices]

full-time /fʊl'taɪm/ *adjective*; *adverb*; *noun*

▻ ***adjective***

Someone who is in **full-time** employment or is a **full-time** employee works for the whole of each week. [*opposite* **part-time**]

▻ ***adverb*** (usually **full time**): *I went back to working full time when my son started school.*

▻ ***noun*** (**full time**) (*uncount*)

In games such as football, hockey and rugby, **full time** is the end of the time normally allowed for a match.

fully /'fʊlɪ/ *adverb*

1 Fully means to the greatest possible extent: *We were not at that time fully aware of the possibilities.* □ *a fully automated process.* [*same as* **completely**] **2** Something is **fully** done when it is completed or finished: *Are you fully qualified yet?* □ *These trees aren't yet fully grown.* [*same as* **completely**] **3** You do something **fully** when you do it without omitting anything: *I'll deal with the question more fully later on.* **4** You use **fully** to emphasize the size of an amount or length of a period: *It was fully twenty minutes before the ambulance arrived.* [*same as* **at least**]

fully-fledged /fʊlɪ'flɛdʒd/ *adjective*

Someone who is a **fully-fledged** member of a profession is a completely qualified or trained member of it: *She's now a fully-fledged lawyer.*

fulsome /'fʊlsəm/ *adjective*

Fulsome praise or compliments are so flattering and exaggerated as to sound rather disgusting and insincere.

fumble /'fʌmbəl/ *verb*: **fumbles**, **fumbling**, **fumbled**

1 You **fumble** when you handle things clumsily or search clumsily with your hands for something: *She fumbled about in the dark for the light switch.* [*same as* **grope**] **2** In games, a player **fumbles** a move when he or she fails to manage it, because of clumsy handling: *He fumbled the catch and the ball dropped to the ground.*

fume /fjuːm/ *noun*; *verb*

▻ ***noun*** (*used in the plural*): **fumes**

Fumes are strong-smelling or poisonous smoke or vapour: *The air was full of petrol fumes.*

▻ *verb* (*informal*): **fumes, fuming, fumed**
You **fume** when you are feeling or expressing anger and impatience: *I was fuming at their inefficiency.* [*same as* **seethe**]

fun /fʌn/ *noun*; *adjective*
▻ *noun* (*uncount*)
1 You have **fun** when you enjoy yourself: *We had a lot of fun deciding on the the colour scheme.* □ *She doesn't get much fun in her life.* **2** An activity that is **fun** is enjoyable or entertaining: *The job's quite fun actually.* □ *It's no fun being ill.* □ *It wasn't much fun clearing up the mess.* **3** A person who is **fun** is amusing to be with: *Our new neighbours are great fun.*
▻ *adjective* (*informal*): *Have a fun time.*
▻ *phrases* **1** Someone who is a **figure of fun** gets laughed at a lot by other people. **2 a** You do or say something **for fun** when you mean it as a joke: *I hid her shoes for fun.* **b** You do something **for fun** or **for the fun of it** when you do it as a pastime or amusement, and not because you have to do it: *We don't set exams for the fun of it, whatever the students may think.* **3** You say something **in fun** when you say it as a joke: *I just said that in fun; I wasn't serious.* **4** You **make fun of** someone or something, or **poke fun at** them when you tease them or make jokes about them, especially unkindly.

function /ˈfʌŋkʃən/ *noun*; *verb*
▻ *noun*: **functions**
1 A person's or thing's **function** is the special job they perform: *The human appendix performs no vital function.* [*same as* **role**] **2** An organized event such as a party or reception can be called a **function**: *She gets an allowance for attending civic functions.* **3** The bodily **functions** are such processes as urinating and defecating. **4** (*computers*) A **function** is a series of tasks that a computer is programmed to perform at the touch of a single key: *the function keys.*
▻ *verb*: **functions, functioning, functioned**
1 A system or a machine **is functioning** when it is working or operating: *Is that cash-dispenser functioning OK?* □ *I'll explain how the committee functions.* **2** A person or thing **functions** as something when they do the job of that thing: *Sometimes the interpreters were called on to function as negotiators.*

functional /ˈfʌŋkʃənəl/ *adjective*
1 Something that is **functional** is designed to be efficient rather than decorative: *a plain, functional-looking kitchen.* **2** A machine is **functional** if it is working as it should: *The new telephone system will be functional from next Monday.* [*same as* **operational**] — *adverb* **functionally:** *The room was furnished functionally, like an office.*

functionary /ˈfʌŋkʃənərɪ/ *noun* (*derogatory*): **functionaries**
A **functionary** is a person who works as a minor official in the government or a similar organization.

fund /fʌnd/ *noun*; *verb*
▻ *noun*: **funds**
1 A **fund** is a sum of money for a special purpose: *She contributed £1000 to the restoration fund.* **2** (*used in the plural*) **Funds** are sums of money available for spending: *We discussed how to raise funds for the repairs.* □ *the difficulties of fund-raising.* **3** (*used in the plural; informal*) You can refer to your own supply of cash as **funds**: *I'd like to come too, but funds are a bit low at present.* **4** Someone has a **fund** of something if they have a large store or supply: *He has a fund of funny stories.*
▻ *verb*: **funds, funding, funded**
People **fund** a project when they provide money for it: *a government-funded scheme.* — *noun* (*uncount*) **funding:** *Your investment in our enterprise provides funding for development.*

fundamental /fʌndəˈmɛntəl/ *adjective*; *noun*
▻ *adjective*
1 Something that is **fundamental** is important and basic: *There appeared to be no very fundamental difference between our attitudes.* **2** You say something is **fundamental** to a thing if it is essential to it: *Mutual trust is fundamental to an enterprise as dangerous as this.*
▻ *noun*: **fundamentals**
The **fundamentals** of something are the basic principles: *He tried to teach us the fundamentals of psychology.*

fundamentalism /fʌndəˈmɛntəlɪzm/ *noun* (*uncount*)
In religion or politics, **fundamentalism** is unquestioning faith in the traditional teachings, especially, amongst Protestants, belief in the literal interpretation of the Bible, or, amongst Muslims, of the Koran. — *noun* **fundamentalist:** *He was attracted to the fundamentalists.* □ *fundamentalist doctrine.*

fundamentally /fʌndəˈmɛntəlɪ/ *adverb*
1 Something that is **fundamentally** true about something concerns its basic, real or essential nature: *Although they made several changes, they remained fundamentallly committed to socialism.* □ (*sentence adverb*) *Fundamentally, this is a criminal, not civil, matter.* **2 Fundamentally** also means to a serious and important extent: *We differed fundamentally on many points.*

funeral /ˈfjuːnərəl/ *noun*: **funerals**
A **funeral** is the ceremony of burying or cremating someone who has died: *The funeral will be held on Friday.* □ *the funeral service.*
▻ *phrase* (*informal*) You tell someone **it's their funeral** or **their own funeral** when you think they have made a bad decision and will only be able to blame themselves for the results.

funereal /fjʊˈnɪərɪəl/ *adjective*
Funereal describes things that are so sad, solemn or slow that they remind you of a funeral: *funereal music* □ *speaking in funereal tones.*

funfair see **fair**[2].

fungus /ˈfʌŋgəs/ *noun*: **funguses** or **fungi** /ˈfʌŋgaɪ/ or /ˈfʌŋdʒaɪ/
A **fungus** is a plant such as a mushroom, toadstool, mould or yeast, that reproduces by spores, not seeds, and has no roots or leaves.

funnel /ˈfʌnəl/ *noun*; *verb*
▻ *noun*: **funnels**
1 A **funnel** is a tube with a cone-shaped opening through which liquid, grain or powder can be poured into a narrow-necked container. **2** The **funnel** of a steamship or steam engine is the chimney through which smoke escapes.
▻ *verb*: **funnels, funnelling, funnelled**
Wind **funnels** somewhere when it rushes there through a narrow space: *A high wind was funnelling through the streets.*

funnily /ˈfʌnɪlɪ/ *adverb*
▻ *phrase* You use **funnily enough** as a sentence adverb when reporting something that is so, or has happened, even if it is surprising, unexpected or unlikely: *Funnily enough, he didn't start skiing until he was in his twenties.*

funny /ˈfʌnɪ/ *adjective*: **funnier, funniest**
1 Something that is **funny** amuses you or makes you laugh: *I heard quite a funny story today.* □ *Children have such a funny way of putting things.* [*same as* **comical, amusing**] **2** You describe something strange, odd, or mysterious as **funny**: *I had a funny suspicion he was lying.* □ *It seemed rather funny that she hadn't been told.* [*same as* **odd**] **3** (*informal*) You say that there has been some **funny** business if you think that something dishonest has been done. **4** You say you are feeling **funny** if you feel ill: *I was feeling funny and thought I*

might faint. **5** (*informal*) Someone who is **funny** in the head is slightly crazy.

fur /fɜː(r)/ *noun*: **furs**
1 (*uncount*) **Fur** is the thick fine soft coat of a hairy animal: *The bear shook itself vigorously and scattered drops from its wet fur.* **2** (*uncount*) **Fur** is also the skin of an animal with the hair attached, or an artificial fabric imitating it, used to make, line or trim clothing: *fur-lined boots* □ *a fur jacket.* **3** A **fur** is a coat, cape or jacket made of fur or of an artificial fabric imitating it. **4** (*uncount*) **Fur** is also **a** a whitish coating on the tongue, generally a sign of illness. **b** a whitish coating that forms on the inside of water pipes and kettles in limestone regions.

furious /ˈfjʊərɪəs/ *adjective*
1 You are **furious** when you are very angry: *My parents were furious with me for failing my exams.* □ *I was furious at having to queue.* **2** **Furious** weather or winds are stormy: *Furious gales lashed the country for days on end.* **3** There is **furious** activity when people are doing things fast and busily, but in rather a disorganized manner. [*same as* **frantic**, **frenzied**] — *adverb* **furiously:** *'Look what you've done now!' he yelled furiously.* □ *She was working furiously to finish her thesis.*

furled /fɜːld/ *adjective*
Flags, sails or umbrellas are **furled** when they are rolled up or folded up, when not being used. [*opposite* **unfurled**]

furnace /ˈfɜːnɪs/ *noun*: **furnaces**
A **furnace** is a closed container in which a fire is made to burn with an intense heat, for *eg* melting metal, heating water or burning rubbish: *This room's like a furnace; can't we open a window?*

furnish /ˈfɜːnɪʃ/ *verb*: **furnishes, furnishing, furnished**
1 You **furnish** a building or room when you to put furniture, carpets and curtains into it: *We furnished the house with stuff we'd bought at auction sales.* [*same as* **provide**] **2** (*formal*) To **furnish** something is to supply it: *Shakespeare's text furnishes us with plenty of examples of this usage.*

furnished /ˈfɜːnɪʃt/ *adjective*
1 **Furnished** accommodation is rented accommodation in the form of an apartment, room or house, with furniture in it already: *We rented a furnished flat for a month while looking for a house to buy.* **2** When you describe a place as **furnished** in a certain way you are referring to the kind or quantity of furniture it has in it: *The monks' cells are plainly furnished with a bed, chair, desk and cupboard.*

furnishings /ˈfɜːnɪʃɪŋz/ *noun* (*plural*)
The **furnishings** of a building are the furniture, fittings, carpets and curtains.

furniture /ˈfɜːnɪtʃə(r)/ *noun* (*uncount*)
Furniture is movable household equipment such as tables, chairs and beds: *This bookcase is a nice piece of furniture.*

> Note that **furniture** is an uncountable noun; you use 'a piece of furniture' to refer to an individual item, such as a chair, table, bed or cupboard.

furore /fʊəˈrɔːreɪ/ (*AmE* **furor** /ˈfjʊərɔː/) *noun* (*used in the singular*)
A **furore** is a general outburst of excitement or anger in reaction to something: *the furore over sackings and dismissals.* [*same as* **uproar**, **outcry**]

furrow /ˈfʌroʊ/ *noun*; *verb*
▻ ***noun***: **furrows**
1 A **furrow** is a groove or trench that farmers cut into the soil with a plough, to plant seeds in. **2** A **furrow** in a person's forehead or cheek is a deep line or wrinkle: *A deep furrow appeared between his dark brows*
▻ ***verb***: **furrows, furrowing, furrowed**
You **furrow** your brow when you make lines in it by frowning; your brow **furrows** when lines appear in it as you frown: *Her forehead furrowed in concentration.*

furry /ˈfɜːrɪ/ *adjective*: **furrier, furriest**
1 A **furry** animal is covered with fur: *The cat pressed its furry body against her leg.* **2** Something **furry** is like fur, or is made of it: *I bought some furry material to make cushions with.*

further /ˈfɜːðə(r)/ *adverb*; *adjective*; *verb*
▻ ***adverb***
1 **Further** is the comparative of **far** and, like **farther**, is used in expressions about distance: *Pluto is further away from the sun than Neptune is.* □ *It was further to the beach than the brochure had indicated.* □ *They live further up the hill.* □ *We found a petrol station further on.* □ *Have we got much further to go?* **2** **Further** also means to a greater extent or degree: *She tried to break away from him but just got further involved.* □ *She was further alarmed to discover the front door standing open.* □ *He's getting even further behind with his work.* **3** Things move on a step or stage **further** when they progress, advance or develop: *We have progressed a stage or two further since you last visited us.* □ *She opened her mouth to speak and got no further.* **4** You go **further** when you say something more extreme than what has already been said: *I'd go further and say that all this money has been spent unnecessarily.* **5** '**Further** on' and '**further** back' are used to refer to the time after or before the time you mean: *Three years further on they had still not decided whether to get married.* □ *We must search further back in the firm's history to find the real cause of its collapse.*
▻ ***adjective***
A **further** thing or quantity is an additional one: *Have you anything further to suggest?* □ *They asked for a further 15 volunteers.* □ *We returned to the meeting room for further discussions.*
▻ ***verb***: **furthers, furthering, furthered**
To **further** something is to help it to advance, progress, develop or succeed: *She was intent on furthering her career by whatever means she could.* □ *This latest attack on defenceless civilians has not furthered the cause of peace.*
▻ ***phrases*** **1** (*formal*) In business letters you use **further to** to refer to a previous letter, communication or discussion: *Further to our telephone conversation yesterday I am sending herewith my cv.* **2** If you say to someone that the information you have given them **must go no further**, you are asking them not to tell it to anyone else. [see also **far**, **farther**]

furtherance /ˈfɜːðərəns/ *noun* (*uncount*; *formal*)
The **furtherance** of something is the process of helping it to progress, advance, develop or succeed: *We discussed what other measures we could take in furtherance of our aims.*

further education /fɜːðə ɛdjʊˈkeɪʃən/ *noun* (*uncount*)
Further education is education for school-leavers, especially those who are not going into higher education at a university or polytechnic.

furthermore /fəːðəˈmɔː(r)/ *adverb* (*sentence adverb*; *formal*)
Furthermore introduces a point that supports or adds to what has already been said: *He should not have used office property, and furthermore, he should not have been in the building at all outside office hours.* [*same as* **moreover**]

furthest /ˈfɜːðɪst/ *adjective or adverb*
1 **Furthest** is the superlative of **far** and, like **farthest**, is used in expressions about distance: *Which planet is furthest from the sun?* □ *in the furthest, most remote, parts of the globe* □ *The furthest she'd ever swum was a couple of lengths of the swimming pool.* **2** **Furthest** is

also used in expressions of degree or extent: *Researchers at Edinburgh University have progressed furthest in this field.* □ *The furthest he would go was to admit that there had been some sort of mistake.* □ *the furthest point to which human endurance can go.*
[see also **far**, **farthest**]

furtive /ˈfɜːtɪv/ *adjective*
You describe someone's behaviour as **furtive** when they act as though they do not want people to see what they are doing: *He gave me a furtive wink.* □ *She looked furtive as soon as I mentioned the subject.* — *adverb* **furtively:** *I glanced furtively at my watch.* — *noun* (*uncount*) **furtiveness:** *the apparent furtiveness of the operation.*

fury /ˈfjʊərɪ/ *noun*
1 (*uncount, or used in the singular*) **Fury** is intense or violent anger: *He flies into a fury if you dare to disagree with him.* [*same as* **rage**] **2** (*uncount; literary*) The **fury** of the weather is its violence: *The fury of the gales subsided after a few days.* **3** (*used in the singular*) A **fury** of activity is rushed, disorganized activity.
▻ ***phrase*** (*informal*) You do something such as fight or run **like fury** when you do it with as much strength or speed as you can: *We spotted a shark and rowed like fury to the shore.* [*same as* **like mad**]

fuse[1] /fjuːz/ *noun; verb*
▻ ***noun***: **fuses**
A **fuse** is a safety device in an electrical plug or circuit, containing a wire that melts and so breaks the circuit when the current becomes too strong; the wire itself is also called a **fuse**: *mend a fuse* □ *change a fuse.*
▻ ***verb***: **fuses, fusing, fused**
1 An electrical circuit or device **fuses** when it stops working because a fuse has melted. **2** Wires, or bits of metal or plastic, **fuse** when they melt and stick together: *The coins had fused together into a solid mass in the intense heat.* **3** Things **fuse** or **are fused** when they blend or combine: *Whirling particles fused to form planets.* [*same as* **merge**]

fuse[2] /fjuːz/ *noun*: **fuses**
A **fuse** is a cord or cable which is attached to something such as a bomb or firework, the end of which is lit so as to give people time to move away to a safe distance before the explosion or detonation.

fuselage /ˈfjuːzəlɑːʒ/ *noun*: **fuselages**
The **fuselage** of an aircraft is its main body, carrying the crew and passengers.

fusion /ˈfjuːʒən/ *noun*
1 (*uncount, or used in the singular*) **Fusion** is the process of melting together, combining or blending: *a successful fusion of new and old ideas.* [*same as* **synthesis**] **2** (*uncount, nuclear physics*) Nuclear **fusion** is the combining of atomic nuclei with a resulting release of energy.

fuss /fʌs/ *noun; verb*
▻ ***noun*** (*uncount, or used in the singular*)
People make a **fuss** about something when they get excited, angry, upset or worried about it, usually unnecessarily, and talk or complain noisily: *There's no need to make such a fuss.* □ *The rules are clear and I want no more fuss about them.*
▻ ***verb***: **fusses, fussing, fussed**
People **fuss** when they talk, act or behave in an unnecessarily excited or worried manner: *Do stop fussing; I'll be all right.* □ *He tends to fuss over unimportant details.*
▻ ***phrase*** (*informal*) You **make a fuss of** someone when you pay a lot of attention to them: *She's one of those people who expect to be praised and made fuss of all the time.*

fussy /ˈfʌsɪ/ *adjective*: **fussier, fussiest**
1 A **fussy** person is too concerned or anxious about unimportant things, or easily gets nervous and excited: *The theatre manager turned out to be a fussy little man.* **2** You are **fussy** about something if you are careful in choosing it: *He's fussy about what he eats.* **3** You describe things such as clothes or furnishings as **fussy** if you think they are over-decorated or too elaborate: *too many fussy frills and fringes.* — *adverb* **fussily:** *He was moving fussily among his guests.* □ *a fussily furnished sitting room.*

futile /ˈfjuːtaɪl/ (*AmE*/ˈfjuːtəl/) *adjective*
You **describe** efforts or actions as **futile** if they are, or are bound to be, unsuccessful: *He knew it was futile to try and persuade her.* [*same as* **pointless**, **useless**] — *noun* (*uncount*) **futility** /fjuːˈtɪlɪtɪ/: *the futility of such an enterprise.* [*same as* **pointlessness**]

futon /ˈfuːtɒn/ or /fuːˈtɒn/ *noun*: **futons**
A **futon** is a cloth-filled mattress intended to be used on the floor and rolled up when not in use. [see picture at **bedroom**]

future /ˈfjuːtʃə(r)/ *noun; adjective*
▻ ***noun*** (*used in the singular*)
1 The **future** is the time that is coming after the present, or the events that are going to occur in that time: *Sometime in the near future we must have a proper discussion.* □ *I haven't considered the future yet.* □ *They claim to foretell the future.* **2** Your **future** is what is going to happen to you, especially in your career: *She never imagined that her future lay anywhere but in dancing.* □ *These scandals have left his political future in some doubt.* **3** Something has a **future** if it is likely to continue and be successful: *There's no future in software that is not user-friendly.* **4** (*grammar*) A verb is in the **future** if it is in the future tense.
▻ ***adjective***
1 Future things are going to exist or happen after the present time: *future generations of children* □ *I hope to see the cathedral on some future occasion.* **2** Your **future** wife or son-in-law is the person who will soon become your wife or son-in-law: *Come and meet our future daughter-in-law.*
▻ ***phrase*** **In future** is used for telling people what you expect to happen in the time after the present: *You will have to work harder in future.* □ *We shall be employing more school-leavers in future.* [*same as* **from now on**]

future tense /fjuːtʃə ˈtɛns/ *noun* (*used in the singular; grammar*)
The **future tense** of a verb is the form used to refer to things that are going to happen in the time after the present.

futuristic /fjuːtʃəˈrɪstɪk/ *adjective*
A **futuristic** design is strange and unusual-looking, and seems to have no relation to traditional forms and shapes: *futuristic buildings.*

fuzz /fʌz/ *noun* (*uncount*)
Fuzz is a mass of fine hair or threads: *His legs were covered with a dark fuzz.*

fuzzy /ˈfʌzɪ/ *adjective*: **fuzzier, fuzziest**
1 Something **fuzzy** is covered with short curly hairs or fuzz: *I found some fuzzy material to make a teddy bear.* **2 Fuzzy** hair forms a mass of tight wiry curls. **3** A **fuzzy** outline is thick and vague rather than clear and distinct: *some fuzzy old photos.* **4** You say your brain feels **fuzzy** when you cannot think clearly: *I tried to focus my fuzzy thoughts.*

G

G or **g** /dʒiː/ *noun*: **Gs** or **g's**
G is the seventh letter of the English alphabet.

gable /ˈgeɪbəl/ *noun*: **gables**
The **gables** of a house or other building are the top parts of the side walls, between the sloping parts of the roof. [see picture at **house**]

gadget /ˈgadʒɪt/ *noun*: **gadgets**
A **gadget** is a small piece of electrical or other equipment, especially one that is clever and useful: *They bought us a new gadget for slicing ham.*

gaffe /gaf/ *noun*: **gaffes**
You commit a **gaffe** when you say or do something that upsets or embarrasses people, often unintentionally: *His first gaffe was asking my mother her age.*

gag /gag/ *verb*; *noun*
▻ ***verb***: **gags, gagging, gagged**
1 To **gag** someone is to put something in or over their mouth to stop them speaking, especially to prevent them from shouting for help: *He had been tied to a chair and gagged.* **2** You **gag** when you choke slightly because you feel you are about to be sick: *disgusting smells that made me gag.*
▻ ***noun***: **gags**
1 A **gag** is something put into or over a person's mouth to keep them quiet. **2** (*informal*) A **gag** is also a joke, especially one told by a professional comedian.

gaiety /ˈgeɪətɪ/ *noun* (*uncount*)
Gaiety is lively happiness or fun: *an atmosphere of gaiety.* [*same as* **cheerfulness**; *opposite* **gloom**]

gaily /ˈgeɪlɪ/ *adverb*
1 You do something **gaily** when you do it in a lively, happy way: *The children skipped gaily along the edge of the water.* **2** (*formal*) Something **gaily** coloured is brightly coloured.

gain /geɪn/ *verb*; *noun*
▻ ***verb***: **gains, gaining, gained**
1 You **gain** something when you get, obtain or earn it: *He gained possession of the house when his father died.* □ *It has gained her the respect of all her colleagues.* [*opposite* **lose**] **2** You **gain** from a situation when you benefit or get some advantage from it: *There is nothing to be gained by complaining* **3** To **gain** something like speed or weight or height is to increase it: *The car seemed to gain speed as it approached the bend.* □ *He's gained five pounds in weight over Christmas.* [*opposite* **lose**] **4** To **gain** in a feeling or quality is to be more affected by it: *They have gained enormously in confidence since they started work.* **5** A watch or clock **gains** when it goes too fast, so that it shows a time later than the real time: *My watch has gained ten minutes since this morning.* [*opposite* **lose**]
▻ ***noun***: **gains**
1 A **gain** is something you obtain or earn: *The thieves were trying to sell their ill-gotten gains.* **2** A **gain** is also an increase: *In order to compete at middleweight, he's looking at a weight gain of over ten pounds.* **3** (*uncount*) **Gain** is benefit, advantage or profit: *Their only interest is financial gain.* [*opposite* **loss**]

> ***phrasal verb***
> You **gain on** someone who is ahead of you when you get closer to them: *The Irish horse was in the lead, but the others were rapidly gaining on it.* □ *The Japanese companies are beginning to gain on their European rivals.*

gait /geɪt/ *noun* (*used in the singular; formal*)
Your **gait** is the way you walk: *He has the typical rolling gait of a sailor.* □ *His gait was unsteady, and he seemed to have trouble focusing on me.*

gala /ˈgɑːlə/ *noun* (*often adjectival*): **galas**
A **gala** is an occasion of special entertainment or a public celebration of some kind, *eg* a carnival: *a gala concert.*

galaxy /ˈgaləksɪ/ *noun*: **galaxies**
A **galaxy** is a very large group of stars and planets, bigger than a solar system.

gale /geɪl/ *noun*: **gales**
A **gale** is a very strong wind: *Shipping has been disrupted by severe gales.*

gall /gɔːl/ *noun*; *verb*
▻ ***noun*** (*uncount; informal*)
You say that someone has the **gall** to do something when they seem to be acting with a lot of nerve or boldness, often rudely or arrogantly: *They did the work badly, and then had the gall to ask for more money.* [*same as* **cheek**]
▻ ***verb***: **galls, galling, galled**
Something **galls** you when it annoys or irritates you, and you feel humiliated: *It galls me to have to ask their permission.*

gallant /ˈgalənt/ *adjective*
1 Gallant behaviour shows bravery or courage: *It was a gallant effort by the losers.* **2** A man might be described as **gallant** when he behaves in a formally polite way towards women.

gallery /ˈgalərɪ/ *noun*: **galleries**
1 A **gallery** is a room or building where works of art are displayed to the public: *a new museum and art gallery.* **2** A **gallery** is also a shop where works of art are displayed for sale. **3** A **gallery** is also a balcony along an inside upper wall, *eg* providing extra seating in a church or where members of the public can sit in a court of law. **4** In a theatre, a **gallery** is a large balcony.

gallon /ˈgalən/ *noun*: **gallons**
1 A **gallon** is a liquid measurement equal to eight pints (4.5 litres in Britain and 3.8 litres in America). **2** (*used in the plural; informal*) **Gallons** of something liquid is a large amount of it: *Gallons of milk had to be poured away.*

gallop /ˈgaləp/ *verb*; *noun*
▻ ***verb***: **gallops, galloping, galloped**
1 A horse **gallops** when it runs at its fastest pace, in which all four legs are off the ground at the same time. **2** To **gallop** is also to run or move very fast: *Cantona galloped unchallenged down the middle of the field.*

▻ ***noun*** (*used in the singular*)
A **gallop** is the fastest pace at which a horse runs: *He trotted for a while, then broke into a gallop.*

gallows /ˈgaloʊz/ *noun*: *plural* **gallows**
1 A **gallows** is a wooden frame on which criminals are put to death by hanging: *They had erected a makeshift gallows in the prison yard.* **2** A criminal who goes to the **gallows** is put to death by hanging.

galore /gəˈlɔː(r)/ *adverb* (*informal, old*)
Galore is used after a noun to refer to a large amount of something or, more usually, a large number of things: *She invited us to a tea party, where there were cakes and biscuits galore.*

galvanize or **galvanise** /ˈgalvənaɪz/ *verb*: **galvanizes, galvanizing, galvanized**
1 To **galvanize** iron or steel is to coat it with a thin layer of zinc to prevent rusting. **2** Something **galvanizes** someone into action when it makes them realize that they have to take action of some kind: *There is no doubt that it was her rousing speech that galvanized the group into action.* — *adjective* **galvanized:** *You can get special galvanized nails for securing the roof slates.* □ *a galvanized-iron roof.*

gambit /ˈgambɪt/ *noun*: **gambits**
A **gambit** is something you say or do, often with some risk, which you hope will achieve a purpose: *The workers' opening gambit was to threaten strike action.*

gamble /ˈgambəl/ *verb*; *noun*
▻ ***verb***: **gambles, gambling, gambled**
1 To **gamble** is to bet money on the result of a card game, horse-race or other contest. **2** You **gamble** when you take a chance or risk: *They decided to gamble on the weather, and went for a picnic.* — *noun* (*uncount*) **gambling:** *A few months of heavy gambling has used up most of the money.*
▻ ***noun***: **gambles**
A **gamble** is a risky action or situation: *She's taking a gamble by talking openly about it.*

game /geɪm/ *noun*; *adjective*
▻ ***noun***: **games**
1 A **game** is any kind of contest in which each player uses their skill to try and defeat the other or others, especially something done for fun or amusement: *Robert doesn't enjoy card games or board games.* **2** A **game** is also an instance or occasion on which people or teams compete in this way: *We played a few games of cards before supper.* □ *She challenged her father to a game of chess.* **3** In some sports, *eg* tennis, a **game** is a division of a match. **4** (*used in the plural, with a singular verb*) At school, **games** is the different sports that pupils are taught how to play: *She was given a note from the doctor excusing her from games.* **5** Any activity might be referred to as a **game**, especially when it involves a struggle for power, or when the people involved are only concerned about winning: *He's new to the game of politics.* □ *From the way he talks, war is just a game to him.* **6** (*uncount, often adjectival*) Birds and animals that are killed for sport are referred to as **game**; their flesh eaten as meat is also **game**: *game pie.*
▻ ***adjective*** (*informal*)
You are **game** for something adventurous when you are willing to do it or be involved in it: *We're organizing a parachute jump this weekend; are you game?*
▻ ***phrases*** **1** You **give the game away** when you accidentally reveal something that should have been kept secret: *He swore he hadn't been out, but his muddy shoes gave the game away.* **2** You **play the game** when you behave in a fair way. **3** If you say to someone who has been doing something dishonest '**the game's up!**', you mean that they have at last been found out.

gamekeeper /ˈgeɪmkiːpə(r)/ *noun*: **gamekeepers**
A **gamekeeper** is someone employed to take care of wild birds and animals on a country estate.

gammon /ˈgamən/ *noun* (*uncount*)
Gammon is ham cut in thick slices: *a gammon steak.*

gamut /ˈgamət/ *noun* (*used in the singular*; *literary*)
The whole **gamut** or the entire **gamut** of things is the whole range of them: *The film takes its audience through the whole gamut of emotions, from elation to absolute despair.*

gang /gaŋ/ *noun*; *verb*
▻ ***noun***: **gangs**
1 A **gang** is a group of criminals or other troublemakers: *He was attacked by a gang of youths.* **2** A **gang** is also any group of people who are friendly with one another and often meet together: *We went for a drink with the usual gang from the office.*
▻ ***verb***: **gangs, ganging, ganged**

> ***phrasal verb***
> When several people **gang up on** another person, they act as a group against that person, especially in a fight or argument.

gangrene /ˈgaŋgriːn/ *noun* (*uncount*)
Gangrene is a state of decay in a part of the body, *eg* the toes or feet, caused by blood not flowing properly to it, as a result of an illness or injury: *At the hospital they found that there was gangrene in two of the toes on her left foot*

gangster /ˈgaŋstə(r)/ *noun*: **gangsters**
A **gangster** is a member of a gang of violent criminals.

gangway /ˈgaŋweɪ/ *noun*: **gangways**
1 A **gangway** is a passage between rows of seats, *eg* in a theatre or on a train: *The train was full, with passengers standing in the gangway.* **2** A **gangway** is also a small movable bridge or platform used for getting on and off a ship.

gaol see **jail**.

gap /gap/ *noun*: **gaps**
1 A **gap** is a hole in something solid, or a space between two things: *They managed to crawl through a narrow gap in the fence.* **2** A **gap** is also a pause or break in time, during which something stops or is not done: *He has begun to play the piano again, after a gap of many years.* **3** There is a **gap** between two things when there is a big difference between them: *We aim to close the gap between the living standards of rich and poor.* **4** There is a **gap** when something is missing that is needed, or when its absence gives someone the chance to provide it: *Holiday homes have filled a big gap in the market.*

gape /geɪp/ *verb*: **gapes, gaping, gaped**
1 You **gape** at something when you stare at it with your mouth wide open, *eg* because you are surprised or impressed: *The crowd stood gaping at the man lying on the pavement.* [*same as* **gawp**] **2** (*informal*) Something **gapes** when it is, or becomes, wide open: *The child was wearing no hat, and her coat gaped open at the front.* — *adjective* **gaping:** *a gaping hole in his sock.*

garage /ˈgarɑːʒ/ or /ˈgarɪdʒ/ *noun*: **garages**
1 A **garage** is a building in which a car is kept, often attached to a private house. [see picture at **house**] **2** A **garage** is also a place where cars are bought, sold and repaired, or where petrol is sold: *His car was then towed to the nearest garage for repair.*

garb /gɑːb/ *noun (uncount; literary)*
Someone's **garb** is the kind of clothes they are wearing: *He looked very rugged and handsome in seaman's garb.*

garbage /'gɑːbɪdʒ/ *noun (uncount)*
1 (*AmE*) **Garbage** consists of things that you throw away to be collected as waste. **2** (*informal*) **Garbage** is also something worthless or of poor quality: *How much did you pay for that garbage?* **3** (*informal*) **Garbage** is also nonsense: *She talks a lot of garbage.* [*same as* **rubbish**; **trash**]

garbled /'gɑːbəld/ *adjective*
You do not understand a **garbled** message because the details are confused or unclear.

garden /'gɑːdən/ *noun*: **gardens**
1 A **garden** is a piece of ground attached to a house, where plants are grown: *She spent the afternoon tidying up the garden.* **2** (*plural*) **Gardens** refers to a large area where many different kinds of plants are grown, usually one that is open to the public: *We visited Edinburgh's splendid botanical gardens.* — *noun (uncount)* **gardening:** *One of her favourite hobbies is gardening.* [for gardening tools, see picture at **tool**]

gargle /'gɑːgəl/ *verb*: **gargles, gargling, gargled**
You **gargle** when you freshen your mouth and throat by blowing air through a liquid held at the back of your mouth: *She'd been gargling with an antiseptic mouthwash.*

garish /'geərɪʃ/ *adjective*
Something that is **garish** is so bright and colourful as to have an unpleasant effect: *She came down wearing a garish pink and yellow outfit.* [*same as* **gaudy**]

garlic /'gɑːlɪk/ *noun (uncount)*
Garlic is a small rounded vegetable with a white, onion-like outer skin and flesh divided into segments, usually crushed or chopped as a flavouring in cooking: *two cloves of garlic.* [see picture at **vegetable**]

garment /'gɑːmənt/ *noun*: **garments**
A **garment** is a piece of clothing, *eg* a shirt or dress.

garnish /'gɑːnɪʃ/ *verb; noun*
▷ ***verb***: **garnishes, garnishing, garnished**
You **garnish** food that is about to be served when you add something to it as a decoration: *The soup can be garnished with a swirl of cream and some chopped parsley.*
▷ ***noun***: **garnishes:** *Add a few whole mint leaves as a garnish.*

garrulous /'garələs/ *adjective (formal)*
A **garrulous** person tends to talk a lot, especially about unimportant things: *On the train I got into conversation with a garrulous old man.* □ *Sophie was being unusually garrulous that evening.* [*same as* **talkative**, **loquacious**; *opposite* **quiet, subdued**]

garter /'gɑːtə(r)/ *noun*: **garters**
A **garter** is a tight band of elastic material formerly worn round each leg to hold up socks or stockings.

gas /gas/ *noun; verb*
▷ ***noun***: **gases**
1 A **gas** is a substance that is neither a solid nor a liquid, such as oxygen: *some of the poisonous gases released through industrial chimneys.* **2** (*uncount, often adjectival*) **Gas** is a substance of this kind used as a fuel for heating, lighting or cooking: *Most homes were soon supplied with natural gas.* □ *an electric hob and a gas oven.* **3** (*uncount; AmE; informal*) **Gas** is also gasoline, or petrol.
▷ ***verb***: **gasses, gassing, gassed**
1 To **gas** someone is to kill them by making them breathe a poisonous gas. **2** (*informal*) People **gas** when they talk, especially for a long time about unimportant things: *She's been gassing on that phone for over half an hour.*

gas chamber /'gas tʃeɪmbə(r)/ *noun*: **gas chambers**
A **gas chamber** is a sealed room which can be filled with poisonous gas, used for killing people or animals.

gas fire /gas 'faɪə(r)/ *noun*: **gas fires**
A **gas fire** is a heater for a room in which heat is produced by a row of small gas flames. [see picture at **living room**]

gash /gaʃ/ *noun; verb*
▷ ***noun***: **gashes**
A **gash** is a deep open cut or wound: *They tried as best they could to bandage the gash in her knee.*
▷ ***verb***: **gashes, gashing, gashed:** *His upper arm was badly gashed.*

gasoline /'gasəliːn/ *noun (uncount; AmE)*
Gasoline is petrol.

gasp /gɑːsp/ *verb; noun*
▷ ***verb***: **gasps, gasping, gasped**
1 You **gasp** when you breathe in suddenly and sharply, *eg* because of surprise or pain: *They gasped in wonder at the splendour of the palace.* **2** You also **gasp** when you struggle to breathe in, *eg* because of illness: *I found him lying at the top of the stairs, gasping for breath.*
▷ ***noun***: **gasps:** *Roberts failed to stifle a gasp of shock.*

gastric /'gastrɪk/ *adjective*
Gastric means relating to the stomach: *gastric juices.*

gastronomic /gastrə'nɒmɪk/ *adjective (formal)*
Gastronomic means relating to food, especially the enjoyment of good food: *a series of gastronomic delights.*

gate /geɪt/ *noun*: **gates**
1 A **gate** is a hinged door or other barrier in an outside wall or fence, *eg* giving entry to a garden. [see picture at **house**] **2** The numbered exits at an airport, where passengers go to get on a plane, are also referred to as **gates**: *Flight 233 to Malaga is now boarding at Gate 44.* **3** (*usually in the singular*) The total number of people attending a sports event or other entertainment is the **gate**; the total money they pay is also the **gate**: *There was a gate of over 35 000 for the last Liverpool match.* □ *We had expected a gate well in excess of £25 000.*

gateau /'gatoʊ/ *noun*: **gateaus** or **gateaux** /'gatoʊz/
A **gateau** is a rich cake filled with cream: *a slice of chocolate gateau.*

gatecrash /'geɪtkraʃ/ *verb (informal)*: **gatecrashes, gatecrashing, gatecrashed**
You **gatecrash** a party or other event when you manage to enter without having been invited: *The group in the corner had obviously gatecrashed.*

gateway /'geɪtweɪ/ *noun*: **gateways**
1 A **gateway** is an entrance where there is a gate, especially a large one. **2** A **gateway** to something is a way of acquiring or achieving it: *A role in one of his films is regarded as the gateway to fame and fortune.*

gather /'gaðə(r)/ *verb*: **gathers, gathering, gathered**
1 Several people **gather** somewhere when they come together in one place: *A small crowd had gathered at the entrance to the building.* □ *The children gathered round to listen to the man's story.* **2** You **gather** things when you bring or collect them together in one place: *She watched Alan gather together his belongings and throw them into a black bag.* □ *He quickly gathered up the papers on his desk and stuffed them into his brief-*

case. □ *information gathered from a number of sources* □ *The last crop of potatoes was gathered in November.* **3** You say you **gather** that something is so when you are reporting about what other people have told you: *I gather that she's been offered a job with another company.* □ *The police have arrested someone, or so I gather.* **4** Something **gathers** speed or pace when it begins to move or progress faster: *Sheila's campaign has gathered momentum in the past few weeks.* [*same as* **gain**]

gathering /ˈgaðərɪŋ/ *noun*: **gatherings**
A **gathering** is a meeting, especially an informal one: *After the church service, there was the regular gathering for tea and cakes.*

gaudy /ˈgɔːdɪ/ *adjective*: **gaudier, gaudiest**
Something **gaudy** is coarsely and brightly coloured or decorated: *gaudy furnishings.* [*same as* **garish**]

gauge /geɪdʒ/ *verb*; *noun*
▻ ***verb***: **gauges, gauging, gauged**
You **gauge** something, such as the size of an object or the likely effect of an action, when you try to judge or estimate it: *It was difficult to gauge the distance from the shore to the island.* □ *They decided it was useless to try to gauge what the committee's reaction would be.*
▻ ***noun***: **gauges**
1 A **gauge** is a measuring instrument: *She glanced at the pressure gauge.* **2** A **gauge** is also one of a series of standard sizes, *eg* of the thickness of wire.

gaunt /gɔːnt/ *adjective*
Someone who is **gaunt** is thin, especially thin-faced, and unhealthy-looking: *Thomson was a stern, gaunt man in his early forties.*

gauntlet /ˈgɔːntlət/ *noun*: **gauntlets**
A **gauntlet** is a metal, or metal-covered, glove worn as part of a suit of armour by mediaeval soldiers.
▻ ***phrases*** You **throw down the gauntlet** when you challenge someone to do something; you **take up the gauntlet** when you accept a challenge made by someone else.

gauze /gɔːz/ *noun* (*uncount*)
Gauze is a kind of thin transparent cotton cloth used to dress wounds: *He cut a piece of gauze from the roll.*

gave /geɪv/ *verb*
Gave is the past tense of **give**.

gawp /gɔːp/ *verb* (*informal*): **gawps, gawping, gawped**
You **gawp** at something when you openly stare at it, especially open-mouthed: *Schoolboys stood gawping at the naked dummies in the shop window.* [*same as* **gape, stare**]

gay /geɪ/ *adjective*; *noun*
▻ ***adjective***; **gayer, gayest**
1 A **gay** man or woman is homosexual: *He wondered if any of them suspected he was gay.* [compare **lesbian**] **2 Gay** describes things relating to homosexual people, especially men: *He took me to my first gay disco.* □ *campaigners for gay rights.* **3** (*old*) **Gay** also means happy and lively: *We left for the party in the gayest of moods.*
▻ ***noun***: **gays**
A **gay** is a homosexual person, usually a man: *the first newspaper written by gays for gays.*

gaze /geɪz/ *verb*; *noun*
▻ ***verb***: **gazes, gazing, gazed**
You **gaze** at something when you stare at it for a long time: *She sat gazing out of the window.*
▻ ***noun*** (*used in the singular*)
You shift your **gaze** when you stop looking at one thing and look at another: *His gaze had settled on a picture on the far wall.*

gazelle /gəˈzɛl/ *noun*: **gazelles**
A **gazelle** is a small light-brown deer of Africa and Asia.

GCE *noun*: **GCEs**
1 GCE is an abbreviation of 'General Certificate of Education', a school examination taken in a particular subject, at **O-level** at age 16 or **A-level** at age 18. **2** A **GCE** is a pass in such an examination: *You've got five GCEs – you're supposed to be clever.*

GCSE *noun*: **GCSEs**
1 GCSE is an abbreviation of 'General Certificate of Secondary Education', a school examination which replaced the GCE O-level in 1988. **2** A **GCSE** is a pass in such an examination: *I only hope he can leave school with at least a couple of GCSEs.*

gear /gɪə(r)/ *noun*; *verb*
▻ ***noun***: **gears**
1 (*count or uncount*) The **gears** in a car or on a bicycle are used to adjust the speed of the wheels; the **gears** in a machine adjust the speed of its moving parts as the speed of its motor or engine changes: *I changed down from fourth gear back into third.* [see picture at **bicycle**] **2** (*uncount*; *informal*) **Gear** is equipment or special clothes that you need for a particular activity: *Remember to bring your football gear.* **3** (*uncount*; *informal*) **Gear** is also clothes in general: *How can he afford smart gear like that?*
▻ ***verb***: **gears, gearing, geared**
Something **is geared** towards the need or purpose it is designed or intended for: *Our new business strategy is geared towards maximum profit.*

gear lever /ˈgɪə liːvə(r)/ *noun*: **gear levers**
The **gear lever** or, in AmE, **gear shift**, is the lever that the driver of a vehicle moves to put the engine into a different gear. [see picture at **car**]

geese /giːs/ *noun*
Geese is the plural of **goose**.

gel /dʒɛl/ *noun*; *verb*
▻ ***noun*** (*uncount*)
Gel refers to any jelly-like substance used in the home or in industry, for example one you use on your hair to keep it in place: *a jar of hair gel.*
▻ ***verb*** (also **jell**): **gels, gelling, gelled**
Something **gels** when suddenly you can understand or imagine it clearly, after a period of uncertainty or confusion.

gelignite /ˈdʒɛlɪgnaɪt/ *noun* (*uncount*)
Gelignite is a powerful explosive, used for example in mining.

gem /dʒɛm/ *noun*: **gems**
1 A **gem** is a precious stone, especially one cut and polished for use in jewellery. **2** (*informal*) You might call someone a **gem** if they are very helpful or kind.

gender /ˈdʒɛndə(r)/ *noun* **genders**
1 A person's **gender** is their sex, the fact of their being either male or female: *These are not gender-specific diseases; that is to say, they attack both men and women.* **2** In some languages, nouns and pronouns are divided into two or three classes called **genders**, which determines the form of adjectives that refer to them.

gene /dʒiːn/ *noun*: **genes**
Your **genes** are the parts of the cells in your body responsible for passing on some of your physical characteristics to your children.

genealogy /dʒiːnɪˈalədʒɪ/ *noun* (*uncount*)
Genealogy is the study of the history of families.

genera /ˈdʒɛnərə/ *noun*
Genera is the plural of **genus**.

general /ˈdʒɛnərəl/ *adjective; noun*

▻ ***adjective***

1 General describes something that applies to all or most of the things or people being considered: *The general opinion of those people present was that the decision had been unfair.* ▫ *A general description of the goods will do.* **2 General** is also used to describe activities, functions or roles that are of various kinds or cannot be described more exactly: *He was hired to carry out general clerical tasks.* **3 General** also describes someone's position when they have overall responsibility in a business or organization: *the general manager.* **4 General** is also used to refer to the main features of something and not the details: *Our general impression was that she was not suitable for the job.*

▻ ***noun*: generals**

A **general** is an army officer of senior rank, and is also used as a title: *The general inspected the troops.* ▫ *the tactics employed by General Patton.*

▻ ***phrases* As a general rule** or **in general** means 'usually' or 'in most cases': *I have to stay late on Tuesdays as a general rule.* ▫ *In general, I prefer red wine to white wine.*

general election /dʒɛnərəl ɪˈlɛkʃən/ *noun*: **general elections**

A **general election** is a national election, in which voters throughout a country elect the members of a national parliament or government.

generalize or **generalise** /ˈdʒɛnərəlaɪz/ *verb*: **generalizes, generalizing, generalized**

You **generalize** when, mistakenly or for the sake of the argument, you apply what you are saying to everybody or everything, without allowing for individual differences. — *noun* **generalization:** *That's just another of your sweeping generalizations.*

general knowledge /dʒɛnərəl ˈnɒlɪdʒ/ *noun (uncount)*

General knowledge is what someone knows about all kinds of things in the world rather than about special subjects.

generally /ˈdʒɛnərəlɪ/ *adverb*

1 Generally means 'usually': *We generally have dinner at eight o'clock.* **2 Generally** also means 'by most people' or 'for most people': *He is generally regarded as the father of modern medicine.* ▫ *The new book is not yet generally available.* **3 Generally** also means 'mostly' or 'for the most part': *The results were generally pleasing.* [*same as* **largely**] **4 Generally** is also used to refer to all or most aspects: *We need more information generally.*

general practitioner see **GP**.

generate /ˈdʒɛnəreɪt/ *verb*: **generates, generating, generated**

Something **is generated** when it is created or produced: *Wave power is now a viable way of generating electricity.* ▫ *Inefficient production techniques have led to a lot of waste being generated.*

generation /dʒɛnəˈreɪʃən/ *noun*: **generations**

1 Your **generation** consists of all the people who are roughly the same age as you, rather than the same age as your parents or your children: *You must remember that people of your father's generation had to live through a war.* ▫ *The younger generation don't seem to have any respect for anything traditional.* **2** A **generation** is a period of roughly 25 to 30 years, the average time between a person's birth and the birth of their children: *Just a few generations ago, this would have been regarded as unacceptable.*

generic /dʒəˈnɛrɪk/ *adjective*

Generic means describing or referring to things in terms of the general class or group they belong to: *'Soft cheeses' is a generic term for anything from cheese spread to Camembert.*

generosity /dʒɛnəˈrɒsɪtɪ/ *noun (uncount)*

Generosity is the quality of being generous: *We would like to thank you for your generosity towards our daughter.*

generous /ˈdʒɛnərəs/ *adjective*

1 Generous people give money or help willingly, especially without expecting anything in return: *It was very generous of you to lend us your car.* ▫ *We are grateful for your generous offer.* [*opposite* **mean, selfish**] **2 Generous** also means large or great, or larger or greater than expected or deserved: *He had expected a more generous portion of Christmas cake.* ▫ *She felt the praise, though not entirely unwarranted, was nevertheless a little generous.* **3** Someone is also **generous** when they tend not to say or think bad or unkind things about people: *She is a woman of generous spirit.*

genetic /dʒəˈnɛtɪk/ *adjective*

Genetic refers to the branch of science or medicine concerned with the way characteristics are passed on from parents to children, or to the processes involved: *The illness would appear to be the result of some genetic defect.* ▫ *advances in genetic engineering.*

genial /ˈdʒiːnɪəl/ *adjective*

A **genial** person is friendly: *We were served beer and sandwiches by our genial host, Brian.* [*same as* **amiable, friendly, jolly**; *opposite* **cold, unfriendly**]

genital /ˈdʒɛnɪtəl/ *adjective*

Genital refers to a person's external sex organs: *The rash had spread all round the genital area.*

genitals /ˈdʒɛnɪtəlz/ *noun (plural)*

A person's **genitals** are their external sex organs.

genius /ˈdʒiːnɪəs/ *noun*: **geniuses**

1 A **genius** is a person of outstanding skill or ability: *In terms of sheer skill, Best was a footballing genius.* **2** (*uncount*) **Genius** is skill or ability of this kind: *They had never before witnessed such genius.*

genocide /ˈdʒɛnəsaɪd/ *noun (uncount)*

Genocide is the murder of people of a particular race or nationality.

genre /ˈʒɑ̃rə/ or /ˈʒɒnrə/ *noun*: **genres**

A **genre** is a particular type or kind of something, usually literature, music or other artistic work: *Westerns are, of course, a unique cinematic genre.*

gent /dʒɛnt/ *noun (informal)*

A **gent** is a gentleman. [see also **gents**]

genteel /dʒɛnˈtiːl/ *adjective*

Genteel behaviour is so polite or delicate that it appears false or insincere, and is often associated with people of the highest social class: *He smiled at the genteel way she held her teacup.*

gentle /ˈdʒɛntəl/ *adjective*: **gentler, gentlest**

1 Gentle describes things that have a pleasant light or soft quality, and are not in any way harsh or forceful: *She lay down in the grass, soothed by the gentle breeze.* ▫ *a gentle caress.* **2** A **gentle** person is quiet, sensitive and kind: *Her uncle was a tall, gentle, scholarly man.* [*opposite* **rough, brash**] **3 Gentle** also means mild or moderate, not harsh or severe: *a gentle reprimand.* — *adverb* **gently:** *She sat gently stroking his face.* ▫ *'I will,' he answered gently.*

gentleman /ˈdʒɛntəlmən/ *noun*: **gentlemen**

1 People often use the term **gentleman** as a polite way of referring to a man: *Would you serve this gentleman, Patsy?* **2** You might refer to a man as a **gentleman** if he is polite and well-mannered, especially towards women, or if he deserves to be respected or trusted: *No formal contract was signed; we conducted the whole affair on a gentleman's agreement.*

gentry /ˈdʒɛntrɪ/ *noun* (*singular*)
The **gentry** consists of people of high social class: *Now she mixes with the gentry at fashionable London parties.*

gents /dʒɛnts/ *noun* (*singular*)
The **gents** is a public toilet for men: *The ladies is through here; the gents is at the top of the stairs.*

genuine /ˈdʒɛnjʊɪn/ *adjective*
1 A **genuine** object really is what it appears to be, or what people claim it is, not artificial or false: *Several art experts have testified that the painting is a genuine Van Gogh.* □ *The seats are genuine American leather.* [*opposite* **fake**, **artificial**] **2** Someone who is described as **genuine** is sincere or honest: *She's the most genuine friend I have.* □ *He made a genuine attempt to give the money back.*

genus /ˈdʒiːnəs/ *noun* (*technical*): **genera**
A **genus** is a formally identified category or class, especially of plants or animals.

geo- /dʒiːoʊ/ *prefix*
Geo- is used to form nouns and adjectives relating to the earth as a planet, or to its physical characteristics: *experts in geochemistry.*

geographical /dʒɪəˈgrafɪkəl/ *adjective*
Geographical means relating to geography, or to those features of the earth studied in geography: *a geographical survey of the area.*

geography /dʒɪˈɒgrəfɪ/ *noun* (*uncount*)
Geography is the scientific study of the earth's surface, in particular of its physical features, climate and population.

geological /dʒɪəˈlɒdʒɪkəl/ *adjective*
Geological means relating to geology, or to those features of the earth studied in geology: *Several major geological changes occurred during this period.*

geology /dʒɪˈɒlədʒɪ/ *noun* (*uncount*)
Geology is the scientific study of the earth's structure, especially its history and development as shown in the formation of rocks.

geometric /dʒɪəˈmɛtrɪk/ or **geometrical** /dʒɪəˈmɛtrɪkəl/ *adjective*
Geometric means relating to geometry, or to the kinds of regular shapes studied in geometry: *They changed the rather geometric layout of the garden by introducing softer, more natural lines and curves.*

geometry /dʒɪˈɒmɪtrɪ/ *noun* (*uncount*)
Geometry is the mathematical study of regular shapes, lines, curves and angles.

geriatric /dʒɛrɪˈatrɪk/ *adjective*
Geriatric refers to very old people, or to their illnesses: *The hospital has three geriatric wards.*

germ /dʒɜːm/ *noun*: **germs**
1 Germs are the tiny creatures that cause disease, which exist everywhere although you cannot see them: *None of the products can kill all the germs that gather in your kitchen or bathroom.* **2** (*literary*) The **germ** of something is its origin or beginning: *the germ of a plan.*

German /ˈdʒɜːmən/ *adjective*; *noun*
▻ ***adjective***
German means concerned with or belonging to Germany, its people, or their language: *She's not actually German; she's Swiss.* □ *German wines* □ *a German dictionary.*
▻ ***noun***: **Germans**
1 A person who was born in, or who is a citizen of, Germany is a **German**: *There were several Germans in the language class.* **2** (*uncount*) **German** is the language of Germany, Austria and parts of Switzerland: *I only speak a little German.*

gesticulate /dʒɛˈstɪkjʊleɪt/ *verb*: **gesticulates, gesticulating, gesticulated**
You **gesticulate** when you move your hands or arms around as you speak: *The way he was gesticulating suggested he was angry about something.* — *noun* (*count or uncount*) **gesticulation** /dʒɛstɪkjʊˈleɪʃən/: *Her words were accompanied by frantic gesticulations.*

gesture /ˈdʒɛstʃə(r)/ *noun*; *verb*
▻ ***noun***: **gestures**
1 You make **gestures** when you move your hands or other parts of your body as a way of expressing something, or to support what you are saying: *In Western countries, the thumb raised up is a gesture of approval or agreement.* □ *She opened her palms and spread her fingers, in a gesture that meant she didn't know the answer.* **2** A **gesture** is also something you do to show your feelings, opinions or intentions: *We should invite them to our house, as a gesture of friendship.*
▻ ***verb***: **gestures, gesturing, gestured**
You **gesture** when you communicate with someone by moving your hands or another part of your body: *She gestured to me that I should not say any more.* □ *Johnson gestured him to sit down in the seat opposite.*

get /gɛt/ *verb*: **gets, getting, got**
(In *AmE* it is usual to say **have gotten**, but **have got** is also used when the meaning is 'have or possess' or 'must')
1 a You **get** something when you obtain it or buy it, or are given it: *She got lots of lovely presents for Christmas.* □ *I got this watch from my parents.* □ *You should get some advice from a solicitor.* □ *They can probably get a grant from the council.* **b** You **get** something for someone when you obtain or fetch it and give it to them: *Would you get me some more tea?* **c** You **get** something like sleep or rest when you have a spell or period of it: *The doctor told me to get more sleep.*
2 You **have got** something when you have it or possess it: *Have you got a car?* □ *She's got long dark hair.* □ *I don't think Jane has got any brothers.* □ *He hasn't got the confidence for this job.* [see also **have**[2]]
3 You can say you **have got** to do something when you must do it or you ought to do it: *We have got to tell them the truth.* □ *He's got to try harder.* [see also **have**[2]]
4 a You **get** to a place when you arrive there after a journey: *They got to Paris on Friday.* □ *I'll need a drink by the time we get to the hotel.* **b** You **get** to a new position when you manage to move to it or reach it: *There was no room to get past them.* □ *I can't get to the cupboard.* **c** You also use **get** to mean 'reach' or 'arrive at' when speaking about a time, or a stage in a process: *She's got to the stage in her life where having children seems the natural thing to do.* □ *We got as far as agreeing that there was a problem, but didn't manage to identify a solution.*
5 a You **get** something down or off or out if you remove it from something like a shelf or container: *I'll get our things out of the car.* □ *Will you get that box off the top shelf?* **b** You say you can **get** something in or on something like a shelf or container when you manage to put it there or find room for it: *I'm sorry, I can't get all this milk in the fridge.*
6 a Get also means 'make' or 'become' when followed by words that refer to states or conditions: *Take care not to get the papers wet.* □ *She's been ill for some time, but is getting better now.* □ *Marjory is beginning to realize that she's getting old.* **b** You **get** in or into trouble or some other difficult situation, or you **get** some-

one else into it, when you become involved, or involve them, in it: *Oh dear, I'm getting in a mess.* □ *I didn't want to get anyone into trouble.*

7 Get is often used with words of action like 'bitten' or 'given' to refer to things that happen to someone or that are done to them: *He'll get smacked if he doesn't behave.* □ *My foot got run over by a car.* □ *Ellen got given a bike for Christmas.*

8 a You **get** something done, *eg* you **get** a piece of work finished, when you manage to do it or you ask or employ someone else to do it for you: *I'd like to get it finished before my holidays.* □ *We've decided to get the house painted.* □ *Our neighbours get some of the European newspapers delivered.* **b** You **get** someone to do something when you ask or employ them to do it: *They're getting a company to landscape their garden.* □ *We could always get Arthur to lend us the money.* **c Get** is also used to describe what happens to things, often by chance or by mistake: *David has got his foot caught in the door.* □ *She's always getting her words muddled up.* □ *It would be better for us not to get involved.*

9 You **get** a disease when you catch it: *We're hoping our little girl doesn't get the flu.*

10 a (*informal*) You **get** doing something when you begin it, usually with urgency or enthusiasm: *You'd better get cleaning that floor before Mum gets back.* □ *We ought to get going for the station fairly soon.* **b** (*informal*) You also **get** to do something when you are allowed to do it or have an opportunity to do it: *My teenage daughter gets to stay out late at weekends.* □ *Then I got to thinking that the situation wasn't so bad after all.* □ *We never did get to see the Eiffel Tower.*

11 You **get** a feeling or experience when you are affected by it: *She gets a lot of enjoyment out of looking after the garden.* □ *Gail got the distinct impression that he was lying.*

12 You **get** a bus or train or other form of public transport somewhere, when you catch or take it: *I decided to stay longer and get the 8 o'clock flight back.*

13 You **get** something like a meaning or joke when you understand it: *It was supposed to be funny, but she clearly didn't get it.* □ *James hasn't really got the point of the exercise.*

14 (*informal*) Something unpleasant or unwelcome **gets** you, or **gets** to you, when you let it annoy or irritate you or it affects you badly: *It really gets me the way she expects the children to keep quiet all the time.* □ *The lack of sleep was beginning to get to her.*

15 (*informal*) **You get** or **we get** is often used to mean 'there are' or 'we have experience of': *You get some customers who expect you to spend an hour with them* □ *In the summer, we get the tourists wanting to cash traveller's cheques.*

phrasal verbs

get about or **get around** (*informal*) **1** You **get about** or **around** if you often go or travel to different places: *She gets about quite a lot as a fashion model.* **2** News or information **gets about** or **around** as more and more people hear about it: *Keep this information to yourself – I wouldn't want it to get about.* □ *The rumour got around that they were planning to close the factory.* [see also **get around**]

get across You **get** an idea or feeling **across** when you manage to make other people understand or realise it: *I think we managed to get our views across.*

get ahead You **get ahead** when you are successful in your career and you reach a senior position: *Hard work is the only way to get ahead.*

get along (*informal*) One person **gets along** with another, or two people **get along**, when they have a friendly relationship: *I suspected she would find it hard to get along with the others.* □ *How are they getting along?*

get around or **get round 1** You **get around** or **round** to doing something when you finally do it, especially after a difficulty or delay: *Steven eventually got round to painting the garden gate.* **2** News or information **gets around** or **round** when more and more people hear about it: *Rumours were getting round about how he mistreated the children.* [see also **get about**] **3** You **get around** or **round** a problem or difficulty when you find a way of avoiding it rather than dealing with it.

get at (*informal*) **1** When you ask or wonder what someone **is getting at** you want them to explain more clearly what they are suggesting or what they mean: *I didn't know what she was getting at when she said we were being unfair.* **2** To **get at** someone is to criticize them repeatedly and unfairly: *He feels that a number of his colleagues have been getting at him.*

get away 1 You **get away** when you escape: *Police made several arrests, but one of the robbers got away.* □ *Thieves got away with over £5,000 worth of jewellery.* [see also **getaway**] **2** You also **get away**: **a** when you leave, especially late or with difficulty: *I'll have to get away by 11 o'clock if I'm to catch the last train.* **b** when you go away for a longer period, such as a holiday: *We're hoping to get away for a couple of weeks in the summer.*

get away with Someone who **gets away with** something illegal or dishonest manages to avoid being caught or punished for it: *He's been getting away with tax fraud for years.*

get by You **get by** when you manage to live or survive without much money, help or other resources: *We were able to get by on a modest pension.*

get down (*informal*) Something **gets** you **down** when it makes you sad or depressed: *The illness is really beginning to get her down.*

get down to You **get down to** something when you begin working seriously at it: *She needs to get down to some serious writing.*

get in 1 A politician or political party **gets in** when they are elected to power. **2** You **get** something **in** when you find the time or opportunity for it: *I'd like to get another hour's work in before dinner.* □ *It was difficult to get a comment in, everyone was talking so furiously.* **3** A train or bus **gets in** when it arrives at its destination: *The last train gets in at midnight.*

get in on (*informal*) You **get in on** an activity when you succeed in taking part in it.

get into (*informal*) **1** You **get into** something that you develop a liking or enthusiasm for: *I started studying Chinese but never really got into it.* **2** You might ask what **has got into** someone if they are behaving in an unusual way, especially when this is unwelcome or disturbing: *I wonder what's got into Peter – he was quite rude to me.*

get off 1 You **get off**, or someone **gets you off**, when you are given little or no punishment for something illegal or dishonest that you have done: *I'd say you got off rather lightly.* □ *The lawyers got him off with a small fine.* **2** You **get** clothes **off** when you take them off or undress: *It's so hot, I must get this thick jersey off.* [*same as* **take off**]

get off with (*informal*) You can say that you **get off with** someone when you attract them into beginning a sexual relationship with you: *She thought I was trying to get off with her boyfriend.*

get on 1 People **get on**, or one person **gets on** with another, when they have a friendly relationship:

They are so alike, but they don't seem to get on. □ *She doesn't really get on with her parents.* **2** You **get on** when you make progress in your career: *It seems that, in order to get on, you have to socialize with the bosses.* **3** (*informal*) If you say that someone **is getting on**, you mean they are rather old. **4** (*informal*) When you ask or wonder how someone **is getting on**, you want to know generally what they are doing, or what progress they are making: *How is David getting on in his new job?* **5** You **get on** a bus or train when you board it at the start of a journey: *Several people got on at the next stop.* □ *Hurry up and get on the bus.* **6** You **get** clothes **on** when you put them on or dress: *She was trying to get her new skirt on.*

get out of 1 You **get out of** a vehicle when you leave it and continue on foot: *They all got out of the car at the station.* **2** You **get out of** something, or **get out of** doing it, when you manage to avoid doing it: *How is it that Dad always gets out of the washing up?*

get over 1 You **get over** something such as an illness, shock or disappointment when you recover from it: *She's never really got over the death of her husband.* **2** You **get over** a problem or a difficulty when you deal with it successfully.

get over with You say you want to **get** something unpleasant **over with** when you mean you want to do it immediately rather than go on worrying about it.

get round You **get round** someone when you persuade them to do what you want, usually by flattering them. [see also **get about**, **get around**].

get through 1 You **get through** work or a task when you finish or complete it: *It'll take me hours to get through all these letters.* **2** You **get through** an amount or supply of something when you use all of it: *It seems a lot of food to be taking, but four of us will easily get through it in a week.* **3 a** You **get through** to someone when you manage to contact them by telephone: *We rang the hotel, but it was difficult to get through.* **b** You **get through**, or **get** something **through**, to someone when you make them understand or realize something: *I can't seem to get through to them how important this is.*

get together 1 People **get together** when they meet informally: *We must get together and discuss these new proposals.* **2** You **get** something **together** when you organize it: *We ought to get some sort of celebration together for her.* [see also **get-together**]

get up 1 You **get up** when you stand from a sitting or lying position, or when you leave your bed after waking: *Everyone got up when she came in the room.* □ *I find it hard to get up on winter mornings.* **2** You **get** someone **up** when you make them get out of bed, usually earlier than they had intended: *She got me up at six o'clock just to watch the sun rise.*

get up to You talk about what someone has been **getting up to** when you are referring to what they have been doing, especially if you think it is something people might disapprove of: *She told amusing stories about what they got up to on holiday.*

getaway /ˈgɛtəweɪ/ *noun* (*often adjectival*): **getaways**
Criminals make a **getaway** when they escape after committing a crime: *They made their getaway in a stolen van.* □ *Police later discovered the getaway van.*

get-together /ˈgɛttəgɛðə(r)/ *noun* (*informal*): **get-togethers**
A **get-together** is an informal meeting or an informal party.

get-up /ˈgɛtʌp/ *noun* (*informal*): **get-ups**
A **get-up** is a strange or unusual outfit: *It was a ridiculous get-up for a teacher.*

geyser /ˈgiːzə(r)/ *noun*: **geysers**
A **geyser** is an underground spring from which, from time to time, hot water and steam shoot up through a hole in the ground.

ghastly /ˈgɑːstlɪ/ *adjective*: **ghastlier**, **ghastliest**
1 (*informal*) You describe something as **ghastly** if it is very unpleasant, or if you dislike it a lot: *He was deeply involved in the whole ghastly business.* □ *I suppose they'll be there as usual, with their ghastly children.* [*same as* **horrible**, **dreadful**; *opposite* **delightful**] **2** Someone who looks **ghastly** looks very ill. **3** Something **ghastly** is very strange and frightening: *She caught a glimpse of a ghastly face at the window.*

ghetto /ˈgɛtoʊ/ *noun*: **ghettos** or **ghettoes**
A **ghetto** is a poor part of a city where people of a particular race, nationality or religion live in large numbers: *Boxing is a way for young black lads to get out of the ghetto.*

ghost /goʊst/ *noun*: **ghosts**
A **ghost** is the spirit of a dead person visible to people still living: *We had letters from many people who claimed to have seen ghosts.* □ *the ghost of his late wife.*

ghostly /ˈgoʊstlɪ/ *adjective*
You might describe some strange and frightening thing that you see or hear as **ghostly**: *He swears he saw some kind of ghostly form at the end of the corridor.*

giant /ˈdʒaɪənt/ *noun*; *adjective*
▻ ***noun***: **giants**
1 In legends and children's stories, a **giant** is an enormously big, frightening, and usually cruel, person. **2** Very talented or important people, and very large and powerful business companies, are often referred to as **giants**: *Greene has never been regarded as a literary giant.* □ *the giants of the chemical industry.*
▻ ***adjective***
1 Giant describes very big things: *a giant portion of pudding.* [*same as* **gigantic**] **2 Giant** is also used to refer to the larger or largest of two or more species of the same animal: *the giant tortoise.*

gibberish /ˈdʒɪbərɪʃ/ *noun* (*uncount*)
When someone is talking in words that don't make sense, *eg* because they are ill or drunk, you might say that they are talking **gibberish**.

gibbon /ˈgɪbən/ *noun*: **gibbons**
A **gibbon** is a small ape with very long arms.

gibe see **jibe**.

giblets /ˈdʒɪbləts/ *noun* (*plural*)
The **giblets** of a chicken or other bird are its heart, liver and other edible internal organs: *He made a turkey stock with some of the meat and the giblets.*

giddy /ˈgɪdɪ/ *adjective*: **giddier**, **giddiest**
1 You are **giddy** when you lose your balance because of an unpleasant feeling that you are spinning round, *eg* because you are ill: *He suddenly felt giddy.* **2** You might also say that you are **giddy** if you feel extremely happy or excited: *Diana was giddy with love.*
[*same as* **dizzy**]

gift /gɪft/ *noun*: **gifts**
1 A **gift** is a present, something that you give to someone: *The clock was a gift from my parents.* □ *I admired the painting, and he said he would like me to have it as a gift from him.* **2** (*especially in the singular*) Someone who has a **gift** for something has a natural ability for doing it: *Steven had this amazing gift for portrait-drawing.*

gifted /ˈgɪftɪd/ *adjective*
Gifted describes someone who is very talented: *a gifted young musician.*

gigantic /dʒaɪˈgantɪk/ *adjective*
Something **gigantic** is extremely large: *She was sitting next to a gigantic pile of ironing.* [*same as* **enormous, huge**]

giggle /ˈgɪgəl/ *verb; noun*
▻ ***verb***: **giggles, giggling, giggled**
You **giggle** when you laugh in a nervous or silly way: *Mr Proctor sent her out of the class for giggling.* ▫ *She opened the door to see a groups of giggling children running off down the street.*
▻ ***noun***: **giggles**
1 A **giggle** is a silly little laugh: *'It's awfully naughty,' she admitted, with a giggle.* **2** (*used in the plural*) When you have the **giggles** you are unable to stop yourself giggling. **3** (*usually in the singular*) You have a **giggle** about something when you laugh about it: *We used to eat our lunchtime sandwiches together and have a good giggle about the way things were run in the office.*

gimmick /ˈgɪmɪk/ *noun*: **gimmicks**
A **gimmick** is something done or given in order to attract publicity or to attract customers: *Is it a useful new product, or just another silly sales gimmick?*

gin /dʒɪn/ *noun*: **gins**
1 (*uncount*) **Gin** is a colourless alcoholic spirit made from grain: *a bottle of gin.* **2** A **gin** is a glass of gin: *I've ordered us a couple of gins.*

ginger /ˈdʒɪndʒə(r)/ *noun; adjective*
▻ ***noun*** (*uncount*)
Ginger is the hot-tasting root of a tropical plant used, often in the form of a powder, as a flavouring in cooking.
▻ ***adjective***
Ginger hair is a bright orange-brown colour.

gingerly /ˈdʒɪndʒəlɪ/ *adverb*
You do something **gingerly** when you do it in a very cautious way: *He put his injured foot on the floor, and gingerly started to put weight on it.* [*same as* **cautiously**; *opposite* **confidently**]

gipsy see **gypsy**.

giraffe /dʒɪˈrɑːf/ *noun*: **giraffes**
A **giraffe** is a tall African animal with a very long neck, long legs and a ginger-coloured coat with regular brown patches.

girder /ˈgɜːdə(r)/ *noun*: **girders**
A **girder** is a long thick iron or steel post used in the construction of buildings and bridges.

girdle /ˈgɜːdəl/ *noun*: **girdles**
A **girdle** is a piece of women's underwear, usually made of elastic material, that fits tightly over the body from the waist to the thighs, and gives a slimmer appearance. [*same as* **corset**]

girl /gɜːl/ *noun*: **girls**
1 A **girl** is a female child: *one of the other girls in her class* ▫ *My youngest girl is six.* [compare **boy**] **2** Women often refer to each other as **girls**, but are sometimes offended when men refer to them as **girls**: *I went to the pub with some of the other girls from the office.*

girlfriend /ˈgɜːlfrɛnd/ *noun*: **girlfriends**
1 A boy or man usually refers to the girl or woman he is having a romantic or sexual relationship with as his **girlfriend**. [compare **boyfriend**] ▫ *'Partner' seems to be the only suitable alternative to the rather juvenile 'girlfriend'.* **2** A woman will often refer to a female friend as a **girlfriend**.

girlish /ˈgɜːlɪʃ/ *adjective*
Girlish might be used to describe a woman's appearance or behaviour if it is attractively youthful: *Janet had an irresistible girlish charm.*

gist /dʒɪst/ *noun* (*singular*)
The **gist** of something written or said is its main point or general meaning: *I didn't understand all the legal jargon, but the gist of the letter is that they refuse to give permission.*

give /gɪv/ *verb*: **gives, giving, gave, given**
1 You **give** someone something **a** when you hand it to them or cause them to have it, *eg* as a present or for them to use or keep: *She gave me a gold watch for my birthday.* ▫ *His mother gave him a large helping of custard.* ▫ *Give me your bags while you get into the car.* **b** when you provide them with it or make it available to them: *They have given us three weeks to finish the work.* ▫ *Give them our best wishes.* ▫ *We can give you an office of your own.* **2** You use **give**: **a** with nouns referring to an action, with the meaning 'perform' or 'carry out' that action: *He gave it a firm pull, and the handle came off.* ▫ *Chris gave a loud yawn.* ▫ *She gave me the most beautiful smile.* ▫ *The ship is given a complete overhaul once a year.* **b** with nouns referring to something said, with the meaning 'tell' or 'communicate': *He was unable to give a good reason for his absence.* ▫ *The company was given bad financial advice.* ▫ *I'm afraid we have to give them some bad news.* ▫ *Most parents gave drugs as their main cause of concern.* **c** as a way of making an estimate or prediction about something: *One expert gave it a value of over £10000.* ▫ *Three independent opinion polls give the Labour Party a convincing lead.* ▫ *Their marriage is unhappy. I give it two years at the most.* **3** Something **gives** you a particular feeling when it causes you to experience it: *The sudden noise gave me a fright.* ▫ *The sight of all those letters gave her an overwhelming desire to run out of the office.* ▫ *His drunken behaviour is giving concern to his friends.* **4** You **give** a party or other celebration when you organize it and act as the host. **5** You **give** thought or attention to something when you concentrate on it: *I hadn't given the idea much thought until now.* ▫ *Please give the matter your full and urgent attention.* **6** Something **gives** when it breaks or collapses: *I was afraid the chair might give under his weight.* [*same as* **give way**] **7** To **give** is to give money, *eg* to a charity: *We were all urged to give generously.*
▻ ***phrases*** **1** You can say you would **give anything** to do or have something when you want it very much: *He would give anything to be able to play the guitar.* **2** (*informal*) You might say **give me** something as a way of showing that you like or prefer it: *I don't much care for classical music – give me jazz any day.* **3 Give or take** is often used to show that an amount is approximate and may be slightly more or slightly less: *The film lasts for two hours, give or take ten minutes.* **4 a** Something **gives way** when it breaks or collapses: *They were afraid the car's suspension might give way under the weight.* **b** You **give way** to someone when you allow them to do something, although you would prefer them not to. **c** One thing, such as a look or feeling, **gives way** to another when the first is replaced by the second: *When Sally arrived, Peter's anxiety gave way to excitement.* **d** When you are driving a road vehicle, you **give way** when you slow down or stop to let traffic from other directions go before you.

phrasal verbs

give away 1 You **give** something **away** when you give it to someone else, often because you no longer want it: *They gave most of her old baby clothes away.* **2** You **give** information **away** when you allow it to become known to other people: *It seems he had been giving away all sorts of valuable information.* **3** You also **give away** personal thoughts or feelings without intending to, when your appearance or behaviour makes it clear what they are: *I wondered what she was thinking – her expression gave very little away.* [see also **give-away**]

give in 1 You **give in** when you admit that you have been defeated, or when you agree to stop opposing or resisting something and allow it: *They were determined not to give in, even though the enemy was besieging the city.* **2** You **give in to** someone or something when you stop arguing or resisting and agree to what they demand: *We are trying hard not to give in to their bullying tactics.*

give off Something **gives off** heat or light or a smell when it produces it or sends it out: *Most light bulbs give off more heat than light.*

give out You **give** things **out** when you distribute them to a number of people: *We stood in the High Street giving out leaflets.*

give up 1 You **give up** something or **give up** doing something when you decide not to do it any longer: *Jean gave up smoking over ten years ago.* □ *I've given up trying to talk sense to him.* **2** You **give up** something helpful or useful when you no longer want it or can no longer justify it: *Why has she given up her work?* □ *Now is not the time to give up hope.* **3** You **give yourself up** when you surrender yourself as a prisoner: *The thieves were cornered by police and forced to give themselves up.*

give-and-take /gɪvən'teɪk/ *noun* (*uncount*)
When there is **give-and-take** between people, each person is willing to listen to and accept the views of the others: *The marriage has suffered from a lack of give-and-take on both sides.*

give-away /'gɪvəweɪ/ *noun* (*informal*): **give-aways**
Something that you do or say is a **give-away** when it reveals to others something else that you had intended to keep secret: *The fact that he blushes whenever you mention her name is a dead give-away.*

given /gɪvən/ *verb; adjective; preposition or conjunction*
▻ ***verb***
Given is the past participle of **give**.
▻ ***adjective***
1 Given means fixed or decided on in advance: *At the given signal, we removed our pistols from their holsters.* □ *At a given time, the children will run forward to greet her.* **2 Given** also means 'particular' or 'being considered, as an example': *We must determine the needs of any given patient with complete disregard for the cost of the treatment involved.* **3** You **are given** to something, or to doing something, when you do it regularly: *Paterson's father was given to bouts of outrageous drunkenness.* □ *He is given to lecturing his staff on their morals, which doesn't make him a very popular boss.*
▻ ***preposition or conjunction***
Given, and **given** that, are ways of introducing a statement that explains or expands something else you say: *Given his lack of experience, his work is remarkably good.* □ *The island was a perfect place to convalesce, given that it was the stresses of city life that had brought on his illness.*

glacier /'glasɪə(r)/ or /'gleɪsɪə(r)/ *noun*: **glaciers**
A **glacier** an enormous moving or expanding mass of ice.

glad /glad/ *adjective*: **gladder, gladdest**
1 You are **glad** about something when you are happy or pleased about it: *We're so glad that you decided to come.* □ *She was glad to hear that Michael had recovered from his illness.* □ *His father was glad of the opportunity to thank everyone who had helped.* [*same as* **happy**; *opposite* **sad, unhappy**] **2** When you say you would be **glad** to do something, you mean that you are willing to do it, and perhaps that you would enjoy doing it: *I'd be glad to give you whatever help I could.*
— *adverb* **gladly:** *We will gladly give you any assistance we can.*

gladden /'gladən/ *verb* (*literary*): **gladdens, gladdening, gladdened**
Something that **gladdens** you makes you happy or pleased: *It gladdened her heart to see Thomas enjoying life again.* [*opposite* **sadden**]

glamorous /'glamərəs/ *adjective*
1 Glamorous people dress and behave in a way intended to make other people think they are attractive and interesting: *rich old men in the company of glamorous young women.* **2** Someone who has a **glamorous** lifestyle does things that only very rich or famous people can do, such as travel regularly to foreign countries or dine in fashionable restaurants.

glamour (*AmE* **glamor**) /'glamə(r)/ *noun* (*uncount*)
Glamour is the quality of being glamorous: *the glamour of the film stars of the 1950s* □ *She enjoys working in Hollywood, with all its glamour.*

glance /glɑːns/ *verb; noun*
▻ ***verb*: glances, glancing, glanced**
1 You **glance** at someone or something when you look at them very briefly: *She only glanced at Sheila for a second, but she knew something was wrong.* **2** You **glance** at something such as a newspaper when you read it quickly and without paying close attention: *I only had time to glance through the report.*
▻ ***noun*: glances:** *She threw a quick glance at Andrew, who was trying not to laugh.*
▻ ***phrase*** When you realize something **at a glance** you realize it immediately, as soon as you look at something or someone: *I could tell at a glance that they had been arguing again.*

phrasal verb

An object **glances off** a surface when it strikes it lightly along its length, with a brushing blow: *Luckily, the hammer had glanced off the table leg, making only a surface scratch.*

glancing /glɑːnsɪŋ/ *adjective*
Something moving through the air gives you a **glancing** blow when it hits you at an angle and moves on: *The stone had caught her a glancing blow on the side of the head, and she found she was bleeding.*

glare /glɛə(r)/ *verb; noun*
▻ ***verb*: glares, glaring, glared**
You **glare** at someone when you stare angrily at them. [*same as* **glower, scowl**]
▻ ***noun*** (*usually in the singular*): **glares**
1 A **glare** is an angry stare: *She felt nervous under his fiery glare.* **2** The **glare** from a light is its unpleasantly strong brightness: *She turned her eyes away from the glare.* □ *the glare of television lights.* **3** People often talk about the **glare** of publicity as a way of referring to the fact that journalists reveal every detail about

people's private lives: *There seemed to be no escape from the glare of publicity.*

glaring /ˈglɛərɪŋ/ *adjective*
Bad qualities are often described as **glaring** when they are very obviously bad: *a case of glaring incompetence.*

glass /glɑːs/ *noun*: **glasses**
1 (*uncount, often adjectival*) **Glass** is the hard transparent substance that windows and bottles are made of: *a new pane of glass to repair the window* □ *a tiny piece of glass stuck in his hand* □ *The older books are displayed in glass cases.* **2** A **glass** is a container for drinking from, made from this substance, usually one without handles: *a collection of wine glasses and sherry glasses.* **3** A **glass** of something is the amount held in such a container: *He's already drunk several glasses of wine.* **4** (*uncount*) **Glass** also refers to articles made of glass: *a collection of cut glass.* **5** (*plural*) **Glasses** are spectacles, two pieces of specially shaped glass in a frame worn over a person's eyes to correct faulty sight: *a pair of glasses* □ *Pass me my reading glasses.*

glaze /gleɪz/ *verb*: **glazes, glazing, glazed**

> ***phrasal verb***
> You say that someone's eyes **glaze over** when you can tell by looking at them that the person is suddenly no longer interested in what they are watching or listening to: *I can see people's eyes glaze over when I tell them I'm an educational psychologist.*

gleam /gliːm/ *verb; noun*
▻ ***verb***: **gleams, gleaming, gleamed**
1 Something **gleams** when it shines brightly because its surface has been cleaned or polished: *They polished the silverware until it gleamed.* **2** Someone's eyes **gleam** when they are bright with a feeling such as interest, satisfaction, anger or greed: *Old John's eyes gleamed at the mention of diamonds.*
▻ ***noun*** (*usually in the singular*): *She was almost dazzled by the gleam of the polished brass.* □ *There was a gleam of malicious satisfaction in his eye.*

glean /gliːn/ *verb*: **gleans, gleaning, gleaned**
If someone asks you what information you've **gleaned** about something, they want to know what you've managed to find out about it: *From what little I did glean from overheard conversations, most people are in favour.*

glee /gliː/ *noun* (*uncount*)
Glee is great delight or excitement: *The children shrieked with glee.* — *adjective* **gleeful:** *gleeful cheers.*

glen /glɛn/ *noun*: **glens**
A **glen** is a long narrow valley, especially one in Scotland.

glib /glɪb/ *adjective*: **glibber, glibbest**
Someone who is **glib** is good at giving quick and convincing solutions or explanations but is suspected by others of being neither sincere nor reliable: *glib politicians.*

glide /glaɪd/ *verb*: **glides, gliding, glided**
1 You **glide** somewhere when you move there smoothly and quietly: *She glided across the dance floor to greet me.* **2** Birds **glide** when they sail through the air without beating their wings.

glider /ˈglaɪdə(r)/ *noun*: **gliders**
A **glider** is a small aeroplane with no engine, kept flying by rising currents of warm air.

glimmer /ˈglɪmə(r)/ *verb; noun*
▻ ***verb***: **glimmers, glimmering, glimmered**
Something **glimmers** when it shines, or reflects light, faintly or irregularly: *The swimming pool glimmered in the moonlight.* [*same as* **shimmer**]
▻ ***noun*** (*usually in the singular*): **glimmers**
1 A **glimmer** of light is a faint, unsteady reflection of it. **2** A **glimmer** of some quality is a small amount of it, a hint or trace: *There was, after all, a glimmer of hope in this desperate situation.*

glimpse /glɪmps/ *verb; noun*
▻ ***verb***: **glimpses, glimpsing, glimpsed**
1 You **glimpse** something when you see it only for a moment and not very clearly: *She glimpsed a little low-roofed house through the trees.* [*same as* **catch sight of**] **2** You also **glimpse** something when you experience it for a very short time: *She might have been content had she not glimpsed something of the life of luxury her wealthy friends led.*
▻ ***noun***: **glimpses:** *I only caught a glimpse of him as we passed on the stairs.* □ *Holidays were a glimpse of how happy life might be.*

glint /glɪnt/ *verb; noun*
▻ ***verb***: **glints, glinting, glinted**
Something **glints** when it reflects flashes of bright light: *His brass doorplate glinted in the sunlight.*
▻ ***noun*** (*usually in the singular*): **glints:** *A glint of silver dazzled me momentarily.* □ *There was a mischievous glint in his eye.*

glisten /ˈglɪsən/ *verb*: **glistens, glistening, glistened**
A wet or icy surface **glistens** when it reflects faint flashes of light: *In the lane, the snow was glistening.*

glitter /ˈglɪtə(r)/ *verb; noun*
▻ ***verb***: **glitters, glittering, glittered**
Something that **glitters** shines, or reflects light, brightly, with occasional flashes: *Her diamond earrings glittered as she danced.* [*same as* **sparkle, flash**]
▻ ***noun*** (*used in the singular*): *It was strange descending from the quiet dark hill into the glitter of the streets.* □ *They were dazzled by the glitter of gold braid and medals.*

glittering /ˈglɪtərɪŋ/ *adjective*
Something might be described as **glittering** when it is very impressive: *It was a glittering performance.* [*same as* **splendid, brilliant**]

gloat /gloʊt/ *verb*: **gloats, gloating, gloated**
Someone **gloats** when they show too much pleasure or satisfaction at their own success or someone else's failure: *Newspapers gloated over the breakdown of the royal marriage.*

global /ˈgloʊbəl/ *adjective*
Global refers to the whole world, or to things that affect or concern the whole world: *It has become fashionable to refer to the world as 'the global village'.* □ *environmental destruction on a global scale.*

globe /gloʊb/ *noun*: **globes**
1 (*used in the singular*) The world is often referred to as the **globe**: *travelling to countries on the other side of the globe.* **2** A **globe** is a sphere with a map of the world on it. **3** A **globe** is also any ball-shaped object: *They watched the bright orange globe of the sun slowly descending in the west.* □ *It has spiky leaves and globe-shaped flowers*

gloom /gluːm/ *noun* (*uncount*)
1 Gloom is a state of near-darkness, as night approaches: *In the gloom, it was hard to tell whether it was a man or a woman.* [*opposite* **brightness**] **2 Gloom** is also a feeling or atmosphere of sadness or despair: *She thought one of her jokes might lift the gloom that*

seemed to engulf them all. [*opposite* **cheerfulness**] — *adjective* **gloomy:** *The house was even larger and gloomier than I remembered.* ▫ *I wondered what had happened; they all looked so gloomy.* [*opposite* **bright**, **cheerful**]

glorified /ˈglɔːrɪfaɪd/ *adjective*
Glorified is used to show that something is far less impressive than it sounds: *The 'study', as they called it, was little more than a glorified boxroom.*

glorious /ˈglɔːrɪəs/ *adjective*
1 Something described as **glorious** is splendidly beautiful: *On display was a glorious array of tapestries.* [*same as* **marvellous**, **splendid**] **2 Glorious** also means extremely happy, and suggests freedom from worries and troubles: *those glorious years after the war.* **3 Glorious** weather is pleasantly hot and sunny.

glory /ˈglɔːrɪ/ *noun*; *verb*
▻ ***noun***: **glories**
1 (*uncount*) **Glory** consists of being greatly admired by many people, for having achieved something outstanding: *We were not fighting for glory.* **2** The **glory** or **glories** of someone or something are their most admirable or attractive features: *She had thick wavy auburn hair, which was indeed her crowning glory.* ▫ *It would take weeks to sample all the glories of Parisian life.*
▻ ***verb***: **glories, glorying, gloried**

> ***phrasal verb***
> You **glory in** something when you feel or show great delight or pride in it: *The ladies were encouraged to glory in their new-found beauty.*

gloss /glɒs/ *noun*; *verb*
▻ ***noun*** (*usually in the singular*): **glosses**
There is a **gloss** on an object when its surface has a shiny brightness: *The table was polished to a high gloss.* [*same as* **sheen**]
▻ ***verb***: **glosses, glossing, glossed**

> ***phrasal verb***
> You **gloss over** an awkward problem or question when you ignore it or deal with it quickly, hoping to take the attention of other people away from it: *It's no use the Minister trying to gloss over his department's mistakes.*

glossy /ˈglɒsɪ/ *adjective*: **glossier, glossiest**
1 A **glossy** surface is smooth and shiny: *Her long hair was glossy and healthy-looking.* ▫ *We can supply prints with a matt or glossy finish.* [*opposite* **dull, matt**] **2 Glossy** magazines are printed on expensive shiny paper: *Their gardens have been featured in a number of glossy magazines of the 'Country Life' kind.*

glove /glʌv/ *noun*: **gloves**
Gloves are coverings for your hands, especially ones that have individual covers for each finger: *a pair of woollen gloves* ▫ *Wear rubber gloves when handling these chemicals.*

glove compartment /ˈglʌv kəmpɑːtmənt/ *noun*: **glove compartments**
The **glove compartment** in a car is a storage space usually in front of the passenger seat [see picture at **car**]

glow /gloʊ/ *verb*; *noun*
▻ ***verb***: **glows, glowing, glowed**
1 Something **glows** when it burns or shines with a dull steady heat or light without flames. **2** Surfaces **glow** when they reflect this kind of light. **3** Someone's face **glows** when it has an attractive reddish or pinkish colour, *eg* when they are very happy or when they have been doing something energetic: *Helen's cheeks glowed with youthful energy.*
▻ ***noun*** (*used in the singular*): *He sat and read by the soft glow of the fire.* ▫ *I was glad to see that she had regained her healthy glow.*

glower /glaʊə(r)/ *verb*: **glowers, glowering, glowered**
Someone **glowers** at you when they stare angrily at you. [*same as* **glare, scowl**]

glowing /ˈgloʊɪŋ/ *adjective*
A **glowing** account of something is full of praise and admiration for it: *Mr Thomas has written a glowing report of her progress.*

glucose /ˈgluːkoʊs/ *noun* (*uncount*)
Glucose is a sugar-like substance in food, that gives you energy when you eat: *The doctor gave him glucose tablets.*

glue /gluː/ *noun*; *verb*
▻ ***noun*** (*uncount*)
Glue is any kind of substance used to stick things together: *a tube of glue.* [*same as* **adhesive**]
▻ ***verb***: **glues, glueing** or **gluing, glued**
1 You **glue** things together when you stick one to the other using glue: *He had somehow managed to glue his fingers to the drawer.* **2** One thing **is glued** to another when it has become stuck to it: *A dirty old coffee cup was glued to his desk.* **3** You **are glued** to something when you are watching it or listening to it with all your attention: *Sandra would sit glued to the radio for hours.*

glum /glʌm/ *adjective*: **glummer, glummest**
Someone who is **glum** is sad or depressed: *There's no need to look so glum.* [*same as* **depressed**; *opposite* **cheerful**]

glutton /ˈglʌtən/ *noun*: **gluttons**
1 A **glutton** is a greedy person who eats too much. **2** You say that someone is a **glutton** for punishment when they seem eager to do or have something that you think is unpleasant or undesirable: *People who go jogging in winter must be gluttons for punishment.* ▫ *He's a glutton for criticism.*

gnarled /nɑːld/ *adjective*
1 A **gnarled** tree has twisted branches and lumps on its bark, because it is very old. **2 Gnarled** hands and fingers are thin and bony, with large knuckles: *The old woman wagged a gnarled finger at me.*

gnash /naʃ/ *verb*: **gnashes, gnashing, gnashed**
You **gnash** your teeth when you grind them together in anger.

gnat /nat/ *noun*: **gnats**
A **gnat** is a very small biting fly, common near water.

gnaw /nɔː/ *verb*: **gnaws, gnawing, gnawed**
1 Animals **gnaw** something, or **gnaw** at it, when they bite it with a scraping action: *The family dog was gnawing away at a bone.* **2** A problem or worry **gnaws** at you when you are unable to get it out of your mind: *She felt the familiar guilt gnawing away at her.*

gnome /noʊm/ *noun*: **gnomes**
In children's stories, a **gnome** is a kind of fairy in the shape of a little old man in a pointed hat; a garden **gnome** is a plaster or plastic figure representing this fairy character, for putting in your garden.

go /goʊ/ *verb*; *noun*
▻ ***verb***: **goes, going, went, gone**

> **gone** or **been**?
> The usual past participle of **go** is **gone**, but **been** is sometimes used. [see **been**]

1 a You **go** somewhere when you walk, move or travel there: *They've gone into town to do some shopping.* □ *We decided not to go to France after all.* □ *Peter went into the garden for some fresh air.* □ *The bus went past without stopping.* **b** You **go** to a building or other place when you visit or attend it, once or regularly: *James decided not to go to the cinema with the others.* □ *She goes to a school near where we live.* □ *If the pain gets any worse, you should go to the doctor's.* **c** Someone or something **goes** when they leave or depart: *I asked her not to go.* □ *When does the next train go?* **d** Roads and paths **go** to the places they lead or extend to: *A narrow path went through the wood to the lake on the other side.* □ *Follow the dirt track that goes across the field between the two farms.* **e** A vehicle **goes** when it is moving under its own power: *The car was not going at the time.* **f** You say that time **goes** fast or slowly when you mean that the hours or minutes seem to be passing quickly or slowly.

2 a You can use **go** to refer to things you do or activities you take part in: *Your mother has gone shopping.* □ *We're going skiing next week.* □ *My parents like to go hill-walking at weekends.* **b** You **go** for an activity when you start to do it: *Jane had gone for an early-morning swim.* □ *I'm exhausted; I'll have to go for a lie-down.* **c** You can also say that someone **goes** to do something, or (*informal*) **goes** and does something, when they have decided to do it and are about to do it: *She went to open the window* □ *I made some coffee, then went and spilt it on the floor.* [see also **going**]

> Notice that '**go** and' is often used to imply disapproval of the thing done: *Why did you go and give away the secret?*

3 a You use **go** to mean 'become': *When she heard the news, her face went white.* □ *This tea's gone cold.* **b Go** is often used with adjectives to refer to unfavourable or unwelcome states or conditions, to show that they continue: *The choice was to steal food or go hungry.* □ *Her comments and suggestions went largely unheard.*

4 You use **go** to refer to how well something is happening or working: *The training exercise was going horribly wrong.* □ *The interview went very well.*

5 a A machine or other device **goes** or **is going** when it is working: *We tried everything we could to make the car go again.* □ *The camera was still going long after the actors had sat down.* **b Go** is used to introduce an action or noise that someone or something makes: *He told me to go like this with my hands.* □ *We have an alarm clock that goes 'Beep! Beep!'*

6 a You say that something **goes** in a place when it is usually kept there or when it is meant to be put there: *Cutlery goes in the top drawer, tea towels in the bottom.* □ *This cap goes on the end of the lens, for protection.* **b** Things **go** together when they make a pleasant or attractive combination: *The hat didn't go with the rest of the outfit.* □ *a light wine that goes particularly well with salads and cooked meats.* **c** One thing **goes** into another when it fits or is contained by it: *My foot won't go into the shoe.* □ *Four into three won't go.* **d** Two or more things **go** together when they are connected or associated in the mind: *Kindness doesn't always go with beauty.* **e** You say that something like an award or honour **goes** to a person when it is given to them: *The job went to someone already employed by the Council.* □ *The Oscar for best actress goes to Jodie Foster.* **f** Something such as a rule or condition **goes** for the person it applies to: *We expect our young girls to behave well in adult company; the same goes for the boys, of course.*

7 You say that a resource such as money or time **goes** on or into something when the resource is used for that purpose: *Over half their income goes on rent.*

8 (*informal*) You can say that something is **going** when it is available or it is being offered: *We decided their offer was the best going.*

▷ ***noun*: goes**

1 A **go** is an attempt at something: *They managed to do it on the third go.* **2** You say it is someone's **go** to do something when they have the next chance or opportunity: *The children wanted to have a go on the swings.* [*same as* **turn**]

▷ ***phrases*** **1** (*informal*) **a** You **have a go** when you try to do something you are not very good at or confident about: *I can't play the piano very well, but I'll have a go.* **b** You **have a go at** someone when you criticize or blame them angrily. **2** You **make a go of** something when you put a lot of effort into making it a success: *They really are trying to make a go of their marriage.* **3** You say there are a certain number of things **to go** when there are that number left: *I've read three chapters and there are six to go.*

> ***phrasal verbs***
>
> **go about**
> **1** You **go about** something in a particular way when you deal with it or handle it in that way: *I couldn't think how to go about breaking the news to her.* **2** You **go about** or **around** or **round** doing something, usually something other people disapprove of, when you do it often: *There's no need for him to go about insulting people like that.* **3** You say that something **is going about** or **around** or **round** when more and more people are talking about it or know about it: *There's a rumour going about that his wife's left him.* **4** When a infectious disease is **going about** or **around** or **round** a lot of people are catching it.
>
> **go ahead 1** Something **goes ahead** when it takes place as planned. **2** You **go ahead** with a plan or idea when you do it as intended. [see also **go-ahead**]
>
> **go along with** You **go along with** a plan or decision when you agree with it and support it.
>
> **go around** see **go about**.
>
> **go back on** You **go back on** a promise or agreement when you decide not to do what you promised or agreed to do.
>
> **go by 1** Time **goes by** when it passes: *Four years went by before I saw her again.* **2** You **go by** something, *eg* someone's advice, when it influences your actions or decisions: *Don't go by what she says – decide for yourself.*
>
> **go down** (*informal*) Something like a remark or piece of humour **goes down** well when people like it or enjoy it: *His jokes didn't go down very well with the older folks.*
>
> **go down with** You **go down with** an illness when you begin to suffer from it: *At the start of the holiday they all went down with measles.*
>
> **go for 1** You **go for** someone when you attack them, physically or with words: *He went for me with a knife.* **2** You **go for** someone or something when you like or are attracted by them: *She goes for him in a big way.* □ *We don't go for classical music, I'm afraid.* **3** You also **go for** something when you choose it: *In the end, I went for the red dress.*
>
> **go in 1** You **go in** when you enter a building or room: *Please do go in.* **2** You **go in** or **into** a building or room when you enter it: *They all went into the dining room for lunch.*
>
> **go in for 1** You **go in for** a contest when you enter it. **2** You **go in for** an activity or occupation when you enjoy it and do it regularly: *He doesn't go in for outdoor sports much.*

go into 1 You **go into** a job or profession when you choose it as a career: *I'd never thought of going into the police force.* **2** You **go into** something when you discuss or explain it in detail: *There's not time to go into the precise reasons for the decision.*
go off 1 A bomb or gun **goes off** when it explodes or is fired. **2** Food **goes off** when it becomes rotten and unfit to eat: *The fridge broke down, and all the milk went off.* **3** An electical device such as a light, or a system controlled by an electrical switch, **goes off** when it stops functioning: *At midnight all the lights and heating went off.* **4** You **go off** someone or something when you stop liking them: *It sounds like she's beginning to go off Simon.* □ *I've gone off the idea completely.* **5** An event **goes off** well when it is successful: *The party went off really well.*
go on 1 You **go on** doing something, or **go on** with something when you continue to do it: *Mark went on working while the others were out.* □ *I'll just go on with my guitar practice.* **2** You **go on** when you continue to talk: *'Please go on,' begged Tim.* **3** (*informal*) You **go on** about something when you talk about it constantly and tediously: *She spent the entire afternoon going on about the film she had seen.* **4** An electrical device such as a light, or a system controlled by an electrical switch, **goes on** when it starts to function: *I heard a click and the lights went on.* **5** (*informal*) You **go on** at someone when you constantly criticize them or urge them to do something: *The children are always going on at her to stop smoking.*
go out 1 You **go out** of a building or room when you leave it. **2 a** A light **goes out** when it is switched off. **b** A fire or something that is burning **goes out** when it stops burning. **3** You **go out** with someone when you have a romantic or sexual relationship with them, but are not living with them: *They've been going out together for years.* **4** You **go out** when you do something socially, such as visit the cinema or the theatre or go to a restaurant: *We don't seem to have the money to go out any more.* **5** Something **goes out** when it is no longer fashionable or popular: *Lavish lifestyles seem to have gone out.* **6** A radio or television programme **goes out** when it is broadcast.
go over 1 You **go over** something when you examine or check it or think about it carefully: *We need to go over these accounts again.* **2** You also **go over** something when you do it or discuss it in detail: *Let's go over the main points of the plan again.*
go round There is enough of something to **go round** when there is enough for everyone. [see also **go about**]
go through 1 You **go through** an amount or supply of something when you use it all up: *When I had the cold I went through several large boxes of paper hankies.* [*same as* **get through**] **2** You **go through** something such as a room or container when you check the contents carefully: *She'd gone through her briefcase twice, and the letter wasn't there.* **3** You **go through** a number of things when you examine or consider each one carefully: *There was a large pile of letters to go through.* **4** You **go through** an unpleasant experience when you suffer it: *You wouldn't believe what some of the prisoners went through.*
go through with You **go through with** something when you decide to do it even though it is difficult or unpleasant: *She's threatened to divorce him but I don't think she'll go through with it.*
go towards An amount of money **goes towards** something when it is used to pay part of the cost: *Their contribution can go towards the travel expenses.*
go under Something such as a business **goes under** when it fails.
go without You **go without** something, especially something needed or expected, when you have to manage without it: *Our parents didn't have the money for Christmas presents, so we went without.* [*same as* **do without**]

goad /goʊd/ *verb*: **goads, goading, goaded**
You **goad** someone into doing something when you repeatedly urge, criticize, ridicule or annoy them so that they feel forced to do it: *She had allowed herself to be goaded into challenging rules that she really thought were acceptable.*

go-ahead /ˈgoʊəhɛd/ *noun* (*used in the singular*)
You are given the **go-ahead** when you are given permission to start doing something: *We had expected to get the go-ahead straight away.* [*same as* **green light**]

goal /goʊl/ *noun*: **goals**
1 In games such as football and hockey, the **goal** is **a** the set of posts that you hit the ball through in order to score a point. **b** an act of scoring a point in this way, or the point scored: *We've seen two spectacular goals so far.* □ *Liverpool lead at half time by two goals to one.* **2** A **goal** is also an aim or purpose: *We've achieved our main goal of securing another 300 jobs.*

goalkeeper /ˈgoʊlkiːpə(r)/ *noun*: **goalkeepers**
In games such as football and hockey, the **goalkeeper** is the player who guards his or her own team's goal.

goat /goʊt/ *noun*: **goats**
A **goat** is an animal of the sheep family, with short horns, kept on farms for its milk and wool: *We spotted a couple of mountain goats.*

gob /gɒb/ *noun* (*informal*): **gobs**
Someone's **gob** is their mouth: *She smacked me in the gob.*

gobble /ˈgɒbəl/ *verb*: **gobbles, gobbling, gobbled**
You **gobble** food when you eat it hurriedly and noisily: *He gobbled down a sandwich before dashing out again.* [*same as* **bolt** down]

go-between /ˈgoʊbɪtwiːn/ *noun*: **go-betweens**
A **go-between** is someone who takes messages between two people or groups who are unable or unwilling to contact each other directly: *Jeanette acted as our go-between.*

goblet /ˈgɒblət/ *noun*: **goblets**
A **goblet** is a drinking-cup with a stem and no handles, especially one made from metal.

gobsmacked /ˈgɒbsmakt/ *adjective* (*informal*)
You can say you are **gobsmacked** when you are extremely surprised or shocked.

god /gɒd/ *noun*: **gods**
1 God is the name given to the being who, many people believe, created the universe and guides or controls the lives of all people: *We pray that God may help us in our time of need.* □ *If there is a God, I hope he will save us.* **2** In many religions, people worship several **gods** who, they believe, each control a particular feature of nature or life: *the Greek god of the sea.* **3** (*informal*) Some people use **God** in expressions of anger, surprise or other strong emotion: *My God, what has happened to you?* □ *Good God, what a mess!* **4** You might refer to someone or something that you greatly admire, or that greatly influences you, as a **god**: *He made money his god.*

▻ ***phrases*** **1 God forbid** is sometimes used as a way of saying that you hope very much that something does not happen: *God forbid that she should ever find out.* **2 God knows** is often used as a way of saying that you don't know something, *eg* how something could have happened: *God knows why she chose to tell him now.* ▫ *'Who do you think they'll choose for the job?' 'God knows; they might choose anyone.'*

goddess /ˈgɒdɛs/ *noun*: **goddesses**
In some religions, a **goddess** is a female god who, people believe, controls a particular feature of nature or life: *She is the Roman goddess of love.*

godparent /ˈgɒdpɛərənt/ *noun*: **godparents**
A **godparent** is a person, often a family friend, responsible for a child's religious education, and sometimes responsible for the child's upbringing if both parents die.

godsend /ˈgɒdsɛnd/ *noun*: **godsends**
A **godsend** is someone or something whose arrival is unexpected but very welcome: *The extra money was a godsend.*

goggles /ˈgɒgəlz/ *noun (plural)*
Goggles are glasses that fit tightly around your eyes for protection, that you might wear *eg* when skiing: *Take a spare pair of goggles.*

going /ˈgoʊɪŋ/ *verb; noun; adjective*
▻ ***verb***
Going is the present participle of **go**. [see also **going to** below]
▻ ***noun*** *(uncount or used in the singular)*
1 Going is progress: *They made good going in the first few hours.* ▫ *'We've nearly finished the first job already.' 'That's not bad going in two hours.'* **2** (*informal*) The **going** is the general situation or conditions that affect the progress you are able to make: *The going began to get tough.* ▫ *The first two hours of climbing were quite hard going.*
▻ ***adjective***
The **going** rate for something is the amount of money people usually pay for it: *They were paid well below the going rate.*
▻ ***phrase*** **Going to** is used with the infinitive form of other verbs to talk about the future. It can be used to mean two different things.
1 It can mean that someone has made a decision to do something in the future: *I'm going to leave work early today.* ▫ *They're going to paint the kitchen first.* ▫ *I'm not going to tell you unless you promise you won't tell anyone else.* ▫ *We're going to go later, when we've finished here.* **2** It can also mean that something will definitely happen in the future, usually quite soon in the future, because the cause of it already exists: *The situation is going to get quite violent if the police don't intervene soon.* ▫ *I think I'm going to be sick.* ▫ *It looks like it's going to rain before long.*

goings-on /goʊɪŋˈzɒn/ *noun (plural)*
Goings-on are things that happen, especially things that you find strange or amusing, or things you disapprove of: *The public don't get to hear about the more sinister goings-on in Parliament.*

gold /goʊld/ *noun; adjective*
▻ ***noun***: **golds 1** (*uncount*) **Gold** is a precious yellow metal used for making jewellery and coins: *The statue was made entirely of gold.* **2** (*uncount*) **Gold** also means objects or coins made of gold: *Thieves got away with several thousand pounds of silver and gold.* **3** (*uncount*) **Gold** is also the yellow colour of the metal: *The pillars are decorated in blue and gold.* **4** A **gold** is a gold medal: *The Austrian athletes are hoping for at least two golds.*
▻ ***adjective***
Something that is **gold** is
1 made of gold: *gold bracelets.* **2** of the colour of gold: *a pot of gold paint.*
▻ ***phrases*** **1** You say that someone has **a heart of gold** if they are very kind. **2** Children are **as good as gold** when they behave well.

golden /ˈgoʊldən/ *adjective*
1 Something **golden** is the colour of gold, especially when it is also shiny: *She took off her hat, revealing beautiful golden hair.* **2 Golden** is often used to describe something very important, valuable or happy: *This is a golden opportunity.* ▫ *Those pre-war years seemed like a golden age.*

golden rule /goʊldən ˈruːl/ *noun*: **golden rules**
A **golden rule** is an essential principle or rule that must be followed or obeyed: *The golden rule in business seems to be self-preservation.*

goldfish /ˈgoʊldfɪʃ/ *noun*: **goldfish**
A **goldfish** is a small fish of a dark orange colour, often kept in aquariums.

gold medal /goʊld ˈmɛdəl/ *noun*: **gold medals**
A **gold medal** is a medal awarded to the winner of a contest, especially a sporting competition.

gold-plated /goʊldˈpleɪtɪd/ *adjective*
Something **gold-plated** is covered with a very thin layer of gold for decoration: *These earrings are gold-plated.*

golf /gɒlf/ *noun (uncount)*
Golf is an outdoor game played on a large area of specially shaped land (a **golf course**), in which you hit a small ball into each of a series of holes using a set of long-handled sticks: *At weekends she usually plays golf.* ▫ *a round of golf.*

golf club /ˈgɒlf klʌb/ *noun*: **golf clubs**
A **golf club** is **1** any of the set of long-handled sticks used to play golf. **2** an association of players of golf, or its buildings with a golf course attached.

gone /gɒn/ *verb; adjective*
▻ ***verb***
Gone is the past participle of **go**.
▻ ***adjective***
Something is **gone** when it has disappeared, or when it no longer exists: *When I looked in the drawer the letter was gone.* ▫ *All the old passion is now gone from his eyes.*

gong /gɒŋ/ *noun*: **gongs**
A **gong** is a hanging metal plate designed to be hit with a stick in order to make a ringing noise: *The gong sounded and the guests made their way to the dining-room.*

good /gʊd/ *adjective; noun; interjection*
▻ ***adjective***: **better, best**
1 Something is **good** if it is enjoyable, pleasant or desirable: *Did you have a good time at the party?* ▫ *She's not been in a very good mood today.* ▫ *It's good to see him smiling again.* **2 a** Someone is **good** at something if they have the talent or ability to do it well: *I was never very good at maths.* ▫ *She's a good swimmer.* **b Good** also means competent or effective: *Peter is very good with the children.* **3 a** Someone is **good** when they are morally virtuous and kind: *She is a very good person.* **b** You say that one person is **good** to another when they are kind and helpful: *My mother was good to me when I was ill.* **c** You say it is **good** of someone to do something when you appreciate it or want to thank them for it: *It was good of you to help.* **4** Something is also **good** if it is of a high standard: *He's always done*

very good work. □ *It's one of the better universities for studying languages.* **5** Something is **good** for you if you benefit from having or doing it, or if it is convenient or suitable: *I think a little break from work would be good for you.* **6** Children who are **good** are well-behaved: *She's been a good girl all day.* **7** You use **good** for emphasis to refer to the large extent or degree of something: *They had spent a good part of their money on food.* □ *Have a good look round the room to make sure you've packed everything.* □ *She waited for a good half hour.* **8** A **good** idea or plan is one that is well thought out and appropriate: *It was a good idea to buy the tickets the day before.* **9** You also use **good** to refer to the best of several similar things that you have: *Put on your good suit.* □ *We'll use the good cups for the tea party.*

▻ ***noun***: **goods**

1 (*used in the plural*) **Goods** are manufactured things that are bought, sold, transported or delivered: *a shop specializing in electrical goods.*

> Note that you do not use **good** in the singular to mean a single thing of this kind.

2 (*uncount*) **a Good** refers to actions or behaviour that are morally right or desirable. **b Good** also refers to the positive, helpful or beneficial effect of someone's actions or behaviour: *She was trying to help, but in the end did more harm than good.*

▻ ***interjection***

Good is often used on its own to show that you approve of or are pleased with something: *'Helena has agreed to help us.' 'Good.'*

▻ ***phrases*** **1** You use **as good as** to mean 'almost' or 'nearly': *We found the animal lying in a ditch, as good as dead.* **2** You say that something **does you good** when you get some benefit from it, especially for your health or well-being: *Do you think a bit of exercise would do you good?* **3** You say something is **for good** when it is for ever and won't change back again: *They left India for good.* **4** Someone can say that something is **for your own good** when it is unpleasant or unwelcome but you will benefit from it. **5** You say that something is **no good** when you don't think it will be effective or worthwhile: *It's no good complaining now.* [*same as* **no use**] **6** You can refer to a remarkable piece of good luck, or an unexpected success, as **too good to be true**. **7** You can ask **what good** does something do or **what is the good of** doing it when you doubt whether it will be of any use: *What good will it do to send them to prison?*

good afternoon /gʊd ɑːftə'nuːn/ *interjection*

Good afternoon is a formal way of saying 'hello', or sometimes 'goodbye', in the afternoon.

goodbye /gʊd'baɪ/ *interjection; noun*

▻ ***interjection***

You say **goodbye** when you leave someone, or when they leave you: *I wanted to say goodbye to him at the station.*

▻ ***noun***: **goodbyes**

A **goodbye** is an act of saying goodbye: *We said our goodbyes at the hotel.*

good evening /gʊd 'iːvnɪŋ/ *interjection*

Good evening is a formal way of saying 'hello', or sometimes 'goodbye', in the evening.

good-looking /gʊd'lʊkɪŋ/ *adjective*

A **good-looking** person has an attractive face: *Her husband was rather good-looking.*

good morning /gʊd 'mɔːnɪŋ/ *interjection*

Good morning is a formal way of saying 'hello', and rarely 'goodbye', in the morning.

good-natured /gʊd'neɪtʃəd/ *adjective*

A **good-natured** person is friendly, helpful and pleasant to other people.

goodness /'gʊdnɪs/ *noun; interjection*

▻ ***noun*** (*uncount*)

1 Goodness is the state or quality of being kind, or of wanting to do things that are morally right: *I believe in the essential goodness of human nature* **2** The **goodness** of food is what makes you healthy when you eat it: *I'll steam the vegetables so they don't lose all their goodness.*

▻ ***interjection***

People use **'goodness'** in various expressions of surprise: *Goodness me! What a heavy box!* □ *My goodness! I didn't realize it was so late.* □ *Goodness gracious! Whatever will he do next?*

▻ ***phrase*** For **for goodness sake** see **sake**.

goodnight /gʊd'naɪt/ *interjection*

You say **goodnight** to someone when you leave them late in the evening, *eg* when you go to bed.

gooey /'guːi/ *adjective* (*informal*): **gooier, gooiest**

Something **gooey** is sticky..

goose /guːs/ *noun*: **geese**

A **goose** is a long-necked bird like a large duck, often kept on farms.

gooseberry /'gʊzbərɪ/ *noun*: **gooseberries**

1 Gooseberries are small, round, green or purple fruits that grow on bushes. [see picture at **fruit**] **2** (*informal*) You might be called a **gooseberry** if you are in the company of two lovers who would prefer to be alone: *I didn't want to play gooseberry to my sister and her boyfriend.* [see picture at **fruit**]

goosepimples /'guːspɪmpəlz/ *noun* (*plural*)

Goosepimples are tiny raised lumps that sometimes appear on your skin when you are cold, frightened or excited.

gore /gɔː(r)/ *verb; noun*

▻ ***verb***: **gores, goring, gored**

Someone who **is gored** by an animal is wounded when the animal attacks them with its horns: *Some of the hunters have been gored to death by the rhinos.*

▻ ***noun*** (*uncount*)

Gore is blood from a wound, especially when it has become thick and sticky.

gorge /gɔːdʒ/ *noun; verb*

▻ ***noun***: **gorges**

A **gorge** is a deep narrow valley, usually one with a river running through it.

▻ ***verb***: **gorges, gorging, gorged**

You **gorge**, or **gorge** yourself, when you eat food greedily until you can eat no more: *While you gorge yourselves on fine food, people in the streets are starving.*

gorgeous /'gɔːdʒəs/ *adjective*

1 Someone who is **gorgeous** is very beautiful or attractive: *Who is that gorgeous little child?* □ *Isn't her hair gorgeous?* **2** Things that are very beautiful or pleasing might also be described as **gorgeous**: *There's a gorgeous view from this window.* □ *The food in the hotel was gorgeous.*

[*same as* **lovely, splendid**]

gorilla /gə'rɪlə/ *noun*: **gorillas**

A **gorilla** is a big, strong, dark brown ape, the largest of all apes.

gorse /gɔːs/ *noun* (*uncount*)

Gorse is a wild bush with yellow flowers and needle-like leaves: *paths lined with gorse* □ *a gorse bush.*

gory /ˈgɔːrɪ/ *adjective*: **gorier, goriest**
A **gory** incident is one in which people are violently injured or killed: *one or two gory scenes at the end of the film.* [*same as* **gruesome**]

gosh /gɒʃ/ *interjection* (*informal*)
People sometimes say **gosh** as a way of expressing surprise or shock: *Gosh! What an enormous house!*

gospel /ˈgɒspəl/ *noun*: **gospels**
1 The **Gospels** are those parts of the Christian bible that describe the life and teachings of Christ. **2** Any set of closely followed principles or rules might be referred to as a **gospel**: *We listened to Doctor Jacques preaching his gospel of a healthy mind and body.* **3** (*uncount*) You might say that something is **gospel** if you believe it is unquestionably true: *The unions are taking it as gospel that the factory will eventually close.* **4** (*uncount*) **Gospel**, or **gospel** music, is lively religious music especially popular among black Christians in America.

gossip /ˈgɒsɪp/ *noun*; *verb*
▻ ***noun*: gossips**
1 (*uncount*) **Gossip** is talk or writing about the private affairs of other people, especially when the comments are nasty, spiteful or untrue: *You shouldn't go around spreading gossip.* **2** You call someone a **gossip** if they talk about other people in this way.
▻ ***verb*: gossips, gossiping, gossiped**
1 To **gossip** is to talk about the private affairs of others, especially in a nasty or critical way. **2** To **gossip** is also to have an informal conversation about unimportant things. [*same as* **chat**]

got /gɒt/ *verb*
Got is the past tense and past participle of **get**. [see also **have got** at **have**]

gotten /ˈgɒtən/ *verb* (*AmE*)
Gotten is often used as the past participle of **get**.

gouge /gaʊdʒ/ *verb*: **gouges, gouging, gouged**

> ***phrasal verb***
> You **gouge** an object **out** when you force it out by pressing at the sides with your fingers or a sharp tool: *Some of the prisoners had had their eyes gouged out.*

gourmet /ˈgʊəmeɪ/ *noun*: **gourmets**
Someone might be described as a **gourmet** if they know a lot about good food and wine and they enjoy cooking and eating.

gout /gaʊt/ *noun* (*uncount*)
Gout is a disease of the blood which causes painful swelling of the joints, especially of the toes.

govern /ˈgʌvən/ *verb*: **governs, governing, governed**
1 A country **is governed** by the group of people who control and direct its social, economic and political affairs: *Most people are unhappy about the way this nation is being governed.* **2** Something **is governed** by what influences or controls it: *There are strict rules governing the selection of candidates.*

governess /ˈgʌvənɛs/ *noun* (*mainly old*): **governesses**
A **governess** is a woman employed by parents to educate their children privately at home, and usually also to supervise their behaviour and leisure pursuits.

government /ˈgʌvəmənt/ *noun*: **governments**
1 (*with a singular or plural verb*) The **government** of a country is the group of people elected to make decisions about its social, economic and political affairs: *This government has failed to keep its election promises.* □ *How can we get out of the economic mess that this goverment have got the country into?* **2** (*uncount*) **Government** is the activity or process of managing the affairs of a country, or the way in which they are managed: *This new legislation is the product of unsound government.* □ *It is an example of Liberal government at its worst.*

governor /ˈgʌvənə(r)/ *noun*: **governors**
1 The **governors** of an institution such as a school or hospital are the group of people who manage its affairs: *They had a meeting with the board of governors.* **2** The head of an institution such as a bank or a prison is often given the title of **governor**. **3** In America, a **governor** is the political head of a state.

gown /gaʊn/ *noun*: **gowns**
1 A **gown** is long dress that women wear on formal occasions: *She has hired a ball gown specially.* **2** A **gown** is also the official garment of people such as lawyers, priests and university teachers, worn loosely over their ordinary clothes.

GP /dʒiːˈpiː/ *noun*: **GPs**
A **GP** is a general practitioner, a local doctor who treats all kinds of minor diseases and illnesses.

grab /grab/ *verb*; *noun*
▻ ***verb*: grabs, grabbing, grabbed**
1 You **grab** something when you seize it suddenly and often with violence: *Rolf grabbed the man's jacket and pulled him to the ground.* □ *Janice grabbed her coat and rushed out of the room.* □ *She grabbed at my hair, but I pulled away.* **2** You also **grab** something when you take it hurriedly or eagerly: *We'll just have time to grab a sandwich.* □ *He should have grabbed the opportunity while it was there.*
▻ ***noun*** (*usually in the singular*): *She made a grab for my arm, but I was too fast for her.*

grace /greɪs/ *noun*; *verb*
▻ ***noun*** (*uncount*)
Grace is the quality of behaving in a very gentle and elegant way: *Classically trained dancers have an extraordinary grace of movement.*
▻ ***verb*** (*formal*): **graces, gracing, graced**
1 Something that **graces** a place or thing makes it elegant and attractive: *fine antique furniture that will grace any home* □ *Top model Naomi Campbell graces the cover of two of the most popular women's magazines this month.* **2** An important person **graces** a certain event or occasion when they attend it: *We are grateful that you were able to grace our little ceremony with your presence.* **3** (*formal*) You use the expressions 'Your **Grace**', 'Her **Grace**' and 'His **Grace**' to address or refer to a duke, duchess or archbishop: *His Grace the Duke Of Atholl attended the opening ceremony.*
▻ ***phrase*** You do something that you are asked, or expected, to do **with a good**, or **bad**, **grace** when you do it showing willingness, or unwillingness: *She did bring us clean plates eventually, but with a very bad grace.*

graceful /ˈgreɪsfʊl/ *adjective*
1 Graceful movements are smooth and elegant: *with a graceful wave of her hand.* **2 Graceful** behaviour is polite. **3 Graceful** also describes things that have a smooth, delicate shape: *the graceful curves of her cheeks.*

gracious /ˈgreɪʃəs/ *adjective*; *interjection*
▻ ***adjective***
1 Gracious behaviour is polite or honourable: *It was very gracious of you to admit that you were wrong.* [*opposite* **ungracious**] **2** Someone who enjoys **gracious** living is wealthy and lives luxuriously.
▻ ***interjection***
People use **'gracious'**, in various expressions of sur-

prise or shock: *Goodness gracious! What a lot of parcels!* □ *Gracious me! How did that happen?*

grade /greɪd/ *noun; verb*
▻ ***noun*: grades**
1 A **grade** is a stage or level on a scale of quality or rank, or a number or letter representing it: *The grade 'A' chickens are slightly more expensive.* □ *We only sell supergrade oil.* □ *Most of our pupils are expecting good grades in this years exams.* □ *all members of staff at managerial grade.* **2** (*AmE*) In schools, a **grade** is a group of classes containing pupils of the same age: *My son is in fifth grade.*
▻ ***verb*: grades, grading, graded**
You **grade** something or someone when you award them a grade according to quality or rank: *The test will be graded A to F, where A is excellent and F indicates failure.* □ *She is graded lower than me, although she arguably does a more important job.*
▻ ***phrase*** (*informal*) You **make the grade** when you succeed by reaching the required or expected standard.

gradient /ˈgreɪdɪənt/ *noun*: **gradients**
The **gradient** of a slope is a measure of how steep it is: *The hill must have a gradient of around 1 in 3.*

gradual /ˈgradʒʊəl/ or /ˈgradjʊəl/ *adjective*
Something **gradual** happens or develops slowly, over a period of time: *a gradual decline in British manufacturing industry.* [*opposite* **sudden**] — *adverb* **gradually:** *I gradually came to realize that my life would have to change.*

graduate *verb; noun*
▻ ***verb*** /ˈgradʒʊeɪt/: **graduates, graduating, graduated**
1 A student **graduates** when they successfully complete a course of study at a college or university and they receive their degree or other award. **2** (*AmE*) A pupil **graduates** when they leave secondary school, having successfully completed the necessary courses. **3** You **graduate** from one thing to another when you change to doing something more important, impressive or serious: *Nancy had quickly graduated from one or two glasses wine to half a bottle of vodka a day.*
▻ ***noun*** /ˈgradʒʊət/: **graduates**
A **graduate** is **1** someone with a degree or other qualification from a university or college. **2** (*AmE*) someone who has left secondary school after successfully completing all the necessary courses.

graduation /gradʒʊˈeɪʃən/ *noun* (*uncount*)
1 Graduation is the fact of successfully completing a course of study at a university or college, or, in the United States, at secondary school. **2 Graduation** is also the ceremony in which graduating students at universities and colleges receive their awards: *We will both be attending Steven's graduation.*

graffiti /grəˈfiːtɪ/ *noun* (*plural*)
Graffiti consists of words or drawings, usually of a humorous, rude or political nature, scratched or painted on walls in public places.

graft[1] /grɑːft/ *verb; noun*
▻ ***verb*: grafts, grafting, grafted**
To **graft** a piece of skin or bone on to another piece is to attach it surgically.
▻ ***noun*: grafts**
A **graft** is a piece of skin or bone surgically attached to another piece, or the surgical operation to attach it: *We'll do a skin graft to replace the damaged tissue.*

graft[2] /grɑːft/ *noun* (*uncount; informal*)
Graft is hard work.

grain /greɪn/ *noun*: **grains**
1 (*uncount*) **Grain** refers to cereal plants in general, or to any single cereal plant; **grain** also refers to the seeds of these plants, used as food. **2** A **grain** of something such as sand is a single tiny piece of it: *Sprinkle just a few grains of salt on top.* **3** A **grain** of something is a very small amount of it: *There isn't a grain of truth in the whole report.* **4** The **grain** of wood is the natural pattern of the lines of growth in it, or their direction: *You should always plane wood with the grain, not against it.*
▻ ***phrase*** Something **goes against the grain** when you don't want to do it or you find it difficult to do, because it is against your principles or natural character: *Try to be pleasant and polite, however much that may go against the grain.*

gram or **gramme** /gram/ *noun*: **grams**
A **gram** is a small measurement of weight equal to about 0.04 ounces.

-gram /gram/ *suffix*
-gram is used to form nouns that refer to something written, recorded or sent in a particular way: *I'll draw you a diagram.* □ *It's easier to phone than to send a telegram.*

grammar /ˈgramə(r)/ *noun*: **grammars**
1 (*uncount*) **Grammar** is the accepted rules by which the words of a language are formed and combined into sentences: *The students have already grasped some of the finer points of English grammar.* **2** (*uncount*) **Grammar** also refers to the way a person's speech or writing obeys or breaks these rules: *Her vocabulary is good but her grammar needs a little work.* **3** (*old*) A **grammar** is a book explaining the grammar of a particular language: *She had lost her Latin grammar.*

grammar school /ˈgramə skuːl/ *noun*: **grammar schools**
In the past, **grammar schools** were secondary schools that taught academic, not technical, subjects to pupils regarded as particularly clever, in preparation for university.

grammatical /grəˈmatɪkəl/ *adjective*
1 Grammatical means relating to grammar: *grammatical rules.* **2** A **grammatical** sentence is one that is correct according to the rules of grammar.

gramme see **gram**.

gramophone /ˈgraməfoʊn/ *noun*: **gramophones**
A **gramophone** is an old-fashioned record-player.

gran /gran/ *noun* (*informal*): **grans**
Your **gran** is your grandmother.

grand /grand/ *adjective; noun*
▻ ***adjective***
1 Something such as a building is **grand** if it is large or impressive in size, appearance or style: *There was a very grand entrance to what was, in fact, quite a modest hotel.* □ *The wedding was a little too grand for my taste.* [*same as* **splendid, impressive, imposing**; *opposite* **humble, plain, simple, unpretentious**] **2 Grand** is also used to describe rich or important people and expensive or important things: *a conference attended by the grand people of politics.* **3 Grand** also describes behaviour that is intended to impress others or gain attention: *Then, in a very grand gesture, she presented him with a cheque.* **4** A **grand** total is a complete or full amount, reached when several smaller amounts are added together: *Our campaign raised the grand total of £83 000.* **5** (*informal*) Some people use **grand** to mean excellent: *The weather was hot, and we all had a grand day out.*
▻ ***noun*** (*informal*): **grand**

A **grand** is a thousand dollars or pounds: *Their new kitchen cost over eight grand.*

grandad /ˈgrandad/ *noun*: **grandads**
Your **grandad** is your grandfather.

grandchild /ˈgrantʃaɪld/ *noun*: **grandchildren**
A **grandchild** is a child of your son or daughter.

granddaughter /ˈgrandɔːtə(r)/ *noun*: **granddaughters**
Your **granddaughter** is the daughter of your son or daughter.

grandeur /ˈgrandjə(r)/ *noun* (*uncount*)
The **grandeur** of something, such as a large building, is its quality of being impressively beautiful. [*same as* **magnificence**]

grandfather /ˈgranfɑːðə(r)/ *noun*: **grandfathers**
Your **grandfather** is the father of your mother or father.

grandfather clock /granfɑːðə(r) ˈklɒk/ *noun*: **grandfather clocks**
A **grandfather clock** is a clock in a tall wooden case, designed to stand on the floor.

grandiose /ˈgrandɪoʊz/ *adjective*
Grandiose is used to describe things that are so large, luxurious or ambitious that they are unattractive or seem ridiculous: *They stopped building those rather grandiose Italian palaces.* □ *She dreamt up some grandiose plan to save his soul.*

grandma /ˈgranmɑː/ *noun* (*informal*): **grandmas**
A **grandma** is a grandmother.

grandpa /ˈgranpɑː/ *noun* (*informal*): **grandpas**
A **grandpa** is a grandfather.

grandson /ˈgransʌn/ *noun*: **grandsons**
Your **grandson** is the son of your daughter or son.

grandstand /ˈgranstand/ *noun*: **grandstands**
A **grandstand** is a large covered stand at a sports ground, providing the best view: *We had excellent seats in the grandstand.*

granite /ˈgranɪt/ *noun* (*uncount*)
Granite is a very hard grey or red rock often used in building.

granny /ˈgranɪ/ *noun* (*informal*): **grannies**
A **granny** is a grandmother.

grant /grɑːnt/ *verb*; *noun*
▻ ***verb***: **grants, granting, granted**
1 You **grant** something such as permission when you give or allow it: *Think of Heaven as a place where all wishes are granted.* □ *The Minister has granted us a few minutes of his valuable time.* □ *Only then will you be granted British citizenship.* [*opposite* **deny**, **refuse**] **2 Grant** is often used as a way of saying you accept that what someone else has said is true: *It is, I grant you, a most embarrassing thing to have to do.* □ *Granted we have a problem here, how to we go about tackling it?*
▻ ***noun***: **grants**
You are given a **grant** when you receive money from a public organization, such as a local council, for a particular purpose: *The average student's maintenance grant has been cut by 5%.* □ *They've applied for a grant towards roof repairs.*
▻ ***phrase***
1 You **take** something **for granted** when you assume that it is true or correct and you don't check or question it: *We took it for granted that they would deliver the one we had ordered.* **2** When you **take** someone **for granted** you fail to appreciate or recognize the effort they make to help or support you: *Many women often feel that their husbands take them for granted.*

granule /ˈgranjuːl/ *noun*: **granules**
Foods and other substances in the form of **granules** are in the form of small grains: *coffee granules.*

grape /greɪp/ *noun*: **grapes**
Grapes are green or dark-purple berries that grow in bunches, eaten as a fruit and pressed to make wine. [see picture at **fruit**]

grapefruit /ˈgreɪpfruːt/ *noun*: **grapefruits** or **grapefruit**
A **grapefruit** is a large round yellow or pink fruit of the lemon family, with slightly sour flesh. [see picture at **fruit**]

grapevine /ˈgreɪpvaɪn/ *noun*: **grapevines**
A **grapevine** is the plant that grapes grow on.
▻ ***phrase*** When you hear about something **on** or **through the grapevine** you hear it mentioned in informal conversations you have with friends or colleagues.

graph /grɑːf/ *noun*: **graphs**
A **graph** is a diagram in which values or amounts are represented by dots, lines or blocks: *His progress was plotted on a graph.*

graphic /ˈgrafɪk/ *adjective*
1 A **graphic** description gives all the details, even if they are unpleasant or shocking: *The film contains one or two fairly graphic sex scenes.* [*same as* **explicit**] **2 Graphic** design is the branch of the arts concerned with drawing, printing and lettering. **3** A **graphic** representation of something shows it in the form of a graph.

graphics /ˈgrafɪks/ *noun* (*plural*)
In a magazine, the **graphics** are the photographs, illustrations and other elements that are not writing.

graphite /ˈgrafaɪt/ *noun* (*uncount*)
Graphite is a black soft form of the mineral carbon, used in various ways in industry and commerce, most commonly in pencils.

grapple /ˈgrapəl/ *verb*: **grapples, grappling, grappled**
1 You **grapple** with someone when you struggle with them physically: *One of the porters was grappling with a pile of suitcases as their owner stood by and watched.* **2** You **grapple** with a difficult problem when you try hard to solve it.

grasp /grɑːsp/ *verb*; *noun*
▻ ***verb***: **grasps, grasping, grasped**
1 You **grasp** something when you take a firm hold of it with your hands. **2** You **grasp** something such as an opportunity when you take it eagerly and immediately: *This is a chance that she should grasp with both hands.* [*same as* **seize**] **3** People **grasp** something when they understand it: *It was clear that Eric hadn't grasped the purpose of it at all.*
▻ ***noun*** (*usually in the singular*): **grasps**
1 Your **grasp** is your ability to hold something firmly in your hand: *I shook his hand, and winced under his powerful grasp.* **2** Something is in your **grasp** when you are able to reach, achieve or obtain it: *The window ledge was just out of my grasp.* □ *A senior management position is clearly within her grasp.* **3** You might say that something is within your **grasp** if you are able to understand it: *Applied mathematics was beyond the grasp of most of her pupils.*

grass /grɑːs/ *noun*; *verb*
▻ ***noun***: **grasses**
1 (*uncount*) **Grass** is any wild plant with green blade-like leaves, that makes up garden lawns and covers the ground in fields, eaten by many animals: *Every blade of grass glistened in the morning dew.* **2 Grasses** are plants with long stems and thin leaves, including bam-

boo and many cereal plants. **3** (*slang*) A **grass** is a person who betrays others, especially to the police.
▻ ***verb*** (*slang*): **grasses, grassing, grassed**
To **grass** on someone is to tell others, especially the police, about their dishonest or criminal behaviour.

grasshopper /ˈgrɑːshɒpə(r)/ *noun*: **grasshoppers**
A **grasshopper** is a small jumping insect that makes a high harsh noise by rubbing its long back legs against its wings.

grass roots /grɑːs ˈruːts/ *noun* (*plural, often adjectival*)
People often talk about **grass roots** as a way of referring to ordinary people or their opinions, as opposed to people in positions of political power: *It's difficult to know what the grass-roots reaction will be.*

grate[1] /greɪt/ *noun*: **grates**
A **grate** is a framework of iron bars for holding coal or wood in an open fireplace.

grate[2] /greɪt/ *verb*: **grates, grating, grated**
1 You **grate** vegetables and other foods when you cut them into thin strips using a grater: *Sprinkle some grated cheese over the top.* [compare **shred**] **2** Something **grates** on a surface when it makes a harsh grinding sound as it rubs against it: *the sound of knives grating on dinner plates.* **3** Something that **grates** on you irritates or annoys you: *It grates to think that the men get paid more than we do for precisely the same work, which I'm sure we do better than they do.*

grateful /ˈgreɪtfʊl/ *adjective*
1 You are **grateful** when you feel you want to thank someone for the help they have given you, or when you give your thanks: *Mr and Mrs Cameron are grateful for all your advice.* □ *We're extremely grateful to you.* □ *She was very grateful when I told her we could help.* [*same as* **appreciative**; *opposite* **ungrateful**] **2** If you say to someone you would be very **grateful** if they would do something, you are asking them to do it: *I'd be so grateful if you could let me have your answer by Friday at the latest.*

grater /ˈgreɪtə(r)/ *noun*: **graters**
A **grater** is a kitchen tool with rough, holed, metal surfaces that vegetables and other food are rubbed against for cutting into thin strips.

gratitude /ˈgratɪtjuːd/ *noun* (*uncount*)
Gratitude is the state or feeling of being grateful; you show **gratitude** when you thank someone.

gratuitous /grəˈtjuːɪtəs/ *adjective*
You might describe behaviour that you disapprove of as **gratuitous** if you think it cannot be justified or excused: *The film was full of scenes of gratuitous violence.*

grave[1] /greɪv/ *noun*: **graves**
1 A **grave** is a hole dug in the ground for burying a dead body in, or the place where a dead body is buried: *We go every week to put flowers on his grave.* **2** (*used in the singular*; *literary*) Death is sometimes referred to as the **grave**: *They live in luxury from the cradle to the grave.*

grave[2] /greɪv/ *adjective*: **graver, gravest**
1 Grave matters are serious or dangerous, and make you worried or concerned. [*opposite* **trivial**, **light**] **2** People are **grave** when they behave in a very serious or solemn way: *She wore a grave expression as she looked up from the letter.* [*same as* **solemn**, **serious**; *opposite* **bright**, **cheerful**]

grave accent /grɑːv ˈaksənt/ *noun*: **grave accents**
A **grave accent** is a mark (`) put over a vowel in certain languages, *eg* French, to show pronunciation.

gravel /ˈgravəl/ *noun* (*uncount, often adjectival*)
Gravel is a mixture of small stones used for the surface of paths and roads: *a gravel path.* [*same as* **grit**]

gravestone /ˈgreɪvstoʊn/ *noun*: **gravestones**
A **gravestone** is a carved stone marking a grave, usually with the dead person's name and dates of birth and death on it.

graveyard /ˈgreɪvjɑːd/ *noun*: **graveyards**
A **graveyard** is a cemetery, a place where dead bodies are buried.

gravitate /ˈgravɪteɪt/ *verb* (*formal*): **gravitates, gravitating, gravitated**
You say that people **gravitate** to or towards a place when they move there gradually, especially if you think they are attracted by something: *By the end of the day, most of the journalists had gravitated to the hotel bar.* □ *The Labour Party has gravitated towards a position of accepting the need for nuclear weapons.*

gravity[1] /ˈgravɪtɪ/ *noun* (*uncount*)
Gravity is the natural force that causes objects to fall to, or stay on, the ground: *Gravity then causes the water to flow down through the pipe.* □ *the force of gravity.*

gravity[2] /ˈgravɪtɪ/ *noun* (*uncount*)
1 The **gravity** of a situation or set of circumstances is its serious or dangerous nature, that makes you concerned or worried. **2 Gravity** is also the quality of being solemn and serious: *There was an unusual degree of gravity in his voice.*

gravy /ˈgreɪvɪ/ *noun* (*uncount*)
Gravy is a sauce served with meat, made by thickening the juices released by the meat during cooking, or made with some artificial substitute.

gravy boat /ˈgreɪvɪ boʊt/ *noun*: **gravy boats**
A **gravy boat** is a sauce boat. [see picture at **tableware**]

gray see **grey**.

graze[1] /greɪz/ *verb*: **grazes, grazing, grazed**
Animals **graze** when they eat grass growing in fields.

graze[2] /greɪz/ *verb*; *noun*
▻ ***verb***: **grazes, grazing, grazed**
You **graze** a part of your body when you break the skin through rubbing it against a hard rough surface.
▻ ***noun***: **grazes:** *a nasty graze on your arm.*

grease /griːs/ *noun*; *verb*
▻ ***noun*** (*uncount*)
Grease is any thick oily substance, especially one used to ease the movement of parts in a machine. [*same as* **oil**]
▻ ***verb***: **greases, greasing, greased:** *We'll need to grease the wheels a little.*

greasy /ˈgriːsɪ/ *adjective*: **greasier, greasiest**
1 Something **greasy** contains or consists of grease, or is covered in grease. **2 Greasy** skin looks slightly moist because the body releases a lot of natural oils into it. [*same as* **oily**] **3** Surfaces such as roads are sometimes described as **greasy** when they are wet and slippery.

great /greɪt/ *adjective*; *interjection*; *noun*
▻ ***adjective***: **greater, greatest**
1 a You use **great** to describe things that are very large in size or extent: *There was a great crowd of people in the square.* [*same as* **huge**] **b Great** is also used to describe things that are very large in quantity or degree: *a great amount of coffee* □ *You'll have great difficulty convincing him.* □ *He lived to a great age.* **2** You also use **great** to describe very impressive or important things, and very talented or successful people: *It was one of the great engineering projects of the last century.* □ *He is undoubtedly one of the greatest living actors.* [*same as* **fine**] **3** (*informal*) **Great** also means

excellent or very enjoyable: *It was a great party.* **4** (*informal*) You might say that someone is **great** at something if they are very clever or talented. **5** You can also use **great** to emphasize other adjectives describing size, especially 'big': *There was a great big box in the middle of the floor.*

▻ ***interjection***

People often say '**great!**' when they are very pleased or satisfied: *'The new cooker has already arrived.' 'Great!'*

▻ ***noun*** (*used in the plural*): **greats**

People and things regarded as the most excellent of their kind are often referred to as **greats**: *He's one of the all-time greats of British athletics.*

great- /greɪt/ *prefix*

Great- is used before nouns referring to family members to indicate a family member one generation older or younger, so that your **great**-grandmother refers to the mother of your grandmother or grandfather, and your **great**-grandson to the son of your grandson or granddaughter.

greatly /'greɪtlɪ/ *adverb* (*intensifying*)

Greatly is used like 'very', to emphasize the degree or extent of something: *We are greatly honoured by your visit.*

greed /gri:d/ *noun* (*uncount*)

1 Greed is the desire to eat lots of food, even though you are not hungry, or the fact of eating it. **2 Greed** also refers to a selfish desire to have more and more of something, *eg* money. — *adjective* **greedy:** *Don't be so greedy – you've already eaten enough for two people.* □ *We're breeding consumers who are becoming greedier and greedier.*

Greek /gri:k/ *adjective*; *noun*

▻ ***adjective***

Greek means concerned with or belonging to the modern country of Greece, or to its people or their language; it is often also used to refer to the society, culture and language of ancient Greece: *My wife holds a Greek passport.* □ *the Greek islands* □ *Poseidon was the Greek equivalent of the Roman god Neptune.*

▻ ***noun*: Greeks**

1 A person who is born in, or is a citizen of, Greece is a **Greek**: *Table 4 has been booked by a party of Greeks.* **2** (*uncount*) **Greek** refers to the language of the modern country of Greece, and sometimes to the language of ancient Greece: *The menu was all in Greek.*

green /gri:n/ *noun*; *adjective*

▻ ***noun*: greens**

1 (*uncount or count*) **Green** is the colour of grass and of the leaves of most plants: *The kitchen cabinets were a light shade of green.* □ *Her painting captures the lush greens and yellows of summer.* □ *I try to avoid wearing green.* **2** An area of short grass is often called a **green**, especially one prepared for a particular purpose: *a bowling-green.* **3** (*plural*) **Greens** are vegetables with edible green leaves and stems.

▻ ***adjective*: greener, greenest**

1 Green things are the same colour as grass and the leaves of most plants: *a long green overcoat* □ *It's more green than blue to my eye.* □ (*with the noun omitted*) *The blue curtains would give the room a cool feeling, so I think the green would be better.* **2 Green** areas have plants and trees growing in them, or they are covered with grass: *The new housing development will incorporate eight large green zones, where building will be forbidden.* **3** A **green** salad consists mainly of lettuce. **4 Green** is sometimes used to describe fruit that is not yet ripe. **5** (*informal*) You might describe someone as **green** if they are young, inexperienced or easily fooled: *He was very green when he first started the job.* **6 Green** is widely used to describe things that are designed to be as harmless as possible to the natural environment, for example by reducing the amount of harmful chemicals released into the air or into rivers: *The council's waste-collection system has benefited from a number of green initiatives.* □ *I'm afraid we're not a very green family.*

greenery /'gri:nərɪ/ *noun* (*uncount*)

Greenery consists of plants and trees: *I like a garden with a lot of greenery.*

greengrocer /'gri:ngroʊsə(r)/ *noun*: **greengrocers**

1 A **greengrocer** is someone who runs a shop selling fruit and vegetables. **2** A **greengrocer** or **greengrocer's** is a greengrocer's shop: *There used to be a greengrocer in the next street.* □ *We stopped at the greengrocer's for some apples.*

greenhouse /'gri:nhaʊs/ *noun*: **greenhouses** /'gri:nhaʊzɪz/

A **greenhouse** is a building with walls and a roof made of glass, used for growing plants which need special protection or conditions.

green light /gri:n 'laɪt/ *noun* (*usually in the singular*; *informal*)

You give someone the **green light** when you give them permission to do something planned: *Our proposals are waiting for the green light from head office.*

greet /gri:t/ *verb*: **greets, greeting, greeted**

1 You **greet** someone when you meet or welcome them as they arrive: *Kevin greeted me with the usual 'Hello, mate!'.* □ *We were warmly greeted by Mrs O'Toole, who offered us a glass of whiskey.* **2 Greet** is also used to refer to the way people react to or receive something they are told or shown: *His remarks were greeted with dismay by the managers.*

greeting /'gri:tɪŋ/ *noun*: **greetings**

1 A **greeting** is a friendly expression or gesture used on meeting or welcoming someone. **2** (*used in the plural*) **Greetings** is a word often used in sending a friendly message: *He sent us a postcard with 'Greetings from Marrakesh' on the front.* □ *Birthday greetings to my grandson.*

grenade /grə'neɪd/ *noun*: **grenades**

A **grenade** is a small bomb thrown by hand or fired from a rifle.

grew /gru:/ *verb*

Grew is the past tense of **grow**.

grey (*AmE* **gray**) /greɪ/ *noun*; *adjective*; *verb*

▻ ***noun*** (*uncount or count*)

Grey is the colour obtained when you mix black with white, the colour of rain clouds and of ash from a fire: *His suit was the usual dull grey.* □ *the greys and deep blues of the wintry ocean.*

▻ ***adjective***

1 Grey things are the same colour as rain clouds and ash. **2** The sky is **grey** when it is cloudy: *one of those grey winter mornings.* [*same as* **overcast, cloudy**] **3 Grey** describes a person's hair when some of it has turned white and some is still the original colour. **4 Grey** is also used to describe people and things that are dull or uninteresting: *He's rather a grey character.*

▻ ***verb*: greys, greying, greyed**

Someone's hair **is greying** when some of it is turning white.

grey area /greɪ 'ɛərɪə/ *noun*: **grey areas**

A **grey area** is a situation or circumstance in which it is not clear what action or decision should be taken: *The issue of staff coffee-breaks has always been something of a grey area, not strictly allowed but not ruled out either.*

greyhound /ˈgreɪhaʊnd/ *noun*: **greyhounds**
A **greyhound** is a tall thin dog that can run very fast, often raced for sport.

grid /grɪd/ *noun*: **grids**
1 A **grid** is a set of numbered squares on a map, used for identifying the position of precise points. **2** A network of something such as electricity cables or water pipes is often referred to as a **grid**. **3** A **grid** is also small framework of metal bars covering the opening to a drain in a road or pavement.

grief /gri:f/ *noun* (*uncount*)
Grief is great sorrow and unhappiness, often on the occasion of someone's death. [*same as* **distress, anguish**]
▻ *phrase* You **come to grief** when you fail, or when you are injured or harmed: *This was the third such scheme to come to grief.* □ *The ship came to grief on the rocks nearby.*

grievance /ˈgri:vəns/ *noun*: **grievances**
A **grievance** is a reason to complain, or the complaint that you make: *The company recognized that the customers had a genuine grievance.* □ *It's our policy to settle grievances as quickly as possible.*

grieve /gri:v/ *verb*: **grieves, grieving, grieved**
1 You **grieve** when you are sad or distressed about something, often someone's death: *She was still grieving for her son.* [*same as* **mourn**] **2** Something that **grieves** you makes you sad or upset: *It grieves me to have to say that the boy is already a confirmed criminal.*

grievous /ˈgri:vəs/ *adjective*
Grievous means very severe or serious: *He was charged with inflicting grievous bodily harm on the woman.* □ *It was a grievous error to make at this stage.*

grill /grɪl/ *verb*; *noun*
▻ *verb*: **grills, grilling, grilled**
1 You **grill** food when you cook it over or usually under a strong heat: *We could grill the chops on the barbecue.* **2** (*informal*) You **grill** someone when you question them repeatedly and for a long time: *Senior detectives had grilled him, but could not get a confession.* [*same as* **interrogate**]
▻ *noun*: **grills**
1 A **grill** is a part of a cooker used for grilling food: *Slip the omelette under the grill to brown it off.* [see picture at **kitchen**] **2** A **grill** is also a dish of grilled food.

grille /grɪl/ *noun*: **grilles**
1 A **grille** is a set of metal bars placed over an opening, *eg* a window **2** The **grille** on a motor vehicle is the set of metal bars covering its radiator. [see picture at **car**]

grilling /ˈgrɪlɪŋ/ *noun* (*informal*): **grillings**
You give someone a **grilling** when you keep questioning them about something. [*same as* **interrogation**]

grim /grɪm/ *adjective*: **grimmer, grimmest**
1 Someone looks **grim** when they look solemn or serious, as if they are thinking about something very unpleasant. **2** You might describe a situation or an incident as **grim** when it is so unpleasant that it shocks or upsets you: *the grim scene in the shop where the bomb exploded.* [*same as* **terrible, dreadful**] **3** (*informal*) Some people use **grim** to describe anything unpleasant or unfortunate: *After all this training, it's a bit grim to be told you're not even in the team.* **4** (*informal*) You might say you are feeling **grim** if you are ill.

grimace /ˈgrɪməs/ or /grɪˈmeɪs/ *noun*; *verb*
▻ *noun*: **grimaces**
A **grimace** is an ugly twisting of the face to express pain or disgust, or to amuse people: *'Not that old joke again!,' she exclaimed, with a grimace.*
▻ *verb*: **grimaces, grimacing, grimaced:** *She tried not to grimace as the needle was pushed into her gum.* [*same as* **pull a face**]

grime /graɪm/ *noun* (*uncount*)
Grime is thick dirt that is difficult to remove because it has been there a long time. — *adjective* **grimy:** *a gang of street children, each one grimier than the last.*

grimy /ˈgraɪmɪ/ See **grime**.

grin /grɪn/ *verb*; *noun*
▻ *verb*: **grins, grinning, grinned**
You **grin** when you smile broadly, showing your teeth.
▻ *noun*: **grins:** *a cheeky grin.*
▻ *phrase* (*informal*) You **grin and bear it** when you suffer something unpleasant without complaining.

grind /graɪnd/ *verb*; *noun*
▻ *verb*: **grinds, grinding, ground**
1 You **grind** something solid when you crush it into tiny pieces or into powder between two hard surfaces: *You can grind most spices by hand.* □ *freshly ground coffee.* **2** You **grind** something when you sharpen or polish it by rubbing it against a special stone or other hard surface: *a grinding tool.* **3** Two hard surfaces **grind** when they rub together with a loud harsh noise: *He drove off from the kerb with a horrible grinding of gears.* [*same as* **grate**] **4** You **grind** your foot or fist into something when you press it there with a twisting action: *Luke ground his heel into the dirt.*
▻ **noun** (*informal*; *singular*)
People often refer to the dull routine of daily working life as the **grind**: *It's back to the grind for me on Monday.*

phrasal verb
You refuse to let problems or troubles **grind** you **down** when you remain cheerful or hopeful despite them.

grip /grɪp/ *verb*; *noun*
▻ *verb*: **grips, gripping, gripped**
1 You **grip** something when you take or keep a firm hold of it: *She gripped my wrist and pulled me back.* □ *He tried to grip the rope between his knees.* [*same as* **clasp**] **2** Something such as a book or film **grips** you when it holds your full attention.
▻ *noun*: **grips**
1 (*used in the singular*) Your **grip** is your ability to hold or squeeze something, usually with your hands, or the action of holding or squeezing it: *Hold the racquet with quite a firm grip.* □ *She was losing her grip on the branch.* **2** A **grip** is a handle or other part designed to be gripped. **3** A hair **grip** is a U-shaped wire pin for keeping the hair in place. **4** (*used in the singular*) You lose your **grip** of something when you are no longer in control of it: *She lost her grip of the situation and the meeting soon descended into chaos.* □ *Such suggestions are wildly untrue; he appears to have completely lost his grip on reality.*
▻ *phrase* You **get to grips with** something when you begin to deal successfully with it.

gripe /graɪp/ *verb*; *noun*
▻ *verb* (*informal*): **gripes, griping, griped**
Someone who **gripes** complains, especially repeatedly. [*same as* **moan**]
▻ *noun* (*informal*): **gripes**
A **gripe** is a complaint: *the usual gripes from staff about poor working conditions.*

gripping /ˈgrɪpɪŋ/ *adjective*
Something such as a book or film is **gripping** if it holds your attention completely. [*same as* **absorbing, exciting**; *opposite* **boring, dull**]

grisly /'grɪzlɪ/ *adjective*: **grislier, grisliest**
A **grisly** scene or incident is disturbing to watch or witness because it involves people being violently injured or killed. [*same as* **ghastly, gruesome**]

gristle /'grɪsəl/ *noun* (*uncount*)
In a piece of meat, **gristle** consists of hard parts that are neither flesh nor fat and are very difficult to chew.

grit /grɪt/ *noun*; *verb*
▻ ***noun*** (*uncount*)
1 **Grit** consists of small hard particles of stone, used as a loose covering for roads and paths. [*same as* **gravel**] **2** (*informal*) **Grit** is also courage and determination: *She has showed a lot of grit throughout.*
▻ ***verb***: **grits, gritting, gritted**
1 Icy roads **are gritted** when a mixture of sand, salt and tiny stones is spread on them, to reduce skidding and make the ice melt quicker. **2** You **grit** your teeth when you press them together tightly, *eg* to overcome pain.

groan /groʊn/ *verb*; *noun*
▻ ***verb***: **groans, groaning, groaned**
1 You **groan** when you make a long deep sound in the back of your throat, expressing *eg* pain or disapproval. **2** Something such as a chair or table **groans** when it makes a long low noise suggesting it is about to collapse: *a desk groaning under the weight of several heavy boxes.*
▻ ***noun***: **groans:** *The suggestion of a day spent shopping was met with groans from the children.* [*opposite* **cheer**]

grocer /'groʊsə(r)/ *noun*: **grocers**
1 A **grocer** is someone who runs a shop selling food and general household goods: *His father was a grocer.* **2** A **grocer** or **grocer's** is a grocer's shop: *That shop used to be a grocer's.*

groceries /'groʊsərɪz/ *noun* (*plural*)
Groceries are items of food bought in a shop: *carrying a bag of groceries.*

groggy /'grɒgɪ/ *adjective* (*informal*): **groggier, groggiest**
You feel **groggy** when you feel weak and dizzy, *eg* as the effect of illness or drinking alcohol. [*same as* **unsteady**; *opposite* **lucid**]

groin /grɔɪn/ *noun* (*used in the singular*)
Your **groin** is the area of your body around your sexual organs, especially in men.

groom /gruːm/ *noun*; *verb*
▻ ***noun***: **grooms**
1 A **groom** is a person who looks after horses and cleans stables. **2** A **groom** is also a bridegroom, a man who is getting married: *Congratulations to the bride and groom.*
▻ ***verb***: **grooms, grooming, groomed**
1 You **groom** a horse or other animal when you wash and especially brush it. **2** Someone who is well **groomed** is clean, neat and smart in appearance, with well-cared-for hair. [*same as* **turned out**] **3** You **groom** someone for a particular job or position when you prepare them for it, by giving them suitable experience and training: *She imagined she was being groomed for a senior management role.* [*same as* **train**]

groove /gruːv/ *noun*: **grooves**
1 A **groove** is a long narrow channel, especially a very regular one cut with a tool: *On some of these old records the grooves are badly worn.* **2** People often use 'the **groove**' as a way of referring to a pleasingly regular rhythm or routine of living or working: *After all the upheaval of moving house, we're looking forward to getting back to the usual groove.*

grope /groʊp/ *verb*: **gropes, groping, groped**
1 You **grope** when you feel about with your hands, being unable to see, *eg* because it is dark: *I groped around for the light switch.* ▫ *Janet groped about in her bag for a pen.* ▫ *We continued to grope along through the fog.* **2** You might say that you **are groping** for something, such as a solution to a problem, when it is difficult to find and you are not sure you will find it at all: *We groped around for answers, but none came.* **3** (*informal*) To **grope** someone is to touch or stroke them in a sexual way: *young couples groping in the back of cars.*

gross /groʊs/ *adjective*; *noun*
▻ ***adjective***
1 **Gross** refers to total amounts or quantities, so that the **gross** weight of a package consists of the combined weights of the contents and the container, and a person's **gross** income is the amount they earn before tax is taken away. [*opposite* **net**; see **net**[2]] **2** **Gross** is used for emphasis to describe extreme cases of actions or behaviour that are strongly disapproved of: *They were accused of gross mismanagement of the affair.* ▫ *committing acts of gross indecency.* **3** Someone's language or behaviour is described as **gross** if it is rude, coarse or vulgar. [*same as* **coarse**; *opposite* **delicate, polite, well-mannered**] **4** (*AmE*; *informal*) **Gross** means disgusting or very unpleasant.
▻ ***noun***: **gross**
A **gross** is an old measure of quantity, 144 of something: *Our free-range eggs are very popular – local market traders have sold over ten gross this year.*

grossly /'groʊslɪ/ *adverb* (*intensifying*)
Grossly means extremely: *Reports of the cost of the project have been grossly exaggerated.*

grotesque /groʊ'tɛsk/ *adjective*
Something **grotesque** looks very strange and unnatural, and either frightens or amuses you: *The illness had aged him terribly, made him almost grotesque.* [*same as* **hideous**]

grotty /'grɒtɪ/ *adjective* (*informal*): **grottier, grottiest**
1 Something **grotty** is unpleasantly dirty or badly cared for: *She had a grotty little flat near the station.* [*same as* **seedy**] **2** You feel **grotty** when you feel ill.

ground[1] /graʊnd/ *noun*; *verb*
▻ ***noun***: **grounds**
1 (*singular or uncount*) The **ground** is the outdoor surface of the earth that you can stand or walk on: *The house had been built on rather stony ground.* ▫ *The ladder collapsed and she fell to the ground.* **2** (*plural or uncount*) The **ground** or **grounds** of a building are the large area of land attached to it or surrounding it: *The castle has splendid grounds.* ▫ *a large country house with a considerable amount of ground.* **3** A **ground** of a special named type is an area of land used for a specific purpose: *a burial ground* ▫ *a football ground.* **4** You cover or go over **ground** when you discuss or deal with a certain range of topics: *The committee covered a lot of new ground at the last meeting.* **5** You make **ground** when you make progress or achieve an advantage; you **lose ground** when someone else such as a rival achieves an advantage over you: *Smaller companies have made a lot of ground in the last year.* ▫ *The book trade may lose ground to electronic publishing in the next few years.* **6** (*used in the plural*) You have **grounds** or there are **grounds** for doing something when there is a good reason or basis for doing it: *There were no grounds for such harsh treatment.*
▻ ***verb***: **grounds, grounding, grounded**
1 An argument or theory or feeling **is grounded** in or on something when this is the basis or reasoning for it: *Their anxiety was grounded in experience.* **2** Someone **is grounded** in a subject when they have a

good knowledge of that subject: *At school they were grounded in Latin and French* [see also **grounding**] **3** A pilot or member of a crew of an aircraft **is grounded** when they are not allowed to fly.

▻ ***phrases*** **1** You say that you **break new ground** when you achieve something new or unusual. **2** (*informal*) You can say that something suits you **down to the ground** when it is perfectly acceptable or convenient. **3** Something gets **off the ground** when it begins to work or proceed according to plan: *The youth club has only been open a week and hasn't really got off the ground yet.* **4** You can use **on the ground** as a way of referring to ordinary people, as opposed to people in positions of power or influence: *What is the opinion on the ground?* **5** You say **on the grounds** of something to refer to a reason or cause: *He was rejected on the grounds of old age.* **6** You **stand your ground** when you stick to your opinion or stand by a decision although other people oppose you. **7** Things are **thin on the ground** if there are very few of them: *Good books are thin on the ground.*

ground² /graʊnd/ *verb*
Ground is the past tense and past participle of **grind**.

ground floor /graʊnd 'flɔ:(r)/ *noun* (*used in the singular*)
The **ground floor** of a building is the floor at, or nearest to, the level of the ground outside: *Our kitchenware department is on the ground floor.*

grounding /'graʊndɪŋ/ *noun* (*used in the singular*)
Someone has a good **grounding** in something when they have learnt the basic facts or skills relating to it: *The job should give her an adequate grounding in management technique.*

groundless /'graʊndləs/ *adjective*
Something **groundless** cannot be justified or excused: *Accusations of mismanagement have proved to be groundless.* [*opposite* **justified**]

group /gru:p/ *noun*; *verb*
▻ ***noun*** (*with a singular or plural verb*): **groups**
1 A **group** of people or things is a number of them gathered, placed or classed together: *A few protesters were standing in a group outside the door.* ▫ *The first group of trees were cut down in May.* ▫ *They did better than all other pupils in their age group.* **2** A **group** is also a band of musicians and singers who play pop music: *a rock group* ▫ *They are a highly respected folk group.*
▻ ***verb***: **groups, grouping, grouped**
You **group** people or things when you put them in a group: *Married men of all ages were grouped together for tax purposes.*

grouse¹ /graʊs/ *noun*: **grouse**
A **grouse** is a medium-sized plump brown bird often shot for sport.

grouse² /graʊs/ *noun* (*informal*): **grouses**
A **grouse** is a complaint or a spell of complaining: *Lack of air conditioning is their latest grouse.*

grove /groʊv/ *noun*: **groves**
A **grove** is a small group of trees, especially fruit trees.

grovel /'grɒvəl/ *verb*: **grovels, grovelling, grovelled**
You **grovel** to someone when you behave in an extremely humble or respectful way towards them, *eg* because you want them to like you or because you want something from them: *I couldn't stand the way my father had to grovel to the bosses.* ▫ *We had to go grovelling to our parents for money.* [*same as* **crawl**]

grow /groʊ/ *verb*: **grows, growing, grew, grown**
1 Living things such as people and plants **grow** when they become larger: *Children grow fast after the age of 2.* ▫ *The trees have grown several metres in the last year.* ▫ *The female lion cubs will grow into expert hunters.* ▫ *Your hair has grown long since you last had it cut.* **2** Living things **grow** parts when these parts gradually develop: *The bear grows an extra-thick winter coat.* ▫ *The trees will grow beautiful pink flowers in the spring.* **3 a** Something such as a business or other organization **grows** when it becomes greater in size or value: *It's amazing how much the Company has grown in the last three years.* **b** You can say that a feeling or emotion **grows** when it becomes stronger and more noticeable: *Their suspicions grew when they saw the broken window.* ▫ *Her confidence is growing all the time.* **c** You **grow** to have a feeling when you begin to have it: *I grew to like and admire them.* **4** You **grow** plants when you cultivate them; plants **grow** in the place where they develop in a living state: *We decided to try growing tomatoes in the open.* ▫ *We didn't want to disturb a bush that had been growing peacefully for years.* **5** You can use **grow** to mean 'become': *At six o'clock it began to grow dark.* ▫ *As winter approached, the days were growing shorter.* **6** A plan or undertaking **grows** from or **grows** out of something when it develops from it: *The scheme grew out of an idea one of the pupils had.* [see also **grow out of**]

phrasal verbs
grow into Children **grow into** clothes that were once too big when they grow enough for the clothes to fit properly.
grow on You can say that something **grows on** you when you gradually begin to like it more: *This music really grows on you.*
grow out of 1 Children **grow out of** clothes when their body grows so much that the clothes no longer fit properly. **2** You **grow out of** something such as a hobby or interest when you gradually stop liking it or wanting to do it, especially when you come to think that it is too childish: *I've rather grown out of late-night parties.*
grow up 1 A person **grows up** when they gradually change from a child into an adult, or they reach the stage of being an adult: *Young Peter is really growing up fast.* ▫ *She's grown up so much since I last saw her.* **2 a** You can also say that someone **grows up** or **is growing up** when they start to behave in an adult way, no matter how old they are. **b** You might tell someone to **grow up** or **start growing up** when you want them to behave in a more mature or less childish way: *Oh, grow up, Martin!*

growl /graʊl/ *verb*; *noun*
▻ ***verb***: **growls, growling, growled**
1 Animals such as dogs and bears **growl** when they make a deep rough sound in their throat, showing anger. **2** You might say that someone **growls** when they speak in an angry or impatient way: *'Nonsense!' he growled.*
▻ ***noun***: **growls:** *They heard a low growl from behind the wall.* ▫ *'Hurry up!', he said, with a growl.*

grown /groʊn/ *verb*; *adjective*
▻ ***verb***
Grown is the past participle of **grow**.
▻ ***adjective***
Grown means mature or adult: *That's no way for a grown woman to behave.* ▫ *The cubs will be fully grown within eight months.*

grown-up /groʊn'ʌp/ *noun*; *adjective*
▻ ***noun***: **grown-ups**
A **grown-up** is an adult: *The grown-ups enjoy themselves as much as the children.*

▻ *adjective:* *We have three grown-up children who all have children of their own.*

growth /grəʊθ/ *noun*: **growths**
1 (*uncount*) **Growth** is the process or rate of growing: *The plant's growth is regulated.* **2** (*uncount*) **Growth** also refers to increases in something, *eg* the profits made by a business organization: *There are good prospects for economic growth.* **3** A **growth** is an unhealthy or diseased lump on or inside someone's body. [*same as* **tumour**]

grub /grʌb/ *noun*: **grubs**
1 A **grub** is a beetle in its first, worm-like stage of development. **2** (*uncount*; *informal*) **Grub** is food.

grubby /'grʌbɪ/ *adjective* (*informal*): **grubbier, grubbiest**
Something **grubby** is dirty: *Wash those grubby hands.*

grudge /grʌdʒ/ *verb*; *noun*
▻ ***verb***: **grudges, grudging, grudged**
You **grudge** someone something when **1** you think it is unfair that they have it, *eg* because they don't deserve it or because you think you yourself should have it: *I don't grudge her the success she's had.* [*same as* **begrudge**] **2** you are unwilling to give it to them, or you give it unwillingly: *She has learnt not to grudge the children the time she spends with them.*
▻ ***noun***: **grudges**
You have or bear a **grudge** against someone when you still feel angry towards them for the unfair or unpleasant way they treated you in the past: *I bear her no grudge.* [*same as* **resentment, hard feelings**]

grudging /'grʌdʒɪŋ/ *adjective*
Something such as respect or approval is **grudging** if it is given unwillingly: *In spite of his ill temper, his courage and flair had earned him the grudging respect of his men.* [*same as* **reluctant**] — *adverb* **grudgingly:** *'I suppose she could stay with us', Tina offered, grudgingly.*

gruelling /'grʊəlɪŋ/ *adjective*
Something such as a task is **gruelling** when it demands a lot of physical effort: *Next comes the gruelling climb up the mountain's northern slope.*

gruesome /'gru:səm/ *adjective*
A **gruesome** scene or incident upsets or disgusts you because it involves people being violently injured or killed. [*same as* **horrific, ghastly**]

gruff /grʌf/ *adjective*
1 A **gruff** voice is deep and harsh-sounding. **2** You might describe the way someone speaks as **gruff** if it sounds unfriendly or angry: *She has a gruff manner which puts people off.* [*same as* **surly**]

grumble /'grʌmbəl/ *verb*; *noun*
▻ ***verb***: **grumbles, grumbling, grumbled**
You **grumble** when you complain in a bad-tempered way: *It's no use grumbling about it.* [*same as* **moan, complain**]
▻ ***noun***: **grumbles:** *There were one or two grumbles from the more militant workers.* [*same as* **complaint**]

grumpy /'grʌmpɪ/ *adjective*: **grumpier, grumpiest**
A **grumpy** person is bad-tempered and complains a lot: *Helena's been particularly grumpy today.* [*opposite* **cheerful, good-natured**]

grunt /grʌnt/ *verb*; *noun*
▻ ***verb***: **grunts, grunting, grunted**
1 Animals such as pigs **grunt** when they make a deep rough sound in the back of their throat. **2** A person **grunts** when they answer by making a similar sound, because they are unwilling to speak fully or because they are displeased or disgusted with what someone has said.
▻ ***noun***: **grunts:** *He recognized the grunt of a wild boar.* □ *Eric replied with his usual grunt.*

guarantee /garən'ti:/ *noun*; *verb*
▻ ***noun***: **guarantees**
1 (*count or uncount*) A **guarantee** is a formal written promise by a manufacturer to repair or replace an article that becomes faulty, within a stated period of time: *All our electrical goods carry a twelve-month guarantee.* □ *We will repair it free of charge while it is still under guarantee.* **2** A **guarantee** is a promise of any kind, or a reason to believe that something will certainly happen: *I can give you my guarantee that none of our workers will lose their jobs.* □ *There's no guarantee that the jury will believe your story.* □ *We're not in a position to give guarantees of re-employment to sacked workers.* [*same as* **assurance**]
▻ ***verb***: **guarantees, guaranteeing, guaranteed**
1 You **guarantee** that something will happen when you promise to make sure that it happens: *We guarantee that letters posted first class will arrive the next day.* □ *The Minister cannot guarantee that all your requests will be granted.* □ *The successful candidate is guaranteed an attractive salary and a promising career.* **2** You **are guaranteed** something when it is certain to happen or be provided: *It seems that you're no longer guaranteed a fair trial.* □ *It's guaranteed to rain before the day is out.* □ *A good education simply doesn't guarantee you a good job.*

guard /gɑ:d/ *verb*; *noun*
▻ ***verb***: **guards, guarding, guarded**
1 You **guard** someone or something when you protect them from danger or attack: *All sides of the house are being guarded.* **2** You **guard** a prisoner when you keep watch over them to prevent them from escaping: *Terrorist suspects are guarded day and night.*
[see also **guarded**]
▻ ***noun***: **guards**
1 (*count or uncount*) A **guard** is a person guarding someone or something, to protect them from danger or attack or to prevent them from escaping: *Security guards patrol the store at all times.* □ *The police had been instructed to give the President's party an armed guard.* □ *The rarer exhibits are kept under constant guard.* **2** On a train, the **guard** is the person in charge of the passengers. **3** A **guard** is a shield that prevents you from accidentally touching something dangerous: *a bicycle with no chain guard* □ *The fireguard was too hot to touch.*
▻ ***phrases*** **1** Something catches you **off guard** when you are not prepared or ready to deal with it: *It was clear that the question had caught the Prime Minister off guard.* **2** You are **on your guard** against something difficult or dangerous when you are prepared for it if it happens: *You have to be on your guard against sudden, severe changes in the weather.*

phrasal verb
You **guard against** something when you try to prevent it from happening by taking care to do something else: *All baby's bottles and other utensils should be sterilized to guard against infection.*

guarded /'gɑ:dɪd/ *adjective*
1 Something is a closely **guarded** secret when the few people who know about it refuse to give any information about it to others. **2** Someone gives a **guarded** answer to a question when they are careful not to reveal their true feelings or opinions, or when they take care not to reveal too much information. [*same as* **cautious**; *opposite* **frank**]

guardian /ˈgɑːdɪən/ *noun*: **guardians**
1 A child's **guardian** is the person legally responsible for bringing up the child, usually because both parents are dead. **2** You might refer to someone as the **guardian** of something if they are responsible for protecting or defending it: *The churches have always set themselves up as guardians of public morality.*

guava /ˈgwɑːvə/ *noun*: **guavas**
A **guava** is a pear-like tropical fruit with pink flesh. [see picture at **fruit**]

guerrilla or **guerilla** /gəˈrɪlə/ *noun*: **guerrillas**
A **guerrilla** is a member of a small independent armed force making surprise attacks, usually for political reasons, *eg* against troops belonging to a government that they are opposed to.

guess /gɛs/ *verb*; *noun*
▻ ***verb***: **guesses, guessing, guessed**
1 You **guess** something when you try to make a judgment about it without having any information: *If asked to guess his age, I would say he was around forty-five.* □ *There was a competition to guess the weight of a huge Christmas pudding.* □ *If you don't know the answer, just guess.* □ *We could only guess at what their reaction might be.* [*same as* **estimate**] **2** You also **guess** something when you judge or estimate it correctly: *I won £10 for guessing the number of pennies in the bottle.* □ *You would never guess that he was over seventy.* □ *I would not have guessed that it would be so cold.* **3** (*AmE*) People often say '**I guess**' as a way of introducing a statement, often an opinion or judgement based on what others have already said: *You all have things to talk about, so I guess I'll just go to bed.* □ *I guess he's the kind of father that wants the best for his children.*
▻ ***noun***: **guesses:** *I didn't know for sure – it was just a guess.*
▻ ***phrase*** (*informal*) When talking about future events, people often use **anybody's guess** as a way of saying that it is impossible to judge what will happen: *It's anybody's guess who will get the job.* □ *Precisely how the workers will vote is anybody's guess.*

guest /gɛst/ *noun*; *adjective*
▻ ***noun***: **guests**
1 In a hotel, the **guests** are the people who pay to stay there. **2** A **guest** is someone you have invited to your home: *Offer our guests a drink, Brian.* **3** When someone invites you to go somewhere with them, *eg* to the theatre, as their **guest**, they are offering to pay for your entertainment.
▻ ***adjective***
Guest describes people invited to give a performance of some kind: *On Tuesday's show, the guest star will be Paul McCartney.* □ *There'll be a guest speaker at next week's meeting.*

guesthouse /ˈgesthaʊs/ *noun*: **guesthouses**
A **guesthouse** is a small hotel.

guffaw /gʌˈfɔː/ *verb*; *noun*
▻ ***verb***: **guffaws, guffawing, guffawed**
You **guffaw** when you laugh loudly.
▻ ***noun***: **guffaws:** *the speaker's gentle tones battling against guffaws from the back row.*

guidance /ˈgaɪdəns/ *noun* (*uncount*)
1 You give someone **guidance** when you help them by giving advice, often based on your own experience: *a marriage-guidance counsellor.* **2** Something is under the **guidance** of the person who directs or leads it: *I'm sure the company will prosper under Sir Peter's expert guidance.*

guide /gaɪd/ *noun*; *verb*
▻ ***noun***: **guides**
1 A **guide** is someone who takes you somewhere when you don't know the way, or who shows you things of interest in a place you have not visited before: *Our guide led us to a hut at the edge of the forest.* □ *The museum's guide has some interesting stories about the artists.* **2** A **guide** is also a guidebook: *The first thing to do was buy a guide.* **3** Other books giving information or instructions are often called **guides**: *They've published a 'guide to stress-free living'.* **4** Something, such as a piece of information, is a **guide** when it helps you to make a judgement or decision: *As a guide to the novice, any new guitar under £80 is likely not to be worth buying.*
▻ ***verb***: **guides, guiding, guided**
1 To **guide** something is to control or direct how it moves or where it goes: *Two men will guide the stone pillar into place.* □ *a guided missile.* **2** You **guide** someone when you show them how to get somewhere, or when you take them yourself: *We were guided into a private room at the back of the bar.* **3** You also **guide** someone when you influence the way they behave: *Be guided by your parents.*

guidebook /ˈgaɪdbʊk/ *noun*: **guidebooks**
A **guidebook** contains information for tourists visiting a particular place.

guideline /ˈgaɪdlaɪn/ *noun*: **guidelines**
Guidelines are suggestions or recommendations: *It is mentioned in the government's guidelines about health and safety in the workplace.*

guild /gɪld/ *noun*: **guilds**
Guild is a name often used in the title of societies and clubs: *the Women's Guild.*

guile /gaɪl/ *noun* (*uncount*)
Guile is the ability to deceive or trick people. [*same as* **cunning, craftiness**]

guillotine /ˈgɪlətiːn/ *noun*: **guillotines**
1 A **guillotine** is an instrument for executing people by cutting their heads off, consisting of a heavy blade that slides down between two posts. **2** A **guillotine** is also a device with a large blade for cutting paper or metal.

guilt /gɪlt/ *noun* (*uncount*)
1 Guilt is the uneasy feeling of knowing you have done something wrong: *It was clear that she had no sense of guilt.* □ *Don't you feel any guilt?* [*same as* **remorse**] **2 Guilt** is also the fact of having done something wrong: *He has admitted his guilt.* [*opposite* **innocence**]

guilty /ˈgɪltɪ/ *adjective*
1 You feel **guilty** about something you have done when you feel that you should not have done it: *Young mothers are still made to feel guilty about working full time.* □ *She feels guilty about not visiting her father when he was ill.* **2** You are **guilty** of doing something when what you do is considered wrong: *He's been guilty in the past of working too hard.* **3** Someone is found **guilty** of a crime when they are officially judged to have committed it: *The jury found him guilty of manslaughter, not of murder.* **4 Guilty** describes the behaviour of someone who shows that they realize they have done something wrong: *a guilty look.* [*opposite* **innocent**] — *adverb* **guiltily:** *He hung his head guiltily.*

guinea /ˈgɪnɪ/ *noun*: **guineas**
A **guinea** is an old British gold coin worth 21 old shillings, or its modern-day value of £1.05: *a prize of a thousand guineas.*

guise /gaɪz/ *noun* (*usually in the singular*)

Guise refers what something appears to be, or what people claim it is, as opposed to what it really is: *They receive a lot of money from big business, under the guise of anonymous donations.* □ *The new university is just the same old polytechnic in a new guise.*

guitar /gɪ'tɑː(r)/ *noun*: **guitars**
A **guitar** is a musical instrument with a body shaped like a figure of eight and strings that are played with the fingers, or an electric version with a body of various shapes: *He's learning to play the guitar.*

gulf /gʌlf/ *noun*: **gulfs**
1 A **gulf** is a large bay: *the Gulf of Mexico.* **2** You might say that there is a **gulf** between things when they are very different from each other: *There is an economic gulf between the two nations that will be difficult to bridge.*

gull /gʌl/ *noun*: **gulls**
A **gull** is a large, common sea-bird. [*same as* **seagull**]

gullible /'gʌləbəl/ *adjective*
A **gullible** person is easily tricked or fooled. [*same as* **credulous**]

gulp /gʌlp/ *verb*; *noun*
▷ ***verb***: **gulps, gulping, gulped**
1 You **gulp** something when you swallow it eagerly or hurriedly in large mouthfuls: *I had a few seconds to gulp down a cup of coffee.* [*opposite* **sip**] **2** You **gulp** when you make a swallowing motion, *eg* because you are nervous or afraid.
▷ ***noun***: **gulps:** *He downed the beer in noisy gulps.* [*opposite* **sip**]

gum¹ /gʌm/ *noun*: **gums**
Your **gums** are the firm fleshy parts of your mouth around the roots of your teeth.

gum² /gʌm/ *noun*; *verb*
▷ ***noun***: **gums**
1 (*uncount*) **Gum** is glue, especially the kind of glue used to stick paper. [*same as* **paste**] **2** Sticky sweets of various kinds are often called **gums**: *a packet of wine gums.* **3** (*uncount*) **Gum** is also chewing-gum.
▷ ***verb***: **gums, gumming, gummed**
One thing **is gummed** to another if it is stuck to it: *He woke to find his eyelids gummed together.* □ *A large label was gummed to the envelope.*

gun /gʌn/ *noun*; *verb*
▷ ***noun***: **guns**
1 A **gun** is any weapon that fires bullets or shells from a metal tube: *a handgun* □ *a machine gun.* **2** A **gun** is also an instrument that sprays a liquid on to a surface: *a paint gun.*
▷ ***verb***: **guns, gunning, gunned**

> ***phrasal verb***
> Someone who **is gunned down** is shot and usually killed.

gunfire /'gʌnfaɪə(r)/ *noun* (*uncount*)
Gunfire is the sound of bullets being fired from a gun.

gunge /gʌndʒ/ *noun* (*uncount*; *informal*)
Gunge is any unpleasantly sticky substance: *a layer of black gunge on the inside of the oven.*

gunman /'gʌnmən/ *noun*: **gunmen**
A **gunman** is an armed criminal: *Two masked gunmen attacked him in his own home.*

gunpoint /'gʌnpɔɪnt/ *noun* (*uncount*)
People are forced to do something at **gunpoint** when someone is threatening to shoot them with a gun if they refuse: *Over twenty customers were held at gunpoint while the robbers emptied the tills.*

gurgle /'gɜːgəl/ *verb*: **gurgles, gurgling, gurgled**
Flowing water **gurgles** when it makes a bubbling noise.

guru /'gʊəruː/ *noun*: **gurus**
1 A **guru** is a Hindu or Sikh religious leader or teacher. **2** Any greatly respected and influential leader or adviser might be referred to as a **guru**: *one of Mrs Thatcher's political gurus.* [*same as* **mentor**]

gush /gʌʃ/ *verb*: **gushes, gushing, gushed**
A liquid **gushes** when it flows out suddenly and violently: *with blood gushing from the wound.*

gust /gʌst/ *noun*: **gusts**
A **gust** of wind is a sudden strong rush of wind: *winds with gusts of over 70 miles per hour.*

gusto /'gʌstoʊ/ *noun* (*uncount*)
You do something with **gusto** when you do it with lively enthusiasm or enjoyment. [*opposite* **apathy**]

gut /gʌt/ *noun*; *adjective*; *verb*
▷ ***noun***: **guts**
1 a (*used in the singular*) In animals, including humans, the **gut** is the long tubelike internal organ through which food passes as it is digested. **b** (*used in the plural; informal*) Your **guts** are the internal organs in the area of your stomach: *He said he had a pain in his guts.* **2** (*used in the plural; informal*) The **guts** of something, especially a machine, are its most important inner working parts **3** (*used in the plural; informal*) You might say that someone has **guts** if they have courage or determination: *He didn't even have the guts to tell me to my face.* **4** (*uncount*) **Gut** is elastic material produced from the intestines of animals, and used *eg* for making violin strings.
▷ ***adjective***
Gut feelings are based on instinct, not reason: *My gut reaction was to accept, although I could see the dangers.* [*same as* **instinctive**]
▷ ***verb***: **guts, gutting, gutted**
A building **is gutted** when the inside of it is completely destroyed by fire.
▷ ***phrase*** (*informal*) You might say that you **hate** someone's **guts** when you dislike them very much.

gutter /'gʌtə(r)/ *noun*: **gutters**
A **gutter** is a channel for carrying away rainwater, fixed to the edge of a roof or built between a pavement and a road. [see pictures at **house, street**]

guy /gaɪ/ *noun* (*informal*): **guys**
1 A **guy** is a man or boy: *the tall guy next to the door.* [*same as* **bloke, fellow**] **2** (*AmE*) You can address or refer to both men and women as **guys**: *You guys pay for the pizzas and we'll get the beer.*

guzzle /'gʌzəl/ *verb* (*informal*): **guzzles, guzzling, guzzled**
You **guzzle** something when you eat or drink it greedily: *I found him sitting on a bench guzzling chips.*

gym /dʒɪm/ *noun*: **gyms**
1 A **gym** is a gymnasium. **2** (*uncount, often adjectival*) **Gym** is gymnastics, especially as a subject taught in schools: *I was never fond of gym as a schoolboy.* □ *a pair of gym shoes.*

gymnasium /dʒɪm'neɪzɪəm/ *noun*: **gymnasiums**
A **gymnasium** is a building or room with equipment for doing physical exercises.

gymnast /'dʒɪmnast/ *noun*: **gymnasts**
A **gymnast** is a person skilled in gymnastics.

gymnastics /dʒɪm'nastɪks/ *noun* (*singular*)
Gymnastics consists of physical exercises that demand great strength and the ability to bend your body in a controlled way.

gypsy or **gipsy** /'dʒɪpsɪ/ *noun*: **gypsies**
Gypsies are a race of brown-skinned people who traditionally travelled around, originally in horse-drawn caravans, rather than settling in one place.

H[1] or **h** /eɪtʃ/: **Hs** or **h's**
H is the eighth letter of the English alphabet.

ha! or **hah** /hɑː/ *interjection*
You say **ha** to express surprise, pleasure or triumph: *Ha! Here's the reference I was looking for.* [see also **ha ha**]

haberdashery /'habədaʃəri/ *noun* (*uncount*)
1 Haberdashery is the things you need for sewing and mending, such as thread, zips, buttons, pins and needles. **2** (*AmE*) **Haberdashery** is men's clothing in a shop or store.

habit /'habɪt/ *noun*: **habits**
1 (*count or uncount*) Your **habits** are things you do regularly or often: *He has an irritating habit of interrupting you when you're telling him something.* □ *It's difficult to break the habit of a lifetime.* **2** A **habit** is also something, usually bad, that you keep doing because you can't stop yourself doing it: *people who bite their nails or have other bad habits.* **3** A drug **habit** or nicotine **habit** is an addiction to a drug or to smoking: *You can go to one of these counsellors who help you to kick your habit.* **4** (*religion*) A **habit** is a piece of clothing like a long loose dress, tied round the waist, that is worn by monks and nuns.
▻ ***phrases*** You **are in the habit of** doing something if you do it often or regularly; you **get into**, or **fall into, the habit**, or **make a habit, of** doing something when you start doing it often or regularly; you **get out of the habit of** doing something when you stop it: *Make a habit of brushing your teeth after every meal.* □ *We had got into the habit of lunching together once a week.* □ *I can't really come up with a good reason why I don't go there any more: I just got out of the habit.*

habitable /'habɪtəbəl/ *adjective*
A place that is **habitable** is in good enough condition for people to live in: *Some of the flats were barely habitable.*

habitat /'habɪtat/ *noun*: **habitats**
An animal's or plant's **habitat** is its usual and natural environment: *These plants don't thrive outside their normal habitat.*

habitation /habɪ'teɪʃən/ *noun*: **habitations**
1 (*uncount*) **Habitation** of a place is the circumstance or activity of living there: *dwellings unfit for human habitation.* **2** (*formal*) A **habitation** is a place where people live: *the caves that served our ancestors as habitations.* [*same as* **dwelling**]

habitual /hə'bɪtʃʊəl/ *adjective*
1 A **habitual** gesture, act or attitude is one that is typical of you: *He made some remark, finishing with his habitual nervous giggle.* [*same as* **usual, customary**] **2** A **habitual** liar often tells lies; a **habitual** drinker frequently drinks too much. — *adverb* **habitually:** *He was habitually drunk by midday.*

hack[1] /hak/ *verb*; **hacks, hacking, hacked**
1 You **hack** something when you cut it or chop it violently or roughly: *He hacked his victims to death with an axe.* □ *They had to hack a path through the jungle.* **2** (*informal*) You **hack** into, or **hack**, a computer's files when you get access to them without permission through your own computer.

hack[2] /hak/ *noun* (*old, informal*): **hacks**
A **hack** is a writer or journalist without much talent who does a lot of boring, badly paid writing work.

hacker /'hakə(r)/ *noun* (*informal*): **hackers**
1 A **hacker** is someone who uses their own computer to get access without permission to files stored in another computer. **2** A **hacker** is also a computer enthusiast.

hacking /'hakɪŋ/ *noun* (*uncount*)
Hacking is the process of using your own computer to get access without permission to files stored in another computer.

hackles /'hakəlz/ *noun* (*plural*)
Hackles are the hairs or feathers on the back of the neck of some animals and birds, that rise up when they are angry.
▻ ***phrase*** Someone's **hackles rise** when they get angry or feel hostile.

hackneyed /'haknɪd/ *adjective*
A **hackneyed** phrase or expression is one that has been used too often and has become boring and meaningless: *love songs with their hackneyed sentiments.* [*same as* **trite**]

hacksaw /'haksɔː/ *noun*: **hacksaws**
A **hacksaw** is a small saw for cutting metal.

had /had/ *verb*
1 Had is the past tense and past participle of **have**. **2** (*formal*) You can start a past conditional clause with **had** instead of *if*: *Had I known* (instead of *if I had known*) *he was in difficulties, I would have helped him.* □ *Had you not warned me, I might have got into serious trouble.*
▻ ***phrase*** For **had better** see **better**.

haddock /'hadək/ *noun* (*count or uncount*): **haddock**
A **haddock** is a small sea fish whose flesh is used as food: *The largest shoals of haddock are found in North Atlantic waters.* □ *a piece of smoked haddock.*

hadn't /'hadənt/ *verb*
Hadn't is the spoken, and informal written, form of **had not**: *I hadn't realized the shops would be shut today.*

haemoglobin (*AmE* **hemaglobin**) /hiːmə'gloʊbɪn/ *noun* (*uncount*)
Haemoglobin is the substance in red blood cells that carries oxygen.

haemophilia (*AmE* **hemophilia**) /hiːmə'fɪlɪə/ *noun* (*uncount*)
Haemophilia is a hereditary disease chiefly of men, in which the sufferer's blood does not clot properly when they are cut or injured, so that they continue to bleed for a long time.

haemophiliac (*AmE* **hemophiliac**) /hiːmə'fɪlɪak/ *noun*: **haemophiliacs**

A **haemophiliac** is a person who has the blood disease haemophilia.

haemorrhage (*AmE* **hemorrhage**) /ˈhɛmərɪdʒ/ *noun*; *verb*

▷ ***noun*** (*count or uncount*): **haemorrhages**
A **haemorrhage** is a case of severe bleeding, usually inside a person's body, especially from a burst blood vessel: *a brain haemorrhage.*

▷ ***verb***: **haemorrhages, haemorrhaging, haemorrhaged**
A person **haemorrhages** when they bleed heavily and severely: *She haemorrhaged after the birth.*

haemorrhoid (*AmE* **hemorrhoids**) /ˈhɛmərɔɪd/ *noun*: **haemorrhoids**
Haemorrhoids are painful swellings that people sometimes get in the veins inside the anus. [*same as* **pile**]

hag /hag/ *noun*: **hags**
A **hag** is **1** (*offensive*) an ugly old woman. **2** a witch.

haggard /ˈhagəd/ *adjective*
You describe someone as **haggard** if they look tired, worried and ill.

haggis /ˈhagɪs/ *noun* (*count or uncount*): **haggises**
A **haggis** is a Scottish dish made from a sheep's or calf's heart, lungs and liver, mixed with oatmeal and boiled in sheep's stomach.

haggle /ˈhagəl/ *verb*: **haggles, haggling, haggled**
You **haggle** when you bargain or argue with someone about the price of something you are buying from them.

ha ha /hɑːˈhɑː/ *interjection*
1 Ha ha is a written representation of the sound of laughter. **2** Sometimes people say **ha ha** when bitterly pretending to be amused: *Oh, ha ha; very clever.*

hail[1] /heɪl/ *noun*; *verb*

▷ ***noun***
1 (*uncount*) **Hail** is frozen raindrops that fall from the sky as small hard white balls. **2** (*used in the singular*) A **hail** of things such as blows or bullets is a great quantity of them falling violently on you at the same time: *There was a continuous hail of arrows from the English archers.*

▷ ***verb***: **hails, hailing, hailed**
You say it **is hailing** when hail is falling.

hail[2] /heɪl/ *verb*: **hails, hailing, hailed**
1 You **hail** someone when you call to them: *He saw her appearing in the distance and hailed her.* **2** You **hail** a taxi when you wave or signal to the driver to stop and pick you up. **3** A person or achievement **is hailed** as something great or important when they are claimed publicly to be that thing: *Critics hailed it as the best new play of the decade.* [*same as* **acclaim**]

hailstone /ˈheɪlstoʊn/ *noun*: **hailstones**
Hailstones are frozen raindrops falling from the sky as small hard white balls.

hailstorm /ˈheɪlstɔːm/ *noun*: **hailstorms**
A **hailstorm** is a shower of hail.

hair /hɛə(r)/ *noun*: **hairs**
1 Hairs are the thread-like objects that grow from the skin of animals, covering humans thickly over the head and thinly over the rest of the body: *The sunlight caught the fine blond hairs on her arms.* **2** (*uncount*) Your **hair** is the mass of hairs that grow on your head: *He had thick curly brown hair.* [see picture at **body**] **3** Fine thread-like projections that grow on plants or insects are also called **hairs**: *The leaves are covered with poisonous hairs.*

▷ ***phrases*** **1** (*informal*) If you tell someone to **keep their hair on** you are asking them to stop getting angry and calm down. **2** (*informal*) You **let your hair down** when you relax and enjoy yourself thoroughly. **3** (*informal*) Something **makes your hair stand on end** if it frightens you: *His driving makes my hair stand on end.* **4** Someone who **does not turn a hair** in a frightening situation remains apparently calm and unworried. **5** If you tell someone they are **splitting hairs** you mean that they are making unnecessarily fine distinctions.

hairbrush /ˈhɛəbrʌʃ/ *noun*: **hairbrushes**
A **hairbrush** is a brush for brushing your hair with.

haircut /ˈhɛəkʌt/ *noun*: **haircuts**
1 You have a **haircut** when someone cuts your hair: *You need a haircut.* **2** Someone's **haircut** is the shape or style in which their hair is cut: *She had one of those short severe haircuts.*

hairdo /ˈhɛəduː/ *noun* (*informal*): **hairdos**
Someone's **hairdo** is the style in which their hair has been cut and arranged: *I didn't recognize her with her new hairdo.* [*same as* **hairstyle**]

hairdresser /ˈhɛədrɛsə(r)/ *noun*: **hairdressers**
1 A **hairdresser** is a person who cuts, washes and styles hair. **2** A **hairdresser** or **hairdresser's** is a hairdresser's shop or place of business: *I've got an appointment at the hairdresser's at 5.15.*

hairdressing /ˈhɛədrɛsɪŋ/ *noun* (*uncount*)
Hairdressing is the profession or art of cutting, washing and arranging hair.

hairdryer or **hairdrier** /ˈhɛədraɪə(r)/ *noun*: **hairdryers**
A **hairdryer** is an electrical device blowing out warm air, which you use to dry your hair with. [see picture at **bathroom**]

hairgrip /ˈhɛəgrɪp/ *noun*: **hairgrips**
A **hairgrip** is a device used by women to hold their hair in place, consisting of a narrow length of bent metal.

hairless /ˈhɛələs/ *adjective*
Hairless means not having any hair: *hairless mammals such as the elephant, rhino and hippo.*

hairline /ˈhɛəlaɪn/ *noun*; *adjective*

▷ ***noun*** (*usually in the singular*): **hairlines**
Your **hairline** is the line along your forehead where your hair begins to grow: *He was barely twenty when his hairline began to recede.*

▷ ***adjective***
A **hairline** crack is a very narrow one.

hairnet /ˈhɛənɛt/ *noun*: **hairnets**
A **hairnet** is a fine net formerly often worn by women over their hair to keep it in place.

hairpin /ˈhɛəpɪn/ *noun*; *adjective*

▷ ***noun***: **hairpins**
A **hairpin** is a thin U-shaped piece of wire used by women to keep their hair in place.

▷ ***adjective***
A **hairpin** bend, especially on a mountain road, is a sharp U-shaped one.

hair-raising /ˈhɛəreɪzɪŋ/ *adjective*
Something that is **hair-raising** is very frightening: *We had a hair-raising descent down the cliff face.*

hair's breadth /hɛəzˈbrɛdθ/ *noun* (*used in the singular*)
A **hair's breadth** is the very narrow gap or margin by which something bad is avoided: *The train managed to stop and disaster was avoided by a hair's breadth.* [*same as* **whisker**]

hair slide /ˈhɛə slaɪd/ *noun*: **hair slides**
A **hair slide** is a plastic or metal hinged clasp, usually decorative, used by girls or women to hold their hair in place.

hairspray /ˈhɛəspreɪ/ *noun* (*uncount*)
Hairspray is a sticky liquid sprayed from a can as a

fine mist, used by women to hold their hairstyle in shape.

hairstyle /ˈhɛəstaɪl/ *noun*: **hairstyles**
Your **hairstyle** is the way your hair is cut and shaped: *I like your new hairstyle* [*same as* **hairdo**]

hairy /ˈhɛərɪ/ *adjective*: **hairier, hairiest**
1 Someone or something **hairy** is covered in hair: *He had very hairy arms and legs.* **2** (*informal*) A **hairy** experience is a frightening or dangerous one: *The climb down the west face of the mountain can be pretty hairy in bad weather.*

halcyon /ˈhalsɪən/ *adjective* (*literary*)
Halcyon days are a peaceful, calm and happy period, *eg* one during your own life, on which you look back with pleasure.

hale /heɪl/ *adjective*
Someone who is **hale** is strong and healthy: *I'm glad to say both my parents are still hale and hearty.*

half (often written ½) /hɑːf/ *determiner*; *pronoun*; *noun*; *adjective*; *adverb*

▻ ***determiner***
1 Half something is one of two equal parts of it that together make the whole; **half** is normally used before another determiner or a possessive pronoun: *The petrol station was half a kilometre further on.* □ *We waited half an hour.* □ *Half a year had passed.* □ *I'll need at least half a dozen* [= six] *copies.* □ *'Have some more tea.' 'Just half a cup, thank you.'* □ *Help yourself to half the food.* □ *He gives half his wages to his mother every week.* □ *Half our team are off ill.* □ *She'd forgotten her sandwiches so I gave her half mine.* **2 Half** is often used rather informally to mean a large number or proportion of something: *Half these books seem to be out of date.* □ *Half Manchester was out on the streets celebrating the victory.* □ *The baby's teething and I was up half the night with her.* **3** Notice how **half** is used in numerical expressions: *The work is going to take one and a half* (or 1½) *weeks.* □ *thirteen and a half* (*or 13* ½) *miles.*

▻ ***pronoun:*** *More than half of the delegates are from abroad.* □ *We'll keep half of the wine for later.* □ *Did your luggage arrive? The airline lost half of ours.* □ *Half of us waited behind.* □ *Half of me still misses him.* □ *Since there are so many of you, let's have half of you performing now, and half later.* □ *The journey takes an hour and a half.* □ *She divided the cake and we took half each.* □ *'How many students finished the course?' 'Roughly half.'*

▻ ***noun***: **halves**
1 (*uncount or count*) **Half** or a **half** is the fraction ½ or 0.5, equal to one divided by two: *nineteen and a half* (or *19*½). □ *Half of 15 is seven and a half* (or 7½). **2** A **half** is one of two equal portions that together make the whole of something: *The plate lay in two halves on the floor.* □ *The group divided into two halves.* □ *We spend the first half of the tutorial practising conversation.* □ *during the latter half of the 19th century.* **3** The first and second **halves** of a match are the two equal periods of play into which it is divided: *New Zealand dominated the first half.* **4** A **half** is a half-price ticket for a child, *eg* on the bus: *One and two halves to Piccadilly, please.* **5** (*informal*) A **half** is half a pint of a drink such as beer: *I'll have a half of cider, please.*

▻ ***adjective:*** *A half pint of lager, please.* □ *We've got another half hour to wait.* □ *A lot has happened in the last half decade.* □ *There was nothing in the fridge except a half lemon.*

▻ ***adverb***
1 You use **half** to mean to the extent of a half: *A half-full glass of water stood on the bedside table.* □ *The theatre was half empty tonight.* □ *We're about half finished.* **2** You also use **half** to mean to a certain extent, or partly: *I half wondered if there'd been a mistake.* □ *He peered at me through half-closed eyes.* □ *I can't come out; I'm only half dressed.* □ *a half-open door.* □ (*informal*) *He was half* [= almost] *dead from exhaustion.* **3** Someone who is **half** one nationality and **half** another, has a parent of each nationality: *I'm half Scottish and half English.* **4** In expressing time, you say it is **half** past five or **half** five when it is 30 minutes past five: *It's almost half past ten.* □ (*informal*) *I'll see you at half six outside the cinema.* **5** (*with a negative*; *informal*) Something that isn't **half** as good or bad as something else, is very much worse or better than it: *Skiing wasn't half as difficult as* [= was much less difficult than] *I was expecting* □ *The countryside was pretty, but not half as beautiful as Scotland.* □ *We won't need half as much food as that.* [*same as* **nearly**] **6** (*with a negative*; *old, informal*) If you say that someone doesn't **half** do something, you mean that they do it to an extreme extent: *She didn't half make a fuss.*

▻ ***phrases*** **1 a** Something is increased **by half** when an amount equal to half of it is added to it; something is decreased, reduced or cut **by half** when an amount equal to half of it is taken away from it: *We've increased profits by half.* **b** (*informal*) If you say someone is too clever, or too kind, **by half**, you mean that their cleverness or kindness could cause trouble for them: *He was too confident by half.* **2** (*with a negative*; *informal*) Someone who never does anything **by halves** does everything enthusiastically and thoroughly. **3** You agree to **go halves** with someone when you decide to share the cost of something equally between you. **4** Something is divided **in half** when it is divided into two equal parts: *I tore the letter in half.* [see also **halve**]

halfback /ˈhɑːfbak/ *noun*: **halfbacks**
In football, hockey and related games, a **halfback** is a player positioned between the forwards and the backs.

half-baked /hɑːfˈbeɪkt/ *adjective* (*informal*)
You describe an idea or plan as **half-baked** if you think it is crazy, stupid or not properly worked out: *another of her half-baked notions.* [*same as* **hare-brained, crackpot**]

half board /hɑːf ˈbɔːd/ *noun* (*uncount*; *BrE*)
A hotel that provides **half board** serves breakfast and an evening meal, but not lunch.

half-brother /ˈhɑːfbrʌðə(r)/ or **half-sister** /ˈhɑːfsɪstə(r)/ *noun*: **half-brothers** or **half-sisters**
A brother or sister who has either the same father, or the same mother, as you do, is your **half-brother** or **half-sister**.

half-caste /ˈhɑːfkɑːst/ *adjective*; *noun*

▻ ***adjective*** (*offensive*)
Someone who is **half-caste** has parents of different races: *half-caste children.*

▻ ***noun***: **half-castes** (*offensive*)
A **half-caste** is someone who has parents of different races.

half day /hɑːf ˈdeɪ/ *noun*: **half days**
A **half day** is a day on which you work only in the morning or only in the afternoon: *I'm taking a half day on Friday.* □ *Wednesday's a half day at some schools.*

half-hearted /hɑːfˈhɑːtɪd/ *adjective*
You are **half-hearted** about something if you are not really interested in it or enthusiastic about it: *He made some half-hearted enquiries.* — *adverb* **half-heartedly:** *Couples were dancing rather half-heartedly round the room.*

half hour /hɑːf ˈaʊə(r)/ *noun*: **half hours**
A **half hour** is a period of thirty minutes: *Buses stop every half hour.* — *adjective or adverb* **half-hourly:** *a*

half-hourly bus-service into town. □ *Trains leave half-hourly for Glasgow.*
▻ ***phrase*** Something happens **on the half hour** if it happens at exactly 30 minutes past any hour.

half life /'hɑːf laɪf/ *noun*: **half lives**
The **half life** of a radioactive substance is the time it takes to lose half its radioactivity.

half-mast /hɑːf 'mɑːst/ *noun*
▻ ***phrase*** A flag is flown **at half-mast** when it is flown from a position halfway down a flagpole, as a sign of respect and mourning for someone important who has just died.

halfpenny /'heɪpnɪ/ *noun* (*history*): **halfpennies** or **halfpence**
A **halfpenny** is an old British coin worth half a penny.

half-price /'hɑːfpraɪs/ *adjective or adverb*
Something that is **half-price** costs only half its usual price; you get something **half-price** when you get it for half its usual price: *half-price goods* □ *We bought the furniture half-price in a sale.*
▻ ***phrase*** You get something **for half price** or **at half price** when you buy it for half its usual price.

half-sister see **half-brother**.

half term /hɑːf 'tɜːm/ *noun* (*uncount or count*; *BrE*): **half terms**
Half term is a short holiday halfway through a school term: *Are you going away for half term?*

half-timbered /hɑːf'tɪmbəd/ *adjective*
A **half-timbered** building is one that has a wooden frame with brick or plaster filling.

half time /hɑːf 'taɪm/ *noun* (*uncount*; *sport*)
Half time is the point halfway through a match when players stop for a few minutes' rest.

halfway /'hɑːfweɪ/ *adverb*; *adjective*
▻ ***adverb***
1 A position that is **halfway** somewhere, or **halfway** between two points, is in the middle between two points: *I was halfway down the steps.* □ *We were already about halfway to Liverpool.* □ *Laxey is halfway between Douglas and Ramsey.* [compare **midway**] **2** You are **halfway** through a period of time, a project, an activity or an event when you are at the middle point of it: *We're now halfway through January.* □ *We stopped for coffee halfway through the meeting.* [*same as* **midway**]
▻ ***adjective:*** *She was still in the lead and running strongly at the halfway mark.*
▻ ***phrase*** You **meet** someone **halfway** when you accept some of their points or demands in order to reach agreement with them.

half-yearly /hɑːf'jɪəlɪ/ *adjective or adverb*
A **half-yearly** event happens every six months, or twice a year: *The bank's half-yearly profits have increased dramatically* □ *These marathons are held half-yearly.* [compare **biennial**]

hall /hɔːl/ *noun*: **halls**
1 A **hall** is a room or passage just inside the entrance to a house, usually giving access to other rooms and the stairs: *Their luggage was piled up in the hall.* **2** A **hall** is also a building or a large room, used for such events as concerts, public meetings or dance classes: *She taught aerobics in the local school hall.* **3** The town **hall** or city **hall** is the building containing the local-government offices. **4** **Hall** is found in names for large country houses: *Tetbury Hall has been turned into a conference centre.* **5** (*count or uncount*; *BrE*) A **hall** is a hall of residence at a university; students live in **hall** when they live in a hall of residence as distinct from in lodgings. [*same as* **dormitory**]

hallelujah /halə'luːjə/ see **alleluia**.

hallmark /'hɔːlmɑːk/ *noun*: **hallmarks**
1 A **hallmark** is an official mark on a gold, silver or platinum article showing the quality of the metal and where the article was made. **2** The **hallmark** of a person's work is a typical feature or quality that makes it recognizable as their work: *the logic and symmetry that are the hallmarks of Bach's music.*

hallo see **hello**.

hall of residence /hɔːl əv 'rɛzɪdəns/ *noun*: **halls of residence**
A **hall of residence** at a university or college is a building containing rooms for students to live in. [*same as* **dormitory**]

hallowed /'haloʊd/ *adjective*
You refer to something as **hallowed** if it is deeply respected: *We wandered through the grounds of the hallowed Oxford colleges.* [*same as* **revered**]

Hallowe'en or **Halloween** /haloʊ'iːn/ *noun* (*uncount*)
Hallowe'en is 31 October, the day before All Saints' Day in the Christian calendar, when according to tradition you can expect to see ghosts and witches wandering about.

hallucinate /hə'luːsɪneɪt/ *verb*: **hallucinates, hallucinating, hallucinated**
You **hallucinate** when you seem to see things that are not really there, *eg* as a result of illness or of taking a drug: *For a minute I thought I was hallucinating.*

hallucination /həluːsɪ'neɪʃən/ *noun* (*count or uncount*): **hallucinations**
You have **hallucinations** when you seem to see things that are not really there, *eg* when you are ill or have taken a drug.

hallway /'hɔːlweɪ/ *noun*: **hallways**
A **hallway** is an entrance hall: *We waited in the hallway with our suitcases till the taxi arrived.*

halo /'heɪloʊ/ *noun*: **halos** or **haloes**
A **halo** is a ring or circle of light round the head of a saint or an angel in religious paintings, indicating that they are holy beings.

halt /hɔːlt/ *verb*; *noun*
▻ ***verb***: **halts, halting, halted**
1 You **halt** or **are halted** when you stop moving and stand still: *An accident has halted traffic in the city centre.* **2** A process **halts** or **is halted** when it stops and cannot continue: *Progress on the project was halted when we ran out of funds.*
▻ ***noun***: **halts**
A **halt** is a short stop, *eg* on a journey: *They completed the journey, with only a couple of halts for refreshment, in a total of eight hours.*
▻ ***phrases*** **1** To **call a halt to** something is to stop it continuing: *It's time to call a halt to these intrusions on our privacy.* **2 a** Something such as a vehicle comes **to a halt** when it stops moving and stands still: *The cars in front slowed down and came to a complete halt.* **b** A process or activity comes, or grinds, **to a halt** when it gets slower and stops completely: *Conversation ground to a halt.*

halter /'hɔːltə(r)/ *noun*: **halters**
A **halter** is a rope or strap that is put over a horse's head, for holding and leading it.

halting /'hɔːltɪŋ/ *adjective*
You speak in a **halting** manner when you speak in an uncertain, hesitating way: *She addressed us in a shy, rather halting voice.* — *adverb* **haltingly:** *He spoke haltingly, as though constantly weighing up his words.*

halve /hɑːv/ *verb*: **halves, halving, halved**

1 You **halve** something when you divide it into two equal parts: *Halve the grapefruit, remove the pips, sprinkle with sugar and serve in individual dishes.* **2** Something **halves** or **is halved** when it is reduced to half its former size or level: *Profits halved during the recession.* [see also **half**]

halves /hɑːvz/ *noun*
Halves is the plural of **half**.

ham¹ /ham/ *noun* (*uncount*)
Ham is smoked, salted meat from the thigh of a pig: *I bought a ham-and-cheese roll.*

ham² /ham/ *noun*; *verb*
▻ ***noun*** (*derogatory*): **hams**
If people call an actor a **ham** they mean that he or she acts in an unsubtle, insensitive, noisy and exaggerated style.
▻ ***verb***: **hams, hamming, hammed**
Actors **ham** their part, or **ham** it up, when they act it in an unsubtle, insensitive, noisy and exaggerated manner.

hamburger /ˈhambɜːgə(r)/ *noun*: **hamburgers**
A **hamburger** is a flat round cake of finely chopped beef, usually fried and served in a bread roll.

hamfisted /ˈhamfɪstɪd/ or **hamhanded** /ˈhamhandɪd/ *adjective* (*informal*)
If you describe a person as **hamfisted** or **hamhanded** you mean that they are physically clumsy: *Someone had made a hamfisted attempt to mend the vase.*

hamlet /ˈhamlət/ *noun*: **hamlets**
A **hamlet** is a small village.

hammer /ˈhamə(r)/ *noun*; *verb*
▻ ***noun***: **hammers**
1 A **hammer** is a tool with a heavy metal head on the end of a handle, that you use for hitting things, *eg* nails into wood. [see picture at **tool**] **2** A device or mechanism with a striking action may be called a **hammer**, *eg* the part connected to a piano key that strikes the wire. **3** (*athletics*) A **hammer** is a metal ball on a long steel chain, that athletes whirl round their heads and throw as far as possible.
▻ ***verb***: **hammers, hammering, hammered**
1 You **hammer** something when you hit it with a hammer: *There are heavy steel pegs that you can hammer into very hard ground.* **2** You **hammer** on a surface when you keep hitting it with your fists: *Someone was hammering on the door.* [*same as* **bang**] **3** (*informal*) To **hammer** something is to condemn it or criticize it severely: *The film was hammered by the critics.* **4** (*informal*) One team **hammers** another when it beats the other thoroughly and soundly. [*same as* **thrash**] **5** (*informal*) You **hammer** an idea into someone when you keep repeating it to them in a determined manner, so that they remember it: *Grammar was hammered into us in our childhood.* **6** You **hammer** away at something when you work at it constantly: *He was still hammering away at his book on English usage.*
▻ ***phrase*** Property **comes under the hammer** when it is sold at an auction sale.

phrasal verb
People **hammer out** an agreement or a compromise when they reach it after difficult discussions and negotiations.

hammock /ˈhamək/ *noun*: **hammocks**
A **hammock** is a long piece of canvas or net that is hung between two supports to serve as a bed. [see picture at **bedroom**]

hamper¹ /ˈhampə(r)/ *verb*: **hampers, hampering, hampered**
To **hamper** someone is to hinder their movement or progress: *Women must have been severely hampered by their long narrow skirts.* [*same as* **hinder**; *opposite* **help, aid**]

hamper² /ˈhampə(r)/ *noun*: **hampers**
A **hamper** is basket with a lid, used for carrying food in, *eg* for a picnic.

hamstring /ˈhamstrɪŋ/ *noun*; *verb*
▻ ***noun***: **hamstrings**
Your **hamstrings** are tendons at the back of your knees: *an old hamstring injury.*
▻ ***verb***: **hamstrings, hamstringing, hamstrung**
To **hamstring** someone is to make it difficult or impossible for them to act in the way they need to: *Small businesses are so hamstrung by EC regulations that some give up operating altogether.*

hand /hand/ *noun*; *verb*
▻ ***noun***: **hands**
1 a Your **hands** are the parts of your body at the end of your arms, with four fingers and a thumb: *What have you got in your left hand?* □ *She passed the back of her hand across her forehead.* □ *She got the children to clap their hands in time to the music.* [see picture at **body**] **b** The **hands** of a clock or watch are the narrow pointers that move round from number to number, showing what time it is: *The long hand tells you the hour and the short hand the minutes.* **c** A worker, *eg* in a factory, on a farm, or on a ship may be called a **hand**. **d** Your **hand** is your handwriting: *I recognized her small neat hand on the envelope.* □ *He writes a good strong hand.* **e** In card games, your **hand** is the set of cards that is dealt to you; you play a **hand** of a card game such as bridge, whist or poker when you play a round of it: *I was dealt a rotten hand.* **f** A **hand** is a unit used for measuring the height of horses, equal to 4 inches (10.16 centimetres). **g** (*old*) A man asks for a woman's **hand**, or her **hand** in marriage, when he asks her to marry him.
2 a (*used in the singular*) You ask someone for a **hand** with something when you ask them to help you with it: *I gave him a hand with the washing-up.* □ *Could you give me hand with* [= help me carry or move] *this table?* **b** You have or take a **hand** in the achieving of something when you are involved in it: *He offered to take a hand in getting the club started.* □ *The feminists had evidently had a hand in the wording of the consitution.* **c** (*used in the plural*) Something is in your **hands** if it is in your control, power or possession: *I'm happy to leave all the organization in your hands.* □ *The matter is now in the hands of the police.* □ *It would be a disaster if that letter fell into the wrong hands.* □ *People must be discouraged from taking the law into their own hands* [= dealing independently with a situation that should be dealt with by those in authority].
3 (*used in the singular*) **Hand** is used in combination with *right* and *left* in indicating position or direction: *May I welcome, on my right hand, Dr Ronald Cain, and on my left, his wife Anna.* □ *The key's in the top left-hand drawer.* □ *Take the second righthand turn.*
▻ ***verb***: **hands, handing, handed**
You **hand** something to someone when you give it to them: *Could you hand me the scissors?* □ *She read the letter and handed it back to me.* [*same as* **pass**]
▻ ***phrases*** **1** You experience or discover something **at first hand** when you experience or discover it yourself, rather than hearing about it from someone else; you hear about something **at second hand** when you are told about it by someone else, rather than discovering it yourself. **2 a** Something is **at hand** or **close at hand** if

it is nearby: *The bus station is close at hand.* **b** Help or assistance is **at hand** when it is quickly available. **3 a** You do something **by hand** when you do it using your hands rather than machinery or an automatic process: *All the furniture is made by hand.* □ *We had to make the corrections by hand as the computer wouldn't do them for us.* **b** A letter comes **by hand** when it is delivered to you by someone, not sent by post. **4** Property or possessions **change hands** when they are sold, or given, by one person to another: *The restaurant has changed hands several times recently.* **5** (*informal*) You have someone **eating out of your hand** when they are willing to do whatever you tell them. **6** You **force** someone's **hand** when you make them act sooner than they intended to, or make them do something they would have preferred not to do. **7** Someone who sets you a task gives you **a free hand** with it if they allow you to do it in any way that you decide is suitable. **8** Something goes **from hand to hand** when one person passes it on to another. **9** Someone who is living **from hand to mouth** has so little money that they can plan only for their immediate needs: *a miserable hand-to-mouth existence.* **10** (*informal*) An audience **gives** a performer **a big hand** when they clap him or her enthusiastically. **11 a** You **get**, or **lay**, **your hands on** something when you manage to obtain it: *I wish I could lay my hands on a copy of that lecture.* **b** You **get**, or **lay**, **your hands** on a person who has done something wrong when you catch them: *Wait till I get my hands on the person who scratched my car.* **12** Someone who is **good with their hands** is clever or artistic at making things. **13** One person is **hand in glove** with another when they are working in close association, often secretly or for a dishonest pupose. **14 a** One person is **hand in hand** with another when they are holding each other's hand: *She was walking along hand in hand with a fellow I hadn't seen before.* **b** Things that go **hand in hand** are closely related: *This kind of crime goes hand in hand with poverty.* **15** For **hand over fist** see **fist**. **16** You beat someone, or win, **hands down** when you win easily. **17** If someone says **'hands off!'** to you, they are asking you not to touch or interfere with something: *Keep your hands off my computer.* **18 a** When a teacher or speaker says **'hands up!'** during a class or meeting, he or she wants people to put a hand up in the air in answer to something: *Hands up those who think they know the answer.* **b** When someone points a gun at you and shouts **'hands up!'**, they are telling you to put your hands in the air so that you cannot get hold of, or use, your own weapon. **19** Soldiers fight **hand to hand** when they fight closely together using knives or swords: *fierce hand-to-hand combat.* **20** You say you **have to hand it to** someone when you feel they deserve praise or credit for something: *You had to hand it to her for protecting the members of her own department.* **21** You **have your hands full** when you are very busy, especially with a number of different jobs. **22** (*old*) Someone offers you **a helping hand** when they offer to help you by doing a task or some work for you. **23** Two people **hold hands** when they hold each other's hand: *It was a strange sight, these two old people going along holding hands with each other.* **24 a** You have a matter **in hand** when you are attending to it, or have it under control: *Don't worry; everything is in hand.* **b** You have time **in hand** when something has not taken as long as you expected and you have some spare time: *We finished early and had two hours in hand till the train left.* **25** You **keep your hand in** at some skill when you continue to practise it: *I don't play as much golf as I did, but I keep my hand in.* **26** You **know** a place or subject **like the back of your hand** when you know it thoroughly. **27** You **lend** someone **a hand** when you help them: *She sometimes lent me a hand with the housework.* **28** You can tell people something **off hand** if you do not need to work it out first, or refer to a source of information. **29** A matter is **off your hands** when you have finished dealing with it, or it is no longer your responsibility: *I was relieved to have the problem off my hands.* **30** Someone who is **an old hand at** something is experienced in it: *He's an old hand at dealing with difficult customers.* **31** Someone or something is **on hand** when they are available to help or be of use: *Library staff are always on hand to help with your queries.* □ *Emergency equipment is on hand at all times.* **32** You use **on the one hand ... on the other hand** to introduce two contrasting circumstances: *On the one hand her temper was likely to cause trouble; on the other we needed her expertise.* **33 a** You have things **on your hands** when you are responsible for dealing with them: *She has a lot on her hands just now.* **b** You have time **on your hands** when you have spare time and need some occupation to fill it. **c** Goods are left **on your hands** when you do not manage to sell them. **34** You are **on your hands and knees** when you are kneeling with your weight equally on your hands and knees. [*same as* **on all fours**] **35 a** You reject a suggestion **out of hand** when you reject it without taking time to consider it. **b** You let things get **out of hand** when you lose control over them: *Discipline problems at the school were getting out of hand.* **36** An opponent **plays into your hands** when they unintentionally do something that gives you the advantage. **37 a** You **rub your hands** when you rub the palm of one hand against the palm of the other, *eg* to warm them. **b** Someone is described as **rubbing their hands** with glee when they are feeling pleased or triumphant about something. **38** Two people **shake hands** when they grasp each other's right hand as a form of greeting: *We shook hands with each other.* □ *I shook his hand.* **39** You **show your hand** when you let people see what your intentions are: *We shall force him to show his hand.* **40 a** You **take** a person **in hand** when you discipline them. **b** You **take** a matter **in hand** when you deal with it. **41** Things are **to hand** when they are near you, ready for use or reference: *I don't have your letter to hand at the moment.* **42** You **try your hand at** a skill when you attempt to learn it: *It's the perfect opportunity to try your hand at windsurfing.* **43** You **turn your hand to** a job or activity when you do it: *These graduates are willing to turn their hands to anything.* **44** You get **the upper hand** in a struggle or argument when you gain an advantage over your opponent. **45** You **wash your hands of** something when you refuse to be responsible for it any more. **46** You do something **with your bare hands** when you do it without the help of weapons or tools: *Rescuers were digging in the rubble with their bare hands to find survivors.*

phrasal verbs

hand down Possessions, stories, traditions or skills **are handed down** when they are given to people of a younger generation: *The brooch had been handed down through our family for many generations.* □ *The art of story-telling is handed down from mother to daughter.* [*same as* **pass down**]

hand in You **hand in** an essay or something you have written when you give it to your teacher or someone in authority: *Your proses should be handed in to me by Friday afternoon.*

hand on You **hand on** something you have received when you give it to someone else: *Could you hand the notice on to the others?* [*same as* **pass on**]

hand out 1 You **hand** things **out** to people when

you give one to each person: *The questionnaires were handed out to the students.* **2** Someone in authority **hands out** something such as equipment or advice when they give it to people: *They were handing out clean needles to drug addicts.* [*same as* **give out**]
hand over 1 You **hand** something **over** to someone when you give it to them: *They handed over their weapons.* [*same as* **surrender**] **2** You **hand over** to someone when you officially give them responsibility for something for which you have been responsible till now: *I hand over to my successor on 1 April.*
hand round 1 You **hand** things **round** to people when you give them one each: *Could you hand round these leaflets for me?* [*same as* **hand out**] **2** People **hand** something **round** when they give it to one another in turn: *The card was handed round for everyone to sign.* [*same as* **pass round**]

hand- /hand/
Hand- is combined with other words to mean **1** done by hand: *handknitted woollens* □ *Are these brooches handmade?* **2** held in the hand, as in *handgun, handrail, hand luggage*. **3** operated by hand, as in *handbrake*.

handbag /ˈhandbag/ *noun*: **handbags**
A woman's **handbag** is a small bag in which she carries such things as her money, keys and make-up.

handbook /ˈhandbʊk/ *noun*: **handbooks**
A **handbook** is a book of instructions or advice about something: *They supply a handbook with the software.* [*same as* **manual**]

handbrake /ˈhandbreɪk/ *noun*: **handbrakes**
The **handbrake** in a motor vehicle is the brake beside the driver's seat that the driver operates with his or her hand.

handclap /ˈhandklap/ *noun* (*used in the singular*)
▷ ***phrase*** An audience gives **a slow handclap** when they clap together in a regular rhythm, usually as an expression of disapproval or impatience.

handcuff /ˈhandkʌf/ *noun*; *verb*
▷ ***noun*** (*used in the plural*)
Handcuffs are a pair of steel rings, joined by a short chain, that the police lock round the wrists of someone they are arresting.
▷ ***verb***: **handcuffs, handcuffing, handcuffed**
The police **handcuff** someone when they put handcuffs on them.

handful /ˈhandfʊl/ *noun*: **handfuls**
1 A **handful** of something is the amount you can hold, or grasp, with your hand: *She scooped up a handful of snow and rolled it into a ball.* **2** (*used in the singular*) A **handful** of people or things is a small number: *A handful of people were already waiting in the hall.* **3** (*used in the singular*; *informal*) You call a person, especially a child, a **handful** if they are difficult to control: *Her two-year-old's a bit of a handful.*

hand-held /ˈhandheld/ *adjective*
A **hand-held** tool is one that you hold in your hand while operating it: *a hand-held hairdryer.*

handicap /ˈhandɪkap/ *noun*: **handicaps**
1 Someone who has a **handicap** has a physical or mental disability that prevents them from living completely normally: *All new public buildings must be designed to accommodate people with handicaps.* **2** A **handicap** is a circumstance that is a disadvantage to you: *A lack of computer skills is certainly a handicap these days.* **3** (*sport*) In a race or other competition, a competitor who is very good is given a **handicap** when he or she is placed at a disadvantage in order to give other competitors a better chance of winning. **4** A golfer's **handicap** is the number by which the total number of strokes they usually play to get round the course is greater than the official total considered necessary.

handicapped /ˈhandɪkapt/ *adjective*; *noun*
▷ ***adjective***
1 A **handicapped** person has a mental or physical disability that prevents them from living completely normally: *Their oldest child was mentally handicapped.* **2** You are **handicapped** by some personal circumstance or characteristic if it is a disadvantage to you: *Handicapped by an inability to realize when he was being rude, he quickly made enemies.*
▷ ***noun*** (*plural*)
The **handicapped** are people with a mental or physical disability: *special holidays for the handicapped.*

handicraft /ˈhandɪkrɑːft/ *noun*: **handicrafts**
1 A **handicraft** is an activity in which you use your hands skilfully to make something: *lacemaking and other traditional handicrafts.* **2** (*used in the plural*) **Handicrafts** are articles made through skilful use of the hands: *The notice said 'Pottery and Other Handicrafts for Sale'.*

handiwork /ˈhandɪwɜːk/ *noun* (*uncount*)
You refer to something that someone has made or done as their **handiwork**: *She had just finished painting the kitchen and asked us to come and admire her handiwork.*

handkerchief /ˈhaŋkətʃɪf/ *noun*: **hankerchiefs**
A **handkerchief** is a small square piece of cloth or soft paper for wiping your nose with. [*same as* **hanky**; see also **tissue**]

handle /ˈhandəl/ *noun*; *verb*
▷ ***noun***: **handles**
The **handle** of a bag or case is the part you hold when carrying it; the **handle** of a door is the part you hold and turn when opening or closing it; the **handle** of a tool is the part you hold when using it; a **handle** on a piece of machinery is a lever you hold and move when operating it: *A broom is a floor brush with a long handle.*
▷ ***verb***: **handles, handling, handled**
1 You **handle** something when you hold it and move it around in your hands: *The archaeological finds must be handled with tremendous care.* **2** You **handle** a device, a piece of machinery or a vehicle when you operate or control it; a vehicle **handles** well if it is easy to operate: *I'd never handled a fire-extinguisher before.* **3** You **handle** a problem or situation when you deal with it: *I thought you handled that little incident most professionally.* **4** (*informal*; *especially AmE*) You are able to **handle** some personal disappointment or other crisis if you refuse to let it upset you: *So you don't want me. OK, I can handle it.* **5** You **handle** a particular part of a business or project if you are responsible for it: *She handles the overseas sales.* **6** You **handle** particular goods if you deal in them: *We don't handle second-hand books now.* **7** You **handle** a topic or subject when you write about it or discuss it: *He handles the problem of authorship quite well.* — *noun* (*uncount*) **handling:** *She won praise for her handling of the strike.*
▷ ***phrase*** (*informal*) Someone **flies off the handle** when they suddenly become uncontrollably angry.

handlebars /ˈhandəlbɑːz/ *noun* (*plural*)
The **handlebars** of a bicycle are the right and left sections of the curved horizontal bar with handles at each end, that you grip when riding and steering.

handler /ˈhandlə(r)/ *noun*: **handlers**
1 A **handler** is a person who trains and controls an animal, especially a dog: *police dogs and their han-*

dlers. **2** Someone whose job is dealing with, carrying or moving something may be called a **handler**: *The baggage-handlers are on strike at Schiphol Airport.*

handmade /hand'meɪd/ *adjective*
Things that are **handmade** are made by hand by someone, not by machine: *handmade silk scarves.*

handout /'handaʊt/ *noun*: **handouts**
1 A **handout** is something such as money, food or clothing that is given free to poor people: *They depend on social-security handouts for survival.* **2** A free leaflet giving information about something is a **handout**: *Do you have any handouts about the jazz festival?* ▫ *You'll find the address on the handout.* **3** The sheets that a speaker distributes to an audience before a lecture, containing material relevant to it, are also **handouts**.

hand-picked /hand'pɪkt/ *adjective*
People are **hand-picked** for a particular task when they are carefully selected for it: *A hand-picked group of students stood ready to talk to the Queen.*

handrail /'handreɪl/ *noun*: **handrails**
A **handrail** is a narrow rail fitted *eg* beside a flight of steps or a steep path, for users to hold on to for safety.

handset /'handset/ *noun*: **handsets**
The **handset** of a telephone is the separate piece that you hold in your hand and talk or listen through: *Lift the handset and dial the number you want.* [*same as* **receiver**; see picture at **office**]

handshake /'handʃeɪk/ *noun*: **handshakes**
A **handshake** is the act of gripping a person's right hand as a greeting: *The members of these secret societies had special handshakes by which they recognized each other.*

handsome /'hansəm/ *adjective*
1 A man who is **handsome** is goodlooking, usually with strong, regular features. [*same as* **good-looking**] **2** People describe a woman as **handsome** if she is good-looking in a strong and dignified, rather than feminine, way. [compare **pretty**, **beautiful**] **3** A **handsome** building is one that is large and well-designed: *the handsome frontage of Queen Street.* [*same as* **imposing**] **4** A **handsome** sum of money is a large or generous one: *She was officially thanked for her handsome donation to the appeal fund.* — *adverb* **handsomely:** *a country house in handsomely laid-out grounds.* ▫ *They were handsomely rewarded for their loyalty.*

hands-on /handz'ɒn/ *adjective*
A **hands-on** demonstration of some system involves the audience in trying it out for themselves, as distinct from merely watching.

handstand /'handstand/ *noun*: **handstands**
You do a **handstand** when you balance your body upside down on your hands with your legs straight up in the air.

handwriting /'handraɪtɪŋ/ *noun* (*uncount*)
Your **handwriting** is your style of writing when you write with a pen or pencil: *I recognized his handwriting on the envelope.*

handwritten /hand'rɪtən/ *adjective*
A letter or other piece of writing is **handwritten** if it has been written with a pen or pencil, not typed or printed.

handy /'handɪ/ *adjective*: **handier**, **handiest**
1 A **handy** tool or device is one that is useful, convenient and easy to use: *A portable computer is so handy.* **2** Something that is **handy** is nearby and available for use or reference: *Is there a dictionary handy?* **3** Someone who is **handy** at something is skilful at it: *He was a likeable lodger, and handy at doing repairs.*

▻ *phrases* **1** Something **comes in handy** if you find it useful on some occasion: *I keep all these bits and pieces in case they come in handy some day.* **2** You **keep** something **handy** if you always have it near you and available for use: *I always kept a pair of haircutting scissors handy.*

handyman /'handɪman/ *noun*: **handymen**
A **handyman** is someone who is good at making and repairing things around the house.

hang /haŋ/ *verb*: **hangs**, **hanging**, **hung** or **hanged**
1 You **hang** a thing on something such as a hook, rail or line when you secure the top part of it there, leaving the rest held loosely above the ground; something **hangs** when it is held loosely in this way, supported at one point: *We hung the washing on the line.* ▫ *Her coat was hanging on the peg as usual.* ▫ *All her dresses were still hanging in the wardrobe.* ▫ *He glanced round at the pictures hanging on the wall.* ▫ *Several animal carcases were hanging from hooks in the ceiling.* ▫ *He had thin fair hair that hung loosely round his face.* ▫ *The old wallpaper hung off the wall in strips.* ▫ *She wore her boots hanging round her neck by their laces.* ▫ *He was left hanging on to the ledge by three fingers.* **2** (**hanged**) To **hang** a person is to kill them by tying a rope round their neck and removing the support from under their feet, so that they die as the rope takes their weight and tightens: *She committed suicide by hanging herself.* ▫ *Bentley was going to hang for a murder committed by his friend.* ▫ *Casement was hanged as a traitor in 1916.* ▫ *They hanged people for the slightest offence in those days.* **3** You can describe a worrying possibility or a threat as **hanging** over you: *The threat of nuclear war hangs over us still.* **4** You **hang** wallpaper when you stick it to the wall. **5** You **hang** a door when you fit it on to its hinges. **6** Clothing **hangs** well if it fits well in the right places.

▻ *phrase* (*informal*) You **get the hang of** something when you understand it: *You'll soon get the hang of it if you keep practising.*

phrasal verbs

hang about or **hang around** (*informal*) **1** You **hang about** or **around** a place when you stay there doing nothing, *eg* when you are waiting for someone or something: *Gangs of boys used to hang about on the street corners.* ▫ *I can't hang about any longer.* ▫ *Journalists had been hanging around the law court all week.* **2** One person **hangs about** or **around** with another if they spend a lot of time together.

hang back You **hang back** when you are unwilling, or too shy, to move forward or join in some activity: *Some of the younger children hung back shyly.* [*same as* **hold back**]

hang on 1 You ask someone to **hang on** when you want them to wait briefly, or stop what they are saying or doing: *Could you hang on a minute while I make a call?* ▫ *Hang on; that doesn't sound right.* [*same as* **hold on**] **2** You **hang on** in a difficult situation when you stay there waiting for help or a change for the better: *We could do nothing but try to hang on till the rescue services arrived.* **3** One thing **hangs on** another if it depends on it: *Acceptance of these proposals hangs on finance, as you know.* **4** (*literary*) You **hang on** someone's words when you listen to them with great attention.

hang on to 1 You **hang on to** something when you hold it tightly: *Here, hang on to my hand.* **2** You **hang on to** something when you keep it: *Hang on to the receipt.* ▫ *At the age of 90 he was still hanging on to the premiership.* [*same as* **hold on to**]

hang out 1 You **hang out** the clothes or the wash-

ing when you hang them outside on a line to dry. **2** (*informal*) You **hang out** of a window when you stretch your head and shoulders out of it.
hang together
1 Facts or statements **hang together** if they support one another or are consistent. **2** People **hang together** when they unite and support one another.
hang up 1 You **hang** something **up** when you put it on something such as a hook or rail so that it is held loosely above the ground from that point; things **are hanging up** when they are held up loosely in this way: *She hung up her jacket.* □ *Some battered pans were hanging up in the kitchen.* **2** You **hang up** at the end of a telephone call when you replace the receiver. **3** You **hang up** on someone when you replace the receiver while they are speaking, or suddenly and without explanation.

hangar /'haŋə(r)/ *noun*: **hangars**
A **hangar** is a large building in which aircraft are kept.

hanger /'haŋə(r)/ *noun*: **hangers**
A **hanger** is a shaped piece of metal, wood or plastic, with a hook, on which to hang clothes. [*same as* **coat-hanger**]

hanger-on /haŋə'ɒn/ *noun*: **hangers-on**
A **hanger-on** is a person who accompanies someone more famous or important out of admiration or a desire to be associated with them: *crowds of friends and hangers-on.*

hang-glider /'haŋglaɪdə(r)/ *noun*: **hang-gliders**
A **hang-glider** is a large light metal frame with cloth stretched across it, with a harness beneath it for the pilot, who makes use of air currents and body movement to guide it and control its height; the pilot is also a **hang-glider**.

hang-gliding /'haŋglaɪdɪŋ/ *noun* (*uncount*)
Hang-gliding is the sport of flying in a hang-glider.

hanging /'haŋɪŋ/ *noun*: **hangings**
1 (*uncount or count*) **Hanging** is the practice of executing people by hanging them; a **hanging** is an occasion when someone is executed by hanging: *'Bring back hanging!' they yelled.* **2** (*usually in the plural*) **Hangings** are such things as curtains or decorative cloths hung on the wall: *These wall-hangings and tapestries helped to keep the rooms warm.*

hangman /'haŋmən/ *noun*: **hangmen**
A **hangman** is an official whose job is to execute people by hanging them.

hangover /'haŋoʊvə(r)/ *noun*: **hangovers**
1 A **hangover** is a bad headache and a sick feeling that you sometimes wake up with when you have drunk a lot of alcohol the night before. **2** A thing that is a **hangover** from the past is something still remaining that relates to circumstances that no longer exist: *Some of the methods we use are a hangover from when we didn't have computers.*

hang-up /'haŋʌp/ *noun* (*informal*): **hang-ups**
You have a **hang-up** about something if you are afraid of it or worry about it: *He had a hang-up about using the telephone.* [*same as* **problem**]

hank /haŋk/ *noun*: **hanks**
A **hank** of something such as wool, rope or string is a loosely wound length of it.

hanker /'haŋkə(r)/ *verb*: **hankers, hankered, hankering**
You **hanker** for or after something when you want it very much: *She was hankering for the ski slopes.* [*same as* **long** for] — *noun* **hankering:** *She had a constant hankering for affection and admiration.*

hanky or **hankie** /haŋkɪ/ *noun* (*informal*): **hankies**
A **hanky** is a handkerchief: *I bought a packet of paper hankies.*

haphazard /hap'hazəd/ *adjective*
Something that is **haphazard** is unplanned or disorganized, rather than planned and organized according to some system: *Their methods of testing seem rather haphazard.* — *adverb* **haphazardly:** *The statistics had been hastily and haphazardly compiled.*

hapless /'hapləs/ *adjective* (*literary*)
A **hapless** person is very unlucky: *These women were the hapless victims of a powerful all-male league.*

happen /'hapən/ *verb*: **happens, happening, happened**
1 Something **happens** when it occurs or is done by chance, or without being planned: *When did all this happen?* □ *Did you see how the accident happened?* □ *We must find out exactly what happened that night at the club.* □ *It so happens that I have the key with me.* **2** Something **happens** when it occurs as the result of some action or event: *I dread to think what would happen if she found out.* □ *I rang the bell but nothing happened.* □ *What happens if you press the 'insert' button?* □ *What happened about that party they were planning?* **3** Something that **happens** to you affects or concerns you directly when it occurs, especially in a bad way: *He's late; whatever can have happened to him?* □ *I thought something awful must have happened to you.* □ *What's been happening to you? Tell me your news.* **4** You **happen** to do something when you do it by chance: *Fortunately I happened to be at home when he had his heart attack.* □ *I happen to be going in your direction, so I can give you a lift.* **5** You say something **happens** to be so as an emphatic way of informing or reminding someone that it is so: *Don't talk about her like that; she happens to be my friend.* □ *I happen to like quiz programmes myself.*
▻ ***phrase*** You use **as it happens** to introduce something unexpected: *As it happens, I've got the information right here.*

happening /'hapənɪŋ/ *noun*: **happenings**
A **happening** is an event or something that happens, especially something unexpected: *There have been a lot of unexplained happenings in the department recently.*

happy /'hapɪ/ *adjective*: **happier, happiest**
1 You are **happy** when you feeling pleased or contented: *a happy smile* □ *She was never very happy at school.* **2** You describe a particular period or place as **happy** if whoever has experienced it has felt happy during it or in it: *We had a happy home.* □ *His university days were his happiest.* **3** You are **happy** about some arrangement or situation if you are satisfied with it: *I'm not happy about these changes.* **4** You are **happy** to do something if you are willing to: *I'm perfectly happy to wait.* □ *I'd be happy to help, of course.* **5 Happy** is often used to mean lucky, fortunate, or suitable in the circumstances: *It was a happy day for our company when he joined us.* **6** You use **happy** in giving greetings for a special occasion: *Happy Birthday!* — *adverb* **happily:** *The kids were playing happily in the garden.* □ (*sentence adverb*) *Happily, she didn't hear his comment.* [*same as* **fortunately**] — *noun* (*uncount*) **happiness:** *moments of supreme happiness.*

happy-go-lucky /hapɪgoʊ'lʌkɪ/ *adjective*
A **happy-go-lucky** person is someone who enjoys life as it passes and does not plan for, or worry about, the future. [*same as* **carefree, easygoing**]

harangue /hə'raŋ/ *noun*; *verb*

▻ ***noun***: **harangues**
You give people a **harangue** when you express your opinion strongly and loudly about something, so as to persuade them to think as you do, or do what you want them to.
▻ ***verb***: **harangues, haranguing, harangued:** *She was never so happy as when on a platform haranguing a crowd.*

harass /ˈharəs/ *verb*: **harasses, harassing, harassed**
Someone **harrasses** you when they keep annoying you, upsetting you or interfering in your life: *She was being harrassed by a mystery caller who kept telephoning her in the middle of the night.* [*same as* **bother**, **pester**] — *noun* (*uncount*) **harassment:** *The inhabitants of the flat frequently complained of police harassment.*

harassed /ˈharəst/ *adjective*
You are **harassed** when you have too much to do and feel worried and anxious: *She was hurrying along with two bags of shopping, looking harassed.*

harassing /ˈharəsɪŋ/ *adjective*
A **harassing** situation makes you feel anxious, worried and under pressure: *I've had a harassing week; too many jobs to do, and endless phone calls to deal with.*

harbinger /ˈhɑːbɪndʒə(r)/ *noun* (*literary*): **harbingers**
A person or thing that is a **harbinger** of something is a sign that it is going to happen: *the sudden caution on the stock market that was the harbinger of a recession.*

harbour (*AmE* **harbor**) /ˈhɑːbə(r)/ *noun*; *verb*
▻ ***noun***: **harbours**
A harbour is a partially enclosed area of water protected by headlands or walls, where ships can shelter or dock: *The steamer backed out of the harbour.*
▻ ***verb***: **harbours, harbouring, harboured**
1 You **harbour** feelings or emotions if you have them and keep them, rather than letting them disappear after a while: *He harboured a grudge against the management over his failure to be promoted.* **2** To **harbour** criminals is to protect them from the police by letting them stay secretly in your house.

hard /hɑːd/ *adjective*; *adverb*
▻ ***adjective***: **harder, hardest**
1 a Something that is **hard** feels firm or solid when you touch it: *The ground was frozen as hard as rock.* □ *a piece of hard stale bread* □ *We sat for two hours on hard uncomfortable chairs.* [*opposite* **soft**] **b** A **hard** push, kick or knock is a strong one: *If a child is choking try giving it a hard slap between the shoulder blades.* [*opposite* **gentle**]
2 a A subject, task or question is **hard** if it is difficult: *I struggled with all my school subjects, but I found maths the hardest.* □ *English is a hard language to speak really well.* □ *It's hard to tell the difference between the copy and the real thing.* □ *It wasn't hard to see* [= it was obvious] *why she liked him.* [*same as* **difficult**; *opposite* **easy**] **b Hard** work involves a lot of effort: *Thank you for all your trouble and hard work.* □ *She works a long hard day.* **c** Equipment that comes in for **hard** use or wear is used frequently, intensively and often roughly. **d** You say someone has a **hard** life or a **hard** time if they have a lot of problems to deal with: *She has a hard time with her elderly mother.* □ *Don't bother me now; I've had a hard day.* [*same as* **difficult, troublesome**; *opposite* **easy**] **e** A **hard** life is also one in which there is too little money or comfort: *We had a hard life as children, as my parents were very poor.* [*same as* **harsh, rigorous**; *opposite* **easy, comfortable**] **f** Circumstances are **hard** on you if they cause you difficulty or suffering: *The regulations are hard on married women with children.* □ *Horse-riding is pretty hard on the bottom till you get used to it.*
3 a A person who is **hard** is unkind, or shows too little affection or sympathy: *His expression was hard and unsympathetic.* □ *She had small hard eyes.* □ *He spoke in a cold, hard tone.* **b** You are **hard** on someone if you behave severely towards them: *Don't be too hard on her; she's only a child.* **c** The difficulties and troubles that you experience in life make you **hard** if they make you tough, strong and independent. [*opposite* **gentle, meek, sensitive**]
4 a You can describe certain things that are unpleasant to the senses as **hard**: *a hard white light.* **b** A **hard** winter is very cold; a **hard** frost is a severe one with temperatures well below freezing. [*opposite* **mild**] **c Hard** water contains large amounts of the minerals calcium or magnesium, which prevent soap from lathering in it. [*opposite* **soft**]
5 a Hard facts are proved, reliable, or known to be true: *What we need here is hard evidence.* **b Hard** drugs are the strongly addictive ones such as heroin and cocaine: *She was on hard drugs for a while.* **c** People who have extreme political opinions can be described as being on the **hard** left or **hard** right.
▻ ***adverb***: **harder, hardest**
1 You try **hard** or work **hard** when you concentrate and make a great effort: *These folk with Alzheimer's can't remember what you tell them no matter how hard they try.* □ *She had worked hard for the scholarship.* □ *I tried hard to make her understand.* **2** You push or hit something **hard** when you do it with force: *He kicked me hard under the table.* **3** You do something such as run or play **hard** if you do it as fast or energetically as you can. **4 Hard-** is used in combination with past participles to mean achieved only with difficulty: *a hard-won victory* □ *hard-earned praise.* — *noun* (*uncount*) **hardness:** *It was more the unfriendliness of her colleagues than the hardness of the work that depressed her.*
▻ ***phrases*** **1** (*informal*) You are **hard at it** if you are working hard or doing something with effort and energy: *He was still hard at it when I left the office.* **2** You feel **hard done by** if you think you have been treated unfairly. **3** For **hard going** see **going**. **4** For **hard of hearing** see **hearing**. **5** One thing follows **hard on** another if it follows the other very closely or soon: *Hard on the break-up of her marriage came her mother's death.* [see also **hard on the heels of** at **heel**] **6** You say you would be **hard put to it**, **hard pushed** or **hard pressed** to do something if it would be difficult to do it: *I'd be hard put to it to think of a better example.* [see also **hard-pressed**] **7** (*informal*) You are **hard up** when you have too little money: *I was so hard up I couldn't afford to go to the cinema.*

hard-and-fast /hɑːdənˈfɑːst/ *adjective*
A **hard-and-fast** rule is one that must not be broken or cannot be changed: *There's no hard-and-fast rule about which method to use.*

hardback /ˈhɑːdbak/ *noun*; *adjective*
▻ ***noun*** (*count or uncount*): **hardbacks**
A **hardback** is a book with a hard cover, as distinct from a paper or plastic cover: *I prefer hardbacks to paperbacks.* □ *published in both hardback and paperback.*
▻ ***adjective:*** *shelves of hardback first editions.*

hardboard /ˈhɑːdbɔːd/ *noun* (*uncount*)
Hardboard is light thin strong board made from small pieces of wood that have been softened and compressed.

hard-boiled /ˈhɑːdbɔɪld/ *adjective*
A **hard-boiled** egg has been boiled in its shell until the yolk is solid.

hard cash /hɑːd'kaʃ/ *noun (uncount)*
Hard cash is coins and bank notes, as distinct from cheques and credit cards.

hard copy /'hɑːdkɒpɪ/ *noun (uncount)*
Hard copy is material printed out from a computer.

hard-core /'hɑːdkɔː(r)/ *adjective*
Hard-core describes the members of a movement who are most strongly loyal and opposed to change, or their views and opinions: *hard-core Conservatives.*

hard currency /hɑːd'kʌrənsɪ/ *noun (count or uncount)*: **hard currencies**
A **hard currency** is a national currency with a stable value, that is easily exchanged for another currency.

hard disk /hɑːd 'dɪsk/ *noun*: **hard disks**
A **hard disk** is a metal disk with a magnetic coating, that is used for storing information in a computer.

harden /'hɑːdən/ *verb*: **hardens, hardening, hardened**
1 A substance **hardens** when it becomes firm or solid: *Leave the clay to harden for a few days.* **2** You **harden** your heart or attitude to something or someone when you become less sympathetic: *The government had hardened its heart towards the sick and unemployed.* **3** Your views or position on some issue **harden** when you become determined not to change them: *Their resistance had hardened.* **4** The trouble and difficulties that you experience in life **harden** you if they make you tougher, or make you less sensitive and sympathetic towards others. — *noun (uncount)* **hardening:** *The violence led to a hardening of attitudes on both sides.*

hardened /'hɑːdənd/ *adjective*
Hardened criminals are people who are so used to committing crimes that they commit them without fear or pity.

hard-headed /'hɑːdhɛdɪd/ *adjective*
A **hard-headed** person is someone who does not let themselves be influenced by feelings such as concern for others in getting what they want: *They are hard-headed business people intent on their careers.* [*same as* **realistic, cynical**]

hard-hearted /'hɑːdhɑːtɪd/ *adjective*
You describe someone as **hard-hearted** if they have no sympathy or pity for others: *I don't want to seem hard-hearted, but I can't give money to every beggar I see.* [*opposite* **soft-hearted**]

hard labour /hɑːd'leɪbə(r)/ *noun (uncount)*
Hard labour is heavy physical work that criminals may have to do as part of their punishment: *He was sentenced to three years' hard labour.*

hard line /hɑːd'laɪn/ *noun (used in the singular)*
You take a **hard line** on something when you decide to deal firmly with it, and refuse to change your mind: *The headteacher is taking a hard line on unpunctuality and truancy this term.*

hard-line /'hɑːdlaɪn/ *adjective*
People who have **hard-line** attitudes stick rigidly to their principles: the *hard-line trade-unionists.*

hard luck /hɑːd'lʌk/ *noun; interjection*
▻ ***noun*** *(uncount)*
Hard luck is bad luck or misfortune: *He came to me with a hard-luck story, wanting to borrow money.*
▻ ***interjection***
You say **'hard luck!'** to someone when you are expressing sympathy with them for not getting or achieving what they wanted.

hardly /'hɑːdlɪ/ *adverb (used like a negative)*
1 Things that are **hardly** so, or that **hardly** happen, are almost not so, or almost don't happen: *I hardly recognized you with your new hairstyle.* ▫ *We've hardly any milk left.* ▫ *I hardly ever see him nowadays.* ▫ *But you hardly know her, do you?* ▫ *Next day I found I could hardly move.* ▫ *She was hardly more than a baby when her mother died.* ▫ *Their standards have hardly improved at all.* [*same as* **barely, scarcely**] **2** You use **hardly** as an emphatic way of saying 'not at all': *You're hardly likely to pick up any bargains as late in the sale as this.* ▫ *We can hardly hope for her support after being so rude to her.* ▫ (*used as an answer*) *'Will he admit his error?' 'Hardly!'* [*same as* **scarcely**] **3** You say that **hardly** had one thing happened when another happened to emphasize how quickly the second event followed the first: *Hardly had he finished saying how dark the sky was when there was a clap of thunder.* [*same as* **barely, scarcely, no sooner**]

hard-pressed /hɑːd'prɛst/ *adjective*
People who are **hard-pressed** have too much to do and suffer a lot of stress and anxiety: *How are teachers, already hard-pressed, supposed to cope with these additional burdens?*

hardship /'hɑːdʃɪp/ *noun (uncount or count)*: **hardships**
You suffer **hardship** when you are in great difficulty or discomfort, *eg* when you haven't enough money to buy food and other necessities: *She led a life of terrible poverty and hardship.*

hard shoulder /hɑːd'ʃoʊldə(r)/ *noun*: **hard shoulders**
The **hard shoulder** on a motorway is a strip along the edge of it where you can park your vehicle in an emergency, *eg* if you have a breakdown.

hardware /'hɑːdwɛə(r)/ *noun (uncount)*
1 Tools and equipment for the house and garden are called **hardware**: *We called at the hardware store to buy a pair of garden shears.* **2** (*computers*) **Hardware** is the electronic machinery used in computing, as distinct from the programs. [see also **software**]

hardwearing /hɑːd'wɛərɪŋ/ *adjective*
Hardwearing clothes and furnishings are well made and last a long time: *hardwearing floor-coverings.* [*same as* **durable**]

hardworking /hɑːd'wɜːkɪŋ/ *adjective*
Hardworking people work hard and conscientiously at their jobs or studies.

hardy /'hɑːdɪ/ *adjective*: **hardier, hardiest**
1 A **hardy** person or animal is strong and tough and able to endure difficult and uncomfortable conditions: *The penguin needs to be hardy to withstand the freezing climate.* **2** A **hardy** plant is able to survive out of doors in winter. — *noun (uncount)* **hardiness:** *a race of mountain-dwellers noted for their hardiness.*

hare /hɛə(r)/ *noun; verb*
▻ ***noun***: **hares**
A **hare** is an animal like a rabbit but larger, with longer legs and ears, which can run very fast.
▻ ***verb*** *(informal)*: **hares, haring, hared**
You **hare** somewhere when you run there very fast: *I hared after her.* ▫ *The deer hared away when they saw us coming.*

harebrained /'hɛəbreɪnd/ *adjective*
You describe a plan as **harebrained** if it seems silly, impractical and unlikely to succeed: *It's just another of his harebrained schemes.* [*same as* **half-baked, crackpot**]

harem /'hɑːriːm/ *noun*: **harems**
1 In some Muslim societies a man's **harem** is his group of wives or mistresses. **2** The part of the house where these women live is also called the **harem**.

haricot /'harɪkoʊ/ *noun (usually in the plural)*: **haricots**

Haricots or **haricot beans** are small white dried beans, used as food.

hark /hɑːk/ *verb*: **harks, harking, harked**

> ***phrasal verb***
> You **hark back** to some past event or situation when you refer to it: *She was constantly harking back to her childhood.*

harlequin /ˈhɑːləkwɪn/ *adjective*
Harlequin describes things that are brightly coloured in lots of different colours.

harm /hɑːm/ *verb; noun*
▻ ***verb***: **harms, harming, harmed**
1 To **harm** a person is to hurt or injure them: *The children were terrified but had not been physically harmed.* **2** To **harm** a thing is to damage or spoil it: *Sunbathing can harm your skin.*
▻ ***noun*** *(uncount)*
Harm is injury or damage; to do someone or something **harm** is to injure or damage them: *These incidents can only do harm to the relationship between our two countries.* □ *Punishing children probably does more harm than good.*
▻ ***phrases*** **1** You say it **will do** someone **no harm** to do something, or it **will not harm** someone to do something, if you think it will be good for them: *It wouldn't harm you to help your mother occasionally.* □ *It'll do him no harm to wait for once.* **2** If you say that **no harm will come to** someone or something, or that they **will come to no harm** you mean that they will not be injured, hurt or damaged: *No harm will come to the china if you pack it properly.* □ *The baby will come to no harm, I promise.* **3** Someone or something that is **out of harm's way** is in a safe place where they cannot be harmed, or cannot cause harm: *At least the children are safely out of harm's way.* □ *Let's lock that gun up out of harm's way.* **4** You say **there is no harm in** doing something if there is no reason why anyone should object to you doing it: *There's no harm in trying, even if we're unlikely to succeed.*

harmful /ˈhɑːmfəl/ *adjective*
Something that is **harmful** has a bad or damaging effect on people or things: *These medicines can have harmful side effects.* — *noun (uncount)* **harmfulness:** *the harmfulness of divorce.*

harmless /ˈhɑːmləs/ *adjective*
1 Something that is **harmless** is safe, *eg* to eat, use or touch: *We use fertilizers that are harmless to the environment.* □ *Most of these snakes are harmless.* **2** A **harmless** activity does not annoy or upset other people: *Flying kites is a harmless enough occupation.* — *adverb* **harmlessly:** *The bullet embedded itself harmlessly in the doorpost.*

harmonica /hɑːˈmɒnɪkə/ *noun*: **harmonicas**
A **harmonica** is a small rectangular musical instrument that you play by moving it from side to side against your lips and blowing and sucking air through it.

harmonious /hɑːˈmoʊnɪəs/ *adjective*
1 In music, notes that are **harmonious** when played together sound pleasant. [*opposite* **discordant**] **2** A combination of colours or shapes is **harmonious** if it is pleasing and satisfactory to the eye: *The flower beds presented a harmonious mixture of pink, blue and purple.* [*opposite* **jarring**] **3** A **harmonious** relationship between people is one that involves peaceful, friendly co-operation and respect for one another: *The atmosphere in our house was never harmonious.* [*same as* **peaceable**; *opposite* **inharmonious, antagonistic, contentious, turbulent**] — *adverb* **harmoniously:** *The various racial elements in the population existed together harmoniously.* □ *We deliberately chose colours that would blend harmoniously.*

harmonize or **harmonise** /ˈhɑːmənaɪz/ *verb*: **harmonizes, harmonizing, harmonized**
1 (*music*) People **harmonize** when they sing or play music together using notes that combine pleasantly with the main tune. **2** Things **harmonize** when they fit in or combine well with one another: *The architects claim to have designed a museum that will harmonize with the surrounding buildings.* [*same as* **blend in**]

harmony /ˈhɑːmənɪ/ *noun*: **harmonies**
1 (*music*) **Harmony** is the combining of notes in a way that sounds pleasant, not discordant. [*opposite* **discord**] **2 Harmony** is the result when colours or shapes are put together in a pleasing or satisfactory arrangement: *the balance and harmony of nature's colours.* **3** People exist or work in **harmony** when they have a peaceful and co-operative relationship and respect one another's attitudes and opinions: *Until this incident they had lived in apparent harmony with their neighbours.*

harness /ˈhɑːnəs/ *noun; verb*
▻ ***noun***: **harnesses**
1 A **harness** is a set of straps and links that are fitted over a horse's head and neck and attached to something such as a cart, carriage or plough that the horse is going to pull. **2** A set of straps that you wear over your body for safety or support in certain activities is also called a **harness**: *The car was already equipped with a baby seat and safety harness*
▻ ***verb***: **harnesses, harnessing, harnessed**
1 You **harness** a horse when you put a harness on it. **2** You **harness** a source of energy, or some other resource, when you adapt or use it for a particular purpose: *devices for harnessing wind and wave power.*
▻ ***phrase*** You say you are **in harness** when you have started work in the job or position you have been appointed to.

harp /hɑːp/ *noun; verb*
▻ ***noun***: **harps**
A **harp** is a musical instrument consisting of a tall triangular wooden frame fitted with vertical strings that you play by pulling or plucking with the fingers. [see picture at **orchestra**]
▻ ***verb***: **harps, harping, harped**

> ***phrasal verb***
> You **harp on** something or **harp on** about it if you continually talk about it: *She does nothing but harp on about the wickedness of her daughter-in-law.* [*same as* **go on about**]

harpoon /hɑːˈpuːn/ *noun; verb*
▻ ***noun***: **harpoons**
A **harpoon** is a spear fastened to a long rope, which is fired from a gun, or thrown, at large sea animals such as whales, to catch or kill them.
▻ ***verb***: **harpoons, harpooning, harpooned:** *They kill the whales by harpooning them.*

harpsichord /ˈhɑːpsɪkɔːd/ *noun*: **harpsichord**
A **harpsichord** is an instrument with a keyboard like a piano, in which the strings are mechanically pulled or plucked when keys are pressed.

harried /ˈharɪd/ *adjective*
Someone looks **harried** when they look anxious and worried: *Her face wore its usual harried expression.*

harrowing /ˈharoʊɪŋ/ *adjective*
A **harrowing** experience is one that upsets, disturbs or distresses you: *It was harrowing to watch her suffering like that.*

harry /ˈharɪ/ *verb*: **harries, harrying, harried**
To **harry** someone is to pursue and worry them continually: *She was harried constantly by reporters.* [*same as* **pester, harass, plague**]

harsh /hɑːʃ/ *adjective*: **harsher, harshest**
1 Harsh surroundings or conditions are severely uncomfortable: *Life as we know it could not exist in so harsh a climate.* [*opposite* **mild, comfortable**] **2 Harsh** words or treatment are cruel or unkind: *I thought the punishment far too harsh.* [*opposite* **mild, lenient, kind**] **3** Lights or colours that are unpleasantly strong, or sounds that are unpleasantly loud and penetrating, are described as **harsh**. — *adverb* **harshly:** *The prisoners had not been harshly treated.* □ *The cell was harshly lit by a single naked bulb.* — *noun* (*uncount*) **harshness:** *The sudden harshness in her tone took me aback.* □ *Winter's harshness gave way to a mild spring.*

harvest /ˈhɑːvɪst/ *noun*; *verb*
▻ ***noun***: **harvests**
1 (*usually in the singular*) The **harvest** is the cutting or gathering of crops after they have ripened, usually in late summer or early autumn: *I can't go on holiday till after the harvest.* **2** The crops picked or gathered are also the **harvest**: *It's been a good harvest this year.*
▻ ***verb***: **harvests, harvesting, harvested**
To **harvest** crops is to cut or gather them: *We employ extra labour to harvest the grain crop.*

has /haz/ or /həz/ *verb*
Has is the third person singular of the present tense of **have**.

has-been /ˈhazbiːn/ *noun* (*informal*): **has-beens**
A **has-been** is someone who was once successful and influential, but is no longer thought to be important.

hash /haʃ/ *noun* (*uncount*)
Hash is a dish of cooked meat and vegetables chopped up together and recooked.
▻ ***phrase*** (*informal*) You **make a hash of** a task or job if you do it very badly: *He couldn't perform the simplest task without making a hash of it.*

hasn't /ˈhazənt/ *verb*
Hasn't is the spoken, and informal written, form of **has not**.

hassle /ˈhasəl/ *noun*; *verb*
▻ ***noun*** (*informal*): **hassles**
1 (*used in the singular*) You call something a **hassle** if it is difficult and inconvenient to do: *It'll be a hassle doing all that photocopying.* **2** (*uncount*) **Hassle** is trouble or inconvenience: *I'd be grateful for a bed for the night, but I don't want to cause any hassle.* **3** (*uncount or count*) **Hassle** is hostility, opposition or argument: *I'll probably get some hassle from my colleagues.*
▻ ***verb*** (*informal*): **hassles, hassling, hassled**
Someone **hassles** you when they annoy or pursue you continually: *I'm being hassled by the tax people again.*

haste /heɪst/ *noun* (*uncount*)
Haste is the doing of things quickly, especially too quickly: *In her haste to get away she had left the key in the door.* [*same as* **hurry**]
▻ ***phrases*** **1** You do something **in haste** if you do it in a hurry: *The letter was evidently written in great haste.* **2** (*old*) You **make haste** when you hurry: *We made haste to pack our belongings.* **3** When people say **'More haste, less speed'** they mean that you do something more efficiently if you take time to do it properly than if you hurry and risk making mistakes that you will have to spend time correcting.

hasten /ˈheɪsən/ *verb*: **hastens, hastened, hastening**
1 To **hasten** a process is to make it faster: *The additional anxiety probably hastened his death.* **2** (*formal*) You **hasten** to do something when you do it immediately: *Let me hasten to reassure you on that point.* □ *I'm not thinking of retiring yet, I hasten to add.* **3** (*literary*) You **hasten** somewhere when you hurry there: *They hastened home out of the rain.*

hasty /ˈheɪstɪ/ *adjective*: **hastier, hastiest**
1 You are **hasty** when you act or decide quickly, especially too quickly, giving yourself no time for consideration: *She regretted her hasty decision to sell the house.* [*same as* **rash, impulsive**] **2** A **hasty** procedure is performed in a hurry, because of lack of time: *She ate a hasty lunch and rushed off to catch the train.* — *adverb* **hastily** /ˈheɪstɪlɪ/: *I hastily slid the letter into a drawer.* □ *She washed and dressed hastily.*

hat /hat/ *noun*: **hats**
1 A **hat** is a covering for your head, especially one that you wear out of doors: *She pulled on a woolly hat.* **2** (*slightly humorous*) If you say you are wearing a particular **hat** you mean you are now acting in that role, as distinct from the roles you act in at other times: *I'm wearing my chairman's hat this evening.*
▻ ***phrases*** **1** (*informal*) You ask someone to **keep** something **under their hat** when you want them to keep it secret. **2** (*informal*) You describe something such as an idea as **old hat** if it is oldfashioned or unoriginal, or already so well known that people are bored with it. **3** You **pass the hat round** when you ask people to contribute money for some cause. **4** (*informal*) You say that you **take your hat off to** someone for doing something if you admire them for doing it. **5** (*informal*) You say that someone **is talking through their hat** if you think they are talking nonsense.

hatch[1] /hatʃ/ *verb*: **hatches, hatching, hatched**
1 A bird, insect or other creature **hatches** or **is hatched** when it breaks out of its egg; an egg **hatches** when it breaks open and the baby creature comes out of it: *The male and female bird take turns to look after the newly hatched young.* □ *The eggs hatch within six weeks.* **2** You **hatch** a scheme or plot when you think of it and develop plans for it, especially secretly: *What plot have you two been hatching behind my back?*

hatch[2] /hatʃ/ *noun*: **hatches**
1 A **hatch** is a door that covers an opening in a ship's deck, or a door in an aircraft or spacecraft. **2** A **hatch** is also an opening in the wall between a kitchen and dining room, through which food can be served and plates passed.

hatchback /ˈhatʃbak/ *noun*: **hatchbacks**
A **hatchback** is a car with a sloping rear door that opens upwards, giving access to the boot.

hatchet /ˈhatʃɪt/ *noun*: **hatchets**
A **hatchet** is a small axe.
▻ ***phrase*** Two people who have quarrelled **bury the hatchet** when they decide to be friends again.

hate /heɪt/ *verb*; *noun*
▻ ***verb***: **hates, hating, hated**
1 You **hate** a person if you strongly dislike them: *He treats me as though he hated me.* □ *She hated herself for being so cowardly.* [*same as* **detest, loathe**] **2** You **hate** something if you dislike it or disapprove of it, or if it upsets you: *I hate any kind of pretence.* □ *She hates cats.* □ *He hates going shopping.* □ *I hate having to wait.* □ *'Is she enjoying her new job?' 'No, she's hating it.'* □ *I hate not being able to help.* □ *I've always hated other people ordering me about.* □ *I hate you being so rude to my mother.* □ *I hate to see you looking so unhappy.* □ *I'd hate to worry him.* □ *I'd hate you to think*

I was being unsympathetic. **3** You say you **hate** to do something when you regret having to do it or are apologizing for doing it: *I hate to disturb you, but the library will be closing in a few minutes.* □ *I hate saying this, but I don't think he can be trusted.*

▻ ***noun*** (*uncount*)

1 Hate is strong dislike for a person or thing: *She turned to me, her eyes full of hate.* □ *There's so much hate in the world.* [*same as* **hatred**] **2** (*informal*) Your **hates** are the things you dislike: *Roses are one of his particular hates.* — *adjective* **hated:** *the much-hated poll tax.*

hateful /ˈheɪtfʊl/ *adjective*

Something or someone **hateful** is unpleasant or horrible: *That was a hateful thing to say.*

hatred /ˈheɪtrɪd/ *noun* (*uncount*)

Hatred is a strong feeling of dislike: *Sometimes her face betrayed real hatred for the child.*

hatter /ˈhatə(r)/ *noun*: **hatters**

A **hatter** is a person who makes or sells hats.

hat trick /ˈhat trɪk/ *noun*: **hat tricks**

You achieve a **hat trick** if you score three successes in a row.

haughty /ˈhɔːtɪ/ *adjective* (*derogatory*): **haughtier, haughtiest**

A **haughty** person is proud and thinks they are better or more important than other people: *His face wore an expression of haughty disapproval.* [*same as* **arrogant**] — *adverb* **haughtily:** *She haughtily refused the invitation.* [*same as* **disdainful**]

haul /hɔːl/ *verb*; *noun*

▻ ***verb***: **hauls, hauling, hauled**

You **haul** something heavy somewhere when you pull or drag it there with a lot of effort: *I managed to haul myself up on to the rock ledge.* [*same as* **heave**]

▻ ***noun***: **hauls**

1 A **haul** is a journey: *I'm getting to bed early to prepare for tomorrow's long haul.* **2** (*used in the singular*) A long **haul** can also be a long struggle towards a goal: *It's going to be long haul back to complete health and mobility.*

> ***phrasal verb***
>
> A person **is hauled up** before a court of law, or other authority, when they have to appear before them for trial, or to be given a scolding or punishment: *She was hauled up before the headmistress for being cheeky to a teacher.*

haulage /ˈhɔːlɪdʒ/ *noun* (*uncount*)

Haulage is the business of transporting goods especially by road, or the cost of this.

haunch /hɔːntʃ/ *noun*: **haunches**

1 Your **haunches** are your bottom and the upper part of your thighs: *She was squatting on her haunches talking to a small child.* **2** A **haunch** of an animal is the upper part of the leg: *He had a haunch of venison in his freezer.*

haunt /hɔːnt/ *verb*; *noun*

▻ ***verb***: **haunts, haunting, haunted**

1 People say a place **is haunted** if they believe that a ghost is frequently seen there: *The west wing of the house is said to be haunted by a girl who died there in her teens.* **2** Unpleasant thoughts **haunt** you if they keep returning to your mind: *She was still haunted by the memory of his death.* **3** A particular problem **haunts** you if it keeps affecting you and spoiling whatever you do: *All her life she was haunted by feelings of inferiority.* [*same as* **plague**]

▻ ***noun***: **haunts**

Your **haunts** are the places you visit frequently: *I didn't know this pub was one of your haunts.*

haunted /ˈhɔːntɪd/ *adjective*

1 A place that is **haunted** is regularly visited by a ghost: *tales of haunted castles.* **2** Someone who looks **haunted** has a worried or troubled expression: *his sad, haunted face.*

haunting /ˈhɔːntɪŋ/ *adjective*

You describe something such as music as **haunting** if it has a strange sad quality that makes a strong, long-lasting impression on you: *a haunting melody.*

have[1] /hav/ *auxiliary verb*: **have** (*short form* **'ve**; *negative short form* **haven't**), **has** (*short form* **'s**; *negative short form* **hasn't**), **having, had** (*short form* **'d**; *negative short form* **hadn't**)

1 Have and **has** are used with the past participles of other verbs to form the perfect tense of those verbs: *How long have you two known each other?* □ *It hasn't been a good summer, has it?* □ *She's worked for us for twenty-two years.* □ *They've changed the dialling code, haven't they?* □ *We've not* (or *we haven't*) *yet explored the countryside round here.* □ *'Has it actually stopped raining?' 'Yes, it has.'* □ *'You've spelt* 'focused' *wrong.' 'No, I haven't.'*

2 Have and **has** are used with *been* and the present participle of other verbs to form the progressive or continuous present perfect tense: *They've been trying to sell their house ever since April.*

> Note that the perfect tense is used
>
> **a** where past circumstances continue into the present: *I've lived here since 1966.*
>
> **b** where an event in the recent past affects the present: *I'm not hungry, thank you; I've just had lunch.*
>
> **c** to refer to an event that happened at some indefinite time in the past, often with adverbs such as *never, ever, often, twice*: *I've often thought he would make a good actor. He's been warned twice already.* Compare the simple past tense, which is used where a definite time is mentioned or is understood: *We moved house in 1992; I last saw her a year ago. Next she added two egg whites.*
>
> **d** with conjunctions such as *if, when, before* and *until*, to refer to the future: *I'll return the book as soon as I've finished reading it. When you've filled in the form, hand it in at the reception desk. If we've managed to contact him by this evening I'll call you. You'll sit here till you've learnt how to behave. Don't be forced into agreeing before you've had time to think about it.*
>
> **e** with expressions such as *it's the first time that ...*: *This is the first time I've crossed the Equator. It's the nicest present anyone has ever given me.*
>
> **f** with *already* and *just*, especially in BrE: *I've already booked* (AmE *I already booked*) *seats. 'I think you should apologize.' 'I just have* (AmE *I just did*).*'*

3 Had is used with the past participles of other verbs to form the past perfect tense of those verbs: *I hadn't been there long when he arrived.* □ *Her death came as a shock as I hadn't known she was ill.* □ *I knew her slightly as we'd met previously at conferences.* □ *Where did you go when you'd finished the shopping?* □ *I'd just put down the telephone when it rang again.* □ *That was the first time I'd seen him angry.*

4 Had is used with *been* and the past participle of other verbs to form the progressive or continuous past perfect tense: *They'd already been going around together for years when they decided to get married.*

> Note that the past perfect is used
> **a** in 'reported' or 'indirect' speech or thought **(i)** to refer to an earlier time: *I realized I'd made a mistake. He told me the match had been cancelled. It was reported that fifty-five people had died in the fighting.* **(ii)** with conjunctions such as *when, before* and *until* to refer to a later time: *She promised to return the book when she'd finished it. I decided to postpone my holiday till I'd written my thesis. We warned the authorities that patients would be sent home before they had fully recovered.*
> **b** in referring to events that could have happened but did not, *eg* in conditional clauses: *If I'd known she was ill, I wouldn't have gone abroad. Had she* [= if she had] *gone to university, she might have done well in the academic world. I wish I'd been kinder to him.*

5 Have is used to form perfect infinitives: *I'm sorry to have kept you waiting so long.* □ *I was hoping to have got the results by this time.* □ *It was stupid of me not to have brought my camera.* [see also uses of **have** with **can, could, may, might, must, need, shall, should, will, would**]
6 You use **having** with the past participle of other verbs to state circumstances that precede, and sometimes explain, the main action of the sentence: *I got to the office early that day, having caught the 7.30 train from Paddington.* □ *Having heard her speak previously, I knew I would enjoy her lecture.* □ *The rest of the family having gone on holiday I had the house to myself.*

have[2] /hav/ *verb*: **have** (short form **'ve**; negative form **haven't**), **has** (short form **'s**; negative form **hasn't**), **having, had** (short form **'d**; negative form **hadn't**)
1 Have is used to express possession: **a** Things that you **have** belong to you, or are in your possession, or are available to you, or are connected with you in some way: *They've a house in the country and a flat in town.* □ *He has a job in publishing.* □ *Who has my box of matches?* □ *She has the bluest eyes I've ever seen.* □ *This copy has a page missing.* □ *She seems to have no friends.* □ *I'll have more time next week.* □ *You've three choices.* □ *I won't have an opportunity till Friday.* □ *I haven't had a moment to look at your report.* **b** In positive statements you also use **have got**: *She's got green eyes and fair hair.* □ *I've got an appointment at 11.15.* □ *You've got a terrible cold.* □ *He's got rather a bad temper.* □ *I've got too much work to do.* **c** You can form questions and negatives with **have, do have** or **have got**: *Have you any seats left for tonight's performance?* □ *Has she anyone to look after her?* □ *Do you have the time on you?* □ *'Has he got any brothers or sisters?' 'Yes, he has.'* □ *What plans have you got for this evening?* □ *Sorry, I haven't the faintest idea.* □ *We do not have sufficient funds to run the department adequately.* □ *I don't have time to see him just now.* □ *I don't have anything to wear.* □ *You don't have a pen with you, do you?* □ *You've got a dictionary there, haven't you?*
d The past tense uses **had** rather than **had got** in positive statements, but usually **did have** in questions and **did not** (or **didn't**) **have** or **hadn't got** in negatives: *He had a bowler hat and a walking stick.* □ *She had a friend with her.* □ *She had a slim, elegant figure.* □ *She had no idea where to go.* □ *I had my own opinion about it.* □ *Did you have enough food with you?* □ *I didn't have a clue where I was.* □ *I found I hadn't got enough money for the fare.* □ *Didn't you have her telephone number?* □ *You had a map, didn't* (or *hadn't*) *you?* □ *You hadn't got my address, had you?*
2 Have is used to express compulsion: **a** You use **have** with *to* and the infinitive of other verbs to express necessity, duty, obligation or compulsion: *I have to look after the children on Wednesdays.* □ *I shall have to be quick, shan't I?* □ *You'll have to read the book yourself, won't you?* □ *I'm going to have to ask you all to contribute £1.* □ *We've been having to save on fuel.* □ *Buy everything now and you won't have to shop later.* **b** In positive statements you also use **have got**: *She's got to take a preliminary test.* **c** Questions and negatives can be formed with **do have** or **have got**: *Does he have to pay for his medical treatment?* □ *Do we have to catch the 9.40 train tomorrow?* □ *Do you have to make that awful noise?* □ *Have we got to clear up this mess ourselves?* □ *We don't have to be there till midday, do we?* □ *It would be nice if you wrote to her, but you don't have to.* □ *'Don't you have to work late tonight?' 'No, I don't.'* □ *He hasn't got to sit the exam again, has he?* **d** The past tense uses **had** in positive statements (**had got** expresses future necessity in the past), **did have** in questions and **did not** (or **didn't**) **have** or **hadn't got** in negatives: *I had to wait half an hour for a bus.* □ *I knew I had to* (or *I'd got to*) *be there by 6.20.* □ *Did you have to hurry?* □ *You didn't have to punish him as severely as that, did you?* □ *Didn't they have to ask permission?* □ *We were told we hadn't got to report the accident to the police.*

> Notice that **do not have to** and **haven't got to** express the lack of obligation or necessity, whereas **must not** expresses prohibition: *You mustn't touch the exhibits. You don't have* (or *you haven't got*) *to come unless you want to.*
> In the present tense, **have to**, and questions and negatives formed with **do have to**, can be used whether the duty or necessity is a repeated one or a particular one; **have got to** is used especially where it is a particular one: *I have to be at my desk by 8 o'clock every morning. Normally I don't have to leave the house till 7.00. Do you have to go shopping today? I've got to ring her tonight.*

3 You use **have** to express actions and experiences, for instance: **a** You **have** food or drink when you eat or swallow it: *Have some tea.* □ *I've just had a coffee, thanks.* □ *What time do you have breakfast?* □ *Have you had your supper yet?* □ *I usually have a sandwich for lunch.* □ *I haven't had a meal all day.* **b** You **have** an illness when you get it and suffer from it for a time: *He had measles very badly.* □ *Have you ever had jaundice?* □ *He had a nervous breakdown in 1982.* **c** A woman **has** a baby when she gives birth to it: *She told me she was going to have a baby in April.* □ *His wife's having a baby soon.* □ *She's just had a little girl.* **d** You **have** a party when you hold or give it: *He had a big party for his 18th birthday.* **e** You **have** people to stay or for a meal when they stay with you, or you give them a meal, in your house: *We had the professor for dinner the other night.* □ *Thanks for having me to stay.* □ *I've had my mother staying with me all week.* **f** You **have** a good time when you enjoy yourself, and a bad time when you suffer: *See you later. Have a good time.* □ *I had a most amusing weekend.* □ *We had a frustrating afternoon.* □ *Did you have a happy childhood?* □ *They had an amazing holiday.* □ *An enjoyable time was had by all.* **g** You **have** certain feelings or qualities when you show them by acting in a particular way: *At last the guide had pity on us and allowed us a rest.* □ *At least she had the decency to apologize.* **h** You use **have** with nouns made from verbs, as a way of expressing the action of the verb: *I had a drink when I got home.* □ *Let's have a rest.* □ *Come on; have a go.* □ *I'll have a try too.* □ *He has a walk every morning.* □ *Did you have your usual swim?* □ *Let me have a think.* □ *I had a good cry and felt much better.* □ *Did you have a nice sleep?* □ *Have you had a proper wash?* □ *Did you have a bath last night?* □ *They were always having quarrels about money.* □ *I was beginning to have doubts about the usefulness of the project.* **i** You use **have** in many other ways as a verb of doing or experiencing: *He's had two operations on his spine.* □ *What effect is this delay going to have on the schedule?* □ *I've just had an idea.* □ *I think we should have a serious discussion.* □ *We've had a bit of disappointment.* □ *He had a bad accident in the autumn.*

4 a You **have** something done when you arrange for it to be done, or cause it to happen: *I'm having my hair cut on Tuesday.* □ *When did you last have the house decorated?* □ *It's time I had the car serviced.* □ *You had me worried for a few minutes.* □ *Let's have everyone on the floor for the last dance.* □ *(especially AmE) I'll have the electrician mend it.* □ *(especially AmE) Have the children form two lines.* [compare **get**] **b** Something that you **have** done to you can happen without you being responsible for it: *He's had his bicycle stolen again.* □ *The cat seemed to like having its tail stroked.* □ *It's a great treat having a meal made for you once in a while.*

5 a You use **have** to mean get or obtain: *As soon as she saw the picture she was determined to have it.* **b** **Have** can mean receive: *Have you had an invitation to the wedding?* □ *The book has had excellent reviews.* **c** You say you will **have** something when you are choosing it: '*Sherry or red wine for you?*' '*I'll have sherry, please.*' [same as **take**] **d** You say you won't **have** something when you refuse to tolerate or accept it: *I won't have such behaviour in the classroom.*

▻ ***phrases*** **1** For **had better** see **better**. **2** (*informal*) You **have been had** if someone has tricked or cheated you. **3** (*informal*) You say someone **has had it** if they are dead, or are going to die, or are ruined, or are too exhausted to go any further or do any more: *He knew he'd had it if the police found out.* **4** (*informal*) Someone **has it in for you** if they dislike you and try to make things difficult for you. **5** Two people **have it out** when they openly express their disagreement or dissatisfaction with each other: *I had it out with her and told her I couldn't put up with her behaviour any longer.*

phrasal verbs

have in or **have round** You **have** people **in** or **round** when you invite them into your home, *eg* to have meal or to repair something: *We're having a few friends in for supper tonight.* □ *When did we last have Peter round?* □ *We had the plumber in last week.*

have on 1 You **have**, or **have got**, something **on** when you are wearing it: *That's a nice dress you've got on.* □ *He had a tweed cap on.* **2** You **have**, or **have got**, something **on** when you have an engagement: *I thought we could go to the concert if you've got nothing else on.* **3** Someone **is having** you **on** if they are teasing you by telling you something untrue: *When she told me she was pregnant I thought she was having me on.*

have up You **are had up** for something when you are charged with an offence and have to appear in a court of law.

haven /ˈheɪvən/ *noun*: **havens**

A place is called a **haven** if people go there for safety, security or peace: *I find the garden a haven of peace after a day in the city.* [*same as* **sanctuary**]

haven't /ˈhavənt/ *verb*

Haven't is the spoken, or informal written, form of **have not**.

haversack /ˈhavəsak/ *noun*: **haversacks**

A **haversack** is a canvas bag that you wear over your shoulder or on your back to carry things when you are out for a walk.

havoc /ˈhavək/ *noun* (*uncount*)

1 Havoc is damage and destruction: *The bomb exploded in a shopping centre, causing widespread havoc.* **2 Havoc** is also disorder and confusion: *There's complete havoc on the underground as a result of the strike.* [*same as* **mayhem**]

▻ ***phrase*** One thing **plays havoc with** another when it confuses or upsets it: *These computer breakdowns are playing havoc with the schedule.*

hawk[1] /hɔːk/ *noun*: **hawks**

A **hawk** is a bird of prey with a short, strong, hooked beak, that feeds on small birds and animals and is thought to have good eyesight.

▻ ***phrase*** You **watch** someone **like a hawk** when you watch them closely in case they do something wrong.

hawk[2] /hɔːk/ *verb*: **hawks, hawking, hawked**

To **hawk** something round is to take it round to people and show it to them, in the hope that they may want to buy it: *He had been hawking his novel round the paperback publishers without success.*

hawthorn /ˈhɔːθɔːn/ *noun* (*uncount or count*): **hawthorns**

A **hawthorn**, or **hawthorn tree**, is a small tree used to form hedges, with pink or white flowers and red berries: *hawthorn blossom.*

hay /heɪ/ *noun* (*uncount*)

Hay is grass that has been cut and dried for storing, *eg* as food for cattle: *bales of hay.*

hay fever /ˈheɪ fiːvə(r)/ *noun* (*uncount*)

Hay fever is an illness like a cold that people get if they are allergic to some kinds of pollen, causing sneezing and watering eyes.

haystack /ˈheɪstak/ *noun*: **haystacks**

A **haystack** is a large, firmly constructed pile of hay.

▻ ***phrase*** You say that searching for a certain thing is **like looking for a needle in a haystack** if it is so difficult that it is unlikely to be successful.

haywire /ˈheɪwaɪə(r)/ *adjective*

▻ ***phrase*** (*informal*) Something **goes haywire** if it goes out of control: *The computer seems to have gone haywire.*

hazard /ˈhazəd/ *noun*; *verb*

▻ ***noun***: **hazards**

A **hazard** is a risk or danger, or something that is a source of danger: *Fog can be a hazard on the motorway.*

▻ ***verb***: **hazards, hazarding, hazarded**

You **hazard** a guess when you make a suggestion that you know may be wrong: *'Guess what it's worth?' 'Two and a half million?' I hazarded.*

hazardous /ˈhazədəs/ *adjective*

Something that is **hazardous** is dangerous: *The climb was considered hazardous in wet weather.*

haze /heɪz/ *noun* (*uncount, or used in the singular*)

Haze is thin mist, often associated with hot weather: *The mountain was dimly visible through the haze.*

hazel /ˈheɪzəl/ *noun*; *adjective*

▻ ***noun*** (*uncount or count*): **hazels**

A **hazel**, or **hazel tree**, is a small tree that produces nuts: *Hazel grew in abundance* □ *a hazel twig.*

▻ ***adjective***

Hazel eyes are brownish-green in colour.

hazelnut /ˈheɪzəlnʌt/ *noun*: **hazelnuts**
A **hazelnut** is the small edible nut of the hazel tree, with a smooth shiny brown shell.

hazy /ˈheɪzɪ/ *adjective*: **hazier**, **haziest**
1 The weather or the view is **hazy** when there is a thin mist or haze in the air: *The mountains rose purple and hazy in the distance.* **2** Your thoughts or memories are **hazy** if they are confused and unclear: *He retained a few hazy recollections of his childhood years in Zambia.* [*same as* **vague**]

he /hiː/ or /hɪ/ *pronoun*; *noun*
▻ ***pronoun*** (*used as the subject of a sentence*)
1 You use **he** to refer to a man, boy or male animal that has already been mentioned: *Jeremy called but he left no message.* ▫ *David's sister was apparently three years older than he was.* ▫ *You can tell a cock because he has a comb.* [see also **him, himself, his**]

> Notice that you can also use *it* to refer to an animal and baby (of either sex), especially one that you do not know.

2 (*old*) Formerly **he** was widely used to refer to such words as *anyone*, *someone*, *no-one*, *person*, *child*, *lawyer*, where the sex was unknown, but *they* or *he or she* are now frequently used instead: *Anyone can buy shares if he has* (or *they have*) *enough money.* ▫ *Contact your local travel agent and he* (or *he or she*) *will advise you.*
▻ ***noun*** (*often used as a prefix*): **hes** or **he's**
A **he** is a male: *Is the lamb a he or a she?* ▫ *a he-goat.* [see also **him, himself, his**]

head /hɛd/ *noun*; *verb*
▻ ***noun***: **heads**
1 Your **head** is the part of your body that has your eyes, nose, mouth, ears and brain in it: *I asked if he was hungry but he just shook his head.* ▫ *She patted the dog's head.* [see picture at **body**] **2** When you refer to someone's **head** you can mean their intelligence, common sense, imagination or awareness: *Do use your head.* ▫ *It's amazing what goes on in children's heads.* **3** The **head** of something is the top of it, or the front, leading or most important end of it, or a part of it like a head in shape and position; the **head** of a bed is the end where you put your head when you lie down: *It was no bigger than the head of a pin.* ▫ *It took them an hour to reach the head of the queue.* ▫ *Father always sat at the head of the table.* **4** The **head** of a river is its source. **5** (*used in the plural, with a singular or plural verb*) **Heads** is the side of a coin that has a ruler's or president's head on it: *We'll toss for it; heads we go, tails we don't.* ▫ *The penny came down heads.* **6** The **head** of an organization is the person in charge of it or in authority over it: *She joined the staff in 1978 and soon rose to be head of the sales force.* [*same as* **chief, leader**] **7** The head teacher of a school can be referred to as the **head**: *The head wants to see you about something.* **8** (*plural* **head**; *formal*) In counting cattle, **head** means individual animals: *600 head of cattle.* **9** In an audio or video apparatus using magnetic tape the **head** is the part that records or reproduces sound or film.
▻ ***verb***: **heads, heading, headed**
1 You **head** an organization or party if you are in charge of it or in authority over it: *the Labour government headed by Clement Attlee.* [*same as* **lead**] **2** You **head** a procession or queue if you are leading it or at the front of it; something **heads** a list if it is at the top of it. **3** You **head** a piece of writing with something when you write a heading or title at the top of it: *She headed the next paragraph 'Financial Problems'.* **4** You **head** in a certain direction when you go in that direction; you **head** for something when you go towards it: *Once inside the shop the children headed straight for the computer games.* **5** You say that someone **is heading** for some situation if the way they are behaving or proceeding is likely to involve them in it, or bring it about for them: *The firm was heading for disaster.* **6** (*football*) Footballers **head** the ball somewhere when they hit it there with their heads.

▻ ***phrases*** **1** You say that some intellectual matter is **above** or **over your head** if it is too difficult for you to understand. **2** Something costs a certain amount **a head** or **per head** if it costs that amount for each person: *Tickets for the excursion are £3.50 a head.* ▫ *They charge visitors £1.50 per head.* **3** Someone **bites**, or **snaps**, **your head off** when they speak to you in an unjustifiably angry or rude way. **4 a** A situation **comes**, or **is brought**, **to a head** when it reaches a crisis and requires urgent action: *Local tensions came to a head yesterday with riots in the streets.* **b** A boil or spot on the body **comes to a head** when it develops a white, pus-filled point. **5** You are covered in something, or dressed in it, **from head to foot** if you are completely covered or dressed in it: *He was covered in bruises from head to foot.* **6** You **give** someone **their head** when you deliberately do not restrict them, but allow them to use their own ideas and imagination, *eg* in developing something. **7 a** Alcohol **goes to your head** when it makes you drunk. **b** Success or praise **goes to your head** when it makes you conceited or too pleased with yourself. **8** (*informal*) You **have a bad head** when you have a headache: *I woke up with a terrible head this morning.* **9 a** You **have a good**, or **poor**, **head for** some intellectual activity if you are good or bad at it: *She had a good head for figures.* **b** For **have a good head for heights** see **height**. **10** One person stands **head and shoulders** above others if they are noticeably very superior to others. **11** (*informal*) You do something such as laugh or shout **your head off** when you do so loudly and in an uncontrolled way: *The audience shrieked their heads off at his jokes.* **12 a** You go **head over heels** when your body rolls over head first, or you perform a forward roll or somersault. **b** (*informal*) You are **head over heels** in love when you have fallen deeply and uncontrollably in love with someone. **13** You **keep your head** in a crisis when you remain calm; you **lose your head** when you panic or let yourself get upset and behave in a foolish or uncontrolled way. **14** (*informal*) You say you can't **make head or tail of** something if you can't understand it: *I couldn't make head or tail of her lecture.* **15** (*informal*) Someone who is **off their head** is crazy or mad: *He was off his head with worry.* **16** (*informal*) You are able to give people facts **off the top of your head** if you can do so without referring to a source of information or working them out first. [*same as* **off hand**] **17** If you say to someone **'on your own head be it'** you mean that they are responsible for anything bad that results from what they are doing. **18** People **put their heads together** over something such as a problem when they discuss it or solve it together. **19** You **take it into your head** to do something when you decide to do it: *He'll probably take it into his head to resign or something stupid.* **20** Success or praise **turns** someone's **head** when it makes them conceited or too pleased with themselves. **21** A horse **wins by a head** when it just wins, by the distance represented by the length of its head.

phrasal verb
head off
1 You **head off** when you go away in a certain direction: *He headed off towards the swimming pool.* **2** You **head** someone **off** when you block their progress forward so that they have to turn aside, or when you distract them from doing what they intend.

headache /ˈhɛdeɪk/ *noun*: **headaches**
1 You have a **headache** when you have a continuous dull pain in your head: *He had gone to bed early with a bad headache.* **2** (*informal*) You call something a **headache** if it causes problems and anxiety: *The shortage of cash is a bit of a headache.* [*same as* **pain**, **nuisance**]

headdress /ˈhɛddrɛs/ *noun*: **headdresses**
A **headdress** is something you wear on your head, especially for a decorative or ceremonial purpose.

headed /ˈhɛdɪd/ *adjective*
Headed writing paper is letter-writing paper with your address printed at the top.

header /ˈhɛdə(r)/ *noun*: **headers**
1 (*informal*) You take a **header** when you fall headfirst, or dive: *She did a header into the swimming pool.* **2** (*football*) A **header** is the action of hitting the ball with your head: *He settled the match with a header into the net.*

headfirst /hɛdˈfɜːst/ *adverb*
You fall or move somewhere **headfirst** when your head is the leading part of you as you fall or move: *She went headfirst down the chute.*

headgear /ˈhɛdgɪə(r)/ *noun* (*uncount*)
Anything you wear on your head can be referred to as **headgear**.

heading /ˈhɛdɪŋ/ *noun*: **headings**
A **heading** is a title written at the top or beginning of a piece of writing, or of a section of it: *She gave Chapter Two the heading 'An Old Flame'.*

headlamp /ˈhɛdlamp/ *noun*: **headlamps**
A **headlamp** is a headlight. [see picture at **car**]

headland /ˈhɛdlənd/ *noun*: **headlands**
A **headland** is a projecting part of a coastline.

headless /ˈhɛdləs/ *adjective*
A **headless** body has no head.

headlight /ˈhɛdlaɪt/ *noun*: **headlights**
A vehicle's **headlights** are the bright and powerful lights that it has on the front of it: *Drivers are advised to use headlights in foggy conditions.*

headline /ˈhɛdlaɪn/ *noun*: **headlines**
1 A **headline** is the title of a newspaper article, printed above the article in large letters. **2** (*used in the plural*) The **headlines** are the chief points in a radio or television news broadcast: *Here are the main headlines again.*
▻ ***phrase*** (*informal*) Someone or something **hits the headlines** when they feature prominently in the news.

headlong /ˈhɛdlɒŋ/ *adjective or adverb*
1 You go **headlong** somewhere when you rush there in an uncontrolled manner: *The cattle were thundering headlong towards the edge of the cliff.* **2** You rush **headlong** into doing something if you do it hastily without giving yourself time to think: *The ordination of women was causing Anglican clergy to rush headlong into the the arms of the Catholic Church.*

headmaster /hɛdˈmɑːstə(r)/ or **headmistress** /hɛdˈmɪstrɪs/ *noun*: **headmasters** or **headmistresses**
The **headmaster** or **headmistress** of a school is the man or woman who is its headteacher.

head-on /hɛdˈɒn/ *adjective or adverb*
1 Vehicles collide **head-on** when the front of one hits the front of the other; fighting animals meet **head-on** when they lower their heads and rush at each other: *a head-on crash.* **2** You have a **head-on** confrontation or disagreement with someone when you oppose them openly and directly; you meet opposition, or a threat or challenge **head-on** when you face it and deal with it in a determined manner.

headphones /ˈhɛdfoʊnz/ *noun* (*plural*)
Headphones are a pair of receivers that you wear over your ears in order to listen to a portable radio or cassette-player without other people hearing.

headquarters /hɛdˈkwɔːtəz/ *noun* (*plural, with a singular or plural verb*)
The **headquarters** of an organization are the offices from which it is administered; the **headquarters** of a military force is the place from which its leaders are controlling its operations: *The charity's headquarters are in Switzerland.* [see also **HQ**]

headrest /ˈhɛdrɛst/ *noun*: **headrests**
A **headrest** is a support for your head, *eg* one fitted to a car seat. [see picture at **car**]

headroom /ˈhɛdruːm/ *noun* (*uncount*)
1 Headroom is the space between people's heads and a roof or ceiling: *For a small car the Micra gives you plenty of headroom.* **2** The **headroom** under a bridge is the distance from the ground to the arch, sometimes stated on the bridge as a warning to drivers of high vehicles.

headscarf /ˈhɛdskɑːf/ *noun*: **headscarves**
A **headscarf** is a woman's scarf, especially a square one made of a thin fabric, designed to be worn over the head and tied under the chin.

headset /ˈhɛdsɛt/ *noun*: **headsets**
A **headset** is a pair of headphones.

headship /ˈhɛdʃɪp/ *noun*: **headships**
A **headship** is the post of headteacher at a school, or the period during which someone is headteacher: *Discipline improved during her headship.*

head start /hɛd ˈstɑːt/ *noun* (*used in the singular*)
You have a **head start** on other people if you have an advantage over them in some competition, or some situation involving competition: *She had spent her early childhood in France so had a head start on the rest of us who were just beginning French.*

headstone /ˈhɛdstoʊn/ *noun*: **headstones**
A **headstone** is a stone placed upright at the end of a grave, on which the name of the dead person is usually carved.

headstrong /ˈhɛdstrɒŋ/ *adjective*
You describe a person as **headstrong** if they are determined to act the way they want to, and refuse to take advice from others: *Young people can be so headstrong and obstinate.* [*same as* **wilful**, **impetuous**, **stubborn**]

headteacher /hɛdˈtiːʃə(r)/ *noun*: **headteachers**
The **headteacher** of a school is the teacher who is in adminstrative charge of it.

headway /ˈhɛdweɪ/ *noun* (*uncount*)
▻ ***phrases***
1 A ship **makes headway** when it moves forward: *The wind was against us all the first day and we made little headway.* **2** You **make headway** when you make progress: *I was beginning to make some headway in sorting out the piles of books.*

headwind /ˈhɛdwɪnd/ *noun*: **headwinds**
A **headwind** is a wind that blows towards you, in the opposite direction to the direction in which you are travelling.

heady /ˈhɛdɪ/ *adjective*: **headier, headiest**
1 You describe an experience as **heady** if it makes you feel energetic and excited, or inspires you with new ideas and self-confidence: *the increase in self-awareness that students experienced in the heady '60s.* [*same as* **exhilarating**] **2** A **heady** drink, perfume or atmosphere has a strong effect on your senses, making you feel excited or slightly drunk. [*same as* **intoxicating**]

heal /hiːl/ *verb*: **heals, healing, healed**
1 An injury or an injured part of the body **heals, heals** up, or **is healed** when it gets better: *The cut healed up in no time.* □ *His hand took several weeks to heal.* **2** Someone who **heals** you when you are ill makes you healthy again: *He claimed to be able to heal the sick.* **3** Pain or sorrow **heals** or **is healed** when it becomes less acute or you feel it less: *Time heals everything.* **4** A conflict or breach between people **heals** or **is healed** when they make friends again. — *noun* **healer:** *Time is the great healer.* □ *People went to her to be cured as she had a great reputation locally as a healer.*

health /hɛlθ/ *noun* (*uncount*)
1 Your **health** is the general condition of your body: *Physically she's in good health but her memory is failing.* □ *mental health.* **2 Health** is also the state of being well: *Their eyes shone with health.* **3** The **health** of an organization is its financial state, and its strength or effectiveness: *the health of the steel industry.*
▻ ***phrase*** You **drink**, or **drink to**, someone's **health** when you drink a toast to them.

health centre /ˈhɛlθ sɛntə(r)/ *noun*: **health centre**
A **health centre** is a centre where the doctors and nurses who serve a particular community see patients and hold clinics.

health food /ˈhɛlθ fuːd/ *noun* (*uncount or count*): **health foods**
Health food is food that has been grown or produced without the use or addition of chemicals, which some people prefer to eat in the belief that it is better for their health.

health service /ˈhɛlθ sɜːvɪs/ *noun* (*used in the singular*)
A country's **health service** is a public service providing free medical care for all its citizens, the cost being covered by taxation.

healthy /ˈhɛlθɪ/ *adjective*: **healthier, heathiest**
1 You are **healthy** when you are well and do not have any illnesses: *strong, healthy children.* □ *I feel a lot healthier since I gave up smoking.* [*opposite* **ill, poorly, unwell**] **2** You describe a characteristic or feature that someone has as **healthy** if it shows they are well: *The walk had given them a healthy appetite.* **3** A **healthy** activity or environment is good for you: *a seaside holiday with plenty of healthy fresh air* □ *a balanced and healthy diet.* **4** An organization is **healthy** if it is successful, especially financially: *a healthy European economy.* **5** People have a **healthy** respect for something dangerous or serious if they have learnt to treat it sensibly so as to avoid trouble: *a healthy respect for authority.* — *adverb* **healthily:** *He doesn't eat very healthily.*

heap /hiːp/ *noun*; *verb*
▻ ***noun***: **heaps**
1 A **heap** of things is a rough or untidy pile or mass of them: *She left her clothes in a heap on the floor.* **2** (*usually in the plural; informal*) **Heaps**, or a **heap**, of something is plenty of it, or a lot of it: *There's heaps of time before the train goes.* [*same as* **loads, stacks, tons**]
▻ ***verb***: **heaps, heaping, heaped**
1 You **heap** things somewhere, or **heap** them up, when you put them somewhere in a rough pile; things **heap** up when they accumulate or collect in piles: *She heaped our plates with food.* □ *He heaped rice on to his dish.* □ *The snow had been heaped up on either side of the path.* □ *Rubbish was beginning to heap up on the streets.* **2** You **heap** criticism or praise on someone or something when you criticize them severely or praise them enthusiastically: *Everyone heaped compliments on her cooking.*

heaped /hiːpt/ *adjective*
1 A **heaped** spoonful of something contains a rounded pile of it: *Mix in two heaped tablespoonfuls of flour.* [compare **level**] **2** A surface that is **heaped** with things has a lot of them in piles on it: *The table was heaped with dirty dishes.*

hear /hɪə(r)/ *verb*: **hears, hearing, heard**
1 You **hear** sounds when you are aware of them through your ears: *I heard a shout in the distance.* □ *Can you hear that ringing sound?* □ *I could hear a stream somewhere nearby.* □ *I thought I heard the door close a minute ago.* □ *We heard people running and shouting outside.* □ *I was interested to hear your name quoted.* □ *She was heard to remark that receptions bored her.* □ *Please could you speak up? I can't hear you.* □ *Mum's over eighty and she doesn't hear very well.* **2** You **hear** news or facts when people tell you them, or they are mentioned on radio or television: *Have you heard the latest news?* □ *We haven't heard all the facts yet.* □ *I don't think I've heard that theory before.* □ *I hear you're leaving the firm.* □ *I've heard that jogging is bad for you.* □ *Have you heard whether she got the job?* □ *We heard about your accident.* □ *She called me as soon as she heard of the trouble I was in.* **3** You say you **have heard** of someone or something if you know they exist: *We had heard of AIDS by then but we didn't know much about it.* □ *Most people have never heard of these minor poets.* **4** You **hear** from someone when they write to you or telephone you: *Have you heard from Robert lately?* □ *We heard from him only last week; he sent us a postcard from Prague.* **5** Someone such as a judge **hears** a case when he or she listens to the facts concerning it and makes a judgement about it: *The case will be heard next week.* □ *Part of a manager's job is to hear complaints.*
▻ ***phrases*** **1** People sometimes say **'do you hear?'** for emphasis when speaking sternly to someone: *You are not to use swearwords in this house, do you hear?* **2** (*rather old, and formal*) People sometimes shout **'hear! hear!'** when they agree with something that a speaker is saying. **3** You say you **won't hear of** something being done if you refuse to allow it: *I offered to drive her to the station but she wouldn't hear of it.*

> ***phrasal verb***
> You **hear** someone **out** when you allow them to finish saying what they want to say.

hearer /ˈhɪərə(r)/ *noun*: **hearers**
Your **hearers** are the people who are listening to you when you are speaking: *She astonished her hearers with an unmistakable display of racial prejudice.* [compare **listener**]

hearing /ˈhɪərɪŋ/ *noun*: **hearings**
1 (*uncount*) **Hearing** is one of the five physical senses; it makes you able to be aware of sounds through the ears: *I may be getting old but my hearing is fine.* **2** Something is said in or within your **hearing** if you are present when it is said, or close enough to hear it being said: *I knew he disapproved because he had often*

said so in my hearing. [compare **earshot**] **3** A **hearing** is a trial of a legal case, or a formal meeting for collecting and discussing the facts relating to some incident or situation: *An official hearing is to be held in a month's time.* **4** You give someone a **hearing** or a fair **hearing** when you give them an opportunity to state and explain their opinion.

▻ ***phrase*** Someone who is **hard of hearing** is deaf.

hearing aid /ˈhɪərɪŋ eɪd/ *noun*: **hearing aids**
A **hearing aid** is a small electrical device for making sounds louder, which deaf people wear in the ear to help them hear better.

hearsay /ˈhɪəseɪ/ *noun* (*uncount*)
Hearsay is things that other people have told you, which you do not yourself know to be true, as distinct from things you have found out for yourself: *Has he definitely resigned, or is it only hearsay?* [*same as* **rumour**]

hearse /hɜːs/ *noun*: **hearses**
A **hearse** is a long car designed for carrying a coffin to a funeral.

heart /hɑːt/ *noun*: **hearts**
1 Your **heart** is the hollow muscular organ inside your chest, that pumps blood around your body: *He could feel his heart beating fast as he lined up with the other runners.* □ *He was given an appointment to see a heart specialist.* □ *a heart-transplant operation.* **2** When you refer to someone's **heart** you often mean their emotions, especially their feelings of love: *affairs of the heart* □ *She captured the hearts of audiences everywhere.* **3** (*literary*) Your **heart** is your breast: *He clasped her to his heart.* **4** Your **heart** is your attitude to others with regard to how sensitive or sympathetic you are towards them; you have a soft **heart** if you are a sympathetic person, and a hard **heart** if you are unsympathetic: *These examiners have no heart, you know.* **5** (*uncount*) **Heart** is courage and determination; you lose **heart** when you feel depressed and discouraged; you take **heart** when you let yourself feel encouraged and optimistic: *I hadn't the heart to start again from the beginning.* □ *No-one had the heart to tell him the truth.* **6** The **heart** of something is its central or most important part: *Her novels seem to get right to the heart of feminist issues.* **7** The **heart** of a place is its centre: *living in the heart of London.* **8** The **heart** of a vegetable such as a cabbage or lettuce is the mass of tightly packed leaves at its centre. **9** A **heart** is a shape representing the human heart and often symbolizing love, with two curved sides meeting in a point at the base: *a white blouse with little pink hearts all over it.* [see picture at **shape**] **10 a** (*used in the plural*) **Hearts** are one of the four suits (♥) in a pack of playing cards: *the jack of hearts* □ *Hearts are trumps.* **b** A **heart** is one of the cards in this suit: *She was holding four hearts.* □ *Her partner led with a heart.*

▻ ***phrases*** **1** You say that someone is a certain type **at heart** if that is what they are really like: *He's a sentimentalist at heart.* **2 a** You **break** someone's **heart** when you make them unhappy, especially when they love you and you don't love them. **b** Something that **breaks your heart** makes you sad: *It broke his heart when his son gave up his medical studies.* **3** You know something **by heart** when you have learnt it so well that you can repeat it: *Each week we were given a poem to learn by heart.* **4** You have **a change of heart** about something when you change your mind or opinion about it: *Having at first refused to sponsor us, they had a change of heart.* **5** (*rather literary*) You say something **from your heart** or **from the bottom of your heart** when you are speaking sincerely. **6** You **have your heart in your mouth** when you are wondering what is going to happen, and are very nervous. **7** You involve yourself in something **heart and soul** when you do so with enthusiasm. [*same as* **wholeheartedly**] **8 Your heart is not in** something you are doing if you do it without enthusiasm: *She tried to practise the piano but her heart wasn't in it.* **9** Something you believe **in your heart of hearts** is what you really or secretly believe: *In his heart of hearts he knows he's a fraud.* **10** You **lose your heart to** someone or something when you fall in love with them: *We lost our hearts to the cottage when we saw it.* **11** You **set your heart on** something you want when you become determined to have it: *She had set her heart on a dancing career.* **12** You **take** something such as advice or a warning **to heart** when you obey it or follow it. [*same as* **take seriously**] **13** You are able to do something **to your heart's content** if you have the opportunity of doing it as much as you want: *At his grandmother's he was allowed to watch television to his heart's content.* **14** (*rather old, and formal*) You do something **with all your heart** when you do it with warmth and sincerity: *I congratulate you with all my heart.*

heartache /ˈhɑːteɪk/ *noun* (*uncount*)
Heartache is sorrow and anxiety.

heart attack /ˈhɑːt ətak/ *noun*: **heart attacks**
Someone has a **heart attack** when one of the arteries supplying blood to the heart muscle is blocked, causing severe pain and sometimes death.

heartbeat /ˈhɑːtbiːt/ *noun*: **heartbeats**
1 (*used in the singular*) Your **heartbeat** is the sound of the regularly repeated pumping action of your heart: *a slow, rhythmical heartbeat.* **2** A **heartbeat** is the sound of a single pumping movement made by the heart: *rapid heartbeats.*

heartbreak /ˈhɑːtbreɪk/ *noun* (*uncount*)
Heartbreak is deep sorrow: *the heartbreak of divorce.*

heartbreaking /ˈhɑːtbreɪkɪŋ/ *adjective*
Something that is **heartbreaking** makes you very sad: *a heartbreaking story.*

heartbroken /ˈhɑːtbroʊkən/ *adjective*
You are **heartbroken** when you are very upset or sad: *He was heartbroken when his dog died.* [*same as* **broken-hearted**]

heartburn /ˈhɑːtbɜːn/ *noun* (*uncount*)
Heartburn is pain in the chest caused by indigestion.

heart disease /ˈhɑːt dɪziːz/ *noun* (*uncount*)
Heart disease is a dangerous condition of the arteries supplying the heart with blood, in which, from various possible causes, they get narrow and may become blocked.

hearten /ˈhɑːtən/ *verb*: **heartens, heartening, heartened**
Something **heartens** you when it encourages you or cheers you up: *I was heartened by the team's performance on Saturday.* — *adjective* **heartening:** *a heartening piece of news.*

heart failure /ˈhɑːt feɪljə(r)/ *noun* (*uncount*)
Someone suffers **heart failure** when their heart stops beating.

heartfelt /ˈhɑːtfɛlt/ *adjective*
Heartfelt describes feelings and gestures that are absolutely sincere: *heartfelt sympathy.*

hearth /hɑːθ/ *noun*: **hearths**
A **hearth** is the floor of a fireplace, or the area surrounding it: *A fire was blazing cheerfully in the hearth.* [see picture at **living room**]

hearthrug /ˈhɑːθrʌg/ *noun*: **hearthrugs**
A **hearthrug** is a floor rug for laying in front of a fireplace. [see picture at **living room**]

heartland /ˈhɑːtland/ *noun* (*often used in the plural*): **heartlands**
The **heartlands** or **heartland** of a region or area is the vital centre of it: *Blairgowrie is a small market town in the agricultural heartland of eastern Scotland.*

heartless /ˈhɑːtləs/ *adjective*
A **heartless** person is cruel or unkind: *It was pretty heartless of the management to make her redundant after 30 years' service.* — *adverb* **heartlessly:** *These beautiful birds are being heartlessly slaughtered.*

heartrending /ˈhɑːtrɛndɪŋ/ *adjective*
Something that is **heartrending** fills you with sadness and pity: *We cannot ignore the heartrending plight of these children.*

hearty /ˈhɑːtɪ/ *adjective*: **heartier, heartiest**
1 Things and people that are **hearty** are friendly and enthusiastic, often rather noisily so: *Our hotel staff will give you a hearty welcome.* **2** A **hearty** meal is a large one. **3 Hearty** feelings are strongly felt ones: *I had a hearty dislike of all politicians.* □ *We returned from the walk with a hearty appetite.* — *adverb* **heartily:** *He slapped me heartily on the back by way of a greeting.* □ *I was heartily sick of her complaints.* — *noun* (*uncount*) **heartiness:** *He greeted me with somewhat excessive heartiness.*

heat /hiːt/ *noun*; *verb*
▻ ***noun***: **heats**
1 (*uncount*) **Heat** is warmth, or the quality of being hot or warm: *The electric fire produces very little heat.* □ *Babies can lose body heat very quickly.* **2** (*uncount, or used in the singular*) You refer to hot weather as the **heat**; the **heat** of the day is the hottest part of a hot day, usually about midday: *You mustn't go out in this heat without a hat.* □ *They were working in the fields in the heat of the day.* **3** (*uncount*) The temperature of something warm or hot is its **heat**: *The milk should be about blood heat.* **4** (*used in the singular*) You use a low or high **heat** when cooking things on a stove if you have the gas or electricity turned up high or turned down low: *Simmer the vegetables over a gentle-to-moderate heat.* **5** (*uncount; literary*) **Heat** is anger or strong feeling: *'Can't you see I'm busy?' she replied with some heat.* **6** (*used in the singular*) Something that happens in the **heat** of some activity happens at the point when feelings of anger or excitement are strongest: *In the heat of the argument I said some rather unforgivable things.* **7** The **heats** in a competition are the preliminary races, rounds or competitions, the winners of which meet each other in the second round: *I won my heat and went on to the next round.*
▻ ***verb***: **heats, heating, heated**
You **heat** something or **heat** it up by raising its temperature, or making it warmer or hotter by some means; things **heat** or **heat** up when they get warmer or hotter: *I'll heat some soup for lunch.* □ *These large houses are difficult to heat in winter.*
▻ ***phrase*** You do or say something stupid or rash **in the heat of the moment** when the excitement or tension of the situation you are involved in causes you to behave that way.

heated /ˈhiːtɪd/ *adjective*
You get **heated** when you get angry or excited: *a heated discussion.* — *adverb* **heatedly:** *Linguists have heatedly debated the origin of this word.*

heater /ˈhiːtə(r)/ *noun*: **heaters**
A **heater** is an apparatus for heating a room or vehicle or for heating the water in a building's hot-water system: *Have you switched on the water-heater?* □ *an electric heater.*

heath /hiːθ/ *noun* (*uncount or count*): **heaths**
A **heath** is a high, wild, uncultivated area of land covered with grass and low-growing bushes: *I took the dog for a walk on the heath.* [*same as* **moor**]

heathen /ˈhiːðən/ *noun*; *adjective*
▻ ***noun*** (*old*): **heathens**
A **heathen** is someone who is not a Christian, or someone who is not a member of one of the main world religions: *Missionaries were sent amongst the heathens to convert them to Christianity.*
▻ ***adjective*** (*old*): *heathen practices.*

heather /ˈhɛðə(r)/ *noun* (*uncount*)
Heather is a plant with small purple or white flowers that grows wild on moors and hills.

heating /ˈhiːtɪŋ/ *noun* (*uncount*)
The **heating** in a place is the apparatus, system or process of keeping it warm: *Heating and lighting bills alone come to £1000 per annum.*

heatwave /ˈhiːtweɪv/ *noun*: **heatwaves**
A **heatwave** is a period of unusually hot weather: *The beach was full of sunbathers taking advantage of the heatwave.*

heave /hiːv/ *verb*; *noun*
▻ ***verb***: **heaves, heaving, heaved** or **hove**
1 You **heave** something that is heavy or hard to move when you pull, push or lift it: *They had to heave the piano on to the stage.* □ *He heaved himself off the bed.* [*same as* **haul**] **2** (*informal*) You **heave** something heavy somewhere when you throw it: *Someone had heaved a brick through the window.* [*same as* **hurl**] **3** You **heave** a sigh when you sigh deeply: *I heaved a sigh of relief.* **4** Things **heave** when they move up and down: *She glanced down at the black heaving water.* **5** To **heave** is to have an urge or need to vomit: *The ship rolled and his stomach heaved.* **6** (**hove**) Something **heaves** into sight when you see it as you approach it, or as it approaches you: *The procession hove into view.*
▻ ***noun***: **heaves:** *I gave another heave on the rope.*
▻ ***phrases*** (*informal*) To **give** someone **the heave** is to sack them or get rid of them; you **get the heave** when you are sacked or got rid of: *I couldn't meet their work targets so I got the heave.* □ *She's given her boyfriend the heave.*

heaven /ˈhɛvən/ *noun*: **heavens**
1 (*uncount*) **Heaven** is the place where God is believed to live, and where good people are believed to go when they die. **2** (*used in the plural*) The **heavens** are the sky: *The stars looked down from the heavens.* **3** (*uncount; informal*) You say that something is **heaven** if you find it very pleasant: *It was heaven being on my own for a change.*
▻ ***phrase***
1 You use '**good heavens**' or '**heavens**' as an interjection, for emphasis or to express surprise: *'Are you angry with me?' 'Good heavens, no.'* □ *Heavens, it's getting late.* **2 a** You use '**heaven knows**' as an emphatic way of saying 'I've no idea': *Heaven knows where we buy tickets.* **b** '**Heaven knows**' sometimes means 'as everyone must know': *I've been extremely patient with her, heaven knows.* **3** For **for heaven's sake** see **sake**. **4** For **thank heavens** see **thank**.

heavenly /ˈhɛvənlɪ/ *adjective*
1 Heavenly describes things and beings that belong to heaven or the heavens: *the sun, the moon and all the heavenly bodies.* **2** (*informal*) You describe something as **heavenly** if you find it very pleasant: *It's heavenly not having to get up and go to work.* [*same as* **delightful, divine**]

heaven-sent /ˈhɛvənsɛnt/ *adjective*
You describe something such as an opportunity as **heaven-sent** if it has occurred unexpectedly but very conveniently: *The conference looked like a heaven-sent opportunity to escape from my family and the office for a while.* [*same as* **providential**]

heavy /ˈhɛvɪ/ *adjective*: **heavier, heaviest**
1 Something that is **heavy** weighs a lot: *I had a rucksack and a heavy suitcase to carry.* □ *That bag of yours looks heavy.* □ *The branches were heavy with fruit.* **2** You ask how **heavy** something is if you want to know what it weighs. **3** Things that are great in quantity or intensity are also **heavy**: *a heavy shower* □ *heavy fighting in the streets* □ *There were heavy civilian casualties.* **4** Someone who is a **heavy** smoker or a **heavy** drinker smokes a lot, or drinks a lot of alcohol. **5** You call someone a **heavy** sleeper if they are difficult to wake; a **heavy** sigh, or **heavy** breathing, is loud and deep. **6** A **heavy** meal is a large one. **7** Things that are **heavy** in appearance look thick and solid: *He had a large, heavy-featured face.* □ *thick, heavy brows.* **8** A substance such as soil that is described as **heavy** is thick and dense in texture; the going on a race course is **heavy** when the ground is wet and soft. **9** A blow or other action involving contact or impact is **heavy** if there is a lot of force or pressure in it: *Her fist caught him a heavy blow on the jaw.* □ *I could hear his heavy tread in the corridor.* **10 Heavy** work is hard physical work requiring a lot of effort: *Digging the garden proved heavy work.* **11** You have a **heavy** day or a **heavy** schedule if you are very busy; you have **heavy** responsibilities if you have a lot of important ones. **12** (*informal*) You describe literature as **heavy** if it rather serious and difficult to understand. **13** (*rather literary*) You have a **heavy** heart when you feel sad. **14** The weather or atmosphere is **heavy** when it feels damp and warm. [*same as* **sultry, humid**] — *adverb* **heavily:** *It rained heavily all day.* □ *He was breathing heavily after his exertions.* □ *Morning came and she was still heavily asleep.* □ *He was short but heavily built.* □ *She sighed heavily.* □ *He was leaning heavily on his stick.*
▻ ***phrase***
1 You describe something you are doing as **heavy going** if progress is slow and difficult: *It was heavy going trying to make conversation with him.* **2** For **make heavy weather of** see **weather**.

heavy-duty /ˈhɛvɪdju:tɪ/ *adjective*
A **heavy-duty** material or machine is designed to stand hard wear or intensive and rough use.

heavy-handed /ˈhɛvɪhandɪd/ *adjective*
Someone who is **heavy-handed** is clumsy or insensitive in their dealings with other people, or is not subtle enough in the way they speak or write: *We shall have to suffer some more of his heavy-handed humour.*

heavy industry /hɛvɪˈɪndəstrɪ/ *noun* (*uncount or count*): **heavy industries**
Heavy industry is the industries such as coalmining and ship-building, that involve the use of heavy machinery or that produce large, heavy products.

heavy metal /hɛvɪ ˈmɛtəl/ *noun* (*uncount*)
Heavy metal is a type of loud fast rock music played on electric instruments.

heavyweight /ˈhɛvɪweɪt/ *noun*: **heavyweights**
1 A **heavyweight** is a boxer of the heaviest class. **2** You sometimes call an important or influential person a **heavyweight**: *She was considered an intellectual heavyweight.*

Hebrew /ˈhi:bru:/ *noun* (*uncount*)
Hebrew is the ancient language of the Jews, revived and spoken in a modern form in Israel.

heck /hɛk/ *interjection* (*swearword, or very informal*)
People sometimes add 'the **heck**' after question words such as *why*, *what* or *who* for emphasis: *Where the heck have you been all this time?* [*same as* **on earth, the hell**]
▻ ***phrase*** (*very informal*) People sometimes use **'a heck of'** to emphasize the size, amount or difficulty of something: *We've got a heck of a lot of work to get through.*

heckle /ˈhɛkəl/ *verb*: **heckles, heckling, heckled**
People **heckle** a public speaker or performer when they interrupt them with loud, rude or critical comments or questions: *She was used to being heckled from the floor.* — *noun* **heckler:** *She stopped in mid-sentence to deal with a couple of persistent hecklers.* — *noun* (*uncount*) **heckling:** *There was a good deal of heckling from the back of the hall.*

hectare /ˈhɛktɛə(r)/ *noun*: **hectares**
A **hectare** is a metric unit of land measurement, equal to 10 000 square metres.

hectic /ˈhɛktɪk/ *adjective*
You have a **hectic** time or schedule when you are very busy and have to do a lot of things in too short a time: *I've had a hectic week.* □ *I'll call you next week when things are a bit less hectic.* — *adverb* **hectically:** *I'm hectically busy.*

he'd /hi:d/
He'd is the spoken, and informal written, form of **1 he had**, typically where **had** is an auxiliary verb: *I thought he'd already left.* **2 he would**: *I thought he'd probably try again.*

hedge /hɛdʒ/ *noun*; *verb*
▻ ***noun***: **hedges**
A **hedge** is a row of bushes planted close together so as to form a solid mass, especially along the edge of a road, garden or field. [see picture at **house**]
▻ ***verb***: **hedges, hedging, hedged**
1 You **hedge** when you answer questions in such a way that you avoid directly stating your opinion or intention: *Get a definite yes or no from her; don't let her hedge.* [*same as* **prevaricate**] **2** Something that **hedges** you in or **hedges** you about restricts or limits you: *She felt marriage was hedging her in and longed to be free again.* [*same as* **hem in**]
▻ ***phrase*** You **hedge your bets** by giving your support to more than one person or scheme, so as to avoid risking a large loss on any particular one.

hedgehog /ˈhɛdʒhɒg/ *noun*: **hedgehogs**
A **hedgehog** is a small brown animal with lots of sharp spikes or prickles growing out of its back.

hedgerow /ˈhɛdʒroʊ/ *noun*: **hedgerows**
A **hedgerow** is a row of bushes and trees forming a hedge, especially along a country road or lane.

hedonism /ˈhi:dənɪzm/ *noun* (*uncount*)
Hedonism is the belief that getting pleasure is the most important aim in life. — *noun* **hedonist:** *The modern generation seem to be a race of unashamed hedonists.* — *adjective* **hedonistic:** *He was leading a life of hedonistic self-indulgence.*

heed /hi:d/ *verb*: **heeds, heeding, heeded**
You **heed** someone's warning or advice if you pay attention to it: *I should have heeded what you said.*
▻ ***phrase*** You **pay heed to** someone's advice or **take heed of** it if you pay attention to it: *Politicians pay little heed to the effects of their decisions on ordinary life.* □ *They whistled at her but she paid them no heed.* □ *We must take heed of the suggestions put forward by the staff council.*

heedless /ˈhiːdləs/ *adjective*
You are **heedless** of something if you take no notice of it, or are apparently unaware of it: *He climbed higher, heedless of the risk he was taking.* — *noun* (*uncount*) **heedlessness:** *the heedlessness of youth.*

heel /hiːl/ *noun*; *verb*
▻ ***noun*: heels**
1 Your **heel** is the rounded back part of your foot: *She had developed a blister on one heel.* [see picture at **body**] **2** The **heel** of a sock or stocking is the part that goes over the heel of your foot. **3** The **heel** of a shoe is the raised part that supports the heel of your foot: *These heels need mending.* □ *Her stiletto heels clicked along the corridor.* [see picture at **clothing**] **4** The **heel** of your hand is the part of your palm near your wrist. — *adjective* **-heeled:** *high-heeled boots.*
▻ ***verb*: heels, heeling, heeled**
To **heel** a shoe is to fix a new heel on it: *I must get these shoes heeled.*
▻ ***phrases*** **1** Your dog walks **at heel** when it walks along close behind you; when you bring it **to heel**, or it comes **to heel**, it comes to you and walks behind you; you bring a person **to heel** when you force them to behave the way you want them to. **2** You **dig your heels in** when you refuse to be persuaded. **3** You are left **kicking your heels** when someone is keeping you waiting. **4** Someone who is **down at heel** looks shabby, untidy and badly-cared-for. **5** One thing comes or follows **hard on the heels of** another if it happens very soon after the other: *Their divorce followed hard on the heels of their son's death.* **6** You are **hot on the heels** of someone if you are following close behind them. **7** (*literary*) You **take to your heels** when you run away. **8** You **turn on your heel** when you turn sharply and suddenly to face the opposite direction: *He turned on his heel and stalked angrily away.*

hefty /ˈhɛftɪ/ *adjective*: **heftier, heftiest** (*informal*)
1 A **hefty** person is large or fat, or heavily or strongly built: *She looks a lot heftier than she used to.* **2** A **hefty** blow is a strong or heavy one: *He gave the cupboard door a hefty kick.* [*same as* **forceful, powerful**] **3** A **hefty** sum is a large amount of money: *We'll have a hefty bill for repairs* [*same as* **substantial**]

heifer /ˈhɛfə(r)/ *noun*: **heifers**
A **heifer** is a young cow.

height /haɪt/ *noun*: **heights**
1 (*uncount or count*) The **height** of something is its measurement from its bottom to its top: *These trees can grow to tremendous heights.* □ *The boy is described as about four foot eight in height.* □ *What's the height of Mount Kenya?* [see picture at **shape**] **2** (*uncount*) **Height** is the quality of being tall: *His height made him conspicuous.* **3** (*count or uncount*) Something that is at a certain **height** is a certain distance above the ground; an aircraft gains **height** when it climbs, and loses **height** when it descends or drops: *We were flying at a height of 10000 metres.* □ *Stretch your arms forward at shoulder height.* **4** (*used in the plural*) The **heights** usually refers to a high place such as the top of a high cliff or hill. **5** (*used in the singular*) Something is at its **height** when it is at its greatest or best, or when it is at its most fierce or intense: *The storm was now at its height.* [*same as* **peak**] **6** (*used in the singular*) Something that is the **height** of a particular quality is an outstanding example of that quality: *Your behaviour towards her was the height of bad manners.* □ *Her clothes are always the height of elegance.* **7** Something that rises to great **heights** becomes very great: *Literature will never reach such heights again.*
▻ ***phrase*** Someone who **has a good head for heights** can look down from a high place without feeling dizzy.

heighten /ˈhaɪtən/ *verb*: **heightens, heightening, heightened**
Things **heighten** or **are heightened** when they are increased: *Their anxiety heightened with each hour that passed.* [*same as* **intensify**]

heinous /ˈheɪnəs/ *adjective*
A **heinous** crime is a very wicked and evil one. [*same as* **abominable**]

heir /ɛə(r)/ *noun*: **heirs**
Your **heir** is the person who will inherit your money, property or title when you die: *She is his sole heir.* □ *Who is the heir to the Spanish throne?*

heiress /ˈɛərɛs/ *noun*: **heiresses**
An **heiress** is a woman who is going to inherit a large amount of money or property.

heirloom /ˈɛəluːm/ *noun*: **heirlooms**
An **heirloom** is an object, *eg* a piece of jewellery, that has belonged to a family for several generations and has been handed down from parents to children: *The brooch was a family heirloom.*

held /hɛld/ *verb*
Held is the past tense and past participle of **hold**.

helicopter /ˈhɛlɪkɒptə(r)/ *noun*: **helicopters**
A **helicopter** is an aircraft that is lifted and powered by a set of rotating blades fixed to its roof.

helium /ˈhiːlɪəm/ *noun* (*uncount*)
Helium is a light non-flammable gas that is used in balloons and airships.

hell /hɛl/ *noun*; *interjection*
▻ ***noun*** (*uncount*)
1 **Hell** is the place where wicked people are believed to go when they die, and where evil spirits or demons are believed to live. **2** (*informal*) You say that all **hell** was let loose, or broke loose, when something happens that upsets people, so that they start arguing angrily or fighting firecely: *All hell broke loose when the coalmine closures were announced.* **3** (*informal*) You call a place or situation **hell** if it is very unpleasant, or full of pain and misery: *He had made her life hell throughout their marriage.*
▻ ***interjection*** (*swearword, or very informal*)
Hell is used as an expression of annoyance: *Oh hell, I've spilt my coffee.*
▻ ***phrases*** (*swearword, or very informal*)
1 Something that is as cold or uncomfortable **as hell** is very cold or uncomfortable: *The place was as bleak as hell.* **2** One person **beats the hell out of** another when they attack and beat them brutally. **3** You do something **for the hell of it** when you do it for fun, or for no good reason: *He said he stole cars just for the hell of it.* **4** You **get the hell out of** somewhere when you leave as fast as you can: *We got the hell out as soon as we smelt burning.* **5** Someone **gives you hell** when they scold you severely or treat you harshly: *He always gave us hell if we failed to come up to standard.* **6** If you tell someone to **go to hell**, you are rudely telling them to go away or stop annoying you. **7** People use **a hell of a** something, or **one hell of a** something to emphasize the size, amount or difficulty of something: *There'll be one hell of a row when they find out.* □ *We've still got a hell of a distance to go.* **8** You **knock hell out of** something or someone when you treat them roughly or harshly: *I bet she knocks hell out of her staff.* **9** You do something **like hell** when you do it fast or vigorously: *It was raining like hell.* **10** People put **the hell** after question words such as *what*, *why* or *who* for emphasis or to express annoyance: *Why the hell don't you listen?*

he'll /hiːl/
He'll is the spoken form, or the informal written form, of **he will**: *He'll be so pleased to see you.*

hellish /ˈhɛlɪʃ/ *adjective* (*informal*)
If you call something **hellish** you mean it is very bad, unpleasant, horrible or difficult: *What hellish weather!* — *adverb* (*intensifying*) **hellishly:** *It's hellishly difficult.*

hello, hallo or **hullo** /həˈloʊ/ *interjection*
Hello is used **1** as a greeting: *Hello, Jo. How are you?* **2** to attract attention: *He let himself in and shouted 'Hello, I'm back.'* **3** in answering the telephone: *'Hello, this is Edenbridge 862144.'* **4** to express surprise, concern or interest at something you notice: *Hello, this looks like an error.*

> **Hello** is the usual greeting in British English. People also use **hi**, as in American English, but it is regarded as more informal than **hello**. When you meet someone for the first time you usually say **how do you do?**

helm /hɛlm/ *noun*: **helms**
The **helm** of a ship is the wheel or other device by which it is steered.
▻ ***phrase*** Someone who is **at the helm** is in a position of control or authority.

helmet /ˈhɛlmɪt/ *noun*: **helmets**
A **helmet** is a hard hat that you wear to protect your head.

help /hɛlp/ *verb*; *noun*; *interjection*
▻ ***verb*****: helps, helping, helped**
1 You **help** someone when you make what they are doing easier by doing some of it yourself, or by advising them how to do it: *We're moving these chairs into the hall. Could you help?* □ *Let me help you put those books back.* □ *I helped her to wash and put away the dishes.* □ *Can you help me with this question?* [*same as* **assist**] **2** You **help** someone somewhere when you support them as they move somewhere: *He helped me into a taxi.* □ *She had to be helped off the bus.* □ *I helped him upstairs.* **3** Something **helps**, or **helps** a problem, if it makes things easier to achieve or bear: *I'll give you something to help the pain.* □ *I tried lying on my side but it didn't help.* □ *I could lend you 50 pence if that would help.* □ *Her deafness doesn't help the situation of course.* **4** A thing **helps** to do something if contributes towards achieving it: *This injection will help you to sleep.* □ *The splendid weather helped to make it a successful occasion.* □ *a style book guaranteed to help you write better.* **5** You **help** yourself to something when you serve yourself with it: *Do help yourself to sherry.* □ *Coffee is in the cupboard; help yourselves.* □ *May I help you to some potatoes?* **6** You say you can't **help** doing something if you cannot stop yourself doing it; if you say you can't **help** a situation you mean that you aren't responsible for it, and shouldn't be blamed: *I couldn't help laughing.* □ *I can't help wondering if we should have waited.* □ *How can I help it if her husband falls in love with me?*
▻ ***noun*** (*uncount*)
1 You give someone **help** when you help them: *Many thanks for all your help.* □ *I'll give you what help I can.* [*same as* **assistance**] **2** (*uncount, or used in the singular*) A person or thing is of **help**, or a **help**, to you if they help you to achieve something, or to bear something: *I'm sorry to have been of so little help to you.* □ *Susan was a great help with the wedding arrangements.* □ *The instruction book was no help at all.* □ *The painkillers were a help.* **3** (*count or uncount*) A domestic **help** or a mother's **help** is a domestic servant; someone who has **help** in the house has one or more domestic servants.
▻ ***interjection***
You shout **'help!'** when you are in danger, to try and attract attention.

> ***phrasal verb***
> You **help** someone **out** when you do some of their work for them, or when you give or lend them money.

helper /ˈhɛlpə(r)/ *noun*: **helpers**
A **helper** is a person who helps you with a job: *We had about fifty voluntary helpers to look after the patients.*

helpful /ˈhɛlpfʊl/ *adjective*
1 Someone who is **helpful** to you helps you by giving you information or advice that you need, or doing a task or some work for you: *Thanks for finding me her address; that was very helpful of you.* **2** Something that is **helpful** makes a job, task or situation easier to deal with: *Wouldn't it be more helpful to consider these points separately?* — *adverb* **helpfully:** *Someone helpfully suggested looking in the telephone directory.* — *noun* (*uncount*) **helpfulness:** *Please pass on my thanks to your staff for their kindness and helpfulness.*

helping /ˈhɛlpɪŋ/ *noun*: **helpings**
A **helping** of food is an individual portion of it that is served to you: *Have another helping of potatoes.* [*same as* **serving**]
▻ ***phrase*** For **a helping hand** see **hand**.

helpless /ˈhɛlpləs/ *adjective*
1 You are **helpless** when you have lost the power to behave or react as you would normally or naturally want to: *She found herself helpless to refuse or resist.* [*same as* **powerless**] **2** Someone who is **helpless** does not have the means to protect, or look after, themselves: *as helpless as a baby.* [*same as* **defenceless**] **3** (*derogatory*) You describe a person as **helpless** if they don't know what to do or how to do it: *I stood around feeling helpless while she gave first aid.* [*same as* **impractical**] — *adverb* **helplessly:** *We looked on helplessly as he slithered further down the cliff.* — *noun* (*uncount*) **helplessness:** *an overwhelming feeling of helplessness.*

hem /hɛm/ *noun*; *verb*
▻ ***noun*****: hems**
The **hem** of a piece of clothing such as a dress or skirt is the bottom edge of it, folded over and sewn.
▻ ***verb*****: hems, hemming, hemmed**
You **hem** cloth, or part of a garment, when you fold its edge over and sew it.

> ***phrasal verb***
> You **are hemmed in** by things when you are surrounded by them, so that escape is difficult or impossible: *They found themselves hemmed in by towering cliffs and waterfalls.*

hemisphere /ˈhɛmɪsfɪə(r)/ *noun*: **hemispheres**
1 A **hemisphere** is one half of a sphere. **2** The northern, southern, western and eastern **hemispheres** of the earth are the northern, southern, western or eastern halves of it: *Singapore is just within the northern hemisphere.* — *adjective* **hemispherical** /hɛmɪˈsfɛrɪkəl/: *A bowl is a more or less hemispherical vessel.*

hemline /ˈhɛmlaɪn/ *noun*: **hemlines**
The **hemline** of a skirt or dress is the level at which its lower edge hangs, relative to the leg: *above-the-knee hemlines*

hemoglobin see **haemoglobin**.

hemophilia see **haemophilia**.

hemorrhoid see **haemorrhoid**.

hemp /hɛmp/ *noun* (*uncount*)
Hemp is a plant from which coarse fibres are obtained that are made into rope and cloth, and the drug marijuana or cannabis is produced.

hen /hɛn/ *noun*: **hens**
1 A **hen** is a female chicken: *We used to keep hens.* **2** The female of any kind of bird is the **hen**.

hence /hɛns/ *adverb*
1 (*sentence adverb*) You use **hence** to mean 'for that reason', or 'because of that fact': *It was a steep and difficult route and hence not too popular with walkers.* **2** A week, month or year **hence** is a week, month or year from the time at which you are speaking: *Goodness knows where I'll be six months hence.*

henceforth /hɛns'fɔːθ/ *adverb* (*old*)
Henceforth means 'from now on', 'from this time on' or 'in future': *Matters of this kind are henceforth to be dealt with by the management.*

henchman /'hɛntʃmən/ *noun*: **henchmen**
The **henchmen** of someone powerful are his or her loyal supporters who will do whatever they are told to do, whether or not it is morally right and honest: *The Prince sent down one of his henchmen with strict orders not to let them in.*

hepatitis /hɛpə'taɪtɪs/ *noun* (*uncount*)
Hepatitis is a serious disease in which the liver becomes inflamed.

her /hɜː(r)/ or /hə(r)/ *pronoun*; *determiner*
▻ ***pronoun***
1 (*used as the object of a verb or preposition*) You use **her** to refer to a woman, girl or female animal that has just been mentioned; you can also refer to a country, ship or car as **her**: *Anna was going my way so I gave her a lift.* ▫ *She looked surprised when I told her.* ▫ *The bullet hit the lioness and I watched her crumple.* ▫ *The yacht was lying at anchor and there seemed to be no-one aboard her.* ▫ *I'm younger than her* (or *than she is*) ▫ *I'm not as tall as her* (or *as she is*). ▫ *'Jean sends you her best wishes.' 'Oh, that's nice of her.'* **2** You find **her** instead of *she* in emphatic uses: *Who's supposed to be in charge? Her or me?* ▫ *'Ginny's got flu.' 'Oh, poor her.'* ▫ *'Which is Sandra?' 'That's her, over by the door.'* [see also **she**]
▻ ***determiner*** (*possessive*)
1 Her means of, or belonging to, the female person or animal, or country ship or car, already mentioned: *Is Jenny enjoying her course?* ▫ *She makes her own clothes.* ▫ *She's like a mother hen fussing over her chicks.* ▫ *Should Britain reduce her spending on defence?* **2 Her** is used in royal and noble titles: *Her Majesty the Queen* ▫ *Her Royal Highness Princess Anne* ▫ *Her Grace the Duchess of Kent.*
[see also **hers, herself**]

herald /'hɛrəld/ *noun*; *verb*
▻ ***noun*** (*literary*): **heralds**
Something that is a sign of what is to come or happen is sometimes called a **herald** of something: *that sudden sharp rain-laden wind that is the herald of a storm.*
▻ ***verb***: **heralds, heralding, heralded**
1 Events **are heralded** when they are announced and publicized in advance: *The treatment was already being heralded as the long-awaited breakthrough.* **2** One event **heralds** another if it is a sign that the other is going to happen: *His arrival heralded the introduction of a new style of management.*

heraldry /'hɛrəldrɪ/ *noun* (*uncount*)
Heraldry is the genealogical study of noble and important families, and the examination and preparation of coats of arms.

herb /hɜːb/ (*AmE* /ɜːb/) *noun*: **herbs**
A **herb** is a plant used to flavour food or to make medicines: *We grew parsley, thyme and other herbs beside the back door.* ▫ *herbs and spices* ▫ *They stock a variety of herb teas.* — *adjective* **herbal:** *Those herbal remedies can be quite effective.*

herculean /hɜːkjʊ'lɪən/ *adjective*
A **herculean** task requires a lot of strength and effort: *It'll be a herculean task to shift all those books.*

herd /hɜːd/ *noun*; *verb*
▻ ***noun*: herds**
1 A **herd** of animals of any particular kind is a large group of them, living and feeding together: *a herd of wild cattle.* [compare **pack**] **2** (*used in the singular*; *derogatory*) The **herd** is the mass or majority of people, regarded as behaving all in the same unthinking way: *Make up your own mind; you don't have to follow the herd.*
▻ ***verb*: herds, herding, herded**
To **herd** animals or people is to make them move together in a herd or group: *People were herded in their thousands on to trains and taken to the concentration camps.*

here /hɪə(r)/ *adverb*; *interjection*
▻ ***adverb***
1 You use **here** to refer to the place where you are: *How long will you be here for?* ▫ *I'll be leaving here at about 6.00.* ▫ *Could you collect the books from here tomorrow?* ▫ *Be back here by lunchtime.* ▫ *Come over here a minute.* ▫ *Hello, it's Anne here; is Mairi in?* ▫ *I'm sorry, Mairi isn't here.* ▫ *It's autumn here.* **2** You use **here** to draw attention to a position near you, that you are pointing at: *Please sign your name just here.* **3 Here** draws attention to something that you are holding, or someone or something that is beside you: *Peter here has made a suggestion.* ▫ *I have here the list of winners.* ▫ *The switch here operates the air-conditioning.* **4** Someone or something that is **here** has just arrived: *Spring is here.* ▫ *Is George here yet?* **5 Here** also refers to the point or stage reached in a discussion or in events that are being described: *I think we should stop here and continue the conversation after tea.* ▫ *Here the writer had crossed out several lines.*
▻ ***interjection***
1 You use **here** to express surprise, anger or concern at what someone is doing or saying: *Here! What do you think you're doing?* ▫ *Here! You mustn't talk like that.* **2** You also use **here** when offering someone something: *Here, take one; they're free.* ▫ *Here, let me help you with your case.*
▻ ***phrases*** **1 a** Something that is happening, or must be done, **here and now**, is happening now, or must be done immediately: *We have urgent matters to deal with here and now.* **b** You make some point **here and now** so that people know what you think before things develop further: *I'm telling you here and now that we can't afford it.* **2** Something that occurs **here and there** occurs in various places: *Industrial trouble had broken out here and there.* **3** You say **'here goes!'** when you are about to do something that you have been preparing yourself for, especially something that needs courage. **4** You use **here is** and **here are** when showing someone what you have obtained or found, or when giving something to someone, or to announce the arrival of someone or something: *Here's your book back.* ▫ *Here are the tickets.* ▫ *Here's that bill I'd lost.* ▫ *'Have you got that leaflet?' 'Here it is.'* ▫ *Here's Mary.* ▫ *Here's the bus coming now.* ▫ *Well, here you are at last.* ▫ *Here's the way to do it.* **5** You introduce a toast to someone or something by raising your glass and saying **'here's to ...'**: *Here's to your success in the new job.*

6 You say '**here we are**' to indicate that you have found what you were looking for: *I can't see it. Oh, yes, here we are.* **7** You say **here you are** when you are giving someone something: *'Could you spare a tissue?' 'Here you are.'* [*same as* **there you go**] **8** Something that is **neither here nor there** doesn't matter, or is not important: *Whether he approves or not is neither here nor there.*

hereabouts /hɪərə'baʊts/ or **hereabout** *adverb*
Hereabouts means near the place where you are: *Are there any public loos hereabouts?*

hereafter /hɪər'ɑːftə(r)/ *adverb* (*formal*)
Hereafter is used, *eg* in documents, to mean after this, or from now on.

hereby /hɪə'baɪ/ *adverb* (*formal*)
You use **hereby** when you are making a statement that implies some act on your part, and is therefore the official announcement of it: *We hereby renounce all claims to the property of the deceased.*

hereditary /hə'rɛdɪtərɪ/ *adjective*
1 Features or characteristics that are **hereditary** can be passed on from parents to their unborn children; illnesses can also be **hereditary**: *hereditary diseases of the nervous system.* **2** A **hereditary** title or rank is one that a child inherits as a right from his or her parents: *Are tribal chiefdoms usually hereditary?*

heredity /hə'rɛdɪtɪ/ *noun* (*uncount*)
Heredity is the process by which features, characteristics and qualities are passed on from parents to children: *How much of their ability is due to heredity and how much to environment would be difficult to say.*

herein /hɪər'ɪn/ *adverb* (*legal or formal*)
Herein is used by writers of documents to mean 'in this document'.

heresy /'hɛrəsɪ/ *noun* (*count or uncount*): **heresies**
A **heresy** is an opinion or belief, especially a religious or political one, that is opposed the standard, official and generally accepted teaching: *Disbelief in Christ's divinity was one of the earliest Christian heresies.*

heretic /'hɛrətɪk/ *noun*: **heretics**
A **heretic** is a person who holds an opinion or belief, especially a religious or political one, that is in disagreement with the official, standard or generally accepted teaching: *She was regarded till recently as one of the party heretics.* — *adjective* **heretical** /hə'rɛtɪkəl/: *heretical beliefs.*

heritage /'hɛrɪtɪdʒ/ *noun* (*used in the singular*)
Your **heritage**, especially as a citizen of your country, is the culture from the past, in the form *eg* of literature, art and architecture, that you have the benefit of enjoying in the present and the task of preserving for the future.

hermit /'hɜːmɪt/ *noun*: **hermits**
A **hermit** is a person who lives alone and keeps apart from society, especially, in the past, so as to be able to pray and think. [*same as* **recluse**]

hernia /'hɜːnɪə/ *noun* (*count or uncount*; *medicine*): **hernias**
You have a **hernia** if part of your bowel or intestine is pushing through the muscle wall of your abdomen.

hero /'hɪəroʊ/ *noun*: **heroes**
1 A **hero** is someone who is admired for their bravery or achievements: *We remember them as heroes who sacrificed their own lives to save their friends.* **2** The **hero** of a story or play is the main male character in it: *Brutus is the real hero of 'Julius Caesar'.* **3** You refer to someone as your **hero** if you admire them a lot: *The footballer Pelé had been one of her childhood heroes.* [see also **heroine**]

heroic /hɪ'roʊɪk/ *adjective*
People or acts that are **heroic** are courageous, or brave and determined: *his heroic battle against cancer.* — *adverb* **heroically:** *The defenders fought heroically.* □ *She struggled heroically to keep going.*

heroin /'hɛroʊɪn/ *noun* (*uncount*)
Heroin is a strong drug that causes addiction, which some people take illegally for pleasure: *He was addicted to heroin for nearly three years.*

heroine /'hɛroʊɪn/ *noun*: **heroines**
1 A **heroine** is a woman whom people admire for her courage or achievements: *sporting heroines of the past.* **2** The **heroine** of a story or play is the main female character: *Beatrice, rather than the confusingly named Hero, is the heroine of 'Much Ado about Nothing'.*

heroism /'hɛroʊɪzm/ *noun* (*uncount*)
Heroism is courage or bravery: *awards for heroism.*

heron /'hɛrən/ *noun*: **herons**
A **heron** is a large fish-eating water bird, with long legs and a long neck.

herring /'hɛrɪŋ/ *noun*: **herring** or **herrings**
A **herring** is a small sea fish with a long silvery body, whose flesh is used as food. [see also **red herring**]

hers /hɜːz/ *pronoun* (*possessive*)
Something that is **hers** belongs to the woman, girl or female animal just mentioned: *I showed her the pen, but she said it wasn't hers.* □ *If you can't find a copy I'm sure Ginny would give you hers.* □ *I must tell Freda I met an acquaintance of hers.* □ *Roland's fingers closed over hers.*

herself /hɜː'sɛlf/ or /hə'sɛlf/ *pronoun* (*reflexive*)
1 You use **herself** as the object of a verb or preposition where a woman, girl or female animal is the subject of the sentence or clause: *She caught sight of herself in the mirror.* □ *She was angry with herself for forgetting.* □ *Auntie had fallen and hurt herself.* □ *Can your little girl dress herself yet?* □ *She found herself a seat at the back.* **2 Herself** can be used for emphasis: *She says herself that she was lucky to pass the exam.* □ *I was hoping to speak to Sue herself, but she was out and I got her secretary.* □ *She knew there were other women like herself who had lost their jobs on getting pregnant.* **3** A girl or woman does something **herself** if she does it without help or interference from anyone: *Did she really draw that herself?* **4** You say that a girl or woman is **herself** when she is in her normal healthy state: *She hasn't been herself lately.* □ *She isn't feeling herself.*
⊳ ***phrase*** For **by herself** see **by**.

he's /hiːz/ or /hɪz/
He's is the spoken, and informal written, form of **1 he is**: *He's just coming.* □ *He's a doctor.* **2 he has**, typically where **has** is an auxiliary verb: *He's finished his thesis at last.* □ *He's got a flat in Queen Street.*

hesitant /'hɛzɪtənt/ *adjective*
You are **hesitant** about doing something when you are anxious or worried about the results of doing it, and so do not do it straightaway: *She felt hesitant about joining them.* [*same as* **uncertain**] — *noun* (*uncount*) **hesitancy:** *I made the suggestion with some hesitancy, not knowing how it would be received.* — *adverb* **hesitantly:** *'Is this seat taken?' he asked hesitantly.*

hesitate /'hɛzɪteɪt/ *verb*: **hesitates, hesitating, hesitated**
1 You **hesitate** before doing something, or while you are doing it, when you pause slightly from a feeling of uncertainty, anxiety or embarrassment: *She opened her mouth to speak and then hesitated.* □ *I watched him hesitate and glance round as he stepped off the pave-*

ment. **2** You say you **hesitate** to do or say something if you are unwilling or reluctant to do it, because you are not sure if it is right or correct: *Please don't hesitate to contact us if there are any problems.*

hesitation /hɛzɪ'teɪʃən/ *noun* (*uncount or count*): **hesitations**
1 Hesitation is the act of pausing slightly in what you are doing: *She addressed me by my name without a moment's hesitation.* □ *After a slight hesitation he continued speaking.* **2 Hesitation** is also unwillingness or reluctance to do something: *I would accept the post without hesitation if I were offered it.* □ *Let's have no more doubts and hesitations over this.*
▻ ***phrase*** You **have no hesitation** in doing or saying something if you know it is the right or appropriate thing to do or say: *And therefore I have no hesitation in asking you to applaud our speaker in the usual way.* □ *I wouldn't have a moment's hesitation in accepting.*

heterogeneous /hɛtəroʊ'dʒiːnɪəs/ *adjective*
A **heterogeneous** collection or group consists of things or people of lots of different kinds: *The more heterogeneous the population, it seemed, the less likelihood there was of racial tension.* [*opposite* **homogeneous**]

heterosexual /hɛtəroʊ'sɛkʃʊəl/ *adjective*; *noun*
▻ ***adjective***
1 Someone who is **heterosexual** is sexually attracted to people of the opposite sex. **2** A **heterosexual** relationship is a sexual relationship between a woman and a man. [*opposite* **homosexual**]
▻ ***noun***: **heterosexuals:** *a society where homosexuals are as welcome as heterosexuals.* — *noun* (*uncount*) **heterosexuality** /hɛtəroʊsɛkʃʊ'alɪtɪ/: *People still tend to regard heterosexuality as the norm.*

het up /hɛt'ʌp/ *adjective* (*informal*)
You get **het up** about something when you get anxious about it: *He was getting all het up over his speech.*

hew /hjuː/ *verb*: **hews, hewing, hewed, hewed** or **hewn**
To **hew** something from wood or stone is to carve or shape it roughly with an axe or other heavy tool: *roughly hewn wooden figures.*

hexagon /'hɛksagən/ *noun*: **hexagons**
A **hexagon** is a six-sided flat shape. [see picture at **shape**] — *adjective* **hexagonal** /hɛk'sagənəl/: *The new office was to be built on a hexagonal plan.*

hey /heɪ/ *interjection* (*informal*)
You use **hey** to attract attention or to express interest or surprise: *Hey, Paul! Look at this!*

heyday /'heɪdeɪ/ *noun*: **heydays**
The **heyday** of a person, place, organization or activity is the time when they are at their most famous, successful, powerful, important, popular or effective: *In her heyday she was the most popular star on Broadway.*

hi /haɪ/ *interjection* (*informal or AmE*)
Hi is used as a greeting or to attract attention: *Hi, Susan. How are you?* □ *Hi, Rita, come here a minute.* [see note at **hello**]

hiatus /haɪ'eɪtəs/ *noun*: **hiatuses**
A **hiatus** is a gap where something is missing, or a pause in which nothing happens: *This had caused a temporary hiatus in the progress of the northern campaign.*

hibernate /'haɪbəneɪt/ *verb*: **hibernates, hibernating, hibernated**
Animals that **hibernate** pass the winter in a sleep-like state: *Few large animals hibernate; bears are the exception.* — *noun* (*uncount*) **hibernation** /haɪbə'neɪʃən/: *After four months' hibernation the animals emerge thin and ravenous.*

hiccup or **hiccough** /'hɪkʌp/ *noun*; *verb*
▻ ***noun***: **hiccups**
A **hiccup** is a sudden sharp sound that you produce in your throat, caused by a contraction of the diaphragm that interrupts your breath; you have **hiccups** when your diaphragm keeps contracting, forcing you to make these sounds regularly, often because you have been eating or drinking too fast: *You'll get hiccups if you gobble your food like that.*
▻ ***verb***: **hiccups, hiccupping, hiccupped:** *She was holding her breath, trying desperately not to hiccup.*

hid /hɪd/ *verb*
Hid is the past tense of **hide**.

hidden /hɪdən/ *verb*; *adjective*
▻ ***verb***
Hidden is the past participle of **hide**.
▻ ***adjective***
1 Things that are **hidden** are easily missed, overlooked or ignored: *There may be hidden expenses we haven't considered.* [*same as* **unseen**] **2** Places that are **hidden** are hard to find: *living in some remote and hidden glen.*

hide[1] /haɪd/ *verb*; *noun*
▻ ***verb***: **hides, hiding, hid, hidden**
1 You **hide** something somewhere when you put it where people cannot see it or easily find it: *I've got to find somewhere to hide these presents from the children.* □ *I couldn't remember where I'd hidden the key.* [*same as* **conceal**] **2** You **hide**, or **hide** yourself, when you deliberately go somewhere where people cannot see you or easily find you; you **are hiding** when you are in that place: *We quickly hid ourselves behind some rocks.* **3** You **hide** facts, or your feelings, from people when you keep them secret: *As a child I would hide my true feelings.* [*same as* **conceal**] **4** One thing **hides** another when it covers or conceals the other, so that it cannot be seen: *The house was hidden from view behind tall trees.*
▻ ***noun***: **hides**
A **hide** is a concealed shelter from which to watch birds and wild animals.

hide[2] /haɪd/ *noun* (*count or uncount*): **hides**
The **hide** of an animal is its skin, used to make leather.

hideous /'hɪdɪəs/ *adjective*
Something that is **hideous** is ugly or foul: *A hideous scar disfigured his mouth and cheek.* — *adverb* **hideously:** *a hideously misshapen head* □ (*intensifying; informal*) *It was all hideously embarrassing.*

hiding[1] /'haɪdɪŋ/ *noun* (*uncount*)
Someone is in **hiding** when they are staying somewhere secretly so that people cannot find them: *He had gone into hiding after receiving a number of death threats.*

hiding[2] /'haɪdɪŋ/ *noun* (*informal*): **hidings**
You give someone a **hiding** when you beat them severely as a punishment: *What that child needs is a good hiding.*

hierarchy /'haɪərɑːkɪ/ *noun*: **hierarchies**
1 People form part of a **hierarchy** when they each have their own position in an organization according to their rank or importance. **2** The people who control an organization are sometimes referred to as the **hierarchy**: *It will be up to the hierarchy to decide.*

hieroglyphics /haɪərə'glɪfɪks/ *noun* (*plural*)
1 Hieroglyphics are symbols or pictures used in a writing system, especially an ancient system, to stand for words or sounds. **2** (*informal*) People sometimes refer to writing or figures that they cannot understand as **hieroglyphics**.

hi-fi /ˈhaɪfaɪ/ *adjective; noun*
▻ ***adjective***
Hi-fi stands for 'high-fidelity' and describes audio equipment that reproduces sound accurately.
▻ ***noun*: hi-fis**
A set of audio equipment that has this high standard of sound reproduction is called a **hi-fi**: *He was playing Wagner very loudly on his hi-fi.* [see picture at **living room**]

high /haɪ/ *adjective; adverb; noun*
▻ ***adjective*: higher, highest**
1 a Things that are **high** measure a lot from bottom to top: *high mountains* □ *surrounded by a high wall.* [*opposite* **low**]

> As a general rule, you use **high** for things that are relatively wide; you use **tall** for people and for narrow objects, but when thinking of the top of something narrow you can use **high**: *that tall girl over there; tall chimneys; tall trees; tall* (or *high*) *buildings; kept a prisoner in a high tower.*

b You use **high** when referring to the measurement of something from bottom to top, or referring to height in a relative way: *a low parapet about two feet high* □ *a six-foot-high fence* □ *How high is Mount Kenya?* □ *The west tower is higher than the east one.* □ *The wall was far too high to climb over.*

> But notice: *She's five feet tall.*

c High describes things that are a long way above the ground, or things that reach, or are positioned, above the usual level: *a high branch* □ *The shelf was too high for him to reach without standing on a chair.* □ *The light switch was quite high up.* □ *a high-necked blouse* [= with a collar or neck section that reaches nearly to the chin] □ *a high-waisted dress.* [= with the waistline above the natural waist] [*opposite* **low**]
2 a High means above the normal or average level, quantity, rate or amount: *He's running a high temperature.* □ *travelling at high speeds* □ *Their prices are pretty high.* □ *I was paying a high rate of income tax.* □ *There's a high risk of failure.* [*opposite* **low**] **b High** describes things of great strength or intensity: *The area of high pressure to the west of Ireland will gradually shift eastwards.* □ *high winds* □ *There was an atmosphere of high tension.* □ *The work demands a high degree of concentration.* [*opposite* **slight, low**]
3 a A **high** number or figure is a comparatively great or large one: *A high proportion of the students come from Japan.* □ *He got high grades in all his exam subjects.* □ *a figure somewhere in the high 90s.* [= 97, 98 or 99] [*opposite* **low**]

> But notice: *She was in her late nineties.*

b A **high** sound is a sound near the top of the possible range of sound: *She spoke in a childishly high voice.* □ *a high-pitched squeal.* [*opposite* **low, deep**] **c** Vehicle-drivers engage a **high** gear when they engage a gear suitable for travelling along a flat or downhill stretch, usually fourth or fifth gear. [*opposite* **low**]
4 a High describes an advanced or complex stage of development: *Mammals are among the higher forms of life.* □ *higher mathematics* □ *high technology.* [*opposite* **low**] **b** In teaching or learning, a **high** level is an advanced one: *higher education* □ *She was moved up to a higher class.* □ *He was planning to go on to take a higher degree.* [*opposite* **low**] **c** A **high** standard is a good one: *high-grade petrol* □ *high-quality materials.* [*opposite* **low, poor**] **d** You use **high** when referring to rank, status, importance or priority: *Doctors and teachers there have a higher standing in the community than they do here.* □ *You must be quite high up in the company by now.* □ *These are not matters of high priority at present.* □ *Prague is high on my list of favourite cities.* □ *high-level discussions* □ *The case will be tried at the High Court next month.* □ *He was murdered on the steps of the high altar.* **e** You have a **high** opinion of someone or something if you approve of them: *Her work was held in high esteem by academics.* **f** People who have **high** moral principles are conscientious about the way they behave and the way they treat others. [*opposite* **low**]
5 a High describes something such as a season when it is at its peak or height: *It's best to avoid these resorts in high summer.* □ *It was high noon and the heat was intense.* **b** When your morale is **high** you are feeling cheerful and confident. [*opposite* **low**; see also **high spirits**] **c** (*informal*) You say a person is **high** when they are unusually or unnaturally lively and excited; someone who is **high** on drugs is in an excited or elated state after taking drugs. **d** Meat or fish that is, or smells, **high**, is beginning to go bad.
▻ ***adverb*: higher, highest**
1 High means at or up to a great height: *We were flying high above Paris.* □ *Throw the ball as high as you can.* **2** People or things that rank or rate **high** are important: *high-ranking diplomats* □ *Washing-up doesn't rate very high in his list of priorities.* [compare **highly**]
▻ ***noun*: highs**
1 A **high** is a maximum: *Sales had reached an all-time high during the autumn.* **2** Weather-announcers call an area of high pressure a **high**. **3** (*informal*) Someone who is on a **high** is in a state of excitement or elation, sometimes as a result of taking drugs.
▻ ***phrases*** **1 a** A boat is **high and dry** if it is out of the water, *eg* on a beach. **b** (*informal*) You leave someone **high and dry** if you leave them to look after themselves but without the means of doing so. **2** You search **high and low** for something when you look everywhere for it: *I've hunted high and low for that missing letter.* **3** (*derogatory*) You call people **high and mighty** if they speak or behave as though they thought themselves better than others: *You're not so virtuous yourself, so there's no need to be so high and mighty.* [*same as* **supercilious, haughty**] **4** For **high time** see **time**. **5 a** (*humorous*) A message or order that comes to you from **on high** comes to you from the people in authority. **b On high** also means in heaven: *praising God on high.* **6** You say that feelings or emotions **are running high** when people are getting angry or upset, *eg* when discussing something.

highbrow /ˈhaɪbraʊ/ *adjective*
You call books, programmes, entertainments or discussions **highbrow** if you consider them too intellectual or academic for the average person to understand or enjoy: *all those highbrow dinner conversations.*

high chair /ˈhaɪ tʃɛə(r)/ *noun*: **high chairs**
A **high chair** is a chair for a baby or young child, fitted with long legs to bring it up to table height.

high-class /haɪˈklɑːs/ *adjective*
High-class things are of good quality, or are good of their kind: *high-class wines.*

higher /ˈhaɪə(r)/ *adjective or adverb*
Higher is the comparative form of **high**: *Can't you throw the ball any higher than that?*

higher education /haɪər ɛdjʊˈkeɪʃən/ *noun (uncount)*
Higher education is instruction beyond the secondary-school level, at universities and colleges: *They have two children, both now in higher education.*

high-handed /haɪ'handɪd/ *adjective*
Someone who is **high-handed** forces their authority on other people without considering those people's feelings: *high-handed behaviour.* [*same as* **domineering**, **overbearing**] — *adverb* **high-handedly:** *I'm sorry if you think I acted high-handedly.* — *noun* (*uncount*) **high-handedness:** *She has a reputation at the BBC for high-handedness.*

high heels /haɪ'hi:lz/ *noun*: (*plural*)
High heels are shoes with tall narrow heels: *She hurried along the passage, high heels clicking.* □ a pair of black patent-leather high heals. [see picture at **clothing**] — *adjective* **high-heeled:** *high-heeled boots.*

high jump /'haɪ dʒʌmp/ *noun* (*used in the singular*)
The **high jump** is an athletic event in which competitors have to jump over a bar, whose height is raised as the competition progresses: *She got the bronze in the high jump.*
▻ ***phrase*** (*informal*) You are **for the high jump** when an unpleasant fate is waiting for you, *eg* death or a severe punishment.

highland /'haɪlənd/ *noun*; *adjective*
▻ ***noun*** (*used in the plural*)
The **highlands** are the mountainous parts of a country: *a walking holiday in the Scottish Highlands.*
▻ ***adjective:*** *the highland scenery.*

highlight /'haɪlaɪt/ *verb*; *noun*
▻ ***verb***: **highlights**, **highlighting**, **highlighted**
1 To **highlight** a problem or other matter is to draw attention to it: *This week's events have certainly highlighted the plight of the Muslim population.* **2** You **highlight** a passage in text when you mark it with a broad-tipped felt pen or **highlighter**.
▻ ***noun***: **highlights**
1 You call an experience a **highlight** if it is the best part of some event, period or activity: *the highlight of the conference.* [*same as* **high point**] **2** People have **highlights** put in their hair when they have small patches or streaks of it dyed blonde.

highly /'haɪlɪ/ *adverb*
1 (*intensifying*) You use **highly** like 'very' for emphasis: *It's highly unlikely that I'll be needed at the meeting.* □ *a highly infectious disease.* **2** You use **highly** to mean 'to or at a high level': *You're too highly qualified for this job.* □ *highly paid officials.* **3** You think **highly** of someone or something if you approve of them: *She speaks very highly of your work.*

highly strung /haɪlɪ 'strʌŋ/ *adjective*
Someone who is **highly strung** is rather nervous and easily gets upset or excited: *He was one of those highly-strung and sensitive children.*

high-minded /haɪ'maɪndɪd/ *adjective*
High-minded people have strong principles and high moral standards: *high-minded moralists.*

Highness /'haɪnɪs/ *noun*
You use **Your Highness** to address a prince or princess, and **His** or **Her Highness** or **Their Highnesses** to refer to them: *Their Highnesses the Prince and Princess of Wales.*

high-pitched /haɪ'pɪtʃt/ *adjective*
A **high-pitched** sound is a high shrill one: *He had a high-pitched nervous giggle.*

high point /'haɪ pɔɪnt/ *noun*: **high points**
The **high point** of some event, experience or period is its climax, or the bit that you enjoy most: *Their performance of Beethoven's Ninth Symphony was the high point of the evening.* [*same as* **highlight**]

high-powered /haɪ'paʊəd/ *adjective*
1 High-powered technical devices or machines are powerful and effective: *using a high-powered telescope.* [*same as* **powerful**] **2** You describe people as **high-powered** if they are clever, energetic, and effective at getting things done. [*same as* **dynamic**] **3 High-powered** activities demand expert knowledge and ability: *a high-powered conference on international finance.*

high-rise /'haɪraɪz/ *adjective*
High-rise buildings are modern buildings in the shape of tall narrow blocks: *Most Singaporeans live in high-rise apartment blocks.*

high-risk /haɪ'rɪsk/ *adjective*
High-risk describes **1** groups that are in particular danger from something: *Women who have started their families late are in the high-risk group.* **2** activities that are particularly dangerous: *climbing and other high-risk sports.*

highroad /'haɪroʊd/ *noun*: **highroads**
A **highroad** is a main road.

high school /'haɪ sku:l/ *noun*: **high schools**
A **high school** is a secondary school **1** in Britain for 11- to 18-year-olds. **2** (*count or uncount*) in the United States for 15- to 18-year-olds.

high spirits /haɪ'spɪrɪts/ *noun* (*plural*)
People who are full of **high spirits** are cheerful, lively, energetic and like having fun. — *adjective* **high-spirited:** *I always enjoyed her company and her high-spirited approach to life.*

high street /'haɪ stri:t/ *noun*: **high streets**
The **high street** is the main street of a town, where the big shops and banks are: *Most of the high-street banks will be raising their interest rates.*

high tea /haɪ'ti:/ *noun* (*uncount or count*; *BrE*): **high teas**
High tea is a large meal eaten in some households and served in some cafés, usually between 5.00 and 6.00 pm, consisting of a cooked main course followed by bread and cakes, with tea to drink.

high tech or **hi tech** /haɪ'tɛk/ *noun*; *adjective*
▻ ***noun*** (*uncount*; *informal*)
High tech is short for 'high technology' and refers to the use of advanced, especially electronic, equipment and devices.
▻ ***adjective*** (**high-tech**): *They can now spot these tissue abnormalities early on, using some sort of hi-tech scanner.*

high tide /haɪ'taɪd/ *noun* (*uncount*)
High tide is the time of day when the sea is at its highest on the beach or coast: *The peninsula is sometimes cut off at high tide.* [*opposite* **low tide**]

high time see **time**.

highway /'haɪweɪ/ *noun*: **highways**
1 (*AmE*) A **highway** is a main road that links towns and cities. **2** (*BrE legal*) The **highway** is any main public road: *The protesters were arrested for obstructing the highway.*

Highway Code /haɪweɪ 'koʊd/ *noun* (*used in the singular*; *BrE*)
The **Highway Code** is an official set of rules for road-users issued by the Department of Transport, or the booklet containing these.

hijack /'haɪdʒak/ *verb*: **hijacks**, **hijacking**, **hijacked**
Someone **hijacks** a plane when they take control of it by force while it is in the air, and make the pilot fly to a destination of their own choice. — *noun* **hijacker:** *The hijackers have been taken into police custody.*

hike /haɪk/ *noun*; *verb*

▷ ***noun***: **hikes**
A **hike** is a long walk in the countryside: *We went for a 14-mile hike on Sunday.*
▷ ***verb***: **hikes, hiking, hiked**
You **hike** when you go for long walks across the countryside: *He had hiked across Europe in his youth.* — *noun* **hiker:** *A party of very wet hikers were just arriving at the hostel.* — *noun* (*uncount*) **hiking:** *She listed hiking as one of her interests.*

hilarious /hɪˈleərɪəs/ *adjective*
Something that is **hilarious** is very funny: *We had some hilarious adventures on our walking trip.* — *adverb* (*intensifying*) **hilariously:** *hilariously funny stories.*

hilarity /hɪˈlarɪtɪ/ *noun* (*uncount*)
Hilarity is laughter and amusement: *The story caused a lot of hilarity.*

hill /hɪl/ *noun*: **hills**
1 A **hill** is a raised and generally rounded piece of the landscape, not as high as a mountain: *the Pentland Hills* □ *a distant range of hills.* **2** A slope on a road is also a **hill**: *We parked on a steep hill.* **3** A **hill** of something is a heap or mound: *anthills.*

hillock /ˈhɪlək/ *noun*: **hillocks**
A **hillock** is a mound or a little hill: *Something of these grassy hillocks could be Bronze-Age burial mounds.*

hillside /ˈhɪlsaɪd/ *noun*: **hillsides**
A **hillside** is the sloping side of a hill: *a south-facing hillside.*

hilltop /ˈhɪltɒp/ *noun* (*often adjectival*): **hilltops**
A **hilltop** is the top of a hill: *the hilltop castles of south-west France.*

hilly /ˈhɪlɪ/ *adjective*: **hillier, hilliest**
A **hilly** area has a lot of hills in it: *I hadn't realized the Isle of Man was so hilly.*

hilt /hɪlt/ *noun*: **hilts**
The **hilt** of a sword or dagger is its handle: *an intricately carved hilt.*
▷ ***phrase*** You back or defend someone **to the hilt** on some issue when you give them as much support as you can: *I'm backing you to the hilt over this dismissal business.*

him /hɪm/ *pronoun*
1 (*used as the object of a verb or preposition*) You use **him** to refer to a man, boy or male animal that has already been mentioned: *Dad had left a message asking me to telephone him.* □ *He said they'd given him permission to leave early.* □ *We'd already heard so much about him.* □ *I saw him open the front door and go in.* □ *'Bill has offered to help.' 'Oh, that's kind of him.'* □ *The bull was bad-tempered and I was scared of him.* □ *I'm not as old as him* (or *as he is*). □ *Are you taller than him* (or *than he is*)? **2** (*old*) Formerly **him** was widely used to refer to such words as *anyone, someone, no-one, person, child, lawyer*, where the sex was unknown, but *them* or *him or her* are now frequently used instead: *Talk to the injured person and make him* (or *them*) *as comfortable as you can.* □ *Watch the child closely and see what interests him* (or *him or her*) *most.* **3** You find **him** instead of **he** in emphatic uses: *Who's making the meal tonight? Me or him?* □ *Bill's off to Spain, lucky him.* □ *'Which is Bill?' 'That's him, in the grey suit.'*

himself /hɪmˈsɛlf/ *pronoun* (*reflexive*)
1 You use **himself** as the object of a verb or preposition where a man, boy or male animal is the subject of the sentence or clause: *He saw himself reflected in the shop window.* □ *Apparently he had taught himself the piano.* □ *Neil's hurt himself running.* □ *Is your son feeding himself already?* □ *He bought himself an ice cream.* **2 Himself** can be used for emphasis: *He admits himself that he was careless.* □ *I got the news about his engagement from Giles himself.* □ *He knew there were other people like himself being made redundant in their 50s.* **3** A man or boy does something **himself** if he does it without help or interference from anyone: *Did he really make that himself?* **4** You say that a man or boy is **himself** when he is in his normal healthy state: *He hasn't been himself lately.* □ *He isn't feeling himself.*
▷ ***phrase*** For **by himself** see **by**.

hind /haɪnd/ *adjective*
A four-legged animal's **hind** parts are at the back of its body: *The horse reared up on its hind legs.* [*same as* **rear**]

hinder /ˈhɪndə(r)/ *verb*: **hinders, hindering, hindered**
Something **hinders** you when it interferes with your progress: *As usual research has been hindered by the lack of funds.* [*same as* **hamper**; *opposite* **help, aid**]

Hindi /ˈhɪndɪ/ *noun* (*uncount*)
Hindi is the main language of northern India: *I was trying to teach myself Hindi.*

hindquarters /ˈhaɪndkwɔːtəz/ *noun* (*plural*)
The **hindquarters** of a four-legged animal are its back parts, including its back legs.

hindrance /ˈhɪndrəns/ *noun*: **hindrances**
1 You call a person or thing a **hindrance** if they interfere with your progress: *I let the children do some of the baking, though they were more of a hindrance than a help.* **2 Hindrance** is interference with the progress of someone or something: *The afternoon's business was then allowed to proceed without further hindrance.*

hindsight /ˈhaɪndsaɪt/ *noun* (*uncount*)
Hindsight is the wisdom you gain after some action or event, from knowing how it turned out, how it went wrong, and therefore how it could have been better organized: *Assessing the incident with the benefit of hindsight, they realized that it had been a mistake to resort to tear gas.*

Hindu /ˈhɪnduː/ or /hɪnˈduː/ *noun*; *adjective*
▷ ***noun***: **Hindus**
A **Hindu** is a person who practises Hinduism.
▷ ***adjective:*** *Hindu beliefs.*

Hinduism /ˈhɪndʊɪzm/ *noun* (*uncount*)
Hinduism is a religion of India that involves the worship of a large number of gods, and teaches that there is life after death.

hinge /hɪndʒ/ *noun*; *verb*
▷ ***noun***: **hinges**
The **hinge** of a door or a lid is the device that attaches it to the door frame or the box, on which it turns freely so as to open or close: *The door seemed to be hanging a bit crookedly on its hinges.* — *adjective* **hinged:** *one of those tables with two hinged flaps.*
▷ ***verb***: **hinges, hinging, hinged**

> ***phrasal verb***
> One circumstance **hinges on** or **upon** another if it depends on it: *I hope to get away to Venice in July, but it all hinges on whether I get my thesis finished in time.*

hint /hɪnt/ *noun*; *verb*
▷ ***noun***: **hints**
1 A **hint** is a suggestion or piece of information that is communicated in an indirect way: *She had given us no hint of her intention to resign.* **2** A **hint** is a piece of advice: *helpful hints for removing stains.* [*same as* **tip, suggestion**] **3** A **hint** of something is a small amount of it: *'OK,' she said, but with a hint of reluctance.* [*same as* **trace**]

▷ ***verb***: **hints, hinting, hinted**
You **hint** at something, or **hint** that something is so, when you suggest or indicate it in an indirect way: *He hinted that there might be redundancies in the next few months.* [*same as* **intimate, indicate**]

hip /hɪp/ *noun*: **hips**
Your **hips** are the two sides of the part of your body between your waist and the top of your legs, or this part at its widest point: *He stood with his hands on his hips.* □ *She fell and broke her hip* [= the top of her thigh bone].

hippie or **hippy** /'hɪpɪ/ *noun* (*old, informal*): **hippies**
Hippies are people who, especially in the 1960s and '70s, rejected the standard way of life in order to live lives based on love and peace, some of them in communities, and many of them wearing their hair long and adopting the colourful fashions of third-world countries.

hippo /'hɪpoʊ/ *noun* (*informal*): **hippos**
A **hippo** is a hippopotamus.

hippopotamus /hɪpə'pɒtəməs/ *noun*: **hippopotamuses** or **hippotami**
A **hippopotamus** is a large African animal with thick loose skin and short legs, that lives near water.

hippy see **hippie**.

hire /haɪə(r)/ *verb; noun*
▷ ***verb***: **hires, hiring, hired**
1 You **hire** something when you pay the owner for the use of it for an arranged period: *I had to hire a van to move all my stuff.*

> In British English you **hire** things for short periods, but **rent** them for longer ones: *The television isn't ours; we rent it.* In British English you always **rent** accommodation: *We're renting a cottage in the Cotswolds for a fortnight.* In American English, **hire** is used in all these senses.

2 You **hire** labourers or workers when you give them employment, usually temporary: *We hired extra labour to get the runway completed.*

> In American English you can **hire** permanent staff: *We thought you'd be good at the job; that's why we hired you.*

▷ ***noun*** (*uncount*)
Hire of something is the act of hiring it, or the fee you pay: *Hire of the hall came to £70 for the two days.*
▷ ***phrases*** **1** Something that is **for hire** is available for hiring: *Mountain Bikes for Hire.* **2** Something that is **on hire** to you is something that you have got temporarily for your use, in return for a fee that you pay the owner.

> ***phrasal verb***
> You **hire** something **out** when you allow people the use of it in return for a fee: *They hire out rowing boats in the summer.*
>
> In general, you **hire out** equipment, but **rent out** or **let** accommodation.

hire-purchase /haɪə'pɜːtʃɪs/ *noun* (*uncount; BrE*)
Hire-purchase is a system of paying for goods after you have taken possession of them, by making small regular payments to the seller until you have paid the full price.

his /hɪz/ *determiner; pronoun*
▷ ***determiner*** (*possessive*)
1 His means of, or belonging to, the male person or animal already mentioned: *Has Peter sold his house yet?* □ *He makes his own bread.* □ *I don't remember his telling me that.* □ *My poor dog's hurt his paw.* **2 His** is used in royal and noble titles: *His Majesty the King* □ *His Royal Highness Prince Charles* □ *His Grace the Duke of Kent.*
▷ ***pronoun*** (*possessive*): *He says the jacket is his.* □ *I'm using my computer, but Peter would lend you his.* □ *I don't know the man personally, but I've met a friend of his.*

hiss /hɪs/ *verb; noun*
▷ ***verb***: **hisses, hissing, hissed**
1 To **hiss** is to make a sound like a long '*s*': *I could hear the pressure cooker hissing on the kitchen stove.* **2** You **hiss** when you whisper something angrily: *'You clown!' she hissed, as loudly as she dared.* **3** An audience **hisses** a performance, or **hisses** someone wicked in a play, when they express their disapproval by making long '*s*' sounds: *The villain was hissed and booed whenever he came on stage.*
▷ ***noun***: **hisses:** *a chorus of hisses and boos.*

historian /hɪ'stɔːrɪən/ *noun*: **historians**
A **historian** is an expert in history, or someone who studies it and writes about it: *political historians.*

historic /hɪ'stɒrɪk/ *adjective*
Historic events are important or significant in history: *that historic day in April 1994 when Black South Africa voted for the first time.*

historical /hɪ'stɒrɪkəl/ *adjective*
1 Historical means relating to history or the events of the past: *historical writers* □ *The castle is recent, so of little historical interest.* **2 Historical** people actually existed and **historical** events actually happened: *Is Macbeth a historical person?* — *adverb* **historically:** *The film tries to be as historically accurate as possible.*

history /'hɪstərɪ/ *noun*: **histories**
1 (*uncount or count*) **History** is past events; the **history** of people or things is what has happened to them in the past: *In the history of Parliament nothing like this has ever occurred before.* □ *They mustn't be allowed to pull these buildings down; they're part of our history.* □ *This desk has an interesting history.* **2** (*uncount*) **History** is the study of past events, *eg* as a school or university subject: *He read history at Aberdeen University.* □ *history lessons.* **3** A **history** of something is a record or account of its past, or of its origins and development: *He was writing a history of the computer.* **4** (*used in the singular; humorous*) Someone or something that has a **history** has an interesting, in some cases unrespectable, past: *People tended to refer to her as a woman with a history.* **5** (*used in the singular; often medicine*) Someone who has a **history** of something has suffered or experienced a lot of it: *He has a history of schizophrenia.* **6** (*old*) A **history** is a play about people and events of the past: *The Comedies, Tragedies and Histories of Shakespeare.*
▷ ***phrases*** **1** Someone **makes history** when they do something important, especially become the first person to do something. **2** You say that someone or something will **go down in history** if you think people in the future will remember them for their achievements or significance.

histrionic /hɪstrɪ'ɒnɪk/ *adjective; noun*
▷ ***adjective***
Histrionic describes behaviour that is so over-emotional and theatrical as to seem insincere: *He gave a histrionic sigh, casting his eyes to heaven.* [*same as* **dramatic**] — *adverb* **histrionically:** *He gestured histrionically.*

▷ ***noun*** (*used in the plural*): **histrionics**
Histrionics are over-emotional, theatrical behaviour: *Her histrionics were beginning to bore me.*

hit /hɪt/ *verb*; *noun*
▷ ***verb***: **hits, hitting, hit**
1 a You **hit** someone or something when you deliberately bring your hand, or something you are holding, against them with force: *Mum, he keeps hitting me.* □ *The victim had been hit over the head with a hammer.* □ *He hit me on the nose.* □ *I hit him in the chest.* □ *Try and hit the ball with the centre of your racquet.* □ *Go on, hit harder!* [*same as* **strike**; compare **punch**, **slap**, **bash**, **thump**, **whack**] **b** (*especially sport*) You **hit** something somewhere when you make it move somewhere by bringing something you are holding, such as a bat, stick or racquet, against it with force: *I can't even hit the ball over the net.* □ *Gower hits the ball to the leg side. One run.* □ *She hit two fantastic shots down the centre line.* **c** One thing **hits** another when it comes into contact with it with force; you **hit** a part of your body on or against something when that part of you comes into contact with it, with force: *Her car hit a wall at 70 mph.* □ *People started throwing stones, and one hit a policeman on the ear.* □ *One climber got hit on the shoulder by a falling rock.* □ *He fell and hit his head on the step.* □ *His head hit the step as he fell.* □ *I hit my foot against a boulder and stumbled.* [*same as* **strike**; compare **knock**] **d** A bomb, bullet or other missile **hits** someone or something, whether or not they are being aimed at, when it reaches them: *The bullet hit the lioness and she crumpled in front of them.* □ *Three of our planes were hit by anti-aircraft fire.* □ *One bomb hit the church and destroyed the tower.*
2 a Something **hits** a person or thing hard or badly when it affects them badly: *The loss of a baby in late pregnancy is bound to hit the mother hard.* □ *The cricketing programme has been badly hit by the weather.* **b** Something such as a thought or realization **hits** you when you suddenly have it: *I was hit by a fresh consideration: where were the visitors going to sleep?* □ *The thought kept hitting me that I could have prevented her death.* [*same as* **strike**] **c** You **hit** something when you meet or encounter it as you progress: *If we walk in that direction we should hit the main road pretty soon.* □ *Life can't always be good; you're bound to hit a bad patch now and then.* [*same as* **meet**]
▷ ***noun***: **hits**
1 A **hit** is an act of hitting: *Give it a good strong hit.* [compare **blow**] **2** A **hit** is a successful shot, or an instance of a missile reaching its target: *The cruiser had received a direct hit in the bows from a torpedo.* □ *You've scored three hits and two misses so far.* [*opposite* **miss**] **3** (*informal*) Something that is a popular success is a **hit**: *This show's going to be a hit.* □ *hit songs of the twenties.* [*opposite* **failure**, **flop**]
▷ ***phrases*** **1** (*informal*) Two people **hit it off** with each other when they like each other and become friendly as soon as they meet: *The two girls hit it off straight away.* **2** You **score a hit** or **make a hit** with someone when you impress them: *She scored a hit with the judges when she came to her final piece.* □ *He certainly likes you; you've obviously made quite a hit there.*

phrasal verbs
hit at To **hit at** something or someone is to make them the target of your attack or criticism: *1968 saw student revolts that hit at the hierarchical organization of society.* □ *I realized she was trying to hit at me particularly in her final comments.*
hit back You **hit back**, or **hit** someone **back** when you attack your attacker in return: *Why don't you hit back?* □ *He hit me and I hit him back.* □ *Her letter hits back at last week's critical article.*
hit on or **hit upon** You **hit on** or **upon** an idea, answer or solution when you think of it: *After much discussion we hit on a plan.* □ *I hit on the answer quite by chance.*
hit out You **hit out** at someone or something when you attack them physically or verbally: *The report hits out at hospital mismanagement.* □ *She hit out at him with her fists and managed to escape.*

hit-and-miss /hɪtən'mɪs/ or **hit-or-miss** /hɪtə'mɪs/ *adjective* (*informal*)
Something that is **hit-and-miss** happens in an unsystematic way, so that you are never certain of a satisfactory result: *Their screening methods are pretty hit-or-miss.*

hit-and-run /hɪtən'rʌn/ *adjective*
A **hit-and-run** driver is a driver who knocks down a pedestrian or cyclist and neither stops to help nor reports the accident.

hitch /hɪtʃ/ *noun*; *verb*
▷ ***noun***: **hitches**
A **hitch** is a slight difficulty or problem: *The launch was delayed by a last-minute hitch.* □ *Fortunately the ceremony went off without a hitch* [= went off smoothly and successfully]. [*same as* **snag**]
▷ ***verb***: **hitches, hitching, hitched**
1 You **hitch** a lift by signalling to a driver to stop and getting a lift towards the place you want to go to; you **hitch** when you hitch-hike: *I hitched a ride with a truck-driver.* □ *After university he spent a year hitching round the world.* **2** You **hitch** one thing on to another when you fasten it to the other: *The ponies were standing ready hitched to the wagon.*

phrasal verb
You **hitch up** something you are wearing when you pull it up: *The trousers were too big for him and he kept having to hitch them up.*

hitch-hike /'hɪtʃhaɪk/ *verb*: **hitch-hikes, hitch-hiking, hitch-hiked**
You **hitch-hike** when you travel by getting free rides in other people's vehicles, asking drivers to stop for you by signalling to them with a raised thumb: *One day we hitch-hiked from Oxford to Stonehenge.* — *noun* **hitch-hiker:** *We picked up a couple of Swedish hitch-hikers.*

hi-tech see **high-tech**.

hither /'hɪðə(r)/ *adverb* (*literary*)
You use **hither** to mean to, or towards, the place where you are: *What brought you hither?*
▷ ***phrase*** (*literary*) Things that move **hither and thither** move in all directions: *We watched the butterflies flying hither and thither.*

hitherto /'hɪðətuː/ *adverb* (*formal*)
Something that has been so **hitherto** has been so until now: *Hitherto the librarian had always been in charge of the keys.*

hit list /'hɪt lɪst/ *noun*: **hit lists**
A **hit list** is a list kept by a terrorist organization of people they want to kill; you can also refer to organizations that are scheduled for closure as being on the **hit list**: *the 32 coal mines on the government's hit list.*

hit man /'hɪt man/ *noun* (*informal*): **hit men**
A **hit man** is a person that someone hires to murder another person for them.

HIV /eɪtʃ aɪ'viː/ *noun* (*uncount*)

HIV is a virus that reduces people's ability to fight infection, and can cause AIDS; someone who is **HIV-positive** has the HIV virus.

hive /haɪv/ *noun*: **hives**
1 A **hive** is a beehive. **2** (*often humorous*) A place that is described as a **hive** of activity or industry is full of people busily doing or making things.

hoard /hɔːd/ *noun*; *verb*
▻ ***noun***: **hoards**
A **hoard** of things is a store of them that you have saved and keep somewhere: *She added the rubber band to the hoard in her desk drawer.*
▻ ***verb***: **hoards, hoarding, hoarded**
You **hoard** things, or **hoard** things up, when you save them, often secretly, and keep them somewhere for future use: *People would buy food they didn't need and hoard it in case of future shortages.*

hoarding /ˈhɔːdɪŋ/ *noun*: **hoardings**
A **hoarding** is a large board, *eg* standing at the side of the road, on which advertisements are displayed.

hoarse /hɔːs/ *adjective*
A **hoarse** voice is rough-sounding and harsh; you are **hoarse** when your voice sounds rough and unclear, *eg* when you have a cold or sore throat: *Sorry, I'm a bit hoarse this morning.* — *adverb* **hoarsely:** *He spoke hoarsely, as if he were an habitual smoker.* — *noun* (*uncount*) **hoarseness:** *What's the best cure for hoarseness?*

hoary /ˈhɔːrɪ/ *adjective*: **hoarier, hoariest**
1 (*literary*) Something that is **hoary** is grey or white: *His hoary locks came down to his shoulders.* **2** A **hoary** subject or joke is an old and boring one: *He repeated all the hoary old anecdotes.*

hoax /hoʊks/ *noun*: **hoaxes**
A **hoax** is the kind of trick in which someone gives a warning of danger that does not exist, or reports an accident or fire that has not occurred: *The bomb warning turned out to be a hoax.*

hob /hɒb/ *noun*: **hobs**
A **hob** is a set of rings or plates on a stove that heat up for cooking on: *a built-in oven and separate hob.*

hobble /ˈhɒbəl/ *verb*: **hobbles, hobbling, hobbled**
1 You **hobble** if you walk with difficulty, with short unsteady steps, *eg* when your legs or feet are injured or painful: *One 104-year-old lady had hobbled half a mile to cast her vote.* **2** To **hobble** an animal is to tie its legs together loosely, to stop it straying.

hobby /ˈhɒbɪ/ *noun*: **hobbies**
A **hobby** is something you do in your spare time for relaxation and enjoyment: *I see you included portrait-drawing in your list of hobbies.* [*same as* **pastime**, **pursuit**]

hobby horse /ˈhɒbɪ hɔːs/ *noun*: **hobby horses**
1 A **hobby horse** is a toy horse, consisting of a horse's head attached to a long stick, which you sit astride and pretend to ride. **2** Your **hobby horse** is the subject you most enjoy talking about, because you have strong opinions about it: *Punctuation is one of my hobby horses.*

hobnob /ˈhɒbnɒb/ *verb* (*usually derogatory*): **hobnobs, hobnobbing, hobnobbed**
You **hobnob** with someone, especially someone more important, or of higher social rank, than you, if you are friends with them and spend time with them: *He's often to be seen hobnobbing with the grand and wealthy.* [*same as* **fraternize**]

hobo /ˈhoʊboʊ/ *noun* (*AmE*): **hobos** or **hoboes**
A **hobo** is someone without work or a home, who wanders from place to place. [*same as* **tramp**]

hock /hɒk/ *noun* (*uncount or count*)
Hock is a German white wine from the Rhine valley: *a bottle of hock.*

hockey /ˈhɒkɪ/ *noun* (*uncount*)
Hockey is a game played by two teams of eleven players with long curved sticks and a small hard ball, on a pitch like a football field with a goal at each end, into which players must hit the ball in order to score. [see also **ice hockey**.]

hodgepodge see **hotchpotch**.

hoe /hoʊ/ *noun*; *verb*
▻ ***noun***: **hoes**
A **hoe** is a long-handled gardening tool with a metal blade at one end, that you use for removing weeds and breaking up soil. [see picture at **tool**]
▻ ***verb***: **hoes, hoeing, hoed**
You **hoe** a bed, or the garden, or a field, when you remove weeds from it or break up the soil with a hoe.

hog /hɒg/ *noun*; *verb*
▻ ***noun***: **hogs**
A **hog** is a castrated male pig.
▻ ***verb*** (*informal*): **hogs, hogging, hogged**
You **hog** something when you use or occupy it selfishly: *He hogs the bathroom for hours.*
▻ ***phrase*** (*informal*) You **go the whole hog** when you do something in the most luxurious or expensive way possible: *She wants to go the whole hog, with a white wedding, marquee, the lot.*

ho ho *interjection*
Ho ho is a written repesentation of laughter.

hoist /hɔɪst/ *verb*; *noun*
▻ ***verb***: **hoists, hoisting, hoisted**
1 You **hoist** something heavy somewhere when you lift it there: *The piano had to be hoisted up through a window.* **2** You **hoist** a flag or sail when you raise it into position with ropes.
▻ ***noun***: **hoists**
A **hoist** is a lift for goods, or some other device for lifting heavy things: *Library books ordered by readers are brought up from the stacks on a hoist.*

hold[1] /hoʊld/ *verb*; *noun*
▻ ***verb***: **holds, holding, held**
1 a You **hold** something when you have your hands, fingers or arms firmly round it; you can also **hold** things in your mouth, between your teeth, or with other parts of you: *She examined the ring, holding it between her thumb and forefinger.* □ *He holds his pen a funny way.* □ *Hold the baby a minute, would you?* □ *She put her arms round him and held him close.* □ *She got on to the bike behind him, put her arms round his waist and held tight.* **b** You **hold** yourself well or badly if you stand, walk and sit in the correct, or incorrect, manner; you **hold** a part of your body in a certain position if you put it in that position and keep it there: *She held herself stiffly upright.* □ *Hold your head up when you walk.* □ *Hold your shoulders back.* □ *Several children were holding their hands up ready to answer.* **c** One thing **holds** another in a certain position when it keeps it fixed or supported in that position: *The book was falling apart, so I tied a bit of string round it to hold it together.* □ *The ceiling was being held up temporarily by a couple of wooden supports.* □ *You have to hold your opponent's shoulders down against the floor for a whole minute.*
2 a One thing **holds** another if it contains it; something **holds** a certain amount if it can contain it: *The tin held some stale-looking biscuits.* □ *The bus holds up to 53 passengers.* □ *My water bottle will only hold a pint.* **b** Something **holds** a certain quality for you if

you feel, or are affected by, that quality in it: *The Chamber of Horrors held a terrible fascination for us as small children.* **c** You wonder what the future **holds** for you when you wonder what is going to happen to you.

3 a You **hold** power, or a post or office, when you have it: *during the years 1970 to 1974, when Heath held office as prime minister* □ *She held a teaching post in a secondary school.* **b** You **hold** a qualification, degree, diploma or certificate if you have gained it: *She holds an MA in the teaching of English as a foreign language.* **c** You **hold** a record for some sporting event or other activity if you have achieved it and no-one else has beaten it: *For two years he held the record for the junior half-mile.*

4 a You **hold** someone, or **hold** them prisoner, when you keep them locked up, or keep them prisoner: *The police have arrested a man and are holding him for questioning.* □ *An intruder had broken into her home and was holding her at gunpoint.* **b** In war, you **hold** a place when you defend it from capture by the enemy: *General Pigot had seized Malta and was holding it for the French.*

5 a If you tell someone you **are holding** them responsible for something you mean that they will be blamed if is not done, or not properly attended to: *We are holding you responsible for the prisoners' safety.* **b** You **hold** someone to their word when you insist that they keep their promise.

6 a You **hold** an opinion or belief if you have it: *I've always held that children have much subtler minds than adults.* □ *Not many people hold that view.* **b** You **hold** something dear or sacred if you regard it as precious or sacred and guard it carefully; you **hold** someone or something in respect or awe if you admire, respect or fear them: *They were witnessing the destructon of their homes and everything they held most dear.* □ *As college principal she was held in some awe by the students.* **c** You **hold** someone responsible, or to blame, for something that has gone wrong, if you think it was their fault.

7 a Something **holds** people's attention when they continue to watch it or be interested in it: *The film didn't hold the children's interest for long.* **b** When you are singing or playing an instrument, you **hold** a note when you make it last or continue: *The sopranos should hold that top note for a bar and a half.* **c** On the telephone, if someone asks you to **hold** the line, or **hold**, they are asking you to wait, *eg* till they connect you, or till they find the person or information you want: *That extension is engaged; will you hold?*

8 a Any kind of supporting structure that looks likely to collapse **holds** if it keeps standing or remains firm: *Miraculously the bridge held and they escaped across it.* **b** You **hold** still or steady when you keep still and don't move: *It was difficult to get the child to hold still while I dressed his injured leg.* **c** Good weather **holds** when it continues. **d** Your luck **holds** when it continues to be good. **e** An offer or invitation **holds** if it remains available for you to accept: *I'd be most grateful for a bed for the night, if your invitation still holds.* [*same as* **stand**] **f** Something **holds** good or true if it remains valid or true, *eg* when circumstances alter: *The insurance arrangements hold good whether or not the woman marries.*

9 a You **hold** an event such as a meeting or party when you organize it and it takes place: *A reception will be held to mark her retirement.* □ *The Prime Minister today held discussions with the Cabinet on a number of issues.* **b** You **hold** a conversation with someone when you talk with them: *He found them holding an animated conversation in a corner of the room.*

▻ ***noun***: **holds**

1 (*used in the singular*) Your **hold** on something is your action of holding it: *She wouldn't relax her hold on his arm even for a second.* □ *He lost his hold on the rope but quickly regained it.* [*same as* **grasp**, **grip**] **2** Climbers' hand**holds** and foot**holds** are the cracks and ledges where they put their fingers and toes to support their weight as they climb. **3 Holds** in wrestling are methods of grasping opponents so that you can gain control over them and throw them. **4** (*used in the singular*) You have a **hold** over someone if you control them, or if you have the means of persuading them, *eg* because you know something bad about them: *Little by little the government tightened its hold over all aspects of Singaporean life.* □ *He seemed to have some mysterious hold over her.* **5** (*uncount*) You get, take, or keep, **hold** of something when you put or keep your hand or fingers tightly round it: *Get hold of that branch and you can pull yourself up.* □ *Keep tight hold of my hand.* □ *She had hold of my sleeve and wouldn't let go.* □ *He grabbed hold of the girl by the shoulders and shook her roughly.* □ *She caught hold of the rope as it swung towards her.* **6** (*uncount*) Something takes **hold** when it gets firmly started or established: *The flames took hold with frightening speed.*

▻ ***phrases*** **1** You **get hold of** something when you obtain it; you **get hold of** a person when you find them or manage to contact them: *I'll see if I can get hold of a copy for you.* □ *I can't get hold of Pat; is she away?* **2** You say '**hold it**' or '**hold everything**' to people when you want them to stop what they are doing: *Hold it! We'll have to start counting again.*

phrasal verbs

hold against You **hold** someone's behaviour **against** them if you regard it as wrong and treat them more severely because of it: *I won't hold it against you if you refuse to take part in the questionnaire.*

hold back 1 You **hold back** from doing something when you are unwilling or reluctant to do it, or hesitate before doing it; something **holds** you **back** when it makes you hesitate: *I'd always previously held back from intervening in the quarrels between my daughter and her husband.* □ *She'd have liked to volunteer but shyness held her back.* **2** You **hold** someone **back** if you prevent them from making full use of their abilities: *He felt that he'd held his wife back and that she'd have been better off without him.* **3** You **hold back** information that someone needs when you don't give it to them: *I felt sure she was holding something back.* [*same as* **withhold**]

hold down You **hold down** a job when you work at it successfully and manage to keep it: *She seemed to be holding down at least three jobs simultaneously.*

hold off 1 You **hold off** attackers when you resist them successfully: *He could hold off his creditors no longer.* **2** The rain **holds off** when it does not rain, especially when you were worried that it was going to. [*same as* **keep off**]

hold on 1 You **hold on** when you keep your hands or arms firmly or tightly round something: *Put your hands on the cross bar and hold on tight.* **2** You ask someone to **hold on**, *eg* on the telephone, when you want them to wait: *Please hold on a minute.* □ *Hold on; I'm not quite ready.* □ *Sorry, we can't hold on any longer.* [*same as* **hang on**]

hold on to You **hold on to** something **a** when you put your hand or fingers tightly round it: *Hold on to my arm.* [*same as* **grip**] **b** when you keep it: *Hold on to that receipt.* □ *He was still managing to hold on to his position in the government.* [*same as* **hang on**]

hold out 1 You **hold out** your hand or something you are holding when you extend it, usually towards someone: *She held out her hand and I took it.* □ *I held out the pen to him.* □ *She held out her hand for the money.* 2 You **hold out** when you manage to survive in spite of difficulties or opposition: *The beseiged population had held out for three weeks without proper food.* 3 You **hold out** for something when you insist on getting it, and refuse to accept anything less: *The women were holding out for equal pay with male employees.*
hold up 1 Something or someone **holds** you **up** when they delay you: *Sorry, I got held up just as I was leaving.* □ *What held you up?* 2 You **hold up** something to people as an example of what they should regard as good or bad when you draw their attention to it, making clear your approval or disapproval: *My sister was always held up to me as a model child.*
hold with You say you do not **hold with** something if you do not approve of it: *Mental arithmetic was good enough for our generation; I don't hold with all these calculators in the classroom.*

hold[2] /hoʊld/ *noun*: **holds**
The **hold** of a ship or aircraft is the place where luggage or cargo is stored.

holdall /'hoʊldɔːl/ *noun*: **holdalls**
A **holdall** is a travelling bag for holding your clothes and belongings.

holder /'hoʊldə(r)/ *noun*: **holders**
1 A **holder** is a specially designed device or container for putting or keeping something in: *We were served with plastic cups of coffee in flimsy holders.* 2 The **holder** of something such as a ticket, licence, certificate or qualification is the person who has it: *Ticket-holders Queue Here.* 3 **Holders** of a certain view or opinion are people who have it: *holders of extreme right-wing views.*

holding /'hoʊldɪŋ/ *noun*; *adjective*
▻ ***noun***: **holdings**
1 A **holding** is a piece of land owned by you or rented from someone else, that you farm or cultivate. 2 Your **holdings** in a company are the shares you own in it.
▻ ***adjective***
1 **Holding** describes a temporary arrangement or a procedure used for dealing with an emergency: *He was using his mother's flat as a holding address.* 2 The **holding** company of a particular industrial concern or number of concerns is the company that owns and controls them, usually without direct involvement in production.

hold-up /'hoʊldʌp/ *noun*: **hold-ups**
1 A **hold-up** is a delay, or something that causes it: *The cable-laying was causing huge traffic hold-ups.* 2 A **hold-up** is an act of threatening someone with a gun to make them hand over money: *The men involved in the hold-up had been caught on video and would be recognized again.*

hole /hoʊl/ *noun*; *verb*
▻ ***noun***: **holes**
1 A **hole** is a hollow place in something solid: *They dug a hole and buried the rubbish.* □ *There's a hole that needs filling in one of your back teeth.* 2 A **hole** is an opening or gap right through something: *Rain was pouring in through a hole in the roof.* 3 A small animal's **hole** is its home or burrow: *rabbit holes* □ *The creature disappeared into its hole.* 4 (*informal*) People sometimes refer to an unpleasant, uncomfortable or uninteresting place as a **hole**: *I hate this hole; I'd leave tomorrow if I could afford to.* [*same as* **dump**] 5 (*golf*) A **hole** is one of the 18 small round numbered hollows into which players must hit the ball; the section of the course preceding each of these, over which the ball must be played, is also called a **hole**.
▻ ***verb***: **holes, holing, holed**
1 A ship **is holed** when a hole is made in it: *The boat had drifted on to rocks and was badly holed.* 2 (*golf*) You **hole**, or **hole** the ball, in a certain number, when you get the ball into a hole after that number of shots: *Have you ever holed in one?*
▻ ***phrases*** 1 (*informal*) Something **makes a hole in** a sum of money when it uses up a lot of it: *That holiday must have made a hole in their savings.* 2 (*informal*) You **pick holes in** something such as a plan or argument when you criticize it or find faults in it.

phrasal verb
(*informal*) Someone **holes up** somewhere when they hide there: *He holed up in a friend's flat till the fuss was over.*

holiday /'hɒlɪdeɪ/ *noun*; *verb*
▻ ***noun***: **holidays**
1 (*count or uncount*) A **holiday** is a period of time that you have away from your work or job, and often away from home, enjoying yourself in some activity or just relaxing: *We're going for a walking holiday in Corsica.* □ *pleasant holiday weather.* [*same as* **vacation**; compare **leave**] 2 (*used in the plural*) The **holidays** are the period between two academic or legal terms, when no classes are held, or cases tried: *I'm going abroad sometime during the summer holidays.* [*same as* **vacation**] 3 A day on which you do not have to go to work, *eg* because it is a religious festival, is also a **holiday**: *Next Monday's a bank holiday.*
▻ ***verb***: **holidays, holidaying, holidayed**
You **holiday** somewhere when you spend a holiday there: *Their house was broken into while they were holidaying in France.*
▻ ***phrase*** You are **on holiday** when you are having a holiday; you go **on holiday** when you go away for a holiday: *She got me to water her plants whenever she went on holiday.*

holiday camp /'hɒlɪdeɪ kamp/ *noun*: **holiday camps**
A **holiday camp** is a place that provides holiday accommodation for a large number of people, and organizes activities and entertainment for them.

holidaymaker /'hɒlɪdeɪmeɪkə(r)/ *noun*: **holidaymaker**
A **holidaymaker** is a person who is having a holiday away from home: *The beach was crowded with holidaymakers.*

holiness /'hoʊliːnəs/ *noun* (*uncount*)
1 **Holiness** is the quality of being holy or sacred: *her purity and holiness of spirit.* 2 You use the title **Your Holiness** to address the Pope, and **His Holiness** to refer to him; these titles are used also for leaders of religions other than Christianity.

holler /'hɒlə(r)/ *verb* (*informal*; *especially AmE*): **hollers, hollering, hollered**
You **holler** when you cry noisily or shout.

hollow /'hɒloʊ/ *adjective*; *noun*; *verb*
▻ ***adjective***
1 Something that is **hollow** has a space or hole inside it: *The tree trunk was hollow.* 2 A **hollow** surface is an inward-curving one: *famine victims with sunken eyes and hollow cheeks.* 3 A **hollow** sound is a deep one with a slight echo: *Our voices sounded hollow in the unfurnished room.* 4 A **hollow** victory is one that was not worth winning, because nothing has been gained

by it. **5** A **hollow** promise is one that you don't intend to keep; opinions and intentions that you express sound **hollow** when people know you don't mean them or cannot fulfil them. [*same as* **empty**] **6 Hollow** laughter is bitter, unamused laughter. — *adverb* **hollowly:** *Her steps echoed hollowly along the corridor.* □ *She laughed hollowly.* — *noun* (*uncount*) **hollowness:** *the hollowness of their triumph.*

▻ ***noun***: **hollows**

A **hollow** is an inward-curving area, or a part of a surface that is lower than the surrounding area: *The farm was hidden from view in a deep hollow in the landscape.* [*same as* **dip, depression**]

▻ ***verb***: **hollows, hollowing, hollowed**

> ***phrasal verb***
> You **hollow out** something solid when you remove the inside of it: *Their canoes are hollowed-out tree-trunks.*

holly /ˈhɒlɪ/ *noun* (*uncount*)

Holly is an evergreen tree or bush with shiny dark prickly-edged leaves and red berries, often used to decorate the house at Christmas.

holocaust /ˈhɒləkɔːst/ *noun*: **holocausts**

1 A **holocaust** is a disaster such as a war or great fire, in which there is death and destruction on a large scale: *the much-feared nuclear holocaust.* **2** The murder of six million Jews by the Nazis during World War 2 is referred to as the **Holocaust**.

hologram /ˈhɒləgram/ *noun*: **holograms**

A **hologram** is a photograph created by laser beams, that appears three-dimensional when looked at from certain angles or in certain kinds of light.

holster /ˈhoʊlstə(r)/ *noun*: **holsters**

A **holster** is a leather holder or case for a gun, usually attached to a belt.

holy /ˈhoʊlɪ/ *adjective*: **holier, holiest**

1 Holy describes things that relate to God or to religion: *the Holy Scriptures* □ *a picture of the Holy Family.* [*same as* **sacred**] **2** Someone who is described as **holy** or as leading a **holy** life lives a life of moral purity and goodness, dedicated to God or to religion.

homage /ˈhɒmɪdʒ/ *noun* (*uncount*)

Homage is deep respect or honour given to someone, or the ceremonies that express this: *We are gathered here to pay homage to the brave who died in two world wars.*

home /hoʊm/ *noun*; *adjective*; *adverb*; *verb*

▻ ***noun***: **homes**

1 (*uncount or count*) Your **home** is the place where you live, where your family are, or where you belong: *Thank you for inviting me to your home.* □ *first-time home-buyers* □ *A whole month in a British home should improve their English.* □ *It's nice to get back to your own home.* □ *Plenty of husbands stay at home and look after the children.* □ *We were only a few miles from home when we had the accident.* □ *A good proportion of their day is spent travelling between home and work.* □ *She gave a home to* [= took into her own home to look after] *numerous stray animals.* □ *children from broken homes* [= whose parents have divorced] □ *He returned to Germany and made his home in Marburg.* □ *A family of rats had made their home under the floorboards.* □ *I must find a home for* [= somewhere to put] *these extra books.* **2** (*uncount, or used in the singular*) Your **home** is also the city, area or country you come from, or where you were born: *She always regarded the island as home.* □ *Latvia is my real home.* □ *My home town is Sheffield.* **3** A **home** is a building where people who have no-one to look after them and are too young, old or ill to look after themselves live and are cared for: *Her early years were spent in a series of children's homes.* □ *old people's homes.* **4** The **home** of something is the place where it began or was invented: *America, the home of jazz.* **5** (*computers*) **Home** is the beginning of the line or the section you are on; you press **home**, or the **home** key, to return there. [*opposite* **end**]

▻ ***adjective***

1 Your **home** life and **home** comforts are your life at home with your family and the comforts you enjoy there. [*same as* **domestic**] **2 Home** affairs are events in your own country as distinct from abroad; goods produced for the **home** market are for sale in your own country. [*same as* **internal**; *opposite* **foreign, overseas**] **3** (*sport*) A team plays a **home** match when they play it on their own ground rather than the opposing team's ground. [*opposite* **away**]

▻ ***adverb***

1 Home means at or to the place where you live: *We got home about 6.30.* □ *I usually go home at the weekends.* □ *The journey home was much quicker than I'd expected.* □ *Is Mick home yet?* □ (*especially AmE*) *We called round but he wasn't home.* □ *recent cases of home-alone kids.* **2** You hammer or drive something such as a nail **home** when you hammer it into place. **3** You drive or hammer a point **home** when you manage to make people recognize or accept it; a point or argument goes **home** when the person at whom it is aimed recognizes and accepts it: *I hinted that she was behaving selfishly and I think the point went home.* **4** Something comes, or is brought, **home** to you when circumstances make you suddenly and strongly aware of it: *The pictures from Rwanda have brought home to us the full horror of the refugees' plight.* **5** In races and in some games, you are **home** when you reach the finishing line: *Her horse romped home to win by four lengths.*

▻ ***phrases*** **1 a** You are **at home** in a particular situation or with particular equipment when you are familiar with it and feel confident and relaxed: *He's at home with computers of any kind.* **b** You feel **at home** when you feel welcome and comfortable: *They gave me a drink and made me feel at home right away.* **c** A team is playing **at home** when it is playing a match on its own ground. [*opposite* **away**] **d** Events **at home** are events in your own country, as distinct from abroad. **2** When you tell a visitor to your house to **make themselves at home** you are inviting them to relax and treat the place as though they lived there: *The children are asleep, so just make yourself at home; we'll be back about 11.30.* **3** (*informal*) If you say that something is **nothing to write home about** you mean it is not very good or interesting.

▻ ***verb***: **homes, homing, homed**

> ***phrasal verb***
> You **home in on** a target when you find it and attack it: *sophisticated missiles that home in on military targets* □ *Try to home in on the weakest points in their argument.* [*same as* **pinpoint**]

home- /hoʊm/

Home-produced things are made or produced by people in their own homes, not in a factory or shop: *home-grown fruit and vegetables.*

homecoming /ˈhoʊmkʌmɪŋ/ *noun* (*count or uncount*): **homecomings**

Someone's **homecoming** is their return home after being away a long time.

home economics /hoʊm ɛkə'nɒmɪks/ *noun* (*uncount*)
Home economics is a school subject that teaches you the skills you need to run a house efficiently.

home ground /hoʊm 'graʊnd/ *noun*: **home grounds**
A team's **home ground** is their own playing field.
▻ ***phrase*** You are **on home ground 1** when you are near your own home, so that your surroundings are familiar and you know where you are. **2** when you are talking about something that you know about.

home help /hoʊm 'hɛlp/ *noun* (*BrE*): **home helps**
A **home help** is a person who is employed, usually by the local authority, to cook and clean for people who are old or ill.

homeland /'hoʊmland/ *noun*: **homelands**
Your **homeland** is your native country.

homeless /'hoʊmləs/ *noun*; *adjective*
▻ ***adjective***
Homeless people have nowhere to live: *Flood damage has left thousands homeless.*
▻ ***noun*** (*with a plural verb*)
The **homeless** are people with nowhere to live: *Tuberculosis was on the increase among London's homeless.* — *noun* (*uncount*) **homelessness:** *the problem of homelessness in all our big cities.*

homely /'hoʊmlɪ/ *adjective*: **homelier**, **homeliest**
1 Homely things are pleasantly simple and ordinary: *The furnishings were homely and comfortable rather than smart.* [*same as* **plain**] **2** A **homely** place or atmosphere is one where you feel welcome and relaxed. **3** (*AmE*) If you describe a person as **homely** you mean they are not good-looking. [*same as* **plain**]

home-made /hoʊm'meɪd/ *adjective*
Home-made things are made by people in their own homes, not in a shop or factory: *home-made marmalade.*

homeopathy see **homoeopathy**.

homeowner /'hoʊmoʊnə(r)/ *noun*: **homeowners**
A **homeowner** is a person who owns their own home.

homesick /'hoʊmsɪk/ *adjective*
You are **homesick** when you are feeling unhappy because you are away from your home and family and you are missing them: *Suddenly I felt homesick for the grey city and its smells.* — *noun* (*uncount*) **homesickness:** *During her first term at university she suffered severe bouts of homesickness.*

homespun /'hoʊmspʌn/ *adjective*
Homespun philosophy, theories or advice are simple and uncomplicated.

homestead /'hoʊmstɛd/ *noun*: **homesteads**
A **homestead** is a house, especially a farmhouse, with land and smaller buildings round it.

home truth /hoʊm 'truːθ/ *noun* (*usually in the plural*): **home truths** /hoʊm 'truːðz/
You learn a few **home truths** when someone tells you unpleasant facts about yourself that they think you ought to know.

homeward /'hoʊmwəd/ *adjective*; *adverb*
▻ ***adjective***
A **homeward** journey is a journey home.
▻ ***adverb*** (also **homewards**)
You travel **homewards** when you go towards your home: *I spotted her walking homewards and gave her a lift.*

homework /'hoʊmwɜːk/ *noun* (*uncount*)
1 Homework is work that teachers give students to do at home: *I've got masses of homework to do.* **2** People say you have done your **homework**, *eg* when you are giving a speech or conducting an interview, if you seem to be well prepared and to have done a lot of research beforehand.

homicidal /hɒmɪ'saɪdəl/ *adjective*
A **homicidal** person is someone who is likely to commit murder: *He's worried that he may have homicidal tendencies.*

homicide /'hɒmɪsaɪd/ *noun* (*uncount or count*; *especially AmE*)
Homicide is murder, or the illegal killing of one person by another: *He will be charged with culpable homicide rather than murder.*

homily /'hɒmɪlɪ/ *noun*: **homilies**
A **homily** is a long dull talk that someone gives you about how to behave. [*same as* **sermon**, **lecture**]

homing /'hoʊmɪŋ/ *adjective*
1 A **homing** device fitted to a missile guides it to its target. **2** A **homing** pigeon is able to return home even when it has been released a long way away; animals with **homing** instincts can remember places and return there.

homoeopathy or **homeopathy** /hoʊmɪ'ɒpəθɪ/ or /hɒmɪ'ɒpəθɪ/ *noun* (*uncount*)
Homoeopathy is a system of treating diseases by giving the patient small quantities of substances that in large quantities would cause a disease similar to the one they have. — *adjective* **homoeopathic** or **homeopathic** /hoʊmɪə'paθɪk/ or /hɒmɪə'paθɪk/: *homoeopathic medicines.*

homogeneous /hɒmə'dʒiːnɪəs/ *adjective*
A **homogeneous** collection or group consists of things or people that are all of the same kind: *The exhibition consisted of a not very homogeneous collection of pictures and sculpture.* [*same as* **comparable**, **consistent**, **uniform**; *opposite* **diverse**, **heterogeneous**] — *noun* (*uncount*) **homogeneity** /hoʊmədʒə'niːətɪ/: *The work has been compiled by a number of different contributors and lacks homogeneity of style.*

homograph /'hɒməgrɑːf/ *noun*: **homographs**
Homographs are words that are spelt the same but pronounced differently, like *lead* [pronounced /liːd/ and meaning 'guide'] and *lead* [pronounced /lɛd/ and meaning 'the metal'].

homonym /'hɒmənɪm/ *noun*: **homonyms**
Homonyms are words that have the same spelling and pronunciation but a different meaning, like *post* [= the mail] and *post* [= a stake or support].

homophone /'hɒməfoʊn/ *noun*: **homophones**
Homophones are words that have the same pronunciation but a different spelling and meaning, like *break* and *brake*.

homosexual /hɒmə'sɛkʃʊəl/ *adjective*; *noun*
▻ ***adjective***
A person who is **homosexual** is sexually attracted to people of the same sex as themselves: *He realized he had always had homosexual inclinations.*
▻ ***noun***: **homosexuals:** *discrimination against homosexuals.* — *noun* (*uncount*) **homosexuality:** *The armed services do not tolerate homosexuality in their ranks.*

hone /hoʊn/ *verb*: **hones**, **honing**, **honed**
1 To **hone** a tool is to sharpen it. **2** You **hone** something when you gradually shape and improve it till it is in the form you want: *a finely honed piece of writing.*

honest /'ɒnɪst/ *adjective*
▻ ***adjective***
1 You are **honest** about something if you tell the truth about it and hide nothing: *He was quite honest about his intention to apply for another job.* □ *Do you like it? I want an honest answer.* □ *What's your honest opinion of*

the book? [*same as* **truthful**, **candid**; *opposite* **dishonest**, **untruthful**] **2** Someone who is **honest** does not cheat or steal, and can be trusted: *I thought he had an honest face.* [*same as* **trustworthy**; *opposite* **dishonest**, **untrustworthy**] **3** An **honest** attempt to do something is a sincere one: *She was now making an honest effort to work harder.*

▻ ***phrase*** You use **to be honest** or **to be perfectly honest** when you are admitting something, or are apologizing for giving your sincere but critical opinion: *To be perfectly honest, I've no experience in this type of work at all.*

honestly /ˈɒnɪstlɪ/ *adverb*

1 You speak **honestly** when you tell the truth: *Did you know about this? Answer me honestly.* **2** You do or achieve something **honestly** if you do or achieve it without cheating or lying: *He could not have obtained these results honestly.* **3** (*sentence adverb*; *informal*) You use **honestly** to emphasize that you are speaking the truth: *I'll do that for you. It's no trouble, honestly.* **4** (*sentence adverb*; *informal*) You use **honestly** to show that you are annoyed: *Honestly, Mike, you could have done the washing-up.*

honesty /ˈɒnɪstɪ/ *noun* (*uncount*)

Honesty is the quality of being honest, truthful or trustworthy: *He realized that the job was too difficult for him, and I admired his honesty in admitting that to us.*

▻ ***phrase*** You use **in all honesty** when you are saying that you cannot deny something, or that you must admit it: *I couldn't in all honesty say I knew nothing about it.*

honey /ˈhʌnɪ/ *noun*: **honeys**

1 (*uncount*) **Honey** is the sweet sticky edible substance that bees produce: *She helped herself to a piece of toast and spread it generously with honey.* **2** (*especially AmE*; *informal*) You can call someone **honey** as an indication of affection; you can refer to someone you like as a **honey**.

honeybee /ˈhʌnɪbiː/ *noun*: **honeybees**

A **honeybee** is a bee that lives in a hive and produces honey.

honeycomb /ˈhʌnɪkoʊm/ *noun* (*count or uncount*): **honeycombs**

A **honeycomb** is the wax structure built by bees, containing rows of cells in which they store honey.

honeymoon /ˈhʌnɪmuːn/ *noun*; *verb*

▻ ***noun***: **honeymoons**

1 A **honeymoon** is a holiday taken by a newly married couple: *We're going abroad for our honeymoon.* **2** The period of goodwill at the start of something such as a business relationship, or a new government's administration, can also be called a **honeymoon**, or **honeymoon** period.

▻ ***verb***: **honeymoons**, **honeymooning**, **honeymooned:** *They honeymooned briefly in Malta.* — *noun* **honeymooner:** *The couple at the other table were clearly honeymooners.*

honeysuckle /ˈhʌnɪsʌkəl/ *noun* (*uncount*)

Honeysuckle is a climbing plant with sweet-smelling pink and yellow flowers.

honk /hɒnk/ *verb*: **honks**, **honking**, **honked**

A vehicle **honks** when its horn is sounded; drivers **honk** their horns, or **honk**, when they sound their horns.

honorary /ˈɒnərərɪ/ *adjective*

1 An **honorary** title or degree, or **honorary** membership of a society, is given to someone as a mark of respect or honour, without their needing the qualifications normally required. **2** An **honorary** job, position or office is one that you carry out without pay: *the post of honorary secretary.*

honour (*AmE* **honor**) /ˈɒnə(r)/ *noun*; *verb*

▻ ***noun***: **honours**

1 (*uncount*) Your **honour** is your good reputation, which you take pride in earning and maintaining by behaving morally and justly, and by performing as well as you can in any activity you undertake; you call someone a man or woman of **honour** if they are well known for their honesty and integrity: *She refused to sacrifice her honour by lying, even to save herself.* □ *He was a hero, a man of honour.* **2** An award that you get for achievement or excellence, especially in public life, is referred to as an **honour**: *Didn't he get some kind of award for bravery in the New Year's honours list?* **3** (*used in the singular*; *formal*) You call a circumstance that indicates other people's respect for you, and makes you proud and happy an **honour**: *It is a great honour to be invited to join your research team.* **4** (*uncount*) Something that is organized or produced in **honour** of some event celebrates it: *He had composed the anthem in honour of the Queen's jubilee.* **5** (*used in the plural*) You gain **honours** in your university degree if you pass exams in your subject at a higher level than is necessary for an ordinary degree: *He has a second-class honours degree from Cambridge.* **6** (*AmE*) In US law courts, you address the judge as 'your **honour**'.

▻ ***verb***: **honours**, **honouring**, **honoured**

1 You **honour** someone when you give them special respect or recognition; if you say you **would be honoured** if a particular thing were to happen to you, you mean that you would feel proud if it did: *I should be honoured if you would accompany me.* **2** (*old*) You **honour** people such as your parents, wife or husband by treating them with the respect that they have a right to. **3** To **honour** someone is also to give them an award for achieving something remarkable, or doing something excellent: *He was honoured by the Swedish Academy for his work in the teaching of literature.* **4** You **honour** a promise by keeping it. **5** You **honour** bills and debts by paying them when they are due.

▻ ***phrases*** **1** (*informal*) You **do the honours** when you perform the task of host by pouring out drinks for your guests or serving them with food. **2** You say you are **honour-bound**, or **in honour bound**, to do something if you feel it is your moral duty: *feel in honour bound to warn you that the operation may be a failure.* **3** You use **'on my honour'** to emphasize that you are telling the truth, or that you can be trusted to fulfil your promise: *I promised them on my honour to be back home by midnight.*

honourable (*AmE* **honorable**) /ˈɒnərəbəl/ *adjective*

1 Honourable people behave justly and morally, treat other people with fairness and respect, and have a reputation for honesty and integrity: *The honourable thing would have been to admit that it was your fault.* [*same as* **decent**] **2** An **honourable** achievement is one that can justly be admired. **3 Honourable** is used in the title of certain members of noble families and certain high officials such as judges, and is used in parliamentary language to refer to other members of parliament: *I refer to the point raised by the honourable member for Devizes.* — *adverb* **honourably:** *As a parliamentarian he served the nation honourably for over 50 years.*

hood /hʊd/ *noun*: **hoods**

1 The **hood** of a garment such as a coat or jacket is a part attached to the neck or collar, that you pull up over your head for warmth: *Her anorak had a fur-lined hood.* **2** A **hood** is also a cover or roof, especially one that can be folded or removed, on a vehicle such as a pram or car, or over a piece of equipment such as a cooker. **3** (*AmE*) A **hood** is the bonnet of a car. [see picture at **car**]

hooded /ˈhʊdɪd/ *adjective*
1 A **hooded** garment has a hood attached to it: *She wore a long hooded cloak.* **2** You describe someone's eyes as **hooded** if their eyelids partly hide their eyes, giving them a look of mystery.

hoodwink /ˈhʊdwɪŋk/ *verb*: **hoodwinks, hoodwinking, hoodwinked**
To **hoodwink** someone is to trick or deceive them: *He had hoodwinked a number of elderly ladies into lending him considerable sums of money.* [*same as* **dupe**]

hoof /huːf/ *noun*: **hoofs** or **hooves**
The **hooves** of animals such as horses, cattle and sheep are the hard parts of their feet.

hook /hʊk/ *noun*; *verb*
▻ ***noun***: **hooks**
1 A **hook** is a piece of metal or plastic bent in the shape of a letter **J**, for hanging things on or attaching things to: *There was a hook on the back of the door and she hung her coat on it.* □ *fishing with a hook and line* □ *a packet of curtain hooks.* **2** Many curved shapes and objects are referred to as **hooks**: *Do you write your fs, gs and js with loops or hooks?* **3** (*sport*) A **hook** is a curved stroke, or a blow delivered with a curved arm.
▻ ***verb***: **hooks, hooking, hooked**
1 You **hook** one thing on to another when you attach it to the other with hooks or a hook; things **hook** up if they are attached to each other with hooks: *She was up a ladder hooking the curtain on to the rail.* □ *These two sections should hook up somehow.* **2** You **hook** your arm, leg or foot round something by curving it like a hook round the thing, so as to hold on to it or pull it somewhere: *He managed to hook one leg over the edge of the ledge and haul himself up on to it.* **3** You **hook** a fish when you catch it using a fishing line and hook.
▻ ***phrases*** **1** A telephone receiver is **off the hook** when it is not sitting on its normal support or rest, so that the telephone is prevented from ringing: *His phone keeps giving the engaged tone; it may be off the hook.* **2** (*informal*) You get **off the hook** when you manage to escape from a difficult situation, *eg* when you avoid being blamed for something.

phrasal verb
Things such as radio stations or computers **are hooked up** when they are connected or linked.

hook and eye /hʊk ənd ˈaɪ/ *noun*: **hooks and eyes**
A piece of clothing that fastens with a **hook and eye** fastens by means of a hook that fits over a bar or through a metal loop.

hooked /ˈhʊkt/ *adjective*
1 A **hooked** object is shaped like a hook: *a hooked beak.* **2** A **hooked** nose is large with a bend or angle near the top. **3** (*informal*) You are **hooked** on something if you are so fond of it or enthusiastic about it that it takes up most of your time and attention: *kids hooked on computer games.* **4** You are **hooked** on drugs if you are addicted to them: *You can easily get hooked on those solvents.*

hooker /ˈhʊkə(r)/ *noun*: **hookers** (*derogatory*; *especially AmE*)
A **hooker** is a prostitute.

hook-up /ˈhʊkʌp/ *noun*: **hook-ups**
A **hook-up** is a temporary linking up of different broadcasting stations, especially a radio and television station for a special broadcast.

hooligan /ˈhuːlɪgən/ *noun*: **hooligans**
A **hooligan** is someone, usually young, who behaves in a noisy, destructive or violent way in public places: *football hooligans.* — *noun* (*uncount*) **hooliganism:** *ways of preventing football hooliganism.*

hoop /huːp/ *noun*: **hoops**
A **hoop** is a large ring made of metal, wood or plastic, used *eg* in gymnastic exercises or in circus tricks: *We each had a hoop and had to practise rolling it along the floor.*

hooray /hʊˈreɪ/, **hurray** /həˈreɪ/ *or* **hurrah** /həˈrɑː/ *interjection*
You shout **hooray** to express pleasure, triumph or approval. [see also **cheer**]

hoot /huːt/ *verb*; *noun*
▻ ***verb***: **hoots, hooting, hooted**
1 A driver **hoots** the horn, or **hoots**, when he or she sounds the horn of a vehicle; a car **hoots** when its driver sounds its horn: *He hooted his horn at some unwary pedestrians.* □ *Suddenly the the street was full of the noise of cars hooting.* **2** An owl **hoots** when it makes its typical long loud call. **3** You **hoot** when you give a loud shout of laughter or scorn: *The audience hooted with laughter.*
▻ ***noun***: **hoots:** *The silence was broken by the hoot of an owl.* □ *I heard the hoot of his horn as he turned out of the driveway into the road.* □ *Hoots of laughter were coming from the room next door.*
▻ ***phrase*** (*informal*) You say you **couldn't care a hoot**, or **two hoots**, about something if it does not worry or concern you at all.

hooter /ˈhuːtə(r)/ *noun*: **hooters**
1 A **hooter** is an instrument or device that makes a loud sound, *eg* as a warning, or, in a factory, as a signal that work is starting or finishing. **2** (*BrE informal*) Your **hooter** is your nose.

Hoover /ˈhuːvə(r)/ *noun*; *verb*
▻ ***noun*** (*trademark*): **Hoovers**
(also **hoover**) A **Hoover** is a vacuum cleaner: *She plugged in the Hoover.*
▻ ***verb*** (usually **hoover**): **hoovers, hoovering, hoovered**
You **hoover** a carpet when you clean it with a vacuum cleaner; you **hoover** a room when you clean its carpet with a vacuum cleaner: *I've hoovered the bedroom already.* [*same as* **vacuum**]

hooves /huːvz/ *noun*
Hooves is the plural of **hoof**.

hop[1] /hɒp/ *verb*; *noun*
▻ ***verb***: **hops, hopping, hopped**
1 You **hop** when you jump on one foot: *He was hopping round the room holding his injured foot.* **2** Birds, small animals and insects **hop** when they jump using both, or all, their legs: *Sparrows were hopping about on the lawn.* **3** (*informal*) You **hop** somewhere when you move there quickly: *Hop into my car and I'll take you there.* **4** You **hop** over or across to a place when you make a quick visit there, especially by air: *I've got to hop over to Paris for a meeting tomorrow.* [*same as* **pop, nip**]
▻ ***noun***: **hops**
A **hop** is an act of hopping: *She gave a little hop of excitement.* □ *Small birds don't walk; they progress in a series of hops.*
▻ ***phrases*** **1** (*informal*) You **catch** someone **on the hop** when you surprise them by doing something unexpectedly, or sooner than they expect, so that they are unprepared: *They may carry out an inspection at any moment, and we mustn't be caught on the hop.* **2** (*BrE offensive*) If you tell someone to **hop it**, you are telling them rudely to go away. **3** (*informal*) You are **hopping mad** when you are very angry.

hop² /hɒp/ *noun* (*usually in the plural*): **hops**
Hops are the flowers of a climbing plant, that are dried and used for flavouring beer.

hope /hoʊp/ *verb*; *noun*
▻ ***verb***: **hopes, hoping, hoped**
You **hope** that something is so, or will happen, if you want it to be so or to happen, and believe that it can be so, or can happen: *I hope to have time to write a longer letter soon.* □ *He hoped he wouldn't make any mistakes.* □ *I hope she doesn't notice the mess.* □ *It's unlikely that they'll find anyone else alive, but we must keep on hoping.* □ *I do hope I didn't disturb you when I came in last night.* □ *I enclose the information leaflet, which I hope is what you wanted.* □ *We're hoping for good weather, of course.* □ *'Will you be able to finish in time?' 'I hope so.'* □ *We may have to cut our holiday short, but I hope not.* □ *We'll see you at the party tonight, I hope?*
▻ ***noun***: **hopes**
1 (*uncount or count, often in the plural*) **Hope** is the feeling that what you want to happen may happen: *He'd given up all hope of finding a job.* □ *I had hopes of seeing her again one day.* □ *The discovery brings fresh hope to victims of Parkinson's Disease.* □ *I see no grounds for hope that agreement is about to be reached.* **2** (*uncount or count*) There is a **hope** of something good or desirable happening if there is a chance that it will happen: *There's little hope of a cure.* □ *He hasn't a hope of being* [= is most unlikely to be] *selected for the team.* **3** Your **hopes** are the things you are wanting to happen: *all our hopes and fears for the future.* **4** (*used in the singular*) You refer to a person or thing that you are depending on entirely to do or produce what you want as your last or only **hope**: *The local library was our last hope.*
▻ ***phrases*** **1** (*formal*) You **hold out hope** to someone when you tell them that what they hope for may happen. **2** You **hope against hope** when you hope for something impossible: *I was hoping against hope that I was mistaken.* **3** You **hope for the best** when you hope that things will turn out the way you want, but are afraid they won't. **4** You do one thing **in the hope of** achieving another if you do it because you hope to achieve the other: *We sat up all night listening to the results in the hope of hearing who'd won.* **5** A circumstance that **raises** your **hopes** makes you believe more strongly that what you want to happen will happen. **6** (*informal*) If you say '**some hope**', '**what a hope**' or '**not a hope**' in response to a suggestion that something may happen, you mean that there is no chance of it happening.

hopeful /ˈhoʊpfəl/ *adjective*; *noun*
▻ ***adjective***
1 You are **hopeful** if you believe that what you want to happen is likely to happen: *The doctors are hopeful that she'll make a full recovery.* [*same as* **confident, optimistic**; *opposite* **pessimistic**] **2** Something that is **hopeful** gives you reason to expect that what you want to happen will happen: *We've had no confirmation as yet, but the situation looks hopeful.* □ *There's a spot of blue sky; that's a hopeful sign.* [*same as* **promising, encouraging**; *opposite* **worrying**]
▻ ***noun***: **hopefuls**
A **hopeful** is someone who has a particular ambition, or is ambitious, or is expected to do well: *He was among the young hopefuls auditioning for the part of Oliver.*

hopefully /ˈhoʊpfəlɪ/ *adverb*
1 You do something **hopefully** when you do it as though you expect that what you want to happen will happen: *'I've run out of cash,' he said, looking hopefully at me.* **2** (*sentence adverb*) People use **hopefully** to mean 'I hope': *Hopefully the weather will improve for the wedding.*

hopeless /ˈhoʊpləs/ *adjective*
1 You feel **hopeless** when you feel you have no chance of improving your situation: *They huddle together in cellars, hopeless and desperate, trying to shelter from the constant bombing.* **2** You describe a situation as **hopeless** if you think things cannot improve; a **hopeless** attempt to do something cannot succeed: *It's hopeless trying to trace the caller after so many months.* **3** (*informal*) Someone who is **hopeless** at something does it very badly: *I was always hopeless at maths.* [*same as* **useless**] **4** (*informal*) You use **hopeless** to emphasize the badness of something: *He left his finances in a hopeless muddle.* □ *Why don't you remember what you're told? You're hopeless!* — *adverb* **hopelessly:** *'It's no good,' he said hopelessly.* □ *He had been hopelessly in love with her almost since childhood.* □ *I'm afraid I'm hopelessly extravagant.* — *noun* (*uncount*) **hopelessness:** *They're filled with hopelessness and despair.* □ *The hopelessness of their quest soon became obvious.*

horde /hɔːd/ *noun* (*often derogatory*): **hordes**
A **horde** is an overwhelming and noisy crowd: *Let's not go to the castle; there'll be hordes of tourists there.*

horizon /həˈraɪzən/ *noun*: **horizons**
1 (*usually in the singular*) The **horizon** is the distant line where the sky meets the land or sea: *A sail appeared on the horizon.* **2** Your **horizons** are the limits of your knowledge, interests or experience: *I've been doing the same job, holidaying in the same place, for years; it's time I widened my horizons.*
▻ ***phrase*** Something that is **on the horizon** is going to happen or be available soon: *A major breakthrough is on the horizon.*

horizontal /hɒrɪˈzɒntəl/ *adjective*
A **horizontal** line or plane is parallel to the ground; something that is **horizontal** is level or flat: *Every horizontal surface in the room was piled high with books.* [*opposite* **vertical**; *same as* **flat, level**] — *adverb* **horizontally:** *The dust cloud spread out horizontally over the town.*

hormone /ˈhɔːmoʊn/ *noun*: **hormones**
A **hormone** is one of a number of chemicals that the body produces, which influence or stimulate growth and development, some of them relating to sexual development and activity. — *adjective* **hormonal** /hɔːˈmoʊnəl/: *In her monthly cycle a woman goes through a series of hormonal changes.*

horn /hɔːn/ *noun*: **horns**
1 The **horn** of a vehicle is the device that makes a loud warning sound, or the button on the steering wheel that you press to operate it; other devices that give warning signals are also called **horns**: *She sounded her horn at the other driver.* □ *a foghorn.* [see picture at **car**] **2** The **horns** of an animal such as a cow, bull, sheep, goat or deer are the two hard pointed objects that grow out of its head. **3** (*uncount*) **Horn** is the material of which an animal's horns are composed, which people carve into tools and ornaments; **horn**-rimmed spectacles have plastic frames that are made to look like horn: *buttons made of horn.* **4** A **horn** is an instrument that you play by blowing into it, traditionally made from an animal's horn and used for signalling: *a collection of ancient hunting horns.* **5** A **horn** or **French horn** is a coiled brass wind instrument. [see picture at **orchestra**] — *adjective* **horned:** *horned animals.*

hornet /'hɔːnɪt/ *noun*: **hornets**
A **hornet** is a stinging insect that looks like a large wasp.

horoscope /'hɒrəskoʊp/ *noun*: **horoscopes**
Your **horoscope** is a prediction of what is going to happen to you in the future, based on the position of the stars and planets at the time of your birth.

horrendous /hə'rɛndəs/ *adjective* (*often informal*)
Something that is described as **horrendous** is shocking or terrible: *Make the slightest mistake and the consequences could be horrendous.* — *adverb* **horrendously:** *The fare is horrendously expensive.*

horrible /'hɒrɪbəl/ *adjective*
1 (*informal*) Something **horrible** is unpleasant or nasty: *That fish smells horrible.* □ *I had a horrible suspicion she was lying.* [*same as* **awful**, **dreadful**] **2 Horrible** things shock or disgust you: *horrible scenes of murder and violence.* **3** (*informal*) **Horrible** is used to emphasize the badness of something: *My life's in a horrible mess.* [*same as* **awful**, **dreadful**] — *adverb* **horribly:** *He grinned horribly, revealing a row of broken teeth.* □ *The weather was horribly cold and wet.* □ *The future is so horribly uncertain.*

horrid /'hɒrɪd/ *adjective* (*informal*)
1 Something that is **horrid** is unpleasant: *a horrid shade of yellow.* **2** A **horrid** person is someone who behaves rudely or cruelly: *What a horrid thing to say!*

horrific /hə'rɪfɪk/ *adjective*
Something that is **horrific** fills you with shock and horror: *There's been a horrific earthquake somewhere in Japan.* — *adverb* **horrifically:** *Some of them were horrifically disfigured.*

horrify /'hɒrɪfaɪ/ *verb*: **horrifies, horrifying, horrified**
You **are horrified** by or at something if it shocks and upsets you: *We were horrified at the conditions they were living in.* — *adjective* **horrifying:** *They were subjected to horrifying tortures.* — *adverb* **horrifyingly:** *The crime had been horrifyingly easy to carry out.*

horror /'hɒrə(r)/ *noun*: **horrors**
1 (*uncount*) **Horror** is a feeling of shock or alarm: *We drew back in horror at the sight.* □ *To my horror he began to weep.* □ *His face betrayed horror at the thought that he might have to pay.* **2** (*used in the singular*) You have a **horror** of something if you dislike it or are afraid of it: *She had a horror of failure.* **3** (*uncount*) The **horror** of something bad is its quality of being terrible or horrible: *The horror of the accident would live with them always.* **4** (*used in the plural*) **Horrors** are terrible experiences: *She recounted some of the horrors she had lived through.* **5** Stories of mystery or **horror** are about such things as monsters, demons, witches and ghosts, and are intended to frighten you: *horror movies.*

horror-stricken /'hɒrəstrɪkən/ or **horror-struck** /'hɒrəstrʌk/ *adjective*
You are **horror-stricken** or **horror-struck** at something that has happened if you are filled with horror at it: *She sat there horror-stricken at this latest turn of events.*

hors d'oeuvre /ɔː'dɜːv/ *noun* (*uncount or count, often in the plural*): **hors d'oeuvres** /ɔː'dɜːvz/
A **hors d'oeuvre** is a salad or savoury dish served before the main course of a meal.

horse /hɔːs/ *noun*: **horses**
1 A **horse** is a large, four-legged animal with a mane and tail, used for riding or for pulling carts, carriages or ploughs. [see also **mare**, **stallion**, **foal**] **2** (*gymnastics*) A **horse** is four-legged gymnastic apparatus with a pair of handles on top, for jumping or vaulting over.

▷ ***phrases*** **1** You can say that someone **is flogging a dead horse** when they go on trying to solve a problem long after they ought to have realized there is no solution. **2** You get information **from the horse's mouth** when you get it directly from a reliable source.

horseback /'hɔːsbak/ *noun* (*uncount*)
▷ ***phrase*** You are **on horseback** when you are riding a horse.

horseman /'hɔːsmən/ or **horsewoman** /'hɔːswʊmən/ *noun*: **horsemen** or **horsewomen**
A **horseman** or **horsewoman** is someone who is riding a horse, or someone who is an expert horse-rider.

horsepower /'hɔːspoʊə(r)/ *noun* (*uncount*)
Horsepower is the unit for measuring the power of an engine, equal to 745.7 watts: *a 16-horsepower engine.*

horseshoe /'hɔːsʃuː/ *noun*: **horseshoes**
A **horseshoe** is a piece of iron curved into the shape of a letter **U** that is nailed to the underside of a horse's hoof, and is regarded as a symbol of luck.

horticulture /'hɔːtɪkʌltʃə(r)/ *noun* (*uncount*)
Horticulture is the science, study and art of gardening, or of growing flowers, fruit and vegetables. — *adjective* **horticultural** /hɔːtɪ'kʌltʃərəl/: *My tomatoes won a prize in the annual horticultural show.*

hose /hoʊz/ *noun*; *verb*
▷ ***noun***: **hoses**
A **hose** or **hosepipe** is a tube or pipe made of plastic, rubber, or heavy canvas, for carrying water and directing it on to things, *eg* on to a garden or plants to water them, or on to burning buildings to extinguish the fire: *The use of garden hoses was banned during the drought.* [see picture at **tool**]
▷ ***verb***: **hoses, hosing, hosed**
You **hose** something when you direct water at it with a hose: *He was outside hosing the lawn.*

> ***phrasal verb***
> You **hose** something **down** when you clean it with water from a hose: *It was good to be able to hose the car down and get all the mud and dust off.*

hosiery /'hoʊzɪərɪ/ *noun* (*uncount*)
Hosiery is a term used in shops for stockings, tights and socks.

hospice /'hɒspɪs/ *noun*: **hospices**
A **hospice** is a small, informally run hospital where people who are dying of incurable diseases are looked after.

hospitable /hɒ'spɪtəbəl/ *adjective*
A **hospitable** person is friendly and welcoming to guests and strangers: *Your parents were so hospitable to me when I first came to Edinburgh and knew nobody.* — *adverb* **hospitably:** *She sat me down and hospitably offered me a drink.*

hospital /'hɒspɪtəl/ *noun*: **hospitals**
A **hospital** is a place where people who are ill or injured are taken to be looked after by doctors and nurses: *He was admitted to hospital suffering from chest pains.* □ *That cut looks as if it needs hospital treatment.*

hospitality /hɒspɪ'talɪtɪ/ *noun* (*uncount*)
Hospitality is the quality of being hospitable, or of being friendly and welcoming to guests and strangers, entertaining them with food or drink, or providing them with accommodation: *Thank you so much for your hospitality last weekend.*

hospitalize /'hɒspɪtəlaɪz/ or **hospitalise** *verb*: **hospitalizes, hospitalizing, hospitalized**

To **hospitalize** someone is to admit them to hospital to stay as long as necessary so that they can be treated for their illness or injury. — *noun* (*uncount*) **hospitalization** /hɒspɪtəlaɪ'zeɪʃən/: *A period of hospitalization would be necessary so that doctors could carry out tests on her.*

host[1] /hoʊst/ *noun*; *verb*

▻ ***noun***: **hosts**

1 Your **host** at a party is the person who has invited you and the other guests, and entertains you with food and drink: *We thanked our hosts and left for home at about 11.30.* **2** The **host** of a television or radio show is the person who introduces guests and performers to the audience, or interviews them. **3** The **host** country, city or organization for an event is the one that provides accommodation and facilities for it; your **host** country or **host** family is the one that provides you with a place to stay if you come as a guest or refugee from another place or country: *Atlanta is to be the host city for the 1996 Olympic Games.* **4** (*medicine or zoology*) The person or animal on which something such as an insect or other organism is living or feeding as a parasite is referred to as its **host**.

▻ ***verb***: **hosts, hosting, hosted**

A country, city or organization **hosts** an event when it provides accommodation and facilities for it: *Manchester failed in its bid to host the 2000 Olympic Games.*

▻ ***phrase*** A country, city or organization **plays host to** an event when it provides accommodation and facilities for it: *The Screen Cinema is playing host to the French-Language Film Festival.*

host[2] /hoʊst/ *noun* (*old*): **hosts**

A **host** of things is a lot of them: *I've got hosts of letters to write.*

hostage /'hɒstɪdʒ/ *noun*: **hostages**

A person or group takes someone **hostage** when they capture them and hold them prisoner, threatening to harm or kill them unless conditions that they make are agreed to, or money that they want is given to them: *hold the passengers and crew hostage.*

hostel /'hɒstəl/ *noun*: **hostels**

1 A **hostel** is a place, usually run by a charity or a local authority, where people can get cheap accommodation, *eg* if they are homeless. **2** A students' or nurses' **hostel** is a place providing accommodation for students at a university or nurses at a hospital.

[see also **youth hostel**]

hostess /'hoʊstəs/ *noun*: **hostesses**

Your **hostess** at a party is the woman who has invited you and the other guests and provided food and drink: *He wanted to leave, and looked round for his hostess to say goodbye.*

hostile /'hɒstaɪl/ *adjective*

1 Someone who is **hostile** is unfriendly: *Her friendly greeting was met by an unsmiling, hostile stare from the children gathered round the car.* **2** You are **hostile** towards an idea or suggestion if you disapprove of it: *He's well known for his hostile attitude towards the trade unions.* **3** In war, the **hostile** forces are those of your enemies. **4** Conditions or an environment that are **hostile** make it difficult for you to do or achieve what you want: *hostile terrain.*

hostility /hɒ'stɪlɪtɪ/ *noun*: **hostilities**

1 (*uncount*) **Hostility** is unfriendliness: *Her parents-in-law scarcely bothered to conceal their hostility.* **2 Hostility** towards an idea or suggestion is opposition or disapproval: *their open hostility to reform of any kind.* **3** (*used in the plural*; *formal*) Your refer to fighting between countries or groups as **hostilities**: *Both sides are seeking an end to hostilities.*

hot /hɒt/ *adjective*; *verb*

▻ ***adjective***: **hotter, hottest**

1 Something that is **hot** has a high temperature: *Is the water hot enough for a bath?* **2** It is **hot** when the surrounding air temperature is high: *nice hot weather* □ *It's far too hot in here; can't we open a window?* □ *The following day was even hotter.* □ *the hottest July on record.* **3** You are **hot** when you feel very warm or too warm: *I got hot in the middle of the night and threw off the blankets.* **4** A person who has a fever feels **hot** when you touch them: *Your forehead feels very hot.* **5 Hot** food has been cooked and is intended to be eaten before it gets cold: *Would you like a hot meal or just a salad?* **6** Strong-tasting spicy food is also described as **hot** because it leaves a burning sensation in your mouth: *You can have your choice of a hot or mild curry.* **7** Someone who has a **hot** temper gets angry easily. [see also **hot-tempered**] **8 Hot** news is fresh, up-to-date news; a **hot** issue is one that everyone is discussing and arguing about. **9** The **hot** favourite for a competition is the competitor thought most likely to win; in betting, a **hot** tip is a reliable piece of information about which competitor is most likely to win. **10** (*informal*) You are **hot** on something if you know a lot about it: *My spelling was never very hot.*

▻ ***phrases*** **1** Someone who **blows hot and cold** keeps changing from being enthusiastic about something to being unenthusiastic. **2** You feel **hot and bothered** when you feel anxious, upset and unable to think clearly: *She's getting all hot and bothered about her daughter's family coming to stay.* **3** (*informal*) You say that someone could **make things hot for** you if you think that they could create an unpleasant situation for you. **4** (*informal*) Something that is **not so hot** is not very good.

▻ ***verb***: **hots, hotting, hotted**

> ***phrasal verb***
> You say things **are hotting up** when a situation or event is becoming more exciting: *The campaigning for the election started slowly but began to hot up after a few days.*

hot air /hɒt'ɛə(r)/ *noun* (*uncount*; *informal*)

People talk a lot of **hot air** if they talk a lot but don't say anything useful.

hotbed /'hɒtbɛd/ *noun*: **hotbeds**

You describe a place as a **hotbed** of some dangerous or dishonest activity if the activity is common there: *The city was becoming a hotbed of vice and crime.*

hotchpotch /'hɒtʃpɒtʃ/ (*AmE* **hodgepodge**) *noun* (*informal*): **hotchpotches**

A **hotchpotch** is a disorganized or confused mixture of different things: *The book is hotchpotch of new and old ideas.*

hot dog /'hɒt dɒg/ *noun*: **hot dogs**

A **hot dog** is a bread roll containing a hot sausage.

hotel /hoʊ'tɛl/ *noun*: **hotels**

A **hotel** is a building where rooms and meals are provided for travellers or people on holiday, in return for payment: *She had paid her bill and checked out of the hotel at about 9.30.*

hotelier /hoʊ'tɛlɪeɪ/ *noun*: **hoteliers**

A **hotelier** is someone who owns or manages a hotel.

hotfoot /hɒt'fʊt/ *adverb*

You go somewhere **hotfoot** if you rush or hurry there.

hothead /'hɒthɛd/ *noun* (*derogatory*): **hotheads**

A **hothead** is someone who acts hastily, without considering what the results may be.

hotheaded /hɒt'hɛdɪd/ *adjective*
A **hotheaded** person acts hastily, without considering what the results may be: *She has some good ideas but is inclined to be impatient and hotheaded.* [*same as* **impetuous**; *opposite* **cautious**]

hothouse /'hɒthaʊs/ *noun*: **hothouses**
A **hothouse** is a heated glass building in which plants that come from tropical climates can be grown. [compare **greenhouse**]

hot line /'hɒt laɪn/ *noun*: **hot lines**
1 A **hot line** is a direct telephone line between two heads of governments, set up so that they can discuss crises and emergencies without delay. **2** The police or other services sometimes set up a **hot line** for the use of members of the public who wish to telephone them with information about a particular incident or situation.

hotly /'hɒtlɪ/ *adverb*
People discuss, argue or deny something **hotly** if they do so in a lively, excited or angry manner: *People say he used to be a Tory voter, a rumour that he hotly denies.* □ *a hotly debated issue.*

hotplate /'hɒtpleɪt/ *noun*: **hotplates**
1 The **hotplate** of a cooker is the flat surface that heats up, on which you cook food. **2** A **hotplate** is also a portable apparatus with a flat surface heated by electricity, on which you can cook food or keep it hot.

hot seat /'hɒt siːt/ *noun* (*used in the singular*)
▻ ***phrase*** (*informal*) You are **in the hot seat** if you are in the position of having to take important and difficult decisions.

hot stuff /hɒt 'stʌf/ *noun* (*uncount*; *informal*)
1 Something or someone that is **hot stuff** is considered excitingly good: *She's hot stuff on the saxophone.* **2** You call someone **hot stuff** if you consider them sexually exciting.

hot-tempered /hɒt'tɛmpəd/ *adjective*
A **hot-tempered** person tends to lose their temper or get angry quickly or easily.

hot-water bottle /hɒt'wɔːtə bɒtəl/ *noun*: **hot-water bottles**
A **hot-water bottle** is a rubber container that you fill with hot water and use to warm your bed.

hound /haʊnd/ *noun*; *verb*
▻ ***noun***: **hounds**
A **hound** or **foxhound** is a breed of dog used for hunting; you often find **-hound** in the names of breeds of dogs of other kinds: *greyhounds.*
▻ ***verb***: **hounds, hounding, hounded**
People **hound** you if they continually chase and bother you: *The rumour of her engagement got about and she was hounded constantly by reporters for several days.*

hour /aʊə(r)/ *noun*: **hours**
1 An **hour** is a unit of time, one of 24 periods of sixty minutes in a day: *News of an earthquake in Chile has been arriving within the last hour.* □ *We've got another hour and a quarter till the train leaves.* □ *It'll take an hour or two to get everything sorted out.* □ *I only had three hours' sleep last night.* □ *It's an hour's walk to the nearest village.* □ *Heathrow is only an hour* [= an hour's journey] *from our house.* □ *Students are required to sit two three-hour papers and a half-hour oral exam.* □ *Off the motorway the official speed limit is 60 miles an hour.* **2** (*used in the plural*) The part of the day during which a particular arrangement is operating is referred to as its **hours**: *If you call outside office hours please leave a message on our answering machine.* □ *Library opening hours are 9.30am to 8.30pm.* □ *new moves to shorten young doctors' working hours.* **3** (*used in the singular*) An early or late **hour** is a time or period early or late in the day: *Sorry to call you at such an early hour.* □ *I'm afraid there's nothing we can do at this late hour; can you wait till tomorrow?* **4** (*used in the singular*; *literary*) Your worst, happiest or proudest **hour** is the worst, happiest or proudest point in your life: *Claverhouse was killed in his finest hour, on the battlefield at Killiecrankie.* [*same as* **moment**] **5** (*used in the singular*; *literary*) You say the **hour** has come for a certain action if it should be carried out now: *The hour has come to make a stand against oppression.* [*same as* **time**]
▻ ***phrases*** **1** Something that happens **after hours** happens after the official closing time of shops or offices: *Calls received after hours are redirected to our main office.* **2** Something that happens **at all hours** happens at any time of the day or night, especially the night: *As a doctor you get used to being called out at all hours.* **3** Something that happens **on the hour** happens as the time reaches *eg* one o'clock, two o'clock, three o'clock and so on: *Trains for Glasgow leave on the hour.* **4** Something that happens **out of hours** happens either before or after the opening or working hours of shops, offices and other establishments: *Children kept breaking into the school out of hours.* **5** Something that happens in **the early hours** or in **the small hours** happens very early in the morning, in the period after midnight: *Well, don't stay awake till the small hours worrying about it!*

hourly /'aʊəlɪ/ *adjective*; *adverb*
▻ ***adjective***
1 An **hourly** happening or event occurs once every hour: *There's an hourly train service to Glasgow.* **2** Your **hourly** pay is the amount of money your earn for an hour's work. **3** **Hourly** can mean constant: *He lived in hourly fear of betrayal.*
▻ ***adverb***
1 Something that happens **hourly** happens once an hour: *Trains leave hourly for Glasgow.* **2** Workers who are paid **hourly** get a certain amount of pay for every hour they work. **3** You do something **hourly** if you do it frequently: *He was in a complete panic, altering his plans hourly.* **4** You expect something **hourly** if you expect it very soon: *There are no definite moves yet, but we expect news hourly.*

house *noun*; *verb*
▻ ***noun*** /haʊs/: **houses** /haʊzɪz/
1 A **house** is a building in which people, especially a family, live: *They're trying to sell their house.* **2** **House** is used in names for buildings with special purposes: *opera houses* □ *a henhouse.* **3** Companies whose business is finance, publishing or design are sometimes called **houses**: *publishing houses* □ *fashion houses.* **4** A country's parliament, or any section of it, or the place where it meets, may be called a **House**: *Their parliament is divided into an upper and lower house.* **5** In a theatre or cinema, the **house** is the part where the audience sit, or the audience itself: *We've been performing to full houses every night.* **6** In reference to ancestry and descent, a **house** is a family, especially a noble, important or ancient family: *the royal house of Stuart.* **7** Sometimes in schools children are divided into groups called **houses**, which compete against each other in games and competitions.
▻ ***verb*** /haʊz/: **houses, housing, housed**
1 People **are housed** when they provided with accommodation, especially in the form of a house or flat: *The family are being temporarily housed in bed-and-breakfast accommodation.* **2** You **house** something somewhere when you keep it there: *The electricity generator was housed in the garage.*

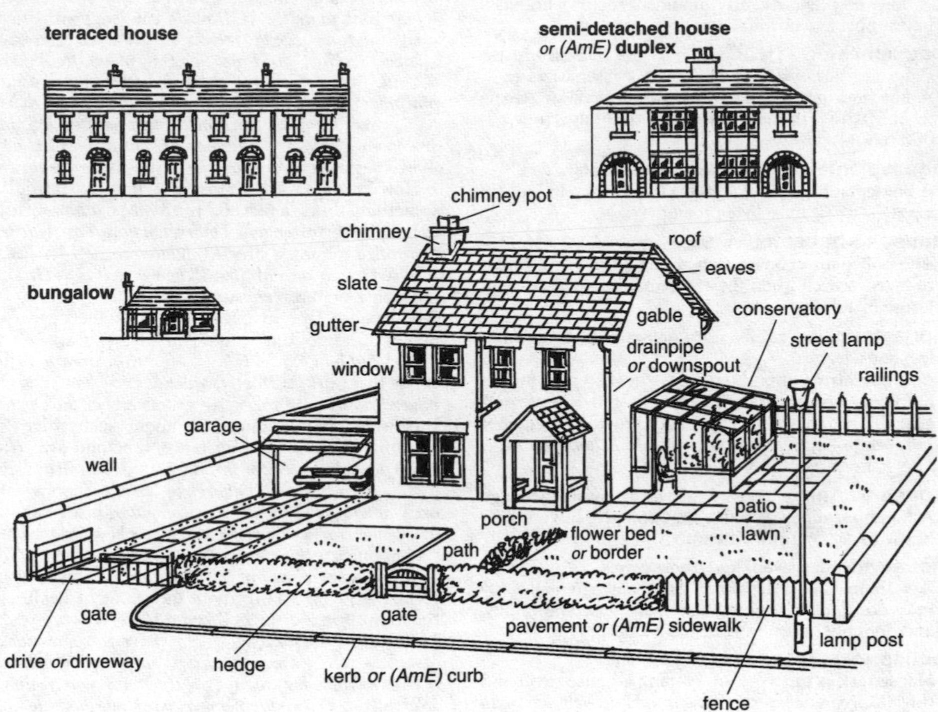

▷ ***phrases*** **1** A performance **brings the house down** if it makes the audience laugh, clap or applaud a lot. **2** To **keep house** is to manage a household, especially to do the cooking, cleaning and shopping: *After his illness his cousin Ellen came to live with him and keep house for him.* **3** (*informal*) Two people get on **like a house on fire** when they quickly become friendly with each other. **4** You get something at a bar or restaurant **on the house** if you get it free. **5** You **set your house in order** when you to organize your personal affairs satisfactorily. **6** You **set up house** when you find a place to live and start living there: *He and his girlfriend have set up house in a flat they've bought in Croydon.*

house agent /haʊs ˈeɪdʒənt/ *noun*: **house agents**
A **house agent** is a person who arranges the buying, selling or renting of houses.

house arrest /haʊs əˈrɛst/ *noun* (*uncount*)
You are put under **house arrest** if you are held prisoner by being prevented from leaving your own house: *She has been under house arrest in Myanmar for four years now.*

houseboat /ˈhaʊsboʊt/ *noun*: **houseboats**
A **houseboat** is a flat-bottomed boat, designed as a permanent home and usually kept moored in the same place on a river or canal.

housebound /ˈhaʊsbaʊnd/ *adjective*
Someone who is **housebound** is unable to leave their house, *eg* because of ill health, old age, or having very young children.

housebreaker /ˈhaʊsbreɪkə(r)/ *noun*: **housebreakers**
A **housebreaker** is someone who enters someone else's house illegally, *eg* by breaking locks, doors or windows, in order to steal the contents. — *noun* (*uncount*) **housebreaking:** *He was convicted of housebreaking.*

household /ˈhaʊshoʊld/ *noun*: **households**
1 A **household** is the family or group of people that live together in a house: *We were all one big happy household.* **2** You refer to your home as the **household** when you think of it as an establishment that needs looking after: *I used to do the weekly shopping for the whole household on a Friday.* □ *household appliances such as dishwashers and cookers.* **3** Something that is a **household** name or word is well known and often mentioned by people: *words like Hoover, that become household names and enter the language.*

householder /ˈhaʊshoʊldə(r)/ *noun*: **householders**
A **householder** is the legal owner or tenant of a house or flat.

housekeeper /ˈhaʊskiːpə(r)/ *noun*: **housekeepers**
A **housekeeper** is someone who is paid to look after the house for someone else, and do the cooking, cleaning and shopping: *The only other member of the household was an elderly housekeeper.*

housekeeping /ˈhaʊskiːpɪŋ/ *noun* (*uncount*)
1 Housekeeping is the task of managing a household, and doing the cooking cleaning and shopping. **2** The money that you set aside for buying food and other

household necessities is sometimes called the **housekeeping**: *I'd spent all the housekeeping by Tuesday.*

houseman /ˈhaʊsmən/ *noun*: **housemen**
A **houseman** is a recently qualified doctor who has a junior post at a hospital and lives there.

housemaster /ˈhaʊsmɑːstə(r)/ or **housemistress** /ˈhaʊsmɪstrɪs/ *noun*: **housemasters** or **housemistresses**
A **housemaster** or **housemistress** is a male or female teacher who is in charge of one of the houses (sense 7) of a school.

houseplant /ˈhaʊsplɑːnt/ *noun*: **houseplants**
A **houseplant** is a plant suitable for growing indoors in a pot. [see picture at **living room**]

house-to-house /haʊstəˈhaʊs/ *adjective*
The police make **house-to-house** enquiries or a **house-to-house** search when they systematically check every house in an area.

housetrain /ˈhaʊstreɪn/ *verb*: **housetrains, housetraining, housetrained**
You **housetrain** an animal that you keep as a household pet when you train it to urinate and defecate outside the house, or in a specially provided container indoors. — *adjective* **housetrained:** *Kittens for sale, fully housetrained.*

house-warming /ˈhaʊswɔːmɪŋ/ *noun*: **house-warmings**
A **housewarming** is a party that you give in your new house to celebrate moving into it.

housewife /ˈhaʊswaɪf/ *noun*: **housewives**
A woman who is described as a **housewife** is usually fully occupied in looking after her house and family, and does not have a job outside her home.

housework /ˈhaʊswɜːk/ *noun* (*uncount*)
Housework is the work of keeping a house clean and tidy: *Margaret comes in once a week to help him with the housework.* [compare **homework**]

housing /ˈhaʊzɪŋ/ *noun*
1 Housing is houses and flats for people to live in: *purpose-designed housing for old people.* **2 Housing** is the job of providing houses for people: *the housing department.*

housing estate /ˈhaʊzɪŋ ɪsteɪt/ *noun*: **housing estates**
A **housing estate** is a group of houses or blocks of flats planned and built all at the same time.

hove /hoʊv/ see **heave**.

hovel /ˈhɒvəl/ *noun*: **hovels**
A **hovel** is a small dirty house or hut, in which people are living.

hover /ˈhɒvə(r)/ *verb*: **hovers, hovering, hovered**
1 A bird, insect or helicopter **hovers** when it stays in the same position in the air: *The rescue helicopter hovered above us while we strapped Jim on to the stretcher.* **2** You **hover** between two states when you are not fully in either; you **hover** between two choices when you cannot decide definitely on either: *For a week she was hovering between life and death.* **3** Someone **hovers** near somewhere if they stay there seeming uncertain what to do, or as though waiting for something: *She looked up to see a small child hovering in the doorway.* [*same as* **linger, hang about**]

hovercraft /ˈhɒvəkrɑːft/ *noun*: **hovercrafts** or **hovercraft**
A **hovercraft** is a craft or vehicle that moves over land or water, staying just above the surface, supported on a layer or cushion of air that is blown underneath it.

how /haʊ/ *adverb and conjunction*
1 a You use **how** to ask about, or refer to, the way something happens or is done, or the method of doing it: *How did it happen?* □ *How shall we plan this?* □ *'How did you get here?' 'How do you think? I got the train of course.'* □ *'David's managed to get the television to work.' 'Oh, how?'* □ *How on earth did you manage to persuade him?* □ *'How's your book progressing?' 'Quite well, actually.'* □ *'How do you like your coffee?' 'Milk and no sugar, thanks.'* □ *How do you spell 'gauge'?* □ *How do I get to Dagenham from here?* □ *Could you show me how to start the washing machine?* □ *The child explained to us in great detail how babies were born.* □ *I can't make any promises; let's just see how we get on.* □ *She may get out of hospital next week, depending on how she responds to treatment.* **b How** is also used almost like *that*, to introduce something that is a fact: *Do you remember how we used to tease her?* □ *Even now I marvel at how those teachers controlled classes of over 40 children each.* □ *We get so involved in our own affairs; I know how it is.* □ *He kept telling me how everyone was against him.*
2 a You use **how** in questions about the degree or extent of some condition or quality: *You say he's an expert, but how expert is he?* □ *How close are you to finishing that work?* □ *Doctors will not know how seriously injured she is until they have examined her thoroughly.* **b How** is used in questions about such things as amount, measurement, distance, time and age: *How much flour do I need for this recipe?* □ *How tall are you?* □ *How far is it from Edinburgh to Glasgow?* □ *How long are you going to be using that computer?* □ *Men as well as women can be reluctant to tell you how old they are.* □ *How much is this ring?* [= What does this ring cost?]
3 a If you ask someone **how** they are, or **how** they are feeling, you are asking about their state of health, or their emotional or mental state: *Hello, how are you? I haven't seen you for ages.* □ *'How have you been since I last saw you?' 'Fine, thanks.'* □ *How's your mother?* □ *How's your leg today?* □ *'How are you feeling?' 'Nervous.'* □ *Did you remember to ask how his wife was?* **b** You ask someone **how** something is or **how** it is going, when you want to know if it is successful, or if they are enjoying it: *'How was your holiday?' 'Great, thanks.'* □ *'How was the exam?' 'OK, I suppose.'* □ *How's the new job going?* □ *'How's this drawing for a first attempt?' 'Not bad.'* □ *I asked how the interview had gone.*
4 a You use **how** with *can* and *could* to express surprise or annoyance: *How can you possibly think he disapproves of you?* □ *How could he have found out?* □ *How can people be so ignorant?* □ *How could you be so careless?* □ *I've no idea how such an error was possible.* **b** You use **how** when exclaiming about some quality, as a form of emphasis: *How blue the sky is!* □ *A picnic! How lovely!* □ *He commented on how efficiently she'd organized the meeting.* □ *We all know how easily accidents happen.*
▷ ***phrases*** **1** (*informal*) You comment **'and how'** to emphasize that something is so, when someone asks you if it is: *'Was she angry?' 'And how!'* **2** For **how about** see **about**. **3** (*informal*) You use **'how come?'** to ask why something has happened: *How come no-one told me about this?* **4** For **how do you do** see **do**. **5** For **how ever** see **however**.

however /haʊˈɛvə(r)/ *adverb; conjunction*
▷ ***adverb***
1 (*sentence adverb*) You use **however** to indicate a contrast in what you are saying with what has been said previously: *He has problems with his reading; however, if he tries hard he should get over them.* □ *It's quite a good article; too long, however.* **2** (*interrogative*) **However** or **how ever** is used as an emphatic form of **how**, often expressing surprise or concern: *However did you get that old radio to work?* □ *How ever are we going to get there in time?* □ *However many times do I*

have to warn you? □ *How ever could she have come to that conclusion?*

▻ ***conjunction***

1 (*conjunction or adverb*) People do something **however** they like, or **however** is convenient or possible, if they do it any way they like, or by any means or method that is convenient or possible: *Pay however you like; cheque, cash, credit card, they're all acceptable here.* **2 However** is used with adjectives, adverbs and words expressing such things as amount, distance and time, to comment that degree or amount make no difference to what you are saying: *You depend largely on the expertise of your staff, however good your software is.* □ *He can't win now, however well he performs in the last round.* □ *I love him, however many failings he has.* □ *It's worth it, however much it costs.* □ *I'm determined to get there tonight, however far it is.* □ *I don't believe I'll ever pass my driving test, however often I try.*

howl /haʊl/ *verb; noun*

▻ ***verb*: howls, howling, howled**

1 Animals, especially those of the dog family such as wolves and jackals, **howl** when they make their long loud cry. **2** To **howl** is to weep loudly and uncontrollably. **3** People **howl** with laughter when they laugh loudly and uncontrollably. **4** You **howl** something when you shout it loudly: *'Don't dare move!' he howled.* **5** The wind **howls** when it blows hard and loudly: *There was a dense blizzard and a howling gale all day.*

▻ ***noun*: howls:** *The animal gave a howl of pain.* □ *Howls of mirth came from the public bar.*

phrasal verb
People **howl down** a speaker when they shout so loudly and angrily that he or she is prevented from speaking.

HQ /eɪtʃ'kjuː/ *noun* (*uncount or count*): **HQs**

HQ is short for **headquarters**: *A message has just come through from HQ.* □ *Where do they have their HQ?*

hub /hʌb/ *noun*: **hubs**

1 The **hub** of a wheel is its central point. **2** A place that is described as the **hub** of an area is its centre of interest and activity: *Douglas is the commercial hub of the island.*

huddle /'hʌdəl/ *verb; noun*

▻ ***verb*: huddles, huddling, huddled**

1 You **huddle** or **are huddled** somewhere when you sit or crouch with your arms round or close to your body: *She sat huddled by the fire.* **2** People **huddle** or **are huddled** together when they are grouped or pressed closely together: *We huddled together in the cellar as the bombs fell.*

▻ ***noun*: huddles**

A **huddle** is a small dense group: *People were standing about in huddles discussing the news.*

hue /hjuː/ *noun* (*literary*): **hues**

A **hue** is a colour: *autumn hues.*

huff /hʌf/ *noun* (*used in the singular*)

You say that someone is in a **huff** if they are behaving in an angry or uncooperative way because they feel offended or insulted.

hug /hʌg/ *verb; noun*

▻ ***verb*: hugs, hugging, hugged**

1 You **hug** someone when you put your arms round them and hold or squeeze them tightly, as a demonstration of affection: *Nowadays it seems to be the fashion even for mere acquaintances to hug each other whenever they say hello or goodbye.* **2** You **hug** an object when you hold it tightly against you: *She sat hugging the parcel all the way home on the train.*

▻ ***noun*: hugs:** *He ran towards her and gave her a big hug.*

huge /hjuːdʒ/ *adjective*

Something that is **huge** is very large: *A huge amount of food is going to be needed to feed the refugees.* — *adverb* (*informal*) **hugely:** *The kids enjoyed themselves hugely.* [= very much] □ *They evidently thought the whole incident hugely funny.* □ *The piano was a hugely extravagant purchase.* [*same as* **enormously**]

huh /hʌ/ *interjection*

1 (*AmE*) **Huh** is sometimes used at the end of a question: *So you want a job here, huh?* **2** (*BrE*) **Huh** is used as an expression of disbelief or disgust.

hulk /hʌlk/ *noun*: **hulks**

1 A **hulk** is an old unused ship. **2** (*informal, derogatory*) If you call a person or thing a **hulk** you mean they are large and clumsy: *She was accompanied by her great hulk of a husband.*

hulking /'hʌlkɪŋ/ *adjective* (*informal, derogatory*)

Hulking describes someone or something that is large and clumsy: *The great hulking creature proved to be a Swedish elk.*

hull /hʌl/ *noun*: **hulls**

The **hull** of a ship or boat is its body.

hullabaloo /hʌləbə'luː/ *noun* (*informal*): **hullabaloos**

A **hullabaloo** is a great noise, or a great fuss: *The residents have been creating a hullabaloo about the new parking regulations.* [*same as* **commotion**]

hullo see **hello**.

hum /hʌm/ *verb; noun*

▻ ***verb*: hums, humming, hummed**

1 You **hum** when you sing with your lips closed: *She could hear Joe humming to himself in the bathroom.* □ *I hummed the tune but still couldn't get the end right.* **2** An engine or machine **hums** when it makes a continuous low sound: *She switched on the computer and it hummed into life.* **3** You say a place **is humming** if it is full of the sound of activity: *It was only 7.00am, but the city centre was already humming with business.* [*same as* **buzz**]

▻ ***noun*** (*used in the singular*): *Through the open window we could hear the distant hum of traffic.*

human /'hjuːmən/ *adjective; noun*

▻ ***adjective***

1 Human means belonging or relating to people: *Police have unearthed human remains in a nearby field.* □ *The bones are believed to be human.* **2 Human** also describes faults that we have as people, as distinct from God's perfection or a machine's accuracy: *Of course we sometimes make mistakes; it's human.* □ *human failings.* **3** Someone who is **human** has the sympathy and concern for others that people, as distinct from animals, are expected to have: *Don't be afraid of the manager; he's quite human.*

▻ ***noun*: humans**

A **human** is a person: *Computers may be capable of complicated analysis but they can't make judgements like humans.*

human being /hjuːmən 'biːɪŋ/ *noun*: **human beings**

A **human being** is a person: *The beach appeared deserted; not a human being in sight.*

humane /hjʊ'meɪn/ *adjective*

Someone who is **humane** is kind and sympathetic, and wants to cause as little suffering as possible to other people and to animals: *What's the most humane method of killing rats and mice?* [*opposite* **inhumane**] — *adverb* **humanely:** *The prisoners had been humanely,* *even kindly, treated.* — *noun* (*uncount*) **humaneness:** *The guillotine was recommended for its humaneness as the official method of execution.*

humanism /'hju:mənɪzm/ *noun* (*uncount*)
Humanism is a non-religious system of morality that has as its basis the belief that humans are capable of behaving and acting morally and justly without any need of a god to guide them. — *noun* **humanist:** *They described themselves as humanists rather than atheists.*

humanitarian /hjʊmanɪ'tɛərɪən/ *adjective*; *noun*
▻ ***adjective***
Humanitarian describes work or activities that are concerned with reducing people's suffering: *humanitarian aid for the war zone.*
▻ ***noun***: **humanitarians**
A **humanitarian** is someone who tries to improve people's welfare and reduce suffering, *eg* through reform or aid.

humanity /hjʊ'manɪtɪ/ *noun*: **humanities**
1 (*uncount*) **Humanity** is the human race: *a deep concern for all humanity.* [*same as* **mankind**] **2** (*uncount*) Your **humanity** is your quality of being human: *What right have they to deny these prisoners their humanity and keep them in cages like animals?* **3** (*uncount*) **Humanity** is sympathetic concern for other people's welfare: *He was governor of a prison, where he was noted for his humanity and good sense.* **4** (*used in the plural*) The **humanities** are school or university subjects that relate to human culture, such as languages, especially Latin and Greek, and literature and philosophy, especially that of the Greeks and Romans.

humankind /hju:mən'kaɪnd/ *noun* (*uncount*)
Humankind is the human race. [*same as* **mankind**]

humanly /'hju:mənlɪ/ *adverb*
▻ ***phrase*** Things that are **humanly possible** are things that human beings can do or achieve within the limited range of their power: *We've done all that is humanly possible; only a miracle can save him now.*

human nature /hju:mən 'neɪtʃə(r)/ *noun* (*uncount*)
Human nature is the range of qualities, characteristics and needs that human beings normally have: *It's human nature to be selfish sometimes.*

human race /hju:mən 'reɪs/ *noun* (*used in the singular*)
The **human race** is mankind, or all people: *the extinction of the entire human race.*

human rights /hju:mən 'raɪts/ *noun* (*used in the plural*)
Human rights are the rights that every person has to justice and freedom.

humble /'hʌmbəl/ *adjective*; *verb*
▻ ***adjective***; **humbler, humblest**
1 Someone who is **humble** believes that they are no better, cleverer or more important than other people: *He was that rare creature, a truly humble politician.* [*same as* **modest**] **2** People of a low social class are sometimes described as **humble**: *The composer's parents were humble peasants.* **3** You use **humble** of everyday objects, usually in contrast to an important use that is made of them: *It was a humble rubber band that got the machine going again.* **4** (*formal*) People use expressions such as 'in my **humble** opinion' or 'in my **humble** view' when they want to express their own opinions politely but definitely. — *noun* (*uncount*) **humbleness:** *the humbleness of his background and origins.* — *adverb* **humbly:** *In the past she would have given in to him humbly.* □ *We must humbly beg God's forgiveness.*
▻ ***verb***: **humbles, humbling, humbled**
1 You **humble** yourself when you sacrifice your pride, *eg* to beg for something, or to apologize: *I refuse to humble myself in front of her by asking for permission to do what I have a perfect right to do.* [*same as* **abase**] **2** You **humble** someone when you do something that makes them feel less proud and confident; you **are humbled** when something makes you lose pride and confidence: *I was much humbled by my failure.*

humbug /'hʌmbʌg/ *noun*: **humbugs**
1 A **humbug** is a hard, sticky, peppermint-flavoured sweet. **2** (*uncount*) If you call something that someone says or writes **humbug** you mean that it is neither sincere nor honest: *all that political humbug.*

humdrum /'hʌmdrʌm/ *adjective*
Things that are **humdrum** are ordinary, dull and boring: *I thought I'd enliven your humdrum existence by paying you a visit.* [*same as* **mundane**; *opposite* **exciting**]

humid /'hju:mɪd/ *adjective*
Weather, a climate or atmosphere that is **humid** is hot and damp: *The days were relentlessly hot, the nights humid.* — *noun* (*uncount*) **humidity** /hju:'mɪdɪtɪ/: *It took a while to adjust to the humidity of Singapore.*

humiliate /hjʊ'mɪlɪeɪt/ *verb*: **humiliates, humiliating, humiliated**
You **humiliate** someone when you damage their pride by making them feel ashamed or seem silly, especially in public: *She longed to humiliate the bully in front of his admirers.* — *adjective* **humiliated:** *Did you have to shout at the waiter? I've never felt so humiliated in my life.* — *adjective* **humiliating:** *It's humiliating to be beaten by your children at Scrabble.* — *noun* (*uncount or count*) **humiliation** /hjʊmɪlɪ'eɪʃən/: *She could not face the humiliation of defeat.* □ *The government had been subjected to many public humilations already.*

humility /hjʊ'mɪlɪtɪ/ *noun* (*uncount*)
Humility is the quality of being humble and thinking yourself no better, cleverer or more important than other people: *She had that humility that you often find in truly great scholars.*

humorist /'hju:mərɪst/ *noun*: **humorists**
A **humorist** is someone who makes jokes or talks amusingly, or writes humorous articles, especially as a profession.

humorous /'hju:mərəs/ *adjective*
A person, a piece or writing or a remark that is **humorous** is amusing or witty: *She used to write humorous articles for a newspaper.* □ *He had a thin face with a humorous expression.* — *adverb* **humorously:** *She humorously refers to her boss as 'the king'.*

humour /'hju:mə(r)/ *noun*; *verb*
▻ ***noun***
1 (*uncount*) **Humour** is the ability to realize when something is funny, and the ability to say amusing things: *He appeared to have no sense of humour.* [see also **sense of humour**] **2** (*uncount*) The **humour** of a situation or remark is its quality of being funny: *I was in no mood to appreciate the humour of my predicament.* **3** (*uncount*) Writing, sayings and remarks that make you laugh are collectively called **humour**. **4** (*used in the singular*) You are in a good **humour** when you are in a cheerful mood, and in a bad **humour** if you are feeling depressed and bad-tempered: *Their son's unexpected success had evidently put them both in a good humour for once.*
▻ ***verb***: **humours, humouring, humoured**
You **humour** someone who is behaving oddly or dangerously by trying to please them, *eg* by agreeing with them, or doing what they want you to do: *She wondered if he was mad, and if she ought to humour him.* [*same as* **indulge**]

humourless /'hju:mələs/ *adjective*
Someone who is **humourless** is very serious, has no sense of humour and cannot appreciate funny remarks or situations: *His writing style was dry and humourless.*

hump /hʌmp/ *noun*; *verb*
▻ ***noun***: **humps**
1 An animal that has a **hump** has a large, rounded lump on its back: *I couldn't remember which camels had two humps and which had only one.* **2** A **hump** in the landscape or in the road is a part that is raised above the rest of the surface: *We had to drive over a serious of humps humorously called 'sleeping policemen'.*
▻ ***verb***: **humps, humping, humped**
You **hump** luggage or something heavy and bulky somewhere when you walk there dragging it or carrying it: *I don't want to hump this bag round town all day.* [*same as* **haul**]

humpbacked /'hʌmpbakt/ *adjective*
1 (**also humpback**) A **humpbacked**, or **humpback**, bridge is usually a small one, with a high curve in the middle. **2** A **humpbacked** animal has a hump on its back.

hunch /hʌntʃ/ *noun*; *verb*
▻ ***noun***: **hunches**
You have a **hunch** that something is so when you feel strongly that it is, though you have no evidence or proof: *I had a hunch that she would invite Maurice.*
▻ ***verb***: **hunches, hunching, hunched**
1 You **hunch** your shoulders when you draw them up towards your ears and forward towards your chest. **2** You **hunch** or **are hunched** somewhere when you sit or crouch with your shoulders drawn forward and your head looking down: *She was hunched in an armchair, her knees covered with a rug.*

hundred /'hʌndrəd/ *noun*; *determiner*; *pronoun*
▻ ***noun***: **hundred** or **hundreds**
A **hundred** or one **hundred** is the number, figure or age of 100: *Five times twenty is one hundred.* ▫ *The total came to five hundred and sixty.* ▫ *(AmE) four hundred thirty two* ▫ *Ten hundreds make a thousand.* ▫ *He'll never learn sense if* [= even if] *he lives to be a hundred.*
▻ ***determiner:*** *It's four hundred and twenty miles from here to Birmingham.* ▫ *The first hundred applicants will receive their replies by tomorrow.*
▻ ***pronoun:*** *We had sixty replies yesterday and another hundred and two today.* ▫ *Yesterday was a proud day for two hundred of the town's schoolchildren.* ▫ (*informal*) *I've got hundreds of letters to write, literally hundreds.*

hundredth (often written **100th**) /'hʌndrədθ/ *determiner*; *pronoun*; *adjective or adverb*; *noun*
▻ ***determiner***
The **hundredth** person or thing is the one that is numbered one hundred in a series: *A centenary is a hundredth anniversary.* ▫ *The 100th Annual General Meeting of the Society of Glassblowers.*
▻ ***pronoun:*** *I've swum eighty lengths and I'm going to stop at the hundredth.*
▻ ***adjective or adverb:*** *He worked out that he was hundredth in the line of succession to the British throne.* ▫ *She came hundredth in the marathon and got a special prize.*
▻ ***noun*** (often written $\frac{1}{100}$)
A **hundredth** of something is one of a hundred equal parts of it: *The device records runners' speeds down to a hundredth of a second.*

hundredweight /'hʌndrədweɪt/ *noun*: **hundredweight** or **hundredweights**
A **hundredweight** is a unit of weight equal to 112 pounds (50.8 kilogrammes) in Britain and 100 pounds (45.4 kilogrammes) in the United States: *two hundredweight of coal.*

hung /hʌŋ/ *verb*; *adjective*
▻ ***verb***
Hung is the past tense and past participle of **hang**.
▻ ***adjective***
In a **hung** parliament no party has a sufficient majority to govern effectively; in a **hung** jury, the members cannot agree on a verdict.
▻ ***phrases*** **1** (*informal*) You are **hung over** if you have a headache or hangover from having drunk too much the night before. **2** (*informal*) You are **hung up** on or about something if you worry about it a lot.

Hungarian /hʌŋ'gɛəriən/ *adjective*; *noun*
▻ ***adjective***
Hungarian means concerned with or belonging to Hungary, its people or their language: *She's Hungarian, not Polish.* ▫ *Hungarian grammar.*
▻ ***noun***: **Hungarians**
1 A person who is born in, or is a citizen of Hungary, is a **Hungarian**: *There were two or three Hungarians at the conference.* **2** (*uncount*) **Hungarian** is the language of Hungary.

hunger /'hʌŋgə(r)/ *noun*; *verb*
▻ ***noun*** (*uncount*)
1 Hunger is the feeling you get when you want or need to eat: *I'm on a diet, but hunger gets the better of me sometimes.* **2 Hunger** is also the lack of food: *People were dying daily of hunger.* **3** A **hunger** for something is a strong desire for it: *a child's hunger for affection.* [*same as* **craving**]
▻ ***verb***: **hungers, hungering, hungered**
You **hunger** for or after something if you want it very much: *Her youngest boy was now at school and she was hungering for some sort of challenge.* [*same as* **crave**]

hungry /'hʌŋgrɪ/ *adjective*: **hungrier, hungriest**
1 You are **hungry** if you want food: *Are you hungry?* ▫ *hungry children.* **2** You are **hungry** for something when you want it very much: *These children are hungry for love.* ▫ *power-hungry politicians.* — *adverb* **hungrily:** *She devoured the bread and cheese hungrily.*
▻ ***phrase*** People **go hungry** when they can get nothing to eat: *If the crops fail, the population goes hungry.*

hunk /hʌŋk/ *noun*: **hunks**
A **hunk** of something is a big piece of it: *He cut himself a hunk of cheese.*

hunt /hʌnt/ *verb*; *noun*
▻ ***verb***: **hunts, hunting, hunted**
1 People **hunt** when they chase and kill wild animals for food, or as a sport; animals **hunt** when they chase and kill other animals for food: *The men were out hunting.* ▫ *They had gone up the hill to hunt deer.* **2** In Britain people **hunt** when they go out in groups on horseback, with a pack of hounds, to chase and kill foxes for sport. **3** You **hunt** an enemy or a criminal if you look for them so as to be able to attack them or capture them: *Police hunting the killer are holding a man for questioning.* **4** You **hunt** for something or someone when you search for them: *I've hunted everywhere for my earring.* ▫ *We've been hunting all over town for the right carpet.* ▫ *We're house-hunting at the moment.* — *noun* (*uncount*) **hunting:** *Hunting was a favourite pastime of King James.* ▫ *a hunting expedition.*
▻ ***noun***: **hunts**
1 A **hunt** is an expedition to chase and kill animals. **2** (*singular*) You have a **hunt** for a person or thing when you look for them: *the hunt for the missing gold.*

> ***phrasal verbs***
> **hunt down** You **hunt** someone or something **down** when you find them after searching hard: *The remaining rebels were hunted down and shot.*
> **hunt out** You **hunt** something **out** when you find it by searching: *I can probably hunt out a copy of that report for you.*

hunter /ˈhʌntə(r)/ *noun*: **hunters**
1 A **hunter** is someone who hunts wild animals for food or sport. **2** You use **hunter** to form words that describe people who are eagerly searching for something: *The bargain-hunters arrived at the sale early.*

huntsman /ˈhʌntsmən/ *noun*: **huntsmen**
A **huntsman** is someone who hunts wild animals for food, or hunts foxes for sport.

hurdle /ˈhɜːdəl/ *noun*: **hurdles**
1 (*usually in the plural*; *athletics*) A **hurdle** is one of a row of fences placed across a race track at regular intervals for runners to jump over in a series of races of various distances, referred to as, *eg* 'the 100-metres **hurdles**'. **2** You can refer to a difficulty that you must overcome, or a challenge that you must face, as a **hurdle**: *She sits her A-level exams in May, so once she's got over that hurdle she can think more clearly about the future.* [*same as* **obstacle**]

hurl /hɜːl/ *verb*: **hurls, hurling, hurled**
1 You **hurl** something somewhere when you throw it with force: *The crowd started hurling stones at the police.* □ *I hurled myself to the ground.* **2** You **hurl** abuse or insults at someone when you shout abuse or insults at them.

hurrah and **hurray** see **hooray**.

hurricane /ˈhʌrɪkən/ *noun*: **hurricanes**
A **hurricane** is a storm in which there is a violent destructive wind, usually blowing at over 120 miles an hour.

hurried /ˈhʌrɪd/ *adjective*
Something that is **hurried** is done quickly, especially too quickly: *He ate a hurried breakfast and rushed off to catch the train.* — *adverb* **hurriedly:** *She glanced hurriedly round the room.*

hurry /ˈhʌrɪ/ *verb*; *noun*
▻ ***verb***: **hurries, hurrying, hurried**
1 You **hurry** when you do something or go somewhere quickly: *She wants this report by 5.30, so I'll have to hurry.* □ *It's late; we'd better hurry.* □ *She hurried off in the direction of the supermarket.* [*same as* **rush**] **2** You **hurry** a person or a process when you try to make them move or progress faster: *Could you hurry your sister a bit? We've got to leave in five minutes.* **3** You **hurry** to do something when you do it as soon as possible: *I hurried to reassure her that there was no real danger.*
▻ ***noun***
1 (*used in the singular*) You are in a **hurry** when you need to get somewhere or do something quickly: *I'm in a bit of a hurry; I'll have to dash.* **2** (*used in the singular*) You do something in a **hurry** if you do it quickly, especially too quickly: *If I pack in a hurry I always forget things.* **3** (*uncount or used in the singular*) **Hurry** is the state of needing to do things quickly: *In my hurry to answer the telephone I knocked over my coffee cup.* [*same as* **rush**]
▻ ***phrases*** **1 a** You say you are **in no hurry**, or **there's no hurry**, if there is plenty of time: *I won't be seeing him till next week so there's no hurry for those photographs.* **b** (*informal*) You say you are **in no hurry** to do something if you would rather not do it: *Having failed to write his essay, he was in no hurry to bump into his tutor.* **2 a** (*informal*) If you say that something will **not** happen **in a hurry** you mean it will not happen for a long time: *It was a major heart attack, so he won't be going back to work in a hurry.* **b** (*informal*) You say you will **not** do something again **in a hurry** if you are unwilling to do it ever again: *Well, we won't be going back to that restaurant in a hurry.* **3** You ask '**what's the hurry?**' when people want something done quickly and you think they are being unreasonable: *Can't the problem wait till I get home? What's the hurry?*

> ***phrasal verb***
> **hurry up**
> **1** You tell someone to **hurry up** when you want them to act or move faster: *Do hurry up; we've got to be there in ten minutes.* **2** You **hurry** a person or process **up** when you make them progress faster: *Is there any way of hurrying up the production stage?*

hurt /hɜːt/ *verb*; *adjective*; *noun*
▻ ***verb***: **hurts, hurting, hurt**
1 You **hurt** yourself, or **hurt** part of your body, when you do something that causes you to be injured: *She fell and hurt herself.* □ *How did you hurt your hand?* **2** You **hurt** someone else when you make them feel pain; something that someone does to you **hurts** if it makes you feel pain: *I'm so sorry; I hope I didn't hurt you?* □ *Let go! You're hurting me!* □ *Ouch, you're hurting!* □ *Ouch, that hurts!* □ *Does this hurt?* □ *Does it hurt when I touch you here?* **3** Part of your body **hurts** or **is hurting** when you feel pain in it: *My foot's hurting.* **4** You **hurt** someone, or **hurt** their feelings, when you upset them by being unkind to them: *I don't want to hurt his feelings, but I'd rather not go out with him.* □ *I could see I'd hurt her, so I apologized quickly.* **5** Something **hurts** a person or thing if it harms them: *It is the pensioners and small savers that will be hurt by the new tax arrangements.*
▻ ***adjective***
1 You are **hurt** if you are injured: *He didn't appear to be seriously hurt.* **2** You are **hurt** when you feel upset because of someone's unkindness or lack of concern for you: *Secretly she felt rather hurt that he hadn't spoken to her.* □ *His face wore a look of hurt innocence.*
▻ ***noun*** (*uncount*)
Hurt is the emotional pain that some unpleasant experience causes you, or the upset feelings you have when you think people have treated you badly: *She continued to feel the hurt of the separation and divorce for several years.*
▻ ***phrase*** (*informal*) If you say **it wouldn't hurt** someone to do something, you mean that they ought to do it: *It wouldn't hurt you to apologize to your mother.*

hurtful /ˈhɜːtfəl/ *adjective*
Words or treatment that are **hurtful** are unkind and make you unhappy: *Emma's remark had been deliberately hurtful and Miss Bates was upset.*

hurtle /ˈhɜːtəl/ *verb*: **hurtles, hurtling, hurtled**
Something **hurtles** when it moves very fast, often in a dangerous or uncontrolled way: *Drivers go hurtling along with no regard for the speed limit*

husband /ˈhʌzbənd/ *noun*: **husbands**
A woman's **husband** is the man she is married to.

husbandry /ˈhʌzbəndrɪ/ *noun* (*uncount*)
Husbandry is
1 farming. **2** the careful management of land, property and resources.

hush /hʌʃ/ *interjection*; *noun*; *verb*
▻ ***interjection***
You say '**hush!**' to someone if you want them to stop talking or be quiet.

▻ ***noun***: **hushes** (*usually in the singular*)
A **hush** is a silence, especially a sudden one: *There was a sudden expectant hush as she stood up to speak.*
▻ ***verb***: **hushes, hushing, hushed**

> ***phrasal verb***
> People in authority **hush** something **up** when they prevent it from becoming publicly known: *She wanted her son's involvement in arms-dealing hushed up as far as possible.*

hushed /'hʌʃt/ *adjective*
1 People talk in **hushed** voices when they talk quietly or whisper: *The cathedral was deserted except for a knot of tourists speaking in hushed tones.* **2** A **hushed** place is noticeably quiet: *He passed along endless hushed corridors.*

hush-hush /hʌʃ'hʌʃ/ *adjective* (*informal*)
Activity or business that is **hush-hush** is secret: *She has one of those very senior hush-hush jobs in the civil service.*

husk /hʌsk/ *noun*: **husks**
Husks are the outer casings or coverings of seeds or grains.

husky /'hʌskɪ/ *adjective*: **huskier, huskiest**
Someone's voice is **husky** if it sounds rough and hoarse: *He replied in that deep, husky growl she found so attractive.*

hustings /'hʌstɪŋz/ *noun* (*plural*; *literary or formal*)
The **hustings** were originally the platform from which candidates for election made their speeches, but the word refers now to the process and activity of campaigning for election.

hustle /'hʌsəl/ *verb*: **hustles, hustling, hustled**
You **hustle** someone somewhere when you push or hurry them there: *After a brief court appearance the accused was hustled back into a waiting van with a blanket over his head.*

hut /hʌt/ *noun*: **huts**
A **hut** is a small house, shelter or shed, usually made of wood, mud or grass.

hutch /hʌtʃ/ *noun*: **hutches**
A **hutch** is a cage, usually made of wood with an opening covered by wire netting, for pets such as rabbits to live in.

hyacinth /'haɪəsɪnθ/ *noun*: **hyacinths**
A **hyacinth** is a plant that grows from a bulb and has lots of small blue, pink or white sweet-smelling flowers on a single strong stem.

hyaena see **hyena**.

hybrid /'haɪbrɪd/ *noun*; *adjective*
▻ ***noun***: **hybrids**
1 A **hybrid** is an animal or plant that has been bred or produced from two or more kinds or species of animal or plant. **2** Anything that is a mixture or combination of elements can be called a **hybrid**: *The software programme appeared to be a hybrid of database and word-processing package.*
▻ ***adjective:*** *hybrid roses* □ *hybrid systems of philosophy that combine elements of both Western and Eastern thought.*

hydrant /'haɪdrənt/ *noun*: **hydrants**
A **hydrant** is a pipe in the street that supplies water for putting out fires.

hydraulic /haɪ'drɔːlɪk/ *adjective*
Hydraulic relates to water or other liquids moving under pressure through pipes, or the use of this pressure to produce power.

hydraulics /haɪ'drɔːlɪks/ *noun* (*uncount*)
Hydraulics is the science dealing with the movement of water and other liquids under pressure through pipes, or the power produced by this pressure.

hydroelectric /haɪdroʊɪ'lɛktrɪk/ *adjective*
Hydroelectric describes electrical energy obtained from flowing water: *hydroelectric power.* — *noun* (*uncount*) **hydroelectricity:** *In mountainous areas energy can be supplied simply and cheaply by hydroelectricity.*

hydrogen /'haɪdrədʒən/ *noun* (*uncount*)
Hydrogen is a gas, the lightest element known, which combines with oxygen to produce water.

hyena or **hyaena** /haɪ'iːnə/ *noun*: **hyenas**
A **hyena** is a dog-like wild animal of Africa and Asia with a cry that sounds rather like human laughter.

hygiene /'haɪdʒiːn/ *noun* (*uncount*)
Hygiene is the practice or scientific study of keeping yourself and your surroundings clean, in order to prevent the spread of disease.

hygienic /haɪ'dʒiːnɪk/ *adjective*
Things that are **hygienic** are clean and free of germs, so as not to allow the spread of disease: *Women were being encouraged to have their babies in the hygienic surroundings of a hospital.* — *adverb* **hygienically:** *hygienically wrapped sweets.*

hymn /hɪm/ *noun*: **hymns**
A **hymn** is a song of praise to God, sung by Christians, especially during church services.

hyper- /haɪpə(r)/ *prefix*
Hyper- is added to adjectives relating to qualities, and indicates that there is too much of the quality; for example, a *hypersensitive* person is over-sensitive, or too sensitive.

hypermarket /'haɪpəmɑːkɪt/ *noun*: **hypermarkets**
A **hypermarket** is a very large supermarket.

hyphen /'haɪfən/ *noun*: **hyphens**
A **hyphen** is the punctuation mark (-), used to join words to form compounds (as in *taxi-driver*, *a two-year-old child*), or at the end of a line to divide a word that continues from the end of that line to the beginning of the next.

hypnosis /hɪp'noʊsɪs/ *noun* (*uncount*)
Hypnosis is hypnotism, the practice of putting someone into a sleep-like state in which they are able to respond to you and obey your suggestions; someone is in a state of **hypnosis**, or under **hypnosis**, when they are in this state: *Some doctors perform these operations using hypnosis instead of anaesthetics, and the patients claim afterwards to have felt no pain.*

hypnotic /hɪp'nɒtɪk/ *adjective*
1 Someone who is in a **hypnotic** state has been hypnotized, or is behaving as if they have been. **2** Something that has a **hypnotic** effect makes you feel as if you are being hypnotized or put to sleep: *The music and the smell of incense were having a hypnotic effect on him.*

hypnotism /'hɪpnətɪzm/ *noun* (*uncount*)
Hypnotism is the practice of hypnotizing people, sometimes as a public entertainment.

hypnotist /'hɪpnətɪst/ *noun*: **hypnotists**
A **hypnotist** is a person who practises hypnotism, sometimes as a public entertainment.

hypnotize or **hypnotise** /'hɪpnətaɪz/ *verb*: **hypnotizes, hypnotizing, hypnotized**
Someone **hypnotizes** you when they put you into a sleep-like state in which you can hear and respond to them, and obey their suggestions: *There were tales of people being hypnotized into committing murders.*

hypochondriac /haɪpə'kɒndrɪak/ *noun*: **hypochondriacs**
A **hypochondriac** is someone who worries too much about their health, and is inclined to think they are ill when they are quite healthy.

hypocrisy /hɪ'pɒkrɪsɪ/ *noun* (*uncount*)
Hypocrisy is the behaviour of someone who is not as righteous, honest, sincere, or concerned for people as they pretend to be: *Such a degree of hypocrisy cannot be tolerated in our public servants.*

hypocrite /'hɪpəkrɪt/ *noun*: **hypocrites**
A **hypocrite** is someone who is not as honest, righteous, sincere or sympathetic as they pretend to be.

hypocritical /hɪpə'krɪtɪkəl/ *adjective*
Someone who is **hypocritical** does not have the feelings or principles that they claim to have: *It would be hypocritical of me to say I was looking forward to her visit.* — *adverb* **hypocritically:** *He privately felt he had behaved rather hypocritically, and was ashamed.*

hypodermic /haɪpoʊ'dɜːmɪk/ *adjective*
A **hypodermic** syringe is an instrument with a hollow needle, for injecting drugs under the skin, into a muscle or vein.

hypothesis /haɪ'pɒθəsɪs/ *noun*: **hypotheses**
A **hypothesis** is a theory that has been worked out as an explanation for something, but has not yet been proved right: *Let's consider the hypothesis that the way words sound influences people's perception of their meaning, and could be a reason for their developing new meanings.*

hypothetical /haɪpə'θetɪkəl/ *adjective*
Hypothetical situations or cases are based on possibilities rather than facts: *Let me give you a hypothetical example.*

hysteria /hɪ'stɪərɪə/ (*AmE* /hɪ'stɛrɪə/) *noun* (*uncount*)
1 Hysteria is a severely disturbed state of the emotions, sometimes causing uncontrollable crying or laughing. **2** Mass **hysteria** is excitement or panic that grows and gets out of control within a crowd of people: *Groups like the Beatles had only to open their mouths to induce hysteria amongst their teenage audience.*

hysterical /hɪ'stɛrɪkəl/ *adjective*
1 A **hysterical** person is suffering from a severe emotional disturbance, often as a result of shock: *The effects of assault can be shock, and a hysterical and nervous condition.* □ *She was laughing uncontrollably and he realized she must be hysterical.* **2** You describe people's behaviour as **hysterical** when they get into a state of panic, or let their excitement or anger get out of control: *hysterical screaming.* **3** (*informal*) You describe something as **hysterical** if it is very funny: *Kids come out with these hysterical remarks sometimes.* [*same as* **hilarious**] — *adverb* **hysterically:** *By now I was in a panic and started yelling hysterically at the children.* □ *The whole incident was hysterically funny.*

hysterics /hɪ'stɛrɪks/ *noun* (*plural*; *rather old, or informal*)
You have **hysterics** when you get into an uncontrollable emotional or excited state: *Please don't tell my mother; she'll have hysterics.*
▻ ***phrase*** (*informal*) Someone who is **in hysterics** is laughing uncontrollably: *She had the audience in hysterics.*

I

I[1] or **i** /aɪ/ *noun*: **Is, i's**
I is the ninth letter of the English alphabet: *How many i's are there in 'infinitive?*

I[2] /aɪ/ *pronoun* (*used as the subject of a verb*)
I is used by the person speaking or writing to refer to himself or herself: *'I haven't seen him for a long time,' said Jean.* □ *'I don't like myself very much,' Tom admitted.* □ *'Who'll tell Amelia?' 'I will.'*

> Notice the following uses: *I bet you don't weigh as much as I do* (or *as me*). *No-one was more disappointed than I was* (or *than me*, or, in formal English, *than I*). *It was I who had to tell her the bad news* (but: *'Who's there?' 'It's me.'*).
> Notice that 'George and I' becomes 'George and me' when used as the object of a verb or preposition: *Thank you for making Jill and me* (not *Jill and I*) *so comfortable. Could you return the form to my secretary or me* (not *my secretary or I*).

[see also **me, my, myself**]

-ibility /ɪbɪlɪtɪ/ *suffix*: **-ibilities**
-ibility is added to adjectives ending in '-ible' to form nouns that refer to qualities or states: *the impossibility of the task* □ *We have no doubts about his eligibility.* □ *This is quite beyond his capabilities.* [see also **-ability**]

-ible /ɪbəl/ *suffix*
-ible is used to form adjectives meaning 'that may be' or 'capable of being': *The board's decision is not reversible.* □ *an inexplicable error.* [see also **-able**]

ice /aɪs/ *noun; verb*
▻ ***noun***: **ices**
1 (*uncount*) **Ice** is frozen water: *roads covered with snow and ice.* **2** (*uncount*) You have **ice** with a drink when you add small, specially-prepared blocks or cubes of ice to the drink to keep it cool: *Would you like ice in your whisky?* **3** (*used in the plural*) Ice cream and other frozen sweets are often referred to as **ices**.
▻ ***verb***: **ices, icing, iced**
You **ice** a cake when you decorate it with icing.
▻ ***phrase*** In a situation where people are behaving in a very shy, reserved or formal way with each other, *eg* because they have not met before, you **break the ice** when you say or do something that makes everyone feel more relaxed.

> ***phrasal verb***
> Something **ices up** or **ices over** when it becomes covered with ice, because the weather is very cold: *All the locks had iced up during the night.*

iceberg /ˈaɪsbɜːg/ *noun*: **icebergs**
An **iceberg** is a huge mass of ice floating in the sea, most of which lies hidden beneath the water: *The theory is still that the ship hit an iceberg.*
▻ ***phrase*** If you say that something, such as a problem you are dealing with, is just **the tip of the iceberg**, you mean that it is just a small part of something much bigger, most of which is still waiting to be discovered or dealt with: *I'm beginning to find out that his truancy is just the tip of the iceberg, and that he's heavily involved in drugs.*

ice cream /aɪsˈkriːm/ *noun* (*uncount or count*): **ice creams**
Ice cream is a sweet, creamy frozen dessert made either from flavoured cream or a substitute, often served in a cone-shaped wafer: *a bowl of ice cream* □ *Mummy bought them an ice cream each.*

ice cube /ˈaɪs kjuːb/ *noun*: **ice cubes**
An **ice cube** is a small block of ice used for cooling drinks.

ice hockey /ˈaɪs hɒkɪ/ *noun* (*uncount*)
Ice hockey is a form of hockey played on ice by players wearing ice skates, with, instead of a ball, a thick hard rubber disc called a 'puck'.

ice lolly /aɪs ˈlɒlɪ/ *noun*: **ice lollies**
An **ice lolly** is a frozen block of ice cream or fruit juice on a stick.

ice skate /ˈaɪs skeɪt/ *noun*: **ice skates**
Ice skates are boots with thick metal blades on the soles, for sliding over ice.

icicle /ˈaɪsɪkəl/ *noun*: **icicles**
An **icicle** is a long hanging spike of ice, formed by water freezing as it drops: *Icicles had formed on the edges of the roof.*

icing /ˈaɪsɪŋ/ *noun* (*uncount*)
Icing is a sweet paste consisting of a flavoured mixture of sugar, water and eggs, used to decorate cakes.
▻ ***phrase*** You can describe an addition to something already complete, or something already very pleasant or enjoyable on its own, as **the icing on the cake**.

icing sugar /ˈaɪsɪŋ ʃʊgə(r)/ *noun* (*uncount*)
Icing sugar is sugar in the form of a very fine powder, used to make icing and also scattered on cakes and other sweets.

icon or **ikon** /ˈaɪkɒn/ *noun*: **icons**
1 An **icon** is a painted wooden panel with a picture of Christ or a saint on it. **2** An **icon** is also a person or thing chosen or regarded as a symbol of something such as a political or other movement: *The ordinary working man is no longer the great icon of Labour politics.*

icy /ˈaɪsɪ/ *adjective*: **icier, iciest**
1 Something **icy** is covered with ice: *icy roads* □ *Drivers are warned of icy conditions on the roads today.* **2** You describe something as **icy** if it is very cold: *the icy waters of the North Sea.* **3** Someone's manner or behaviour is described as **icy** if it is very unfriendly: *She gave me an icy stare.* — *adverb* **icily:** *'What kept you?' he enquired icily.*

ID /aɪˈdiː/ *noun* (*uncount, often adjectival*)
When a person asks you for **ID**, they want you to show them some official document that will prove

who you are, such as a passport or driving licence: *Do you have any ID with you?* □ *We should issue all members of staff with ID cards.* □ *an ID badge.*

I'd /aɪd/ *verb*
I'd is the spoken, and informal written, form of **1 I had**, in cases where 'have' is used as an auxiliary verb: *I'd left my wallet in the restaurant.* **2 I would**: *I'd give you the money myself, if I had it.* □ *I'd not have told him unless he'd asked.*

idea /ai'dɪə/ *noun*: **ideas**
1 An **idea** is a plan, suggestion, or a possible move or course of action, *eg* for solving a problem: *All ideas and suggestions are welcome.* □ *Someone had the idea of recording the talk.* □ *I've got an idea; couldn't we get her address through the University?* □ *That's a good idea.* □ *Well, it was your idea.* □ *I've thought of an idea for a novel.* □ *It might be a good idea to learn some Czech before going to Prague.* □ *I don't like the idea of leaving the children alone in the house all day.* **2** An **idea** is an opinion about how things should be, or about what something should be like: *He has some strange ideas about how to treat women.* □ *old-fashioned ideas on grammar-learning* □ *Walking about in thick mist is not my idea of fun.* [*same as* **notion**] **3** (*used in the singular*) The **idea** of something is its aim or purpose: *The idea of the game is to win as many cards as possible.* □ *The whole idea of this weekend break was to get you to relax.* [*same as* **purpose**] **4** (*used in the singular*) You have or get the **idea** that something is so if you think it is so from what you have seen or heard: *I don't know how you got the idea that they were arriving this weekend.* □ *I had an idea you might be needing help.* □ *What on earth gave you that idea?* [*same as* **impression**] **5** (*uncount or used in the singular*) You have an **idea** of something if you know about it, or have some experience, understanding or appreciation of it: *She already had some idea of the work involved.* □ *Have you any idea how much a second-hand printer might cost?* □ *She'll be late; she never had any idea of time.*
▻ ***phrases*** **1** Someone **gets the idea** when they understand how to do something, or understand what they are being told. **2** You say **'That's the idea!'** when someone shows that they have understood what you are telling them or what you want them to do. **3** You say you **have no idea** if you do not know something: *'What time does his train arrive?' 'I've no idea.'* □ *I'd no idea there would be so many people here.*

ideal /aɪ'dɪəl/ *adjective*; *noun*
▻ ***adjective***
Ideal describes people and things that are perfectly suitable and exactly what is wanted or needed, whether or not they really exist: *She's absolutely ideal for a job like this.* □ *It's the ideal solution to our problem.* □ *Janice would not be my ideal woman.* □ *Her ideal home would be somewhere sunny.*
▻ ***noun***: **ideals**
1 An **ideal** is something, especially an idea or concept, that seems perfect to you, and that you try to aim for: *The ideal of amateur excellence in sport is becoming a thing of the past.* □ *A gold medal would of course be my ideal, but I'll be satisfied with any medal.* **2** (*used in the plural*) Your **ideals** are the principles or standards of behaviour according to which you try to live: *people with high ideals.* □ *Your trouble is that you have no ideals.*

idealise see **idealize**.

idealism /aɪ'dɪəlɪzm/ *noun* (*uncount*)
Idealism is the belief that ideal things are possible, and especially the refusal to accept that problems, difficulties and disappointments are more likely: *We were inspired by her youthful idealism.* [*opposite* **realism**] — *noun* **idealist** /aɪ'dɪəlɪst/: *Henry had always been an idealist.* [*opposite* **realist**] — *adjective* **idealistic** /aɪdɪə'lɪstɪk/: *Isn't that a rather idealistic approach?* [*opposite* **realistic**]

idealize or **idealise** /aɪ'dɪəlaɪz/ *verb*: **idealizes, idealizing, idealized**
You **idealize** something or someone when you think of them as being more perfect or ideal than they really are. [*same as* **glorify**] — *adjective* **idealized:** *She has this rather idealized notion of married life.* [*same as* **glorified**]

ideally /aɪ'dɪəlɪ/ *adverb*
1 (*sentence adverb*) **Ideally** is used when talking about what is desirable, as distinct from what is actually the case, or what may be possible: *Ideally, someone with more experience should have been given the job.* □ *They would ideally want to move in before Christmas.* **2 Ideally** means 'perfectly': *The cottage is ideally located for exploring the beautiful South Devon coast.* □ *He's ideally suited to family life.*

identical /aɪ'dɛntɪkəl/ *adjective*
1 Identical describes two or more things that are exactly alike or very similar: *This is an identical situation to the one we faced last year.* □ *The women were dressed in identical outfits.* [*opposite* **different**; compare **same**, **similar**] **2 Identical** twins are both the same sex and look so alike that it is difficult to tell which is which. [*opposite* **non-identical**]

identification /aɪdɛntɪfɪ'keɪʃən/ *noun* (*uncount*)
1 When someone asks you for **identification** they want you to show them some official document, such as a passport or driving licence, that proves who you are: *I don't normally carry any identification.* [*same as* **papers**] **2 Identification** is also the process of finding out who someone is or what something is, or the fact of being able to find out: *The body's advanced state of decay has made identification impossible.*

identify /aɪ'dɛntɪfaɪ/ *verb*: **identifies, identifying, identified**
1 You **identify** someone or something when you find out, recognize or state who or what they are: *Police have so far failed to identify the gunman.* □ *Our witness has identified the man she saw running from the car.* □ *The origin of the problem has been identified as a lack of resources.* □ *The victim has been identified as John Morgan, aged 33.* □ *We managed to identify the piece of bone as part of the lower jaw.* **2** You **identify** with someone when you feel sympathy and understanding for them because their situation is similar to your own in some way: *You can't expect readers to identify with a hero whose only problem is what to spend his money on.* [*same as* **relate to**] **3** People and things **are identified** with each other when they are thought of as being closely related or associated: *In the public's mind, the name Jaguar is still identified with quality and excellence in motor cars.*

identity /aɪ'dɛntɪtɪ/ *noun* (*usually in the singular*): **identities**
1 The **identity** of a person or thing is who or what they are: *I should now like to ask our celebrity guest to open this envelope and reveal the identity of the winner.* **2** Your **identity** also consists of those characteristics that you share with other people in the same racial, religious or other group, that make you aware of what kind of person you are: *Perhaps the English as a race no longer have a cultural identity.*

identity card /aɪ'dɛntɪtɪ kɑːd/ *noun*: **identity cards**
An **identity card** is a card bearing information about a

illiterate /ɪˈlɪtərət/ *adjective*
An **illiterate** person is unable to read and write: *A worrying percentage of school-leavers are technically illiterate.* [*opposite* **literate**] — *noun* (*uncount*) **illiteracy** /ɪˈlɪtərəsɪ/: *Are schools equipped to handle the problem of adolescent illiteracy?* [*opposite* **literacy**]

ill-mannered /ɪlˈmanəd/ *adjective*
An **ill-mannered** person behaves in a rude or impolite way. [*opposite* **polite**]

illness /ˈɪlnɪs/ *noun*: **illnesses**
1 (*uncount*) **Illness** is the state of being in poor health: *He's had several weeks off work through illness.* [*opposite* **(good) health**] **2** An **illness** is a particular disease: *She had a strange illness that was finally diagnosed as Sjögren's syndrome.*

illogical /ɪˈlɒdʒɪkəl/ *adjective*
Something such as a plan or argument is **illogical** if it makes no sense because the final parts do not follow on reasonably from the earlier parts: *It is illogical to claim that good weather is guaranteed during the rainy season.* [*opposite* **logical**]

ill-timed /ɪlˈtaɪmd/ *adjective*
An action or remark that is **ill-timed** is done or made at an unsuitable or unfortunate time: *The minister's involvement in a sex scandal could not have been more ill-timed, coming as it does in the middle of the government's 'family values' campaign.* ▫ *His visit was described as inopportune and ill-timed.* [*same as* **inopportune**; *opposite* **well-timed**]

ill-treat /ɪlˈtriːt/ *verb*: **ill-treats, ill-treating, ill-treated**
You **ill-treat** someone when you treat them badly or cruelly: *It was alleged that some of the residents had been ill-treated.* [*same as* **abuse**] — *noun* (*uncount*) **ill-treatment**: *There was clear evidence of abuse and ill-treatment by staff.*

illuminate /ɪˈluːmɪneɪt/ *verb*: **illuminates, illuminating, illuminated**
1 You **illuminate** something when you shine a light or lights on it: *It would look better if we illuminated the back half of the stage only.* [*same as* **light up**] **2** (*formal*) You also **illuminate** something when you explain it or make it easier to understand: *His critical essays illuminated the more obscure examples of Pound's poetry.* [*same as* **clarify**] — *adjective* **illuminating:** *I've been finding the lectures quite illuminating.* [*same as* **enlightening**]

illumination /ɪluːmɪˈneɪʃən/ *noun*: **illuminations**
1 (*uncount*) **Illumination** is lighting, or the number or kind of lights used: *Fluorescent lights give a rather dazzling illumination.* **2** (*used in the plural*) **Illuminations** are coloured lights hung in streets for decoration.

illusion /ɪˈluːʒən/ *noun*: **illusions**
An **illusion** is **1** (*usually in the singular*) a false belief or impression: *She's under the illusion that everyone in the office thinks she's wonderful.* ▫ *They wore smart suits to help create the illusion that they were serious businessmen.* ▫ *Mirrors on the wall create an illusion of space.* [*same as* **impression**] **2** a false or misleading appearance that deceives your eyes: *an optical illusion.* **3** a magic trick in which the audience is persuaded to believe they are seeing something that is not really happening.
▻ ***phrase*** If you say you **have no illusions** about something, you mean you have no falsely optimistic ideas about it: *She had no illusions about the task she had set herself; it was not going to be easy.*

illusionist /ɪˈluːʒənɪst/ *noun*: **illusionists**
An **illusionist** is a magician who performs illusions.

illusory /ɪˈluːzərɪ/ *adjective* (*formal*)
Something that is **illusory** seems possible or true but in reality is impossible, or mistaken: *Our assumption that we have recalled incidents exactly is to some extent illusory.*

illustrate /ˈɪləstreɪt/ *verb*: **illustrates, illustrating, illustrated**
1 You **illustrate** something you are saying when you support it or make it clearer by giving examples: *I can illustrate that last point by telling a little story.* ▫ *Their lack of enthusiasm illustrates the fact that they're extremely self-centred.* [*same as* **demonstrate**] **2** To **illustrate** something such as a book or magazine is to add pictures or diagrams.

illustration /ɪləˈstreɪʃən/ *noun*: **illustrations**
1 Illustrations are pictures or diagrams, *eg* in books and magazines. **2** Something that is an **illustration** of what you are saying serves as a proof or as an example: *That was just one illustration of their cruelty.*

illustrious /ɪˈlʌstrɪəs/ *adjective* (*formal*)
Someone who is **illustrious** is greatly admired and respected for their achievements by people in general: *She was always in the shadow of her more illustrious team mate.* ▫ *The book charts his illustrious political career.* [*same as* **celebrated, distinguished**]

ill-will /ɪlˈwɪl/ *noun* (*uncount*)
Ill-will is unfriendly feelings towards someone, or the wish to do them harm: *In spite of all that's happened, I bear him no ill-will.*

I'm /aɪm/
I'm is the spoken, and informal written, form of **I am**.

image /ˈɪmɪdʒ/ *noun*: **images**
1 Your **image** of something is the impression you have of it, or what you imagine it to be: *My lasting image of Greece is of a country of wide open spaces.* ▫ *She has this image of me as a man who can handle any situation.* ▫ *The word 'executive' conjures up images of sharp-suited men having business lunches.* **2** Your **image** consists of how you behave and the kind of clothes you wear, as a way of showing other people what kind of person you are: *In the mid seventies, he decided to change his image.* ▫ *She's having a bit of an image crisis.* **3** (*formal*) **Images** are pictures, *eg* the pictures on a television screen or photographs in a magazine: *the impression created by a combination of sound and image.*

imaginable /ɪˈmadʒɪnəbəl/ *adjective*
Imaginable is used in descriptions of extreme things, and means 'that you can think of or imagine': *It was the most disgusting sight imaginable!* ▫ *What would happen if it were to strike the hardest imaginable surface?*

imaginary /ɪˈmadʒɪnərɪ/ *adjective*
Imaginary describes things that exist only in your mind or imagination, not in reality: *The doctors reckon her illness is imaginary.* ▫ *The children played for ages with an imaginary teaset.* [*opposite* **real**]

imagination /ɪmadʒɪˈneɪʃən/ *noun* (*uncount or used in the singular*)
1 Your **imagination** is the part of your mind that forms mental pictures or impressions of things, especially things that you have never seen or that don't really exist: *I suspect that the whole story is a product of his imagination.* ▫ *Young Lucy has a very active imagination.* ▫ *Is it my imagination, or is there a noise coming from the bathroom?* **2** Someone who has **imagination** has the ability to think of new or original things: *Solving this kind of problem requires more than a little imagination.* [*same as* **creativity**]

imaginative /ɪˈmadʒɪnətɪv/ *adjective*
1 Something **imaginative** has been planned or created

by someone with the ability to think of new and original ideas: *an imaginative combination of colours.* [*opposite* **dull**, **pedestrian**] **2** An **imaginative** person is creative, and good at thinking of new and original ideas: *Britain's most imaginative young novelist.* [*opposite* **unimaginative**]

imagine /ɪ'madʒɪn/ *verb*: **imagines, imagining, imagined**
1 You **imagine** something, *eg* an unlikely situation, when you form a picture of it in your mind: *Imagine you can fly.* □ *Imagine for a moment that you didn't have a wife and family.* □ *I tried to imagine what life would be like without him.* □ *Just imagine the scene: blue sky, golden sands, absolute peace.* □ *Can you imagine having to shake hands with hundreds of strangers every day?* □ *I can't imagine myself ever wanting to join a fitness club, though I can imagine other people wanting to.* [*same as* **picture**, **envisage**] **2** You **imagine** something when you think you are seeing, hearing, or experiencing it, although actually you are not doing so: *Are you sure you didn't just imagine the voice in the room?* □ *'Everybody's staring at me.' 'No, they aren't; you're just imagining it.'* **3** You use **imagine** to mean 'suppose', 'expect' or 'think': *He's much smaller in real life than I had imagined he would be.* □ *I imagine he's missed the train.* □ *We imagined that you two would want to be alone together.* □ *'Will Tom want to come too?' 'I imagine so.'* □ *'Will she have gone to bed by now?' 'I imagine not* (or *I don't imagine so).'* [*same as* **suppose**, **expect**; see note at **think**] **4** You can say '**Imagine** a certain thing happening' in order to express surprise that it did happen: *Imagine her saying that!* [*same as* **fancy**]
▻ ***phrase*** You use '**I can't imagine**' like 'I have no idea', to mean that you really don't know: *I can't imagine what he meant.*

imbalance /ɪm'baləns/ *noun* (*usually in the singular*): **imbalances**
There is an **imbalance** when things are not arranged fairly or equally: *There is clearly an imbalance in the funding given to state-run prisons and privately managed institutions.*

imbecile /ɪmbə'si:l/ *noun*: **imbeciles**
If you call someone an **imbecile** you mean they are stupid or foolish: *Look what the imbecile did to my flowers!* [*same as* **idiot**]

imitate /'ɪmɪteɪt/ *verb*: **imitates, imitating, imitated**
1 You **imitate** someone when you do what they do: *Some of the larger companies are imitating the Japanese in their working practices.* □ *Here, he is clearly imitating Joyce's literary style.* [*same as* **copy**] **2** You also **imitate** someone when you try to speak or behave the way they do, in order to be amusing: *He can imitate George Bush brilliantly.* [*same as* **mimic**]

imitation /ɪmɪ'teɪʃən/ *noun*; *adjective*
▻ ***noun***: **imitations**
1 You do an **imitation** of someone when you try to speak or behave like them as a way of being funny: *Have you heard his imitation of Sylvester Stallone?* [*same as* **impression**] **2** (*uncount*) **Imitation** is the activity or the process of copying from someone or something else: *Some plastic products, such as shoes, come with marks on them in imitation of the stitching you'd get on real leather.* □ *'My word!' she exclaimed, in unmistakable imitation of her mother.*
▻ ***adjective***
Imitation describes something cheaply made to look or function like something else more expensive: *The car seats are upholstered in imitation leather.*

immaculate /ɪ'makjʊlət/ *adjective*
1 Someone or something whose appearance is **immaculate** is very clean, neat and tidy: *She keeps that house immaculate.* [*same as* **spotless**] **2 Immaculate** also describes something that is perfectly correct, with no mistakes: *an immaculate performance.* [*same as* **flawless**]

immaterial /ɪmə'tɪərɪəl/ *adjective*
Something that is **immaterial** is not important or not relevant: *It's immaterial whether you agree or not.* □ *He collects old books of all kinds; their condition is immaterial to him.* [*same as* **irrelevant**; *opposite* **important**]

immature /ɪmə'tjʊə(r)/ *adjective*
1 Something **immature** is not yet fully grown or fully developed: *The immature tiger already has the hunting instinct.* **2** Someone who is **immature** behaves in a silly, childish way: *He was one of those rather immature people who can see no-one's needs but their own.* [*opposite* **mature**]

immeasurably /ɪ'mɛʒərəblɪ/ *adverb* (*intensifying*)
Immeasurably means 'extremely' or 'enormously': *They are immeasurably more advanced than we are.*

immediacy /ɪ'mi:dɪəsɪ/ *noun* (*uncount*)
You might describe things such as paintings, photographs and passages of writing as having **immediacy** if they instantly make a very strong impression on you, so that you feel involved in what they are portraying.

immediate /ɪ'mi:dɪət/ *adjective*
1 Immediate describes things that happen or are done at once and without delay: *I want an immediate report of its progress.* □ *His immediate reaction was to deny it.* **2 Immediate** is often used to describe people or things that are nearest or next in space, time or relationship: *No firearms were found in the immediate vicinity.* □ *members of his immediate family.* [*same as* **close**] **3 Immediate** also describes things that need to be dealt with first, before anything else: *Our immediate concern is to eliminate the danger of further explosions.*

immediately /ɪ'mi:dɪətlɪ/ *adverb*; *conjunction*
▻ ***adverb***
1 You do something **immediately** when you do it at once or without delay: *We must leave immediately or we shall be late.* □ *She said yes, and then changed her mind almost immediately.* [*same as* **at once**, **straight away**] **2** Something that is **immediately** obvious, apparent or recognizable is quickly and easily noticed, understood or recognized: *Even after a gap of 35 years he was immediately recognizable.* □ *It was not immediately evident that something was wrong.* [*same as* **instantly**] **3** You are **immediately** involved in a situation if it affects you directly or closely: *I've spoken to the people immediately affected by the redundancy announcements.* **4** A thing that is **immediately** in front of, behind, before, after or beside another thing, is next to it in space or time: *I had a very tall man sitting immediately in front of me, so I couldn't see.* □ *I always check in my pocket for my keys immediately before leaving the house.*
▻ ***conjunction***
A thing that happens **immediately** another thing does, happens as soon as the other has happened: *Immediately I saw her face I knew she had bad news.* □ *I realized what a stupid remark it was immediately I'd made it.* [*same as* **as soon as**]

immense /ɪ'mɛns/ *adjective*
Immense means very large or very great: *an immense castle at the edge of the sea* □ *She has immense respect for him as a writer.* [*same as* **enormous**]

immensely /ɪˈmɛnslɪ/ *adverb* (*intensifying*)
Immensely means greatly: *We enjoyed ourselves immensely.* □ *They're immensely grateful to you.* [*same as* **enormously**]

immerse /ɪˈmɜːs/ *verb*: **immerses, immersing, immersed**
1 You **immerse** something in water or another liquid when you put it completely under the surface of the water: *Knives with wooden handles should not be immersed in water.* [*same as* **submerge**] **2** You say that someone **is immersed** in something if it occupies them completely, taking all their effort and concentration: *Jon is immersed in his work at the moment.* [*same as* **absorb**] — *noun* (*uncount*) **immersion** /ɪˈmɜːʃən/: *Avoid immersion in salt water.* □ *her complete immersion in all things French.*

immigrant /ˈɪmɪgrənt/ *noun* (*often adjectival*): **immigrants**
An **immigrant** is someone who has come to live permanently in a country after leaving their home country: *immigrant workers.* [see also **emigrant**]

immigration /ɪmɪˈgreɪʃən/ *noun* (*uncount*)
1 Immigration is the act of coming into a foreign country in order to settle permanently in it: *new laws on immigration.* [see also **emigration**] **2 Immigration** is also the place at an airport, sea port or other point of entry where officials check the passports of people coming into a country: *We had expected trouble at immigration.*

imminent /ˈɪmɪnənt/ *adjective*
Something **imminent** will happen or arrive very soon: *The process had to be speeded up in view of her imminent departure* □ *Civil war seemed imminent.*

immobile /ɪˈmoʊbaɪl/ *adjective*
1 Something **immobile** is not able to move or be moved: *A fitted kitchen is, of course, immobile; it stays when you sell the house.* **2** Someone or something that is **immobile** is completely still or motionless: *Janet stood immobile, gazing at the stained-glass window.* [*same as* **stationary**] — *noun* (*uncount*) **immobility** /ɪmoʊˈbɪlɪtɪ/: *She was sitting bolt upright in the chair and I was immediately struck by her look of immobility.*

immobilize or **immobilise** /ɪˈmoʊbɪlaɪz/ *verb*: **immobilizes, immobilizing, immobilized**
Something **is immobilized** when it is prevented from moving or from working: *Air attacks have immobilized much of the enemy's tank force.* [*same as* **paralyze**]

immodest /ɪˈmɒdəst/ *adjective* (*formal*)
Immodest describes the appearance or behaviour of someone who reveals parts of their body that are normally covered up, especially if this embarrasses or offends others: *a rather immodest red dress that attracted considerable attention.* [*opposite* **modest**]

immoral /ɪˈmɒrəl/ *adjective*
Immoral behaviour is wrong or evil: *It is quite immoral to tax old people on their heating bills.* □ *the immoral exposure of children to violence of all kinds.* [*opposite* **moral**] — *noun* (*uncount*) **immorality** /ɪməˈralɪtɪ/: *the immorality of charges for health care.*
[see also **amoral**]

immortal /ɪˈmɔːtəl/ *adjective*
1 Someone who is **immortal** lives for ever and never dies. [*opposite* **mortal**] **2 Immortal** is often used to describe people and things who will always be remembered: *when Churchill uttered those immortal words, 'We will never surrender'.* — *noun* (*uncount*) **immortality** /ɪmɔːˈtalɪtɪ/: *They believed the plant held the secret of immortality.* □ *The statue is his way of securing immortality.* [*opposite* **mortality**]

immortalize or **immortalise** /ɪˈmɔːtəlaɪz/ *verb*: **immortalizes, immortalizing, immortalized**
Something or someone **is immortalized** when their inclusion in something such as a book or film ensures that people will remember them for a long time: *Her beauty is immortalized in numerous films, notably 'Gilda'.*

immune /ɪˈmjuːn/ *adjective*
1 You are **immune** to a particular disease if you cannot catch it, either because your body resists it naturally, or because you have been protected medically: *It seemed for a while that women were immune to Aids.* **2** You are **immune** to, or **immune** from, something when you are not affected by it, or you are protected from it and cannot be harmed by it: *Men are not immune to feelings of guilt, you know.* □ *Nobody connected to the victim can be immune from police questioning.* [*same as* **free**] — *noun* (*uncount*) **immunity** /ɪˈmjuːnɪtɪ/: *Drugs can supplement the body's natural immunity.* □ *her immunity to criticism of all kinds.*

immunize or **immunise** /ˈɪmjʊnaɪz/ *verb*: **immunizes, immunizing, immunized**
You **are immunized** against a particular disease when you are made immune to it, often by being given a mild dose of the disease to force your body to create its own resistance. [*same as* **vaccinate, inoculate**]

impact /ɪmˈpakt/ *noun* (*usually in the singular*)
1 Impact is the action of one object hitting another object, or the force that they hit each other with: *The bomb is designed to explode on impact.* □ *The windows shattered with the impact.* **2** The **impact** that something has on you is the effect it has or the impression it makes: *His criticisms have made little impact on our resolve to pursue the campaign.* □ *That first meeting had a very strong impact on me.*

impair /ɪmˈpɛə(r)/ *verb*: **impairs, impairing, impaired**
To **impair** something is to damage it, or reduce its quality, strength or effectiveness: *Her beauty was slightly impaired by a faint scar on the left cheek.* □ *He's arguing that noise in the factory has impaired his hearing.* [*opposite* **enhance**]

impale /ɪmˈpeɪl/ *verb*: **impales, impaling, impaled**
Something **is impaled** on a pointed object when it is speared by it: *He fell, and was impaled on his own sword.*

impart /ɪmˈpɑːt/ *verb* (*formal*): **imparts, imparting, imparted**
1 You **impart** information or knowledge when you give it to someone. **2** To **impart** a particular quality to something is to give it that quality: *Yellow walls impart a warm, sunny feeling to any room.*

impartial /ɪmˈpɑːʃəl/ *adjective*
You are **impartial** when you give a fair opinion or judgement that does not favour one particular person or side: *Her involvement doesn't allow her to give an impartial assessment.* [*same as* **unbiased**; *opposite* **biased**] — *noun* (*uncount*) **impartiality** /ɪmpɑːʃɪˈalɪtɪ/: *Atkins' impartiality as a judge is essential.*

impassable /ɪmˈpɑːsəbəl/ *adjective*
A road is **impassable** when you cannot travel along it because it is blocked, *eg* by snow or floods. [*opposite* **passable, navigable**]

impasse /amˈpas/ *noun* (*usually in the singular*): **impasses**
You reach an **impasse**, *eg* in a discussion or negotiation, when no more progress is possible or no solution can be found: *There doesn't seem to be a way out of this impasse.*

impassive /ɪmˈpasɪv/ *adjective*
You are **impassive** when you show no feeling or emo-

tion: *Her face was totally impassive.* [*same as* **composed**] — *adverb* **impassively:** *He listened impassively to my story of childhood hardship.* [*same as* **unemotionally**]

impatient /ɪm'peɪʃənt/ *adjective*
1 You are **impatient** when you feel angry about being forced to wait: *There was a long delay and several passengers grew impatient.* □ *He's a rather impatient young man.* **2** You are **impatient** with people when you are irritated by them because they don't understand or learn things as quickly as you would like them to. **3** You are **impatient** for something when you are eager for it to happen immediately, and perhaps worried that, if it doesn't happen soon, it might not happen at all: *The students are impatient for change.* □ *Jennifer is a little impatient to get started.* [*opposite* **patient**] — *adverb* **impatiently:** *He paced the room impatiently.* [*opposite* **patiently**] — *noun* (*uncount*) **impatience:** *I detected a hint of impatience in his voice.* [*opposite* **patience**]

impeccable /ɪm'pɛkəbəl/ *adjective*
Something that is **impeccable** is perfect: *The locomotive is still in impeccable condition externally.* □ *The children's behaviour was impeccable at all times.* □ *Her attendance record has been impeccable this term.* [*same as* **flawless**]

impede /ɪm'piːd/ *verb*: **impedes, impeding, impeded**
You **impede** something or someone when you make it difficult or impossible for them to move or progress: *Recent developments have been impeded by a shortage of funds.* [*same as* **hinder**; *opposite* **help**]

impediment /ɪm'pɛdɪmənt/ *noun*: **impediments**
1 An **impediment** is something that makes it difficult to move or progress: *Some critics argue that our reliance on cars is an impediment to an effective transport policy.* **2** Someone who has a speech **impediment** cannot say certain sounds properly. [*same as* **defect**]

impel /ɪm'pɛl/ *verb*: **impels, impelling, impelled**
You **are impelled** to do something when you feel you must do it: *Overwhelming curiosity impelled me to visit her one more time.* [*same as* **move**]

impending /ɪm'pɛndɪŋ/ *adjective*
Impending describes something that is about to happen, especially something dangerous or unpleasant: *a feeling of impending doom.* [*same as* **imminent**; see also **pending**]

impenetrable /ɪm'pɛnɪtrəbəl/ *adjective*
1 Something that is **impenetrable** cannot be entered or passed through: *a dense, impenetrable forest.* [*opposite* **penetrable**] **2** You also describe something as **impenetrable** if it is impossible to understand: *pages of impenetrable legal jargon.* [*same as* **incomprehensible**]

imperative /ɪm'pɛrətɪv/ *adjective*; *noun*
▻ ***adjective***
Something that is **imperative** is absolutely essential: *It's imperative that we contact them tonight.* [*same as* **vital**]
▻ ***noun*** (*grammar*; *used in the singular*)
The **imperative** is the form of verbs used for giving orders, *eg* the form *be* of the verb **be** in 'Please be sensible': *Is the verb in the imperative?*

imperceptible /ɪmpə'sɛptɪbəl/ *adjective*
Something such as a sound or movement is **imperceptible** when it is too faint or slight to be noticed: *an almost imperceptible change of expression.*

imperfect /ɪm'pɜːfɪkt/ *adjective*; *noun*
▻ ***adjective***
Something is **imperfect** if it has faults or flaws in it: *The cups are reduced in price because some of them are slightly imperfect.* [*same as* **faulty**]
▻ ***noun*** (*grammar*; *used in the singular*)
The **imperfect**, or the **imperfect tense**, is the tense used to describe continuing or incomplete actions or states in the past, as in *I <u>was working</u> in the library all yesterday.*

imperfection /ɪmpə'fɛkʃən/ *noun*: **imperfections**
An **imperfection** is a fault, flaw or weakness, which makes someone or something imperfect: *A tendency to be lazy was his only imperfection.* [*same as* **failing**]

imperial /ɪm'pɪərɪəl/ *adjective*
1 Imperial means relating to an empire, or to an emperor or empress: *Napoleon's imperial ambitions* □ *living conditions in Imperial Rome* □ *the Imperial Palace.* **2 Imperial** refers to the system of measurement in which length is measured in feet and inches, weight is measured in pounds and ounces, and volume is measured in pints and gallons. [compare **metric**]

imperialism /ɪm'pɪərɪəlɪzm/ *noun* (*uncount*)
Imperialism is the policy or practice of taking control, by force, of less powerful countries and ruling over them: *the past imperialism of countries such as Britain, France, Spain and Portugal* □ *European museums are often accused of cultural imperialism.* — *adjective* **imperialist:** *imperialist tendencies.*

imperious /ɪm'pɪərɪəs/ *adjective*
You describe someone as **imperious** if their behaviour shows that they think others should obey them: *His face usually wore an imperious expression.* [*same as* **bossy, authoritarian**]

impersonal /ɪm'pɜːsənəl/ *adjective*
Someone who gives **impersonal** service or treatment treats every customer or guest the same, rather than treating them as individuals with different wishes and needs: *the impersonal atmosphere of a large hotel.* □ *the questionnaire approach can be sterile and impersonal.* [*opposite* **friendly**]

impersonate /ɪm'pɜːsəneɪt/ *verb*: **impersonates, impersonating, impersonated**
1 You **impersonate** someone, usually someone well known, when you copy their behaviour as a way of amusing or entertaining others: *Have you seen him impersonate the headmaster?* [*same as* **imitate**] **2** You also **impersonate** someone when you pretend to be them, in order to deceive others: *She was charged with impersonating a police officer.* — *noun* **impersonation** /ɪmpɜːsə'neɪʃən/: *She does a brilliant impersonation of Mrs Thatcher.* [*same as* **impression**]

impertinent /ɪm'pɜːtɪnənt/ *adjective*
Someone is **impertinent** when they fail to show proper respect for someone else, usually in the way they speak to that person: *Jessica was an impertinent girl.* □ *Your question is impertinent.* [*same as* **rude**] — *noun* (*uncount*) **impertinence:** *I will not tolerate such impertinence!* [*same as* **rudeness**]

impervious /ɪm'pɜːvɪəs/ *adjective*
1 You are **impervious** to something when you are not affected or influenced by it: *You never quite become impervious to criticism.* **2** Something is **impervious** to water if water cannot pass through it: *The outer surface of the jacket is completely impervious to rain.*
[*same as* **resistant**]

impetuous /ɪm'pɛtjʊəs/ *adjective*
Someone who is **impetuous** does things immediately, without waiting to think about the consequences: *It was an impetuous, spur-of-the-moment decision.* [*same as* **impulsive**; *opposite* **cautious**]

impetus /ˈɪmpətəs/ *noun* (*uncount or used in the singular*)
The **impetus** for an action or event is what makes you do it, or what makes it happen: *A series of complaints from customers was the impetus for this survey.* □ *One or two positive results have given the campaign fresh impetus.* [*same as* **momentum**]

impinge /ɪmˈpɪndʒ/ *verb*: **impinges**, **impinging**, **impinged**
One thing **impinges** on another if it affects it or interferes with it in some way: *At times of crisis my work schedule inevitably impinges on my private life.* [*same as* **encroach**]

implacable /ɪmˈplakəbəl/ *adjective* (*formal*)
Someone who is **implacable** is too angry or resentful to be calmed or pacified: *He had worked himself up into an implacable rage.*

implant *verb*; *noun*
▻ ***verb*** /ɪmˈplɑːnt/: **implants, implanting, implanted**
1 To **implant** something in a person's body is to fix it there, *eg* using surgery: *A tiny transmitter is implanted into the bird's chest.* **2** Something such as an idea or belief **is implanted** in a person's mind when it is fixed there permanently: *Has her Catholic childhood implanted in her these feelings of guilt?*
▻ ***noun*** /ˈɪmplɑːnt/: **implants**
An **implant** is something implanted in a person's body: *They wondered if hormone implants might be the answer.*

implausible /ɪmˈplɔːzɪbəl/ *adjective*
Something **implausible** is difficult to believe because it seems very unlikely to be true: *a ridiculously implausible excuse.* [*same as* **improbable**]

implement *noun*; *verb*
▻ ***noun*** /ˈɪmpləmənt/: **implements**
Implements are tools or utensils: *a rack of gardening implements.*
▻ ***verb*** /ˈɪmpləmɛnt/: **implements**, **implementing**, **implemented**
You **implement** something such as a plan when you carry it out or do it: *The new parking regulations will be implemented in the spring.* — *noun* (*uncount*) **implementation** /ɪmpləmənˈteɪʃən/: *the implementation of alternative policies.*

implicate /ˈɪmplɪkeɪt/ *verb*: **implicates**, **implicating**, **implicated**
Something **implicates** someone in a crime or other affair when it shows or suggests that they are involved: *The discovery of his footprints at the scene certainly implicates him.* □ *Several members of the victim's family have been implicated.* [*opposite* **absolve**]

implication /ɪmplɪˈkeɪʃən/ *noun*: **implications**
The **implications** of what someone says or does consist of what is revealed or suggested by it, rather than what is directly shown or expressed: *She stood up and offered me her seat, the implication being that I was an old man.* □ *Are we fully aware of the wider implications of this decision?* [*same as* **suggestion, significance**]
▻ ***phrase*** You use **by implication** when talking about something that is suggested or hinted at, rather than stated or expressed directly: *The report insists that production costs must be reduced and, by implication, that some workers will lose their jobs.*

implicit /ɪmˈplɪsɪt/ *adjective*
Implicit describes something that is suggested, not stated directly: *It was implicit in her criticism that she thought he could have done it better.* □ *the implicit snobbery contained in remarks about the importance of a 'good' education.* [*opposite* **explicit**]

implicitly /ɪmˈplɪsɪtlɪ/ *adverb*
You believe something **implicitly** when you have no doubt at all that it is true: *I trust all the servants implicitly.* [*same as* **absolutely**]

implore /ɪmˈplɔː(r)/ *verb* (*formal*): **implores, imploring, implored**
You **implore** someone to do something when you beg them to do it: *'Please, just help him one more time, please!,' she implored.* [*same as* **entreat**]

imply /ɪmˈplaɪ/ *verb*: **implies, implying, implied**
1 You **imply** something when you suggest it or express it indirectly: *Are you implying that I can't do my job properly?* □ *The offer implied she was an old woman in need of help.* **2** One thing **implies** another when it suggests that it will follow as a result: *Increasing profits implies cutting costs, which in turn implies cutting jobs.*

impolite /ɪmpəˈlaɪt/ *adjective*
Someone who is **impolite** is rude: *It would be impolite of you to refuse.* [*opposite* **polite**]

import *verb*; *noun*
▻ ***verb*** /ɪmˈpɔːt/: **imports, importing, imported**
To **import** goods is to bring them from another country: *All our cooked meat is imported from France and Italy.* □ *They are refusing to buy imported fish.* [*opposite* **export**]
▻ ***noun*** /ˈɪmpɔːt/: **imports**
Imports are goods imported from other countries: *a rise in the cost of imports.* [*opposite* **exports**]

important /ɪmˈpɔːtənt/ *adjective*
1 Something is **important** when it has great value, influence or effect: *Knowing how to listen is the counsellor's most important skill.* □ *It seems that most men feel their job is more important than their marriage.* □ *It's important to me that the children like me.* □ *It was important for her self-confidence that the lecture was a success.* [*opposite* **unimportant**, **significant**] **2** An **important** person has high rank or status: *She was not very important in the organization as a whole.* [*opposite* **unimportant**, **insignificant**] — *noun* (*uncount*) **importance**: *We were asked to assess the importance of the exercise.* [*opposite* **unimportance**] — *adverb* **importantly**: *How are you, and, more importantly, how are the children?*

impose /ɪmˈpoʊz/ *verb*: **imposes, imposing, imposed**
1 You **impose** something on someone when you force them to accept or suffer it: *I wouldn't want to impose my religious beliefs on anyone.* □ *The new tax will not be imposed on people's savings.* **2** You **impose** on someone when you cause them bother or inconvenience: *I hate to impose on you, but my car won't start and I wondered if you would give me a lift.* □ *It's a kind offer, but I wouldn't want to impose.* [*same as* **intrude**] — *noun* (*uncount or used in the singular*) **imposition** /ɪmpəˈzɪʃən/: *the imposition of value-added tax on children's clothes* □ *I know it's an imposition, but would you look after my dog for a few days?*

imposing /ɪmˈpoʊzɪŋ/ *adjective*
Someone or something **imposing** has a very impressive appearance: *Her father was a tall, imposing man with clear blue eyes.* □ *The long driveway led up to an imposing mansion.* [*same as* **striking**]

impossible /ɪmˈpɒsɪbəl/ *adjective*
1 Something that is **impossible** cannot be done or cannot happen: *I was so excited I found it impossible to concentrate.* □ *It seems impossible that she could have walked 20 miles in under 3 hours.* □ *It's impossible for anyone to survive more than a few minutes without air.* □ *an impossible suggestion* □ *I could meet you on Wednesday, but Tuesday is impossible for me.* **2** You

describe a person or situation as **impossible** if they are difficult to deal with: *The children were misbehaving and being absolutely impossible.* □ *She's an impossible woman to try and satisfy.* □ *We were in an impossible situation.* — *noun* (*uncount*) **impossibility** /ɪmpɒsɪˈbɪlɪtɪ/: *It was the sheer impossibility of the task that made it attractive.* — *adverb* **impossibly:** *The moon looks impossibly large tonight.* □ *He's impossibly arrogant.*

impostor /ɪmˈpɒstə(r)/ *noun*: **impostors**
An **impostor** is a person who pretends to be someone else in order to deceive others.

impoverished /ɪmˈpɒvərɪʃt/ *adjective* (*formal*)
Impoverished means poorer than before, whether in terms of money or some other quality or value: *trade with some of the world's more impoverished countries* □ *Today's youngsters do seem to be culturally impoverished.* [*opposite* **rich**]

impractical /ɪmˈpraktɪkəl/ *adjective*
Something **impractical** is not practical, reasonable or sensible: *one or two fairly impractical suggestions.* [*opposite* **practical**]

imprecise /ɪmprəˈsaɪs/ *adjective*
Something **imprecise** is not precise, accurate or clear: *The information proved to be wholly imprecise.* □ *I've only got a very imprecise notion of what's involved.* [*opposite* **precise**]

impregnate /ˈɪmprɛgneɪt/ *verb* (*formal*): **impregnates, impregnating, impregnated**
Something such as a cloth **is impregnated** with a liquid or other substance when the substance has spread throughout it.

impress /ɪmˈprɛs/ *verb*: **impresses, impressing, impressed**
1 You **are impressed** by something you see, hear or experience when you admire it or wonder at it: *Visitors are impressed by the sheer size of the factory.* □ *My parents were obviously impressed by his courteous manner and wealthy appearance.* □ *What impressed me was the speed with which they dealt with complaints.* **2** You **impress** something on or upon someone when you make them understand that it is very important: *Doctors try to impress upon new parents the need for hygiene in the home.*

impression /ɪmˈprɛʃən/ *noun*: **impressions**
1 The **impression** you have of something or someone consists of the effect they have on you, or the way they look or seem to you: *Visiting Czechoslovakia that spring, I had the impression of a country about to be reborn.* □ *My first impression of him was that he didn't like himself very much.* □ *She thinks she made quite a good impression on the judges.* **2** Someone gives you the **impression** that something is true when they allow or encourage you to believe it, often when it is not really true: *They gave us the impression they would be finished within a few days.* □ *She was given the impression that the job was hers if she wanted it.* **3** You do an **impression** of someone, usually someone famous, when you try to look and talk like them as a way of amusing or entertaining others. [*same as* **imitation, impersonation**]
▻ ***phrases*** **1** Someone who **makes an impression** causes others to notice and remember them because they have outstanding features or qualities: *None of the candidates made much of an impression.* **2** You are **under the impression** that something is true when you believe that it is true, usually because someone has suggested that it is true: *I was under the impression that you were staying until Tuesday.*

impressionable /ɪmˈprɛʃənəbəl/ *adjective*
An **impressionable** person is easily impressed or influenced by others: *Only the most impressionable of customers would believe that.*

impressive /ɪmˈprɛsɪv/ *adjective*
Something that you see, hear or experience is **impressive** when you admire it or wonder at it: *Her calmness under pressure was extremely impressive.* □ *The house has very impressive gardens.* — *adverb* **impressively:** *an impressively large ballroom.*

imprint /ˈɪmprɪnt/ *noun*: **imprints**
An **imprint** is a mark left when something has been pressed onto a surface: *Without realizing it, the thief had left the imprint of his hand in the wet paint.*

imprison /ɪmˈprɪzən/ *verb*: **imprisons, imprisoning, imprisoned**
To **imprison** someone is to put them in prison as a punishment.

imprisonment /ɪmˈprɪzənmənt/ *noun* (*uncount or used in the singular*)
Imprisonment is the state of being in prison, or the punishment of being kept in prison: *She was sentenced to 20 years' imprisonment.* □ *After such a long imprisonment, life on the outside seemed overwhelmingly busy.*

improbable /ɪmˈprɒbəbəl/ *adjective*
1 Something **improbable** is unlikely to happen or be true: *another highly improbable excuse.* □ *It's improbable that they'll raise sufficient money.* **2** You describe something as **improbable** if it looks ridiculous or very unusual: *dressed in the most improbable three-piece suit.*
[*same as* **unlikely**]

impromptu /ɪmˈprɒmptjuː/ *adjective*
Something **impromptu** happens when people suddenly decide to do it, without preparing or planning it in advance: *It was an evening of impromptu speeches from unlikely well-wishers.* [*same as* **spontaneous**]

improper /ɪmˈprɒpə(r)/ *adjective*
Improper behaviour is rude or shocking because it is not considered correct or suitable: *A smile would have been polite; laughter seemed improper.* [*same as* **unsuitable**]

improve /ɪmˈpruːv/ *verb*: **improves, improving, improved**
1 Something **improves** when it becomes better; you **improve** it when you make it better: *Her health has improved immeasurably since she stopped smoking.* □ *The match will not be played at all unless the weather improves considerably.* □ *Your school marks will have to improve if you want to go to college.* □ *The addition of cleaning agents has improved the performance of our petrol.* □ *regular visits to the gym to improve her fitness.* **2** You **are improving** when you are recovering after an illness. [*opposite* **deteriorate**]

> ***phrasal verb***
> You **improve on** something you have done when you do it better a second time; you **improve on** something someone else has done when you make it better by changing it or by doing it differently: *She'll find it difficult to improve on her first-round score.* □ *Last year's performance must be improved on.*

improvement /ɪmˈpruːvmənt/ *noun* (*uncount or count*): **improvements**
Improvement is change that makes something or someone better: *I'm afraid there's been no improvement in her health.* □ *This might lead to the improvement of living conditions for thousands of our citizens.* □ *Even a tent would be an improvement on sleeping in the street.*

improvise /ˈɪmprəvaɪz/ *verb*: **improvises, improvising, improvised**
1 You **improvise** when you perform something as you think of it, without having prepared it in advance: *Every jazz musician learns how to improvise.* [*same as* **ad lib**] **2** You **improvise** something when you make or provide it using whatever materials you find at the time, rather than using special materials prepared in advance: *With a few tables and some old crates, we were able to improvise a small stage.* — *noun* (*uncount or count*) **improvisation** /ɪmprəvaɪˈzeɪʃən/: *actors skilled in improvisation.* — *adjective* **improvised:** *They carried their belongings in improvised carts.*

imprudent /ɪmˈpruːdənt/ *adjective* (*formal*)
Imprudent behaviour shows a lack of good sense or caution: *I think it would be imprudent to climb in trainers; you'd better get proper boots.* [*same as* **unwise**, **rash**; *opposite* **prudent**]

impudent /ˈɪmpjʊdənt/ *adjective*
Someone who is **impudent** behaves rudely, without showing proper respect to those who deserve it: *He could have strangled this impudent upstart, who seemed bent on humiliating him.* [*same as* **impertinent**; *opposite* **polite**] — *noun* (*uncount*) **impudence:** *I was surprised that she allowed such impudence to go unchecked.* [*same as* **impertinence**; *opposite* **politeness**]

impulse /ˈɪmpʌls/ *noun*: **impulses**
You have an **impulse** to do something when you suddenly feel that you want to do it: *Madeleine felt a sudden impulse to punch him in the face.* [*same as* **urge**]
▻ ***phrase*** You do something **on impulse** when you suddenly decide to do it, without planning it and usually without thinking about the consequences.

impulsive /ɪmˈpʌlsɪv/ *adjective*
Someone who is **impulsive** tends to suddenly decide to do things, rather than planning to do them, usually without thinking about the consequences: *She flung her arms round his neck in gratitude; it was an impulsive gesture that she later regretted.* [*same as* **impetuous**]

impunity /ɪmˈpjuːnɪtɪ/ *noun* (*uncount; formal*)
You do something wrong with **impunity** when you are not punished for doing it, or when you do not suffer the bad consequences of it: *The larger companies flout the law with impunity.*

impure /ɪmˈpjʊə(r)/ *adjective*
1 Things connected with sex might be described as **impure** by someone who regards them as morally wrong: *The girls were warned of the dangers of having impure thoughts.* [*same as* **corrupt**] **2** An **impure** substance has other things mixed with it which spoil its quality: *An impure metal would break under the strain.* [*opposite* **pure**]

impurity /ɪmˈpjʊərɪtɪ/ *noun*: **impurities**
Impurities in a substance are other things mixed with it that spoil its quality: *Serious engine damage can result from impurities in the petrol.*

in /ɪn/ *preposition; adverb; adjective*
▻ ***preposition***
1 a Something is **in** something else if it is enclosed by it or surrounded by it: *The knives are in the top drawer.* □ *We keep the candles in a box under the stairs.* □ *Do you take sugar in your coffee?* □ *an object wrapped in brown paper.* **b** You are **in** certain clothes or colours when you are wearing them: *She arrived in a sweater and jeans.* □ *That's his wife in the straw hat.* □ *dressed entirely in black.* □ *You look good in red.* **c** Something is **in** a place if that is where it is: *The children were told to stay in their room.* □ *They have a small pond in the middle of their garden.* □ *a large company with offices in London, Paris and New York* □ *a man selling flowers in the street* □ *We spent the weekend at their house in the country.* □ *Jean felt obliged to visit him while he was in hospital.* □ *She arrived in a taxi.* □ *As she bent forward she felt a sudden pain in her back.* **d** You are **in** the sun or rain when you are exposed to it: *I walked home in the pouring rain.* □ *Don't lie in the sun for too long.* **e** Goods are **in** a shop window if they are being displayed just behind it, so that you can look through the glass at them. **f** You look at yourself **in** the mirror when you look at your reflection there.
2 a Someone or something is **in** a group if they are part of it: *Please wait in the queue.* □ *Am I in the team for next week?* □ *Over fifty runners will compete in the first race.* **b** Something that is **in** a book, play, picture or film can be found or seen there: *Please read the explanation in chapter 2.* □ *Who are the couple in this photo?* □ *The tower in the painting is presumably a fanciful representation of the Tower of London.* □ *You remember in the film, where you see the red coat lying on top of the pile?*
3 In is also used when referring to time, to mean **a** during a certain period, such as a season, year or month: *She'll be arriving sometime in the afternoon.* □ *The mountains look spectacular in winter.* □ *Alison is joining the company in October.* □ *He died in 1975.* **b** taking no more than the length of time stated: *They shot the whole film in two weeks.* **c** after a certain period has passed: *The rains are expected in a couple of weeks.* □ *I'll attend to you in a few minutes.*
4 a Things are **in** a certain shape or arrangement if that is the way they are arranged: *The children were asked to stand in a circle and hold hands.* □ *We stood in a line with our backs to the wall.* □ *They advanced in rows, six abreast.* □ *The papers were still in a heap on my desk.* **b** Someone or something is **in** a certain state, situation or position if that is their position, state or situation: *I'm in a hurry.* □ *By then I was in a state of panic.* □ *a few pieces of furniture in very poor condition* □ *We stood in silence while the verdict was read.* □ *I'd like a word with you in private.* □ *We were in considerable danger.* □ *He realized he was in no position to refuse.* □ *They were young and in love.* **c** Something happens **in** a certain situation if it happens during it or because of it: *In the confusion that followed, three of the prisoners escaped.* □ *We cannot envisage a situation in which we would be forced to increase taxes.* **d** You do something **in** a certain state of emotion or **in** a move to achieve something if that is what makes you do it: *In my agitation I knocked over the lamp.* □ *I tried to smile brightly in an attempt to conceal my anger.* **e** Something that is said or written **in** a certain way is expressed or presented in that way or form: *The message was in code.* □ *Here's their report, written in the usual incomprehensible jargon.* □ *Some things can be expressed better in French than in English.* □ *names listed in alphabetical order.* □ *Please put your suggestions in writing.*
5 You use **in** to specify **a** a particular subject or area of activity: *significant advances in cancer research* □ *She'd like a career in television.* **b** the particular matter, point or detail that your statement applies to: *In physique he resembled his father.* □ *She was a marvellous mother in every way.* □ *She tended to be arrogant in her dealings with others.* **c** the colour of something or the colours that are available for something: *I'm looking for a suit in pale grey.* □ *The new Nissan Micra comes in blue, bright red, black or white.* **d** to specify the dimension to which a measurement applies: *about 10 metres in width.*
6 You use **in** with numbers and amounts **a** to specify how many parts something has after division: *I cut the pie in three.* **b** to express proportion: *Of those ques-*

tioned, one in three was dissatisfied with government policy. □ *The scheme has no more than a one-in-ten chance of success.* **c** to indicate roughly how many people or things are involved all at once in doing something: *Tourists still flock to Stratford in their thousands.* □ *Bananas arrive in shiploads from the Caribbean.* □ *Guests were drifting into the room in twos and threes.* **d** to indicate someone's approximate age: *a man in his fifties* □ *She was in her early-to-mid thirties.*
7 You use **in** with the present participle to refer to the process or circumstance of doing something: *You use prepositions in describing* [= when you are describing] *the position of people or things.* □ *In unlocking* [= during the process of unlocking] *the door she had bent the key.* □ *He realized that, in refusing* [= as a consequence of refusing] *the invitation, he had offended the whole village.* **8** You have something such as a friend or enemy **in** a certain person if they are your friend or enemy: *She realised that in Jack she had made a formidable enemy.* □ *I think we have found in Freda a worthy successor to our retiring president.*

▻ ***adverb***
1 In means at home, at your place of work, or inside a room or building: *I used to stay in on my own while the others went to the pub.* □ *The managing director won't be in till tomorrow.* □ *She knocked several times, but there seemed to be nobody in.* □ *The door slammed shut, and I realized I was locked in.* [*opposite* **out**] **2 In** is used with verbs of moving or admitting to mean to or towards the inside of something: *Come in!* □ *Go straight in; Mr Jenkins is expecting you.* □ *Aren't you going to ask me in?* □ *I can't let you in without a pass.* □ *Come on in! The water's lovely and warm.* □ *The bus stopped and I got in.* □ *The weight of snow was too much and the roof fell in* [= collapsed]. □ *I opened my case and thrust the jacket in.* [*opposite* **out**] **3 In** also means to or towards the place where you are, or the place mentioned: *Just complete the form and send it in to our London office.* □ *The tide comes in* [= advances to its highest point on the shore] *about 6 o'clock.* □ *Her plane was late in* [= late arriving] *at Heathrow.* □ *I stopped at the library to hand in some books.* □ *The man at the bookshop said they would be getting more copies in next week.* **4** In games such as tennis, the ball is **in** when it has landed within the area of the court where it can be played: *His second service went in.*

▻ ***adjective*** (*informal*)
Something is **in** when it is fashionable: *Armenian cuisine is now the in thing.* □ *Earrings are no longer in for men.*

▻ ***phrases*** **1** You **are in for** something such as a surprise when you are going to experience or suffer it: *I'm afraid she's in for a shock when she sees the results.* □ *If he's expecting to get money from me he's in for a big disappointment.* **2** (*informal*) You **are in on** something when you are involved in it, or when you know about it: *I should have liked to have been in on the planning.* **3** (*informal*) Someone who **has it in for** you tries to create problems for you because they dislike you: *For some reason the warehouse manager has got it in for me.* **4** You use **in that** to introduce an explanation of something you have just said: *He's a true friend, in that he's always honest with me.* **5** (*informal*) You are **in with** someone, especially someone important, when you are on friendly terms with them: *She appeared to be in with all the directors.*

in- /ɪn/ *prefix*
In- is used before many nouns, adjectives and adverbs to form words that mean the opposite: *She's not the only pupil guilty of inattention.* □ *inaccurate reporting of the facts* □ *The word had been spelled incorrectly.*

inability /ɪnəˈbɪlɪtɪ/ *noun* (*uncount*)
Your **inability** to do something is the fact that you are not able to do it: *Teachers are worried by the inability of today's pupils to concentrate for any length of time.* [*opposite* **ability**]

inaccessible /ɪnəkˈsɛsɪbəl/ *adjective*
1 Something **inaccessible** is difficult or impossible to approach, reach or obtain: *The summit is inaccessible to all but the most experienced climbers.* □ *Women often find that higher management positions are simply inaccessible.* **2** You also describe something as **inaccessible** if it is difficult or impossible to understand: *Modern art is often criticized for being inaccessible.* — *noun* (*uncount*) **inaccessibility** /ɪnaksɛsɪˈbɪlɪtɪ/: *The inaccessibility of the region has deterred potential visitors.*

inaccurate /ɪnˈakjʊrət/ *adjective*
Something **inaccurate** is not correct or accurate, and contains mistakes: *Some of the earlier calculations were inaccurate.* □ *Inaccurate recording of time led to disputes about who exactly had won the race.* [*same as* **imprecise**; *opposite* **accurate**] — *noun* (*uncount or count*) **inaccuracy:** *the inaccuracy of some of their measurements* □ *The report contains one or two minor inaccuracies.*

inaction /ɪnˈakʃən/ *noun* (*uncount*)
You can accuse someone of **inaction** if they are doing nothing in a situation where action needs to be taken: *We would like councillors to explain their inaction.*

inactive /ɪnˈaktɪv/ *adjective*
Someone who is **inactive** is not doing anything: *Weekends are quite dull; we're a pretty inactive family.* □ *Our fleet of lorries has been inactive for months.* [*opposite* **active**] — *noun* (*uncount*) **inactivity** /ɪnakˈtɪvɪtɪ/: *The huge lunch was followed by several hours of inactivity.* [*opposite* **activity**]

inadequate /ɪnˈadɪkwət/ *adjective*
1 Something is **inadequate** if there is not enough of it, or if you need or want something better: *Supplies of food were inadequate for our needs.* □ *We were offered a rather inadequate replacement.* [*opposite* **adequate**] **2** Someone who feels **inadequate** feels that they do things in general, or something in particular, badly: *She made me feel sexually inadequate.* □ *I thought, perhaps unfairly, that Pauline was an inadequate wife.* — *noun* (*uncount or count*) **inadequacy** /ɪnˈadɪkwəsɪ/: *We were shocked by the inadequacy of their medical facilities.* □ *He went on to list my inadequacies as a business partner.*

inadvertently /ɪnədˈvɜːtəntlɪ/ *adverb*
You do something **inadvertently** when you do it by accident, without wanting or intending to do it: *I had inadvertently stood on the child's foot.* [*same as* **unintentionally**; *opposite* **deliberately**]

inadvisable /ɪnədˈvaɪzəbəl/ *adjective* (*formal*)
You say that something is **inadvisable** when you think that it should not be done, usually because it is dangerous or likely to fail: *We are agreed that asking him outright would be inadvisable.* □ *It would be inadvisable for you to stop taking the medicine altogether.* [*opposite* **advisable**]

inane /ɪˈneɪn/ *adjective*
Inane behaviour is silly or stupid: *We have learned not to listen to her inane remarks.*

inanimate /ɪnˈanɪmət/ *adjective*
Inanimate describes things that are not living: *She often shouts at tables, chairs and other inanimate objects.* [*opposite* **animate**]

inapplicable /ɪnəˈplɪkəbəl/ *adjective*
Something **inapplicable** cannot be applied to a particular situation because it is not relevant or suitable: *Note that Question 4 on this form will be inapplicable in certain cases.* [*opposite* **applicable**]

inappropriate /ɪnə'proʊprɪət/ *adjective*
Something **inappropriate** is not suitable or appropriate, usually because it is not useful or not what is considered to be right or proper: *The tools I had with me were completely inappropriate for the job.* □ *Her remarks were inappropriate to the circumstances.* [*opposite* **appropriate, suitable**]

inarticulate /ɪnɑː'tɪkjʊlət/ *adjective*
Someone who is **inarticulate** has difficulty in choosing the right words to express what they want to say, and they express themselves badly. [*opposite* **articulate**]

inaudible /ɪn'ɔːdɪbəl/ *adjective*
A sound that is **inaudible** is not loud enough to be heard: *a note which is inaudible to the human ear.* [*opposite* **audible**]

inaugural /ɪ'nɔːgjʊrəl/ *adjective*
Inaugural events officially mark the beginning of something: *The new chairman will make her inaugural speech on Friday.*

inaugurate /ɪn'ɔːgjəreɪt/ *verb*: **inaugurates, inaugurating, inaugurated**
1 A new scheme or system **is inaugurated** when it is put into operation. **2** A new president or other leader **is inaugurated** when they are officially installed in office in a special ceremony. — *noun* (*uncount*) **inauguration** /ɪnɔːgjə'reɪʃən/: *We had an invitation to attend the inauguration ceremony.*

inbred /ɪn'brɛd/ *adjective*
Inbred feelings or opinions are ones you feel or hold so strongly that they are an unchangeable part of your personality: *They have an almost inbred hatred of their Arab neighbours.* [*same as* **ingrained**]

incalculable /ɪn'kalkjʊləbəl/ *adjective*
The size or extent of something is **incalculable** if it is too great to judge or calculate: *This has done incalculable harm to the peace process.*

incapable /ɪn'keɪpəbəl/ *adjective*
1 You are **incapable** of doing something if you don't have the skill, talent or ability necessary to do it: *He seems incapable of accepting opinions different from his own.* □ *I think Janet would be incapable of organizing such a big affair.* [*opposite* **capable**] **2 Incapable** also means physically unable to do something, *eg* because of illness or drunkenness: *She lay in bed all day, weak and incapable.*

incapacitate /ɪnkə'pasɪteɪt/ *verb*: **incapacitates, incapacitating, incapacitated**
You **are incapacitated** by something that takes away your strength, power or ability: *Most of the patients have been more or less incapacitated by their illness.*

incarnation /ɪnkɑː'neɪʃən/ *noun*: **incarnations**
1 (*used in the singular*) You can describe someone as the **incarnation** of a particular quality, such as beauty or honour, if their appearance or behaviour is a perfect example of it: *Uncle Humphrey was the incarnation of good manners.* **2** An **incarnation** is a person or animal regarded, by the followers of some religions, as a physical form that a spirit exists as, the spirit continuing to take new forms or **incarnations** as the old ones die: *She claims she was a tiger in a previous incarnation.*

incendiary /ɪn'sɛndɪərɪ/ *adjective*
An **incendiary** bomb is designed to start a fire when it explodes: *Police experts discovered a number of incendiary devices.*

incense[1] /'ɪnsɛns/ *noun* (*uncount*)
Incense is a substance that produces a pleasant smell when burned, used *eg* during religious services.

incense[2] /ɪn'sɛns/ *verb* (*formal*): **incenses, incensing, incensed**
You **are incensed** by something if it makes you extremely angry: *His refusal to negotiate has incensed his employees.* [*same as* **infuriate**]

incentive /ɪn'sɛntɪv/ *noun*: **incentives**
An **incentive** is something, usually the promise of a reward or other benefit, that encourages or persuades you to do something else: *Remove the prospect of promotion, and there is no incentive for people to work harder.* [*same as* **motivation**]

incessant /ɪn'sɛsənt/ *adjective*
Something **incessant** goes on and on without stopping: *the incessant drumming of rain on the windows.* [*same as* **continuous**]

incest /'ɪnsɛst/ *noun* (*uncount*)
Incest is the crime of having sex with a close relative such as a brother or sister. — *adverb* **incestuous** /ɪn'sɛstjʊəs/: *an incestuous relationship.*

inch /ɪntʃ/ *noun*; *verb*
▻ ***noun***: **inches**
1 An **inch** is a measure of length equal to one twelfth of a foot or 2.54 centimetres: *My little girl has grown over four inches this year.* □ *A six-inch ruler would be handier than a twelve-inch one.* **2** An **inch** is also a small distance, area or space: *Every inch of the area has been searched by police.*
▻ ***verb***: **inches, inching, inched**
You **inch** somewhere when you move there slowly and carefully: *We had to inch the car through the narrowest of gates.*

incidence /'ɪnsɪdəns/ *noun* (*singular*)
The **incidence** of something is how often it happens or occurs: *There seems to be a particularly high incidence of divorce amongst couples who marry within a year of meeting.* [*same as* **frequency**]

incident /'ɪnsɪdənt/ *noun*: **incidents**
An **incident** is something that happens, especially something involving death, injury or other unpleasantness: *In a separate incident, five people were killed when a minibus collided with an ambulance.* □ *It was a rather embarrassing incident.*

incidental /ɪnsɪ'dɛntəl/ *adjective*
Something **incidental** is connected to something else more important: *Any other benefits will really be incidental to the main aim of the scheme.* □ *She wrote much of the film's incidental music, as well as its theme tune.*

incidentally /ɪnsɪ'dɛntəlɪ/ *adverb* (*sentence adverb*)
You use **incidentally** as a way of introducing a comment that is not connected to what you have just been talking about: *Incidentally, those pictures you sent me were wonderful.* [*same as* **by the way**]

incinerator /ɪn'sɪnəreɪtə(r)/ *noun*: **incinerators**
An **incinerator** is a large industrial oven for burning rubbish.

incision /ɪn'sɪʒən/ *noun* (*technical*): **incisions**
An **incision** is a cut, especially one made by a surgeon.

incisive /ɪn'saɪsɪv/ *adjective* (*formal*)
You describe something that someone says or writes as **incisive** if it seems to state the truth in a clear, clever or forceful way: *in her incisive summing-up of the situation.* [*same as* **astute**]

incite /ɪn'saɪt/ *verb*: **incites, inciting, incited**
You **incite** people to behave in a certain way when you encourage, urge or provoke them: *The students had been incited to riot by Communist-minded workers.* □ *There was severe punishment for anyone inciting anti-government feeling.* [*same as* **encourage**; *opposite* **dis-**

courage] — *noun (uncount)* **incitement:** *The charge of incitement to murder was brought against his mistress.*

inclination /ɪŋklɪ'neɪʃən/ *noun*: **inclinations**
An **inclination** to do something is a feeling that you want to do it: *I have neither the time nor the inclination to help with anything connected with the church.* □ *You may like that sort of thing; it depends where your inclinations lie.*

incline *verb; noun*
▻ ***verb*** /ɪn'klaɪn/ (*formal*): **inclines, inclining, inclined**
You **incline** your head or body when you bend it forwards or downwards: *She stood for some time with her whole torso uncomfortably inclined at the waist.*
▻ ***noun*** /'ɪnklaɪn/: **inclines**
An **incline** is a slope or hill: *He changed down into second gear and accelerated into the incline.*

inclined /ɪn'klaɪnd/ *adjective*
1 You are **inclined** to behave in a particular way when you usually behave like that: *Rats are inclined to become aggressive when cornered.* □ *I'm inclined to be a little grumpy in the mornings.* **2 Inclined** is also used to describe the kind of talent or ability a person has: *The girls were always very artistically inclined.* **3** People often use **inclined** as a way of expressing an opinion: *I'm inclined to disagree with the Professor on that point.*

include /ɪn'klu:d/ *verb*: **includes, including, included**
One thing **includes** another **a** when the other is part of it, or is one of its features: *The list of her works includes the bestselling novel 'Games Women Play'.* □ *The team includes five players in their first international.* □ *Europe, and that includes Britain, has a vital role in world affairs.* **b** when the other is covered by it or contained in it: *The rent, which is £200 a month, includes all heating and electricity costs.* □ *Packing and postage are included in the price.* [*opposite* **exclude**] — *adjective* **included:** *Everyone, myself included, voted for the proposed reforms.* □ *We had a great time, the dog included.* □ *It is essential that all EEC countries, Britain included, should work together.* [*opposite* **excluded**] — *preposition* **including:** *All 125 passengers were killed, including three Britons.* □ *The debt now amounted to $40 000, including interest.* □ *We need the support of at least five board members, not including the chairman.* [*opposite* **excluding**]

inclusion /ɪn'klu:ʒən/ *noun (used in the singular)*
The **inclusion** of something is the act of including it, or the fact that it is included: *We are arguing in favour of the inclusion of some kind of escape clause.* □ *A number of delegates were opposed to its inclusion.* [*opposite* **exclusion**]

inclusive /ɪn'klu:sɪv/ *adjective*
1 Inclusive means including everything, with nothing left out: *holidays in Greece for an all-inclusive price of £199 for two weeks* □ *Is the price inclusive of road tax?* **2** You use **inclusive** when speaking about a range of things to show that the limits you mention are included as well, not just the things in between: *I'm on holiday from Monday to Friday inclusive.*

incognito /ɪnkɒg'ni:toʊ/ *adjective and adverb*
Someone who is **incognito** is hiding their identity, *eg* by using a disguise and a false name: *The pair are thought to be travelling incognito.*

incoherent /ɪnkoʊ'hɪərənt/ *adjective*
Someone who is **incoherent** speaks in an unclear way, not forming words properly, *eg* because they are ill, drunk, or very angry or excited: *He was incoherent with rage.* □ *She could give the police only a very disjointed and incoherent account of what had happened to her.* [*opposite* **coherent**] — *adverb* **incoherently:** *She began to tell her story, incoherently at first, but more rationally as she became calmer.* — *noun (uncount)* **incoherence:** *incoherence brought on by distress.*

income /'ɪnkʌm/ *noun (uncount)*
Your **income** is all the money you receive, *eg* your wages and the interest from any savings you have: *She took on evening work to supplement her income.* □ *rises in income tax.*

incomparable /ɪn'kɒmpərəbəl/ *adjective*
Incomparable means exceptional: *a woman of incomparable beauty*

incompatible /ɪnkəm'patɪbəl/ *adjective*
People and things that are **incompatible** are so different from each other that they cannot live or exist together: *As lovers we were well suited; as marriage partners we were totally incompatible.* □ *It became apparent that his methods were incompatible with the kind of standards we had set for the company.* [*opposite* **compatible**] — *noun (uncount)* **incompatibility** /ɪnkəmpatɪ'bɪlɪtɪ/: *We had to recognize the basic incompatibility that existed between our styles of football.*

incompetent /ɪn'kɒmpɪtənt/ *adjective*
Someone who is **incompetent** lacks the necessary skill or ability to do their job, or some other task, properly: *What do you do with people who are incompetent at their job?* □ *He was a good solicitor, but an incompetent barrister.* [*opposite* **capable, competent**] — *adverb* **incompetently:** *The repairs had been incompetently carried out.* — *noun (uncount)* **incompetence:** *He accused the government of economic incompetence.* [*opposite* **competence**]

incomplete /ɪnkəm'pli:t/ *adjective*
1 Something **incomplete** has bits of it missing: *This list of names is incomplete.* **2 Incomplete** also describes something that has not been finished: *The new airport is still lying incomplete after investment in the project was withdrawn over three years ago.*
[*opposite* **complete**]

incomprehensible /ɪnkɒmprɪ'hɛnsɪbəl/ *adjective*
Something that is **incomprehensible** is difficult or impossible to understand: *I was relieved to discover that his lectures were just as incomprehensible to the other students.* [*opposite* **comprehensible**]

incomprehension /ɪnkɒmprɪ'hɛnʃən/ *noun (uncount)*
Incomprehension is the state of not understanding something: *the look of incomprehension on his face.*

inconceivable /ɪnkən'si:vəbəl/ *adjective*
You describe something as **inconceivable** if you can't imagine that it will ever happen, or you can't believe that it might be true: *It was inconceivable that her mother wished her any harm.* [*same as* **unimaginable**; *opposite* **conceivable**]

inconclusive /ɪnkəŋ'klu:sɪv/ *adjective*
Something that is **inconclusive** does not lead to a definite conclusion, result or decision: *Negotiations on the issue of pay were inconclusive.* [*opposite* **conclusive**]

incongruous /ɪn'kɒŋgrʊəs/ *adjective*
Incongruous describes things that appear strange because they are very different from their surroundings, or are not suited to their situation: *He was a rather incongruous figure in his dinner jacket.* — *noun (uncount)* **incongruity** /ɪnkɒŋ'gru:ɪtɪ/: *It was incongruity of her remarks on such a sober occasion that made us all laugh.*

inconsiderate /ɪnkən'sɪdərət/ *adjective*
Someone who is **inconsiderate** does not care about the feelings or wishes of other people, or about how their

own behaviour affects others: *It was very inconsiderate of him.* [*opposite* **thoughtful, considerate**]

inconsistent /ɪnkən'sɪstənt/ *adjective*
1 Someone's behaviour is **inconsistent** when they do not always behave the same way in the same situation, suggesting that they do not have firm principles or opinions: *The Minister has expressed rather inconsistent views on a number of related issues.* **2** Something you say or do is **inconsistent** with the principles or standards you claim to have when it does not reasonably or logically match them: *I would argue that the decision to develop the site is inconsistent with the government's professed environmental sensitivity.*
[*opposite* **consistent**] — *noun* (*uncount or count*) **inconsistency:** *He was attacked in the press for his inconsistency.* □ *There are a number of inconsistencies in the report.* [*opposite* **consistency**]

inconspicuous /ɪnkən'spɪkjʊəs/ *adjective*
You do something **inconspicuous** when what you do is not easily noticed, usually because you are trying to avoid attracting attention: *Our store detectives make themselves as inconspicuous as possible.* [*opposite* **conspicuous**]

inconvenience /ɪnkən'viːnɪəns/ *noun; verb*
▻ ***noun*** (*uncount or count*): **inconveniences**
Inconvenience is minor trouble or difficulty: *I don't want to cause you any inconvenience.* □ *It's no inconvenience to me to give you a lift.* □ *Having to cook for an extra person was an inconvenience I could have done without.* [*same as* **nuisance**]
▻ ***verb***: **inconveniences, inconveniencing, inconvenienced:** *I hope I'm not inconveniencing you too much.*

inconvenient /ɪnkən'viːnɪənt/ *adjective*
Something is **inconvenient** when it causes you slight trouble or difficulty: *Would it be inconvenient if I came to see you this evening?* □ *I hope I haven't called at an inconvenient moment.* [*opposite* **convenient**]

incorporate /ɪn'kɔːpəreɪt/ *verb*: **incorporates, incorporating, incorporated**
One thing **incorporates** another thing when it includes or has it as one of its parts: *a health club incorporating a gym, sauna and steam room* □ *The latest technological advances have been incorporated into our wine production.*

incorrect /ɪnkə'rɛkt/ *adjective*
1 Something **incorrect** is not correct or accurate: *You lose two points for an incorrect answer.* **2** Something is also **incorrect** when it is wrong according to normal or accepted standards: *incorrect grammar.* [*opposite* **correct**]

increase *verb; noun*
▻ ***verb*** /ɪn'kriːs/: **increases, increasing, increased**
Something **increases** when it becomes greater in size or extent: *The number of tourists visiting these islands has increased dramatically in recent years.* □ *We are hoping that the campaign will increase the public's awareness of the dangers involved.* [*opposite* **decrease**]
▻ ***noun*** /'ɪnkriːs/: **increases:** *There has been an increase of nearly 20% in the number of reported thefts.* [*opposite* **decrease**]
▻ ***phrase*** Something that is **on the increase** is becoming larger or more frequent: *It's generally accepted that violent crime is on the increase.* — *adjective* **increasing:** *Increasing numbers of teenagers are rejecting the drugs culture.* [*opposite* **decreasing**] — *adverb* **increasingly:** *People are becoming increasingly aware that our natural environment needs to be protected by law.*

incredible /ɪn'krɛdɪbəl/ *adjective*
1 Something is **incredible** when it is difficult or impossible to believe: *He gave us some wholly incredible excuse about having got lost on his way to work.* [*same as* **unbelievable**; *opposite* **believable, credible**] **2** (*informal*) **Incredible** also means amazing or surprising, or amazingly large or great: *It's incredible to think that, just a few weeks ago, there was nothing here except mud.* □ *This man has walked an incredible distance in an effort to raise money for charity.* — *adverb* (*intensifying*) **incredibly:** *They have these incredibly long ears.*

incredulous /ɪn'krɛdjʊləs/ *adjective*
You are **incredulous** if you cannot believe what someone is saying because it sounds impossible or extremely unlikely: *Don't sound so incredulous; I am capable of doing the job!* — *noun* (*uncount*) **incredulity** /ɪnkrə'djuːlɪtɪ/: *I had clearly not managed to disguise my incredulity.*

increment /'ɪnkrəmənt/ *noun*: **increments**
An **increment** is an increase from one point or level to the next one on a fixed scale, especially a scale of salaries.

incriminate /ɪn'krɪmɪneɪt/ *verb*: **incriminates, incriminating, incriminated**
Something that **incriminates** someone proves that they are guilty of committing a crime or other wrongdoing: *They were ordered to destroy any documents that might incriminate the President.* [*same as* **implicate**] — *adjective* **incriminating:** *They've uncovered several pieces of incriminating evidence.*

incubator /'ɪnkjʊbeɪtə(r)/ *noun*: **incubators**
An **incubator** is a box-like apparatus that newborn babies who are very ill or very tiny are placed inside for special medical treatment.

incumbent /ɪn'kʌmbənt/ *adjective; noun*
▻ ***adjective*** (*formal*)
You say it is **incumbent** on someone to do something if they are expected to do it because it is a duty or responsibility: *It is incumbent on all doctors to respect the confidentiality of information about their patients.*
▻ ***noun*** (*formal*): **incumbents**
The **incumbent** is the person who currently occupies a particular official position: *It is quite usual, in the early part of a presidential campaign, for the challenger to be more popular than the incumbent.*

incur /ɪn'kɜː(r)/ *verb*: **incurs, incurring, incurred**
You **incur** something unpleasant or unwanted when you suffer it as a direct result of something you have done: *Any member of your team breaking the rules will incur a heavy penalty.* □ *Simpson had once more incurred the displeasure of the headmaster.*

incurable /ɪn'kjʊərəbəl/ *adjective*
1 An **incurable** disease cannot be cured: *Nobody has actually admitted that the cancer is incurable.* [*same as* **terminal**; *opposite* **curable**] **2 Incurable** is often also used to describe someone whose personality or habits can never be changed: *Ralph was an incurable romantic.* [*same as* **incorrigible**]

indebted /ɪn'dɛtɪd/ *adjective* (*formal*)
You are **indebted** to someone when you are grateful to them for something they have done for you: *I am indebted to the Minister for bringing this matter to my attention.* [*same as* **obliged**]

indecent /ɪn'diːsənt/ *adjective*
1 Indecent describes the behaviour of someone who uses sex or nakedness to shock, offend or attack someone else: *He had carried out a number of indecent assaults on young women.* **2** You also describe what someone says or does as **indecent** if you think it is bad or impolite behaviour: *They proceeded to divide up the dead woman's belongings with indecent haste.* [*same as* **unseemly**] — *noun* (*uncount*) **indecency:** *He was*

charged with gross indecency in a public place. □ *the indecency of his remarks.*

indecision /ɪndɪ'sɪʒən/ *noun* (*uncount*)
Indecision is the state of not being sure what you should do: *This is not a time for indecision.* [*same as* **hesitation**; *opposite* **decisiveness**]

indecisive /ɪndɪ'saɪsɪv/ *adjective*
An **indecisive** person is unable to make decisions quickly about what they should do. [*opposite* **decisive**]

indeed /ɪn'diːd/ *adverb*
1 Indeed is used at the end of a clause to emphasize an adjective or adverb, normally in combination with 'very': *We're very sorry indeed if we've offended you.* □ *Thank you very much indeed.* □ *It's very unusual indeed for this to happen.* **2** (*sentence adverb*) **Indeed** is also used **a** when agreeing with or confirming something: *'Is it the ninth today?' 'It is indeed.'* **b** when adding another comment that supports or extends what you have just said: *As a company, they're not very stable financially; indeed, they're possibly facing bankruptcy.* **3 Indeed** is often used to express surprise, disbelief, anger or scorn at what someone has just said: *'He thinks you're too easily persuaded.' 'Does he indeed!'*

indefensible /ɪndɪ'fɛnsɪbəl/ *adjective*
Behaviour that is **indefensible** is too bad to be justified or excused: *For a Minister of the Crown to disregard the law so blatantly was indefensible.* [*opposite* **justified**]

indefinable /ɪndɪ'faɪnəbəl/ *adjective*
Something such as a quality is **indefinable** when it is difficult to describe clearly or accurately: *In such situations, people often have an undefinable feeling of having lost something important.*

indefinite /ɪn'dɛfɪnət/ *adjective*
When you begin something for an **indefinite** period you have not decided when you will stop or end it: *an indefinite ban on foreign imports.* [*opposite* **limited**]

indefinite article /ɪndɛfɪnət 'ɑːtɪkəl/ *noun*: **indefinite articles**
In English grammar, the **indefinite articles** are the words 'a' and 'an'.

indefinite pronoun /ɪndɛfɪnɪt 'proʊnaʊn/ *noun* (*grammar*): **indefinite pronouns**
The **indefinite pronouns** are *anybody*, *anyone*, *somebody*, *someone*, *something*, *everybody*, *everyone*, *everything*, *nobody*, *no-one*, *nothing*, which you use when you are referring generally to people or things, meaning no particular person or thing.

> Adjectives can be used with the indefinite pronouns but notice that they follow the pronouns: *Did you meet anyone interesting? It's nothing unusual.*

indefinitely /ɪn'dɛfənɪtlɪ/ *adverb*
Something will continue **indefinitely** when nobody has decided when it should stop or end, and it may continue for ever: *Clearly, our resources will not last indefinitely.*

indelicate /ɪn'dɛlɪkət/ *adjective* (*formal*)
You describe what someone says or does as **indelicate** if it slightly rude or impolite: *He felt it would have been indelicate to ask how she was feeling.*

indentation /ɪndɛn'teɪʃən/ *noun*: **indentations**
1 An **indentation** is a mark left when a small area of a surface has been pushed down or in, or when a small part of the surface has been cut away. **2** An **indentation** on a page of text is a place where there is a space at the beginning of a line.

independent /ɪndɪ'pɛndənt/ *adjective*
1 An **independent** country has its own government and is not ruled or controlled by another. **2** You are **independent** when you make your own decisions about your life, without relying on others for help, advice or other support: *The children are encouraged to be independent.* □ *The law should recognize that many women are now financially independent of their husbands.* [*same as* **self-reliant**; *opposite* **dependent**] **3** Something is **independent** when it happens or exists separately from other things, and is not influenced by or connected to anything else: *In over a dozen independent incidents, patients in the area complained of unusual bouts of headaches and vomiting.* □ *The surveys were quite independent of each other.* [*same as* **separate**] **4 Independent** institutions such as schools and hospitals do not receive money from the government. [*opposite* **state**] **5** Someone who is **independent** is not involved in something, and so they can be trusted to give a fair judgement or opinion of it: *They want an independent inquiry into the affair.* [*same as* **objective**] — *noun* (*uncount*) **independence:** *political and economic independence* □ *Getting married needn't mean losing your independence.* □ *The independence of the survey cannot be relied on.* — *adverb* **independently:** *The same conclusions were reached quite independently.* □ *Quite independently of each other, we organized parties for the same night.*

indescribable /ɪndɪ'skraɪbəbəl/ *adjective*
Something **indescribable** is so extreme or shocking that you cannot find the right words to describe it accurately: *My sense of grief was indescribable.* □ *the indescribable sight of all those mangled bodies.* — *adverb* (*intensifying*) **indescribably:** *Thomson's performance was indescribably bad.*

indestructible /ɪndɪ'strʌktɪbəl/ *adjective*
Something that is **indestructible** is so strong or tough that nothing and no-one can destroy it or break through it: *The new Challenger tanks were supposed to be virtually indestructible.*

indeterminate /ɪndɪ'tɜːmɪnɪt/ *adjective*
You describe something as **indeterminate** if you don't know exactly *eg* what it is or how much it is: *We discovered a number of creatures of indeterminate species.* □ *Phil has decided to stay on in Paris, for an indeterminate period.*

index /'ɪndɛks/ *noun*; *verb*
▻ ***noun***: **indexes** or **indices**
An **index** is **1** an alphabetical list, usually at the end of a book, of the names of people or subjects dealt with in it, with the number of the page that each one appears on. **2** an alphabetical set of cards giving information about a collection of things, *eg* books in a library. **3** a scale used for measuring changes in something, *eg* changes in the prices of goods sold in shops: *the retail price index.*
▻ ***verb***: **indexes, indexing, indexed**
To **index** something such as a book or a collection is to create an index of all the items contained in it: *She spent the afternoon indexing her record collection.*

index finger /'ɪndɛks fɪŋə(r)/ *noun*: **index fingers**
Your **index finger** is the finger next to your thumb. [*same as* **forefinger**; see picture at **body**]

index-linked /ɪndɛks'lɪnkt/ *adjective*
Things such as wages are **index-linked** when they are increased as the cost of living rises, and by the same amount.

indicate /'ɪndɪkeɪt/ *verb*: **indicates, indicating, indicated**
1 One thing **indicates** another if it shows, suggests or

represents it: *A red light indicates that another train is on the track ahead.* □ *Our survey indicates that men are happy to carry out household tasks.* □ *She lowered her eyes, indicating her refusal to be associated with the decision.* **2** Someone driving a car **indicates** when they turn on one of their indicators: *The lorry was indicating left and I pulled out to overtake it* **3** (*formal*) You **indicate** something when you point to it: *'Please sit down', she said, indicating a large armchair by the fire.* **4** (*formal*) You **indicate** something when you say it or make it known, perhaps indirectly: *They have indicated that they would not oppose any attempt to take over the company.* □ *I have indicated my intentions to their legal representatives.*

indication /ɪndɪ'keɪʃən/ *noun*: **indications**
There is an **indication** of what is going to happen when you can judge what will happen by what people are saying or how they are behaving: *There are indications that the discussions are about to break down.* □ *So far, we have seen no indication that the President is willing to change his mind.* □ *The Minister this morning gave the clearest indication yet that he recognizes he may have to resign.* [*same as* **sign**]

indicative /ɪn'dɪkətɪv/ *adjective* (*formal*)
One thing is **indicative** of another when it shows or suggests that other thing is the case: *The rise in crime is perhaps indicative of a general moral decline in society.*

indicator /'ɪndɪkeɪtə(r)/ *noun*: **indicators**
The **indicators** on a car are the lights that flash to show that the car is about to change direction. [see picture at **car**]

indices /'ɪndɪsiːz/ *noun*
Indices is one of the plural forms of **index**.

indictment /ɪn'daɪtmənt/ *noun*: **indictments**
You say that something is an **indictment** of something else when it shows or proves how bad it is: *The results of this survey are an indictment of our public health service.*

indifferent /ɪn'dɪfərənt/ *adjective*
1 You are **indifferent** to something when you are not interested in it or concerned about it: *I think most actors soon become indifferent to newspaper criticism.* [*same as* **impervious**, **unconcerned**] **2** You describe something as **indifferent** if it is only of average quality: *He gave a rather indifferent performance.* [*same as* **mediocre**] — *noun* (*uncount*) **indifference**: *Self-interest implies indifference to the problems and concerns of others.*

indigenous /ɪn'dɪdʒənəs/ *adjective*
Indigenous describes plants, animals and races of people that have existed in a place from the beginning, as distinct from those brought or settled from other places: *The domestic cat isn't actually indigenous to Europe.* □ *the rights of the indigenous peoples.* [*same as* **native**]

indigestion /ɪndɪ'dʒɛstʃən/ *noun* (*uncount*)
Indigestion is discomfort or pain in your stomach or chest caused when you have difficulty digesting food.

indignant /ɪn'dɪgnənt/ *adjective*
You are **indignant** when you are angry because someone has not acted reasonably or fairly, often towards you: *She was most indignant when I told her you were too busy to see her.* — *noun* (*uncount*) **indignation** /ɪndɪg'neɪʃən/: *They had not expected him to react with such indignation.*

indigo /'ɪndɪgoʊ/ *noun* (*uncount, often adjectival*)
Indigo is a dark purplish-blue colour: *a long indigo sweater.*

indirect /ɪndɪ'rɛkt/ *adjective*
1 There is an **indirect** relationship between two things when they are linked in a secondary rather than immediate way: *A prolonged rail strike has all sorts of indirect consequences, such as, for example, a sharp reduction in tourism.* **2** You take an **indirect** route between two places when you travel a longer distance than you need to. [*opposite* **direct**] — *adverb* **indirectly**: *She feels indirectly responsible for what happened.*

indirect object /ɪndɪrɛkt 'ɒbdʒɛkt/ *noun* (*grammar*): **indirect objects**
An **indirect object** is an object representing the person or thing who benefits from the action of the verb, as distinct from the person or thing that has the action of the verb done directly to them, as in: *I bought my mother a watch. Give Simon a chance to speak. Could you tell this lady what time the next bus is?* [see also **direct object**]

indirect speech /ɪndɪrɛkt'spiːtʃ/ *noun* (*uncount*)
Indirect speech consists of a person's words reported by someone else, with changes of person and tense, *eg* the direct speech form 'I will do it' becomes 'She said she would do it' in indirect speech. [*same as* **reported speech**; see also **direct speech**]

indiscreet /ɪndɪs'kriːt/ *adjective*
You are **indiscreet** if you do or say openly what you should have kept secret: *The perfect lover takes care not to be indiscreet.* [*opposite* **discreet**]

indiscretion /ɪndɪs'krɛʃən/ *noun* (*uncount or count*): **indiscretions**
Indiscretion is the quality of being indiscreet: *One of her major faults was indiscretion.* □ *One or two minor indiscretions on her part had made him a little suspicious.* [*opposite* **discretion**]

indiscriminate /ɪndɪs'krɪmɪnət/ *adjective*
Indiscriminate describes the actions or behaviour of someone who does not make careful choices or decisions: *She was somewhat indiscriminate in her choice of friends.* □ *A gang of vandals had broken into the gardens and caused indiscriminate destruction of plants and trees.* [*opposite* **selective**]

indispensable /ɪndɪs'pɛnsəbəl/ *adjective*
Something **indispensable** is absolutely necessary or essential: *I don't suppose any single member of staff is indispensable.* [*opposite* **dispensable**]

individual /ɪndɪ'vɪdjʊəl/ *adjective*; *noun*
▷ ***adjective***
Individual means relating to a single person or thing, or to each one separately: *We will interview each of you on an individual basis.* □ *The treatment you are offered depends upon the assessment of the individual doctor.* □ *Sow the seeds in individual pots.* □ *We have family-size and individual pies.*
▷ ***noun*** (*informal*): **individuals**
An **individual** is a person: *Coley was an odd-looking individual.*

individuality /ɪndɪvɪdjʊ'alɪtɪ/ *noun* (*uncount*)
Individuality is the quality of being different from all others, or the circumstance of each one in a group being different from the rest: *It is his individuality as an artist that has made him famous.* [*same as* **originality**]

indoctrinate /ɪn'dɒktrɪneɪt/ *verb*: **indoctrinates, indoctrinating, indoctrinated**
To **indoctrinate** someone is to persuade them to hold particular beliefs or opinions so strongly that they refuse to accept any others: *It is not the duty of parents to indoctrinate; merely to give guidance.* [*same as* **brainwash**] — *noun* (*uncount*) **indoctrination** /ɪndɒktrɪ'neɪʃən/: *They had been practising a kind of religious indoctrination.*

indolent /ˈɪndələnt/ *adjective* (*formal*)
Indolent means lazy: *a row of indolent, semi-naked young men lying in the sun.* [*opposite* **active**, **industrious**]

indoor /ˈɪndɔ:(r)/ *adjective*
Indoor describes things that exist, belong or happen inside a building, not outside in the open air: *an indoor swimming pool.* [*opposite* **outdoor**]

indoors /ɪnˈdɔ:z/ *adverb*
Indoors means in or into a building: *The heavy rain forced us to spend the day indoors.* □ *It had grown cold and we moved the table indoors.* [*opposite* **outdoors**]

induce /ɪnˈdju:s/ *verb*: **induces, inducing, induced**
1 You **induce** someone to do something when you persuade or influence them to do it: *Unscrupulous colleagues had induced him to betray the Chief.* **2** Something **induces** a particular state or feeling when it causes it: *Working at home often induces a sense of isolation.* [*same as* **bring about**]

inducement /ɪnˈdju:smənt/ *noun*: **inducements**
An **inducement** is something offered to someone as a way of persuading them to do something. [*same as* **incentive**]

indulge /ɪnˈdʌldʒ/ *verb*: **indulges, indulging, indulged**
1 You **indulge** in something when you allow yourself the pleasure of doing it or having it: *Anyone indulging in casual sex should be aware of the risks involved.* □ *She spent the weekend indulging her passion for gardening.* □ *He decided to indulge himself and open another bottle.* **2** You **indulge** someone when you allow them to do or have what they want, or when you give it to them: *If he starts to tell his old war stories, just indulge him.* [*same as* **humour**]

indulgence /ɪnˈdʌldʒəns/ *noun* (*formal*): **indulgences**
An **indulgence** is something that you allow yourself the pleasure of doing or having: *Fine wines are my only real indulgence.*

indulgent /ɪnˈdʌldʒənt/ *adjective* (*formal*)
Someone who is **indulgent** allows others to do or have what they want, perhaps too much: *Reginald was, it seemed, an indulgent husband who ignored his wife's 'affairs'.* [*opposite* **strict**]

industrial /ɪnˈdʌstrɪəl/ *adjective*
1 Industrial means relating to or used in industry: *chemicals for industrial use.* **2** An **industrial** country has highly developed industry: *Germany has been traditionally regarded as Europe's greatest industrial nation.*

industrial estate /ɪnˈdʌstrɪəl ɪsteɪt/ *noun*: **industrial estates**
An **industrial estate** is a separate area in or near a town, where there are a lot of factories and other businesses.

industrialist /ɪnˈdʌstrɪəlɪst/ *noun*: **industrialists**
An **industrialist** is someone who owns one or more large factories or other businesses.

industrialized or **industrialised** /ɪnˈdʌstrɪəlaɪzd/ *adjective*
An **industrialized** country has a lot of highly developed industries.

industrious /ɪnˈdʌstrɪəs/ *adjective*
An **industrious** person works very hard: *She spent an industrious morning in the garden.*

industry /ˈɪndəstrɪ/ *noun*: **industries**
1 (*uncount*) **Industry** is the business of making things, usually on a large scale in factories: *They've recruited top managers from all branches of industry.* □ *the decline of British industry.* **2** An **industry** consists of all the factories or businesses that produce goods or services of a particular kind: *the tourist industry.* **3** (*uncount; formal*) **Industry** is hard work. *Due tribute was paid to their industry and dedication.*

inebriated /ɪˈni:brɪeɪtɪd/ *adjective*
Someone who is **inebriated** is very drunk.

inedible /ɪnˈɛdɪbəl/ *adjective*
Something **inedible** is not fit or suitable to be eaten: *The bread was a little stale, but not inedible.* [*opposite* **edible**]

ineffective /ɪnɪˈfɛktɪv/ *adjective*
Something that is **ineffective** has no effect, or does not have the desired or intended effect: *Attempts to persuade her proved ineffective.* [*opposite* **effective**]

ineffectual /ɪnɪˈfɛktʃʊəl/ *adjective*
1 Something that is **ineffectual** does not achieve what it is intended to achieve: *ineffectual methods* □ *the brave, but unfortunately ineffectual, efforts of the rescuers* **2** An **ineffectual** person lacks the ability or courage to do what is necessary: *She was a nice person to work for, if a little ineffectual and lacking in spirit.*

inefficient /ɪnɪˈfɪʃənt/ *adjective*
Someone or something that is **inefficient** carries out tasks or produces results slowly and in a way that wastes time, energy or resources: *The old engines were very inefficient.* □ *inefficient working methods.* [*opposite* **efficient**] — *noun* (*uncount or count*) **inefficiency:** *We are constantly having to combat the inefficiencies of an outdated system.*

inept /ɪnˈɛpt/ *adjective* (*formal*)
You might describe someone as **inept** if they lack skill or ability: *the rather inept way he deals with the press.*

ineptitude /ɪˈnɛptɪtju:d/ *noun* (*uncount; formal*)
Ineptitude is the quality of being inept: *She was criticized for what others saw as her diplomatic ineptitude.*

inequality /ɪnɪˈkwɒlɪtɪ/ *noun* (*uncount or count*): **inequalities**
Inequality is a difference between two things, especially an unfair difference in what different people have or are given: *We live in a world of inequality of wealth and opportunity.* □ *the glaring inequalities of the system.* [*opposite* **equality**]

inescapable /ɪnɪˈskeɪpəbəl/ *adjective*
Inescapable facts are ones you must accept or admit are true: *We reached the inescapable conclusion that some workers would have to be sacked.*

inevitable /ɪnˈɛvɪtəbəl/ *adjective*; *noun*
▷ ***adjective***
1 Something is **inevitable** when it cannot be avoided and is certain to happen: *It's inevitable that you will feel in some way responsible.* □ *Complete closure of the factory now seems inevitable.* [*opposite* **avoidable**] **2** You also describe something that happens boringly often or regularly as **inevitable**: *On Sunday, we went for the inevitable walk in the park.*
▷ ***noun*** (*used in the singular*)
You refer to something that is certain to happen, or that you think of as a strong possibility, as the **inevitable**: *A policeman's wife spends her whole married life preparing herself for the inevitable.* — *noun* (*uncount*) **inevitability** /ɪnɛvɪtəˈbɪlɪtɪ/: *the inevitability of failure.* — *adverb* (*sentence adverb*) **inevitably:** *Inevitably, she arrived late and missed the train.*

inexcusable /ɪnɛkˈskju:zəbəl/ *adjective*
Something **inexcusable** is too bad to be excused, justified or tolerated: *scenes of inexcusable rudeness.* [*opposite*, **justified, excusable**]

inexhaustible /ɪnɪgˈzɔ:stɪbəl/ *adjective*
A supply of something is **inexhaustible** when there is

so much of it that it can never be used up: *Fossil fuels such as oil and gas are now known not to be inexhaustible.*

inexorable /ɪn'ɛksərəbəl/ *adjective* (*formal*)
Something **inexorable** cannot be stopped: *British manufacturing industry seems to be in an inexorable decline.* — *adverb* **inexorably:** *We are sliding inexorably towards financial ruin.*

inexpensive /ɪnɛk'spɛnsɪv/ *adjective*
Something **inexpensive** does not cost much to buy. [*same as* **affordable**; *opposite* **expensive**]

inexperience /ɪnɛk'spɪərɪəns/ *noun* (*uncount*)
Inexperience is lack of experience, or lack of skill or knowledge gained from experience. [*opposite* **experience**] — *adjective* **inexperienced:** *It would be madness for an inexperienced climber to set out in this weather.* [*opposite* **experienced**]

inexplicable /ɪn'ɛksplɪkəbəl/ *adjective*
Something **inexplicable** is impossible to explain or understand: *the inexplicable disappearance of the schoolgirl.* [*same as* **baffling**]

inextricably /ɪnɛk'strɪkəblɪ/ *adverb*
Two things are **inextricably** linked when you cannot separate them: *The government still refuses to accept that rising poverty and rising crime are inextricably linked.*

infallible /ɪn'falɪbəl/ *adjective*
Someone or something that is **infallible** is always right and never makes a mistake: *Like most of my friends, I assumed our teachers were infallible.*

infamous /'ɪnfəməs/ *adjective*
Infamous describes people or things that are well known for being bad or unpleasant: *on that infamous day when war was declared.* [*same as* **notorious**]

infancy /'ɪnfənsɪ/ *noun* (*uncount*)
1 Your **infancy** is the period when you are a very young child: *the number of deaths in infancy.* **2** Something is in its **infancy** when it has only just started or begun to develop: *The new machines are still in their infancy; some problems must be anticipated.*

infant /'ɪnfənt/ *noun*: **infants**
An **infant** is a baby or very young child.

infantile /'ɪnfəntaɪl/ *adjective*
1 You describe someone or their behaviour as **infantile** if they are very silly and childish: *grown men making infantile little jokes.* **2** An **infantile** disease or illness is one that affects very young children.

infantry /'ɪnfəntrɪ/ *noun* (*uncount or used in the singular*)
Infantry refers to the part of an army consisting of soldiers who fight on foot, not in tanks or other vehicles.

infant school /'ɪnfənt sku:l/ *noun*: **infant schools**
In Britain, an **infant school** is a school for children between the ages of five and seven or eight.

infatuated /ɪn'fatjʊeɪtɪd/ *adjective*
To be **infatuated** with someone is to have very strong feelings of love for them often when you hardly know them at all. — *noun* (*uncount or count*) **infatuation** /ɪnfatjʊ'eɪʃən/: *Is it love or just infatuation?* □ *We initially dismissed it as a teenage infatuation.*

infect /ɪn'fɛkt/ *verb*: **infects, infecting, infected**
1 Someone **is infected** when they catch a disease or illness, or when their body is attacked by germs that can cause diseases: *It was so common in the last century for whole families to become infected with tuberculosis.* □ *You cannot be infected by shaking hands with a sufferer.* □ *The wound will become infected if it is not dressed immediately.* **2** The way you feel or behave **infects** someone you are with when they begin to feel or behave the same way: *Johnson's gloom had infected the whole staffroom.*

infection /ɪn'fɛkʃən/ *noun* (*uncount or count*): **infections**
1 (*uncount*) **Infection** is the process of becoming infected, or the state of being infected: *a simple way to guard against infection.* **2** An **infection** is an illness caused by germs: *The doctor said it was some kind of mild throat infection.*

infectious /ɪn'fɛkʃəs/ *adjective*
1 An **infectious** disease is one you can catch by being with a person who has it, even if you don't touch them. [compare **contagious**] **2** A person is **infectious** when they are infected by germs that they can pass on to other people: *I've had this cold for at least a week, so I don't think I can be infectious any more.* **3** The way you feel or behave is **infectious** when the people you are with begin to feel or behave the same way: *Joan's optimism was infectious.* □ *He had an infectious laugh.*

infer /ɪn'fɜ:(r)/ *verb*: **infers, inferring, inferred**
You **infer** something when you conclude that it is so, from facts or information you have been given: *Are we to infer from what you say that you are opposed to the scheme?* □ *Much of what we inferred, from a few brief conversations, was later proved accurate.* [*same as* **conclude, deduce, understand**]

> **Infer** is sometimes used to mean 'imply' or 'suggest': *Are you inferring that I'm a liar?* This use is considered incorrect by some people.

inference /'ɪnfərəns/ *noun*: **inferences**
An **inference** is a conclusion you reach, based on information you have been given: *That is my statement; draw from it what inferences you will.*

inferior /ɪn'fɪərɪə(r)/ *adjective*; *noun*
▻ ***adjective***
1 Something that is **inferior** is of poor quality, or of poorer quality than the thing you are comparing it with: *Our coffee is noticeably richer in taste than the inferior brands.* □ *It is certainly inferior to the comparable German engine.* **2** Someone who is **inferior** to you has lower rank or status. **3** You feel **inferior** to someone when you think they are better or more important than you in some way. [*opposite* **superior**]
▻ ***noun***: **inferiors**
Someone's **inferiors** are people lower in rank or status, or people they consider to be less important: *We couldn't allow her to marry someone who was socially her inferior.* [*opposite* **superior**] — *noun* (*uncount*) **inferiority** /ɪnfɪərɪ'ɒrɪtɪ/: *She had grown up with a terrible sense of inferiority.* [*opposite* **superiority**]

infernal /ɪn'fɜ:nəl/ *adjective* (*old, informal*)
People sometimes use **infernal** to refer to things that are annoying or upsetting them: *What an infernal mess we're in!*

inferno /ɪn'fɜ:noʊ/ *noun* (*literary*): **infernos**
A huge, destructive fire is often referred to as an **inferno**.

infertile /ɪn'fɜ:taɪl/ *adjective*
1 Infertile soil does not produce good crops. [*same as* **barren**; *opposite* **fertile**] **2** Someone who is **infertile** is unable to have or produce babies. [*same as* **sterile, barren**; *opposite* **fertile**] — *noun* (*uncount*) **infertility** /ɪnfə'tɪlɪtɪ/: *Doctors have suggested infertility treatment.* [*opposite* **fertility**]

infested /ɪn'fɛstɪd/ *adjective*
A place is **infested** with rats or other harmful or dan-

gerous creatures when they exist there in large numbers: *The roof timbers were infested with woodlice.*

infidelity /ɪnfɪˈdɛlɪtɪ/ *noun* (*uncount*)
Someone guilty of **infidelity** has sex with someone other than the person they are married to or in a steady relationship with. [*opposite* **fidelity**]

infiltrate /ˈɪnfɪltreɪt/ *verb*: **infiltrates, infiltrating, infiltrated**
Someone **infiltrates** an organization controlled by an enemy or rival when they join it in order secretly to ruin it or steal information.

infinite /ˈɪnfɪnət/ *adjective*
1 Something that is **infinite** has no end in time or space: *Scientists refuse to accept that the universe is infinite.* [*opposite* **finite**] **2** You might also describe something as **infinite** if it extremely large in amount or extent: *She has an infinite knowledge of her subject.* — *adverb* **infinitely:** *The problem is infinitely larger than we imagined.*

infinitesimal /ɪnfɪnɪˈtɛsɪməl/ *adjective*
Something **infinitesimal** is extremely small. [*same as* **minute**]

infinitive /ɪnˈfɪnɪtɪv/ *noun* (*usually in the singular*)
The **infinitive** is the basic form of a verb, such as *be*, *have* and *do*, as opposed to inflections, such as *is*, *has* and *does*.

> The infinitive is often used with *to*, following another verb, noun, or adjective, as in *I wanted to scream*; *a strong impulse to jump*; *It is essential to sign both parts of the form*. It can also be used without *to* after certain verbs, as in *You must come* and *I saw him leave*.

infinity /ɪnˈfɪnɪtɪ/ *noun* (*uncount*)
Infinity exists in time or space where there is no end, so that time or space continues for ever: *The clear blue sea stretched away into infinity.*

infirm /ɪnˈfɜːm/ *adjective*
Someone who is **infirm** is very weak through being ill or old. — *noun* (*uncount or count*) **infirmity** /ɪnˈfɜːmɪtɪ/: *In spite of her physical infirmity, she still has a sharp mind.* □ *How does she cope with her infirmities?*

infirmary /ɪnˈfɜːmərɪ/ *noun*: **infirmaries**
Infirmary is a title used by some hospitals: *North Staffordshire Royal Infirmary.*

inflamed /ɪnˈfleɪmd/ *adjective*
A part of your body that is **inflamed** is swollen and sore through being injured or diseased.

inflammable /ɪnˈflaməbəl/ *adjective*
An **inflammable** material or substance is easily set on fire: *Petrol is, of course, highly inflammable.* [*same as* **flammable**]

inflammation /ɪnfləˈmeɪʃən/ *noun* (*uncount or used in the singular*)
An **inflammation** is an area on your body that has become sore, red and swollen through injury or infection: *The problem is caused by inflammation of the membranes inside the nose.* [*same as* **swelling**]

inflammatory /ɪnˈflamətərɪ/ *adjective* (*formal*)
What someone says or does is **inflammatory** when it is likely to make people very angry: *an inflammatory remark.*

inflatable /ɪnˈfleɪtəbəl/ *adjective*
An **inflatable** object is made ready for use by being filled with air: *They crossed the river in an inflatable dinghy.*

inflate /ɪnˈfleɪt/ *verb*: **inflates, inflating, inflated**
You **inflate** something when you make it ready for use by filling it with air: *The lifejacket automatically inflates when you pull this cord.* [*same as* **blow up**; *opposite* **deflate**]

inflated /ɪnˈfleɪtɪd/ *adjective*
1 Inflated describes things, such as prices or wages, that are unreasonably high: *The workers take a pay cut while the directors award themselves grossly inflated salary increases.* **2 Inflated** also describes the behaviour of someone who thinks they are much more important than they really are: *It shows she has a rather inflated opinion of herself.*

inflation /ɪnˈfleɪʃən/ *noun* (*uncount*)
Inflation exists when there is a general increase in the cost of things people buy: *The economic policies of this government have brought inflation down to just over 3%.*

inflection or **inflexion** /ɪnˈflɛkʃən/ *noun*: **inflections**
1 (*uncount*) **Inflection** is change in the loudness or tone of your voice as you speak. **2** An **inflection** is a change in the basic form of a word, that shows its grammatical relationship to other words in the sentence; the changed form is also called an **inflection**; the inflections of the verb *fall*, for instance, are *falls*, *falling*, *fell* and *fallen*.

inflexible /ɪnˈflɛksɪbəl/ *adjective*
Something that is **inflexible** cannot be changed or altered; an **inflexible** person is unwilling to change their plans or opinions: *The rules are designed to be inflexible.* [*opposite* **flexible**]

inflexion see **inflection**.

inflict /ɪnˈflɪkt/ *verb*: **inflicts, inflicting, inflicted**
You **inflict** something unpleasant on someone when you force them to suffer it: *She didn't want to inflict her troubles on the others.*

influence /ˈɪnflʊəns/ *noun*; *verb*
▷ ***noun***: **influences**
1 (*uncount or count*) You have **influence** over someone if they tend to follow your advice, agree with your opinions or copy your behaviour or the way you do things: *He'll use his influence with the manager to get something done about it.* □ *She's in a position of considerable political influence.* □ *One or two idiots can have a disruptive influence on the whole class.* □ *As a musician, who would you say has been your main influence?* **2** Something has an **influence** on things that it affects or changes: *The book discusses the influence of the war on the poetry of the period.*
▷ ***verb***: **influences, influencing, influenced**
You **influence** people and things that you affect or change: *I didn't want to be influenced by the way previous actors had played the part.* □ *The activities of terrorists have never been allowed to influence government policy.*
▷ ***phrase*** (*informal*) You can say that someone is **under the influence** when they are drunk.

influential /ɪnflʊˈɛnʃəl/ *adjective*
Influential describes people and things that have an influence on others: *one of the most influential rock musicians of our time.*

influenza /ɪnflʊˈɛnzə/ *noun* (*uncount*; *formal*)
Influenza is flu, an illness causing a general feeling of weakness, usually with a fever and sometimes with a sore throat and running nose: *She's had a very severe bout of influenza.*

influx /ˈɪnflʌks/ *noun* (*used in the singular*)
There is an **influx** of people or things when great numbers of them arrive or appear in a place: *We're witnessing the usual influx of tourists to the island.*

info /'ɪnfoʊ/ *noun* (*uncount*; *informal*)
Info is information: *Did they give you any info on the new book?*

inform /ɪn'fɔːm/ *verb*: **informs informing, informed**
You **inform** someone of something when you tell them about it: *Have you informed the police that there's been an accident?* [*same as* **notify**]

informal /ɪn'fɔːməl/ *adjective*
1 Informal occasions and events are ones where you can wear casual clothes and behave in a relaxed, friendly way: *an informal dinner with a few friends.* **2 Informal** language is the kind of language you use when speaking casually to people you know well; words that are normally used in a casual context are labelled (*informal*) in this dictionary. — *noun* (*uncount*) **informality** /ɪnfɔː'malɪtɪ/: *We put on some music to inject a tone of informality into what had become a rather solemn evening.*

informant /ɪn'fɔːmənt/ *noun*: **informants**
1 Your **informant** on a certain subject is someone who gives you information about it: *They're putting on an extra train at the weekend, or so my informant at British Rail gave me to understand.* **2** An **informant** is also an informer.

information /ɪnfə'meɪʃən/ *noun* (*uncount*)
Information is knowledge, facts or news: *I can't give you any information about the precise nature of the crime.* □ *Do you have any information on hotels in the area?* □ *We were able to provide him with some useful travel information.*

informative /ɪn'fɔːmətɪv/ *adjective*
You describe something such as a book or lecture as **informative** if you learn useful or interesting things from it.

informed /ɪn'fɔːmd/ *adjective*
Someone who is well **informed** knows a lot about something; an **informed** guess about a situation is one made using the knowledge you have of that situation.

informer /ɪn'fɔːmə(r)/ *noun*: **informers**
An **informer** is a person who tells the police about someone who has committed a crime: *a police informer.*

infrastructure /'ɪnfrəstrʌktʃə(r)/ *noun* (*uncount*)
The **infrastructure** of a country or city consists of services such as roads, railways, bridges, factories and schools that are needed to allow it to function properly.

infrequent /ɪn'friːkwənt/ *adjective*
Something that is **infrequent** happens only rarely or occasionally: *Visits to the hospital became increasingly infrequent.* [*opposite* **frequent**]

infringe /ɪn'frɪndʒ/ *verb*: **infringes, infringing, infringed**
Something **infringes** on your rights or your freedom when it prevents you from doing something you have the right to do, or makes it more difficult: *People see the introduction of identity cards as infringing on their civil liberties.* [*same as* **violate**] — *noun* **infringement:** *This is a serious infringement on public freedom.*

infuriate /ɪn'fjʊərɪeɪt/ *verb*: **infuriates, infuriating, infuriated**
Something that **infuriates** you makes you very angry: *It has infuriated the women to learn that the men get paid more for doing the same work.* [*same as* **incense**[2]] — *adjective* **infuriating:** *an infuriating series of delays and mistakes.* [*same as* **exasperating**]

ingenious /ɪn'dʒiːnɪəs/ *adjective*
Something such as a plan is **ingenious** if it is very clever and original: *a range of ingenious gadgets.*

ingenuity /ɪndʒə'njuːɪtɪ/ *noun* (*uncount*)
Ingenuity is cleverness in thinking of original ways of doing things: *You have to admire the sheer ingenuity of the man.*

ingratiate /ɪn'greɪʃɪeɪt/ *verb*: **ingratiates, ingratiating, ingratiated**
To **ingratiate** yourself with someone in a position of power or influence is to try to make friends with them because their friendship would be useful. — *adjective* **ingratiating:** *She has an ingratiating manner with the managers that I find irritating.*

ingratitude /ɪn'gratɪtjuːd/ *noun* (*uncount*)
Ingratitude is the fact of not being grateful when you should be: *Parents often find the ingratitude of their children hard to bear.* [*opposite* **gratitude**]

ingredient /ɪn'griːdɪənt/ *noun*: **ingredients**
The **ingredients** of something are all the separate things that are combined to make it: *The secret of good cooking is always to use fresh ingredients.* □ *This film has all the classic ingredients of a good thriller.*

inhabit /ɪn'habɪt/ *verb*: **inhabits, inhabiting, inhabited**
The people or animals that **inhabit** a place live there: *a string of villages inhabited mostly by farmworkers.*

inhabitant /ɪn'habɪtənt/ *noun*: **inhabitants**
The **inhabitants** of a place are the people who live there permanently: *a city of some three million inhabitants.*

inhale /ɪn'heɪl/ *verb*: **inhales, inhaling, inhaled**
You **inhale** something such as air or a gas when you breathe it in: *The fumes can be poisonous if inhaled.* [see also **exhale**]

inherent /ɪn'hɪərənt/ *adjective*
Qualities that are **inherent** in something exist in it as permanent features that cannot be changed or removed: *I'm afraid that inequalities of this kind are inherent in our economic system.* — *adverb* **inherently:** *The scheme is inherently flawed.*

inherit /ɪn'herɪt/ *verb*: **inherits, inheriting, inherited**
1 You **inherit** property or other wealth when you receive it from someone when they die. **2** You **inherit** personal qualities that your parents have when you are born with them: *We were hoping she would inherit her mother's blue eyes.* □ *He seems to have inherited his father's quick temper.* **3** You **inherit** things when they are left for you by the person who occupied your house, job or other position before you: *This is a problem we inherited from the old Labour government.*

inheritance /ɪn'herɪtəns/ *noun* (*uncount or singular*)
Your **inheritance** consists of the property or other wealth you inherit from someone who dies.

inhibit /ɪn'hɪbɪt/ *verb*: **inhibits, inhibiting, inhibited**
One thing **inhibits** another if it slows it down or prevents its development: *The plant's growth has been inhibited by a lack of sunlight.* [*same as* **hinder**; *opposite* **encourage**]

inhibited /ɪn'hɪbɪtɪd/ *adjective*
You feel **inhibited** when you are embarrassed or uneasy about something, and it prevents you from behaving in an open and relaxed way: *A religious upbringing needn't leave a child inhibited about sex.* [*opposite* **uninhibited**]

inhibition /ɪnhɪ'bɪʃən/ *noun*: **inhibitions**
Inhibitions are feelings of embarrassment or uneasiness about something, that prevent you from behaving in an open and relaxed way: *a woman with no sexual inhibitions.*

inhospitable /ɪnhɒ'spɪtəbəl/ *adjective*
1 Someone's behaviour is **inhospitable** if they are not

friendly and welcoming: *Would you think it inhospitable of me if I returned to work this afternoon?* [*opposite* **hospitable**] **2** In an **inhospitable** place you are exposed to harsh weather or other unpleasantness: *The jungles of South America are the most inhospitable places on earth.*

inhuman /ɪn'hjuːmən/ *adjective*
Inhuman behaviour is extremely cruel: *It's inhuman, the way these children are treated.* — *noun* (*uncount*) **inhumanity** /ɪnhjuː'manɪtɪ/: *our inhumanity to fellow creatures.*

inhumane /ɪnhjʊ'meɪn/ *adjective*
Inhumane treatment of animals is extremely cruel: *inhumane slaughterhouse practices.* [*same as* **brutal**; *opposite* **humane**]

inimitable /ɪn'ɪmɪtəbəl/ *adjective*
You describe someone's excellent or admirable qualities or abilities as **inimitable** if they are unique to that person, something that you instantly recognize as belonging to them: *He made the announcement in his own inimitable style.* [*same as* **distinctive**]

initial /ɪ'nɪʃəl/ *adjective*; *noun*; *verb*
▻ ***adjective***
Initial refers to things that happen or exist at the beginning: *My initial reaction was anger.* ▫ *in the initial stages.* [*same as* **first**]
▻ ***noun***: **initials**
Your **initials** are the letters that begin your first name and other names: *She had my initials engraved on the ring.*
▻ ***verb***: **initials, initialling** (*AmE* **initialing**), **initialled** (*AmE* **initialed**)
You **initial** something such as a document when you write your initials on it, *eg* to show that you have seen or received it.

initially /ɪ'nɪʃəlɪ/ *adverb*
Initially means 'at first' or 'in the beginning': *I was initially reluctant to agree.* ▫ *Initially, we thought we would need at least five people.*

initiate *verb*; *noun*
▻ ***verb*** /ɪ'nɪʃɪeɪt/: **initiates, initiating, initiated**
1 You **initiate** something when you cause it to begin: *This initiated a rethink of the whole system.* [*same as* **prompt**] **2** Someone **is initiated** into an organization or society when they are accepted as a new member, often by successfully passing a test of some kind.
▻ ***noun*** /ɪ'nɪʃɪət/: **initiates**
An **initiate** is someone who has recently been, or is soon to be, initiated. [*same as* **beginner**] — *noun* (*uncount or used in the singular*) **initiation** /ɪnɪʃɪ'eɪʃən/: *the initiation of new housing schemes.* ▫ *mysterious stories of strange initiation ceremonies.* [*same as* **institution**]

initiative /ɪ'nɪʃətɪv/ *noun*: **initiatives**
1 (*uncount*) Someone who has **initiative** is able to take decisions quickly, or able to think of ways of solving problems, without asking the help or advice of others: *She started the business on her own initiative.* ▫ *You'll be on your own; you'll have to use your initiative.* [*same as* **resourcefulness**] **2** An **initiative** is a first step or move towards achieving something: *This is an important initiative in the fight against violent crime.* ▫ *Don't stand around waiting for someone else to take the initiative.*

inject /ɪn'dʒɛkt/ *verb*: **injects, injecting, injected**
1 Doctors **inject** a liquid medicine into your body when they force it in using a special hollow needle called a syringe: *We'll inject it into the thigh.* ▫ *Half the patients were injected with the new drug.* **2** To **inject** something such as a quality into something is to introduce or add it: *We put on some jazz records to inject a bit of life into the party.* ▫ *Forgive me for injecting a pessimistic note into the conversation.*

injection /ɪn'dʒɛkʃən/ *noun*: **injections**
You have an **injection** when a doctor injects a liquid medicine into your body.

injure /'ɪndʒə(r)/ *verb*: **injures, injuring, injured**
You **are injured** when part of your body is hurt or damaged: *toys with sharp parts that children could injure themselves on.*

injury /'ɪndʒərɪ/ *noun* (*count or uncount*): **injuries**
You suffer an **injury** when part of your body is hurt or damaged: *She's recovering from head injuries.* ▫ *Most crashes result in serious injury and death.*

injury time /'ɪndʒərɪ taɪm/ *noun* (*uncount*)
Injury time is playing time added to the end of a football or rugby match to make up for time taken to treat injured players during the match.

injustice /ɪn'dʒʌstɪs/ *noun* (*uncount or count*): **injustices**
Injustice occurs when someone is treated unfairly: *the injustice of a system which takes money away from those least able to pay it* ▫ *The report highlights the injustices of the benefit scheme.* [*same as* **unfairness**]
▻ ***phrase*** You **do** someone **an injustice** when you have a bad opinion of them that they don't deserve: *I was made to feel that I was doing Alan a considerable injustice.*

ink /ɪŋk/ *noun* (*uncount*)
Ink is a coloured liquid used for writing, printing and drawing: *Should he write in pencil or in ink?* [see picture at **office**]

inkling /'ɪŋklɪŋ/ *noun* (*singular*)
You have an **inkling** that something is true when you suspect that it might be true: *I had an inkling that the chairman was about to make an important announcement.* ▫ *Sheila had no inkling of what awaited her.* [*same as* **idea**]

inland /'ɪnland/ or /ɪn'land/ *adjective or adverb*
Inland means in or towards areas that are away from the coast: *The inland* (/'ɪnlənd/) *towns, being more sheltered, are greener.* ▫ *The further inland* (/ɪn'land/) *you go, the taller the trees become.*

in-laws /'ɪnlɔːz/ *noun* (*plural*)
Your **in-laws** are your husband's or wife's parents: *We've been invited to spend Christmas with my in-laws.*

inmate /'ɪnmeɪt/ *noun*: **inmates**
The **inmates** of a prison are the prisoners kept there; patients in certain hospitals are also called **inmates**.

inn /ɪn/ *noun*: **inns**
An **inn** is a pub or small hotel, especially an old one in the country or a remote place.

innate /ɪ'neɪt/ *adjective*
Innate qualities and talents are ones you are born with, or ones that seem very natural to you: *The whole family seems to have an innate talent for offending people.* [*same as* **natural**]

inner /'ɪnə(r)/ *adjective*
1 Inner describes things that are inside others: *tyres that have no inner tubes* ▫ *The inner wheel revolves in the opposite direction to the outer.* [*opposite* **outer**] **2 Inner** thoughts and feelings are ones you keep secret or hidden.

inner city *noun* (*often adjectival*): **inner cities**
An **inner city** is the central area of a city, often densely populated and with poor housing and other facilities: *a scheme to revive Britain's inner cities* ▫ *an inner-city shopping centre.*

innermost /'ɪnəmoʊst/ *adjective*
Your **innermost** thoughts and feelings are the most personal ones that you discuss with nobody.

inning /'ɪnɪŋ/ *noun*: **innings**
In the sport of baseball, an **inning** is the period of a game during which one particular player or team bats.

innings /'ɪnɪŋz/ *noun*: *plural* **innings**
In cricket, an **innings** is the period of a game during which one particular player or team bats.

innocent /'ɪnəsənt/ *adjective*; *noun*
▻ ***adjective***
1 Someone who is **innocent** is not guilty of committing a crime or other wrongdoing: *How many times has the law convicted an innocent person?* □ *He's absolutely innocent of this crime, I'm sure of that.* □ *She's been found innocent on all the charges made against her.* [*opposite* **guilty**] **2** An **innocent** victim is someone not directly involved in a war, fight or other argument, who does not deserve to be killed or harmed: *the bombing of innocent civilians.* **3** Someone who is **innocent** has no experience of how unpleasant people, and life in general, can be, and tends to trust everyone: *She was quite an innocent teenager.* [*same as* **naïve**; *opposite* **worldly**] **4** When something you say or do offends or embarrasses someone, it is **innocent** if you didn't mean to offend or embarrass them and you didn't realize that you had: *My remarks were entirely innocent.* [*same as* **well-intentioned**]
▻ ***noun***: **innocents**
An **innocent** is someone with no experience of how unpleasant people and life can be. — *noun* (*uncount*) **innocence** /ɪnəsəns/: *I think the jury will be convinced of his innocence.* □ *the innocence of youth* □ *I'm sure she asked the question in all innocence.*

innocuous /ɪ'nɒkjʊəs/ *adjective*
An **innocuous** substance is harmless; what you say or do is **innocuous** if it avoids offending or upsetting anyone: *Most household cleaning liquids contain fairly innocuous chemicals.* □ *Surprisingly, it was quite an innocuous little film.* [*opposite* **harmful**]

innovation /ɪnə'veɪʃən/ *noun*: **innovations**
1 An **innovation** is something entirely new, especially a new method of doing something. **2** (*uncount*) **Innovation** is the introduction of new things, especially new methods. [*same as* **modernization**]

innovative /'ɪnəvətɪv/ *adjective*
Something **innovative** is entirely new and original: *innovative production techniques.*

innuendo /ɪnjʊ'endoʊ/ *noun*: **innuendos** or **innuendoes**
An **innuendo** is a remark that suggests something rude or unpleasant: *He was fond of making sexual innuendos in front of the younger women.* [*same as* **insinuation**]

innumerable /ɪ'nju:mərəbəl/ *adjective*
Innumerable means a great many: *They received innumerable letters on the subject.* [*same as* **uncountable**]

innumerate /ɪ'nju:mərət/ *adjective*
Someone who is **innumerate** has a very poor knowledge of arithmetic or mathematics. [*opposite* **numerate**]

inoculate /ɪ'nɒkjʊleɪt/ *verb*: **inoculates, inoculating, inoculated**
To **inoculate** someone is to protect them from a particular disease by injecting a mild form of the disease into their body, encouraging the body to resist the stronger form: *Every child is inoculated against all the serious diseases.* [*same as* **vaccinate**] — *noun* (*count or uncount*) **inoculation** /ɪnɒkjʊ'leɪʃən/: *You get three inoculations on each visit.* □ *a programme of inoculation.* [*same as* **vaccination**]

inoffensive /ɪnə'fɛnsɪv/ *adjective*
Something or someone **inoffensive** is not likely to offend or upset anyone: *He was a quiet, gentle, inoffensive sort of person.* □ *It was a perfectly inoffensive remark.* [*opposite* **offensive**]

inopportune /ɪn'ɒpətju:n/ *adjective*
Something **inopportune** causes trouble or embarrassment because it happens at an unsuitable time: *She arrived at a rather inopportune moment.* [*same as* **inconvenient**; *opposite* **well-timed, opportune**]

inordinate /ɪn'ɔ:dɪnət/ *adjective* (*formal*)
Inordinate means very great, especially greater than is reasonable or acceptable: *after what I consider to be an inordinate delay.* [*same as* **excessive**] — *adverb* **inordinately:** *Their children seemed inordinately confident.* [*same as* **excessively**]

inorganic /ɪnɔ:'ganɪk/ *adjective*
Inorganic substances are things such as stone or metal, that do not consist of, or contain, living matter. [*opposite* **organic**]

inquest /ɪn'kwɛst/ *noun*: **inquests**
An **inquest** is an official investigation to find out how someone died: *The inquest into his death revealed he'd been poisoned.*

inquire or **enquire** /ɪn'kwaɪə(r)/ *verb*: **inquires, inquiring, inquired**
You **inquire** about something when you ask for information about it: *She inquired at the travel agent's about the cost of a flight to Paris.* □ *We should inquire whether they serve vegetarian meals.* □ *'What time does it leave?' she inquired.*

> ***phrasal verbs***
> **inquire after** You **inquire after** someone when you ask for news about them: *She always inquires after the children.*
> **inquire into** You **inquire into** something when you investigate it thoroughly: *The Prime Minister's office is inquiring into how the information was leaked.*

inquiring /ɪn'kwaɪərɪŋ/ *adjective*
Someone with an **inquiring** mind is eager to discover or learn new things.

inquiry or **enquiry** /ɪn'kwɪrɪ/ *noun* (*count or uncount*): **inquiries**
You make **inquiries** about something when you ask for information about it: *We made a few inquiries about alternative train times.* □ *A man in his thirties is helping the police with their inquiries.* □ *We will have to pursue a different line of inquiry.*

inquisitive /ɪn'kwɪzɪtɪv/ *adjective*
An **inquisitive** person is interested in finding out things, especially a little too interested in other people's affairs: *I'm sorry to sound inquisitive, but we need to know.* [*same as* **curious**]

insane /ɪn'seɪn/ *adjective*
1 Someone who is **insane** is mad or mentally ill: *horrific experiences that drove the men insane.* [*opposite* **sane**] **2** If you call someone **insane** you mean that they are behaving foolishly: *You would be insane to refuse such an offer.* □ *The plan was quite insane.* — *noun* (*uncount*) **insanity** /ɪn'sanɪtɪ/: *She suffered from phases of insanity.* □ *Are you not aware of the insanity of what you're proposing?* [*opposite* **sanity**]

insatiable /ɪn'seɪʃəbəl/ *adjective*
Someone who has an **insatiable** appetite or desire for something wants lots of it, regularly or all the time: *He was one of those men with an insatiable need for success.*

inscribed /ɪn'skraɪbd/ *adjective*
Words that are **inscribed** on an object are carved or written on it; an object is **inscribed** with words if they are carved or written on it: *He showed me a trophy with his name inscribed on it.* □ *On the door was a brass plate inscribed with the name 'E H Hughes'.* [*same as* **engrave**]

inscription /ɪn'skrɪpʃən/ *noun*: **inscriptions**
An **inscription** consists of words written, printed or carved on something: *The book carried the inscription 'To Johnny, from your friend Larry'.*

inscrutable /ɪn'skruːtəbəl/ *adjective*
You describe someone as **inscrutable** if they reveal nothing about their thoughts or feelings: *She always has the same inscrutable smile.*

insect /'ɪnsɛkt/ *noun*: **insects**
Insects are small creatures, typically with six legs and wings, such as flies, beetles and butterflies.

insecticide /ɪn'sɛktɪsaɪd/ *noun* (*count or uncount*): **insecticides**
An **insecticide** is a chemical substance for killing insects. [*same as* **pesticide**]

insecure /ɪnsɪ'kjʊə(r)/ *adjective*
1 Someone who feels **insecure** thinks that, in some way, they are not as good as others, and is perhaps worried that others don't like or respect them: *We couldn't understand why she was so insecure.* **2** Something that is **insecure** is not fixed or safe: *Is that luggage on the roof tied down firmly enough? It looks rather insecure.* □ *The future of the company is very insecure.* [*opposite* **secure**] — *noun* (*uncount*) **insecurity** /ɪnsɪ'kjʊərɪtɪ/: *a deep sense of insecurity* □ *a period of economic insecurity.* [*opposite* **security**]

insensitive /ɪn'sɛnsɪtɪv/ *adjective*
Someone who is **insensitive** tends not to notice how other people are feeling and not to realize when others are likely to be upset: *Angela was just about the most insensitive person you could meet.* □ *It seems the father is rather insensitive to the son's emotional needs.* [*opposite* **sensitive**] — *noun* (*uncount*) **insensitivity** /ɪnsɛnsɪ'tɪvɪtɪ/: *We all marvelled at her insensitivity.* [*opposite* **sensitivity**]

inseparable /ɪn'sɛpərəbəl/ *adjective*
1 Friends who are **inseparable** are always together: *Even at school they were inseparable.* **2** Two things that are **inseparable** are so closely linked that one cannot be considered in isolation from the other: *She argues that politics and philosophy are inseparable disciplines.*

insert /ɪn'sɜːt/ *verb*: **inserts, inserting, inserted**
You **insert** something into something else when you put, place or fit it inside that other thing: *Insert the coin into the machine.* □ *An extra paragraph was inserted near the end.* [*same as* **place**]

inshore /ɪn'ʃɔː(r)/ or /'ɪnʃɔː(r)/ *adjective or adverb*
Inshore means in or on the sea but near or towards the shore: *one or two of the inshore islands* □ *We decided to move further inshore.* [compare **offshore**]

inside /ɪn'saɪd/ *preposition; adverb; adjective; noun*
▻ ***preposition***
1 One thing is **inside** another if it is enclosed by it: *Once inside the hotel I sat down in the foyer and felt safer.* □ *The tyre-pressure gauge is inside the right-hand glove compartment.* □ *Several times recently I'd managed to lock my key inside the car.* [*same as* **in**] **2** One thing goes **inside** another when it moves into it and is enclosed by it: *The dolls fit one inside the other.* □ *She ran inside the house.* [*same as* **into**] **3** Feelings that are **inside** you are in your body, heart or mind: *She felt the resentment increasing inside her.* [*same as* **within**] **4** You are **inside** an organization if you belong to it: *A number of senior people inside the company have expressed misgivings.* **5** Something that is done **inside** a certain period of time takes less than that time: *You can board a train in London and be in Edinburgh inside four hours.* □ *I'm unlikely to finish the job inside three days.*
▻ ***adverb***
1 The adverb **inside** reflects senses 1-3 of the preposition: *Open the parcel and see what's inside.* □ *The weather was so bad that we stayed inside all day.* □ *I settled down on the patio and then realized I'd left the newspaper inside.* □ *She opened the case and found the ring inside.* □ *Come inside; it's cold in the garden.* □ *A plateful of soup will make you feel nice and warm inside.* □ *Inside she felt hurt and jealous.* **2** (*informal*) Someone who is **inside** is in prison. [*opposite* **outside**]
▻ ***adjective***
1 Inside describes things contained within, or on the inner part or surface of, something: *Most of the houses in the street had inside toilets by then.* □ *She slid the letter into her inside pocket.* **2** The **inside** lanes of a road are those closest to the edge of it. [*opposite* **outside**] **3 Inside** information about a concern is provided by someone who is involved with it and therefore knows about it; a crime against an organization that is described as an **inside** job is planned or carried out by someone within the organization.
▻ ***noun*: insides**
1 The **inside** of something is the inner part or surface of it: *Opening the cabinet, we see that the inside is also highly decorated.* □ *pans that are copper on the outside and stainless steel on the inside.* [*opposite* **outside**] **2** (*used in the plural; informal*) Your **insides** are your internal organs, especially your stomach: *She's in hospital having something done to her insides.*
▻ ***phrase*** Something that is **inside out** has the inside surface turned to face outwards: *He appeared to be wearing his shirt inside out.*

insider /ɪn'saɪdə(r)/ *noun*: **insiders**
An **insider** is a member of an organization or group, who is able to provide reliable information about it. [*opposite* **outsider**]

insidious /ɪn'sɪdɪəs/ *adjective*
Insidious refers to unpleasant things that develop gradually, without being noticed, and cause great harm or damage: *The education they receive is little more than insidious brainwashing.*

insight /'ɪnsaɪt/ *noun* (*uncount or count*): **insights**
Someone with **insight** is able quickly and clearly to understand the real nature of complex situations or problems: *She was a leader of unparalleled political insight.* □ *The lectures contain some fascinating literary insights.*

insignia /ɪn'sɪgnɪə/ *noun*: **insignia**
The **insignia** of a group or organization is its official badge or emblem.

insignificant /ɪnsɪg'nɪfɪkənt/ *adjective*
Something **insignificant** has little or no importance or value: *The number of people opposed was fairly insignificant.* □ *They donated a not insignificant amount of money.* [*opposite* **significant**] — *noun* (*uncount*) **insignificance** /ɪnsɪg'nɪfɪkəns/: *the comparative insignificance of the sums of money involved.* [*opposite* **significance**]

insincere /ɪnsɪn'sɪə(r)/ *adjective*
Insincere means not sincere: *She tried not to sound insincere.* □ *He gave me an insincere-looking smile.*

insinuate /ɪn'sɪnjʊeɪt/ *verb*: **insinuates, insinuating, insinuated**

1 You **insinuate** something unpleasant when you suggest or hint that it is true: *newspaper reports insinuating that she'd had an affair with a married man.* [*same as* **imply**] **2** You **insinuate** yourself into a position of influence when you achieve it gradually, using cleverly planned and often unpleasant methods: *Over a period of months, we watched her insinuate herself into the manager's favour.* [*same as* **ingratiate yourself**] — *noun* **insinuation** /ɪnsɪnjʊ'eɪʃən/: *I've learned to pay no attention to media insinuations about my private life.*

insipid /ɪn'sɪpɪd/ *adjective*
Insipid is used to describe people and things that are dull and uninteresting: *It was a fairly insipid performance.* ▫ *She served up a rather insipid lamb stew.* [*same as* **dull**; *opposite* **appetizing, tasty**]

insist /ɪn'sɪst/ *verb*: **insists, insisting, insisted**
1 You **insist** that something is true when you state firmly that it is true, refusing to be persuaded that it is not: *She insists she hasn't seen him for months.* ▫ *'But I've told you I wasn't there,' Hale insisted.* [*same as* **assert, stress**] **2** You **insist** on something when you state firmly that you want to have or do it, refusing to accept any alternative: *He insisted on walking me right to the door, saying you couldn't be too careful at night.* ▫ *We are a company that insists on punctuality among the staff.*

insistence /ɪn'sɪstəns/ *noun* (*uncount*)
When you refer to someone's **insistence** on something, you are talking about the fact that they insist on doing or having it: *the extra work created by his insistence on having a clean shirt every day.*

insistent /ɪn'sɪstənt/ *adjective*
Someone is **insistent** when they insist on having or doing something: *On that point at least, she was most insistent.* [*same as* **emphatic**]

insolent /'ɪnsələnt/ *adjective*
Someone who is **insolent** shows a lack of proper respect for someone or something: *I find such insolent behaviour unpardonable.* [*same as* **rude**; *opposite* **polite**] — *noun* (*uncount*) **insolence:** *I will not tolerate his insolence a second longer.* [*same as* **rudeness**; *opposite* **politeness**]

insoluble /ɪn'sɒljʊbəl/ *adjective* (*formal*)
An **insoluble** problem is too difficult to be solved: *Yes, it's a problem, but it's not insoluble.*

insolvent /ɪn'sɒlvənt/ *adjective*
The owners of a business company are **insolvent** when they do not have enough money to pay back what they have borrowed. [*same as* **bankrupt**; *opposite* **solvent**]

insomnia /ɪn'sɒmnɪə/ *noun* (*uncount*)
Someone suffering from **insomnia** is regularly unable to sleep at night.

insomniac /ɪn'sɒmnɪak/ *noun*: **insomniacs**
An **insomniac** is someone suffering from insomnia.

inspect /ɪn'spɛkt/ *verb*: **inspects, inspecting, inspected**
You **inspect** something when you look at or examine it closely, often to check for faults or mistakes: *We make monthly visits to inspect the standards of hygiene in hotel kitchens.* ▫ *Police inspected the windows for fingerprints.* — *noun* (*count or uncount*) **inspection** /ɪn'spɛkʃən/: *Tourist Board officials carry out inspections of all caravan sites listed in the brochure.* ▫ *On closer inspection, it was obvious that the handle had been repaired.*

inspector /ɪn'spɛktə(r)/ *noun*: **inspectors**
1 An **inspector** is an official employed to inspect something, checking that rules or regulations are being followed: *Her husband's a tax inspector.* **2** In the police force, an **inspector** is an officer of middle rank.

inspiration /ɪnspɪ'reɪʃən/ *noun*: **inspirations**
1 (*uncount or used in the singular*) You get **inspiration** for something, especially a piece of creative work such as a painting or a poem, when you have an idea that makes you want to do it: *The main inspiration for the film came from a collection of Irish folk tales I was reading.* ▫ *For long periods, I would stare at a blank sheet of paper, searching for inspiration.* **2** An **inspiration** is a good idea: *That was an inspiration, getting out those jigsaws for the children.*

inspire /ɪn'spaɪə(r)/ *verb*: **inspires, inspiring, inspired**
1 Something or someone **inspires** you to do something when they give you the desire to do it: *The trip to Italy had inspired her to start painting again.* ▫ *One feels that this series of poems must have been inspired by a passionate love affair.* [*same as* **motivate**] **2** You **inspire** a particular feeling in someone when your behaviour makes them feel that way: *You need a teacher who inspires self-confidence in her pupils.* [*same as* **arouse**]

inspired /ɪn'spaɪəd/ *adjective*
You might describe someone as **inspired** if they are exceptionally talented at something: *She is an inspired writer who deserves every success.* [*same as* **brilliant**]

inspiring /ɪn'spaɪərɪŋ/ *adjective*
You might describe something as **inspiring** if it is very exciting or interesting: *Your average television viewer doesn't find the game of chess a particularly inspiring spectacle.* [*opposite* **dull**]

instability /ɪnstə'bɪlɪtɪ/ *noun* (*uncount*)
Instability is the condition of not being steady or stable: *a period of economic instability.* [*opposite* **stability**; see also **unstable**]

install /ɪn'stɔːl/ *verb*: **installs, installing, installed**
1 You **install** equipment or machinery when you put it in place and make it ready for use: *the cost of installing a new telephone system.* **2** (*formal*) You **install** yourself somewhere when you settle yourself comfortably or happily there: *Dempsey had installed himself in a large armchair by the fire.* ▫ *Within a few days, we were safely installed in our new hideaway.*

installation /ɪnstə'leɪʃən/ *noun*: **installations**
1 (*uncount*) The **installation** of equipment or machinery is the process of installing it: *There will be no installation or repair charges.* **2** An **installation** is a place where equipment or machinery of a particular kind, or relating to a particular activity, is used or ready to use: *We spotted what looked like an enemy missile installation.*

instalment (*AmE* **installment**) /ɪn'stɔːlmənt/ *noun*: **instalments**
1 You pay for something in **instalments** when you make a series of small payments for it, over an agreed period of time, rather than paying the whole price when you buy it. **2** Something that is published or broadcast in **instalments** appears as a series of parts at regular intervals: *Don't forget to listen to next week's exciting instalment.*

instance /'ɪnstəns/ *noun*: **instances**
An **instance** of something is a single example of it, or a single occasion on which it happens: *In this instance, we feel that the rules can be broken.* ▫ *There have been several instances of serious bullying in this school this year.*
▻ ***phrase*** **For instance** is used to introduce an example or examples of something you have just been talking about: *The money could be used to help the Church, by,*

for instance, paying for repairs to the roof. [*same as* **for example**]

instant /'ɪnstənt/ *adjective; noun*

▻ ***adjective***

1 Instant describes things that happen immediately or straight away: *The film was an instant success.* **2 Instant** also describes meals and drinks that you can prepare very quickly and easily: *a jar of instant coffee.*

▻ ***noun*** (*usually in the singular*): **instants**

1 An **instant** is a moment, a very brief period of time: *We must not for an instant forget why we are doing this.* □ *And then, in an instant, she disappeared.* **2** When one thing happens the **instant** that another happens, it happens immediately after it, without delay: *Phone me the instant you receive any news.* **3** When someone demands that something should be done this **instant**, they want you to do it immediately: *I insist on seeing the manager this instant.*

instantaneous /ɪnstən'teɪnɪəs/ *adjective*

Something **instantaneous** happens or is done very quickly: *The doctors assured her that death must have been instantaneous.* [*same as* **immediate**]

instead /ɪn'stɛd/ *adverb*

You do or select one thing **instead** of another when you do it or select it rather than, or in place of, the other; one thing happens **instead** of another if it, as distinct from the other, is what happens: *Instead of continuing up the M90, branch off towards Crieff on the A977.* □ *Most of us would like to spend the day out in the sun instead of imprisoned in the office.* □ *Would you mind if my husband came instead of me?* □ *I suggested lunch at the pub instead of the Cafe Royal.* □ *Instead of improving the traffic situation the new bypass has made matters worse.* □ *My remark was intended to comfort her but instead it upset her even more.* □ *The cinema had nothing on worth seeing so we just stayed in and watched television instead.* □ *There's no fruit salad left; would you like ice cream instead?* [compare **in place of, rather than**]

instep /'ɪnstɛp/ *noun*: **insteps**

Your **instep** is the upper surface of your foot that curves upwards from your toes to your ankle. [see picture at **body**]

instigate /'ɪnstɪgeɪt/ *verb* (*formal*): **instigates, instigating, instigated**

You **instigate** something when you cause it to happen, especially when you order others to do it or carry it out: *The committee has instigated an inquiry into the affair.* — *noun* (*uncount*) **instigation** /ɪnstɪ'geɪʃən/: *A thorough investigation of the claims is being carried out at the instigation of the local MP.*

instil (*AmE* **instill**) /ɪn'stɪl/ *verb*: **instils** (*AmE* **instills**), **instilling, instilled**

You **instil** a particular feeling in someone when you cause them to have that feeling: *There's no question that military service instils a sense of discipline in a young man.*

instinct /'ɪnstɪŋkt/ *noun* (*uncount or count*): **instincts**

Instinct is what causes you to behave or react the way you do, naturally and without having to think: *It is the mother's instinct to protect her young.* □ *Sharon's first instinct was to punch him in the face, but she resisted it.* □ *I knew by instinct that he had come to deliver bad news.*

instinctive /ɪn'stɪŋktɪv/ *adjective*

Instinctive describes the natural way you feel or react, without thinking or reasoning: *It was hard for me to control my instinctive jealousy.* — *adverb* **instinctively:** *I instinctively knew that something was wrong.*

institute /'ɪnstɪtjuːt/ *noun; verb*

▻ ***noun***: **institutes**

Institute is a name often used by organizations connected with education, or research of some kind: *the University of Manchester Institute of Science and Technology.*

▻ ***verb*** (*formal*): **institutes, instituting, instituted**

You **institute** something when you establish it or set it up: *It was then clear that we could proceed to institute a nationwide Health Service that was free for everyone.* [*same as* **introduce**]

institution /ɪnstɪ'tjuːʃən/ *noun*: **institutions**

1 An **institution** is a large company or organization, especially one owned or managed by a government: *The banks are still losing custom to building societies and other financial institutions.* □ *We're approaching schools, colleges and other educational institutions.* □ *contrasting the modern, hi-tech prisons with some of the crumbling Victorian institutions.* [*same as* **establishment**] **2** Hospitals for mentally ill people are sometimes referred to as **institutions**.

instruct /ɪn'strʌkt/ *verb*: **instructs, instructing, instructed**

1 You **instruct** someone to do something when you tell them to do it: *We've been instructed not to allow him to speak with his solicitor.* [same as **order**, **direct**] **2** You **instruct** someone when you teach them or give them training: *The maths teacher also instructed us in rugby.*

instruction /ɪn'strʌkʃən/ *noun*: **instructions**

1 You give someone **instructions** to do something when you tell them to do it or say that they should do it: *The doctor can only help you if you follow his instructions.* [*same as* **order**, **direction**] **2 Instructions** consist of information on how to do something, usually printed in the form of a booklet: *Please read the instructions carefully before attempting to use this machine.* [*same as* **directions**] **3** (*uncount; formal*) **Instruction** is teaching: *religious instruction.*

instructive /ɪn'strʌktɪv/ *adjective*

Something that is **instructive** gives you helpful information: *It's a very instructive little book.*

instructor /ɪn'strʌktə(r)/ *noun*: **instructors**

An **instructor** is someone who teaches people how to do something practical: *The children will be taught by a qualified swimming instructor.* □ *a driving instructor.*

instrument /ɪnstrə'mɛnt/ *noun*: **instruments**

1 An **instrument** is a tool, especially one used for delicate scientific work or measurement: *surgical instruments.* **2** An **instrument**, or musical **instrument**, is a device that you play music on, such as a piano or a guitar. **3** (*formal*) Someone or something that is an **instrument** of some process is the means used to carry it out: *Parliament seemed an inefficient instrument of change compared with a public campaign of civil disobedience.*

instrumental /ɪnstrə'mɛntəl/ *adjective*

1 Someone or something that is **instrumental** in some process enables it to happen: *There's no question that his campaign was instrumental in getting the government to review the law.* [*opposite* **obstructive**] **2 Instrumental** music is performed by musical instruments as distinct from voices.

insubstantial /ɪnsəb'stanʃəl/ *adjective* (*formal*)

Insubstantial describes things that are not solid, strong or satisfying: *We wondered whether such a flimsy, insubstantial vessel could really transport all those cars.* □ *The dinner was tasty, if a little insubstantial.* [*opposite* **substantial**]

insufferable /ɪn'sʌfərəbəl/ *adjective*

Someone or something that is **insufferable** is extremely annoying: *I refused to spend the evening with the insufferable idiot.* [*same as* **unbearable**]

insufficient /ɪnsəˈfɪʃənt/ *adjective*
Insufficient describes something that there is not enough of: *There are insufficient funds in your account to pay for it.* [*opposite* **sufficient**]

insular /ˈɪnsjʊlə(r)/ *adjective* (*formal*)
You describe someone as **insular** if they don't like meeting new people or listening to new ideas or opinions: *the disadvantages of having rather insular parents.*

insulate /ˈɪnsjʊleɪt/ *verb*: **insulates, insulating, insulated**
1 You **insulate** something when you cover it with a material that keeps heat in and cold out: *They'd used foam rubber to insulate the water pipes.* **2** You **insulate** an electrical appliance when you put a covering of rubber on the part of it you touch, to prevent injury from electric shock. — *noun* (*uncount*) **insulation** /ɪnsjʊˈleɪʃən/: *Old blankets had been wrapped around the water tank for insulation.*

insult *verb; noun*
▻ ***verb*** /ɪnˈsʌlt/: **insults, insulting, insulted**
You **insult** someone when you speak rudely to them, or behave in a way that shows you don't respect them: *The two ministers openly insulted each other.* ▫ *I was afraid that, if I refused, she would feel insulted.*
▻ ***noun*** /ˈɪnsʌlt/: **insults:** *She shouted insults at the boys.* ▫ *Would she take it as an insult if I asked to be alone?* — *adjective* **insulting:** *She used some fairly insulting language.*
▻ ***phrase*** Something that **adds insult to injury** makes a bad or unpleasant situation even worse: *He backed into my car; then, to add insult to injury, drove off without apologizing.*

insurance /ɪnˈʃʊərəns/ *noun*
1 (*uncount, often adjectival*) **Insurance** is a guarantee that you will receive money if something is lost or damaged, or receive a replacement for it, or have repairs paid for, by a financial company in return for regular payments you make to them: *Don't forget we'll have to take out insurance on the new car.* ▫ *life insurance* ▫ *She works for an insurance company.* ▫ *an insurance policy.* **2** An **insurance** against an unpleasant situation is something you do which will make the situation easier to deal with if it happens: *They installed their own generator as an insurance against power cuts.*

insure /ɪnˈʃʊə(r)/ *verb*: **insures, insuring, insured**
1 You **insure** something such as your property or possessions when you take out insurance on it: *Was the stolen jewellery insured?* [*same as* **cover**] **2** You do something to **insure** against an unpleasant situation when what you do will make the situation easier to deal with if it happens: *We'd laid drainage pipes around the farm to insure against flooding.*

insurmountable /ɪnsəˈmaʊntəbəl/ *adjective* (*formal*)
An **insurmountable** problem is too difficult to solve or overcome.

insurrection /ɪnsəˈrɛkʃən/ *noun* (*count or uncount*)
An **insurrection** is a violent attempt by a group of people to overthrow the rulers of their country: *plans to deal with armed insurrection.*

intact /ɪnˈtakt/ *adjective*
Something that remains **intact** is not broken, damaged or harmed: *In test crashes, the passenger compartment remained intact.* ▫ *We had left the negotiations with our pride still intact.*

intake /ˈɪnteɪk/ *noun* (*usually in the singular*): **intakes**
1 Your **intake** of something is the amount you consume: *Doctors advised him to reduce his alcohol intake.* ▫ *This process speeds up the engine's intake of petrol.* [*same as* **consumption**] **2** The **intake** of people to an organization or institution at any particular time is the number joining it at that time: *We estimate that 75% of this year's intake of pupils will go on to university.*

intangible /ɪnˈtandʒɪbəl/ *adjective* (*formal*)
You describe something such as an idea as **intangible** if it is believed to exist, although it cannot actually be touched or seen: *the rather intangible notion of the Holy Spirit.* [*opposite* **tangible**]

integral /ˈɪntɪgrəl/ *adjective*
Something that is an **integral** part of something else is a necessary part, needed to make the other thing complete: *The notion of human imperfection is integral to all religions.*

integrate /ˈɪntɪgreɪt/ *verb*: **integrates, integrating, integrated**
1 To **integrate** things is to fit them together to form something larger, or make them a part of something larger: *By that time, the new tunnel will be fully integrated into our rail network.* **2** To **integrate** different groups of people is to bring them together, especially so that they will live together happily or peacefully: *It's clear that some racial minorities are not fully integrated into the community.* — *noun* (*uncount*) **integration** /ɪntɪˈgreɪʃən/: *It is feared that we will never achieve the full integration of the black and white populations.*

integrity /ɪnˈtɛgrɪtɪ/ *noun* (*uncount*)
Someone who has **integrity** always behaves honestly and according to firm moral values and principles: *a woman of admirable integrity.* [*same as* **virtue**]

intellect /ˈɪntəlɛkt/ *noun* (*uncount*)
A person's **intellect** is their ability to think, reason and understand, especially when they do this very quickly and clearly: *She is a filmmaker of some considerable intellect.*

intellectual /ɪntəˈlɛktʃʊəl/ *adjective; noun*
▻ ***adjective***
1 Intellectual means involving or requiring the ability to think and understand: *The job wasn't giving her enough intellectual stimulation.* ▫ *his incredible intellectual capacity.* **2 Intellectual** is sometimes used to describe things that only very clever people can understand or appreciate: *The film was a bit too intellectual for my taste.*
▻ ***noun***: **intellectuals**
An **intellectual** is someone who enjoys and is skilled in thinking about difficult or complex ideas.

intelligence /ɪnˈtɛlɪdʒəns/ *noun* (*uncount*)
1 Intelligence is the ability to learn or understand: *Even as a small child she displayed remarkable intelligence.* ▫ *I wouldn't insult your intelligence by explaining how it works.* **2 Intelligence** is also secret information gathered about a military or political enemy, or the process of gathering it: *the intelligence services.*

intelligent /ɪnˈtɛlɪdʒənt/ *adjective*
1 An **intelligent** person is able to learn and understand things quickly and easily; **intelligent** also describes actions or behaviour that reflect this ability: *Some of the students are not particularly intelligent.* ▫ *That wasn't a very intelligent thing to do.* [*opposite* **unintelligent**] **2** (*computers*) An **intelligent** computer or other machine is able to adjust to changes in the situations it is programmed to deal with. — *adverb* **intelligently:** *The children dealt with the crisis most intelligently.*

intelligible /ɪnˈtɛlɪdʒəbəl/ *adjective*
Something is **intelligible** when it is clear enough to

understand: *This kind of explanation is simply not intelligible to a young child.* [*opposite* **unintelligible**]

intend /ɪn'tɛnd/ *verb*: **intends, intending, intended**
1 You **intend**, or **are intending**, to do something when you have decided, or have planned, to do it: *She's intending to apply for another job.* □ *How far do you intend walking today?* □ *We spent far more money than we had intended to.* □ *I realized I'd spoken louder than I intended.* **2** You say you did not **intend** to do something if you did not do it deliberately: *I'm sorry if he's upset; I didn't intend to insult him.* [*same as* **mean**] **3** You **intend** something to happen, or to have a particular result or role, if that is the way you have planned or designed it: *I hadn't intended my lecture to go on for so long.* □ *He had probably never intended that his song should be adopted as a national anthem.* □ *The theatre tickets were intended as a birthday present.* [*same as* **mean**] **4** Something **is intended** for a certain person or function if it has been designed or planned for them: *This dictionary is really intended for the intermediate learner.* □ *There was only one recorded message and it was evidently intended for my son.* □ *The bullet had been intended for me.* □ *May I remind you that the ramps are intended solely for the use of the disabled?* [*same as* **meant**] — *adjective* **intended:** *To judge from her subsequent behaviour, my scolding had had the intended effect.* □ *This was not the result intended.* □ *The bomb had missed its intended target.* □ *He will have to cancel his intended visit.*

intense /ɪn'tɛns/ *adjective*
1 Intense means very great or extreme: *the intense heat from the furnace.* **2** You describe someone as **intense** if they usually behave in a very serious or thoughtful way: *You're an actor who is usually cast in rather intense roles.* — *noun* (*uncount*) **intensity** /ɪn'tɛnsɪtɪ/: *You can't imagine the sheer intensity of the cold.*

intensify /ɪn'tɛnsɪfaɪ/ *verb*: **intensifies, intensifying, intensified**
Something **intensifies** when it becomes greater or more extreme: *Opposition to the proposals had intensified by this time.* [*same as* **strengthen**]

intensifying /ɪn'tɛnsɪfaɪɪŋ/ *adjective*
In this dictionary, **intensifying** describes adverbs used with adjectives and other adverbs to mean 'very'.

intensive /ɪn'tɛnsɪv/ *adjective*
1 Intensive describes activities carried out with great effort or concentration, often over a short period of time: *She took a very intensive three-month course in teaching English.* **2 Intensive** is often used with nouns to form compound adjectives that mean 'using or needing a lot of something': *The old manufacturing processes were now regarded as too labour-intensive.*

intensive care /ɪntɛnsɪv 'kɛə(r)/ *noun* (*uncount*)
Intensive care is continuous medical treatment given by a team of doctors and nurses to very seriously ill patients who are in danger of dying; the department of a hospital where this treatment is provided is also called **intensive care**: *She'll be in intensive care for a day or so at least.*

intent /ɪn'tɛnt/ *noun*; *adjective*
▻ ***noun*** (*uncount*)
Your **intent** to do something is the fact that you have decided to do it: *The company has declared its intent to prosecute those involved.* □ *He was charged with intent to commit murder.* [*same as* **intention**]
▻ ***adjective***
1 You are **intent** on doing something when you are determined to do it: *She seems intent upon crushing the power of the trade unions.* **2 Intent** describes someone who is concentrating all their attention on something: *a roomful of students wearing intent expressions.*
▻ ***phrase*** When something is true **to all intents and purposes** it is, if not absolutely or strictly true, so close to the truth that there is no practical difference: *It became clear that, to all intents and purposes, the company was bankrupt.*

intention /ɪn'tɛnʃən/ *noun* (*count or uncount*): **intentions**
You have the **intention** of doing something when you have decided you will do it: *I was hurt that she didn't tell me of her intention to leave.* □ *It was not my intention to cause you any distress.* □ *Ralph had no intention of accepting the offer.* □ *Do you have any amorous intentions towards my daughter?*

intentional /ɪn'tɛnʃənəl/ *adjective*
Something you do is **intentional** if you do it meaning or intending to do it: *I'm sorry if I upset you; it wasn't intentional.* [*same as* **deliberate**; *opposite* **unintentional**] — *adverb* **intentionally:** *Are you being intentionally insulting?* [*same as* **deliberately**; *opposite* **unintentionally**]

inter- /ɪntə(r)/ *prefix*
Inter- is used before adjectives to form compound adjectives meaning between or among two or more different things: *We expect a certain degree of interdepartmental co-operation.* □ *We are reducing the prices of some of our intercontinental flights.*

intercept /ɪntə'sɛpt/ *verb*: **intercepts, intercepting, intercepted**
You **intercept** someone or something that is moving or travelling when you stop them: *The thieves were intercepted at the airport.* □ *This will allow us to intercept attacking aircraft long before they reach our airspace.*

interchange /ɪntə'tʃeɪndʒ/ *verb*; *noun*
▻ ***verb***: **interchanges, interchanging, interchanged**
You **interchange** two things when you exchange one for the other; two things **interchange** when each takes the place of the other: *These parts can be interchanged without affecting the machine's performance.*
▻ ***noun***: **interchanges**
An **interchange** is a place where two or more major roads or motorways meet.

interchangeable /ɪntə'tʃeɪndʒəbəl/ *adjective*
When two things are **interchangeable** you could change one for the other and still achieve the same effect or result, because both have the same value, nature or meaning: *In most people's minds, the notions of success and wealth are interchangeable.*

intercom /'ɪntəkɒm/ *noun*: **intercoms**
An **intercom** is a system of microphones and speakers that enables people in different parts of a building to talk to each other: *My secretary buzzed me on the intercom, to say that Thomas had arrived.*

intercontinental /ɪntəkɒntɪ'nɛntəl/ *adjective*
Intercontinental means travelling between or connecting different continents: *They possess a number of intercontinental ballistic missiles.*

intercourse /'ɪntəkɔːs/ *noun* (*uncount*)
Two people have **intercourse**, or **sexual intercourse**, when they have sex with each other: *When did you and your husband last have intercourse?*

interest /'ɪntərəst/ or /'ɪntərɛst/ *noun*; *verb*
▻ ***noun***: **interests**
1 (*uncount or used in the singular*)
You have, or take, an **interest** in something if you are keen to know more about it, to do it, or to be involved in it: *I used to take a mild interest in dance.* □ *He obviously has no interest in going to university.* □ *Teaching*

methods were to blame for killing children's interest in Shakespeare. □ *Members were showing considerable interest in the scheme.* □ *I lost interest when the discussion turned to football.* **2** (*uncount or used in the singular*) There is **interest** in something, or it attracts **interest**, if it attracts people's attention or curiosity: *There was much interest in the couple's wedding plans.* □ *It's difficult to account for the growing interest in learning Gaelic.* **3** (*uncount*) Something that is of **interest** is remarkable or unusual: *There's nothing of any interest to report.* **4** (*often used in the plural*) Your **interests** are the things you enjoy doing, learning about, or following, especially in your spare time: *He had few interests outside sport and television.* □ *Embroidery has always been an interest of mine.* **5** (*count or uncount*) You have an **interest** in something happening if you will benefit from it happening and therefore want it to happen: *We all have an interest in the success of this venture.* □ *The company has no interest at all in seeing the workforce dissatisfied.* □ *My solicitor will, of course, seek to protect my interests.* **6** (*used in the plural*) You have **interests** in the business world if you own shares or companies, or hold directorships: *MPs must declare their interests.* **7** (*uncount*) **Interest** is extra money you pay back as a charge for borrowing money; **interest** is also money you receive from a bank or other institution that you have invested money with: *If you take the loan over a longer period, the rate of interest rises to 23%.* □ *The total repayments, interest included, amount to over £11 000.* □ *Building societies offer savers a better rate of interest.*

▻ ***verb***: **interests, interesting, interested**

1 Something that **interests** you attracts or holds your attention, or rouses your curiosity: *His face interested her.* □ *Their love life does not interest me in the least.* □ *The work no longer interested him.* **2** (*formal*) When you ask someone if you can **interest** them in something, you are trying to persuade them to have it or buy it: *Could I interest you in a glass of wine?* □ *Perhaps we can interest you in one of our cut-price holidays?* — *adjective* **interested:** *He's recently become very interested in golf.* □ *We should be most interested to hear about your work for the Resistance if you would care to address us on the subject.* □ *Would you be interested in joining us?* [= would you like to join us?] □ *I'm only interested in* [= concerned with] *ensuring that everyone is treated fairly.* □ *It was Jill's inspired teaching that kept the children so interested.* — *adjective* **interesting:** *The lectures were not particularly interesting or useful.* □ *She's a most interesting person to talk to.*

▻ ***phrases*** **1** Something that is **in your interests** will benefit you: *It is in your own best interests to be as quick as possible.* **2** You do something **in the interests** of a certain thing if you do it in order to maintain or obtain that thing: *In the interests of world peace, we must put national aspirations second.*

interestingly /ˈɪntrəstɪŋlɪ/ *sentence adverb*

You use **interestingly** as a way of introducing something you think another person will be interested to hear: *Interestingly enough, this has never been done on live television before.*

interfere /ɪntəˈfɪə(r)/ *verb*: **interferes, interfering, interfered**

1 You **interfere** when you involve yourself in the affairs of someone who doesn't want your help or advice: *It's difficult for parents not to interfere in their children's lives.* **2** You **interfere** with something when you disturb it or have a harmful effect on it: *I could tell that someone had interfered with the papers I'd left on the desk.* □ *I need a job that won't interfere too much with my family life.* [*same as* **meddle, conflict**] — *adjective* **interfering:** *I must admit to being a rather interfering parent.*

interference /ɪntəˈfɪərəns/ *noun* (*uncount*)

1 Interference is the act of interfering: *Her parents' constant interference in our affairs irritated me.* [*same as* **meddling**] **2 Interference** is also the unwanted disturbance of the sound from a radio or the picture on a television, caused *eg* by severe weather conditions.

interim /ˈɪntərɪm/ *adjective*

Interim describes action taken, or things provided, temporarily, until something better or more final can be done or obtained: *These are really just interim measures.* [*same as* **provisional**]

interior /ɪnˈtɪərɪə(r)/ *adjective*; *noun*

▻ ***adjective***

1 Interior describes things that are on the inside of buildings: *Some of the interior walls need replastering.* □ *a specialist in interior design.* [*opposite* **exterior**] **2** In politics and government, **interior** means concerned with affairs in the home country, rather than with affairs abroad: *The old Minister of the Interior was replaced by the Home Secretary.*

▻ ***noun*** (*usually in the singular*)

The **interior** of a building or other thing is the inside of it: *The car's sleek lines are matched by its elegant interior.* [*opposite* **exterior**]

interjection /ɪntəˈdʒɛkʃən/ *noun* (*grammar*): **interjections**

An **interjection** is a word like 'gosh!', 'blow!' or 'ouch!', that you use, often in a loud voice, to express feelings such as surprise, disappointment or pain. [*same as* **exclamation**]

interlock /ɪntəˈlɒk/ *verb*: **interlocks, interlocking, interlocked**

Things that **interlock** are connected together by means of parts which fit into each other: *The pieces interlock like a jigsaw.*

interloper /ˈɪntəloʊpə(r)/ *noun*: **interlopers**

An **interloper** is a person who enters a place uninvited, having no right to be there: *This is the most glamorous of Hollywood parties, from which all would-be interlopers are politely turned away.* [*same as* **intruder, gatecrasher**]

interlude /ˈɪntəluːd/ *noun*: **interludes**

1 An **interlude** is a short break between parts of a play, opera or other performance: *I don't usually leave my seat during the interlude.* [*same as* **interval**] **2** An **interlude** is also a short period spent doing something different: *She had several romantic interludes in her twenties.*

intermediary /ɪntəˈmiːdɪərɪ/ *noun*: **intermediaries**

An **intermediary** is a person who passes messages between two people or groups, often to try to settle a disagreement. [*same as* **mediator**]

intermediate /ɪntəˈmiːdɪət/ *adjective*

Intermediate describes things that are in the middle, *eg* between the beginning and end of a process, or half way on a scale of ability or achievement: *for students at intermediate level.* □ *He's at that difficult intermediate stage between childhood and adulthood.* [compare **transitional**]

interminable /ɪnˈtɜːmɪnəbəl/ *adjective* (*formal*)

You describe something as **interminable** if it lasts such a long time that you think it will never end. [same as **endless**] — *adverb* **interminably:** *We listened to the men droning on interminably about politics and business.*

intermission /ɪntəˈmɪʃən/ *noun*: **intermissions**

An **intermission** is a short break between two parts of

a play, film or other performance. [*same as* **interlude**, **interval**]

intermittent /ɪntə'mɪtənt/ *adjective*
Something that is **intermittent** happens only occasionally, stopping for a while and then starting again: *The north of the country will have intermittent rain.* [*opposite* **continuous**]

internal /ɪn'tɜːnəl/ *adjective*
1 Internal describes things inside a building or other place: *From the internal photographs we saw, the standard of decor is very high indeed.* □ *It's a disease that affects all the major internal organs.* **2 Internal** also means relating to a country's domestic affairs, as opposed to its relations with foreign countries. **3 Internal** also refers to people, events or affairs within an organization: *We are carrying out an internal inquiry into the disappearance of the files.*
[*opposite* **external**]

international /ɪntə'naʃənəl/ *adjective; noun*
▻ ***adjective***
International means involving, affecting, or carried on between, two or more countries: *both domestic and international flights* □ *a truly international film festival.*
▻ ***noun*: internationals**
An **international** is a sports match between two national teams, or a player in it: *a rugby international between Scotland and England* □ *The team includes three Scotland internationals.*

interplay /'ɪntəpleɪ/ *noun* (*uncount*)
The **interplay** between two or more things is the effect or influence each one has on the other: *The painter has successfully captured the interplay between light and water.*

interpret /ɪn'tɜːprət/ *verb*: **interprets, interpreting, interpreted**
1 You **interpret** something in a certain way when you consider or understand it to mean a certain thing: *She interprets this dream as an unconscious desire to be young again.* □ *Were we to interpret her silence as disapproval?* □ *How was I to interpret this lack of communication?* **2** To **interpret** is to act as an interpreter: *I interpreted for top businessmen at a number of international conferences.* — *noun* (*uncount or count*) **interpretation** /ɪntɜːprə'teɪʃən/: *What is your interpretation of the Chancellor's decision to cut interest rates at this precise moment?* □ *His remarks seemed deliberately vague, as if they were inviting individual interpretation.* □ *It's interesting to read their different interpretations of what the author intended.*

interpreter /ɪn'tɜːprɪtə(r)/ *noun*: **interpreters**
An **interpreter** is someone who enables two people who speak different languages to communicate, by translating in turn the words of each person to the other: *We spoke to him through an interpreter.*

interrelated /ɪntərɪ'leɪtɪd/ *adjective*
Two or more things are **interrelated** when there is a connection or relationship between them in which one directly affects the other or others: *He found that the two problems were interrelated.*

interrogate /ɪn'tɛrəgeɪt/ *verb*: **interrogates, interrogating, interrogated**
To **interrogate** someone is to question them closely and thoroughly for a long time, sometimes using threatening behaviour: *Three suspects were interrogated at the local police station.* [*same as* **grill**] — *noun* (*count or uncount*) **interrogation** /ɪntɛrə'geɪʃən/: *a long and often tense interrogation* □ *confessions made during police interrogation.*

interrogative /ɪntə'rɒgətɪv/ *adjective* (*grammar*)
Interrogative pronouns, determiners and adverbs are words such as *what*, *who*, *which* and *where*, that are used to ask questions.

interrupt /ɪntə'rʌpt/ *verb*: **interrupts, interrupting, interrupted**
1 You **interrupt** someone when you speak while they are still talking: *I'm sorry to interrupt, but you're not really answering the question.* □ *'But that's not true!' interrupted Robert.* [*same as* **butt in**] **2** You **interrupt** an activity when you say or do something that causes it to stop temporarily: *Nobody was allowed to interrupt them while a meeting was in progress.* □ *His promising career was interrupted by the war.* □ *I interrupted my studies in 1940 to join the army.* [*same as* **disturb**, **cut short**] — *noun* (*count or uncount*) **interruption** /ɪntə'rʌpʃən/: *We don't want any more interruptions.* □ *Might I be allowed to speak without interruption?*

intersect /ɪntə'sɛkt/ *verb*: **intersects, intersecting, intersected**
Roads or paths **intersect** when they meet and cross each other. — *noun* **intersection** /'ɪntəsɛkʃən/: *The house was close to a busy intersection.* □ *at the intersection of West Bridge Street and Carlton Avenue.* [*same as* **junction**]

interspersed /ɪntə'spɜːst/ *adjective*
An area or surface is **interspersed** with things that are in or on it at various points far apart: *The plain was interspersed with tiny farming communities.* [*same as* **dotted**]

intertwined /ɪntə'twaɪnd/ *adjective*
Two or more things are **intertwined** when they are twisted or wrapped around each other: *lovers with their arms intertwined.*

interval /'ɪntəvəl/ *noun*: **intervals**
1 An **interval** is a short break between parts of a play, film or other performance: *In the interval, everyone heads for the bar.* [*same as* **interlude**] **2** An **interval** is also a period of time between two events or states: *their return to competition skating after an interval of four years.* [*same as* **gap**]
▻ ***phrase***
1 Something that happens **at intervals** happens occasionally; something that exists **at intervals** exists here and there, with large spaces in between: *The interview continued, with Smith breaking off at intervals to consult his notes.* □ *Trees had been planted at intervals along the waterfront.* **2 At intervals** is also used to state the precise gap in time or distance between things: *We visited the hospital at three-hour intervals, to check on his progress.* □ *Marker posts had been erected at intervals of a few hundred yards.*

intervene /ɪntə'viːn/ *verb*: **intervenes, intervening, intervened**
You **intervene** in a situation when you involve yourself in it, often to stop people fighting or arguing: *I'm afraid the law prevents us from intervening in the case of a domestic quarrel.* □ *Her solicitor then intervened to bring the interview to a close.* [*same as* **step in**] — *noun* (*uncount or count*) **intervention** /ɪntə'vɛnʃən/: *This prevents government intervention in the affairs of what are now private companies.* □ *We've had to listen to some fairly abusive interventions from people in the public gallery.*

intervening /ɪntə'viːnɪŋ/ *adjective*
An **intervening** period of time comes between two events: *Both Conservative governments had big majorities; the intervening Labour government had a much harder task.*

interview /'ɪntəvjuː/ *noun; verb*
▻ ***noun*: interviews**
1 An **interview** is a formal meeting at which someone applying for a job is asked questions, as a way of judg-

ing how suitable they are: *I've been asked to go for a second interview.* □ *She's had a couple of job interviews, but no offers.* **2** An **interview** is also a conversation between a journalist and a famous person, broadcast or published: *In this week's programme, an interview with Kevin Costner.* □ *Radio interviews are generally more relaxed than television ones.*
▷ ***verb***: **interviews, interviewing, interviewed:** *She's being interviewed next week for the Chief Executive's job.* □ *That's the secret when you're interviewing the big stars.*

intestine /ɪn'tɛstɪn/ *noun* (*usually in the plural*): **intestines**
Your **intestines** are the tube-like organs in your body that food passes through after leaving your stomach.

intimacy /'ɪntɪməsɪ/ *noun* (*uncount*)
1 When there is **intimacy** between people they have a very close friendship. [*same as* **closeness**] **2** (*euphemistic*) **Intimacy** is also sex: *She claimed there had been no intimacy between them.*

intimate *adjective*; *noun*; *verb*
▷ ***adjective*** /'ɪntɪmət/
1 An **intimate** friend is someone you have a very close friendship with: *Yes, I know her quite well, but she's not an intimate friend of mine.* □ *The girls met at university and became quite intimate I believe?* [*same as* **close**] **2 Intimate** also describes things that are very private or personal: *The diary, naturally enough, contains intimate details of her private life.* **3** You describe a place as **intimate** if it is small and has a friendly, relaxed atmosphere. [*same as* **cosy**] **4** (*euphemistic*) When two people are **intimate** with each other, they have a sexual relationship.
▷ ***noun*** /'ɪntɪmət/ (*literary*): **intimates**
Your **intimates** are your close friends.
▷ ***verb*** /'ɪntɪmeɪt/ (*formal*): **intimates, intimating, intimated**
You **intimate** something when you tell it to someone, usually in an indirect way: *She has intimated that she would be willing to help.* [*same as* **hint**]

intimidate /ɪn'tɪmɪdeɪt/ *verb*: **intimidates, intimidating, intimidated**
1 Someone **intimidates** you into doing something when they frighten you into doing it, usually by making threats: *This government will not be intimidated into giving up its historical rights.* [*same as* **coerce**] **2** You **are intimidated** by someone or something if they make you feel frightened and uneasy, or take away your self-confidence: *An ordinary working-class lad, I had to try hard not to be intimidated by the aristocratic company I was suddenly keeping.* — *adjective* **intimidating:** *The thought of meeting her was a thoroughly intimidating prospect.* — *noun* (*uncount*) **intimidation** /ɪntɪmɪ'deɪʃən/: *Many immigrant families suffer intolerable intimidation on a daily basis.*

into /'ɪntuː/ *preposition*
1 One thing goes **into** another, or is put **into** it, when it moves, or is moved, from outside it to inside it, or from on or above its surface to below its surface: *She thrust the letter quickly into a drawer.* □ *The ball trickled into the hole.* □ *He got into his car and drove off.* □ *I saw her going into the fish shop.* □ *We crossed the border into Belgium.* □ *They crawled out of the tunnel into the light.* □ *Bodies were being thrown into the river.* □ *He dipped his finger into the mixture.* □ *moisturizing cream that penetrates deep into your skin.* **2** One thing gets **into** another, or is put **into** it, when it is added to it so that it becomes part of it: *Dangerous chemicals had found their way into the cooking oil.* □ *Have you paid that cheque into your account yet?* **3** You bump **into** something when you collide with it: *A young man bumped into me and made me spill my drink.* □ *The van swerved out of control and crashed into a wall.* □ *A taxi ran into the back of me* [= my car] *today.* **4** You get **into** clothes when you put them on: *I got into my jeans.* □ *I think I'll change into something cooler.* **5** One thing changes, or is changed, **into** another form or shape when it develops, or is given, a different form or shape: *Yet another once-peaceful village has beenturned into a bustling tourist centre.* □ *As soon as she kissed the frog he changed back into a prince.* □ *Her poems have been translated into most of the major languages.* □ *I told the children to get into a circle.* □ *At the airport I changed most of my cash back into dollars.* **6 Into** follows verbs of dividing: *Tear your piece of paper into 10 narrow strips.* □ *The latest scheme proposes that the country should be divided into fifty-two administrative districts.* **7** You get **into** a certain state or situation when you begin to be in it: *Several swimmers got into difficulties and had to be rescued.* □ *There's no need to get into such a panic.* **8** An enquiry **into** something is an examination of it: *There will be an official enquiry into the accident.* □ *Much research has already been done into British eating habits.* □ *Scientists are looking into ways of preventing the problem.* **9** (*informal*) You are **into** something if you are interested in it or enthusiastic about it: *She's into classical music and all that.*

intolerable /ɪn'tɒlərəbəl/ *adjective*
Something **intolerable** is too bad or unpleasant to accept or put up with: *She's been under an intolerable strain lately.* □ *His rudeness is quite intolerable.* [*opposite* **tolerable**]

intolerant /ɪn'tɒlərənt/ *adjective*
An **intolerant** person refuses to accept ideas, beliefs or behaviour that is different from their own: *The British are still, by and large, very intolerant of foreigners.* [*opposite* **tolerant**] — *noun* (*uncount*) **intolerance:** *racial intolerance* □ *the well-known intolerance of the French for any innovations or intrusions into the language.* [*opposite* **tolerance**]

intonation /ɪntə'neɪʃən/ *noun* (*uncount*)
Intonation is the rise and fall of your voice when you speak: *You'll notice that young children learn to match not only the parent's words but their intonation as well.*

intoxicated /ɪn'tɒksɪkeɪtɪd/ *adjective*
1 (*formal*) Someone who is **intoxicated** is drunk. [*opposite* **sober**] **2** (*literary*) Someone who is **intoxicated** by something is greatly excited by it, often so much so that they behave unreasonably or foolishly: *As students, we were intoxicated by his theories and thought he had the answer to everything.* □ *The soldiers, intoxicated with victory, danced in the streets for hours.* [*same as* **exhilarated**]

intoxicating /ɪn'tɒksɪkeɪtɪŋ/ *adjective*
1 Intoxicating drink is alcohol: *the sale of intoxicating liquor to children.* **2** You describe something as **intoxicating** if it is very exciting, and could cause you to behave foolishly: *To think I was going to spend the evening alone with her; it was an intoxicating prospect.*

intractable /ɪn'traktəbəl/ *adjective* (*formal*)
1 An **intractable** person is difficult to deal with because they refuse to change their views or opinions. [*same as* **stubborn, obstinate**] **2** An **intractable** problem seems impossible to solve.

intransigent /ɪn'trɑːnsɪdʒənt/ *adjective*
An **intransigent** person refuses to change their views or opinions, or do what people ask them to. [*same as* **stubborn, obstinate**] — *noun* (*uncount*) **intransigence:** *The whole idea of European union is threatened by the intransigence of the British.* [*same as* **stubbornness**]

intransitive /ɪn'tranzɪtɪv/ *adjective* (*grammar*)
An **intransitive** verb is a verb that does not have an object, *eg* the verbs *try* and *speak* in the sentences *You can do it if you try* and *I spoke to Neil about it.* [Compare **transitive**]

in-tray /'ɪntreɪ/ *noun*: **intrays**
Your **in-tray** in your office is the tray or container in which you keep letters and papers waiting to be dealt with. [see picture at **office**]

intrepid /ɪn'trɛpɪd/ *adjective* (*literary, often humorous*)
An **intrepid** person bravely takes risks without worrying about danger or difficulty: *Our intrepid reporter is at the scene of the crime.* [*same as* **brave, fearless, courageous**]

intricate /'ɪntrɪkət/ *adjective*
Something **intricate** is made up of a complicated series of small parts or details: *the intricate workings of clocks of this period* □ *They don't appreciate just how intricate international negotiations of this kind are.* [*same as* **complex**] — *noun* (*uncount or count*) **intricacy** /'ɪntrɪkəsɪ/: *the intricacy of the problem that faced us* □ *anyone familiar with the intricacies of Westminster politics.* [*same as* **complexity**]

intrigue *noun*; *verb*
▻ ***noun*** /'ɪntri:g/ or /ɪn'tri:g/ (*uncount*)
Intrigue consists of secret plans or plots, especially to do something harmful or unpleasant: *The true history of this affair is a tale of scandal and intrigue.*
▻ ***verb*** /ɪn'tri:g/: **intrigues, intriguing, intrigued**
Something **intrigues** you when you are very curious to find out more about it: *As a woman, she didn't attract me in the least; as a politician, she intrigued me.* □ *Intrigued by what little I had been told, I set out to discover more.* [*same as* **fascinate**] — *adjective* **intriguing**: *It was an intriguing tale of jealousy and corruption.* □ *I found the prospect of an evening in his company intriguing.* [*same as* **fascinating**; *opposite* **boring**]

intrinsic /ɪn'trɪnsɪk/ *adjective*
Intrinsic describes the basic qualities or characteristics of something, that give it its nature or identity: *The jewels have very little intrinsic value; however, they are of considerable sentimental value.*

introduce /ɪntrə'dju:s/ *verb*: **introduces, introducing, introduced**
1 You **introduce** one person to another when you tell each person the other person's name, so that they can begin to get to know each other: *She introduced him as 'the man who had changed her life'.* □ *Would you introduce me to your friend?* □ *Allow me to introduce myself; my name is Harold Carter.* **2** To **introduce** someone or something is to present them to an audience: *They were introduced as the world's greatest rock and roll band.* □ *The programme is introduced by Carl Davies.* **3** You **introduce** someone to something when you cause them to experience it for the first time; you **introduce** something somewhere when you take it to that place for the first time: *It was my mother who introduced me to classical music.* □ *The first species of rose were introduced to this country around 300 years ago.* **4** You also **introduce** something when you bring it into operation, practice or use for the first time: *Was it a mistake to introduce the tax on heating and other bills?* □ *We're introducing higher rates of interest for long-term savers.* [*same as* **institute**; *opposite* **withdraw**]

introduction /ɪntrə'dʌkʃən/ *noun*: **introductions**
1 An **introduction** is the act of introducing two people to each other, or of introducing a performer to an audience: *I was hoping for an introduction to his friend, the professor.* □ *Next, a singer who needs no introduction.* **2** In a book, the **introduction** is a section at the beginning, explaining what it is about and perhaps giving background information. **3** Books that explain the basic principles of a subject often have **introduction** in their title: *a quotation from his book 'An Introduction to Post-War British Cinema'.* **4** (*uncount*) The **introduction** of something is the fact of bringing it to a place, or bringing it into use or practice, for the first time: *the year that saw the introduction of a student loan scheme.* [*same as* **institution**; *opposite* **withdrawal**] **5** Your **introduction** to something is the first experience you have of it: *The films of Godard were supposed to serve as an introduction to French Cinema.*

introductory /ɪntrə'dʌktərɪ/ *adjective*
Introductory describes things that are intended to serve as an introduction to a subject, often to be followed by a fuller explanation: *We run an introductory course on mediaeval German poetry.* □ *There were a few brief introductory remarks before the lecture began in earnest.* [*same as* **preliminary**]

introvert /'ɪntrəvɜ:t/ *noun*: **introverts**
An **introvert** is an introverted person. [*opposite* **extrovert**]

introverted /'ɪntrəvɜ:tɪd/ *adjective*
An **introverted** person is typically quiet and shy, and prefers spending time alone rather than mixing with others: *It seems odd that his wife should be so introverted.* [*opposite* **extroverted**]

intrude /ɪn'tru:d/ *verb*: **intrudes, intruding, intruded**
You **intrude** on someone when you disturb them on a private or personal occasion, when your presence is unwanted and unwelcome: *I'm sorry for intruding; I came to see if you would like some tea.* □ *It wouldn't be right for us to intrude on them in their time of grief.*

intruder /ɪn'tru:də(r)/ *noun* (*formal*): **intruders**
An **intruder** is someone who enters a place illegally or by force in order to commit a crime: *Police say the intruder must have had a key.*

intrusion /ɪn'tru:ʒən/ *noun* (*count or uncount*)
An **intrusion** is an act of intruding on someone: *I apologise for this intrusion; it will not happen again.* □ *The time didn't seem right for the intrusion of another baby into our lives.*

intrusive /ɪn'tru:sɪv/ *adjective*
Intrusive describes unwelcome people and things that disturb your peace or privacy: *I was irritated by the intrusive interest they showed in our affairs.*

intuition /ɪntjʊ'ɪʃən/ *noun* (*uncount or count*)
Intuition is your ability to realize or suspect something without having any definite knowledge, evidence or proof: *I was content to be guided by intuition, and not take the risk.* □ *What does your famous female intuition tell you?* □ *All my intuitions were against it.* [*same as* **instinct**; *opposite* **reason**]

inundate /ɪn'ʌndeɪt/ *verb*: **inundates, inundating, inundated**
1 You **are inundated** with things when you have huge numbers or amounts of them to deal with: *The office has been inudated with requests for photographs of the royal couple.* [*same as* **flood**] **2** An area of land **is inundated** when it is flooded.
▻ ***noun*** (*uncount*): *the periodic inundation of the delta region.*

invade /ɪn'veɪd/ *verb*: **invades, invading, invaded**
1 To **invade** a country is to enter it by force with an army: *Shortly afterwards, Hitler invaded Poland.* [*opposite* **withdraw**] **2** When large numbers of people come or go to a place you can say that they **invade** it: *In the summer, these islands are invaded by hundreds of thousands of crabs coming onshore to lay their eggs.*

3 Someone **invades** your privacy when they disturb you when you want to be alone: *Most children said parents too often invaded their personal space.* — *noun* **invader**: *the threat of invaders from outer space.* — *adjective* **invading**: *invading armies.*

invalid[1] /ˈɪnvəlɪd/ *noun*: **invalids**
An **invalid** is someone who is seriously ill, or disabled, and needs to be constantly cared for by someone else: *At the slightest sign of illness his mother would treat him like an invalid.* — *noun* (*uncount*) **invalidity** /ɪnvəˈlɪdɪtɪ/: *In cases of death or invalidity, payments are waived.* □ *an invalidity pension.*

invalid[2] /ɪnˈvalɪd/ *adjective*
1 An official document or agreement is **invalid** when it is not, or is no longer, legally proper and acceptable: *Didn't you realize that the ticket was invalid?* □ *It was decided that the rules had been broken, and the contract was declared invalid.* [*opposite* **valid**] 2 An **invalid** argument or theory is based on false reasoning and is not correct or reliable: *It is a basic flaw which makes the conclusions of the experiment totally invalid.* — *noun* (*uncount*) **invalidity** /ɪnvəˈlɪdɪtɪ/: *the invalidity of their theories.* [*opposite* **validity**]

invalidate /ɪnˈvalɪdeɪt/ *verb* (*formal*): **invalidates, invalidating, invalidated**
To **invalidate** something is to make it invalid: *This simple fact invalidates any claim he may make on the property.* [*opposite* **validate**]

invalidity see **invalid**[1], **invalid**[2].

invaluable /ɪnˈvaljʊəbəl/ *adjective*
You describe something as **invaluable** if it is extremely valuable or useful: *She has made an invaluable contribution to medical research.* [*opposite* **worthless**]

invariably /ɪnˈvɛərɪəblɪ/ *adverb*
Something that **invariably** happens always happens, or almost always: *In the evenings, he is invariably drunk by about 8 o'clock.* [*same as* **inevitably**]

invasion /ɪnˈveɪʒən/ *noun* (*count or uncount*): **invasions**
1 An **invasion** occurs when an army enters a foreign country by force: *the invasion of north Africa.* 2 You can describe the arrival of large numbers of people as an **invasion**: *She wasn't prepared for the invasion of her house by hordes of screaming, hungry children.*

invent /ɪnˈvɛnt/ *verb*: **invents, inventing, invented**
1 To **invent** something is to be the first person to make or use it: *Scots were responsible for inventing many of our modern household machines.* □ *It was Ford who invented the production line method of manufacturing cars.* 2 You **invent** something such as an excuse when what you say is untrue: *The boys invented stories about how brave their fathers had been during the war.* [*same as* **make up**] — *noun* (*count or uncount*) **invention** /ɪnˈvɛnʃən/: *the washing-machine and other labour-saving inventions* □ *Her greatest achievement was the invention of new breeding methods.* □ *She dismissed the story as pure invention.* — *noun* **inventor:** *He is generally acknowledged to be the inventor of the modern camera.*

inventive /ɪnˈvɛntɪv/ *adjective*
An **inventive** person is good at inventing things, or at thinking of new and original ways of doing things: *She has a mind that is sharp and inventive.* [*same as* **creative, original**]

inventory /ˈɪnvəntərɪ/ *noun*: **inventories**
An **inventory** is a formal and complete list of the objects in a particular place, *eg* of furniture and other possessions in a house: *The landlord has sent you a copy of the inventory he's made.*

inverse /ˈɪnvɜːs/ *noun* (*singular; formal*)
The **inverse** of something is the direct opposite of it: *Gothic architecture seems to me to be the inverse of good taste.*

invert /ɪnˈvɜːt/ *verb* (*formal*): **inverts, inverting, inverted**
You **invert** something when you turn it upside down or inside out: *The so-called sculpture appeared to be little more than an inverted bucket.* [*same as* **up-end**]

invertebrate /ɪnˈvɜːtəbrət/ *noun* (*technical*): **invertebrates**
An **invertebrate** is a creature that does not have a backbone, such as a worm or a fly.

inverted comma /ɪnvɜːtɪd ˈkɒmə/ *noun*: **inverted commas**
Inverted commas are the punctuation marks (" and ", or ' and '), used to show where speech or a quotation begins and ends.

invest /ɪnˈvɛst/ *verb*: **invests, investing, invested**
1 You **invest** money in a company or business when you give or lend money to it, hoping to make a profit: *Most of the money was invested in shares in British companies.* □ *The banks want to reward those savers investing the most money.* 2 You **invest** in something when you buy it, especially when you pay more for something that you hope will last longer than the cheaper versions available: *Isn't it time we invested in a new car?* □ *It's worth investing in a decent pair of walking boots.* 3 You might say that you **invest** time, effort or energy in something when you work hard to try to make it succeed.

investigate /ɪnˈvɛstɪgeɪt/ *verb*: **investigates, investigating, investigated**
To **investigate** something is to try to find out information about it, *eg* how it happened, especially officially: *Experts from the fire department are investigating the cause of the blaze.* □ *We heard a noise in the kitchen, and my husband went through to investigate.* [*same as* **look into**] — *noun* (*count or uncount*) **investigation** /ɪnvɛstɪˈgeɪʃən/: *The company is carrying out a thorough investigation of the affair.* □ *It seems that a member of their staff is under investigation by the fraud squad.* — *noun* **investigator**: *Our team of investigators is already on the scene.*

investigative /ɪnˈvɛstɪgətɪv/ *adjective*
Investigative describes activities in which people try to find out all the facts about something: *You have become an acknowledged expert in the field of investigative journalism.*

investment /ɪnˈvɛstmənt/ *noun*: **investments**
1 (*uncount or count*) **Investment** is money invested: *one of the ways we are encouraging inward investment in our company* □ *We also have to protect the investments of our shareholders.* 2 An **investment** is also something you have bought or spent money on, especially something you consider to be a good use of your money: *Improving our children's education has to be a worthwhile investment.*

inveterate /ɪnˈvɛtərət/ *adjective* (*formal*)
Inveterate describes someone whose behaviour or habits have always been the same and will never change, especially when others disapprove of them: *Philip was an inveterate gambler.* [*same as* **confirmed**]

invidious /ɪnˈvɪdɪəs/ *adjective*
Invidious describes the actions of someone whose behaviour is likely to cause others to criticize or dislike them, because it is unfair, or seems to be: *They have placed me in a rather invidious position.* □ *She has been given the somewhat invidious task of judging her colleagues' work.*

invigorating /ɪn'vɪgəreɪtɪŋ/ *adjective*
Something **invigorating** fills you with energy: *an invigorating walk along the beach.* [*same as* **bracing**; *opposite* **tiring**]

invincible /ɪn'vɪnsɪbəl/ *adjective*
Someone who is **invincible** cannot be defeated: *the city of Liverpool, with its invincible football team.* [*same as* **unbeatable**]

invisible /ɪn'vɪzɪbəl/ *adjective*
Something **invisible** cannot be seen, because it is extremely small or it has been hidden: *The average house is crawling with all sorts of insects invisible to the human eye.* □ *The boards are fitted to each other using an invisible nailing technique.* □ *The story's main character is a man who makes himself completely invisible.* [*opposite* **visible**]

invitation /ɪnvɪ'teɪʃən/ *noun*: **invitations**
1 An **invitation** is a request to a person to come or go somewhere, *eg* to a party: *Thank you for your kind invitation; I regret I am unable to accept.* **2** An **invitation** is also a card or paper that the request is written on: *We should get some invitations printed right away.* **3** Behaviour that seems to encourage people to do something can be described as an **invitation** to do it: *Leaving your car unlocked is an open invitation to thieves.*

invite /ɪn'vaɪt/ *verb*: **invites, inviting, invited**
1 You **invite** someone to something such as a party when you tell them you would like them to come: *They've invited us over to their house for dinner.* □ *I thought he was going to invite me out to the theatre.* □ *They've invited me to attend a session of tests and interviews.* **2** You **invite** something such as criticism when you encourage it from others: *At various points during the programme, members of the audience are invited to comment.* **3** Action or behaviour that seems likely to result in something unwanted or undesirable can be said to **invite** it: *Remarks like that just invite trouble.*

inviting /ɪn'vaɪtɪŋ/ *adjective*
Something **inviting** is attractive or tempting: *The seafood dish looked very inviting.* □ *She gave him a long, inviting look.* [*same as* **tempting, seductive**]

invoice /'ɪnvɔɪs/ *noun*; *verb*
▻ ***noun***: **invoices**
An **invoice** is a list of goods that a company has sent to you, showing how much money you need to pay them. [*same as* **bill**]
▻ ***verb***: **invoices, invoicing, invoiced:** *They've invoiced us for the table but not the chairs.* [*same as* **bill**]

invoke /ɪn'voʊk/ *verb* (*formal*): **invokes, invoking, invoked**
To **invoke** something such as a law is to state it as a reason or explanation, or for support: *When pressured, surgeons often invoke their sworn duty to preserve life.*

involuntary /ɪn'vɒləntərɪ/ *adjective*
An **involuntary** action or movement is one you perform without intending to, unable to control it. [*opposite* **voluntary**] — *adverb* **involuntarily** /ɪn'vɒləntərɪlɪ/: *Suddenly and involuntarily, she slapped him across the face.* [*opposite* **voluntarily**]

involve /ɪn'vɒlv/ *verb*: **involves, involving, involved**
1 Something **involves** a person or thing if it includes them, or if they are a necessary part of it: *I couldn't do a job that involved a lot of lifting.* □ *A teacher's role also involves talking to children and listening to their problems.* □ *I don't think we need involve the directors at this stage.* [*same as* **entail**] **2** Something that **involves** you concerns or affects you. **3** You **involve** someone in something when you cause them to take part in it or to be affected by it: *I'd rather you didn't involve me in your family quarrels.* — *noun* (*uncount*) **involvement:** *They claimed to have had no involvement in the sale of arms.* □ *He was a target because of his involvement with the security forces.*

involved /ɪn'vɒlvd/ *adjective*
1 You are **involved** in something that you take part in: *Parents don't want their children to get involved with drugs.* □ *Rosemary is not involved in the actual production process.* **2** The things **involved** in something are the necessary or required parts or elements: *We didn't know what was involved in making an official complaint.* □ *She explained the different tasks involved.* **3** You describe something as **involved** if it is very complicated: *The whole situation with her job and her husband became a bit involved.* [*same as* **complex**] **4** When you have a romantic or sexual relationship with someone you can say that you are **involved** with them: *She was briefly involved with an officer serving under her father.*

inward /'ɪnwəd/ or **inwards** /'ɪnwədz/ *adverb*
Inwards means to or towards the inside or the middle: *The gate was suddenly blown inward and struck him on the chin.* □ *Then your partner turns to face inwards.* [*opposite* **outward(s)**]

inwardly /'ɪnwədlɪ/ *adverb*
Inwardly is often used in descriptions of feelings that are kept hidden or secret: *I was inwardly thrilled at the idea.* [*opposite* **outwardly**]

iota /aɪ'oʊtə/ *noun* (*singular*)
A tiny part or amount is sometimes called an **iota**: *This has made not one iota of a difference.* □ *She hasn't improved an iota.*

irascible /ɪ'rasɪbəl/ *adjective* (*formal*)
An **irascible** person is easily made angry: *My grandfather was rather irascible.* [*same as* **bad-tempered**; *opposite* **placid**]

irate /aɪə'reɪt/ *adjective* (*formal*)
Someone who is **irate** is very angry: *The assistant manager was sent to deal with an irate guest.* [*same as* **furious**; *opposite* **calm**]

iridescent /ɪrɪ'dɛsənt/ *adjective* (*literary*)
Iridescent describes something that has many bright colours which seem to change or flow into each other: *Through the water, we could see the fish's iridescent skin.*

iris /'aɪərɪs/ *noun*: **irises**
1 The **iris** is the coloured part of your eye. **2** **Irises** are tall plants with long, sword-shaped leaves and blue, yellow or white flowers.

irk /ɜːk/ *verb*: **irks, irking, irked**
Something that **irks** you annoys or irritates you: *It irked me that she should be given all the credit.*

irksome /'ɜːksəm/ *adjective*
Something **irksome** is annoying or irritating: *Visits to my grandmother became an irksome duty.*

iron /'aɪən/ *noun*; *verb*
▻ ***noun***: **irons**
1 (*uncount, often adjectival*) **Iron** is a heavy grey metal widely used in industry and engineering, tiny amounts of which are also found in food: *a pair of tall iron gates* □ *She'll need to increase the level of iron in her diet.* **2** An **iron** is a household tool for smoothing the creases out of newly washed clothes, originally in the form of a shaped piece of iron heated on a fire, now usually an electrical device. **3** (*uncount*) **Iron** also

refers to or describes firmness of character: *Your mother has a will of iron.* □ *his iron self-discipline.*
▻ *verb*: **irons, ironing, ironed**
You **iron** newly washed clothes when you smooth out the creases with an iron.

> ***phrasal verb***
> You **iron out** difficulties or problems when you solve them or get rid of them.

ironic /aɪ'rɒnɪk/ *adjective*
You say that a situation is **ironic** when it is slightly strange or amusing because what happens is the opposite of what you expect: *It's ironic that Jackson, the slowest kid in the class, should end up as this multimillionaire businessman.* — *sentence adverb* **ironically:** *Ironically, it is often the poorer people who give the most.*

ironing /'aɪənɪŋ/ *noun* (*uncount*)
Ironing consists of clothes or other household linen that need to be ironed, or have just been ironed: *There's a pile of ironing waiting for me when I get home.*

ironmonger /'aɪənmʌŋgə(r)/ *noun*: **ironmongers** (*old*)
An **ironmonger** is a person who owns or works in a hardware shop; you refer to the shop itself as an **ironmonger's**.

irony /'ɑɪərənɪ/ *noun*: **ironies**
1 (*uncount*) When you speak with **irony**, you say the opposite of what you mean, in order to be amusing or to make someone appear ridiculous: *'Aren't you clever?' she said, with heavy irony.* □ *I wondered if there was a hint of irony in the compliment.* **2** (*uncount or count*) **Irony** exists in a situation when you find it strange or amusing that what happens is the opposite of what you expect: *The irony of it is that she was once thought to be the person least likely to succeed.* □ *It's one of life's little ironies that hard work often gets you nowhere.*

irrational /ɪ'raʃənəl/ *adjective*
Irrational behaviour shows a lack of good sense or clear thinking: *Like many of our fears, this one was completely irrational.* [*opposite* **rational**]

irreconcilable /ɪrɛkən'saɪləbəl/ *adjective* (*formal*)
Things such as ideas or opinions are **irreconcilable** when they are so different from each other that you cannot accept both of them: *Such narrow-minded views are wholly irreconcilable with the way the Party intends to treat this issue.* [*opposite* **reconcilable**]

irrefutable /ɪrɪ'fjuːtəbəl/ *adjective* (*formal*)
What someone says is **irrefutable** if it cannot be denied, or proved false or wrong: *It is an irrefutable fact that the Prime Minister lied to Parliament.* [*same as* **undeniable**]

irregular /ɪ'rɛgjʊlə(r)/ *adjective*
1 Something that is **irregular** does not happen or occur at regular or equal intervals, but with unequal spaces between occurrences: *We phoned the doctor when her breathing became irregular.* **2** The surface or shape of something is **irregular** if it is not smooth, even or balanced: *an irregular pattern.* **3** **Irregular** behaviour goes against rules, custom or accepted standards: *Some of their accounting practices were most irregular.* **4** (*grammar*) An **irregular** verb, noun or adjective changes its form in ways different from the usual patterns in the language.
[*opposite* **regular**] — *noun* (*uncount or count*) **irregularity** /ɪrɛgjʊ'larɪtɪ/: *the irregularity of his visits* □ *We identified a number of irregularities in their application of the rules.*

irrelevance /ɪ'rɛləvəns/ *noun* (*uncount*)
The **irrelevance** of something is the fact that it is irrelevant: *I was not so much irritated by the vulgarity of his comment as by its irrelevance.* [*opposite* **relevance**]

irrelevancy /ɪ'rɛləvənsɪ/ *noun*: **irrelevancies**
1 (*uncount*) **Irrelevancy** is irrelevance: *the irrelevancy of the conclusions they draw.* **2** An **irrelevancy** is something irrelevant: *Don't waste your energy thinking about such irrelevancies.*

irrelevant /ɪ'rɛləvənt/ *adjective*
Something **irrelevant** does not have any effect on, or connection with, the matter you are discussing or dealing with: *Your own personal wishes are irrelevant to us; the decision is ours.* [*opposite* **relevant**]

irreparable /ɪ'rɛpərəbəl/ *adjective* (*formal*)
Irreparable damage is so serious that it cannot be restored or put right: *The scandal had done irreparable harm to the government's credibility.*

irreplaceable /ɪrɪ'pleɪsəbəl/ *adjective*
Something **irreplaceable** is so valuable or rare that it could not be replaced if it became lost or damaged. [*opposite* **replaceable**]

irrepressible /ɪrɪ'presɪbəl/ *adjective*
An **irrepressible** person is always lively, cheerful and enthusiastic, even in very difficult situations.

irreproachable /ɪrɪ'proʊtʃəbəl/ *adjective*
Someone's behaviour is **irreproachable** if it is so good, proper or correct that it can't rightly be criticized. [*same as* **faultless**]

irresistible /ɪrɪ'zɪstəbəl/ *adjective*
1 When you have an **irresistible** desire or wish to do or have something you feel very urgently that you must do or have it: *The urge to slap him was almost irresistible.* □ *an apricot flan and an irresistible chocolate gateau.* **2** You say that you find someone **irresistible** if you think they are sexually very attractive: *He is apparently irresistible to women.*

irrespective /ɪrɪ'spɛktɪv/ *adjective*
Something is true **irrespective** of other things when those other things do not affect or change it: *The law demands that workers be treated the same, irrespective of sex or age.* □ *Everyone receives our thanks, irrespective of how much they have been able to contribute.* [*same as* **regardless**]

irresponsible /ɪrɪ'spɒnsɪbəl/ *adjective*
An **irresponsible** person does not seriously consider the results or effects of their behaviour: *It's shocking to think that my parents could have been so irresponsible.* □ *It was irresponsible of you to leave her alone for so long.* [*opposite* **responsible**] — *adverb* **irresponsibly:** *I realized that I had acted irresponsibly.*

irreverent /ɪ'rɛvərənt/ *adjective*
Irreverent behaviour shows a lack of proper respect for someone or something: *His speech was spiced with irreverent comments about the church.* [*opposite* **reverent**] — *noun* (*uncount*) **irreverence:** *the shocking irreverence of such a thought.* [*opposite* **reverence**]

irreversible /ɪrɪ'vɜːsɪbəl/ *adjective*
In an **irreversible** situation or process, you cannot stop, change, or return to the way things originally were: *It seems that the decision is irreversible.* [*same as* **irrevocable**; *opposite* **reversible**]

irrevocable /ɪ'rɛvəkəbəl/ *adjective*
Actions that are **irrevocable** cannot be changed: *It is an irrevocable decision.* [*same as* **irreversible**; *opposite* **reversible**]

irrigate /ˈɪrɪgeɪt/ *verb*: **irrigates, irrigating, irrigated**
To **irrigate** land is to direct water on to it so that crops can grow: *The fields were irrigated by means of a system of pipes and ditches.* — *noun* (*uncount*) **irrigation** /ɪrɪˈgeɪʃən/: *digging irrigation channels.*

irritable /ˈɪrɪtəbəl/ *adjective*
An **irritable** person is easily annoyed or made angry: *You're very irritable this morning.* [*same as* **touchy**]

irritate /ˈɪrɪteɪt/ *verb*: **irritates, irritating, irritated**
1 Something that **irritates** you makes you slightly angry or annoyed: *I was a bit irritated by some of his personal habits.* [*same as* **annoy**] **2** Something also **irritates** you when it makes part of your body sore or itchy: *As a baby, his skin was irritated by woollen clothes.* — *adjective* **irritating:** *the irritating noises she makes when she eats.* — *noun* (*uncount or count*) **irritation** /ɪrɪˈteɪʃən/: *'Hurry up!' she said, not without irritation.* □ *The lateness of the train was yet another irritation.* [*same as* **annoyance**]

is /ɪz/ *verb*
Is is the form of the present tense of the verb **be** that is used with *he, she* and *it*.

-ise See **-ize**.

-ish /ɪʃ/ *suffix*
-ish is used to form adjectives that mean **1** slightly or fairly: *reddish hair* □ *a tallish woman.* **2** approximately, about or roughly: *I'd say he was fiftyish.* **3** having the appearance or other qualities of: *His mother has a beautiful, girlish face.*

Islam /ˈɪzlɑːm/ *noun* (*uncount*)
Islam is the religion of Muslims, who worship one God and follow the teachings of the prophet Mohammed. — *adjective* **Islamic** /ɪzˈlamɪk/: *the Islamic culture.*

island /ˈaɪlənd/ *noun*: **islands**
An **island** is a piece of land completely surrounded by water: *No cars are allowed on the island.* □ *the islands of Skiathos and Skopelos* □ *the Falkland Islands.*

islander /ˈaɪləndə(r)/ *noun*: **islanders**
An **islander** is someone who lives on an island: *The Shetland Islanders were very friendly.*

isle /aɪl/ *noun* (*literary*): **isles**
An **isle** is an island: *the reference to Ireland as the Emerald Isle.*

-ism /ɪzm/ *suffix*: **-isms**
-ism is used to form nouns that refer to **1** a formal set of beliefs, ideas or principles: *Support for Socialism seemed to be on the decline.* □ *She's one of the champions of modern feminism.* **2** a quality or state: *heroism.* **3** unfair treatment of someone because of their race, sex or other personal characteristic: *This is the worst kind of ageism.*

isn't /ˈɪzənt/
Isn't is the spoken, and informal written, form of **is not**.

isolate /ˈaɪsəleɪt/ *verb*: **isolates, isolating, isolated**
1 You **isolate** something when you separate it from other things, *eg* in order to examine or consider it closely: *Could these cells be isolated from the surrounding tissue?* **2** To **isolate** a sick person or animal is to keep them away from others, so their illness does not spread. **3** You **isolate** people when your behaviour makes them dislike you and not want to be with you or support you; you **are isolated** when this happens: *Through all this silliness, she has managed to isolate nearly all her friends.* □ *She has isolated herself from the rest of the committee.* **4** To **isolate** yourself is also to make or keep yourself separate or different from other people: *They wanted to isolate themselves from the evils of urban life.* □ *The boy has no friends; you get the feeling that his upper-class background has isolated him.* — *adjective* **isolated:** *an isolated cottage on the moors* □ *The big city is also so impersonal that you can at times feel totally isolated.* □ *I don't think it will happen again; this was just an isolated incident.* — *noun* (*uncount*) **isolation** /ɑɪsəˈleɪʃən/: *The infected animals are kept in isolation.* □ *This issue must be considered in isolation from all other concerns.* □ *I frequently had a horrible sense of my own isolation from the world.*

issue /ˈɪʃuː/ *noun; verb*
▻ ***noun***: **issues**
1 An **issue** is something that people are discussing or considering: *The government has done little to address the issue of homelessness.* □ *I hope to raise the issue at tomorrow's meeting.* □ *Your own personal views are not really the issue.* [*same as* **matter**, **subject**] **2** An **issue** of a newspaper or magazine is a copy of it printed at a particular time: *The full interview will appear in next month's issue.* [*same as* **edition**]
▻ ***verb***: **issues, issuing, issued**
1 You **issue** something when you give or send it out, especially officially or formally: *The President has issued a statement to the Press, denying any involvement in the affair.* □ *Invitations have been issued to all Academy members.* **2** To **issue** someone with something is to supply them with it, especially officially or formally: *Each airman is issued with three uniforms.*
▻ ***phrases*** **1** What is **at issue** is the subject being discussed or argued about: *His abilities as headmaster are not at issue here.* **2** You **make an issue of** something when you treat it as very important, and something to be argued about.

-ist /ɪst/ *suffix*: **-ists**
-ist is used to form nouns, which are also often adjectival, that refer to **1** a person who believes in or follows a formal system of ideas or principles: *Most of us were communists at one time or another.* □ *a landmark in feminist literature.* **2** a person who carries out an activity or practises an art: *one of the greatest novelists this century.* **3** a person who treats others unfairly because of their race, sex or other personal characteristic: *Some of her friends are out-and-out racists.* □ *a rather sexist joke.*

it /ɪt/ *pronoun*
1 It is used **a** (*as the subject of a verb or the object of a verb or preposition*) to refer a thing, animal or small child: *You can't buy a boat and not give it a name.* □ *The ceasefire has now been in force for three days; how much longer can it last?* □ *Honesty is not the best policy if it causes unnecessary pain.* □ *There's the post office; you walked right past it.* □ *She picked up the puppy and cradled it in her arms.* □ *A baby's no trouble when it's asleep.* □ *You should read it; it's an excellent book.* □ *Put your ticket in your pocket; I'm afraid of it* (or *its*) *getting left behind.* **b** to ask, or refer to, the identity of someone who is present, or who is speaking on the telephone: *'Who's there?' 'It's me.'* □ *'Hallo, it's Mike here.'* **c** to refer to something such as a circumstance, fact, situation or proposal: *She was getting tired, but wouldn't admit it.* □ *You've spelt my name wrong; it doesn't matter, though.* □ *It's a most difficult situation.* □ *How's it going?* □ *If it's possible, could you be ready to start by 7.00?* □ *Take no notice when he screams; he just does it to get attention.* □ *I don't like it* [= I don't like being] *in London.* □ *The children hated it when he was angry.* **d** to refer to the words *something, anything, nothing, everything, eg* in question tags: *Something's bound to go wrong, isn't it?* □ *Is everything as it should be?*
2 It is used as the subject of a clause stating, describing, or asking about **a** the weather, temperature, time,

date or distance: *It's so cold today.* □ *It's quite windy up on the moors.* □ *Has it begun to snow yet?* □ *It must be at least 40° in here.* □ *It's half past ten and we still haven't had any breakfast.* □ *I keep forgetting what day it is.* □ *Is it the 23rd today?* □ *I reckon it's at least another forty miles to Cambridge.* **b** environment or surroundings: *It's lovely and peaceful here.* □ *It was completely dark inside the cave.*
3 You use **it a** to refer forward to, and comment on, a matter or circumstance you are about to mention: *It's lovely to see you again.* □ *The doctor thought it would be good for you to have a holiday.* □ *It'd be a shame not to see the exhibition.* □ *I find it difficult to keep my enthusiasm going.* □ *Is it OK if I leave early today?* □ *It isn't as though they weren't warned.* □ *It's no good sitting there complaining.* □ *It's a wonder you weren't hurt.* □ *It's extraordinary what doctors can do nowadays.* □ *It amazes me how he goes on ignoring her misbehaviour.* □ *It's most unfortunate, the way things have turned out.* □ *I thought it odd that he hadn't telephoned.* □ *Let me make it quite clear that personally I disagree.* □ *Don't you find it strange returning after so long?* □ *I make it a custom to telephone them on their birthdays.* □ *We can leave it to them to decide.* □ *I take it that you agree?* **b** in passive constructions such as '**it** is thought', to introduce a clause: *It was believed that he'd escaped to France.* □ *It has never been established whether Burns actually did meet Scott.* **c** in impersonal constructions such as '**it** seems', to introduce a clause: *It occurs to me that the shops may be closed today.* □ *It appeared that he'd gone out without telling anyone.* □ *It seems as if he deliberately misled us.* □ *It so happens that I'm going too.* **d** in constructions such as '**it** is' and '**it** was', followed by a clause, to emphasize a particular part of what you want to say: *It wasn't till I saw his face that I realized something had gone badly wrong.* □ *It's the waste that appals one.* □ *It would be the housing department that you'd have to contact.* □ *It's Jack I worry about.*
▻ ***phrases*** **1** You say **'That's it!'** to mean **a** that you've come to the end of something, *eg* something you are telling people or showing them: *I think that's it for just now.* **b** that nothing more can be done: *That's it unless someone can give us a lift.* **c** to indicate that the important point has been mentioned: *'Can't we telephone for help?' 'That's just it; the line's dead.'* **2** (*informal*) You say **'This is it!'** when you reach the moment that you have been waiting for, *eg* the moment of action.
[see also **its, itself**]

Italian /ɪ'talɪən/ *adjective*; *noun*
▻ ***adjective***
Italian means concerned with or belonging to Italy, its people, or their language: *His first wife was Italian.* □ *Italian business practices* □ *an Italian dictionary.*
▻ ***noun***: **Italians**
1 An **Italian** is a person who was born in, or who is a citizen of, Italy: *The Italians in the group saw it differently.* **2** (*uncount*) **Italian** is the language of Italy, and parts of Switzerland: *Some of her books have been translated into Italian.*

italics /ɪ'talɪks/ *noun* (*plural*)
Italics are printed letters that slope upwards to the right, *like these*, and like the letters used for the examples in this dictionary.

itch /ɪtʃ/ *verb*; *noun*
▻ ***verb***: **itches, itching, itched**
1 When a part of your body **itches** you have the feeling of wanting to scratch the skin there: *Woollen socks always make my feet itch.* **2** (*informal*) You say you **are itching** to do something when you are very eager or impatient to do it: *The children were itching to get started.*
▻ ***noun***: **itches:** *I've got this terrible itch on my neck.* □ *Men of this age often get the itch for a sexual experience outside marriage.*

itchy /'ɪtʃɪ/ *adjective*: **itchier, itchiest**
A part of you is **itchy** if you have a feeling there that makes you want to scratch: *His legs get terribly itchy in cold weather.* □ *I've got an itchy spot on my back.*

it'd /'ɪtəd/
It'd is the spoken, and informal written, form of **1 it had**, where 'have' is an auxiliary verb: *I realized that it'd been years since I'd seen him.* **2 it would**: *Don't you think it'd be better to leave now?*

item /'aɪtəm/ *noun*: **items**
1 An **item** is one of several things in a group or collection: *She listed every item of furniture in the place.* □ *some of the more interesting items in the window.* **2** An **item** is also an individual piece of information or news: *There was a fascinating item in 'The Observer'.*

itemize or **itemise** /'aɪtəmaɪz/ *verb*: **itemizes, itemizing, itemized**
Things that **are itemized** are listed or mentioned separately, *eg* on a bill.

itinerant /ɪ'tɪnərənt/ *adjective* (*formal*)
Itinerant describes people whose work involves them travelling from place to place: *a small firm of itinerant teachers going round the local villages.*

itinerary /ɑɪ'tɪnərərɪ/ *noun*: **itineraries**
An **itinerary** is a plan of the route for a journey or trip, usually with details of places you will stop at or visit. [*same as* **route**]

it'll /'ɪtəl/
It'll is the spoken, and informal written, form of **it will**: *I think it'll be difficult to get them to agree.*

its /ɪts/ *determiner* (*possessive*)
Its is the possessive form of **it**, and describes something that belongs to or relates to the thing, animal or child already mentioned: *Do you think that sheep has hurt its leg?* □ *A baby should be allowed to vary its mealtimes.* □ *The government must be persuaded to alter its position.* □ *Because of its situation in the mountains, Simla was considered a healthy place to spend the hot season.* □ *It was posted a week ago; I'm surprised at its not reaching you by now.* [compare **it's**]

it's /ɪts/
It's is the spoken, and informal written, form of **1 it is**: *It's obvious that they never intended to.* **2 it has**, where 'have' is an auxiliary verb: *I think it's proved that we were right from the beginning.*

itself /ɪt'sɛlf/ *pronoun* (*reflexive*)
1 You use **itself** as the object of a verb or preposition, in reference to a thing, animal or child, where the subject of the verb is the same thing, animal or child: *Sharp objects should be removed so that the baby doesn't hurt itself on them.* □ *The washing machine will switch itself off when it's finished.* □ *It's good to see the motor industry gaining some confidence in itself once again.* □ *Watch how a cat licks itself clean.* **2** If a thing, animal or child does something **itself** it does it without help: *'How did the dog get in?' 'It can open the gate itself.'* **3 Itself** is also used after the subject or object of a clause to make your reference to it sound more specific or exclusive: *The food itself was fine; it was the atmosphere of the restaurant that we didn't care for.* □ *I haven't visited the school itself, but I've met the headmaster.*
▻ ***phrase*** For **by itself** see **by**.

I've /aɪv/
I've is the spoken, and informal written, form, of **I have**, especially where 'have' is an auxiliary verb: *I've*

never been to Paris in the spring. □ *I've a feeling I've told you this before.*

ivory /ˈaɪvərɪ/ *noun (uncount, often adjectival)*
1 Ivory is the hard, white, bony substance that forms the tusks of elephants and certain other animals: *one or two carvings in ivory* □ *a knife with an ivory handle.*
2 Ivory is also a creamy-white colour: *The wedding dress was ivory.*

ivy /ˈaɪvɪ/ *noun (uncount)*
Ivy is a plant with dark-green leaves, that grows up walls and trees.

-ize or **-ise** /aɪz/ *suffix*
-ize is often added to adjectives to form verbs meaning 'to make or become': *Perhaps the amount of work done by the different groups should be equalized.* □ *some of the world's most industrialized countries.*

J

J or **j** /dʒeɪ/: **Js** or **j's** /dʒeɪz/
J is the tenth letter of the English alphabet: *'Jail', with a J, is now a commoner spelling than 'gaol', with a G.*

jab /dʒab/ *verb*; *noun*
▻ ***verb***: **jabs, jabbing, jabbed**
You **jab** someone or something with something pointed when you push it into them; you **jab** something pointed somewhere when you push it into something or someone: *She kept jabbing me in the knee with her index finger as she spoke.* □ *She jabbed the gun into my back and hissed 'Move!'* [*same as* **poke, prod**]
▻ ***noun***: **jabs**
1 A **jab** is the action of pushing something pointed into something or someone: *She gave him a sharp jab with her elbow.* [*same as* **poke, prod**] **2** (*informal*) A **jab** is an injection of a drug into your body to prevent or treat illness: *He'll need a second polio jab when he's twelve.*

jack /dʒak/ *noun*; *verb*
▻ ***noun***: **jacks**
1 A **jack** is a device for lifting heavy objects, *eg* motor vehicles, off the ground. **2** The **jack** in a pack of cards is the card with a picture of a young man on it, between the ten and queen in value: *the jack of diamonds*
▻ ***verb***: **jacks, jacking, jacked**

> ***phrasal verb***
> You **jack up** a vehicle or other heavy object when you raise it off the ground using a jack.

jackal /'dʒakəl/ *noun*: **jackals**
A **jackal** is a dog-like wild animal of Africa and Asia, that feeds on creatures killed by other animals.

jacket /'dʒakɪt/ *noun*: **jackets**
1 A **jacket** is a short coat reaching down to about hip level, usually with long sleeves: *He was wearing his old tweed jacket and flannel trousers.* [see picture at **clothing**] **2** The **jacket** or **dustjacket** of a hardback book is its loose paper cover: *It's the jacket that sells the book.* **3** You cook and serve a potato in its **jacket** by baking it in the oven and serving it without peeling it: *Supper was a potato in its jacket, filled with grated cheese.*

jack-knife /'dʒaknaɪf/ *verb*: **jack-knifes, jack-knifing, jack-knifed**
An articulated vehicle **jack-knifes** when it goes out of control and the trailer swings round against the cab, *eg* when it has to stop suddenly.

jackpot /'dʒakpɒt/ *noun*: **jackpots**
You win the **jackpot** in a game or lottery when you win the the maximum prize, usually consisting of everybody else's stakes or bets.

jade /dʒeɪd/ *noun* (*uncount, often adjectival*)
1 Jade is a green stone used in jewellery, and for making ornaments: *a jade statuette.* **2 Jade** is a bright blue-green colour: *For her official visit the Queen wore a jade silk dress.*

jaded /'dʒeɪdɪd/ *adjective*
You feel **jaded** if you feel tired and bored: *jaded employees* □ *You look a bit jaded; can't you take a short holiday?* [*same as* **weary**; *opposite* **refreshed**]

jagged /'dʒagɪ d/ *adjective*
A **jagged** surface or outline is rough and uneven, with a lot of sharp points: *jagged rocks* □ *There was a jagged, gaping hole in the floor.*

jaguar /'dʒagjʊə(r)/ *noun*: **jaguars**
A **jaguar** is a large animal of the cat family, with a yellow coat covered with black circular marks, that is native to South America.

jail or **gaol** /dʒeɪl/ *noun*; *verb*
▻ ***noun*** (*count or uncount*): **jails**
A **jail** is a prison: *He was sent to jail for four years.* □ *She was given a six-month jail sentence.* □ *Conditions in Britain's jails have come under criticism.*
▻ ***verb***: **jails, jailing, jailed**
People **are jailed** when they are put in prison: *These men should be jailed for life.* [*same as* **imprison**; *opposite* **free**]

jailer or **gaoler** /'dʒeɪlə(r)/ *noun*: **jailers**
A **jailer** is the person in charge of the prisoners in a jail.

jam¹ /dʒam/ *noun* (*uncount*)
Jam is a thick sticky food made from fruit boiled with sugar, that you spread on bread or toast: *a pot of raspberry jam* □ *There was nothing in the house to eat except bread and jam.*

jam² /dʒam/ *verb*; *noun*
▻ ***verb***: **jams, jamming, jammed**
1 A road or other place **is jammed** with people or vehicles if it is so full of them that they can hardly move: *The roads out of the city were jammed with people in cars and on foot, trying to escape.* [*same as* **block**] **2** You **jam** things or people into a place when you pack them in tightly together: *Too many spectators were being jammed into one part of the stand.* **3** You **jam** something somewhere when you push it there hard: *He jammed his fingers into his ears.* [*same as* **stick**] **4** Something **is jammed** somewhere if it is stuck there and cannot move: *He had got his head jammed between the railings.* [*same as* **stick**] **5** Machinery **jams** when it gets stuck and stops working: *The steering wheel had jammed.* **6** To **jam** a radio signal is to cause interference, especially deliberately, so that it cannot be received clearly.
▻ ***noun***: **jams**
A traffic **jam** is a situation, especially at a street junction, where vehicles trying to move in different directions have become so closely packed together that movement stops.

> ***phrasal verb***
> A driver **jams on** the brake when he or she puts it on suddenly and with force.

jam-packed /dʒam'pakd/ *adjective* (*informal*)
A place that is **jam-packed** is very crowded with people or things: *The middle of town is always jam-packed during the Festival.*

jangle /'dʒaŋgəl/ *verb*: **jangles, jangling, jangled**
Bells **jangle** when they ring harshly; metal objects such as keys **jangle** when they strike against one another and produce a ringing noise; you **jangle** metal things when you make a ringing noise with them: *The prison warder appeared, keys jangling at his waist.*

janitor /'dʒanɪtə(r)/ (*especially AmE*) *noun*: **janitors**
A **janitor** is someone who looks after a large building, especially a public one. [*same as* **caretaker**]

January /'dʒanjʊərɪ/ *noun* (*uncount*)
January is the first month of the year, coming after December and before February: *We started the project last January.* □ *The next meeting will be on the fourteenth of January* (written *14 January*). □ *January the twenty-fourth* (written *January 24*) □ *There's usually a fair amount of snow in January.* □ *freezing January weather.*

Japanese /dʒapə'ni:z/ *adjective*; *noun*
▻ ***adjective***
Japanese means concerned with or belonging to Japan, its people or their language: *At least half the EFL students were Japanese.* □ *Japanese cars* □ *Japanese national costume* □ *written in Japanese script.*
▻ ***noun***
1 (*uncount*) **Japanese** is the language of Japan: *She's trying to teach herself Japanese.* **2** (*plural*) The Japanese are the people of Japan.

jar[1] /dʒɑ:(r)/ *noun*: **jars**
A **jar** is a wide-mouthed cylindrical glass container, typically used for foods such as jam or honey: *While the jam is coming to the boil, warm 12 large jam jars in the oven.*

jar[2] /dʒɑ:(r)/ *verb*; *noun*
▻ ***verb***: **jars, jarring, jarred**
1 Something **jars**, or **jars** on you, if it makes an unpleasantly harsh impression: *He had a loud, contemptuous laugh which jarred in the ears of the listeners.* [*same as* **grate**] **2** A sudden jerk or bump **jars** a part of your body if the shaking action causes pain or injury: *Running on ordinary roads can jar your spine.*
▻ ***noun***: **jars:** *These frequent jars and jolts to the skeleton can lead to long-term damage.*

jargon /'dʒɑ:gən/ *noun* (*uncount*)
Jargon is the technical or specialized vocabulary used by people involved in a particular trade, profession or activity: *medical jargon.*

jarring /'dʒɑ:rɪŋ/ *adjective*
Something that is **jarring** has a disturbing effect on you, because it looks or sounds harsh, or is unsuitable in its particular surroundings or situation: *a jarring tone of voice* □ *A concrete office block had arisen at one side of the square, and the effect was jarring.*

jaundice /'dʒɔ:ndɪs/ *noun* (*uncount*)
Jaundice is an illness that affects your liver and causes your skin and the whites of your eyes to turn yellow.

jaunt /dʒɔ:nt/ *noun*: **jaunts**
You go on a **jaunt** somewhere when you travel there for a short visit, especially for pleasure: *Her job seems to allow her the occasional jaunt to Paris.* [*same as* **trip**]

jaunty /'dʒɔ:ntɪ/ *adjective*: **jauntier, jauntiest**
1 Jaunty behaviour is confident, cheerful and carefree: *His appearance was youthful, his manner jaunty.* [*same as* **sprightly**] **2** A **jaunty** way of dressing is smart and stylish: *She wore a man's tweed cap, tilted at a jaunty angle.*

javelin /'dʒavəlɪn/ *noun*: **javelins**
A **javelin** is a light spear for throwing as a weapon or in sport.

jaw /dʒɔ:/ *noun*: **jaws**
1 (*often in the plural*) Your **jaws** are the upper and lower parts of your skull in which your teeth are set: *The disease causes deformity of the lower jaw.* □ *The dog had its jaws round the child's arm and wouldn't let go.* **2** Your **jaw** is the lower part of your face, containing your lower lip and chin: *She had a firm, well-rounded jaw.* [see picture at **body**]

jazz /dʒaz/ *noun*; *verb*
▻ ***noun*** (*uncount*)
Jazz is popular music of Black American origin, with strong rhythms, that people perform with individual variations and improvisations: *The saxophone is the supreme jazz instrument.*
▻ ***verb***: **jazzes, jazzing, jazzed**

> ***phrasal verb***
> (*informal*) You **jazz** something **up** when you do something to make it look or seem brighter or livelier: *I suppose we could jazz the walls up with some posters.*

jealous /'dʒɛləs/ *adjective*
1 You are **jealous** of someone else or their possessions, success or talents if you feel a bitter dislike of them because you are not as *eg* good-looking, wealthy, successful or clever as they are: *It's not uncommon for mothers to be jealous of their daughters.*

> Being **jealous**, and being **envious**, of someone else both involve wishing that you had their qualities, possessions or opportunities, but when you are **jealous** of someone you also hate them for being better or luckier than you.

2 Jealous husbands, wives or lovers easily suspect their partners of being unfaithful to them, and suspect other people of being rivals: *He injured her seriously in one of his jealous rages.* **3** (*literary*) You are **jealous** of something that you have, such as a right or privilege, if you anxiously guard it. — *adverb* **jealously:** *The hiding place of the jewel was a jealously guarded secret.*

jealousy /'dʒɛləsɪ/ *noun* (*uncount or count*)
1 Jealousy is a feeling of bitter dislike you have for someone who has qualities, possessions or opportunities that you wish you had yourself: *Parents must guard against setting up any causes for jealousy between their children.* □ *the petty jealousies and rivalries typical of office life.* [*same as* **envy, resentment**] **2** In a relationship between lovers, marriage partners or friends, **jealousy** is bitter hatred of rivals, and intolerance of any unfaithfulness: *Jealousy is the surest destroyer of a relationship.*

jeans /dʒi:nz/ *noun* (*plural*)
Jeans are casual trousers made of a thick coarse cotton called denim: *A new pair of jeans can cost you anything up to £70 these days.*

jeep /dʒi:p/ *noun*: **jeeps**
A **jeep** is a light military vehicle capable of travelling over rough country.

jeer /dʒɪə(r)/ *verb*; *noun*
▻ ***verb***: **jeers, jeering, jeered**
1 People **jeer** a speaker or performer when they show their disapproval by shouting insults at them: *Labour MPs booed and jeered this morning in Parliament when John Major put forward his new proposals for the*

National Health Service. [*same as* **heckle**] **2** People **jeer** at someone when they laugh unkindly at them or make rude and insulting remarks to them: *His colleagues jeered at him when he refused to go on strike.* [*same as* **taunt**]

▻ ***noun*** (*usually in the plural*): **jeers**

A **jeer** is an insulting or unkind remark. [*same as* **taunt**]

jell /dʒɛl/ or **gel** *verb*: **jells, jelling, jelled**

1 A plan or idea **jells** when it gets clearer and more organized. [*same as* **take shape**] **2** A liquid **jells** when it sets, or becomes thicker and firmer, like jelly.

jelly /ˈdʒɛlɪ/ *noun* (*uncount or count*): **jellies**

1 Jelly is a dessert consisting mainly of fruit juice, thickened or set with gelatine: *jelly and ice cream* ▫ *Help yourself to some jelly.* **2 Jelly** is also **a** a clear jam made by boiling and straining fruit: *blackcurrant jelly.* **b** any thick clear food or substance: *The soup comes out of the tin in the form of jelly.* **3** You say your legs feel like **jelly** if you feel very nervous.

jellyfish /ˈdʒɛlɪfɪʃ/ *noun*: **jellyfish** or **jellyfishes**

A **jellyfish** is a sea creature with a jelly-like body, some species of which have long ribbon-like stinging parts.

jeopardize or **jeopardise** /ˈdʒɛpədaɪz/ *verb*: **jeopardizes, jeopardizing, jeopardized**

You **jeopardize** something when you risk getting it harmed, lost or destroyed: *Any renewal of the violence will jeopardize the success of the peace negotiations.* [*same as* **endanger**]

jeopardy /ˈdʒɛpədɪ/ *noun* (*uncount*)

Something that is in **jeopardy** is in danger of harm, loss or destruction: *The closure of the shipyard will put many jobs in jeopardy.* ▫ *Don't put your own life in jeopardy by taking foolish risks.* [*same as* **danger**]

jerk /dʒɜːk/ *verb*; *noun*

▻ ***verb***: **jerks, jerking, jerked**

1 You **jerk** something when you pull it with a sharp movement: *He grabbed hold of my arm and jerked me to my feet.* ▫ *I jerked on the brakes.* **2** You **jerk** when you move suddenly and sharply: *I let go of the branch and it jerked back.* ▫ *When a dog's body jerks like that, is it dreaming?*

▻ ***noun***: **jerks:** *She sat up with a jerk.* ▫ *I gave the reins a jerk and the horse slowly set off.*

jerky /dʒɜːkɪ/ *adjective*: **jerkier, jerkiest**

Jerky movements are uncontrolled and sudden: *He had a strange jerky walk.* — *adverb* **jerkily:** *We drove jerkily along the uneven track.*

jersey /ˈdʒɜːzɪ/ *noun*: **jerseys**

1 A **jersey** is a knitted garment that you wear over the upper part of your body, and put on by pulling over your head. [*same as* **pullover, sweater**; see picture at **clothing**] **2** (*uncount*) **Jersey** is a fine knitted fabric made of *eg* wool, silk or cotton, used for making clothing: *shirts made of cotton jersey.*

Jerusalem artichoke /dʒəˈruːsələm ˈɑːtɪtʃoʊk/ *noun*: **Jerusalem artichokes**

A **Jerusalem artichoke** is a potato-like root vegetable, with a stronger taste than a potato. [see picture at **vegetable**].

jest /dʒɛst/ *noun* (*old, or literary*): **jests**

A **jest** is a joke or amusing remark: *His pupils smiled dutifully at his jests.*

▻ ***phrase*** You say something **in jest** when you say it to be witty or amusing, and do not mean it to be taken seriously: *Outrageous as his remark was, he did not, to judge from his expression, appear to have spoken in jest.*

Jesus /ˈdʒiːzəs/ *noun*

Jesus, or **Jesus Christ**, was the founder of Christianity, and is believed by Christians to be the son of God: *At Christmas we commemorate the birth of Jesus.*

jet[1] /dʒɛt/ *noun* (*uncount*)

Jet is a hard black stone that is polished and used in jewellery or made into ornaments: *a jet necklace.*

jet[2] /dʒɛt/ *noun*; *verb*

▻ ***noun***: **jets**

1 A **jet** is a strong fast stream of liquid, gas or air, forced under pressure from a narrow opening: *Powerful jets of water were directed at the blaze.* **2** The opening through which a jet of liquid or gas is forced is also called a **jet**: *The gas jets on the stove were always getting blocked.* **3** A **jet**, **jet aircraft** or **jet plane** is a large fast aircraft powered by a jet engine.

▻ ***verb*** (*informal*): **jets, jetting, jetted**

You **jet** somewhere when you travel there by jet aircraft: *She always seems to be jetting off to some distant part of the world.*

jet-black /dʒɛtˈblak/ *adjective*

Something that is **jet-black** is very deep black in colour: *She had glossy, jet-black hair.*

jet engine /dʒɛt ˈɛndʒɪn/ *noun*: **jet engines**

A **jet engine** is an engine that gets its power by sucking air in at the front and forcing it out behind.

jet lag /ˈdʒɛt lag/ *noun* (*uncount*)

Jet lag is the tiredness that results from the body's inability to adjust to the rapid changes of time zone that go with high-speed, long-distance air travel: *She was still suffering from jet lag a week later.* — *adjective* **jet-lagged:** *I'm still feeling a bit jet-lagged*

jet-propelled /dʒɛtprəˈpɛld/ *adjective*

A **jet-propelled** aircraft is powered by jet engines.

jet set /ˈdʒɛt sɛt/ *noun* (*used in the singular*; *informal*)

The **jet set** are wealthy people who lead a life of fast travel and expensive pleasure; a **jet-setter** is a member of the jet set.

jettison /ˈdʒɛtɪsən/ *verb*: **jettisons**, **jettisoning**, **jettisoned**

The crew of an aircraft or ship **jettison** cargo in an emergency when they throw it overboard in order to make the ship or aircraft lighter.

jetty /ˈdʒɛtɪ/ *noun*: **jetties**

A **jetty** is **1** a stone or wooden platform or landing-stage projecting into the sea, lake or river, where boats can be tied so that people can get on and off. **2** a stone barrier built out into the sea to protect a harbour from currents and high waves.

Jew /dʒuː/ *noun*: **Jews**

A **Jew** is **1** a member of the Hebrew race. **2** (*religion*) someone who practises Judaism.

jewel /dʒʊəl/ *noun*: **jewels**

1 A **jewel** is a precious stone used in a personal ornament such as a necklace, brooch or ring: *brooches set with precious jewels.* **2** Someone's **jewels** are their personal ornaments or jewellery, made with precious stones and metals: *She kept her jewels in the bank.* ▫ *The thieves had forced the lid of her jewel box open.*

jewelled /ˈdʒʊəld/ *adjective*

Things that are **jewelled** are decorated with precious stones: *a jewelled crown.*

jeweller /ˈdʒʊələ(r)/ *noun*: **jewellers**

1 A **jeweller** is a person who deals in, makes or repairs jewellery, watches, and objects of gold and silver. **2** A **jeweller's** is a jeweller's shop: *Could you collect my watch from the jeweller's on your way home?*

jewellery (*AmE* **jewelry**) /ˈdʒʊəlrɪ/ *noun* (*uncount*)

Jewellery is personal ornaments such as bracelets,

necklaces, brooches, rings, and earrings: *Don't take your best jewellery on holiday with you; put it in the bank.*

Jewish /'dʒuːɪʃ/ *adjective*
Jewish means relating or belonging to the race of Jews or to Judaism: *the Jewish nation* □ *Jewish customs.*

jibe /dʒaɪb/ *noun*: **jibes**
A **jibe** is an unkind or sarcastic remark.

jig /dʒɪg/ *noun; verb*
▻ ***noun*: jigs**
A **jig** is a lively traditional dance of the kind formerly performed by country people.
▻ ***verb*: jigs, jigging, jigged**
People or things **jig** about, or **jig** up and down, when they keep moving or jumping about, or up and down.

jiggle /'dʒɪgəl/ *verb*: **jiggles, jiggling, jiggled**
Something **jiggles** when it moves from side to side, or up and down; you **jiggle** something when you move it from side to side, or up and down: *She poked a knitting needle into the lock and jiggled it about.*

jigsaw /'dʒɪgsɔː/ *noun*: **jigsaws**
A **jigsaw**, or **jigsaw puzzle**, is a picture stuck on to wood or cardboard and cut into small pieces, which you fit together to make the picture again.

jingle /'dʒɪŋgəl/ *verb; noun*
▻ ***verb*: jingles, jingling, jingled**
Metallic objects such as coins or keys **jingle** when they strike against one another and produce a ringing noise: *His loose change jingled in his pocket as he ran.*
▻ ***noun*: jingles**
1 (*used in the singular*) A **jingle** is a ringing sound made by metallic objects, such as coins or keys, striking against one another: *the jingle of keys.* **2** A **jingle** is also a simple rhyming verse or song: *The children knew all the jingles from the TV commercials.*

jinx /dʒɪŋks/ *noun*: **jinxes**
You say that something has a **jinx** on it if it seems constantly to suffer from bad luck: *When, after a series of problems, our leading actor fell ill, I really began to believe the production had a jinx on it.* — *adjective* **jinxed:** *The project was jinxed from the start; everything went wrong that could go wrong.*

jittery /'dʒɪtərɪ/ *adjective*
You feel **jittery** when you feel very nervous and anxious: *The government is bound to be jittery about race relations, with the election so soon.* [*same as* **edgy, anxious**]

job /dʒɒb/ *noun*: **jobs**
1 Your **job** is your employment, or the work you do regularly to earn money: *He found a job as a nightwatchman.* □ *I may lose my job if they make staff cuts.* □ *She realized she'd been in the same job for fifteen years.* **2** A **job** is a task or a piece or work that needs to be done: *I've got a few jobs to finish; they'll probably take another couple of hours.* □ *household jobs such as making the beds and washing the dishes.* **3** If you say that it is, or is not, someone's **job** to do something, you mean that they are, or are not, the person responsible for doing it: *It isn't my job to check that all the windows are closed at night.*
▻ ***phrases*** **1** (*informal*) You say that someone **is doing a good job** if they are doing something well: *He's doing a good job as foreman, and the men like him.* **2** Something that **does the job** achieves what is required: *A four-inch screw would probably do the job.* **3** You **give** something **up as a bad job** if you abandon it because you think it is impossible or not worth the trouble. **4** (*informal*) You **have a job** doing something if it is difficult to do: *You'll have a job persuading them to give you more money.* □ *I had a job getting the door open.* **5** (*informal*) If you say **it's a good job** that something is so, you mean that it's lucky or fortunate that it is: *It's a good job your mother's not here to see the mess.* **6** (*informal*) Something that is **just the job** is exactly what you need or require: *A walking holiday sounds just the job.* **7** You **make a good job of** something if you do it well: *You've made a lovely job of ironing my shirts.* □ *The workmen have made a nice job of the kitchen.* **8** You have to **make the best of a bad job** when you have to do your best in difficult circumstances.

job centre /'dʒɒb sɛntə(r)/ *noun*: **job centres**
A **job centre** is a government office displaying information on available jobs.

jobless /'dʒɒbləs/ *adjective; noun*
▻ ***adjective***
People who are **jobless** would like a job but cannot find one: *thousands of jobless university graduates.* [*same as* **unemployed**]
▻ ***noun*** (*plural*)
The **jobless** are people who want jobs and cannot find them: *As soon as they graduate they join the ranks of Britain's jobless.* [*same as* **unemployed**]

job-sharing /'dʒɒb-ʃɛərɪŋ/ *noun* (*uncount*)
Job-sharing is the practice of sharing the tasks of one full-time job between two or more part-time workers.

jockey /'dʒɒkɪ/ *noun; verb*
▻ ***noun*: jockeys**
A **jockey** is a someone who rides horses, especially professionally, in horse races.
▻ ***verb*: jockeys, jockeying, jockeyed**
▻ ***phrase*** In a competitive situation, people **jockey for position** when by various means they try to push colleagues or rivals out of their way and get themselves into the best position for promotion or advancement.

jocular /'dʒɒkjʊlə(r)/ *adjective*
You are in a **jocular** mood when you make jokes or try to be amusing; a **jocular** remark is intended to be funny: *There were the usual jocular contributions in the visitors' book.* [*same as* **witty**; *opposite* **serious**] — *adverb* **jocularly:** *'We had summer yesterday,' someone commented jocularly.*

jodhpurs /'dʒɒdpəz/ *noun* (*plural*)
Jodhpurs are horse-riding trousers that are loose-fitting over the buttocks and thighs and tight-fitting from knee to ankle: *a pair of jodhpurs.*

jog /dʒɒg/ *verb; noun*
▻ ***verb*: jogs, jogging, jogged**
1 People **jog** or go **jogging** when they go running at a gentle, steady pace, for exercise: *I used to go jogging regularly before breakfast.* **2** People **jog** along when they progress slowly and steadily. **3** You **jog** someone or something when you knock or bump them slightly: *He jogged my elbow and made me spill my coffee.* [*same as* **jolt**, **knock**] **4** Someone or something **jogs** your memory when they make you remember something. — *noun* **joggers:** *The park was empty except for a few early-morning joggers.* — *noun* (*uncount*) **jogging:** *She listed her forms of exercise as jogging, aerobics and swimming.*
▻ ***noun*: jogs:** *He usually goes for a jog round the park in the evening.* □ *The photo gave my memory a jog.*

joggle /'dʒɒgəl/ *verb*: **joggles, joggling, joggled**
Something **joggles** when it shakes or wobbles; you **joggle** something when you shake it: *Stop joggling the table.*

join /dʒɔɪn/ *verb; noun*
▻ ***verb*: joins, joining, joined**
1 You **join** things when you connect or attach them to each other; things that **are joined** are attached or connected to each other: *Join these two wires together and*

join the red one to the red terminal. □ *At low tide the island is joined to the mainland.* [*same as* **attach, connect, link**] **2** You join two points when you connect them with a line: *Join point A to point B.* □ *the line joining points C and D.* **3** One road or river **joins** another where the two meet: *The River Tilt joins the River Garry at Blair Atholl.* □ *The two motorways join at Perth.* □ *Drive on till you join the Plymouth road.* [*same as* **meet, converge** with] **4** You **join** a queue when you go and wait at the end of it. **5** You **join** someone when you come into their company: *I'll join you later in the dining room.* □ *She joined them for supper.* □ *We were soon joined by Philip and his wife.* **6** You **join** activities when you take part in them: *Come and join the celebrations.* **7** You **join** a society, class, school or business firm when you become a member of it: *She joined the firm in the late '70s.* □ *You can join the golf club as a junior member at a reduced fee.*

▻ ***noun*: joins**

A **join** is the place where two things or parts are fastened, attached or connected: *The joins between the sleeves and the body of the garment should be invisible.* □ *The pipe started leaking at the join.* [*same as* **seam, joint**]

phrasal verbs

join in You **join in** something when you take part in it: *Soon everyone was joining in the discussion.* □ *She used to watch the other children playing but wouldn't join in.*

join up 1 You **join** things **up** when you connect or attach them: *I think you've joined the back and front up wrongly.* **2** Someone **joins up** when they become a member of the army, navy or air force: *She joined up in 1940 and was immediately posted abroad.* [*same as* **enlist**]

join with If you invite people to **join with** you in doing something, you want them to do it with you: *Please rise and join with me now in drinking a toast to the bride and groom.*

joiner /ˈdʒɔɪnə(r)/ *noun*: **joiners**

A **joiner** is a craftsman who makes and fits wooden structures in buildings, such as doors, window frames, stairs, cupboards and shelves.

joint /dʒɔɪnt/ *noun*; *adjective*

▻ ***noun*: joints**

1 A **joint** is the place where two parts or pieces are joined or attached to each other: *The pipes were old and leaking at the joints.* [*same as* **join, seam**] **2** Your **joints** are the parts of your skeleton, such as your knee or elbow, where two bones are connected, with a certain range of movement: *Wear and tear on the joints can result in arthritis in old age.* **3** A **joint** of meat is a large piece of meat for roasting.

▻ ***adjective***

1 Joint things are shared by people, done together with other people, or have a combined purpose or function: *Most of our meals are a joint effort.* □ *She had taken the money out of the joint account she had with her husband.* **2 Joint** owners of something share it; **joint** organizers of something organize it together: *He appointed his son and daughter joint executors of his will.* — *adverb* **jointly:** *The copyright was jointly owned by the author and publisher.* □ *a meeting jointly organized by the Classical Association and the English Society.*

▻ ***phrase*** You put a part of you such as your shoulder or knee **out of joint** when you dislocate it, or cause the bones to come out of their proper position.

joke /dʒoʊk/ *noun*; *verb*

▻ ***noun*: jokes**

1 A **joke** is a funny story, especially one that gets passed round and repeated a lot: *Have you heard the latest joke about the Common Market?* □ *Some people are better at telling jokes than others.* **2** A **joke** is anything you say or do to make people laugh; you make or crack **jokes** when you say things to make people laugh; you see a **joke** when you understand it: *It was only a joke; I'm sorry if I hurt your feelings.* **3** If you refer to a person or thing as a **joke** you mean that they are ridiculous or useless: *Public health care was turning into a joke.*

▻ ***verb*: jokes, joking, joked**

1 You **joke** when you tell funny stories or say or do things to make people laugh: *You shouldn't joke about death.* **2** Someone **is joking** when they are being amusing, not serious: *Don't get worried; I'm only joking.*

▻ ***phrases* 1** (*informal*) A situation that is **beyond a joke** is out of control or becoming impossible to bear: *The state of these streets is getting beyond a joke.* **2** You say **'you're joking'** or **'you must be joking'** to someone when they have just said something surprising. **3** You say **'joking apart'** or **'joking aside'** when you want to say something serious. **4** (*informal*) Something that is **no joke** is unpleasant or difficult: *It's no joke trying to teach 30 five-year-olds when you have a splitting headache.* **5** You **see the joke** when you realize that the awkward or unpleasant situation you are in is quite funny. **6** Someone who can **take a joke** is able to laugh at jokes that other people make about them.

joker /ˈdʒoʊkə(r)/ *noun*: **jokers**

1 The **joker** in a pack of cards is an extra card, with a picture of a jester on it, which is used in certain games. **2** You call someone a **joker** if they make a lot of jokes, or speak and behave amusingly and make you laugh. [*same as* **clown**]

jokingly /ˈdʒoʊkɪŋlɪ/ *adverb*

You say or do something **jokingly** when you say or do it without being serious, to amuse people: *Someone jokingly suggested a swim in the rain.*

jollity /ˈdʒɒlɪtɪ/ *noun* (*uncount*; *old*)

Jollity is cheerfulness and good humour: *an evening of great jollity.*

jolly /ˈdʒɒlɪ/ *adjective*; *adverb*

▻ ***adjective*: jollier, jolliest**

1 A **jolly** person is cheerful and happy: *The head teacher was large and jolly.* [*same as* **merry**; *opposite* **sad**] **2** (*old*) A **jolly** occasion is lively, merry and enjoyable: *There were the usual speeches and jokes at the reception; it was all very jolly.*

▻ ***adverb*** (*BrE*; *intensifying*; *informal*)

People use **jolly** like 'very': *It was jolly nice of him to save places for us.*

▻ ***phrase*** (*BrE*; *informal*) People use **jolly well** for emphasis: *I don't care if you're hurt; you jolly well deserve to be.*

jolt /dʒoʊlt/ *verb*; *noun*

▻ ***verb*: jolts, jolting, jolted**

1 A vehicle **jolts** when it shakes or sways: *The train jolted suddenly and my book slipped off my lap.* □ *We jolted along the stony track in our hired Land Rover.* [*same as* **lurch**] **2** You **jolt** something when you knock it, bump it or shake it: *She jolted my elbow and I nearly dropped the tray.* [*same as* **knock**]

▻ ***noun*: jolts**

1 A **jolt** is a shake or bump: *The train gave a jolt and began to move.* **2** A **jolt** is also an emotional shock: *The news of her accident had given me a jolt.*

jostle /ˈdʒɒsəl/ *verb*: **jostles, jostling, jostled**

1 People **jostle**, or **jostle** one another, when they push against one another in a crowd, sometimes in an angry or hostile manner: *crowds of jostling shoppers* □ *People jostled against us.* □ *We were jostled off the pavement.* □ *The Prime Minister is reported to have been jostled by the crowd at Newbury today.* **2** People **jostle** for something such as notice or attention when they compete for it: *up-and-coming young skaters all jostling for recognition.*

jot /dʒɒt/ *verb*: **jots, jotting, jotted**
You **jot** something, or **jot** it down, when you write it quickly: *I jotted her address on a receipt I found in my pocket.* □ *Could you jot down this number for me?*

journal /ˈdʒɜːnəl/ *noun*: **journals**
1 A **journal** is a magazine, especially one dealing with a specialized subject: *a copy of the British Medical Journal* □ *scientific journals.* **2** A **journal** is a diary in which you write about your daily activities: *Ideally everyone should keep a journal.*

journalism /ˈdʒɜːnəlɪzm/ *noun* (*uncount*)
Journalism is the profession of writing news stories or articles for newspapers and magazines, or for radio and television: *She had always wanted to go into journalism.*

journalist /ˈdʒɜːnəlɪst/ *noun*: **journalists**
A **journalist** is a person whose profession is writing news stories or articles for newspapers, magazines, radio or television: *He was a journalist on the Evening News.* [*same as* **reporter**] — *adjective* **journalistic** /dʒɜːnəˈlɪstɪk/: *He had had some journalistic experience on the student newspaper.* □ *Her writing style was lively, almost journalistic.*

journey /ˈdʒɜːnɪ/ *noun*; *verb*
▷ ***noun***: **journeys**
You make a **journey** when you travel from one place to another: *the two-hour journey to work in the mornings and home again in the evenings.* □ *Would you like to wash and change after your journey?* □ *Take the following precautions if you're planning to go on a long journey.*
▷ ***verb*** (*literary*): **journeys, journeying, journeyed**
You **journey** somewhere when you travel there: *We journeyed on, stopping at the occasional village to buy food.*
▷ ***phrase*** You **break your journey** somewhere when you stop there for a rest: *We decided to break our journey at Washington before travelling on to Vancouver.* [*same as* **stop off**]

jovial /ˈdʒoʊvɪəl/ *adjective*
Someone described as **jovial** is cheerful and good-humoured, and usually a man: *She remembered her grandfather as a jovial, bearded man.* □ *His expression was jovial and welcoming.* [*same as* **jolly**] — *noun* (*uncount*) **joviality** /dʒoʊvɪˈalɪtɪ/: *His joviality is what I remember best about him.* — *adverb* **jovially:** *He smiled jovially round at the assembled guests.*

jowl /dʒaʊl/ *noun* (*usually in the plural*): **jowls**
Your **jowls** are the lower part of your cheeks and the flesh round your jawbone: *He looked older, and somewhat heavier about the jowls.*

joy /dʒɔɪ/ *noun*: **joys**
1 (*uncount*) **Joy** is a feeling of happiness: *When I heard she was safe I could find no words to express my joy adequately.* □ *His parents could not conceal their joy at his success.* **2** Something that is a **joy** gives you pleasure and happiness: *One of the joys of childhood is freedom from responsibility.* □ *At the age of fifty he discovered the joy of mountaineering.* □ *Our grandchildren are a great joy to us.*

joyful /ˈdʒɔɪfʊl/ *adjective*
1 You are **joyful** when you are very happy: *The missing child has been found safe and well and is back with his joyful family.* □ *joyful faces.* □ *joyful celebrations.* **2 Joyful** events or news make you very happy: *He told me the joyful news about his forthcoming marriage.* — *adverb* **joyfully:** *The dog greeted us joyfully.*

joyless /ˈdʒɔɪləs/ *adjective* (*literary*)
1 A **joyless** situation is one in which people have no pleasure or happiness: *Ours was a bleak and joyless household.* **2 Joyless** people do not enjoy life: *The nuns who taught them seemed stern and joyless.*
[*same as* **gloomy, cheerless**; *opposite* **joyful**]

joyous /ˈdʒɔɪəs/ *adjective* (*literary*)
People are **joyous** when they are feeling happy or full of joy: *Their laughter was wild and joyous.* — *adverb* **joyously:** *joyously celebrating Christ's birth.*

joyride /ˈdʒɔɪraɪd/ *noun*; *verb*
▷ ***noun***: **joyrides**
Someone goes for a **joyride** when they drive around fast and dangerously in a vehicle they have just stolen.
▷ ***verb***: **joyrides, joyriding, joyrode, joyridden:** *They go joyriding and get involved in these fearful crashes.* — *noun* **joyrider:** *a pair of 14-year-old joyriders.*

JP /dʒeɪˈpiː/ *noun*: **JPs** /dʒeɪˈpiːz/
A **JP** is a Justice of the Peace: *He had already appeared before the local JP on some minor charge.*

jubilant /ˈdʒuːbɪlənt/ *adjective*
You are **jubilant** when you are delighted with your success or the success of your side or team: *The streets were full of jubilant crowds celebrating the victory.* □ *The Conservatives were in jubilant mood as the conference opened.* [*same as* **triumphant**] — *adverb* **jubilantly:** *Fans thronged the streets, singing jubilantly.* [*same as* **triumphantly**]

jubilation /dʒuːbɪˈleɪʃən/ *noun* (*uncount*)
Jubilation is rejoicing at, and celebration of, success or victory: *The announcement was greeted with wild jubilation.*

jubilee /ˈdʒuːbɪliː/ *noun*: **jubilees**
A **jubilee** is a special anniversary, especially the 25th, 50th or 60th (respectively a **silver**, **golden**, and **diamond jubilee**) of an important event, *eg* the succession of the monarch.

Judaism /ˈdʒuːdeɪɪzəm/ *noun* (*uncount*)
Judaism is the religion of the Jews, which has its basis in the Old Testament, or their traditional religious and cultural practices.

judge /dʒʌdʒ/ *noun*; *verb*
▷ ***noun***: **judges**
1 A **judge** is a senior lawyer who supervises the trying of cases in a law court, guides the jury, and decides what should be done as a result of their decision: *The judge sentenced him to three years' imprisonment.* **2** In a competition, the **judges** are the people appointed to decide the winner: *The judges unanimously awarded first prize to Pamela's creation.* [*same as* **adjudicator**] **3** Someone who is a good or poor **judge** of things or people is good or bad at estimating their quality or worth: *She prided herself on being a good judge of character.* □ *I'm rather a poor judge of wines.* **4** You insist on being the **judge** of something when you are determined to be the person who decides about it: *Let me be the judge of whether my mother needs to go into an old people's home.*
▷ ***verb***: **judges, judging, judged**
1 Someone **judges** a legal case in a court of law when they act as judge of it: *It has not yet been announced who will judge the case.* **2** You **judge** a competition when you decide the winner of it: *The drama competition was judged by the writer L. A. G. Strong.* [*same as* **adjudicate**] **3** You **judge** something when you form an opinion about it: *It was difficult to judge whether she*

meant what she said. ▫ *You must decide for yourself; I'm not in a position* [= I'm not the right person] *to judge what's best for you.* ▫ *I judged it safer to pretend to be asleep.* ▫ *She was judged fit to travel by the local doctor.* **4** You **judge** something when you estimate it: *It's difficult to judge his age.* ▫ *It must be about four metres deep, but it's impossible to judge accurately.* **5** You **judge** someone when you criticize them or express disapproval of them: *If you're not perfect yourself, don't judge others.*

▻ ***phrase*** You say **'to judge from** or **by** something', or **'judging from** or **by** something' when you are giving a reason for your opinion: *She must have had an attractive personality, to judge from her popularity.*

judgement or **judgment** /ˈdʒʌdʒmənt/ *noun*: **judgements**
1 You make a **judgement** about something when you form an opinion about it: *She's the right person for the job, in our judgement.* **2** In a court of law, the **judgement** is the decision made on the case by the judge or the court: *She will give her judgement today in the motorway murder trial.* [*same as* **verdict**] **3** (*uncount*) **Judgement** is the ability to make wise or sensible decisions, good guesses, or reliable estimations: *He lacks judgement.* ▫ *Faulty judgement in overtaking is a major cause of accidents.*

▻ ***phrases*** **1** You do something **against your better judgement** when you are persuaded to do it although you believe it would be more sensible not to. **2 a** A judge or court of law **passes judgement** on a case or on an accused person when they make their decision. **b** You **pass judgement** on someone or something when you express your opinion of them or criticize them. **3** You **reserve judgement** when you wait till you know more about something before giving your opinion on it.

judicial /dʒʊˈdɪʃəl/ *adjective*
Judicial means relating to courts of law, judges, or their decisions: *a fair and reliable judicial system.*

judiciary /dʒʊˈdɪʃərɪ/ *noun*: **judiciaries**
The **judiciary** of a country is the branch of government concerned with the legal system and the administration of justice.

judicious /dʒʊˈdɪʃəs/ *adjective*
Judicious behaviour, or a **judicious** action, is wise and sensible, and often has the aim of avoiding trouble: *It might be a judicious move at this stage to increase their wages.* [*opposite* **injudicious**, **foolish**] — *adverb* **judiciously:** *'Let's see what the others think,' said he judiciously.* [*opposite* **foolishly**]

judo /ˈdʒuːdoʊ/ *noun* (*uncount*)
Judo is a Japanese form of wrestling that aims at using minimum physical effort.

jug /dʒʌg/ *noun*: **jugs**
1 A **jug** is a deep container for liquids with a handle and a point shaped for pouring: *Could you pass the milk jug, please?* ▫ *a tall glass jug.* **2** A **jug** of something is also the liquid, or the amount of liquid, contained in it: *He emptied a whole jug of water over her head.*

juggernaut /ˈdʒʌgənɔːt/ *noun* (*BrE*): **juggernauts**
A **juggernaut** is a very large lorry.

juggle /ˈdʒʌgəl/ *verb*: **juggles, juggling, juggled**
1 People **juggle** when they keep several objects in the air at the same time by skilful throwing and catching: *She bought herself some coloured balls to practise juggling with.* **2** You **juggle** facts, figures, possibilities and alternatives when you keep adjusting and re-arranging them till you produce the result or pattern that you want: *We shall have to juggle the figures to allow for an extension to the schedule.* [*same as* **manipulate**]

juggler /ˈdʒʌglə(r)/ *noun*: **jugglers**
A **juggler** is a person who juggles with objects as a performance or entertainment.

juice /dʒuːs/ *noun*: **juices**
1 (*uncount*) **Juice** is the liquid that is contained in fruit or vegetables, or a drink made from this liquid: *a glass of orange juice* ▫ *tomato juice* ▫ *Squeeze lemon juice over the fish.* **2** (*used in the plural*) The body's **juices** are its natural fluids, *eg* those in the stomach that help digestion; the fluid that comes out of roasted meat is referred to as its **juices**: *digestive juices* ▫ *Roasting meat in foil helps to preserve its juices.*

juicy /ˈdʒuːsɪ/ *adjective*: **juicier, juiciest**
1 A **juicy** fruit or vegetable contains a lot of juice: *fat juicy tomatoes.* **2** (*informal*) A **juicy** piece of news usually involves scandal.

jukebox /ˈdʒuːkbɒks/ *noun*: **jukeboxes**
A **jukebox** is a record-player in a public place such as a bar, which you operate by putting in a coin and selecting the record you want played.

July /dʒʊˈlaɪ/ *noun* (*uncount*)
July is the seventh month of the year, coming after June and before August: *The book is due to be published in July 1995.* ▫ *They stayed with us last July.* ▫ *We meet next on the fifteenth of July* (written *15 July*). ▫ *July the tenth* (written *July 10*) ▫ *The wedding took place in hot July sunshine.*

jumble /ˈdʒʌmbəl/ *verb; noun*

▻ ***verb***: **jumbles, jumbling, jumbled**
1 You **jumble** things together when you mix or throw them together in a disorganized manner: *Her clothes and shoes were jumbled together in the cupboard.* **2** You **jumble** things up when you mix or confuse them: *puzzles in which words or letters have been jumbled up.* [*same as* **mix up**]

▻ ***noun***
1 (*used in the singular*) A **jumble** of things is a confused mass of them: *a jumble of shapes and colours.* **2** (*uncount*) **Jumble** is unwanted possessions collected, or suitable, for a jumble sale.

jumble sale /ˈdʒʌmbəl seɪl/ *noun*: **jumble sales**
A **jumble sale** is a sale of unwanted possessions, *eg* used clothing, usually held to raise money for charity.

jumbo /ˈdʒʌmboʊ/ *adjective; noun*

▻ ***adjective***
Jumbo describes an extra-large size of something: *A jumbo packet of cornflakes.*

▻ ***noun***: **jumbos**
A **jumbo** or **jumbo jet** is a large jet aircraft capable of carrying several hundred passengers.

jump /dʒʌmp/ *verb; noun*

▻ ***verb***: **jumps, jumping, jumped**
1 You **jump** somewhere when you leave the surface you are standing or sitting on with a strong push into the air: *She jumped down from the wall.* ▫ *He jumped the remaining few feet and landed in a bog.* ▫ *Jumping and diving into the pool are forbidden.* ▫ *We had to jump over the puddles.* **2** You **jump** something when you jump over it: *This time her horse jumped the fence successfully.* ▫ *We walked on, jumping streams as we came to them.* **3** You **jump** somewhere when you move there quickly: *I jumped into a taxi.* ▫ *He jumped to his feet and offered me his chair.* **4** You **jump** when your body makes a sudden movement from fright or surprise: *The sound made me jump.* **5** The price or level of something **jumps** when it rises suddenly: *Deaths from the disease had jumped to a frightening 40 in March.* **6** In reading a book you **jump** passages or **jump** to a certain point when you omit parts: *You can jump the next chapter.* ▫ *I jumped to the end of the chapter.*

[*same as* **skip**] **7** People **jump** a queue when they go to the front of it before it is their turn.

▷ ***noun***: **jumps**

1 A **jump** is an act of jumping or a distance to be jumped: *Even if we climbed the wall we'd have a ten-foot jump down on the other side.* **2** (*sport*; *used in the singular*) In athletics, **jump** is used in the name of jumping events: *the high jump* □ *the long jump.* **3** A **jump** in amount, cost, price or value is a sudden increase: *an enormous jump in profits.* **4** A **jump** is a sudden movement you make when something frightens you: *She gave a little jump of surprise.*

▷ ***phrases*** **1** For **jump out of your skin** see **skin**. **2** You **jump the gun** when you do something before the proper or appropriate time. **3** For **jump to conclusions** see **conclusion**. **4** (*informal*) You tell someone to **jump to it** when you have given them an order and want them to carry it out quickly. **5** You **keep one jump ahead** of a rival or opponent when you guess what they will do next and prepare yourself to deal with it.

phrasal verbs
jump at You **jump at** a suggestion or offer when you accept it eagerly.
jump on Someone **jumps on** you when they attack you physically or verbally.

jumper /'dʒʌmpə(r)/ *noun*: **jumpers**
1 A **jumper** is a knitted garment that you pull on over your head and wear on the top half of your body: *a long-sleeved woollen jumper.* [*same as* **jersey**, **pullover**, **sweater**; see picture at **clothing**] **2** (*AmE*) A **jumper** is a pinafore dress.

jumpy /'dʒʌmpɪ/ *adjective*: **jumpier**, **jumpiest**
Someone who is **jumpy** is nervous or anxious about something: *The delay was making me jumpy.* [*same as* **edgy**; *opposite* **calm**, **relaxed**]

junction /'dʒʌŋkʃən/ *noun*: **junctions**
A **junction** is a place where roads or railway lines meet: *The accident occurred at the junction between Frederick Street and George Street.* □ *You should exit from the motorway at Junction 14.* [*same as* **intersection**]

juncture /'dʒʌŋktʃə(r)/ *noun*: **junctures**
You refer to a particular important stage in a series of events as a **juncture**: *We can't possibly give up at this juncture.*

June /dʒu:n/ *noun* (*uncount*)
June is the sixth month of the year, coming after May and before July: *We're off to Prague in June.* □ *I'll see you on the ninth of June* (written *9 June*). □ *June the twelfth* (written *June 12*). □ *They're planning a June wedding.*

jungle /'dʒʌŋgəl/ *noun*: **jungles**
1 (*count or uncount*) A **jungle** is a dense tropical forest: *the jungles of South America* □ *We picked our way through dense jungle.* **2** (*used in the singular*) People refer to a complex and confusing mass of things as a **jungle** of things: *We had to work our way through the jungle of building regulations.*

junior /'dʒu:nɪə(r)/ *adjective*; *noun*

▷ ***adjective***

1 Junior describes people of low, or lower, rank within a profession or organization: *the junior office staff* □ *He has a junior ministerial post.* □ *She's junior to me in rank.* **2** In Britain, **junior** describes schools or education for children between the ages of 7 and 11: *the junior pupils.* **3 Junior** is sometimes used after a man's name to distinguish him from an older man, usually his father, who has the same name: *James Dwight Junior.*
[*opposite* **senior**]

▷ ***noun***: **juniors**

1 Someone who is your **junior** is younger than you: *George was my junior by several years.* □ *He's nine years my junior.* **2** The **juniors** at a school are the pupils in the junior section of the school, in Britain usually aged between 7 and 11: *The juniors go home at 2.30.*
[*opposite* **senior**]

junk /dʒʌŋk/ *noun*; *adjective*

▷ ***noun*** (*uncount*; *informal*)

1 Junk is rubbish, or useless, worthless objects: *There's loads of junk to clear away.* **2 Junk** is also old or second-hand articles that are being sold cheaply: *a junk shop.*

▷ ***adjective*** (*informal*)

1 Junk food is easy to produce but not good for your health. **2 Junk** mail is advertising material that is sent to you, that you have no use for, or don't want to read.

junkie /'dʒʌŋkɪ/ *noun* (*informal*): **junkies**
A **junkie** is a drug addict.

jurisdiction /dʒʊərɪs'dɪkʃən/ *noun* (*uncount*)
Someone in authority has **jurisdiction** over particular matters, or over a particular area, if their administrative powers cover or include them: *Libraries come under the jurisdiction of the local authority.*

juror /dʒʊərə(r)/ *noun*: **jurors**
A **juror** is a member of a jury: *The jurors took four hours to reach a verdict.*

jury /'dʒʊərɪ/ *noun* (*with a singular or plural verb*): **juries**
1 The **jury** in a legal case is a group of usually 12 people who have sworn to give an honest verdict according to the evidence presented to the court. **2** A group of people selected to judge a contest is also called a **jury**. [*same as* **panel**]

just[1] /dʒʌst/ *adjective*
Things or people that are **just** are fair and reasonable: *As head teacher she was firm but just.* □ *To be just, he was only trying to help.* □ *It was a perfectly just decision.* □ *There can be no just and adequate reward for such dedicated work.* □ *They have a just claim to the money.* [*opposite* **unjust**, **unfair**, **unreasonable**] — *adverb* **justly:** *We are not being treated justly.*

just[2] /dʒʌst/ *adverb*
1 a Something that has **just**, or only **just**, happened, happened a short time ago: *I'm sorry, Peter's just left.* □ *I've only just heard the awful news.* □ *I'd just put down the telephone when it rang again.* □ (*AmE*) *'What's the time?' 'I just told you.'* **b** You are **just** doing something if you are doing it at present and will soon be finished: *I'm just making supper; do stay and eat with us.* **c** You are **just** going to do something, or are **just** about to do it, if you are going to do it very soon: *I'm just going to fetch some milk.* □ *I was just about to call you myself when you phoned.* **d** One thing happens **just** as another is happening if they happen at the same time: *Just when he was recovering from this first shock, his mother died.* □ *Just as we were sitting down to eat, the doorbell rang.*
2 a Just means exactly or precisely: *Thanks, that's just the information I wanted.* □ *You're just like your mother.* □ *It's just like Frank not to want to cause any bother.* □ *She's just the same; just as obstinate as she always was.* □ *Just how much money do you owe them?* **b** You refer to a person, thing or place that is absolutely suitable for some purpose as **just** the person, thing or place: *I know just the book you need.* □ *I've found just the person for the job.*

3 a Something that is **just**, or only **just**, so, is almost not so: *The water was just warm enough for a bath.* □ *The stone only just missed my ear.* □ *It looks too small, but it might just fit.* **b Just** is used in expressing amount, distance or time, with the meaning 'exactly, but no more': *It's just two o'clock now.* □ *He's just six feet.*

4 Just is used in various ways for emphasis: *Just listen to those birds!* □ *Just think where we'll be this time next week.* □ *That's just terrific!* □ *I can just imagine you tramping through the jungle.* □ *That just isn't true!*

5 a Just means 'only' or 'merely': *Don't be angry; she's just a child.* □ *This isn't just a novel; it's a philosophy of life.* □ *I've received ten complaints today, and that's just a small proportion of the total.* **b** You use **just** generally to make things seem small, unimportant or easy, often for the sake of politeness: *You just add cold water.* □ *I just don't feel very well.* □ *Could I just remind you about tomorrow's meeting?* □ *Can you wait just a couple of minutes?*

▻ ***phrases*** **1** Something is **just about** so if it is nearly or almost so: *We're just about ready.* □ *You're just about my size, I think.* **2** You say **'just a minute'**, **'just a moment'**, or **'just a second'** when you want to ask people to wait briefly: *Just a moment, I'll check her address for you.* **3 Just now** means **a** at the present time: *I'm rather busy just now; can I ring you back?* **b** a short time ago: *He rang just now sounding worried.* □ *Where's my notebook? I had it just now.* **4** You have everything **just so** when you have arranged everything exactly as you want it. **5** For **just the same** see **same**. **6 Just then** means **a** at that time or moment: *I didn't like to mention it just then.* **b** immediately after that: *Just then the door opened and in came Janet.* **7 Not just yet** means sometime soon but not immediately: *He's not planning to retire just yet.*

justice /ˈdʒʌstɪs/ *noun*: **justices**

1 (*uncount*) **Justice** is the quality of fairness in the way people are treated: *Everyone has a right to justice.* □ *Where's your sense of justice?* □ *At last justice had been done.* [*opposite* **injustice**] **2** (*uncount*) The proper administration of the law is referred to as **justice**: *There has been a miscarriage of justice.* **3** (*uncount*) **Justice** is also the quality of being reasonable: *There was some justice in her criticisms.* □ *The justice of their claim is certainly not disputed.* [*opposite* **injustice**] **4 Justice** is used in the title of a judge: *Mr Justice Saunders.* **5** (*AmE*) A **justice** is a judge.

▻ ***phrases*** **1** Criminals **are brought to justice** when they are arrested, tried, sentenced and punished. **2 a** To **do justice to** someone or something, or **do** them **justice**, is to deal with them properly, or present them at their best: *Her biography doesn't do justice to him as a social reformer.* □ *That photograph doesn't do her justice.* **b** You **do yourself justice** in a competition or performance when you do as well as you are capable of doing. **c** You say **'to do** someone or something **justice'**, or **'in justice to** someone or something' when you want to correct an unfair impression: *In justice to her, she did try to get help.*

Justice of the Peace /dʒʌstɪs əv ðə ˈpiːs/ *noun*: **Justices of the Peace**

In Britain, a **Justice of the Peace** is a person with the authority to judge minor criminal cases. [*same as* **magistrate**]

justifiable /dʒʌstɪˈfaɪəbəl/ *adjective*

Something that is **justifiable** can be defended, or shown to be acceptable, because there is a good reason for it: *I believe these price increases are justifiable.* □ *She replied with justifiable fury.* [*same as* **unjustified**] — *adverb* **justifiably:** *She was justifiably upset.*

justification /dʒʌstɪfɪˈkeɪʃən/ *noun* (*uncount or count*): **justifications**

A **justification** for something that might otherwise not be acceptable is a good reason for it, or a satisfactory explanation: *There's never any justification for ill-mannered behaviour.* □ *They appear to have dismissed him without much justification.* [*same as* **grounds**]

justify /ˈdʒʌstɪfaɪ/ *verb*: **justifies, justifying, justified**

1 You **justify** an action or decision when you show that it is necessary, or that there is a good reason for it: *The closure of these mines cannot be justified on the grounds of economy.* □ *How can you justify spending all that money?* [*same as* **defend**] **2** You try to **justify** yourself when you try to give satisfactory reasons for your actions or behaviour. [*same as* **explain**] — *adjective* **justified:** *You were quite justified in complaining to the management.* □ *Lying in such cases is justified.*

jut /dʒʌt/ *verb*: **juts, jutting, jutted**

> ***phrasal verb***
> Something that **juts out** projects or sticks out from a surface: *He glanced up to see a rock ledge jutting out above him.*

jute /dʒuːt/ *noun* (*uncount*)

Jute is fibre from certain Southeast Asian plants, used for making sacks and ropes.

juvenile /ˈdʒuːvənaɪl/ *noun*; *adjective*

▻ ***noun***: **juveniles**

A **juvenile** is a young person who is not yet an adult: *a horrifying increase in murders committed by juveniles.* [*same as* **minor**; *opposite* **adult**]

▻ ***adjective***

1 (*often legal*) **Juvenile** describes activities and procedures relating to young people who are not yet adults: *a high rate of juvenile crime* □ *juvenile offenders* □ *He appeared before a juvenile court on a charge of robbery.* **2** (*derogatory*) You describe someone's behaviour as **juvenile** if you think it is silly and childish: *I've had enough of Paul and his juvenile jokes.* [*same as* **immature**]

juxtapose /dʒʌkstəˈpoʊz/ *verb*: **juxtaposes, juxtaposing, juxtaposed**

You **juxtapose** things when you place them side by side, often for contrast; things **are juxtaposed** when they are side by side: *Paintings ancient and modern are juxtaposed to interesting effect at the new gallery.* — *noun* (*uncount or count*) **juxtaposition:** *Wealth and poverty are in stark juxtaposition.* □ *fascinating juxtapositions.*

K or **k** /keɪ/ *noun*: **Ks, k's**
1 K is the eleventh letter of the English alphabet: *'Know' begins with a K.* **2 K** means one thousand: *She earns £20K a year.* **3 K** is also a kilobyte, the amount of space taken by 1024 bytes in a computer memory, used as a way of measuring the amount of memory a computer has: *This computer has 40K of hard-disk space.*

kaleidoscope /kəˈlaɪdəskoʊp/ *noun*: **kaleidoscopes**
1 A **kaleidoscope** is a tube fitted with mirrors, containing loose fragments of coloured glass which are reflected in the mirrors to form constantly changing patterns when the tube is shaken or turned. **2** A colourful and constantly changing scene, pattern of colours or series of events can be called a **kaleidoscope**: *The market was a kaleidoscope of colour.*

kangaroo /kaŋgəˈruː/ *noun*: **kangaroos**
A **kangaroo** is an Australian animal that moves by jumping on its large powerful back legs, and carries its young in a pouch on its stomach.

karate /kəˈrɑːtɪ/ *noun* (*uncount*)
Karate is a system of self-defence, using the hands and feet to punch and kick.

kebab /kəˈbab/ *noun*: **kebabs**
A **kebab** is a dish of small pieces of meat and sometimes vegetables put on a metal stick or skewer and grilled.

keel /kiːl/ *verb*: **keels, keeling, keeled**

> ***phrasal verb***
> (*informal*) To **keel over** is to fall over, faint or collapse: *Several soldiers keeled over in the heat.*

keen /kiːn/ *adjective*: **keener, keenest**
1 You are **keen** about something if you want to do it, or want it to happen: *We are especially keen to attract young people.* □ *The patient's relatives were keen for him to be an organ-donor.* □ *She is keen that we make every effort to achieve maximum attendance.* □ *We did invite him, but he didn't seem very keen on coming.*
2 You are **keen** on an activity if you enjoy it and spend a lot of time on it: *He's a keen swimmer.* □ *She's getting keener on rock-climbing than she used to be.*
3 People are **keen** when they show interest and enthusiasm: *She has a lovely class of five-year-olds, very keen and enthusiastic.* **4** You have a **keen** interest in something, or a **keen** desire for it, if you are very interested in it, or want it very much: *He took a keen interest in the education of his children.* **5** (*informal*) You are **keen** on someone if you are fond of them or attracted to them romantically: *He's keen on a girl at school.*
6 Your sight or hearing is **keen** if you see or hear well; you have a **keen** understanding of something if you understand it thoroughly. [*same as* **sharp**] **7** A **keen** wind is is a strong cold one. [*same as* **biting**]
8 Competition or rivalry is **keen** when the competitors are all of a high standard. **9** A knife or blade is **keen** if it is sharp. — *adverb* **keenly:** *She felt her disappointment keenly.* □ *I can't say I was very keenly interested in the topic.* □ *a keenly contested match.*

keep /kiːp/ *verb*; *noun*
▻ ***verb*: keeps, keeping, kept**
1 a You **keep** something when you continue to have it: *I'll lend you my scarf but you can't keep it.* □ *You can keep the book; I've finished with it.* □ *I won't be able to keep my job if we move.* [*same as* **hold on to**] **b** You **keep** things when you don't throw them away or get rid of them: *He keeps all his theatre tickets as souvenirs.* **c** You **keep** something somewhere if you put it there when it is not being used: *The tools are kept in the garage.* □ *Where do you keep the sugar?* □ *I always keep a notebook in my bag.*
2 a To **keep** people or things somewhere, or in a certain state, is to make them stay there, or stay like that: *They usually keep you in hospital for about three days after your operation.* □ *He kept his hand on my shoulder.* □ *Keep her off school till the rash clears up.* □ *I thought smoking was supposed to keep mosquitoes away.* □ *We were kept awake all night by the noise from the disco.* □ *I'm so sorry. I was kept late at work.* □ *He apologized for keeping her waiting.* □ *They successfully kept the news secret.* □ *We usually keep the front door locked.* **b** You **keep** off, out of, or away from a place when you stay off, out off, or away from it; you **keep** in a certain state when you stay like that: *There was a notice on the door saying 'Keep out'.* □ *They were warned to keep away from the cliff edge.* □ *Keep still a minute while I take your photo.* □ *I was so sleepy I couldn't keep awake.* **c** People or things **keep** you when they make you late for something: *I'm sorry if I've kept you.* □ *What kept you?* [*same as* **hold up**, **delay**, **detain**]
3 You **keep** doing something when you continue to do it, or do it repeatedly: *He managed to keep smiling in spite of the pain he was in.* □ *You should see your doctor if you keep fainting like that.* □ *I keep forgetting to get a new light bulb.* □ *Don't keep interrupting me!*
4 a People who **keep** animals own them and care for them, as pets or for their use: *She makes a little money by keeping hens and selling the eggs.* [*same as* **support**] **b** Someone who **keeps** a shop or hotel owns it and runs it. **c** You **keep** someone when you provide them with the housing, food and clothing that they need: *He makes just enough money to keep his family.*
5 a You ask someone how they **are keeping** when you want to know if they are well. **b** Food **keeps** when it remains in a condition suitable for eating: *Cheese should keep for several days if it is stored in the fridge.* □ *Lettuce doesn't keep well.* [*same as* **last**]
6 a You **keep** a diary or journal if you record your daily activities in one; you **keep** a record or note of something if you write it down regularly: *Keep a note of your expenses.* **b** You use **keep** with several nouns that represent actions or activities, to express continuous or repeated action: *The nurses kept an hourly*

check on his pulse and temperature. ▫ *It's impossible to keep control of the situation.* ▫ *Keep a good lookout for pickpockets.*
7 a You **keep** a secret when you tell it to nobody: *Can you keep a secret?* **b** You **keep** a promise or your word when you act in the way you promised you would: *He can be relied on to keep his word.* **c** You **keep** an appointment when you arrive for it in the right place at the right time.

▻ ***noun*** (*uncount*)
Your **keep** is the cost of your food and other daily needs: *He used to hand over most of his wages to his mother to pay for his keep.* ▫ *You can stay and earn your keep by looking after the baby.*

▻ ***phrases*** **1** (*informal*) You give something to someone **for keeps** when you intend them to keep it: *'You can have the bike if you like.' 'For keeps, you mean?'* **2** You **keep to yourself**, or **keep yourself to yourself**, when you avoid the company of other people: *She was always a very quiet neighbour and kept herself to herself.* **3** You **keep** something **to yourself** when you do not tell anyone about it: *She kept her problems to herself.*

phrasal verbs
keep at You **keep at** something when you continue to work hard at it: *She didn't find maths easy but she kept at it and began to make progress.* [*same as* **stick at**]
keep back **1** You **keep** something **back** when you do not give people all the information they want: *He reported the accident to us, but we got the impression he was keeping something back.* ▫ *The police accused him of keeping back important information.* [*same as* **withold**] **2** You **keep back** laughter or tears when you control yourself and manage not to laugh or cry. [*same as* **suppress**, **stifle**] **3** You **keep back** when you stand some distance away from something: *Keep back and let the ambulance through.* [*same as* **stand** back]
keep down **1** You **keep** something **down** when you try to limit its growth or increase: *The government is not doing enough to keep food prices down.* [*same as* **control**, **restrict**] **2** People **keep down** food they have just eaten if they do not vomit: *He can't keep anything down.*
keep from **1** You **keep** someone **from** doing something when you stop them doing it: *She clung on to the rail to keep herself from falling.* [*same as* **prevent**] **2** You **keep** a fact **from** someone when you do not tell them about it: *Are you keeping something from me?*
keep off You **keep off** something when you avoid it: *People using the park are requested to keep off the grass..* ▫ *We kept off* [= avoided discussing] *the subject of money in case it caused an argument.* ▫ *Keep off fatty foods for the time being.*
keep on **1** You **keep on** doing something when you continue to do it or do it repeatedly: *I had to keep on walking in spite of the blisters.* ▫ *His own watch was broken and he kept on asking her the time.* **2** Someone **keeps on** about something when they continue to talk about it, or talk about it often: *He will keep on about my bad driving.* [*same as* **go on**, **harp on**] **3** Someone **keeps on** at you when they continually remind you about something that they think is your responsibility: *She keeps on at me to clean the car.* [*same as* **go on**, **nag**]
keep to **1** You **keep to** something when you do not go away from it: *Keep to the path and you won't get your shoes muddy.* ▫ *Our discussion time is limited, so we must keep to the subject.* [*same as* **stick to**] **2** You **keep to** a plan or schedule when you do exactly what is indicated in it and do not alter it. [*same as* **stick to**] **3** You **keep** something **to** a certain amount when you limit it to that amount: *Pocket money should be kept to about £5 per child per week.* [*same as* **restrict**] **4** You **keep** someone **to** a decision or promise when you make them do what they have decided or promised: *He had said he was willing to marry the girl and they were determined to keep him to it.*
keep up **1** One person or thing **keeps up** with another that is moving or progressing when they move or progress at the same speed as the other: *She walked so fast that I had to run to keep up with her.* ▫ *Salaries are increased regularly to keep up with inflation.* **2** You **keep up** with things that are happening if you make sure you know about them: *I do try to keep up with the latest developments.* **3** You **keep** something **up** when you continue to achieve it: *I knew he couldn't keep that pace up for long.* **4** People say **'Keep** it **up!'** to encourage you to continue to work or try as hard as you have been doing: *Your work has improved a lot - keep it up!* **5** You **keep up** some activity when you continue it without stopping; something **keeps up** when it continues: *He kept up a continuous flow of complaints throughout the car journey.* ▫ *If the hot weather keeps up, there could be a drought.*

keeper /kiːpə(r)/ *noun*: **keepers**
1 A **keeper** is a person who cares for animals in a zoo or for a collection in a museum. **2** The word **keeper** can also be combined with other words to mean a person who is in charge of that particular thing: *a shopkeeper* ▫ *a beekeeper* ▫ *a goalkeeper.*

keep-fit /kiːp'fɪt/ *noun* (*uncount*)
Keep-fit is a series or system of exercises for keeping the body in good condition.

keeping /'kiːpɪŋ/ *noun* (*uncount*)
Something that is in your **keeping** is in your care: *The jewellery is in my keeping.* ▫ *The woodland is now in the keeping of Leicestershire County Council.*
▻ ***phrases*** **1** One thing is **in keeping with** another if it is suitable for it or does not fit in with it: *You need furniture which is in keeping with the style of the house.* **2** Something that is **out of keeping with** something else is not suitable for it or does not fit in with it: *Don't wear your jeans tomorrow; they'd be out of keeping with the seriousness of the occasion.*

keepsake /'kiːpseɪk/ *noun*: **keepsakes**
A **keepsake** is a small gift kept in memory of the giver: *She gave me her brooch as a keepsake.*

kennel /'kɛnəl/ *noun*: **kennels**
A **kennel** is a small hut for a dog *eg* in a garden or yard.

kept /kɛpt/ *verb*
Kept is the past tense and past participle of **keep**.

kerb (*AmE* **curb**) /kɜːb/ *noun*: **kerbs**
The **kerb** is the row of stones forming the edging of a pavement or sidewalk: *The driver drove impatiently out from the kerb.* ▫ *I managed to stop her before she stepped off the kerb.* ▫ *The van mounted the kerb and struck a pedestrian.* [see pictures at **street**]

kernel /'kɜːnəl/ *noun*: **kernels**
1 The **kernel** is the part of a nut inside the shell, or the soft inner part of the stone of a plum or peach. **2** The **kernel** of something such as an argument or discussion is the important or essential part of it. [*same as* **heart**]

kerosene or **kerosine** /ˈkɛrəsiːn/ *noun* (*uncount*; *AmE*)
Kerosene is paraffin.

kestrel /ˈkɛstrəl/ *noun*: **kestrels**
A **kestrel** is a bird that hunts small animals and other birds for food.

ketchup /ˈkɛtʃəp/ *noun* (*uncount*)
Ketchup is a thick cold sauce made from tomatoes, vinegar and spices, used on *eg* fish and chips: *bottles of tomato ketchup.*

kettle /ˈkɛtəl/ *noun*: **kettles**
A **kettle** is a covered metal pot with a spout and handle, for boiling water in: *I'll put the kettle on.*

key /kiː/ *noun*; *adjective*; *verb*
▻ ***noun***: **keys**
1 A **key** is a piece of metal cut into a particular shape, that turns a lock, stops or starts an engine or winds a clock: *She lost the key to her front door.* ▫ *car keys.* **2** A **key** is also one of a series of buttons or levers that you press with your fingers to sound the notes on a musical instrument, or to print or display a character on a computer, typewriter or calculator: *Some of the keys on this piano are missing.* **3** In music, a **key** is a system of notes related to one another in a scale: *The piece is written in the key of G major.* **4** (*used in the singular*) The **key** to something such as a mystery is the thing that explains it: *The accident holds the key to her changed behaviour.* **5** (*used in the singular*) The **key** to success is a thing that helps you achieve it: *A good education is the key to success in life.* **6** A **key** to puzzles or exercises is a set of answers at the back of a book. **7** A **key** to a map or diagram is a table explaining the signs and symbols used.
▻ ***adjective***
A **key** person or thing is one that is important and necessary: *He plays a key role in the running of the organization.*
▻ ***verb***: **keys, keying, keyed**
You **key** information or data into a computer when you type it using a keyboard: *She keyed in her password.* ▫ *Have you keyed the corrections to the questionnaire yet?*
▻ ***phrase*** For **under lock and key** see **lock**.

keyboard /ˈkiːbɔːd/ *noun*: **keyboards**
1 The **keyboard** of a typewriter or computer terminal is the set of keys that you press when you type. **2** The **keyboard** of a musical instrument is the set of keys you press to play the notes. [see picture at **office**]

keyboarding /ˈkiːbɔːdɪŋ/ *noun*: (uncount)
Keyboarding is the process of entering data into a computer using a keyboard: *keyboarding skills.*

keyhole /ˈkiːhoʊl/ *noun*: **keyholes**
A **keyhole** is the hole in a lock into which you put the key.

keynote /ˈkiːnoʊt/ *noun*: **keynotes**
1 The **keynote** of a musical scale or key is the note on which it is based. **2** (*used in the singular, often adjectival*) The **keynote** of something such as a speech or policy is its central and most important theme or idea: *in his keynote speech to the conference* ▫ *two keynote speakers from America.*

keyring /ˈkiːrɪŋ/ *noun*: **keyrings**
A **keyring** is a ring for keeping keys on.

khaki /ˈkɑːkɪ/ *noun* (*uncount, often adjectival*)
1 Khaki is a brownish-green colour: *She was smartly turned out in khaki and black.* ▫ *a pair of khaki shorts.* **2 Khaki** is also a strong cloth of this colour, widely used for military uniforms: *soldiers in khaki* ▫ *khaki uniforms.*

kibbutz /kɪˈbʊts/ *noun*: **kibbutzim** /kɪˈbʊtsɪm/
A **kibbutz** is a farm or factory in Israel, owned and run jointly by the people who live and work there.

kick /kɪk/ *verb*; *noun*
▻ ***verb***: **kicks, kicking, kicked**
1 You **kick** something or someone when you hit them with your foot, especially with your toe: *He was kicking a ball along the pavement.* ▫ *The man had been kicked and beaten.* ▫ *She was carrying glasses in both hands and had to kick the door open.* **2** You **kick**, or **kick** your legs, when you move your legs energetically in the air or in the water, with a shaking or swinging action: *The baby was lying on the floor kicking.* ▫ *Swimmers sometimes concentrate so hard on their arm movements that they forget to kick their legs.* **3** (*informal*) You **kick** a habit when you give it up or stop it: *He's trying to kick smoking.* [*same as* **quit, pack in**]
▻ ***noun***: **kicks**
1 You give something or someone a **kick** when you kick them: *She gave his ankle a sharp kick under the table as a reminder.* **2** (*informal*) You get a **kick** out of doing something if it gives you a feeling of excitement or pleasure; you do something for **kicks** if you do it because it gives you a lot of pleasure and excitement: *Naturally you get a kick out of winning an argument.* ▫ *These kids happen to get their kicks stealing cars.* ▫ *Others beat up old ladies for kicks.* [*same as* **thrill**]

phrasal verbs
kick about or **kick around** (*informal*) Something that **is kicking around** or **kicking about** is lying somewhere and not being used: *There are plenty more knives and forks kicking about in a box upstairs, which you're welcome to use.*
kick off 1 A football match, or the players in it, **kick off** when play begins: *We kicked off late.* [see also **kick-off**] **2** (*informal*) You **kick off** with some activity when you start an event with it: *We kicked off with coffee and an introductory chat.* ▫ *I suppose we should kick off by learning one another's names.*
kick out (*informal*) To **kick** someone **out** of somewhere is to force them to leave: *She kicked out one of her tenants for making too much noise.* ▫ *He's been kicked out of his job.* [*same as* **throw out**]
kick up You **kick up** a fuss or a row about something when you behave angrily, especially unnecessarily: *He kicked up a fuss when I told him I would be half an hour late.*

kick-off /ˈkɪkɒf/ *noun*: **kick-offs**
A **kick-off** is the start of a football match, or the time at which it begins: *The kick-off was delayed because of rain.*

kid[1] /kɪd/ *noun*; *adjective*
▻ ***noun***: **kids**
1 (*informal*) A **kid** is a child: *She has three kids.* **2** A **kid** is also a young goat.
▻ ***adjective*** (*informal*)
Your **kid** sister and your **kid** brother are your younger sister and brother.

kid[2] /kɪd/ *verb*: **kids, kidding, kidded** (*informal*)
1 You **kid** someone if you tell them things that are not true, as a joke: *They hid his car and then kidded him that it had been stolen.* **2** You **kid** yourself when you deceive yourself: *She's kidding herself if she thinks she is going to find a better job than this.*
▻ ***phrase*** You say **'you're kidding'** or **'you must be kidding'** to someone who has told you something that you can hardly believe.

kidnap /ˈkɪdnap/ *verb*: **kidnaps, kidnapping** (*AmE* **kidnaping**), **kidnapped** (*AmE* **kidnaped**)
To **kidnap** someone is to capture them and keep them

prisoner illegally, usually demanding money for their release: *He was kidnapped by terrorists.* — *noun* **kidnapper:** *The police couldn't find the kidnappers.* — *noun* (*uncount or count*) **kidnapping:** *There were several kidnappings in the country last year.*

kidney /ˈkɪdnɪ/ *noun*: **kidneys**
Your **kidneys** are the two organs in your body that remove waste products from your blood and produce urine: *a kidney transplant.*

kill /kɪl/ *verb*; *noun*
▻ *verb*: **kills, killing, killed**
1 To **kill** someone or something means to cause them to die: *He killed the ants with poison.* □ *She was killed in an accident.* □ *My brother killed himself.* **2** (*informal*) Something that is **killing** you is causing you pain: *My feet are killing me.* □ *These shoes are killing me.* **3** (*informal*) Something **kills** an activity when it causes it to end or fail: *His remark killed the conversation.* **4** A drug that **kills** pain reduces it.

> Notice some differences between the various words for killing. **Kill** is a general word for causing someone or something to die: *The fire killed several people.* One person **murders** another when they kill them deliberately: *The terrorists murdered seven of the hostages.* When a lot of people are killed at the same time, especially in a particularly cruel way, they are **slaughtered** or **massacred**: *The army massacred hundreds of innocent civilians. Millions of people were slaughtered in the war.* Animals are **slaughtered** for food: *They slaughtered several sheep to provide food during the festival.* A person who is killed for political reasons is **assassinated**: *The president was assassinated last year.*

▻ *noun* (*usually in the singular*)
1 The **kill** is the act of killing a bird or animal that has been hunted. **2** The **kill** is also the bird or animal killed by a hunter: *The lioness stood over her kill.*
▻ *phrase* For **kill time** see **time**.

> ***phrasal verb***
> Something **is killed off** when it is destroyed completely: *The frost killed off the fruit.*

killer /ˈkɪlə(r)/ *noun*: **killers**
A **killer** is a person, animal or thing that kills: *Malaria is a killer in many parts of the world.*

killing /ˈkɪlɪŋ/ *noun*: **killings**
A **killing** is a murder: *There were several brutal killings in the city last weekend.*
▻ *phrase* (*informal*) You **make a killing** when you make a lot of money quickly: *Investors lost heavily on cocoa but made a killing on cotton.*

kilo /ˈkiːloʊ/ *noun*: **kilos**
A **kilo** is a kilogram: *He bought several kilos of sugar.*

kilobyte /ˈkɪləbaɪt/ *noun*: **kilobytes**
A **kilobyte** is 1024 bytes, used as a way of measuring the amount of memory a computer has.

kilogram or **kilogramme** /ˈkɪləgram/ *noun*: **kilograms** or **kilogrammes** (often written **kg**)
A **kilogram** is a measurement of weight equal to 1000 grams or 2.2 pounds: *How much does he weigh in kilograms?*

kilometre (*AmE* **kilometer**) /ˈkɪləmiːtə(r)/ or /kɪˈlɒmɪtə(r)/ *noun*: **kilometres**
A **kilometre** is a measurement of distance equal to 1000 metres or 0.62 miles: *The sea is four kilometres away from the village.* □ *The car was travelling at sixty kilometres an hour.* □ *a twenty-kilometre walk.*

kilt /kɪlt/ *noun*: **kilts**
A **kilt** is a pleated knee-length skirt, worn by women and girls, and by men as part of Scottish Highland dress.

kimono /kɪˈmoʊnoʊ/ *noun*: **kimonos**
A **kimono** is a long loose wide-sleeved Japanese garment.

kin /kɪn/ *noun* (*plural*; *formal*)
Your **kin** are you relations.
▻ *phrases*
1 For **next of kin** see its own entry. **2** For **kith and kin** see **kith**.

kind[1] /kaɪnd/ *noun*: **kinds**
1 You refer to a certain **kind** of thing when you mean one of the types or classes of that thing, or when you are thinking of the thing in terms of its particular qualities: *Most kinds of cheese are fattening.* □ *There's a funny kind of worm over here; come and look.* □ *He's off work with an infection of some kind.* □ *Her children are grown up and doing all kinds of interesting things.* □ *We think of her as a kind of legal consultant.* □ *Her problems were not the kind she wanted to discuss with her parents.* □ *'What kind of person was your father?' 'He was gentle and clever.'* □ *This is not the kind of Europe we are seeking.* □ *If I had that kind of money* [= as much money as that] *I wouldn't be working.* [*same as* **sort, type**]

> People often use the form *those* (or *these*) *kind of* with a plural noun, but it sounds better, and still has the meaning you want, if you use *that* (or *this*) *kind of*, with a singular noun: *I've never enjoyed that kind of book* (rather than *those kind of books*). With nouns that are always plural in form, such as *tights*, you can use the expressions *tights like these*, or *tights of this kind.* [see also **sort, type**]

2 You can refer to a person as a particular **kind** when describing their personality. *I'm not the pushy kind.*
▻ *phrases*
1 You use **a kind of** when giving a rough description or an indefinite idea: *The curtains are a kind of pinkish orange.* □ *I had a kind of feeling that something was wrong.* **2** (*informal*; *especially AmE*) **Kind of** is used to mean 'rather' or 'a little': *I was feeling kind of low.* □ *He was standing around kind of suspiciously.* □ *I kind of hoped he'd dance with me.* [*same as* **sort of**] **3 a** You pay someone **in kind** when you give them goods or services instead of money: *She said straight away she couldn't afford the rent, but offered to pay them in kind by doing jobs round the house.* **b** You repay someone who has treated you badly **in kind** if you treat them badly in return. **4** For **nothing of the kind** see **nothing**. **5** Something described as a thing **of a kind** is not a very good one: *I've worked out a timetable of a kind.*

kind[2] /kaɪnd/ *adjective*: **kinder, kindest**
A **kind** person is a person who is friendly, helpful and caring: *Always be kind to animals.* □ *It was kind of you to help me.* □ *He had a kind smile.* [*opposite* **unkind, cruel**]
▻ *phrases* You use **be so kind as to** and **be kind enough to** when you ask someone politely to do something for you: *Would you be so kind as to open the door for me?*

kindergarten /ˈkɪndəgɑːtən/ *noun*: **kindergartens**
A **kindergarten** is a school for children under the age of five or six. [*same as* **nursery**; compare **creche**]

kind-hearted /kaɪndˈhɑːtɪd/ *adjective*
A **kind-hearted** person is kind, caring and sympathetic.

kindle /ˈkɪndəl/ *verb*: **kindles, kindling, kindled**
1 You **kindle** something when you make it start burning: *They kindled a fire using paper and twigs.* **2** Something **kindles** an idea or feeling when it encourages or strengthens it; a feeling **kindles** when it is roused: *She blew him a kiss, perhaps only to kindle the jealousy of rival ladies.* □ *She felt a small warmth of pride kindle in her.*

kindling /ˈkɪndlɪŋ/ *noun* (*uncount*)
Kindling is the dry wood and leaves that you use to start a fire.

kindly /ˈkaɪndlɪ/ *adverb*; *adjective*
▻ ***adverb***
1 You do something **kindly** when you do it in a way which expresses kindness: *She smiled kindly at the child.* [*opposite* **unkindly**, **cruelly**] **2** If you tell someone **kindly** to do something you are telling them sternly or angrily to do it: *Kindly put that photograph back where you found it.* **3** You ask someone if they would **kindly** do something when you are politely requesting them to do it: *Would you kindly pass me the salt?* [*same as* **please**]
▻ ***adjective***: **kindlier, kindliest**
A **kindly** person or thing is kind, gentle and friendly: *a kindly smile* □ *a kindly face.* [*same as* **kind**; *opposite* **unkind**, **cruel**]
▻ ***phrases*** **1** You **don't take kindly to** something when you do not like it or do not approve of it: *He doesn't take kindly to criticism.* **2** You **look kindly on** something when you approve of it: *The government usually look kindly on this kind of approach.*

kindness /ˈkaɪndnəs/ *noun*: **kindnesses**
1 (*uncount*) **Kindness** is the quality of being kind: *He thanked them for their kindness.* **2** A **kindness** is a kind action: *It would be a kindness to help her while her husband is in hospital.*

kindred spirit /kɪndrəd ˈspɪrɪt/ *noun*: **kindred spirits**
Someone who is a **kindred spirit** is a person who has the same interests and opinions as you: *She recognized a kindred spirit in Henri.*

king /kɪŋ/ *noun*: **kings**
1 A **king** is a male ruler of a country who is not elected but is usually the son of the previous ruler: *Prince Charles will become king when his mother dies.* □ *King Henry III.* **2** The **king** of a group is the most important or strongest male member of it: *The lion is the king of the beasts.* **3** (*cards*) The **king** is the playing card bearing a picture of a king, between the queen and the ace in value: *The king of diamonds.* **4** (*chess*) In chess, the **king** is the most important piece: *the black king.*

kingdom /ˈkɪŋdəm/ *noun*: **kingdoms**
1 A **kingdom** is a region ruled by a king or queen. **2** A **kingdom** is also one of the three groups into which things in the natural world are divided; animals, birds and fish form the **animal kingdom**, plants, trees and flowers form the **plant kingdom** and stones and minerals form the **mineral kingdom**.

kingfisher /ˈkɪŋfɪʃə(r)/ *noun*: **kingfishers**
A **kingfisher** is a bird with brilliant blue and orange plumage that dives for fish in rivers and lakes.

kingpin /ˈkɪŋpɪn/ *noun*: **kingpins**
The **kingpin** of an organization is the most important person in it.

king-size /ˈkɪŋsaɪz/ or **king-sized** /ˈkɪŋsaɪzd/ *adjective*
Something that is **king-size** is larger than average: *king-size cigarettes* □ *a king-sized bed.*

kink /kɪŋk/ *noun*: **kinks**
A **kink** is a bend or twist in hair or in a piece of string, rope or wire.

kinky /ˈkɪŋkɪ/ *adjective* (*informal*): **kinkier, kinkiest**
Kinky behaviour is behaviour, especially sexual behaviour, that is strange or odd in some way.

kinship /ˈkɪnʃɪp/ *noun* (*uncount*)
Kinship is the relationship between members of a family: *the bond of kinship.*

kiosk /ˈkiːɒsk/ *noun*: **kiosks**
1 A **kiosk** is a small enclosed stall with an open window, that sells things such as sweets, newspapers, drinks and sandwiches: *She bought a magazine and a bar of chocolate at the kiosk on the station platform.* **2** A public telephone box is also called a **kiosk**. [see picture at **street**]

kipper /ˈkɪpə(r)/ *noun*: **kippers**
A **kipper** is a herring that has been salted and smoked.

kiss /kɪs/ *verb*; *noun*
▻ ***verb***: **kisses, kissing, kissed**
1 You **kiss** someone when you touch them with your lips, as a greeting or sign of affection: *She kissed him on the cheek.* □ *He kissed his wife goodbye.* **2** Two people **kiss** when they kiss each other on the lips: *They kissed goodbye.* **3** (*literary*) Something **kisses** something else when it touches it gently or lightly: *sun-kissed peaches.*
▻ ***noun***: **kisses**
A **kiss** is a touch with the lips: *He gave her a kiss goodnight.*
▻ ***phrase*** You give a person who has stopped breathing the **kiss of life** when you breathe into their mouth to try and make them start breathing again: *She saved his life by giving him the kiss of life.*

kit /kɪt/ *noun*; *verb*
▻ ***noun***: **kits**
1 A **kit** is a group of instruments or a set of equipment needed for a particular purpose and kept together: *The first-aid kit was kept under the passenger seat.* □ *Have you packed your shaving kit?* **2** (*uncount*) An athlete's, soldier's or footballer's **kit** is the clothing and equipment they need: *He had his football kit with him in a holdall.* [*same as* **tackle**, **gear**] **3** A set of parts that can be put together to make something is also called a **kit**: *He built his car from a kit.*
▻ ***verb***: **kits, kitting, kitted**

phrasal verb
kit out You **kit** someone **out** when you provide them with the clothes and equipment needed for a particular occupation or job: *She must kit herself out for her trip to Africa.* [*same as* **equip**, **fit out**]

kitchen /ˈkɪtʃən/ *noun*: **kitchens**
A **kitchen** is a room where you prepare and cook food.

kite /kaɪt/ *noun*: **kites**
A **kite** is a light frame covered with paper or some other light material that people fly in the air for fun, keeping hold of and controlling it as it flies by means of a long string.

kith and kin /kɪθ ənd ˈkɪn/ *noun* (*plural*; *old*)
Your **kith and kin** are your friends and relations.

kitten /ˈkɪtən/ *noun*: **kittens**
A **kitten** is a young cat.

kitty /ˈkɪtɪ/ *noun*: **kitties** (*usually in the singular*)
A **kitty** is an amount of money collected by a group of people for use by them all: *They each put £3 into the kitty to pay for their coffee and sandwiches.*

kiwi /ˈkiːwiː/ *noun*: **kiwis**
A **kiwi** is a bird which cannot fly, that lives in New Zealand.

kitchen

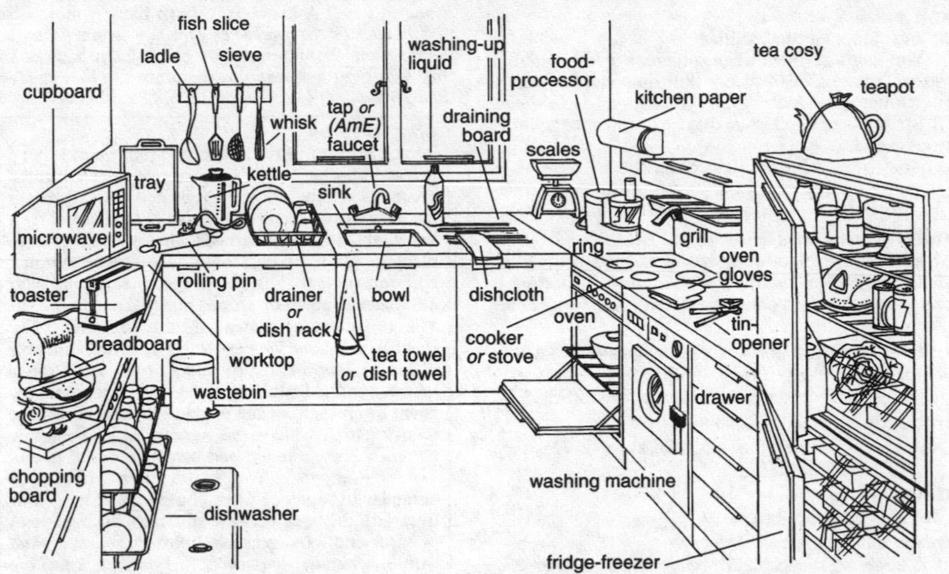

kiwi fruit /'ki:wi: fru:t/ *noun*: **kiwi fruit** or **kiwi fruits**
A **kiwi** fruit is an oval fruit with furry brown skin and dark green juicy flesh. [see picture at **fruit**]

knack /nak/ *noun* (*used in the singular*; *informal*)
You have the **knack** of doing something if you can do it easily and skilfully: *Knitting is quite easy once you've got the knack.* [*same as* **hang**]

knead /ni:d/ *verb*: **kneads, kneading, kneaded**
You **knead** something such as dough, bread or pasta when you press it hard with your hands and fingers to make it smooth and elastic and ready to cook.

knee /ni:/ *noun*: **knees**
1 Your **knees** are the joints in the middle of your legs: *She banged her knee on the table.* **2** The **knee** of a garment is the part covering the knee: *All her trousers have patches at the knees.* **3** Something is on your **knee** when it is resting on the upper surface of your thighs when you are sitting down: *The child sat on her mother's knee.*
▻ ***phrases*** **1** You **bring** people **to their knees** when you weaken, defeat or destroy them: *The country has been brought to its knees by debt and war.* **2** You are **on your knees** when you are kneeling: *He was on his knees washing the floor.*

kneecap /'ni:kap/ *noun*: **kneecaps**
The **kneecap** is the triangular bone covering the front of the knee joint.

knee-deep /ni:'di:p/ *adjective or adverb*
You are **knee-deep** in something when it reaches up to your knees: *She was knee-deep in water.* ▫ *He was standing knee-deep in mud.*

kneel /ni:l/ *verb*: **kneels, kneeling, knelt** or **kneeled**
(**Kneeled** and **knelt** can both be used as either the past tense or the past participle.)
1 You are **kneeling** when your legs are bent and your knees are touching the ground: *He was kneeling on the carpet.* **2** You **kneel**, or **kneel** down, when you bend your legs so that your knees touch the ground: *He knelt in front of the fire.* ▫ *She knelt down to pray.*

knee-length /'ni:-lɛŋθ/ *adjective*
Something that is **knee-length** comes down as far as, or up as high as, the knees: *a knee-length skirt* ▫ *knee-length socks.*

knelt /nɛlt/ *verb*
Knelt is the past tense and past participle of **kneel**.

knew /nju:/ *verb*
Knew is the past tense of **know**.

knickers /'nɪkəz/ *noun* (*plural*)
Knickers are an undergarment for women and girls, covering the bottom, and with separate holes for the legs: *two clean pairs of knickers.* [same as **pants**]

knick-knack /'nɪknak/ *noun*: **knick-knacks**
A **knick-knack** is a small ornament: *His house is full of knick-knacks from the different places he has visited.*

knife /naɪf/ *noun*; *verb*
▻ ***noun***: **knives**
A **knife** is a cutting instrument or weapon, usually in the form of a blade fitted into a handle: *knives, forks and spoons* ▫ *He was armed with a knife.* ▫ *a bread knife* ▫ *a vegetable knife.* [see picture at **tableware**]
▻ ***verb***: **knifes, knifing, knifed**
To **knife** someone means to stab them or kill them with a knife: *He was knifed on his way home from the cinema.*
▻ ***phrase*** (*informal*) Someone who **has their knife into you** is always trying or hoping to harm you: *He's had his knife into me ever since I got the job he wanted.*

knight /naɪt/ *noun*; *verb*
▻ ***noun***: **knights**
1 In medieval times, a **knight** was a man of noble rank who served his king or lord and who was trained to fight on horseback. **2** A **knight** is a man who has been given a noble rank and the title 'Sir' as a reward for service to his country or government: *He was made a knight in 1979.* **3** (*chess*) A **knight** is a piece shaped like a horse's head.
▻ ***verb***: **knights, knighting, knighted**
The king or queen **knights** a man when they give him the rank of knight and the title 'Sir'.

knighthood /ˈnaɪthʊd/ *noun*: **knighthoods**
A **knighthood** is the rank of a knight: *He was given a knighthood last year.*

knit /nɪt/ *verb*; *adjective*
▷ ***verb***: **knits, knitting, knitted**
1 You **knit** a garment when you make it from wool or some other thread using knitting needles or a machine: *I'm knitting my daughter a cardigan.* **2** Broken bones **knit** when they grow together again.
▷ ***adjective***
People are closely **knit**, tightly **knit** or close-**knit** when they are united: *The people in the village are a close-knit community.* — *adjective* **knitted:** *a knitted jumper.*

knitting /ˈnɪtɪŋ/ *noun* (*uncount*)
1 Knitting is a garment or article which is being knitted: *She put her knitting away in a bag.* **2 Knitting** is also the action of a person who knits: *He spends hours knitting.*

knitting needle /ˈnɪtɪŋ niːdəl/ *noun*: **knitting needles**
A **knitting needle** is a long thin plastic or metal stick with a point at one end, used in pairs for knitting.

knitwear /ˈnɪtwɛə(r)/ *noun* (*uncount*)
Knitwear is clothing that has been knitted: *This shop doesn't sell knitwear.*

knives /naɪvz/ *noun*
Knives is the plural of **knife**.

knob /nɒb/ *noun*: **knobs**
1 A **knob** is a round handle on a door or drawer: *She turned the knob and opened the door.* **2** A **knob** on mechanical or electrical equipment is a button that you press or turn to operate it: *The radio has a knob to control the volume and another to control the tone.* **3** A **knob** is also a hard rounded lump at the end of a stick or on a flat surface: *He banged on the door with the knob at the end of his umbrella.* **4** A **knob** of something is a small roundish lump: *a knob of butter.*

knobbly /ˈnɒblɪ/ *adjective*: **knobblier, knobbliest**
Something **knobbly** has a surface covered with lumps: *knobbly knees.*

knock /nɒk/ *verb*; *noun*
▷ ***verb***: **knocks, knocking, knocked**
1 You **knock** at a door or window when you hit or tap it several times with your knuckles, in order to get the attention of the person inside: *I knocked at the door and a voice said, 'Come in.'* □ *Try knocking on the window.* □ *Knock harder; they might not have heard you.* **2** You **knock** something, or **knock** it somewhere, when you hit it so that that it shakes, or moves somewhere, or falls over: *He stood up suddenly, knocking his chair over.* □ *I accidentally knocked my glass off the table.* □ *Someone knocked my elbow and I spilt my drink.* **3** You **knock** someone somewhere, or **knock** them unconscious, by hitting them so hard that they fall, or become unconscious: *He threatened to knock me down if I insulted him again.* □ *The blast was so fierce it knocked us off our feet.* □ *The blow knocked him senseless.* **4** You **knock** a part of your body on or against something when you accidentally let that part of you come sharply into contact with it, sometimes hurting yourself: *She knocked her head against the step when she fell.* [*same as* **bang, bump**] **5** People have a certain kind of behaviour or attitude **knocked** into or out of them when they are forced, usually by some experience, to stop behaving or thinking in a certain way: *It's time she had some common sense knocked into her.* □ *The rigorous training and the uncertainty of work had knocked the enthusiasm for acting out of him.* **6** (*informal*) You **knock** someone or something when you criticize them, often unfairly: *She was always knocking her colleagues' efforts.*
▷ ***noun***: **knocks**
1 A **knock** is the sound of someone knocking on a door or window: *There was a knock at the door and in came Susan.* **2** A **knock** is a sharp blow: *I must have got a knock on the head when I fell downstairs.* [*same as* **bang, bump**] **3** (*informal*) You can refer to a piece of bad luck or an unpleasant experience as a **knock**: *He's had a number of knocks recently, but he's survived.*

phrasal verbs

knock about or **knock around** (*informal*) **1** One person **knocks** another **about**, or **knocks** them **around**, when they hit them repeatedly: *I'm sure he's the kind of man who knocks his wife about.* **2** You **knock about** or **knock around** when you travel from place to place, or pass time, in a casual manner, without any very serious purpose; someone who **has knocked about** or **around** has had experience of a large variety of places and circumstances: *She spent a year knocking about France* (or *knocking about in France*). □ *I've knocked about; I know what's what.* **3** People or things that **are knocking about** are present in the place or situation you are referring to: *As students we were nearly all socialists, but there was also the odd communist and liberal knocking about.* **4** You **knock about** or **knock around** with someone when you spend a lot of your time with them, *eg* because you are their boyfriend or girlfriend: *At weekends I mostly knock around with my friends from school.* □ *Who's he knocking about with these days?*

knock back (*informal*) You **knock** a drink **back** when you drink it quickly or drink a lot of it: *He knocked back two glasses of whisky in less than three minutes.* □ *I think she's been knocking back the gin lately.*

knock down **1** A vehicle or its driver **knocks** someone **down** when they hit them so that they fall and get hurt or killed: *He was in serious trouble for knocking down a pedestrian on a pedestrian crossing.* □ *She was knocked down by a lorry.* [*same as* **run over**] **2** To **knock down** a building or part of a building is to remove it or destroy it deliberately: *A row of houses had to be knocked down to make way for the new road.* □ *We're planning to knock the dividing wall down so as to make one large room.* [*same as* **take down, pull down, demolish**]

knock off (*informal*) **1** You **knock** an amount **off** something when you reduce its price by that amount: *He knocked £75 off the car because it had a dent in one door.* **2** You **knock off**, or **knock off** work, when you stop work for the day: *Some people used to knock off early on Fridays.* **3** Someone **knocks** something **off** when they steal it: *Watch the customers and make sure they aren't knocking off the CDs.* [*same as* **nick**]

knock out **1** People **are knocked out** when they are hit so hard on the head that they become unconscious: *The punch knocked him out.* [see also **knockout**] **2** A competitor or team **is knocked out** of a competition when they are defeated at one of its stages and do not take any further part in it: *We were knocked out in the third round.* [*same as* **eliminate**; see also **knockout**] **3** Something such as alcohol or a drug **knocks** you **out** when it makes you sleepy or unconscious: *They gave me an injection, which knocked me out for the next few hours.*

knock up (*informal*) You **knock** something **up** when you make it quickly: *She was one of those people who could knock up a dress in an evening.*

knocker /ˈnɒkə(r)/ *noun*: **knockers**
A **knocker** or **doorknocker** is a heavy hinged piece of metal fixed to a door, used for knocking.

knock-kneed /nɒk'ni:d/ *adjective*
A **knock-kneed** person has legs that are too close together at the knee, and too far apart at the ankle.

knock-on effect /nɒkɒn ɪ'fɛkt/ *noun*: **knock-on effects**
A **knock-on effect** is an indirect effect that an action has: *Putting up the price of petrol will have a knock-on effect on transport costs.*

knockout /'nɒkaʊt/ *noun*: **knockouts**
1 A **knockout** is a blow from an opponent that makes a boxer unconscious. **2** A **knockout** is a competition in which only the winning teams or competitors go forward to the next round.

knot /nɒt/ *noun*; *verb*
▻ ***noun***: **knots**
1 A **knot** is a join or tie in a piece of string, rope or ribbon made by looping the ends around each other and pulling tight, used especially to join two pieces of string, rope or ribbon together: *He took the trouser legs and tied them in a knot.* □ *She couldn't undo the knot in the ribbon.* **2** A **knot** in hair or a piece of string, rope or ribbon is a part that is or has become twisted around itself to form a tight loop: *Her long hair often gets into knots.* **3** A **knot** of people is a small group. **4** A **knot** in a tree or piece of wood is a hard lump where a branch used to grow. **5** A **knot** is a measurement of speed at sea equal to one nautical mile (1.85 km) an hour: *The ship was travelling at a speed of 12 knots.* **6** A **knot** in your stomach is a tight feeling caused by nervousness: *I always get a knot in my stomach before exams.*
▻ ***verb***: **knots, knotting, knotted**
1 You **knot** a piece of string, rope or ribbon when you loop the ends round each other and pull tight: *She knotted the ends together.* □ *He knotted the scarf round his neck.* [*same as* **tie**] **2** Something **knots** when it becomes tangled: *The ship's rigging has become knotted.*

knotty /'nɒtɪ/ *adjective*: **knottier, knottiest**
A **knotty** problem is one that is difficult to solve.

know /noʊ/ *verb*: **knows, knowing, knew, known**
1 You **know** something when you have it in your head, and have no doubt that it is correct: *I don't know her telephone number.* □ *I didn't know the Italian word for 'size', so I just guessed.* □ *All we knew about him was that he'd trained as a social worker.* □ *She's known to be in favour of reform.* □ *I know which idea Jack will prefer.* □ *'Is she seriously injured?' 'We don't know yet.'* □ *Do you know how to thread this machine?*

> Notice that you say you *know how to* do something if you are able to do it: *Don't you know how to swim* (not *know to swim*) yet?

2 You **know** about something, or **know** of it, if you have heard about it: *I knew about the takeover.* □ *Did you know of this proposal before now?* [*same as* **be aware of**] **3** You **know** a person if you have met them and talked to them, usually enough to have become familiar with them: *They hadn't known each other for very long when they got engaged.* □ *Robin, do you know my sister? Marian, this is Robin.* □ *I know someone who could help.* [*same as* **be acquainted with**] **4** You **know** a place if you have been there and are familiar with it; you **know** things such as literary or musical works if you have read them or heard them, and are familiar with them: *I lived for a while in Warsaw, so I know it well.* □ *Oh, yes, I know the restaurant you mean.* □ *I know most of his symphonies.* □ *I don't think I know that word.* [*same as* **be acquainted with**] **5** You **know** something such as a poem, a speech, or your part in a play, if you have learnt it and remember it: *How much poetry do you know by heart?* **6** You **know** a language if you have learnt it, and can speak it and understand it: *Do you know any Russian?* □ *I knew only a few words of Malay.* **7** You **know** about a subject if you have studied it and learnt the facts about it: *She knows a lot about old movies.* **8** (*in the passive*) Someone or something **is known** as something if that is what people call them: *The huge white house on the corner was always known as 'the Wedding Cake'.*
▻ ***phrases*** **1** You **get to know** a person, place or thing when you become familiar with them and find out what they are like: *I got to know Southampton well when I was a student there.* □ *I liked her immediately and looked forward to getting to know her.* **2** (*informal*) People say **'heaven knows'**, **'God knows'** or **'goodness knows'** as an emphatic way of saying they don't know something: *I've said I'll help him but heaven knows how I'll find the time.* □ *'Where's Janet?' 'Goodness knows.'* **3** You use **'I know' a** to agree with someone, or to acknowledge a fact: *'You'll be late if you don't hurry.' 'I know.'* □ *She's only young, I know, but she should have learnt to behave by now.* **b** to announce that you have had an idea: *What shall we do to celebrate? I know, we'll go to the Indian restaurant.* **4** (*informal*) A person who is **in the know** about something is one of the few people who have information about it. **5** For **know backwards** see **backward**. **6** You say a particular person **knows best** if they are the person most likely to understand what should be done: *When it comes to understanding babies, mothers usually know best.* **7 a** You say that someone ought to **know better** if you think they should behave better, or more sensibly: *'Don't tell lies; you're big enough to know better.'* **b** Someone who **knows better** than others has information that they do not have, and therefore can judge the situation better: *He thought it would be easy, but I knew better.* **c** You **know better** than to do something if you realize you should not do it: *I knew better than to betray any signs of fear.* **8** You **let** someone **know** something when you inform them about it: *Let me know if you're going to be late.* **9** You say **'you know' a** to introduce a person or thing that you are just going to say something about: *You know the people at the end house? Well, they've got themselves a puppy.* **b** to add information that helps to identify something: *I was in the bookshop this morning; you know, the one on South Street.* **c** for emphasis, *eg* in scolding or advising: *You're being a bit silly, you know.* **d** merely as a conversational habit, to hold your hearer's attention: *She's so pleased with herself, you know, and she's got no reason to be.* **10** You say **'You never know'** to indicate that what has been suggested is not impossible: *'Do you think you might visit us in Australia one day?' 'You never know.'*

know-all /'noʊɔ:l/ *noun*: **know-alls** (*derogatory*)
A **know-all** is a person who claims to know more than other people.

know-how /'noʊhaʊ/ *noun* (*uncount*; *informal*)
Know-how is special skill or knowledge, usually in scientific or technical subjects: *We need an employee with the know-how to operate the company computer system.*

knowing /'noʊɪŋ/ *adjective*
A **knowing** gesture or comment shows that you understand something that is secret or has not been expressed directly: *In the office, there were knowing smiles at the sight of them leaving together.* □ *He gave me a knowing look.*
▻ ***phrase*** You say **there's no knowing** when it is impossible to say what will happen: *'Is the firm likely to survive?' 'There's no knowing at this stage.'*

knowingly /ˈnoʊɪŋlɪ/ *adverb*
1 You do something **knowingly** when you do it on purpose: *I would never knowingly upset you.* **2** You smile or look **knowingly** when you understand something which is secret or which has not been directly expressed: *The man passed him the package and winked knowingly.*

knowledge /ˈnɒlɪdʒ/ *noun* (*uncount*)
Knowledge is information or understanding about something: *scientific knowledge* □ *Her knowledge of French is very poor.* □ *I have no knowledge of computing.*
▻ ***phrase*** You say **to the best of my knowledge** when you think something is true but are not certain that it is: *To the best of my knowledge, all of the children have passed this exam.*

knowledgeable /ˈnɒlɪdʒəbəl/ *adjective*
A person who is **knowledgeable** knows a lot or is well-informed about a subject: *He is very knowledgeable about plants.*

known /noʊn/ *verb*
Known is the past participle of **know**.

knuckle /ˈnʌkəl/ *noun*; *verb*
▻ ***noun*****: knuckles**
Your **knuckles** are the bones which join your fingers to your hand, at the place where the fingers bend. [see picture at **body**]
▻ *verb*: **knuckles, knuckling, knuckled**

phrasal verbs
knuckle down You **knuckle down**, or **knuckle down** to work, when you begin to work hard: *You'll have to knuckle down to some hard work if you want to pass the exam.*
knuckle under (*informal*) You **knuckle under** when you are forced to obey or give way to someone.

koala /koʊˈɑːlə/ *noun*: **koalas**
A **koala**, or **koala bear**, is a small bear-like Australian animal with thick grey fur and large ears, that lives in trees.

Koran /kɔːˈrɑːn/ *noun*: **Korans**
1 (*used in the singular*) The **Koran** is the holy book of Islam. **2** A **Koran** is a copy of this book.

kosher /ˈkoʊʃə(r)/ *adjective*
Kosher food is food which has been prepared according to Jewish law: *kosher meat.*

kowtow /kɑʊˈtɑʊ/ *verb*: **kowtows, kowtowing, kowtowed**
You **kowtow** to someone when you behave in a very respectful way towards them: *She dislikes kow-towing to people in authority.*

L

L or **l** /ɛl/ *noun*: **Ls, l's**
L is the twelfth letter of the English alphabet.

lab /lab/ *noun* (*informal*): **labs**
A **lab** is a laboratory: *The blood will be sent to the lab to be analysed.*

label /ˈleɪbəl/ *noun*; *verb*
▻ ***noun***: **labels**
1 A **label** is a small written note attached to something such as a parcel, a piece of luggage, a piece of clothing, or an item for sale in a shop, giving details of things such as its contents, owner, destination, size or price: *He put labels on all his suitcases.* □ *She picked out a dress with a size-16 label and went off to the fitting room to try it on.* **2** People give you a **label** when they describe you, or think of you, in that way: *She resented the label 'housewife'.*
▻ ***verb***: **labels, labelling** (*AmE* **labeling**), **labelled** (*AmE* **labeled**)
1 You **label** something when you put a label on it: *Please ensure that your luggage is securely locked and clearly labelled.* □ *She eventually found the book she wanted on a shelf labelled 'outdoor activities'.* **2** People **label** you as something when they describe you, or regard you, in that way: *Now I'm labelled as a liar for good.* □ *I object to being labelled a 'character actress'.* [*same as* **brand, dub**]

labor see **labour**.

laboratory /ləˈbɒrətərɪ/ *noun*: **laboratories**
A **laboratory** is a room or building specially equipped for scientific experiments, research or teaching science. [see also **lab, language laboratory**]

laborious /ləˈbɔːrɪəs/ *adjective*
Something that is **laborious** takes a lot of hard work or effort: *a laborious task.* [*opposite* **easy, effortless**] — *adverb* **laboriously:** *a laboriously written book.*

labour (*AmE* **labor**) /ˈleɪbə(r)/ *noun*; *verb*
▻ ***noun***: **labours**
1 (*uncount or count*) **Labour** is hard physical or mental work: *He had worked as a builder, but since his illness was no longer capable of hard manual labour.* □ *The rewards that tutors receive for their labours are not merely financial.* **2** (*uncount*) Workers thought of as a group or class are called **labour**: *The country has a shortage of skilled labour.* **3** (*uncount*) The work done by a group of workers is also **labour**: *The workers may withdraw their labour if their demands for a pay rise are not met.* **4** (*uncount*) **Labour** is the process of giving birth to a baby: *She was in labour for six and a half hours.* **5** (*used in the singular, with a singular or plural verb*; *BrE*) **Labour** refers to the **Labour Party**, the political party representing the working people and aiming at social equality: *Labour are* (or *is*) *hoping to win the next general election.*
▻ ***verb***: **labours, labouring, laboured**
1 You **labour** when you work hard, especially with your hands: *A crew of twenty laboured from dawn to dusk in two shifts to keep the boat moving.* **2** You **labour** at or over something when you do it with difficulty: *She laboured over the report for several hours.* **3** You **labour** somewhere when you move with difficulty: *She was labouring along the road carrying a bag of shopping in each hand.* □ *I got stuck behind a procession of lorries labouring up the hill.* **4** You **labour** under a mistaken notion, a delusion or misapprehension when you keep on believing something that is not the case: *He was evidently labouring under the misapprehension that finding a job in London would be easy.* **5** You **labour** a point that you are making when you keep mentioning it or talking about it in too much detail.

laboured /ˈleɪbəd/ *adjective*
Something that is **laboured** looks as if it is achieved with difficulty: *the sound of laboured breathing.* □ *her rather laboured written style.*

labourer /ˈleɪbərə(r)/ *noun*: **labourers**
A **labourer** is a worker who does heavy physical work such as digging.

labour-saving /ˈleɪbə seɪvɪŋ/ *adjective*
A **labour-saving** device is a machine which reduces the amount of work or effort needed to do a particular task: *Washing machines, vacuum cleaners and dishwashers are all labour-saving devices.*

labyrinth /ˈlabɪrɪnθ/ *noun*: **labyrinths**
A **labyrinth** is a complicated network of passages which it is very difficult to find your way through: *a labyrinth of narrow winding streets.* [*same as* **maze**]

lace /leɪs/ *noun*; *verb*
▻ ***noun***: **laces**
1 (*uncount*) **Lace** is a delicate material made from fine thread woven into net-like patterns: *gloves decorated with lace* □ *lace curtains.* **2** (*often in the plural*) A **lace** is a string or cord drawn through holes, especially the kind used for tying shoes: *a new pair of bootlaces* □ *Wait for me; my laces have come undone.*
▻ ***verb***: **laces, lacing, laced**
1 You **lace** shoes or boots, or **lace** them up, when you tie their laces: *It takes ages to lace these boots.* □ *She bent down to lace up her trainers.* **2** You **lace** a drink when you flavour or strengthen it with alcohol, or put a drug in it.

lacerate /ˈlasəreɪt/ *verb*: **lacerates, lacerating, lacerated**
Something **lacerates** your skin when it tears or cuts it roughly: *His back had been lacerated by the whip.* — *noun* **laceration** /lasəˈreɪʃən/: *There were bruises and lacerations all over his body.*

lace-up /ˈleɪs ʌp/ *noun* (*usually in the plural*): **lace-ups**
A pair of **lace-ups** is a pair of shoes, especially leather ones, fastened with laces.

lack /lak/ *noun*; *verb*
▻ ***noun*** (*uncount; or used in the singular*)
There is a **lack** of something if it is missing, or there is not enough of it: *Lack of time is the main problem.* □ *I couldn't bear the lack of freedom any longer.* □ *Our policies suffer from a lack of fresh ideas.* [*same as* **absence, dearth**]

▻ ***verb***: **lacks, lacking, lacked**
1 You **lack** something, or **are lacking** in it, when you need it and do not have it: *She certainly isn't lacking in confidence.* ▫ *They would have preferred to educate the children privately, but lacked the means to do so.* **2** Something **is lacking** if it is missing, or if there is not enough of it: *The thing that's lacking here is somewhere for the kids to play.* ▫ *areas where rain is lacking.*
▻ ***phrases*** **1** Something that happens **for**, or **through**, **lack of** something else happens because it is missing, or there is not enough of it: *The idea had to be abandoned for lack of support.* **2** You say there is **no lack of** something if there is plenty of it, especially too much: *There was no lack of interest among the staff.* ▫ *There's never any lack of applicants to choose from.*

lackey /ˈlakɪ/ *noun* (*derogatory*): **lackeys**
A **lackey** is a servant, or a person who behaves like one by humbly obeying someone else's orders, or doing unpleasant jobs for them: *Her husband would follow her round like a lackey, ready to obey her least whim.*

laconic /ləˈkɒnɪk/ *adjective*
A person who is **laconic** uses very few words to say what they want to say: *I could never get more than a laconic 'Suit yourself' from him when I asked his advice.* [*same as* **terse**] — *adverb* **laconically:** *'Too bad,' he replied laconically.* [*same as* **tersely**, **shortly**]

lacquer /ˈlakə(r)/ *noun*; *verb*
▻ ***noun*** (*uncount*)
Lacquer is **1** a type of paint that is applied to wood or metal to form a hard shiny covering. **2** a clear liquid that people spray on their hair to keep it tidy and in place: *a canister of hair lacquer.* [*same as* **hair-spray**]
▻ ***verb***: **lacquers, lacquering, lacquered**
You **lacquer** something when you cover or coat it with lacquer: *His hair, which he used to lacquer, was combed over a bald expanse at the front.* ▫ *The white kitchen has high-gloss lacquered units.*

lacy /ˈleɪsɪ/ *adjective*: **lacier, laciest**
Something that is **lacy** is made of lace, decorated with it, or looks like lace: *lacy table mats* ▫ *lacy underwear* ▫ *a lacy jumper.*

lad /lad/ *noun*: **lads**
A **lad** is a boy or young man.

ladder /ˈladə(r)/ *noun*; *verb*
▻ ***noun***: **ladders**
1 A **ladder** is a piece of equipment that you climb up in order to reach up to a higher level, basically consisting of two upright posts with equally spaced rungs or steps fitted between them: *Sorry I took so long to pick up the phone; I was up the ladder changing a light bulb.* **2** A **ladder** in tights or stockings is a long narrow gap in the stitching where the stitches have come undone above or below a hole. **3** (*usually in the singular*) Social, academic or professional progress in its various stages can be referred to as a **ladder**: *Her husband was progressing steadily up the academic ladder and was, we understood from her, in line for a professorship.*
▻ ***verb***: **ladders, laddering, laddered**
You **ladder** your stockings or tights, or they **ladder**, when you get a hole in them which turns into a ladder as the stitches come undone: *Look, you've laddered your tights.* ▫ *My tights have gone and laddered in two places.*

laden /ˈleɪdən/ *adjective*
1 You are **laden** with things when you are carrying a lot of them: *She arrived back home laden with shopping.* ▫ *Let me help you; you're absolutely laden.* [*same as* **loaded**] **2** A tree is **laden** with fruit when there is a lot of fruit on it: *laden plum trees.*

ladies /ˈleɪdɪz/ *noun* (*singular*)
The **ladies** is a public toilet for women: *Where's the nearest ladies, I wonder?*

ladle /ˈleɪdəl/ *noun*; *verb*
▻ ***noun***: **ladles**
A **ladle** is a large spoon with a long handle and deep bowl, for serving *eg* soup. [see picture at **kitchen**, **tableware**]
▻ ***verb***: **ladles, ladling, ladled**
You **ladle** something such as soup, or **ladle** it out, when you serve it with a ladle: *She was in the kitchen, ladling porridge into bowls.* ▫ *I ladled out the soup to the guests.*

lady /ˈleɪdɪ/ *noun*: **ladies**
1 People use **lady** as a polite word for a woman: *Ask the lady at the desk to help you if you can't find the book you want.* ▫ *the old lady who lives next door* ▫ *I know a French lady who might give you lessons.* ▫ *No, it was a lady doctor I saw last time.* **2** A woman who is referred to as a **lady** behaves in the well-mannered and dignified way that people associate with the upper classes: *You could tell she was a lady from the way she spoke.* **3** (*rather old*) A **lady** is a woman from a noble or aristocratic family: *The hall will be full of lords and ladies, and there'll be music and dancing.* [see also **lord**] **4 Lady** is a title used before the names of certain women who have the rank of a peer, or whose husbands have knighthoods; 'my **lady**' is sometimes used to address women of noble rank: *Lady Olga Maitland spoke next.* ▫ *It's a call for you, my lady.* [see also **lord**, **knight**] **5** Things relating to or intended for women sometimes have **ladies'** or **lady's** in their name: *Cheltenham Ladies' College* ▫ *The ladies' shoe department is on the third floor.* **6** You can address a group of women as **'ladies'**, usually when you are getting their attention; you address a mixed gathering as **'Ladies** and Gentlemen': *Ladies, perhaps we could begin the proceedings.*

ladybird /ˈleɪdɪbɜːd/ *noun*: **ladybirds**
A **ladybird** is a small red beetle with black spots.

ladylike /ˈleɪdɪlaɪk/ *adjective*
A **ladylike** woman behaves in a polite and dignified way.

ladyship /ˈleɪdɪʃɪp/ *noun*: **ladyships**
You use 'your **ladyship**, 'her **ladyship**' and 'their **ladyships**' to address or refer to women who have the rank of a peer: *We are most grateful to your ladyship for agreeing to attend.* ▫ *Her ladyship will see you now.*

lag[1] /lag/ *noun*; *verb*
▻ ***noun***: **lags** (*usually in the singular*)
A time **lag** is a delay or a period of waiting between events: *There's usually a short time lag before the treatment takes effect, but you should feel the benefit of it in a week or so.* ▫ *There's at least a two-month lag beween ordering goods and receiving them.*
▻ ***verb***: **lags, lagging, lagged**

phrasal verb
One person or thing **lags behind** another when they move or progress slower, and get left behind: *The children were getting tired and beginning to lag behind.* ▫ *Salaries in Britain lag behind those in many other European countries.*

lag[2] /lag/ *verb*: **lags, lagging, lagged**
You **lag** something such as a boiler or water pipes, or the inside of a roof, when you cover them with a thick material so as to stop heat escaping.

lager /ˈlɑːgə(r)/ *noun*: **lagers**
1 (*uncount*) **Lager** is a type of light beer. **2** A **lager** is a bottle or glass of lager: *He asked the waiter for two lagers and a glass of brandy.*

lagoon /ləˈguːn/ *noun*: **lagoons**
A **lagoon** is a shallow area of calm water separated from the sea by sandbanks or rocks.

laid /leɪd/ *verb*
Laid is the past tense and past participle of **lay**.

laid up /leɪd ˈʌp/ *adjective*
You are **laid up** when you are ill or injured and have to stay in bed: *I was laid up for three weeks with pneumonia this last winter.*

lain /leɪn/ *verb*
Lain is the past participle of **lie**[2].

lair /lɛə(r)/ *noun*: **lairs**
An animal's **lair** is the place, usually underground and well-concealed, where it lives.

lake /leɪk/ *noun*: **lakes**
A **lake** is a large area of fresh water surrounded by land: *pollution of our lakes and rivers* ▫ *We had rented a cottage beside Lake Windermere.*

lamb /lam/ *noun*: **lambs**
1 A **lamb** is a young sheep. **2** (*uncount*) **Lamb** is the meat of a lamb: *roast lamb with mint sauce.*

lame /leɪm/ *adjective*: **lamer, lamest**
1 A person or animal that is **lame** is unable to walk properly, usually because their legs, or one of their legs, has been injured, or weakened by illness: *The hip operation had left her slightly lame.* ▫ *The large field was occupied by a solitary lame donkey.* **2** A **lame** excuse or argument is one that does not sound very good or convincing: *I made the rather lame excuse that my alarm had failed to go off.* — *adverb* **lamely**: *'Well, it isn't my fault,' he said lamely.* — *noun* (*uncount*) **lameness**: *The operation may leave you with a certain degree of lameness, but it will hardly be noticeable to other people.*

lament /ləˈmɛnt/ *verb*; *noun*
▻ ***verb***: **laments, lamenting, lamented**
You **lament** something when you feel sad about it or express your sadness or regret: *She's still lamenting the death of her cat.* [*same as* **mourn**, **grieve**; *opposite* **celebrate, rejoice**]
▻ ***noun***: **laments**
A **lament** is an expression of sadness or regret, sometimes in the form of a poem or song: *a Lament for the Dead.*

lamentable /ˈlaməntəbəl/ *adjective*
Something that is **lamentable** is very disappointing or bad: *The old cinema was in a lamentable condition.* ▫ *Most people's performance in the general knowledge test was lamentable.* — *adverb* (*intensifying*) **lamentably:** *There was lamentably little support for carers.*

lamp /lamp/ *noun*: **lamps**
A **lamp** is a piece of equipment for producing a steady light, usually by means of a bulb which uses electricity, or by burning gas or oil. [see picture at **bedroom, living room**]

lamp post /ˈlamp poʊst/ *noun*: **lamp posts**
A **lamp post** is a tall concrete or metal pole with a light at the top, standing at the edge of a raod or street. [see picture at **house, street**]

lampshade /ˈlampʃeɪd/ *noun*: **lampshades**
A **lampshade** is a cover placed over a lamp or light bulb for the purpose of decoration and to soften or direct the light coming from it. [see picture at **living room**]

land /land/ *noun*; *verb*
▻ ***noun***: **lands**
1 (*uncount or used in the singular*) **Land** is that part of the earth's surface not covered by water: *In those days, goods were transported more commonly by water than by land.* ▫ *Our ship was now only a few miles from dry land.* ▫ *The land along the west coast is being eaten away by the sea.* **2** (*uncount or used in the singular*) **Land** is ground, especially in terms of the uses that can be made of it; people who work on the **land** farm it: *a plot of building land* ▫ *They've bought some land to keep sheep on.* ▫ *acres of farmland* ▫ *people who cultivate the land for a living.* **3** (*often in the plural*) You refer to the area of land that someone owns as their **land** or **lands**: *His lands extend as far as the river.* **4** A **land** is a country: *people in faraway lands* ▫ *Canada is my native land.*
▻ ***verb***: **lands, landing, landed**
1 a An aircraft, or the people travelling in it, **land** somewhere when the aircraft arrives there after a flight: *She's due to land at Heathrow this afternoon.* ▫ *The plane landed early.* **b** A pilot **lands** an aircraft when he or she brings it down to earth: *She was forced to land the plane on the lake.* **2** You **land** somewhere when you come to rest there after flying or falling: *She fell off the ladder and landed in the flower bed.* ▫ *A bird flew down and landed on the roof.* ▫ *I slipped again but this time managed to land on my feet.* **3** To **land** goods, cargo or passengers is to unload them after a journey, especially one by ship. **4** (*informal*) You **land**, or **land** yourself, in a difficult situation when you get into it; someone **lands** you in a difficult situation when they are the cause of your getting into it: *You're going to land yourself in an intolerable situation if you don't assert yourself now.* ▫ *He's always landing me in trouble.* ▫ *Eventually he landed in jail.* **5** Someone **lands** you with a problem or something unwanted when they leave you to deal with it: *I found myself landed with the bill for the whole meal.*

phrasal verb
(*informal*) You **land up** in a particular place or situation when you arrive there, especially without particularly intending to, after a journey or a series of events: *After months of travelling she landed up in Istanbul.* ▫ *I didn't want to land up teaching English in some remote place.* [*same as* **end up**]

landed /ˈlandɪd/ *adjective*
A **landed** person owns a lot of land: *a landed family.*

landing /ˈlandɪŋ/ *noun*: **landings**
1 (*count or uncount*) **Landing** is the process of coming to shore or to ground after a flight: *Pilots are trained to deal with emergency landings.* ▫ *Landing was impossible at Chicago because of the fog.* [compare **takeoff**] **2** A **landing** is a level area at the top of the staircase or between flights of steps. **3** A **landing**, or **landing stage**, is a platform where passengers either get on to or leave a boat.

landlady /ˈlandleɪdɪ/ *noun*: **landladies**
1 Someone's **landlady** is the woman in whose house they rent a room or flat, or who owns the house in which they live, and to whom they pay rent: *I've spoken to his landlady, and she says he did not come home last night.* **2** The **landlady** of a pub is the woman who owns or manages it.

landlocked /ˈlandlɒkt/ *adjective*
A country that is **landlocked** is completely surrounded by land and has no sea coast.

landlord /ˈlandlɔːd/ *noun*: **landlords**
1 Someone's **landlord** is the man who owns the

house in which they rent a room or flat, or owns the house in which they live, and to whom they pay rent. **2** The **landlord** of a pub is the man who owns or manages it.

landmark /ˈlandmɑːk/ *noun*: **landmarks**
1 A **landmark** is a very noticeable building or other feature in a city or in a landscape, that helps you find your position: *In the distance was Jurby church, a familiar white landmark on the northwest coast.* **2** An important event or stage in the development of something is also called a **landmark**: *landmarks in the history of science, such as the invention of the telescope.* [*same as* **milestone**, **turning point**]

landscape /ˈlandskeɪp/ *noun*: **landscapes**
1 The **landscape** is the area and features of land that you can see when you look around: *From Mdina's walls we looked out on Malta's bare brown landscape, dotted with clusters of bright yellow stone buildings in various stages of completion.* **2** A **landscape** is a painting of a countryside scene: *The walls were hung with watercolour landscapes.*

landslide /ˈlandslaɪd/ *noun*: **landslides**
1 A **landslide** is a fall of land or rock down the side of a hill or cliff. [compare **avalanche**] **2** (*often adjectival*) In an election, a **landslide** victory is one in which the winning party or candidate gets a very large proportion of the votes: *Blair and his men are no doubt expecting a Labour landslide.*

lane /leɪn/ *noun*: **lanes**
A **lane** is **1** a narrow road or street in the country or in a town: *He turned left along an unfamiliar little lane.* **2** one of the marked divisions on a wide road or motorway: *I was just moving into the fast lane to overtake.* **3** one of the marked divisions of an athletics track or swimming pool, for the use of an individual competitor in a race: *Britain's Sharon Gould is in the far lane.*

language /ˈlaŋgwɪdʒ/ *noun*: **languages**
1 (*uncount*) **Language** is the ability to use speech to communicate: *It's important to diagnose deafness early, otherwise the child will have difficulty acquiring language.* **2** A **language** is the speech of a particular nation or group of people: *He's studying Oriental languages.* □ *How many languages can you speak?* **3** (*uncount*) The **language** of a particular written or spoken communication is the way words are used in it: *I would have known him anywhere, this man with the big belly, colourful language, and beaming red face.* **4** (*uncount or used in the singular*) A form of communication that doesn't use words can also be referred to as a **language**: *Whales and dolphins have their own highly developed language.* □ *I learnt sign language as part of my teacher-training course.* **5** (*uncount or used in the singular*) The vocabulary used by particular groups, *eg* of specialists in a certain subject, is the **language** of that group: *I don't understand all that legal language; can't you explain it to me more simply?* □ *the constantly changing and developing language of the street.* **6** (*computers*) A system of words, signs and symbols used to write computer programs is called a **language**: *a programming language.*

language laboratory /ˈlaŋgwɪdʒ ləbɒrətərɪ/ *noun*: **language laboratories**
A **language laboratory** is a room, *eg* in a school or university, that has equipment such as tape recorders to help students learn foreign languages.

languid /ˈlaŋgwɪd/ *adjective*
A **languid** person does everything rather slowly, and shows little energy or liveliness: *She favoured me with a languid smile.* [*same as* **lethargic**, **apathetic**; *opposite* **lively**, **energetic**] — *adverb* **languidly:** *He ate his meal languidly.*

languish /ˈlaŋgwɪʃ/ *verb* (*literary*): **languishes**, **languishing**, **languished**
People **languish** when they lose health and strength, usually from having to stay in an unhappy or confined situation: *people whose lives are being wasted as they languish year after year in prison.*

languor /ˈlaŋgə(r)/ *noun* (*uncount*; *literary*)
Languor is a feeling of weakness, tiredness and lack of enthusiasm or interest.

lanky /laŋkɪ/ *adjective*: **lankier**, **lankiest**
A **lanky** person is tall and thin and moves awkwardly.

lantern /ˈlantən/ *noun*: **lanterns**
A **lantern** is a kind of lamp used mainly in past times, consisting of a candle or oil lamp burning inside a metal-framed, glass-sided container, with a handle to hang it up or carry it by.

lap[1] /lap/ *noun*: **laps**
Your **lap** is the flat, horizontal area formed by your thighs when you are sitting down: *She sat with the baby on her lap.*

lap[2] /lap/ *verb*: **laps**, **lapping**, **lapped**
1 An animal **laps** a liquid when it drinks by scooping liquid up with its tongue: *the faint sound made by the cat as it lapped its milk.* **2** Water **laps** against something when it flows against it with a light splashing sound: *The sea lapped against the side of the boat.*

> ***phrasal verb***
> **lap up** **1** An animal **laps up** a drink when it drinks it, especially eagerly, using its tongue to scoop it up: *The dog lapped up the spilt beer with apparent enjoyment.* **2** People **lap up** something such as praise, gossip or information when they enjoy hearing it, and accept it eagerly: *She stood at the front of the stage, arms spread wide, lapping up the applause.* □ *It's all nonsense, but people lap it up all the same.*

lap[3] /lap/ *noun*; *verb*
▻ ***noun***: **laps**
A **lap** is one circuit of a racecourse or other track: *He was overtaken on the final lap.*
▻ ***verb***: **laps**, **lapping**, **lapped**
You **lap** another runner on a race track when you overtake them while they are still on their previous lap.

lapel /ləˈpɛl/ *noun*: **lapels**
The **lapels** of a jacket are the two sections that are joined to the collar and folded back against your chest: *He was wearing a little silver cross pinned to his lapel.*

lapse /laps/ *noun*; *verb*
▻ ***noun***: **lapses**
1 A **lapse** is an unusual instance of bad behaviour from someone who normally behaves well: *We'll forget yesterday's incident; I'm sure it was just an unfortunate lapse on your part.* **2** You have a **lapse** of concentration when you stop concentrating, so that you are not performing at your best: *McEnroe suffered an unexpected lapse and succumbed to the efforts of Connors.* **3** You have a **lapse** of memory when you can't remember something that you usually know perfectly well: *You get these terrible lapses of memory when you're trying to introduce one person to another, and find you you've forgotten the name of one of them.* **4** (*used in the singular*) **a** A **lapse** of time is an amount of time that has passed: *There was to be a lapse of two*

years before they met again. □ *She seemed unconscious of the time lapse between his visits.* [*same as* **gap**] **b** A **lapse** of a certain amount of time is also a break of that length in some activity: *Except for a lapse of a few weeks, associated with some crisis over a deadline, she had visited the health club pretty regularly.*

▻ ***verb*: lapses, lapsing, lapsed**

1 You **lapse** into a particular, often less desirable, way of behaving or talking when you start behaving or talking in that way: *He lapsed into a depressed silence.* □ *I'm afraid I've lapsed back into my old unhealthy eating patterns.* □ *When excited about something she would lapse into Polish.* **2** An arrangement or contract **lapses** when it comes to an end; your membership of a society lapses when you fail to pay your membership fee: *I'd lost interest in the Pictish Society and decided to let my membership lapse.*

lapsed /lapst/ *adjective*

Lapsed describes people who were once a certain thing, but have stopped being that thing: *I learnt that he was a lapsed Catholic.* □ *I'm a lapsed vegetarian.*

laptop /'laptɒp/ *noun*: **laptops**

A **laptop**, or **laptop computer**, is a small portable computer intended for use away from the office: *They didn't seem to mind me using the laptop on the plane.*

larch /lɑːtʃ/ *noun*: **larches**

A **larch** is a tall tree with needle-like leaves and cones.

lard /lɑːd/ *noun* (*uncount*)

Lard is soft white fat from pigs, used in cooking.

larder /'lɑːdə(r)/ *noun*: **larders**

A **larder** is a cool room or cupboard where food is stored.

large /lɑːdʒ/ *adjective*: **larger, largest**

Something that is **large** is big or above average in physical size, or great or above average in amount or quantity: *They own a large car.* □ *He was a large man; it took four of us to lift him.* □ *She has a large family.* □ *He disappeared owing the company a large amount of money.* [*opposite* **small**] — *noun* (*uncount*) **largeness:** *I was startled by the largeness of the figure and thought there had been a mistake.*

Notice that **large** is more formal than **big** and is generally preferred to it in referring to the sizes of goods on sale, and in talking about amounts or quantities: *Do you have these boots in a larger size? A large number of people were already assembled in the hall.* [compare **big, great**]

▻ ***phrases*** **1 a** If you refer to people **at large** you mean most people or people in general: *I know that the public at large aren't interested in this issue.* **b** A dangerous person or animal that is **at large** has escaped from prison or captivity and has not yet been recaptured: *They were warned that a convicted murderer was at large in the area.* **2** Something that is so **by and large** is so in a general way: *By and large it was a successful holiday.*

largely /'lɑːdʒlɪ/ *adverb*

1 Something that is **largely** true is almost completely true: *Incidents like this one go largely unnoticed by the media.* **2 Largely** is used to introduce the chief reason for something: *I had to admit that my success had been largely due to luck.* □ *I had not contacted her again, largely because I did not want to get involved in her problems.*

large-scale /'lɑːdʒskeɪl/ *adjective*

1 Large-scale events or activities affect a wide area: *A large-scale-search for survivors has been mounted.* **2** A **large-scale** map shows an area of land on a large enough scale for small details to be represented on it: *We managed to procure a large-scale map of Mount Mulanje.*

lark[1] /lɑːk/ *noun*: **larks**

A **lark** is a small brown bird that nests on the ground, and sings sweetly as it flies high overhead.

lark[2] /lɑːk/ *noun* (*usually in the singular*; *informal*): **larks**

People do something for a **lark** when they do it for fun or as a joke.

phrasal verb

(*informal*) You **lark about** or **lark around** when you do silly things for fun.

larva /'lɑːvə/ *noun*: **larvae** /'lɑːvɪ/

A **larva** is an insect in a worm-like state before it develops into the winged adult.

laryngitis /larɪn'dʒaɪtɪs/ *noun* (*uncount*)

Laryngitis is a painful inflamed condition affecting your larynx.

larynx /'larɪŋks/ *noun*: **larynxes**

Your **larynx** is the hollow organ in your throat, containing your vocal cords, the folds of tissue that vibrate to produce your voice.

lasagne /lə'zanjə/ *noun* (*uncount*)

Lasagne is pasta in the form of wide flat strips, or a dish consisting of layers of these alternating with layers of meat and tomatoes and covered with cheese sauce.

laser /'leɪsə(r)/ *noun*: **lasers**

A **laser** is an intensely bright and powerful beam of light, used to cut hard materials, and also used in surgery to perform operations.

lash /laʃ/ *noun*; *verb*

▻ ***noun*: lashes**

1 (*usually in the plural*) Your **lashes** are the tiny hairs that grow along the edge of your eyelids. [*same as* **eyelash**] **2** A **lash** is **a** the strip of leather at the end of a whip: *The tip of the lash caught his leg and made it sting.* **b** a stroke with a whip on a person's back, as a punishment: *He was sentenced to twelve lashes.*

▻ ***verb*: lashes, lashing, lashed**

1 To **lash** someone is to strike them with a whip, especially as a punishment. **2** Wind, waves or rain **lash** something when they beat against it violently: *She could hear the rain lashing against the windows.* **3** A fish **lashes** around or **lashes** its tail when it moves violently, waving its tail: *The shark was lashing about in the water.*

phrasal verbs

lash together You **lash** two things **together**, or **lash** one thing **to** another, when you tie them together tightly: *He lashed the boxes together.* □ *He lashed the buoy to the side of the boat.*

lash out 1 You **lash out** at someone when you suddenly try to hit them: *He lashed out at me with a knife.* **2** You also **lash out** at someone or something when you criticize them fiercely.

lass /las/ *noun*: **lasses**

A **lass** is a girl or young woman.

lasso /lə'suː/ *noun*; *verb*

▻ ***noun*: lassos** or **lassoes**

A **lasso** is a long rope with a loop which tightens when the rope is pulled, used *eg* for catching animals.

▻ ***verb*: lassoes, lassoing, lassoed**

You **lasso** an animal when you catch it with a lasso.

last¹ /lɑːst/ *determiner or adjective; pronoun; adverb*

▻ ***determiner*** or ***adjective***

1 a Last describes the most recent occasion, period of time, event or thing, or the one before the present one: *I saw her only last week.* □ *We went to France for our holidays last year.* □ *The last book I read was a biography.* □ *Our last party was a disaster.* [see also note at **latest**]

> Notice that when you are referring to events that relate to a point in the past rather than to the present, you usually replace **last** with *the* and *before*, or *the previous*: *I'd been in Devon the weekend before* (or *the previous weekend*). *He had sounded so depressed in his previous* (or *last*) *letter*.
> Notice also that although you can refer to the night before today as *last night*, you have to say *yesterday morning*, *yesterday afternoon* and *yesterday evening*.

b 'The **last**' is used with a particular length of time to mean that length of time up to the present: *He's been working in Birmingham for the last three years.* □ *I've been in bed ill for the last week.* [*same as* **past**]
2 The **last** thing is **a** the one that comes at the end of a series or row of things: *We caught the last train back to town.* □ *Their house is the last one on this side of the lane.* □ *My interview was last.* [*opposite* **first**] **b** the only one that is left: *He ate the last cake.* □ *Workmen were busy removing the last remains of the crashed plane.* □ *I'm giving you one last chance to apologize.*
3 You can refer to an unlikely or unsuitable person or thing as the **last** person to do something, or to do something to, or the **last** thing to do: *I'm afraid I'm the last person to give you advice.* □ *She's the last person I'd want to upset.* □ *If you've got a sore throat, singing is the last thing you should be doing.*

▻ ***pronoun:*** *She was the last to arrive.* □ *They were the last to board the plane.* □ *This is the last* [= all that remains] *of the milk.* □ *The last I heard of him* [= the last news I received about him] *was that he had found a job in Spain.* □ *He walked out and that was the last we saw of him* [= we never saw him again]. □ *I'd be the last* [= the person least likely] *to criticize his efforts.*

▻ ***adverb***

1 Something that happens **last** happens after everything else, or comes at the end: *She spoke last in the debate.* □ *He came last in the race.* [*opposite* **first**] **2** Something that **last** happened on a particular occasion has not happened since then: *I last went to Italy in 1986.* □ *When did you last see your father?* **3** (*sentence adverb*) **Last** can also be used to introduce a final point: *Last, I'd like to thank my parents.* [*same as* **lastly**; *opposite* **first, firstly**]

▻ ***phrases*** **1** Something that happens **at last** or **at long last** happens after a long time, or after a long period of waiting: *At last I can relax.* □ *At long last the guests departed.* **2** The week, year or time **before last** is the week, year or occasion before the most recent one: *We visited America the year before last.* □ *I think we mentioned this in the tutorial before last.* **3** You use expressions such as '**down to the last** detail, penny or person' to mean that everything or everybody is included, however unimportant: *He knew exactly how much money he had, down to the last penny.* **4** For **last but not least** see **least**. **5** You use **last but two, last but three** and so on to indicate that a thing or person is that many places before the final one in a series; or you can use **second last, third last** and so on to indicate that a thing or person is that many places before the end: *She lost her passport on the last day but one* (or *the second last day*) [= on the day before the last day] *of her holiday.* □ *She was the last but three* (or *fourth last*) *in the queue.* **6** You do something **last thing** when you do it after doing everything else, especially before leaving or going to bed: *My husband always locked up last thing at night.* [*opposite* **first thing**] **7** You leave something **till last**, or something waits **till last**, when you deal with it after you have dealt with everything else: *The ironing can wait till last.*

last² /lɑːst/ *verb*: **lasts, lasting, lasted**

1 Something **lasts** when it continues to exist or happen: *The warm weather only lasted a couple of weeks.* □ *I wish the holiday could last forever.* **2** Something such as food **lasts** when it remains in good condition: *This bread will only last one more day.* **3** An amount of something **lasts** for a period of time when there is enough of it to meet your needs during that period of time: *I've got enough milk to last us two days.* □ *There isn't enough bread to last till Thursday.*

lasting /ˈlɑːstɪŋ/ *adjective*

Something that is **lasting** exists or continues for a long time or permanently: *a lasting friendship.* [*same as* **abiding**; *opposite* **short-lived**]

lastly /ˈlɑːstlɪ/ *adverb*

1 (*sentence adverb*) You use **lastly** to introduce a final point that is connected to those you have already mentioned: *Lastly, I'd like to thank everyone who helped organize the tea and coffee.* [*same as* **finally**]
2 Lastly is also used to introduce the last action or event in a series: *He peeled the potatoes, scrubbed the carrots and put the meat in the oven. Lastly, he prepared the salad.* [*same as* **finally**]

last-minute /lɑːstˈmɪnɪt/ *adjective*

Something that is **last-minute** is made, done or given at the latest possible moment: *She still had some last-minute Christmas presents to buy.*

latch /latʃ/ *noun; verb*

▻ ***noun***: **latches**

1 A **latch** is a fastening for a door consisting of a bar which is lowered or raised by a lever or string. **2** A **latch** is also a lock for a door which can be opened from the inside by a handle, but from the outside only by using a key.

▻ ***verb***: **latches, latching, latched**

You **latch** a door or gate when you fasten it: *She went out and latched the door.*

▻ ***phrase*** A door that is **on the latch** is shut but not locked.

> ***phrasal verb***
> **latch on to 1** You **latch on to** someone if you attach yourself to them, usually because you find them interesting or useful: *He latched on to her and followed her everywhere* **2** You **latch on to** something when you understand it or realize what it means: *It took her a moment to latch on to what they were arguing about.*

late /leɪt/ *adjective or adverb; adjective*

▻ ***adjective or adverb***: **later, latest**

1 Something or someone that is **late** comes, arrives or happens after others, or after the expected, normal or proper time: *The train was late.* □ *I'm sorry to be so late.* □ *I expect to be home late.* □ *We had a late breakfast at about 11.00 am.* □ *I apologize for my late application.* □ *She arrived late for her appointment.* □ *The film started late.* □ *I got up very late this morning.* □ *I've been having too many late nights.* [*opposite* **early**]
2 Late also means far on in the day or night or nearly at the end of something: *She got home by late after-*

noon. □ *Her baby was born late in 1992.* □ *I usually get a late bus home on Fridays.* □ *It's getting late; I must go.* □ *Isn't it a bit too late to telephone them?* □ *He started playing tennis late in life.* □ *Her late compositions are less easy to interpret.* [*opposite* **early**]

▻ ***adjective*** (*only before a noun*)
Late is used in referring to someone who has died, especially recently: *Her late husband was a teacher.*

▻ ***phrases*** **1 As late as** draws attention to a surprisingly recent or late date or time: *In Germany, even as late as 1960 trousers were thought rather daring for women.* **2** (*formal*) Something that has been happening **of late** has been happening recently: *He hasn't been feeling very well of late.* [*same as* **lately**, **recently**] **3 a** It is **too late** for something, or to do something, if that thing is no longer possible or suitable: *It's too late to change the arrangements now.* □ *The doctor reached her too late to save her life.* **b** You realize or notice something **too late** if you do so when the harm you could have prevented by realizing earlier has already been done: *I asked about her parents, remembering too late that her father had died only a month previously.*
[see also **later**, **latest**]

latecomer /ˈleɪtkʌmə(r)/ *noun*: **latecomers**
A **latecomer** is someone who arrives for a performance or meeting after it has already begun.

lately /ˈleɪtlɪ/ *adverb*
Something that has happened **lately** has happened in the recent past or not long ago: *I haven't seen him very much lately.* [*same as* **recently**]

latent /ˈleɪtənt/ *adjective*
Something that is **latent** is present but hidden and not yet developed: *a latent talent for languages.*

later /ˈleɪtə(r)/ *adjective or adverb*
1 Later is the comparative form of **late**: *I got to the theatre after the play had started, and Peter was even later.* □ *We set off later than we'd intended to.* **2** One thing happens **later** than another if it happens after it; '**later**' and '**later** on' mean after the present time, or after the time you are referring to: *These poems were written much later than the ones we've just read.* □ *I went into hospital and the baby was born four hours later.* □ *I haven't time now; I'll deal with it later.* □ *I can ring you later on if you're busy now.* □ *I was planning to go out later on this evening.* □ *Some points we must consider now; others will be relevant at a later stage.* **3 Later** also refers to the last part of a period of time, *eg* your life: *in the later part of the century* □ *They develop bronchial trouble in later life.*

▻ ***phrase*** For **sooner or later** see **sooner**.

latest /ˈleɪtɪst/ *adjective; noun*

▻ ***adjective***
1 Latest is the superlative form of **late**: *The latest date on which we can accept applications is 31 January.* **2** Something that is the most recent of its kind, or the most up-to-date can be described as the **latest** one: *Her latest book is about her travels in Egypt.* □ *I've prepared three versions of this document and this one is the latest.* □ *the latest fashions in swimwear* □ *What's the latest news?*

> Like **latest**, **last** can mean 'most recent', but **last** often has the meaning 'the most recent before the present one': *What is her latest book about? I didn't enjoy his last film but this one is an improvement.*

▻ ***noun*** (*used in the singular*)
The **latest** is the most recent or most up-to-date news or information: *Have you heard the latest?*

▻ ***phrase*** Something that must, or will, happen or be done by a certain time **at the latest** must or will happen or be done at or before that time, and not after: *I have to return these books to the library by Friday at the latest.*

lathe /leɪð/ *noun*: **lathes**
A **lathe** is a machine which holds wood and metal while it is being cut and shaped.

lather /ˈlɑːðə(r)/ *noun; verb*

▻ ***noun*** (*uncount or used in the singular*)
Lather is the white foam that is produced when soap is mixed with water.

▻ ***verb***: **lathers, lathering, lathered**
1 Soap **lathers** in water when it produces a mass of small bubbles or foam: *This washing powder doesn't lather very well.* **2** You **lather** something when you rub it with soap to form a lather, or cover it with lather.

Latin /ˈlatɪn/ *noun* (uncount)
Latin is the language that was spoken by the ancient Romans.

latitude /ˈlatɪtjuːd/ *noun*: **latitudes**
1 The **latitude** of a place is its distance north or south of the equator, measured in degrees: *The latitude of the island is twenty degrees north.* [compare **longitude**] **2** (*uncount; formal*) **Latitude** the freedom to choose how to behave or act: *She doesn't allow her children any latitude.*

latter /ˈlatə(r)/ *adjective; noun*

▻ ***adjective***
The **latter** part of something is the part that is nearer to the end: *She didn't enjoy the latter part of the holiday.*

▻ ***noun*** (*singular or plural*) You use 'the **latter**' to refer to the second of two people, things, or groups just mentioned: *The college offered courses in Russian and Chinese, and I decided to enrol for the latter.* □ *We've had replies from Dickinsons and from Arnolds, and the latter are prepared to offer us a discount.* [compare **former**]

latterly /ˈlatəlɪ/ *adverb*
Something that has happened or been done **latterly**, has happened or been done recently: *She hasn't been feeling very well latterly.*

lattice /ˈlatɪs/ *noun*: **lattices**
A **lattice** is an open frame made from crossed narrow strips of wood or metal, used *eg* for gates and fences, or for decoration.

laudable /ˈlɔːdəbəl/ *adjective* (*formal*)
Something that is **laudable** is worthy of praise: *This is a laudable first attempt at portrait painting.* [*same as* **praiseworthy**, **creditable**]

laugh /lɑːf/ *verb; noun*

▻ ***verb***: **laughs, laughing, laughed**
You **laugh** when you make the sound with your voice that shows you are amused: *You don't have to laugh at my jokes.* □ *They couldn't stop laughing.*

▻ ***noun***: **laughs**
A **laugh** is an act of laughing, or the sound you make when laughing: *They had a good laugh watching the children playing on the beach.* □ *His jokes never get many laughs.*

▻ ***phrases*** **1** You do something **for a laugh** or **for laughs** when you do it for fun or as a joke: *She hid his shoes for a laugh.* **2** Someone **has the last laugh** when they are finally proved right or succeed in the end.

> ***phrasal verbs***
> **laugh at** You **laugh at** someone or something when you make fun of them: *You shouldn't laugh at people who have to wear glasses.*
> **laugh off** You **laugh off** something such as an injury, embarrassment or serious problem when you treat it as a joke.

laughable /ˈlɑːfəbəl/ *adjective*
Something that is **laughable** is so bad that it deserves to be laughed at: *He made a laughable attempt at ordering breakfast in French.* [*same as* **ludicrous**]

laughing /ˈlɑːfɪŋ/ *noun* (*uncount*)
Laughing is laughter.
▻ ***phrase*** Something is described as being **no laughing matter** when it is very serious: *This disease is no laughing matter.*

laughing stock /ˈlɑːfɪŋ stɒk/ *noun* (*singular*)
Something that is in danger of becoming a **laughing stock** is likely to be laughed at or ridiculed: *We should become a laughing stock if we published the book in this state.*

laughter /ˈlɑːftə(r)/ *noun* (*uncount*)
Laughter is the act or sound of laughing: *Everyone roared with laughter.*

launch[1] /lɔːntʃ/ *verb*; *noun*
▻ ***verb***: **launches, launching, launched**
1 A ship **is launched** when it is allowed to slide into the water, especially for the first time; someone celebrated **launches** a new ship when they name it in a special ceremony just before it enters the water: *The Queen launched the new liner.* **2** A spacecraft or missile **is launched** when it is sent into the air by means of rocket power. **3** To **launch** something such as an attack or campaign means to start it. **4** A new product **is launched** when it becomes available to the public; a new company **is launched** when it begins to operate.
▻ ***noun***: **launches**
A **launch** is an act of launching something such as a ship or spacecraft.

> ***phrasal verb***
> You **launch into** something such as a speech or story when you begin it: *She launched into the long and complicated story of how she had managed to get lost in spite of having a map.*

launch[2] /lɔːntʃ/ *noun*: **launches**
A **launch** is a large motorboat.

launder /ˈlɔːndə(r)/ *verb*: **launders, laundering, laundered**
You **launder** things such as clothes, sheets and towels when you wash and iron them.

launderette /lɔːndəˈret/ *noun*: **launderettes**
A **launderette** is a shop where customers may wash clothes in coin-operated washing machines.

laundry /ˈlɔːndrɪ/ *noun*: **laundries**
1 A **laundry** is a place where clothes, sheets and towels are washed, especially in return for payment: *He works in the hospital laundry.* **2** (*uncount*) **Laundry** is the clothes, sheets and towels which have been, or are going to be, washed: *It'll take me a couple of hours to do my laundry.* [*same as* **washing**]

laurel /ˈlɒrəl/ *noun*: **laurels**
A **laurel** is a small evergreen tree with smooth, dark, shiny leaves.
▻ ***phrase*** Someone who has been successful is said to **rest on their laurels** if they rely on their reputation instead of trying to progress further.

lava /ˈlɑːvə/ *noun* (*uncount*)
Lava is the hot liquid rock which flows from a volcano, and becomes solid as it cools.

lavatory /ˈlavətrɪ/ *noun*: **lavatories**
A **lavatory** is **1** a toilet. **2** a room containing one or more toilets and washbasins.

lavender /ˈlavəndə(r)/ *noun* (*uncount*)
Lavender is **1** a plant with sweet-smelling pale bluish-purple flowers. **2** the pale purple colour of these flowers.

lavish /ˈlavɪʃ/ *adjective*; *verb*
▻ ***adjective***
1 A **lavish** person is someone who spends a lot of money or spends it generously: *She is lavish in her gifts to charity.* **2** **Lavish** also describes something that is large in amount, especially when the amount is excessive: *lavish praise* □ *a lavish meal with several courses.* **3** Something that is **lavish** looks rich and luxurious, as if a lot of money has been spent on it: *a bedroom with lavish decoration.* — *adverb* **lavishly:** *a lavishly decorated house.*
▻ ***verb***: **lavishes, lavishing, lavished**

> ***phrasal verb***
> You **lavish** money, time, affection or praise **on** someone when you give them a large or generous amount of it: *She lavishes love and affection on all her grandchildren.*

law /lɔː/ *noun*: **laws**
1 The **laws** of a country are the rules that allow or forbid certain actions: *a new law against speeding.* **2** (*uncount or used in the singular*) The **law** is the system of rules that govern how people live and how a country or state is run: *It's against the law in some countries to drink alcohol.* □ *Murder is against the law.* □ *people who knowingly break the law* □ *You must by law pay taxes.* **3** (*uncount*) **Law** is a collection of such rules as a subject for study: *She's studying law.* □ *a law degree.* **4** (*uncount or used in the singular*) **Law**, or **the law**, is the group of people who work professionally with these rules, *eg* advising people and representing them in court: *He works for a law firm.* **5** (*uncount*) A group of rules relating to a particular activity is a particular type of **law**: *family law* □ *He was to be tried under military law.* **6** (*used in the singular*; *informal*) 'The **law**' is the police: *You'll have the law on you if you park there.* **7** A **law** is a rule, *eg* in science, which says that under certain conditions certain things will always happen: *the laws of nature* □ *the law of gravity.*
▻ ***phrases*** **1** **Law and order** is a situation in which the law is obeyed and respected: *There has been a breakdown in law and order in some cities.* **2** If you **lay down the law**, you give your opinions and orders in a forceful and demanding way because you think you are right and everyone else is wrong.

law-abiding /ˈlɔːəbaɪdɪŋ/ *adjective*
A **law-abiding** person is someone who obeys the law.

lawcourt /ˈlɔːkɔːt/ *noun*: **lawcourts**
A **lawcourt** or **court of law** is a place where a judge and jury hear cases and decide if people are guilty or innocent of the crimes they have been accused of.

lawful /ˈlɔːfəl/ *adjective* (*formal*)
Something that is allowed by or according to law is **lawful**: *a lawful business agreement.* [*same as* **legal, legitimate**; *opposite* **unlawful, illegal**] — *adverb* **lawfully:** *The house is now lawfully yours.*

lawless /ˈlɔːləs/ *adjective* (*formal*)
Lawless actions or people break the law, especially violently. — *noun* (*uncount*) **lawlessness:** *a growth in lawlessness.*

lawn /lɔːn/ *noun*: **lawns**
A **lawn** is an area of smooth grass, especially as part of a garden: *I ought to mow the lawn.*

lawnmower /ˈlɔːnmoʊə(r)/ *noun*: **lawnmowers**
A **lawnmower** is a machine for cutting grass in a garden. [see picture at **tool**]

lawsuit /'lɔːsuːt/ *noun*: **lawsuits**
A **lawsuit** is an argument or disagreement between two people or companies, taken to a lawcourt to be settled.

lawyer /'lɔːjə(r)/ *noun*: **lawyers**
A **lawyer** is a person who has studied law and whose job is to give legal advice and help, and to represent people in court. [see also **attorney, barrister, solicitor**]

lax /laks/ *adjective*
You call a system or someone's behaviour **lax** when the rules or morals that control it are not being obeyed or followed strictly: *The company's standards are becoming far too lax.* [*opposite* **strict**]

laxative /'laksətɪv/ *noun*: **laxatives**
A **laxative** is a medicine which makes it easier to pass solid waste matter from the body.

lay[1] /leɪ/ *verb*: **lays, laying, laid**
1 You **lay** something somewhere, or in a certain position, when you place it there so that it lies flat or rests there: *We laid the two rugs on the floor side by side to compare them.* □ *I laid the baby on her back.* □ *Fresh flowers had been laid on her grave.* □ *He laid his hand against her cheek.* □ *I laid down my pen.* **2** You **lay** things that go on or under the ground, such as carpets or cables, when you fit them in position: *The council are laying new electricity cables in our area.* □ *We're planning to lay the new carpet at the weekend.* □ *At last the villa's foundations had been laid, and the building work could speed ahead.* **3** You **lay** something such as a trap to catch an animal or to trick a person into betraying themselves, when you prepare it and make it ready to put into operation: *The police laid a trap to catch him.* □ *The best-laid plans can go wrong.* **4** You **lay** a table when you put plates and cutlery on it ready for a meal: *Could you lay three places for dinner?* **5** You **lay** a fire when you pile up wood, paper or coal on it, ready for lighting. **6** A bird **lays** eggs when it produces them from its body. **7** You **lay** the blame for something on someone when you blame them for it, or decide that they are responsible for it. **8** You **lay** emphasis on something when you insist on it, or give it special importance: *I can't lay enough stress on the need for joint effort.*
▻ ***phrases*** A circumstance **lays you open to** criticism or attack if it puts you in danger of being criticized or attacked.

phrasal verbs
lay aside You **lay** something **aside** when you keep it to deal with, or use, later: *Lay aside some spare cash for use in emergencies.*
lay before You **lay** something such as a proposal or problem **before** someone when you present it to them for their consideration or advice: *New plans are to be laid before the committee.*
lay down 1 A rule, or someone in authority, **lays down** what should be done when they state officially what must be done: *The government have issued a new booklet laying down guidelines for safety at work.* □ *Conditions for membership are laid down in the club rules.* **2** Someone **lays down** their life when they die fighting for a cause or to save someone else. [*same as* **sacrifice**]
lay in You **lay** something **in** when you buy a supply of it and store it somewhere: *I laid in a good supply of food in case the snow cut us off from the shops.*
lay into (*informal*) Someone **lays into** you when they attack or criticize you.
lay off 1 A company **lays** people **off** when it stops employing them: *The factory has had to lay off fifty employees.* [*same as* make **redundant**; see also **layoff**] **2** (*informal*) If you tell someone who is annoying you or attacking you to **lay off**, you are telling them to stop doing it.
lay on You **lay** something **on** when you provide or supply it: *Up till now the management has always laid on a Christmas party for the staff.*
lay out 1 You **lay** things **out** when you spread them out in an orderly arrangement: *She laid all her photographs out on the floor.* □ *He would methodically lay out all his clothes for the morning.* **2** Things such as gardens, towns and streets **are laid out** when they are designed and arranged according to a certain plan: *splendidly laid-out gardens.* [see also **layout**] **3** (*informal*) Someone **is laid out** when they are knocked unconscious: *The blow laid him out flat on the floor.*

lay[2] /leɪ/ *verb*
Lay is the past tense of the verb **lie**.

lay[3] /leɪ/ *adjective*
A **lay** member of a church is a person who belongs to that church but is not a member of the clergy: *a lay preacher.*

layabout /'leɪəbaʊt/ *noun*: **layabouts** (*informal, derogatory*)
A **layabout** is a lazy person.

lay-by /'leɪbaɪ/ *noun* (*BrE*): **lay-bys**
A **lay-by** is a small area at the side of a road where drivers may stop out of the way of the traffic.

layer /'leɪə(r)/ *noun*: **layers**
A **layer** is a thickness or covering on something or between two other things: *This dish is made up of layers of pasta, tomato sauce and cheese.* □ *She put on several layers of clothes to keep herself warm.*

layman /'leɪmən/ *noun*: **laymen**
A **layman** is a person who does not have specialized or professional knowledge of a particular subject. [*same as* **amateur**]

layoff /'leɪɒf/ *noun*: **layoffs**
There are **layoffs** in a company when it stops employing people because there is no work for them to do: *The company blamed the layoffs on the recession.* [*same as* **redundancies**]

layout /'leɪaʊt/ *noun*: **layouts**
A **layout** is an arrangement or plan showing how eg land or buildings are to be organized: *This layout shows the position of the new hosptial and car park.*

laze /leɪz/ *verb*: **lazes, lazing, lazed**

phrasal verb
You **laze around** when you spend your time doing nothing or just relaxing: *She lazed around on the beach all afternoon.*

lazy /'leɪzɪ/ *adjective*: **lazier, laziest**
1 A **lazy** person is someone who does not like doing things that take effort. [*opposite* **active, energetic**] **2** A **lazy** action is one done slowly or without effort: *a lazy smile.* [*same as* **languid**] **3** A **lazy** period of time is time when you do nothing or which you spend relaxing: *She spent a lazy afternoon on the beach.* — *adverb* **lazily:** *She sat lazily in her chair in the garden.* — *noun* (*uncount*) **laziness:** *It's only laziness that stops him from doing any work in the garden.*

lead[1] /liːd/ *verb; noun*
▻ ***verb***: **leads, leading, led**
1 a You **lead** a group of people that is moving somewhere when you go in front of them: *He led his team up on to the platform to collect their medals.* □ *The pro-*

cession was led by a pipe band. **b** You **lead** people somewhere when you take them there: *I noticed him walking along the High Street, leading a little girl by the hand.* □ *She led me upstairs to my room.* □ *Guides shouting information in every possible language were leading their parties round the gallery.* **c** You **are leading** in a game, race or competition when you are winning: *Oxford is leading by half a length.* □ *She led for two miles and then fell back.* **d** Someone who **leads** the field in a particular subject is the greatest authority on it, or has done the most advanced research on it: *Our own university leads the world in engineering research.* **e** You **lead** an activity, project, seminar or discussion if you are the person who controls and guides it. [see also **leading**]

2 a A road, path, passage, or something such as a wire or pipe, **leads** somewhere if it goes there: *A narrow path led through the woods.* □ *North Street and South Street both lead to the Cathedral.* □ *This cable must lead somewhere.* **b** A door or gate **leads** somewhere if you get there by going through it: *An archway led into the quadrangle.* **c** One thing **leads** to another if the second thing develops from, or is caused by, the first: *We now know that prolonged sunbathing can lead to the growth of skin tumours.* □ *The discovery that we had music in common led to many pleasant evenings together at the Proms.* □ *It was this clue that led us with certainty to the murderer.* **d** Someone or something **leads** you to do something if they are responsible for your doing it: *The management led us to believe that there would be no further redundancies.* □ *Problems at work have led me to reconsider my future.* □ *What led to your interest in African languages?*

3 You **lead** a particular kind of life if that is the kind of life you have: *Some people lead such exciting lives.* □ *For some months she led a miserable existence in a tiny basement flat.*

▷ ***noun*: leads**

1 (*used in the singular*) You give people a **lead** if you do something that sets an example for them to follow: *We ought to be following the lead set by Denmark.* □ *We should be giving a lead in sending out peace-keeping forces, instead of watching as the two sides try to exterminate each other.* **2** (*used in the singular*) You are in the **lead** in a race or competition when you are winning; you have a **lead** of a certain distance or amount if that is the distance or amount by which you are winning: *Britain's Sally Gunnell is in the lead.* □ *In the final 50 metres she lost the lead to her strongest rival.* □ *Dawn and Paul have established a lead of four points.* **3** The **lead** in a play or film is the most important role in it, or the person who is chosen for it: *The lead is taken as usual by Kenneth Branagh.* □ *the male and female leads.* **4** A **lead** is a clue or a piece of information that may help to solve a problem or mystery: *The police are still looking for leads in the motorway mystery.* **5** A **lead** is also **a** a wire attached to an electrical device through which power is supplied to make it operate. **b** a strap or chain for attaching to a dog's collar so that you can control it.

▷ ***phrases*** **1** You **lead the way** when you go in front of other people, *eg* to show them where to go: *She led the way up the mountain.* □ *This country leads the way in cancer research.* **2** You **take the lead** when you do things before other people do them: *The Russians took the lead in the space race in 1957 when they put a satellite into orbit.*

phrasal verbs

lead off 1 You **lead off** something such as a discussion when you begin it: *We'll introduce ourselves first; Roger, would you like to lead off?* **2** A road or passage **leads off** from somewhere if it starts there; one room **leads off** another if it is entered from the other: *The road leading off to the right will take you to the beach.* □ *The normal pattern of student accommodation is a large sitting room with two bedrooms leading off it.*

lead up to 1 A series of events **leads up to** a particular situation if one develops from another in such a way as to cause it: *the events leading up to World War I.* **2** You **lead up to** a particular subject in a conversation when you carefully direct the conversation towards it: *I wondered what you were leading up to.*

lead² /lɛd/ *noun*: **leads**

1 (*uncount*) **Lead** is a soft, heavy, bluish-grey metal: *These pipes are made of lead.* □ *lead pipes.* **2** (*count or uncount*) The thin stick of grey or coloured material in the centre of a pencil is its **lead**.

leaden /ˈlɛdən/ *adjective*

1 A **leaden** sky or sea is dull grey in colour. **2 Leaden** movements are heavy or slow. [*same as* **cumbersome**] **3** Something that is dull and often sad can also be described as **leaden**.

leader /ˈliːdə(r)/ *noun*: **leaders**

1 A **leader** is a person, animal or thing that leads, guides, organizes or is in charge of others: *She hopes to become leader of a political party.* [*same as* **head**] **2** The **leader** is the person or horse that is winning a race or competition: *She was the leader during the first half of the race.*

leadership /ˈliːdəʃɪp/ *noun*

1 (*uncount*) **Leadership** is the position of leader: *Who will take over the leadership now that he has retired?* **2** (*uncount*) **Leadership** is the ability to lead others: *She shows leadership qualities.* **3** (*with a singular or plural verb*) The **leadership** of a group is the person or people who are in charge of it: *The leadership should represent members' interests.* [*same as* **management**]

leading /ˈliːdɪŋ/ *adjective*

1 The **leading** person, thing or part in a film, is the one that is most important: *He is one of Scotland's leading playwrights.* **2** The **leading** person, team or car is the one in front or in first position.

leading question /liːdɪŋ ˈkwɛstʃən/ *noun*: **leading questions**

You ask a **leading question** when the way that you ask the question suggests what answer you want to receive: *The judge told the lawyer not to ask the witness leading questions.*

leaf /liːf/ *noun*; *verb*

▷ ***noun*: leaves** /liːvs/

1 A **leaf** is one of the thin flat parts, usually green in colour, growing from the stem and branches of a plant: *This tree doesn't lose its leaves in winter.* **2** A **leaf** is also a single sheet of paper forming two pages in a book.

▷ ***phrases*** **1** A tree or plant that is **in leaf** is covered with leaves. **2** You say you are going to **turn over a new leaf** when you say that you are going to try and behave in a better or more serious way.

▷ ***verb*: leafs, leafing, leafed**

phrasal verb

You **leaf through** a book or the pages of a book when you turn the pages quickly and look briefly at what is written or printed on them: *She leafed through her magazine.*

leaflet /ˈliːflət/ *noun*: **leaflets**
A **leaflet** is a single sheet of paper, or several sheets of paper folded together, giving information or advertising products, and usually given to people free of charge.

leafy /ˈliːfɪ/ *adjective*: **leafier, leafiest**
1 A **leafy** plant or tree has a lot of leaves: *green leafy vegetables.* **2** A **leafy** place is one that has a lot of trees and plants: *a quiet, leafy lane.*

league /liːg/ *noun*: **leagues**
1 A **league** is a group of people, countries or states that work together or have a common interest: *the League of Nations.* [*same as* **alliance**] **2** A **league** is also a group of sports clubs which compete for a championship: *the Football League.* **3** Someone's **league** is their class or standard: *He just isn't in her league.*
▻ ***phrase*** You are **in league with** someone when you agree to work with them, usually in secret or for some bad purpose: *She was accused of being in league with the murderer.*

leak /liːk/ *noun*; *verb*
▻ ***noun*: leaks**
1 A **leak** is a small crack or hole which allows liquid or gas to pass in or out: *He's got to repair the leak in the garage roof.* **2** A **leak** is also the liquid or gas which has escaped through a crack or hole: *There's been a gas leak.* **3** There is a **leak** when news or information that should be kept secret is made known to the public: *There has been a security leak.*
▻ ***verb*: leaks, leaking, leaked**
1 Something such as a container, pipe or roof **leaks** when it has a small crack or hole through which a liquid or gas can pass in or out: *The garage roof leaks.* ▫ *This pipe is leaking gas.* **2** A liquid or gas **leaks** when it passes in or out of a small crack or hole in *eg* a container, pipe or roof: *The air was slowly leaking out of the tyre.* [*same as* **escape**] **3** Someone **leaks** secret news or information when they tell it to the public: *He leaked the news of the royal divorce to the press.*

> ***phrasal verb***
> Secret news or information **leaks out** when it becomes known to the public: *The news of their divorce leaked out.*

leakage /ˈliːkɪdʒ/ *noun*: **leakages**
There is a **leakage** when an amount of liquid or gas passes in or out of *eg* a container, pipe or roof through a small crack or hole.

leaky /ˈliːkɪ/ *adjective*: **leakier, leakiest**
A **leaky** container, pipe or roof is one that has a small crack or hole through which liquid or gas can pass in or out: *a leaky roof.*

lean¹ /liːn/ *verb*: **leans, leaning, leaned** or **leant** (**leant** and **leaned** are both used as the past tense and past participle)
1 You **lean** in a particular direction when your body is sloping in that direction: *She leant back in the chair.* ▫ *The children were leaning out of the window.* ▫ *She leaned over the bridge to look at the boats passing beneath it.* ▫ *He leant over to talk to me.* ▫ *You'll see better if you lean over a bit.* **2** You **lean** on something when you rest on it for support; you **lean** one thing on another when you rest it on or against it for support: *She leant on the table to stop herself from falling.* ▫ *He leant his bike against the wall.* **3** You **lean** on or upon someone when you rely on them for help or are supported by them: *He leans on his wife a lot.* [*same as* **depend** on, **rely** on] **4** You **lean** towards something when you prefer it or approve of it: *I rather lean towards painting the bedroom walls orange.*

> ***phrasal verb***
> (*informal*) You **lean on** someone when you put pressure on them to try to make them act in a certain way: *I'm sure he'll agree to give you the money if you lean on him a bit.* [*same as* **pressurize**]

lean² /liːn/ *adjective*: **leaner, leanest**
1 A **lean** person or animal is thin: *a lean athlete.* **2 Lean** meat does not contain much fat. **3 Lean** years are years of hardship, when people have little food and make little money.

leaning /ˈliːnɪŋ/ *noun*: **leanings**
You have a **leaning** for something when you like it, prefer it or believe in it: *She has a leaning towards medicine and may decide to become a doctor.* ▫ *They have different political leanings.*

leant /lɛnt/ *verb*
Leant is the past tense and past participle of **lean**¹.

leap /liːp/ *noun*; *verb*
▻ ***noun*: leaps**
1 You take a **leap** when you jump suddenly or quickly: *She took a flying leap into the swimming pool.* [*same as* **jump**] **2** A **leap** in something such as prices is a sudden or great increase in them: *a leap in the price of petrol.*
▻ ***verb*: leaps, leaping, leaped** or **leapt** (**leapt** and **leaped** are both used as the past tense and past participle)
1 You **leap** when you jump high in the air or over a long distance: *The dancer leapt into the air.* ▫ *He leaped over the river.* **2** You **leap** when you jump or move suddenly or with force: *He leaped into a taxi and asked to be driven to the hospital.* **3** When something such as prices increase suddenly, quickly or greatly, you say that they **leap**: *Petrol prices have leapt in the past few years.*
▻ ***phrases*** **1** You take **a leap in the dark** when you act or decide something without knowing what the consequence may be: *She didn't know him well and took a leap in the dark when she decided to marry him.* **2** When something moves forward or progresses quickly and successfully, it progresses **by leaps and bounds**: *Her health improved by leaps and bounds after the operation.*

> ***phrasal verb***
> **leap at** You **leap at** something when you accept it eagerly: *She leapt at the chance to spend her summer working in Australia.* [*same as* **jump at**]

leap year /ˈliːp jɪə(r)/ *noun*: **leap years**
A **leap year** is a year with 366 days (instead of 365), the extra day being 29 February.

learn /lɜːn/ *verb*: **learns, learning, learned** or **learnt** (**learnt** and **learned** are both used as the past tense and past participle)
1 You **learn** something when you gain knowledge of it or skill in it through training and study: *Lots of people have never learnt to swim.* ▫ *I've just learnt how to stand on my head.* ▫ *How long have you been learning Italian?* ▫ *What did you learn at school today?* ▫ *We learnt why leaves turn brown and fall off.* ▫ *Everyone should learn what to do in certain emergencies.* **2** You **learn** something such as a poem or your part in a play by repeating it so often to yourself that you remember it: *I've got to learn three passages by heart.* [*same as* **memorize**; see also **by heart** at **heart**] **3** You **learn** a particular attitude or way of behaving when you develop that attitude, or start behaving in that way: *He should learn how to say no.* ▫ *She had never learnt*

to assert herself. □ *You must learn not to worry.* □ *I learnt that my husband was not to be trusted.* □ *learnt behaviour patterns.* **4** (*formal*) You **learn** of or about something when you discover it or are told about it: *He was surprised to learn that his wife was expecting a baby.* □ *I was so sorry to learn of his death.* □ *His behaviour suggests that he didn't learn about the accident till the next morning.* □ *How did you learn the truth?*

learned /ˈlɜːnɪd/ *adjective*
1 A **learned** person is respected for having studied a lot: *a learned professor.* **2 Learned** books or magazines have been written by, or for, learned people: *learned journals.*

learner /ˈlɜːnə(r)/ *noun*: **learners**
A **learner** is a person who is learning something: *He's a fast learner.* □ *a learner driver.*

learning /ˈlɜːnɪŋ/ *noun* (*uncount*)
Learning is knowledge gained through study: *a woman of great learning.*

learnt /ˈlɜːnt/ *verb*
Learnt is the past tense and past participle of **learn**.

lease /liːs/ *noun; verb*
▷ ***noun***: **leases**
A **lease** is a legal agreement by which the owner of a building or piece of land lets another person use it for a period of time in return for rent: *The lease for the flat expires next year.* □ *a 10-year lease.*
▷ ***verb***: **leases, leasing, leased**
You **lease** a building or piece of land **1** when you are allowed to use it in return for rent: *She leases her flat from the council.* [*same as* **rent**] **2** when you own it and let someone else live in it in return for rent: *He leases his field to a farmer.* [*same as* **rent out, let**]
▷ ***phrase*** Someone gets **a new lease of life** when they feel livelier, healthier or have more energy than before, often after a rest: *He got a new lease of life after his heart operation.*

leash /liːʃ/ *noun*: **leashes**
A **leash** is a strip of leather or chain used for leading or holding a dog or other animal: *Dogs must be kept on a leash.* [*same as* **lead**]

least /liːst/ *determiner; pronoun; adverb*
▷ ***determiner***
1 'Least' and 'the **least**' are used with uncount nouns to mean the smallest quantity of something: *Of the three candidates, she had least experience of working with computers.* □ *The babies are the first to die, because they have the least resistance to disease.* [*opposite* **most**] **2** 'The **least**' is sometimes used with singular count nouns to mean the smallest: *She hadn't the least intention of apologizing.* □ *He's terribly nervous; the least little thing upsets him.*

> **Least** is the superlative form of **little** and is therefore normally used with uncount nouns. Use **fewest** with plural count nouns: *She has the least money and the fewest worries.*

▷ ***pronoun:*** *You appear to have most pudding and I've got the least.* □ *every single one of us, from the greatest to the least* [= the most unimportant]. □ *Money is the least of my worries just now.* □ *He offered to risk his life, believing that of all of us he had least to lose.*
▷ ***adverb***
1 When something is **least** the case it is hardly the case at all: *Troubles come when you least expect them.* □ *Late evening is a time when I feel least like dealing with problems.* **2** Someone or something that does something **least** or the **least** does it less than anyone or anything else: *I liked Phyllis; of the whole group she was certainly the one who complained the least.* □ *Decide which item matters least and deal with it last.* **3 'Least'** and 'the **least**' can be used before adjectives and other adverbs: *I don't mind which wallpaper we have; just choose the least awful.* □ *Give the job to Jean; she's the least likely to make a fuss.* □ *He was the one who performed least confidently in the interview.* [*opposite* **most**]
▷ ***phrases*** **1 At least** is used **a** to describe an amount that is the smallest that is likely, though the actual amount is probably more: *He must weigh at least 300 pounds.* □ *Even a second-hand car will cost at least £2000.* **b** to suggest the minimum, or smallest thing, that ought to be done, although more should really be done: *You could at least apologize.* □ *Even if you don't visit her in hospital, you should at least send her a card.* □ *Why don't you at least enquire at the lost-property office?* **c** to point out the single advantage that something has: *My car may be old and battered but at least it goes.* **d** to correct something you have just said, *eg* when you have just had a doubt about it: *Oh yes, I've seen that film; at least, I think I have.* **2 Last but not least** describes a person or thing that is mentioned or introduced last but is nevertheless important: *And last but not least we have the matter of salary increases to discuss.* **3** You use **the least bit, in the least** and **in the very least** to emphasize a negative: *She didn't seem in the least concerned.* □ *I'm not the least bit interested in her career.* □ *He doesn't attract me in the very least.* **4 Least of all** emphasizes a particular person or thing to which a negative statement applies: *No-one was prepared for the shock, least of all me.* □ *You mustn't worry about a thing, least of all my safety.* **5 Not least** introduces an important example: *It happens in all the big cities, not least in Liverpool.* **6 The least** someone **can do** is the minimum that they should do, even if they don't do anything more: *If we can't stop teenagers from having sex, the least we can do is tell them about the dangers.* **7** If something is so **to say the least**, the situation is actually more extreme than that: *It's a nuisance, to say the least.*

leather /ˈlɛðə(r)/ *noun* (*uncount*)
Leather is the skin of an animal, treated to make it smooth, and used to make shoes, bags and clothes.

leathery /ˈlɛðərɪ/ *adjective*
Something that is **leathery** is tough like leather: *leathery skin.*

leave[1] /liːv/ *verb*: **leaves, leaving, left**
1 a You **leave** a place or person when you go away from them: *She left home at the usual time to catch her bus.* □ *The train leaves Paddington at 5.35.* □ *I do hate leaving you.* □ *I left my desk for a moment to see what all the noise was about.* **b** You **leave** your husband or wife, or the person with whom you live and have a sexual relationship when you stop living with them and end the relationship: *This time he's left her for good.* **c** You **leave** an institution such as school or university when you stop attending it; you **leave** your job when you resign from it: *He had to leave school at 12 and start earning his living.* □ *She left her job to have a baby.* **2 a** You **leave** something somewhere when you go away and forget to take it with you: *She left her purse in the cafe.* □ *I must have left the tickets at the office.* **b** You **leave** someone or something somewhere, or in a particular situation, if they stay there when you go away: *I decided to leave the car at home.* □ *I can't remember where I left my keys.* □ *I left Alison putting on her make-up in the ladies' room.* □ *I don't like leaving her in that state.* **c** You **leave** someone or something in a particular condition if you are responsible

for putting them into it: *Remember to leave your bedroom tidy.* □ *Who left the window open?* □ *Don't leave the door unlocked.* □ *What do you expect if you leave your car parked on a yellow line?* □ *Her so-called explanation has left us all doubly confused.* □ *The accident left him with a limp.* **d** Something **leaves** a mark if it makes it: *That glass has left a mark on the table.* □ *The operation won't leave a big scar.* **e** You **leave** a gap or space somewhere when you make it intentionally: *Leave a space on the postcard for me to add a message.* □ *When writing an essay, leave a margin wide enough for your tutor's comments.* **f** You **leave** a matter or task till another time when you stop dealing with it, expecting to come back to it: *Let's leave the question of responsibility for the moment and pass on to the matter of compensation.* □ *I can leave the ironing till this evening.* □ *I glanced through the mail and decided to leave the bills till the last.* **g** A quantity of something **is left**, or **is left** over, if it has not all been used: *Is there any milk left?* □ *I've got no money left.* □ *There are some sausages left over from the barbecue.*

3 a You **leave** someone something, or **leave** it for them, when you put it somewhere for them to find or collect: *Leave me your address before you go.* □ *She's left you a note.* □ *I'm just leaving this package for him.* □ *Did he leave any message?* □ *I've left food for you in the fridge.* **b** You **leave** something with someone when you give it to them: *Leave the keys with my neighbour if I'm not in when you're ready to go.* **c** You **leave** something to someone when you let them have the responsibility of dealing with it: *She leaves all the gardening to her husband.* □ *Leave the problem to me.* **d** You **leave** a quantity of something for someone when you do not use all of it but save some of it for them: *I've left you half the pizza.* **e** You **leave** property or money to someone when you arrange in your will for it to be given to them when you die: *My grandmother left me her ring and watch.* □ *He left his house to his sister.* □ *They were left jewellery and money in their uncle's will.*

▻ ***phrases*** If you tell someone who is bothering or attacking someone else to **leave** them **alone**, you are telling them to stop doing it.

phrasal verbs

leave behind You **leave** someone or something **behind 1** When you go away and do not take them with you, *eg* because you have forgotten to: *I arrived at the meeting to find I'd left my notes behind.* □ *I'm afraid we'll have to leave the dog behind at home.* **2** When you go away from them for ever: *I'd left my schooldays far behind.* **3** When you progress much faster than them: *She was leaving the other runners well behind.*

leave off 1 You **leave** something **off** your list when you do not include it: *She left potatoes off her shopping list.* **2** You **leave off** doing something when you stop doing it: *She continued reading from where she had left off.*

leave out You **leave** something or someone **out** of something when you do not include them: *She was left out of the tennis team.* □ *The film left out some of the minor characters in the book.* □ *I told her what you'd said, leaving out the bit about her husband.*

leave over (*used in the passive*) A certain amount of something **is left over** if it remains after the rest has been used: *There's still some drink left over from the party.*

leave² /liːv/ *noun* (*uncount*)

1 Leave is a period of time away from work or military duties: *He has one month's leave each year.* □ *She is on maternity leave* [= leave given to her because she is going to have, or has recently had, a baby]. □ *He is on sick leave* [= leave given to him because he is ill]. **2** (*formal*) **Leave** is official permission to do something: *The judge granted him leave to appeal against the court's verdict.*

leaves /liːvz/ *noun*

Leaves is the plural of **leaf**.

lecherous /ˈlɛtʃərəs/ *adjective*

A **lecherous** person has or shows great sexual desire, especially in ways which offend or upset other people.

lectern /ˈlɛktən/ *noun*: **lecterns**

A **lectern** is a stand with a sloping surface for holding a book or notes to be read from when talking to an audience.

lecture /ˈlɛktʃə(r)/ *noun*; *verb*

▻ ***noun*: lectures**

1 A **lecture** is a formal talk on a particular subject given to an audience, *eg* at university: *a history lecture.* **2** If someone gives you a **lecture**, they scold or criticize you. [*same as* **reprimand, rebuke**]

▻ ***verb*: lectures, lecturing, lectured**

1 Someone **lectures** on some subject when they give or read a talk they have prepared about it. **2** Someone **lectures** you if they scold or criticize you at length: *His parents lectured him about getting home late.* [*same as* **scold, tell off**]

lecturer /ˈlɛktʃərə(r)/ *noun*: **lecturers**

A **lecturer** is a person who lectures, especially to students at college or university. [compare **teacher**]

led /lɛd/ *verb*

Led is the past tense and past participle of **lead¹**.

ledge /lɛdʒ/ *noun*: **ledges**

1 A **ledge** is a narrow shelf below a window. **2** A **ledge** on the side of a mountain or cliff is a narrow shelf-like piece of rock.

ledger /ˈlɛdʒə(r)/ *noun*: **ledgers**

A **ledger** is a book in an office or shop, which gives details of the money spent and received.

leek /liːk/ *noun*: **leeks**

A **leek** is a long, thin vegetable with broad, flat, dark green leaves and a white base. [see picture at **vegetable**]

leer /lɪə(r)/ *noun*; *verb*

▻ ***noun*: leers**

A **leer** is an unpleasant grin or smile which suggests sexual interest.

▻ ***verb*: leers, leering, leered:** *Don't leer at me like that!* [*same as* **ogle**]

leeway /ˈliːweɪ/ *noun* (*uncount*)

Leeway is the small amount of additional time, space or money that allows you to change your mind or plans if necessary: *I've allowed half an hour's leeway for the journey in case the traffic is bad.*

left¹ /lɛft/ *verb*

Left is the past tense and past participle of **leave¹**.

left² /lɛft/ *noun*; *adjective or adverb*

▻ ***noun***

1 (*uncount*; *or used in the singular*) **Left** is the direction, side or position that is opposite to right, or is towards the west when you are facing north: *Take the second turning to the left.* □ *Green fields stretched away to our left.* □ *Our house is the third on the left.* □ *We drive on the left in this country.* □ *Maggie was sitting on my left.* [*opposite* **right**] **2** (*with a singular or plural verb*; *politics*) The **left** is the socialist position as opposed to the capitalist one, or the people and groups that support socialism: *Her political sympathies had moved further to the left.* □ *The Left are regrouping after last week's defeat.* [*opposite* **right**]

▻ ***adjective or adverb:*** *He fell and broke his left arm.* ▫ *Do you write with your left hand?* ▫ *She complained of a pain in her left side.* ▫ *Keep left round the roundabout.* ▫ *Turn left at the next set of traffic lights.* ▫ *Look right and left before crossing.* ▫ *His political opinions are somewhat left of centre.* [*opposite* **right**]

Notice that you refer to either of a pair of body parts as, *eg*, *the left ear* or *my right foot*, but when you are referring to things positioned on the left or right you commonly use the adjectives **left-hand** and **right-hand**: *It's in the left-hand* (not *left*) *drawer*; *the right-hand* (rather than *right*) *side of the road.*

left-hand /lɛft'hand/ *adjective*
Left-hand describes something which is on or towards the left: *the left-hand side of the page.*

left-handed /lɛft'handɪd/ *adjective*
1 A **left-handed** person uses their left hand to perform manual activities such as writing and throwing: *a left-handed tennis player.* **2** A **left-handed** object is designed to be used by left-handed people, or the left hand: *left-handed scissors.*

left-luggage office /lɛft'lʌgɪdʒ ɒfɪs/ *noun*: **left-luggage offices**
A **left-luggage office** is a place at a railway or coach station where travellers may leave luggage safely for a short period of time.

leftovers /'lɛftoʊvəz/ *noun* (*plural*)
Leftovers are pieces of food that have not been finished at a meal.

left wing *noun* (*used in the singular*)
The **left wing** of a political party are the members that hold the most socialist opinions: *the left wing of the Labour Party.* — *adjective* **left-wing:** *left-wing politicians.*

leg /lɛg/ *noun*: **legs**
1 A **leg** is one of the limbs on which animals, birds and people walk and stand. [see picture at **body**] **2** (*count or uncount*) A **leg** is also an animal's or bird's leg used as food: *roast leg of lamb.* **3** The **leg** of a garment is the part that covers one of a person's legs: *He rolled up his trouser legs.* **4** The **leg** of a chair or table is one of the long narrow parts that support its weight. **5** A **leg** of a long journey is one stage of it: *the first leg of a journey across America.*
▻ ***phrases*** (*informal*)
1 You say that someone **doesn't have a leg to stand on** if you think that their behaviour or opinions cannot be supported by facts or evidence. **2 a** Something is **on its last legs** if it is in bad condition and likely to collapse or break down soon: *His old car is on its last legs.* **b** Someone is **on their last legs** if they are ill or weak and likely to die soon. **3** You **pull** someone's **leg** when you try to make them believe something which is not true, especially as a joke. **4** When you tell someone to **shake a leg**, you tell them to hurry up. **5** You **stretch your legs** when you go for a walk.

legacy /'lɛgəsɪ/ *noun*: **legacies**
1 A **legacy** is something such as money, property or jewellery that is given to you by the owner when they die. [*same as* **inheritance**] **2** A **legacy** is a usually bad situation caused by someone or something that went before: *The war left a legacy of poverty and famine.*

legal /'liːgəl/ *adjective*
1 An act or situation that is **legal** is allowed by the law: *It isn't legal to drive a car without a licence.* ▫ *This agreement is perfectly legal.* [*same as* **lawful**, **legitimate**; *opposite* **illegal**] **2 Legal** is used to describe something that relates to the law or lawyers: *the legal profession* ▫ *legal advice* ▫ *take legal action* ▫ *the legal system.* — *adverb* **legally:** *They are not legally married.* ▫ *You are legally responsible for keeping your car in good condition.*

legality /lɪ'galɪtɪ/ *noun* (*uncount*)
You talk about the **legality** of a situation when you discuss whether it is legal or not: *It is for the courts to decide on the legality of their marriage.*

legalize /'liːgəlaɪz/ or **legalise** *verb*: **legalizes, legalizing, legalized**
A situation or act **is legalized** if a law is passed to make it legal: *The government has refused to legalize the use of some drugs.* [*same as* **authorise**]

legend /'lɛdʒənd/ *noun*: **legends**
1 A **legend** is a traditional story which may or may not be true: *the legend of King Arthur and the Knights of the Round Table.* **2** (*uncount*) A collection of such stories can be called **legend**: *According to legend, Robin Hood lived in Sherwood Forest.* ▫ *Chinese legend.* [*same as* **myth**] **3** A famous person that popular stories are told about, and who is greatly admired, can also be called a **legend**: *She was a legend in her own lifetime.*

legendary /'lɛdʒəndərɪ/ *adjective*
1 A **legendary** person, thing or event is talked about in legends: *Arthur is a legendary king of Britain.* **2** Something is **legendary** when it is very famous: *Her generosity is legendary.*

-legged /lɛgd/ or / 'lɛgɪd/ *adjective*
You use **-legged** combined with a number or other words to form adjectives relating to number or type of legs: *four-legged creatures* ▫ *hairy-legged spiders.*

legible /'lɛdʒɪbəl/ *adjective*
Handwriting or printing that is **legible** is clear enough to be read: *The letter had got wet and was no longer legible.* [*opposite* **illegible**; compare **readable**]

legion /'liːdʒən/ *noun*; *adjective*
▻ ***noun***: **legions**
1 A **legion** is a group of soldiers, one of several sections in some armies: *the French Foreign Legion.* **2** A **legion** is also a large number: *legions of foreign tourists.*
▻ ***adjective*** (*formal*)
You can say things are **legion** if there are a large number of them: *Books on this subject are legion.*

legislate /'lɛdʒɪsleɪt/ *verb* (*formal*): **legislates, legislating, legislated**
A government, parliament or state **legislates** when it makes a law or laws: *The government may decide to legislate against smoking in public places.*

legislation /lɛdʒɪ'sleɪʃən/ *noun* (*uncount*; *formal*)
A group of laws can be called **legislation**: *The European parliament wants to introduce legislation preventing children from working.*

legislative /'lɛdʒɪslətɪv/ *adjective* (*formal*)
Something that relates to laws and law-making can be described as **legislative**: *a legislative assembly* ▫ *the government's legislative powers.*

legislator /'lɛdʒɪsleɪtə(r)/ *noun* (*formal*): **legislators**
A **legislator** is a person who is involved in law-making.

legislature /'lɛdʒɪsleɪtʃə(r)/ *noun* (*formal*): **legislatures**
The **legislature** is the part of the government which has the power to make laws.

legitimate /lə'dʒɪtɪmət/ *adjective*
1 Something that is **legitimate** is lawful or acceptable: *He has a legitimate cause for complaint.* ▫ *Those without a legitimate reason for being on the premises are*

requested to leave. [*opposite* **illegal, illegitimate, unlawful**] **2** A person who is born to parents who are married to each other can be described as **legitimate**. [*opposite* **illegitimate**] — *noun* (*uncount*) **legitimacy** /lə'dʒɪtɪməsɪ/: *There is some doubt about the legitimacy of their marriage.* — *adverb* **legitimately:** *She is legitimately concerned about her son's health.*

leisure /'lɛʒə(r)/ *noun* (*uncount*)
Leisure is the time when you do not have to work, and which you can spend doing things you enjoy: *You'll have a lot more leisure when you retire.* □ *leisure activities.*
▷ ***phrase*** You do something **at leisure** or **at your leisure** when you do it at a convenient time and without hurrying: *I don't want the book back so you can finish reading it at your leisure.*

leisurely /'lɛʒəlɪ/ *adjective*; *adverb*
▷ ***adjective***
Something is **leisurely** when it is done in a relaxed way and is not hurried: *a leisurely break from work.*
▷ ***adverb:*** *We'll just walk leisurely round the gardens.*

lemon /'lɛmən/ *noun* (*count or uncount, often adjectival*)
1 A **lemon** is a thick-skinned, yellow, oval fruit with a sour taste: *a slice of lemon* □ *lemon juice.* [see picture at **fruit**] **2 Lemon** or **lemon yellow** is the pale greenish-yellow colour of a lemon: *brown walls with a lemon ceiling* □ *lemon-yellow curtains.*

lemonade /lɛmə'neɪd/ *noun*: **lemonades**
1 (*uncount*) **Lemonade** is a fizzy or still drink flavoured with or made from lemons. **2** A **lemonade** is a serving of this: *She bought two lemonades and one glass of wine.*

lend /lɛnd/ *verb*: **lends, lending, lent**
1 You **lend** someone money, or something that you own, when you let them have it or use it for a limited period: *I've lent him my car for a week.* □ *The bank agreed to lend him £4000.* □ *If you lend money to your children don't rely on getting it back.* □ *I've learnt never to lend my books.* [*same as* **loan**; *opposite* **borrow**] **2** (*literary*) One thing **lends** a particular quality to another if it gives it that quality: *His dignified manner lends authority to whatever he says.* **3** (*literary*) You **lend** advice or support to someone when you give it to them. **4** (*formal*) Something **lends** itself to being used or dealt with in a certain way if it can readily or easily be used or dealt with in that way: *There's a certain kind of novel that lends itself to adaptation as a television serial.*

length /lɛŋθ/ *noun*: **lengths**
1 (*count or uncount*) The **length** of an object is the distance from one end of it to the other: *What's the length of the cable?* □ *The roots grow to the amazing length of three metres.* □ *Our garden is no more than about 12 metres in length.* □ *Choose blades of grass of various different lengths.* **2** (*count or uncount*) The **length** of something is the amount of time it takes or lasts: *I'll see you in mid July or a little later, depending on the length of my stay in Madrid.* □ *You can't expect small children to sit still for any length of time.* [compare **duration**] **3** (*uncount*) **Length** is the quality of being long: *I'm amazed at the length of your hair!* □ *The length of your essay suggests an enthusiasm for the subject.* **4** A **length** of something long and narrow is a piece of it: *Cut a length of string and lay it parallel to the edge of the table.* **5** You swim a **length** of a swimming pool when you swim once from one end to the other: *I swam 50 lengths this morning.* **6** In a boat race or horse race, a boat or horse is ahead by a **length** if it is ahead by the distance representing its own length: *Oxford won by six lengths.* □ *Mr Frosty is overtaking Jack-the-Lad; he's half a length, no, a length ahead now.* **7** To travel, or look along, the **length** of something is to travel the whole way along it, or look all the way along it: *standing on Calton Hill and looking down the length of Princes Street* □ *We drove the length of Lake Malawi.*
▷ ***phrases*** **1 a** You describe something **at length** when you describe it in great detail: *He wrote to her at great length about his new job.* **b** You speak **at length** when you speak for a long time: *He seemed quite happy to discuss personal matters loudly and at length over the telephone.* **c** Something happens **at length** when it finally happens: *They came at length to a telephone box and phoned for help.* [*same as* **at last**] **2** You **go to great lengths** to do or achieve something when you take a lot of trouble over it; someone who is prepared to **go to any lengths** to achieve something is determined to achieve it by whatever means may be necessary: *He's the kind of person who would go to any lengths to get promotion.* □ *Now look after this book; I went to great lengths to get a copy for you.* **3** If you say there is no need to **go to the length of** doing something, you mean it would be too extreme a step in the circumstances: *I don't think we need go to the length of telephoning the police; not yet, anyway.* **4** Something that happens **throughout the length and breadth of** an area happens everywhere in it.

lengthen /'lɛŋθən/ *verb*: **lengthens, lengthening, lengthened**
You **lengthen** something, or something **lengthens**, when you make it longer, or it becomes longer: *This skirt needs lengthening.*

lengthways /'lɛŋθweɪz/ or **lengthwise** /'lɛŋθwaɪz/ *adverb*
Lengthways or **lengthwise** means in the direction along the length of something: *fold the sheets lengthways.*

lengthy /'lɛŋθɪ/ *adjective*: **lengthier, lengthiest**
Something that is **lengthy** is long, and often too long: *lengthy explanations.* [*opposite* **short, brief**]

lenient /'li:nɪənt/ *adjective*
A person in authority or something such as a fine or punishment is **lenient** when it is not as severe as it could have been: *When a judge is too lenient, it shakes the public's faith in the legal system.* — *adverb* **leniently:** *The judge dealt leniently with him.*

lens /lɛnz/ *noun*: **lenses**
A **lens** is **1** a thin piece of glass or clear plastic that is curved on one or both sides, used in cameras, telescopes and glasses to make an image look larger, smaller or clearer. [see also **contact lens**] **2** a clear substance behind the coloured part of the eye, which directs light through it.

Lent /lɛnt/ *noun* (*uncount*)
In the Christian calendar, **Lent** is the period of forty days before Easter, during which many Christians give up some items of food or pleasure.

lent /lɛnt/ *verb*
Lent is the past tense and past participle of **lend**.

lentil /'lɛntɪl/ *noun* (*often adjectival*): **lentils**
A **lentil** is a small round orange, brown or green seed, eaten as food: *lentil soup.*

leopard /'lɛpəd/ *noun*: **leopards**
A **leopard** is a large animal of the cat family, with a yellowish-brown coat and black spots, found in Africa and Asia.

leotard /'lɪətɑ:d/ *noun*: **leotards**
A **leotard** is a tight-fitting garment worn especially by women for dancing and doing exercises.

leper /ˈlɛpə(r)/ *noun*: **lepers**
1 A **leper** is a person suffering from leprosy. **2** A social **leper** is a person who has done something that has shocked other people, and who is avoided because of it.

leprosy /ˈlɛprəsɪ/ *noun* (*uncount*)
Leprosy is a skin disease which can be passed from one person to another, and which causes serious and permanent damage to the body, including the loss of fingers, toes or limbs.

lesbian /ˈlɛzbɪən/ *noun* (*often adjectival*): **lesbians**
A **lesbian** is a woman who is sexually attracted to other women: *a lesbian relationship.*

less /lɛs/ *determiner*; *pronoun*; *adverb*; *preposition*
▻ ***determiner***
Less means 'a smaller amount of' or 'not so much': *You could put a little less sugar in your coffee.* ▫ *The shopping takes far less time now that I have a car.* ▫ *I've got less cash than I thought I had.* ▫ *What we need is less haste and more accuracy.* [*opposite* **more**]

Less is the comparative of **little**, and so is used with uncount nouns. Use **fewer** before plural count nouns: *The fewer children, the less expense.*

▻ ***pronoun*** (*sometimes used with count nouns*)
Less is a smaller amount of something: *You'll have to pay the full price; they won't accept any less.* ▫ *Masses of money pours into these charities, but less of it than you'd believe actually gets to those in need.* ▫ *I've got less of this job left to do than I realized.* ▫ *It's not good, but it's less of a disaster than we'd feared.* ▫ *We see much less of my parents* [= we don't see them nearly as often] *since we moved away.* [*opposite* **more**]

Notice that with specified quantities **less** is usually preferred to **fewer**: *They live less than three miles away. I bought it for less than £20. We had five hours or less to do the job in.*

▻ ***adverb***
1 Something that is so **less** than it was, or **less** than something else, is so to a smaller degree: *He paints a lot less now that he is getting older.* ▫ *Spelling mistakes are thought to matter less than grammatical ones.* **2 Less** is also used before adjectives and other adverbs: *She's much less bossy than her colleague.* ▫ *I see him a lot less often nowadays.* ▫ *She views these problems less philosophically than you do.* [*opposite* **more**]
▻ ***preposition***
Less can mean 'without' or 'minus': *She earns £450 a month less tax.*
▻ ***phrases*** **1 Less and less** describes something that is decreasing all the time: *There's less and less enthusiasm for work of this kind.* ▫ *As time went by I found I had less and less in common with her.* ▫ *He visited his parents less and less.* **2 a Less than** a certain amount means under that amount: *I had less than 50 pence in my purse.* **b Less than** can be used as an emphatic form of 'not': *My eyesight is less than perfect.* [*same as* **far from**] **3** For **more or less** see **more. 4** (*often humorous*) You add **'no less'** after mentioning someone or something, to emphasize their importance: *When you get to my age you receive a telegram from the Queen, no less.* **5 No less than** draws attention to the surprising largeness of an amount: *There were no less than 600 people at the meeting.*

-less /ləs/ *suffix*
-Less is used to make adjectives and is added **1** to nouns to mean 'not having, lacking, without': *heartless* ▫ *meaningless* ▫ *hopeless.* **2** to verbs to mean 'not affected by the action of the verb' or 'not doing the action of the verb': *countless people* ▫ *tireless* ▫ *ceaseless.*

lessen /ˈlɛsən/ *verb*: **lessens, lessening, lessened**
You **lessen** something when you make it smaller or less; something **lessens** when it becomes smaller or less: *These drugs will help lessen the pain.* ▫ *Her financial problems have lessened since she got a job.* [*same as* **reduce, diminish**]

lesser /ˈlɛsə(r)/ *adjective*
Lesser describes things that are not so great in importance, amount or degree as other things you are considering: *Auden, Eliot and a few lesser poets* ▫ *burglary and other lesser crimes* ▫ *We're all involved, to a greater or lesser extent.* ▫ *Some of these lesser-known writers are worth reading.*
▻ ***phrase*** **The lesser of two evils** is the less bad or harmful of two bad or harmful things.

lesson /ˈlɛsn/ *noun*: **lessons**
1 A **lesson** is a short period of time when you learn or teach something: *She has a French lesson every afternoon.* ▫ *He gives guitar lessons.* ▫ *I've decided to take dancing lessons.* **2** Something that you have learnt, especially something that is a warning or example to you, is also called a **lesson**: *Let his unhappiness be a lesson to you!* ▫ *Let's hope she learns her lesson from this disaster.* **3** A **lesson** is also a short passage read from the Bible during a service.
▻ ***phrase*** If you **teach** someone **a lesson** you try to make sure they do not do something bad or wrong again by punishing them for it.

lest /lɛst/ *conjunction* (*formal*)
1 You do something **lest** something unpleasant or unwanted should happen when you do something to try and prevent it from happening: *Speak quietly lest they should hear us.* **2 Lest** can also be used instead of 'that': *She was worried lest the car should break down.*

let /lɛt/ *verb*: **lets, letting, let**
1 When you **let** something happen, you allow or cause it to happen: *I'm afraid I've let the garden get rather untidy.* ▫ *Throw the ball up and let it bounce.* **2** You **let** someone do something when you allow them to do it: *We usually let the kids stay up late at weekends.* ▫ *Stop interrupting and let me finish what I was saying.* **3** You **let** someone somewhere, *eg* in, out, through or past, when you allow them to pass in that direction: *I knocked at the door and a young man let me in.* ▫ *We had to wait at the gate because the guards wouldn't let us through.* ▫ *Would somebody let the cat out?* ▫ *The coach stopped to let passengers off.* **4** One thing **lets** another *eg* in, out or through if the other thing can get into it, out of it or through it: *My walking boots have started letting in water.* ▫ *The windows were too tiny to let much sunlight through.* **5** You use **let a** in expressing warnings: *They're threatening to take the children away from me, but just let them try!* **b** to say you do not care what happens: *Let them think what they like; I know myself that I'm in the right.* **c** to say what ought to happen: *Let them wait their turn, like everybody else.* **6** You **let** a room, a house, or land when you allow someone else to use it in return for the payment of a rent: *We used to let the basement to students.* ▫ *A notice in one window read 'Rooms to Let'.*
▻ ***phrases*** **1 a** If you tell someone who is annoying someone else, or attacking them, to **let** them **alone**, or **let** them **be**, you are telling them to stop doing it. **b** If one thing is not so, **let alone** another, the second thing cannot be so, since it is the less likely or possible of the two: *There's no room for her, let alone her children and*

animals. ▫ *I can't even sing, let alone sight-read.* **2 a** You **let go** of someone or something when you stop holding them: *Let go of me.* ▫ *Let go of my coat.* ▫ *Please let go!* ▫ *Don't let go of your end of the rope.* ▫ *The child suddenly let go of her hand and ran across the street.* **b** You **let** a person or animal **go** when you allow them to leave, or free them: *The police questioned him for four hours and then let him go.* **3** You **let** someone **know** something when you tell them about it: *Let me know if you want me to get tickets.* **4** You use **let me** when you are offering to do something, or saying that you are going to do it: *Let me carry your case for you.* ▫ *Let me begin by saying how pleased we are to welcome you as tonight's speaker.* **5** You use **let's** or **let us** to suggest something that you and the people you are addressing should do: *Let's start.* ▫ *Let's wait another five minutes.* ▫ *Let us take time to consider the issue fully.*

Notice that the negative of **let's** and **let us** is **let's not** and **let us not**, or, more informally, **don't let's**: *Let's not quarrel about it. We don't need to get there till 5.00, but don't let's be later than that. Let us not forget their sacrifice.*

6 You say **let's see** or **let me see** when you are thinking or trying to remember something: *Now let me see; where did I put my car keys?* ▫ *It happened, let's see, about six weeks ago.*

phrasal verbs

let down 1 You **let** someone **down** if you disappoint them or do not help them when you should: *She felt that her husband had let her down.* [see also **letdown**] **2** You **let down** something such as a tyre when you allow the air inside it to escape. **3** You **let down** a piece of clothing, or its hem, when you make it longer: *She's grown out of all her dresses so I'm busy letting them down.*

let in for (*informal*) You wonder what you have **let** yourself **in for** when you realize you may have involved yourself in something difficult: *She was very vague about today's programme, so I've no idea what we've been let in for.*

let in on (*informal*) You **let** someone **in on** or **into** something such as a plan when you tell them about it: *They wouldn't let me in on their so-called future strategies.*

let off 1 You **let** someone who has done something wrong **off** if you do not punish them, or if you punish them only mildly: *I'll let you off this time.* ▫ *He was let off with a £50 fine.* **2** Someone is **let off** work or duties when they are told they do not have to do them: *I'll let you off your essay so that you can catch up on your reading.* **3** You **let off** a gun when you fire it; you **let off** a bomb when you make it explode.

let up 1 Something **lets up** when it becomes less strong or violent: *There'll be serious flooding if the rain doesn't let up soon.* [*same as* **abate**; see also **let-up**] **2** You **let up** if you stop working as hard, or being as busy, as you have been, and relax: *You'll be ill if you don't let up a bit.*

letdown /ˈlɛtdaʊn/ *noun*: **letdowns**
A **letdown** is a disappointment: *Most stars are a bit of a letdown in the flesh.*

lethal /ˈliːθəl/ *adjective*
A **lethal** substance is one that can kill: *a lethal weapon.*

lethargic /ləˈθɑːdʒɪk/ *adjective*
A person who is **lethargic** has no interest, enthusiasm or energy: *The procession of lethargic clerks climbed the steps to their office.*

lethargy /ˈlɛθədʒɪ/ *noun* (*uncount*)
Lethargy is lack of interest, enthusiasm or energy.

let's /lɛts/
Let's is the spoken, and informal written, form of **let us**. [see **let**]

letter /ˈlɛtə(r)/ *noun*: **letters**
1 A **letter** is a written or printed mark or symbol used to express a speech sound: *'A' is the first letter of the English alphabet.* **2** A **letter** is also a written or printed message usually sent by post in an envelope: *She wrote a letter to her friend living in Denmark.* ▫ *He got a letter from his doctor.*
▻ ***phrase*** You do something **to the letter** when you do it exactly as you are told to do it: *They followed his instructions to the letter.*

letter box /ˈlɛtə bɒks/ *noun*: **letter boxes**
1 A **letter box** is a slot in a door or wall through which letters are delivered to a building: *The parcel was too big to go through the letter box.* **2** A **letter box** is also a large metal box with a slot in the front, where people may post letters.

lettering /ˈlɛtərɪŋ/ *noun* (*uncount*)
Lettering is letters which have been drawn or painted, usually in a particular style: *The ingredients are listed in small lettering on the back of the packet.*

lettuce /ˈlɛtɪs/ *noun*: **lettuces**
A **lettuce** is a green plant with large leaves, eaten in salads. [see picture at **vegetable**]

let-up /ˈlɛt ʌp/ *noun*: **let-ups** (*count or uncount*)
There is a **let-up** when something becomes less strong or violent: *There should be a let-up in the rain soon.* [see also **let up** sense 1]

leukaemia (*AmE* **leukemia**) /ljʊˈkiːmɪə/ *noun* (*uncount*)
Leukaemia is a very serious disease which can kill people, in which the blood has too many white cells.

level /ˈlɛvəl/ *noun*; *adjective*; *adjective or adverb*; *verb*
▻ ***noun*** (*count or uncount*)
1 Something is at, above or below a certain **level** if it is at, above or below that height: *The rooms at ground level get a lot of traffic noise.* ▫ *The town is four hundred metres above sea level.* ▫ *Keep your arms stretched out at shoulder level.* ▫ *The house was built against a steep hillside with the ground floor on three different levels.* **2** (*used in the singular*) You can refer an area or surface that is parallel to the ground as the **level**: *It's a nice easy walk, all on the level; no steep hills.* **3** The **level** of liquid in a container, or of an area of water, is the height of its surface: *The river level kept rising.* ▫ *the difference between the summer and winter water levels.* ▫ *Check the vehicle's oil level regularly.* **4** The **level** of something is also **a** its position on a scale, *eg* of importance, difficulty or quality: *top-level negotiations* ▫ *discussions at local and national level* ▫ *intermediate-level students* ▫ *She teaches dancing at an advanced level.* ▫ *extraordinary levels of achievement.* **b** the point of view that you regard a situation from: *On a practical level the new system will take a few days to get used to.* **c** how much it amounts to: *a high level of unemployment* ▫ *Record production levels have been achieved.* ▫ *Refugee numbers have reached crisis level.* ▫ *intolerable noise levels.*
▻ ***adjective***
1 An object or surface that is **level a** is absolutely horizontal: *You haven't got that shelf quite level.* **b** has a smooth, flat, even surface: *The kitchen floor isn't very level.* [*same as* **even**] **2** You take a **level** spoonful of *eg* flour or sugar when you fill the spoon so that the contents come up only as far as the top of its sides: *a level teaspoonful of baking powder.* [see also **heaped**] **3** You speak in a **level** tone if you speak calmly and unemo-

tionally. [compare **even**] **4** Someone looks somewhere with a **level** gaze when they look there calmly and steadily.

▻ ***adjective* or *adverb***

1 Two or more things are **level** when they are at the same height or standard, or when they are absolutely side by side: *I'd like to get the tops of the pictures level with each other.* ▫ *The runners were level as they approached the first hurdle.* ▫ *Our schoolmarks stayed more or less level, though she was a better athlete than me.* [compare **equal**] **2** One thing draws **level** with another when it approaches closer to it until the two things are side by side: *Two cyclists drew level with us at the traffic lights.* **3** One thing remains **level** with another if it increases at the same rate: *Pay increases must keep level with inflation.*

▻ ***verb*: levels, levelling** (*AmE* **leveling**), **levelled** (*AmE* **leveled**)

1 You **level** something such as a piece of ground when you make it flat and smooth: *Use a rake to level the soil before planting.* **2** Something **levels** the score if it makes competitors' scores equal: *Two points to Jane, which levels the score at 15 points each.* **3** Buildings and other standing objects **are levelled** when they are knocked down to the ground or destroyed: *Much of the town centre was levelled in the bombing.* ▫ *Acres of woodland will be levelled to make way for the new road.* **4** You **level** something such as a criticism, accusation or charge at or against someone when you criticize them, accuse them of something, or charge them with something: *Serious criticism has been levelled at the police.* ▫ *Negligence was one of the charges levelled against her.* **5** Someone **levels** a gun at you if they aim it at you.

▻ ***phrases*** **1** (*informal*) You **do your level best** when you try to do something as well as you can: *I always did my level best to please her.* **2** You say that a piece of business is **on the level** if it is fair and honest.

> ***phrasal verbs***
> Something **levels off** or **levels out** when it become flat or horizontal after rising or falling, or when it remains steady after increasing or decreasing: *The road climbed steeply and then levelled out.* ▫ *Unemployment figures are levelling off at last.*

level crossing /lɛvəl ˈkrɒsɪŋ/ *noun* (*BrE*): **level crossings**

A **level crossing** is a place where a road crosses a railway on the same level.

level-headed /lɛvəlˈhɛdɪd/ *adjective*

A person who is sensible and calm can be described as **level-headed.**

lever /ˈliːvə(r)/ *noun*; *verb*

▻ ***noun*: levers**

1 A **lever** is a handle that you pull or push to operate a machine: *This gear lever's a bit stiff.* **2** A **lever** for moving things is a strong bar, one end of which is placed under the object or lid to be opened while you push down on the other. **3** Anything that can be used to gain an advantage, or force someone to do something, is also called a **lever**: *They used the threat of strikes as a lever to make the management discuss pay rises.*

▻ ***verb*: levers, levering, levered**

You **lever** something to the proper position when you move or open it using a lever: *He levered the door open.*

leverage /ˈliːvərɪdʒ/ *noun* (*uncount*)

Leverage is **1** the force or power gained by using a lever. **2** power, influence or advantage over someone.

levity /ˈlɛvɪtɪ/ *noun* (*uncount*; *formal*)

Levity is lack of seriousness.

levy /ˈlɛvɪ/ *verb*; *noun*

▻ ***verb*: levies, levying, levied**

A government **levies** something such as a tax when it raises or collects it: *levy a fine.*

▻ ***noun*: levies**

A **levy** is a sum of money that is paid *eg* in tax to the government.

liability /laɪəˈbɪlɪtɪ/ *noun*: **liabilities**

1 (*uncount*; *legal*) You have a **liability** for something when you are legally responsible for it: *liability for her husband's debts.* **2** (*usually in the plural*) The money that a company or person owes are their **liabilities**. [see also **asset**] **3** (*informal*) A **liability** is a person or thing that is or causes a problem: *This car is so old and battered it is a liability.*

liable /ˈlaɪəbəl/ *adjective*

1 (*legal*) You are **liable** for something such as a debt if you are legally responsible for it. **2** A person or thing that is **liable** to something is likely to suffer from it: *Both of the children are liable to travel sickness.* ▫ *areas liable to flooding.* [*same as* **susceptible**] **3** Something that is **liable** to happen is likely to happen: *It's liable to snow heavily.* [*same as* **likely**]

liaise /lɪˈeɪz/ *verb*: **liaises, liaising, liaised**

1 People or groups **liaise** with each other when they have a close working relationship and tell each other what they are doing: *The company must liaise with the police on the question of security.* **2** A person **liaises** between two or more people or groups when they tell each group or person what the others are doing: *Her job is to liaise between the author and the publisher.*

liaison /lɪˈeɪzɒn/ *noun*: **liaisons**

1 (*uncount*) **Liaison** is communication or co-operation between different groups or organizations: *liaison between the army and government.* **2** A **liaison** is a secret sexual or romantic relationship, usually between people who are married to other people. [*same as* **affair**]

liar /laɪə(r)/ *noun*: **liars**

A **liar** is a person who tells lies.

lib /lɪb/ *noun* (*uncount*; *informal*)

Lib is a short form of liberation: *women's lib* ▫ *gay lib.*

libel /ˈlaɪbəl/ *noun* (*uncount or count*): **libels**

Libel, or a **libel**, is the publication of a written, false statement which damages a person's good reputation: *sue the newspaper for libel.* [compare **slander**]

libellous (*AmE* **libelous**) /ˈlaɪbələs/ *adjective*

Something that is **libellous** contains a written false statement which damages a person's good reputation: *This newspaper article is libellous.* [*same as* **slanderous**]

liberal /ˈlɪbərəl/ *adjective*; *noun*

▻ ***adjective***

1 A **liberal** amount or supply of something is a generous amount or supply; a **liberal** person is someone who gives things, especially money, generously: *a liberal supply of cakes and sandwiches.* ▫ *He has always been a liberal supporter of charity.* [*opposite* **mean**] **2** A **liberal** person is one who respects and is tolerant of different opinions and behaviour: *a liberal attitude towards different religions.* [*opposite* **narrow-minded, blinkered**]

▻ ***noun*: liberals**

1 A **Liberal** is member of a political party that supports social and political reform. **2** A **liberal** is also any person who thinks in a liberal way.

liberalize or **liberalise** /ˈlɪbərəlaɪz/ *verb*: **liberalizes, liberalizing, liberalized**
A law is **liberalized** when it is made less strict: *The government has decided to liberalize the law on the use of drugs.* — *noun* (*uncount*) **liberalization** /lɪbərəlaɪzeɪʃən/: *liberalization of the drugs laws.*

liberally /ˈlɪbərəlɪ/ *adverb*
Liberally means generously, in large quantities or freely: *She helped herself liberally to cake.* □ *They give liberally to charity.*

liberate /ˈlɪbəreɪt/ *verb* (*formal*): **liberates, liberating, liberated**
1 You **liberate** a person or animal when you set them free: *The government has agreed to liberate all political prisoners.* **2** If an army **liberates** a country, it frees it from the control of an enemy country or state. — *noun* (*uncount; formal*) **liberation** /lɪbəˈreɪʃən/: *wars of liberation.*

liberated /ˈlɪbəreɪtɪd/ *adjective*
A **liberated** person is someone who acts according to modern ideas about what is correct sexual and moral behaviour: *a liberated young woman.*

liberty /ˈlɪbətɪ/ *noun*: **liberties**
1 a (*uncount*) **Liberty** is freedom to act, think and speak as you want, especially without government control: *Individual liberty is a basic human right.* **b Liberty** is also freedom to go where you want and do what you want because you are not imprisoned or a slave. **2** (*used in the plural*) Your **liberties** are the rights or privileges that you have: *civil liberties.*
▻ ***phrases*** **1 a** A person who is **at liberty** has escaped from prison. **b** You are **at liberty** to do something when you are allowed or permitted to do it. **2** Someone **takes the liberty** of doing something when they do it without permission: *I took the liberty of discussing your case with my friends.*

librarian /laɪˈbrɛərɪən/ *noun*: **librarians**
A **librarian** is a person employed in, or in charge of, a library: *If you can't find the book you need you should ask the librarian for help.*

library /ˈlaɪbrərɪ/ *noun*: **libraries**
1 A **library** is a room or building where a collection of books and newspapers, or things such as films or records, is kept to be used by members. **2** A **library** is also a collection of books, or a similar collection of things such as films or records: *a record library.*

lice /laɪs/ *noun*
Lice is the plural of **louse**: *He had head lice.*

licence (*AmE* **license**) /ˈlaɪsəns/ *noun*: **licences**
1 A **licence** is a document that gives you official permission to own something such as a dog, gun or television, or to do something such as sell alcohol: *Don't forget to bring your driving licence.* □ *They were granted a licence to develop the land.* [*same as* **permit**] **2** (*uncount; mainly literary*) **Licence** is freedom to behave or act as you wish: *We were lucky; we were brought up in the countryside and had licence to roam as we pleased.* **3** (*uncount*) Artistic **licence** is an artist's forgivable practice of altering the real appearance of a subject in his or her representation of it, for the sake of creating a more striking effect.

license /ˈlaɪsəns/ *verb*: **licenses, licensing, licensed**
A government or organization in authority **licenses** a person or activity when they give official permission for a person to do something or official permission for something to happen: *The government has refused to license the use of some drugs.* [*same as* **authorise**]

licensed /ˈlaɪsənst/ *adjective*
1 A hotel or restaurant that is **licensed** is legally allowed to sell alcohol to customers. **2** A person, thing or activity that is **licensed** has an official licence: *a licensed pilot.*

licentious /laɪˈsɛnʃəs/ *adjective*
A **licentious** person behaves in an immoral way, especially in their sexual behaviour.

lick /lɪk/ *verb; noun*
▻ ***verb***: **licks, licking, licked**
1 You **lick** something when you pass your tongue over it, usually to taste, moisten or clean it: *She licked the chocolate off the biscuit.* □ *He licked the stamp and stuck it on the envelope.* **2** (*informal*) You **lick** someone if you defeat them easily in a competition or game.
▻ ***noun***: **licks**
1 A **lick** is an act of passing your tongue over something: *She gave the ice cream a couple of licks.* **2** (*informal*) A small amount of something can also be called a **lick**: *a lick of paint.*
▻ ***phrases*** **1** For **lick your lips** see **lip**. **2** (*informal*) You **lick** something **into shape** when you make it more efficient or improve it. **3** You **lick your wounds** when you are recovering after having been thoroughly defeated or humiliated.

licorice see **liquorice**.

lid /lɪd/ *noun*: **lids**
1 A **lid** is a cover for a pot or box, that can either be removed completely or lifted up on one side. **2** Your **lids** are your eyelids.

lie[1] /laɪ/ *noun; verb*
▻ ***noun***: **lies**
A **lie** is a statement you make that you know is not true: *He hated himself for telling lies.*
▻ ***verb***: **lies, lying, lied**
You **lie** when you say things that you know are not true: *He lied about his qualifications to get the job.*

lie[2] /laɪ/ *verb*: **lies, lying, lay, lain**
1 You **lie** somewhere when you are in, or get into, a flat or horizontal position: *He was lying asleep in bed.* □ *I lay sick in my bunk.* □ *She lay flat on the sand.* □ *Was he lying on his back or his side?* □ *He lay there wondering what to do.* □ *Go and lie on the sofa for a while.* **2** An object **lies** somewhere if it is in a horizontal position in that place: *Several letters were lying on the doormat.* □ *The violin was lying unused on a shelf.* □ *Her book lay open at page 202.* □ *A map was lying spread out on the floor.* **3** A place **lies** somewhere if that is where it is situated: *The village lay about three miles from the sea.* □ *Innerpeffray Library lies between Crieff and Auchterarder on the B8062.* □ *low-lying regions.* **4** (*literary*) Something **lies** in a certain state if it is in that state: *The town lay in ruins after the bombing.* □ *Her dreams of a dancing career lay shattered.* **5** Something you are trying to discover or explain **lies** somewhere if that is where you can find it, or if that is the explanation for it: *Apparently the truth lay somewhere between the two statements.* □ *The beauty of the plan lay in its simplicity.* **6** Something that **lies** ahead of you is going to happen in the future: *Who knows what problems lie before us?*
▻ ***phrase*** Someone **lies in wait for** you when they hide themselves and wait for you to come past, usually so that they can harm you in some way: *They would lie in wait for us after school and follow us home, pulling our hair and yelling abuse.*

phrasal verbs
lie about or **lie around** **1** You **lie about** or **around** when you spend your time relaxing or doing nothing: *We just lay around on the beach all afternoon.* **2** Things that **are lying about** or **around** have been left somewhere in an untidy, disorganized state: *She left her books lying about on the floor.*

lie back You **lie back** when you lean back on something that supports you: *She lay back against the cushions.*
lie behind One thing **lies behind** another if it is the cause of it, or explains it: *Parental ambition lies behind many childhood problems.*
lie down You **lie down** when you get into a flat or horizontal position, especially to sleep or have a rest: *I lay down on the grass and went to sleep.* [see also **lie-down**]
lie with The responsibility for something **lies with** a person if it is their responsibility: *The real blame lies with the parents.*

lie-down /ˈlaɪdaʊn/ *noun* (*singular*)
You have a **lie-down** when you lie somewhere and rest: *He had a lie-down on the bed.* [see also **lie down**]

lie-in /laɪˈɪn/ *noun* (*used in the singular*)
You have a **lie-in** if you stay in bed later than usual in the morning: *She has a lie-in on Sundays.*

lieutenant (*BrE*) /lɛfˈtɛnənt/, (*AmE* /luːˈtɛnənt/) *noun*: **lieutenants**
A **lieutenant** is a junior officer in the army or navy.

life /laɪf/ *noun*: **lives** /laɪvz/
1 a (*uncount*) **Life** is the quality that humans, animals and plants have when they are not dead, which distinguishes them from objects, materials and substances, and is responsible for their growth and development: *the borderline between life and death* □ *disasters that cause widespread loss of life* □ *The priority is to save life.* [*opposite* **death**] **b** (*uncount*) You refer to living things as **life**: *Is there life on Mars?* □ *marine life* □ *the plant life of the island* □ *wildlife.* **c** (*used in the plural*) You refer to the number of people who die or are saved from death in a disaster or accident as that number of **lives**: *The ship sank with the loss of many lives.* □ *Her timely warning undoubtedly saved hundreds of lives.* **d** Your **life** is the state of your being alive: *He risked his life to rescue her.* □ *Know your first aid; you may be able to save somebody's life.* **e** Your **life** is also the period during which you are alive; you can refer to particular parts of it as *eg* your *married life* or your *adult life*; you can also refer to areas of it as *eg* your *private life* or your *social life*: *She spent her whole life in London.* □ *He doesn't want to have to remain abroad for the rest of his life.* □ *I've been a pacifist all my life.* □ *I've never in my life been so frightened.* □ *What a busy life you lead!* □ *Their married life was very brief.* □ *people who remain in the same job all their working lives* □ *He passed much of his adult life in a wheelchair.* □ *I object to the press intruding into my private life.* □ *She had a busy social life.* **f** The **life** of something such as a machine or piece of equipment is the length of time it lasts or functions satisfactorily: *These washing machines have a limited life.* □ *long-life batteries.* **g** A **life** of someone is a written account of their life: *She's writing a life of Jane Austen.* □ *I've been reading her life of John Clare.* **h** (*uncount*) A convicted criminal is sentenced to **life** when he or she is sent to prison for the rest of their life or for a very long time.
2 a (*uncount or used in the singular*) **Life** is people's experiences, activities and the things that happen to them; you can refer to an area of experience or activity as *eg college life*, *the life of a university*, or *the outdoor life*: *Life is easier now than it was 100 years ago.* □ *How's life been treating you?* □ *Married life was better than she'd expected.* **b** A person or place that is full of **life** is busy and full of energy or activity.
▻ ***phrases*** **1** You **bring** a subject **to life** when you talk about it or present it in a lively way that makes people interested in it. **2** A person or thing **comes to life** when they start being lively or interesting: *The play came to life in the second half.* **3** (*informal*) You hold on to something **for dear life** when you hold on to it tightly because it would be dangerous to let go: *He was hanging on to the rope for dear life.* **4 For life** means until death: *He'll probably be disabled for life.* □ *imprisoned for life.* **5** (*informal*) If you say you cannot understand or remember something **for the life of you** you mean that you cannot do so however hard you try. **6** You **lose your life** when you die: *He lost his life in a road accident.* **7** Something that is **a matter of life and death** is an emergency in which someone may die unless action is taken urgently. **8** To **take** someone's **life** is to kill them; someone who **takes their own life** kills themselves. **9** You **take your life in your hands** when you take a serious risk that could result in your death. **10** Someone who is **the life and soul of** a group or of an activity is someone whose cheerfulness and liveliness encourage everyone else to be cheerful and lively: *She used to be the life and soul of the club.*

lifebelt /ˈlaɪfbɛlt/ *noun*: **lifebelts**
A **lifebelt** is a ring or belt which floats, used to support people who have fallen into the water and are in danger of drowning.

lifeboat /ˈlaɪfboʊt/ *noun*: **lifeboats**
1 A **lifeboat** is a small boat for rescuing people in trouble at sea. **2** A **lifeboat** is also one of several small boats carried by a large ship, used to escape from the ship in an emergency.

lifebuoy /ˈlaɪf saɪkəl/ *noun*: **lifebuoys**
A **lifebuoy** is a lifebelt.

life cycle /ˈlaɪfboʊt/ *noun*: **life cycles**
The **life cycle** of an animal or plant is the various stages of development that it passes through during its life.

life expectancy /laɪf ɪkˈspɛktənsɪ/ *noun* (*count or uncount*): **life expectancies**
A person's **life expectancy** is the number of years that they can expect to live: *a life expectancy of 75 years.*

lifeguard /ˈlaɪfgɑːd/ *noun*: **lifeguards**
A **lifeguard** is an expert swimmer employed at a swimming pool or beach to rescue people in danger of drowning.

life jacket /ˈlaɪf dʒakɪt/ *noun*: **life jackets**
A **life jacket** is a sleeveless jacket that can be filled with air, worn to support you in the water.

lifeless /ˈlaɪfləs/ *adjective*
1 A person or animal that is **lifeless** is dead or unconscious. **2** People, places or things that are **lifeless** are dull and boring: *a lifeless performance in the play.* [*opposite* **lively, alive**].

lifelike /ˈlaɪflaɪk/ *adjective*
Something that is **lifelike** is very like the person or thing it represents: *a lifelike portrait.* [*same as* **true-to-life**]

lifeline /ˈlaɪflaɪn/ *noun*: **lifelines**
1 A **lifeline** is a rope used to support people in dangerous operations or to save lives. **2** A person's **lifeline** is something that is important because it is their only way of communicating, or because it allows some activity to take place: *The telephone is her lifeline.*

lifelong /ˈlaɪflɒŋ/ *adjective*
A **lifelong** friendship, ambition or desire is one that lasts the whole of your life.

life-size /ˈlaɪfsaɪz/ or **life-sized** /ˈlaɪfsaɪzd/ *adjective*
Life-size models, paintings or sculptures are the same size as the real person or thing.

lifespan /ˈlaɪfspan/ *noun*: **lifespans**
The **lifespan** of a person, animal or plant is the length of time that they are alive.

lifestyle /ˈlaɪfstaɪl/ *noun*: **lifestyles**
A person's **lifestyle** is the way they live and the conditions they live in: *a simple lifestyle.*

lifetime /ˈlaɪftaɪm/ *noun*: **lifetimes**
1 Your **lifetime** is the length of time you are alive: *He's seen a lot of changes in his lifetime.* □ *She'd spent a lifetime in politics.* **2** Something's **lifetime** is the length of time it exists: *in the lifetime of this government.*
▻ ***phrase*** If you get the **chance of a lifetime** you get an opportunity to do something exciting which you'll probably never get again.

lift /lɪft/ *verb*; *noun*
▻ ***verb***: **lifts, lifting, lifted**
1 You **lift** something when you move it into the air, especially from a surface: *She lifted the case off the ground to see how heavy it was.* □ *He lifted the baby out of her cot.* □ *We'll have to lift the boxes down from the top of the cupboard.* □ *He lifted the telescope to his eye.* [*same as* **raise**] **2** You **lift** a part of your body when you move it upwards or to a higher position: *Lift your arms out to the sides.* □ *She could hardly lift her head off the pillow.* □ *He lifted himself out of the armchair.* □ *Lift those knees higher!* [*same as* **raise**] **3** You **lift** your head or your eyes when you look up: *She replied without lifting her eyes from her work.* [*same as* **raise**] **4** Fog, mist or cloud **lifts** when it clears away or disappears. **5** Someone in authority **lifts** a rule that forbids something when they cancel it: *The 50-mph speed restriction is due to be lifted.* □ *TV channels refused to lift the ban on cigarette advertising.* **6** Something **lifts** your spirits if it makes you more cheerful. **7** (*informal*) If you **lift** a piece of writing or music that someone else has written you use it in your own work as though you had written it yourself: *Composers in those days were always lifting tunes from each other's work.*
▻ ***noun***: **lifts**
1 A **lift** is a compartment that moves between floors in a tall building, carrying people and things up or down: *Take the lift to the sixth floor.* **2** You give someone a **lift** when you help them by taking them somewhere in your vehicle: *She used to give me a lift to the tutorial on her motorbike.* □ *Never accept lifts from strangers.* **3** (*used in the singular*) Something gives you a **lift** when it makes you feel happy: *Winning the competition gave me quite a lift.*

> ***phrasal verb***
> A spacecraft **lifts off** when it rises up from the ground at the beginning of a flight. [see also **lift-off**]

lift-off /ˈlɪftɒf/ *noun* (*count or uncount*): **lift-offs**
Lift-off, or a **lift-off**, is the moment when a spacecraft rises up off the ground at the beginning of a flight.

ligament /ˈlɪgəmənt/ *noun*: **ligaments**
A **ligament** is a band of tough tissue that joins bones together.

light[1] /laɪt/ *noun*; *adjective*; *verb*
▻ ***noun***: **lights**
1 (*uncount*) **Light** is the brightness that comes from the sun, moon, flames or a lamp, that makes things able to be seen; natural **light** is daylight: *The fire gave him just enough light to read by.* □ *She opened the curtains and light flooded into the room.* □ *They blinked as they crawled out of the tunnel into the light.* [*opposite* **dark, darkness**] **2** A **light** is anything that produces light, such as an electric lamp or bulb: *Could someone switch the light on?* □ *street lights.* **3** (*usually in the plural*) You refer to traffic lights as the **lights**: *turn left at the lights.* □ *The lights were green.* **4** You give someone a **light** when you give them a match or lighter for their cigarette. **5** (*used in the singular*) You see something in a particular **light** when you regard it or think about it in that way: *After discussing the problem she was able to see it in a new light.* **6** Something appears, or is presented, in a good or bad **light** if it gives, or is presented so as to give, a good or bad impression: *Rome's conquests appear in a good light in the history books.* □ *The incident has shown him in a most damaging light.* □ *The press usually presented the princess and her views in a favourable light.* **7** There is a particular **light** in someone's eyes when they have a particular expression: *There was no mistaking the murderous light in his eyes.* □ *The light in her eyes showed only too clearly how happy she was.* [*same as* **look**]
▻ ***adjective***: **lighter, lightest**
1 You say it is **light** when the sky is bright because it is daytime: *At 3.00 am it was already getting light.* □ *It was just light enough for us to see our way.* □ *the long light summer evenings.* **2** A room or building that is **light** gets a lot of natural light in it, usually because it has large windows: *I was taken up to her large, light, airy office.* [*opposite* **dark**] **3 Light** colours are pale colours that are closer to white than black: *wearing a light-blue overall.* □ *His hair was blonde and his eyes light green.* [*same as* **pale**; *opposite* **dark**]
▻ ***verb***: **lights, lighting, lit** or **lighted**

> **Lighted** and **lit** can both be used as the past tense and past participle of the verb, though **lit** is more usual. **Lighted** is the form normally used as an adjective before a noun: *a lighted candle* (but *a brightly lit room*).

1 A place **is lit** by *eg* a lamp if that is the source of the light in it; **lighted** windows are the windows of a building in which the lights are on, seen from outside: *a narrow cell lit only by a small high window* □ *a dimly lit entrance.* **2** You **light** something, or it **lights**, when you make it start burning: *We lit the oil lamps.* □ *A watchman came into the hut and lit a log fire for us.* □ *Someone had dropped a lighted match on the carpet.* □ *The stove wouldn't light.*
▻ ***phrases*** **1** Something **is brought to light** or **comes to light** when it is discovered, or people get to know about it: *New evidence of police misconduct had come to light.* **2** One thing **casts, sheds** or **throws light on** another if it helps you to understand it: *Her biography to some extent sheds new light on the character of a strange man.* **3** (*informal*) Someone **goes out like a light** when they fall asleep as soon as they get into bed. **4** Someone is **in your light** when they are positioned so that they prevent the light from a lamp or window from reaching you. **5** You make a judgement or decision **in the light of** something if you take it into consideration: *In the light of recent difficulties with the alarm system it will be best if we withdraw all keys held by members of staff.* **6** You **see the light** when you suddenly understand or realize something. **7** You **set light to** something when you make it start burning: *A couple of boys had set light to the shed.*

> ***phrasal verb***
> **light up 1** One thing **lights up** another when it makes it bright with light: *The fire lit up the sky.* **2** Someone's face or eyes **light up** when an expression of liveliness or happiness comes into them: *Her eyes lit up when I mentioned his name.* **3** (*informal*) Someone **lights up** when they light a cigarette or pipe and begin to smoke it.

light² /laɪt/ *adjective*; *adverb*

▻ ***adjective***: **lighter**, **lightest**

1 Something that is **light a** does not weigh much and is easy to lift or carry: *a light metal such as aluminium* □ *My suitcase feels lighter than yours.* [*opposite* **heavy**] **b** is small in amount, degree or extent: *A light rain was falling.* □ *The traffic is always lighter on Sundays.* □ *We're planning a light revision of the dictionary in a year's time.* [*opposite* **heavy**] **2** A **light** wind is a gentle one: *a light westerly breeze.* [*opposite* **strong**] **3 Light** clothing is made of thin material: *wearing only a light summer dress* [*opposite* **heavy**, **thick**] **4 Light** equipment and machinery is easily moved about or manoeuvred: *a light aircraft* □ *light-armed troops.* [*opposite* **heavy**] **5 Light** work or exercise is easy to do and does not need much effort. [*opposite* **heavy**] **6** A **light** punishment is one that is not severe: *He'll probably get off with a light sentence in view of his age.* [*same as* **mild**, **lenient**; *opposite* **harsh**, **severe**] **7 Light** movements are graceful and quick, performed without effort or force; you are **light** on your feet if you move about gently and quietly: *Keep the skipping very light.* □ *He gave her a light kiss on the cheek.* **8** Books or music that are **light** are intended for amusement and relaxation, and are not serious or difficult to understand: *Pack some light reading for the journey.* □ *There seemed to be nothing but news or light entertainment on television.* **9 Light** food is easy to digest: *We usually have just a light meal in the evenings. — adverb* **lightly**: *He stroked her hair lightly.* □ *flicking a duster lightly over the furniture.* □ *She stepped lightly down from the carriage. — noun* (*uncount*) **lightness**: *Keep clothing and equipment to a minimum; lightness is everything when you're going backpacking.* □ *grace and lightness of movement.*

▻ ***adverb***

1 You travel **light** when you take very little luggage with you. **2** Something that weighs **light** is not heavy to carry.

▻ ***phrase*** You **make light of** something serious if you talk about it as though it is not important: *She used to make light of her illness.* □ *We should not make light of the very real difficulties.*

light³ /laɪt/ *verb*: **lights**, **lighting**, **lit** or **lighted**

You **light** on or upon something when you notice or discover it: *Suddenly his eye lit upon the paper knife.*

light bulb /ˈlaɪt bʌlb/ *noun*: **light bulbs**

A **light bulb** is a piece of hollow, pear-shaped glass in a lamp, that gives out light.

lighten¹ /ˈlaɪtən/ *verb*: **lightens**, **lightening**, **lightened**

1 You **lighten** something, or something **lightens**, when you make it, or it becomes, brighter: *The sky lightened after the rain.* [*opposite* **darken**] **2** Your face, voice or mood **lightens** when it becomes brighter or livelier because you are happier.

lighten² /ˈlaɪtən/ *verb*: **lightens**, **lightening**, **lightened**

You **lighten** something, or something **lightens**, when you make it, or it becomes, less heavy: *This bag is too heavy for the plane; you need to lighten it.*

lighter¹ /ˈlaɪtə(r)/ *adjective*

Lighter is the comparative form of the **light**¹ and **light**².

lighter² /ˈlaɪtə(r)/ *noun*: **lighters**

A **lighter** is a small device that produces a flame, used for lighting *eg* cigarettes.

light-fingered /ˈlaɪtfɪŋgərd/ *adjective*

You can say that someone is **light-fingered** if they steal things.

light-headed /ˈlaɪthɛdɪd/ *adjective*

You feel **light-headed** if your head feels as if it is spinning and you feel as if you may faint. [*same as* **dizzy**]

light-hearted /ˈlaɪthɑːtɪd/ *adjective*

1 You are **light-hearted** if you are happy and are not worried about anything: *a light-hearted mood.* [*opposite* **downhearted**] **2** Something that is **light-hearted** is amusing and cheerful: *a light-hearted discussion of the subject. — adverb* **light-heartedly:** *She laughed light-heartedly.*

lighthouse /ˈlaɪthaʊs/ *noun*: **lighthouses**

A **lighthouse** is a tall building on the coast with a flashing light which guides ships or warns them of rocks.

lighting /ˈlaɪtɪŋ/ *noun* (*uncount*)

Lighting is the quality of the light, or the type of equipment for providing light, in a place: *street lighting* □ *subdued lighting* □ *artificial lighting.*

lightly /ˈlaɪtlɪ/ *adverb*

1 You do something **lightly** when you do it gently: *She tapped him lightly on the arm.* **2** You treat something **lightly** when you do not treat it seriously: *He speaks lightly of his debts but he is actually very worried about them.*

▻ ***phrases*** Someone **gets off lightly** if they escape without serious punishment, damage or harm.

lightning /ˈlaɪtnɪŋ/ *noun*; *adjective*

▻ ***noun*** (*uncount*)

Lightning is a flash of light in the sky caused by electricity, especially during a storm.

▻ ***adjective***

Lightning movements are very quick and sudden: *She ran up the stairs with lightning speed.* □ *a lightning attack.*

lightning-conductor /ˈlaɪtnɪŋ kənˈdʌktə(r)/ *noun*: **lightning-conductors**

A **lightning-conductor** is a metal rod attached to a building or a ship's mast, which protects it from damage by lightning by taking the lightning harmlessly to the ground or into the sea.

lightning rod /ˈlaɪtnɪŋ rɒd/ (*AmE*) *noun*: **lightning rods**

A **lightning rod** is a lightning-conductor.

lightweight /ˈlaɪtweɪt/ *adjective*

1 Something that is **lightweight** weighs less than is usual: *a lightweight suit for the summer.* **2** Something can be described as **lightweight** if it is not important or influential, and is for amusement rather than any serious purpose: *He took some lightweight magazines and books to read during the flight.*

light year /ˈlaɪt jɪə(r)/ *noun*: **light years**

1 A **light year** is the distance light travels in a year, being nearly six million million miles. **2** (*informal*; *used in the plural*) You can say that something that happened recently seems **light years** away when it seems to have happened a long time ago.

likable see **likeable**.

like¹ /laɪk/ *preposition*; *conjunction*

▻ ***preposition***

1 a A person or thing that is, or behaves, **like** another is similar to them or behaves in a similar way: *It was a big black bird, like a crow.* □ *She looks very like her mother.* □ *At night a cat sometimes sounds like a baby crying.* □ *It felt like a summer's day.* □ *You're behaving like a two-year-old.* □ *Stop acting like a coward.* [= stop being so cowardly]. □ *Your third gear acts like a brake.* **b** You use **like** in expressions called similes, that compare one thing to another: *He was shaking like a leaf.* □ *He smokes like a chimney* [= He smokes a lot of cigarettes or cigars]. **c** You use expressions such as 'that sounds **like**', or 'it looks **like**' to say what you think is happening or is the case: *That sounds like* [= I think I hear] *Robert coming up the stairs now.* □ *That looks like* [= I think I see] *our bus at last.* □ *This tastes like* [= I think this is] *salt, not sugar.* □ *That sounds like* [= I think that is] *a good idea.* □ *It feels like rain* [= I think it's going to rain]. □ *It looks like being a busy week.* [see also **feel**]

2 You use **like** with *what* to ask for a description of someone or something: *What is he like?* □ *We now know what many of the dinosaurs looked like.* □ *What does caviar taste like?* □ *What's it like working underground?* □ *I can hardly remember what it was like having a job.*

3 a Like can introduce examples of what you have mentioned, and so means the same as 'such as': *She wants to go somewhere exciting, like Africa or South America.* □ *outdoor sports like running and climbing.* **b** People or things '**like** this', '**like** that' or '**like** them' are people or things of this or that kind: *Situations like this need careful handling.* □ *I can't stand people like her.* **c** You use '**like** this' or '**like** that' to mean in this or that way: *Do it like this.* **d** '**Like** this' and '**like** that' can refer to the degree to which something is done, and so mean 'so much': *There's no need for us to quarrel like this.* □ *Do stop shouting like that!* **e** You do something **like** someone else when you copy them or do it in the way that they do it, or do it as well as or to the same extent as they do: *Do it like me.* □ *She can't draw like her sister.* □ *He swears just like his predecessor.* **f** You use **like** to mention another person or thing in the same situation as the one you are talking about: *Like the rest of us, he's worried.*

4 Behaviour that is **like** someone is behaviour that you expect from them because it is typical of them: *It would be just like him to change his mind at the last minute.* □ *That kind of generosity is so like her.*

▷ ***conjunction*** (*informal*; *especially AmE*) **1 Like** is sometimes used to mean 'as', 'in the same manner as', 'to the same extent as' or 'as well or expertly as': *The leaves are turning brown like they do every year.* □ *He drinks just like his father did.* □ *He can't play the piano like his sister can.* **2 Like** can also mean 'as if': *He acts like he owns the place.* □ *You look like you need a hot drink.*

▷ ***phrases*** **1** You use **and the like** to mean 'and other things of the same sort': *Always carry your passport, money and the like with you.* **2** You **compare like with like** when you compare one thing with another of the same kind. **3** You ask a child to do something **like a good boy** or **girl** as a way of persuading them to do what you want: *Eat up your fish like a good girl.* **4** (*informal*) You use **like so** when demonstrating something to someone: *Place the spoon and fork like so.* **5** A person or thing that is **nothing like** another is completely different from them: *She's nothing like her photographs.* □ *The house isn't anything like what I was expecting.* **6** (*especially with a negative*) **The likes of** a certain person or thing is the kind of person or thing they are: *I would never trust the likes of him.* □ *fearful storms, the likes of which we'd never before witnessed.*

like² /laɪk/ *verb*; *noun*

▷ ***verb***: **likes, liking, liked**

1 a You **like** something if you are fond of it or pleased with it, or if you enjoy it or prefer it: *I like travel books.* □ *He doesn't like the new house.* □ *What do you like best about her?* □ *She likes her coffee without sugar.* □ *Don't you like dancing?* □ *They don't like having to concentrate on anything difficult.* □ *Do you like me brushing your hair?* □ *She doesn't like anyone being late for her lectures.* □ *I don't like your* (or *you*) *criticizing me in public.* □ *We have to pay for dental treatment whether we like it or not.* □ *How are you liking university?* [*opposite* **dislike**; see note at **love**] **b** You **like** someone if you are fond of them, sometimes as distinct from loving them: *I liked him but I never loved him.* [*opposite* **dislike**] **c** You **like** to do something, or **like** something to happen if you normally choose to do it, or normally prefer it to happen: *He always liked to lay out his clothes ready for the morning.* □ *She likes to get some exercise every day.* □ *They liked the children to finish their homework before watching television.* □ *I do like everyone to be satisfied.* **d** You say you don't **like** to do something, or don't **like** doing it, if you do not want to do it, or are reluctant to: *I don't like disturbing them after 10.00 pm.* □ *I didn't like to tell him the truth in case it upset him.*

2 You express, or enquire about, wishes and preferences, and make offers and suggestions, using **a** 'would **like**' and 'should **like**': *I should like a copy of the report.* □ *Where would you like to go tonight?* □ *Which desk would you like?* □ *Would you like me to help you?* □ *I'd like to get to the library today.* □ *Would you like to help?* □ *I would like to come and visit you if I may.* □ *He says he'd like the essays handed in by Friday.* □ *Would you like* [= please will you] *wait here?* □ *I should have liked to stay.* □ *I'd like to have spoken to him before he left.* [see note at **love**] **b** expressions such as 'if you **like**': *I'll give you a lift, if you like.* □ *We can start as early as you like.* □ *Tell her she can come whenever she likes.* [*same as* **wish**, **want**; compare **please**]

3 You also use 'if you **like**' **a** to agree to a suggestion: *'Shall we go out for a meal tonight?' 'If you like.'* **b** to offer your hearers some word or expression that they may prefer: *It was a misleading thing to say; dishonest, if you like.*

▷ ***noun*** (*used in the plural*): **likes**

Your **likes** are the things that you like. [*opposite* **dislikes**]

-like /laɪk/ *suffix*

-like is added to a noun to form an adjective to describe something that is like, of or suitable for the thing the noun refers to: *His behaviour is childlike.* □ *a lifelike portrait.*

likeable or **likable** /'laɪkəbəl/ *adjective*

A **likeable** person or thing is easy to like and pleasant: *a friendly, likeable young woman.*

likelihood /'laɪklɪhʊd/ *noun* (*used in the singular*)

When you talk about the **likelihood** of something happening, you talk about how probable or likely it is to happen: *There is a strong likelihood that it will snow tomorrow.* □ *There is every likelihood of rain.* [*same as* **probability**]

likely /'laɪklɪ/ *adjective*; *adverb*

▷ ***adjective***: **likelier, likeliest**

1 Something that is **likely** is expected or probable; you are **likely** to do something, or to have done something if you will probably do it, or have probably done it: *Apparently snow is likely tomorrow.* □ *The experts are busy predicting the likely results of next week's poll.* □ *It now seems likely that I was right after all.* □ *It's quite likely that the strain would kill him.* □ *His explanation didn't seem very likely.* □ *That's a likely tale!* [= that's probably a lie] □ *Is it likely to rain?* □ *Don't worry, I'm not likely to forget your birthday.* □ *Things are bad and likely to get worse.* □ *Which car is least likely to be needed this afternoon?* □ *the girl most likely to succeed* □ *They're likely to have thought about this already.* [*opposite* **unlikely**; compare **certain**, **sure**]

2 Likely describes a person or thing that is suitable for a purpose or job: *I've found a likely man for the job.* □ *We've had one or two likely applicants.* [*same as* **suit-**

able; *opposite* **unlikely**, **unsuitable**]
▻ ***adverb*** (*sentence adverb*)
You use **likely** with words such as *very*, *most* and *quite* to mean 'probably': *This is most likely the spelling rule you've been taught.* ▫ *The post will very likely have been filled by now.* ▫ *More than likely she's missed the bus.*
▻ ***phrase*** (*informal*) If you say '**Not likely!**' you mean 'No!' or 'Certainly not!': *'Would you have him back?' 'Not likely!'*

like-minded /laɪkˈmaɪndɪd/ *adjective*
People who are **like-minded** have similar opinions, tastes or intentions: *yourself and like-minded friends.*

liken /ˈlaɪkən/ *verb*: **likens**, **likening**, **likened**
You **liken** one thing to something else when you say that it is similar to it: *The flavour of these apples has been likened to that of pears.* [*same as* **compare**]

likeness /ˈlaɪknəs/ *noun* (*usually in the singular*): **likenesses**
If one person or thing has or bears a **likeness** to another, they look like them: *The pen bore a remarkable likeness to the one I'd lost.* ▫ *The brothers have a strong family likeness.*

likewise /ˈlaɪkwaɪz/ *adverb*
When someone does something and you do **likewise**, you do the same thing as they do: *I'm getting extra travel insurance and I suggest you do likewise.*

liking /ˈlaɪkɪŋ/ *noun* (*used in the singular*)
You have a **liking** for someone or something when you like or prefer them: *Most children have a liking for chocolates.*
▻ ***phrases*** **1** If something is *eg* too big **for your liking**, it is bigger than you want it to be: *This bed is too soft for her liking.* **2** (*formal*) When something is **to your liking**, you are pleased or satisfied with it: *The new house isn't to his liking.*

lilac /ˈlaɪlək/ *noun*: **lilacs**
1 (*count or uncount*) **Lilac**, or a **lilac**, is a small tree with bunches of white or pale pinkish-purple, sweet-smelling flowers. **2** (*uncount, often adjectival*) **Lilac** is a pale pinkish-purple colour: *a lilac blouse.*

lilt /lɪlt/ *noun*: **lilts**
A **lilt** is a light, swinging rhythm in *eg* a voice or tune: *He speaks with a soft Irish lilt.*

lilting /ˈlɪltɪŋ/ *adjective*
A voice or tune that rises and falls in a pleasantly rhythmical way can be described as **lilting**: *The lilting voice of the folk singer drifted over the floodlit lawn.*

lily /ˈlɪlɪ/ *noun*: **lilies**
A **lily** is a plant with white or coloured trumpet-shaped flowers growing at the end of a tall stem.

limb /lɪm/ *noun*: **limbs**
1 Your **limbs** are your arms and legs. **2** A **limb** of a tree is one of its main branches.
▻ ***phrase*** A person who is **out on a limb** is in a dangerous and isolated position, usually because of having ideas or opinions that are not accepted by other people.

limber /ˈlɪmbə(r)/ *verb*: **limbers**, **limbering**, **limbered**

> ***phrasal verb***
> You **limber up** when you do exercises to warm your muscles before taking part in a sport.

limbo[1] /ˈlɪmboʊ/ *noun* (*uncount*)
▻ ***phrase*** You are **in limbo** when you are in a state of uncertainty and confusion about what is going to happen next.

limbo[2] /ˈlɪmboʊ/ *noun* (*used in the singular*)
The **limbo** is a West Indian dance in which the dancer leans backwards to dance under a rope or bar which is moved lower and lower towards the floor.

lime[1] /laɪm/ *noun*: **limes**
1 A **lime** is a small, round, green fruit with a sour, lemon-like flavour. **2** (*uncount, often adjectival*) **Lime** or **lime green** is the green colour of this fruit.

lime[2] /laɪm/ *noun*: **limes**
A **lime**, or **lime tree**, is a tree with rough bark, pale green, heart-shaped leaves and yellow blossom.

lime[3] /laɪm/ *noun* (*uncount*)
Lime is a white substance that is used for making cement and spreading on soil to improve its quality.

limelight /ˈlaɪmlaɪt/ *noun* (*used in the singular*)
Someone who is in the **limelight** is getting a lot of public attention, either because they are famous, or because they have done something remarkable. [*same as* **spotlight**]

limerick /ˈlɪmərɪk/ *noun*: **limericks**
A **limerick** is a humorous poem of five lines with a special rhyming scheme.

limestone /ˈlaɪmstoʊn/ *noun* (*uncount*)
Limestone is a white-coloured rock used in building and to make cement.

limit /ˈlɪmɪt/ *noun*; *verb*
▻ ***noun***: **limits**
1 A **limit** is a point or line that may not be passed: *No-one is allowed within a two-mile limit of the palace.* **2** A **limit** is the greatest or smallest extent, amount or degree that is allowed or is possible: *the speed limit* ▫ *There are no limits to what you can achieve.* ▫ *government spending limits.* [*same as* **restriction**]
▻ ***verb***: **limits**, **limiting**, **limited**
1 You **limit** something when you keep it below a certain amount or level: *She limits her spending on books to £10 a week.* **2** If someone or something **limits** you, they allow you only to have a small or restricted amount or number of things. [*same as* **restrict**]: *You must limit yourself to two suitcases if you want to travel by plane.*
▻ ***phrases*** **1** (*informal*) You can say that someone or something is **the limit** when you are annoyed with them. **2** You are not allowed in a place that is **off limits**. **3** You say **within limits** when something you have said applies to a certain extent or with a moderate degree of freedom only: *You can spend as much as you like, within limits!*

limitation /lɪmɪˈteɪʃən/ *noun*: **limitations**
1 (*usually in the plural*) A person's **limitations** are the extent of their ability, which sets a limit on what they can achieve: *know your limitations* ▫ *Acupuncture is good for some medical conditions but it has its limitations.* **2** A **limitation** is a condition that controls or limits what you can do: *There is a limitation on what the company can spend on publicity this year.* **3** (*uncount*) **Limitation** is control or restriction, especially of the growth or development of something: *arms limitation talks.*

limited /ˈlɪmɪtɪd/ *adjective*
1 Something that is **limited** is not large in size or amount: *There are only a limited number of spaces in the car park.* [*opposite* **unlimited**] **2** A **limited** company is one in which the shareholders are responsible for a part of the company's debt.

> **Limited** is usually written **Ltd** after the name of a company: *Marks and Spencer Ltd.*

limitless /ˈlɪmɪtləs/ *adjective*
Something that is **limitless** is very large: *The possibili-*

ties are limitless. [*same as* **infinite**; *opposite* **limited, restricted**]

limousine /ˈlɪməziːn/ *noun*: **limousines**
A **limousine** is a large, expensive and luxurious motor car.

limp[1] /lɪmp/ *verb*; *noun*
▻ ***verb***: **limps, limping, limped**
1 A person or animal **limps** when they walk with an awkward or uneven step, because one leg is weak or injured: *She limped down the road.* **2** A damaged ship or aircraft **limps** when it moves with difficulty.
▻ ***noun*** (*usually in the singular*): **limps**
A **limp** is an uneven, awkward way of walking: *He has walked with a limp ever since he broke his leg.*

limp[2] /lɪmp/ *adjective*: **limper, limpest**
1 Something that is **limp** is not stiff but is soft and hangs loosely. **2** A person who is **limp** has no energy or strength: *a cold, limp hand.* — *adverb* **limply**: *He lay limply on the bed.* — *noun* (*uncount*) **limpness**: *the limpness of the material.*

limpet /ˈlɪmpɪt/ *noun*: **limpets**
A **limpet** is a cone-shaped shellfish that fixes itself firmly to rocks and stones.

line[1] /laɪn/ *noun*; *verb*
▻ ***noun***: **lines**
1 a A **line** is a long thin mark on a surface: *Draw a straight line diagonally across your sheet of paper.* ▫ *You can't park on double yellow lines.* ▫ *He signed his name on the dotted line as instructed.* ▫ *There was some doubt as to which horse was first over the finishing line.* ▫ *Her mouth was set in a grim determined line.* **b** (*often in the plural*) The **lines** on a person's face are the creases or wrinkles in it: *Deep lines ran from either side of his nose to the corners of his mouth.* **c** (*often in the plural*) You can refer to the shape, outline and general design of an object as its **lines**: *People liked the ship's strong clean lines.* **d** A rope, cable, wire or string with a specific purpose is referred to as a **line**: *I had removed the washing from the machine and was just hanging it outside on the line.* ▫ *nylon fishing lines* ▫ *The storm had brought down the telephone lines.* **e** The **line** between two groups, classes or sets of circumstances is the point where the one changes or develops into the other: *the dividing line between genius and madness* ▫ *people who live below the poverty line.* **f** (*usually in the plural*) In war, each side's **lines** are the front edge of the area they occupy: *The plan was to drop a party by parachute behind enemy lines.*
2 a A **line** of people or things is several of them standing or placed one behind the other, or side by side in a row: *Get yourselves into lines of eight.* ▫ *We drove along between two lines of cypress trees.* **b** (*AmE*) A **line** is a queue. **c** (*usually in the singular*) A **line** of people is a series of people that exist one after the other, *eg* in each generation of a family, or as holders of a particular post: *the Angevin line of kings* ▫ *She got her musical ability from her father; in fact she came from a long line of musicians.*
3 a A **line** is a row of written or printed words: *What does the last line in the book say?* ▫ *a six-line poem.* **b** (*usually in the plural*) Actors' **lines** are the words they must learn for their part in a play or film: *She always had difficulty remembering her lines.* ▫ *Line-learning has never been a problem for me.*
4 You use **line** to refer to directions and routes, *eg* **a** the direction in which something is moving or travelling: *You're standing in my line of vision.* ▫ *She was caught in the line of fire as she passed one of the gun positions and died immediately.* ▫ *A row of trees marks the line of the old road.* **b** a railway track: *Repairs to the Edinburgh-Glasgow line will mean delays to passenger services.* **c** a route along which vehicles such as trains or buses travel regularly: *You can get there on the Underground, using the Victoria Line.* **d** (*often in the plural*) a route along which supplies and messages are sent, *eg* during a military operation: *It was vital to keep the lines of communication open.* ▫ *We attacked the enemy's supply lines.*
5 a Your **line** of work or interest is the kind of work you do, or the kind of thing you are interested in: *What's your line of business?* ▫ *Are you in the banking line yourself?* **b** The **line** you take on a particular subject is your attitude or policy towards it: *The Government takes a firm line on juvenile crime.* ▫ *I take the line that she's old enough to organize her own life.* ▫ *What's the official line on overtime pay?* [see also **party line**] **c** A **line** of thought, enquiry, argument, research or development is a series of considerations or activities in which one thing leads to another: *We'll try a new line of investigation.* ▫ *I see that we've been thinking along slightly different lines.* **d** A **line** of goods is a particular type of product made or sold by a business company: *They've recently launched a new line in chocolate biscuits.* **e** Something in a particular **line** is an item in a particular class of things or area of activity: *That's the shop to go to if you need anything in the skiing line.*
▻ ***verb***: **lines, lining, lined**
People or things **line** something such as a road when they stand in rows along its sides: *Crowds lined the streets leading to the cathedral.* ▫ *a tree-lined avenue.* [see also **line**[2], **lined, lining**]
▻ ***phrases*** **1** Something that happens somewhere **along the line** happens at some point in a process: *The investigating team had made mistakes all along the line.* **2** You describe something as being **along**, or **on, the lines of** something else if that is what it is roughly like: *We're planning a children's dictionary on similar lines to an encyclopaedia.* ▫ *It will be along the lines of a student's workbook.* **3** You **draw the line** at something when you refuse to do it, because it goes beyond what you are willing to do: *I don't mind helping her clean the house but I draw the line at tidying her garden.* **4** (*informal*) You **drop** someone **a line** when you send them a note or a short letter. **5 a** People or vehicles stand or wait **in line** when they are in a queue: *Cars were already waiting in line to board the ferry.* **b** One thing is **in line** with others when it forms a straight row with them: *He moved the chair back into line.* **c** One person or group is **in line** with others when they agree with the others and act in the same way; an action or move that is **in line** with a particular policy follows or obeys it: *Britain needs to be brought into line with the rest of Europe on this issue.* **6** You are **in line for** something when you are likely to get it: *She thinks she's in line for promotion.* **7** You **keep someone in line** when you make them behave as they ought to behave. **8** (*computers*) You are **on line** when the terminal you are working at is connected directly to a computer system that allows you to input and access data. **9** Something such as your job or reputation is **on the line** if you are in danger of losing it. **10** For **on the lines of** see **along the lines of** above. **11** You are **on the right lines** if you are acting or working in a way that is likely to bring successful results: *My supervisor thinks my research is on the right lines so far.* **12 a** One thing is **out of line** with others if it is not in a straight line with them: *The dancers got a bit out of line at one stage.* **b** One person or group is **out of line** with others when they disagree with the others, or act differently from them: *His thinking is out of line with company policy.* **13** You **read between the lines** when you understand what is

implied by what someone says, although they do not express it openly: *Reading between the lines, I realized that she wasn't enjoying the job as much as she'd expected to.* **14** You **toe the line** when you behave as you ought to.

> ***phrasal verb***
> **line up** **1** People **line up** when they form a straight line or queue; you **line** people **up** when you put them into a straight line or queue. **2** You **line** something **up** when you organize or arrange it: *She has lined herself up a new job.* □ *A singer has been lined up for the party.* [see also **line-up**]

line² /laɪn/ *verb*: **lines, lining, lined**
1 You **line** something such as a garment or drawer when you cover its inside surface with a layer of fabric or paper: *drawers lined with newspaper* □ *fur-lined gloves.* [see also **lining**] **2** One thing **lines** another when it forms a layer covering its inside surface: *I waited in her small book-lined study.* □ *The disease damages the membrane lining the bowels.*

linear /ˈlɪnɪə(r)/ *adjective* (*formal*)
1 Something that is in the form of or is made of a line or lines, can be described as **linear**: *wallpaper with linear patterns.* **2** In a **linear** process one thing leads directly to the next, and so on.

lined /laɪnd/ *adjective*
1 If a person's skin is **lined**, it has lines and wrinkles on it: *a face lined with age and worry.* **2** **Lined** paper has straight lines marked on it.

linen /ˈlɪnɪn/ *noun* (*uncount*)
1 (*often adjectival*) **Linen** is a type of cloth used *eg* for making sheets, tablecloths and clothes: *a lightweight linen suit.* **2** **Linen** is household articles such as sheets and tablecloths: *bed linen.* **3** A person's **linen** is their underwear.

liner¹ /ˈlaɪnə(r)/ *noun*: **liners**
A **liner** is a large passenger ship or aircraft.

liner² /ˈlaɪnə(r)/ *noun*: **liners**
A **liner** is a bag put inside a bin or dustbin to keep it clean: *a bin liner.*

linesman /ˈlaɪnzmən/ *noun*: **linesmen**
A **linesman** is an official in some sports, *eg* soccer, cricket and tennis, whose job is to tell the referee when the ball has gone over the boundary line of the pitch or court.

line-up /ˈlaɪnʌp/ *noun*: **line-ups**
1 A **line-up** is a list of people chosen for a sports team, or appearing in a show: *The line-up for tonight's show includes the actor Derek Jacobi.* **2** A **line-up** is also a list of programmes on a television or radio station: *Tonight's line-up on Channel 4 includes coverage of the World Chess Championships.*

linger /ˈlɪŋgə(r)/ *verb*: **lingers, lingering, lingered**
1 A person or thing **lingers** when they are slow to depart: *The smell of fried onions lingered for some days.* □ *Equality may exist officially; in practice the old prejudices linger on.* **2** You **linger**, or **linger** over something, when you spend a long time with it or doing it: *They lingered on the verandah till darkness fell.* □ *She lingered behind, unwilling to leave.* □ *They lingered over lunch.* — *adjective* **lingering:** *a lingering smell of onions.*

lingerie /ˈlanʒərɪ/ *noun* (*formal uncount*)
Lingerie is women's underwear and nightclothes.

linguist /ˈlɪŋgwɪst/ *noun*: **linguists**
A **linguist** is **1** a person who has good knowledge of languages. **2** a person who teaches or studies linguistics.

linguistic /lɪŋˈgwɪstɪk/ *adjective*
Linguistic developments and ideas relate to **1** language: *the linguistic development of young children.* **2** linguistics: *current linguistic theory.* — *adverb* **linguistically:** *Television serves as a unifying influence in a linguistically divided country.*

linguistics /lɪŋˈgwɪstɪks/ *noun* (*uncount*)
Linguistics is the scientific study of the structures and development of a particular language or a group of languages, and language in general.

lining /ˈlaɪnɪŋ/ *noun*: **linings**
The **lining** in something such as a garment or box is a piece of material which covers its inside surface: *a fur lining.* [see also **line²**]

link /lɪŋk/ *noun*; *verb*
▻ ***noun*: links**
1 A **link** is one of the rings in a chain. **2** A **link** is also any person or thing that connects two other people, things or places: *a rail link to the airport* □ *a telephone link.* **3** There is a **link** between things when there is a connection between them: *There is a link between unemployment and poverty.* □ *The company has close links with local schools.*
▻ ***verb*: links, linking, linked**
1 Two things **are linked** when there is a connection between them, especially one of cause and effect: *Heart disease can be linked to smoking.* [*same as* **connect**] **2** Two places, things or people **are linked** when there there is a physical connection, or a channel of communication, between them: *the motorway linking Glagow and Edinburgh* □ *computer-users linked by e-mail.* [*same as* **connect**] **2** You **link** two things when you put part of one through the other: *He linked his arm through hers.* □ *We walked along with arms linked.*

> ***phrasal verb***
> To **link up** two people, places or things is to connect or join them in some way: *The Edinburgh office is linked up with the London office by computer.* [see also **link-up**]

link-up /ˈlɪŋkʌp/ *noun*: **link-ups**
A **link-up** is a connection: *We have a computer link-up with the Paris office.* [see also **link up**]

lino /ˈlaɪnoʊ/ *noun* (*uncount informal*)
Lino is the same as linoleum.

linoleum /lɪˈnoʊlɪəm/ *noun* (*uncount*)
Linoleum is a smooth, hard-wearing covering for floors, made of cloth with a shiny surface.

lion /laɪən/ *noun*: **lions**
A **lion** is **1** a large, flesh-eating animal of the cat family, with a yellow coat. **2** the male of this species, with long hair on the head and shoulders.
▻ ***phrase*** The **lion's share** is the largest part of something: *He always gets the lion's share of the cake.*

lioness /ˈlaɪənɛs/ *noun*: **lionesses**
A **lioness** is a female lion.

lip /lɪp/ *noun*: **lips**
1 Your **lips** are the folds of flesh which form the top and bottom edges of the mouth. [see picture at **body**] **2** The **lip** of something such as a cup or glass is its rim or edge.
▻ ***phrases*** **1** You **keep a stiff upper lip** if you hide your feelings when you are upset or worried. **2** You **lick your lips** when you pass your tongue over your lips in anticipation of something good to eat. **3** Something is

on everyone's lips when a lot of people are talking about it: *His name is on everyone's lips* [= everyone is talking about him]. **4** You **put your finger to your lips** when you place your raised forefinger against them, to indicate the need for silence or secrecy.

lip-read /ˈlɪpri:d/ *verb*: **lip-reads, lip-reading, lip-read**
You **lip-read** if you understand what someone is saying by watching the movement of their lips: *Many deaf people learn to lip-read.* — *noun* (*uncount*) **lip-reading:** *She is good at lip-reading.*

lip service /ˈlɪpsɜ:vɪs/ *noun* (*uncount*)
Someone who pays **lip service** to an idea or principle pretends to support or uphold it without really doing so: *The government pays occasional lip service to the idea of prison reform.*

lipstick /ˈlɪpstɪk/ *noun*: **lipsticks**
1 (*uncount*) **Lipstick** is colouring for the lips: *She always wears pink lipstick.* **2** A **lipstick** is stick of this.

liqueur /lɪˈkjʊə(r)/ *noun* (*count or uncount*): **liqueurs**
Liqueur, or a **liqueur**, is any of several strong, sweet alcoholic drinks, often drunk at the end of a meal.

liquid /ˈlɪkwɪd/ *noun*; *adjective*
▻ ***noun*** (*count or uncount*): **liquids**
A **liquid** is a substance like water that flows and can be poured, as distinct from being a solid or a gas: *The crystals had turned to liquid overnight.* ▫ *a thick oily liquid.*
▻ ***adjective***
A substance that is **liquid** is able to flow and be poured, and is neither a solid nor a gas: *liquid nitrogen.*

liquidate /ˈlɪkwɪdeɪt/ *verb*: **liquidates, liquidating, liquidated**
1 (*informal*) If someone **liquidates** their enemies or opponents, they get rid of them, usually by killing them: *The President ordered all his opponents to be liquidated.* **2** An unsuccessful company or business **is liquidated** when it is closed down and its property sold to pay its debts. — *noun* (*uncount*) **liquidation** /lɪkwɪˈdeɪʃən/: *The company has gone into liquidation.*

liquidize or **liquidise** /ˈlɪkwɪdaɪz/ *verb*: **liquidizes, liquidizing, liquidized**
You **liquidize** solid food when you make it into a liquid or smooth cream: *He liquidized the vegetables to make soup.*

liquidizer or **liquidiser** /ˈlɪkwɪdaɪzə(r)/ *noun*: **liquidizers**
A **liquidizer** is a machine used in cookery to crush solid food into a liquid or smooth cream.

liquor /ˈlɪkə(r)/ *noun* (*especially AmE*) (*uncount*)
Liquor is strong alcoholic drink.

liquorice or **licorice** /ˈlɪkərɪs/ *noun* (*uncount*)
Liquorice is a firm black sticky sweet with a strong flavour.

lisp /lɪsp/ *verb*; *noun*
▻ ***verb***: **lisps, lisping, lisped**
Someone **lisps** if they pronounce the sounds *s* and *z* as if they were the sound *th*.
▻ ***noun*** (*usually in the singular*): **lisps**
Someone who speaks with a **lisp** pronounces *s* and *z* as *th*.

list /lɪst/ *noun*; *verb*
▻ ***noun***: **lists**
A **list** is a set or series of names, numbers or things written down or said one after the other: *a shopping list* ▫ *Add her name to the list.*
▻ ***verb***: **lists, listing, listed**
1 You **list** things when you write or say them one after the other: *The back page of the magazine lists all the week's television programmes.* **2** Something **is listed** when it is present on a list: *His name and address are listed in our files.* [*same as* **record**]

listed building /lɪstɪd ˈbɪldɪŋ/ *noun*: **listed buildings**
A **listed building** is one that may not be destroyed or changed because of its interesting architecture or history.

listen /ˈlɪsən/ *verb*: **listens, listening, listened**
1 You **listen** to a person speaking or to a sound such as music when you pay attention to them: *We listened in respectful silence to what she had to say.* ▫ *I hope you're listening, because this is important.* ▫ *She doesn't seem to listen to the radio much.* ▫ *I decided to listen to a Beethoven concerto instead.* **2** You **listen**, or **listen** out, for something when you wait expectantly to hear it: *He sat listening for the sound of her key in the door.* ▫ *Listen out for the baby crying, won't you?* **3** You **listen** to someone when you accept what they say or follow their advice: *I warned him but he wouldn't listen.*

> ***phrasal verb***
> You **listen in** to a private conversation, *eg* on the telephone, when you listen to it secretly: *I became aware that she was listening in on the extension*

listener /ˈlɪsənə(r)/ *noun*: **listeners**
A **listener** is a person who listens, *eg* to a radio programme or to something you are saying: *The programme has received complaints from listeners.* ▫ *She told the story of her adventures to an enthusiastic group of listeners.* [compare **viewer**]

listless /ˈlɪstləs/ *adjective*
You are **listless** if you are tired and have no energy or interest: *Her illness left her feeling listless.* — *adverb* **listlessly:** *He wandered listlessly round the house.*

lit /lɪt/ *verb*
Lit is the past tense and past participle of **light**[1].

liter /ˈli:tə(r)/ (*AmE*) *noun*: **liters**
A **liter** is a litre.

literacy /ˈlɪtərəsɪ/ *noun* (*uncount*)
Literacy is the ability to read and write: *The government wants to improve standards of literacy amongst adults.*

literal /ˈlɪtərəl/ *adjective*
1 The **literal** sense of a word is its exact and usual meaning. [compare **figurative, metaphorical**] **2** A **literal** translation is one which follows the words of the original exactly without considering the general meaning or style of the text. **3** If you say that something is the **literal** truth, you are emphasizing that it is true.

literally /ˈlɪtərəlɪ/ *adverb*
1 You can use **literally** to emphasize that something is really true: *There are literally millions of children in the world who are starving.* **2** (*informal*) **Literally** is sometimes added to an exaggerated statement: *We were literally freezing to death.* **3** You translate something **literally** when you translate each word without considering the general meaning: *In English the French phrase 'crème anglaise' literally means 'English cream', but its proper translation is 'custard'.*
▻ ***phrase*** You **take** something **literally** when you think that a statement means exactly what the words in it suggest it means: *You shouldn't take everything he says literally.*

literary /ˈlɪtərərɪ/ *adjective*
1 Literary things which are concerned with literature or the writing of books: *literary criticism.* **2** A **literary** person knows a lot about literature. **3 Literary** words

or phrases are found especially in poetry and older literature, rather than in everyday language; words of this kind are labelled (*literary*) in this dictionary: *'Languor' is a literary word for 'tiredness'.*

literate /ˈlɪtərət/ *adjective*
1 **Literate** people are able to read and write. [*opposite* **illiterate**] **2** People that are well-educated are also described as **literate**: *children from highly literate families.* **3** You can be described as **literate** if you are experienced in a particular field or with particular things: *Candidates must be computer-literate.*

literature /ˈlɪtərətʃə(r)/ *noun* (*uncount*)
1 You use the term **literature** to refer to novels, poetry and plays, especially if they have high artistic quality that will ensure that they last: *Italian literature* □ *medieval literature.* **2** The **literature** on a subject is all the books and articles about it: *There is quite a lot of literature available on the history of computers.* **3** (*informal*) **Literature** is also printed leaflets which advertise things or give you advice: *The bank produces literature advising customers of the services it can provide them with.*

litigation /lɪtɪˈgeɪʃən/ *noun* (*uncount; formal or legal*)
Litigation is the fighting or defending of a case in a civil court.

litre /ˈliːtə(r)/ *noun*: **litres**
A **litre** is a metric measure of weight for liquids equal to about 1.75 pints: *a litre of water.*

litter /ˈlɪtə(r)/ *noun*; *verb*
▻ ***noun***: **litters**
1 (*uncount*) **Litter** is a mess of paper and rubbish left in a public place. **2** A **litter** is a group of animals born to the same mother at the same time: *My cat has had a litter of kittens.*
▻ ***verb***: **litters, littering, littered**
Objects **litter** a place, or a place **is littered** with them, when they lie or are scattered around untidily: *books littering a room* □ *a desk littered with papers.*

litter bin /ˈlɪtə bɪn/ *noun*: **litter bins**
A **litter bin** is a container for rubbish. [see picture at **street**]

little /ˈlɪtəl/ *adjective*; *adverb*; *determiner*; *pronoun*
▻ ***adjective*** (*usually only before a noun*)

> **Littler** and **littlest** are informal and rarely used; you use **smaller** and **smallest** instead.

1 **Little** things are small in size: *remote little villages* □ *She wore a little green hat.* □ *People were standing about in little groups.* [*opposite* **big, large**]

> Notice that although **little** and **small** both refer to size, **little** when used after other adjectives can express in addition an attitude such as affection, dislike or amusement: *He's such a sweet little baby. She's one of those nosy little women. I was given a jewel box with its own little key. We used to laugh at some of his funny little habits.*

2 A **little** child is a very young one: *All the other little boys and girls will be in bed.* □ *When I was little I went to bed at six.* **3** Your **little** brother or sister is a brother or sister that is younger than you: *She was leading her little brother by the hand.* [*same as* **younger**] **4** A **little** distance, period of time, or act of doing something, is a short one: *Would you mind waiting a little while?* □ *We live a little way out of town.* □ *She had a little weep and felt better.* [*same as* **short**] **5** **Little** describes things that are not very important: *We all have our little problems.* □ *I witnessed an odd little incident the other day.* **6** Your **little** finger is the smallest finger on your hand; your **little** toe is the smallest toe on your foot. [see picture at **body**]
▻ ***adverb***: **less, least**
1 'A **little**' means 'to some extent' or 'slightly': *I did sympathize with her a little; didn't you?* □ *The flight via Brussels is a little less expensive.* □ *I was beginning to feel just a little anxious.* [*same as* **a bit**] **2** (*used like a negative*) **Little** means 'not much' or 'not often': *Tennyson is read very little nowadays, is he?* □ *a little-known composer* □ *Some teachers earned little more than the school cleaners.* □ *Little did I think* [= I had no idea] *I might one day have my own TV programme.* [*same as* **barely, hardly**; *opposite* **a lot**]
▻ ***determiner*** (*used with uncount nouns*): **less, least**
1 'A **little**' means 'a small amount of' or 'a certain amount of': *I've got a little cash left.* □ *You know a little Spanish, don't you?* [*opposite* **a lot** of] **2** (*used like a negative*) **Little** means 'not much': *She has very little chance of recovery, has she?* □ *You can see how little difference there is between them.* □ *You have far too little confidence in yourself.* □ *We've got so little time left.*
▻ ***pronoun*** (*sometimes used with count nouns*): *'Is there any milk left?' 'Yes, a little.'* □ *Taste a little of this.* □ *Other people complained about police harrassment but we experienced very little ourselves.* □ *Once on the job she showed little of the ability she had claimed to have.* □ *I see very little of my brothers and sisters.* [= I see them rarely]
▻ ***phrases*** **1** **As little as** draws attention to an amount that is surprisingly small: *Premature babies weighing as little as 12 ounces have been known to survive.* **2** Something that happens **little by little** happens gradually: *Little by little his health improved.*
[see also **least, less, lesser**]

live[1] /lɪv/ *verb*: **lives, living, lived**
1 You **live** in a particular place if that is where your home is: *Where do you live?* □ *She lives in Madrid.* □ *We live on the other side of town.* □ *I live at 40 Green Street.* □ *I don't think I'd like to live in such a large house.* □ *My mother's sister lived with us till she got married.* **2** You **are living** if you are alive: *Are your grandparents still living?* □ *She lived to be 103.* □ *They lived to see the end of Apartheid.* □ *He hasn't got long to live.* □ *I feel he no longer has the will to live.* **3** You **live** a certain kind of life, or **live** in certain conditions or circumstances, if that is the way you pass your life: *She earns enough to live comfortably.* □ *He has lived his whole life in the service of others.* □ *We live unsatisfactory lives in so many ways.* □ *It's a materialist world that we live in.* □ *People just don't live according to their principles.* **4** You **live** by doing something if that is the way you make enough money to buy what is necessary for survival: *They live mainly by stealing.* **5** (*informal*) You **live** when you enjoy life: *I want to be able to live a little while I'm still young.* □ *He really knows how to live.*
▻ ***phrases*** (*informal*) You **live it up** when you have an enjoyable time, especially with an exciting social life.

phrasal verbs

live down If you have made an embarrassing mistake, or failed in something, and you say you'll never **live it down**, you mean that people will never forget about it: *I'll never live it down if I fail my driving test again.*

live for You **live for** something when it is the most important thing in your life: *She lives for her children.*

live in You **live in** when you are resident in the place where you work or study: *A lot of students decide to live in during their first year at college.* [see also **live-in**]

live off You **live off** someone or something if they provide you with money to buy the things you need: *He's still living off his parents.*
live on 1 You **live on** a certain amount of money if that is the amount you have to spend on housing, food and clothes: *They have only £30 a week to live on.* 2 You **live on** a certain kind of food when that is the only kind of food you eat: *He has to live mainly on fruit and vegetables.* 3 A person **lives on** when they go on living: *His widow lived on into her nineties.* 4 Something **lives on** if people go on remembering it: *The disaster lives on in people's memories.*
live out Students **live out** when they are not resident in college or university accommodation, but live elsewhere.
live together People who are having a sexual relationship **live together** when they live in the same house as if they were married.
live up to Someone or something **lives up to** your expectations if they are as good as you expected them to be: *She couldn't live up to her parents' expectations.*
live with 1 You **live with** someone you are having a sexual relationship with when you share a house with them. 2 If you **live with** something unpleasant, you continue to suffer from it or remember it: *He will have to live with the mistake for the rest of his life.* □ *You must learn to live with the pain.*

live² /laɪv/ *adjective*; *adverb*
▻ ***adjective***
1 **Live** animals are alive and not dead: *He saw a live snake in the garden.* 2 A radio or television broadcast that is **live** is heard or seen as the event takes place: *live music.* 3 A **live** recording is made during a performance rather than in a studio. 4 A wire or piece of electrical equipment is **live** when it is connected to a source of electrical power. 5 **Live** coals are still glowing or burning. 6 **Live** bombs or bullets have not yet exploded.
▻ ***adverb***
You do something **live** when you do it during or as a live performance rather than recording it to be broadcast at a later date: *He prefers performing live on stage to making television programmes.* □ *We'll be able to hear the opera live on the radio.*

lived-in /ˈlɪvdɪn/ *adjective*
A room or garment that is **lived-in** has a comfortable, homely feeling.

live-in /ˈlɪvɪn/ *adjective*
A **live-in** partner lives in the same house as the person they are having a sexual relationship with.

livelihood /ˈlaɪvlɪhʊd/ *noun*: **livelihoods**
Your **livelihood** is the way you earn enough money to pay for housing, food and clothes: *Art is her livelihood.* □ *He may lose his livelihood.*

lively /ˈlaɪvlɪ/ *adjective*: **livelier, liveliest**
1 People are **lively** when they behave in an energetic and cheerful way: *She has two lively sons.* [*opposite* **apathetic**] 2 A place or event is **lively** if there are a lot of interesting or exciting things happening there. [*opposite* **dull**] 3 A **lively** feeling is one that is strong and enthusiastic: *He took a lively interest in chess.* 4 A debate or discussion can be described as **lively** when a lot of people have things to say: *a lively debate between politicians from different parties.* 5 Someone who has a **lively** mind is quick and intelligent in understanding things and working things out.

liven /ˈlaɪvən/ *verb*: **livens, livening, livened**

phrasal verb
liven up 1 You **liven** a place or event **up**, or it **livens up**, when you make it, or it becomes, livelier or more interesting or exciting: *Some pictures on the walls should liven this room up a bit.* 2 You **liven up**, or something **livens** you **up**, when you become, or it makes you, livelier or happier and more energetic: *She needs to liven up a bit.* □ *The holiday has livened him up a lot.* [*same as* **perk up**]

liver /ˈlɪvə(r)/ *noun*: **livers**
1 Your **liver** is a large organ in the body which has several important functions, including cleaning the blood. 2 (*uncount*) **Liver** is this organ in some animals, used as food.

lives /laɪvz/ *noun*
Lives is the plural of **life**.

livestock /ˈlaɪvstɒk/ *noun* (*uncount*)
Livestock is animals kept on a farm, especially horses, cattle, sheep, and pigs.

livid /ˈlɪvɪd/ *adjective*
1 (*informal*) Someone who is **livid** is extremely angry: *He was absolutely livid.* 2 **Livid** bruises are dark blue and purple.

living /ˈlɪvɪŋ/ *adjective*; *noun*
▻ ***adjective***
A **living** person, animal or plant is alive: *He has no living relatives.* □ *Biology is the study of living things.*
▻ ***noun***
1 (*used in the singular*) You do something for a **living** when you do it to earn money to pay for housing, food and clothes: *What does she do for a living?* □ *He earns his living teaching the piano.* 2 (*uncount, often adjectival*) You can use **living** to talk about the way someone lives or the quality of their life: *the need for better living standards.* □ *We need to improve the living conditions in these old flats.* 3 (*uncount*) The cost of **living** is the amount of money people spend on food, clothing and housing; your standard of **living** is your level of wealth and comfort.

living room /ˈlɪvɪŋ ruːm/ *noun*: **living rooms**
A **living room** is a room in a house where people can sit and relax. [see picture on next page]

lizard /ˈlɪzəd/ *noun*: **lizards**
A **lizard** is a reptile with a long body and tail, four legs, and a rough skin.

'll /l/ or /əl/ *verb*
'll is a short form of 'shall' and 'will' used in speech and informal writing: *I'll come and see you tomorrow.*

llama /ˈlɑːmə/ *noun*: **llamas**
A **llama** is a S American animal related to the camel, kept for its wool and to carry heavy loads.

load /loʊd/ *noun*; *verb*
▻ ***noun*: loads**
1 A **load** is something heavy that is being carried somewhere: *The lorry delivered a load of coal to the factory.* 2 A **load** is also a number of people that a vehicle can carry at one time: *a coach-load of children.* 3 (*informal*) If you have **loads** of, or a **load** of, something, you have a large amount of it: *They have loads of money.* □ *That film is a load of rubbish.* □ *'Is there any of that cake left?' 'Yes, loads.'* 4 A **load** of washing is a number of dirty clothes that can be washed at the same time. 5 The **load** on an electrical circuit is the power that it carries.

living room

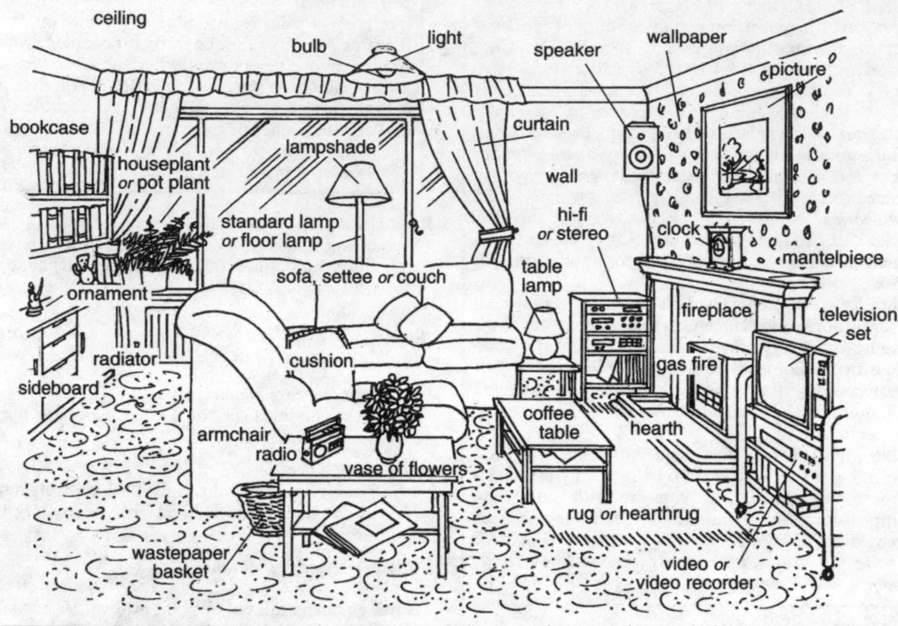

▻ ***verb***: **loads, loading, loaded**

1 You **load** a vehicle, ship or container, or **load** things into it, when you put things into it: *They loaded the furniture into the van.* ▫ *He loaded the car with boxes and cases.* **2** If you **load** someone with something, you give them generous amounts of it: *They loaded her with gifts for the children.* **3** If you **load** a gun, you put bullets into it. **4** When you **load** a camera, tape recorder or video recorder, or **load** film or tape into it, you put film or tape into it. **5** When you **load** a program or data, you put it in a computer's main memory so that it may be used. **6** When you **load** information stored on a disk or tape into a computer, you put it into the computer so that it may be used.

loaded /ˈloudɪd/ *adjective*

1 (*informal*) A person who has a lot of money can be described as **loaded**. **2** A **loaded** question or remark is one that has more meaning or significance than it seems to have. **3** You can say that a system is **loaded** in favour of someone when it gives them an advantage: *The whole system of exams is loaded against underprivileged pupils.* **4** If a vehicle is **loaded**, it is carrying a load: *a coach loaded with children.* **5** A person can be described as **loaded** when they are carrying a lot of things: *She was loaded down with heavy bags of shopping.* **6** A gun is **loaded** when it has bullets in it. **7** A camera is **loaded** when it has film in it.

loaf[1] /louf/ *noun*: **loaves**

A **loaf** is bread that has been shaped and baked in one piece: *two loaves of bread.*

loaf[2] /louf/ *verb*: **loafs, loafing, loafed**

> ***phrasal verbs***
> **loaf about** or **loaf around** If you **loaf about** or **loaf around**, you spend your time doing nothing and being lazy. [*same as* **idle**]

loan /loun/ *noun*; *verb*

▻ ***noun***: **loans**

1 A **loan** is money that you borrow, especially if it must be paid back with interest: *a bank loan.* **2** (*used in the singular*) Someone gives you the **loan** of something when they lend it to you: *I asked him for a loan of his car.*

▻ ***verb***: **loans, loaning, loaned**

If someone **loans** you something, they lend it to you: *My mother loaned me the money to go on holiday.*

▻ ***phrase*** Something is **on loan** when it is given as a loan or has been borrowed: *These videos are on loan from the local library.*

loath or **loth** /louθ/ *adjective*

You are **loath** to do something when you are not willing to do it: *I am loath to lend him any more money until he finds another job.* [*same as* **reluctant, unwilling**; *opposite* **willing, keen**]

loathe /louð/ *verb*: **loathes, loathing, loathed**

You say that you **loathe** something if you dislike it or are disgusted by it: *I absolutely loathe having to queue.* [*same as* **detest, hate**]

loathing /ˈlouðɪŋ/ *noun* (*uncount*)

Loathing is a feeling of great dislike or disgust: *a loathing for fish* ▫ *I remember my maths teacher with loathing.*

loathsome /ˈlouðsəm/ *adjective*

If you describe someone as something as **loathsome**, you dislike them strongly: *She's a loathsome individual.* ▫ *Why do you have to watch that loathsome programme?* [*same as* **nasty, obnoxious**]

loaves /louvz/ *noun*

Loaves is the plural of **loaf**[1].

lob /lɒb/ *verb*; *noun*

▻ ***verb***: **lobs, lobbing, lobbed**

You **lob** something such as a ball somewhere when you get it there by hitting or tossing it high into the air: *He couldn't believe his luck as he lobbed the ball over the goalkeeper's head into the net.* ▫ *I managed to get my racquet to the ball just in time to lob it back over the net.*
▻ ***noun*: lobs:** *The Frenchman wins that point with a lob to the back court.*

lobby /'lɒbɪ/ *noun; verb*
▻ ***noun*: lobbies**
1 A **lobby** is an entrance hall immediately inside a main door, which leads to other rooms, corridors and staircases: *the hotel lobby.* **2** A **lobby** is a group of people who try to influence the Government or politicians in favour of a particular cause: *the anti-smoking lobby.*
▻ ***verb*: lobbies, lobbying, lobbied**
If you **lobby** a politician or member of the government, you try to influence them in favour of a particular cause: *We will continue to lobby MPs for an environmentally friendly national transport system.*

lobe /loʊb/ *noun*: **lobes**
1 The **lobe** is the soft round part at the bottom of the ear. [*same as* **earlobe**] **2** A **lobe** is a division of an organ in the body, especially of the lungs or brain.

lobster /'lɒbstə(r)/ *noun*: **lobsters**
1 A **lobster** is a large sea animal with a hard shell, two large claws and eight legs. **2** (*uncount*) **Lobster** is its flesh eaten as food.

local /'loʊkəl/ *adjective; noun*
▻ ***adjective***
1 Something that is **local** serves or is for a particular place, especially the place where you live: *the local council* ▫ *a local newspaper* ▫ *the local bus service.* **2** (*medicine*) A **local** anaesthetic affects only a small area of the body. — *adverb* **locally:** *She lives and works locally.* ▫ *He does most of his shopping locally.*
▻ ***noun*: locals**
1 The **locals** are the people living in a particular area. **2** Your **local** is the public house near your home that you visit most regularly.

locality /loʊ'kalɪtɪ/ *noun*: **localities**
A **locality** is a district or neighbourhood.

localized or **localised** /'loʊkəlaɪzd/ *adjective*
Something that is **localized** is restricted to a particular place or area: *localized pain in the lower back.*

locate /loʊ'keɪt/ *verb*: **locates, locating, located**
1 You **locate** someone or something when you find their exact position: *I couldn't locate the school on the map.* **2** Something **is located** in a particular place when that is where it is found or placed: *The school is located next to the station.*

location /loʊ'keɪʃən/ *noun*: **locations**
A **location** is a particular position or situation: *a good location for a campsite* ▫ *The factory is moving to a new location.*
▻ ***phrase*** A film or programme that is made **on location** is made outside the studio: *a film shot on location in Spain.*

loch /lɒk/ *noun*: **lochs**
In Scotland, a **loch** is a lake, or an area of sea surrounded by land on three sides: *Loch Lomond.* ▫ *Loch Nevis is a sea loch.*

lock /lɒk/ *noun; verb*
▻ ***noun*: locks**
1 A **lock** is a small device for fastening *eg* doors, windows and suitcases, which has a bolt which needs a key to move it: *He's had new locks fitted on all his windows.* **2** A **lock** is also a stretch of water closed by gates on a canal or river, where the water level may be raised or lowered, allowing boats to pass between higher and lower sections of the canal or river. **3** A **lock** of hair is a piece of hair, or a curl: *She pushed back a stray lock of hair from her forehead.* ▫ *I cut a lock of the baby's hair and put it in an envelope.*
▻ ***verb*: locks, locking, locked**
1 You **lock** something such as a door, window or suitcase when you fasten it by turning a key in its lock: *She forgot to lock the car door.* **2** You **lock** things into a room, safe, container, drawer or cupboard when you put them into it and lock it: *She locked the papers in her desk.* ▫ *He locked the drugs away in a cupboard.* ▫ *My passport is locked in my drawer.* **3** A door **locks** when you are able to lock it with a key: *This suitcase won't lock any more.* **4** Something **locks** or **is locked** when it becomes fixed or fastened so that it cannot move: *The wheels have locked and the car won't move.* **5** You can say that people **are locked** in *eg* battle when they are fighting fiercely: *The children were locked in argument over who should go on the swing next.*
▻ ***phrases*** **1** You have something **under lock and key** when you have it securely locked up; you have a person **under lock and key** when you have locked them up in prison. **2** If you win or lose something **lock, stock and barrel**, you win or lose all of it.

phrasal verbs
lock in If you **lock** someone **in**, you put someone inside a room or building and stop them from getting out by locking the doors while they are inside.
lock out If you **lock** someone **out**, you stop them from getting into a building or room by locking the doors while they are outside; you **lock** yourself **out** when you go out of a door that locks automatically and forget to take your key with you: *She found she was locked out of the house.*
lock up **1** If you **lock** someone **up**, you put them in a safe or secure place, especially in prison, and stop them from leaving by locking all the doors: *He spent the night locked up in the local police station.* **2** You **lock up**, or **lock up** a building, when you lock all the doors and windows securely.

locker /'lɒkə(r)/ *noun*: **lockers**
A **locker** is a small cupboard which can be locked, and which is used for storing things such as sports equipment or luggage.

locket /'lɒkɪt/ *noun*: **lockets**
A **locket** is a piece of jewellery in the form of a small case that holds a person's photograph or a piece of hair, worn on a chain round your neck.

locomotive /loʊkə'moʊtɪv/ *noun*: **locomotives**
A **locomotive** is a railway engine that pulls trains.

locust /'loʊkəst/ *noun*: **locusts**
Locusts are large insects which travel in large groups and eat and destroy crops and vegetation.

lodge /lɒdʒ/ *noun; verb*
▻ ***noun*: lodges**
A **lodge** is **1** a small house at the gate to the grounds of a large house. **2** a small house in the country used by hunters or sportsmen: *a hunting-lodge.*
▻ ***verb*: lodges, lodging, lodged**
1 You **lodge** in someone's house when you live there, often only for a short period of time, and pay them rent. **2** If you **lodge** something such as a complaint, you make an official complaint: *He lodged a formal protest with the police.* **3** Something **lodges**, or **is lodged**, somewhere when it is firmly fixed there: *The*

bullet is lodged at the base of the skull. **4** You **lodge** something somewhere when you put it there for safety: *money lodged in the bank.*

lodger /ˈlɒdʒə(r)/ *noun*: **lodgers**
A **lodger** is a person who rents accommodation in someone else's home, often only for a short period of time.

lodging /ˈlɒdʒɪŋ/ *noun*: **lodgings**
1 (*used in the plural*) Your **lodgings** are the rooms or room that you rent in someone else's home. **2** (*uncount*) **Lodging** is a place where you can stay, but usually only for a short period of time: *a night's board and lodging.*

loft /lɒft/ *noun*: **lofts**
A **loft** is a room or space between the roof and main part of the house.

lofty /ˈlɒftɪ/ *adjective* (*literary*): **loftier, loftiest**
1 A building or place is **lofty** if it is very tall or has a very high ceiling. **2 Lofty** ideals are very noble or important. **3** A person who behaves in a proud and unfriendly way behaves in a **lofty** way. — *adverb* **loftily:** *It was her habit to speak and act loftily.*

log /lɒg/ *noun*; *verb*
▻ ***noun***: **logs**
1 A **log** is a part of a tree trunk or a thick branch, especially when it is used as firewood: *She threw another log on the fire.* **2** A **log** is also an official record of events that occur during a journey, especially one made by a ship or aircraft: *The captain entered the weather report in his log.* [*same as* **record**] **3** A **log** is a logarithm.
▻ ***verb***: **logs, logging, logged**
You **log** information when you write it down in an official record: *He logs the number of cars using the road.* [*same as* **record**]
▻ ***phrase*** If you **are sleeping like a log**, you are sleeping very deeply or soundly.

> ***phrasal verbs***
> **log in** or **log on** You **log in** or **log on** when you gain access to a computer system by typing your personal code.
> **log out** or **log off** You **log out** or **log off** when you type in a command to show that you have finished using a computer system.

logarithm /ˈlɒgərɪðəm/ *noun*: **logarithms**
A **logarithm** is the number of times a base, usually 10, must be multiplied by itself to produce a given number: *The logarithm of 1000 to the base 10 is 3, because 10×10×10 = 1000.*

loggerheads /lɒgəhɛdz/ *noun* (*plural*)
▻ ***phrase*** You are **at loggerheads** with someone if you argue or disagree with them violently: *They have been at loggerheads ever since he was promoted.*

logic /ˈlɒdʒɪk/ *noun* (*uncount*)
1 Logic is the science of reasoning correctly. **2** Individual, personal or a particular kind of **logic** is an individual, personal or particular way of reasoning or thinking: *feminine logic* □ *I don't follow your logic.* **3** The **logic** of a series of events or probabilities is the way one follows inevitably from another: *It almost defies logic that anyone could do anything so stupid.* □ *the inexorable logic by which wage rises follow price rises.*

logical /ˈlɒdʒɪkəl/ *adjective*
1 Something is **logical** when it follows reasonably or sensibly from facts or events: *the logical implications of this event* □ *a logical decision* □ *the logical thing to do next.* [*opposite* **illogical**] **2** An argument is **logical** when it has been reasoned according to the rules of logic: *a logical analysis of the problems.* [*opposite* **illogical**] — *adverb* **logically:** *Think about this problem logically.* □ (*sentence adverb*) *You ought, logically, to be the next to be promoted.*

logistic /ləˈdʒɪstɪk/ or **logistical** /ləˈdʒɪstɪkəl/ *adjective*
Something that relates to the organizing of a large-scale or complicated operation or event can be described as **logistic** or **logistical**: *the logistical problems of arranging an expedition to Malawi for several hundred school children.*

logistics /ləˈdʒɪstɪks/ *noun* (*plural*)
The organizing of all the people and things needed for a large-scale or complicated event or operation can be called the **logistics**: *The logistics of arranging such a large party are very complicated.*

logo /ˈloʊgoʊ/ *noun*: **logos**
A **logo** is a small design used as the symbol of an organization: *stationery printed with the company logo.*

-logy /lədʒɪ/ *suffix*
Words are formed with the ending **-logy** to mean the science or study of something: *geology* □ *anthropology.*

loincloth /ˈlɔɪnklɒθ/ *noun*: **loincloths**
A **loincloth** is a length of cloth worn by men in some, especially hot, countries to cover their buttocks and sex organs. [see picture at **clothing**]

loins /lɔɪnz/ *noun* (*plural*; *old or literary*)
Your **loins** are the area of your body from your waist to the top of your thighs.

loiter /ˈlɔɪtə(r)/ *verb*: **loiters, loitering, loitered**
If you **are loitering**, you are standing around or passing your time doing nothing in particular: *Five teenagers were loitering in front of the newsagent's, drinking shandy and smoking.* [*same as* **linger**]

loll /lɒl/ *verb*: **lolls, lolling, lolled**
1 If you **loll** about, or **loll** somewhere, you lie or sit about lazily: *tourists lolling around on the beach.* **2** Your head or tongue **lolls** when it hangs down or out loosely.

lollipop /ˈlɒlɪpɒp/ *noun*: **lollipops**
A **lollipop** is a large mass of hard, boiled sugar on a stick, eaten as a sweet.

lolly /ˈlɒlɪ/ *noun* (*informal*): **lollies**
1 A **lolly** is a lollipop. **2** A **lolly** or **ice lolly** is an ice cream or flavoured water ice on a stick.

lone /loʊn/ *adjective*
A **lone** person or thing is one that is on its own or without a companion: *A lone rider came galloping towards them.*

lonely /ˈloʊnlɪ/ *adjective*: **lonelier, loneliest**
1 A **lonely** person is sad because they have no companions or friends. **2** If you lead a **lonely** life or existence, you live on your own and have no friends or companions. **3** A place is **lonely** when very few people go there or live near it: *a lonely road leading to the old church.* — *noun* (*uncount*) **loneliness:** *the loneliness of the cottage by the shore.*

loner /loʊnə(r)/ *noun*: **loners**
A **loner** is a person who prefers to be alone and who avoids close relationships.

lonesome /ˈloʊnsəm/ *adjective* (*AmE*)
1 A person is **lonesome** when they are sad and lonely. **2** A **lonesome** place is isolated and lacks human company. [*same as* **lonely, desolate**].

long[1] /lɒŋ/ *adjective; adverb*
▻ ***adjective***: **longer, longest**
1 Something that is **long** measures a lot, or is a big distance, from one end to the other: *It's supposed to be an advantage to have long legs.* □ *The queue didn't look too long.* □ *It's quite a long way to walk.* □ *The other route is prettier and it isn't much longer.* [*opposite* **short**]

Notice that though you can describe people as **short,** you cannot say they are **long**; use **tall** instead: *You'll find something to suit you, whether you're short or tall.*

2 You ask how **long** something is when you want to know its length, or how much it measures from one end to the other; something that is, *eg*, 20 metres **long**, measures that much from one end to the other: *The average double bed is about 6 feet long and 4.5 feet wide.* □ *a 50-metre-long swimming pool.* **3** A **long** period or event lasts or takes a lot of time: *He's waited a long time for this moment.* □ *We had a long wait at the airport.* □ *There are long delays in both directions.* □ *His lecture was far too long.* □ *We get a short break in October and a longer one at Christmas.* □ *The seminar wasn't as long as I was expecting it to be.* [*opposite* **short**] **4** You ask how **long** an event is when you want to know its length, or how long it lasts from beginning to end; something that is, *eg*, two hours **long**, takes that amount of time: *'How long will the church service be?' 'About an hour.'* □ *a 20-minute-long oral exam.* □ *The film is about 110 minutes long.* **5** A **long** book is one that contains a lot of text: *a long novel such as 'War and Peace'.* **6** You describe a period such as a day or week as **long** if a lot happens in it, or if it is boring or tiring: *How was I going to endure the long hours of waiting?* □ *It's been a long, tiring day.* **7** A **long** dress or **long** trousers come down to your feet: *Should I wear a short skirt or my long one?* [*opposite* **short**; compare **full-length**] **8** You can refer to a large, cool, non-alcoholic drink as a **long** drink. **9** (*phonetics*) A sound is **long** if it has the greater of two recognized lengths, such as the *i* in *pile*, as opposed to the *i* in *pill*. [*opposite* **short**] **10** People have **long** faces when they look depressed or sad: *There's no need to go around with such a long face.*
▻ ***adverb***: **longer, longest**
1 **Long** means 'a long time' or 'for a long time'; you use 'how **long**?' in questions about amounts of time: *Have you been waiting long?* □ *I hadn't been there long when the telephone rang.* □ *I can't stay much longer.* □ *I apologize for keeping you waiting so long.* □ *'How long have you lived in Manchester?' '25 years.'* □ *'How long did the meeting last?' 'About three hours.'* □ *The job didn't take as long as I thought it would.* □ *It won't be long till she starts going to school.*

Notice that the adverb **long** is used mainly with negatives and in questions; in positive statements you use 'a long time' or 'for a long time': *I've lived here a long time.*

2 You do something all day **long** or all night **long** when you do it throughout the whole day or night: *I worked at this essay all night long.* **3** People who wear their hair **long** have long hair. **4** You say that *eg* jackets or skirts are being worn **long** if long jackets or skirts are fashionable.
▻ ***phrases*** **1 a** One thing is so **as long as** or **so long as** another is so if the first is so only while the other is so: *We were perfectly warm as long as the sun was shining.* **b** You also use **as long as** and **so long as** to mean 'on condition that': *'Have dinner with me.' 'OK, so long as you let me pay for the wine.'* **2** Something that happens **before long** or **before very long** or **before too long** happens soon: *She'll be walking before too long.* **3** **For long** is used with negatives and in questions to mean 'for a long time': *Have you been waiting for long?* □ *I can't stay for long.* **4** For **in the long run** see **run**. **5** Something **no longer** happens, or **does not** happen **any longer**, if it used to happen in the past but has stopped happening: *He always used to visit me on Saturdays, but not any longer.* □ *She is no longer well enough to get out of bed.* **6** (*informal*) **'So long'** means 'goodbye'.
[compare **length**]

long[2] /lɒŋ/ *verb*: **longs, longing, longed**
You **long** for something or to do something when you want it or want to do it very much: *She's longing to go to university.* □ *I was longing for a cool shower after my run.*

long-distance /lɒŋ'dɪstəns/ *adjective*
Long-distance means covering, travelling or operating between or over long distances: *a long-distance runner* □ *long-distance telephone calls.*

long-drawn-out /lɒŋdrɔːn'aʊt/ *adjective*
If something is **long-drawn-out**, it takes more time than it needs to: *a long-drawn-out industrial dispute.*

longevity /lɒn'dʒevɪtɪ/ *noun (uncount; formal)*
Longevity is great length of life: *Improvements in diet have led to an increase in longevity.*

longing /'lɒŋɪŋ/ *noun (count or uncount)*
A **longing** for something is a strong desire for it: *He felt a nostalgic longing for his homeland.* □ *She looked at the baby with longing.* — *adverb* **longingly:** *The children looked longingly at the toys.*

longitude /'lɒŋɪtjuːd/ *noun*: **longitudes**
The **longitude** of a place is its distance east or west of an imaginary line passing from north to south through Greenwich, shown on maps as 0°: *The longitude of Kiev is 30° east.* [compare **latitude**]

long jump /'lɒŋ dʒʌmp/ *noun (used in the singular)*
The **long jump** is an athletics contest in which competitors jump as far as possible along the ground from a running start. [compare **high jump**]

long-life /'lɒŋlaɪf/ *adjective*
Long-life batteries or milk last longer than usual.

long-lived /lɒŋ'lɪvd/ *adjective*
A thing that is **long-lived** lives or lasts for a long time. [*opposite* **short-lived, ephemeral**]

long-range /lɒŋ'reɪnʒ/ *adjective*
1 A **long-range** missile is able to reach to distant targets; **long-range** aircraft can travel very long distances: *long-range bombers.* **2** A **long-range** weather forecast or prediction is concerned with what will develop far into the future.

long-sighted /lɒŋ'saɪtɪd/ *adjective*
You are **long-sighted** when you are able to see things far away clearly, but not things close to you. [*opposite* **short-sighted, near-sighted**]

long-standing /lɒŋ'standɪŋ/ *adjective*
A **long-standing** arrangement, agreement or feud is one that has existed or continued for a long time: *The company has a long-standing contract to supply them with coal.*

long-suffering /lɒŋ'sʌfərɪŋ/ *adjective*
A **long-suffering** person patiently bears trouble and problems.

long-term /lɒŋ'tɜːm/ *adjective*
Long-term describes things that will continue to be valid or effective in the future: *the company's long-term plans* □ *the long-term effects of the drug.* [*opposite* **short-term**; see also **in the long term** at **term**]

long wave /ˈlɒŋ weɪv/ *noun* (*uncount*)
Long wave is radio broadcasting using wavelengths over 1000 metres: *The station broadcasts on 1500 metres long wave.* [compare **medium wave**, **short wave**]

long-winded /lɒŋˈwɪndɪd/ *adjective*
A piece of writing or speech that is **long-winded** is longer than necessary, or uses too many words to express something. [*same as* **verbose**, **wordy**; *opposite* **concise**, **succinct**]

loo /luː/ *noun* (*BrE informal*)
A **loo** is a lavatory. [*same as* **toilet**]

look /lʊk/ *verb*; *interjection*; *noun*
▻ ***verb***: **looks**, **looking**, **looked**
1 a You **look** in a certain direction when your turn your eyes in that direction; you **look** at something when you turn your eyes so that you can see it: *He looked up from his work.* ▫ *He was still looking out of the window.* ▫ *We looked at each other in dismay.* ▫ *She looked down at her watch.* ▫ *They looked away in embarrassment.* **b** A building, room or window **looks** in a certain direction if it faces that way: *The dormitory windows looked out on the playing fields.* ▫ *The front of the cottage looks north.* **c** You **look** at something when you examine it: *Let me look at that cut on your forehead.* ▫ *I haven't had a chance to look at the report yet.* **d** You **look** at something when you investigate it or consider it: *We need to look at the long-term implications of this plan.* **e** You say you **are looking** at some option or possible procedure if you think it will be necessary or desirable: *You should be looking at a weight loss of at least 30 pounds.* ▫ *We're looking at the end of August for publication.* **f** You **look** at something from a certain point of view when that is the way you regard it: *People look at marriage very differently, depending to some extent on what religion they are.*
2 You say that someone or something **looks** a certain way **a** when describing their appearance or expression: *He looks like his father.* ▫ *What does she look like?* ▫ *You look nice in red.* ▫ *He came in looking agitated.* ▫ *You look as if you need a holiday.* ▫ *How does that look to you?* **b** when saying how they seem to you: *Things are looking a bit depressing.* ▫ *That looks an interesting book.* ▫ *This looks like an exciting project.* ▫ *That looks like* [= I think that is] *our bus in the distance.* ▫ *It looks like rain.* [= I think it's going to rain] ▫ *It looks like being another hot sunny day.* ▫ *It looks as if he's going to be late again.* [see also **like**]
3 You **look** for something when you try to find it: *They're looking for a new house.* ▫ *He's been looking for a job for five months.* ▫ *We're looking for graduates with a teaching qualification.* ▫ *I looked everywhere for that cheque.* [*same as* **seek**] **4** You say '**Look**' to draw attention to things, *eg* an instance of something, or to the present situation, especially when you are surprised, anxious or angry about it: *Look at lawyers, for example.* ▫ *But look how much money you save by walking everywhere.* ▫ *Now look what you've done!* ▫ *Do look where you're going!* ▫ *Just look where your short cut has led us!*
▻ ***interjection*** You use '**Look!**' and '**Look** here!' to protest, complain, scold or rebuke: *Look, this just isn't fair!* ▫ *Look, Mary, I know you're angry, but shouting won't do any good.*
▻ ***noun***: **looks**
1 (*usually in the singular*) You have or take a **look** at something when you look at it or examine it: *Take a look at this illustration.* ▫ *Has the doctor had a look at you this morning?* ▫ *Have a good look through these photographs.* **2** You give someone a **look** when you look at them with a particular expression on your face: *She gave me one of her warning looks.* **3** (*usually in the singular*) You refer to the **look** of someone or something when you are talking about how they look or seem: *I don't like the look of the weather.* ▫ *The school had the over-elaborate look of a building that might once have been a hotel.* ▫ *She had a timid look in her eyes.* **4** (*used in the plural*) If you refer to a person's **looks** you are talking about how attractive, handsome or beautiful they are: *It's such a mistake to marry anyone for their looks.* ▫ *He hates the idea of getting old and losing his looks.*
▻ ***phrases*** **1** If you say that something is so **by the look of**, or **the looks of**, a thing, you are stating an opinion based on appearance: *We're in for some snow by the look of the sky.* ▫ *The garden hasn't been tidied for years by the looks of it.* [compare **to judge from**, **judging from**] **2** Someone who is **not looking themselves** is looking ill: *I'm glad to see you looking more yourself.*

phrasal verbs
look after You **look after** someone or something when you take care of them or are responsible for them: *Her husband looks after the baby when she goes to work.*
look ahead You **look ahead** when you think about, or plan for, the future.
look back or **look back on 1** You **look back**, or **look back on** something, when you think about the past: *She looks back on her childhood with affection.* **2** You say someone has **never looked back** if they have been very successful: *She opened her first shop at the age of twenty and never looked back.*
look down on You **look down on** someone or something if you regard them as not important enough, or not good enough: *It's amazing to think how goods from Japan were once looked down on.*
look forward to You **look forward to** something that is going to happen when you feel happy because you know you are going to enjoy it: *She's looking forward to the birth of her baby.*
look into You **look into** something when you investigate it: *I've offered to look into the problem for him.*
look on 1 You **look on** when you watch something without taking part: *She looked on proudly as her son was given his medal.* **2** You **look on** or **upon** something or someone as a certain thing if you regard them as that thing: *He looks upon marriage as an unnecessary restriction on freedom.*
look out You say '**look out!**' to warn someone of danger: *Look out! There's a car coming!* [see also **lookout**]
look out for You **look out for** someone or something when you pay attention so as to make sure you see them when they are there: *I'll look out for that book in the second-hand shops.* [see also **lookout**]
look over You **look over** something, or **look** it **over**, when you examine it: *We've looked over several flats in this part of town.* ▫ *Could you briefly look over this report for me?* ▫ *Why don't you let the doctor look you over to make sure you haven't broken anything?*
look round 1 You **look round** when you look at lots of things before deciding which to buy: *It's a good idea to look round before deciding which car to get.* **2** You **look round** a place or building when you visit it: *Let's look round the castle this afternoon.*
look through You **look through** things when you examine them one by one: *I looked through my clothes but found nothing suitable for the funeral.*
look to 1 You **look to** someone for something, or to do something, when you expect them to provide something or do something for you: *She has always*

looked to her parents for support. □ *They look to the state to give them money to buy food.* **2** You **look to** the future when you consider it.
look up 1 You **look** information **up** when you search for it in a reference book: *She looked up the spelling in the dictionary.* □ *Look it up in an encyclopedia.* **2** (*informal*) You **look** someone **up** when you visit them. **3** You say that things **are looking up** when they are improving: *The weather is beginning to look up.*
look up to You **look up to** someone that you admire and respect.

lookalike /lʊkəˈlaɪk/ *noun*: **lookalikes**
Your **lookalike** is a person who looks a lot like you.

look-in /ˈlʊk ɪn/ *noun* (*used in the singular, with a negative*)
You don't get a **look-in** when you never have a chance to join in or are never included, in something: *I never get a look-in when it comes to playing with the computer games.* □ *She talks so much the others hardly get a look-in.*

lookout /ˈlʊkaʊt/ *noun*: **lookouts**
A **lookout** is **1 a** a person watching for danger, *eg* on board a ship: *I asked Alex to act as lookout.* **b** (*often adjectival*) a place that gives you a good view all round, from which you can watch for danger: *We would see his signal clearly from the lookout post on top of the rock.* **2** (*informal*) If you tell someone who is doing something dangerous or stupid that the undesirable consequences are their **lookout**, you mean that if they do happen, they have only themselves to blame: *It's your lookout if the police catch you.* □ *If you want to throw all your money away in the casino, that's your lookout.*
▻ ***phrase*** You **are on the lookout**, or **keep a lookout**, for someone or something when you are watching to make sure you see them when they appear: *She kept a lookout for the bus.* □ *He's on the lookout for a new job.*

loom[1] /luːm/ *noun*: **looms**
A **loom** is a machine for weaving thread into cloth.

loom[2] /luːm/ *verb*: **looms, looming, loomed**
1 Something **looms**, or **looms up**, when it appears as an unclear shape or mass, usually in some threatening or frightening form: *The ship loomed out of the mist.* **2** An event or problem **looms** when it will soon happen, especially in some threatening or frightening way: *Her exams are looming.*

loony /ˈluːnɪ/ *adjective*; *noun*
▻ ***adjective*** (*informal*): **loonier, looniest**
If you describe a person or their ideas as **loony** you mean they are crazy: *these extremists with their loony ideas.*
▻ ***noun*** (*informal*): **loonies:** *The local council is run by loonies.*

loop /luːp/ *noun*; *verb*
▻ ***noun***: **loops**
A **loop** is the oval-shaped coil in *eg* a piece of string or rope, which forms as it crosses over itself.
▻ ***verb***: **loops, looping, looped**
1 You **loop** something when you fasten it with or enclose it in a loop: *She looped the scarf round her neck.* **2** Something **loops** when it forms a loop or loops, or moves in loop-like patterns.

loophole /ˈluːphoʊl/ *noun*: **loopholes**
A **loophole** is a way of avoiding obeying a rule or law without actually breaking it: *a loophole in the law which lets him avoid paying tax.*

loose /luːs/ *adjective*: **looser, loosest**
1 Something is **loose** when **a** it is not firmly fixed in place: *The shelf has come loose from the wall.* □ *The window is loose and rattles in the wind.* **b** it is not held together with anything else: *loose sheets of paper* □ *it's cheaper if you buy sweets loose rather than in a packet.* **2** A thing or animal is **loose** when it is not tied up or shut in: *Her long hair was loose round her shoulders.* □ *The boat has got loose from its mooring.* □ *He let the rabbits loose in the field.* **3 Loose** clothes are not tight or close-fitting. **4** A **loose** translation is not exact. [*opposite* **literal**] — *adverb* **loosely:** *His shirt hung loosely on his body.*
▻ ***phrases*** **1** You are **at a loose end** when you have nothing to do. **2** A dangerous person or criminal is **on the loose** when they have escaped from prison or control.

loose-leaf /luːsˈliːf/ *adjective*
A **loose-leaf** folder or binder has a cover which opens to allow pages to be added and taken out.

loosen /ˈluːsən/ *verb*: **loosens, loosening, loosened**
You **loosen** something, or it **loosens**, when you make it, or it becomes, less firm, fixed or tight: *He loosened his belt.* □ *This screw has loosened.* [*same as* **slacken**; *opposite* **tighten**]

phrasal verb
You **loosen up**, or something **loosens** you **up**, when you become, or something makes you, less tense, rigid or stiff: *Do some exercises to loosen up your muscles before the race begins.* □ *A long hot bath helped her loosen up after a tiring day.*

loot /luːt/ *noun*; *verb*
▻ ***noun*** (*uncount*)
Loot is stolen goods and money, especially those stolen from the enemy in wartime.
▻ ***verb***: **loots, looting, looted**
People **loot** *eg* shops and houses when they steal money or goods from them, especially during periods of violence or war: *A lot of shops were looted during the riots.* [*same as* **ransack**] — *noun* **looter:** *The looters stole videos and cameras.* — *noun* (*uncount*) **looting:** *The police could do nothing to stop the looting.*

lop /lɒp/ *verb*: **lops, lopping, lopped**

phrasal verb
1 You **lop** branches **off** a tree when you cut them off. **2** You **lop off** the unnecessary parts of something when you cut them off or get rid of them.

lope /loʊp/ *verb*: **lopes, loping, loped**
A person or animal **lopes** when they run with long, easy, steps.

lopsided /lɒpˈsaɪdɪd/ *adjective*
Something is **lopsided** when it is uneven because it has one side smaller or lower than the other: *a lopsided smile.* [*same as* **crooked**; *opposite* **symmetrical, balanced, even**]

loquacious /loʊˈkweɪʃəs/ *adjective* (*formal*)
A **loquacious** person talks a lot. [*same as* **talkative, garrulous**; *opposite* **quiet, reticent**]

lord /lɔːd/ *noun*: **lords**
1 Lord is a title used before the names of men who have the rank of peer, and occurs in the names of certain important offices; 'my **lord**' is used to address some men of the rank of peer, and also to address a bishop or a judge: *Lord Alfred Douglas* □ *Lord Linley* □ *The Lord Mayor of London* □ *the Lord Chancellor*

□ *'Will you take your coffee in the lounge, my lord?'* [see also **lady**] **2** (*rather old*) A **lord** is a man of noble or aristocratic rank: *a magnificent gathering of lords and ladies.* [see also **lady**] **3** (*used in the plural, with a singular or plural verb*) In Britain, the members of the upper house in Parliament are called **the Lords**: *The Lords have* (or *has*) *voted against the bill.* **4** A **lord** is also a master or ruler. **5** (*religion*) Christians refer to God or Christ as the **Lord**: *May the Lord save you and protect you.*

▷ ***phrases*** **1** (*informal*) People use **'Lord!'**, **'Good Lord!'**, and **'Oh Lord!'** as expressions of surprise or dismay. **2** (*informal*) Someone **lords it over you** when they behave towards you as though they were more important than you.

lordship /lɔːdʃɪp/ *noun*: **lordships**
You use 'your **lordship**', 'his **lordship**' and 'their **lordships**' to address or refer to some men of the rank of peer: *His lordship will take that call.* □ *Would your lordship kindly sign these letters?* □ *May we express our gratitude to your lordship?* □ *Their Lordships were still discussing the Bill.*

lore /lɔː(r)/ *noun* (*uncount*)
Lore is the whole body of knowledge, beliefs and traditions on a particular subject or in a particular culture: *Jewish lore.*

lorry /ˈlɒrɪ/ *noun*: **lorries**
A **lorry** is a large, heavy vehicle for transporting heavy loads by road. [*same as* **truck**; see picture at **vehicle**]

lose /luːz/ *verb*: **loses, losing, lost**
1 You **lose** something when you cannot find it, *eg* because you have forgotten where you put it: *I've completely lost that cheque you sent me.* [*same as* **mislay**] **2** You **lose** something, especially something important to you, when you no longer have it, *eg* because it has been taken away from you or destroyed: *He lost a leg in the war.* □ *She's afraid of losing her job.* □ *She has lost the use of her right arm.* □ *A lot of precious exhibits were lost in the fire.* **3** You **lose** something when you have less of it than before: *You look thinner; have you lost weight?* □ *I'm beginning to lose patience with him.* **4** A business **loses** money, or a person **loses** money over some transaction, if they make less money than they spend. **5** You **lose** a close friend or relative when they die: *She lost her father at the age of twelve.* □ *She lost the baby at four months.* [= her baby died when she was four months pregnant] **6** You **lose** time or an opportunity when you waste it: *If the patient deteriorates, you should lose no time in calling the doctor.* [= call the doctor as soon as possible] □ *Apply now or you may lose your chance of a free gift.* **7** You **lose** an argument, battle or game when you are defeated and your opponent wins: *Suppose Labour lose the election again?* □ *Gloucestershire lost to Herefordshire by 6 wickets.* □ *I lost by 4 points to 5.* **8** You **lose** your way when you go in the wrong direction and get lost: *We lost our way in the centre of Birmingham and were half an hour late.* **9** A clock or watch **loses** time when it goes too slowly: *My watch is losing at least 2 minutes a day.* [*opposite* **gain**] **10** (*informal*) You **lose** someone when they cannot understand you: *I'm afraid you've lost me; could you explain that again?*

▷ ***phrases*** **1** You **have nothing to lose** by acting in a certain way if it cannot harm you to do so: *Why don't you apply? You've nothing to lose.* **2** You **lose yourself in** something when it takes all your attention: *She finds it easy to lose herself in music.* □ *He was lost in thought.*

> ***phrasal verb***
> (*informal*) You **lose out** if you suffer a loss or are at a disadvantage: *She lost out on the deal.* □ *If you charge an enormous entrance fee a lot of people won't be able to afford it, and they'll lose out.*

loser /ˈluːzə(r)/ *noun*: **losers**
1 The **loser** of a game, argument or battle is the person who does not win. [*opposite* **winner**] **2** (*informal*) A **loser** is a person who seems likely to always fail and be unsuccessful. **3** If you are the **loser** in any event or situation, you are the person who will suffer most because of it: *She'll be the loser if she decides not to accept that job.*

loss /lɒs/ *noun*: **losses**
1 Loss is the act of losing something, or the fact of its being lost: *Have you reported the loss of your purse to the police?* □ *weight loss.* [*opposite* **gain**] **2** (*usually in the singular*) A **loss** is a disadvantage caused by losing someone or something: *If she leaves it will be a great loss to the company.* **3** A **loss** is the amount of money lost by a company: *We made a loss of several hundred pounds last year.* [*same as* **deficit**; *opposite* **profit**] **4** You suffer a **loss** when someone, especially a close friend or relative, dies: *She never got over the loss of her son.* □ *We suffered heavy losses in the war.* [= a lot of people were killed] **5** (*uncount*) **Loss** of life is the death of a lot of people at a single time: *The accident caused great loss of life.*

▷ ***phrases*** **1** You are **at a loss** when you are puzzled and do not know what to do or say: *I was at a loss for words.* **2** You **cut your losses** when you stop doing something that is making a situation worse: *It would be better to cut your losses and start the whole thing over again.* [see also **dead loss**]

lost /lɒst/ *verb*; *adjective*
▷ ***verb***
Lost is the past tense and past participle of **lose**.
▷ ***adjective***
1 Something is **lost** when it is missing and you cannot find it: *The keys to the garage have got lost.* **2** You are **lost** when you cannot find your way or have gone in the wrong direction: *I got lost on the way to the station.* **3** You are also **lost** when you are confused or puzzled: *I'm a bit lost; could you go over that point again?* **4** A person **is lost** if they are killed: *soldiers lost in battle.*

▷ ***phrases*** **1** (*slang*) **'Get lost!'** is a rude way of telling someone to go away. **2** You can say that something is **lost on** someone when they do not use, understand or appreciate it properly: *Good wine is lost on him.*

lost cause /lɒst ˈkɔːz/ *noun*: **lost causes**
A **lost cause** is an aim or ideal that will never be achieved.

lot /lɒt/ *determiner*; *pronoun*; *adverb*; *noun*
▷ ***determiner***
'A **lot** of' and '**lots** of' are used with uncount nouns, plural count nouns and sometimes singular count nouns to mean 'a large number of' or 'a large amount of': *Lots of food gets thrown away at the end of each day.* □ *There's a lot of truth in that.* □ *A lot of books have been written on the subject* □ *There are always lots of cats wandering about in this street.* □ *I still see a lot of my family.* [= I often see them] □ *A lot of that statement is mere repetition.* □ *Lots more replies arrived this morning.* □ *'Is the ice cream finished?' 'No, there's lots more in the freezer.'* □ *There's a lot less money around.*

Notice that if the noun is uncount or singular the verb is singular; if the noun is plural the verb is plural: *A lot of people disagree with that. Lots of food is wasted.*
Notice also that 'a **lot** of' and '**lots** of' are generally used in positive statements, where *many* and *much* often sound formal and unnatural; you use *many* and *much* in negative sentences and in questions: *There isn't much food left. 'Were there many mistakes to correct?' 'Well, there were a lot of misprints.'*

▻ ***pronoun***
1 'A **lot**' and '**lots**' are used to mean a large number or amount: *I think we can do a lot to help.* □ *Some staff are staying on but a lot are leaving.* □ *Lots of them have found other jobs.* □ *A lot of us are dissatified with working conditions.* □ *'Is there any milk in the fridge?' 'Yes, lots.'* □ *Lots of it is potentially useful.* □ *A lot of what you say is true.* **2** 'the **lot**' or 'the whole **lot**' means the whole of a quantity or group just mentioned: *I started out with about £70 this morning and I seem to have spent the lot.* □ *There was a pound of cheese in there yesterday and the whole lot has disappeared.* □ *I got these strawberries at the supermarket and the whole lot are bad.*
▻ ***adverb***
'A **lot**' is used as an adverb **a** before comparatives to mean 'much': *She's been a lot happier since she found a new job.* □ *This year's holiday was a lot less expensive than last year's.* □ *You'd get there a lot more quickly if you went by train.* **b** with verbs to mean 'a great deal' or 'often': *I like him a lot.* □ *We see her a lot at weekends.*
▻ ***noun***: **lots**
1 You can refer a certain group of things or people as 'a **lot**': *The new students are quite a promising lot.* □ *I've bought two lots of table napkins, one green and one blue, so that we can alternate them along the table.* **2** (*rather old*) Your **lot** is the sort of life you have: *I live quietly, but I'm contented with my lot.* **3** A **lot** is an object or group of objects sold at an auction: *I bid for Lots 21 and 35.* **4** (*AmE*) A parking **lot** is acarpark.
▻ ***phrase*** A group of people of a certain number **draw lots** for something when they decide who is to have it or do it by putting a set of things of the same number, of which one is different from the others, into a container, so that when they each take out one of the things, the person who gets the one that is different is the person who is chosen.

loth /loʊθ/ *adjective*
Loth is the same as **loath**.

lotion /ˈloʊʃən/ *noun*: **lotions**
A **lotion** is a liquid for *eg* healing or cleaning the skin: *suntan lotion.*

lottery /ˈlɒtərɪ/ *noun*: **lotteries**
1 A **lottery** is a way of raising money by selling tickets and giving prizes for those tickets chosen at random. **2** A **lottery** is also anything which is thought of as being decided by chance.

loud /lɑʊd/ *adjective or adverb*: **louder, loudest**
1 A **loud** noise produces a large amount of sound: *Loud music was coming from the caravan.* □ *She had one of those loud, authoritative voices.* □ *Could you turn the radio up a bit louder?* □ *Let's see who can shout the loudest.* □ *Her voice rang out loud and clear over the telephone.*

Notice that although **loud** is frequently used as an adverb, some people prefer to use **loudly**: *She laughed so loud* (or *loudly*) *that everyone jumped. He yelled her name as loud as* (or *as loudly as*) *he could.*

2 Someone who is **loud** in their approval or disapproval of something expresses their approval or disapproval strongly: *Lady Olga was loud in her condemnation of the use of marijuana as a pain-killer.* [*same as* **vehement**] **3** You describe colours or patterns as **loud** if they are tastelessly bright: *Isn't your tie a bit on the loud side?* [*same as* **garish**]
▻ ***phrase***
1 Something that is stated **loud and clear** is stated so that it can be easily understood. **2** People complain **loud and long** about something when they complain bitterly about it. **3** You say something **out loud** when you speak it, as distinct from thinking it or recording it mentally: *He read part of the letter out loud.*

loudly /ˈlɑʊdlɪ/ *adverb*
You do something **loudly** when you do it in a way that makes a lot of noise: *crying loudly* □ *Speak more loudly or the people at the back won't be able to hear.* [compare **loud**]

loud-mouthed /ˈlɑʊdmaʊðd/ *adjective* (*informal*)
A person who is **loud-mouthed** talks a lot in a noisy, forceful and unpleasant way.

loudspeaker /lɑʊdˈspiːkə(r)/ *noun*: **loudspeakers**
A **loudspeaker** is a piece of audio equipment that turns electrical signals into sound.

lounge /lɑʊndʒ/ *noun; verb*
▻ ***noun***: **lounges**
1 A **lounge** is room where you can sit and relax, in a house or hotel. **2** An airport **lounge** is a large room where passengers sit while waiting for their flights: *the departure lounge.* **3** (*BrE*) A **lounge**, or **lounge bar**, is a comfortable, more expensive bar in a public house or hotel.
▻ ***verb***: **lounges, lounging, lounged**
You **lounge** somewhere when you sit or lie there lazily and comfortably: *She lounged on a rug in the garden.* [*same as* **recline, laze**]

phrasal verb
You **lounge about** or **lounge around** when you pass your time doing nothing: *He spends most of his time lounging around the house.*

louse /lɑʊs/ *noun*: **lice**
A **louse** is a small insect which sucks the blood of the animal or person it is living on.

lousy /ˈlɑʊzɪ/ *adjective* (*informal*): **lousier, lousiest**
1 Something that is **lousy** is very bad or unpleasant: *a lousy film.* **2** You can say that you feel **lousy** when you feel ill: *You'll feel lousy in the morning if you don't get any sleep.*

lout /lɑʊt/ *noun*: **louts**
A **lout** is a young man who behaves in a bad-mannered, rough and unpleasant way. [*same as* **yob**]

lovable or **loveable** /ˈlʌvəbəl/ *adjective*
Someone is **lovable** when they are easy to love or like a lot: *a lovable child.*

love /lʌv/ *verb; noun*
▻ ***verb***: **loves, loving, loved**
1 You **love** someone when, as well as being attracted to them sexually and romantically, you have a deep affection for them: *She told him she didn't love him enough to marry him.* **2** You **love** your family and people who are close to you, or people you admire, if you are fond of them and are concerned about their welfare and happiness: *Of course mothers love their babies.* □ *People like to feel loved.* □ *She loved my sister more than me.* □ *He may be unscrupulous but the*

people love him. [*opposite* **hate**, **dislike**] **3** You **love** something such as your country if you want to be loyal to it and protect it. **4** You say you **love** something if you enjoy it or like it a lot: *I love this hot weather.* □ *They love living in the country.* □ *She used to love cooking and dressmaking.* □ *We loved meeting all your family last weekend.* □ *I love you telling me about your childhood.* □ *I love to get up early in the summer.* □ *'How's she enjoying her job?' 'She's really loving it.'* □ *He loved it when she smiled.* **5** You express desires and wishes using 'would **love**' or 'should **love**': *I'd love to visit you in Canada one day.* □ *'Would you like to come to this film with me?' 'I should love to.'* □ *I'd have loved to join you, but I've another engagement.*

> Notice that in senses 3 and 4 **love** usually occurs in positive statements; **like** is used with negatives or in questions: *'Do you like walking?' 'Yes, I love it.' 'Do you think he'd like to come?' 'I'm sure he'd love to.'* But **love** is possible in questions expecting the answer 'yes': *Don't you love being in control?*

▻ ***noun***: **loves**

1 (*uncount*) **Love** is a deep feeling of affection for someone to whom you are sexually and romantically attracted: *Your parents choose your husband; marrying for love is out of the question.* **2** (*uncount*) **Love** is also deep affection for people close to you, such as your family, or for someone you admire, and concern for their welfare and happiness: *Children need love and security.* □ *She had won the love of fellow Tories.* [*opposite* **hate**, **hatred**] **3** (*uncount*) **Love** for your country or native land is loyalty towards it, or patriotism. **4** (*uncount or used in the singular*) People have a **love** for something if they have a strong liking for it: *her love of bright colours* □ *She's driven entirely by ambition and the love of power.* [*opposite* **dislike**] **5** (*usually in the singular*) The thing that someone is most fond of can be referred to as their great or real **love**, or as the **love** of their life: *Opera is his real love.* **6** (*especially old*) People sometimes refer to, or address, someone they love, or are fond of, as their **love**: *Margaret, my love, come and sit beside me.* □ *I gave my love a cherry.* **7** (*BrE*; *informal*) Some people address others, including strangers, and especially women and children, as **love**: *'Can I help you, love?'* **8** (*uncount*) People often finish a letter to a friend or relation with '**love**,' or '**love** from', or 'with **love** from' before signing their name: *'Lots of love, Susan.'* **9** (*uncount*) In tennis, **love** is a score of no points: *Thomson leads 30 love.* [= Thomson has 30 points and the other player has none]

▻ ***phrases*** **1** One person **falls in love** with another when they feel sexually attracted, and deeply affectionate, towards them: *He confessed that he had fallen in love with her.* □ *when two people fall in love.* **2** You **send** a person **your love**, or ask someone to **give** them **your love**, when you ask someone to give them an affectionate greeting from you: *Give my love to your sister when you see her next.* **3** You are **in love** with someone when you are strongly attracted to them sexually and romantically, and feel a deep affection for them: *We realized we were in love with each other.* □ *Much can be forgiven to two young people in love.* **4** Two people **make love** when they have sex: *He had made love to 1003 women in Spain alone.*

loveable see **lovable**.

love affair /ˈlʌv əfɛər/ *noun*: **love affairs**

A **love affair** is a romantic and sexual relationship between two people who are not married to each other.

loveless /ˈlʌvləs/ *adjective*

A **loveless** relationship is one in which the people do not, or no longer, love each other: *a loveless marriage.*

love letter /ˈlʌv lɛtə(r)/ *noun*: **love letters**

You write a **love letter** to tell someone that you love them.

lovely /ˈlʌvlɪ/ *adjective*: **lovelier**, **loveliest**

1 Someone or something that is **lovely** is beautiful or attractive: *a lovely face* □ *She always looks lovely.* **2** (*informal*) Something that is **lovely** is enjoyable or pleasing: *a lovely walk on the beach* □ *It was lovely to see you again.* — *noun* (*uncount*) **loveliness:** *Her loveliness has increased with age.*

love-making /ˈlʌvmeɪkɪŋ/ *noun* (*uncount*)

Love-making is romantic and sexual activities between sexual partners.

lover /ˈlʌvə(r)/ *noun*: **lovers**

1 Your **lover** is the person you are having a romantic and sexual relationship with, and that you are not married to. **2** (*used in the plural*) **Lovers** are two people who are in love or who are having a romantic and sexual relationship. **3** A **lover** of something is a person who enjoys or likes it a lot: *a lover of fine wines* □ *dog-lovers.*

loving /ˈlʌvɪŋ/ *adjective*

1 A **loving** act shows love or affectation: *a loving glance at his wife* □ *He gives his plants tender loving care.* [*same as* **affectionate**] **2** A **loving** person feels and shows love or affection: *a loving husband and father.* — *adverb* **lovingly:** *He looked at her lovingly.* □ *She cared lovingly for her invalid husband.*

low /loʊ/ *adjective or adverb*; *adjective*; *noun*

▻ ***adjective or adverb***: **lower**, **lowest**

1 Something that is **low** is **a** close to the ground: *The ceiling was so low I used to bump my head on it.* □ *low clouds.* □ *I think I've hung this picture rather too low.* □ *Residents complain continually of aircraft flying low over the town.* □ *The ball bounced lower and lower.* □ *He opened the door and bowed low.* **b** close to the bottom of something: *Her name is quite low on the list.* □ *The pain seemed to be lower down my back than usual.* **2** Someone or something is **low** on or in something if they haven't got much of it: *We're getting a bit low on coffee.* □ *The car's low on petrol.* □ *We were running low on fuel.* □ *cigarettes that are low in tar.* **3** A rank or position that is **low** is near the bottom: *a low-ranking officer* □ *He could never marry a low-born commoner.* □ *one of the lowest grades of technician.* **4** You use **low** to describe people or behaviour that you disapprove of or consider dishonest or not respectable: *That was a low trick to play.* □ *I hope I never sink so low as to betray a friend.* **5** A woman's dress or blouse is **low** if it leaves her neck and upper chest bare: *a low-necked top* □ *Her dress was cut daringly low.* **6** A sound is **low** if **a** it is soft or doesn't make much noise: *They spoke in low voices.* □ *Turn the sound lower or you'll wake the baby.* **b** it is deep: *She struck the lowest note on the piano.* □ *How low can you sing?*

▻ ***adjective***: **lower**, **lowest**

1 Something that is **low** **a** measures a short distance from bottom to top: *a low bush* □ *The wall was low enough to look over.* **b** is small in amount, level, value or degree: *low-fat margarines.* □ *Temperatures have been lower than usual for the time of year.* □ *surviving on very low wages.* **2** Temperatures in *eg* the **low** twenties are between twenty and twenty-five degrees. [*compare* **early**] **3** A quality or standard is **low** if it is poor or bad: *They've become used to a very low standard of living.* □ *low-quality workmanship.* **4** You have a **low** opinion of someone if you disapprove of them. **5** You feel **low** when you are feeling ill or depressed. **6** When driving, you engage a **low** gear when you engage first or second gear, *eg* when going uphill.

▻ ***noun*** (*usually in the singular*): **lows**

A **low** is a low position or level on a scale: *Prices have fallen to a record low.* ▫ *Relations between our two countries are at an all-time low.* [*opposite* **high**]

▻ ***phrases*** **1** You are **laid low** when you are ill: *I've been laid low with flu.* **2** You **are lying low** if you are keeping quiet or hiding from public notice: *She's been lying low since the news of her divorce broke in the press.*

low-cut /loʊ'kʌt/ *adjective*

A woman's dress or blouse is **low-cut** when it does not cover her neck and the top part of her chest.

low-down /'loʊdaʊn/ *noun* (*singular*; *informal*)

▻ ***phrase*** You **give** someone **the low-down on** something when you give them information about it; you **get the low-down on** it when someone gives information to you: *I'll give you the low-down on what was discussed at the meeting.*

lower /'loʊə(r)/ *adjective*; *verb*

▻ ***adjective***

1 Lower is the comparative form of **low**. **2 Lower** describes **a** the bottom one of two things: *The lower jaw was mising.* **b** the less important or less senior of two sections of an organization: *Their parliament, like ours, consists of an upper and lower house.* **c** the bottom part of something: *lower-back pain.* **d** the less important or less senior part of an organization: *in the lower ranks of the civil service.* [*opposite* **upper**]

▻ ***verb***: **lowers, lowering, lowered**

1 You **lower** something when you move it slowly downwards: *The injured climber was lowered to safety.* ▫ *She lowered herself into an armchair.* ▫ *The flag was lowered to half-mast.* [*opposite* **raise**] **2** Amounts **are lowered** when they are reduced: *They voted against lowering the age of consent.* [*opposite* **raise**] **3** You **lower** your voice, or the volume on the radio, when you make it quieter. **4** You **lower** your eyes when you look down. [*opposite* **raise**]

lower class /loʊə klɑːs/ *noun*: **lower classes**

The **lower classes** are the lowest social class, below middle class: *The lower classes have a poorer standard of living.* ▫ *lower-class families.*

low-key /loʊ'kiː/ *adjective*

Something is **low-key** when it is controlled and quiet: *a low-key wedding with only six guests.*

lowlands /loʊ'ləndz/ *noun* (*plural*)

The **lowlands** are an area of land that is flat and at sea level, especially in comparison with more mountainous areas: *the Scottish Lowlands.* [*opposite* **highlands**]

lowly /'loʊlɪ/ *adjective*: **lowlier, lowliest**

Someone or something that is **lowly** has a low rank or position: *I'm only a lowly employee, not one of the managers.* [*same as* **humble**]

low-paid /loʊ'peɪd/ *adjective*

People are **low-paid** when they do not earn much money; jobs are **low-paid** when people doing them are not paid much.

low tide /loʊ 'taɪd/ *noun* (*uncount*)

Low tide is the time when the sea is at its lowest level. [*opposite* **high tide**]

loyal /'lɔɪəl/ *adjective*

You are **loyal** to people when you never stop supporting them: *a loyal supporter of the local football team.* [*same as* **faithful**; *opposite* **disloyal**] — *adverb* **loyally**: *She supported her husband loyally through all his problems.*

loyalty /'lɔɪəltɪ/ *noun*: **loyalties**

1 (*uncount*) **Loyalty** is faithful support of *eg* your friends: *his loyalty to his local football team.* **2** (*usually in the plural*) Your **loyalties** are feelings of faithful friendship and support, especially for a particular person or thing: *divided loyalties* ▫ *You must decide where your loyalties lie.*

lozenge /'lɒzɪndʒ/ *noun*: **lozenges**

1 A **lozenge** is a small sweet or tablet that you suck *eg* to make a sore throat feel better. **2** A **lozenge** is a diamond shape.

LP /ɛl 'piː/ *noun*: **LPs**

An **LP** is a record which plays for 20 to 30 minutes on each side.

L-plate /'ɛlpleɪt/ *noun*: **L-plates**

An **L-plate** is a small, square, white sign with a red letter *L* on it, put on cars being driven by learners.

LSD /ɛlɛs'diː/ *noun* (*uncount*)

LSD is a powerful drug which makes people think they see things that are not really there.

lubricate /'luːbrɪkeɪt/ *verb*: **lubricates, lubricating, lubricated**

You **lubricate** something such as an engine or machinery when you cover it with oil or grease to make it work smoothly. [*same as* **oil**] — *noun* (*uncount*) **lubrication** /'luːbrɪkeɪʃən/: *the engine's lubrication system.*

lucid /'luːsɪd/ *adjective*

1 Writing or words that are **lucid** are easily understood and clear. **2** A person or their mind is **lucid** when they are able to think clearly, especially after a period of illness or mental confusion: *There are only short periods when she is lucid.* [*same as* **sane**, **reasonable**] — *noun* (*uncount*) **lucidity** /luː'sɪdɪtɪ/: *His writing lacks lucidity.* ▫ *her periods of lucidity.* — *adverb* **lucidly**: *Try to write and think lucidly.*

luck /lʌk/ *noun* (*uncount*)

1 Luck is success that comes by chance: *He got that job through luck rather than hard work.* **2 Luck** is also good fortune: *Let me wish you luck.* **3 Luck** is also those events in life which cannot be controlled and seem to happen by chance: *You seem to have been having a lot of bad luck lately*

▻ ***phrases*** **1** You say **bad luck** or **hard luck** to someone when something unfortunate has happened to them or they have failed to get or do something they wanted. **2** If you are **down on your luck**, you are having problems and things are not going well for you. **3** You wish someone **good luck** or **the best of luck** when you want them to be successful: *I wished him the best of luck for the future.* ▫ *Good luck with the interview!* **4** You are **in luck** when you are lucky or fortunate, especially about a particular thing: *If you want some more cake, you're in luck.* [= because there is still some left] **5** (*informal*) Someone **is pushing their luck** if they are risking total failure by trying to gain too much. **6** You **try your luck** at something when you try it: *She decided to try her luck at acting.* **7** You can add **with luck** or **with any luck** at the end of a statement that you hope will be true: *I should get this work finished tomorrow, with luck.* **8** (*informal*) **Worse luck** means 'unfortunately': *I've got to work late tonight, worse luck.*

luckily /'lʌkɪlɪ/ *adverb* (*sentence adverb*)

You use **luckily** to show that you are glad that something is the case or has happened: *Luckily, he came to my rescue.* [*same as* **fortunately**; *opposite* **unfortunately**, **unluckily**]

luckless /'lʌklɛs/ *adjective*

A person or scheme is **luckless** when they are unlucky, unsuccessful or unfortunate: *The luckless owner woke to find his car gone.* ▫ *Their luckless expedition to the South Pole.*

lucky /ˈlʌkɪ/ *adjective*: **luckier, luckiest**
1 You are **lucky** when you have good luck or are fortunate: *I'm lucky to have such a good job.* [*opposite* **unlucky**] **2** A situation or event is **lucky** when it has good results or effects: *It's lucky for you that I arrived when I did.* □ *It's your lucky day!* □ *a lucky escape.* [*opposite* **unlucky**] **3** You regard something such as a possession as **lucky** if you believe it brings you good luck or success: *His lucky number is 13.* □ *a lucky charm.* [*opposite* **unlucky**]
▻ ***phrase*** (*informal*) **1** You can say **you'll be lucky** to someone when you think it is very unlikely that they will get something: *You'll be lucky to get off with a fine.* **2** You **strike lucky**, or **strike it lucky**, when you have good luck in some respect: *At least you've struck it lucky with the weather.*

lucrative /ˈlu:krətɪv/ *adjective* (*formal*)
Something is **lucrative** when it makes a lot of money: *a lucrative business deal.* [*same as* **profitable**]

ludicrous /ˈlu:dɪkrəs/ *adjective*
Something that is described as **ludicrous** is completely ridiculous or very foolish: *a ludicrous idea.* [*same as* **crazy**] — *adverb* **ludicrously:** *ludicrously expensive clothes.*

lug /lʌg/ *verb* (*informal*): **lugs, lugging, lugged**
You **lug** something, especially something heavy, when you pull or drag it with difficulty: *She lugged the heavy bags up the stairs.*

luggage /ˈlʌgɪdʒ/ *noun* (*uncount*)
Luggage is a traveller's suitcases and bags: *pieces of luggage* □ *Check your luggage in at the desk.* [*same as* **baggage**; see also **left-luggage office**]

lugubrious /lʊˈgu:brɪəs/ *adjective* (*formal*)
Something that is **lugubrious** is sad and gloomy: *a lugubrious song.* [*same as* **dreary, mournful**; *opposite* **cheerful, happy**]

lukewarm /lu:kˈwɔ:m/ *adjective*
1 Something that is **lukewarm** is only slightly warm: *lukewarm water.* [*same as* **tepid**] **2** You can say that someone is **lukewarm** when they are not very interested, enthusiastic or pleased: *He's lukewarm about the idea.* □ *a lukewarm response.*

lull /lʌl/ *verb*; *noun*
▻ ***verb***: **lulls, lulling, lulled**
1 You **lull** someone when you make them calm or sleepy: *She lulled the baby to sleep.* **2** Something or someone **lulls** you when they deceive you into feeling safe and not under threat: *They were lulled into a false sense of security.*
▻ ***noun*** (*usually in the singular*): **lulls**
A **lull** is a period of calm and quiet, or of less activity: *a lull in the fighting.*
▻ ***phrase*** **The lull before the storm** is a period of quiet and peace before something unpleasant begins or before a very busy period.

lullaby /ˈlʌləbaɪ/ *noun*: **lullabies**
A **lullaby** is a gentle song that you sing to help a child fall asleep.

lumber¹ /ˈlʌmbə(r)/ *noun*; *verb*
▻ ***noun*** (*uncount*)
1 (*BrE*) **Lumber** is old and unwanted things, especially articles of furniture, that aren't being used any more. **2** (*AmE*) **Lumber** is the same as timber.
▻ ***verb***: **lumbers, lumbering, lumbered**

> ***phrasal verb***
> (*informal*) You **are lumbered with** a job or task when you are given one you do not want: *I always get lumbered with the washing up.*

lumber² /ˈlʌmbə(r)/ *verb*: **lumbers, lumbering, lumbered**
A person or animal **lumbers** when they move heavily, slowly and clumsily: *He lumbered round the house.*

lumberjack /lʌmbəˈdʒak/ *noun*: **lumberjacks**
A **lumberjack** is a person employed to cut down, saw up and move trees.

luminous /ˈlu:mɪnəs/ *adjective*
Something that is **luminous** glows or shines in the dark: *luminous paint.*

lump¹ /lʌmp/ *noun*; *verb*
▻ ***noun***: **lumps**
1 A **lump** is a small, solid, shapeless piece of something. **2** A **lump** in or on part of the body is a small, hard swelling or tumour. [*same as* **growth, cyst**] **3** A **lump** of sugar is a small, cube-shaped piece of it: *Would you like one lump or two?* **4** If you have a **lump** in your throat, you have a feeling of tightening or swelling in it caused by feelings such as sadness and pity.
▻ ***verb***: **lumps, lumping, lumped**
You **lump** people or things together when you treat them all in the same way, or as if they were a single whole: *All of these expenses can be lumped together.* [*same as* **group**]

lump² /lʌmp/ *verb* (*informal*)
▻ ***phrase*** You can say that someone will **have to lump it** if they must accept or put up with a bad or difficult situation without complaining.

lump sum /lʌmp ˈsʌm/ *noun*: **lump sums**
A **lump sum** is a large amount of money paid at one time and not paid as small amounts over a period of time: *The pension scheme will give you a lump sum when you retire as well as monthly payments.*

lumpy /ˈlʌmpɪ/ *adjective*: **lumpier, lumpiest**
Something that is **lumpy** has or is full of lumps: *a lumpy bed.*

lunacy /ˈlu:nəsɪ/ *noun* (*uncount*)
Lunacy is
1 great foolishness or stupidity: *It was lunacy to go climbing without the proper boots.* **2** severe mental illness. [*opposite* **sanity**]

lunar /ˈlu:nə(r)/ *adjective*
Lunar means of, like, for use on or caused by the moon: *a lunar eclipse* □ *the lunar surface* □ *a lunar spacecraft.*

lunatic /ˈlu:nətɪk/ *noun*; *adjective*
▻ ***noun***: **lunatics**
1 You can call someone a **lunatic** when they behave in a foolish or stupid way: *Only a lunatic would drive so fast and dangerously.* [*same as* **madman**] **2** (*old*) A **lunatic** is a person suffering from a severe mental illness.
▻ ***adjective***
You can describe something such as an idea or plan as **lunatic** when you think is is foolish or stupid. [*same as* **crazy, insane, mad**; *opposite* **sane, sensible**]

lunatic asylum /ˈlu:nətɪk əsaɪləm/ *noun* (*old, offensive*): **lunatic asylums**
A **lunatic asylum** was a home or hospital for people with mental illnesses.

lunch /lʌntʃ/ *noun*; *verb*
▻ ***noun*** (*count or uncount*): **lunches**
Lunch is a meal eaten in the middle of the day between breakfast and dinner: *Where shall we go for lunch?* □ *Lunch is served between twelve and two.* □ *We'll have an early lunch.*
▻ ***verb***: **lunches, lunching, lunched**
You **lunch** when you eat lunch, usually in a restaurant: *We lunched on sandwiches and coffee, and then continued on our way.*

luncheon /ˈlʌntʃən/ *noun* (*count or uncount*): **luncheons**
A **luncheon** is a formal lunch: *We shall serve the fish at luncheon.*

lunchtime /ˈlʌntʃtaɪm/ *noun* (*count or uncount*): **lunchtimes**
Lunchtime is the time in the middle of the day when you have lunch: *I'll meet you at lunchtime.*

lung /lʌŋ/ *noun*: **lungs**
Your **lungs** are the two organs inside your chest that are used for breathing: *lung cancer.*

lunge /lʌndʒ/ *verb; noun*
▻ ***verb***: **lunges, lunging, lunged**
You **lunge** at something when you make a sudden strong movement forwards: *She lunged towards the door.* ▫ *He lunged at me with a knife.*
▻ ***noun*** (*usually in the singular*): **lunges**
Someone makes a **lunge** at you when they move towards you suddenly.

lurch[1] /lɜːtʃ/ *verb; noun*
▻ ***verb***: **lurches, lurching, lurched**
You **lurch** if you move unsteadily, especially rolling slightly to one side: *The boat lurched towards the rocks.* [*same as* **reel, stagger**]
▻ ***noun*** (*usually in the singular*): **lurches**
A **lurch** is a sudden roll to one side: *The boat gave a lurch.*

lurch[2] /lɜːtʃ/ *noun* (*uncount*)
▻ ***phrase*** (*informal*) You **leave** someone **in the lurch** if you withdraw your help or support and leave them in a difficult situation: *He left me in the lurch with all the cleaning to do.*

lure /lʊə(r)/ or /ljʊə(r)/ *verb; noun*
▻ ***verb***: **lures, luring, lured**
To **lure** someone means to tempt or attract them to go somewhere or do something, often by offering some reward: *Companies are using promises of high salaries and a secure future as a lure to university leavers.* [*same as* **entice**]
▻ ***noun*** (*usually in the singular*): **lures**
A **lure** is anything which attracts or tempts you, or the attractive or tempting quality something has: *the irresistible lure of the big city.* [*same as* **attraction, temptation**]

lurid /ˈlʊərɪd/ *adjective* (*derogatory*)
1 Things are **lurid** when they are unpleasantly bright: *lurid colours.* [*same as* **garish**] **2** Something that is **lurid** is shocking or unpleasant because it is violent or disgusting: *The newpaper gave all the lurid details of the killings.* — *adverb* **luridly:** *a luridly coloured dress.*

lurk /lɜːk/ *verb*: **lurks, lurking, lurked**
1 An animal or person **is lurking** when they are waiting secretly or in hiding, especially for some criminal or evil purpose: *There was a man lurking in the bushes.* **2** Something such as a suspicion **lurks** *eg* in your mind when it remains there: *He had a lurking suspicion that she was really innocent.*

luscious /ˈlʌʃəs/ *adjective*
1 **Luscious** food is richly sweet and juicy. [*same as* **succulent**] **2** (*informal*) You can describe someone or something as **luscious** when you find them attractive in a sensual way.

lush /lʌʃ/ *adjective*: **lusher, lushest**
1 Grass and plants are **lush** when they are green and healthy and growing well. [*same as* **luxuriant**] **2** A place is **lush** when it is rich and luxurious: *a lush hotel in Nice.* [*same as* **plush**]

lust /lʌst/ *noun; verb*
▻ ***noun***: **lusts**
1 (*uncount*) **Lust** is strong sexual desire. **2** (*count, usually in the singular*) A **lust** for something is a feeling of enthusiasm for it: *a lust for life* ▫ *the lust for power.* [*same as* **passion**]
▻ ***verb***: **lusts, lusting, lusted**
You **lust** for or after something if you have a strong, especially sexual, desire for it: *She lusted for power and money.* ▫ *He lusted after her body.* [*same as* **yearn for**]

lustful /ˈlʌstfʊl/ *adjective*
Lustful thoughts, or **lustful** people, are full of, or show, great sexual desire.

lustre /ˈlʌstə(r)/ *noun* (*literary; uncount*)
1 The **lustre** of something is the shiny appearance its surface has in reflected light: *Her hair had a marvellous coppery lustre.* [*same as* **glow**] **2** A circumstance may give **lustre** to something if it adds glamour or interest to it: *The presence of a number of distinguished actors added a little lustre to the occasion.* [*same as* **glamour**] — *adjective* **lustrous** /ˈlʌstrəs/: *You too can have a head of lustrous curls.*

lusty /ˈlʌstɪ/ *adjective*: **lustier, lustiest**
Lusty means strong, healthy and full of energy: *Suddenly the lusty cry of a newborn baby sounded from the bedroom.* — *adverb* **lustily:** *The churchgoers joined in the hymns lustily, with heart and voice.*

luxuriant /lʌgˈʒʊərɪənt/ *adjective*
Things such as plants, trees and hair are **luxuriant** when they grow richly and thickly: *long, luxuriant chestnut hair.* — *adverb* **luxuriantly:** *plants growing luxuriantly in the jungle.*

luxuriate /lʌgˈʒʊərɪeɪt/ *verb*: **luxuriates, luxuriating, luxuriated**
You **luxuriate** in something when you enjoy it greatly, especially in a relaxed or lazy way: *She spent the evening luxuriating in a warm bath.*

luxurious /lʌgˈzjʊərɪəs/ *adjective*
Things that are **luxurious** **1** are comfortable and expensive: *a luxurious hotel.* **2** give or express enjoyment and comfort: *a deep, luxurious bath* ▫ *She gave a luxurious sigh.* — *adverb* **luxuriously:** *a luxuriously furnished house* ▫ *She lay luxuriously in the warm bath.*

luxury /ˈlʌkʃərɪ/ *noun*: **luxuries**
1 (*uncount, often adjectival*) **Luxury** is great comfort, especially when it is provided by expensive, beautiful surroundings and objects: *He lives in great luxury.* ▫ *a luxury hotel.* **2** A **luxury** is a pleasant, often expensive thing which is not necessary and which you cannot often have: *A new car is a luxury.* [*opposite* **essential**] **3** (*usually in the singular*) A **luxury** is a pleasure that you do not often have: *An evening in by myself is a real luxury.*

-ly /lɪ/ *suffix*
-ly is used **1** to form adverbs from adjectives: *cleverly* ▫ *happily.* **2** to form adverbs and adjectives meaning 'at intervals of': *daily* [= every day] ▫ *hourly* [= every hour]. **3** to form adjectives meaning 'like': *brotherly* ▫ *fatherly.*

lychee /ˈlaɪtʃiː/ *noun*: **lychees**
A **lychee** is a small fruit with a rough brown skin and sweet white juicy flesh. [see picture at **fruit**]

lying /ˈlaɪɪŋ/ *verb; noun; adjective verb*
▻ ***verb***
Lying is the present participle of **lie[1]** and **lie[2]**.
▻ ***noun*** (*uncount*)
Lying is the activity of telling lies or speaking dishonestly: *Are you accusing me of lying?*
▻ ***adjective***
A **lying** person is dishonest: *I refuse to tell those lying reporters anything.*

lynch /lɪntʃ/ *verb*: **lynches, lynching, lynched**
A crowd of people **lynch** someone if they attack and kill them because they believe them to be guilty of a crime.

lynx /lɪŋks/ *noun*: **lynxes**
A **lynx** is an animal of the cat family, with a grey-brown coat, long legs and a short tail.

lyric /'lɪrɪk/ *adjective*
Lyric poetry, or a **lyric** poet, expresses strong personal feelings. [see also **lyrical, lyrics**]

lyrical /'lɪrɪkəl/ *adjective*
1 Something that is **lyrical** has a poetic or musical quality: *Her letters were full of lyrical descriptions of places and occasions.* □ *a lyrical writing style.* **2** You become **lyrical** about something when you talk or write enthusiastically about it. — *adverb* **lyrically:** *He writes lyrically.*

lyrics /'lɪrɪks/ *noun* (*plural*)
The **lyrics** of a song are its words: *Lennon and McCartney wrote both the music and the lyrics for many Beatles' hits.*

M

M or **m** /ɛm/ *noun*: **Ms** or **m's**
1 M is the thirteenth letter of the English alphabet: *'Lamb' ends with a b, not an m.* **2 m** is a written abbreviation of 'metre' or 'metres': *The bed's about 2.5m wide.*

ma /mɑː/ *noun* (*informal*)
Some people call their mother **Ma**: *Hello, Ma.*

ma'am /mɑːm/ *noun*
Ma'am is an abbreviation of 'madam', and is used as a polite form of address to a woman, especially to a queen or princess.

mac /mak/ *noun* (*informal*): **macs**
A **mac** is a mackintosh: *the man in the grey mac.*

macabre /mə'kaːbrə/ *adjective*
Macabre things are strange and frightening, and usually involve death or evil acts: *a macabre tale of devil worship.* [*same as* **grisly**]

macaroni /makə'rouni/ *noun* (*uncount*)
Macaroni is pasta in the form of short tubes.

machete /mə'ʃɛti/ *noun*: **machetes**
A **machete** is a long, heavy knife with a broad blade, used as a weapon or a cutting tool.

machination /maʃɪ'neɪʃən/ *noun* (*usually in the plural*; *formal*): **machinations**
Machinations are secret plans or actions designed to achieve something dishonest or harmful: *She had been a victim of the machinations of senior figures within the Party.*

machine /mə'ʃiːn/ *noun*: **machines**
1 A **machine** is any powered device with moving parts, designed to perform a particular task: *Are your cows milked by hand or by machine?* □ *a photocopying machine.* **2** A group of people organized to perform a particular task is sometimes referred to as a **machine**: *the party's campaign machine.* **3** (*informal*) A motorcycle or other motor vehicle is often referred to as a **machine**: *These bikes are really powerful machines.*

machine gun /mə'ʃiːn gʌn/ *noun*: **machine guns**
A **machine gun** is an automatic gun that fires bullets in quick successon.

machinery /mə'ʃiːnəri/ *noun* (*uncount*)
1 Machinery is machines in general: *the high capital cost of farm machinery and buildings* □ *Men and machinery arrived with a great deal of noise and bustle* **2** Any combination of processes, systems or people that keeps anything working might also be referred to as **machinery**: *Many solicitors fear that the whole machinery of law is becoming too expensive to run.* □ *The machinery and procedures adequate to manage 5000 are entirely inappropriate for 50 000.*

machismo /ma'tʃɪzmou/ *noun* (*uncount*)
Machismo is an extreme form of the behaviour or opinions considered typical of men, especially respect for physical strength and aggression: *Staff and inmates at the prison meet in an atmosphere of machismo, of men being tough.*

macho /'matʃou/ *adjective* (*informal*)
People describe a man as **macho** if his behaviour or attitudes display a male aggressiveness: *He has some fairly macho views on the role of women in society.*

macintosh see **mackintosh**.

mack /mak/ *noun* (*informal*): **macks**
A **mack** is a mackintosh.

mackerel /'makərəl/ *noun* (*count or uncount*): **mackerel** or **mackerels**
A **mackerel** is a small sea fish with a bluish-green striped body, whose flesh is used as food: *Mackerel are a popular fish in northern Europe.* □ *I prefer smoked mackerel.*

mackintosh or **macintosh** /'makɪntɒʃ/ *noun*: **mackintoshes**
A **mackintosh** is a full-length raincoat made from a waterproof material. [see picture at **clothing**]

mad /mad/ *adjective*: **madder**, **maddest**
1 Someone who is **mad** is mentally ill, and behaves in a strange, unstable, perhaps violent way: *For a while, he seriously believed he was going mad.* [*same as* **crazy**] **2** You call someone **mad** if they behave foolishly: *You must be mad to go walking in that weather.* [*same as* **crazy, idiotic**] **3** (*informal*) **Mad** also means very angry: *He'll go mad when you tell him we lost it.* □ *You're not mad at me, are you?* **4** (*informal*) You say you are **mad** about something or someone when you like them very much. [*same as* **crazy**] **5** You describe confused, hurried or excited behaviour as **mad**: *As soon as we saw the gun, we all made a mad dash for the door.*
▻ ***phrase*** (*informal*) You do something **like mad** when you do it with great energy or enthusiasm: *We had to run like mad to catch the train.* □ *He sat in his bedroom hammering away like mad at his typewriter.* — *noun* (*uncount*) **madness:** *There is a history of madness in their family.* □ *It would be sheer madness to climb it without ropes.*

madam /'madəm/ *noun*
Women are called **Madam** by people behaving in a formal or polite way, *eg* writing a letter or serving in a shop: *The letter began, 'Dear Madam, We regret to inform you...', and I didn't read the rest.* □ *If I might make a suggestion, Madam Chairman.*

madden /'madən/ *verb*: **maddens**, **maddening**, **maddened**
Something that **maddens** you irritates you or makes you angry: *The rest of us were maddened by his success.* [*same as* **enrage, infuriate**] — *adjective* **maddening:** *The children can be quite maddening at times.*

made /meɪd/ *verb*
Made is the past tense and past participle of **make**.
▻ ***phrases*** **1** (*informal*) You say that someone **has it made** or **has got it made** when they are in a very lucky situation, especially when their success or happiness seems certain to continue. **2** (*informal*) You say that something was **made for** someone if it fits or suits

them perfectly: *He tried on a leather jacket that I thought was made for him.* □ *She's an excellent teacher; she was made for the job.* **3** For **made from, made of, made out of** and **made with** see note at **make**.

-made /meɪd/ *suffix*
-made combines with other words to form adjectives describing how or where something was made: *a range of handmade gifts* □ *They sell mostly foreign-made goods.*

madhouse /'madhaʊs/ *noun* (*usually in the singular*)
You describe a place as a **madhouse** if there is a lot of noise or confusion: *It's like a madhouse in here most of the time.* □ *the politics of the madhouse.*

madly /'madlɪ/ *adverb*
1 You do something **madly** when you do it with great energy or enthusiasm, or in a great hurry: *I searched around madly for somewhere to hide it.* **2 Madly** also means passionately: *You know I love you madly.* □ *They fell madly in love.*

madman /'madmən/ *noun*: **madmen**
1 People sometimes call a mentally ill man a **madman**, especially if he tends to be violent. [*same as* **lunatic, maniac**] **2** People also call a man who behaves in a wild or foolish way a **madman**: *Her brother is that madman who drove on the frozen river in his car.*

mag /mag/ *noun* (*informal*): **mags**
A **mag** is a magazine (sense 1).

magazine /magə'ziːn/ *noun*: **magazines**
1 A **magazine** is a collection of news or other articles published regularly, smaller but usually thicker than a newspaper, and usually with lots of photographs, illustrations and advertisements: *some of the glossier women's magazines.* **2** Regular television and radio programmes presenting reports on a variety of subjects are sometimes referred to as **magazines**: *BBC 2's arts magazine, 'The Late Show'.*

maggot /'magət/ *noun*: **maggots**
A **maggot** is a tiny worm-like creature, the immature form of a fly.

magic /'madʒɪk/ *noun*; *adjective*
▻ ***noun*** (*uncount*)
1 Magic is the power that forces outside nature have to make strange things happen, *eg* making things disappear, as they often do in stories: *As if by magic, a man appeared by the tree.* **2 Magic** is also the art or practice of performing entertaining illusions and tricks in which impossible things appear to happen: *My uncle taught me a few bits of magic.* **3** The **magic** of something is its wonderful or charming quality: *I'll never forget the special magic of that evening.*
▻ ***adjective***
1 Magic refers to the power of forces outside nature to do strange things: *The witches cast a magic spell.* **2 Magic** also refers to tricks and illusions in which impossible things seem to happen: *They've hired someone who does magic tricks.* **3** (*informal*) People often say that something is **magic** when it is excellent: *That was a magic film!*

magical /'madʒɪkəl/ *adjective*
You describe something as **magical** if it has a wonderful or charming quality: *memories of that magical night we spent on the lake in an open boat.*

magician /mə'dʒɪʃən/ *noun*: **magicians**
1 A **magician** is someone who performs illusions and tricks in which impossible things appear to happen. **2** A **magician** is also a man with supernatural powers, *eg* in children's stories.

magistrate /'madʒɪstreɪt/ *noun*: **magistrates**
A **magistrate** is a judge in court of law where minor crimes are examined.

magnanimous /mag'nanɪməs/ *adjective* (*formal*)
You describe someone, or their behaviour, as **magnanimous** if they show kindness or generosity in a situation where others might have been jealous, bitter or unkind: *In an admirably magnanimous gesture, he shook Tony by the hand and congratulated him.*
▻ ***noun*** (*uncount*; *formal*) **magnanimity** /magnə'nɪmətɪ/: *We were overwhelmed by her magnanimity.*

magnate /'magneɪt/ *noun*: **magnates**
A **magnate** is a very rich and powerful person in business or industry: *an American oil magnate*

magnet /'magnɪt/ *noun*: **magnets**
A **magnet** is a piece of iron or other metal that attracts other iron objects to it, and also points in a north-south direction when you let it hang free.

magnetic /mag'nɛtɪk/ *adjective*
1 A **magnetic** object behaves like a magnet, attracting other objects made of iron and other metals: *This simple bomb has a magnetic surface which allows it to cling to the underside of the target vehicle.* **2 Magnetic** is often also used to describe someone who has charming or attractive qualities: *She has a lively, magnetic personality.* [*same as* **attractive, fascinating charismatic**] **3 Magnetic** tape is the kind of plastic tape used for sound and video recording.

magnetism /'magnətɪzm/ *noun* (*uncount*)
1 Magnetism is the power that a magnet has to attract iron and other metals. **2** You can also describe someone's charming or attractive qualities as **magnetism**: *Women see in him a kind of raw, sexual magnetism.* [*same as* **allure, charisma**]

magnification /magnɪfɪ'keɪʃən/ *noun*: **magnifications**
1 (*uncount*) **Magnification** is the process of making objects appear larger or closer, or the power that instruments such as microscopes and binoculars have to do this. **2** (*count or uncount*) **Magnification** is also how much larger or closer than reality an object is made to appear: *We viewed it under a magnification of 10.*

magnificent /mag'nɪfɪsənt/ *adjective*
1 You describe something as **magnificent** if it is very impressive or beautiful: *On the top of the hill sits a magnificent castle.* [*same as* **splendid**] **2** (*informal*) People often use **magnificent** to mean excellent or very good: *It's a magnificent theatre for this kind of play.*
— *adverb* **magnificently:** *She coped magnificently with the crisis.*

magnify /'magnɪfaɪ/ *verb*: **magnifies, magnifying, magnified**
1 To **magnify** an object is to make it appear larger or closer than it really is, *eg* using a microscope or telescope. **2** When you **magnify** something you make it seem more important than it really is: *The government has accused several prominent charities of magnifying the problem of homelessness.* [*same as* **exaggerate**]

magnifying glass /'magnɪfaɪɪŋ glɑːs/ *noun*: **magnifying glasses**
A **magnifying glass** is a hand-held lens that makes things appear larger than they really are, used for examining very small objects or written text.

magnitude /'magnɪtjuːd/ *noun* (*uncount*; *formal*)
The **magnitude** of something is its great size, extent or importance: *We mustn't underestimate the magnitude of the problems that face us.*

magpie /'magpaɪ/ *noun*: **magpies**
A **magpie** is a medium-sized, black-and-white bird with a long tail.

mahogany /mə'hɒgənɪ/ *noun* (*uncount, often adjectival*)
Mahogany is a hard, reddish-brown wood used to make furniture: *two mahogany wardrobes.*

maid /meɪd/ *noun*: **maids**
A **maid** is a woman who does cleaning and other domestic jobs in a house or hotel.

maiden /'meɪdən/ *noun*; *adjective*
▻ ***noun*** (*literary*): **maidens**
A **maiden** is a young unmarried woman: *a painting of the Roman gods surrounded by beautiful maidens.*
▻ ***adjective***
Maiden describes the first journey made by a new ship, aeroplane or other vehicle: *Her maiden voyage was happily uneventful.* □ *a maiden flight.*

maiden name /'meɪdən neɪm/ *noun*: **maiden names**
A married woman's **maiden name** is the surname she had before she got married and took her husband's name.

mail /meɪl/ *noun*; *verb*
▻ ***noun*** (*uncount*)
1 Mail consists of letters and parcels sent by post: *Did we receive any mail this morning?* **2** The **mail** is the postal system, the system used for sending letters and parcels: *Sending it by courier will be quicker than sending it by mail.*
▻ ***verb***: **mails, mailing, mailed**
You **mail** something when you send it by mail: *How long would it take if I mailed it to him?*
[*same as* **post**]

mailing list /'meɪlɪŋ lɪst/ *noun*: **mailing lists**
A **mailing list** is a list of the people to whom an organization regularly sends information: *We'll put you on our mailing list.*

mail order /meɪl 'ɔːdə(r)/ *noun* (*uncount, often adjectival*)
Mail order is a system of buying and selling goods by post, in which customers choose goods from a company's catalogue: *a mail-order catalogue.*

maim /meɪm/ *verb*: **maims, maiming, maimed**
To **maim** someone is to injure them seriously, usually causing permanent damage to one or more of their limbs: *enough ammunition to kill and maim thousands* □ *More than 300 000 soldiers were killed, maimed or taken prisoner.* [*same as* **cripple**]

main /meɪn/ *adjective*; *noun*
▻ ***adjective***
Main means most important, principal or chief: *We have identified the main cause of the disease.* □ *guards at the main entrance and all the side entrances.*
▻ ***noun***: **mains**
1 (*plural, often adjectival*) The **mains** are the pipes that supply water or gas to a house or other building, or the cables that supply electricity: *The farmhouse doesn't even have mains water.* □ *We can plug it into the mains while the batteries are recharging.* **2** A **main** is a large gas or water pipe leading into a house or other building.
▻ ***phrase*** **In the main** means mostly or generally: *Our customers are, in the main, foreign businessmen.* □ *In the main, we think the scheme has been successful.* [*same as* **for the most part**]

main clause /'meɪn klɔːz/ *noun* (*grammar*): **main clauses**
A **main clause** is a clause that can stand independently as a complete sentence.

mainframe /'meɪnfreɪm/ *noun* (*technical*): **mainframes**
A **mainframe** is a large powerful computer, especially one that several smaller computers are linked to.

mainland /'meɪnlənd/ *noun* (*used in the singular, often adjectival*)
The **mainland** is the biggest single mass of land belonging to a country, rather than any nearby island or islands that form part of the same country: *Some parts of mainland Spain are now more popular with tourists than Majorca and the other islands.*

mainly /'meɪnlɪ/ *adverb*
Mainly means mostly or in most cases: *He was chosen mainly because he's young.* □ *Our customers are mainly people in business.* [*same as* **principally**]

mainstream /'meɪnstriːm/ *noun* (*used in the singular, often adjectival*)
The **mainstream** consists of the most popular and most traditional ideas, methods and styles in any activity: *His films range from the unashamedly mainstream to the truly avant-garde.* □ *What is the opinion within the more mainstream political movements?*

maintain /meɪn'teɪn/ *verb*: **maintains, maintaining, maintained**
1 You **maintain** something when you keep it in existence, not letting it fail or stop, or when you keep it at the same level, not letting it rise or fall: *We hope the bank's interest in the scheme can be maintained.* □ *The Blaksco Group intend to maintain their position as market leader.* **2** You **maintain** something when you keep it in good condition or keep it working well, *eg* by regular cleaning and repairing: *A house this size must cost a fortune to maintain.* □ *All gas boilers should be regularly maintained.* **3** To **maintain** someone is to give them the money they need to live on: *the cost of maintaining two grown-up children at university.* [*same as* **support**] **4** You **maintain** that something is the case when you continue to insist that it is true, or when you often state it as an opinion: *Seagrove maintains that his son never left the house that evening.* □ *My father always maintained that life should be enjoyed.* [*same as* **assert, claim**]

maintenance /'meɪntənəns/ *noun* (*uncount*)
1 Maintenance is the process of keeping something in good condition or making sure that it is still working efficiently: *Each tenant pays a monthly sum towards the maintenance of the stairway and the garden.* □ *The college runs classes in car maintenance.* **2 Maintenance** is also money to pay for a person's living costs: *Successful students will receive a grant to pay college fees and maintenance.* □ *It is still true, in most divorce cases, that the court will order the man to pay maintenance to his ex-wife.*

maisonette /meɪzə'nɛt/ *noun*: **maisonettes**
A **maisonette** is a flat or apartment on two floors, often with its own direct entrance to the outside.

maize /meɪz/ *noun* (*uncount*)
Maize is a tall cereal plant that the edible yellow grain called sweetcorn grows on.

majestic /mə'dʒɛstɪk/ *adjective*
Something that is described as **majestic** is very large and impressive: *The main focus of the house is a majestic central staircase.* — *adverb* **majestically:** *This avenue of trees sweeps majestically round to west side of the castle.*

Majesty /'madʒəstɪ/ *noun*: **Majesties**
Majesty is a title you use when you speak to or about a king or queen: *Would Your Majesty like to see the gardens?* □ *I spoke to His Majesty about it this morning.* □ *This is the coach that will carry Their Majesties to the palace.*

major /'meɪdʒə(r)/ *adjective*; *noun*; *verb*
▻ ***adjective***
Major describes things that are great, greater or greatest in size or importance: *She spent the major part of her childhood abroad.* □ *The major distinction between*

them is their age. □ *It could develop into a major problem.* [*opposite* **minor**]

▻ ***noun***: **majors**

A **major** is an army officer of middle rank: *You'll be sharing a tent with Major Burns.*

▻ ***verb*** (*especially AmE*): **majors, majoring, majored**

A student **majors** in their main subject of study: *She majored in Psychology, with subsidiaries in Sociology and Philosophy.*

majority /mə'dʒɒrɪtɪ/ *noun*: **majorities**

1 (*used in the singular*) The **majority** of people or things is the greatest number of them or the largest group of them: *The majority of Scots voted against the government.* □ *The vast majority of students were opposed to the loans scheme.* **2** In a vote or election, a **majority** consists of the difference between the number of votes gained by the winner and the number gained by the candidate who comes second: *The Labour challenger is fighting to overturn a Conservative majority of over 10500.*

▻ ***phrase*** People or things are **in the majority** or **in a majority** when most other people or things are the same as them and they form the largest group: *Opponents of the government's transport policy are definitely in the majority.*

[*opposite* **minority**]

make /meɪk/ *verb; noun*

▻ ***verb***: **makes, making, made**

1 a You **make** something when you form, create or produce it, *eg* by shaping or combining materials: *This is the skirt I made in my first dressmaking class.* □ *I'll make the sandwiches.* □ *Shall I make us a cup of tea?* □ *They're making a television series based on his life.* □ *I could make you a set of bookshelves out of these bits of wood.* □ *The earliest knives were made of flint.*

> You use **made of** in reference to the material used: *chairs made of moulded plastic.* You use **made from** and **made out of** in reference to the process of manufacture or production: *Paper is made from wood. Her skirt appeared to have been made out of an old blanket.* You use **made with** in reference to ingredients: *a cake made with the finest Californian dried fruit.*

b One thing **is made** into another when it is changed into the other by some process: *We've made the barn into a cottage.* □ *They make their failed politicians into lords.* **c** Circumstances **make** a particular thing of someone if they turn them into that thing: *Their eighteen months' national service made men of them.* □ *The film manages to make a hero of this rather unremarkable man.* **d** You say that someone or something will **make** a certain thing if you think they have the qualities required to be that thing: *This material will make a nice dress.* □ *Books make an excellent present for young children.* □ *He was told he would never make a professional footballer.* **e** Someone or something **is made** a certain thing when they are given that post or function: *He was made company secretary at the last general meeting.* □ *We decided to make Minden our headquarters.* **f** One thing **makes** another if it is responsible for its success: *The trip to the theatre really made my birthday.* □ *What made the film for me was the beautiful soundtrack.* **g** You **make** a bed when you tidy it and pull up the covers again after it has been slept in: *The children should make their own beds.*

2 a One person or thing **makes** another do or be something if they cause them to do or be that thing: *Waiting for Emily had made them miss their train.* □ *What makes you think that?* □ *His hurt expression made me feel ashamed.* □ *A few days' holiday will make you feel more relaxed.* □ *Short hair makes you look younger.* □ *You weren't the only one to fail, if that makes you any happier.* □ *He made it quite clear that he supported us.* **b** Something or someone **makes** you do something when they force you to do it: *Make the children sit down and keep quiet.* □ *One look at the stormy sky made us change our minds.* □ *I didn't want to come; she made me.*

3 a You use **make** with nouns of action or activity, with a meaning like that of a verb; *eg*, if you **make** an attempt to do something, you attempt to do it: *The thieves made their escape in a stolen van.* □ *Alan made no attempt to stop the man.* □ *It's time we made a start.* □ *Stop making such a fuss!* □ *I may have made the wrong decision.* □ *Could I make a suggestion?* □ *We made an arrangement to meet that Wednesday.* □ *Have the board made an appointment yet?* □ *We'd better make some excuse.* □ *People were always making use of her apartment.* □ *Unpunctuality will make a bad impression.* □ *I've got a couple of phone calls to make.* □ *She hated making speeches.* □ *Do make an effort to be cheerful.* □ *We made the journey in less than two hours.* □ *It was clear that a serious error had been made.* □ *They made me an offer I couldn't refuse.* □ *Make peace, not war.* **b** You **make** a sound when you produce it or cause it: *I wish the children wouldn't make so much noise.* □ *He cupped his hands over his mouth and made a hooting sound.*

4 a You **make** money when you gain or earn it: *They expected to make a profit on the house sale.* □ *I don't imagine he makes much more than £100 a week.* □ *Their overseas investments have made them a fortune.* **b** Two or more quantities **make** a certain sum if that is what they add up to: *4 plus 4 makes* (or *make*) *8.* □ *3 and 5 make* (or *makes*) *8.* □ *There's another. That makes the fifth.* □ *Two halves make a whole.* **c** You **make** the answer to some calculation a particular amount if that is the result of your calculation: *Using your tape, I make the length just over 3 metres.* □ *I think my watch has stopped; what time do you make it?* **d** You **make** a destination when you reach it or arrive there; you **make** something such as a boat, train or plane when you arrive at the place it is leaving from in time to travel on it: *We had planned to make Connemara before nightfall.* □ *If we hurry, we could make the earlier train.*

▻ ***noun***: **makes**

The **make** of an object is the name of the company that made or produced it: *What make of car is that?* □ *She was in a smart jacket, obviously one of the more expensive makes.* [compare **brand**]

▻ ***phrases*** **1** For **have got it made** see **made**. **2** You **make do** with something inferior when you accept it, or make the best use of it, because nothing better is available: *The children had to make do with second-hand clothes.* □ *There's no fresh milk; we'll have to make do with the powdered variety.* **3** (*informal*) You **make it** when **a** you are successful in doing or being something: *Do you think she could make it as a professional singer?* **b** you survive: *For a while up there on the rock, I thought we weren't going to make it.* **c** you manage to reach a place: *We made it to the airport 15 minutes before the plane left.* **d** you manage to attend an event that you have been invited to: *Frank won't be able to make it; he's been held up at work.* **4** You **make it up to** someone you have disappointed when you do something for them as a way of apologizing.

> ***phrasal verbs***
>
> **make for 1** You **make for** a place when you move towards it: *We didn't tell them we were really making for Athens.* □ *He jumped up and made hastily for the door.* [*same as* **head** for] **2** Something **makes for** a

certain situation if that situation is likely to be the result of it: *Fine weather made for an enjoyable holiday.*

make of What you **make of** something is the opinion you form of it, or the impression you get of it, or what you understand it to mean: *So, what do you make of the new manager?* □ *I didn't know what to make of her strange response.*

make off (*informal*) You **make off** when you leave, especially hurriedly or secretly: *The thieves made off in a van.*

make off with (*informal*) You **make off with** something when you steal it: *Anyone might walk in and make off with the family silver.*

make out 1 You can **make** something **out** when you are able to see, hear or understand it, usually with difficulty: *I could make out the faint outline of a car through the fog.* □ *I couldn't make out the words of the song.* □ *Could you make out from what he said whether he agrees with us or not?* [*same as* **discern**, **distinguish**] **2** You **make out** that something is so when you try to convince people that it is: *She's been making out that checking the windows was not her responsibility.* □ *The programme made her out to be concerned only with holding on to power.* □ *It's not as difficult as some people make out.* [*same as* **claim**, **imply**, **suggest**, **maintain**] **3** You **make out** a cheque when you write in the necessary details on it: *Could you make the cheque out to Breakages Ltd?*

make up 1 You **make up** something such as a story or explanation when you invent it, sometimes with the intention of deceiving people: *Is his wife really a friend of the Princess, or is he making it up?* **2** Someone **makes** themselves **up** when they put cosmetics on their face: *her heavily made-up face.* [see also **make-up**] **3** You **make** something **up** when you prepare it by putting various things together: *The kitchen staff will be happy to make up packed lunches for any guests that require them.* **4** Something **is made up** of various things if they combine to form it: *Each team is made up of two men and two women.* □ *the seventeen regional offices that make up local adminstration.* **5** You **make up** something when you add the number or amount of things that are missing, to make it complete: *We need another player to make up the team.* **6** People who have had a quarrel **make up** or **make it up** when they settle their differences and become friends again. [see also **make it up to** above] **7** Something **makes up** for something else that is lacking or lost if it replaces it and restores the balance: *We'll have to work hard to make up for lost time.*

maker /ˈmeɪkə(r)/ *noun*: **makers**
The **maker** of something is the person who has made it: *The early Russian film-makers had a different method.* □ *She now works for Jaguar, makers of some of the world's finest cars.* □ *We raised your point with the programme-makers themselves.*

makeshift /ˈmeɪkʃɪft/ *adjective*
Something **makeshift** is a temporary substitute made with whatever materials are available: *We constructed a makeshift bridge with some old planks of wood.* □ *The electricity failed; no surprise, since the wiring was decidedly makeshift.*

make-up /ˈmeɪkʌp/ *noun* (*uncount*)
1 Make-up consists of things such as lipstick, face powder and other cosmetics put on the face. **2** The **make-up** of something or someone is their character or nature: *She argued that the average jury's make-up was overwhelmingly middle-class.* □ *Such petty emotions are simply not part of her make-up.*

making /ˈmeɪkɪŋ/ *noun* (*uncount*)
Making is the act or process of producing or forming something: *courses in film-making* □ *We've all been heavily involved in the making of a new radio series.*
▻ ***phrases* 1** An experience or event that **will be the making of** a person or thing will be the most important influence on their development: *Her early experience in the classroom was the making of her as a child psychologist.* **2** A person or thing that **has the makings of** something has the qualities or abilities needed to develop into that thing: *None of these stories had the makings of a full-length feature film.* □ *She seems to think I have the makings of a poet.* **3 In the making** describes a person or thing that is developing into something: *local conflicts that are a civil war in the making* □ *Most political commentators regard him as a Prime Minister in the making.* **4** Something, especially a problem or failure, is **of your own making** when you have caused it by your own actions.

mal- /mal/ *prefix*
Mal- is used before nouns and adjectives to mean 'bad or badly' or 'wrong or wrongly': *a clear example of maladministration* □ *This has resulted in fingers and toes being malformed.*

malady /ˈmalədɪ/ *noun* (*literary*): **maladies**
A **malady** is an illness or a disease.

malaise /maˈleɪz/ *noun* (*uncount*; *formal*)
Malaise is a general feeling of uneasiness or unhappiness: *Uncertainty about the future is the root cause of the malaise gripping British society.*

malaria /məˈlɛərɪə/ *noun* (*uncount*)
Malaria is a serious disease caused by the bite of a mosquito, in which you suffer periods of fever and extreme cold.

male /meɪl/ *adjective*; *noun*
▻ ***adjective***
1 A **male** animal is of the sex that does not give birth to young: *The male lion does very little of the hunting.* **2 Male** also describes men or boys, or things that involve or relate to them: *The male members of the group had a different view.* □ *Women were no longer prepared to tolerate this kind of male domination.* □ *Is the professor male or female?*
▻ ***noun***: **males:** *In many birds, the male is by far the most brightly coloured.* □ *the typical beer-drinking British male in jeans and a T-shirt.*

male chauvinist /meɪl ˈʃoʊvənɪst/ *noun*: **male chauvinists**
A **male chauvinist** is a man who believes that men are superior to women: *She accused me of being a male chauvinist.* — *noun* (*uncount*) **male chauvinism:** *That's the worse kind of male chauvinism.*

malevolent /məˈlɛvələnt/ *adjective*
Malevolent describes people who want to hurt or harm others: *It was, in the words of the judge, a malevolent act which must be severely punished.* [*same as* **evil**, **vicious**] — *noun* (*uncount*) **malevolence:** *an act of sheer malevolence.* [*same as* **evil**, **viciousness**]

malfunction /malˈfʌŋkʃən/ *verb*; *noun*
▻ ***verb***: **malfunctions**, **malfunctioning**, **malfunctioned**
A computer or other machine **malfunctions** when it fails to work properly or it breaks down.
▻ ***noun*** (*count or uncount*): **malfunctions:** *time lost through the malfunction of the printing presses.*

malice /ˈmalɪs/ *noun* (*uncount*)
Malice is the desire or the intention to harm or hurt

others: *There was a degree of malice in her tone as she made the remark* □ *I bore him no malice.* [*same as* **spitefulness, vindictiveness**]

malicious /məˈlɪʃəs/ *adjective*
A **malicious** person wants or intends to offend someone or hurt their feelings: *Someone has been spreading malicious gossip about me.* □ *They all seemed to take a malicious delight in my troubles.* [*same as* **spiteful, vindictive**]

malign /məˈlaɪn/ *verb* (*formal*): **maligns, maligning, maligned**
You **malign** someone when you say or write unpleasant things about them: *He is the much-maligned manager of their national football team.*

malignant /məˈlɪgnənt/ *adjective*
1 Malignant cancers and other diseases can cause death: *Luckily, the tumour wasn't malignant.* [compare **benign**] **2** (*formal*) A **malignant** person or action is malevolent.

malinger /məˈlɪŋgə(r)/ *verb*: **malingers, malingering, malingered**
Someone who **is malingering** is pretending to be ill in order to avoid work. — *noun* **malingerer:** *He's such a malingerer!*

mall /mɔːl/ *noun* (*especially AmE*): **malls**
A **mall**, or **shopping mall**, is a shopping centre.

malnutrition /malnjuˈtrɪʃən/ *noun* (*uncount*)
Someone suffering from **malnutrition** is seriously ill because they have not eaten properly for a long time: *Thousands have already died of malnutrition.*

malpractice /malˈpraktɪs/ *noun* (*uncount*)
Someone such as a doctor or a lawyer charged with **malpractice** has behaved dishonestly or improperly and has broken the rules of their profession.

malt /mɔːlt/ *noun* (*uncount*)
Malt is a substance made from barley or other grains, used in making beer and other alcoholic drinks.

mama /məˈmɑː/ *noun* (*mainly old*)
Some people call their mother **mama**: *Have you spoken to your mama yet?* □ *Listen to me, Mama.*

mammal /ˈmaməl/ *noun*: **mammals**
Mammals are the kinds of animals that give birth to babies and feed them with milk they produce inside their bodies, rather than laying eggs: *including whales, elephants and the other larger mammals.*

mammoth /ˈmaməθ/ *adjective*
Mammoth means extremely large: *The bridge itself is a mammoth construction.* □ *We faced a mammoth task.*

man /man/ *noun*; *verb*
▷ ***noun***: **men**
1 A **man** is **a** an adult male human being: *Her husband's a very nice man.* □ *men, women and children.* **b** a human being of either sex: *distant lands inhabited by strange men* □ *sorrows that every man must bear.* **2** (*uncount*) **Man** is sometimes used to refer to human beings generally: *What right has man to kill and ill-treat his fellow creatures?* □ *the deadliest poison known to man.* [*same as* **mankind**]

> Many people avoid using **man** in senses 1b and 2, and use *people* or *human beings* instead.

3 (*informal*) Some women refer to their husband or boyfriend as their **man**: *The women had to run the household while their men were at sea.* □ *She's looking for a new man.* **4** In the army, ordinary soldiers, as opposed to officers, are sometimes referred to as the **men**; in industry, the ordinary workers as distinct from the management, are refered to as the **men**. **5** (*informal*) People sometimes address a man as '**Man**', especially impatiently: *Come on, man, pull yourself together.*
▷ ***verb***: **mans, manning, manned**
People **man** something when they run it or operate it: *The office is only manned during normal working hours.* □ *We need someone to man the boiler.*

-man /man/ *suffix*
-man is added to nouns and adjectives to form nouns meaning: **1** a man who performs, or is involved with, a particular activity: *Geoff used to be a postman.* □ *Her cousin is a fisherman.* **2** a man from a particular country or region: *a team of Scotsmen and Irishmen* □ *You can tell Paul is a Yorkshireman.*

manage /ˈmanɪdʒ/ *verb*: **manages, managing, managed**
1 a You **manage** to do something when you succeed in doing or producing it: *Did you manage to finish it on time?* □ *I'm not sure we'll be able to manage it without help.* **b** You also **manage** to do something stupid or unfortunate when you do it: *How on earth did we manage to miss each other at the station.* **2** Someone who **manages** a shop, a business or an organization is in charge or in control of it. **3** To **manage** is to survive on very little money: *Times have been hard before, but we always managed.*

manageable /ˈmanɪdʒəbəl/ *adjective*
Something that is **manageable** can be done, or dealt with, without too much difficulty: *Does she think that amount of work is manageable in a week?* □ *The garden's a nice manageable size.*

management /ˈmanɪdʒmənt/ *noun*
1 (*uncount*) **Management** is the practice of controlling a business or other activity: *She has good experience in restaurant management.* □ *The management of the Council's education budget is a daunting task.* □ *The university now offers degrees in management science.* **2** (*with a singular or plural verb*) The managers of a company are often referred to as the **management**: *negotiations between management and workers.*

manager /ˈmanɪdʒə(r)/ *noun*: **managers**
The **manager** is the person responsible for directing or controlling a business or other activity: *We complained to the hotel manager about it.* □ *She's the organization's personnel manager.*

manageress /manɪdʒəˈrɛs/ *noun*: **manageresses**
A **manageress** is a woman who runs a shop or restaurant.

> A woman who has a management post in business is usually called a **manager**.

managerial /manəˈdʒɪərɪəl/ *adjective*
Managerial means relating to a manager or to management: *Together they form a highly competent managerial team.* □ *He doesn't really have much managerial experience.*

managing director /manədʒɪŋ dɪˈrɛktə(r)/ *noun*: **managing directors**
The **managing director** of a firm is the director who is in charge of the way it is run, organized and developed.

mandarin /ˈmandərɪn/ *noun*: **mandarins**
A **mandarin**, or **mandarin orange**, is a small, easily-peeled orange-like fruit.

mandate /ˈmandeɪt/ *noun*: **mandates**
1 The **mandate** of a politician or political party is their right to govern because they have won an elec-

tion. **2** A **mandate** is also a written instruction to a bank or other organization, or the printed form it is written on.

mandatory /ˈmandətərɪ/ *adjective*
Something is **mandatory** when rules or laws state that you must do it: *The absence of chemicals of any kind is mandatory in German beer-making.*

mane /meɪn/ *noun*: **manes**
A **mane** is a mass of long hair growing from the neck of a horse, lion or other animal.

maneuver see **manoeuvre**.

mangle /ˈmaŋgəl/ *verb*: **mangles, mangling, mangled**
Something **is mangled** when it is severely damaged by being badly crushed or twisted: *The bear had broken free, leaving its cage a mangled mass of metal.*

mango /ˈmaŋgoʊ/ *noun*: **mangos** or **mangoes**
A **mango** is a large, yellowish, pear-shaped fruit. [see picture at **fruit**]

manhandle /manˈhandəl/ *verb*: **manhandles, manhandling, manhandled**
You **manhandle** someone when you treat them roughly, *eg* by pushing or pulling them: *The woman who manhandled the Prince was quickly arrested.*

manhole /ˈmanhoʊl/ *noun*: **manholes**
A **manhole** is a covered opening in the surface of a road, providing access to the drains beneath.

manhood /ˈmanhʊd/ *noun (uncount)*
1 Manhood is the state of being a man, rather than a boy, especially of being sexually mature: *She made one or two comments that called his manhood into question.* **2** A man's **manhood** is the period of his life during which he is a man, rather than a boy: *Looking back, I see that time as the eve of my manhood.*

manhunt /ˈmanhʌnt/ *noun*: **manhunts**
A **manhunt** is an organized search for someone, especially an escaped criminal.

mania /ˈmeɪnɪə/ *noun*: **manias**
1 Someone who has a **mania** for something has a strong, almost uncontrollable liking for it: *She seems to have developed a mania for regular routine in her life.* [*same as* **obsession**] **2** A **mania** is also a form of mental illness in which there is over-excited, sometimes violent behaviour.

maniac /ˈmeɪnɪak/ *noun*: **maniacs**
People often call someone who behaves wildly or violently a **maniac**: *He was driving like a maniac.* □ *Suddenly this maniac started shouting at him and waving his arms.*

manic /ˈmanɪk/ *adjective*
Manic describes actions that are performed very fast and energetically: *I spent a manic half hour dashing round the shops.*

manicure /ˈmanɪkjʊə(r)/ *noun*: **manicures**
When you have a **manicure**, someone, usually a trained professional, cuts and polishes your fingernails.

manifest /ˈmanɪfɛst/ *verb*; *adjective*
▻ ***verb*** *(formal)*: **manifests, manifesting, manifested**
A quality or characteristic **manifests** itself in a person's actions or behaviour when it is revealed or displayed in that way: *With the arrival of a new baby, jealousy in the older child often manifests itself as a complete emotional detachment from the family.*
▻ ***adjective*** *(formal)*
Something is **manifest** when it is obvious or evident: *her colleagues' manifest reluctance to support her.* — *adverb* **manifestly:** *They were manifestly envious of the success of our scheme.*

manifestation /manɪfɛˈsteɪʃən/ *noun (formal)*: **manifestations**
Actions or behaviour are a **manifestation** of some quality or characteristic when they reveal or display it: *Lifestyle is a manifestation of a number of behavioural factors such as motivation, personality and culture.*

manifesto /manɪˈfɛstoʊ/ *noun*: **manifestos** or **manifestoes**
A **manifesto** is a written statement of the policies or intentions of a political party or candidate: *This will be outlined in our manifesto, to be published next week.*

manifold /ˈmanɪfoʊld/ *adjective (literary)*
Manifold means of many different kinds: *The benefits to residents will be manifold.* □ *It was her manifold social graces which first attracted me.*

manipulate /məˈnɪpjʊleɪt/ *verb*: **manipulates, manipulating, manipulated**
You **manipulate** someone when you cleverly cause them to behave in a way that benefits you; you **manipulate** a situation when you cleverly cause it to develop in a way that benefits you: *Many of the workers felt that they had simply been manipulated by the Party.* □ *It was clear that they had tried to manipulate voting procedures on that particular day.* — *noun (uncount)* **manipulation** /mənɪpjʊˈleɪʃən/: *Newspapers uncovered his shameful manipulation of the whole affair.* — *adjective* **manipulative** /məˈnɪpjʊlətɪv/: *Don't underestimate the manipulative influence of advertising.*

mankind /manˈkaɪnd/ *noun (uncount)*
Human beings in general are sometimes referred to as **mankind**: *the worst natural disaster ever witnessed by mankind.*

manly /ˈmanlɪ/ *adjective*
People describe a man's appearance or behaviour as **manly** if they think it shows qualities such as strength or courage, that are traditionally associated with men: *He lifted her on to his broad, manly shoulders.*

man-made /manˈmeɪd/ *adjective*
Man-made things are manufactured or made by people, rather than occurring or existing naturally: *man-made fibres* □ *The little lake behind the house, though man-made, was an attractive feature.* [*same as* **synthetic, artificial**]

manner /ˈmanə(r)/ *noun*: **manners**
1 Your **manner** is the way you talk and behave, which shows what kind of person you are: *The old man had a rather abrupt, military manner.* **2** Someone who has good **manners** behaves politely towards others; someone who has bad or no **manners** behaves rudely or impolitely towards others: *Nothing could excuse such bad manners.* □ *The little boy has no manners at all.* **3** *(used in the singular)* The **manner** in which you do something is the way that you do it: *They had been arranged in a fairly haphazard manner.* □ *She was dressed in the Chinese manner.* **4** *(used in the singular; literary)* 'All **manner** of things' means all kinds of them: *markets selling all manner of exotic fruit and vegetables.*
▻ ***phrase*** You use **in a manner of speaking** to show that a word or phrase you have used is not quite the proper or correct one, but it gives a good description of what you mean: *She was, in a manner of speaking, the journalists' moral guardian.*

mannerism /ˈmanərɪzm/ *noun*: **mannerisms**
You refer to a particular element of the way someone speaks or behaves as a **mannerism** if it is strange or unusual: *She had one or two odd mannerisms that frightened the children.*

mannish /ˈmanɪʃ/ *adjective*
You describe a woman's appearance or behaviour as **mannish** if you think it is more typical of, or suitable for, a man: *She wore her hair in a short, mannish style.*

manoeuvre (*AmE* **maneuver**) /mə'nuːvə(r)/ *noun*; *verb*
▻ ***noun***: **manoeuvres**
1 A **manoeuvre** is a difficult movement that requires skill: *Reversing any vehicle round a corner is quite a tricky manoeuvre.* **2** A **manoeuvre** is also something clever that you do in order to cause a situation to develop in a particular way: *Getting the two leaders around the same negotiating table is the result of some fairly crafty diplomatic manoeuvres.* **3** Military **manoeuvres** consist of moving large numbers of troops, vehicles and equipment, often as an exercise.
▻ ***verb***: **manoeuvres, manoeuvring, manoeuvred**
You **manoeuvre** something somewhere when you move it there carefully, accurately and with skill: *I had to manoeuvre the car into the tiniest of spaces.*

manor /'manə(r)/ *noun*: **manors**
Manor is a name given to some large, old private houses: *plans to restore Grange Manor.*

manpower /'manpɑʊə(r)/ *noun* (*uncount*)
Manpower is the staff, or the number of workers or other employees needed for a particular type of work: *We simply don't have the manpower to cope with such a heavy workload.*

mansion /'manʃən/ *noun*: **mansions**
1 A **mansion** is a large private house: *We spent the weekend at their mansion in the country.* **2 Mansions** is a word sometimes used in the name of blocks of luxury flats: *8 Grosvenor Mansions.*

manslaughter /'manslɔːtə(r)/ *noun* (*uncount*)
Manslaughter is the crime of killing someone without intending to: *You are charged with manslaughter.* [compare **murder**]

mantelpiece /'mantəlpiːs/ *noun*: **mantelpieces**
A **mantelpiece** is an ornamental frame around a fireplace, especially the top part which forms a shelf: *a clock on the mantelpiece.* [see picture at **living-room**]

manual /'manjʊəl/ *adjective*; *noun*
▻ ***adjective***
1 Manual work is work you do with your hands, using physical skills or strength; a **manual** worker is someone who does this kind of work. **2** A machine or system that is **manual** is not automatic, and it needs to be operated or performed by someone: *The older manual presses are being replaced by semi-automatic ones.* — *adverb* **manually:** *Most of the machines are manually operated.*
▻ ***noun***: **manuals**
A **manual** is a book of instructions on how to do something: *The diagrams in the manual were no help at all.*

manufacture /manjʊ'faktʃə(r)/ *verb*; *noun*
▻ ***verb***: **manufactures, manufacturing, manufactured**
1 To **manufacture** objects is to make or produce them, especially in large quantities in a factory using machinery: *We've been manufacturing cars in this city for nearly a hundred years.* **2** Something such as an excuse or explanation **has been manufactured** when it not true or genuine: *The police had manufactured most of their evidence.*
▻ ***noun*** (*uncount*) *the manufacture of dolls and other toys.* — *noun* **manufacturer:** *a firm of pipe manufacturers.*

manure /mə'njʊə(r)/ *noun* (*uncount*)
Manure is any substance, especially solid waste released by animals, that you dig into soil to help plants grow: *a few bags of horse manure* ▫ *These fast-growing plants can be dug in as a green manure.*

manuscript /'manjʊskrɪpt/ *noun*: **manuscripts**
1 The **manuscript** of a book or other work is the original form in which the author writes or types it, before handing it over for printing and publication: *The publisher wants my finished manuscript on his desk by next week.* **2** Old books or documents written by hand, before printing was invented, are usually called **manuscripts**.

many /'mɛnɪ/ *determiner*; *pronoun*
▻ ***determiner***: **more, most**
1 (*used with plural count nouns*) **Many** people or things means a lot of them, or a large number of them: *Many parents still prefer to send their children to private schools.* ▫ *one of the many advantages of living in the country* ▫ *The bus was carrying far too many passengers.* ▫ *There are so many interesting things to see in Paris.* ▫ *Have you got many letters to write?* ▫ *Not many* [= only a few] *people applied.* ▫ *I didn't find very many errors.* [= I found only a few] ▫ *It'll never be perfect, however many hours you spend on it.* [*opposite* **few**]

> Notice that in positive statements **many** is rather formal, and **a lot of** and **lots of** are more commonly used, especially in conversation. **Many** is common with negatives and in questions, and is used with words such as *so, too* and *as*: *We've had a lot of donations, but not many offers of help. Take as many brochures as you need.*

2 Many is used with *how* in questions about quantities of people or things: *How many people could we get into your car?* ▫ *I didn't know how many more tickets to buy.*
▻ ***pronoun***: **more, most:** *Many of us in the health professions are worried about the proposed changes.* ▫ *Could you count up and see how many of them there are?* ▫ *A good many of the students own a car.* ▫ *Here are the leaflets; if there are too many, could you give the extra ones back?* ▫ *'I suppose there were a lot of objections?' 'No, not many.'*

> Notice that the pronoun **many** is never used by itself at the end of a positive statement: *There are a lot* (not *there are many*). *We bought lots* (not *many*). But it is acceptable to say: *There are a great many. I have too many.*

▻ ***phrases***
1 As many as draws attention to a surprisingly large number: *As many as thirty local businesses have expressed an interest in the scheme.* **2 A great many** and **a good many** mean a lot: *A great many people have benefited from our research.* ▫ *A good many of the complaints were perfectly justified.*
[see also **more, most, much, few**]

map /map/ *noun*; *verb*
▻ ***noun***: **maps**
A **map** is a diagram of a country, town or other place, showing the position of features such as hills, rivers and roads as if you were looking at them from above, used for finding your way: *We need an up-to-date road map.* ▫ *I asked where I could buy a map of the area.*
▻ ***verb***: **maps, mapping, mapped**

> ***phrasal verb***
> Something **is mapped out** when all the details of it have been planned and decided in advance: *Julian's got his banking career all mapped out.*

maple /'meɪpəl/ *noun*: **maples**
A **maple** tree, or **maple**, is a tree with broad, flat leaves.

mar /mɑː(r)/ *verb*: **mars, marring, marred**
To **mar** something is to spoil it in some way: *This unfortunate episode marred what was an otherwise bril-*

liant career. □ *The view was somewhat marred by the electricity pylons marching across the hillside.*

marathon /'marəθən/ *noun*; *adjective*
▻ ***noun*: marathons**
A **marathon** is a race in which runners cover a distance of 26 miles (42 kilometres), usually through the streets of a town or city: *the Edinburgh Marathon.*
▻ ***adjective***
Marathon describes long and difficult tasks or activities that need a lot of energy and effort: *taking his theatre company on a marathon tour of the country.*

marble /'mɑːbəl/ *noun*: **marbles**
1 (*uncount, often adjectival*) **Marble** is a hard rock with bands of different colour, polished smooth for use in buildings: *The fireplace was a single piece of marble.* □ *a row of marble statues.* **2 Marbles** are small hard balls of coloured glass, used in a children's game; the game is also called **marbles**.

March /mɑːtʃ/ *noun* (*uncount*)
March is the third month of the year, coming after February and before April: *I must fill in my tax form by next March.* □ *My birthday is the twenty-ninth of March (*written *29 March).* □ *March the eighth (*written *March 8)* □ *We don't really expect snow in March.* □ *March weather is usually warmer than this.* [see also note at **date**]

march /mɑːtʃ/ *verb*; *noun*
▻ ***verb*: marches, marching, marched**
1 A group of soldiers **march** when they walk in an upright formal manner, all at the same regular pace. **2** You **march** somewhere when you walk there quickly and with a particular intention or purpose: *She marched into the office and demanded to see the manager.* **3** When crowds of people walk through the streets to show they support or oppose something, such as a new law, you say that they **are marching**: *Thousands turned out to march to the town square.* **4** You **march** someone somewhere when you hold them in a firm grip and force them to walk there: *I saw two police officers march him away.*
▻ ***noun*: marches**
1 A **march** is an organized gathering of people walking through the streets to show that they support or oppose something: *a protest march* □ *the Jarrow March.* **2** (*literary*) The **march** of something is its steady and unstoppable progress: *the march of technology.*

mare /mɛə(r)/ *noun*: **mares**
A **mare** is an adult female horse.

margarine /mɑːdʒə'riːn/ *noun* (*uncount*)
Margarine is a butter-like substance made from vegetable oils or animal fats: *a tub of margarine.*

margin /'mɑːdʒɪn/ *noun*: **margins**
1 On a page of writing or print, the **margin** is the blank area around the outside: *She had scribbled some notes in the margin.* **2** A **margin** is also an extra amount of something, available if you need it: *We've allowed ourselves a margin of about an hour, in case the train is late.* **3** In an election or other contest, a **margin** is the difference between the number of votes or points gained by the winner and the number gained by the person or group in second place: *We lost by a very narrow margin.*

marginal /'mɑːdʒɪnəl/ *adjective*
1 Something that is **marginal** is not important or significant, because it is not the main concern or event: *Within the UK educational scene, EFL is a very marginal activity and educationalists have very little idea of its nature.* **2** In political elections, a **marginal** constituency is an area in which the political representative won at the last election by only a small majority of votes.

marginally /'mɑːdʒɪnəlɪ/ *adverb*
Marginally means 'slightly' or 'to a small degree': *It is marginally colder than it was this time last year.*

marigold /'marɪgoʊld/ *noun*: **marigolds**
A **marigold** is a yellow or orange flower.

marijuana or **marihuana** /marɪ'wɑːnə/ *noun* (*uncount*)
Marijuana is a drug, illegal in some countries, that people smoke in the form of a cigarette.

marina /mə'riːnə/ *noun*: **marinas**
A **marina** is a harbour for private pleasure boats.

marinate /'marɪneɪt/ *verb*: **marinates, marinating, marinated**
When you **marinate** meat or fish you put it for a while into a liquid usually consisting of a mixture of oil, vinegar, spices and wine, in order to flavour it or make it tender.

marine /mə'riːn/ *adjective*; *noun*
▻ ***adjective***
Marine describes things relating to the sea: *the Centre for Marine Research* □ *She's a marine biologist.*
▻ ***noun*: marines**
A **marine** is a soldier trained to fight on land or at sea.

marital /'marɪtəl/ *adjective*
Marital means relating to marriage: *a period of marital bliss.*

maritime /'marɪtaɪm/ *adjective*
Maritime describes things relating to ships and the sea: *an expert in maritime law.*

mark /mɑːk/ *noun*; *verb*
▻ ***noun*: marks**
1 A **mark** is something such as a scratch or a stain on a surface: *There's a dirty mark on your jacket.* □ *The glass had left a mark on the table.* □ *greasy fingermarks.* **2** A **mark** is a written or printed sign or symbol representing something: *One of the marks looked like the letter Z.* □ *The phrase was in quotation marks.* **3** A teacher, examiner or judge awards a student or a competitor a **mark** or a certain number of **marks** when they assess their work or performance, or give it a letter or number representing its standard: *You pass with distinction if you get 120 marks or over.* □ *'What mark did you get for your essay?' 'B+.'* **4** You behave in a certain way as a **mark** of something if your behaviour is intended to indicate that thing: *There are still men who lift their hats to women as a mark of respect.* □ *We should like, as a mark of our appreciation, to offer you this small gift.* **5** Something that has the **marks** of a certain thing has the typical appearance of that thing: *The break-in bore all the marks of an amateur job.* □ *Her work shows marks of haste.* **6** Something reaches a particular **mark** when it reaches that level or stage: *if inflation were to rise above the 10% mark* □ *As the race reaches the halfway mark, no horse looks a clear winner.*
▻ ***verb*: marks, marking, marked**
1 A surface that **is marked** has been spoiled by something such as a scratch or stain: *The table was badly marked.* **2** You **mark** something when you write a symbol or label on it: *Mark your preference with a cross.* □ *The envelope was marked 'private and confidential'.* **3** A certain thing **marks** a spot if it indicates the position of something: *The change in crop colour marks the site of a prehistoric dwelling.* **4** An event that **marks** a stage in something is associated with a significant change in it: *Their victory in the European Championships marked an upturn in their fortunes.*

5 Teachers and examiners **mark** students' work when they read it and indicate its standard, or indicate if a particular answer in it is right or wrong, by putting a symbol, letter or number on it: *I've got 120 exam scripts to mark.* □ *Why did you mark this sum wrong?* **6** You **mark** a particular occasion by doing something if you celebrate or commemorate it in that way: *An exhibition will be held to mark the centenary of his death.* **7** Something **is marked** by a certain quality if that quality is a typical feature of it: *the sensitive and precise use of words that marks all her writing.* **8** Something **marks** you as a particular kind of person if it makes others regard you as that kind of person: *Her lack of aggression marked her as a typical loser.* **9** In games such as football, you **mark** an opposing player when you stay close to them to stop them getting the ball or scoring.

▻ ***phrases*** **1** You **make your mark** or **leave your mark** on something when you have a significant influence on it: *a young writer who will undoubtedly soon make his mark on the publishing world* □ *I'm content to have left some mark, however minor, on the study of the subject.* **2** You **are marking time** when you are doing something unimportant while waiting for a particular thing to happen. **3** You are **quick** or **slow off the mark** if you react promptly, or slowly, to a situation: *She was always quick off the mark whenever an opportunity presented itself of promoting her own interests.* **4** A guess is **wide of the mark** if it is quite wrong.

phrasal verbs

mark down Goods for sale **are marked down** or **marked up** when their price is reduced or increased.

mark off **1** You **mark off** items on a list when you mark them with a symbol to show that they have been dealt with. **2** You **mark** something **off** when you divide it with lines or measurements: *Mark off the vertical line in centimetres.*

mark out **1** You **mark out** something such as a games pitch, or an area of land to be used as one, when you put the appropriate lines on it. **2** A quality or feature of someone or something **marks** them **out** if it makes them different from other people or things: *It was his very quietness that marked him out.*

marked /mɑːkt/ *adjective*
Marked means obvious or noticeable: *There is a marked change in the attitude of modern women.* — *adverb* **markedly** /ˈmɑːkɪdlɪ/: *It's not markedly different from the first one we saw.*

marker /ˈmɑːkə(r)/ *noun*: **markers**
1 A **marker** is anything used to mark the position of something: *Markers placed at 300-metre intervals keep the riders on the right route.* **2** A **marker**, or **marker pen**, is a pen with a thick point, for writing on classroom boards and other large areas.

market /ˈmɑːkɪt/ *noun*; *verb*
▻ ***noun***: **markets**
1 A **market** is a place where goods of various kinds are sold, especially by traders who set up temporary tables, or stalls, in the street: *a fruit and vegetable market* □ *Wednesday is market day in the town square.* **2** **Market** is used in many ways to refer to the people who buy things, *eg* people of a particular age or in a particular area, to how much is bought or sold, and to how willing people are to buy goods of a particular kind: *Their records aim unashamedly at the teenage market.* □ *The housing market in Scotland has always remained fairly buoyant.* □ *The international currency markets were quite slow today.* □ *Do you think there is the market for another fast-food restaurant?*

▻ ***verb***: **markets, marketing, marketed**
To **market** a particular product is to organize, and put into practice, different methods of selling it: *The new film has been quite aggressively marketed.*

▻ ***phrase*** Something is **on the market** when it is on sale and available for you to buy: *Electric cars have, of course, been on the market for some years.* □ *They're hoping the new drug will come onto the market next year.*

marketable /ˈmɑːkɪtəbəl/ *adjective*
Something is **marketable** when you think it is likely that people will want to buy it: *He is certainly the most marketable asset in Rugby League.* □ *translating inventions into marketable products.*

marketing /ˈmɑːkɪtɪŋ/ *noun* (*uncount, often adjectival*)
Marketing consists of the business techniques involved in selling things: *She's gone to college to study marketing.* □ *We need to develop a new marketing strategy.* □ *a marketing executive.*

market place /ˈmɑːkɪt pleɪs/ *noun*: **market places**
1 A **market place** in a town is an open space where markets are held, or where they used to be held. **2** People often refer to the world, as a place where things are bought and sold, as the **market place**: *It's an attractive product in theory, but how will it perform in the market place?*

marking /ˈmɑːkɪŋ/ *noun*: **markings** (*usually in the plural*)
Markings are coloured areas that form a pattern on the surface of something, *eg* an animal's skin: *The cheetah's markings are more regular, more rounded, like spots.*

marksman /ˈmɑːksmən/ *noun*: **marksmen**
A **marksman** is someone, usually a soldier or a police officer, trained to shoot a gun very accurately.

marmalade /ˈmɑːməleɪd/ *noun* (*uncount*)
Marmalade is jam made from oranges or any similar fruit.

maroon[1] /məˈruːn/ *noun*; *adjective*
▻ ***noun*** (*uncount*)
Maroon is a dark, purplish-red colour: *We chose a deep shade of maroon for the curtains.*
▻ ***adjective:*** *a maroon dress.*

maroon[2] /məˈruːn/ *verb*: **maroons, marooning, marooned**
You **are marooned** somewhere unpleasant when you are unable to leave or escape: *As flood water continues to sweep through the streets, many local residents are still marooned on the rooftops of their houses.*

marquee /mɑːˈkiː/ *noun*: **marquees**
A **marquee** is a very large tent used for an outdoor event such as a circus or fair.

marquis or **marquess** /ˈmɑːkwɪs/ *noun*: **marquises**
A **marquis** is a nobleman of middle rank.

marriage /ˈmærɪdʒ/ *noun*: **marriages**
1 (*uncount or count*) **Marriage** is the state or relationship of being husband and wife: *A couple should not enter into marriage without thinking about it seriously.* □ *the marriage ceremony* □ *Bring a copy of your marriage licence.* □ *We have always had a very happy marriage.* **2** A **marriage** is also a wedding, the ceremony of becoming husband and wife.

married /ˈmærɪd/ *adjective*
1 A **married** person has a husband or wife: *comparisons between married and unmarried mothers.* **2** **Married** also means relating to marriage: *How are you enjoying married life?* **3** You get **married** when you marry someone: *They've decided to get married next*

summer. □ *We'll probably get married at the registry office, rather than have a big church wedding.*

marrow /'marou/ *noun*: **marrows**
1 A **marrow** is a large, long, rounded vegetable with thick green skin. [see picture at **vegetable**] **2** (*uncount*) **Marrow**, or bone **marrow**, is a substance that forms the inside of bones in people and animals: *a disease of the bone marrow.*

marry /'marɪ/ *verb*: **marries, marrying, married**
1 You **marry** someone when you become their husband or wife: *I hate the thought of him marrying our daughter.* □ *The couple have declared their intention to marry.* **2** A priest **marries** a couple when he or she performs the ceremony in which they become husband and wife. **3** (*formal*) To **marry** things, or **marry** them together, is to join one to the other correctly or suitably: *That still leaves the problem of how to marry a busy career with a home life.*

marsh /mɑːʃ/ *noun* (*count or uncount*): **marshes**
A **marsh** is an area of land that is permanently soft and wet: *The farm bordered a long marsh.* □ *Most of the surrounding land is marsh.* — *adjective* **marshy**: **marshier, marshiest** /mɑːʃɪ/: *It would be useless to plant in such marshy conditions.*

marshal /'mɑːʃəl/ *noun*; *verb*
▻ ***noun***: **marshals**
1 In the armed forces, a **marshal** is an officer of any of several senior ranks: *His father was an air vice-marshal.* □ *Field Marshal Montgomery.* **2** At a large public event such as a music concert, a **marshal** is an official who controls the movement of crowds of people. **3** In America, a **marshal** is the chief police officer or fire officer in a city or other area.
▻ ***verb***: **marshals, marshalling** (*AmE* **marshaling**), **marshalled** (*AmE* **marshaled**)
You **marshal** people or things when you gather them together in an organized way: *Outside the concert hall, thousands of vehicles were being marshalled into the various parking areas.* □ *a successful report which marshals opinions effectively.*

marshmallow /mɑːʃ'malou/ *noun*: **marshmallows**
A **marshmallow** is a soft, spongy pink or white sweet.

martial /'mɑːʃəl/ *adjective*
Martial describes things that refer or relate to the armed forces or to military affairs: *Martial law has come into force and soldiers are already out on the streets.* □ *The airmen could face a court-martial for disobeying orders.*

martial art /mɑːʃəl 'ɑːt/ *noun* (*usually in the plural*): **martial arts**
Martial arts are fighting sports or techniques of self-defence, such as karate and judo.

martyr /'mɑːtə(r)/ *noun*: **martyrs**
A **martyr** is someone who is killed or made to suffer because they refuse to give up their religious beliefs.

marvel /'mɑːvəl/ *noun*; *verb*
▻ ***noun***: **marvels**
A **marvel** is an astonishing or wonderful person or thing: *It's a marvel that some of them managed to survive the attack.* □ *The painting remains one of the marvels of modern art.*
▻ ***verb***: **marvels, marvelling** (*AmE* **marveling**), **marvelled** (*AmE* **marveled**)
You **marvel** at something when it astonishes you or fills you with wonder: *The rest of us marvelled at the calm, rational way she accepted this dreadful tragedy.*

marvellous (*AmE* **marvelous**) /'mɑːvələs/ *adjective*
Something **marvellous** is excellent or very good indeed: *She gives a marvellous performance as the old queen.* □ *That's marvellous news!* — *adverb* **marvellously:** *She coped marvellously well with the whole thing.*

marzipan /'mɑːzɪpan/ *noun* (*uncount*)
Marzipan is a sweet paste made with sugar and crushed nuts, used to decorate cakes and to make sweets.

mascara /ma'skɑːrə/ *noun* (*uncount*)
Mascara is make-up that is brushed on to eyelashes to make them darker, thicker and more noticeable.

mascot /'maskət/ *noun*: **mascots**
A **mascot** is something, often a child or an animal, chosen by a group to be a symbol of good luck: *As a boy, it was my dream to be the mascot for our local football team.*

masculine /'maskjʊlɪn/ *adjective*
1 Masculine describes things that relate to men, or things that are typical of men, rather than women, or more suitable for men than women: *That kind of aggression is a standard masculine response.* □ *She was wearing a rather masculine suit.* **2** (*grammar*) In some languages, **masculine** nouns are nouns that belong to the gender that contains words referring to males: *'Waiter' and 'drake' are masculine nouns.*

masculinity /maskjʊ'lɪnɪtɪ/ *noun* (*uncount*)
Masculinity is the quality of being a man, especially the fact of having features or characteristics that people typically admire in men: *Some men feel that talking about their emotions somehow undermines their masculinity.*

mash /maʃ/ *verb*; *noun*
▻ ***verb***: **mashes, mashing, mashed**
1 You **mash** vegetables that have been cooked when you crush them into a soft mass: *served with mashed potato.* **2** (*informal*) To **mash** anything is to crush or beat it: *His face was all mashed up in the accident.*
▻ ***noun*** (*uncount*; *informal*)
Mash is mashed potato: *sausages and mash.*

mask /mɑːsk/ *noun*; *verb*
▻ ***noun***: **masks**
1 A **mask** is a covering for the face, or part of the face, worn for amusement, for protection, or as a disguise: *She helped the children to make Hallowe'en masks for the party.* □ *The welding mask protects your eyes from sparks.* □ *lying in a hospital bed wearing an oxygen mask.* **2** Anything that hides or disguises the truth can be described as a **mask**: *All that jolly behaviour is just a mask.* [*same as* **front**]
▻ ***verb***: **masks, masking, masked**
Something **is masked** by something else that covers and hides or disguises it: *The house was masked by the thickest of fog.* □ *Our deepest emotions tend to be masked by our subconscious desire not to bother others with them.*

masochism /'masəkɪzm/ *noun* (*uncount*)
1 Masochism is getting sexual pleasure from allowing yourself to be physically hurt by another person. **2 Masochism** is also wanting and enjoying suffering of any kind. — *noun* **masochist:** *Only a real masochist would chose to spend her life with him.* — *adjective* **masochistic** /masə'kɪstɪk/: *There is a rather masochistic tendency to invite this kind of punishment.*

mason /'meɪsən/ *noun*: **masons**
A **mason** is a person trained in the craft of shaping and carving stone to be used in buildings.

masonry /'meɪsənrɪ/ *noun* (*uncount*)
1 Masonry consists of the parts of a building made of stone or bricks: *She was struck by a piece of falling masonry.* **2 Masonry** is also the craft of a mason.

masquerade /maskə'reɪd/ *verb*: **masquerades, masquerading, masqueraded**
Someone **masquerades** as a particular kind of person, *eg* a doctor or a police officer, when they pretend to be that kind of person: *The thieves gain entry to people's houses by masquerading as telephone engineers.*

mass /mas/ *noun*; *adjective*; *verb*
▻ ***noun***: **masses**
1 A **mass** of something is a large quantity of it; a **mass** of things is a large number of them: *She had a mass of heavy dark hair.* □ *He turned his attention to the disorganized mass of scripts on his desk.* **2** (*used in the plural; informal*) **Masses** of something is a large quantity of it: □ *There are masses of potatoes left; would you like some more?* □ *I've got to read masses of books for my history course.* **3** A **mass** of liquid, air, gas, or a solid substance, is an amount of it, of no particular shape: *A mass of cloud was building up on the horizon.* □ *The gigantic land masses of the world are constantly on the move.* **4** A surface that is described as a **mass** of something is covered with it: *Her back was a mass of cuts and bruises.* **5** (*uncount*; *technical*) **Mass** is a measure of the quantity of matter in an object: *There is a tendency to confuse mass and weight.* **6** (*used in the plural*) Ordinary people are sometimes referred to as the **masses**: *The paintings were intended to be 'art for the masses'.* **7** (*uncount or count*) In some Christian churches, **Mass** is a religious ceremony in which people remember Jesus Christ's last meal by taking bread and wine that symbolize his body and blood. [*same as* **Holy Communion**]
▻ ***adjective***
Mass describes things that involve large numbers of people: *a mass meeting* □ *a mass murderer* □ *a mass protest.*
▻ ***verb***: **masses, massing, massed**
Large numbers of people or things **mass** when they gather together: *Crowds of protesters massed in George Square.*

massacre /'masəkə(r)/ *noun*; *verb*
▻ ***noun***: **massacres**
A **massacre** is the cruel and violent killing of large numbers of people: *We are getting reports of the indiscriminate massacre of civilians by enemy troops.*
▻ ***verb***: **massacres, massacring, massacred:** *There were grim tales of whole villages being massacred.*

massage /'masɑːʒ/ *noun*; *verb*
▻ ***noun*** (*uncount or count*)
Massage is a method of easing pain or stiffness in parts of the body by rubbing it firmly with the hands: *Have you tried massage?* □ *We then give your back a gentle massage.*
▻ ***verb***: **massages, massaging, massaged**
1 To **massage** a part of the body it to treat it with massage: *You could try gently massaging the thigh.* **2** To **massage** something, such as the results of a survey, is to alter it in order to produce a false impression: *The government has been accused of massaging the unemployment figures.*

massive /'masɪv/ *adjective*
Something **massive** is very big in size or extent: *The house itself is massive.* □ *She must be on a massive salary.* □ *massive reductions in prices.* — *adverb* **massively:** *Production of the new model has been massively increased to meet demands.*

mass media /mas 'miːdɪə/ *noun* (*plural, with a singular or plural verb*)
The **mass media** are television, radio and newspapers, the forms of communication that reach large numbers of people: *The mass media are regarded by all parties as an important political tool.*

mass noun /'mas naʊn/ *noun* (*grammar*): **mass nouns**
A **mass noun** is an uncount noun such as *cheese*, *wine*, *wool* or *wood*, that refers to a substance or material; some mass nouns can be used as count nouns (eg *fine wines*, *a soft cheese*) when a variety or brand is being referred to.

mass-produce /masprə'djuːs/ *verb*: **mass-produces, mass-producing, mass-produced**
To **mass-produce** an object is to manufacture large quantities of it in a factory, usually by machine: *Cars that were once hand-built are now mass-produced.* — *noun* (*uncount*) **mass production:** *the latest techniques of mass production.*

mast /mɑːst/ *noun*: **masts**
A **mast** is an upright wooden or metal pole, especially one supporting the sails of a ship, or a radio or television aerial.

master /'mɑːstə(r)/ *noun*; *adjective*; *verb*
▻ ***noun***: **masters**
1 You are the **master** of something that you own or control, especially if you are a man: *The husband was traditionally referred to as the 'master of the house'.* □ *Slaves were expected to be courteous to their master at all times.* □ *a dog and its master.* **2** A man with outstanding skill in a particular activity can be described as a **master** of it: *Our criminal is clearly a master of disguise.* **3** The male teachers in some schools are called **masters**: *I didn't like the Maths master much.* **4** Someone with the title '**Master** of Arts' or '**Master** of Science' has an advanced degree in the arts or sciences. [compare **bachelor, doctor**]
▻ ***adjective***
1 Master is a title given to highly skilled craftsmen who are qualified to teach others their craft: *His father is a master baker.* **2** The **master** bedroom in a house is the main or principal one. **3** A **master** switch, or other device referred to by the description '**master**', is the one that controls the operation of several smaller ones.
▻ ***verb***: **masters, mastering, mastered**
1 You **master** something when you become skilled in it and are able to make use of it successfully: *We expect our students to have mastered the basics of English grammar.* **2** To **master** feelings or emotions is to control them: *You must learn to master your impatience.*

masterful /'mɑːstəfʊl/ *adjective*
You describe someone's behaviour as **masterful** if it shows that they want to, or are able to, control people or situations: *He can be quite masterful when he wants to.*

masterly /'mɑːstəlɪ/ *adjective*
You describe something that someone does as **masterly** if it shows great skill or talent: *his masterly handling of an awkward situation.*

mastermind /'mɑːstəmaɪnd/ *noun*; *verb*
▻ ***noun***: **masterminds**
The **mastermind** of a clever scheme or plan is the person who thinks of it and makes sure it is carried out properly.
▻ ***verb***: **masterminds, masterminding, masterminded:** *It was Jenkins who masterminded the bank robbery.*

masterpiece /'mɑːstəpiːs/ *noun*: **masterpieces**
1 A **masterpiece** is an exceptionally good book, painting or other work of art: *The film is a masterpiece of cinematic art.* **2** Something described as a person's **masterpiece** is the greatest work of art that person ever produced: *Hitchcock's masterpiece is, of course, the 1960 film 'Psycho'.*

mastery /'mɑːstərɪ/ *noun* (*uncount*)
1 Your **mastery** of something is your ability to do it

excellently: *We were amazed by the young child's mastery of the game.* **2 Mastery** of something is also control of it: *The dominant lion is willing to fight for mastery over his territory.*

masturbate /'mastəbeɪt/ *verb*: **masturbates, masturbating, masturbated**
People **masturbate** when they rub or stroke their own or their partner's sexual organs as a way of getting sexual pleasure. — *noun (uncount)* **masturbation** /mastə'beɪʃən/: *Masturbation was considered a terrible sin.*

mat /mat/ *noun*: **mats**
1 A **mat** is a flat piece of any carpet-like material, used as a decorative or protective floor-covering: *Wipe your dirty feet on the doormat.* □ *Exotic-looking mats and rugs were scattered about the floor.* **2** A **mat** is a small piece of fabric or harder material used to protect a table or other surface from heat or scratches: *They gave us a set of cork table mats.* [see also **matt**]

match¹ /matʃ/ *noun*: **matches**
A **match** is a device that produces a flame, *eg* for lighting a cigarette, in the form of a short thin piece of wood coated at the end with a substance that burns when you rub it against a rough surface: *I heard a sound like someone striking a match.* □ *a box of matches.*

match² /matʃ/ *noun; verb*
▷ ***noun*: matches**
1 A **match** is an organized game in any sport or other activity: *a boxing match* □ *a chess match* □ *It's some years since we played a match against them.* □ *They haven't lost a match so far this season.* □ *She won her second-round match.* □ *The match was drawn.* **2** (*used in the singular*) Two things are a good **match** if they have the same colour or pattern and therefore go well together: *The jacket and trousers you're wearing aren't a very good match.* **3** (*old*) A marriage, especially an arranged one, or a person to be obtained in marriage, can be referred to as a **match**: *negotiations concerning the royal match* □ *He'll make a fine match for one of our girls.* **4** (*used in the singular*) One person or thing is a **match** for another if they can equal them; a person or thing that is no **match** for another is inferior to them: *Our product is a match for anything similar presently available on the market.* □ *My brothers were no match for me when it came to arguing.*
▷ ***verb*: matches, matching, matched**
1 One thing **matches** another if it has the same colour or design as the other: *Those shoes would match your dress nicely.* □ *The carpet and curtains don't match.* □ *a light grey suit with a hat to match.* **2** You **match** one thing with or to another when you recognize that there is a connection between them, and put them together: *Match the faces to the names to win a prize.* **3** You say that two people, *eg* a married couple, are well **matched** if you think their personalities fit well together. **4** You can **match** something when you are able to equal it, *eg* in quality or level: *We can match their product but not their prices.*
▷ ***phrase*** You say that someone has **met their match** when they meet someone who is their equal in some skill or quality.

matchbox /'matʃbɒks/ *noun*: **matchboxes**
A **matchbox** is a small cardboard box for holding matches: *tiny houses like matchboxes.*

matching /'matʃɪŋ/ *adjective*
Matching describes something that combines well with something else, usually because it has the same colour or pattern: *a new duvet cover and matching curtains.*

mate /meɪt/ *noun; verb*
▷ ***noun*: mates**
1 (*informal*) People, especially men, often refer to their friends as their **mates**, and often use **mate** as a way of addressing another man: *I went to the pub with a few mates.* □ *Can you tell me the time, mate?* **2 Mate** also forms compound nouns that refer to a person that you share something with: *She's one of my flatmates.* □ *Alan is a workmate of mine.* **3** An animal's **mate** is its sexual partner.
▷ ***verb*: mates, mating, mated**
Animals **mate** when they have sex with each other.

material /mə'tɪərɪəl/ *noun; adjective*
▷ ***noun***
1 (*uncount or count*) **Material** is cloth or fabric: *trousers made of a cotton material* □ *three metres of curtain material.* **2** (*count or uncount*) **Materials** are substances that things can be made out of: *building materials.* **3** (*used in the plural*) **Materials** are instruments or tools needed for a particular activity: *a shop selling artist's materials.* **4** (*uncount*) **Material** is also ideas and information used to make something such as a book or television programme.
▷ ***adjective***
Material means relating to objects, possessions and physical comfort, rather than to emotional or spiritual happiness: *material comforts.*

materialistic /mətɪərɪə'lɪstɪk/ *adjective*
You describe a person or their attitudes as **materialistic** if they think too much about objects and possessions and not enough about emotional or spiritual happiness.

materialize or **materialise** /mə'tɪərɪəlaɪz/ *verb*: **materializes, materializing, materialized**
Something **materializes** when it happens or appears: *We'll have to wait and see if the promised pay rise ever materializes.* □ *Suddenly there he was as if he had materialized out of thin air.*

materially /mə'tɪərɪəlɪ/ *adverb*
1 (*formal*) **Materially** means to a large or important extent: *It's not materially different from the earlier version.* **2 Materially** also means relating to objects, possessions or physical comfort, rather than to emotional or spiritual well-being: *Materially, they want for nothing; but are they happy?*

maternal /mə'tɜːnəl/ *adjective*
Maternal describes things that relate to, or are typical of, mothers: *Do some women have a more developed maternal instinct than others?* □ *I was never very maternal; children just didn't interest me.*

maternity /mə'tɜːnɪtɪ/ *adjective*
Maternity means relating to pregnancy or giving birth: *a maternity clinic* □ *Some women who take maternity leave never go back to work.*

math /maθ/ *noun (uncount; AmE)*
Math is mathematics.

mathematical /maθə'matɪkəl/ *adjective*
Mathematical means relating to, or using, mathematics: *mathematical calculations.*

mathematician /maθəmə'tɪʃən/ *noun*: **mathematicians**
A **mathematician** is a student of, or an expert in, mathematics.

mathematics /maθə'matɪks/ *noun (uncount)*
Mathematics is the science dealing with measurements, numbers, quantities and shapes, usually expressed in the form of symbols: *a student of mathematics* □ *a mathematics textbook.*

maths /maθs/ *noun (uncount)*
Maths is mathematics.

matinée or **matinee** /'matɪneɪ/ *noun*: **matinées**
A **matinée** is a performance of a play, or a showing of a film, in the afternoon rather than the evening.

matrimony /ˈmatrɪmənɪ/ *noun* (*uncount*; *formal*)
Matrimony is the state of being married: *You are here to be joined in holy matrimony.*

matron /ˈmeɪtrən/ *noun*: **matrons**
In some hospitals, the **matron** is the female nurse in charge of all other nurses.

matt or **mat** (*AmE* **matte**) /mat/ *adjective*
Matt paint gives a dull surface without gloss or shine.

matted /ˈmatɪd/ *adjective*
Something such as hair is **matted** when the separate parts or lengths of it are twisted together, forming an untidy mass.

matter /ˈmatə(r)/ *noun*; *verb*
▻ ***noun***: **matters**
1 A **matter** is anything such as a situation, incident, affair or issue that you have to deal with: *I'd like to speak to you about a rather personal matter.* □ *There's still the matter of fees to discuss.* □ *That is a matter for the court to decide.* □ *various political matters.* **2** (*used in the plural*) You refer to the present situation, or to the one you are discussing, as **matters**: *Matters have taken a worrying turn.* □ *It won't help matters if you lose your nerve.* □ *To make matters worse, the banks were all shut.* [*same as* **things**] **3** (*used in the singular*) Something is the **matter** when something is wrong, or there is a problem: *I could see she had been crying, and I asked her what the matter was.* □ *You look upset; is anything the matter?* □ *What's the matter with your leg?* □ *There's nothing the matter with me; I'm perfectly OK.* [compare **wrong**] **4** (*uncount*) **Matter** is a general term for all substances, or can refer to any particular substance: *Ancient philosophers were much concerned with composition of matter.* □ *decayed vegetable matter.* **5** (*uncount*) Any written or broadcast material, or its content, can be referred to as **matter** of a certain kind: *books, magazines and other reading matter* □ *The subject matter of the programme didn't interest me much.*
▻ ***verb***: **matters, mattering, mattered**
1 Something **matters** to you if it is important to you: *Her ambitions and career are the only things that matter to her.* □ *Your opinion matters, so tell me what you think.* **2** Something does not **matter** if it is not important, because it makes no difference to the situation: *It doesn't matter whether you arrive on Friday or Saturday.* □ *The spelling doesn't matter.*
▻ ***phrases*** **1 a** Something that can be done in **a matter of** days or weeks only takes that amount of time to do: *They can build you a house in a matter of days.* □ *We could be in Paris in a matter of a few hours.* **b** Something that is just **a matter of** doing something has to be dealt with by doing that thing: *It's just a matter of knowing whom to apply to for help.* □ *Learning the guitar is just a matter of practice, like anything else.* **2** For **a matter of opinion** see **opinion**. **3** Something that is just **a matter of time** is certain to happen at some point in the future: *They'll find a cure; it's only a matter of time.* **4** If you say that something is **another matter** or **a different matter**, you mean it is an entirely different thing: *Enjoying your work is one thing; liking your colleagues is another matter.* **5** You do something **as a matter of** policy or principle if one or the other is your reason for doing it: *We offer them early retirement as a matter of policy.* □ *You must insist on it as a matter of principle.* **6** For **as a matter of course** see **course**. **7** For **as a matter of fact** see **fact**. **8 For that matter** introduces a second statement that extends the first: *My wife was very angry; so was I, for that matter.* **9** You say **'it doesn't matter' a** to reassure someone when they apologize to you: *'I'm so sorry I'm late.' 'It's OK, it doesn't matter.'* **b** to indicate that you have no particular preference: *'Tea or coffee?' 'It doesn't matter.'* **10** You use **no matter** before *what*, *how*, *where*, *when* and so on to give them the same meaning as *whatever*, *however*, *wherever*, *whenever* and so on, indicating that something remains so in all possible circumstances: *They won't hear you, no matter how* [= however] *loud you shout.* □ *No matter what* [= whatever] *the problem is, she always seems able to help.*
11 You use **'the truth**, or **the fact**, **of the matter'** to emphasize what you say: *The fact of the matter is she's afraid of failure.*

matter-of-fact /matərəvˈfakt/ *adjective*
A person, or their behaviour, is **matter-of-fact** when they react to an exciting or upsetting event in a calm way, as if it were a normal or everyday event: *'By the way', she said, all matter-of-fact, 'I'm leaving you'.*

matting /ˈmatɪŋ/ *noun* (*uncount*)
Matting is material, especially stiff, rough woven fibres, used for making mats.

mattress /ˈmatrəs/ *noun*: **mattresses**
A **mattress** is a large flat cushion-like pad, the part of a bed that you sleep on: *an old feather-filled mattress.* [see picture at **bedroom**]

mature /məˈtjʊə(r)/ *adjective*; *verb*
▻ ***adjective***
1 You describe someone as **mature** when they behave in the kind of sensible and reasonable way that you expect all adults to behave in: *She's a very mature young woman.* □ *It's not a very mature attitude, is it?* **2 Mature** cheese or wine has been kept long enough to develop a full, strong flavour before being sold. — *noun* (*uncount*) **maturity** /məˈtjʊərɪtɪ/: *The young ape will reach maturity in just over a year.* □ *He's shown impressive maturity in his handling of the affair.*
▻ ***verb***: **matures, maturing, matured**
1 A young person **matures** when they become an adult, physically or emotionally: *Colin is maturing into a handsome young man.* **2** Wine or cheese **matures** when it develops a full, strong flavour after being kept for a while.

maul /mɔːl/ *verb*: **mauls, mauling, mauled**
An animal **mauls** someone when it attacks them fiercely, causing severe injuries: *One of the zookeepers was badly mauled by a lion.*

mausoleum /mɔːsəˈlɪəm/ *noun*: **mausoleums**
A **mausoleum** is a small building with the grave of a rich or famous person inside.

mauve /moʊv/ *adjective*
Something **mauve** is pale purple in colour: *a pair of mauve gloves.*

maverick /ˈmavərɪk/ *noun* (*often adjectival*): **mavericks**
Someone who is described as a **maverick** tends to choose their own way of doing things, not caring about traditions or customs: *I went along to interview this maverick businessman himself.*

max /maks/ *noun* (*informal*)
Max is an abbreviation of 'maximum': *They'll lend us 1000 dollars max.*

maxim /ˈmaksɪm/ *noun*: **maxims**
A **maxim** is a short saying that expresses a general truth or principle: *My mother's favourite maxim was 'The Devil makes work for idle hands'.*

maximize or **maximise** /ˈmaksɪmaɪz/ *verb*: **maximizes, maximizing, maximized**
You **maximize** something when you make it as great as possible: *Yellow curtains would maximize the summery effect.* □ *It's clear their first priority must be to maximize company profits.*

maximum /ˈmaksɪməm/ *adjective*; *noun*

▻ *adjective*
Maximum means greatest possible: *The maximum amount of time must be given to our overseas projects.* ▫ *Maximum levels of investment have gone into this new venture.*
▻ ***noun*** *(used in the singular) We've been allowed a maximum of seven days to get it finished.*

May /meɪ/ *noun (uncount)*
May is the fifth month of the year, coming after April and before June: *We don't move house till next May.* ▫ *Kathleen's birthday is on the fifth of May (*written 5 *May).* ▫ *May the eighth (*written *May 8)* ▫ *You can still get some nasty frosts well into May.* ▫ *the traditional May festival in the village.*

may /meɪ/ *modal verb*
(*negative form* **may not**, *past tense* **might** (see separate entry))
1 (*more formal than* **can**) **May** is used **a** to ask permission: *Please may I use your telephone?* ▫ *Hallo. May I speak to James?* ▫ *May I smoke?* ▫ *May I use the car this evening?* ▫ *May I accept your offer provisionally?* **b** to give permission: *You may unfasten your seatbelts and smoke if you wish.* ▫ *'May I leave the table?' 'Of course you may.'* **c** to make a polite offer: *May I assist you?* **d** to express your intention or opinion in an indirect way: *May I interrupt you for a minute?* ▫ *May I make a suggestion?* ▫ *You're looking very glamorous, if I may say so.* ▫ *It was a stupid and, may I say, dangerous thing to do.* **e** with *not* to refuse permission or say what is not allowed: *'May I borrow the car?' 'No, you may not.'* ▫ *Drinks may not be taken into the auditorium.*
2 a Something that **may** be so is possible or likely, now or in the future: *She looks quite like him; she may be his sister.* ▫ *You may change your mind when you hear the price.* ▫ *Pauline may not be here tomorrow; she's hoping to take a few days' holiday.* **b** You use '**may** have' with a past participle to express the possibility that something has happened, or that it will have happened by some future time: *We could try telephoning them but they may already have left home.* ▫ *'Was it you that made the suggestion?' 'It may have been; I can't remember.'* ▫ *I may have managed to contact her by tomorrow evening.*

> For an unreal possibility in the past, you should use '**might** have' rather than '**may** have': *If you'd come a minute later we might not have* (rather than *may not have) survived.*

3 You can say that something **may** be so, meaning that although it is so, there is another more important fact to consider: *She may be the boss, but she's still an idiot.* ▫ *You may think it's silly, but it works.* ▫ *Knowledgeable as he may seem on the surface he doesn't actually know very much.* **4** (*formal*) You do one thing so that another **may** happen when you do the first so as to allow the second to happen: *They have moved to the country so that the children may enjoy the benefits of an outdoor life.* **5** Something **may** be achieved if it can be achieved: *The deterioration process in bone may be halted by hormone-replacement therapy.* **6** (*formal*) You use **may** to express wishes: *May you both be very happy!* ▫ *The sales figures are most impressive; long may it last!*
▻ ***phrases*** **1** You say you **may as well** do something if there is no point in not doing it: *It's obvious she's not going to answer the door; we may as well leave.* **2 a** Something that **may well** be so, or happen, or have happened, is likely to be so, or happen, or have happened: *You may well be right.* ▫ *She may well change her plans.* ▫ *They may well have decided to leave early.* **b** You tell people they **may well** be reacting in a certain way when you think their reaction is justified: *You may well look horrified.* ▫ *'Where will you go if you resign?' 'You may well ask.'*

maybe /ˈmeɪbiː/ *adverb (sentence adverb)*
Maybe means 'possibly' or 'perhaps' and is used
1 to say that something may be so: *Maybe he'll come if you ask him yourself.* ▫ *Maybe I was wrong to tell her.* ▫ *Maybe I should wear something more daring.* **2** to show you are guessing: *He's a little older than you, I think; four or five years, maybe.*

> Be careful to distinguish between the single-word adverb **maybe** and the two-word verb combination **may be**: *Maybe you're right. You may be right.*

mayhem /ˈmeɪhɛm/ *noun (uncount)*
Mayhem is a state of great confusion, noise and disorder: *There was absolute mayhem outside the courtroom.*

mayonnaise /meɪəˈneɪz/ *noun (uncount)*
Mayonnaise is a thick creamy sauce made with eggs and oil and eaten cold with salads and other foods: *We should have bought a bigger jar of mayonnaise.*

mayor /mɛə(r)/ *noun*: **mayors**
The **mayor** of a town is the person elected to act as its official leader, especially on ceremonial occasions.

maze /meɪz/ *noun*: **mazes**
1 In a large garden, a **maze** is a confusing network of paths each bordered by high walls or hedges, designed as a game to test how well you can find your way. **2** A very confusing or complicated system or process is often referred to as a **maze**: *Real justice is lost on the way through the tortuous legal maze.*

me /miː/ *pronoun (used as the object of a verb or preposition, and in certain other positions)*
A person speaking or writing refers to himself or herself as **me**: *I asked him to give me the money.* ▫ *Didn't you hear me coming in?* ▫ *He bumped into me and apologized.* ▫ *I'm sorry; that was careless of me* ▫ *'Hello, Mark; it's me, John.'* ▫ *'Which is you in this photo?' 'That's me, in the front row.'* ▫ *I think she's a bit older than me* (or *than I am*). ▫ *She couldn't walk as fast as me* (or *as I could*). ▫ *They've asked Margaret and me to be witnesses.* ▫ *It's me she wants to talk to, not you.* ▫ *It's Philip who's been chosen, not me.* ▫ *'Who wants to try it first?' 'Me* (or *I do*).*'* ▫ *'I'm hungry.' 'Me too* (or *I am too*).*'*
[see also **my, myself**]

meadow /ˈmɛdoʊ/ *noun*: **meadows**
A **meadow** is a field of grass.

meagre (*AmE* **meager**) /ˈmiːgə(r)/ *adjective*
Something is **meagre** when there is only a small quantity or amount of it: *I wondered how we would survive on such apparently meagre supplies?* ▫ *She's paid a fairly meagre salary.*

meal /miːl/ *noun*: **meals**
A **meal** is an occasion when you eat food, or the food that you eat: *Lunch is my favourite meal of the day.* ▫ *a light meal of an omelette and salad.*

mean[1] /miːn/ *verb*: **means, meaning, meant**
1 You ask what something such as a word, expression or gesture **means** when you want it explained to you: *What does 'duress' mean?* ▫ *It sounded like a French word; I didn't know what it meant.* ▫ *In Greece tilting your chin upwards means 'no'.* **2** You ask a person what

they **mean** when you want them to explain what they intend to say, or to what they are referring: *Did you mean that you'd both like a ticket?* □ *'Michael's disappeared.' 'What do you mean he's disappeared?'* □ *That's what I thought you meant.* □ *Why can't people say what they mean?* □ *Which gallery do you mean?* □ *I know the shop you mean.* □ *She wondered if his silence meant agreement or disagreement.* **3** One thing **means** another if it indicates that it is so or that it is likely: *There was a dark blue car in the drive; that meant that Dad had returned.* □ *Lower profits mean redundancies.* □ *Cold cloudless evenings mean overnight frost.* **4** Things that **mean** a lot to you are important to you: *Your approval means a lot to me.* □ *It means nothing to me whether she admires me or despises me.* [compare **matter**] **5** You say you **mean** what you say to emphasize that you are not joking, pretending, exaggerating or being polite, but are being quite serious: *Please come round whenever you want to. I mean it.* □ *I mean what I say, Tom; any more noise and you go straight to bed.* □ *There are thousands, and I mean thousands, of people who think just that.* **6** You **mean** something, or **mean** to do it, if you intend it to happen, or intend to do it: *I didn't mean to offend you.* □ *I meant to stop at the shops on the way home, but I forgot.* □ *I'm sure he didn't mean the children any harm.* □ *She means trouble; I can tell from her expression.* [*same as* **intend**] **7** Something or someone that **is meant** to do or be something is **a** intended to do or be that thing: *What's that meant to be a picture of?* □ *Sorry. It was meant to be funny.* □ *'It doesn't rhyme.' 'It's not meant to.'* □ *The bullet had been meant for me.* **b** expected to do or be that thing: *I think this is where we're meant to sit.* □ *You're not meant to talk in here.* □ *It was meant to be warm and sunny today.* **c** thought to be or reported to be that thing: *It's meant to be a very exciting film.* □ *She's meant to be one of the world's most beautiful women, but I can't see why.* **d** destined to do or be that thing: *I believe we were meant to meet.* □ *They're obviously meant for each other.* □ *I don't think you were meant to be a teacher.* [compare **supposed**]

▻ ***phrases*** **1** You say **I mean** when **a** you are adding something that explains what you have just said: *Is he handsome? Her father, I mean.* **b** you are adding something that corrects what you have just said: *Are you bringing Heather? Sorry, I mean Hazel.* **2** People **mean well** if they have kindly or good intentions, even if they upset or hurt others.

mean² /miːn/ *adjective*: **meaner, meanest**

1 Someone who is **mean** is not generous, especially in not wanting to spend money: *She is so mean with money.* □ *It was rather mean of you not to offer him a lift.* [*same as* **stingy**] **2** Someone who is **mean** behaves in a nasty or spiteful way: *Don't be so mean to your little brother.* [*same as* **spiteful**] **3** You also call someone **mean** if they behave in a violent or vicious way: *The bears can turn mean if provoked.* **4** (*informal*) Some people describe things that are very good as **mean**: *Eric makes a mean potato salad.* — *noun* (*uncount*) **meanness** or /ˈmiːnnəs/: *My husband's meanness with money was becoming a public embarrassment.*

▻ ***phrase*** (*informal*) **No mean** is used to describe

1 someone who is very good at something: *Shirley was no mean singer.* **2** something that is very difficult to achieve: *Organizing such a successful event was no mean task.*

meaning /ˈmiːnɪŋ/ *noun*: **meanings**

1 The **meaning** of something is what it refers to, indicates or expresses: *The dictionary lists all the different meanings of the most common words in the language.* □ *Perhaps the film isn't supposed to have a meaning; it's just meant to be pleasant to watch.* **2** The **meaning** of something is also its importance or purpose: *We all have our own ideas about the meaning of life.*

meaningful /ˈmiːnɪŋfəl/ *adjective*

1 Something such as a gesture, or the expression on someone's face, is **meaningful** when it is intended to express something: *The couple then exchange a meaningful look and move towards the bedroom.* **2** You describe something as **meaningful** if you think it is useful or important: *There are no real meaningful conclusions to be drawn from these tests.* □ *That was his only meaningful relationship with a woman.*

meaningless /ˈmiːnɪŋləs/ *adjective*

1 You describe something as **meaningless** if you think it has no purpose or importance: *Life can seem meaningless at times.* [*same as* **pointless**] **2** Something that is **meaningless** has no meaning: *a load of meaningless administrative jargon.*

means /miːnz/ *noun*: *plural* **means**

1 A **means** of doing something is a method or way of doing it, or a device or instrument for doing it: *There are various means we can try.* □ *They discovered a simple means of erecting the boulders.* □ *I've no means of contacting her before tomorrow.* □ *The car's our only means of transport.* □ *She was determined to get the top by any means available.* □ *We have the authority and the means to enforce it.* □ *Mankind now has the means to destroy the whole planet.* **2** (*used in the plural*) Your **means** are your money or income: *She's a woman of considerable means.* □ *They obviously have means.*

▻ ***phrases*** **1** Something that is **a means to an end** is something that people do not for enjoyment but to achieve something: *I regard the computer course as a means to an end.* **2** You say **by all means** as a polite way of giving permission: *'Could I use your phone?' 'By all means.'* □ *By all means call me if you need help.* **3** Something is done **by means of** a certain method or device if it is done using it: *They crossed by means of a rope bridge.* **4** **By no means** means 'not at all' or 'definitely not': *It is by no means certain that they'll give us a grant.* □ *We haven't by any means finished.*

meant /mɛnt/ *verb*

Meant is the past tense and past participle of **mean**.

meantime /ˈmiːntaɪm/ *sentence adverb*

Meantime, or in the **meantime**, refers to the period of time between now and some future event you have referred to: *The others will arrive soon; in the meantime, we must try to stay calm.* □ *These developments will be discussed in next week's lecture; meantime, let's look at the book's history.*

meanwhile /ˈmiːnwaɪl/ *sentence adverb*

Meanwhile is used to show that two things exist or are happening at the same time, often different or opposing things: *I phoned for an ambulance; meanwhile, Andy was trying to bandage the wound as best he could.* □ *Public employees are told not to expect pay increases; meanwhile, company directors continue to award themselves huge bonuses.*

measles /ˈmiːzəlz/ *noun* (*uncount*)

Measles is an infectious disease, common in children, with red spots appearing on the skin, and a fever: *None of the children has ever had measles.*

measly /ˈmiːzlɪ/ *adjective* (*informal*)

Measly describes things that are very small in amount or value: *That left us with a measly ten pounds each.* □ *just a lamb chop and a few measly potatoes.* [*same as* **paltry**]

measurable /ˈmɛʒərəbəl/ *adjective*

Measurable describes things that have some value or importance, although usually not much: *There's no measurable difference between them.*

measure /'mɛʒə(r)/ *verb; noun*
▻ ***verb*: measures, measuring, measured**
1 You **measure** something when you find out qualities such as how long or how heavy it is: *The children then measured the length of the fish with a ruler.* □ *You need to measure the distance from the door to the window.* □ *They measured my chest at 44 inches.* □ *The weight of the apples is measured in kilograms.* □ *The problem arises because there is no fixed scale against which you can measure how much work a person does.* **2** Something **measures** a number of units, such as metres or inches, when its size is expressed in this way: *The garden measured thirty yards from the wall to the back door.* □ *an earthquake measuring 5 on the Richter Scale* □ *winds measuring over 70 knots.*
▻ ***noun*: measures**
1 A **measure** of something is an amount of it, especially a standard amount: *She poured herself a large measure of vodka.* □ *In British society, we expect our achievers to have a measure of humility, however small.* **2** A **measure** is also an action, something you do in order to achieve a certain aim: *Drastic measures will have to be taken if we are to avoid bankruptcy.*
▻ ***phrase*** You do or have something extra **for good measure** when what you do or have seems necessary to make a situation complete: *I was pleased with the new suit, and bought a new shirt and tie for good measure.*

> ***phrasal verb***
> Someone or something that **measures up** reaches a required or desired standard of some kind: *She's a competent manager, but I'm not sure she'd measure up to the new position.* □ *Compared with last year's results, how do this year's students measure up?*

measured /'mɛʒəd/ *adjective*
Measured describes a slow and careful way of doing something: *The Minister replied in his usual measured tone.*

measurement /'mɛʒəmənt/ *noun*: **measurements**
1 A **measurement** is a calculation of the size of something: *We will visit your house to take the precise measurements of the window to be replaced.* **2** Your **measurements** are the size of one or more parts of your body, especially as they relate to the size of clothes: *Do you know your chest measurement?*

meat /mi:t/ *noun* (*uncount*)
Meat is the flesh of dead animals used as food, sometimes not including fish or chicken.

mechanic /mɪ'kanɪk/ *noun*: **mechanics**
A **mechanic** is someone who repairs or maintains machinery: *a car mechanic.* [see also **mechanics**]

mechanical /mɪ'kanɪkəl/ *adjective*
1 Mechanical refers to machines, or to tasks performed by machines: *a mechanical bottling system.* **2** Someone's actions or behaviour are described as **mechanical** if they don't seem to be thinking about what they are doing, or if they seem able to do it without thinking: *a brief, mechanical handshake* □ *She worked at a steady, mechanical pace.*

mechanics /mɪ'kanɪks/ *noun*
1 (*plural*) When you talk about the **mechanics** of something, you are referring to the processes or systems involved in making it work: *I'm not really familiar with the mechanics of taking someone to court.* **2** (*uncount; physics*) **Mechanics** is the study of the effect of physical forces on moving or stationary objects: *wave mechanics.* [see also **mechanic**]

mechanism /'mɛkənɪzm/ *noun*: **mechanisms**
1 A **mechanism** is a working part of a machine or other device, or its system of working parts: *There seems to be a fault with the safe's locking mechanism.* **2** People's automatic reactions to particular situations are sometimes referred to as **mechanisms**: *Laughter is a common defence mechanism.*

mechanized or **mechanised** /'mɛkənaɪzd/ *adjective*
Something such as an industrial process is **mechanized** when it is carried out by machines rather than people: *Car production has become increasingly mechanized.*

medal /'mɛdəl/ *noun*: **medals**
A **medal** is a small metal disc given as a prize or an award, *eg* to the winner of a sporting competition: *old soldiers with rows of medals pinned to their chest.* □ *an Olympic medal.*

medallion /mə'dalɪən/ *noun*: **medallions**
A **medallion** is a large, medal-like piece of jewellery worn round the neck on a chain.

medallist (*AmE* **medalist**) /'mɛdəlɪst/ *noun*: **medallists**
A **medallist** is a person who has been given a medal, especially a sportsperson: *Britain's team includes three gold medallists at the last Olympics.*

meddle /'mɛdəl/ *verb*: **meddles, meddling, meddled**
You **meddle** when you involve yourself in something that does not concern you: *a grown woman whose parents still meddle in her affairs* □ *I don't want the children meddling with my papers.*

media /'mi:dɪə/ *noun* (*plural, with a singular or plural verb, often adjectival*)
People often refer to television, radio and newspapers as the **media**: *The Minister has been criticized in the media for not acting sooner.* □ *The media don't seem ever to have had a very good opinion of his acting.* □ *There has been intense media speculation about her private life.* [see also **medium**]

mediaeval or **medieval** /mɛdɪ'i:vəl/ *adjective*
Mediaeval refers to a period of European history from around the year 1100 to the year 1450, known as the Middle Ages: *one of our finest mediaeval cathedrals.*

mediate /'mi:dɪeɪt/ *verb*: **mediates, mediating, mediated**
You **mediate** between two people or groups when you try to settle an argument or dispute between them. — *noun* (*uncount*) **mediation** /mi:dɪ'eɪʃən/: *All attempts at mediation have so far failed.* — *noun* **mediator:** *United Nations mediators have arrived in the war-torn province, with instructions to secure a lasting peace.*

medic /'mɛdɪk/ *noun* (*informal*): **medics**
A **medic** is a doctor or a medical student.

medical /'mɛdɪkəl/ *adjective; noun*
▻ ***adjective***
Medical refers to doctors, or to the science or practice of medicine: *An elite medical team have been flown to the war zone.* □ *advances in medical technology* □ *Bring the child to the medical centre.*
▻ ***noun*: medicals**
A **medical** is a doctor's general examination of a person to discover their state of health.

medication /mɛdɪ'keɪʃən/ *noun* (*uncount; formal*)
Medication is medicine that a doctor gives to a patient: *Are you taking the medication?*

medicinal /mɪ'dɪsɪnəl/ *adjective*
Medicinal relates to the curing of illnesses or diseases: *a range of medicinal herbs* □ *I have a glass of whisky at night, for medicinal purposes.*

medicine /'mɛdsɪn/ or /'mɛdɪsɪn/ *noun*: **medicines**
1 Medicines are substances used to treat or prevent diseases or illnesses, especially those you swallow: *Do*

you sell cough medicine specifically for children? □ *There's another jar in the medicine cupboard.* **2** (*uncount*) **Medicine** is the science or practice of treating or preventing illnesses: *university degrees in law and medicine* □ *drugs widely used in preventive medicine.*

medieval see **mediaeval**.

mediocre /miːdɪ'oʊkə(r)/ *adjective*
Something that is **mediocre** is of a rather poor standard, at best only ordinary or average: *Carter, on the other hand, gave a fairly mediocre performance.* — *noun* (*uncount*) **mediocrity** /miːdɪ'ɒkrɪtɪ/: *If British tennis is ever to rise above the mediocrity it has been wallowing in for decades, juniors will have to be given greater access to courts and coaching.*

meditate /'mɛdɪteɪt/ *verb*: **meditates, meditating, meditated**
1 You **meditate** on something when you think about it carefully: *Sheila spent the afternoon meditating on her career prospects.* **2** Someone who **meditates** spends long periods of time being very still, quiet and relaxed, often for religious reasons. — *noun* **meditation** /mɛdɪ'teɪʃən/: *She teaches yoga and meditation at the health club.*

medium /'miːdɪəm/ *noun*; *adjective*
▷ ***noun***: **mediums** or **media**
1 (**mediums** *or* **media**) A **medium** is a way of communicating news or information, *eg* television or radio, or a way of expressing something, such as a painting: *The cinema is perhaps the most versatile photographic medium.* **2** (**mediums**) A **medium** is also a person who claims they can communicate with the spirits of dead people.
▷ ***adjective***
Medium describes things that are roughly half way between two extremes, especially of qualities such as size, so are neither large nor small: *a woman of medium height* □ *a medium-sized stadium.*

medium wave /'miːdɪəm weɪv/ *noun* (*uncount*)
Medium wave is a range of radio waves that programmes are broadcast on, with wavelengths between 200 and 1000 metres. [compare **long wave, short wave**]

meek /miːk/ *adjective*
A **meek** person behaves in a gentle way, and tends not to oppose or disagree with others. — *adverb* **meekly:** *'Of course I'll do it, if you want me to,' David replied, meekly.*

meet /miːt/ *verb*: **meets, meeting, met**
1 You **meet** someone **a** when you see them by chance somewhere and have a conversation with them: *I met Jill in the supermarket today.* [*same as* **bump into**] **b** when you talk to them and get to know them for the first time: *I met an old friend of yours at the conference.* □ *How did you meet your husband?* □ *They met at a party.* □ *You look familiar. Have we met before?* **c** when you are introduced to them: *Sally, come over here and meet Robert.* □ *I'd like you to meet my parents.* **d** when you each go to the same place at the same time by arrangement, in order, *eg*, to have a meal or a talk: *I've arranged to meet Roy for a discussion tomorrow.* □ *We used to meet every Tuesday for lunch.* **2** A group or body of people **meet** when they assemble or gather together for a certain purpose: *The Heads of Department meet every Thursday to discuss college affairs.* [*same as* **assemble**] **3** You **meet** someone at the station or airport, or you **meet** their train, bus or plane, when you go to the station or airport to collect them as they arrive there: *My husband is meeting me at the station.* □ *We drove to Swansea to meet her train.* **4** You **meet** an attitude or a problem when you experience it: *I'd never met such arrogance before.* □ *You meet friendliness wherever you go in Turkey.* □ *We're bound to meet a few obstacles.* [*same as* **encounter**] **5** You **meet** a challenge or difficulty when you deal with it, especially successfully: *We are prepared to meet the complications as they occur.* [*same as* **confront, tackle**] **6** You **meet** the cost of something when you pay for it: *He decided that he could meet the cost of a private operation, if necessary.* **7** Something that **meets** a need or requirement fulfils it: *I think £5000 should meet our immediate needs.* [*same as* **satisfy, fulfil**] **8** The point where things such as lines **meet** is the point where they join, cross or come into contact with each other: *There's a bus stop just where the path meets the road.* [*same as* **join, cross**] **9** Something moving **meets** something else when it hits it: *Her head met the pavement with a resounding crack.* **10** Two people's eyes **meet** when they look at each other at the same moment: *Her eyes met mine for a brief second and she grinned.*

phrasal verbs
meet up You **meet up** with someone when you each go to the same place at the same time by arrangement, to do something together: *We parted in Cologne, arranging to meet up again in Venice a week later.*
meet with 1 (*especially AmE*) You **meet with** people when you come together for a discussion: *She is meeting with her solicitors this morning.* **2** Something **meets with**, or **is met with** a certain reaction or response if that is the way people react or respond to it: *My suggestion met with contempt.* □ *Reports of atrocities had initially been met with disbelief.* **3** Someone or something **meets with** success or failure when they succeed or fail: *Her first novel met with considerable success.*

meeting /'miːtɪŋ/ *noun*: **meetings**
1 A **meeting** is an occasion when people come together for a particular purpose, usually in order to discuss something: *The company holds its Annual General Meeting every June.* □ *The chairman of the finance committee has called a meeting for next week.* □ *This is the most important athletics meeting of the whole sporting calendar.* **2** (*formal*) A **meeting** is also an occasion when you meet someone: *We kissed on our first meeting.*

mega- /'mɛgə/ *prefix*
1 (*technical*) **Mega-** forms nouns that refer to a million units of something: *a computer with 50 megabytes of memory.* **2** **Mega-** also means large or great, and informally, greatly: *She's one of American cinema's megastars.* □ *The last lecture was mega-boring.*

megalomaniac /mɛgəloʊ'meɪnɪak/ *noun*: **megalomaniacs**
A **megalomaniac** is someone who wants to have as much power or influence as possible.

megaphone /'mɛgəfoʊn/ *noun*: **megaphones**
A **megaphone** is a device shaped like an open cone, or the open end of a trumpet, that you speak through to make your voice sound louder, *eg* when you are speaking to a crowd of people.

melancholy /'mɛləŋkɒlɪ/ *adjective* (*literary*)
A **melancholy** person feels sad; you describe something as **melancholy** if it makes you feel sad: *There was a melancholy note in his voice.* □ *It was a dark, melancholy room.*

mellow /'mɛloʊ/ *adjective*; *verb*
▷ ***adjective***: **mellower, mellowest**

1 Mellow describes things that are pleasantly soft and gentle: *a walk in the mellow evening sunlight* □ *The first guitar has a mellower sound.* □ *a rich and mellow wine.* **2** You feel **mellow** when you feel pleasantly relaxed, *eg* because you are slightly drunk.
▷ ***verb***: **mellows, mellowing, mellowed**
People **mellow** when they become calmer, more relaxed, happier, and easier to deal with, *eg* as they grow older: *Her temper has certainly not mellowed with age.*

melodrama /'mɛlədrɑ:mə/ *noun* (*count or uncount*): **melodramas**
A **melodrama** is a play or film in which the situations, events and characters are more extreme than in real life: *The film is a classic piece of melodrama.*

melodramatic /mɛlədrə'matɪk/ *adjective*
You describe someone's behaviour as **melodramatic** if it seems falsely or insincerely extreme: *There's no need to be so melodramatic about it.*

melody /'mɛlədɪ/ *noun*: **melodies**
A **melody** is a tune, especially the basic tune of a song without the notes added around it: *a haunting melody played by a guitarist on a small stage beneath the flood-lit trees.*

melon /'mɛlən/ *noun*: **melons**
A **melon** is a large rounded fruit with a thick skin, sweet juicy flesh and many seeds: *She cut me a huge slice of melon.* [see picture at **fruit**]

melt /mɛlt/ *verb*: **melts, melting, melted**
1 Something solid such as ice or metal **melts** when it becomes soft or liquid, usually as a result of being heated: *The butter had melted in the sun.* **2** Something that slowly or gradually disappears can be said to **melt**, or **melt** away: *Any support he had once had amongst his colleagues had melted away.*

melting pot /'mɛltɪŋ pɒt/ *noun* (*usually in the singular*)
You describe a place or a situation in which different beliefs, ideas or cultures are mixed as a **melting pot**: *There existed a sort of political melting pot from which a government emerged.*

member /'mɛmbə(r)/ *noun*: **members**
1 (*often adjectival*) A **member** of something such as a class, group or organization is one of the people, animals or things that belong to it: *Are you a member of this golf club?* □ *Women members should have the same rights as the men.* □ *These countries are not members of the UN Security Council.* □ *discussions between the member states of the European Union* □ *the youngest member of the family* □ *The lynx is a member of the cat family.* **2** The **member** for a certain place is the member of parliament for that place: *the member for Hillhead.* **3** (*formal, rather old*) Your limbs are sometimes referred to as **members**; the 'male **member**' is the penis.

membership /'mɛmbəʃɪp/ *noun* (*uncount*)
1 Membership of an organization is the state of being a member of it: *I've made no secret of my membership of several political groupings.* **2** The members of an organization, or the number of them, are sometimes referred to as the **membership**: *Membership of the Party has risen to over three million.*

membrane /'mɛmbreɪn/ *noun*: **membranes**
A **membrane** is a thin layer of skin covering, connecting or lining an inner organ of your body.

memento /mə'mɛntoʊ/ *noun*: **mementos** or **mementoes**
A **memento** is an object that you keep to remind you of the past: *a collection of seashells that were all mementos of her childhood holidays.* [*same as* **souvenir**]

memo /'mɛmoʊ/ *noun*: **memos**
A **memo** is an official note you send to someone, usually someone who works in the same company or organization as you: *I had a memo from the Director of Housing about the cost of repairs to council flats.*

memoirs /'mɛmwɑ:z/ *noun* (*plural*)
A person who writes their **memoirs** writes a book about their life: *the recently published memoirs of her political career.*

memorable /'mɛmərəbəl/ *adjective*
A **memorable** event or occasion is one you can, or you will, easily remember because it was special or important in some way: *It will be a truly memorable an colourful day.* □ *the man who created some of the Sixties' most memorable images.*

memorandum /mɛmə'randəm/ *noun*: **memorandums** or **memoranda**
A **memorandum** is an official note of something sent to a colleague within an organization.

memorial /mə'mɔ:rɪəl/ *noun*; *adjective*
▷ ***noun***: **memorials**
A **memorial** is something built, *eg* a statue, as a way of remembering and honouring a person or an event.
▷ ***adjective: Teams will compete for the George Ward memorial trophy.***

memorize or **memorise** /'mɛməraɪz/ *verb*: **memorizes, memorizing, memorized**
You **memorize** something when you learn it thoroughly, so that you will be able to remember every detail of it: *Memorize the code and destroy this piece of paper.*

memory /'mɛmərɪ/ *noun* (*uncount or count*): **memories**
1 Memory is the power that your mind has to remember things: *He was able to recite the whole poem from memory.* □ *I have a terrible memory for names, but an excellent memory for faces.* **2** Your **memory** is also the store, in your mind, of all the things that you remember; a **memory** is something that you remember: *I searched my memory for the name of the book.* □ *She has a vague memory of being carried on her father's shoulders along a beach.*
▷ ***phrase*** Something is done **in memory of** a dead person when it is done as a way of remembering them: *A monument was erected in the town square, in memory of the people who died in the fire.*

men /mɛn/ *noun*
Men is the plural form of **man**.

menace /'mɛnəs/ *noun*; *verb*
▷ ***noun***: **menaces**
1 You describe someone or something as a **menace** if they cause trouble or harm, or they are dangerous in some way: *Drugs of this kind are a menace to society.* **2** (*uncount*) **Menace** is the quality of threatening trouble, harm or violence: *I was unnerved by the menace in her voice.*
▷ ***verb***: **menaces, menacing, menaced:** *Our children's children will still be menaced by the threat of nuclear war.* □ *A gang of youths were menacing people on the bus.* — *adjective* **menacing:** *the menacing way he stared at us.*

mend /mɛnd/ *verb*: **mends, mending, mended**
You **mend** something broken or damaged when you fix or repair it, so that it works again or can be used again: *I must mend the garden gate this weekend.* □ *There's a hole in the roof that needs mending.*
▷ ***phrase*** (*informal*) You say that someone ill is **on the mend** when they are getting better.

menial /'mi:nɪəl/ *adjective*
Menial jobs require little skill or training and are boring to do: *scraping a living from the most menial tasks.*

meningitis /mɛnɪn'dʒaɪtɪs/ *noun* (*uncount*)
Meningitis is a serious disease of the brain that sometimes kills people.

menopause /'mɛnəpɔ:z/ *noun* (*singular*)
The **menopause** is the end of menstruation, or the time in a woman's life when this happens, usually around the age of 50: *She's going through the menopause.*

menstrual /'mɛnstrʊəl/ *adjective*
Menstrual means relating to menstruation.

menstruate /'mɛnstrʊeɪt/ *verb*: **menstruates, menstruating, menstruated**
A woman or girl **menstruates** when blood comes from her womb at the time of her monthly period.

menstruation /mɛnstrʊ'eɪʃən/ *noun* (*uncount*)
Menstruation is the process, occurring every month, in which blood comes from the womb of a girl or woman. [*same as* **period**]

mental /'mɛntəl/ *adjective*
1 Mental means relating to, or done using, the mind or the intelligence: *children with a mental handicap* □ *You were never much good at mental arithmetic.* **2 Mental** also refers to people with illnesses of the mind: *a mental hospital.* **3** (*informal*) **Mental** also means stupid or foolish: *Anyone who pays that price must be mental.* — *adverb* **mentally:** *Although she's now physically very weak, mentally she's still fairly sharp.* □ *He made demands on her mentally and emotionally.*

mentality /mɛn'talɪtɪ/ *noun*: **mentalities**
Your **mentality** consists of the attitudes and opinions that you tend to have: *Can you understand the mentality of someone who likes to watch animals fighting each other?*

mention /'mɛnʃən/ *verb*; *noun*
▻ ***verb***: **mentions, mentioning, mentioned**
You **mention** something when you write or, more usually, speak about it, perhaps only briefly or indirectly: *You mentioned your childhood; tell us more about it.* □ *In her book, she mentions that she didn't really have any close friends in Parliament.* □ *I forgot to mention to Claude that we were considering changing our plans.* □ *Did I mention that I've been offered a job in Hong Kong?*
▻ ***noun*** (*count or uncount*): **mentions**
A **mention** is an act of referring to something when speaking or writing: *The report makes no mention of the fact that the bank has withdrawn financial support.* □ *The review praises the actors and the costumes, but the director doesn't even get a mention.*
▻ ***phrases*** **1** People say **don't mention it** as a way of replying politely to someone who has just thanked them. **2** People often say **not to mention** before they add something else to what they have already said: *This relationship has stripped me of everything; my money, my home and my friends, not to mention my chances of ever working again.*

mentor /'mɛntɔ:(r)/ *noun* (*formal*): **mentors**
A person's **mentor** is someone who gives them advice or guidance: *The most indispensable member of our party was Dorothy, who acted as our guide and mentor.*

menu /'mɛnju:/ *noun*: **menus**
A **menu** is a list of the different foods available in a restaurant; a restaurant's range of foods is also referred to as a **menu**: *Could we see the menu, please?* □ *The Oyster Bar actually has a very varied menu.*

mercenary /'mɜ:sənərɪ/ *adjective*; *noun*
▻ ***adjective*** (*derogatory*)
You describe someone as **mercenary** if they seem only to be interested in money, and in ways of getting more money: *I'm afraid my motives were purely mercenary.*
▻ ***noun***: **mercenaries**
A **mercenary** is a soldier who fights for any country or group that is willing to pay him.

merchandise /'mɜ:tʃəndaɪz/ *noun* (*uncount*)
Merchandise is goods that are bought and sold: *We are only interested in top-quality merchandise.*

merchant /'mɜ:tʃənt/ *noun*; *adjective*
▻ ***noun***: **merchants**
A **merchant** is someone who buys and sells goods in large quantities: *a firm of timber merchants.*
▻ ***adjective***
Merchant ships are used for trade, not for war: *the merchant navy.*

merchant bank /mɜ:tʃənt 'baŋk/ *noun*: **merchant banks**
A **merchant bank** is a bank whose main activity is lending money to industry.

merciful /'mɜ:sɪfəl/ *adjective*
1 Someone who is **merciful** is willing to forgive, or tends not to want to give out severe punishment: *Let's hope the judge will be merciful.* **2** You describe something that eases or relieves pain, trouble or difficulty as **merciful**: *There are certainly some patients for whom death comes as a merciful release.*

mercifully /'mɜ:sɪflɪ/ *sentence adverb*
Mercifully shows that you are glad or grateful for something: *We arrived at the station late but, mercifully, the train had been delayed.*

merciless /'mɜ:sɪləs/ *adjective*
A **merciless** person cruelly refuses to forgive others or show them kindness: *We are merciless in our pursuit of criminals.*

mercury /'mɜ:kjʊrɪ/ *noun* (*uncount*)
Mercury is a silvery-white metal commonly used in liquid form, *eg* in thermometers.

mercy /'mɜ:sɪ/ *noun*: **mercies**
1 (*uncount*) Someone who shows **mercy** is kind and willing to forgive in situations where punishment is possible or justified. **2** You refer to something as a **mercy** when you are lucky or fortunate that it exists or has happened: *It was a mercy that we were able to afford it at the time.* [compare **blessing, godsend**]
▻ ***phrase*** When you are **at the mercy of** someone, they have complete control over you and can treat you as badly or unfairly as they wish.

mere /mɪə(r)/ *adjective* (*used only before a noun*): **merest**

> **Merest** is used for emphasis rather than as a superlative.

1 You use **mere** to emphasize the unimportance of something: *Nowadays the sovereign is a mere figurehead; the real power is vested in parliament and the prime minister.* □ *The job was already hers, and the interview was the merest formality.* **2** You use **mere** before a quantity to emphasize how small it is: *All those improvements we made have added a mere £2000 to the value of the house.* **3 Mere** is also used to emphasize that, although something is apparently slight or unimportant, it creates a very strong impression or effect: *The mere sight of a sausage made him feel ill.* □ *She would become distressed at the merest mention of divorce or separation.*

merely /ˈmɪəlɪ/ *adverb*
1 Something that is **merely** a certain thing is simply and only that thing, and not anything more important or significant: *We don't have to do it; it was merely an idea.* □ *I'm merely one of the editors.* □ *I suggested a walk, merely for something to do.* □ *I was merely trying to be helpful.* □ *It isn't merely because he's rich that I'm marrying him.* **2** 'Not **merely**' emphasizes the unimportance of a certain circumstance in comparison with another: *He isn't merely a bad speller; he's downright illiterate.* **3 Merely** emphasizes how small an amount is: *The insurance will cost you merely £12.* □ *Its maximum penalty is merely two years' imprisonment.*
[*same as* **only**, **just**]

merge /mɜːdʒ/ *verb*: **merges, merging, merged**
Two or more things **merge** when they combine with each other or they become mixed together: *Regional and district councils will be merged to form single authorities.* □ *We are merging with a Canadian publishing company.* □ *bands of colour that were so similar that they seemed to merge into each other* □ *The zebra's stripes help it to merge into its natural landscape of tall grass and bushes.*

merger /ˈmɜːdʒə(r)/ *noun*: **mergers**
A **merger** occurs when two or more business companies join to form a single large company.

meringue /məˈraŋ/ *noun*: **meringues**
A **meringue** is a kind of sweet cake made from a flavoured mixture of sugar and egg whites: *Sarah's baked a lemon meringue pie.*

merit /ˈmɛrɪt/ *noun*; *verb*
▻ ***noun***: **merits**
1 (*uncount*; *formal*) Something has **merit** when it has some value or importance: *Marks are awarded for the skater's technical skill and for artistic merit.* **2** The **merits** of something are the reasons why it is good or desirable: *The merits of the scheme far outweigh its disadvantages.*
▻ ***verb*** (*formal*): **merits, meriting, merited**
To **merit** something is to deserve it: *Some of her earlier poems merit a critical reassessment.* □ *The film didn't attract enough attention to merit showing it for another week.*
▻ ***phrase*** You judge something **on its merits** when you form an opinion of it by considering or examining it in an objective way, without being influenced by your personal feelings: *Each candidate is considered on his or her own merits.*

mermaid /ˈmɜːmeɪd/ *noun*: **mermaids**
In stories and legends, a **mermaid** is a sea creature with a woman's head and upper body, and a fish's tail.

merrily /ˈmɛrɪlɪ/ *adverb*
1 Merrily means in a merry way: *The children laughed merrily.* **2** When you **merrily** do something, you do it without thinking properly about it, especially about difficulties that may occur: *They travelled on for weeks, merrily spending more and more money.*

merriment /ˈmɛrɪmənt/ *noun* (*uncount*)
Merriment is lively and cheerful behaviour, especially laughter.

merry /ˈmɛrɪ/ *adjective*: **merrier, merriest**
1 People are **merry** when they are lively and cheerful; something that is **merry** makes you feel lively and cheerful: *We joined up with a merry crowd of carol-singers in the street.* □ *a merry song.* **2** (*informal*) **Merry** also means slightly drunk: *After the second sherry, I began to feel quite merry.*

Merry Christmas /mɛrɪ ˈkrɪsməs/ *interjection*
People say **Merry Christmas** as a way of greeting each other at Christmas.

merry-go-round /ˈmɛrɪgoʊraʊnd/ *noun*: **merry-go-rounds**
At fairgrounds, a **merry-go-round** is an amusement consisting of a revolving platform fitted with rising and falling seats in the form of horses or other figures. [see also **carousel**]

mesh /mɛʃ/ *noun* (*uncount*)
Mesh is any substance, *eg* wire or thread, in the form of a net: *We made a fence out of wooden posts and wire mesh.*

mesmerize or **mesmerise** /ˈmɛzməraɪz/ *verb*: **mesmerizes, mesmerizing, mesmerized**
You **are mesmerized** by something when it is so impressive or attractive that it holds all your attention: *Audiences all over the country have been mesmerized by their performance.* [*same as* **fascinate**]

mess /mɛs/ *noun*; *verb*
▻ ***noun*** (*uncount or used in the singular*)
1 A **mess** is an untidy or dirty state of things: *The children are in the kitchen making a mess.* □ *I spilt a tray of coffee all over the floor, and it took ages to clean up the mess.* □ *How much mess was there after the party?* □ *Ryan's bedroom is always in such a mess.* □ *Her face was in a bit of a mess after the accident.* □ *The forceps made a mess of the baby's head.* **2** You can refer to a place as a **mess** when it it is dirty and untidy: *The whole house is a mess.* **3** You describe a situation as a **mess** if it involves a lot of problems: *Our finances got into a bit of a mess, and the only way out of it was to borrow more money.* **4** In the armed forces, a dining room is called a **mess**: *the officers' mess.*
▻ ***phrase*** You **make a mess of** something you are doing when you do it badly: *I made a mess of that last exam.* [*same as* **botch**]
▻ ***verb***: **messes, messing, messed**

phrasal verbs
mess about or **mess around** (*informal*) **1** You **mess about** or **around** when you spend time doing silly or foolish things: *The teacher told them off for messing about in the toilets.* **2** When you **mess** someone **about** or**mess** them **around** you treat them badly or unfairly: *I wish they'd stop messing me about and make their minds up what job they want me to do.*
mess up You **mess** something **up** when you make it untidy or dirty, or when you spoil or damage it: *Don't mess up my dress; I've just ironed it.* □ *This has really messed up our plans.*
mess with (*informal*) You **mess with** someone when you involve yourself in an argument or conflict with them: *the kind of violent man that you know not to mess with.*

message /ˈmɛsɪdʒ/ *noun*: **messages**
1 A **message** is a spoken or written communication sent from one person to another: *We sent a message to our head office, warning them of his visit.* □ *He's not here at the moment; I'll leave a message for him to phone you when he gets back.* □ *If she's not there, give one of her colleagues this message.* **2** In something such as a book or a film, the **message** is the idea, theory or principle offered: *The play's message seems to be that life isn't always fair.* □ *Some of the best poetry contains no message at all, but simply records a personal experience.*
▻ ***phrase*** (*informal*) You **get the message** when you understand what someone has been suggesting or indirectly indicating: *If we don't reply to their letters they'll eventually get the message.*

messenger /ˈmɛsɪndʒə(r)/ *noun*: **messengers**
A **messenger** is a person who carries communications between people: *Hermes, the messenger of the gods.*

messy /ˈmɛsɪ/ *adjective*: **messier, messiest**
1 Messy activities make you or your surroundings dirty and untidy: *Painting with children can be quite messy.* **2** A **messy** person leaves an untidy mess wherever they go: *She was one of those messy cooks.* **3** A place that is **messy** is dirty or untidy: *This is my son's messy bedroom.* **4** A **messy** situation is a confused and unpleasant one: *Things got a bit messy when he started an affair with another woman.*

met /mɛt/ *verb*
Met is the past tense and past participle of **meet**.

metabolism /məˈtabəlɪzm/ *noun* (*used in the singular*)
Your **metabolism** is the system of chemical processes in your body that digest food and convert it into energy and waste matter: *Your metabolism needs a kick to start it in the morning, so always eat a healthy breakfast.*

metal /ˈmɛtəl/ *noun* (*often adjectival*): **metals**
Metals are substances such as iron and steel, usually hard and shiny: *Some of the parts are plastic and some are metal.* □ *a metal box.*

metallic /məˈtalɪk/ *adjective*
Metallic describes things that look or sound like metal: *paint with a metallic finish* □ *It was a harsh, almost metallic noise.*

metalwork /ˈmɛtəlwɜːk/ *noun* (*uncount*)
1 Metalwork is the craft or practice of making objects out of metal: *Metalwork was his favourite subject at school.* **2** Objects made out of metal are sometimes referred to as **metalwork**.

metamorphose /mɛtəˈmɔːfoʊz/ *verb* (*formal*)
Something **metamorphoses** when its form or nature changes completely and it becomes something else: *It was as if this dull, unintelligent boy had metamorphosed overnight into an artistic genius.*

metamorphosis /mɛtəˈmɔːfəsɪs/ *noun*: **metamorphoses** /mɛtəˈmɔːfəsiːz/
A **metamorphosis** is a complete change of form or nature, a change into something else: *I was startled by such a metamorphosis: the ugly, awkward young girl had blossomed into a beautiful woman.*

metaphor /ˈmɛtəfɔː(r)/ *noun*: **metaphors**
A **metaphor** is an expression in which you describe the qualities of a person, action or thing by referring to them as something else with similar qualities, *eg* when you refer to an angry, impatient and frustrated person as 'a caged tiger', or something difficult to find as 'a needle in a haystack'.

metaphorically /mɛtəˈfɒrɪkəlɪ/ *adverb*
You say something **metaphorically** when you use words not in their usual or real sense but only as an imaginative way of describing something: *I felt isolated in this empty, ice-covered wilderness: out in the cold, both literally and metaphorically.*

mete /miːt/ *verb* (*formal*): **metes, meting, meted**

> ***phrasal verb***
> To **mete out** punishment is to give it out: *Stricter sentences have been meted out to relatively minor criminals.*

meteor /ˈmiːtɪə(r)/ *noun*: **meteors**
A **meteor** is a huge mass of rock travelling through space, sometimes visible in the sky as a bright moving light.

meteoric /miːtɪˈɒrɪk/ *adjective*
Meteoric describes extremely rapid progress, especially to a position of success, power or fame: *the singer's meteoric rise to stardom.*

meteorite /ˈmiːtɪəraɪt/ *noun*: **meteorites**
A **meteorite** is a meteor that has fallen out of the sky onto the earth.

meteorological /miːtɪərəˈlɒdʒɪkəl/ *adjective*
Meteorological means relating to the weather or to weather forecasting: *recent meteorological surveys.*

meter /ˈmiːtə(r)/ *noun*: **meters**
A **meter** is an instrument for measuring and recording levels, quantities or amounts, *eg* the amount of electricity, gas or water used in a house: *The gas man came to read the meter.*

methane /ˈmiːθeɪn/ *noun* (*uncount*)
Methane is a gas that you can't see or smell, that occurs naturally in coal mines and marshes.

method /ˈmɛθəd/ *noun*: **methods**
1 A **method** is a way of doing something, especially an ordered set of actions or processes: *They use different teaching methods.* **2** (*uncount*) You refer to good planning or efficient organization as **method**: *Management of the factory was totally lacking in method.*

methodical /mɛˈθɒdɪkəl/ *adjective*
A **methodical** person tends to do things in an ordered, efficient way: *She's very methodical in the kitchen.* □ *We need a more methodical approach.* — *adverb* **methodically:** *I watched as he worked his way methodically through the tasks on the list.*

meths /mɛθs/ *noun* (*uncount*; *informal*)
Meths is methylated spirits.

methylated spirits /mɛθɪleɪtɪd ˈspɪrɪts/ *noun* (*uncount*)
Methylated spirits is a type of alcohol used as fuel in lamps and heaters.

meticulous /məˈtɪkjʊləs/ *adjective*
You are **meticulous** about something when you take great care to do it perfectly, paying attention to every detail: *Her work has always been meticulous.* □ *He's a meticulous dresser; trousers neatly pressed, shirt ironed to perfection, and tie smartly tied.*

metre (*AmE* **meter**) /ˈmiːtə(r)/ *noun*: **metres**
A **metre** is a unit of length equal to 100 centimetres or about 39 inches: *The room measured five metres by three and a half.*

metric /ˈmɛtrɪk/ *adjective*
The **metric** system of measurement has metres, grammes and litres as its basic units: *Do you mean the metric tonne or the imperial ton?*

metro /ˈmɛtroʊ/ *noun*: **metros**
In some cities, the underground railway system is called the **metro**.

metropolis /məˈtrɒpəlɪs/ *noun* (*formal*): **metropolises**
People sometimes refer to a large city, especially a country's capital city, as the **metropolis**.

metropolitan /mɛtrəˈpɒlɪtən/ *adjective*
Metropolitan means relating to, situated in, or typical of a large city: *the Metropolitan Police Force* □ *We miss the theatres, restaurants and other aspects of metropolitan life.*

mew /mjuː/ *verb*: **mews, mewing, mewed**
A cat **mews** when it miaows or makes its typical noise.

mews /mjuːz/ *noun* (*singular*)
A **mews** is a small yard or square surrounded by houses or flats, a word sometimes used in street-names.

miaow /mɪ'aʊ/ *verb; noun*
▻ ***verb***: **miaows, miaowing, miaowed**
A cat **miaows** when it makes its typical noise.
▻ ***noun***: **miaows:** *Through my sleep I could hear Jason's soft miaow outside the window.*

mice /maɪs/ *noun*
Mice is the plural form of **mouse**.

mickey /'mɪkɪ/ *noun*
▻ ***phrase*** Someone **takes the mickey** out of you when they mock you or make fun of you: *There's no need to take the mickey.*

micro- /'maɪkroʊ/ *prefix*
Micro- forms nouns that refer to a small version or type of something: *a microcomputer* □ *experts in microelectronics.*

microbe /'maɪkroʊb/ *noun*: **microbes**
Microbes are tiny organisms that exist everywhere but that you can only see by using a microscope.

microchip /'maɪkroʊtʃɪp/ *noun*: **microchips**
A **microchip** is a tiny component in computers and other electric appliances, with several tiny electrical circuits on it.

microcosm /'maɪkroʊkɒzm/ *noun*: **microcosms**
You describe something as a **microcosm** of something larger that it is a part of if it contains all the features of the larger thing, as if it were a smaller copy: *Student demonstrations in Paris were a microcosm of the frustration felt by young people all over the world.*

microphone /'maɪkrəfoʊn/ *noun*: **microphones**
A **microphone** is a device that gathers sounds, *eg* a singer's voice, so that they can be recorded, or made louder for playing to an audience.

microscope /'maɪkrəskoʊp/ *noun*: **microscopes**
A **microscope** is an instrument with a system of lenses for looking at and examining things so tiny that you can't ordinarily see them: *These new plant cells were studied under the microscope.*

microscopic /maɪkrə'skɒpɪk/ *adjective*
Microscopic things are extremely small: *The average bed is full of microscopic creatures of all sorts.* □ *The problem was caused by a microscopic crack in the glass.*

microwave /'maɪkrəweɪv/ *noun; verb*
▻ ***noun***: **microwaves**
A **microwave oven**, or **microwave**, is an oven that cooks food very quickly using invisible electrical and magnetic waves, rather than ordinary heat: *Just pop it into the microwave for a couple of minutes.* [see picture at **kitchen**]
▻ ***verb***: **microwaves, microwaving, microwaved**
You **microwave** food when you cook it in a microwave oven.

mid- /mɪd/ *prefix*
Mid- forms nouns and adjectives that refer to the middle of something: *His birthday is some time in mid-March.* □ *She interrupted me in mid sentence.* □ *a beautiful midsummer morning.*

mid-air /mɪd'ɛə(r)/ *noun (uncount)*
In **mid-air** means in the air, as opposed to on the ground: *She jumped to catch the ball in mid-air.*

midday /mɪd'deɪ/ *noun (uncount, often adjectival)*
Midday is noon, twelve o'clock in the middle of the day: *It must have been around midday before we set off.* □ *a light midday snack.*

middle /'mɪdəl/ *noun; adjective*
▻ ***noun*** *(usually in the singular)*: **middles**
1 The **middle** of something is the point, position, part or area furthest from the sides or edges: *She put the vase of flowers down in the middle of the table.* □ *The ball struck her in the middle of her forehead.* □ *The motorway will go right through the middle of her farmland.* □ *It was a narrow country road without a white line down the middle.* □ *When the bed starts sagging you tend to roll towards the middle.* □ *You sit in the middle and then we can both talk to you.* [*same as* **centre**] **2** The **middle** of a period of time is the point halfway through it: *She expects to be home about the middle of September.* **3** Something that happens in the **middle** of an event happens during it: *I was born in the middle of a thunderstorm.* □ *He collapsed right in the middle of the ceremony.* **4** (*informal*) Your **middle** is your waist: *She was wearing her sweater tied round her middle.* □ *I thought he was getting a bit fat round the middle.*
▻ ***adjective***
1 Middle describes a thing positioned between two others, or at the halfway point in a row or series, or happening after the beginning and before the end of a period of time: *Your middle finger is your longest one.* □ *I'll be on holiday for the middle two weeks of August.* **2 Middle** also means intermediate, as distinct from junior and senior: *He'll be starting at the middle school in September.* □ *middle management.* **3** A **middle** way or course is moderate one, as distinct from an extreme one: *You're either for us or against us; there's no middle way.*
▻ ***phrases*** You **are in the middle of** something, or of doing it, when you are busy with it: *Could I phone you back? We're in the middle of dinner.* □ *I was just in the middle of writing her a letter when she rang.*

middle-aged /mɪdəl'eɪdʒd/ *adjective*
A **middle-aged** person is between the ages of about 40 and 60: *We were addressed by a woman: middle-aged, tall and very attractive.*

Middle Ages /mɪdəl 'eɪdʒɪz/ *noun (plural)*
The **Middle Ages** refers to the period of history, especially European history, roughly between the years 1100 and 1450: *living conditions in the Middle Ages.*

middle class /mɪdəl 'klɑːs/ *noun (often adjectival)*: **middle classes**
The **middle class** refers to the social class of people between the working class and the upper class, including educated people with professional careers; people of this kind are often referred to as the **middle classes**: *It has been criticized as 'art for the middle classes'.* □ *She had a very middle-class upbringing.*

Middle East /mɪdəl 'iːst/ *noun (used in the singular)*
The **Middle East** consists of all the countries between, but not including, Tunisia and Pakistan: *political turmoil in the Middle East.* — *adjective* **Middle-Eastern:** *some of the richer Middle-Eastern countries.*

middle name /mɪdəl 'neɪm/ *noun*: **middle names**
A person's **middle name** is the name that comes between their first name and their family name: *Her middle name is Elizabeth.*

middle-of-the-road /mɪdələvðə'roʊd/ *adjective*
You describe something as **middle-of-the-road** if it is moderate, not extreme, especially if it is likely to appeal to people with the kind of traditional tastes or opinions that you think are a little boring: *This is easy-listening, middle-of-the-road music.*

middle school /'mɪdəl skuːl/ *noun*: **middle schools**
A **middle school** is a school for children between the ages of 8 or 9 and 12 or 13.

midge /mɪdʒ/ *noun*: **midges**
Midges are any tiny flying insects that bite people.

midget /'mɪdʒɪt/ *noun*: **midgets**
A **midget** is an unusually small person.

midnight /ˈmɪdnaɪt/ *noun* (*uncount, often adjectival*)
Midnight is twelve o'clock at night: *We arrived in Kerry just after midnight.* ▫ *We used to sneak down to the kitchen for midnight feasts.*

midriff /ˈmɪdrɪf/ *noun*: **midriffs**
Your **midriff** is the part of your body between your chest and your waist.

midst /mɪdst/
▻ ***phrases*** **1** You are **in the midst of** several people or things when you are surrounded by them: *The baby was sitting on the floor in the midst of a huge pile of washing.* [*same as* **amidst**] **2** You are **in the midst of** doing something when you are busy with it: *I was in the midst of getting the children to bed when the telephone rang.* [*same as* **in the middle of**] **3** You refer to someone as being **in your midst** when they are among the people who are present in the same room as you: *Ladies and gentlemen, we have a truly great writer in our midst this evening.*

midstream /ˈmɪdstriːm/
▻ ***phrase*** Someone interrupts you **in midstream** when they interrupt you while you are speaking or doing something and haven't nearly finished.

midsummer /mɪdˈsʌmə(r)/ *noun* (*uncount, often adjectival*)
Midsummer is the period of time in the middle of summer: *another beautiful midsummer day.*

midway /mɪdˈweɪ/ *adverb*
Midway means at a middle point between two places, or in the middle of a period of time: *The village is midway between Boulogne and Le Touquet.* ▫ *He became ill midway through the holiday.*

midweek /mɪdˈwiːk/ *adjective or adverb*
Something happens **midweek** when it happens in the middle of the week, on or around Wednesday: *We like to do the shopping midweek.* ▫ *The midweek match has been cancelled.*

midwife /ˈmɪdwaɪf/ *noun*: **midwives**
A **midwife** is a nurse who gives care and advice to pregnant women and helps during the birth of their baby.

might[1] /maɪt/ *modal verb*
(*negative forms* **might not** or **mightn't**)
1 You use **might a** as the past tense of **may** in reported speech referring to the asking and granting of permission: *I asked if I might leave early.* ▫ *I told him he might borrow the car.* **b** (*more formal than* **may**, **can** *or* **could**) to ask permission politely, or make a polite request or offer, or express your intention or opinion indirectly: *I wonder if I might open the window?* ▫ *Might I see you for a few minutes?* ▫ *Might I give you some advice?* ▫ *If I might mention the fact, this is your responsibility.* ▫ *It's an unrealistic and, might I add, irresponsible scheme.*
2 You use **might a** as the past tense of **may** to express possibility in reported speech: *She told me she might be late.* ▫ *I realized I mightn't ever see him again.* **b** to express possibility in the present and the future, with less certainty than is indicated by **may**: *It might rain, mightn't it?* ▫ *I might join you later if I'm feeling better.* ▫ *They might win a medal this year.* ▫ *I might not get to work tomorrow if the rail strike continues.* **c** to express possibility of an unreal kind: *If he offered I might accept.* ▫ *What chilly weather! It might be the depths of winter* [though of course it isn't]. **d** to suggest what someone could do: *You might enquire at the bus station.* **e** to complain that someone is not doing something: *You might help me carry this luggage.*
3 You use '**might** have' with a past participle **a** to express an unreal possibility in the past, where something that could have happened did not actually happen: *If you'd asked more politely, I might have been more willing to help.* ▫ *We might not have had all this trouble if she'd given us some warning.*

Some people use '**may** have' instead of '**might** have' to express unreal possibility in the past, but '**might** have' is better English: *If you had warned us in time you might have* (not *may have*) *saved us all this trouble.*

b to complain that someone did not do something that they should have done: *You might have asked me before borrowing money from my purse.* ▫ *You might have confided in us; we're here to help.* ▫ *They might have apologized!* **c** like '**may** have', to express the possibility that something has happened, or that it will have happened by some future time: *'They're very late.' 'Yes, they might have lost their way; they didn't have a map.'* ▫ *He might have changed his mind by this time next week.* ▫ *'Did you leave the dog's lead in the car?' 'I might have done; I don't remember.'* **d** in expressions such as 'I **might** have known' or 'I **might** have guessed' to comment that what has happened is typical, or was to be expected: *I might have guessed he'd get drunk.* ▫ *I might have realized she'd do something stupid.*
▻ ***phrases*** **1 a** You say you **might as well** do something if there is no point in not doing it: *I might as well give you the money now, seeing you'll be needing it so soon.* **b** If you say that something **might as well** be so you are complaining that it would make no difference if were so: *He never notices my hairstyle anyway; I might as well be bald.* ▫ *Did you hear me? Honestly, I might as well talk to the moon.* **2** You use **might well** in various ways: *I might well have said that* [= it's very possible I did]. ▫ *She might well be on her way already* [= it's very possible she is]. ▫ *You might well be surprised* [= your surprise is quite justified]. ▫ *He might well have refused* [= it's surprising that he didn't].
[see also **may**, **could**]

might[2] /maɪt/ *noun* (*uncount literary*)
Might is power or strength: *I pulled with all my might, but the door didn't move an inch.* ▫ *a company as large as theirs, with all that industrial might.*

mighty /ˈmaɪtɪ/ *adjective*; *adverb*
▻ ***adjective***: **mightier**, **mightiest**
Mighty describes something very large and powerful: *In the 18th century, it was the world's mightiest army.* ▫ *Experienced sailors know that there is no mightier force than the ocean.* — *adverb* **mightily:** *I was mightily* [= extremely] *relieved.* ▫ *I had to get him to drive me to work, which he did, complaining mightily* [= furiously] *all the way.*
▻ ***adverb*** (*intensifying*; *AmE*; *informal*)
Mighty means very: *She's a mighty pretty young woman.*

migraine /ˈmiːgreɪn/ *noun* (*count or uncount*)
A **migraine** is an extremely severe headache, often with feelings of sickness: *She's recovering from a migraine.* ▫ *Migraine makes you feel a lot worse than just off-colour.*

migrant /ˈmaɪgrənt/ *noun* (*often adjectival*): **migrants**
A **migrant** is a person who moves from place to place, especially looking for work: *These figures don't take account of migrant workers.*

migrate /maɪ'greɪt/ *verb*: **migrates, migrating, migrated**
1 Animals, especially birds, **migrate** when they travel from one country or region to another at certain times of the year: *The geese migrate south in winter.* **2** People who **migrate** move from place to place, especially looking for work. — *noun* (*uncount*) **migration** /maɪ'greɪʃən/: *the mass migration from rural communities to the cities.*

mike /maɪk/ *noun* (*informal*): **mikes**
A **mike** is a microphone.

mild /maɪld/ *adjective*: **milder, mildest**
1 Mild tastes or flavours are not sharp or strong: *I prefer a milder cheese.* **2 Mild** describes things, such as pain or punishment, that are not severe or great: *a relatively mild form of the disease.* **3 Mild** also describes things that don't have a strong or powerful effect: *The milder soap powder is handy for delicate woollen garments.* **4 Mild** weather is fairly warm, especially warmer than expected. **5** You describe someone who is quiet and gentle as having a **mild** personality: *She has inherited my husband's milder nature, I'm glad to say.*
▻ ***noun*** (uncount) *There was a pleasant mildness about the weather.*

mildew /'mɪldjuː/ *noun* (*uncount*)
Mildew is a disease of plants, which causes a harmful white spongy substance to grow on them.

mildly /'maɪldlɪ/ *adverb*
1 Mildly means in a mild or calm manner: *'I believe you'll find you're wrong,' she said mildly.* **2** You use **mildly** to mean 'slightly': *You may feel mildly ill the day after the injection, but it should pass off quickly.*
▻ ***phrase*** You use '**to put it mildly**' to indicate that you are not expressing yourself as strongly as you could do in the circumstances: *Well, it's a nuisance, to put it mildly.*

mile /maɪl/ *noun*: **miles**
1 A **mile** is a unit of distance equal to 1760 yards or 1.6 kilometres: *It's at least ten miles to the next village.* **2** (*informal*) A great distance is often referred to as a **mile** or **miles**: *We walked for miles without seeing another soul.* □ *The arrow missed the target by a mile.*
▻ ***phrase*** (*informal*) You say that someone **is miles away** when they are thinking so deeply about something else that they are not aware of what is happening around them or what someone is saying to them.

mileage /'maɪlɪdʒ/ *noun* (*uncount*)
1 Mileage is the number of miles you have travelled: *It's not a very old car, but the mileage is quite high.* **2 Mileage** is also the number of miles a vehicle will travel on a fixed amount of fuel: *We get better mileage with the Renault.* **3** (*informal*) You refer to how often you can make use of something for your own benefit or advantage as **mileage**: *'Were you angry that he forgot your birthday?' 'Not when I realize how much mileage I can get out of how guilty he feels.'*

milestone /'maɪlstoun/ *noun*: **milestones**
You refer to a very important event or change in the development of something as a **milestone**: *Having a baby is perhaps the first significant milestone in any relationship.* [*same as* **landmark**]

milieu /'miːljɜː/ *noun* (*literary*): **milieus** or **milieux**
You refer to your surroundings, especially the kind of people you typically spend your time with and the kind of places you typically go to, as your **milieu**: *She felt more comfortable in this artistic milieu.* [*same as* **environment, ambience**]

militant /'mɪlɪtənt/ *adjective*
Militant describes someone who takes positive, often aggressive action to achieve political or social change: *the more militant wing of the Party.* — *noun* (*uncount*) **militancy:** *They have been criticized for their militancy.*

military /'mɪlɪtərɪ/ *adjective*; *noun*
▻ ***adjective***
Military means relating to a country's armed forces: *The President has not ruled out the possibility of military action.* □ *a senior military commander.* — *adverb* **militarily:** *They are much weaker militarily.*
▻ ***noun*** (*singular, with a plural verb*)
Armed forces, especially the most senior officers, are sometimes referred to as the **military**: *The military have not been consulted at this stage.*

militate /'mɪlɪteɪt/ *verb* (*formal*): **militates, militating, militated**
A fact, event or situation **militates** against something when it is a disadvantage or drawback: *There's no reason why her age should militate against her finding another job.*

militia /mɪ'lɪʃə/ *noun* (*count or uncount*): **militias**
A **militia** is any fighting force made up of ordinary members of the public, not professional soldiers: *The hilltops were occupied by Serb militia.*

milk /mɪlk/ *noun*; *verb*
▻ ***noun*** (*uncount*)
1 Milk is a white liquid produced by cows and some other female animals as food for their young, that people also drink and use to make butter and cheese: *cartons of milk on supermarket shelves* □ *a glass of milk* □ *She prefers goats' milk.* **2 Milk** is also **a** the liquid that women produce in their breasts, for feeding their babies with. **b** the whitish liquid inside a coconut.
▻ ***verb***: **milks, milking, milked**
1 To **milk** a cow or other female animal is to take milk from it. **2** (*informal*) You **milk** someone or something when you obtain money, information or other benefit from them, cleverly or cruelly: *glamorous young women milking their rich, foolish old husbands* □ *They tried to milk the situation as much as possible, of course.*

milkman /'mɪlkmən/ *noun*: **milkmen**
A **milkman** is a man who delivers milk to people's houses.

milkshake /'mɪlkʃeɪk/ *noun*: **milkshakes**
A **milkshake** is a drink consisting of a flavoured mixture of milk and ice cream.

milky /'mɪlkɪ/ *adjective*: **milkier, milkiest**
1 Something that is **milky** is a pale, whitish colour: *her soft, milky skin.* **2** A **milky** drink contains a lot of milk: *milky coffee.*

mill /mɪl/ *noun*; *verb*
▻ ***noun***: **mills**
1 A **mill** is a building where grain is turned into flour. [see also **windmill**] **2** A device for grinding salt or pepper is also a **mill**: *a pepper mill.* **3** Factories that produce goods of certain kinds, especially wool or steel, are sometimes referred to as **mills**: *after they closed down the woollen mills.*
▻ ***verb***: **mills, milling, milled**

phrasal verb
(*informal*) You say that a crowd of people **are milling about** or **around** when they are moving idly about, especially when they are waiting for something to happen.

millennium /mɪ'lɛnɪəm/ *noun*: **millenia** or **milleniums**
A **millenium** is a period of a thousand years: *looking back at political history as we approach the next millenium.*

milli- /ˈmɪlɪ/ *prefix*
Milli- forms nouns that refer to a thousandth part of something: *a millisecond* □ *50 millilitres.*

milligram or **milligramme** /ˈmɪlɪgram/ *noun*: **milligrams**
A **milligram** is a unit of weight equal to one thousandth of a gram.

millimetre (*AmE* **millimeter**) /ˈmɪlɪmiːtə(r)/ *noun*: **millimetres**
A **millimetre** is a unit of length equal to one thousandth of a metre: *Each cabinet is 600 millimetres wide.*

million /ˈmɪlɪən/ *noun*; *determiner*; *pronoun*
▻ ***noun***: **million** or **millions**
A **million** or one **million** is the number or quantity 1 000 000: *A thousand thousands are a million.*
▻ ***determiner:*** *spacecraft that will travel over a million miles.*
▻ ***pronoun:*** *Of the city's 8 million citizens, over a million are unemployed.* □ (*informal*) *Millions of people told us they liked the band.*
▻ ***phrase*** You say that someone or something you like or admire very much is **one in a million** if you think there are very few others as good as them: *'You've got a good wife there, Alan.' 'I know; she's one in a million.'*

millionaire /mɪljəˈnɛə(r)/ *noun*: **millionaires**
A **millionaire** is a person whose wealth amounts to a million pounds or dollars, or usually more.

millionth /ˈmɪlɪənθ/ *determiner*; *noun*
▻ ***determiner***
The **millionth** person or thing is the one numbered 1 000 000 in a series: *The millionth customer came through the supermarket doors today.*
▻ ***noun***: **millionths**
A **millionth** of something is one of a million equal parts of it: *sophisticated devices capable of measuring a thousandth of a millimetre, which is one millionth of a metre.*

millstone /ˈmɪlstoʊn/ *noun*: **millstones**
You describe an unpleasant duty or responsibility that prevents you from doing what you would like as a **millstone**, or a **millstone** round your neck: *For too long, old people have been regarded as the millstone around the neck of society.*

mime /maɪm/ *noun*; *verb*
▻ ***noun*** (*uncount or count*)
Mime is acting using movements and gestures alone, without words: *a mime artist* □ *He did an imaginative mime of a man replacing a burst tyre.*
▻ ***verb***: **mimes, miming, mimed**
1 You **mime** an action or activity when you perform the movements or gestures involved in doing it, rather than describing it in words. **2** A singer **mimes** when they move their mouth, without singing, to match a recording of a song played at the same time, giving the impression that they are singing.

mimic /ˈmɪmɪk/ *verb*; *noun*
▻ ***verb***: **mimics, mimicking, mimicked**
You **mimic** someone when you speak or act like them as a way of amusing or entertaining people.
▻ ***noun***: **mimics**
A **mimic** is someone skilled in mimicking others. — *noun* (*uncount*) **mimicry** /ˈmɪmɪkrɪ/: *my daughter's talent for mimicry.*

mince /mɪns/ *noun*; *verb*
▻ ***noun*** (*uncount*)
Mince is meat, usually beef, that has been cut into very small pieces: *half a pound of steak mince.*
▻ ***verb***: **minces, mincing, minced**
1 To **mince** meat is to shred it finely. **2** People **mince** when they walk or speak in an exaggeratedly delicate way: *Albert minced across the room with his hand to his forehead.* — *adjective* **mincing:** *His mincing little voice really irritates me.*
▻ ***phrase*** Someone who **does not mince their words** speaks plainly and openly, even though what they say may offend or embarrass others: *Let's not mince words; I don't like you and you don't like me.*

mincemeat /ˈmɪnsmiːt/ *noun* (*uncount*)
Mincemeat is a spiced mixture of dried fruits, used as a filling for pies.
▻ ***phrase*** (*informal*) To **make mincemeat of** someone is to defeat them thoroughly: *If they don't tighten up their defence, the first-division team will make mincemeat of them.*

mind /maɪnd/ *noun*; *verb*
▻ ***noun***: **minds**
Your **mind** is your brain, or your capacity to think, understand, reason and remember, often thought of as a place where ideas, memories and feelings exist: *She may be old and frail but her mind is as sharp as ever.* □ *You need a special kind of mind to be a crossword-setter.* □ *She has a most logical mind.* □ *Their minds are filled with desperate thoughts.* [*same as* **brain, head**]
▻ ***verb***: **minds, minding, minded**
1 You **mind** something if it upsets or annoys you; you ask people if they would **mind** doing something, or if they **mind** you doing something, as a way of making requests or asking permission: *He never seems to mind the heat.* □ *I don't mind working late occasionally.* □ *She won't mind what you wear, as long as you come.* □ *Would you mind moving along slightly?* [= please would you move along?] □ *Do you mind if I smoke?* □ *I've brought my sister along; I hope you don't mind.* □ *You've got a dirty mark on your cheek, if you don't mind my* (or *me*) *mentioning it.* **2** You tell someone to **mind** something as a warning to be careful of it or about it: *I'm always telling the children to mind the traffic.* □ *You really ought to mind your language in front of the children.* □ *Mind the step.* □ *Mind your jacket; there's wet paint here.* □ *Mind where you leave your bag; anyone could steal it.* **3** You say '**Mind** you do something' to someone to remind them to do it: *Mind you switch the fire off when you go out.* □ *Mind you remember to listen to that concert on Radio 3.* **4** You **mind** someone or something when you look after them: *A neighbour is minding the children for the afternoon.* □ *Could you mind the shop for me while I make a phone call?*
▻ ***phrases*** **1** A thought or feeling that is **at the back of your mind** is a vague but persistent one: *I had an idea at the back of my mind that there was something I promised to do this evening.* **2** You **bear** or **keep** something **in mind** when you take it into consideration: *Bear in mind that they're only children.* □ *You should keep that in mind when you apply for another job.* **3** You **cast your mind back** to a certain period or event when you remember or recall it. **4** You **change your mind** when you alter your opinion, or change a decision or choice you have made: *I've changed my mind again; I want the blue one.* **5** An idea or memory **comes** or **springs to mind** when you think of it, or it occurs to you: *Note down any good examples that spring to mind.* **6** A thought or idea **crosses your mind** when it occurs to you: *It crossed my mind that he might be at the pub.* **7** (*offensive*) You say '**Do you mind?**' to someone to express annoyance at what they are doing: *Do you mind? That's my jacket you're sitting on.* **8** You say '**I don't mind**' to express a lack of preference when some-

one offers you a choice: *'Tea or coffee?' 'Either; I don't mind.'* **9** You say you **have a mind to** do something if you have a vague intention of doing it, or if you feel like doing it: *I had a mind to visit the costume museum while I was there.* □ *I've a good mind to refuse, since you ask so rudely.* □ *You could easily finish your thesis if you had half a mind to.*
10 Something that you **have in mind** is something that you want, or that you intend to have or do: *Have you got any particular design in mind?* □ *'Shouldn't we have a special celebration for his 70th birthday?' 'What sort of thing did you have in mind?'*
11 You see something **in your mind's eye** when you have a mental picture of it. **12** People are **in their right mind** when they are quite sane and rational. **13** You say you are **in two minds** about something when you cannot decide whether or not you want it or want to do it: *I think she's in two minds whether to accept or not.* **14** You **make up your mind** when you make a decision or form a definite opinion: *I can't make up my mind whether or not I like him.* **15** Your **mind** is **on** something when you are thinking about it or concentrating on it: *I fear my mind is not on the job this morning.* □ *Her mind was evidently on higher things.* **16** People say **'mind you'** as a way of emphasizing a point, or adding a contrasting one: *Mind you, I never thought it was a very practical scheme.* □ *He's a nice lad; not academically bright, mind you, but always helpful and cheerful.* **17** You say **never mind** to someone **a** to cheer them up or comfort them: *Never mind; you did your best.* **b** to reassure them when they are apologizing: *Never mind; it was a very cheap plate.* **c** to tell them not to do something, either because it is unnecessary, or because you intend to do it yourself: *Never mind about the plants now; I'll water them later.*
18 Something is **on your mind** if you are anxious about it: *I can't think about that now; I've got too much else on my mind.* **19** You keep **an open mind** about something if you are willing to consider new ideas about it and change your own; you have **a closed mind** if you refuse to consider any new ideas once you have formed your own opinion. **20** You **put your mind to** doing something when you start thinking about how to do it: *It's high time we put our minds to planning the wedding.* **21** Something **slips your mind** when you forget to do it, or forget to deal with it: *I'm sorry I forgot to tell him; it completely slipped my mind.*
22 You **speak your mind** when you state your opinion frankly. **23** Your **state of mind** is your mental and emotional state at any particular time: *He was in no state of mind to discuss things rationally.*
24 Something that **takes your mind off** your problems makes you for-get them temporarily and relax.
25 Something is so **to your mind** if that is your opinion or judgement: *To my mind George's is the more sensible plan.* **26** When you are relieved about something, and no longer have to worry about it, you can say it is **a weight** or **a load off your mind**. **27** If you say you **wouldn't mind** something you mean you would very much like it: *I wouldn't mind a free Mediterranean cruise myself.*

> ***phrasal verb***
> **mind out** You say **'mind out!'** to someone to tell them to be careful: *Mind out! There's a car coming!'*

mindful /'maɪndfʊl/ *adjective* (*formal*)
You are **mindful** of something when you think about it or consider it when doing something else: *As teachers, we should be more mindful of the needs of our pupils.*

mindless /'maɪndləs/ *adjective*
1 Mindless actions are pointless destructive ones: *the mindless destruction of public buildings.* **2** You can also describe a very boring and repetitive job or task as **mindless**.

mine[1] /maɪn/ *pronoun* (*possessive*)
Mine is used by the person speaking or writing to refer to something that belongs to or relates to himself or herself: *'Whose is this newspaper?' 'It's mine, but you can read it.'* □ *His hair's longer than mine.* □ *Your desk looks different from mine.* □ *I happened to be talking about it to a colleague of mine.* [= one of my colleagues] □ *She's not a particular friend of mine.* □ *His hand touched mine.* □ *Her eyes are blue and mine are green.*

mine[2] /maɪn/ *noun; verb*
▷ ***noun*: mines**
1 A **mine** is a place where things such as coal, metals or precious stones are dug up out of the ground: *the gold mines of South Africa.* **2** A **mine** is also a bomb that explodes when touched, either floating in water or laid just beneath the surface of the ground.
▷ ***verb*: mines, mining, mined:** *Tin has been mined in this county for over two hundred years.*

minefield /'maɪnfiːld/ *noun*: **minefields**
1 A **minefield** is an area of land or water in which explosive mines have been laid. **2** You describe a situation involving many difficult, perhaps hidden, problems or dangers as a **minefield**: *The process of buying a house can be an absolute minefield if you don't get good advice.*

miner /'maɪnə(r)/ *noun*: **miners**
A **miner** is a person who works in a mine, especially a coal mine.

mineral /'mɪnərəl/ *noun*: **minerals**
Minerals are solid substances found naturally in rocks and soil, such as salt or coal: *an area rich in mineral deposits.*

mineral water /'mɪnərəl wɔːtə(r)/ *noun* (*uncount*)
Mineral water is water taken from underground, often sold in bottles as a healthy drink.

mingle /'mɪŋgəl/ *verb*: **mingles, mingling, mingled**
1 Different things **are mingled** when they are mixed together: *Kitchen smells mingled with the odours from the street.* **2** To **mingle** at a party is to move from person to person, briefly talking to each.

mini- /'mɪnɪ/ *prefix*
Mini- forms nouns that refer to a small or short type of something: *a mini-submarine* □ *The girls all wore miniskirts.*

miniature /'mɪnɪtʃə(r)/ *adjective*
Miniature describes something that is a small copy, version or model of a larger thing: *My favourite toy of all was the miniature railway.* □ *a miniature poodle.*

minibus /'mɪnɪbʌs/ *noun*: **minibuses**
A **minibus** is a small bus, usually with between twelve and fifteen seats.

minimal /'mɪnɪməl/ *adjective*
Minimal means very small in amount or extent: *employing someone with minimal experience* □ *It was all achieved with minimal fuss.*

minimize or **minimise** /'mɪnɪmaɪz/ *verb*: **minimizes, minimizing, minimized**
1 You **minimize** something when you reduce it to the smallest size or extent possible: *We must minimize the risk of other children being exposed to it.* **2** You also **minimize** something when you treat it as not being very important or less important than it really is: *The*

Minister was keen to minimize differences of opinion between himself and the Prime Minister.

minimum /ˈmɪnɪməm/ *noun; adjective*
▻ ***noun*: minimums**
The **minimum** is the lowest possible number, value, quantity or degree, or the lowest reached or allowed: *Government spending must be kept to a minimum.* □ *Three weeks is the minimum we need to finish the film.* □ *A minimum of 24 hours notice must be given if you wish to cancel your appointment.*
▻ ***adjective:*** *The minimum recorded temperature was minus 34 degrees centigrade.* □ *The minimum investment is £200.*

minister /ˈmɪnɪstə(r)/ *noun; verb*
▻ ***noun*: ministers**
1 A **minister** is someone in charge of a government department: *the Minister for Foreign Affairs* □ *a prominent minister in the Thatcher cabinet.* **2** In some branches of the Christian church, a priest is called a **minister**.
▻ ***verb*** (*formal*): **ministers, ministering, ministered**
You **minister** to someone, or to someone's needs, when you provide help, or carry out some kind of service, for them: *doctors who spend their lives ministering to the sick.*

ministerial /mɪnɪˈstɪərɪəl/ *adjective*
Ministerial means relating to a government minister or ministers: *Enquiries were made at ministerial level.*

ministry /ˈmɪnɪstrɪ/ *noun*: **ministries**
1 A **ministry** is a government department: *the Ministry of the Environment* □ *officials in the Social Security Ministry.* **2** The profession of a religious minister is often referred to as the **ministry**: *She had even thought of entering the ministry.*

mink /mɪŋk/ *noun*: **mink**
1 A **mink** is a small furry animal. **2** (*uncount, often adjectival*) **Mink** is its highly valued fur, used for making coats and other garments: *a mink coat.*

minor /ˈmaɪnə(r)/ *adjective; noun*
▻ ***adjective***
Minor describes things that have little importance or value: *He made one or two minor changes to my article.* □ *It had a relatively minor influence on her life.* □ *one of Ireland's minor poets.*
▻ ***noun*: minors**
A **minor** is a person below the age at which people are legally regarded as adults: *banning the sale of cigarettes to minors.*

minority /mɪˈnɒrɪtɪ/ or /maɪˈnɒrɪtɪ/ *noun*: **minorities**
1 You refer to a small group of people, especially the smaller of two groups, as a **minority**: *A minority of pupils thought the idea was unworkable.* □ *There are some people opposed to the scheme, but they are in a minority.* **2** A **minority** also consists of people who are different, usually in race or religion, from most of the people in a country or region: *We particularly welcome applicants from London's ethnic minorities.*

mint[1] /mɪnt/ *noun*: **mints**
1 (*uncount*) **Mint** is a plant with strong-smelling purplish-green leaves used as a flavouring in cooking. **2 Mints** are sweets with the flavour of mint.

mint[2] /mɪnt/ *noun; verb*
▻ ***noun*: mints**
1 A **mint** is a place where coins are produced under the authority of a country's government: *the Royal Mint.* **2** (*informal*) People sometimes refer to a very large sum of money as a **mint**: *That new house must have cost them a mint.*
▻ ***verb*: mints, minting, minted**
Coins **are minted** when they are produced in a mint.
▻ ***phrase*** Something that is **in mint condition** is in excellent condition, as if it had never been used.

minus /ˈmaɪnəs/ *preposition; noun; adjective*
▻ ***preposition***
1 Minus is used to show that one number or amount is taken away or subtracted from another: *13 minus 5 is 8.* **2** (*informal*) **Minus** also means without: *They arrived late, minus the children.*
▻ ***noun*: minuses**
1 A **minus**, or **minus sign**, is the mathematical symbol (-), indicating a negative quantity, or indicating that a following quantity is to be taken away. **2** (*informal*) A disadvantage can also be referred to as a **minus**: *It's a nice house; though the lack of off-street parking is a bit of a minus.*
▻ ***adjective***
1 Minus indicates that a quantity is negative or less than zero: *temperatures as low as minus twenty-three centigrade.* **2** In a system of marking a student's work, **minus** indicates a grade slightly below, so that a B minus is slightly lower than a B, but slightly higher than a C plus: *She gave me a B minus for my essay.*

minuscule /ˈmɪnəskjuːl/ *adjective* (*formal*)
Minuscule means extremely small: *He was complaining about a minuscule stain on his shirt.*

minute[1] /ˈmɪnɪt/ *noun*: **minutes**
1 A **minute** is a unit of time, equal to sixty seconds, or to a sixtieth part of an hour: *the first man to run a mile in under four minutes.* □ *I'll meet you back here in ten minutes' time.* □ *I was a few minutes early.* □ *Three minutes later the telephone rang.* □ *The time is six minutes to six.* **2** (*used in the singular*) You often use 'a **minute**' to mean a very short time: *Wait a minute; I'm not ready yet.* □ *I'll be back in a minute.* □ *It won't take a minute.* □ *Let me finish this; I'll only be a minute.* [*same as* **moment**] **3** (*used in the singular*) Something that happens at a particular **minute** happens at a particular point in time: *At that minute, I realized the danger I was in.* [*same as* **moment**] **4** (*used in the plural*) The **minutes** of a formal meeting consist of an official written record of what is said at that meeting: *Copies of the minutes will be made available to all members.*
▻ ***phrases*** **1** You say that something may happen at **any minute** or **moment** if it is likely to happen very soon: *I expect him back any minute now.* □ *She was going to spot the mistake at any minute.* **2** For **at the minute** see **moment**. **3** For **not for one minute** see **moment**. **4** You do something at **the last minute** or **moment** when you do it just before it is too late: *Don't leave it till the last minute to get the tickets; get them well in advance.* □ *We escaped at the last minute from the collapsing building.* **5** You do something **the minute** something else happens when you do it as soon as it happens: *Phone me the minute you hear any news.* [*same as* **the moment**] **6** You say that something must be done **this minute** if it must be done immediately: *We must leave this minute or we'll be late.* □ *Come here this minute.*

minute[2] /maɪˈnjuːt/ *adjective*
Something **minute** is very small: *Pigeons and ducks have an in-built barometer capable of detecting minute air-pressure changes.*

minutely /maɪˈnjuːtlɪ/ *adverb*
Minutely means considering every little detail: *The contracts have been minutely drawn up.*

miracle /ˈmɪrəkəl/ *noun*: **miracles**
1 A **miracle** is an act or event that breaks the laws of nature, that people believe is performed or caused directly by God or a god: *Jesus's well-known miracle of turning water into wine.* **2** (*informal*) People often refer

to an amazing or wonderful event, especially something that happens unexpectedly, as a **miracle**: *It was a miracle that the ship survived such a storm.* □ *These plants are real miracles of nature.*

miraculous /mɪ'rakjʊləs/ *adjective*
Something **miraculous** is wonderful or amazing, especially when it happens unexpectedly: *Helena made a miraculous recovery.*

mirage /'mɪrɑːʒ/ *noun*: **mirages**
1 In hot countries, you see a **mirage** when you see something that is not really there, usually a distant mass of water, a false image created when very hot air mixes with sunlight. **2** Something imaginary, or something you cannot or did not achieve or obtain, can be referred to as a **mirage**.

mirror /'mɪrə(r)/ *noun*; *verb*
▻ ***noun***: **mirrors**
A **mirror** is a glass surface that produces reflections, so that you see an image of yourself when you look at it: *She sat combing her hair in the mirror.* [see picture at **bathroom, bedroom, car**]
▻ ***verb***: **mirrors, mirroring, mirrored**
One thing **mirrors** another thing, usually something it is connected with, when it has the same features or qualities: *Hostility between working class and middle class was mirrored in traditional worker-management conflicts.*

mirth /mɜːθ/ *noun* (*uncount*; *literary*)
Mirth is the laughter of people who are enjoying themselves. [*same as* **merriment**]

mis- /mɪs/ *prefix*
Mis- forms words with the meaning 'wrong' or 'wrongly', or 'bad' or 'badly': *I won't tolerate this kind of misbehaviour.* □ *You have been misinformed; the wedding is tomorrow.*

misadventure /mɪsəd'vɛntʃə(r)/ *noun* (*count or uncount; formal*)
A **misadventure** is an unfortunate happening, an example of bad luck: *death by misadventure.*

misapprehension /mɪsaprɪ'hɛnʃən/ *noun* (*formal*): **misapprehensions**
You are under a **misapprehension** when you think or believe something that is not true: *I was under the misapprehension that this was to have been a business trip, not the holiday it has turned out to be.*

misappropriation /mɪsəproʊprɪ'eɪʃən/ *noun* (*uncount; formal*)
The **misappropriation** of money occurs when someone belonging to an organization uses its money for their own purposes.

misbehave /mɪsbɪ'heɪv/ *verb*: **misbehaves, misbehaving, misbehaved**
People, especially children, **misbehave** when they behave badly, or refuse to co-operate: *The girls have been quarrelling and misbehaving the whole day.* □ *There was a rumour that he'd been misbehaving with someone else's wife.* □ *What's the matter? Is the car misbehaving again?* — *noun* (*uncount*) **misbehaviour** (*AmE* **misbehavior**) /mɪsbɪ'heivjə(r)/: *Any misbehaviour will be severely dealt with.*

miscalculate /mɪs'kalkjʊleɪt/ *verb*: **miscalculates, miscalculating, miscalculated**
You **miscalculate** when you make a wrong guess about something: *They seem to have miscalculated what the public reaction would be.* — *noun* **miscalculation** /mɪskalkjʊ'leɪʃən/: *It was a serious miscalculation.*

miscarriage /'mɪskarɪdʒ/ *noun*: **miscarriages**
When a pregnant woman has a **miscarriage**, her body releases the baby too early for it to be able to live.

miscarry /mɪs'karɪ/ *verb*: **miscarries, miscarrying, miscarried**
When a woman **miscarries** she has a miscarriage.

miscellaneous /mɪsə'leɪnɪəs/ *adjective*
A **miscellaneous** collection of things contains things of various different kinds: *a few miscellaneous items of jewellery.*

mischief /'mɪstʃɪf/ *noun* (*uncount*)
1 When children get into **mischief** they behave naughtily, but cause no serious harm: *I could hear them making mischief in the next room.* **2 Mischief** is also the desire to do embarrassing or slightly shocking things that will amuse people: *His soft voice was full of mischief.*

mischievous /'mɪstʃɪvəs/ *adjective*
1 A **mischievous** child is often naughty, but causes no serious harm. **2** A **mischievous** person is full of mischief: *a mischievous smile.*

misconception /mɪskən'sɛpʃən/ *noun*: **misconceptions**
You have a **misconception** about something when you have a wrong idea or belief about it: *It's a common misconception that all physiotherapists are very fit.*

misconduct /mɪs'kɒndʌkt/ *noun* (*uncount; formal*)
Misconduct is improper behaviour by a professional person, that breaks the rules of their profession: *They accused him of gross misconduct.*

misconstrue /mɪskən'struː/ *verb* (*formal*): **misconstrues, misconstruing, misconstrued**
Something **is misconstrued** by someone who misunderstands what it means or indicates: *My comments about her beauty seem to have been misconstrued as a proposal of marriage.*

misdemeanour (*AmE* **misdemeanor**) /mɪsdɪ'miːnə(r)/ *noun* (*formal*): **misdemeanours**
A **misdemeanour** is a wrongdoing, an example of bad or unacceptable behaviour not serious enough to be called a crime.

miser /'maɪzə(r)/ *noun*: **misers**
A **miser** is a person who is very unwilling to spend money, especially one whose main interest is saving money.

miserable /'mɪzərəbəl/ *adjective*
1 Someone who is **miserable** is very unhappy; people also describe someone as **miserable** if they are often bad-tempered: *I couldn't bear to sit looking at his miserable face.* **2 Miserable** also describes things that make you feel unhappy, depressed or uncomfortable: *It was another miserable February morning.* □ *She showed me to a dark, miserable little room on the second floor.* □ *It was the last in a long line of miserable defeats.*

miserly /'maɪzəlɪ/ *adjective*
A **miserly** person is mean, and hates spending money: *Aren't you being a bit miserly? Surely you can afford to lend him more than that?*

misery /'mɪzərɪ/ *noun*: **miseries**
1 (*uncount or count*) **Misery** is great unhappiness; a **misery** is something that causes great unhappiness: *She told of the misery suffered by the villagers.* □ *the miseries of that inter-war period.* **2** (*uncount*) The state of being very poor is sometimes referred to as **misery**: *Ordinary people were born into a life of misery.* **3** (*informal*) You call someone a **misery** if they are always sad or bad-tempered.

misfire /mɪs'faɪə(r)/ *verb*: **misfires, misfiring, misfired**
A plan **misfires** when it goes wrong and has the wrong result: *Her little scheme had misfired.*

misfit /ˈmɪsfɪt/ *noun*: **misfits**
A **misfit** is a person whose attitudes and behaviour are very different from most other people and who does not mix well with them.

misfortune /mɪsˈfɔːtʃʊn/ *noun* (*uncount or count*)
Misfortune is bad luck: *I had the misfortune to be seated next to him on the train.* ▫ *The whole project seemed dogged by misfortune.*

misgiving /mɪsˈɡɪvɪŋ/ *noun*: **misgivings** (*used in the plural*)
You have **misgivings** about something when you have doubts or suspicions about it, *eg* because you think it may fail: *I was beginning to have misgivings about my choice.*

misguided /mɪsˈɡɑɪdɪd/ *adjective*
Someone who is **misguided** acts according to mistaken ideas or bad judgement: *He was an intelligent, if rather misguided, young man.* ▫ *Their actions were a little misguided, to say the least.*

mishap /ˈmɪshap/ *noun*: **mishaps**
A **mishap** is a minor accident or other unfortunate happening: *She becomes depressed at the slightest mishap.*

misinform /mɪsɪnˈfɔːm/ *verb*: **misinforms, misinforming, misinformed**
You **are misinformed** when someone gives you incorrect or misleading information: *You have been misinformed; the woman was my sister, not my wife.*

misinterpret /mɪsɪnˈtɜːprət/ *verb*: **misinterpret, misinterpreting, misinterpreted**
You **misinterpret** something when you misunderstand what it means or indicates: *My comments were misinterpreted as a wish to withdraw from the agreement.* — *noun* (*uncount or count*) **misinterpretation** /mɪsɪntɜːprɪˈteɪʃən/: *You need to be careful; such gestures could be open to misinterpretation.* ▫ *a misinterpretation of what had been said.*

misjudge /mɪsˈdʒʌdʒ/ *verb*: **misjudges, misjudging, misjudged**
You **misjudge** something when you judge it badly or wrongly; you **misjudge** someone when you have an unfairly bad opinion of them: *We had misjudged our audience, and given them a play that was too revolutionary for their taste.* ▫ *I realise now that I had misjudged him.* — *noun* (*uncount or count*) **misjudgement** or **misjudgment** /mɪsˈdʒʌdʒmənt/

mislay /mɪsˈleɪ/ *verb*: **mislays, mislaying, mislaid**
You **mislay** something when you to lose it, usually temporarily, especially because you can't remember where you put it.

mislead /mɪsˈliːd/ *verb*: **misleads, misleading, misled**
You **mislead** someone when you cause them to believe something that is not true: *She had been misled into thinking that Marcia didn't like her.* — *adjective* **misleading:** *We were given misleading instructions.*

misled /mɪsˈlɛd/ *verb*
Misled is the past tense and past participle of **mislead**.

misnomer /mɪsˈnoʊmə(r)/ *noun*: **misnomers**
A **misnomer** is an unsuitable name given to someone or something, or a word that describes someone or something badly: *This makes the term 'free market economy' seem something of a misnomer.*

misogynist /mɪˈsɒdʒɪnɪst/ *noun*: **misogynists**
A **misogynist** is a person who hates women.

misplaced /mɪsˈpleɪst/ *adjective*
Something such as energy or trust is **misplaced** when it is directed towards or given to the wrong person or thing: *all that misplaced guilt.*

misprint /ˈmɪsprɪnt/ *noun*: **misprints**
A **misprint** is a mistake in printing.

Miss /mɪs/ *noun*: **Misses**
1 **Miss** is a title used before the name of a girl or an unmarried woman: *'May I introduce Miss Elizabeth Bancroft.' 'How do you do, Miss Bancroft.'* ▫ *We're having dinner with the Misses Wilton.* **2** (*BrE; informal*) Schoolchildren sometimes address their female teachers as '**Miss**': *Why have you marked this sum wrong Miss?* [see also **Sir**]

miss /mɪs/ *verb; noun*
▻ ***verb***: **misses, missing, missed**
1 You **miss** a thing that you are aiming at, or aiming something at, or trying to catch, when you fail to hit it or catch it: *He threw a book at me but fortunately missed.* ▫ *She put out a hand to catch the ball but missed.* ▫ *My first shot missed the target altogether.* ▫ *A stone whizzed passed, just missing my ear.* ▫ *The bullet had missed his heart by inches.* **2** You **miss** an experience, event or activity when **a** you do not attend it for some reason: *I'm afraid I'll have to miss next week's class.* ▫ *I daren't miss another tutorial.* ▫ *She had missed a lot of schooling through illness.* **b** you do not arrive in time for it: *We missed the first ten minutes of the film.* ▫ *'I'm afraid I missed your speech.' 'Oh well, you didn't miss much* [= it wasn't very good].*'* ▫ *You've just missed seeing yourself on television.* **3** You just **miss** being harmed in some way if you only just avoid it or escape it: *She came rushing across the road and only just missed being run over by a bus.* **4** You **miss** a bus, train or plane when you do not get to it in time to travel on it: *If you don't hurry up you'll miss your train.* [*opposite* **catch**] **5** You **miss** something when you fail to hear or see it: *The phone box is right next to the garage; you can't miss it.* ▫ *Sorry, I missed your name; could you repeat it?* ▫ *She may be ninety, but she doesn't miss much.* [= she is very alert and observant] **6** You **miss** something when you first realize it is missing: *When did you miss your purse?* **7** You **miss** a chance or opportunity when you fail to take advantage of it: *You don't want to miss the chance of a free trip to California.* **8** You **miss** a person when you are sad because they are no longer with you; you **miss** a thing when you regret not having it or doing it any longer: *I'm so homesick; I'm missing you all terribly.* ▫ *Have you missed me?* ▫ *The children miss the fields and the freedom to wander.* ▫ *We miss seeing the grandchildren.* ▫ *What do you miss most about your old life?*
▻ ***phrases*** **1** (*informal*) You **give** something **a miss** when you decide not to do it, have it or attend it: *I think I'll give tomorrow's lecture a miss.* ▫ *I'd eaten too much already, so decided to give the dessert a miss.* **2 a** If you just fail to hit what you are aiming at, or if you almost, but do not quite, succeed in doing something, you call the result **a near miss**: *The Liberals have had few successes and a lot of near misses.* **b A near miss** between vehicles or aircraft is an encounter that is nearly a collision.

> ***phrasal verb***
> **miss out** **1** You **miss** something **out** when you fail to include it or decide not to include it: *When I read through the form, I noticed that he'd missed out his date of birth.* ▫ *Have I missed anyone out?* ▫ *Don't miss out a single detail.* **2** You **miss out** on something that others enjoy when you don't receive it or don't take part in it: *You mustn't miss out on all the free food.* ▫ *I don't want my children to feel that they're missing out.*

misshapen /mɪsˈʃeɪpən/ *adjective*
Something **misshapen** does not have the natural or

intended shape: *Misshapen stems and leaves are a sign that fungus has attacked the plant.*

missile /'mɪsaɪl/ *noun*: **missiles**
1 A **missile** is a flying bomb: *The submarines carry a number of surface-to-air missiles.* **2** (*formal*) Any object that is thrown or fired as a weapon can be called a **missile**: *The police were pelted with stones and other missiles.*

missing /'mɪsɪŋ/ *adjective*
Something is **missing** when it is not where it should be, because someone has taken it or because it has not been provided: *The police have asked for a list of everything that's missing.* □ *The company said they would send replacements for the missing parts.*

mission /'mɪʃən/ *noun*: **missions**
1 A **mission** is a purpose for which a person or group of people is sent somewhere, especially to a foreign country; the group of people sent is also a **mission**: *They set off on their mission to bring back new plant species.* □ *We spoke to members of the diplomatic mission.* □ *Allied warplanes carried out a number of bombing missions over this area.* **2** Someone who feels they have a **mission** to do something has decided to spend all their time and energy on achieving it, so that it becomes their main purpose in life: *He is a tireless worker for human rights, a man with a mission.* **3** A **mission** is also a group of missionaries, or the building where they work.

missionary /'mɪʃənərɪ/ *noun*: **missionaries**
A **missionary** is a member of a Christian organization working to improve the lives of poor people in a foreign country, and teaching them about Christianity.

misspent /mɪs'spent/ *adjective*
Time or money that has been **misspent** has been used foolishly or wastefully: *the results of a misspent youth.*

mist /mɪst/ *noun*; *verb*
▻ ***noun*** (*uncount*)
Mist consists of tiny drops of water in the air, like thin fog: *The hills were shrouded in mist.*
▻ ***verb***: **mists, misting, misted**
A glass surface **mists**, or **mists** up, or **mists** over, when it becomes covered with tiny drops of water so that you cannot see through it properly: *Alan's glasses were all misted up.*

mistake /mɪs'teɪk/ *verb*; *noun*
▻ ***verb***: **mistakes, mistaking, mistook, mistaken**
You **mistake** something or someone when you think they are something or someone else: *She mistook my silence for disapproval.* □ *I'm sorry; I mistook you for a colleague of my wife's.*
▻ ***noun*** (*count or uncount*): **mistakes**
A **mistake** is something wrong that you do or say, or something that you regret or did not intend: *You have copied it faithfully, with no mistakes.* □ *I made the mistake of agreeing without asking her first.* □ *I opened your letter by mistake.*
▻ ***phrase*** You say there is **no mistaking** someone or something if they are absolutely obvious or recognizable: *There was no mistaking her intentions; she was obviously going to close down the factory at the first opportunity.*

mistaken /mɪ'steɪkən/ *adjective*
You are **mistaken** when you are wrong about something, and your opinions or beliefs are **mistaken** when they are wrong: *I'm afraid you are mistaken; nobody of that name lives here.* □ *It was a case of mistaken identity.* — *adverb* **mistakenly:** *I had mistakenly assumed that she would be coming as well.*

mister see **Mr.**

mistletoe /'mɪsəltoʊ/ *noun* (*uncount*)
Mistletoe is a plant with small white berries, often used to decorate houses at Christmas: *I persuaded her to kiss me under the mistletoe.*

mistook /mɪs'tʊk/ *verb*
Mistook is the past tense of **mistake**.

mistress /'mɪstrəs/ *noun*: **mistresses**
1 A married man's **mistress** is a second woman he is having a sexual relationship with: *I'd been his mistress for years.* **2** Women teachers in some schools are called **mistresses**: *I was encouraged by the English mistress.* **3** The **mistress** of a large house, especially one with servants working in it, is the woman in charge of running it.

mistrust /mɪs'trʌst/ *verb*; *noun*
▻ ***verb***: **mistrusts, mistrusting, mistrusted**
You **mistrust** someone when you don't trust them or you are suspicious of them: *They tend to mistrust the government's motives, whatever they are.*
▻ ***noun*** (*uncount*): *Workers have traditionally regarded management with deep mistrust.*

misty /'mɪstɪ/ *adjective*: **mistier, mistiest**
1 It is **misty** when there is mist in the air: *a misty March morning.* □ *It was very misty on the motorway.* **2** People's eyes are **misty** when they have tears in them: *I always go a bit misty-eyed when I hear that tune.*

misunderstand /mɪsʌndə'stand/ *verb*: **misunderstands, misunderstanding, misunderstood**
You **misunderstand** someone when you think you have understood them, but in fact you have not: *My comments were clearly misunderstood.*

misunderstanding /mɪsʌndə'standɪŋ/ *noun*: **misunderstandings**
1 There is a **misunderstanding** when someone does not understand what someone else means: *There's been a slight misunderstanding; I wasn't suggesting it was your fault.* **2** (*euphemistic*) Two people have a **misunderstanding** when they argue or quarrel.

misuse *noun*; *verb*
▻ ***noun*** /mɪs'juːs/ (*uncount or count*)
The **misuse** of something is the act of using it wrongly, often in a way that breaks rules or laws: *the misuse of public money.*
▻ ***verb*** /mɪs'juːz/: **misuses, misusing, misused:** *Some of the tools had been badly misused.*

mitigating /'mɪtɪgeɪtɪŋ/ *adjective* (*formal*)
A **mitigating** circumstance is a reason or excuse that makes someone who has committed a crime seem less responsible or less guilty.

mitten /'mɪtən/ *noun* (*often in the plural*): **mittens**
Mittens are gloves with one covering for the thumb and a large covering for all the other fingers together.

mix /mɪks/ *verb*; *noun*
▻ ***verb***: **mixes, mixing, mixed**
1 You **mix** substances when you put them together to form a single mass, especially by stirring: *Mix the eggs with the butter and flour.* □ *You mix together sand, cement and water.* **2** You **mix** different things when you combine them, put them together or do them at the same time: *It's not a good idea to mix business with pleasure.* □ *For the furnishings, she mixed browns and yellows to give the room an autumn feeling.* **3** Things **mix** when they can be put together to form a single mass, or an attractive, suitable or wise combination: *Our experiments prove that water and oil do not mix.* □ *We all know that alcohol and driving don't mix.* **4** You **mix** with people when you meet them socially;

someone who **mixes** well feels at ease meeting different people in social situations: *I don't think she really mixes with any of her colleagues.* □ *He was a shy man who didn't mix easily.*

▻ ***noun*: mixes**

1 A **mix** is a specially prepared powder that you add water or other liquid to in order to make something, usually food: *a cake mix.* **2** A **mix** is also any combination of different things: *They selected pupils with a mix of abilities.*

> ***phrasal verb***
>
> **mix up** **1** You **mix up** two people or things when you identify them wrongly and think one is the other: *I always mix him up with his brother.* **2** You **mix** things **up** when you upset their usual or correct order: *Your papers fell on the floor and I may have mixed them up in retrieving them.*
> [see also **mix-up**]

mixed /mɪkst/ *adjective*

1 **Mixed** describes groups or collections containing things of different kinds: *a mixed grill.* **2** **Mixed** also describes things that relate to or include people of both sexes: *Some halls of residence were mixed, and some were single-sex.* **3** **Mixed** is often used to describe things that involve people of different races: *a mixed marriage.* **4** You have **mixed** feelings about something when you like some parts or aspects of it, but dislike others.

mixed bag /mɪkst 'bag/ *noun* (*used in the singular*; *informal*)

You describe something as a **mixed bag** if it has both good and bad parts, or if it contains people or things of different kinds or different standards.

mixture /'mɪkstʃə(r)/ *noun*: **mixtures**

1 A **mixture** is a combination of different substances, either one you have mixed yourself or one prepared for a particular purpose: *Add milk to the mixture of flour and eggs.* □ *a bottle of cough mixture.* **2** Any combination can be called a **mixture**: *I left Charlottesville with a mixture of sadness and relief.*

mix-up /'mɪksʌp/ *noun* (*informal*): **mix-ups**

A **mix-up** is a mistake caused by confusion or misunderstanding: *There was a mix-up with the bags and our luggage was put on a different plane.*

mo /moʊ/ *noun* (*used in the singular*; *informal*)

A **mo** is a moment, a short while: *Wait a mo while I get my bag from the office.* [compare **sec**]

moan /moʊn/ *verb*; *noun*

▻ ***verb*: moans, moaning, moaned**

1 You **moan** when you make a long low noise expressing sadness, grief or pain, or sometimes sexual pleasure. **2** The wind **moans** when it makes a long sad wild noise. **3** (*informal*) People **moan** when they complain, especially without good reason about something unimportant: *There's no use moaning about the weather.* □ *The children kept moaning that they were cold.*

▻ ***noun*: moans:** *the moans and groans of patients in the next room.*

moat /moʊt/ *noun*: **moats**

A **moat** is a deep, wide channel, often filled with water, round a castle to prevent people attacking it.

mob /mɒb/ *noun*; *verb*

▻ ***noun*: mobs**

1 A **mob** is a large crowd of people, especially people behaving violently: *Angry mobs stormed the parliament building.* **2** (*informal, rather old*) A group or gang can be referred to as a **mob**: *There were the usual protest from the animal liberation mob.*

▻ ***verb*: mobs, mobbing, mobbed**

1 A crowd of people **mob** someone when they gather round them round curiously or admiringly: *pop stars being mobbed by teenage girls.* **2** A place **is mobbed** when it is very busy and full of people: *The pub was mobbed and it took ages to get served.*

mobile /'moʊbaɪl/ *adjective*; *noun*

▻ ***adjective***

1 Something that is **mobile** can move or be moved easily: *Modern furniture is lighter and more mobile.* **2** You are **mobile** when you are able or willing to travel to different places, especially to settle in a new house or job: *A married man with a family is clearly a lot less mobile than a single student.* **3** A **mobile** shop or other service is provided by a vehicle travelling from place to place.

▻ ***noun*: mobiles**

A **mobile** is a hanging decoration moved around by air currents. — *noun* (*uncount*) **mobility** /moʊ'bɪlɪtɪ/: *the increased mobility provided by better transport.*

mobilize or **mobilise** /'moʊbɪlaɪz/ *verb*: **mobilizes, mobilizing, mobilized**

1 To **mobilize** people is to organize them so that they are ready to take action of some kind: *Opponents of the Council's road-building proposals are mobilizing support amongst local residents.* **2** To **mobilize** troops is to organize them ready for war.

moccasin /'mɒkəsɪn/ *noun*: **moccasins**

A **moccasin** is a kind of slipper or soft shoe with a low heel.

mock /mɒk/ *verb*; *adjective*

▻ ***verb*: mocks, mocking, mocked**

You **mock** someone when you try to make them appear silly, by copying their speech or behaviour, or by making jokes about them: *The other children mocked her.* □ *He can't help the way he looks; you mustn't mock.*

▻ ***adjective***

1 **Mock** describes things that are not real or genuine: *expressions of mock sincerity* □ *rooms full of mock Elizabethan furniture.* [*same as* **sham, imitation**] **2** In schools a **mock** examination is a practice for the real one coming later.

mockery /'mɒkərɪ/ *noun*

1 (*uncount*) **Mockery** is the attitude of someone who tries to make someone or something appear foolish: *Her smile had more than a hint of mockery in it.* **2** (*used in the singular*) You refer to a ridiculously poor or failed version of something as a **mockery**: *Elections in these countries are something of a mockery.* □ *It makes a mockery of our attempts to give the children a good education.*

mock-up /'mɒkʌp/ *noun*: **mock-ups**

A **mock-up** is a detailed model of something: *Tests were carried out on a mock-up of the space shuttle.*

modal verb /moʊdəl 'vɜːb/ *noun*: **modal verbs**

A **modal verb** is used with other verbs to express ideas such as possibility, probability or obligation. The **modal verbs** are *can, could, may, might, must, ought to, shall, should, will* and *would*; the verbs *dare, need* and *used to* are **modal** in some senses.

mod cons /mɒd 'kɒnz/ *noun* (*plural*; *informal*)

Mod cons are modern conveniences, facilities such as central heating that make many modern houses comfortable to live in.

mode /moʊd/ *noun*: **modes**

A **mode** is a way, method or style: *alternative modes of transport* □ *women's clothes in the Chinese mode.*

model /ˈmɒdəl/ *noun*; *verb*
▷ ***noun***: **models**
1 (*often adjectival*) A **model** is a small version of something that will be built later, made to show how the real thing will look or work; a **model** is also a small copy of something used as a toy or for decoration: *Take a look at this working model of the engine.* □ *a collection of model trains.* **2** A **model** is also one of several types or designs of a manufactured object: *The 1985 model had a more rounded shape.* □ *The more expensive models have quieter motors.* **3** A **model** is a person who displays clothes by wearing them, whether at a fashion show or in photographs in a magazine. **4** A **model** is also someone that an artist paints, or a photographer takes pictures of. **5** You can refer to anything that other people copy as a **model**: *They have a parliament styled on the British model.* **6** (*often adjectival*) **Model** is often used to refer to someone who has qualities you admire, or who is excellent in some way: *None of the staff would betray me; they are all models of loyalty.* □ *Janice was the model partner; loving, sensitive, fun to be with.*
▷ ***verb***: **models, modelling, modelled**
1 You **model** yourself on someone you admire when you try to be like them: *I've tried to be an original singer, not modelling myself on any one person.* **2** To **model** is to work as a model: *I modelled clothes in Paris for a few months.* □ *She has modelled for the world's greatest photographers.* **3** You **model** something such as clay when you shape it. — *noun* (*uncount*) **modelling:** *a career in fashion modelling.*

moderate *adjective*; *noun*; *verb*
▷ ***adjective*** /ˈmɒdərət/
1 Moderate describes things that are not extreme, or not strong or violent: *He has quite moderate political opinions.* □ *The winds will be light to moderate, becoming stronger later in the day.* **2 Moderate** also means medium or average: *a pupil of moderate intelligence.*
▷ ***noun*** /ˈmɒdərət/: **moderates**
A **moderate** is a person with moderate political views: *some of the moderates in the Conservative Party.*
▷ ***verb*** /ˈmɒdəreɪt/: **moderates, moderating, moderated**
To **moderate** something is to make it less extreme, strong or violent: *You will moderate your tone of voice when speaking to me!* □ *The wind has moderated a little.*

moderately /ˈmɒdərətlɪ/ *adverb*
Moderately means 'slightly', or 'quite' or 'fairly': *It's only moderately more expensive than the other.* □ *a moderately attractive young woman.*

moderating /ˈmɒdəreɪtɪŋ/ *adjective*
In this dictionary, **moderating** describes adverbs such as *fairly*, *rather*, *quite*, and *pretty*, which can reduce the force of the the adjective or adverb they are used with, instead of intensifying it, as *very* does.

moderation /mɒdəˈreɪʃən/ *noun* (*uncount*)
You show **moderation** when you don't allow your behaviour to become extreme: *Don't drink too much; try to exercise a little moderation.* □ *It would be more sensible to take exercise in moderation.*

modern /ˈmɒdən/ *adjective*
1 Modern describes things that belong or relate to the present or to recent times, rather than to the past or to history: *Standards are different in modern political life.* □ *a study of European culture, both ancient and modern.* **2** Something **modern** is, or makes use of, the very latest techniques, equipment or styles: *a very modern kitchen.* — *noun* (*uncount*) **modernity** /məˈdɜːnɪtɪ/: *We were impressed by the modernity of their business facilities.*

modernize or **modernise** /ˈmɒdənaɪz/ *verb*: **modernizes, modernizing, modernized**
To **modernize** something is to make it modern by introducing new equipment or techniques: *plans to modernize the bottling operation.* — *noun* (*uncount*) **modernization** /mɒdənaɪˈzeɪʃən/: *the modernization of our manufacturing processes.*

modest /ˈmɒdɪst/ *adjective*
1 A **modest** person is not too proud of their abilities or achievements: *She would be too modest to admit that it was her idea.* [*same as* **humble**; *opposite* **conceited, immodest**] **2 Modest** also describes things that are fairly small, and often not very expensive: *a modest income* □ *a modest gift.* — *adverb* **modestly:** *She spoke very modestly about her involvement in charity work.*

modesty /ˈmɒdɪstɪ/ *noun* (*uncount*)
1 Modesty is the quality of not being too proud of your abilities or achievements: *Try to show a little more modesty.* **2** People sometimes use **modesty** to refer to the fact that someone, especially a woman, is wearing clothes that don't reveal much of their body: *She quickly wrapped herself in a towel to preserve her modesty.*

modicum /ˈmɒdɪkəm/ *noun* (*used in the singular*; *formal*)
A **modicum** of something is a small amount of it: *Try to develop at least a modicum of good taste.*

modification /mɒdɪfɪˈkeɪʃən/ *noun* (*count or uncount*): **modifications**
A **modification** is a slight change that you make in order to improve something: *There have been a few modifications to the design of the wing.* □ *It would need very little modification.*

modify /ˈmɒdɪfaɪ/ *verb*: **modifies, modifying, modified**
You **modify** something when you make small changes in order to improve it: *The system has been modified to allow for better air circulation.*

module /ˈmɒdjuːl/ *noun*: **modules**
A **module** is a separate unit that combines with others to form a larger unit, structure or system: *Degree courses are divided into modules, each module representing a term's work.*

mohair /ˈmoʊheə(r)/ *noun* (*uncount*, *often adjectival*)
Mohair is a very soft fluffy kind of wool often used to make jumpers: *a luxurious mohair rug.*

moist /mɔɪst/ *adjective*
1 Something **moist** is slightly wet: *I shook his moist hand.* [*same as* **damp**] **2** Foods such as cakes are **moist** when they are pleasantly soft and fresh, not dry. [*opposite* **stale**]

moisten /ˈmɔɪsən/ *verb*: **moistens, moistening, moistened**
You **moisten** something when you wet it slightly: *a drink of water to moisten my lips.*

moisture /ˈmɔɪstʃə(r)/ *noun* (*uncount*)
Moisture is wetness, especially tiny drops of water in the air or on a surface.

molar /ˈmoʊlə(r)/ *noun*: **molars**
Molars are the large square teeth at the back of your mouth.

mold see **mould**.

moldy see **mouldy**.

mole[1] /moʊl/ *noun*: **moles**
A **mole** is a raised dark permanent spot on a person's skin, especially on their face.

mole² /moʊl/ *noun*: **moles**
1 A **mole** is a small animal with tiny eyes and soft dark fur, that digs tunnels underground. **2** A person working inside an organization and passing secret information to people outside it is sometimes called a **mole**.

molecule /ˈmɒlɪkjuːl/ *noun* (*technical*): **molecules**
A **molecule** is the smallest unit that a chemical substance can be divided into without losing its basic nature, consisting of two or more atoms.

molehill /ˈmoʊlhɪl/ *noun*: **molehills**
A **molehill** is a little pile of soil thrown up by a mole digging a tunnel.
▻ ***phrase*** You say that someone **is making a mountain out of a molehill** if they are treating something very unimportant as if it were very serious or important.

molest /məˈlɛst/ *verb*: **molests, molesting, molested**
1 To **molest** someone, especially a child or a woman, is to touch them in a sexual way that they don't want and don't like. [compare **rape**] **2** (*formal*) To **molest** someone is also to attack them and physically harm them.

molt see **moult**.

molten /ˈmoʊltən/ *adjective*
Molten describes normally solid substances such as metal and rock that are in the form of a liquid, because they have been heated: *volcanos spewing out molten lava.*

mom /mɒm/ *noun* (*AmE*; *informal*): **moms**
Some people call their mother **mom**: *I'll have to ask my mom.* □ *Let's go later, Mom.*

moment /ˈmoʊmənt/ *noun*: **moments**
1 A **moment** is a very short time: *I'll be back in a moment.* □ *Moments later the plane was airborne.* □ *For one moment I thought you were serious.* □ *Have you got a moment? I need to discuss something urgently.* □ *The ambulance arrived not a moment too soon.* [= just in time] [*same as* **minute**] **2** A particular **moment** is a particular point in time: *At that precise moment I realized the truth.* □ *The next moment she had disappeared.* □ *This is an important moment in the history of our two countries.* □ *That was my proudest moment.*
▻ ***phrases*** **1** For **any moment** see **minute**. **2** You use **at the moment** or **at the minute** to refer to present circumstances: *I'm rather busy at the moment; could I call you back?* □ *That's all we know at the moment.* **3 For the moment** also refers to present circumstances, with the suggestion that more will happen, be done, or be needed, in the future: *The Prime Minister's position seems safe, for the moment at least.* □ *Let's leave the subject for the moment and return to it later.* □ *That's enough examples for the moment.* **4** If you say you do **not for one moment** or **minute** believe a person or what they say, you mean you do not believe them at all: *I didn't for a moment think she'd carry out her threat.* □ *I don't believe you for a moment.* **5** For **the last moment** see **minute**. **6** You do one thing **the moment** another happens if you do it as soon as the other happens: *She asked me to contact her the moment they returned.* □ *I loved the house the moment I saw it.* [*same as* **the minute**] **7** You say that someone or something **has their moments** if they have been successful or interesting on a few occasions at least: *The play has its moments but on the whole it's pretty dull.* □ *'Was Dad ever much of a romantic?' 'Oh, he had his moments.'*

momentary /ˈmoʊməntərɪ/ *adjective*
Something **momentary** lasts for only a moment: *a momentary loss of consciousness.* — *adverb* **momentarily** /ˈmoʊməntərɪlɪ/: *He paused momentarily as he tried to remember what happened next.*

momentous /məˈmɛntəs/ *adjective*
A **momentous** event has great importance for the future: *The election of South Africa's first black president is a momentous occasion.*

momentum /məˈmɛntəm/ *noun* (*uncount*)
1 The **momentum** of a moving object is the force it has to continue moving: *Once over the top of the hill, the bikes gather considerable momentum on the way down.* **2 Momentum** is also the speed that something develops or progresses at: *The election campaign gained momentum.*

monarch /ˈmɒnək/ *noun*: **monarchs**
A **monarch** is a king, queen or other royal person who rules a country.

monarchy /ˈmɒnəkɪ/ *noun* (*uncount or count*): **monarchies**
Monarchy is a system of government in which a monarch is the official ruler of a country, even if they have very little real power; a country with such a system is a **monarchy**.

monastery /ˈmɒnəstrɪ/ *noun*: **monasteries**
A **monastery** is the home of a community of monks.

Monday /ˈmʌndɪ/ *noun* (*uncount or count*): **Mondays**
Monday is the first day of the week, coming after Sunday and before Tuesday: *Our holiday ends on Monday.* □ *We usually do the shopping on a Monday* (or *on Mondays*). □ (*AmE*) *The office is closed Mondays.* □ *We discussed it in last Monday's class.* □ *We need to be up early on Monday morning.*

monetary /ˈmʌnɪtərɪ/ *adjective*
Monetary means relating to money, especially to the function of money in an economic system: *the government's tighter monetary controls.*

money /ˈmʌnɪ/ *noun* (*uncount*)
Money consists of coins or banknotes used to buy things; wealth in general is often referred to as **money**: *I didn't even have enough money for a cup of tea.* □ *Would the hotel change Spanish money back into pounds for me?* □ *The more money a man has, the more she is interested in him.*
▻ ***phrases*** **1** (*informal*) You **get your money's worth** when you get full value for the money, or sometimes the time or effort, you have spent. **2** To **make money** is to earn or gain a profit: *another scheme to make quick money* □ *The enterprise was no longer making money and had to be closed down.*

-monger /ˈmʌŋgə(r)/ *suffix*
1 -monger forms nouns that mean a person who sells goods of a particular kind: *fishmonger.* **2 -monger** is also used to form nouns meaning someone who spreads unpleasant information: *scandalmonger* □ *gossipmonger.*

mongrel /ˈmʌŋgrəl/ *noun*: **mongrels**
A **mongrel** is a dog of mixed breed, whose parents were different breeds.

monitor /ˈmɒnɪtə(r)/ *noun*; *verb*
▻ ***noun***: **monitors**
1 A **monitor** is an instrument that measures or records something: *We can check your heart rate by looking at the monitor.* **2** A **monitor** is also a television screen showing the picture being filmed by a camera, rather than one receiving broadcast programmes. [see picture at **office**]
▻ ***verb***: **monitors, monitoring, monitored**
You **monitor** something when you make regular checks on its development or progress: *The patient's condition is being closely monitored by a team of doctors.*

monk /mʌŋk/ *noun*: **monks**
A **monk** is a member of a community of men who spend their lives in religious worship.

monkey /'mʌŋkɪ/ *noun; verb*
▻ ***noun*: monkeys**
A **monkey** is a medium-sized animal with a long tail, that climbs trees.
▻ ***verb* (*informal*): monkeys, monkeying, monkeyed**

phrasal verb
(*informal*) You **monkey about** or **around** when you enjoy behaving in a lively, silly way.

mono- /'mɒnoʊ/ *prefix*
Mono- forms nouns and adjectives that mean 'one' or 'single', so that a **monoplane** is an aeroplane with one set of wings only, and a **monosyllabic** word contains one syllable only.

monogamy /mə'nɒgəmɪ/ *noun (uncount)*
Monogamy refers to the practice of having only one husband or wife at any one time.

monologue /'mɒnəlɒg/ *noun*: **monologues**
A **monologue** is an occasion on which one person speaks for a long time uninterrupted, especially a character alone in a film or play. [compare **dialogue**]

monopolize or **monopolise** /mə'nɒpəlaɪz/ *verb*: **monopolizes, monopolizing, monopolized**
1 You **monopolize** something when you alone control, use or dominate it, excluding all others: *They were able to monopolize trade in furs for a number of years.* **2** You **monopolize** a person when you keep talking to them, so that other people don't get a chance to do so; you **monopolize** the conversation when you talk a lot yourself, so that no-one else is able to speak: *Flavia managed to monopolize the guest of honour for the rest of the evening.*

monopoly /mə'nɒpəlɪ/ *noun*: **monopolies**
1 You have a **monopoly** on something when you are the only person who possesses, controls or uses it: *You don't have a monopoly on the truth!* **2** A business company has a **monopoly** when it is the only one selling a particular product or providing a particular service; the company itself, and the industry they control, is also referred to as a **monopoly**: *These have been state-run monopolies for too long.*

monotonous /mə'nɒtənəs/ *adjective*
Something is **monotonous** when it always follows the same boring pattern or routine, never changing or varying: *fairly monotonous factory work.*

monotony /mə'nɒtənɪ/ *noun (uncount)*
Monotony is boring regularity in a routine or pattern, with no interesting changes or variations: *We all need a holiday to help break the monotony of working life.*

monsoon /mɒn'su:n/ *noun*: **monsoons**
1 The **monsoon** is a season of heavy rain in the summer in some hot countries. **2** (*informal*) People sometimes refer to a heavy fall of rain as a **monsoon**.

monster /'mɒnstə(r)/ *noun; adjective*
▻ ***noun*: monsters**
1 In stories, a **monster** is any large and frightening creature: *tourists hoping to catch a glimpse of the Loch Ness monster.* **2** People refer to a very cruel or evil person as a **monster**: *I don't know why she stays married to that monster.*
▻ ***adjective***
Monster means very large: *monster portions of food.*

monstrosity /mɒn'strɒsɪtɪ/ *noun*: **monstrosities**
People refer to something large and ugly as a **monstrosity**: *The Eiffel Tower was regarded as a hideous monstrosity when it was first built.*

monstrous /'mɒnstrəs/ *adjective*
1 You can describe something that is cruelly unfair as **monstrous**: *the monstrous decision to take these children away from their parents.* **2** Something is also **monstrous** when it is extremely large: *He has responsibility for flying this monstrous aircraft.*

month /mʌnθ/ *noun*: **months**
1 A **month** is any of the twelve named periods that a year is divided into: *March is the third month of the year.* □ *Campaigning continued throughout the summer months.* □ *towards the end of the month of July* □ *We'll visit them again next month.* □ *You could earn up to £3000 a month.* **2** A **month** is also a period of roughly four weeks or 30 days: *They left the island a few months later.* □ *It doubles in size in just a couple of months.*

monthly /'mʌnθlɪ/ *adjective or adverb*
Something is **monthly** when it happens once a month or every month: *the monthly meeting of the Council Finance Committee* □ *Would you like to be paid weekly or monthly?*

monument /'mɒnjʊmənt/ *noun*: **monuments**
1 A **monument** is something built to remind people of a person or an event: *They erected a monument to the men who died in the Great War.* **2** A **monument** is also any ancient building or structure preserved for its historical value.

monumental /mɒnjʊ'mɛntəl/ *adjective*
Monumental means very large or great, or extreme: *the monumental incompetence of a government department.*

moo /mu:/ *verb*: **moos, mooing, mooed**
A cow **moos** when it makes its typical low long sound.

mood /mu:d/ *noun*: **moods**
1 The **mood** you are in is the way you are feeling in your mind, particularly whether you are cheerful, or whether you are angry and impatient: *He's in quite a good mood, in spite of everything.* □ *Something had put her in a bad mood.* □ *Eleanor wasn't in the mood for dancing.* **2** Someone who is in a **mood** feels angry and impatient for a while: *I disappear into the garden when she's in one of her moods.* **3** You can refer to the general attitude or opinion of a group of people as their **mood**: *The mood in the factory is one of determination.*

moody /'mu:dɪ/ *adjective*: **moodier, moodiest**
1 A **moody** person tends to change mood often and quickly, from cheerful to angry and impatient: *Diane's always been a bit moody.* **2** A person who is **moody** is **a** in a bad mood and behaving in an angry and impatient way: *You're a moody old devil this morning!* **b** has quick changes of mood, and is often in a bad mood.

moon /mu:n/ *noun*: **moons**
The **moon** is the planet-like object that moves once round the Earth each month, that you can see as a full or partial circle in the sky, usually at night; Other planets also have **moons** travelling round them: *Who could have known that we would put a man on the Moon?* □ *Is there a full moon tonight?*
▻ ***phrases*** **1** You do something **once in a blue moon** if you hardly ever do it. **2** (*informal*) You say that you are **over the moon** if you are very pleased or happy about something: *We're over the moon about the way it's all turned out.*

moonlight /'mu:nlaɪt/ *noun; verb*
▻ ***noun* (*uncount, often adjectival*)**
Moonlight is light that shines from the moon at night: *a moonlight walk along the beach.*

▻ ***verb*** (*informal*): **moonlights, moonlighting, moonlighted**
To **moonlight** is to work secretly at a second job, usually avoiding paying tax on the money you earn: *Having to take on part-time jobs, or moonlighting, was not viewed by academics as an acceptable solution to their problems.*

moor[1] /mɔ:(r)/ *noun*: **moors**
A **moor** is an area of wild land high above the surrounding area: *a walk on the North Yorkshire moors.*

moor[2] /mɔ:(r)/ *verb*: **moors, mooring, moored**
To **moor** a boat is to tie it to a post or other fixed place with a rope: *down by the rocks where the boat was moored.*

moorland /'mɔ:land/ *noun* (*uncount*)
Moorland is wild open countryside in a high place.

moose /mu:s/ *noun*: **moose**
A **moose** is a large deer with flat rounded horns.

mop /mɒp/ *noun*; *verb*
▻ ***noun***: **mops**
1 A **mop** is a tool for washing floors, consisting of a large sponge or a set of thick threads on a long handle. **2** You refer to a thick untidy mass of hair as a **mop** of hair.
▻ ***verb***: **mops, mopping, mopped**
1 To **mop** a floor is to wash it with a mop. **2** You **mop** a wet or damp surface when you wipe it; you **mop** up liquid from a surface when you remove it by wiping: *men in suits mopping the sweat from their necks with handkerchiefs* □ *We watched the child mop up the gravy on his plate with a piece of bread.*

mope /moʊp/ *verb*: **mopes, moping, moped**
You **mope**, or **mope** about, when you behave in a bored and depressed mood, not wanting to do anything: *It's no use moping about the house.*

moped /'moʊpɛd/ *noun*: **mopeds**
A **moped** is a lightweight motorcycle with a small engine, especially one started using pedals.

moral /'mɒrəl/ *adjective*; *noun*
▻ ***adjective***
1 Moral means relating to the principles of good and evil, or right and wrong: *Is it true that today's young people have lower moral standards than we had?* **2** You describe someone as **moral** if they always behave in a way that people think is good, right or proper. [*opposite* **immoral**] **3** You give someone **moral** support when you encourage them and show that you approve of what they are doing.
▻ ***noun***: **morals**
1 (*plural*) **Morals** are the opinions people have about what is right and wrong: *Of course parents should be responsible for a child's morals!* □ *It's not true that all young people have no morals.* **2** The **moral** of a story or an event is what it teaches you about the way you should behave: *The moral of this little episode seems to be 'Don't rely on your colleagues for support'.* — *adverb* **morally:** *I have always tried to behave morally.* □ *It would be morally wrong to accept money for a job a haven't done.*

morale /mə'rɑ:l/ *noun* (*uncount*)
The **morale** of a group of people is how confident they feel, or how successful they think they will be: *Morale in the nursing profession is at an all-time low.*

moralise see **moralize.**

morality /mə'ralɪtɪ/ *noun* (*uncount*)
Morality is the quality of being right or proper, according to accepted standards of good and bad behaviour: *We must question the morality of killing animals at all.*

moralize or **moralise** /'mɒrəlaɪz/ *verb*: **moralizes, moralizing, moralized**
Someone who **moralizes** talks about good and proper behaviour, especially in a way that criticizes how someone else is behaving: *The pupils don't want to listen to old folks moralizing about sex.*

moratorium /mɒrə'tɔ:rɪəm/ *noun* (*formal*): **moratoriums**
There is a **moratorium** on a certain kind of activity when the people involved in it agree not to do it for a fixed period of time: *We could not agree to a moratorium on arms sales.*

morbid /'mɔ:bɪd/ *adjective*
Morbid people tend to think a lot about sad or unpleasant things, especially death: *Don't let's get too morbid.* □ *a morbid conversation.*

more /mɔ:(r)/ *determiner*; *pronoun*; *adverb*
▻ ***determiner*** (*used with plural count nouns and with uncount nouns*)
1 More is the comparative of **many** and **much** and means a greater quantity or amount: *Rather more people have applied than last year.* □ *There was more money in the kitty than we thought.* □ *He has more money than sense.* □ *They have far more staff than we do.* **2 More** also means an additional quantity or amount: *How many more chairs shall we need?* □ *Could you get me five more copies?* □ *I won't need any more help today.*
▻ ***pronoun:*** *More than 83% of those eligible to vote turned up.* □ *She earns more in an afternoon than I earn in a week.* □ *I see a bit more of my mother* [= I see my mother more often] *now that she's moved into town.* □ *There have been 25 deaths from the virus so far and many more are expected.* □ *Isn't there any more of that nice cheese?* □ *What more could we do to help?* □ *After that I heard no more of her.* [= I received no more news of her]
▻ ***adverb***
1 More is used to form the comparatives of adjectives that do not form their comparatives with *-er*, and to form the comparatives of adverbs ending in *-ly*, and certain others: *I've never met a more charming man.* □ *She's more confident than she used to be.* □ *He's become a little more relaxed with age.* □ *You could have expressed that more tactfully!* □ *It happens more often than you'd expect.* **2 More** is the comparative of **much** and means to a greater degree: *He used to buy her expensive presents in the hope that it would make her like him more.* □ *I didn't admire her second book any more than I had her first.* **3 More** is also used to mean 'further' or 'again'; something that isn't so any **more** has stopped being so: *We can talk more about this tomorrow.* □ *Try doing that once or twice more for practice.* □ *I didn't want to live with him any more.* □ *He doesn't come and visit us any more.* □ *She disappeared mysteriously and we saw her no more.* [compare **any longer**] **4** Something is **more**, or **more** of, one thing than another if it is closer to being the first thing than the second: *It's to be more a holiday than a business trip.* □ *She was more like a friend than a teacher.* □ *It's more of an encyclopaedia than a dictionary.* □ *He was evidently more frightened than injured.*
▻ ***phrases*** **1 More and more** indicates a continuing increase in something: *More and more people are choosing to stay in Britain for their holidays.* □ *What impresses me more and more is the way she manages to stay calm in a crisis.* □ *It became more and more obvious that he couldn't cope.* **2 More or less** means **a** almost: *We're more or less finished.* **b** about or approximately: *It took two hours, more or less.* **3 a More than** a certain number means over that number: *More than two hundred people applied.* **b** Something is **more than** a certain thing if it has

more importance and significance than that thing: *Nowadays the sovereign is no more than a figurehead.* **4 What is more** is used to introduce a second statement relating to or extending the first: *He thinks he's capable of doing the job and, what's more, so do I.*

moreover /mɔːˈroʊvə(r)/ *adverb* (*formal*)
Moreover introduces a second statement that extends or supports the first one: *We are not in a position to stop them; moreover, we would not wish to.* [*same as* **furthermore**]

morgue /mɔːg/ *noun*: **morgues**
A **morgue** is a building where dead bodies are kept until they are buried or cremated. [see also **mortuary**]

morning /ˈmɔːnɪŋ/ *noun* (*often adjectival*): **mornings**
The **morning** is the part of the day from when you get out of bed to midday or lunchtime, or from midnight to midday: *I phoned several times during the morning.* □ *Come and see me tomorrow morning.* □ *I do my best work in the mornings.* □ *Friday morning would be a good time for me.* □ *Would you like a morning newspaper?* □ *I read it with my morning coffee.* □ *We stayed up until 3 o'clock in the morning.*

moron /ˈmɔːrɒn/ *noun* (*informal*): **morons**
If you call someone a **moron** you mean they are very stupid: *Don't do that, you moron!* □ *that group of morons he calls his friends.*

morose /məˈroʊs/ *adjective*
You describe someone as **morose** if they are quiet in a way that suggests they are unfriendly or bad-tempered: *Jim was a particularly morose individual.*

morphine /ˈmɔːfiːn/ *noun* (*uncount*)
Morphine is a drug that relieves pain.

morsel /ˈmɔːsəl/ *noun*: **morsels**
A **morsel** is a small piece, especially of food: *a few tasty morsels.*

mortal /ˈmɔːtəl/ *adjective; noun*
▻ ***adjective***
1 When you say that people are **mortal**, you mean that they are certain to die at some future time and cannot live forever: *There are times when he forgets he is mortal too.* [*opposite* **immortal**] **2** A **mortal** wound is one that causes death; people who are in **mortal** combat are trying to kill each other. **3** A **mortal** enemy is the enemy you fear or hate the most: *It was then that he realized that he'd made a mortal enemy of Briggs..* **4 Mortal** is sometimes used for emphasis: *They removed every mortal thing from the room.*
▻ ***noun***: **mortals**
You can refer to ordinary people as **mortals**, in contrast to a particular person who is regarded as great: *She clearly didn't want to speak to us mere mortals.*

mortality /mɔːˈtalɪtɪ/ *noun* (*uncount*)
1 Mortality is the state of being mortal, or the fact that people die: *It makes you acutely aware of your own mortality.* **2** The **mortality** among certain groups, *eg* over a certain period, is the number of them that die: *During the '40s infant mortality fell steadily.*

mortar /ˈmɔːtə(r)/ *noun*: **mortars**
1 (*uncount*) **Mortar** is a mixture of sand, water and cement, used in building to stick bricks together. **2** A **mortar** is a gun that fires shells over short distances: *the sound of mortar fire.*

mortgage /ˈmɔːgɪdʒ/ *noun; verb*
▻ ***noun***: **mortgages**
A **mortgage** is a loan of money, from a bank or building society, for buying a house or other property; the amount of money you repay each month to the bank or building society is also your **mortgage**: *Getting a mortgage would be cheaper than rent in the long run.* □ *Our mortgage has gone up by over £20 a month.*
▻ ***verb***: **mortgages, mortgaging, mortgaged**
You **mortgage** your house or other property when you give ownership of it to a bank or building society in return for a loan of money: *They had to remortgage their house to pay off his business debts.*

mortified /ˈmɔːtɪfaɪd/ *adjective*
You say you are **mortified** when you are very embarrassed or ashamed: *I was absolutely mortified when he pointed out my mistake.*

mortuary /ˈmɔːtjʊərɪ/ *noun*: **mortuaries**
A **mortuary** is a building or room where dead bodies are kept until they are buried or cremated. [see also **morgue**]

mosaic /moʊˈzeɪɪk/ *noun*: **mosaics**
A **mosaic** is a design formed by fitting together small pieces of coloured stone or glass.

Moslem see **Muslim**.

mosque /mɒsk/ *noun*: **mosques**
A **mosque** is a Muslim place of worship.

mosquito /mɒˈskiːtoʊ/ *noun*: **mosquitos** or **mosquitoes**
A **mosquito** is a small long-legged flying insect that bites people and sucks their blood.

moss /mɒs/ *noun* (*uncount*)
Moss is a small flowerless plant that grows as a thick mass in damp places, *eg* on rocks. — *adjective* **mossy**: **mossier, mossiest:** *The north wall was damp and mossy.*

most /moʊst/ *determiner; pronoun; adverb*
▻ ***determiner*** (*used with plural count nouns and with uncount nouns*)
1 Most people or things is nearly all of them, or the majority of them; **most** something is nearly all of it, or the bulk of it: *Most people like to have a bet now and then.* □ *anxieties that affect most mothers* □ *It's cheaper than most modern cars of its size.* □ *Most paper nowadays is made from wood.* **2 'Most'** or 'the **most**' is the superlative of **many** and **much** and means more than anyone or anything else: *The person holding the most cards wins.* □ *It's the planning stage that requires most effort and ingenuity.* [*opposite* **fewest, least**]
▻ ***pronoun***
1 Most of a group of people or things is nearly all of them, or the majority of them; **most** of a thing is nearly all of it, or the bulk of it: *Most of my friends are vegetarians.* □ *Most of us wanted to go home and get to bed.* □ *Most of the country will have rain.* □ *I had to rewrite most of what she'd written.* **2 'Most'** or 'the **most**' is the superlative of **many** and **much** and means more than anyone or anything else: *I've told the blackberry-pickers that there'll be a prize for the person who collects the most.* □ *I probably spend most on fuel.* [*opposite* **fewest, least**] **3** 'The **most**' also means the largest amount that is possible or available: *The most she would admit was that they had had a disagreement.*
▻ ***adverb***
1 You use **most** to form the superlatives of adjectives that do not form their superlatives with *-est*, and to form the superlatives of adverbs ending in *-ly*, and certain others: *She appeared to be the most interesting person in the room.* □ *It was the most cleverly devised escape plan ever.* □ *The phenomenon occurs most often in the early morning when there is cloud and mist around.* [*opposite* **least**] **2 'Most'** or 'the **most**' is the superlative of **much** and means more than anything or anyone else, or to the greatest degree: *What I liked about him most was his honesty.* □ *Which kind of exercise do you enjoy the most?* □ *That was what I was most*

afraid of. □ *I'm fond of the others but I respect you the most.* [*opposite* **least**] **3** (*intensifying; slightly formal*) '**Most**' and 'the **most**' are used to mean 'very' or 'extremely': *It's been a most interesting conversation.* □ *I've had the most frustrating day.* □ *Thank you; that was most enjoyable.* □ *You dealt most skilfully with that difficulty.* □ *I most certainly agree.*
▻ ***phrases*** **1 At most** or **at the most** means no more than, and probably not as much or many as, the amount mentioned: *It'll take me five minutes at most to have a shower and change.* □ *There were 30 people there at the most.* [compare **at least**] **2** You **make the most of** something when you get as much benefit or use as possible out of it: *We spent Sunday in the garden, making the most of the sunshine.*

-most /moʊst/ *suffix*
-most forms adjectives that mean furthest in a particular direction: *at the northernmost tip of the island* □ *Nobody has ever penetrated the innermost reaches of the jungle.*

mostly /ˈmoʊstlɪ/ *adverb*
Mostly means generally, in most cases or in most parts: *The area is mostly farmland.* □ *He goes fishing mostly at weekends.* □ *We mostly like to stay in and watch television.*

MOT /ɛmoʊˈtiː/ *noun* (*BrE*): **MOTs**
When you take your car in for an **MOT**, a qualified mechanic checks it to make sure it is officially safe to drive, and gives you an official certificate to prove it: *My last car failed its MOT.*

motel /moʊˈtɛl/ *noun*: **motels**
A **motel** is a hotel for motorists, usually consisting of rooms on a single storey, each with space outside to park a car.

moth /mɒθ/ *noun*: **moths**
A **moth** is a butterfly-like insect that is active at night and is attracted by light.

moth-eaten /ˈmɒθiːtən/ *adjective*
Old worn things, especially clothes, are sometimes described as **moth-eaten**: *a flimsy table and a couple of moth-eaten chairs.*

mother /ˈmʌðə(r)/ *noun; verb*
▻ ***noun***: **mothers**
Your **mother** is your female parent, the woman who gave birth to you: *Do you think he looks like his mother?* □ *Help me with this tray, Mother.*
▻ ***verb***: **mothers, mothering, mothered**
You **mother** someone when you treat them with great, or perhaps too much, care and protection: *Something vulnerable about him makes women want to mother him.*

motherhood /ˈmʌðəhʊd/ *noun* (*uncount*)
Motherhood is the state of being a mother: *I don't think she was really prepared for motherhood.*

mother-in-law /ˈmʌðərɪnlɔː/ *noun*: **mothers-in-law**
A person's **mother-in-law** is the mother of their husband or wife.

motherly /ˈmʌðəlɪ/ *adjective*
A **motherly** woman behaves towards someone with great care and protection, like a mother: *She had a kind, almost motherly way with the younger men.*

motif /moʊˈtiːf/ *noun*: **motifs**
A **motif** is a shape or design, often a single shape repeated many times to form a pattern.

motion /ˈmoʊʃən/ *noun; verb*
▻ ***noun***: **motions**
1 (*uncount*) **Motion** is the state of moving: *Don't try to get off while the train is still in motion.* **2** A **motion** is a movement: *She made a beckoning motion with her hand.* □ *The rolling motion of the boat made me feel sick.* **3** At a formal meeting, a **motion** is a suggestion that is formally discussed and voted on.
▻ ***verb***: **motions, motioning, motioned**
You **motion** to someone when you move your hand or other part of your body as a signal for them to do something: *Frank motioned to us to join him.*
▻ ***phrase*** You say that someone is **going through the motions** when they are pretending to do something, or they are doing it without sincerity or enthusiasm: *Their marriage was all but at an end; they were now just going through the motions.*

motionless /ˈmoʊʃənləs/ *adjective*
Something that is **motionless** is not moving: *The patients sat staring out of the window, quite motionless.*

motion picture /ˈmoʊʃən pɪktʃə(r)/ *noun* (*AmE*): **motion pictures**
A **motion picture** is a cinema film.

motivate /ˈmoʊtɪveɪt/ *verb*: **motivates, motivating, motivated**
1 You **are motivated** by things such as feelings when they cause you to act in a particular way: *Most of them were motivated by greed alone.* **2** You **motivate** someone when you make them feel interested and enthusiastic: *a lively young teacher who can motivate her pupils.* — *noun* (*uncount or singular*) **motivation** /moʊtɪˈveɪʃən/: *It seems that the only motivation for this crime was jealousy.* □ *The reason for their failure certainly isn't lack of motivation.*

motive /ˈmoʊtɪv/ *noun*: **motives**
A **motive** is a reason why a person does something: *This appears to be a crime without a motive.* □ *Do you have any reason to suspect her motives?*

motley /ˈmɒtlɪ/ *adjective*
A **motley** group of people or things is made up of many different kinds: *The firefighters' team were a motley crew.*

motor /ˈmoʊtə(r)/ *noun; adjective; verb*
▻ ***noun***: **motors**
1 A **motor** is the part of a machine that produces movement: *An electric motor lowers the blinds as the temperature rises.* **2** (*slang*) A **motor** is also a car: *What do you think of my new motor?*
▻ ***adjective***
1 Motor means relating to cars or other road vehicles: *a motor show.* **2 Motor** also means driven by a motor: *a motor boat.*
▻ ***verb***: **motors, motoring, motored**
1 (*old*) To **motor** is to travel by car: *We motored down to Monte Carlo.* **2** (*informal*) You are **are motoring** when you are travelling very fast: *The car was really motoring when it hit the bend.*

motorbike /ˈmoʊtəbaɪk/ *noun* (*informal*): **motorbikes**
A **motorbike** is a motorcycle. [see picture at **vehicle**]

motor car *noun*: **motor cars**
A **motor car** is a car.

motorcycle /ˈmoʊtəsaɪkəl/ *noun*: **motorcycles**
A **motorcycle** is a two-wheeled road vehicle with an engine.

motorcyclist /ˈmoʊtəsaɪklɪst/ *noun*: **motorcyclists**
A **motorcyclist** is a person who rides a motorcycle.

motorist /ˈmoʊtərɪst/ *noun*: **motorists**
A **motorist** is a person who drives a car.

motorized or **motorised** /ˈmoʊtəraɪzd/ *adjective*
A **motorized** vehicle or other device is powered or operated by a motor: *The motorized valve was faulty.*

motorway /ˈmoʊtəweɪ/ *noun*: **motorways**
A **motorway** is a major road for fast-moving traffic, linking major towns and cities. [see also **freeway**]

mottled /ˈmɒtəld/ *adjective*
Something that is **mottled** has patches of different colour: *mottled skin.*

motto /ˈmɒtoʊ/ *noun*: **mottos** or **mottoes**
A **motto** is a phrase adopted as a principle of behaviour: *Their company motto was 'We exist to serve'.*

mould[1] (*AmE* **mold**) /moʊld/ *noun* (*uncount*)
Mould is a plant that grows as a soft white mass on substances, especially food, kept in warm and damp conditions: *kitchen cupboards filled with the disgusting smell of mould.* — *adjective* **mouldy:** *The bedroom smelt damp and the walls were mouldy.*

mould[2] (*AmE* **mold**) /moʊld/ *noun*; *verb*
▻ ***noun***: **moulds**
1 A **mould** is a hollow shaped container that a liquid substance such as clay is poured into, hardening to produce an object the same shape as the container. **2** If you say that one person or thing is in the **mould** of another, you mean that they display similar patterns of action and behaviour: *He's a player very much in the McEnroe mould.*
▻ ***verb***: **moulds, moulding, moulded**
1 You **mould** a substance when you shape it, usually with your hands rather than a mould: *Mould the dough into individual rolls.* **2** You **mould** someone or something when you have a controlling influence on the way they develop: *The new team coach will be expected to mould them into a championship side.* ▫ *Teachers are just as influential as parents in moulding a young individual.*

moult (*AmE* **molt**) /moʊlt/ *verb*: **moults, moulting, moulted**
An animal **moults** when it loses its feathers, hair or skin to allow for a new growth.

mound /maʊnd/ *noun*: **mounds**
1 A **mound** is a small bank or pile of earth, whether natural or man-made: *We pitched the tent on a grassy mound.* **2** A **mound** is also a heap or pile of anything: *mounds of dirty laundry.*

Mount /maʊnt/ *noun*: **Mounts**
Mount is used to mean 'mountain' in place-names: *the top of Mount Everest* ▫ *a district known as Mount Pleasant.*

mount /maʊnt/ *verb*: **mounts, mounting, mounted**
1 You **mount** organized action of some kind, such as an attack, when you carry it out: *Opposition parties are mounting a campaign against government taxation proposals.* **2** You say that something **is mounting** when it is increasing, especially rapidly or to a high level: *More people collapsed as the temperature inside the prison mounted.* **3** To **mount** an object is to put in a frame or on a background in order to display it: *Your photographs always look better mounted.* **4** (*formal*) You **mount** stairs when you go up them; you **mount** a horse when you get on it: *A trained fire-fighter can mount a ladder like this in seconds.* ▫ *She promptly mounted a chair and pulled the painting off the wall.*

> ***phrasal verb***
> Something **mounts up** when it increases in amount: *Our savings will soon mount up if we don't touch them.*

mountain /ˈmaʊntɪn/ *noun*: **mountains**
1 (*often adjectival*) A **mountain** is a very high steep hill, often of bare rock: *She spends the weekends climbing mountains.* ▫ *the rugged mountain landscape.* **2** (*informal*) You refer to a huge mass or quantity of something as a **mountain** of it: *There were mountains of papers to be sorted.*
▻ ***phrase*** For **make a mountain out of a molehill** see **molehill**.

mountaineer /maʊntɪˈnɪə(r)/ *noun*: **mountaineers**
A **mountaineer** is a person skilled in climbing mountains.

mountaineering /maʊntɪˈnɪərɪŋ/ *noun* (*uncount*)
Mountaineering is the sport or pastime of climbing mountains.

mountainous /ˈmaʊntɪnəs/ *adjective*
A **mountainous** region contains many mountains.

mounted /ˈmaʊntɪd/ *adjective*
Mounted police or soldiers ride horses.

mourn /mɔːn/ *verb*: **mourns, mourning, mourned**
1 To **mourn** is to feel or show deep sorrow because someone has died: *It would be indecent to question her while she is still mourning her husband.* ▫ *I remember the children spent weeks mourning for the family dog.* **2** You **mourn** for something when you feel very sad because you don't have or experience it any longer: *It's does no good to mourn for the success of bygone years.*

mourner /ˈmɔːnə(r)/ *noun*: **mourners**
A **mourner** is someone who attends a funeral: *There was only a handful of mourners at Gillamoor Church, as Uncle George had rarely gone out of the little dale.*

mournful /ˈmɔːnfʊl/ *adjective*
Mournful describes people who feel or express sadness or grief, and things that suggest sadness or grief: *Even the dog seemed to wear a permanently mournful expression.* ▫ *The attic room was a dark, mournful place.*

mourning /ˈmɔːnɪŋ/ *noun* (*uncount*)
Mourning is deep sorrow that you feel or show because someone has died.
▻ ***phrase***
1 A person who is **in mourning** for someone who has died continues to feel or show deep sorrow because of their death. **2** You also say that someone is **in mourning** when they are wearing something, especially black clothes, as a formal sign that a member of their family has died.

mouse /maʊs/ *noun*: **mice**
1 A **mouse** is a small, long-tailed, furry animal that lives in the wild and in houses: *Let's hope the cat keeps those mice away.* **2** (*computers*) A **mouse** is a device that you move about on a desk surface in order to move the cursor on a computer screen, and which you also use to perform various operations. [see picture at **office**]

mousse /muːs/ *noun* (*count or uncount*): **mousses**
A **mousse** is a light cold dessert made by mixing eggs, cream and flavouring: *Who would like some more chocolate mousse?*

moustache /məˈstɑːʃ/ (*AmE* **mustache** /ˈmʌstaʃ/) *noun*: **moustaches**
A **moustache** is a line of unshaved hair above a man's upper lip: *I remember Mark when he used to have a moustache.*

mousy /ˈmaʊsɪ/ *adjective*
Mousy hair is a dull, light-brown colour.

mouth *noun*; *verb*
▻ ***noun*** /maʊθ/: **mouths** /maʊðz/
1 Your **mouth** is the opening in your head that you

speak through, that contains your teeth and tongue, and is surrounded by your lips; when people refer to the shape of your **mouth** they are talking about the shape of your lips: *Did the doctor look inside your mouth?* □ *Could you open your mouth a little wider?* □ *I wouldn't say Jeremy has a sad mouth.* [see picture at **body**] **2** The **mouth** of something, such as a cave or a bottle, is the opening to it. **3** The **mouth** of a river is where it meets the sea.
▻ ***verb*** /maʊð/: **mouths, mouthing, mouthed**
You **mouth** words when you move your lips to form the words, but you make no sound: *She mouthed 'I love you' to the camera.*

mouthful /'maʊθfʊl/ *noun*: **mouthfuls**
1 A **mouthful** is an amount of food or drink that you put in your mouth at one time: *I'll have to speak between mouthfuls.* **2** (*informal*) A **mouthful** is also a word or phrase that is difficult to say: *Her full title is a bit of a mouthful.*

mouth organ /'maʊθ ɔːgən/ *noun*: **mouth organs**
A **mouth organ** is a harmonica.

mouthpiece /'maʊθpiːs/ *noun*: **mouthpieces**
1 A **mouthpiece** is the part of something, such as a musical instrument or a telephone receiver, that you hold in or against your mouth. [see picture at **office**] **2** A person, or sometimes a magazine, expressing the views of a group or organization is sometimes referred to as their **mouthpiece**: *She seems to have become the mouthpiece of the Left of the party.*

mouthwatering /'maʊθwɔːtərɪŋ/ *adjective*
Mouthwatering food looks or smells very inviting and makes you feel like eating.

movable or **moveable** /'muːvəbəl/ *adjective*
Something **movable** is not fixed in one place and can be moved. [*opposite* **immovable**; compare **portable**]

move /muːv/ *verb*; *noun*
▻ ***verb***: **moves, moving, moved**
1 You **move** something when you take it from one place or position and put it in another; it **moves** when it goes from one place or position to another: *Could you move your car?* □ *Help me move this table over to the wall.* □ *I thought I saw the door handle move.* □ *The glacier moves forward at the rate of 30 centimetres a year.* **2** You **move** when you go from one place to another, or change your position; you **move** a part of you when you change its position: *Ssh! Can you hear someone moving about?* □ *Far below me I could see people moving to and fro in the square.* □ *He moved a couple of paces forward.* □ *Could you all move along one seat?* □ *I woke up next morning so stiff I couldn't move.* □ *She moved gracefully, like a dancer.* □ *He had a funny way of moving his eyes without moving his head.* □ *I can't move my wrist.* **3** You **move** when you act, take action, or start doing something or going somewhere: *It's getting late; it's time I moved.* □ *You should move now so as to make the best of the economic situation.* **4** You **move**, or **move** house, when you go and live in another house, taking your belongings and furniture with you: *We'd like to move back into town in a year or so.* □ *They moved away about six months ago.* □ *You could sell the house and move to a ground-floor flat.* □ *the worries of moving house* □ *We hereby notify customers that we shall be moving premises on 5 April to 11 Sunningdale Street.* **5** People **move** or **are moved** when they change jobs or their place of work: *I've been moved to a different department.* □ *His company has moved him to Germany.* □ *I decided to move into the entertainment world.* **6** You **move** towards a certain state or position when you progress or develop in that direction: *South Africa seems to be moving towards a political solution.* □ *They've moved closer to our point of view.* □ *The world has moved into the computer age and there's no going back.* **7** You say things **are moving** if progress is being made or the situation is developing quickly: *We need to keep the campaign moving to attract the support we need.* □ *Events were moving too quickly for me.* □ *Everything seems to be moving ahead satisfactorily.* **8** (*formal*) What **moves** you to do something is what makes you do it: *What ever could have moved her to write such an article?* **9** Something **moves** you if it makes you feel deep emotion, especially sadness: *The last act of the opera never fails to move me.* [*same as* **affect**] — *adjective* **moved:** *We were all very moved by his words.* □ *For a moment I was too moved to answer.*
▻ ***noun***: **moves**
1 (*usually in the singular*) You make a **move** when you change your position or go from one place or position to another: *He was watching every move she made.* [*same as* **movement**] **2** A **move** is also an act, or the process, of changing your house or your job: *The grandfather clock got broken during the move.* □ *The move to administrative work had been a big mistake.* **3** You can refer to some action you take as a **move**: *It would be a wise move to test the market first.* [*same as* **step**] **4** In board games such as chess or draughts it is your **move** when it is your turn to change the position of a piece or counter on the board: *how to win in 10 moves.*
▻ ***phrases*** **1** Someone watches **your every move** when they watch everything you do. **2** (*informal*) If someone tells you to **get a move on** they want you to hurry up. **3** If you say it's time you **made a move** you mean that it's time you went where you have to go, or did what you have to do. **4** You are **on the move** when you are moving, progressing, or travelling from one place to another: *extra-light suitcases for the busy executive who is always on the move.*

phrasal verbs
move down Someone **moves down** or **is moved down** when they go back to a lower rank, grade, level or position: *She missed a lot of school work through illness and had to be moved down a year.*
move in **1** You **move in** when you begin to occupy a new house or other building: *The new neighbours are moving in next week.* □ *We'll be moving into our new offices soon.* **2** Troops or police **move in** when they surround a place, position or target ready to make an attack or make arrests: *Mounted police were ordered to move in on the rioters.*
move off A vehicle **moves off** when it starts moving after being stationary.
move on **1** You **move on** when you leave one place and go to another: *Two days in Florence was enough; we decided to move on to Greece.* **2** You **move on** from one thing to the next when you stop doing one thing and begin dealing with the next: *Moving on to the question of the concert, we still need volunteers to sell tickets.*
move out You **move out** when you leave your house to go and live somewhere else: *We're moving out of the flat in April.* □ *They've moved out of this area altogether.*
move up **1** People in a row or line **move up** when they move so that they are standing or sitting more closely together, usually so as to make room for others. **2** You **move up** or **are moved up** when you progress to a higher grade, rank or level or position: *He moves up to the senior school next term.*

moveable see **movable**.

movement /'mu:vmənt/ *noun*: **movements**
1 (*count or uncount*) A **movement** is the act of moving your body or a part of it: *The skilled actor can create emotions with very slight movements of his face.* **2** A group or organization, especially one with a political aim, is often called a **movement**: *associations within the Labour movement.* **3** A person's **movements** are what they do during a particular time: *The police have asked for an account of her movements between midnight and 3 o'clock.*

movie /'mu:vɪ/ *noun*: **movies**
1 A **movie** is a cinema film: *an old gangster movie.* **2** Some people call the cinema in general the **movies**: *We spent our day off at the movies.*

moving /'mu:vɪŋ/ *adjective*
You describe something as **moving** if it causes you to feel strong emotions, usually sadness: *a moving farewell.* [*same as* **touching, stirring**]

mow /moʊ/ *verb*: **mows, mowing, mowed, mown**
You **mow** grass when you cut it, usually with a special machine called a **mower** or a **lawnmower**.

MP /ɛm'pi:/ *noun*: **MPs**
An **MP** is a Member of Parliament, a person elected as the political representative of people in a particular area: *the new Conservative MP for Stirling.*

Mr /'mɪstə(r)/ *noun*
1 Mr is the ordinary title given to a man, used before his name: *I spoke to Mr Jones about it.* □ *May I introduce Mr Philip Short.* **2 Mr** is often used before other official titles such as 'chairman' when addressing a man formally: *Can I speak to you for a moment, Mr President?*

Mrs /'mɪsɪz/ *noun*
Mrs is the ordinary title used before the name of a married woman: *Mrs Wilkins will attend to you.* □ *You are invited to the home of Mrs Mary Armitage.*

Ms /mɪz/ *noun*
Ms is a title that is used before the name of a woman whether or not she is married: *Dear Ms Brown.*

much /mʌtʃ/ *determiner; pronoun; adverb*
▻ ***determiner*** (*used with uncount nouns*): **more, most**
1 Much means a lot, or a large amount: *Much dedicated effort has gone into the production.* □ *After much discussion we at last reached a solution.* □ *He hasn't got much common sense* [= he has very little]. □ *Did you have much trouble finding your way?* □ *I've far too much work to do.* □ *There's so much discontent in the country.* [*opposite* **little**]

> Notice that in positive statements **much** is rather formal, and **a lot of, lots of** and expressions such as **a great deal of** and **plenty of** are more commonly used, especially in conversation; **much** is common with negatives and in questions, and is used with words such as *so, too* and *as*: *We've got lots of milk but not much bread. Take as much paper as you need.*

2 Much is used with *how* to ask about the amount of something: *How much time would you need to finish the job?* □ *I wasn't sure how much more food we'd need for the weekend.*
▻ ***pronoun***: **more, most:** *I agree with much of what he says.* □ *Much of their material is repetitive.* □ *We didn't get very much to eat.* [= we got very little] □ *I've got too much; I didn't want as much as this.* □ *Much of the town is without electricity tonight.* □ *It wasn't much of a lecture.* [= it was a poor lecture] □ *I don't see as much of my brother* [= I don't see him as often] *as I'd like to.* [*opposite* **little**]

> Notice that the pronoun **much** is never used by itself at the end of a positive statement: *There is a lot* (not *there is much*). *I need a great deal* (not *I need much*). But you can say: *There is too much. I need so much.*

▻ ***adverb***: **more, most**
1 Much emphasizes comparatives and superlatives, and the word *too*: *The other girls seemed very much more confident than she felt.* □ *We got here much more quickly than we were expecting to.* □ *It's much less cold than it was.* □ *Her mother was much the cleverer of her parents.* □ *She was much the best-dressed person there.* □ *He spoke much the most wittily of the three.* □ *It's much too late to telephone her.* [*same as* **far, by far**] **2** You say that one thing is **much** the same as another if you think the two things are very similar: *I imagined that riding a horse would be much the same as riding a bike.* □ *It was a day much like any other.* □ *She looks much as she did 20 years ago.* **3 Much** means greatly, or to a great extent: *I very much agree with you.* □ *I'm very much looking forward to your talk.* □ *I never liked sport much.* [= I disliked sport] □ *We didn't think much of* [= we were not impressed by] *the concert.* □ *Do you miss your job much?* □ *Thank you very much.* □ *I love him so much.* □ *She was too much upset to speak.* [*opposite* **little**]

> Notice that **much** by itself is used chiefly with negatives and in questions; in positive statements you use it with words such as *very, so* or *too*. But **much** can be used, rather formally, as an intensifying adverb with certain adjectives and past participles: *She was much distressed to find that the man was still following her. I'm much impressed by her. She's now enjoying a much-deserved holiday.*

4 Much is used with *how* in questions about the degree or frequency of an activity: *How much do you use the fitness club?*
▻ ***phrases*** **1** (*informal*) You describe something as **a bit much** if you think it is very unfair or unreasonable: *I thought the way he spoke to you was a bit much.* **2** If you say **'I thought as much'** you mean that what you expected to be so is so. **3 Much as** is used as an emphatic form of 'although': *Much as I'd like to help, I'm afraid I can't.* **4** Something that happens **much to** your horror, amusement, disgust or delight greatly horrifies you, amuses you, disgusts you or delights you: *Much to our amusement, the bird picked up the handkerchief and flew away with it in its beak.* **5** (*informal*) **Nothing much** means nothing that is worth mentioning: *'What did you do today?' 'Nothing much.'* **6** Something that is **not so much** one thing as another is closer to being the second thing: *It wasn't so much a business trip as a holiday.* □ *not so much a novel, more a documentary account.* **7** Someone does **not do so much as** a certain thing if they do not even do that thing: *She left without so much as a backward glance.* **8** (*informal*) Something that is **not up to much** is not very good: *The food isn't up to much.* **9** If you say **'So much for'** something, you mean that it is worthless: *So much for his speed if his work is full of errors.* **10** Something that is **too much** for someone is too difficult for them to manage or bear: *The walk would probably be too much for him.*
[see also **more, most**]

muck /mʌk/ *noun; verb*
▻ ***noun*** (*uncount; informal*)
1 Muck is dirt: *Your hands are covered in muck from the garden.* **2 Muck** is also solid waste released by animals: *Cow's muck is the gardener's traditional soil conditioner.*

▻ ***verb*** (*informal*): **mucks, mucking, mucked**

> ***phrasal verbs***
> **muck about** You **muck about** or **muck around** when you behave in a silly way: *He got told off by the teacher for mucking about in class.*
> **muck in** Several people **muck in** when they all work together to achieve something: *We might as well muck in with the rest of them.*
> **muck up** You **muck** something **up** when you do it very badly and fail at it: *She thinks she's mucked up her exams.*

mucky /'mʌkɪ/ *adjective* (*informal*): **muckier, muckiest**
1 Something is **mucky** when it is very dirty: *Take those mucky boots off before you come in.* **2 Mucky** books or films describe or show sex in detail, intended as entertainment. [*same as* **dirty, pornographic**]

mucus /'mju:kəs/ *noun* (*uncount*)
Mucus is the thick sticky liquid produced in various parts of your body, *eg* your nose.

mud /mʌd/ *noun* (*uncount*)
Mud is soft wet soil: *Her feet were stuck in the mud.*

muddle /'mʌdəl/ *verb*; *noun*
▻ ***verb***: **muddles, muddling, muddled**
You **muddle** things, or **muddle** them up, when you put them into a disordered, confused state, or when you confuse them in your mind: *Somehow my notes got muddled up with other papers.* ▫ *I always get the two Johns muddled up.*
▻ ***noun*** (*used in the singular*) *The arrangements for his arrival were a bit of a muddle.* ▫ *The company accounts were in a right muddle.*

> ***phrasal verb***
> You **muddle through** when you succeed in spite of foolish mistakes or lack of organization.

muddy /'mʌdɪ/ *adjective*: **muddier, muddiest**
1 Something that is **muddy** is covered in mud: *a muddy path* ▫ *My shoes are a bit muddy.* **2 Muddy** colours are various shades of dull brown.

mudguard /'mʌdgɑ:d/ *noun*: **mudguards**
A **mudguard** is a curved piece of metal or plastic that partly covers a wheel, and that stops water or mud from being thrown up behind it. [see picture at **bicycle**]

muesli /'mju:zlɪ/ *noun* (*uncount*)
Muesli is a breakfast food consisting of a mixture of crushed grain, nuts and dried fruit, eaten with cold milk.

muffin /'mʌfɪn/ *noun*: **muffins**
A **muffin** is a small round flat bread roll usually eaten hot with butter: *tea and muffins.*

muffled /'mʌfəld/ *adjective*
A **muffled** noise is made quieter by being blocked or covered by something: *muffled voices from the next room.*

mug[1] /mʌg/ *noun*: **mugs**
A **mug** is a tall drinking-cup with a handle, used without a saucer; a **mug** is also the drink contained in, or the amount contained in, this kind of cup: *I've already had three mugs of coffee this morning.* [see picture at **tableware**]

mug[2] /mʌg/ *verb*: **mugs, mugging, mugged**
Someone who **is mugged** is attacked and robbed violently or under threat of violence. — *noun* **mugger:** *The muggers left him with a broken wrist.* — *noun* **mugging:** *There have been a number of muggings in the area.*

mug[3] /mʌg/ *noun* (*informal*): **mugs**
Someone's face is sometimes referred to as their **mug**: *Just look at his ugly mug!*

mug[4] /mʌg/ *noun* (*informal*): **mugs**
If you call someone a **mug** you mean they have been easily fooled by someone: *And, like a mug, I agreed.*

muggy /'mʌgɪ/ *adjective*: **muggier, muggiest**
Muggy weather is unpleasantly warm and damp. [*same as* **humid, close**]

mule /mju:l/ *noun*: **mules**
A **mule** is a horse-like animal whose parents were a horse and a donkey.

mull /mʌl/ *verb*: **mulls, mulling, mulled**

> ***phrasal verb***
> You **mull** something **over** when you spend time thinking about it carefully: *I sat down to mull over what she had said.*

multi- /mʌltɪ/ *prefix*
Multi- means 'many': *a multicoloured shirt* ▫ *Most of the top players are multimillionaires.*

multilateral /mʌltɪ'latərəl/ *adjective*
Multilateral discussions or decisions involve several people or groups. [compare **bilateral, unilateral**]

multinational /mʌltɪ'naʃənəl/ *adjective*
A **multinational** company operates in several different countries.

multiple /'mʌltɪpəl/ *adjective*
Multiple describes things that have, involve or affect many parts, things or people: *Several of the victims received multiple injuries.* ▫ *a multiple-lane motorway.*

multiple-choice /mʌltɪpəl'tʃɔɪs/ *adjective*
In a **multiple-choice** test, you choose your answer from several possible answers provided.

multiple sclerosis /mʌltɪpəl sklə'roʊsɪs/ *noun* (*uncount*)
Multiple sclerosis is a serious disease that attacks a person's nervous system, making them permanently unable to move parts of their body.

multiplication /mʌltɪplɪ'keɪʃən/ *noun* (*uncount*)
Multiplication is the process of multiplying one number by another.

multiplication sign /mʌltɪplɪ'keɪʃən saɪn/ *noun*: **multiplication signs**
A **multiplication sign** is the symbol ×, used between two numbers to indicate that they are to be multiplied.

multiplicity /mʌltɪ'plɪsɪtɪ/ *noun* (*used in the singular*; *formal*)
A **multiplicity** of things is a large number or variety of them: *the impressive multiplicity of talents she has to offer.*

multiply /'mʌltɪplaɪ/ *verb*: **multiplies, multiplying, multiplied**
1 You **multiply** one number when you add it to itself as many times as is indicated by a second number, so that 3 multiplied by 4 is 12 (3 + 3 + 3 + 3). **2** Things **multiply** when they increase in number, especially greatly: *The weeds just multiplied, and before long the garden was a jungle.* **3** Animals **multiply** when they breed, increasing the number of them.

multitude /'mʌltɪtju:d/ *noun* (*singular*)
1 (*formal*) A **multitude** of things is a huge number of them: *So there are a multitude of reasons for you to join a trade union.* **2** (*literary*) A **multitude** is also a huge crowd of people.

mum /mʌm/ *noun*: **mums**
Your **mum** is your mother: *a room where mums can feed their babies in peace* ▫ *Hurry up, Mum!*

mumble /ˈmʌmbəl/ *verb*: **mumbles, mumbling, mumbled**
You **mumble** when you speak unclearly, especially with your mouth partly closed, *eg* because you are eating: *He's a shy boy who has a tendency to mumble.* □ *She mumbled an apology.*

mummy[1] /ˈmʌmɪ/ *noun*: **mummies**
Mummy is a child's word for mother: *Go and ask your mummy.* □ *Can I have another biscuit, Mummy?*

mummy[2] /ˈmʌmɪ/ *noun*: **mummies**
A **mummy** is a person's dead body preserved with spices and wrapped in strips of cloth, especially one buried long ago: *Egyptian mummies.*

mumps /mʌmps/ *noun* (*uncount*)
Mumps is a disease that causes painful swelling of the parts of your neck near your ears.

munch /mʌntʃ/ *verb*: **munches, munching, munched**
You **munch** something when you chew it with a steady movement of your jaws, especially noisily: *The dog sat in the corner, munching on a bone.*

mundane /mʌnˈdeɪn/ *adjective*
Something **mundane** is dull and uninteresting because it is ordinary or familiar: *The women were traditionally given the less creative, more mundane tasks like cleaning the plant pots.*

municipal /mjʊˈnɪsɪpəl/ *adjective*
Municipal means relating to or operated by the local government of a town or region: *offices inside the municipal buildings* □ *This is a municipal park to which the public has open access.*

mural /ˈmjʊərəl/ *noun*: **murals**
A **mural** is a painting painted directly on to a wall.

murder /ˈmɜːdə(r)/ *noun*; *verb*
▻ ***noun***: **murders**
1 (*uncount or count*) **Murder** is the crime of deliberately killing a person: *This was a particularly vicious murder.* **2** (*uncount*; *informal*) People sometimes refer to something very severe or unpleasant as **murder**: *Sorry I'm late; the traffic in town was murder.*
▻ ***verb***: **murders, murdering, murdered**
To **murder** someone is to kill them deliberately: *He was convicted of murdering the Yorkshire schoolgirl.* — *noun* **murderer:** *The police are no nearer finding the murderer.* □ *His murderers were caught and hanged.*
▻ ***phrase*** (*informal*) Someone who **gets away with murder** is allowed to behave badly without being punished or scolded.

murky /ˈmɜːkɪ/ *adjective*: **murkier, murkiest**
1 A **murky** place is dark and frightening: *We followed him down a murky corridor.* **2 Murky** water is dark and dirty. **3** (*often humorous*) You describe as **murky** something that little is known about, but that is likely to be unpleasant or sinister: *Gradually, more of her murky past was revealed.* □ *Come on, let's hear a few more of your murky secrets.*

murmur /ˈmɜːmə(r)/ *noun*; *verb*
▻ ***noun***: **murmurs**
A **murmur** is a quiet continuous sound, *eg* of running water or low voices: *the murmur of the breeze in the trees.*
▻ ***verb***: **murmurs, murmuring, murmured**
You **murmur** when you speak so softly and quietly that people can hardly hear you: *Jack murmured polite congratulations.*

muscle /ˈmʌsəl/ *noun*; *verb*
▻ ***noun***: **muscles**
1 Your **muscles** are the parts of your body that move your limbs and organs, that you can make bigger and stronger by exercising: *Men with big muscles don't seem to be fashionable any more.* **2** (*uncount*) **Muscle** is power or influence: *the City of London with all its financial muscle.*
▻ ***verb*** (*informal*): **muscles, muscling, muscled**

> ***phrasal verb***
> You **muscle in** when you involve yourself in something that does not concern you, or take a share of something that you have no right to: *We didn't want the parents muscling in on our plans.*

muscular /ˈmʌskjʊlə(r)/ *adjective*
1 Muscular means relating to your muscles: *Is there any muscular pain?* **2** A **muscular** person has large, well-developed muscles: *Most of the runners are very muscular.*

muse /mjuːz/ *verb* (*literary*): **muses, musing, mused**
You **muse** when you spend time thinking about something, usually something not very serious: *She lay musing, eyes on the ceiling.*

museum /mjuːˈzɪəm/ *noun*: **museums**
A **museum** is a place where objects of artistic, scientific or historic interest are displayed to the public: *a new museum of Scottish art.* □ *the Science Museum.*

mush /mʌʃ/ *noun* (*singular*)
A **mush** is a soft, half-liquid mass of anything: *He tried not to look at the disgusting mush on his plate.*

mushroom /ˈmʌʃrʊm/ *noun*; *verb*
▻ ***noun***: **mushrooms**
Mushrooms are small funguses, usually white or brown, with a short stem and a fleshy, umbrella-shaped top part; many types of mushroom are edible. [see picture at **vegetable**]
▻ ***verb***: **mushrooms, mushrooming, mushroomed**
Something **mushrooms** when it develops or increases surprisingly quickly: *The housing estate has mushroomed since I was here last.*

mushy /ˈmʌʃɪ/ *adjective* (*informal*): **mushier, mushiest**
1 Something that is **mushy** is in a soft, half-liquid state: *The beans had been cooked for so long that they had gone all mushy.* **2** A film or a piece of writing is described as **mushy** if it is sentimental in a silly or embarrassing way.

music /ˈmjuːzɪk/ *noun* (*uncount*)
1 Music is organized patterns of sound, either sung or produced with instruments: *classical and popular music.* **2 Music** is also the art or practice or creating such sound: *a music teacher.*

musical /ˈmjuːzɪkəl/ *adjective*; *noun*
▻ ***adjective***
1 Musical means relating to music: *a long and distinguished musical career.* **2** A **musical** sound is pleasant to hear. [*same as* **tuneful, melodious**] **3** Someone who is **musical** is talented at playing music.
▻ ***noun***: **musicals**
A **musical** is a play or film in which there is a lot of singing and dancing.

musician /mjuːˈzɪʃən/ *noun*: **musicians**
A **musician** is a person who plays music, whether as a job or a pastime: *professional musicians.*

Muslim or **Moslem** /ˈmʊzlɪm/ *noun* (*often adjectival*): **Muslims**
A **Muslim** is a follower of the religion of Islam: *a group made up of Jews, Christians and Muslims* □ *Friday is the Muslim holy day.*

muslin /ˈmʌzlɪn/ *noun* (*uncount*)
Muslin is thin cotton cloth.

mussel /'mʌsəl/ *noun*: **mussels**
Mussels are edible shellfish with a long, rounded, blackish shell.

must /mʌst/ *verb*; *noun*
▻ ***modal verb***
(*negative forms* **must not** or **mustn't**)
1 People **must** do something if they have to do it, *eg* if it is necessary, if it is their duty, if a law or rule compels them, or if they have no choice: *We must cut our costs if we are to remain competitive.* □ *The violence must stop.* □ *Britain must pull its weight.* □ *You must not run in the corridors.* □ *Why mustn't we mention the subject?* □ *The drawing must be all your own work.* □ *We must all die.*

Something that you **must not** do is something you are forbidden to do, or not allowed to do; use **do not have to** or **needn't** to express the lack of necessity or obligation: *I don't have to agree with everything you say. You needn't come if you don't want to.*

2 You say you **must** do something if you need to do it or think you ought to do it, and you intend to do it or are determined to do it: *I must finish my essay this evening.* □ *I must take more exercise.* □ *I mustn't eat so much, must I?* □ *I must remember to tell them, mustn't I?*
3 You tell someone they **must** do something **a** when you are giving them orders or instructions: *You must drop everything and come.* □ *You mustn't tell a soul.* **b** when you are giving them a vague invitation: *You must come and spend a weekend with us.* **c** if you think they would enjoy it: *You must read her other novels.*
4 You phrase questions with **must** **a** to express annoyance or impatience at someone's behaviour: *Must you have the radio on while I'm trying to work?* □ *Why must you complain all the time?* **b** to plead with someone, *eg* to change their mind or excuse you from something: *Must you go so soon?* □ *Must I really get up now?*
5 You introduce your opinion with expressions such as '**I must** say' and '**I must** admit': *You've done a splendid job, I must say.* □ *I must admit that her work has improved.* □ *I'm afraid I must disagree.*
6 You say that something **must** be so if you think it is unlikely not to be so; something that **must** have happened is very likely to have happened: *You must be Charles.* □ *You must be very proud of your daughter.* □ *They must have arrived by now, mustn't they?* □ *I must have dropped my keys when I got out of the car.*
▻ ***noun*** (*used in the singular; informal*)
Something that is a **must** is necessary or essential: *Fitness is a must in this game.* □ *These story tapes are a must for long journeys with children.*
▻ ***phrases*** **1** You say '**if you must**' when you cannot persuade someone not to do something that you think is silly: *Write and apologize if you must, but it's quite unnecessary.* **2** You say '**if you must know**' to express annoyance at someone's curiosity: *I'm spending the weekend with friends, if you must know.*

mustache See **moustache**.

mustard /'mʌstəd/ *noun* (*uncount*)
Mustard is a thick, strong-tasting, yellowish-brown paste often eaten with meat.

muster /'mʌstə(r)/ *verb*: **musters, mustering, mustered**
You **muster** a quality such as strength or patience when you try to find within yourself as much of it as you can, in order to deal with a situation: *With all the courage I could muster, I told him to get out.*

mustn't /'mʌsənt/ *verb* (*informal*)
Mustn't is the spoken, and informal written, form of **must not**.

must've /'mʌstəv/ *verb* (*informal*)
Must've is the spoken and informal written, form of **must have**, when 'have' is used as an auxiliary verb: *We must've left it at the shop.*

musty /'mʌstɪ/ *adjective*
Something **musty** smells old and damp: *She led us down to a musty cellar.* □ *a musty smell.*

mute /mju:t/ *adjective*
1 A **mute** person is not able to speak. **2** Someone is **mute** when they are quite silent: *Lionel stood, mute, staring at the wall.* **3** **Mute** emotions or reactions are felt but not expressed in words.

muted /'mju:tɪd/ *adjective*
1 A **muted** sound or colour is soft, not harsh. **2** You describe feelings or reactions as **muted** if you can tell from the way they are expressed that they are not very strong: *Their enthusiasm was a little muted.*

mutilate /'mju:tɪleɪt/ *verb*: **mutilates, mutilating, mutilated**
1 Someone **is mutilated** when they suffer severe injuries, especially when one or more of their limbs are cut off: *Policemen arriving on the scene were shocked by the sight of so many mutilated bodies.* **2** To **mutilate** something is to damage it severely: *The flower beds had been mutilated beyond recognition.* — *noun* (*uncount or count*) **mutilation** /mju:tɪ'leɪʃən/: *The body had been been subjected to horrible mutilation.*

mutiny /'mju:tɪnɪ/ *noun*; *verb*
▻ ***noun*** (*uncount or count*): **mutinies**
Mutiny is the act of rebelling against people in authority, especially in the armed forces: *It seems we have a mutiny on our hands.*
▻ ***verb***: **mutinies, mutinying, mutinied:** *The rest of the crew were planning to mutiny.*

mutter /'mʌtə(r)/ *verb*: **mutters, muttering, muttered**
You **mutter** something when you say it quietly, often in an angry or irritated tone of voice: *She muttered that she never had any time to herself.* □ *He went off muttering to himself about the unfairness of life.*

mutton /'mʌtən/ *noun* (*uncount*)
Mutton is the flesh of an adult sheep, used as food.
▻ ***phrase*** (*informal*) People describe an older woman as **mutton dressed as lamb** if they think she is trying to look much younger than she really is, *eg* by wearing youthful clothes and a lot of make-up.

mutual /'mju:tʃuəl/ *adjective*
1 **Mutual** feelings are felt by each of two or more people about the other or others: *They had a relationship of mutual respect and admiration.* □ *I disliked Williams intensely, and I suspected that the feeling was mutual.* **2** **Mutual** also describes something shared by each of two or more: *a mutual friend.* [*same as* **common**]

muzzle /'mʌzəl/ *noun*; *verb*
▻ ***noun***: **muzzles**
1 The **muzzle** of an animal such as a dog is its nose and mouth, the part that sticks out from its face. **2** A **muzzle** is a set of straps fitted round an animal's mouth to prevent it biting people. **3** The open end of a gun, where the bullet comes out, is the **muzzle**.
▻ ***verb***: **muzzles, muzzling, muzzled**
1 To **muzzle** an animal such as a dog is to put a muzzle around its mouth. **2** Someone who **is muzzled** is prevented from speaking openly and honestly: *a junior minister who claims that senior party officials muzzled him.* [*same as* **silence, gag**]

my /maɪ/ *determiner* (*possessive*)
1 The person speaking or writing uses **my** to refer to things that belong or relate to himself or herself: *I seem to have twisted my ankle.* □ *My parents were both doctors.* □ *I gave her my telephone number.* □ *How old are you, if you don't mind my* (or *me*) *asking?* **2** (*formal or old*) You use **my** in some titles and forms of address, *eg* at the beginning of a letter: *My dear Peter* ... □ *You're in luck today, my friend.* □ *No, my lord.*

myriad /ˈmɪrɪəd/ *noun* (*singular, often adjectival literary*)
A **myriad** of things is a very great number of them: *a myriad of stars in the night sky* □ *her myriad admirers.*

myself /maɪˈsɛlf/ *pronoun* (*reflexive*)
1 A person speaking or writing uses **myself** as the object of a verb or preposition when *I* is the subject: *I decided to smarten myself up a bit.* □ *I fell down and hurt myself.* □ *I felt quite proud of myself.* □ *I haven't had a minute to myself all day.* **2** You add **myself** after *I* for emphasis: *I myself disapprove.* □ *I don't like her much myself.* □ *I'm not feeling very well myself.* **3** Sometimes **myself** is used as an emphatic form of *me*: *No-one was keener than myself.* □ *She's a mathematician like myself.* **4** If you say 'I did it **myself**' you mean that you did it independently, without help or participation by anyone else: *I made the cake myself.* □ *Let me speak to her myself.* **5** You say 'I'm not **myself**' when you are not feeling well: *I haven't been myself recently.* □ *At last I'm beginning to feel myself again.*
▷ ***phrase*** For **by myself** see **by**.

mysterious /mɪˈstɪərɪəs/ *adjective*
1 Something **mysterious** is difficult or impossible to understand or explain: *What mysterious forces caused it to explode at that very moment?* □ *I find the whole affair of his death rather mysterious.* **2** You say someone is being **mysterious** about something when they avoid talking about it, making you even more curious.
— *adverb* **mysteriously:** *When we got back, the car had mysteriously vanished.* □ *Why is he behaving so mysteriously?*

mystery /ˈmɪstərɪ/ *noun*: **mysteries**
1 A **mystery** is something that people cannot, or have not been able to, understand or explain: *Her sudden death remains a mystery to us all.* □ *the mystery of the creation of the universe.* **2** (*uncount*) **Mystery** is the quality of being difficult or impossible to explain or understand, or of being strange and making people curious: *Her private life remained shrouded in mystery.*

mystical /ˈmɪstɪkəl/ *adjective*
Mystical means relating to or involving the spiritual world and spiritual powers: *He is said to have had some kind of mystical experience.*

mystify /ˈmɪstɪfaɪ/ *verb*: **mystifies, mystifying, mystified**
You **are mystified** by something that you cannot understand or explain at all: *His sudden change of mind has mystified us all.* [*same as* **bewilder**, **perplex**, **puzzle**]

myth /mɪθ/ *noun*: **myths**
1 (*count or uncount*) **Myths** are ancient stories telling of gods and heroes: *These explanations belong in the realm of myth and legend, not scientific fact.* **2** You can refer to something people wrongly believe to be true as a **myth**: *the widespread myth that lightning never strikes in the same place twice.*

mythical /ˈmɪθɪkəl/ *adjective*
1 A **mythical** creature is one that exists only in myths. **2** You can refer to something that is regarded as existing, but which does not really exist, as **mythical**: *We seem to live our lives in search of some mythical state of perfection.* [*same as* **fabulous**]

mythology /mɪˈθɒlədʒɪ/ *noun* (*uncount*)
Ancient myths in general are often referred to as **mythology**: *characters from Greek mythology.*

N

N or **n** /ɛn/ *noun*: **Ns** or **n's**
N is the fourteenth letter of the English alphabet: *There's an n at the end of 'solemn'.*

naff /naf/ *adjective* (*informal*)
If you describe something as **naff** you mean it looks cheap, of poor quality and not very stylish: *He turned up for the interview in a really naff suit he'd had for years.*

nag /nag/ *verb*: **nags, nagging, nagged**
1 Someone **nags** you when they repeatedly criticize you or find fault with you: *She keeps nagging me about drinking too much beer.* □ *My parents were always nagging at me to do my homework.* **2** An unpleasant feeling **nags** you when it constantly troubles you: *I had a nagging suspicion that I was being tricked.* □ *The pain came back and nagged at her shoulder.*

nail /neɪl/ *noun*; *verb*
▻ ***noun***: **nails**
1 Your **nails** are the hard coverings on the upper side of the ends of your fingers and toes: *She had painted her fingernails.* □ *a small pair of clippers for cutting toenails.* **2** A **nail** is also a small thin metal bar with one pointed end, that you force into a surface, *eg* to join two pieces of wood together, by hitting it with a hammer: *a bag of masonry nails.*
▻ ***verb***: **nails, nailing, nailed**
You **nail** something when you attach or join it using nails: *They had nailed the plaque to the wall.* □ *Boards had been nailed over the windows.*
▻ ***phrase*** You say that someone **has hit the nail on the head** if they have described or identified something precisely or accurately.

naive or **naïve** /naɪ'iːv/ *adjective*
Someone who is **naive** assumes that people are good and situations are simple, because they have had no experience of how cruel people can be or how difficult and complicated life sometimes is: *They had a very naive approach to business, which was bound to lead them into trouble.* — *adverb* **naively:** *I continued naively to believe that he had really wanted to help me.* — *noun* (*uncount*) **naivety** or **naïvety** /naɪ'iːvətɪ/: *I was embarrassed by my own naivety.*

naked /'neɪkɪd/ *adjective*
1 A person who is **naked** is wearing no clothes: *the sight of their naked bodies.* [*same as* **bare**, **nude**; *opposite* **clothed**] **2 Naked** is often used to describe strong feelings, especially bad or unpleasant feelings, that a person makes no attempt to hide or control: *I found their naked ambition quite disgusting.* □ *She was motivated by naked greed.* **3** A **naked** light or flame is one you can see plainly or touch, because it is not covered or protected in any way: *the light from a single naked bulb.* **4** You look at something with the **naked** eye when you don't use a telescope, microscope or other instrument: *These tiny creatures are quite invisible to the naked eye.* — *noun* (*uncount*) **nakedness:** *As children, we were taught not to be embarrassed by our own nakedness.*

name /neɪm/ *noun*; *verb*
▻ ***noun***: **names**
1 The **name** of a person, place or thing is the word or words used to refer to and identify them: *The name of the dead man is being withheld till relatives are informed.* □ *What's your boss's name?* □ *Her name's Jane Tyrie.* □ *I couldn't remember the name of the town.* □ *The plant's botanical name is Aquilegia, but most of us refer to it by its popular name 'columbine'.* □ *How did you come by the name of Tuzi?* □ *I preferred it to the name my parents gave me.* □ *Coaldale, as the name suggests, was an old mining village.* **2** A person's reputation can be referred to as their **name**: *It's incidents like this that give English football fans a bad name.* □ *He's prepared to go to court in order to clear his name.* [*same as* **reputation**] **3** A famous or important person or company can be referred to as a **name**: *All the big names in fashion will be there.* □ *You're quite a name in the literary world now.*
▻ ***verb***: **names, naming, named**
1 You **name** someone or something when you give them a name; you **name** them after a person or thing when you give them the person or thing's name: *We decided to name the baby Laurence, after his grandfather.* [*same as* **call**] **2** You **name** someone when you mention or identify them by name: *We were asked to name three poets whose work we admired.* □ *He refused to name the other members of the gang.* **3** You **name** a date or price when you suggest it: *When I asked what salary they were offering, they told me to name my own figure.* — *adjective* **named:** *Her contact was a man named Peter Sykes.* [*same as* **called**]
▻ ***phrases*** **1** You mention or know someone or something **by name** when you say their name, or can say what it is: *She could address every member of the work force by name.* □ *He didn't actually refer to you by name.* **2** You use **by name** and **by the name of** to supply someone's name: *another lecturer, Brunton by name* □ *a cabaret dancer by the name of Ethel.* **3** You **call** someone **names** when you insult or abuse them by using unpleasant terms to refer to them or describe them. **4** Something that exists **in name only** does not have the status indicated by its name: *It's a capital city in name only.* **5** You do something **in the name of** a principle or belief if that is the reason why you do it: *History has seen millions of people tortured and put to death in the name of religion.* **6** Something that is reserved **in your name** has been reserved officially for you: *The seats were booked in the name of Henderson.* **7** You **make a name for yourself**, or **make your name**, when you become well known or famous for something that you do: *He was beginning to make a name for himself as a fast bowler.* □ *She had already made her name as a singer by the age of 19.* **8** You do something **under** a certain **name** if you use that name while you do it: *He was travelling under a false name.*

name-dropping /'neɪmdrɒpɪŋ/ *noun* (*uncount*)
Name-dropping is the practice of referring to well-known people as if they were your friends, in order to impress others.

nameless /ˈneɪmləs/ *adjective*
You use **nameless** when talking about someone or something that you don't want to identify or specify: *A friend of mine, who shall remain nameless, was discovered with no clothes on.*

namely /ˈneɪmlɪ/ *adverb* (*sentence adverb*)
You use **namely** to introduce an explanation of, or additional information about, someone or something you have just mentioned: *It was given to two other members of the group, namely Mckinnon and Endicott.* □ *This disguised her intention; namely, to turn her colleagues against the boss.*

namesake /ˈneɪmseɪk/ *noun*: **namesakes**
You can refer to someone who has the same name as you as your **namesake**.

nana /ˈnanə/ or **nan** /ˈnan/ *noun* (*informal*): **nanas**
Some people call their grandmother **nana** or **nan**: *It was a present from my nana.* □ *Would you like more tea, Nan?* [*same as* **granny**, **grandma**]

nanny /ˈnanɪ/ *noun*: **nannies**
A **nanny** is a person employed to look after or bring up a child in its own home.

nap /nap/ *noun*; *verb*
▻ ***noun***: **naps**
A **nap** is a short sleep that you have during the day: *Why don't you have a little nap.?*
▻ ***verb***: **naps, napping, napped**
You **nap** when you have a nap: *We were able to get some rest while the children were napping.*
▻ ***phrase*** (*informal*) You **catch** someone **napping** when they are not prepared for something you do to them: *In the case of the first goal, the defenders were caught napping.*

nape /neɪp/ *noun* (*used in the singular*)
The **nape** of your neck is the back of your neck.

napkin /ˈnapkɪn/ *noun*: **napkins**
A **napkin** is a piece of cloth or paper for wiping your fingers and mouth on during a meal. [*same as* **serviette**; see picture at **tableware**]

nappy /ˈnapɪ/ *noun*: **nappies**
A **nappy** is a piece of towelling or other soft cloth, or a pad of paper, fastened round a baby's bottom to soak up the solid and liquid waste it releases: *a pack of disposable nappies.*

narcotic /nɑːˈkɒtɪk/ *noun*: **narcotics**
Narcotics are drugs that relieve pain or make you feel sleepy, or any drug that people take for pleasure, usually illegally.

narration /nəˈreɪʃən/ *noun* (*uncount*)
1 The **narration** of a story is the process or manner of telling it: *The theme is supported by skilful narration and sensitive character-drawing.* **2** In a film, the **narration** is the spoken commentary that accompanies it.

narrative /ˈnarətɪv/ *noun*: **narratives**
A **narrative** is a story, or the parts of a book, film or play that deal with telling a story: *It is a fascinating narrative.* □ *Too long a descriptive paragraph slows down the narrative.*

narrator /nəˈreɪtə(r)/ *noun*: **narrators**
The **narrator** of a story is the person telling it.

narrow /ˈnaroʊ/ *adjective*; *verb*
▻ ***adjective***: **narrower, narrowest**
1 Something **narrow** is not very wide, especially in comparison with how long it is: *A narrow path led to the bottom of the garden.* □ *The road was too narrow for overtaking.* **2 Narrow** is used in many ways to suggest a failure to consider all aspects or possibilities, or a failure to consider or accept new and different views, attitudes or tastes: *The essay takes a rather narrow view of British cinema.* □ *Her parents would never allow it; they're very narrow-minded.* **3 Narrow** also means only just achieved: *a narrow victory* □ *a narrow escape.* — *adverb* **narrowly:** *They were narrowly defeated in last year's final.* — *noun* (*uncount*) **narrowness**: *the extreme narrowness of their views.*
▻ ***verb***: **narrows, narrowing, narrowed**
Something **narrows** when it becomes narrow: *The road narrows from both sides.* □ *This way, our choices are drastically narrowed.* □ *the narrowing gap between the political parties.*

phrasal verb
You **narrow** things **down** when you reduce or limit the number of them as choices or possibilities: *Over a hundred applicants will be narrowed down to a shortlist of five candidates.*

nasal /ˈneɪzəl/ *adjective*
1 Nasal means relating to the nose: *the lining of the nasal cavity.* **2 Nasal** sounds are made through the nose: *She spoke in a rather nasal tone.*

nasty /ˈnɑːstɪ/ *adjective*: **nastier, nastiest**
1 Something **nasty** is unpleasant, disgusting or offensive: *It left a nasty taste in my mouth.* □ *nasty little pamphlets stirring up racial hatred.* [*opposite* **pleasant**] **2** Someone who is **nasty** behaves in a cruel or unkind way towards others: *That's a nasty thing to say about your own son.* □ *She complained that the other children were nasty to her.* [*same as* **mean**; *opposite* **nice**] **3** A **nasty** injury is serious; a **nasty** situation is difficult or unpleasant, usually because it involves strong or violent disagreement or argument: *a nasty wound* □ *It looked like things might turn nasty.* — *adverb* **nastily:** *I apologized for speaking nastily about her mother.*

nation /ˈneɪʃən/ *noun*: **nations**
1 A **nation** is a country, especially one thought of as a separate political and social unit: *one of the world's most powerful trading nations.* **2** You sometimes refer to the people of a country as the **nation**: *In tomorrow's election, the nation decides who is to run the country.*

national /ˈnaʃnəl/ or /ˈnaʃənəl/ *adjective*; *noun*
▻ ***adjective***
1 National means relating to a whole country, rather than to a single area or region, or to a single country, rather than to several countries: *government at local and national level* □ *a roundup of today's national and international news.* **2 National** also describes things relating to the people of a particular country: *the national flag of Malta* □ *Preoccupation with health seems to be a national characteristic.* — *adverb* **nationally:** *She's competed both at county level and nationally.*
▻ ***noun***: **nationals**
You can refer to a citizen of a particular country as a **national**: *Foreign nationals were not eligible for these visas.* □ *an Egyptian national.*

national anthem /naʃnəl ˈanθəm/ *noun*: **national anthems**
A country's **national anthem** is its official song.

national insurance /naʃnəl ɪnˈʃʊərəns/ *noun* (*uncount*)
National insurance is a kind of tax paid by employers and employees, to provide money for people who become ill or unemployed, and to provide pensions for people who retire.

nationalism /'naʃnəlɪzm/ *noun* (*uncount*)
1 Nationalism is the desire for political independence for your country, and the efforts made to achieve it: *Is this a victory for Irish nationalism?* **2 Nationalism** is also great pride in your own country, especially of an extreme kind that makes you believe that other nations are inferior: *feelings of nationalism.* [*same as* **patriotism**] — *noun and adjective* **nationalist:** *His father's an ardent nationalist.* □ *the nationalist tendencies of the right-wing of the party.*

nationality /naʃə'nalɪtɪ/ *noun* (*count or uncount*): **nationalities**
Nationality refers to a person's status as a citizen of a particular country: *The children are eligible for both French and British nationality.* □ *What nationality are her parents?*

nationalize or **nationalise** /'naʃnəlaɪz/ *verb*: **nationalizes, nationalizing, nationalized**
To **nationalize** an industry is to bring it under the ownership and control of a country's government: *Cuts in government subsidies have forced the nationalized industries to increase their prices.* — *noun* (*uncount*) **nationalization** /naʃnəlaɪ'zeɪʃən/: *the nationalization of the car industry* □ *a policy of nationalization.*

national service /naʃnəl 'sɜːvɪs/ *noun* (*uncount*)
National service is a period of compulsory service in the armed forces: *There is still national service in these countries.* □ *He did his national service in Aden.*

nationwide /neɪʃən'waɪd/ *adjective and adverb*
Nationwide describes things that exist throughout a whole country, in every area: *a nationwide search to find the most talented musician* □ *I've visited businesses nationwide, and they all say the same thing.*

native /'neɪtɪv/ *adjective*; *noun*
▻ ***adjective***
1 Your **native** country is where you were born and brought up; your **native** language is the one you first learned to speak and the one you speak most of the time: *back to my native Germany* □ *a dictionary for foreign and native speakers of English.* **2** Something such as a plant or an animal is **native** to a particular place when it exists there naturally and originally, rather than being brought from another place: *Many of the trees that make up Scotland's forests are not actually native.*
▻ ***noun***: **natives**
1 A **native** of a country is a person who was born and brought up there. **2** (*old, offensive*) In some non-European countries, white European people who settled there later sometimes refer to the original black inhabitants as **natives**.

natter /'natə(r)/ *verb*; *noun*
▻ ***verb*** (*informal*): **natters, nattering, nattered**
You **natter** to someone when you have an informal conversation with them: *We left them nattering about the war.* [*same as* **chat**]
▻ ***noun*** (*used in the singular, informal*): *They had a natter about football and the elections.* [*same as* **chat**]

natural /'natʃrəl/ or /'natʃərəl/ *adjective*; *noun*
▻ ***adjective***
1 Someone's behaviour is **natural** when it is normal and unsurprising, because it is the way people usually behave: *It's only natural that you should feel a little envious.* □ *It's not natural for a mother to behave like that.* □ *She responded with natural hostility.* **2** Your **natural** skills or talents are the things you do so well or easily that you seem to have been born with the ability: *She has a natural flair for coping with children.* □ *Painting seemed natural to him.* □ *He is a natural teacher.* **3 Natural** also means relating to nature, or existing as part of nature and not made or altered by people: *the natural sciences* □ *areas of outstanding natural beauty* □ *earthquakes, floods and other natural disasters* □ *natural and man-made fibres.* **4** You can say that someone has a **natural** manner if they behave in an open, sincere way rather than trying to give a false impression of the kind of person they are: *He has an easy, natural charm.* **5** Someone who dies of **natural** causes dies because they were ill, rather than as a result of a crime or accident: *She died a natural death at the age of 84.* **6** Your **natural** parents are your real, biological parents. — *adverb* **naturally:** *She fitted quite naturally into her new community.* □ *You look very nervous; try to act more naturally.* □ *She is a naturally gifted artist.* [see also **naturally** in its own separate entry]
▻ ***noun*** (*used in the singular; informal*)
You can describe someone as a **natural** if they have a natural ability or skill.

naturalist /'natʃrəlɪst/ *noun*: **naturalists**
A **naturalist** is a person who studies plants and animals.

naturally /'natʃrəlɪ/ *adverb* (*sentence adverb*)
You use **naturally** to talk about things that don't surprise you because they are normal and you expect them; as a reply, **naturally** means 'of course': *He was naturally very shocked at the news.* □ *She heard a scream, so, naturally, she ran downstairs to see what had happened.* □ *'Will you be voting against the bill?' 'Naturally; it's an undemocratic proposal.'* [*same as* **of course**; see also **naturally** at **natural**]

nature /'neɪtʃə(r)/ *noun*: **natures**
1 (*uncount*) **Nature** is the physical world of plants and animals and forces such as the weather, not including things made or changed by people: *For many of the city children, this visit to a farm will be their first experience of nature.* □ *The development of caterpillars into butterflies is one of Nature's most fascinating mysteries.* **2** (*used in the singular or uncount*) The **nature** of something is its basic quality, or what it consists of: *the romantic nature of much of his poetry* □ *This depends on the nature and seriousness of the accident.* □ *It is by nature a very sensitive issue.* **3** (*used in the singular or uncount*) A person's **nature** is their character, or the kind of person they are: *It's against his nature to be impatient.* □ *She has a very calm nature.* □ *It's not in her nature to be cruel to animals.* □ *He is by nature rather an aggressive person.* [*same as* **character**]
▻ ***phrase*** Something is **second nature** to you if you can do it very easily, without having to think about it or try very hard.

naturist /'neɪtʃərɪst/ *noun* (*often adjectival*): **naturists**
A **naturist** is a person who likes to be naked, especially someone who goes to special camps or other areas for people who don't like wearing clothes: *We had stumbled on to a naturist beach.* [*same as* **nudist**]

naughty /'nɔːtɪ/ *adjective*: **naughtier, naughtiest**
1 A **naughty** child is one who behaves badly: *I told them off for being naughty.* [*same as* **badly-behaved**; *opposite* **good**, **well-behaved**] **2** People sometimes describe things such as books or films as **naughty** when they are mildly embarrassing or shocking because they deal with sex: *The play had one or two naughty scenes.* [*same as* **saucy, risqué**]

nausea /'nɔːzɪə/ *noun* (*uncount*)
Nausea is the feeling that you are about to be sick: *I was overcome by nausea.*

nauseating /'nɔːzɪeɪtɪŋ/ *adjective*
1 Something **nauseating** makes you feel that you are

about to be sick: *streets full of nauseating smells.* [*same as* **sickening**] **2** You can describe something as **nauseating** if you find it disgusting or offensive: *She vowed not to let that impertinent man get away with such nauseating behaviour.* [*same as* **detestable**]

nautical /'nɔːtɪkəl/ *adjective*
Nautical means relating to ships, sailors and the sea: *a life devoted to nautical pursuits* □ *several nautical miles.* [*same as* **maritime**]

naval /'neɪvəl/ *adjective*
Naval means relating to a navy, or to ships generally: *He looked smart in his naval uniform.*

navel /'neɪvəl/ *noun*: **navels**
Your **navel** is the small round hollow in your lower abdomen, the point where the cord connecting you to your mother was cut when you were born.

navigate /'navɪgeɪt/ *verb*: **navigates, navigating, navigated**
To **navigate** is to direct the course of a ship, aircraft or other vehicle, using maps and other instruments: *Jenkins was chosen as pilot, and I agreed to navigate.* □ *This part of the river is notoriously difficult to navigate.* — *noun* (*uncount*) **navigation** /navɪ'geɪʃən/: *A sandstorm blew up, making navigation almost impossible.* — *noun* **navigator**: *He was the most experienced navigator I had ever flown with.*

navy /'neɪvɪ/ *noun*: **navies**
1 A country's **navy** is the armed force that fights in ships: *He wanted to join the navy.* □ *the Royal Navy.* **2** (*uncount, often adjectival*) **Navy**, or **navy** blue, is a dark blue colour: *I'll wear my navy raincoat.* □ *Are these tights navy blue or black?*

near /nɪə(r)/ *preposition or adverb; adjective or adverb; adjective; verb*
▻ ***preposition or adverb***: **nearer, nearest**
1 One thing is **near**, or **near** to, another if it is only a short distance from it: *We found a café near the bus station.* □ *I spoke to the man standing nearest to me.* □ *Don't go any nearer the edge than you need to.* □ *I wish you lived nearer to us.* □ *The animal approached a little nearer.* □ *We sat in the third row, near enough to see the sweat on his face.* **2** Something that occurs **near**, or **near** to, a certain time happens just before or after it: *We'll decide a bit nearer the time.* □ *The nearer it got to the audition, the more nervous I was becoming.* □ *in a scene near the end of the play* □ *It's too near the beginning of term to assess their progress.* **3** Someone or something is **near**, or **near** to, a particular state, condition, point or level when they are close to it or have almost reached it: *Mrs Roberts was evidently near to tears.* □ *I was very near to losing my temper.* □ *Our nerves were near breaking point.* □ *Her guess was nearer the truth than she realized.* □ *This is the nearest we've come to a solution so far.* □ *It set the curtains on fire, with near-disastrous results.* □ *The level of investment was nearer £4 million than £3 million.* □ *They've given us some money, but nowhere near enough.*
▻ ***adjective or adverb***: **nearer, nearest**
An event or time that is **near** or coming **nearer** is going to come soon: *The dreaded ordeal drew nearer and nearer.* □ *An end to the violence is said to be near.*
▻ ***adjective***: **nearer, nearest**
1 Near describes things that are a short distance away from you: *The nearest shop is over two miles away.* □ *They're near neighbours of my parents.* □ *Focus on the nearer figure.* **2** Your **near** relatives are the people you are most closely related to, such as your brothers, sisters, parents and grandparents. **3 Near** describes a situation that can almost, but not quite, be classified as something: *an atmosphere of near panic* □ *a situation of near chaos* □ *in a state of near collapse* □ *another near disaster.* **4** The **near** side of a vehicle is the side next to the kerb, that is, its left side in countries where people drive on the left. — *noun* (*uncount*) **nearness:** *His physical nearness disturbed her.* □ *Nearness to the shops is an important factor.*
▻ ***verb***: **nears, nearing, neared**
1 You **near** a place when you approach it: *As we neared the coast I could see the white villas scattered along the clifftop.* **2** Someone or something **is nearing** a time or a stage when they are reaching it: *teenagers nearing school-leaving age* □ *The motorway is now nearing completion.*
▻ ***phrases*** **1** If you say that some incident was **a near thing** you mean that it was almost a disaster or accident: *The bus swerved in time, but it was a near thing.* [compare **a near miss** at **miss**] **2** Something that is the case **near enough**, or **as near as makes no difference**, is almost the case: *It'll cost you £3000 or near enough.* **3** For **nowhere near** see **nowhere**. **4** Something that is **the nearest thing** to a certain kind of thing is the most similar thing to it that is available: *This was the nearest thing to a screwdriver I could find.*

nearby /nɪə'baɪ/ *adjective and adverb*
Nearby places are quite close to where you are, or to the place you are talking about: *We stopped for refreshment at a nearby village.* □ *All the towns nearby were overrun with tourists.* □ *The sun was setting and, nearby, we could hear the fishermen setting out for the night.*

nearly /'nɪəlɪ/ *adverb*
Something that **nearly** happens, or is **nearly** so, does not quite happen, or is not completely so: *He was stung by a jellyfish and very nearly died.* □ *I was nearly late for my appointment because of the traffic jam.* □ *They're pretty nearly bankrupt.* □ *It wasn't until nearly a month later that I received a reply.* □ *It was five o'clock, and nearly time to leave.* □ *He's very nearly as tall as his father already.* □ *They nearly always send a cheque.* □ *Nearly everyone on the course said they had enjoyed it.* [*same as* **almost**]
▻ ***phrase*** You use **not nearly** as an emphatic form of 'not', where something is *eg* not as good as something else, or not as much as it should be: *I tried on a size 8, but it wasn't nearly big enough.* □ *'Is there enough?' 'Not nearly.'* □ *Their sports facilities aren't nearly as good as those in American universities.* □ *I'm afraid I haven't nearly finished.* □ *The book isn't nearly complete.* [*same as* **nothing like, nowhere near**]

near-sighted /nɪə'saɪtɪd/ *adjective*
You are **near-sighted** if you can only see clearly things that are fairly close to you. [*same as* **short-sighted**; *opposite* **long-sighted**]

neat /niːt/ *adjective*: **neater, neatest**
1 Something that is **neat** is tidy, clean and arranged in an ordered way: *He keeps his clothes very neat.* □ *The room was neat and tidy.* [*opposite* **untidy, messy**] **2** Something that is **neat** is also pleasingly small or regular: *I recognized Phil's neat handwriting.* □ *Arlene was pretty, with a neat little figure.* **3** You drink alcohol, especially an alcoholic spirit, **neat** when you drink it without water or other drinks added to it: *a couple of neat vodkas.* [*same as* **straight**; compare **on the rocks**] **4** (*AmE; informal*) **Neat** also means excellent: *The film was really neat!* — *adverb* **neatly:** *Albert was always neatly dressed.*

necessarily /nɛsə'sɛrɪlɪ/ *adverb*
You use **necessarily** to talk about facts or certainties: *'It's obvious they've decided not to come.' 'Not necessarily; they may simply have got lost.'* □ *Men aren't necessarily physically stronger than women.* □ *Our*

choice will necessarily be the candidate we consider best for the job.

necessary /'nɛsəsəri/ *adjective*
1 Something that is **necessary** is needed or is essential so as to ensure the result you want: *She'd have to obtain the necessary equipment.* □ *They don't have the skills necessary for the job.* □ *comforts necessary to our wellbeing* □ *Of course it's not necessary for a nursery nurse to be a woman.* □ *It will be necessary for us to review your contract at the end of each year.* □ *Is it really necessary to check everything all over again?* □ *We can stay an extra day if necessary.* □ *We mustn't spend any more money than is necessary.* □ *You seem to me to be working harder than necessary.* **2** A **necessary** connection or condition is one that must exist: *the necessary relationship between politics and economics.*

necessitate /nə'sɛsıteıt/ *verb* (*formal*): **necessitates, necessitating, necessitated**
One thing **necessitates** another when it makes it necessary or unavoidable: *Disputes like this necessitate sharp judgment on the part of the manager.* □ *Had those comments alone necessitated his resignation?*

necessity /nə'sɛsıtı/ *noun*: **necessities**
1 A **necessity** is something necessary or essential: *food and other necessities.* **2** (*uncount or used in the singular*) **Necessity** is the need to do or have something, or a circumstance that makes something necessary or unavoidable: *She works out of necessity rather than choice.* □ *We must of necessity draw the conclusion that the company itself was to blame.* □ *There is no necessity to rush.*

neck /nɛk/ *noun*: **necks**
1 Your **neck** is the part of your body between your head and your shoulders: *She stroked the dog's neck.* □ *Water was dripping on the back of my neck.* [see picture at **body**] **2** The **neck** of a garment is the part that fits around your neck. **3** The **neck** of a bottle is the long narrow part leading to the open end.
▷ ***phrases*** **1** (*informal*) Someone who **is breathing down your neck** is watching you closely or checking what you are doing, especially so closely that you feel nervous or uneasy. **2** (*informal*) Someone who **gets it in the neck** is severely scolded or punished. **3** Two or more competitors who are **neck and neck** are exactly level, with nobody clearly winning. **4** (*informal*) You **risk your neck** when what you do exposes you to some kind of danger: *Politically, he risked his neck to save my career.* **5** (*informal*) You **stick your neck out** when what you do puts you in a situation where you might fail, or might be criticized or attacked. **6** (*informal*) You are **up to your neck** when you are very busy with something, or deeply involved in something: *I'm up to my neck in paperwork at the moment; can I call you back?* □ *Although they denied any involvement with the robbery, it was clear that they were in it up to their necks.*

necklace /'nɛkləs/ *noun*: **necklaces**
A **necklace** is a string of beads or jewels, or a decorative chain, that a woman wears around her neck: *a pearl necklace.*

necktie /'nɛktaı/ *noun* (*AmE*): **neckties**
A **necktie** is a tie.

need /ni:d/ *verb*; *modal verb*; *noun*
▷ ***verb***: **needs, needing, needed**
1 You **need** something if it is necessary for you to have it: *Contact us if you need our advice.* □ *All they needed was a bit of love.* **2** You **need** to do something if it is necessary for you to do it: *I need to finish this work by five o'clock.* □ *Grandparents need to feel useful.* □ *How often do we need to check the temperature?* □ *You don't need to be an expert to see that it wouldn't work.* □ *You don't need to stay if you don't want to.* □ *You didn't need to get so angry.* **3** Something **needs** dealing with in a certain way if it is necessary to deal with it in that way: *Tomato plants need regular feeding and watering.* □ *My hair needs washing at least every two days.* □ *That jacket needs cleaning.* □ *various questions that need attention.* **4** Something **needs** doing when it is necessary to do it: *There are so many jobs that need doing urgently.*
▷ ***modal verb***
(*negative forms* **need not** and **needn't**)
Need is used with negatives, in questions expecting the answer 'no', and with words like *hardly*:
1 to talk about what it is not necessary for someone to do, or what there is no good reason for them to do: *You needn't get so nervous.* □ *They needn't have behaved so rudely.* □ *I don't think we need inform the parents at this early stage.* □ *Need you have the radio on so loud?* □ *'Need you wait for written confirmation?' 'No, I suppose I needn't.'* □ *You needn't have gone to so much trouble.* □ *I scarcely need to warn you of the danger.* □ *I need hardly add that we regret your decision.*

> Distinguish between **needn't** and **mustn't**: *You needn't* [= it is unnecessary to] *tell the entire truth, but you mustn't* [= it is wrong to] *lie.*

2 to talk about what can be avoided, or, with *have*, what could have been avoided or prevented: *They need never know.* □ *It needn't be an expensive repair; you could do it yourself.* □ *It was one of those accidents that need not have happened.* □ *I needn't have taken so much trouble with the report, since nobody bothered to read it.*

> Notice that with reference to the present, there is no difference in meaning between the modal and the ordinary verb: *You needn't* (or *you don't need to*) *stay*. But with reference to the past there can be a difference: *I didn't need to get up early after all* [= it was unnecessary to get up early, so I didn't]. *I needn't have got up early after all* [= I got up early unnecessarily].

▷ ***noun***: **needs**
1 Your **needs** are things you need to have: *The local shop supplies all our needs.* □ *a relationship that satisfies one's emotional needs.* **2** (*uncount or used in the singular*) You have the **need** for something when you want or desire it strongly, when you lack it, or when it is necessary for you to do or have it: *She feels no need of male companionship.* □ *If you feel the need to talk, give me a call.* □ *Some of the children were in urgent need of medical treatment.* □ *There's no need for you to stay.* [= it isn't necessary for you to stay] □ *There is no need to shout.* [= please stop shouting]
▷ ***phrase*** **If need be** or **if needs be** means 'if it should become necessary': *I'll work all day and all night to finish it, if need be.*

needle /'ni:dəl/ *noun*; *verb*
▷ ***noun***: **needles**
1 A **needle** is an instrument for sewing, in the form of a thin steel pin pointed at one end with a hole for the thread at the other end. **2** A **needle**, or knitting **needle**, is a similar instrument for knitting, but longer and thicker and often made of plastic. **3** A **needle** is also a hypodermic syringe, an instrument for injecting liquids into the body. **4** On instruments that show measurements on a dial, *eg* a compass, the **needle** is the moving pointer. **5** On a record player, the **needle** is the tiny, pointed piece of diamond that transfers the

sound from the record. **6** A **needle** is also the needle-shaped leaf of a tree such as the pine or fir.

▻ ***verb*** (*informal*): **needles, needling, needled**

Someone who **needles** you deliberately annoys or irritates you by repeatedly making criticisms or other unkind remarks: *It seems her mother has being needling her about her weight.*

needless /ˈniːdləs/ *adjective*

Something **needless** is unnecessary or can be avoided: *You have caused your parents needless days of worry.* — *adverb* **needlessly:** *I'm afraid you have been needlessly inconvenienced.*

▻ ***phrase*** People often use **needless to say** before saying something that they think others might already know or may have realized or expected: *Since the pay offer was less than had been demanded, it was, needless to say, rejected by the unions.*

needn't /ˈniːdənt/ *verb* (*informal*)

Needn't is the usual spoken, and informal written, form of **need not**.

needy /ˈniːdɪ/ *adjective*; *noun*

▻ ***adjective***: **needier, neediest**

People who are **needy** are very poor, without a proper place to live, proper food or proper clothes: *The children of Bogota are certainly a very needy case.*

▻ ***noun*** (*plural*)

You can refer to needy people as the **needy**.

negative /ˈnɛgətɪv/ *adjective*; *noun*

▻ ***adjective***

1 A **negative** statement means or says 'no', denying, refusing or rejecting something: *Our suggestions met with a negative response.* ▫ *The scandal can only have a negative impact on our campaign.* **2** You can say that someone has a **negative** attitude if they lack enthusiasm, hope or faith: *They must be feeling very negative after such a bad defeat.* **3** A **negative** number is less than zero. **4** A medical test is **negative** when it shows that what was tested for, for example pregnancy or a disease, is not present or does not exist.

[*opposite* **positive**] — *adverb* **negatively:** *They reacted negatively to most of the work in the exhibition.* [*opposite* **positively**]

▻ ***noun***: **negatives**

1 In photography, a **negative** is the image that the camera first produces, with light and dark areas opposite to the way they are in the final photograph. **2** (*grammar*) A **negative** is a word or expression that means 'not', 'no'; some words, such as *hardly*, *scarcely*, *barely*, behave like *not* in some ways and are labelled (*used like a negative*) in this dictionary. **3** (*used in the singular*) You answer a question in the **negative** when you say 'no'.

neglect /nɪˈglɛkt/ *verb*; *noun*

▻ ***verb***: **neglects, neglecting, neglected**

1 You **neglect** someone or something when you don't give them proper care and attention: *It was clear that some of the children in the home had been neglected.* **2** (*formal*) You **neglect** to do something when you don't do it, for example because you have forgotten: *They neglected to inform you of an increase in bank charges.* ▫ *He was accused of neglecting his duties.* ▫ *He neglected to remember their wedding anniversary.* [*same as* **fail**]

▻ ***noun*** (*uncount*)

Neglect is lack of proper care, or the state of being in very poor condition that results from lack of care: *Some of the outbuildings had suffered neglect.* ▫ *The farmhouse had fallen into neglect.*

negligent /ˈnɛglɪdʒənt/ *adjective*

Someone who is **negligent** fails to give proper care and attention to someone or something, or fails to do something they ought to do. [*opposite* **attentive, careful, scrupulous**] — *noun* (*uncount*) **negligence** /ˈnɛglɪdʒəns/: *She was charged with pofessional negligence.*

negligible /ˈnɛglɪdʒəbəl/ *adjective*

Something that is **negligible** is so small or unimportant that you can ignore it: *It would have a negligible effect on their standard of living.* ▫ *The amounts involved are negligible.* [*same as* **insignificant**]

negotiable /nɪˈgoʊʃəbəl/ *adjective*

Something is **negotiable** when it will only be fixed or decided on after it has been discussed: *Salary is negotiable, within the range £35 000 to £45 000.*

negotiate /nɪˈgoʊʃɪeɪt/ *verb*: **negotiates, negotiating, negotiated**

1 You **negotiate** with someone when you have discussions with them in order that you can both agree about something or make a joint decision: *The peace accord was negotiated jointly by representatives from the warring parties and United Nations advisers.* ▫ *We will negotiate for a pay increase of 3.5%.* **2** You **negotiate** an obstacle or a difficulty when you pass it safely or deal with it successfully. — *noun* (*count or uncount*) **negotiation** /nɪgoʊʃɪˈeɪʃən/: *We have entered into negotiations with the managers.* ▫ *After lengthy negotiation, a settlement has still not been achieved.* — *noun* **negotiator:** *a group of experienced United Nations negotiators.*

Negro /ˈniːgroʊ/ *noun* (*often adjectival*; *rather offensive*): **Negroes**

People who belong to the black-skinned race of people originally from Africa are sometimes referred to as **Negroes**: *the Negro people of the modern West Indies.*

neighbour (*AmE* **neighbor**) /ˈneɪbə(r)/ *noun*: **neighbours**

1 Your **neighbours** are the people who live in houses close to yours: *my next-door neighbour.* **2** A person or thing placed next to another is their **neighbour**: *She turned to her neighbour and asked to borrow his programme.* ▫ *Zambia and its smaller neighbour Malawi.*

neighbourhood (*AmE* **neighborhood**) /ˈneɪbəhʊd/ *noun* (*often adjectival*): **neighbourhoods**

A **neighbourhood** is an area within a town or city; your **neighbourhood** is the area you live in: *This is a fairly quiet neighbourhood.* ▫ *the neighbourhood grocer's shop.*

▻ ***phrase*** **In the neighbourhood of** means roughly, approximately or about: *an annual salary in the neighbourhood of £40 000.*

neighbouring (*AmE* **neighboring**) /ˈneɪbərɪŋ/ *adjective*

Neighbouring describes places and things that are nearby: *The strike has affected transport systems in a number of neighbouring districts.*

neighbourly (*AmE* **neighborly**) /ˈneɪbəlɪ/ *adjective*

The people who live near you are **neighbourly** if they are friendly or willing to give help: *It was a very neighbourly gesture.*

neither /ˈnaɪðə(r)/ or /ˈniːðə(r)/ *determiner*; *pronoun*; *conjunction*

▻ ***determiner*** (*used with singular count nouns and a singular verb*)

Neither person, animal or thing means not the one nor the other of two: *Neither proposal was acceptable to the committee.* ▫ *Neither woman is prepared to comment on what was said in private.* ▫ *We accepted neither offer in the end* (or, less emphatically, *we didn't accept either offer*).

▻ ***pronoun*** (*with a singular or plural verb*) *Neither of* *the paintings was an original.* ▫ *Neither of us are* (or *is*) *planning to go.* ▫ *Both passengers were injured, neither of them seriously.* ▫ *I saw round two flats, but neither were* (or *was*) *suitable.*

▻ ***conjunction***

Neither is used **1** to introduce the first of two, or sometimes several, possibilities, both or all of which are denied, with **nor** introducing the second or a subsequent possibility: *'Do you know where he's gone?' 'I neither know nor care.'* ▫ *That would be neither wise nor practical.* ▫ *An arrangement of that sort would neither be fair nor desirable.* ▫ *He had neither washed, dressed, nor breakfasted.* ▫ *Neither she nor her partner was* (or *were*) *free to come.*

> Notice that where you have a combination of *eg* third and first person, or second and third person, a plural verb sounds better: *Neither Roger nor I are sure. Neither you nor he have been put on the short list.*

2 to introduce a second negative statement: *'I've never been to Paris before.' 'Neither have I.'* ▫ *If she wasn't going to reveal her age, neither was I.* ▫ *I didn't say no, but neither did I agree.*

> Notice the difference in word order when you use the parallel expression *not* (*n't*) *either*: *'I can't swim.' 'Neither can I'* or *'I can't either.'*
> Notice also that you can use **nor** instead of **neither**: *'I don't know her.' 'Neither do I* (or *Nor do I*).*'* [see also **so**]

[compare **either**, **nor**]

neo- /ˈniːoʊ/ or /ˈneɪoʊ/ *prefix*

Neo- is added to nouns and adjectives with the meaning 'a new or modern form': *buildings in a neoclassical design* ▫ *They were dismissed as neo-Fascists.*

neon light /niːɒn ˈlaɪt/ *noun*: **neon lights**

A **neon light** is a light consisting of a tube filled with a colourless gas that glows brightly when electricity is passed through it, often used in street signs and advertisements. [see picture at **street**]

nephew /ˈnɛfjuː/ or /ˈnɛvjuː/ *noun*: **nephews**

A person's **nephew** is the son of their brother or sister. [compare **niece**]

nerve /nɜːv/ *noun*: **nerves**

1 The **nerves** in your body are the thousands of thread-like fibres that carry messages about feelings and sensations between your brain other parts of your body: *This might cause damage to the nerve endings.* **2** (*uncount*) **Nerve** is courage: *We didn't have the nerve to actually do it.* **3** (*uncount*) **Nerve** is also willingness to be rude or bold, or show a lack of respect: *Then she had the nerve to ask me for money!* ▫ *Can you believe her nerve?* **4** (*used in the plural*) People often refer to a nervous or anxious state as **nerves**: *A drink of brandy would calm your nerves.* ▫ *He has always suffered from nerves.*

▻ ***phrases*** **1** (*informal*) Something that **gets on** your **nerves** annoys or irritates you. **2** You **lose** your **nerve** when you lose your courage or calmness and you begin to be afraid or to panic.

nerve-racking /ˈnɜːvrakɪŋ/ *adjective*

A **nerve-racking** experience is something that makes you feel extremely anxious or worried: *The first five minutes were pretty nerve-racking.*

nervous /ˈnɜːvəs/ *adjective*

1 A **nervous** person is easily frightened or upset. **2** You are feeling **nervous** when you are worried, frightened or uneasy: *I'm always nervous before a big performance.* ▫ *She feels a bit nervous about walking home alone.* [*same as* **anxious**] **3 Nervous** illnesses make you feel tense and unrelaxed. — *adverb* **nervously:** *I edged my way nervously along the window ledge.* ▫ *She smiled, rather nervously, I thought.* — *noun* (*uncount*) **nervousness:** *I had that familiar pre-interview nervousness.*

nervous breakdown /nɜːvəs ˈbreɪkdaʊn/ *noun*: **nervous breakdowns**

A person who suffers a **nervous breakdown** spends a long period, usually following a very stressful experience, feeling so nervous or anxious that they are unable to think clearly or perform ordinary tasks such as talking to people.

-ness /nəs/ *suffix*

-ness is added to adjectives to form nouns referring to a state or condition: *the slowness of progress* ▫ *They emerged from the darkness into the daylight.* ▫ *a period of great happiness.*

nest /nɛst/ *noun*; *verb*

▻ ***noun***: **nests**

A **nest** is a structure that birds build to lay their eggs in and bring up their young, using grass, twigs and other natural materials; a **nest** is also the home that some other animals, such as rats or wasps, build for themselves.

▻ ***verb***: **nests, nesting, nested:** *The sparrows had nested in our hedge.*

nestle /ˈnɛsəl/ *verb*: **nestles, nestling, nestled**

1 You **nestle** somewhere warm or comfortable when you settle yourself there: *The children climbed into bed and nestled against us.* **2** You can say that something **nestles** in a place where it seems sheltered or hidden: *From the top of the hill we could just see the village nestling in the valley.*

net[1] /nɛt/ *noun*; *verb*

▻ ***noun***: **nets**

1 (*uncount*) **Net** is material consisting of threads twisted or woven together to form a series of crossed lines with spaces in between. **2** A **net** is a piece of this material used in any of a variety of ways, for example for catching fish, or for hitting the ball over in tennis or badminton: *Use a net to protect the crops from attack by birds.*

▻ ***verb***: **nets, netting, netted**

You **net** something when you catch it in a net, or when you manage to get or obtain it in any way: *We netted our biggest ever catch of fish.* ▫ *He's managed to net himself a deal worth over £3 million.*

net[2] /nɛt/ *adjective*; *verb*

▻ ***adjective***

1 A **net** profit is the profit that remains after all expenses and taxes have been paid: *Their net income is just over £1200 a month.* **2** The **net** weight of something is its weight not including the package or container it is in.

▻ ***verb***: **nets, netting, netted**

You **net** the amount of profit that is left after all expenses and taxes have been paid.

netball /ˈnɛtbɔːl/ *noun* (*uncount*)

Netball is a game similar to basketball, usually played by women.

netting /nɛtiŋ/ *noun* (*uncount*)

Netting is material or fabric made by twisting, knotting or weaving string, thread or wire in a regular pattern: *fences made of wire netting.*

nettle /ˈnɛtəl/ *noun*: **nettles**

Nettles are wild plants with spiky leaves that sting you if you touch them.

network /ˈnɛtwɜːk/ *noun*: **networks**
1 A **network** is a system or pattern of things that looks like a mass of lines that cross each other: *a network of streets.* **2** A **network** is also a number of offices, organizations or pieces of equipment connected to, and communicating with, each other: *a telecommunications network* □ *The information is transferred to each computer on the network.*

neurotic /njʊˈrɒtɪk/ *adjective*
You can say that someone is **neurotic** if they are very anxious or nervous about something, for no good reason: *Every time the phone rang, I expected it to be the boss telling me I was sacked; I had become neurotic.* [*same as* **obsessive**]

neutral /ˈnjuːtrəl/ *adjective; noun*
▻ ***adjective***
1 A person or group that remains **neutral** does not support either side in a quarrel or war: *Switzerland was a neutral country.* □ *We were on neutral territory.* [*opposite* **biased**] **2 Neutral** is used in many ways to describe things, for example colours, that are not strong or definite but are rather light or vague: *John's was a fairly neutral reaction; I had expected more emotion.* **3** In an electrical circuit, the **neutral** wire is attached to the live wire carrying the electrical charge, in order to complete the circuit.
▻ ***noun*** (*uncount*)
When a car or other vehicle is in **neutral**, none of the gears is connected to the engine, so it cannot move.

never /ˈnɛvə(r)/ *adverb*
1 Never means **a** not ever, or not at any time: *I'll never understand algebra.* □ *I've never been abroad.* □ *She never writes or telephones.* □ *I never get up before 10.00.* □ *It's never too late to learn.* □ *Never do that again!* □ *Never have I experienced such rudeness!* **b** not under any circumstances: *The end can never justify the means.*

> Notice that you can use the less emphatic *not* (*n't*) *ever* instead of **never**, except where **never** introduces the sentence: *I've never* (or *I haven't ever*) *thought about that.* But: *Never give up hope.*

2 Never is often used as a negative with the past tense, meaning simply 'did not': *I never realized that.* □ *I waited for hours, but he never came.* **3** (*informal*) **Never** is also used, with the meaning 'not', to express surprise or disbelief: *That's never his mother, is it?*
▻ ***phrases*** **1 Never ever** is used as an emphatic form of **never**: *We never ever waste any food in this family.* **2 Well I never!** is an expression of astonishment.

nevertheless /nɛvəðəˈlɛs/ *adverb* (*sentence adverb*)
Nevertheless means 'in spite of that' or 'however': *This is a difficult problem; nevertheless, we will overcome it.* □ *It's an unpleasant job; it needs to be done, nevertheless.*

new /njuː/ *adjective; adverb*: **newer, newest**
▻ ***adjective***
1 Something that is **new** a has been recently bought, made or built, or is in the process of being made or built: *They're building a new supermarket outside the town.* □ *Have I shown you my new watch?* [opposite **old**] **b** has never existed before, or has just been invented: *the newest techniques in dentistry.* **c** has just been discovered: *They called the new planet Neptune.* **d** has not been owned before by anyone: *dealers in new and used cars.* □ *They cost over £100 new.* □ *It was built new for us in 1969.* **e** replaces something that has been lost, damaged or used up: *Here's a new roll of kitchen paper.* □ *I'll be needing a new hair-dryer if they can't mend my old one.* □ *We're expecting a new supply next week.* □ *The most recent results have given us new hope.* [compare **fresh**] **f** replaces a person or thing in a particular role or capacity: *I haven't met her new husband yet.* □ *the new prime minister* □ *The hotel is under new management.* **g** has only recently become a certain thing: *For new parents, the first few weeks with the baby can be quite frightening.* **h** is different from what you have now or what you had before: *He's looking for a new job.* □ *We didn't learn anything new.* **2** You are **new** to something, or something is **new** to you, when you have never experienced it before: *This kind of competitiveness was new to me.* □ *She's new to the work.* **3** A **new** period of time is one that is about to start: *at the start of each new day* □ *the beginning of a new age.* — *noun* (*uncount*) **newness:** *the newness, for us all, of the situation.*
▻ ***adverb***
New is combined with past participles to refer to what has happened only recently: *a newborn baby.*

newfangled /njuːˈfaŋgəld/ *adjective* (*informal*)
You describe something very new and modern as **newfangled** if you don't like it or approve of it, often because it seems ridiculously complicated and represents no real improvement: *I don't hold with these newfangled theories about sympathizing with the criminals instead of the victims.* □ *a newfangled gadget for unscrewing the tops off bottles.*

newly /ˈnjuːlɪ/ *adverb*
You use **newly** before past participles to refer to what has only recently happened or been done: *the smell of newly-mown grass* □ *The room was newly painted.*

newly-weds /ˈnjuːlɪwɛdz/ *noun* (*plural; informal*)
You can refer to a recently married couple as **newly-weds**: *It was time to leave the newly-weds alone.*

news /njuːz/ *noun* (*uncount*)
1 News is information about something that has recently happened: *The good news is that I've been given a promotion.* □ *I'm afraid I've got some bad news for you; the bank has refused your application for a loan.* **2** (*often adjectival*) **News** is also information about recent events in the world, reported on radio or television, or in newspapers; the **news** is a radio or television programme giving news: *the national and international news from the BBC* □ *I heard about it on the news.* □ *the 9 o'clock news bulletin.*
▻ ***phrase*** (*informal*) You say **that's news to me** when someone tells you something you didn't know, especially something very surprising or something you think others should have told you earlier.

newsagent /ˈnjuːzeɪdʒənt/ or **newsagent's** *noun*: **newsagents**
A **newsagent** or **newsagent's** is a shop selling newspapers and magazines, and usually other things such as sweets and cigarettes.

newsflash /ˈnjuːzflaʃ/ *noun*: **newsflashes**
A **newsflash** is a brief announcement of important news interrupting a radio or television programme.

newsletter /ˈnjuːzlɛtə(r)/ *noun*: **newsletters**
A **newsletter** is a simple newspaper containing information about a club or society, sent regularly to its members.

newspaper /ˈnjuːspeɪpə(r)/ *noun*: **newspapers**
1 A **newspaper** is a collection of reports about recent events, printed on a set of folded sheets of paper, usually produced daily or weekly: *an advert in a local newspaper* □ *last Monday's issue of a national newspaper* □ (*adjectival*) *a newspaper reporter.* **2** (*uncount*) **Newspaper** is old newspapers: *We wrapped the more breakable objects in newspaper.*

newt /njuːt/ *noun*: **newt**
A **newt** is a small lizard-like animal with a long body and tail and short legs, that lives both in water and on land.

New Testament /njuː 'tɛstəmənt/ *noun*
The **New Testament** is the second part of the Christian Bible, containing the Gospels and the letters written by St Paul. [see also **Old Testament**]

New Year /njuː'jɪə(r)/ *noun* (*uncount or used in the singular*)
The **New Year** is the first day of the year, usually 1 January, with **New Year's Eve** being the last day of the old year and **New Year's Day** the first day of the new year; **New Year** is also the traditional period of celebration around this time, or January in general: *We spent the New Year with my parents.* □ *Are you doing anything special for New Year?* □ *They're having a New Year's party.* □ *Happy New Year!* □ *Did you have any time off last New Year?* □ *We'll be recruiting in the New Year.*

next /nɛkst/ *determiner or adjective; pronoun; adverb*
▻ ***determiner or adjective***
1 The **next** person, thing, event or period of time is the one that immediately follows the present one or the one just past: *Read the next name on the list.* □ *I decided I would leave the very next day.* □ *I'll be seeing him next week.* □ *We go on holiday next Monday.* □ *How about Friday next* [= next Friday] *for lunch?* □ *I'll be away for the next two days.* □ *Next time you see him, tell him to phone me.* □ *The next question comes from Mrs Laura Mills.* □ *Who's next on the waiting list?* □ *What's next on the programme?*

In the context of time, **next** commonly refers to the immediate future; you use expressions such as *the following* in referring to the past or the more distant future: *He departed the following* (or *the next*) *day. I went to stay with her the following March. I'm busy next Wednesday, but I can meet you the Wednesday after that.*
You use '**next**' rather than 'the **next**' when referring by name to days, months or seasons, or to periods of time, in the immediate future: *next Thursday, next February, next summer, next week, next month.* But use '**the next**' to refer to a length of time in the immediate future: *The next few months will be frantic.*

2 The **next** person or place is the one nearest to you, or the one you come to first: *There are some free seats in the next compartment.* □ *Pass the message on to the next person in the row.* □ *Take the next turning on the left.* [compare **neighbouring**]
▻ ***pronoun:*** *One minute I was sweating and the next I was freezing cold.* □ *I'll see you the week after next.* [= not next week, but the week after it] □ *Are they coming this weekend or next?* □ *Their house is the next but one.* [= not the next one, but the one after it]
▻ ***adverb***
1 Next means immediately after this, or after the thing or event just mentioned: *Next, let's look at the schedule.* □ *We tried the window next.* □ *What do we do next?* □ *What happened next?* **2 Next** also means on the next occasion: *When I next saw her, she had changed the colour of her hair.* **3 Next** is used with a superlative to describe something secondary in order of degree: *It's the next-longest river after the Amazon.* □ *Their next-best performance was in the European championships in Stuttgart.*
▻ ***phrases*** **1** The houses **next door** to you are the houses on either side of yours: *They live next door to my parents.* □ *The post office is next door to the bank.* □ *We saw that the house next door was for sale.* □ *I went next door to borrow some milk.* □ *Our next-door neighbours were a young couple.* **2** For **next of kin** see **kin**. **3 a** One thing is **next to** another if it is beside it: *The Oxfam shop is next to the fishmonger's.* □ *There was a bookcase next to the wardrobe.* □ *Next to me stood a tall red-haired man.* **b** You use **next to** with the sense 'almost' before words that have a negative meaning: *He was wearing next to no clothes.* □ *They know next to nothing about cattle farming.* □ *These coins are next to worthless.* [*same as* **practically**, **virtually**]

next of kin /nɛkst əv 'kɪn/ *noun* (*singular or uncount*)
Your **next of kin** is the person, or the people, most closely related to you: *Write your name and the name of your next of kin.* □ *His name is not being released until his next of kin have been informed.*

nibble /'nɪbəl/ *verb; noun*
▻ ***verb***: **nibbles, nibbling, nibbled**
You **nibble** something when you take small bites out of it, or when you bite it gently: *She had little appetite, and sat nibbling at her food.* □ *The dogs nibbled each other's ears playfully.*
▻ ***noun***: **nibbles:** *I had a couple of nibbles of one of her cream cakes.* □ *She bought crisps, peanuts, and a few other nibbles.*

nice /nɑɪs/ *adjective*: **nicer, nicest**
1 You call something **nice** if you think it is pleasant, good, attractive or satisfactory: *We hope the weather will be a little nicer next week.* □ *Oh, don't you look nice!* □ *You look nice in that suit.* □ *Did you have a nice time at the zoo?* □ *It was a nice relaxing holiday.* □ *Saturday was nice and warm.* □ *It was so nice to meet you.* □ *It would be nice to see you again sometime soon.* □ *Wouldn't it be nice if we could arrange a family get-together?* **2** You call someone **nice** if they are kind, pleasant and friendly, and you like them: *People are so nice here.* □ *My father was not a very nice man.* □ *He seemed nice enough to me.* **3** You say that it is **nice** of someone to do something if you think they have been kind, helpful or considerate in doing it: *It was so nice of you to write.* □ *It's nice of you to say so.* □ *How nice of you to remember!* □ *Thank you for your nice letter.* □ *That wasn't a very nice thing to say.* **4** You are **nice** to someone when you treat them kindly and politely: *The police were quite nice to me.* □ *I was trying my best to be nice to her.* — adverb **nicely:** *We're trying to teach the children to ask for things nicely.* □ *She stands and moves nicely.* □ *The holiday was progressing quite nicely.* □ *If you don't have any cash, a cheque will do nicely.*

Notice that **nice** and **nice and** are often used to intensify adjectives and adverbs, with the meaning 'pleasantly': *There was a nice cool breeze. It's nice and quiet once the children have gone to bed. Everything was going nice and smoothly.*

nicety /'naɪsətɪ/ *noun*: **niceties**
Niceties are very small details: *I wasn't familiar with the niceties of table-setting.*

niche /niːʃ/ *noun*: **niches**
You can refer to a job or other activity as your **niche** if you feel perfectly suited to it and enjoy doing it very much: *She seems to have found her niche, in teaching.*

nick /nɪk/ *noun; verb*
▻ ***noun***: **nicks**
1 A **nick** is a small cut: *There was a tiny nick in his chin where the razor had slipped.* **2** (*used in the singular; slang*) People, especially criminals, sometimes refer to

a police station as the **nick**: *They took me down the nick.*
▻ ***verb***: **nicks, nicking, nicked**
1 You **nick** something when you make a small cut in it. **2** (*slang*) Someone who **nicks** something steals it: *Kids had nicked apples from my stall before.* **3** (*slang*) To **nick** someone also means to arrest them: *Okay, son; you're nicked!*
▻ ***phrases*** **1** (*informal*) You can say that something is **in good nick** if it is in good condition. **2** (*informal*) Something happens **in the nick of time** when it happens at the last possible moment, just in time: *I thought the dog had got me, then I managed to close the door in the nick of time.*

nickel /ˈnɪkəl/ *noun*: **nickels**
1 (*uncount*) **Nickel** is a greyish-white metal often mixed with other metals. **2** In America and Canada, a **nickel** is a coin worth five cents.

nickname /ˈnɪkneɪm/ *noun*; *verb*
▻ ***noun***: **nicknames**
A **nickname** is a funny, affectionate or insulting name you give to a person or thing: *At school, my nickname was Coco, because I had a face like a clown's.*
▻ ***verb***: **nicknames, nicknaming, nicknamed:** *The first engine he designed was nicknamed 'Old Faithful'.*

nicotine /ˈnɪkətiːn/ *noun* (*uncount*)
Nicotine is the poisonous substance contained in tobacco.

niece /niːs/ *noun*: **nieces**
A person's **niece** is the daughter of their sister or brother. [compare **nephew**]

nifty /ˈnɪftɪ/ *adjective* (*informal*): **niftier, niftiest**
People often use **nifty** to describe something they like, especially something that is pleasingly clever or attractively stylish: *And then, with a nifty flick of his left foot, he was past the defender.* □ *I had to admit that his new idea sounded pretty nifty.*

niggle /ˈnɪgəl/ *verb*: **niggles, niggling, niggled**
Something **niggles** you when it worries or irritates you slightly but continually: *What had been niggling him was the knowledge that the others thought he was unprofessional.* [*same as* **nag**] — *adjective* **niggling:** *a niggling doubt at the back of your mind.* [*same as* **nagging**]

night /naɪt/ *noun* (*uncount or count*): **nights**
The **night** is **1** the period of darkness between the time the sun goes down and the time it rises, during which most people sleep: *animals that are active at night* □ *They stayed up all night writing the speech.* □ *Three nights ago, somebody broke into our house.* □ *Could I stay the night with you on Thursday?* □ *I spent a few nights in Prague.* □ *What do you charge per night for a double room?* □ *One night, she heard a strange noise downstairs.* □ *It must have rained during* (or *in*) *the night.* □ *Did you hear the thunder last night?* □ *a dark, stormy night* □ *I woke in the middle of the night.* □ *Night after night she had the same dream.* □ *She works nights.* [= she has a regular job that she does during the night] **2** the evening, or the time between afternoon and bedtime: *We all go down to the club on Friday nights.* □ *I was at home the night before last.* □ *Wednesday night was always washing night in our house.* □ *I've got a meeting tomorrow night.*

nightclub /ˈnaɪtklʌb/ *noun*: **nightclubs**
A **nightclub** is a club, open until late at night, for drinking, dancing and other entertainment.

nightdress /ˈnaɪtdrɛs/ *noun*: **nightdresses**
A **nightdress** is a woman's loose dress for sleeping in.

nightfall /ˈnaɪtfɔːl/ *noun* (*uncount*)
Nightfall is the time when the sun goes down and night begins. [compare **dusk**]

nightgown /ˈnaɪtgaʊn/ *noun*: **nightgowns**
A **nightgown** is a nightdress.

nightie /ˈnaɪtɪ/ *noun* (*informal*): **nighties**
A **nightie** is a nightdress.

nightmare /ˈnaɪtmɛə(r)/ *noun*: **nightmares**
1 A **nightmare** is a frightening dream: *Watching horror films gives me nightmares.* □ *I had a nightmare about falling off a cliff.* **2** You can describe a very unpleasant or frightening experience as a **nightmare**: *Driving in the rush-hour traffic is a nightmare.*

night school /ˈnaɪt skuːl/ *noun* (*uncount*)
Adults who go to **night school** attend educational courses in the evening: *I studied accountancy at night school.*

night-time /ˈnaɪt taɪm/ *noun* (*uncount*)
Night-time is the period of darkness between the time the sun goes down and the time it rises again. [compare **daytime**]

nil /nɪl/ *noun* (*uncount*)
In games, **nil** is a score of nothing or no points: *They beat us three-nil.* □ *With only five minutes remaining, the score is still nil-nil.*

nimble /ˈnɪmbəl/ *adjective*: **nimbler, nimblest**
Someone who is **nimble** moves quickly and quietly or lightly, with little effort: *He watched her nimble fingers clicking the knitting-needles.* [*same as* **agile**; *opposite* **clumsy**]

nine /naɪn/ *noun*; *adjective*; *determiner*; *pronoun*
▻ ***noun***: **nines**
1 (*uncount or count*) **Nine** is **a** the number or figure 9: *Three times three is nine.* □ *Five nines are forty-five.* □ *A nine looks like an upside-down six.* **b** a piece of clothing whose size is represented by the number 9, or a person who wears clothes of this size: *These slippers are nines.* □ *Your father takes a nine in hats.* □ *I'm an eight in ordinary shoes but a nine in riding boots.* **2** (*uncount*) **Nine** is **a** the age of 9: *She started learning French at nine.* **b** the time of 9 o'clock: *We should aim to set off around nine.* **3** A **nine** is a playing-card with 9 symbols: *The card he picked was the nine of clubs.*
▻ ***adjective***
Someone who is **nine** is nine years old: *John will be nine next April.* □ *Children under nine travel free.*
▻ ***determiner:*** *A whisky could cost as much as nine dollars.* □ *It lasted for nine and a half weeks.* □ *the nine-hour flight to Zimbabwe* □ *my nine-year-old daughter.*
▻ ***pronoun:*** *Nine of us voted in favour.* □ *We planted nine seeds and we got nine plants, but then all nine died.*

nineteen /naɪnˈtiːn/ *noun*; *adjective*; *determiner*; *pronoun*
▻ ***noun***: **nineteens**
1 (*uncount or count*) **Nineteen** is the number or figure 19: *Twelve and seven are nineteen.* □ *I couldn't tell if it was a nineteen or a sixty-one.* **2** (*uncount*) **Nineteen** is the age of 19: *The extra year meant she didn't leave school until nineteen.*
▻ ***adjective***
Someone who is **nineteen** is nineteen years old: *She got married when she was nineteen.*
▻ ***determiner:*** *The first nineteen years were the best.* □ *You can expect a nineteen-year-old girl to know all about it.*
▻ ***pronoun:*** *Out of twenty students, nineteen failed the course.*

nineteenth /naɪnˈtiːnθ/ *determiner*; *pronoun*; *adjective or adverb*; *noun*: **nineteenths**

1 (often written **19th**) The **nineteenth** person or thing is the one numbered nineteen in a series. **2** (often written $\frac{1}{19}$) A **nineteenth** of something is one of nineteen equal parts.

ninetieth /ˈnaɪntɪəθ/ *determiner; pronoun; adjective or adverb; noun*: **ninetieths**
1 (often written **90th**) The **ninetieth** person or thing is the one numbered ninety in a series. **2** (often written $\frac{1}{90}$) A **ninetieth** of something is one of ninety equal parts of it.

ninety /ˈnaɪntɪ/ *noun; adjective; determiner; pronoun*
▷ ***noun***: **nineties**
1 (*uncount or count*) **Ninety** is the number or figure 90. **2** (*uncount*) **Ninety** is the age of 90. **3** (*used in the plural*) Someone who is in their **nineties** is aged between 90 and 99. **4** (*used in the plural*) The temperature is in the **nineties** when it is between 90 and 99 degrees Fahrenheit. **5** (*used in the plural*) The **nineties** are the period between the ninetieth year of a century and the end of that century.
▷ ***adjective***
Someone who is **ninety** is ninety years old.
▷ ***determiner:*** *his ninety-year-old grandmother.*
▷ ***pronoun:*** *Three people were killed and over ninety injured.*

ninth (often written **9th**) /naɪnθ/ *determiner; pronoun; adjective or adverb; noun*
▷ ***determiner***
The **ninth** person or thing is the one numbered nine in a series: *towards the end of the ninth month.*
▷ ***pronoun:*** *This is the ninth of their albums to reach number one in the charts.* □ *She's the ninth from the left in the front row.* □ *His birthday is on the 9th of June.* [see also note at **date**]
▷ ***adjective or adverb:*** *I was* (or *came*) *ninth in the photographic competition.* □ *His horse came in ninth.*
▷ ***noun*** (often written $\frac{1}{9}$): **ninths**
A **ninth** of something is one of nine equal parts of it: *A ninth of the population owned 89% of the country's wealth.*

nip /nɪp/ *verb; noun*
▷ ***verb***: **nips, nipping, nipped**
1 You **nip** something when you pinch or squeeze it sharply: *Carefully nip off older flowers to encourage new growth.* **2** An animal **nips** you when it gives you a sharp little bite. **3** (*informal*) You **nip** somewhere nearby when you go there quickly and only for a short time: *I nipped along the road to see if the shop was still open.* [*same as* **pop**]
▷ ***noun***: **nips:** *The dog gave me a nasty nip on the ankle.*
▷ ***phrase*** You can say there's **a nip in the air** when it feels cold and fresh. [*same as* **chill**]

nipple /ˈnɪpəl/ *noun*: **nipples**
Your **nipples** are the two round, projecting points on your chest or breasts: *Women who breast-feed their babies often get sore nipples.*

nippy /ˈnɪpɪ/ *adjective* (*informal*): **nippier, nippiest**
1 You can say it is **nippy** when the weather is cold. [*same as* **chilly**] **2** Something such as a car is **nippy** if it is fast or quick-moving. [opposite **sluggish**]

nitrogen /ˈnaɪtrədʒən/ *noun* (*uncount*)
Nitrogen is a colourless gas that makes up most of the air we breathe and is present in all living things: *The plants are then unable to take up nitrogen from the soil.*

no[1] /noʊ/ *interjection*
No is used **1** as a negative reply, to deny something, to refuse an offer or refuse permission, or to disagree with something: *'Have you finished that job?' 'No, I haven't.'* □ *'Don't you miss acting?' 'No, not any more.'* □ *'It must have been you that left the tap running.' 'No, it wasn't!'* □ *'Would you like some more potatoes?' 'No, thank you.'* □ *'May I watch television?' 'No, not until you've finished your homework.'* □ *'It's quite a difficult journey, isn't it?' 'No, I wouldn't say so.'* [*opposite* **yes**] **2** to agree with a negative statement, or a question that expects a negative answer: *'You don't take milk in your coffee, do you?' 'No, I don't.'* □ *'There's nothing unusual about that.' 'No, I suppose not.'* [*opposite* **yes**] **3** to make a correction to something you have said: *There are about 30, no, maybe 35.* **4** to warn someone, or plead with them, not to do something: *'I'll tell your mother.' 'No, please don't!'* **5** to express horror, disbelief, surprise or concern at something you have realized, or been told: *Oh no! I've forgotten my purse!* □ *'I ran over a dog today.' 'No, how awful!'* □ *'Did you hear that she's engaged?' 'No! Really?'* □ *'Apparently her husband has left her.' 'No! He hasn't, has he?'*
▷ ***phrase*** Someone who will **not take no for an answer** goes on trying to persuade you to agree to something even though you have already refused to.

no[2] /noʊ/ *determiner; adverb*
▷ ***determiner***
No is used **1** with uncount nouns and with singular and plural count nouns to mean 'not any' or 'not even one': *No other car gives you this level of luxury.* □ *No book this century has made such an impact.* □ *No children will be admitted unless accompanied by an adult.* □ *No previous experience is necessary.* □ *No two flats have quite the same design.* □ *There is absolutely no need to panic.* □ *There's no time to waste.* □ *We meant no harm.* □ *Is there no way of solving the problem?* □ *I'm afraid we've got no more copies.* □ *There were no biscuits left.*

> Notice that you can use the more informal *not* (*n't*) *any* instead of *no*, except where *no* and the noun it qualifies introduce the sentence as its subject: *There weren't any biscuits left. We didn't mean any harm.* But: *No students turned up.*

2 in the construction 'there is **no** doing something', to say that it is impossible to do that thing: *I shall have to talk to her about it; there's no avoiding the issue.* [= the issue must be dealt with] □ *There was no mistaking the threat in her tone.* [= the threat was only too clear] **3** frequently in notices to indicate that something is not allowed: *No Smoking* □ *No photography* □ *No parking* □ *No overnight caravans* □ *No entry.* **4** in expressions such as 'She's **no** fool' as an emphatic way of stating the opposite: *He may be young, but he's no child when it comes to business.* □ *Convincing my father would be no easy task.*
▷ ***adverb***
No is used before comparative adjectives and adverbs **1** to draw attention to a surprisingly large or small amount, a surprisingly long or short time, and so on: *At the age of 26 he was earning no less than £35 000.* □ *a crowd of no fewer than 100 000 spectators* □ *There were no more than half a dozen of us at the class.* □ *The crossword came into existence no earlier than the '20s.* □ *It's no bigger than a pinhead.* **2** to mean 'not the least bit'; **no** can also be used with *different* and *differently* in this sense: *We're still no closer to finding a solution.* □ *She seemed to be behaving no differently from usual.* □ *She hasn't got worse, but she's certainly no better.* □ *We got no further that evening.* □ *His explanation left me no clearer.*

> Notice that you can use the less emphatic *not* (*n't*) *any* instead of *no*: *She isn't any better.*

[compare **none, any, some, every**]

nobility /noʊˈbɪlɪtɪ/ *noun* (*uncount or used in the singular*)
Nobility is the state of belonging to the highest class of people in society; the people in this class are often referred to as the **nobility**. [*same as* **aristocracy**]

noble /ˈnoʊbəl/ *adjective*; *noun*
▻ ***adjective***: **nobler, noblest**
1 Someone who is **noble** behaves in a brave, honourable or generous way: *It was a noble gesture.* **2 Noble** also describes people who belong to the highest social class: *Is she of noble birth?* [*same as* **aristocratic**] **3** You can describe something as **noble** when it looks very impressive, especially if it has a classic or traditional style: *An elegant avenue leads you up to the house's noble facade.*
▻ ***noun***: **nobles**
A **noble** is a person of noble rank: *mixing with royalty and nobles.* [*same as* **aristocrat**]

nobody /ˈnoʊbədɪ/ *pronoun*; *noun*
▻ ***pronoun***
1 Nobody and **no-one** mean 'no person' or 'not anybody': *Nobody asked her for her opinion.* □ *There was no-one at home.* □ *I told nobody of my plans to visit Germany.* □ *There's no-one else I can confide in.* □ *Nobody in particular struck me as suitable.* **2** If you tell someone they are **nobody**, or **no-one** special, you mean they are unimportant.

> Notice that you can use the less emphatic *not* (*n't*) *anybody* or *not* (*n't*) *anyone* instead of **nobody** or **no-one**, except where **nobody** or **no-one** introduces the sentence as its subject: *There was nobody* (or *there wasn't anybody*) *around.* But: *No-one noticed her.* Notice also that although **nobody** and **no-one** are singular, both are often followed by the pronoun *they*, which takes a plural verb: *No-one's allowed in yet, are they?*

▻ ***noun***: **nobodies**
A **nobody** is a person of no importance: *They evidently regarded me as a nobody.*
[see also **anybody, somebody, everybody**]

nod /nɒd/ *verb*: **nods, nodding, nodded**
1 You **nod** when you move your head, usually up and down, either once or several times, to express agreement or as an informal greeting: *He nodded his head in agreement.* **2** (*informal*) You can say someone **is nodding** when their head keeps falling forwards because they are sleepy; they **nod** off when they fall asleep.

noise /nɔɪz/ *noun*: **noises**
1 A **noise** is a sound: *I heard a noise like a plate being smashed.* □ *like the noise a cat makes.* **2** (*uncount or count*) **Noise** consists of unpleasant, loud sounds that disturb you: *Can't the children make less noise?* □ *I can't hear you for the noise of the traffic.* [*opposite* **silence**]

noisy /ˈnɔɪzɪ/ *adjective*: **noisier, noisiest**
A **noisy** person makes a lot of noise; a **noisy** place is full of noise: *The fridge seems a bit noisy tonight.* □ *The pub would be too noisy for the younger ones.* [*opposite* **quiet**]

nominal /ˈnɒmɪnəl/ *adjective*
1 You use **nominal** to describe what someone or something is supposed to be, because that is what they are called, usually suggesting that, in reality, that is not what they are at all: *The Queen is the nominal head of the Church, but she has no real power to influence policy.* **2** A **nominal** amount is very small in comparison to the actual cost or value of something: *We were charged only a nominal rent.* [*same as* **minimal**] — *adverb* **nominally:** *Although nominally in charge of the operation, the General played a very minor role.* [*same as* **theoretically**]

nominate /ˈnɒmɪneɪt/ *verb*: **nominates, nominating, nominated**
You **nominate** someone for a job or other position when you suggest formally that it should be given to them, or when you choose them to have it: *Sheila was nominated president of the bowling club. Someone nominated Peter as club secretary.* — *noun* (*count or uncount*) **nomination** /nɒmɪˈneɪʃən/: *We are inviting nominations for the post of Chancellor.* □ *after the nomination of Henry Oswald to the post of chairman.*

nominee /nɒmɪˈniː/ *noun*: **nominees**
A **nominee** is a person nominated, especially one of the candidates for a position or job.

non- /nɒn/ *prefix*
Non- is used **1** with adjectives, with the meaning 'not' or 'the opposite of': *All non-essential personnel were given the day off.* □ *a range of alcoholic and non-alcoholic drinks.* **2** with nouns ending in *-er* and *-ing*, to refer to people who don't do or take part in something, or to places where something is not done: *This table is reserved for non-smokers.* □ *Non-swimmers are advised to stay in the shallow part of the pool.* □ *seats in the non-smoking section of the aircraft.* **3** with other nouns, to refer to the fact that something is not done: *a policy of non-cooperation with government* □ *They were sent to prison for non-payment of debts.*

nonchalant /ˈnɒnʃələnt/ *adjective*
Someone who behaves in a **nonchalant** way appears to be calmly uninterested in, or unconcerned about, something: *He managed to appear nonchalant when Tom said he had spent the night with Karen.* [*same as* **blasé**; *opposite* **excited, enthusiastic**] — *noun* (*uncount*) **nonchalance** /ˈnɒnʃələns/: *We were impressed by his nonchalance.*

non-committal /nɒnkəˈmɪtəl/ *adjective*
You are **non-committal** when you avoid expressing any definite opinion or preference: *The minister gave a typically non-committal reply.*

nonconformist /nɒnkənˈfɔːmɪst/ *noun* (*often adjectival*): **nonconformists**
A **nonconformist** is someone who refuses to do what is traditional or generally expected, or simply someone who behaves in a strange or unusual way: *She has rather a nonconformist approach to education that worried her colleagues.*

nondescript /ˈnɒndɪskrɪpt/ *adjective*
Something **nondescript** is very ordinary and dull, with no noticeable qualities that you can describe it by: *It was just another nondescript suburban bungalow.*

none /nʌn/ *pronoun*
None means 'not any' and corresponds to the determiner *no* as the pronoun *any* corresponds to the determiner *any*; you use **none** **1** (*with a singular or plural verb*) to refer to plural count nouns or pronouns: *None of his injuries were very serious.* □ *None of them has the courage to admit they're wrong.* □ *His cheerful manner fooled none of us.* □ *We looked in the cupboard for biscuits, but there were none left.* □ *I've hunted for references but have found none so far.*

> Notice that **none** refers to a possible group of three or more; use **neither** when referring to only two: *I sent them all a form, but none have applied. They both offered to help, but neither of them did in the end.*

2 (*with a singular verb*) to refer to uncountable nouns and certain singular countable nouns: *I'd offer you* *coffee, but there's none left.* □ *'Did you have trouble finding the house?' 'No, absolutely none.'* □ *It's a good story, but practically none of it is true.*

▷ ***phrases*** **1 None too** is used before adjectives and adverbs to mean their opposites: *His health has been none too good* [= has been bad] *recently.* □ *She was treated none too sympathetically* [= she was treated unsympathetically] *by the board.* □ *I was none too certain that I would cope.* **2 None the** is used with comparative adjectives and adverbs to mean 'not the least bit', to indicate that the experience referred to has made no difference to the situation: *They appeared none the worse for their terrifying ordeal.* [= they seemed not to have been harmed by it] □ *I was none the wiser after hearing his explanation.*

> Notice that you can in many cases use the less emphatic *not* (*n't*) *any* instead of **none**, but not where **none** introduces the sentence as its subject: *There's none* (or *there isn't any*) *left. He was none* (or *he wasn't any*) *the wiser*. But: *None of it was true.*

[see also **any, some, all**]

nonentity /nɒn'entɪtɪ/ *noun*: **nonentities**
You can refer to someone as a **nonentity** if you think they are unimportant or worthless. [*same as* **nobody**]

nonetheless /nʌnðə'lɛs/ *adverb* (*formal*; *sentence adverb*)
Nonetheless means 'in spite of that' or 'nevertheless': *It would not be easy; nonetheless, he intended to try his best.* □ *There have been one or two delays; it will open on time, nonetheless.* [*same as* **however**]

non-existent /nɒnɪg'zɪstənt/ *adjective*
Something that is **non-existent** does not exist: *in the small rural communities where cinemas and theatres are non-existent.*

nonplussed /nɒn'plʌst/ *adjective*
You are **nonplussed** when you are puzzled, and don't know what to do or say next. [*same as* **dumbfounded**]

nonsense /'nɒnsəns/ *noun*; *interjection*
▷ ***noun*** (*uncount*)
1 Nonsense is words or ideas that you think are untrue or stupid, or that don't make sense: *Most of their theories were a load of nonsense.* **2 Nonsense** is also silly behaviour: *Stop that nonsense, you boys!*
▷ ***interjection***
If you say **nonsense!** in response to what someone says, you mean it is untrue or stupid.

nonsensical /nɒn'sɛnsɪkəl/ *adjective*
You can say that something is **nonsensical** if you think it is stupid or it doesn't make sense: *It would be nonsensical to pay someone to do it, and then do it yourself.*

non-stop /nɒn'stɒp/ *adjective or adverb*
Non-stop means without a break, pause or stop: *the non-stop hammering in the room above* □ *It has rained non-stop for three days.* [*same as* **continuous, continuously**]

noodles /'nu:dəlz/ *noun* (*plural*)
Noodles are thin, string-like pieces of pasta made with egg.

nook /nʊk/ *noun*: **nooks**
A **nook** is a corner or space, especially in the phrase **every nook and cranny**, which means every part of a room: *He mopped the floor and dusted in every nook and cranny.*

noon /nu:n/ *noun* (*uncount, often adjectival*)
Noon is twelve o'clock in the daytime, or midday: *She eats her lunch at noon.* □ *We caught the noon train from the Gare de Lyon.* [*opposite* **midnight**]

no-one or **no one** /'nouwʌn/ *pronoun*
The uses of **no-one** are shown in the entry for **nobody**.

> Notice the difference between **no-one** (meaning 'no person') and **no one** (which can refer to things or people, and means 'no single'): *No-one told me. No one solution works for everybody.*

noose /nu:s/ *noun*: **nooses**
A **noose** is a ring of rope with a sliding knot at the end, that tightens when the end of the rope is pulled, used for killing by hanging.

nor /nɔ:(r)/ *conjunction*
Nor is used **1** after **neither**, to introduce the second or a subsequent possibility, where both or all possibilities are denied: *I neither know nor care where she's gone.* □ *I'd been neither to Spain, France, nor Italy before.* □ *Neither Budapest nor Prague is on the itinerary.* □ *Neither Frank nor I were able to provide the answer.* [see note at **neither** for information on plural and singular verbs with **neither ... nor**] **2** to introduce a second or further negative statement: *If you don't tell them, nor shall I.* □ *'I haven't seen the film yet.' 'Nor me* (or *Nor have I*).' □ *'No more chips for me, thanks.' 'Nor for me.'* □ *She didn't want to go herself, nor did she want him to go without her.* □ *I didn't see him that night, nor the following night, nor at all during the next few weeks.*
[see also **neither, or**]

norm /nɔ:m/ *noun*: **norms**
1 (*used in the singular*) You can say that something is the **norm** if it is what people normally or traditionally do: *It has become the norm to send your young children to a nursery or to a childminder.* **2 Norms** are usual or accepted ways of behaving: *I wasn't familiar with their social norms.*

normal /'nɔ:məl/ *adjective*
1 Something **normal** is usual, typical or expected: *Is it normal for him to leave without telling you where he is going?* □ *He was a normal young boy, with all the normal hobbies a young boy has.* **2** Sometimes **normal** has the meaning 'natural', suggesting that what is not **normal** is against nature in some way and should be criticized as morally wrong: *It's simply not normal for a mother to reject a child in that way.*

normality /nɔ:'malɪtɪ/ *noun* (*uncount*)
Normality is the state or condition in which things are as they usually are: *I had been glad of the holiday, but now I was ready to get back to normality.*

normally /'nɔ:məlɪ/ *adverb*
1 (*sentence adverb*) **Normally** means usually or typically: *Normally, I prefer to have my shower before my breakfast.* □ *I don't normally eat a big lunch.* **2 Normally** also means in a normal way: *We were glad to see him behaving normally again.*

north /nɔ:θ/ *noun*; *adverb*; *adjective*
▷ ***noun*** (*used in the singular*)
1 The **north**, is the direction to your left when you face the sunrise (east): *A range of hills became visible to the north of us.* □ *We got in the car and drove out of the city to the north.* □ *The wind had shifted round from north to east.* **2** The **north** is the part of a country or other area that lies towards the north: *Cotton manufacturing continued to expand in the industrial north.* □ *You should visit the north of Scotland.*
▷ ***adverb***
North means to the north: *We were on the motorway, travelling north.* □ *Singapore lies north of the equator.* □ *The north-facing slopes were still covered with snow.*

▻ *adjective*
A part of a place with the name or description **north** is a part towards the north: *Repairs have already begun on the north wall.* □ *We've been trying to buy a flat in North Edinburgh.*

northbound /ˈnɔːθbaʊnd/ *adjective*
1 Northbound traffic is travelling north. **2** The **northbound** carriageway of a motorway is the one used by traffic travelling north.

northeast /nɔːθˈiːst/ *noun; adverb; adjective*
▻ *noun* (*used in the singular*)
1 The **northeast** is the direction between north and east: *A strange glow lit up the sky to the northeast.* **2** The **northeast** is the part of a country or other area that lies towards the northeast: *Newcastle and the Northeast.*
▻ *adverb*
Northeast means to the northeast: *The path leads northeast towards the valley.*
▻ *adjective*
1 A part of a place with the description **northeast** is the part towards the northeast: *cracks in the northeast tower.* **2** A **northeast** wind blows from the northeast.

northeasterly /nɔːθˈiːstəlɪ/ *adjective*
1 A **northeasterly** direction or region lies towards the northeast. **2** A **northeasterly** wind blows from the northeast.

northeastern /nɔːθˈiːstən/ *adjective*
Northeastern means in, or belonging to, the northeast of a country or other area: *the Northeastern region* □ *northeastern customs.*

northerly /ˈnɔːðəlɪ/ *adjective*
1 A **northerly** direction or region lies towards the north: *the island's most northerly point* □ *We seem to be heading in a northerly direction.* **2** A **northerly** wind blows from the north.

northern /ˈnɔːðən/ *adjective*
Northern means in, or belonging to, the north of a country or other area: *the cold northern climate* □ *Northern districts will have some rain.*

northerner /ˈnɔːðənə(r)/ *noun*: **northerners**
A **northerner** is a person who lives in, or comes from, the north of a country or other area: *Northerners come across as being more friendly than people from the south.*

northward /ˈnɔːθwəd/ *adverb; adjective*
▻ *adverb*
Northward or **northwards** means towards the north: *We cycled northwards for several miles.*
▻ ***adjective:*** *the northward journey.*

northwest /nɔːθˈwɛst/ *noun; adverb; adjective*
▻ *noun* (*used in the singular*)
1 The **northwest**, is the direction between north and west: *Looking to the northwest, we can see some interesting star constellations.* **2** The **northwest** is the part of a country or other area that lies towards the northwest: *There will be rain in Manchester and much of the northwest.* [for more examples, see **northeast**]

nose /noʊz/ *noun; verb*
▻ *noun*: **noses**
1 Your **nose** is the part of your face that you use to smell, and that you can breathe through: *He had a thin face and a long, pointed nose.* [see picture at **body**] **2** The front or projecting part of something, especially an aircraft, is often referred to as the **nose**.
▻ *verb*: **noses, nosing, nosed**

phrasal verb
You **nose about** or **around** in a place, especially somewhere you don't belong or have not been invited to, when you look for something there or simply look around because you are curious: *A couple of journalists were nosing around outside.*

▻ *phrases* **1** You **blow your nose** when you clear it of mucus by sharply blowing air through it. **2** (*informal*) You can say that something **gets up** your **nose** when it annoys or irritates you. **3** (*informal*) You can say that you **have a nose for** something when you are skilled at recognizing or identifying it: *a journalist with a nose for a good story.* **4** (*informal*) You can say you **pay through the nose** for something when you pay an unreasonably high price for it. **5** (*informal*) You **turn** your **nose up at** something when you refuse it because you don't think it is good enough: *You can't turn your nose up at a job opportunity like this!* **6** (*informal*) Something is **under** your **nose** when it is very obviously in front of you; something happens **under** your **nose** when it happens close to you, and is not hidden from you, and you should notice it.

nosey see **nosy**.

nostalgia /nɒˈstaldʒə/ *noun* (*uncount*)
Nostalgia consists of remembering happy times in the past, often also feeling slightly sad because they are gone: *I wasn't sure I could stand another evening of nostalgia.* — *adjective* **nostalgic:** *He was naturally nostalgic, even sentimental, and respected established institutions.* □ *The programme takes a nostalgic look at the career of one of our best-loved comedians.*

nostril /ˈnɒstrɪl/ *noun*: **nostrils**
Your **nostrils** are the two openings in your nose, that you breathe and smell through. [see picture at **body**]

nosy or **nosey** /ˈnoʊzɪ/ *adjective* (*derogatory*): **nosier, nosiest**
You can describe someone as **nosy** if they are too curious about things that don't concern them: *How would we keep it a secret from our nosy neighbours?* □ *Don't be so nosy, Timothy!*

not /nɒt/ *adverb* (often shortened to **n't**, especially in conversation and in informal English)
Not is used **1** to make negative statements **a** with the verbs *be* and *have*: *It's not fair.* □ *It isn't fair.* □ *I'm willing but he isn't.* □ *They're free but I'm not.* □ *We haven't any more news.* **b** with auxiliary and modal verbs: *I haven't finished yet.* □ *You won't succeed.* □ *They'd enjoy it, but I wouldn't.* □ *She might not want to see you.* □ *I could not think what to say.* **c** with the auxiliary verb *do* where there is no other auxiliary or modal verb: *Don't expect him to agree.* □ *We didn't see her at all.* □ *'You cheated!' 'I did not!'*

Remember that **not** is used with words like *any*, *anyone* and *anywhere* rather than with a second negative: *We don't have any* (not *we don't have no*) *sugar*.

d before participles formed with *-ing* and infinitives preceded by *to*: *Not wishing to disturb them, I tiptoed out again.* □ *I was nervous, not having met him before.* □ *I pleaded with him not to mention it.* □ *It was difficult not to laugh.* **e** before verbs of thinking and intending, and the verb *want*, to give a negative sense to the part of your statement that comes after the verb: *I don't think he's right.* [= I think he is not right] □ *I don't want to disappoint her.* [= I would rather not disappoint her] □ *I don't expect to be late tonight.*
2 (often **n't**) to construct questions **a** in the form of

question tags after a positive statement: *We visited it last year, didn't we?* □ *They've bought a new one, haven't they?* □ (*old or Scottish*) *We should make certain, should we not?* **b** making a straightforward enquiry, or expressing surprise or annoyance: *Didn't you manage to find it?* □ *Hasn't he got another one somewhere?* □ *Isn't she awake yet?* □ *Hasn't he got the brains to see how impossible that is?* **c** making a polite suggestion: *Couldn't we go tomorrow instead?* □ *Wouldn't it be better if you telephoned first?* □ *Ought we not to warn them?* □ *Why don't we take the car?*

3 in place of a negative clause **a** after verbs of thinking and reporting: *I may have lost it, but I hope not.* [= but I hope I haven't lost it] □ *'Has he arrived yet?' 'It appears not.'* □ *'Did he pass?' 'I'm afraid not.'* [compare **so**] **b** after sentence adverbs: *'Did she get the job?' 'Unfortunately not.'* □ *'Are there enough?' 'Evidently not.'* **c** after words such as *if*, *or* and *why*: *We'll probably get there in time, but if not, we can catch the next train.* □ *We'll see you again next Christmas, if not before.* □ *Are you coming with us or not?* □ *'I didn't go after all.' 'Oh, why not?'* **d** to make a correction or distinction: *You say 'lice', not 'louses'.* □ *It's in the fridge, not on the shelf.* □ *I wondered why they had chosen him and not me.*

4 a to make a particular word or phrase negative: *Not everyone is* [= few people are] *as generous as you.* □ *Not many* [= few] *people in your position would have done that.* □ *Not enough* [= too little] *time was spent on the planning stage.* □ *Ideally the total should be not less than 25 and not more than 30.* □ *I spent a not very successful day at the races.* □ *'Did you have a good time?' 'Not very.'* □ *'Was the weather perfect?''Not all the time.'* □ *'Could I see you this afternoon?' 'Well, not before 3.00 pm.'* □ *'Is 'staff' singular?' 'Not always.'* **b** with *a* and *one* to emphasize the complete absence or lack of something: *We made not a sound climbing out of the window.* □ *Not a single leaf was left on the tree.* □ *Not one student turned up.* □ *I didn't understand a word of the lecture.* □ *'Did you find any mistakes?' 'No, not even a misprint.'* **c** to mean 'barely', or 'no more than': *He stood bang in front of me with his face not two inches from mine.*

5 to introduce a less important point in contrast to a more important one, or to the real one: *He felt betrayed not just by his friends, but by his family as well.* □ *Not only was he a talented sportsman; he was also a highly respected academic.* □ *We refused, not because we didn't want to come, but because we thought it was inappropriate to.*

▷ ***phrases*** **1 Not at all** is used **a** as a polite way of responding to someone, *eg* when they thank you or apologize for causing inconvenience: *'Thanks for the lift.' 'Not at all.'* □ *'Would you mind moving back a bit?' 'Not at all.'* □ *'I'm so sorry.''Not at all.'* **b** as an emphatic way of saying 'no': *'Isn't that a ridiculous suggestion?' 'Not at all; I think it's very sensible.'* **2 Not that** introduces a negative clause that reduces the importance of what you say in the main statement: *I've corrected this section; not that there were many errors in it.* **3** For **not to mention** see **mention**. **4** For **not very** see **very**.

notable /ˈnoʊtəbəl/ *adjective*
Something that is **notable** is important or worth mentioning: *The critics have, with a few notable exceptions, received his new play very well.* — adverb (*sentence adverb*) **notably:** *This technique is increasingly used by modern composers, notably British ones.*

notch /nɒtʃ/ *noun*: **notches**
A **notch** is a small, V-shaped cut: *He caught another fish, and cut another notch in his stick.*

note /noʊt/ *noun*; *verb*
▷ ***noun*: notes**
1 A **note** is a short, informal letter: *There's a note on your desk asking you to call your husband.* **2 Notes** are written records of something: *I copied his notes from the last two lectures.* □ *Some listened attentively to what he said, and others scribbled notes.* □ *She made a note of the important points.* □ *You may take notes, if you wish.* **3** In a book, a **note** is a brief comment explaining something or giving a reference to another place in the book. **4** A **note** is also a banknote, a piece of paper used as money: *coins and notes.* **5** (*uncount or count*) You take **note** of something when you pay attention to it or notice it: *Nobody took note of what he had said.* □ *Some of these buildings are particularly worthy of note.* □ *I kept a mental note of everything I had seen.* **6** A **note** is also a musical sound, or a written symbol representing it. **7 Note** is also used in many ways to mean an impression, a feeling or a mood: *There was a note of panic in her voice.* □ *The film ends on a happy note.*
▷ ***verb*: notes, noting, noted**
1 You **note** something when you notice it, and sometimes mention it or tell others: *You will note that the tone of the poem changes towards the end.* □ *Note the absence of primary colours in the painting.* □ *The minister noted that this question had been asked before.* **2** You **note** something, or **note** something down, when you make a usually written note of it: *She noted down the time of the meeting in her diary.*

noted /ˈnoʊtɪd/ *adjective*
A person or a place is **noted** for a quality they have when they are famous because they have it: *Switzerland is noted for its beautiful scenery and clean air.* [*same as* **renowned**]

nothing /ˈnʌθɪŋ/ *pronoun*; *adverb*
▷ ***pronoun***
1 Nothing means 'no things' or 'not anything': *I looked at her for reassurance, but she said nothing.* □ *There was nothing to eat in the cupboard, so I looked in the fridge.* □ *There's nothing to get anxious about.* □ *Nothing exciting ever happens here.* □ *There's nothing seriously wrong with her, I hope?* □ *'What are you doing this afternoon?' 'Nothing in particular.'* □ *I've got nothing else to report.* □ *Nothing I do ever turns out right.* □ *'Have a drink.' 'Thanks, there's nothing I'd like better just now.'* **2** You say that something is **nothing** if it is not serious, important or worth mentioning: *'What's the matter?' 'Oh, it's nothing.'* □ *'It was very kind of you to give him a lift.' 'That's OK, it was nothing.'* □ *It's nothing nowadays to fly to Paris and back in the same day.*
▷ ***adverb*** **Nothing** is used before *like* to mean 'not in the least' or 'not nearly': *She's nothing like her photographs.* □ *The work is nothing like done.*

> Notice that you can use the less emphatic *not* (*n't*) *anything* instead of **nothing**, except where **nothing** introduces the sentence as its subject: *I've got nothing* (or *I haven't got anything*) *else to offer. We're nothing like* (or *aren't anything like*) *finished.* But: *Nothing much was happening.*

▷ ***phrases***
1 a You get something **for nothing** if you get it without having to pay for it: *Children travel for nothing.* **b** Something is done **for nothing** if it is done for no good reason, or without any useful result: *They were dying in their thousands for nothing.* □ *All that hard work for nothing!* **2 Nothing but** a certain thing means that thing and only that thing: *There's nothing but rub-*

bish on television. □ *I could hear nothing but a vague buzzing sound.* **3** (*informal*) If you say **'nothing doing'** to someone who has requested or proposed something, you are rudely refusing to consider their request or proposal. **4** If you say that there is **nothing for it but** to do a certain thing, you mean that that is the only possible thing to do, even though you would rather not do it: *There was nothing for it but to wait.* **5** You use **nothing if not** to emphasize a description: *He was nothing if not* [= he was very] *generous.* **6** If you say, in reference to a story or report, that there is **nothing in it**, you mean that it isn't true. **7** You use **nothing of the sort** or **kind** as an emphatic negative: *'You were spying on us.' 'I was doing nothing of the sort!'* **8** If you say, in reference to a task, that there is **nothing to it**, you mean that it is very easy.
[compare **anything, something, everything**]

notice /ˈnoʊtɪs/ *noun; verb*
▻ ***noun*: notices**
1 A **notice** is an announcement displayed or delivered publicly: *Above the bar, there was a notice warning you not to ask for credit.* □ *Did you read the notice in the paper about council tax payments?* **2** (*uncount; formal*) Something comes to your **notice** when you realize it, or when someone tells you about it: *It has come to our notice that certain members have still not paid their subscription.* □ *I'm sure that fact has not escaped his notice.* □ *You should have brought it to the notice of the police immediately.* **3** (*uncount*) You are given **notice** of something when someone tells or warns you that it is going to happen: *Have you given them notice of your intention to leave?* □ *The strikes will continue until further notice.* □ *You can't just leave your job like that; you have to give at least a month's notice.* □ *If you'd given me more notice I could have prepared something better.* □ *It all happened at such short notice that none of us were really ready for it.* □ *We were prepared to leave for Europe at a moment's notice.*
▻ ***verb*: notices, noticing, noticed**
You **notice** something when you realize it, observe it, or become aware of it: *I noticed that she didn't have her wedding ring on.* □ *I hadn't noticed how tall he was until now.* □ *Did you notice the mark on his shirt?* □ *He wondered if they had noticed any change in his behaviour.*
▻ ***phrases*** **1** You **take notice** of something when you pay attention to it: *You should take notice of the advice your parents have given you.* □ *They're just trying to scare you; take no notice.* [*same as* **pay attention**] **2** For **not take a blind bit of notice** see **blind**.

noticeable /ˈnoʊtɪsəbəl/ *adjective*
Something **noticeable** is easy to see or recognize: *There's been no noticeable improvement in the service.* □ *It was noticeable that her husband never made any of the decisions.* — *adverb* **noticeably:** *He was noticeably more relaxed after she had gone.*

notification /noʊtɪfɪˈkeɪʃən/ *noun* (*uncount; formal*)
Someone gives you **notification** of something when they tell you about it, especially formally or officially: *You will receive notification of our decision in due course.*

notify /ˈnoʊtɪfaɪ/ *verb*: **notifies, notifying, notified**
Someone **notifies** you of something when they tell you about it, especially formally or officially: *You will be notified of any change in bank charges.* □ *If your passport is stolen, you should notify the police immediately.*

notion /ˈnoʊʃən/ *noun*: **notions**
A **notion** is a belief, understanding or impression: *He had a fairly romantic notion of what life as a writer would be like.* □ *I had the rather misguided notion that you might actually love me.* [*same as* **idea**]

notoriety /noʊtəˈraɪətɪ/ *noun* (*uncount*)
Notoriety is the quality of being notorious: *They had gained notoriety as one of the most violent gangs in Chicago.*

notorious /noʊˈtɔːrɪəs/ *adjective*
Someone or something that is **notorious** is well-known for having some bad or undesirable quality: *This was nothing compared with the notorious Bloom case, in which seven people had been convicted of serious fraud.* □ *London, it seems, has become notorious for dirty streets and poor public services.* — *adverb* **notoriously:** *The south coast is notoriously overcrowded in summer.*

notwithstanding /nɒtwɪðˈstandɪŋ/ *preposition* (*formal*)
Notwithstanding means 'in spite of': *Notwithstanding his extreme youth, his work was brilliant and highly influential.* [*same as* **despite**]

nought /nɔːt/ *noun* (*count or uncount*)
Nought is zero, or the figure 0: *It has increased by nought point two per cent.* □ *a three and two noughts.*

noun /naʊn/ *noun*: **nouns**
1 A **noun** is a word used to refer to a person, thing or quality. See also the entries **count**, **uncount**, **collective**, **mass noun**, **proper noun** **2** Notice how a lot of nouns can be used like an adjective before another noun (*winter clothing, a skiing outfit*). **3** Notice how words like *piece* and *pair*, and words of measurement, are used with uncount and plural nouns (*a clean pair of shorts, some pieces of furniture, one kilo of flour*).

nourish /ˈnʌrɪʃ/ *verb*: **nourishes, nourishing, nourished**
To **nourish** people or animals is to provide them with food: *Some of the children had been poorly nourished.* — *noun* (*uncount*) **nourishment** /ˈnʌrɪʃmənt/: *health problems created by a lack of proper nourishment.*

nourishing /ˈnʌrɪʃɪŋ/ *adjective*
Food that is **nourishing** contains substances that make you strong and healthy: *It may taste good, but it's not particularly nourishing.*

novel[1] /ˈnɒvəl/ *noun*: **novels**
A **novel** is a book that tells a fictional story: *Have you read any of Dickens's novels?* □ *I'm reading a novel by Graham Greene at the moment.*

novel[2] /ˈnɒvəl/ *adjective*
Something **novel** is completely new or original, and sometimes rather strange or unusual: *They have a fairly novel approach to education.* □ *Someone had had the novel idea of painting the windows black.*

novelist /ˈnɒvəlɪst/ *noun*: **novelists**
A **novelist** is a person who writes novels.

novelty /ˈnɒvəltɪ/ *noun*: **novelties**
1 (*uncount*) **Novelty** is the quality of being new, original or interestingly different: *At first I enjoyed living abroad, but the novelty soon wore off.* **2** You can refer to something you have never seen or experienced before as a **novelty**: *In this part of the world, mothers who did full-time work were a bit of a novelty.* **3** **Novelties** are small cheap toys or souvenirs.

November /noʊˈvɛmbə(r)/ *noun* (*uncount*)
November is the eleventh month of the year, coming after October and before December: *My contract runs out next November.* □ *His birthday is the twenty-ninth of November* (written *29 November*). □ *November the second* (written *November 2*) □ *You can expect the weather to be pretty cold in November.* □ *a frosty November morning.* [see also note at **date**]

novice /ˈnɒvɪs/ *noun*: **novices**
A **novice** is a beginner, someone who has had no previous experience of what they are doing: *In the world of business, I'm something of a novice.*

now /naʊ/ *adverb; conjunction*
▻ ***adverb***
1 You use **now** to mean **a** 'at the present time' or 'the present time': *The time is now four minutes past five.* □ *I am now sitting in the hall where this historic meeting will take place.* □ *It is now just over three hours since they landed on the moon.* □ *From now on, you will be expected to make all the decisions yourself.* □ *Now is the time to make your statement.* □ *I thought they would have arrived by now.* □ *Until now, she has never had the opportunity to say what she really thinks.* □ *They've been perfectly satisfied up till now.* □ *It's happened plenty of times before now.* **b** immediately: *I'd like you to do it now, not next week!*
2 You also use **now** to mean **a** 'then', 'next', or 'at that point', when relating a story or a series of events: *He now turned from journalism to fiction.* □ *She had now achieved exactly what she wanted.* **b** up to the present time, or 'so far': *She has now been teaching for over 13 years.* □ *He'd now been gone six hours, far longer than he'd said he'd be.* **c** because of what has just happened: *I was going to let you into a secret, but I won't now, seeing as you've been so nasty.*
3 You use **now** informally in conversation, *eg* to give liveliness to a statement or comment, or emphasis to a request or instruction: *Now although it was dark he could just see his way.* □ *Now please don't misunderstand me.* □ *Now just be patient.* □ *'I've decided to leave school.' 'Oh, have you now?'* □ *Off you go, now; I must have some peace.* □ *Careful, now!* □ *Well now, what next?* □ *Now, let's go on to the next point.*
▻ ***conjunction***
You use **'now'** or **'now** that' to introduce a circumstance that makes it possible for a new stage to begin, or necessary for a change to be made: *Now we're all here, let's begin.* □ *I'm thinking of getting a job now that the children are older.* □ *I was going to go back today, but now that Mum's got flu I'd better stay a bit longer.*
▻ ***phrases*** **1 a** Something that happened **just now** happened a short time ago: *I saw him getting off a bus just now.* **b** What is happening **just now** is what is happening at the present moment: *I'm busy just now; can I call you back later?* **2** Something that happens **now and again**, **now and then** or **every now and then**, happens occasionally: *We used to meet now and then for coffee.* **3** You say **'Now, now'** to people to calm them down or stop them behaving in a certain way: *Now, now; there's nothing to be frightened of.* □ *Now, now; be reasonable.*

nowadays /'naʊədeɪz/ *adverb*
Nowadays means in these present times: *Nowadays, men are expected to play their part in running the household.* □ *Children nowadays don't have any respect for anything.*

nowhere /'noʊwɛə(r)/ *adverb*
1 Nowhere means 'no place', 'in or to no place', or 'not anywhere': *She's very old and goes nowhere these days.* □ *Nowhere have I discovered any reference to this.* □ *There was nowhere for us to shelter.* □ *I could think of nowhere else to look.* □ *'Where are you going?' 'Nowhere special.'* □ *We wanted to eat out but could find nowhere cheap enough.* **2 Nowhere** can refer to situations, circumstances or aspects: *Her ability as a writer is nowhere more evident than in her precise use of language.*

> Notice that you can use the less emphatic *not* (*n't*) *anywhere* instead of **nowhere**, except where **nowhere** introduces the sentence: *She goes nowhere* (or *she doesn't go anywhere*) *nowadays.* But: *Nowhere was this more obvious than in her portrait-painting.*

▻ ***phrases*** **1** Someone or something appears **from nowhere** or **out of nowhere** when they appear suddenly and unexpectedly: *A car came from nowhere and hit them on the crossing.* □ *He managed to produce a meal out of nowhere.* **2** You say you **are getting nowhere** when you are making no progress. **3** (*informal*) A place that is **in the middle of nowhere** is a long way from any large town. **4** (*informal*) **Nowhere near** is an emphatic form of 'not' and means the same as 'not nearly': *We've nowhere near enough money.* □ *Edinburgh is nowhere near as well-preserved as Bath.* **5** Something that is **nowhere to be seen** cannot be found or has completely disappeared: *The nurse I'd just spoken to was nowhere to be seen.*

noxious /'nɒkʃəs/ *adjective*
Noxious substances are harmful or poisonous: *noxious fumes.* [*same as* **toxic**]

nozzle /'nɒzəl/ *noun*: **nozzles**
A **nozzle** is a part fitted to the end of a pipe, to control the flow of liquid from it.

n't /ənt/ see **not**.

nuance /'nju:ɒ:ns/ *noun*: **nuances**
A **nuance** is a slight difference in something such as a colour or the meaning of a word.

nuclear /'nju:klɪə(r)/ *adjective*
Nuclear means relating to, producing, or using, the extremely powerful form of energy created when atoms are split or forced together: *a nuclear power station* □ *nuclear energy* □ *conventional and nuclear weapons.* [*same as* **atomic**]

nuclear-free /nju:klɪə'fri:/ *adjective*
A **nuclear-free** zone is an area where nuclear weapons and nuclear energy are not allowed.

nuclear reactor /nju:klɪə rɪ'aktə(r)/ *noun*: **nuclear reactors**
A **nuclear reactor** is a large machine for producing nuclear energy.

nude /nju:d/ *adjective; noun*
▻ ***adjective***
Someone who is **nude** is wearing no clothes: *pictures of nude women.* [*same as* **naked**; *opposite* **clothed**]
▻ ***noun***: **nudes**
A **nude** is a painting or a statue of a nude person.

nudge /nʌdʒ/ *verb; noun*
▻ ***verb***: **nudges, nudging, nudged**
You **nudge** someone when you give them a short, gentle push, especially with your elbow, to get their attention or to encourage them to do something.
▻ ***noun***: **nudges:** *If your father falls asleep, give him a nudge.*

nudist /'nju:dɪst/ *noun* (*often adjectival*): **nudists**
A **nudist** is a person who likes to be naked, especially someone who goes to special camps and other areas for people who don't like wearing clothes: *a nudist beach.* [*same as* **naturist**]

nudity /'nju:dɪtɪ/ *noun* (*uncount*)
Nudity is the state of being nude or wearing no clothes: *We were no longer embarrassed by nudity.*

nuisance /'nju:səns/ *noun* (*usually in the singular*)
A **nuisance** is someone or something that annoys you or causes you trouble: *This cold weather's a bit of a nuisance.* □ *The boy seemed determined to make a nuisance of himself.* [cause trouble]

numb /nʌm/ *adjective*
1 Part of your body is **numb** when there is no feeling in it and you feel as if it is not actually there: *Her fingers were numb, her hands aching with the cold.* **2** You

can say you are **numb**, especially when you have had a shock, when you are unable to think, or feel any emotion: *Freda was numb with shock.*

number /'nʌmbə(r)/ *noun; verb*

▻ ***noun*: numbers**

1 (*count or uncount*) **Numbers** are words such as 'one', 'eight' and 'two hundred', and symbols such as 12, 1003 and 0.75, along with other words and symbols such as 'fifth' and '2nd', that are used to count or calculate quantities, and to talk about the positions of things in a series: *She wrote a number four on the blackboard.* □ *a three-figure number* □ *understanding the concept of number.* **2** (often **No.** or **no.**) Something or someone that is one of a series can be referred to as *eg* **number** 5 or **No.** 228: *the people who live at No. 39* □ *Runner number 21 is beginning to pull ahead of the others.* **3** Your **number** is any of several personal sets of figures or digits, *eg* those on any of your credit cards, or the ones that people have to dial to telephone you: *Could I have you Visa number, please?* □ *I'll call you. What's your number?* □ *Have you looked up her telephone number?* **4** You refer to the **number** of people or things in a situation when you are talking about how many are involved in it: *The number of deaths has risen to 50.* □ *An impressive number of people have written to express their support.* □ *a disappointingly small number of applications* □ *The book sold in vast numbers.*

Notice that '**a number**' of things takes a plural verb, but '**the number**' of things takes a singular verb: *A vast number of tasks remain to be done. The number of tasks involved is fairly small.* [see also note at **amount**]

5 Any of the issues of a magazine can be referred to as a **number**; a back **number** is any issue before the present one: *They can supply back numbers of any periodical.* □ *some old numbers of 'The Scots magazine'.* **6** (*informal*) A piece of popular music is often referred to as a **number**.

▻ ***verb*: numbers, numbering, numbered**

1 You **number** something when you give it a number or mark a number on it, so that it can be identified: *Remember to number the pages.* **2** A group that **numbers** a certain quantity consists of as many as that: *A crowd numbering several hundred had gathered to greet her.* **3** Someone or something **is numbered** among a certain group if they are considered worthy of belonging to it: *It must be numbered among the century's greatest novels.* □ *I numbered her amongst my most intimate friends.*

▻ ***phrases*** **1 A number of** things or people is several of them: *There are a number of things to discuss.* □ *A number of delegates have expressed dissatisfaction with the arrangements.* [see note at sense 4 of the noun **number** above] **2 Any number of** particular things is a large quantity of them: *There are any number of ways a problem like this can be tackled.* **3** Someone whose **days are numbered** is likely to die very soon.

number one /nʌmbə 'wʌn/ *adjective* (*informal*)

Number one describes what is best, most important, or most popular: *Give it number-one priority.* □ *She is the number-one writer on everyone's list.*

number plate /'nʌmbə pleɪt/ *noun*: **number plates**

On a car or other vehicle, the **number plates** are the signs, one on the front and one on the back, showing the number that the car is identified by. [*same as* **registration number**; see picture at **car**]

numeracy /'nju:mərəsɪ/ *noun* (*uncount*)

Numeracy is the ability to use numbers to do calculations.

numeral /'nju:mərəl/ *noun*: **numerals**

A **numeral** is a symbol that represents a number.

numerate /'nju:mərət/ *adjective*

A person who is **numerate** knows how to use numbers to do calculations.

numerical /nju:'merɪkəl/ *adjective*

Numerical means relating to, or expressed using, numbers: *arranged in numerical order.*

numerous /'nju:mərəs/ *adjective*

Numerous means many or a lot; people or things are **numerous** when there are many of them: *He's a member of numerous environmental organizations.* □ *Numerous people wrote to me saying how sorry they were.* □ *The smaller hotels and hostels were more numerous.*

nun /nʌn/ *noun*: **nuns**

A **nun** is a member of a female religious community.

nurse /nɜ:s/ *noun; verb*

▻ ***noun*: nurses**

A **nurse** is a person trained to look after ill or injured people, usually in a hospital.

▻ ***verb*: nurses, nursing, nursed**

To **nurse** someone is to look after them when they are ill, not necessarily as a trained nurse in a hospital: *She nursed her father for the last five years of his life.* □ *He was taken in by a group of monks who nursed him back to health.*

nursery /'nɜ:sn/ *noun*: **nurseries**

1 A **nursery** is a place where parents can take their children to be looked after, while they are at work. **2** Some people refer to a young child's bedroom as a **nursery**. **3** A **nursery** is also a place where plants are grown for sale.

nursery rhyme /'nɜ:sn raɪm/ *noun*: **nursery rhymes**

A **nursery rhyme** is a short simple traditional song for children.

nursery school /'nɜ:sn sku:l/ *noun*: **nursery schools**

A **nursery school** is a school for children between three and five years old.

nursing /'nɜ:sɪŋ/ *noun* (*uncount*)

Nursing is the work or profession of a nurse: *a career in nursing.*

nursing home /'nɜ:sɪŋ houm/ *noun*: **nursing homes**

A **nursing home** is a small private hospital or home, especially for old people.

nurture /'nɜ:tʃə(r)/ *verb* (*formal*): **nurtures, nurturing, nurtured**

1 You **nurture** a growing child, animal or plant when you look after them. **2** You **nurture** something such as a plan or an idea when you encourage its development.

nut /nʌt/ *noun*: **nuts**

1 Nuts are the fruits of certain trees, consisting of a hard shell with a firm inner part that you can eat: *She bought a bag of mixed nuts.* **2** A **nut** is also a small piece of metal with a hole through it, for screwing on the end of a bolt to fasten pieces of wood or metal together. **3** (*informal*) If you call someone a **nut** you mean they are mad or foolish.

nutrient /'nju:trɪənt/ *noun*: **nutrients**

Nutrients are substances in soil that plants feed on, or substances contained in food that give you energy and make you healthy.

nutritious /nju:'trɪʃəs/ *adjective*

Nutritious food contains plenty of the kind of substances that give you energy and make you healthy.

nuzzle /ˈnʌzəl/ *verb*: **nuzzles, nuzzling, nuzzled**
An animal, for example a dog, **nuzzles** you when it rubs its nose and mouth against you affectionately.

nylon /ˈnaɪlɒn/ *noun* (*uncount, often adjectival*)
Nylon is a strong, man-made fabric used for making clothes and other things: *nylon stockings* □ *Is the carpet made of wool or nylon?*

O[1] or **o** /oʊ/ *noun*: **Os** or **o's**
1 O is the fifteenth letter of the English alphabet: *There are two Os in 'good'.* □ *Name a city beginning with 'O'.* **2 O** is also used in speech to mean 'zero' or 'nought'. [see note at **zero**]

O[2] /oʊ/ *interjection*
O is used in exclamations to express strong feelings such as surprise, admiration, pleasure, anger or fear: *O God!* □ *O, what a beautiful view!* [see also **oh**]

oaf /oʊf/ *noun*: **oafs**
If you call a man or boy an **oaf**, you think they are awkward and stupid: *Be more careful, you clumsy oaf!*

oak /oʊk/ *noun* (*often adjectival*): **oaks**
1 An **oak** or **oak tree** is a tree common in northern parts of the world: *The way led through an oak wood.* **2** (*uncount*) **Oak** is the hard wood of the oak tree, used *eg* for making furniture: *doors made of solid oak* □ *oak panelling.*

OAP /oʊ eɪ 'piː/ *noun* (*BrE*; *informal*): **OAPs**
An **OAP** is an old age pensioner: *The tour company offers special rates for children and OAPs.* [see note at **senior citizen**]

oar /ɔː(r)/ *noun*: **oars**
An **oar** is a long pole with a broad, flat blade at one end that is used for rowing a boat. Oars are usually used in pairs. [compare **paddle**]
▻ ***phrase*** (*informal*) If you say that someone **puts, shoves** or **sticks their oar in**, you mean that they interfere, especially by offering their opinion when it is not wanted.

oasis /oʊ'eɪsɪs/ *noun*: **oases** /oʊ'eɪsiːz/
1 An **oasis** is a small area in a desert where water is found and plants grow. **2** Any pleasant or restful place or situation in the middle of hard work, problems, or continual activity can also be referred to as an **oasis**: *The garden was an oasis of tranquillity in the middle of the bustling city.*

oatcake /'oʊtkeɪk/ *noun*: **oatcakes**
An **oatcake** is a flat dry biscuit made from oatmeal: *We ended the meal with cheese and oatcakes.*

oath /oʊθ/ *noun*: **oaths** /oʊðz/
1 An **oath** is a solemn promise that someone makes, *eg* to tell the truth or be loyal, and often naming God as a witness: *They swore an oath of allegiance to the king.* **2** (*old*) An **oath** is also a swearword, especially one that uses the name of God or religion improperly: *He uttered a stream of oaths as he struggled to pull on his boots.* [*same as* **curse**]
▻ ***phrase*** (*legal*) In a court of law, someone who is **on** or **under oath** has made a solemn promise to tell the truth: *The witness was on oath to tell the truth.* □ *Evidence to the senate committee was given under oath.*

oatmeal /'oʊtmiːl/ *noun* (*uncount*)
1 Oatmeal is a coarse flour made from ground oats and used for making cakes and porridge: *a packet of oatmeal.* **2** (*often adjectival*) **Oatmeal** is also a very pale brownish cream colour: *a patterned carpet with a background of the palest oatmeal.* □ *an oatmeal skirt with matching jacket.*

oats /oʊts/ *noun* (*plural*)
Oats are a type of cereal whose grain is used as food for people and animals: *a good crop of oats* □ *The farmers grew oats and barley.* □ *porridge oats.*

obdurate /'ɒbdjʊrət/ *adjective* (*formal, usually derogatory*)
Someone who is **obdurate** stubbornly or determinedly refuses to change their mind or their beliefs despite attempts by others to influence them or persuade them to do so: *She pleaded with him, but he remained obdurate.* □ *Her obdurate refusal to accept the reformed religion led to her imprisonment.* [*same as* **stubborn**]

obedience /ə'biːdɪəns/ *noun* (*uncount*)
Obedience is the act of obeying orders from someone in a position of authority or power, or willingness to obey their orders: *She always showed respect and obedience to her parents.*

obedient /ə'biːdɪənt/ *adjective*
A person or animal who is **obedient** does what they are told or ordered to do or is willing to obey: *an obedient child* □ *Their dog is very obedient.* [*opposite* **disobedient**] — *adverb* **obediently:** *He ordered me to give him the books, and, obediently, I handed them over.* □ *The dog followed obediently at his master's heels.*

obese /oʊ'biːs/ *adjective* (*formal, technical*)
A person who is **obese** is very fat. — *noun* (*uncount*) **obesity:** *Obesity can cause serious health problems.*

obey /ə'beɪ/ or /oʊ'beɪ/ *verb*: **obeys, obeying, obeyed**
You **obey** when you do what you are told or commanded to do by someone else, especially someone in authority: *The children were disruptive and wouldn't obey their teachers.* □ *The soldier said that he was just obeying orders.* □ *He told the dog to sit, and it obeyed immediately.* [*opposite* **disobey**]

obituary /ə'bɪtʊərɪ/ *noun*: **obituaries**
An **obituary** is a formal announcement or report of a person's death, *eg* in a newspaper, often giving details of their life and work: *an obituary in the* Times □ *an obituary notice* □ *an obituary column.*

object[1] /'ɒbdʒɛkt/ *noun*: **objects**
1 An **object** is a thing that exists physically, and can be seen and touched, but is not alive: *He handed her a small round object wrapped in tissue paper.* □ *a bronze bangle, one of the many interesting objects found on this prehistoric site.* □ *back in the world of material objects.* □ *What's this object for?* [*same as* **thing**] **2** Your **object** in doing something is your aim: *My object in asking was merely to make sure I'd understood you correctly.* □ *But what's your object in all this?* □ *Show the grants committee that you have a clear and definite object in view.* □ *The object of the presentation was to underline the uniqueness of our product.* [*same*

as **aim**, **intention**] **3** The **object** of your thoughts or desires is the person or thing you are thinking about or wanting: *It was at that very moment that the object of his fantasies appeared in the doorway.* **4** The **object** of a particular feeling or reaction among people is the person or thing it is directed towards: *Things are in a bad way when the prime minister becomes an object of ridicule.* ▫ *Some pretty women have a brain too, and object to being treated purely as sex objects.* **5** (*grammar*) The **object** of a verb or preposition is the noun, noun phrase or pronoun affected by the action of the verb (*eg*: *I booked three seats. Wilson's resignation amazed everyone*) or governed by the preposition (*eg*: *We were amazed at his departure from office*). In the sentence '*He read me his resignation speech*' the **direct object** is '*his resignation speech*' and the **indirect object** is '*me*'. [see also **direct object**, **indirect object**, compare **subject**]

▻ ***phrases*** **1** If you say in reference to someone being able to afford something that money or expense is **no object**, you mean that they can easily afford it: *She manages a lot of foreign travel, expense no object, apparently.* **2** The **object of the exercise** is the aim of what is being organized or carried out: *Right, the object of the exercise is to get over as many obstacles as you can in five minutes.*

object² /əb'dʒɛkt/ *verb*: **objects, objecting, objected**

1 You **object** to something if you dislike it or disapprove of it: *I'd like to introduce a tidying rota for the kitchen, provided no-one objects.* ▫ *Most of us object to the proposed development on environmental grounds.* ▫ *I object strongly to people smoking in restaurants.* ▫ *Of course we don't object to giving a certain amount to charity, but we do object to doing the local authority's job for them.* **2** You **object** when you state or indicate that you dislike something or disapprove of it: *I objected that no time had been allowed for checking the text over.* ▫ *He objected loudly and bitterly to being woken up so early.* ▫ *'But I haven't had my five minutes' relaxation,' objected Jennifer.* — *noun* **objector:** *We shall be talking to Phyllis Fleming, one of the main objectors to the plan.*

objection /əb'dʒɛkʃən/ *noun*: **objections**

1 An **objection** is a statement or feeling of opposition or disapproval: *Objections to the building of the new road were raised at the public meeting.* ▫ *He made his objection to their marriage very clear.* **2** An **objection** is also a reason or argument made against something: *I can see no objection to the scheme.* ▫ *The only real objection against him is that he is very young to be in charge of a large department.*

objectionable /əb'dʒɛkʃənəbəl/ *adjective*

Someone's behaviour or manner is **objectionable** when it is very unpleasant and likely to cause offence: *I find his attitude thoroughly objectionable.*

objective /əb'dʒɛktɪv/ *noun*; *adjective*

▻ ***noun***: **objectives**

You have an **objective** when you have something that you want to achieve: *One of the government's main objectives is to reduce unemployment.* ▫ *Is he just trying to be awkward or does he have some more sinister objective in mind?* [*same as* **aim, goal**]

▻ ***adjective***

You describe someone as **objective** when they make a decision or form a conclusion based on the facts only and do not allow themselves to be influenced by their own personal feelings or experiences: *It is difficult to be objective when dealing with one's family.* ▫ *an objective view of British history.* [*opposite* **subjective**] — *adverb* **objectively:** *Someone who is not so deeply involved in the argument is more likely to consider the facts objectively.* — *noun* (*uncount*) **objectivity** /ɒbdʒɛk'tɪvətɪ/: *The tribunal will consider their claim with complete objectivity.*

obligation /ɒblɪ'geɪʃən/ *noun*: **obligations**

1 An **obligation** is something you must do because it is your moral or legal duty or because you have promised to do it: *She wasn't able to take up their offer because of family obligations.* ▫ *He felt an obligation to the people who had helped him.* **2** (*uncount*) **Obligation** is the binding power of such a duty: *They weren't under any obligation to accept his terms.*

obligatory /ə'blɪgətərɪ/ *adjective* (*formal*)

Something that is **obligatory** must be done because it is required by a law, rule or custom: *Evening dress is not obligatory.* [*same as* **compulsory**; *opposite* **optional, voluntary**]

oblige /ə'blaidʒ/ *verb*: **obliges, obliging, obliged**

1 (*usually in the passive*) Someone **is obliged** to do something when they are forced to do it or feel that they must do because it is their duty: *You are not obliged to say anything, but anything you do say will be taken down in evidence.* **2** To **oblige** someone means to be helpful by doing what they ask you to do: *Please oblige me by leaving at once.* ▫ *'Ask John about it; he's always happy to oblige a friend.'*

obliged /ə'blaɪdʒd/ *adjective*

When you say you are **obliged** to someone, you are grateful to them for something they have done for you: *I'm much obliged to you for all your help.*

obliging /ə'blaɪdʒɪŋ/ *adjective*

An **obliging** person is someone who is always willing to help others: *I've always found him to be very obliging.* ▫ *He has very obliging neighbours.*

oblique /ə'bli:k/ *adjective*; *noun*

▻ ***adjective***

1 An **oblique** line slopes at an angle rather than being vertical or horizontal. **2** If someone makes an **oblique** reference to something they refer to it indirectly without going straight to the point: *He made several oblique references to her past record in dealing with financial matters.*

▻ ***noun***: **obliques**

An **oblique** or **oblique stroke** is a mark (/) used in mathematics and in writing to separate numbers, letters or words. — *adverb* **obliquely:** *He referred obliquely to their former relationship.*

obliterate /ə'blɪtəreɪt/ *verb* (*formal*): **obliterates, obliterating, obliterated**

1 Something **obliterates** what it destroys completely: *A full-scale nuclear attack would obliterate many major towns and cities.* [*same as* **wipe out**] **2** To **obliterate** also means to cover or blot out completely: *A dense cloud of dust and smoke obliterated the sun.* [*same as* **blot out**]

oblivion /ə'blɪvɪən/ *noun* (*uncount*)

1 Oblivion is the state of being unconscious or completely unaware of what is going on around you: *a sleeping pill that brings almost instant oblivion.* **2 Oblivion** is also the state of being forgotten: *After a brief period of popularity, the movement and its leaders sank into oblivion.*

oblivious /ə'blɪvɪəs/ *adjective*

You are **oblivious** of something when you do not notice it or are unaware of it: *She seemed to be quite oblivious of the danger.* ▫ *The drunk man lay on the park bench, oblivious to what was going on around him.*

oblong /'ɒblɒŋ/ *noun*; *adjective*

▻ ***noun***: **oblongs**

An **oblong** is a shape that has four straight sides, four

right angles, and is longer than it is broad: *She cut the cake into neat oblongs.* [compare **rectangle, square**]
▻ ***adjective:*** *Place the sheets of pasta in an oblong dish.*

obnoxious /əb'nɒkʃəs/ *adjective*
If you describe someone or something as **obnoxious**, you mean that they are very unpleasant, disagreeable or offensive: *Their children are obnoxious little monsters.* □ *obnoxious behaviour.*

oboe /'oʊboʊ/ *noun*: **oboes**
An **oboe** is a musical instrument consisting of a hollow wooden tube fitted with a double reed. It is played by blowing air into the top of the reed: *an oboe player* □ *He is learning to play the oboe.* [see picture at **orchestra**]

obscene /əb'si:n/ *adjective*
Something that is **obscene** is disgusting or offensive, often because it deals with or shows sex in a way that most people find shocking: *an obscene publication* □ *an obscene phone call* □ *He spent an obscene amount of money on clothes and luxury cars.* [*same as* **indecent**]

obscenity /əb'sɛnɪtɪ/ *noun*: **obscenities**
1 (*uncount*) **Obscenity** is the state of being shocking, indecent or disgusting: *the obscenity of war.* [*same as* **atrocity**] **2** An **obscenity** is a word or act that is extremely offensive or disgusting: *The youths shouted obscenities at the police.*

obscure /əb'skjʊə(r)/ *adjective; verb*
▻ ***adjective***
Something that is **obscure** is **1** not well known: *He studied some of the more obscure Latin poets.* □ *an obscure island in the Pacific.* **2** not easy to understand: *His remarks were a trifle obscure.* **3** not easy to see: *He could see them only as obscure shapes moving towards him through the mist.*
▻ ***verb***: **obscures, obscuring, obscured**
To **obscure** something means to hide it from view or make it difficult to understand: *Their view was obscured by a thick hedge.* □ *The true meaning of his statement was obscured by vague and ambiguous language.*

obscurity /əb'skʊərɪtɪ/ *noun* (*uncount*)
1 Obscurity is the state of being unknown or forgotten: *For most of his life, he lived in obscurity in a small village in the country.* **2 Obscurity** is also the state of being difficult to see or understand: *small creatures taking advantage of the obscurity of the night to forage in the jungle* □ *the obscurity of his philosophical arguments.*

obsequious /əb'si:kwɪəs/ *adjective* (*formal, usually derogatory*)
Someone who is **obsequious** is too eager to serve you or agree with you: *He had a fawning and obsequious manner.* [*same as* **smarmy**] — *adverb* **obsequiously:** *His assistant bowed and nodded obsequiously.*

observance /əb'zɜ:vəns/ *noun* (*uncount or count; formal*): **observances**
1 (*uncount*) **Observance** of a law or custom is the act of obeying or following it: *strict observance of the law* □ *the observance of traditional Chinese ritual.* **2** An **observance** is an act performed as part of a ceremony, especially a religious ceremony: *religious observances.*

observant /əb'zɜ:vənt/ *adjective*
Someone who is **observant** is quick at noticing things, especially things that are not usually noticed: *An observant passer-by had noticed the man and could describe him to the police.* □ *I'm surprised you noticed that; you must be very observant.*

observation /ɒbzə'veɪʃən/ *noun*: **observations**
1 (*uncount*) **Observation** is the act of observing or watching closely and carefully, or the state of being observed or watched closely and carefully: *the study and observation of wildlife* □ *They planned to leave by the back door to escape observation.* □ *He didn't have any major injury but was kept in hospital overnight under observation.* **2** (*uncount*) **Observation** is also the ability to notice things and remember them accurately: *a game designed to test their powers of observation.* **3** (*formal*) If you make an **observation** you make a remark or comment about something: *He made one or two observations about the weather and then lapsed into silence.* **4** (*used in the plural*) Someone's **observations** about something are the pieces of information that they have collected and recorded by studying or watching it: *He published his observations in a scientific journal.*

observatory /əb'zɜ:vətərɪ/ *noun*: **observatories**
An **observatory** is a room or building that has been specially equipped for observing and studying the stars and planets.

observe /əb'zɜ:v/ *verb*: **observes, observing, observed**
1 (*formal*) You **observe** a person or thing when you see or notice them: *I observed a small boy darting into the doorway.* **2** To **observe** also means to watch carefully: *He spent several months observing and photographing the animals in their natural habitat.* **3** You **observe** something, such as a law, rule or custom, when you obey or follow it: *The two sides agreed to observe a temporary ceasefire.* □ *Visitors to our country are required to respect our customs and observe our laws.* **4** (*formal*) To **observe** also means to make a remark or comment about something: *He observed that the weather was very mild for February.* □ *'It's a very original work,' he observed approvingly.*

observer /əb'zɜ:və(r)/ *noun*: **observers**
1 An **observer** is someone who watches or studies something: *a keen observer of nature.* **2** An **observer** is a person who goes or is sent to a place where *eg* a conference, meeting or election is being held in order to watch the proceedings but not to take part in them: *He was one of a team of international observers appointed to see that the elections were conducted freely and fairly.*

obsess /əb'sɛs/ *verb* (*usually in the passive*): **obsesses, obsessing, obsessed**
If a person or thing **obsesses** you or you **are obsessed** by them, that person or thing fills your mind so that you find it difficult to think about anyone or anything else: *She is obsessed with winning.* □ *He is becoming obsessed with that woman.*

obsession /əb'sɛʃən/ *noun*: **obsessions**
If someone thinks about or does a particular thing all or most of the time and seems unable to stop, you can say that they have an **obsession** about that thing: *His interest in keeping fit has developed into an obsession.*

obsessional /əb'sɛʃənəl/ *adjective*
Obsessional means the same as obsessive: *He's obsessional about keeping his flat tidy.* □ *an obsessional interest in football.*

obsessive /əb'sɛsɪv/ *adjective*
You say that someone or their behaviour is **obsessive** if they continually think or behave in a particular way and seem unable to stop it: *He is obsessive about punctuality.* □ *obsessive tidiness.* — *adverb* **obsessively:** *She's obsessively neat.*

obsolescent /ɒbsə'lɛsənt/ *adjective*
Something that is **obsolescent** is becoming out of date or going out of use: *an obsolescent machine.*

obsolete /'ɒbsəli:t/ or /ɒbsə'li:t/ *adjective*
Something that is **obsolete** it is no longer used or needed: *The introduction of diesel locomotives made steam engines obsolete.* □ *an obsolete word.*

obstacle /'ɒbstəkəl/ *noun*: **obstacles**
An **obstacle** is something that stands in your way making it difficult for you, or preventing you, from going where you want to go or doing what you want to do: *They tried to place obstacles in his path.* □ *They had to overcome many obstacles before they could get the project started.* □ *The continuing dispute over territory was a major obstacle to achieving peace in the region.* □ *an obstacle race* (= a race in which runners have to climb or jump over, or crawl through, various obstacles). [*same as* **barrier, hindrance**]

obstetrician /ɒbstə'trɪʃən/ *noun*: **obstetricians**
An **obstetrician** is a doctor qualified in obstetrics.

obstetrics /əb'stɛtrɪks/ *noun* (*uncount*)
Obstetrics is the branch of medicine and surgery which is concerned with the birth of children and the care of the mother during pregnancy and childbirth.

obstinate /'ɒbstɪnət/ *adjective*
1 An **obstinate** person refuses, or cannot be persuaded, to change their opinion or their chosen course of action: *an obstinate old man* □ *Johnny's getting so obstinate; he's going to be just like his father!* **2** You can also use **obstinate** to describe something that is difficult to deal with, defeat or remove: *obstinate resistance* □ *a special cleaner designed to remove obstinate stains.* [*same as* **stubborn**] — *noun* (*uncount*) **obstinacy** /'ɒbstɪnəsɪ/: *She was infuriated by his obstinacy.* [*same as* **stubbornness**]

obstreperous /əb'strɛpərəs/ *adjective* (*formal or humorous*)
You can describe someone or their behaviour as **obstreperous** if they are noisy, disruptive and difficult to control: *His behaviour tends to become obstreperous after a few drinks.* [*same as* **boisterous, unruly**]

obstruct /əb'srʌkt/ *verb*: **obstructs, obstructing, obstructed**
1 When something **obstructs** a road or route, it blocks it and prevents people or things from moving past or through: *A broken-down truck obstructed the traffic on the motorway.* □ *The residents objected to the new building because it would obstruct their view.* [*same as* **block**] **2** To **obstruct** something means to prevent or hinder its movement or progress: *The opposition party did everything they could to obstruct the passage of the bill through parliament.*

obstruction /əb'strʌkʃən/ *noun*: **obstructions**
1 An **obstruction** is something that blocks a road or route and prevents people or things from passing or getting through. **2** (*uncount*) **Obstruction** is the act or process of preventing something from happening or making progress: *If you don't move your vehicle immediately you will be charged with obstruction of the highway.*

obstructive /əb'strʌktɪv/ *adjective*
If you say that someone is being **obstructive**, they are deliberately trying to prevent something from happening or progressing: *We will never make any progress if he continues to behave in such an obstructive manner.* [*opposite* **helpful**]

obtain /əb'teɪn/ *verb*: **obtains, obtaining, obtained**
You **obtain** something when you get it: *Where can we obtain a copy of the report?* □ *How was this information obtained?*

obtainable /əb'teɪnəbəl/ *adjective*
Something that is **obtainable** can be got or obtained: *The ingredients are easily obtainable in any supermarket or grocer's shop.* [*opposite* **unobtainable**]

obtrusive /əb'tru:sɪv/ *adjective*
Something that is **obtrusive** is noticeable or prominent in an unpleasant way: *an obtrusive modern development built on the edge of a conservation area.* [*opposite* **unobtrusive**] — *adverb* **obtrusively:** *satellite dishes placed obtrusively on the front of the building.*

obtuse /əb'tju:s/ *adjective*
1 (*formal, derogatory*) If you say that someone is or is being **obtuse**, you mean that they are stupid and annoyingly slow to understand: *He was being deliberately obtuse, just to irritate me.* **2** In geometry, an **obtuse** angle is an angle greater than 90° and less than 180°.

obverse /'ɒbvɜ:s/ *noun* (*singular*)
1 (*technical*) The **obverse** of a coin or medal is the side with the head or main design on it. [*opposite* **reverse**] **2** (*formal*) The **obverse** of a fact, situation or argument is its opposite or the opposite view of it: *The image portrayed was just the obverse of reality.*

obvious /'ɒbvɪəs/ *adjective*
1 Something that is **obvious** is easily or clearly seen or understood: *an obvious error* □ *There are obvious differences in the appearance and texture of the two materials.* □ *He makes it obvious that he doesn't like her.* □ *He's broken his leg, so for obvious reasons he won't be able to come for a walk.* **2** You can also use **obvious** to describe a statement or remark that someone makes which you think is unnecessary because it is already clearly understood or recognized: *'He doesn't seem to want to join in.' 'That's obvious!'*
▷ ***phrase*** When you say that someone **is stating the obvious**, you mean that what they are saying is unnecessary because everyone knows it already.

obviously /'ɒbvɪəslɪ/ *adverb*
1 You use **obviously** when you want to indicate that something can easily be seen or understood: *He's obviously in great pain.* **2** (*sentence adverb*) People use **obviously** when they want to show or emphasize that what they are saying is already understood or recognized: *We obviously can't do anything without first getting his permission.* □ *Obviously you will want to avoid any unnecessary expense.* [*same as* **clearly**; compare **apparently, evidently**]

occasion /ə'keɪʒən/ *noun*; *verb*
▷ ***noun*: occasions**
1 An **occasion** is a particular time when something happens: *I've met your boss on several occasions.* **2** An **occasion** is also a special event or celebration: *The opening of the new village shop was quite an occasion.* □ *She's bought her wedding dress and is all ready for the big occasion.* **3** (*uncount or used in the singular*) The **occasion** for doing something is the suitable opportunity or the right time to do it: *He can be very forceful when the occasion arises.* □ *She has never had occasion to scold any of the children.*
▷ ***verb*** (*formal*): **occasions, occasioning, occasioned**
To **occasion** something means to cause it: *What occasioned his change of opinion?* □ *His resignation was occasioned by sudden illness.*
▷ ***phrases*** **1** If something happens **on occasion**, it happens from time to time but not very often: *He has been known to lose his temper on occasion.* **2** If you **rise to the occasion**, you make the extra effort necessary to deal with unusual circumstances: *Whenever she faces a challenge, she always rises to the occasion.*

occasional /ə'keɪʒənəl/ *adjective*
Something that is **occasional** happens or is done

sometimes but not very often: *sunshine with occasional showers (or with the occasional shower)* □ *birds that are occasional visitors to Britain.* □ *He usually drinks beer, but also has the occasional glass of wine.* [*opposite* **frequent**] — *adverb* **occasionally**: *'Do you go to the theatre much?' 'Occasionally, when we can afford it.'* □ *He visits London occasionally.*

occult /ə'kʌlt/ or /'ɒkʌlt/ *noun; adjective*
▷ ***noun*** *(used in the singular)*
The **occult** is magic and the supernatural: *He is interested in the occult.*
▷ ***adjective:*** *occult powers* □ *She dabbles in the occult arts including palmistry and witchcraft.*

occupancy /'ɒkjʊpənsɪ/ *noun (uncount)*
Occupancy is the act or period of time of actually living or working in a house or building: *They turned the flats into offices and had to apply to the local authority for change of occupancy.* □ *an occupancy of three years.*

occupant /'ɒkjʊpənt/ *noun*: **occupants**
1 The **occupant** of a house or flat is the person actually living in it, but not necessarily owning it: *There's a new occupant in the house next door.* [see also **occupier**] **2** The **occupants** of a place or space are the people in it: *The only occupants of the village were a few old people who were too frail to leave.* □ *The bus crashed into a wall killing a pedestrian and two of the occupants.*

occupation /ɒkjʊ'peɪʃən/ *noun*: **occupations**
1 Your **occupation** is your job or profession: *Please state your name, address and occupation.* □ *'What's your present occupation?' 'I'm a van driver.'* **2** An **occupation** is also something that someone does for pleasure or in their free time: *Reading is one of his favourite occupations.* **3** *(uncount)* The **occupation** of a house or room is the period of time during which it is lived in: *The houses have been completely renovated and are now ready for occupation.* **4** *(uncount)* The **occupation** of a country is the control of that country by the army of another country: *He lived in France during the German occupation.*

occupational /ɒkjʊ'peɪʃənəl/ *adjective*
1 Occupational means of or connected with a person's job or profession: *an occupational pension.* **2** If you say that something is an **occupational** risk or hazard, you mean that it is a risk or danger that is, or must be accepted as, part of a particular job or activity: *Injuries are an occupational hazard for professional footballers.*

occupier /'ɒkjʊpaɪə(r)/ *noun*: **occupiers**
The **occupier** of a house, building or piece of land is the person who lives or works there, as either a tenant or owner: *The letter was addressed to the present occupier of the flat.*

occupy /'ɒkjʊpaɪ/ *verb*: **occupies, occupying, occupied**
1 People who **occupy** a building live or work there: *a large Victorian house occupied by students* □ *They will occupy the second and third floors of the office building.* **2** If you say that something **occupies** a position, space or time, you mean that it fills it: *A large map occupied the whole of one wall.* □ *Thoughts of her home and family occupied her waking hours.* **3** *(in the passive)* When a bed or seat **is occupied** someone is using it: *Is this seat occupied?* **4 a** If soldiers **occupy** a country or town, they move into it and take control of it by force: *All the main towns and villages in the region were occupied by rebel soldiers.* [*same as* **invade**] **b** If people who are protesting about something **occupy** a building, they move into it and refuse to move out again until their demands are met or they are forced to leave: *The sacked workers occupied the factory.* **5** You **occupy** yourself or your time when you do something that keeps you busy or fills your time: *He keeps himself occupied with gardening and reading.* □ *He needs to occupy his mind by taking up an interest or hobby.* **6** When someone or something **occupies** a particular place or position in an organization, system or process, they are in or have that place or position: *His young cousins occupied an important place in his affections.*

occur /ə'kɜː(r)/ *verb*: **occurs, occurring, occurred**
1 When an event **occurs**, it takes place or happens: *Earthquakes occur most frequently along faults in the earth's crust.* □ *The explosion occurred only minutes after the area had been cleared of people.* **2** To **occur** also means to exist or be found: *Scurvy commonly occurred amongst sailors whose diet did not include fresh fruit and vegetables.* **3** An idea **occurs** to you when it comes into your mind: *It occurred to me that he might not be telling the truth.*

occurrence /ə'kʌrəns/ *noun (formal)*: **occurrences**
1 An **occurrence** is something that happens: *These events are becoming an everyday occurrence.* **2** *(uncount)* The **occurrence** of something is the fact that it happens or exists or the process of it happening or existing: *the occurrence of disputes between the various factions.*

ocean /'oʊʃən/ *noun*: **oceans**
1 The **ocean** is the sea. [see note at **sea**] **2** (**Ocean**) The **oceans** of the world are the five largest areas of salt water on the Earth; the Atlantic Ocean, Indian Ocean, Pacific Ocean, Arctic Ocean and Antarctic Ocean. **3** *(often used in the plural; informal)* If you say that there is an **ocean** of a thing, or there are **oceans** of it, you mean that there is a very large amount of it or very large numbers of it, covering a wide area: *oceans of people.*

o'clock /ə'klɒk/ *adverb*
When you are stating what the time is, you can use **o'clock** after the numbers one to twelve: *He was wakened at five o'clock in the morning.* □ *The children get out of school at four o'clock.*

> You only use **o'clock** when you are talking about the exact hour, *eg* 'It's one o'clock'. You say 'It's one fifteen' not 'It's one fifteen o'clock', and 'It's quarter past twelve' not 'It's quarter past twelve o'clock'.

octagon /'ɒktəgən/ *noun*: **octagons**
An **octagon** is a flat shape with eight straight sides and eight angles.

octagonal /ɒk'tagənəl/ *adjective*
An **octagonal** object is one that has eight straight sides: *a watch with an octagonal face.*

octane /'ɒkteɪn/ *noun (uncount, often adjectival, technical)*
The **octane** of a fuel, such as petrol, is its power or quality, indicated by a number (**octane number** or **octane rating**). The higher the number the better the quality of the fuel: *high-octane fuel.*

octave /'ɒktɪv/ *noun*: **octaves**
An **octave** is the range of sound, or the series of notes, between the first note and the eighth note on a musical scale.

octet /ɒk'tɛt/ *noun*: **octets**
1 An **octet** is a group of eight musicians that play together. **2** An **octet** is also a piece of music composed for a group of eight musicians.

October /ɒk'toʊbə(r)/ *noun* (*uncount*)
October is the tenth month of the year, coming after September and before November: *The book will be published in hardback in May, and in paperback the following October.* □ *Their wedding anniversary is on the fifteenth of October* (written *15 October*). □ *October the fifth* (written *October 5*) □ *The weather begins to get colder in October.* □ *The roof of their house was damaged in the October gales.* [see also note at **date**]

octopus /'ɒktəpəs/ *noun*: **octopuses**
An **octopus** is an animal that lives in the sea. It has a soft body and eight legs called tentacles which it uses to catch food. [compare **squid**]

odd /ɒd/ *adjective*: **odder**, **oddest**
1 You describe someone or something as **odd** if you think they are strange or unusual: *He had an odd face, a bit like a bird's.* □ *Did you notice anything odd about her behaviour?* □ *It's very odd that he hasn't contacted us.* □ *This coffee smells odd.* □ *an odd-shaped room.* [*same as* **strange**, **unusual**, **peculiar**, **curious**, **queer**] **2** An **odd** occasion on which something happens, or an **odd** thing or person that something applies to, is one that occurs or exists irregularly here and there, or that you do not need to specify: *I always carry a book with me, for the odd moment when I've got nothing to do.* □ *Her English is pretty good even if she does get the odd pronunciation wrong.* □ *There's always the odd child who causes trouble.* □ *We can find some odd jobs for her to do.* [compare **occasional**] **3 Odd** bits of something are pieces left over unused: *I've got some odd bits of material you can have.* **4 Odd** numbers are numbers such as 7, 19 and 93, that cannot be divided exactly by the number two: *The odd-numbered houses ran along the left side.* [*opposite* **even**] **5** Two things are **odd** if they do not belong to the same pair: *She appeared to be wearing odd earrings.* **6** An **odd** sock or glove is one of a pair from which the other is missing: *a drawerful of odd socks.* **7** You use **odd** after a number to make it sound vague or approximate: *She must be 50 odd by now.* □ *We received 500 odd replies.* — *adverb* **oddly:** *Now you mention it, she has been behaving oddly.* □ (*sentence adverb*) *Oddly enough, I didn't even recognize her.* — *noun* **oddness:** *The oddness of the coincidence didn't strike me immediately.* [*same as* **strangeness**; see also **oddity**]
▻ ***phrase*** Someone or something that is **the odd one out** or **the odd man out** in any group is the one that is noticeably different from the rest: *He was made to feel the odd man out as far as age was concerned, since everyone else was at least 15 years younger than him.* □ *Look at these four pictures and say which is the odd one out.*

oddity /'ɒdɪtɪ/ *noun*: **oddities**
1 An **oddity** is a strange or unusual person or thing: *He's a bit of an oddity.* **2** (*uncount*) **Oddity** is also the state of being strange or unusual: *the oddity of his appearance.* [*same as* **oddness**]

oddment /'ɒdmənt/ *noun*: **oddments**
Oddments are pieces that are left over from something much larger: *She made the quilt from oddments of material.* [*same as* **remnant**]

odds /ɒdz/ *noun* (*plural*)
1 In gambling, the **odds** are the difference between the amount of a bet and the amount that will be paid to the person making the bet if he or she wins. Therefore, if something that you bet on has odds of '25 to 1', and you win the bet, you will receive twenty five times the amount of your bet. **2** If you say that the **odds** are that something will happen, you mean that it is very likely to happen: *'I wonder why he's so late?' 'The odds are that his train was delayed.'* **3** If you say that the **odds** are against something happening, you mean that it is very unlikely to happen: *'Do you think it will snow before Christmas?' 'It might, but the odds are against it'.* **4** If you say that the **odds** are in someone's or something's favour, you mean that they are in an advantageous position: *Though they may be able to reach a settlement, the odds are not in their favour.*
▻ ***phrases*** **1** Something happens or is done **against all the odds** when it happens or is done in spite of great difficulty or disadvantage: *They won against all the odds.* **2** You **are at odds with** someone when you are in disagreement with or in opposition to them: *They have been at odds with their neighbours for years.* □ *His statement is at odds with other witnesses' evidence.* **3** (*informal*) You say **it makes no odds** when you want to make it clear that a fact or action will make no difference to a particular situation: *It makes no odds whether we go by train or by car; we won't get to London in time for the meeting.* **4** (*informal*) Some people refer to small objects of many different shapes or kinds and of little value or importance as **odds and ends** or **odds and sods**: *The basket was filled with odds and ends of wool.* **5** (*informal*) **Over the odds** means more than is required, expected or necessary: *I was charged over the odds for the repair to my car.*

odds-on /ɒdz'ɒn/ *adjective*
1 There is an **odds-on** chance of something happening when it is very likely to happen: *Judging by what he said last night, it's odds-on that he won't turn up.* **2** When a horse entered in a race is the **odds-on** favourite, it is one calculated to be most likely to win.

ode /oʊd/ *noun*: **odes**
An **ode** is a type of long poem addressed to a particular person or thing.

odious /'oʊdɪəs/ *adjective* (*formal*)
An **odious** person or thing is extremely unpleasant or offensive: *an odious little man* □ *He was odious in the extreme.* □ *an odious smell.* [*same as* **loathsome**]

odour (*AmE* **odor**) /'oʊdə(r)/ *noun*: **odours** (*formal*)
An **odour** is a smell, which may be pleasant or unpleasant but which is usually strong and easily recognized: *body odour* (=the smell of stale sweat) □ *The delicious odour of frying bacon met them as they came in.* □ *an unpleasant fishy odour in the fridge.*

of /ɒv/ or /əv/ *preposition*
You use **of** to express various relationships between things, *eg*:
1 where one thing belongs to another **a** as a physical part: *the arm of the chair* □ *the base of his skull* □ *the back of the house* □ *the fruit of the coconut palm.* **b** as a member: *members of the club* □ *citizens of Rome.* **c** as something associated with it, in various different ways: *the beliefs of our ancestors* □ *the law of the land* □ *the diseases of childhood* □ *the king and queen of France* □ *the poetry of the 19th century* □ *the revolution of 1916* □ *the property boom of the 1980s* □ *the aim of the expedition* □ *the whole point of the operation* □ *the causes of war* □ *cancer of the brain* □ *the results of the poll.*

> Notice that when you are talking about what belongs to or relates to a person, as distinct from a thing, you are more likely to use the possessive **'s**: *Howard's keyboard* (not *the keyboard of Howard*); *my father's plans* (not *the plans of my father*).

Notice also that in some cases the noun preceded by *of* can instead be used as an adjective: *19th-century poetry; brain cancer; childhood diseases.* [see also sense 7e]

d as its creation or product: *the poems of Burns* □ *the collected works of Shakespeare* □ *an amazing work of nature.*
2 when you are specifying **a** quantities: *two pounds of apples* □ *a litre of wine* □ *a cup of sugar* □ *a lorryload of sand* □ *a pile of snow* □ *a lot of trouble* □ *plenty of excitement* □ *some of the food* □ *none of the staff* □ *most of us* □ *the bulk of her fortune.* **b** contents: *a box of matches* □ *a book of poetry* □ *a field of corn.* **c** the things composing a group: *a bunch of flowers* □ *a crowd of people* □ *an army of ants.* **d** materials and substances in terms of units: *a blade of grass* □ *a piece of paper* □ *a lump of coal* □ *a drop of water* □ *a bar of chocolate* □ *a slice of bread.* **e** the shape or mass something appears in: *a bank of cloud* □ *a ring of fire* □ *a shaft of sunlight.* **f** the subject of an account: *the tale of two bad mice* □ *an account of the incident.* **g** the class of the thing you are referring to: *the city of Aberdeen* □ *the problem of vandalism* □ *the science of genetics* □ *the issue of equal pay* □ *feelings of annoyance* □ *in a state of decay* □ *at the age of 14* □ *Her hair was the colour of ripe corn.* **h** a quantity in terms of a certain dimension: *a certain length of time* □ *I bought a width of tweed.* **i** what constitutes something: *a gift of money* □ *a wage rise of 5%.* **j** the material used for something: *a dress of purest silk.* **k** the things that make up a combination: *a blend of herbs and spices.*
3 to describe a person or thing in terms of **a** their qualities: *a man of principle* □ *a painting of great value* □ *children of unusual talent.* **b** their possessions, reputation or rank: *a woman of substance* □ *men of high standing.* **c** their physical characteristics: *people of average build* □ *a man of nondescript appearance.* **d** their age: *a boy of twelve.*
4 when specifying **a** dates: *the 19th of January.* **b** a period of time in a series: *the fourth year of the war* □ *the third month of the year* □ *on the second morning of their stay in London* □ *the last decade of his life.* **c** anything by its place or position: *on the first page of the report* □ *the second half of the play* □ *the right side of her neck.* **d** the point when or where something occurs: *on the morning of their wedding* □ *at the moment of his birth* □ *in the hour of triumph* □ *at the site of the accident.* **e** a point, level or extreme: *the beginning of the meeting* □ *the middle of the night* □ *the height of bad manners* □ *the depths of despair.*
5 in expressing distance from a certain point, *eg* **a** in space, with *within*: *The army had advanced to within two kilometres of the capital.* □ *We're within sight of victory.* **b** in time, with *within*: *He became ill within minutes of* [= minutes after] *eating the mushroom.* **c** (*AmE*) in stating how long it is before the exact hour: *It's a quarter of four* (= 3.45, or 'quarter to four').
6 with words expressing action, **a** to link the action with the thing performing the action: *the rising of the sun* □ *the massing of troops along the border* □ *the constant movement of traffic* □ *the flight of the condor* □ *the arrival of Flight JE 604* □ *the downfall of Rome.* **b** to link the action with the thing it affects: *the destruction of Troy* □ *the raising of Lazarus* □ *the defeat of Carthage* □ *a review of the facts.* **c** to link someone who does something with the thing they do: *the writer of the note* □ *the author of several novels.*
7 in combination **a** with certain verbs, to express various relations: *I think of you constantly* □ *I'm thinking of resigning.* □ *The house smells of stale tobacco.* □ *This tastes slightly of lemon.* □ *She reminds me of someone.* □ *They accused me of cheating.* □ *She had been robbed of her dignity.* □ *He was cured of his addiction.* □ *Let go of me!* □ *hundreds dying of starvation.* **b** with nouns representing verbs or expressing attitudes: *their hopes of a settlement* □ *her dislike of compromise.* **c** with certain adjectives expressing various attitudes or relations: *I'm frightened of spiders.* □ *Be wary of flatterers.* □ *We were bored of waiting.* □ *I'm aware of his disapproval.* □ *Aren't you ashamed of your behaviour?* □ *I'm proud of you.* □ *She's too sure of herself.* □ *They're certain of victory.* □ *The sky was full of birds.* **d** with certain adjectives, to express your opinion of people's behaviour: *It was kind of you to ask me.* □ *It was stupid of him to leave the car unlocked.* □ *That was most thoughtful of you.* **e** with possessive pronouns and nouns; *eg* if someone is a friend **of** yours, they are your friend: *some acquaintances of mine* □ *a scheme of the council's for saving water.*
▻ ***phrases*** **1** For **of all** see **all**. **2** (*old or literary*) Something that you do **of a** morning or **of an** evening is something you do in the morning or evening, usually as a habit: *He liked to go for a long walk of a Sunday.*

off /ɒf/ *adverb*; *preposition or adverb*; *preposition*; *adverb or adjective*; *preposition, adverb or adjective*; *adjective*
▻ ***adverb***
1 Something moves or goes **off** when it moves or goes away from where it has been: *He drove off.* □ *Just as I got to the bus stop, the bus started moving off.* □ *The plane took off at 11.42.* □ *I shouted and the dog ran off.* [compare **away**] **2** You are **off** somewhere when you are leaving to go there; you are **off** doing something when you are away doing it: *We're off to France next week.* □ *I'm off now; Goodbye.* □ *Goodnight. I'm off to bed.* □ *We must be off in five minutes.* □ *He's off attending a conference in Oxford.* [*same as* **away**] **3** A place that you are going to, or approaching, is a certain distance **off** if it is that distance away: *We had rowed fast and the island was now only 100 metres off.* □ *The summit still looked miles off.* [*same as* **away**] **4** An event is a certain length of time **off**, if it is going to occur at the end of that length of time: *The exams were still three weeks off.* [*same as* **away**] **5 Off** is used in expressions for falling asleep: *I must have dozed off briefly.* □ *I took ages to get off to sleep.* □ *He used to drop off in his armchair.* **6** An area that is *eg* fenced, walled or partitioned **off** is surrounded or made separate, by a fence, wall or partition: *The police cordoned off the whole district.* □ *She's got a bookcase dividing off her study area from the rest of the sitting room.* **7** Someone who is well **off** has plenty of money; someone who is badly **off** does not have enough; if you are well or badly **off** for something, you have plenty of it, or not enough: *I'm slightly better off financially than I used to be.* □ *We're not very well off for restaurants in this part of town.* **8** You use **off** with words like *finish* to give an extra sense of finality to them: *He finished the work off.* □ *She finished off the chocolates.* □ *The chemical kills off any germs.*
▻ ***preposition or adverb***
1 You cut or break one thing **off** another when you remove it from the other by cutting or breaking: *I discovered the baby tearing the backs off my books.* □ *We sawed at least 20 centimetres off the legs of the bed.* □ *It was just an old jug with the handle broken off.* □ *Be firm with the hairdresser and don't let her cut too much off.* **2** A thing comes, falls or breaks **off** something to which it was attached when it becomes separated from it: *A button's come off your jacket.* □ *The paint was peeling off the walls.* □ *We'd better pick this fruit before it falls off.* **3** You take **off** a piece of clothing when you

remove it from your body; you take a thing such as a cover **off** something when you remove it: *Do take off your coat.* ▫ *It was very hot and I decided to leave my jacket off.* ▫ *He took the cover off his typewriter.* ▫ *Don't forget to peel the plastic film off first.* [*opposite* **on**] **4** You get **off** a bus, train, boat or plane when you leave it or get out of it; you also get **off** a horse or bicycle when you climb down from it: *He got off the train at Crewe.* ▫ *I'll be getting off at the next stop.* ▫ *We were allowed off the ship for a few hours at Igoumenitsa.* ▫ *He stopped pedalling and got off.* [*opposite* **on, on to**]

Notice that though you can either get **off** or **out of** a bus, train, boat or plane, you only get **out of** a car.

5 A person or vehicle turns **off** the road they are travelling along when they turn aside from it, down another road: *Turn off at the war memorial.* ▫ *Turn off the M90 at Milnathort.* [*opposite* **on to**] **6** You take an amount of money **off** the price of goods or services when you reduce the price by that amount: *There's up to a third off the standard price if you book through us.* ▫ *He said he would take £20 off if we paid cash.* **7** You keep **off** something when you stay away from it or avoid it: *Keep off the grass.* ▫ *Danger. Keep off.* ▫ *We'd better keep off the subject of holidays.*

▻ ***preposition***

1 One thing moves, or is moved, **off** another thing, when it moves or is moved so that it is no longer touching it or covering it: *The snow had all melted off the roof.* ▫ *Please get that dog off the sofa.* ▫ *The children spent the afternoon walking along the wall and jumping off it.* [*opposite* **on, on to**] **2** You take something **off** a horizontal surface that supports it, or **off** a vertical surface to which it is attached, when you remove it, or get it from there: *She stretched up to get a book off the top shelf.* ▫ *We'll have to take all the pictures off the wall.* ▫ *We drank out of plastic cups and ate off* (or *ate our meals off*) *paper plates.* [*opposite* **on**] **3** Something that is **off** a coast is in the area of sea surrounding it: *The oil tanker sank off the south coast.* ▫ *an island off Australia.* **4** A street or road that is **off** another joins it; a building or place that is **off** a certain street is in a street or road that joins it: *in a lane off Fleet Street.* ▫ *We live just off the main square.* [compare **on**] **5** You are **off** something **a** when you no longer like it; you are **off** your food when you cannot eat, *eg* because you are ill: *I'm off aerobics at the moment.* ▫ *The cat's off its food.* **b** when you have stopped taking it or using it: *How long have you been off the tablets?* ▫ *The doctor took me off that treatment.* [compare **on**]

▻ ***adverb or adjective***

1 A machine or apparatus is turned **off**, or is **off**, when it is not working or operating: *Switch the engine off.* ▫ *Turn the radio off.* ▫ *Make sure all the lights are off before leaving.* [*opposite* **on**] **2** An event is called **off**, or is **off**, when it is cancelled: *The match was rained off.* ▫ *Is tomorrow's meeting on or off?* **3** Something that has gone **off** is not up to its former standard: *The restaurant changed hands and went off considerably.* **4** Food goes **off**, or is **off**, when it goes bad and becomes unfit to eat: *I think these prawns are off.* ▫ *Milk quickly goes off if it is not kept cool.* **5** An item on a restaurant's menu is **off** if it is no longer available as a choice to customers: *Sorry, the fish is off.*

▻ ***preposition, adverb or adjective***

You take time **off**, or **off** work, or you are **off** work or school, when you spend time away from your place of work, or from school: *I've got the whole of next week off.* ▫ *I'm taking a few days off work.* ▫ *She's been off school since February.* ▫ *He's been off for several weeks with a bad back.* ▫ *She's off ill.*

▻ ***adjective***

1 The **off** side of a vehicle is the side that is nearer to the centre of the road when it is being driven. [*opposite* **near**] **2** The **off** season, *eg* at a resort, is the time of year when there is no, or not much, activity. **3** You have an **off** day when you can't do anything right.

▻ ***phrases*** **1** (*informal*) You describe someone's behaviour as **a bit off** if you consider it impolite or unfair. **2** Something that happens **off and on** or **on and off** happens occasionally.

offal /ˈɒfəl/ *noun* (*uncount*)

Offal is the heart, brains, liver, kidneys and other internal organs of an animal that are used as food.

off-beat /ɒfˈbiːt/ *adjective* (*informal*)

Something that is **off-beat** is unusual or unconventional: *an off-beat comedy* ▫ *I like his films; they're rather quirky and off-beat.*

off-chance /ˈof tʃɑːns/ *noun*

▻ ***phrase*** You **do** something **on the off-chance** when you hope it will be useful or successful but do not expect it to be: *She went to the doctor's surgery on the off-chance that she would be able to see him between appointments.*

off-colour /ɒfˈkʌlə(r)/ *adjective* (*BrE*)

If someone is **off-colour**, they are not looking or feeling very well: *He's been off-colour since the beginning of the week.* ▫ *I think I'll stay in bed; I'm feeling a bit off-colour this morning.*

offence (*AmE* **offense**) /əˈfɛns/ *noun*: **offences**

1 An **offence** is a crime: *The last year has seen a reduction in traffic offences.* ▫ *He categorically denied carrying out any of the alleged offences.* ▫ *They are on trial for drugs offences.* ▫ *Her performance was an offence against good taste.* **2** (*uncount*) **Offence** is displeasure, annoyance or resentment: *His remarks caused great offence.* ▫ *I meant no offence.*

▻ ***phrases*** **1** Someone who **gives offence** does or says something that causes someone else to feel annoyed, upset or resentful: *His remarks gave offence to some of the women in the audience.* **2** You **take offence** when you are annoyed or upset by something that someone has said or done: *He instantly took offence at the suggestion that he might have made a mistake.*

offend /əˈfɛnd/ *verb*: **offends, offending, offended**

1 You **offend** someone when you upset them or hurt their feelings: *I hope I won't offend them by refusing their invitation.* ▫ *His speech offended many of the more conservative members of the audience.* **2** To **offend** also means to commit a crime: *If he offends a second time, he will be sent to jail.* **3** (*formal*) You **offend against** something when you act in a way that goes against convention, custom or moral behaviour: *His so-called art offends against good taste.* — *adjective* **offended:** *She looked offended when he said that she was a little too old for the part.* [*opposite* **pleased**]

offender /əˈfɛndə(r)/ *noun*: **offenders**

1 An **offender** is someone who has committed a crime: *He was a first offender, so he was not given a prison sentence.* ▫ *Persistent offenders will be heavily fined.* **2** Any person or thing that offends or causes offence can be referred to as an **offender**: *an offender against the true religion.*

offending /əˈfɛndɪŋ/ *adjective*

An **offending** thing is something that causes displeasure, discomfort or inconvenience: *He protested to the editor and the offending article was withdrawn before the magazine was published.*

offensive /əˈfɛnsɪv/ *adjective*; *noun*

▻ ***adjective***

1 Offensive behaviour is insulting or rude and causes people to be offended; words that may offend people, or that are usually used with the intention of offending them, are labelled (*offensive*) in this dictionary: *I found his manner extremely offensive.* ▫ *He made a highly offensive remark about her father.* [*opposite* **inoffensive**] **2** An **offensive** weapon is one that is used for attacking. **3** An **offensive** position is one from which an attack is made. [*opposite* **defensive**]

▻ ***noun*: offensives**

An **offensive** is a strong and continued attack or effort: *The general ordered a full-scale offensive against enemy positions.* ▫ *a peace offensive.* — *adverb* **offensively:** *She apologized for speaking offensively about their religious beliefs.* — *noun* (*uncount*) **offensiveness:** *the offensiveness of his remarks.*

▻ ***phrases*** **1** If someone **goes on the offensive**, they make a strong attack or prepare to make an attack against someone or something: *The police are going on the offensive against drug dealers.* **2** Someone who **takes the offensive** attacks first before their opponent can attack them.

offer /ˈɒfə(r)/ *verb*; *noun*

▻ ***verb*: offers, offering, offered**

1 You **offer** something to someone if you ask them if they would like to accept it or have it: *He's been offered a job in Hong Kong.* ▫ *May I offer you a lift into town?* ▫ *I got up and offered her my seat.* ▫ *I felt obliged to offer him a cup of coffee.* ▫ *We're under no obligation to offer them further work.* **2** You **offer** to do something when you say you are willing to do it: *He offered to drive me to the airport.* ▫ *'I could post it on my way home,' offered Jack.* ▫ *I don't think we need any more help, but thanks for offering.* **3** You **offer** something such as advice, an opinion, or information when you give it: *I can offer no explanation for this.* ▫ *A number of bystanders offered suggestions.* ▫ *Do they offer any evidence to support their claim?* **4** A person or thing **offers** something if they can provide it: *The elections offer the people some hope for a better future.* ▫ *The college offers expert training in technical as well as academic subjects.* ▫ *Homes that offer the children a secure environment to grow up in.* ▫ *Unpaid volunteers have a lot to offer.* ▫ *What have we got to offer that other agencies haven't?* ▫ *the drug that offers the best protection against malaria.* **5** You **offer** someone something such as affection when you show it to them: *Foster parents can undoubtedly offer them the affection and friendship they lack.* ▫ *All he had to offer her was his love.* **6** Something that **is offered** for sale at a particular price, can be bought for that amount: *The facsimile edition is now being offered at £20.* ▫ *One travel agent was offering trips down the Danube for £50.* **7** You **offer** a sum of money for something when you say you are willing to pay that amount for it: *It depends how much you're prepared to offer for a genuine orginal.* ▫ *I can't offer more than £300.* **8** Someone **offers** something such as resistance when they show it or express it: *To my relief they offered no further objections.*

▻ ***noun*: offers**

1 An **offer** of something is a statement or indication that you are willing to provide it: *Apparently she'd already refused several offers of marriage.* ▫ *We decided to accept his offer of accommodation for the night.* ▫ *I was grateful for her offer of companionship.* ▫ *We don't need any more contributions, but thanks for the offer.* ▫ *I'd have jumped at the offer.* **2** You make an **offer** for something you want to buy when you say how much you are willing to pay for it: *No-one had yet made him a decent offer for the land.* ▫ *We've had one or two firm offers for the property.* ▫ *'How much do you want for it?' 'How about making me an offer?'* **3** A special **offer** in a shop is a product that is being sold especially cheaply: *She was quick to spot the cheap offers and snap them up.*

▻ ***phrases*** **1 a** If something is **on offer** it is available: *Hang-gliding is just one of the exciting activities on offer the centre.* ▫ *What's on offer by way of entertainment tonight?* ▫ *at The Dragon, where a very varied menu is on offer.* **b** If a product is **on offer** it is for sale, especially at a reduced price: *These biscuits are on special offer this week.* **2** Someone advertising something for sale at a certain price **or nearest offer** is prepared to accept the highest offer they receive if no-one is willing to pay the suggested price.

offering /ˈɒfərɪŋ/ *noun*: **offerings**

1 An **offering** is anything that is given as a gift or contribution: *She made an offering of flowers and fruit, which was accepted with delight.* **2** An **offering** is also something offered as a sacrifice to a god.

offhand /ɒfˈhand/ *adjective*; *adverb*

▻ ***adjective***

Someone who behaves in an **offhand** manner acts or speaks to you in a way that seems unfriendly and impolite: *He was very offhand with me.* [*same as* **abrupt**]

▻ ***adverb***

Offhand means without having or taking time to think carefully: *Offhand, I would say that there were at least twenty restaurants in the town.* ▫ *Can you tell me offhand how much we might expect to pay?*

office /ˈɒfɪs/ *noun*: **offices**

1 An **office** is a room, a set of rooms or a building where people do written work, accounts or administration, especially for a business or organization: *They are moving to new offices nearer the centre of town.* ▫ *He has a small office at home.* ▫ *The manager's office is at the end of the hall.* ▫ *He left for the office as usual.* [see picture on next page] **2** An **office** is an administrative department of government: *a tax office* ▫ *a passport office* ▫ *the Scottish Office.* **3** An **office** is a small room or building which offers people a service of some kind: *a ticket office* ▫ *an information office.* [see also **box office**, **post office**] **4** (*count or uncount*) If someone holds an **office** or is in **office**, they have been elected or appointed to a position of authority or responsibility, especially in the government or in public service: *Secretary of State is an important office with many responsibilities.* ▫ *The President of the United States holds office for four years.* ▫ *the office of mayor.* **5** (*uncount*) The political party in **office** is the one which forms the government: *The Labour Party had been out of office for fifteen years.*

office-bearer /ˈɒfɪsbɛərə(r)/ *noun*: **office-bearers**

An **office-bearer** or **office-holder** is someone who has an office or official position in an organization or in the state.

officer /ˈɒfɪsə(r)/ *noun*: **officers**

1 An **officer** in the army, navy or airforce is a person in a position of responsibility, especially one that is in command of the ordinary soldiers, sailors or airmen and officers of more junior rank: *a naval officer* ▫ *an officer in the merchant navy* ▫ *a non-commissioned officer* ▫ *the officers and men of the First Battalion.* **2** People who hold a position of authority or resposibility in a government department or other large organization are sometimes called **officers**: *a bank officer* ▫ *an environmental health officer* ▫ *a prison officer.* [compare **official**] **3** Members of the police force are also sometimes referred to as **officers**: *Excuse me, officer, can you direct me to the railway station?* ▫ *The officer in charge of the investigation is Detective Inspector Willis.*

office

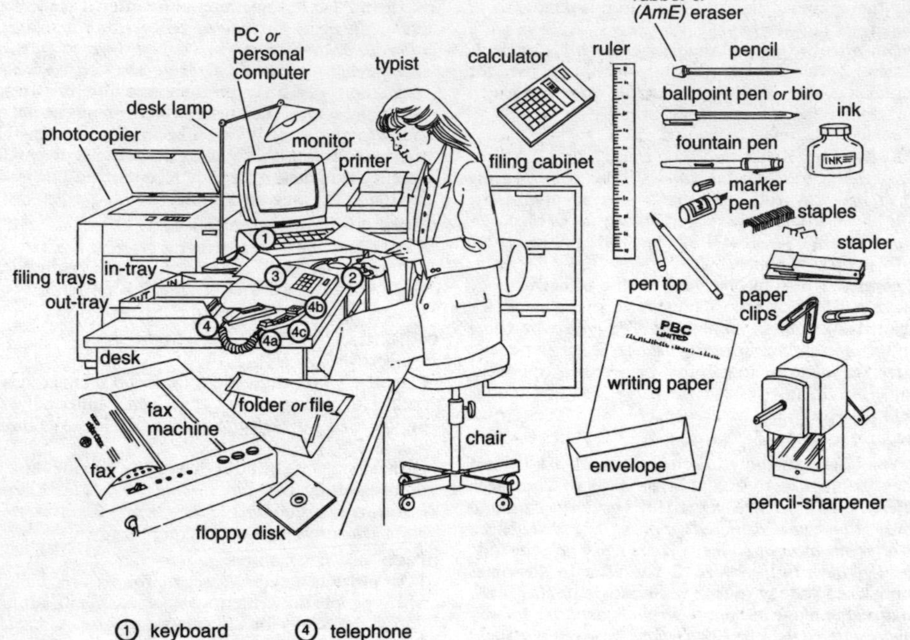

official /ə'fɪʃəl/ *adjective; noun*
▻ ***adjective***
1 Something that is **official** is approved or authorized by a person or people in authority or by the government: *an official report* □ *You'll have to get official permission to cut down these trees.* □ *English is the official language in many countries throughout the world.* [*opposite* **unofficial**] **2 Official** is also used to describe things that are used by or done by a person in a position of authority: *The mayor arrived in his official car.* □ *The Queen is to make an official visit to Russia.* **3** Something becomes **official** when it is announced publicly or recognized formally: *Have they made their engagement official yet?* □ *The new motorway has been open to traffic for a month though the official opening isn't until Monday.* [*opposite* **unofficial**]
▻ ***noun*: officials**
An **official** is someone who holds a position of authority or responsibility in an organization: *a public official* □ *a trade union official.* [compare **officer**]

officialdom /ə'fɪʃəldəm/ *noun* (*uncount; often derogatory*)
Officialdom is used to refer to the work of officials as a group, especially those that work in a government department or other large organization, whose methods or procedures are regarded by many people as being unnecessarily slow, complicated or unhelpful to the general public.

officially /ə'fɪʃəlɪ/ *adverb*
1 Something that is done **officially** is done publicly or formally: *The Channel Tunnel was officially opened by the Queen and President Mitterand in May 1994.* **2** (*sentence adverb*) **Officially** is also used to refer to a reason or explanation that is given publicly but which may not actually be true: *Officially, he is on leave but he has actually been suspended from work.* [*opposite* **unofficially**]

officiate /ə'fɪʃɪeɪt/ *verb*: **officiates, officiating, officiated**
The person who **officiates** at a ceremony or event performs or conducts the official duties that are part of that particular ceremony or event: *They are to be married in the cathedral, and the bishop will be officiating.*

officious /ə'fɪʃəs/ *adjective* (*derogatory*)
Someone who is **officious** is too ready to give other people orders: *An officious little man told us that we would have to move our bicycles.*

offing /'ɒfɪŋ/ *noun* (*uncount*)
▻ ***phrase*** Something that is **in the offing** is likely to come or happen soon: *He said he thought there was a storm in the offing.*

off-licence /'ɒflaɪsəns/ *noun* (*BrE*): **off-licences**
An **off-licence** is a shop where alcohol is sold to be taken away and drunk elsewhere.

offload /ɒf'loʊd/ *verb*: **offloads, offloading, offloaded**
If you **offload** something that you do not want, you get rid of it by giving it to someone else: *He managed to offload all his old records on to his friend's teenage son.*

off-peak /'ɒf piːk/ *adjective*
Off-peak periods of time are the times when there is lowest demand for something, such as electricity sup-

ply, and it is made available at a lower cost: *off-peak rates.*

off-putting /ɒfˈpʊtɪŋ/ *adjective* (*informal*)
If something is **off-putting**, it is unpleasant and makes you dislike it or not want to try it: *He has a very off-putting manner.* □ *Her description of the holiday resort was rather off-putting.* [see also **put off** at **put**]

offset /ɒfˈsɛt/ *verb*: **offsets, offsetting, offset**
If one thing **is offset** by another, its effect is balanced or made up for by that other thing: *price rises offset by tax cuts* □ *The occasional side-effects of the drug are more than offset by the benefits it brings to the majority of patients.*

offshoot /ˈɒfʃuːt/ *noun*: **offshoots**
An **offshoot** is something new that has grown or developed from another thing: *an offshoot from the plant's main stem* □ *The company is an offshoot of a large American multinational.*

offshore /ɒfʃɔː(r)/ *adjective; adverb*
▻ ***adjective***
1 Offshore is used to describe things that are situated in or on the sea, not far from the coast: *an offshore drilling platform* □ *an offshore island.* **2** An **offshore** wind blows away from the coast out to sea: *offshore breezes.*
▻ ***adverb:*** *He is working offshore on a North Sea oil platform.* [compare **inshore, onshore**]

offside *adjective; adverb; noun*
▻ ***adjective*** /ɒfˈsaɪd/
In games such as football and rugby, a player is **offside** when he or she is in an illegal position between the ball and the opponents' goal: *plans to change the off-side rule.*
▻ ***adverb*** /ɒfˈsaɪd/: *One of the forwards had moved off-side and the goal was disallowed.* [compare **onside**]
▻ ***noun*** /ˈɒfsaɪd/ (*used in the singular*)
The **offside** of a vehicle is the side nearest the centre of the road. In Britain the **offside** is the right-hand side: *The rear offside tyre of your car is flat.* [*opposite* **near** side]

offspring /ˈɒfsprɪŋ/ *noun* (*singular or plural; formal or humorous*)
1 Some people refer to their child or children as their **offspring**: *He is the offspring of a distinguished soldier and a famous writer.* □ *Our youngest offspring shows signs of being a musician.* □ *Don't tell me they intend to bring their ghastly offspring with them.* **2** The young of an animal are also sometimes called **offspring**: *A rabbit can have up to thirty offspring in one breeding season.*

off-white /ɒfˈwaɪt/ *noun; adjective*
▻ ***noun*** (*used in the singular*)
Off-white is a yellowish or greyish white colour: *'What colour will you paint the bedroom.' 'We're considering an off-white or pale grey.'*
▻ ***adjective***
Off-white things are cream, yellowish or greyish white: *an off-white wedding dress* □ *The bedspread is off-white with lace trimmings.*

often /ˈɒfən/ or /ˈɒftən/ *adverb*: **oftener, oftenest**

> The comparative and superlative 'more **often**' and 'most **often**' tend to be used in preference to **oftener** and **oftenest**.

1 a Something that happens **often** happens lots of times; something that is **often** so is so a lot of the time: *We go for walks in the hills fairly often.* □ *The river often dries up completely.* □ *I can often hear them arguing through the wall.* □ *She's often too stiff to walk.* □ *'Are you often in pain?' 'Not very often as bad as this.'* [*same as* **frequently**] **b Often** is used in saying or asking how many times something happens, or for how much of the time it is so: *'How often does the ferry sail?' 'Twice a day.'* □ *I visit her as often as I can.* □ *He's drunk oftener than he'll admit.* [*same as* **frequently**] **2 Often** also means in many cases: *The children are often* [= lots of the children are] *seriously malnourished.* □ *Women have often* [= many women have] *had to sacrifice their careers to look after their families.* □ *In Shakespeare the word is often ironical.* □ *Losing a bit of weight will often cure arthritis.* [*same as* **frequently**]
▻ ***phrases*** **1** Something that happens **as often as not** happens on at least half of the occasions that you are referring to, or in at least half of the cases; something that happens **more often than not** happens on most of the occasions, or in most of the cases, you are referring to: *When I telephone her I get the answerphone as often as not.* □ *More often than not all the patient wants is a bit of comfort and encouragement.* **2** Something that happens **every so often** happens occasionally: *They stopped every so often to rest.* □ *We get a letter from him every so often.* **3** Someone indulges in a silly or annoying habit **once too often** when it has unpleasant or disastrous results: *I wish you wouldn't overtake on a corner like that; you'll do it once too often.*

ogle /ˈoʊgəl/ *verb* (*derogatory*): **ogles, ogling, ogled**
If someone **ogles** someone else, they look or stare at that them in a way that expresses sexual desire: *More and more often she would catch him ogling other women.*

ogre /ˈoʊgə(r)/ *noun*: **ogres**
1 In fairy stories, an **ogre** is a cruel ugly frightening giant that eats people. **2** A person who behaves in a cruel or frightening way is also sometimes called an **ogre**: *His father is a bit of an ogre.*

oh /oʊ/ *interjection*
1 Oh is used in exclamations to express surprise, admiration, pleasure, anger or fear: *Oh! What a fright you gave me!* [see also **O**[2]] **2 Oh** is also used when you are speaking to a person, especially when you want to attract his or her attention: *Oh Mary, would you come through here for a moment, please?* □ *Oh, I nearly forgot; there's a meeting on Friday at six.*

oil /ɔɪl/ *noun; verb*
▻ ***noun*: oils**
1 (*uncount*) **Oil** is any smooth thick liquid that burns easily and does not mix with water. Oil that is found under the ground is used as a fuel and for making the moving parts of machinery work smoothly. Other types of oil are obtained from plants or animals and are used mainly in cooking: *North Sea oil* □ *The wells produce thousands of barrels of oil a day.* □ *olive oil* □ *sunflower oil* □ *coconut oil* □ *whale oil.* **2** (*uncount*) **Oil** is also a smooth, often scented, liquid that you rub into your hair or skin or put into your bath: *hair oil* □ *bath oil* □ *suntan oil.* **3** (*used in the plural*) **Oils** are oil paints: *He usually paints in oils.* **4** (*usually in the plural*) **Oils** are also pictures painted with oil paints.
▻ ***verb*: oils, oiling, oiled**
1 You **oil** the moving parts of a machine when you put oil on or into it to make it work smoothly: *I must oil the hinges of the front door; it squeaks terribly.* **2** If you **oil** your skin or hair, you rub oil on or into it to make it smooth or shiny.

oilfield /ˈɔɪlfiːld/ *noun*: **oilfields**
An **oilfield** is an area where oil is found in the ground or under the sea: *an oilfield in the North Sea.*

oil-fired /ˈɔɪlfaɪəd/ *adjective*
An **oil-fired** heating system is one that burns oil to produce heat: *oil-fired central heating.*

oil paint /ˈɔɪl peɪnt/ *noun* (*uncount or count*): **oil paints**
Oil paint is paint made by mixing coloured powder with oil. Oil paints are used by artists.

oil painting /ˈɔɪl peɪntɪŋ/ *noun*: **oil paintings**
1 An **oil painting** is a picture painted with oil paints. **2** (*uncount*) **Oil painting** is the activity or art of painting using oil paints.

oil rig /ˈɔɪl rɪg/ *noun*: **oil rigs**
An **oil rig** is a large structure with equipment and machinery for getting oil from underground, especially from the seabed.

oilskin /ˈɔɪlskɪn/ *noun* (*uncount or count*): **oilskins**
1 Oilskin is a thick cotton cloth treated with oil to make it waterproof. **2 Oilskins** are a suit of clothes made from this cloth: *They were given life jackets and oilskins to put on before going out to sea.*

oil tanker /ˈɔɪl tæŋkə(r)/ *noun*: **oil tankers**
(also **tanker**) An **oil tanker** is a ship with large containers for carrying oil.

oil well /ˈɔɪl wɛl/ *noun*: **oil wells**
An **oil well** is a hole drilled into the ground or the seabed in order to obtain oil.

oily /ˈɔɪlɪ/ *adjective*: **oilier, oiliest**
1 Something that is **oily** contains or resembles oil: *An oily film spread over the surface of the water.* □ *an oily fish.* **2** Something that is **oily** is covered with oil: *The mechanic rubbed his hands on an oily rag.* **3** (*derogatory*) If you describe a person or their behaviour as **oily**, you think that they are unpleasant because they flatter people and are too friendly or polite to be sincere: *He gave her an oily smile.* [*same as* **obsequious**]

oink /ɔɪŋk/ *noun* (*used in the singular*)
Oink is a word used to represent the sound that a pig makes.

ointment /ˈɔɪntmənt/ *noun* (*uncount or count*): **ointments**
Ointment is a thick greasy substance that is rubbed on the skin to help heal roughness or a wound, or as a cosmetic. [*same as* **cream**]
▻ ***phrase*** For **fly in the ointment** see **fly**.

OK see **okay**.

okay or **OK** /oʊˈkeɪ/ *interjection*; *adjective*; *adverb*; *verb*; *noun*
▻ ***interjection*** (*informal*)
1 You say **'okay' a** when you are agreeing to a proposal or arrangement: *'How about lunch at the pub?' 'Yes, OK; I'll see you there about one.'* **b** when you are accepting what someone says: *Okay, so it was stupid.* **c** to indicate that you are ready for the next stage of discussion or action: *OK, let's get started.* □ *OK, here we go.* □ *Okay, try again now.* **2** You use **'Okay?'**, sometimes impatiently, to make sure that you are being understood: *I'm just going out for a few minutes. OK?'* □ *See you later. OK?* □ *Just do as you're told, okay?* □ *Leave me alone, OK?* □ *I know what I'm doing, OK?* □ *I've already said I'll do it, okay?*
▻ ***adjective*** (*informal*)
1 You say that something is **okay** if it is all right, satisfactory or acceptable: *'Was it a good conference?' 'It was OK, I suppose.'* □ *We'll set off about nine o'clock, if that's OK with you.* □ *That's okay by me.* □ *You have to let children know that it's OK for them to use their own words.* □ *'Sorry to interrupt.' 'It's OK, I'd finished.'* □ *Is it OK to come in?* □ *Does this tie look OK?* **2** A person is **okay** if they are safe and well, or as cheerful as usual: *'Have you hurt yourself?' 'No, I'm quite OK, thanks.'* □ *You'll feel OK in a few minutes.* □ *She sounded okay on the telephone.* □ *I was having a little cry. I'm OK again now.*
▻ ***adverb:*** *He survived the operation itself okay.* □ *I take it you got home OK after the party?* □ *This method usually works okay.*
▻ ***verb***: **okays** or **OK's**, **okaying** or **OK'ing**, **okayed** or **OK'ed**
Someone in authority **okays** something when they give official permission for it: *The proposal had been okayed by the committee.* □ *I only hope they okay my expenses claim.*
▻ ***noun***: **okays** or **OK's**
Someone in authority gives something the **okay** when they give permission for it: *We can't buy any more equipment till we've had the OK from head office.*

okra /ˈɒkrə/ *noun* (*uncount*)
(also called **gumbo** *or* **lady's fingers**) **Okra** is a type of tropical plant with long thin green seed pods that are eaten as a vegetable. [see picture at **vegetable**]

old /oʊld/ *adjective*; *noun*
▻ ***adjective***: **older, oldest**
1 a People or animals that are **old** have lived a long time and are no longer young: *Her old father lived with her.* □ *hotels full of old people* □ *homes for old horses* □ *when you're old and can't run any more.* □ *I don't exactly feel old.* [*opposite* **young**; compare **elderly**] **b** You use **old** in referring to, or asking, the age of someone or something; someone or something that is a certain number of years **old** has lived or existed for that length of time: *How old are you?* □ *since I was 13 years old* □ *their month-old baby* □ *her 82-year-old mother* □ *buildings that are hundreds of years old* □ *You're old enough to know better.* □ *He's a year older than me.* □ *my older* (or *elder*) *brother.* □ *Marianne was the oldest* (or *eldest*). [see also **elder, eldest**, see also **old**, *noun*, sense 2, below]
2 Things that are **old a** have existed for a long time: *gigantic trees that are the oldest living things on earth* □ *old customs.* [compare **ancient**] **b** belong to the past; words and senses that are not used much nowadays are labelled (*old*) in this dictionary: *old books and manuscripts* □ *looking at old photographs* □ *reading through some of my old essays* □ *in the old days.* [*opposite* **recent**] **c** are in poor condition because of long use or great age: *He was wearing a shabby old jacket.* □ *old ragged carpets* □ *I kept some old clothes for gardening in.* □ *hospitals that are old and ill-equipped.* [*opposite* **new**]
3 Old also describes things **a** that are not being used any more because they are out of date: *Some of the old farming methods were actually quite efficient.* [*opposite* **modern**] **b** that have been replaced, *eg* because of age or damage through long use: *We got a new car in April and gave the old one to our son.* [*opposite* **new**] **c** that were previously a certain thing, but have been replaced in that capacity: *I met one of your old boyfriends.* □ *Our old house had no garden.* □ *old pupils of the school.* [*same as* **previous, former**; *opposite* **present, current**] **d** that you are familiar with from your past experience: *She'd lost none of her old thoroughness.* □ *He's gone back to his old habits.* □ *lecturers who give students the same old stuff year after year* □ *making the same old excuse.*
4 a Old friends are friends that you have had for a long time: *one of my oldest acquaintances.* **b** (*informal*) **Old** is sometimes used merely as a term of affection: *good old Bill* □ *silly old you.*
▻ ***noun***: **-olds**
1 (*plural*) The **old** are old people: *The old are our responsibility.* [*same as* **elderly**] **2** You can refer to a person or animal, especially a horse, as *eg* a fifteen-year-**old** or a three-year-**old**: *Two-year-olds are the hardest to control.*
▻ ***phrase*** For **any old** see **any**.

old age /oʊld'eɪdʒ/ *noun* (*uncount*)
Old age is the part of someone's life when they are old: *In his old age, he was looked after by his granddaughter.*

old-age pension /oʊld eɪdʒ'pɛnʃən/ *noun*: **old-age pensions**
If someone receives an **old-age pension**, they are paid a sum of money regularly by the state after they reach a certain age.

old-age pensioner /oʊld eɪdʒ'pɛnʃənə(r)/ *noun*: **old-age pensioners**
(also **pensioner**) An **old-age pensioner** is someone who receives a pension from the state after they reach a certain age. [see note at **senior citizen**]

olden /'oʊldən/ *adjective* (*old*)
▻ ***phrase*** If something happened or was done in **olden days** or in **olden times**, it happened or was done long ago in the past.

old-fashioned /oʊld'fæʃənd/ *adjective*
1 If something is **old-fashioned** it is of a style or design that belongs to the past and is no longer commonly used or worn: *old-fashioned furniture* □ *Her clothes were old-fashioned.* [*same as* **out-of-date**] **2** Someone who is **old-fashioned** is in favour of or behaves according to the habits and standards of the past: *She had an old-fashioned view of marriage.*

old flame /oʊld 'fleɪm/ *noun* (*informal*): **old flames**
An **old flame** is someone with whom you were once in love.

old hand /oʊld 'hand/ *noun*: **old hands**
If you say that someone is an **old hand** at something, you mean that they are skilled at it because they have been doing it for a long time: *He's an old hand at political intrigue.*

old hat see **hat**.

old lady /oʊld 'leɪdɪ/ *noun* (*slang*)
Some people call their wife or mother their **old lady**.

old maid /oʊld 'meɪd/ *noun* (*informal, derogatory*)
An **old maid** is a woman who has never married and is thought of as being unlikely ever to marry.

old man /oʊld man/ *noun* (*used in the singular*)
1 (*informal*) Some people call their husband or father their **old man**. **2 Old man** is also an affectionate form of address used by a man or a boy when talking to another man or boy.

old master /oʊld 'mɑːstə(r)/ *noun*: **old masters**
An **old master** is **a** an important painter from the past, especially from the period stretching from the Renaissance to about 1800. **b** a painting by one of these painters.

old school /'oʊld skuːl/ *noun* (*used in the singular*)
If someone is described as being of the **old school**, they are traditional or old-fashioned in their attitudes or values: *an actress of the old school.*

Old Testament /oʊld 'tɛstəmənt/ *noun*
The **Old Testament** is the first part of the Christian Bible, containing the Hebrew scriptures. [see also **New Testament**]

old wives' tale /oʊld 'wəɪvz teɪl/ *noun*: **old wives' tales**
An **old wives' tale** is a belief or theory that is based on tradition rather than known scientific fact.

old woman /oʊld 'wʊmən/ *noun* (*slang*)
1 Some people refer to their wife or mother as their **old woman**. **2** (*derogatory*) If you call someone, especially a man, an **old woman**, you think that they are very fussy.

old-world /'oʊld wɜːld/ *adjective*
Old-world is used to describe things that are from an earlier time, especially when they are regarded as being attractive because they are not modern: *The village has a certain old-world charm.* [*same as* **picturesque**]

O-level /'oʊ lɛvəl/ *noun*: **O-levels**
(in full **Ordinary level**) An **O-level** was a qualification in a particular subject formerly taken by secondary school students in Britain. O-levels have been replaced in England and Wales by GCSEs, and in Scotland by Standard Grades: *She was studying for her O-levels.* □ *He has five O-levels.* □ *O-level French.*

olive /'ɒlɪv/ *noun*; *adjective*
▻ ***noun***: **olives**
1 An **olive** is a small oval green or black fruit with a bitter taste. Olives are eaten as food or are pressed to obtain olive oil. **2** An **olive** or **olive tree** is a small tree on which these fruits grow. **3 Olive** or **olive green** is the dull yellowish-green colour of the olive fruit before it ripens: *Her uniform was a smart olive green.*
▻ ***adjective***
Olive or **olive green** things are of this dull yellowish-green colour: *an olive green jacket.*

olive oil /ɒlɪv'ɔɪl/ *noun* (*uncount*)
Olive oil is the oil pressed from ripe olives, used in cooking and for making dressings for salads.

-ology See **-logy**.

Olympic /ə'lɪmpɪk/ *adjective*; *noun*
▻ ***adjective***
Olympic means of or concerned with the Olympic Games: *an Olympic athlete* □ *an Olympic medal* □ *the International Olympic Committee.*
▻ ***noun*** (*plural*)
The **Olympics** are the Olympic Games: *He won a gold medal at the winter Olympics.* □ *The Olympics are held every four years.*

Olympic Games /əlɪmpɪk'geɪmz/ *noun* (*plural*)
The **Olympic Games** are the international athletic and sporting competitions held every four years in a different country.

ombudsman /'ɒmbʊdzmən/ *noun*: **ombudsmen**
An **ombudsman** is an official appointed by the government to investigate complaints made by ordinary citizens against public authorities.

omelette (*AmE* **omelet**) /'ɒmlət/ *noun*: **omelettes**
An **omelette** is a food made with eggs that have been beaten together and cooked in a flat, usually round, pan, often with other foods, such as cheese or vegetables, added.

omen /'oʊmən/ *noun*: **omens**
An **omen** is a sign that something, either good or bad, is going to happen in the future: *a good omen* □ *He took it as a bad omen that he hadn't received a reply to his letter by the end of the week.*

ominous /'ɒmɪnəs/ *adjective*
Something that is **ominous** gives a suggestion or warning that something bad or unpleasant is about to happen: *Ominous black clouds were gathering on the horizon.* □ *The morning had dawned cloudy and ominous.* □ *an ominous silence.* [*same as* **threatening**] — *adverb* **ominously:** *It was ominously quiet.*

omission /ə'mɪʃən/ or /oʊ'mɪʃən/ *noun*: **omissions**
1 An **omission** is something that has not been included or has not been done: *There were several omissions in the form which you submitted.* □ *Neglecting to make the proper checks was a serious omission on his part.* **2** (*uncount*) **Omission** is the act of not including or not doing something: *He was irritated by the omission of any reference to his discovery.*

omit /ə'mɪt/ or /oʊ'mɪt/ *verb*: **omits, omitting, omitted**
1 You **omit** something when you leave it out, either by mistake or deliberately: *He omitted the last verse of the poem.* **2** (*formal*) If you **omit** to do something, you do not do it: *He omitted to tell me that there would be no other women in the expedition.* [*same as* **fail**]

omni- /'ɒmnɪ/ *prefix*
Omni- is used before nouns and adjectives to mean 'all', 'everyone', 'everywhere' or 'everything'.

omnibus /'ɒmnɪbəs/ *noun*
▻ ***noun***: **omnibuses**
1 (*old*) An **omnibus** is a bus. **2** An **omnibus** is also a book containing a number of novels or stories by a single author. [compare **anthology**] **3** A television or radio broadcast which brings together a number of programmes originally broadcast separately is also called an **omnibus**.

omnipotent /ɒm'nɪpətənt/ *adjective* (*formal*)
Someone who is **omnipotent** has unlimited or very great power over people or things: *an omnipotent ruler* □ *God is regarded as being omnipotent.*

omnivorous /ɒm'nɪvərəs/ *adjective*
An **omnivorous** animal eats all types of food, including both meat and plants: *Bears are omnivorous.* [compare **carnivorous**]

on /ɒn/ *preposition*; *adverb or preposition*; *adverb or adjective*; *adverb*
▻ ***preposition***
1 One thing is **on** another **a** if it is supported by it: *the books on the top shelf* □ *He left the letter lying on the table.* □ *Most of us were sitting on the floor.* □ *The vowels* a, e, i, o *and* u *all sit on the line.* [see also **on top of** below] **b** if it covers it: *There was no carpet on the stairs.* **c** if it marks its surface: *She had a bruise on her arm.* □ *There's a dirty mark on your skirt.* **d** if it is attached to it: *a single picture hanging on the wall* □ *The sheets were drying on the line.* □ *There was no stamp on the envelope.* □ *All dogs to be kept on leads.*
2 a One thing is dropped, thrown, put, or falls **on** another when it moves or is moved so that it rests on it: *The table got tipped over and everything fell on* (or *on to) the floor.* □ *Could you put the lid back on* (or *on to) the jar?* [see also **on to** below] **b** You are **on** a part of your body if your weight is being supported by it: *Should you put babies to sleep on their fronts or their backs?* □ *She couldn't put any weight on her left ankle.* □ *The cat landed on its paws.*
3 a You have an expression **on** your face if you have that expression: *There was a look of amusement on her face.* **b** You have something **on** you if you are carrying it with you, *eg* in your pockets: *I didn't have enough money on me.* **c** Something that is **on** paper is printed or written there: *I wrote down her number on the back of a receipt.* □ *See map on page 6.* □ *Pinned to the notice board was an envelope with her name on it.* **d** Something that is **on** a list, schedule, timetable or agenda appears there, or is among the things to be dealt with: *Is my name on the list?* □ *What's next on the schedule?* **e** Someone who is **on** the board of a company, **on** the local council, or **on** a committee, is a member of it. **f** You are **on** a course of study when you are attending it or taking part in it: *She made friends with another student on the course.* **g** You are **on** a journey when you are going somewhere: *I was just on my way to the shops.*
4 a A building is **on** something such as a road if it is situated beside it and faces towards it: *a hotel on the seafront* □ *the shops on the high street.* **b On** is commonly used in referring to other locations: *He works on a farm.* □ *Do you enjoy living on an island?*

> Notice that the inhabitants even of small islands often refer to themselves as living **in** the island: *I've spent most of my life in the Isle of Man. They leave because they can find no work in the Island.*

5 a Something happens **on** a certain day or date if it happens then: *He died on 29 May.* □ *We're off to France on Wednesday.* □ *on the final day of her holiday.* **b** A thing that happens **on** another thing happening happens immediately after it, often because of it: *I was a bit upset on hearing the news.* □ *We advise you to contact your union immediately on being made redundant* □ *He telephoned her on his return.* □ *The guards would probably shoot him on sight.* **c** You do something **on** certain grounds if that is your reason for doing it: *On what grounds could you think that?* □ *The police can arrest people on suspicion.*
6 A book, piece of writing, or programme that is **on** a particular subject is about it: *a book on Chinese cookery* □ *a programme on urban violence* □ *She addressed us on the subject of recycling.*
7 a Something that affects someone or something in some way has that effect **on** them: *Her teaching had a lasting influence on the children.* **b** You hurt yourself **on** something when you are injured as a result of coming into contact with it: *He cut himself on a piece of broken glass.* **c** Something such as a building is **on** fire if it is burning: *A couple of boys had set the shed on fire.*
8 a You store information **on** a computer and record pictures and sound **on** tape. **b** A programme is **on** television or **on** the radio when it is being broadcast there; you appear or speak **on** television or **on** the radio when you can be seen or heard there: *I was watching the news on television.* □ *Did you hear her speaking on the radio?* **c** Music that is played **on** a particular instrument is played using that instrument: *I tried to work out the tune on the piano.* **d** You are **on** the telephone when you are using it to talk to someone.
9 a You are working **on** a particular task when you are dealing with it: *He's working on a new project.* □ *We need more people on this job.* **b** You spend money **on** something when you use some of your money to buy it or pay for it; you spend time **on** something when you use some of your time to deal with it: *He spends a lot on clothes.* □ *Don't spend too long on the first question.* **c** You put money **on** something when you make a bet on it: *He put £500 on a horse in the Grand National.* **d** There is a tax **on** something if tax has to be paid as a percentage of its value or cost: *The tax on fuel is likely to increase.* □ *You have to pay tax on unearned income.* **e** You make a profit **on** something if you sell it for more money than you paid for it, or get back more money for it than you spend. **f** If you say that something that has to be paid for, such as food or drinks for people, is **on** you, you mean that you are willing to pay for it: *The drinks are on me.* □ *He had his operation on the National Health Service.* **g** You say that a joke is **on** someone if it is against them.
10 a Someone is **on** a drug when they are taking it regularly; you are **on** a course of treatment when you are receiving regular treatment for something: *The doctor has put me on some new pills.* **b** You are **on** a diet if you are trying to lose weight or improve your health by eating only certain foods. **c** You are living **on** a certain sum of money or a certain type of income if you are using it to pay for the things you need: *She's living on a student grant.* □ *They don't earn enough to live on.* **d** You are living **on** a certain type of food if you are eating only that food: *He lives on breakfast cereals and orange juice.* **e** Something works, or is organized, **on** a certain system if that is the way it

works: *The device works on the same principle as a watch.*

▷ ***adverb or preposition***

1 You put a piece of clothing **on** when you cover part of your body with it; you have something **on** when you are wearing it: *She put on her jacket.* □ *I had no clothes on.* □ *That's a smart dress you've got on.* □ *with a crown instead of a hat on your head.* **2** You put one thing **on** another when you cover the other with it: *We'd better put clean sheets on* (or *on to*) *the bed.* □ *I've put a clean pillowslip on for you.* □ *The bed had no covers on.* **3** You stick or sew one thing **on** another when you attach the one to the other by sticking or sewing: *She was busy sewing name tapes on* (or *on to*) *the children's clothes.* □ *The button came off but I sewed it on again.* □ *a pyjama jacket with only one button on* □ *an envelope with no stamp on* □ *The anorak had no name on.* **4** You get **on** a bus, train or plane when you get into it in order to travel somewhere in it: *I got on* (or *on to*) *the coach.* □ *The bus doesn't stop here unless anyone wants to get on or off.* □ *There were more than two hundred people on the plane.* □ *He was on the 5 o'clock train.* **5** You are **on** a horse, bicycle or motorbike when you are riding it: *He arrived on a motorbike.* □ *She got on* (or *on to*) *her bike and rode off.* □ *I fell off the horse but managed to climb on again.*

▷ ***adverb or adjective***

1 You turn a machine or apparatus **on**, when you make it start working; it is **on** when it is working: *The oven switches itself on and off automatically.* □ *Shall I turn the radio on?* □ *The television's on all the time.* □ *She likes having the radio on when she's studying.* □ *Who left the lights on?* □ *Is the washing machine still on?* **2** A television or radio programme, or a film or play, is **on** when it is being broadcast, presented or performed: *What films are on this week?* □ *'Wolves' is on at the Odeon till Friday.* □ *They're putting on an opera at the King's Theatre.* **3** (*informal*) You keep **on** about something, or are always **on** about it, if you keep talking about it; people say they don't know what you are **on** about if they don't understand what you are saying. **4** (*informal*) If you say that something is not **on,** you mean that it is not possible, practicable or acceptable: *That kind of behaviour just isn't on.* □ *There was a suggestion that the company might pay, but I'm afraid that's not on.*

▷ ***adverb***

1 On expresses progress, or movement forward or ahead: *We had a rest and then walked on again.* □ *You go on ahead. I'll catch you up.* □ *Things have moved on since your childhood.* **2 On** is used with *earlier* and *later* to mean before or after the present moment, or the time mentioned: *I'll see you later on.* □ *I'd noticed it earlier on.* **3** You keep **on** doing something when you continue to do it: *He kept on reading.* □ *She just went on with what she was doing.*

▷ ***phrases*** **1** You **have** a lot **on** when you are busy: *Have you got much on this week?* **2** The time, or a measurement, is **just on** something if it is almost exactly that: *It's just on six.* □ *I make the length just on 5 metres.* **3** Something that happens **on and off** or **off and on** happens occasionally: *We used to see her on and off.* **4** Something that goes **on and on** continues for a long time, or for a long way: *The meeting went on and on.* □ *The track wound on and on through the hills.* **5 a** One thing moves, or is moved, **on to** or **onto** another thing when it moves so that it the other is underneath it or supporting it: *She fell off the wall on to some rocks.* □ *The baby had reached the stage of wanting to climb up on to the furniture.* □ *He got on to his motorbike.* □ *He lifted her on to his shoulders.* □ *She threw herself on to* (or *on*) *the sofa.* □ *She lowered herself slowly on to the chair.* □ *We carried him out on to the verandah.* **b** You get **on to** a bus, train, plane or boat when you get into it to travel somewhere: *We were allowed back on to the plane half an hour later.*

> Notice that although you can get either **on to** or **into** a bus, train, boat or plane, you can only get **into** a car.

c You fasten one thing **on to** another when you attach the one to the other: *His job was to stick price labels on to the goods.* **d** People move from one subject **on to** another when they start discussing it: *Let's get on to the next topic.* **e** You hold **on to** something when you hold it firmly: *She clung on to the seat.* **f** (*informal*) If you say you are **on to** something, especially something wrong or illegal, you mean that you have become aware of it or have discovered it: *The police are on to the drugs racket.* **g** If you get **on to** someone, you contact them: *I've already been on to the suppliers twice this week.* **6** For **on top of** see **top.**

once /wʌns/ *adverb; conjunction*

▷ ***adverb***

1 Things that happen **once** happen just one time, or just on one occasion: *Press the button once and hold it down for a few seconds.* □ *I want to be able to get this right just once.* □ *I only met his mother once.* □ *'How often have you done this?' 'Once, twice, maybe three times.'* **2** Something that happens *eg* **once** a month, or **once** every two weeks, happens regularly one time every month or every two weeks: *The Pythian games were held at Delphi once every four years.* □ *He visits the New York office once a year.* **3** Something that was **once** so, was so at some time, or on a particular occasion, in the past: *We once had a cat called Sam.* □ *The school had once been a railway hotel.* □ *the hill town of Malvern, once celebrated for its healing waters* □ *I once won a prize for my handwriting.*

▷ ***conjunction***

Something that happens **once** something else has happened, happens straight after it, or soon after it: *I'll enjoy the work once I've got used to it.* □ *Once lunch is over you can meet your fellow guests and chat informally.* [*same as* **as soon as**]

▷ ***phrases*** **1** Something that happens **all at once** happens suddenly: *I was just walking along the street when all at once there was this terrible bang.* **2 a** Something that happens **at once** happens immediately: *Stop this noise at once!* □ *I realized at once that I'd said the wrong thing.* **b** You do several things **at once** if you do them all at the same time, or all on one occasion: *I'll help you when I've finished this, but I can't do six things at once.* □ *You can either sing or whistle, but it's quite difficult to do both at once.* □ *I can't hear you if you all talk at once.* □ *Now you're not to eat all those chocolates at once; keep some for tomorrow.* **3** You let something happen **just for once**, or **just this once**, if this is to be the only occasion on which it happens: *Surely you can be lazy just for once?* □ *I'm letting them stay up late just this once to watch the fireworks.* **4** Something that happens **more than once** happens several times: *He's been told more than once not to go upstairs in his walking boots.* **5 a** You do something **once again** or **once more** when you do it again: *Try that once again, to make sure you can do it right.* □ *Do that once more and I'll smack you!* **b** Something happens **once again** or **once more** when it happens again after an interval: *Once again we'll be relying on your support for the success of the fête.* □ *Christmas will soon be here once more.* **6** You deal with something **once and for all**, or **once for all**, when you settle it finally, so that there is no need for further discussion or action: *Let's get out* *the dictionary and settle this dispute once and for all.* **7** For **once in a while** see **while.** **8** Something that happens **once or twice** within a certain period happens a few times: *I've only visited them once or twice in the last ten years.* **9** For **once too often** see **often.** **10** For **once upon a time** see **time.**

once-over /ˈwʌnsoʊvə(r)/ *noun* (*used in the singular; informal*)
If you give something the **once-over** you examine it quickly: *He gave the car the once-over and found no faults.*

oncoming /ˈɒnkʌmɪŋ/ *adjective*
Something is **oncoming** when it is moving towards you: *oncoming traffic.*

one /wʌn/ *noun; adjective; determiner; pronoun*
▻ ***noun*: ones**
1 One is **a** (*uncount or count*) the number or figure 1: *He can count from one to twenty in French.* ▫ *One plus two is three.* ▫ *Two ones are two.* ▫ *That's a one, not an I.* **b** a piece of clothing or a shoe size represented by the number 1: *These trainers are ones, but I need twos.* **2** (*uncount*) **One** is **a** the age of 1: *He started walking at one, and talking at one and a half.* **b** the time of 1 o'clock: *We'll have lunch at half past one.* ▫ *He phoned me at one in the morning.*
▻ ***adjective*** Someone who is **one** is one year old: *She'll be one on Saturday.* ▫ *babies aged one or less.*
▻ ***determiner***
1 One person or thing is a single person or thing: *There's only one train per day.* ▫ *One person in 40 is a twin.* ▫ *He's one year old today.* ▫ *one-week-old puppies* ▫ *toys for one-year-olds* ▫ *The population of the island is at least one million.* ▫ *One more or less won't make any difference.* **2** You normally use **a** or **an** in referring to singular things or people, but you can use **one** instead **a** for emphasis, with the meaning 'a single': *He composed this symphony in one week.* [Compare *I'll see you in a week.*] **b** for contrast with other numbers: *There were about one hundred people in favour and two hundred against.* [Compare *There were about a hundred people there.*] **c** before someone's name, to show that you haven't heard of them before: *The chairman was one Peter Phillips.* **3 One** day is an indefinite or unspecified day in the future or past: *Maybe we'll meet again one day.* ▫ *There was a fearful thunderstorm one night.* **4** The **one** person or thing is the only person or thing for a certain purpose or job: *He's the one man who can help us.* **5 One** is used with *the other* to contrast two people or things: *Stand on one foot and point the other.* ▫ *driving from one side of the country to the other.* **6** Page **One**, Chapter **One** and Scene **One** are the first page, chapter or scene. **7** (*literary*) People are of **one** mind when they agree with one another about something.
▻ ***pronoun*: ones**
1 One refers to a single person or thing: *I thought I'd sold them all, but there's one left.* ▫ *Masses of people have applied, but unfortunately we can only appoint one.* **2 One** of a group of things or people is a member of it, or a single or particular member of it: *One of my colleagues recommends it.* ▫ *If you haven't got a book to read you can borrow one of mine.* ▫ *She's one of those people who are good at everything.* ▫ *Not one of them has visited her.* **3** You use **one** and **ones** to refer to singular and plural count nouns just mentioned: *I couldn't find my copy and had to buy a new one.* ▫ *There are no china plates left, but I've got some paper ones.* ▫ *This bed's quite nice and firm, but I prefer the other one.* ▫ *If you like really comfortable shoes, these ones are made of very soft leather.* ▫ *Which one is your brother?* ▫ *He's the one on the left.* ▫ *Her children are very well-behaved, if they're the ones I'm thinking of.* ▫ *Our house is the one with a dark grey roof.* ▫ *There were a hundred questions, but I could only answer the ones about literature.* ▫ *The really ill ones don't make a fuss.* ▫ *I'm afraid I'm the guilty one.*

> You usually use **mine**, **yours** rather than *my one*, *your one* and so on: *Mine* (not *my one*) *is in the cupboard.*

4 (*informal*) You are a **one** for doing something if you like doing it, or do it a lot: *They're great ones for having parties.* ▫ *He's quite a one for practical jokes, isn't he?* ▫ *I'm not one to refuse an invitation like that.* **5** You use 'the **one**' with 'the **other**' to refer to, or contrast, two people or things: *I didn't care for either man; the one was too noisy and the other too quiet.* **6** (*rather formal*) **One** is also a personal pronoun used mostly to refer to people in general, including yourself, but sometimes used to refer to yourself in an indirect way: *One can't do better than that.* ▫ *words that one doesn't use every day* ▫ *Vigorous exercise is good for one.* ▫ *One must look after oneself and one's interests.* ▫ *One feels so helpless.*

> Notice that you use **somebody** or **someone**, not **one**, to refer to a particular, but unidentified, person: *Did somebody mention ice cream?*

▻ ***phrases***
1 You say you have **a hundred and one**, or **a thousand and one**, things to do if you have a lot of things to do. **2** You say, in reference to two or more possibilities, that it's **all one** to you, if you don't care which happens: *It's all one whether she goes or stays.* **3** Two people are **at one**, or **at one** with each other, if they are in agreement. **4** (*informal*) You are **one up on** someone else when you have an advantage over them. **5** You say 'I, **for one**' to mean you at least, whether anyone else supports you or not: *I for one don't agree.* **6** For **one after the other** see **other**, and for and **one on top of the other** see **top**. **7** (*rather old*) **One and all** is everyone: *entertainment for one and all.* **8** You use '**the one and only**' as an emphatic form of 'the only': *This is the one and only time of day that I get some peace.* **9** For **one another** see **another**. **10 One by one** means one after the other: *They queued up one by one to be injected.* **11** (*informal*) **One or two** means a few: *There have been one or two complaints.*

one-man /ˈwʌn man/ *adjective*
A **one-man** business, operation or performance is one that is run, carried out or done by one person.

one-night stand /wʌn naɪt ˈstand/ *noun*: **one-night stands**
1 A **one-night stand** is a performance given only once in any place with the next performance taking place somewhere else: *The tour by the pop group group included several one-night stands in small theatres and clubs.* **2** (*informal*) A **one-night stand** is also a sexual relationship which lasts for only one night.

one-off /wʌn ˈɒf/ *noun* (*informal; often adjectival*): **one-offs**
A **one-off** is **a** something which is made or happens on one occasion only: *The car is a one-off.* ▫ *a one-off opportunity.* **b** a person who is unlike anyone else: *He's a one-off.*

one-parent family /ˈwʌn peərənt ˈfamɪlɪ/ *noun*: **one-parent families**
A **one-parent family** is a family in which the children are looked after by one parent only.

one-piece /'wʌn piːs/ *adjective*
One-piece things are made in a single piece as opposed to separate parts: *a one-piece suit.*

onerous /'oʊnərəs/ *adjective*
Work or a task that is **onerous** is difficult to do and requires a lot of effort: *an onerous burden* □ *I was given the onerous task of reorganizing all the files.*

oneself /wʌn'sɛlf/ *pronoun*
Oneself is the reflexive form of 'one'. It is used by a speaker or writer as the object of a preposition or verb in a clause or sentence where 'one' is the subject or a previous object: *When one is expected to get through so much work in such as short time, it is important to discipline oneself.*

one-sided /wʌn'saɪdɪd/ *adjective*
1 A **one-sided** competition or contest is one in which one person or side has a great advantage over the other: *The match was a bit one-sided; the visiting team was much more experienced than the home side.* **2** A **one-sided** discussion, argument or view is one that takes into account or considers only some of the facts involved in a situation. [*same as* **biased**] — *noun* (*uncount*) **one-sidedness:** *the one-sidedness of his argument.*

one-time /'wʌntaɪm/ *adjective*
One-time means former. It is used to refer to people who used to do a particular job or were involved in a particular activity in the past: *a one-time soldier in the French army.*

one-to-one /wʌntə'wʌn/ *adjective*
One-to-one is used to describe activities in which a person is involved with only one other person: *one-to-one teaching.*

one-track mind /wʌntrak 'maɪnd/ *noun* (*informal*): **one-track minds**
Someone who has a **one-track mind** thinks about one thing or subject all the time: *All he ever talks about is football; he has a one-track mind.*

one-upmanship /wʌn'ʌpmənʃɪp/ *noun* (*uncount*; *informal*)
One-upmanship is the art of gaining and keeping social or professional advantage over other people.

one-way /'wʌnweɪ/ *adjective*
1 On a **one-way** street traffic moves in one direction only. **2** If you get a **one-way** ticket, you travel to a place but do not travel back again. [*same as* **single**]

one-woman /'wʌn wʊmən/ *adjective*
If a female artist puts on a **one-woman** show or exhibition, they perform alone or exhibit only their own work.

ongoing /'ɒngoʊɪŋ/ *adjective*
Something that is **ongoing** is continuing or is in progress: *an ongoing situation* □ *The negotiations are ongoing.*

onion /'ʌnjən/ *noun*: **onions**
An **onion** is a round vegetable with a strong taste and smell. It is white or reddish-purple inside with a thin dry brown or purple skin. [see picture at **vegetable**]
▷ ***phrase*** (*informal*) If you say that someone **knows their onions** you mean that they know their subject well or can do their job well.

on-line /'ɒnlaɪn/ *adjective* (*technical*)
On-line is used to describe a piece of equipment or data that is directly connected to and/or controlled by a computer: *on-line information in the library* □ *an on-line encyclopedia.*

onlooker /'ɒnlʊkə(r)/ *noun*: **onlookers**
An **onlooker** is someone who watches something happening but does not take part in it: *The police had to get through a large crowd of onlookers before they could break up the fight.*

only /'oʊnlɪ/ *adjective*; *adverb*; *conjunction*
▷ ***adjective***
1 You refer to something or someone as the **only** one if there are no others that what you are saying applies to: *This is the only method that really works.* □ *Peter and I were the only ones to pass the test first time.* □ *It's the only house with green window frames; you can't miss it.* □ *Next weekend is our only chance to see them before they return to Australia.* **2** Something or someone that is the **only** one is the best or most suitable: *She's the only girl for me.* □ *They're the only people for the job.* □ *Flying is the only way to travel.*
▷ ***adverb***

> The rule that **only** should come immediately before or after the word it emphasizes is not much obeyed in spoken English, or even in written English; its commonest position is before the verb, or after the auxiliary verb; but there is usually no doubt about its meaning, or the word or words it refers to, which in spoken English are often stressed.

1 You use **only a** to emphasize that what you say applies to one person, thing or circumstance and not to any other: *They only speak Urdu.* (Or, more formally, *they speak only Urdu*) □ *I only get time to read when* (or, more formally, *I get time to read only when*) *I'm on holiday.* □ *Only Jane Austen could have written that.* □ *'Read-only' files are for reference only, and cannot be edited.* [compare **just**] **b** to emphasize how small an amount is: *I've only got a few pounds with me.* □ *It only takes five minutes to walk to the station.* □ *A bus tour of the city costs you only £1.* □ *The baby was tiny and weighed only five pounds.* □ *This'll only take a moment.* [compare **just**] **c** to emphasize that something is unimportant, and not a cause for concern, admiration, alarm or anger: *Fortunately it was only a cold and nothing more serious.* □ *He was only a minor poet.* □ *The stones are only imitations.* □ *'What's that noise?' 'It's only the wind.'* □ *It's OK; I'm only joking.* □ *She was only trying to help.* □ *I only want everyone to be happy.* **d** to insist that something is still at too early a stage for action or concern: *Why are you up so early? It's only six o'clock.* □ *He's only a child; you can't expect him to understand.* [compare **just**] **e** to emphasize how recently something happened: *I was talking to her only yesterday.* □ *This drug has only recently come on the market.* □ *He went out only a minute ago.* □ *I've only just got home.* [see also **only just** below] **f** to state the result that something is bound to have: *If I come sailing I'll only be sick.* □ *Telling her the truth will only make things worse.* □ *The situation can only improve.* **2** You can **only** do something when that is the one possible course: *We can only wait and hope for the best.* □ *I could only agree with her.* **3** Something that is **only** natural is not unexpected or unusual: *We ought to pay him something; that's only reasonable.* □ *It's only to be expected that she should feel a bit homesick.* **4** You say that one thing will happen **only** if another does, to emphasize that the second circumstance must be the case for the first to happen: *Bees only sting if they're frightened.* □ *'How about coming round for a meal tonight?' 'Well, only if you let me bring the wine.'* **5** You say you **only** wish that something, often something impossible, were so, or **only** hope that something is or will be the case, if you wish it or hope it very strongly: *I only wish I'd spent more time with her.* □ *I only wish he'd telephone and at least we'd know where he is.* □ *I only hope I've passed.* **6** You do one thing **only** to do another when the second thing is the surprising, unfortunate or unwelcome result: *We got ourselves to the rendezvous at 12.30 only to find that the bus had left early.* □ *He had once tried inviting her out, only to meet with a rather cool response.* **7** If you have **only** to do one thing in order to do or achieve another, the second thing is easily done: *You have only to turn on the television to see reports of violence all over the world.* □ *I'm here to help; you have only to ask me.*

▻ ***conjunction*** (*informal*)

You use **only** like *but*: *Come if you want to, only don't complain if you're bored.* □ *I'd write myself, only I don't have her address.* □ *Flying must be like swimming, only better.*

▻ ***phrases*** **1** For **if only** see **if**. **2** You use **not only** to introduce the first of two circumstances of which the second is more surprising or significant than the first: *They had not only omitted essential details; they'd actually faked some of the statistics as well.* **3** Something is **only just** so when it almost not so: *Her work was only just passable.* □ *'Can you hear me?' 'Only just.'* [*same as* **barely**] **4 Only too** emphasizes that something is so to a particularly great, or even unwelcome, extent: *He seemed only too pleased to accept our offer.* □ *In normal circumstances, I'd be only too willing to assist.* □ *My embarrassment must have been only too obvious.* [compare **all too**]

only child /ounlı 'tʃaıld/ *noun*: **only children**

An **only child** is one that has no brothers or sisters.

onrush /'ɒnrʌʃ/ *noun* (*used in the singular; formal*)

An **onrush** is a sudden strong movement forward or a sudden flow of something: *an onrush of emotion* □ *The police were overwhelmed by the sudden onrush of hundreds of football supporters.*

onset /'ɒnsɛt/ *noun* (*used in the singular*)

The beginning or first attack of something unpleasant is sometimes referred to as its **onset**: *The symptoms are characteristic of the onset of influenza.* □ *They are ill prepared for the onset of winter.*

onshore /'ɒnʃɔ:(r)/ *adjective; adverb*

▻ ***adjective***

Onshore is used to describe **1** a wind that is blowing or moving towards the shore. **2** something that is situated on the shore or the land, rather than on the sea: *onshore oil installations.*

▻ ***adverb:*** *The breeze was blowing onshore.* □ *oil workers based onshore.* [compare **offshore**]

onside /ɒn'saıd/ *adjective* or *adverb*

In sports such as football and hockey, a player who is **onside** is in a position where the ball may legally be played, especially because the required number of players of the opposing team are between him or her and the goal: *The striker was onside when he scored.* □ *The referee declared the player to be onside and allowed the goal.* [compare **offside**]

onslaught /'ɒnslɔ:t/ *noun*: **onslaughts**

An **onslaught** is a fierce attack: *They were well-equipped to withstand the enemy onslaught.* □ *He coped well with the onslaught of questions from newspaper and television reporters.*

onto see **on to** at **on**.

onus /'ounəs/ *noun* (*used in the singular; formal*)

When the **onus** is on someone to do something, it is their responsibility or duty to do it: *The onus will be on you to prove that the allegations you have made are true.*

onward /'ɒnwəd/ *adjective; adverb*

▻ ***adverb*** (also **onwards**)

1 Something happens from a certain time or point **onwards** or **onward** when it starts happening then and goes on happening: *The flowers should appear from mid-March onwards.* □ *the systematic records that were kept from 1855 onwards* □ *He'll be available for consultation from 4 o'clock onwards.* □ *From now onward a lifeguard will be on duty at all times.* □ *From this point onwards the tone of her diary changes.* **2** To move **onwards** or **onward** is **a** to continue to move forward: *They pressed onwards and upwards toward the frontier.* □ *We stumbled onward, close to exhaustion.* **b** to progress or develop: *Meanwhile technology sweeps onwards.*

▻ ***adjective:*** *the onward march of science* □ *the onward development of this type of research* □ *Tour members should assemble at nine o'clock for the onward journey to Perth.*

oodles /'u:dəlz/ *noun* (*plural; informal*)

If you say that there are **oodles** of a thing, you mean that there are great quantities of it: *I like my pancakes with oodles of maple syrup.* [*same as* **loads, heaps**]

ooh /u:/ *interjection*

If someone says **ooh**, they are expressing pleasure, surprise, excitement or pain: *Ooh, look at that wonderful chocolate cake!* □ *Ooh, that hurt!*

oops /u:ps/ or /ʊps/ *interjection* (*informal*)

People say **oops** when they have made a mistake or when they have dropped something: *Lady, oops, sorry, I mean Princess Diana.* □ *Oops, sorry, are you okay?*

ooze /u:z/ *verb*: **oozes, oozing, oozed**

1 You can say that a thick liquid **oozes** from something, or a thing **oozes** a thick liquid, when the liquid flows or leaks out slowly from it: *The cut on his hand was oozing blood.* □ *an oily liquid oozing up through the ground.* **2** (*often derogatory*) If you say that someone **oozes** a particular quality or feeling, you mean that it seems to flow out of them: *He stood in a circle of ladies, oozing charm and making all the other young men jealous.*

op /ɒp/ *noun*: **ops** (*informal*)

An **op** is a surgical or military operation: *She's having her op tomorrow morning.*

opaque /ou'peık/ *adjective*

1 If an object, material or substance is **opaque**, you cannot see through it: *The glass in the bathroom window is opaque.* □ *The bottle was filled with an opaque liquid.* **2** (*formal*) When a statement or piece of writing is described as **opaque** it is difficult to understand: *The next passage is somewhat opaque.* [compare **transparent**; *opposite* **clear**]

open /'oupən/ *verb; adjective*

▻ ***verb***: **opens, opening, opened**

1 a You **open** something such as a door, or it **opens**, when you move it, or it moves, so that it no longer fills or covers a gap; you **open** containers of any kind when you adjust their position, or move or remove a part of them, so that you can reach their contents: *She went over to the window and opened the curtains.* □ *Would you mind if I opened the window?* □ *The door opened and in walked George.* □ *I lifted down the first-aid box and opened the lid.* □ *He took off his tie and opened his top button.* □ *The cupboard wouldn't open.* □ *He opened a drawer in his desk and took out an envelope.* □ *Could you open this bottle for me?* □ *We opened a tin of beans.* □ *I'm so sorry; I opened your letter by mistake.* [*opposite* **close, shut**] **b** You **open** a book when you separate its covers and reveal its pages: *I picked up a magazine and opened it.* □ *Open your textbooks at page 214.* □ *The dictionary opened at the entry 'monarch'.* [*opposite* **close, shut**] **c** You **open** something folded when you unfold it or spread it out: *I opened my umbrella.*

□ *He sat down and opened a newspaper.* [*opposite* **fold**] **d** You **open** something such as a road when you remove what has been blocking it: *Snow ploughs have worked all night to open the roads.* □ *The southbound carriageway has been re-opened to traffic.* [*opposite* **close**, **block**] **e** A door or room **opens** on to or into somewhere if you can get there directly through that door or from that room: *The street door opened straight into the sitting room.* **f** Something **opens** the way to progress when it makes it easier: *discoveries that have opened the way to further research.* [*opposite* **close**, **block**]

2 a You **open** your mouth when you part your lips or teeth; you **open** your eyes when you raise your eyelids: *She opened her mouth as if to say something.* □ *When next I opened my eyes it was broad daylight.* [*opposite* **close**, **shut**] **b** A flower **opens** when it spreads out its petals; a bud **opens** when it bursts and the flower or leaf inside it spreads out. [*opposite* **close**]

3 a Offices, shops and other public buildings **open** or **are opened** when their entrances are unlocked so that customers or visitors can come in: *The post office opens at nine o'clock.* [*opposite* **close, shut**] **b** You **open** a new shop or office when you equip it and begin business in it: *They've opened several branches in our area.* [*opposite* **close**] **c** Someone important **opens** something newly built when they declare it ready for use, in an official ceremony: *The road bridge was opened by the Queen in September '64.* **d** You **open** an account with a bank or building society when you pay some of your money into it, to be invested or kept for when you need it. [*opposite* **close**]

4 a An event such as a conference or debate **opens** when its proceedings begin; you **open** it when you speak first: *Who would care to open the discussion?* □ *The conference opened with a reception for delegates.* [*opposite* **close**, **finish**] **b** A play or opera **opens** when the first performance of a series is given: *'Men Should Weep' opens in Glasgow on Friday.* [*opposite* **close**]

▻ ***adjective***

1 a Things are **open** when they are not shut or closed: *Someone must have left the front door open.* □ *The window was wide open.* □ *Drawers had been pulled open and their contents thrown out.* □ *The kittens' eyes aren't open yet.* □ *She stared at me open-mouthed.* □ *His diary lay open on the desk.* □ *We've got a bottle of red wine open ready.* □ *I couldn't get the tin open.* [*opposite* **closed, shut**] **b** Roads are **open** when they are not blocked: *There was an accident earlier on the A9 but the road is reported to be open again.* [*opposite* **closed**, **blocked**] **c** You wear your clothing **open** when you don't fasten it: *She had a purple coat which she always wore open.* □ *It was Saturday and he was in an open-necked shirt.*

2 a Shops and offices are **open** when people are working there and customers or visitors can go in: *The National Library is open from 9.30 am.* □ *We're open seven days a week.* □ *The bank will be open for business as usual on Tuesday.* [*opposite* **closed**, **shut**] **b** A place is **open** to the public if people are allowed in: *The house and grounds are open to the public at weekends.* [*opposite* **closed**, **private**] **c** Something that has been newly built is **open** when it is officially ready for use: *When is the tunnel going to be open?* □ *She declared the new hospital wing open.* **d** An **open** meeting or competition is one that anyone can attend or take part in: *We're entering a team for the Open Championships.* [*opposite* **closed**]

3 a An area is **open** if it is not enclosed, or if nothing blocks your view or way across it: *out on the open sea* □ *an open view* □ *open countryside* □ *You start longing for the wide open spaces.* **b** **Open** describes things that are not covered or enclosed: *They sailed 4000 miles in a tiny open boat.* □ *driving along in an open sports car* □ *We cooked over an open log fire.* □ *open sewers running along the street.* **c** An **open** wound or sore is one where raw flesh is exposed; you cut *eg* your leg or head **open** when you get a deep wound in it: *He fell downstairs and cut his head open.* **d** Loosely woven cloth is sometimes described as having an **open** weave. [*opposite* **close**]

4 a Someone described as **open** is honest, and doesn't hide anything: *She's such a nice open person.* □ *He's always been quite open about his criminal record.* □ *I'll be open with you.* [*same as* **frank**, **candid**] **b** People's attitude to one another is one of *eg* **open** hostility when they do not try to hide or disguise it: *They stared at me with open dislike.* [*same as* **undisguised**, **frank**] **c** An **open** secret is one that everyone knows about. **d** With a system of **open** government the public are kept informed about how the country is run, and what decisions are being taken.

5 a You have an **open** mind, or are **open** to new ideas, if you are willing to change your opinions and consider new ideas: *sensible, open-minded parents.* □ *I'm open to suggestions if anyone has a better idea.* **b** A matter that is still **open** to debate or discussion is not considered settled, and is likely to go on being discussed and disagreed over. **c** A statement that is **open** to misinterpretation is not clear, and is likely to be misunderstood. [*same as* **liable**] **d** A question or matter that remains **open** is one about which a decision has not yet been made: *Whether or not he'll go to the polls is still an open question.* □ *I'd rather keep my options open than decide straight away.* **e** A course of action is **open** to you if it is something you could do: *There are a number of courses open to you.* [*same as* **available**] **f** An **open** invitation is either an invitation to anyone who wishes to accept it, or an invitation to someone to accept when they want to: *You know you have an open invitation to our cottage.*

▻ ***phrases*** **1** You do things **in the open** when you do them out of doors, not inside a building: *Meals taste better in the open.* **2** A matter that has been kept hidden is brought **into the open** when people are told about it: *The whole story was now out in the open.*

phrasal verbs

open out 1 You **open out** something when you unfold it or spread it out: *We opened the map out on the table.* **2** A road or passage **opens out** when it widens.

open up 1 You **open up** a shop or place of business when you unlock its doors so that people can get in: *They open the school up at 8.00.* **2** An area **is opened up** when it is made easier to get to, or easier to have trading links with: *when Japan was first opened up to trade in the 19th century* □ *a system of marked footpaths that opens up the countryside to less adventurous walkers.* **3** A circumstance **opens up** opportunities to you, or opportunities **open up**, when they become available to you: *You'll be surprised at the career prospects that open up.* **4** (*informal*) Someone **opens up** when they begin to talk more freely.

open air /oupən 'ɛə(r)/ *noun* (*uncount*)
You are in the **open air** when you are outside rather than in an enclosed space or building: *The service of remembrance was held in the open air.* — *adjective* **open-air:** *an open-air concert.* [*opposite* **indoor**]

open-and-shut /oupən ənd 'ʃʌt/ *adjective*
Open-and-shut means easily proved, decided or solved: *It was an open-and-shut case, and the defendants were found guilty.* [*same as* **straightforward**]

open book /oupən 'bʊk/ *noun* (*used in the singular*)

If you say that a person or their life is an **open book**, you mean that they have no secrets and are easily understood.

opencast /ˈoupənkɑːst/ *adjective*
An **opencast** mine is one in which minerals, especially coal, are dug from an open hole in the ground and not from deep underground shafts.

open day /ˈoupən deɪ/ *noun*: **open days**
When a school or other institution has an **open day**, members of the public are allowed to visit it and look around it.

open-ended /oupən ˈɛndɪd/ *adjective*
If something is **open-ended**, it has no restrictions or limits, or no clear aims, set in advance: *an open-ended discussion between the management and unions* □ *The contract will be open-ended.*

opener /ˈoupənə(r)/ *noun*: **openers**
An **opener** is a device for opening something: *a bottle-opener* □ *a can-opener.*

open-handed /oupən ˈhandɪd/ *adjective*
Someone or something can be described as **open-handed** when they are generous, or it is freely given: *an open-handed gesture of friendship.*

open house /oupən ˈhaus/ *noun* (*uncount*)
If you keep **open house** you are willing to welcome and entertain visitors in your home at any time: *It's always open house at the Camerons.*

opening /ˈoupənɪŋ/ *noun*; *adjective*
▻ ***noun*: openings**
1 An **opening** is a hole or a gap in something through which things can pass: *The sun suddenly appeared through an opening in the clouds.* □ *The cow stuck its head through an opening in the hedge.* **2** (*usually used in the singular*) The **opening** of something is the act of making it open, especially officially: *the opening of a new stretch of motorway.* **3** An **opening** is an opportunity or a favourable set of circumstances: *a good opening for any enterprising businessman.* **4** An **opening** is also a job or position which has not yet been filled: *We have an opening for a qualified accountant at our head office.* □ *There are very few openings for people with your qualifications.* [*same as* **vacancy**] **5** The **opening** of a book or play is the first part or beginning of it: *The opera has a very dramatic opening.*
▻ ***adjective***
The **opening** part of something is the first part or beginning of it: *his opening remarks* □ *the opening chapter.*

opening hours /ˈoupənɪŋ auəz/ *noun* (*plural*)
A pub's, shop's, bank's or other premises' **opening hours** are the times when it is open to the public: *The library's opening hours are from 9am to 8pm, Monday to Saturday.*

opening time /ˈoupənɪŋ taɪm/ *noun* (*uncount*)
Opening time is the time of day at which a public house, bar, or hotel can begin to sell alcoholic drinks.

openly /ˈoupənlɪ/ *adverb*
If you do something **openly**, you do it in a direct and honest way, without trying to hide anything: *He talked quite openly about his problems.* [*opposite* **secretively**]

open-minded /oupən ˈmaɪndɪd/ *adjective*
Someone who is **open-minded** is willing to consider or receive new ideas, opinions or arguments: *an open-minded attitude* □ *His parents are very open-minded.* [see also **open**] [*same as* **broad-minded**; *opposite* **narrow-minded**]

open-mouthed /oupən ˈmauðd/ *adjective* or *adverb*
If someone is **open-mouthed**, they have their mouth wide open because they are surprised or shocked by what they hear or see: *The children stared open-mouthed at the antics of the clowns.* [*same as* **dumbfounded, spellbound**]

openness /ˈoupənnəs/ *noun* (*uncount*)
Openness is honesty or frankness: *They were taken aback by his openness about his criminal record.*

open-plan /oupən ˈplan/ *adjective*
Open-plan areas or buildings have no internal walls and form one large room rather than a number of smaller rooms: *an open-plan office* □ *an open-plan kitchen and dining area.*

Open University /oupən juːnɪˈvɜːsɪtɪ/ *noun* (*uncount*)
The **Open University** is a British university which offers study courses to degree level to people who do not have the entrance qualifications to get into other universities or are unable to do a full-time university course. Students are taught through radio and television programmes and send in and receive course work by post.

opera /ˈɒpərə/ *noun*: **operas**
1 An **opera** is a musical play in which many of the words are sung: Fidelio *is an opera by Beethoven.* □ *Mozart wrote several popular operas.* **2** (*uncount*) **Opera** is these musical plays considered together as a form of art: *Italian opera* □ *She has sung in opera and as a concert artist.* [see also **operetta, soap opera**]

operable /ˈɒpərəbəl/ *adjective*
If a disease or medical condition is **operable**, it can be treated by means of a surgical operation: *The tumour had grown so large, it was no longer operable.* [*opposite* **inoperable**]

opera house /ˈɒpərə haus/ *noun*: **opera houses**
An **opera house** is a theatre specially built for the performance of operas.

operate /ˈɒpəreɪt/ *verb*: **operates, operating, operated**
1 You **operate** a machine or a machine **is operated** when you make it work or it is made to work: *How does the laser printer operate?* □ *The trainees are learning how to operate the machines safely.* **2** The way in which something **operates** is the way in which it acts or produces an effect: *There are several factors operating in the economy which make it difficult to predict the future.* **3** To **operate** also means to manage, direct or conduct something, especially a business: *The company operates in several European countries.* □ *The drug ring is operated from a base in South America.* **4** When a surgeon **operates**, he or she cuts open a patient's body in order to repair or remove a damaged or diseased part: *The surgeon operated to replace the damaged artery.* □ *He was operated on to remove a blood clot from his brain.*

operatic /ɒpəˈratɪk/ *adjective*
Operatic means of or for opera: *an operatic voice* □ *an operatic society* □ *an operatic score.*

operating system /ˈɒpəreɪtɪŋ sɪstəm/ *noun* (*technical*): **operating systems**
An **operating system** is a set of programs which control the basic functions of a computer.

operating table /ˈɒpəreɪtɪŋ teɪbəl/ *noun*: **operating tables**
An **operating table** is a special table on which surgical operations are carried out.

operating theatre /ˈɒpəreɪtɪŋ θɪətə(r)/ *noun*: **operating theatres**
An **operating theatre** is a specially-equipped room in a hospital where surgical operations are done.

operation /ɒpə'reɪʃən/ *noun*: **operations**
1 An **operation** is an activity or something that is done, such as managing or conducting a business or part of a business: *The company's overseas operations include mining and oil exploration.* ▫ *Fitting all the parts together is quite a complicated operation.* **2** An **operation** is also a highly organized activity which involves the movement or coordinated action of many people or things: *He planned the whole thing like a military operation.* ▫ *When it was discovered they were missing, a massive rescue operation was mounted.* **3** If a surgeon performs an **operation**, he or she cuts into a patient's body to treat a damaged or diseased part: *He will need a small operation to correct his vision.* ▫ *a hip operation.* **4** (*uncount*) The **operation** of something is the process or action of working or the way in which it is made to work: *The operation of these machines is carried out by highly trained personnel.* **5** (*technical*) In mathematics, an **operation** is a process, such as addition and subtraction, used to get an answer to a problem. **6** (*uncount*) Something that is in **operation** is working or having an effect: *All workers should stand clear of the machine while it is in operation.* **7** (*uncount*) When something comes into **operation** it begins to work or have an effect: *New procedures will come into operation later in the year.*

operational /ɒpə'reɪʃənəl/ *adjective*
1 A machine or system is **operational** when it is able or ready to work: *The dam will not be fully operational until 1995.* **2 Operational** also means of or concerned with operations: *operational costs* ▫ *They have been experiencing some operational difficulties.*

operative /'ɒpərətɪv/ *adjective*; *noun*
▻ ***adjective***
1 Something is **operative** when it is working or having an effect: *When is the new law due to become operative?* ▫ *The Channel Tunnel will be operative from the middle of 1994.* [*opposite* **inoperative**; compare **operational**] **2** An **operative** word is one that is most suitable or significant: *'He's crazy about that woman.' 'Yes, crazy being the operative word.'*
▻ ***noun***: **operatives** (*formal or euphemistic*)
An **operative** is a worker, especially one who has special skills: *All our operatives are trained to the highest standards.*

operator /'ɒpəreɪtə(r)/ *noun*: **operators**
1 An **operator** is a person who operates a particular machine or piece of equipment: *a radio operator* ▫ *a computer operator.* **2** An **operator** is also a person at a telephone exchange, or at a switchboard in an office building or hotel, whose job it is to connect telephone calls: *'Operator, I seem to have been cut off; can you reconnect me.'* **3** A person or company that runs certain types of business is also called an **operator**: *a tour operator.*

operetta /ɒpə'rɛtə/ *noun*: **operettas**
An **operetta** is a short cheerful or amusing opera which usually includes dancing and in which many of the words are spoken rather than sung.

ophthalmic /ɒf'θalmɪk/ *adjective*
Opthalmic means of or relating to the eye.

opiate /'oʊpɪət/ *noun*: **opiates**
An **opiate** is a drug that contains opium, used to relieve pain or make you sleep.

opinion /ə'pɪnjən/ *noun*: **opinions**
1 Your **opinion** is what you think about someone or something, based on your personal judgement: *What's your opinion of his latest play?* ▫ *I have a bad opinion of him.* **2** (*uncount*) **Opinion** is the beliefs and views held by a particular group of people or by people in general: *Public opinion is in favour of capital punishment.*
▻ ***phrases*** **1** If two people have **a difference of opinion** about something, they disagree or argue about it. **2** If you say that something is **a matter of opinion**, you mean that it is something that is not clearly proved and is therefore a matter of personal judgement. **3** A **second opinion** is a judgement or diagnosis made by a second person, especially a doctor. **4** If you say you **are of the opinion that** something is the case, you mean that you think or believe that it is the case.

opinionated /ə'pɪnjəneɪtɪd/ *adjective* (*derogatory*)
An **opinionated** person is someone who holds very strong opinions and refuses to accept that they may be wrong: *I found him over-confident and opinionated.*

opinion poll /ə'pɪnjən poʊl/ *noun*: **opinion polls**
An **opinion poll** is an organized process in which a random sample of people are asked their opinion on a particular subject, especially on political issues.

opium /'oʊpɪəm/ *noun* (*uncount*)
Opium is a drug made from juice from the seeds of the opium poppy, used in medicine in various forms to cause sleep and to relieve pain.

opponent /ə'poʊnənt/ *noun*: **opponents**
1 Your **opponent** is the person you are competing against in *eg* a game, argument or fight: *His next opponent will be the reigning world heavyweight champion.* ▫ *a brutal attempt to silence their political opponents.* **2** An **opponent** of something is someone who disapproves of it and tries to change it or stop it happening: *He's been a life-long opponent of socialist policies.* ▫ *a march staged by opponents of the nuclear arms race.* [*opposite* **proponent**]

opportune /'ɒpətjuːn/ *adjective* (*formal*)
You can use **opportune** to describe something that happens or comes at the most suitable or convenient time: *His intervention at that particular point was most opportune.* ▫ *He chose an opportune moment to make the announcement.* [*opposite* **inopportune**]

opportunist /ɒpə'tjuːnɪst/ *noun* (*often adjectival*; *derogatory*): **opportunists**
An **opportunist** is someone who recognizes and uses every chance or opportunity that occurs in order to gain success or an advantage for themselves: *a political opportunist* ▫ *an opportunist thief.* — *noun* (*uncount*) **opportunism:** *He became prime minister through a combination of luck and political opportunism.*

opportunity /ɒpə'tjuːnɪtɪ/ *noun* (*count or uncount*): **opportunities**
An **opportunity** is a chance to do something or a time when circumstances allow you to do it: *You will be given an opportunity to ask questions at the end of the lecture.* ▫ *I'd like to take the opportunity to thank you.* ▫ *an area with few employment opportunities* ▫ *He missed an excellent opportunity to score a goal.* [*same as* **chance**]

oppose /ə'poʊz/ *verb*: **opposes, opposing, opposed**
If you **oppose** a person's actions, plans or beliefs, you disagree with them and try to prevent or change what they want to do using force or argument: *local organizations that oppose the government's plans to build a new motorway.* [*same as* **resist**; *opposite* **support**]

opposed /ə'poʊzd/ *adjective*
1 If you are **opposed** to something, you are against it or disagree with it: *He was opposed to any form of corporal punishment.* **2** When two things are **opposed** to each other, they are opposite to each other or completely different from each other: *His approach was diametrically opposed to the teaching methods used by his predecessor.*

▻ ***phrase*** You use **as opposed to** when you want to indicate clearly that something you are talking about is separate or distinct from, or in contrast to, something else: *personal as opposed to business expenditure.*

opposing /ə'poʊzɪŋ/ *adjective*
Opposing things are in opposition to each other or are different from each other: *A penalty was awarded to the opposing team.* □ *Let's also consider the opposing argument before we make any decision.*

opposite /'ɒpəzɪt/ *preposition; adverb or adjective; adjective; noun*
▻ ***preposition***
1 One thing is **opposite** another if it faces it across a space, or is on the other side of something such as a street, river or table: *I was sitting opposite Morris at dinner.* □ *I kept catching the eye of the lady opposite me.* □ *The post office is opposite the bookshop.* **2** An actress plays or stars **opposite** the leading male actor when she has the leading female part; a male actor plays **opposite** the leading actress when he has the leading male part: *She plays opposite her real-life partner in 'Shadowlands'.*
▻ ***adverb or adjective:*** *They've made friends with the children living opposite.* [= living on the other side of the street] □ *The passenger seated opposite looked rather familiar.* □ *There's a little church in the field opposite.* □ *It's directly opposite to the fire station.*
▻ ***adjective***
1 The **opposite** side of something is the side furthest away from you, or the other side; the **opposite** ends or sides of something are its two ends, or two facing sides of it: *He was fishing from the opposite bank.* □ *living on the opposite side of the world* □ *The boys and girls stood in little groups at opposite ends of the hall.* [compare **other**] **2** People go off in **opposite** directions when they part and move away from each other: *They spoke briefly, then turned and walked off in opposite directions.* [*opposite* **same**] **3 Opposite** things are as different as possible from each other: *She thought it would be easy, but I took the opposite view.* □ *We showed her the photos to cheer her up, but they seemed to have the opposite effect.* [*opposite* **same**] **4** The **opposite** sex is the sex that you don't belong to yourself: *We spend seven years in a girls' boarding school, well protected from the opposite sex.*
▻ ***noun*: opposites**
One thing is the **opposite** of another if it is as different as possible from it: *My parents were opposites in many ways: she sociable and talkative, and he silent and antisocial.* □ *'Under' is the opposite of 'over', and 'below' is the opposite of 'above'.* □ *'Was she pleased with her performance?' 'No, quite the opposite.'* [see also **antonym**]

opposite number /ɒpəzɪt 'nʌmbə(r)/ *noun*: **opposite numbers**
Someone's **opposite number** is the person with an equivalent position or job in *eg* another company, political party, or country: *The British Foreign Secretary will be discussing the problem with his Japanese opposite number at the summit.* [*same as* **counterpart**]

opposition /ɒpə'zɪʃən/ *noun*
1 (*uncount*) When there is **opposition** to something, a person or group of people do not approve of it or agree with it, and try to change it or stop it happening: *The plan is likely to meet with fierce opposition from local residents.* □ *There's a lot of local opposition to the proposed development.* [*same as* **resistance**] **2** (*with a singular or plural verb*) The person or group of people you are competing against or in conflict with are often referred to as the **opposition**: *With their star player injured, they were no match for the opposition.* □ *study the opposition's tactics.* **3 a** (*with a singular or plural verb*) In a parliament, the **opposition** are the politicians or political parties who oppose the party in government. **b** (*uncount, or used with a singular or plural verb*) In Britain, the political party with the greatest number of members or supporters in Parliament after the party in government forms the official **Opposition**: *The Labour Party had been in Opposition for fifteen years.* □ *an Opposition spokesman* □ *the leader of the Opposition.*

oppress /ə'prɛs/ *verb*: **oppresses, oppressing, oppressed** (*often in the passive*)
1 If a person or group of people in authority **oppress** other people, they rule over them or treat them in a cruel or unjust way that allows them no freedom to do what they want: *The military government oppressed the people.* **2** If something **oppresses** you, it makes you feel worried and depressed: *The silence oppressed him.* — *adjective* **oppressed:** *an organization that campaigns for the rights of oppressed people everywhere.*

oppression /ə'prɛʃən/ *noun* (*uncount*)
1 Oppression is the state or action of oppressing people or the state of being oppressed: *systematic oppression of religious minorities* □ *They had suffered years of oppression under successive governments.* **2 Oppression** is also a feeling of worry or depression: *The high brick walls and bars on the windows created a feeling of oppression which he found very disturbing.*

oppressive /ə'prɛsɪv/ *adjective*
1 Systems, laws or rules are **oppressive** when they are cruel and unjust and do not allow people freedom to do what they want: *an oppressive regime* □ *oppressive new laws that prevent people from travelling freely.* **2** A situation or condition can be described as **oppressive** when it is very uncomfortable and hard to bear: *The heat was so oppressive, they felt they could hardly breathe.* — *adverb* **oppressively:** *There was no air conditioning and the room became oppressively hot.*

oppressor /ə'prɛsə(r)/ *noun*: **oppressors**
An **oppressor** is someone who oppresses others: *There was no means of escape from their oppressors.*

opt /ɒpt/ *verb*: **opts, opting, opted**
When you **opt** to do something, you choose or decide to do it instead of something else: *He could have taken a job in his father's firm, but instead he opted to go into the army.*

> ***phrasal verbs***
> **opt for** When you **opt for** something, you choose it rather than any of the other possibilities that are available: *After taking time to consider, she opted for the course of action he had first suggested.*
> **opt out** You **opt out** when you choose or decide not to do something or take part in something: *You made a promise to them, and you can't opt out now.* □ *schools that have opted out of local authority control.*

optic /'ɒptɪk/ *adjective*
Optic means of or concerning the eye or vision: *the optic nerve.*

optical /'ɒptɪkəl/ *adjective*
1 Optical means of or concerned with the sense of sight: *an optical effect.* **2 Optical** instruments are for looking through: *The firm makes microscopes, telescopes and other optical instruments.*

optical illusion /ɒptɪkəl ɪ'luːʒən/ *noun*: **optical illusions**
An **optical illusion** is something that deceives the eye

and makes the person looking at it think it is something that it is not: *The road seemed to go up rather than downhill, but it was just an optical illusion.*

optician /ɒp'tɪʃən/ *noun*: **opticians**
1 An **optician** is someone who tests people's eyesight and makes and sells glasses and contact lenses. **2** An **optician** or **optician's** is an optician's place of business or practice: *There's an optician in the High Street.* □ *He made an appointment at the optician's.*

optics /'ɒptɪks/ *noun* (*uncount*)
Optics is the scientific study of light and vision.

optimal see **optimum**.

optimism /'ɒptɪmɪzm/ *noun* (*uncount*)
Optimism is the state of believing that future events will turn out well, or the tendency to take a bright, hopeful view of things and expect the best possible outcome: *He was full of optimism about the future.* [*opposite* **pessimism**] — *noun* **optimist:** *He's always been an optimist.* □ *The optimists in the party think that they will win the next general election easily.*

optimistic /ɒptɪ'mɪstɪk/ *adjective*
Someone who is **optimistic** expects or believes that future events will turn out well or have the best possible outcome: *The doctor said he was optimistic that the little boy would make a full recovery.* [*opposite* **pessimistic**] — *adverb* **optimistically:** *He left his umbrella at home, believing optimistically that it wouldn't rain.*

optimum /'ɒptɪməm/ *adjective* (*formal*)
(also **optimal**) **Optimum** conditions are the best or most favourable: *A heated greenhouse provides the optimum conditions for growing young and tender plants.*

option /'ɒpʃən/ *noun*: **options**
1 An **option** is something that is chosen or may be chosen in preference to others: *There weren't many other options open to him.* □ *Do I have an option, or must I do what he tells me to do?* □ *She was given two equally difficult options: remain and be kept under house arrest, or leave and never return.* [*same as* **alternative**] **2** (*uncount or used in the singular*) If you have or are given the **option** to do something, you have or are given the freedom or right to choose whether you do it or not: *He did it because he felt he had no other option.*
▻ *phrases* If you **keep** or **leave your options open**, you avoid making a choice or decision now, so that you are free to do so at a later time when you have more information or have to make a choice: *Don't commit yourself yet; keep your options open until you have seen what else is available.*

optional /'ɒpʃənəl/ *adjective*
If something is **optional** you can choose whether or not you have it or do it: *For this evening's concert, formal dress is optional.* □ *an optional subject at school* □ *Leather upholstery is an optional extra on this model of car.* (=it is available but will cost extra) [*opposite* **compulsory, obligatory**]

opulent /'ɒpjələnt/ *adjective*
Opulent means having or showing great wealth: *an opulent lifestyle* □ *He wore a cream silk shirt abd dark casual trousers; his black BMW too, was opulent.* — *noun* (*uncount*) **opulence:** *the opulence of the imperial court.*

or /ɔː(r)/ *conjunction*
You use **or 1** (*often in questions and after negatives*) as a link between alternatives and possibilities where there are two, and between the last two where there are several: *You can write 'judgement' or 'judgment'; both are correct.* □ *Ask Jane or Carol.* □ *There's a choice of tea, coffee or hot chocolate.* □ *in times of doubt or despair* □ *when you're tired or feeling depressed* □ *Do you want fried or boiled potatoes?* □ *Are you coming with me or staying here?* □ *Do you have any friends or relations in the US?* □ *I don't want to talk about it or hear it mentioned.* □ *They have no hope, future or self-respect.*

> Notice that where **or** links singular nouns as the subject, a plural verb is sometimes used instead of a singular, especially in informal English, and you usually use a plural verb where there is combination of *eg* third and first person, or second and third: *A book or a crossword helps* (or *help*) *to pass the time. Alice or I are usually available to deal with queries.*

2 to introduce the second of two alternatives where the first is introduced by *whether* or *either*: *She was so exhausted she didn't know whether she was coming or going.* □ *He'll have to sign whether he wants to or not.* □ *She's either missed the train or stayed late at the office.* □ *Either you or Peter is* (or *are*) *going to be asked to do a presentation.* **3** between numbers to indicate an approximate amount: *He walks into town two or three times a week.* [see also **or two** at **two**] **4** sometimes with **else**, to state what the result will be of not doing what you suggest: *Hold my hand or we may get separated.* □ *I must dash or else I'll be late.* **5** to introduce an alternative for a word you have just used: *He was brought up in Rhodesia, or Zimbabwe as it is now known.* **6** to correct something you have just said: *She's in her bedroom, or she was three minutes ago.* □ *I'm working on it now, or at least I've just started.* □ *She's my cousin, or rather my second cousin.* **7** to introduce a doubt you have just had: *We've finished at last; or have we?* **8** to justify or explain something you have just said: *She can't be angry with you or she wouldn't have invited you.*
▻ *phrases* **1** For **or else** see **else**. **2** For **or other** see **other**. **3** For **or rather** see **rather**. **4** For **or so** see **so**. **5** For **or two** see **two**.
[see also **nor**]

-or /ə(r)/ *suffix*
-or is used to form nouns from verbs to indicate the person or thing that performs the action of the verb: *actor* □ *elevator.*

oral /'ɔːrəl/ *adjective*; *noun*
▻ *adjective*
1 Oral is used to describe things that are spoken rather than written: *an oral tradition* □ *an oral examination.* **2 Oral** also means of or taken in through the mouth: *oral hygiene* □ *an oral contraceptive.* — *adverb* **orally:** *He gave his answers orally.* □ *The tablets are to be taken orally.*
▻ *noun*: **orals**
An **oral** is a spoken test or examination.

orange /'ɒrɪndʒ/ *noun*; *adjective*
▻ *noun*: **oranges**
1 An **orange** is a round, juicy fruit with a thick reddish-yellow skin and sharp, sweet taste. [see picture at **fruit**] **2** An **orange** or an **orange tree** is an evergreen tree on which this fruit grows. **3** (*uncount*) **Orange** is the reddish-yellow colour of the skin of this fruit: *a bright orange* □ *a pattern of browns and oranges* □ *Her favourite colour is orange.* **4** An **orange** is a glass of orange-flavoured drink: *'Would you like a glass of wine?' 'No, thank you, I'll just have an orange.'* □ *a drink of orange.*
▻ *adjective*
1 Orange things are of the colour of an orange's skin:

They're orange, not yellow. □ *an enormous orange sun.* **2 Orange** also means made with or flavoured with orange: *orange marmalade* □ *an orange drink.*

oration /ə'reɪʃən/ *noun*: **orations** (*formal*)
An **oration** is a formal and solemn public speech, especially one that is made in fine or beautiful language.

orator /'ɒrətə(r)/ *noun*: **orators**
An **orator** is a person who is good at making public speeches: *Though he was a very clever politician, he had never been a great orator.*

oratorio /ɒrə'tɔːrɪoʊ/ *noun*: **oratorios**
An **oratorio** is a long musical work with singing but without scenery or acting, usually about some story from the Bible or other religious subject.

oratory /'ɒrətərɪ/ *noun* (*uncount*)
Oratory is the art of speaking well in public, especially using fine or formal language: *I had to admire his oratory though I didn't agree with his policies.* [*same as* **eloquence**]

orb /ɔːb/ *noun*: **orbs**
1 An **orb** is a ball decorated with jewels and with a cross on top, that is carried by a king or queen at their coronation and other important ceremonies. **2** (*literary*) **Orb** is also sometimes used to refer to an object that is shaped like a ball, such as the sun, a planet or the eyeball.

orbit /'ɔːbɪt/ *noun*; *verb*
▻ ***noun*** (*count or uncount*): **orbits**
An **orbit** is a curved path that is followed by a solid object, such as a moon, planet or spacecraft, that is moving round a planet or star: *the orbits of Uranus and Neptune* □ *The spacecraft made three complete orbits of the Earth.* □ *The astronauts successfully repaired the telescope while it was in orbit.*
▻ ***verb***: **orbits, orbiting, orbited**
A solid object, such as a planet, satellite or spacecraft **orbits** a sun, moon or planet when it moves round and round it: *All the planets orbit the Sun in the same direction.*

orbital /'ɔːbɪtəl/ *adjective*
1 Orbital means of or going round in an orbit: *the orbital path of Neptune.* **2** An **orbital** road runs in a complete circle or loop round a large city.

orchard /'ɔːtʃəd/ *noun*: **orchards**
An **orchard** is a garden or piece of land where fruit trees are grown: *It was a small orchard, with some apple and pear trees and long grass.*

orchestra /'ɔːkɪstrə/ *noun*: **orchestras**
An **orchestra** is a group, usually a large group, of musicians who play a variety of instruments and are led by a conductor: *The orchestra played 'God save the Queen'.* □ *a chamber orchestra* □ *a symphony orchestra* □ *The singer tours with his own small orchestra.* □ *the London Philharmonic Orchestra.*

An orchestra usually plays classical music. Jazz and pop music are played by a band or group.

orchestral /ɔː'kɛstrəl/ *adjective*
Orchestral means of, for, or played by an orchestra: *orchestral music* □ *an orchestral arrangement.*

orchestrate /'ɔːkɪstreɪt/ *verb*: **orchestrates, orchestrating, orchestrated**
1 To **orchestrate** a piece of music means to arrange or compose it in various parts for an orchestra. [*same as* **arrange**] **2** To **orchestrate** something is to organize or arrange its various parts in order to get the best result or effect: *He was responsible for orchestrating the whole presidential campaign.* — *adjective* **orchestrated:** *a cleverly orchestrated publicity campaign.*

orchid /'ɔːkɪd/ *noun*: **orchids**
An **orchid** is a plant with beautiful flowers divided into three parts with one lip-shaped petal which is much larger than the others.

ordain /ɔː'deɪn/ *verb*: **ordains, ordaining, ordained**
1 When someone **is ordained**, they are made a priest or minister in a religious service: *The first women were ordained in the Church of England in 1994.* □ *He was ordained as a priest.* **2** (*formal*) If someone in a position of power or authority **ordains** that something should be done, they order or command that it should be done: *The king ordained that they should be tried for treason.* [*same as* **decree**]

ordeal /ɔː'diːl/ *noun*: **ordeals**
An **ordeal** is a difficult or painful experience, especially one that goes on for some time: *They had been through a terrible ordeal.* □ *The former hostages took many months to recover from their ordeal.*

order /'ɔːdə(r)/ *verb*; *noun*
▻ ***verb***: **orders, ordering, ordered**
1 Someone in authority **orders** people to do something when they tell them to do it and expect to be obeyed: *She ordered us to stop writing and hand in our papers.* □ *I'd been ordered by the doctor to stay in bed.* □ *'Sign here,' she ordered.* □ *He ordered the men to be shot and the women and children to be taken prisoner.* □ *The bank had ordered that the money should be paid to him only on proof of identity.* □ *An offical inquiry had been ordered into the affair.* [compare **tell, command**] **2** Someone **orders** you somewhere when they tell you to go there: *He spoke to the tenants and ordered them out of the house by the following Friday.* □ *The regiment had been ordered to Northern Ireland.* **3** You **order** goods that you are going to pay for from a manufacturer or supplier when you ask them to make them for you or send them to you: *I've ordered new chair covers from Sproules.* □ *The book you want is not in stock, but we can order it for you.* □ *Would you order me a copy too?* **4** You **order** food or drink in a restaurant or bar when you ask the person serving you to bring it to you: *The waiter inquired if we were ready to order.* □ *I phoned room service and ordered some sandwiches.* □ *I've ordered you a tomato juice.* **5** You **order** a taxi when you arrange for one to come for you: *I've ordered a cab for 7 o'clock.* □ *Could you order a taxi to take me to the airport?* **6** You **order** something when you arrange or organize it satisfactorily: *I need a moment to order my thoughts.* □ *Some people never manage to order their lives properly.* [*same as* **arrange, compose, organize**]
▻ ***noun***: **orders**
1 (*often in the plural*) An **order** is a command or instruction to do something, given by someone in authority: *We had not yet received the order to advance.* □ *You have been given your orders; please carry them out efficiently.* □ *I was only obeying orders.* □ *The hospital had been closed on the orders of the local authority.* □ *'Go to bed, and that's an order!'* [*same as* **command, instruction**]
2 a You place, or put in, an **order** for goods with a manufacturer or supplier when you ask them to make them for you or send them to you: *I'd like to place an order for stationery, please.* □ *I think Jane was dealing with your order.* □ *resulting in serious delays to the processing of export orders* □ *I regret that we cannot meet your order.* □ *Please ensure that your order form is filled in correctly.* **b** The goods that are being supplied are also referred to as your **order**: *Your order will be ready for collection on Saturday.* □ *We shall deliver your*

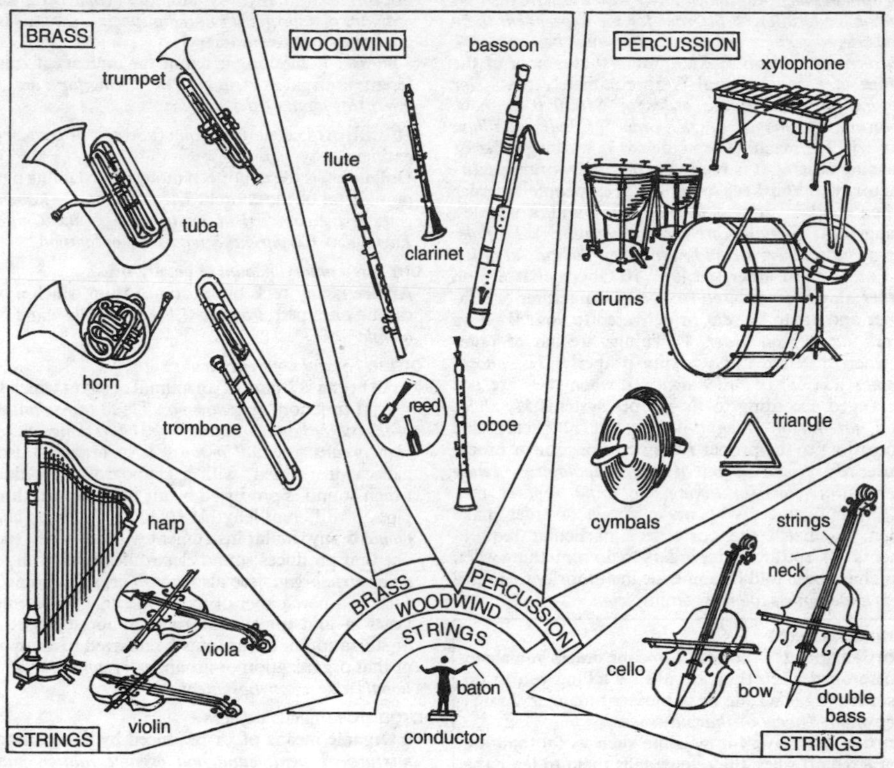

order this afternoon. **c** At a restaurant a waiter or waitress takes your **order** when you tell them what food or drink you would like. **d** (*BrE count or uncount*) An **order** is also a form or slip with instructions to a bank or post office to pay the person presenting it a certain amount of money: *You can pay by international money order* □ *She regularly sent me a postal order for my birthday.*
3 (*uncount or used in the singular*) Things are put in a particular **order** when they placed, arranged or dealt with one after another according to some system: *Our names were read out in alphabetical order.* □ *The dictionary lists meanings in order of frequency.* □ *Put your aims in order of importance.* □ *They announce the winner and runners-up in reverse order.* □ *The programme had now been re-arranged in a different order.* **4** There is **order** somewhere when **a** (*uncount*) things are properly organized, or are in their proper places, or are dealt with at the proper time: *She spent her first morning reducing my filing system to some sort of order* □ *It was time I introduced a little order into my chaotic existence.* [*opposite* **disorder**, **chaos**] **b** (*uncount*) people obey laws or rules and live together peacefully without fighting or causing disturbances: *The police were called in to restore order.* □ *less and less respect for law and order.* [*opposite* **disorder**] **5** (*uncount*) At a meeting, or in parliament, **order** is the conducting of business according to the rules: *One member intervened on a point of order.* **6** (*used in the singular*) The way things are organized in any society, *eg* with respect to what and who is considered important, can be referred to as an **order** of a certain kind: *The old order had changed.* □ *challenging the established social order.*

7 a (*used in the singular*) Something that is of a superior or inferior **order** is of good or bad quality: *He was accustomed to accommodation of a rather more luxurious order.* **b** (*with a singular or plural verb*) An **order** is a group of people, especially monks or nuns, who lead their lives according to a particular set of religious or other rules: *a monastic order founded by St Bruno of Cologne.* □ *The Order have recently received back several of the palaces taken over by the communists.* **c** (*BrE*) People are awarded honours with the title 'the **Order** of something' for distinguished service to their country or its culture: *He was awarded the Order of Merit in 1925.*

▻ ***phrases*** **1** (*informal*) You call something that you are expected to do **a tall order** if it seems rather unreasonable. **2** Something that is to be done, or that is forbidden, **by order of** someone in authority has been made compulsory, or forbidden, by that person or body: *No entry for Unauthorized Persons. By Order.* **3** A meeting is **called to order** when the chairman requests those attending it to conduct themselves according to the rules of procedure. **4** Things are **in order a** when they are tidy or properly organized: *I should put my financial affairs in order.* **b** when they are arranged one after the other according to some system: *I've put the slides in order, so don't change them round.* **c** when there is nothing wrong with them: *Her passport and other personal documents appeared to be in order* □ *Would it be in order for me to inform my wife and family about the proposed move?* **5** You do something **in order to** achieve some result when you do it with that purpose: *I had to shout in order to make myself heard above the noise of the waterfall.* □ *I tiptoed past* *their door in order not to wake them.* ▫ *We came to Britain in order that the children should receive the best possible education.* ▫ *In order for the experiment to be considered genuine the participants must be non-native speakers of English.* **6** An amount that is **in** or **of the order of** a certain total is approximately that: *Her salary must be in the order of $100000 by now.* ▫ *awarded damages of the order of half a million pounds.* **7** A machine or vehicle is **in working order** or **running order** if it is ready for use and working satisfactorily. **8** You **keep order** or **keep** people **in order** when you keep control of a situation and of people's behaviour: *The police are here to keep order.* ▫ *I'd make an awful teacher; I could never keep the kids in order.* **9** For **law and order** see **law**. **10** Goods that are **on order** have been ordered from a manufacturer or supplier and are to be sent or delivered to you: *We have fresh supplies on order.* **11** Things are **out of order** **a** when they are not working properly: *The photocopier was out of order again.* **b** when they are not arranged according to the proper system: *My slides had got out of order.* **c** if they are not acceptable according to the proper rules of behaviour or procedure: *My remark was out of order. I apologize.* ▫ *I may be out of order in taking the initiative over this.* **12** Manufacturers who make goods **to order** make them to match the customer's particular requirements. **13** You are **under orders** to do something when you have been told by someone in authority to do it: *I was under orders to arrest on suspicion.*

phrasal verbs

order about *or* **around** Someone **orders** you **about** or **around** when they are always telling you to do something in a rude or unpleasant manner: *I won't be ordered about by that silly man.*

order off Players in a game such as football **are ordered off** when the referee tells them to leave the field, *eg* because they have behaved badly or committed a serious foul.

ordered /'ɔːdəd/ *adjective*
Something that is **ordered** is well organized and arranged: *a well-ordered society.*

orderly /'ɔːdəlɪ/ *adjective*; *noun*

▻ ***adjective***
1 Something that is **orderly** is well organized or arranged: *The office records are neat and orderly.* **2** Someone who is **orderly** organizes and arranges things neatly and efficiently: *She is very orderly in her habits.* **3 Orderly** also means well-behaved and peaceful: *They formed an orderly queue.* ▫ *an orderly crowd.* [*opposite* **disorderly**]

▻ ***noun***: **orderlies**
1 In a hospital, an **orderly** is a male attendant or helper who has no medical qualifications and who does various jobs, such as moving patients. **2** In the army, an **orderly** is a soldier who carries an officer's orders and messages.

ordinal /'ɔːdɪnəl/ *noun*: **ordinals**
An **ordinal**, or **ordinal number**, is a number which shows a position in a sequence rather than quantity: *'First', 'second', 'eleventh', and 'hundredth' are ordinals.* [compare **cardinal number**]

ordinarily /ɔːdɪ'nɛrɪlɪ/ *adverb*
Ordinarily means **a** in an ordinary way: *They were behaving quite ordinarily.* **b** (*sentence adverb*) usually or generally: *The lambs would ordinarily be sent to market when they were three to six months old.* ▫ *'Does it get very windy here?' 'Not ordinarily.'*

ordinary /'ɔːdɪnrɪ/ *adjective*
Something is **ordinary** when it is usual or normal and not different in any way: *ordinary people* ▫ *It's just an ordinary restaurant; it's nothing special.* [*same as* **familiar**; compare **extraordinary**]

▻ ***phrases*** Something is **out of the ordinary** if it is different, unusual or strange: *I'm looking for a dress that is a little bit out of the ordinary.*

ordination /ɔːdɪ'neɪʃən/ *noun* (*uncount or count*): **ordinations**
Ordination is the act or ceremony of ordaining a priest or minister of the church: *The ordination of women has caused a great deal of controversy in the Church of England.* ▫ *His parents attended his ordination.*

ore /ɔː(r)/ *noun* (*uncount or count*): **ores**
An **ore** is any rock or substance from which a metal can be obtained: *iron ore* ▫ *Bauxite is the main ore of aluminium.*

organ /'ɔːgən/ *noun*: **organs**
1 An **organ** is a part of an animal or plant which has a special function: *It is now possible to transplant many of the major human organs.* ▫ *the heart, lungs and other vital organs* ▫ *sexual organs.* **2** An **organ** is also **a** a musical instrument with a keyboard and pedals, in which sound is produced by air being forced through pipes of different lengths: *He plays the organ and the piano.* **b** any similar instrument without pipes, such as one that produces sound electronically or with reeds: *an electric organ.* [see also **mouth organ**] **3** Something such as a newspaper or magazine, that represents the views of and spreads information about a particular organization or group, may be referred to as an **organ** of that organization or group: *an organ of the international trade union movement.*

organic /ɔː'ganɪk/ *adjective*
1 Organic means of or produced by living things. (*a mixture of peat, sand and organic matter, such as manure or compost.*) [*opposite* **inorganic**] **2 Organic** also means of or concerning the organs of the body: *an organic disease* ▫ *The illness doesn't appear to be organic.* **3** (*formal*) **Organic** structures or systems are made up of related parts each with a special function in making the whole structure or system work. **4 Organic** food is produced by **organic** gardening or agriculture which uses natural methods, without artificial chemicals, to fertilize the soil and control pests and diseases: *organic vegetables* ▫ *organic farming.* — *adverb* **organically:** *There's nothing organically wrong with him.* ▫ *They farm organically.* ▫ *organically grown potatoes.*

organisation see **organization**.

organisational see **organizational**.

organise see **organize**.

organised see **organized**.

organism /'ɔːgənɪzm/ *noun*: **organisms**
An **organism** is **1** a living thing, often a very small one that cannot be seen unless you look at it through a microscope: *the organism that causes malaria* ▫ *viruses and other harmful organisms.* **2** a single plant or animal made up of a number of parts that work together: *a coral reef made up of thousands of individual living organisms.*

organist /'ɔːgənɪst/ *noun*: **organists**
An **organist** is a person who plays the organ: *He is the church organist.*

organization or **organisation** /ɔːgənaɪ'zeɪʃən/ *noun*: **organizations**
1 An **organization** is a group of people working together in an organized way for a specific purpose:

She is a member of several voluntary organizations. □ *a trade union organization* □ *He's the head of a huge international organization.* **2** (*uncount*) The **organization** of something is the activity of arranging it or making it happen: *The expedition will require a lot of organization.* **3 Organization** is also the state or condition of being organized: *The examiner will be assessing the organization and presentation of your work as well as its content.*

organizational or **organisational** /ɔ:gənɪ'zeɪʃənəl/ *adjective*
1 Someone who has good **organizational** skills, is good at organizing and arranging things. **2 Organizational** is also used to decribe things that are related to organizations: *They have organizational links with several groups operating on the Continent.*

organize or **organise** /'ɔ:gənaɪz/ *verb*: **organizes, organizing, organized**
1 If you **organize** a collection of things, you arrange them into an efficient system or to give them an orderly structure: *She organized his papers so that he could find each one easily.* □ *The children were organized into groups according to ability.* **2** If you **organize** an event, you make arrangements or preparations for it which usually involve some time and effort: *The school had organized a trip to the seaside.* □ *He is organizing a surprise party for her birthday.* **3** When a group of workers **organize** or someone **organizes** them, they form themselves or are formed into an organization, especially a trade union, so that they have more power to negotiate with their employers: *He organized the workers into a trade union.* — *noun* **organizer:** *He's a brilliant organizer.* □ *a trade union organizer.*

organized or **organised** /'ɔ:gənaɪzd/ *adjective*
1 Organized events or activities have been planned or arranged: *a well-organized tour* □ *organized crime.* **2** If you say that someone is an **organized** person, you mean that they work in an orderly and efficient way: *She's so organized, she always knows where everything is.* [*opposite* **disorganized**]

orgasm /'ɔ:gazm/ *noun*: **orgasms**
An **orgasm** is the highest point of sexual excitement.

orgy /'ɔ:dʒɪ/ *noun*: **orgies**
1 An **orgy** is a wild party where people get involved in sexual activities, often after drinking large amounts of alcohol. **2** You can also refer to any activity that is done in an excessive or extreme way as an **orgy**: *an orgy of shopping.*

Orient /'ɔ:rɪənt/ *noun* (*used in the singular*; *formal or literary*)
The **Orient** is the East, especially countries of the Far East, such as China and Japan: *spices of the Orient.*

orient see **orientate**.

oriental /ɔ:rɪ'ɛntəl/ *adjective*
Oriental things come from, or are associated with, the Orient, especially China and Japan: *His features were vaguely oriental.* □ *oriental cookery* □ *oriental languages.*

orientate /'ɔ:rɪənteɪt/ *verb*: **orientates, orientating, orientated**
(also *AmE* **orient** /'ɔ:rɪɛnt/)
1 You **orientate** yourself when you find out where you are by using a compass or by looking at a map or at features of the surrounding landscape: *They stopped on the brow of the hill and tried to orientate themselves by identifying various landmarks.* **2** Someone or something that **is orientated** towards a certain thing aims at it, or is inclined towards it: *She's more career-orientated than her sister.* □ *The course is orientated towards older women who have not worked for some years.* — *noun* (*uncount*) **orientation** /ɔ:rɪən'teɪʃən/: *Individuals are entitled to equal respect, regardless of their sexual orientation.*

orienteering /ɔ:rɪən'tɪərɪŋ/ *noun* (*uncount*)
Orienteering is a sport in which contestants run over an unknown course, especially through forests and across country, finding their way with a map and compass.

orifice /'ɒrɪfɪs/ *noun*: **orifices** (*formal*)
An **orifice** is an opening or hole, especially in the body.

origin /'ɒrɪdʒɪn/ *noun* (*count or uncount*): **origins**
1 The place or source from which something first comes or begins can be referred to as its **origin** or **origins**: *a custom of unknown origin* □ *They are trying to trace the origin of the pollution.* □ *a word of Greek origin* □ *a theory about the origins of the universe.* **2** You can also refer to the family, class, country or race that a person comes from as his or her **origin** or **origins**: *Her family is of Scandinavian origin.* □ *He tried to keep his humble origins a secret.*

original /ə'rɪdʒɪnəl/ *adjective*; *noun*
▻ ***adjective***
1 Original things are things that have existed from the beginning or were the first or earliest: *The original owner of the house was an architect.* □ *The original inhabitants of the islands were thought to have been people of Polynesian descent.* **2** You can also use **original** to describe something that has been newly created or formed or which has never been done or thought of before: *He paints in a very original way.* □ *That's a very original idea.* [*opposite* **unoriginal**] **3 Original** is also used to describe a person who is able to produce new ideas: *He is an original thinker.* **4** An **original** document or work of art is the first that was made and from which copies or reproductions may have been made: *This isn't the original manuscript; it's just a facsimile.* □ *The play is an adaptation of an original work by an unknown American writer.*
▻ ***noun***: **originals**
1 An **original** is the first example of something which is copied, reproduced or translated to produce others. **2** If you say that someone is an **original**, you mean there is no other person like them.

originality /ərɪdʒɪ'nalɪtɪ/ *noun* (*uncount*)
Originality is the quality of being new and different: *His writing lacks originality.*

originally /ə'rɪdʒɪnəlɪ/ *adverb*
1 Originally means in or from the beginning: *He has lived in England all his life, though his family is from Ireland originally.* □ *The walled garden was originally used for growing fruit and vegetables.* **2 Originally** also means in a new and different way: *She dresses very originally.*

originate /ə'rɪdʒɪneɪt/ *verb*: **originates, originating, originated**
1 Something **originated** at a particular place or time when it began or came into existence there or then: *The practice originated in the Middle Ages.* **2** Someone **originates** something when they are the first to do it or they create it: *He originated the fashion.* [*same as* **introduce**]

ornament /'ɔ:nəmənt/ *noun*: **ornaments**
An **ornament** is an object that people put on display in their homes because it is attractive to look at: *porcelain figures and other ornaments* □ *She was dusting the ornaments on the mantelpiece.* [see picture at **living-room**]

ornamental /ɔ:nə'mɛntəl/ *adjective*
Ornamental things are things whose main purpose is

to decorate or to look attractive rather than for any practical use: *an ornamental pond* □ *an ornamental sword.*

ornamentation /ɔːnəmɛnˈteɪʃən/ *noun* (*uncount*)
1 Ornamentation is the process of decorating: *The ornamentation of the building was carried out by skilled craftsmen.* **2 Ornamentation** is also the state of being decorated: *iron gates with elaborate ornamentation.*

ornate /ɔːˈneɪt/ *adjective*
Something that is **ornate** has a lot of decoration: *The temple walls were covered with ornate carvings.* □ *The women wore ornate headdresses made from solid silver decorated with beads.*

ornithology /ɔːnɪˈθɒlədʒɪ/ *noun* (*uncount*)
Ornithology is the scientific study of birds and their behaviour: *He is interested in ornithology.* — *noun* **ornithologist:** *ornithologists and bird watchers.*

orphan /ˈɔːfən/ *noun; verb*
▷ ***noun***: **orphans**
An **orphan** is a person, especially a child, whose parents are both dead: *His parents were killed leaving him an orphan.* □ *a charity for widows and orphans.*
▷ ***verb*** (*in the passive*): **orphaned**
A person, especially a child, **is orphaned** when he or she is caused to become an orphan by the death of both his or her parents: *She was orphaned at the age of six and lived with foster parents until she was sixteen.*

orphanage /ˈɔːfənɪdʒ/ *noun*: **orphanages**
An **orphanage** is an institution that provides a home for orphan children.

orthodox /ˈɔːθədɒks/ *adjective*
1 Orthodox methods, practices or ideas are those which are established or generally accepted: *orthodox medicine* □ *an orthodox approach.* [*same as* **conventional**; *opposite* **unorthodox**] **2 Orthodox** is also used to describe people that follow the older, more traditional practices of their religion: *an orthodox Jew* □ *the Greek Orthodox Church.*

orthodoxy /ˈɔːθədɒksɪ/ *noun*: **orthodoxies**
1 (*uncount*) **Orthodoxy** is the state of being orthodox or of holding orthodox beliefs. **2** An **orthodoxy** is a traditional belief or a generally accepted opinion about something.

oscillate /ˈɒsɪleɪt/ *verb* (*formal*): **oscillates, oscillating, oscillated**
1 To **oscillate** means to move from one position to another and back again regularly and repeatedly. **2** When someone **oscillates** between two feelings, opinions or types of behaviour, they keep changing from one to the other: *His mood oscillated between elation and severe depression.* [*same as* **swing**]

ostensible /ɒˈstɛnsɪbəl/ *adjective* (*formal*)
An **ostensible** reason or cause is the one that is stated or claimed but which may not necessarily be the true one: *The ostensible purpose of the conference was to foster good relations between the various states.* [*same as* **supposed**] — *adverb* **ostensibly:** *His arrest was ostensibly for a criminal offence, but was really for political reasons.* [*same as* **supposedly**]

ostentation /ɒstɛnˈteɪʃən/ *noun* (*uncount; formal*)
Ostentation is behaviour which makes a public or open display of wealth, knowledge or importance that is intended to attract attention or admiration.

ostentatious /ɒstɛnˈteɪʃəs/ *adjective* (*formal*)
Something that is **ostentatious** is designed or intended to attract attention or admiration: *an ostentatious display of wealth* □ *ostentatious jewellery.* [*same as* **showy, flamboyant**] — *adverb* **ostentatiously:** *He was dressed ostentatiously in the brightest and most expensive fabrics.* [*same as* **flamboyantly**]

ostracize or **ostracise** /ˈɒstrəsaɪz/ *verb* (*formal*): **ostracizes, ostracizing, ostracized**
To **ostracize** a person means to deliberately exclude that person from a group or from society by refusing to speak to them or be friendly with them: *He was ostracized by his former workmates for refusing to join the strike.* [*same as* **shun**; *opposite* **accept**]

ostrich /ˈɒstrɪtʃ/ *noun*: **ostriches**
An **ostrich** is a large African bird with a long neck and legs and beautiful feathers. Ostriches can run very quickly but cannot fly.

other /ˈʌðə(r)/ *determiner; pronoun*
▷ ***determiner***
1 Other people or **other** things are people or things in addition to, or different from, the one or ones already mentioned, or the rest of any particular class of people or things: *She isn't like other women.* □ *There were a few other people waiting.* □ *I did it that way because there was no other way of doing it.* □ *The desk was full of old lists, letters and other papers.* □ *things made of plastic or some other synthetic material* □ *nursing and other similar work* □ *There's no other business to discuss, is there?* □ *Are there any other questions?* □ *What other languages do you speak besides English?*

> Notice that you never use **other** by itself with a singular count noun to refer to something additional or different; you use **another**, or you use **other** with a determiner: *There's another way we can try. Could I ask one other question?*

2 'Other people' can mean your fellow men and women: *You don't care nearly enough about other people.* **3** The **other** people or things in a group are the rest of them: *She gets teased by the other children in the class.* □ *He gave me his atlas and dictionary but all his other books were sold.* **4** The **other** person or thing is the second of two: *Where's my other shoe?* □ *I'm sure I had two copies; someone must have borrowed the other one.* □ *the other* [= the opposite] *side of the road.* **5** Something that happened 'the **other** day' or 'the **other** week' happened a few days or weeks ago: *I was talking to her only the other day.*
▷ ***pronoun:*** *Try to think of others* [= other people] *more.* □ *Some children develop more quickly than others.* □ *These ideas are fine, but there are others we can consider.* □ *Auden, Macneice and others.* □ *Could you tell the others to hurry up?* □ *Will these trousers do? My others are all at the cleaner's.* □ *I was holding the baby in one arm and a pile of washing in the other.* □ *We have two daughters, one of whom is a doctor and the other a physiotherapist.*
▷ ***phrases*** **1** For **each other** see **each**. **2** Something that happens **every other** week, month or year happens in alternate ones, *eg* a festival held every other year might be held in the years 1989, 1991, 1993, 1995, and so on. You can apply **every other** to alternate items in any kind of series: *I visit her every other day.* □ *They tried to brighten up the street by painting every other house pink.* **3** For **in other words** see **word**. **4** You say that someone is **none other than** a certain person to emphasize how surprising or impressive that is: *The guest speaker is none other than the Prince of Wales.* □ *The caller turned out to be none other than her long-lost uncle.* **5** Things that happen **one after the other** follow each other quickly: *Members of staff came into her office one after the other to congratulate her.* □ *When you've visited several galleries one after the other you forget which pictures are in which.* [see also

one after another at another] 6 **One or other** refers to either person or thing of two, or any person or thing in a larger group, when it does not matter which one it is: *Leave one or other tap running for a few minutes.* □ *One or other of our members will certainly give you a lift.* 7 For **on the other hand** see **hand**. 8 Nothing or no-one **other than** a certain thing or person means that thing or that person only: *I haven't had time to look at anything other than the first page of the report.* □ *You need take no action other than to keep me informed of any developments.* □ *There's no-one in the house other than my grandmother.* □ *He could scarcely be other than* [= he was bound to be] *amazed.* [*same as* **except, apart from**] 9 You add **or other** after words like *someone, somewhere* and *sometime* to make them seem even vaguer: *I've seen that face somewhere or other before.* 10 If you cannot **tell one** of two things or people **from the other** you cannot distinguish between them, because they are so alike.

otherwise /ˈʌðəwaɪz/ *adverb*
1 **Otherwise** means 'if not' or 'or else': *We better leave now, otherwise we will be late.* 2 **Otherwise** also means 'in other ways' or 'apart from that': *The rooms were rather small, but otherwise the hotel was very pleasant.* □ *He had a few scratches but was otherwise unhurt.* 3 **Otherwise** also means 'in a different way' or 'differently': *He was incapable of behaving otherwise.* □ *She believes he is completely honest, but I know otherwise.*
▻ ***phrase*** You use **or otherwise** when you are referring to things that are not the same as the thing you have just mentioned: *I welcome comments, critical or otherwise, from my colleagues.*

otter /ˈɒtə(r)/ *noun*: **otters**
An **otter** is an animal with smooth brown fur and webbed feet with claws. Otters hunt for their food in rivers and the sea, eating fish and shellfish.

ouch /aʊtʃ/ *interjection*
People say **ouch** when they feel a sharp sudden pain: *Ouch, that hurt!* [*same as* **ow**]

ought /ɔːt/ *modal verb* (*always used with* **to** *before the infinitive of other verbs*) (negative forms **ought not** or **oughtn't**)
1 You say someone **ought** to do something if you think **a** it would be the right thing to do: *I don't want to apologize, but I suppose I ought to.* □ *People like that ought to be locked up.* □ *You ought to be ashamed of yourself.* □ *She ought not to neglect her family.* □ *Oughtn't you to get your parents' permission?* [*same as* **should**] **b** it would be correct, or consistent with the rules: *'Oughtn't there to be a 'u' in 'manoeuvre'?' 'Oh, so there ought.'* □ *There ought to be a space between those two paragraphs.* [*same as* **should**] **c** it would be sensible, or a good idea, to do it: *You really ought to see a doctor about that cough.* □ *Ought we to lock our cases?* □ *You ought not to leave it till too late.* □ *Perhaps we ought to discuss this in more detail?* [*same as* **should**] **d** it would be an enjoyable thing to do: *It's a film you ought not to miss.* □ *You ought to try it; it's terrific!* [*same as* **should**]
2 You say that something **ought** to be so, or **ought** to happen **a** if you think it is probably so, or will probably happen: *They ought to be well on their way by now.* □ *On present performance, the French team ought to win.* □ *I posted the cheque today, so you ought to get it tomorrow.* [*same as* **should**] **b** if there is no reason why it should not be so, or not happen, according to the facts you have available to you: *This ought to be a simple task, but it isn't.* [*same as* **should**]
3 You say someone '**ought** to have' done something, or that something '**ought** to have' happened, when you are referring to the past: *I'm sorry; I ought to have told you sooner.* □ *She ought not to have spoken to you like that.* □ *Oughtn't we to have inserted the disk first?* □ *You ought to have seen her face when she heard!* □ *They ought to have arrived by now.* □ *According to the recipe the jelly ought to have set two hours ago.* □ *There were six pints in the fridge, which ought to have been plenty.* [*same as* **should** have] [compare **must, need, have** to]

ounce /aʊns/ *noun*: **ounces**
1 An **ounce** is a unit of weight used in Britain and the USA that is equal to 28.35 grams: *There are sixteen ounces in a pound.* □ *an ounce of butter* □ *Do these scales measure in ounces or grams?* [see also **fluid ounce**] 2 A very small amount of something is also sometimes referred to as an **ounce**: *I didn't have a ounce of energy left.* □ *Anyone with an ounce of common sense would be able to work it out.*

our /aʊə(r)/ *determiner* (*possessive*)
You use **our** to refer to things that belong or relate to you and one or more other people, sometimes including the person you are addressing: *My husband and I usually take our holidays separately.* □ *We've had our lunch.* □ *Is this the kind of world we want our children to grow up in?* □ *It was our last chance.* □ *Do you mind our* (or *us*) *taking a few photographs?*

ours /aʊəz/ *pronoun* (*possessive*)
You use **ours** to refer to something that belongs to you and one or more other people, sometimes including the person you are addressing: *Their children are a bit older than ours; ours haven't left school yet.* □ *'Is this your classroom?' 'No, ours is further down the corridor.'* □ *He's a distant relative of ours.* □ *in this country of ours.*

ourselves /aʊəˈsɛlvz/ *pronoun* (*reflexive*)
1 You use **ourselves a** as the object of a verb or preposition where the subject of the verb is 'we': *There was no-one serving so we helped ourselves.* □ *We really enjoy ourselves when we go out together.* □ *Jane and I had the whole house to ourselves.* **b** for emphasis, or as an emphatic form of 'us': *We'd better go round there ourselves and see what's happening.* □ *We ourselves don't do much travelling, but our son is often abroad on business.* □ *Lots of people less well off than ourselves seem to manage to have foreign holidays.* 2 If you say 'We did it **ourselves**' you mean that you and one or more other people did it without help or participation by anyone else: *'Did you employ a builder for the extension?' 'No, we built it entirely ourselves.'*
For **by ourselves** see **by**.

-ous /əs/ *suffix*
-ous is used to form adjectives that mean having a certain nature, quality or character, such as **spacious**, meaning having a lot of space.

oust /aʊst/ *verb*: **ousts, ousting, ousted**
To **oust** someone from their position or job means to force them out of it: *She was ousted from her position as leader by a group of right-wing councillors.* □ *The main aim of the generals was to oust the elected government and form a military dictatorship.* [*opposite* **install**]

out /aʊt/ *adverb; adverb or adjective*
▻ ***adverb***

Notice that **out** is an adverb only, not a preposition; use the phrase '**out** of' as the preposition.

1 a You go **out** of a place, or get **out** of something like a vehicle, when you leave it so that you are not inside it any more: *She walked out of the room.* □ *The door opened and out came Bill.* □ *I ran out into the street.* □ *I want everyone out of the office by six.* □ *We couldn't find the way out.* □ *The bus stopped and one or two people got out.* □ *I got out of bed and stretched.* [*opposite* **in, into**] **b** You are **out**, or you have gone **out**, when you are not at home, or not at your place of work: *I called but you were out.* □ *She'll be out all afternoon.* □ *I was only out for a minute.* □ *I think he's gone out for a walk.* □ *They were burgled while they were out of the house.* [*opposite* **in**] **c** You also go **out** when you do something such as go to a theatre or restaurant: *Let's go out for dinner tonight.* □ *I'm going out with Peter this evening.* **d** You look **out** of a window from inside a building when you look through it at things outside: *I glanced out of the window to see if the rain had stopped.* □ *We gazed out at the sunset.* □ *He drew the curtains and looked out.* [*opposite* **in**] **e Out** is used like *outside* or *out of doors* to mean not inside or indoors: *It's lovely and warm out today.* □ *They had to sleep out for a second night.* □ *The children have been out in the fresh air all day.* [*opposite* **inside**] **f** You live a certain distance **out**, or **out** of town, if you live that far from the centre of a town or city: *Their house is miles out.* **g** You are kept **out** of somewhere when you are prevented from getting in: *Keep the other children out of his bedroom.* □ *a high fence for keeping out the wild animals* □ *Private. Keep out.* [*opposite* **in**] **h** You are **out** of the wind or rain when you have found shelter from it: *Let's find somewhere out of the wind to sit down.* [*opposite* **in**] **i** You are **out** of danger or trouble when you are no longer exposed to it or involved in it: *He could never stay out of trouble for long.* [*opposite* **in, into**]

2 a You get something **out** of a container or other place when you remove it from there; it comes **out** when it leaves that place or becomes detached: *We'll have to move all the furniture out of the sitting room.* □ *I lifted the cat out of her basket.* □ *She opened the drawer and took out a pack of cards.* □ *The policeman took out his notebook.* □ *Get out your dictionaries.* □ *I called at the library and got out 'Hard Times'.* □ *I'll have to go to the bank and get out some money.* □ *Someone had torn a page out of the book.* □ *I copied the recipe out of her cookery book.* □ *I've got some wine, if you don't mind drinking out of plastic cups.* □ *My wallet must have fallen out of my pocket.* □ *The plug wouldn't come out of the socket.* □ *Could you get this splinter out of my finger?* [*opposite* **in, into**] **b** Something such as a mark or stain comes **out** of a fabric or surface when it disappears from it: *There was a greasy mark on my skirt which I couldn't get out.* □ *I rubbed out the pencilled comment.* **c** You get information **out** of someone if you persuade them to tell you it: *We couldn't get much out of him.* [*same as* **from**] **d** You get pleasure or some other good thing **out** of something that you do or are involved in if it that is what it provides: *She got a lot of satisfaction out of seeing her book in print.* □ *Nothing much came out of the discussion.* [*same as* **from**]

3 a A certain number of things **out** of an amount or total is that proportion of the amount or total: *One out of three marriages* [= a third of all marriages] *ends in divorce.* □ *You get ten out of ten* [= full marks] *for effort.* **b** Something is paid for **out** of some money source if that money is used to pay for it: *They have to pay for books out of their student grants.* **c** One thing is made **out** of another if the second has been used to make the first: *The best-quality paper is made out of rags.* □ *She made us party frocks out of her old ball dress.* [*same as* **from**] **d** You do something **out** of something such as shame or pity if that is what makes you do it: *I only visit them out of a sense of duty.* □ *She told him purely out of spite.* [*same as* **from**]

4 a You are **out** of something, or have run **out** of it when you have used up your supply of it: *I'm out of instant coffee.* [see also **run out** at **run**] **b** You are **out** of work when you have no job. [*opposite* **in**] **c** You are **out** of a team or other selected group when you are excluded from it: *He had been left out of the team.* [*opposite* **in**] **d** Things are **out** of order, or **out** of some other kind of proper arrangement or condition, when they not organized or working as they should be: *The cards had got out of alphabetical order.* □ *I realized I was out of step.* □ *singing out of tune* □ *I'm very out of practice.* [*opposite* **in**] **e** Something that is **out** of a certain range is beyond it: *Pupils may not go out of bounds.* □ *a performance quite out of the ordinary* □ *The best apples were just out of reach.* [*opposite* **within**] **f** Someone tricks or cheats you **out** of something when they stop you having it by some dishonest piece of behaviour: *We felt we'd been done out of our trip abroad.*

5 Out conveys various other senses in phrases and phrasal verbs, *eg* **a** spreading and distributing (*hand out, send out, spread out*). **b** deleting (*cross out*). **c** excluding (*leave out*). **d** completing, finishing or exhausting (*work out, tire out, run out*). **e** emerging (*come out, bring out*). **f** projecting (*stick out, poke out*). **g** using a loud voice (*call out, speak out, say something out loud*).

▻ ***adverb or adjective***

1 a Something that burns is **out** when it is no longer burning: *She blew the candle out.* □ *The fire's gone out.* □ *He put his cigarette out.* □ *A fire engine arrived and put the blaze out.* **b** A light is **out** if it is no longer shining: *There'd been a power cut and all the lights were out.* [*opposite* **on**] **c** A flower is **out** when its petals are at their full extent: *The snowdrops are just coming out.* □ *The daffodils aren't out yet.* **d** A book is **out** when it is published: *Her first book of poetry came out last spring.* **e** The sun, moon or stars are **out** when they are visible in the sky: *By eleven o'clock the sun was out and it was really hot.* □ *The moon came out from behind a cloud.* **f** The tide is **out** when the sea is at its furthest from the shore: *Is the tide going out or coming in?* [*opposite* **in**] **g** Workers are **out** when they are on strike.

2 a A calculation is **out** by a certain amount if that is the amount by which it is wrong: *Your total is out by three.* □ *The numbers are slightly out.* [*same as* **inaccurate, wrong**] **b** Something is **out** when it is no longer fashionable: *Tight jumpers are out.* □ *Flared jeans went out years ago.* [*opposite* **in**] **c** An idea, date or suggestion is **out** if it is not possible: *Next weekend is out; I'm visiting my parents.* [*same as* **impossible**] **d** In a game such as tennis, the ball is **out** if it lands in a part of the court where it cannot be played: *My first serve went out.* **e** Someone is **out** to do something or **out** for something when they are determined to achieve it: *He's out to make as much money as he can.* □ *She's out for revenge.* □ *People nowadays are just out for themselves.*

▻ ***phrases*** **1** You get **out and about** when you get away from your house and lead a sociable life, *eg* after being ill: *It's good to see you out and about again.* **2** You feel **out of it** when you feel that people are excluding you from their activities. **3** If you say **'out with it!'** to someone, you want to hear what they have to say.

out-and-out /aʊt and ˈaʊt/ *adjective*
Out-and-out means complete or thorough: *an out-and-out liar.*

outback /ˈaʊtbak/ *noun* (*used in the singular*)

The **outback** is the part of a country, especially the inland part of Australia, that is a long way away from cities and the areas where most people live: *a cattle station in the outback.*

outboard /'aʊtbɔːd/ *noun*: **outboards**
An **outboard**, or **outboard motor**, is a motor or engine that can be fixed to the back of a small boat.

outbreak /'aʊtbreɪk/ *noun*: **outbreaks**
An **outbreak** of something bad or unpleasant is a sudden appearance or occurrence of it: *There was an outbreak of cholera in the camp.* ▫ *sporadic outbreaks of violence.*

outbuilding /'aʊtbɪldɪŋ/ *noun*: **outbuildings**
An **outbuilding** is a building such as a barn, stable or garage that is separate from but within the grounds of a main building or house: *a farmhouse with several outbuildings.* [compare **outhouse**]

outburst /'aʊtbɜːst/ *noun*: **outbursts**
An **outburst** is **1** a sudden, violent expression of strong emotion, especially anger: *Apologise immediately for that disgraceful outburst!* ▫ *Nothing can justify such a disgraceful outburst of rage.* **2** a sudden period of great or violent activity: *a spontaneous outburst of cheering.*

outcast /'aʊtkɑːst/ *noun*: **outcasts**
An **outcast** is a person who has been rejected by his or her friends or by society: *a social outcast* ▫ *They were treated as outcasts.*

outclass /aʊtklɑːs/ *verb*: **outclasses, outclassing, outclassed**
Someone or something **outclasses** another person or thing that they are much better than: *They were outclassed by the team from Birmingham.* [*same as* **outshine, outdo**]

outcome /'aʊtkʌm/ *noun*: **outcomes**
An **outcome** is a result or consequence: *a satisfactory outcome* ▫ *The outcome of their meeting was an agreement on trade.*

outcrop /'aʊtkrɒp/ *noun*: **outcrops**
1 An **outcrop** is a rock or group of rocks which sticks out above the surface of the ground: *an outcrop of limestone* ▫ *They climbed to the top of a rocky outcrop.* **2** An **outcrop** is also a number of things that appear on the surface of something: *an outcrop of spots on his forehead.*

outcry /'aʊtkraɪ/ *noun* (*usually in the singular*): **outcries**
An **outcry** is a strong reaction or protest by a large number of people: *The decision produced a public outcry.*

outdated /aʊt'deɪtɪd/ *adjective*
Something that is **outdated** is out of fashion or is no longer used: *outdated methods* ▫ *His ideas are a little outdated.* [see also **out-of-date**]

outdistance /aʊt'dɪstəns/ *verb*: **outdistances, outdistancing, outdistanced**
A runner or competitor **outdistances** other runners or competitors in a race when he or she runs faster or further than them and leaves them behind: *He outdistanced his nearest rival by more than half a kilometre.*

outdo /aʊt'duː/ *verb*: **outdoes** /aʊt'dʌz/: **outdoing, outdid** /aʊt'dɪd/: **outdone** /aʊt'dʌn/
You **outdo** someone else when you do much better than them: *He was aiming to outdo the school long-jump champion.* ▫ *He outdid all the other students in his year.* ▫ *His friend bought a cottage in France, and not to be outdone, he bought a villa in Italy.*

outdoor /'aʊtdɔː(r)/ *adjective*
1 Outdoor activities or events happen or are done in the open air rather than inside a building: *an outdoor concert* ▫ *It is mainly an outdoor job.* **2 Outdoor** things are situated in or suitable for the open air: *outdoor clothes* ▫ *an outdoor swimming pool.* **3** If you describe someone as an **outdoor** person, you mean that they spend, or prefer to spend, a lot of time in the open air. [*opposite* **indoor**]

outdoors /aʊt'dɔːz/ *adverb*
(also **out of doors**) Something that happens or is done **outdoors**, happens or is done in the open air, not inside a building: *The children aren't allowed to play outdoors when it is raining.* [*opposite* **indoors**]

outer /'aʊtə(r)/ *adjective*
1 Outer means on the outside: *She peeled off the outer layers of the onion.* **2 Outer** also means further from the centre or middle: *outer London.* [*opposite* **inner**]

outermost /'aʊtəmoʊst/ *adjective*
Outermost means furthest from the centre or middle: *the orbit of the outermost planets* ▫ *the outermost regions of space.* [*opposite* **innermost**]

outer space /aʊtə 'speɪs/ *noun* (*uncount*)
Outer space is the area beyond the Earth's atmosphere where the stars are: *visitors from outer space.*

outfall /'aʊtfɔːl/ *noun*: **outfalls**
An **outfall** is the place where water from a sewer or stream flows out, especially into the sea.

outfit /'aʊtfɪt/ *noun*: **outfits**
1 An **outfit** is a set of clothes that are worn together: *She bought a new outfit for the wedding.* **2** (*informal*) Some people refer to a business or an organization as an **outfit**: *He works for an outfit based in Hong Kong.*

outflow /'aʊtfloʊ/ *noun*: **outflows**
An **outflow** is a quantity of something that flows or moves out of one place into another: *In October, there was a large outflow of funds from building societies.*

outgoing /aʊt'goʊɪŋ/ *adjective*; *noun*
▻ ***adjective***
1 If you say that someone is **outgoing** or has an **outgoing** personality, you mean they are friendly and interested in meeting and talking to other people. [*opposite* **introvert**] **2** /'aʊtgoʊɪŋ/ **Outgoing** is also used to describe someone who is leaving a job, or something that is leaving a place: *the outgoing president* ▫ *All outgoing flights have been cancelled.* [*opposite* **incoming**]
▻ ***noun*** /'aʊtgoʊɪŋz/ (*used in the plural*): **outgoings**
Your **outgoings** are the amounts of money that you spend: *His outgoings have been exceeding his income.* [*same as* **expenditure**]

outgrow /aʊt'groʊ/ *verb*: **outgrows, outgrowing, outgrew** /aʊt'gruː/, **outgrown** /aʊt'groʊn/
1 You **outgrow** things, such as shoes or clothes, when you grow too large for them. **2** When you **outgrow** things, such as childhood illnesses or childish behaviour, you become too old or mature for them: *Don't worry too much about his tantrums; he will outgrow them eventually.* [*same as* **grow out of**]

outhouse /'aʊthaʊs/ *noun*: **outhouses**
An **outhouse** is a building such as a shed that is built close to a house: *They keep the coal in a little outhouse.* [compare **outbuilding**]

outing /'aʊtɪŋ/ *noun*: **outings**
An **outing** is a short journey or trip away from your home, school or place of work, made for pleasure: *They went on an outing to the seaside.* ▫ *a school outing* ▫ *a works outing.* [*same as* **trip**]

outlandish /aʊt'landɪʃ/ *adjective*
You can describe someone's or something's appearance or behaviour as **outlandish** if it is very strange and unusual: *He wore the most outlandish clothes.* ▫ *Their ideas are outlandish.* [*same as* **eccentric**]

outlast /aʊt'lɑːst/ *verb*: **outlasts, outlasting, outlasted**
To **outlast** means to last or live longer than someone or something: *These buildings have outlasted several generations of inhabitants.* [compare **outlive**]

outlaw /'aʊtlɔː/ *noun*; *verb*
▻ ***noun***: **outlaws** (*old*)
An **outlaw** is a person who has broken the law and who lives outside society trying to avoid capture or punishment: *a band of outlaws* □ *He was declared an outlaw.*
▻ ***verb***: **outlaws, outlawing, outlawed**
Something that **is outlawed** is made illegal: *legislation that outlaws the keeping and breeding of certain dangerous dogs* □ *The production and sale of alcohol was outlawed.*

outlay /'aʊtleɪ/ *noun* (*usually in the singular*): **outlays**
An **outlay** is money that is spent, especially money that is invested or spent in order to start a business or project: *a guaranteed income of £500 per annum for an initial capital outlay of £5000.*

outlet /'aʊtlɛt/ *noun*: **outlets**
1 An **outlet** is a hole, pipe or passage through which something, *eg* water or steam, can flow out or escape. **2** An **outlet** is also an activity which allows you to use or release energy or strong feelings: *Sport provides children with an outlet for their energies.* **3** An **outlet** is also a market or shop in which the goods produced by a particular manufacturer are sold: *a retail outlet* □ *The company has opened several new outlets throughout the United Kingdom.*

outline /'aʊtlaɪn/ *noun*; *verb*
▻ ***noun***: **outlines**
1 An **outline** is a line forming or marking the outer edge or shape of an object: *Snow masked the outlines of eaves, gutters and railings.* □ *They could see the outline of a large sailing ship through the mist.* **2** An **outline** is also a statement or description of the main points or most important facts about something, without the details: *Can you give me a brief outline of what will be discussed at the meeting?*
▻ ***verb***: **outlines, outlining, outlined**
1 An object **is outlined** when its general shape or outer edge is seen or drawn: *The three figures could be seen clearly outlined against the sky.* □ *He drew a design for the garden, outlining the positions of the flowerbeds and paths.* **2** You **outline** an idea or plan when you give a general description of its main points or features.

outlive /aʊt'lɪv/ *verb*: **outlives, outliving, outlived**
You **outlive** someone when you live or survive longer than they do: *He outlived his older brother by fifteen years.* [compare **outlast**]

outlook /'aʊtlʊk/ *noun*: **outlooks**
1 An **outlook** is a view on which you look out: *A house with a pleasant outlook over farmland and rolling hills.* **2** Your **outlook** is your attitude or way of looking at things: *The experience has changed his whole outlook on life.* □ *Travel has broadened his outlook and made him more tolerant.* **3** (*used in the singular*) The **outlook** for a particular thing or situation is the way in which it seems likely to develop in the future: *The outlook for the economy is bleak.*

outlying /'aʊtlaɪɪŋ/ *adjective*
Outlying places are far away from the centre of a town or city: *Children from the outlying villages were taken to school by bus.*

outmanoeuvre (*AmE* **outmaneuver**) /aʊtmə'nuːvə(r)/ *verb*: **outmanoeuvres, outmanoeuvring, outmanoeuvred**
If you are **outmanoeuvred** by someone, they put you in a position of disadvantage by making more skilful or effective movements than you do.

outmoded /aʊt'moʊdɪd/ *adjective*
Something that is **outmoded** is out of date and no longer in fashion: *outmoded ideas.*

outnumber /aʊt'nʌmbə(r)/ *verb* (*especially in the passive*): **outnumbered**
A group of people or things **is outnumbered** by another when it has fewer people or things than the other group: *The police were outnumbered ten to one by the rioters.*

out of bounds See **bound**.

out of date /aʊt əv 'deɪt/ *adjective*
Something that is **out of date** is no longer used or useful because it is not modern: *Their attitudes are completely out of date.* □ *an out-of-date timetable.* [*same as* **outmoded**; *opposite* **fashionable, new**]

out of doors see **outdoors**.

out of pocket see **pocket**.

out-of-the-way /aʊt əv ðə 'weɪ/ *adjective*
Out-of-the-way places are not easy to get to and are not often visited as a result: *He has always lived in out-of-the-way places.*

out of work /aʊt əv 'wɜːk/
Someone who is **out of work** has no job: *out-of-work actors.*

outpatient /'aʊtpeɪʃənt/ *noun*: **outpatients**
An **outpatient** is a patient who visits a hospital for treatment but does not stay there overnight.

outpost /'aʊtpoʊst/ *noun* (*humorous*): **outposts**
You can refer to a place that is far away from towns and cities, or a place in a faraway country, as an **outpost**: *He was transferred to some distant outpost in the north of Scotland.*

output /'aʊtpʊt/ *noun* (*uncount or count*): **outputs**
1 The amount that a worker, machine, factory or area of industry produces is called its **output**: *a decline in industrial output due to the recession* □ *The factory has an output of 500 units per day.* [*same as* **production**] **2** The **output** of a computer is the information it produces in either printed or coded form after processing.

outrage /'aʊtreɪdʒ/ *noun*; *verb*
▻ ***noun***: **outrages**
1 An **outrage** is an event or act whose violence, cruelty or lack of justice shocks people and makes them very angry: *outrages committed against innocent civilians* □ *His behaviour was an outrage against public decency.* **2** (*uncount*) If you have a feeling or sense of **outrage**, you are very shocked and angry.
▻ ***verb*** /'aʊtreɪdʒ/: **outrages, outraging, outraged**
If something **outrages** you, it makes you feel very shocked and angry: *He was outraged by the suggestion that he had been telling lies.*

outrageous /aʊt'reɪdʒəs/ *adjective*
1 If you say that something is **outrageous**, you mean that you find it very shocking and immoral: *outrageous behaviour* □ *That children should be allowed to suffer in that way is outrageous.* □ *These prices are outrageous.* [*same as* **disgraceful**] **2 Outrageous** is also used to describe things that are very unusual or intended to shock people: *an outrageous hat* □ *an outrageous performer.* —*adverb* **outrageously:** *You behaved outrageously.* □ *The dress designer's clothes are outrageously expensive.*

outran see **outrun**.

outright /aʊt'raɪt/ *adverb*; *adjective*
▻ ***adverb***
1 Outright means immediately or instantly: *The soldier stepped on a mine and was killed outright.* **2 Outright** also means completely, totally or clearly:

He can afford to buy the land outright (without having to borrow money to buy it). ▫ *She won the competition outright.* **3 Outright** is also used to describe something that is done openly and directly without hiding anything: *I asked him outright if he was going to resign.*

▻ ***adjective*** /'aʊtraɪt/

Outright means **1** complete: *an outright lie.* **2** clear: *the outright winner.* **3** open or honest: *outright hostility.*

outrun /aʊt'rʌn/ *verb*: **outruns, outrunning, outran** /aʊt'ran/, **outrun**

1 If you **outrun** someone, you run faster or further than they do: *The fox outran the hounds and escaped unhurt.* **2** To **outrun** something also means to do better than or go beyond it: *His enthusiasm outran his ability to complete the task.* [*same as* **exceed**]

outset /'aʊtset/ *noun* (*used in the singular*)

▻ ***phrase*** If something happens or is done **at** or **from the outset**, it happens or is done at the beginning or start of a period of time or process: *He knew at the outset how risky the venture was likely to be.* ▫ *The residents have been involved in the project from the outset.*

outshine /aʊt'ʃaɪn/ *verb*: **outshines, outshining, outshone** /aʊt'ʃɒn/

If one person or thing **outshines** another, they are very much better than the other: *At drawing and painting, she outshone all the other students in her year.* [*same as* **outclass**]

outside /aʊt'saɪd/ *preposition*; *adverb*; *noun*; *adjective*

▻ ***preposition*** (*AmE* also **outside of**)

1 You are **outside** a building when you are close to it but not in it: *The strange car had been parked outside our house for several days.* [*opposite* **inside**] **2** You are **outside** a room when you are close to the door into it: *A queue was forming outside the bathroom.* ▫ *A newspaper had been left outside the door.* [*opposite* **inside**] **3** You are **outside** a city, country or area if you are not in it: *special concessions for members living outside London* ▫ *They bought a house just outside Glasgow.* ▫ *Outside Britain, Elgar's works are not well known.* [*opposite* **in**] **4** People **outside** a community or organization do not belong to it, or are not involved in it: *No-one outside the family had been told.* ▫ *countries outside the European Union.* [*opposite* **within**] **5** Something that is **outside** a particular range is not included in it: *Occasionally a doctor will encounter symptoms quite outside the scope of his or her experience.* [*opposite* **within**] **6** Things that happen **outside** a certain period of time do not happen during it: *A limited number of keys are available for those wishing to use the office outside working hours.* [*opposite* **inside, within**]

▻ ***adverb:*** *Is it cold outside? Do I need a coat?* ▫ *Is it still raining outside?* ▫ *There's a man outside leaning against the lamp post.* ▫ *She'd gone into the the shop leaving the pram outside.* ▫ *I emerged from his hospital room to find his daughter waiting outside.* [*opposite* **inside**]

▻ ***noun*** (*used in the singular*)

The **outside** of something is its outer side or surface, or the area surrounding it: *We couldn't open the door; there appeared to be no handle on the outside.* ▫ *Full instructions are printed on the outside of the packet.* ▫ *We're getting the outside of the house painted.* ▫ *I'd had a good look at the house from the outside.* ▫ *She usually contrived to seem calm on the outside at least.* [*opposite* **inside**; compare **exterior**]

▻ ***adjective*** /'aʊtsaɪd/

1 Outside describes **a** the outer side or surface of something: *We planned to spend the day whitewashing the outside walls of the cottage.* [*same as* **exterior**; *opposite* **inside**] **b** things not inside a building but associated with it or attached to it: *Have you turned off the outside light?* ▫ *We had an outside toilet in those days.* [*opposite* **inside**] **c** activities or other things that are not part of the organization or group you are referring to: *He enjoyed his work but had plenty of outside interests, such as his golf and his acting.* ▫ *Most publishers have to rely on outside help with editing and printing.* **2** By 'the **outside** world' you mean the things that exist and happen other than in your own home environment or the community you live in: *Boys grew up in boarding schools, knowing nothing of the outside world.* **3** The **outside** lane on a motorway carriageway is the one nearest the central division. [*opposite* **inside**] **4** If there is an **outside** chance of something happening, it may happen but is unlikely to: *There's an outside chance that she'll phone.* ▫ *only an outside chance of winning.* **5** An **outside** radio or television broadcast is one made away from the broadcasting studio.

▻ ***phrases*** When you estimate an amount at a certain number or figure **at the outside**, you mean that it cannot be more than that, and may be less: *I don't expect to be away long: ten days at the outside.* ▫ *A new part would cost £20 at the outside.* ▫ *'How many were there?' 'Oh, 50 at the outside.'*

outsider /aʊt'saɪdə(r)/ *noun*: **outsiders**

1 An **outsider** is a person who is not part of a group, or who refuses to accept the general values of society. [compare **insider**] **2** A competitor in a race or contest who is not expected to win is also sometimes called an **outsider**.

outsize /'aʊtsaɪz/ *adjective*

1 (also **outsized**) Something that is **outsize** or **outsized** is much larger than the normal or standard size: *The clown wore a funny hat and a pair of outsized shoes.* **2 Outsize** clothes are made specially for people who are larger than average: *A large woman of 95 kilos, she fought for the manufacture of outsize clothes at modest prices.*

outskirts /'aʊtskɜːts/ *noun* (*plural*)

The **outskirts** of a city or town are the parts that are furthest from the centre: *They are based in one of the industrial estates on the outskirts of Birmingham.*

outsmart /aʊt'smɑːt/ *verb* (*informal*): **outsmarts, outsmarting, outsmarted**

You **outsmart** another person when you succeed in defeating them or gaining an advantage over them by being cleverer or more cunning than they are: *The criminals outsmarted the police and escaped abroad.* [*same as* **outwit**]

outspoken /aʊt'spoʊkən/ *adjective*

Someone who is **outspoken** says openly exactly what they think or feel: *an outspoken critic of the government* ▫ *He was outspoken in his criticism.* [*same as* **frank**]

outstanding /aʊt'standɪŋ/ *adjective*

1 If a person or thing is described as **outstanding**, they are exceptionally good, especially when compared with others: *She's an outstanding musician.* ▫ *an outstanding example of its type* ▫ *Last night's performance was outstanding.* [*same as* **exceptional**] **2 Outstanding** is also used to describe something that is very obvious or of the greatest importance: *The outstanding feature of his writing is his original use of language.* **3** Something is **outstanding** if it has not yet been paid or dealt with: *He used the money to pay all his outstanding debts.* ▫ *We have a few outstanding points to deal with before the agreement can be signed.*

outstandingly /aʊt'standɪŋlɪ/ *adverb* (*intensifying*)

You can use **outstandingly** to show that the particular

quality or action you are referring to is exceptional: *She's an outstandingly gifted pianist.* □ *Even though it was his first public concert, he performed outstandingly (well).* [*same as* **exceptionally**]

outstay /aʊt'steɪ/ *verb*: **outstays, outstaying, outstayed**
If you **outstay** other people, you stay at a place longer than they do: *They outstayed all the other guests at the party and didn't leave until midnight.*
▻ *phrase* You **outstay your welcome** when you visit someone, especially at their home, and do not leave when they want or expect you to leave.

outstretched /aʊt'strɛʃt/ *adjective*
If your limbs, especially your arms, are **outstretched,** they are stretched or spread out as far as possible from your body: *She stood with outstretched arms waiting to welcome them.*

outstrip /aʊt'strɪp/ *verb*: **outstrips, outstripping, outstripped**
One thing **outstrips** another when it goes or develops faster or becomes greater in amount or importance than the other thing, leaving it behind: *Prices rose as demand outstripped production.* [*same as* **exceed**]

out-tray /'aʊttreɪ/ *noun*: **out-trays**
Your **out-tray** in your office is the tray or container into which you put letters or papers ready for posting or passing on. [see picture at **office**]

outward /'aʊtwəd/ *adjective*
1 Outward is used to describe things that are on or facing towards the outside: *The stone was roughly hewn on its outward face and smooth on the inside.* **2** Something's **outward** appearance is the way that it seems or is perceived, though it may not be the actual or true one: *There had been no outward sign that she was in any distress.* □ *To all outward appearances, she seemed calm and relaxed.* [compare **inward**] **3** An **outward** journey is one made away from a place that you are going to return to later: *The sea was calm on the outward voyage.* [*opposite* **homeward, return**; see also **outwards**]

outwardly /'aʊtwədlɪ/ *adverb*
If a person or thing displays a certain quality or feeling **outwardly**, that quality or feeling is the one that they have or appear to have when seen from the outside: *He was outwardly cheerful despite being terribly sad.* [*opposite* **inwardly**]

outwards /'aʊtwədz/ *adverb*
(also *especially AmE* **outward**)
Something that faces or moves **outwards**, faces or moves towards the outside or away from a central point: *The door opens outwards.* □ *They began their search near the village moving slowly outwards to cover the surrounding hills.* [*opposite* **inwards**]

outweigh /aʊt'weɪ/ *verb*: **outweighs, outweighing, outweighed**
If one thing **outweighs** another, it is of greater value or importance than that other thing: *The advantages of the scheme far outweigh its disadvantages.*

outwit /aʊtwɪt/ *verb*: **outwits, outwitting, outwitted**
You **outwit** someone when you defeat them or gain an advantage over them by being cleverer than they are: *Though the police had laid an elaborate trap, the criminals managed to outwit them and escape.*

outworn /aʊt'wɔːn/ *adjective*
An **outworn** method, custom or idea is no longer useful because it is old-fashioned or has been used too often: *minority parties campaigning against what they regard as an outworn system of voting.* [*same as* **outdated**]

oval /'oʊvəl/ *adjective*; *noun*
▻ ***adjective***
Oval things are shaped like an egg, so that they are wider across or around the middle than at each end: *an oval plate.*
▻ ***noun*: ovals**
An **oval** is an object with this shape: *Her face was a perfect oval.* [see picture at **shape**]

ovary /'oʊvərɪ/ *noun*: **ovaries**
1 An **ovary** is one of the two organs that produce eggs in women and other female animals. **2** The female part of a plant that produces seeds is also called an **ovary**.

ovation /ə'veɪʃən/ *noun*: **ovations**
An **ovation** is a long period of applause and cheering showing approval or welcome.
▻ *phrase* When people, who have been sitting down, give someone **a standing ovation**, they stand up to clap and cheer.

oven /'ʌvən/ *noun*: **ovens**
An **oven** is an enclosed box-like space with a door, that is heated up for baking or roasting food. [see picture at **kitchen**]
▻ *phrase* If you say that a room is **like an oven**, you mean that it uncomfortably hot.

oven glove /'ʌvən glʌv/ *noun*: **oven gloves**
Oven gloves are special gloves made of a thick material that you use for removing hot food from an oven. [see picture at **kitchen**]

ovenproof /'ʌvənpruːf/ *adjective*
Ovenproof dishes or plates are specially made so that they will not crack or break when they are put into a hot oven.

oven-ready /'ʌvən rɛdɪ/ *adjective*
Oven-ready food, especially poultry, needs no preparation and can be put straight into the oven to be cooked.

over /'oʊvə(r)/ *preposition*; *adverb*; *noun*
▻ ***preposition***
1 One thing is **over** another **a** if it is higher than it, or directly above it: *They live in the flat over ours.* □ *There was a weird carving over the door.* □ *He held a piece of mistletoe over her head* □ *seven over two divided by ten over seven.* [$= \frac{7}{2} \div \frac{10}{7}$] [*opposite* **under**; see note at **above**] **b** if it extends above it, *eg* as a protection: *people without a roof over their heads* □ *He held an umbrella over us.* [*opposite* **under**] **c** if it covers it: *She was wearing a raincoat over her summer dress.* □ *Put your hand over the answers and see how many can get right.* □ *White cloths had been spread over the tables.* □ *He pulled the blankets up over his head.* □ *I poured cream over my fruit.* □ *A blush spread over her face.* **d** if it is being supported by it and is hanging down on each side: *She hung her jacket over the back of her chair.* □ *He put his towel over the radiator to dry.*
2 a Something moves **over** a surface when it moves across it: *He strode over the fields.* □ *Her fingers moved deftly over the keys.* [*same as* **across**] **b** One thing goes **over** another when it goes from one side of it to the other: *We were now flying over the Alps.* □ *We passed over the Equator at about 5.30.* □ *There's a footbridge further on that takes you over the river.* □ *They ran along jumping over the puddles.* [compare **across**] **c** You get **over** a barrier such as a wall when you get to the other side of it by climbing or jumping across the top: *He vaulted over the railings and got away.* □ *I threw the ball back over the wall to her.* □ *We took the route over the mountain ridge.* [*opposite* **under**] **d** You fall **over** something when it trips you up: *I fell over a*

box in the dark and landed painfully on my knees. **e** You fall **over** an edge such as a cliff when you drop from it: *He deliberately drove his car over a cliff.* **f** You bend or lean **over** something when you bend yourself so that the upper part of your body is above it: *She leant over the bed to kiss him goodnight.* **g** You look **over** a set of things, or something written, when you examine them: *I glanced quickly over the report.* □ *Her eye passed over the furniture.* **h** You talk to someone or look at something **over** some object when you talk or look across the top of it: *They'd had the occasional conversation over the garden wall.* □ *She was regarding me coldly over the top of her spectacles.* **i** You have a view **over** something when it extends in front of you: *The front of the house looked out over the school playing fields.* **j** Something is **over** a street or river if it is on the other side of it: *They used to live just over the road from us.* [*same as* **across**] **k** You can tell someone something **over** the telephone, or hear something **over** the radio: *I can't talk about it over the telephone.* [*same as* **on**]

3 a Something is **over** a certain amount if it is more than it: *The fare comes to over £200.* □ *men over the age of 60.* □ *The journey took us just over a week.* □ *It happened over a year ago.* [see note at **above**] **b** Something that happens **over** a certain period, or **over** a meal, happens during it: *She's staying with us over the Christmas break.* □ *I was ill over the weekend.* □ *Tell me about it over lunch.* □ *We can discuss it over a drink.* □ *The new strategies will be developed over several years.* **c** People agree and disagree, or feel and react a certain way, **over** something, when they agree or disagree about it, or feel and react that way regarding it: *Let's not argue over details just yet.* □ *There's nothing to get into a rage over.* □ *She'd taken a lot of trouble over her speech.* [*same as* **about**] **d** You take a certain time **over** a job when you take that time to do it: *Don't spend too long over your essay.* **e** You have power, control or influence **over** someone or something if you can control or influence them: *I have no influence over their decisions.* □ *the strange power that he exercised over women* □ *You must sometimes exert your authority over your staff.* **f** The person **over** you at your place of work is in charge of you: *They had someone called a 'project manager' over them.* **g** You are **over** an illness, injury or shock when you have recovered from it: *He's still ill, but he's over the worst.*

▻ ***adverb***

1 Over as an adverb reflects the senses that the preposition has of **a** crossing, or being on the other side of, a space, gap, dividing line or barrier: *He went over to the door.* □ *Come over here and look at this.* □ *She passed the letter over to me.* □ *when we crossed over from Malawi into Zambia.* □ *We flew over from the Island last night.* □ *How long are your Canadian friends going to be over here for?* □ *But there's a high fence; how will you get over?* □ *She's standing over by the window.* □ *There's a postbox on the corner over there.* [compare **across**] **b** extending outwards in some direction: *My back hurts when I bend over to the left.* **c** being more than a certain amount: *Children of 12 and over pay full fare.* **d** discussing or thinking about something, or examining something: *Think this over carefully.* □ *We'll talk it over later.* □ *Could you read this over for me and check the spelling?*

2 a Something falls **over** or is knocked **over** when it falls or is knocked from a standing position into a lying one: *I fell over on the pavement.* □ *He knocked the lamp over in his haste.* **b** Something rolls **over** or is turned **over** when it rolls or is turned on to its other side: *I'd turned over two pages at once.* □ *She rolled over and yawned.* □ *My pack rolled over and over down the hill.*

3 a An event or period is **over** when it is finished: *Thank goodness the exams are over.* □ *She was finished; her career was over.* **b** Something that is left **over** from an amount is what remains of it when the rest has been used or dealt with: *We've got some potatoes left over from lunch.* **c** You repeat an action several times **over** when you do it again that number of times: *I had to say it twice over before she heard me.* **d** (*AmE*) You start or begin **over** when you start again from the beginning. **e** You change **over** from one thing to another when you have or choose the second rather than the first: *When did you change over from gas to electricity?* □ *He went over to the Liberals in 1906.* □ *We may be able to win her over to our side.*

▻ ***noun*: overs**

(*cricket*) An **over** is a series of six or eight balls bowled by one bowler from one end of the pitch.

▻ ***phrases*** **1 a** One thing is **all over** another when it is spread across it: *Someone has spilt milk all over the floor* □ *You've got jam all over your face.* **b** (*informal, derogatory*) Someone is **all over** you when they are being very friendly and attentive to you, usually so that you'll do something they want. **c** Something is **all over** when it is finished: *It appeared that the panic was all over and everyone could go home.* **d** You do something **all over** again when you repeat it from the beginning: *Have we got to key the material all over again?* **2** You **get** something difficult or unpleasant **over with** when you attend to it satisfactorily, so that it can be forgotten; something is **over and done with** when it has been dealt with and can be forgotten: *I'll be glad when we've got the checking over with.* **3** Things or amounts **over and above** something are in addition to it: *You now pay a £5 airport tax over and above your already excessive fare.* **4** Something happens **over and over again** when it keeps happening: *I've had to correct her punctuation over and over again.*

over- /ˈouvə(r)/ *prefix*

1 Over- is used before nouns, verbs, adjectives and adverbs to mean 'too much' or 'excessive': *overcook* □ *overconfident* □ *overpopulation* □ *over-protective.* **2 Over-** is also used to indicate that something is **a** 'above', 'beyond' or 'across': *overlord* □ *overhang* □ *overland.* **b** 'covering' or 'outer': *overcoat.* **c** 'additional': *overtime.*

overall *noun; adjective; adverb*

▻ ***noun*** /ˈouvərɔːl/: **overalls**

1 An **overall** is a garment like a coat that you wear over your clothes to protect them while you are working. **2** (*plural*) **Overalls** are a one-piece garment made up of a part (with or without sleeves) to cover your upper body and trousers to cover your legs. Overalls are worn to keep your clothes clean while you are working.

▻ ***adjective*** /ˈouvərɔːl/

Overall means including everything: *He added up all the sets of figures to arrive at the overall total.* □ *The overall length of the two sections is 42 metres.*

▻ ***adverb*** /ouvərˈɔːl/

1 Overall means including everything: *What is the length overall?* **2** (*sentence adverb*) You also use **overall** to indicate that you mean something as a whole or a situation in general: *Overall, your son's schoolwork has been satisfactory.* [*same as* **on the whole, by and large**]

overawe /ouvərˈɔː/ *verb* (*usually in the passive*): **overawes, overawing, overawed**

You are **overawed** by something when you are so impressed by it that it makes you feel a little afraid: *He was a little overawed by the splendid surroundings and the sophisticated people.*

overbalance /ouvəˈbaləns/ *verb*: **overbalances, overbalancing, overbalanced**

You **overbalance** when you fall over or nearly fall over, because you are not standing or sitting in a steady position: *The boy had been walking along the top of the wall when he overbalanced and fell to the ground.*

overbearing /oʊvəˈbɛərɪŋ/ *adjective* (*derogatory*)
Someone who is **overbearing** tries to tell others what to do or forces them to do what he or she wants without thinking about their feelings: *He was a self-opinionated and sometimes painfully overbearing extrovert.* [*same as* **domineering**]

overboard /ˈoʊvəˈbɔːd/ *adverb*
A person or object falls or is washed **overboard** when they fall or are washed over the side of a ship or boat into the water.
▻ ***phrases*** **1** (*informal*) You **go overboard for** or **about** someone or something when you become very or too enthusiastic about that person or thing. **2** (*informal*) You **throw** something **overboard** when you abandon it or stop supporting it because you think it is no longer useful: *The party has thrown some of its more radical policies overboard in an attempt to win the next election.*

overcast /ˈoʊvəkɑːst/ *adjective*
If you say that it is **overcast**, you mean that the sky is dark with clouds: *In the afternoon it became overcast and they felt a few spots of rain.* [*opposite* **bright, sunny**]

overcharge /oʊvəˈtʃɑːdʒ/ *verb*: **overcharges, overcharging, overcharged**
You are **overcharged** when you are asked to pay too much money for something: *The shopkeeper overcharged us for the bread.* □ *He complained that he had been overcharged by £10.* [*opposite* **undercharge**]

overcoat /ˈoʊvəkoʊt/ *noun*: **overcoats**
An **overcoat** is a warm, heavy coat worn over other clothes in cold weather.

overcome /oʊvəˈkʌm/ *verb*: **overcomes, overcoming, overcame** /oʊvəˈkeɪm/, **overcome**
1 You **overcome** something, such as a difficulty or fear, when you succeed in defeating it or controlling it: *She struggled to overcome her feelings of revulsion.* □ *They overcame all the difficulties that had been placed in their path.* **2** (*usually in the passive*) You **are overcome** by something when it affects you so strongly that it makes you feel weak or ill or causes you to lose control: *She was overcome with remorse.* □ *They were overcome by the fumes.*

overcrowded /oʊvəˈkraʊdɪd/ *adjective*
A place that is **overcrowded** has too many people or things in it: *our overcrowded world* □ *The train was overcrowded.*

overcrowding /oʊvəˈkraʊdɪŋ/ *noun* (*uncount*)
Overcrowding is the state of having too many people in one place: *The council plans to take steps to reduce overcrowding in the poorer areas of the city.*

overdo /oʊvəˈduː/ *verb*: **overdoes** /oʊvəˈdʌz/: **overdoing, overdid** /oʊvəˈdɪd/, **overdone** /oʊvəˈdʌn/
You **overdo** something when you do, perform or express it in an exaggerated manner or use too much of it: *He rather overdid the role of the tragic victim.* □ *I enjoyed the film but I think they overdid the gruesome details.*
▻ ***phrase*** If someone says that you have been **overdoing it** or **overdoing things**, they mean that you have been working too hard or have been doing more than you can manage physically or mentally.

overdone /oʊvəˈdʌn/ *adjective*
Food that is **overdone** has been cooked for too long. [*opposite* **underdone**]

overdose /ˈoʊvədoʊs/ *noun*: **overdoses**
Someone takes or is given an **overdose** of a drug when they take or are given more of it than is safe: *She tried to commit suicide by taking a massive overdose of sleeping tablets.*

overdraft /ˈoʊvədrɑːft/ *noun*: **overdrafts**
An **overdraft** is an amount of money that you have spent, or are allowed to spend, that is greater than the amount that is in your bank account: *He made an appointment with the bank manager to arrange an overdraft of £500.* □ *an automatic overdraft facility of £250* □ *I've never had an overdraft.*

overdrawn /oʊvəˈdrɔːn/ *adjective*
You are **overdrawn** when you have spent more money than you have in your bank account: *Your account is overdrawn by £150.*

overdue /oʊvəˈdjuː/ *adjective*
Something that is **overdue** is late in arriving or has not happened, been completed or paid at the time when it should have been or was expected: *Her baby is two weeks overdue.* □ *an overdue account* □ *These changes were long overdue.*

overestimate /oʊvərˈɛstɪmeɪt/ *verb*: **overestimates, overestimating, overestimated**
1 You **overestimate** the amount, value or importance of something when you think it is greater than it really is: *I overestimated the number of rolls of wallpaper it would take to cover the hall.* **2** You **overestimate** someone's abilities or skills when you think that they are more able or skilful than they really are. [*opposite* **underestimate**]

overflow *verb*; *noun*
▻ ***verb*** /oʊvəˈfloʊ/: **overflows, overflowing, overflowed**
1 A liquid **overflows** when it has filled a container to the top and is now spilling over the sides. **2** To be **overflowing** with something is to be too full of it, or so full that some of it spills out: *Her desk was overflowing with unanswered letters.* □ *She was overflowing with gratitude.*
▻ ***noun*** /ˈoʊvəfloʊ/: **overflows**
1 An **overflow** is a pipe or hole through which excess liquid can escape. **2** The **overflow** from something is the amount which overflows or the act of flowing over.

overgrown /oʊvəˈgroʊn/ *adjective*
A place that is **overgrown** is covered with plants that have grown too large or too fast because they have not been controlled: *The old kitchen garden was overgrown with weeds.*

overhang /oʊvəˈhaŋ/ *verb*; *noun*
▻ ***verb***: **overhangs, overhanging, overhung**
To **overhang** something means to stick out from it or to hang out over it: *The stream was overhung by the drooping branches of ancient willow trees.*
▻ ***noun*** /ˈoʊvəhaŋ/: **overhangs**
1 An **overhang** is something that sticks out from the main part: *They sheltered under a rocky overhang.* **2** (*uncount*) The amount by which something sticks out over something else is the **overhang**: *The roof has been designed with a three foot overhang.*

overhaul *verb*; *noun*
▻ ***verb*** /oʊvəˈhɔːl/: **overhauls, overhauling, overhauled**
1 You **overhaul** something, such as a piece of equipment, when you examine it carefully and thoroughly and make any repairs or changes that are necessary: *The steamer has had its engines completely overhauled.* [*same as* **service**] **2** A vehicle **overhauls** another vehicle when it comes up from behind and passes the other vehicle. [*same as* **overtake**]

▻ ***noun*** /'ouvəhɔ:l/
An **overhaul** is a thorough examination followed by any necessary changes or repairs: *a major overhaul of the National Health Service.*

overhead *adjective; adverb*
▻ ***adjective*** /'ouvəhɛd/
Overhead means above your head or above the ground: *He switched on the overhead light.* ▫ *an overhead cable* ▫ *an overhead railway.*
▻ ***adverb*** /ouvə'hɛd/: *vultures circling overhead* ▫ *Overhead, clouds drifted slowly across a midsummer sky.*

overheads /'ouvəhɛdz/ *noun (plural)*
The regular expenses involved in running a business, such as rent, heat, light and salaries, are its **overheads**.

overhear /ouvə'hɪə(r)/ *verb*: **overhears**, **overhearing**, **overheard** /ouvəh'hɜ:d/
You **overhear** somebody when you hear what they are saying, either by accident or on purpose, when they are not speaking to you: *I overheard John telling Peter that he was going abroad.* ▫ *He stood nearby and was obviously trying to overhear our conversation.*

overheat /ouvə'hi:t/ *verb*: **overheats**, **overheating**, **overheated**
Something **overheats** when it becomes too hot: *He switched off the engine because it was overheating.*

overhung /ouvə'hʌŋ/ *verb*
Overhung is the past tense and past participle of **overhang**.

overjoyed /ouvə'dʒɔɪd/ *adjective*
You are **overjoyed** when you are filled with great happiness: *His mother was overjoyed when he returned safely.* [*same as* **delighted**]

overlaid see **overlay**.

overland *adjective; adverb*
▻ ***adjective*** /'ouvəland/
An **overland** journey is made across land rather than by sea or air: *an overland trek.*
▻ ***adverb*** /ouvə'land/: *They are going to travel overland to India.*

overlap /ouvə'lap/ *verb; noun*
▻ ***verb***: **overlaps**, **overlapping**, **overlapped**
1 Two things **overlap** when a part of one thing covers part of the other: *The tiles on the roof overlap.* ▫ *a pattern of overlapping circles.* **2** To **overlap** also means to have something in common, such as the same area of interest or activity or the same period of time: *The times when the two doctors were on duty never overlapped.* [*same as* **coincide**]
▻ ***noun*** /'ouvəlap/: **overlaps**: *Leave an overlap of 25cm.* ▫ *There was an overlap between the end of the night shift and the beginning of the day shift.*

overlay /ouvə'leɪ/ *verb (usually in the passive)*: **overlays**, **overlaying**, **overlaid**
Something **is overlaid** with something else when it is covered, usually thinly, with a layer of that other thing: *wood overlaid with ivory.*

overleaf /ouvə'li:f/ *adverb*
Overleaf is used as an instruction to the reader of a book or magazine to indicate that something may be found on the other side of the page: *See the tables overleaf.*

overload /ouvə'loud/ *verb*: **overloads**, **overloading**, **overloaded**
1 (*often in the passive*) When a vehicle **is overloaded**, it has too many people or things in it or on it: *The overloaded car was dangerously close to the ground.* **2** You **are overloaded** with work or problems when you are given more work or problems that you are able to cope with. **3** You **overload** an electrical circuit when you cause too much electrical current to pass through it by connecting more electrical appliances to it than it is designed to cope with.

overlook /ouvə'luk/ *verb*: **overlooks**, **overlooking**, **overlooked**
1 You say that something, such as a house or window, **overlooks** a place when it provides a clear view of that place from a higher position: *a cottage overlooking the harbour* ▫ *The windows of their hotel room overlooked Central Park.* **2** You **overlook** something when you fail to see it or notice it: *These small details are frequently overlooked, but can turn out to be very important.* ▫ *He apologised for having overlooked the payment.* [*same as* **miss**] **3** Someone **overlooks** something that someone else has done wrong when they decide to ignore it and do not penalize or criticize them for it: *I've decided to overlook your bad behaviour this time, but don't let it happen again or you will be severely punished.* [*same as* **disregard**, **ignore**]

overly /'ouvəlɪ/ *adverb (formal)*
Overly means too or too much: *I'm not overly concerned about the situation.* ▫ *She tends to be overly cautious.*

overnight *adverb; adjective*
▻ ***adverb*** /ouvə'naɪt/
Overnight means **1** for or during the night: *They parked overnight in a layby.* ▫ *Do you intend to stay overnight?* **2** (*informal*) suddenly or very quickly: *He became a celebrity overnight.* ▫ *Nobody expects the changes to happen overnight.*
▻ ***adjective*** /'ouvənaɪt/
Overnight means
1 for or during the night: *an overnight stay* ▫ *an overnight stop in Edinburgh* ▫ *He packed an overnight bag with his pyjamas and shaving things.* **2** (*informal*) sudden. *an overnight success.*

overpass /'ouvəpɑ:s/ *noun (AmE)*: **overpasses**
An **overpass** is a road that carries traffic over another road. [*same as* **flyover**; compare **underpass**]

overpopulated /ouvə'pɒpjuleɪtɪd/ *adjective*
An area or country is **overpopulated** when it has too many people living in it: *The city was overpopulated with thousands living in shanty towns around its edges.* [*same as* **overcrowded**]

overpopulation /ouvəpɒpju'leɪʃən/ *noun (uncount)*
When there is **overpopulation** in a place, there are too many people living in it: *Overpopulation is one of the major problems facing the world.*

overpower /ouvə'pauə(r)/ *verb*: **overpowers**, **overpowering**, **overpowered**
Someone or something **overpowers** you when they defeat you because they are stronger than you are: *The man was cornered in an alley and was soon overpowered by two large policemen.* ▫ *The man tried to save the children from the burning building but he was overpowered by the heat and smoke.* [*same as* **overwhelm**]

overpowering /ouvə'pauərɪŋ/ *adjective*
An **overpowering** smell or feeling is one that is extremely strong: *An overpowering smell of sulphur filled the air.* ▫ *an overpowering feeling of grief.* [*same as* **overwhelming**]

overran see **overrun**.

overrate /ouvə'reɪt/ *verb (often in the passive)*: **overrates**, **overrating**, **overrated**
You **overrate** something when you think it is better or more important than it really is: *I think his books are overrated.* [*opposite* **underrate**]

override /oʊvə'raɪd/ *verb*: **overrides, overriding, overrode** /oʊvə'roʊd/, **overridden** /oʊvə'rɪdən/
1 You **override** someone when you ignore their decisions or actions because you have more authority than they do: *He simply overrode their objections and continued with the meeting.* **2** One thing **overrides** another when it is considered to be more important than that other thing: *The welfare of the patients overrides all other considerations.* [*same as* **outweigh**]

overriding /oʊvə'raɪdɪŋ/ *adjective*
Overriding means more important than anything else: *a matter of overriding importance* □ *Their overriding consideration is the need to maintain peace in the area.*

overrode see **override**.

overrule /oʊvə'ru:l/ *verb*: **overrules, overruling, overruled**
Someone, especially someone in authority, **overrules** a decision or action when they decide that it is wrong or not valid: *The judge overruled the defence lawyer's objection.* □ *The President has the power to overrule the parliament in certain circumstances.*

overrun /oʊvə'rʌn/ *verb*: **overruns, overrunning, overran** /oʊvə'ran/, **overrun**
1 Animals or plants, especially of a kind that are unwanted, **overrun** an area when they spread through it and occupy it in large numbers: *The camp was overrun with rats.* **2** An army **overruns** an area or country when it invades and takes complete control of it: *The Mongol hordes overran vast areas from Asia to Northern Europe.* [*same as* **occupy**] **3** Something **overruns** when it goes beyond a fixed limit, especially of time or money: *The programme overran by ten minutes.* □ *The delays have caused us to overrun our budget for the contract.*

oversaw see **oversee**.

overseas *adverb; adjective*
▻ ***adverb*** /oʊvə'si:z/
Overseas means to, in or from a foreign country or countries that you have to cross the sea to get to: *They have gone to live overseas.* [*same as* **abroad**]
▻ ***adjective*** /'oʊvəsi:z/: *overseas news* □ *an overseas student* (=one who has come from a foreign country to study in your country). [*same as* **foreign**]

oversee /oʊvə'si:/ *verb*: **oversees, overseeing, oversaw** /oʊvə'sɔ:/: **overseen**
A person who **oversees** a job or activity watches or supervises the people who are doing it to make sure it is done properly: *A consultant engineer has been employed to oversee the project.*

overshadow /oʊvə'ʃadoʊ/ *verb*: **overshadows, overshadowing, overshadowed**
1 You can say that someone or something **is overshadowed** by another person or thing when they are made to seem less important by that other person or thing: *Because she is usually so quiet, she is overshadowed by her more talkative sister.* **2** When something, such as a tall building or plant, **overshadows** something else, it casts a shadow over that other thing because it is stands between it and the light: *The little village was overshadowed by the huge castle on the hill.* **3** An event or situation **is overshadowed** by something unpleasant when it is made less happy because of it: *Their normally high spirits were overshadowed by the threat of war.*

overshoot /oʊvə'ʃu:t/ *verb*: **overshoots, overshooting, overshot** /oʊvəʃɒt/
You **overshoot** the point or place that you are aiming at or trying to reach when you go or travel beyond it: *He overshot the target by ten yards with his first arrow.* □ *The plane overshot the runway and crashed into the sea.*

oversight /'oʊvəsaɪt/ *noun*: **oversights**
An **oversight** is something that you fail to notice or do which you should have noticed or done: *The error was made because of an oversight on my part.*

oversimplify /oʊvə'sɪmplɪfaɪ/ *verb*: **oversimplifies, oversimplifying, oversimplified**
You **oversimplify** something when you explain it so simply that its true meaning is lost or distorted: *Recent press reports have tended to oversimplify the problems that were faced by the people directly involved.* — *adjective* **oversimplified:** *an oversimplified interpretation of the facts.*

oversleep /oʊvə'sli:p/ *verb*: **oversleeps, oversleeping, overslept** /oʊvə'slɛpt/
You **oversleep** when you sleep for longer than you intended to: *I was late for the lecture because I overslept.*

overspill /'oʊvəspɪl/ *noun* (*uncount, often adjectival*)
The **overspill** from a city or town are the people who have left it to live elsewhere because of overcrowding or because their former homes have been demolished: *The new town was built for the overspill created when Glasgow's Victorian slums were demolished.* □ *an overspill housing estate.*

overstate /oʊvə'steɪt/ *verb*: **overstates, overstating, overstated**
You **overstate** something when you explain or express it too strongly, making it seem much better, much worse, or more important than it really is: *She overstated her case to such an extent that noone believed her.* □ *The importance of a healthy diet in childhood cannot be overstated.* [*opposite* **understate**]

overstep /oʊvə'stɛp/ *verb*: **oversteps, overstepping, overstepped**
▻ ***phrase*** If someone **oversteps the mark**, they do or say more than they should or more than is wise, reasonable, acceptable or proper: *He overstepped the mark when he made a joke about her divorce.*

overt /oʊ'vɜ:t/ *adjective*
Something that is **overt** is not secret or hidden but is done or shown publicly or openly: *He was taken aback by the overt hostility of the locals.* [*same as* **manifest**; *opposite* **covert**] — *adverb* **overtly:** *The newspaper article was overtly critical of the regime.* [*same as* **manifestly**]

overtake /oʊvə'teɪk/ *verb*: **overtakes, overtaking, overtook** /oʊvətʊk/: **overtaken** /oʊvə'teɪkən/
1 You **overtake** a vehicle or person that is moving in the same direction when you catch up with and go past them: *He overtook the slow-moving lorry on a straight stretch of the road.* □ *It is dangerous to overtake on a bend.* □ *The British runner was overtaken on the final lap by the Kenyan.* **2** One thing **overtakes** another when it draws level with that thing and begins to do better than it: *The Labour Party has overtaken the Conservatives in the opinion polls.* **3** An event or change in conditions **overtakes** you when it reaches or happens to you suddenly and unexpectedly: *Their plans were overtaken by events.* □ *When they reached the Bay of Biscay they were overtaken by bad weather and had to make for the nearest port.* **4** An unpleasant feeling **overtakes** you when it affects you suddenly and very strongly: *He was overtaken by a feeling of revulsion.*

overthrow *verb; noun*
▻ ***verb*** /oʊvə'θroʊ/: **overthrows, overthrowing, overthrew** /oʊvə'θru:/: **overthrown** /oʊvə'θroʊn/
1 A government or leader **is overthrown** when they are removed from power by force: *The generals were accused of trying to overthrow the democratically-*

elected government. **2** A fixed or established plan, idea or standard **is overthrown** when it is overturned or replaced with a new one: *As soon as he was appointed, he overthrew all our existing plans.*

▻ ***noun*** /ˈoʊvəθroʊ/ (*used in the singular*)

The **overthrow** of a government or leader is the act of removing them from power by force: *the overthrow of the communist dictatorship in Romania.*

overtime /ˈoʊvətaɪm/ *noun; adverb*

▻ ***noun*** (*uncount*)

1 Overtime is time that you spend working at your job after or in addition to your usual working hours: *The boss regularly asks him to do overtime.* ▫ *I worked nearly fifteen hours overtime last week.* **2 Overtime** is also the money paid for this extra time worked: *The overtime rate is one and a half times the basic hourly rate.*

▻ ***adverb:*** *We'll have to work overtime to get this finished by the due date.* ▫ *He was paid overtime when he worked through his lunch hours.*

overtone /ˈoʊvətoʊn/ *noun* (*usually plural*): **overtones**

Something has **overtones** of a particular quality or feeling when that quality or feeling is suggested or hinted at without being shown or stated clearly: *a novel with strong political overtones* ▫ *Their public statements had threatening overtones.* [*same as* **connotation**; compare **undertone**]

overtook see **overtake**.

overture /ˈoʊvətjʊə(r)/ *noun*: **overtures**

1 An **overture** is a piece of music written an as introduction to a long musical piece, such as an opera or ballet. **2** (*usually in the plural*) You make **overtures** to someone when you make friendly approaches or proposals to them, usually because you want to start a relationship or reach an agreement with them: *She was taken aback when he said he loved her because he had never made any romantic overtures in the past.*

overturn /oʊvəˈtɜːn/ *verb*: **overturns, overturning, overturned**

1 When you **overturn** something or when it **overturns**, you turn it over or it turns over, so that it is upside down: *The car hit a patch of ice and overturned.* ▫ *The lamp was overturned and the room was plunged into darkness.* **2** Someone **overturns** a decision that has been made previously when they change it or reverse it: *They appealed to the House of Lords to try to get the decision overturned.* **3** To **overturn** a government or political system means to bring it to an end or destroy it: *Their aim was to overturn the military regime and restore democracy to the country.* [*same as* **overthrow**]

overview /ˈoʊvəvjuː/ *noun* (*formal*): **overviews**

An **overview** of a situation is an account or description which gives a general picture of it without any unnecessary details: *The chairman's report is an overview of the company's performance in the last year.*

overweight /oʊvəˈweɪt/ *adjective*

1 Someone who is **overweight** is too fat: *an overweight teenager* ▫ *She is very overweight.* [*opposite* **underweight**] **2** Something that is **overweight** is too heavy or is heavier than the weight allowed: *The baggage allowance on the plane was 40 kilograms and his suitcases were 5 kilograms overweight.*

overwhelm /oʊvəˈwɛlm/ *verb*: **overwhelms, overwhelming, overwhelmed**

1 (*usually in the passive*) You **are overwhelmed** by something when you are made completely helpless by it: *She sank to her knees, overwhelmed by feelings of relief and gratitude.* **2** One group of people **overwhelms** another when they defeat them or gain complete control over them by greater force or numbers: *The rebel army attacked in such numbers that they quickly overwhelmed the small number of troops who had remained loyal to the government.* [*same as* **overcome**]

overwhelming /oʊvəˈwɛlmɪŋ/ *adjective*

1 Something that is **overwhelming** affects you so strongly that you are overcome or made helpless by it: *She felt an overwhelming sense of despair.* ▫ *The constant media attention can be a little overwhelming for someone who is not used to it.* **2 Overwhelming** is also used to describe things that are very great or form by far the greatest part of something: *an overwhelming victory* ▫ *The poll shows that an overwhelming majority of people are against the government's proposals.* [*opposite* **insignificant**] — *adverb* **overwhelmingly:** *You have been overwhelmingly generous.* ▫ *In the referendum, the people voted overwhelmingly in favour of the treaty.*

overwork /oʊvəˈwɜːk/ *verb; noun*

▻ ***verb***: **overworks, overworking, overworked**

1 Someone **overworks** or they **are overworked** when they work or are made to work too hard or too long: *You look exhausted; I think you've been overworking.* ▫ *He is overworked and underpaid.* **2** You **overwork** something when you use it too much so that it loses its effectiveness: *I think the author has overworked the theme of alienation.* ▫ *The soil has been overworked and nothing will grow on it.*

▻ ***noun*** (*uncount*)

Overwork is the act of working too hard or too long: *She died young of poverty and overwork.* — *adjective* **overworked:** *a broken-down overworked horse* ▫ *an overworked phrase.*

overwrought /oʊvəˈrɔːt/ *adjective*

You are **overwrought** when you are too upset or emotional to be in control of what you are doing: *She was so tired and overwrought that she didn't know what she was saying.* ▫ *The overwrought child was too emotional to listen to reason.*

ow /aʊ/ *interjection*

People say **'Ow!'** when they feel a sudden, usually slight, pain: *'Ow! That was sore!'* [*same as* **ouch**]

owe /oʊ/ *verb*: **owes, owing, owed**

1 You **owe** someone money when you have borrowed it from them and not yet paid it back, or have received goods or services from them that you have not yet paid for: *John still owes me that £500 I lent him in 1990.* ▫ *How much do I owe you for the shopping?* ▫ *You owe me for the taxi.* ▫ *They suddenly vanished abroad, owing large sums to most of the local tradespeople.* **2** Money **is owing** to someone if they have lent it to you, or if they have provided goods or services, and you have not yet paid them: *In addition there's the £50 owing to the church for the hire of the hall.* **3** You **owe** someone a favour when they have done something for you and deserve something from you in return. **4** You **owe** someone something such as an apology, gratitude, or loyalty if they deserve it from you: *I think you owe me an explanation for the way you treated me.* ▫ *We owe them a great debt of gratitude.* ▫ *the respect you owe your parents* ▫ *I owe my party support, yes, but not unquestioning loyalty.* ▫ *We owe it to our fans to perform well.* ▫ *You owe it to yourself to keep fit and well.* **5** Someone or something **owes** something such as a quality, skill, advantage or their existence to a person or circumstance if it is because of them that they have it: *I felt I owed my success chiefly to Ewen's tuition.* ▫ *Norway owes its prosperity to its rich natural resources.* ▫ *To what do we owe the pleasure of your company?* [= why are you here?] ▫ *I owe that* *doctor my life.* ▫ *if the world's species owe their origin to God.* **6** One thing **owes** a certain amount to another if it is based on it, or imitates it, to that extent: *Obviously his poetry owes a little to Eliot.*

▻ ***phrase*** Something happens or is the case **owing to** some circumstance if that is what causes it: *We missed each other at the station, owing to some misunderstanding about the meeting point.* ▫ *Owing to last night's train derailment serious delays are expected this morning.* [*same as* **because** of; compare **due** to]

owl /ɑʊl/ *noun*: **owls**

An **owl** is a bird with a round flat face, large eyes, and a short hooked beak that eats small animals such as mice caught at night.

own /oʊn/ *determiner; pronoun; verb*

▻ ***determiner***

1 Your **own** things belong to you and to no-one else: *She has her own flat at the back of the house.* ▫ *How could she betray her own brother?* ▫ *I didn't believe it until I saw it with my own eyes.* **2** Your **own** qualities, characteristics or opinions are your particular ones that are typical of you, or individual to you: *his own distinctive style of composition* ▫ *We all have our own preferences.* **3** You make your **own** bed, or find your **own** way, if you do so without help or interference from anyone else: *She makes all her own clothes.* ▫ *May I leave you to get your own supper?* ▫ *Are these paintings your own handiwork?*

Own must be preceded by a possessive pronoun, or the possessive form of a noun: *I'd like to have my own* (not *an own*) *business one day. This is Anne's own copy, not a departmental one. The entry must be entirely the child's own work.*

▻ ***pronoun:*** *'Could I share your music?' 'Why, haven't you brought your own with you?* ▫ *She had one or two expressions that were very much her own.* ▫ *Parade costumes were not issued to us; we were expected to make our own.*

▻ ***verb***: **owns, owning, owned**

If you **own** something, you have bought it or been given it, and it is your property: *Many more people now own their own homes.* ▫ *Who owns the big red car?* ▫ *an apartment block owned by the university.*

▻ ***phrases***

1 You **get your own back** on someone who has done you harm or played a trick on you when you do something to harm or trick them in return. **2** You **hold your own** in a struggle or contest when you are not defeated: *The firm has been holding its own in the face of cut-throat competition.* ▫ *She's perfectly capable of holding her own in any argument.* ▫ *The doctors report that she's still on the danger list but she's holding her own.* **3** Something **of your own** is something that belongs to you, or is your responsibility, alone: *I was longing for a room of my own.* ▫ *I'll help you later if I can; just now I've got problems of my own.* **4 a** You are **on your own** when there is no-one else with you: *He lives on his own.* ▫ *The child was being left on her own for hours at a time.* ▫ *I'd rather not go to the dance on my own; I do wish you'd come with me.* [*same as* **alone, by yourself**] **b** You do something **on your own** when you do it without help or interference from anyone: *We'll be able to manage on our own now, thanks.* ▫ *I've given you all the help I can; you're on your own from now on.* [*same as* **by yourself**]

phrasal verb

Someone who has done something wrong **owns up** when they admit that they have done it: *No-one would own up to damaging the photocopier.* ▫ *I was too scared to own up.* [compare **admit, confess**]

owner /ˈoʊnə(r)/ *noun*: **owners**

An **owner** is a person who owns something: *Are you a dog owner?* ▫ *The police are trying to trace the owner of the car used in the raid.*

owner-occupier /oʊnərˈɒkjʊpaɪə(r)/ *noun* (*BrE*): **owner-occupiers**

An **owner-occupier** is a person who owns the house or flat that he or she is living in. [compare **tenant**]

ownership /ˈoʊnəʃɪp/ *noun* (*uncount*)

Ownership is the state of owning something: *The British steel industry was transferred out of public and into private ownership.* ▫ *land ownership* ▫ *The business is under new ownership.*

ox /ɒks/ *noun*: **oxen** /ˈɒksən/

An **ox** is an adult bull that has been castrated. Oxen are sometimes used for pulling carts and farm machinery, for carrying loads, and for food.

oxygen /ˈɒksɪdʒən/ *noun* (*uncount*)

Oxygen is a gas with no colour, taste or smell, which is present in the air and in water. Plants and animals cannot live without oxygen.

oyster /ˈɔɪstə(r)/ *noun*: **oysters**

An **oyster** is a shellfish used, either cooked or raw, as food. Some oysters make pearls inside their shells.

▻ ***phrase*** You can say to someone **the world is your oyster** when you mean that all of life's opportunities and pleasures are available for them to enjoy.

ozone /ˈoʊzoʊn/ *noun* (*uncount*)

Ozone is a form of oxygen with a strong smell.

ozone-friendly /oʊzoʊn ˈfrɛndlɪ/ *adjective*

Products, especially products in aerosol sprays, are **ozone-friendly** when they do not contain chemicals that could damage the ozone layer.

ozone layer /ˈoʊzoʊn leɪə(r)/ *noun* (*uncount*)

The **ozone layer** is a layer of ozone, high above the earth's surface, that helps to protect the earth from harmful rays from the sun.

P

P or **p** /piː/: **Ps** or **p's**
P is the 16th letter of the English alphabet: *'Phrase' begins with a p.*
▻ ***phrase*** (*often humorous*) People **mind their p's and q's** when they behave politely and remember to say 'please' and 'thank you'.

PA /piː 'eɪ/ *noun*: **PAs**
1 PA is a widely used abbreviation for 'personal assistant': *She has worked as a secretary, and as a PA.* □ *a course for office managers and PAs.* **2 PA** is also an abbreviation for 'public-address' (system): *He made the announcement over the PA system.*

pa /pɑː/ *noun* (*informal, old*): **pas**
Some people refer to their father as **pa**: *'Pa, when can I have a new bicycle?' asked John.* □ *'Be sure to ask your pa,' she said.* [see also **papa**]

pace /peɪs/ *noun; verb*
▻ ***noun***: **paces**
1 a A **pace** is a single step: *He took two paces forward.* **b** A **pace** is also the length of a single step or the distance covered by it: *He stopped a few paces away from the cliff edge.* **2** (*uncount or used in the singular*) Your **pace** is the speed at which you move, especially when walking or running: *at normal walking pace* □ *He set off at a brisk pace.* □ *They strolled around the park at a leisurely pace.* □ *Roadworks had slowed the motorway traffic down to a snail's pace.* **3** (*uncount*) The **pace** of something is its speed or rate of movement, progress, development, or activity: *the rapid pace of reform in education* □ *He now lives in the country because he couldn't stand the pace of city life.*
▻ ***verb***: **paces, pacing, paced**
1 Someone **paces** when they walk with steady or regular steps, especially when they walk to and fro in or over a small area: *The sentries paced up and down in front of the gate.* □ *He paced nervously up and down the hall.* □ *He was waiting impatiently, pacing the floor and frequently looking at his watch.* **2 a** When someone **paces** you, they set or regulate the speed at which you do something: *He cycled alongside, pacing me as I ran.* □ *In rowing competitions, a coxswain's main role is to pace the rowers.* **b** If you **pace** yourself during a race, activity, or task you make adjustments to your speed or rate of progress so that you are able to complete it without running out of energy or time: *If she paces herself in the early stages, she should finish the race in record time.*
▻ ***phrases*** **1** If you do something **at your own pace**, you do it at a rate or speed that you can manage comfortably: *The pupils are allowed to progress at their own pace.* **2** If you **go through** or **show your paces**, you demonstrate your skills in a particular activity: *She has to go through her paces at every audition.* **3 a** You **keep pace with** someone when you keep up with them by going as fast, or as slowly, as they do: *I managed to keep pace with him throughout the race.* **b** One thing **keeps pace with** another when it progresses or increases at the same rate or changes at the same time: *In recent years, wage rises have kept pace with the rate of inflation.* **4** You **put** someone **through their paces** by making them demonstrate their skills or abilities in a particular activity: *The director is putting the new members of the dance company through their paces.* □ *The young skaters were put through their paces by the coach.* **5** A competitor in a race or contest **sets the pace** when they lead in the early stages, and so determine the rate or speed the others have to go at: *The Russian athlete set the pace for the first two laps.* □ *The leaders set a crippling pace, and the rest of the field was soon left far behind.* [see also **pacesetter**]

> ***phrasal verbs***
> **pace out** When you **pace out** a length or area, you measure it by making a series of steps of equal length: *He paced out the area of the garden that was to be covered with grass.* □ *He measured the hall roughly by pacing out its length and breadth.*
> **pace off** When you **pace** a length or distance **off**, you measure it by counting the number of equally spaced steps you take to cover it: *He placed the fence posts at regular intervals by pacing off five metres between them.*

pacemaker /'peɪsmeɪkə(r)/ *noun*: **pacemakers**
A **pacemaker** is **1** an electronic device that is fitted surgically on or near the heart which helps it to beat normally. **2** another term for a pacesetter.

pacesetter /'peɪssetə(r)/ *noun*: **pacesetters**
A **pacesetter** is a leader that determines the speed or rate of progress which others have to keep up with in a race or contest: *The firm has always been a pacesetter in the electronics industry.* [see also **set the pace** at **pace**]

pacifism /'pasɪfɪzm/ *noun* (*uncount*)
Pacifism is the belief that all war is wrong and that peaceful means should be used to settle disputes.

pacifist /'pasɪfɪst/ *noun* (*often adjectival*): **pacifists**
A **pacifist** is someone who believes that all war is wrong and who therefore refuses to take part in making war: *After his experiences in the First World War, he became a pacifist.* □ *They refused to fight because of their pacifist beliefs.*

pacify /'pasɪfaɪ/ *verb*: **pacifies, pacifying, pacified**
1 If you **pacify** someone, you calm and soothe them so that they are no longer distressed or angry: *Imagination is needed to distract and pacify a crying child.* □ *The little boy made such a fuss that she had to give him sweets to pacify him.* [*same as* **calm down**] **2** To **pacify** an area or country where there is war or unrest means to restore or establish peace there: *All the attempts made by the international community to pacify the region failed.* **3** (*euphemistic*) To **pacify** also means to restore order and subdue any protest or resistance by force or threats: *Police armed with batons were used to pacify the rioting students.* — *noun* (*uncount*) **pacification** /pasɪfɪ'keɪʃən/: *Brutal force was used in the pacification of indigenous tribes.*

pack /pak/ *noun*; *verb*
▻ ***noun***: **packs**
1 A **pack** is **a** a collection of things tied together or put into a container so that they may carried: *He heaved an enormous pack on to his shoulders.* □ *All their equipment was put into packs and loaded on mules.* **b** a rucksack: *walkers with packs on their backs* □ *He searched in his pack for dry socks.* **2** A **pack** of cards is a complete set of playing-cards: *The game is played with a standard pack of 52 playing-cards.* □ *He shuffled the pack and dealt the cards.* **3** A compact package of equipment for a special purpose is also sometimes known as a **pack**: *a first-aid pack* □ *A starter pack containing a basic beer-making kit and step-by-step instructions.* **4** (*AmE*) A **pack** of things is a packet of them: *a pack of cigarettes.* **5** A **pack** is **a** a group of animals of the same kind that hunt together: *a pack of hounds* □ *a wolf-pack* □ *Wild dogs and wolves hunt in packs.* **b** a troop of Brownie Guides or Cub Scouts. **c** a group made up of the forwards in a rugby team. **6** (*derogatory*) A **pack** is also used for a group or collection of people or things that are considered to be criminal or dishonest: *a pack of thieves* □ *He told the police a pack of lies.*
▻ ***verb***: **packs, packing, packed**
1 You **pack** a container such as a suitcase, bag or box when you put things into it so that they may be transported or carried: *He packed all his books into a tea chest.* □ *machine parts packed into wooden boxes for export* □ *Have you packed the suntan lotion?* [*opposite* **unpack**] **2** (*in the passive*) You can say a place **is packed** with people or things when it is completely crowded or filled with them: *a special train packed with English and Welsh football supporters* □ *The House of Commons was packed for yesterday's debate.* **3** (*AmE*; *informal*) Someone who **packs** a gun makes a habit of carrying one: *It is not unusual to find ordinary citizens packing guns.*
▻ ***phrases*** **1** (*informal*) If you tell someone to **pack it in** you tell them rudely or impatiently to stop doing something: *'I can't stand that noise you're making. Pack it in!'* **2** (*informal*) You **send** someone **packing** when you dismiss them firmly and without ceremony: *If he bothers you at home again, send him packing.*

phrasal verbs
pack in 1 Someone **packs** a lot **in** or **into** a short space of time when they succeed in doing a great many things: *You seemed to have packed a lot into your weekend in Paris.* □ *They plan to pack as many excursions as possible into the three days.* **2** (*informal*) You **pack** something **in** when you stop doing it: *He's decided to pack his job in and go abroad.* □ *Do you know why she's packing in her job?* [*same as* **jack in, chuck**]
pack off You **pack** someone **off** somewhere when you send them there without wasting any time: *He was packed off to boarding school as soon as he was seven years old.* [*same as* **send off, bundle off**]
pack out You can say a place **is packed out** if it is as full as it is possible to be: *The cinema was packed out for the premiere of his latest film.* [*same as* **mob**]
pack up 1 a You **pack up** your belongings when you put them in a suitcase, bag or other container so that you may take them with you when you are leaving: *He packed up all his belongings in a battered suitcase and left the same day.* **b** You **pack up** at the end of a working day when you tidy your desk or work area and put everything away before you leave: *'The lesson is over,' said the teacher. 'It's time to pack up, children.'* [*same as* **clear up**] **2** (*informal*) You can say that something **has packed up** if it has broken down or stopped working altogether: *The car's engine packed up when they were a mile away from home.* □ *His kidneys have packed up completely and he needs a transplant urgently.*

package /ˈpakɪdʒ/ *noun*; *verb*
▻ ***noun***: **packages**
1 A **package** is a small parcel wrapped in paper: *a mysterious package wrapped in plain brown paper* □ *The postman couldn't get the package through her letterbox.* **2** A **package** is also a number of things that are offered together for sale or acceptance: *If you buy this model, a year's free car insurance is part of the package.* □ *This was part of the Chancellor's economic stabilization package, announced in May.* [see also **package deal**]
▻ ***verb*** (*usually in the passive*): **packages, packaging, packaged**
Something **is packaged** when it is put in a packet or box or wrapped up in a parcel before it is sold, sent, or given to someone: *The eggs are graded and packaged by machine.* □ *The perfume was beautifully packaged.* [see also **packaging**]

package deal /ˈpakɪdʒ diːl/ *noun*: **package deals**
A **package deal** is a number of related proposals or arrangements that must be accepted as a whole or not at all.

package holiday /pakɪdʒ ˈhɒlɪdeɪ/ or **package tour** /ˈpakɪdʒ tʊə(r)/ *noun*: **package holidays** or **tours**
A **package holiday** or **package tour** is a holiday or tour arranged by a travel agent for which you pay a fixed price to include travel and accommodation.

packaging /ˈpakɪdʒɪŋ/ *noun* (*uncount*)
The paper, cardboard, plastic, or other material that is used to wrap and pack something before it is sold or sent somewhere is its **packaging**: *bottles of perfume in expensive packaging* □ *It took a long time to remove all the layers of packaging.* [*same as* **packing**]

packed lunch /pakt ˈlʌntʃ/ *noun*: **packed lunches**
A **packed lunch** is food which you put in a box or similar container and take with you to work or school to eat as your lunch: *a packed lunch of sandwiches and fruit* □ *He doesn't use the canteen at work because he usually takes a packed lunch.*

packer /ˈpakə(r)/ *noun*: **packers**
A **packer** is someone whose job it is to pack things into containers ready for sale or distribution: *He works as a packer in the meat processing plant.*

packet /ˈpakɪt/ *noun*: **packets**
1 A **packet** is a small bag, box or other container in which a quantity of something is sold. It is often used to refer to the container and its contents: *He bought a packet of the new soap powder.* □ *a packet of seeds* □ *an empty cigarette packet* □ *He likes chocolate biscuits so much he often eats a whole packet.* **2** A **packet** is also a small flat parcel or package: *The documents were delivered in a sealed packet.* **3** (*informal*) When someone says that something cost a **packet**, or that someone is earning a **packet**, they mean that it cost, or they are earning, a large amount of money: *The house must have cost him a packet.* □ *He can afford a new car; he's earning a packet in his new job.* [*same as* **fortune, bomb**]

packing /ˈpakɪŋ/ *noun* (*uncount*)
1 Packing is any material used for wrapping or for protecting things from being damaged while they are being transported or stored: *There will be a small extra charge for postage and packing.* □ *You will have to put some more packing in around the china to stop it rattling about.* [*same as* **packaging**] **2 Packing** is also the process of putting things into a bag, suitcase, box,

or other suitable container so that they may be carried or sent somewhere: *He's in charge of packing and distribution.* □ *My clothes are washed and ironed and ready for packing.* □ *Have you done your packing for the holiday?*

packing case /ˈpakɪŋ keɪs/ *noun*: **packing cases**
A **packing case** is a wooden crate in which things are transported or stored: *When they emigrated they travelled by air, but their packing cases had to go by ship.*

pact /pakt/ *noun*: **pacts**
A **pact** is a formal agreement between two or more people, groups, or countries: *The Prince and Princess of Wales have made a pact to cover up their differences in public.* □ *It was discovered that the dead couple had made a suicide pact.* □ *The four countries signed a non-aggression pact.* [compare **contract, deal**]

pad[1] /pad/ *noun*; *verb*
▻ ***noun***: **pads**
1 A **pad** is a thick piece of material used to cushion, shape, protect or clean something: *The skateboarder escaped serious injury because he was wearing knee pads.* □ *a jacket with large shoulder pads* □ *Batsmen in cricket wear pads to protect their legs.* □ *She cleaned the wound with a pad of cotton wool soaked in iodine.* **2** A **pad** is also a number of sheets of paper fixed together along one edge so that each sheet may be torn off when it has been used: *a writing pad* □ *a notepad* □ *a pad of ruled paper.* **3** A **pad** is **a** a flat piece of ground or a specially-built flat-topped structure, often marked with a cross or the letter H, where helicopters can land and take off: *ships equipped with helicopter pads.* **b** a level surface or flat-topped structure from which rockets or missiles are launched: *a rocket launched from a mobile pad.* **4** The soft, fleshy parts on the bottom of the feet of certain animals, *eg* cats or dogs, are called **pads.**
▻ ***verb*** (*in the passive*): **pads, padding, padded**
Something **is padded** when it is covered or filled with a soft material to make it more comfortable or to protect it: *a padded bra* □ *The players legs are well padded to protect them from injury.* [see also **padding**]

phrasal verb
pad out 1 You **pad** a piece of writing or speech **out** when you add things to it which are not strictly necessary in order to make it longer: *He padded his essay out with a lot of quotations.* □ *Her first draft of the letter seemed too short, so she padded it out with descriptions of the weather.* □ *Can you pad your speech out a little so that it will last for half an hour?* [*opposite* **condense, shorten, cut down**] **2** To **pad** something **out** also means to fill it out with soft material so that it is the right size: *The actor's cheeks have been padded out with cotton wool to make him appear fatter.*

pad[2] /pad/ *verb*: **pads, padding, padded**
Someone or something **pads** when they walk softly so that their footsteps cannot be heard: *He was padding around the flat in his bare feet.* □ *The dog sniffed the air as he padded along.* □ *The lion padded about its enclosure.*

padding /ˈpadɪŋ/ *noun* (*uncount*)
Padding is soft material that is used to shape, fill, or protect something: *The padding in the sofa is made from polyurethane foam.* □ *American footballers with all-over padding* □ *a jacket with padding in the shoulders* □ *He wore a costume with lots of padding around the middle to make him look fat.* [compare **stuffing, filling**]

paddle[1] /ˈpadəl/ *noun*; *verb*
▻ ***noun***: **paddles**
A **paddle** is a short light oar with a wide part at one or both ends that is used to move a boat, especially a canoe, through the water.
▻ ***verb***: **paddles, paddling, paddled**
You **paddle** a boat when you move it through the water using a paddle or paddles, or something used like a paddle: *They paddled furiously to stop the canoe going over the waterfall.* □ *They had to use their hands to paddle the raft to the shore.*

paddle[2] /ˈpadəl/ *verb*; *noun*
▻ ***verb***: **paddles, paddling, paddled**
You **paddle** when you walk barefoot in shallow water: *The children went paddling in the sea* □ *The water's too cold for paddling.*
▻ ***noun*** (*used in the singular*); *The water looks lovely, so I'm going for a paddle.*

paddock /ˈpadək/ *noun*: **paddocks**
1 A **paddock** is a small field, usually close to a house or stable, for keeping horses in: *They usually keep the donkeys in the lower paddock.* **2** A **paddock** is also a special enclosure at a race track where horses are saddled and walked round before a race.

paddy /ˈpadɪ/ *noun*: **paddies**
A **paddy**, or **paddy field**, is a flooded field in which rice is grown.

padlock /ˈpadlɒk/ *noun*; *verb*
▻ ***noun***: **padlocks**
A **padlock** is a lock with a U-shaped bar that pivots at one side so that it can be passed through a ring or chain and locked in position.
▻ ***verb***: **padlocks, padlocking, padlocked**
You **padlock** something when you lock it or fasten it to something else using a padlock: *The gate was padlocked.* □ *He padlocked his bicycle to the railings.*

paediatric (*AmE* **pediatric**) /piːdɪˈatrɪk/ *adjective*
A **paediatric** ward in a hospital is one in which small children are treated; a **paediatric** nurse is a nurse who has special training in paediatrics, or who works in a paediatric ward.

paediatrician (*AmE* **pediatrician**) /piːdɪəˈtrɪʃən/ *noun*: **paediatricians**
A **paediatrician** is a doctor who specializes in studying and treating children's illnesses: *a consultant paediatrician* □ *The newborn baby was examined by a paediatrician.*

paediatrics (*AmE* **pediatrics**) /ˈpiːdɪˈatrɪks/ *noun* (*singular*)
Paediatrics is the branch of medicine that deals with children and their illnesses.

pagan /ˈpeɪgən/ *adjective*; *noun*
▻ ***adjective***
Pagan is used to describe certain religious beliefs and practices, particularly those that do not belong to any of the major world religions: *pagan rituals* □ *a old pagan festival celebrating the coming of Spring.*
▻ ***noun***: **pagans**
People whose beliefs do not belong to any of the major world religions or who have no religious beliefs are sometimes called **pagans**: *The ancient Romans were pagans.* — *noun* (*uncount*) **paganism:** *the paganism of the pre-Christian era in Britain.*
[compare **heathen**]

page[1] /peɪdʒ/ *noun*: **pages**
1 a A **page** is one side of the pieces of paper in a book, magazine, or newspaper: *The map of Scotland is on page 24.* □ *See the illustration on the facing page.* □ *a full-page advertisement* □ *Football results are on the*

back page of the newspaper. **b** A **page** is also one of the pieces of paper in a book, magazine, or newspaper: *a copy of the Bible with two pages missing* □ *She tore a page out of her diary to write him a note.* **2** (*literary*) An episode or series of related events in history or in a person's life is sometimes called a **page**: *He had turned a page in the book of life.* □ *The conquest of Mexico began a new page in the nation's history.* [*same as* **chapter**]

page[2] /peɪdʒ/ *noun*; *verb*

▻ ***noun***: **pages**

1 A **page** is a boy who works in a hotel and whose job it is to carry messages and luggage. **2** (also **pageboy**) In historical times, a **page** or **pageboy** was a boy who attended a knight, usually as part of his own training for knighthood. **3** (also **pageboy**) A **page** or **pageboy** is a small boy who is one of the bride's attendants at a wedding.

▻ ***verb***: **pages, paging, paged**

Someone **is paged** when they are called or summoned over a public-address system or via an electronic pager: *There isn't a doctor on the ward at the moment, but I'll page Doctor Peters in the casualty department.* □ *If I'm not in the office when you call, get the receptionist to page me.* □ *There was no reply from his hotel room, so I had him paged.*

pageant /ˈpadʒənt/ *noun*: **pageants**

1 A **pageant** is a form of outdoor public entertainment with people dressed in rich costumes, often acting out various scenes from history or literature, in a colourful procession: *She was chosen to play Queen Elizabeth the First in the village pageant.* □ *a historical pageant.* [compare **parade**] **2** A **pageant** is also any splendid or colourful show or spectacle: *a pageant of colour.*

pageantry /ˈpadʒəntrɪ/ *noun* (*uncount*)

Pageantry is the impressive and colourful display which forms part of a grand public show or ceremony: *the pageantry of Elizabeth I's coronation.* [*same as* **pomp, splendour**]

pageboy /ˈpeɪdʒbɔɪ/ *noun*: **pageboys**

1 A **pageboy** is a page. [see **page**[2], senses 2 and 3] **2** A **pageboy** is also a type of smooth medium-length hairstyle in which the ends of the hair are turned under and there is a long fringe from the crown of the head to the forehead.

pager /ˈpeɪdʒə(r)/ *noun*: **pagers**

A **pager** is an electronic communication system which is used to call or summon people through a small radio receiver which they carry with them. Pagers are widely used in hospitals and some types are designed to display a short message or to make a bleeping sound so that the person carrying it is aware that someone is trying to get in touch with them: *a radio pager* □ *a mobile phone equipped with a pager.*

paid /peɪd/ *verb*; *adjective*

▻ ***verb***

Paid is the past tense and past participle of **pay**.

▻ ***adjective***

1 You do **paid** work when you receive money for the work that you do: *Have you had any paid employment in the last six months?* □ *a paid assassin* □ *a low-paid job* □ *He has a well-paid job in industry.* **2 Paid** holiday or **paid** leave is a holiday or period of leave from work during which you are paid your normal wages or salary: *She earns a high salary and has six weeks paid leave a year.* [*opposite* **unpaid**]

paid-up /ˈpeɪdʌp/ *adjective*

Paid-up members of a society, club, or political party are members who have paid in full the money or subscription required to be a member: *He is a paid-up member of the British Communist Party.* □ *Only paid-up members may use the club's facilities.* [see also **pay up** at **pay**]

pail /peɪl/ *noun*: **pails**

1 A **pail** is a bucket: *He carried the water from the well in a metal pail.* **2** A **pail** of something is the pail and its contents or just the contents: *She walked across the field with a pail of milk in each hand:* □ *Mix one pail of sand with two pails of cement.*

pain /peɪn/ *noun*; *verb*

▻ ***noun***: **pains**

1 (*uncount or count*) You have **pain** or a **pain** when you have an unpleasant feeling of discomfort in part of your body because you are ill or have been hurt: *He has stabbing pains in his chest.* □ *The constant pain in his back makes him irritable.* □ *He suffers from back pain.* □ *It is common to get aches and pains in your joints as you get older.* □ *Are you in pain?* □ *I can't stand pain.* □ *The doctor gave him an injection to relieve the pain.* **2** (*uncount*) **Pain** is also the unhappiness or distress which someone feels when something unpleasant or upsetting happens or when someone else is cruel or inconsiderate: *She never recovered from the pain of her husband's death.* □ *He has caused his parents untold pain and suffering.* [*same as* **hurt**] **3** (*informal, derogatory*) **a** You can call someone a **pain**, or a **pain in the neck**, if you think they are irritating or annoying: *She is a real pain!* [*same as* **nuisance, pest**] **b** You can also refer to a task or situation as a **pain**, or a **pain in the neck**, because you think it is tiresome or difficult: *I hate ironing. It's a pain!* □ *Having to take two different buses to work is a pain in the neck.* [*same as* **nuisance, bother, drag, bore**]

▻ ***verb***: **pains, paining, pained**

Something **pains** you if it makes you feel unhappy or distressed: *It pains me to have to tell you that you have failed the exam again.* □ *It pains her when her son ignores her advice.* [*same as* **hurt, grieve**]

▻ ***phrases*** **1** (*formal*) Someone **is at pains**, or **takes pains**, to do something when they take great trouble and care to do it properly and thoroughly: *She was at pains to make it understood that all the children received equal rations.* □ *He took great pains to ensure that the party was a success.* **2** If you say someone got a particular thing **for their pains** you mean that it was a poor or unfair reward for all their trouble and effort in doing something: *She was always kind towards him, and all she got for her pains was abuse and ridicule.* **3** (*formal*) Someone is **on** or **under pain of** a particular punishment if they are at risk of receiving that punishment if they do something that is forbidden or against a stated rule or law: *He was driven from the palace and forbidden to return on pain of death.* □ *He was sworn to secrecy under pain of instant dismissal from his position at the ministry.*

pained /peɪnd/ *adjective*

If someone looks or sounds **pained**, they show by their expression or tone of voice that they are upset or offended: *He listened to the singers rehearsing with a pained expression on his face.* □ *I wasn't criticizing you, so you needn't sound so pained.*

painful /ˈpeɪnfəl/ *adjective*

1 A part of the body is **painful** when it hurts: *His arm was so painful he couldn't sleep.* □ *a painful injury* □ *Is your knee painful?* [*same as* **sore**] **2** Something is **painful** when it causes or involves physical pain: *Arthritis is a painful condition.* □ *The treatment is likely to be very painful.* [*opposite* **painless**] **3** You can describe something that causes unhappiness or is upsetting as **painful**: *He had the painful duty of telling* *the parents that their son was dead.* □ *They have just been through a very painful divorce.* □ *Growing up is sometimes a very painful process.* [*same as* **distressing**] **4** You can also describe something that is difficult or involves a lot of effort or hard work as **painful**: *Their progress through the dense jungle was slow and painful.* [*same as* **arduous**] — *adverb* **painfully**: *He rose painfully and limped to the door.* □ *Medical facilities were painfully inadequate and many children died in infancy.* □ *Their progress was painfully slow because of the rough tracks and the bad weather conditions.*

painkiller /ˈpeɪnkɪlə(r)/ *noun*: **painkillers**
A **painkiller** is a drug that reduces or gets rid of pain: *Morphine is an effective painkiller.*

painless /ˈpeɪnləs/ *adjective*
1 Something is **painless** when it involves or causes no physical pain or discomfort: *painless childbirth* □ *Dental treatment is usually quite painless nowadays.* [*opposite* **painful**] **2** (*informal*) You can also describe something as **painless** if it is easy to do or involves very little effort or hard work: *a relatively painless way to lose weight* □ *I was dreading the exam, but it turned out to be quite painless.* — *adverb* **painlessly**: *The surgery was carried out painlessly using local anaesthetic.* □ *They bought their tickets, got through the customs, and boarded the plane, all quite painlessly.*

painstaking /ˈpeɪnzteɪkɪŋ/ *adjective*
A person described as **painstaking** takes a great deal of trouble to do things carefully and thoroughly: *The book on African tribal customs involved the author in years of painstaking research.* □ *His approach to his studies has always been painstaking.* [*same as* **meticulous**; *opposite* **careless, negligent**]

paint /peɪnt/ *noun*; *verb*
▻ ***noun*: paints**
1 (*uncount, often adjectival*) **Paint** is a colouring substance in the form of liquid or paste which is applied to a surface, usually with a brush or roller, to decorate or protect it: *paint for exterior walls* □ *a tin of gloss paint* □ *a paint manufacturer* □ *She mixed some white into the green paint to get the shade she wanted.* □ *He had to scrape off several layers of old paint before he exposed the original woodwork.* □ *Don't touch the walls until the paint has dried.* **2 Paints** are tubes, bottles, or solid tablets of colouring matter for creating pictures or designs: *acrylic paints* □ *oil paints* □ *poster paints* □ *He took his paints and brushes with him on holiday.*
▻ ***verb*: paints, painting, painted**
1 You **paint** something, such as a wall or woodwork, when you cover it with a layer, or several layers, of paint: *He has painted all the window frames green.* □ *We can't use the sitting room while the men are painting the ceiling.* □ *What colour are you going to paint the kitchen?* **2** You **paint** when you make a picture or design on paper, canvas or any other suitable surface using paints: *He enjoys painting outdoors.* □ *She learnt how to draw and paint in art college.* □ *She paints with oils.* □ *The design was painted using watercolours.* **3** You **paint** someone or something when you make a picture of them using paints: *His wife was his favourite subject, and he painted her many times.* □ *He had his portrait painted by a famous artist.* □ *She enjoys painting flowers.* **4** A woman **paints** her face or her nails when she puts make-up or nail varnish on: *Her lips and nails were painted a bright red.*

paintbox /ˈpeɪntbɒks/ *noun*: **paintboxes**
A **paintbox** is a box or case containing paints in a variety of colours for painting pictures: *Is there a cobalt blue in your paintbox?*

paintbrush /ˈpeɪntbrʌʃ/ *noun*: **paintbrushes**
A **paintbrush** is a brush used for applying paint: *He is using a roller rather than a paintbrush for the walls.* □ *You should always clean your paintbrushes thoroughly.*

painter /ˈpeɪntə(r)/ *noun*: **painters**
A **painter** is **1** an artist who paints pictures: *a portrait painter* □ *He has always wanted to be a painter.* **2** someone whose job is painting the inside and outside of houses and other buildings: *a house painter* □ *We are having the painters in next week to do the sitting room.*

painting /ˈpeɪntɪŋ/ *noun*: **paintings**
1 A **painting** is a painted picture: *an oil painting* □ *a painting by Constable* □ *His paintings are found in galleries throughout the world.* **2** (*uncount*) **a Painting** is the art of creating pictures in paint: *an evening class in drawing and painting* □ *He has taken up painting in his spare time.* **b Painting** is also the activity or process of applying paint, *eg* to walls and woodwork to decorate and protect them: *He did all the painting and decorating himself.* □ *I enjoy hanging wallpaper, but I hate painting.*

pair /peə(r)/ *noun*; *verb*
▻ ***noun*: pairs**
1 (*usually with a singular verb*) A **pair** of things is **a** a set of two things that are the same size or shape and are used, or designed for use, together: *two pairs of woollen gloves* □ *Wear thick socks and take a spare pair with you in your pack.* □ *The male has an extra pair of legs at its front end.* □ *Every pair of eyes was turned towards her.* □ *I bought a pair of contact lenses but I've never worn them.* **b** an object such as a tool or piece of clothing consisting of two joined, corresponding parts: *a pair of nail scissors* □ *There's a clean pair of underpants in the drawer.* □ *He needs two pairs of glasses.* **c** any two things that are being considered together for some reason: *Take a pair of examples from English, one abstract, one concrete.* [*same as* **couple**]
2 (*with a singular or plural verb*) **a** Two people who are associated in some way, or just happen to be together, can be referred to as a **pair**: *The pair are pictured above setting off on their honeymoon.* □ *Tansy and Jules made an odd pair as they stepped among the gravestones.* □ *We gazed at each other like a pair of fools.* □ *the superb dancing of the Dublin pair, Michael O'Connor and Sharon McCann* □ *They came second in the pairs competition.* [*same as* **couple**] **b** A **pair** of creatures, especially birds, is a male and a female that are mates: *When they mate the pair intertwine their bodies.*
▻ ***verb*: pairs, pairing, paired**
To **pair** or **be paired** is to be grouped together in twos, pairs, or couples, or as mates: *Fully sighted pupils are paired with visually handicapped ones.* □ *Killer whales pair for life.*
▻ ***phrase*** If people or things are **in pairs** they are grouped in twos, pairs or couples: *There will be a variety of activities for you to carry out individually, in pairs, and in groups.* □ *China dogs like these were usually made in pairs.*

phrasal verbs
pair off People **pair off** or **are paired off** when they associate, or are grouped, together in twos, pairs or couples: *She had evidently paired off Damien and Clare in her mind.* □ *You'll all meet at the rendezvous point, then pair off.*
pair up One person or creature **pairs up** with another when they join together as a couple or as mates: *Perhaps we could pair up and share a room, to save money.* □ *The birds only pair up shortly before breeding.*

pajamas see **pyjamas**.

pal /pal/ *noun; verb*
▻ ***noun*** (*informal*): **pals**
1 Your **pal** is your friend: *They have always been great pals.* ▫ *He is bringing his new pal home for tea.* ▫ *Be a pal and lend me your ruler.* **2** Some people use **pal** as a rude or aggressive form of address to a man or boy: *Don't get clever with me, pal!*
▻ ***verb*** (*informal*): **pals, palling, palled**

> ***phrasal verbs***
> **pal around** People, especially children or young adults, **pal around** together when they are friends with each other and spend time together: *He pals around with the boys from the village.* ▫ *Who do you pal around with at boarding school?*
> **pal up** You **pal up** with someone when you become friends with them: *Has he palled up with any of the children at school yet?*

palace /ˈpaləs/ *noun*: **palaces**
A **palace** is **1** a large, grand house that is the home or official residence of a king or queen, bishop, archbishop or president: *the presidential palace* ▫ *They are changing guard at Buckingham Palace.* ▫ *Lambeth Palace.* **2** any grand or magnificent house or building: *Their house is like a little palace!*

palatable /ˈpalətəbəl/ *adjective* (*formal*)
1 If you describe food or drink as **palatable** you mean that it has a pleasant taste: *This wine is most palatable.* ▫ *a very palatable Beaujolais* ▫ *Though the hotel wasn't what I'm used to, the food was quite palatable.* [*same as* **appetizing**] **2** If you describe a fact or idea as **palatable** you mean that it is acceptable or agreeable: *The truth is not always very palatable.*
[*opposite* **unpalatable**]

palate /ˈpalət/ *noun* (*uncount or used in the singular*)
1 Your **palate** is the top of the inside of your mouth, made up of the **hard palate** at the front and the **soft palate** at the back. **2** Someone's **palate** is also their sense of taste, especially their ability to judge good food and wines: *He has developed a good palate for fine wine.* ▫ *My palate is not refined enough to distinguish between good and bad wine.*

palatial /pəˈleɪʃəl/ *adjective*
A house or other building that is described as **palatial** is grand and splendid like a palace: *a palatial mansion* ▫ *The hotel was palatial and the service first class.*

palaver /pəˈlɑːvə(r)/ *noun* (*uncount or used in the singular; informal*)
Palaver is unnecessary fuss, often including a lot of talking about the way something is, or should be, done: *They would get the job done just as well without all the palaver of weekly committee meetings.* ▫ *What a palaver!*

pale /peɪl/ *adjective; verb*
▻ ***adjective***: **paler, palest**
1 A person or their face looks or goes **pale** when their skin colour is or becomes a lighter colour than normal because they are ill, frightened, or shocked: *You look a little pale: do you feel all right?* ▫ *When she heard the news, she turned deathly pale and looked as if she was going to faint.* [compare **pallid**] **2** Colours that are **pale** are of a whitish tone that is not bright or vivid: *pale green leaves* ▫ *a pale pink dress* ▫ *Is this carpet available in a paler blue?* ▫ *a rose of palest pink* ▫ *She suits pale colours.* [*same as* **light**; *opposite* **dark**] **3** Light that is described as **pale** is dim and faint: *a pale moon* ▫ *the pale light of dawn.*
▻ ***verb***: **pales, paling, paled**
1 Someone's face **pales** when they lose some of their normal colour, usually as a result of fear or shock: *She paled visibly when she was given the result of the test.* **2** Something **pales** when its brightness or importance fades: *Their financial problems pale into insignificance compared with the poverty of their tenants.* — *adverb* **palely**: *The moon shone palely down on the travellers as they hurried through the night.* — *noun* **paleness**: *Many thought her a great beauty because of the blackness of her hair and the paleness of her skin.* [compare **pallor**]

palette /ˈpalət/ *noun*: **palettes**
1 A **palette** is a flat piece of wood or plastic, usually with a hole for the thumb to hold it by, on which an artist mixes colours while painting. **2** A **palette** is also the assortment or range of colours used by a particular artist or school of painting: *Rembrandt's palette was darker and more sombre in his later paintings.*

palette knife /ˈpalət naɪf/ *noun*: **palette knives**
A **palette knife** is
1 a knife with a blade that can be bent easily used by artists for mixing and applying paint. **2** a round-ended knife with such a blade used in cookery for spreading or mixing ingredients.

paling /ˈpeɪlɪŋ/ *noun* (*usually in the plural*): **palings**
Palings are a series of thin, pointed pieces of wood or metal fixed together to form a solid fence: *The park was surrounded by high metal palings.* [compare **railings**]

pall[1] /pɔːl/ *noun*: **palls**
1 A **pall** is a dark-coloured cloth that is sometimes used to cover a coffin at a funeral. **2** A thick cloud of something, such as smoke, that hangs over or covers an area is also called a **pall**: *A great pall of smoke rose from the burning city.* ▫ *A pall of gloom descended on the village when the mine closed.* [*same as* **shroud, cloak**]

pall[2] /pɔːl/ *verb* (*formal*): **palls, palling, palled**
Something **palls** when it becomes boring or less interesting: *His comic antics begin to pall after a while.* ▫ *She found that their conversation soon palled on her.*

pallbearer /ˈpɔːbeərə(r)/ *noun*: **pallbearers**
A **pallbearer** is one of the people who carry the coffin or walk beside it at a funeral.

pallet /ˈpalət/ *noun*: **pallets**
A **pallet** is a small wooden platform or tray on which goods are stacked so that they can be lifted or moved by a fork-lift truck: *a pallet of bricks.*

pallid /ˈpalɪd/ *adjective* (*formal* or *literary*)
Pallid is used to describe people or things that are unnaturally or unhealthily pale: *His skin had a pallid, sickly appearance.* ▫ *slices of pallid tinned meat with limp lettuce.*

pallor /ˈpalə(r)/ *noun* (*uncount; formal*)
Pallor is unnatural or unhealthy paleness of the skin: *There was a general air of pallor and limp weariness about her.* ▫ *The sleepless night had added to her pallor and the haunted look in her eye.*

palm[1] /pɑːm/ *noun; verb*
▻ ***noun***: **palms**
Your **palms** are the flat inner surfaces of your hands between the wrist and the fingers: *She held the little bird gently in the palm of her hand.* ▫ *They held out their hands with the palms upwards.* ▫ *When he took her hand, his palm felt damp and unpleasant.* ▫ *gloves with leather palms.* [see picture at **body**]

▻ ***verb*: palms, palming, palmed**

A magician or conjurer **palms** something when he or she hides it in the palm of their hand so that the audience cannot see it: *He palmed the red ball so that it seemed to disappear.*

> ***phrasal verb***
> **palm off** (*informal, derogatory*) **1** Someone **palms** an unwanted or inferior thing **off** on someone else when they get rid of it by persuading the other person to take it or buy it: *He tried to palm an old cooker off on me with a promise that it would go on working for years.* **2** Someone **palms** somebody **off** with something when they dishonestly try to persuade them to accept it: *I won't let him palm me off with any more excuses.*
> [*same as* **fob off**]

palm² /pɑːm/ *noun*: **palms**

A **palm**, or a **palm tree**, is any of several types of tree that grow in warm or tropical climates. Palms have a mass of broad blade-like leaves growing from the top of a trunk without branches: *a date palm* □ *coconut palms* □ *There was an avenue of tall palms between the seafront hotels and the beach.*

palpable /'palpəbəl/ *adjective*

1 (*formal*) Something that is **palpable** is easily noticed or felt: *a palpable lie* □ *the palpable flaws in his argument* □ *'A hit, a very palpable hit.'* [*same as* **obvious, evident**] **2** (*medicine*) Something, such as a lump or an organ in the body, is described as **palpable** when it can be felt or detected by touch: *a palpable growth in the lower intestine.* — *adverb* (*formal*) **palpably**: *His entire statement was palpably untrue.*

palpitate /'palpɪteɪt/ *verb*: **palpitates, palpitating, palpitated**

Someone's heart **palpitates** when it beats very quickly or irregularly causing an unpleasant feeling: *Her heart was palpitating with fear.*

palpitation /palpɪ'teɪʃən/ *noun*: **palpitations**

You have **palpitations** if your heart beats very rapidly for a time, usually because you are afraid or anxious or because your heart is under too much strain: *The doctor asked if he had ever had chest pains or palpitations after exercise.* □ *The thought of running a marathon gives me palpitations!*

paltry /'pɔːltrɪ/ *adjective* (*formal*): **paltrier, paltriest**

You can describe something, such as an amount, as **paltry** if you think it is small and unimportant or inadequate for the purpose: *She was paid a paltry sum for her work.* □ *He paid a paltry £5 for the painting.* □ *The small bedroom had a paltry view of the sea and harbour.* [*same as* **meagre, mean, trifling**]

pamper /'pampə(r)/ *verb*: **pampers, pampering, pampered**

You **pamper** someone when you treat them with too much kindness and do too much for them, or give special things to them: *The little boy was pampered by his mother.* □ *I'm going to pamper myself by going to hairdresser this weekend.* [*same as* **spoil**] — *adjective* **pampered:** *a pampered pet.*

pamphlet /'pamflət/ *noun*: **pamphlets**

A **pamphlet** is a thin book with a paper cover which gives information on, or deals with, a particular subject: *political pamphlets* □ *The doctor gave her a pamphlet on the various methods of birth control.* □ *Does the tourist office have any pamphlets dealing with local history?* [*same as* **leaflet**; compare **brochure**]

pan¹ /pan/ *noun*: **pans**

1 A **pan** is a container, usually made of metal and with a handle or handles, that is used for cooking things in: *Put the meat and vegetables into a pan with the stock and cook over a low heat for one hour.* □ *a pan of boiling water* □ *a frying-pan* □ *pots and pans made of copper.* **2** A **pan** is also any of various kinds of shallow or bowl-shaped containers used for various purposes: *a lavatory pan* □ *a bedpan* □ *a dustpan.*

pan² /pan/ *verb*: **pans, panning, panned**

A film or television camera operator **pans** when he or she moves the camera to the right or left while filming to follow a moving object or show a wide view of a scene: *It reduces the need to pan the camera to follow the subject.* □ *a panning shot.*

pan- /pan/ *prefix*

Pan- is used before adjectives and means 'all of' or 'the whole of': *Pan-African* □ *Pan-American* □ *pandemic.*

panacea /panə'sɪə/ *noun*: **panaceas**

A **panacea** is something that is supposed to cure all illnesses or solve all problems: *There is no single panacea for all the problems of humanity.* □ *a panacea for all the country's economic difficulties.*

panache /pə'naʃ/ *noun* (*uncount*)

When somebody does something with **panache** they do it with spirited and stylish self-confidence: *They performed the tango with great panache.* [*same as* **dash**]

pancake /'pankeɪk/ *noun*: **pancakes**

A **pancake** is a very thin round cake made from a mixture of milk, flour and eggs and cooked on both sides in a frying-pan or on a griddle: *There are pancakes with sweet or savoury fillings on the menu.* □ *He's an expert at tossing pancakes.*

Pancake Day /'pankeɪk deɪ/ *noun* (*uncount*)

Pancake Day is another name for Shrove Tuesday, a day on which it is traditional to make and eat pancakes.

panda /'pandə/ *noun*: **pandas**

(also **giant panda**) A **panda** is a large black and white bear-like animal that lives in the bamboo forests in the mountains of SW China. Pandas are extremely rare and are protected in the areas of China where they are still found.

pandemonium /pandə'moʊnɪəm/ *noun* (*uncount*)

Pandemonium is a state of great noise and wild confusion: *Pandemonium broke out as soon as the teacher left the classroom.* □ *There was pandemonium in the theatre when it was announced that the concert was cancelled.* [*same as* **uproar**; *opposite* **calm, order, peace**]

pander /'pandə(r)/ *verb*: **panders, pandering, pandered**

> ***phrasal verb***
> You **pander to** someone when you give or tell them something that they want or like, even when it may be wrong to do so: *She panders to his slightest whim.* □ *He made a speech pandering to the extremists in the party.* [*same as* **indulge**]

pane /peɪn/ *noun*: **panes**

A **pane** is a flat sheet of glass fitted into a window or door: *a pane of frosted glass* □ *a windowpane.*

panel /'panəl/ *noun*; *verb*

▻ ***noun*: panels**

1 A **panel** is a flat rectangular piece of wood or some other material that forms a section of *eg* a wall or door: *He fitted a new glass panel in the front door.* **2** A **panel** is also a piece of cloth, often of a different colour or fabric, that is set into an article of clothing: *a white skirt with panels of red and green* □ *a plain* *white dress with an embroidered panel down the front.* **3** The separate metal sections that form the bodywork of a vehicle are called **panels**: *The door-panels on the driver's side of the car were dented in the crash.* **4** A **panel** is a board with switches or instruments for controlling or operating a machine, a piece of equipment, or an aircraft: *an instrument panel* □ *a control panel.* **5** (*with a singular or plural verb*) A **panel** is a group of people selected for a special purpose, *eg* to judge a contest or to take part in a discussion, quiz or other game in front of an audience: *The panel is made up of MPs from the three main political parties.* □ *The competition will be judged by a panel of experts.* □ *a panel of twelve jurors* □ *Shall we find out what the panel thinks (*or *think)?* □ *a panel game.*

▻ ***verb***: **panels, panelling** (*AmE* **paneling**), **panelled** (*AmE* **paneled**)

You **panel** a door or a wall when you fit or decorate it with panels: *The hall is to be panelled in oak.* — *adjective* **panelled:** *an oak-panelled study.*

panelling (*AmE* **paneling**) /ˈpanəlɪŋ/ *noun* (*uncount*)
Panelling is wood or other material for panels in walls or doors: *The panelling in the hall is made of oak.*

panellist (*AmE* **panelist**) /ˈpanəlɪst/ *noun*: **panellists**
A **panellist** is a member of a panel (sense 5): *Let's ask the other panellists for their opinions.* □ *The panellists tonight are all distinguished experts in their respective fields.*

pang /paŋ/ *noun*: **pangs**
A **pang** is a sudden strong feeling or physical pain caused by *eg* hunger or guilt: *As the day wore on he began to feel pangs of hunger.* □ *She felt a pang of remorse as she watched him hurry away.*

panic /ˈpanɪk/ *noun*; *verb*

▻ ***noun*** (*uncount or count*): **panics**

Panic is a feeling of great fear or anxiety which causes the person or people affected by it to lose their ability to think clearly or act in a reasonable or logical way: *When the volcano began to erupt, panic spread through the village.* □ *The rumours of war caused widespread panic.* □ *She was in a state of total panic.* □ *They rushed about in a mad panic.*

▻ ***verb***: **panics, panicking, panicked**

Someone **panics**, or **is panicked** by something, when they have, or something causes them to have, a feeling of fear or anxiety which is so great they cannot think or act normally: *She panics whenever she's asked to speak in public.* □ *If you just keep calm and don't panic, we'll get there in time.* □ *He was panicked into making the wrong decision.* □ *The shots panicked the horses and several riders were thrown.*

panicky /ˈpanɪkɪ/ *adjective* (*informal*)
Someone who is **panicky** is, or has a tendency to become, extremely anxious or afraid: *She gets a bit panicky before interviews.*

panic-stricken /ˈpanɪkstrɪkən/ *adjective*
Someone who is **panic-stricken** is filled with terror or anxiety: *He helped to calm the panic-stricken horses.* □ *She rushed around panic-stricken, trying to stop the water getting in.*

pannier /ˈpanɪə(r)/ *noun*: **panniers**
A **pannier** is one of a pair of baskets or bags carried on either side of a horse's or donkey's back or on either side of the rear wheel of a bicycle or motor bike.

panorama /panəˈrɑːmə/ *noun*: **panoramas**
1 A **panorama** is an all-round view of a wide area of land: *Seen from the top of the mountain, the rainforest stretched away into the distance on all sides in a breathtaking panorama.* **2** A **panorama** is also an overall survey or representation of a subject: *a panorama of European history from Roman times to the present day.* — *adjective* **panoramic** /panəˈramɪk/: *a panoramic view of London.*

panpipes /ˈpanpaɪps/ *noun* (*plural*)
Panpipes are a musical instrument made up of a series of reeds or pipes of different lengths fixed together and played by blowing across their open ends.

pansy /ˈpanzɪ/ *noun*: **pansies**
1 A **pansy** is a small garden flower with broad flat brightly-coloured petals. **2** (*offensive slang*) Some people call a man or a boy a **pansy** if they think he looks or behaves like a woman or a girl, or is a homosexual.

pant /pant/ *verb*: **pants, panting, panted**
A person or animal **pants** when they breathe quickly and loudly, *eg* because they have been running or because it is very hot: *He staggered, exhausted and panting, over the finish line.* □ *The dogs lay down in the shade, panting.*

panther /ˈpanθə(r)/ *noun*: **panthers**
1 A leopard, especially one with a black rather than a spotted coat, is called a **panther** or a **black panther**. **2** (*AmE*) A puma is also sometimes called a **panther** in Canada and the US.

panties /ˈpantɪz/ *noun* (*plural*)
Panties are pants for women and girls: *a pair of panties.*

pantihose or **pantyhose** /ˈpantɪhoʊz/ *noun* (*plural*; *AmE*)
Pantihose or **pantyhose** are women's tights.

pantomime /ˈpantəmaɪm/ *noun*: **pantomimes**
A **pantomime** is a musical play for children performed at or around Christmas. Pantomimes are usually based on popular fairy stories and include songs, dancing and comedy acts: *One of the stars of the Christmas pantomime at Blackpool.* □ *He has appeared in 'Jack and the Beanstalk', 'Cinderella', and other popular pantomimes.*

pantry /ˈpantrɪ/ *noun*: **pantries**
1 A **pantry** is a small room where food is stored. In a house, a pantry is usually close to or leading off a kitchen: *She put the jars of pickles on the top shelf in the pantry.* **2** In some hotels and large houses, a **pantry** is also a small room where glass, silver and tableware is kept: *a butler's pantry.*

pants /pants/ *noun* (*plural*)
1 (*BrE*) **Pants** are an undergarment worn to cover the buttocks and lower part of the body: *a clean pair of pants.* [*same as* **knickers, panties, underpants;** see picture at **clothing**] **2** (*AmE*) **Pants** are trousers: *schoolboys in short pants* □ *striped pants* □ *He found the piece of paper in his pants pocket.* [see picture at **clothing**]

pantyhose see **pantihose**.

pap /pap/ *noun* (*uncount*; *derogatory*)
You can refer to a book, magazine, newspaper or television programme as **pap** if you think that it is completely lacking in merit or interest: *Why do you watch this awful pap?* [*same as* **rubbish, drivel, trash**]

papa /pəˈpɑː/ *noun* (*informal, old*): **papas**
Some people call or refer to their father as **papa**: *My papa is a banker.* □ *'Papa, do hurry or we will be late,' said Emily.* □ *Our papas have been friends since they were small boys.*

papal /ˈpeɪpəl/ *adjective*
Papal means of, from, concerned with, or relating to the pope: *a papal dispensation* □ *a papal procession.*

papaya /pəˈpaɪə/ *noun*: **papayas**
A **papaya** is a large yellow fruit with sweet orange flesh which grows on a tropical palm-like tree. [*same as* **pawpaw**; see picture at **fruit**]

paper /ˈpeɪpə(r)/ *noun*; *verb*
▻ ***noun***: **papers**
1 (*uncount*) **Paper** is a material made in thin sheets and used for writing, printing and drawing on, and for wrapping things in: *a sheet of paper* □ *wrapping paper* □ *a brown paper bag* □ *writing paper* □ *We've run out of paper for the printer.* **2** A **paper** is a newspaper: *I saw the article in yesterday's paper.* □ *Which paper does that journalist work for?* □ *It is front-page news in all the papers.* **3** (*uncount or count*) Wallpaper, or a particular type or pattern of wallpaper, is also called **paper**, or a **paper**: *We have to buy paper and paint to decorate the living room.* □ *a book of samples with more than 50 different papers.* **4** (*plural*) **a Papers** are pieces of paper with information written, printed or typed on them: *He gathered up all his papers and put them back in his briefcase.* **b** Your **papers** are official documents showing your identity or giving you permission to travel to or work in another country: *an illegal immigrant with forged papers* □ *The soldiers stopped the bus and demanded to see everyone's papers.* **5 a** A **paper** is a set of questions on a certain subject for a written examination: *Was there a question on Shakespeare's sonnets in the English paper?* □ *He failed his Latin paper.* **b** A **paper** is also a piece of written material on an academic subject, especially one that is to be read to an audience or intended for publication: *His paper on ancient Egyptian pyramid scripts was very well received.*
▻ ***verb***: **papers, papering, papered**
You **paper** a wall or a room when you decorate it with wallpaper: *When are you going to start papering the hall?*
▻ ***phrases*** **1** A plan, idea, or proposal can be described as looking good **on paper** when it has been worked out well in theory but may not necessarily work in practice. **2 a** You put your ideas or thoughts down **on paper** when you write them down: *Get some of your proposals down on paper so that you can present them at the next meeting.* **b** Something is **on paper** when there is evidence in writing that it is true or that it exists: *The agreement was only made verbally; there is nothing on paper.*

> ***phrasal verb***
> You **paper over** a disagreement, fault or difficulty when you hide or disguise it so that you can give the impression that there is agreement or that all is well. [*same as* **cover up**]

paperback /ˈpeɪpəbak/ *noun* (*uncount or count*): **paperbacks**
A **paperback** is a book with a paper or thin cardboard binding: *He bought three paperbacks to read on the journey.* □ *a paperback edition of 'Jane Eyre'* □ *When will his new book be available in paperback?* [compare **hardback**]

paper boy /ˈpeɪpə bɔɪ/ *noun*: **paper boys**
A **paper boy** is a boy who sells newspapers in the street or delivers them to people's homes.

paper clip /ˈpeɪpə klɪp/ *noun*: **paper clips**
A **paper clip** is a metal clip formed from bent wire, for holding papers together. [see picture at **office**]

paper knife /ˈpeɪpə naɪf/ *noun*: **paper knives**
A **paper knife** is a knife or knife-like object with a cutting edge used *eg* for opening envelopes.

paper money /ˈpeɪpə mʌnɪ/ *noun* (*uncount*)
Paper money is money in the form of bank notes, rather than coins.

paper shop /ˈpeɪpə ʃɒp/ *noun*: **paper shops**
A **paper shop** is a shop that sells newspapers and magazines.

paperweight /ˈpeɪpəweɪt/ *noun*: **paperweights**
A **paperweight** is a small heavy, often ornamental, object that is placed on top of loose papers to prevent them from being scattered or blown away: *a glass paperweight.*

paperwork /ˈpeɪpəwɜːk/ *noun* (*uncount*)
Paperwork is the written work that forms part of someone's job, *eg* keeping records and files and writing letters and reports: *I've got a lot of paperwork to catch up on.* □ *His secretary deals with a lot of the routine paperwork.*

papery /ˈpeɪpərɪ/ *adjective*
Something that is **papery** is thin and dry in texture like paper: *the papery outer skin of an onion.*

papier mâché /papɪeɪˈmaʃeɪ/ *noun* (*uncount*)
Papier mâché is a light material made of chopped up pieces of paper mixed with glue that can be moulded into shape while wet to make models, ornaments, bowls and boxes: *a model of a dinosaur in papier mâché* □ *a papier-mâché box.*

paprika /ˈaprɪkə/ *noun* (*uncount*)
Paprika is a red powder made from a type of sweet pepper and used as a seasoning for food.

papyrus /pəˈpaɪrəs/ *noun*: **papyri** /pəˈpaɪraɪ/ or **papyruses**
1 (*uncount*) **Papyrus** is a tall reed-like water plant that grows in North Africa. **2** (*uncount*) **Papyrus** is a type of paper made, especially by the ancient Egyptians, Romans and Greeks, from the stems of this plant. **3** A **papyrus** is an ancient manuscript written on this paper: *The entire papyrus contains 190 chapters, dealing in detail with the Egyptian cult of the dead.* □ *Scholars found a wealth of information in the innumerable papyri that were recovered.*

par /pɑː(r)/ *noun* (*used in the singular*)
In golf, **par** is the number of strokes considered necessary for a good golfer to complete a hole or course: *What is par for the next hole?* □ *a par 5 hole* □ *His last round was two over par.*
▻ ***phrases*** **1** (*informal*) **a** Something can be described as **below par** or **not up to par** if it is not up to the usual or required standard: *Your work has not been up to par recently.* □ *His game was below par all last season.* **b** You are feeling **below par** if you are feeling unwell: *He had been feeling a bit below par for some time.* **2** Something is **on a par with** something else if it is equivalent to that thing or of equal quality or importance: *As a footballer, he is on a par with many first division players.* **3** (*informal*) Something can be described as being **par for the course** if it is only to be expected or is typical: *The company has to fight hard for every order, but that's par for the course nowadays.*

parable /ˈparəbəl/ *noun*: **parables**
A **parable** is a short story, especially in the Bible, intended to teach a moral or religious lesson.

parachute /ˈparəʃuːt/ *noun*; *verb*
▻ ***noun***: **parachutes**
A **parachute** is a device which allows people or objects to fall slowly to the ground when dropped from an aircraft or from a great height. A parachute is made from a large umbrella-like circle of cloth attached by strings or cords to a harness: *He strapped his parachute on his back.* □ *a parachute drop behind enemy lines.*

▷ ***verb***: **parachutes, parachuting, parachuted**
You **parachute** when you drop to the ground from an aircraft using a parachute: *The commandos parachuted into occupied France.* □ *Emergency supplies will have to be parachuted in to the region when winter comes.* — *noun* **parachutist:** *stunt parachutists.*

parade /pə'reɪd/ *noun*; *verb*
▷ ***noun***: **parades**
1 A **parade** is an event when a group of people or vehicles move through the streets or some other public place in a procession: *a fashion parade* □ *The annual carnival parade through the streets of Rio.* □ *The Commonwealth Games began with a parade of all the athletes taking part.* **2** A group of soldiers gathered together in rank for formal marching or inspection is a **parade**: *a drill parade* □ *The commanding officer will inspect the parade at two o'clock.* □ *The entire regiment is on parade for its centenary celebrations.* **3** You make a **parade** of your skill, knowledge or feelings when you make a public display of them to attract attention or admiration: *Don't make such a parade of your feelings; it tends to cause embarrassment.* [*same as* **show**] **4 Parade** is also used in certain placenames, such as a promenade or shopping street: *Alexandra Parade.*
▷ ***verb***: **parades, parading, paraded**
1 When a group of people or soldiers **parade** they walk or march in procession: *Scottish regiments parading down the Mall* □ *The circus paraded through the centre of the town.* **2** You **parade** something when you make a display of it, intended to attract attention or admiration: *ladies parading extraordinary and original hats in the royal enclosure at Ascot* □ *The other students get irritated when she parades her knowledge in class.* [*same as* **flaunt, show off**]

paradise /'parədaɪs/ *noun*: **paradises**
1 (*used in the singular*) **Paradise** is the wonderful place which some people believe good people go to when they die. [*same as* **heaven**] **2** (*usually in the singular*) A **paradise** is a perfect place or a state of perfect happiness: *a paradise for birdwatchers* □ *an island paradise in the South Seas* □ *It's sheer paradise to be home again and be able to relax.*

paradox /'parədɒks/ *noun*: **paradoxes**
1 A **paradox** is a statement including two elements which on first sight appear to contradict each other, but which is nevertheless true: *'More haste, less speed' is a paradox.* **2** A **paradox** is also used to refer to a person or situation in which two or more apparently opposite ideas or qualities are combined: *It is a paradox that such an intelligent man should apparently have such little common sense.* **3** (*uncount*) **Paradox** is the use of such statements by writers and poets: *Paradox was a favourite device of the metaphysical poets.* [compare **irony**]

paradoxical /parə'dɒksɪkəl/ *adjective*
A situation is **paradoxical** when it combines two apparently contradictory elements: *It is paradoxical that so many should be homeless when there are many empty houses in the area.* — *adverb* (*sentence adverb*) **paradoxically**: *Paradoxically, his efforts to simplify the system seem to have produced more complications than ever.*

paraffin /'parəfɪn/ *noun* (*uncount*; *BrE*)
Paraffin, or paraffin oil, is a type of fuel oil obtained from petroleum or coal and used *eg* in domestic heaters and lamps: *a paraffin lamp.*

paragon /'parəgən/ *noun*: **paragons**
You can call someone a **paragon** if you think they are a completely perfect person or that some aspect of their behaviour is perfect: *She has always been a paragon of virtue.*

paragraph /'parəgrɑːf/ *noun*: **paragraphs**
1 A **paragraph** is a section of a piece of writing or printed text made up of one or more sentences with the first sentence starting on a new line: *Start a new paragraph.* □ *The details are set out in the following paragraph.* **2** A **paragraph** is also a short report in a newspaper.

parakeet /'parəkiːt/ *noun*: **parakeets**
A **parakeet** is a kind of small parrot with a long tail.

parallel /'parəlɛl/ *adjective*; *adverb*; *noun*; *verb*
▷ ***adjective***
1 Straight lines or planes are **parallel** when they go in the same direction and are the same distance apart at every point along their length: *The trees were planted in parallel lines.* □ *The road is parallel to the existing railway line.* **2** A **parallel** situation or circumstance is one which happens at the same time as, or corresponds in some way to, another: *From the time that they left university, the friends have had parallel careers in different areas of the same industry.* □ *parallel developments in the space programmes of both countries.*
▷ ***adverb***
Something that travels or runs **parallel** with something else travels or runs alongside it but always about the same distance away from it: *They rode parallel to the river for about ten miles.*
▷ ***noun***: **parallels**
1 A **parallel**, or **parallel line**, is a straight line that goes in the same direction as and at a constant distance from another. **2** A situation, event or circumstance which happens at the same time as, or is similar in some way to, another may be referred to as its **parallel**: *In his speech, he attempted to draw a parallel between the high level of unemployment and the rising crime rate.* **3** A **parallel**, or a **parallel of latitude**, is one of the imaginary lines that circle the earth at an equal distance from the equator: *the 49th parallel.*
▷ ***verb***: **parallels, paralleling** (*BrE* **parallelling**), **paralleled** (*BrE* **parallelled**)
Something **parallels** something else when it matches it or coincides with it: *The dramatic growth in the level of consumer credit paralleled a boom in property values.* □ *His political career exactly paralleled that of the Chancellor of the Exchequer.*
▷ ***phrase*** Something can be described as being **without parallel** if it has never been equalled or has no equal: *A discovery without parallel in modern medicine.* [*same as* **unparalleled**]

parallelogram /parə'lɛləgram/ *noun*: **parallelograms**
A **parallelogram** is a four-sided geometrical figure with opposite sides parallel to each other.

paralyse (*AmE* **paralyze**) /'parəlaɪz/ *verb*: **paralyses, paralysing, paralysed**
1 Something **paralyses** you when it stops the normal feeling or movement in your body, or in part of your body: *Damage to the sciatic nerve paralysed his right leg.* □ *The scorpion paralyses its prey with its sting.* □ *He was paralysed from the neck down in a road accident.* □ *She was paralysed with fear and could do nothing to defend herself.* **2** Something **is paralysed** when it is prevented from acting or working normally by some event or situation, or comes to a complete stop because of it: *The strike paralysed the transport system.* □ *The whole system was paralysed when the main computer broke down.* [*same as* **immobilize, bring to a standstill**]

paralysis /pə'raləsɪs/ *noun* (*uncount*)
1 Paralysis is the loss of the power of movement or of

feeling in a part of the body: *Nerve damage has caused paralysis in his legs.* □ *She suffers from recurring paralysis in her hands and fingers.* **2 Paralysis** is also loss or lack of ability to move or work normally: *The organization is suffering from a sort of creeping paralysis which is stifling new ideas.*

paramedic /parəˈmɛdɪk/ *noun*: **paramedics**
A **paramedic** is someone, such as a member of an ambulance crew, who has been specially trained to give emergency medical treatment to patients before they are seen by a qualified doctor or are admitted to hospital.

parameter /pəˈramɪtə(r)/ *noun* (*used in the plural*): **parameters**
Parameters are limiting factors or characteristics which affect the way in which something can be done or made: *They have to operate within certain parameters.*

paramilitary /parəˈmɪlɪtərɪ/ *adjective*
A **paramilitary** group or organization is one that is organized like, but is not part of, the official armed forces.

paramount /ˈparəmoʊnt/ *adjective* (*formal*)
Something that is **paramount**, or of **paramount** importance, is greater in importance or significance than anything else: *The safety of the civilian population of the area should be paramount.* □ *This issue is of paramount importance.*

paranoia /parəˈnɔɪə/ *noun* (*uncount*)
1 Paranoia is a mental illness in which a person wrongly believes that he or she is being badly treated by others or that he or she is somebody very important. **2** (*informal*) **Paranoia** is also an abnormal tendency to be suspicious and distrustful of others.

paranoiac /parəˈnɔɪak/ *noun*; *adjective*
▷ *noun*: **paranoiacs**
A **paranoiac** is someone suffering from paranoia
▷ ***adjective***: He has been diagnosed as being paranoiac.

paranoid /ˈparənɔɪd/ *adjective*
Someone who is **paranoid** is suffering from paranoia or is extremely suspicious or distrustful of other people: *He's a paranoid schizophrenic.* □ *None of this was likely; surely she was just being paranoid.*

parapet /ˈparəpɪt/ *noun*: **parapets**
A **parapet** is a low wall along the edge of a bridge, balcony, or roof: *He leaned over the parapet to watch the boats go under the bridge.*

paraphernalia /parəfəˈneɪlɪə/ *noun* (*uncount*)
Paraphernalia is a large number of small articles of various kinds, especially personal belongings or things needed for a particular hobby or activity: *The television crews packed up all their paraphernalia and left.* [*same as* **gear**]

paraphrase /ˈparəfreɪz/ *noun*; *verb*
▷ ***noun***: **paraphrases**
A **paraphrase** of something, such as a statement or piece of writing, is a way of saying or writing it in different words so that it is easier to understand.
▷ ***verb***: **paraphrases**, **paraphrasing**, **paraphrased**
To **paraphrase** something is to express it in different words so that it is easier to understand.

paraplegic /parəˈpliːdʒɪk/ *adjective*
Someone who is **paraplegic** is paralysed from the waist down and is unable to move their legs.

parasite /ˈparəsaɪt/ *noun*: **parasites**
1 A **parasite** is an animal or a plant that lives on, and gets its food from, another animal or plant. **2** (*derogatory*) Someone who is supported by another person or other people without making any effort to work or earn their own living may be called a **parasite**. [*same as* **sponger**, **scrounger**]

parasitic /parəˈsɪtɪk/ or **parasitical** /parəˈsɪtɪkəl/ *adjective*
1 A **parasitic** animal or plant is one that lives and feeds off another animal or plant: *a parasitic worm* □ *The tapeworm is parasitic on humans.* **2** A **parasitic** disease is one that is caused by a parasite.

parasol /ˈparəsɒl/ *noun*: **parasols**
A **parasol** is a light umbrella used as a protection against the sun. [*same as* **sunshade**]

paratrooper /ˈparətruːpə(r)/ *noun*: **paratroopers**
A **paratrooper** is a soldier who is specially trained to drop from an aeroplane using a parachute.

paratroops /ˈparətruːps/ *noun* (*plural*)
Paratroops are soldiers that are specially trained to drop into enemy territory or a battle area by parachute.

parcel /ˈpɑːsəl/ *noun*; *verb*
▷ ***noun***: **parcels**
1 A **parcel** is something wrapped in paper or cardboard and tied with string or sticky tape: *a brown paper parcel* □ *a parcel of books* □ *parcel post* [=a postal service for sending parcels]. **2** A **parcel** of land is a portion of land, especially one that is offered for sale.
▷ ***phrase*** For **part and parcel** see **part**.
▷ ***verb***: **parcels**, **parcelling** (*AmE* **parceling**), **parcelled** (*AmE* **parceled**)

> ***phrasal verb***
> You **parcel** something **up** when you wrap it up in a parcel: *He parcelled up the books and sent them to his friend.*

parched /pɑːtʃt/ *adjective*
1 When soil and plants are **parched** they are very dry because the weather has been very hot and no rain has fallen. **2** You can say that you are **parched** if you are so thirsty that your mouth and throat are dry.

parchment /ˈpɑːtʃmənt/ *noun* (*uncount*)
Parchment is a material used, especially long ago, for writing on. Parchment was made from the skin of goats or sheep.

pardon /ˈpɑːdən/ *verb*; *noun*
▷ ***verb***: **pardons**, **pardoning**, **pardoned**
1 To **pardon** someone is to forgive or excuse them for a fault or offence: *Pardon me for interrupting your meeting, but I have an important message for the chairman.* **2** Someone who has been sentenced to be punished for a crime **is pardoned** if the punishment is cancelled: *He was pardoned before the death sentence could be carried out.* [*same as* **reprieve**]
▷ ***noun***: **pardons**
Someone who has been sentenced to be punished for a crime receives a **pardon** when their punishment is cancelled.
▷ ***phrases*** People say **'I beg your pardon'** or **'pardon'** or **'pardon me' a** to apologize for their mistake or rudeness: *'I do beg your pardon, I didn't know that this was your seat.'* **b** in a questioning voice, as a polite way of asking someone to repeat something that they have not heard properly, or have not understood.

pardonable /ˈpɑːdənəbəl/ *adjective*
Something is **pardonable** when it can be excused or forgiven: *a pardonable error.* [*same as* **excusable**, **forgiveable**; *opposite* **unpardonable**]

pare /pɛə/ *verb*: **pares, paring, pared**
You **pare** something when you trim or peel off its outer edge, layer or skin using *eg* a sharp knife: *He was paring his fingernails with a penknife.* □ *Pare the apple and cut it into slices.*

phrasal verbs
pare down You **pare down** something, such as your expenses, when you reduce it: *The company is paring down its labour and other costs.*
pare off To **pare** something **off** something else means to remove it in thin strips using *eg* a sharp knife: *He pared the hard skin off his feet.*

parent /ˈpɛərənt/ *noun*: **parents**
1 Your **parents** are your father and mother: *She told her parents she was leaving home.* □ *He only has one parent still living.* □ *She's a single parent.* **2** A **parent** is also someone who has adopted, or is guardian to, a child: *their adoptive parents.* **3** A **parent** plant, animal or organization is one which has created others or from which others have been produced: *a parent company* □ *You can separate the small plantlets by cutting the stems that join them to the parent plant.*

parenthesis /pəˈrɛnθəsɪs/ *noun*: **parentheses** /pəˈrɛnθəsiːz/
1 (*used in the plural*); **Parentheses** are round brackets. [see **bracket**]. **2** A word or words introduced in speech or writing as an added explanation or thought is a **parenthesis**. When written, such words are enclosed in a pair of round brackets, as in the following example: *The storm (the worst in living memory) caused millions of pounds worth of damage.*

parenthood /ˈpɛərənthʊd/ *noun* (*uncount*)
Parenthood is the state or condition of being a parent: *She was experiencing parenthood for the first time.*

parenting /ˈpɛərəntɪŋ/ *noun* (*uncount*)
Parenting is the care taken of children by a parent or parents: *parenting skills.*

parent-teacher association /pɛərəntˈtiːtʃər əsoʊsɪeɪʃən/ *noun*: **parent-teacher associations**
(often shortened to **PTA**) A **parent-teacher association** is an organization made up of parents and teachers of children that attend a particular school.

parish /ˈparɪʃ/ *noun*: **parishes**
1 A **parish** is a district or area with its own church and priest or minister: *the parish of St Mary's* □ *a parish priest* □ *a parish church.* **2** (also **civil parish**) A **parish** is a small division of a county with its own local government: *a parish council* □ *parish councillors.*

parishioner /pəˈrɪʃənə(r)/ *noun*: **parishioners**
A **parishioner** is a person who lives in a parish (sense 1), especially one that regulars attends the parish church: *The rector is visiting an elderly parishioner.*

parity /ˈparɪtɪ/ *noun* (*uncount*)
There is **parity** between two things when they are equal: *Women are demanding parity* (*of pay*) *with men.* [*same as* **equality**]

park /pɑːk/ *noun*; *verb*
▻ ***noun***: **parks**
1 A **park** is a public area in a town or city with grass and trees, used for sport and leisure. **2** A **park** is also an area of land kept or designed for a particular purpose: *a play park* □ *a wildlife park* □ *an amusement park.* [see also **car park**] **3** A large area of woodland and grass surrounding and belonging to a large country house is also called a **park**.
▻ ***verb***: **parks, parking, parked**
1 You **park** a vehicle when you stop and leave it somewhere for a period of time: *He parked his car in front of the house.* □ *The lorry was parked by the side of the road.* □ *The sign says 'No parking'.* □ *You can't park here.* **2** (*informal*) You can say you **park** something somewhere when you place it or leave it there for a period of time, often causing inconvenience or irritation to others: *I wish you wouldn't park your briefcase on top of my desk.* □ *He parked himself down in the best chair.* □ *We can park the children with my mother for the afternoon.*

parka /ˈpɑːkə/ *noun*: **parkas**
A **parka** is a type of long warm jacket with a hood.

parking lot /ˈpɑːkɪŋ lɒt/ *noun* (*AmE*): **parking lots**
A **parking lot** is a car park.

parking meter /ˈpɑːkɪŋ miːtə(r)/ *noun*: **parking meters**
A **parking meter** is a metal box with a slot into which you put coins to pay for parking your car in the space next to it. [see picture at **street**]

parking ticket /ˈpɑːkɪŋ tɪkɪt/ *noun*: **parking ticket**
A **parking ticket** is an official piece of paper which instructs you to pay a fine within a certain period of time because you have parked your car in a place where it is not allowed. Parking tickets are issued by traffic wardens and the police.

parkland /ˈpɑːklənd/ *noun* (*uncount*)
Parkland is land with grass and trees growing on it, especially the land surrounding and forming part of a large country estate.

parlance /ˈpɑːləns/ *noun* (*uncount*; *formal*)
Parlance is a particular way of speaking or using words: *in legal parlance* □ *in common parlance.* [*same as* **phraseology**]

parliament /ˈpɑːləmənt/ *noun*: **parliaments**
1 A country's **parliament** is the group of people who discuss and make its laws: *laws passed by the French and German parliaments* □ *Iceland's parliament is the oldest in the world.* **2** (*used in the singular*) In the United Kingdom, **Parliament** is the law-making assembly made up of the House of Lords and the House of Commons: *a Member of Parliament* □ *He is standing for Parliament.* □ *the Houses of Parliament.* **3** A **parliament** is the period of time that a particular parliament does its work, between its official opening and closing: *the present parliament;* □ *These matters will continue to be discussed by future parliaments.*

parliamentary /pɑːləˈmɛntərɪ/ *adjective*
1 Parliamentary means of, for or concerned with parliament: *a parliamentary committee* □ *a parliamentary candidate* □ *a parliamentary session.* **2 Parliamentary** also means used in or suitable for parliament: *parliamentary procedures.* [*opposite* **unparliamentary**]

parlour (*AmE* **parlor**) /ˈpɑːlə(r)/ *noun*: **parlours**
1 A **parlour** is a room in a private house used for sitting in and for receiving guests. **2** A **parlour** is a shop which sells a particular thing or provides a particular service to its customers: *an ice-cream parlour* □ *a beauty parlour* □ *a funeral parlour.*

parlous /ˈpɑːləs/ *adjective* (*formal*)
Something that is in a **parlous** state or condition is in a very bad or dangerous state or condition: *the parlous state of the royal finances.* [*same as* **dire**]

parochial /pəˈroʊkɪəl/ *adjective* (*often derogatory*)
If you describe someone or something as **parochial**, you mean that they are interested only in their own local affairs and not in wider, more important issues: *a parochial attitude* □ *He tends to be very parochial in his outlook.* [*same as* **insular, provincial**]

parody /ˈparədɪ/ *noun*; *verb*
▻ ***noun***: **parodies**
1 A **parody** is a piece of writing, drama or music that

is a humorous imitation of a writer's or musician's work or style: *'Don Quixote' was a parody of medieval romances.* [compare **satire**] **2** (*derogatory*) You can refer to something that you think is a very poor or unsuccessful example or copy of a particular thing as a **parody** of that thing: *a parody of a marriage* □ *a parody of the truth.* [*same as* **travesty**]
▻ ***verb*: parodies, parodying, parodied**
To **parody** someone or something is to copy their work or style in a humorous way.

parole /pə'roʊl/ *noun* (*uncount*)
Prisoners who are given **parole** are let out of prison before the end of their sentence on condition that they behave well after they have been freed: *He was granted parole after serving ten years of a fifteen year sentence.*
▻ ***phrase*** A prisoner who is **on parole** has been given parole.

paroxysm /'parəksɪzm/ *noun*: **paroxysms**
1 A **paroxysm** is an uncontrollable movement of your body caused by *eg* pain, laughter or coughing: *They rolled about in paroxysms of mirth.* **2** A **paroxysm** of rage is a sudden uncontrolled outburst of rage: *She stamped her feet and screamed in a paroxysm of rage.* [*same as* **fit**]

parquet /'pɑːkeɪ/ *noun* (*uncount*)
Parquet, or **parquet flooring**, is flooring made up of small rectangular blocks of wood fitted together and arranged in a geometric pattern.

parrot /'parət/ *noun*; *verb*
▻ ***noun*: parrots**
A **parrot** is a tropical bird with a curved beak and brightly-coloured or grey feathers. Some parrots that are kept as pets are able to copy human speech.
▻ ***verb*: parrots, parroting, parroted**
If someone **parrots** what another person says or does, they repeat their words or copy their actions without thinking.
▻ ***phrase*** Someone repeats or learns something **parrot fashion** when they repeat or learn it without understanding what it means: *She couldn't speak German, but she had learned a few German songs parrot fashion.*

parry /'parɪ/ *verb*: **parries, parrying, parried**
1 You **parry** a blow from someone who is trying to hit you when you push their arm or weapon aside. [*same as* **fend off**] **2** You **parry** a question when you skilfully avoid answering it or dealing with it. [*same as* **dodge, evade**]

parsimonious /pɑːsɪ'moʊnɪəs/ *adjective* (*formal*)
Someone who is **parsimonious** is extremely careful with money and unwilling to spend it: *They have always had a parsimonious attitude towards wages.* [*same as* **mean, miserly, stingy**]

parsley /'pɑːslɪ/ *noun* (*uncount*)
Parsley is a small plant with curly green leaves that are used for flavouring or decorating food.

parsnip /'pɑːsnɪp/ *noun*: **parsnips**
A **parsnip** is a white or cream-coloured vegetable shaped like a carrot that grows under the ground.

parson /'pɑːsən/ *noun*: **parsons**
A **parson** is any Christian priest, especially a vicar or rector in the Church of England.

parsonage /'pɑːsənɪdʒ/ *noun*: **parsonages**
A **parsonage** is a parson's house.

part /pɑːt/ *noun*; *verb*
▻ ***noun*: parts**
1 a (*count or uncount*) A **part** of a thing is a piece, bit or portion of it: *I passed the early part of my life in Ireland.* □ *They spend part of the year abroad.* □ *An earth tremor had caused parts of the building to collapse.* □ *I'll leave the complicated part of the work to you.* □ *The film was OK in parts.* **b** (*count or uncount*) One of the **parts** of something is one of the pieces of which it consists; one thing is **part** of another if it belongs to it: *the various organs and parts of the body* □ *The shop sold spare parts for motor bikes.* □ *Sports and games form part of the school curriculum.* □ *The disabled need to feel part of the community.* **c** (*used in the singular*) The best or worst **part** of a situation is the best or worst circumstance in it: *The worst part of being unemployed is never having any money.*
2 a A **part** of a town, country or the world is an area or region in it: *people from the wealthy part of town.* □ *I know that part of Germany well.* □ *The promise of gold drew men from all parts of the world.* **b** (*used in the plural*) You can refer to the area you are in as 'these **parts**': *I don't come from these parts myself.*
3 a A **part** is one of the sections that something may be divided into: *The subject can be split into two parts.* **b** A book, programme or course of study may be divided into several **parts**: *You will study the anatomy of the insect in Part 4 of your course.* **c** The proportions in which things are present in a mixture can be described as so many **parts** of one to so many **parts** of the other: *Dilute the bleach in the proportion one part bleach to ten parts water.*
4 a A **part** in a play or film is one of the roles in it: *One of the boy actors played the part of Juliet.* **b** A singer's or instrumental player's **part** is the music that he or she has to perform in a musical composition *eg* for choir or orchestra: *The altos and tenors are still unsure of their parts.* □ *He practised the trumpet part.* **c** (*used in the singular*) Your **part** in an event is the extent to which you are involved in it: *He was feeling guilty about the part he'd had in the deception.*
▻ ***verb*: parts, parting, parted**
1 People **part** when they leave one another: *Maggie gave Jean a hug as they parted at the street door.* □ *He couldn't bear to part from her.* □ *Who will have the children if you and your husband decide to part?* **2** Something **parts** people, or they **are parted**, if they are separated and cannot be together: *She had never been parted for long from her family.* □ *Death parted them at last.* **3 a** Crowds or clouds **part** when they separate and a gap opens in them. **b** You **part** your lips or **part** the curtains when you open them. **4** You **part** your hair by dividing it and combing the two sections away from the dividing line or 'parting': *I usually part my hair on the left.*
▻ ***phrases*** **1** The **best** or **better part of** a year or other period is most of it: *She had been waiting for the best part of three years for an operation.* **2** Someone **does their part** when they help or co-operate in the way that they ought to: *Nowadays fathers are expected to do their part in looking after the children.* **3** You say that **for your part** you think something when you are stating your personal opinion: *I, for my part, have difficulty accepting that view.* [*same as* **personally**] **4** Something that is true **for the most part** is usually the case: *For the most part our students want to learn English for business purposes.* [*same as* **mostly, generally**] **5 In part** means to some extent: *His lack of confidence was in part a result of his strict upbringing.* [*same as* **partly**] **6** A person's action or behaviour can be described as a particular kind of action or behaviour **on their part**: *It was a mistake on my part to give him our address.* **7** People or things that are described as **part** one thing and **part** another are a mixture of both things: *She's part Irish and part Italian.* **8** One thing is **part and parcel** of another if it belongs to it: *Drugs are part and parcel of their everyday life.* **9** Someone or

something **plays a part** in something if they are involved in it and have an influence on it: *I know what a big part she has played in your life.* □ *Some mothers play little part in household budgeting.* □ *The rise in the value of the pound played a major part in crippling Britain's export programme.* **10** You **take** a joke or criticism **in good part** if you are not upset or annoyed by it: *He took the rebuke in good part.* **11** You **take part** in something when you join in or are involved in it: *They take no part in village life.* **12** You **take** someone's **part** in a quarrel or argument when you defend them against others' attacks: *His mother always took his part when his father criticized him.*
13 You say you **want no part** of a scheme or plan if you want to keep out of it, *eg* because you think it is wrong.

phrasal verb
You **part with** something when you give it to someone else or sell it: *There were several pieces of furniture she couldn't bear to part with.* □ *He hates parting with his cash.*

partial /'pɑːʃəl/ *adjective*
1 Partial means incomplete or limited: *These measures can provide only a partial solution to the problem.* □ *The two sides have reached partial agreement.* [*opposite* **complete, absolute**] **2** You are **partial** to something if you like it: *He was partial to shellfish.* [*same as* **fond of**] **3** You have a **partial** attitude to something if your judgement of it is prejudiced or unfair: *He gives a partial and misleading account of the situation.* [*opposite* **impartial**] — *adverb* **partially:** *It was partially true.* □ *The road was partially blocked.* [*same as* **partly**; *opposite* **completely, wholly**]

partiality /pɑːʃɪ'alɪtɪ/ *noun*
1 (*uncount*) **Partiality** is unfair favour shown to one side or person in a competition or trial by a person acting as judge. [*same as* **bias, favouritism**; *opposite* **impartiality**] **2** (*used in the singular*) You have a **partiality** for something if you like it: *her well-known partiality for long difficult words.* [*same as* **fondness, liking, weakness**]

participant /pɑː'tɪsɪpənt/ *noun*: **participants**
A **participant** in an activity joins in it or takes part in it: *He had been an active participant in the 1989 coup.*

participate /pɑː'tɪsɪpeɪt/ *verb*: **participates, participating, participated**
You **participate** in some activity if you join in it or are involved in it: *Junior and senior staff participate in a profit-sharing scheme.* □ *people that participate in active sports.* [*same as* **take part**] — *noun* (*uncount*) **participation** /pɑːtɪsɪ'peɪʃən/ : *Lack of child care is an enormous obstacle to women's participation in the work force.*

participle /'pɑːtɪsɪpəl/ *noun* (*grammar*): **participles**
A **participle** is a word formed from a verb and used as an adjective or to form tenses. [see **past participle, present participle**].

particle /'pɑːtɪkəl/ *noun*: **particles**
1 A **particle** is a tiny piece or amount: *particles of dust* □ *Particles of food get stuck between the teeth.* **2** In physics, a **particle** is a unit of matter smaller than an atom, *eg* an electron.

particular /pɑː'tɪkjʊlə(r)/ *adjective*; *noun*
▻ ***adjective***
1 Particular people or things are **a** specific ones that you can identify: *This particular model contains an ingenious cooling device.* □ *There was a particular child who kept causing trouble.* □ *What particular topics would you like to discuss?* □ *Had you any particular person in mind?* □ *'Why did you ask?' 'Oh, no particular reason.'* □ *Is there anything particular to report?* [*same as* **specific**; compare **certain**; see also **in particular** below] **b** specific ones that you don't need to identify: *Once a particular stone was recognized as precious, it tended to remain so.* □ *special people with a particular destiny to fulfil* □ *That would depend on the particular groups and individuals involved.* [compare **certain**] **2** The **particular** qualities, interests, possessions, attitudes or circumstances of people or things are those that belong individually to them: *My own particular academic subject is geography.* □ *We have had plenty of scope for demonstrating our particular talent.* □ *Each educationist will be asked to justify his or her particular approach.* [*same as* **individual**] **3 Particular** also means more or greater than usual: *He dressed slowly, having particular difficulty with his socks.* □ *sociologists who place particular emphasis on behaviour that can be directly observed* □ *It's a matter of no particular importance.* [*same as* **special, especial**] **4** People are **particular** about something if they are difficult to satisfy *eg* when choosing that thing: *He's very particular about his ties.* □ *She's very particular about keeping the place tidy.* [*same as* **fastidious, fussy**]
▻ ***noun*** (*used in the plural*): **particulars**
Particulars are details, especially personal ones: *We need your personal particulars: name, date of birth, next of kin, home address, telephone number.* □ *Full particulars about the seminar are available from the office.*
▻ ***phrases*** **1** You use **in particular** to make what you are saying apply especially to a certain person, thing or group: *Teenagers are now more prepared to use contraceptives, those over sixteen in particular.* [*same as* **especially, particularly**] **2 In particular** is used like **particular**, after words like *anything*, *nowhere* and *somebody*: *Were you going anywhere in particular?* □ *I've nothing in particular to do today.*

particularly /pə'tikjʊləlɪ/ *adverb*
1 You use **particularly** to make what you are saying apply especially to one person, thing, group or situation: *Asians, particularly Pakistanis, are more concentrated in industry than West Indians.* □ *But eggs, particularly those with large rich yolks, make excellent eating.* □ *We can hear some of the sounds bats make, particularly when we are young and our ears are sharp.* □ *The Italian government was particularly disappointed by the outcome.* □ *We particularly hated the music teacher.* [*same as* **especially**] **2** (*intensifying*) **Particularly** also means 'more than usually' or 'especially': *It was a particularly outrageous joke.* □ *Nor was she particularly thrilled at being considered one of the world's leading sex symbols.* [*same as* **exceptionally, especially**]

parting /'pɑːtɪŋ/ *noun*: **partings**
1 (*usually uncount*) **Parting** is the act of leaving someone: *the sadness of parting* □ *Each parting seemed more difficult that the last.* **2** Your **parting** is the dividing line you make in your hair when you comb some of it to one side and some to the other: *My parting is on the left.*

partisan /'pɑːtɪzan/ *adjective*; *noun*
▻ ***adjective***
1 Someone who is **partisan** is strongly loyal to a particular person or cause, often without having considered all the issues carefully: *It's important to support environmental causes, but let's not get too partisan.* **2** A **partisan** opinion is based more on loyalty than reason: *partisan attitudes.* [*same as* **biased, prejudiced**]

▻ ***noun*: partisans**
1 A **partisan** is an enthusiastic supporter of a party, person or cause: *the militant left and its partisans.* [*same as* **adherent, champion, follower**] **2 Partisans** are resistance fighters in a country occupied by an enemy army.

partition /pɑːˈtɪʃən/ *noun*; *verb*
▻ ***noun*: partitions**
A **partition** is a thin wall or screen that divides a room or other indoor space: *Glass partitions divided the room into individual offices.*
▻ ***verb*: partitions, partitioning, partitioned**
1 A country **is partitioned** when it is divided into separate independent states. **2** You **partition** a room by dividing it with thin walls or screens.

> ***phrasal verb***
> You **partition off** part of a room by putting a thin wall or screen round it: *The toilet has been partitioned off from the rest of the bathroom.*

partly /ˈpɑːtlɪ/ *adverb*
Partly means in some ways or to a certain extent: *I was partly to blame for the accident.* ▫ *His problem is partly emotional and partly medical.*

partner /ˈpɑːtnə(r)/ *noun*; *verb*
▻ ***noun*: partners**
1 A **partner** in a firm or business is one of two or more people who jointly own or run it: *She is one of five partners in a firm of lawyers.* **2** Your **partner** in a dance is the person you are dancing with: *Take your partners for a waltz.* **3** Your **partner** in *eg* tennis or card games is the person with whom you make a two-person team. **4** Your **partner** is also the person you are married to or have a sexual relationship with. **5** Countries or organizations that are members of an association or have signed a joint agreement are **partners**: *Britain should be less hostile towards her European partners.*
▻ ***verb*: partners, partnering, partnered**
You **partner** someone when you are their partner in a dance or game.

partnership /ˈpɑːtnəʃɪp/ *noun*: **partnerships**
1 (*uncount or count*) A **partnership** is a relationship in which two or more people or groups work together as partners: *Marriage is a partnership.* ▫ *They decided to go into partnership.* **2** In business, a **partnership** is the rank or status of a partner: *She was offered a partnership at the age of 30.*

part of speech /pɑːt əv ˈspiːtʃ/ *noun*: **parts of speech**
The **parts of speech** are nouns, verbs, adjectives and other grammatical classes: *What part of speech is 'sad'?*

partridge /ˈpɑːtrɪdʒ/ *noun*: **partridges**
A **partridge** is a plump grey and brown bird that nests on the ground.

part-time /pɑːtˈtaɪm/ *adjective*; *adverb*
▻ ***adjective***
Someone who is in **part-time** employment or is a **part-time** employee works for only part of the full working day or week.
▻ ***adverb*** (*also* **part time**): *She worked part time when her children were small.* — *noun* **part-timer:** *Six of the teachers on the staff are part-timers.*

party /ˈpɑːtɪ/ *noun*; *verb*
▻ ***noun*: parties**
1 A **party** is a social event at which people gather together to eat, drink or dance, often to celebrate something: *We're holding an end-of-term party.* ▫ *Why don't you invite her to your birthday party?* **2** A group of people involved in a certain activity together is a **party**: *He guides parties of tourists round the castle.* ▫ *We'll organize a working party to get the job done.* **3** A political **party** is a group of people united by common political aims and usually organized on a national scale, some of whose members stand as candidates for election to parliament: *The Labour Party was returned to power in the 1950 election.* **4** (*legal*) The **parties** in a contract, agreement or law case are the people concerned in it: *All three parties must sign the contract.* [see also **third party** at **third**]
▻ ***verb*** (*informal*): **parties, partying, partied**
To **party** is to attend parties or to celebrate as if you were at a party: *They were out partying all night.*
▻ ***phrase*** You are **party to** or **a party to** an agreement, decision or action if you know about it or are involved in it, and usually therefore approve of it: *I was not party to his dismissal.*

party line /pɑːtɪ ˈlaɪn/ *noun*: **party lines**
The **party line** is the official opinion of a political party on any particular issue: *We are expected to follow the party line even when we disagree with it.*

pass /pɑːs/ *verb*; *noun*
▻ ***verb*: passes, passing, passed**
1 a To **pass** a place is to reach it and go beyond it: *I pass his house on my way home.* ▫ *The bus has just passed.* **b** You **pass** someone who is coming towards you when you meet them and go on in your own direction: *The road was just wide enough for two cars to pass each other.* ▫ *They exchanged 'Hi's' as they passed in the corridor.* ▫ *Look at people's faces as you pass them.*
2 a You **pass** people or vehicles that are moving ahead of you by moving faster and getting past them: *She soon passed the other runners.* ▫ *He pulled out to pass a lorry and ran head-on into an oncoming car.* ▫ *Never pass on a corner.* [*same as* **overtake**] **b** You **pass** your target or expectations if you do better than you were expecting, or trying, to do. [*same as* **exceed, surpass**] **c** You **pass** a limit if you go over it: *'Another drink?' 'Thanks, but I've already passed my usual limit.'* [*same as* **exceed**] **d** Something that **passes** belief is incredible: *Her laziness passes belief.*
3 a To **pass** is to move, progress, get through or go: *She passed quickly along the corridor.* ▫ *Consider how food passes through our bodies.* ▫ *The road passes through mountainous country.* ▫ *The crowd parted to let the ambulance pass.* ▫ *The frontier guards refused to let them pass.* ▫ *Nothing has passed my lips* [= I've eaten nothing] *since that cup of tea this morning.* **b** You **pass** one thing over or through another by making it go or flow over or through that thing: *Pass a long piece of string through each hole.* ▫ *The blood must be passed through a filter.* **c** You **pass** something, such as your hand, over something when you move it over smoothly and lightly: *She passed a hand across her forehead.* ▫ *He passed his tongue over his cracked lips.* ▫ *She passed a damp rag over the table.* **d** You **pass** from one state to the other when you progress from the one to the other: *In that short time she had passed from childhood to adulthood.* **e** Something, such as a feeling, **passes** when it disappears after a while: *His fear gradually passed.* **f** (*formal*) You **pass** water when you urinate; people **pass** blood when it is present in their urine or faeces.
4 a You **pass** a test or examination by reaching the required standard in it: *Have you passed your driving test?* ▫ *I never thought I'd pass.* **b** An examiner **passes** a candidate if he or she awards the candidate the marks required for success. **c** A law, bill or resolution **passes**, or **is passed** by an assembly or council, when it is agreed to: *The President's bill will not pass.* **d** A product, film, programme or book that **has been passed** by

an authority is considered fit for people to use, view, read or hear. **e** Something that is satisfactory, but only just so, **will pass**: *Your shoes need cleaning but I suppose they'll pass.*

5 a (*formal*) You say something **has passed** when it has happened or occurred: *We were never told what had passed in the meeting.* ▫ *I said nothing about the conversation that had passed between us.* **b** Time **passes** when it goes by: *A month passed.* **c** You **pass** a certain period of time somewhere or somehow when you spend it in some place or manner: *He passed his whole life in his native village.* **d** You **pass** the time doing something when you spend it in that activity: *What shall we do to pass the time till dinner?*

6 a You **pass** something to someone else when you give or hand it to them: *Could you pass me the matches?* **b** News or a message **passes** or **is passed** from person to person when one person tells it to another: *The joke passed quickly round the table.* **c** You **pass** a ball to another player in a game by throwing, kicking or hitting it to them: *We were given a lesson on how to pass the ball.* ▫ *Burgon broke through the Bangor defence and passed to Minnis.* **d** Property **passes** to someone when they inherit it or it comes into their possession: *If Ann remarried the estate would pass to her second husband.*

7 a You **pass** a remark when you make one: *Until they leave your house, your guests are in no position to pass critical remarks on your cooking.* **b** You **pass** judgement on something when you form or state your own firm and usually critical opinion on it: *Has society the right to pass judgement on matters of morals?* **c** The judge in a court of law **passes** sentence on a convicted person when he or she announces what their punishment will be: *Judge Eustace Johns was due to pass sentence on Agnes Martin.*

8 a A remark, comment or behaviour is allowed to **pass** when it is accepted without objection or ignored: *I'm not sure about rhyming 'perestroika' with 'balalaika', but I'll let it pass.* ▫ *Her attempt at humour passed unnoticed.* **b** Something **passes** for or as something when it is accepted as, or mistaken for, that thing: *insults that pass for wit.* **c** You decide to **pass** in a quiz or card game when you choose not to answer or make a bid.

▻ ***noun***: **passes**

1 A **pass** is a route through a gap in a mountain range. **2** A **pass** is an official card or paper permitting you *eg* to go somewhere, or use some kind of transport without buying a ticket: *They issued her with a prison-visitor's pass.* ▫ *I'd lost my bus pass.* **3** You gain a **pass** in an examination or test if you reach the required standard in it: *She got good passes in her written papers.* **4** In sport, a **pass** is the action of throwing, kicking or hitting the ball to another player in your team. **5** In quiz games or card games, a **pass** is a decision not to answer or not to bid.

▻ ***phrases*** **1** (*literary*) Something **comes to pass** when it happens: *I wondered how it came to pass that a thinking man could have all the prejudices of his unthinking parents.* **2** (*informal*) Someone who **makes a pass** at you indicates by word or action that they would like a sexual relationship with you. **3** You say that things have **reached** or **come to a pretty pass** if you think the situation is bad.

phrasal verbs

pass away 1 A feeling **passes away** when it disappears: *The pain gradually passed away.* **2** (*euphemistic*) You say someone **has passed away** when they have died.

pass by 1 People, things or time **pass by** when they go past: *The bus passes right by our door.* ▫ *Did you see a black car pass by just now?* ▫ *The weeks passed by and there was still no news.* **2** You **pass** things or people **by** if you ignore them or pay no attention to them: *Don't pass the cathedral by; it deserves a visit.* ▫ *You might pass her by unnoticed; her appearance is not out of the ordinary.* ▫ *She decided that if life was not to pass her by, she must socialize with her own circle of friends.*

pass down Stories, customs, physical characteristics or abilities **are passed down** when they are taught to, or reappear in, a younger generation: *lace-making skills that are passed down from mother to daughter.*

pass off 1 A feeling **passes off** when it disappears: *His feeling of nausea gradually passed off.* **2** An event **passes off** *eg* well or badly if it goes well or badly: *The demonstration passed off peaceably.* **3** People **pass** one thing **off** as another when they make others believe that it is that thing: *She tried to pass her tactless remark off as a joke.* ▫ *They had little trouble passing the fake banknotes off as the real thing.* ▫ *You can't go on passing yourself off as a student.*

pass on 1 You **pass on** something you have received when you give it to someone else: *He passed on the news to his colleagues.* ▫ *OK, I'll pass on your message.* ▫ *The gene for the disease is passed on through the female line to subsequent generations of males.* **2** You **pass on** from one place or subject to another when you progress from one to the next: *We shall pass on the next item on the agenda.* [*same as* **proceed**] **3** (*euphemistic*) You say someone **has passed on** when they have died. [*same as* **pass away**]

pass out 1 (*informal*) To **pass out** is to faint: *He felt as if he was about to pass out.* **2** Students or cadets being trained at a military or police college **pass out** when they successfully finish their course: *the passing-out ceremony.*

pass over 1 Someone **is passed over** for a job if they are not selected for it, especially when a younger or less experienced person is chosen instead: *He had twice been passed over for promotion.* **2** You **pass over** a subject when you do not mention it or discuss it: *The first twelve years of Jesus's life are passed over in silence.* [*same as* **ignore, omit, overlook**]

pass round or **around** People **pass** something round when they give or hand it to one another in turn: *Pass the stories round so that everyone has a chance to read them.* ▫ *The photographs were passed round the office.* [*same as* **circulate**]

pass up (*informal*) You **pass up** an opportunity or chance when you decide not to use it: *I can never pass up a bargain!* ▫ *It seemed too good an opportunity to pass up.* [*same as* **forego, sacrifice**]

passable /'pɑːsəbəl/ *adjective*

1 Passable means satisfactory but only just so, or, informally, quite good. *Your essay was passable.* ▫ *quite a passable performance.* **2** A road or river that is **passable** can be travelled along or crossed. [*opposite* **impassable**]

passage /'pasɪdʒ/ *noun*: **passages**

1 A **passage** is a narrow way, especially one with walls along both sides connecting rooms or parts of a building: *She was hurrying along the passage when I met her.* [*same as* **corridor**] **2** You force a **passage** through something when you make your way through it with difficulty: *He had to force a passage through the crowd of onlookers.* **3** (*formal*) Openings in the body are sometimes called **passages**: *If you find someone unconscious make sure their air passage is open.* **4** A **passage** of text or music is a short section from a piece of writing or a musical composition: *Read the following passage.* **5** A **passage** by air or sea is a passenger's journey aboard a ship or aircraft, or the cost of this: *He's saving up for his passage to the US.* **6** (*uncount*) **Passage** is the process or action of passing: *He'll recover with the passage of time.* □ *Small villages suffer considerably from the constant passage of heavy traffic.*

passenger /'pasɪndʒə/ *noun*: **passengers**
A **passenger** is a traveller in a vehicle, ship or aircraft that is driven, sailed or piloted by someone else: *The minibus holds 15 passengers.*

passer-by /pɑːsə'baɪ/ *noun*: **passers-by**
A **passer-by** is someone who happens to be walking past, *eg* when something is happening: *Fortunately, a passer-by heard her screams and the attacker fled.*

passing /'pɑːsɪŋ/ *adjective*
1 A **passing** feeling or activity lasts only for a short time: *Her refusal to eat was fortunately only a passing phase.* **2** You give something a **passing** glance or make a **passing** reference to it while you are concentrating on something else. [*same as* **casual**]
▻ ***phrase*** You do or mention something **in passing** while you are doing or talking about something else: *In passing, let me draw your attention to this unusual word.*

passion /'paʃən/ *noun*: **passions**
1 (*uncount or count*) **Passion** is strong feeling or emotion, *eg* love, hatred, anger or desire, especially sexual love and desire: *She had never before loved anyone with such passion.* □ *Passions flared as soon as money was mentioned.* **2** Someone who has a **passion** for something likes it very much: *Her passion for dancing was interfering with her schoolwork.* □ *Music is his overwhelming passion.* [*same as* **enthusiasm**]

passionate /'paʃənət/ *adjective*
Passionate people have strong feelings, emotions or enthusiasms and express them in their language and behaviour: *a passionate lover* □ *She gave a passionate speech on unemployment.* □ *He was passionate about the need for educational reform.* □ *a passionate supporter of women's rights.* [*same as* **enthusiastic**]
— *adverb* **passionately:** *She loved her children passionately.* □ *I've never been passionately fond of exercise.*

passive /'pasɪv/ *adjective*; *noun*
▻ ***adjective***
1 Someone who remains **passive** does not react to or resist whatever is done to them: *The child lay passive while the doctor examined her wound.* **2** A **passive** person lacks liveliness and energy and is willing to be led by others. [*same as* **apathetic, unenterprising**] **3** (*grammar*) The **passive** form of a verb is the form used when the subject is affected by the action rather than performs it, as in 'She was knocked over by a car' and 'The heather is being burned'. [see also **active**]
— *adverb* **passively:** *He passively accepted the court's condemnation.*
▻ ***noun*** (*used in the singular*; *grammar*)
The **passive** is the passive form of a verb. The verb is in the passive in: *He* <u>*is being moved*</u> *to another department.*

Passover /'pɑːsoʊvə(r)/ *noun* (*uncount*)
Passover is an eight-day Jewish spring festival celebrating the freeing of the Jews from slavery in Egypt.

passport /'pɑːspɔːt/ *noun*: **passports**
1 A **passport** is a small official book issued to you by the government, showing your identity and nationality and giving you permission to enter foreign countries: *They were asked to show their passports at the frontier.* **2** A particular advantage that you have may be called a **passport** to something: *A university degree is your passport to a good job.* [*same as* **key**]

password /'pɑːswɜːd/ *noun*: **passwords**
A **password** is a secret word you have to know and repeat before you are allowed to go into a place, or must type into a computer before you can use the computer system.

past /pɑːst/ *adjective*; *noun*; *preposition*; *adverb*
▻ ***adjective***
1 Past events and ages are those of an earlier time: *We must forget our past differences with Russia.* □ *Suspicions arise from past experience.* □ *In centuries past, these offenders would have been hanged.* **2** The **past** week, year or other period of time is the one just before the present: *For the past century Britain, France and Germany have been clearly the most powerful European states.* □ *I haven't slept for the past three nights.* [*same as* **last**] **3** A **past** president or other office-holder is a former or previous one: *He praised past editors of the newspaper for their tolerant views.* **4** A situation that is **past** is over or finished: *I suppose we can relax now that the crisis is past.*
▻ ***noun*** (*used in the singular*)
1 The **past** is the time before the present, or the events that happened during it: *You can't alter the past.* □ *People are all too ready to forget the recent past.* □ *famous figures of the past, such as Nero, Napoleon and Marco Polo* □ *She had once in the past tried to stab a policeman.* [compare **present**, **future**] **2** Your **past** is whatever has happened to you before the present time: *She falsified details of her past.* □ *scenes from Britain's imperial past* □ *A society that ignores its past deserves no future.* **3** (*grammar*) A verb is in the **past** if it is in the past tense. [compare **present**, **future**]
▻ ***preposition***
1 Someone or something goes **past** something else when they go up to and beyond it: *Walking past trees and hedgerows we heard more birdsong.* □ *He glanced past me at the clock.* **2** Something or somewhere is **past** somewhere else if it is situated beyond it: *The chemist's is just past the post office.* **3 Past** means 'after' or 'over' in expressions about time and age: *The clock said twenty past three.* □ *He's well past seventy.* **4** You are **past** something if you are too old or sensible for it or have got to a stage beyond it: *He's past rock-climbing now.* □ *I thought you were past childish jokes.* **5** Someone who is **past** *eg* help or cure has no chance of being helped or cured, or could not benefit from help or treatment. **6** Something that is **past** belief or description is fantastic or incredible: *His insolence is past belief.*
▻ ***adverb***
1 People, things or time go **past** when they pass by: *She stood helplessly on the pavement as the taxi shot past.* □ *Three years went past.* **2 Past** can be used without the hour in expressions of time: *Is it half past already?*
▻ ***phrases*** **1** (*derogatory*) You say someone is **past it** if you think they have lost the energy and ability that they had at a earlier age or time. **2** Something that is **a thing of the past** no longer exists, or is no longer considered important: *The family is evidently a thing of the past.* **3** (*informal*) You say you **wouldn't put it past** someone to do something, if you think they are quite likely to do it: *I wouldn't put it past him to change his mind.*

The past participle of **pass** is **passed**; it is used to form the perfect tense: *A whole year has passed since I last saw her*. The adjectival form is **past**: *I haven't seen her during the past year*.

pasta /ˈpastə/ *noun* (*uncount*)
Pasta is a food made with flour, water and eggs in a variety of different shapes: *spaghetti, macaroni and other forms of pasta.*

paste /peɪst/ *noun*; *verb*
▻ ***noun***: **pastes**
1 (*uncount or count*) A **paste** is a stiff sticky mixture: *toothpaste* □ *Mix the powder and liquid to form a paste.* **2** (*uncount or count*) Foods made from ground meat or fish for spreading on bread or biscuits are **pastes**: *She spread some fish paste on the cracker.*
▻ ***verb***: **pastes, pasting, pasted**
You **paste** something to something else when you stick it with glue: *The protesters had pasted notices all over the walls.*

pastel /ˈpastəl/ *adjective*; *noun*
▻ ***adjective***
Pastel colours are pale delicate colours: *The apartment was decorated in pastel shades of blue and pink.*
▻ ***noun***: **pastels**
1 A **pastel** is a coloured stick of chalk-like material for drawing with. **2** A picture drawn with pastels is called a **pastel**.

pasteurized or **pasteurised** /ˈpɑːstʃəraɪzd/ *adjective*
Pasteurized milk has had all the harmful bacteria in it destroyed using a special heating process.

pastime /ˈpɑːstaɪm/ *noun*: **pastimes**
A **pastime** is something you enjoy doing in your spare time: *Why don't you go in for a gentle pastime like embroidery.* [*same as* **hobby**]

pastoral /ˈpɑːstərəl/ *adjective*; *noun*
▻ ***adjective***
1 Pastoral means of or connected with the countryside or country life. **2 Pastoral** also means of or concerned with people's general or personal needs rather than their religious or educational needs: *a guidance teacher responsible for the pastoral care of pupils.*

past participle /pɑːst ˈpɑːtɪsɪpəl/ *noun* (*grammar*): **past participles**
The **past participle** of the verb is the form ending in '-ed', '-en' or '-t' which is used to form the perfect tense (*they have arrived*), the passive form (*we were warmed*), and is an adjective before nouns (*their astonished faces*)

past perfect /pɑːst ˈpɜːfɪkt/ *noun* (*used in the singular*; *grammar*)
(also **pluperfect**) The **past perfect** is the tense of a verb that shows that the action described by the verb was finished before a particular time or event in the past. In English the past perfect is formed with *had* and a past participle, as in the following examples: *When I rang the office, his secretary told me that he had gone home.* □ *We had made a meal, and were just sitting down to eat it when the doorbell rang.*

pastry /ˈpeɪstrɪ/ *noun*: **pastries**
1 (*uncount*) **Pastry** is a type of food made by mixing flour, fat and water to form a dough which is then baked in an oven. Pastry is used to make pies. **2** A **pastry** is a small cake, tart or pie made with sweet pastry: *a Danish pastry.*

past tense /pɑːst ˈtɛns/ *noun*: (*used in the singular*)
You use the **past tense** of a verb to refer to things that happened or existed before the present: *The weather was warm.* □ *I looked round me.*

pasture /ˈpɑːstʃə(r)/ *noun*; *verb*
▻ ***noun***: **pastures**
1 (*uncount or count*) **Pasture** or a **pasture** is land or an area of land with grass and other plants growing on it that is suitable for grazing farm animals on: *The farm has twenty hectares of pasture.* □ *a landscape of rolling pastures dotted with farm buildings.* **2** (*uncount*) **Pasture** is grass and other plants suitable as food for farm animals: *Grass with a lot of clover makes good pasture.*
▻ ***verb***: **pastures, pasturing, pastured**
Farmers, shepherds or herdsmen **pasture** their animals when they put them to graze in a pasture.

pasty[1] /ˈpeɪstɪ/ *adjective*: **pastier, pastiest**
Someone is **pasty** or has a **pasty** face if their skin is unhealthily and unpleasantly pale: *a pasty complexion.*

pasty[2] /ˈpastɪ/ *noun*: **pasties**
A **pasty** is a kind of pie consisting of pastry folded round a savoury or sweet filling: *a Cornish pasty.*

pat /pat/ *verb*; *noun*; *adjective*
▻ ***verb***: **pats, patting, patted**
1 You **pat** something when you hit or tap it lightly with your fingers or the palm of your hand: *He patted her on the head.* □ *She was patting the dog when it bit her.* □ *The minister patted her hand sympathetically.* **2** You **pat** something into shape when you use repeated light blows of the palm of your hand or a flat instrument to make the shape you want: *He patted the wet sand into a little mound.* □ *She patted her hair down.*
▻ ***noun***: **pats**
1 A **pat** is a light, especially affectionate, touch or tap made with the palm of the hand: *She gave the dog a pat.* **2** A **pat** of butter is a small flat piece of butter.
▻ ***adjective*** A **pat** answer or comment is one that is made quickly as if it had been prepared beforehand.
▻ ***phrases*** **1** Someone gives you **a pat on the back** when they congratulate or praise you. **2** You **have** or **know** something **off pat** when you have memorized it and know it perfectly.

patch /patʃ/ *noun*; *verb*
▻ ***noun***: **patches**
1 A **patch** is a piece of material sewn or stuck on to cover a hole or strengthen a worn area: *He wore a jacket with leather patches on the elbows.* **2** A small area of earth or soil, especially one that is used to grow a particular crop, is also called a **patch**: *a vegetable patch* □ *a cabbage patch* □ *a melon patch.* **3** A **patch** is also a small piece of material that is used to cover and protect an injured eye: *an eye patch* □ *He wore a black patch over one eye.* **4** A **patch** is also a small area of something that is different in colour or in some other way from its surroundings: *patches of ice* □ *a patch of sunlight* □ *The dog is black with patches of white.* □ *a damp patch on the ceiling.* **5** (*informal*) A phase or period of time of a particular kind is also sometimes referred to as a **patch**: *Their marriage is going through a bad patch.* □ *The economy has hit a difficult patch.* [*same as* **spell**] **6** (*slang*) Policemen often call the area that they patrol or cover their **patch**.
▻ ***verb***: **patches, patching, patched**
You **patch** a hole in something, such as a piece of clothing, when you sew or stick a patch or patches on it: *He had to patch the hole in the knee of his trousers.*
▻ ***phrase*** (*informal*) You can say something is **not a patch on** another thing when it is not nearly as good as that other thing: *That film wasn't a patch on the one we saw last week.*

phrasal verb
patch up 1 You **patch up** a quarrel or disagreement that you have been having with someone if you both agree not to quarrel or disagree any more:

Have they patched up their quarrel yet? **2** When you **patch** something that has been damaged **up,** you repair or mend it so that it can be used again: *The soldiers who had not been too badly wounded were patched up and sent back to the front.*

patchwork /'patʃwək/ *noun*
1 (*uncount*) **Patchwork** is a type of sewing in which small pieces of different coloured or patterned fabrics are sewn together: *a quilt made in patchwork* □ *a patchwork quilt.* **2** (*used in the singular*) You can refer to an area as a **patchwork** if it is made up of several parts or pieces: *a patchwork of fields.*

patchy /'patʃɪ/ *adjective*: **patchier, patchiest**
1 Something that is **patchy** occurs in small quantities and is not spread evenly: *There will be patchy fog in low-lying areas.* **2 Patchy** is also used to describe something that is incomplete or that is good or correct only in parts: *My knowledge of French is a bit patchy.* □ *a patchy performance.* [*same as* **erratic, variable**; *opposite* **consistent, uniform**]

pâté /'pateɪ/ *noun* (*uncount or count*): **pâtés**
Pâté is a food made from meat, fish or vegetables mixed with various herbs and flavourings and ground or blended into a thick paste: *pâté made with chicken livers flavoured with brandy* □ *duck pâté.*

patent /'peɪtənt/ *noun*; *verb*; *adjective*
▻ ***noun*: patents**
1 A **patent** is an official licence from the government which gives a person or business the right to be the only one to make and sell a new product for a certain period of time. **2** A **patent** is also the right so given or the product covered by such a licence. **3** (*uncount*) **Patent** is patent leather.
▻ ***verb*: patents, patenting, patented**
To **patent** something, such as an idea, invention or new product, is to obtain a patent for it.
▻ ***adjective***
1 (*formal*) **Patent** is used to describe or refer to feelings or qualities that are obvious or evident: *It is patent nonsense.* □ *his patent lack of enthusiasm* □ *It was patent that she disliked him intensely.* [*same as* **manifest**] **2** A **patent** product is one that is protected by a patent: *patent medicines.* — *adverb* **patently:** *It is patently obvious that she was lying.*

patent leather /peɪtənt 'lɛθə(r)/ *noun* (*uncount*)
Patent leather or **patent** is a kind of leather that has a very shiny surface. Patent leather is used to make shoes and handbags.

paternal /pə'tɜːnəl/ *adjective*
1 Paternal is used to describe things that relate or are appropriate to a father: *paternal love* □ *paternal authority.* [compare **fatherly**] **2** Your **paternal** relatives or ancestors are those that are related to you on your father's side of your family: *his paternal grandmother.* [see also **maternal**]

path /pɑːθ/ *noun*: **paths**
1 (also **pathway**) A **path** is a track or way across a piece of land made or used by people walking: *a path over the mountains* □ *a path leading through the forest* □ *a gravel path* □ *She could see the postman coming up the garden path.* [see picture at **house**] **2** An open or clear space ahead that allows you to move forward is also called a **path**: *There were several cars blocking his path.* [*same as* **way**] **3** A **path** is also the line along which something moves or is travelling: *The fire raged through the forest destroying everything in its path.* □ *the path of Jupiter* □ *The child was thrown into the path of an oncoming vehicle.* **4** A **path** is a particular course of action or way of doing something: *They are on a path to ruin.* □ *He must be helped so that he doesn't take the wrong path in life.* [*same as* **road**]
▻ ***phrases*** **1** (*informal*) You can say that someone **beats a path to your door** if they compete with others for your services. **2** You can say that someone has **crossed your path** or **your paths crossed** if you met that person by chance.

pathetic /pə'θɛtɪk/ *adjective*
1 Something that is **pathetic** causes you to feel pity or sadness: *Their cries were pathetic.* □ *He was moved by the children's pathetic little faces.* □ *a pathetic story of suffering and abuse.* [*same as* **moving, heart-rending, poignant**] **2** (*informal, derogatory*) You can say that someone or something is **pathetic** if you mean that they are useless or hopelessly inadequate: *She's a pathetic actress.* □ *a pathetic performance.* □ *Can't you do anything without my help? You're pathetic!* [*same as* **feeble, worthless**] — *adverb* **patheticallly:** *She was sobbing pathetically.*

pathological /paθə'lɒdʒɪkəl/ *adjective*
1 Pathological means relating to pathology. **2** (*informal*) You can describe someone's behaviour as **pathological** if it is unreasonable or unnatural: *She has a pathological fear of dirt.* **3** (*informal*) A **pathological** liar is someone who is in the habit of telling lies.

pathologist /pə'θɒlədʒɪst/ *noun*: **pathologists**
A **pathologist** is a person who is an expert in pathology, and who examines people who have died to discover the reason for their deaths.

pathology /pə'θɒlədʒɪ/ *noun* (*uncount*)
Pathology is the branch of medicine concerned with the study of the diseases.

pathos /'peɪθɒs/ *noun* (*uncount*)
Pathos is a quality in a situation, a person, or something that is said or written that causes people to feel sadness or pity: *His performance was full of pathos.*

patience /'peɪʃəns/ *noun* (*uncount*)
1 Patience is the ability to stay calm without complaining or becoming angry when you have to wait or endure something for a long time: *You must have a lot of patience to work with small children.* □ *She has lost patience with him.* □ *He's got no patience with people who give up without a fight.* [*same as* **perseverance, tolerance**; *opposite* **impatience**] **2 Patience** is a card game for one player in which each card that is turned over has to be fitted into a certain sequence.

patient /'peɪʃənt/ *adjective*; *noun*
▻ ***adjective***
Someone who is **patient** is able to stay calm or self-controlled, especially when they have to wait for a long time or endure a difficult or annoying situation: *He's very patient with the children.* □ *Just be patient; the bus will be along soon.* [*same as* **long-suffering, tolerant**; *opposite* **impatient**] — *adverb* **patiently:** *He listened patiently to a long list of complaints.*
▻ ***noun*: patients**
A **patient** is a person who is being treated by, or is registered with, a doctor or dentist: *hospital patients* □ *I've been a patient of Dr Clark's for ten years.* □ *He's a patient in a mental hospital.* □ *The doctor will see the next patient now.*

patio /'patɪoʊ/ *noun*: **patios**
A **patio** is an open paved area beside or at the back of a house: *On warm summer evenings, they had their meals outside on the patio.* [see picture at **house**]

patriarch /'peɪtrɪɑːk/ *noun*: **patriarchs**
1 A **patriarch** is a man who is the head of a family or

tribe: *the venerable patriarch of the clan.* **2** In the Eastern Orthodox and Roman Catholic Churches, a **patriarch** is a high-ranking bishop: *The title of Patriarch was bestowed on the archbishop of Moscow in the late sixteenth century.*

patriarchal /peɪtrɪ'ɑːkəl/ *adjective*
A **patriarchal** society, organization or system is one that is ruled or controlled by men or patriarchs: *patriarchal authority in the Coptic Church* □ *the patriarchal system of clanship in the Scottish Highlands.*

patriarchy /'peɪtrɪɑːkɪ/ *noun*: **patriarchies**
A **patriarchy** is a society in which a man is head of the family and descent is traced through the male line.

patriot /'patrɪət/ or /'peɪtrɪət/ *noun*: **patriots**
Someone who loves and is loyal to his or her country is a **patriot**: *He was a true patriot whose greatest wish was to see his country freed from tyranny.* □ *French patriots.*

patriotic /patrɪ'ɒtɪk/ or /peɪtrɪ'ɒtɪk/ *adjective*
Someone who is **patriotic** loves his or her country country and is loyal to it: *He has always been very patriotic.* □ *They sang 'Rule Britannia' and other popular patriotic songs.* □ *He felt it was his patriotic duty to join the army as soon as war was declared.*

patriotism /'patrɪətɪzm/ or /'peɪtrɪətɪzm/ *noun* (*uncount*)
Patriotism is love for and loyalty to your country: *Their patriotism cannot be doubted.*

patrol /pə'troʊl/ *verb*; *noun*
▻ ***verb***: **patrols, patrolling, patrolled**
Soldiers, policemen or security guards **patrol** a building or an area when they walk or move around it in a vehicle to see that that there is no trouble and that noone is trying to get in or out illegally: *police cars patrolling the city centre* □ *The grounds are patrolled by armed guards with dogs.* □ *A security guard patrols the building every half hour.*
▻ ***noun***: **patrols**
1 A **patrol** is a person or vehicle or a group of people or vehicles that patrol an area: *While the army were camped for the night, patrols were sent out every hour.* □ *a night patrol* □ *Did the last patrol have anything to report?* **2** A **patrol** is also the act of patrolling a building or an area: *The guard makes regular patrols of the perimeter fence.* □ *A nuclear submarine on patrol in the South Atlantic.*

patron /'peɪtrən/ *noun*: **patrons**
1 A **patron** is **a** a person who supports an artist, musician or writer by giving them money or by buying their work: *a patron of the arts.* [*same as* **sponsor**] **b** a person, usually someone who is well-known, who supports a charity or other good cause, by lending their name or devoting some of their time to its activities: *The princess is patron of several well-known charities.* **2** A **patron** is also someone who is a regular customer of a shop, restaurant or theatre: *He has been a patron of this pub for twenty years.* □ *There's a notice in the theatre car park which says 'Patrons Only'.*

patronage /'patrənɪdʒ/ *noun* (*uncount*)
1 Patronage is **a** the support and money given by a patron to the arts or to a charity: *He has had private patronage throughout his artistic career.* **b** the trade and custom given to a shop, restaurant or theatre by one of its patrons: *We greatly value your continued patronage of our establishment.* **2** (*often derogatory*) **Patronage** is also the power or the right to appoint people to, or recommend them for, important positions: *The creation of new life peers has been in the past largely a matter of political patronage.*

patronize or **patronise** /'patrənaɪz/ (*AmE* /'peɪtrənaɪz/) *verb*: **patronizes, patronizing, patronized**
1 Someone **patronizes** you when they treat you in a way that seems kind and friendly, but which shows that they think they are better than you: *Since his promotion, he thinks he can patronize all the junior clerks.* □ *'I can't bear it when men patronize me,' she said angrily.* [*same as* **talk down to**] **2** (*formal*) You **patronize** a shop, restaurant or theatre when you give it your custom: *He and his family have patronized our shop for as long as we can remember.* □ *They no longer patronize the local shopkeepers and merchants.* — *adjective* **patronizing**: *His patronizing manner makes my blood boil!* [*same as* **condescending**] — *adverb* **patronizingly**: *She remarked patronizingly that she was sure the work was very good; for a beginner.*

patron saint /peɪtrən 'seɪnt/ *noun*: **patron saints**
The **patron saint** of a country, or of a group of people involved in a particular activity, is the saint believed to provide help and protection to that country or group: *Saint Andrew is the patron saint of Scotland and of Russia.* □ *Saint Thomas Aquinas, patron saint of students.*

patter[1] /'patə(r)/ *verb*; *noun*
▻ ***verb***: **patters, pattering, pattered**
Drops of water **patter**, or a person's or animals's footsteps **patter**, when they make light rapid tapping noises as they fall on or against a hard surface: *Fat raindrops pattered on the tin roof of the shack.* □ *She could hear mice pattering along behind the skirting-board in the hall.*
▻ ***noun*** (*used in the singular*)
The **patter** of raindrops or footsteps is the light rapid tapping sound they make when they hit a hard surface: *the patter of tiny feet* □ *a patter of raindrops.*

patter[2] /'patə(r)/ *noun*: **patters**
1 (*uncount*) **Patter** is the continuous amusing speech used by some entertainers in their acts, or the very fast persuasive talk that a salesman has learned and uses to try to sell you something: *The magician kept up the flow of patter throughout his act.* □ *The saleman's patter was very convincing.* **2 Patter** is also used to refer to the jargon or speech of a particular group or area: *Glasgow patter.*

pattern /'patən/ *noun*; *verb*
▻ ***noun***: **patterns**
1 A **pattern** is a model, guide or set of instructions for making something: *a knitting pattern* □ *She uses a paper pattern when she is making a skirt or a dress.* **2** A decorative design, or an arrangement of lines and shapes, repeated several times over a surface, is also called a **pattern**: *a pattern of geometric shapes* □ *Do you like the pattern on this wallpaper?* □ *A rug with a traditional oriental pattern.* □ *Their footprints made an irregular pattern in the wet sand.* **3** A **pattern** is also the particular way in which something happens, develops or is organized: *Discuss the pattern of events that led up to the First World War.* □ *His behaviour pattern seems to be following a predictable course.* □ *Work patterns in manufacturing industry have had to change radically in recent years.*
▻ ***verb***: **patterns, patterning, patterned**
Lines or shapes **pattern** a surface when they form a pattern that covers or partly covers it: *windowpanes patterned with frost* □ *a white dress patterned with red roses.*

phrasal verbs
Someone **patterns** themselves **on** another person when they copy what that person has done or follow the example that they have set: *As a military stategist, he has patterned himself on Napoleon.* □ *The new magazine's format is patterned on the old* Picture Post. [*same as* **model on**]

patterned /ˈpatənd/ *adjective*
A **patterned** fabric or wallpaper is one that has a decorative design. [*opposite* **plain**]

paunch /ˈpɔːntʃ/ *noun*: **paunches**
If a person, especially a man, has a **paunch**, they have a fat stomach: *You should go on a diet; you're getting as bit of a paunch.*

pauper /ˈpɔːpə(r)/ *noun* (*old*): **paupers**
A **pauper** is a very poor person: *He died a pauper.* □ *He was buried in a pauper's grave.*

pause /pɔːz/ *noun*; *verb*
▻ ***noun***: **pauses**
A **pause** is a short period of time when you stop doing something or stop speaking: *There was a pause in the conversation.* □ *She talked for twenty minutes without a pause.*
▻ ***verb***: **pauses, pausing, paused**
1 You **pause** when you stop doing something or stop speaking for a short period: *They paused to look at the scenery.* □ *He read the poem without once pausing for breath.* **2** To **pause** also means to hesitate: *She paused before opening the door.*
▻ ***phrase*** If something **gives you pause** it causes you stop and think carefully about what you are doing: *I hope my complaint will give them some pause (for thought).*

pave /peɪv/ *verb*: **paves, paving, paved**
You **pave** a surface, or a surface **is paved**, when you cover it or it is covered with a hard material, especially paving stones: *He paved the path with concrete slabs.* □ *The path is paved.*
▻ ***phrase*** Something **paves the way for** something else when it makes its introduction or development easier: *His visit to Moscow has paved the way for closer cooperation in the future.*

pavement /ˈpeɪvmənt/ *noun*: **pavements**
A **pavement** is a raised paved path along the side or sides of a road or street that is used for people to walk on. [see pictures at **house, street**]

pavilion /pəˈvɪlɪən/ *noun*: **pavilions**
1 A **pavilion** is a building at a sports ground in which players change their clothes and store equipment: *a cricket pavilion.* **2** A **pavilion** is also a large ornamental building used for concerts and other forms of public entertainment: *the Brighton Pavilion.*

paving /ˈpeɪvɪŋ/ *noun*: **pavings**
1 (*uncount*) **Paving** is **a** any material, *eg* stones or slabs, used to pave a surface: *concrete paving.* **b** a surface that has been paved: *The paving on the patio needs to be replaced.* **2 Pavings** are paving stones.

paving stone /ˈpeɪvɪŋ stoʊn/ *noun*: **paving stones**
Paving stones are pieces of flat stone fitted close together to form a path or pavement.

paw /pɔː/ *noun*; *verb*
▻ ***noun***: **paws**
1 A **paw** is the foot of an animal with claws or nails, such as a dog, cat, bear or monkey: *a lion's paw* □ *The bear held the fish in its paws while it ate.* [compare **hoof**] **2** (*informal, humorous or derogatory*) Sometimes people refer to a person's hands as **paws**: *Take your paws off me!*
▻ ***verb***: **paws, pawing, pawed**
1 a An animal **paws** something when it feels it or scratches it with its paw: *The cat pawed at the mouse, but didn't kill it.* **b** A horse or a bull **paws** the ground when it scrapes the ground with its hoof. **2** Someone **paws** another person when they touch that person in a rough, awkward, or familiar way: *Stop pawing me!* [*same as* **manhandle, molest**]

pawn¹ /pɔːn/ *verb*: **pawns, pawning, pawned**
You **pawn** an article of value when you leave it with a pawnbroker in exchange for a sum of money which he lends you. If you cannot pay the money back within a certain period the pawnbroker will keep the article that you have pawned.
▻ ***phrase*** Something that is **in pawn** is being held by a pawnbroker as security against a loan that he has made.

pawn² /pɔːn/ *noun*: **pawns**
1 A **pawn** is a chess piece of the lowest value. Each player has eight pawns at the start of a game. **2** You can refer to someone as a **pawn** if they are being controlled or manipulated by others: *They were regarded as mere pawns in the game of international espionage.* [*same as* **puppet**]

pawnbroker /ˈpɔːnbroʊkə(r)/ *noun*: **pawnbrokers**
A **pawnbroker** is a person who lends money in exchange for pawned articles.

pawnshop /ˈpɔːnʃɒp/ *noun*: **pawnshop**
A **pawnshop** is a pawnbroker's place of business.

pawpaw /ˈpɔːpɔː/ **pawpaws.**
A **pawpaw** is a papaya [see picture at **fruit**]

pay /peɪ/ *verb*; *noun*
▻ ***verb***: **pays, paying, paid**
1 a You **pay** money to someone when you give them money for something you are buying, or money that you owe them; you **pay** a bill or debt when you settle it, or give someone the money you owe them: *What do you have to pay for a pair of men's shoes, for example?* □ *Guests pay £20 per person for bed and breakfast.* □ *He went over to the bar and paid for the coffees.* □ *She used to send money to pay for my education.* □ *Did I pay the taxi-driver too much, do you think?* □ *I paid by credit card.* □ *I don't let any woman pay when she's with me.* □ *I had to pay the publisher to print the book.* □ *Tourists don't mind paying to see the castle.* □ *Individuals pay income tax on their earnings from labour and other sources.* □ *He was ordered to pay a fine of £500.* □ *I can't pay the rent here any more.* □ *She had just enough to pay her grocery bill.* □ *His debts have been paid in full.* **b** Your employers **pay** you when they give you your money, wages or salary in return for your work: *They haven't paid our wages for three weeks.* □ *Most of the men are paid by the week.* □ *Each pharmacist is paid £8.40 per hour.* □ *Pay us each 1000 roubles a month and we'll build your house for you.* □ *And does she pay her farmworkers well?* □ *The firm pays quite generously.* [see also **paid**] **c** A job, business, deal or investment **pays,** or **pays** a certain amount, if you make a profit, or make a certain amount in profit, from it: *They had to close the restaurant because it wasn't paying.* □ *She wanted a temporary job that would pay well.* □ *The Balmoral deal pays 9.74% on amounts over £25000.*
2 a Something that you do **pays** if it brings you benefits or advantages: *It pays to read the instructions carefully.* □ *It never pays to show you're nervous.* **b** You **pay** for something you have done, or that has happened, when you suffer because of it: *They should pay for their crimes with their lives.* □ *I'll make them pay for this insult.* □ *Why should we be made to pay for his stupidity?* □ *That's the price you pay for being so unwary.*
3 You **pay** people such things as attention, a visit or a compliment when you give them your attention, visit them, or compliment them: *She said I was always out drinking and didn't pay her enough attention.* □ *She felt ready to pay her morning visit to Aunt Tossie.* □ *That was the nicest compliment you could have paid me.* □ *I'd like to pay a warm tribute to my publishers.* □ *Quite a*

crowd had gathered at the crematorium to pay their last respects [= say farewell] *to this strange Englishman.*

▻ ***noun*** *(uncount)*

Your **pay** is the money you get as your wages or salary: *Doctors and nurses were threatening to strike for better pay and conditions.*

▻ ***phrases*** **1** Someone who is **in the pay of** a person or organization is employed and paid by that person or organization, usually for carrying out secret or dishonest work. **2** For **pay your way** see **way**. **3** (*informal*) To **put paid to** something such as a plan or scheme is to prevent it from being carried out.

phrasal verbs

pay back 1 You **pay back** money that someone has lent you when you return it to them: *Thanks; I'll pay you back tomorrow.* □ *She may have to pay back the whole or part of the grant.* **2** You **pay** someone **back** for something bad they have done to you when you get your revenge and make them suffer for it. [*same as* **revenge** yourself on]

pay in or **pay into** You **pay** money **in**, or **pay** it **into** *eg* a bank or building society, when you put it into your account.

pay off 1 A business or organization **pays off** workers when it makes them redundant. **2** Something you do **pays off** if it has profitable results: *This looks like being an occasion when hard work will pay off later rather than sooner.* [see also **payoff**] **3** You **pay off** a debt when you return to someone all the money you owe them: *He had to sell his lands to pay off her debts.*

pay out You **pay out** money for something when you spend it, especially in large quantities, on that thing: *Employers complained that they had to pay out more money for no increase in productivity.*

pay up (*informal*) You **pay up** when you give someone the money you owe them, especially when you do so unwillingly: *Most drivers pay up straight away, but some try to bluff it out.* [see also **paid-up**]

payable /ˈpeɪəbəl/ *adjective*

1 A sum of money is **payable** if it can or must be paid: *The second instalment is payable on or before 1 July.* **2** A cheque is made **payable** to someone when it has their name written on it to show that they are the person who is to receive the money: *Cheques and money orders should be made payable to 'Smith & Mills Limited'.*

payee /peɪˈiː/ *noun* (*usually in the singular*): **payees**

A **payee** is someone to whom money is paid or a cheque or money order is made out.

payer /ˈpeɪə(r)/ *noun*: **payers**

If a person or a business is a good or bad **payer**, they pay their employees well or badly, or they pay their bills promptly or take too long to pay.

payload /ˈpeɪloʊd/ *noun*: **payloads**

1 A ship's or aircraft's **payload** is the part of its load for which payment is received, *eg* the goods and passengers which it carries. **2** A satellite's or spaceship's **payload** is the equipment that it carries excluding its fuel. **3** The **payload** of a missile is the amount of explosive power or the number of warheads on that missile.

payment /ˈpeɪmənt/ *noun*: **payments**

1 A **payment** is a sum of money paid: *He made two mortgage payments before he went on holiday.* □ *When is the next payment due?* □ *The contract allows for interim payments to be made on a fortnightly basis.* **2** (*uncount*) **Payment** is the act of paying money to someone or the process of being paid: *The bill was issued two months ago, and we must now ask for immediate payment.* □ *What are your terms of payment?* □ *At the auction, payment is by certified cheque or cash.*

payoff /ˈpeɪɒf/ *noun* (*informal*): **payoffs**

1 A **payoff** is a good or successful result from a course of action or policy which involved a certain amount of risk or uncertainty: *The payoff for his years of patient research was a Nobel Prize.* [*same as* **reward**] **2** A **payoff** is also a bribe: *He had to give her a substantial payoff to stop her speaking to the newspapers.*

payroll /ˈpeɪroʊl/ *noun*: **payrolls**

1 A list of all the people employed and paid by a particular company or organization is its **payroll**: *We have more than 500 full-time workers on the payroll.* □ *Small businesses with less than 50 people on their payrolls are exempt from the tax.* **2** A **payroll** is also the total amount of money required for employees' wages or salaries: *a payroll of more than £100 000 per month* □ *Because of lack of orders, the company is struggling to meet its monthly payroll.*

PC /piːˈsiː/ *noun*: **PCs**

1 PC is an abbreviation for 'personal computer': *He uses a PC for all his accounts and business records.* □ *All the work stations are equipped with PCs.* [see picture at **office**] **2** (*BrE*) **PC** is also an abbreviation for 'police constable': *PC Forbes* □ *a police sergeant and two PCs.*

pea /piː/ *noun*: **peas**

Peas are small round green seeds that are eaten as a vegetable. Peas grow in pods on a type of climbing plant: *tinned peas* □ *garden peas* □ *marrowfat peas* □ *pea soup* □ *Would you like peas with your fish?*

peace /piːs/ *noun* (*uncount or used in the singular*)

1 Peace is the state or condition of freedom from war or violence: *There has been peace in Europe for fifty years.* □ *After two years of war, the people longed for peace.* [*opposite* **war**] **2** (*used in the singular*) A treaty or agreement ending a war is a **peace**: *A peace was signed between the local tribes and the government.* **3 Peace** is the state or condition of calm or quiet: *He goes to the country for a little peace.* □ *Would you please stop making that noise and let us have some peace.* □ *peace of mind.*

▻ ***phrases*** **1** You are **at peace** if you are no longer troubled or suffering as you were. **2** Policemen or soldiers **keep the peace** when they preserve law and order or prevent violence. **3** Someone tries to **keep the peace** when they try to stop or prevent fighting and quarrelling. **4** When two or more countries that have been at war **make peace**, they agree to stop the war. **5** You **make your peace with** someone when you end a fight or quarrel and become reconciled.

peaceable /ˈpiːsəbəl/ *adjective*

Someone who is **peaceable** wants or tries to live in peace with others: *peaceable tribes.* [*opposite* **warlike**] — *adverb* **peaceably:** *Can't we settle the dispute peaceably?*

peaceful /ˈpiːsfʊl/ *adjective*

1 Something that is **peaceful** is calm and quiet: *a peaceful scene* □ *The house is very peaceful when the children are at school.* [*same as* **tranquil**] **2** If the expression on someone's face is **peaceful** it is untroubled and free from worry or suffering. [*opposite* **anxious**] **3** A **peaceful** country or region is free from war, violence, disturbance or disorder: *a peaceful nation.* — *adverb* **peacefully:** *He slept peacefully.* □ *The two communities lived together peacefully.* — *noun* **peacefulness:** *The peacefulness of the island was its main attraction for him.*

peacetime /'pi:staɪm/ *noun* (*uncount*)
Peacetime is any period that is free from war: *The army continues to recruit and train soldiers in peacetime.* [*opposite* **wartime**]

peach /pi:ʃ/ *noun*: **peaches**
1 A **peach** is a round fruit with velvety yellowish-pink skin, juicy yellow flesh and a large stone. [see picture at **fruit**] **2 Peach** is also a yellowish-pink colour, like the skin of a peach: *a pale peach.*
▻ ***adjective***
Peach things are a yellowish-pink colour: *peach curtains* □ *The wallpaper is peach with a white stripe.* □ (*with the noun omitted*) *The orange carpet is very striking, but the peach will match the decor of the room better.*

peacock /'pi:kɒk/ *noun*: **peacocks**
A **peacock** is a large bird of the pheasant family. The male has brightly-coloured blue and green feathers and a long tail that it can spread out like a fan.

peak /pi:k/ *noun*; *verb*
▻ ***noun*: peaks**
1 A **peak** is a mountain or the top part of a mountain that forms a point: *There is snow on the mountain peaks.* □ *The jagged peaks of the Cuillins rose out of the mist.* **2** A **peak** is a high point or maximum: *Demand for electicity reaches a peak at around 6 pm* □ *She was at the peak of her career.* [*same as* **height**] **3** A **peak** is the front part of a cap that projects over the forehead.
▻ ***verb*: peaks, peaking, peaked**
Something **peaks** when it reaches a high point or maximum: *The shares peaked at 595 pence.* □ *Their share of the vote peaked at 23%.* □ *The athletes trained hard so that they peaked* [=they reached their level of greatest power or fitness] *just before the race.* — *adjective* **peaked:** *a peaked cap.*

peaky /'pi:kɪ/ *adjective* (*informal*): **peakier, peakiest**
You can say that someone is looking **peaky** if you think they are pale and ill-looking: *Are you feeling alright? You look a bit peaky.*

peal /pi:l/ *noun*; *verb*
▻ ***noun*: peals**
1 A **peal** is the ringing of a bell or set of bells. **2** A **peal** is also a set of bells, each with a different note. **3** A **peal** of laughter or thunder is a sudden loud burst of laughter or thunder.
▻ ***verb*: peals, pealing, pealed**
1 A bell or set of bells **peals** when it sounds in a peal: *When the war ended, the church bells pealed out over the countryside.* **2** To **peal** a bell is to cause it to ring or sound: *He ordered the cathedral bells to be pealed in celebration.*

peanut /'pi:nʌt/ *noun*: **peanuts**
(also **groundnut**) A **peanut** is a type of nut that ripens under the ground in a pod-like shell.

pear /pɛə(r)/ *noun*: **pears**
1 A **pear** is a fruit that is rounded at the bottom and narrows towards the top or stem. Pears have greenish- or yellowish-brown skin and white flesh. [see picture at **fruit**] **2** A **pear** or a **pear tree** is a tree on which this fruit grows.

pearl /pɜ:l/ *noun* (*often adjectival*): **pearls**
1 A **pearl** is a precious shining white rounded stone produced by an oyster inside its shell: *She wore a single strand of pearls.* □ *a pearl necklace.* **2** (*uncount*) **Pearl** is also the material 'mother-of-pearl': *knives with pearl handles.*

pearly /'pɜ:lɪ/ *adjective*: **pearlier, pearliest**
Something that is **pearly** is white in colour like a pearl: *She has pearly teeth.* □ *pearly-white skin.*

peasant /'pɛzənt/ *noun*: **peasants**
1 (*often adjectival*) In the rural areas of some countries, a **peasant** is a farmer that owns a small piece of land which he works himself: *French peasants.* □ *a peasant farmer.* **2** (*derogatory*) You can call someone a **peasant** if you think they are rough and bad-mannered or know nothing about art and culture.

peasantry /'pɛzəntrɪ/ *noun* (*uncount*)
The **peasantry** of a country is all the peasants as a social class or group: *Chairman Mao appealed to the Chinese peasantry to back his revolution.*

peat /pi:t/ *noun*: **peats**
1 (*uncount*) **Peat** is a material made up of partly-rotted dead plants that is found in marshy areas and is used in gardening and as a fuel: *a peat bog* □ *He dug some peat into the garden.* **2 Peats** are cut blocks of this material which are dried and burned as fuel, *eg* in parts of Scotland and Ireland.

peaty /'pi:tɪ/ *adjective*: **peatier, peatiest**
Something is **peaty** when it contains peat: *a peaty soil* □ *a whisky with a peaty flavour* □ *This water tastes peaty.*

pebble /'pɛbəl/ *noun*: **pebbles**
A **pebble** is a small stone that has been worn smooth by water: *He picked up a pebble from the beach and threw it into the sea.*

pebbly /'pɛblɪ/ *adjective*: **pebblier, pebbliest**
A **pebbly** beach is one that is covered with pebbles.

peccadillo /pɛkə'dɪloʊ/ *noun*: **peccadilloes** or **peccadillos**
A **peccadillo** is a small unimportant fault or offence: *She tolerated her husband's little peccadilloes.* [*same as* **misdemeanour**]

peck /pɛk/ *verb*; *noun*
▻ ***verb*: pecks, pecking, pecked**
1 A bird **pecks** when it strikes with its beak or picks food up in its beak: *The eagle chick pecked his hand.* □ *The chickens were pecking up the split corn.* □ *The bird was pecking at the window.* □ *The bones has been pecked clean by crows.* **2** You can say that someone **is pecking** at their food if they are eating only little pieces of it without much enjoyment. **3** To **peck** also means to kiss quickly and lightly without much affection: *He pecked her on the cheek.*
▻ ***noun*: pecks**
1 A bird gives something a **peck** when it gives it a tap or nip with its beak. **2** A **peck** is also a quick light kiss: *She gave him a peck on the cheek.*

pecker /'pɛkə(r)/ *noun*
▻ ***phrase*** (*informal*) If someone tells you to **keep your pecker up** they mean that you should keep your spirits up and try to stay cheerful.

peckish /'pɛkɪʃ/ *adjective* (*informal*)
You can say that you are feeling **peckish** if you are a little hungry.

peculiar /pɪ'kju:lɪə(r)/ *adjective*
1 Peculiar means strange or odd: *a peculiar little man* □ *He's been to all sorts of peculiar situations.* □ *There's always a light burning next door, but no-one ever goes in or out; it's most peculiar.* **2** (*informal*) You can say that you are feeling **peculiar** if you are feeling unwell. [*same as* **queer**] **3** Something is **peculiar** to a particular person, thing or place when it belongs only to that person, thing, or place: *a species peculiar to Africa* □ *music peculiar to the French-speaking population of Louisiana.* [*same as* **exclusive**] **4 Peculiar** also means

special or particular: *a matter of peculiar interest* □ *He has his own peculiar way of doing things.* — *adverb* **peculiarly:** *He is behaving very peculiarly.*

peculiarity /pɪkjuːlɪ'arɪtɪ/ *noun*: **peculiarities**
1 (*uncount*) **Peculiarity** is the quality of being strange or odd. **2** A **peculiarity** is a distinctive feature or characteristic: *This method of cooking is a pecularity of the region.* **3** A **peculiarity** is also an odd or strange thing, quality, or habit: *One of his little peculiarities is wearing his hat in bed.*

pedal /'pɛdəl/ *noun; verb*
▻ ***noun***: **pedals**
1 (*often adjectival*) A **pedal** is a lever which drives a machine or vehicle when it is pressed down by a foot or the feet: *a pedal car.* [see picture at **bicycle**] **2** A **pedal** is also a lever on a musical instrument operated by the foot: *Use the soft pedal when you are playing this passage.*
▻ ***verb***: **pedals, pedalling** (*AmE* **pedaling**), **pedalled** (*AmE* **pedaled**)
You **pedal** something when you move or operate it using a pedal or pedals: *He came pedalling up the hill on his bicycle.* □ *You'll have to pedal faster if you want to catch up with the others.*

pedantic /pɪ'dantɪk/ *adjective*
Someone who is **pedantic** is too concerned with correctness of details or rules, especially in teaching or learning: '*It's not the correct use of the word.*' '*Oh, don't be so pedantic; you know what I meant.*'

peddle /'pɛdəl/ *verb*: **peddles, peddling, peddled**
1 Someone that **peddles** goes from place to place selling small goods: *He was peddling brushes from door to door.* [*same as* **hawk**] **2** (*informal*) Someone that **peddles** drugs deals in or sells illegal drugs: *He was arrested for peddling cocaine.* **3** (*informal*) If someone **peddles** *eg* an idea or theory, they talk about it to as many people as possible in order to try to get it accepted: *He's been peddling his pet theory around the scientific establishment.*

peddler /'pɛdlə(r)/ *noun*: **peddlers**
1 A **peddler** is someone who deals in illegal drugs: *a dope peddler.* **2** (*AmE*) A **peddler** is the same as a pedlar.

pedestal /'pɛdɪstəl/ *noun*: **pedestals**
A **pedestal** is a base on which something, such as a statue or pillar, stands.
▻ ***phrase*** If you **put someone on a pedestal** you admire them or worship them, especially when you believe they have no faults.

pedestrian /pə'dɛstrɪən/ *noun; adjective*
▻ ***noun***: **pedestrians**
A **pedestrian** is a person who travels on foot, especially in a street: *His car skidded out of control and he hit a pedestrian.* □ *a bridge for pedestrians only.* [see picture at **street**]
▻ ***adjective***
1 Pedestrian means of or for pedestrians: *a pedestrian walkway.* **2** If you say that something is **pedestrian**, you think it is dull and lacking in imagination: *a pedestrian performance* □ *His last novel was pretty pedestrian.* [*same as* **uninspired**]

pedestrian crossing /pədɛstrɪən 'krɒsɪŋ/ *noun*: **pedestrian crossings**
A **pedestrian crossing** is a part of a road specially marked with white lines or flashing lights where vehicles must stop to allows pedestrians to cross. [see picture at **street**; see also **pelican crossing**]

pedestrian precinct /pədɛstrɪən 'priːsɪŋt/ *noun*: **pedestrian precincts**
A **predestrian precinct** is a shopping street where no motor vehicles are allowed.

pediatrics see **paediatrics**.

pedigree /'pɛdɪgriː/ *noun; adjective*
▻ ***noun***: **pedigrees**
1 Your **pedigree** is your background or ancestry. **2** If an animal has a **pedigree**, there is a record showing that all its ancestors were of the same breed.
▻ ***adjective***
A **pedigree** animal is one that is pure-bred, being descended from a long line of known ancestors of the same breed: *a pedigree dog.*

pedlar /'pɛdlə(r)/ *noun*: **pedlars**
A **pedlar** is a person who goes from place to place selling small goods.

pee /piː/ *verb; noun*
▻ ***verb*** (*informal*): **pees, peeing, peed**
To **pee** is to urinate: *The dog peed on the carpet.*
▻ ***noun*** (*informal*)
1 (*uncount*) **Pee** is urine: *a smell of pee.* **2** (*used in the singular*) A **pee** is an act of urinating: *have/take a pee* □ *need a pee.*

peek /piːk/ *verb; noun*
▻ ***verb***: **peeks, peeking, peeked**
To **peek** means to look quickly, especially in secret: *She peeked into the basket when her mother wasn't looking.* □ *Cover your eyes, and no peeking!*
▻ ***noun***: **peeks**
A **peek** is a quick look, especially one taken without other people knowing about it: *I took a quick peek in the mirror to see if my tie was straight.* [*same as* **peep**]

peel /piːl/ *verb; noun*
▻ ***verb***: **peels, peeling, peeled**
1 You **peel** a vegetable or piece of fruit when you strip or cut the outer skin or rind off it: *She peeled the potatoes.* □ *peel an apple.* **2** You **peel** an outer covering off or away when you strip it off or away: *The bark can be peeled off easily.* □ *peel away the outer layers of the onion.* **3** The outer layer or covering on a surface **peels** when it comes off, especially in small strips or flakes: *The wallpaper was peeling off the walls.* □ *The skin on her nose is peeling where she got sunburnt.*
▻ ***noun*** (*uncount*)
Peel is the skin or rind of certain fruit or vegetables: *orange peel* □ *lemon peel.*

phrasal verb
peel off 1 You **peel** something **off** a surface when you pull it off carefully, usually in one piece: *She peeled off the face pack.* □ *He peeled the plastic protective covering off the new mirror.* **2** You **peel off**, or **peel off** a piece of clothing, when you undress, or remove a piece of clothing, *eg* because you are hot: *He peeled off and dived into the water.* □ *She peeled off her sweater.*

peelings /'piːlɪŋz/ *noun* (*plural*)
Peelings are strips of peel removed from a fruit or vegetable: *potato peelings.*

peep[1] /piːp/ *verb; noun*
▻ ***verb***: **peeps, peeping, peeped**
1 You **peep** when you look quickly or secretly, especially through hole or from a hiding place: *She peeped through the curtains.* □ *He was caught peeping through the keyhole.* **2** Something that **peeps** out or through something else, appears or begins to appear: *sunlight peeping through the clouds* □ *Daffodils and other spring flowers were just beginning to peep through the soil.*
▻ ***noun*** (*used in the singular*)
A **peep** is a quick look made in secret, often through a hole or from a hiding place. [*same as* **peek**]

peep[2] /piːp/ *noun* (*usually in the singular*): **peeps**
1 A **peep** is a short weak high-pitched sound made by a baby bird. [*same as* **cheep**] **2** (*informal*) A **peep** is also a sound, especially something spoken: *I don't want to hear another peep out of you!* [*same as* **cheep**]

peer[1] /pɪə(r)/ *noun*: **peers**
1 A **peer** is a male member of the nobility. The five noble ranks in Britain are duke, marquess, earl, viscount and baron. British peers are entitled to sit in the House of Lords. **2** Your **peers** are the people who are your equals in age, class, rank or status: *a jury of one's peers* □ *He has been heavily influenced by peer pressure.*

peer[2] /pɪə(r)/ *verb*: **peers, peering, peered**
Someone **peers** when they look carefully or closely at someone or something, as if they are having difficulty seeing: *He peered at her over his glasses.* □ *They were peering through the dirty window, trying to see what was inside.*

peerage /ˈpɪərɪdʒ/ *noun*: **peerages**
1 A **peerage** is the title or rank of a peer: *He was granted a peerage.* **2** (*with singular or plural verb*) The members of the nobility as a group are the **peerage**: *He was raised to the peerage.*

peeress /pɪəˈrɛs/ *noun*: **peeresses**
A **peeress** is a female peer (sense 1) or the wife of a peer. The five noble ranks for women in Britain are duchess, marchioness, countess, viscountess, and baroness. A woman who is a peeress is her own right is entitled to sit in the House of Lords.

peer group /ˈpɪə gruːp/ *noun*: **peer groups**
Your **peer group** is all the people of around the same age or status as yourself, especially when they influence your attitudes and behaviour: *Children are greatly influenced by their peer groups.* □ *peer-group pressure.*

peerless /ˈpɪələs/ *adjective* (*formal*)
Something that is **peerless** has no equal and is better or greater than any other: *her peerless beauty.* [*same as* **unrivalled, incomparable**]

peeved /piːvd/ *adjective* (*informal*)
Someone is **peeved** when they are angry or offended: *He had a peeved expression on his face.*

peevish /ˈpiːvɪʃ/ *adjective*
Someone who is **peevish** is bad-tempered and easily annoyed by small unimportant things: *He's always a bit peevish when he is feeling ill.* [*same as* **irritable, touchy**] — *adverb* **peevishly:** *'Where's my supper?' she asked peevishly.*

peg /pɛg/ *noun*; *verb*
▻ ***noun***: **pegs**
1 A **peg** is a hook or short piece of wood, metal or plastic fixed to a wall and used for hanging things on: *He hung his jacket up on the peg on the back of the door.* **2** (also **clothes peg**) A **peg** is also a wooden or plastic clip for fastening washed clothes to a line to dry. **3** (also **tent peg**) A **peg** is also a short piece of wood or metal that is hammered into the ground to keep one of the ropes of a tent in place.
▻ ***verb***: **pegs, pegging, pegged**
1 To **peg** washing is to fasten it to a line with a peg or pegs: *She pegged out the washing.* **2** If prices or incomes **are pegged** at a certain level, they are kept at that level: *Pensions are pegged to the rate of inflation.* [*same as* **be frozen**]
▻ ***phrases*** **1** You buy clothes **off the peg** when you buy them ready made and ready to wear, rather than having them made specially for you: *He buys all his suits off the peg.* □ *an off-the-peg suit.* **2** You can say someone is **a square peg in a round hole** if you think they do not fit in well in their job or environment. **3** (*informal*) You **take someone down a peg**, or **down a peg or two**, when you show them that they are not as important as they think they are.

> ***phrasal verb***
> **peg out 1** You **peg** an area **out** when you mark it out using wooden or metal pegs stuck or hammered into the ground. **2** (*informal*) You can say that someone **has pegged out** when they have died.

pejorative /pɪˈdʒɒrətɪv/ *adjective*
A **pejorative** word, phrase or expression is one that expresses criticism or suggests that something is of little value or importance. [*same as* **derogatory, disparaging**] — *adverb* **pejoratively:** *The word is used pejoratively.*

pelican /ˈpɛlɪkən/ *noun*: **pelican** or **pelicans**
A **pelican** is a large water bird that lives in Africa and other warm countries. It feeds on fish and stores them in a deep baglike part that hangs down under its beak.

pelican crossing /pɛlɪkən ˈkrɒsɪŋ/ *noun*: **pelican crossings**
A **pelican crossing** is a pedestrian crossing with traffic lights that are operated by pedestrians.

pellet /ˈpɛlɪt/ *noun*: **pellets**
A **pellet** is a small round tightly-packed mass of material *eg* that has been formed by pressing or rolling: *shotgun pellets* □ *The schoolboys were firing paper pellets at each other.*

pelmet /ˈpɛlmɪt/ *noun* (*BrE*): **pelmets**
A **pelmet** is a narrow piece of wood or cloth that is fitted along the top of a window to hide the rail on which curtains hang.

pelt[1] /pɛlt/ *verb*: **pelts, pelting, pelted**
1 Someone **pelts** another person with something when they repeatedly throw missiles at them in order to attack them: *The crowd pelted the speaker with rotten eggs so that he had to leave the platform.* □ *They pelted each other with snowballs.* [*same as* **bombard**] **2** Rain or hail **pelts** down when it falls very fast and heavily: *The rain was pelting down.* [*same as* **teem, bucket**] **3** To **pelt** also means to run very fast, usually in a particular direction: *He came pelting down the hill.* □ *They were pelting along the road.* [*same as* **race, belt, tear**]
▻ ***phrase*** Someone or something goes **at full pelt** when it goes or travels as fast as possible: *The boys came running down the road at full pelt.*

pelt[2] /pɛlt/ *noun*: **pelts**
A **pelt** is the skin of a dead animal, especially with the fur or hair still on it: *a beaver pelt.*

pelvic /ˈpɛlvɪk/ *adjective*
Pelvic means of or belonging to the pelvis: *a pelvic bone* □ *a pelvic fracture.*

pelvis /ˈpɛlvɪs/ *noun*: **pelvises** or **pelves**
Your **pelvis** is the bowl-shaped framework of bones around your hips, to which your leg bones are joined.

pen[1] /pɛn/ *noun*; *verb*
▻ ***noun***: **pens**
A **pen** is an instrument that you use to write or draw in ink: *a fountain pen* □ *a felt-tipped pen* □ *a ballpoint pen* [see picture at **office**]
▻ ***verb*** (*formal or literary*): **pens, penning, penned**
Someone **pens** something, such as a letter or poem, when they write it: *She penned a brief letter of apology.*
▻ ***phrase*** (*formal*) You **put pen to paper** when you begin to write something, such as a letter.

pen² /pɛn/ *noun*; *verb*
▻ ***noun*: pens**
A **pen** is a small piece of land surrounded by a fence, used especialy for keeping an animal or animals in: *a sheep pen.*
▻ ***verb*: pens, penning, penned**

> ***phrasal verbs***
> Someone or something **is penned in** or **penned up** when they are confined or shut up in a small space: *The farmer penned the cattle up for the winter.* □ *The walls were high and she felt penned in by them.*

penal /ˈpiːnəl/ *adjective*
Penal means of or relating to, or used for, punishment, especially by law: *a penal colony* □ *penal reform* □ *a penal code.*

penalize or **penalise** /ˈpiːnəlaɪz/ *verb* (*especially in the passive*): **penalizes, penalizing, penalized**
1 In sports and games, a player or team **is penalized** for breaking a rule when they are punished by giving their opponents an advantage: *The team was penalized when one of their forwards deliberately handled the ball.* **2** Someone who **is penalized** by something is placed at a disadvantage, often unfairly: *Profitable companies are being penalized under the new tax rules.*

penalty /ˈpɛnəltɪ/ *noun*: **penalties**
1 A **penalty** is a punishment for breaking a law, rule or contract: *The penalty for murder is life imprisonment.* □ *the death penalty* □ *Parking without a permit incurs an automatic penalty of £20.* □ *The contract has a penalty clause for late completion.* **2** A **penalty** is also a disadvantage or unfair position caused by an action or circumstances: *One of the penalties of fame is the constant attention of the media.* **3** In sports and games, a **penalty** is an advantage awarded to the opposing side because the other team has broken a rule: *a penalty kick* [=a free shot at the opposing team's goal in football or rugby].

penance /ˈpɛnəns/ *noun* (*uncount*)
Penance is the action of punishing yourself to show that you are sorry for something that you have done wrong: *do penance for one's sins* □ *an act of penance* □ *As penance for losing her temper, she was especially nice to him all evening.*

pence /pɛns/ *noun*
Pence is the plural of penny.

penchant /ˈpɒnʃɒn/ (*AmE* /ˈpɛntʃənt/) *noun* (*used in the singular*)
You have a **penchant** for a particular thing if you have a liking or taste for it: *He has a penchant for expensive suits.*

pencil /ˈpɛnsəl/ *noun*; *verb*
▻ ***noun*: pencils**
1 A **pencil** is an instrument for drawing and writing with consisting of a hollow wooden shaft containing a stick of graphite or coloured chalk. [see picture at **office**] **2** (*uncount*) Something that is drawn or written using this instrument is drawn or written in **pencil**: *a pencil sketch.* **3** Pencil-like instruments, eg for applying make-up, are referred to as **pencils**: *an eyebrow pencil.* **4** A **pencil** of light is a very narrow beam of it; people or things that are **pencil**-thin are very thin: *pencil-slim models.*
▻ ***verb*: pencils, pencilling** (*AmE* **penciling**), **pencilled** (*AmE* **penciled**)
You **pencil** a note when you write it in pencil: *a pencilled message.*

> ***phrasal verb***
> If you **pencil** an appointment or arrangement **in** you include it in a diary or list, with the possibility of changing it later: *I know you're not certain that you will be available, but I've pencilled the meeting in for 5 May.*

pendant /ˈpɛndənt/ *noun*: **pendants**
A **pendant** is a piece of jewellery or an ornament that hangs down: *She wore a gold pendant* [=a necklace with a decorative ornament hanging from it].

pending /ˈpɛndɪŋ/ *adjective*; *preposition*
▻ ***adjective*** (*formal*)
1 Something that is **pending** is waiting to be decided or dealt with: *Put the papers in the pending file.* □ *a pending lawsuit.* **2 Pending** is also used to describe something that is about to happen: *The decision is pending.* [*same as* **imminent, impending**]
▻ ***preposition***
Something is done **pending** some event in the future when it is done while waiting for that event to happen: *He was held in prison pending trial.*

pendulous /ˈpɛndjʊləs/ *adjective* (*formal*)
Something that is **pendulous** hangs down loosely so that it swings from side to side.

pendulum /ˈpɛndjʊləm/ *noun*: **pendulums**
A **pendulum** is a weight hung from a fixed point so that it swings freely from side to side, especially the swinging weight that regulates the mechanism of a clock.

penetrate /ˈpɛnətreɪt/ *verb*: **penetrates, penetrating, penetrated**
1 To **penetrate** something means to enter or force a way into or through it: *The blade penetrated his heart.* □ *A piercing shriek penetrated the silence.* □ *The bitter wind penetrates even the thickest clothing.* □ *A shell penetrated the outer wall of the fortress.* **2** Someone **penetrates** something that is difficult to get into when they succeed in finding a way in: *Government agents have penetrated the terrorist organization.* □ *They are hoping to penetrate the European market.* **3** A disguise or mystery **is penetrated** when it is seen through or solved. **4** To **penetrate** something is to understand it fully: *The news didn't penetrate at first.*

penetrating /ˈpɛnətreɪtɪŋ/ *adjective*
1 A **penetrating** sound is so sharp and clear that it reaches places a considerable distance away: *a penetrating whistle* □ *He had a loud penetrating voice.* **2 Penetrating** also means searching or having the ability to see or understand quickly and clearly: *a penetrating question* □ *a penetrating mind* □ *a penetrating look.*

penetration /pɛnəˈtreɪʃən/ *noun* (*uncount*)
1 Penetration is the process of penetrating or being penetrated: *penetration of the Japanese market.* **2 Penetration** is also the ability to understand quickly and clearly. [*same as* **insight**]

penfriend /ˈpɛnfrɛnd/ *noun*: **penfriends**
A **penfriend** or **penpal** is someone, especially someone that you have never met and who lives in a foreign country, that you write letters to regularly and who writes back to you.

penguin /ˈpɛŋgwɪn/ *noun*: **penguins**
A **penquin** is a black and white sea bird that lives in the Antartic. Penguins cannot fly and use their wings to swim under water.

penicillin /pɛnɪˈsɪlin/ *noun* (*uncount*)
Penicillin is a substance that is used as a medicine to treat illnesses and infections caused by bacteria.

peninsula /pəˈnɪnsjʊlə/ *noun*: **peninsulas**
A **peninsula** is a piece of land that is almost completely surrounded by water but is joined at one end to

a larger land mass: *the Iberian peninsula* □ *the Malay peninsula.*

penis /ˈpiːnɪs/ *noun*: **penises**
A **penis** is the outer sex organ of male animals. In humans and other mammals, the **penis** is used for urinating and for having sex.

penitent /ˈpɛnɪtənt/ *adjective*
Someone who is **penitent** feels or shows that they are very sorry for something that they have done wrong: *penitent sinners.* [*same as* **repentant**; *opposite* **impenitent**] — *adverb* **penitently:** *He hung his head penitently.*

penitentiary /pɛnɪˈtɛnʃərɪ/ *noun*: **penitentiaries**
A **penitentiary** is a federal or state prison in the United States.

penknife /ˈpɛnnaɪf/ *noun*: **penknives**
A **penknife** is a pocket knife with blades that fold into the handle.

pen name /ˈpɛn neɪm/ *noun*: **pen names**
A **pen name** is a name used by a writer instead of his or her real name. [compare **nickname, pseudonym**]

pennant /ˈpɛnənt/ *noun*: **pennants**
A **pennant** is a small narrow flag that tapers to a point, used especially on ships for signalling and identification.

penniless /ˈpɛnɪləs/ *adjective*
Someone who is **penniless** has little or no money: *He died penniless.* □ *The refugees arrived in the United States, penniless and with only the clothes they stood up in.* [*same as* **destitute, poverty-stricken**; *opposite* **rich, wealthy**]

penny /ˈpɛnɪ/ *noun*: **pence** or **pennies**
1 (*plural* **pence**) A **penny** is a small bronze British coin whose value is one hundredth of £1.

> The singular form used in speech or writing is a (or one) **penny,** or one **pence,** or (*informal*) one **p.** If you are talking or writing about a coin or amount that is greater that one you use **pence** or (*informal*) **p.**

2 (*plural* **pennies** or **pence**) In Britain before 1971, a **penny** was a bronze coin equal to $\frac{1}{12}$ of a shilling or $\frac{1}{240}$ of £1. **3** (*AmE; plural* **pennies**) A **penny** is one cent or a coin worth one cent.
▻ ***phrases*** **1** (*informal*) You can say **the penny dropped** to refer to the moment when someone understood or realized something that they had not understood or realized before: *He looked blank for a moment, and then the penny dropped.* **2** You can say that something cost **a pretty penny** if it cost a very large sum of money: *That house must have cost her a pretty penny.* **3** (*informal, euphemistic*) Some people say that they are going to **spend a penny** when they are going to the lavatory or are going to urinate. **4** You can say that things are **two** or **ten a penny** if they are very common or very easy to obtain.

penny-pinching /ˈpɛnɪpɪntʃɪŋ/ *adjective* (*derogatory*)
Someone who is **penny-pinching** is too careful with, and unwilling to spend, money. [*same as* **mean, miserly, parsimonious, stingy, tight-fisted**; *opposite* **generous, open-handed**]

penpusher /ˈpɛnpʊʃə(r)/ *noun* (*derogatory*): **penpushers**
A **penpusher** is someone whose job involves a lot of paperwork, especially a clerk or minor official.

pension /ˈpɛnʃən/ *noun*; *verb*
▻ ***noun***: **pensions**
1 A **pension** is a sum of money paid weekly or monthly by the government to a person who is retired, disabled or widowed: *a widow's pension* □ *an old-age pension* □ *a war pension.* **2** A **pension** is also a sum of money paid weekly or monthly by an employer or insurance company to someone that is retired: *an occupational pension* □ *a personal pension.*
▻ ***verb***: **pensions, pensioning, pensioned**

> ***phrasal verb***
> Someone **is pensioned off** when they are forced or allowed to retire from their job or work but are given a pension: *He was pensioned off to make way for a younger man.*

pensionable /ˈpɛnʃənəbəl/ *adjective*
Pensionable means relating to a person's right or entitlement to receive a pension: *He is 64 and nearly of pensionable age.* □ *pensionable employment.*

pensioner /ˈpɛnʃənə(r)/ *noun*: **pensioners**
A **pensioner** is a person who receives a pension: *Chelsea pensioners* □ *an old-age pensioner.*

pensive /ˈpɛnsɪv/ *adjective*
Someone is or looks **pensive** if they are thinking deeply about something, especially in a sad or serious way: *He was in a pensive mood.* □ *You're looking very pensive; is something the matter?* [*same as* **thoughtful**] — *adverb* **pensively:** *He was staring pensively at the ceiling.*

pentagon /ˈpɛntəgən/ *noun*: **pentagons**
A **pentagon** is a solid shape with five sides and five angles. [see picture at **shape**]

pentathlon /pɛnˈtaθlən/ *noun*: **pentathlons**
A **pentathlon** is an athletic competition in which all contestants must compete in five different events. The **modern pentathlon** is made up of swimming, cross-country riding and running, fencing and pistol-shooting. [compare **decathlon**]

Pentecost /ˈpɛntɪkɒst/ *noun* (*uncount*)
1 Pentecost is a Christian festival held on the seventh Sunday after Easter. **2 Pentecost** is also a Jewish harvest festival on the fiftieth day after the second day of Passover.

penthouse /ˈpɛnthaʊs/ *noun*: **penthouses**
A **penthouse** is house or flat built on to the roof of a tall building.

pent-up /pɛntˈʌp/ *adjective*
Energies or emotions that are **pent-up** are not allowed to be released or expressed: *pent-up rage* □ *She took the boys to the park so that they could get rid of some of their pent-up energy.* [*same as* **bottled-up**]

penultimate /pɛnˈʌltɪmət/ *adjective*
Penultimate is used to refer to something that is the last but one in a series: *The marathon is the penultimate race in the Olympics.*

penury /ˈpɛnjʊrɪ/ *noun* (*uncount; formal*)
Penury is extreme poverty.

people /piːpəl/ *noun*; *verb*
▻ ***noun***
1 (*plural*) **People** are any human beings, men, women or children: *A couple of people got into the lift with him.* □ *There are quite a few elderly people living round here.* □ *dwellings designed for young people* □ *the problems of black people and ethnic minorities* □ *As many people as possible should be interviewed, to get a proper cross-section of opinion.* □ *We've got a lot of people applying for research fellowships just now.*

> **People** is used as the plural of **person** except in official or legal contexts, where the formal plural **persons** is preferred.

2 (*plural*) You use **people** to refer generally to men and women, or to refer to those within a certain group: *I'm not saying people aren't racist, but things have changed.* □ *People on the bus were talking about the number of police cars around.* □ *People ask me why I don't get a flat and live on my own.* □ *Two contradictory notices came round the office, and naturally people were confused.* **3** The **people** are the ordinary citizens of a country, as distinct from *eg* the aristocracy or the government: *By 'popular rule' I mean rule of the people by the people.* **4** A **people** is a nation or race: *The French are a fairly responsible people, after all.* □ *the Arctic peoples of Siberian Russia, Greenland, Alaska and Canada* □ *It seems that primitive peoples ate human flesh for two reasons.*
▻ ***verb***: **peoples, peopling, peopled**
A place **is peopled** by a particular group of people if they live there: *The surrounding countryside was peopled by Slavs.* □ *It seemed a dead, seedy place now, peopled by hangers-on and time-wasters.* [*same as* **populate**]

pep /pɛp/ *noun*; *verb*
▻ ***noun*** (*uncount*; *informal*)
If someone has **pep** they are full of energy and vitality.
▻ ***verb***: **peps, pepping, pepped**

> ***phrasal verb***
> You **pep** something **up** when you make it more lively or interesting: *A holiday would be just the thing to pep me up.* □ *He added some wine to the stew to pep it up.* [*same as* **enliven, liven up**]

pepper /'pɛpə(r)/ *noun*; *verb*
▻ ***noun***: **peppers**
1 (*uncount*) **Pepper** is a powder with a hot taste that is used for flavouring food: *salt and pepper* □ *black pepper.* **2** A **pepper** is a red, green, orange, yellow or black fruit that is hollow inside and is eaten as a vegetable. [see picture at **vegetable**]
▻ ***verb***: **peppers, peppering, peppered**
1 You **pepper** your food when you add pepper to it. **2** (*informal*) Something that **is peppered** with other things has a large number of those other things in it: *His language is peppered with swearwords.* □ *The letter is peppered with typing errors.* [*same as* **full of**]

peppercorn /'pɛpəkɔːn/ *noun*: **peppercorns**
Peppercorns are the dried berries of the pepper plant that are ground up to make pepper (sense 1).

peppermill /'pɛpəmɪl/ *noun*: **peppermills**
A **peppermill** is a device for grinding peppercorns. [see picture at **tableware**]

peppermint /'pɛpəmɪnt/ *noun*: **peppermints**
1 (*uncount*, *often adjectival*) **Peppermint** is a strong flavouring that is used in sweets and medicines. Peppermint comes from the leaves of a plant of the same name: *peppermint tea.* **2 Peppermints** are sweets flavoured with peppermint. [see also **mint**]

pepper pot /'pɛpə(r) pɒt/ *noun*: **pepper pots**
A **pepper pot** is a small container, with several small holes in its top, for holding ground pepper [see picture at **tableware**]

peppery /'pɛpərɪ/ *adjective*
1 Food or a drink that is **peppery** has a lot of pepper in it, or it tastes hot and spicy as if it has a lot of pepper in it. **2** You can say that a person is **peppery** if you think that they are hot-tempered or easily made angry. [*same as* **fiery**]

pep talk /'pɛp tɔːk/ *noun*: **pep talks**
Someone gives or is given a **pep-talk** when they give or listen to a short talk intended to encourage harder work or greater effort: *The players were given a pep talk by their manager before the match.*

per /pɜː(r)/ *preposition*
1 Per means 'out of every': *two infant deaths per thousand live births.* **2 Per** also means 'for every' or 'for each': *The cost of the meal works out at £5 per head.* □ *If potatoes at 20 pence per kilo, how much will 15 kilos cost?* **3 Per** also means 'during every' or 'during each': *The train travels at sixty miles per hour.* □ *The factory produces 100 cars per week.*
▻ ***phrases*** **1** Something is done **as per** something else when it is done according to that thing: *proceed as per instructions.* **2** (*informal*) Something happens **as per usual** when it happens as it has always done in the past: *The train was late, as per usual.*

per annum /pɜːr 'anəm/ *adverb*
Per annum means for or in each year: *a salary of £25 000 per annum.*

perceive /pə'siːv/ *verb*: **perceives, perceiving, perceived**
1 You **perceive** something when you notice it or become aware of it: *I perceived a change in their attitude.* □ *The doctors failed to perceive that his condition was deteriorating.* [*same as* **observe, recognize**] **2** Something **is perceived** when it is understood, viewed or interpreted in a certain way: *How do you perceive your role in the organization?* □ *Their actions were perceived as treasonable.* [*same as* **regard**]

per cent /pə'sɛnt/ *adverb*
1 Per cent means in or for every 100: *twenty per cent.*

> When it is written down **per cent** is often represented by the symbol **%**, as in *75%*.

2 Per cent also means on a scale of 1 to 100: *I'm 90 per cent certain.*

percentage /pə'sɛntɪdʒ/ *noun*: **percentages**
1 A **percentage** is an amount or number in each hundred: *The rate of inflation is expressed as a percentage.* **2** (*with a singular or plural verb*) A **percentage** of something is a proportion of that thing: *What percentage of students get a job immediately after leaving college?* □ *A high percentage of the world's cereal production is used to feed farm animals.*

perceptible /pə'sɛptəbəl/ *adjective*
Something that is **perceptible** can be observed or noticed: *The change was barely perceptible.* □ *a perceptible improvement.* [*same as* **detectable, noticeable**; *opposite* **imperceptible, undetectable**]

perception /pə'sɛpʃən/ *noun* (*uncount or count*): **perceptions**
1 (*uncount*) **Perception** is **a** the ability to see, hear or understand: *increase your powers of perception.* **b** the quality of understanding: *His work shows great perception.* **2** A **perception** is a particular way of looking at or interpreting something: *They have a different perception of how business should be conducted.* [*same as* **view**]

perceptive /pə'sɛptɪv/ *adjective*
Someone who is **perceptive** is quick to notice and understand things: *He's very perceptive.* □ *a perceptive comment.* [*same as* **sharp, shrewd**]

perch /pɜːtʃ/ *noun*; *verb*
▻ ***noun***: **perches**
1 A **perch** is a branch or other narrow support above the ground that a bird rests on. **2** A **perch** is also a high position where someone sits or something is placed: *From his perch on the top of the mast, he could see far into the distance.*

▻ ***verb***: **perches, perching, perched**
1 Birds **perch** when they rest from flying on a branch or other support above the ground. **2** To **perch** also means to sit or be placed on the edge of something or in a high place, especially where there is a danger or risk of falling: *She was perched on a high stool by the bar.* □ *The climbers were perched precariously on a narrow ledge.*

percolator /'pɜːkəleɪtə(r)/ *noun*: **percolators**
A **percolator** is a pot for making coffee in which boiling water is forced through ground coffee beans.

percussion /pə'kʌʃən/ *noun* (*used in the singular, with a singular or plural verb*)
The **percussion** is the section of an orchestra which includes all the musical instruments that are played by hitting with a stick or hammer or the hand, such as drums, cymbals and xylophone. [see picture at **orchestra**]

percussionist /pə'kʌʃənɪst/ *noun*: **percussionists**
A **percussionist** is a musician who plays percussion instruments.

peremptory /pə'rɛmtərɪ/ *adjective* (*formal*)
1 A **peremptory** order or command is one that cannot be disobeyed or questioned: *They received a peremptory summons to attend the hearing.* [*same as* **summary**] **2** Someone's behaviour is **peremptory** if it shows that they expect to be obeyed without question: *He dismissed them with a peremptory wave of the hand.* [*same as* **autocratic, dictatorial, high-handed, imperious**] — *adverb* **peremptorily:** *They were dismissed peremptorily.*

perennial /pə'rɛnɪəl/ *adjective*; *noun*
▻ ***adjective***
1 A **perennial** plant lives for at least two years. **2** A **perennial** situation or problem happens again and again or lasts for a long time: *the perennial problem of inner-city decay.*
▻ ***noun***: **perennials**
A **perennial** is a perennial plant: *Michelmas daisies and other perennials* □ *a hardy perennial.* [compare **annual, biennial**]

perfect *adjective*; *noun*; *verb*
▻ ***adjective*** /'pɜːfɪkt/
1 Something that is **perfect** is complete and has no parts missing or damaged: *The vase is in perfect condition.* □ *His teeth are perfect.* **2** Something that is **perfect** has no faults or flaws: *He speaks perfect English.* [*same as* **flawless, impeccable**] **3 Perfect** is also used to describe something that is excellent or the very best of its kind: *the perfect crime* □ *She was the perfect wife and mother.* [*same as* **model**] **4 Perfect** also means exact or precise: *a perfect circle* □ *a perfect copy.* [*opposite* **imperfect**] **5** (*informal*) You can also use **perfect** to mean absolute or utter: *That's perfect nonsense.* □ *He's a perfect fool.* [*same as* **complete**]
▻ ***noun*** /'pɜːfɪkt/ (*uncount*; *grammar*)
The **perfect**, or the **perfect tense**, is the tense of a verb formed in English by the auxiliary verb *have* and past participle of the main verb to refer to conditions existing, or actions completed **a** before the present (*I have read it, they've known about it was ages*). **b** before a point in the past (*She had bought a copy*). **c** before a point in the future (*We shall have left by tomorrow evening*).
▻ ***verb*** /pə'fɛkt/: **perfects, perfecting, perfected**
You **perfect** something when you make it perfect or improve it ao that it is as good as possible: *He practised for hours to perfect his technique.*

perfection /pə'fɛkʃən/ *noun* (*uncount*)
1 Perfection is the state or quality of being perfect: *In his latest work, he has, I believe, achieved perfection.* □ *This cheesecake is absolute perfection.* **2** The **perfection** of something is the process of making it perfect or complete: *She is working hard on the perfection of her technique.* [compare **imperfection**]
▻ ***phrases***
1 Something is done **to perfection** when it is done exactly as it should be and could not be done any better: *The meat was cooked to perfection.* **2** Something suits someone **to perfection** if it is exactly what they want or need: *They found a new office in the city centre that suits their needs to perfection.*

perfectionist /pə'fɛkʃənɪst/ *noun*: **perfectionists**
Someone who is a **perfectionist** does things or expects things to be done to the highest possible standard and refuses to accept anything less: *His teacher, who is a perfectionist, makes him practise for hours at a time.*

perfectly /'pɜːfɪktlɪ/ *adverb*
1 Something is done **perfectly** when it is done in a perfect way without any mistakes or flaws: *She sang the aria perfectly.* [*same as* **faultlessly**] **2 Perfectly** also means very well or completely: *They suit each other perfectly.* □ *He understood me perfectly.* [*opposite* **imperfectly**] **3** (*intensifying*) **Perfectly** is also used for emphasis before adjectives and adverbs to mean 'completely' or 'absolutely': *'How are you feeling now?' 'Perfectly well, thank you.'* □ *To be perfectly honest, I am not very fond of parties.* □ *That's a perfectly ridiculous suggestion!* □ *Things were perfectly satisfactory as they were.* □ *I made it perfectly clear.* □ *She took the news perfectly calmly.* [compare **quite**]

perforate /'pɜːfəreɪt/ *verb*: **perforates, perforating, perforated**
Something **perforates** something else when it pierces it or makes a hole or holes in it: *The broken rib perforated his lung.* □ *After printing, the sheets of stamps are perforated by machine.* — *adjective* **perforated:** *He has a perforated eardrum.* □ *Tear the sheet along the perforated line.*

perforation /pɜːfə'reɪʃən/ *noun*: **perforations**
1 A **perforation** is a small hole made in something: *The needle is used to make a series of tiny perforations in the skin.* □ *Postage stamps without any perforations may be valuable.* **2** (*uncount*) **Perforation** is the process of making a hole or holes in something.

perform /pə'fɔːm/ *verb*: **performs, performing, performed**
1 You **perform** a task, a duty, a service or an action when you do it or carry it out: *A distinguished heart surgeon will perform the operation.* □ *Jesus is said to have performed many miracles.* □ *The police perform a vital service to the community.* **2** You **perform** something, such as a play, a piece of music or a dance, when you do it in front of an audience: *The school orchestra and choir will perform Handel's 'Messiah' at the Christmas concert.* □ *The band be performing at various venues throughout Britain.* □ *Will you perform some of your magic tricks at the children's party?* **3 a** Something **performs** when it works or functions in the way that it should or is intended to do: *The car performed well until the final stages of the rally.* □ *The company has performed badly over the last six months, and its shares are at an all-time low.* **b** (*informal*) A person **performs** when they work or carry out a particular activity or task in the way that is expected or required: *He doesn't perform well under pressure.* □ *If the team performs next season they should avoid relegation to the second division.*

performance /pə'fɔːməns/ *noun*: **performances**

1 A **performance** is something that is performed in front of an audience, *eg* a play, a part in a play, a piece of music, a dance or other entertainment: *a performance of Hamlet* □ *His performance in the new production of Hamlet received wide critical acclaim.* □ *She does concert performances as well as opera.* **2** A certain type of **performance** is the standard achieved by a person or group of people in carrying out a particular job or activity: *Their performance in the Olympics was second to none.* □ *After several bad performances, the team found their form again.* **3** (*used in the singular*) The **performance** of a task, duty, service or action is the carrying out or doing of it: *He was charged with obstructing the police in the performance of their duty.* **4 Performance** is also a measure of the efficiency with which something works: *a high-performance racing car.* **5** (*informal, derogatory*) You can refer to someone's behaviour in public as a **performance** if you think it is unacceptable, outrageous or silly: *The demonstrators had to be carried out of the council chamber by the police. What a performance!* [*same as* **carry-on**]

performer /pə'fɔ:mə(r)/ *noun*: **performers**
1 A **performer** is a someone who performs in front of an audience or in public, especially someone who acts or sings or does some other form of entertainment: *a circus performer* □ *The opera company has lost one of its star performers.* **2** Someone who is a stated type of **performer** does something or operates in that way: *a seasoned performer in the House of Commons* □ *The president was a skilful performer in front of the television cameras.*

perfume /'pɜ:fju:m/ *noun*; *verb*
▻ ***noun*** (*uncount or count*): **perfumes**
1 A **perfume** is a smell, usually a pleasant one: *The roses had a heady perfume.* □ *The sweet perfume of gardenias filled the room.* [*same as* **aroma, fragrance**] **2 Perfume** is a pleasant-smelling liquid or cream, often made from flowers, that a woman puts on her body to make it smell nice: *a bottle of French perfume* □ *Which of these perfumes do you prefer?* □ *He could still smell her perfume after she had left the room.*
▻ ***verb*** /'pɜ:fju:m/ (*AmE* /pə'fju:m/): **perfumes, perfuming, perfumed**
1 You **perfume** something when you put perfume on or in it: *She perfumed her hair with oil of roses.* **2** (*formal or literary*) Something **perfumes** something else when it fills it with a pleasant smell: *The scent of roses perfumed the air.*

perfunctory /pə'fʌŋktərı/ *adjective* (*formal*)
1 A **perfunctory** action is one that is done quickly without any obvious care, thought or feeling: *His only greeting was a perfunctory nod as he passed.* **2** If a person's actions or manner towards others is **perfunctory** they behave in this way: *His perfunctory manner often causes offence.* [*same as* **cursory, offhand**]

perhaps /pə'haps/ *adverb* (*sentence adverb*)
1 You use **perhaps** to indicate that you are not certain whether what you are saying is true, likely, or possible; you can use it in conversation to agree reluctantly: *She hesitated, perhaps wondering which answer would be more acceptable.* □ *Lots of people mistrust machines, perhaps because they've had bad experiences with them.* □ *Perhaps it would be dangerous to tell her.* □ *Perhaps he'll come back this way.* □ *With £1000 we could afford perhaps 300 mats.* □ *'Do you think you'll buy it?' 'I don't know; perhaps I shall.'* □ *'I don't have to do what you say.' 'Perhaps not, but you can at least be polite.'* □ *'It's a bit warmer today.' 'Well, perhaps so.'* [*same as* **maybe**] **2** You can use **perhaps** to add politeness to a suggestion, request, offer or opinion: *Margot, it's getting late; perhaps we could hear the rest of your news tomorrow?* □ *Perhaps you should think again about selling the place.* □ *Perhaps you would be kind enough, Madame Sherman, to ask me no further questions.* □ *That's perhaps the best solution for the meantime.* [*same as* **maybe**]

peril /'pɛrəl/ *noun* (*formal or literary*): **perils**
1 (*uncount*) **Peril** is great danger, especially of being injured or killed: *in dire peril* □ *His rash action placed them in peril of their lives.* □ *those in peril on the sea.* **2** (*used in the plural*) **Perils** are dangers or hazards, especially those associated with a particular activity or situation: *the perils of the sea* □ *Defend us from all perils and dangers of this night.*
▻ ***phrase*** Someone can tell you that you do something **at your peril** when they mean that you will be in great danger if you do it: *Ignore this warning at your peril!*

perilous /'pɛrələs/ *adjective* (*formal or literary*)
Something that is **perilous** is dangerous: *They made the perilous journey across the Alps in winter.* □ *Anyone who had displeased the king found themselves in a perilous position.* [*same as* **hazardous, precarious**] — *adverb* **perilously:** *They came perilously close to financial ruin.*

perimeter /pə'rımıtə(r)/ *noun*: **perimeters**
1 (*also adjectival*) The **perimeter** of any enclosed space or special area of ground is its outer edge, boundary or border: *Sentries guarding the perimeter of the military airfield.* □ *A high fence was built around the perimeter of the prison camp.* □ *Anti-nuclear demonstrators scaled the perimeter fence.* **2** The **perimeter** of a flat shape such as a circle or a square is the length around its outer edge: *Find the perimeter of this square to the nearest centimetre.* [*same as* **circumference**]

period /'pıərıəd/ *noun*; *adjective*
▻ ***noun***: **periods**
1 A **period** is a length of time with a beginning and an end: *a short period of silence* □ *a three-month period* □ *a period of economic growth* □ *There were long periods when he was unemployed.* □ *The weather on Wednesday will be mainly dry with sunny periods.* **2** A **period** is also a phase or stage in history or in someone's life: *the Regency period* □ *a geological period* □ *They are going through a difficult period in their marriage.* **3** A **period** is one of the divisions of equal length in a school day or week during which a lesson is given in a particular subject: *a study period* □ *a free period* □ *We have two French periods and a chemistry period this morning.* **4 a** A **period** is a full stop. [see **Punctuation** in Appendices] **b** (*informal*) People sometimes say **period** at the end of a statement to mean that is the end of the matter or a decision will not be changed: *They won't lend us any more money, period.* □ *You will have no more parties in this house, period.* **5** (*also adjectival*) A woman's **period** is the bleeding from her womb that happens for a few days each month: *She has missed a period.* □ *Her periods are irregular.* □ *period pains.*
▻ ***adjective***
A **period** costume or a piece of **period** furniture is one that was made in, or is designed in the style of, a historical period: *This desk is a period piece.*

periodic /pıərı'ɒdık/ or **periodical** /pıərı'ɒdıkəl/ *adjective*
Periodic means happening at intervals, especially at regular intervals: *He gets periodic bouts of malaria.* □ *The weather will be dull with periodic showers.* [*same as* **occasional**]

periodical /pɪərɪ'ɒdɪkəl/ *noun; adjective*
▷ ***noun*: periodicals**
A **periodical** is a magazine published at regular intervals, *eg* weekly, monthly or quarterly: *The reference library has various newspapers and periodicals.*
▷ ***adjective***
Periodical means at regular intervals or every now and then: *You will need periodical check-ups for the next five years.* [*same as* **periodic**] — *adverb* **periodically:** *He goes to America periodically.*

peripheral /pə'rɪfərəl/ *adjective*
1 Peripheral means of or belonging to the outer edge or outer surface of something: *peripheral nerves* □ *peripheral housing estates.* **2** Something is said to be **peripheral** to something else if it is thought not to be of much importance or significance when considering the matter as a whole: *The issue of subsidies is peripheral to the question of agricultural reform.* [*same as* **marginal**, **secondary**; *opposite* **central**, **crucial**]

periphery /pə'rɪfərɪ/ *noun*: **peripheries**
The **periphery** of something is the edge, fringe, border or boundary of it: *a circular lawn with trees planted around the periphery* □ *They were living on the periphery of society.* [*same as* **margin**; *opposite* **centre**]

periscope /'perɪskoʊp/ *noun*: **periscopes**
A **periscope** is an apparatus consisting of an arrangement of mirrors and lenses mounted in a tube through which the user can get a view of what is happening above. Periscopes are used in submarines to get an all-round view of the surface of the water when they are submerged.

perish /'perɪʃ/ *verb*: **perishes, perishing, perished**
1 (*formal*) Someone or something **perishes** when they die: *Nearly 700 men perished when the ship sank.* **2** A material such as rubber **perishes** when it decays or rots: *The rubber hoses in the engine are perished and should be replaced.*

perishable /'perɪʃəbəl/ *adjective*
Perishable goods are those, especially food, that rot or go bad quickly: *Fresh meat, fish and other perishable foods should be kept in a refrigerator.*

perishing /'perɪʃɪŋ/ *adjective* (*informal*)
You can describe something, especially the weather, as **perishing** when it is very cold: *My hands are perishing.* □ *Be sure to put on your scarf and hat; it's absolutely perishing outside!* [*same as* **freezing**] — *adverb* **perishingly:** *perishingly cold.*

perjury /'pɜːdʒərɪ/ *noun*: **perjuries**
1 (*uncount*) **Perjury** is the crime of lying in a court of law after swearing to tell the truth: *Jones was found guilty of committing perjury at the trial.* **2** A **perjury** is a lie told while under oath to tell the truth, especially in a court of law.

perk[1] /pɜːk/ *verb*: **perks, perking, perked**

> ***phrasal verb***
> Someone who has been ill or unhappy **perks up** when they become more cheerful and lively: *She soon perked up when she heard there was to be a party.* □ *He has been very miserable for the last few days and we thought a trip to the seaside might perk him up.* [*same as* **cheer up**, **buck up**]

perk[2] /pɜːk/ *noun* (*informal*): **perks**
A **perk** is a benefit or advantage which you get in addition to your wages or salary or as a direct result of your particular job or position: *As a director, his perks include a car and free foreign travel.* □ *One of the perks of being self-employed is being able to decide when you will work.*

perky /'pɜːkɪ/ *adjective*: **perkier, perkiest**
Someone who is **perky** is cheerful and full of energy: *Despite his recent illness, he seems quite perky.* [*same as* **cheery**]

perm /pɜːm/ *noun; verb*
▷ ***noun*: perms**
A **perm** is a hair treatment using chemicals that give a long-lasting wave or curl: *She goes to the hairdresser every six weeks for a perm.*
▷ ***verb*: perms, perming, permed**
Someone **perms** their hair when they give it a long-lasting curl or wave using this hair treatment: *She has had her hair permed.*

permanence /'pɜːmənəns/ *noun* (*uncount*)
Permanence is the state of continuing or remaining for a long time or for ever: *The permanence of their settlements was dependent on their ability to grow their own food.*

permanent /'pɜːmənənt/ *adjective*
1 Permanent means lasting, or expected to last, for a long time or for ever: *a permanent settlement* □ *The scar will be permanent.* □ *Does he have a permanent job?* □ *The pollution will probably have a permanent effect on marine life.* □ *Do you have a permanent address to which correspondence can be sent?* [*opposite* **temporary**] **2 Permanent** also means that which does not change: *The hills and the sea were the only permanent features in a changing landscape.* □ *They seem to be in a permanent state of war.* [*same as* **enduring**, **perpetual**] — *adverb* **permanently:** *They are going to live there permanently.* □ *He will be permanently disabled.*

permeable /'pɜːmɪəbəl/ *adjective* (*formal*)
A **permeable** material is one through which liquids and gases can pass: *a permeable membrane.* [*opposite* **impermeable**]

permeate /'pɜːmɪeɪt/ *verb*: **permeates, permeating, permeated**
1 A liquid **permeates** through a porous material when it passes or seeps through it: *Water permeating through the limestone had created underground streams.* **2** Something such as a smell **permeates** a room or other space when it spreads through it or fills it: *A strong smell of disinfectant permeated the hospital wards.* □ *A sense of despair had permeated throughout the entire mining community.*

permissible /pə'mɪsəbəl/ *adjective* (*formal*)
Something is **permissible** if it can be allowed under the rules or the law: *The maximum permissible load for road vehicles is 30 tonnes.* □ *It is no longer permissible for the goalkeeper to pick up a ball that has been passed back by one of his own team.* [*same as* **allowable**; *opposite* **forbidden, prohibited**]

permission /pə'mɪʃən/ *noun* (*uncount*)
Someone gives their **permission** for something when they allow it to be done: *You must get your parents' written permission to go on the trip.* □ *He wouldn't give me permission to go.*

permissive /pə'mɪsɪv/ *adjective*
Permissive means having or allowing a lot of freedom, especially in sexual matters: *a permissive attitude* □ *the permissive society.* [*same as* **liberal**, **tolerant**; *opposite* **oppressive, puritanical**] — *noun* (*uncount*) **permissiveness:** *The permissiveness of the 1960s.*

permit *verb; noun*
▷ ***verb*** /pə'mɪt/ (*formal*): **permits, permitting, permitted**
1 You **permit** something when you give your consent to it or allow it: *Will you permit me to accompany you?*

□ *Parking is not permitted between the hours of 8 a.m. and 4 p.m.* **2** One thing **permits** another if it makes it possible for the other thing to happen: *We are going to have a barbecue, weather permitting.* □ *While they are in Greece, they are going to visit as many ancient monuments as time permits.*
[*same as* **allow**]
▻ ***noun*** /ˈpɜːmɪt/: **permits**
A **permit** is an official document which says that you are allowed to do a particular thing: *You will need a permit to fish on this river.* □ *a parking permit* □ *a travel permit* □ *His work permit is only for six months.* [compare **licence, pass**]

permutation /pɜːmjʊˈteɪʃən/ *noun* (*formal*): **permutations**
A **permutation** is any of the possible ways in which a number or set of things can be arranged in order: *The permutations of A, B and C are ABC, ACB, BAC, BCA, CAB, and CBA.* □ *the numbers 1, 2, 3, 4, 5 and permutations thereof* □ *He tried various colour permutations before finally deciding on red, white and yellow.*

pernicious /pəˈnɪʃəs/ *adjective* (*formal or literary*)
Something that is **pernicious** has a very harmful or destructive effect: *the pernicious influence of the drug culture on certain vulnerable groups in society* □ *Their pernicious lies destroyed his reputation.* [*opposite* **harmless, innocuous**]

pernickety /pəˈnɪkətɪ/ *adjective* (*informal, often derogatory*)
If you describe someone as **pernickety,** you mean that you think they are fussy and pay too much attention to small and unimportant details: *Don't be so pernickety!* □ *He's very pernickety about his appearance.* [*same as* **fastidious, finicky**]

perpendicular /pɜːpəndɪkjʊlə(r)/ *adjective*
1 Something that is **perpendicular** stands or rises staight upwards and does not lean or slope to one side or the other: *a perpendicular line* □ *Ice from the glacier had broken off forming massive perpendicular cliffs where it met the sea.* **2** A line or surface is **perpendicular** to another line or surface when it is at right angles to it: *Draw a line perpendicular to the base of the triangle.* [compare **horizontal, vertical**]

perpetrate /ˈpɜːpɪtreɪt/ *verb* (*formal*): **perpetrates, perpetrating, perpetrated**
Someone **perpetrates** a crime or offence when they carry it out or are guilty of it: *They perpetrated one of the largest frauds in legal history.* □ *Who perpetrated that ghastly monstrosity that some people like to call a sculpture?* — *noun* **perpetrator:** *The perpetrators went free because the police didn't have enough evidence against them.*

perpetual /pəˈpɛtʃʊəl/ *adjective*
1 Perpetual means never ending or permanent: *in a state of perpetual fear* □ *deep-sea fishes living in perpetual darkness.* [*same as* **eternal, everlasting**] **2 Perpetual** also means continuous: *the perpetual roar of the traffic* □ *She got tired of their perpetual bickering.* [*same as* **constant**]

perpetuate /pəˈpɛtʃʊeɪt/ *verb* (*formal*): **perpetuates, perpetuating, perpetuated**
Something is **perpetuated** when it is caused to continue or continue to be known: *perpetuate a myth* □ *The feud was perpetuated over many generations.* □ *The monument was intended to perpetuate the memory of a great wartime leader.* □ *Bees and ants have evolved complex social behaviour as a means of perpetuating their genes.*

perpetuity /pɜːpɪˈtʃuːətɪ/ *noun* (*uncount; formal or legal*)
▻ ***phrase*** Something is to be done **in perpetuity** if it is intended to last for ever: *All these lands shall henceforth belong to the person here named and to his descendants in perpetuity.*

perplexed /pəˈplɛkst/ *adjective*
Someone is **perplexed** when they do not understand something or are confused by it: *She had to explain the situation to the perplexed villagers.* □ *He studied the letter with a slightly perplexed look on his face.* □ *I have no idea what was intended by his remarks; I'm perplexed.* [*same as* **baffled**]

perplexing /pəˈplɛksɪŋ/ *adjective*
A situation is **perplexing** if it is confusing or difficult to understand: *The report contained a number of puzzling and perplexing statements.* [*same as* **puzzling**]

perplexity /pəˈplɛksɪtɪ/ *noun* (*uncount; formal*)
Perplexity is the state of being confused or unable to understand something: *He felt considerable perplexity as to which course to take.*

persecute /ˈpɜːsɪkjuːt/ *verb*: **persecutes, persecuting, persecuted**
1 Someone **persecutes** you if they cause you to suffer by treating you cruelly or unfairly, especially because of your political or religious beliefs: *The Nazis persecuted the Jews and other non-Aryan peoples.* □ *They were persecuted for their beliefs.* [compare **victimize**] **2** To **persecute** someone also means to continually annoy or harass them: *The cattle were being persecuted by flies and biting insects.* □ *He claimed he was being persecuted by the police.* — *noun* (*uncount or count*) **persecution** /pɜːsɪˈkjuːʃən/: *the systematic persecution of Roman Catholics* □ *the persecutions suffered by their race over the centuries.* — *noun* **persecutor:** *No matter where he went, he could not escape his persecutors.*

persevere /pɜːsɪˈvɪə(r)/ *verb*: **perseveres, persevering, persevered**
You **persevere** when you continue as you have been doing, especially when doing something that is difficult or unpleasant: *You will succeed eventually if you persevere with your studies.* □ *Does your lawyer think it is worth persevering with the claim.* □ *He is going to persevere with the treatment despite all the setbacks he has experienced.* [*same as* **carry on, go on**] — *noun* (*uncount*) **perseverance:** *He doesn't have much success but you have to admire his perseverance.* □ *It takes perseverance as well as talent to become a successful writer.*

persist /pəˈsɪst/ *verb*: **persists, persisting, persisted**
1 You **persist** in a course of action or type of behaviour when you continue with it even when other people oppose you or say that you are wrong: *If you persist with this, I won't be responsible for the consequences.* □ *He will persist in calling all women 'my dear'.* □ *She persists in the belief that she has royal blood.* **2** Something **persists** when it continues for a long time: *Mist and fog will persist throughout the day in low-lying regions.* □ *Belief in magic has persisted even in the most sophisticated societies.* — *noun* (*uncount*) **persistence**: *Their persistence paid off when they were given permission to appeal to the House of Lords.* □ *The persistence of the new strain of influenza is giving cause for concern.*

persistent /pəˈsɪstənt/ *adjective*
1 Someone who is **persistent** continues with a course of action and refuses to give up: *Even though I made it clear that I didn't want to buy anything, the salesman was very persistent.* □ *a persistent offender.* **2** Something is **persistent** when it continues for a long

time or happens frequently: *a persistent cough* □ *There were persistent rumours about the bank's financial stability.* [*same as* **constant**] — *adverb* **persistently:** *He is persistently late for meetings.*

person /'pɜːsən/ *noun*: **persons** or **people**

The plural **persons** is used only in formal or legal language; **people** is normally used as the plural of **person**, and **person** is generally regarded as its singular.

1 (*plural* **people**) A **person** is a human being, a man, woman or child: *Have you ever seen a dead person before?* □ *In the following riots one person died and 60 were injured.* □ *Have you got room for another person in your car?* □ *I want to speak to the person in charge of sales.* □ *A media person needs a variety of skills.* □ *Joe, you're just the person I was looking for.* □ *Mr Wray was the nicest person he had met in years.* □ *She's the kind of person that people ask to parties.* □ *You're a practical sort of person.* □ *I'm really an outdoor person.* □ *He was evidently a person of some determination.* □ *An actor may play a different person every night.* □ *She now seemed more a person than a policewoman.* □ *A woman may find she's a different person when she's pregnant.*

Notice that though **person** is singular, it is often followed by the pronoun *they*, which takes a plural verb: *I'm not the sort of person who gets what they want and then rejects it. A person has a right to live how they please* (or, more formally, *how he or she pleases*).

2 (*plural* **persons**; *formal or legal*) A **person** is someone unknown or unnamed: *A verdict of murder by person or persons unknown was returned at the inquest.* □ *the register of missing persons* □ *The 1969 Act prohibits the tattooing of persons under 18.* □ *I declare the said person duly elected to Parliament.* **3** (*plural* **persons**; *formal*) Your **person** is your body, usually including the clothes you are wearing: *He had the drugs concealed somewhere on his person.* **4** (*used in the singular*; *grammar*) Pronouns and verb forms fall into one of three classes: the **first person**, meaning the speaker, or the speaker and others, as in *I am* and *we are*, the **second person**, meaning the person or people being spoken to, as in *you are*; and the **third person**, meaning someone or something being talked about but not being spoken to directly, as in *he*, *she* or *it is*, and *they are*.

▻ ***phrases*** **1 a** You do something **in person** when you do it yourself, as distinct from another person doing it for you: *He decided to deliver it in person.* □ *If you wish you may appear in person before the court.* **b** You meet, see or hear someone **in person** when you are present to see or hear them, as distinct from seeing or hearing them on television or radio, or hearing about them: *You'll be able to meet him in person tomorrow.* [*same as* **face to face**] **2** You use **in the person of** before naming someone, to mean that they are what you are referring to: *A royal substitute was already available, in the person of the young Prince Edward.*

-person /'pɜːsən/ *suffix*
-person is used with other nouns to form nouns that refer to someone who does a particular job or has a particular role. It is often used instead of *-man* or *-woman* to avoid having to specify the sex of the person concerned: *chairperson* □ *He was appointed official spokesperson by the new regime.*

personable /'pɜːsənəbəl/ *adjective*
Someone who is **personable** has a pleasant appearance and manner: *a personable young man.*

personal /'pɜːsənəl/ *adjective*
1 Something is **personal** if it comes from or belongs to an individual person rather than a group or organization: *If I may be allowed to express a personal opinion, I don't think the plan has been properly thought through.* □ *His personal wealth amounts to more than ten million dollars.* □ *The former cabinet minister made a personal statement in the House of Commons.* □ *a member of the prince's personal bodyguard* □ *The chairman of the company made a personal donation to the appeal.* [compare **private**, **individual**] **2** Something is **personal** if it is done by the particular individual concerned rather than by someone who is their representative: *The pop singer made a rare personal appearance.* □ *I will give your application my personal attention.* **3** A **personal** service is one done or made specially for a particular person: *Will you do it as a personal favour to me?* □ *The company offers a personal service to all its customers.* **4 Personal** also means of or concerned with someone's private, rather than their public or professional, life: *What he does in his personal life is no business of ours.* □ *personal relationships* □ *a personal bank account* □ *The envelope was marked 'Personal', so I didn't open it.* □ *I want to speak to you on a personal matter.* **5** If someone makes a **personal** remark or comment, they are critical of or rude about somebody else's appearance or character: *The argument was becoming a little too personal.* **6 Personal** also means concerned with or relating to the body: *personal hygiene.* [compare **impersonal**]

personal assistant /pɜːsənəl ə'sɪstənt/ *noun*: **personal assistants**
(often shortened to **PA**) A **personal assistant** is a secretary, especially of a senior executive or manager.

personal computer /pɜːsənəl kəm'pjuːtə(r)/ *noun*: **personal computers**
(often shortened to **PC**) A **personal computer** is a small desk computer that is used by an individual operator for *eg* word-processing and storage of information. [see picture at **office**]

personality /pɜːsə'nalɪtɪ/ *noun*: **personalities**
1 Your **personality** is your nature and character as a whole: *He has a very strong personality.* □ *They have three children, all with quite different personalities.* **2** (*uncount*) Someone has **personality** if they have a strong or attractive character: *She's got lots of personality.* □ *He's very handsome, but he doesn't seem to have much personality.* **3** A **personality** is a famous person, especially in the world of entertainment or sport: *a television personality* □ *some of football's best-known personalities.* [*same as* **celebrity**, **star**]

personalized /'pɜːsənəlaɪzd/ *adjective*
Something that belongs to you is **personalized** when it has your name, address or initials marked on it: *personalized notepaper* □ *He has personalized numberplates on his car.*

personally /'pɜːsənəlɪ/ *adverb*
1 (*sentence adverb*) You use **personally** when you want to indicate that you are giving your own opinion: *Personally, I don't approve of what they are doing.* □ *They all agreed that the meal was excellent, but personally I was disappointed with it.* **2** You do something **personally** when you do it yourself without anyone else acting for you: *The manager deals with important clients personally.* **3** Something that concerns you **personally** concerns you as an individual and not other people: *He is being held personally responsible for the*

mistake. □ *I don't know him personally, but I've heard all about him from my neighbour.*

personal pronoun /pɜːsənəl 'prounaʊn/ *noun* (*grammar*): **personal pronouns**
Personal pronouns are the pronouns that are used when talking or writing about a person or thing that has been mentioned already. The personal pronouns *I, you, she, it, we, you,* and *they* are used to refer to the subject of a clause or sentence. Those used to refer to the direct or indirect object of a verb or preposition are *me, you, him, her, it, us, you* and *them*: *In these sentences the personal pronouns are underlined: I hit him. She welcomed us warmly.* □ *'I have lost a blue pencil. Have you seen it?'* [see also **possessive**]

personify /pə'sɒnɪfaɪ/ *verb*: **personifies, personifying, personified**
1 Someone **personifies** a particular quality when they are an example in human form, or a perfect example, of that quality: *She's patience personified.* □ *She personifies evil.* [*same as* **embody**] **2** If something such as an abstract quality **is personified**, *eg* in literature or art, it is thought of or represented as a human or as having human qualities: *A massive stone statue personifying the power of the state.* [*same as* **embody**] — *noun* (*uncount or count*) **personification** /pəsɒnɪfɪ'keɪʃən/: *She is the personification of goodness.* □ *The figures are personifications of the seven deadly sins.*

personnel /pɜːsə'nɛl/ *noun*
1 (*plural*) **Personnel** are all the people employed in a business company, in the army, navy or airforce, or in a public office: *a memo to all personnel* □ *A modern army needs highly skilled personnel.* □ *security personnel.* **2** (*uncount, with a singular or plural verb*) **Personnel**, or the **personnel department**, is a department within a large organization which deals with employees, especially with new appointments and any complaints or difficulties the employees may have: *Personnel has* (or *have*) *received your application form.*

perspective /pə'spɛktɪv/ *noun*: **perspectives**
1 A **perspective** is a particular way of thinking about something, especially when influenced by personal experience or circumstances: *Try to look at it from a woman's perspective.* □ *Fatherhood gave him an entirely new perspective on life.* [*same as* **viewpoint, standpoint, point of view**] **2** (*uncount*) In art, **perspective** is the method of drawing objects or figures on a flat surface so that they seem to be solid and things in the background appear to be further away than those in the foreground.
▻ ***phrase*** You are able to see something **in perspective**, or you get something **into perspective**, when you are able to judge sensibly its real importance in relation to other things: *The problem needs to be looked at in its proper perspective.* □ *She needs to face up to her problems and get them into perspective.* [compare **proportion**]

perspiration /pɜːspə'reɪʃən/ *noun* (*uncount*)
Perspiration is the salty liquid which comes out of the sweat glands in your skin when you are hot or frightened: *His whole body was dripping with perspiration.* [*same as* **sweat**]

perspire /pə'spaɪə(r)/ *verb* (*formal*): **perspires, perspiring, perspired**
A person **perspires** when a salty liquid is released from sweat glands on to the surface of their skin: *He was perspiring freely by the time he reached the top of the hill.* □ *He wiped his perspiring brow with a large spotted handkerchief.*

Perspire is a more polite form than **sweat**.

persuade /pə'sweɪd/ *verb*: **persuades, persuading, persuaded**
1 You **persuade** someone to do something when you cause them to do it by giving them a good reason or reasons to do it: *We couldn't persuade him to come with us.* □ *They tried to persuade her to open the door.* □ *After some time, she was persuaded to leave.* [*opposite* **dissuade**] **2** You **persuade** somebody that something is true when you cause them to believe it: *She was persuaded that the allegations were true.* □ *She was persuaded of the truth of his allegations.* [*same as* **convince**]

persuasion /pə'sweɪʒən/ *noun*: **persuasions**
1 (*uncount*) **Persuasion** is the act or skill of persuading someone to do something or to believe something: *He had to use all his powers of persuasion to get her to agree.* □ *It didn't take a lot of persuasion to convince him.* **2** People who hold a set of, *eg* religious or political, beliefs are often said to be of a particular **persuasion**: *people of different religious persuasions.* [compare **leaning, tendency**]

persuasive /pə'sweɪzɪv/ *adjective*
Someone or something is **persuasive** if they have the ability or power to persuade you to do something or believe something: *He's very persuasive.* □ *a persuasive argument.* [*same as* **convincing, plausible**] — *adverb* **persuasively:** *He argued his case very persuasively.* — *noun* (*uncount*) **persuasiveness:** *The persuasiveness of their argument cannot be denied.*

pert /pɜːt/ *adjective*
Someone, especially a girl or a woman, who is **pert** is slightly disrespectful in an amusing way: *a pert little madam* □ *She gave him a pert little smile.*

pertain /pə'teɪn/ *verb* (*formal*): **pertains, pertaining, pertained**
Something that **pertains** to something else belongs to or concerns it: *The meeting will discuss the annual report and matters pertaining to it.* □ *information pertaining to the case.* [*same as* **relate**]

pertinent /'pɜːtɪnənt/ *adjective* (*formal*)
Something that is **pertinent** is relevant to or directly connected with something else: *a pertinent question.*

perturb /pə'tɜːb/ *verb* (*formal*): **perturbs, perturbing, perturbed**
Something that **perturbs** you causes you to be worried or agitated: *He was perturbed to hear that there had been no news of them for several days.* □ *a perturbing experience.* [*same as* **disturb**]

peruse /pə'ruːz/ *verb* (*formal*): **peruses, perusing, perused**
1 You **peruse** a piece of writing when you read it carefully and thoroughly: *His lawyer perused the documents.* **2** (*often humorous*) To **peruse** something also means to read it quickly without concentrating: *He was standing by the counter casually perusing the magazines on display.*

pervade /pə'veɪd/ *verb* (*formal*): **pervades, pervading, pervades**
Something that **pervades** a place or thing spreads throughout or affects every part of it: *A smell of wood smoke pervaded the little hollow.* □ *a pervading sense of despair.*

pervasive /pə'veɪsɪv/ *adjective*
Something that is **pervasive** tends to spread and be present everywhere: *a pervasive smell of disinfectant* □ *an all-pervasive sense of gloom and despondency.*

perverse /pə'vɜːs/ *adjective*
Someone who is **perverse** deliberately behaves in a way that is unreasonable, unacceptable or wrong: *Why*

must you always be so stubborn and perverse? □ *He takes a perverse pleasure in upsetting his mother.* □ *a perverse decision.* — *adverb* **perversely:** *Perversely, they continued to make the same product though it had become obsolete long ago.*

perversion /pəˈvɜːʃən/ *noun*: **perversions**
1 (*uncount or count*) **Perversion** is the process of changing or twisting something into a form that is no longer recognisable: *perversion of the facts* □ *a perversion of the truth.* **2** (*count or uncount*) A **perversion** is an abnormal or unnatural desire or activity, especially a sexual one: *sexual perversion.*

perversity /pəˈvɜːsɪtɪ/ *noun* (*uncount or count*): **perversities**
Perversity, or a **perversity**, is stubborn refusal to behave in an acceptable or reasonable way: *Sometimes his perversity drives them to distraction.* □ *She's very old, so we tolerate her little perversities.*

pervert *verb*; *noun*
▷ ***verb*** /pəˈvɜːt/: **perverts, perverting, perverted**
1 Something **is perverted** by someone or something when it is changed or turned away from its proper or normal use or form: *He was accused of attempting to pervert the course of justice.* □ *Their natural loyalty was perverted into rampant nationalism.* [compare **distort**] **2** One person **perverts** another when they cause them to turn away from what is natural or right: *She argued that too much violence on television perverts young minds.* [*same as* **corrupt, deprave**]
▷ ***noun*** /ˈpɜːvɜːt/: **perverts**
A **pervert** is someone whose moral, especially sexual, behaviour is unnatural or abnormal.

peseta /pəˈseɪtə/ *noun*: **pesetas**
The **peseta** is the standard unit of currency used in Spain: *How many pesetas are there to a pound sterling?*

pessimism /ˈpɛsɪmɪsm/ *noun* (*uncount*)
Pessimism is the state of expecting or believing that only bad things will happen, or the tendency to see only the bad side of things: *Such hope is in dazzling contrast to the mood of sombre pessimism expressed in the early novels.* □ *There was widespread pessimism about the future of democracy.* [*opposite* **optimism**; compare **defeatism**] — *noun* **pessimist:** *What a pessimist you are!* □ *There are pessimists who believe the country will never return to prosperity.*

pessimistic /pɛsɪˈmɪstɪk/ *adjective*
Someone who is **pessimistic** sees only the bad side of things or believes that only bad things will happen: *He's very pessimistic about his prospects of finding a job.* □ *a pessimistic forecast.* [*opposite* **optimistic**; compare **defeatist**] — *adverb* **pessimistically:** *He predicted, somewhat pessimistically, that there would be a rapid increase in the level of unemployment.*

pest /pɛst/ *noun*: **pests**
1 An insect or animal that is harmful to plants, crops or livestock is a **pest**: *locusts and other pests* □ *The rabbit has become a pest since it was introduced to Australia.* **2** If you call someone a **pest** you mean that they are a nuisance: *He makes a pest of himself by constantly asking silly questions.* □ *Go away, you little pest!*

pester /ˈpɛstə(r)/ *verb*: **pesters, pestering, pestered**
Someone or something **pesters** you when they annoy you or bother you, especially by asking repeated questions: *Will you please stop pestering me with questions?* □ *In the summer, the cattle are pestered by biting flies.*

pesticide /ˈpɛstɪsaɪd/ *noun*: **pesticides**
Pesticide is any chemical used, especially on food crops, for killing insects or other pests: *spray the fruit trees with pesticide* □ *They grow all their crops without using any chemical pesticides.* [compare **insecticide**]

pet /pɛt/ *noun*; *adjective*; *verb*
▷ ***noun***: **pets**
1 (*often adjectival*) A tame animal or bird kept as a companion is a **pet**: *The teacher asked the children to write about their pets.* □ *Cats and dogs are popular pets.* □ *a pet shop* □ *pet food.* **2** A **pet** is also a person who is treated as someone's favourite: *She is the teacher's pet.* □ *As the youngest child, her father made something of a pet of her.* **3** You can call someone a **pet** if you think they are a kind or lovable person: *Be a pet and bring me my newspaper.* □ *He's very patient with the children; he's such a pet.* [*same as* **angel, dear**] **4 Pet** is sometimes used as a term of affection, especially when talking to a child or a young woman: *That was very nice, pet.* [*same as* **dear**]
▷ ***adjective***
1 A **pet** animal or bird is one that has been tamed or is kept as a pet: *a pet lamb* □ *He has a pet parrot.* **2** Someone's **pet** project, subject or opinion is their favourite one or the one which specially concerns them: *a pet theory* □ *Shopping is one of my pet hates.*
▷ ***verb***: **pets, petting, petted**
1 You **pet** an animal when you pat or stroke it: *The little boy was petting the calves.* **2** You **pet** someone when you make a fuss of them and treat them indulgently: *He was petted by all the courtiers.* **3** Two people **pet** when they touch and caress each other's bodies for sexual pleasure.

petal /ˈpɛtəl/ *noun*: **petals**
A **petal** is any of the thin coloured parts forming the head of a flower: *rose petals.*

peter /ˈpiːtə(r)/: **peters, petering, petered**

> ***phrasal verb***
> Something **peters out** when it finishes or comes to an end gradually: *The path peters out when it reaches the wood.* □ *The conversation gradually petered out and they sat in uncomfortable silence.*

petite /pəˈtiːt/ *adjective*
A woman or girl who is **petite** is small and slim: *a petite blonde* □ *She's petite and very pretty.*

petition /pəˈtɪʃən/ *noun*; *verb*
▷ ***noun***: **petitions**
1 A **petition** is a written document signed by a number of people which asks *eg* the government to take some action: *Will you sign our petition?* □ *a petition against the new road* □ *They delivered the petition to 10 Downing Street.* **2** (*formal*) A **petition** is any appeal to a higher authority, such as a prayer to God. **3** (*legal*) A **petition** is also a formal application to a court for some procedure to be set in motion.
▷ ***verb***: **petitions, petitioning, petitioned**
1 You **petition** someone in authority when you address a petition to them. **2** You **petition** a court or other authority for something when you ask them to grant a request or set some procedure in motion: *She has petitioned for divorce.* □ *He is going to petition parliament for a change in the law.*

petrol /ˈpɛtrəl/ *noun* (*uncount*)
Petrol is a liquid used as fuel for motor vehicles: *lead-free petrol* □ *a gallon of petrol.*

petrol cap /ˈpɛtrəl kap/ *noun*: **petrol caps**
A **petrol cap** is a protective cap over the opening in the petrol tank of a motor vehicle. [see picture at **car**]

petroleum /pəˈtroʊlɪəm/ *noun* (*uncount*)
Petroleum is the dark-coloured mineral oil found under the surface of the earth or under the sea bed. Petroleum is refined to make fuels such as petrol and paraffin.

petrol station /'pɛtrəl steɪʃən/ *noun*: **petrol stations**
A **petrol station** is a filling-station.

petticoat /'pɛtɪkoʊt/ *noun*: **petticoats**
A **petticoat** is a piece of clothing worn under a skirt or dress: *a flannel petticoat.*

petty /'pɛtɪ/ *adjective*: **pettier, pettiest**
1 A **petty** thing is one that is small and unimportant: *petty details* □ *His problems seemed petty in comparison to theirs.* [*same as* **little, trivial**] **2** You can say that someone's behaviour is **petty** if you think that it is unpleasant or unkind for a foolish or unimportant reason: *She wished she had not been so petty when he had called.* □ *petty jealousies.* [*same as* **small-minded**]

petty cash /pɛtɪ 'kaʃ/ *noun* (*uncount*)
Petty cash is money in notes and coins kept for small everyday expenses in the office of a business company: *Draw money out of petty cash to buy the envelopes and postage stamps.*

petulant /'pɛtʃʊlənt/ *adjective*
Someone who is **petulant** is bad-tempered or upset for an unimportant reason or for no reason at all: *She is behaving like a petulant child.* [*same as* **sulky**] — *adverb* **petulantly:** *'I don't want your advice,' she said petulantly.* — *noun* (*uncount*) **petulance:** *She threw the books down in a fit of petulance.*

pew /pjuː/ *noun*: **pews**
A **pew** is one of the long wooden seats with backs that people sit on in church: *the family pew.*

pewter /'pjuːtə(r)/ *noun*; *adjective*
▻ ***noun*** (*uncount*)
1 Pewter is a grey metal made by mixing tin and lead: *Though he is best known as a goldsmith, he also works in silver and pewter.* **2 Pewter** also means objects made of pewter: *a sale of 17th-century pewter and silver.*
▻ ***adjective***
Something that is **pewter** is made of pewter: *a pewter tankard* □ *Is the plate pewter or silver?*

phantom /'fantəm/ *noun*; *adjective*
▻ ***noun*** (*often adjectival*): **phantoms**
A **phantom** is a shadowy shape of a dead person that seems to appear on earth: *His dreams were inhabited by ghosts and phantoms.* □ *a phantom horseman.*
▻ ***adjective***
Phantom describes something that you think is real but which exists only in your imagination: *a phantom presence* □ *a phantom pregnancy* [=a condition in which a woman has all the symptoms of pregancy but is not actually pregnant].

pharaoh /'fɛəroʊ/ *noun*: **pharaohs**
The **pharaohs** were the rulers of ancient Egypt: *Tutankhamen was an Egyptian pharaoh.* □ *in the time of Pharaoh Ramses III.*

pharmaceutical /fɑːmə'sjuːtɪkəl/ *adjective*
Pharmaceutical means connected with the production of drugs and medicines: *the pharmaceutical industry.*

pharmacist /'fɑːməsɪst/ *noun*: **pharmacists**
A **pharmacist** is a person qualified to prepare and sell medicines. [*same as* **chemist**]

pharmacy /'fɑːməsɪ/ *noun*: **pharmacies**
1 A **pharmacy** is a shop where medicines and drugs are prepared and sold. [*same as* **chemist's (shop), drugstore**] **2** (*uncount*) **Pharmacy** is the preparation and giving out of medicines and drugs.

phase /feɪz/ *noun*; *verb*
▻ ***noun***: **phases**
A **phase** is a stage or period in the development of something: *a critical phase in the economic cycle* □ *The first and second phase of the building programme has been completed.* □ *a new phase in the development of nuclear weapons* □ *He'll grow out of it; it's just a phase* [=a stage in childhood or adolescence].
▻ ***verb***: **phases, phasing, phased**

phrasal verbs
phase in Something **is phased in** when it is introduced slowly or gradually over a period of time: *The tax changes will be phased in over the next two years.* □ *They are going to phase the changes in over five years.*
phase out Something **is phased out** when it is taken away or removed slowly or gradually over a period of time: *Mortgage tax relief will be phased out over a ten year period.*

PhD /piːeɪtʃ'diː/ *noun*: **PhDs**
PhD is an abbreviation for 'Doctor of Philosophy', a university degree that is awarded to people who have done advanced research in a particular subject: *He's doing a PhD in applied mathematics.* □ *They both have PhDs.* □ *Andrew Martin, MA, PhD.*

pheasant /'fɛzənt/ *noun*: **pheasant** or **pheasants**
1 A **pheasant** is a long-tailed bird. The male has brightly coloured feathers. Pheasants are often shot for sport and for food: *two pheasants* □ *a brace of pheasant.* **2** (*uncount*) **Pheasant** is the flesh of this bird eaten as food: *roast pheasant* □ *pheasant soup.*

phenomena see **phenomenon.**

phenomenal /fə'nɒmɪnəl/ *adjective*
Something that is **phenomenal** is unusual or remarkable because it is so good or so great: *The play was a phenomenal success all round the country.* □ *He has a phenomenal appetite.* □ *Her memory is phenomenal.* [*same as* **fantastic, amazing, exceptional**] — *adverb* **phenomenally:** *He is a phenomenally gifted musician.*

phenomenon /fə'nɒmɪnən/ *noun*: **phenomena** /fə'nɒmɪnə/
A **phenomenon** is something that is seen to happen or exist, especially something that is unusual or of scientific interest: *Hurricanes are a relatively common phenomenon in the Caribbean.* □ *Stress-related illness is a recent phenomenon.* □ *Thunder and lightning are natural phenomena.*

phew /fjuː/ *interjection*
Phew is the written form of the whistling sound that you make by breathing in or out quickly, *eg* when you are hot, surprised, shocked or relieved: *'Phew, it's hot in there.'* □ *'Phew, that was a close thing!'*

philanderer /fɪ'landərə(r)/ *noun* (*derogatory*): **philanderers**
A **philanderer** is a man who amuses himself by having casual love affairs with women.

philanthropist /fɪ'lanθrəpɪst/ *noun*: **philanthropists**
A **philanthropist** is someone who helps others, especially by giving money to people who need it: *Andrew Carnegie, the well-known Scottish philanthropist.*

philanthropy /fɪ'lanθrəpɪ/ *noun* (*uncount*)
Philanthropy is concern for mankind, especially the giving of money to charitable causes and people who need it. — *adjective* **philanthropic** /fɪlən'θrɒpɪk/: *a philanthropic act.*

-phile /faɪl/ or **-phil** /fɪl/ *suffix*
-phile is used to form nouns and adjectives that mean (a person who is) fond of or attracted to something, such as *bibliophile*, meaning (someone who is) very fond of books, and *Francophile*, meaning (someone who is) fond of France and the French.

-philia /'fɪlɪə/ *suffix*
1 **-philia** is used to form nouns that mean a tendency to do something, such as *haemophilia*, meaning a tendency to bleed. **2** **-philia** is also used to form nouns that mean an unnatural or abnormal love of or fondness for something, such as *paedophilia*, meaning fondness for or preference for sexual relations with children. [compare **-phobia**]

-philiac /'fɪlɪak/ *suffix*
-philiac is used to form nouns and adjectives that mean (someone) having a tendency to do something (especially something abnormal), such as *haemophiliac*, meaning (someone) having a tendency to bleed abnormally.

philistine /'fɪlɪstaɪn/ *noun*: **philistines**
If you call someone a **philistine**, you mean that they dislike or are not able to appreciate good art, literature or music.

philosopher /fɪ'lɒsəfə(r)/ *noun*: **philosophers**
A **philosopher** is a person who studies philosophy, especially one who develops a particular set of doctrines or theories: *the German philosopher, Immanuel Kant.*

philosophical /fɪlə'sɒfɪkəl/ *adjective*
1 **Philosophical** means of or concerning philosophy. **2** You are **philosophical** about something, such as a danger or disappointment, when you remain calm and do not get upset by it: *He was philosophical about the failure of his business.* □ *They adopted a philosophical attitude to the threat of war.* — *adverb* **philisophically:** *They accepted their fate quite philosophically.*

philosophize or **philosphise** /fɪ'lɒsəfaɪz/ *verb*: **philosophizes, philosophizing, philosophized**
Someone **philosophizes** when they think or argue like a philosopher and form philosophical theories.

philosophy /fɪ'lɒsəfɪ/ *noun*: **philosophies**
1 (*uncount*) **Philosophy** is the study of ideas and beliefs and the search for truth about the nature of the universe and human existence through reasoned thought and argument. **2** A **philosophy** is a belief or set of beliefs that tries to explain the meaning of life or which provides a guide for behaviour: *the philosophy of the early humanists* □ *'Live and let live', that's my philosophy.* [compare **ideology**, **doctrine**]

phlegm /flɛm/ *noun* (*uncount*)
Phlegm is a thick, yellowish substance produced in your nose, throat and lungs when you have a cold.

phlegmatic /flɛg'matɪk/ *adjective* (*formal*)
Someone who is **phlegmatic** is calm and not easily excited or upset: *He is a phlegmatic character.*

phobia /'foʊbɪə/ *noun*: **phobias**
A **phobia** is a very strong fear or hatred which you cannot explain: *She has a phobia about flying.*

-phobia /'foʊbɪə/ *suffix*
-phobia is used to form nouns that mean hatred or fear of something, such as *agoraphobia* meaning fear of open spaces, and *homophobia*, meaning hatred of homosexuals and homosexuality. [compare **-philia**]

-phobic /'foʊbɪk/ *suffix*
-phobic is used to form adjectives that mean having or creating a very strong dislike or fear of something, such as *claustrophobic*, meaning having or creating a fear of enclosed spaces. [compare **-philiac**]

phone /foʊn/ *noun*; *verb*
▻ ***noun*** (*informal*): **phones**
1 (*uncount*) The **phone** is the telephone: *You will be able to contact him by phone from Thursday onwards.* □ *We can't discuss this over the phone; we will have to arrange a meeting.* **2** A **phone** is a telephone: *Is there a phone in the bedroom?* □ *My phone is ringing.* □ *Will you answer the phone, please?*
▻ ***verb***: **phones, phoning, phoned**
To **phone** is to telephone: *Phone me tomorrow.* □ *Did anyone phone while I was out of the office?* □ *He phoned the police.* □ *John phoned to invite you to his birthday party.* [*same as* **call, ring**]
▻ ***phrase*** You are **on the phone** when **1** you are using the telephone: *Would you wait outside for a moment; he's on the phone.* **2** you have a telephone in your home so that you may be contacted by phone: *They're not on the phone.*

> ***phrasal verb***
> You **phone** someone **up** when you dial their telephone number and speak to them on the phone: *I phoned him up to ask his advice.* [*same as* **call up, ring up**]

phone booth /'foʊn buːð/ *noun*: **phone booths**
A **phone booth** is a small space containing a telephone and separated from a larger public area by thin walls: *There's a public phone booth in the hotel lobby.*

phone box /'foʊn bɒks/ *noun*: **phone boxes**
A **phone box** is a telephone box: *There's a phone box outside the station.*

phone call /'foʊn kɔːl/ *noun*: **phone calls**
A **phone call** is a telephone call: *Have there been any phone calls for me?* □ *I'm just going to make a quick phone call.*

phonecard /'foʊnkɑːd/ *noun*: **phonecards**
A **phonecard** is a small plastic card that you can use instead of cash to pay for calls in a public telephone box.

phone-in /'foʊnɪn/ *noun*: **phone-ins**
A **phone-in** is a radio or television programme during which listeners or viewers may ask questions or give their comments or opinions by telephone: *a phone-in programme.*

phonetic /fə'nɛtɪk/ *adjective*
Phonetic means **1** of or connected with the sound or sounds made when pronouncing a word or the sounds used in languages. **2** using a system for writing the words in a language with a symbol representing each different speech sound: *a phonetic alphabet* □ *a phonetic spelling.* — *adverb* **phonetically:** *How do you write 'elephant' phonetically?*

phonetics /fɛ'nɛtɪks/ *noun* (*uncount*; *technical*)
Phonetics is the study of human speech sounds, how they are made, transmitted and received.

phoney or **phony** /'foʊnɪ/ *adjective*; *noun*
▻ ***adjective*** (*informal, derogatory*): **phonier, phoniest**
1 Something that is **phoney** is false or is not what it appears to be: *a phoney English accent.* [*same as* **fake, bogus**] **2** Someone who is **phoney** is insincere or pretends to be something that they are not: *He said he thought all politicians were phoney.* □ *Her phoney manner really irritates me.* [*same as* **false**]
▻ ***noun*** (*informal, derogatory*): **phoneys:** *The passport is a phoney.* □ *He pretends to be an old-fashioned English gentleman; he's such a phoney!* [*same as* **fake, fraud**]

phony see **phoney**.

phosphorescent /fɒsfə'rɛsənt/ *adjective*
Something that is **phosphorescent** shines faintly in the dark but gives out little or no heat: *a phosphorescent glow.*

photo /ˈfoʊtoʊ/ *noun*: **photos** (*informal*)
A **photo** is a photograph: *a passport photo* □ *Did you take any photos while you were on holiday?*

photo- /ˈfoʊtoʊ/ *prefix*
1 (*technical*) **Photo-** is used before nouns and adjectives to mean of, making use of, or reacting to light: *photography* □ *photosynthesis* □ *a photoelectric cell* □ *photosensitive paper.* **2 Photo-** is also used before nouns to mean a method or technique which makes use of photography or photographs: *photomontage* □ *photojournalism* □ *photogravure.*

photocopier /ˈfoʊtoʊkɒpɪə(r)/ *noun*: **photocopiers**
A **photocopier** is a machine that makes a quick copy or copies of something, such as a piece of paper with writing or printing on it, by taking a photograph or a series of photographs of it. [see picture at **office**]

photocopy /ˈfoʊtoʊkɒpɪ/ *noun*; *verb*
▻ ***noun***: **photocopies**
A **photocopy** is a copy of something, such as a piece of paper with writing or printing on it, that is made on a photocopier: *He has a photocopy of the original letter.*
▻ ***verb***: **photocopies, photocopying, photocopied**
You **photocopy** something when you make a copy of it using a photocopier: *I need to photocopy this letter before it can be sent out.*

photogenic /foʊtəˈdʒenɪk/ *adjective*
Someone or something is **photogenic** if they look attractive in photographs: *They were looking for a naturally attractive and photogenic child to represent the soap company.* □ *The south of the island is particularly photogenic and often features on posters.*

photograph /ˈfoʊtoʊgrɑːf/ *noun*; *verb*
▻ ***noun***: **photographs**
A **photograph** is a picture taken with a camera: *a photograph of her parents* □ *That's a good photograph of you.* □ *He is standing in the back row in the school photograph.* □ *I want to take some photographs of the garden.*
▻ ***verb***: **photographs, photographing, photographed**
You **photograph** something when you use a camera to get a picture of it: *The deer are very shy and difficult to photograph.* □ *They were photographed outside Buckingham Palace.* □ *one of the most photographed tourist attractions in Britain.*

photographer /fəˈtɒgrəfə(r)/ *noun*: **photographers**
A **photographer** is someone who takes photographs, especially someone whose profession is taking photographs: *a keen amateur photographer* □ *a sports photographer* □ *a newspaper photographer.*

photography /fəˈtɒgrəfɪ/ *noun* (*uncount*)
Photography is the art or process of taking photographs with a camera: *Photography is one of his hobbies.* □ *stills photography* □ *wildlife photography.*

Photostat /ˈfoʊtəstat/ *noun*; *verb*
▻ ***noun*** (*trademark*): **Photostats**
A **Photostat** is a copy of a document made on a particular type of photocopier.
▻ ***verb*** (usually **photostat**): **photostats, photostatting, photostatted**
To **photostat** something is to make a Photostat of it.

phrasal verb /freɪzəl ˈvɜːb/ *noun*: **phrasal verbs**
A **phrasal verb** is a phrase made up of two or three words: a verb combined with an adverb or a preposition, or a verb combined with an adverb and a preposition. Phrasal verbs are very common in English, and their meaning may be quite different from the meaning of the ordinary verb, *eg* you may know the individual meanings of the words **make** and **off**, but you may not be able to guess that **to make off** means 'to leave or escape'. Some phrasal verbs have the adverb or preposition following immediately after the verb, as in 'He **owned up**' and 'He **looks after** the children'; others have the object of the verb placed between the verb and the other parts of the phrasal verb, as in 'He **laid** the book **down**.' Phrasal verbs with their meanings and examples of their usage are shown in this dictionary in special boxes at the end of the entry for the ordinary verb.

phrase /freɪz/ *noun*; *verb*
▻ ***noun*** (*grammar*): **phrases**
1 A **phrase** is a small group of words expressing a single idea that may be used on its own or as part of a sentence, *eg a bunch of flowers, at the last minute.* **2** A **phrase** is also a group of words which, when used together, have a different meaning from the usual meanings of the individual words. Phrases (or idioms) and their meanings are included in this dictionary under the heading 'phrase' or 'phrases' and may be found under the headword entry for the most important noun in the phrase, or, when there is no noun, another important word, *eg* the meaning of the phrase **out on a limb** may be found at **limb**, and the meaning of the phrase **agree to differ** is given at **differ** (with a cross reference at **agree**).
▻ ***verb***: **phrases , phrasing, phrased**
You **phrase** something in a particular way when you choose the words to express it in that way: *His reply was carefully phrased to avoid giving the impression that he was too eager.*

phrase book /ˈfreɪz bʊk/ *noun*: **phrase books**
A **phrase book** is a book, used by people when they travel abroad, containing useful words and phrases in a foreign language with a translation of each word or phrase in the user's own language: *an Italian phrase book.*

phraseology /freɪzɪˈɒlədʒɪ/ *noun* (*uncount*)
The particular **phraseology** used by a person or a particular group of people is the way in which they choose, arrange or use words and phrases to express themselves: *He uses the phraseology typical of sports commentators.* □ *legal phraseology.* [*same as* **language, idiom**]

physical /ˈfɪzɪkəl/ *adjective*
1 Physical means of or for a person's body, rather than their mind: *physical exercise* □ *physical strength* □ *physical contact* □ *a physical disability* □ *their physical and emotional needs.* **2 Physical** also means **a** of or concerning real things that can be seen or felt: *the physical world.* **b** of or relating to nature, natural features or to the laws of nature: *physical geography* □ *It's a physical impossibility for most living things to survive in these temperatures.* **c** of or connected with physics or the laws of physics: *physical chemistry.* — *adverb* **physically:** *He is physically fit.*

physician /fɪˈzɪʃən/ *noun*: **physicians**
A **physician** is a doctor, especially one who treats people with medicine rather than performing surgery.

physicist /ˈfɪzɪsɪst/ *noun*: **physicists**
A **physicist** is a person who studies physics: *a nuclear physicist.*

physics /ˈfɪzɪks/ *noun* (*singular*)
Physics is branch of science concerned with the study of natural forces such as heat, light, sound, electricity, and magnetism.

physiology /fɪzɪˈɒlədʒɪ/ *noun*
1 (*uncount*) **Physiology** is the study of the way in which the bodies of living things work, *eg* how they breathe, how they take in and use food, and how they

grow. **2** (*singular*) The **physiology** of an animal or plant is the way in which it works: *He is studying the physiology of sharks.* —*adjective* **physiological** /fɪzɪəˈlɒdʒɪkəl/: *The circulation of blood is a physiological process.*

physiotherapist /fɪzɪoʊˈθɛrəpɪst/ *noun*: **physiotherapists**
A **physiotherapist** is a person who is treats people using physiotherapy.

physiotherapy /fɪzɪoʊˈθɛrəpɪ/ *noun* (*uncount*)
Physiotherapy is the treatment of injury and disease by massage, physical exercise and heat, rather than with drugs.

physique /fɪˈziːk/ *noun* (*uncount or count*): **physiques**
Someone's **physique** is the shape, size and muscular development of their body: *His physique is ideal for gymnastics, small but powerfully built.*

pianist /ˈpiːənɪst/ *noun*: **pianists**
A **pianist** is a person who plays the piano: *She is a trained pianist.* □ *a famous pianist.*

piano /pɪˈanoʊ/ *noun*: **pianos**
A **piano** is a large musical instrument wih a row of black and white keys. When you press down on the keys with your fingers little hammers strike wire strings inside the piano and different notes are made: *a grand piano* □ *Do you play the piano?*

pianoforte /pɪanoʊˈfɔːtɪ/ *noun*: **pianofortes**
Pianoforte is the full formal term for a piano.

piccolo /ˈpɪkəloʊ/ *noun*: **piccolos**
A **piccolo** is a musical instrument similar to, but smaller and more high-piched than, the flute.

pick[1] (*core*) /pɪk/ *verb*; *noun*
▻ ***verb***: **picks, picking, picked**
1 You **pick** a particular person or thing when you to choose or select them: *Pick any card from the pack.* □ *As a manager he had a talent for picking a good team.* □ *Next time I pick a secretary I'll be more careful!* □ *You've certainly picked a good day for your visit.* **2** You **pick** flowers or fruit when you break or pull them off the plant or tree on which they are growing: *There's nothing better than being able to pick a juicy apple from your own tree.* □ *I've picked some daffodils for you.* □ *The children and I went blackberry-picking that afternoon.* **3** You **pick** an object from a place when you take it or remove it from there, especially with your finger and thumb: *He picked a stray grey hair off his cardigan.* □ *She picked a match out of the ashtray.* □ *One by one I picked the pieces of glass out of the wound.* **4** To **pick** a lock is to open it using a piece of wire instead of a key: *He'd taught them how to pick a lock, steal a car, and shoplift.* **5** People **pick** their noses when they scrape matter out with their fingernails; you **pick** your teeth when you remove bits of food with a sharp point; you **pick** a spot or pimple when you scrape off the scab: *I used to pick my spots and make them worse.* □ *Woolley picked his teeth with a matchstick.* **6** You **pick** a fight or quarrel with someone when you deliberately annoy or provoke them into fighting or quarrelling with you: *She was deliberately trying to pick a fight with him.* **7** You **pick** your way across difficult ground when you walk carefully across it, avoiding obstacles and dangers: *He picked his way along the muddy track to where he'd left the car.*
▻ ***noun*** (*used in the singular*)
1 You have, or take, your **pick** of things or people when you are free to choose whichever you want: *They can take their pick of the best graduates from the best universities.* □ *You can have your pick of any of our horses for breeding.* **2** The **pick** of a group of things are the best ones: *The apples we sell are the pick of the crop.* □ *The pick of the girls get married.* □ *Lewis and Jarvis were the pick of England's attack.*
▻ ***phrases*** **1** You **have a bone to pick with someone** when they have done something that has made you angry or upset, and you want to question them about it. **2** You **pick and choose** when you select or choose very carefully the things you want, and reject the rest: *I'm in no hurry; I can afford to pick and choose.* **3** For **pick holes in** see **hole**. **4** For **pick someone's brains** see **brain**. **5** For **pick someone's pocket** see **pocket**. **6** For **pick up the pieces** see **piece**.

phrasal verbs

pick at **1** You **pick at** your food when you eat very little of it: *It's good to meet a woman who doesn't pick at her food and moan about diets.* **2** You **pick at** something such as a pimple or a scab when you remove bits of it with your fingernails.

pick off Individuals in a group of *eg* soldiers **are picked off** by a gunman or gunmen when they are shot down one by one: *They worked under the grim threat that armed and dangerous rebels could pick them off at any time.*

pick on Someone **picks on** you if they select you without good reason to treat badly or unfairly: *He tends to pick on new people a bit at first, to bring them into line.*

pick out **1** You **pick** something **out** when you select it from a group: *It's impossible to pick out any single painting for more praise than the others.* **2** You **pick** someone or something **out** from a crowd or mass when you recognize or identify them: *He ran his eye over the sea of faces, trying to pick out his daughter Karen.* □ *It was difficult to pick out his features beneath the layer of grime covering his face.*

pick up **1** You **pick** something **up** when you lift it, using your hands or fingers: *I crawled out of bed to pick up a blanket that had fallen on the floor.* □ *The baby began to howl and Jennifer picked him up again.* □ *If you need advice, you have only to pick up the phone, or call in to see us.* **2** You **pick** yourself **up** when you stand up again after falling: *She picked herself up off the dusty ground.* **3** If you **pick** someone or something **up**, you go and fetch them from the place where they are waiting to be collected: *She picked the children up from school.* □ *Could you call at Mrs Brennan's and pick up a loaf of bread?* □ *I've arranged for you to pick her up from her hotel at four o'clock.* □ *Her employer was to pick her up by car.* **4** You **pick up** something such as a skill or language when you learn it casually through observation and practice, rather than through formal training and conscious effort: *I've picked up some Spanish, and other languages too.* □ *I had picked up a bit of surgery from him.* **5** You **pick up** a habit when you copy other people who have it. **6** You **pick up** a disease when you come into contact with the thing that infects you. **7** You **pick up** things like news and ideas when you gather them from various sources: *I picked up an interesting piece of gossip the other day.* □ *She never went shopping without picking up a bargain of some sort.* **8** You **pick up** a radio or television transmission when you receive it on your equipment: *I might be able to pick up Radio 5 when conditions are good.* **9** Someone **is picked up** by the police when they are arrested and taken to a police station: *He was picked up by the police for drunken driving.* **10** You **pick up** when you recover from an illness, or when your health improves; something that has been in a bad state **picks up** when it improves: *It was a good month before she began to*

pick up. □ *The Japanese economy will soon pick up again.* **11** A vehicle or vessel **picks up** speed when it starts going faster; the wind **picks up** when its force increases: *The car picked up speed and shot off into the distance.* □ *The yacht began to pick up speed.* □ *The wind had started to pick up again.*
12 (*informal*) Someone who tries to **pick** you **up** tries to make your acquaintance in the hope of having a sexual relationship with you: *Among them she noticed the man in the grey suit who had tried to pick her up earlier.*

pick² /pɪk/ *noun*: **picks**
A **pick** is a pickaxe: *The workman was carrying a pick and shovel.*

pickaxe (*AmE* **pickax**) /'pɪkaks/ *noun*: **pickaxes**
A **pickaxe** is a tool consisting of a curved iron head pointed at one or both ends, and fixed to a long handle. Pickaxes are used for breaking up hard surfaces or rocks.

picker /'pɪkə(r)/ *noun*: **pickers**
A **picker** is a person who harvests fruit or other crops: *hop pickers.*

picket /'pɪkɪt/ *verb*; *noun*
▻ ***verb***: **pickets, picketing, picketed**
A group of striking workers **picket** their work place when they stand outside it and try to persuade other workers not to go in: *They picketed the factory.*
▻ ***noun***: **pickets**
A **picket** is (any one of) a group of striking workers that stand outside their place of work and try to persuade other employees not to go in: *The union had organized pickets at all the company's depots.*

picket line /'pɪkɪt laɪn/ *noun*: **picket lines**
A **picket line** is a line of striking workers who stand outside the entrance to a factory or other workplace and try to prevent other workers going in: *The lorry drivers refused to cross the picket line.*

pickings /'pɪkɪŋz/ *noun* (*plural*; *informal*)
Rich or easy **pickings** are things, such as profits or goods, that are in plentiful supply and are easy to get or take: *The large herds crossing the river provided easy pickings for the crocodiles.* □ *Rich pickings were available to the crews of privateers prepared to indulge in a little piracy.*

pickle /'pɪkəl/ *noun*; *verb*
▻ ***noun***: **pickles**
1 (*count or uncount*) **Pickles** are foods made from fruit or vegetables that are put vinegar or salt water so that they can be kept for a long time: *lime pickle* □ *We had freshly-baked bread with cheese and pickles.* **2** (*usually in the singular*; *informal*) If someone is in a **pickle** they are in a difficult situation or a state of confusion: *He's got himself into a bit of a pickle.* [*same as* **state**]
▻ ***verb***: **pickles, pickling, pickled**
You **pickle** a food, such as fruit, vegetables or meat, when you preserve it by putting it in vinegar or salt water: *Silverskin onions are the best kind for pickling.* □ *The beef has been pickled in brine.* — *adjective* **pickled:** *pickled cucumbers* □ *pickled herrings.*

pick-me-up /'pɪkmɪʌp/ *noun* (*informal*): **pick-me-ups**
A **pick-me-up** is something, such as a drink, which restores a person's energy, health or cheerfulness: *She drinks an occasional glass of fortified wine as a pick-me-up.*

pickpocket /'pɪkpɒkɪt/ *noun*: **pickpockets**
A **pickpocket** is a thief who steals things from people's pockets: *They were warned to beware of pickpockets in the crowded streets.*

pick-up /'pɪkʌp/ *noun*: **pick-ups**
A **pick-up** is a type of small open-backed lorry or van that can be easily loaded and unloaded: *They loaded the boxes into a pick-up truck.*

picky /'pɪkɪ/ *adjective* (*informal*): **pickier, pickiest**
You can describe a person as **picky** if you think they are difficult to please or too fussy: *Why must you be so picky?* [*same as* **pernickety, finicky**]

picnic /'pɪknɪk/ *noun*; *verb*
▻ ***noun*** (*often adjectival*): **picnics**
A **picnic** is an informal meal which you carry with you and eat in the open air, *eg* as part of a trip or outing to the beach or the countryside: *If we take a picnic, we can spend the whole day at the beach.* □ *a picnic lunch* □ *a picnic basket* □ *There are special picnic areas along the forest trail.*
▻ ***verb***: **picnics, picnicking, picnicked**
You **picnic** when you have such a meal in the open air: *We picnicked beside a pretty little stream.* — *noun* **picknicker:** *The woods in summer are full of hickers and picknickers.*

pictorial /pɪk'tɔːrɪəl/ *adjective*
Pictorial means **1** in a picture or pictures or consisting of a picture or pictures: *They took many photographs so that they would have a pictorial record of their journey.* **2** having or including pictures: *a pictorial calendar.* — *adverb* **pictorially:** *The story was told pictorially.*

picture /'pɪktʃə(r)/ *noun*; *verb*
▻ ***noun***: **pictures**
1 A **picture** is a representation of something on a flat surface: *a picture of a kitten* □ *There were a lot of pictures on the walls.* [see picture at **living room**] **2** A **picture** is also a photograph: *Take a picture of the house.* □ *He keeps a picture of his wife in his wallet.* **3** A **picture** is also an image or view: *He had a clear picture in his mind of the man who had attacked him.* □ *This plan will give you a picture of how the offices will look.* **4** A **picture** is also a situation or outlook: *a gloomy financial picture.* **5** You can say that someone is the **picture** of some quality when you mean that they are a visible example of that quality: *She was a picture of happiness.* [*same as* **personification, embodiment, model**] **6** (*informal*) You can say that someone looks a **picture** if you think that they look very pretty or attractive. **7** (*uncount*) The image received on a television screen is called the **picture**. **8** A **picture** is a film, especially one made for the cinema: *He made his first picture in 1934.* **9** (*used in the plural*; *informal*) People often say that they are going to the **pictures** when they are going to the cinema.
▻ ***verb***: **pictures, picturing, pictured**
1 You **picture** something when you form an image or view of it in your mind: *It's a bit of a mess at the moment, but just picture what it will be like when it is finished.* **2** Something or someone **is pictured** in a certain way when they are represented or shown in that way in a picture or photograph: *They are pictured standing in front of the Taj Mahal.*
▻ ***phrases*** **1** (*informal*) You can say that you **get the picture**, when someone who has been describing something, to show that you understand or can see what they mean. **2** Someone or something that is **pretty as a picture is** very pretty. **3** (*informal*) You **put** someone **in the picture** when you give them all the information that they need to know about. **4** (*informal*) If you say that someone is **in** or **out of the picture**, you mean that they are involved, or are no longer involved, in a situation that you are discussing.

picturesque /pɪktʃə'rɛsk/ *adjective*
A **picturesque** place or building is one that is attractive and interesting to look at, especially if it is old-fashioned or unspoilt: *They live in a picturesque village in the Cotswolds.* [compare **quaint, scenic**]

piddling /ˈpɪdlɪŋ/ *adjective* (*informal, derogatory*)
You can describe something as **piddling** if you think that it is small and unimportant: *He won't be interested in piddling little details like that.* [*same as* **trivial**]

pie /paɪ/ *noun*: **pies** (*count or uncount*)
A **pie** is a kind of food consisting of meat, vegetables or fruit baked in a case of pastry: *an apple pie* □ *She made mince pies.* □ *We had pork pie and salad for lunch.*
▻ ***phrases*** **1** (*informal*) You can say that something was **easy as pie** if you think it was very easy. **2** A promise, plan or hope for the future is **pie in the sky** if it is very unlikely to happen.

piece /piːs/ *noun*; *verb*
▻ ***noun***: **pieces**
1 A **piece** of something is **a** a bit of it that has been broken, cut, or torn, off: *He'd cut the sole of his foot on a piece of broken glass.* □ *She laid the brooch on a piece of black velvet for us to see.* □ *The sign had been painted on an old piece of board.* □ *She tore the letter into several pieces.* **b** an individual bit or portion of it; *eg* a sheet of paper is a **piece** of paper, and a slice of bread is a **piece** of bread: *For dessert I allowed myself a single piece of chocolate.* □ *There was time for a mug of tea and a piece of cake.* □ *They used to hang up a piece of seaweed as a weather-forecasting device.* □ *The body was found on a piece of waste ground.* □ *Piece by piece the Conti estates, insignificant at first, were added to by purchase.* **c** one of several parts that are designed to fit together to make a whole item: *Solving the problem would be like assembling the pieces of a jigsaw puzzle.* □ *Fold the fabric and pin on the pattern pieces as shown in the diagram.* **d** an individual member of a class of things represented by a collective noun; *eg* a chair or table is a **piece** of furniture, an apple or orange is a **piece** of fruit, and a cup or plate is a **piece** of crockery: *One traditional piece of clothing worn here by the men is a conical knitted cap with ear flaps.* □ *There was a cracked mug, a steam iron, and some odd pieces of cutlery.* □ *The ring had been her favourite piece of jewellery.* **e** an individual item or instance of something; *eg* a fact can be referred to as a **piece** of information: *I've got a piece of advice for you.* □ *Not one piece of evidence has ever come to light to support this view.* □ *I had a piece of business to transact in the city.* □ *Thanks for your report; it's an excellent piece of work.* □ *Code each piece of data as you enter it.* □ *This was a clumsy piece of diplomacy.* □ *What a piece of nonsense!* □ *It's a familiar enough piece of music.*
2 a A **piece** by someone, *eg* in a newspaper, is an article by them: *There was a wonderful piece by TP O'Mahoney in the Cork Evening Echo.* □ *He used the expression in a recent Spectator piece.* **b** A short musical composition, or an artistic work, or a literary work such as a poem, is referred to as a **piece**: *She'd played the piece often before, and knew it by heart.* □ *The sculpture I mean is a little-known piece by Frink.* **c** The figures or objects used in certain board games are **pieces**: *At the little table sat two old men, playing chess with unusual wooden pieces.* **d** A coin can be called a **piece**: *a hoard of gold pieces* □ *a fifty-penny* (or *fifty-pence*, or *50p*) *piece* □ *The machine rejected his ten-cent piece.* **e** You use **-piece** when specifying the number of items that make up a set: *an 18-piece teaset* □ *a 30-piece orchestra.*
▻ ***phrases*** **1** (*informal*) You **go to pieces** when you get so anxious or upset that you completely lose your ability to deal with things, or perform, as you usually do: *the story of a model housewife who went to pieces as one disaster followed another.* **2** Someone or something survives things such as danger or an accident **in one piece** if they are unhurt or undamaged by them: *He's badly cut up by the broken glass, but he's more or less in one piece.* □ *Let's just hope the car gets there in one piece.* **3** You **pick up the pieces** after some crisis when you try to get the situation back to normal again: *Counselling may not be available, and the social worker is often left to pick up the pieces.* **4** You **say your piece** when you say something that you think needs saying, *eg* during a discussion: *You've said your piece already.* **5** Something is smashed **to pieces** when it is broken into a number of pieces, or very badly damaged; something falls **to pieces** when it collapses or disintegrates: *Several cups toppled to the floor and smashed to pieces.* □ *He came in, slammed the door, and without a word started to pull the room to pieces.* □ *The people of Vicenza are trying to save their basilica, which is falling to pieces.* [*same as* **apart**] **6** You take something **to pieces** when you separate it into the individual parts that make it up; something comes **to pieces** if it can be separated into parts and reassembled: *He learnt to take a car to pieces.* □ *The table comes to pieces, so can be packed away and stored.* [*same as* **apart**] **7** Someone **pulls** or **tears you** or **your** work **to pieces** when they talk about you in a destructive way, or criticize your work harshly: *Communists not only declare that God is dead, but savagely tear him to pieces.*
▻ ***verb***: **pieces, piecing, pieced**

> ***phrasal verb***
> **piece together** **1** You **piece together** something such as a story or the truth when you gradually collect all the relevant facts and understand how they fit together: *We want to trace everyone who was at the party, to try and piece together the last hours of his life.* **2** You **piece together** something broken up into fragments when you mend it, or re-form it, by fitting them all together again: *The plaster lay scattered about when Rodin died, and it wasn't clear how he would have wanted it pieced together.*

piecework /ˈpiːswɜːk/ *noun* (*uncount*)
Someone who does **piecework** is paid for the amount of work they do rather than the number of hours they work: *Farm workers on piecework can only earn a decent wage if the weather is good.*

pier /pɪə(r)/ *noun*: **piers**
1 A **pier** is a platform built of stone, wood or metal stretching from the shore into a lake or the sea where boats can stop and take on or put down passengers and goods. **2** A **pier** at a seaside town is a similar structure used as a place of entertainment for visitors.

pierce /pɪəs/ *verb*: **pierces, piercing, pierced**
You **pierce** something when you push a sharp object into and through it, forming a hole: *He pierced the top of the carton with a pair of scissors.* □ *The arrow had pierced one of his lungs.*

piercing /ˈpɪəsɪŋ/ *adjective*
1 You can say someone's eyes are **piercing** if they are very bright and seem able to look through things, especially to know what you are thinking: *He had piercing blue eyes.* **2** A **piercing** wind is one that is so cold it seems to cut through you. [*same as* **bitter, cutting**] **3** A **piercing** scream or other noise is sharp and clear in an unpleasant way: *The latest alarms emit a piercing bleep to momentarily stun the attacker.* [*same as* **ear-splitting**]

piety /ˈpaɪətɪ/ *noun* (*uncount*)
Piety is the quality of having strong religious belief and a sense of religious duty.

The adjective related to **piety** is **pious**.

piffle /ˈpɪfəl/ *noun* (*uncount*; *informal*, *derogatory*)
You can call something that someone has said or written **piffle** if you think it is nonsense or rubbish: *He talks a lot of piffle.* [*same as* **rot**]

piffling /ˈpɪflɪŋ/ *adjective* (*informal*, *derogatory*)
If someone describes something as **piffling** they mean that it is ridiculously small and unimportant: *They were charging a piffling sum.* [*same as* **petty**, **trivial**]

pig /pɪg/ *noun*: **pigs**
1 A **pig** is a plump short-legged animal with a curly tail and pink or black skin. Pigs are often kept on farms for their meat which, when it is eaten as food, is called pork, ham or bacon: *a pig farm* □ *The farmer keeps dairy cattle and a few pigs.* [see also **boar**, **piglet**, **sow**] **2** (*offensive*) If you call someone a **pig**, you think they are greedy, dirty, selfish, or unkind. [compare **animal**, **beast**, **swine**]

pigeonhole /ˈpɪdʒɪnhoʊl/ *noun*: **pigeonholes**
A **pigeonhole** is one of a set of compartments, *eg* in a desk or in a frame on a wall, for putting letters or papers in: *All messages and letters for members of staff will be placed in their individual pigeonholes at reception.* □ *The music press tried to box us in the 'country music' pigeonhole.*

piggyback /ˈpɪgɪbak/ *noun*: **piggybacks**
Someone gives you a **piggyback** when they carry you on their back with your legs supported by their arms.

piggybank /ˈpɪgɪbank/ *noun*: **piggybanks**
A **piggybank** is a small container, often but not always in the shape of a pig, that children use for saving money in.

pigheaded /pɪgˈhɛdɪd/ *adjective* (*informal*, *derogatory*)
A person who is never willing to change their mind or opinion, even when they are shown to be wrong, is sometimes described as **pigheaded**: *He can be really pigheaded at times.* [*same as* **stubborn**, **obstinate**]

piglet /ˈpɪglət/ *noun*: **piglets**
A **piglet** is a baby pig.

pigment /ˈpɪgmənt/ *noun* (*count or uncount*): **pigments**
A **pigment** is a substance that gives something such as a plant or someone's skin its colour: *paints made from natural pigments* □ *Hair goes grey or white when it loses its pigment.*

pigsty /ˈpɪgstaɪ/ *noun*: **pigsties**
1 A **pigsty** is partly-covered pen on a farm where pigs are kept. **2** (*informal*) If you say that the place where someone lives is a **pigsty**, you mean that it is very dirty and untidy. [*same as* **tip**, **dump**]

pigtail /ˈpɪgteɪl/ *noun*: **pigtails**
A **pigtail** is a length of hair divided into three, twisted or woven together, and worn hanging at the sides or back of the head. [compare **plait**]

pilchard /ˈpɪltʃəd/ *noun*: **pilchards**
A **pilchard** is a small sea fish of the herring family whose flesh is used as food: *She bought two tins of pilchards.*

pile[1] /paɪl/ *noun*; *verb*
▷ ***noun***: **piles**
1 A **pile** is a number of things lying on top of each other: *a pile of books.* **2** A **pile** is also a quantity of something in a heap or mound: *a pile of sand.* **3** (*often plural*; *informal*) When you say that you have **piles** of a particular thing, you mean you have a large or sufficient quantity of that thing: *She's got piles of clothes.* □ *'Have you got enough money.' 'Oh yes, piles.'* [*same as* **loads**, **tons**, **stacks**] **4** (*used in the singular*; *informal*) You can say that someone has made their **pile** doing a particular thing if they have made their fortune from that business or activity: *He made his pile in the property business.* **5** (*informal*) You can refer to a very large and imposing building or house as a **pile**: *He lived in a mouldering pile deep in the countryside.*
▷ ***verb***: **piles**, **piling**, **piled**
1 You **pile** things, or **pile** them up, when you place them one on top of the other to form a pile: *He piled the bricks up.* □ *They piled the boxes one on top of the other.* [*same as* **stack**] **2** You **pile** something on to something else when you load it with a pile or heap of that thing: *She piled vegetables on to his plate.* [*same as* **heap**] **3** A place **is piled** with things when it is filled or covered with those things: *The room was piled high with boxes full of books.* **4** People **pile** into or out of a place when they come or go in a disorderly crowd: *He stopped the bus and they all piled off.* □ *They piled into the lift.*

pile[2] /paɪl/ *noun* (*uncount*)
The **pile** on a carpet or on velvet is the upright threads that give it a soft raised surface.

pile[3] /paɪl/ *noun* (*usually in the plural*; *informal*): **piles**
Piles are haemorrhoids.

pile-up /ˈpaɪlʌp/ *noun*: **pile-ups**
A **pile-up** happens when several vehicles crash into each other on a road: *a pile-up involving 30 vehicles.*

pilfer /ˈpɪlfə(r)/ *verb*: **pilfers**, **pilfering**, **pilfered**
Someone **pilfers** when they steal small items or small amounts of something, especially from their place of work: *He was caught pilfering pens and stationery from his office.*

pilgrim /ˈpɪlgrɪm/ *noun*: **pilgrims**
A **pilgrim** is a person who makes a journey to a holy place as an act of religious faith: *Every year, thousands of pilgrims visit Jerusalem.*

pilgrimage /ˈpɪlgrɪmɪdʒ/ *noun* (*count or uncount*): **pilgrimages**
A **pilgrimage** is a journey to a shrine or other holy place, or to a place celebrated or made special by its associations: *He made several pilgrimages to the Holy Land.* □ *Santiago de Compostela in Spain has been a place of pilgrimage since the 9th century.*

pill /pɪl/ *noun*: **pills**
1 A **pill** is a small round piece of medicine that you swallow without chewing: *a bottle of pills* □ *She took a sleeping pill.* [compare **tablet**] **2** (*uncount*) The **pill** is a type of pill that some women take regularly so that they do not become pregnant: *She's on the pill.*

pillar /ˈpɪlə(r)/ *noun*: **pillars**
1 A **pillar** is an upright post of wood, stone, metal or concrete used in building as a support or for decoration: *He was leaning against a pillar near the door.* [*same as* **column**] **2** A **pillar** is also any tall vertical structure or mass, *eg* of rock or smoke: *In the Bible, Lot's wife was turned into a pillar of salt.* □ *A pillar of fire rose up through the floor and decimated the upper levels.* **3** You can say that someone is a **pillar** of a group or organization if they are an active supporter or important member of it: *He has always been regarded as a pillar of the community.*
▷ ***phrase*** You go, or are sent, **from pillar to post** when you go or are sent from one place to another without receiving the help you need at any one of them.

pillar box /ˈpɪlə bɒks/ *noun* (*BrE*): **pillar boxes**
A **pillar box** is a tall, round red box with a narrow slit in it, in which letters can be posted for collection at

regular times by a postman. Pillar boxes are found in streets. [compare **letterbox**, **postbox**]

pillion /ˈpɪljən/ *noun*; *adverb*
▻ ***noun***: **pillions**
A **pillion** is a seat for a passenger on a motorbike or horse, behind the rider.
▻ ***adverb***
You ride **pillion** on a motorbike when you sit behind the rider.

pillow /ˈpɪloʊ/ *noun*: **pillows**
A **pillow** is a large cushion for the head, especially one on which you rest your head while you are in bed. [see picture at **bedroom**]

pillowcase /ˈpɪloʊkeɪs/ *noun*: **pillowcases**
A **pillowcase**, or **pillowslip**, is a washable cover for a pillow. [see picture at **bedroom**]

pilot /ˈpaɪlət/ *noun*; *adjective*; *verb*
▻ ***noun***: **pilots**
1 A **pilot** is a person trained to fly an aircraft: *an airline pilot* □ *a helicopter pilot* □ *He is a fighter pilot in the RAF.* **2** A **pilot** is also a person with special knowledge of a particular area of water, *eg* in a river or harbour, who is employed to guide ships through it.
▻ ***adjective***
A **pilot** scheme or study is one done on a small scale as an experiment or test to establish whether a larger scheme is likely to succeed. [*same as* **trial**]
▻ ***verb***: **pilots, piloting, piloted**
1 Someone **pilots** an aircraft or ship when they fly it or guide it: *He has been piloting helicopters for ten years.* □ *He piloted the container ship into the harbour.* **2** You **pilot** someone or something when you guide or steer them or it through something: *He piloted her skilfully through the crowds.* □ *The minister responsible for piloting the legislation through the House of Commons.*

pilot light /ˈpaɪlət laɪt/ *noun*: **pilot lights**
1 A **pilot light** is a small permanently-lit gas flame, *eg* on a gas cooker or boiler, that lights the main burners when they are turned on. **2** A **pilot light** is also a light on an electrical apparatus that shows when it is switched on.

pimp /pɪmp/ *noun* (*informal*): **pimps**
A **pimp** is a man who controls and finds customers for prostitutes, and takes a large part of the money that they earn.

pimple /ˈpɪmpəl/ *noun*: **pimples**
A **pimple** is a small red swelling or spot on the skin: *She had a pimple on the end of her nose.*

pimply /ˈpɪmplɪ/ *adjective*: **pimplier, pimpliest**
Someone's skin is **pimply** when it is covered with pimples: *a pimply youth.*

pin /pɪn/ *noun*; *verb*
▻ ***noun***: **pins**
1 A **pin** is a short thin piece of metal with a sharp point and small round head used for fastening together or holding in place pieces of cloth or paper. **2** (*AmE*) A **pin** is a brooch. **3** A **pin** is a piece of wood or metal used for fastening things together, for marking a position, or as a support: *a packet of hairpins* □ *the leg that was broken has scars where the pins were.* **4** The **pins** on an electric plug are the round or square pieces of metal that fit into the holes in an electric socket. **5** (*usually in the plural*; *informal*) Your **pins** are your legs: *He's up on his pins again.*
▻ ***verb***: **pins, pinning, pinned**
1 You **pin** something when you fasten or attach it to another thing with a pin or pins: *She pinned up the hem.* □ *He pinned the poster up on the back of the door.* □ *The seams haven't been sewn up yet, they've only been pinned.* **2** Someone or something **pins** you in a particular position when they hold or trap you in that position with their weight: *He was pinned to the ground by a fallen tree.* **3** (*informal*) Someone **pins** the blame for something on you when they say that you did it or caused it: *Don't try to pin the blame on me!* **4** You **pin** your hopes on something or someone when you hope that that thing or person will bring the result that you want because there is no other way it will happen.
▻ ***phrases*** (*informal*) You can say you would do something **for two pins** if you mean that you would do it with very little persuasion.

phrasal verb
pin down **1** You **pin** something **down** if you are able to describe, understand or identify exactly what it is: *There's a peculiar atmosphere in here, but I can't pin it down.* [*same as* **put one's finger on**] **2** You **pin** somebody **down** to do something when you get them to do it, especially at a particular time: *He said he would come some time next week, but I managed to pin him down to Tuesday.*

pinafore /ˈpɪnəfɔː(r)/ *noun*: **pinafores**
1 A **pinafore** is a kind of apron worn to cover and protect your clothes above and below the waist: *The children wore plastic pinafores when they were painting at the nursery school.* **2** A **pinafore** is also a kind of sleeveless dress which women and girls wear over a blouse or sweater: *a school pinafore.*

pincer /ˈpɪnsə(r)/ *noun*: **pincers**
1 (*used in the plural*) **Pincers**, or a pair of **pincers**, are a hinged tool with claw-like jaws for gripping things. **2** The hinged end of a crab's or lobster's claw, adapted for gripping, is it **pincer**.

pinch /pɪntʃ/ *verb*; *noun*
▻ ***verb***: **pinches, pinching, pinched**
1 You **pinch** someone when you squeeze or nip a part of their body between your finger and thumb: *She pinched her baby brother and he began to scream.* **2** Your shoes **pinch** if they squeeze your feet in an uncomfortable or painful way. **3** (*informal*) To **pinch** something is to steal it or take it without permission: *He pinched my ruler.* [*same as* **nick, swipe**]
▻ ***noun***: **pinches**
1 A **pinch** is a nip or a squeeze: *He gave her cheek an affectionate pinch.* **2** A **pinch** of something is the quantity that you can hold between your finger and thumb: *Add a pinch of salt.*
▻ ***phrases*** **1** You say you can do something **at a pinch**, or **if it comes to the pinch**, when you mean you can do it if absolutely necessary: *We should be able to feed two extra people at a pinch.* □ *If it comes to the pinch, we can get Peter to stand in for John.* **2** Someone who is **feeling the pinch** is having problems because of lack of money: *Since interest rates rose, many companies are feeling the pinch.*

pinched /pɪntʃt/ *adjective*
Someone's face is **pinched** when it looks pale and thin, *eg* because of cold or illness: *Homeless children, with pinched little faces, begging in the streets.*

pincushion /ˈpɪnkʊʃən/ *noun*: **pincushions**
A **pincushion** is a very small cushion or pad that you stick pins and needles into when you are not using them.

pine[1] /paɪn/ *noun* (*often adjectival*): **pines**
1 A **pine**, or **pine tree**, is a tall tree that has thin needle-like leaves and round or tapering woody fruits: *the pine forests of Northern Europe.* **2** (*uncount*) **Pine** is the pale-coloured soft wood of pine trees, used *eg* for

making furniture and in building: *A kitchen table made of pine.* □ *red pine* □ *pine panelling.*

pine² /paɪn/ *verb*: **pines, pining, pined**
When you **pine** you miss, or long for, someone or something so much that it makes you sad: *He spent the first six months at boarding school pining for his mother.* [compare **yearn**]

phrasal verb
Someone **pines away** when they are so unhappy that they gradually become weaker and weaker, and eventually die: *She died only six months after her husband was killed; she simply pined away.*

pineapple /'paɪnapəl/ *noun* (*often adjectival*): **pineapples**
A **pineapple** is a large fruit that is yellow and juicy inside and has a thick brown skin. Pineapples grow in hot countries: *a piece of pineapple* □ *pineapple juice.* [see picture at **fruit**]

ping /pɪŋ/ *noun*; *verb*
▻ ***noun***: **pings**
A **ping** is a short sharp ringing sound such as is made by lightly hitting a metal or glass object with something hard or when a stretched wire is pulled and released: *When the lift doors open you will hear a ping.* □ *The guitar string broke with a loud ping.*
▻ ***verb***: **pings, pinging, pinged**
Something **pings**, or **is pinged**, when it makes or is caused to make this sound: *The crystal glass pinged when he flicked it with his fingernail.* □ *He sat idly pinging the elastic band.*

ping-pong /'pɪŋpɒŋ/ *noun* (*uncount*; *informal*)
Ping-pong is the game of table tennis: *They had a game of ping-pong.*

pink /pɪŋk/ *noun*; *adjective*
▻ ***noun*** (*uncount or count*): **pinks**
Pink is a pale red colour, or is any shade of this colour: *Her hat was a gorgeous shade of pink.* □ *We decorated the bedroom in pinks and blues.* □ *She suits pink.* □ *The rug was a pale pink with a pattern of white roses.*
▻ ***adjective***: **pinker, pinkest**
1 Something that is **pink** is pale red in colour: *pink cherry blossom* □ *a pink and white bedroom* □ (*with the noun omitted*) *The black hat is very smart, but I think the pink would be better for a wedding.* **2** Someone goes **pink** when their skin becomes slightly redder than usual: *She went pink with embarrassment.*
▻ ***phrase*** (*informal*) You can say that you are **in the pink** when you are in the best of health: *'How are you?' 'In the pink, thank you.'.*

pinkish /'pɪŋkɪʃ/ *adjective*
Something that is **pinkish** is slightly pink or rather pink in colour: *a pinkish blue* □ *Are you feeling all right? Your cheeks look a bit pinkish.*

pinnacle /'pɪnəkəl/ *noun*: **pinnacles**
1 A **pinnacle** is a thin pointed ornament made of stone or metal on the highest part of *eg* a church or a castle. **2** A **pinnacle** is also a pointed piece of stone or rock on the top of a mountain: *the towering pinnacles of the Himalayas.* **3** (*usually in the singular*) Someone who reaches the **pinnacle** of success or achievement reaches the highest point possible: *The gold medal was the pinnacle of his sporting career.* [*same as* **peak, high point**]

pinpoint /'pɪnpɔɪnt/ *verb*: **pinpoints, pinpointing, pinpointed**
1 You **pinpoint** the position of something when you find its exact position: *The destroyer pinpointed the submarine's position using sonar.* **2** You **pinpoint** something when you discover or explain exactly what it is: *We haven't been able to pinpoint the cause of your back pain.*

pins and needles /pɪnz ən 'niːdəlz/ *noun* (*plural*)
You get **pins and needles** in a part of your body when you feel sharp little pains there because the flow of blood is returning to it after being stopped or restricted for a time: *I got pins and needles in my legs after kneeling down for so long.*

pinstripe /'pɪnstraɪp/ *noun* (*often adjectival*): **pinstripes**
A **pinstripe** is a narrow stripe in cloth, or a cloth with such a stripe: *The suit is made of navy wool with a white pinstripe.* □ *He decided to wear the navy pinstripe.* [=a navy suit with a pinstripe] — *adjective* **pinstriped:** *a pinstriped suit.*

pint /paɪnt/ *noun*: **pints**
1 A **pint** is a liquid measurement, equal to about 0.57 of a litre: *Two pints of milk, please.* **2** (*informal*) A **pint** is a pint of beer, especially one served in a pub: *He always drinks pints.*

pin-up /'pɪnʌp/ *noun* (*often adjectival*; *informal*): **pin-ups**
A **pin-up** is a picture of an attractive woman or man that you pin on your wall: *The walls of his cell were covered with pin-ups and pictures of motorbikes.* □ *a pin-up girl.*

pioneer /paɪə'nɪə(r)/ *noun*; *verb*
▻ ***noun***: **pioneers**
A **pioneer** is **1** someone who is one of the first people to go to or settle in a country or part of a country which is uninhabited or considered to be uncivilized: *the American pioneers.* **2** someone who is the first to do something: *He was one of the pioneers in the field of genetic engineering.*
▻ ***verb***: **pioneers, pioneering, pioneered**
A person or organization **pioneers** something when it is one of the first to do it: *Christian Barnard pioneered heart transplant surgery.* □ *They were awarded the Nobel Prize for their pioneering work in the field.*

pious /paɪəs/ *adjective*
A **pious** person is someone who has strong religious feelings and a strong sense of religious duty: *Catherine of Aragon was a pious woman.* □ *She is extremely pious.* [see also **piety**]

pip¹ /pɪp/ *noun*: **pips**
A **pip** is the small seed of a fruit such as an apple, pear, orange or grape.

pip² /pɪp/ *verb*: **pips, pipping, pipped**
▻ ***phrase*** (*informal*) Someone **is pipped at the post** when they are overtaken by someone else in the very last stages of a race or contest.

pipe /paɪp/ *noun*; *verb*
▻ ***noun***: **pipes**
1 A **pipe** is a hollow tube made of metal or plastic, through which water, gas or oil can flow: *a lead pipe* □ *a gas pipe* □ *The outlet pipe from the washing machine carries water into the drain.* [see also **drainpipe**] **2** A **pipe** is **a** an object consisting of a narrow tube with a small cup-shaped bowl on one end, for smoking tobacco: *He doesn't smoke cigarettes but he sometimes smokes a pipe.* **b** the amount of tobacco smoked in a pipe: *He smokes up to four pipes a day.* **3** A **pipe** is a musical instrument consisting of a simple wooden or metal tube with holes. You blow into the tube and make notes by putting you fingers over the holes. **4** (*used in the plural*) The **pipes** are bagpipes:

Do you play the pipes? □ the pipes and drums of the King's Own Scottish Borderers.
▻ ***verb*: pipes, piping, piped**
1 Gas or liquid **is piped** when it is carried or transferred from one place to another through pipes: *Natural gas is piped ashore from the North Sea.* **2** Someone **pipes** something when they say it in a high voice: *'Miss, I know the answer!' piped the little boy, jumping up and down to attract the teacher's attention.* **3** Someone who **pipes** plays a pipe or the bagpipes: *The boy was piping away merrily. □ He learned to pipe when he was in a Highland regiment.*

> ***phrasal verbs***
> **pipe down** (*informal*) If someone tells you to **pipe down** they tell you firmly to be quiet or to stop talking: *If you don't pipe down immediately, you'll all be kept in after school!* [*same as* **shut up**]
> **pipe up** Someone **pipes up** when they speak unexpectedly or break the silence by saying something: *The teacher asked the class what the capital of Norway was, and after a long pause young Jones piped up, 'Oslo, sir.'*

piped music /paɪpt 'mju:zɪk/ *noun* (*uncount*)
Piped music is the recorded music that is played through loudspeakers in some restaurants, bars and other public places.

pipe dream /'paɪp dri:m/ *noun*: **pipe dreams**
A **pipe dream** is an idea or a plan that someone has that will never happen or be carried out: *He knew that his hope for an idyllic life in the country was just a pipe dream.*

pipeline /'paɪplaɪn/ *noun*: **pipelines**
A **pipeline** is a series of connected pipes used to carry gas, water or oil from one place to another, often underground: *a gas pipeline.*
▻ ***phrase*** You can say something is **in the pipeline** when it is being planned or prepared: *There are more redundancies in the pipeline.*

piper /'paɪpə(r)/ *noun*: **pipers**
A **piper** is someone who plays the bagpipes: *The McCrimmonds were a famous family of Scottish pipers.*

piping /'paɪpɪŋ/ *noun*; *adjective*
▻ ***noun*** (*uncount*)
1 **Piping** is a length of pipe, or a system or series of pipes for carrying gas or liquid: *copper piping □ They removed the old lead piping and replaced it with plastic.* **2** (*often adjectival*) **Piping** is also the art of playing the bagpipes: *a school of piping □ a piping competition.*
▻ ***adjective***
Someone speaks in a **piping** voice if they speak in a high voice.
▻ ***phrase*** Food or water that is **piping hot** is very hot: *a bowl of piping hot soup □ You can have a bath anytime; the water is piping hot.*

piquant /'pi:kɒnt/ *adjective*
1 Food that is **piquant** has a pleasantly sharp or spicy taste: *a piquant sauce made with tomatoes, ginger, garlic and chilli peppers.* [*opposite* **bland**] **2** You can describe something that is exciting and stimulating to the mind as **piquant**: *a particularly piquant piece of gossip.* — *noun* (*uncount*) **piquancy:** *A little vinegar adds piquancy to a sauce. □ The risk of being discovered gave the plan added piquancy.*

pique /pi:k/ *noun* (*uncount*)
Pique is anger or frustration shown by someone whose pride has been hurt: *After making several mistakes, she threw down her violin in a fit of pique.*

piracy /'paɪrəsɪ/ *noun* (*uncount*)
1 **Piracy** is robbery carried out by pirates: *an act of piracy □ The captain was accused of piracy on the high seas.* **2** **Piracy** is also the illegal copying of things such as video tapes and computer programs.

pirate /'paɪrət/ *noun*; *verb*
▻ ***noun*** (*often adjectival*): **pirates**
1 A **pirate** is someone who attacks and robs ships at sea: *Their treasure was carried off by pirates. □ a pirate ship.* **2** A **pirate** is also someone who illegally copies and sells things such as video tapes and computer programs: *a software pirate □ a pirate copy of a video game.*
▻ ***verb*: pirates, pirating, pirated**
Someone who **pirates** a video, music recording, book or computer program, copies and sells it illegally.

pirouette /pɪrʊ'ɛt/ *noun*: **pirouettes**
In dancing, especially ballet, a **pirouette** is a very fast spin or turn made on one toe or on the front of the foot.

piss /pɪs/ *verb*; *noun*
▻ ***verb*** (*vulgar slang*): **pisses, pissing, pissed**
1 To **piss** is to urinate. **2** People sometimes say it **is pissing** when it is raining.
▻ ***noun*** (*vulgar slang*)
1 (*uncount*) **Piss** is urine. **2** (*used in the singular*) Someone has a **piss** when they urinate.
▻ ***phrase*** You **take the piss** when you make fun of someone or something.

> ***phrasal verbs***
> **piss about** or **around** (*vulgar slang*) Someone **pisses about** or **around** when they waste time. [*same as* **muck about**]
> **piss down** (*vulgar slang*) If someone says it is **pissing down** they mean it is raining very hard.
> **piss off** (*vulgar slang*) **1** If someone tells you to **piss off** they tell you very rudely to go away. **2** If something **pisses** you **off** it annoys or bores you.

pissed /pɪst/ *adjective* (*vulgar slang*)
Someone who is **pissed** is very drunk.

pistol /'pɪstəl/ *noun*: **pistols**
A **pistol** is a small gun held in one hand when fired: *He was armed with a pair of steel pistols.*

pit /pɪt/ *noun*: **pits**
1 A **pit** is a deep hole made in the ground: *He dug a pit in the garden and filled it with sand.* **2** A **pit** is also a small shallow hole on the surface of *eg* glass or metal. **3** A coalmine is sometimes known as a **pit**: *He worked down the pit all his life.* **4** (*plural*) At a motor-racing track, **the pits** are the areas beside the track where vehicles can stop for *eg* fuel or new tyres during a race. **5** (*usually in the singular*) The **pit** or the **orchestra pit** is the area in front of and below a theatre stage, where musicians play.
▻ ***verb*: pits, pitting, pitted**
1 A surface becomes **pitted** when it is marked with holes: *The surface of the moon is pitted with craters.* **2** Someone's skin **is pitted** when it is permanently marked with small shallow scars from *eg* acne or smallpox.
▻ ***phrases*** **1** (*informal*) When you say someone's behaviour, or a situation, **is the pits**, you mean that it is very bad or the worst possible. **2** You have an unpleasant feeling **in the pit of your stomach** when you have that feeling, usually caused by anxiety or fear, low down inside your stomach: *He had a gnawing feeling of anxiety in the pit of his stomach.* **3** For **pit one's wits against** see **wit**.

> ***phrasal verb***
> Someone or something **is pitted against** somebody or something else when they are set against each other in a fight or contest: *The wrestlers were pitted against opponents of equal size and weight.*

pitch /pɪtʃ/ *verb; noun*
▻ ***verb*: pitches, pitching, pitched**
1 You **pitch** camp or a tent when you set up a camp or erect a tent and fix it in place: *They pitched camp for the night.* ▫ *He pitched his tent by the stream.* **2** In *eg* cricket or golf, a player **pitches** a ball if they aim and throw or hit it to reach a certain point or fall in a certain way. **3** A baseball player **pitches** when they throw the ball towards the person with the bat, for them to try and hit and score runs. [compare **bowl**[2]] **4** Something **is pitched** forward or backward when it is caused to fall heavily forwards or backwards: *The driver suddenly put on the brakes and she was pitched forward onto the floor of the bus.* **5** When a ship or aircraft **pitches**, it moves along with the front and back ends going up and down: *The boat pitched and rolled as it made its way through the heavy seas.* **6** A roof or other surface **is pitched** at a certain angle when it slopes at that angle: *The roof of the barn was pitched at a steep angle to give the greatest loft space.* **7** A piece of music or a voice **is pitched** at a certain level when it is set at a certain level of highness or lowness: *The song should be pitched in a higher key.* ▫ *She pitched her voice lower so that she sounded less strident.* **8** You **pitch** something, such as a talk, at a certain level when you express or present it at a level or in a style that will be understood or appreciated by the audience at whom it is directed: *His lecture was pitched at a level that could be understood by people who were not experts in the field.*
▻ ***noun*: pitches**
1 A **pitch** is an area of ground specially marked out and used for playing any of various games, such as football, hockey or cricket: *The team only had ten players on the pitch for the second half.* **2** (*uncount*) **Pitch** is **a** the degree of highness or lowness of a voice or musical note. **b** the quality of a sound in music. **3** (*uncount or used in the singular*) Something reaches a particular **pitch** if it reaches a particular level or degree of intensity: *His frustration reached such a pitch that he punched the wall.* ▫ *The excitement of the fans reached fever pitch when the team scored for the second time.* **4** A street trader's **pitch** is the place in a street where he or she sets up their stall.

> ***phrasal verb***
> **pitch in** (*informal*) You **pitch in** when you join in or make a contribution to something.
> **pitch into** (*informal*) Someone **pitches into** someone else when they attack them or start a fight or argument: *She pitched into the other directors for ignoring her advice.*

pitch-black /pɪtʃ'blak/ or **pitch-dark** /pɪtʃ'dɑːk/ *adjective*
If a place or the night is described as **pitch-black** or **pitch-dark**, it is completely black or dark: *Take a torch with you; it's pitch-black outside.*

pitched battle /pɪtʃt'batəl/ *noun*: **pitched battles**
A **pitched battle** is a fierce and violent fight or argument: *There were pitched battles between the police and gangs of youths who were rampaging through the city centre.*

pitcher /'pɪtʃə(r)/ *noun*: **pitchers**
A **pitcher** is a large jug for holding liquids, made of clay and with one or two handles.

pitchfork /'pɪtʃfɔːk/ *noun*: **pitchforks**
A **pitchfork** is a long-handled farm tool with two or three sharp prongs, used for lifting and throwing hay or grass.

piteous /'pɪtɪəs/ *adjective* (*formal or literary*)
Something that is **piteous** makes you feel great pity or sadness: *the piteous cries of the wounded and dying.* [see also **pitiful**, **pitiable**] — *adverb* **piteously:** *The dying man whimpered piteously.*

pitfall /'pɪtfɔːl/ *noun*: **pitfalls**
A **pitfall** is an unexpected danger or difficulty, or a mistake that can easily be made: *a dictionary designed to help students overcome some of the pitfalls in English spelling and grammar.*

pith /pɪθ/ *noun* (*uncount*)
Pith is the soft white substance between the skin and the flesh of an orange or other citrus fruit.

pithy /'pɪθɪ/ *adjective*: **pithier, pithiest**
You can describe something that is said or written as **pithy** if it is expressed clearly and cleverly without using too many words: *a pithy comment.*

pitiable /'pɪtɪəbəl/ *adjective*
Someone who is **pitiable** is in such a sad or unfortunate state or situation that they are to be pitied. [see also **pitiful, piteous**]

pitiful /'pɪtɪfʊl/ *adjective*
1 Someone or something that is **pitiful** is so sad or pathetic that you are caused to feel pity for them: *Their cries of pain were pitiful.* [see also **piteous, pitiable**] **2** Something that is so poor or bad that it deserves or causes you to feel contempt can also be described as **pitiful**: *His handwriting is pitiful in the extreme.* ▫ *They were paid a pitiful amount of money.* [*same as* **pathetic, despicable**] — *adverb* **pitifully:** *The dog was pitifully thin.*

pitiless /'pɪtɪləs/ *adjective*
Someone who is **pitiless** shows no pity or mercy: *a pitiless tyrant.* [*same as* **merciless, heartless**]

pity /'pɪtɪ/ *noun; verb*
▻ ***noun***
1 (*uncount*) You feel **pity** when you feel sorrow for the sufferings and troubles of others: *He was filled with pity for the unfortunate prisoners.* **2** A **pity** is a cause of sorrow or regret: *It's a pity that you won't be able to attend in person.* ▫ *'He died before he could visit his sister again.' 'Yes, it's a great pity.'*
▻ ***verb*: pities, pitying, pitied**
You **pity** someone when you feel or show you are very sorry for them: *She's more to be pitied than condemned.*
▻ ***phrases*** **1** You **have** or **take pity on** someone when you feel or show pity for them *eg* by giving them something that they badly need or want: *She took pity on the beggar and gave him some small coins.* ▫ *'Have pity on a crippled old man,' he said.* **2** (*sentence adverb; informal*) You can use **more's the pity** in a statement instead of 'unfortunately' or 'I'm sorry to say': *He can never be punished for his crimes, more's the pity.*

pitying /'pɪtɪɪŋ/ *adjective*
If you give someone a **pitying** look, it shows that you feel pity and slight contempt for them: *He gave her a pitying smile.* — *adverb* **pityingly:** *She looked at him pityingly.*

pivot /'pɪvət/ *noun; verb*

▻ ***noun*: pivots**

1 A **pivot** is the pin, shaft or central point on which something turns or balances. **2** A **pivot** is also the central or most important person or thing on which everyone or everything else depends: *Her art was the pivot of her life and everything else was of secondary importance.* [*same as* **hub, focus**]

▻ ***verb*: pivots, pivoting, pivoted**

1 Someone or something **pivots** when it turns or revolves on a central point: *He pivoted abruptly on his heel and marched off in the opposite direction* **2** If something **pivots** on something else it depends on it: *The success of the venture will pivot on the availability of capital.*

pixie or **pixy** /ˈpɪksɪ/ *noun*: **pixies**

A **pixie** is a kind of small fairy who is believed to play tricks on people.

pizza /ˈpiːtsə/ *noun* (*count or uncount*): **pizzas**

A **pizza** is a flat round piece of dough baked with a mixture of cheese, tomatoes and herbs on top: *a cheese and tomato pizza* ▫ *They ordered pizza and salad for lunch.*

placard /ˈplakɑːd/ *noun*: **placards**

A **placard** is a board with a notice, advertisement, slogan, or message of protest written or printed on it that is carried or displayed in public: *The marchers carried placards printed with anti-nuclear slogans.*

placate /pləˈkeɪt/ or /pleɪˈkeɪt/ *verb*: **placates, placating, placated**

You **placate** someone who is angry or resentful when you say or do things that cause them to feel less angry or resentful: *The latest Brussels' initiative seems designed to placate noisy pressure groups.* [*same as* **appease**]

place /pleɪs/ *noun*; *verb*

▻ ***noun*: places**

1 A **place** is any area, position or point; it can refer to such things as **a** a region, city, building, room, or business premises: *We can try to make the world a better place.* ▫ *exciting places like New York* ▫ *They travelled from place to place entertaining villagers with songs, ballads and drama.* ▫ *Can you help me? I'm looking for a place called Ballacondra.* ▫ *You can so easily lose your way in a strange place.* ▫ *This is a picturesque, wooded place.* ▫ *He remembered the house as being a gloomy place.* ▫ *The kitchen was a great echoing place.* ▫ *She's the only person in this place who understands computers.* **b** (*used in the singular*) your environment at any particular time: *It's nice having someone cheerful about the place.* ▫ *We need some flowers round the place.* **c** a point or position for doing something, or where something happens: *No sound came from the place where he lay.* ▫ *I need to know his date and place of birth.* ▫ *Pass our advert round your place of work.* ▫ *We got a list of pubs and eating places from the tourist office.* ▫ *Suppose they discovered his hiding place?* ▫ *damp and dirty dwelling places* ▫ *We used the cellar as a meeting place.* ▫ *Send one copy to your insurers and keep one yourself in a safe place.* ▫ *Store them in a a cool dry place.* ▫ *He found a good place to pull off the road.* **d** the position where something belongs or is kept: *It was a lonely person's house, with everything neatly in its place.* ▫ *I returned the photo to its place on the mantelpiece.* ▫ *The floor is not the place for newspapers.* ▫ *Someone's obviously borrowed it and put it back in the wrong place.* ▫ *Have you got a place where you keep rubber bands?* **e** a seat or position that is given or assigned to you: *She motioned me to take my place beside her at the desk.* ▫ *Please go back to your places.* ▫ *I lost my place in the queue.* ▫ *There's a spare place at our table.* ▫ *Shall I keep you a place?*

Notice the similar use of **room**, which is uncountable and means space, or enough space, for something: *Is there room in your car for me? Have you got enough room for your legs?*. [compare also **space**]

f a space on a table with *eg* a knife, fork and spoon arranged ready for one person to sit and eat a meal: *Brigitte was laying* (or *setting*) *another place.* **g** (*informal*) your own home or lodging: *Shall we meet at my place?* ▫ *I'd like to buy a little place in the country.* **h** a point or area *eg* on the surface of something: *Show me the place where it's sore.* **i** the point you have reached in something you are reading; you lose your **place** when you can't remember where you stopped reading: *He was trying to keep his place in the book.*

2 a (*AmE; used in the singular*) **Place** is often used like *-where* after words such as *any*, *some* and *no*: *'Can I drive you some place?' he offered.* **b Place** is used as a name for a street or square: *He owned the house next to Christie's in Rillington Place.* **c** A decimal **place** is any of the positions that a number can have to the right of a decimal point.

3 a (*used in the singular*) A good **place** to do something is the right point in time, or during some procedure, to do it: *This is not the place to enter into a discussion of Wittgenstein's view.* ▫ *The best place to start, with a new technology like desk-top publishing, is at the beginning.* [*same as* **point**] **b** Someone's or something's **place** in a community, system or situation is the role or function they have in it; someone who knows their **place** realizes how humble they are, and behaves appropriately; you say it is not your **place** to do something if it is not one of your duties, and would be an unsuitable thing to do: *I've worked here long enough to know my place.* ▫ *They've evidently got friends in high places.* [= influential and powerful friends who can arrange things for them] ▫ *Try changing places with a farm labourer and see how you like it.* ▫ *It's not my place to tell the junior staff to work harder.* ▫ *Counselling now has an important place in the life of our society.* ▫ *I like chaos; it has its place.* [*same as* **position, duty, role, function**] **c** You have a **place** *eg* at a college, or on some course or tour, or in some group, if you have been selected or accepted for it: *He won a place at Keble College to read Modern History.* ▫ *Are there any places left for the Budapest trip?* ▫ *Dolly couldn't give her a place in the chorus.* **d** You are in, *eg* second or third **place** in a competition if that is your position in the order of competitors at the end of the competition or at any point during it: *He finished the championship in third place.* ▫ *Anna could only manage seventh place.* ▫ *The French are lying in fifth place at the moment.* [*same as* **position**]

▻ ***verb*: places, placing, placed**

1 You **place** something somewhere when you put it there: *He placed the glass on a tray and bore it away.* ▫ *She placed a finger on her lips.* ▫ *Lie on your back and place your hands on your tummy.* ▫ *The dog placed a dirty paw on his knee.* [*same as* **put**] **2** You **place** someone somewhere when you find accommodation or a job for them: *We've managed to place most of the refugees with local families.* **3** You **place** someone in a certain state or situation when you involve them in it: *I refused their offer, not wanting to be placed at a disadvantage.* ▫ *Learners can now be placed in a situation where they must use language as an instrument.* [*same as* **put**] **4** Someone or something **places** *eg* responsibility or blame on you when they cause it to be given to you: *Rising musical standards have placed a heavy responsibility upon these singers.* ▫ *Explanations such as this tend to place the blame on teachers.* ▫ *I place absolute confidence in my team of workers.* **5** You **place**

emphasis or a value on something if you consider it important: *The company will continue to place great emphasis on staff training.* □ *I place no value on claims of that sort.* **6** You are unable to **place** someone if you recognize them but cannot remember where you met them, or what their name is: *There was something familiar about his face although she couldn't place him.* [compare **identify**] **7** You **place** something such as an order, advertisement or bet when you ask for goods to be ordered, or for an advertisement to be published, or for a bet to be recorded: *To place your order by telephone, call any time, including weekends.* □ *One logging company placed a full-page ad in the Borneo Post.* **8** A competitor who **is placed** *eg* fifth or twentieth, comes fifth or twentieth in the final result; a competitor who **is placed** comes first, second or third.

▷ ***phrases*** **1** Something that is **all over the place** is present throughout the area you are referring to: *There was blood all over the place.* □ *There's no-one here except tourists swarming all over the place.* □ *Workers flocked to Middlesborough from all over the place.* **2** Things **fall into place** when you begin to understand a particular situation: *The details are falling into place as a result of this morning's discoveries.* **3** Something that is **in place** is **a** in the correct position: *Use clamps to hold the wood in place.* [*same as* in **position**] **b** ready or available for using or putting into practice: *We now have safeguards in place against this sort of fraud.* **4** Something that is provided **in place of**, or **in the place of**, something else, is provided instead of it: *In place of the trained lab assistant he'd asked for, he'd been landed with an amateur and a child.* [*same as* **instead of**] **5** Something that happens or is so **in places** happens or is so in some parts and not in others: *The fog is likely to be thick in places.* □ *His autobiography is quite interesting in places.* [*same as* **in parts**, **here and there**] **6 a** You refer to what happened **in the first place** when you are mentioning some circumstance that is fundamental to the situation that has developed: *Why did you get engaged to him in the first place?* **b** You use **in the first place** and **in the second place** to introduce points or reasons in order of importance: *In the first place, we're not in a position to choose.* [*same as* **firstly**, **secondly**] **7** Someone says that **in your place** they would do a certain thing when they are giving you advice: *In your place I'd accept the money and drop the complaint.* [*same as* **if I were you**] **8 a** Something that is **out of place** it is not in its correct position: *He never had a hair out of place.* **b** Something or someone that seems **out of place** seems not to belong to their environment: *The picture looked out of place.* □ *He felt awkward and out of place.* □ *She felt a sense of relief that she knew was out of place.* [compare **incongruous**, **inappropriate**] **9** You **put** someone **in their place** when you make then realize that they are not as important as they think they are: *Her remark was evidently intended to put him in his place.* [*same as* **snub**, **humble**, **humiliate**]

10 a Something **takes place** when it happens: *When did this accident take place?* □ *Where do our meetings take place?* □ *Because of government policy, little house-building has taken place.* [*same as* **happen**, **occur**, be **carried out**] **b** A person or thing that **takes the place of** another person or thing is provided, or does something, instead of them: *We've got a young woman off sick, and you can take her place.* □ *Nothing really takes the place of pure cotton.* [*same as* **replace**]

11 One person or thing has to **take second place** to another when they are treated as less important than the other: *Fun would have to take second place to the serious business of home-making.* [*same as* be **subordinated** to]

placement /ˈpleɪsmənt/ *noun*: **placements**
1 (*uncount*) **Placement** is the act or process of placing or positioning something. **2** A **placement** is a temporary job which provides someone with experience in the work that they are training for.

place name /ˈpleɪs neɪm/ *noun*: **place names**
Place names are names of towns, cities, villages, regions or countries, and of geographical features, such as mountains and rivers.

place setting /ˈpleɪs setɪŋ/ *noun*: **place settings**
A **place setting** is an arrangement of cutlery, glasses and crockery for the use of one person when eating at a table [see picture at **tableware**]

placid /ˈplasɪd/ *adjective*
1 A **placid** person or animal is one that is not easily made upset or excited: *She's a placid little girl.* □ *The pony is quite placid and will allow anyone on its back.* **2** Something that is **placid** is calm and peaceful: *The hotel is set in the placid surroundings of rural Devon.* — *adverb* **placidly:** *The cows ignored the dog completely, and placidly went on chewing the cud.*

plague /pleɪg/ *noun*; *verb*
▷ ***noun***: **plagues**
1 A **plague** is an attack of any of several diseases that spread quickly to and kill a large number of people. **2** A **plague** is also a large number of pests that come into a area at one time and cause damage or inconvenience: *a plague of rats* □ *a plague of locusts* □ *a plague of tourists.*
▷ ***verb***: **plagues**, **plaguing**, **plagued**
1 If something **plagues** you, it causes you continual trouble, suffering or discomfort: *She's been plagued by severe headaches for years.* □ *The project has been plagued by bad weather.* **2** When you **plague** someone, you keep annoying them, especially by repeatedly asking them questions or making demands: *The children had been plaguing her with questions all morning.*

plaice /pleɪs/ *noun* (*count or uncount*): **plaice**
A **plaice** is a flat brown fish with orange spots whose flesh is used as food: *He caught two plaice.* □ *grilled plaice.*

plain /pleɪn/ *adjective*; *noun*; *adverb*
▷ ***adjective***: **plainer**, **plainest**
1 Plain things have no pattern or decoration or are all of one colour: *a plain carpet* □ *a plain brown envelope.* **2 Plain** is also used to describe things that are simple or ordinary in style: *good plain cooking* □ *She wore a plain black dress and no jewellery.* □ *The front of the building is richly decorated but the back is quite plain.* **3** Something that is **plain**, or **plain** to see, is obvious or clear: *It was plain that she didn't like him.* **4 Plain** statements are straightforward and easily understood: *Why can't the instructions be written in plain English?* **5** If someone is **plain** with you, they are frank and open with you and don't try to deceive or mislead you: *To be perfectly plain, I don't think your work is good enough.* **6** If you say a person, especially a girl or woman, is **plain**, you mean that they are not pretty or good-looking: *She's very plain.* □ *a rather plain child.* **7 Plain** is also sometimes used for emphasis before a noun to mean 'sheer' or 'complete': *It was just plain selfishness on his part.* □ *That's just plain nonsense!* **8 Plain** flour is a type of flour that does not contain a chemical to make cakes rise, and that is used for making *eg* bread, biscuits and pastry. [compare **self-raising flour**]
▷ ***noun***: **plains**
1 A **plain** is a large level area of land: *a grassy plain* □ *The rain in Spain falls mainly in the plain.* **2** (*uncount*) In knitting, **plain** is a simple stitch made

by passing the wool round the front of the needle: *knit two plain, one purl.* [see also **purl**]

▻ ***adverb***

Plain is sometimes used before an adjective to mean 'utterly' or 'completely': *It's just plain ridiculous.* ▫ *That would be just plain silly.*

▻ ***phrases*** **1** If you **make yourself plain**, you make your meaning clear and easy to understand: *You can't go; do I make myself plain?* **2** For **plain sailing** see **sailing**.

plain clothes /pleɪn 'kloʊðz/ *noun* (*plural*)
Police officers in **plain clothes** wear ordinary clothes while they are on duty rather than a uniform: *He was arrested by two policemen in plain clothes.* — *adjective* **plain-clothes:** *a plain-clothes policeman.*

plainly /'pleɪnlɪ/ *adverb*
1 Plainly means in a plain manner: *She was dressed quite plainly in navy blue and white.* **2** (*sentence adverb*) You can use **plainly** to indicate that something is clearly or obviously the case: *There's plainly no other explanation for it.* ▫ *From the evidence we've seen, he's plainly guilty.*

plaintiff /'pleɪntɪf/ *noun*: **plaintiffs** (*formal or legal*)
A **plaintiff** is a person who brings a legal action against someone else in a court of law: *Who is the plaintiff in this case?* [compare **defendant**]

plaintive /'pleɪntɪv/ *adjective*
A **plaintive** sound or voice is full of sadness or suffering: *A plaintive Beetles love song poured out of the speakers.* ▫ *His tone was plaintive rather than angry.* — *adverb* **plaintively:** *'My head hurts,' she said plaintively.*

plait /plat/ *erb*; *noun*

▻ ***verb***: **plaits, plaiting, plaited**

You **plait** hair, straw or rope when you twist or weave three or more lengths of it over and under each other to form a single thick length: *She plaited her hair.*

▻ ***noun***: **plaits**

A **plait** is a rope-like length of hair made by plaiting. [compare **braid**]

plan /plan/ *noun*; *verb*

▻ ***noun***: **plans**

1 A **plan** is an arrangement or method for doing something that has been carefully considered or thought out in detail beforehand: *He had devised a cunning plan to escape.* ▫ *a plan to produce energy from waste* ▫ *They made plans for their wedding.* **2 Plans** are intentions: *Do you have any holiday plans?* ▫ *He was forced to change his plans.* **3** A **plan** is a way of arranging or organizing something, especially one that is written down or shown on a list, sketch or drawing: *a seating plan* ▫ *Before they began the project, they devised a plan of action.* **4** A **plan** is also a map or drawing showing the layout of buildings or streets: *a street plan of Edinburgh.* **5** A **plan** is a drawing of a floor of a building as if seen from above, showing the shape of rooms, the position of walls and doors, and measurements.

▻ ***verb***: **plans, planning, planned**

1 You **plan** something when you arrange how to do it carefully in advance. **2** To **plan** means to make plans: *If we are going to manage this successfully we'll have to plan ahead.* **3** If you **plan** to do something, you intend to do it: *What do you plan to do when the children have left home?* **4** If something **is planned** for, it is allowed for in advance: *They weren't planning on going abroad this year.* ▫ *They didn't plan for such big rise in interest rates.* **5** When you **plan** something that you are going to make, you design it or decide how its parts will be arranged: *The kitchen was planned with plenty of cupboard space.* ▫ *She spent some time planning the garden before making alterations.*

plane¹ /pleɪn/ *noun* (*often adjectival*): **planes**
A **plane** is an aeroplane: *The plane landed in thick fog.* ▫ *Their plane leaves at 10 o'clock.* ▫ *a plane crash* ▫ *a plane ticket.*

plane² /pleɪn/ *noun*: **planes**
1 A **plane** is a flat or level surface: *A cube has six planes.* **2** If you say something is on a particular **plane**, you mean that it is on a particular level of existence, development, or thought: *on a higher intellectual and spiritual plane.*

plane³ /pleɪn/ *noun*; *verb*

▻ ***noun***: **planes**

A **plane** is a tool with a sharp blade set into a flat surface used for making wood smooth by cutting away very thin layers from its surface. [see picture at **tool**]

▻ ***verb***: **planes, planing, planed**

> ***phrasal verbs***
> **plane away** or **plane off** You **plane away** or **plane off** uneven or excess parts from wood when you remove them with a plane.
> **plane down** You **plane** wood **down** when you make it smooth with a plane.

planet /'planɪt/ *noun*: **planets**
A **planet** is a large round object in space that moves around a star, such as the Sun. The nine **planets** of our solar system are Mercury, Venus, Earth, Mars, Jupiter, Saturn, Uranus, Neptune and Pluto: *Earth is a planet.* ▫ *Is there life on other planets?*

planetarium /planə'tɛərɪəm/ *noun*: **planetariums**
A **planetarium** is **1** an apparatus that shows the position and movements of the planets and stars by shining spots of light on to the inside of a curved ceiling. **2** a building with such an apparatus.

planetary /'planɪtərɪ/ *adjective*
Planetary means of or concerning planets: *planetary movements* ▫ *planetary exploration.*

plank /plaŋk/ *noun*: **planks**
A **plank** is a long narrow piece of sawn wood used in building *eg* for making floors.

planner /'planə(r)/ *noun*: **planners**
A **planner** is a person who draws up plans and designs: *a town planner.*

planning /'planɪŋ/ *noun* (*uncount*)
1 Planning is the fact or process of making plans for something: *This project will need careful planning.* [see also **family planning**] **2 Planning** is the control by a local authority over the way land is used in a particular area or what new buildings or alterations to existing buildings should be allowed.

plant /plɑːnt/ *noun*; *verb*

▻ ***noun***: **plants**

1 A **plant** is a living thing that usually grows in the ground and has roots, a stem and leaves: *a strawberry plant* ▫ *garden plants* ▫ *They had to water the young plants regularly.* **2** A factory or building where an industrial process takes place or power is generated is also called a **plant**: *a steel plant* ▫ *a nuclear plant.* **3** (*uncount*) **Plant** is the machinery and equipment used in an industrial or manufacturing process, or in building or road construction: *heavy plant.*

▻ ***verb***: **plants, planting, planted**

1 You **plant** seeds or plants when you put them in the ground to grow: *The farmer planted wheat.* ▫ *She planted the shrubs along the wall.* ▫ *Plant the seeds in a mixture of peat and sand.* **2** If an area of ground **is planted** it has plants or seeds put in it: *The hillside had been planted with conifers.* ▫ *The borders had been* *planted out with annuals.* **3** If an idea or doubt **is planted** in someone's mind, it is put there by someone else. **4** If something **is planted** it is placed or fixed firmly or forcefully in or on something: *He planted the box down.* □ *She planted a kiss on his forehead.* □ *He planted himself squarely down in her doorway and demanded to know what all the fuss was about.* **5** If someone **plants** something in a place, they put it there secretly so that no one knows it is there: *The terrorists planted a bomb under the car.* **6** If someone **plants** something such as illegal drugs or a weapon on someone, they put it deliberately among that person's belongings so that when it is found the person will be wrongly accused of a crime: *He accused the police of planting the evidence.* **7** If a spy or informer **is planted** in a group or organization, they are sent to join that group or organization so that they can discover secrets or other things about it.

phrasal verb
You **plant out** seedlings or small plants that have been grown in a tray or pot when you put them in the ground outside with enough space to grow.

plantation /plɑːn'teɪʃən/ *noun*: **plantations**
1 A **plantation** is a large piece of land, especially in warm countries, used for growing crops such as tea, coffee, rubber and cotton on a large scale. **2** A **plantation** is also a large area of land planted with a certain kind of tree: *a plantation of fir.*

planter /'plɑːntə(r)/ *noun*: **planters**
1 A **planter** is the owner or manager of a plantation: *a tea planter.* **2** A **planter** is also a container in which plants are grown.

plaque[1] /plɑːk/ *noun*: **plaques**
A **plaque** is a flat piece of metal or stone that is fixed to a wall and has the name or description of a famous person that lived there or an event that happened there: *They put up a plaque in memory of the people who had died in the explosion.*

plaque[2] /plɑːk/ *noun (uncount)*
Plaque is a substance that forms on the surface of your teeth and encourages the growth of harmful bacteria.

plasma /'plazmə/ *noun (uncount)*
Plasma is the clear liquid part of blood in which the blood cells float.

plaster /'plɑːstə(r)/ *noun*; *verb*
▻ ***noun***: **plasters**
1 (*uncount*) **Plaster** is a material consisting of lime, sand and water, that is applied to walls when soft and which dries to form a hard smooth surface. **2** (*uncount*) **Plaster** is plaster of Paris. **3** A **plaster** or a **sticking plaster** is a piece of sticky tape, usually with a protective pad attached, used for covering a small wound.
▻ ***verb***: **plasters, plastering, plastered**
1 You **plaster** walls when you apply wet plaster to them. **2** (*informal*) If you **plaster** a surface with something, you coat or cover it thickly with that thing: *Her bedroom walls were plastered with posters.* □ *His hair was plastered with oil.* **3** If something **is plastered** down or **plastered** to a surface, it is made to lie flat or is stuck to that surface with a wet or sticky substance: *His hair had been plastered down with water.* □ *They came in from the rain with their clothes plastered to their bodies.*

plastered /'plɑːstəd/ *adjective (slang)*
If you say someone is **plastered**, you mean they are very drunk.

plasterer /'plɑːstərə(r)/ *noun*: **plasterers**
A **plasterer** is a person who applies plaster to walls and ceilings.

plaster of Paris /plɑːstər əv 'parɪs/ *noun (uncount)*
Plaster of Paris is a type of plaster made from fine white powder mixed with water. **Plaster of Paris** dries quickly and is used for making plaster casts, and in sculpture.

plastic /'plastɪk/ *noun*; *adjective*
▻ ***noun***: **plastics**
1 (*uncount or count*) **Plastic** is a light hard-wearing artificial material made from chemicals that can be moulded when it is soft and keeps it shape when it is hard. It is used to make a wide variety of objects: *The box is made of plastic.* □ *the plastics industry.* **2** (*uncount*; *informal*) If you pay for something using **plastic**, you pay for it with a credit card: *Do you take plastic?*
▻ ***adjective***
1 A **plastic** object is made of plastic: *a plastic bag* □ *plastic toys* □ *The table top isn't wood, it's plastic.* **2** (*technical*) Something that is **plastic** can be moulded or shaped easily: *Wax is a plastic substance.* **3** (*informal, derogatory*) If you describe something as **plastic**, you mean that it is artificial or contains artificial substances: *plastic food.*

Plasticine /'plastɪsiːn/ *noun (trademark; uncount)*
Plasticine is a soft substance, similar to clay, used by children for making small models and shapes.

plastic surgery /plastɪk 'sɜːdʒərɪ/ *noun (uncount)*
Plastic surgery is the practice of doing surgical operations to repair damaged or diseased body tissue or to improve a person's appearance: *He was so badly burned he will need extensive plastic surgery.* □ *She looked so different that I wondered if she'd had plastic surgery.*

plate /pleɪt/ *noun*: **plates**
1 A **plate** is a shallow dish for serving food on: *a paper plate* □ *a side plate* □ *a dinner plate* □ *plates and cups.* **2** (also **plateful**) A **plate** or a **plateful** is the amount that a plate can hold: *She gave the cat a plateful of scraps.* □ *She offered him a scone and he ate the whole plateful.* □ *He was so hungry he ate two platefuls of soup.* **3** A **plate** is a shallow container used for taking the collection in a church. **4** A **plate** is also a flat thin sheet of some hard substance especially metal: *a steel plate.* **5** A **plate** is a flat piece of metal or plastic with letters or information printed or engraved on it: *The brass plate on the door said 'Charles P. Wentworth, Solicitor and Notary'.* **6** (*uncount*) **Plate** is articles made of a valuable material such as gold or silver: *The queen had brought all her jewels and plate from France.* **7** (*uncount*) **Plate** is also an ordinary metal with a thin covering of gold, silver or tin applied to its surface: *gold plate.* **8** A **plate** is a picture printed on shiny paper in a book. **9** In photography, a **plate** is a sheet of glass with a special coating of chemicals that are sensitive to light.
10 In printing, a **plate** is a sheet of metal with an image engraved on it, or a print taken from it. **11** A **plate** or a **dental plate** is piece of plastic specially moulded to fit the mouth and fitted with false teeth.
▻ ***phrases*** **1** (*informal*) If you **have a lot on your plate**, you have a lot of things to do or attend to. **2** (*informal*) If someone is **handed** something **on a plate** they get or are given it without having to try too hard.

plateau /'platoʊ/ *noun*: **plateaus** or **plateaux** /'platoʊz/
1 A **plateau** is a large area of fairly flat land that is higher than the land around it on at least one side:

From the valley floor, the land rose several hundred feet to a grassy plateau. **2** If something has reached a **plateau**, it has reached a stable condition after having risen, often sharply.

plate glass /pleɪt 'glɑːs/ *noun* (*uncount*)
Plate glass is glass in the form of large thick sheets used *eg* for shop windows and mirrors.

platform /'platfɔːm/ *noun*: **platforms**
1 A **platform** is a raised floor from which people who are speaking or performing can be seen or heard easily: *a concert platform* □ *At the conference, the party officials were given seats on the platform.* **2** A railway **platform** is the raised walkway alongside the track at a railway station from which passengers can get into trains. **3** A **platform** is a floating structure used, especially in the oil industry, as a base for drilling under the sea bed. **4** A political party's **platform** is its main ideas or aims, especially those which are stated before a general election: *The party must formulate a credible political platform from which to fight the forthcoming election.*

platinum /'platɪnəm/ *noun*; *adjective*
▻ ***noun*** (*uncount*)
Platinum is a precious silvery-white metal often used in making jewellery and for mixing with other metals to form alloys: *Her wedding ring is made of platinum.*
▻ ***adjective***
Platinum objects are made of platinum: *a platinum watch* □ *Is the bracelet silver or platinum?*

platitude /'platɪtjuːd/ *noun*: **platitudes** (*formal*; *derogatory*)
A **platitude** is a statement that has been made many times before and is therefore no longer meaningful or interesting: *His speech was full of platitudes about the importance of family values.* [compare **cliché**]

platonic /plə'tɒnɪk/ *adjective*
If your relationship with someone is **platonic,** it is very close or friendly but does not involve sex.

platoon /plə'tuːn/ *noun* (*with a singular or plural verb*): **platoons**
In the army, a **platoon** is a division of a company.

platter /'platə(r)/ *noun*: **platters**
A **platter** is a large flat dish used for serving food.

plausible /'plɔːzɪbəl/ *adjective*
1 If a statement or argument is **plausible**, it seems to be reasonable and true. [*same as* **believable**; *opposite* **implausible**] **2** A **plausible** person is someone who is skilled in producing convincing arguments or statements, especially in order to deceive others.

play /pleɪ/ *verb*; *noun*
▻ ***verb***: **plays, playing, played**
1 a Children **play** when they spend time amusing themselves with toys or games: *He was in the porch, playing with his train set.* □ *I'm sorry, I can't let you play with matches.* □ *I never had anyone to play with.* □ *She and I used to play together when we were little.* □ *I was sent out to play in the garden.* □ *Joe always makes time to play with his kids.* **b** You **play** with something when you fiddle with it or move it about, *eg* in your fingers: *He leant forward, playing with his pen.* **c** Someone **plays** a trick or joke on you when they trick you or deceive you for their amusement: *He was convinced someone was playing a trick on him.*
2 a You **play** a particular game, or **play** a match, when you take part in it: *He plays football on Saturdays.* □ *He usually plays in midfield.* □ *Do you play golf?* □ *She's playing in the first-eleven hockey team.* □ *I saw her play at Wimbledon once.* □ *We used to play a lot of chess.* **b** You **play** a person or team, or **play** against them, when they are your opponents in a match: *Aberdeen are playing Celtic in the semi-final.* □ *It's a great feeling to be playing against some of the finest golfers in the world.* **c** You **play** the ball, or **play** a shot, *eg* in tennis or football, when you hit or kick the ball: *She played the next shot straight down the middle.* **d** In card games, you **play** a card when you place it face upwards on the table.
3 a You **play** a musical instrument, or **play** a tune on it, when you produce music from it: *He used to play the violin.* □ *Do play me a tune on your guitar.* □ *I didn't start playing in bands till I was 23.* **b** You **play** a record or tape when you listen to it on a record-player, tape recorder or cassette-player; audio equipment **is playing** when it is operating; music **is playing** when it is being broadcast or reproduced on audio equipment: *You can set your security system so that lights come on and radios play at different times while you're out.* □ *There was some pretty music playing in the background.*
4 a An actor or actress **plays** a part or role in a play or film when he or she acts that part: *He saw 58-year-old Sarah Bernhardt playing a 21-year-old.* □ *She's recently been playing in Ibsen's 'A Doll's House'.* **b** A show or film **is playing** at a certain theatre or cinema when it is being performed or shown there. **c** You **play**, or **play** it, a certain way when you behave in that way, especially deliberately; you **play** *eg* the fool, or the host, when you behave like a fool, or act as host: *Just play it cool and admit nothing.* □ *They like to play tough.* □ *You really think you can play God with people's lives, don't you?* □ *You needn't play the innocent* [= pretend not to know what I'm talking about] *with me.* **d** Someone or something **plays** a role or part in something if they are involved in it, or have an influence on it: *Alan Sugar undoubtedly played a key role in bringing PCs to the masses.* □ *Poor eating habits play a major part in causing ill health.*
5 a Light **plays** on a surface when it moves over it quickly and unsteadily: *Sunlight filtered through the trees and played on her hair, emphasizing its brightness.* **b** An expression **plays** across someone's face when it appears, or keeps reappearing, briefly there: *A smile played across his lips.* **c** To **play** water or a hose on a surface is to aim or direct it there; a fountain **is playing** when it is working.
▻ ***noun***: **plays**
1 A **play** is a story written for performance by actors in a theatre or on radio or television: *'An Enemy of the People' is one of his most relevant plays for today.* □ *The novel was turned into a stage play by the author herself.* **2** (*uncount*) **Play** is the activity of amusing yourself or playing games: *He would sit on a park bench and watch the children at play.* **3** (*uncount*) **Play** is the action during a game: *Rain stopped play.* □ *There was some excellent play by the visiting side.*
▻ ***phrases*** **1** Something **comes**, or **is brought**, **into play** when it is introduced into a situation: *Once again the threat of outright war was brought into play.* □ *Certain social factors come into play here.* **2** You **make great play** of some circumstance when you particularly emphasize it: *She made great play of her familiarity with car engines.*

phrasal verbs
play along You **play along** with someone when you keep them happy by pretending to co-operate or agree with them.
play at 1 Someone who **is playing at** some activity **a** is not doing it in a serious or responsible way: *We were just playing at being in love.* **b** is giving them-

selves a function that is not officially theirs: *We had to queue outside the dance hall while the stewards played at being customs officials and went through everyone's pockets and handbags.* **2** You ask what someone **is playing at** when you are annoyed with them for doing something foolish or wrong: *What on earth do the district council think they're playing at?*
play back You **play back** a film or sound recording when you watch it or listen to it immediately after doing the filming or recording.
play down You **play** something **down** when you try to make it seem unimportant: *She tended to play down her disabilities and not look after herself well enough.*
play off against To **play** one person **off against** another is deliberately to try and make them quarrel or be suspicious of each other.
play on Someone **plays on** or **upon** your feelings, good nature or weaknesses when they take advantage of them for their own benefit: *He knew just how to play on the prejudices of his hearers.*
play out (*used in the passive*; *informal*) An idea that **is played out** no longer has any further usefulness or relevance.
play up **1** (*informal*) **2** A machine that **is playing up** is not working properly. **3** A part of your body, especially a diseased or injured part, that **is playing up**, or **playing** you **up**, is giving you a lot of pain: *Is your ankle playing up again?* **4** Children who **are playing up** are behaving badly and refusing to co-operate.

playboy /ˈpleɪbɔɪ/ *noun*: **playboys**
A **playboy** is a wealthy man who does no work and spends his time enjoying himself.

player /ˈpleɪə(r)/ *noun*: **players**
1 A **player** is someone who takes part in a game or sport: *a hockey player* □ *a football player* □ *a card player.* **2** A **player** is also a performer on a musical instrument: *a piano player.* **3** (*old*) A **player** is also an actor.

playful /ˈpleɪfʊl/ *adjective*
1 Someone who is **playful** is full of fun: *as playful as a kitten.* **2** A **playful** remark or action is one that is not intended to be serious: *He gave her a playful shove.* — *adverb* **playfully:** *He teased her playfully.* — *noun* (*uncount*) **playfulness**: *His playfulness was one of his more endearing qualities.*

playground /ˈpleɪgraʊnd/ *noun*: **playgrounds**
1 A **playground** is an area where children can play, *eg* around a school building. **2** When a place, such as a holiday resort, is called a **playground**, it means that people go there to have fun: *a millionaires' playground* □ *The South of France used to be the playground of the rich and famous.*

playgroup /ˈpleɪgruːp/ *noun*: **playgroups**
A **playgroup** is a number of children who meet and play together in a group organized and supervised by their parents or a suitably qualified adult.

playhouse /ˈpleɪhaʊs/ *noun*: **playhouses** (*old*)
A **playhouse** is a theatre: *the Edinburgh Playhouse.*

playing card /ˈpleɪɪŋ kɑːd/ *noun*: **playing cards**
A **playing card** is a card (sense 3).

playing field /ˈpleɪɪŋ fiːld/ *noun*: **playing fields**
A **playing field** is an area of ground prepared and marked out for playing games such as football.

playmate /ˈpleɪmeɪt/ *noun*: **playmates**
A **playmate** is someone who joins you, or who is your companion, in play: *The little boy was sorry to leave his playmates.*

play on words /pleɪ ɒn ˈwɜːdz/ *noun* (*used in the singular*)
A **play on words** is a pun.

playpen /ˈpleɪpen/ *noun*: **playpens**
A **playpen** is a wooden or plastic frame placed on the floor inside which a baby can play safely.

plaything /ˈpleɪθɪŋ/ *noun*: **playthings**
A **plaything** is a toy.

playwright /ˈpleɪraɪt/ *noun*: **playwrights**
A **playwright** is someone who writes plays.

plea /pliː/ *noun*: **pleas**
1 A **plea** is an urgent or emotional request: *He ignored her pleas for mercy.* **2** If someone accused of a crime makes a **plea**, they or their lawyer makes a statement in a court of law saying whether they are guilty or not.

plead /pliːd/ *verb*: **pleads**, **pleading**, **pleaded** (*AmE*, *Scottish* **pled**)
1 If you **plead** with someone to do something, you beg them to do it in an urgent or emotional way: *He pleaded for forgiveness.* □ *They pleaded with him not to get rid of the kittens.* **2** If a person accused of a crime **pleads** guilty or not guilty, they or their lawyer states in a court of law that they are guilty or not guilty. **3** If someone **pleads** for someone else, they argue or speak in defence or support of that person: *He appointed a barrister to plead his case in court.* **4** If you **plead** a particular thing as a reason for an action, you give it as your excuse: *He pleaded ignorance.*

pleasant /ˈplɛzənt/ *adjective*
1 Something that is **pleasant** gives you a feeling of enjoyment or happiness: *We had a very pleasant chat about the old days.* □ *'It's John and Mary! What a pleasant surprise!'* □ *The weather was warm and dry with a pleasant breeze blowing from the sea.* [*opposite* **unpleasant**] **2** If a person is **pleasant**, they are friendly and likeable: *What a pleasant woman Mrs Forbes is.* □ *He wasn't very pleasant to me.* [*opposite* **unpleasant**] — *adverb* **pleasantly:** *I was pleasantly surprised by my son's exam results.*

please /pliːz/ *verb*; *interjection or adverb*
▻ *verb*: **pleases, pleasing, pleased**
1 Something or someone **pleases** you when they make you feel satisfied, contented or happy: *The resulting compromise pleased nobody.* □ *It pleases me that he still seems to want my advice.* □ *My father was such a difficult man to please.* □ *She tended to be apologetic and over-eager to please.* [*opposite* **displease**; see also **pleased**] **2** People do what they **please**, or do as they **please**, when they act as they want; you can have what you **please** when you can have whatever you want: *Do whatever you please; I shan't mind.* □ *My parents allowed me come and go as I pleased.* □ *You can get anything you please from her if you know how to ask.* [*same as* **want**]
▻ ***interjection or adverb*** (*sentence adverb*)
1 You say '**please**' or ' yes, **please**' when you are politely accepting an offer, or something that is being offered to you: *'More toast?' 'Yes, please.'* □ *'Shall I make you a copy?' 'Oh, please, if you would.'* [compare **thanks, thank you** at **thank**] **2** You use **please a** when politely asking someone to do something: *Would you repeat that, please?* □ *Could you please return your keys to the office?* □ *Please don't leave dirty dishes in the sink.* **b** when politely asking for something, or asking to do something: *Please could I leave the room?* □ *Could I speak to Brian, please?* □ *May I please have your name?* □ *'How do you take your coffee?' 'Black,*

please.' **c** when requesting information: *Please, sir, how do you spell that?* ▫ *Who's speaking, please?* **d** to express a protest or appeal: *Please, no swearing.* ▫ *Silence, please.* ▫ *Please be patient.* ▫ *Please don't cry.* ▫ *Please believe me.* ▫ *May I finish, please?*

▻ ***phrases*** **1** (*formal*) You say '**if you please**' very formally when asking for someone's attention, or making a request: *Follow me, if you please.* ▫ *The sugar, Gerald, if you please.* **2** (*informal*) If you say '**please yourself**' to someone, you want to show that you do not care or mind what they do: *'I don't think I'll come tonight.' 'Please yourself.'*

pleased /pli:zd/ *adjective*

1 If you are **pleased** you are happy or satisfied: *I was very pleased to see them.* ▫ *He deserved to win; I'm very pleased for him.* ▫ *He was pleased with the way the garden looked.* ▫ *She wasn't pleased when he told her he'd lost the tickets.* [*opposite* **displeased**] **2 Pleased** also means glad or delighted: *'I'm your new neighbour.' 'Pleased to meet you.'* ▫ *'He's feeling much better now.' 'I'm so pleased.'*

▻ ***phrase*** (*often derogatory*) If someone **is pleased with themselves** they are too satisfied with what they have done.

pleasing /'pli:zɪŋ/ *adjective*

Something that is **pleasing** gives pleasure or satisfaction: *a most pleasing wine* ▫ *a pleasing painting* ▫ *It was a very pleasing result.* [*opposite* **displeasing**]

pleasurable /'plɛʒərəbl/ *adjective*

Something that is **pleasurable** is enjoyable or pleasant: *a pleasurable experience.*

pleasure /'plɛʒə(r)/ *noun; adjective*

▻ ***noun*: pleasures**

1 (*uncount*) **Pleasure** is a feeling of enjoyment or satisfaction: *She took pleasure in helping others.* **2** A **pleasure** is something that gives or produces such a feeling: *Gardening is one of her greatest pleasures.* ▫ *Will we have the pleasure of your company this evening?* **3** (*used in the singular*) Your **pleasure** is your wish, preference or inclination: *What's your pleasure; wine or beer?* ▫ (*formal*) *We await your pleasure.* **4** (*uncount*) **Pleasure** is time spent enjoying yourself rather than working: *combine business with pleasure.*

▻ ***adjective***

Pleasure is used to describe things that are used for or done for pleasure: *a pleasure boat* ▫ *a pleasure trip.*

▻ ***phrases*** **1** (*used as an answer*) If you reply to something by saying **my pleasure**, it means 'you're welcome', 'not at all' or 'it's no trouble': *'Thank you for bringing me home.' 'My pleasure.'* **2** (*used as an answer*) If you reply to a request by saying **with pleasure**, it means 'gladly', 'willingly' or 'of course': *'Will you join us for dinner?' 'With pleasure.'*

pleat /pli:t/ *noun*: **pleats**

A **pleat** is a fold that is sewn or pressed into a piece of cloth: *a skirt with pleats.*

pleated /'pli:tɪd/ *adjective*

A **pleated** piece of clothing is one with folds sewn or pressed into the cloth: *a pleated skirt.*

pled /plɛd/ *verb*

Pled is the past tense and past participle of **plead** used in American English and Scottish English.

pledge /plɛdʒ/ *noun; verb*

▻ ***noun*: pledges**

1 A **pledge** is a solemn promise: *Do I have your pledge that you won't try to escape?* **2** A **pledge** is something left, *eg* at a pawnbrokers, as security for money lent.

▻ ***verb*: pledges, pledging, pledged**

1 If someone **pledges** to do something, they solemnly promise to do it: *He pledged his support in the coming election.* ▫ *The government has pledged to reduce taxation.* **2** If you **pledge** yourself to someone or something, you bind or commit yourself to support or follow a particular person or group: *He pledged himself to God.*

plentiful /'plɛntɪfʊl/ *adjective*

If something is **plentiful** there is a good supply or more than enough of it: *Vegetables are cheap and plentiful at this time of year.* ▫ *When he went into hospital, he made sure he had a plentiful supply of books and magazines.* — *adverb* **plentifully:** *The shortages were apparently over and the shops were plentifully stocked with food.*

plenty /plɛntɪ/ *pronoun or determiner; adverb; noun*

▻ ***pronoun or determiner***

Plenty of things or people, or **plenty** of a thing, is as many or as much as you need, or a substantial number or amount: *There are plenty of chairs for everyone.* ▫ *I had plenty of work to keep me busy.* ▫ *She's certainly had plenty of experience.* ▫ *Plenty of articles have been written about it.* ▫ *'Have you got enough room there?' 'Plenty, thanks.'* ▫ *There's plenty more of that pie if you want it.* ▫ *'Have we run out of paper clips?' 'No, there are plenty more.'* ▫ *Always give kids plenty to do.* ▫ *I've never met a woman who wanted an abortion, but plenty who felt they had no alternative.* [compare a **lot, lots**]

> Notice that if the noun used with or referred to by **plenty** is uncount, the verb is singular; if the noun is plural, the verb is plural: *Plenty of research has been done on it. There are plenty who agree with her.* Notice also that **plenty** is usually found in positive sentences; in negative sentences *enough* is more likely to be used: *The children hadn't got enough to do and got bored.*

▻ ***adverb*** (*informal*)

Something that is *eg* **plenty** big enough, or **plenty** wide enough, is easily as big or wide as you need it to be.

▻ ***noun*** (*uncount*)

A time of **plenty** is a period of wealth, when people have a good supply of all the necessities of life: *Nowadays, in times of plenty, we eat only those things that we enjoy the taste of.*

▻ ***phrase*** Things are available, or occur, **in plenty**, when there are a lot of them: *There are shops in plenty, banks, hotels and guesthouses.* ▫ *There were wars in plenty.*

pliable /'plaɪəbəl/ *adjective*

1 Something that is **pliable** can be bent or shaped easily without breaking: *pliable pieces of wood.* **2** Someone who is **pliable** can be easily influenced, persuaded or controlled by others.

pliant /plaɪənt/ *adjective*

1 Something that is **pliant** bends easily without breaking. **2** Someone who is **pliant** is easily influenced or controlled by other people.

pliers /'plaɪəz/ *noun* (*plural*)

Pliers are, or a pair of **pliers** is, a tool used for gripping things, pulling out nails, or for bending or cutting wire. [see picture at **tool**]

plight /plaɪt/ *noun* (*used in the singular; formal*)

If someone is in a bad or difficult condition or state, you can refer to that state or condition as their **plight**: *They were deeply moved by the plight of the starving children.* ▫ *She can't get a job and is in an awful plight financially.*

plimsoll /'plɪmsəl/ *noun* (*old*): **plimsolls**

Plimsolls are light rubber-soled canvas shoes worn for indoor sports, especially gymnastics. [*same as* **pumps, sneakers**]

plinth /plɪnθ/ *noun*: **plinths**
A **plinth** is a block of stone on which a statue, sculpture or pillar stands: *Statues of Lenin and Stalin had been knocked off their plinths.*

plod /plɒd/ *verb*: **plods, plodding, plodded**
1 Someone **plods** when they walk slowly as if they are tired or their feet are heavy: *She came plodding up the hill.* □ *They plodded on for miles through driving rain and sleet.* **2** If you **plod** along or on with something, you do it slowly and steadily but without much enthusiasm: *'How are you getting on?' 'Oh, I'm plodding along just as usual.'* □ *The paperwork seems never-ending, but he just plods on regardless.*

plonk[1] /plɒŋk/ *noun*; *verb*; *adverb*
▷ ***noun*** (*informal*; *singular*)
Plonk is the sound made by something dropping heavily: *The chimneypot fell to the ground with a plonk.*
▷ ***verb*** (*informal*): **plonks, plonking, plonked**
1 If you **plonk** something down, you put it down heavily: *He plonked the books down on the table.* **2** If you **plonk** yourself down, you sit down heavily: *He plonked himself down beside the fire.*
▷ ***adverb:*** *The ornament toppled over and fell plonk at her feet.*

plonk[2] /plɒŋk/ *noun* (*uncount*; *BrE*; *informal*)
Some people call cheap wine **plonk**: *I bought a couple of bottles of plonk to take to the party.*

plop /plɒp/ *noun*; *verb*; *adverb*
▷ ***noun***: **plops**
A **plop** is the sound of a small object dropping into water: *The chestnut fell off the tree and landed with a plop in a puddle.*
▷ ***verb***: **plops, plopping, plopped**
If something **plops** it falls or drops with this sound: *The frog plopped back into the pond.*
▷ ***adverb:*** *His hat blew off and fell plop into the water.*

plot[1] /plɒt/ *noun*; *verb*
▷ ***noun***: **plots**
1 A **plot** is a secret plan, especially one made with others to do something illegal or evil: *a terrorist plot* □ *a plot to overthrow the government* □ *They hatched a plot to kill the king.* [*same as* **conspiracy**] **2** A **plot** is also a set of connected events in the story of a play, film or novel: *a film with a complicated plot.*
▷ ***verb***: **plots, plotting, plotted**
If a group of people **plot**, they plan to do something, especially something illegal or evil: *They plotted Darnley's murder.* □ *I worry that they will plot against me.* □ *They plotted together to bring about the downfall of the government.*

plot[2] /plɒt/ *noun*: **plots**
A **plot** is an area of ground specially marked out or used for a particular purpose: *a building plot* □ *a vegetable plot.*
▷ ***verb***: **plots, plotting, plotted**
1 If a person **plots** the position of a ship or aircraft, they mark it on a map or chart to show its course or the progress it has made: *The enemy aircraft's course was plotted at airforce headquarters.* **2** If you **plot** something on a graph, you make a curve or line by connecting up several points on the graph.

plough (*AmE* **plow**) /plaʊ/ *noun*; *verb*
▷ ***noun***: **ploughs**
1 A **plough** is a piece of equipment used in farming for turning the soil. Modern ploughs have one or more curved steel blades and are usually pulled by tractors. **2** A **plough** is also any similar piece of equipment, especially one for pushing snow off roads: *a snow plough.*
▷ ***verb***: **ploughs, ploughing, ploughed**
To **plough** is to break up the surface of the soil and turn it over using a plough: *plough a field* □ *The moorland has been ploughed up to grow conifers.*

phrasal verbs
plough back If profits are **ploughed back** into a business they are reinvested in the business that made them.
plough into If a vehicle **ploughs into** another vehicle or some other obstacle, it crashes into it violently: *The van skidded and ploughed into the back of a lorry.*
plough through **1** When something **ploughs through** something else, it forces a way through it: *The ship ploughed through the waves.* **2** If you say you are **ploughing through** work, especially paperwork, you mean you are working your way through it slowly or with some difficulty: *He had to plough through a mountain of paperwork.*

plow see **plough**.

ploy /plɔɪ/ *noun*: **ploys**
A **ploy** is a carefully thought-out plan or method of doing something intended to gain an advantage or a particular result: *The boys came up with a ploy which would enable them to have an afternoon off school.* [*same as* **tactic**]

pluck /plʌk/ *verb*; *noun*
▷ ***verb***: **plucks, plucking, plucked**
1 You **pluck** a hen, turkey or some other bird when you pull the feathers off before cooking it. **2** (*literary*) If you **pluck** fruit or flowers, you pick them from a plant or tree: *He plucked an apple from the branch above his head.* **3** If you **pluck** something out, you remove it by pulling it sharply: *She plucked out a grey hair.* **4** If someone **plucks** their eyebrows, they shape them by removing some of the hairs with tweezers. **5** You **pluck** a stringed instrument, such as a guitar, when you pull and release the strings with your fingertips or a plectrum. [compare **pick**] **6** To **pluck** at something means to take hold of it and pull it: *The little boy plucked at his father's sleeve.* **7** (*often in the passive*) If someone or something **is plucked** from somewhere, they are removed from that place suddenly or just in time: *He was plucked from the jaws of death.*
▷ ***noun*** (*uncount*; *informal*; *rather old*)
Pluck is courage: *He showed a lot of pluck.*
▷ ***phrase*** You **pluck up the courage** to do something when you summon up enough courage to do it: *She plucked up the courage to tell her father that she had failed her exams.*

plucky /ˈplʌkɪ/ *adjective* (*informal*): **pluckier, pluckiest**
A **plucky** person is brave and determined: *a plucky performance.*

plug /plʌg/ *noun*; *verb*
▷ ***noun***: **plugs**
1 A **plug** is a piece of rubber or plastic shaped to fit over and block a hole, *eg* the drain hole in a bath or sink. [see picture at **bathroom**] **2** A **plug** is also any device or piece of material used to cover or block a hole: *an earplug.* **3** A **plug** is **a** a plastic or rubber object with two or three metal pins, fitted to the end of the flex of an electrical apparatus, and pushed into a socket to connect with the power supply. **b** an electric socket. **4** (*informal*) A piece of favourable publicity about a product such as a record or book given on a radio or television programme is called a **plug**. **5** A **plug** is also a spark plug: *The mechanic changed the plugs when he serviced the car.*

▻ ***verb***: **plugs, plugging, plugged**
1 If you **plug** something up, you block, close or fill it with a plug: *He plugged the hole with a piece of sacking.* **2** (*informal*) If someone **plugs** a product, such as a record or book, they talk about it on televison or radio in order to publicize it.

> ***phrasal verbs***
> **plug away** (*informal*) If you **plug away** at something, you work at it steadily in order to finish it successfully: *He has been plugging away at Beethoven's Fifth for weeks.*
> **plug in** If you **plug in** an electrical appliance, you connect it to the power supply by means of an electrical plug.

plughole /ˈplʌghoʊl/ *noun* (*usually used in the singular*): **plugholes**
The **plughole** in a sink or bath is the hole through which water flows into the wastepipe.

plum /plʌm/ *noun*; *adjective*
▻ ***noun***: **plums**
1 A **plum** is an oval red, purple, green or yellow fruit with soft, juicy flesh and a stone. [see picture at **fruit**] **2** A **plum** or a **plum tree** is the tree on which this fruit grows.
▻ ***adjective*** (*informal*)
A **plum** job or a **plum** part in a play or film, is a very good job or part that many people would like to get.

plumage /ˈpluːmɪdʒ/ *noun* (*uncount*)
A bird's **plumage** is the feathers covering its body.

plumb /plʌm/ *verb*: **plumbs, plumbing, plumbed**
▻ ***phrase*** If you say that someone or something **plumbs the depths** of an unpleasant feeling or bad behaviour, you mean that they reach the lowest point of that feeling or behaviour: *plumb the depths of bad taste* □ *She plumbed the depths of despair when her husband left her.*

> ***phrasal verb***
> You **plumb in** a washing machine or dishwasher, when you connect it to the water supply or waste pipe.

plumber /ˈplʌmə(r)/ *noun*: **plumber**
A **plumber** is a person whose job is fitting and repairing pipes, drains and other equipment that carries or uses water or gas.

plumbing /ˈplʌmɪŋ/ *noun* (*uncount*)
1 The **plumbing** in a building is the system of water and gas pipes in it. **2 Plumbing** is also the work of a plumber.

plume /pluːm/ *noun*: **plumes**
1 A **plume** is a large feather or bunch of feathers worn as an ornament *eg* on a hat or helmet. **2** A **plume** is also something that rises into the air in a shape like a large feather: *a plume of smoke.*

plummet /ˈplʌmɪt/ *verb*: **plummets, plummeting, plummeted**
To **plummet** means to fall or drop very quickly or suddenly: *The eagle came plummeting down from the sky and grabbed the rabbit in its talons.* □ *Food prices are set to plummet.* □ *The party's popularity has plummeted in the past few weeks.*

plump[1] /plʌmp/ *adjective*; *verb*
▻ ***adjective***: **plumper, plumpest**
Someone who is **plump** is slightly fat or has a rounded shape: *a baby with nice plump cheeks* □ *a plump chicken* □ *She's getting a bit plump around the middle.*
▻ ***verb***: **plumps, plumping, plumped**

> ***phrasal verbs***
> If you **plump up** or **plump out** a cushion or pillow, you shake and squeeze it until it has a rounded shape.

plump[2] /plʌmp/ *verb*: **plumps, plumping, plumped**

> ***phrasal verbs***
> **plump down** If you **plump** something **down**, you put it down suddenly or let it drop or fall heavily or carelessly: *He plumped the sacks of coal down outside the back door.* □ *She plumbed herself down on the sofa.*
> **plump for** If you **plump for** something, you choose it from a selection available, especially after a period of hesitation or careful thought.

plunder /ˈplʌndə(r)/ *verb*; *noun*
▻ ***verb***: **plunders, plundering, plundered**
To **plunder** means to steal valuable goods or property from a place, especially in time of war: *The Spanish plundered gold and precious stones from the Aztec cities that they conquered.* □ *Many of the pharaohs' tombs had been plundered by grave robbers.*
▻ ***noun*** (*uncount*)
1 Plunder is the action of plundering. **2 Plunder** is also goods that are stolen. [*same as* **loot**]

plunge /plʌndʒ/ *verb*; *noun*
▻ ***verb***: **plunges, plunging, plunged**
1 Someone or something **plunges** if they move, are made to move or are thrown suddenly in a certain direction, especially downwards: *He ran to the edge of the swimming pool and plunged in.* □ *The car plunged over the cliff.* **2** If something is **plunged** into something else, it is thrust or pushed suddenly or with force all the way into that other thing: *She plunged the knife into his chest.* □ *The chef plunged the lobsters into boiling water.* **3** If someone or something **is plunged** into a particular state or condition, it is brought or forced suddenly into that particular state or condition: *The country was plunged into civil war.* □ *The room was plunged into darkness.* **4** If you **plunge** in or into a particular activity, you get quickly involved in it, often without much preparation or warning: *He had never organized a concert before, but he just plunged in and got on with it.* **5** Something, such as a ship, **plunges** when its forward and goes up and down violently as it moves forward: *The little fishing boat plunged up and down as it battled through the waves.* □ *The horse plunged and kicked as it struggled to be free of the rope.*
▻ ***noun***: **plunges**
A **plunge** is the action of plunging, especially the action of diving head first into water.
▻ ***phrase*** (*informal*) When you **take the plunge** you decide to do something that is difficult, especially after hesitating or thinking about it for some time: *When are you going to take the plunge and get married?*

plunger /ˈplʌndʒə(r)/ *noun*: **plungers**
A **plunger** is an instrument consisting of a round rubber cup on the end of a stick that is used for clearing blocked drains and sinks. The rubber cup is pushed up and down over the drain hole causing suction which removes the blockage.

pluperfect /pluːˈpɜːfɪkt/ see **past perfect**.

plural /ˈplʊərəl/ *noun*; *adjective*
▻ ***noun***: **plurals** (*grammar*)
A **plural** is the form of a noun, pronoun, determiner, adjective or verb used to refer to more than one per-

son or thing: *'Mice' is the plural of 'mouse'.* □ *The verb is in the plural.* [opposite **singular**]

▻ ***adjective***

1 (*grammar*) A **plural** word is a word in or having this form: *This noun can be followed by a singular or plural verb.* □ *Many plural nouns in English end in 's'.* [opposite **singular**] **2 Plural** means consisting of more than one person or thing or consisting of different kinds of people or things: *a plural society.*

plus /plʌs/ *preposition; adjective; noun; conjunction*

▻ ***preposition***

1 Plus means 'with the addition of': *Three plus five is eight.* **2** (*informal*) **Plus** also means 'and also' or 'as well as': *There's the four of us, plus two children and a dog.*

▻ ***adjective***

1 Plus is used after a number or quantity to show that the actual number or quantity is more than the number given: *He earns £30 000 plus.* □ *Everyone who goes there is 60 plus.* **2 Plus** is also used to indicate that a number is greater than zero: *The temperature is plus 30 degrees throughout the summer months.* **3** A **plus** factor is one that gives an advantage or extra benefit. **4** A **plus** grade or mark for school or college work is a slightly higher grade or mark: *He got a B for his maths paper and a B plus for his history essay.*

▻ ***noun*: pluses**

1 A **plus** or **plus sign** sign is a sign (+) showing that two or more numbers are to be added together or used to show that a number is greater than zero. **2** (*informal*) A **plus** is a positive or good quality that is a welcome addition or added advantage: *The experience he has gained will be a great plus when he is applying for jobs.*

▻ ***conjunction*** (*informal*)

Some people use **plus** to mean 'in addition to which' after a statement about something and before another statement about the same thing: *It's too wet to go for a walk, plus I don't have a raincoat.*

plush /plʌʃ/ *adjective*

Something that is **plush** is very smart, luxurious and expensive: *a plush hotel.*

plutonium /plʊ'toʊnɪəm/ *noun* (*uncount*)

Plutonium is a radioactive substance obtained from uranium that is used in nuclear weapons and as a fuel in nuclear power stations.

ply[1] /plaɪ/ *noun* (*uncount*)

1 Ply is a measure of the thickness of yarn or rope according to the number of strands it is made from: *three-ply wool* □ *This wool is of a different ply.* **2 Ply** is also a measure of the thickness of plywood according to the number of thin layers of wood it is made from.

ply[2] /plaɪ/ *verb*: **plies, plying, plied**

1 When a ship or bus **plies** a route, especially between two places, it travels regularly on that route: *British ships plying the world's oceans* □ *passenger ferries that ply between Dover and Calais.* **2** A taxi driver **plies** for hire when he or she drives around or waits at a particular place looking for passengers. **3** (*old*) If someone **plies** a trade, they do a particular type of skilled work, especially regularly. **4** (*old*) If someone **plies** a tool, they work steadily using that tool: *She sat quietly in a corner, plying her needle.*

> ***phrasal verb***
>
> If you **ply** someone **with** food, drink or questions, you keep offering or giving them food or drink, or asking them questions: *As an honoured guest, he was plied with delicacies and the best wines.* □ *The boy plied his father with questions about his experiences in the war.*

plywood /'plaɪwʊd/ *noun* (*uncount, often adjectival*)

Plywood is a wooden material made up of thin layers of wood glued together: *sheets of plywood* □ *a box made of plywood* □ *a plywood table.*

pneumatic /njʊ'matɪk/ *adjective*

1 Pneumatic means containing or filled with air: *pneumatic tyres.* **2** A **pneumatic** drill or pump is worked or driven by compressed air.

pneumonia /njʊ'moʊnɪə/ *noun* (*uncount*)

Pneumonia is a serious illness which affects one or both lungs and makes breathing difficult: *The old man died of pneumonia.*

poach[1] /poʊtʃ/ *verb*: **poaches, poaching, poached**

You **poach** an egg when you cook it, without its shell, in or over boiling water; you **poach** fish when you cook it gently in a pan of hot milk or other liquid. — *adjective* **poached:** *She had a poached egg on toast for breakfast.*

poach[2] /poʊtʃ/ *verb*: **poaches, poaching, poached**

1 Someone **poaches** when they hunt and catch fish, game birds or animals without permission on somebody else's property: *He was caught poaching.* □ *He went out at night to poach pheasants.* **2** If someone **poaches** a rival's staff or ideas, they take and use their staff or ideas in a dishonest way: *One of our competitors has poached our best engineers.*

poacher /'poʊtʃə(r)/ *noun*: **poachers**

A **poacher** is someone who hunts and catches fish, game birds or animals without permission on somebody else's property.

PO box /piː oʊ 'bɒks/ *noun*: **PO boxes**

A **PO box** or **post office box** is a numbered box at a post office, to which someone's mail can be sent and from which they can collect it.

pocket /'pɒkɪt/ *noun; adjective; verb*

▻ ***noun*: pockets**

1 A **pocket** is an extra piece of cloth sewn into a piece of clothing to form an enclosed section for carrying small things in: *He walked along with his hands in his trouser pockets.* □ *She found the key in her jacket pocket* [see picture at **clothing**]. **2** A **pocket** is also any container for small or thin articles fitted *eg* to the inside of a suitcase, a car door, or the back of an aircraft seat. **3** (*usually in the singular*) Someone's **pocket** is their supply of money or income: *He paid for it out of his own pocket.* □ *The medical expenses were a drain on her pocket.* □ *The travel company offers holidays to suit every pocket.* **4** A **pocket** is a small area or group that is separated from others like it: *As they travelled through the valley, they came across pockets of mist.* □ *There were still pockets of resistance in the rural areas.* **5** On a snooker or billiard table, the **pockets** are the bag-like nets or pieces of material hanging from the holes at the sides of the table, into which the balls are played.

▻ ***adjective***

Pocket is used to describe something that is small enough to fit into a pocket: *a pocket dictionary* □ *a pocket calculator* □ *a pocket handkerchief.*

▻ ***verb*: pockets, pocketing, pocketed**

1 If you **pocket** something, you put it in your pocket: *He pocketed the train tickets.* **2** (*informal*) To **pocket** also means to take and keep money, especially dishonestly: *She gave him £20 to buy the children Easter eggs, but he pocketed most of it.* **3** In snooker or billiards, you **pocket** a ball when you hit it into a pocket: *He pocketed the black* (or *the black ball*).

▻ ***phrases*** **1** If you **have** someone **in your pocket**, you have complete power or influence over them and can make them do what you want: *He has two US senators in his pocket.* **2** (*informal*) If two people **live in each**

other's pockets they are together too much. **3** If you say you are **out of pocket**, you mean that you have lost money as a result of something: *The driver of the car that crashed into me wasn't insured, and I'm out of pocket by £500.* **4** If someone **picks your pocket**, they steal *eg* your wallet from your pocket. **5** If someone **puts their hand in their pocket**, they spend or give money for something: *He lets everyone buy him drinks but he never puts his hand in his pocket.*

pocketbook /'pɒkɪtbʊk/ *noun*: **pocketbooks**
1 (*AmE*) A **pocketbook is a** a wallet for carrying money and papers. **b** a woman's small handbag or purse. **2** A **pocketbook** is also a small notebook.

pocketful /'pɒkɪtfʊl/ *noun*: **pocketfuls**
A **pocketful** is the amount that a pocket will hold: *a pocketful of sweets.*

pocket knife /'pɒkɪt naɪf/ *noun*: **pocket knives**
A **pocket knife** is a penknife.

pod /pɒd/ *noun*: **pods**
A **pod** is the long green part on *eg* pea and bean plants inside which the seeds grow.

podgy /'pɒdʒɪ/ *adjective* (*informal*): **podgier, podgiest**
Someone who is **podgy** is fat: *podgy fingers* □ *He was quite podgy as a child.*

podium /'poʊdɪəm/ *noun*: **podiums** or **podia** /'poʊdɪə/
A **podium** is a small platform for *eg* a public speaker, entertainer or orchestra conductor to stand on: *The conductor stepped on to the podium and bowed to the audience.*

poem /'poʊɪm/ *noun*: **poems**
A **poem** is a piece of writing arranged in patterns of lines and sounds. **Poems** express some feeling, thought or human experience in imaginative language: *a poem by Keats* □ *She writes poems.*

poet /'poʊɪt/ *noun*: **poets**
A **poet** is someone who writes poems: *He is a writer and poet.* □ *Wordsworth, Keats and Shelley are amongst the most famous English poets.*

poetess /poʊɪ'tɛs/ *noun*: **poetesses**
A **poetess** is another word for a woman poet, though nowadays it is very rarely used.

poetic /poʊ'ɛtɪk/ or **poetical** /poʊ'ɛtɪkəl/ *adjective*
Poetic or **poetical** means **1** having beauty or imagination like poetry: *the poetic grace of her dancing.* **2** of or like poets or poetry, or written in verse: *the poetic works of Milton.*

poetry /'poʊətrɪ/ *noun* (*uncount*)
1 (*often adjectival*) **Poetry** is poems considered as a group or as a form of literature: *a book of English poetry* □ *modern poetry* □ *He writes poetry.* □ *a poetry reading* □ *a poetry book.* **2** A quality such as beauty or grace that is pleasing to your senses may be referred to as **poetry**: *Their performance of the ballet was sheer poetry.*

poignancy /'pɔɪnjənsɪ/ *noun* (*uncount; formal*)
Poignancy is the state of quality of being poignant.

poignant /'pɔɪnjənt/ *adjective*
Something that is **poignant** affects your feelings deeply causing *eg* great sadness or pity: *a poignant farewell* □ *The letter was a poignant reminder of happier times.* — *adverb* **poignantly:** *He talked poignantly about the sufferings of victims of the holocaust.*

point /pɔɪnt/ *noun; verb*
▷ ***noun*: points**
1 a The **point** of something such as a knife, needle or pin is its sharp end or tip: *He dug the point of his penknife into the wood.* □ *I sharpened the stick to a point.* [*same as* **tip**] **b** A **point** is a part of the coast that projects into the sea: *He'd left his boat in a cove round the point.* [*same as* **headland**]
2 a The **point** or **decimal point** in a number is the dot that comes before the decimal fraction: *twelve point five* (written *12.5*) □ *To multiply a decimal number by 10, move the point one place to the right.* **b** In punctuation, a **point**, or **full point**, is a full stop. **c** A **point** is an exact position or location, *eg* on a graph, diagram, plan or map, or a dot marking it: *Line AB intersects line XY at point C.* □ *Using a pencil join points F and G.* **d** The **points** of the compass are the 32 directions marked on it, especially north, south, east and west, or the actual directions that these represent: *Men were approaching on foot and on horseback from all points of the compass.* [= from all directions] **e** A **point** on a scale is a position or level on it: *Metals have different melting points.* □ *100° Celsius is the boiling point of water.*
3 a A **point** is a place or location, *eg* within an area or on a surface: *A point on the skin can be stimulated by contact.* □ *The highest point in the district is White Stones, 2500 ft.* □ *There were weak points in the structure.* □ *The leaf is about 5 cm at its widest point.* **b** A place where something happens can be referred to as a **point** of a certain kind: *We had reached the point where the trees began.* □ *Malham had always been a favourite stopping-off point for me.* □ *Slateford used to be a major crossing point on the river.* □ *the transportation of chilled food from the point of production to the point of sale* □ *electronic point-of-sale data.* **c** A **point** in time is a particular moment or stage, *eg* in a procedure, or in the development of a situation: *You reach a point where you can't sleep in spite of your tiredness.* □ *Up to this point he'd remained a background figure.* □ *Perhaps I could arrange a consultation with her at some convenient point?* □ *That's all I need to say at this point.* □ *Anna said at one point, 'Jill's not eating.'* □ *The situation had reached crisis point.* □ *Midsummer has become the high point* [= the climax] *of operatic year in London.*
4 a You get or score a **point** in a game or competition when get a single mark to add to your total score: *The rest of the team try to throw the ball to the catcher, and if they succeed they get a point.* □ *Leeds are second, five points behind Middlesborough.* **b** Your good points and bad points are the good and bad aspects of your character and behaviour: *Perhaps you have awful faults to counterbalance your few good points.* □ *Her perseverence is a point in her favour.*
5 a You make a **point** in an argument or discussion when you mention something that is relevant to it; people say that you have a **point** or that they can see your **point** when they acknowledge the significance of what you have said; you raise a **point** when you mention something you think people should consider: *I see her point.* □ *That's an excellent point.* □ *She didn't feel like arguing the point any further.* □ *You've proved your point about me not knowing enough to be manager.* □ *Could I make a brief point here?* □ *The book fails, but it does make a point.* □ *I could raise a point or two about discipline.* □ *Sorry, just one more point.* **b** A **point** is a detail to be considered, understood or dealt with: *She took him through the agreement point by point.* □ *I just want to check a few small points.* □ *Could you clarify that point?* □ *Occasionally someone will say something that illuminates a point of grammar for you.* □ *We have had no instructions on this point.* **c** (*used in the singular*) When discussing something, you refer to the main factor or issue as the **point**; something that misses the **point** does not deal with it properly: *That's not the point.* □ *His argument misses the point.* □ *The point is that most parents would prefer their babies not*

to be defective. **d** (*uncount or used in the singular*) The **point** of some activity or procedure is its purpose; if there's no **point** in doing something it is not worth doing: *What's the point of that?* □ *The whole point of putting them on a boat is that they can't get off and swim home.* □ *I can't see the point of expending all that energy when I'm perfectly happy as I am.* □ *The point of laboratory work was to prove the truth of a theory.* □ *Children shouldn't be made to obey rules that they can't see the point of.* □ *There's not much point in getting angry.* □ *If we didn't have troubles to sort out there would be no point to our existence.* **e** The **point** of a joke or remark is something that the hearer has to understand in order to realize its significance: *I don't get the point of that cartoon.*

6 a (*electricity*) An electrical point is a socket in a wall into which a plug can be put: *The power points and ceiling lights had already been installed.* **b** (*used in the plural*) A set of **points** on a railway line is an adjustable section that allows trains to cross over an intersecting line, and can be swung round to direct them on to another line.

▻ ***verb*: points, pointing, pointed**

1 You **point** at or to someone or something when you use your index finger or some other long thin object to show your hearer whom or what you are referring to: *The lecturer can point to objects and diagrams on the screen.* □ *You mustn't point at people like that.* □ *'Oh God,' gasped Julie, pointing towards the kitchen.* □ *I couldn't see what she was pointing at.* **2** You **point** something at or towards a person or thing when you aim it at them: *'Why have you brought him?' she asked, pointing her bony finger at Frank.* □ *You wake up and there's a guy pointing a gun at your head.* **3** Something **points** in a certain direction if it is turned, or is facing, in that direction: *He waited, gun at the ready, its barrel pointing towards the ceiling.* □ *Pitch your tent with the entrance pointing away from the wind.* □ *I followed his pointing finger.* **4** Circumstances **point** to a certain person or thing if they indicate that person or thing as likely to have been responsible for them, or for something else that has happened: *Staff unpunctuality points to poor managerial control.* □ *All the evidence points to Simons.* **5** Someone who is dancing **points** their toes when they stretch their foot and toes to form a point.

▻ ***phrases*** **1** Something that someone says during a discussion that is **beside the point** is irrelevant to main issue. **2** For **a case in point** see **case**. **3 a** Having started to speak, you **come** or **get to the point** when you say the thing that is relevant to the present discussion or situation: *To come straight to the point, I came down here to make a suggestion.* □ *I waited for him to get to the point.* **b** If you say you couldn't do something when it **came** or **got to the point**, you mean that you couldn't do it when the right time came to do it: *When it came to the point I couldn't bring myself to tell her.* **4** You **make a point of** doing something, or **make it a point to** do something, when you make a special effort to do it: *The writer makes a point of stressing the limitations of her data.* **5** You are **on the point of** doing something when you are just going to do it: *Benjamin was on the point of driving his sword through his opponent's breast.* □ *The young Scot was on the point of fulfilling the potential she had shown in the amateur game.* **6** For **point of fact** see **fact**. **7** For **point of no return** see **return**. **8** For **point of order** see under **order**. **9** For **point of view** see separate entry. **10** In a debate, one person tries to **score points off** another when they attack minor or unimportant details of their argument in the hope of impressing hearers. **11** Something that is **a sore point** with you is a personal matter or issue about which you have had arguments with people, or received criticism, and feel sensitive: *My clothes were becoming a sore point.* **12** You **stretch a point** in special circumstances when you allow something that is not normally allowed: *There's actually an entrance fee, but I think we can stretch a point in your case.* **13** If you say **'I take your point'** to someone you are discussing something with, you mean that you acknowledge that what they say is relevant or true: *I take your point, but what about the wider issues?* **14** Something that is **to the point** is relevant: *Your CV should be factual and to the point.* **15** You describe a person or thing as being or doing something **to the point of** some extreme state if they progress as far as that state: *employers who work their staff to the point of exhaustion* □ *She was conscientious to the point of obsession.* **16** Something that is true **up to a point** is partly true: *Up to a point, the House of Commons expects the House of Lords to do this job.*

phrasal verb

point out 1 You **point** something **out** to someone when you indicate it to them in some way: *He began to recognize familiar places, and eagerly pointed them out to Rose.* **2** You **point out** something when you mention it to people for consideration: *It is necessary to point out that there does not seem to be any decisive evidence for this.*

point-blank /pɔɪnt'blaŋk/ *adjective; adverb*

▻ ***adjective***

1 If a shot is fired at **point-blank** range it is fired from a position very close to the target. **2** A **point-blank** question or refusal is direct, complete and often rather rude.

▻ ***adverb***

1 Point-blank means at very close range: *The gun had been fired, point-blank, at the man's chest.* **2 Point-blank** also means in a very direct or rude manner: *I asked him for a few days off but he refused point-blank.*

pointed /'pɔɪntɪd/ *adjective*

1 An object that is **pointed** has a point at one end: *a pointed stick* □ *a pointed hat.* **2** A **pointed** statement or look is intended to express a particular meaning in a very direct way, or is directed against a particular person or thing: *a pointed remark* □ *She made a few pointed references to his lack of courtesy.* — *adverb* **pointedly:** *He was staring quite pointedly at Peter when he made the remark.*

pointer /'pɔɪntə(r)/ *noun*: **pointers**

1 A **pointer** is a thin stick or rod of wood or metal used to point to positions on a wall map, chart or blackboard: *The teacher used a pointer to indicate the position of various cities on the map.* **2** A **pointer** is also a thin piece of metal or plastic that moves to indicate figures on a measuring instrument. **3** (*informal*) If someone gives you a **pointer** to something they give you a piece of advice about how something is or should be done: *I don't know anything about business taxation, and I'd be grateful if you would give me a few pointers.*

pointless /'pɔɪntlɪs/ *adjective*

Something that is **pointless** has no use, meaning or purpose: *It would be pointless to go on searching in the dark.* □ *a pointless remark.* — *adverb* **pointlessly**: *she rather pointlessly tried to make him change his mind.* — *noun* (*uncount*) **pointlessness:** *They tried to convince him of the pointlessness of his actions.*

point of view /pɔɪnt əv 'vjuː/ *noun*: **points of view**

Your **point of view** is your particular opinion or attitude to something based on your own experience or feelings: *Try to see it from my point of view.* [see also **viewpoint**]

poise /pɔɪz/ *noun* (*uncount*)
Poise is a calm, dignified, self-confident and self-controlled manner or way of behaving: *Those in the first group had a poise and confidence that the rest of us did not.* □ *Despite being shouted at and booed, she didn't lose her poise for a single moment.*

poised /pɔɪzd/ *adjective*
1 If someone or their behaviour is **poised** they are calm, dignified and self-controlled: *She looked stunningly elegant, as poised and graceful as she had ever been.* **2** If something is **poised** it is completely still as if it is hanging in the air, or it is in a state of balance or tension ready to move or fall at any moment: *She took out her notebook, pencil poised at the ready.* □ *George sat there quietly, his finger poised over the TV remote control.*

poison /ˈpɔɪzən/ *noun*; *verb*
▻ ***noun*** (*uncount or count*): **poisons**
Poison is any substance that causes illness, death or damage when it is taken into the body or tissues of an animal or plant: *She committed suicide by taking poison.* □ *poisons such as arsenic.* □ *a deadly poison* □ *rat poison.* [compare **venom**]
▻ ***verb***: **poisons, poisoning, poisoned**
1 A person or animal **is poisoned** when they are made ill or killed with poison: *Birds of prey were being poisoned by pesticides.* □ *The foxes were poisoned with arsenic.* **2** If *eg* food or drink **is poisoned**, it has poison added to it: *The queen's drink had been poisoned.* **3** If water, land, or air **is poisoned** it is damaged or contaminated with harmful substances such as chemicals: *rivers poisoned by effluents* □ *exhaust gases poisoning the air.* **4** If something **poisons** something else, it has a dangerous or damaging influence or effect on that other thing: *He has poisoned his children's minds against her.* □ *Their relationship was poisoned by the quarrel.* — *adjective* **poisoned:** *a poisoned drink* □ *He has a poisoned finger.* [=his finger has become infected]

poisoner /ˈpɔɪzənə(r)/ *noun*: **poisoners**
A **poisoner** is someone who has used poison to murder someone: *a notorious poisoner.*

poisonous /ˈpɔɪzənəs/ *adjective*
1 A **poisonous** substance is one that causes illness or death if swallowed or absorbed: *The berries of that bush are poisonous.* □ *a cloud of poisonous gas.* **2** A **poisonous** animal is one that produces a poison that it uses as a means of killing its prey or attacking its enemies: *The viper is the only poisonous British snake.* **3** Something that is extremely harmful, *eg* to morals or opinions, may be described as **poisonous**: *the poisonous doctrine of racial superiority.* **4** (*informal*) If you describe someone or their actions as **poisonous**, you mean that they are nasty or malicious: *He's a poisonous little brute.* □ *She gave him a poisonous look.*

poke /poʊk/ *verb*: **pokes, poking, poked**
1 If you **poke** someone or something, you push or prod them with your finger or a sharp object: *She poked him in the ribs.* □ *Be careful what you're doing with that stick; you nearly poked me in the eye.* **2** If you **poke** something into a hole or space, you push or thrust it into that hole or space: *He poked a piece of wire mesh into the hole.* □ *chimpanzees using sticks to poke into termite moulds.* **3** Something that **pokes** out of or through something else projects out of or through that thing: *He poked his head out of the door.* □ *Her big toe was poking through a hole in her sock.*

> ***phrasal verbs***
> If you **poke about** or **poke around** for something, you look or search for it amongst other things: *He was poking around in the attic looking for his stamp collection.*

poker[1] /ˈpoʊkə(r)/ *noun*: **pokers**
A **poker** is a heavy metal rod that you use for stirring a fire in order to make it burn better.

poker[2] /ˈpoʊkə(r)/ *noun* (*uncount*)
Poker is a card game, usually played for money.

poky /ˈpoʊkɪ/ *adjective* (*informal, derogatory*): **pokier, pokiest**
If you say that a room or house is **poky**, you mean it is uncomfortably small.

polar /ˈpoʊlə(r)/ *adjective*
1 Polar is used to describe things that come from, happen in, or are situated at or near, the North or South Pole: *a polar expedition* □ *polar latitudes* □ *the polar ice-caps.* **2** (*formal*) **Polar** opposites or extremes are complete or absolute opposites or extremes.

polar bear /poʊlə(r) ˈbɛə(r)/ *noun*: **polar bears**
A **polar bear** is a type of large white bear found in the Arctic.

polarize /ˈpoʊləraɪz/ or **polarise** *verb*: **polarizes, polarizing, polarized**
If people **are polarized** they divide or are caused to divide into groups with completely opposite views, principles, or opinions: *The issue has polarized public opinion.* □ *The violence has had the effect of increasing hostility on both sides, and so polarizing attitudes.* — *noun* (*uncount*) **polarization** /poʊləraɪˈzeɪʃən/: *the polarization of political attitudes.*

pole[1] /poʊl/ *noun*: **poles**
The **poles** are either of the two points at the exact top and bottom of a planet, especially the North and South Pole on the Earth and the areas around them.
▻ ***phrase*** (*informal*) If you say that people or their opinions are **poles apart**, you mean that they are as different or as far apart as is possible.

pole[2] /poʊl/ *noun*: **poles**
A **pole** is a long thin piece of wood or metal fixed in the ground as a support for something, or used to push a boat or skier along: *a telegraph pole* □ *a flag pole* □ *tent poles* □ *a barge pole.*

pole-vault /ˈpoʊlvɔːlt/ *noun* (*uncount or count*)
The **pole-vault** is an athletic event in which competitors try to jump over a high horizontal bar using a pole to push themselves off the ground. — *noun* **pole-vaulter:** *Olympic pole-vaulters.*

police /pəˈliːs/ *noun*; *verb*
▻ ***noun*** (*with a plural verb*)
1 (*often adjectival*) The **police** are the body of men and women employed by the government of a country to catch criminals, prevent crime, keep public order, and see that laws are obeyed: *He wants to join the police.* □ *I'll call the police if you don't stop bothering me.* □ *a police car.* **2 Police** are members of this body: *Over 200 police were on duty at the football match.*
▻ ***verb***: **polices, policing, policed**
1 To **police** an area means to keep law and order in it using the police or the army: *troops of the United Nations policing war-torn Lebanon.* **2** To **police** also means to control or keep a watch on something, *eg* to make sure it is done fairly or as it should be: *a body appointed to police the nuclear industry.*

police constable /pəliːs 'kɑːnstəbəl/ *noun*: **police constables**
A **police constable** or **constable** is a police officer of the lowest rank.

policeman /pə'liːsmən/ *noun*: **policemen**
A **policeman** is a male police officer.

police officer /pə'liːs ɒfɪsə(r)/ *noun*: **police officers**
A **police officer** is a male or female member of a police force.

police station /pə'liːssteɪʃən/ *noun*: **police stations**
A **police station** is the office of a local police force: *He has to report to his local police station once a week.*

policewoman /pə'liːswʊmən/ *noun*: **policewomen**
A **policewoman** is a female police officer.

policy[1] /'pɒlɪsɪ/ *noun (uncount or count)*: **policies**
A **policy** is **a** a plan of action or set of aims, decided on by a group, such as a political party, company or other organization: *government policy* □ *economic policy* □ *privatization of state-owned industries and other Conservative policies.* **b** a principle or set of principles on which to base decisions or conduct: *Honesty is the best policy.*

policy[2] /'pɒlɪsɪ/ *noun*: **policies**
A **policy**, or an **insurance policy**, is a document which contains the terms of a contract with an insurance company.

polio /'poʊlɪoʊ/ *noun (uncount)*
Polio is a serious infectious disease affecting the brain and the nerves of the spine which can sometimes result in permanent paralysis.

poliomyelitis /poʊlɪoʊmaɪə'laɪtɪs/ *noun (uncount; formal)*
Poliomyelitis is the full form of **polio**.

polish /pɒlɪʃ/ *noun; verb*
▷ ***noun***: **polishes**
1 (*uncount or count*) **Polish**, or a **polish**, is a liquid, powder or paste that you rub on the surface of an object to clean it and make it shine: *shoe polish* □ *furniture polish.* **2** If something has a **polish** it has a smooth shiny surface made by rubbing: *There's a marvellous polish on this old table.* **3** A **polish** is an act of polishing: *Give your shoes a good polish.* **4** (*uncount*) A person or thing that has **polish** is refined: *He's very intelligent, but he lacks charm and polish.* □ *He gave a good performance, but it lacked polish.*
▷ ***verb***: **polishes, polishing, polished**
You **polish** something when you make it smooth and shiny by rubbing: *He polished his shoes.* □ *She dusted and polished the furniture.*

phrasal verbs
polish off (*informal*) If you **polish** something **off**, you finish it quickly and easily: *He polished off the last of the wine.*
polish up If you **polish up** a skill or technique, you improve it by practising: *He went to a night class to polish up on his French.*

polished /'pɒlɪʃt/ *adjective*
1 A **polished** surface is one that is shiny from polishing: *polished wood.* **2** **Polished** manners or **polished** behaviour is polite and refined. **3** A **polished** performance or artistic work is done with great skill and refinement.

polite /pə'laɪt/ *adjective*: **politer, politest**
1 Someone who is **polite** has or shows good manners and consideration for other people: *He's very polite.* □ *a polite remark* □ *It's more polite to say 'yes, thank you' than 'okay'.* □ *It's not polite to interrupt when someone else is speaking.* [*opposite* **impolite**] **2** **Polite** also means well-bred, well-educated and refined: *polite society.* — *adverb* **politely:** *He thanked them politely.* — *noun (uncount)* **politeness**: *He thanked her with his customary politeness.*

politic /'pɒlɪtɪk/ *adjective (formal)*
If you say that something is **politic**, you mean it is the wisest or most sensible thing to do in the circumstances: *a politic action* □ *When they began to argue amongst themselves, he thought it politic to quietly leave.* [*same as* **prudent**; see also **politics**]

political /pə'lɪtɪkəl/ *adjective*
1 **Political** means of or connected with politics and government: *a political party* □ *the BBC's political editor* □ *political freedom* □ *Attempts to find a political solution to problems in Northern Ireland have so far failed.* **2** Someone who is **political** is interested in or involved in politics: *He's not very political.* — *adverb* **politically:** *Can the problem be solved politically?*

political asylum /pəlɪtɪkəl ə'saɪləm/ *noun (uncount)*
Political asylum is protection given by a government to a foreigner who has left his or her own country for political reasons.

political prisoner /pəlɪtɪkəl 'prɪzənə(r)/ *noun*: **political prisoners**
A **political prisoner** is a person who has been imprisoned because they disagree with or oppose their own government or its policies.

politician /pɒlɪ'tɪʃən/ *noun*: **politicians**
A **politician** is someone whose job is in politics, especially a member of parliament or the government: *Labour politicians* □ *His ambition is to be a politician.*

politicize /pə'lɪtɪsaɪz/ or **politicise** *verb*: **politicizes, politicizing, politicized**
If someone or something **is politicized**, it is given a political character or made more political: *As the trade union movement grew, it became more and more politicized.*

politics /'pɒlɪtɪks/ *noun*
1 (*uncount, with a singular or plural verb*) **Politics** is political affairs, especially the work of governing a country: *party politics* □ *He wants to go into politics.* □ *Do you think politics is a good career for a woman?* **2** (*uncount*) **Politics** is the science or study of the ways in which countries are governed: *He's studying history and politics at university.* **3** (*plural*) Your **politics** are your political views or beliefs: *What are your politics?* **4** (*uncount*) **Politics** is also any activity or manoeuvre aimed at achieving power or advantage over others within a particular group or organization: *office politics* □ *I'm not interested in who has succeeded is doing what to whom; it's all just politics.*

poll /poʊl/ *noun; verb*
▷ ***noun***: **polls**
1 A **poll** is a political election in which votes are given in writing: *victory at the polls* □ *The result of the poll will be known some time around 2 a.m.* **2** The number of votes cast and recorded at an election is a **poll**: *a heavy poll.* **3** A **poll** or **opinion poll** is a survey designed to find out public opinion on a particular matter by questioning a number of people chosen at random.
▷ ***verb***: **polls, polling, polled**
1 If you **are polled** on something, you are asked to give your opinion as part of a survey: *Nearly two thirds of the people polled said that smoking should be banned.* **2** If a political party **polls** a certain number of votes, they receive that number of votes at an election.

pollen /'pɒlən/ *noun (uncount)*

Pollen is the fine yellow powder formed in flowers. It is carried to other flowers of the same species by insects or the wind, and fertilizes them so that they produce seeds.

pollinate /ˈpɒlɪneɪt/ *verb*: **pollinates, pollinating, pollinated**
If a flower **is pollinated** by an insect or some other means, pollen is carried to it from another flower of the same species causing it to be fertilized and thus produce seeds. — *noun* (*uncount*) **pollination** /pɒlɪˈneɪʃən/: *pollination by bees*.

polling station /poʊlɪŋ ˈsteɪʃən/ *noun*: **polling stations**
A **polling station** is a building or place where all the people in an area can cast their votes in an election.

pollutant /pəˈluːtənt/ *noun*: **pollutants**
A **pollutant** is a substance that causes pollution: *lead and other pollutants from vehicle exhausts.*

pollute /pəˈluːt/ *verb*: **pollutes, polluting, polluted**
To **pollute** something, especially water or the air, means to make it dirty by adding unpleasant or harmful substances: *Waste from the chemical factory polluted the river.* □ *The water is polluted and dangerous for bathers.*

pollution /pəˈluːʃən/ *noun* (*uncount*)
1 Pollution is the process of polluting or the state of being polluted: *the pollution of Britain's beaches.* **2 Pollution** is also the dangerous or harmful substances that pollute the water, land or air.

polo /ˈpoʊloʊ/ *noun* (*uncount*)
Polo is a ball game in which players on horseback use long-handled hammers to hit the ball along the ground.

polo neck /ˈpoʊloʊ nɛk/ *noun*: **polo necks**
1 A **polo neck** is a high, close-fitting neck band on a sweater or shirt, worn folded over. **2** A **polo neck** is also a sweater or shirt with such a neck. [see picture at **clothing**] — *adjective* **polo-necked:** *a polo-necked sweater.*

poly /ˈpɒlɪ/ *noun*: **polys** (*informal*)
A **poly** is a polytechnic: *He's a student at the poly.*

poly- /pɒlɪ/ or /pəˈlɪ/ *prefix*
Poly- is used with nouns or adjectives to mean 'many' or 'much' of something: *polysyllabic.* [=having several syllables]

polyester /ˈpɒlɪɛstə(r)/ *noun* (*uncount, often adjectival*)
Polyester is a type of man-made fabric used for making clothes.

polygon /ˈpɒlɪgɒn/ *noun*: **polygons**
A **polygon** is a solid shape with many, especially more than five, sides.

polystyrene /pɒlɪˈstaɪəriːn/ *noun* (*uncount*)
Polystyrene is a very light, plastic substance used as a packing and insulating material.

polytechnic /pɒlɪˈtɛknɪk/ *noun*: **polytechnics**
In Britain, a **polytechnic** is a college where you can go to study after leaving school, especially if you want to study more practical courses than those which are offered by a traditional university. Since 1992, **polytechnics** have had the same status as, and most are now called, universities.

polythene /ˈpɒlɪθiːn/ *noun* (*uncount, often adjectival*)
Polythene is a very thin plastic material used for making protective coverings, bags, and light containers: *a polythene bag* □ *He covered the earth with sheets of black polythene to stop the weeds growing.*

polyunsaturated /pɒlɪʌnˈsatjəreɪtɪd/ *adjective* (*technical*)
Polyunsaturated margarines and oils are made from fish or vegetable oils and fats and are thought to be healthier than those made from animal fats.

pomegranate /ˈpɒmɪgranɪt/ *noun*: **pomegranates**
A **pomegranate** is a round fruit with a thick reddish-brown skin. Inside the skin there are a large number of small seeds surrounded by red flesh. [see picture at **fruit**]

pomp /pɒmp/ *noun* (*uncount*)
Pomp is splendid or magnificent display, especially when associated with a public ceremony or occasion: *the pomp and ceremony of the coronation of the Prince of Wales.*

pompous /ˈpɒmpəs/ *adjective* (*derogatory*)
1 A **pompous** person is someone whose manner is very grand and self-important: *a pompous little man.* **2** If speech or writing is **pompous** it is full of long and important-sounding words. — *adverb* **pompously**: *'I believe every young man benefits from being in the army, as I did,' he said pompously.* — *noun* (*uncount*) **pomposity** /pɒmˈpɒsɪtɪ/ or **pompousness**: *She was irritated by the pomposity of his manner.*

pond /pɒnd/ *noun*: **ponds**
A **pond** is a small area of water that is smaller than a lake and larger than a pool. Artificial ponds are often made for animals to drink at or as an ornamental feature in a garden: *He was thrown into the village pond.* □ *They have a fish pond in their garden.*

ponder /ˈpɒndə(r)/ *verb* (*formal or literary*): **ponders, pondering, pondered**
Someone **ponders** when they think about something carefully or for a long time, especially when they are trying to make a decision or form a conclusion: *He pondered for a few moments before he made his reply.* □ *He said he would like some time to ponder the question.* □ *They spend a lot of time pondering on* (or *over*) *the meaning of human existence.*

ponderous /ˈpɒndərəs/ *adjective* (*formal or literary*)
1 You can describe someone's speaking or writing style as **ponderous** when you think it is competely lacking in interest or imagination. **2 Ponderous** also means heavy and awkward: *His movements were slow and ponderous.* — *adverb* **ponderously:** *He moved ponderously towards the door.*

pong /pɒŋ/ *noun; verb*
▻ ***noun*** (*BrE; informal*): **pongs**
A **pong** is a strong unpleasant smell: *What a pong!* □ *There's a dreadful pong coming from your socks.*
▻ ***verb*** (*BrE; informal*): **pongs, ponging, ponged**
If something **pongs** it has a strong unpleasant smell: *The changing-room pongs of stale sweat.* [*same as* **stink**]

pontoon[1] /pɒnˈtuːn/ *noun* (*technical*): **pontoons**
A **pontoon** is one of a number of floating platforms or flat-bottomed boats that are joined together to form a support for a temporary roadway *eg* across a river: *a pontoon bridge.*

pontoon[2] /pɒnˈtuːn/ *noun* (*uncount*)
Pontoon is a card game in which the aim is to collect sets of cards that add up to 21 and no more.

pony /ˈpoʊnɪ/ *noun*: **ponies**
A **pony** is a type of small horse: *a Shetland pony* □ *The children learnt to ride on small ponies.*

ponytail /ˈpoʊnɪteɪl/ *noun*: **ponytails**
A **ponytail** is a hairstyle in which the hair is gathered up at the back of the head and tied so that it hangs down like a tail: *She wore her hair in a ponytail.*

poodle /'pu:dəl/ *noun*: **poodles**
A **poodle** is a type of dog with a thick curly coat.

pooh /pu:/ *interjection* (*informal*)
Pooh is used as an exclamation of disgust at an unpleasant smell: *Pooh, that fish smells rotten!*

pool[1] /pu:l/ *noun*: **pools**
1 A **pool** is **a** a small area of still water: *a rock pool* **b** an area of slow-moving water in a stream or river: *a deep pool at the base of the waterfall* □ *He caught a salmon in the pool near the bridge.* **2** A **pool** is also a small puddle of any liquid, especially liquid that has been spilt: *pools of blood* □ *a pool of oil.* **3** A **pool** is also a swimming-pool: *They were splashing around in the pool.*

pool[2] /pu:l/ *noun*; *verb*
▷ ***noun***: **pools**
1 A **pool** is a collection or group of *eg* money, people or vehicles that forms a fund, stock or supply that can be used by several people or organizations: *They put money into a general pool for living expenses.* □ *a typing pool.* **2** (*plural*) The **pools** or the **football pools** is a form of gambling in which a large number of people bet on the results of football matches and their combined bets forms a fund from which winners are paid. **3** (*uncount*) **Pool** is a game similar to snooker that is played with a white ball and usually 15 numbered coloured balls on a special table with pockets around its edge. The aim is to hit the coloured balls in the correct order into particular pockets using a long stick to hit the white ball against the coloured balls.
▷ ***verb***: **pools, pooling, pooled**
If a number of people or organizations **pool** money or other resources, they put it together in a common fund or supply which can be used by everyone or for a special purpose.

poor /pʊə(r)/ or /pɔ:(r)/ *adjective*: **poorer, poorest**
1 Someone who is **poor** has very little money and a low standard of living: *Poor people live shorter lives and have more illnesses.* □ *After all, he was poor and Dempster was rich.* □ *The so-called tax reforms will actually leave us 5% poorer.* [*opposite* **rich**] **2 Poor** countries or areas are inhabited by people with very little money: *He was born in a poor district of London.* □ *Weapons go to the poorest countries and money to the richest.* [*opposite* **rich**] **3** A place or thing that is **poor** in a resource or quality has very little of it: *This is an area relatively poor in metals.* □ *The available plant material is poor in nutritional value.* [*opposite* **rich**] **4 Poor** also describes things that are **a** of a low standard: *Standards of hygiene were poor.* □ *Because of poor health he was educated at home.* □ *buildings that are in a poor state of repair* □ *people with poor employment prospects* □ *It's been a poor summer.* □ *The book was printed on poor-quality paper.* [*opposite* **good**] **b** unsatisfactorily small in quantity: *There was a poor attendance.* □ *The crop yield was very poor.* □ *He let his eyes adjust to the poor light.* [*opposite* **good**] **5** Someone or something that is a **poor** performer at some activity is not good at it: *You're a poor liar, Fran.* □ *Rose, his tone implied, was a poor cook and a worse mother.* □ *Glass is a poor conductor of heat.* [*opposite* **good**] **6** You refer to someone as *eg* 'the poor man', or address someone as *eg* 'poor you', to express pity or sympathy: *The baby died in its sleep, poor little soul.* □ *She's got a lot of worries, poor Beth.* □ *So they blame the poor old social worker.* □ *Poor Mum, you must be tired.* □ *'He lost his wife recently.' 'Oh, poor him.'* □ *You're hurting my poor arm.*
▷ ***noun*** (*plural*)
The **poor** are poor people: *Don't underestimate the difficulty the poor have in finding work.* □ *The Bell Street tenements were built to house the poorest of the poor.*

poorly /'pʊəlɪ/ or /'pɔ:lɪ/ *adverb*; *adjective*
▷ ***adverb***
Poorly means badly or inadequately: *The shares have performed poorly in the last year.* □ *a poorly-paid job.*
▷ ***adjective*** (*informal*)
If someone is or is feeling **poorly** they are ill or are feeling ill: *She's poorly.* □ *He's feeling a bit poorly today* □ *poorly-housed immigrants* □ *a poorly-attended meeting.*

pop[1] /pɒp/ *noun*; *adverb*; *verb*
▷ ***noun***: **pops**
A **pop** is a short sharp noise, like a small explosion: *The cork came out of the champagne bottle with a loud pop.*
▷ ***adverb***
If something goes **pop** it makes this sound: *The cork went pop.*
▷ ***verb***: **pops, popping, popped**
1 You **pop** something or something **pops** when you cause it to make a pop or it makes a pop: *He popped the balloon.* □ *The champagne corks were popping.* **2** If something **pops** out it springs out or sticks out suddenly: *The rabbit popped its head out of its burrow.* **3** If your eyes **pop**, you open them very wide so that they appear to stick out: *His eyes nearly popped out of his head with surprise.* **4** (*informal*) You **pop** something into a place when you put it there quickly: *I'm just going to pop this thermometer under your tongue.* □ *I'll pop a train timetable through your letterbox this evening.* **5** (*informal*) If you say that you are going to **pop** to a place you mean that you are going there quickly: *I'm just popping next door for a few minutes.* □ *I'm popping out for a second.* □ *Can you pop round today and pick up the parcel?*

phrasal verb
If something **pops up** it appears or occurs suddenly and usually unexpectedly: *He pops up in the most unexpected places.*

pop[2] /pɒp/ *noun* (*uncount, often adjectival*)
Pop or **pop music** is modern music that usually has a strong beat and is often played with electronic equipment. **Pop** is especially popular amongst young people: *rock and pop* □ *a pop group* □ *a pop singer.*

pop[3] /pɒp/ *noun* (*AmE; informal*)
Some young people refer to their father or an old man as **pop**.

popcorn /'pɒpkɔ:n/ *noun* (*uncount*)
Popcorn is a food made from maize grains that are heated until they burst and become light and fluffy.

pope /poʊp/ *noun*: **popes**
The **pope** is the head of the Roman Catholic Church: *the first non-Italian pope* □ *Pope John Paul.*

poplar /'pɒplə(r)/ *noun*: **poplars**
A **poplar** is a type of tree. Poplars are members of the willow family and are tall and slender.

popper /'pɒpə(r)/ *noun* (*informal*): **poppers**
A **popper** is another word for a press stud.

poppy /'pɒpɪ/ *noun*: **poppies**
A **poppy** is a wild flower with large flat-petalled red flowers and a hairy stem. **Poppies** grow in fields and several varieties are also grown as garden plants.

populace /'pɒpjʊləs/ *noun* (*used in the singular*; *with a singular or plural verb*; *formal*)
The ordinary people of a country or area are sometimes referred to as the **populace**: *There were rumblings of discontent amongst the populace.* □ *The measures are intended to win the support of the populace.*

popular /ˈpɒpjʊlə(r)/ *adjective*
1 If something is **popular** it is liked or enjoyed by many people: *Angling is one of the most popular pastimes in Britain.* □ *These video games are especially popular among teenage boys.* **2** If a person is **popular** he or she is liked and admired by a lot of people: *He was a popular choice as head boy.* □ *She was very popular with the other students.* [*opposite* **unpopular**] **3** A **popular** belief or idea is one that is accepted or supported by many people: *a popular theory* □ *Contrary to popular belief, some parts of Scotland have relatively low rainfall.* **4 Popular** is also used to describe something that can be easily read or understood by ordinary people and is not aimed at specialists in a particular subject: *a popular history of science* □ *the popular press.* **5 Popular** also means of or involving the people in general: *the popular vote* □ *The show will be staged for an extra week by popular demand.*

popularity /pɒpjʊˈlærɪtɪ/ *noun* (*uncount*)
Popularity is the quality or state of being liked, admired or enjoyed by many people: *The sport has gained in popularity over the last ten years.* □ *Even after twenty years, his popularity with television and radio audiences is undiminished.*

popularize /ˈpɒpjʊləraɪz/ or **popularise** *verb*: **popularizes, popularizing, popularized**
1 To **popularize** something means to make it interesting to or liked by a lot of people: *She did a lot to popularize the monarchy.* **2** To **popularize** something also means to make it available in an easily understandable form so that it has a wider appeal amongst ordinary people: *His book helped to popularize the new theories about the creation of the universe.*

popularly /ˈpɒpjʊləlɪ/ *adverb*
Popularly means by many or most people: *Louis Armstrong, popularly known as 'Satchmo'* □ *a popularly held belief* □ *It is popularly believed that St Patrick was Irish, though he actually came from Scotland.*

populate /ˈpɒpjʊleɪt/ *verb*: **populates, populating, populated**
1 (*usually in the passive*) If an area or country **is populated** with people or animals, those people or animals live there: *The desert regions are sparsely populated, with only a few nomadic tribes.* **2** If an area or country **is populated** by people or animals, those people or animals move to and settle in that area or country: *The area was first populated by settlers from Europe.* □ *In summer, the beaches are populated with colonies of breeding seals.*

population /pɒpjʊˈleɪʃən/ *noun* (*usually in the singular*): **populations**
1 The **population** of a particular area or country is the number of people that live there: *What is the population of China?* □ *a population of two million.* **2** (*with a singular or plural verb*) A **population** is all the people living in a particular area or country: *More than a third of the country's population lives on or under the poverty line.* □ *The local population objected strongly to the proposed development.* **3** (*with a singular or plural verb*) A **population** is also all the people or animals of a particular type that live in an area: *the immigrant population* □ *the working population* □ *the Gaelic-speaking population* □ *the elephant population of Malawi.*

populous /ˈpɒpjʊləs/ *adjective*
A **populous** region or country has a large number of people living in it.

porcelain /ˈpɔːslɪn/ *noun* (*uncount*)
Porcelain is a hard white substance made by heating a special type of clay. It is used to make cups, plates and ornaments: *The dinner service is made of porcelain.* □ *a porcelain figure* □ *A sale of fine Chinese porcelain.*

porch /pɔːtʃ/ *noun*: **porches**
1 A **porch** is a structure which forms a covered entrance to the doorway of a building such as a house or a church. [see picture at **house**] **2** (*AmE*) A **porch** is the same as a verandah.

porcupine /ˈpɔːkjʊpaɪn/ *noun*: **porcupines**
A **porcupine** is an animal whose body and tail are covered with long, sharp spikes which it uses to protect itself when it is attacked.

pore[1] /pɔː(r)/ *noun*: **pores**
A **pore** is one of the tiny openings in your skin or on the surface of a plant through which liquids can pass: *He was sweating from every pore.*

pore[2] /pɔː(r)/ *verb*: **pores, poring, pored**

> ***phrasal verb***
> If you **pore over** something such as a book you study it with great concentration.

pork /pɔːk/ *noun* (*uncount, often adjectival*)
Pork is the meat from a pig: *We had roast pork with apple sauce.* □ *pork sausages* □ *a pork chop.* [compare **bacon, ham**]

porn /pɔːn/ *noun* (*informal*)
Porn means the same as pornography.

pornography /pɔːˈnɒgrəfɪ/ *noun* (*uncount*)
Pornography is films, pictures or books intended to cause sexual excitement. **Pornography** is offensive to many people because it contains scenes or descriptions of sexual acts. —*adjective* **pornographic** /pɔːnəˈgrafɪk/: *pornographic films* □ *The magazine is pornographic.*

porous /pɔːrəs/ *adjective*
A material that is **porous** allows liquids or gases to pass through it: *The soil in the garden is clay, so I'm adding sand to make it more porous.* □ *porous limestone.*

porpoise /ˈpɔːpəs/ *noun*: **porpoises**
A **porpoise** is an animal that lives in the sea. **Porpoises** are similar to dolphins but have a shorter, rounder nose.

porridge /ˈpɒrɪdʒ/ *noun* (*uncount*)
Porridge is a food made by boiling oatmeal in water or milk until it forms a thick soft mass. **Porridge** is often eaten for breakfast.

port[1] /pɔːt/ *noun*: **ports**
1 (*count or uncount*) A **port** is a place where ships load and unload cargo and passengers, or shelter during stormy weather: *a seaport* □ *a fishing port* □ *ships coming into and leaving port* □ *The naval fleet stayed in port.* [*same as* **harbour**] **2** A **port** is also a town or city on a river or by the sea that has a harbour: *Liverpool is a port.*

port[2] /pɔːt/ *noun* (*uncount, often adjectival*)
Port is the side of a ship or aircraft that is on the left when you are facing the front: *The captain ordered the helmsman to steer hard to port.* □ *a cabin on the port side.* [compare **starboard**]

port[3] /pɔːt/ *noun* (*uncount*)
Port is a type of strong dark red or brownish wine, originally made in Portugal: *a bottle of port.*

portable /ˈpɔːtəbəl/ *adjective*
Something that is **portable** can be carried or moved easily: *a portable typewriter* □ *a portable phone* □ *The thieves made off with everything that was portable.*

portacrib /ˈpɔːtəkrɪb/ *noun* (*AmE*): **portacribs**
A **portacrib** is a carrycot. [see picture at **bedroom**]

portal /ˈpɔːtəl/ *noun*: **portals** (*often used in the plural; literary*)
A **portal** is an entrance, gateway or doorway, especially a large or grand one: *Over the years, many illustrious guests have entered its portals.*

portcullis /pɔːtˈkʌlɪs/ *noun*: **portcullises**
In former times, a **portcullis** was a strong vertical iron or wooden grating that was raised and lowered in a town gateway or castle entrance.

portentous /pɔːˈtɛntəs/ *adjective* (*formal*)
Something that is **portentous** acts as a warning or indication of something that will happen in the future: *portentous events.*

porter /ˈpɔːtə(r)/ *noun*: **porters**
A **porter** is **1** a doorman, caretaker or janitor at a college, office or factory. **2** a person employed to carry luggage at *eg* a railway station or hotel.

portfolio /pɔːtˈfoʊlɪoʊ/ *noun*: **portfolios**
1 A **portfolio** is a flat case for carrying papers or drawings. **2** An artist's or photographer's **portfolio** is a collection of drawings, paintings or photographs that represent his or her work. **3** A set of investments owned by a person or institution is also called a **portfolio**.

porthole /ˈpɔːthoʊl/ *noun*: **portholes**
A **porthole** is a small round window such as is found on the side of a ship or aircraft.

portico /ˈpɔːtɪkoʊ/ *noun*: **porticos** or **porticoes**
A **portico** is a covered area or porch at the entrance to a building with columns supporting the roof.

portion /ˈpɔːʃən/ *noun; verb*
▻ ***noun***: **portions**
1 A **portion** is one of several pieces or parts that something can be divided into: *I'm due to collect my portion of the money tomorrow.* [compare **share**] **2** A **portion** of food is an amount of food served to someone at one time: *Would you like another portion of cheese?* [*same as* **helping, serving**]
▻ ***verb***: **portions, portioning, portioned**

phrasal verb
You **portion** something **out** if you share it out portion by portion: *The building work has been portioned out to several companies.*

portly /ˈpɔːtlɪ/ *adjective* (*rather old*): **portlier, portliest**
If someone, especially a man, is described as **portly**, they have a fat body: *a portly old gentleman.*

portrait /ˈpɔːtrɪt/ or /ˈpɔːtreɪt/ *noun*: **portraits**
1 A **portrait** is a drawing, painting or photograph of a person: *a portrait of the Queen.* □ *Holbein painted many portraits of members of the royal court.* **2** A **portrait** is also a description in words of someone or something: *a portrait of English rural life.*

portray /pɔːˈtreɪ/ *verb*: **portrays, portraying, portrayed**
1 An artist or writer **portrays** someone or something when they produce a picture or written description of that person or thing, often in a particular way: *He portrayed Venice as a busy bustling city.* □ *In the biography, the king was portrayed as bullying and autocratic.* **2** If an actor **portrays** a particular person or emotion in a play or film they act the part of that person or represent that emotion: *He portrayed Henry VIII very convincingly.* □ *She portrayed fear by shrinking back with her hands held up.*

portrayal /pɔːˈtreɪəl/ *noun*: **portrayals**
A **portrayal** is a description or representation of someone or something: *His portrayal of a madman was both convincing and disturbing.* □ *George Eliot's complex and sensitive portrayal of middle England.*

pose /poʊz/ *noun; verb*
▻ ***noun***: **poses**
1 A **pose** is a particular position or way of holding your body: *The portrait painter tried to get him to adopt a relaxed pose.* □ *She was photographed in various poses.* **2** (*derogatory*) A **pose** is also an exaggerated or artificial way of behaving intended to impress or deceive other people: *His concern for their welfare is just a pose.*
▻ ***verb***: **poses, posing, posed**
1 When you **pose** or **are posed** for a photograph or portrait you stay in a particular position while the photograph is being taken or the picture is being painted: *They posed for the camera.* □ *She posed in the nude.* □ *She arranged herself in another pose, her legs tucked under her like a cat.* **2** (*derogatory*) If you say that someone **is posing** you mean that they are behaving in an exaggerated or artificial way in order to impress other people: *He spends his evenings posing in fashionable nightclubs.* **3** If someone **poses** as someone or something, they pretend to be that person or thing in order to deceive other people: *A burglar posing as a delivery man.* **4** (*formal*) You **pose** a question when you ask it. **5** If something **poses** a problem or a threat, it creates or presents that problem or threat: *The railway strike will pose problems for commuters.* □ *Tigers rarely pose any threat to humans.*
▻ ***phrase*** If you **strike a pose** you take up a particular position, especially an impressive one.

poser /ˈpoʊzə(r)/ *noun*: **posers**
1 (*derogatory*) If you call someone a **poser** you think they are putting on an act to try to impress others. **2** (*informal*) You can refer to a puzzle or a problem that is difficult to solve as a **poser**: *That's a bit of a poser!*

posh /pɒʃ/ *adjective* (*informal*)
1 A **posh** place or thing is expensive, smart and stylish: *posh clothes* □ *a posh hotel.* **2** If you say that someone is **posh** you mean that they are upper-class: *She speaks with a posh accent.*

position /pəˈzɪʃən/ *noun; verb*
▻ ***noun***: **positions**
1 A **position** is a place where something or someone is: *From his position at the back of the room, he could watch the audience's reactions.* □ *The position of the footprints led him to conclude that someone had jumped out of the window.* □ *Plant the shrub in a sunny position.* [*same as* **location**] **2** A **position** is also something's correct or usual place: *He put the clock back in position on top of the mantelpiece.* □ *The block of stone had slipped out of position.* **3** A **position** is a way of sitting, standing, lying, facing, being held or placed: *He was lying in an awkward position.* **4** A place that is occupied by soldiers and used as a base for attacking or defending themselves against an enemy is also called a **position**: *They captured the enemy position on the hillside.* □ *a defensive position.* **5** Your **position** on an issue is your opinion or viewpoint: *What's the party's position on law and order?* □ *I take the position that all drivers should be banned from residential areas.* **6** A **position** is a job or post: *He holds a senior position at the bank.* □ *She got a new position as governess to the duke's children.* **7** Your **position** in society is your rank, status or importance in society: *He has wealth and position.* □ *He has a position to uphold.* **8** Someone's place in the finishing order or at an ear-

lier stage in a contest is their **position**: *The British driver is lying in fourth position.* **9** In team games, such as football, hockey and rugby, a player's **position** is the place on the pitch where they begin play from: *the centre-forward position* □ *a position in mid-field.*
10 A **position** is also the situation you are in at a particular time: *They are not in a position to help.* □ *Their financial position is a little precarious.*
▻ ***verb***: **positions, positioning, positioned**
If you **position** something or **position** it somewhere, you place it or put it somewhere: *The policeman positioned himself outside the door.* □ *She positioned the desk so that the light would fall on it.*
▻ ***phrases*** **1** When you say that someone is **in a position** to do something, you mean that they are able to do it: *He's in a position to buy the company outright.* **2** If you say that someone is **in no position** to do something, you mean that they are not able to do it or have no right to do it: *She doesn't take any exercise so she's in no position to criticize me.*

positive /ˈpɒzɪtɪv/ *adjective*
1 If you are **positive** about something, you are completely sure or certain about it: *I'm positive I locked the door.* □ (*used as an answer*) *'Are you sure you won't have another cake?' 'Positive.'* **2** Something that is **positive** is definite and cannot be doubted: *The police have positive proof of her guilt.* □ *They don't have a positive identification yet.* **3** A **positive** response or reply shows or expresses agreement, approval or encouragement. [*opposite* **negative**] **4** If you have a **positive** attitude to things, you are confident or hopeful that things will turn out well: *She's feeling a bit more positive now.* [*opposite* **negative**] **5** A **positive** action or a **positive** decision is one that deals with a task or problem in a practical or constructive way: *a positive suggestion.* [*opposite* **negative**] **6** **Positive** qualities or values are good ones that help or improve life or society. [*opposite* **negative**] **7** **Positive** instructions are clear and easily understood: *positive directions.* **8** (*informal; intensifying*) You can use **positive** before a noun to mean 'complete' or 'real': *It's a positive scandal that she wasn't given the proper treatment.* □ *She takes positive pleasure in seeing him suffer.* **9** If a result of a chemical test is **positive**, it confirms that a particular substance is present: *The pregnancy test was positive.* [*opposite* **negative**] **10** **Positive** is used to refer to quantities that are greater than zero: *ten is a positive number.* [*opposite* **negative**] **11** (*grammar*) **Positive** is used to indicate that an adjective or adverb is in a simple form as distinct from the comparative or superlative forms: *'Bad' is the positive form of the adjective, 'worse' is the comparative form, and 'worst' is the superlative form.*

positively /ˈpɒzɪtɪvlɪ/ *adverb*
1 (*intensifying*) **Positively** means 'absolutely' or 'extremely': *He was positively livid.* [=extremely angry] **2** (*sentence adverb*) You use **positively** when you want to emphasize that you really mean what you say: *This is positively the last time that I will lend you money.*

possess /pəˈzɛs/ *verb*: **possesses, possessing, possessed**
1 To **possess** means to have or to own: *She gave everything she possessed to the poor.* □ *He possesses several Picassos and a Degas.* **2** If you are **possessed** by an emotion, feeling or evil spirit, that emotion, feeling or spirit controls your actions: *They believed that she was possessed by the devil.* □ *What possessed you to behave like that?*

possession /pəˈzɛʃən/ *noun*: **possessions**
1 (*uncount*) **Possession** is the condition of having, holding or owning something: *Important new evidence has come into my possession.* □ *When her parents died she found herself in possession of a large fortune.* □ *My solicitor is in possession of all the relevant facts.* □ *He took possession of the property the following week.* **2** (*uncount*) **Possession** is the crime of having or holding something illegally: *He was charged with possession of firearms.* □ *possession of illegal drugs.* **3** (*uncount*) In football, **possession** is the control of the ball by one or other team in a match: *The German team had possession for most of the match.* **4** A **possession** is something that is owned: *He was ordered to pack up all his possessions and move out.* □ *personal possessions.* **5** A country's **possessions** are other countries or regions that it governs or controls: *India was one of Britain's former colonial possessions.*

possessive /pəˈzɛsɪv/ *adjective; noun*
▻ ***adjective***
1 If you are **possessive** about things that you own, you are unwilling to share them or allow them to be used by other people: *I'm possessive about my car.* **2** If someone is **possessive** about another person, they want all that person's attention and love and get upset or jealous if they give attention or love to anybody else: *a possessive husband.* **3** (*grammar*) **Possessive** is used to describe words that show who or what a person or thing belongs to; the **possessive** determiners are *my, your, his, her, its, our, their*, and the **possessive** pronouns are *mine, yours, his, hers, its, ours* and *theirs.* 'Robert's' is the **possessive** form of 'Robert'. [see also **personal pronoun**]: *a possessive pronoun.*
▻ ***noun*** (*uncount; grammar*)
The **possessive** is the possessive form of a word. — *adverb* **possessively:** *The little boy clung possessively to his teddy bear.* — *noun* (*uncount*) **possessiveness:** *His possessiveness is driving her mad.*

possessor /pəˈzɛsə(r)/ *noun* (*usually in the singular; formal*): **possessors**
A **possessor** is a person who has or owns something: *He is the possessor of extensive estates.*

possibility /pɒsɪˈbɪlɪtɪ/ *noun*: **possibilities**
1 (*count or uncount*) There is a **possibility** that something is so, or a **possibility** of it happening, if it may be so, or may happen: *We should consider the possibility that he may still be alive.* □ *There's no possibility of my being appointed.* □ *The Sheikh dismissed any possibility of an exchange of hostages.* [compare **probability**] **2** Something that may happen is a **possibility**: *A Spring election is a possibility.* [*opposite* **impossibility**] **3** The **possibility** of doing a certain thing is an option that is available to you: *He'd never thought about the possibility of going to university.* □ *Creating an extra room by building a partition is certainly one possibility.* □ *The advent of youth hostels meant that holidays in the countryside became a possibility for thousands previously denied them.* **4** (*uncount*) Something described as being within the realms or bounds of **possibility** could happen, be done, or be true: *Such a thing is not beyond the bounds of possibility.* **5** (*used in the plural*) Someone or something that has **possibilities** has the potential for successful development: *Celia saw at once that the place had possibilities.*

possible /ˈpɒsɪbəl/ *adjective; noun*
▻ ***adjective***
1 a Something that is **possible** can be done or managed, or can happen, or can be the case: *The 1980 Act made it possible for parents to send their children to a school of their choice.* □ *Would it be possible to deliver the furniture on Saturday?* □ *Increased wealth makes possible a more relaxed attitude to work.* □ *She hadn't known it was possible to feel so frightened.* □ *In the context the word has two possible meanings.* □ *Either the fifth or the seventh of April would be possible for me.*

[*opposite* **impossible**] **b** You use **possible** in place of a whole clause in several constructions: *They've done everything possible* [= everything they can] *to make me feel welcome.* □ *Where possible* [= wherever you can] *give your answers in decimal form.* □ *Avoid using stereotyped ideas if possible.* [= if you can] □ *Rest your legs whenever possible .* □ *I want to get pregnant again as soon as possible.* □ *We're arranging for the best possible care.* □ *The enlargement of the EC has come at the worst possible time as far as the global economy is concerned.* □ *We have the clearest possible evidence that this actually happened.*

2 Something that is **possible a** may happen: *It's possible that we'll see a further slowing of the ageing process.* □ *They report on the possible effects on the earth of the warming-up of its atmosphere.* **b** may be the case, or may be true or correct: *It's quite possible that I was wrong.* □ *There are other possible explanations.* [*opposite* **impossible**; compare **probable**]

3 A **possible** *eg* manager or organizer is someone who can be selected for the role, or might volunteer for it; a **possible** troublemaker is someone who might cause trouble: *The expedition leaders are now looking round for possible sponsors.* [compare **probable**] **4** You use **possible** in expressing amazement, disbelief or horror at something: *What possible excuse can he have for such behaviour?*

▻ ***noun***: **possibles**

You describe someone or something as a **possible** if you think they are suitable for selection for some purpose: *Mr Dickie is one of the possibles for the 3.0'clock race.* □ *She was top of my list of possibles for the job.*

possibly /ˈpɒsɪblɪ/ *adverb*

1 (*sentence adverb*) **Possibly** is used like *perhaps*: *Something had moved out there in the trees, possibly a bird.* □ *That was possibly her best-ever performance.* □ *'Are you thinking of going into town?' 'Possibly.'* □ *'This isn't the quickest way.' 'Possibly not, but it's the safest.'* [compare **probably**]

2 You use **possibly** with *can* and *could* **a** to make polite requests: *Could I possibly have a word with you?* □ *Could you possibly make less noise?* **b** in wondering whether something is likely: *Could there possibly be a link between them?* □ *He couldn't possibly still be alive.* □ *So Sir Thomas could not possibly have committed suicide.* □ *The thing can't possibly exist.* **c** in talking about what can or cannot be done, managed or expected: *We can't possibly get there by nightfall.* □ *I couldn't possibly do what you ask.* □ *I've kept the bill as low as I possibly can, Miss Glover.* □ *And if I possibly can, I'm going to stop you wrecking his life.* □ *Do everything you possibly can to avoid a delay.* **d** to express amazement, disbelief or horror at something: *Who could possibly have told him?* □ *How can that possibly have any useful effect?* □ *What could a ten-year-old boy possibly have against me?* □ *How can people possibly not know which party they support?*

post[1] /poʊst/ *noun*: **posts**

1 A **post** is a piece of wood or metal fixed upright in the ground as *eg* a support or marker: *fence posts* □ *a gate post.* **2** (*singular*) The place where a race starts and finishes is also called the **post**: *the winning-post* □ *The horses assembled at the starting-post.*

▻ ***phrases*** **1** For **from pillar to post** see **pillar**. **2** For **pip somebody at the post** see **pip**.

post[2] /poʊst/ *noun*; *verb* **posts**

▻ ***noun***:

1 A **post** is a job or position of paid employment in a company or organization: *a teaching post* □ *He resigned from his post as sales manager.* □ *He was given a post in the new government.* **2** A **post** is also a place where a person, especially a member of the armed services, is on duty: *The sentry never left his post.* **3** A place occupied and defended by soldiers or a settlement in an remote area is also called a **post**: *a frontier post* □ *a trading post in the Yukon.*

▻ ***verb***: **posts, posting, posted**

If someone **is posted** somewhere, they are sent there by the organization that they work for to take up a job or a responsibility: *The officer was posted to the general's staff.* □ *The diplomat was posted to the embassy in Paris.*

post[3] /poʊst/ *noun*; *verb*

▻ ***noun***: **posts**

1 (*uncount*) The **post** is the official system for collecting and delivering letters and parcels: *The documents are in the post.* □ *Your order will reach you by post within 28 days.* □ *The parcel was lost in the post.* **2** (*uncount*; *in the singular*) The **post** is all the letters and parcels delivered to a single address or individual: *Was there any post for me this morning?* □ *His secretary opens all his post.* **3** A **post** is any of the regular collections and deliveries of letters and parcels: *I want the letter finished in time to catch the next post.* □ *The cheque will probably arrive by the second post.* □ *How many posts are there on a Saturday?* **4** (*used in the singular*) If you take a letter or parcel to the **post** you take it to a place where letters and parcels are collected, such as a postbox or post office.

[*same as* **mail**]

▻ ***verb***: **posts, posting, posted**

You **post** a letter or parcel when you send it by post: *Could you post this letter for me?* □ *The letter was posted in London.* □ *If you aren't able to collect the documents they can be posted to you.* [*same as* **mail**]

▻ ***phrase*** If you **keep** someone **posted** you keep them informed about a situation by giving them the latest news or details of any developments: *He asked them to keep him posted about the planning application.*

post- /poʊst/ *prefix*

Post- is used before nouns, adjectives and verbs to mean 'after': *postgraduate* □ *the postwar government* □ *a post-industrial society* □ *postdate.* [compare **ante-**, **pre-**]

postage /ˈpoʊstɪdʒ/ *noun* (*uncount*)

Postage is the amount that you must pay to send a letter or parcel through the post: *A small additional charge will be made for postage and packing.* □ *What will the postage be if I send this letter by airmail?*

postage stamp /ˈpoʊstɪdʒ stamp/ *noun*: **postage stamps**

A **postage stamp** is a small printed label stuck on a letter or parcel showing that the postage has been paid. [see also **stamp**]

postal /ˈpoʊstəl/ *adjective*

Postal means **a** of or relating to the post office or the public service of collecting and delivering letters and parcels: *postal charges* □ *postal workers.* **b** sent by post: *a postal vote* □ *Postal applications should be received not later than 30th March.*

postal code /ˈpoʊstəl koʊd/ *noun*: **postal codes**

A **postal code** is a postcode.

postal order /ˈpoʊstəl ɔːdə(r)/ *noun*: **postal orders**

A **postal order** is a piece of paper that you can buy at a post office that represents a certain sum of money. A postal order is a safe way of sending money through the post and can be cashed at a post office by the person to whom it is sent.

postbag /ˈpoʊstbag/ *noun*: **postbags**

1 A **postbag** is a bag used by a postman to carry letters and small parcels. **2** The collection of letters received at a particular time by *eg* a radio or television programme, magazine, or public figure is often referred to as their **postbag**. [*same as* **mailbag**]

postbox /ˈpoustbɒks/ *noun*: **postboxes**
A **postbox** is a box in a public place where letters can be posted. [see also **letter box, pillar box**]

postcard /ˈpoustkɑːd/ *noun*: **postcards**
A **postcard** is a card for writing messages on, often with a picture on one side, designed for sending through the post without an envelope: *We'll send you a postcard when we get to Australia.*

postcode /ˈpoustkoud/ *noun*: **postcodes**
A **postcode** is a special series of letters and numbers which you add at the end of an address and which helps the post office to sort letters and parcels. [see also **zip code**]

poster /ˈpoustə(r)/ *noun*: **posters**
1 A **poster** is a large notice displayed in a public place and often advertising something: *a theatre poster* □ *a poster campaign by the Conservative party.* **2** A **poster** is also a large printed picture: *Her bedroom wall was covered in posters.*

posterity /pɒˈsterɪtɪ/ *noun* (*uncount; formal*)
Posterity is the future and all the people, such as your children and grandchildren, who will be living then: *The works of art should be preserved for posterity.*

postgraduate /poustˈgradjuːət/ *noun; adjective*
▻ ***noun***: **postgraduates**
A **postgraduate** is a person who has obtained a first degree at a university and is studying or doing research for an advanced degree or qualification.
▻ ***adjective:*** *postgraduate students* □ *postgraduate studies.*
[compare **graduate, undergraduate**]

posthumous /ˈpɒstjʊməs/ *adjective*
Posthumous refers to something that happens or is given after a person's death: *a posthumous pardon* □ *a posthumous award for bravery.* — *adverb* **posthumously:** *Samuel Butler's autobiographical novel 'The Way of All Flesh' was published posthumously in 1903.*

postman /ˈpoustmən/ *noun*: **postmen**
A **postman** is a person whose job is to collect and deliver letters and parcels. [compare **mailman**]

postmark /ˈpoustmɑːk/ *noun*: **postmarks**
A **postmark** is a mark printed on a letter or parcel by the post office showing the date and place of posting.

postmaster /ˈpoustmɑːstə(r)/ *noun* (*old*): **postmasters**
A **postmaster** is a man in charge of a post office.

postmistress /ˈpoustmɪstrɪs/ *noun* (*old*): **postmistresses**
A **postmistress** is a woman in charge of a post office.

post mortem /poustˈmɔːtəm/ *noun*: **post mortems**
A **post mortem** is a medical examination of a dead person to find out the cause of their death. [*same as* **autopsy**]

post office /ˈpoust ɒfɪs/ *noun*: **post offices**
1 A **post office** is a building or part of a shop where you can post letters and parcels, buy stamps, and use various other postal services. **2** The **Post Office** is the public department or national organization in charge of postal services.

postpone /poustˈpoun/ *verb*: **postpones, postponing, postponed**
You **postpone** something when you arrange for it to happen at a later time than the time you had originally planned: *We will have to postpone the meeting until next week.* □ *The flight was postponed because of high winds.* □ *The concert hasn't been cancelled, it has just been postponed.*

postponement /pəstˈpounmənt/ *noun* (*uncount or count*): **postponements**
Postponement is the act of putting something off until a later time: *He announced the postponement of the concert.* □ *flights were severally disrupted with many cancellations and postponements.*

postscript /ˈpoustskrɪpt/ *noun*: **postscripts**
A **postscript** is a short message written at the end of a letter after the writer's signature. The message usually begins with the abbreviation 'PS': *She ended her letter with a postscript letting him know that she would be in New York for a fortnight.* □ *PS, can you send me some money?*

posture /ˈpɒstʃə(r)/ *noun; verb*
▻ ***noun***: **postures**
1 (*uncount*) Your **posture** is the way in which you stand, sit or walk: *A fashion model must have good posture.* □ *Bad posture often leads to backache.* **2** A particular position or attitude of the body can be referred to as a **posture**: *He had been sitting in an awkward posture.* □ *She was photographed in a reclining posture.* **3** A **posture** is also an attitude that you have towards a particular issue: *The government has adopted a more liberal posture on immigration.*
▻ ***verb*** (*derogatory*): **postures, posturing, postured**
When you say that someone **is posturing** you mean that they are talking or behaving in an insincere or artificial way in order to create a particular impression: *The Tories are posturing when it comes to the Maastricht agreement.*

postwar /poustˈwɔː(r)/ *adjective*
Postwar means of or belonging to the period following a war, especially the Second World War from 1939-45: *postwar rationing* □ *postwar housing.*

posy /ˈpouzɪ/ *noun*: **posies**
A **posy** is a small bunch of flowers: *The bridesmaids carried posies of violets.*

pot /pɒt/ *noun; verb*
▻ ***noun***: **pots**
1 A **pot** is a deep round container used for cooking: *pots and pans* □ *a soup pot.* **2** A **pot** is also any of various round containers used for a particular purpose: *a paint pot* □ *a flowerpot* □ *a teapot* □ *a pot for jam.* **3** A **pot** is the amount held by such a container: *a pot of tea* □ *a pot of honey.*
▻ ***verb***: **pots, potting, potted**
You **pot** a plant when you put it into a flowerpot or plant pot filled with earth so that it can grow there.
▻ ***phrase*** (*informal*) If you say that something has **gone to pot** you mean that it has been spoilt or ruined.

potato /pəˈteɪtou/ *noun* (*uncount or count*): **potatoes**
A **potato** is a round white or yellowish vegetable with a brown, yellow or red skin. **Potatoes** grow underground: *meat and potatoes* □ *mashed potato* □ *roast potatoes.* [see picture at **vegetable**]

potent /ˈpoutənt/ *adjective*
1 Something that is **potent** is strong and powerful: *a potent argument* □ *a potent weapon.* **2** A **potent** drug or poison has a very strong effect: *a potent mixture.* **3** A man who is **potent** is capable of sexual intercourse. — *noun* **potency** (*uncount*) /ˈpoutənsɪ/: *Scientists are carrying out tests to measure the potency of the drug.*

potential /pəˈtɛnʃəl/ *adjective; noun*
▻ ***adjective***
Potential is used to describe something that is possible, or capable of developing into or being developed into a particular thing: *a potential health hazard* □ *The*

book is a potential bestseller. □ *He has been identified by the media as a potential cabinet minister.* □ *a potential source of renewable energy.*

▻ ***noun*** (*uncount*)

Potential is the range of qualities that a person or thing has that can be developed: *He will have to be encouraged if he is going to fulfil his potential.* □ *She has the potential to be a great singer.* □ *He bought the land because he could see that it had development potential.* — *adverb* **potentially:** *a potentially explosive mixture.*

pothole /ˈpɒthoʊl/ *noun*: **potholes**
1 A **pothole** is a hole in the surface of a road caused by the constant movement of traffic: *The road was full of potholes.* **2** A **pothole** is a cave or deep hole that has been created by water wearing away soft rock such as limestone.

potion /ˈpoʊʃən/ *noun*: **potions**
A **potion** is a drink containing medicine, poison or some substance that is supposed to have magic powers.

pot plant /ˈpɒt plɑːnt/ *noun*: **pot plants**
Pot plants are plants grown indoors in containers. [see picture at **living room**]

potter¹ /ˈpɒtə(r)/ *noun*: **potters**
A **potter** is a person who makes pottery.

potter² /ˈpɒtə(r)/ *verb*: **potters, pottering, pottered**
1 If you **potter** about, you do various small unimportant jobs: *He was pottering about in the garden.* **2** If something **potters** along, it travels or progresses in an unhurried way: *We're going to potter down to the pub.*

pottery /ˈpɒtərɪ/ *noun* (*uncount or count*): **potteries**
1 (*often adjectival*) **Pottery** is containers and other objects made of baked clay: *a pottery jug* □ *The shop sells pottery figures and other bric-à-brac.* **2** (*often adjectival*) **Pottery** is the art of making such objects: *a pottery class.* **3** A **pottery** is a factory or workshop where such objects are made: *the local pottery.*

potty¹ /ˈpɒtɪ/ *adjective* (*informal*): **pottier, pottiest**
1 If you say that someone is **potty** you mean that they are mad or crazy: *He's quite potty, you know.* □ *That idea is completely potty.* **2** If someone is **potty** about someone or something they love or like that person or thing very much: *He's potty about her.* □ *She's potty about horses.*

potty² /ˈpɒtɪ/ *noun* (*informal*): **potties**
A **potty** is a deep usually plastic pot that a small child uses as a toilet.

pouch /paʊtʃ/ *noun*: **pouches**
1 Kangaroos and some other animals have a pocket of skin called a **pouch** on the lower part of their bodies that they use to carry their babies in. **2** A **pouch** is also the name given to the fold of flesh on each side of *eg* a hamster's mouth that it uses for storing food.

poultry /ˈpoʊltrɪ/ *noun*
1 (*plural*) **Poultry** are birds such as hens, ducks or geese that are kept for their eggs or meat. **2** (*uncount*) **Poultry** is the meat of these birds.

pounce /paʊns/ *verb*: **pounces, pouncing, pounced**
1 If an animal **pounces**, it leaps or jumps suddenly in order to attack or catch hold of something: *The lioness crouched in the long grass, ready to pounce.* □ *The kitten pounced on the mouse and tossed it into the air.* □ *The burglars were pounced on by the police as soon as they came out of the house.* **2** If someone **pounces** on something, such as a mistake or fault, they point it out or find it very quickly: *The defence lawyer pounced on the apparent inconsistency in her evidence.*

pound¹ /paʊnd/ *noun*: **pounds**
1 The **pound** or **pound sterling** is the standard unit of currency used in the United Kingdom. One pound is divided into 100 pence: *It costs a pound.* □ *He lent me ten pounds.* □ *a ten-pound note* □ *devaluation of the pound.* **2** The **pound** is also the standard unit of currency used in several other countries, *eg* Malta, Cyprus, Egypt and Ireland. **3** A **pound** is also a measure of weight used in Britain, America and some other countries. One pound is equal to 16 ounces or 453 grammes: *two pounds of carrots* □ *She lost forty pounds on the new diet.*

pound² /paʊnd/ *verb*: **pounds, pounding, pounded**
1 If you **pound** something, or **pound** on or at it, you hit or strike it heavily and repeatedly: *He was pounding his opponent with his fists.* □ *He had been pounding at the door for fifteen minutes before someone answered it.* **2** If you **pound** something out, you produce it or cause it to be produced by repeatedly hitting or striking something: *The drummers were pounding out the beat with wooden hammers.* □ *She pounded out articles on her typewriter.* **3** To **pound** also means to walk or run with heavy thudding steps: *He came pounding along the road.* **4** If you **pound** something, such as grain, you crush or grind it into a powder: *The ship was being pounded against the rocks*

pour /pɔː(r)/ *verb*: **pours, pouring, poured**
1 If a liquid **pours** or **is poured**, it flows or is made to flow, especially downwards, in a continuous stream: *Sweat was pouring down his face.* □ *Rainwater poured over the edge of the blocked gutter.* **2** If a container such as a jug **pours** in a certain way, it allows liquid to flow out of it in that way: *The teapot doesn't pour very well.* **3** If you **pour** someone a drink, you serve them a drink by pouring it out of a bottle into a glass: *Can I pour you a drink?* □ *Would you pour me a glass of wine, please.* **4** (*informal*) If you say it **is pouring**, or it is **pouring down**, you mean it is raining heavily: *Take an umbrella; it's pouring outside.* □ *It poured down all through the match.* **5** If people or animals **pour** in or out of somewhere, they come into or go out of a place in large numbers: *people pouring out of the cinema* □ *The rats came pouring out of every nook and cranny when the piper began to play.* **6** To **pour** also means to flow or be produced in large quantities or in a continuous stream: *Donations poured in.* □ *Words poured from her pen.* **7** If you **pour** out your feelings, you express or reveal them without hesitating: *All of a sudden, there she was, pouring out her troubles to me as if I was her closest friend.* **8** If you **pour** something into something else, you put a large amount of it in: *They had to pour money into the business to keep it afloat.* □ *She poured all her energies into the performance.*

pout /paʊt/ *verb*; *noun*

▻ ***verb***: **pouts, pouting, pouted**

When someone **pouts** they push their lips or their lower lip forward, as a sign that they are annoyed or as a means of looking sexually attractive: *When she was told off, the little girl pouted.* □ *The film star posed and pouted for the cameras.*

▻ ***noun***: **pouts**

A **pout** is the action of pouting or a pouting expression: *She wore a sullen pout.*

poverty /ˈpɒvətɪ/ *noun* (*uncount*)
1 Poverty is the state of being poor: *They lived in extreme poverty.* **2 Poverty** also means poor quality or the state of being inferior: *The poverty of the soil meant they could grow only the hardiest crops.* **3** (*uncount or used in the singular; formal*) **Poverty** or a **poverty** of something is scarcity or lack of that thing: *Their policies display a desperate poverty of new ideas.*

poverty-stricken /ˈpɒvətɪ strɪkən/ *adjective*
If you are **poverty-stricken** you are suffering because you have very little money: *poverty-stricken students* □ *The peasants were poverty-stricken.*

powder /ˈpaʊdə(r)/ *noun; verb*
▻ ***noun*: powders**
1 (*uncount or count*) A **powder** is any dry substance in the form of very small dust-like particles or grains: *a white powder* □ *The spices were ground to a fine powder.* □ *The snow was like powder.* **2** (*uncount*) **Powder** is a cosmetic patted on to the skin to give it a soft, smooth appearance: *face powder* □ *She uses lipstick and a little powder.* **3** (*uncount*) **Powder** is also talcum powder.
▻ ***verb*: powders, powdering, powdered**
If you **powder** your face or body, you apply face powder or talcum powder to it: *She powdered her nose.* □ *The baby has been bathed and powdered.* — *adjective* **powdered:** *a powdered wig* □ *powdered milk.* [=milk that has been dried and made into powder]

power /paʊə(r)/ *noun; adjective; verb*
▻ ***noun*: powers**
1 a (*uncount*) Someone or something that has **power** is able to control people and what they do: *Within our society, power is in the hands of a few individuals.* □ *power-hungry people who enjoy ordering others around* □ *It was one of several attempts to undermine the power of the Prime Minister.* □ *It's amazing, the power that a tiny baby exercises over its parents.* □ *the power of love to make a fool of a man.* **b** (*uncount*) Groups that have **power** within a society can influence the way it it is run and organized: *the feminist threat to male power* □ *the shift of power to students.* **c** (*uncount*) A political party or person takes **power** or comes to **power** when they take charge of the government of a country; they are in **power** while they are governing it; they fall from **power** when they are defeated and another party or person takes charge: *On returning to power in 1979, the Conservatives began to reduce spending in the public sector.* □ *The Communist Khmer Rouge took power in 1975.* □ *After Kruschev's fall from power in 1964, the atmosphere was calmer.* **d** (*count or uncount*) Someone in authority has the **power** to do something if they have the legal right to do it: *The courts have no power to order anyone to give evidence.* □ *The 1967 Act conferred power to release a life prisoner on the Secretary of State.* □ *The prime minister has the power to instruct the Civil Service on the conduct of its task.* □ *The use of police powers may actually provoke incidents.* [compare **right**, **authority**]
2 a Your physical and mental **powers** are your physical and mental abilities and faculties: *Whales have excellent powers of hearing.* □ *Her understanding and powers of reasoning may be reduced.* □ *I lost the power to concentrate.* □ *people with remarkable powers of endurance.* [compare **ability**, **faculty**, **capacity**] **b** Things may have certain **powers**: *plants with healing powers* □ *the power of poetry to stimulate thought.* **c** (*uncount*) People do everything in their **power** to achieve something when they do everything they possibly can to achieve it: *Pogo never refused any of her requests if it was within his power to satisfy her.* □ *We're doing everything in our power to get the hostages released.* □ *She's done everything in her power to stir up trouble.*
3 a (*uncount*) Military **power** is the possession of powerful weapons and a strong successful army; naval **power** or sea **power** is the possession of a strong successful navy. **b** A **power** is a state that has military strength and an influential role in world affairs: *Britain and other former colonial powers* □ *alliances between Third-World countries and the Western powers* □ *Spain failed to take advantage of her position as a naval power to establish political control over her vast empire.* **c** (*usually in the singular*) A person who is referred to as *eg* the real **power**, or the **power** behind someone or something, is the person who really controls things: *Richelieu was the real power behind the French throne.*
4 a (*uncount*) **Power** is physical energy or force: *She was wrenched from the rock by the power of the water.* [*same as* **force**, **strength**] **b** (*uncount*) **Power** is energy obtained from various sources or by various means, *eg* by burning fuel, for producing heat and light, and running machinery: *electrical power* □ *nuclear power* □ *This is one area where solar power could help.* □ *She realized the engine was losing power.* [compare **energy**] **c** (*uncount*) You refer to electricity as **power**: *Check the wiring of your device before connecting it to the power supply.* □ *Switch off the power before cleaning the machine.* □ *Tonight's power failure has left whole districts without heat or light.*
▻ ***adjective***
A **power** tool is one that is driven by mechanical or electrical power: *Have you used a power drill before?*
▻ ***verb*: powers, powering, powered**
1 A machine that **is powered** by a certain type of energy works or runs by means of it: *Two million car-owners use vehicles powered by sugar-cane alcohol.* [*same as* **fuel**] **2** (*informal*) A person or vehicle **powers** somewhere when they move there fast: *I looked back as we powered away up the hill.*
▻ ***phrases*** **1** (*informal*) Something such as a drink or a holiday **does you a power of good** if you feel much better after it: *It's whisky, and it's doing me a power of good.* **2** You use **the powers that be** to refer vaguely to the people who have control or authority, *eg* the government of a country or the management of a business.

power cut /ˈpaʊə(r) kʌt/ *noun*: **power cuts**
A **power cut** is a break in the electricity supply.

powerful /ˈpaʊəfʊl/ *adjective*
1 Someone who is **powerful** is able to control or influence other people or events: *a powerful ruler* □ *The government believed that the trade unions had become too powerful.* □ *You have made a powerful enemy.* **2** If something is **powerful** it is very strong: *The hyena has powerful jaws for chewing and crushing bones.* □ *a powerful smell* □ *The explosion was so powerful it blew the roof off the house.* — *adverb* **powerfully:** *His breath smelt powerfully of garlic.* □ *a powerfully-built athlete.*

powerless /ˈpaʊələs/ *adjective*
1 Someone is **powerless** to do something when they are completely unable to do it: *She stood by, powerless to prevent the soldiers dragging away her husband.* **2 Powerless** also means having no power to control or influence other people or events: *a powerless head of state.* — *noun* (*uncount*) **powerlessness:** *the powerlessness of a lone protestor.*

power station /ˈpaʊəsteɪʃən/ *noun*: **power stations**
A **power station** is a place where electricity is generated [=made]: *a nuclear power station.*

practicable /ˈpraktɪkəbəl/ *adjective* (*formal*)
Something that is **practicable** can be done, used or successfully carried out: *a practicable scheme* □ *His suggestion may be imaginative, but I'm afraid it just isn't practicable.* [*same as* **workable**; *opposite* **impracticable**]

practical /ˈpraktɪkəl/ *adjective; noun*
▻ ***adjective***
1 Practical means concerned with action with some purpose or result rather than ideas or theory: *You*

should put your knowledge to some practical use. [compare **theoretical**] **2** If something is **practical**, it is very useful, especially for a particular purpose: *practical ideas* □ *Those shoes aren't very practical for gardening.* [*opposite* **impractical**] **3** A **practical** person is someone who makes sensible decisions and is good at dealing with problems. [*opposite* **impractical**] **4** A **practical** person is also someone that is good at doing manual jobs: *I'm not very practical; I can't even change a light bulb.* [*opposite* **impractical**]

▻ ***noun***: **practicals**

A **practical** is a lesson or examination in which you make things or do things rather than write or talk about them: *He has a chemistry practical this morning.*

practicality /praktɪ'kalɪtɪ/ *noun*: **practicalities**

1 (*uncount*) **Practicality** is the quality or state of being sensible and realistic: *They were concerned about the practicality of such a complicated scheme.* **2** (*usually in the plural*) The **practicalities** of a scheme or situation are the practical matters associated with it rather than ideas: *His proposal seems all right in theory, but we should discuss the practicalities before we adopt it as official company policy.*

practical joke /praktɪkəl 'dʒoʊk/ *noun*: **practical jokes**

A **practical joke** is a trick played on someone which involves doing something that will make them look silly: *She tied his shoe laces together as a practical joke.*

practically /'praktɪklɪ/ *adverb*

1 Practically means 'almost' or 'very nearly': *During their summer holiday, the sun shone practically every day.* □ *She practically begged him for a job.* □ *Crimes of violence are practically unknown in the remote villages.* **2 Practically** also means in a practical manner: *They solved the problem very practically.*

practice (*AmE* also **practise**) /'praktɪs/ *noun*: **practices**

1 (*uncount*) **Practice** is the actual process of doing things, as distinct from theory and reasoning; you put ideas and theories into **practice** when you try them to see if they work: *Difficulties are bound to emerge when the reforms are put into practice.* □ *put one's ideas into practice.* **2** (*uncount or count*) A habit, custom, or something that is done regularly is a **practice**: *I'll pay this time, as long as you don't make a regular practice of leaving your purse at home* □ *Saving money this way is accepted business practice.* □ *The binding of women's feet was a common practice in China until quite recently.* **3** (*uncount or count*) **Practice** is also regularly repeated exercise to improve your technique or skill in something, such as an art or sport: *To play the violin well requires a lot of practice.* □ *She does an hour's practice every evening.* □ *There's a football practice on Wednesday.* **4** (*uncount*) The work done by doctors or lawyers is referred to as the **practice** of medicine or the law: *He has been in practice since 1965.* **5** The place where a doctor or lawyer, or a group of doctors or lawyers, do their work is called a **practice**: *a group practice* □ *His practice is in Churchill Street.* □ *a country practice.* **6** (*uncount*) The **practice** of a religion is the particular activities associated with that religion.

▻ ***phrase***

1 a What happens **in practice** is what actually happens, as distinct from what ought to happen, *eg* in theory, or according to the rules: *You've supposed to sign when you borrow the key; in practice hardly anyone does.* **b** If you keep **in practice**, you spend a lot of time practising something so that you maintain a certain level of skill at it. **2** If you say you are **out of practice** in doing something, you mean that you cannot do it as well as you used to because you have not spent time practising it.

practise (*AmE* also **practice**) /'praktɪs/ *verb*: **practises, practising, practised**

1 If you **practise** something, you keep doing it regularly in order to improve your skill or technique: *He practised several tunes.* □ *She's been practising her speech for weeks.* **2** When people **practise** something such as a religion, they take part in the activities associated with it: *She practises witchcraft.* □ *They weren't allowed to practise their religion openly.* **3** When something **is practised** by a person or group of people, they do it regularly as a habit or custom: *Circumcision is practised for reasons of religion or hygiene by many groups and races around the world.* **4** To **practise** means to work as a doctor or lawyer: *He practises in an inner-city area.*

practised (*AmE* **practiced**) /'praktɪst/ *adjective*

Someone who is **practised** at doing something is expert at doing it because they have had a lot of experience: *He is a practised performer in front of the television cameras.* □ *a practised liar.*

practitioner /prak'tɪʃənə(r)/ *noun* (*formal*): **practitioners**

A **practitioner** is a person who works at a profession, especially the medical profession. [see also **general practitioner**]

pragmatic /prag'matɪk/ *adjective* (*formal*)

A **pragmatic** approach to dealing with something is concerned with what is sensible and realistic in the actual circumstances rather than following a principle or theory: *a pragmatic solution* □ *Though she was a Roman Catholic, Mary, Queen of Scots, adopted a pragmatic approach to the reformed church in Scotland.* — *adverb* **pragmatically** *The problem needs to be approached pragmatically.*

pragmatism /'pragmətɪzm/ *noun* (*uncount; formal*)

Pragmatism is thinking about or dealing with problems in a practical, matter-of-fact way. — *noun* **pragmatist**: *Though they may have strong principles, they are also pragmatists.*

prairie /'preərɪ/ *noun*: **prairies**

A **prairie** is a wide area of level grassland with very few trees, especially in North America.

praise /preɪz/ *verb; noun*

▻ ***verb***: **praises, praising, praised**

1 You **praise** someone or something when you speak of them or write about them with admiration or approval: *The government minister praised the efforts of the security forces in combating terrorism.* □ *The policeman was praised for his courage and quick thinking.* □ *His latest film has been praised by the critics.* **2** To **praise** God is to worship and glorify God with hymns and thanksgiving *eg* in a church: *Praise the Lord!*

▻ ***noun*** (*uncount*)

1 Praise is the expression of admiration or approval: *high praise* □ *His efforts received a lot of praise.* **2 Praise** is also the worship of God: *a hymn of praise.*

▻ ***phrase*** If you **sing the praises** of someone or something, you praise them enthusiastically.

praiseworthy /'preɪzwɜːðɪ/ *adjective*

Something that is **praiseworthy** deserves praise: *His first novel was a very praiseworthy effort.*

pram /prɑːm/ *noun*: **prams**

A **pram** is a four-wheeled carriage for a baby, pushed by someone on foot.

prance /prɑːns/ *verb*: **prances, prancing, pranced**

1 When a horse **prances** it moves with quick springing steps. **2** If someone **prances** they move about happily or proudly with quick steps as if they were dancing or jumping: *He came prancing into the room.* □ *She was prancing about the beach in a very revealing swimsuit.*

prank /praŋk/ *noun*: **pranks**
A **prank** is a playful or mischievous trick or a practical joke: *a childish prank* □ *He was always playing pranks on his sisters.*

prat /prat/ *noun*: **prats** (*offensive slang*)
If you call someone a **prat** you think they are stupid: *What a prat!*

prawn /prɔːn/ *noun*: **prawns**
A **prawn** is a type of shellfish similar to a shrimp but larger. **Prawns** are eaten as food and they turn pink when you cook them.

pray /preɪ/ *verb*: **prays, praying, prayed**
1 When people **pray** they speak to God or a god in order to ask for something or to give thanks: *pray to the Almighty* □ *They knelt down to pray.* □ *He prayed for forgiveness.* **2** If someone says that they **are praying** for something they mean that they are hoping for it very strongly: *The sports day is on Saturday, and we are praying for good weather.*

prayer /preə(r)/ *noun*: **prayers**
1 A **prayer** is a solemn request to God or a god, often in a fixed form of words: *Have you said your prayers?* □ *the Lord's Prayer* □ *a prayer for forgiveness* □ *He said a prayer for all the victims of the plane crash.* **2** (*uncount*) **Prayer** is the activity of praying: *She spent much of her time in prayer.*

pre- /prɪ/ *prefix*
Pre- is used with verbs, nouns, adjectives and adverbs to describe something **a** that has taken place before a particular date, time or period: *prewar* □ *the pre-Christian era* □ *prematurely.* **b** that has been done in advance: *a prearranged meeting* □ *The chicken has been pre-cooked.* [compare **ante-, post-**]

preach /priːtʃ/ *verb*: **preaches, preaching, preached**
1 A member of the clergy **preaches** when they give a sermon [=a talk on a religious or moral subject], usually as part of a religious service: *The evangelist preached in the open air to huge crowds.* □ *He preached about loving your neighbour.* **2** If someone **preaches** to you or at you, they give you unwanted advice in a boring and irritating way: *She's always preaching at me about the importance of good manners.* **3** When someone **preaches** a particular thing, they try to advise or persuade other people to do or accept that thing: *to preach caution* □ *She preaches economy in all the council meetings.*
▻ ***phrase*** If you **practise what you preach** you always do yourself what you tell others to do: *He is continually reminding the children to put on their seatbelts, but he doesn't always practise what he preaches.*

preamble /prɪ'ambəl/ *noun* (*count or uncount*): **preambles**
A **preamble** is a spoken or written introduction, often explaining the purpose of the document, lecture or speech that follows: *There is a short preamble to the report dealing with the main points that the committee had to consider.* □ *He launched into his resignation statement without any preamble.*

precarious /prɪ'keərɪəs/ *adjective*
1 Something that is **precarious** is unsafe or dangerous: *The old staircase looks a bit precarious.* **2** **Precarious** is also used to describe something that is uncertain or insecure: *The future of the industry is looking increasingly precarious.* □ *Except for the most successful, acting can be a precarious career.* — *adverb* **precariously:** *The young birds were perched precariously on narrow ledges on the cliff.* □ *They lived somewhat precariously on the money he earned from painting the occasional portrait.*

precaution /prɪ'kɔːʃən/ *noun*: **precautions**
A **precaution** is something that is done in advance in order to avoid risk or danger or to prevent problems: *Wearing a hat is a sensible precaution in hot sunshine.* □ *The climbers took the precaution of telling the local policeman when they expected to return.* □ *fire precautions.* — *adjective* **precautionary**: *precautionary measures.*

precede /prɪ'siːd/ *verb*: **precedes, preceding, preceded**
1 If something **precedes** something else it comes or goes before it: *In the months that preceded her operation, she had become progressively more crippled.* □ *The earthquake was preceded by several minor tremors.* □ *The queen entered the abbey, preceded by the bishops and other dignitaries.* **2** If you **precede** an action or statement with something else, you do or say that thing before you begin: *He preceded his talk with a practical demonstration.* — *adjective* **preceding:** *The dates may be found on the preceding page.*

precedence /'priːsɪdəns/ *noun* (*uncount*)
1 When something takes **precedence** over another thing, it is put or dealt with before that thing, because it is considered to be more important: *The children's welfare should take precedence over all other considerations.* **2** If one person has **precedence** over another, they have the right to come before that person because of their rank: *Does a duke come before a marquis in the order of precedence?*

precedent /'presɪdənt/ *noun*: **precedents**
1 A **precedent** is a past action, especially a legal decision, that can be used as an example or rule for present or future action: *The judge's ruling set a legal precedent.* **2** A **precedent** is also something that has happened before: *The appointment of a female commander of a navy warship is without precedent.* □ *The prince broke with precedent when he married a commoner.*

precept /'priːsept/ *noun* (*formal*): **precepts**
A **precept** is a rule or principle that helps to guide your behaviour or thinking: *moral precepts* □ *Children are taught the basic precepts of the Christian religion in Sunday school.* □ *He has always lived by the precept 'Make hay while the sun shines'.*

precinct /'priːsɪŋkt/ *noun*: **precincts**
1 (*often plural*) A **precinct** or the **precincts** of *eg* a cathedral, college or other large building is the area of land enclosed within its boundary or walls: *They were buried in a small chapel in the castle precincts.* **2** (*BrE*) An area of a town or city that is designed for a particular use is also called a **precinct**: *a pedestrian precinct* □ *a shopping precinct.* **3** In the United States, a **precinct** is any of the districts into which a city is divided, especially for election administration and policing purposes.

precious /'preʃəs/ *adjective*
1 Something that is **precious** is valuable because it is rare or scarce: *precious jewels* □ *Water is a precious resource in desert regions.* □ *We're wasting precious time.* **2** You can also describe something as **precious** when it is treasured or loved very much: *Her son was very precious to her.* □ *Her photographs are amongst her most precious possessions.* **3** (*derogatory*) You can describe someone's manner or style of talking or writing as **precious**, if you think it is unnaturally formal or affected: *a precious young man.* **4** You can use **precious** ironically to describe a person or thing that you think is terrible: *Him and his precious brats!*

precious metal /preʃəs 'metəl/ *noun*: **precious metals**
A **precious metal** is a valuable metal such as gold, silver or platinum.

precious stone /prɛʃəs 'stoun/ *noun*: **precious stones**
A **precious stone** is a rare and valuable stone often used in jewellery: *diamonds, emeralds and other precious stones.*

precipice /'prɛsɪpɪs/ *noun*: **precipices**
A **precipice** is a very steep and dangerous side of a mountain, cliff or high rock: *a precipice hundreds of feet high.*

precipitate *verb*; *adjective*
▻ ***verb*** /prɪ'sɪpɪteɪt/ (*formal*): **precipitates, precipitating, precipitated**
To **precipitate** means to cause to happen suddenly or sooner: *The economic crisis precipitated the downfall of the government.* □ *His resignation was precipitated by revelations published in all the newspapers.*
▻ ***adjective*** /prɪ'sɪpɪtət/ (*formal*)
An action can be described as **precipitate** if it is done too quickly without proper thought or care. [*same as* **impulsive**]

precipitous /prɪ'sɪpɪtəs/ *adjective* (*formal*)
1 Precipitous can be used to describe an area of land that is dangerously high and steep: *A precipitous path was the only route to the mountain village.* **2 Precipitous** also has the same meaning as precipitate.

précis /'preɪsɪ/ *noun* (*uncount or count*): **précis** /'preɪsɪ/
A **précis** is a shortened form of a speech or piece of writing containing the most important points but not the details. [compare **summary**]

precise /prɪ'saɪs/ *adjective*
1 Precise means exact: *at this precise moment* □ *I don't have a precise figure.* □ *I'd like to build a house on this precise spot.* **2 Precise** is also used to describe something that is clear, detailed or accurate: *precise instructions* □ *a precise record of all their financial transactions* □ *precise timing* □ *Can you supply me with precise measurements?* **3** Someone who is **precise** is very careful or correct about small details: *She is very neat and precise.* □ *He has a very precise mind.*

precisely /prɪ'saɪslɪ/ *adverb*
1 Precisely means exactly: *At the first stroke, it will be one o'clock precisely.* **2 Precisely** also means carefully or in a precise manner: *He asked the question again, speaking slowly and precisely.* **3** (*used as an answer*) You can say **'precisely'** meaning 'you are right' or 'that is quite so' when you want to show that you agree with the statement just made by another person: *'If we don't get our visas before the end of the week, we'll have to cancel our trip.' 'Precisely.'*

precision /prɪ'sɪʒən/ *noun* (*uncount*)
If something is done with **precision** it is done with exactness and accuracy: *His work shows great precision and attention to detail.*

preclude /prɪ'klu:d/ *verb* (*formal*): **precludes, precluding, precluded**
If something, such as an event or action, **precludes** something else, it makes that thing impossible or prevents it from happening: *They accepted the loss without protest so as not to preclude the possibility of being awarded future contracts.* □ *Everything will be written down to preclude any future misunderstandings.*

precocious /prɪ'kouʃəs/ *adjective*
1 If a child is described as **precocious**, he or she behaves in a way that makes them seem older than they are. **2** A **precocious** talent, ability or interest is one that has developed very early or at an earlier stage than is usual.

preconceived /pri:kən'si:vd/ *adjective*
A **preconceived** idea or opinion about someone or something is one that you already hold without having enough real knowledge or experience of the person or thing concerned: *Before he got married he had a lot of preconceived ideas about how his wife ought to behave.*

preconception /pri:kən'sɛpʃən/ *noun*: **preconceptions**
A **preconception** is an idea or opinion that you have formed about someone or something before you have any real knowledge or experience of them or it. [compare **misconception**]

precursor /prɪ'kɜ:sə(r)/ *noun* (*formal*): **precursors**
A **precursor** is something that comes before and is a sign of an approaching event.

pre-date /pri:'deɪt/ *verb*: **pre-dates, pre-dating, pre-dated**
One thing **pre-dates** another when it occurs or exists at an earlier date: *Balloons pre-date aircraft.*

predator /'prɛdətə(r)/ *noun*: **predators**
A **predator** is a bird or animal that kills and eats others: *lions, leopards and other large predators.*

predatory /'prɛdətərɪ/ *adjective*
1 Predatory animals kill and eat others. **2 Predatory** people take advantage of other people's weakness or kindness to gain something for themselves.

predecessor /'pri:dəsɛsə(r)/ *noun*: **predecessors**
1 Your **predecessor** is the person who had your job or position before you: *I got this job when my predecessor retired.* **2** The **predecessor** of *eg* a machine or product is the previous version or model: *Modern production cars have better steering and suspension than their predecessors of the 1950s and 60s.*

predestination /pri:dɛstɪ'neɪʃən/ *noun* (*uncount*; *religion*)
Predestination is the belief that everything has been decided by God and people can do nothing to change their fate.

predestined /pri:'dɛstɪnd/ *adjective*
You are **predestined** to do something when you believe God or fate has caused it to happen to you: *They believed they were predestined to meet.* [*same as* **fated**]

predetermined /pri:dɪ'tɜ:mɪnd/ *adjective* (*formal*)
Something is **predetermined** when it is fixed in advance and you can do nothing to change it: *The colour of a person's hair and eyes are predetermined by the genes they inherit from their parents.*

predicament /prɪ'dɪkəmənt/ *noun*: **predicaments**
A **predicament** is a difficult or unpleasant situation which you are not sure what to do about.

predicate /'prɛdɪkeɪt/ *noun* (*grammar*): **predicates**
The **predicate** is the word or words in a sentence or clause that tell you something about the subject. In the sentence *The men knew what to do*, '*knew what to do*' is the **predicate**.

predicative /prɪ'dɪkətɪv/ *adjective* (*grammar*)
An adjective is **predicative** when it comes after the verb. In the phrase *She's asleep*, '*asleep*' is **predicative**. [compare **attributive**]

predict /prɪ'dɪkt/ *verb*: **predicts, predicting, predicted**
You **predict** something when you say that it will happen: *I predict that they will be divorced within two years.* [*same as* **foretell, prophesy**]

predictable /prɪ'dɪktəbəl/ *adjective*
1 Something is **predictable** when you know that it is going to happen: *The monsoon was predictable.* **2** You can say that something is **predictable** when it is dull and boring because it always happens: *I knew he would be angry with me; his behaviour is always so pre-*

dictable. [*opposite* **unpredictable**] — *adverb* **predictably:** *The train was, predictably, half an hour late.*

prediction /prɪ'dɪkʃən/ *noun*: **predictions**
1 A **prediction** is a statement of what you believe will happen: *The newspapers are all making predictions about the election.* **2** (*uncount*) **Prediction** is the act of making predictions: *The number of uncertain voters makes accurate prediction of the election result very difficult.*

predilection /pri:dɪ'lɛkʃən/ *noun* (*formal*): **predilections**
You have a **predilection** for something when you have a special liking for it.

predisposed /pri:dɪs'poʊzd/ *adjective*
You are **predisposed** to act, react or think in a certain way if something has influenced you and caused you to act in that way: *The examiners will be predisposed in your favour if your handwriting is clear and neat.*

predisposition /pri:dɪspə'zɪʃən/ *noun* (*formal*): **predispositions**
You have a **predisposition** to act in a certain way when your family history and background have caused you to act in that way: *She has inherited a predisposition to depression from her father.*

predominance /prɪ'dɒmɪnəns/ *noun* (*uncount*)
1 There is a **predominance** of something when there is a lot more of it than of any other thing: *There is a predominance of women among the company's new employees.* **2** Something has **predominance** when it has the most influence or power: *Japanese companies have predominance in the world electronics market.*

predominant /prɪ'dɒmɪnənt/ *adjective*
Something is **predominant** when there is more of it, or it has more power or influence, than anything else: *Beethoven was the predominant composer of the early 19th century.* ▫ *Marriage is a predominant theme in the novels of Jane Austen.*

predominantly /prɪ'dɒmɪnəntlɪ/ *adverb*
Predominantly means 'mostly' or 'mainly': *Her books are predominantly about life in Africa.*

predominate /prɪ'dɒmɪneɪt/ *verb*: **predominates, predominating, predominated**
One thing **predominates** over another when there is more of it, or it has more power or influence than that other thing: *Girls predominate over boys in this class.*

pre-eminent /prɪ'ɛmɪnənt/ *adjective* (*formal*)
Someone or something is **pre-eminent** when they are much better or much more important than any other person or thing: *He is one of the most pre-eminent politicians in his party.* — **noun** (*uncount*; *formal*) **pre-eminence:** *Everybody recognizes his pre-eminence in the field of family law.*

pre-empt /prɪ'ɛmpt/ *verb*: **pre-empts, pre-empting, pre-empted**
You **pre-empt** someone if you do or say what they were planning to do or say before they have a chance, and so make their action pointless: *I don't want to pre-empt anything the Minister is going to say.* — *adjective* **pre-emptive:** *They completely discount the possibility of pre-emptive attacks by Russia.*

preen /pri:n/ *verb*: **preens, preening, preened**
1 A bird **preens** its feathers when it cleans and smooths them. **2** A person **preens** when they spend a lot of time tidying their hair and arranging their clothes: *She spends hours preening herself.*

prefab /'pri:fab/ *noun*: **prefabs**
A **prefab** is a house built of parts made in a factory that can be put together quickly.

prefabricated /pri:'fabrɪkeɪtɪd/ *adjective*
A **prefabricated** building is built of parts made in a factory that can be put together quickly.

preface /'prɛfɪs/ *noun*; *verb*
▻ ***noun***: **prefaces**
A **preface** is an introduction at the beginning of *eg* a book or speech. [*same as* **foreword**]
▻ ***verb***: **prefaces, prefacing, prefaced**
You **preface** *eg* a speech or action when you say or do something else first as an introduction: *She prefaced her speech with a few words of welcome to the guests.*

prefect /'pri:fɛkt/ *noun*: **prefects**
In some schools, a **prefect** is a senior pupil with special duties and some powers over younger pupils.

prefer /prɪ'fɜ:(r)/ *verb*: **prefers, preferring, preferred**
You **prefer** one thing to another if you like it better than the other, and so will choose it when you have the choice; you can use **prefer** in a variety of constructions: *Apparently he prefers mature women to young girls.* ▫ *We prefer to control such people rather than be controlled by them.* ▫ *I much prefer being assessed as I go along, rather than having big exams at the end of the year.* ▫ *I'll make tea, or would you prefer coffee?* ▫ *This is the interpretation I prefer.* ▫ *A form is provided overleaf, but you may write a letter if you prefer.* ▫ *There are still women who prefer not to think about money.* ▫ *Some people like using commas, and some prefer not to.* ▫ *They'd prefer sex education to be undertaken by the school.* ▫ *I should prefer that we did it the easy way.* ▫ *Maybe you'd prefer it if I left you alone?* ▫ *My preferred method is to press F8 and use the dialogue box.*
▻ ***phrase*** For **prefer charges against** see **charge**.

preferable /'prɛfərəbəl/ *adjective*
Something is **preferable** when it is more desirable or suitable, or better: *A quick death is obviously preferable to years of pain and suffering.* — *adverb* (*sentence adverb*) **preferably:** *He needs advice, preferably from a professional.*

preference /'prɛfərəns/ *noun*: **preferences**
1 (*count or uncount*) You have a **preference** for something when you prefer it to something else: *I have a preference for tea rather than coffee.* ▫ *She chose the pink dress in preference to the purple one.* ▫ *Your personal preferences are important when you choose a new car.* **2** (*uncount*) You give **preference** to someone when you consider them favourably or prefer them: *The company will give preference to applicants with experience.*

preferential /prɛfə'rɛnʃəl/ *adjective*
You give **preferential** treatment to someone when you treat them better or consider them more favourably than someone else: *The elderly should get preferential treatment on public transport.*

preferment /prɪ'fɜ:mənt/ *noun* (*uncount*; *formal*)
Preferment is promotion to a more responsible position: *his hopes for preferment once he had made his mark.*

prefix /'pri:fɪks/ *noun*: **prefixes** (*grammar*)
A **prefix** is an element such as *un-*, *re-*, *non-* or *de-* added to the beginning of a word to create a new word. [compare **suffix**]

pregnancy /'prɛgnənsɪ/ *noun* (*count or uncount*): **pregnancies**
Pregnancy is the condition of being pregnant or the time during which a woman is pregnant: *She kept well throughout her pregnancy.* ▫ *She's had three pregnancies.*

pregnant /'prɛgnənt/ *adjective*
1 A woman or female animal is **pregnant** when she is carrying an unborn child or young in her womb: *She is pregnant with her second child.* ▫ *She is six months*

pregnant. **2** A remark, pause or silence can be described as **pregnant** when it has an important meaning which is clear but which is not actually expressed.

prehistoric /priːhɪ'stɒrɪk/ *adjective*
Prehistoric things or people existed or belong to the time before there were written historical records: *These caves contain evidence of prehistoric man.* □ *prehistoric cave paintings.*

prejudge /priː'dʒʌdʒ/ *verb*: **prejudges, prejudging, prejudged**
You **prejudge** a person or situation when you form an opinion of them before you know all the important or relevant facts: *Jury members should try not to prejudge the defendant on the basis of reports of the crime in the newspapers.*

prejudice /'prɛdʒʊdɪs/ *noun*; *verb*
▷ ***noun*** (*uncount or count*): **prejudices**
Prejudice is a usually unfair or unreasonable opinion or dislike of a person or thing, based on lack of knowledge: *racial prejudice* □ *have strong prejudices* □ *a prejudice against Jews.*
▷ ***verb***: **prejudices, prejudicing, prejudiced**
One thing **prejudices** another when it harms it or puts it in danger: *Bad handwriting prejudices your chances of passing the exam.*

prejudiced /'prɛdʒʊdɪst/ *adjective*
You are **prejudiced** when you have an unfair or unreasonable opinion or dislike of someone or something, based on lack of knowledge: *racially prejudiced attitudes* □ *There are some people in the Church who are prejudiced against homosexuals.*

prejudicial /prɛdʒʊ'dɪʃəl/ *adjective*
An action is **prejudicial** to something when it harms it or puts it in danger: *Smoking is prejudicial to health.*

preliminary /prɪ'lɪmɪnərɪ/ *adjective*; *noun*
▷ ***adjective***
A **preliminary** action comes before or at the beginning of the main event, often to introduce or prepare for it: *There will be preliminary races to select competitors for the final.*
▷ ***noun*** (*usually in the plural*): **preliminaries**
The **preliminaries** are the things done to prepare for the main event.

prelude /'prɛljuːd/ *noun*: **preludes**
1 One event is the **prelude** to another when it occurs before it and prepares the way for it: *The quarrel over land was the prelude to war between the countries.* □ *talks that are being seen as a prelude to peace.* **2** (*music*) A **prelude** is a short passage or movement at the beginning of a piece of music.

premature /'prɛmətjʊə(r)/ *adjective*
1 A **premature** baby is born before the expected date of its birth: *Her baby was six weeks premature.* **2** Something that is **premature** happens before the usual or expected time: *her premature death in her early forties* □ *The sun causes premature ageing of the skin.* **3** A decision or action is **premature** when it is taken or done too early before the proper or suitable time: *a premature farewell.* — *adverb* **prematurely:** *The baby was born prematurely.* □ *a decision taken prematurely.*

premeditated /priː'mɛdɪteɪtɪd/ *adjective*
A **premeditated** act is planned before it is done: *premeditated murder.*

premier /'prɛmɪə(r)/ *noun*; *adjective*
▷ ***noun***: **premiers**
A **premier** is a prime minister: *the Spanish premier.*
▷ ***adjective***
Premier describes the most important or leading thing in a group: *Britain's premier industrial city.*

premiere /'prɛmɪɛə(r)/ *noun*: **premieres**
The **premiere** of *eg* a play or film is its first public performance: *a world premiere.*

premiership /'prɛmɪəʃɪp/ *noun* (*used in the singular or uncount*): **premierships**
The **premiership** is the position of premier or prime minister or the period during which someone is prime minister: *laws passed during her premiership.*

premise or **premiss** /'prɛmɪs/ *noun* (*formal*): **premises**
A **premise** is something that you accept as true and use as a basis for another idea or way of thinking: *This conclusion is only reasonable if your original premise was correct.*

premises /'prɛmɪsɪz/ *noun* (*plural*)
The **premises** a company or business occupies are the buildings and land it uses: *The company is looking for new premises.* □ *The shop sells food but doesn't allow it to be eaten on the premises.*

premium /'priːmɪəm/ *noun*: **premiums**
1 A **premium** is an amount of money paid regularly, *eg* for insurance: *Your car insurance premium is due in March.* **2** A **premium** is an extra sum added to wages or to interest paid by *eg* a bank or building society: *You'll be paid a premium if you finish the job early.*
▷ ***phrase*** Something is **at a premium** if there is very little of it or less than is needed, and it is therefore sold at a higher price than usual or is very difficult to obtain: *Hotel rooms are at a premium in August and cost more than they do in March.* □ *Skilled workers are at a premium so the company should make every effort to keep them.*

premonition /prɛmə'nɪʃən/ *noun*: **premonitions**
You have a **premonition** if you have a strange feeling that something will happen before it actually does: *She had a premonition about her grandfather's death one month before he died.* □ *a premonition of the accident.*

prenatal /priː'neɪtəl/ *adjective*
Prenatal care or classes are for pregnant women. [compare **antenatal**]

preoccupation /prɪɒkjʊ'peɪʃən/ *noun*: **preoccupations**
A **preoccupation** is something that you think about all or most of the time: *Buying clothes is one of his main preoccupations.* □ *She has a preoccupation with death.*

preoccupied /prɪ'ɒkjʊpaɪd/ *adjective*
You are **preoccupied** when you think so much about one thing that you ignore most other things: *He is preoccupied with his computer games.* □ *I saw her in the street yesterday but she was too preoccupied to notice me.*

preoccupy /prɪ'ɒkjʊpaɪ/ *verb*: **preoccupies, preoccupying, preoccupied**
Something **preoccupies** you when you think about it all, or a lot of, the time: *The problem of juvenile crime is one that preoccupies many politicians.*

pre-packed /priː'pakt/ *adjective*
Food is **pre-packed** when it is packed or wrapped before being to sent to the shop where it is sold.

prepaid /priː'peɪd/ *adjective*
An envelope or letter is **prepaid** when the postage is paid by the person who will receive it and not by the person sending it: *The company sent me a prepaid envelope for me to return my order form in.*

preparation /prɛpə'reɪʃən/ *noun*: **preparations**
1 (*uncount*) You do **preparation** when you get something ready or prepare for it: *A wedding involves a lot of preparation.* □ *Plans for the new factory are in*

preparation. [= being prepared] □ *She is responsible for the preparation of all the food.* **2** (*usually in the plural*) **Preparations** for an event are things done to get ready for it: *preparations for the birth of a baby.* **3** A **preparation** is anything made by mixing substances together, especially for use as a medicine or cosmetic: *The pharmacist produced a preparation to soothe burnt skin.*

preparatory /prɪ'parətərɪ/ *adjective*
Preparatory actions get ready or prepare for something else: *a preparatory report on the traffic problems.*

preparatory school /prɪ'parətərɪ sku:l/ *noun*: **preparatory schools**
A **preparatory school** is a prep school.

prepare /prɪ'pɛə(r)/ *verb*: **prepares, preparing, prepared**
1 You **prepare** someone, something or yourself for some future event when you get them ready or into a fit state to receive or deal with it: *Prepare yourself for a shock.* □ *He prepared to jump.* □ *They prepared for their holiday.* □ *I must prepare a room for my guests.* □ *Parents should prepare their children for adult life.* **2** You **prepare** a meal or food when you get it ready to be eaten: *prepare a flask of coffee.*

prepared /prɪ'pɛəd/ *adjective*
1 Something is **prepared** when it is made ready in advance: *a prepared statement.* **2** You are **prepared** for something when you are ready for it and can deal with it: *Many students could be better prepared for college life.* **3** You are **prepared** to do something when you are willing to do it: *I'm not prepared to lend him any more money.*

preponderance /prɪ'pɒndərəns/ *noun* (*uncount; formal*)
There is a **preponderance** of one type of thing when there is more of it than of any other type in a group: *There was a preponderance of young men in the karate class.* — *adjective* **preponderant** /prɪ'pɒndərənt/: *Young men are preponderant in karate and judo classes.*

preposition /prɛpə'zɪʃən/ *noun* (*grammar*): **prepositions**
A **preposition** is a word such as *to, from, into, by, with* and *against*, that shows *eg* position, movement, means and time.

> Prepositions are usually followed: (1) by a noun or noun phrase, as in *She gave the book to George.* and *I helped her with the cleaning and tidying;* (2) by a pronoun, as in *I gave it to him;* or (3) by a verb ending in *-ing*, as in *He devotes his spare time to gardening.*

preposterous /prɪ'pɒstərəs/ *adjective*
Something can be described as **preposterous** when you think it is silly, ridiculous or unreasonable: *a preposterous idea.*

prep school /'prɛp sku:l/ *noun*: **prep schools**
A **prep school** is a private school for children aged between seven and thirteen.

prerequisite /pri:'rɛkwɪzɪt/ *noun* (*formal*): **prerequisites**
A **prerequisite** is something that must happen or exist for something else to be possible: *Good exam passes in science subjects are a prerequisite for studying medicine.* □ *A good diet is a prerequisite of good health.*

prerogative /prɪ'rɒgətɪv/ *noun* (*formal*): **prerogatives**
Your **prerogative** is a right, privilege or power that only you have: *It is the bride's prerogative to fix the day for her wedding.* □ *Expensive cars are the prerogative of the rich and famous.*

prescribe /prɪ'skraɪb/ *verb*: **prescribes, prescribing, prescribed**
1 A doctor **prescribes** a drug or medicine for you when they tell you which drug or medicine you should take to cure an illness: *My doctor prescribed painkillers for my headache.* **2** (*formal*) Something such as a law **prescribes** something when it states formally or officially that it must be done or carried out: *The law prescribes that your will must be signed in the presence of witnesses.*

prescription /prɪ'skrɪpʃən/ *noun*: **prescriptions**
1 A **prescription** is a piece of paper on which your doctor writes the name of the drug or medicine that you must take to cure some illness: *She took her prescription to the chemist.* **2** A **prescription** is also the drug or medicine that your doctor has told you to take.
▻ ***phrase*** A drug is available **on prescription** when you can get it from a chemist only if your doctor writes a prescription for it.

presence /'prɛzəns/ *noun*: **presences**
1 (*uncount*) A person's or thing's **presence** somewhere is the circumstance of their being there: *Johnny's continued presence in the room was threatening.* □ *He coughed to announce his presence.* □ *Will my presence be required at the meeting?* □ *difficulty in breathing due to the presence of fluid in the lungs.* [*opposite* **absence**] **2** (*uncount or used in the singular*) Someone with **presence** has an impressive appearance and manner: *She has so much presence.* □ *Lister was a man with a keen eye and forceful presence* **3** (*usually in the singular*) A **presence** is a being that you are aware of, especially one that you cannot see: *I sensed a hostile presence in the room.* □ *For some Death appears as a real presence.*
▻ ***phrases*** **1** You are **in** someone's **presence** when you are in the same place as they are: *I slowly learnt to relax in her presence.* □ *Be careful what you say in his presence.* □ *The will must be signed in the presence of two witnesses.* **2** You have the **presence of mind** to do something when you act quickly and sensibly in an awkward situation: *Fortunately we had the presence of mind to turn the radio on to another station.* □ *With her usual presence of mind she changed the subject.*

present[1] /'prɛzənt/ *adjective; noun*
▻ ***adjective***
1 Someone is **present** somewhere, or **present** at an event, if they are there; something is **present** somewhere if it is there: *She was never at ease when he was present.* □ *I was unfortunately unable to be present at the degree ceremony.* □ *To the delight of everyone present, she stood up and made a little speech of her own.* □ *Small amounts of these gases are present in the atmosphere.* [*opposite* **absent**] **2 Present** describes things, people or office-bearers that exist now, as distinct from those of the past or future: *the present Principal of the college* □ *the present population of Britain* □ *geological activity both past and present* □ *I know nothing about the present situation in Cuba.* □ *I wouldn't be good company in my present mood.* [*same as* **current**]
▻ ***noun*** (*used in the singular*)
1 The **present** is the time now, or the events that are now taking place: *She's a person who lives in the present.* □ *We're often told that the past was nobler than the present.* □ *Future conditions and demands may be different from those of the present.* [compare **past, future**] **2** (*grammar*) A verb that is in the **present** is in the present tense.
▻ ***phrases*** **1** You use **at present** to mean 'now' or 'at the moment': *Many more people could benefit from a university education than are able to at present.* □ *He's at present working for a PhD.* □ *I'd rather not change jobs at present.* [*same as* **at the moment**] **2** Circumstances

that exist **for the present** exist now, but are likely to be altered: *He's to be kept in hospital for the present.* □ *Let's drop the subject for the present.* [same as **for the moment**] **3 The present day** is modern times: *beer-brewing methods that have survived from ancient times to the present day.* [see also **present-day**]

present² /ˈprɛzənt/ *noun*: **presents**
A **present** is something that you give someone, *eg* for their birthday, or when you visit them: *I've got a present for you.* □ *Thanks for the Christmas present.* □ *They gave me a bottle of champagne as a farewell present.* □ *Why don't you open your presents?*

present³ /prɪˈzɛnt/ *verb*: **presents, presenting, presented**
1 You **present** someone with something, or **present** it to them, when you give it to them, especially at a formal ceremony: *Mrs Anne Miller presented a cheque for £338 to the matron of the hospice.* □ *The Society presented her with a silver brooch.* □ *The winner will be presented with the Driver-of-the-Year trophy.* □ *Right on schedule Mary-Claude presented him with a daughter, Sarah.* **2** You **present** a person to someone important when you introduce them officially: *May I present Mr Nicholas Urfe.* □ *Allow me to present myself.* **3** Someone who **presents** a radio or television programme introduces the various parts of it, or introduces the speakers on it; a company **presents** a play when it performs it for an audience: *the recent BBC2 three-part series presented by Anthony Clare* □ *'Blithe Spirit' by Noel Coward will be presented by Coolmine Drama Circle.* **4** Something that **presents** a problem or difficulty is difficult to deal with: *The structure of the universe presents a challenge to our understanding.* □ *the small crises that babies so frequently present us with.* **5** You **present** something such as information when you communicate it to people: *Present your ideas as if you had something unique to offer.* □ *On 20 March the Chancellor of the Exchequer, Mr John Major, presented his first budget.* □ *She presents her argument with admirable clarity.* **6** You **present** someone that you are writing or talking about in a certain way when you give that impression of them: *Sophocles presents Oedipus as a noble character doomed to error and misery despite his wisdom.* **7** You **present** yourself somewhere when you appear there, especially when you have officially been instructed to do so: *Next day he presented himself in Branson's office to announce that he was leaving.* **8** An idea **presents** itself when you think of it; an opportunity **presents** itself when it occurs, especially unexpectedly: *In 1341 the opportunity presented itself to intervene in Brittany.*

presentable /prɪˈzɛntəbəl/ *adjective*
Someone or something that is **presentable** is smart or tidy enough to be seen in public: *He rose, washed, and made himself as presentable as possible.*

presentation /prɛzənˈteɪʃən/ *noun*: **presentations**
1 (*uncount*) **Presentation** is the act of presenting something: *the presentation of photographic material in the book.* **2** (*uncount*) **Presentation** is the way in which something is presented, explained or advertised and the impression it makes on people: *She can cook well but her presentation is not very good.* □ *Bad presentation may lose you marks in the art exam.* **3** A **presentation** is **a** a formal ceremony at which prizes or awards are presented: *He missed the presentation through bad health.* **b** a formal talk or lecture: *He went to a presentation on life in Africa.* **4** In the theatre, a **presentation** is a play or show performed before an audience.

present-day /prɛzənt ˈdeɪ/ *adjective*
Present-day describes people, things and situations that exist now: *life in present-day Israel.* [see also **the present day** at **present¹**]

presenter /prɪˈzɛntə(r)/ *noun*: **presenters**
A **presenter** is a person who introduces the guests and items on a radio or television programme.

presently /ˈprɛzəntlɪ/ *adverb*
1 Something will happen **presently** when it will happen soon or in a short time: *He'll be here presently.* **2** (*also sentence adverb*) You can use **presently** when one action follows another after a short time: *They sat in the sun for a while. Presently, they went for a swim in the sea.* **3** You are **presently** doing something when you are doing it at the moment or now: *She's presently in a meeting with the management committee.*

> **Presently** usually goes at the end of the sentence when it means 'soon', at the beginning when it means 'after a short time' and after the verb when it means 'now'.

present participle /prɛzənt ˈpɑːtɪsɪpəl/ *noun*: **present participles**
The **present participle** is the form of the verb that ends in *-ing*, and is used with the verb *be* to form the continuous tenses, *eg He is walking along the road* and *She was singing songs in French.*

present tense /prɛzənt ˈtɛns/ *noun* (*used in the singular*)
You use the **present tense** of a verb to refer to things that are happening now, or situations that exist now: *I* <u>*enjoy*</u> *my food.* □ *He* <u>*runs*</u> *very quickly.* □ *They* <u>*don't speak*</u> *any Greek.*

preservation /prɛzəˈveɪʃən/ *noun* (*uncount*)
The **preservation** of something is the process of keeping it in good condition: *The preservation of the rainforests.*

preservative /prɪˈzɜːvətɪv/ *noun*: **preservatives**
A **preservative** is a substance that keeps *eg* food, wood and metal in good condition: *Some tinned food is full of preservatives.*

preserve /prɪˈzɜːv/ *verb*; *noun*
▷ ***verb***: **preserves, preserving, preserved**
1 You **preserve** something when you save it from loss, damage or decay: *Scientists are trying to develop a chemical that will preserve the ancient paintings found on many cave walls.* **2** You **preserve** *eg* a situation or peace when you take care that it doesn't change or isn't lost: *try hard to preserve someone's good opinion of you.* **3** You **preserve** food when you treat it in some way, *eg* by freezing it or by cooking it in sugar or vinegar, so that it will not decay.
▷ ***noun***: **preserves**
A **preserve** is a food prepared by cooking fruit or vegetables with sugar or vinegar so they don't decay: *apricot preserve.*

preset /priːˈsɛt/ *verb*: **presets, presetting, preset**
You **preset** a piece of electronic equipment when you set the controls so that it will operate at the required time: *The camera can be preset.*

preside /prɪˈzaɪd/ *verb* (*formal*): **presides, presiding, presided**
You **preside** at or over a meeting or formal event when you are in charge of it: *He phoned me up to ask if I would preside over a press briefing.* — *adjective* **presiding:** *the presiding judge.*

presidency /ˈprɛzɪdənsɪ/ *noun*: **presidencies**
The **presidency** is the position of being president or the period of time during which someone is president: *He was elected to the presidency.* □ *laws passed during his presidency.*

president /ˈprɛzɪdənt/ *noun*: **presidents**
1 The **president** is the elected head of state in a republic: *the president of France* □ *President Clinton.* **2** The **president** of a society is the person occupying the highest position in it: *the president of the drama society* □ *the president of the board of trade.*

presidential /prɛzɪˈdɛnʃəl/ *adjective*
Presidential things or activities are for or done by a president: *the presidential tour of Britain* □ *the presidential residence.*

press /prɛs/ *verb*; *noun*
▻ ***verb***: **presses, pressing, pressed**
1 a You **press** something when you push it or squeeze it, *eg* with your fingers: *He pressed her hand affectionately.* □ *I pressed the bruise to see if it still hurt.* **b** You **press** *eg* a button or bell when you push it steadily, usually with your finger: *I pressed the doorbell of Number 28.* □ *Press the Return key.* **c** You **press** one thing against another when you hold it or push it firmly against the other: *The pistol was pressed against his cheek.* □ *She pressed her ear against the door.* □ *They pressed their noses flat against the glass.* □ *Ted pressed a finger to his lips.* □ *He looked at her, pressing the tips of his fingers together.* **d** You **press** something into a certain position when you push it firmly there: *Pack the soil round the roots and press it down firmly.* □ *Someone pressed a note into her hand.* **e** You **press** on something, when you push down on it, *eg* with a hand or foot: *She pressed harder on the accelerator pedal, urging the car on.* **f** People **press** somewhere when they crowd there: *Cameras clicked as spectators pressed round the eighteenth hole.* [*same as* **crowd**] **g** You **press** clothes when you iron them: *Turn the garment right side out and press the hemline.* □ *His trousers had been newly washed and pressed.* [*same as* **iron**] **h** Fruit **is pressed** when it is crushed to extract the juice: *They needed help with gathering the crop and pressing the grapes.* [*same as* **crush**]
2 a You **press** for something when you try to get people to agree to it: *We must press for a return to traditional methods of teaching.* □ *The Opposition were pressing for an early election.* **b** You **press** *eg* a gift, food or drink on someone when you insist that they accept it: *He was going round pressing more drinks on everyone.* **c** You **press** a person to do something when you try to persuade them to do it: *They pressed him to accept the offer.* [*same as* **beg**] **d** You **press** someone on some matter when you repeatedly question them about it: *Fortunately the newspaperman did not press him on the point.* □ *She didn't ask what my plans were, or press me for details.* **e** You **press** something such as a point, a demand, or a claim, when you insist on it being considered or dealt with: *She intended to press her case for compensation.* **f** You **press** charges when you officially accuse someone of committing a crime against you, and bring a case against them that has to be decided in a court of law: *The victims of rape may not want to press charges.*
▻ ***noun***: **presses**
1 You give something a **press** when you press it or squeeze it: *He gave her hand a little press.* **2** (*used in the singular*) The **Press** is **a** the newspapers: *The event was covered in the local press.* □ *press reports of renewed violence* □ *A press release was issued by Buckingham Palace this morning.* **b** (*with a singular or plural verb*) journalists: *Press photographers were invited to be present.* □ *In an interview with the press he declared himself willing to negotiate.* □ *The press were delighted to have yet another scandal to report.* **3** A printing **press** is a machine for printing books, newspapers or magazines; a printing and publishing organization may also be called a **press**: *new reference works from Oxford University Press.*
▻ ***phrases*** Someone or something **gets a good press** when they are praised by the media; they **get a bad press** when the media criticize them: *Slimming diets have been getting a bad press recently.* □ *The crime reporter was a friend of mine, and would give the police a good press.*

> ***phrasal verbs***
> **press ahead** You **press ahead** with something you intend to do when you carry it out fast and firmly: *The Education Minister is keen to press ahead with reforms.*
> **press on** You **press on** with something you are doing when you continue with it in a determined way; you **press on** somewhere when you continue your journey there without delay: *We decided to press on towards Toulouse without stopping.*

press conference /ˈprɛs kɒnfərəns/ *noun*: **press conferences**
A **press conference** is an interview given to reporters by a politician or a person in the news, *eg* to announce something or to answer questions: *hold a press conference* □ *give a press conference.*

pressed /prɛst/ *adjective*
You are **pressed** for time or money when you do not have enough of it: *I can't stay long; I'm very pressed for time today.*

pressing /ˈprɛsɪŋ/ *adjective*
Something is **pressing** when it must be done immediately: *a pressing engagement.*

press release /ˈprɛs rɪˈliːs/ *noun*: **press releases**
A **press release** is an official written statement given to reporters: *The palace issued a press release announcing the prince's marriage.*

press stud /ˈprɛs stʌd/ *noun*: **press studs**
A **press stud** is a small, metal button-like fastener, one part of which is pressed into the other.

press-up /ˈprɛsʌp/ *noun*: **press-ups**
You do **press-ups** by lying face downwards on the floor and pushing your body up on your arms, keeping your body and legs straight.

pressure /ˈprɛʃə(r)/ *noun*; *verb*
▻ ***noun***: **pressures**
1 (*uncount*) **Pressure** is the force produced by pressing on something: *She could feel the pressure of his hand or her arm.* **2** (*uncount*) **Pressure** is also the force that a gas or liquid has when it presses against a surface: *The wall isn't strong enough to take the pressure of the sea.* [see also **blood pressure**] **3** (*uncount*) You put **pressure** on someone when you force or try to persuade them to do something: *They brought pressure to bear on her to resign.* □ *We are under pressure to sell our house.* **4** (*uncount*) You work under **pressure** when you must work quickly and hard: *We are under pressure to get the job finished by next Monday.* **5** (*usually in the plural*) **Pressures** are things that cause problems, stress and worry: *the pressures of family life.*
▻ ***verb***: **pressures, pressuring, pressured**
You **pressure** someone to do something when you try to force or persuade them to do it: *He was pressured into resigning.* [*same as* **pressurize**]

pressure cooker /ˈprɛʃə(r) kʊkə(r)/ *noun*: **pressure cookers**
A **pressure cooker** is a pan with an airtight lid, which cooks food quickly using steam at high pressure.

pressure group /ˈprɛʃə(r) gruːp/ *noun*: **pressure groups**

A **pressure group** is a number of people who join together to influence public opinion and government policy on some issue: *He belongs to a pressure group urging a ban on advertising cigarettes and tobacco.*

pressurize /'prɛʃəraɪz/ or **pressurise** *verb*: **pressurizes, pressurizing, pressurized**
You **pressurize** someone into doing something when you try to force or persuade them to do it: *She was pressurized into selling her house.* [*same as* **pressure**]

prestige /prɛ'stiːʒ/ *noun* (*uncount*)
1 An organization has **prestige** when it is generally admired and respected for its quality and success: *the prestige of universities like Oxford and Cambridge.* **2** A job or position gives you **prestige** when it makes you important and influential: *Her new job will give her more prestige.*

prestigious /prɛ'stɪdʒəs/ *adjective*
Something is **prestigious** when it is generally admired and respected, and is important and influential: *She teaches at one of the most prestigious universities in Canada.*

presumably /prɪ'zjuːməblɪ/ *adverb* (*sentence adverb*)
You use **presumably** when you suppose that something is the case, but are not certain that it is: *Presumably the flight has been delayed by the bad weather.* □ *This story is presumably meant to be funny.*

presume /prɪ'zjuːm/ *verb*: **presumes, presuming, presumed**
1 You **presume** that something is the case when you have some reason to think it is but have no certain proof of it: *When you didn't answer the telephone, I presumed you were out, naturally.* □ *She is presumed to be working in Germany.* □ *Several hundred soldiers are missing, presumed dead.* [*same as* **suppose**; see note at **assume**] **2** (*with a negative*) You can say that you would not **presume** to do something when you would not attempt or dare to do it: *I wouldn't presume to advise the experts.*

presumption /prɪ'zʌmpʃən/ *noun*: **presumptions**
A **presumption** is something that you think is the case but have no proof of: *She remarried on the presumption that her first husband was dead.*

presumptuous /prɪ'zʌmptjʊəs/ *adjective* (*derogatory*)
Someone is **presumptuous** when they rudely do something they have no right or authority to do: *It was presumptuous of you to say I would lend him money without asking me first.*

presuppose /priːsə'poʊz/ *verb*: **presupposes, presupposing, presupposed**
One thing **presupposes** a second thing when it must exist or be true before that second thing can exist or be true: *Your plan presupposes that the company has money to invest.*

presupposition /priːsʌpə'zɪʃən/ *noun* (*formal*): **presuppositions**
A **presupposition** is something assumed to be true: *Your report on the crime is based on the presupposition that the witness has told you everything he saw.*

pretence (*AmE* **pretense**) /prɪ'tɛns/ *noun* (*uncount or used in the singular*): **pretences**
Pretence or a **pretence** is behaviour intended to make people believe something that is not true: *She smiled with a pretence of affection.* □ *He really is ill; it isn't all pretence.* □ *She made a pretence of reading so he wouldn't disturb her.* □ *His anger is just pretence.*
▻ ***phrase*** You do something **under false pretences** when you act in a way that hides your real intentions from people: *She got the job under false pretences; she isn't really qualified at all!*

pretend /prɪ'tɛnd/ *verb*: **pretends, pretending, pretended**
1 You **pretend** that something is the case when you act as if it is, usually to deliberately deceive people: *She pretended to be asleep.* □ *He isn't really ill; he's only pretending.* □ *She pretended not to know what to do.* **2** Children **pretend** when they imagine a game: *The girls pretended to be riding horses.*

pretension /prɪ'tɛnʃən/ *noun*: **pretensions**
A person with **pretensions** believes they are, or pretends to be, more important than they really are: *I make no pretensions to great musical talent, but I do enjoy playing the piano.* □ *a house with pretensions to elegance.*

pretentious /prɪ'tɛnʃəs/ *adjective*
A person or thing is **pretentious** when they try to seem, or are presented as being, more important or influential than they really are: *His manner was arty and pretentious.* □ *one of the most pretentious novels published this year.*

pretext /'priːtɛkst/ *noun*: **pretexts**
A **pretext** is a false reason for doing something, given to hide the real one: *Extremists, it was claimed, had used the march as an excuse for attacking police officers.*

pretty /'prɪtɪ/ *adjective*; *adverb*
▻ ***adjective***: **prettier, prettiest**
1 You describe a woman or girl as **pretty** if she is nice-looking, especially if her face is attractive in a neat, delicate way: *Bob had brought Samantha, a pretty blonde girl.* □ *She looks much prettier with her hair cut short.* □ *Though not conventionally pretty, she dressed elegantly.*

> Conventionally, *good-looking* and *handsome* are used rather than **pretty** to describe men.

2 Pretty things and places are nice to look at, especially in a traditional or conventional way: *She enjoyed wearing pretty clothes.* □ *The cottage was pretty to look at, but it was small and poky inside.* — *adverb* **prettily:** *The apartment was prettily furnished.* □ *She laughed prettily.* — *noun* (*uncount*) **prettiness:** *The village had a picture-postcard prettiness.*
▻ ***adverb*** (*moderating or intensifying*)
You use **pretty** before adjectives and adverbs, more informally than *rather* and with a meaning slightly closer to 'very': *Things were pretty bad in Britain, Howard discovered.* □ *We've got a pretty good idea who the leader is.* □ *He had some pretty strong reasons for hating her.* □ *The answer's pretty obvious.* □ *I've been watching her pretty closely recently.* □ *That was pretty* [= almost] *certainly an exaggeration.* □ *I'm pretty* [= almost] *sure that's him.* [see note at **rather**, compare **quite, fairly**]
▻ ***phrases*** **1** (*informal*) Something that is **pretty much** so is so to a great extent: *They're all pretty much alike.* **2** Something that is **pretty nearly** so, or **pretty well** so, is almost so: *That's everything we need, pretty nearly.* □ *His paralysis is pretty well total.* **3** (*informal*) You are **sitting pretty** when you are not affected by the problems that affect other people, or you have an advantage that they don't have.

prevail /prɪ'veɪl/ *verb*: **prevails, prevailing, prevailed**
1 Something **prevails** when it succeeds in having most influence or importance, or in becoming generally accepted: *Justice prevailed in the end.* **2** A belief or custom **prevails** when it is common: *a tradition that has prevailed since the Middle Ages.* **3** You **prevail** on someone to do something when you persuade them to do it: *Let me prevail on you to stay to dinner.*

prevailing /prɪ'veɪlɪŋ/ *adjective*

1 A **prevailing** mood or opinion is generally held or commonly found: *the prevailing fashion for short skirts.* **2** The **prevailing** wind in a region is the wind that blows, often from a particular direction, for most of the time.

prevalent /ˈprɛvələnt/ *adjective*
Something is **prevalent** if it is common or widespread: *a prevalent belief in life after death* □ *areas where poverty and disease are prevalent.* — *noun* (*uncount*) **prevalence**: *the prevalence of the rose in English gardens.*

prevaricate /prɪˈvarɪkeɪt/ *verb*: **prevaricates, prevaricating, prevaricated**
You **prevaricate** if you avoid speaking the truth or giving a direct answer: *The North Korean government is prevaricating in order to move and conceal evidence.*

prevent /prɪˈvɛnt/ *verb*: **prevents, preventing, prevented**
1 You **prevent** someone from doing something, or **prevent** them doing it, when you stop them doing it before they can do it: *She pushed aside a man who was trying to prevent her from leaving.* □ *They did everything they could to prevent Allende assuming power.* □ *He had to prevent the 2.45 train from entering the tunnel.* □ *He took no steps actually to prevent my departure.* [*same as* **stop**] **2** Someone or something **prevents** something, or **prevents** it from happening, or **prevents** it happening, when they avoid it, or ensure that it does not happen: *Europeans wanted to prevent a war, not fight one.* □ *Prohibition does not work in preventing alcoholism.* □ *The tragedy could have been prevented.* □ *She had to grip the saddle to prevent herself from being thrown forward.* □ *The surface was covered with wire netting, presumably to prevent birds nesting there.* [*same as* **stop, avoid, avert**] **3** Circumstances **prevent** something, or **prevent** it from happening, or **prevent** it happening, when they interfere with its being able to happen: *Bad weather prevented us reaching the summit.* □ *Fire was spreading up the staircase and preventing her escape.* □ *Her ill health did not prevent her from painting.* [*same as* **stop**] — *adjective* **preventable:** *Nine thousand children a day die from one of six preventable diseases.*

preventative see **preventive.**

prevention /prɪˈvɛnʃən/ *noun* (*uncount*)
Prevention is action or behaviour that stops something from happening: *the prevention of disease* □ *crime prevention.*

preventive /prɪˈvɛntɪv/ or **preventative** /prɪˈvɛntətɪv/ *adjective*
1 Preventive measures are intended to stop something from happening or occurring: *preventive measures to reduce crime.* **2 Preventive** medicine is intended to prevent disease or bad health.

preview /ˈpriːvjuː/ *noun*: **previews**
A **preview** is an advance showing of *eg* a film, play or exhibition before presentation to the general public: *I haven't been to the exhibition since it opened but I did go to the preview.*

previous /ˈpriːvɪəs/ *adjective*
1 A **previous** occasion or event is one that happened earlier or in the past: *He has no previous experience of computers.* □ *She has a daughter from a previous marriage.* **2 Previous** also describes a person or thing that comes immediately before the present one: *the previous evening* □ *the previous chairman.*

previously /ˈpriːvɪəslɪ/ *adverb*
1 You use **previously** to describe something that was the case at some time in the past: *She previously worked in our London office.* **2 Previously** is also used to indicate how long ago something was the case: *He had worked for us five years previously.* [= five years ago]

pre-war /priːˈwɔː/ *adjective*
Pre-war things or events belong to the period before a war, especially before World War II: *pre-war fashions.*

prey /preɪ/ *noun*; *verb*
▷ ***noun*** (*uncount*)
A bird's or animal's **prey** is the creatures that it hunts and kills as food.
▷ ***verb***: **preys, preying, preyed**

> ***phrasal verb***
> **prey on 1** A bird or animal **preys on** another when it hunts and kills it as food. **2** Something **preys on** your mind when it worries you: *The argument preyed on her mind for the rest of the evening.* □ *preyed on by anxieties.*

price /praɪs/ *noun*; *verb*
▷ ***noun***: **prices**
1 (*count or uncount*) The **price** of something is the amount of money you must pay to buy it: *Tea and biscuits will be served at a price of 40p per person.* □ *I believe the property is worth the price.* □ *Laser printers are dropping in price.* □ *Rubber prices fell steadily during 1989.* □ *a rise in the price of oil* □ *We're faced with price increases of up to 25%.* □ *the relationship between price and demand.* [see note at **cost**] **2** (*used in the singular*) The **price** of something that you want is what you suffer in order to get it: *Unwelcome publicity is the price you pay for fame.* □ *Freedom has its price.*
▷ ***verb***: **prices, pricing, priced**
Something **is priced** at a certain amount if that is what you must pay to buy it: *The watches in this design range are reasonably priced at £14.50.*
▷ ***phrases* 1 a** Something that you want **at any price** is something you are so determined to have that you are willing to suffer anything, or cause any amount of suffering, to achieve it: *He wanted access to Gibraltar, but not at any price.* **b** Something that you don't want **at any price** is something you don't want at all: *In those days I didn't want a regular job at any price.* **2 a** Something can be obtained **at a price** if it is very expensive: *Privacy and convenience are available at a price.* **b** You achieve something **at a price** if you suffer in the process of achieving it: *Victory was achieved, but at a price.*

priceless /ˈpraɪslɪs/ *adjective*
1 Something is **priceless** when it is very valuable: *a priceless work of art.* **2** (*informal*) Something that is described as **priceless** is funny: *a priceless account of how he came to miss the train.*

pricey or **pricy** /ˈpraɪsɪ/ *adjective* (*informal*): **pricier, priciest**
Things that are **pricey** are expensive: *That car's a bit too pricey for me.*

prick /prɪk/ *verb*; *noun*
▷ ***verb***: **pricks, pricking, pricked**
1 You **prick** something when you make a small hole in it with a fine point: *prick yourself on a pin* □ *She pricked holes in the potato skins with a fork.* **2** Something sharp **pricks** you when it sticks into your skin causing you pain: *The nettles pricked her arms.* **3** Tears **prick** your eyes, or your eyes **prick**, when they sting because you are about to cry.
▷ ***noun***: **pricks**
A **prick** is a hole or wound made by a small, sharp object: *sharp pricks from the thorns on the rose stems.*

> ***phrasal verb***
> **prick up** (*informal*) **1** An animal **pricks up its ears**, or its ears **prick up**, when they stand straight in response to a sound. **2** You **prick up your ears** when you begin to listen more carefully because you have heard something interesting: *She pricked up her ears when she heard he was buying a new car.*

prickle /ˈprɪkəl/ *noun*; *verb*
▻ ***noun***: **prickles**
1 A **prickle** is a sharp point or thorn-like growth on a plant or creature: *a hedgehog's prickles.* **2** You feel a **prickle** when you feel as if lots of small sharp points are pricking you: *a prickle of fear.*
▻ ***verb***: **prickles, prickling, prickled**
Your skin **prickles** when it feels as if lots of small sharp points are pricking it, either because something is touching it or because of some strong emotion: *Wool makes my skin prickle.* □ *Her skin prickled with pleasure.*

prickly /ˈprɪklɪ/ *adjective*: **pricklier, prickliest**
1 A **prickly** plant or creature has a lot of prickles on its skin: *a prickly hedgehog.* **2** (*informal*) A person is **prickly** when they get angry or upset easily or quickly: *She can be a bit prickly sometimes.*

pride /praɪd/ *noun*; *verb*
▻ ***noun*** (*uncount*)
1 Pride is a feeling of pleasure and satisfaction at your own or someone else's accomplishments, possessions or qualities: *a feeling of pride that her son had qualified as a doctor.* □ *She looked at her new baby daughter with pride.* **2 Pride** is also a feeling of personal dignity and self-respect: *Her pride prevented her from admitting she was disappointed.* □ *maternal pride.*
▻ ***verb***: **prides, priding, prided**
You **pride** yourself on a skill or quality when you think highly of it: *She prides herself on being able to speak three foreign languages.*
▻ ***phrases*** **1** Your **pride and joy** is a person or thing that you are proud of and that is valuable to you: *Her garden is her pride and joy.* **2** You give **pride of place** to the most important thing in a group or collection: *She gave pride of place on her shelves to a glass vase from Venice.* **3** You **swallow your pride** when you decide you must do something you are ashamed of: *She swallowed her pride and admitted that she needed help.* **4 a** You **take pride in** something when you are proud of it: *She took pride in her son's success.* **b** You **take pride in** something when you try to do it well or work hard on it: *I take pride in doing my work well.* □ *They take pride in their garden.* **5 The pride of** a collection is the most valuable or best item in it.

priest /priːst/ *noun*: **priests**
1 A **priest** is an ordained minister in the Roman Catholic and Orthodox churches, and in some Protestant churches. **2** A **priest** is a man with duties associated with worship in some non-Christian churches: *a Buddhist priest.*

priestess /priːˈstɛs/ *noun*: **priestesses**
A **priestess** is a female priest in non-Christian churches.

priesthood /ˈpriːsthʊd/ *noun* (*used in the singular*)
1 The **priesthood** is the position of being a priest. **2** Priests as a group are members of the **priesthood**: *enter the priesthood.*

priestly /ˈpriːstlɪ/ *adjective*
Priestly actions or things are done by or belong to a priest: *priestly duties.*

prig /prɪg/ *noun* (*old*): **prigs**
A **prig** is a person who always behaves correctly and is quick to criticize and find fault with the behaviour of others. — *adjective* **priggish**: *priggish behaviour.*

prim /prɪm/ *adjective*
A person is **prim** when they are easily shocked by the informal or rude behaviour of others: *a prim, old-fashioned teacher.* — *adverb* **primly:** *She sat primly, listening to his jokes with disapproval.*

prima ballerina /priːmə baləˈriːnə/ *noun*: **prima ballerinas**
A **prima ballerina** is the leading female dancer in a ballet company.

primacy /ˈpraɪməsɪ/ *noun* (*uncount*)
Something has **primacy** when it is first in importance, order or rank: *Japanese primacy in the Far East.*

prima donna /priːmə ˈdɒnə/ *noun*: **prima donnas**
1 A **prima donna** is a leading female opera singer. **2** A **prima donna** is also a person who thinks he or she is very important, is difficult to please, and whose moods change suddenly: *My boss is a bit of a prima donna.*

primaeval see **primeval.**

primarily /ˈpraɪmərɪlɪ/ *adverb*
Primarily means 'chiefly' or 'mainly', and is used to indicate the most important feature or element: *She is primarily interested in the development of health care in rural Mexico.* □ *The problem is caused primarily by a lack of money.*

primary /ˈpraɪmərɪ/ *adjective*; *noun*
▻ ***adjective***
1 Something is of **primary** importance when it is most important: *Our primary concern was to ensure all children could read by the age of eleven.* □ *Your primary task is to get the company running efficiently.* **2 Primary** education is for children aged between 5 and 11: *primary schools.* [see also **secondary**]
▻ ***noun***: **primaries**
1 A **primary** is a primary school. **2** (*AmE*) A **primary** is a preliminary election in a state in which party members vote for a candidate for political office in that party, or for the candidate to stand for president: *If he wins this primary he is sure to get the Republican nomination.*

primary colour /praɪmərɪ ˈkʌlə(r)/ *noun*: **primary colours**
The **primary colours** are the three colours that can be mixed together to make all the other colours, being red, blue and yellow in painting and red, blue and green in photography.

primate /ˈpraɪmeɪt/ *noun*: **primates**
A **primate** is a member of the group of intelligent mammals that includes monkeys, apes and humans.

prime /praɪm/ *adjective*; *noun*; *verb*
▻ ***adjective***
1 Something is **prime** when it is **a** the most important thing: *A knowledge of languages is a prime requirement for a career in translating.* **b** of the best quality: *prime beef* □ *a prime building site.* **2** A **prime** example of something is a typical example of it.
▻ ***noun*** (*used in the singular*)
The **prime** is the period in a person's or thing's existence when they are at their best, strongest, most productive or most active: *She'd been an excellent dancer in her prime.* □ *old vehicles past their prime* □ *A young woman in the prime of life.*
▻ ***verb***: **primes, priming, primed**
1 You **prime** someone when you give them important or necessary information in advance: *Having been primed by Draper back at the hotel, he handled the journalists with apparent calm.* [*same as* **brief**] **2** You

prime *eg* wood when you cover it with a special substance before painting it.

prime minister /praɪm ˈmɪnɪstə(r)/ *noun*: **prime ministers**
The **prime minister** is the chief minister of a government: *the Prime Minister's visit to Ireland.*

prime number /praɪm ˈnʌmbə(r)/ *noun*: **prime numbers**
A **prime number** is a number that is exactly divisible only by itself and 1: *3, 5 and 7 are prime numbers.*

primeval or **primaeval** /praɪˈmiːvəl/ *adjective*
Primeval describes things that belong to or date from the earliest period in the earth's history: *primeval rainforests.*

primitive /ˈprɪmɪtɪv/ *adjective*
1 Primitive people or things belong to the earliest stages of development: *primitive stone tools* □ *an example of primitive computers.* **2 Primitive** people live in a society that is usually simple and is not developed, and is not industrialized: *Too many people still live in primitive conditions.* □ *primitive tribes in isolated parts of South America.*

primrose /ˈprɪmrouz/ *noun*: **primroses**
A **primrose** is a small, low-growing wild plant with pale yellow flowers that appear in spring.

prince /prɪns/ *noun*: **princes**
1 A **prince** is the son of a king or queen, or some other male member of the royal family: *The Queen's husband is Prince Philip and her youngest son is Prince Edward.* **2** A **prince** is also a male ruler of a small state or country: *Prince Rainier of Monaco.*

princely /ˈprɪnslɪ/ *adjective*
1 Princely things belong to or are suitable for a prince. **2** A **princely** sum of money is a large or generous one: *His donation to the charity was princely.*

princess /ˈprɪnsɛs/ *noun*: **princesses**
A **princess** is a female member of a royal family, usually either the daughter of a king or queen or the wife or daughter of a prince.

principal /ˈprɪnsɪpəl/ *adjective*; *noun*
▻ ***adjective***
Something is described as **principal** when it is the most important or main thing: *the principal reason for moving house* □ *the principal female character in the opera.*
▻ ***noun*: principals**
The **principal** of a school, college or university is the person who is in charge of it.

principality /prɪnsɪˈpalɪtɪ/ *noun*: **principalities**
A **principality** is a small state or country ruled by a prince: *the principality of Monaco.*

principally /ˈprɪnsɪplɪ/ *adverb*
Principally means 'mostly' or 'mainly': *She teaches languages, principally French and Spanish.* □ *This type of car is sold principally to young women drivers.*

principle /ˈprɪnsɪpəl/ *noun*: **principles**
1 A **principle** is a general truth or rule that something is based on: *the principles of French cooking* □ *a school organized on liberal principles.* **2** (*count or uncount*) A **principle** is a general rule that guides your behaviour, based on your religious and moral beliefs: *He has high principles.* □ *a woman of principle.* **3** A **principle** is also a general scientific law, especially one that explains how something works: *a mathematical principle.*
▻ ***phrases*** **1** You agree to something **in principal** when you agree with it in general but not with all its details: *The workers agree with the arrangement in principle but would like further discussion of some minor points.* **2** You do something **on principle** when a particular religious or moral belief you have causes you to do it: *I disagree with divorce on principle.*

principled /ˈprɪnsɪpəld/ *adjective*
Principled behaviour shows, or is influenced by, having, high religious or moral beliefs.

print /prɪnt/ *verb*; *noun*
▻ ***verb*: prints, printing, printed**
1 You **print** words or pictures when you produce a copy of them on paper in ink, using *eg* a printing press or other machine: *The newspaper printed pictures of the wedding.* **2** You **print** a book, article or newspaper when you publish it: *The magazine printed several recipes for fruit cake.* **3** You **print** when you write with letters that are separate and not joined up: *Print your name in capital letters at the top of the form.* **4** You **print** designs on fabric when you mark them on it using dye.
▻ ***noun*: prints**
1 A **print** is a mark made on a surface by the pressure of something in contact with it: *Her feet left prints on the sand.* □ *footprints* □ *fingerprints.* **2** (*uncount*) The **print** in a newspaper, magazine or book is the words and numbers that are produced mechanically: *books in large print for the partially-sighted.* □ *small print.* **3** (*uncount*) **Print** is writing done with each letter written separately. **4** A **print** is a design printed from an engraved wood block or metal plate: *There are several framed prints on the wall.* **5** A **print** is a positive photograph made from a negative: *She collected her prints from the chemist.*
▻ ***phrases*** **1** A speech or opinion is **in print** when it is published in an article, book or newspaper: *The results of the study are in print in a scientific journal.* **2** A book is **in print** when it is available from a publisher. It is **out of print** when it is no longer available from a publisher: *Is the book still in print?* □ *It's been out of print for a couple of years.*

> ***phrasal verb***
> You **print out** data from a computer when you produce a printed copy of it: *The files are being printed out now.* □ *print the tables out.* [see also **printout**]

printer /ˈprɪntə(r)/ *noun*: **printers**
1 A **printer** is a person or business that prints books or newspapers. **2** A **printer** is also a machine that prints data from a computer. [see picture at **office**]

printing /ˈprɪntɪŋ/ *noun* (*uncount*)
Printing is the art or business of producing books or newspapers in print: *the development of printing in the late fifteenth century.*

printing press /ˈprɪntɪŋ prɛs/ *noun*: **printing presses**
A **printing press** is a machine that prints books and newspapers.

printout /ˈprɪntaʊt/ *noun*: **printouts**
A **printout** is printed copy of data held in a computer: *I need a printout of all these files.* [see also **print out**]

prior /praɪə(r)/ *adjective*
1 A **prior** engagement has already been arranged for the time in question: *She couldn't attend the meeting because she had a prior engagement.* **2 Prior** knowledge is knowledge that you have about something before it occurs: *No prior knowledge of computing is necessary as full training will be given when you start the job.* **3** A **prior** claim is more urgent or important than other claims: *have prior claims on your time.*

▻ ***phrase*** (*formal*) One thing happens **prior to** another when it happens just before it: *The pilot checked the weather conditions prior to departure.*

prioritize or **prioritise** /praɪˈɒrɪtaɪz/ *verb*: **prioritizes, prioritizing, prioritized**
You **prioritize** tasks when you decide which are the most important and must be dealt with first.

priority /praɪˈɒrɪtɪ/ *noun*: **priorities**
1 (*uncount*) One person or thing has **priority** when they have the right to be dealt with or be put first: *People with experience will be given priority.* ▫ *Ambulances have priority over cars.* **2** A **priority** is something that must be dealt with before anything else or as soon as possible: *Earning enough money to keep his family is a high priority.* ▫ *a top priority* ▫ *Holidays abroad are no longer a priority for me.*
▻ ***phrase*** You **get your priorities right** when you deal with things in the proper order according to how important they are: *The health service should get its priorities right and concentrate on making people better, rather than trying to save money.*

prise or **prize** /praɪz/ *verb*: **prises, prising, prised**
You **prise** something open, off or out when you force it open, off or out usually using some flat or sharp implement as a lever: *She prised open the lid.* ▫ *He prised the shell off the rock.*

prism /ˈprɪzm/ *noun*: **prisms**
1 A **prism** is an object made of clear glass that separates a beam of white light into the colours of the rainbow. **2** (*geometry*) A **prism** is a solid figure with matching ends, *eg* both triangles, and parallel sides. [see picture at **shape**]

prison /ˈprɪzən/ *noun*: **prisons**
1 A **prison** is a public building where criminals are kept as a punishment: *She was sent to prison for robbery.* ▫ *Her brother is in prison.* ▫ *escape from prison.* **2** You can describe something as a **prison** when you feel it restricts your life in some way and makes you unhappy: *She feels her marriage has become a prison.*

prisoner /ˈprɪzənə(r)/ *noun*: **prisoners**
1 A **prisoner** is a person who is under arrest or is kept in prison as a punishment: *police hunting the escaped prisoners.* **2** A **prisoner** is also a person who has been captured by the enemy, especially during a war.
▻ ***phrase*** You **take** someone **prisoner** when you capture them.

prisoner of war /prɪzənə(r) əv ˈwɔː/ *noun*: **prisoners of war**
A **prisoner of war** is a soldier taken prisoner during a war.

pristine /ˈprɪstiːn/ *adjective*
Something is **pristine** when it is fresh, clean and so well looked after that it looks as if it has never been used: *a car in pristine condition.*

privacy /ˈprɪvəsɪ/ *noun* (*uncount*)
You have **privacy** when you are able, or have the right, to be alone when you want to be: *There's no privacy in our house.* ▫ *She asked the press to respect her privacy.* ▫ *What you do in privacy is nothing to do with me.* ▫ *the privacy of your own home.*

private /ˈpraɪvət/ *adjective*; *noun*
▻ ***adjective***
1 Something that is **private** is available for the use of only a few people and not everyone: *All hotel rooms have a private bathroom.* [*opposite* **public**] **2 Private** discussions are kept secret from people in general: *a private interview with the pope.* [*same as* **confidential**; *opposite* **public**] **3 Private** activities relate to your personal life and not to your job or profession: *He likes to keep his work separate from his private life.* **4** Your **private** thoughts, opinions and plans are personal and usually not shared with other people: *He doesn't let his wife read his private letters.* **5** A person is **private** when they are quiet and do not share their thoughts and feelings with other people. **6** A place is **private** when you can be there alone. **7 Private** industry or companies are owned by a person or group of people and not by the state or government, and provide services that you must pay for: *a private hospital* ▫ *private education* ▫ *a private bus service between the station and the airport.* [*opposite* **public**] — *adverb* **privately:** *We need to talk privately.* ▫ *a privately run bus service* ▫ *She's paying for her children to be educated privately.* ▫ *I'm privately very worried about him.*
▻ ***noun***: **privates**
A **private** is a soldier with the lowest army rank.
▻ ***phrase*** You do something **in private** when you do it in secret or without other people there: *Could I talk to you in private for a few minutes, please?*

private detective /praɪvət dɪˈtɛktɪv/ *noun*: **private detectives**
A **private detective** is a person who investigates crimes and does detective work, but not as a member of a police force: *She hired a private detective to try to find her missing husband.*

private enterprise /praɪvət ˈɛntəpraɪz/ *noun* (*uncount*)
Private enterprise is the management and financing of industry by people or groups of people rather than by the state or government: *It is government policy to encourage private enterprise.*

private school /praɪvət ˈskuːl/ *noun*: **private schools**
A **private school** is a school which parents must pay to send their children to, and which is not part of the state school system. [see also **public school**]

privation /praɪˈveɪʃən/ *noun* (*count or uncount*): **privations**
You suffer **privation** if you do not have the things that you need or that make life comfortable and pleasant: *the privations of life in the far north of Canada.*

privatize or **privatise** /ˈpraɪvətaɪz/ *verb*: **privatizes, privatizing, privatized**
A government **privatizes** a nationally owned company or business when it gives up control of it by selling it to private individuals and organizations: *The government is planning to privatize the railways.*

privet /ˈprɪvɪt/ *noun* (*uncount*)
Privet is a type of bush used to make hedges.

privilege /ˈprɪvɪlɪdʒ/ *noun*: **privileges**
1 A **privilege** is a special right given to an individual or a few people, that brings some advantage that other people don't have: *Older school pupils enjoy special privileges.* **2** You can describe something as a **privilege** when it is a pleasure or honour that few people have: *I was delighted to have the privilege of meeting the Queen.*

privileged /ˈprɪvɪlɪdʒd/ *adjective*
A **privileged** person has advantages, opportunities and sometimes wealth that other people do not have: *the privileged classes* ▫ *Travel on Concorde is only available to the privileged few who can afford it.*

privy /ˈprɪvɪ/ *adjective* (*formal*)
You are **privy** to *eg* a secret or secret discussion when you are allowed to know about it or be involved in it: *I'm afraid I'm not privy to his domestic arrangements.*

prize[1] /praɪz/ *noun*; *adjective*; *verb*
▻ ***noun***: **prizes**
A **prize** is something won in a competition or given as a reward for good work or an achievement: *win first prize in the crossword competition* ▫ *win the school prize for music* ▫ *the Nobel prize for peace.*

▻ ***adjective***
You can use **prize** to describe things that you value highly: *That painting is her prize possession.*
▻ ***verb***: **prizes, prizing, prized**
You **prize** something when you value it highly: *She prizes honesty above all other human qualities.* ▫ *This painting is his most prized possession.*

prize² see **prise**.

pro¹ /prəʊ/ *noun*
▻ ***phrase*** **The pros and cons** of something are the reasons in favour of and against it: *He's been considering the pros and cons of moving to London from the country.*

pro² /prəʊ/ *noun* (*informal*): **pros**
A **pro** is a professional sportsman or sportswoman: *a tennis pro.*

pro- /prəʊ/ *prefix*
Pro- forms adjectives that describe people or things that support or are in favour of something: *the government's pro-European policies* ▫ *a pro-Labour newspaper.*

probability /prɒbə'bɪlɪtɪ/ *noun*: **probabilities**
1 (*count or uncount*) The **probability** of something happening is the question of how likely it is to happen: *The probability of contracting HIV through receiving blood is now virtually zero.* ▫ *With this method of calculation there is a significant probability of error.* ▫ *theories based on probabilities.* [*opposite* **improbability**; compare **possibility**] **2** (*count or uncount*) The **probability** that something is so, or will happen, is the circumstance that it is likely to be so, or to happen: *The probability is that the murderer washed himself in the kitchen.* ▫ *There was now a high probability that a job would be available in the near future.* [*same as* **likelihood**]
▻ ***phrase*** Something that is so, or will happen, **in all probability**, is likely to be so, or to happen: *In all probability he failed to understand the consequences of his actions.* ▫ *An old person in reasonable health would in all probability be assessed as too fit to qualify for a home help.*

probable /'prɒbəbəl/ *adjective*
1 Something that is **probable** is likely to be so or to happen: *It seems probable that the tendency to addiction has a genetic element.* ▫ *It's probable he didn't realize the police had the letter.* ▫ *Modern ways of living make it probable that all of us will go through periods of stress.* ▫ *My superiors are pleased with me, and promotion seems probable.* ▫ *constituencies where a Conservative victory is probable.* [*same as* **likely**; *opposite* **improbable**; compare **possible**] **2** A **probable** outcome or result is a likely one: *The probable result for Britain would be a rise in sea level.* ▫ *Sir John was widely thought of as a probable successor to Lord Hailsham.* [*same as* **likely**] **3** A **probable** explanation or guess is likely to be the real one: *The probable cause of the fire was a faulty plug socket.* ▫ *It's possible to arrive at a probable date for the birth of Jesus.* [*same as* **likely**]

probably /'prɒbəblɪ/ *adverb* (*sentence adverb*)
Something that is **probably** so, or will **probably** happen, is likely to be so, or is likely to happen: *He had four sons and three daughters, probably all by his first wife.* ▫ *The hands were probably not painted by him.* ▫ *'Was it an eagle?' 'Yes, probably.'* ▫ *It's probably just a coincidence.* ▫ *'Where's Rob?' 'In bed, probably.'* ▫ *She's probably outside, listening.* ▫ *I'll probably see her later.* ▫ *It probably won't last long.* ▫ *The librarian will probably be able to tell you where to find it.* ▫ *'Will you be taking some time off this month?' 'Probably.'* ▫ *'Would that work?' 'Probably not.'* [*same as* almost **certainly**; compare **possibly**]

probation /prə'beɪʃən/ *noun* (*uncount*)
1 Probation is the system which allows criminals to stay out of prison under supervision, on condition that they behave well and meet a probation officer at regular intervals: *He was put on probation for six months.* **2** A new employee is on **probation** when they are working for a trial period to show that they can do the job properly.

probation officer /prə'beɪʃən ɒfɪsə(r)/ *noun*: **probation officers**
A **probation officer** is a person whose job is to supervise the behaviour of criminals on probation.

probe /prəʊb/ *noun*; *verb*
▻ ***noun***: **probes**
1 A **probe** is a long thin instrument used by doctors and dentists to examine *eg* a wound or part of the body. **2** A **probe** is an investigation: *a police probe into drug-dealing.*
▻ ***verb***: **probes, probing, probed**
1 You **probe** when you ask questions or carry out an investigation: *The police probed the circumstances surrounding his death.* ▫ *You'll have to probe his mind to discover what he thinks.* **2** You **probe** something when you examine it with a probe: *He probed through the pile of sand looking for shells.*

problem /'prɒbləm/ *noun*; *adjective*
▻ ***noun***: **problems**
1 A **problem** is a situation, matter or person that it is difficult to understand or deal with: *They have money problems.* ▫ *the problem of unemployment* ▫ *Her children are a problem.* **2** A **problem** is a puzzle or mathematical question set for solving: *The answers to the problems are given at the back of the book.*
▻ ***adjective***
Problem children are difficult to deal with, usually because their behaviour is bad.
▻ ***phrase*** (*informal*) You can describe something as **no problem** when you can do it easily: *'Do you think you can manage on your own?' 'No problem.'*

problematic /prɒblə'matɪk/ or **problematical** /prɒblə'matɪkəl/ *adjective*
Something that is **problematic** causes problems: *Racial integration proves problematic in some societies.*

procedure /prə'siːdʒə(r)/ *noun* (*count or uncount*): **procedures**
Procedure or a **procedure** is the correct or usual way of doing something or the usual order followed when doing it: *You should follow legal procedure closely.* ▫ *What's the company procedure in cases like this?*

proceed /prə'siːd/ *verb*: **proceeds, proceeding, proceeded**
1 You **proceed** with something when you begin it after doing something else, or continue after stopping: *We can't proceed any further until we've assessed work done so far.* ▫ *I can't proceed with my work until my computer is fixed.* ▫ *Please proceed.* **2** An activity **proceeds** when it continues without stopping: *Work on the new houses was proceeding according to plan.* **3** (*formal*) You **proceed** in a particular direction when you travel in that direction: *The car proceeded along the road.*

proceedings /prə'siːdɪŋz/ *noun* (*plural*)
1 The **proceedings** are the things done or said at an organized meeting or event: *She read about the council proceedings in the newspaper.* **2** (*formal*) Legal **proceedings** are legal action: *He began divorce proceedings*

against his wife.

proceeds /'prousi:dz/ *noun* (*plural*)
The **proceeds** from *eg* a sale or fund-raising event are the money made from it: *All proceeds from the jumble sale will go to charity.*

process /'prousɛs/ *noun*; *verb*
▻ ***noun***: **processes**
1 A **process** is a series of operations performed to produce or achieve something: *the process of producing paper from wood.* □ *the manufacturing process.* □ *Learning a foreign language can be a slow process.* **2** A **process** is also a series of natural stages passed through bringing development or change: *the process by which steam becomes water, and by which water becomes ice.*
▻ ***verb***: **processes, processing, processed**
1 You **process** something when you deal with it in the proper or required way: *process photographic film* □ *I won't start processing applications until next week.* **2** Food **is processed** when it is prepared for sale, *eg* by being packed in cans or bottles or by being treated with chemicals. **3** You **process** information when you analyse it by computer. — *adjective* **processed:** *He bought several cans of processed peas.*
▻ ***phrases*** **1** When you are talking about something that has happened or has been done, and you talk about something else that happened or was done **in the process**, you mean that the second event happened during the first or as a result of the first: *I was trying to park the car and knocked the fence over in the process.* **2** You are **in the process of** something when you are still doing it: *I'm in the process of decorating my house.*

procession /prə'sɛʃən/ *noun*: **processions**
A **procession** is a line of moving people or vehicles, usually as part of a ceremony or formal event: *A procession followed the coffin from the church to the grave.*

proclaim /prə'kleɪm/ *verb* (*formal*): **proclaims, proclaiming, proclaimed**
You **proclaim** something when you announce it publicly: *The government proclaimed a period of mourning following the King's death.*

proclamation /prɒklə'meɪʃən/ *noun* (*formal*): **proclamations**
A **proclamation** is an official public announcement of something that is important to everyone in the country: *The government issued a proclamation announcing the King's death.*

procreate /'proukrɪeɪt/ *verb* (*formal*): **procreates, procreating, procreated**
People or animals **procreate** when they produce babies or young animals. — *noun* (*uncount*) **procreation** /proukrɪ'eɪʃən/: *study the process of procreation in fish.*

procure /prə'kjuə(r)/ *verb* (*formal*): **procures, procuring, procured**
You **procure** something when you manage to obtain it: *procure more food and water.*

prod /prɒd/ *verb*; *noun*
▻ ***verb***: **prods, prodding, prodded**
1 You **prod** someone or something when you push them with your finger or a similar object: *She prodded the bread with a knife.* □ *He prodded me in the back with his umbrella.* **2** You **prod** someone when you urge them to start doing what they should be doing: *He needs prodding into action.*
▻ ***noun***: **prods**
1 You give someone or something a **prod** when you push them with your finger or a similar object: *She gave him a prod in the stomach with her walking stick.* **2** You also give someone a **prod** when you urge them to start doing what they should be doing: *It took several prods from his parents before he got out of bed.*

prodigal /'prɒdɪgəl/ *adjective* (*literary*)
A **prodigal** son or daughter is one that left their family home to live away from it but who has now returned after failing to do well.

prodigious /prə'dɪdʒəs/ *adjective* (*formal*)
Something is **prodigious** when it is **1** extraordinary or marvellous: *Her talent is prodigious.* **2** enormous: *prodigious wealth.* — *adverb* **prodigiously:** *She is prodigiously talented.* □ *a prodigiously wealthy man.*

prodigy /'prɒdɪdʒɪ/ *noun*: **prodigies**
A **prodigy** is a person, especially a child, who is exceptionally clever or talented.

produce *verb*; *noun*
▻ ***verb*** /prə'dju:s/: **produces, producing, produced**
1 To **produce** a reaction, result or effect means to cause it to happen or to prompt it: *The rail strike produced terrible delays.* □ *Her singing produced laughter and applause.* □ *His suggestion produced a positive response.* **2** You **produce** something when you cause it to be seen: *She can't produce any evidence against him.* □ *He produced several good reasons backing up his views.* **3** Things or people **produce** something when it comes from them, usually as a result of a natural process: *The sun produces heat and light.* **4** A person or thing **produces** goods or products when they make them: *The company produces video recorders.* □ *Bees produce honey.* **5** A place **produces** *eg* crops or fruit when they are grown there: *France produces a lot of wine.* **6** People or animals **produce** children or young animals when they bear them: *Trees produce leaves.* **7** You **produce** a play, film or radio or television programme when you arrange how it should be done and give instructions to people taking part: *He has produced both operas and films.*
▻ ***noun*** /'prɒdju:s/ (*uncount*)
Produce is food or a product that is produced from land or animals: *fresh farm produce* □ *Scottish produce includes salmon and honey.*

producer /prə'dju:sə(r)/ *noun*: **producers**
1 A **producer** is a person who arranges to put on or make a play, film or radio or television programme *eg* by organizing the people and equipment needed and gives instructions to people taking part. [compare **director**] **2** A **producer** is a person, company or country that grows or makes a large amount of some food or product: *France is a major producer of wine.* □ *The Japanese are important producers of cameras and video recorders.*

product /'prɒdʌkt/ *noun*: **products**
1 A **product** is something that is produced, *eg* through manufacture or agriculture: *The company makes household products like soap powder and furniture polish.* □ *Wine and cheese are major French products.* **2** One thing is the **product** of another when it is the result of it: *This article was the product of hours of thought.* □ *Unemployment is the product of the government's economic policy.*

production /prə'dʌkʃən/ *noun*: **productions**
1 (*uncount*) **Production** is the act of making, growing or producing: *France is famous for the production of cheese and wine.* □ *The new model of car goes into production next year.* □ *Rising production costs will mean an increase in prices.* □ *mass production.* **2** (*uncount*) **Production** is also the quantity of something produced: *an increase in oil production.* **3** A **production** is a particular version of *eg* a play, opera or ballet: *a new production of 'The Marriage of Figaro'.*

productive /prəˈdʌktɪv/ *adjective*
1 Someone or something is **productive** when they produce a lot: *His orchards haven't been very productive this year.* □ *The company needs to become more productive.* **2** A meeting or conversation is **productive** when it is useful and produces good results: *a productive discussion.*

productivity /prɒdʌkˈtɪvɪtɪ/ *noun* (*uncount*)
Productivity is the rate at which goods are produced and how efficiently they are produced: *Britain needs to increase its productivity to prosper.*

prof /prɒf/ *noun* (*informal*): **profs**
A **prof** is a professor: *All the essays will be marked by the prof.* □ *Prof Caie.*

profane /prəˈfeɪn/ *adjective*
Something is **profane** when it does not show the proper respect to religious or holy things: *In some paintings the symbol is profane; in others it is sacred.*

profess /prəˈfɛs/ *verb*: **professes, professing, professed**
1 You **profess** to be or to have something when you claim to be or have it: *I must profess ignorance.* □ *She doesn't profess to be an expert.* □ *He professed not to have seen her.* **2** You **profess** an opinion or belief when you state it openly: *She professed her horror at the crime.*

profession /prəˈfɛʃən/ *noun*: **professions**
1 A **profession** is an occupation, especially one that requires specialist academic and practical training, such as medicine, law, teaching and engineering: *He wants a career in one of the professions, probably either law or journalism.* **2** (*with a singular or plural verb*) All of the people working in one particular profession are called the **profession**: *the medical profession.*

professional /prəˈfɛʃənəl/ *adjective*; *noun*
▻ ***adjective***
1 Professional means of, for or from someone who belongs to a trained profession: *a lawyer's professional skills* □ *You need professional advice.* **2** Someone is **professional** when they do their job with skill and care: *His work is always professional.* □ *She needs a more professional attitude if she is to be a successful teacher.* **3** A **professional** person earns money doing what other people do as a hobby or pastime: *a professional actor* □ *a professional footballer.* [*opposite* **amateur**] — *adverb* **professionally:** *Lawyers must be professionally qualified.* □ *play football professionally.*
▻ ***noun***: **professionals**
1 A **professional** is a person who works in one of the professions: *nurses, doctors, lawyers and other professionals.* **2** A **professional** is someone who does their job skilfully and with care: *He is a real professional.* **3** A **professional** is a person who earns money doing what other people do as a hobby or pastime: *I'm an amateur footballer but my brother is a professional.* [*opposite* **amateur**]

professionalism /prəˈfɛʃənəlɪzm/ *noun* (*uncount*)
A person's **professionalism** is the skill, care, experience and knowledge that they show when doing something: *The school play was produced and acted with considerable professionalism by the pupils.*

professor /prəˈfɛsə(r)/ *noun*: **professors**
1 In British universities and colleges, a **professor** is a teacher with the highest rank: *He used to be professor of French at St Andrews University.* **2** In North American and Canadian universities and colleges, a **professor** is a teacher: *a literature professor.*

proffer /ˈprɒfə(r)/ *verb* (*formal*): **proffers, proffering, proffered**
You **proffer** something to someone when you hold it out for them to take: *proffer them a drink.*

proficient /prəˈfɪʃənt/ *adjective*
You are **proficient** in something when you do it well or with skill: *She's a proficient skier.* □ *He is proficient in several European languages.* — *noun* (*uncount*) **proficiency** /prəˈfɪʃənsɪ/: *her proficiency in skiing* □ *a certificate of proficiency in French* □ *a cycling proficiency test.* — *adverb* **proficiently:** *She skis proficiently.*

profile /ˈproʊfaɪl/ *noun*: **profiles**
1 A person's **profile** is a view of their face seen from the side and not the front. **2** A **profile** of someone is a brief description of their life, experience and character: *The television programme presented profiles of some of the most important poets living in Spain.*
▻ ***phrases*** **1** You see someone **in profile** when you see them from the side: *She is having her portrait painted in profile.* **2** You **keep a low profile** when you behave so that people do not notice you: *The princess kept a low profile at her friend's wedding.*

profit /ˈprɒfɪt/ *noun*; *verb*
▻ ***noun*** (*count or uncount*): **profits**
Profit or a **profit** is money that you make when you sell something for more than you paid for it: *I made a good profit from the sale of my car.* □ *The company has increased its profits this year.* □ *a profit of £500* □ *I don't expect the restaurant will make much profit in its first year.*
▻ ***verb*** (*formal*): **profits, profiting, profited**
You **profit** from something when you gain some benefit from it, not necessarily a financial one: *You should profit from the sale of the house.* □ *I hope you'll be able to profit by my mistakes.*

profitable /ˈprɒfɪtəbəl/ *adjective*
1 A business or company is **profitable** when it makes a profit: *Farming is not very profitable any more.* □ *The company has had a more profitable year this year.* **2** Something is **profitable** when it is useful: *a profitable discussion* □ *I didn't find the talk very profitable.* — *adverb* **profitably:** *The company cannot operate profitably in a recession.* □ *Try to invest your money profitably.* □ *I like to spend my weekends profitably.*

profound /prəˈfaʊnd/ *adjective*
1 Profound describes something that is very great, strong or intense: *His death was a profound shock.* □ *Losing her job had a profound effect on her life.* □ *profound deafness.* **2** A comment or remark is **profound** when it shows great understanding or knowledge: *a profound statement on the nature of god.* — *adverb* **profoundly:** *The news was profoundly disturbing.*

profuse /prəˈfjuːs/ *adjective*
Something is **profuse** when it occurs in large amounts: *offered profuse apologies* □ *profuse bleeding.* — *adverb* **profusely:** *He apologized profusely.* □ *The wound was bleeding profusely.*

profusion /prəˈfjuːʒən/ *noun* (*used in the singular or uncount; formal*)
There is a **profusion** of something when there is a lot of it: *a profusion of new books about the war* □ *roses growing in profusion in the garden.*

prognosis /prɒgˈnoʊsɪs/ *noun* (*formal*): **prognoses** /prɒgˈnoʊsiːz/
A **prognosis** is a judgement about how something will develop, especially a doctor's opinion as to how a patient's illness will develop and how likely the patient is to recover: *His doctor has told him the prognosis is poor.*

program /'prougram/ *noun*; *verb*
▻ ***noun***: **programs**
1 A **program** is a set of instructions that a computer needs to be able to perform some task: *write a program to analyse the data* ▫ *load the program into the computer.* **2** (*AmE*) A **program** is a programme.
▻ ***verb***: **programs, programming, programmed**
You **program** a computer when you give it the instructions it needs to be able to perform a task.

programme (*AmE* **program**) /'prougram/ *noun*; *verb*
▻ ***noun***: **programmes**
1 A radio or television **programme** is a show or item that is broadcast on radio or television: *I like to watch cooking and gardening programmes.* **2** A **programme** is a series of events that has been planned or has to be done: *What's the programmme for this morning?* ▫ *a programme of lectures and seminars* ▫ *the government's programme to reform the health service.* **3** A theatre or concert **programme** is a leaflet that gives information about the performance and the people taking part.
▻ ***verb***: **programmes, programming, programmed**
You **programme** a machine when you set the controls so that it operates at the required time: *The heating system is programmed to come on at 7.00 p.m.* ▫ *She programmed the video to record the film.*
[see also **program**]

programmer (*AmE* **programer**) /'prougramə(r)/ *noun*: **programmers**
A **programmer** is someone whose job involves writing computer programs.

progress *noun*; *verb*
▻ ***noun*** /'prougrɛs/ (*uncount*)
1 Progress is movement towards something or towards conpleting it: *I'm only making slow progress with my music.* ▫ *She's making steady progress with her maths.* ▫ *We have made very little progress towards finding a solution to the problem.* ▫ *The traffic was heavy and our progress home was slow.* ▫ *I'll be in soon to check on your progress.* ▫ *a progress report.* **2 Progress** is also the advances or developments that improve society or life: *Scientists are beginning to make progress in the treatment of cancer.*
▻ ***verb*** /prə'grɛs/: **progresses, progressing, progressed**
1 Something **progresses** when it advances, develops or improves: *My Spanish is progressing.* ▫ *Medical knowledge is progressing quickly.* **2** Something **progresses** when it moves forwards or continues: *He got more and more bored as the meeting progressed.* **3** You **progress** from one thing to another when you move naturally from the first to the second: *After discussing marriage, it seemed natural to progress to discussing children.*
▻ ***phrase*** Something is **in progress** when it is taking place: *Building work on the new swimming pool is still in progress.*

progression /prə'grɛʃən/ *noun* (*count or uncount*; *formal*): **progressions**
1 Progression is the process of moving forwards or advancing in stages: *a logical progression of ideas* ▫ *Progression from one stage to another is gradual.* **2** A **progression** is series of things that follow each other: *a progression of events.*

progressive /prə'grɛsɪv/ *adjective*
1 A process is **progressive** when it moves forward or advances gradually by stages over a period of time: *a progressive increase in the number of staff.* **2** A person or thing is **progressive** when they use or prefer advanced or modern ideas and methods: *a school run on progressive lines.* — *adverb* **progressively:** *The weather got progressively worse.*

prohibit /prə'hɪbɪt/ *verb*: **prohibits, prohibiting, prohibited**
Something **is prohibited** when it is forbidden by law: *new laws to prohibit smoking in public buildings and on public transport* ▫ *The law prohibits children from buying alcohol.*

prohibition /prouɪ'bɪʃən/ *noun*: **prohibitions**
1 (*formal*) A **prohibition** is a law or order forbidding something: *a prohibition on the import of British beef.* **2** (*uncount*) **Prohibition** is the act of forbidding it: *the prohibition of smoking in public places.*

prohibitive /prə'hɪbɪtɪv/ *adjective*
The cost of something is **prohibitive** when it is so high you cannot afford it: *A prohibitive tax on bequests would make the problem worse.* ▫ *They'd thought of fibreglass, but the cost was prohibitive.*

project *noun*; *verb*
▻ ***noun*** /'prɒdʒɛkt/: **projects**
1 A **project** is a plan, scheme or proposal, usually one that involves a lot of people and a lot of work: *a project to build new roads between the town and several remote villages.* **2** A **project** is also a piece of work by a pupil or student that involves research and a written report: *I'm doing a project on the history of the cinema.*
▻ ***verb*** /prə'dʒɛkt/: **projects, projecting, projected**
1 (*usually in the passive*) Something **is projected** when it is planned or suggested for the future: *her projected visit to Cuba.* **2** (*usually in the passive*) A future amount or number **is projected** when it is estimated or forecast: *Rail fares are projected to rise by 10%.* **3** (*formal*) Something **projects** when it stands out from an edge or surface: *The balcony projects from the south side of the house.* **4** You **project** light or images on a surface when you cause them to appear there: *He projected his holiday slides on the wall.* **5** You **project** yourself in a certain way when you try to make yourself appear in that way to other people: *He projected himself as kind, caring and thoughtful.*

projection /prə'dʒɛkʃən/ *noun*: **projections**
1 A **projection** is an estimate or a forecast of a future amount or number: *sales projections for the next five years.* **2** (*uncount*) **Projection** is the showing of a film or slides on a screen: *film projection.* **3** A **projection** is something that stands out from a surface.

projector /prə'dʒɛktə(r)/ *noun*: **projectors**
A **projector** is a machine for projecting films or slides on to a screen.

proletarian /proulə'tɛərɪən/ *adjective* (*technical*)
Proletarian means relating to the proletariat: *the proletarian masses* ▫ *a proletarian newspaper.*

proletariat /proulə'tɛərɪət/ *noun* (*used in the singular*; *technical*)
The **proletariat** is made up of members of the working class, especially industrial workers: *a book about the proletariat's struggle for political power.*

proliferate /prə'lɪfəreɪt/ *verb*: **proliferates, proliferating, proliferated**
Things **proliferate** when they rapidly increase in numbers: *The number of English language courses for foreigners has proliferated in recent years.* — *noun* (*uncount*) **proliferation** /prəlɪfə'reɪʃən/: *the proliferation of language courses for foreigners.*

prolific /prə'lɪfɪk/ *adjective*
A writer, composer or artist is **prolific** when they continually produce new work: *Haydn was a prolific composer of symphonies.* — *adverb* **prolifically:** *work prolifically.*

prologue (*AmE* **prolog**) /'proulɒg/ *noun*: **prologues**
1 A **prologue** is a speech or piece of writing that intro-

duces a play or book: *the prologue to Shakespeare's play 'Romeo and Juliet'.* [compare **epilogue**] **2** An event is a **prologue** to another, usually more important, event or set of events when it comes before it or leads up to it: *The dispute was the prologue to a battle that lasted several months.*

prolong /prə'lɒŋ/ *verb*: **prolongs, prolonging, prolonged**
You **prolong** *eg* an event or situation when you make it last longer: *She didn't prolong her visit beyond a couple of hours.*

prolonged /prə'lɒŋd/ *adjective*
Something is **prolonged** when it continues for a long time or for longer than expected: *her prolonged absence from school.*

promenade /prɒmə'nɑːd/ *noun*: **promenades**
A **promenade** is a broad path or pavement, usually along a sea front.

prominent /'prɒmɪnənt/ *adjective*
1 A **prominent** person has an important or influential position or role: *a prominent politician* □ *a prominent member of the community.* **2** Something that is **prominent** is easy to see or noticeable: *The hill is a prominent landmark.* **3** Part of your face is **prominent** if it stands out or protrudes beyond the surface: *a prominent chin* □ *prominent eyes* □ *prominent teeth.* — *noun* (*uncount*) **prominence**: *his rise to prominence in the Labour Party.* — *adverb* **prominently:** *The parking ticket should be displayed prominently on the windscreen.*

promiscuous /prə'mɪskjʊəs/ *adjective* (*derogatory*)
Someone who is **promiscuous** has sexual intercourse with a lot of people: *a promiscuous lifestyle.* — *noun* (*uncount*) **promiscuity** /prɒmɪ'skjuːɪtɪ/: *lead a life of promiscuity.*

promise /'prɒmɪs/ *verb*; *noun*
▻ ***verb***: **promises, promising, promised**
1 You **promise** to do something, or promise someone you will do it, when you tell them that you will definitely do it: *He had promised his secretary faithfully that he would be on time.* □ *I promise you it won't happen again.* □ *I've promised to be at the theatre by eight o'clock.* □ *Promise not to get into a political argument with my father.* □ *I won't forget, I promise.* □ *'I'll be there,' she promised.* **2** You **promise** someone something when you tell them you will definitely give it to them: *Nellie promised me one of her dresses when she bought a new one.* □ *A Bristol engineering firm had promised him a job.* □ *We were unable to promise our support.* **3** Someone in authority **promises** something, or **promises** it for a certain time, when they say they will provide it: *The government promised a referendum.* □ *A pay rise was promised for 1991.* **4** You **promise** yourself something when you decide or resolve to do it: *I promised myself I'd never smoke again.* □ *Tess had promised herself she would never marry.* **5** One thing **promises** another if it seems likely to produce it: *We chose a 12-mile route that promised spectacular views.* □ *It's a challenge that promises growth and achievement.* **6** Something **promises** to be of a certain quality if it looks likely to have that quality: *This promises to be his toughest task yet.* □ *The book promises to be highly readable.*
▻ ***noun***: **promises**
1 You make a **promise** when you tell someone that you will definitely do something or give them something: *I can't make any promises yet.* □ *She kept her promise.* □ *I hate breaking promises.* □ *What happened to all those promises of help he had received?* □ *He left with a promise to return on his first free Sunday.* **2** (*used in the singular*) There is a **promise** of something if there is a sign of it happening: *The day dawned still and misty, with a promise of autumn sunshine.* **3** (*uncount or used in the singular*) Someone or something that shows **promise** shows signs of being successful: *She was already showing promise as a designer.* □ *He never fulfilled his early promise.*

promising /'prɒmɪsɪŋ/ *adjective*
Someone or something is **promising** when they look likely to be excellent or successful: *This book looks promising.* □ *a promising young dancer.*

promote /prə'moʊt/ *verb*: **promotes, promoting, promoted**
1 Someone **is promoted** when they are given a more senior position: *The lieutenant was promoted to captain.* **2** You **promote** something when **a** you work to spread or encourage it: *diplomats promoting peace.* **b** you work to try to make it more popular, especially through advertising: *promote health education in schools* □ *The area has been promoted as a tourist resort.* **3** One thing **promotes** another when it contributes to it: *Exercise promotes health.*

promoter /prə'moʊtə(r)/ *noun*: **promoters**
A **promoter** is a person who organizes or provides the money for *eg* a sporting event or concert: *The newspaper was the promoter of the chess championship.* □ *a concert promoter.*

promotion /prə'moʊʃən/ *noun*: **promotions**
1 (*count or uncount*) You are given **promotion**, or a **promotion**, when you are given a more senior position: *She has applied for promotion.* □ *This job will be a promotion for him.* **2** (*uncount*) The **promotion** of something is action taken to try to make it more successful or popular: *the promotion of a new type of car* □ *a government ban on the promotion of alcohol.* **3** A **promotion** is a campaign advertising a particular product: *a promotion to encourage people to buy her new novel.*

prompt /prɒmpt/ *adjective*; *adverb*; *verb*
▻ ***adjective***
1 A **prompt** action is done immediately or without delay: *a prompt reply to her letter* □ *require prompt attention.* **2** A person is **prompt** when they act quickly, immediately or without waiting: *She was prompt in her offers of help.* **3** A person is **prompt** when they arrive at the right time: *Do try to be prompt tomorrow.*
▻ ***adverb***
You can use **prompt** to show that something will happen at an exact time: *You must be here by 2.15 prompt.* □ *The film will start at 8 p.m. prompt.* [compare **promptly**]
▻ ***verb***: **prompts, prompting, prompted**
1 You **prompt** someone to do something if you suggest they do it, cause them to do it or remind them to do it: *Reading a book about Spain prompted him to go there on holiday.* □ *She prompted me to call a staff meeting.* **2** You **prompt** someone who is speaking, especially an actor, when you help them to remember what they must say next by saying a few words for them: *The lawyer prompted her witness by asking him what happened next.* □ *'And then?' he prompted after a short pause.* □ *I'm going to prompt at the performance tomorrow.*

promptly /'prɒmptlɪ/ *adverb*
1 Something happens **promptly** when it happens at the correct time: *The train arrived promptly at 6.30 p.m.* **2** You do something **promptly** when you do it immediately or without delay: *He fell over and promptly burst into tears.* [compare **prompt**]

prone /proʊn/ *adjective*
1 You are **prone** to something when you suffer from it or are likely to do it: *He is prone to bronchitis.* □ *accident-prone.* □ *I am prone to make mistakes.* **2** You are

prone when you are lying flat, especially face downwards.

prong /prɒŋ/ *noun*: **prongs**
1 A **prong** is a point or spike, especially one of those on the head of a fork. **2** (*military*) The **prongs** of an attacking force are the various sections as they approach the target from different directions. — *adjective* **pronged**: *a three-pronged attack*. [see picture at **tool**]

pronoun /ˈprounaun/ *noun* (*grammar*): **pronouns**
1 Pronouns are words that are used to refer to nouns and noun phrases. See the entries in this dictionary for **personal pronoun**, **possessive**, **reflexive pronoun**, **relative**, **indefinite pronoun**, **interrogative** and **demonstrative**. **2** A lot of determiners can be used as pronouns, *eg all, both, some*. See these words. **3** Pronouns are not usually used with adjectives or determiners, but *one* and *ones* are an exception: *I'll have those ones. Is there a cheaper one*?

pronounce /prəˈnauns/ *verb*: **pronounces, pronouncing, pronounced**
1 You **pronounce** words or letters when you say them in the way they are usually said: *She can't pronounce 'th' properly.* □ *His name is foreign; can you pronounce it?* **2** (*formal*) You **pronounce** something when you state it officially or formally: *The jury pronounced her innocent.* □ *The minister pronounced them husband and wife.* **3** (*formal*) You **pronounce** on something when you give your opinion or verdict on it: *He isn't qualified to pronounce on this matter.*

pronounced /prəˈnaunsd/ *adjective*
Something that is **pronounced** is noticeable: *He walks with a pronounced limp.*

pronouncement /prəˈnaunsmənt/ *noun*: **pronouncements**
A **pronouncement** is a formal or official announcement or statement.

pronunciation /prənʌnsɪˈeɪʃən/ *noun*: **pronunciations**
1 (*count or uncount*) The **pronunciation** of a word or letter is the way it is usually pronounced: *the standard pronunciation of the word.* **2** (*usually in the singular*) Your **pronunciation** is the way you pronounce words and letters: *an educated, middle-class pronunciation.*

proof /pru:f/ *noun*; *adjective*
▻ ***noun*** (*count or uncount*): **proofs**
Proof is evidence that shows that something is true or a fact, or exists: *We have no proof that he is still alive.* □ *Do you have any proof?* □ *Where's the proof?*
▻ ***adjective***
One thing is **proof** against another when it is able not to be or designed not to be damaged by a particular thing. **Proof** is often used in combination with another word, usually a noun: *The roof needs to be proof against storms.* □ *waterproof* □ *fireproof.*

prop[1] /prɒp/ *noun*; *verb*
▻ ***noun***: **props**
1 A **prop** is a rigid, usually upright support: *a clothes prop.* [= for holding a rope of washing to dry] **2** A **prop** is also a person or thing that you depend on for help or support: *The company couldn't survive without the bank as a prop.*
▻ ***verb***: **props, propping, propped**
You **prop** one thing against another when you lean it on it: *She propped her bike against the wall.* □ *prop the window open with a book.*

> ***phrasal verb***
> **prop up 1** You **prop** something or someone **up** when you support them or keep them upright by leaning them on something: *use planks of wood to prop the roof up* □ *She sat in bed, propped up with cushions.* **2** One person or group **props up** another when they support or help it financially: *Loans from the bank are propping the company up.* □ *The government is being propped up by money sent from supporters living abroad.*

prop[2] /prɒp/ *noun* (*usually in the plural*): **props**
The **props** are the items and objects used in a film or play: *One of the props needed for 'Hamlet' is a skull.*

propaganda /prɒpəˈgandə/ *noun* (*uncount*; *often derogatory*)
Propaganda is usually false or exaggerated information, rumours and opinions that are presented to try to influence public feeling: *political propaganda produced by the government's opponents.*

propagandist /prɒpəˈgandɪst/ *noun* (*usually derogatory*): **propagandists**
A **propagandist** is a person who prepares or publishes propaganda in support of a particular idea or person.

propagate /ˈprɒpəgeɪt/ *verb*: **propagates, propagating, propagated**
1 (*technical*) You **propagate** plants when you grow them from seed or from a small part cut off another plant. **2** (*formal*) Someone **propagates** ideas when they try to spread them and make them popular. — *noun* (*uncount*) **propagation** /prɒpəˈgeɪʃən/: *the propagation of plants.*

propel /prəˈpɛl/ *verb*: **propels, propelling, propelled**
You **propel** someone or something when you drive or push them forwards: *A sailing boat is propelled by the wind.* □ *She propelled him towards the door.* □ *A desire to work with children propelled him into teaching.*

propeller /prəˈpɛlə(r)/ *noun*: **propellers**
A **propeller** is a device with blades that turn to propel a ship or an aircraft.

propensity /prəˈpɛnsɪtɪ/ *noun*: **propensities**
Someone has a **propensity** to act in a particular, usually bad, way when they have a tendency to act in this way: *He has a propensity towards violence.* □ *a propensity for complaining* □ *a propensity to act without thinking.*

proper /ˈprɒpə(r)/ *adjective*
1 Proper describes something that is real or genuine: *We haven't had a proper holiday for years.* □ *The injury to your arm needs proper medical attention.* **2** The **proper** thing is the one that is correct or suitable: *Put the book back in its proper place on the shelf.* □ *at the proper time.* **3** The **proper** way to behave is socially accepted or respectable: *It isn't proper to speak with your mouth full of food.* **4** You use **proper** after a noun to show that you are referring strictly to it and not to things related or close to it: *She lives in the suburbs, not in the city proper.*

properly /ˈprɒpəlɪ/ *adverb*
1 You do something **properly** when you do it correctly: *My computer hasn't worked properly since I dropped it on the floor.* **2** You behave **properly** when you behave in a suitable and polite way: *Children must behave properly in restaurants.*

proper noun /prɒpə(r) ˈnaun/ or **proper name** /prɒpə(r) ˈneɪm/ *noun* (*grammar*): **proper nouns**
A **proper noun** is the name of a particular person, place or thing: *'George', 'Kent', The 'Eiffel Tower,' and 'New York' are all proper nouns.*

property /ˈprɒpətɪ/ *noun*: **properties**
1 (*uncount*) Your **property** is all the things you own: *That book is my property.* □ *Whose property is this?* **2** (*uncount*) **Property** is land and buildings: *A lot of*

property in the city centre was destroyed in the war. **3** A **property** is a building or piece of land: *He owns several properties near the beach.*

prophecy /ˈprɒfəsɪ/ *noun*: **prophecies**
A **prophecy** is a statement saying what will happen in the future: *a prophecy foretelling the end of the world.* [*same as* **prediction**]

prophesy /ˈprɒfɪsaɪ/ *verb*: **prophesies, prophesying, prophesied**
You **prophesy** something or that something will happen when you say that you believe it will happen: *She prophesied the war.* □ *He prophesied that the government would increase tax.* [*same as* **foretell, predict**]

prophet /ˈprɒfɪt/ *noun*: **prophets**
1 A **prophet** is a person who is believed to have been chosen by God to express God's will, reveal God's intentions and guide the followers of a religion. **2** A **prophet** is someone who claims to be able to tell what will happen in the future: *prophets of doom.*

prophetic /prəˈfɛtɪk/ *adjective*
Something is **prophetic** when it correctly tells what will happen in the future: *His novel proved to be prophetic.*

propitiate /prəˈpɪʃɪeɪt/ *verb* (*formal*): **propitiates, propitiating, propitiated**
You **propitiate** an angry person when you try to make them less angry by doing something you hope will please them.

propitious /prəˈpɪʃəs/ *adjective* (*formal*)
Something is **propitious** if it is favourable and likely to bring success: *a propitious moment to sell the house* □ *The government chose a propitious time for the election.*

proponent /prəˈpoʊnənt/ *noun*: **proponents**
A **proponent** of something is someone who supports it: *a proponent of recycling.* [compare **opponent**]

proportion /prəˈpɔːʃən/ *noun*: **proportions**
1 A **proportion** of an amount or total is part of it: *A large proportion of the population is aged over 50.* **2** The **proportion** of one element or group in relation to the whole or total is the size of it: *Only a small proportion of lawyers are women.* **3** (*count or uncount*) The **proportion** of one part or amount to another is the size of one part in relation to another: *gas and air mixed in a proportion of two parts to one* □ *get the proportions right* □ *mix orange juice and lemonade in equal proportion.* **4** (*used in the plural*) The **proportions** of something are its measurements and size: *The new church is a building of huge proportions.*
▷ ***phrases*** **1** Things **get out of proportion** when you spend more time thinking or worrying about them than is necessary: *She tends to let minor problems get out of proportion.* **2** Something is **in proportion** when the relationship between its individual parts is correct: *Your drawing isn't in proportion; the dog is almost as large as the cow.* **3 a** One thing is *eg* small or large **in proportion to** another when it is small or large in comparison with it: *She has long legs in proportion to her body.* **b** One thing grows **in proportion to** another when it grows at the same rate: *Her salary has not increased in proportion to the cost of living.* **4** One thing is **out of all proportion** to another when it is larger, more important or more serious than it needs to be in comparison with it: *Her anger with him is out of all proportion to what he did to upset her.* **5** You have a **sense of proportion** when you can judge which things are really important and which are not: *He's lost all sense of proportion and spent more on one shirt than he did on two suits.*

proportional /prəˈpɔːʃənəl/ *adjective*
One thing is **proportional** to another when it grows at the same rate as it, and when it always matches or corresponds with it by the same amount: *The number of people catching this disease are proportional to the size of the population.* □ *a salary increase proportional to the inflation rate.* — *adverb* **proportionally:** *Women have proportionally larger brains than men.*

proportionate /prəˈpɔːʃənət/ *adjective*
Proportionate means proportional: *The wages will be proportionate to the work done.* — *adverb* **proportionately:** *Britain spends proportionately less money on aid to poor countries than America does.*

proposal /prəˈpoʊzəl/ *noun*: **proposals**
1 A **proposal** is a plan or suggestion: *The council have to consider a proposal to build a new shopping centre.* □ *a peace proposal.* **2** You receive a **proposal** when someone asks you to marry them.

propose /prəˈpoʊz/ *verb*: **proposes, proposing, proposed**
1 You **propose** *eg* a plan when you suggest people consider it: *She proposed a break for coffee.* □ *She proposed stopping for coffee.* □ *He proposed that they stop early.* **2** You **propose** to do something when you intend to do it: *I don't propose to sell my house.* □ *I don't propose helping him unless he asks me to.* **3** You **propose** someone when you suggest they be considered for a position: *I'd like to propose George for president.* **4** You **propose** a motion in a debate when you introduce it and begin the discussion of it: *She proposed the motion 'Children are the country's future'.* **5** You **propose** a toast or someone's health when you announce that people will drink to someone's health. **6** You **propose** to someone when you ask them to marry you: *He'd only known her for three weeks before he proposed.* □ *propose marriage.* — *adjective* **proposed:** *her proposed holiday in Malawi* □ *the proposed peace plan.*

proposition /prɒpəˈzɪʃən/ *noun*; *verb*
▷ ***noun***: **propositions**
1 A **proposition** is a proposal or suggestion: *He wanted to sell his car so I made him a proposition.* [= I offered to buy it] □ *a strange proposition.* **2** A **proposition** is a statement expressing an opinion or judgement: *We have no evidence to support the proposition that he is lying.*
▷ ***verb***: (*euphemistic, informal*) **propositions, propositioning, propositioned**
One person **propositions** another if they ask them to have sexual intercourse with them.

proprietary /prəˈpraɪətərɪ/ *adjective* (*formal*)
A **proprietary** product is sold under a tradename: *a proprietary cough mixture.*

proprietor /prəˈpraɪətə(r)/ *noun*: **proprietors**
The **proprietor** of a shop, hotel or business is the owner.

proprietress /prəˈpraɪətrəs/ *noun*: **proprietresses**
The **proprietress** of a shop, hotel or business is the woman who owns it.

propriety /prəˈpraɪətɪ/ *noun* (*uncount*; *formal*)
You behave with **propriety** when you behave in a way that is morally or socially acceptable: *He always behaves with perfect propriety, especially towards women.*

prosaic /proʊˈzeɪɪk/ *adjective*
Something that is **prosaic** is dull, ordinary and uninteresting: *a rather prosaic film.*

pros and cons see **pro**[1].

prose /proʊz/ *noun* (*uncount*)
Prose is ordinary written or spoken language in contrast to verse or poetry: *write in prose.*

prosecute /ˈprɒsɪkjuːt/ *verb*: **prosecutes, prosecuting, prosecuted**
A person **is prosecuted** if they are charged with a crime and tried in a court of law: *He was prosecuted for dangerous driving.*

prosecution /prɒsɪˈkjuːʃən/ *noun*: **prosecutions**
1 (*count or uncount*) **Prosecution** is the process of charging someone with a crime and trying them in a court of law: *You could face criminal prosecution for dangerous driving.* □ *bring a prosecution against the builders.* **2** (*with a singular or plural verb*) The **prosecution** are the lawyers who try to prove someone is guilty of a crime in a court of law.

prosecutor /prɒsɪkjuːtə(r)/ *noun* (*AmE*): **prosecutors**
A **prosecutor** is a lawyer who accuses someone of a crime and tries to prove they are guilty.

prospect *noun*; *verb*
▷ ***noun*** /ˈprɒspɛkt/: **prospects**
1 (*usually in the singular*) There is a **prospect** of something if it is likely to happen or occur: *the prospect of rain* □ *There's not much prospect of her getting the job.* **2** (*usually in the singular*) A **prospect** is something which you expect will happen: *I don't like the prospect of having to give up work when I get old.* **3** (*used in the plural*) Your **prospects** are your chances of success or opportunities for improvement: *Her prospects are excellent if she passes her exams.* □ *a job with prospects.* **4** (*formal*) A **prospect** is a broad view: *a prospect of the bay.*
▷ ***verb*** /prəˈspɛkt/: **prospects, prospecting, prospected**
You **prospect** for *eg* gold, silver or oil if you search land or under water for it.

prospective /prəˈspɛktɪv/ *adjective*
Someone is described as **prospective** if they hope, expect or are likely to be something: *a prospective buyer for the house* □ *The college had applications from nearly 200 prospective students.*

prospectus /prəˈspɛktəs/ *noun*: **prospectuses**
A **prospectus** is a booklet or document giving information about a school or university, or a business proposal.

prosper /ˈprɒspə(r)/ *verb*: **prospers, prospering, prospered**
A person or business **prospers** when it is successful financially: *It can take a couple of years before a new business begins to prosper.*

prosperity /prɒˈspɛrɪtɪ/ *noun* (*uncount*)
Prosperity is the state of being successful, especially financially: *a period of prosperity.*

prosperous /ˈprɒspərəs/ *adjective*
A **prosperous** person is wealthy and successful.

prostitute /ˈprɒstɪtjuːt/ *noun*; *verb*
▷ ***noun***: **prostitutes**
A **prostitute** is someone who has sexual intercourse with men in return for money.
▷ ***verb***: **prostitutes, prostituting, prostituted**
You **prostitute** yourself or your talents if you use them for things that are not honourable or admirable.

prostitution /prɒstɪˈtjuːʃən/ *noun* (*uncount*)
Prostitution is the work of people who have sexual intercourse with men in return for money.

prostrate *adjective*; *verb*
▷ ***adjective*** /ˈprɒstreɪt/
1 Someone is **prostrate** when they are lying on their stomach with their face downwards, *eg* as a sign of being humble or ashamed. **2** Someone is **prostrate** when they are exhausted by *eg* illness or grief.
▷ ***verb*** /prɒˈstreɪt/: **prostrates, prostrating, prostrated**
You **prostrate** yourself when you lie on your stomach with your face downwards, *eg* as a sign of being humble or ashamed.

protagonist /prəˈtagənɪst/ *noun* (*formal*): **protagonists**
1 A **protagonist** in a play, film or story is the main character in it. **2** A **protagonist** of some idea or movement is a supporter of it: *He's a leading protagonist of nuclear energy.*

protect /prəˈtɛkt/ *verb*: **protects, protecting, protected**
You **protect** someone or something when you guard them from harm, injury or danger: *You'll need a thick coat to protect you from the cold.* □ *She wore gloves to protect the delicate skin on her hands.* □ *These computers need protecting from dust and dirt.*

protection /prəˈtɛkʃən/ *noun* (*uncount*)
Something gives **protection** when it stops someone or something from being harmed, injured or put in danger: *An umbrella offers some protection against the rain.* □ *The trees protect the house from the full force of the wind.*

protective /prəˈtɛktɪv/ *adjective*
1 A **protective** object gives or is designed to give protection: *protective clothing.* **2** You are **protective** towards someone when you want to keep them safe: *People always feel protective towards their children.*

protégé or **protégée** /ˈprɒtɪʒeɪ/ *noun*: **protégés**

> This word is spelt **protégée** when the person concerned is a woman.

Someone is the **protégé** of an older, more experienced person when that person helps and guides them.

protein /ˈproʊtiːn/ *noun* (*count or uncount*): **proteins**
Protein or a **protein** is a substance that helps the body grow and remain healthy, found in *eg* eggs, milk, fish, meat, beans and grains.

protest *verb*; *noun*
▷ ***verb*** /prəˈtɛst/: **protests, protesting, protested**
1 You **protest** about, at or against something when you express your objection to it or disapproval of it: *They protested against the new law.* □ *She protested at the way she had been treated.* □ *If you think you've been charged too much, you should protest.* □ *He protested to his boss.* **2** (*AmE*) You **protest** a decision or measure when you challenge or object to it: *The unions are protesting the company's decision to sack 20 workers.* **3** You **protest** that something is the case when you declare that it is, especially in reply to an accusation: *He protested that he hadn't been told about the meeting.* □ *She protested her innocence.*
▷ ***noun*** /ˈproʊtɛst/: **protests**
A **protest** is an act of expressing disapproval or objecting to something: *The government expected protests against its proposals.* □ *The prisoners rioted in protest at conditions.* □ *The workers held a protest.* — *noun* **protester**: *Several of the protesters were arrested by the police.*
▷ ***phrase*** You do something **under protest** when you do it unwillingly.

Protestant /ˈprɒtɪstənt/ *noun* (*often adjectival*): **Protestants**
A **Protestant** is a member of any of the Christian churches that separated from the Roman Catholic Church in the 16th century: *Protestants and Catholics* □ *a Protestant minister.*

protestation /prɒtəˈsteɪʃən/ *noun* (*formal*): **protestations**
A **protestation** is a formal, solemn or strong declaration or statement: *protestations of friendship.*

protocol /'proutəkɒl/ *noun* (*uncount*)
Protocol is a system of fixed rules that govern behaviour and how things are done in formal situations: *diplomatic protocol* □ *follow protocol closely.*

proton /'proutɒn/ *noun* (*physics*): **protons**
A **proton** is an atomic particle with a positive electrical charge. [compare **electron**]

prototype /'proutətaɪp/ *noun*: **prototypes**
A **prototype** is the first or an original model that is made of a new *eg* vehicle, aircraft or machine, that later models are developed from: *the prototype of a much more powerful computer.*

protracted /prə'traktɪd/ *adjective*
Something is **protracted** when it lasts longer than usual or longer than expected: *I was beginning to worry about her protracted absence.* □ *a protracted coffee break.*

protractor /prə'traktə(r)/ *noun*: **protractors**
A **protractor** is an instrument in the form of a semicircle, used for drawing and measuring angles.

protrude /prə'tru:d/ *verb* (*formal*): **protrudes**, **protruding**, **protruded**
Something **protrudes** when it sticks out: *His legs were protruding from under the table.* □ *protruding teeth.*

proud /praud/ *adjective*
1 You feel **proud** when you respect or admire what you or someone else has done or own: *She was very proud when her son qualified as a doctor.* □ *I am proud to have been chosen to represent the school in the competition.* □ *You should be proud of him.* □ *He's very proud of his new car.* **2** (*derogatory*) A person is **proud** when they have too high an opinion of themselves: *She is too proud to accept help.* [*same as* **arrogant**, **conceited**; *opposite* **humble**] **3** You say you are **proud** when you are pleased or honoured: *I was proud to be invited.* — *adverb* **proudly:** *She smiled proudly at her son.* □ *He walked proudly up to receive his award.*

prove /pru:v/ *verb*: **proves, proving, proved, proven**

> **Proved** and **proven** are both used as the past participle.

1 You **prove** that something is true, correct or a fact when you show that it definitely is true or correct: *The evidence proved his innocence.* □ *Your passport proves your nationality.* □ *His theory was proved wrong.* **2** You **prove** to be something when experience shows that you are it: *He has proved himself reliable.* □ *She has proved to be an excellent singer.* — *adjective* **proven:** *drugs of proven effectiveness* □ *She is a proven liar.*

proverb /'prɒvɜ:b/ *noun*: **proverbs**
A **proverb** is a short statement that gives advice or expresses something people suppose is true: ... *the old proverb about a stitch in time saving nine.*

proverbial /prə'vɜ:bɪəl/ *adjective*
You can use **proverbial** to show that something is referred to in a proverb and well known: *a cat's proverbial nine lives.*

provide /prə'vaɪd/ *verb*: **provides, providing, provided**
Something that is needed **is provided**, or someone **provides** it, when it is given or supplied: *His parents provided the money for his car.* □ *They provided him with the money.* □ *The day at the beach provided hours of enjoyment.*

> ***phrasal verb***
> **provide for 1** You **provide for** someone when you supply the money and other things they need to live: *If he loses his job he won't be able to provide for his family.* **2** You **provide for** an event or situation when you prepare for it in advance: *The estimate of the cost of building a new garage provided for a 5% rise in the cost of wood.*

provided /prə'vaɪdɪd/ or **providing** *conjunction*
Something that can happen **provided** or **provided** that, or **providing** or **providing** that, something else happens, cannot happen unless the second thing does: *Mavis Weeks is another possibility, providing that she hasn't already been snapped up by another company.* □ *Providing I had no objection, Matron wanted me to work on until my holiday.* □ *We could squeeze in another 2000 people, providing we erected temporary seating.* □ *It is legal to bring fish into the UK, provided that you obtain an import licence first.*

providence /'prɒvɪdəns/ *noun* (*uncount; literary*)
Providence is God or a mysterious power or force that operates to keep you from harm: *divine providence.*

providential /prɒvɪ'denʃəl/ *adjective* (*formal*)
Something is **providential** when it is lucky or happens just when it is needed: *His arrival was providential.*

providing /prə'vaɪdɪŋ/ see **provided**

province /'prɒvɪns/ *noun*: **provinces**
1 A **province** is a division of a country that has its own local government and administrative system. **2** (*usually in the plural*) The **provinces** are the parts of a country away from the capital: *a young man from the provinces.* **3** (*used in the singular; formal*) Something is your particular **province** when you know a lot about it or are responsible for it: *a task outside my province.*

provincial /prə'vɪnʃəl/ *adjective*
1 Provincial things belong or relate to the parts of a country away from the capital: *speak with a provincial accent.* **2** A person or thing is **provincial** when they are narrow in outlook: *a provincial attitude to marriage and divorce.* [*same as* **parochial**; *opposite* **sophisticated**]

provision /prə'vɪʒən/ *noun*: **provisions**
1 (*uncount*) The **provision** of goods and services is the act of making them available: *the provision of food and clothing to the homeless.* **2** (*uncount*) You make **provision** for someone when you provide the things they need to live or function properly: *The school has no provision for disabled pupils.* **3** (*uncount*) You make **provision** for a future event when you prepare for it: *She is concerned to make proper provision for the birth of her baby.* **4** (*used in the plural*) **Provisions** are food and other necessary items: *buy enough provisions to last during the two-week camping trip.* **5** A **provision** in a legal document is a condition or requirement in it: *He made provisions for all his grandchildren in his will.*

provisional /prə'vɪʒənəl/ *adjective*
Something that is **provisional** is subject to certain conditions or requires that certain conditions be met before it can go ahead: *a provisional offer of a job* □ *a provisional driving license.* — *adverb* **provisionally:** *He accepted their offer, but only provisionally.*

proviso /prə'vaɪzou/ *noun*: **provisos**
A **proviso** is a condition in an agreement that must be fulfilled before you will act: *She's agreed to go out to dinner with me, but with the proviso that she'll pay.*

provocation /prɒvə'keɪʃən/ *noun* (*count or uncount*): **provocations**
Someone does something as **provocation** when they do it to deliberately annoy someone else: *She refused to react to his provocation.* □ *She bursts into tears at the least provocation.* □ *His comments aren't helpful; they're blatant provocation.*

provocative /prəˈvɒkətɪv/ *adjective*
1 Something is **provocative** when it is deliberately designed to make people angry: *a provocative book on the pope.* **2** **Provocative** behaviour or clothing is designed to be sexually exciting: *a provocative smile.* — *adverb* **provocatively:** *He smiled provocatively.*

provoke /prəˈvoʊk/ *verb*: **provokes, provoking, provoked**
1 You **provoke** someone when you make them angry or annoyed, especially deliberately: *If you provoke the dog, he'll bite you.* □ *She can get very angry when provoked.* **2** Something **provokes** a reaction when it causes it: *The government's plans provoked a storm of protest.*

provoking /prəˈvoʊkɪŋ/ *adjective*
A person or thing is **provoking** when they are annoying.

prow /praʊ/ *noun*: **prows**
The **prow** of a boat or ship is the projecting front part.

prowess /ˈpraʊɪs/ *noun* (*uncount; formal*)
You **prowess** is your skill or ability: *She shows great prowess as a musician.*

prowl /praʊl/ *verb*: **prowls, prowling, prowled**
People or animals **prowl** around when they move about quietly, *eg* when hunting or looking for something: *a fox prowling around the chicken houses* □ *gangs of boys prowling the streets.*
▻ ***phrase*** A person or animal is **on the prowl** when they are hunting or looking for something.

proximity /prɒkˈsɪmɪtɪ/ *noun* (*uncount*)
Proximity is nearness: *the proximity of Mexico to Brazil* □ *He lives in close proximity to the station.* [= near the station]

proxy /ˈprɒksɪ/ *noun*: **proxies**
Your **proxy** is the person you legally allow to act or vote for you: *I've asked my sister to be my proxy and register my vote for me.* □ *vote by proxy.*

prude /pruːd/ *noun*: **prudes**
A **prude** is a person who is easily shocked by the naked human body and sexual intercourse: *His sister was too much of a prude to talk about these things.*

prudent /ˈpruːdənt/ *adjective*
A **prudent** person is sensible, wise or careful: *She considered it prudent to keep a spare set of car keys at her brother's house.* □ *It's prudent to carry an umbrella if you think it might rain.* [*opposite* **imprudent**] — **noun** (*uncount; formal*) **prudence**: *I admire your prudence in keeping a spare set of car keys at your brother's house.* — *adverb* **prudently:** *behave prudently.*

prudish /ˈpruːdɪʃ/ *adjective*
A **prudish** person is easily shocked by the naked human body and sexual intercourse: *a prudish desire to sit on the beach fully dressed.*

prune¹ /pruːn/ *verb*: **prunes, pruning, pruned**
You **prune** a tree or plant when you cut off some of its branches: *The rose bush needs pruning.*

prune² /pruːn/ *noun*: **prunes**
A **prune** is a dried plum: *prunes and custard.*

pry /praɪ/ *verb*: **pries, prying, pried**
You **pry** or **pry** into something when you try to find out about the personal affairs of others: *reporters prying into her private life* □ *I caught him prying in my desk.* □ *I told him to stop prying.* [*same as* **snoop**]

psalm /sɑːm/ *noun*: **psalms**
A **psalm** is a holy song, especially one from the Book of Psalms in the Bible.

pseudo- /sjuːdoʊ/ or /suːdoʊ/ *prefix*
Pseudo- is used to form adjectives and nouns that describe something that is pretending to be, or is falsely like, something else: *pseudo-intellectuals* □ *pseudo-scientific language.*

pseudonym /ˈsjuːdənɪm/ or /ˈsuːdənɪm/ *noun*: **pseudonyms**
A **pseudonym** is a false name used by an author: *Mary Ann Evans wrote under the pseudonym 'George Eliot'.*

psych /saɪk/ *verb* (*informal*): **psychs, psyching, psyched**

> ***phrasal verb***
> You **psych** yourself **up** for something when you prepare mentally for it: *She psyched herself up for the exam.*

psyche /ˈsaɪkɪ/ *noun*: **psyches**
Your **psyche** is your mind, especially with regard to the deep feelings and attitudes that govern your opinions and behaviour.

psychedelic /saɪkəˈdɛlɪk/ *adjective*
1 **Psychedelic** drugs produce a state of mind which makes someone imagine strange sights and visions. **2** **Psychedelic** clothes and pictures have clear, vivid colours: *She was wearing a black shirt and psychedelic skirt.*

psychiatric /saɪkɪˈatrɪk/ *adjective*
Psychiatric means **1** relating to psychiatry: *a psychiatric unit in the hospital.* **2** relating to or involving mental illness: *a psychiatric problem* □ *a psychiatric patient.*

psychiatrist /saɪˈkaɪətrɪst/ *noun*: **psychiatrists**
A **psychiatrist** is a doctor who specializes in treating patients with mental illnesses.

psychiatry /saɪˈkaɪətrɪ/ *noun* (*uncount*)
Psychiatry is the study and treatment of mental illness.

psychic /ˈsaɪkɪk/ *adjective*
A person who is **psychic** has unusual mental powers that cannot be explained, such as being able to see into the future or being able to tell what people are thinking.

psychoanalyse (*AmE* **psychoanalyze**) /saɪkoʊˈanəlaɪz/ *verb*: **psychoanalyses, psychoanalysing, psychoanalysed**
A doctor **psychoanalyses** a patient when they treat them using psychoanalysis.

psychoanalysis /saɪkoʊəˈnalɪsɪs/ *noun* (*uncount*)
Psychoanalysis is the study and treatment of mental illness by talking about the patient's past life, experiences and feelings to identify the usually hidden cause of their illness.

psychoanalyst /saɪkoʊˈanəlɪst/ *noun*: **psychoanalysts**
A **psychoanalyst** is a person who treats patients using psychoanalysis.

psychological /saɪkəˈlɒdʒɪkəl/ *adjective*
Psychological means **1** relating to the mind and how it works: *suffer psychological damage as a result of the war* □ *study the psychological differences between the twins.* **2** relating to psychology: *psychological tests.* — *adverb* **psychologically:** *You need to be tough psychologically to help people affected by war.*

psychologist /saɪˈkɒlədʒɪst/ *noun*: **psychologists**
A **psychologist** is a person who has studied and is specialized in psychology.

psychology /saɪˈkɒlədʒɪ/ *noun*
1 (*uncount*) **Psychology** is the study of the human mind and the reasons for human behaviour. **2** (*used in the singular*) A person's **psychology** is the particular type of mind they have and the behaviour this produces: *gang psychology.*

psychopath /ˈsaɪkoʊpaθ/ *noun*: **psychopaths**
A **psychopath** is a person who is suffering from such a severe mental illness that it makes them dangerous and violent towards others. — *adjective* **psychopathic** /saɪkoʊˈpaθɪk/: *psychopathic behaviour.*

psychosis /saɪˈkoʊsɪs/ *noun*: **psychoses** /saɪˈkoʊsiːz/
A **psychosis** is a severe mental disorder causing the sufferer to lose touch with reality.

psychosomatic /saɪkoʊsəˈmatɪk/ *adjective*
A **psychosomatic** illness is one that has no physical cause but is caused by mental or emotional problems.

psychotherapist /saɪkoʊˈθɛrəpɪst/ *noun*: **psychotherapists**
A **psychotherapist** is a doctor who treats patients using psychotherapy.

psychotherapy /saɪkoʊˈθɛrəpɪ/ *noun* (*uncount*)
Psychotherapy is the treatment of mental or nervous illness using psychological methods rather than surgery or drugs.

psychotic /saɪˈkɒtɪk/ *adjective*
A person who is **psychotic** has a severe mental illness.

pub /pʌb/ *noun*: **pubs**
A **pub** is a place where alcoholic drinks may be bought and drunk. [same as **public house**]

puberty /ˈpjuːbətɪ/ *noun* (*uncount*)
Puberty is the stage in life during which a child's body begins to develop into that of an adult: *reach puberty.*

public /ˈpʌblɪk/ *adjective*; *noun*
▻ ***adjective***
1 Something that is **public** relates to or is of all the people in a country or community: *Pollution is a hazard to public health.* □ *public opinion.* [*opposite* **private**] **2** A **public** area or service is provided for the use of everyone: *public transport* □ *public parks* □ *a public library.* [*opposite* **private**] **3 Public** actions, events or meetings are made, done or held openly so that everyone can be aware of what is happening or said: *a public announcement* □ *a public enquiry into the proposed new road.* [*opposite* **private**] **4** Facts are **public** when everyone knows them and they are not kept secret: *It is public knowledge that she is getting a divorce.* □ *when the facts became public* □ *make your views public* □ *The report into the train accident was not made public.* [*opposite* **secret**] **5 Public** figures, or people who lead **public** lives, are people who are well known as they are mentioned a lot in newspapers and magazines and on the television. **6** A **public** place is not private or isolated: *It's too public to talk secretly here.* [*opposite* **private**] — *adverb* **publicly:** *She admitted publicly that she was expecting a baby.* [*opposite* **privately**]
▻ ***noun*** (*with a singular or plural verb*)
1 The **public** are all the people in a country or community: *The castle is open to the public.* □ *Is the public ever consulted?* □ *Members of the public are not permitted beyond this point.* **2** You can refer to sections of the population involved in particular activities as a certain kind of **public**: *the opera-going public.*
▻ ***phrase*** You do something **in public** when you do it in the presence of other people: *He doesn't like talking about his problems in public.*

publican /ˈpʌblɪkən/ *noun*: **publicans**
A **publican** is a person who owns or manages a pub.

publication /pʌblɪˈkeɪʃən/ *noun*: **publications**
1 (*uncount*) **Publication** is the act of publishing a book, magazine or newspaper: *His article has been accepted for publication.* **2** A **publication** is a book, magazine, newspaper or other printed and published work. **3** (*uncount*) **Publication** is the act of making something known to the public: *Students have to wait three weeks before the publication of the exam results.*

public company /pʌblɪk ˈkʌmpənɪ/ *noun*: **public companies**
A **public company** or **public limited company** is a company whose shares can be bought by members of the public.

public convenience /pʌblɪk kənˈviːnɪəns/ *noun* (*BrE*): **public conveniences**
A **public convenience** is a toilet in a public place that anyone can use.

public house /pʌblɪk ˈhaʊs/ *noun* (*formal*): **public houses**
A **public house** is a pub.

publicity /pʌˈblɪsɪtɪ/ *noun* (*uncount*)
1 Publicity is advertising or actions designed to increase public interest in something: *publicity for her new book* □ *a publicity campaign.* **2 Publicity** is also the public interest or attention that a person or thing attracts: *The film star's visit to London attracted a lot of publicity.* □ *politicians seeking publicity* □ *avoid publicity.*

publicize or **publicise** /ˈpʌblɪsaɪz/ *verb*: **publicizes, publicizing, publicized**
You **publicize** a fact or event when you give people information about it: *Her political opinions have been well publicized in the newspapers.* [*same as* **advertise**]

public relations /pʌblɪk rɪˈleɪʃənz/ *noun*
1 (*uncount*) **Public relations** is the job of producing a good relationship between a company or business and the public: *She works in public relations.* **2** (*plural*) **Public relations** are the state of relationship between a company or business with the public: *It's good for public relations.*

public school /pʌblɪk ˈskuːl/ *noun* (*count or uncount*): **public schools**
1 In Britain, a **public school** is a secondary school that is not part of the state system and that parents must pay for if they want their children to go there. [*same as* **private school**] **2** In the US, a **public school** is a school that any child can go to and that gets its money from the government.

public transport /pʌblɪk ˈtranspɔːt/ *noun* (*uncount*)
Public transport is the buses and trains provided by the state or by local authorities for members of the public to use: *travel by public transport.*

publish /ˈpʌblɪʃ/ *verb*: **publishes, publishing, published**
1 A company **publishes** *eg* books or newspapers when it prints them and sells them to the public: *Larousse publishes dictionaries and encyclopedias.* □ *Her book on Sylvia Plath was published in 1992.* **2** A piece of writing **is published** when it is printed in a newspaper or magazine: *have a letter published in a newspaper.* **3** A person **publishes** a book or article that they have written when a company prints and sells it for them: *He's published several articles on Chaucer.* **4** (*formal*) A piece of information **is published** when it is announced publicly: *They have not yet published their engagement.*

publisher /ˈpʌblɪʃə(r)/ *noun*: **publishers**
A **publisher** is a person or company that publishes books, newspapers or magazines.

publishing /ˈpʌblɪʃɪŋ/ *noun* (*uncount*)
Publishing is the business of printing and selling books, newspapers and magazines: *He works in publishing.*

puce /pjuːs/ *noun* (*uncount*, *often adjectival*)
Puce is a deep pinkish purple colour.

pucker /ˈpʌkə(r)/ *verb*: **puckers, puckering, puckered**
Your face or part of your face **puckers** when it forms into creases, folds or wrinkles: *Her face puckered and she began to cry.* □ *He puckered his lips ready to kiss her.*

pudding /ˈpʊdɪŋ/ *noun*: **puddings**
1 (*count or uncount*) A **pudding** is any of several sweet or savoury foods made with flour and eggs and cooked by steaming, boiling or baking: *eat jam pudding and custard* □ *a plum pudding* □ *roast beef and Yorkshire pudding.* **2** (*uncount*; *BrE*) The **pudding** is the sweet food served at the end of a meal: *What would you like for pudding?*

puddle /ˈpʌdəl/ *noun*: **puddles**
A **puddle** is a small pool of liquid, especially of rainwater: *children splashing in the puddles* □ *a puddle of milk on the kitchen floor.*

puerile /ˈpjʊəraɪl/ *adjective* (*formal*)
Something that is **puerile** is childish or silly. [*same as* **immature**]

puff /pʌf/ *noun*; *verb*
▻ ***noun***: **puffs**
1 A **puff** of air or wind is a small rush of air or wind, or the sound made by it: *a puff of smoke.* **2** You take a **puff** when you breathe smoke from a cigarette into your mouth and then out again: *Rebecca took several puffs on the cigar.*
▻ ***verb***: **puffs, puffing, puffed**
1 You **puff** on *eg* a cigarette when you breathe smoke in from it and then out again: *He sat puffing his pipe.* □ *puff on a cigar.* **2** You **puff** *eg* smoke when you blow it out: *He puffed cigarette smoke in her face.* **3** (*usually in the passive*) You **are puffing** when you are breathing quickly, *eg* because you have been working hard or running: *She was puffing hard as she ran up the hill.* **4** Smoke or steam **puffs** when it comes out of *eg* a chimney in small blasts. **5** A vehicle such as a train **puffs** along when it moves slowly, often with short bursts of steam: *The train puffed up the side of the hill.*

phrasal verbs
You **puff** something **up** or **puff** it **out** when you make it become larger, *eg* by filling it with air, or cause it to swell: *The swan puffed out its feathers.* □ *His eye was all puffed up where the man had hit him.*

puffed /pʌft/ *adjective* (*informal*)
You are **puffed** or **puffed** out when you are breathing heavily or with difficulty because you have been *eg* working hard or running: *She felt puffed after running up the stairs.* □ *He was puffed out by the time he'd climbed to the top of the cliffs.*

puffin /ˈpʌfɪn/ *noun*: **puffins**
A **puffin** is a black and white sea bird with a large brightly coloured beak.

puff pastry /pʌf ˈpeɪstrɪ/ *noun* (*uncount*)
Puff pastry is light flaky pastry made with a lot of butter or margarine.

puffy /ˈpʌfɪ/ *adjective*: **puffier, puffiest**
Part of the body is **puffy** when it is soft and swollen, often as a result of injury: *Her eyes were puffy because she had been crying.*

puke /pjuːk/ *verb*; *noun* (*slang*)
▻ ***verb***: **pukes, puking, puked**
Someone **pukes** when they vomit: *He puked all over the floor.*
▻ ***noun*** (*uncount*)
Puke is vomit.

pull /pʊl/ *verb*; *noun*
▻ ***verb***: **pulls, pulling, pulled**
1 You **pull** something when you take hold of it and draw or force it towards you or towards a point that is near you: *He found a chair and pulled it towards the sofa.* □ *Barclay pulled a pen from his pocket.* □ *He turned to the bookshelves and pulled down an art book.* □ *She began to pull all her daughter's clothes from the wardrobe.* □ *She pulled back the blankets and patted the pillow.* □ *He checked his watch, then pulled a timetable from his jacket pocket.* **2** You **pull** something like a lever or trigger when you move it either towards you or away from the point at which it is fixed, to operate it or make something work: *The bottom opened when a lever was pulled.* □ *Woolley reached up and pulled the switch on the alarm.* □ *I was calling Sweetman's bluff, confident that he would not dare pull the trigger.* **3** You **pull** something like a tooth, or a cork from a bottle, by applying force to remove it: *The boat bumped the bank just as Kate pulled the cork from the bottle.* □ *It's no more serious than having your tooth pulled out.* **4** A vehicle or its driver **pulls** a trailer or caravan when the vehicle is attached to it and draws it along behind: *A tractor drove past, pulling a trailer loaded with bales of hay.* **5** You **pull** curtains or a blind when you open or close them across a window or other opening: *Stephen strolled over to the window and pulled up the blind.* □ *I switched on the light and pulled the curtains.* **6** You **pull** at something when you take hold of it and tug it or move it with force towards you, usually in a quick action and letting it go again: *Little Danny pulled at Ruth's skirt, wanting her to talk to him.* □ *She was pulling at the fringe of the curtain.* **7** You **pull** something apart, or to pieces, or to bits, when you tear it or break it up roughly or violently into small pieces: *Slowly he pulled a flower to pieces with his long fingers.* **8** You **pull** a part of your body, usually your arm or leg, in a certain direction when you move or jerk it suddenly in that direction, *eg* as a quick reaction: *The teacher pulled her hand away, frowning at a smear of paint.* **9** You **pull** yourself out of something like a bath or other quantity of water in which you are immersed when you use your arms to draw yourself up out of it: *Julia pulled herself out of the water, rubbed herself with the towel, and went to dress.* **10** You **pull** a muscle when you stretch or strain it: *Hampson pulled a calf muscle when he stepped up his training.* **11** You say that someone like an entertainer or speaker **pulls** a crowd or a large number of people when a large number come to see or support them: *Jugglers pull the largest crowds at the circus.* **12** Someone **pulls** a gun or other weapon on you when they suddenly produce the weapon and threaten you with it: *A couple of sailors pulled knives on each other in the car park one night.*
▻ ***noun***: **pulls**
1 You give something or someone a **pull** when you pull them, especially quickly or sharply: *She gave the cord a pull, and the light went on.* □ *His reply was to give her a sharp pull forward.* **2** A **pull** is also a tab or loop attached to the top or side of a container, which you pull to open the container. **3** Someone takes a **pull** of a drink, or a **pull** on a cigarette, when they swallow some of their drink, or suck in smoke from their cigarette: *He took a final pull of his beer.* □ *Kate took a long pull on her cigarette and sighed.* **4** (*uncount*) **Pull** is the power to attract people; a speaker is said to have **pull** if a large number of people come to listen. **5** (*uncount*) **Pull** is also the power to influence other people, especially those in a position of authority: *They have some pull with the immigration department.* □ *The board was influenced by the continuing pull of large profits.*

▻ *phrases* **1** For **pull a face** see **face**. **2** For **pull** someone's **leg** see **leg**.

phrasal verbs

pull away 1 A vehicle or its driver **pulls away** when the vehicle starts moving after being stationary for a while, *eg* at the side of the road or at traffic lights: *The car pulled away into the wide street.* **2** A person **pulls away** when they move back suddenly in alarm or surprise: *Lily pulled away from him and screamed.*

pull back You **pull back** from something when you decide not to do it or not to be involved in it: *Jane disagreed, but pulled back from starting an argument*

pull down A building or other structure **is pulled down** when it is deliberately taken down or demolished, *eg* to clear land or because it is unsafe: *People pull down lovely old houses because they're falling to pieces.* □ *Most of the ancient city walls were pulled down twenty years ago.*

pull in or **pull into 1** A vehicle or its driver **pulls in**, or **pulls into** a place, when the vehicle leaves the road it has been travelling on and turns off or stops, *eg* at the side of the road or at a filling station: *She pulled in on the opposite side of the road, and switched off the engine.* □ *Pull into the side a minute and let's talk.* □ *Eventually they pulled into the lane behind the house.* **2** A train **pulls into** a station when it arrives there: *The train pulled into Woodburn, and Clare stepped up out of the carriage.*

pull off 1 You **pull** something **off** when you succeed in it or manage to achieve it: *Sometimes I would pull it off and other times nothing went right.* □ *They were triumphant at having pulled off the deal.* **2** You **pull** clothes **off** when you take them off in a hurry: *She helped him pull off his raincoat.* **3** A vehicle or its driver **pulls off** the road when the vehicle leaves the road and parks, or joins another road: *He pulled off the main highway into a side road.*

pull on You **pull** clothes **on** when you put them on in a hurry.

pull out 1 A vehicle or its driver **pulls out** when it moves out from from the side of the road, or moves to the centre of the road in order to overtake another vehicle going in the same direction. **2** A train **pulls out** when it leaves a station: *Just as the train pulled out of the station, a lorryload of soldiers drove in.* **3** Someone **pulls out** of an agreement or undertaking when they withdraw from it: *The news that Earle had pulled out of the race left everyone aghast.* □ *The Company announced its intention to pull out of Ireland.*

pull over A vehicle or its driver **pulls over** when it moves closer to the side of the road, usually to park or to let other vehicles overtake: *'Pull over and park,' Lorton said.*

pull together 1 People **pull together** when they work together to achieve a common aim or purpose: *Everyone on the team has pulled together well and worked conscientiously.* **2** You try to **pull yourself together** when you try to get your emotional feelings under control so that you can act more rationally: *He seemed to be trying to pull himself together.*

pull through Someone **pulls through** when they recover from an illness or injury, or when they survive or overcome their personal troubles and difficulties; you **pull** someone **through** when you help them to recover: *Dad did pull through; his toughness saw to that.* □ *It was Rosemary who really pulled me through.* □ *If you are finding the work impossible, perhaps your tutors can pull you through.*

pull up 1 You **pull** yourself **up** when you are sitting or lying down, by using your arms to press against something so as to bring your body into a more upright position: *Slowly he pulled himself up to a sitting position against the pillows.* **2** You **pull** someone **up** when you scold or reprimand them: *They were pulled up for being late.* **3** You **pull up** plants when you remove them from the ground by their roots. **4** You **pull** yourself **up** when you suddenly stop yourself doing or saying something: *Edwards began to explain, then pulled himself up with a start.* **5** A vehicle or its driver **pulls up** at a certain place when the vehicle stops there: *Evelyn heard a car pull up and poked her head through the curtains.*

pulley /ˈpʊlɪ/ *noun*: **pulleys**
A **pulley** is a device for lifting and lowering weights or loads, that works by means of a wheel with a hollow or grooved rim, through which the rope attached to the load runs.

pullover /ˈpʊloʊvə(r)/ *noun*: **pullovers**
A **pullover** is a knitted garment for the upper part of your body, usually with sleeves. [*same as* same as **jumper**, **sweater**; see picture at **clothing**]

pulp /ˈpʌlp/ *noun*
1 (*uncount*) **Pulp** is the soft flesh of certain fruits or vegetables. **2** (*uncount or used in the singular*) Food or other substances are reduced to a **pulp** when they are softened to a thick semi-liquid state by beating or mashing: *The cheaper kind of paper is made from wood pulp.* □ *Mash the raspberries to a pulp.*

pulpit /ˈpʊlpɪt/ *noun*: **pulpits**
A **pulpit** is a small raised platform in a church, where the minister or other member of the clergy stands when preaching to the congregation.

pulsate /pʌlˈseɪt/ *verb*: **pulsates, pulsating, pulsating**
Something **pulsates** when it moves or vibrates with a strong, regular rhythm or beat: *loud pulsating music* □ *The creature's throat was visibly pulsating.* [*same as* **throb**, **pulse**]

pulse[1] /pʌls/ *noun*; *verb*
▻ ***noun*** (*usually in the singular*): **pulses**
Your **pulse** is the regular movement of your heart and arteries in pumping blood through your body, felt as a beat where an artery nears the skin surface, *eg* at the wrist: *Your pulse rate slows down when you rest.*
▻ ***verb***: **pulses, pulsing, pulsed**
Something **pulses** when it moves or vibrates with a strong, regular rhythm or beat. [*same as* **throb**, **pulsate**]
▻ ***phrase*** You **take** someone's **pulse** by feeling their wrist with your fingertips, to find out how fast their heart is beating.

pulse[2] /pʌls/ *noun* (*usually in the plural*): **pulses**
Pulses are edible seeds such as beans, peas and lentils: *Try to include a variety of pulses among the vegetables you eat.*

pulverize or **pulverise** /ˈpʌlvəraɪz/ *verb*: **pulverizes, pulverizing, pulverized**
1 You **pulverize** something when you crush it to dust or powder: *Birds swallow a good deal of grit, which helps to pulverize any nuts and seeds that they eat whole.* **2** (*informal*) You **pulverize** your opponents in a competition when you defeat them decisively: *Henry Cecil's horse pulverized its rivals to win the Racing Post Trophy.*

puma /'pjuːmə/ *noun*: **pumas**
A **puma** is a wild animal of the cat family, with a reddish brown coat, that lives in America.

pummel /'pʌməl/ *verb*: **pummels, pummelling** (*AmE* **pummeling**), **pummelled** (*AmE* **pummeled**)
To **pummel** someone or something is to beat them hard and repeatedly with your fists: *She lay face down, screaming and kicking and pummelling the sofa with her fists.*

pump /pʌmp/ *noun*; *verb*
▷ ***noun***: **pumps**
1 A **pump** is **a** a device for forcing or driving liquids or gases through, into or out of something. **b** a device standing *eg* in a public street, with a handle that you pull up and down to raise water from beneath the ground: *They had to fetch water every day from the village pump.* **2** A bicycle **pump** is a narrow cylindrical device for forcing air into a tyre. [see picture at **bicycle**] **3** A petrol **pump** is a device with a hose, from which to fill your car with petrol.
▷ ***verb***: **pumps, pumping, pumped**
1 Liquids or gases **are pumped** somewhere when they are forced or driven there by means of pumps: *The main problem concerns the cost of pumping water up the 1000-metre gradient to the city.* □ *The heart performs the function of pumping blood through the body.* **2** You **pump** a tyre up when you force air into it with a pump. **3** You **pump** money into something when you spend a lot of money on it: *It was hoped that pumping money into sport would increase the nation's general fitness.* **4** Someone who has swallowed a poisonous substance has their stomach **pumped** by a doctor or nurse in order to force the contents out of it. **5** (*informal*) You **pump** someone when you ask them a lot of questions to try to get information from them: *Was he just making polite conversation, or was he pumping me for information?*

pumpkin /'pʌmpkɪn/ *noun* (*count or uncount*): **pumpkins**
A **pumpkin** is a large round vegetable with thick yellow skin and soft orange-coloured flesh: *a slice of pumpkin pie.* [see picture at **vegetable**]

pumps /pʌmps/ *noun* (*plural*)
Pumps are canvas sports shoes with rubber soles. [*same as* **plimsolls**]

pun /pʌn/ *noun*: **puns**
A **pun** is a type of joke using words that have more than one meaning, or words that have a similar sound but a different meaning, *eg* 'A pun is a punishable offence'. [*same as* **play on words**]

punch¹ /pʌntʃ/ *verb*; *noun*
▷ ***verb***: **punches, punching, punched**
You **punch** someone or something when you hit them with your fist: *She punched him on the nose.* □ *Someone punched him in the belly and he doubled up.*
▷ ***noun***: **punches**
1 You give someone or something a **punch** when you hit them with your fist: *His next punch sent her flying against the cooker.* **2** (*uncount*) A piece of writing or a speech has **punch** if it is lively and convincing: *Where there is no dialogue to liven it up his narrative lacks punch.*

punch² /pʌntʃ/ *noun*; *verb*
▷ ***noun***: **punches**
A **punch** is a tool for making holes in materials such as paper, leather or metal.
▷ ***verb***: **punches, punching, punched**
You **punch** a hole in something by pushing or pressing something sharp through it; you **punch** something such as a card when you make a hole in it with a punch: *Punch a few holes in the container to allow a little ventilation.* □ *The conductor punched our tickets.*

punch³ /pʌntʃ/ *noun* (*uncount*)
Punch is a drink made by adding ingredients such as spirits, sugar, spice and fruit juice to wine, and is often drunk hot: *a bowl of rum punch.*

punchline /'pʌntʃlaɪn/ *noun*: **punchlines**
The **punchline** of a funny story or joke is the important last bit of it, which contains the point and makes you laugh.

punch-up /'pʌntʃʌp/ *noun* (*informal*): **punch-ups**
A **punch-up** is a fight in which people hit or punch each other: *He'd been involved in another punch-up in the school playground.*

punctilious /pʌŋk'tɪlɪəs/ *adjective* (*formal*)
A **punctilious** person is careful about carrying out their duties correctly, especially their social ones: *He never forgot our birthdays; he was always most punctilious about that.* [*opposite* **lax**]

punctual /'pʌŋtʃʊəl/ *adjective*
Someone who is **punctual** arrives, and does things, at the right time, and is not late: *The lecture starts at ten, and I expect you to be punctual.* □ *She's usually such a punctual person.* [*opposite* **late, unpunctual**] — *noun* (*uncount*) **punctuality** /pʌŋktʃʊ'alɪtɪ/: *Evidence of good attendance and punctuality at school indicates to employers that you are responsible and conscientious.* — *adverb* **punctually:** *Our guest arrived punctually at 7.30.*

punctuate /'pʌŋktʃʊeɪt/ *verb*: **punctuates, punctuating, punctuated**
1 You **punctuate** a piece of writing when you put punctuation marks in it. **2** (*literary*) An activity **is punctuated** by something when it is repeatedly interrupted by it: *He revealed his uneasiness by his rather fast speech, punctuated by a high, too-frequent laugh.*

punctuation /pʌŋktʃʊ'eɪʃən/ *noun* (*uncount*)
Punctuation is the system of marks, including *eg* full stops and commas, used in writing to make its meaning clear for the reader: *Could you read through these sheets and correct the punctuation?*

punctuation mark /pʌŋktʃʊ'eɪʃən mɑːk/ *noun*: **punctuation marks**
Punctuation marks are the marks such as full stops, commas, question marks and quotation marks that are used in writing to help make its meaning clear for the reader. [See the appendix pages for guidance on punctuation in English]

puncture /'pʌŋktʃə(r)/ *noun*; *verb*
▷ ***noun***: **punctures**
A **puncture** is a small hole made in something by a sharp point: *I got a puncture in my back tyre on the way home.*
▷ ***verb***: **punctures, puncturing, punctured**
To **puncture** something is to make a small hole in it: *The point of the knife had punctured his lung.* □ *I must have punctured my tyre on that broken glass down the road.*

pundit /'pʌndɪt/ *noun*: **pundits**
A **pundit** is a person who knows a lot about a particular subject and is frequently asked to give an opinion about it: *Only a year ago the pundits were shaking their heads and prophesying that the Democrats would never again provide a President.* [*same as* **expert**]

pungent /'pʌndʒənt/ *adjective*
1 A **pungent** taste or smell is sharp and strong; something that is **pungent** has a strong, often unpleasant, smell or taste: *The chimney was pouring out pungent*

green smoke. [*same as* **acrid**; *opposite* **mild**] **2** (*formal*) **Pungent** talk or writing is cleverly and powerfully expressed, often containing sharp criticism of something: *She put her view in a series of pungent and forceful articles.* [*same as* **cogent**, **caustic**] — *noun* (*uncount*) **pungency:** *It lacked the usual pungency of Indian food.*

punish /ˈpʌnɪʃ/ *verb*: **punishes, punishing, punished**
1 To **punish** people is to make them suffer because they have done something wrong: *We may not punish criminals to a greater extent than their crimes are felt to deserve.* □ *We were never actually punished for disobedience.* □ *It was forbidden to punish children by locking them up.* □ *Slave masters ran around punishing any one who slowed down.* **2** You **punish** a crime or offence if you punish people who commit it: *Murder has to be punished.* □ *They established a legal system with the exclusive authority to punish crime.*

punishable /ˈpʌnɪʃəbəl/ *adjective*
A crime or offence is **punishable** if people are punished for committing it: *Perjury is a serious and punishable offence.* □ *In those days most crimes were punishable by death.*

punishing /ˈpʌnɪʃɪŋ/ *adjective*
A **punishing** activity, experience or routine makes you weak and exhausted: *The punishing 3-mile ascent to the top of the pass still lay ahead of them.* □ *He had set himself a punishing schedule.*

punishment /ˈpʌnɪʃmənt/ *noun*: **punishments**
1 (*uncount*) **Punishment** is the act of punishing someone, or the process of being punished: *Methods of punishment are now less dramatic, but the principle of suffering remains the same.* □ *These soldiers should face punishment for their crimes.* **2** A **punishment** is any method, or instance, of punishing someone: *A nine-match ban was felt to be a fair punishment for his latest outrage on the pitch.* □ *Illnesses were regarded as a punishment from God.* **3** (*uncount*; *informal*) **Punishment** is rough physical treatment: *We took a lot of punishment from the wind and driving snow as we neared the summit.*

punitive /ˈpjuːnɪtɪv/ *adjective*
1 Punitive actions are intended to punish wrongdoing as severely as possible: *The government will take punitive measures against drug dealers.* **2 Punitive** arrangements of any kind are harsh or severe: *punitive levels of taxation.*

punk /pʌŋk/ *noun*: **punks**
1 (*uncount*, *often adjectival*) **Punk** or **punk rock** is a type of loud and aggressive music, popular with young people in the 1970s and 1980s, which represented a rebellion against the usual polite and conventional ways of behaving and dressing: *a punk band.* **2** A **punk** or **punk rocker** is a person who likes punk rock and dresses in the unconventional clothes associated with it.

punnet /ˈpʌnət/ *noun*: **punnets**
A **punnet** is a small cardboard or plastic basket or container, designed to hold soft fruit: *a punnet of strawberries.*

punt /pʌnt/ *noun*: **punts**
A **punt** is a long flat-bottomed open boat with square ends, that you use especially on a river, and move by pushing a long pole against the river bed.

punter /ˈpʌntə(r)/ *noun* (*informal*): **punters**
1 A **punter** is someone who bets on horses. **2** Customers, clients and ordinary members of the public are referred to by some people as **punters**.

puny /ˈpjuːnɪ/ *adjective*: **punier, puniest**
Someone or something that is **puny** is small and weak: *I was a puny little guy who didn't have the strength or courage to do anything.* □ *The men stood jeering at the villagers' puny efforts to save their houses.*

pup /pʌp/ *noun*: **pups**
1 A **pup** is a young dog. [*same as* **puppy**] **2** The young of a seal, wolf or rat are also called **pups**.

pupil[1] /ˈpjuːpɪl/ *noun*: **pupils**
1 The **pupils** of a school are the children who attend it: *a school with nearly 2000 pupils.* **2** A teacher's **pupils** are the people he or she is teaching or has taught; the **pupil** of someone such as a painter or musician is someone who has studied under them: *Titian's best-known pupils, Veronese and Tintoretto.*

pupil[2] /ˈpjuːpɪl/ *noun*: **pupils**
The **pupil** in your eye is the small round black opening in the middle of it, through which light passes.

puppet /ˈpʌpət/ *noun*: **puppets**
1 A **puppet** is a doll that is designed to move, either when you pull strings attached to its limbs, or when you fit it over your hand and move your fingers. **2** (*often adjectival*) A person or country that is described as a **puppet** has no real independence, but acts in obedience to a more powerful person or country: *They installed puppet governments throughout their conquered territories.* □ *a puppet state.*

puppy /ˈpʌpɪ/ *noun*: **puppies**
A **puppy** is a young dog. [*same as* **pup**]

purchase /ˈpɜːtʃəs/ (*formal*) *verb*; *noun*
▻ ***verb***: **purchases, purchasing, purchased**
You **purchase** something when you buy it: *I purchased the car only a couple of years ago.*
▻ ***noun***: **purchases**
1 A **purchase** is something that you have bought: *His purchases included shampoo, soap and toothpaste.* **2** (*uncount*) **Purchase** is the act of buying something: *Keep your receipt as proof of purchase.* — *noun* **purchaser:** *I spent the morning showing prospective purchasers round the property.*

pure /pjʊə(r)/ *adjective*
1 Something that is **pure** is not mixed with anything else: *Our two-tone T-shirt is made from pure cotton.* □ *The snow was pure white against the blue sky.* **2** Substances that are **pure** are clean and contain nothing harmful: *pure mountain air* □ *We have a right to pure drinking water.* [*same as* **clean**; *opposite* **polluted**, **contaminated**] **3** You can refer to things such as emotions or qualities as *eg* **pure** hatred or **pure** beauty, to emphasize their strength or intensity, or to emphasize that you mean that particular emotion or quality and no other: *a smile of pure happiness* □ *There was a gleam of pure malice in his eye.* □ *Shs had make the remark out of pure jealousy.* □ *a scene of pure beauty* □ *It's all pure rubbish.* [*same as* **sheer**] **4** (*literary*) A person described as **pure** has no evil or sinful thoughts and usually little sexual experience: *There are few more wholesome things in nature than a pure country girl.* □ *She sat there in silence, no doubt thinking her pure thoughts.* [*same as* **virtuous**, **chaste**; *opposite* **immoral**, **sinful**] **5** A **pure** sound is clear and pleasant to hear: *She listened, and began to enjoy the pure voices of the Sisters.* **6** (*informal*) Something that happens by **pure** chance happens completely by chance: *It was by pure chance that I happened to spot her.* □ *That may be pure coincidence of course.* **7 Pure** mathematics or science deals with the theory of the subject, as distinct from how it can be used in practical ways. — *noun* (*uncount*) **purity:** *There were doubts about the purity of the heroin.* □ *The piece was played with great beauty and purity of tone.* □ *The varying degrees of purity of native gold involved different melting points.* □ *With the*

purity of the very young he wondered how anyone could be unfaithful.
▻ ***phrase*** **Pure and simple** means 'and nothing else': *That man wants revenge, pure and simple.*

purée /ˈpjʊəreɪ/ *noun; verb*
▻ ***noun*** (*count or uncount*): **purées**
A **purée** consists of fruit or vegetables made into a smooth, thick liquid by mashing or blending: *Blend the spinach and potato into a purée.* □ *Add a tablespoonful of tomato purée.*
▻ ***verb***: **purées, puréeing, puréed**
You **purée** fruit or vegetables when you mash or blend them into a purée.

purely /ˈpʊəlɪ/ *adverb*
Purely emphasizes that only one thing is involved in a particular circumstance: *It's a purely personal decision.* □ *This is purely a matter of choice.* □ *The arches are purely decorative.* □ *It had been intended, purely and simply, as an insult.*

purgatory /ˈpɜːgətərɪ/ *noun* (*uncount*)
1 In the Roman Catholic church, **Purgatory** is a place or state that your soul passes into after death, where it suffers for your sins before going to heaven. **2** (*humorous, informal*) You can describe any experience that causes you discomfort or suffering as **purgatory**: *To an overweight and ungainly child like Ellie, school gym classes were purgatory.*

purge /pɜːdʒ/ *verb; noun*
▻ ***verb***: **purges, purging, purged**
1 You **purge** yourself, or **are purged**, of unworthy or undesirable thoughts or emotions when you get rid of them from your mind: *She at last felt purged of the terrible guilt she had suffered since his death.* □ *Purge such thoughts from your mind.* **2** To **purge** *eg* a political party or other organization is to get rid of all those members of it who are considered dangerous or undesirable: *In exasperation the Army purged Parliament of all but their own supporters.*
▻ ***noun***: **purges:** *The procedure amounted to a total purge of communists from all positions of responsibility.* □ *the Stalinist purges of the 1930s.*

purify /ˈpjʊərɪfaɪ/ *verb*: **purifies, purifying, purified**
You **purify** something when you make it pure by removing dirt and harmful substances from it: *You can get tablets to purify the water and make it safe to drink.* — *noun* (*uncount*) **purification** /pjʊərɪfɪˈkeɪʃən/: *The place was evidently a water-purification plant.*

purist /ˈpjʊərɪst/ *noun*: **purists**
Purists are people who insist that things should be said or done in a particular way that they regard as correct: *Some purists think Handel's music shouldn't be played on modern instruments.*

puritan /pjʊərɪtən/ *noun and adjective* (*usually derogatory*): **puritans**
A **puritan**, or a person with **puritan** attitudes, is someone who lives according to strict moral and religious principles and who thinks pleasure and luxury are wrong: *They had a somewhat puritan upbringing: no television, and little else in the way of entertainment.* — *adjective* **puritanical** /pjʊərɪˈtanɪkəl/: *puritanical attitudes to sex.*

purity /ˈpjʊərətɪ/ see **pure**.

purl /pɜːl/ *noun* (*uncount*)
Purl is one of the two basic stitches used in knitting. [see also **plain**]

purple /ˈpɜːpəl/ *noun; adjective*
▻ ***noun*** (*uncount or count*)
Purple is a colour that is a mixture of red and blue, or any shade of this colour: *She thought of purple as an old lady's colour.* □ *In the summer the flower bed was a mass of reds and purples.* □ *The sky turning a deep purple.*
▻ ***adjective:*** *There was a large purple bruise over her left eye.* □ *He was purple in the face with exertion.*

purport *verb; noun* (*formal*)
▻ ***verb*** /pəˈpɔːt/: **purports, purporting, purported**
Something that **purports** to be or do a certain thing is claimed to be or do that thing: *the 'Eikon Basilike', a work purporting to have been written by Charles I.*
▻ ***noun*** /ˈpɜːpɔːt/ (*used in the singular*)
The **purport** of something that is said or written is its general meaning or point: *He was not astute enough to realize the purport of Oliver's carefullly thought-out questions* [*same as* same as **significance, gist**]

purpose /ˈpɜːpəs/ *noun*: **purposes**
1 Your **purpose** in doing something is the thing you want to achieve by doing it: *My original purpose in writing this was to provoke debate.* □ *Our purpose in Bosnia is to maintain peace.* [*same as* **aim**] **2** The purpose of something is the reason for which it is done, or the function for which it is designed: *Is the purpose of a single European currency to assist us in improving living standards?* □ *The purpose of a sleeping bag is to insulate the body from the surrounding cold.* **3** (*often in the plural*) Something is used for a certain **purpose** if that is the use that is made of it: *They told us that our rented accommodation was required for business purposes.* □ *You have to sign a book to say that the poison is for household purposes only.* □ *It was built as a nursing home, but was never used for that purpose.* **4** (*uncount*) **Purpose** is the awareness of an aim, combined with the determination to achieve it: *A sense of common purpose and identity is essential to teamwork.* [*same as* **resolve**] **5** Your **purpose** in life is the thing you care most about achieving: *A commercial organization's purpose in life is not of course to please its employees.*
▻ ***phrases*** **1** You do something **on purpose** when you do it deliberately: *I killed him on purpose* □ *Nobody gives way on purpose.* [*same as* **purposely, deliberately**] **2** Something **serves a purpose** if it is useful: *The clothes are pretty loose, but they serve their purpose and I'm glad to have them.* **3** You use something **to good purpose** if you find a good use for it: *Its very rigidity can be used to good purpose.* **4** You do something **to little purpose** or **to no purpose** if it produces no useful results. **5** For **to all intents and purposes** see **intent**.

purpose-built /pɜːpəsˈbɪlt/ *adjective*
Something that is **purpose-built** is designed for a particular specialized use: *a purpose-built medical centre.*

purposeful /ˈpɜːpəsfʊl/ *adjective*
Someone behaves in a **purposeful** manner when they look full of determination: *He walked into the office looking purposeful.* □ *She was wearing a purposeful expression.* [*same as* **determined**] — *adverb* **purposefully:** *Damien was walking softly but purposefully along the gallery.*

purposely /ˈpɜːpəslɪ/ *adverb*
You do something **purposely** when you do it deliberately: *Whitlock purposely fired wide.* □ *The kids purposely use words their parents can't understand.* [*same as* **on purpose, deliberately**; *opposite* **accidentally**]

purr /pɜː(r)/ *verb; noun*
▻ ***verb***: **purrs, purring, purred**
1 A cat **purrs** when it makes its typical low vibrating noise, associated with contentment. **2** A machine or engine **purrs** when it is working smoothly and makes a satisfactory vibrating noise. **3** People **purr** when they speak in a soft tone that expresses delight or satisfac-

tion: *'I never expected to have an aristocrat in the family,' she purred.*
▻ ***noun*** (*usually in the singular*): **purrs**: *I could hear the purr of a car engine in the drive.*

purse /pɜːs/ *noun; verb*
▻ ***noun***: **purses**
1 A **purse** is a small container for money, for carrying in a pocket or handbag. **2** (*AmE*) A woman's **purse** is her handbag.
▻ ***verb***: **purses, pursing, pursed**
You **purse** your lips when you draw them together, especially as a sign of disapproval.

purser /pɜːsə(r)/ *noun*: **pursers**
A **purser** is a ship's officer responsible for keeping the accounts and, on a passenger ship, for the welfare of passengers.

pursue /pə'sjuː/ *verb* (*formal*): **pursues, pursuing, pursued**
1 You **pursue** someone or something when you follow them in order to catch them: *He was tearing down the street carrying a sledgehammer, hotly pursued by two policemen.* □ *She was bored at finding herself forever pursued by men.* [*same as* **chase**] **2** People **pursue** a certain policy when they act according to it: *The government was intending to pursue a policy of austerity in public and private expenditure.* **3** You **pursue** a goal or aim when you work hard to achieve it: *Managements are thus able to pursue a variety of objectives.* **4** You **pursue** an activity or career when you are busy with it: *His attempt to pursue a medical career was shortlived.* □ *She wanted more freedom to pursue her many interests.* **5** You **pursue** a certain subject when you try to investigate it: *There was no reason for him to pursue the matter any further.*

pursuit /pɜː'sjuːt/ *noun*: **pursuits**
1 (*uncount*) The **pursuit** of someone or something is the activity of chasing them: *There was a lot of barking and I glanced up to see a dog in headlong pursuit of a cat.* **2** (*uncount*) The **pursuit** of something you want is the activity of trying to achieve it: *He'd gone to Africa in pursuit of adventure.* □ *the pursuit of fame and success.* **3** (*usually in the plural*) Your **pursuits** are your interests and leisure activities: *She listed reading and walking among her favourite pursuits.* [*same as* **interest, pastime, hobby**]
▻ ***phrase*** You are **in hot pursuit** of someone or something when you are chasing them and determined to catch them: *The police were following in hot pursuit.*

purvey /pə'veɪ/ *verb* (*formal*): **purveys, purveying, purveyed**
A shopkeeper or supplier who **purveys** certain goods sells them.

pus /pʌs/ *noun* (*uncount*)
Pus is the thick, yellowish liquid that forms in infected wounds.

push /pʊʃ/ *verb; noun*
▻ ***verb***: **pushes, pushing, pushed**
1 a You **push** something when you apply pressure to it to move it forward or into some specified position or direction: *We pushed the bikes up a steep slope.* □ *She could hear him pushing the two armchairs close to the heater.* □ *He took a stick and pushed it into the hole.* □ *She unlocked the door, pushed it open, and stood aside.* □ *Did he fall or was he pushed?* **b** You **push** your way somewhere, or **push** forward, when you get somewhere by pushing people or obstacles out of the way: *They pushed their way through the gathering crowd.* □ *Lawrence pushed forward to another interior office.* **c** You also **push** forward or ahead, or **push** something forward, when you make progress in other ways: *These are the areas of policy now being pushed forward.* **d** You **push** past someone or something when you go past them in a rough, inconsiderate manner: *Adam pushed past him, out of the kitchen door.* **e** You **push** something like a button or a switch to operate it or make something work: *I pushed the button marked 'doors' and watched the gold-plated doors swing open.* **f** You **push** against something, or **push** down on it, when you exert pressure or force on it: *He pushed against the door with his shoulder.* □ *Push down on the clutch pedal.*
2a Something or someone is said to **push** prices or values up or down when they cause them to rise or fall: *The Bank of England had pushed up interest rates.* **b** A person or circumstance **pushes** you into a situation, or into doing something, when they force you into it: *The effect will be to push ethnic minorities into low-paid jobs.* □ *I had to push him into taking his annual leave.* **c** You **push** someone when you put pressure on them to work hard and be successful: *You push yourself too hard.* **d** You **push** for something when you recommend it strongly or want to see it accepted: *The Japanese are in no hurry to push for the resumption of commercial whaling.* **e** To **push** an idea or commercial product is to promote it actively and advertise it widely. **f** To **push** drugs is to sell them illegally. **g** (*informal*) You say you **are pushed** when you are in a hurry and short of time; if you **are pushed** for time or money you are short of it: *I'll call you back; I'm a bit pushed just now.* **h** (*informal*) Someone who **is pushing** *eg* forty or fifty is approaching that age, being already in their late thirties or forties.
▻ ***noun***: **pushes**
1 You give something or someone a **push** when you push them: *The car wouldn't start this morning but my neighbour kindly gave me a push.* □ *Nurses materialize at the push of a bell.* **2** (*uncount*) Someone who has **push** has determination and the ability to influence people and get things done.
▻ ***phrases*** **1** You say you could do something **at a push** if you could just manage to do it if it became necessary. **2** (*informal*) **a** You **get the push** or **are given the push** when you are dismissed from your job. **b** A boyfriend or girlfriend **gives you the push** when they end their relationship with you.

phrasal verbs
push along (*informal*) You say you are going to **push along** when you are about to leave.
push around (*informal*) To **push** someone **around** is to bully them or treat them roughly.
push in (*informal*) When someone **pushes in**, they take a place in a queue or group that they are not entitled to.
push off (*informal*) You say you are going to **push off** when you are about to leave; if you tell someone to **push off** you are telling them rudely to go away.
push on Someone or something **pushes on** when they continue in a certain direction: *Well, we'd better be pushing on.* □ *The railway pushed on to Birmingham.*
push over You **push** something or someone **over** when you knock them down or cause them to fall to the ground. [see also **pushover**]
push through You **push** a proposal or idea **through** when you persist in getting it accepted.

push-button /'pʊʃ bʌtən/ *adjective*
A **push-button** machine is operated by pressing a button.

pushchair /'pʊʃtʃɛə(r)/ *noun*: **pushchairs**
A **pushchair** is a small folding chair on wheels used for pushing a young child around.

pusher /ˈpʊʃə(r)/ *noun* (*informal*): **pushers**
A **pusher** is a person who sells illegal drugs.

pushover /ˈpʊʃoʊvə(r)/ *noun* (*informal*): **pushovers**
1 A **pushover** is a task that is easily accomplished or done: *He's clever and has worked hard all year so he'll probably find exam a pushover.* **2** A person who is a **pushover** is a person who can be easily persuaded or influenced: *I'll ask my father to lend me the money; he's a real pushover.*

pushy /ˈpʊʃɪ/ *adjective*: **pushier**, **pushiest**
A person who is **pushy** behaves a forceful, bossy way to get what they want, or to get attention: *You'll have to be pushy if you want to act in films.* [*same as* **aggressive**; *opposite* **quiet**, **restrained**]

puss /pʊs/ *noun* (*informal*): **pusses**
You call **puss** when you call a cat to you: *Here, puss!*

pussy /ˈpʊsɪ/ *noun* (*informal*): **pussies**
A **pussy** is a cat.

put /pʊt/ *verb*: **puts**, **putting**, **put**
1 a You **put** something in a particular place or position when you move or place it there: *She put a cloth on the tray.* □ *He put a coin into her small hand.* □ *He absent-mindedly put too much sugar in his tea.* □ *Put the soup in a food-processor.* □ *She put the whistle to her lips.* □ *He put a bath towel round himself.* □ *She put her arm round him.* □ *Put your head back and close your eyes.* □ *They put up their hands to shield their faces.* □ *He threatened to put a bullet through my head.* □ *Put couple of holes in it, for the legs.* □ *I put a 'Don't Disturb' notice on my door.* □ *I'll put the application forms in the post tonight.* □ *Perhaps you could put an advert in the local paper?* **b** You **put** one thing on another when you apply it, fit it or fix it there: *I'd better put a bandage on that wound at once.* □ *She put a dab of perfume behind her ears.* □ *Put less paint on the brush.* □ *We had to put locks on all the windows.*
2 To **put** a tax, duty or charge on something is to add it to its price; you **put** an amount of money on the price of something when you increase its price by that amount: *The reference is to the tax that Pitt the Elder put on gin.* □ *They're putting two pence on a pint of beer.* [compare **impose**] **3** You **put** money on something when you bet on it: *The horse he'd intended to put money on won by a length.* **a** Something **puts** pressure or a strain on you when it causes you to be affected by it: *Joe's illness put a strain on us all.* □ *It's funny how a silence puts pressure on people to start talking.* [*same as* **impose**] **b** You **put** an end or a stop to something, or a **put** check on it, when you stop it or control it: *Mussolini wanted to put a quick end to the war.* □ *The abuses were put a stop to.* **c** You **put** faith in something, or **put** reliance on it, when you believe in it or rely on it; you **put** emphasis on something when you stress or emphasize it: *Banks put too much faith in their computers.* **d** You **put** money, energy or time into an activity or cause if you spend them on it: *We've put considerable effort into producing the framework document.* □ *Sir Lionel put a great deal of money into film production.* [compare **invest**]
4 a You **put** things in a certain order when you classify or arrange them in that way; you **put** one thing before another if you regard it as more important than the other: *Put these sentences in the right order.* □ *Women get criticized for putting their careers before their families.* □ *people who put their work first* □ *She tends to put everyone before herself.* **b** You **put** the number or extent of something at a certain amount when you estimate it to be about that amount: *Other sources put the number of dead at 85.* **c** You **put** a question to someone when you ask them it; you **put** a suggestion or proposal to someone when you offer it to them for consideration: *Permit me instead to put some questions to you.* **d** You **put** thoughts into words when you express them; you put something into another language when you translate it; you **put** what you say in a certain way when you express it that way: *That could have been more tactfully put, couldn't it?* □ *Francis Latham put the point even more clearly.* □ *To put it more simply, the benefit of the bill will be to increase respect for women.* □ *It wasn't easy to put her feelings into words.* **e** You **put** something when you write it: *Put your answer on a postcard, please.* □ *Having started on the letter, she couldn't think what to put.* **f** You **put** a plan or idea into practice, effect or operation when you carry it out: *Meanwhile Plan B was being put into effect.* □ *Measures were put into operation to discourage black immigration.* **g** You **put** something such as a skill or talent to use when you use it in something you are doing: *At least you'll be able to put your training to good use.*
5 a You **put** someone somewhere when you cause them to go there and stay there for a certain time: *Dad put me to bed.* □ *They put me in the prison hospital.* □ *The children were put in foster homes.* □ *She put me in a taxi and told the driver where to take me.* □ *those '60s scientists who put people into space and on the moon.* **b** To **put** someone into a situation or state is to cause them to be in it: *Marshal Tolonen put me in charge of the investigation.* □ *You've put me in an embarrassing position.* □ *The woman's wagging tongue might have put him in danger.* □ *The news had put him in an excellent mood.*
▻ ***phrases*** **1** For **hard put to it** see **hard**. **2** You **put it to** someone **that** something is so when you suggest it formally to them: *I put it to him that he had not been telling us the whole truth.* **3** For **stay put** see **stay**.

phrasal verbs
put across or **put over** You **put** ideas **across** well, or **put** them **over** well, if you express them in a way that makes them clear to your listeners or readers: *He did try in his lectures to put across some of his underlying convictions.* □ *You put your point over perfectly clearly.*
put aside You **put** something **aside** **a** when you separate it from other things for some purpose: *She unpacked her luggage and put aside things to be taken upstairs.* **b** when you save it for future: *I'd been putting money aside for my holiday.* [*same as* **save**] **c** when you abandon it: *Publishers should put aside their prejudices.* [*same as* **discard**]
put away **1** You **put** something **away** when you put it into the place where it is kept: *She opened the drawer to put away the knives and spoons.* **2** (*informal*) Someone who can **put** food or drink **away** can eat or drink a lot. **3** (*informal*) People **are put away** when they are sent to prison or a mental hospital.
put back **1** You **put** something **back** when you return it to its proper place, or the place it came from: *He put the stone back where he had found it.* □ *She put back the receiver.* **2** To **put** a scheduled event or procedure **back** is to postpone it or delay it: *His case was put back a week, till the following Tuesday, to allow a solicitor to represent him* [*same as* **postpone**] **3** You **put** a clock **back** when you adjust it so that it shows an earlier time: *Remember to put your clocks back an hour.*
put by You **put** something **by** when you save it for future use: *He'd put money by for just such an emergency.* [*same as* **save**]
put down **1** You **put** something **down** when you place it *eg* on the floor or on a table: *She put down the tray.* **2** The police or army **put down** a revolt or

rebellion when they use force to stop it: *The riots were put down by the Yugoslav National Army.* **3** (*informal*) You **put** someone **down** when you criticize them and make them feel stupid: *She evidently enjoyed putting her husband down in public.* [see also **put-down**] **4** An animal **is put down** when it is killed painlessly, *eg* when it is ill, or is considered dangerous: *My puppy had something wrong with him and the vet wanted to put him down.* **5** You **put down** *eg* suggestions or ideas when you write them on paper. **6** An aircraft **puts down** somewhere when it lands there. **7** You **put** your name **down** for something when you add it to the list of people planning to do that thing: *I put myself down for the trip to Rievaulx.*

put down to You **put** one thing **down to** another if you think the first is caused by the second: *Scorn was evident in her voice, and I put it down to stress.*

put forward **1** You **put forward** an idea when you suggest it for consideration: *Merry put forward his plans for dealing with the troublemakers.* □ *Your name has been put forward for treasurer.* **2** You **put** a clock **forward** when you adjust it so that it shows a later time: *Tomorrow we put the clocks forward one hour.* **3** You **put** a planned event **forward** when you arrange for it to happen earlier than scheduled: *The rising was timed for 10 April, but was put forward to 27 March.* [*opposite* **bring forward**]

put in **1** You **put in** time or effort when you spend it in some activity: *She puts in four hours' violin practice daily.* □ *They put a great deal of their own time into gaining these qualifications.* **2** You **put in** *eg* a claim when you make it officially: *Don't forget to put in your claim for expenses.* **3** You **put in** for something when you formally apply for it: *I was considering putting in for early retirement.* **4** Someone **puts in** a remark when they make it: *'You can't bite it,' put in Franco.*

put off **1** You **put** an electrical device **off** when you switch it off and stop it working: *Could you put the light off?* [*same as* **switch off, turn off**; *opposite* **put on, switch on, turn on**] **2** You **put** a job **off** when you delay doing it: *It was a task he'd been putting off for far too long.* **3** You **put off** a planned event when you cancel it or postpone it: *I would have to put off my journey for the present.* [*same as* **postpone**] **4** You **put** someone **off** **a** when you cancel an invitation you have given them or some other appointment or arrangement you have with them: *If you're no better tomorrow we must put the Russells off.* **b** when you make them wait for something that they want: *She put him off with a kiss.* **c** when you stop them concentrating on something: *Don't hum; you're putting me off.* **5** To **put** someone **off** something is **a** to stop them doing it: *This snowstorm might put them off coming.* **b** to make them dislike it, or not want it: *'I've been put off my dinner,' said Camilla.* □ *People won't eat the fruit; they're put off by its smell.*

put on **1** You **put** clothes **on** when you dress yourself in them: *Now put a coat on and run outside to play.* [*opposite* **take off**] **2** You **put on** weight when you get fatter: *She never seems to put on an ounce of weight.* □ *I've put on at least half a stone over the holiday.* [*same as* **gain**; *opposite* **lose**] **3** You **put on** a certain kind of behaviour you behave deliberately in a way that is unnatural to you: *We used to put on silly voices and tell silly jokes.* □ *You have to put on a show of toughness.* **4** You **put** a device **on** when you start it working: *Shall I put the television on?* □ *She put the brake on.* [*opposite* **put off, switch off**] **5** You **put on** a record, tape or compact disc when you start it playing: *He went to put a record on.* **6** People **put on** a play, show or concert when they perform it for an audience: *Marius Steen continued to put on shows throughout the war.* **7** A transport company **puts on** a service when it provides it: *They're putting on extra trains over the holiday period.* **8** You **put** food **on** when you begin to cook it: *I haven't put lunch on yet.*

put on to (*informal*) Someone or something **puts** you **on to** something when you hear about it or discover it from them: *A friend put me on to these biscuits.* □ *What first put them on to Ames's spying activities?*

put out **1** You **put out** your hand when you stretch it out, away from your body: *She put out her hand to take the envelope.* □ *He put out his arms and she ran into them.* [*same as* **extend**] **2** You **put** things **out** when you lay them somewhere ready for use: *A clean shirt had been put out for him.* □ *We remembered to put out cookies and milk for Santa.* **3** You **put out** a statement or announcement when you make it publicly, or broadcast it: *The Soviet authorities put out a statement that the UK was seventeenth in the world economic league.* **4** You **put out** a light when you press a switch to stop it shining: *Stephen leant over and put out the bedside light.* [*same as* **extinguish**; *opposite* **turn on**] **5** You **put out** *eg* a fire, candle or cigarette when you stop it burning. [*same as* **extinguish**; *opposite* **light**]: *I threw water over him, desperately trying to put out the flames.* **6** You **put out** *eg* your back or shoulder when you injure it by straining the muscles or displacing the bones: *He put his back out trying to move the piano.* **7** You **put** yourself **out** when you do something for someone even though it causes you trouble or extra work: *He'd already put himself out by agreeing to see Dougal at short notice.* **8** You **are put out** when you are annoyed by something: *He was particularly put out by the absence of a telephone.*

put over see **put across**.

put through **1** You **put** a caller **through** on the telephone when you connect them with the person they want to speak to: *I rang the bank and asked to be put through to the overseas department.* □ *'Mrs Ogilvie for you, sir.' 'Oh, put her through, would you?'* **2** Someone **puts** you **through** an unpleasant experience when they make you suffer it: *She put him through the most intensive analysis.*

put together **1** You **put** something **together** when you join all its separate parts together: *He rose, apprehensively clutching the section of rods he'd managed to put together.* **2** You **put together** a piece of work when you prepare it: *I was asked to put together an analysis of cross-border trade.* **3** You **put together** an event when you organize it: *Last year we put together a summer reading campaign.* **4** You say that one thing excels or is worth several other things **put together** if even in combination they cannot beat it: *I get more work done on a Sunday than in the whole of the rest of the week put together.*

put up **1** You **put up** a building or other structure when you build it: *We'll put up a statue to you, Mary.* [*same as* **erect**] **2** You **put up** something such as an umbrella when you unfold it and raise it ready for use: *I put up my hood.* □ *We managed to put up the small sail.* **3** You **put up** something such as a poster or notice when you attach it to a wall or noticeboard: *He put up a 'For Sale' sign.* **4** Prices **are put up** when they are increased: *We've had to put up the price of your Brownie magazine.* **5** You **put up**

money for some cause when you provide money for it: *Two bankers were persuaded to put up a lot of money to fund the scheme.* **6** You **put up** a struggle, fight or resistance when you resist something in a determined way: *The unions put up a spirited resistance to the so-called reforms.* **7** You **put** someone **up** when you give them accommodation in your house, especially a bed for the night: *I called Margaret to ask if she would put me up for a few nights.*

put up to One person **puts** another **up to** something wrong, silly or dishonest when they encourage them to do it: *I hope you didn't think I'd put him up to it.*

put up with You **put up with** something unpleasant or unsatisfactory when you accept it or tolerate it: *Syl, I won't put up with all this nonsense.* □ *Nowadays a wife doesn't have to put up with an unsatisfactory marriage in the way her mother might have done.*

put-down /ˈpʊtdaʊn/ *noun* (*informal*): **put-downs**
A **put-down** is something that you say that makes someone appear foolish or stupid, or that criticizes them.

putrefy /ˈpjuːtrɪfaɪ/ *verb*: **putrifies, putrifying, putrified**
Something **putrifies** when it rots or decays, producing an offensive smell.

putrid /ˈpjuːtrɪd/ *adjective*
Something is **putrid** when it is rotten and has an offensive smell.

putt /pʌt/ *verb* (*golf*): **putts, putting, putted**
You **putt** when you hit the ball gently forward along the ground towards the hole: *putt the ball into the hole.*

putty /ˈpʌtɪ/ *noun* (*uncount*)
Putty is a paste used *eg* for fixing glass in window frames and filling holes in wood.

put-up job /pʊtʌp ˈdʒɒb/ *noun* (*informal*): **put-up jobs**
A **put-up job** is something arranged to give someone a false impression or idea.

puzzle /ˈpʌzəl/ *verb*; *noun*

▻ ***verb***: **puzzles, puzzling, puzzled**
1 Something or someone **puzzles** you when you find them confusing and cannot understand them: *There is one thing about all this that still puzzles me.* □ *The police are still puzzling about the cause of the accident.* □ *It puzzles me why she agreed to come when she is so busy.* [*same as* **baffle**] **2** You **puzzle** over something when you try hard to understand it or find an answer: *He spent hours puzzling over a maths problem.*

▻ ***noun***: **puzzles**
1 A **puzzle** is a game or toy which gives you a problem to solve or that tests *eg* your knowledge, memory or skill: *the puzzle page in the newspaper* □ *a crossword puzzle.* **2** A **puzzle** is a problem or situation that is hard to understand or confusing. — *adjective* **puzzling:** *a puzzling situation* □ *I find this whole subject very puzzling.*

phrasal verb
You **puzzle** something **out** when you understand it or find the answer to it after thinking hard.

pyjamas (*AmE* **pajamas**) /pəˈdʒɑːməz/ *noun* (*plural*)
Pyjamas are a loose jacket or top and loose trousers worn for sleeping in: *a pair of pyjamas.* — **pyjama** or **pajama** /pəˈdʒɑːmə/ *noun* (*often adjectival*) *pyjama trousers* □ *a pyjama top.*

pylon /ˈpaɪlən/ *noun*: **pylons**
A **pylon** is a tall metal tower that supports electric power cables.

pyramid /ˈpɪrəmɪd/ *noun*: **pyramids**
1 The **pyramids** are the huge ancient Egyptian royal tombs built on a square base, with four sloping triangular sides meeting in a point. **2** A **pyramid** is a shape with a square or triangular base and sloping sides. [see picture at **shape**]

Pyrex /ˈpaɪərɛks/ *noun* (*trademark*; *uncount*)
Pyrex is a type of glass used to make bowls and dishes that can be used in ovens.

python /ˈpaɪθən/ *noun*: **pythons**
A **python** is a large non-poisonous snake that kills its prey by crushing it.

Q

Q or **q** /kjuː/ *noun*: **Qs** or **q's**
Q is the 17th letter of the English alphabet.

quack[1] /kwak/ *verb*: **quacks, quacking, quacked**
A duck **quacks** when it makes its typical cry.

quack[2] /kwak/ *noun* (*informal*): **quacks**
1 (*derogatory*) You call a doctor, or someone else in the medical or healing profession, a **quack** if you don't think he or she has much real knowledge or skill: *She goes to some quack who sticks pins in her legs and tells her it'll cure her bad back.* **2** Some people refer to any doctor, especially a general practitioner, as a **quack**: *I went to the local quack to have my blood pressure checked.*

quad /kwɒd/ *noun* (*informal*): **quads**
Quads are quadruplets.

quadrangle /'kwɒdraŋgəl/ *noun*: **quadrangles**
A **quadrangle** is a yard surrounded by buildings, especially in a school or college.

quadruped /'kwɒdrʊpɛd/ *noun* (*formal*): **quadrupeds**
A **quadruped** is any animal with four legs.

quadruple /kwɒd'ruːpəl/ *verb*: **quadruples, quadrupling, quadrupled**
A number or amount **quadruples** when it is multiplied by four or when it becomes four times larger: *Profits are expected to quadruple in the second year.* □ *We could quadruple our sales figures by the end of the year.*

quadruplet /'kwɒdrʊplət/ *noun*: **quadruplets**
A **quadruplet** is one of four children born to the same mother at the same time.

quaff /kwɑːf/ *verb* (*old or humourous*): **quaffs, quaffing, quaffed**
You **quaff** a drink when you drink it eagerly or thirstily: *The terrace was full of rich young women quaffing champagne.*

quail /kweɪl/ *verb*; *noun*
▻ ***verb*** (*formal*): **quails, quailing, quailed**
You **quail** if you feel frightened or show that you are frightened: *She quailed at the sound of his angry voice.*
▻ ***noun***: **quail** or **quails**
A **quail** is a small bird often shot for sport, and eaten as food.

quaint /kweɪnt/ *adjective*: **quainter, quaintest**
Something **quaint** is pleasantly or amusingly odd and old-fashioned: *We passed through a string of quaint little villages.* □ *She found the idea rather quaint.*

quake /kweɪk/ *verb*; *noun*
▻ ***verb***: **quakes, quaking, quaked**
You **quake** when you shake or tremble with fear: *His raised voice had the children quaking in their boots.*
▻ ***noun*** (*informal*): **quakes**
A **quake** is an earthquake.

qualification /kwɒlɪfɪ'keɪʃən/ *noun*: **qualifications**
1 Your **qualifications** are the recognized skills you have, shown by the examinations you have passed: *The advert read, 'Trainee accountant wanted; no qualifications or experience necessary'.* **2** You can refer to any skill or ability as a **qualification**: *Patience is an essential qualification for this job.* **3** (*count or uncount*) A **qualification** is also a comment you add, that limits or lessens what you have just said: *'You are quite a good student', he said, before adding the deflating qualification, 'considering you're not particularly bright.'* □ *She is without qualification the best manager we have ever had.*

qualify /'kwɒlɪfaɪ/ *verb*: **qualifies, qualifying, qualified**
1 You **qualify** when you complete a training course or pass an examination that gives you some kind of professional status: *It was another four years before I would qualify as a lawyer.* □ *a qualified accountant.* **2** Something **qualifies** you for a job or task when it makes you suitable for it or able to do it: *His army experience should qualify him to handle a bunch of rowdy teenagers.* □ *As a single man, you're hardly qualified to comment on the pressures facing working mothers.* **3** You **qualify** for something when you have a right to have or receive it, according to certain rules: *People living within a three-mile radius don't qualify for a travelling allowance.* **4** In a competition, especially a sporting contest, you **qualify** when, in an early stage, you reach the standard required to allow you to take part in a later stage: *This is the first time the Scottish team has qualified for the semi-final.*

quality /'kwɒlɪtɪ/ *noun*: **qualities**
1 (*uncount*) The **quality** of something is how good it is: *Don't rush through your work; it's quality that counts, not quantity.* □ *poor-quality workmanship* □ *a top-quality watch.* **2** (*uncount; often adjectival*) Something has **quality** if it is of a high standard: *We have a reputation for quality.* □ *one of the quality newspapers.* **3** A person's **qualities** are the characteristics that make up their personality, especially the good and positive ones, and their abilities and talents; a thing's **qualities** are its physical or other characteristics: *Among her admirable personal qualities was a genuine desire to help others.* □ *Patience has never been a quality of mine.* □ *The place had a haunted, dream-like quality.* □ *People define substances in terms of qualities such as colour, shape, size, hardness and heaviness.*

qualm /kwɑːm/ *noun* (*usually in the plural*): **qualms**
You have **qualms** about something you do when you are not sure if you should do it, because you think it might not be right, especially morally: *He has no qualms about dismissing staff who can't do the job.* [*same as* **doubt, misgivings, scruple**]

quandary /'kwɒndərɪ/ *noun* (*often used in the singular*): **quandaries**
You are in a **quandary** about something when you cannot decide whether or not you should do it: *It seems you're in a bit of a quandary.* [*same as* **dilemma**]

quantity /'kwɒntɪtɪ/ *noun*: **quantities**
1 A **quantity** is an amount that can be measured or counted: *The recipe tells you the exact quantities you need of the various ingredients.* □ *Measure out the quantities carefully.* □ *the operation of adding a num-*

ber of quantities together. **2** (*often in the plural*) '**Quantities**' or 'a **quantity**' of something can be any unspecified amount of it: *Use only a small quantity of washing-up liquid.* □ *A large quantity of ammunition has been stolen.* □ *Gold was discovered in tiny quantities.* □ *Raw cotton was imported in enormous quantities.* □ *The police recovered a quantity of the stolen jewellery within 24 hours.* □ *quantities of clothing belonging to the victims.* [see note at **amount**] **3** (*uncount*) **Quantity** is how much there is of something, often as distinct from its quality, or how good it is: *There has been a sharp improvement in the quality and quantity of training available to school-leavers.*

▻ ***phrase***

1 People describe a person or thing as **an unknown quantity** if they know nothing, or very little, about them. **2** Something that is bought, sold or produced **in quantity** is bought, sold or produced on a large scale, or in large amounts: *The cooking oil was purchased in quantity by the wholesalers for distribution to the supermarkets.*

quarantine /ˈkwɒrəntiːn/ *noun; verb*

▻ ***noun*** (*uncount*)

A person or animal that may have a disease that can spread to others is kept in **quarantine** when they are kept separate from others for a time, to prevent the disease from spreading: *Britain's strict quarantine regulations.*

▻ ***verb***: **quarantines**, **quarantining**, **quarantined:** *The dog had to be quarantined for two months.*

quarrel /ˈkwɒrəl/ *noun; verb*

▻ ***noun***: **quarrels**

1 A **quarrel** is an angry disagreement or argument: *It was clear that they had had some sort of quarrel.* **2** You can say you have no **quarrel** with someone when they have done nothing you disagree with or object to: *He pointed out that the government had no quarrel with the workers themselves; it was the union which was posing problems.*

▻ ***verb***: **quarrels**, **quarrelling** (*AmE* **quarreling**), **quarrelled** (*AmE* **quarreled**): *We quarrelled, and I left without saying where I was going.* □ *I would quarrel with the conclusions you have drawn.*

quarrelsome /ˈkwɒrəlsəm/ *adjective*

A **quarrelsome** person often becomes involved in quarrels or arguments.

quarry /ˈkwɒrɪ/ *noun*: **quarries**

A **quarry** is an area of land where stone or a mineral is dug up out of the ground: *The abandoned car was found in a nearby slate quarry.*

quart /kwɔːt/ *noun*: **quarts**

A **quart** is a liquid measurement equal to two pints (1.1 litres).

quarter (often written ¼) /ˈkwɔːtə(r)/ *noun*: **quarters**

1 (*count or uncount; often adjectival*) A **quarter** of something is one of four equal parts of it: *Could you get me quarter of a pound of cheese?* □ *You need about a quarter pound of flour.* □ *Over a quarter of those questioned reported some form of abuse.* □ *We'll be back within quarter of an hour.* □ *The next quarter hour will be crucial.* □ *We waited for an hour and a quarter.* □ *The journey takes two and a quarter hours.* □ *three-quarters of an hour* □ *She lives only about three-quarters of a mile away.* □ *a quarter century later.* **2** (*uncount or used in the singular*) In telling the time, '**quarter** to' or 'a **quarter** to' (or, in AmE 'a **quarter** of') a particular hour is 15 minutes before it; '**quarter** past' or 'a **quarter** past' (or, in AmE 'a **quarter** after') a particular hour is 15 minutes after it: *We arrived at quarter to four.* □ *The train left at a quarter to midnight.* □ *The time is now quarter past six.* □ (*AmE*) *My watch says a quarter after eleven.*

> American English tends to use the forms 'six-fifteen (6.15)' and 'six-forty-five (6.45)' in preference to the forms with **quarter**.

3 A **quarter** is any of the periods of three months that a year is often divided into: *Profits for the second quarter were down 25%.* **4** A **quarter** of something is quarter of a pound, or four ounces, of it: *The smoked ham is 53p a quarter.* □ *I'll have a quarter of mushrooms, please.* **5** A particular **quarter** of a city is a district of it, often one in which people from a particular racial or national group live: *She has an apartment in the Spanish quarter.* **6** A reaction or response in certain **quarters**, or from a certain **quarter**, is a reaction or response from certain people: *They expected disapproval in some quarters.* □ *She'll certainly get no sympathy from that quarter.* **7** (*used in the plural; especially military*) Somebody's **quarters** are the room or set of rooms provided for them to live in: *The army moved me temporarily to married quarters.* [compare **lodgings**] **8** In America and Canada a **quarter** is a coin worth twenty-five cents.

▻ ***phrase*** You see someone or something **at close quarters** when you see them from a position very near them: *At close quarters his face looked lined and old.*

quarterly /ˈkwɔːtəlɪ/ *adjective or adverb*

Quarterly means done, produced or happening once every three months: *a quarterly journal* □ *I bought a copy of 'Literature Quarterly'.* □ *We would have meetings initially on a monthly basis, then quarterly.*

quartet /kwɔːˈtɛt/ *noun*: **quartets**

A **quartet** is a group of four musicians, or a piece of music written for four musicians: *She's joined a string quartet.* □ *That tune comes from Mozart's 'Quartet in A flat'.*

quartz /kwɔːts/ *noun* (*uncount*)

Quartz is a mineral found in the form of crystals, widely used in electronic equipment such as watches.

quash /kwɒʃ/ *verb*: **quashes**, **quashing**, **quashed**

A person in authority **quashes** a decision when they state officially that it is no longer legal or valid: *The appeal judge quashed his conviction for dangerous driving.*

quasi- /ˈkweɪsaɪ/ or /ˈkwɑːziː/ *prefix*

Quasi- is used to form nouns and adjectives, with the meaning 'nearly, but not quite': *They are regarded as quasi-experts.* □ *She has a quasi-official role.*

quaver /ˈkweɪvə(r)/ *verb*: **quavers**, **quavering**, **quavered**

Your voice **quavers** when it trembles, *eg* because you are upset or nervous.

quay /kiː/ *noun*: **quays**

A **quay** is the edge of a harbour or port, next to the water, where ships are loaded and unloaded: *They are stored in one of the sheds along the quay.* □ *She was waiting at the quayside.*

queasy /ˈkwiːzɪ/ *adjective*: **queasier**, **queasiest**

You feel **queasy** when you feel that you are going to be sick: *The sight of blood always made him feel a bit queasy.*

queen /kwiːn/ *noun*: **queens**

1 A **queen** is a woman who is the official ruler of a country, inheriting the position by birth: *The ceremony will be attended by Queen Elizabeth II and her husband, the Duke of Edinburgh.* **2** A woman who marries a king is also given the title of **queen**: *Would the Princess of Wales automatically become queen?* **3** You can refer to a woman as **queen** of something if she is outstandingly talented at it, better than any other woman: *a farewell wave from Navratilova, queen of Wimbledon.* **4** A **queen** is also a large female insect, especially a bee, that lays large numbers of eggs. **5** In chess, the **queen** is the most powerful piece, able to move forwards, backwards, sideways or diagonally. **6** In cards, a **queen** is a playing card with the picture of a queen on it.

queer /kwɪə(r)/ *adjective*: **queerer, queerest**
1 Something **queer** is odd, strange or unusual: *Thomas was a queer-looking man of about forty.* □ *It gave me a queer feeling to be in the same room as a murderer.* □ *His skin was strangely smooth, and the colour was decidedly queer.* [*same as* **funny**, **peculiar**] **2** You can say that you are feeling **queer** if you are feeling slightly ill, as if you are going to faint or be sick. **3** (*offensive slang*) Some people use **queer** to describe homosexual men: *I don't want any of his queer friends in this house!*

quell /kwɛl/ *verb*: **quells, quelling, quelled**
1 To **quell** something, especially other people's violent behaviour, is to put an end to it: *Soldiers were called in to quell the riots.* □ *They were hoping this offer would quell any opposition to their plans.* [*same as* **suppress**] **2** You **quell** unwanted feelings when you try hard not to feel or express them: *This did little to quell my fears.*

quench /kwɛntʃ/ *verb*: **quenches, quenching, quenched**
You **quench** your thirst when you drink something that stops you feeling thirsty: *Only sensational reports like this can quench the public's thirst for scandalous stories.*

query /ˈkwɪərɪ/ *noun*; *verb*
▻ ***noun***: **queries**
1 A **query** is a question, especially one that expresses doubt or suspicion: *There was a query as to whether she should be allowed to take the exam since her grades were not good.* **2** A **query** is also a request for information: *Does anyone have any queries regarding travel arrangements?*
▻ ***verb***: **queries, querying, queried**
You **query** something when you ask a question about it that expresses doubt or suspicion: *When I queried the bill, the waiter admitted we had been overcharged and apologized.* □ *I queried whether his previous experience was really relevant to this job.*

quest /kwɛst/ *noun* (*formal*): **quests**
A search for something, especially a long and difficult search, is often referred to as a **quest**: *He has travelled half way round the world in his quest for the truth about his son's death.*

question /ˈkwɛstʃən/ *noun*; *verb*
▻ ***noun***: **questions**
1 You ask someone a **question** when you ask them for information or ask them to tell you something: *I expect an honest answer to a straightforward question.* □ *She refused to answer my question directly.* □ *Members of the audience put questions to the minister on a number of issues.* □ *Someone asked a question about parking facilities.* □ *The question of whether the scheme was a sensible one was never asked.* **2** (*count or uncount*) There is some **question** about something if there is some doubt, suspicion or uncertainty about it: *There appears to be some question as to whether she is eligible for a grant at all.* □ *This latest incident raises questions about their loyalty.* □ *There is no question that* [= there is no doubt that] *he's capable of doing the job.* [*same as* **doubt**] **3** A **question** is also a matter or issue that needs to be discussed: *She raised the question of safety in children's playgrounds.* □ *Heads of government are again meeting to discuss the Northern Ireland question.* □ *A number of questions came up during the debate.* [*same as* **issue**] **4** (*used in the singular*) If you say about some situation that it is a **question** of a particular thing, you mean that the situation has to do with, or is about, that thing: *It's not a question of money; there will always be enough money for this kind of project.* □ *This is a question of principle.* [*same as* **matter**] **5** A **question** is also a problem set in a test or an examination for candidates to deal with: *Answer one question from each section.* □ *I couldn't do Question 5 at all.*
▻ ***verb***: **questions, questioning, questioned**
1 You **question** someone when you ask them in a detailed or intensive way about something: *When I questioned him about the money, he said he had won it in a bet.* □ *The police are holding a man for questioning.*

> Note that you **ask** someone something when you put a question to them; you **question** someone when you ask them a lot of questions about something.

2 You **question** something when you express doubt about it: *I can't help questioning her motives.* □ *I question the need for an extra member of staff.* — adjective **questioning:** *He gave me a questioning glance.*
▻ ***phrases*** **1** Something that is **beyond question** is absolutely certain, and there is no doubt about it: *I knew beyond question who was responsible for the rumour.* □ *His loyalty is beyond question.* **2** You **call** something **into question** if you express doubts about it: *The importance of the institution of marriage has been called into question in the last 30 years.* **3 a** The person or thing **in question** is the person or thing being discussed or referred to: *Where were you on the night in question?* **b** Something is **in question** if people have doubts about it: *Her ability is not in question.* □ *Again, the necessity of some of his expenditure comes into question.* **4** There is **no question of** your doing something, or of something happening, if you have no intention of doing it, or if there is no possibility of it happening: *There is no question of my resigning.* □ *There's no question of the firm closing down.* □ *There was no question of her being allowed to walk home alone.* **5** Something that is **open to question** is still not certain or agreed upon: *It's open to question whether most women want a child.* **6** Something that is **out of the question** is impossible or cannot be done: *Buying a second car is quite out of the question.* **7** You accept something **without question** when you accept it without objecting, protesting or asking any questions: *They agreed without question.*

questionable /ˈkwɛstʃənəbəl/ *adjective*
Something is **questionable** when people suspect it might not be good, correct, proper or worthwhile: *Her motives seem questionable.* □ *schemes of questionable benefit to local residents.*

question mark /ˈkwɛstʃən mɑːk/ *noun*: **question marks**
1 A **question mark** is the punctuation mark (?), placed after a question. [see appendix on **Punctuation**] **2** You can say there is a **question mark** over something when people have doubts about it: *A big question mark now hangs over the future of the company.*

questionnaire /kwɛstʃəˈnɛə(r)/ *noun*: **questionnaires**
A **questionnaire** is a printed set of questions answered by many different people, used as a way of collecting information about the habits or opinions of people in general: *Please fill in the questionnaire overleaf.*

queue /kjuː/ *noun*; *verb*
▻ ***noun***: **queues**
A **queue** is a line of people or vehicles waiting for something: *We joined the queue, and it was not long*

before we were served. ▫ *All those waiting for tickets please form an orderly queue.* ▫ *Heavy queues of traffic are building up on the approach to the Kingston Bridge.*
▻ ***verb***: **queues**, **queuing**, **queued:** *Some people have been queuing since yesterday.* ▫ *They queued up for over two hours, only to be told there were no tickets left.*

quibble /ˈkwɪbəl/ *verb*: **quibbles**, **quibbling**, **quibbled**
People who **quibble** over something unimportant argue about it or object to it: *When the bill arrived, they all started quibbling about who had ordered coffee and who hadn't.*

quiche /kiːʃ/ *noun*: **quiches**
A **quiche** is a savoury pie with no top, with a filling made from eggs and other chopped foods.

quick /kwɪk/ *adjective*: **quicker**, **quickest**
1 Quick movements are performed with speed: *He turned the pastry over with a quick flick of the wrist.* ▫ *I could hear her quick light step in the corridor.* [*same as* **rapid**, **swift**] **2** A **quick** action or procedure takes only a short time: *I had a quick glance at the morning paper before leaving.* ▫ *I'd like a quick word with you.* ▫ *Have you time for a quick cup of coffee?* [compare **brief**] **3** Something that you perform or undertake, such as a journey, is **quick** if it doesn't take you long; you are **quick** doing something if you take only a short time to do it: *The rail journey is reasonably quick.* ▫ *It's quicker to go by underground.* ▫ *Let's see how quick you can be getting undressed and into bed.* ▫ *Goodness, that was quick!* ▫ *You've been very quick getting here.* ▫ *She's a quick worker.* **4** You are **quick** to do something when you do it immediately or without delay: *Cabinet members were quick to express their sorrow at the tragic news.* ▫ *That must be about the quickest decision I've ever made.* **5** You are **quick** to react in some way if you do so too hastily: *She's always been quick to take offence.* — *adverb* **quickly:** *I quickly told her what had happened.* ▫ *I'd like this dealt with as quickly as possible.* ▫ *We got here as quickly as we could.* ▫ *She responded quickly to the new drug.* ▫ *You'll get there much more quickly if you take a taxi.*
▻ ***phrase*** (*informal*) If someone tells you to do something **and be quick about it**, they are telling you rudely to hurry.

quicken /ˈkwɪkən/ *verb*: **quickens**, **quickening**, **quickened**
Something **quickens** when it begins to move or happen quicker than before: *We usually find the heart rate quickens for a short while after the drug is administered.*

quicksand /ˈkwɪksand/ *noun* (*uncount*)
Quicksand is loose, wet sand that sucks you down if you walk on it.

quick-witted /kwɪkˈwɪtəd/ *adjective*
You are **quick-witted** if you are intelligent and can think of the answers to problems quickly. [*same as* **sharp**; *opposite* **slow-witted**]

quid /kwɪd/ *noun* (*BrE*) (*informal*): **quid**
A **quid** is a pound in money: *They can earn a hundred quid a day on some sites.* ▫ *a ten-quid note.*

quiet /ˈkwaɪət/ *adjective*; *noun*
▻ ***adjective***: **quieter**, **quietest**
1 Something that is **quiet** makes little noise: *The new washing machine is nice and quiet.* ▫ *She spoke in a quiet but authoritative voice.* [*opposite* **noisy**, **loud**] **2** A **quiet** place is a place where there is little or no noise: *We moved to the quieter atmosphere of the lounge.* [*opposite* **noisy**] **3** You are **quiet** when you say nothing, or make no noise: *He told the boys at the back to be quiet.* ▫ *I had nothing to add, so I remained quiet.* [*same as* **silent**] **4** A **quiet** person has a calm, controlled manner and does not communicate readily with others: *She was one of those quiet, efficient people.* [*same as* **reserved**, **unobtrusive**] **5** A **quiet** place or a **quiet** period is one in which there is little activity or excitement: *a quiet little village* ▫ *I just want a nice quiet restful holiday.* [*same as* **peaceful**] **6** Business or trade is **quiet** when there is little of it: *There's usually a quiet couple of months before the Christmas rush.* ▫ *Trading in shares has been quiet.* [*opposite* **busy**] **7** A **quiet** event is one that only a few people attend, with little ceremony or formality: *We had a very quiet wedding.* ▫ *The funeral was a quiet affair.* [*opposite* **big**, **large**] **8 Quiet** colours are colours such as grey and beige, as distinct from bright or noticeable colours such as red and orange. — *adverb* **quietly:** *'Wait here,' he said quietly.* ▫ *Just listen quietly.* ▫ *I slipped quietly out of the room while nobody was looking.* ▫ *He quietly but deliberately prepared his revenge.*
▻ ***noun*** (*uncount*)
Quiet is silence, or an absence of excitement and activity: *Sometimes we like to exchange the bustle of city life for the peace and quiet of the countryside.* ▫ *Let's have some quiet in here.* [*same as* **silence**, **peace**; *opposite* **noise**, **excitement**]
▻ ***phrases* 1** You **keep quiet about** something, or **keep it quiet**, if you say nothing about it, but keep it secret: *I decided to keep quiet about what had happened.* **2** People do things **on the quiet** when they do them secretly: *He occasionally did a bit of drug-dealing on the quiet.*

quieten /ˈkwaɪətən/ *verb*: **quietens**, **quietening**, **quietened**
Something **quietens**, or **quietens** down, when it becomes calmer or less noisy: *We try to quieten the children down before bedtime.*

quilt /kwɪlt/ *noun*: **quilts**
A **quilt** is a warm, thick bedcover filled with feathers or a similar man-made material. [compare **duvet**]

quip /kwɪp/ *noun*; *verb*
▻ ***noun***: **quips**
A **quip** is a clever or amusing remark.
▻ ***verb***: **quips**, **quipping**, **quipped:** *'The reports of my death have been greatly exaggerated', he quipped.*

quirk /kwɜːk/ *noun*: **quirks**
1 A **quirk** is a strange habit or a strange way of behaving: *At first they tried to correct her, but after a while they accepted it as one of her little quirks.* **2** People often refer to a strange or unfortunate accident or coincidence as a **quirk** of fate: *By some quirk of fate, she was out of town on the one day of the year he had chosen to visit.*

quit /kwɪt/ *verb*: **quits**, **quitting**, **quit**
1 You **quit** something such as a job when you leave it: *She sent me a note saying that she had quit the movie business for ever.* ▫ *You won't have to fire me because I quit!* **2** You **quit** something such as a habit when you stop doing it and give it up: *That was the week I quit smoking.*

quite /kwaɪt/ *adverb*
1 (*moderating or intensifying*) The meaning of **quite** ranges from 'not very' or 'only moderately' when stressed and spoken in a high tone, to 'fairly', 'pretty' or 'more than usually' when you stress the following word: *That's <u>quite</u>* [= not particularly] *good.* ▫ *That's quite <u>good</u>* [= pretty good]. ▫ *It's been quite a nice day.* ▫ *We had quite pleasant weather.* ▫ *They're quite agreeable people.* ▫ *We found the way quite easily.* ▫ *They left quite early this morning.* [compare **rather**, **fairly**, **pretty**; see note at **rather**] **2** With verbs, **quite** has a similar range of meanings, from 'not particularly' to

'greatly': *I quite enjoyed my trip to France.* □ *She quite admires you.* **3** You use **quite** with 'a' before singular count nouns to mean 'considerable'; **quite** also emphasizes expressions like *a lot*: *You've got quite some problem there.* □ *That's quite a horse.* [= that's a splendid horse] □ *It's been quite a week.* [= an extraordinary, or a very busy, week] □ *Quite a few* [= a large number of] *people turned up.* [compare **rather**] **4** You use **quite**, with the meaning 'absolutely' or 'completely', for emphasis: *He remained quite motionless.* □ *It's quite normal.* □ *It's all quite simple.* □ *Are you quite sure?* □ *You're quite right.* □ *It's quite OK.* □ *That's a quite brilliant suggestion.* □ *with quite disastrous results* □ *She's quite the best candidate.* □ *'Are you angry?' 'No, quite the opposite'.* □ *That was quite the wrong thing to suggest.* □ *I quite agree with you.* □ *I've quite finished, thank you.* □ *That news has quite spoilt my day.* □ *Quite honestly, I don't care what he thinks of me.* □ *We've quite obviously lost our way.* [*same as* **absolutely**, **completely**; compare **perfectly**]

Notice a difference in word order between senses 1 and 4: *quite a good idea* [= a reasonably good idea]; *a quite brilliant suggestion* [= an absolutely brilliant suggestion].

5 With a negative, **quite** means 'not, although almost', or 'not exactly', or is used merely to reduce the force of the negative: *It isn't quite wide enough.* □ *Today wasn't quite as wet as yesterday.* □ *'Have you finished?' 'Not quite.'* □ *Things were never quite the same after that.* □ *I wasn't sure quite what was expected of me.* □ *Sorry, I didn't quite catch your name.* **6** (*used as an answer*) You answer **'Quite'** or **'Quite so'** to express agreement: *'We can only await developments.' 'Quite.'* □ *'We can do nothing further at present.' 'No, quite.'* [*same as* **absolutely**]

quits /ˈkwɪts/ *adjective* (*informal*)
Two people are **quits** when neither person owes the other anything and both are even or equal: *If you pay for the damage to my car, we'll call it quits.*

quiver /ˈkwɪvə(r)/ *verb*: **quivers, quivering, quivered**
Something, especially part of your body, **quivers** when it trembles or shakes slightly: *Her bottom lip quivered, and her eyes filled with tears.*

quiz /kwɪz/ *noun*; *verb*
▻ ***noun***: **quizzes**
A **quiz** is a competition in which people are asked questions to test their knowledge: *the popular television sports quiz, 'A Question of Sport'* □ *quiz programmes on the radio.*
▻ ***verb***: **quizzes, quizzing, quizzed**
You **quiz** someone when you ask them questions, especially in a forceful or aggressive way: *I had no wish to be quizzed about my private life.* [*same as* **interrogate, cross-examine**]

quizzical /ˈkwɪzɪkəl/ *adjective*
You give someone a **quizzical** look when your expression shows that you don't understand what they say, or that you suspect that what they say isn't true. [*same as* **questioning**]

quorum /ˈkwɔːrəm/ *noun* (*used in the singular*)
An official or formal meeting has a **quorum** if there are enough people present to allow business to be carried out, and to make any decisions taken legal: *Some of the union members walked out of the meeting, with the result that there was no quorum and a vote on strike action couldn't be taken.*

quota /ˈkwoʊtə/ *noun*: **quotas**
A **quota** is a number or amount allowed or required, or a share of something given to someone: *Some of the farms are not producing their milk quota.* □ *What do we do once we've completed our quota of work?*

quotation /kwoʊˈteɪʃən/ *noun*: **quotations**
1 A **quotation** is something someone has written or said, repeated or mentioned by someone else: *I've not heard the phrase before, but it sounds like a quotation from the Bible.* **2** Someone who gives you a **quotation** tells you how much they would charge to do a particular job for you: *We got quotations from several local builders.* [compare **estimate**]

quotation marks /kwoʊˈteɪʃən mɑːkz/ *noun* (*plural*)
Quotation marks are the punctuation marks (" " or ' '), used to show the beginning and end of speech, or of a quotation. [see appendix on **Punctuation**]

quote /kwoʊt/ *verb*; *noun*
▻ ***verb***: **quotes, quoting, quoted**
1 You **quote** what someone has said or written when you repeat their exact words: *He spent the evening quoting passages of Shakespeare to try and impress her.* □ *He continued his speech, frequently quoting from the Bible.* □ *You were quoted in the 'Daily Telegraph' as saying that you thought the Prime Minister was an incompetent idiot.* **2** Someone who **quotes** you a price for work tells you how much money they would charge for doing the work for you: *Three companies have quoted for the roof repairs.* □ *Sinclair is quoting £500 to replace the glass alone.*
▻ ***noun***: **quotes**
1 A **quote** is a quotation: *I think it's a quote from an Oscar Wilde play.* □ *Applications for Home Improvement grants must be accompanied by quotes from at least three companies.* **2** (*used in the plural*) **Quotes** are quotation marks: *Could you read the word in quotes?*

R or **r** /ɑː(r)/ *noun*: **Rs** or **r's**
R is the eighteenth letter of the English alphabet: *The English seem to be incapable of pronouncing the 'r' in 'Ireland'.*

rabbi /ˈrabaɪ/ *noun*: **rabbis**
A **rabbi** is a Jewish religious minister.

rabbit /ˈrabɪt/ *noun*: **rabbits**
A **rabbit** is a smallish, long-eared, furry animal that lives in holes in the ground.

rabble /ˈrabəl/ *noun* (*used in the singular*)
You might refer to a noisy, disorderly crowd of people as a **rabble**.

rabies /ˈreɪbiːz/ *noun* (*uncount*)
Rabies is a disease of the nervous system that causes madness and usually death, that people catch by being bitten by an infected animal.

race[1] /reɪs/ *noun*; *verb*
▷ ***noun***: **races**
1 A **race** is a contest between for example runners, horses or cars to find out who is the fastest: *This next race is run over two miles.* ▫ *a horse race.* **2** A contest of any kind, for example between people who want to be the first to do or get something, is also a **race**: *The 60s was the decade of the 'Race into Space', between the United States and the Soviet Union.* ▫ *the nuclear arms race.*
▷ ***verb***: **races, racing, raced**
1 You **race** when you take part in a race: *She's never raced over this distance before.* ▫ *I'll race you to the postbox.* **2** To **race** an animal or a vehicle is to enter it in a race: *Will you be racing him again this season?* **3** You **race** somewhere when you move fast: *We all raced along the road to the ice-cream shop at the end.* **4** You say your heart **is racing** when it is beating very fast, usually because you are excited: *There was a time when my heart would race every time someone mentioned his name.*

race[2] /reɪs/ *noun*: **races**
All the people of the world can be divided into **races**, according to physical features such as skin colour: *an unknown African race of people* ▫ *We will consider you irrespective of your race, religion or sexual orientation.*

racecourse /ˈreɪskɔːs/ *noun*: **racecourses**
A **racecourse** is a track that horses race on.

racehorse /ˈreɪshɔːs/ *noun*: **racehorses**
A **racehorse** is a horse specially bred and trained for racing.

race relations /reɪs rɪˈleɪʃənz/ *noun* (*plural*)
You refer to the attitudes that people of different races in the same community or country have towards each other as **race relations**: *The police are working hard to improve race relations.*

racial /ˈreɪʃəl/ *adjective*
Racial means relating to a person's race, or to different races of people: *companies guilty of racial discrimination* ▫ *disturbing levels of racial hatred.* — *adverb* **racially:** *This seems to have been a racially motivated attack.*

racialism /ˈreɪʃəlɪzm/ *noun* (*uncount*)
Racialism is racism.

racing /ˈreɪsɪŋ/ *noun* (*uncount*)
Racing is the sport of racing animals or vehicles: *an evening's greyhound racing* ▫ *one of motor racing's most glamorous drivers.*

racism /ˈreɪsɪzm/ *noun* (*uncount*)
Racism is dislike of all people who are of a different race, or cruel or unfair treatment of them: *Of course we must combat racism in all its forms.* — *noun and adjective* **racist:** *His father's an out-and-out racist.* ▫ *a barrage of racist abuse.*

rack /rak/ *noun*; *verb*
▷ ***noun***: **racks**
A **rack** is a framework with rails, shelves, hooks or other fastenings, for holding or storing things: *I put the suitcase on the luggage rack above my seat.* ▫ *We could get a roof rack for the car.*
▷ ***verb*** (*literary*): **racks, racking, racked**
You **are racked** by something when it causes you great pain or suffering: *I knew that it was cowardice that had led me to betray her, and I was still racked by guilt over the incident.* ▫ *She spent the remainder of her days shut up alone in her apartment, racked with pain.*
▷ ***phrase*** (*informal*) You **rack your brains** when you try as hard as you can to think of something: *We spent a whole morning racking our brains for a good name to give the new product.*

racket[1] or **racquet** /ˈrakɪt/ *noun*: **rackets**
A **racket** is an oval frame with strings stretched across it, used for hitting the ball in tennis, squash and other games: *a badminton racket.*

racket[2] /ˈrakɪt/ *noun* (*used in the singular*; *informal*)
1 A **racket** is a loud, confused noise or disturbance: *Who's making that racket?* [*same as* **din**] **2** A **racket** is also an illegal scheme for making money: *They were running some sort of racket.*

racquet see **racket**[1].

racy /ˈreɪsɪ/ *adjective*: **racier, raciest**
Something such as a story, film or style of writing is described as **racy** if it is lively, exciting, amusing and slightly shocking: *This is the raciest novel she has written yet.*

radar /ˈreɪdɑː(r)/ *noun* (*uncount*)
Radar is a system that uses radio waves to find the position of aircraft and ships: *Even the smallest submarines are equipped with radar.*

radiant /ˈreɪdɪənt/ *adjective* (*literary*)
People are **radiant** when they are so full of joy that it can be seen in their faces: *Your daughter looks radiant today.* — *noun* (*uncount*) **radiance:** *She looked so beautiful that evening; she had the radiance of a bride.*

radiate /ˈreɪdɪeɪt/ *verb*: **radiates, radiating, radiated**
1 Something that **radiates** heat or light produces it and sends it out. [*same as* **emit**] **2** People **radiate** feel-

ings such as happiness or optimism if their behaviour shows clearly that they feel that way: *The children radiated such vitality that we all felt uplifted.* **3** Things **radiate** from a central point when they form a pattern of lines like the spokes of a wheel: *The main square has a number of impressive avenues radiating from it.*

radiation /reɪdɪ'eɪʃən/ *noun* (*uncount*)
Radiation is radioactive energy, that can harm or kill people if they are exposed to it: *The number of likely deaths from cancer caused by radiation is still small.*

radiator /'reɪdɪeɪtə(r)/ *noun*: **radiators**
1 Radiators are the parts of a central heating system that release heat into a room or rooms, each consisting of a series of pipes, often in the form of a flat panel, fitted to a wall. [see picture at **living room**] **2** The **radiator** in a vehicle is a similar device for cooling the engine. [see picture at **car**]

radical /'radɪkəl/ *adjective*; *noun*
▷ ***adjective***
1 Radical means relating to the basic nature or form of something: *radical changes in government policy.* [*same as* **fundamental**] **2 Radical** also describes people who want to make big changes, for example changes to the political system: *the radical wing of the party.* [*same as* **extremist**] — *adverb* **radically:** *The final product was radically different from what we had originally envisaged.*
▷ ***noun***: **radicals:** *Most of my fellow students were ardent radicals.*

radii /'reɪdɪaɪ/ *noun*
Radii is the plural of **radius**.

radio /'reɪdɪoʊ/ *noun*; *verb*
▷ ***noun***: **radios**
1 (*uncount, often adjectival*) **Radio** is a system of broadcasting sound by converting it into electrical signals that are sent through the air, not along wires: *Because of the high mountains, communication by radio was impossible.* ▫ *a radio station broadcasting radio programmes of all kinds.* **2** A **radio** is an electrical device which receives, transmits or broadcasts radio signals: *She listens to the news on the radio.* ▫ *Each lorry is equipped with a short-wave radio, for communication between drivers.* [see picture at **living room**]
▷ ***verb***: **radios, radioing, radioed**
You **radio** someone when you communicate with them by radio: *The police officer had radioed the station for assistance.*

radioactive /reɪdɪoʊ'aktɪv/ *adjective*
A **radioactive** substance sends out a very powerful form of energy called **radioactivity**, that can be extremely harmful: *They measured disturbing levels of radioactivity in the atmosphere around the nuclear power station.*

radish /'radɪʃ/ *noun*: **radishes**
A **radish** is a small rounded vegetable eaten raw in salads. [see picture at **vegetable**]

radius /'reɪdɪəs/ *noun*: **radii**
1 The **radius** of a circle is the distance from its centre to its outside edge, or a line drawn between these two points. [see picture at **shape**] **2** The size of an area surrounding a particular place is often referred to as a **radius** of a particular distance from that place: *Everyone living within a radius of four miles from the explosion was evacuated from their home.*

raffle /'rafəl/ *noun*; *verb*
▷ ***noun***: **raffles**
A **raffle** is a competition to win a prize, in which each competitor buys a numbered ticket and the winner is the person whose number is selected at random: *They regularly organize raffles to raise money for charity.* [*same as* **lottery**]
▷ ***verb***: **raffles, raffling, raffled**
You **raffle** something, or **raffle** it off, when you offer it as the prize in a raffle.

raft /rɑːft/ *noun*: **rafts**
A **raft** is a simple boat made by tying pieces of wood together to form a flat platform to sit on.

rafter /'rɑːftə(r)/ *noun*: **rafters**
Rafters are the sloping pieces of wood that form the framework of a roof.

rag /rag/ *noun*: **rags**
1 A **rag** is a piece of cloth used for cleaning, especially a piece torn off old clothes: *Wipe the blades clean with an oily rag.* **2 Rags** are dirty, old, torn clothes: *children dressed in rags.* **3** (*informal*) A poor-quality newspaper, or one that you disapprove of, can be referred to as a **rag**: *I wouldn't believe anything I read in that rag.*
▷ ***phrase*** (*informal*) To **lose your rag** is to lose your temper and become very angry.

rage /reɪdʒ/ *noun*; *verb*
▷ ***noun***
1 (*uncount or used in the singular*) **Rage** is violent anger: *I was consumed by rage.* ▫ *I've never seen him in such a rage.* [*same as* **fury**] **2** (*informal*) Something that is all the **rage** is very popular, usually only for a short time: *I remember that baggy trousers were all the rage that summer.*
▷ ***verb***: **rages, raging, raged:** *'Get out of here!', she raged.*

ragged /'ragɪd/ *adjective*
1 Ragged clothes are old, worn and torn; you describe someone's appearance as **ragged** if they are dressed in clothes like this: *A ragged little boy stood in the doorway.* [*same as* **tatty**] **2** A **ragged** edge is rough and irregular: *I want nice neat columns, not these ragged lines.* [*same as* **jagged**]

raid /reɪd/ *noun*; *verb*
▷ ***noun***: **raids**
1 A **raid** is a sudden unexpected attack: *We carried out a number of bombing raids over Germany.* **2** A **raid** is also a sudden unexpected visit by the police, who force their way into a building, searching for suspected criminals or stolen goods: *A dawn raid resulted in three arrests.*
▷ ***verb***: **raids, raiding, raided:** *Villages were raided and houses burnt down.* ▫ *Uniformed officers raided the warehouse.* — *noun* **raider:** *Gangs of raiders swept through the town.*

rail /reɪl/ *noun*: **rails**
1 A **rail** is a horizontal bar for hanging things on: *Staff in the shop said she tried on every dress on the rail.* ▫ *a towel rail.* [*same as* **rack**] **2** The long steel bars forming the track that trains travel on are called **rails**. **3** (*uncount, often adjectival*) You travel by **rail** when you travel by train: *the rising cost of rail travel.*

railing /'reɪlɪŋ/ *noun* (*usually in the plural*): **railings**
A fence made of vertical metal bars is usually referred to as **railings**; one of the individual metal bars can be referred to as a **railing**: *I had to climb over the railings.* ▫ *a missing railing.*

railway /'reɪlweɪ/ *noun* (*count or uncount, often adjectival*)
1 A **railway** is a track for trains to travel on, formed by two parallel steel rails fixed to wooden bars: *The house is quite close to the railway.* ▫ *a short railway journey.* **2** A **railway** is also a system of such tracks, plus all the trains, buildings and people required for it to operate: *the regional railway companies.*

rain /reɪn/ *noun; verb*
▻ ***noun*** *(uncount)*
Rain is water falling from the clouds in drops: *The rain eased off and the weather turned brighter.* ▫ *a particularly heavy fall of rain.*
▻ ***verb***: **rains, raining, rained**
You say it **is raining** when rain falls from the clouds: *I hope it doesn't rain tomorrow.*

> ***phrasal verbs***
> **rain down** Something **rains down** when a lot of it falls from above: *They sat in the trenches with bullets raining down on them.*
> **rain off** Something, especially a sports match, **is rained off** when rain prevents it from taking place: *We might have known the picnic would be rained off.*

raincoat /ˈreɪnkoʊt/ *noun*: **raincoats**
A **raincoat** is a light waterproof coat, especially one without a hood, worn to keep out the rain. [see picture at **clothing**]

rainfall /ˈreɪnfɔːl/ *noun (uncount)*
Rainfall is the amount of rain that falls in a certain place over a certain period of time: *statistics for average rainfall.*

rainforest /ˈreɪnfɒrɪst/ *noun* (*count or uncount*): **rainforests**
A **rainforest** is a dense tropical forest with lots of tall trees, in an area with very heavy rainfall.

rainy /ˈreɪnɪ/ *adjective*: **rainier, rainiest**
You say it is **rainy** when there is a lot of rain: *It's been very rainy lately.* ▫ *another rainy day.* [*same as* **wet**]

raise /reɪz/ *verb; noun*
▻ ***verb***: **raises, raising, raised**
1 You **raise** something when you move it or lift it to a higher position or level: *We'll have to raise the back of the car off the ground.* ▫ *She raised the blinds and sun poured into the room.* ▫ *There was great excitement as the wreck was raised from the sea bed.* ▫ *If you know the answer raise your hand.* ▫ *He raised his eyebrows in surprise.* [*same as* **lift**; *opposite* **lower**] **2** You **raise** yourself when you move your body, *eg* from lying, into a sitting or standing position: *She raised herself on her elbow and reached out for the clock.* [*opposite* **lower**] **3** You **raise** something when you increase its level or amount: *One of the Council's main objects is to raise the standard of local facilities.* ▫ *We'll have to raise the rent again.* [*opposite* **reduce**] **4** You **raise** your voice when you start speaking more loudly, usually from anger: *Don't raise your voice in front of the children.* ▫ *I heard raised voices in the next room.* [*opposite* **lower**] **5** You **raise** a subject or an objection, especially at a formal meeting, when you mention it or suggest that it should be considered or discussed: *I raised the issue of overtime pay.* ▫ *No objections to the proposals were raised.* ▫ *That raises other questions that we can't discuss now.* **6** You **raise** money when you obtain it in some way, *eg* by borrowing it from a bank: *We couldn't even raise enough to pay a deposit.* **7** You **raise** money for a charity or other cause when you collect it by asking people to give it to you: *We're holding a sponsored swim to raise money for new sports equipment.* **8** You **raise** children when you look after them until they are grown up: *She had raised three children single-handed.* [*same as* **bring up**] **9** To **raise** crops is to grow them; to **raise** animals is to breed them.
[compare **rise**]
▻ ***noun*** *(AmE)*: **raises**
A **raise** is an increase in wages or salary. [*same as* **rise**]

raised /reɪzd/ *adjective*
Something that is **raised** is higher than the thing or things around it: *The swimming pool is built on a raised area at the back of the garden.*

raisin /ˈreɪzən/ *noun*: **raisins**
A **raisin** is a dried grape.

rake /reɪk/ *noun; verb*
▻ ***noun***: **rakes**
A **rake** is a garden tool consisting of a comb-like head attached to a long handle, used for smoothing or breaking up soil, and for gathering leaves and other objects. [see picture at **tools**]
▻ ***verb***: **rakes, raking, raked:** *I usually rake the grass cuttings into little piles.* ▫ *It'll take him hours to rake up all those leaves.* [see also **rake up** below]

> ***phrasal verbs***
> **rake in** (*informal*) Someone who **is raking in** money is earning lots of it, usually without much effort: *If our investments pay off we'll be raking it in.*
> **rake up** (*informal*) You **rake up** the past when you talk about unpleasant things that happened, that people would prefer to forget: *I told him not to go raking up all that business again.* [*same as* **dredge up**]

rally /ˈralɪ/ *noun; verb*
▻ ***noun***: **rallies**
1 A **rally** is a large gathering of people outdoors, especially with a political aim: *an anti-fascist rally in the park.* **2** A **rally** is also a car race on a course that includes ordinary roads and forest tracks. **3** In sports like tennis, a **rally** is the period of play between each point, especially the number of times the ball is hit: *That was the longest rally of the match so far.*
▻ ***verb***: **rallies, rallying, rallied**
1 People **rally** when they come together to show support for, or opposition to, something; you **rally** them when you bring them together: *There are signs that the Cabinet are rallying to the Prime Minister.* ▫ *The minister is hoping to rally enough support to get the bill passed.* **2** People **rally** when they become well after being ill, or when they recover their energies, spirits or abilities: *Beth rallied for a while, but suffered a relapse and died within a few days.* ▫ *Then Edberg rallied, and looked like winning the match at one stage.*

ram /ram/ *noun; verb*
▻ ***noun***: **rams**
A **ram** is an adult male sheep.
▻ ***verb***: **rams, ramming, rammed**
1 You **ram** something somewhere when you push it there hard: *Jones rammed his shoulder into the door.* ▫ *She grabbed the papers angrily and rammed them into her briefcase.* [*same as* **thrust**] **2** One vehicle **rams** another when it crashes into it, especially deliberately.

ramble /ˈrambəl/ *verb; noun*
▻ ***verb***: **rambles, rambling, rambled**
Someone **rambles**, or **rambles** on, when they speak or write in an aimless or confused way: *We sat next to an old man who rambled on about the war and hot summers.* — *adjective* **rambling:** *a rather rambling speech.*
▻ ***noun***: **rambles**
A **ramble** is a long walk in the countryside, for pleasure: *She's taken the children on a nature ramble.* — *noun* **rambler:** *At weekends, the fields were full of ramblers.*

ramp /ramp/ *noun*: **ramps**
A **ramp** is a sloping surface between two different levels, especially one used instead of steps: *We'll need wheelchair ramps at every entrance.*

rampage /ram'peɪdʒ/ *verb*: **rampages, rampaging, rampaged**
People or animals **rampage** when they rush about in a wild, angry, violent way: *Efforts were made to prevent the buffalo rampaging through the village.* [*same as* **run wild**]
▻ *phrase* People or animals **go on the rampage** when they rampage, causing damage and destruction: *Soccer hooligans went on the rampage through the streets of Amsterdam.*

rampant /'rampənt/ *adjective*
Something such as a disease is described as **rampant** when it is spreading quickly and is affecting large numbers of people: *The army seemed on the brink of defeat and despair was rampant among the men.* [*same as* **widespread**]

ramshackle /'ramʃakəl/ *adjective*
A **ramshackle** building is in very bad condition, with pieces falling off: *an old farm with a number of ramshackle outbuildings.* [*same as* **dilapidated**]

ran /ran/ *verb*
Ran is the past tense of **run**.

ranch /rɑːntʃ/ *noun*: **ranches**
A **ranch** is a large farm, especially one in North America, where cattle or horses are reared.

rancid /'ransɪd/ *adjective*
Rancid food, especially butter, tastes or smells sour. [*same as* **rank**]

random /'randəm/ *adjective*
Random describes things that happen or are done without a definite plan, system or purpose: *The computer makes a random selection of names from the list.* □ *It seems that the houses burgled were chosen quite at random.* — *adverb* **randomly:** *The plants will look better randomly dotted about the garden.*

randy /'randɪ/ *adjective* (*informal*): **randier, randiest**
Someone who feels **randy** is sexually excited and keen to have sex.

rang /raŋ/ *verb*
Rang is the past tense of **ring**.

range /reɪndʒ/ *noun*; *verb*
▻ ***noun***: **ranges**
1 A **range** of things is a number of different ones, especially of the same broadly similar type: *Over 300 people were questioned, and a whole range of opinions emerged.* □ *They were given a range of topics to choose from.* [*same as* **variety**] **2** A **range** is also a number of items or products forming a distinct series: *We tested every freezer in the medium price range.* □ *children in the age range 10 to 16.* **3 Range** is also used to refer to the maximum distance that something can reach or travel: *The larger cannons had a range of nearly half a mile.* □ *long-range missiles* □ *These new aircraft have a range of over five thousand miles, which is Chicago and back without refuelling.* □ *We thought the airport was out of range of their rifles, but it's actually well within range.* **4** A **range** is an area where you can practise shooting guns; a driving **range** is an area where you can practise hitting golf balls. **5** A mountain **range** is a distinct row of mountains.
▻ ***verb***: **ranges, ranging, ranged**
Things **range** when they vary or change between stated limits or extremes: *We have jackets ranging from £35 to over £500.* □ *Opinions ranged from those who thought that no whales should be killed at all to those who didn't care.* [*same as* **extend**]

ranger /'reɪndʒə(r)/ *noun*: **rangers**
A **ranger** is someone whose job is looking after a forest or large park.

rank[1] /raŋk/ *noun*; *verb*
▻ ***noun***: **ranks**
1 Your **rank** is your position, grade or level of seniority within an organization, or sometimes within society: *an officer of junior rank* □ *It involves managers from the very highest ranks of the company.* □ *They would never let her marry a man of inferior social rank.* **2** (*used in the plural*) The lowest grades within an organization are often referred to as the **ranks**, or the **rank and file**: *She had risen from the ranks to the very top of her profession in under five years.* □ *Political leaders so often isolate themselves from the rank and file in the party.* **3** (*used in the plural*) When you become part of a group, you can say you have joined its **ranks**: *a young actor aspiring to the ranks of the rich and famous.*
▻ ***verb***: **ranks, ranking, ranked**
When you say where someone or something **ranks**, you are talking about their position, grade or status in relation to others, or to how you judge them in comparison to others: *A brilliant grass-court player, she is now ranked fifth in the world.* □ *For me, it ranks as the best British film of the post-war period.*

rank[2] /raŋk/ *adjective*
1 Something that is **rank** has a strong unpleasant smell: *His body was rank with stale sweat.* □ *the rank odour of rotting onions.* **2 Rank** is also used to describe an extreme example of behaviour that you disapprove of: *a case of rank disobedience* □ *That's rank bad management.* **3 Rank** is also used for emphasis, with the meaning 'complete' or 'absolute': *a rank beginner.*

rankle /'raŋkəl/ *verb*: **rankles, rankling, rankled**
Something that **rankles** makes you feel angry, annoyed or bitter when you think about it: *Their refusal to help still rankles.*

ransack /'ransak/ *verb*: **ransacks, ransacking, ransacked**
To **ransack** a place is to search through it violently, damaging and destroying many of the things in it: *When we got back, the caravan had been ransacked and the television had been stolen.*

ransom /'ransəm/ *noun*: **ransoms**
A **ransom** is money paid in return for the release of a kidnapped person: *The police have advised us to pay the ransom demanded.*
▻ *phrase* To **hold** someone **to ransom** is **1** to keep them as a prisoner until a ransom is paid: *Their daughter was held to ransom for over three weeks.* **2** to force them to do something, using threats: *With such military superiority, a country could hold the whole world to ransom.*

rant /rant/ *verb*: **rants, ranting, ranted**
Someone who **rants** speaks in a loud, angry way: *We could hear drunken men ranting and raving.*

rap /rap/ *noun*; *verb*
▻ ***noun***: **raps**
1 A **rap** is a quick, sharp tap or blow: *several raps on the table with his pen.* **2** (*uncount*) **Rap** is a kind of pop music with words sung in a way that sounds like ordinary talking.
▻ *phrase* (*informal*) You **take the rap** when you take the blame and are punished, often for something you didn't do.

rape[1] /reɪp/ *noun*; *verb*
▻ ***noun*** (*uncount or count*): **rapes**
Rape is the crime of forcing someone to have sex against their will, usually committed by a man against a woman: *a particularly brutal rape.*
▻ ***verb***: **rapes, raping, raped:** *The victim had been badly beaten and raped.*

rape² /reɪp/ *noun* (*uncount*)
Rape is a plant with bright yellow flowers, grown as food for sheep and for its seeds which are used to make a cooking oil.

rapid /ˈrapɪd/ *adjective*; *noun*
▻ ***adjective***
Rapid means moving, acting or happening very quickly: *the rapid progress of building work* ▫ *with a rapid swing of his arm.* [*same as* **swift**; *opposite* **slow**] — *adverb* **rapidly:** *moving rapidly on to the next item on our list.*
▻ ***noun*** (*used in the plural*): **rapids**
Rapids are parts of a river where the water flows very quickly, usually over dangerous rocks.

rapist /ˈreɪpɪst/ *noun*: **rapists**
A **rapist** is a person who has committed rape, usually a man who has raped a woman.

rapport /raˈpɔː(r)/ *noun* (*used in the singular*)
There is said to be a **rapport** between people who enjoy living or working together if they understand each other's personality and fit in with each other well: *Bush had enjoyed a personal rapport with Gorbachev.* ▫ *the rapport that develops between human and animal.* [*same as* **bond, understanding**]

rapture /ˈraptʃə(r)/ *noun*: **raptures**
You go into **raptures** over something when you speak about it with great enthusiasm or excitement.

rapturous /ˈraptʃərəs/ *adjective* (*literary*)
Someone who gets a **rapturous** reception is greeted with great enthusiasm by a crowd or audience: *the rapturous applause that followed the performance.*

rare¹ /rɛə(r)/ *adjective*: **rarer, rarest**
Something that is **rare** is not often done or found, or does not occur very often, and it is therefore regarded as particularly interesting or valuable: *a dealer in rare antiques* ▫ *She has that quality of humility so rare in famous people.* ▫ *It's rare to find a pair of these china dogs in such perfect condition.* — *adverb* (*used like a negative*) **rarely:** *We rarely go out in the week.* ▫ *Rarely have I seen any patient who seemed closer to death.* [*same as* **seldom**]

rare² /rɛə(r)/ *adjective*: **rarer, rarest**
Rare meat is cooked on the outside but still raw on the inside.

raring /ˈrɛərɪŋ/ *adjective*
People are **raring**, or **raring** to go, when they are full of energy or enthusiasm for some planned activity. [*same as* **keen, impatient**]

rarity /ˈrɛərɪtɪ/ *noun*: **rarities**
1 (*uncount*) **Rarity** is the state of being rare: *antique furniture of such rarity.* **2** A **rarity** is something which is very interesting or valuable because it is very rare.

rascal /ˈrɑːskəl/ *noun*: **rascals**
1 People call a badly behaved or cheeky child a **rascal**: *Come here, you little rascal!* **2** (*old*) A dishonest person is also referred to as a **rascal**: *I don't trust that old rascal who runs the newspaper stall.*

rash¹ /raʃ/ *adjective*
A person who is **rash** does foolish things hastily, without waiting to think about the results or consequences: *Don't make any rash decisions.* [*same as* **impulsive**] — *adverb* **rashly:** *I had rather rashly agreed to marry her.*

rash² /raʃ/ *noun*: **rashes**
A **rash** is an area of redness or red spots on your skin caused by an illness or disease: *Ian had broken out in a dreadful rash.*

rasher /ˈraʃə(r)/ *noun*: **rashers**
A **rasher** of bacon is a thin slice of it.

raspberry /ˈrɑːzbərɪ/ *noun*: **raspberries**
1 Raspberries are small edible red berries that grow on bushes and are often used to make jam. **2** You blow a **raspberry** when you make a rude or offensive noise by sticking out your tongue and blowing through your lips.

rasping /ˈrɑːspɪŋ/ *adjective*
A **rasping** noise is harsh and high-pitched: *She had a rasping voice that grated on my nerves.*

rat /rat/ *noun*: **rats**
1 A **rat** is a small furry animal like a large, long-tailed mouse, often found in or near water: *The sewers were full of rats.* **2** (*informal, derogatory*) People sometimes refer to a person they dislike as a **rat**, especially if the person has behaved dishonestly or disloyally.

rate /reɪt/ *noun*; *verb*
▻ ***noun***: **rates**
1 You often use **rate** when speaking about how fast something happens or how often it happens: *The rate of progress has been rather slow.* ▫ *Businesses are closing all over the country at a rate of fifty a week.* ▫ *The city has one of the highest suicide rates in Europe.* **2** You also often use **rate** when speaking about money, for example about how much interest or tax you pay as a percentage: *The rate of exchange is 8.4 francs to the pound.* ▫ *a savings account with a high interest rate.* **3** (*used in the plural*) The tax people pay for the services provided by local government, such as road repairs and rubbish collection, was formerly called **rates**: *I'm entitled to good service; I pay my rates like everyone else.* **4** You also use **rate** to refer to the standard of something; *eg*, things that are 'first **rate**' are excellent and things that are 'third **rate**' or 'fourth **rate**' are very poor: *He calls himself a musician, but he's just a third-rate trumpet-player.* [*same as* **-class**]
▻ ***verb***: **rates, rating, rated**
You use **rate** when speaking about how good you, or people in general, think someone or something is: *I'd rate it as the best book on the subject for years.* ▫ *You know we rate you very highly as a teacher.* ▫ *Albert was rated a better-than-average painter, nothing more.* [*same as* **judge**]
▻ ***phrases*** **1** You use **at any rate a** when you are adding something to correct what you have just said and make it more accurate: *Most of them, at any rate half of them, were opposed to it.* **b** when you are making a general statement containing the most relevant or important details of what you have just said: *He's visiting a niece or a cousin or something; a female relative, at any rate.* **2 At this rate** means 'if what is happening now continues to happen for some time': *This is the third traffic jam we've got caught in; at this rate, we'll miss the plane.*

ratepayer /ˈreɪtpeɪə(r)/ *noun*: **ratepayers**
You sometimes refer to people as **ratepayers** when you want to emphasize that they are citizens whose lives are affected by the policies of local and national governments: *But what will ratepayers think of the increase in council tax?*

rather /ˈrɑːðə(r)/ *adverb*
1 (*moderating or intensifying*) **Rather** has a range of meanings, from 'a bit' when said without stress, to 'pretty', 'very' or 'very much' when stressed: *You look rather tired.* ▫ *a bird rather like an owl* ▫ *We've done rather more than half.* ▫ *It's rather colder today.* ▫ *He's rather too pleased with himself.* ▫ *I had rather unwisely left the money on the kitchen table.* ▫ *I think he's rather attractive.* ▫ *I felt I'd handled the situation rather well.* ▫ *I heard some rather interesting news today.* ▫ *Indexing can be rather boring work.* ▫ *one or two rather silly undergraduates* ▫ *a rather shy* (or *rather a shy*) *young man.*

> **Rather** and **pretty** have a more intensifying effect than **quite** and **fairly** (which moderate the more they are stressed). **Rather** is often used to criticize, but may also express surprised approval: *rather inferior workmanship; I was rather impressed.*

2 You use **rather** with 'a' before certain singular nouns, to mean 'considerable' or 'significant', and for emphasis before *a lot*: *It seems rather a waste of talent.* □ *There's been rather a demand for the book lately.* □ *We've got rather a problem here.* □ *I've got rather a lot to do this evening.* [compare **quite**] **3** You can use **rather** with certain verbs, to mean both 'to a certain extent' and 'very much': *I've rather wasted your time, I'm afraid.* □ *That's rather spoilt our plans.* □ *I was rather hoping to meet her again.* □ *I rather liked what he wrote.* □ *if she's telling the truth, which I rather doubt.* **4** (*sentence adverb*) **a** You use 'or **rather**' to make a correction to what you have just said: *We're expecting a visit from my parents, or rather my mother and stepfather.* **b Rather** introduces what is actually so, in contrast to what is not so: *She was no longer the affectionate mother they'd known; rather, she'd turned into a quarrelsome old woman who seemed not to recognize them.*

▻ ***phrases*** **1 a** One thing is the case **rather than** another if the first is so and not the second: *It's an encyclopaedia rather than a dictionary.* □ *This is a cause for alarm rather than celebration.* **b** You choose one thing, or choose to do one thing, **rather than** another, if you choose the first in preference to the second: *For the walls, we chose yellow rather than blue, which would have made the room too dark.* □ *Rather than risk offending him, I accepted the invitation reluctantly.* □ *Rather than checking the whole population, we should concentrate on the high-risk groups.* **2** If you say you **would rather** do something, or **would rather** something happened, you mean you would prefer it: *'Do you mind if I smoke?' 'Well I'd rather you didn't.'* □ *I would much rather be out of doors than inside, even if it is raining.* □ *We'd far rather keep the money than spend it on something we don't need.* □ *I'd really rather not have to answer a lot of awkward questions.* □ *I'd rather you wrote nothing at all than wrote rubbish.* □ *Would you rather the children came with you instead?*

ratify /ˈratɪfaɪ/ *verb* (*formal*): **ratifies, ratifying, ratified**
To **ratify** something such as a formal contract is to give official agreement to it, usually by signing it: *The peace treaty has not yet been ratified by both sides.* — *noun* (*uncount*) **ratification** /ratɪfɪˈkeɪʃən/: *This could delay ratification of the trade agreements.*

ratio /ˈreɪʃɪoʊ/ *noun*: **ratios**
A **ratio** is a way of expressing how much or many of something exists in comparison to the amount or number of something else: *You mix sand and cement in the ratio 4 to 1, so 4 times as much sand as cement.* □ *The ratio of Christian children to Muslim children is slightly over 2 to 1.* □ *The older universities tend to have a higher teacher/student ratio.* [*same as* **proportion**]

ration /ˈraʃən/ *noun*; *verb*
▻ ***noun***: **rations**
1 Your **ration** of something is a limited amount of it you are allowed to have, because there is not much of it generally available: *They had already used up their sugar ration for the week.* [*same as* **quota**] **2** (*used in the plural*) A soldier's **rations** consist of the food he or she is given for one day.
▻ ***verb***: **rations, rationing, rationed**
Something **is rationed** when each person is only allowed a limited amount of it, because there is not much available.

rational /ˈraʃənəl/ *adjective*
Someone who is **rational** is able to make proper, sensible judgments and decisions; you say that someone is not **rational** when they are unable to think in this way, *eg* because they are too emotionally upset or they are mentally ill: *Would you describe this as rational behaviour?* [*same as* **balanced**, **reasonable**; *opposite* **irrational**] — *adverb* **rationally:** *Let's try to look at the problem rationally.*

rationalize or **rationalise** /ˈraʃənəlaɪz/ *verb*: **rationalizes, rationalizing, rationalized**
1 You **rationalize** something that has happened when you find reasons that explain or justify it, so that you can accept it: *There seems to be no way of rationalizing the sudden death of a child.* □ *We try to rationalize our greed and jealousy by saying that they are products of the society we live in.* [*same as* **justify**] **2** To **rationalize** an industry or organization is to make it more efficient and profitable by reorganizing it, and especially by sacking workers. [*same as* **streamline**]

rat race /ˈrat reɪs/ *noun* (*used in the singular; informal*)
People sometimes describe society, or the kind of job they do, as a **rat race** as a way of referring to how fiercely the people in it compete with each other.

rattle /ˈratəl/ *verb*; *noun*
▻ ***verb***: **rattles, rattling, rattled**
1 Something **rattles** when it makes a series of short, sharp, hard sounds, such as the sounds made when the wind keeps blowing a loose door or gate: *The wheels of the old cart rattled over the cobblestones.* [*same as* **clatter**] **2** (*informal*) Something **rattles** you when it makes you anxious or nervous: *The question had clearly rattled him.* [*same as* **disturb**, **shake**]
▻ ***noun***: **rattles**
A **rattle** is a baby's toy that makes a rattling noise when the baby shakes it.

> ***phrasal verbs***
> **rattle off** (*informal*) You **rattle off** something that you say or do if you say or do it very quickly and without having to think: *She rattled off a list of her party's tax proposals.* □ *He has rattled off another story in the same mould as every other book he's written.* [*same as* **reel off**]
> **rattle through** (*informal*) You **rattle through** something when you do it quickly: *He started by rattling through the main points of last week's lecture.*

ratty /ˈratɪ/ *adjective* (*informal*): **rattier, rattiest**
Someone who is **ratty** is in a bad temper: *What's wrong with Morris? He was terribly ratty with me just now.* [*same as* **touchy, short-tempered**]

raucous /ˈrɔːkəs/ *adjective*
A **raucous** voice sounds very rough and harsh, and is usually rather loud: *the sound of raucous laughter.*

raunchy /ˈrɔːntʃɪ/ *adjective* (*informal*): **raunchier, raunchiest**
Raunchy behaviour, stories or films have a strong sexual content: *Jagger gave his usual raunchy performance.*

ravage /ˈravɪdʒ/ *verb*; *noun*
▻ ***verb***: **ravages, ravaging, ravaged**
Something that **is ravaged** is so badly damaged that it is almost destroyed completely: *the history of a nation ravaged by civil war.*
▻ ***noun*** (*literary*): **ravages**
The **ravages** of something are the very damaging or destructive effects of it: *photographs of faces that bear the ravages of time.*

rave /reɪv/ *verb; adjective; noun*
▻ ***verb*: raves, raving, raved**
1 (*informal*) You **rave** about something when you talk about it with great enthusiasm or passion: *'The best book written this decade!', raved the Sunday Times.* **2** You say someone **is raving** when they are talking in an angry, uncontrolled way, suggesting that they are slightly mad. [*same as* **rant**]
▻ ***adjective*** (*informal*)
A journalist who writes a **rave** review of something praises it very highly: *The play has received rave notices.*
▻ ***noun*** (*informal*): **raves**
A **rave** is an organized party held in a large building, where young people dance to pop music, and sometimes take illegal drugs.
▻ ***phrase*** (*informal*) People **rave it up** when they enjoy themselves in a loud, lively way, *eg* at a party.

raven /'reɪvən/ *noun*: **ravens**
A **raven** is a large black bird that belongs to the crow family.

ravenous /'ravənəs/ *adjective*
You say you are **ravenous** when you are very hungry: *a band of ravenous children.* □ *What's for lunch? I'm ravenous.* [*same as* **starving**]

rave-up /'reɪv ʌp/ *noun* (*informal*): **rave-ups**
A **rave-up** is a lively party or celebration: *It was time we had a bit of a rave-up.*

ravine /rə'viːn/ *noun*: **ravines**
A **ravine** is a deep, narrow, steep-sided valley or channel.

ravishing /'ravɪʃɪŋ/ *adjective*
You describe someone as **ravishing** if they are very beautiful or attractive: *with his ravishing wife, Arlene.* □ *I believe it was Auberon Waugh who described Tony Blair as 'quite ravishing'.*

raw /rɔː/ *adjective*
1 Raw food is not cooked: *You can eat lots of vegetables raw.* [*same as* **uncooked**; *opposite* **cooked**] **2** A **raw** substance is still in its original, natural state, before being processed: *raw cotton.* [*same as* **unprocessed**; *opposite* **refined**] **3** Someone who is described as **raw** has no experience or training: *a bunch of raw recruits.* **4** Part of your body is **raw** when the skin has been removed in an accident, leaving it sore: *The teacher bathed his raw knee.* **5 Raw** weather is uncomfortably cold, wet and windy.

raw deal /rɔː'diːl/ *noun* (*used in the singular; informal*)
Someone who has been given, or has had, a **raw deal** has been treated unfairly, or has suffered a lot: *Old people get a raw deal; far more attention should be paid to their needs.*

raw materials /rɔː mə'tɪərɪəlz/ *noun* (*plural*)
Raw materials are natural substances used in a manufacturing process to make something.

ray /reɪ/ *noun*: **rays**
1 A **ray** is a beam of light: *A few rays of sunshine were squeezing through the gaps in the shutters.* □ *All these suntan creams protect the skin from harmful ultraviolet rays.* **2** A **ray** of something such as hope is a small amount of it or the beginnings of it: *These gestures are tiny rays of communication between baby and mother.* [*same as* **glimmer**]

raze /reɪz/ *verb* (*literary*): **razes, razing, razed**
A place **is razed** when all the buildings in it are destroyed completely: *All the villages within a 3-mile radius have been razed to the ground.*

razor /'reɪzə(r)/ *noun*: **razors**
A **razor** is a tool with a blade or blades, used for shaving parts of your body: *an electric razor.* [see picture at **bathroom**]

re /riː/ *preposition* (*formal*)
Re is used especially in written communications to mean 'about' or 'concerning': *Have we received any communication from them re the sale of shares?* □ *Re your request for a copy of the report: it is being sent to you by this morning's post.*

re- /riː/ or /rɪ/ *prefix*
Re- forms words that refer to the repeating of an action, and means **1** again in the same way: *I reread the report to see if I had missed anything important.* **2** again and in a different or improved way: *You'll have to rewrite the last paragraph to make it less critical.* **3** back or into a previous state: *She replaced the book on the shelf.*

reach /riːtʃ/ *verb; noun*
▻ ***verb*: reaches, reaching, reached**
1 You **reach** a place when you arrive there, or get as far as there: *We hoped to reach the island before nightfall.* □ *By the third day, they had only reached Brindisi.* **2** You can **reach** something that you are able to touch or get hold of: *If I stand on a stool, I can reach the ceiling.* **3** Something **reaches** the point or level that it projects as far as or extends to: *The hem of the skirt reached just below the knee.* □ *The shiny, blonde hair reached down to her waist.* □ *The new train reaches speeds of up to 150 miles per hour.* □ *When you reach your parents' age, you'll understand what it is to suffer.* [*same as* **attain**] **4** You **reach** your hand or other part of your body when you stretch it out to try to touch or get hold of something: *Could you reach into that bag and pass me a pen?* **5** You **reach** someone when you contact them or communicate with them, especially by telephone: *I've been trying to reach you all day.* □ *News of the crash hadn't reached her by then.* **6** People **reach** an agreement or a decision when they finally make it, especially after a long period of discussion or thought: *It's unlikely that an agreement will be reached within the next few days.*
▻ ***noun*: reaches**
1 (*uncount*) Something is within **reach** when you can reach it; it is out of **reach** if you can't: *Keep all household cleaning liquids well out of reach of children.* □ *The house is within easy reach of the town centre and all its amenities.* □ *Does an agreement seem within reach?* □ *Expensive holidays of this kind are simply out of reach for people on our salary.* [*same as* **grasp**] **2** (*used in the plural*) People often talk about the **reaches** of a place as a way of referring to the different parts or areas of it: *the inner reaches of the forest.*

react /rɪ'akt/ *verb*: **reacts, reacting, reacted**
1 The way you **react** to what someone has done or said is the way you behave or the way you feel as a result, often referring to how well you control your temper or your emotions: *'How did she react to the news?' 'She reacted quite well, under the circumstances.'* □ *They didn't react very positively to my suggestion.* [*same as* **respond**] **2** You **react** against the way other people want or expect you to behave when you protest by behaving in an opposite or very different way: *Some might argue that his drugs-and-drink lifestyle was his way of reacting against a very strict upbringing.* **3** One chemical substance **reacts** with another when the mixing causes them to change and form a third substance.
— *noun* **reaction** /riː'akʃən/: *This provoked a very angry reaction from the Minister.* □ *Thanks to his very sharp reactions, he was able to stop the car in time.* □ *Could you say it was a reaction against custom and tradition?* □ *a chemical reaction.* [*same as* **response**]

reactionary /rɪ'akʃənrɪ/ *adjective; noun*
▻ ***adjective***
People who are **reactionary** tend to oppose changes to

the way things have traditionally been done, especially political or social changes: *a speaker from the reactionary wing of the Party.* [*same as* **conservative**]

▻ ***noun***: **reactionaries:** *This won't please the right-wing reactionaries.*

reactor /rɪ'aktə(r)/ *noun*: **reactors**

A **reactor** is a nuclear reactor.

read /ri:d/ *verb*; *noun*

▻ ***verb***: **reads, reading, read** /rɛd/

1 You **read** printed or written words, symbols or diagrams when you look at and understand them: *His writing's so difficult to read.* □ *I haven't had a chance to read the report yet.* □ *I read about it in this morning's newspaper.* □ *Did you read that the sports complex is closing down?* □ *He spends most of his spare time reading.* □ *She drove while I read the map.* □ *Are you good at reading music?* **2** You **read** something when you say aloud what is written or printed: *Could you read me that last sentence again?* □ *I used to sit by her bed and read aloud to her.* □ *He read the children a story every night.* **3** A piece of writing **reads** in a certain way **a** if that is what it says: *There was a message pinned to the door, reading as follows: 'Sorry to miss you; will call later. A.'* □ *The sign read 'No exit'.* [*same as* **say**] **b** if that is its style, or the impression it makes: *Her letters always read like articles from a women's magazine.* □ *Your material reads excellently.* **4** You **read** an instrument such as a thermometer or meter when you look at it and note the measurement or figure it records; an instrument **reads** a certain measurement or amount if that is what it is recording or registering: *A man called to read the electricity meter.* □ *The thermometer somewhat alarmingly read 41.* **5** You say that you can **read** someone's mind when you know what they are thinking: *She smiled, seeming to read my thoughts.* **6** A student **reading** a particular subject is studying that subject at college or university: *She read maths at Oxford.* [*same as* **study**]

▻ ***noun*** (*usually in the singular*): **reads**

A book that is a good **read** is one that is interesting and enjoyable to read.

▻ ***phrase*** You say that you **are taking** something **as read** when you assume that it is the case: *I'd taken it as read that dogs would not be permitted in the restaurant.*

phrasal verbs

read into You **read** something **into** what someone says or does when you see some extra meaning in it: *You're reading too much into his refusal.* □ *Please don't read any criticism into what I'm about to say.* [*same as* **interpret**]

read up on You **read up on** a subject when you find out a lot about it by reading.

readable /'ri:dəbəl/ *adjective*

1 You describe a book as **readable** if it is enjoyable or interesting: *It's a highly readable journal.* **2** A machine-**readable** or computer-**readable** text can be read by computer.

reader /'ri:də(r)/ *noun*: **readers**

A **reader** is a person who reads, especially someone who reads a particular newspaper or other publication: *This offer is only open to readers of 'The Times'.* □ *This book keeps the reader in suspense up to the very last page.*

readily /'rɛdɪlɪ/ *adverb*

1 You **readily** do something when you do it willingly: *They readily agreed to help.* [*same as* **gladly**, **eagerly**] **2 Readily** also means quickly and with little effort: *Replacement cartridges are readily available from your local stationer.*

readiness /'rɛdɪnəs/ *noun* (*uncount*)

1 Readiness is the state of being ready and prepared: *The horses had been fed and groomed, in readiness for the long journey.* [*same as* **preparation**] **2** Your **readiness** to do something is the fact that you are willing to do it, often only if it becomes necessary: *The king was heartened by the readiness of his troops to fight.* [*same as* **willingness**; *opposite* **reluctance**]

reading /'ri:dɪŋ/ *noun*: **readings**

1 (*uncount*) **Reading** is the activity of looking at and understanding printed words in books and other publications: *Reading has become her favourite pastime.* **2** A **reading** on a gauge or other measuring instrument is the measurement shown: *The thermometer gives a reading for the maximum temperature reached during the day.* **3** A **reading** is a text or passage that someone reads to an audience: *There will be a few poetry readings before we serve the wine.*

ready /'rɛdɪ/ *adjective*; *adverb*

▻ ***adjective***

1 You are **ready** for something when you have prepared yourself to deal with or do it, or when others have prepared or trained you: *I helped her to get the children ready for bed.* □ *I'm not sure he's ready for this level of responsibility.* □ *Are we all ready to go?* □ *I'll call you when dinner is ready.* □ *Is the report ready for the printer?* **2** You are **ready** to do something when you are willing or eager to do it: *The children are always ready to help.* □ *She's a bit too ready to criticize others.* **3** You are **ready** to do something when you are about to do it or you will do it very soon: *This plant is just ready to flower.*

▻ ***adverb***

Ready is often used to describe things prepared or made in advance, so that they can be used immediately: *ready-cooked meals* □ *The shed is delivered ready-built.*

real /rɪəl/ *adjective*; *adverb*

▻ ***adjective***

1 A **real** thing or person actually exists, as distinct from existing only in imagination, theory or pretence: *In the real world things don't happen like that.* □ *She has to deal with real people who have real problems.* □ *War is becoming a very real possibility.* □ *To a child these things can seem very real.* [*opposite* **imaginary**, **abstract**, **unreal**; compare **actual**] **2** Something that is **real** is genuine, as distinct from being an imitation, copy or a piece of pretence: *seats upholstered in real leather.* □ *These fabric flowers look quite effective, but I'd prefer the real thing.* □ *The fear in her eyes was real.* **3 Real** describes what is actually the case as distinct from what people may say or think: *my real reason for leaving* □ *That's not his real name.* **4 Real** can mean 'in the true sense of the word', but is sometimes used just for emphasis: *She was never a real mother to me.* □ *We knew we had a real crisis on our hands.* □ *She's a real menace.*

▻ ***adverb*** (*AmE*; *intensifying*)

Real means 'really' or 'very': *We're real proud of you.*

▻ ***phrase*** (*informal*) Something that is **for real** is actually happening, or is intentional, serious or genuine: *This time I've left him for real and I'm not coming back.* □ *Was that fight for real?*

real estate /'rɪəl ɪsteɪt/ *noun* (*AmE*; *uncount*)

Real estate is property in the form of houses or land.

realise see **realize**.

realism /'rɪəlɪzm/ *noun* (*uncount*)

In art, books and films, **realism** is the style that aims to show things as they really are.

realist /'rɪəlɪst/ *noun*: **realists**

People who are **realists** deal in a practical way with situations as they actually are, rather than pretending they are different. [*same as* **pragmatist**; *opposite* **idealist**]

realistic /rɪəˈlɪstɪk/ *adjective*
1 Something in a book or film is **realistic** when it is so similar to real life that you could believe it was real: *I didn't think the fight scenes were very realistic.* □ *a realistic portrayal of a family in crisis.* [*opposite* **unrealistic**] **2** You are **realistic** when you deal practically with a situation as it is, rather than pretending it is different: *We have to be realistic; she might not get the job.* [*opposite* **idealistic**]

reality /rɪˈalɪtɪ/ *noun* (*uncount or count*): **realities**
People often refer to real or true situations as **reality**, especially when they are more unpleasant than some people pretend: *political leaders who are distant from the harsh realities of poverty and unemployment* □ *I tell you that Evil is a reality, not something dreamt up by the Church.* □ *We must face up to reality and accept that we've failed.* [*same as* **fact, truth**]
▻ ***phrase***
1 In reality means in real life, rather than *eg* in books or films: *He is much smaller in reality than he looks on the television.* **2** You also use **in reality** to introduce a true statement as a contrast to something false or inaccurate that has just been said: *They were claiming record profits when, in reality, the company was close to bankruptcy.* [*same as* **in fact, actually**]

realize or **realise** /ˈrɪəlaɪz/ *verb*: **realizes, realizing, realized**
1 You **realize** something at the moment when you know or understand it: *I realized then that she had never really loved me.* □ *Roger never realized how important my friends were to me.* □ *They didn't realize the seriousness of what had happened.* □ *It was far more dangerous than any of us realized.* **2** Things such as hopes or plans **are realized** when what you have hoped for or planned happens or comes true: *When I married Helen, all my dreams were realized.* [*same as* **fulfil**] — *noun* **realization** /rɪəlaɪˈzeɪʃən/: *the sudden realization that I had offended him* □ *The opening ceremony will be the realization of four years' hard work.*

really /ˈrɪəlɪ/ *adverb*; *interjection*
▻ ***adverb***
1 (*especially informal*) You use **really a** to emphasize what you are saying: *She really will have to work harder.* □ *I'm really not prepared to tolerate this kind of behaviour any longer.* □ *I'm grateful; I really mean that.* **b** (*intensifying*) to emphasize an adjective or adverb, with a meaning like 'very': *I thought the film was really exciting.* □ *This has been a really enjoyable holiday.* □ *The sauce can be prepared really quickly.* **2** You use **really** when referring to, or stating, the true facts about something, especially in contrast to the impression given: *He's not really my uncle; he's just a friend of my parents.* □ *Is she really as busy as she says?* □ *I don't think we'll ever know what really happened.* □ *That's not really what I meant.* [*same as* **actually**] **3** You add **really** to a question to which you expect the answer 'no': *Do you really think he would ever deliberately hurt you?* **4** People often use **really** after *not* as a polite or less severe way of saying 'no' or making a negative statement: *'Don't you think it's lovely?' 'Not really, no.'* □ *I don't really like whisky very much.* □ *I haven't really thought about it.* **5** (*used as an answer*) If you respond to what someone says with '**Really?**' you are expressing **a** surprise, disbelief, or a request for confirmation: *'He earns over £50 000 a year.' 'No, really?'* □ *'He evidently approves.' 'Does he really?'* **b** polite interest: *'And my other son is a biochemist.' 'Really?'* **6** (*sentence adverb*) You use **really** to mean 'in fact': *Really, things are no better than they were.*
▻ ***interjection***
'**Really!**' expresses anger or annoyance: *Really! Of all the stupid things to do!*

realm /rɛlm/ *noun*: **realms**
1 (*formal*) People often refer to the **realm** of something when they are talking about something as a particular subject or topic: *These experiments belong more to the realm of biochemistry than pure biology.* [*same as* **domain, sphere**] **2** (*literary*) A **realm** is also a country or land, especially one ruled by a king or queen: *He was the bravest knight of the realm.*

reappear /riːəˈpɪə(r)/ *verb*: **reappears, reappearing, reappeared**
Someone or something **reappears** when they come back after being away, or after not being seen or experienced for a while: *Shannon reappeared at the airport, where he was captured by police.* □ *Perennial weeds will keep reappearing if they are not removed at the root.*

rear[1] /rɪə(r)/ *noun* (*usually in the singular, often adjectival*): **rears**
1 The **rear** of something is the back part of it, or the area at the back of it: *Inspections of the rear of the aircraft showed signs of structural damage.* □ *towards the rear of the hall* □ *One of its rear wheels had worked loose.* [*same as* **back**] **2** (*informal*) Your **rear** is your buttocks, the part of your body that you sit on: *They just sit on their rears and do nothing all day.* [*same as* **backside**]
▻ ***phrase*** The person **bringing up the rear** is the last one in a line of people moving together.

rear[2] /rɪə(r)/ *verb*: **rears, rearing, reared**
1 To **rear** children is to look after them until they are grown up. [*same as* **bring up**] **2** To **rear** animals is to breed them; to **rear** crops is to grow them. **3** A horse or other animal **rears**, or **rears** up, when it stands on its back legs and lifts its front legs into the air, especially when it has been frightened or startled.
▻ ***phrase*** When a certain unpleasant situation develops or recurs, you can say that it has **reared its ugly head**: *Once again, senseless racial hatred has reared its ugly head in our cities.*

rearrange /riːəˈreɪndʒ/ *verb*: **rearranges, rearranging, rearranged**
You **rearrange** things when you change their position or order; you **rearrange** something when you change the position or order of the things in it: *We could rearrange the plants in this border to let more light in at the back.* □ *If she rearranged her schedule slightly, she might be able to see you for lunch.* [*same as* **adjust**]

reason /ˈriːzən/ *noun*; *verb*
▻ ***noun*: reasons**
1 The **reason** for something is the situation or circumstance that causes it to happen or exist, or explains why it does: *What was the reason for all that commotion?* □ *He'd better have a good reason for being so late!* □ *I can think of no reason why it shouldn't work.* □ *The real reason why I left early was that I was feeling sick.* □ *There were plenty of good reasons for our decision.* □ *You have every reason for anxiety.* □ *I had no reason to doubt her word.* **2** (*uncount*) **Reason** is your ability to think clearly, and form opinions and judgements: *Has she lost all reason?* □ *Your decision should be based entirely on reason; sentiment and emotion must play no part.* [*same as* **rationality**] **3** (*uncount*; *formal*) You have **reason** to think, believe or feel something if there are good reasons why you do: *We have reason to believe that you have been handling stolen property.* □ *She felt very offended, and with good reason.* □ *He has little reason to feel so pleased with himself.* [*same as* **grounds**]

▻ ***verb***: **reasons, reasoning, reasoned**
You **reason** when you are thinking carefully in the process of forming an opinion, judgement or conclusion: *'He's very unlikely to remember that,' she reasoned.* □ *I reasoned that there would be no advantage in paying for extra insurance.* [*same as* **conclude**]
▻ ***phrases*** **1** If you say that something happened **for some reason**, you mean that it happened but you can't explain why it did: *They thought we were brother and sister, for some reason.* □ *For some reason, I've been asked to speak at the conference.* **2** If you say that **it stands to reason** that something should happen, you mean that it was to be expected: *It stands to reason that she would prefer the company of her own family.* **3 Within reason** means within the limits of what most people would consider sensible or acceptable: *Choose any present you like, within reason of course.*

phrasal verbs
reason out You **reason** something **out** when you solve the problems relating to it by careful thought and argument: *Let's sit down and reason this out calmly.* [*same as* **work out**]
reason with You **reason with** someone when you argue with them to try and persuade them to do or not do something, or try and convince them about something: *Trained negotiators were sent in to reason with the hijackers.*

reasonable /ˈriːzənəbəl/ *adjective*
1 Someone is being **reasonable** when they are behaving in a sensible, fair or acceptable way that is not foolish or extreme: *Be reasonable, Anne; you can't expect them to work on Sundays as well.* □ *It's simply not reasonable to want it all now.* □ *Their prices were far more reasonable than the high-street shops.* **2** There is a **reasonable** amount of something when there is quite a lot of it: *He handled it with a reasonable amount of tact.* □ *It would appeal to a reasonable number of our customers.* — *adverb* **reasonably:** *I refuse to listen to you; you're not reacting at all reasonably.* □ *(moderating) A reasonably large crowd watched an entertaining match.* [*same as* **fairly**]

reassurance /riːəˈʃʊərəns/ *noun*: **reassurances**
You give someone **reassurances** when you say things that reassure them: *We were given no reassurances that we would get our money back.*

reassure /riːəˈʃʊə(r)/ *verb*: **reassures, reassuring, reassured**
You **reassure** someone when you say things that stop them feeling worried or anxious and give them hope or confidence: *We would like to reassure parents that their children would never be allowed to play in the water unsupervised.* — *adjective* **reassuring:** *We received a very reassuring letter from our solicitors.* [*same as* **encouraging**]

rebate /ˈriːbeɪt/ *noun*: **rebates**
You are given a **rebate** when you get back some of the money you have paid, usually because someone discovers later that you have paid too much: *We got a £50 rent rebate.*

rebel *noun*; *verb*
▻ ***noun*** /ˈrɛbəl/ (*often adjectival*): **rebels**
1 A **rebel** is a person who opposes or fights against the government or others in authority: *It's unlikely that the Prime Minister has done enough to win the support of the Euro-rebels within his party.* □ *Rebel armies have advanced towards the capital.* **2** Someone who is a **rebel** refuses to accept normal rules and conventions, and chooses to behave differently from other people.
▻ ***verb*** /rɪˈbɛl/: **rebels, rebelling, rebelled:** *the early Protestants who rebelled against the Catholic Church* □ *She's reached the age at which children begin to rebel.*

rebellion /rɪˈbɛljən/ *noun* (*count or uncount*): **rebellions**
A **rebellion** is an act of rebelling: *one of the leaders of the student rebellion* □ *Single protests like this could easily lead to full-scale rebellion.* [*same as* **uprising**]

rebellious /rɪˈbɛljəs/ *adjective*
A **rebellious** person is one who rebels, or who tends to rebel: *The child is growing increasingly rebellious.*

rebirth /riːˈbɜːθ/ *noun* (*usually in the singular*): **rebirths**
There is a **rebirth** of something when people begin to do it or believe it again: *the rebirth of Communism in some Central European countries.* [*same as* **renaissance, revival**]

rebuke /rɪˈbjuːk/ *verb*; *noun*
▻ ***verb***: **rebukes, rebuking, rebuked**
You **rebuke** someone when you speak severely to them because they have done something wrong: *She was sharply rebuked for her conduct by the headmistress.* [*same as* **reprimand, tell off**]
▻ ***noun***: **rebukes:** *She had not expected to receive such a fierce rebuke.* [*same as* **reprimand, telling off**]

recap /ˈriːkap/ *verb*: **recaps, recapping, recapped**
You **recap** when you mention or state something again, to remind people of it: *Let's recap the main conclusions we can draw from these experiments.* [*same as* **review**]

recede /rɪˈsiːd/ *verb*: **recedes, receding, receded**
1 Something that **recedes** moves back or backwards, into the distance: *The train pulled away, and her face and her waving arm receded.* [*same as* **retreat**; *opposite* **approach**] **2** A man's hair **is receding** when he is losing hair at the front of his head and becoming bald.

receipt /rɪˈsiːt/ *noun*: **receipts**
1 A **receipt** is a piece of paper stating that money or goods have been received: *We'll need to see your receipt, as proof that you bought the shoes from this shop.* **2** (*uncount*; *formal*) **Receipt** is the fact that you have received something: *We will write to acknowledge receipt of the money.*

receive /rɪˈsiːv/ *verb*: **receives, receiving, received**
1 You **receive** something when someone gives it to you, or when you get it after they have sent it to you: *We've received some very generous gifts.* □ *Have you received a copy of our latest report?* □ *If you send it first class, with luck I'll receive it tomorrow.* **2** You often use **receive** as a way of saying that you experience or suffer something, or something happens to you: *A number of the students received quite severe injuries.* □ *They received stern criticism for their lack of sensitivity.* [*same as* **sustain, suffer**] **3** The way you **receive** something is how you react or respond when it is given or done to you: *She is likely to receive the news very angrily.* □ *My suggestions were very well received.* **4** (*formal*) To **receive** guests is to welcome or greet them, especially formally: *The Prince will receive them in his study.*

received /rɪˈsiːvd/ *adjective*
People often use **received** when they are talking about the opinions or beliefs of people in general: *It used to be the received wisdom that children should be taught to be independent.*

receiver /rɪˈsiːvə(r)/ *noun*: **receivers**
On a telephone, the **receiver** is the part that you hold: *Lift the receiver first, then insert your money.* [*same as* **handset**]

recent /ˈriːsənt/ *adjective*
Recent describes things that happened or were done a

short time ago: *the recent increase in her popularity* □ *Some of the changes are quite recent.* — *adverb* **recently:** *He's been quite relaxed recently.* □ *Recently, I had the misfortune to meet his brother.* □ *Parts of it were built as recently as the 19th century.*

receptacle /rɪ'sɛptɪkəl/ *noun* (*formal*): **receptacles**
A **receptacle** is a container.

reception /rɪ'sɛpʃən/ *noun*: **receptions**
1 (*uncount*) In places such as hotels and hospitals, **reception** is the place where guests or visitors are welcomed, and where you make enquiries: *I'll ask at reception.* □ *There was nobody at the reception desk.* **2** You also use **reception** when you are talking about how people react or respond to something: *Our proposals met with a hostile reception from the committee.* □ *The Queen received an enthusiastic reception from staff and patients.* **3** A **reception** is also a formal party to welcome guests or celebrate something, for example a wedding. **4** (*uncount*) The **reception** from your radio or television is how clear the sound or picture is: *We often get poor reception because of the bad weather.*

receptionist /rɪ'sɛpʃənɪst/ *noun*: **receptionists**
A **receptionist** is a person employed, for example in a hotel or factory, to welcome visitors and guests and answer the telephone.

receptive /rɪ'sɛptɪv/ *adjective*
Someone who is **receptive** is willing to listen to and accept suggestions and new ideas: *We like to think we are receptive to anything our staff suggest.* [*same as* **approachable, sympathetic**]

recess *noun*: **recesses**
1 /'riːsɛs/ A **recess** is a small area that exists where part of a wall stands further back than the rest: *a private little table set in a recess.* **2** /'riːsɛs/ (*used in the plural*; *literary*) The **recesses** of something are the inner, secret, hidden areas of it: *Unpleasant memories lingered in the dark recesses of her mind.* **3** /rɪ'sɛs/ A **recess** is a temporary break from work, especially in Parliament or a law court.

recession /rɪ'sɛʃən/ *noun* (*uncount or count*): **recessions**
A country is in **recession** when factories and businesses are closing, unemployment is increasing and people in general have less money: *This is the deepest recession this country has ever seen.*

recipe /'rɛsɪpɪ/ *noun*: **recipes**
1 A **recipe** is a set of instructions on how to prepare and cook a particular kind of meal, with a list of its ingredients: *a recipe book* □ *I'll give you my recipe for vegetable curry.* **2** You refer to a situation or an action as a **recipe** for *eg* trouble or disaster if you think it is just the thing to cause it: *Taking the children shopping was a recipe for disaster.*

recipient /rɪ'sɪpɪənt/ *noun* (*formal*): **recipients**
The **recipient** of something is the person who receives it.

reciprocal /rɪ'sɪprəkəl/ *adjective*
Reciprocal describes things done by each of two people or groups to the other, or something one of them does in return: *We insisted that the terms of any trade agreement must be reciprocal.* □ *It was just a reciprocal gesture of goodwill.*

reciprocate /rɪ'sɪprəkeɪt/ *verb* (*formal*): **reciprocates, reciprocating, reciprocated**
You **reciprocate** when you behave towards someone in the same way that they have behaved towards you: *We felt that our affection was not reciprocated.*

recital /rɪ'saɪtəl/ *noun*: **recitals**
A **recital** is a public performance of music, songs or poetry, usually by one person or a small number of people.

recite /rɪ'saɪt/ *verb*: **recites, reciting, recited**
You **recite** something, such as a poem, when you say it aloud from memory: *Laura's father began by reciting a few lines from Shakespeare.*

reckless /'rɛkləs/ *adjective*
A **reckless** person does not think, or does not care, about how dangerous or harmful their behaviour might be: *He was charged with reckless driving.* □ *She shows a reckless disregard for her parents' feelings.* □ *Such men are inclined to be reckless.* [*same as* **careless, rash, thoughtless**; *opposite* **cautious**] — *adverb* **recklessly:** *The car sped recklessly through a busy shopping street.* — *noun* **recklessness:** *an attitude of recklessness.*

reckon /'rɛkən/ *verb*: **reckons, reckoning, reckoned**
1 (*informal*) You say you **reckon** something is so if you think it is; you **reckon** something may happen if you expect it to: *I reckon she's pregnant.* □ *The doctors reckon his chances of a full recovery pretty high.* [= they think he has a good chance of recovering] □ *None of us reckoned that he'd bring his wife.* □ *'Is this the house?' 'I reckon so.'* □ *'I don't suppose you'll get away this weekend, then?' 'I reckon not.'* □ *He's reckoned to be one of the best plastic surgeons for this kind of job.* [compare **suppose, expect, think**] **2** You **reckon** something when you calculate it: *The police have reckoned that a house is burgled every three minutes.* □ *She quickly reckoned the sum in her head.*

phrasal verbs

reckon on You **reckon on** something happening when you expect it to, and base your plans on it: *We reckon on getting the first stage finished by the end of August.* □ *I hadn't reckoned on having her as a neighbour as well as a colleague.*

reckon up You **reckon up** an amount when you calculate its total: *The waitress came over and reckoned up our bill for us.*

reckon with **1** You say you **had not reckoned with** something, or you had **reckoned without** it, if you did not realize that it existed or would happen, and so did not consider it: *They had reckoned without the opposition of some of their fairer-minded employees.* [*same as* **anticipate, bargain for**] **2** You describe someone as a person **to be reckoned with** if you respect their ability.

reckoning /'rɛkənɪŋ/ *noun* (*usually in the singular*): **reckonings**
A **reckoning** is a calculation: *By my reckoning, we must be about eight miles from Canterbury.*

reclaim /rɪ'kleɪm/ *verb*: **reclaims, reclaiming, reclaimed**
1 (*formal*) You **reclaim** something when you collect it or take it back: *luggage not reclaimed by passengers at the airport.* **2** To **reclaim** waste land is to make it suitable to be used for something, for example building houses on.
[*same as* **retrieve, salvage**]

recline /rɪ'klaɪn/ *verb* (*formal*): **reclines, reclining, reclined**
You **recline** when you sit or lie with your back at an angle: *I could massage you in a reclining position.*

recluse /rɪ'kluːs/ *noun*: **recluses**
A **recluse** is a person who lives alone and prefers not to mix with other people.

recognition /rɛkəg'nɪʃən/ *noun* (*uncount*)
Recognition is the act of recognizing someone or something: *Even after all these years, there was a glimmer of recognition in his eyes.* □ *There seemed to be no recognition of the fact that I had been working hard all day.*
▷ *phrase* Something that changes **beyond recognition** or **out of all recognition** changes so much that people can no longer recognize it.

recognize or **recognise** /'rɛkəgnaɪz/ *verb*: **recognizes, recognizing, recognized**
1 You **recognize** who or what you are able to identify because you know them already or you have been told about them: *I recognized Jessica from my mother's description of her.* □ *I'm not sure I could recognize the taste again.* **2** You **recognize** something when you accept or admit that it exists or is true: *We recognize that the mistake was ours.* □ *The government has failed to recognize the need for investment in employment training.* **3** Something **is recognized** when people in a particular place accept that it is valid or it has some legal force: *Her academic qualifications were not recognized by any of the British universities.* □ *South Africa may well be recognized as a member of the Commonwealth once more.* **4** Someone's achievements **are recognized** when people formally show their appreciation or thanks, for example by giving an award.
[*same as* **acknowledge**]

recoil /rɪ'kɔɪl/ *verb*: **recoils, recoiling, recoiled**
You **recoil** from someone or something when you immediately feel very frightened or disgusted by it when you see it or think about it, and perhaps move back as if to get away: *Most doctors recoil at the idea of accountants running the health service.* □ *I recoiled in horror from her outstretched arm.* [*same as* **shrink**]

recollect /rɛkə'lɛkt/ *verb* (*formal*): **recollects, recollecting, recollected**
You **recollect** something when you remember it: *I recollect that it was a cold Tuesday morning.* □ *The witness does not recollect what time it was.* [*same as* **recall**] — *noun* **recollection** /rɛkə'lɛkʃən/: *I have no recollection of his face at all.* [*same as* **memory**]

recommend /rɛkə'mɛnd/ *verb*: **recommends, recommending, recommended**
You **recommend** that someone does something when you advise them to do it, because you think it is wise; you **recommend** something to someone when you advise them to get, buy or experience it, because you think it is good: *The bank recommends that the loan be taken over a period of ten years.* □ *It's a book my mother recommended to me.* □ *I'm looking for a quiet holiday spot; where would you recommend?* [*same as* **suggest**] — *noun* (*count or uncount*) **recommendation** /rɛkəmɛn'deɪʃən/: *The successful candidate will be selected on the recommendation of the personnel officer.* □ *I made a few recommendations in my letter.*

reconcile /'rɛkənsaɪl/ *verb*: **reconciles, reconciling, reconciled**
1 You **reconcile** yourself to something unpleasant when you accept that you will have to do it or deal with it: *He isn't really reconciled to the idea of spending two weeks in hospital.* **2** You **reconcile** two or more different or opposing aims, views or beliefs when you find a way of accepting both or all of them: *It was impossible to reconcile my socialist principles with the notion of owning my own business.* **3** You **are reconciled** with someone when you are friendly with them again, after a quarrel or argument.

reconciliation /rɛkənsɪlɪ'eɪʃən/ *noun* (*uncount*)
Reconciliation is the fact of being friendly with someone again, after an argument, dispute or conflict: *There seems little hope of reconciliation.*

reconstruct /riːkən'strʌkt/ *verb*: **reconstructs, reconstructing, reconstructed**
You **reconstruct** something, for example a crime, when you create a description or idea of how it happened by putting all the known details together. [*same as* **recreate**] — *noun* **reconstruction** /riːkɛn'strʌkʃən/: *police reconstructions of the incident.*

record *noun*; *verb*; *adjective*
▷ ***noun*** /'rɛkɔːd/: **records**
1 A **record** of something is a permanent account of it, for example written down or stored on a computer, as proof that it happened: *We have a taped record of the conversation.* □ *You should keep a record of all your business expenses.* □ *an inspection of local crime records.* [*same as* **file**] **2** A **record** is a round flat piece of plastic that music and other sound is stored on: *We spent the evening listening to old jazz records.* □ *I'll play that last record again.* **3** In competitions and contests, especially in sport, the **record** is the best performance ever, which has never yet been beaten: *That jump of over ten metres sets a new world record.* □ *She's broken Janner's record of 3 minutes 56.* **4** A **record** is also a description or list of a person's achievements, or of the crimes they have committed: *army officers with distinguished service records* □ *The company has an impressive record of achievement.* □ *Does she have a criminal record?* [*same as* **background**]
▷ ***verb*** /rɪ'kɔːd/: **records, recording, recorded**
1 To **record** something such as music or a television programme is to copy it onto a record or a tape, so that it can be heard or seen again later: *The sound is better when you record from a CD onto a tape than from tape to tape.* □ *The band recorded their first album in 1962.* □ *The President recorded all conversations that took place in the Oval Office.* **2** You also **record** something when you write it down: *I know because I recorded the incident in my diary that night.* □ *The affair is well recorded in her political memoirs.*
▷ ***adjective*** /'rɛkɔːd/
Record describes standards or levels that are higher, lower, better or worse than ever before: *The value of shares in British companies is at a record low.* □ *A record number of patients are being treated in our hospitals.*
▷ ***phrases*** **1** You say you are telling people something **for the record** when you want what you say to be publicly known and remembered: *I want it known, for the record, that we offered him help, which he refused.* **2** You say that what you are telling someone is **off the record** when you don't want them to tell anyone else or make the information public: *It is claimed he told a 'Times' journalist, strictly off the record, that he was thinking of resigning.* **3** You use **on record a** as a way of talking about what someone has said publicly, so that others know about it and can prove they said it: *The minister is on record as saying that unemployment was just a minor problem.* **b** when you are talking about information that you keep, so you may look at it or refer to it in future: *We have no jobs at the moment, but we'll keep your details on record.* **c** when you are talking about the highest or lowest standards or levels anyone has ever recorded: *We've just experienced the wettest April on record.* **4** You **set the record straight** when you tell the truth about something in order to correct people's false beliefs or impressions.

recorder /rɪ'kɔːdə(r)/ *noun*: **recorders**
1 A **recorder** is a musical instrument in the form of a straight wooden or plastic tube with a mouthpiece

and holes which are covered by the player's fingers. **2** Any machine that records sound or pictures, such as a tape recorder or video recorder, can be referred to as a **recorder**.

recording /rɪˈkɔːdɪŋ/ *noun*: **recordings**
A **recording** of sounds or pictures is a record, tape or video of them: *one of the finest recordings of Beethoven's 'Fifth Symphony'.*

record player /ˈrɛkɔːd pleɪə(r)/ *noun*: **record players**
A **record player** is an apparatus that you play records on, in order to listen to the sound or music recorded on them.

recount /rɪˈkaʊnt/ *verb* (*formal*): **recounts, recounting, recounted**
You **recount** a story when you tell it; you **recount** something that happens when you tell people about it: *This bizarre incident is recounted in some detail in her autobiography.* [*same as* **relate**]

re-count *verb*; *noun*
▻ ***verb*** /riːˈkaʊnt/: **re-counts, re-counting, re-counted**
You **re-count** things, especially votes in an election, when you count them again.
▻ ***noun*** /ˈriːkaʊnt/: **re-counts:** *There will have to be a re-count.*

recoup /rɪˈkuːp/ *verb*: **recoups, recouping, recouped**
You **recoup** something, especially money you have spent or lost, when you get it back: *The initial £50,000 is unlikely to be recouped.* [*same as* **recover**]

recourse /rɪˈkɔːs/ *noun* (*uncount or count*; *formal*)
You have **recourse** to something when you use it, especially in an emergency or a case of extreme need: *If matters get worse, we shall have recourse to the courts.* □ *The police were the only recourse we had left.*

recover /rɪˈkʌvə(r)/ *verb*: **recovers, recovering, recovered**
1 Recover is used in many ways when you are talking about returning to good health after being ill, injured or upset: *She's recovering from a stomach complaint.* □ *It'll be a few weeks before he is completely recovered.* □ *The patient has not yet recovered consciousness.* □ *I'm afraid he's unlikely to recover full use of the damaged limb.* □ *It was clearly a shock, but Michael quickly recovered his composure.* [*same as* **restore**] **2** You **recover** something that has been lost, stolen or used up when you get it back: *The aircraft's flight recorder has been recovered from the wreckage.* □ *We predict that the initial cost of machinery would be recovered within the first three years.* — *adjective* **recoverable:** *This money is recoverable by law.* — *noun* (*count or uncount*) **recovery:** *We expect most of the patients to make a full recovery.* □ *the recovery of a number of stolen items* □ *a period of depression followed by a period of economic recovery.*

recreate /riːkrɪˈeɪt/ *verb*: **recreates, recreating, recreated**
You **recreate** something when you create it again, so that others can see or experience it again: *The play successfully recreates the atmosphere of wartime London.*

recreation /rɛkrɪˈeɪʃən/ *noun* (*uncount*)
Recreation consists of enjoyable things you do in your spare time: *And for recreation, I enjoy tennis and gardening.* □ *the council's Leisure and Recreation Department.* — *adjective* **recreational:** *the development of areas of the farm for recreational purposes.*

recreation ground /rɛkrɪˈeɪʃən graʊnd/ *noun*: **recreation grounds**
A **recreation ground** is an area of land with facilities for people to play sports and games.

recrimination /rɪkrɪmɪˈneɪʃən/ *noun* (*uncount or count*): **recriminations**
There is **recrimination** when two people accuse each other of behaving badly or doing something wrong: *The negotiations quickly descended into exchanges of recriminations.*

recruit /rɪˈkruːt/ *verb*; *noun*
▻ ***verb***: **recruits, recruiting, recruited**
1 An organization **recruits** people when it attracts them into becoming members of it: *The Trades Union movement has to look to new ways of recruiting members.* **2** You **recruit** someone for a particular job or task when you persuade them to help you or do it for you: *Local church members have been recruited for the routine painting jobs.* [*same as* **muster, enlist**]
▻ ***noun***: **recruits**
A **recruit** is someone who has recently joined an organization, especially one of the armed forces or the police force.

recruitment /rɪˈkruːtmənt/ *noun* (*uncount*)
Recruitment refers to the activity of attracting people to become members of organizations; **recruitment** also refers to the business of finding jobs for people, or finding workers for companies: *The army reported a sharp drop in levels of recruitment.* □ *She's sent off letters to all the big recruitment agencies.*

rectangle /ˈrɛktaŋgəl/ *noun*: **rectangles**
A **rectangle** is a four-sided shape with opposite sides of equal length and four right angles. [*same as* **oblong**; see picture at **shape**] — *adjective* **rectangular** /rɛkˈtaŋgjʊlə(r)/: *a curving lawn leading to a number of rectangular vegetable beds* □ *The car park would be better made rectangular.*

rectify /ˈrɛktɪfaɪ/ *verb*: **rectifies, rectifying, rectified**
You **rectify** something wrong when you put it right: *The mistake was soon rectified.* [*same as* **amend**]

rector /ˈrɛktə(r)/ *noun*: **rectors**
In the Church of England, a priest is sometimes called a **rector**. [see also **vicar**]

rectory /ˈrɛktərɪ/ *noun*: **rectories**
The house that a priest lives in is sometimes called a **rectory**. [see also **vicarage**]

recuperate /rɪˈkuːpəreɪt/ *verb* (*formal*): **recuperates, recuperating, recuperated**
You **recuperate** when you become well again after being ill. — *noun* (*uncount*) **recuperation** /rɪkuːpəˈreɪʃən/: *This holiday was intended for rest and recuperation.* [*same as* **recovery**]

recur /rɪˈkɜː(r)/ *verb*: **recurs, recurring, recurred**
Something that **recurs** happens again, either once or several times: *These same feelings of guilt recurred over and over again.* [*same as* **return**]

recurrence /rɪˈkʌrəns/ *noun* (*formal*): **recurrences**
A **recurrence** of something is when it happens again: *There were to be frequent recurrences of this passionate debate.*

recurrent /rɪˈkʌrənt/ *adjective* (*formal*)
Recurrent means happening or appearing many times: *Bad weather was, of course, a recurrent problem.*

recurring /rɪˈkɜːrɪŋ/ *adjective*
Recurring means happening or appearing many times: *She described the details of a recurring nightmare.*

recycle /riːˈsaɪkəl/ *verb*: **recycles, recycling, recycled**
Things made of materials such as paper or glass **are recycled** when, after they have been used, they are processed and made into something that can be used again; you **recycle** used things when you save them so

that they can be processed and used again: *You can recycle your kitchen waste as garden compost.* □ *We recycle all our bottles and cans.* □ *toilet tissue made from recycled paper.*

red /rɛd/ *noun; adjective*
▻ ***noun*** (*uncount or count*): **reds**
Red is the colour of blood, or any shade of this colour: *It was painted a dazzling red.* □ *the reds and oranges of the more exotic plants.*
▻ ***adjective***: **redder, reddest**
1 Something **red** is the colour of blood: *red lipstick* □ *Her eyes were red with tiredness.* □ *Helen's face went red whenever anyone mentioned his name.* **2 Red** hair is an orange-brown colour.
▻ ***phrase*** Your bank account is **in the red** when you have spent more money than you have, and you owe the bank money: *The company was several thousand pounds in the red.*

redden /'rɛdən/ *verb*: **reddens, reddening, reddened**
Something **reddens** when it becomes red: *I kissed her on the cheek and her face reddened.*

reddish /'rɛdɪʃ/ *adjective*
Something **reddish** is a kind of red colour: *a tall tree with thin reddish leaves.*

redeem /rɪ'di:m/ *verb*: **redeems, redeeming, redeemed**
Something bad or unpleasant **is redeemed** when there is at least a small part or feature of it that is good, making it not completely bad: *This is a dreadful film, redeemed only slightly by Eastwood's solid acting.* □ *It was a thoroughly disastrous holiday, with nothing to redeem it.* □ *He would try to redeem himself by helping more with the children and the jobs around the house.* — *adjective* **redeeming:** *His mother was cruel and nasty, with no redeeming qualities.*

red-handed /rɛd'handɪd/ *adjective*
You catch someone **red-handed** when you catch them as they are doing something wrong or illegal: *We waited for them to smash the window then caught them red-handed.*

red herring /rɛd 'hɛrɪŋ/ *noun*: **red herrings**
A **red herring** is something that is intended to mislead people and give them the wrong impression or make them reach the wrong conclusions about something: *A good crime story contains a number of real clues and one or two red herrings.*

redress /rɪ'drɛs/ *noun; verb*
▻ ***noun*** (*uncount; formal*)
Redress is something done or given, for example an apology or an amount of money, to make up for a loss or wrong that someone has suffered: *We will seek redress in the courts.* [*same as* **compensation**]
▻ ***verb*** (*formal*): **redresses, redressing, redressed**
You **redress** the balance when you make an unfair or unequal situation fair or equal: *Giving their department an extra member of staff would redress the balance.*

red tape /rɛd 'teɪp/ *noun* (*uncount*)
People often refer to official rules and procedures as **red tape** when they think they are too complicated and cause problems and delays: *We had to fight our way through miles of red tape.*

reduce /rɪ'dju:s/ *verb*: **reduces, reducing, reduced**
1 You **reduce** something when you make it smaller in amount, number or extent: *Our budget has been reduced by over 6%.* □ *We have reduced the number of reception staff from eight to five.* □ *This reduces the temperature to a pleasant 68 degrees.* [*same as* **decrease**; *opposite* **increase**] **2** You also use **reduce** when you are talking about changes to a bad, unpleasant or undesirable state or form: *The constant criticism reduced her to tears on one occasion.* □ *As a result of illness, he is reduced to eating all his food with a spoon.* □ *Many of the youngsters are reduced to sleeping on the streets.* [*same as* **force**]

reduction /rɪ'dʌkʃən/ *noun* (*count or uncount*): **reductions**
There is a **reduction** in something when you make it smaller in amount, number or extent: *sharp reductions in living standards* □ *Reduction of the workforce is always the quickest way of cutting costs.* [*same as* **drop**; *opposite* **increase**]

redundancy /rɪ'dʌndənsɪ/ *noun* (*uncount or count; often adjectival*): **redundancies**
Redundancy is the state of no longer having a job; there are **redundancies** when people in a factory or business company lose their job: *For workers with families to support, redundancy will be a severe blow.* □ *A number of redundancies are forecast for the spring.* □ *That depends on the level of redundancy pay I'm offered.*

redundant /rɪ'dʌndənt/ *adjective*
1 You are made **redundant** when you lose your job: *We had regular holidays abroad before I was made redundant.* **2** Something that is **redundant** is no longer useful, or is not needed and so can be dispensed with or got rid of: *The old hand-operated presses are now redundant, replaced by larger, faster, semi-automatic machines.* □ *In the phrase 'the discussions in which he had participated in' the second 'in' is redundant.*

reed /ri:d/ *noun*: **reeds**
Reeds are plants that grow in or near water, with tall thin hollow stems used to make baskets, and used in the mouthpiece of some musical intruments. [see picture at **orchestra**]

reef /ri:f/ *noun*: **reefs**
A **reef** is a line of rocks, or a bank of sand, just above or below the surface of the sea.

reek /ri:k/ *verb; noun*
▻ ***verb***: **reeks, reeking, reeked**
Something that **reeks** has a very strong, unpleasant smell: *His clothes reeked of fish.* [*same as* **stink**]
▻ ***noun*** (*used in the singular*): *He brought the reek of the farmyard right into the kitchen.* [*same as* **stench**]

reel /ri:l/ *noun; verb*
▻ ***noun***: **reels**
1 A **reel** is any kind of cylinder that a long strip of something, for example fishing line or cinema film, is wrapped around: *a garden hose complete with reel and attachments* □ *One of the reels jammed and the video tape snapped.* [*same as* **spool**] **2** A **reel** is also a kind of fast folk dance.
▻ ***verb***: **reels, reeling, reeled**
1 You say that your head **is reeling** if you have a lot of things to think about: *Dozens of opportunities suddenly opened up, and my mind was reeling.* [*same as* **swim, spin**] **2** You **reel** when you walk unsteadily, as if you are about to fall, for example because you are ill: *She began to reel and then she fainted.*

> ***phrasal verb***
> You **reel** things **off** when you say them quickly and without having to think: *The boy stood up and reeled off the names of the kings and queens of England.*

refectory /rɪ'fɛktərɪ/ *noun*: **refectories**
A **refectory** is a large dining hall, especially one in a college or university. [*same as* **canteen**]

refer /rɪ'fɜː(r)/ *verb*: **refers, referring, referred**
1 You **refer** to something when you mention it: *I would prefer it if you did not refer to my past.* □ *We had better not refer to the company by name.* **2** You use **refer** when talking about a name or title that is given to someone or something: *This period is usually referred to as the post-war period.* □ *She always refers to Jean as 'that Irish woman'.* □ *In this context, the term 'veteran' refers to cars built before 1905.* [*same as* **allude**] **3** You **refer** to a source of information, such as a book, when you look there in order to find out something: *I would need to refer to my notes before I could give you the precise date.* [*same as* **consult**] **4** You **refer** someone to some other place or person when you direct them there, so that they can get further information or treatment: *I refer the court to the case of Bowles versus Markham.* □ *My own doctor referred me to a specialist at the hospital.* □ *The customer has been referred to this department by a member of staff at reception.*

referee /rɛfə'riː/ *noun*: **referees**
In some sports, the **referee** is the official who makes decisions and makes sure that the players obey the rules.

reference /'rɛfərəns/ *noun* (*count or uncount*): **references**
1 (*uncount*) **Reference** is the act of referring to a source of information in order to find out something: *She was able to speak at length without reference to notes of any kind.* □ (*often adjectival*) *a range of reference books.* **2** (*uncount or count*) You make **reference** to something when you mention it or refer to it: *There is little reference to the incident in his autobiography.* □ *She makes a few brief references to her family and her time at school.* [*same as* **allusion**] **3** A **reference** is something that shows you where else to look for information, for example the page number of another place in a book: *cross-references of the style "For 'gaol' see 'jail'".* **4** A **reference** is also a written report on a person's character, talents and abilities: *Her previous employer gives her an excellent reference.*
▷ ***phrases*** In referring to something, you can say, '**In reference to**', or '**with reference to**'; people often write **with reference to** in a formal reply to a formal letter: *With reference to your letter of 29 March, I regret to inform you that we have not yet located your file.*

referendum /rɛfə'rɛndəm/ *noun*: **referendums** or **referenda** /rɛfə'rɛndə/
A country's government holds a **referendum** when they give the people the chance to state whether they support or oppose what the government is proposing to do.

refined /rɪ'faɪnd/ *adjective*
1 A **refined** substance such as oil is in a pure state after all the dirt and other waste has been removed from it. [*same as* **purified**] **2** You describe someone as **refined** if they have good manners and they are polite in a rather formal way: *a very refined young man.*

refinement /rɪ'faɪnmənt/ *noun*: **refinements**
Refinements are slight changes that you make in order to improve or perfect something.

refinery /rɪ'faɪnərɪ/ *noun*: **refineries**
A **refinery** is a factory where raw materials such as sugar and oil are refined.

reflect /rɪ'flɛkt/ *verb*: **reflects, reflecting, reflected**
1 A mirror or similar surface **reflects** something when you see its image in the mirror or on the surface: *moonlight reflected in the water.* **2** When light or heat strikes a surface, it **is reflected** when, rather than passing through the surface or being absorbed by it, it is sent back. **3** Something **reflects** what it expresses, demonstrates or proves: *Rising prices reflect the rise in demand for these goods.* □ *It was an interview that reflected his true political beliefs.* [*same as* **indicate**] **4** You **reflect** on something when you think about it carefully: *It will give you time to reflect on your future prospects.* □ *I reflected that it had been quite unfair of her to treat me that way.* — *noun* (*count or uncount*) **reflection** /ri'flɛkʃən/: *She stared at her reflection in the mirror.* □ *The principle of the reflection of light is used to heat the whole greenhouse.* □ *These abominable policies are a true reflection of the government's political and moral judgement.* □ *Let us pause for reflection.* □ *On reflection, I decided that I had been wrong to oppose it.* — *noun* **reflector**: *All bicycles should be fitted with reflectors.* [see picture at **bicycle**]

reflective /rɪ'flɛktɪv/ *adjective* (*formal*)
Someone who is **reflective** is thinking deeply about something: *Joanne was in a reflective mood.* [*same as* **pensive**]

reflex /'riːflɛks/ *noun*: **reflexes**
1 A **reflex** is an automatic, uncontrollable response to something, for example a sharp kicking movement when someone taps your knee, or a feeling you always get when you think about a particular thing: *This is the standard guilt reflex.* [*same as* **response**] **2** You have good **reflexes** if you are able to react immediately to something sudden and unexpected, especially by moving your body quickly: *You need good reflexes to drive a car at high speed.*

reflexive pronoun /rɪflɛksɪv 'proʊnaʊn/ *noun* (*grammar*): **reflexive pronouns**
The **reflexive pronouns** are *myself, yourself, herself, himself, itself, ourselves, yourselves, themselves*, and are used as the object of a verb, and of some prepositions, when the subject of the sentence is the same person: *Have you hurt yourself? I looked at myself in the mirror.*

reform /rɪ'fɔːm/ *verb*; *noun*
▷ ***verb***: **reforms, reforming, reformed**
1 You **reform** something when you make major changes to improve it: *The law relating to victims' rights needs to be reformed.* **2** Someone who **is reformed** has given up their bad habits, or has stopped leading a life of crime: *He claims to be a reformed man.*
▷ ***noun*** (*uncount or count*): **reforms:** *the reform of immigration law* □ *important legal reforms.*

refrain[1] /rɪ'freɪn/ *verb* (*formal*): **refrains, refraining, refrained**
You **refrain** from doing something when you don't do it, or when you prevent yourself from doing it: *Members of the jury will refrain from speaking to witnesses.* □ *I felt like slapping his face, but I refrained.*

refrain[2] /rɪ'freɪn/ *noun* (*usually in the singular*): **refrains**
The **refrain** in a song is the chorus, the part that you repeat several times.

refresh /rɪ'frɛʃ/ *verb*: **refreshes, refreshing, refreshed**
1 Something **refreshes** you when it gives you new energy or strength after you have been tired, or when it makes you feel comfortably cool after you have been unpleasantly hot: *We were refreshed by a brisk walk along the beach.* [*same as* **revive**] **2** You **refresh** your memory when you remind yourself of something by reading about it, seeing it or listening to it again: *You don't remember what you said? Let me refresh your memory.* [*same as* **jog**]

refreshing /rɪ'frɛʃɪŋ/ *adjective*
1 Something that refreshes you is **refreshing**: *What you need is a refreshing bath.* [*same as* **invigorating**]

2 You describe something as **refreshing** if it is pleasantly different, unexpected or new: *It makes a refreshing change from the usual routine.*

refreshments /rɪˈfrɛʃmənts/ *noun* (*plural*)
Refreshments are drinks and snacks: *Are refreshments available inside the park itself?*

refrigerator /rɪˈfrɪdʒəreɪtə(r)/ *noun*: **refrigerators**
A **refrigerator** is an electrical kitchen device like a large cupboard, that you put food in to keep it cool and fresh. [*same as* **fridge**]

refuge /ˈrɛfjuːdʒ/ *noun* (*uncount or count; literary*)
You take **refuge** when you protect yourself from something harmful or unpleasant, especially by going somewhere safe: *There was no bomb shelter, so we took refuge in the cellar.* □ *In a world he regarded as evil, prayer was his only refuge.* [compare **cover**]

refugee /rɛfjʊˈdʒiː/ *noun*: **refugees**
A **refugee** is a person who comes to a foreign country for protection from people in their own country who want to kill or harm them, usually because of their religious or political beliefs.

refund *noun; verb*
▷ ***noun*** /ˈriːfʌnd/ (*usually in the singular*): **refunds**
You are given a **refund** when you get back money that you have paid: *The performance was so bad that some people in the audience demanded a refund.*
▷ ***verb*** /riːˈfʌnd/: **refunds, refunding, refunded**: *We'll be expecting them to refund our money.* [*same as* **reimburse**]

refusal See **refuse**[1].

refuse[1] /rɪˈfjuːz/ *verb*: **refuses, refusing, refused**
1 You **refuse** to do something that you are asked, advised, ordered or expected to do when you deliberately do not do it, or say that you will not do it: *I asked if I could borrow her car, but she refused.* □ *I refuse to accept the blame for something that was someone else's fault.* □ *She refused to reveal the name of her informant.* □ *I hope you will not refuse our request.* □ *I don't want to, but I daren't refuse.* [opposite **agree**] **2** You **refuse** something such as an invitation or an offer when you do not accept it: *He refused my offer of help.* □ *A number of young men wanted to marry her, but she had refused them all.* □ *She refused all proposals of marriage.* □ *I hate having to refuse such a nice invitation.* □ *She refused my assistance.* [compare **decline, reject**] **3** Someone **refuses** you something when they do not give it to you or allow you to have it: *We were refused an interview with the Prime Minister.* □ *They refused us permission to go in.* □ *He was refused entry.* [*same as* **deny**] — *noun* (*count or uncount*) **refusal** /rɪˈfjuːzəl/: *The court has noted the prisoner's refusal to co-operate with police.* □ *Please do not ask for credit as a refusal often offends.* □ *All our requests met with refusal.* □ *We sent out 150 invitations and have so far had 75 acceptances and 7 refusals.*

refuse[2] /ˈrɛfjuːs/ *noun* (*uncount*)
Refuse is waste or rubbish, things people throw away: *piles of refuse lying at the side of the road* □ *the council department responsible for domestic refuse collection.*

regard /rɪˈgɑːd/ *verb; noun*
▷ ***verb***: **regards, regarding, regarded**
1 You **regard** a person or thing as something if you think of them as that thing: *My mother still regards me as a child.* □ *She's regarded as being the leading authority in this field.* □ *Till now I had regarded myself as one of his closest friends.* □ *They must be regarded as capable of making up their own minds.* [compare **consider**] **2** You **regard** a thing or person with a particular feeling if you have that feeling about them: *She was regarded with a certain affection by her colleagues.* □ *I had learnt to regard everything she did with suspicion.* [*same as* **view**] **3** People who are highly **regarded** are respected by others: *She used to be quite highly regarded as a writer.*
▷ ***noun***: **regards**
1 (*uncount or used in the singular*) You have a high **regard** for someone or something if you respect them: *I have no very high regard for politicians.* □ *Her work is held in very high regard by her fellow researchers.* [*same as* **esteem**] **2** (*used in the plural*) If you ask one person to give your **regards** to another, you are asking them to pass on your good wishes to the other; you can end a letter with expressions such as 'kind **regards**' or 'with warm **regards**': *Please give him my regards when you see him.* □ *'Kind regards, Michael'*
▷ ***phrases*** You use the expressions **as regards, in regard to**, and **with regard to** to introduce or refer to the particular matter that you want to say something about; you use **in this**, or **that, regard** to refer to a matter just mentioned: *As regards the patient's mental health, there has been little improvement.* □ *With regard to your first query, have you not already had a satisfactory explanation from this department?* □ *The bank gave us little useful advice in regard to setting up a business plan.* □ *I should mention in this regard that a number of clients have already complained to me.* [*same as* **with reference to, in reference to, regarding**]

regarding /rɪˈgɑːdɪŋ/ *preposition*
You use **regarding** to introduce or refer to the particular matter that you want to say something about: *None of us have any doubts regarding your ability to do the work.* □ *Regarding the matter of the dustbins, I think the problem is solved.* [*same as* **in regard to, concerning, about**]

regardless /rɪˈgɑːdləs/ *adjective or adverb*
You do something **regardless**, or **regardless** of the consequences, when you do it ignoring the factors that could have stopped you; something happens **regardless of** something else when it happens in spite of it: *She feels like giving up her job, regardless of the consequences.* □ *We warned them them that there wasn't time to get to the summit and back before dark, but they went on regardless.* □ *The plans are likely to go ahead regardless of local opposition.*

regime or **régime** /reɪˈʒiːm/ *noun*: **regimes**
1 A **regime** is a system of government, or a particular government itself: *the collapse of the Communist regime.* **2** You can also refer to a routine, for example the way you organize your working day, as a **regime**: *Top-class skaters have an extremely rigid daily regime of training and practice.* [*same as* **routine**]

regimented /ˈrɛdʒɪmɛntɪd/ *adjective*
You describe a place or system as **regimented** if it is organized or ordered very strictly, perhaps too strictly: *They have a very regimented home routine in which the children are not allowed to take toys out of their rooms, or watch television on weekdays.* □ *We've seen a move away from regimented package holidays.* [*same as* **disciplined, strict**]

region /ˈriːdʒən/ *noun*: **regions**
1 A **region** is a large area of land, for example one of the named parts that a country is divided into: *wines from the Bordeaux region* □ *plants that thrive in mountainous regions.* **2** An area of the body, round or near a specific part, is sometimes referred to as a **region**: *the abdominal region.*
▷ ***phrase*** **In the region of** means approximately or about: *We're expecting crowds in the region of ten or twelve thousand.*

regional /ˈriːdʒənəl/ *adjective*
Regional means relating to the regions of a country, or to a particular region: *meetings at both regional and national level* □ *I detect in your voice a slight regional accent.*

register /ˈrɛdʒɪstə(r)/ *noun; verb*
▻ ***noun*: registers**
A **register** is a written list or record of something, for example people's names, or the book it is written in: *You are not on the doctor's register of patients.* □ *I'll check in the register.*
▻ ***verb*: registers, registering, registered**
1 You **register** for something when you formally declare that you want to join or take part by putting your name on an official list: *Students must register by 5 o'clock on Wednesday.* [*same as* **enrol**] **2** You **register** something when you give information about it to an official, who records the information on a list: *Have you registered the birth of your child?* **3** A measuring instrument **registers** the measurement that it shows or records: *We'll make a note of the lowest temperature registered.* [*same as* **record**] **4** (*formal*) You **register** your feelings or opinions when you tell others about them, especially in a formal way: *I wrote to their Head Office to register my complaint.*

registration /rɛdʒɪˈstreɪʃən/ *noun* (*uncount*)
Registration is the act or process of recording something on an official list.

registration number /rɛdʒɪˈstreɪʃən nʌmbə(r)/ *noun*: **registration numbers**
The **registration number** on a car or other vehicle is the set of numbers and letters that identify it. [see picture at **car**]

registry /ˈrɛdʒɪstrɪ/ *noun*: **registries**
A **registry** is a place where official records are kept.

registry office /ˈrɛdʒɪstrɪ ɒfɪs/ *noun*: **registry offices**
A **registry office** is a place where official records of all the births, marriages and deaths in a town or district are kept, and where people can get married without having a religious service.

regret /rɪˈgrɛt/ *verb; noun*
▻ ***verb*: regrets, regretting, regretted**
1 You **regret** something when you wish that you had not done it, or that it had not happened: *I regret their decision to increase train fares.* □ *Do you regret leaving school so young?* □ *She doesn't regret what she said.* **2** People sometimes use **regret** as a formal way of saying they are sorry, or when they are refusing something: *The shop will be closed on Friday; we regret any inconvenience caused.* □ *I regret that I will be unable to attend your wedding.*
▻ ***noun*** (*count or uncount*): **regrets:** *Do you have any regrets about the way things have turned out?* □ *It was with a sense of regret that I started that first letter.* □ *Peter was not able to come, and sends his regrets.* — *adjective* **regretful:** *She shows no signs of being regretful.*

regrettable /rɪˈgrɛtəbəl/ *adjective*
You refer to something as **regrettable** if you wish it had not happened, or you are sorry that it happened: *It was a most regrettable omission.* [*same as* **unfortunate**] — *adverb* (*sentence adverb*) **regrettably:** *I have to inform you, regrettably, that there are no vacancies at present.* [*same as* **unfortunately**]

regular /ˈrɛgjʊlə(r)/ *adjective; noun*
▻ ***adjective***
1 Regular describes things that are often done, or that always happen at the same time or after the same period of time: *We visit our parents at regular intervals.* □ *She's a regular visitor to this part of the world.* [*same as* **frequent**; *opposite* **irregular**] **2** (*especially AmE*) **Regular** also means usual or normal: *My regular dentist was away on holiday.* □ *Six o'clock is our regular time for tea.* □ *Treehorn was relieved to be back to his own regular size again.* **3 Regular** also means of ordinary size, especially not the largest size available: *a regular portion of chips.* **4 Regular** also describes something that has a steady rhythm or an even pattern: *The patient's breathing had become more regular.* □ *He had those very regular features of the classically handsome man.* **5** You make the different forms of a **regular** verb according to fixed rules or patterns.
▻ ***noun*: regulars**
A **regular** is someone who regularly goes to the same pub, shop or similar place as a customer. — *noun* (*uncount*) **regularity** /rɛgjʊˈlarɪtɪ/: *We made weekend trips to museums and galleries with boring regularity.* — *adverb* **regularly:** *I visited him regularly during his first weeks in hopsital.*

regulate /ˈrɛgjʊleɪt/ *verb*: **regulates, regulating, regulated**
1 You **regulate** a machine or appliance when you use the controls to adjust or fix the way it works: *You set the thermostats to regulate the temperature in each room.* [*same as* **control**] **2** The way something **is regulated** is the way it is controlled by rules or laws.

regulation /rɛgjʊˈleɪʃən/ *noun* (*count or uncount*): **regulations**
Regulations are rules or laws: *We can't allow that; it's against regulations.* □ *It must be controlled by strict regulation.*

rehabilitation /riːhabɪlɪˈteɪʃən/ *noun* (*uncount*)
Rehabilitation refers to things done to give people normal lives and make them part of normal society, especially people coming out of prison or people trying to stop taking illegal drugs: *a drug rehabilitation centre.*

rehearsal /rɪˈhɜːsəl/ *noun* (*count or uncount*): **rehearsals**
A **rehearsal** is a practice of something that is to be performed in public, such as a play: *We did the second piece entirely without rehearsal.*

rehearse /rɪˈhɜːs/ *verb*: **rehearses, rehearsing, rehearsed**
1 You **rehearse** something when you practise it before performing it in front of an audience: *I'd like us to rehearse the second scene again.* **2** You **rehearse** things you are going to say, such as reasons or excuses, when you prepare yourself by repeating them in your mind: *He was sitting on the step, rehearsing his latest explanation.*

reign /reɪn/ *verb; noun*
▻ ***verb*: reigns, reigning, reigned**
1 A king or queen who **reigns** rules a country: *the reigning monarch at the time.* **2** You say that a particular quality, such as hope or fear, **reigns** when most people are feeling or expressing it: *In the office, a sense of desperation still reigned.* [*same as* **prevail**]
▻ ***noun*: reigns**: *the reign of Elizabeth II.*

reimburse /riːɪmˈbɜːs/ *verb*: **reimburses, reimbursing, reimbursed**
You **reimburse** someone when you pay them back the money they have spent or lost: *We will of course reimburse your travelling expenses.* □ *They insisted that we reimburse them for the damage our children had caused in their garden.*

rein /reɪn/ *noun*: **reins**
Reins are straps attached to a horse's head, that the rider uses to control the horse.
▻ ***phrases*** **1** You **give** someone **a free rein** when you allow them total freedom to do what they want or make their own decisions: *My deputy has been given a*

free rein to set whatever price he thinks appropriate. **2** You **keep a tight rein on** something when you control or limit it strictly.

reincarnation /riːɪŋkɑːˈneɪʃən/ *noun* (*uncount*)
Reincarnation is the idea that the soul or spirit of a dead person is born again into a new and different person: *Do they believe in reincarnation?*

reindeer /ˈreɪndɪə(r)/ *noun*: **reindeer** or **reindeers**
A **reindeer** is a large deer that lives in northern countries: *the image of Santa Claus on a sleigh pulled by reindeer.*

reinforce /riːɪnˈfɔːs/ *verb*: **reinforces, reinforcing, reinforced**
1 You **reinforce** something when you make it stronger and harder to break or damage: *The base is made of reinforced concrete.* [*same as* **toughen**; *opposite* **weaken**] **2** Something that **reinforces** an argument or theory supports it and makes it more convincing; something that **reinforces** the way you feel makes the feeling stronger: *The witnesses comments did nothing to reinforce our case.* □ *We praise the children regularly to reinforce their sense of self-worth.* [*same as* **strengthen**; *opposite* **undermine**]

reinstate /riːɪnˈsteɪt/ *verb*: **reinstates, reinstating, reinstated**
Someone who **is reinstated** is given back the job, position or status they used to have: *His supporters want him reinstated as Chairman.* [*same as* **reappoint**]

reiterate /riːˈɪtəreɪt/ *verb*: **reiterates, reiterating, reiterated**
You **reiterate** something when you say it again, especially several times: *In answer to your question, I can only reiterate my organization's position on the matter.*

reject *verb*; *noun*
▻ ***verb*** /rɪˈdʒɛkt/: **rejects, rejecting, rejected**
1 You **reject** something when you refuse to accept it, agree to it or believe it: *Voters have clearly rejected the government's proposals for Europe.* □ *As parents, we hope our children won't reject the values we try to give them.* **2** When you apply for a job, you **are rejected** if you are not given the job. [*opposite* **accept**] — *noun* (*count or uncount*) **rejection** /rɪˈdʒɛkʃən/: *He tells of his childhood rejection of his mother's Catholicism.* □ *My suggestions were met with a firm rejection.* □ *He applied for several jobs but all he ever received were rejections.* [*opposite* **acceptance**]
▻ ***noun*** /ˈriːdʒɛkt/: **rejects**
A **reject** is a product that has not been made properly and is not considered good enough to sell: *At the factory, you can buy rejects very cheaply.*

rejoice /rɪˈdʒɔɪs/ *verb* (*literary*): **rejoices, rejoicing, rejoiced**
You **rejoice** when you feel or show great happiness: *We rejoice in the success of our troops.*

relapse *noun*; *verb*
▻ ***noun*** /rɪˈlaps/ or /ˈriːlaps/: **relapses**
An ill person who is getting better has a **relapse** when they suddenly become ill again.
▻ ***verb*** /rɪˈlaps/: **relapses, relapsing, relapsed**
Someone **relapses** into a former bad or undesirable state when they go into that state again: *By that time, the whole country had relapsed into chaos.*

relate /rɪˈleɪt/ *verb*: **relates, relating, related**
1 You **are related** to the people in your family: *His name is Jones as well, but we're not related.* □ *I'm related to him on my mother's side; he is my mother's cousin.* **2** One thing **relates** to another when the two are connected or linked in some way; something **relates** to what it is about or what it concerns: *You can't prove that violent crime is related to violence on television.* □ *These themes are closely related.* □ *Your question relates back to what we were discussing last week.* □ *We asked for copies of all letters relating to the sale of shares.* **3** You say that you can **relate** to someone if you understand how they think and feel, because they have a similar personality to your own: *I don't really relate to any of my colleagues.* [*same as* **identify with**] **4** (*formal*) You **relate** a story when you tell it: *He was able to relate the whole incident in French, without hesitation.* [*same as* **recount**]

relation /rɪˈleɪʃən/ *noun*: **relations**
1 There is a **relation** between things when they are linked or connected: *This bears no relation to what we were talking about earlier.* [*same as* **connection**] **2** Your **relations** are your relatives, the people who belong to your family: *I'm a relation of his by marriage.* [*same as* **relative**] **3** There are good **relations** between people who are friendly towards each other and enjoy working or living together: *We enjoy very close relations with a number of government ministers.* □ *Relations between them were in a state of decline.*
▻ ***phrase*** You use **in relation to** when you are comparing things: *At 65, he's quite young in relation to previous Presidents.* □ *What is my precise status in relation to the others in the office?* [*same as* **compared with**]

relationship /rɪˈleɪʃənʃɪp/ *noun*: **relationships**
1 There is a **relationship** between things that are linked or connected in some way: *Sociologists see a relationship between poverty and crime.* [*same as* **connection**] **2** People or groups have a good **relationship** with each other when they behave in a friendly way towards each other and enjoy working together: *We wouldn't want to damage the special relationship that exists between our two governments.* **3** You are in a **relationship** with someone who is your sexual or romantic partner: *She's had a few brief relationships since her husband died.*

relative /ˈrɛlətɪv/ *noun*; *adjective*
▻ ***noun***: **relatives**
Your **relatives** are the people who belong to your family: *We've just invited our parents and a handful of close relatives.* [*same as* **relation**]
▻ ***adjective***
1 You use **relative** when you are comparing people or things: *We measured the relative speeds of a car and a train.* **2** There is a **relative** quality somewhere if there is a fair degree of it there, in comparison with elsewhere: *He longed to get back to the relative calm of the office.* [*same as* **comparative**] **3** Something is **relative** when you can't measure it, and can only judge or express it in a comparison with something else: *'Hot' and 'cold' are relative terms.* □ *Happiness is relative, of course.* **4** (*grammar*) The **relative** pronouns are *who, whom, whose, which* and *that*, and they introduce a **relative** clause, part of a sentence that defines or gives more information about the subject or object of a verb.

relatively /ˈrɛlətɪvlɪ/ *adverb* (*moderating*)
Relatively means 'fairly', 'quite' or 'to some extent': *The afternoon was relatively warm.*

relax /rɪˈlaks/ *verb*: **relaxes, relaxing, relaxed**
1 You **relax** when you become less nervous, worried or tense: *You must learn to relax and forget about your problems at work.* □ *A week's holiday would really relax me.* □ *I find listening to music very relaxing.* [*same as* **unwind**] **2** You also **relax** when you rest completely from work or effort of any kind: *She spent the afternoon relaxing in the garden.* □ *I find listening to music very relaxing.* **3** You **relax** something when you make it less strict or severe: *Could the admission rules be relaxed a lit-*

tle? □ *They have a very relaxed attitude to child discipline.* **4** You **relax** a part of your body when you stop holding it in a stiff or tight position and let it become loose.

relaxation /riːlak'seɪʃən/ *noun* (*uncount*)
Relaxation is rest from work or things that worry or trouble you: *We should all get a bit more relaxation.*

relay *noun*; *verb*
▻ ***noun*** /'riːleɪ/: **relays**
A **relay**, or **relay** race, is a race between teams of people, with each member of the team starting as the previous member finishes.
▻ ***verb*** /rɪ'leɪ/ (*formal*): **relays, relaying, relayed**
You **relay** something you have been told when you tell it to someone else: *We'll relay the news to the Cabinet office.* [*same as* **communicate, transmit**]

release /rɪ'liːs/ *verb*; *noun*
▻ ***verb***: **releases, releasing, released**
1 You **release** a person who is held prisoner when you free them: *Every animal in the zoo had been released from its cage.* **2** You **release** someone from something difficult or unpleasant, such as a duty, when you free them from it: *We were at last released from the burden of responsibility.* [*same as* **free**] **3** Something such as a book or a film **is released** when it is made available for people to see: *A copy of the letter has been released to the press and other media.* **4** You **release** something when you stop holding or gripping it; you **release** a device that holds or grips something when you turn off the mechanism that holds or grips: *I clawed at his face and he released my wrist.* □ *Release the hand brake slowly as you accelerate.* [*same as* **let go**]
▻ ***noun*** (*count or uncount*): **releases:** *the release of dangerous criminals into society* □ *Death came as a welcome release from years of pain.* □ *I have a copy of the press release.* □ *Now for more information about this week's cinema releases.* □ *Now showing in London, the film will be on general release next month.*

relegate /'rɛlɪgeɪt/ *verb*: **relegates, relegating, relegated**
You **relegate** someone when you move them down to a lower grade, position or status: *The bottom three teams will be relegated to the third division.* □ *The women were relegated to the kitchen, to leave the men to discuss business.* [*same as* **consign**; *opposite* **promote**]

relentless /rɪ'lɛntləs/ *adjective*
Relentless describes things that continue on and on without stopping, or without ever becoming weaker or less intense: *the relentless pounding of the noises in my head* □ *Our fight against crime must be determined and relentless.* [*same as* **persistent**]

relevant /'rɛləvənt/ *adjective*
Something is **relevant** when it is directly connected with something, especially with what is currently happening or currently being discussed: *I'll give you a list of relevant textbooks.* □ *Your question is not really relevant to the matter in hand.* □ *Most people feel that debate about the European Parliament is not relevant to their daily lives.* [*opposite* **irrelevant**] — *noun* (*uncount*) **relevance:** *It's difficult to see the relevance of these issues to the lives of university students.* [*opposite* **irrelevance**]

reliable /rɪ'laɪəbəl/ *adjective*
A **reliable** person is someone you can depend on, someone who will do what you ask or what they promise they will do; **reliable** information is very probably true or correct; a **reliable** machine or device does not often break down: *As a witness, I don't think he would be very reliable.* □ *We've received information from a very reliable source.* □ *My first car was far more reliable.* [*opposite* **unreliable**]

reliant /rɪ'laɪənt/ *adjective*
You are **reliant** on something when you need it or depend on it, and cannot easily work or survive without it: *As a charitable organization, we are reliant on donations of money from members of the public.* □ *The baby is entirely reliant on its parents, for food, warmth, love.* [*same as* **dependent**] — *noun* (*uncount*) **reliance:** *I'm sometimes frightened by our reliance on computer technology.* [*same as* **dependence**]

relic /'rɛlɪk/ *noun*: **relics**
1 Relics are objects from past periods in history: *ancient relics.* **2** You say that something, such as a belief or custom, is a **relic** of some past time when you are emphasizing how unsuited it is to the present: *Such politeness is a relic of a bygone era.* [*same as* **vestige**]

relief /rɪ'liːf/ *noun*
1 (*uncount or used in the singular*) **Relief** is the feeling of calmness and happiness because something unpleasant has not happened or has stopped happening: *a huge sigh of relief* □ *It was a relief to be outside in the fresh air again.* **2** (*uncount, often adjectival*) **Relief** is also help given, usually in the form of food, clothes and medicine, to people who need it: *Relief supplies were flown into the war zone.*

relieve /rɪ'liːv/ *verb*: **relieves, relieving, relieved**
1 To **relieve** pain or an unpleasant feeling is to lessen it or make it stop: *I went for a walk to relieve the boredom.* **2** (*formal*) You **relieve** someone of something, usually something unwanted or unpleasant, when you take it away from them: *I offered to relieve her of the heavy bag.*
▻ ***phrase*** (*euphemistic*) You **relieve yourself** when you release liquid or solid waste from your body: *A dog was relieving itself against my car.*

relieved /rɪ'liːvd/ *adjective*
You are **relieved** when you begin to feel at ease because something unpleasant has not happened or has stopped happening: *I was relieved to see that you had not forgotten to bring the key.* □ *She felt relieved that their first meeting had gone smoothly.*

religion /rɪ'lɪdʒən/ *noun* (*uncount or count*): **religions**
Religion is belief in, or the worship of, a god or gods: *People clearly think that religion has no place in modern life.* □ *the Christian and Muslim religions.*

religious /rɪ'lɪdʒəs/ *adjective*
1 Religious describes things relating to religion: *religious beliefs* □ *the religious content of the marriage ceremony.* **2** You describe someone as **religious** if they follow their particular religion very strictly: *My grandfather was a very religious man.*

religiously /rɪ'lɪdʒəslɪ/ *adverb*
You do something **religiously** when you are careful to do it regularly: *I used to clean the car religiously every Saturday morning.*

relinquish /rɪ'lɪŋkwɪʃ/ *verb* (*formal*): **relinquishes, relinquishing, relinquished**
You **relinquish** something, such as your right to do or have something, when you give it up: *She has decided to relinquish the chairmanship, and let a younger person take it over.* [*same as* **renounce**]

relish /'rɛlɪʃ/ *verb*; *noun*
▻ ***verb***: **relishes, relishing, relished**
1 You **relish** something when you enjoy it very much: *She relishes any opportunity to speak in public.* **2** You say that you **relish** the prospect of something when you want it to happen soon because you know you will enjoy it: *I didn't relish the idea of travelling all that distance by bus.*

▻ ***noun*** (*uncount*)
Certain kinds of sharp-tasting sauce that you eat cold with other food are called **relish**: *a jar of sweetcorn relish.*

relive /riːˈlɪv/ *verb*: **relives, reliving, relived**
You **relive** something when you experience it again, especially in your imagination: *I have relived that moment many times.*

reluctant /rɪˈlʌktənt/ *adjective*
You are **reluctant** to do something when you don't want to do it or you feel you ought not to do it, even if you do it in the end: *I am reluctant to mention the subject again, but I feel it must be discussed.* [*same as* **loath**; *opposite* **willing**] — *noun* (*uncount*) **reluctance:** *It was with reluctance that I accepted their invitation.* □ *We are disappointed by their reluctance to help.* — *adverb* **reluctantly:** *She reluctantly agreed to accompany them as far as Bologna.* [*same as* **willingly**]

rely /rɪˈlaɪ/ *verb*: **relies, relying, relied**
1 You **rely** on something that you need or depend on: *The church relies heavily on money donated by members of the public.* **2** You can **rely** on someone when they can be trusted, and you are sure they will do what they should do or what you ask them to do: *Can they be relied upon to do it properly?* □ *I wonder if I can rely on your support in next week's election.* [*same as* **depend**]

remain /rɪˈmeɪn/ *verb*: **remains, remaining, remained**
1 What **remains** is what is left when something else, or another part, has been lost, taken away or used up: *After the bombing, all that remained of the house was a pile of bricks and rubble.* □ *The remaining members of the team of 1946 are now all very old.* **2** To **remain** is to stay in the same place or the same state, not moving or changing: *I remained at her bedside throughout the operation.* □ *She remains reluctant to give any advice at all.* **3** Something that **remains** to be done has not yet been done and still needs to be done: *The precise date remains to be decided.* □ *All that remains for me to do is to thank you all for coming.*

remainder /rɪˈmeɪndə(r)/ *noun* (*used in the singular*)
The **remainder** of something is the part or the amount left after the rest has been done, lost, used up or dealt with: *We spent the remainder of the holiday lying on beaches.* □ *Three potatoes each will be enough; the remainder we can use for a salad.* [*same as* **rest**]

remains /rɪˈmeɪnz/ *noun* (*plural*)
1 Remains are parts left after other parts have been taken away, lost, used up or destroyed: *a table littered with the remains of the previous evening's dinner* □ *The cotton remains are reprocessed to make cleaning cloths.* [*same as* **remnants, scraps**] **2 Remains** are also objects from past periods in history, found or dug up: *the discovery of Roman remains.* **3** The body of a dead person is often called their **remains**: *Her remains will be flown back to this country for burial.*

remake /ˈriːmeɪk/ *noun*: **remakes**
A **remake** is a new version of an old film, usually, but not always, with the same title: *The film is essentially a remake of 'Twelve Angry Men'.*

remand /rɪˈmɑːnd/ *verb*; *noun*
▻ ***verb***: **remands, remanding, remanded**
A court judge **remands** a person accused of a crime when they order the person to come back to court at a later date because the trial cannot be held immediately, often also ordering them to stay in prison until the trial: *He was remanded in custody.*
▻ ***noun*** (*uncount*)
A person accused of a crime is on **remand** when they have been ordered to return to a court for trial at some future time, and often held in prison until that time.

remark /rɪˈmɑːk/ *noun*; *verb*
▻ ***noun***: **remarks**
Remarks are things you say: *He made some casual remark about the way I was dressed.* [*same as* **comment**]
▻ ***verb***: **remarks, remarking, remarked**
Remark is used to refer to things that people say: *I remarked that I hadn't seen him for a few weeks.* □ *Alice had remarked on how grown-up the children were looking.* □ *'It's been a pleasant evening', Hubert remarked.* [*same as* **comment, mention**]

remarkable /rɪˈmɑːkəbəl/ *adjective*
Remarkable describes things, usually qualities, that are extreme, exceptional or impressive; a **remarkable** person has such qualities: *She handled the affair with remarkable self-confidence.* □ *They move at remarkable speed for such big animals.* □ *He is a politician with a remarkable breadth of knowledge.* [*same as* **amazing**] — *adverb* (*intensifying*) **remarkably:** *She prepared it remarkably quickly.* □ *You answered a difficult question remarkably well.* [*same as* **extremely**]

remedy /ˈrɛmədɪ/ *noun*; *verb*
▻ ***noun***: **remedies**
1 A **remedy** is a drug or other treatment that cures a disease or illness: *The leaves were rubbed on the skin as a remedy for sunburn.* [*same as* **cure, treatment**] **2** You also describe something that solves a problem or gets rid of something unwanted as a **remedy**: *a remedy for the country's economic problems.*
▻ ***verb***: **remedies, remedying, remedied**
You **remedy** something when you correct it or put it right: *It's an unfair situation that could be remedied by increasing the pay of office staff.* [*same as* **put right**]

remember /rɪˈmɛmbə(r)/ *verb*: **remembers, remembering, remembered**
1 You **remember**, or can **remember**, something from the past when you still have an impression of it and can bring it back into your mind: *Can you remember her name?* □ *I remember very little of my childhood.* □ *She remembered nothing about the accident.* □ *Remember the marvellous fruit pies she used to make?* □ *Do you remember the time we lost our way in the fog?* □ *I remember it was raining heavily.* □ *I can remember staying at that hotel when I was four.* □ *We all remembered his* (or *him*) *remarking on the time.* □ *I'm afraid I can't remember what day that was.* □ *She's working in Leeds or Halifax, I don't remember which.* [*same as* **recall, recollect**] **2** You **remember** to do something when you do it as you intended; you **remember** something when you don't forget to deal with it; you say '**Remember**' to people as a way of reminding them about something: *I must remember to switch the oven off before we leave.* □ *Remember to lock the door behind you.* □ *Did you remember to send her a postcard?* □ *He promised he'd let her know, so I hope he remembers to.* □ *You will remember Granny's birthday, won't you?* □ *Now, have I remembered everything?* □ *Remember the shops will be shut on Monday.* □ *Guy comes back on Friday, remember.* [*opposite* **forget**] **3** You ask one person to **remember** you to another as a way of asking them to pass on your good wishes to the other: *Please remember me to your parents when you next see them.*

remembrance /rɪˈmɛmbrəns/ *noun* (*uncount*)
Something that is done in **remembrance** of a dead person is done as a way of showing that people still think about them: *Flowers were laid on the pavement, in remembrance of those killed in the disaster.* [*same as* **commemoration**]

remind /rɪˈmaɪnd/ *verb*: **reminds, reminding, reminded**
1 You **remind** someone about a certain thing when

you do or say something that makes them remember it: *I would have forgotten my appointment if my secretary hadn't reminded me about it.* □ *Remind me on Friday to get more bread for the weekend.* □ *I reminded her that she had promised to take presents for the children.* □ *Remind me nearer the time.* □ *'Could you bring your tape next time?' 'Yes, but you'll have to remind me to.'* **2** One thing **reminds** you of another if there is a similarity or connection between the two that makes you think of the other: *She reminds me of her mother at that age, especially when she smiles.* □ *The smell of lilac always reminds me of our old house.* □ *What does that picture remind you of?* □ *That reminds me; what became of that book you were planning to write?*

reminder /rɪ'maɪndə(r)/ *noun*: **reminders**
A **reminder** is a note reminding someone to do something: *We sent them a reminder about the unpaid bill.*

reminisce /rɛmɪ'nɪs/ *verb*: **reminisces, reminiscing, reminisced**
You **reminisce** when you think, talk or write about things you remember from the past, usually happy times: *Most of the meal was spent reminiscing about our school days.*

reminiscence /rɛmɪ'nɪsəns/ *noun*: **reminiscences**
Reminiscences are remembered experiences that you think, talk or write about: *They exchanged reminiscences for the first few hours.*

reminiscent /rɛmɪ'nɪsənt/ *adjective*
Something is **reminiscent** of something else that it is similar to and makes you think of: *paintings in a style reminiscent of van Gogh.*

remnant /'rɛmnənt/ *noun*: **remnants**
A **remnant** is a small piece or amount of something left after the rest of it has been used, lost or destroyed: *Remnants of curtain fabric were used to make cushion covers.* □ *This strange tradition is a remnant of the medieval laws relating to the ownership of property.*

remorse /rɪ'mɔːs/ *noun* (*uncount*)
Remorse is a deep feeling of guilt for something wrong or bad that you have done: *He wrote me a letter filled with remorse.* [*same as* **anguish, guilt**]

remote /rɪ'moʊt/ *adjective*: **remoter, remotest**
1 A **remote** place is far away from the kinds of places that most people live in or travel to, and so is quiet or difficult to get to: *a cottage on a remote hillside.* [*same as* **isolated**] **2** You say that the chance of something happening is **remote** if it is very unlikely to happen: *I suppose there's a remote possibility that she'll get the job.* □ *You don't even have the remotest chance of success.* [*same as* **slight**] **3** Someone is **remote** from things that they have very little experience of or rarely have to deal with: *Politicians have become increasingly remote from the realities of the ordinary person's life.* **4** You might describe someone as **remote** if they behave in an unfriendly or uninterested way, showing that they don't want to be involved: *She had a remote manner that made her difficult to talk to.* [*same as* **distant**; *opposite* **warm**] — *noun* (*uncount*) **remoteness:** *It was the remoteness of the island that attracted us to it.* [see also **remotely**]

remote control /rɪmoʊt kən'troʊl/ *noun* (*uncount or count*): **remote controls**
An electrical device, such as a television, that has **remote control** can be operated from a distance, for example from your chair, using a small control box you hold in your hand; the box itself is also called a **remote control**. — *adjective* **remote-controlled:** *Most modern music systems are remote-controlled.*

remotely /rɪ'moʊtlɪ/ *adverb* (*intensifying*)
Remotely is often used with a negative for emphasis: *He wasn't remotely interested in what we had to say.* □ *There isn't anything remotely similar available in this country.*

removal /rɪ'muːvəl/ *noun*: **removals**
1 (*uncount*) The **removal** of something is the act of removing it: *They have agreed to the removal of all trade barriers by next month.* [*same as* **withdrawal**] **2** (*count or uncount, often adjectival*) A **removal** is the act of moving to a new home: *All our furniture was loaded into a removal van and taken to the depot.*

remove /rɪ'muːv/ *verb*: **removes, removing, removed**
You **remove** something when you take it away or get rid of it; you **remove** clothes when you take them off: *We were instructed to remove all the tablecloths from the tables.* □ *When I removed my hand from the bag, it was covered in red ink.* □ *The committee voted in favour of removing the restrictions on access to the club for non-members.* □ *The new washing-powders can remove even the toughest stains.* □ *It was customary to remove your shoes before going inside.*

renaissance /rɪ'neɪsəns/ or /rɪ'neɪsɒns/ *noun* (*used in the singular; formal*)
There is a **renaissance** of something when it becomes popular again, after not being popular for some time: *Classical music is enjoying something of a renaissance.* [*same as* **revival, rebirth**]

render /'rɛndə(r)/ *verb* (*formal*): **renders, rendering, rendered**
People use **render** to say that something is changed from one state or condition to another: *Dampness has rendered the house unfit to live in.* □ *The drug will render the tiger harmless for up to two hours.* □ *He was rendered unconscious by a blow on the back of the neck.* [*same as* **make**]

rendering /'rɛndərɪŋ/ *noun* (*formal*): **renderings**
A **rendering** of something such as a song is a performance of it.

rendezvous /'rɒndeɪvuː/ or /'rɒndɪvuː/ *noun*: **rendezvous** /'rɒndeɪvuːz/
1 A **rendezvous** is an arranged meeting between people, especially a private or secret meeting: *I don't want any more of these secret rendezvous.* **2** The place where people meet in this way is sometimes also called a **rendezvous**: *We've found an excellent rendezvous.* □ *It's a familiar landmark, and a popular rendezvous with tourists.*

rendition /rɛn'dɪʃən/ *noun* (*formal*): **renditions**
A **rendition** of something such as a song is a performance of it: *We had to listen to my uncle's familiar rendition of 'White Christmas'.*

renew /rɪ'njuː/ *verb*: **renews, renewing, renewed**
1 You **renew** something such as a licence or a pass when you make it valid for a further period of time: *I must get my passport renewed.* **2** You also **renew** something when you start doing it again, after a pause or break, often putting more effort or energy into it this second time: *During the interview, he renewed his criticism of the party leadership.* □ *She was able to tackle the task with renewed vigour and enthusiasm.* — *noun* (*uncount*) **renewal** /rɪ'njuːəl/: *The renewal of your driving licence could take up to four weeks.* □ *My contract is due for renewal at the end of the year.* □ *A breakdown in peace talks could lead to a renewal of hostilities between the two nations.*

renounce /rɪ'naʊns/ *verb* (*formal*): **renounces, renouncing, renounced**
You **renounce** something when you say you will no longer do it, be involved in it or believe in it: *Before the terrorists can sit at the negotiating table, they must*

renounce violence. ▫ *By this time, he had renounced the Communism that had dominated his early political career.* [*same as* **give up**; see also **renunciation**]

renovate /ˈrɛnəveɪt/ *verb*: **renovates, renovating, renovated**
Someone who **renovates** an old building repairs it so that it is in a good enough condition to be used again. [*same as* **do up**] — *noun* (*uncount*) **renovation** /rɛnəˈveɪʃən/: *the renovation of the old fish market.*

renowned /rɪˈnaʊnd/ *adjective*
Someone or something is **renowned** for having a particular quality when they are famous because many people have heard about how good this quality is: *Irish guest houses were renowned for their warm welcome and their good food.* [*same as* **reputed**]

rent /rɛnt/ *noun*; *verb*
▻ ***noun*** (*uncount*)
Rent is money you pay to the owner of a house or other building in return for your living in it or using it: *Many families can't even afford to pay the rent.*
▻ ***verb***: **rents, renting, rented**
1 You **rent** a house or other building, or sometimes a car or a piece of equipment, when you pay its owner money so that you can live in it or use it: *We rented motorbikes for a week, so we could travel round the island.* **2** You **rent** something you own, or **rent** it out, when you allow others to use it if they pay you money: *I'm afraid all the other apartments have already been rented out.* [see note at **hire**]

rental /ˈrɛntəl/ *noun*: **rentals**
1 (*uncount, often adjectival*) **Rental** is the act or practice of renting out things people own: *Ivan had arranged the rental of a car for the whole holiday.* ▫ *a television rental company.* [*same as* **hire**] **2** (*uncount or count*) **Rental** is also the amount of rent you pay: *Would a rental of £50 a month be fair?*

renunciation /rɪnʌnsɪˈeɪʃən/ *noun* (*uncount; formal*)
The **renunciation** of something is the act of saying that you will no longer do it, be involved in it or believe in it: *This followed their renunciation of trade links with Japan.*

rep /rɛp/ *noun* (*informal*): **reps**
A **rep** is a representative, someone who sells the products and services of a particular business company, often by travelling round to other companies who might want to buy them: *She's a sales rep for a computer firm.*

repair /rɪˈpɛə(r)/ *verb*; *noun*
▻ ***verb***: **repairs, repairing, repaired**
1 You **repair** something that is damaged or broken when you put it back into good, working condition: *The problem with plastic components is that they can't be repaired.* ▫ *How much will it cost to repair the washing-machine?* ▫ *Can the fault be repaired?* [*same as* **mend**] **2** (*formal*) You **repair** something wrong that has been done when you do something to make it better: *How can this unfortunate situation be repaired?* [*same as* **remedy**]
▻ ***noun***: **repairs**
1 (*count or uncount, often adjectival*) You carry out **repairs** on something when you repair it: *It was so badly damaged as to be beyond repair.* ▫ *a television repair man.* **2** (*uncount; formal*) Something that is in bad **repair** is in a poor or damaged condition and needs repairing; it is in good **repair** when it is in good condition: *The house was in a very poor state of repair.*

repartee /rɛpɑːˈtiː/ *noun* (*uncount*)
Repartee is conversation in which people rapidly exchange clever or humorous comments: *I enjoyed the lively repartee in the office.*

repay /rɪˈpeɪ/ *verb*: **repays, repaying, repaid**
1 You **repay** money you have borrowed when you pay it back: *The loan will be repaid over three years.* [*same as* **pay back**] **2** You **repay** someone for something they have done for you, usually something good, when you do something for them in return: *How can we ever repay his kindness?* [*same as* **return**]

repayment /rɪˈpeɪmənt/ *noun*: **repayments**
Repayments are amounts of money you pay back at fixed intervals, as a way of paying back a larger sum of money you have borrowed.

repeat /rɪˈpiːt/ *verb*; *noun*
▻ ***verb***: **repeats, repeating, repeated**
1 You **repeat** something when you say it again: *She repeated her criticisms of management in an article in the company magazine.* ▫ *'You will never win!', he repeated. 'Never!'* [*same as* **reiterate**] **2** You **repeat** what someone has told you when you tell someone else, often when you ought not to: *Don't repeat that story in front of the children.* **3** You also **repeat** something when you do it again: *We guarantee that this error will not be repeated.* **4** A television or radio programme **is repeated** when it is broadcast again. **5** You **repeat** yourself when you say the same thing again, usually on several occasions: *At the risk of repeating myself, there will be no pay increases.*
▻ ***noun*** (*often adjectival*): **repeats**
A **repeat** is something repeated, especially a television or radio programme broadcast again: *We don't want a repeat of last year's disaster.* ▫ *The advertised programme has been replaced by a repeat of the World Cup Final.* ▫ *a number of repeat performances.* [see also **repetition**]

repeated /rɪˈpiːtɪd/ *adjective*
Repeated describes things that are done or said several times: *After repeated attempts to contact him by phone, I finally went round to his office.* — *adverb* **repeatedly:** *We have repeatedly requested that staff should not be allowed to smoke in the offices.* [*same as* **again and again**]

repel /rɪˈpɛl/ *verb*: **repels, repelling, repelled**
You say that you **are repelled** by something if you think it is disgusting or very unpleasant: *She was repelled by the prospect of having to kiss her Uncle Tom.* [*same as* **disgust**]

repellent /rɪˈpɛlənt/ *noun*; *adjective*
▻ ***noun*** (*uncount*)
Chemical substances used to keep something away are sometimes called **repellent**: *She sprayed insect repellent all over her arms and legs.*
▻ ***adjective*** (*formal*)
You decribe something as **repellent** if you think it is disgusting or very unpleasant: *The thought of an afternoon in his company was repellent to me.* [*opposite* **attractive**]

repercussion /riːpəˈkʌʃən/ *noun* (*usually in the plural*): **repercussions**
The **repercussions** of something that happens are what happens afterwards, as a result: *Years later, we are still seeing repercussions of the currency crisis of the 1970s.*

repertoire /ˈrɛpətwɑː(r)/ *noun* (*usually in the singular*): **repertoires**
A performer's **repertoire** consists of all the pieces they know and can perform: *That particular song is not in my repertoire.* ▫ *an orchestra with an extensive repertoire of concertos.*

repetition /rɛpəˈtɪʃən/ *noun* (*usually in the singular or uncount*): **repetitions**
A **repetition** of something is when it happens again, or when you say or do it again: *I wouldn't want a repeti-*

tion of last month's poor performance. ▫ *He managed to speak without hesitation or repetition.*

repetitive /rɪ'pɛtɪtɪv/ *adjective*
Something **repetitive** is boring because the same things are repeated many times in it: *fairly mundane, repetitive work* ▫ *a rather repetitive speech.* [*same as* **monotonous**]

replace /rɪ'pleɪs/ *verb*: **replaces, replacing, replaced**
1 You **replace** something when you put it back in its previous or proper position: *With some telephones, you have to replace the receiver before dialling a second time.* **2** You use **replace** when you are talking about people or things that take the place of others: *He has replaced Sir John Fosset as chairman.* ▫ *We would need to replace the broken lock with a new one.* ▫ *Harry bought a new one to replace the one he'd broken.*

replacement /rɪ'pleɪsmənt/ *noun*: **replacements**
1 (*often adjectival*) A **replacement** is a person or thing that replaces another: *I'll make you a replacement for the one I lost.* ▫ *a replacement teacher.* **2** (*uncount*) **Replacement** refers to the fact of replacing one person or thing with another: *the replacement of state-run pension schemes with private ones.*

replay *verb*; *noun*
▻ ***verb*** /riː'pleɪ/: **replays, replaying, replayed**
A sporting match **is replayed** when it is played again, usually because there was no clear winner the first time: *The second semi-final will be replayed in two weeks.*
▻ ***noun*** /'riːpleɪ/: **replays**
1 A **replay** is a sporting match played again: *I remember him scoring in the second-round replay.* **2** In a television broadcast of a sporting match, you are shown a **replay** when an incident in the match is shown again, usually immediately after it happens: *Watching the action replay, we can see that the ball did in fact cross the line.*

replenish /rɪ'plɛnɪʃ/ *verb* (*formal*): **replenishes, replenishing, replenished**
You **replenish** your supply or stock of something when you get more of it, to replace what has been used: *We went into town to replenish our winter reserves.* [*same as* **restock, renew**]

replica /'rɛplɪkə/ *noun*: **replicas**
A **replica** of something is a model of it, usually much smaller than the original: *cast-iron replicas of warplanes.* [*same as* **model, reproduction**]

reply /rɪ'plaɪ/ *verb*; *noun*
▻ ***verb***: **replies, replying, replied**
1 You **reply** when you answer someone who has spoken or written to you: *I replied by saying that it was too late to change our plans.* ▫ *'Of course I do,' replied Francis. 'I think it's a great idea.'* ▫ *You haven't replied to my question yet.* ▫ *He replied with a nod.* ▫ *Have you replied to their invitation?* ▫ *I wrote months ago to complain, but they never replied.* **2** (*literary*; *especially sports journalism*) You **reply** to an attack when you fight back: *He replied by serving two aces in succession.*
▻ ***noun*** (*count or uncount*): **replies:** *In your reply to my last letter, you mentioned a possible meeting.* ▫ *We've had a large number of replies to our advertisement.* ▫ *She raised her eyebrows by way of reply.* ▫ *In reply to your question I can only report that we are still awaiting developments.* [*same as* **response**]

report /rɪ'pɔːt/ *noun*; *verb*
▻ ***noun***: **reports**
A **report** is a written account of something, for example a pupil's progress at school, or a firm's business dealings in a particular year: *In his report to Parliament, Lord Taylor makes over seventy recommendations.* ▫ *Investors are sent annual progress reports.* ▫ *Some newspaper reports of the incident claim government troops killed hundreds of students.* [*same as* **account**]
▻ ***verb***: **reports, reporting, reported**
1 You **report** what has happened when you tell people about it: *You should have reported the incident to the police immediately.* ▫ *British radio is reporting that there are no survivors of the crash.* ▫ *It is reported in the newspapers that you earn over £5 million a year.* **2** You **report** someone when you make an official complaint about them to a person in authority: *I could have reported you to the manager for hitting another member of staff.* **3** You **report** to a person or a place when you go there because you have been asked or ordered: *Guests are requested to report to hotel reception on arrival.* ▫ *I reported for duty at Nancy barracks the next morning.* **4** (*formal*) At your place of work, you **report** to the person who is your boss: *There are three assistant managers who report to me.*

reportedly /rɪ'pɔːtɪdlɪ/ *adverb* (*sentence adverb*)
You say that something is **reportedly** true if people have said it is true, but you don't know that it definitely is: *He has reportedly considered resigning on a number of occasions.* [*same as* **apparently**]

reporter /rɪ'pɔːtə(r)/ *noun*: **reporters**
A **reporter** is a person who writes articles and reports for a newspaper, or for broadcasts on television or radio. [*same as* **journalist**]

repose /rɪ'poʊz/ *noun* (*uncount*; *literary*)
You are in **repose** when you are resting or relaxing.

reprehensible /rɛprɪ'hɛnsəbəl/ *adjective* (*formal*)
You describe something as **reprehensible** if you think people ought to disapprove of it, because it is morally wrong: *These were entirely reprehensible acts.* [*same as* **disgraceful**]

represent /rɛprɪ'zɛnt/ *verb*: **represents, representing, represented**
1 Something **represents** what it means, expresses or acts as a symbol of: *The letters of the alphabet represent speech sounds.* ▫ *The American dollar is usually represented by the sign '$'.* ▫ *Personal wealth is often represented in the size of your house or your car.* [*same as* **denote**] **2** You **represent** people when you speak or act on their behalf of: *I have been elected to represent the citizens of this town.* **3** A thing **represents** what it is, what it consists of, or what it is the result of: *The Prime Minister's comments represent a significant shift in the government's position.* ▫ *This book represents years of research on the subject.* [*same as* **constitute**] **4** The way you **represent** something is how you describe it or what kind of thing you say it is: *They somehow managed to represent this absolute failure as a remarkable success.*

representation /rɛprɪzɛn'teɪʃən/ *noun*: **representations**
1 (*formal*) You refer to a painting or other artistic work as a **representation** of something: *The cave walls are covered with primitive representations of animals.* **2** (*uncount*) You have **representation** in a place such as a parliament when someone in that place represents your views or opinions: *It seems that homeless people have no representation within the council.* **3** (*used in the plural*; *formal*) You make **representations** to someone in authority when you tell them about something or complain about something: *The Director General receives representations on a variety of consumer issues.*

representative /rɛprɪ'zɛntətɪv/ *adjective*; *noun*
▻ ***adjective***
Something is **representative** when it is typical or it is a

good example: *I don't think this is a very representative case; most of the many thousands of our customers are very satisfied.* □ *Is this representative of the kind of complaints you receive?*

▻ ***noun***: **representatives**

A **representative** is a person who represents others, for example who acts in a country's parliament on behalf of others or who sells the goods or services of a business company.

repressed /rɪ'prɛst/ *adjective*

Someone who is **repressed** tries to hide or deny their natural feelings, especially sexual desires; you also describe the feelings as **repressed**: *It resulted in my being rather sexually repressed.* □ *This kind of behaviour often stems from a kind of repressed guilt.*

repression /rɪ'prɛʃən/ *noun (uncount)*

1 Repression is the very strict controlling of people, not allowing them to do things such as vote in elections or attend religious worship. **2 Repression** is also the way that some people hide or deny their natural feelings, especially their sexual desires.

repressive /rɪ'prɛsɪv/ *adjective*

A **repressive** government controls the citizens of a country very strictly, not allowing them to do ordinary things such as attend religious worship. [*same as* **dictatorial**]

reprieve /rɪ'priːv/ *verb; noun*

▻ ***verb***: **reprieves, reprieving, reprieved**

Someone **is reprieved** when the punishment or other unpleasantness they are due to receive or experience is delayed or cancelled.

▻ **noun** (*usually in the singular*): **reprieves**: *It earned us a reprieve of a few weeks.*

reprimand /'rɛprɪmɑːnd/ *verb; noun*

▻ ***verb***: **reprimands, reprimanding, reprimanded**

You **reprimand** someone when you tell them, especially formally or officially, that they should have not done something. [*same as* **rebuke**]

▻ **noun**: **reprimands:** *She was given a severe reprimand from the manager.*

reproach /rɪ'proutʃ/ *verb; noun*

▻ ***verb***: **reproaches, reproaching, reproached**

You **reproach** someone for doing something bad or wrong when you tell them you disapprove or you are disappointed: *You mustn't reproach yourself too much; you made a genuine mistake.* [*same as* **criticize**]

▻ **noun** (*uncount; formal*) *a look of reproach.* — *adjective* **reproachful:** *She wrote me a rather reproachful letter.*

reproduce /riːprə'djuːs/ *verb*: **reproduces, reproducing, reproduced**

1 You **reproduce** something when you make or produce it again, or copy it: *We doubted that the tension of the film could be reproduced in a stage play.* □ *He was able to reproduce my signature with frightening accuracy.* [*same as* **recreate**] **2** People and animals **reproduce** when they have babies; plants **reproduce** when they produce new plants of the same kind.

reproduction /riːprə'dʌkʃən/ *noun*: **reproductions**

1 (*often adjectival*) A copy of something, especially a work of art, is often called a **reproduction**: *makers of reproduction furniture.* [*same as* **replica**; *opposite* **original**] **2** (*uncount*) **Reproduction** is the process in which people, animals and plants produce others like themselves.

reptile /'rɛptaɪl/ *noun*: **reptiles**

Reptiles are animals whose skin consists of scales or bony plates, such as snakes, lizards and crocodiles.

republic /rɪ'pʌblɪk/ *noun*: **republics**

A **republic** is a country with no king or queen, ruled by a government of elected people, with the head of government usually given the title 'president': *We're not arguing that Scotland should become an independent republic.* □ *the People's Republic of China.*

repugnant /rɪ'pʌgnənt/ *adjective*

You describe something as **repugnant** if you think it is disgusting or extremely unpleasant: *Its basic policies were repugnant to many trade unions.* □ *It was an intimacy she found repugnant at first.* [same as **abhorrent**]

repulsive /rɪ'pʌlsɪv/ *adjective*

You describe something as **repulsive** if you find it disgusting, perhaps so disgusting that it makes you feel slightly sick: *He has some quite repulsive habits.* [*same as* **offensive**]

reputable /'rɛpjʊtəbəl/ *adjective*

A **reputable** company is one that people in general believe to provide good products or services: *Is their solicitor reputable?*

reputation /rɛpjʊ'teɪʃən/ *noun*: **reputations**

The **reputation** of someone or something is the opinion that people in general have of them: *He has the reputation of being a very tough player.* □ *a restaurant with a reputation for good food and excellent service* □ *They felt the article would damage the company's good reputation.* [*same as* **name**]

reputed /rɪ'pjuːtɪd/ *adjective*

You say that something is **reputed** to be true when people in general say that it is true: *She is reputed to be earning over £500 000 a year.* [*same as* **deemed, thought, believed**] — *adverb* (*sentence adverb*) **reputedly:** *She is reputedly the most talented member of the government.*

request /rɪ'kwɛst/ *verb; noun*

▻ ***verb***: **requests, requesting, requested**

You **request** something when you ask for it, especially formally or officially: *I requested assistance from fellow officers in the area.* □ *The manager has requested that you meet him here.*

▻ **noun** (*count or uncount*): **requests:** *We've received an urgent request for more money.* □ *I've made several requests for the opening to be delayed.* □ *At the request of my friend, Sherlock Holmes, I went by train to Norwood.* [*same as* **appeal**]

▻ ***phrase*** Something is done **on request** if it is done when people ask for it: *A copy of the policy document may be sent on request.*

require /rɪ'kwaɪə(r)/ *verb* (*formal*): **requires, requiring, required**

1 You say that you **require** something if you need it, or you simply want to have it: *We will require tables and chairs to be set out before we arrive.* □ *Do you require me to give you assistance of any kind?* □ *In the writing of future reports, greater attention to detail will be required.* **2** You **are required** to do something when someone asks or orders you to do it: *We require you to be in the office by 8 o'clock.* □ *Pupils are required to study at least one foreign language.* □ *Here is a list of books that are required reading for the history course.*

requirement /rɪ'kwaɪəmənt/ *noun*: **requirements**

A **requirement** is something needed or asked for: *Patience is definitely a requirement for a career in teaching.* □ *Inspectors closed down the restaurant because it didn't meet government hygiene requirements.* [*same as* **specification**]

rescue /'rɛskjuː/ *verb; noun*

▻ ***verb***: **rescues, rescuing, rescued**

You **rescue** someone when you take them out of a dangerous or unpleasant situation: *Firefighters managed to rescue the children trapped in the burning house.*

□ *They aim to rescue the women from a life of violence and prostitution.* [*same as* **save**]
▻ ***noun*** (*count or uncount, often adjectival*): **rescues:** *We were stranded on the island, with no hope of rescue.* □ *We carried out a fairly complex rescue operation.* — *noun* **rescuer:** *Rescuers from the centre are hoping to reach the stranded climbers by evening.*

research *noun; verb*
▻ ***noun*** /rɪ'sɜːtʃ/ or /'riːsɜːtʃ/ (*uncount*)
You carry out **research** into something when you study it carefully in order to find out about it: *research by government departments into the causes of crime* □ *We did some research on people's voting habits.*
▻ ***verb*** /rɪ'sɜːtʃ/: **researches, researching, researched:** *The factual errors in the book show that the subject was not properly researched.*

resemblance /rɪ'zɛmbləns/ *noun* (*usually in the singular or uncount*): **resemblances**
There is a **resemblance** between people or things that resemble each other or are similar: *Her evidence bears no resemblance to what other witnesses have told us.* [*same as* **likeness**]

resemble /rɪ'zɛmbəl/ *verb*: **resembles, resembling, resembled**
People or things **resemble** each other when they are similar: *I'd say he resembles his mother more than his father.* □ *The situation resembled nothing we'd experienced before.* [*same as* **look like**]

resent /rɪ'zɛnt/ *verb*: **resents, resenting, resented**
You **resent** something when you are angry or bitter about it: *We all resented the fact that she was given promotion so early.* □ *I couldn't help feeling that the others resented me, resented my being in charge of them.* [*same as* **grudge, object to**] — *adjective* **resentful:** *She was clearly resentful at having to take orders from someone so young.* □ *I don't feel in the least resentful towards him.* [*same as* **grudging**] — *noun* (*uncount*) **resentment:** *feelings of resentment* □ *I can't explain my resentment towards Keith.*

reservation /rɛzə'veɪʃən/ *noun*: **reservations**
1 You make a **reservation** when you book or reserve something you want to use in future: *I bought my train ticket and made a reservation at the same time.* □ *My reservation was for 9 o'clock, and I insist that you find me a free table now.* [*same as* **booking**] **2** (*count or uncount*) You say that you have **reservations** about something if you are not sure that is it right, good or wise: *Do you have any reservations at all about the scheme?* □ *We were confident all had been properly arranged and we signed the contract without reservation.* [*same as* **doubts**]

reserve /rɪ'zɜːv/ *verb; noun*
▻ ***verb***: **reserves, reserving, reserved**
You **reserve** something for future use, such as a seat in a theatre or a table in a restaurant, when you arrange for it to be kept free for you; something **is reserved** for certain people when other people are not allowed to use it: *'We'd like a table for four, please.' 'Have you reserved?'* □ *I'm afraid this table has already been reserved.* □ *This offer is reserved for existing members only.* □ *He spoke with an intimacy usually reserved for wives or lovers.* [*same as* **book, save, keep**]
▻ ***noun***: **reserves**
1 (*count or uncount*) A **reserve** is a supply of something kept back or set aside, to be used later or whenever you need it: *the nation's gold reserves* □ *We had a few bottles in reserve, in case the guests were feeling particularly thirsty.* [*same as* **stock**] **2** A **reserve** is an area of land set aside for a particular purpose, especially for the protection of animals: *a nature reserve.* **3** (*uncount*) Someone who shows **reserve** does not show their feelings openly. [*same as* **reticence**]

reserved /rɪ'zɜːvd/ *adjective*
You describe someone as **reserved** if they do not show their feelings or opinions openly, suggesting that they are perhaps slightly unfriendly: *Her companion was a rather reserved American woman.* [*same as* **aloof**]

reservoir /'rɛzəvwɑː(r)/ *noun*: **reservoir**
A **reservoir** is a large lake, often man-made, where water is collected and stored.

reside /rɪ'zaɪd/ *verb* (*formal*): **resides, residing, resided**
1 You **reside** in the place where you live: *Are you Terence Powell and do you reside at 34 Ripon Court?* [*same as* **dwell**] **2** You say that something, such as power or authority, **resides** in the person who possesses it: *The real political weight resides in the President.*

residence /'rɛzɪdəns/ *noun* (*count or uncount; formal*): **residences**
A house is sometimes referred to as a **residence** or a place of **residence**: *It's not often that such a desirable residence comes on to the property market.* □ *the Queen's official residence.*
▻ ***phrases*** **1** Someone, especially an important person, is **in residence** when they are living in a particular place: *The national flag flies over the palace whenever the King is in residence.* **2** A professional artist, such as a writer, is **in residence** in a particular place, such as a university, when they are working there for a period of time, and the people in that place can speak to them and ask their advice: *The local council has taken on a poet in residence, based at the library.*

resident /'rɛzɪdənt/ *noun; adjective*
▻ ***noun***: **residents**
A **resident** of a house or a place is a person who lives there: *The people living in the flats formed a residents' committee.*
▻ ***adjective***
1 You are **resident** in a place when you live there: *Have you ever been resident abroad for longer than one year?* **2 Resident** also describes someone who lives where they work: *Students approached the resident tutor for advice.* [*same as* **live-in**]

residential /rɛzɪ'dɛnʃəl/ *adjective*
1 A **residential** area contains mostly houses, with very few businesses or factories. **2 Residential** also describes places that people live in: *a residential college* □ *day care centres and residential homes for the elderly.*

residue /'rɛzɪdjuː/ *noun* (*formal*): **residues**
A **residue** is an amount left after the rest has gone or been used up: *just a residue of oil in the bottom of the tank.* [*same as* **remainder**]

resign /rɪ'zaɪn/ *verb*: **resigns, resigning, resigned**
1 You **resign** when you give up your job or another position you occupy: *She's threatened to resign from the committee altogether unless there are changes.* **2** You **resign** yourself to something unwanted or unpleasant when you accept that you will have to tolerate it or deal with it: *Julia answered civilly, and resigned herself to half an hour's polite conversation.* □ *I think he is resigned to the likelihood that he will never be a genius.*

resignation /rɛzɪg'neɪʃən/ *noun*: **resignations**
1 (*uncount or count*) You hand in your **resignation** when you resign from your job: *Opposition ministers were demanding his resignation.* □ *a letter of resignation.* **2** (*uncount*) **Resignation** is the fact of accepting that you will have to tolerate or deal with something unpleasant: *Her tone was one of resignation.* [*same as* **submission**]

resilient /rɪ'zɪlɪənt/ *adjective*
Resilient describes people and things that are able to

survive harsh or damaging treatment: *one of our more resilient politicians* □ *There's no question that the cheaper boots are less resilient than the good-quality ones.* [*same as* **tough**]

resin /ˈrɛzɪn/ *noun* (*uncount*)
Resin is a sticky solid or semi-solid substance produced by certain trees, or an artificial substitute, used in making plastics.

resist /rɪˈzɪst/ *verb*: **resists, resisting, resisted**
1 You **resist** something when you oppose it and try to stop it happening: *We will strongly resist any attempt to close down our business.* □ *The Minister has resisted demands for his resignation.* [*same as* **fight**] **2** A substance **resists** a certain damaging influence when it remains undamaged by it: *new metals that resist corrosion.* [*same as* **withstand**] **3** You **resist** something when you don't allow yourself to do or have what is tempting or attracting you: *He just can't resist chocolate.* □ *I have so far resisted the temptation to sack him.* — *noun* (*uncount*) **resistance:** *Any attempt to influence our decision will be met with the strongest resistance.* □ *It helps to boost the body's resistance to disease.* — *adjective* **resistant:** *The traditionalists have never been more resistant to change.* □ *Some sun creams are water-resistant.*

resolute /ˈrɛzəluːt/ *adjective* (*formal*)
Someone who is **resolute** is very determined not to change their mind or give up: *The unions are resolute; only a complete agreement to their demands can prevent a strike.* □ *his resolute refusal to accept our terms.* [*same as* **steadfast**]

resolution /rɛzəˈluːʃən/ *noun*: **resolutions**
1 You make a **resolution** to do something when you make a firm decision to do it: *I've already broken my New Year's resolution to stop smoking.* **2** A **resolution** is also a formal or official decision made after people have given their opinions, often by voting: *The conference passed a resolution supporting a ban on nuclear testing.* **3** (*uncount*; *formal*) The **resolution** of a problem is the act of solving it. [*same as* **settlement**] **4** (*uncount*) **Resolution** is the quality of being resolute, determined not to change your mind or give up. [see also **resolve, tenacity**]

resolve /rɪˈzɒlv/ *verb*; *noun*
▷ ***verb***: **resolves, resolving, resolved**
1 You **resolve** to do something when you make a firm decision to do it: *I had resolved to confront Michael about it.* [*same as* **determine**] **2** (*formal*) You **resolve** a problem or difficulty when you solve it or deal successfully with it: *I wondered if such differences of opinion could be resolved.*
▷ ***noun*** (uncount; *formal*)
Resolve is great determination: *You have to admire his resolve.* [*same as* **conviction**]

resort /rɪˈzɔːt/ *verb*; *noun*
▷ ***verb***: **resorts, resorting, resorted**
You **resort** to doing something when you do it only because other methods or approaches have failed, and you would prefer not to have to do it; you also use **resort** as a way of showing that you disapprove of what someone else is doing: *If the child feels the teacher does not care, he will often resort to misbehaving simply to get attention.* □ *You cannot deal with organizations that have resorted to violence.*
▷ ***noun***: **resorts**
A **resort** is a place where many people go for their holidays: *a popular seaside resort.*
▷ ***phrase*** You do something **as a last resort** or **in the last resort** when you do it only because all other methods or approaches have failed: *We could ask our parents for the money, as a last resort.*

resounding /rɪˈzaʊndɪŋ/ *adjective*
A **resounding** success or victory is complete or thorough. [*same as* **decisive**]

resource /rɪˈzɔːs/ or /rɪˈsɔːs/ *noun* (*usually in the plural*): **resources**
Resources are substances or qualities that you possess and are able to use: *Such countries might soon use up all their natural mineral resources.* □ *It would take all my resources of patience and self-control to survive the day.*

resourceful /rɪˈzɔːsfəl/ or /rɪˈsɔːsfəl/ *adjective*
A **resourceful** person is good at finding ways of doing things, especially of solving problems: *The more resourceful teacher needs few materials to keep the children interested.* [*same as* **imaginative**]

respect /rɪˈspɛkt/ *noun*; *verb*
▷ ***noun***: **respects**
1 (*uncount*) You have **respect** for someone when you recognize that they deserve to be admired or obeyed, or that you should pay attention to their wishes, opinions or needs: *You have to earn the respect of your colleagues.* □ *I think you could show your parents a little more respect.* □ *These thugs had no respect for the law.* [*same as* **consideration**] **2** You often use **respect** as a way of making clear what your comments refer or relate to: *He had a tendency to lose his temper but, in every other respect, he was a good father.* □ *In this respect, we are a weak nation.* □ *With respect to the European elections, I don't think the Conservatives have the slightest chance of winning.*
▷ ***verb***: **respects, respecting, respected:** *We respected him as an adviser, but never thought him a leader.* □ *She was a highly respected member of the college.* □ *No matter what we think, we should respect the wishes of his family.* [*same as* **consider**]
▷ ***phrases*** **1** People often say they **pay** their **last respects** to someone who has died when they attend their funeral or visit their grave. **2** You say **'with respect'** when you are politely disagreeing with someone: *But, with respect, I think you have misunderstood my point.*

respectable /rɪˈspɛktəbəl/ *adjective*
1 Someone who is described as **respectable** looks or behaves like a decent, honest person; **respectable** behaviour is the kind that most people approve of: *He comes from a perfectly respectable family.* □ *At one time, it was not thought respectable for a woman to show her bare arms in public.* [*same as* **decent**] **2 Respectable** also describes levels, amounts or standards that are moderate or average, but good enough to be proud of: *It was a fairly respectable performance.* □ *My salary was, if not impressive, at least respectable.* [*same as* **acceptable**]

respectful /rɪˈspɛktfəl/ *adjective*
You are **respectful** towards someone when you show them respect: *I expect a more respectful attitude from my children.*

respective /rɪˈspɛktɪv/ *adjective*
Respective means belonging to or relating to each person or thing mentioned: *They're very good at their respective jobs, but I'm not sure they'd perform well doing each other's.* — *adverb* **respectively:** *John, Ian and Alan were given £10, £5 and £1 respectively.*

respiration /rɛspəˈreɪʃən/ *noun* (*uncount*; *technical*)
Respiration is breathing: *We're monitoring his heart beat and his respiration.*

respite /ˈrɛspaɪt/ or /ˈrɛspɪt/ *noun* (*uncount*; *formal*)
Respite is rest or relief from something unpleasant or

difficult: *The pain continued without respite for about two hours.*

resplendent /rɪˈsplɛndənt/ *adjective* (*literary*)
You describe someone as **resplendent** in a certain outfit if they are very smart and well dressed: *Alice, resplendent in her blue evening gown, attracted the eyes of everyone in the room.* [*same as* **dazzling**]

respond /rɪˈspɒnd/ *verb*: **responds, responding, responded**
You **respond** when you say or do something as a reaction or reply to what someone else has said or done: *'How do you respond to that criticism?' 'I respond by saying that we made the best of a bad situation.'* □ *When the parent slaps the child, the child will often respond by hitting back.* □ *The disease is responding very well to treatment.* [*same as* **react**]

response /rɪˈspɒns/ *noun* (*count or uncount*): **responses**
A **response** is something you say or do as a reaction or reply to what someone else has said or done: *Our response to the question was to reinforce our commitment to a United Europe.* □ *The decision was hastily taken in response to recent criticism.* [*same as* **reaction**]

responsibility /rɪspɒnsɪˈbɪlɪtɪ/ *noun*: **responsibilities**
1 (*uncount or count*) You have **responsibility** for something when you are expected to deal with it or take care of it: *I gave responsibility for foreign accounts to Mike, who accepted it willingly.* □ *I'm not the person to complain to; this is not my responsibility.* □ *I have a responsibility to my children to give them my love and my attention.* [*same as* **duty**] **2 Responsibilities** are duties: *How will she cope with the responsibilities of parenthood?* **3** (*uncount*) You accept **responsibility** for something that goes wrong when you agree that it is your fault and you should be blamed: *I don't think my department should assume responsibility.*

responsible /rɪˈspɒnsəbəl/ *adjective*
1 You are **responsible** for something when you are expected to deal with it or take care of it: *Sheila is responsible for ordering new books.* □ *Teachers are responsible for the welfare of children in their care.* **2** You are **responsible** for something that goes wrong when it is your fault and you are to blame; the cause of, or the reason for, something is what is **responsible** for it: *Which of you is responsible for this mess?* □ *If it fails, we'll hold you personally responsible.* □ *We can't simply say that poverty is solely responsible for crime; there are clearly other influences.* **3** A **responsible** job involves many important duties and decisions: *This is a very responsible position.* **4** A **responsible** person is someone you can trust to behave sensibly. [*same as* **conscientious**] — *adverb* **responsibly:** *She has acted thoroughly responsibly throughout.*

responsive /rɪˈspɒnsɪv/ *adjective*
Someone who is **responsive** reacts quickly and with great energy, emotion or effect: *He's the most responsive partner a dancer could want.* □ *The disease was much more responsive to the second drug.* □ *The steering on this car is much more responsive.* [*same as* **sensitive**]

rest[1] /rɛst/ *noun*; *verb*
▻ ***noun***
1 (*uncount or count*) You have a **rest** when you spend time doing nothing active: *Let's get some rest before the next match.* **2** Something used as a support, especially for a part of your body, is often called a **rest**: *a car seat with an adjustable headrest.*
▻ ***verb***: **rests, resting, rested**
1 You **rest** when you spend time doing nothing active: *You should be resting in bed.* □ *Do you feel rested after that sleep?* □ *Put the bags down and rest your arms for a while.* **2** One thing **rests** on another when it lies on or against it: *She lay next to me with her head resting on my chest.* □ *The spade was resting against a wall.* **3** One thing **rests** on another if it depends on it: *My whole argument rests on the fact that she never intended to do it.* **4** You say that you want to let something **rest** when you don't want to discuss it any more or do any more about it: *Let the matter rest there.*
▻ ***phrase*** You are **at rest** if you are no longer worrying: *We hoped this news would set your mind at rest.* □ *It would put my mind at rest to know that she had arrived safely.*

rest[2] /rɛst/ *noun* (*used in the singular*)
The **rest** of something, or the **rest** of a group, is the remaining part or members of it: *I'd rather not spend the rest of my working life in an office.* □ *The rest of the country will have showers and sunny intervals.* □ *You think your husband is different and then you discover he's just like all the rest.* □ *She took the guests home while the rest of us washed up.* [compare **remainder**]

restaurant /ˈrɛstərɒnt/ *noun*: **restaurants**
A **restaurant** is a place where you can buy and eat a meal: *one of the restaurants in the high street* □ *Does the hotel have its own restaurant?* □ *a fast-food restaurant.*

restful /ˈrɛstfəl/ *adjective*
Something that is **restful** makes you feel calm or relaxed: *The gardens have a very restful atmosphere.* □ *We spent a restful afternoon reading the papers.* [*same as* **relaxing**]

restless /ˈrɛstləs/ *adjective*
You are **restless** when you are unable to stay still or quiet, because you are nervous or worried, or because you are bored and want to do something: *I get restless if I stay in the same job for too long.* □ *We had a very restless night's sleep.* [*same as* **agitated**; *opposite* **calm**] — *noun* (*uncount*) **restlessness:** *There was an atmosphere of restlessness in the room.* [*same as* **agitation**]

restore /rɪˈstɔː(r)/ *verb*: **restores, restoring, restored**
1 You **restore** something old and dirty or broken when you clean or repair it to bring it back into its original condition: *A number of disused council buildings are being restored.* □ *She restores old paintings at the museum.* [*same as* **renovate**] **2** You **restore** something when you bring it back, especially so that normal or proper conditions return: *The headmaster was called to restore order in the classroom.* □ *Her health should be fully restored within a few weeks.* □ *Hope for the future has been restored.* **3** (*formal*) You **restore** something lost or stolen to someone when you give it back to them. — *noun* (*uncount*) **restoration** /rɛstəˈreɪʃən/: *the restoration of historic monuments* □ *We are working towards the restoration of peace on our streets.* [*same as* **recovery**]

restrain /rɪˈstreɪn/ *verb*: **restrains, restraining, restrained**
1 You **restrain** someone when you prevent them from doing something: *We are restrained by law from taking the matter further.* □ *He couldn't restrain himself from telling the truth.* **2** You **restrain** something when you keep it under control and prevent it from growing or spreading: *His anger was barely restrained.*

restraint /rɪˈstreɪnt/ *noun*: **restraints**
1 Restraints are controls or limitations, things that prevent you from doing something: *There are certainly legal restraints on their freedom.* [*same as* **restriction**] **2** (*uncount*) You show **restraint** when you keep your anger or other emotions under control and don't

show them: *'Let's try again', she urged, not without restraint.*

restrict /rɪ'strɪkt/ *verb*: **restricts, restricting, restricted**
You **restrict** something when you limit or control it: *Non-members are restricted to one ticket each.* □ *We decided not to restrict the number of applications, in order to give everyone a chance.* □ *Rather than attempt to give a worldwide view, I will restrict myself to what is known and thought in this country alone.* □ *The number of possibilities is therefore quite restricted.* [*same as* **confine**]

restriction /rɪ'strɪkʃən/ *noun*: **restrictions**
1 Restrictions are rules that control or limit something: *Are there restrictions on the number of people who can apply?* **2** You describe something that prevents you from acting or behaving in a certain way as a **restriction**: *Parenthood certainly places restrictions on what you can do with your evenings.* [*same as* **limitation**]

result /rɪ'zʌlt/ *noun*; *verb*
▻ ***noun***: **results**
1 The **result** of something is what happens because of it: *She commented on my hair, with the result that I became even more self-conscious.* □ *As a result of staying an extra day, I was able to gain some valuable information.* □ *I tried to dye my own hair, with frightening results.* [*same as* **effect**] **2** The **result** of a contest, especially a sports match, is a statement of the points that were scored by each player or team, or simply a statement of who won. **3** A student's exam **results** are the marks or grades they achieve: *You need better results in the summer if you're going to university.*
▻ ***verb***: **results, resulting, resulted**
1 One thing **results** from another when it happens because of it: *You could argue that her sense of insecurity results from growing up in an unstable family environment.* [*same as* **arise, stem**] **2** Something **results** in what happens because of it: *Carelessness usually results in mistakes.* □ *the blow on the head and the resulting headache.*

resultant /rɪ'zʌltənt/ *adjective* (*formal*)
Resultant describes things that happen because of others: *increased levels of funding and the resultant improvements in hospital treatment.*

resume /rɪ'zjuːm/ *verb*: **resumes, resuming, resumed**
1 Something **resumes** when it begins again or returns: *Normal service will be resumed as soon as possible.* □ *The performance will resume after a short interval.* **2** (*formal*) You **resume** your seat when you return to it.

résumé /'rɛzəmeɪ/ *noun* (*AmE*): **résumés**
Your **résumé** is your CV.

resumption /rɪ'zʌmpʃən/ *noun* (*uncount or used in the singular*)
There is a **resumption** of something when it begins again: *the resumption of peace talks between the warring factions.*

resurgence /rɪ'sɜːdʒəns/ *noun* (*used in the singular*)
There is a **resurgence** of something when it begins to happen again, often in a stronger or more intense form than before: *the resurgence of violence in the townships.*

resurrect /rɛzə'rɛkt/ *verb*: **resurrects, resurrecting, resurrected**
1 A person **is resurrected** when they are brought back to life after being dead. **2** You say that something **has been resurrected** when it is brought back into use or operation again, after people thought it had finished or been forgotten for good: *They resurrected the old idea of building a supermarket there.* [*same as* **revive**] — *noun* (*uncount*) **resurrection** /rɛzə'rɛkʃən/: *the resurrection of long-abandoned customs and traditions.*

resuscitate /rɪ'sʌsɪteɪt/ *verb*: **resuscitates, resuscitating, resuscitated**
You **resuscitate** someone who is unconscious when you bring them back to consciousness: *They were trained to resuscitate accident victims.*

retail /'riːteɪl/ *adjective or adverb*
Retail goods are sold in shops to ordinary customers, rather than by factories to businesses or people who own shops: *a retail price that was three times the wholesale price* □ *If it costs £30 retail, the wholesale price could be as little as £5 or £6.*

retain /rɪ'teɪn/ *verb* (*formal*): **retains, retaining, retained**
You **retain** something when you keep it: *They've managed to retain possession of the ball.* □ *She's retained some degree of pride in her family's achievements.* □ *Wooden greenhouses retain heat better than aluminium ones.* [*opposite* **release**; see also **retention**]

retaliate /rɪ'talɪeɪt/ *verb*: **retaliates, retaliating, retaliated**
You **retaliate** when you react to an attack of some kind by attacking in a similar way: *She accused him of robbing his customers, and he retaliated by saying she was deceiving the people who read her newspaper articles.* — *noun* (*uncount*) **retaliation** /rɪtalɪ'eɪʃən/: *They admitted planting the bomb in retaliation for recent attacks in Loyalist areas.*

retarded /rɪ'tɑːdɪd/ *adjective* (*rather old*)
Someone who has a much lower level of intelligence than people normally have is sometimes described as **retarded**: *a group of mentally retarded children.*

retch /rɛtʃ/ *verb*: **retches, retching, retched**
You **retch** when your stomach, throat and mouth make the movements of being sick, but you are not actually sick: *The foul smell made us retch.*

retention /rɪ'tɛnʃən/ *noun* (*uncount; formal*)
The **retention** of something is the act of keeping or retaining it: *We support the retention of the right to consult a lawyer if you've been accused of a crime.*

rethink /riː'θɪŋk/ *verb*: **rethinks, rethinking, rethought**
You **rethink** something when you think of ways you could change it: *We urge the government to rethink its policy on immigration.*

reticent /'rɛtɪsənt/ *adjective*
You are **reticent** about something when you don't say very much about it, especially if you don't say what you really think about it or don't tell everything you know about it: *I was a shy and reticent student in those days.* □ *Some companies are rather reticent in giving information on their working methods.* — *noun* (*uncount*) **reticence:** *We were a little surprised by her reticence.*

retire /rɪ'taɪə(r)/ *verb*: **retires, retiring, retired**
1 You **retire** when you stop working for ever, usually because you are old enough to receive a pension: *She plans to retire at 50.* □ *They wondered if some of the older workers could be retired early.* □ *Our third contestant is a retired teacher.* **2** (*formal*) To **retire** is to go to bed. **3** (*formal*) You **retire** somewhere when you leave one room or place to go to another: *The men retired to the billiard room.*

retirement /rɪ'taɪəmənt/ *noun* (*uncount*)
Your **retirement** is the point when you permanently stop working, or the period of your life after this point: *She came to me just a few weeks before my retirement.* □ *How will you spend your retirement?* □ *Have you organized a retirement pension?*

retiring /rɪ'taɪərɪŋ/ *adjective* (*formal*)
You describe someone as **retiring** if they are shy and

tend not to like talking to or meeting other people: *His wife was a quiet, retiring young woman.* [*same as* **shy**]

retort /rɪ'tɔːt/ *verb*; *noun*

▻ ***verb***: **retorts, retorting, retorted**

You **retort** when you answer someone sharply or angrily: *'I certainly will not!', he retorted.* ▫ *Marjorie retorted that she did not wish to be involved.*

▻ ***noun***: **retorts:** *I was taken aback by the ferocity of her retort.*

retract /rɪ'trakt/ *verb*: **retracts, retracting, retracted**

1 You **retract** something you have said when you say that you did not seriously mean it, or you accept that you should not have said it: *Will the minister retract his unjustified criticism of the party chairman?* [*same as* **withdraw**] **2** Something, especially part of an animal's body, **retracts** when it it is able to be pulled back or inside so that it no longer sticks out: *It retracts like a cat's claws.* —*adjective* **retractable** /rɪ'traktəbəl/: *a razor with a retractable blade.*

retreat /rɪ'triːt/ *verb*; *noun*

▻ ***verb***: **retreats, retreating, retreated**

1 You **retreat** when you move back or move away: *The attacker moves towards her and she retreats onto the balcony.* **2** Soldiers **retreat** when they move back from enemies who are moving forward to attack them. **3** You say that someone **retreats** when they decide not to do what they said or promised they would do: *Here is a government yet again retreating from its obligations to this country.* [*same as* **shrink**]

▻ ***noun***: **retreats**

1 A **retreat** is an act of retreating: *As the dog approached, we beat a hasty retreat to the other side of the wall.* ▫ *For the Fifth Army, this was a humiliating retreat.* ▫ *It represents a dishonourable retreat from promises that were given to our members.* **2** You might describe a quiet, private place as a **retreat**: *They spent the weekend in their mountain retreat in Virginia.*

▻ ***phrase*** (*often humorous*) You **beat a retreat** when you run away from someone or something: *He beat a hasty retreat when he saw me approaching.*

retribution /rɛtrɪ'bjuːʃən/ *noun* (*uncount*; *formal*)

Retribution is punishment you deserve: *For those who sin, there will be retribution from God Almighty.*

retrieve /rɪ'triːv/ *verb* (*formal*): **retrieves, retrieving, retrieved**

1 You **retrieve** something when you get it back after losing it or leaving it somewhere: *They managed to retrieve her handbag from the dog's mouth.* **2** You **retrieve** the situation when you do something that makes it better or brings it back to normal: *A delicious dinner retrieved what had been an otherwise disastrous day.* [*same as* **save**]

retrograde /'rɛtrəgreɪd/ *adjective*

You describe an action as **retrograde** if you think it makes a situation worse, not better: *The reintroduction of any prison-like establishment for children is certainly a retrograde step.* [*opposite* **progressive**]

retrospective /rɛtrə'spɛktɪv/ *adjective* (*technical*)

A **retrospective** law affects things that happened before the time the law was introduced: *Are these new regulations retrospective?*

return /rɪ'tɜːn/ *verb*; *noun*; *adjective*

▻ ***verb***: **returns, returning, returned**

1 a You **return** to a place when you go back there after being away: *Which year did you return to Britain?* ▫ *Robert returned home shortly after midnight.* ▫ *We fly out on Thursday and return the following Tuesday.* ▫ *I returned to my car to find a policeman standing beside it.* ▫ *He went out jogging and never returned.* **b** A situation, condition or feeling **returns** when it comes back again after being absent for some time: *Towards the end of April the cold weather returned.* ▫ *If the nausea returns, take another tablet.* ▫ *The search will be resumed as soon as daylight returns.* **c** You **return** to something when you begin doing it or discussing it again, after a pause or break: *I had a quick drink with them and then returned to my essay.* ▫ *He returned to his digging after tea.* ▫ *We'll return to the subject of dream interpretation in next week's class.* ▫ *Teachers are returning to teaching grammar.* **d** A person or thing **returns** to a previous state when they get back into that state again: *Labour returned to power in 1964.* ▫ *Things are returning to normal again.* ▫ *I'm glad to see you've returned to your senses.*

2 a You **return** something you have borrowed or taken when you give it back; you **return** something sent to you when you send it back; you **return** something to its place when you put it back there after removing it: *She still hasn't returned the jacket I lent her.* ▫ *Books should be returned to the library within three weeks.* ▫ *Please return the completed order form to us in the envelope provided.* ▫ *She returned the letter to its envelope.* ▫ *Please return reference books to their shelves after use.* **b** You **return** someone's feelings if you feel the same about them as they do about you: *He was perfectly aware that she returned his affection.* **c** You **return** someone's action or gesture when you do the same to or for them as they have just done to or for you: *Thanks so much for your help; I hope to return the favour soon.* ▫ *She realized he was gazing curiously across at her and she returned his gaze briefly.* **d** In a game such as tennis, you **return** the ball when you hit it back to your opponent.

3 (*legal*) In a court of law, a jury **returns** a verdict when they say what their verdict is: *The jury returned a verdict of guilty.*

▻ ***noun***: **returns**

1 (*used in the singular*) A **return** is an act of coming back, of returning to a state or activity, or of giving or sending something back: *On my return to the house I found the front door unlocked.* ▫ *Many still wish for the return of Communism.* ▫ *We must pray for her return to complete health.* ▫ *the return to grammar-teaching in schools* ▫ *The kidnappers are demanding £1 million for the return of the hostages.* **2** (*count or uncount*; *tennis*) A **return** is a shot sending the ball back to your opponent: *She hit some amazing returns.* ▫ *practising her return of service.* **3** A **return** is also a return ticket: *I bought a second-class return to Long Eaton.* **4** (*uncount or count*) The **return** on money you invest is the profit you make: *We had expected a higher rate of return.* ▫ *The returns on our investment are not as high as we expected.*

▻ ***adjective***

1 A **return** ticket allows you to travel to a place and back again. **2** Your **return** journey is your journey home, or back to the place you started from. **3** You make a **return** shot in tennis when you hit the ball back to your opponent.

▻ ***phrases*** **1** You reply to a letter **by return** when, as soon as you receive it, you write a reply and post it. **2** You do something **in return for** what someone has done for you if you do it because of what they did for you: *I don't expect anything in return.* **3** You say '**Many happy returns**' or '**Many happy returns of the day**' to someone on their birthday to wish them a happy birthday. **4** You reach the **point of no return** in some activity when you have to continue with it because it is too late to stop or give up.

reunion /rɪ'juːnjən/ *noun*: **reunions**

A **reunion** is a meeting of people, for example relatives

or friends, who have not seen each other for some time: *Christmas is always something of a family reunion.*

reunite /riːjʊˈnaɪt/ *verb*: **reunites, reuniting, reunited**
People **are reunited** when they meet after not seeing each other for some time: *You'll soon be reunited with your wife and family.*

rev /rɛv/ *verb* (*informal*): **revs, revving, revved**
You **rev** the engine of a car or other vehicle when you press the accelerator to make the engine run faster, usually when the car itself is not moving: *Outside in the street, a car was revving up.*

reveal /rɪˈviːl/ *verb*: **reveals, revealing, revealed**
1 You **reveal** something when you tell it to people: *The details of the policy have not yet been revealed.* □ *She revealed to me that she was planning to leave her husband.* [*same as* **divulge, announce**] **2** You **reveal** something when you show it or allow it to be seen: *He opened his shirt a little, revealing a large scar on his chest.* □ *Jemima has revealed a talent for solving people's marital problems.*
[*same as* **display**; *opposite* **conceal**]

revealing /rɪˈviːlɪŋ/ *adjective*
1 What someone does or says is **revealing** when it reveals something that you did not know: *a very revealing interview.* **2** Clothes, usually a woman's clothes, are **revealing** if they reveal parts of the body that are normally covered up: *a rather revealing dress.*

revel /ˈrɛvəl/ *verb*: **revels, revelling** (*AmE* **reveling**), **revelled** (*AmE* **reveled**)

> ***phrasal verb***
> You **revel in** something that you delight in or enjoy very much: *The children revelled in all the excitement.* [*same as* **delight in**]

revelation /rɛvəˈleɪʃən/ *noun*: **revelations**
You can refer to something surprising or particularly interesting that you find out as a **revelation**; you also describe an experience that reveals something like this as a **revelation**: *His autobiography contains some startling revelations about his private life.* □ *My week down the mine was nothing short of a revelation.*

revelry /ˈrɛvəlrɪ/ *noun* (*literary, old*)
Revelry is noisy, lively fun or enjoyment: *an evening of drunken revelry.*

revenge /rɪˈvɛndʒ/ *noun*; *verb*
▻ ***noun*** (*uncount*)
You get your **revenge** on someone who has harmed you when you harm them in return: *What good would it do to take revenge on them?* □ *All I knew was that I wanted revenge.*
▻ ***verb***: **revenges, revenging, revenged:** *She promised to revenge herself on her father's killers.*

revenue /ˈrɛvənjuː/ *noun* (*uncount; technical*)
Revenue is money you earn from doing work, or money that an organization such as a business company or a government receives from people: *The magazine has had to cope with a fall in the level of revenue from subscriptions.* [*same as* **income**]

reverberate /rɪˈvɜːbəreɪt/ *verb*: **reverberates, reverberating, reverberated**
1 A sound **reverberates** when it produces several loud echoes: *The noise of the explosion reverberated through the streets.* **2** (*literary*) You say that an event or incident **reverberates** when it creates such a strong impression or effect that everyone is talking about it: *The news of her resignation has reverberated throughout the parliament building.*

revere /rɪˈvɪə(r)/ *verb* (*formal*): **reveres, revering, revered**
Someone **is revered** when others respect and admire them very much: *an evening with his revered former college master.*

Reverend /ˈrɛvərənd/ *adjective*
Reverend is a title used before the name of a priest: *The service will be conducted by the Reverend John McCallum.*

reversal see **reverse**.

reverse /rɪˈvɜːs/ *verb*; *noun*; *adjective*
▻ ***verb***: **reverses, reversing, reversed**
1 You use **reverse** in many different ways to refer to changes from one position, state or direction to its opposite: *The order has been completely reversed, with the last now coming first and first coming last.* □ *The flow of water through the gates can be reversed.* □ *Traditional family roles were reversed, so that the father found himself looking after the house and the children.* □ *Is there any way that this decision could be reversed?* **2** You **reverse** a car or other vehicle when you drive it backwards: *The lorry reversed into a postbox.* — *noun* (*uncount or count*) **reversal:** *a humiliating reversal of government policy* □ *psychologists monitoring experiments in role-reversal.*
▻ ***noun*** (*used in the singular*)
The **reverse** of something is the opposite or contrary of it: *Men are supposed to be strong, but most women know that the reverse is often true.*
▻ ***adjective:*** *The cards were in reverse order.*
▻ ***phrases*** **1** Things happens **in reverse** when they happen in an order opposite to the usual or expected order: *By running the film in reverse, we create the impression that the man is catching the table.* [*same as* **backwards**] **2** You **reverse the charges** when you make a telephone call that is paid for by the person you are calling, not by you yourself.

reversible /rɪˈvɜːsɪbəl/ *adjective*
A decision or process that is **reversible** can be cancelled so that the situation returns to its previous state: *Ideally women would like a reliable sterilization operation that would be easily reversible.* □ *The decision is reversible should you at any time change your mind.*

revert /rɪˈvɜːt/ *verb* (*formal*): **reverts, reverting, reverted**
Something **reverts** to a former state or condition when it goes back to it: *After the laird's death, ownership of the house reverted to my family.* □ *Many ex-prisoners revert to a life of crime.* [*same as* **return**]

review /rɪˈvjuː/ *noun*; *verb*
▻ ***noun***: **reviews**
1 (*count or uncount*) You carry out a **review** of something when you examine it in order to check its progress and decide whether any changes need to be made: *A review of civil service spending is already taking place.* □ *The whole taxation system is under review at present.* □ *My contract comes up for review at the end of September.* [*same as* **survey, reconsideration**] **2** A **review** of something such as a book or a film is a newspaper article in which a critic gives their opinion of it: *The play has received fairly good reviews.* □ *She writes book reviews for 'The Times'.*
▻ ***verb***: **reviews, reviewing, reviewed:** *The milk-bottling system will need to be reviewed.* □ *After reviewing the situation carefully, we have decided that some members will be asked to leave.* □ *I was given the job of reviewing all the films that appeared during the festival.*

revise /rɪˈvaɪz/ *verb*: **revises, revising, revised**
1 You **revise** something when you examine it again to check for faults and make changes to correct or

improve it: *Our atlases have had to be revised to take account of the changing political situation in Eastern Europe.* **2** You **revise** for an exam when you prepare for it by re-reading notes and texts: *She's staying at home to revise.*

revision /rɪ'vɪʒən/ *noun*
1 (*uncount or used in the singular*) The **revision** of something is the act of revising it: *It was clear that a complete revision of factory regulations was needed.* [*same as* **update**] **2** (*uncount*) **Revision** is preparation for an exam by re-reading notes and texts: *How much revision do you need to do?*

revitalize or **revitalise** /riː'vaɪtəlaɪz/ *verb*: **revitalizes, revitalizing, revitalized**
To **revitalize** something is to make it more lively, active or appealing, often in order to make people more interested in it: *This has revitalized the whole political campaign.* [*same as* **revive**]

revival /rɪ'vaɪvəl/ *noun*: **revivals**
There is a **revival** of something when it becomes active or popular again: *Classical music is enjoying something of a revival at the moment.* □ *We are witnessing a revival of interest in herbal medicine.* [*same as* **renaissance**]

revive /rɪ'vaɪv/ *verb*: **revives, reviving, revived**
1 To **revive** something is to make it active, interesting or popular again: *Some of the more traditional customs are being revived.* **2** You **revive** someone who is unconscious when you bring them back to consciousness: *Attempts to revive him proved unsuccessful and he was declared dead at 6.05 pm.*

revoke /rɪ'voʊk/ *verb*: **revokes, revoking, revoked**
To **revoke** something is to cancel it or make it no longer valid: *He had his licence revoked.*

revolt /rɪ'voʊlt/ *noun* (*count or uncount*): **revolts**
A **revolt** is an attempt by people to take political power away from the existing government, using force and violence: *There were signs that an armed revolt was being planned.* □ *the sight of students and workers in revolt together.* [*same as* **rebellion**]

revolting /rɪ'voʊltɪŋ/ *adjective*
You describe something as **revolting** if you think it is very nasty or offensive, or if it is disgusting: *He's a nasty revolting little man who is a danger to decent people.* □ *The whole cupboard began to smell positively revolting.* [*same as* **disgusting**]

revolution /rɛvə'luːʃən/ *noun* (*count or uncount*): **revolutions**
1 A **revolution** is an act of using force and violence to change an existing government or political system: *In the 18th century, we had the French Revolution.* □ *fringe political groups advocating revolution.* **2** A **revolution** is also a complete change in anything, especially in the methods or equipment used in it: *The Thatcher government brought about a revolution in traditional relations between politicians and the unions.* □ *a technological revolution.*

revolutionary /rɛvə'luːʃənrɪ/ *adjective*; *noun*
▻ ***adjective***
1 Revolutionary ideas or methods are entirely new and different, bringing about a complete change in something: *His use of colours and textiles was revolutionary.*
2 Revolutionary activities are designed to bring about a political revolution: *They published a number of revolutionary pamphlets.*
▻ ***noun***: **revolutionaries:** *You have been described as a revolutionary; do you think that's fair?*

revolutionize or **revolutionise** /rɛvə'luːʃənaɪz/ *verb*: **revolutionizes, revolutionizing, revolutionized**
To **revolutionize** something is to introduce many new and different methods or ideas that change it completely: *The discovery of the silicon chip revolutionized the computer industry.* [*same as* **transform**]

revolve /rɪ'vɒlv/ *verb*: **revolves, revolving, revolved**
1 Something that **revolves** moves or turns around a central point: *It was discovered that the Earth revolved around the Sun.* □ *the revolving door at the entrance to the building.* [*same as* **rotate**] **2** Something **revolves** around what is the most important feature or part of it: *Employers imagine that everyone's life revolves around their job.* □ *The essay revolves around the theme of betrayal.*

revolver /rɪ'vɒlvə(r)/ *noun*: **revolvers**
A **revolver** is a hand-held gun: *I reached into the drawer for my revolver.*

revulsion /rɪ'vʌlʃən/ *noun* (*uncount; formal*)
You feel **revulsion** for something that you think is extremely nasty or completely disgusting: *These are crimes that society regards with complete revulsion.* [*same as* **disgust**]

reward /rɪ'wɔːd/ *noun*; *verb*
▻ ***noun*** (*count or uncount*): **rewards**
A **reward** is something you get or are given in return for something good or useful you have done: *I don't need money; knowing I do a useful job is reward enough.* □ *The victim's family have offered a reward of £5000 for important information about the killer.*
▻ ***verb***: **rewards, rewarding, rewarded:** *The officer is to be rewarded for his efforts with promotion to the rank of Inspector.* □ *We give love, attention and comfort to our children and are rewarded with disobedience and bad behaviour.*

rewarding /rɪ'wɔːdɪŋ/ *adjective*
Something is **rewarding** when it gives you personal pleasure or satisfaction: *It can be a very rewarding job.* [*same as* **fulfilling**]

rhetoric /'rɛtərɪk/ *noun* (*uncount*)
Speech or writing that contains long, formal or literary words and phrases is sometimes referred to as **rhetoric**, especially if it has very little real meaning and is intended simply to impress people: *the usual political rhetoric.*

rhetorical /rɪ'tɒrɪkəl/ *adjective*
A **rhetorical** question is used to make an impressive-sounding statement, and is not meant to be answered: *You have misunderstood me; my question was a rhetorical one.*

rheumatism /'ruːmətɪzm/ *noun* (*uncount*)
Rheumatism is a disease that causes painful swelling of a person's joints and muscles, making them sore to move.

rhino /'raɪnoʊ/ *noun* (*informal*): **rhinos**
A **rhino** is a rhinoceros.

rhinoceros /raɪ'nɒsərəs/ *noun*: **rhinoceroses**
A **rhinoceros** is a large, plant-eating animal with thick grey skin and one or two horns on its nose, found in Africa and Asia.

rhombus /'rɒmbəs/ *noun*: **rhombuses** or **rhombi** /'rɒmbaɪ/
A **rhombus** is a flat shape with four straight sides and four angles that are not right angles. [*same as* **diamond**; see picture at **shape**]

rhubarb /'ruːbɑːb/ *noun* (*uncount*)
Rhubarb is a plant with large flat leaves, and red stems that are eaten as a fruit, often cooked: *a jar of rhubarb jam.*

rhyme /raɪm/ *verb*; *noun*
▻ ***verb***: **rhymes, rhyming, rhymed**
Words that **rhyme** sound like each other, especially

words whose last sounds are the same: *Only the most useless poet would rhyme 'ghost' with 'toast'.*
▷ ***noun*** (*count or uncount*): **rhymes**
A **rhyme** is a word that sounds like another, or a pair of words that have a similar sound; **rhyme** is poetry in which rhymes are used.

rhythm /rɪðm/ *noun* (*count or uncount*): **rhythms**
A **rhythm** is a regular, repeated pattern of sounds or movements, or any kind of regular, repeated pattern: *The rhythm of the poem speeds up in the last verse.* □ *a dancer with an excellent sense of rhythm* □ *Both players seemed to lose their concentration and their rhythm in the second game.*

rhythmic /'rɪðmɪk/ *adjective*
A **rhythmic** sound or movement is repeated to form a regular pattern: *We listened to the rhythmic beating of the rain on the windows.*

rib /rɪb/ *noun*: **ribs**
Your **ribs** are the curved bones that form your chest: *He had been kicked in the stomach and ribs.*

ribbon /'rɪbən/ *noun* (*count or uncount*): **ribbons**
A **ribbon** is a long narrow strip of fabric used for decorating clothes, or tying up hair and parcels: *a piece of pink ribbon.*

rib cage /'rɪb keɪdʒ/ *noun*: **rib cages**
Your **rib cage** is the set of ribs that form your chest.

rice /raɪs/ *noun* (*uncount*)
Rice is a kind of food in the form of small brown or white grains that swell when you cook them: *a bowl of boiled rice.*

rich /rɪtʃ/ *adjective*: **richer**, **richest**
1 Someone who is **rich** has a lot of money, property or possessions: *She's looking for a rich husband.* [*same as* **wealthy**; *opposite* **poor**] **2 Rich** food contains a lot of fat or sugar: *The pudding was a little too rich for me.* **3** To be **rich** in something is to contain a lot of it: *It was discovered that the bed of the North Sea was rich in oil.* □ *an area rich with bird life.* **4 Rich** soil contains a lot of the minerals that make plants grow well. [*opposite* **infertile**] **5** Bright, deep colours are sometimes described as **rich**: *curtains of rich red velvet.* — *noun* (*uncount*) **richness:** *the richness of mineral deposits in the area* □ *We were impressed by the richness of plant growth.*

riches /'rɪtʃɪz/ *noun* (*plural*; *literary*)
You refer to large amounts of money or very valuable things as **riches**.

richly /'rɪtʃlɪ/ *adverb*
1 Richly means with rich colours or impressive designs: *a large, richly decorated fruit bowl.* **2** You say that what someone receives is **richly** deserved if you think they fully deserve it: *The rewards and recognition that he so richly deserved came late in life to him.*

rickety /'rɪkətɪ/ *adjective*
You describe something such as a piece of furniture as **rickety** if it is so old or badly made that it seems likely to collapse: *We wondered if such a rickety bridge would take the weight of the truck.* [*same as* **precarious**]

rid /rɪd/ *verb*; *adjective*
▷ ***verb***: **rids**, **ridding**, **rid**
1 You **rid** a place of something unpleasant or unwanted when you manage to remove it: *Scientists are working night and day to rid the world of this dreadful virus.* **2** You **rid** yourself of unacceptable feelings or characteristics when you do something to stop yourself having them: *We must try to rid ourselves of all hatred and prejudice.* [*same as* **purge**]
▷ ***adjective***
You are **rid** of something troublesome when you no longer have it: *I'm glad to be rid of the responsibility.* □ *It was a relief to be rid of his company.* [*opposite* **burdened**]
▷ ***phrase*** You **get rid of** something that you do not want when you do something so as not to have it any longer: *It would do you good to get rid of some of that excess weight.* □ *We got rid of that old sofa by sending it to the saleroom.*

riddance /'rɪdəns/ *noun* (*uncount*; *informal*)
You say 'good **riddance**' when you are glad you have got rid of something or someone: *I say it's good riddance to anyone who's refused to fight with us.*

ridden /'rɪdən/ *verb*
Ridden is the past participle of **ride**.

riddle /'rɪdəl/ *noun*: **riddles**
1 A **riddle** is a puzzle with words, often in the form of a question mysteriously or misleadingingly describing something to be identified: *He was an odd character who spoke in riddles.* **2** You refer to someone or something as a **riddle** if they are mysterious or difficult to understand: *How the murderer had entered the house was a complete riddle.* [*same as* **mystery**, **enigma**]

ride /raɪd/ *verb*; *noun*
▷ ***verb***: **rides**, **riding**, **rode**, **ridden**
1 You **ride** a horse or a bicycle when you sit on it and control the way it moves: *He went riding across the field on the farmer's donkey.* □ *Have you ever ridden a motorbike?* **2** You **ride** on or in a vehicle when you travel on or in it: *I climbed inside while Holmes elected to ride up beside the coachman.* □ (*AmE*) *I rode the subway to the Lower East Side.* — *noun* **rider:** *One of the horses had unseated its rider.* □ *He's the most successful motorcycle rider this decade.*
▷ ***noun***: **rides**
1 You go for a **ride** on a horse or bicycle when you ride it: *We went for a ride on one of his old motorbikes.* □ *Halifax was only a ten-minute train ride away.* **2** A vehicle that gives a smooth **ride** is comfortable to travel in because you don't feel it moving: *It was a much bumpier ride in the old tractors.* **3** A **ride** is also a fairground entertainment in the form of some moving object that you ride on.
▷ ***phrase*** (*informal*) You say that someone **has taken** you **for a ride** if they have cheated or deceived you in some way.

> ***phrasal verb***
> Clothes **ride up** when they are pulled up out of position when you move your body: *My trousers kept riding up, exposing an expanse of white leg.*

ridge /rɪdʒ/ *noun*: **ridges**
1 A **ridge** is a narrow strip of land higher than the ground on either side of it, for example along the top of a mountain: *Then came the long climb up the icy north ridge.* **2** A **ridge** is also the top edge of something, especially the edge formed where the two sloping surfaces of a roof meet.

ridicule /'rɪdɪkjuːl/ *verb*; *noun*
▷ ***verb***: **ridicules**, **ridiculing**, **ridiculed**
You **ridicule** something when you criticize it as being silly or foolish: *It seems that some of the other boys were ridiculing his hairstyle.* [*same as* **mock**]
▷ ***noun*** (*uncount*) *My request for a bank loan was met with ridicule.* [*same as* **derision**]

rife /raɪf/ *adjective*
Something is **rife** when it is very common or wide-

spread: *The claim is that such racist attitudes are rife within the police force itself.* [*same as* **widespread**]

rifle[1] /ˈraɪfəl/ *noun*: **rifles**
A **rifle** is a powerful, accurate gun with a long barrel, that you hold against your shoulder to fire.

rifle[2] /ˈraɪfəl/ *verb*: **rifles, rifling, rifled**
1 Someone who **rifles** something searches through it and steals things from it: *I found Al rifling my desk.* **2** You **rifle** through things when you search through them quickly, looking for something: *It only took a few seconds to rifle through the files.* [*same as* **rummage**]

rift /rɪft/ *noun*: **rifts**
1 There is a **rift** between people when the friendship they had is broken by an argument or quarrel: *A rift had opened between Bejing and Moscow.* [*same as* **split**] **2** A **rift** is also a large, long crack or split in an area of land. [*same as* **fault**]

rig /rɪg/ *verb*; *noun*
▻ ***verb*** (*informal*): **rigs, rigging, rigged**
Someone who **rigs** something dishonestly controls the way it happens, so that it benefits them: *There were claims that the election had been rigged.* [*same as* **tamper with**]
▻ ***noun***: **rigs**
1 A **rig** is a large, platform-like structure that holds equipment for taking oil or gas from under the ground: *an oil rig.* **2** (*slang*) You refer to a set of equipment or clothes as your **rig**.

> ***phrasal verb*** (*informal*)
> You **rig** something **up** when you build it up from different parts: *The tent was soon rigged up.* □ *We managed to rig up a new aerial using copper wire and a coat hanger.* [*same as* **improvise**]

right[1] /raɪt/ *adjective*; *adverb*; *noun*; *verb*; *interjection*
▻ ***adjective***
1 Something is **right** if it is correct or accurate: *4 times 18 is 64; is that right?* □ *That total doesn't look right.* □ *the right answer* □ *Is that clock right?* □ *Do you have the right time?* □ *'You spell 'benefited' with one t, don't you?' 'That's right.'* [*same as* **correct**; *opposite* **wrong**] **2** You are **right** about something if what you think or say about it is correct: *You were right about 'manoeuvre'; it has got a 'u' in it.* □ *You're quite right; thanks for reminding me.* [*same as* **correct**; *opposite* **wrong**] **3** A choice or decision is **right** if it is the best, most suitable, or most appropriate one: *I hope I've made the right decision.* □ *Who would be the right person to advise me?* □ *I'm anxious to do the right thing.* □ *I don't think that hat looks right on you.* [*opposite* **wrong**] **4** You say that something is not **right** if you think there is a problem: *Things aren't right in that family.* [*opposite* **wrong**] **5** Something is in its **right** place when it is in the place where it is usually kept, or where it belongs: *I wish people would put things back in their right places.* [*same as* **proper**; *opposite* **wrong**] **6** You are **right** to do something if it is legally or morally justified: *You're right to resist unfair pressure.* □ *Can it be right for the emergency services to go on strike?* [*opposite* **wrong**] **7** The **right** side of a fabric or a piece of clothing is the side that is intended to be seen, or that faces outwards: *The mend won't show when the trousers are turned right side out.* [*opposite* **wrong**] **8** A **right** angle is a 90-degree angle, formed when a vertical line extends from a horizontal base. [compare **acute**, **obtuse**; see picture at **shape**] **9** The **right** people are the people who are socially important or have power and influence: *Success in the medical world depends, as elsewhere, on knowing the right people.* [*opposite* **wrong**] **10** (*informal*) **Right** emphasizes certain nouns such as 'mess' and 'fool': *I feel a right idiot.* [*same as* **absolute, complete**] — *adverb* **rightly:** *As you rightly point out, the statement is misleading.* □ *She quite rightly reported the matter to the police.*
▻ ***adverb***
Right is used **1** to emphasize that you mean exactly the place or moment mentioned: *She was standing right on the edge.* □ *Don't move; stay right there.* □ *He collapsed right in the middle of the meeting.* **2** to mean 'immediately' or 'without delay': *My new job starts right after Christmas.* □ *I'll be right back.* [*same as* **straight**] **3** to mean 'all the way': *The ring road takes you right round the town.* □ *It dropped right to the bottom.* [*same as* **straight**] **4** to mean 'correctly' or 'properly': *Can't you do anything right?* □ *I hope I've screwed it on right.* □ *Have I spelt your name right?* □ *I probably didn't pronounce it right.* [*opposite* **wrong**]
▻ ***noun***: **rights**
1 You have a **right** to something, or a **right** to do something, if it is morally or legally proper for you to have it or do it: *Everyone has a right to their own opinion.* □ *People have a right to worship as they choose.* □ *Women have died in the struggle for equal rights.* **2** (*uncount*) **Right** is what is just or morally good: *She appears to lack any sense of right and wrong.* □ *You have right on your side.* [*opposite* **wrong**]
▻ ***verb***: **rights, righting, righted**
1 You **right** something that has fallen or tipped over when you place it upright again; something **rights** itself when it returns to the upright position: *The rider was thrown sideways but managed to right himself.* **2** You **right** a wrong when you do something to reverse an unfair situation, or compensate for harm done.
▻ ***interjection***
You say **'Right'** **1** to agree to a request: *'You could clean the vegetables, Mike.' 'Right.'* **2** to acknowledge a piece of information: *'She isn't arriving till tomorrow.' 'Oh, right.'* **3** to get people's attention, *eg* at a new stage in the proceedings: *Right, what's next?* □ *Right, who wants more coffee?* **4** to obtain agreement or confirmation: *This is the front-door key, right?*
▻ ***phrases*** **1** You use **by rights** to suggest what should be the case, although it isn't: *By rights she ought to be sent to prison.* **2** You **get** something **right** when you deal with it correctly: *I hope they've got the date right this time.* **3** Things **go right** for you when you are successful. **4** You say someone **has no right to** do something if you think they ought not to do it: *She had no right to speak to you like that.* **5** You are **in the right** when what you are doing is morally or legally right. **6** You have a position or claim **in your own right** if you are entitled to it through your own ability or qualifications, rather than through other people's: *Lady Macbeth could have been queen in her own right.* **7** You **put** or **set** things **right** when you do something to adjust a bad or unfair situation, or compensate for harm done. **8** You **reserve the right to** do something when you announce that you will do it whenever necessary: *We reserve the right to appoint our own consultants.* **9** Something that is to be done **right away** or **right now** is to be done immediately. **10** The **rights and wrongs** of a situation are the moral issues involved in it. **11** You say in reference to someone's misfortune that it **serves them right** if you think that they deserved it: *It serves you right for interfering.* **12** You are **within your rights** in doing something if you are not breaking the law by doing it.

right[2] /raɪt/ *noun*; *adjective*; *adverb*
▻ ***noun***
1 (*used in the singular*) **Right** is the direction opposite to left; you turn to your **right** when you turn east after

facing north: *On my right is a man who needs no introduction.* □ *The car had to swerve to the right to avoid him.* □ *To our right is Magdalen College.* □ *Take the first turning to your right.* □ *Remember to drive on the right when you get off the ferry.* **2** (*with a singular or plural verb*) The **Right** refers to the people who support capitalism rather than socialism, or to their position: *The Right have suffered a severe defeat.* □ *members on the far right of the party.*

▻ ***adjective***
Your **right** side or your **right** hand is the one on the right: *One of the fingers on his right hand was missing.* □ *He had to have his right kidney removed.*

> Notice that although you refer to a part of the body that is one of a pair as, *eg*, *his right eye*, *my right big toe*, you usually use **right-hand** to refer to other things placed on the right: *the right-hand top drawer.*

▻ ***adverb:*** *We turned right just past the hotel.* □ *Look right, left, and right again before crossing.*

righteous /ˈraɪtʃəs/ *adjective* (*formal*)
You describe someone as **righteous** if they behave in a way that is morally very good or correct: *He was a righteous man.* [*same as* **virtuous**] — *noun* (*uncount*) **righteousness:** *Don't stray from the path of righteousness.* [*same as* **goodness**]

rightful /ˈraɪtfʊl/ *adjective* (*formal*)
Rightful describes things that people have a right, or deserve, to do or have: *The stolen items were returned to their rightful owner.* □ *My rightful place is as head of the household.* — *adverb* **rightfully:** *I am only claiming what is rightfully mine.*

right-hand /ˈraɪt hand/ *adjective*
Right-hand describes things on the right side: *The right-hand mirror was broken.* □ *the painting on the right-hand side of the window.*

right-handed /ˈraɪt handɪd/ *adjective*
A **right-handed** person tends to prefer using their right hand to do things with, rather than their left hand: *Many of the world's top tennis-players are not right-handed.*

rightly /ˈraɪtlɪ/ *adverb* (*sentence adverb*)
You use **rightly** when you are talking about behaviour that is fair, or is legally or morally proper or correct: *He should rightly have been given the first choice.* □ *Jan has rightly pointed out that we should consider the family's wishes first.*

right-minded /ˈraɪt maɪndɪd/ *adjective*
A **right-minded** person is someone who has fair, honest or sensible attitudes or opinions: *No right-minded person would think this was reasonable.*

right of way /raɪt əv ˈweɪ/ *noun*: **rights of way**
1 A **right of way** is a public road or path going through privately owned land. **2** (*uncount*) As a driver at a junction, you have **right of way** when vehicles coming from other directions must allow you to pass first. [*same as* **priority**]

right wing /ˈraɪt wɪŋ/ *noun* (*used in the singular, often adjectival*)
The **right wing** of a political party is the group of people who have the most conservative views: *This has angered some right-wing members.*

rigid /ˈrɪdʒɪd/ *adjective*
1 Something **rigid** is completely stiff and does not or cannot bend: *I stood in the dark doorway, rigid with fear.* □ *Her wrist was quite rigid; she had clearly been dead for several hours.* **2 Rigid** also describes people who are not willing to change their decisions, opinions or usual behaviour: *She was thoroughly rigid in her daily routine.* **3 Rigid** rules cannot be changed or ignored. [*opposite* **flexible**] — *noun* (*uncount*) **rigidity** /rɪˈdʒɪdɪtɪ/: *We were impressed by the rigidity of the model.* □ *The minister's rigidity on this issue frustrated and irritated his opponents.* [*opposite* **flexibility**] — *adverb* **rigidly:** *a custom which has been rigidly observed for decades.*

rigmarole /ˈrɪgməroʊl/ *noun* (*used in the singular*)
You refer to an irritatingly long, complicated series of actions or procedures as a **rigmarole**: *I had to go through the whole rigmarole of re-applying for the licence.*

rigorous /ˈrɪgərəs/ *adjective*
Rigorous describes things that are done in a very careful, thorough or strict way: *Every aircraft undergoes the most rigorous mechanical inspection before take-off.* □ *I hadn't expected them to be quite so rigorous in applying the rules.* [*same as* **thorough**]

rigours (*AmE* **rigors**) /ˈrɪgəz/ *noun* (*plural*; *literary*)
You refer to harsh or severe conditions as **rigours**: *We were not prepared for the rigours of an Alaskan winter.*

rim /rɪm/ *noun*: **rims**
1 The **rim** of something such as a cup or glass is its top edge: *Pour water into the glass until it is just level with the rim.* **2** The **rim** of something such as a wheel is its outside edge: *She wore an odd-looking pair of glasses with green rims.*

rind /raɪnd/ *noun* (*uncount or used in the singular*)
1 Rind is the hard outer covering on cheese or bacon: *Trim off the rind.* **2** The **rind** of fruits such as lemon is the skin or peel.

ring[1] /rɪŋ/ *noun*; *verb*
▻ ***noun***: **rings**
1 A **ring** is a small circle of gold, silver or some other metal, that you wear on your finger: *a wedding ring.* **2** Anything in the shape of a circle can be referred to as a **ring**: *Then slide the curtain rings on to the pole.* □ *The children sat in a ring round her.* **3** A **ring** is also a square area marked off by ropes, where boxers or wrestlers fight: *a boxing ring.* **4** The **rings** on a cooker are the circular plates or burners that you cook food on. [see picture at **kitchen**] **5** You refer to a group of people as a **ring**, especially different groups of criminals working together: *Customs officials claim to have smashed the biggest drugs ring in Europe.*
▻ ***verb***: **rings, ringing, ringed**
You **ring** something written or printed when you draw a circle round it, to draw attention to it or make a note of it: *Ring the letter that corresponds to your chosen answer.*
▻ ***phrase*** (*informal*) You **run rings round** an opponent when you beat them with very little effort or show that you are far better than them.

ring[2] /rɪŋ/ *verb*; *noun*
▻ ***verb***: **rings, ringing, rang, rung**
1 An object **rings** when it makes a sound like a bell: *Good-quality glass rings when you tap it with your finger.* □ *The doorbell rang and I rushed to see who it was.* □ *The noise of the factory was still ringing in my ears hours later.* **2** You **ring** someone when you telephone them: *Just ring him up and ask him.* □ *I'm rather busy at the moment; can I ring you back later?* □ *I rang this morning, but there was no answer.* [*same as* **call**] **3** (*literary*) You say a place **is ringing** with sound when there is a lot of it: *The whole house was ringing with the sound of children laughing and shouting.* [*same as* **resound**] **4** You might say that what someone says **rings** true if you have the impression that it's true: *For most of us, all politicians' promises ring false.*

▻ ***noun*** (*used in the singular*): *the familiar, clear ring of our church bell* ▫ *You could write them a letter, or give them a ring.* ▫ *I didn't recognize his face, although his voice had a familiar ring to it.*

ringleader /ˈrɪŋliːdə(r)/ *noun*: **ringleaders**
The leader of a gang of criminals or troublemakers is often referred to as the **ringleader**.

ring road /ˈrɪŋ roʊd/ *noun*: **ring roads**
A **ring road** is a road that goes round a town or city, allowing drivers to pass it without going through it. [*same as* **circular**]

rink /rɪŋk/ *noun*: **rinks**
A **rink** is a large smooth surface for skating on, or the building containing it: *We spent Wednesday afternoons at the ice rink.*

rinse /rɪns/ *verb*: **rinses, rinsing, rinsed**
You **rinse** something when you put water on it to remove the soap you have washed it with, or when you wash it quickly using only water, with no soap: *Rinse your mouth out to get rid of all the toothpaste.* ▫ *Just rinse the fruit under the tap.*

riot /ˈraɪət/ *noun*; *verb*
▻ ***noun***: **riots**
There is a **riot** when crowds of people behave violently in the streets or a public place.
▻ ***verb***: **riots, rioting, rioted:** *If the students had rioted, many would certainly have been seriously injured.*
▻ ***phrase*** To **run riot** is to behave in a wild and uncontrolled way: *They let their children run riot in our garden.* — *adjective* **riotous** /ˈraɪətəs/: *The west wing was taken over by a riotous mob of prisoners.*

rip /rɪp/ *verb*; *noun*
▻ ***verb***: **rips, ripping, ripped**
1 You **rip** something when you tear it roughly or violently: *I ripped my trousers climbing over the fence.* ▫ *Her dress caught on a nail and ripped in several places.* ▫ *Rip me off a strip of paper.* ▫ *She ripped up the letter into little pieces.* **2** You **rip** something away from someone when you take it away from them suddenly and violently: *She ripped the notebook from my hand.* [*same as* **grab**]
▻ ***noun***: **rips:** *I heard a loud rip and looked back to see part of my jacket hanging in the tree.*

> ***phrasal verb***
> (*informal*) Someone **rips** you **off** when they cheat you, especially by charging you too much money for something or taking money from you dishonestly: *I always come out with the feeling that I've been ripped off.* [*same as* **swindle**]

ripe /raɪp/ *adjective*: **riper, ripest**
1 When fruit, and sometimes cheese, is **ripe** it has fully matured and is ready to be eaten: *a bowl of ripe peaches.* **2** You are **ripe** for something when you are ready or suitable for it; something is **ripe** when it is about to happen: *It struck me that Alison was ripe for promotion.* ▫ *British politics is now ripe for change.*

ripen /ˈraɪpən/ *verb*: **ripens, ripening, ripened**
Fruit or vegetables **ripen** when they become ripe or ready to eat: *a basket of sun-ripened tomatoes.*

rip-off /ˈrɪpɒf/ *noun* (*informal*): **rip-offs**
You say that something is a **rip-off** if you think it is unreasonably expensive: *At £18 a ticket, the show is a complete rip-off.* [*same as* **con, swindle**]

ripple /ˈrɪpəl/ *noun*; *verb*
▻ ***noun***: **ripples**
1 Ripples are tiny waves produced when the surface of water is disturbed. **2** A gentle sound that rises and falls can be described as a **ripple** of sound: *ripples of laughter.*
▻ ***verb***: **ripples, rippling, rippled:** *The pond rippled soothingly.*

rise /raɪz/ *verb*; *noun*
▻ ***verb***: **rises, rising, rose, risen**
1 Something **rises** when it moves upwards: *A column of black smoke rose into the air.* ▫ *Hundreds of birds suddenly rose into the sky from the tree tops.* **2** A sound **rises** from a group when it comes from them: *A murmur rose from the crowd.* **3** Something tall **rises** in front of you when it comes into view or appears in front of you: *The castle wall rose before them.* **4** Land **rises** when it slopes upwards: *Ahead, the ground rose rapidly.* **5** A sound **rises** when it becomes louder: *Her voice rose to a hysterical scream.* **6** The sun or moon **rises** when it appears above the horizon. **7** A river **rises** at a particular place if that is its source, or the place where it begins to flow: *The Rhine rises in Switzerland.* **8** The level of something **rises** when it gets higher: *The river had risen by at least two feet in the night.* **9** An amount **rises** when it increases: *The number of people unemployed rose by over 10 000 last month.* ▫ *with temperatures rising to 19 degrees by midday* ▫ *Prices have risen by 40%.* **10** (*literary*) You **rise** when you stand up from a lying, sitting or kneeling position; you also **rise** when you get out of bed in the morning: *He rose from his chair angrily.* ▫ *We rose at about nine and went down for breakfast.* **11** Someone **rises** in their profession when they reach a higher rank; things **rise** in popularity when they become more popular: *She rapidly rose to the position of director.* ▫ *Within a month of publication her book had risen to the top of the bestseller list.* **12** The citizens of a country **rise**, or **rise** up, when they rebel against those in authority and start fighting them: *He urged them to rise up against the capitalist bosses and take possession of the factories.* **13** You **rise** to a challenge, or to an occasion, when you manage to deal with it successfully.
▻ ***noun***: **rises**
1 (*used in the singular*) Someone's rise is their progress to a position of popularity or power: *No-one could explain his sudden rise to fame.* **2** A rise in something is an increase in it: *the rise in unemployment* ▫ *Yearly they award themselves enormous pay rises.*
▻ ***phrase*** One thing **gives rise to** another if it causes it: *Her remarks had given rise to uncertainty among her constituents.*

> ***phrasal verb***
> You **rise above** some unpleasant circumstance when you don't allow yourself to be affected by it: *She somehow managed to rise above the criticisms and survive.*

risk /rɪsk/ *noun*; *verb*
▻ ***noun***: **risks**
1 (*count or uncount*) There is a **risk** that something unpleasant will happen when it might happen: *Plant them outside after the risk of frost has passed.* ▫ *You have to accept that there are risks involved in any investment.* ▫ *Fabrics like this create a serious fire risk.* ▫ *At the risk of sounding unkind, I don't think he's good enough for the job.* ▫ *If we don't accept his offer, we run the risk of offending him.* ▫ *It would be taking too great a risk to buy it before we've seen it.* [*same as* **danger**]
2 You refer to a person or thing as a **risk** if they might not achieve the result you want: *In such a politically sensitive area, I think sending Alan would be a risk.*

▻ ***verb***: **risks, risking, risked**
You **risk** something when what you do might cause it to be harmed, damaged or lost, or might be dangerous: *I wouldn't risk the old car on such treacherous roads.* □ *We are asking you to risk your lives for the security of your country.* □ *I wouldn't risk my job by supporting the strike.* □ *Could we risk leaving the decision to the last minute?* [*same as* **chance**]
▻ ***phrase*** Something is **at risk** when it is in a situation where it might be harmed, damaged or lost: *If you don't repay the loan, your home is at risk.* □ *In such an exposed position, the young trees were at risk of storm damage.* [*same as* **in danger**]

risky /ˈrɪskɪ/ *adjective*: **riskier, riskiest**
Something you do is **risky** when there is a possibility of danger, harm, damage or failure: *Investing on the stock exchange can be a risky business.* [*same as* **dangerous**; *opposite* **safe**]

risqué /rɪsˈkeɪ/ *adjective*
Risqué stories or jokes are stories or jokes about sex.

rite /raɪt/ *noun*: **rites**
A **rite** is a ceremony, especially a ceremony that has some religious connection: *New members of the secret society had to go through certain initiation rites.*

ritual /ˈrɪtʃʊəl/ *noun*; *adjective*
▻ ***noun*** (*count or uncount*): **rituals**
A **ritual** is a set of actions performed on certain special occasions as a custom or tradition: *The wedding ceremony was full of mystery and ritual.*
▻ ***adjective***
Ritual describes things done as part of a ritual, or simply things you do regularly, or things you expect people to do because they always do them: *the ritual sacrifice of a lamb* □ *Holidaymakers descended on the beach for the ritual period of sunbathing.* [*same as* **customary, habitual**]

rival /ˈraɪvəl/ *noun*; *verb*
▻ ***noun*** (*often adjectival*): **rivals**
A **rival** is a person or organization that competes with another in some way: *a match between fierce rivals* □ *Many of the rival newspapers have cut their prices dramatically.* [*same as* **competitor**]
▻ ***verb***: **rivals, rivalling** (*AmE* **rivaling**), **rivalled** (*AmE* **rivaled**)
One thing **rivals** another when it is as good as it, or nearly so: *Shop-bought vegetables can't rival the ones you grow yourself.* □ *No other fruit rivals the lemon for flavour.* [*same as* **compete**; *opposite* **cooperate**]

rivalry /ˈraɪvəlrɪ/ *noun* (*uncount or used in the plural*): **rivalries**
There is **rivalry** between people or organizations that compete against each other: *It's nice to see such friendly rivalry on the tennis court.* □ *It's difficult for them to forget their past rivalries.* [*opposite* **cooperation**]

river /ˈrɪvə(r)/ *noun* (*often adjectival*): **rivers**
A **river** is a large natural stream of water: *five miles down the river where we had left the boat* □ *the River Trent* □ *some of the canal boats and larger river craft.*

rivet /ˈrɪvɪt/ *noun*; *verb*
▻ ***noun***: **rivets**
A **rivet** is a metal fastener like a short, fat nail, driven into metal parts to fix them together.
▻ ***verb***: **rivets, riveting, riveted**
You **are riveted** by something that holds all your attention and interest: *The stories kept the younger children riveted.* [*same as* **fascinate, grip, enthral**] — *adjective* **riveting:** *The last half hour of the film was absolutely riveting.*

road /roʊd/ *noun*: **roads**
1 (*count or uncount*) A **road** is a wide path, often with a special hard surface, for vehicles to travel on from one place to another: *We got lost somewhere on the road from Stirling to Edinburgh.* □ *A dead bird was lying in the middle of the road.* □ *We travelled by road as far as Chester.* □ *a side street just off Langdon Road.* **2** A **road** is also a route or way of getting somewhere: *Is there a shorter road?* □ *Can you tell me the road to Gloucester?* □ *a singer on the road to international success.* **3** (*used in the singular*; *informal*) Something is in your **road** when it is in your way, or hindering your progress: *Hang on and I'll move all these boxes out of the road.* [*same as* **way**]
▻ ***phrase*** You are **on the road** when you are travelling: *We've been on the road since 6 this morning.*

roadside /ˈroʊdsaɪd/ *noun* (*used in the singular, often adjectival*)
The **roadside** is the strip or area of ground beside or along a road: *A variety of wildflowers grow at the roadside.* □ *roadside telephones.*

roadworks /ˈroʊdwɜːks/ *noun* (*plural*)
Roadworks are repairs to roads: *There are roadworks on the Kingston Bridge, so drivers can expect long delays there.*

roam /roʊm/ *verb*: **roams, roaming, roamed**
You **roam** when you wander, or travel around without a fixed purpose or destination: *In the evenings, we roamed along the beach until bedtime.* □ *There's nothing for him to do except roam the streets.*

roar /rɔː(r)/ *verb*; *noun*
▻ ***verb***: **roars, roaring, roared**
1 Animals such as lions **roar** when they give their loud, deep, rough cry. **2** Things that **roar** make a loud noise: *Traffic roared past in the street below.* **3** Someone **roars** at you when they shout at you, especially angrily: *'Get out of my house!' Jasper roared.* □ *There's no need to roar down the telephone like that.* [*same as* **bellow**]
▻ ***noun***: **roars:** *the roar of the tiger.*

roaring /ˈrɔːrɪŋ/ *adjective*
1 A business company does a **roaring** trade when they sell a lot: *We are doing a roaring trade in Spanish holidays.* **2** Something that is a **roaring** success is very successful.

roast /roʊst/ *verb*; *adjective*; *noun*
▻ ***verb***: **roasts, roasting, roasted**
1 You **roast** meat or other food when you cook it in an oven or over a fire. **2** Other foods such as nuts and coffee beans **are roasted** when they are browned and dried in an oven or over a fire.
▻ ***adjective***
Roast foods have been roasted: *roast potatoes.*
▻ ***noun***: **roasts**
A **roast** is a piece of roasted meat.

roasting /ˈroʊstɪŋ/ *adjective or adverb* (*informal*)
You say that something is **roasting**, or **roasting** hot, if it is very hot: *It was absolutely roasting in the greenhouse.* □ *I'm roasting in this overcoat.* □ *a roasting hot day.* [*same as* **sweltering**]

rob /rɒb/ *verb*: **robs, robbing, robbed**
1 Someone who **robs** you steals something from you: *They had robbed me of my passport and my wallet.* □ *His first big job was robbing a local bank.* **2** Someone also **robs** you of something when they prevent you from having or getting it: *She had robbed me of the opportunity to speak to Louise alone.* [*same as* **deprive**] — *noun* **robber:** *a bank robber.* — *noun* (*count or uncount*) **robbery**: *The robbery must have been carried out at night.* □ *They were charged with armed robbery.*

robe /roʊb/ *noun*: **robes**
1 A **robe** is a dressing gown or bathrobe: *Still dripping from the pool, she pulled on her robe.* **2** (*used in the plural*) An important office-bearer's ceremonial **robes** are a set of garments, usually long and elaborate, that he or she wears for special occasions: *The archbishop arrived in his robes.*

robin /ˈrɒbɪn/ *noun*: **robins**
A **robin** is a small brown bird with a red breast.

robot /ˈroʊbɒt/ *noun*: **robots**
1 In science fiction stories and films, a **robot** is a machine that looks and functions like a person. **2** In industry, a **robot** is an automatic machine that can be programmed to perform certain tasks.

robust /roʊˈbʌst/ *adjective*
1 A **robust** person is strong and healthy: *Most premature babies are quite robust by six months.* **2** Something that is **robust** is strongly built or constructed: *The chair didn't seem robust enough to take his weight.* [*same as* **sturdy**]

rock¹ /rɒk/ *noun*: **rocks**
1 (*uncount or count*) **Rock** is the hard mineral that the earth is made of: *She cut her ankle on a sharp fragment of rock.* ▫ *Huge rocks came rolling down the hillside.* **2** (*uncount*) **Rock** is also a hard sweet in the form of long, cylindrical sticks, brightly coloured: *He broke his tooth on a stick of rock.*
▻ ***phrases*** (*informal*) **1** A marriage or other relationship is **on the rocks** when the people involved are unhappy with each other and would like to separate. **2** You say that you want your alcoholic drink **on the rocks** when you would like ice cubes in it. [compare **neat**]

rock² /rɒk/ *verb*; *adjective*; *noun*
▻ ***verb***: **rocks, rocking, rocked**
1 To **rock** is to move or swing gently backwards and forwards or from side to side; you **rock** a baby when you hold them and comfort them by moving them in this way. **2** Something **rocks** you when it upsets or shocks you greatly: *The whole political world was rocked by the news of his death.* [*same as* **stagger**, **astound**]
▻ ***adjective***
Rock music is a form of popular music with a strong beat, usually played on electrical instruments: *one of the great rock guitarists.*
▻ ***noun*** (*uncount*)
Rock is rock music: *You've been described as the king of rock.*

rock and roll /rɒk ən ˈroʊl/ *noun* (*uncount, often adjectival*)
Rock and roll is a kind of popular music with a lively beat and simple melodies, that rock music is developed from: *the world's greatest rock and roll band.*

rockery /ˈrɒkərɪ/ *noun*: **rockeries**
A **rockery** is a garden, or part of one, in which small plants are grown among large stones or rocks.

rocket /ˈrɒkɪt/ *noun*; *verb*
▻ ***noun***: **rockets**
1 A **rocket** is a large cylindrical vehicle for travelling from Earth into space. [*same as* **spacecraft**] **2** A **rocket** is also a kind of large missile: *We destroyed an enemy rocket-launcher.* **3** A **rocket** is also a cylindrical firework that goes high into the air before exploding.
▻ ***verb*** (*informal*): **rockets, rocketing, rocketed**
Something **rockets** when it increases suddenly and very rapidly: *Property prices rocketed.* [*same as* **shoot up**]

rocking chair /ˈrɒkɪŋ tʃɛə(r)/ *noun*: **rocking chairs**
A **rocking chair** is a chair which rocks backwards and forwards on two curved supports.

rocking horse /ˈrɒkɪŋ hɔːs/ *noun*: **rocking horses**
A **rocking horse** is a child's toy horse fixed to two curved supports, that the child can sit on and rock backwards and forwards.

rocky /ˈrɒkɪ/ *adjective*
1 A **rocky** area has many rocks: *a stretch of rocky moorland.* [*same as* **rugged**] **2** (*informal*) You say that the progress of something is **rocky** if there are a lot of problems and obstacles: *They've had rather a rocky marriage.* [*same as* **shaky**; *opposite* **steady**]

rod /rɒd/ *noun*: **rods**
A **rod** is a long thin pole or bar, especially made of wood or metal: *a fishing rod.*

rode /roʊd/ *verb*
Rode is the past tense of **ride**.

rodent /ˈroʊdənt/ *noun*: **rodents**
A **rodent** is any of a class of small, furry animals with sharp teeth, such as mice, rats and rabbits.

rogue /roʊg/ *noun* (*old*): **rogues**
A **rogue** is a person who behaves in a cheating, dishonest way; you also call someone a **rogue** if they like having fun or playing tricks: *Maurice was a very likeable rogue.* [*same as* **scoundrel**] — *adjective* **roguish:** *He has a kind of roguish charm.* [*same as* **mischievous**]

role or **rôle** /roʊl/ *noun*: **roles**
1 The **role** of someone or something is their position or function: *Your role as mother involves patience, tolerance and senstivity.* ▫ *The police play the principal role in enforcing the laws we create.* ▫ *It was believed that Britain could play a key role as sponsor of these developments.* [*same as* **function**] **2** An actor's **role** is the part they play in a film or play: *Gielgud and Olivier alternated in the roles of Romeo and Mercutio.*

roll /roʊl/ *verb*; *noun*
▻ ***verb***: **rolls, rolling, rolled**
1 Something that **rolls** along on a surface moves along it by turning over itself again and again; you also say that a vehicle, or other object with wheels, **rolls** when it moves: *The ball rolled down the slope and into the pond.* ▫ *She rolled the ball across the grass to her brother.* ▫ *The brakes failed and I felt the car begin to roll back down the hill.* ▫ *He had turned over in his sleep and rolled completely out of the bed.* **2** You **roll** something into a cylinder or a ball when you form it into that shape with your hands, by pressing or folding: *Roll the dough into two large balls.* ▫ *I hit him on the head with a rolled-up newspaper.* ▫ *We rolled up our sleeves and started work.*
▻ ***noun***: **rolls**
1 A **roll** is a small loaf of bread eaten as a snack: *Would you like the ham as a sandwich or on a roll?* **2** A **roll** of something flat, such as paper or fabric, is a length of it rolled into a cylinder: *a van with rolls of carpet in the back.* **3** A list of something, especially people's names, is sometimes called a **roll**: *They get your name from the electoral roll.* [*same as* **register**]

> ***phrasal verbs***
> **roll in** (*informal*) You say things **are rolling in** when they arrive in large quantities: *Once the new restaurant is open, customers will come rolling in.* [*same as* **pour in**]
> **roll up** (*informal*) You **roll up** somewhere when you arrive: *Graham rolled up half way through the speeches.*

roller /ˈroʊlə(r)/ *noun*: **rollers**
Many cylindrical objects are called **rollers**, such as the

hollow tubes tied into hair to curl it, or a large iron cylinder pulled over ground to flatten it.

rollercoaster /'roʊləkoʊstə(r)/ *noun*: **rollercoasters**
A **rollercoaster** is an exciting fairground entertainment in which you sit in cars that ride very fast on a raised railway with sharp bends and steep drops.

roller skate /'roʊlə skeɪt/ *noun*: **roller skates**
Roller skates are boots with a set of wheels attached to the bottom, for skating on surfaces of wood or concrete.

rolling pin /'roʊlɪŋ pɪn/ *noun*: **rolling pins**
A **rolling pin** is a cylindrical kitchen tool that you roll over pastry to make it flat and thin. [see picture at **kitchen**]

romance /roʊ'mans/ or /rə'mans/ *noun*: **romances**
1 (*literary*) A **romance** is a loving relationship, especially between people who are not married to each other: *She's had a number of brief romances since Frederic.* **2** (*uncount*) **Romance** is an intense kind of love, the kind felt by people who are just discovering that they love each other: *a marriage that has lost all its romance.* **3** (*uncount*) **Romance** is also the quality of causing strong or intense feelings, especially of excitement: *There is none of the romance of the book in the film.* [*same as* **passion**] **4** A **romance** is a story about love. [*same as* **love story**]

Roman numeral /roʊmən 'nju:mərəl/ *noun*: **Roman numerals**
Roman numerals are the letters used to represent numbers in the system developed by the ancient Romans, in which, for example I = 1 and V = 5.

romantic /roʊ'mantɪk/ or /rə'mantɪk/ *adjective*; *noun*
▻ ***adjective***
1 Romantic means concerned with love, or producing feelings of love, especially an innocent, ideal kind of love: *There is no romantic interest in the film.* ▫ *It's been described as a romantic comedy.* ▫ *a romantic candlelit meal for two* ▫ *Her husband is so romantic.* [*same as* **sentimental**] **2** You describe someone as **romantic** if they have an innocent, ideal view of life, believing that great things can easily be achieved: *Isn't that rather a romantic notion?* [*opposite* **practical**]
▻ ***noun***: **romantics:** *Stephen was an incurable romantic.* — *adverb* **romantically:** *She's not attached to anyone romantically.*

romanticized or **romanticised** /roʊ'mantɪsaɪzd/ or /rə'mantɪsaɪzd/ *adjective*
You have a **romanticized** view of something if you think about it as easier, happier or more pleasant than it really is, not considering its problems or difficulties. [*same as* **idealized**]

romp /rɒmp/ *verb*; *noun*
▻ ***verb***: **romps, romping, romped**
People, usually children, **romp** when they play in a lively, energetic way: *a pair of deer romping about by the lake.*
▻ ***noun***: **romps:** *The boys had a good old romp in the garden.*

roof /ru:f/ *noun*: **roofs**
1 The **roof** of something such as a building or vehicle is the part that covers the top of it: *Did he want the house built with a flat or a pitched roof?* ▫ *There was a hole in the tent roof.* [see picture at **house**] **2** The **roof** of your mouth is the top inner surface. **3** A home is sometimes referred to as a **roof**: *two families under one roof* ▫ *You're not sleeping together while you're under my roof.*
▻ ***phrases*** **1** (*informal*) An amount that **goes through the roof** increases very quickly to a high level: *That was the year that house prices went through the roof.* [*same as* **shoot up**] **2** (*informal*) Someone **hits the roof** when they lose their temper and start shouting: *Dad'll hit the roof when you tell him.* [*same as* **go mad**]

roof rack /'ru:f rak/ *noun*: **roof racks**
A **roof rack** is a metal frame that you can fix to the roof of your car, for carrying luggage on.

rook /rʊk/ *noun*: **rooks**
A **rook** is a large black bird that builds its nest in the tops of trees.

room /ru:m/ *noun*: **rooms**
1 A **room** is one of the areas that the inside of a building is divided into, with its own ceiling, floor, walls and door: *We've got three rooms downstairs and four bedrooms.* ▫ *He came into the room and shut the door.* ▫ *Their hotel room faced the sea.* ▫ *Could I book a double room for Wednesday night?* **2** (*uncount*) There is **room** for something if there is enough space for it: *There's room for another bed in here.* ▫ *There was no room on the table to put the tray down.* ▫ *I haven't got much room to put my clothes.* ▫ *She moved along the bench to make room for me.* ▫ *A 19th-century square was pulled down to make more room for university buildings.* ▫ *Buy their shoes slightly too large so that there's room for growth.* [see note at **place**] **3** (*uncount*) There is **room** somewhere for some sort of activity or behaviour if it can be permitted or encouraged there: *There is no room in this club for racist attitudes.* ▫ *There's plenty of room for more English teaching.* [*same as* **scope**] **4** (*uncount*) If you say about something that there is **room** for improvement, you mean that it isn't good enough. — *adjective* **-roomed:** *a three-roomed flat.*

roommate /'ru:mmeɪt/ *noun*: **roommates**
Your **roommate** is a person you share a room with, for example as a student; in American English, your **roommate** is a person you share a flat with.

roomy /'ru:mɪ/ *adjective*: **roomier, roomiest**
A place is **roomy** when there is a lot of room or space inside it: *The first car had a roomier interior.* [*same as* **spacious**; *opposite* **cramped**]

roost /ru:st/ *noun*; *verb*
▻ ***noun***: **roosts**
A **roost** is a place where a bird, especially a farmyard bird, has its nest.
▻ ***verb***: **roosts, roosting, roosted**
Birds **roost** in the place where they spend the night.
▻ ***phrase*** (*informal*) The person who **rules the roost** dominates or controls all others.

root /ru:t/ *noun*; *verb*
▻ ***noun***: **roots**
1 The **roots** of a plant are the underground parts that keep it firm and take in water and minerals from the soil. **2** The **root** of a tooth, hair or nail is the part beneath the skin that attaches it to the body. **3** (*often adjectival*) The **root** of something such as a problem is its basic cause, source or origin: *Nobody knew what was at the root of their hostility towards each other.* ▫ *The root cause of all this misery was a silly family dispute.* **4** Your **roots** are your family origins: *He set about tracing his roots.* ▫ *It seems my roots lie in a farming community in the south of France.* **5** Your **roots** are also your feelings of belonging to a particular place: *I felt that I had abandoned my roots.*
▻ ***verb***: **roots, rooting, rooted**
1 Something **is rooted** in what is its cause, source or origin: *All her emotional problems are rooted in an inability to accept that she's not perfect.* [*same as* **entrenched**] **2** You **root** around somewhere when you search for something there, usually roughly and with-

out care: *Through the window, I watched him rooting about in the drawers and on the bookshelves.* [*same as* **rummage**]

rope /roʊp/ *noun*; *verb*
▻ ***noun*** (*count or uncount*): **ropes**
A **rope** is a length of strong thick cord made by twisting fibres together: *The boat was tied to the tree with a rope.* □ *a piece of rope.*
▻ ***phrase*** You **know the ropes** when you have a thorough knowledge and experience of what needs to be done in a particular circumstance or for a particular job.
▻ ***verb***: **ropes, roping, roped**

> ***phrasal verbs***
> **rope in** (*informal*) You **rope** someone **in** when you persuade them to do something or take part in something: *I got roped into helping with the barbecue.*
> **rope off** An area **is roped off** when it is surrounded by a circle of ropes supported on posts, to keep people out.

ropy or **ropey** /ˈroʊpɪ/ *adjective* (*informal*): **ropier, ropiest**
People sometimes say something is **ropy** when it is not very good, especially when it is of poor quality: *a fairly ropy performance* □ *The food was okay, but the wine was a bit ropy.* [*same as* **rough**]

rosary /ˈroʊzərɪ/ *noun*: **rosaries**
A **rosary** is a string of beads that people of certain religions count prayers on as they say them; a set of prayers counted in this way is also a **rosary**.

rose[1] /roʊz/ *noun*; *adjective*
▻ ***noun***: **roses**
A **rose** is a popular garden plant with prickly stems and large, sweet-smelling flowers; the flowers are also **roses**: *We've planted a climbing rose by the back door.* □ *He presented her with a beautiful bouquet of red roses.*
▻ ***adjective***
Something that is **rose** is a pale pink colour: *a white pattern on a rose background.*

rose[2] /roʊz/ *verb*
Rose is the past tense of **rise**.

rosette /roʊˈzɛt/ *noun*: **rosettes**
A **rosette** is a rose-shaped badge or decoration made of coloured ribbon, awarded as a prize or worn to show support for a group or organization, for example a football team or a political party.

roster /ˈrɒstə(r)/ *noun*: **rosters**
A **roster** is a rota.

rostrum /ˈrɒstrəm/ *noun*: **rostrums**
A **rostrum** is a platform that someone stands on to speak to an audience. [*same as* **podium**]

rosy /ˈroʊzɪ/ *adjective*: **rosier, rosiest**
1 Something that is **rosy** is an attractive pink colour: *The children were all rosy-cheeked after their walk in the snow.* **2** You say that a situation is **rosy** if there are reasons to be hopeful or cheerful: *The future for their business is not exactly rosy.* [*same as* **promising**]

rot /rɒt/ *verb*; *noun*
▻ ***verb***: **rots, rotting, rotted**
Food, wood and other living materials **rot** when they become diseased and begin to break down or decay: *Her teeth were rotting away.* □ *The leaves will eventually rot down to form compost.* [*same as* **decay**]
▻ ***noun*** (*uncount*)
1 **Rot** is disease that leads to decay: *The roof had leaked and rot had begun to set in.* [*same as* **decay**] **2** (*informal*) **Rot** is also nonsense or rubbish: *Don't talk such rot!*

rota /ˈroʊtə/ *noun*: **rotas**
A **rota** is a list of duties to be done and names of people who are to take turns in doing them: *I'm on the rota for Friday night.* [*same as* **roster**]

rotary /ˈroʊtərɪ/ *adjective*
Rotary movement is the turning or spinning movement of a wheel: *the rotary motion of the blades.* [*same as* **rotating**]

rotate /roʊˈteɪt/ *verb*: **rotates, rotating, rotated**
1 Something that **rotates** turns or spins like a wheel: *A rotating arm circulates water around the chamber.* **2** You **rotate** things when you change their order or position according to a fixed pattern or sequence; they **rotate** when they change in this way: *Rotating vegetable crops helps to reduce the risk of disease.* □ *It was agreed that the Presidency would rotate among members of the major groups.* □ *The explorers have a range of main meals which they rotate to provide variety and nutritional balance.* — *noun* (*uncount*) **rotation** /roʊˈteɪʃən/: *air currents produced by the rotation of the blades* □ *a method of crop rotation.*

rotor /ˈroʊtə(r)/ *noun*: **rotors**
A **rotor** is a rotating part of a machine, especially the set of rotating blades that propel a helicopter.

rotten /ˈrɒtən/ *adjective*
1 Food, wood and other living materials are **rotten** when they have become diseased, decayed, or are falling to pieces: *The box contained three rotten eggs.* **2** (*informal*) You describe something as **rotten** if it is of very poor quality: *The second film was rotten.* □ *That's a rotten idea.* [*same as* **dreadful**] **3** (*informal*) **Rotten** also means unpleasant, unfair or unkind; you say you feel **rotten** if you feel ill: *We've had some rotten weather this summer.* □ *That was a rotten way to behave.* **4** (*informal*) People sometimes use **rotten** for emphasis, to describe something they dislike: *I don't want any of your rotten old sandwiches!*

rough /rʌf/ *adjective*: **rougher, roughest**
1 A surface that is **rough** is not smooth, even or regular: *The skin on his hands was quite rough.* □ *The cart bumped over the rough track.* **2** Someone who behaves in a **rough** way uses too much force or strength, not taking care to be gentle or delicate: *Don't worry about being rough; babies are actually more robust than you think.* □ *His fellow prisoners subjected him to rough treatment.* **3** (*informal*) Something that is **rough** requires hard work or effort, or involves great difficulties or problems: *She's had a rough day at work.* **4** (*informal*) A situation that is **rough** is unpleasant, unfair or hard to bear: *It's rough on the wife to be left alone with four children to bring up.* **5** A **rough** guess or calculation is only approximate; a **rough** drawing or description gives only the main points or features, not the small details: *At a rough estimate, I would say £10 000.* □ *Could you give us a rough outline of your plans?* **6** **Rough** weather is windy and stormy: *The sea can be a bit rough, even in summer.* **7** (*informal*) If you say you are feeling **rough** you mean you feel ill: *We must have drunk a huge amount; I've got a really rough head this morning.* **8** A **rough** area is a place where there is a lot of crime and violence. — *adverb* **roughly:** *Teachers shouldn't handle the children so roughly.* □ *I would guess it was roughly 20 yards to the back fence.*
▻ ***phrases*** **1** (*informal*) You **rough it** when you spend some time without the comforts that you are used to having: *We decided to rough it in the tent for a few*

nights, to save money. **2** People who **sleep rough** sleep outdoors, usually because they have no home to go to: *For most of the holiday, we slept rough in the park.*

> ***phrasal verb***
> **rough up** (*informal*) Someone **roughs** you **up** when they hurt you by physically attacking you. [*same as* **beat up**]

rough-and-ready /rʌf ənd ˈredɪ/ *adjective*
You describe something as **rough-and-ready** if it has been made or prepared hurriedly or without the proper materials: *It was a bit of a rough-and-ready speech, but it roused the crowd.* [*same as* **unpolished**]

roulette /ruːlet/ *noun* (*uncount*)
Roulette is a gambling game in which a ball is dropped on to a spinning wheel divided into numbered sections: *a game of roulette.*

round /raʊnd/ *adjective*; *preposition*; *preposition or adverb*; *adverb*; *noun*; *verb*
▻ ***adjective***: **rounder, roundest**
1 Something that is **round** is **a** the shape of a circle: *a round table.* [*same as* **circular**] **b** the shape of a ball, or approximately this shape: *The earth is round.* □ *big round boulders.* [*compare* **spherical**] **c** curved: *The Norman arch is round rather than pointed.* **2** A **round** number or figure is a number such as 20, 30, 100 or 1000, as distinct from the numbers in between them, or just above or below them: *The total is 47, so just count it as a round 50.*
▻ ***preposition*** (also **around**)
1 One thing is **round** another if it encloses or surrounds it: *The book had a piece of brown paper wrapped round it.* □ *He had a line round each leg where the tops of his socks had been.* □ *We sat down round the table.* □ *She put her arms round his neck.* □ *A wall had been built round the city in medieval times.* **2** The distance **round** something is its circumference, or the length of its edge or boundary: *As a young girl I was a mere 24 inches round the waist.* □ *We measured the distance round the garden.* **3** One thing goes **round** another when it travels in a circle with the other in the middle: *The planets circle round the sun.* □ *They ran round the fire dancing and shouting.* **4** Something that occurs or exists **round** an area occurs or exists in various parts of it: *They have offices all round the world.* □ *A fashion show like this serves as a guide to what's happening round Europe.* [compare **over**] **5** The area **round** a place is the local district: *There's nothing round here for the children to do.* **6** You go **round** something such as an exhibition, or a house you are thinking of buying or renting, when you go from object to object, or room to room, looking at them: *Have you been round the museum lately?* □ *We've been looking round various flats.* **7** You go **round** a corner when you come to it and change direction: *A car came round the corner too fast and knocked him down.* **8** You find a way **round** a problem or difficulty when you find a solution to it.
▻ ***preposition or adverb*** (also **around**)
1 You look **round** you, or **round** the place you are in, when you look at the things surrounding you: *I glanced round at the various pictures and ornaments.* [*same as* **about**] **2** Things or people are, or move, **round** a place when they move here and there in it: *We walked round the town and did a bit of shopping.* □ *A wasp was flying round the room.* □ *People were sitting round chatting.* □ *We drove round for a while, trying to decide where to go.* [*same as* **about**] **3** People gather **round** you when they surround you closely: *Gather round and I'll tell you a story.* **4** Something is passed **round** from person to person when one person hands it on to another: *They passed the plate round.* □ *The message went round the office.*
▻ ***adverb*** (also **around**)
1 Something goes **round** when it spins, revolves or travels in a circular direction: *The wheel kept spinning round.* **2** You turn or look **round** when you turn to face in the opposite direction: *I called his name and he spun round.* **3** You go **round** to someone's house when you visit them: *Do come round this evening.* □ *We're going round to Janet's to play Scrabble.*
▻ ***noun***: **rounds**
1 In a competition, a **round** is a set of games whose winners play against each other in the next **round**, until only two players or teams are left. **2** A **round** of bread is a slice of it. **3** A **round** of things such as talks, meetings or negotiations is a set or series of them: *A further round of peace talks will begin in the spring.* **4** A delivery **round** is the regular route taken by someone such as a milkman or postman. **5** (*used in the plural*) Doctors make, or go on, their **rounds** when they go visiting their various patients: *I'm afraid she's out on her rounds at the moment.* **6** In boxing or wrestling, a **round** is one of the short periods during which the contestants fight. **7** You buy a **round** of drinks when you buy a drink for everybody in the group you are with: *It must be my round; same again, everyone?* **8** A **round** of applause is a burst of clapping: *He stopped speaking, clearly expecting a round of applause.* **9** A **round** of ammunition is the amount of it fired from a gun at one shot: *We fired several rounds over their heads.*
▻ ***verb***: **rounds, rounding, rounded**
You **round** a corner when you come to it and change direction: *As it rounded the corner the bus mounted the pavement.*
▻ ***phrases*** **1** (*informal*) People such as tourists **do the rounds** when they visit all the usual places. **2 Round about** means **a** approximately: *The meeting attracted round about fifty people.* **b** in the area surrounding the place mentioned: *methods used by most of the farms round about here* □ *She made friends with the children living round about.* **3** Your head goes **round and round** when you feel dizzy. **4** Something that is the right **way round** is in the right position, with the front to the front and the top to the top: *You're holding your chopsticks the wrong way round.*

> ***phrasal verb***
> **round up** You **round up** people or animals when you gather them in one place. or collect them together: *The police have rounded up all the usual suspects.* [see also **round-up**]

roundabout /ˈraʊndəbaʊt/ *noun*; *adjective*
▻ ***noun***: **roundabouts**
1 In a children's playground, a **roundabout** is a revolving platform, sometimes with seats, for children to ride on. **2** A **roundabout** is also a circular road junction where several roads meet, with all traffic travelling in the same direction round a central island: *You go straight on at the second roundabout.*
▻ ***adjective***
You do or say something in a **roundabout** way when you do it in a way that is not direct or straightforward, perhaps because you are unsure or cautious: *He was telling me in a roundabout way that I was too fat.* [*same as* **indirect, evasive**]

rounded /ˈraʊndɪd/ *adjective*
Something **rounded** is curved, with no sharp edges or points.

rounders /ˈraʊndəz/ *noun* (*uncount*)

Rounders is a team game similar to baseball, played on a smaller field with a smaller bat.

roundly /'raʊndlɪ/ *adverb* (*formal*)
Roundly means plainly, thoroughly, and often rudely: *They were roundly criticized by the committee for their failure to take responsibility.*

round trip /raʊnd 'trɪp/ *noun*: **round trips**
A **round trip** is a trip to a place and back again: *It's a round trip of nearly five hundred miles.* [*same as* **return trip**]

round-up /'raʊnd ʌp/ *noun*: **round-ups**
A **round-up** of facts or information is a summary of them: *Let's go back to the studio for the latest news round-up.* [see also **round up** at **round**]

rouse /raʊz/ *verb*: **rouses, rousing, roused**
1 You **rouse** someone when you wake them up: *She couldn't be roused so we sent for a doctor.* **2** Something **rouses** you when it causes strong feelings or emotions in you, which often make you want to take action of some kind: *The generals rode past, rousing their troops.* □ *Normally placid, he could be frightening when roused to anger.* □ *Her sudden promotion has roused suspicions amongst fellow workers.* [*same as* **stir up**; see also **arouse**] — *adjective* **rousing:** *a very rousing national anthem.* [*same as* **stirring**]

route /ruːt/ *noun*; *verb*
▷ ***noun***: **routes**
1 The **route** of a bus or train is the way it travels on a regular journey from one place to another: *a different bus route.* **2** The **route** you take is the particular line of roads you travel along to get to a place: *There is a shorter route, via Haddington.* [*same as* **way**] **3** You refer to a way of achieving something as a **route** to it: *Getting your own television show was the shortest route to fame and fortune.*
▷ ***verb***: **routes, routing, routed**
Traffic **is routed** a certain way when it is directed to travel that way: *Because of the festival, city-bound traffic has been routed along the bypass.*

routine /ruː'tiːn/ *noun*: **routines**
1 (*count or uncount, often adjectival*) A **routine** is a regular or fixed way of doing things, often so regular that it has become dull or boring: *Shaving was clearly not part of his bathtime routine.* □ *a life of soul-destroying routine* □ *We carried out a routine inspection of all its mechanical parts.* □ *The job is really just a dull series of fairly routine tasks.* **2** In dancing or other types of performance, a **routine** is a series of movements that you learn.

row[1] /roʊ/ *noun*: **rows**
A **row** of things is a number of them arranged in a line: *Inside the theatre, several rows of seats were empty.* □ *A woman in the row in front of me wore a hat which completely blocked my view of the screen.* □ *Sow the seeds in rows four inches apart.*
▷ ***phrase*** Several things happen **in a row** when they happen one after the other, with no breaks or changes in between: *That's their eighth victory in a row.*

row[2] /roʊ/ *verb*: **rows, rowing, rowed**
You **row** a boat you are sitting in when you move it by pulling large poles called oars through the water: *I rowed slowly across to the bank, where they were standing.* □ *He rowed us across to the other side.*

row[3] /raʊ/ *noun*; *verb*
▷ ***noun***: **rows**
1 A **row** is a noisy quarrel or argument, or a disagreement of any kind: *It sounded like the people in the next room were having a row.* □ *A row broke out over who was most eligible to lead the party.* [*same as* **argument**]
2 (*informal*) You describe a loud, unpleasant noise or disturbance as a **row**: *The children were making a hell of a row.*
▷ ***verb***: **rows, rowing, rowed**
People **row** when they quarrel noisily with each other: *I don't think we have ever really rowed with each other.* [*same as* **argue**]

rowboat /'roʊboʊt/ *noun* (*AmE*): **rowboats**
A **rowboat** is a rowing boat.

rowdy /'raʊdɪ/ *adjective*: **rowdier, rowdiest**
People who are **rowdy** behave in a noisy, rough, perhaps violent way: *The more beer they drank, the rowdier they became.*

rowing boat /'roʊɪŋ boʊt/ *noun*: **rowing boats**
A **rowing boat** is a small, simple boat that you move by rowing.

royal /rɔɪəl/ *adjective*; *noun*
▷ ***adjective***
1 Royal describes kings, queens and other members of their family, and things relating to them: *The whole country loves a royal wedding.* □ *The royal party will be arriving shortly.* **2** Organizations that have the word **Royal** in their title have been established by a king or queen, or are supported by them: *the Royal Geographical Society.*
▷ ***noun*** (*informal*): **royals**
Members of a royal family are sometimes referred to as **royals**: *She wondered if any of the royals would be attending.*

royalty /'rɔɪəltɪ/ *noun*: **royalties**
1 (*uncount*) Members of a royal family are often referred to as **royalty**: *She'd never been in the company of royalty before.* **2** (*used in the plural*) **Royalties** are payments of money made to a person who has written a book or a song, every time the book is sold or the song performed in public.

rub /rʌb/ *verb*; *noun*
▷ ***verb***: **rubs, rubbing, rubbed**
1 You **rub** something when you move your hand, or a cloth or other object, back and forwards over the surface of it, usually pressing down: *Coat the shoes with polish, then rub hard with a soft cloth to give a shine.* □ *He looked tired, and sat rubbing his eyes.* □ *Rub the cream into your skin.* **2** Things **rub** against each other when they move backwards and forwards while pressing against each other: *There was a bruise where the shoe had been rubbing against his heel.*
▷ ***noun*** (*used in the singular*) *Give it a rub with a damp cloth.*
▷ ***phrase*** (*informal*) You say that someone **is rubbing it in** when they continue to talk about something concerning you that you find unpleasant or embarrassing, for example a mistake that you have made: *I know it was stupid; there's no need to rub it in!*

phrasal verbs
rub off on Someone's qualities or habits **rub off on** you if you acquire or develop them yourself after spending time with that person: *I was worried that the atmosphere of ruthlessness might rub off on Peter.*
rub out You **rub** something **out** when you remove it by rubbing, especially something written or drawn, with a rubber: *You can see where he tried to rub out the last few words.* [*same as* **erase**]

rubber /'rʌbə(r)/ *noun*: **rubbers**
1 (*uncount, often adjectival*) **Rubber** is a strong elastic substance made from a sticky liquid released by some

trees, or made chemically: *sports shoes with soles made of rubber* □ *Wear rubber gloves to protect your hands.* **2** A **rubber** is a small piece of rubber or plastic used for rubbing out pencil or ink marks on paper. [*same as* **eraser**; see picture at **office**] — *adjective* **rubbery:** *The stems of the plant were thick and rubbery.*

rubber band /rʌbə 'band/ *noun*: **rubber bands**
A **rubber band** is a small thin circle of rubber wrapped around things to hold them together. [*same as* **elastic band**]

rubbish /'rʌbɪʃ/ *noun* (*uncount*)
1 Rubbish is waste, things that have been thrown away as unwanted or used: *the collection of household rubbish* □ *a rubbish bin.* [*same as* **waste**] **2 Rubbish** is also nonsense: *I wouldn't believe any of that rubbish.* **3** You also refer to things of poor quality as **rubbish**: *Most of the films were pure rubbish.* □ *They sell a lot of cheap rubbish.* [*same as* **trash**]

rubble /'rʌbəl/ *noun* (*uncount*)
1 Rubble consists of the broken stones, bricks, and pieces of wood and plaster left when a building is destroyed or knocked down: *The houses were reduced to rubble.* **2 Rubble** is also small, rough stones used in building.

ruby /'ru:bɪ/ *noun*: **rubies**
A **ruby** is a dark-red stone used as a jewel: *decorated with diamonds and rubies* □ *her ruby-red lips.*

rucksack /'rʌksak/ *noun*: **rucksacks**
A **rucksack** is a bag that you carry on your back, with straps that fit over your shoulders, *eg* when you are walking in the country or climbing mountains.

rudder /'rʌdə(r)/ *noun*: **rudders**
1 On a boat, the **rudder** is the flat piece of wood or metal below the water at the back, moved by a handle to steer the boat. **2** On an aeroplane, the **rudder** is the movable part of the aeroplane's tail, that controls movement from side to side.

ruddy /'rʌdɪ/ *adjective*: **ruddier, ruddiest**
1 Something that is **ruddy** is a deep pink colour: *the apple's ruddy skin* □ *Her cheeks were a healthy-looking ruddy colour.* **2** Some people use **ruddy** as a mild swearword, instead of saying 'bloody': *My ruddy finger's stuck!*

rude /ru:d/ *adjective*: **ruder, rudest**
1 Someone's behaviour is **rude** when they show a lack of politeness or courtesy: *It would be rude to refuse.* □ *He was told off for being rude to a teacher.* [*same as* **impolite**; *opposite* **polite**] **2** You describe things that deal with sex as **rude** if you think they are embarrassing or slightly offensive: *a few rude jokes.* [*same as* **crude**] **3 Rude** also describes unpleasant things that happen suddenly and unexpectedly: *My first job was a rude awakening to the harsh realities of life.* — *adverb* **rudely:** *children behaving rudely in public* □ *I was made rudely aware of my responsibilities as a parent.*

rudiments /'ru:dɪmənts/ *noun* (*plural*)
The **rudiments** of something are the first basic facts or techniques that you learn relating to it: *He showed me the rudiments of the game.* [*same as* **basics**]

rueful /'ru:fəl/ *adjective*
A **rueful** expression on someone's face shows regret or sorrow: *a rueful smile.*

ruffian /'rʌfɪən/ *noun* (*old*): **ruffians**
Someone who is referred to as a **ruffian** behaves in a rough, violent way: *a busload of young ruffians armed with sticks.* [*same as* **thug**]

ruffled /'rʌfəld/ *adjective*
1 Something such as hair or clothing is **ruffled** when it has been made untidy. [*same as* **messed up**] **2** Someone is **ruffled** when they have lost their calmness and have become nervous, confused or irritated: *I've never once seen Claude ruffled.* [*same as* **disconcerted**]

rug /rʌg/ *noun*: **rugs**
1 A **rug** is a thick, heavy mat or small carpet for covering part of a floor. [see picture at **living room**] **2** A **rug** is also a thick blanket that you wrap around your legs or shoulders to keep warm.

rugby /'rʌgbɪ/ *noun* (*uncount, often adjectival*)
Rugby is an outdoor game played with an oval ball on a large field, in which players run holding the ball in their hands: *a game of rugby* □ *an international rugby match.*

rugged /'rʌgɪd/ *adjective*
1 A **rugged** area of land is rough and uneven, with many rocks. [*same as* **rocky**] **2** You describe a man as **rugged** if his face has an attractively rough quality that suggests physical strength.

ruin /'ru:ɪn/ *noun*; *verb*
▻ ***noun*: ruins**
1 (*used in the plural*) **Ruins** are the pieces left after something has been broken or destroyed, or has decayed or collapsed: *the ruins of an ancient civilization* □ *My life lay in ruins.* **2** (*uncount*; *formal*) **Ruin** is the state of having lost all money or wealth: *The company was heading for ruin.*
▻ ***verb*: ruins, ruining, ruined**
1 You **ruin** something when you spoil it, or when you damage or destroy it: *This wind will ruin my hairstyle.* □ *revelations about his private life that might ruin his career.* **2** To **ruin** someone is to cause them to lose all their money or wealth: *Maintaining such a large house would ruin us.* [*same as* **destroy**]

rule /ru:l/ *noun*; *verb*
▻ ***noun*: rules**
1 A **rule** is an order or instruction concerning what is allowed and not allowed: *The rules of the game forbid any use of the hands.* □ *I don't think it's against the rules.* □ *Under rule 4, a player can be banned from the next three matches.* **2** (*uncount*) **Rule** is government or control, for example by politicians or a monarch: *Things were different under King Edward's rule.* [*same as* **leadership, reign**] **3** (*used in the singular*) You say that something is a **rule**, or the **rule**, if it is a general principle or custom, or a popular fashion: *I make it a rule always to be punctual.* □ *Concern for the environment became the rule among politicians.*
▻ ***verb*: rules, ruling, ruled**
1 To **rule** a country is to govern or control it. **2** A court or judge **rules** when they make an official decision: *The judge ruled that the evidence was not permissible.* **3** You say that something **rules** when it is very common or widespread: *During the first weeks of war, chaos ruled.* [*same as* **prevail**]
▻ ***phrase*** You **bend the rules** when you do something that the rules don't strictly allow.

> ***phrasal verb***
> **rule out 1** You **rule** something **out** when you decide that it is not a choice, option or possibility: *Total surrender was ruled out from the start.* [*same as* **eliminate**] **2** One thing **rules out** another when it prevents it or makes it no longer possible: *We voted against it, effectively ruling out future support from our European partners.*

ruler /'ru:lə(r)/ *noun*: **rulers**
1 A **ruler** is a person who rules or governs: *Once ruler of half the world, he was now a tired old general.* **2** A **ruler** is also a strip of wood, metal or plastic with straight edges, used for drawing straight lines and for measuring length. [see picture at **office**]

ruling /'ru:lɪŋ/ *noun; adjective*
▻ ***noun***: **rulings**
A **ruling** is an official decision, for example by a court. [*same as* **verdict, pronouncement**]
▻ ***adjective***
Ruling describes a person or group that controls an organization or body: *The ruling committee took the opposite view.* [*same as* **governing, commanding**]

rum /rʌm/ *noun (uncount)*
Rum is an alcoholic spirit made from sugar cane: *a bottle of rum.*

rumble /'rʌmbəl/ *verb; noun*
▻ ***verb***: **rumbles, rumbling, rumbled**
1 Something **rumbles** when it makes a deep, low, continuous sound like a series of heavy blows: *The sky rumbled with thunder.* **2** (*informal*) You say you **have rumbled** someone when you have discovered something about them that they were trying to hide: *When he asked us to open our bags, we knew we'd been rumbled.*
▻ ***noun:*** *the rumble of cartwheels on the cobblestones.*

ruminate /'ru:mɪneɪt/ *verb (formal, slightly humorous)*: **ruminates, ruminating, ruminated**
To **ruminate** is to think carefully and seriously about something: *Their predecessors in the House had ruminated on the issue some years previously.* □ *I'll stay here and ruminate while you ladies compare your purchases.* [*same as* **mull, reflect**]

rummage /'rʌmɪdʒ/ *verb*: **rummages, rummaging, rummaged**
You **rummage** somewhere when you search in a rough, untidy way: *I rummaged about in my bag for a pen.* □ *I had to rummage through all the cupboards to find it.* [*same as* **root around**]

rummy /'rʌmɪ/ *noun (uncount)*
Rummy is a card game in which each player tries to collect sets or sequences of three or more cards: *a game of rummy.*

rumour (*AmE* **rumor**) /'ru:mə(r)/ *noun (count or uncount)*: **rumours**
A **rumour** is a piece of information passed from person to person, which may or may not be true: *There's a rumour going round the office that he's been offered the director's job.* □ *These news stories are the product of rumour and speculation.*

rumoured (*AmE* **rumored**) /'ru:məd/ *adjective*
You say it **is rumoured** that something is true when people are saying that it's true, although it may not be true: *It is rumoured that she is going to have a baby.* □ *He is rumoured to have turned the offer down.* [*same as* **reported**]

rump /rʌmp/ *noun*: **rumps**
1 (*often adjectival*) An animal's **rump** consists of the area around its tail or above its back legs: *It's best to use rump steak.* **2** (*informal*) Your buttocks can be referred as your **rump**: *She gave me a slap on the rump.* [*same as* **backside**]

rumpled /'rʌmpəld/ *adjective*
Something such as clothing or hair is **rumpled** when it is no longer smooth and flat and has been made untidy. [*same as* **crumpled, creased**]

rumpus /'rʌmpəs/ *noun (used in the singular)*
There is a **rumpus** when a lot of people are arguing noisily: *a controversial speech that caused a bit of a rumpus.* [*same as* **commotion**]

run /rʌn/ *verb; noun*
▻ ***verb***: **runs, running, ran, run**
1 a You **run** when you move quickly, with both feet off the ground between each step: *We had to run for the bus.* □ *She ran upstairs.* □ *He liked to run at least a mile before breakfast.* □ *Do you still go running in the mornings?* **b** You **run** a race, or **run** in one, when you take part in it: *Are you going to run in the marathon?* □ *Some of these horses aren't running today.* □ *That's the best race I've run this year.* **c** You **run** somewhere when you rush there: *You can't keep running to your Mum every time you hurt yourself.* **d** You **run** from something when you try to avoid it: *I run from embarrassing discussions like that.* **e** You **run** somewhere when you travel quickly there: *I must run up to London this afternoon.* **f** You get someone to **run** an errand when you ask them go and get, or do, something for you. **g** Candidates **run** for a post when they offer themselves for election to it: *He has decided not to run for President.* [*same as* **stand**]
2 a Things **run** when they move on wheels or on rails: *The brake was left off and the car ran quite a distance downhill.* **b** Trains and buses **run** or **are run** when they provide public transport on a regular route: *That bus doesn't run on a Sunday.* □ *They run extra train services over the Christmas period.* **c** You **run** someone somewhere when you take them there in your car: *Let me run you to the station.* [*same as* **drive**] **d** You **run** a vehicle somewhere when you drive it there: *He ran the locomotive into a siding.* **e** You **run** a car if you own and drive one: *I don't run a car any longer.* □ *The car was getting too expensive to run.*
3 a Machinery **runs** or **is run** when it operates: *Run the engine for a few minutes to let it warm up.* □ *A gas fridge is less expensive to run than an electric one.* **b** Machinery **runs** on, or off, a certain type of energy, or on a certain type of fuel, if that is what makes it work: *Laptop computers will run off mains electricity or a battery.* □ *All modern cars run on unleaded petrol.* [*same as* **work**] **c** A machine, especially a vehicle, **is running** well or badly when it is working satisfactorily or unsatisfactorily: *The car has been running better since its last service.*
4 a You **run** something such as a scheme, operation or project when you organize it; it **is running** when it is proceeding or progressing: *The distribution scheme has been running smoothly so far.* □ *We're running another course for learners in the spring.* **b** Something **is running** late when it is taking longer than, or happening later than, the time advertised or planned; something **is running** on time when it is proceeding punctually: *Because of the extended news bulletin, programmes are running a little late this evening* □ *The 6.40 train from Glasgow is running approximately 20 minutes late.* □ *All train services in and out of Kings Cross are now running on time.* **c** You **run** something such as a business when you manage it: *They run a small restaurant in the High Street.* □ *We always thought running our own business would be fun.* [*same as* **manage**] **d** You **run** a test or experiment when you carry it out; you **run** a computer program when you put it into operation. [*same as* **operate**] **e** Programmes that **are running** on the radio or television are being broadcast: *one of the serials currently running on television.* **f** A play or other entertainment **runs** for a certain number of weeks or months if it is performed for that length of time: *The play was very popular in New York, where it ran for over four months.* **g** A newspaper **runs** a story or feature when it includes it. **h** Something such as a lease or contract **runs** for a certain length of time if that is the time it lasts, or is valid, for: *The contract runs from April to September.* [*same as* **last**]
5 a Liquid **runs** when it flows: *The sweat was running down his face.* □ *Running water is usually safe to drink.* □ *A little stream ran past the cottage.* [*same as* **flow**]

b Something such as a river **is running** with a liquid when it is full of it: *rivers running with blood.* [*same as* **flow**] **c** You **run** water when you let it flow by turning a tap on: *I ran some more cold water into the bath.* □ *Someone had left the kitchen tap running, so I turned it off.* □ *I'm just running a bath for the children.* **d** The colour of a fabric **runs** if it flows out of it when you wash it: *Indian cottons should be washed in cold water, otherwise the colours may run.* **e** Stitches in a knitted garment **run** when they come undone one by one in a vertical line and form a ladder.

6 a You **run** something such as your hand over or through something else when you move it over or through smoothly and lightly: *She ran her fingers through his hair.* □ *He ran a finger down the list.* □ *Let me run an iron over those trousers.* □ *Could you run your eye over this essay to see if there are any spelling mistakes?* [compare **pass**] **b** Something such as a road **runs** somewhere if it leads that way: *The road to Shrewsbury runs through several pretty villages.* □ *A cycle track ran alongside the road.* □ *A high wall ran round the entire estate.* [compare **pass, lead**] **c** A feeling **runs** somewhere when it passes or spreads quickly: *A shiver ran down her spine.* □ *Excitement ran through the audience.* **d** Features and characteristics, such as brown eyes or musical ability, **run** in certain families if they are noticeable in generation after generation of its members. **e** Something written **runs** in a certain way if that is what it says: *The wire ran: 'Heading south. Amundsen'.* [*same as* **read**]

7 a You **run** a risk when you take one: *I didn't want to run the risk of missing the plane.* **b** You **run** a temperature when you are ill and have a fever: *She was running a temperature of 39.* **c** Something such as inflation or unemployment **is running** at a certain level if it has reached it: *with inflation running at 8%.*

▻ ***noun***: **runs**

1 a (*used in the singular*) You move at a **run** when you run: *She broke into a run.* **b** A **run** is a race or a period of running for exercise: *a cross-country run.* **c** A **run** somewhere is a trip or journey in a vehicle: *Would you like to come for a run in the car?* □ *The run into town normally took about 30 minutes.* **d** (*usually in the singular*) A **run** is also a regular route travelled by a bus or train: *He had been a driver on the London-to-Glasgow run for several years.* **e** A ski **run** is a downhill course that people use regularly. **f** In games such as cricket and baseball, a **run** is a point scored by running a set distance after hitting the ball. **g** A **run** in a knitted garment such as a pair of tights is a vertical line of stitches that have come undone. [*same as* **ladder**]

2 a (*usually in the singular*) A play or show has a **run** of a certain length if it is performed for that length of time: *The play had a run of six weeks.* □ *after a successful run on Broadway.* **b** (*used in the singular*) You experience a **run** of something when you experience a period of it: *I've had a run of bad luck recently.* □ *They'd had a run of defeats.* [compare **series**] **c** The usual **run** of something is the usual kind or mixture: *the usual run of new students.*

3 a You are given the **run** of a place when you are given permission to go anywhere, or use anything, in it: *They kindly gave us the run of their apartment.* **b** There is a **run** on some kind of product when everyone is buying it or wanting it. [compare **demand**]

▻ ***phrases*** **1** You think about something **in the long run** when you consider its long-term effects, and **in the short run** when you consider its immediate effects: *It'd be wiser in the long run to get the repairs done now, even if the delay is a nuisance.* **2** A person who is **on the run** is trying to escape or hide from an enemy, the authorities, or the police. **3** You **run for it** or **make a run for it** when you try to escape. **4** A scheme or project that is **up and running** is actually going ahead, as distinct from being planned.

phrasal verbs

run across You **run across** someone when you meet them unexpectedly: *We ran across each other several times in the Far East.*

run along You tell children to **run along** when you want them to go away and leave you in peace.

run away 1 You **run away** when you try to escape by running: *The thieves were caught as they were running away.* **2** Children **run away** *eg* from home or from an institution when they leave without telling anyone, usually because they are unhappy there: *She ran away to London at the age of 14.* [see also **runaway**] **3** You **run away** from something that you don't want to deal with when you try to avoid it: *men who run away from their responsibilities as fathers.* **4** You let your feelings **run away** with you when you don't control them as you should, and behave foolishly: *We rather let our emotions run away with us.* **5** You **run away** with a mistaken idea if you start believing it: *Don't run away with the idea that this is going to be a quick job.*

run down 1 You **run** someone or something **down** when you criticize them unfairly: *Don't run yourself down all the time; have a little pride in your achievements.* **2** A business or organization that **is being run down** is being reduced in size and in its range of activities. [see also **run-down**]

run into 1 You **run into** someone when you meet them unexpectedly. **2** A vehicle **runs into** something when it bumps into it or collides with it: *Her car ran into a wall.* **3** You **run into** difficulties when you are unexpectedly faced with them and have to deal with them: *Quite early on in the project we ran into serious problems.* **4** Something **runs into** a certain amount if it reaches that amount: *debts running into thousands of pounds.* **5** One thing **runs into** another if it joins with the other so that you cannot distinguish them: *The colours all ran into one another.*

run off (*informal*) **1** You **run off** with someone when you go away with them secretly in order to live with them or marry them: *Her husband ran off with another woman.* **2** You **run off** copies of something when you make them, *eg* on a copying machine.

run on Something **runs on** when it continues for longer than people expect or want: *I was afraid that the speeches would run on a bit.*

run out 1 You **run out** of something when you have used it all up and there is none left; something **runs out** when there is none left: *We knew we might run out of money before the end of the holiday.* □ *Our good luck had evidently run out.* **2** Something such as a passport, licence, lease or contract **runs out** when it reaches its time limit and is no longer valid: *I hadn't noticed that my passport had run out.* □ *The contract runs out at the end of the year.*

run over 1 A vehicle **runs** someone **over** when it knocks them down and kills or injures them: *I was nearly run over on a pedestrian crossing today.* **2** You **run over** something when you check it, *eg* in order to correct it, or to remember it: *Let's run over the main points again.*

run through 1 You **run through** something when you practise or rehearse it: *We'll run through Scene Two once again.* **2** You **run through** a list or a number of points when you mention all the items in

order. **3** A quality, feature or characteristic **runs through** something if it is noticeable throughout it: *the despair that runs through all his plays.*
run to Something **runs to** a certain amount if it reaches that amount: *This particular biography runs to 957 pages.*
run up **1** You **run up** debts or bills when you buy a lot of expensive things that have to be paid for: *By the end of the meal, we had run up a bill of over £100.* **2** You **run up** against problems when you are faced with them and have to deal with them: *We've no idea of the kind of difficulties we're likely to run up against.* [see also **run-up**]

runaway /ˈrʌnəweɪ/ *noun; adjective*
▻ ***noun***: **runaways**
A **runaway** is someone who has run away, especially a child who has secretly left home. [see also **run away** at **run**]
▻ ***adjective***
1 A **runaway** vehicle is moving out of control, with no driver to control or stop it. **2** **Runaway** is also used to refer to how great the extent of something is: *Her first book was a runaway success in America.* ▫ *a runaway victory.*

run-down /rʌnˈdaʊn/ *adjective*
1 Someone is **run-down** when they are very tired and weak, and perhaps unhealthy or unwell as a result: *My patients often complain of feeling run-down.* [*same as* **drained**] **2** A **run-down** building is in a very bad condition, needing many repairs. [*same as* **broken-down**] [see also **run down** at **run**]

rung[1] /rʌŋ/ *noun*: **rungs**
The **rungs** on a ladder are the horizontal parts you stand on.

rung[2] /rʌŋ/ *verb*
Rung is the past participle of **ring**.

run-in /ˈrʌn ɪn/ *noun* (*informal*): **run-ins**
A **run-in** is a quarrel or argument: *I had a bit of a run-in with one of the directors over this very issue.* [*same as* **confrontation**]

runner bean /ˈrʌnə biːn/ *noun* (*usually in the plural*): **runner beans**
Runner beans are long green pods that grow on a climbing plant, and are eaten as a vegetable. [see picture at **vegetable**]

runner-up /rʌnərˈʌp/ *noun*: **runners-up**
In a competition or contest, the **runner-up** is the person who finishes in second place.

running /ˈrʌnɪŋ/ *noun; adjective*
▻ ***noun*** (*uncount, often adjectival*)
1 (*uncount*) **Running** is the sport or activity of running: *a pair of running shoes.* **2** The **running** of something is the act of managing, organizing or operating it: *She looks after the day-to-day running of three residential homes.* ▫ *a rise in our running costs.* [*same as* **management**]
▻ ***adjective***
Running describes things that are continuing, or that continue without a break or change: *It's difficult to keep up a running commentary for any length of time.* ▫ *I hadn't seen anyone in the house for several days running.*
▻ ***phrases*** You say you are **in the running** when you have a chance of winning; you are **out of the running** when you have no chance of winning: *In spite of a poor performance in the first round, Ballesteros is still very much in the running for the championship.*

runny /ˈrʌnɪ/ *adjective*: **runnier**, **runniest**
1 A substance is **runny** when it is in the form of a thin, watery liquid: *Heat the jam until it is runny.* **2** Your nose is **runny** when mucus keeps flowing from it, for example because you have a cold.

run-of-the-mill /rʌnəvðəˈmɪl/ *adjective*
You describe something as **run-of-the-mill** if it is only ordinary or average, not particularly good or special: *They offer a fairly run-of-the-mill range of pub food.* [*same as* **commonplace**, **everyday**]

run-up /ˈrʌnʌp/ *noun* (*used in the singular*)
The **run-up** to an important event is the period of time immediately before it, or the sequence of events that lead up to it: *We don't want any strenuous training sessions in the run-up to the final.* [see also **run up** at **run**]

runway /ˈrʌnweɪ/ *noun*: **runways**
At an airport, a **runway** is a road-like surface that aircraft take off from and land on: *There had been snow on the runway.*

rupture /ˈrʌptʃə(r)/ *noun; verb*
▻ ***noun***: **ruptures**
1 A **rupture** is an injury in which part of a muscle or joint is torn apart. [*same as* **tear**] **2** (*formal*) A **rupture** is also a break in something, for example in a friendship: *What could have provoked such a rupture between them?* [*same as* **split**]
▻ ***verb***: **ruptures**, **rupturing**, **ruptured:** *If I stretched my leg any further, I might rupture myself.*

rural /ˈrʊərəl/ *adjective*
Rural describes places in the countryside, or things relating to such places: *in our rural communities* ▫ *rural pursuits such as fishing and shooting.*

ruse /ruːz/ *noun* (*formal*): **ruses**
A **ruse** is a clever trick or plan intended to deceive someone. [*same as* **ploy**, **trick**]

rush /rʌʃ/ *verb; noun*
▻ ***verb***: **rushes**, **rushing**, **rushed**
1 You **rush** somewhere when you go there in a hurry: *I heard a scream and I rushed downstairs to see what had happened.* ▫ *If I rushed round to see him now, I might still be back in time for Donald.* ▫ *They rushed him to hospital immediately.* ▫ *People all over the country are rushing to buy a copy of her new book.* [*same as* **race**, **dash**] **2** You **rush** something when you do it too quickly or hurriedly: *I didn't want to have to rush it at the last minute.* ▫ *Don't let them rush you into making a foolish decision.* **3** You **rush** someone when you attack them suddenly, hoping to surprise them.
▻ ***noun*** (*used in the singular*)
1 You are in a **rush** when you are rushing, or when there is a reason why you should rush: *Don't be in such a rush all the time.* ▫ *Everyone was in a rush to get the best seats.* ▫ *There's no rush; the train doesn't leave for another half hour.* **2** There is a **rush** somewhere, or a **rush** for something, when large numbers of people are rushing to get somewhere, or get something: *There was a rush for the door.* ▫ *We hadn't anticipated such a rush for tickets.* ▫ *in the days of the gold rush.* [*same as* **stampede**] **3** People often refer to a period of very busy activity as the **rush**, especially the periods of the day when large numbers of people travel to and from work: *I went to the bank early, to avoid the lunchtime rush.* ▫ *We could leave at 4 o'clock and beat the rush.*

rushes /ˈrʌʃɪz/ *noun* (*plural*)
Rushes are tall grass-like plants that grow in or near water.

rush hour /ˈrʌʃ aʊə(r)/ *noun* (*uncount or count, often adjectival*): **rush hours**

Rush hour is the period at the beginning and the end of the day when traffic is busiest because people are travelling to and from work: *We got caught in the rush-hour traffic.*

Russian /ˈrʌʃən/ *adjective*; *noun*

▷ ***adjective***

Russian means concerned with or belonging to Russia, its people, or their language: *His wife is Russian.* □ *Russian novels of the 19th century* □ *a Russian dictionary.*

▷ ***noun***: **Russians**

1 A **Russian** is a person who is born in, or is a citizen of, Russia: *A party of Russians were sitting at the next table.* **2** (*uncount*) **Russian** is the language of Russia and some neighbouring countries: *He was trying to teach himself Russian.*

rust /rʌst/ *noun*; *verb*

▷ ***noun*** (*uncount*)

Rust is a reddish-brown substance that forms on iron and other metals exposed to water and air, slowly causing decay. [*same as* **corrosion**]

▷ ***verb***: **rusts, rusting, rusted:** *The bolts had rusted up and were impossible to move.* [*same as* **corrode**]

rustic /ˈrʌstɪk/ *adjective*

Rustic means simple or rough, in a way typical of people who live in the countryside: *The house had a certain rustic charm.* □ *The furniture was heavy and rustic.*

rustle /ˈrʌsəl/ *verb*; *noun*

▷ ***verb***: **rustles, rustling, rustled**

Something **rustles** when it makes a soft sound like dry leaves rubbing together: *I could hear the rustling of a newspaper.*

▷ ***noun*** (*used in the singular*): *I remember the rustle of the dress as she walked down the aisle.*

phrasal verb

You **rustle** something **up**, especially a meal, when you prepare it quickly using whatever materials are available: *I'm sure I could rustle up a few sandwiches later.*

rusty /ˈrʌstɪ/ *adjective*: **rustier, rustiest**

1 Rusty metal has rust on it: *The car was basically in good condition, if a little rusty in places.* **2** Your skill or knowledge is **rusty** when it is not as good as it used to be, because you have not used it for a while: *Ordering a coffee was all I could manage with my rusty French.*

rut /rʌt/ *noun* (*singular*)

You say you are in a **rut** when you have become fixed in a boring routine: *Before long, I would feel I was in a rut, so I would leave my job and move on.*

ruthless /ˈruːθləs/ *adjective*

A **ruthless** person takes whatever action is practical or necessary, without thinking or caring about how unfair, harsh or cruel it might be: *You have to accept that ruthless decisions are being taken every day.* □ *It scared me to think that I might become as ruthless as he was.* [*same as* **remorseless, heartless**] — *noun* (*uncount*) **ruthlessness:** *I was shocked and dismayed by the sheer ruthlessness of the legal profession.*

rye /raɪ/ *noun* (*uncount, often adjectival*)

Rye is a grass-like cereal plant whose grain is used for making bread and whisky, and as food for animals: *rye bread.*

S

'S or **s** /ɛs/ *noun*: **S's** or **s's** /ˈɛsɪz/
S is the nineteenth letter of the English alphabet: *'Sure' begins with an S.* □ *There are four s's in Mississippi.*

's[1] /z/ or /s/ *suffix*
1 's is added to singular nouns, and to plural nouns that do not end in 's', to form the possessive: *John's car* □ *the children's toys.* **2 's** is also added to some numbers, letters, symbols and abbreviations to form plurals: *a row of X's.*

's[2] /z/ or /s/ *verb*
's is a short form of 'is' or 'has' used in informal speech and writing: *He's not here.* □ *Mary's going shopping.* □ *What's he doing here?* □ *He's got chicken-pox.* □ *She's gone on holiday.* □ *The boat looks very smart now that it's had a new coat of paint.*

-s or **-es** *suffix*
1 -s or **-es** is used to form the plurals of most nouns, as in *cats, tables* and *churches*. **2 -s** is also used to form the plurals of abbreviations that are made up of capital letters: *JPs* □ *CFCs.* **3 -s** or **-es** is used to form the third person singular of the present tense of verbs, as in *walks, jumps* and *reaches*.

Sabbath /ˈsabəθ/ *noun* (*used in the singular*)
The **Sabbath** is the day of the week set aside for rest and worship in certain religions; Saturday amongst Jews and Sunday amongst most Christians.

sabotage /ˈsabətɑːʒ/ *noun*; *verb*
▻ ***noun*** (*uncount*)
1 Sabotage is the deliberate damage or destruction of buildings, machinery or equipment carried out secretly to disrupt or weaken an enemy or political system: *partisans involved in sabotage of the enemy's supply lines.* **2 Sabotage** is also secret action that is intended to disrupt a plan or prevent it being carried out: *industrial sabotage.*
▻ ***verb***: **sabotages, sabotaging, sabotaged**
To **sabotage** a plan is to disrupt it or prevent it from being carried out: *He seems determined to sabotage the whole project.*

saccharin /ˈsakərɪn/ *noun* (*uncount*)
Saccharin is a very sweet chemical that is used as a non-fattening substitute for sugar by people who want to lose weight or who are not allowed to eat sugar. — *adjective* **saccharine** /ˈsakəraɪn/: *a saccharine-sweet smile* [=one that is too sweet or pleasant to be genuine].

sachet /ˈsaʃeɪ/ *noun*: **sachets**
A **sachet** is a small sealed plastic or paper packet containing a small quantity of liquid or powder: *a sachet of shampoo.*

sack /sak/ *noun*; *verb*
▻ ***noun***: **sacks**
1 A **sack** is a large bag made from coarse cloth, paper or plastic, used to carry or store things in. **2** (also **sackful, sackfuls**) A **sack** or **sackful** is the amount contained in such a bag: *a sack of potatoes* □ *sacks of coal* □ *They removed sackfuls of litter after the concert.*
▻ ***verb***: **sacks, sacking, sacked** (*informal*)
If your employer **sacks** you, they say you can no longer work for them, *eg* because your work or behaviour has not been up to the required standard or because you are no longer needed: *The company sacked all the workers who went out on strike.* [*same as* **fire**]
▻ ***phrases*** (*informal*) You **are given sack** or **get the sack**, when your employer dismisses you from your job: *They gave him the sack for stealing from the till.* □ *He got the sack from his first job for smoking in the toilets.*

sacking /ˈsakɪŋ/ *noun* (*uncount*)
Sacking is a type of coarse cloth used to make sacks: *He covered the pile of cut logs with a piece of sacking.*

sacrament /ˈsakrəmənt/ *noun*: **sacraments**
The **sacraments** are any of various Christian ceremonies thought of as being especially sacred, *eg* marriage, baptism or communion.

sacred /ˈseɪkrɪd/ *adjective*
1 Sacred places, objects or rituals are devoted to God or a god and are therefore regarded with deep and solemn respect. **2 Sacred** is also used to describe things that are connected with religion or worship: *sacred music.* **3** When someone regards *eg* a rule or duty as **sacred** they believe that it is so important that it must not be challenged or changed: *She saw it as her sacred duty to ensure that the children were taught respect for others.*
▻ ***phrase*** A place, object or ritual that is **sacred to** the followers of a particular religion is regarded as holy or of special religious significance to them.

sacrifice /ˈsakrɪfaɪs/ *noun*; *verb*
▻ ***noun***: **sacrifices**
1 (*uncount or count*) **Sacrifice** is the process of making an offering to God or a god in the belief that some benefit may be obtained or to prevent something bad happening; a **sacrifice** is something offered to God or a god, especially a person or animal that is ceremonially killed. **2** (*uncount or count*) **Sacrifice** or a **sacrifice** is the giving up or giving away of something valuable for the sake of another person or for some other purpose that is thought good.
▻ ***verb***: **sacrifices, sacrificing, sacrificed**
1 If something **is sacrificed**, it is offered to God or a god as a sacrifice. **2** If you **sacrifice** something that you value, you give it up or give it away for someone else's sake or for some other purpose that you believe is good.

sacrificial /sakrɪˈfɪʃəl/ *adjective* (*formal*)
Sacrificial means of or connected with sacrifice, or used as a religious sacrifice: *a sacrificial lamb.*

sacrilege /ˈsakrɪlɪdʒ/ *noun* (*uncount or used in the singular*)
Sacrilege or a **sacrilege** is the act of causing deliberate damage to, or treating with disrespect, something

holy or something regarded with great respect by other people. — *adjective* **sacrilegious** /sakrɪ'lɪdʒəs/: *It is considered sacrilegious to go into the temple with your head uncovered.* [*opposite* **reverent**, **pious**]

sacrosanct /'sakroʊsaŋkt/ *adjective*
Something that is **sacrosanct** is regarded as being too holy or too important to be treated with disrespect: *He is never available on Saturdays or Sundays; he regards the weekends he spends with his family as sacrosanct.*

sad /sad/ *adjective*: **sadder**, **saddest**
1 If you are **sad**, you are feeling unhappy: *Why does he look so sad?* □ *I was very sad when I had to leave.* [*opposite* **happy**] **2** Something **sad** **a** makes you feel grief or unhappiness: *I've just heard the sad news of your grandmother's death.* □ *The closing of the mine was the saddest day in the village's history.* **b** expresses or suggests unhappiness: *sad music* □ *The dog had large sad eyes.* **3** A **sad** state or situation is one that is very unfortunate or very bad: *The children in the orphanage were in a very sad state when they were discovered by aid workers.* □ *It's a sad fact that it has proved impossible to bring lasting peace to the region.* [*same as* **deplorable**] — *adverb* **sadly:** *She nodded her head sadly.* □ *The house has been sadly neglected.* □ (*sentence adverb*) *Sadly, she died before help arrived.* — *noun* (*uncount or count*) **sadness:** *She was filled with sadness at the news.* □ *The fact that she could not see her grandchildren was one of the great sadnesses of her life.* [*opposite* **happiness**]

sadden /'sadən/ *verb*: **saddens**, **saddening**, **saddened** (*often in the passive*)
You **are saddened** by something, when it makes you feel sad: *He was greatly saddened to hear of the death of his old schoolfriend.*

saddle /'sadəl/ *noun*; *verb*
▻ ***noun***: **saddles**
A **saddle** is **1** a seat, often made of leather, that you put on a horse's back so that you can ride it. A saddle is held on by straps which you tie under the horse's belly. **2** a fixed seat on a bicycle or motorcycle. [see picture at **bicycle**]
▻ ***verb***: **saddles**, **saddling**, **saddled**
You **saddle** a horse or pony when you put a saddle on it.
▻ ***phrase*** Someone who is **in the saddle** is **a** on horseback. **b** in control or working effectively in a job or role: *After such a long illness, it will take him some time to get back in the saddle.*

> ***phrasal verbs***
> **saddle up** A horse rider or jockey **saddles up** when they put a saddle on their horse so that they can ride it: *The cowboys saddled up and rode out of town.*
> **saddle with** You are **saddled with** something, such as unpleasant or difficult work or responsibility, when you have it or are given it though you do not want it: *We don't want to be saddled with two young children on such a long and difficult journey.* [*same as* **lumber with**]

sadism /'seɪdɪzm/ *noun* (*uncount*)
1 **Sadism** is the practice of getting sexual pleasure by inflicting pain on another person. **2** Used more generally, **sadism** also means the practice of getting pleasure or satisfaction from being cruel to, or hurting, other people. [compare **masochism**]

sadist /'seɪdɪst/ *noun*: **sadists**
A **sadist** is someone who gets pleasure from inflicting pain and suffering on others: *These horrific murders must be the work of a sadist.* □ *Our football coach is a real sadist; he makes us run ten miles every weekend.* [compare **masochist**]

sadistic /sə'dɪstɪk/ *adjective*
You describe a person or their behaviour as **sadistic** when they get, or seem to get, pleasure from inflicting pain and suffering on others.

s.a.e. /ɛs eɪ iː/ *noun*: **s.a.e.s**
An **s.a.e.** is a stamped addressed envelope: *For a copy of the script write to the BBC enclosing an s.a.e.*

safari /sə'fɑːrɪ/ *noun* (*count or uncount*): **safaris**
A **safari** is an expedition or tour during which people hunt or watch wild animals, especially in Africa: *an African safari* □ *They're on safari in Tanzania.*

safe /seɪf/ *adjective*; *noun*
▻ ***adjective***: **safer**, **safest**
1 **Safe** is used to describe situations or actions that do not involve danger or risk: *The procedure is quite safe and only involves a small operation.* □ *That ladder doesn't look very safe to me.* **2** You are **safe** when you get out of, or are taken out of, a dangerous situation unharmed: *They were overjoyed to hear that he was safe after so many weeks of uncertainty.* **3** A **safe** place gives protection from possible harm or danger: *The reedbed is a relatively safe place for the birds to raise their chicks.* □ *a safe haven for Kurdish refugees.* [*same as* **secure**; *opposite* **unsafe**, **dangerous**] **4** A **safe** bet or a **safe** investment involves no risk of loss.
▻ ***noun***: **safes**
A **safe** is a strongly built metal box in which valuables can be locked away: *She put her diamonds in the hotel safe overnight.*
▻ ***phrases*** **1** You take a precaution **to be on the safe side** when you take it so as to be doubly cautious; if you take a certain course of action **to be on the safe side**, you choose that course of action as the safer alternative to another: *There should be plenty of accommodation available, but I would book early just to be on the safe side.* □ *If these pills are making you feel sick, you had better stop taking them, to be on the safe side.* **2** If someone or something is **in safe hands**, they are with or are being looked after by someone who can be relied upon to keep them safe: *Don't worry about your son; he's in safe hands.* **3** You **play safe** when you take no risks: *If you want to play safe put your money in a building society rather that risking it on the stock market.* **4** If someone comes back **safe and sound**, they return from a journey or dangerous situation without having been injured or harmed: *They were tremendously relieved when the police brought their small son back safe and sound.* — *adverb* **safely:** *The plane landed safely despite the high wind.* □ *The children were safely tucked up in bed.*

safeguard /'seɪfgɑːd/ *noun*; *verb*
▻ ***noun***: **safeguards**
A **safeguard** is a means of providing protection against danger or harm: *an agreement in which there are certain safeguards to prevent disabled workers from being discriminated against.* [*same as* **precaution**]
▻ ***verb***: **safeguards**, **safeguarding**, **safeguarded**
To **safeguard** something is to protect it from danger or harm: *The government has done very little to safeguard jobs in traditional industries.*

safekeeping /seɪf'kiːpɪŋ/ *noun* (*uncount*)
If you put something somewhere for **safekeeping**, or it is in that person's **safekeeping**, you put it in a safe place, or someone keeps it safe: *The deeds are at the lawyer's office for safekeeping.*

safety /'seɪftɪ/ *noun* (*uncount*)
Safety is the quality or circumstance of being safe: *The police were concerned for her safety.* □ *The birds can feed in the area in perfect safety.*

safety belt /'seɪftɪ bɛlt/ *noun*: **safety belts**
A **safety belt** is a strap or straps that are tied around a person's body to prevent them falling or being injured, especially a seat belt in a car or plane.

safety catch /'seɪftɪ katʃ/ *noun*: **safety catches**
A **safety catch** is **1** a device that prevents a gun from being fired accidentally. **2** a small lock on *eg* a bracelet or necklace that prevents it from opening accidentally.

safety net /'seɪftɪ nɛt/ *noun*: **safety nets**
1 A **safety net** is a large net positioned underneath circus performers, especially trapeze artists, that will catch them if they accidentally fall. **2** (*usually in the singular*) You can also refer to any measure that will protect people from financial difficulty or ruin as a **safety net**: *Some young people have fallen through the social security safety net and are completely destitute.*

safety pin /'seɪftɪ pɪn/ *noun*: **safety pins**
A **safety pin** is a U-shaped metal pin with a guard fitted over the point that you use for fastening things together.

safety valve /'seɪftɪ valv/ *noun*: **safety valves**
1 A **safety valve** is a device designed to open and release gas or liquid if the pressure level in a machine becomes dangerously high. **2** You can also refer to a means by which strong emotions, such as anger or frustration, can be harmlessly released as a **safety valve**. [*same as* **outlet**]

sag /sag/ *verb*: **sags, sagging, sagged**
1 Something **sags**, when it sinks or bends downwards because it is carrying too much weight or because it has lost its original firmness: *The tent sagged under the weight of the rainwater.* □ *The bed is so old it sags in the middle.* □ *The skin on her face has sagged into folds and wrinkles.* [*same as* **droop**] **2** If prices **sag**, or the level of something **sags**, it falls, especially for a short time.

saga /'sɑːgə/ *noun*: **sagas**
A **saga** is a long story, especially a work of fiction about several generations of the same family: *the long-running saga of the royal family's private lives.*

sage /seɪdʒ/ *noun*; *adjective*
▻ ***noun***: **sages**
1 (*uncount*) **Sage** is a plant with grey-green leaves used as a herb in cooking. **2** (*literary*) A **sage** is a person, especially someone old, who is regarded as being very wise.
▻ ***adjective*** (*literary*)
If someone, especially someone old, is described as **sage**, they are very wise: *a sage old man.* — *adverb* **sagely:** *The old man listened to their report, saying nothing, but nodding his head sagely every so often.*

said /sɛd/ *verb*
Said is the past tense and past participle of **say**.

sail /seɪl/ *noun*; *verb*
▻ ***noun***: **sails**
1 A **sail** is a sheet of canvas attached to a mast on a boat or ship spread to catch the wind and used to carry the boat or ship through the water. **2** A **sail** is a trip in a boat or ship (with or without sails) or the distance travelled by boat or ship: *Let's go for a sail.* □ *It was only a short sail to the island.* **3** A windmill's **sails** are its broad flat blades that catch the wind.
▻ ***verb***: **sails, sailing, sailed**
1 You **sail** when you travel by boat or ship: *They sailed across the Pacific in small open boats.* **2** You **sail** a boat or a ship when you steer it through the water using a sail or sails to catch the wind: *The children sailed the Swallow to the island.* **3** A boat or ship **sails** when it leaves a port or harbour: *The ferry sails at noon.* **4** If someone **sails** into or out of a place, they come in or go out moving in a dramatic or stately manner like a ship with all its sails spread; if a person or thing **sails** past you it moves past you smoothly and quickly as if it is being carried by the wind: *Miss Taylor sailed into the room where she was immediately surrounded by a large group of adoring fans.* □ *A piece of the roof sailed past him, missing him by inches.*
▻ ***phrase*** When people **set sail**, they begin a journey by boat or ship: *They set sail for the Azores.*

> ***phrasal verb***
> If you **sail through** a test or examination, you pass it easily: *He sailed through his final exams.*

sailboard /'seɪlbɔːd/ *noun*: **sailboards**
A **sailboard** is another name for a windsurfer.

sailing /'seɪlɪŋ/ *noun*: **sailings**
1 (*uncount*) **Sailing** is the sport or activity of sailing small boats: *Sailing is his favourite hobby.* □ *Activities at the summer camp include sailing and canoeing.* **2** A **sailing** is a voyage made by a boat or ship carrying passengers from one place to another: *There are regular sailings from the mainland to all the Greek islands.*
▻ ***phrase*** When you describe a task that you have to do or complete as **plain sailing**, you mean it is straightforward and easy to do.

sailing boat /'seɪlɪŋ boʊt/ *noun*: **sailing boats**
A **sailing boat** is a boat equipped with sails.

sailor /'seɪlə(r)/ *noun*: **sailors**
A **sailor** is any member of a ship's crew, especially one who is not an officer: *soldiers, sailors, and airmen* □ *He's a sailor in the Greek navy.*
▻ ***phrase*** Someone who is a **good sailor** is able to travel on boats or ships in bad weather without being seasick.

saint /seɪnt/ *noun*: **saints**
1 A **saint** is a person who is officially recognized after their death by a Christian church as having lived an especially holy life and therefore being worthy of honour and praise for ever: *Sir Thomas More was made a saint in 1935.* □ *Saint Columba brought Christianity to the Picts, the Scots and the Northern English.* **2** (*informal*) If you call someone a **saint**, you mean they are an exceptionally good and kind person: *She must be a saint to put up with all his bad habits.*

saintly /'seɪntlɪ/ *adjective*: **saintlier, saintliest**
A **saintly** person is very good or very holy; a **saintly** thing shows that a person is very good or very holy: *a saintly life* □ *a saintly smile.*

sake /seɪk/ *noun* (*usually in the singular*): **sakes**
1 You do something for someone's **sake** if their needs are the reason why you do it: *They decided to stay married for the sake of the children.* □ *Please don't prepare an elaborate meal just for my sake.* **2** Something that you hope will happen, or that would be a good thing to happen, for someone's **sake**, would be a good thing from their point of view: *I hoped for her sake that she would die before she became even more crippled.* □ *I believe it will be best, for both our sakes, if we separate now.* □ *Let's hope you're right, for all our sakes.* **3** You do something, or enjoy doing it, for its own **sake** if you do it because you enjoy it, not for any other purpose: *I just enjoy studying for its own sake.* **4** You do something for the **sake** of it, or for the **sake** of doing it, when you do it because you want to, and have no better reason: *She tends to disagree with me*

just for the sake of it. □ *They're just arguing for the sake of arguing.* **5** You do something for the **sake** of a particular thing if you do it in order to maintain or achieve that thing: *He made such a fuss that I gave him what he wanted for the sake of peace.* **6** People assume something for the **sake** of argument when they treat it as true in order to discuss something that depends on its being true: *Let's just say, for the sake of argument, that the government decided to reduce the basic rate of tax by 2%.*

▻ ***phrases*** **1** (*informal*) People use **for goodness sake, for heaven's sake, for Pete's sake**, and the stronger or more offensive **for Christ's sake** and **for God's sake**, to express impatience or anger, or to add emphasis to a question, order or request: *Can't you do it yourself, for heaven's sake?* □ *Don't start that argument again, for God's sake.* **2** For **old times' sake** see **time**.

salad /ˈsaləd/ *noun* (*uncount or count*): **salads**
Salad or a **salad** is a mixture of raw, or occasionally cooked, vegetables, often served with a dressing and sometimes also including other foods such as cheese, meat or fish: *grilled steak with tomato salad* □ *a buffet with cold meats and various salads.* [see also **fruit salad**]

salami /səˈlɑːmɪ/ *noun* (*uncount or count*): **salamis**
Salami is a type of spicy sausage, usually served cold in thin slices.

salaried /ˈsalərɪd/ *adjective*
Salaried is used to describe people to whom, or jobs for which, a salary is paid: *salaried workers* □ *salaried employment.*

salary /ˈsalərɪ/ *noun* (*count or uncount*): **salaries**
You are paid a **salary**, when you receive a fixed payment for the work that you do. People who do non-manual work are usually paid an annual salary of a specified amount made up of regular monthly payments: *a salary of £20000 a year* □ *an increase in salary for civil servants* □ *households with two salaries coming in.* [compare **wage**]

sale /seɪl/ *noun*: **sales**
1 (*uncount*) The **sale** of goods or services is the act or practice of selling them for money. **2** An item sold is a **sale**: *That couple seemed very interested in the house; do you think we've made a sale?* **3** (*plural*) The **sales** of an individual business or of a sector of industry are the value of the items it sells: *Sales are up in the first quarter.* □ *retail sales* □ *a downturn in manufacturing sales.* **4** When a shop or store has a **sale**, its goods, or some of its goods, are offered at reduced prices for a limited period: *the January sales* □ *Does the store normally have a summer sale?* **5** A **sale** is any event at which goods can be bought: *an auction sale* □ *a book sale* □ *a jumble sale.* **6** (*plural*) **Sales** are the operations associated with, or the staff responsible for, selling the goods or services of a particular business organization: *He works in sales.*

▻ ***phrases*** **1** If something, especially something that is owned privately, is **for sale**, or is **put up for sale**, it is offered to be sold: *There has been a 'For Sale' sign on the house for three months.* □ *The estate is being put up for sale.* **2** Goods that are **on sale** are available for buying, especially in a shop: *His biography of the Prince of Wales goes on sale next month.*

saleroom /ˈseɪlruːm/ *noun*: **salerooms**
A **saleroom** is a large room in which public auctions are held, or goods to be auctioned are displayed.

sales clerk *noun* (*AmE*): **sales clerks**
A **sales clerk** is a shop assistant.

salesman /ˈseɪlzmən/ *noun*: **salesmen**
A **salesman** is a person who tries to sell, or whose job it is to sell, goods to customers: *a car salesman* □ *a travelling salesman.*

salesmanship /ˈseɪlzmənʃɪp/ *noun* (*uncount*)
Salesmanship is the skill or techniques used in persuading people to buy things.

salesperson /ˈseɪlzpɜːsən/ *noun*: **salespeople**
A **salesperson** is a shop assistant or a sales representative.

sales representative /ˈseɪlz rɛprɪzɛntətɪv/ *noun*: **sales representatives**
(often shortened to **sales rep**) A **sales representative** is a person employed by a company to sell their products.

sales talk /ˈseɪlz tɔːk/ *noun* (*uncount*)
Sales talk is the persuasive talk used by *eg* salesmen, salespeople or sales representatives intended to convince customers that they should buy something.

salient /ˈseɪlɪənt/ *adjective* (*formal*)
The **salient** features or points of something are those which are most important or noticeable: *a short report dealing with the salient points of the proposed legislation.* [*same as* **marked, significant**]

saliva /səˈlaɪvə/ *noun* (*uncount*)
Saliva is the watery liquid produced in your mouth that helps you to chew and digest food.

sallow /ˈsaloʊ/ *adjective*
A person with a **sallow** complexion has pale, yellowish-brown, unhealthy-looking skin.

salmon /ˈsamən/ *noun*: **salmon**
1 (*count*) A **salmon** is a large sea fish with a silvery skin that swims up rivers to lay its eggs: *He caught two salmon.* **2** (*uncount, often adjectival*) **Salmon** is the flesh of this fish, eaten as food: *tinned salmon* □ *poached salmon* □ *salmon steaks.* **3** (*uncount*) **Salmon**, or **salmon pink**, is a orange-pink colour, like the flesh of a salmon.

salmonella /salməˈnɛlə/ *noun* (*uncount*)
Salmonella is a type of bacteria that can cause food poisoning.

salon /ˈsalɒn/ *noun*: **salons**
A **salon** is **1** a shop where services, such as hairdressing and beauty treatments, are provided: *a hairdressing salon* □ *a beauty salon.* **2** a shop where stylish and expensive clothes are sold.

saloon /səˈluːn/ *noun*: **saloons**
1 A **saloon** is a large public room on a passenger ship, *eg* for functions or some other specified purpose. **2** (*old*) A **saloon**, or **saloon bar**, is a lounge bar. **3** (*AmE*) A **saloon** is any bar where alcohol is sold. **4** A **saloon**, or **saloon car**, is any motor car that is not an estate, coupé, convertible or sports model. [see also **sedan**]

salt /sɒlt/ *noun*; *verb*; *adjective*

▻ ***noun***: **salts**
1 (*uncount*) **Salt** is a substance consisting of small white crystals of sodium chloride, which occurs naturally as a mineral (**rock-salt**) or in solution in sea water (**sea-salt**). Salt is used to season and preserve food: *add a pinch of salt* □ *The sauce needs more salt and pepper.* □ *Pass the salt, please.* **2** (*used in the plural*) **Salts** are any substance resembling salt in appearance or taste, *eg* those used as a tonic or medicine: *Epsom salts.*

▻ ***verb***: **salts, salting, salted**
1 You **salt** food when you add salt to it: *Have you salted the potatoes?* **2** An icy road **is salted** when it is covered with a thin scattering of salt to melt the ice:

Council workmen have been working through the night, salting the roads before the morning rush hour.

▷ ***adjective***

1 Salt food is preserved with salt: *salt pork.* **2 Salt** water is water that contains salt. [compare **fresh**]

▷ ***phrases* 1** You **rub salt in** or **into** someone's **wounds** when you do or say something that adds to the discomfort or distress that they are already feeling. **2** If you refer to other people or another person as **the salt of the earth**, you consider them to be worthy of respect because they always do what is required or expected of them without complaining or making any unnecessary fuss. **3** You **take** something **with a pinch of salt** if you treat it with suspicion or have doubts about whether it is actually true: *I take everything he says with a very large pinch of salt.* **4** A person who is **worth his** or **her salt** is competent and worthy of respect: *No detective worth his salt would have missed such an obvious clue.*

> ***phrasal verb***
> You **salt** something **away**, when you store it up for future use, often secretly or dishonestly: *He had millions salted away in Swiss bank accounts.* [*same as* **amass, stash**]

salt cellar /ˈsɒlt sɛlə(r)/ *noun*: **salt cellars**
A **salt cellar** is a small container for salt used at the table during mealtimes. [see picture at **tableware**]

salted /ˈsɒltɪd/ *adjective*
Salted foods are preserved in or flavoured with salt: *salted herrings* □ *salted peanuts.*

saltwater /ˈsɒltwɔːtə(r)/ *adjective*
Saltwater fish, animals or plants live or grow in salty water or in the sea. [compare **freshwater**]

salty /ˈsɒltɪ/ *adjective*: **saltier, saltiest**
Something that is **salty** contains salt or tastes, especially too strongly, of salt: *salty air* □ *This bacon is terribly salty.*

salubrious /səˈluːbrɪəs/ *adjective* (*formal*)
If you describe a place as **salubrious**, you mean that is pleasant and respectable: *A drop in salary would mean moving to a less salubrious part of town.*

salutary /ˈsaljʊtərɪ/ *adjective* (*formal*)
A **salutary** experience, or a **salutary** lesson, is one that has, or is intended to have, a good effect on future behaviour, even though it may seem very unpleasant at the time: *Listening to those criticisms has taught me a humbling and salutary lesson.*

salute /səˈluːt/ *verb*; *noun*
▷ ***verb***: **salutes, saluting, saluted**
1 If a member of the police or the armed forces **salutes** an officer or some other important person, they pay formal respect to them by making a set gesture with their arm or with a weapon: *The naval cadets saluted the commodore and marched out of the arena.* **2** (*rather formal*) If you **salute** someone or their actions, you pay tribute to them: *We salute your bravery.* **3** You **salute** someone when you greet them: *He saluted them with a cheerful 'Good morning.'*
▷ ***noun***: **salutes**
1 A **salute** is **a** a gesture of respect used by the military and various other organizations or individuals in which usually the right arm is raised and bent with the hand held flat to the side of the head or the forehead which is touched with the ends of the fingers. **b** any similar gesture, *eg* with the right arm extended in front of the body. **2** (*rather formal*) A **salute** is also a greeting.

salvage /ˈsalvɪdʒ/ *verb*; *noun*
▷ ***verb***: **salvages, salvaging, salvaged**
1 To **salvage** a wrecked or sunken ship, or its contents, is to recover it from the sea or the seabed. **2** You **salvage** items from a fire or a flood, when you rescue them. **3** If you take some action to **salvage** your pride or honour, you do it in order to preserve your pride or honour: *He just managed to salvage his pride by winning second place.*
▷ ***noun*** (*uncount, often adjectival*)
1 Salvage is the activity or business of recovering wrecked or sunken ships, or property from wrecked or sunken ships. **2 Salvage** is also the monetary value of a wrecked or sunken ship when it is recovered.

salvation /salˈveɪʃən/ *noun*
1 (*uncount*) **Salvation** is the act of saving a person or thing from danger or harm: *Their main task was salvation of as many of the civilian population as was possible in the circumstances.* **2** (*used in the singular*) Someone or something that is your **salvation** is a person or thing that saves you from harm. **3** (*uncount*; *religion*) **Salvation** is the freeing of the human soul from the influence of sin, or its consequences.

salve /salv/ *noun*; *verb*
▷ ***noun*** (*uncount or count*): **salves**
Salve or a **salve** is ointment used to soothe or heal dry or damaged skin: *lip salve.*
▷ ***verb***: **salves, salving, salved**
If there is something that you feel guilty or worried about, you **salve** your conscience by doing something that helps you to feel more at ease about it.

same /seɪm/ *adjective or pronoun*; *pronoun*; *adverb*
▷ ***adjective or pronoun***
1 Things are the **same** thing if they are exactly alike, or very similar to each other: *I realized I was wearing the same jacket as Barbara.* □ *The two cases are exactly the same.* **2** Two or more people do the **same** thing, or have the **same** experience, if they both or all do that thing or have that experience: *We shared many of the same interests.* □ *He and I are doing the same sort of job.* □ *I feel the same way as you do about the alterations.* □ *We were all treated in the same manner.* **3** The **same** thing happens when the thing that happened before happens again: *I daresay I would make the same mistakes all over again.* **4** Things that are *eg* the **same** colour, age, height or width, are both or all that colour, age, height or width: *My sister is about the same weight as me* (or *as I am*). □ *The two cars are roughly the same price.* □ *The price of the ticket is the same, whichever route you go by.* □ *We painted the ceiling the same colour as the doors.* **5** The **same** thing or person is that particular thing or person **a** in every case: *They all three have the same surname, though they aren't related.* □ *I went to same school as she did.* □ *She never seems to be with the same man twice.* □ *Words that have the same meaning are known as 'synonyms'.* **b** throughout the whole of a certain period: *He wore the same pair of socks for a fortnight.* □ *They've lived in the same house for thirty years.* **6** Something remains the **same** if it doesn't change: *She still had the same over-optimistic outlook.* □ *The place had the same polished smell that I remembered* (or *as I remembered*) *it having.* □ *You still look the same after all these years.* □ *You can't expect things to stay the same.* **7** The **same** person or thing is the one you have mentioned previously: *I could make the same point about pre-school education.*
▷ ***pronoun:*** *'I'll have the fish, I think.' 'Yes, I'll have the same.'* □ *You know I'd do the same for you.* □ *I probably weigh the same as you.* □ *You might say the same about*

fishing. □ *It's the same with* (= the same thing applies to) *fashion.* □ *Does 'continuous' mean the same as 'continual'?* [see also **synonym**]

▻ ***adverb*** (*informal*): *We love each of you the same.* □ *Everyone's treated the same here.* □ *I found he felt the same about me as I felt about him.*

▻ ***phrases*** **1 All the same** or **just the same** means 'nevertheless'; you use **'thanks all the same'** to refuse an offer politely: *He seems well qualified for the job; all the same, we should check his references.* □ *The flight may be delayed but you have to check in before 10.30 just the same.* □ *I won't need a lift this morning, thanks all the same.* **2** For **at the same time** see **time**. **3** You say that something **is all the same to you** if it will make no difference to you and therefore you have no objection to it: *If it's all the same to you, I think I'll go to bed early.* **4** Someone or something is **much the same** if they, or their condition, has altered very little: *'How's your mother today?' 'Much the same.'* □ *The village is much the same as it was when I was a boy.* **5** Things or circumstances are **not the same** if they are not as good or enjoyable as the previous, or other, things or circumstances you are comparing them with: *Christmas was never the same after he died.* **6** People say **'Same again'** when they are requesting or ordering another drink of the kind they have just had.

sameness /ˈseɪmnɪs/ *noun* (*uncount*)
Sameness is the state of being the same, especially in the sense of being boring because of lack of variety: *the sameness of household chores* □ *The sameness of the landscape meant that it was difficult to tell exactly where we were without using a compass.*

sample /ˈsɑːmpəl/ *noun*; *verb*
▻ ***noun***: **samples**
1 A **sample** of something is a small part of it used to represent the whole: *a random sample of the voting public.* **2** A **sample** of a new product is intended to show customers what the product is like: *a free sample of the new washing powder.* **3** When a doctor takes a **sample** of your blood, urine or body tissue, he or she removes a small quantity of it in order that it may be tested for the presence of something, such as a particular disease. [*same as* **specimen**]
▻ ***verb***: **samples, sampling, sampled**
1 You **sample** something, when you take or try a small part of it to find out what it is like: *He sampled wines from several countries before deciding on a case of French Burgundy.* [*same as* **taste**] **2** You **sample** a situation when you get some experience of it: *After sampling life abroad, he found he preferred home.*

sanatorium /sanəˈtɔːrɪəm/ *noun*: **sanatoriums** or **sanatoria**
A **sanatorium** is a hospital that cares for people who need treatment or rest for a long period of time: *He had chronic mental illness and spent years in a Swiss sanatorium.*

sanctify /ˈsaŋktɪfaɪ/ *verb*: **sanctifies, sanctifying, sanctified**
1 To **sanctify** something is to make it holy or free it from sin: *a life sanctified by prayer and service to others.* **2** To **sanctify** something is to make it legal and binding, especially in the eyes of the Church.

sanctimonious /saŋktɪˈmoʊnɪəs/ *adjective* (*derogatory*)
A **sanctimonious** person is someone who is always pointing out how much more virtuous, sensible or religiously dutiful they are than other people: *a sanctimonious smile* □ *What a sanctimonious old bore he is!* [*same as* **moralizing**]

sanction /ˈsaŋkʃən/ *noun*; *verb*
▻ ***noun***: **sanctions**
1 (*uncount*) **Sanction** for an action is official permission or approval for it: *The proposed changes to the Act will require the Sanction of Parliament.* **2 Sanctions** are any economic or military measure taken by, usually several, nations to persuade another to adopt a particular policy or conform to international law: *International sanctions against South Africa were lifted when the apartheid system was dismantled.* **3** A **sanction** is any reason or means, involving either a penalty or reward, which stops people from disobeying a rule, law or a social custom.
▻ ***verb***: **sanctions, sanctioning, sanctioned**
If someone in authority **sanctions** something, they give their formal permission for, or authorize, it.

sanctity /ˈsaŋktɪtɪ/ *noun* (*uncount*)
Sanctity is the quality or condition of being holy or sacred, especially in the sense of deserving respect: *the sanctity of marriage.*

sanctuary /ˈsaŋktjʊərɪ/ *noun*: **sanctuaries**
1 A **sanctuary** is a holy or sacred place, *eg* a church, mosque or temple. **2** The **sanctuary** in a church or temple is the most sacred area within it, *eg* around an altar. **3** A **sanctuary** is also a place, especially in former times a church, where a person is protected from arrest, attack or any other form of interference by others. **4** (*uncount*) **Sanctuary** is the protection or refuge offered in such a place or the right to offer protection in this way: *She fled, seeking the sanctuary of the garden.* **5** A **sanctuary** is also a nature reserve in which the animals or plants are protected: *She runs a sanctuary for injured and abandoned animals.*

sand /sand/ *noun*; *verb*
▻ ***noun***: **sands**
1 (*uncount*) **Sand** is a mass of very small pieces of rock and other minerals that have been worn down by the action of the sea or the wind. Sand is found on beaches, in river-beds and deserts: *a mixture of sand and cement* □ *Add some sand to the compost to improve the drainage.* **2** (*plural*) A large area covered with sand, especially at the seashore, is often referred to as **sands** or the **sands**.
▻ ***verb***: **sands, sanding, sanded**
You **sand** the surface of wood when you make it smooth by rubbing or polishing it with sandpaper or a sander.

sandal /ˈsandəl/ *noun*: **sandals**
Sandals are light, open shoes with straps worn when the weather is warm.

sandbank /ˈsandbaŋk/ *noun*: **sandbanks**
A **sandbank** is a bank of sand in a river or sea, formed by currents and often exposed at low tides.

sandcastle /ˈsandkɑːsəl/ *noun*: **sandcastles**
A **sandcastle** is a pile of damp sand formed into the approximate shape of a castle by children when they are playing on the beach.

sand-dune /ˈsand djuːn/ *noun*: **sand-dunes**
A **sand-dune** is a bank or hill of sand on or near a beach. [*same as* **dune**]

sander /ˈsandə(r)/ *noun*: **sanders**
A **sander** is a tool or machine driven by electric power with a fast-moving disc or rough surface like sandpaper used to make wood or metal smoother.

sandpaper /ˈsandpeɪpə(r)/ *noun* (*uncount*)
Sandpaper is strong paper with a layer of sand glued to one side, used for smoothing and polishing wood and metal surfaces.

sandpit /ˈsandpɪt/ *noun*: **sandpits**
A **sandpit** is a shallow pit in the ground filled with sand for children to play in.

sandshoe /ˈsandʃuː/ *noun*: **sandshoes**
Sandshoes are soft light shoes, often with rubber soles, worn on the beach or for indoor sports.

sandstone /ˈsandstoun/ *noun* (*uncount*)
Sandstone is a type of soft rock formed from many layers of sand pressed together, widely used in building.

sandwich /ˈsandwɪdʒ/ or /ˈsandwɪtʃ/ *noun*; *verb*
▷ ***noun***: **sandwiches**
A **sandwich** is a snack consisting of two slices of bread or a roll with a filling of cheese, meat or some other food.
▷ ***verb***: **sandwiches, sandwiching, sandwiched**
When a person or thing **is sandwiched** between two other people or things, they are placed or pressed into a very narrow space between them: *On the train, the small boy was sandwiched between two large ladies.*

sandwich course /ˈsandwɪdʒ kɔːs/ *noun*: **sandwich courses**
A **sandwich course** is an educational course in which periods of study take place between periods of work experience in business or industry.

sandy /ˈsandɪ/ *adjective*: **sandier, sandiest**
1 Sandy means containing or covered with sand: *sandy soil* □ *a sandy beach.* **2 Sandy** hair is the light reddish-brown colour of sand.

sane /seɪn/ *adjective*: **saner, sanest**
1 A **sane** person is someone who is not mentally ill. [*opposite* **insane, lunatic**] **2 Sane** actions or judgements are sensible and based on good reasonable thinking: *a sane decision.*

sang /saŋ/ *verb*
Sang is the past tense of **sing**.

sanguine /ˈsaŋgwɪn/ *adjective* (*formal*)
If you are **sanguine** about a situation, you are quite cheerful about it and full of hope that it will turn out the way that you want it to.

sanitarium /sanɪˈtɛərɪəm/ *noun*: **sanitariums** or **sanitaria**
Sanitarium means the same as sanatorium.

sanitary /ˈsanɪtərɪ/ or /ˈsanɪtrɪ/ *adjective*
1 Sanitary means hygienic and free from dirt or other things that may cause disease or ill health: *Conditions in the field hospital were far from sanitary and many wounded men developed infections.* [*opposite* **insanitary**] **2 Sanitary** products are designed to protect health, especially with regard to disposal of waste and sewage.

sanitary towel /ˈsanɪtrɪ tauəl/ *noun*: **sanitary towels**
A **sanitary towel** is an absorbent pad worn by a woman to soak up blood during her periods.

sanitation /sanɪˈteɪʃən/ *noun* (*uncount*)
Sanitation is the process of, or the systems for, protecting people's health, especially providing clean water and hygienic removal and disposal of sewage.

sanity /ˈsanɪtɪ/ *noun* (*uncount*)
Sanity is **1** the state or quality of being sane: *Sometimes, he felt he was losing his sanity.* [=he was going mad] [*opposite* **insanity**] **2** good sense: *He tried to introduce some sanity into the chaotic situation that had arisen.*

sank /saŋk/ *verb*
Sank is the past tense of **sink**.

Santa Claus /ˈsantə klɔːz/ *noun*
Santa Claus or **Santa** is another name for Father Christmas: *What did Santa bring you?*

sap /sap/ *noun*; *verb*
▷ ***noun*** (*uncount*)
Sap is the thin liquid that carries food and minerals around the tissues of plants and trees.
▷ ***verb***: **saps, sapping, sapped**
If something **saps** your strength or energy, it gradually drains or exhausts it over a period of time: *The long climb saps the cyclists' strength and slows them down to walking pace.*

sapling /ˈsaplɪŋ/ *noun*: **saplings**
A **sapling** is a young tree.

sapphire /ˈsafaɪə(r)/ *noun*: **sapphires**
1 (*count or uncount, often adjectival*) A **sapphire** is a dark blue transparent precious stone often used in jewellery: *a ring set with diamonds and sapphires* □ *a sapphire necklace.* **2** (*uncount*) **Sapphire**, or **sapphire blue**, is the dark blue colour of this stone: *a sapphire sea* □ *Her eyes were a deep sapphire blue.*

sarcasm /ˈsɑːkazm/ *noun* (*uncount*)
Sarcasm is the use, in speech or writing, of words or expressions that actually mean the opposite of what they appear to mean, with the aim of mocking or showing contempt for someone or hurting their feelings in a bitterly amusing way: *'That was a really clever thing to do,' she said with heavy sarcasm.*

sarcastic /sɑːˈkastɪk/ *adjective*
A **sarcastic** person is someone who tends to use sarcasm; **sarcastic** remarks or expressions contain or show sarcasm: *Don't be so sarcastic!* □ *'So this is your best effort, is it?' she asked with a sarcastic smile.* [*same as* **acid**] — *adverb* **sarcastically:** *'I really appreciated being kept waiting for two hours,' she said sarcastically.*

sardine /sɑːˈdiːn/ *noun*: **sardines**
A **sardine** is a type of small sea fish used as food. Sardines are eaten fresh or packed tightly in small tins and preserved in oil.

sardonic /sɑːˈdɒnɪk/ *adjective*
Someone who is **sardonic** has a mocking or scornful attitude to other people or the things that they do: *a sardonic smile.* — *adverb* **sardonically:** *He laughed sardonically.*

sari /ˈsɑːrɪ/ *noun*: **saris**
A **sari** is a traditional piece of clothing worn by Hindu women, consisting of a single long piece of fabric wound round the body and draped over one shoulder and sometimes the head. [see picture at **clothing**]

sarong /səˈrɒŋ/ *noun*: **sarongs**
A **sarong** is a piece of clothing worn by Malaysian men and women, consisting of a single piece of fabric wrapped around the body to cover it from the waist or chest down. [see picture at **clothing**]

sartorial /sɑːˈtɔːrɪəl/ *adjective* (*formal*)
Sartorial means relating to clothes and the way they are made and worn: *sartorial elegance.*

sash /saʃ/ *noun*: **sashes**
1 A **sash** is a broad band of cloth worn round the waist or over one shoulder, usually as part of a uniform. **2** A **sash** is also either of the two glazed frames forming a sash window.

sash cord /ˈsaʃ kɔːd/ *noun*: **sash cords**
A **sash cord** is a cord connecting the system of weights and pulleys by which a sash window is opened and held open.

sash window /saʃ ˈwɪndou/ *noun*: **sash windows**
A **sash window** is a type of window made up of two frames (**sashes**) which can slide up and down over each other.

sat /sat/ *verb*
Sat is the past tense and past participle of **sit**.

Satan /ˈseɪtən/ *noun*
Satan is another name for the Devil, the most important evil spirit and the enemy of God.

satanic /səˈtanɪk/ *adjective*
1 Satanic means of or relating to Satan: *satanic rites.* **2** (*literary*) A **satanic** person is extremely cruel or evil.

satchel /ˈsatʃəl/ *noun*: **satchels**
A **satchel** is a small bag made of canvas or leather, usually with a shoulder strap, especially one that is used to carry schoolbooks.

satellite /ˈsatəlaɪt/ *noun*: **satellites**
1 A **satellite** is an object in space that moves round a larger planet or star, as the Earth moves round the Sun. **2** A **satellite** is also a man-made device sent into space to orbit the Earth for some purpose, *eg* to take pictures of the Earth's surface or to transmit television or radio signals to and from the Earth: *a live broadcast via satellite.* **3** A nation or state that is politically or economically dependent on a larger more powerful one can also be referred to as a **satellite** of that more powerful state: *the former USSR and its satellites.*

satellite dish /ˈsatəlaɪt dɪʃ/ *noun*: **satellite dishes**
A **satellite dish** is a round dish-shaped aerial used for receiving television programmes broadcast via satellite.

satellite television /satəlaɪt ˈtɛlɪvɪʒən/ or **satellite TV** *noun* (*uncount*)
Satellite television or **satellite TV** is a television system in which programmes are broadcast via satellites.

satin /ˈsatɪn/ *noun* (*uncount, often adjectival*)
Satin is a type of smooth shiny cloth made from silk or similar man-made fibres: *a length of black satin* □ *a satin cushion.*

satire /ˈsataɪə(r)/ *noun*: **satires**
1 (*uncount*) **Satire** is a variety of humour in which stupid or wicked behaviour is attacked or criticized by making fun of it: *the use of satire in English literature.* **2** A **satire** is any work of literature, a film, or a play, using this kind of humour: *a political satire.*

satirical /səˈtɪrɪkəl/ *adjective*
Something that is **satirical** contains or uses satire to attack or criticize someone or something: *a satirical magazine* □ *a satirical remark* □ *a satirical poem* □ *a satirical cartoon.*

satirist /ˈsatɪrɪst/ *noun*: **satirists**
A **satirist** is a person who writes satires or uses satire: *the two great 18th-century satirists, Swift and Pope.*

satirize or **satirise** /ˈsatɪraɪz/ *verb*: **satirizes, satirizing, satirized**
To **satirize** someone or something means to attack or criticize them using satire: *a play satirizing middle-class morality.*

satisfaction /satɪsˈfakʃən/ *noun*: **satisfactions**
1 (*uncount*) **Satisfaction** is the contented feeling you get when you have, or have achieved, what you want or need: *Her success gave her parents a lot of satisfaction.* [*opposite* **dissatisfaction**] **2** (*count*) A **satisfaction** is something that gives a feeling of pleasure or contentment: *the immense satisfactions of parenthood.* **3** (*uncount*) **Satisfaction** of a need, desire or expectation is the fulfilment of it: *She dedicated herself to the satisfaction of all his selfish demands.* **4** If you demand or get **satisfaction**, you demand or get an adequate apology or compensation for a complaint that you have made: *If I don't get any satisfaction, I will take my complaint to a higher authority.*

satisfactory /satɪsˈfaktərɪ/ *adjective*
1 Something is **satisfactory** when it is good enough but not outstanding: *His progress in mathematics has been satisfactory but his language skills are poor.* **2** Something is **satisfactory** when it fulfils a need, desire or expectation: *'Is everything satisfactory?' the head waiter asked as he passed their table.* □ *He was sacked because he didn't give a satisfactory explanation for his conduct.* [*opposite* **unsatisfactory**] — *adverb* **satisfactorily:** *He completed the test satisfactorily.*

satisfied /ˈsatɪsfaɪd/ *adjective*
1 If you are **satisfied** you feel satisfaction or are contented: *'My son is always top of his class,' she said with a satisfied smile.* **2** People sometimes say ironically 'I hope you're **satisfied**' to someone else, or ask 'Are you **satisfied** now?', when that person has done something bad or destructive: *'You've broken your mother's heart! I hope you're satisfied!'* [*opposite* **dissatisfied**]

satisfy /ˈsatɪsfaɪ/ *verb*: **satisfies, satisfying, satisfied**
1 Something **satisfies** a need, desire or expectation when it fulfils it: *New forms of energy will be needed to satisfy the demands of an ever-increasing population.* [*same as* **meet**] **2** Something **satisfies** you when it gives you what you want or need: *No matter what you do, you'll find that nothing will satisfy her.* **3** If an explanation **satisfies** someone, it convinces them: *Your evidence alone is unlikely to satisfy the court of his innocence.* □ *I was satisfied that his motives were entirely honourable.* **4** A meal **satisfies** you when it fills you up and you do not want to eat anything else: *A simple meal of bread and cheese was enough to satisfy them.*

satisfying /ˈsatɪsfaɪɪŋ/ *adjective*
1 Something that is **satisfying** gives you a feeling of pleasure and satisfaction: *Winning the Oscar was a very satisfying experience.* **2** A **satisfying** meal is one in which there is enough food to fill you up. [*same as* **filling**]

satsuma /satˈsuːmə/ *noun*: **satsumas**
A **satsuma** is a small seedless fruit similar to an orange.

saturate /ˈsatʃʊreɪt/ *verb*: **saturates, saturating, saturated**
1 Something **is saturated** with a liquid when it is made soaking wet: *Water poured through the bedroom ceiling saturating the bedding and the carpet.* □ *He was caught in a thunderstorm and his clothes were saturated.* [*same as* **soak**] **2** To **saturate** something also means to fill or cover it completely so that no more can be added: *The constituency was saturated with leaflets by all the main political parties.* [*same as* **inundate, overwhelm**] — *noun* (*uncount*) **saturation** /satʃʊˈreɪʃən/: *The market has reached saturation point.* [=there are so many products available that it is becoming difficult to sell them all]

Saturday /ˈsatədɪ/ *noun* (*uncount or count*): **Saturdays**
Saturday is the seventh day of the week, coming after Friday and before Sunday: *I'm flying to the States on Saturday.* □ *They go swimming on a Saturday* (or *on Saturdays*). □ (*AmE*) *He always visits his mother Saturdays.* □ *The fifth of the month is next Saturday.* □ *She works on Saturday mornings.*

sauce /sɔːs/ *noun* (*uncount or count*): **sauces**
Sauce or a **sauce** is any seasoned liquid that food is cooked in or served with: *bolognese sauce* □ *prawns with a chilli sauce* □ *He likes lots of tomato sauce on his hamburgers.*

sauce boat /ˈsɔːs boʊt/ *noun*: **sauce boats**
A **sauce boat** is a long shallow jug for serving sauce. [see picture at **tableware**]

saucepan /ˈsɔːspən/ *noun*: **saucepans**
A **saucepan** is a deep round cooking pot with a long handle and often a lid, used for boiling or stewing food.

saucer /ˈsɔːsə(r)/ *noun*: **saucers**
A **saucer** is a small round dish with an upward curving edge that is used for putting a tea or coffee cup on: *He gave the cat a saucer of milk.* [see picture at **tableware**]

saucy /ˈsɔːsɪ/ *adjective* (*informal*): **saucier, sauciest**
A **saucy** person or thing is cheeky or disrespectful in a harmless and amusing way: *She's a saucy little minx.*

sauna /ˈsɔːnə/ *noun*: **saunas**
A **sauna** is **1** a Finnish-style steam bath with the steam being created by pouring water on hot coals. **2** a building or room equipped for this type of steam bath.

saunter /ˈsɔːntə(r)/ *verb*: **saunters, sauntering, sauntered**
You **saunter** when you walk slowly and casually; you **saunter** somewhere when you walk there in a slow and relaxed fashion: *He came sauntering along with his hands in his pockets.* □ *They sauntered down to the seafront.*

sausage /ˈsɒsɪdʒ/ *noun*: **sausages**
1 (*uncount*) **Sausage**, or **sausage meat**, is a mixture of minced meat with seasonings that is forced into a thin tube-shaped casing and formed into sections: *garlic sausage.* **2** A **sausage** is one of these tube-shaped sections: *pork sausages* □ *We cooked sausages over an open fire.*

sausage roll /sɒsɪdʒ ˈroʊl/ *noun*: **sausage rolls**
A **sausage roll** is a small amount of sausage meat covered with pastry that you bake in an oven.

sauté /ˈsoʊteɪ/ *verb*; *adjective*
▻ ***verb***: **sautés, sautéing** or **sautéeing, sautéd** or **sautéed**
You **sauté** food when you fry it quickly and lightly in hot butter or oil: *Sauté the mushrooms in a mixture of olive oil and butter.*
▻ ***adjective:*** *sauté potatoes*

savage /ˈsavɪdʒ/ *adjective*; *noun*; *verb*
▻ ***adjective***
Something that is **savage** is fierce and cruel: *He has a savage temper.* □ *He was the victim of a savage attack.* □ *a savage wolf.* [*same as* **ferocious**]
▻ ***noun***: **savages**
1 (*old, offensive*) People who are members of a tribe or group considered to be primitive or uncivilized are sometimes referred to as **savages**. **2** (*derogatory or humorous*) If you refer to people as **savages**, you think their behaviour is uncivilized: *their children are little savages.* [*same as* **monster**]
▻ ***verb***: **savages, savaging, savaged**
1 If you **are savaged** by an animal, *eg* a dog, it attacks you fiercely, biting you and causing you severe injury. [*same as* **maul**] **2** If someone **savages** another person or their actions, they criticize them severely using harsh and cruel language: *The new play was savaged by the critics.* [*same as* **attack**] — *adverb* **savagely:** *He was savagely beaten.* □ *They were savagely attacked in the popular press.*

savagery /ˈsavɪdʒrɪ/ *noun* (*uncount*)
Savagery is extreme cruelty or fierceness: *They were shocked by the savagery of the attack.* [*same as* **ferocity**]

save /seɪv/ *verb*; *noun*; *preposition*
▻ ***verb***: **saves, saving, saved**
1 You **save** someone or something when you rescue them from danger, or prevent them from dying, or being killed, destroyed, injured, damaged or lost: *Doctors fought all night to save her life.* □ *They got to us just in time to save us all from drowning.* □ *She just managed to save herself from falling.* □ *Despite the efforts of the firemen the building couldn't be saved.* □ *An appeal has been launched to save the painting for the nation.* [= to prevent it from being sold to a foreign buyer] **2** You **save** things when you keep them instead of getting rid of them, usually for some purpose: *We used to save all those cardboard tubes for the children to make things out of.* [*same as* **preserve**] **3** You **save** something for someone when you keep or reserve it for them: *Could you save me a place?* [*same as* **reserve**] **4** You **save** money when you keep it instead of spending it, usually so that you can use it later for something; you **save** for something when you put some money aside regularly until you have enough to pay for it: *He saves half his pocket money every week.* □ *I'm saving for a proper holiday.* [see also **save up**] **5** You also **save** money by buying the things you need more cheaply, or buying cheaper alternatives: *Do I save anything by buying this brand?* □ *Shop at Shopround; save up to 30% on household goods.* [*opposite* **waste, lose**] **6** You **save** such things as water and fuel by using them economically and avoiding waste: *Save electricity by switching off lights.* □ *the campaign to save paper.* [*same as* **economize** on; *opposite* **waste**] **7** You **save** time by finding quicker ways of doing things: *You might save time if you went through the city centre.* □ *It will save time if you all read the report before the meeting.* **8** Something **saves** such things as trouble, work or effort if it makes them unnecessary or helps to avoid them: *You'd save yourself a lot of extra work if you bought a dishwasher.* □ *I'm only trying to save you unnecessary trouble.* □ *They telephoned this morning, which saved me the bother of writing to them.* □ *Help me carry the shopping up, would you? It'll save me making another trip down to the car.* [compare **avoid**] **9** (*sport*) In football or hockey a goalkeeper **saves** a shot when he or she prevents the ball from getting into the goal: *He saved two out of the five penalties.* **10** (*religion*) People **are saved** or their souls **are saved** when they are freed from their sins and the consequences of them. **11** You **save** information that you have keyed into a computer when you give the computer an instruction to store it in its memory or on a disk or tape: *Select 'Save' from the menu.*
▻ ***noun*** (*sport*): **saves**
In football or hockey, a **save** is the action of preventing the ball from entering your goal: *'What a save!'* □ *He made some amazing saves.*
▻ ***preposition*** (*formal or old*)
Save or '**save** for' means the same as 'except' and draws attention to something that the statement you are making does not apply to: *No further assistance will be provided save in cases of severe poverty.* □ *Save for the odd sheep the hillside seemed bare of life.*
▻ ***phrase*** For **save face** see **face**.

phrasal verb
You **save up** when you avoid spending money, or set some aside regularly, so as to have enough to buy or pay for something: *We're saving up for a trip to the States.* □ *She's been saving up to buy a car.*

saver /ˈseɪvə(r)/ *noun*: **savers**
A **saver** is someone who saves money, especially in a bank or building society: *high interest rates for regular savers.*

saving /ˈseɪvɪŋ/ *noun*: **savings**
1 If you make a **saving** or **savings** in something, you reduce the amount of money that you spend on that thing: *We need to make some savings in our household expenses.* □ *By buying in bulk, he made a saving of £50.* **2** (*plural*) Your **savings** are the money

that you have saved up: *He lost his life savings in the burglary.*

saviour (*AmE* **savior**) /ˈseɪvjə(r)/ *noun*: **saviours**
1 A **saviour** is a person who rescues someone or something from danger or destruction: *He was regarded as the saviour of the nation.* **2** In Christianity, the **Saviour** is Jesus Christ, who saves people from sin.

savour (*AmE* **savor**) /ˈseɪvə(r)/ *verb*: **savours, savouring, savoured**
1 You **savour** food or drink when you eat or drink it slowly in order to enjoy or appreciate its full taste or quality: *He ate the pastry slowly, savouring every mouthful.* [*same as* **relish**] **2** If you **savour** an experience or achievement, you take time to enjoy the feelings of pleasure it gives you: *This was one of the truly great days of Irish sport, one to savour for years to come.*

savoury (*AmE* **savory**) /ˈseɪvərɪ/ *adjective*; *noun*
▻ ***adjective***
1 **Savoury** foods have a salty or sharp, rather than a sweet, taste or smell: *a savoury pancake.* **2** If you describe something such as a piece of news or gossip as **savoury**, you mean that it is one that you relish or take pleasure in. [*same as* **appetizing**] **3** (*usually used in negative statements*) If something is **savoury**, it is pleasant, attractive or morally acceptable: *He's not a very savoury character.* [*opposite* **unsavoury**]
▻ ***noun***: **savouries**
Savouries are foods with a savoury taste, especially those made with salty or sharp tasting ingredients, such as cheese, pickles or pâté, and served with alcoholic drinks or before a meal.

saw[1] /sɔː/ *verb*
Saw is the past tense of **see**.

saw[2] /sɔː/ *noun*; *verb*
▻ ***noun***: **saws**
A **saw** is any of various tools having a thin metal blade with a row of V-shaped teeth along one edge used for cutting wood or metal. [see picture at **tool**]
▻ ***verb***: **saws, sawing, sawed, sawn** (*AmE* **sawed**)
You **saw** something when you cut it with a saw: *He sawed the logs up.* □ *The dead branch will have to be sawn off.* □ *The trees were cut down and taken away to be sawn into planks.*

sawdust /ˈsɔːdʌst/ *noun* (*uncount*)
Sawdust is dust made up of tiny pieces of wood produced when wood is sawn.

sawmill /ˈsɔːmɪl/ *noun*: **sawmills**
A **sawmill** is a place where large mechanical saws cut timber into pieces for use in *eg* building and paper-making.

sawn /sɔːn/ *verb*
Sawn is the past participle of **saw**.

> Note that in American English, **sawed** is used as both the past tense and past participle of **saw**.

sax /saks/ *noun* (*count or uncount*; *informal*): **saxes**
A **sax** is a saxophone: *a tenor sax* □ *He plays sax (or the sax) in a jazz band.*

saxophone /ˈsaksəfoʊn/ *noun* (*count or uncount*): **saxophones**
A **saxophone** is a musical instrument with a long curved metal body. You play it by blowing into it and pressing keys with your fingers: *a saxophone player* □ *She plays saxophone (or the saxophone) in an all-girl jazz band.*

saxophonist /sakˈsɒfənɪst/ *noun*: **saxophonists**
A **saxophonist** is a person who plays the saxophone: *a jazz saxophonist.*

say /seɪ/ *verb*; *noun*
▻ ***verb***: **says** /seɪz/ or /sɛz/, **saying, said**
1 You **say** something when you speak or utter words aloud: *'Do come too,' he said, so I said 'OK.'* □ *'That's not the point,' said George.* □ *What were you going to say?* □ *Sorry, I didn't hear what you said.* □ *I've said I'm sorry.* □ *I did ask them but they said no.* □ *Say hallo to Granny.* **2** You **say** something when you state it: *She said she'd be late.* □ *Peter said there might be trouble.* □ *'Can Janet come?' 'She said so.'* □ *That's not what she said to me.* □ *I enquired whether we needed to book in advance, but she said not.* □ *We asked him to phone and he said he would.* □ *There's a staff meeting at 4.30, so Susan says.* □ *He didn't say what time he'd be back.* □ *Has she said yet whether she can help?* □ *'How did she find out?' 'She didn't say.'*

> **Say** and **tell** are both used to report speech, but **tell** usually takes an object in the form of the person receiving the information: *He said he'd be late.* But: *He told me he'd be late.*

3 If someone asks you something and you refuse to **say**, you won't tell them what they want to know: *'Where have you been?' 'I'd rather not say.'* □ *She did ask him, but he wouldn't say.* **4** You **say** something to yourself when you think it: *I said to myself 'What's the use of trying?'* **5** You **say** something you have learnt, such as a prayer or poem, when you repeat it: *We learnt to say the Lord's Prayer.* □ *He asked me to say grace.* **6** What you **say** in a letter or book is what you write: *She wrote to say thank you.* □ *'A little learning is a dangerous thing', as Pope says.* □ *It says here that the practice stopped in the last century.* **7** Something such as a map, sign, clock, instrument **says** something if it indicates it: *The clock in the kitchen said ten o'clock.* □ *What does that sign say?* □ *That's not what the map says.* **8** You often use **say** in expressing your opinion or feelings: *You've done a good job, I must say.* □ *He should see to it himself, that's what I say.* □ *May I just say how grateful I am?* □ *I think I can safely say we're in agreement about this.* □ *I can't say I like him.* [= I don't like him] □ *No-one can say I haven't tried.* **9** What you **are saying** is what you are trying to communicate to people when you are speaking or writing: *What are you trying to say?* □ *She spoke for an hour but didn't actually say much.* □ *What is the poet saying here about fame?* **10** You use expressions such as 'I couldn't **say**' when you don't know the answer to something: *'When will he be back?' 'I couldn't say.'* □ *It's difficult to say which way is better.* □ *There's no saying* [= no-one knows] *when there may be another round of redundancies.*
11 People **say** something is so, or it **is said** to be so, if it is claimed or reported to be so: *The house is said to be haunted.* □ *She's said to have been at least 95 when she died.* □ *They say he's lost his memory.* □ *'Is the recession getting worse?' 'So people say.'*
12 You use **say** to introduce a possibility, so as to discuss what follows if it does occur: *Say he doesn't come, what do we do then?* □ *Let's say you finish this in three weeks; that takes us to the end of March; but just say you take longer ...* [*same as* **suppose**] **13** **Say** also introduces possible examples or approximate amounts: *if you were looking for something for the garden, say an electric mower* □ *That will take, say, six weeks.*
▻ ***noun*** (*used in the singular*)
You have a **say** in something that is to be decided if you have a chance, or the right, to express an opinion

about it and so to influence the decision; someone has their **say** when they express their own opinion: *We have no say in how the money's spent.* ▫ *You've had your say already.*

▻ ***phrases*** **1** Someone who **doesn't have much to say**, or **doesn't have much to say for themselves**, does not speak very much. **2 a** You use '**you don't say!**' to express surprise, or mock surprise, at something you are told: '*Eating all that junk food is bad for you.*' '*You don't say!*' **b** You use '**don't say**' when wondering if some undesirable possibility is the case: *Don't say I've left my keys behind!* **3** Something that **goes without saying** is obvious or does not need stating: *It goes without saying that we shall pay your expenses.* **4** Something that **has a lot**, or **something, to be said for it** has advantages, or can be recommended: *Weight training is fine, but there's a lot to be said simply for a brisk walk.* ▫ *There's something to be said for booking early.* **5** You comment '**I'll say this for**' a certain person or thing to introduce some point in their favour, especially after they have been criticized: *I'll say this for him, he never gives up.* **6** (*informal*) You use the expression '**I wouldn't say no**' to indicate, or hint, that you would like something: *'Have another piece of cake.' 'I wouldn't say no; it's so delicious.'* ▫ *I wouldn't say no to a hot shower.* **7** You use **not to say** to introduce a more extreme term which you think suits the circumstances better than one just used: *The price was high, not to say extortionate.* **8** For **so to say** see **so to speak** at **speak**. **9** You use '**that is to say**' to repeat what you have said in a clearer form: *I was outside, that's to say in the garden, when I heard a loud bang.* **10** You use '**to say nothing of**' to introduce something that your statement applies to even more: *The organization will be horrific, to say nothing of the expense.*

saying /ˈseɪɪŋ/ *noun*: **sayings**
A **saying** is a phrase or sentence that people use often and which usually gives wise advice about something: *'Watch the pennies, and the pounds will look after themselves', as the saying goes.* [compare **proverb**]

scab /skab/ *noun*: **scabs**
1 A **scab** is a crust of dried blood formed over a healing wound. **2** (*derogatory*) Workers who have gone on strike often refer to those people who continue to work at the place where the strike is being staged as **scabs**.

scaffold /ˈskafəld/ *noun*: **scaffolds**
1 A **scaffold** is a framework of metal poles and wooden boards built around a building or other tall structure and used by workmen as a temporary platform while they are doing repairs, painting, or building work. **2** A **scaffold** is also a raised platform used, especially in the past, to kill criminals by hanging or cutting off their heads.

scaffolding /ˈskafəldɪŋ/ *noun* (*uncount*)
1 **Scaffolding** is a scaffold. (sense 1). **2** **Scaffolding** is also the poles and boards used for building scaffolds.

scald /skɔːld/ *verb*; *noun*
▻ ***verb***: **scalds, scalding, scalded**
1 If very hot liquid or steam **scalds** you, it burns you: *The hot tea scalded her tongue.* ▫ *A baby was scalded in the bath after his brother turned on the hot tap.* **2** You **scald** milk when you heat it to just below boiling point.
▻ ***noun***: **scalds**
A **scald** is a burn caused by contact with very hot liquid or steam: *ointment for scalds and burns.*

scalding /ˈskɔːldɪŋ/ *adjective or adverb*
If something is **scalding**, or **scalding hot**, it is hot enough to scald: *She gave him a mug of scalding soup to thaw him out.* ▫ *The water was scalding hot.*

scale /skeɪl/ *noun*; *verb*
▻ ***noun***: **scales**
1 A **scale** is a series of markings or divisions at regular known intervals, for use in measuring, or a system of such markings or divisions: *the Richter scale.* **2** A **scale** is a measuring instrument with these markings. [see also **scales**] **3** The **scale** of a model or drawing is its size relative to the actual size of the thing it represents. **4** (*music*) A **scale** is a complete sequence of notes, especially those between two octaves. **5** A wage or salary **scale** is a graded system according to which the level of a particular employee's wages or salary is fixed relative to others. **6** (*uncount*) The **scale** of something is its extent or level relative to others of the same type: *theatre on a grand scale.* **7** (*usually in the plural*) **Scales** are any of the small thin plates that cover the skin of fish and reptiles.
▻ ***verb***: **scales, scaling, scaled**
You **scale** a vertical or near-vertical surface when you climb it: *They scaled the wall using ropes made from torn-up sheets.*
▻ ***phrase*** If a model or drawing is done **to scale**, it is done with all sizes and distances in correct proportion to the real thing.

phrasal verbs
scale down If an activity or operation **is scaled down**, it is decreased: *The UN may have to scale down its involvement in some of the world's trouble spots.*
scale up If an activity or operation **is scaled up**, it is increased: *The sales department will have to be scaled up to meet the increased demand.*

scales /skeɪlz/ *noun* (*plural*)
Scales are an instrument for weighing: *a set of scales.* [see picture at **kitchen**]
▻ ***phrase***
1 If a factor or circumstance **tips** or **turns the scales** in favour of a particular decision, it is the one that causes that decision to be made. **2** If someone or something **tips** or **turns the scales** at a specific weight, that is what they weigh: *The American contender tipped the scales at 250 pounds.*

scallop /ˈskɒləp/ or /ˈskaləp/ *noun*; *verb*
▻ ***noun***: **scallops**
1 A **scallop** is an edible shellfish with a pair of hinged, fan-shaped shells. **2** **Scallops** are a series of curves that together form a wavy edge, *eg* on fabric.
▻ ***verb***: **scallops, scalloping, scalloped**
You **scallop** the edge of something, especially fabric, when you shape it in a series of small curves.

scalp /skalp/ *noun*; *verb*
▻ ***noun***: **scalps**
1 Your **scalp** is the skin on the top of your head where hair grows: *an itchy scalp.* **2** A **scalp** is also part of this piece of skin with the hair attached which American Indian warriors, in former times, cut from their enemies' heads as a sign of victory.
▻ ***verb***: **scalps, scalping, scalped**
To **scalp** someone means to cut off their scalp.

scalpel /ˈskalpəl/ *noun*: **scalpels**
A **scalpel** is a small knife with a thin, very sharp blade. Scalpels are used in surgical operations to cut into a patient's body.

scaly /ˈskeɪlɪ/ *adjective*: **scalier, scaliest**
A surface that is **scaly** is covered with small, thin, stiff pieces of skin: *The skin on her body was dry and scaly.*

scamper /ˈskampə(r)/ *verb*: **scampers, scampering, scampered**

When a child or a small animal **scampers**, they run quickly taking short steps, especially while they are playing or when they have been suddenly frightened: *The baby rabbits scampered back into their burrow.*

scampi /'skampɪ/ *noun* (*plural*; *BrE*)
Scampi are large prawns that are cooked and eaten as food. They are usually covered with a mixture of flour and egg (**batter**), or breadcrumbs, and fried in hot oil.

scan /skan/ *verb*; *noun*
▻ ***verb***: **scans, scanning, scanned**
1 You **scan** a page or a piece of writing when you look at it and read through it quickly: *She scanned the jobs section hoping to find something that would suit her.* [*same as* **glance through**] **2** You **scan** an area when you examine it carefully by looking all around it using your eyes or some other means, such as radar: *She stood on a box and scanned the sea of uniformed figures below trying to find her husband.* ▫ *radar scanning the skies for enemy aircraft.* [*same as* **scrutinize, survey**] **3** (*medicine*) Any of several electronic devices using beams of light or sound are used in hospitals to **scan** your body or part of your body so as to build up an image of your internal organs or of an unborn baby in the womb: *The machine scans the whole body and produces a three-dimensional image on the computer screen for the doctors to analyse and make a diagnosis.* **4** A poem **scans** when it conforms to a pattern of rhythm; you **scan** a piece of poetry when you examine its pattern of rhythm: *The next two lines don't scan.*
▻ ***noun***: **scans**
1 A **scan** is an act of scanning: *Can you give these pages a quick scan and mark any errors you find.* **2** In medicine, a **scan** is an image of the body or part of the body produced by scanning: *Most British women have an ultrasound scan early in their pregnancy.*

scandal /'skandəl/ *noun*: **scandals**
1 (*uncount or count*) **Scandal** is the widespread public discussion and disapproval of behaviour or a situation considered to be shocking or immoral; a **scandal** is a situation or behaviour that causes this: *He should have resigned at the first hint of scandal.* ▫ *a scandal concerning a government minister.* **2** You can also refer to any situation or event that you consider to be very bad or wrong as a **scandal**: *It's a scandal that some old people don't have enough money to heat their homes adequately in winter.* [*same as* **disgrace**] **3** (*uncount*) **Scandal** is also malicious gossip: *She told me some juicy scandal.*

scandalize or **scandalise** /'skandəlaɪz/ *verb*: **scandalizes, scandalizing, scandalized**
If someone **is scandalized** by something, they are extremely shocked or offended by it: *Her family was scandalized when she made no attempt to hide her affair with a married man.*

scandalous /'skandələs/ *adjective*
When you describe something or someone's behaviour as **scandalous**, you think that it is disgraceful or outrageous: *It's scandalous that the beautiful old house should have been allowed to become a ruin.* — *adverb* **scandalously:** *It is scandalously expensive.*

Scandinavian /skandɪ'neɪvɪən/ *adjective*; *noun*
▻ ***adjective***
Scandinavian means concerned with or belonging to Scandinavia, that is the countries of Sweden, Norway and Denmark collectively, sometimes also including Finland and Iceland, their people or their languages: *He's of Scandinavian origin.* ▫ *Scandinavian traditions and customs.*
▻ ***noun***: **Scandinavians**
1 A **Scandinavian** is a person who comes from one of the Scandinavian countries: *He's a Scandinavian; a Swede, I believe.* **2** (*uncount*) **Scandinavian** is the name given to the group of languages spoken in and around the Scandinavian countries.

scanner /'skanə(r)/ *noun*: **scanners**
A **scanner** is an instrument that is passed over an object either to identify or examine it or build up a picture of its internal structure. Scanners use a beam of light, X-rays or sound waves, and have various uses, *eg* in medical diagnosis and examination.

scant /skant/ *adjective*
1 Someone who has **scant** experience or knowledge of something, has very little or insufficient experience or knowledge of it: *I only have a scant knowledge of Latin and even less of Greek.* [*same as* **sparse, minimal**; *opposite* **ample, adequate**] **2** When something is given or receives **scant** attention, it is given or receives very little or inadequate attention.

scanty /'skantɪ/ *adjective*: **scantier, scantiest**
Something that is **scanty** is nearly too small or hardly big enough in size or amount for its purpose: *scanty clothing* ▫ *a scanty meal.* [*opposite* **plentiful, substantial**] — *adverb* **scantily:** *pictures of scantily-clad young women.* [=with very few clothes on]

scapegoat /'skeɪpgoʊt/ *noun*: **scapegoats**
If someone is, or is made, a **scapegoat**, they are made to take the blame or punishment for the mistakes or failures of other people: *It's so unfair that he should be made the scapegoat when it wasn't his fault.*

scar /skɑ:(r)/ *noun*; *verb*
▻ ***noun***: **scars**
1 A **scar** is a mark left on the skin after a wound or sore has healed: *On his passport, he lists his distinguishing marks as a scar on his left cheek, and a glass eye.* **2** If an unpleasant experience leaves a **scar**, it has a permanent damaging effect on your mind: *the psychological scar caused by this terrible childhood experience.*
▻ ***verb***: **scars, scarring, scarred**
If someone's skin **is scarred**, it has a permanent mark or marks on it where a wound or sore has healed: *The burns were so severe that he will be scarred for life.* ▫ *The landscape was scarred where great areas of forest had been felled and the vegetation burned.*

scarce /skɛəs/ *adjective*
Something that is **scarce** is hard to find because there is very little of it or not enough of it to meet demand: *During the war, fresh fruit was extremely scarce.* ▫ *We must find effective ways of preserving the Earth's increasingly scarce resources of oil and gas.* [*opposite* **abundant, plentiful**]
▻ ***phrase*** (*informal*) If someone **makes themselves scarce**, they leave quickly usually to avoid trouble or someone they do not want to meet: *'Here comes a policeman!' said the boy who was lookout. 'We'd better make ourselves scarce.'*

scarcely /'skɛəslɪ/ *adverb* (*used like a negative*)
1 Something that is **scarcely** so, or that **scarcely** happens, is almost not so, or almost doesn't happen: *Could you speak up? I can scarcely hear you.* ▫ *Fresh fruit was scarcely ever available.* ▫ *I can scarcely remember when I last ate home-baked bread.* [*same as* **barely, hardly**; compare 'only **just**'] **2** You use **scarcely** as an emphatic form of 'not': *That was scarcely the most tactful thing to say.* ▫ *Office-cleaning was scarcely the career I'd set my heart on.* ▫ (*used as an answer*) *'Will it do?' 'Scarcely!'* [*same as* **hardly**] **3** You say that **scarcely** had one thing happened when another did to emphasize how quickly the second event followed the

first: *He had scarcely put the telephone down when it rang again.*

scarcity /ˈskɛəsɪtɪ/ *noun (uncount or count)*: **scarcities**
Scarcity or a **scarcity** is lack of sufficient supplies or a shortage of a particular thing: *They grew their own vegetables to combat wartime scarcity.* □ *a scarcity of clean water.*

scare /skɛə(r)/ *verb; noun*
▷ ***verb***: **scares, scaring, scared**
If someone or something **scares** you, they startle you or make you feel frightened: *Don't creep up on me like that. You scared me!* □ *It scares him when you talk about cancer.* [*same as* **alarm**]
▷ ***noun***: **scares**
1 If someone or something gives you a **scare**, they give you a fright: *I got such a scare when the wind blew the back door open.* **2** A **scare** is a sudden sense of alarm or fear felt amongst a population or group of people caused by the spread of news of, or information about, something unpleasant or dangerous: *a bomb scare.*
▷ ***phrase*** Someone or something **scares the life**, or **the hell**, or **the wits, out of** you, when they make you feel very frightened.

> ***phrasal verb***
> **scare away** or **scare off** You **scare away** people or animals, or **scare** them **off**, when you frighten them so that they go away: *Their loud voices scared away the birds that were feeding in the garden.* □ *They've split up; I think the prospect of marriage scared him off.*

scarecrow /ˈskɛəkroʊ/ *noun*: **scarecrows**
A **scarecrow** is a rough model of a human figure dressed in old clothes and set up in a field to scare birds away and prevent them eating the crops.

scared /ˈskɛəd/ *adjective*
If someone is **scared**, or **scared** of something, they are frightened, or frightened by it: *She was too scared to jump off the high diving board.* □ *I'm scared of spiders.* □ *The children were all scared of the headmaster.* □ *She lay with the bedclothes pulled up to her chin, too scared to move.* [*same as* **afraid**]
▷ ***phrase*** If someone is **scared stiff**, or **scared to death**, they are very frightened: *I'm scared stiff of heights.*

scarf /skɑːf/ *noun*: **scarfs** or **scarves**
A **scarf** is a long strip or square of cloth that is worn around the neck, shoulders or head for warmth or decoration: *He put on his overcoat and wrapped a long woollen scarf around his neck.* □ *a silk scarf* □ *a football scarf.* [=one displaying the colours of a particular team]

scarlet /ˈskɑːlət/ *noun; adjective*
▷ ***noun*** *(uncount)*
Scarlet is a bright red colour: *a black cloak edged with scarlet.*
▷ ***adjective:*** *She blushed scarlet.* □ *a scarlet petticoat* □ *(with the noun omitted) She chose two lengths of velvet, a dark blue and a scarlet.*

scarlet fever /skɑːlət ˈfiːvə(r)/ *noun (uncount)*
Scarlet fever is an infectious disease which causes inflammation of the nose, throat and mouth, a red rash on the body, and fever.

scarves /skɑːvz/ *noun*
Scarves is the plural of **scarf**.

scary /ˈskɛərɪ/ *adjective*: **scarier, scariest** *(informal)*
Something that is **scary** causes you to feel frightened: *a scary film* □ *one of the scariest stories I have ever read.* [*same as* **frightening**]

scathing /ˈskeɪðɪŋ/ *adjective*
Someone is **scathing** about something, or makes a **scathing** comment or remark about it when they criticize it scornfully or in a hurtful way: *He was scathing about the government's economic policy.* [*same as* **scornful**; *opposite* **complimentary**] — *adverb* **scathingly:** *He talked scathingly about the team's performance.*

scatter /ˈskatə(r)/ *verb*: **scatters, scattering, scattered**
1 You **scatter** things when you throw or drop them so that they are spread over a wide area: *All the drawers had been opened and their contents scattered on the floor.* □ *Scatter the grass seed evenly over the prepared soil.* [*same as* **strew**] **2** People in a group **scatter** when they separate and rush off in different directions: *The soldiers fired a round of rubber bullets and the crowd scattered.* — *adjective* **scattered:** *The weather forecast is for sunshine with scattered showers.*

scatterbrain /ˈskatəbreɪn/ *noun (informal)*: **scatterbrains**
If you call someone a **scatterbrain**, you mean that they are a forgetful, disorganized, but usually likeable, person: *She always forgets her keys; she's such a scatterbrain!* — *adjective* **scatterbrained:** *She's completely scatterbrained.*

scattering /ˈskatərɪŋ/ *noun*: **scatterings**
A **scattering** of something is a small quantity or thin layer of it thrown or spread over a wide area: *a thin scattering of snow.*

scavenge /ˈskavɪndʒ/ *verb*: **scavenges, scavenging, scavenged**
To **scavenge** means to search amongst waste or rubbish for things that can be used or eaten: *They tried to make a living by selling things they had scavenged from the city rubbish dumps.* □ *stray dogs scavenging food from the dustbins.*

scavenger /ˈskavɪndʒə(r)/ *noun*: **scavengers**
1 Wild animals or birds that feed mainly on the flesh of dead animals and on other waste material are **scavengers**: *The lions had to guard their kill from vultures, hyenas and other scavengers* **2** A **scavenger** is also a person who searches among rubbish for usable things.

scenario /sɪˈnɑːrɪoʊ/ *noun*: **scenarios**
1 A **scenario** is a written description or outline of what happens in a play or film. **2** A **scenario** is also a description of the way that events or a situation may develop in the future: *He presented them with the likely scenario if preventative measures were not taken immediately.*

scene /siːn/ *noun*: **scenes**
1 *(usually in the singular)* The **scene** of an event is the setting in which it takes place: *evidence found at the scene of the crime.* □ *Napoleon surveyed the scene of battle.* **2** In a play or film, a **scene** is one of parts or sections in which action happens in the same place. [see also **act**] **3** A **scene** is also a landscape or situation, as seen or viewed by someone: *The great ships gathered in the harbour made an impressive scene.* □ *a scene of chaos and panic.* **4** If someone makes a **scene**, they make an embarrassing display of emotion in public: *Please don't make a scene.* [*same as* **commotion, fuss**] **5** *(used in the singular; informal)* People often refer to a particular **scene** when they are talking about a particular area of activity: *the current music scene* □ *He's heavily involved in the drugs scene.* **6** *(informal)* People also refer to a particular thing, area of interest

or activity that they like or prefer as their **scene**: *I don't enjoy guided tours; roaming where the fancy takes me is more my scene.*
▻ ***phrases*** **1** If you have a **change of scene**, you go somewhere different after being or working in a place for a long time. **2** If something happens or is done **behind the scenes**, it is done or happens out of the sight of the public so that they do not know about it. **3** Someone or something **comes on the scene** when it arrives or becomes part of the current situation. **4** You **set the scene** when you describe the situation in which an event takes place: *Just to set the scene: we were on holiday in Greece; it was early morning and the sun was shining; we had just got up and were about to have breakfast, when....*

scenery /ˈsiːnərɪ/ *noun* (*uncount*)
1 **Scenery** is the appearance of the countryside, especially when it is beautiful or impressive: *They go to the Rockies for the air and the magnificent scenery.* [*same as* **landscape**] **2** **Scenery** is also the items making up a stage or film set.

scenic /ˈsiːnɪk/ *adjective*
Scenic means having beautiful or impressive scenery: *the scenic route to the Highlands.*

scent /sɛnt/ *noun*; *verb*
▻ ***noun***: **scents**
1 (*uncount or count*) An animal's or plant's **scent** is the distinctive smell that it has: *the scent of violets* □ *The wolves recognize each other mainly by scent.* **2** A **scent** is also a trail of this left behind: *The hounds can follow a man's scent hours after he has passed that way.* **3** (*used in the singular*) If someone is on the **scent** of an important discovery, they have made a series of findings that lead or point to it. **4** (*uncount*; *BrE*; *rather old*) **Scent** is perfume: *a bottle of scent.*
▻ ***verb***: **scents, scenting, scented**
1 When an animal **scents** something, it discovers or becomes aware of it through its sense of smell: *The great tiger sniffed the air, scenting the deer as they grazed in the clearing.* **2** If you **scent** something, especially something bad, you get a feeling, by instinct or intuition, that it is happening or a fact: *I scent betrayal.* [*same as* **detect**] **3** Something **scents** something such as the air when it gives it a smell, especially a pleasant one: *a warm summer evening scented with lavender and lilies.* — *adjective* **scented:** *scented roses.*

sceptic (*AmE* **skeptic**) /ˈskeptɪk/ *noun*: **sceptics**
A **sceptic** is a person who has doubts about a theory, idea or claim that many other people believe is true or right: *Sceptics claimed that the mysterious photos were a hoax.*

sceptical (*AmE* **skeptical**) /ˈskɛptɪkəl/ *adjective*
Someone is **sceptical** about something when they have doubts about it being true: *He is absolutely convinced that the plan will work, but I'm still a bit sceptical about it.*

scepticism (*AmE* **skepticism**) /ˈskɛptɪsɪzm/ *noun* (*uncount*)
Scepticism is a doubting state or attitude: *His claims for the new drug were regarded with scepticism by many doctors.*

schedule /ˈʃɛdjuːl/ or /ˈskɛdjuːl/ *noun*; *verb*
▻ ***noun***: **schedules**
1 A **schedule** is a plan or timetable listing activities or events and the times when they should each happen or be done: *We have to complete the work on a very tight schedule.* □ *a flight schedule.* **2** A **schedule** is also a written list of things, or details about a thing: *I'm interested in the house so I asked the estate agent to send me a copy of the schedule.*
▻ ***verb***: **schedules, scheduling, scheduled**
1 Events **are scheduled** when they are planned to happen or be done at a specific time: *When is the president's plane scheduled to arrive?* **2** You **schedule** something when you put it on a schedule. [*same as* **timetable**]
▻ ***phrases*** Something that happens or is completed **ahead of schedule** happens or is completed earlier than the time planned; if something is **behind schedule** it has not happened or been completed at the proper time according to a schedule; if something is done or happens **on schedule** or **according to schedule**, it is done or happens at the time planned.

scheme /skiːm/ *noun*; *verb*
▻ ***noun***: **schemes**
1 If you have a **scheme** for doing something, you have a plan of action: *He came up with a mad scheme to sail the Atlantic in a bathtub.* **2** A **scheme** is also a system or programme: *a pension scheme* □ *The company operates a bonus scheme in which workers can share in the profits.* **3** A **scheme** is also a careful arrangement of different parts or things: *I don't like the colour scheme in their living room.* **4** (*rather old*) A **scheme** is also a secret plan to cause harm or damage. [*same as* **plot**]
▻ ***verb***: **schemes, scheming, schemed**
Someone **schemes** when they plan or act secretly, often to cause harm or damage: *She was accused of scheming with certain noblemen to murder Elizabeth.* [*same as* **plot**]
▻ ***phrase*** When someone refers to **the scheme of things**, they are referring to the way the world or the universe seems to be organized, perhaps by God or some other unknown force: *How important are we in the larger scheme of things?*

schilling /ˈʃɪlɪŋ/ *noun*: **schillings**
The **schilling** is the standard unit of currency in Austria.

schizophrenia /skɪtsəˈfriːnɪə/ *noun* (*uncount*)
Schizophrenia is a severe mental illness in which the sufferer becomes confused about what is real and what they imagine is real, often leading to a complete withdrawal from other people into a world of the imagination.

schizophrenic /skɪtsəˈfrɛnɪk/ *noun*; *adjective*
▻ ***noun***: **schizophrenics**
A **schizophrenic** is someone who is suffering from schizophrenia.
▻ ***adjective:*** *schizophrenic behaviour.*

scholar /ˈskɒlə(r)/ *noun*: **scholars**
1 A **scholar** is a person who studies and knows a great deal about an academic subject: *a scholar of Greek* □ *a distinguished classical scholar.* [*same as* **academic**] **2** A **scholar** is also a person who has won a scholarship: *a Rhodes scholar.* **3** If a schoolchild or student is a good **scholar**, he or she is good at studying.

scholarly /ˈskɒləlɪ/ *adjective*
1 A **scholarly** person has a lot of knowledge about an academic subject because they have spent a lot of time studying it. **2** A **scholarly** book or other work is one that shows that the person who has written it has great knowledge of, or has made a detailed study of, its subject: *a scholarly work.*

scholarship /ˈskɒləʃɪp/ *noun*: **scholarships**
1 A **scholarship** is a sum of money that is made available to a good student so that they can pay for their studies at a school or university: *She won a scholarship to the Massachusetts Institute of Technology.* [*same as* **award**, **bursary**] **2** (*uncount*) **Scholarship** is serious study, usually of an academic subject, or the methods used by scholars.

scholastic /skɒ'lastɪk/ *adjective (formal)*
Scholastic means of schools and education: *They were proud of their son's scholastic achievements.* [*same as* **academic**]

school /sku:l/ *noun*
1 (*uncount or count*) **School** or a **school** is a place where children and teenagers go to be educated: *He started school when he was four.* □ *Their children attend the village school.* □ *Is it a good school?* □ *Do you enjoy school?* □ *He went to school in India.* **2** (*uncount*) **School** is also the period of the day or the period of the year that you spend at school: *School finishes for the summer holidays at the end of June.* □ *He had to stay behind after school.* □ *She did a paper round every morning before school.* **3** (*with a singular or plural verb*) All the pupils, students and teachers in a school are known collectively as the **school**: *The whole school was (or were) gathered in the assembly hall.* **4 a** A group of *eg* artists or philosophers who have worked together under the same teacher or have the same style or ideas is known as a **school**. **b** A group of people meeting together regularly for some other purpose is also called a **school**: *a card school.* **5** A **school** of fish or dolphins is a large number of fish or dolphins swimming together in a group. [see also **secondary school, Sunday school**]
▻ ***phrase*** A particular **school of thought** is the beliefs shared by a specific group of people.

school age /'sku:l eɪdʒ/ *noun (uncount)*
School age is the age when a child must attend school. In Britain, this is between the ages of 5 and 16, but it varies from country to country: *children of school age.*

schoolboy /'sku:lbɔɪ/ *noun*: **schoolboys**
A **schoolboy** is a boy who goes to school.

schoolchild /'sku:ltʃaɪld/ *noun*: **schoolchildren**
A **schoolchild** is a child who goes to school: *a large party of schoolchildren.*

schooldays /'sku:ldeɪz/ *noun (plural)*
A person's **schooldays** are the period when they attend school: *His schooldays were the happiest days of his life.*

schoolgirl /'sku:lgɜ:l/ *noun*: **schoolgirls**
A **schoolgirl** is a girl who goes to school.

schooling /'sku:lɪŋ/ *noun (uncount)*
Your **schooling** is the education or instruction that you receive at school: *She had only five years of formal schooling.*

school-leaver /'sku:l-li:və(r)/ *noun*: **school-leavers**
A **school-leaver** is a young person who is just about to leave or has recently left school: *a training scheme for unemployed school-leavers.*

schoolmaster /'sku:lmɑ:stə(r)/ *noun (old)*: **schoolmasters**
A **schoolmaster** is a male schoolteacher or head of a school: *She married the village schoolmaster.*

schoolmistress /sku:l'mɪstrɪs/ *noun (old)*: **schoolmistresses**
A **schoolmistress** is a female schoolteacher or head of a school.

schoolteacher /'sku:lti:tʃə(r)/ *noun*: **schoolteachers**
A **schoolteacher** is a teacher in a school.

schoolwork /'sku:lwɜ:k/ *noun (uncount)*
Schoolwork is the work that a child does while at school or as homework.

science /'saɪəns/ *noun*: **sciences**
1 (*uncount*) **Science** is the study of the natural world and the things that happen in it, through observation and experiment; **science** is also the knowledge gained by such study. **2** A **science** is any of the branches of science, such as physics, chemistry and biology, which deal with a particular area of the natural world. **3** A **science** is also any area of knowledge which is arranged or obtained according to formal principles: *political science*

science fiction /saɪəns 'fɪkʃən/ *noun (uncount)*
Science fiction is stories or films that are set in the future or other parts of the universe, often dealing with space travel, life on other planets, and technological developments that the writer imagines may exist at the time or place portrayed.

scientific /saɪən'tɪfɪk/ *adjective*
Scientific is used **1** to describe things that are concerned with or used in science: *scientific instruments* □ *a scientific textbook* □ *scientific research.* **2** to describe something that is done based on expert knowledge or a system of rules and tests, like the rules and principles used in science: *a scientific approach to food production* □ *It may not be very scientific, but it works very well.* — *adverb* **scientifically:** *It's still just a theory and hasn't yet been proved scientifically.*

scientist /'saɪəntɪst/ *noun*: **scientists**
A **scientist** is a person who studies or works in one or more of the sciences: *a famous scientist.*

scintillating /'sɪntɪleɪtɪŋ/ *adjective*
You can describe a person or what they say as **scintillating** if they are very witty and clever: *an example of his scintillating wit.* [*same as* **sparkling**]

scissors /'sɪzəz/ *noun (plural)*
Scissors are a cutting tool consisting of two blades joined in the middle which open in the shape of an X and cut when they close. Scissors are opened and closed using the thumb and fingers of one hand which you put through loops or holes in the handles of each blade: *a pair of scissors.* [see picture at **bathroom**]

scoff /skɒf/ *verb*: **scoffs, scoffing, scoffed**
1 You **scoff**, or **scoff** at something, when you speak or behave in a way that expresses scorn or contempt for it: *'Is that the best you can do?' he scoffed.* □ *He scoffed at my attempt to write poetry.* **2** (*informal*) If you **scoff** food, you eat it quickly and greedily. [*same as* **gobble, bolt**]

scold /skoʊld/ *verb*: **scolds, scolding, scolded**
If you **scold** someone, you speak to them angrily or in a complaining manner because they have done something wrong: *I was often very naughty, but my mother rarely scolded me.* [*same as* **tell off**]

scone /skɒn/ or /skoʊn/ *noun*: **scones**
A **scone** is a small round flattish plain cake made from flour and fat, often halved and spread with butter and jam.

scoop /sku:p/ *verb; noun*
▻ ***verb*****: scoops, scooping, scooped**
1 You **scoop** something up **a** when you make a cup-like shape with your hand or hands and lift it with a quick circular movement. **b** when you pick it up with a scoop: *She scooped the coffee into the pot.* **2** A machine, especially a mechanical digger, **scoops** something up when it lifts it using a hollow shovel-like part.
▻ ***noun*****: scoops**
1 A **scoop** is **a** any of various spoon-like implements for handling or serving food: *an ice cream scoop.* **b** a hollow shovel-like part of a mechanical digger. **c** a quantity that is scooped: *Would you like one or two scoops of ice cream?* **2** A **scoop** is also an important or exciting news story printed or broadcast by one newspaper, television or radio station before any other has had the opportunity to print or broadcast it.

phrasal verb
You **scoop** a part of something **out** when you remove it with a scooping or digging action or using a spoon-like tool: *Prepare the avocado by removing the stone and scooping out the flesh with a spoon.*

scooter /ˈskuːtə(r)/ *noun*: **scooters**
1 A **scooter** is a toy vehicle consisting of a board on a two-wheeled frame with tall handlebars, which a child moves along the ground by pushing against the ground with one foot while standing on the board with the other. **2** (also **motor-scooter**) A **scooter** is also a type of light motorcycle with a small engine and a protective front shield curving back at the bottom to form a supporting board for the feet which joins the casing containing the engine at the back of the vehicle.

scope /skoʊp/ *noun*
1 (*used in the singular*) A subject, topic or activity's **scope** is the whole range of things that it deals with or includes; a person's **scope** is the limit or range of their abilities or capabilities: *These matters are outside the scope of this inquiry.* □ *It's an interesting book, if somewhat limited in scope.* □ *Olympic competition should be well within his scope as an athlete.* **2** (*uncount*) If there is **scope** for something in a particular set of circumstances, there is freedom or the opportunity to act in a certain way: *The system is far from perfect and there's plenty of scope for improvement.*

scorch /skɔːtʃ/ *verb*: **scorches, scorching, scorched**
1 If you **scorch** something, or it **scorches**, you burn it or it burns on the surface leaving a usually brown mark: *The iron was too hot, and I scorched my best silk blouse.* **2** Plants **are scorched** when they dry up and wither, *eg* when the sun is very hot: *patches of scorched grass.* — *adjective* **scorching:** *It's been a scorching day.* [*same as* **blistering**]

score /skɔː(r)/ *verb*; *noun*
▻ ***verb***: **scores, scoring, scored**
1 a A person or team **scores** a point or points when they gain a point or points in a game, competition or test: *He scored 150 out of a possible 200 points.* **b** In football, hockey or rugby, a team or individual player **scores**, or they **score** a goal, when they succeed in putting the ball over the opposing team's goal line; in cricket, a batsman **scores** when he makes a run or series of runs: *'Now the centre-half is lining up for a shot at goal...Is he going to score?...Yes, he's scored!'* □ *Which British batsman has scored the greatest number of centuries in test cricket?* **2** The person **scoring** a game, competition or test is the person who keeps a record of the total number of points gained by each player or competitor: *Who's scoring the match?* **3** Someone or something **scores** high or low for some quality or attribute when they are judged or regarded as having that quality or attribute in a high or low degree: *He may not be the best student we have ever had, but his work scores high for effort and enthusiasm.* **4** In card games and board games like Scrabble, a single card (or combination of cards) or a single letter (or combination of letters making up a word), **scores** a certain number of points when it is equivalent to that number of points: *black king scores three* □ *What does the word 'zebra' score?* **5** If something with a point or sharp edge **scores** a surface, or if you **score** a surface with something sharp, you make shallow cuts or scratches in it: *Use a chopping board so that you don't score the top of the table.* [*same as* **scrape**] **6 a** A written piece of music is **scored** when it is broken down into parts for individual instruments or voices or is adapted for instruments or voices other than those for which it was originally written: *a composition scored for violin and cello.* **b** A film or play **is scored** when music is composed or adapted specially for that film or play. [*same as* **arrange, orchestrate**]
▻ ***noun***: **scores**
1 A **score** is a number of points, goals or runs scored: *A number of children have had very high scores in the intelligence test.* □ *Our team's score was 250, making us the overall winners.* □ *What was the score* [=how many goals did each team score] *in Saturday's cup final?* **2** A **score** in the surface of something is a shallow cut or scratch in it: *Before you put the joint of pork in the oven make scores in the skin using a sharp knife.* **3** A **score** is **a** a written copy of music showing the parts for individual instruments or voices. **b** written music specially composed or adapted for a film or play: *a film score.* **4** A **score** is a set of twenty: *three score year and ten.* [=70 years] **5** (*used in the plural*) You talk about there being **scores** of people or things when there are a great many of them, but too many for you to count accurately: *Scores of young actresses turned up for the auditions.* **6** (*used in the singular*; *informal*) When someone wants to find out what the current state of affairs is concerning something, or the reason for a particular situation that exists, they might ask what the **score** is: *What's the score here? Is he being arrested or not?* □ *He hasn't signed the contract yet. Will you ring him please and find out what the score is?*
▻ ***phrases*** **1** If you have a **score to settle** with someone, you have a grudge, grievance or complaint against them that you want to settle or resolve. **2** Someone **keeps score** when they make a note of the points won by the different players or competitors in a game or competition: *The boys asked their sister to keep score for them.* **3** (*informal*) You **know the score** if you know about or understand a particular situation and so can do what is required: *I won't tell the police anything; don't worry, I know the score.* **4** You use **on this** or **that score** when you are referring to some factor that has already been mentioned either by you or the person you are talking to: *He seems to be doing very well at school, so we have no worries on that score.* [=we don't have to worry about his schoolwork] **5** People **settle old scores** when they take some action to settle grudges or grievances that they have had for a long time against the other people concerned: *It is difficult to guarantee that the cease fire will hold when so many people feel they have old scores to settle, going back for generations.*

phrasal verbs
score off 1 Something that has been written down **is scored off** when a line is drawn through it to show that it has been dealt with or is no longer required: *I've packed all my night things so you can score them off your list.* [*same as* **cross off**] **2** One person **scores off** another when they gain an advantage over that other person, *eg* by saying something clever or insulting that the other person cannot match.
score out You **score** a piece of writing or printing **out** when you draw a line through it so that it can no longer be read, especially because it is not correct: *'Oh dear, I've signed my name in the wrong place.' 'Don't worry, just score it out.'* [*same as* **cross out**]

scoreboard /ˈskɔːbɔːd/ *noun*: **scoreboards**
A **scoreboard** is a board on which the score in a game is displayed, and which is altered as the score changes.

scorn /skɔːn/ *noun*; *verb*
▻ ***noun*** *(uncount)*
If someone feels or shows **scorn** for someone or something, they feel or show contempt for them: *She gave him a look of utter scorn.* ▫ *'What good will that do you?' he asked with bitter scorn.*
▻ ***verb***: **scorns, scorning, scorned** *(rather formal or literary)*
When you **scorn** somebody or something, you reject them with contempt: *He scorned making any form of apology.* ▫ *She scorned his advances.* [*same as* **sneer at**]

scornful /ˈskɔːnfəl/ *adjective*
Someone who is **scornful** feels or shows scorn: *a scornful remark* ▫ *He was scornful of their fears.* [*same as* **sneering, contemptuous**] — *adverb* **scornfully:** *He laughed scornfully.* [*same as* **sneeringly, contemptuously**]

scorpion /ˈskɔːpɪən/ *noun*: **scorpions**
A **scorpion** is a small creature that lives in desert regions. It has a body like an insect, four pairs of legs, and a long tail with a poisonous sting on the end.

Scot /skɒt/ *noun*: **Scots**
A **Scot** is a person who comes from Scotland.

Scotch /skɒtʃ/ *noun*; *adjective*
▻ ***noun***: **Scotches**
1 *(uncount)* **Scotch** is whisky made in Scotland: *a bottle of Scotch.* **2** (also **scotch**) A **Scotch** is a glass of Scotch whisky: *a Scotch on the rocks* [=with ice].
▻ ***adjective***
Scotch is used to describe things that are made in or come from Scotland: *Scotch broth* [=a type of thick soup made with barley and vegetables]. [see note at **Scottish**]

Scotch whisky /skɒtʃ ˈwɪskɪ/ *noun (uncount or count)*: **Scotch whiskies**
Scotch whisky is whisky distilled in Scotland from barley or other grain.

scot-free /skɒtˈfriː/ *adjective*
If someone goes, escapes or gets off **scot-free**, they are unpunished or unharmed: *The suspect got off scot-free because the police could not gather enough evidence to convict him.*

Scots /skɒts/ *adjective*; *noun*
▻ ***adjective***
Scots means of Scotland, its people or its dialect of English: *Scots law.* ▫ *The play was entirely in Scots dialect.*
▻ ***noun*** *(uncount)*
Scots is any of the dialects related to English used in Scotland, especially Lowland Scotland: *Burns wrote many of his poems in broad Scots.* [see note at **Scottish**]

Scotsman /ˈskɒtsmən/ *noun*: **Scotsmen**
A **Scotsman** is a man who comes from Scotland.

Scotswoman /ˈskɒtswʊmən/ *noun*: **Scotswomen**
A **Scotswoman** is a woman who comes from Scotland.

Scottish /ˈskɒtɪʃ/ *adjective*
Scottish means concerned with, belonging to or situated in Scotland: *He's of Scottish ancestry.* ▫ *His parents are Scottish.* ▫ *the Scottish Highlands* ▫ *a Scottish parliament.*

> Though the adjectives **Scottish, Scots** and **Scotch** all mean of or from Scotland, **Scots** is now usually only used of Scottish people, their law or their dialect of English, and **Scotch** only to describe things that are made in Scotland. It should be noted that Scottish people do not like to be described as **Scotch.**

scoundrel /ˈskaʊndrəl/ *noun (old)*: **scoundrels**
A **scoundrel** is a man who behaves very badly, especially one who cheats or deceives other people: *He's an utter scoundrel.* [*same as* **rogue**]

scour /skaʊə(r)/ *verb*: **scours, scouring, scoured**
1 If you **scour** a surface, you clean it by hard rubbing or scrubbing. **2** If you **scour** an area for someone or something, you make a thorough search of it looking for that person or thing: *They scoured the hillsides looking for the missing dog.* [*same as* **comb**]

scourge /skɜːdʒ/ *noun*: **scourges**
Something that is a **scourge** is a cause of great suffering or harm to many people or to a particular group of people: *... Falcone, Italian prosecutor and scourge of the Mafia* ▫ *Cancer is the scourge of Western society.*

scout /skaʊt/ *noun*; *verb*
▻ ***noun***: **scouts**
1 A **scout** is a person, either a soldier or someone with special knowledge of an area, who is sent out to track or watch an enemy and report back to a military unit. **2** A **scout** or a **talent scout** is a person whose job is to discover and recruit talented people, especially in the fields of sport and entertainment. **3** (often **Scout, Boy Scout**) A **Scout** is a young person who is a member of the Scout Association, a worldwide organization for boys, and now also girls, which teaches outdoor skills and encourages young people to develop as independent and useful members of the community. **4** *(informal)* If you have a **scout** for something, you make a search for it: *I returned from a lengthy scout round the area.*
▻ ***verb***: **scouts, scouting, scouted**
1 If someone **scouts** for, *eg* a football team, they act as a talent scout for them. **2** *(informal)* If you **scout** around or about for something you search for it: *I'll scout around a bit and see if I can find some decent secondhand furniture.*

scowl /skaʊl/ *verb*; *noun*
▻ ***verb***: **scowls, scowling, scowled**
If someone **scowls**, they wrinkle their brow to show that they are angry or in a bad mood: *He scowled at her over his newspaper.*
▻ ***noun***: **scowls:** *'This soup is cold', he said with a scowl.* [compare **frown**]

scrabble /ˈskrabəl/ *verb*: **scrabbles, scrabbling, scrabbled**
If you **scrabble** around or about in something, you move your fingers with scratching movements or noises trying to find or get hold of something: *He was on his knees, scrabbling about in the sand trying to find his glasses.* [*same as* **grope**]

scramble /ˈskrambəl/ *verb*; *noun*
▻ ***verb***: **scrambles, scrambling, scrambled**
1 You **scramble** somewhere when you climb or crawl there using your hands and feet to grip or support you as you go: *They had to scramble down a steep bank to reach the road.* ▫ *The boy scrambled over the wall.* [*same as* **clamber**] **2** If a crowd of people **scrambles** for something, they push and struggle against each other to reach or get it: *The boys scrambled in the gutter to get the coins he had thrown.* [*same as* **jostle**] **3** You **scramble** eggs when you beat their yolks and whites together so that they form a soft mass when they cook. **4** A number of things **are scrambled** when they are thrown or jumbled together in a disorganized or disordered heap or mass. **5** A message or a broadcast signal **is scrambled** when it is written or transmitted in code or otherwise distorted so that only those that know the code or that have a special device for decod-

ing it can read it or receive it. **6** An aircraft or its crew **scrambles** when it takes off immediately in response to an emergency.

▻ ***noun***: **scrambles**

1 A **scramble** is a violent struggle to beat others in reaching or getting something: *an undignified scramble for tickets.* [*same as* **rush**] **2** A **scramble** is also a difficult climb or walk in which you have to use your hands as well as your feet: *Getting over those rocks will be a bit of a scramble.* **3** When an aircraft takes off immediately in an emergency or its crew rushes to it in order to take off immediately, it is referred to as a **scramble**.

scrambled egg /skrambəld 'ɛg/ *noun*: **scrambled eggs**
Scrambled egg is the yolk and white of eggs beaten together and cooked in a pan.

scrap /skrap/ *noun*; *verb*

▻ ***noun***: **scraps**

1 A **scrap** of something is a small piece or fragment of it: *She wrote his address down on a scrap of paper.* **2** (*often with a negative*) A **scrap** is the smallest possible piece or amount of something: *There wasn't a scrap of evidence against him.* [*same as* **trace, grain**] **3** (*uncount*) **Scrap** is waste material of any sort, especially waste metal for recycling or re-use: *The car is being sold for scrap.* **4** (*plural*) **Scraps** are leftover pieces of food: *She fed the pigs on scraps.* **5** (*informal*) A **scrap** is also a fight or quarrel: *The two boys had a bit of a scrap in the school playground.* [*same as* **brawl, squabble**]

▻ ***verb***: **scraps, scrapping, scrapped**

If you **scrap** something you discard it because it is useless or abandon it because it is unworkable: *I think we had better scrap the idea.* [*same as* **drop**]

scrapbook /'skrapbʊk/ *noun*: **scrapbooks**
A **scrapbook** is a book with blank pages which you fill up with newspaper cuttings, pictures and photographs that you want to keep or display together.

scrape /skreɪp/ *verb*; *noun*

▻ ***verb***: **scrapes, scraping, scraped**

1 You **scrape** something, especially a hard object, when you push or drag it along a hard or rough surface: *He drove too close to the wall and scraped the car's wing.* **2** Something **scrapes** something else when it moves or is moved along it with a scratching or dragging action: *Be careful that the side of the boat doesn't scrape the jetty.* **3** You **scrape** something from a surface when you remove it with a scratching or dragging action, usually with a sharp-edged tool: *He scraped the dirt out from under his fingernails with a penknife.* ▫ *Scrape off the old layers of paint.* **4** You **scrape** something when you damage it by scratching it against or dragging it along a hard or rough surface: *He fell and scraped his knees on the gravel.*

▻ ***noun***: **scrapes**

1 A **scrape** is an act or the action of dragging or scratching along a hard surface. **2** A **scrape** is also a damaged area caused by scraping. **3** (*informal*) If you get into a **scrape**, you get into a difficult or embarrassing situation: *He's always getting into scrapes of one sort or another.* **4** (*informal*) A **scrape** is also a fight or quarrel.

▻ ***phrases*** For **scrimp and scrape** see **scrimp**.

phrasal verbs

scrape through or **scrape by** If you **scrape through** or **scrape by**, you manage to do something or succeed in doing it with great difficulty or narrowly avoiding failure: *He just managed to scrape through his final exams.* ▫ *She just manages to scrape by on the money she earns from selling her paintings.*

scrape together or **scrape up** If you **scrape together** enough money for a particular purpose, or you **scrape** it **up**, you collect it in small amounts with great effort or difficulty: *If we can scrape together enough cash we intend to renew the old windows next year.*

scrap heap /'skrap hiːp/ *noun*: **scrap heaps**
1 A **scrap heap** is a place where unwanted objects, *eg* old furniture and cars, are piled up. **2** Someone or something is on the **scrap heap** when they are discarded or rejected because they are no longer useful: *Young men increasingly face the daunting prospect of being thrown on the scrap heap in these times of rising unemployment.*

scratch /skratʃ/ *verb*; *noun*

▻ ***verb***: **scratches, scratching, scratched**

1 You **scratch** something when you rub or drag a sharp or pointed object along its surface, causing damage or making marks: *He reversed into a hawthorn hedge, scratching the car's paintwork.* **2** You **scratch** a mark on something when you make it by a rubbing or dragging action with a sharp or pointed object: *The old masons often scratched their initials on stones in the buildings they worked on.* **3** You **scratch** yourself when you scrape your skin lightly with your fingernails, especially to relieve itching: *He scratched his nose thoughtfully.* **4** You **scratch** an item off a list when you cross it out or cancel it. [*same as* **cross off**] **5** To **scratch** also means to make a grating or scraping sound: *She could hear the dog scratching at the back door.*

▻ ***noun***: **scratches**

A **scratch** is an act of scratching, or a mark or sound made by scratching: *The cat wants you to give his ears a scratch.* ▫ *How did you get the scratches on your face?* ▫ *the skirl of the pipes and the scratch of the fiddle.*

▻ ***phrases*** **1** You do something **from scratch** or start it **from scratch** when you start it from the very beginning, often after having failed in a previous attempt. **2** If you say that something **scratches the surface** of an issue or problem, you mean that it deals only superficially with it. **3** (*informal*) If someone or something is or comes **up to scratch** they meet or reach the required or expected standard.

scrawl /skrɔːl/ *verb*; *noun*

▻ ***verb***: **scrawls, scrawling, scrawled**

You **scrawl** when you write or draw untidily or hurriedly: *He scrawled his name on the wall with chalk.* [*same as* **scribble**]

▻ ***noun***: **scrawls**

A **scrawl** is untidy or illegible handwriting: *Surely you don't call this scrawl handwriting.* [*same as* **scribble**]

scrawny /'skrɔːnɪ/ *adjective*: **scrawnier, scrawniest**
Scrawny means very thin and bony: *a few scrawny chickens* ▫ *The old woman stretched out her scrawny arms.*

scream /skriːm/ *verb*; *noun*

▻ ***verb***: **screams, screaming, screamed**

1 When someone **screams** they utter a very loud high-pitched cry, because they are frightened, angry, or feel pain: *She screamed with pain.* ▫ *Her screams alerted the neighbours.* **2** You **scream** with laughter when you laugh very loudly or hysterically. **3** If something that is moving very fast **screams** past or through something, it goes past or through it making a loud high-pitched sound: *bullets screaming past his head* ▫ *The train screamed through the tunnel.* **4** If you say that a colour or pattern **screams** at you, you mean that it is intensely and unpleasantly bright: *The curtains scream at you.*

▷ ***noun***: **screams**

1 A **scream** is a loud high-pitched cry or other sound: *No-one heard her screams for help.* ▫ *a scream of pain* [compare **screech, shriek**] **2** (*informal*) If you say that someone or something is a **scream**, you think they are extremely amusing: *Your brother is a real scream.* ▫ *We moved his bed into the garden while he was asleep; it was a scream!*

scree /skriː/ *noun* (*uncount or count*): **screes**

Scree is a mass of loose stones covering a hill or mountain slope; a **scree** is a slope covered with such a mass of stones.

screech /skriːtʃ/ *noun*; *verb*

▷ ***noun***: **screeches**

A **screech** is a loud harsh high-pitched cry or sound: *the distinctive screech of the barn owl* ▫ *The car accelerated away from the traffic lights with a screech of tyres.*

▷ ***verb***: **screeches, screeching, screeched**

1 When someone or something **screeches** they make a loud harsh high-pitched cry. **2** If a machine or vehicle **screeches**, it makes an unpleasant high-pitched noise: *The car came up the driveway very fast and screeched to a halt outside the front door.*

screed /ˈskriːd/ *noun*: (*informal*) **screeds**

You can refer to a very long piece of writing which uses many pages as a **screed** or **screeds**: *He had written screeds of unintelligible nonsense.* ▫ *I had to read screeds of very boring statistics.*

screen /ˈskriːn/ *noun*; *verb*

▷ ***noun***: **screens**

1 A **screen** is an upright frame, often made up of several folding panels, used to divide a part of a room off to provide people with privacy or to protect them from cold draughts or heat from a fire: *an elaborate black-and-gold Chinese screen* ▫ *a fire screen.* **2** Something that acts as a **screen** protects you from being seen or shelters you from *eg* high winds: *They planted a screen of fast-growing conifers to protect the garden from the wind.* **3** A **screen** is **a** an upright surface on which films are shown in the cinema. **b** the part of a television set on which the picture appears: *This ever-popular TV comedy will be returning to your screens in the autumn.* **c** the part of a visual display unit connected to a computer on which information is displayed. **4** (*used in the singular*) **a** Cinema films as a medium are sometimes referred to as the **screen**: *adapt a novel for the screen* ▫ *stars of stage and screen.* [=famous actors who appear in the theatre and in cinema films] **b** Television as a medium is sometimes referred to as the small **screen** to distinguish it from cinema. **c** Data held on computer is displayed on **screen** when it can be viewed on a visual display unit.

▷ ***verb***: **screens, screening, screened**

1 Someone or something **is screened** when they are hidden from view or sheltered by a screen, or by something that acts as a screen: *The garden was screened from the worst effects of the wind by a high hedge.* ▫ *Her face was screened by a thick veil.* ▫ *He used the larger trees to screen himself from the view of any passing police cars.* **2** A film or television programme **is screened** when it is shown in the cinema or on television: *His latest film will be screened in the autumn.* **3** Certain organizations **screen** people when they investigate them to test whether they meet a required standard and are not likely to be disloyal or become a security risk. **4** People **are screened** by doctors and health workers when they are examined to determine whether they are suffering from a particular disease: *It is essential to screen women regularly for cervical cancer.*

> ***phrasal verb***
>
> You **screen** part of a room **off** when you make it into a separate area by putting up a screen or partition: *Backstage, the dancers' changing area was screened off by a heavy curtain.*

screenplay /ˈskriːnpleɪ/ *noun*: **screenplays**

A **screenplay** is the text of a film, including the actors' dialogue and directions for the action.

screw /skruː/ *noun*; *verb*

▷ ***noun***: **screws**

1 A **screw** is a small piece of metal with a pointed end, similar in shape to a nail, but with a spiral ridge on its shaft and a slot in its head. Screws are used to fix two pieces of *eg* wood together and are driven in using a screwdriver. **2** A **screw** is also any object that is similar in shape or which works by turning like a screw, *eg* a ship's propeller.

▷ ***verb***: **screws, screwing, screwed**

1 You **screw** one thing to another when you fix the one to the other using screws: *He screwed the hook firmly to the door.* **2** You **screw** one thing on to the other, or you **screw** them together, when you fasten one to the other using a twisting or turning movement: *Screw the lid on tightly.* ▫ *Does this connection screw in or push in?* [*opposite* **unscrew**] **3** (*informal*) To **screw** someone means to cheat or swindle them or to make them give you something by using force or threats: *landowners who screwed all they could out of the local peasants.*

▷ ***phrases*** **1** (*informal*) If you say that someone **has their head screwed on** or **screwed on the right way**, you mean that they are sensible and know how to look after themselves. **2** (*informal*) If you say that someone **has a screw loose**, you think they are slightly mad or crazy.

> ***phrasal verb***
>
> **screw up 1** If you **screw up** your face or your eyes, you twist your face or make your eyes narrower, usually because of pain, distress, or great effort or in order to see better or focus on something: *Her face was screwed up in an angry frown.* ▫ *His eyesight had deteriorated so much he had to screw up his eyes to read the newspaper.* **2** If you **screw** paper or other material **up**, you press or twist it with your fingers into a rough ball shape: *He found the letter in the wastepaper basket, screwed up into a ball.* **3** You **screw up** your courage when you make a great effort to stop yourself being afraid: *She couldn't screw up enough courage to ask him for a loan.* [*same as* **muster up**] **4** (*informal*) **a** You **screw up** or **screw** something **up** when you make a mistake or error of judgement which causes something to be ruined or to fail. [*same as* **botch**] **b** If someone **is screwed up** or someone has **screwed** them **up**, they are or have been emotionally damaged or upset.

screwdriver /ˈskruːdraɪvə(r)/ *noun*: **screwdrivers**

A **screwdriver** is a hand-held tool with a metal shaft whose shaped end fits into the slot on a screw's head, and is used to twist it into position. [see picture at **tool**]

scribble /ˈskrɪbəl/ *verb*; *noun*

▷ ***verb***: **scribbles, scribbling, scribbled**

1 To **scribble** means to write quickly or untidily: *I scribbled down his address on the back of an envelope.*

[*same as* **scrawl**] **2** If you **scribble** on something, you draw meaningless lines or shapes on it: *His little brother had scribbled all over his school books with a red crayon.*
▷ ***noun***: **scribbles**
1 If your handwriting is a **scribble**, it is untidy or illegible. [*same as* **scrawl**] **2 Scribbles** are meaningless written lines or shapes.

scrimp /skrɪmp/ *verb*: **scrimps, scrimping, scrimped**
▷ ***phrase*** You **scrimp and save** or **scrimp and scrape** when you spend as little money as possible by living cheaply so as to have enough left over to pay for something specific at a later time: *She scrimped and saved so that she could afford to send her son to a good school.*

script /skrɪpt/ *noun*: **scripts**
1 The **script** for a play, film or television or radio broadcast is the written or printed version of the words that are to be spoken in it. **2** A **script** is a system of characters used for writing: *Chinese script* □ *Arabic script.* **3** (*uncount*) You can also refer to handwriting as **script**: *She found a note in his minute script.*

scripture /ˈskrɪptʃə(r)/ *noun* (*uncount or count*): **scriptures**
1 The sacred writings of a religion are referred to as **scripture** or its **scriptures**: *ancient Hindu scripture.* **2** Christians also refer to the Bible as **Scripture** or the **Scriptures**.

scriptwriter /ˈskrɪptraɪtə(r)/ *noun*: **scriptwriters**
A **scriptwriter** is a person who writes scripts for films.

scroll /skroʊl/ *noun*; *verb*
▷ ***noun***: **scrolls**
A **scroll** is a long roll of paper or parchment with writing on it, now usually only used for ceremonial or official purposes: *He was presented with a scroll officially making him a freeman of the city.* □ *the Dead Sea Scrolls.*
▷ ***verb***: **scrolls, scrolling, scrolled**
If you display the text or other data from a computer file on a computer screen by **scrolling** up or down, you move the text or data up or down so that you can look at other parts of the same file.

scrounge /skraʊndʒ/ *verb* (*informal*): **scrounges, scrounging, scrounged**
If you **scrounge**, or **scrounge** off or from someone else, you get the things you want or need by begging or persuading them to give them to you: *He's always scrounging other people's cigarettes.* □ *She doesn't buy food; she just scrounges off her flatmates.* [*same as* **cadge, sponge**]

scrounger /ˈskraʊndʒə(r)/ *noun*: **scroungers**
A **scrounger** is a person who gets the things they want or need, not by working or paying for them, but by begging or persuading other people to give them to them. [*same as* **sponger**]

scrub /skrʌb/ *verb*; *noun*
▷ ***verb***: **scrubs, scrubbing, scrubbed**
1 You **scrub** something when you rub it hard, *eg* with a brush, in order to remove dirt from its surface: *She scrubbed the kitchen table with warm soapy water.* □ *Go into the bathroom and scrub those dirty fingernails.* **2** If you **scrub** dirt or a stain off something, you remove it by hard rubbing: *Once she had scrubbed the dirt off the old vase she knew for certain that it was valuable.*
▷ ***noun***
1 (*used in the singular*) If you give something a **scrub** you remove the dirt from it by hard rubbing: *He needs to wash his hair and give his face a good scrub.* **2** (*uncount*) **Scrub** is low bushes and short trees forming a thick covering in an area with poor soil (**scrubland**).

scruff /skrʌf/ *noun*: **scruffs**
▷ ***phrase*** If someone holds a person or an animal, such as a cat, **by the scruff of the neck**, they hold them by the collar or by the skin on the back of their neck.

scruffy /ˈskrʌfɪ/ *adjective*: **scruffier, scruffiest**
Someone or something **scruffy** is dirty and untidy: *He wore a scruffy old pair of trainers.* □ *a scruffy little town.*

scrum /skrʌm/ *noun*: **scrums**
In rugby, a **scrum** is the part of the game where groups of players from both teams form a circle by joining arms, and with their heads down try to win the ball by pushing against the players from the opposing team.

scrumptious /ˈskrʌmpʃəs/ *adjective* (*informal*)
When someone, especially a child, describes food as **scrumptious**, they mean it is delicious: *This cake is scrumptious!*

scruples /ˈskru:pəlz/ *noun* (*plural*)
If you have **scruples**, you have moral principles which make you unwilling to do anything that you believe is wrong according to these principles: *He had no scruples about taking money from his elderly mother.* □ *a ruthless tycoon, completely lacking in scruples.*

scrupulous /ˈskru:pjələs/ *adjective*
1 If a person is **scrupulous**, or **scrupulous** about details, they pay careful attention to even the smallest details: *He's scrupulous about keeping accurate accounts.* [*same as* **meticulous**] **2** Someone who is **scrupulous** takes care not to do anything that is unfair, dishonest or morally wrong: *A less scrupulous individual would not have told her about the money.* [*opposite* **unscrupulous**] — *adverb* **scrupulously:** *scrupulously honest.*

scrutinize or **scrutinise** /ˈskru:tɪnaɪz/ *verb*: **scrutinizes, scrutinizing, scrutinized**
If you **scrutinize** something, you examine it carefully or look at it closely: *The school inspectors will be scrutinizing every aspect of the teachers' as well as the children's performance.* □ *She scrutinized his face for any trace of emotion.* [*same as* **inspect**]

scrutiny /ˈskru:tɪnɪ/ *noun* (*uncount*)
Scrutiny is a close and thorough examination or inspection: *Every aspect of her life was subjected to close public scrutiny.* □ *The test was carried out under the scrutiny of independent observers.*

scuba-diving /ˈsku:bədaɪvɪŋ/ *noun* (*uncount*)
Scuba-diving is the sport or activity of swimming underwater using special equipment, consisting of tanks of compressed air carried on the back and connected to a mouthpiece, allowing the swimmer to breathe.

scuff /skʌf/ *verb*: **scuffs, scuffing, scuffed**
1 If you **scuff** something, you make scratches on it or scrape off some of its polished or smooth surface, by rubbing it with or against something hard: *He has scuffed the toes of his brand new boots.* [*same as* **scrape**] **2** If you **scuff** your feet, you walk without lifting your feet off the ground properly. [*same as* **drag**]

scuffle /ˈskʌfəl/ *noun*: **scuffles**
A **scuffle** is a confused fight or struggle: *As the crowd tried to move through the streets, scuffles broke out between some of the marchers and the police.*

scullery /ˈskʌlərɪ/ *noun*: **sculleries**

A **scullery** is a small room attached to a kitchen where certain kitchen work, such as washing dishes and chopping vegetables, is done.

sculpt /skʌlpt/ *verb*: **sculpts, sculpting, sculpted**
An artist or craftsman who **sculpts** carves or models solid objects or figures using *eg* clay or stone; a solid object **is sculpted** when it is made by carving or modelling a material such as clay or stone: *He doesn't paint; he sculpts.* □ *the figure of a youth sculpted from Carrara marble.*

sculptor /ˈskʌlptə(r)/ *noun*: **sculptors**
A **sculptor** is an artist who makes sculpture: *pieces by Epstein and other famous sculptors.*

sculpture /ˈskʌlptʃə(r)/ *noun*: **sculptures**
1 (*uncount*) **Sculpture** is the art of carving or modelling solid objects using clay, wood, stone, plaster, or other materials: *She studied painting and sculpture at art college.* **2** (*uncount or count*) **Sculpture** or a **sculpture** is works of art or a work of art made in this way: *an exhibition of modern American sculpture* □ *sculptures by Henry Moore and Barbara Hepworth.*

sculptured /ˈskʌlptʃəd/ *adjective*
1 Sculptured things have been made by carving or modelling: *sculptured stone ornaments.* **2** You describe the features on a person's face as **sculptured** when they are so regular and well formed that they look like those typically seen on classical statues.

scum /skʌm/ *noun* (*uncount*)
1 Scum is a covering of dirt or usually unpleasant waste material floating on the surface of a liquid: *The water was covered with an oily scum.* □ *Bring the jam to the boil removing any scum that forms.* **2** (*informal, derogatory*) If you refer to a person or group of people as **scum**, or **scum of the earth**, you think they are very bad, disgusting or worthless.

scupper /ˈskʌpə(r)/ *noun*; *verb*
▻ ***noun***: **scuppers**
On a ship, the **scuppers** are holes or pipes through which water drains from the deck.
▻ ***verb***: **scuppers, scuppering, scuppered**
1 When someone **scuppers** a ship, they sink it deliberately. [*same as* **scuttle**] **2** (*informal*) If something **scuppers** a plan, it ruins it: *Our holiday plans will be scuppered if the strike continues.*

scurrilous /ˈskʌrɪləs/ *adjective*
If you make a **scurrilous** remark or write something **scurrilous** about someone, you insult them unfairly and in a way that is likely to damage their reputation. [*same as* **slanderous**]

scurry /ˈskʌrɪ/ *verb*: **scurries, scurrying, scurried**
To **scurry** means to move hurriedly, especially with short quick steps: *The ants scurried about searching for food.* □ *Shots rang out and everyone scurried for shelter.* [*same as* **scuttle**]

scuttle /ˈskʌtəl/ *verb*: **scuttles, scuttling, scuttled**
1 A small creature **scuttles** somewhere when it moves there with rapid short steps; a person **scuttles** along if they move rapidly like a small creature would: *The beetle scuttled under the stone.* □ *She scuttled along muttering to herself.* [*same as* **scurry**] **2** When someone **scuttles** a boat or a ship they deliberately make a hole in it so that it sinks. [*same as* **scupper**]

scythe /saɪð/ *noun*; *verb*
▻ ***noun***: **scythes**
A **scythe** is a tool with a handle and a long curved blade, used for cutting grass or tall crops by hand.
▻ ***verb***: **scythes, scything, scythed**
You **scythe** grass when you cut it with a scythe.

sea /siː/ *noun*: **seas**
1 (*uncount or used in the singular*) **Sea** or the **sea** is the great mass of salt water that covers most of the Earth's surface and surrounds its land masses: *Australia is surrounded on all sides by sea.* [same as **ocean**] **2** A **sea** is any named part of this, usually smaller than an ocean: *the Baltic Sea* □ *the North Sea.* **3** A **sea** is also a large inland saltwater lake: *the Dead Sea* □ *the Caspian Sea.* **4** You talk about a particular type of **sea** when you are describing the condition of an area of salt water, especially with regard to its degree of calmness or roughness: *a calm sea* □ *the stormy seas around the Cape of Good Hope.* **5** You can refer to any vast expanse or crowd as a **sea**: *He looked down on a sea of upturned faces.*
▻ ***phrases*** **1** If you are **all at sea**, you are in a completely disorganized state or have no idea what to do next: *I'm all at sea with this knitting pattern.* **2** You are **at sea** when you are in a boat or ship on the sea: *a weather forecast for ships at sea.* **3** You travel, or travel to a place, **by sea**, when you travel there across the sea on a boat or ship: *The more remote villages on the peninsula are only accessible by sea.* **4** If a place is **by the sea**, it is situated close to or next to the sea: *a cottage by the sea.* **5** If someone **goes to sea**, they become a sailor in the navy: *He went to sea when he was only a boy.* **6** If something happens **out to sea**, it happens on or in the sea at some distance from the land: *Storm clouds were gathering out to sea.* **7** You **put to sea** or **put out to sea** when you start a journey by sea: *They put to sea in a flimsy raft.*

seabed /ˈsiːbɛd/ *noun* (*singular*)
The **seabed** is the bottom or floor of the sea: *creatures that live on the seabed.*

seabird /ˈsiːbɜːd/ *noun*: **seabirds**
A **seabird** is any bird that lives on or near, and finds its food in, the sea: *a large colony of gannets, gulls and other seabirds.*

seaboard /ˈsiːbɔːd/ *noun*: **seaboards**
A **seaboard** is the part of a country or continent that borders the sea: *along the eastern seaboard of the USA.*

sea change /ˈsiː tʃeɪndʒ/ *noun* (*used in the singular; especially literary*)
If you say that something has undergone a **sea change**, you mean that it has changed completely.

seafaring /ˈsiːfɛərɪŋ/ *adjective*
A **seafaring** man is a sailor; a **seafaring** people or nation use seagoing ships to travel, trade and earn a living.

seafood /ˈsiːfuːd/ *noun* (*uncount, often adjectival*)
Seafood is shellfish and other fish from the sea that are eaten as food: *I'm very fond of seafood.* □ *a restaurant specializing in seafood* □ *a seafood restaurant.*

seagoing /ˈsiːgoʊɪŋ/ *adjective*
Seagoing ships and boats are designed or equipped for travelling on the sea, rather than on lakes, rivers and canals: *a large seagoing yacht.*

seagull /ˈsiːgʌl/ same as **gull**.

seal[1] /siːl/ *noun*; *verb*
▻ ***noun***: **seals**
1 A **seal** is a device, such as a strip of plastic or metal, that is fixed over the opening to a container and which must be broken before the container can be opened. **2** A **seal** is also a piece of rubber or other material which keeps a joint airtight or watertight: *The rubber seal on my car door is letting in water.* **3** A **seal** is **a** an official mark stamped on a piece of wax or other material and attached to a document as proof that the

document is authentic. **b** an engraved metal stamp or ring for making this mark: *the royal seal.*
▻ ***verb***: **seals, sealing, sealed**
1 You **seal** a joint, opening or gap when you close it or make it airtight or watertight with a seal: *Seal the jars and store in a cool cupboard.* **2** You **seal** an envelope when you close it by sticking the open edges together or by fixing a wax seal to it. **3** Something **is sealed** when it is decided or settled: *With the final defeat at Culloden, the fate of the Jacobite cause was sealed.* □ *The bargain was sealed when the buyer gave the seller an open-handed slap on his outstretched palm.* **4** You **seal** wood, brick or other material when you apply a substance to its surface which will protect it from damage.
▻ ***phrases*** **1** If someone **gives** a project or plan **their seal of approval**, they say or do something that shows that they are in favour of what is being proposed. **2** Something that **sets the seal on** something else makes that other thing definite or confirms it in a formal or appropriate way: *The hardship they endured together set the seal on what was to be a lifelong friendship.*

phrasal verbs
seal in Something **is sealed in** when it is trapped, or kept inside a container, so that it cannot escape: *The coffee is freeze-dried to seal in the flavour.*
seal off An area **is sealed off** when a barrier or tight ring is formed around it so that nothing or no-one can enter or escape from it: *Police sealed the area off so that the gang had no hope of escape.* [*same as* **close off**]

seal² /siːl/ *noun*: **seals**
A **seal** is an animal that lives mainly in the sea but which breathes air and comes onto the land to breed. It has a small head, a shiny coat, and very short limbs with flippers: *a grey seal.*

sea level /ˈsiː lɛvəl/ *noun* (*used in the singular*)
Sea level is the average level of the sea's surface between high and low tides. It is used as the point from which the height of land is measured: *The summit is 4000 feet above sea level.*

sea lion /ˈsiː laɪən/ *noun*: **sea lions**
A **sea lion** is a type of large seal found in the Pacific Ocean.

seam /siːm/ *noun*: **seams**
1 A **seam** is a join between two edges, especially one that is sewn or welded: *The jacket has burst along the back seam.* **2** A **seam** of coal or ore is a band or layer of it in the earth or in rocks. [*same as* **stratum**]

seaman /ˈsiːmən/ *noun*: **seamen**
A **seaman** is a sailor below the rank of officer: *a merchant seaman.* [=a sailor in the merchant navy]

seamanship /ˈsiːmənʃɪp/ *noun* (*uncount*)
Seamanship is the skill of sailing and navigating ships at sea.

séance or **seance** /ˈseɪɑːns/ *noun*: **séances**
A **séance** is a meeting at which people try to contact and obtain messages from the spirits of dead people.

seaplane /ˈsiːpleɪn/ *noun*: **seaplanes**
A **seaplane** is an aircraft that is designed to take off from, and land on water. Seaplanes have two long floats in place of wheels.

seaport /ˈsiːpɔːt/ *noun*: **seaports**
A **seaport** is a port on the coast used by seagoing ships.

search /sɜːtʃ/ *verb*; *noun*
▻ ***verb***: **searches, searching, searched**
1 You **search** for something, when you look carefully for it; you **search** an area when you look or walk over it looking carefully for something: *'Give me your phone number,' she said, searching in her bag for a pen and a piece of paper.* □ *He searched everywhere for the missing letters.* □ *Her eyes searched his face for any sign of emotion.* **2** If you **are searched**, or your luggage **is searched**, someone looks in your clothing or luggage to check whether you are concealing something there: *The police searched them for weapons.* **3** You **search** *eg* your conscience when you examine it closely.
▻ ***noun***: **searches**
A **search** is an act of searching: *They made a thorough search of the woods and surrounding countryside.*
▻ ***phrase*** If you go **in search of** something, you look for it or seek it out: *He went to sea in search of adventure.*

searching /ˈsɜːtʃɪŋ/ *adjective*
1 A **searching** inquiry or examination is one that tries to discover the truth by looking very closely or carefully at every detail. [*same as* **thorough**; *opposite* **superficial**] **2** If someone gives you a **searching** look, they look at you closely, usually in order to try and find out from your expression what you are thinking. [*same as* **quizzical**]

search party /ˈsɜːtʃ pɑːtɪ/ *noun*: **search parties**
A **search party** is a group of people taking part in an organized search for a missing person or thing.

search warrant /ˈsɜːtʃ wɒrənt/ *noun*: **search warrants**
A **search warrant** is an official document giving the police permission to search a house or other building, *eg* for stolen goods.

searing /ˈsɪərɪŋ/ *adjective*
1 A **searing** pain is a very severe pain, that feels like burning. **2 Searing** heat is so hot that it scorches or burns: *the searing heat of the desert.*

seascape /ˈsiːskeɪp/ *noun*: **seascapes**
A **seascape** is a picture or painting of a scene at sea.

seashell /ˈsiːʃɛl/ *noun*: **seashells**
Seashells are the empty shells of sea creatures, often found washed up on beaches.

seashore /ˈsiːʃɔː(r)/ *noun* (*uncount*)
The **seashore** is the land next to the sea, especially the area with sand and rocks that the sea reaches in a storm or at a very high tide: *They walked along the seashore.* [*same as* **shore**]

seasick /ˈsiːsɪk/ *adjective*
If you are **seasick** when you are on a boat or ship, you vomit or feel unwell because of the movement of the boat or ship. — *noun* (*uncount*) **seasickness:** *Do you suffer from seasickness?*

seaside /ˈsiːsaɪd/ *noun* (*uncount, often adjectival*)
The **seaside** is a place beside the sea, especially where people go on holiday: *a trip to the seaside* □ *a seaside hotel.*

season /ˈsiːzən/ *noun*; *verb*
▻ ***noun***: **seasons**
1 The **seasons** are the four main periods into which the year is divided, that is spring, summer, autumn and winter. **2** The period of the year during which a particular sport is played or some other activity is carried out is that sport's or activity's **season**: *the fishing season* □ *the football season* □ *the holiday season.* **3 a** Any period of time which is characterized by a particular quality or level of activity is also referred to as a particular **season**: *the rainy season* □ *our busy season* □ *the growing season.* **b** A period of time when a particular fruit or vegetable ripens or is in plentiful supply is its **season**: *the strawberry season.*

▻ *verb*: **seasons, seasoning, seasoned**
1 You **season** food when you flavour it by adding salt, pepper or other spices. **2** Timber **is seasoned** when it is prepared for use by slowly drying it so that it becomes hard.
▻ ***phrases* 1 a** When certain crops such as fruit and vegetables are **in season**, they have grown or ripened enough to be harvested and eaten. **b** When certain birds and animals are **in season**, you can hunt or shoot them legally, according to the time of year. **c** A female animal that is **in season** is ready to mate. **2 Out of season** is used to refer to **a** foods, especially crops such as fruits and vegetables, that are not available because it is the wrong time of year. **b** game animals and birds that cannot be legally hunted because it is the wrong time of year.

seasonal /ˈsiːzənəl/ *adjective*
1 Seasonal work or employment is only available at certain times of the year, especially the spring or summer. **2** If you describe the weather as **seasonal**, it is typical of a particular season.

seasoned /ˈsiːzənd/ *adjective*
Seasoned is used to describe people who have a lot of experience in a particular field or activity: *a seasoned traveller* □ *He is a seasoned campaigner of several general elections.* [*same as* **experienced**]

seasoning /ˈsiːzənɪŋ/ *noun* (*uncount or count*): **seasonings**
Seasoning or a **seasoning** is any substance, such as salt, pepper or other spices, that is used to season food.

season ticket /ˈsiːzən tɪkɪt/ *noun*: **season tickets**
If you buy a **season ticket** for *eg* a train or a football ground it entitles you to a specified or unlimited number of journeys or visits during a given period: *a season-ticket holder.*

seat /siːt/ *noun*; *verb*
▻ ***noun***: **seats**
1 A **seat** is **a** an object used or designed for sitting on: *a garden seat.* **b** the part of such an object on which you sit: *a chair with a leather seat.* **c** a place for sitting, *eg* in a cinema or theatre, which you pay for as you go in or in advance: *All the seats for the concert are sold out.* **2** Your **seat** is your bottom, the part of your body on which you sit. **3** (*usually in the singular*) The **seat** of a piece of clothing, such as a pair of trousers, is the part which covers your bottom. **4** If someone has a **seat** in parliament, local government or on a committee they have a place or position there: *He lost his seat at the last election.* □ *The Liberal Democrats gained three seats and lost one.* □ *a seat on the council* □ *He was offered the chairman's seat.* **5** A **seat** of something is an established centre of it: *Washington is the seat of government in the United States.* □ *Oxford, Cambridge and other seats of learning.* **6** A large house belonging to an old or important family is also sometimes referred to that family's **seat**, or, if it is in the country, their country **seat**.
▻ ***verb***: **seats, seating, seating**
1 You **seat** someone in a particular place, when you assign that place to them, *eg* at a dinner table: *She seated the bishop next to her aunt.* □ *He was seated at the other end of the table from the host.* **2** If a place or a vehicle **seats** a certain number of people, it has seats or spaces for that number of people: *The dining room seats two hundred.* [*same as* **accommodate**] **3** Something **is seated** in a particular place or position when it is placed there: *exotic African masks seated on the windowsill.* **4** If you **seat** something in or on something, or it **is seated** there, it is fitted firmly and accurately in that place or material: *The supports were seated in concrete.* [*same as* **set**]
▻ ***phrases* 1** If someone asks you to **be seated**, they ask you to sit down; if you **are seated** you are sitting down, not standing: *All passengers should remain seated during take-off.* **2** If you ask someone to **take a seat**, you ask them to sit down. **3** If you **take your seat**, you sit down in the space allocated to you: *The show will begin when everyone has taken their seat.*

seat belt /ˈsiːt bɛlt/ *noun*: **seat belts**
A **seat belt** is a belt attached to the seat in a car, bus or plane that prevents a passenger from being thrown violently forward in the event of a crash. [see picture at **car**] [*same as* **safety belt**]

-seater /ˈsiːtə(r)/ *prefix*
-seater is used after a number to mean 'having seats for' that number of people: *a three-seater sofa.*

seating /ˈsiːtɪŋ/ *noun* (*uncount*)
The **seating** in a place, such as a restaurant, is the type or number of seats available or the way that the seats are arranged: *The hotel dining-room has seating for 70 guests.* □ *a seating plan.*

seaweed /ˈsiːwiːd/ *noun* (*uncount*)
Seaweed is any of several types of plant that grow in the sea.

seaworthy /ˈsiːwɜːðɪ/ *adjective*
A **seaworthy** boat or ship is in good enough condition to be sailed on the sea. [*opposite* **unseaworthy**]

sec /sɛk/ *noun* (*BrE*; *informal*)
▻ ***phrase*** If someone asks you to **hang on a sec** or **wait a sec**, they ask you to wait or stop for a brief moment: *Will you hang on a sec while I get my diary.* □ *Wait a sec. What was that number you just gave me?*

secluded /sɪˈkluːdɪd/ *adjective*
A **secluded** place is quiet, private and hidden from view or disturbance by people or noise: *a house in the secluded Sussex countryside* □ *a seat in a secluded corner of the garden* □ *The valley was quiet and secluded.*
— *noun* (*uncount*) **seclusion** /sɪˈkluːʒən/: *The nuns lived in total seclusion.*

second[1] (often written **2nd**) /ˈsɛkənd/ *determiner*; *pronoun*; *adjective or adverb*; *adverb*; *noun*; *verb*
▻ ***determiner***
1 The **second** person or thing is the one that is numbered two in a series: *They go on holiday in the second week of July.* □ *His wife has just given birth to their second child.* □ *We succeeded at our second attempt.* **2** The **second** person or thing in position or order is the one behind or next after the first or front one: *They got seats in the second row.* □ *the second person in the queue.* **3** A **second** thing or person is another one, or an extra one: *I certainly won't invite him a second time.* □ *You won't get a second chance.* □ *He's being hailed as a second Elvis Presley.* □ *people who own a second house.* **4** Something that happens every **second** week, month or year happens in alternate ones: *The ferry only sails to the island every second Tuesday.* **5 Second** describes something that is next best after the first, or less good or important than the first: *Our roses won a second prize this year.* □ *We were just beaten into second place.* □ *You only need a second-class stamp for local mail.* □ *I'm usually a second violin.* **6 Second** gear in a motor vehicle or on a bicycle is the next gear above the lowest gear: *Move into second gear as the car gathers speed.*
▻ ***pronoun:*** *This programme is the second in a series of three.* □ *He is the second from the right in the front row.* □ *Her birthday is on the 2nd of August.* [see note at **date**] □ *in the reign of Charles the Second* (written *Charles II*).
▻ ***adjective or adverb:*** *He was second in the final exams.*

▫ *She came second in the reading competition.* ▫ *I was standing second in the queue.*

▻ ***adverb***

1 You do something **second a** if you are the next person to do it after the first: *Do you want to jump first or second?* **b** if you do it as the next task after the first: *I'll leave the ironing till second.* **2** (*sentence adverb*) You use '**second**' in giving a list of things: *We've got plenty of excuses: first, it's too far; second, you're too busy; third...*

▻ ***noun***: **seconds**

1 (*uncount*) You are in **second** when you have engaged second gear *eg* in a motor vehicle: *Are you in first or second?* **2** A **second** is a second-class honours degree: *She was disappointed because she only got a second.* **3** A **second** is a person who acts as attendant to a boxer during a match. **4** (*usually in the plural*) **Seconds** are damaged or flawed goods sold at reduced prices: *These wine glasses are seconds.* **5** (*used in the plural; informal*) You have **seconds** when you have another helping of the food you have just eaten: *Anyone for seconds?*

▻ ***verb***: **seconds, seconding, seconded**

In a formal meeting or debate, when someone **seconds** someone else's proposal, they declare their support for it, so that a vote may be taken on it.

▻ ***phrases*** **1** If one thing is **second only to** another, the other thing is the only one that is better than it: *Singapore, second only to France for gourmet food.* **2** Something that is **second to none** is better than any other: *Our curries are second to none.* ▫ *As a political commentator he's second to none.*

second[2] /'sɛkənd/ *noun*: **seconds**

1 A **second** is a period of time equal to a sixtieth of a minute: *The spacecraft will take off in precisely 10 minutes and thirty seconds.* **2** You can use '**a second**' to mean a brief moment: *Can you wait a second?* ▫ *He hesitated for a few seconds.* [*same as* **moment**]

second[3] /sɪ'kɒnd/ *verb*: **seconds, seconding, seconded** (*usually in the passive*)

If you **are seconded** to work in a different post or place, you are transferred there temporarily from your usual post or the place where you usually work: *He has been seconded to the New York office for six months.* — *noun* (*uncount or count*) **secondment:** *a staff officer on secondment from an infantry regiment.*

secondary /'sɛkəndərı/ *adjective*

1 Secondary is used to describe something that is not of the first importance or is of lesser importance than the principal or primary concern: *That is a secondary consideration.* **2 Secondary** is also used to describe things that develop from something that came first or before: *He had measles and developed a secondary infection which affected his hearing.* ▫ *a secondary tumour.* [=a tumour that develops from, but at a different site from, the original tumour] **3 Secondary** education is for children between the ages of 11 or 12 and 18 who have completed their education at primary school.

secondary school /'sɛkəndərı sku:l/ *noun* (*BrE*): **secondary schools**

A **secondary school** is a school for children between the ages of 11 or 12 and 18, where subjects are taught at a more advanced level than at primary school.

second best (when used as an adjective **second-best**) /sɛkənd 'bɛst/ *noun; adjective*

▻ ***noun*** (*used in the singular*)

The **second best** is the person or thing that is next after the best, and that may not be as good as you would like: *He was the second best in his class at maths.*

▻ ***adjective:*** *He wore his second-best suit.*

▻ ***phrase*** (*informal*) If you **come off second best** in a fight or competition with another person, you lose.

second-class /sɛkənd'klɑ:s/ *adjective; adverb*

▻ ***adjective***

1 A person or thing that is **second-class** is not as good or as important as the best or top class: *a second-class service.* **2** A **second-class** degree is a degree awarded for academic performance that is in the class next after or below the first or highest class. **3 Second-class** postage is the cheaper class of postage in which mail takes longer to be delivered than if it was sent by first-class postage. **4** If people are treated like **second-class** citizens, they are treated as though they are not as important as other people: *Pensioners complained that they were made to feel like second-class citizens.*

▻ ***adverb:*** *I want to send these letters second-class.*

second cousin /sɛkənd 'kʌzən/ *noun*: **second cousins**

You can apply the term **second cousin** to your first cousin's child, or to your parent's first cousin.

second floor /sɛkənd 'flɔ:(r)/ *noun* (*used in the singular*)

1 (*BrE*) The **second floor** in a building is the floor that is two floors above the ground floor: *a room on the second floor* ▫ *a second-floor flat.* **2** (*AmE*) The **second floor** is the floor that is next above the ground floor.

second hand /'sɛkənd hand/ *noun*: **second hands**

The **second hand** on a watch or clock is the pointer that measures the time in seconds.

second-hand /sɛkənd'hand/ *adjective; adverb*

▻ ***adjective***

Second-hand things have been previously owned or used by someone else: *second-hand clothes* ▫ *a second-hand book shop.*

▻ ***adverb***

1 If you get or buy things **second-hand**, they have been owned or used by someone else before you: *They bought all their furniture second-hand.* **2** If you get news or information **second-hand**, you do not receive it directly from the person or people concerned, but from someone else: *He didn't tell me himself, I heard it second-hand.*

secondly /'sɛkəndlı/ *adverb* (*sentence adverb*)

You use **secondly** to introduce the second in a list of things: *I don't think she would be suitable for the job: first, because she is very young; and secondly, she doesn't speak French.*

second nature /sɛkənd 'neɪtʃə(r)/ *noun* (*uncount*)

Something that is **second nature** to you is so firmly fixed as a habit that you do it without having to think about it or without seeming to have to put much effort into it: *Being cautious was second nature to him.*

second person /sɛkənd 'pɜ:sən/ *noun* (*used in the singular; grammar*)

In speech analysis, the **second person** is the term used to refer to the person or people being spoken to, represented by the pronoun *you.* [see also **first person, third person**]

second-rate /sɛkənd'reɪt/ *adjective*

If you describe something as **second-rate**, you mean that it is not of the best quality or standard: *a second-rate novelist* ▫ *The service was good but the food was pretty second-rate.* [*same as* **inferior**]

second sight /sɛkənd 'saɪt/ *noun* (*uncount*)

Someone with **second sight** has the power, or is believed to have the power, to see into the future or to know about things happening elsewhere.

second thoughts /sɛkənd 'θɔ:tz/ *noun* (*plural*)
When someone has **second thoughts** about a decision they have made, they begin to have doubts about it and wonder whether it is the right thing to do: *She seems to be having second thoughts about getting married.*
▻ ***phrase*** You say **on second thoughts** when you change your mind suddenly about something you have been talking about or asking someone about: *I think I'll go out to the cinema. No, on second thoughts, I'd better stay in and finish the housework.*

secrecy /'si:krəsɪ/ *noun* (*uncount*)
Secrecy is the state or fact of being secret, or the ability or tendency to keep information secret: *The plan must be carried out in total secrecy.* □ *the secrecy of senior civil servants.*

secret /'si:krət/ *adjective; noun*
▻ ***adjective***
1 Something that is **secret** is hidden from or is not made known to other people: *Mary called it her secret garden.* □ *a secret passage* □ *secret government files.* **2** If an organization is **secret**, its activities are unknown or are not observed by people outside the organization: *a secret society.* **3 Secret** is also used to describe things that are concealed or that conceal something from others: *She gave a secret smile.* — *adverb* **secretly:** *She wrote to him secretly.* □ *He was secretly flattered.*
▻ ***noun*: secrets**
1 A **secret** is a piece of information that is not revealed, or which may not to be revealed, to others: *'What's in the parcel?' 'It's a secret.'* □ *Can you keep a secret?* □ *government secrets.* **2** A **secret** is also an unknown or unexplained fact: *unlock the secrets of the universe* □ *find the secret of eternal youth.*
▻ ***phrase*** If you do something **in secret** you do it without revealing what you are doing to others: *He visited her in secret.*

secret agent /si:krət 'eɪdʒənt/ *noun*: **secret agents**
A **secret agent** is someone who works for a government and tries to get secret information about the governments of other countries. [*same as* **spy**]

secretarial /sɛkrə'tɛərɪəl/ *adjective*
1 Secretarial work is typing or wordprocessing, taking shorthand, and the various other clerical and administrative duties of a secretary. **2** A **secretarial** college is one that provides training for people who want to do secretarial work.

secretariat /sɛkrə'tɛərɪət/ *noun*: **secretariats**
A **secretariat** is the administrative department of any large international organization: *the United Nations Secretariat.*

secretary /'sɛkrətərɪ/ *noun*: **secretaries**
1 A **secretary** is **a** a person employed to type letters, keep files and record business arrangements and meetings for another person or a group of people in an office: *If I'm not in the office when you call, you can leave a message with my secretary.* [compare **personal assistant**] **b** a person who keeps the records and does business administration for a club, society, business firm or other organization: *Please submit you application for membership to the club secretary.* □ *a company secretary.* **2** In Britain and some other countries, a **Secretary** is **a** Secretary of State: *Foreign ministers from several Commonwealth nations are to meet the British Foreign Secretary.* □ *the Defence Secretary* (or *the Secretary of Defence*). **b** a senior civil servant in charge of the administration of a government department: *the Cabinet Secretary.*

Secretary of State /sɛkrətərɪ əv 'steɪt/ *noun*: **Secretaries of State**
1 In the UK, a **Secretary of State** is a government minister in charge of one of the large departments of state, such as education, employment, health, or defence. **2** In the US, the **Secretary of State** is the head of the department dealing with foreign affairs.

secrete /sɪ'kri:t/ *verb*: **secretes, secreting, secreted**
1 If a part of an animal, plant or person **secretes** a substance, it makes it and and releases it: *The plant secretes a sticky liquid that attracts flies.* □ *The liver secretes bile.* **2** (*formal*) If you **secrete** something somewhere, you hide it or conceal it there: *A large quantity of cash had been secreted under a floorboard in her bedroom.* — *noun* (*uncount or count*) **secretion** /sɪ'kri:ʃən/: *The secretion of bile is one of the major functions of the liver.* □ *secretions from various internal organs.*

secretive /'si:krətɪv/ *adjective*
A **secretive** person is fond of secrecy or tends to keep things secret from other people: *He was always terribly secretive about his past.*

secret service /si:krət 'sɜ:vɪs/ *noun*: **secret services**
The **secret service** of a country is the government department responsible for espionage and matters of national security: *The President is accompanied wherever he goes by members of the secret service.*

sect /sɛkt/ *noun*: **sects**
A **sect** is a group of people within a larger, especially religious group, whose views and practices are different from, and are often regarded as extreme by, the remainder of the group: *the extremist sects, like the Cameronians, who, with more moderate presbyterians, became known as the Covenanters.*

sectarian /sɛk'tɛərɪən/ *adjective*
1 Sectarian means of, relating to or belonging to a sect. **2 Sectarian** also means having, showing or caused by hostility towards those outside your own group or belonging to a particular group: *sectarian violence* □ *a sectarian murder.* — *noun* (*uncount*) **sectarianism**: *sectarianism in Northern Ireland.*

section /'sɛkʃən/ *noun*: **sections**
1 A **section** of something is any of the parts into which it is or can be divided, or from which it is constructed: *You'll find biographies in the non-fiction section.* □ *The building was made in sections and fitted together on site.* **2** A **section** is also a number of soldiers that form a subdivision of an army platoon. **3** (*uncount or count*) The surface formed by cutting through a solid object such as a geometric figure is known as a **section**; a solid object that is viewed or displayed in **section** is viewed or displayed by cutting it, or as if it has been cut through, to show some internal surface or structure: *a section of a cylinder* □ *The diagram shows the structure of the bone in section.*

sector /'sɛktə(r)/ *noun*: **sectors**
1 A **sector** is a part of an area divided up for military purposes: *the American sector.* **2** A **sector** is also a separate part into which any sphere of activity, *eg* a nation's economy, can be divided: *the public sector* [=the part of a nation's economy owned and run by the state] □ *the private sector.* [=the part of a nation's economy owned or run by private companies and individuals] **3** (*maths*) A **sector** is a portion of a circle formed by two radii and the part of the circumference lying between them.

secular /'sɛkjʊlə(r)/ *adjective*
Secular is used to describe things that are not religious or connected with the church: *secular music* □ *a practice condemned by both church and secular authorities.*

secure /sɪ'kjʊə(r)/ *adjective*; *verb*
▻ ***adjective***
1 When someone feels **secure** they feel safe and happy and are not worried that anything bad will happen to them. [*opposite* **insecure**] **2** If a place is **secure**, it is well protected against attack, danger or loss: *Fit good locks to your windows and doors to make your house secure.* **3** Something that is **secure** is firmly fixed or attached: *Is that rope secure?* **4** A **secure** job or investment is one that is not likely to be lost or taken away.
▻ ***verb***: **secures, securing, secured**
1 You **secure** something when you fasten or attach it firmly to something else: *The cables were secured by heavy metal bolts driven into the rock.* [*opposite* **unfasten**] **2** (*formal*) You **secure** something when you get it or you are guaranteed to get it: *He campaigned vigorously in colleges and universities to secure the votes of young people.* [*opposite* **lose**] **3** You **secure** a place when you protect it in some way from danger or risk: *When the first wave of troops had secured the beachheads, the army moved against the enemy positions inland.* — *adverb* **securely:** *Make sure the rope is tied securely.*

security /sɪ'kjʊərɪtɪ/ *noun*: **securities**
1 (*uncount*) **Security** is the condition of being protected from or free from harm, danger or loss: *Small children need the security of a loving family.* ▫ *financial security* ▫ *national security* ▫ *We will have to review our security arrangements.* [*opposite* **insecurity**] **2** (*uncount or count*) **Security** or a **security** is something given as a guarantee, *eg* of repayment of a loan: *The bank asked him for security for the loan.* **3** (*usually plural*) **Securities** are certificates which show ownership of stocks and shares, or, the value represented by these certificates: *£200000 in government securities.*

sedan /sɪ'dan/ *noun* (*AmE*): **sedans**
A **sedan** is a saloon car: *a Plymouth sedan.*

sedate /sɪ'deɪt/ *adjective*; *verb*
▻ ***adjective***
1 A **sedate** person is quiet, calm and dignified in the way they behave: *Since she got married, she's much more sedate.* [*same as* **composed**] **2** If someone or something moves at a **sedate** pace, they move rather slowly without unnecessary or undignified hurry. [*opposite* **hasty**, **undignified**] — *adverb* **sedately:** *The Rolls Royce moved sedately down the drive.*
▻ ***verb***: **sedates, sedating, sedated**
A doctor **sedates** a patient when he or she gives them a drug or drugs which make them less nervous or agitated: *She had to be kept sedated for twenty four hours.*

sedation /sɪ'deɪʃən/ *noun* (*uncount*)
Someone who is under **sedation** has been given drugs to make them calmer or less agitated: *Severely disturbed patients may be kept under sedation for long periods.*

sedative /'sɛdətɪv/ *noun*: **sedatives**
A **sedative** is a drug that has a calming or soothing effect: *The doctor gave her a sedative to calm her nerves.*

sedentary /'sɛdəntərɪ/ *adjective*
A **sedentary** job or way of life is one in which you sit down most of the time and take very little exercise: *Because he has a sedentary job, he likes to be active in his spare time.* [*same as* **inactive**; *opposite* **active**]

sediment /'sɛdɪmənt/ *noun* (*uncount or count*): **sediments**
Sediment or a **sediment** is **1** a solid substance that settles at the bottom of a liquid: *decant the wine to get rid of any sediment.* **2** a layer of mud, sand, small stones or other material that has been carried along by water, wind or ice and left somewhere: *rocks made up of sandy sediments built up over millions of years.* [*same as* **deposit**]

seduce /sɪ'djuːs/ *verb*: **seduces, seducing, seduced**
1 If someone **seduces** another person, they persuade or succeed in tempting that other person to have sex with them. **2** If you **are seduced** by something, you are tempted or persuaded by it into doing or thinking something wrong or foolish: *The prospect of making quick profit seduced him into buying the shares.* [*same as* **lure**] — *noun* (*uncount or count*) **seduction** /sɪ'dʌkʃən/: *his seduction of an innocent young woman* ▫ *She was drawn there by the many seductions of city life.*

seductive /sɪ'dʌktɪv/ *adjective*
Seductive means tempting, charming or attractive, especially sexually attractive: *a seductive voice* ▫ *He was unable to resist her seductive charms.* ▫ *It's a very seductive offer, but I'm quite happy in my present job.* — *adverb* **seductively:** *She smiled seductively.* [*same as* **invitingly**]

see /siː/ *verb*: **sees, seeing, saw, seen**
1 a You **see** something when you notice it, observe it, witness it or look at it: *I'm afraid our dog goes mad whenever it sees a cat.* ▫ *I haven't seen their new baby yet.* ▫ *We're taking her to London to see the sights.* ▫ *I've seen him several times on television.* ▫ *She saw a piece of paper lying on the floor, and bent to pick it up.* ▫ *He saw a look of amazement on her face.* ▫ *I saw her hesitate.* ▫ *Did you actually see them attacking her?* ▫ *He was seen leaving the house at 4.30.* ▫ *His hand was seen to move to his pocket.* **b** You can **see** if you have the power of sight, or are in circumstances where you can use it; you **see**, or can **see**, something when it is within your range of vision, or comes into view: *They come out of hospital able to see for the first time in many years.* ▫ *He can hardly see at all without his lenses in.* ▫ *She's been seeing better since the operation.* ▫ *He was too small to see over the wall.* ▫ *You can see into their garden from the bus.* ▫ *It was so dark we couldn't see a thing.* ▫ *I see* (or *can see*) *Peter over there.* ▫ *Can* (or *Do*) *you see her anywhere?* ▫ *We could see her waving to us.* ▫ *I can't see what he's holding.* **c** You **see** a play, film or television programme when you watch it: *We'd just been to see 'Macbeth'.* ▫ *Did you happen to see the six o'clock news last night?*
2 a You **see** someone when you meet them or spend time in their company: *I haven't seen him since we were in school together.* ▫ *I'm seeing my mother this weekend.* ▫ *Have you seen much of Peter lately?* ▫ *He called round to see me the other day.* **b** Two people **are seeing** each other when they having a romantic relationship and spending a lot of time together: *They broke up a while ago and she's been seeing someone new.* [*same as* **go out with**] **c** You **see** someone such as a doctor, or they **see** you, when you consult them or go to them for advice: *He's been seeing a psychiatrist.* ▫ *An appointment was made for her to see the specialist.* ▫ *You ought to see someone about that ankle.* ▫ *The dentist will see you now.* ▫ *How long is it since you were seen by a doctor?* **d** You **see** someone in authority, or they **see** you, when you go and talk to them about something: *See me at the end of the morning.* ▫ *She was told to go and see the college principal.* ▫ *We asked to see the manager.* ▫ *Could I see you for a few minutes in my office?* **e** You agree to **see** people when you are willing to meet them, or to receive them as visitors: *She refused to see him when he called at her house.* **f** You **see** someone somewhere when you accompany or escort them there: *May I see you home?* ▫ *I'll see you to the gate.*

□ *Don't bother to see me out.* □ *I'll see myself out.* [= I'll find the way out by myself]
3 You **see** something such as a fact or circumstance **a** when you notice it: *I see from his application that he went to Cambridge.* □ *I could see that she was upset.* □ *As you can see, the box is empty.* □ *I couldn't help seeing how nervous he was.* □ *They must have seen my embarrassment.* □ *'They're digging up the road again.' 'So I see.'* **b** when you realize it: *We were beginning to see that we'd made a mistake.* □ *I saw that it was hopeless to try.* **c** when you understand it: *The two sides must balance, if you see what I mean.* □ *I'm afraid I don't see.* □ *'Pull the two cords simultaneously.' 'Oh, I see.'* □ *'I haven't managed to write my essay yet.' 'I see.'* □ *I don't see why I can't come too.* □ *He obviously didn't see the joke.* □ *I see no point in getting angry about it.*
4 You **see** what the situation is **a** when you investigate it: *I'll go and see if the milk has been delivered.* □ *I'm just seeing if these boots would fit me.* □ *Could you see how they're getting on?* □ *I'd better see what she wants.* □ *We'll see what we can do for you.* **b** when you witness it or discover it from reading or television: *You saw what happened to the husband who raped his wife?* □ *Next week we shall see how the difficulty was resolved.* **c** when you observe it, *eg* so that you can make a decision: *We'll have to wait and see how he settles down at school.* □ *Let's see whether the new system works.* **d** You **see** if you can do something when you try to do it: *See if you can close this zip.* □ *I'll see if I can help.* **e** You **see** that something is done when you take action to make sure it is done: *See you learn those verbs by next week.* □ *Please see that I'm not disturbed for the next hour.* [see also **see to** below]
5 You can **see** something **a** when you have a visual memory of it: *I can still see her face when she was told she'd won.* **b** when you can imagine or foresee it happening: *I can't see you as a civil servant in a grey suit somehow.* □ *I can just see them altering their plans at the last moment.* □ *I don't see the rate of inflation falling much in the foreseeable future.* **c** You **see** someone or something in a particular way if that is how you regard them: *My mother still sees us as little kids.* □ *We see it more as our home than as a weekend cottage.* □ *The situation as I see it is quite simple.* **d** What you **see** in someone are the things that you find attractive about them: *I don't know what you see in him; he seems pretty ordinary to me.*
6 a You can talk about people **seeing** events if they are around or alive when they happen; a period of time **sees** certain events if they happen during it: *We are seeing a gradual return to economic prosperity.* □ *the century that saw not only the agricultural revolution but also the start of the industrial revolution.* **b** You say you want to **see** something happening if you want it to happen: *I don't want to see you wasting your life.* □ *How would you like to see the socialist movement developing?*
7 See is used in books and other printed material to tell the reader to look at information given somewhere else, *eg* on another page: *For the Atholl régime see page 55.*
▷ ***phrases*** **1** You use **as far as I can see** when expressing your own opinion about a situation: *There's no need for further action, as far as I can see.* **2** (*used as an answer*) You say **'I'll see'** or **'we'll see'** to avoid giving a definite answer to a request: *'Can I go to Germany with the choir?' 'We'll see.'* **3** You say **'let me see'** or **'let's see'** when you are working something out: *That makes, let me see, 520.* □ *Let's see, I think she may have put it in the desk.* **4 'See you'**, **'See you later'** and **'See you around'** are informal ways of saying goodbye. **5** You say **'you see'** to draw your listener's attention to what you are trying to explain: *You see I never had any formal musical training.* □ *But that would be unnecessary, you see.*

phrasal verbs
see about 1 You **see about** something when you attend to it: *I'll see about getting you set up with your own computer.* □ *Who would be willing to see about the tickets?* **2** If you say 'We'll **see about** that' in reference to something that someone intends to do, you mean that you'll do your best to stop them: *'She refuses to pay.' 'We'll soon see about that.'*
see off 1 You **see** someone **off** when you go with them to the airport or railway station from which they are leaving, so as to say goodbye to them there. **2** (*informal*) You **see** someone **off** when you get rid of them: *Photographers were collecting round the gate but I saw them off pretty quickly.*
see through 1 You **see through** something such as a transparent surface when you can see what is on the other side of it: *The windows were so dirty you couldn't see through them.* [see also **see-through**] **2** You **see through** someone who is trying to hide their real intentions, or **see through** a trick or a lie, when you are not deceived by them: *I'm surprised that more people don't see through her.* □ *Unfortunately they saw through my little stratagem.* **3** You **see** a task **through** when you go on helping with it until you are satisfied it has been fully and successfully completed: *We're going to see this job through.* **4** You **see** someone **through** a difficult time when you support them until it is over. **5** You say that a supply of something will **see** you **through**, or **see** you **through** a certain period, if it is enough to last the time you need it for: *I hoped the cash I had with me would see me through the holiday.*
see to 1 You **see to** something that needs to be dealt with when you deal with it: *Will you see to the travel arrangements?* □ *A doctor examined him and saw to the cut on his head.* **2** You **see to** it that something is done when you take action to make sure it is done: *Please see to it that you get here punctually.*

seed /siːd/ *noun*; *verb*
▷ ***noun***: **seeds** or **seed**
1 (*count or uncount*) **Seeds** or **seed** are the things that a plant produces from which new plants grow: *Sow the seed about two inches deep and about eight inches apart.* □ *seed-eating birds* □ *sunflower seeds.* [see picture at **fruit**] **2** (*used in the plural*) The **seeds** of something are its source or origin: *the seeds of rebellion.* **3** In sport, a **seed** is a seeded player: *The second seed was knocked out in the first round.*
▷ ***verb***: **seeds, seeding, seeded**
1 A plant **seeds** when it produces seeds. **2** You **seed** an area when you plant seeds in it: *seed the lawn with a mixture of ryegrass and fescue.* **3** You **seed** a fruit when you remove the seeds from it: *seed the grapes.* **4** In sport, a player **is seeded** in a tournament when they are giving a ranking according to his or her likelihood of winning: *He was seeded fourth.*
▷ ***phrase***
1 If a plant **goes** or **runs to seed**, it grows rapidly and untidily just before it produces seeds. **2** (*informal*) If a person has **gone** or **run to seed** they have allowed themselves to get untidy, fat or unhealthy because they have not paid enough attention to themselves.

seedless /ˈsiːdləs/ *adjective*
Seedless fruits have no seeds in them: *seedless grapes.*

seedling /ˈsiːdlɪŋ/ *noun*: **seedlings**
A **seedling** is a young plant that has grown from a seed.

seedy /ˈsiːdɪ/ *adjective* (*informal*): **seedier, seediest**
1 If you are feeling **seedy**, you are feeling slightly ill: *I felt a bit seedy this morning when I got up.* **2** If you say that a place is **seedy**, you mean that it is dirty, in bad condition and not respectable: *a seedy little shop in a back street.*

seeing /ˈsiːɪŋ/ *conjunction* (*informal*)
'**Seeing**', '**seeing** that' and sometimes '**seeing** as' are used with the meaning 'since' or 'because' to introduce the reason for saying or doing something: *We thought we'd pay you a visit, seeing we were in the area.* □ *Seeing that a lot of you are against the proposal, I suggest we look at other alternatives.*

seek /siːk/ *verb* (*formal*): **seeks, seeking, sought**
1 You **seek** something when you search for it: *The President has announced that he will not be seeking re-election at the end of his first term.* **2** You **seek** something when you try to get or achieve it: *He's seeking employment.* **3** When you **seek** someone's opinion or advice, you ask for it.

phrasal verb
If you **seek** someone or something **out**, you search for them and find them: *He sought them out so that he could ask their advice.*

seem /siːm/ *verb*: **seems, seeming, seemed**
1 Someone or something **seems** to be a certain thing if they give, or you get, the impression that they are that thing: *She seems a nice sensible girl.* □ *They seemed so enthusiastic.* □ *You didn't seem* (or *you seemed not to be*) *very interested.* □ *He seemed to be some sort of international lawyer.* □ *She seemed like* [= she seemed to be, or she seemed] *the sort of person you could trust.*

You could replace **seem** with **appear** in any of the examples above, but notice that you would not use *like* after **appear**. Visual impressions can be conveyed also by **look**, which is often followed by *like*: *She looks the athletic type. That looks* (or *looks like*) *the easier route.*

2 Something **seems** to be so if it gives the impression of being so: *The smoke seemed to be coming from the roof.* □ *There seem to be more problems than ever.* □ *They don't seem to* (or *they seem not to*) *realize the inconvenience they're causing.* □ *She seems to be getting more forgetful.* □ *He seemed not to recognize me.* □ *I seem to be upsetting everyone today.* [*same as* **appear**] **3** You use **seem a** to report what you know from the available facts: *There seems to have been a delay at their end.* □ *It seems that we've been successful after all.* □ *'Is it true she's leaving?' 'It seems so.'* □ *'Doesn't he approve?' 'It seems not.'* [*same as* **appear**; compare **apparently**] **b** to register an exaggerated or fanciful impression: *Goodness, did it happen as long ago as that? It seems like yesterday.* □ *At the time it seemed as if* (or *as though*) *my whole world had been shattered.* □ *It seemed just like old times again.* □ *It seems ages since I last saw you.* **c** to ask someone's opinion or express your own: *That seems the wisest course.* □ *Does that seem reasonable to you?* □ *There didn't seem to be any point in continuing the discussion.* □ *It seems odd that he left no message.* □ *She seems to me to be fussing about nothing.* [*same as* **appear**] **d** to indicate uncertainty regarding some situation: *Things seem calm, at least for the present.* [*same as* **appear**] **4** You say you **seem** to remember or know something if you think you do: *I seem to recognize that man.* □ *I seem to know you from somewhere.* □ *I seem to recollect that we took a vote on it.* **5** You say you can't **seem** to do something if you find that you can't: *I can't seem to* (or *I seem unable to*) *get rid of this cold.*

seeming /ˈsiːmɪŋ/ *adjective* (*formal*)
Seeming means apparent: *his seeming generosity.* — *adverb* **seemingly:** *a seemingly endless stream of refugees* □ (*sentence adverb*) *Seemingly, what happened was he threatened to resign.* □ *'Is it true?' 'Seemingly it is.'*

seen /siːn/ *verb*
Seen is the past participle of **see**.

seep /siːp/ *verb*: **seeps, seeping, seeped**
A liquid **seeps** through or out of something when it flows through or out of it very slowly: *Oil seeping out of the pipe had formed a puddle on the ground.* □ *Water had seeped through a crack in the wall.*

seesaw /ˈsiːsɔː/ *noun*: **seesaws**
A **seesaw** is an outdoor toy consisting of horizontal board balanced in the middle, on which people, especially children, sit, one on either end, and propel each other up and down by pushing off the ground with their feet.

seethe /siːð/ *verb*: **seethes, seething, seethed**
1 When you **are seething**, you are very angry: *He was absolutely seething (with rage).* [*same as* **fume**] **2** If a place **is seething** with people, it is full of people moving around: *The city centre was seething with shoppers.* [*same as* **teem**]

see-through /ˈsiːθruː/ *adjective*
A **see-through** piece of clothing is made of very thin cloth so that you can see the wearer's body or underclothes through it: *She wore a see-through blouse.* [*same as* **transparent**; *opposite* **opaque**]

segment /ˈsɛgmənt/ *noun*: **segments**
A **segment** is a part, section or division of something: *Divide the orange into segments.* □ *An insect's body is divided into segments* □ *The surgeon removed a small segment of bowel.*

segregate /ˈsɛgrɪgeɪt/ *verb*: **segregates, segregating, segregated**
You **segregate** groups of people or animals when you separate them or keep them apart from others or from each other: *The young bulls were segregated from the cows.* □ *a segregated community.* [compare **integrate**] — *noun* (*uncount*) **segregation** /sɛgrɪˈgeɪʃən/: *the segregation of Protestants from Roman Catholics.*

seize /siːz/ *verb*: **seizes, seizing, seized**
1 a You **seize** something when you grab it or take hold of it suddenly, forcefully or eagerly: *He seized his friend's hand and shook it.* □ *The policeman seized the boy by the collar.* **b** You **seize** a chance or opportunity when you take it eagerly and without hesitation: *You should seize the opportunity with both hands.* [*same as* **grasp**] **2** (*in the passive*) If someone **is seized** by a feeling or thought, they are affected suddenly and deeply by it or it takes control of their mind or body: *The whole country was seized by panic at the news.* □ *He was seized by the sudden desire to run away.* **3** If someone **seizes** power they take it by force. **4** If something **is seized** by the police or someone else in authority, they take possession of it by official order or authority: *The consignment of illegal drugs was seized by customs officers in an undercover operation.* [*same as* **confiscate**; *opposite* **let go**]

phrasal verbs
seize on or **upon** When someone **seizes on** or **upon** something, such as an idea or opportunity, they accept it with enthusiasm or take it eagerly: *He*

seized upon the suggestion as a way of getting out of his financial difficulties.
seize up **1** If an engine or other machinery **seizes up**, it stops working because it does not have enough oil to keep its parts moving smoothly or it has been used too much. **2** If joints **seize up**, they suddenly become stiff and you cannot move easily, usually because you have strained them: *My knees have seized up with too much bending.*

seizure /'siːʒə(r)/ *noun*: **seizures**
1 (*uncount*) The **seizure** of something is the act of taking it or taking control of it, often by force or using the force of law: *the seizure of large quantities of illegal drugs by customs officers.* [*same as* **confiscation**] **2** If someone has a **seizure**, they have a sudden attack of an illness, *eg* a heart attack, which disables them temporarily or permanently.

seldom /'sɛldəm/ *adverb* (*used like a negative*)
If something **seldom** happens, it does not often happen: *The pine marten is very seldom seen in the wild.* □ *He seldom, if ever, writes, though he does telephone once a week.* [*same as* **rarely**]

select /sə'lɛkt/ *verb*; *adjective*
▷ ***verb***: **selects, selecting, selected**
You **select** something when you choose it from amongst several available: *She was selected for the school hockey team.* □ *After looking carefully through the racks, he selected a brightly-patterned tie.* □ *The members of the committee have been carefully selected.* [*same as* **choose**]
▷ ***adjective***
1 Things are described as **select** when they have been carefully chosen because they are of the highest quality: *a select range of garden furniture.* [*same as* **choice**] **2** **Select** places are places to which entrance or membership is restricted, usually to those people who can afford it or who are of sufficiently high social class: *He lives in a select area of the suburbs.* [*same as* **exclusive**]

selection /sɪ'lɛkʃən/ *noun*: **selections**
1 (*uncount*) **Selection** is the act or process of selecting or being selected: *His selection as a parliamentary candidate was controversial.* □ *All candidates must go through the selection process.* **2** A **selection** is a thing or set of things that have been chosen from amongst others: *He ordered a selection of goods from the company's catalogue.* [*same as* **assortment**] **3** A **selection** is a range from which to choose: *The company offers a good selection of package holidays at reasonable prices.* **4** (*uncount*) **Selection** or **natural selection** is the process by which certain animals or plants survive while others do not, leading, according to evolutionary theory, to the development of certain physical characteristics.

selective /sɪ'lɛktɪv/ *adjective*
1 If you are **selective** you are careful in choosing things: *He's very selective about the company he keeps.* [*same as* **particular**] **2** Something that is **selective** has an effect only on certain things: *a selective weedkiller.*

self /sɛlf/ *noun* (*usually with a possessive adjective, followed by an adjective*): **selves**
Your **self** is the real you, or the person that you are, with all your qualities and attitudes: *It wasn't till they'd been married for a few weeks that he revealed his true self.* □ *Lots of actors have forgotten how to be their real selves.* □ *By the next day she was her old sunny self again.* □ *She put her whole self into her work.*

self- /sɛlf/ *prefix*
1 **Self-** is used to form nouns and adjectives that refer to something that is of, by, for, in, to, or in relation to yourself: *self-doubt* □ *a self-inflicted wound.* **2** **Self-** is also used to form adjectives that describe something that performs some action automatically: *self-closing doors.*

self-addressed /sɛlfə'drɛt/ *adjective*
A **self-addressed** envelope is one which the sender addresses to himself or herself so that something can be returned to their address.

self-appointed /sɛlfə'pɔɪntɪd/ *adjective* (*usually derogatory*)
Self-appointed is used to describe someone who chooses themselves for a particular job or role, without being asked or chosen by others: *a self-appointed judge of public morals.*

self-assured /sɛlfə'ʃʊəd/ *adjective*
A **self-assured** person is confident in their own talents and abilities: *a very self-assured young man.* [*same as* **assured, self-confident**] — *noun* (*uncount*) **self-assurance:** *She walked onto the stage with great dignity and self-assurance.*

self-catering /sɛlf'keɪtərɪŋ/ *adjective* (*BrE*)
A **self-catering** holiday or **self-catering** holiday accommodation is a holiday or accommodation in which you provide and prepare your own meals.

self-centred (*AmE* **self-centered**) /sɛlf'sɛntəd/ *adjective*
A **self-centred** person thinks only about themselves and does not consider other people. [compare **selfish**]

self-coloured (*AmE* **self-colored**) /sɛlf'kʌləd/ *adjective*
Self-coloured fabrics are the same colour all over and are not patterned: *a self-coloured carpet.*

self-confessed /sɛlfkən'fɛst/ *adjective*
Self-confessed is used to describe someone who openly admits that they have a particular fault or bad habit: *a self-confessed chocolate addict.*

self-confident /sɛlf'kɒnfɪdənt/ *adjective*
A **self-confident** person is sure of their own value and ability to succeed: *Do you think he's self-confident enough to stand up and give a speech in front of such a large crowd?* [*same as* **self-assured**] — *noun* (*uncount*) **self-confidence:** *She lacks the self-confidence to apply for promotion.*

self-conscious /sɛlf'kɒnʃəs/ *adjective*
If you are **self-conscious** or **self-conscious** about something, you feel nervous and uncomfortable when you are with other people because you think they are looking at and criticizing or judging you: *She's too shy and self-conscious to sing in public.* □ *He's very self-conscious about his weight.* — *adverb* **self-consciously:** *He was self-consciously aware of his shabby clothes.*

self-contained /sɛlfkən'teɪnd/ *adjective*
1 A **self-contained** flat has its own private front door, kitchen and bathroom. **2** If you refer to someone as a **self-contained** person, you mean that they are independent and do not seem to need emotional support from other people.

self-control /sɛlfkən'troʊl/ *noun* (*uncount*)
Your **self-control** is the ability you have to control your own strong feelings and impulses so that other people are not aware of them: *He completely lost his self-control and banged on the table with his fist.* □ *I needed all my self-control to stop myself hitting him.*

self-defence (*AmE* **self-defense**) /sɛlfdɪ'fɛns/ *noun* (*uncount*)

Self-defence is the act of defending yourself from someone who is trying to attack you, or any of the various techniques which you can learn in order to do so: *He shot the man in self-defence* [in order to protect himself from being killed or injured by him]. □ *a class teaching self-defence for women.*

self-drive /sɛlf'draɪv/ *adjective*
A **self-drive** vehicle is one which you hire and drive yourself.

self-employed /sɛlfɪm'plɔɪd/ *adjective*
If you are **self-employed**, you work for yourself rather than for an employer, organizing your own working hours, rates of pay and accounts.

self-esteem /sɛlfɪ'stiːm/ *noun (uncount)*
Your **self-esteem** is your good opinion of yourself or your respect for yourself: *He suffers from a lack of self-esteem.*

self-evident /sɛlf'ɛvɪdənt/ *adjective (formal)*
Something that is **self-evident** is so clear that there is no need for further explanation or proof: *It is self-evident that the world's resources cannot meet the needs of an ever-expanding human population.* [*same as* **obvious**]

self-explanatory /sɛlfɪk'splanətərɪ/ *adjective*
Something that is **self-explanatory** is easily understood and needs no further explanation: *The instructions are self-explanatory.*

self-government /sɛlf'gʌvəmənt/ *noun (uncount)*
Self-government is government of a country or nation by the people of that country or nation rather than by others: *They are campaigning for self-government for Scotland.*

self-important /sɛlfɪm'pɔːtənt/ *adjective*
A **self-important** person has too high an opinion of their own importance: *a self-important little man with a large briefcase.* [*same as* **arrogant**, **pompous**]

self-imposed /sɛlfɪm'poʊzd/ *adjective*
Something that is **self-imposed** is forced or imposed on a person by himself or herself, not by others: *He lived in self-imposed exile.*

self-indulgent /sɛlfɪn'dʌldʒənt/ *adjective*
A **self-indulgent** person allows themselves, or is too ready to allow themselves, to have or do things that they want or enjoy: *He has a tendency to be self-indulgent.* [*opposite* **abstemious**] — *noun (uncount)* **self-indulgence:** *We had a week of pure self-indulgence at a luxury hotel.* [*same as* **excess**]

self-interest /sɛlf'ɪntrɛst/ *noun (uncount)*
Self-interest is the attitude or fact of being concerned only about the things that you want or need or about things that are to your own advantage: *He acted purely out of self-interest.* [*same as* **selfishness**]

selfish /'sɛlfɪʃ/ *adjective*
A **selfish** person thinks only about themselves and not about what other people may want or need: *What a selfish little boy you are!* □ *That's a very selfish attitude.* □ *Don't be so selfish; give her one of your sweets.* [*opposite* **generous**, **unselfish**] — *adverb* **selfishly:** *He selfishly ate all the chocolates, leaving none for the others.* — *noun (uncount)* **selfishness:** *I was shocked at his selfishness.*

selfless /'sɛlfləs/ *adjective*
Selfless is used to describe **1** a person who thinks of other people's needs or wants before their own. **2** an act in which such a person gives up something in order that someone else may benefit. [*opposite* **selfish**]

self-made /sɛlf'meɪd/ *adjective*
A **self-made** man or a **self-made** millionaire has become successful or wealthy through their own efforts.

self-pity /sɛlf'pɪtɪ/ *noun (uncount)*
Self-pity is the tendency to feel sorry for yourself when things go wrong.

self-portrait /sɛlf'pɔːtrət/ or /sɛlf'pɔːtreɪt/ *noun*: **self-portraits**
A **self-portrait** is a painting or drawing that an artist does of himself or herself: *Rembrandt painted many self-portraits throughout his life.*

self-possessed /sɛlfpə'zɛst/ *adjective*
Someone who is **self-possessed** is calm and able to act in a confident way, especially in a difficult situation: *a self-possessed young woman.* [*same as* **composed**]

self-raising flour /sɛlf'reɪzɪŋ flaʊə(r)/ (*AmE* **self-rising flour**) *noun (uncount)*
Self-raising flour is flour used in baking containing an ingredient that makes dough or pastry rise when it is cooked.

self-reliant /sɛlfrɪ'laɪənt/ *adjective*
If you are **self-reliant**, you are independent and do not need to ask for help or support from other people.

self-respect /sɛlfrɪ'spɛkt/ *noun (uncount)*
Self-respect is your respect for yourself and concern for your dignity and reputation: *You should have more self-respect than to allow yourself to be treated in that way.* — *adjective* **self-respecting:** *No self-respecting journalist would work for that so-called newspaper.*

self-righteous /sɛlf'raɪtʃəs/ *adjective*
A **self-righteous** person has too high an opinion of their own goodness, thinking that they are always right and other people are wrong. [*same as* **smug**, **superior**]

self-sacrifice /sɛlf'sakrɪfaɪs/ *noun (uncount)*
Self-sacrifice is the act of giving up what you have or what you want to do, in order to help others or to achieve something in the future: *In order to succeed, the scheme will require hard work and self-sacrifice by everyone concerned.*

self-satisfied /sɛlf'satɪsfaɪd/ *adjective*
A **self-satisfied** person feels, or shows in a way that is irritating to other people, that they are very pleased or satisfied with themselves or their achievements: *'The teacher says my work is always the best in the class,' she said with a self-satisfied smile.* [*same as* **smug**]

self-service /sɛlf'sɜːvɪs/ *noun (uncount, often adjectival)*
Self-service is a system, *eg* in a restaurant, shop or garage, in which customers serve themselves rather than being served by somebody else: *It's self-service in the works canteen.* □ *a self-service restaurant.*

self-sufficient /sɛlfsə'fɪʃənt/ *adjective*
A **self-sufficient** country or group of people is one which is able to produce or provide everything it needs without having to bring things in from outside: *The monastery is a completely self-sufficient community.* □ *The country has been self-sufficient in most cereals since the war.*

sell /sɛl/ *verb*: **sells, selling, sold**
1 You **sell** something when you give it to someone in exchange for money: *He sold his car and bought a motorbike.* □ *They sold the land to a property developer.* **2** You **sell** things when you make them available for buying: *The shop sells trinkets and handicrafts.* □ *Do you sell stamps?* **3** If something **is sold** at a particular price, it is available for buying at that price; if something **sells** for a stated price the person

who has bought it has paid that price for it: *Melons are selling at 50p today.* □ *What are houses like this selling for these days?* **4** Something that **sells** is bought by customers or is in demand: *His paintings don't sell.* □ *This line of cosmetics sells well.* **5** If you **sell** something you encourage or persuade people to buy it; you **sell** an idea or a scheme when you persuade people to accept it: *These T-shirts sell themselves.* □ *The government is trying to sell the idea that state ownership of industry is bad for the economy.*

phrasal verbs
sell off If you **sell** goods **off**, you offer them for sale at a cheaper price than usual so that they will sell quickly.
sell out **1** If goods that are offered for sale **sell out**, they are all bought: *We can't get enough of these toys, they sell out so fast.* **2** If you **sell out**, or **sell** someone **out**, you betray your principles or betray your friends or associates, often for some personal gain: *His early pictures were some of the most original I have ever seen, before he sold out to the mass market.* □ *He was supposed to represent us but he sold us out for a job in management.* [see also **sell-out**]
sell up You **sell up** when you sell your house or business: *He says he's going to sell up and move abroad.*

sell-by date /ˈsɛlbaɪ deɪt/ *noun*: **sell-by dates**
A **sell-by date** is a date marked on many packaged foods that shows the last date on which that item may be displayed for sale.

seller /ˈsɛlə(r)/ *noun*: **sellers**
A **seller** is someone who offers something for sale.

Sellotape /ˈsɛləteɪp/ *noun* (*trademark; uncount*)
Sellotape is a type of transparent sticky tape, used especially for sticking pieces of paper together.

sell-out /ˈsɛlaʊt/ *noun*: **sell-outs**
A concert or other event is a **sell-out** when all the tickets for it have been sold. [see also **sell out**]

selves /sɛlvz/ *noun*
Selves is the plural of **self**.

semblance /ˈsɛmbləns/ *noun* (*uncount or used in the singular; formal*)
You say something is a **semblance** of a particular state or condition or has some **semblance** of that state or condition when it is or has an outward appearance of, or apparent likeness to, that state or condition: *He tried to bring some semblance of order to the proceedings.*

semen /ˈsiːmən/ *noun* (*uncount*)
Semen is the whitish liquid containing sperm that is produced in the male sex glands.

semi- /ˈsɛmɪ/ *prefix*
Semi- is used before nouns and adjectives to mean 'half' or 'partly': *quavers and semiquavers* □ *semiconscious.*

semicircle /ˈsɛmɪsɜːkəl/ *noun*: **semicircles**
A **semicircle** is half of a circle: *The children sat in a semicircle round the teacher's chair.* [see picture at **shape**]

semicolon /sɛmɪˈkoʊlɒn/ *noun*: **semicolons**
A **semicolon** is a punctuation mark (;) used in writing or printing to separate items in a list or different parts of a sentence.

semi-detached /sɛmɪdɪˈtatʃt/ *adjective*
A **semi-detached** house is a house that is joined to another house on one side: (*with the noun omitted*) *They live in a semi-detached.* [see picture at **house**]

semifinal /sɛmɪˈfaɪnəl/ *noun*: **semifinals**
A **semifinal** is either of two matches in a competition, the winners of which play against each other in the final: *Sweden reached the semifinal of the 1994 World Cup.*

semifinalist /sɛmɪˈfaɪnəlɪst/ *noun*: **semifinalists**
A **semifinalist** is one of the players or teams of players in the semi-finals of a competition.

seminar /ˈsɛmɪnɑː(r)/ *noun*: **seminars**
A **seminar** is **1** a class in a university or college in which a small number of students discuss or study a particular topic with a tutor or teacher. **2** any meeting in which a particular subject is taught or discussed: *a business seminar.*

semi-precious /sɛmɪˈprɛʃəs/ *adjective*
A **semi-precious** stone is a gemstone that is considered to be less valuable than a precious stone: *turquoises, amethysts and other semi-precious stones.*

semi-skilled /sɛmɪˈskɪld/ *adjective*
A **semi-skilled** job is one which requires less advanced training or skills than those needed for a skilled job or trade.

senate /ˈsɛnət/ *noun* (*with a singular or plural verb*): **senates**
1 In some countries, such as the USA and Australia, the **Senate** is the smaller and higher-ranking of the two law-making bodies of central government. **2** The governing council in some British universities is called the **senate**. **3** (*singular*) In ancient Rome, the **Senate** was the highest law-making and administrative council.

senator (when used with a name **Senator**) /ˈsɛnətə(r)/ *noun*: **senators**
A **senator** is a member of a Senate: *Senator Kennedy.*

send /sɛnd/ *verb*: **sends, sending, sent**
1 You **send** something to someone when you post it, or have it delivered, to them; you **send** something somewhere when you arrange for it to be taken there: *I'm sending you those papers by this morning's post.* □ *Did you remember to send Granny a postcard?* □ *I'll have the form sent round to you straight away.* □ *You'll be sent a copy of the policy document.* □ *The goods were faulty and we sent them back.* □ *Our luggage was sent home by sea.* □ *She had breakfast sent up to her room.* □ *Everyone sends their love to you.* **2** You **send** someone somewhere **a** when you tell them to go there: *He was sick at school so his teacher sent him home.* □ *I was spanked and sent to bed.* □ *She'd been sent along to the shop to collect the newspaper.* □ *I sent him away and told him to call back later.* □ *Could you send a plumber round?* □ *She was examined and sent to the eye clinic.* □ *They sent me on various training courses.* **b** when you arrange for them to go there and stay for a period: *I was sent away to boarding school in England.* □ *They couldn't afford to send me to college.* □ *He was sent to prison for twenty years.* **3** Something **sends** out things such as light or signals when they come from it: *The space probe has been sending some amazing pictures back to earth.* □ *the heat and light sent out by the sun.* **4** Something such as a blow or other happening **sends** you somewhere when it forces you in that direction, or causes you to move there: *He collided with me in the corridor and sent me flying.* □ *The rain sent everyone scurrying indoors.* **5** Something **sends** you into a particular state when it makes you pass into that state: *The heat from the fire sent him to sleep.* □ *The noise was sending the dog frantic.* [compare **drive**]

phrasal verbs

send for or **send away for** or **send off for** **1** You **send for** goods, or **send away for** them, or **send off for** them, when you send an order to the supplier by post: *We've sent away for some plants that we can't get locally.* □ *I sent for three copies of the report.* **2** You **send for** someone when you ask them to come to you: *If you suspect a heart attack send for the ambulance immediately.* □ *It's reported that the Prime Minister has sent for him to demand his resignation.* [*same as* **summon**] **3** You **send for** something when you order it to be brought or delivered: *I've sent for some champagne to be brought to the room.*

send in You **send** something **in** when you submit it by post: *I sent in my application two weeks ago.* □ *Send all your suggestions in to us.*

send off **1** You **send** a parcel or letter **off** when you post it: *The package was sent off yesterday.* **2** If a player in a game such as football, rugby or hockey **is sent off**, they are ordered to leave the field, *eg* for committing a foul.

send on **1** If you **send** a letter or parcel **on**, you re-address and re-post it so that it reaches the person for whom it is intended: *Could you send on any mail that arrives for me?* **2** You **send** a person or thing **on**, or **send** them **on** ahead, when you arrange for them to go or be taken to the place you are going to before you get there: *I was sent on ahead to find accommodation.*

send up (*informal*) To **send** someone or something **up** is to imitate them in a way that makes them look ridiculous.

senile /ˈsiːnaɪl/ *adjective*
Someone who is or becomes **senile** can no longer remember things or look after themselves properly because their mind has become weak and confused with old age. — *noun* (*uncount*) **senility** /səˈnɪlɪtɪ/: *in an advanced state of senility.*

senior /ˈsiːnɪə(r)/ *adjective; noun*
▻ ***adjective***
1 Someone who is **senior** to you is higher in rank or authority than you are: *Always salute a senior officer.* □ *senior civil servants.* [=high-ranking civil servants] **2** Someone who is **senior** to you is older than you are: *He's senior to me by five years.* **3** **Senior** school is for schoolchildren over the age of 11 or 12. **4** **Senior** is also used after a person's name to show that they are the older of two people, usually father and son, with the same name: *John Willis, Senior.*
▻ ***noun*: seniors**
1 Your **senior** is a person who is older or of a higher rank than you are: *He's ten years my senior.* **2** A **senior** is a pupil in a senior school, especially one who is in the last two or three years of senior school. **3** (*AmE*) A **senior** is a student in their final year at high school.

senior citizen /siːnɪə ˈsɪtɪzən/ *noun*: **senior citizens**
A **senior citizen** is an elderly person, especially one who has reached retirement age.

Note that it is considered by many people to be more respectful and polite to use **senior citizens** rather than **pensioners** or **old-age pensioners** when referring to people who are over retirement age.

seniority /siːnɪˈɒrɪtɪ/ *noun* (*uncount*)
1 **Seniority** is the state or condition of being older or higher in rank: *The officers were seated at the table in order of seniority* **2** **Seniority** is also the higher position or advantage over others that comes to someone who has long service in an organization or group: *Other Tory MPs of comparable seniority have been awarded knighthoods.*

sensation /sɛnˈseɪʃən/ *noun*: **sensations**
1 (*uncount*) **Sensation** is the ability to feel or be aware of the physical existence or characteristics of things or of their contact with other things through the senses. **2** A **sensation** is a physical feeling, especially one coming from the sense of touch: *a burning sensation in my chest.* **3** A **sensation** is a general feeling, often one that you cannot describe exactly: *Travelling upside down was a most peculiar sensation.* **4** A **sensation** is a widespread feeling of excitement, shock or lively interest; something causes a **sensation** when it produces such a feeling: *The show was a sensation.* □ *His announcement caused quite a sensation.* [*same as* **stir**]

sensational /sɛnˈseɪʃənəl/ *adjective*
1 Things that are **sensational** cause or are intended to cause widespread excitement, intense interest or shock: *sensational headlines* □ *a sensational robbery.* **2** (*informal*) If you describe something as **sensational**, you think that it is wonderful or marvellous: *a sensational performance* □ *He arrived with a sensational blonde on his arm.* [*same as* **fabulous**]

sense /sɛns/ *noun; verb*
▻ ***noun*: senses**
1 Your **senses** are the five physical powers of sight, touch, taste, hearing and smell: *Dogs have a highly developed sense of smell.* □ *Her sense of hearing was particularly acute.* **2** (*uncount, or used in the singular*) A **sense** of something is **a** an awareness or understanding of that thing, or a regard for it: *A comedian must have a good sense of timing.* □ *She had a poor sense of direction and was always getting lost.* □ *Her business sense was always reliable.* □ *I couldn't help admiring his dress sense.* □ *You need a sense of humour in this job.* □ *You always did have a sense of style.* □ *I began to lose all sense of reality.* □ *people who have a strong sense of duty* □ *Where's your sense of justice?* **b** a feeling of that thing: *People need to do something that gives them a sense of achievement.* □ *We both felt a sense of satisfaction at our morning's work.* □ *I had a vague sense of unease about the whole thing.* □ *Maybe the chain isn't that strong, but it gives me a sense of security.* **3** (*uncount*) **Sense** or **common sense** is the ability to make wise and practical judgements and decisions, and to behave sensibly: *I hope she has enough sense to stay where she is and not go wandering.* □ *He had the sense to call an ambulance.* □ *Some people have more money than sense.* **4** (*used in the singular*) The **sense** of *eg* a piece of writing is its general meaning: *She understood the general sense of the passage, though some of the words were unfamiliar.* **5** The **senses** of a word are its different meanings: *I was using 'unhappy' in the sense of 'unfortunate'.* □ *the various senses of 'poor'* □ *He's a gentleman in every sense of the word.* [= he's a real gentleman]
▻ ***verb*: senses, sensing, sensed**
You **sense** something when you realize it or become aware of it without it being very obvious: *Sensing my disapproval, he started to explain.* □ *I sensed that someone was following me.*
▻ ***phrases*** **1** **a** You **come to your senses** or **are brought to your senses** when you start behaving sensibly after a period of foolishness; people say you **have taken leave of your senses** when you do something crazy. **b** (*old*) You also **come to your senses** when you regain consciousness, *eg* after fainting. **2** Something that is so **in a sense** is partly so, or is so in one way: *In a sense I'd have preferred to end the relationship then and there.* □ *So we have, in a sense, come back to where we started.*

3 Something **makes sense** if it can be understood: *The words he heard himself utter seemed to make no sense.* **4** You **make sense** of something when you work out what it means: *It took me a while to make any sense of the message.* **5** An action or decision **makes sense** if it is wise and practical: *It makes sound sense to have your car serviced regularly.* **6** You say there is **no sense in** doing something if there's no advantage or point in doing it: *There's no sense in forcing people to do things they don't want to do.* **7** People **talk sense** when they speak wisely and sensibly, or make practical suggestions: *He's a useful member of the committee; he talks a lot of sense.*

senseless /'sɛnsləs/ *adjective*
1 Someone is **senseless** when they are unconscious or stunned: *He lifted the child's senseless body into the ambulance.* □ *He was knocked senseless by a blow to the head.* **2** If you describe a situation or action as **senseless** you mean it is foolish and without purpose: *a senseless argument.* [*same as* **ridiculous**, **meaningless**; *opposite* **sensible**]

sense of humour /sɛns əv 'hjuːmə(r)/ *noun* (*uncount, or used in the singular*)
If someone has a **sense of humour**, they are able to see the funny side of things or are able to appreciate jokes: *You should know better than to play a trick on her; she's got no sense of humour.* □ *You need to have a sense of humour to work in this place.* □ *He's got a peculiar sense of humour.*

sensibility /sɛnsɪ'bɪlɪtɪ/ *noun*: **sensibilities**
1 (*uncount*) **Sensibility** is the ability to feel or have sensations. **2** Your **sensibilities** are your feelings, especially when they are easily hurt or offended.

sensible /'sɛnsɪbəl/ *adjective*
Sensible people are wise and practical and do not behave foolishly: *I think you can trust him; he's a sensible lad.* □ *It was sensible of you to get his offer in writing.* [*same as* **wise**; *opposite* **foolish**, **reckless**] — *adverb* **sensibly:** *She sensibly phoned for a doctor immediately.*

sensitive /'sɛnsɪtɪv/ *adjective*
1 If something is **sensitive** it responds quickly, strongly or painfully, or is able to feel or respond to something: *sensitive hearing* □ *The skin around the wound is still a bit sensitive.* **2** A **sensitive** person is someone whose feelings are easily hurt: *He's very sensitive about his odd appearance.* **3** A **sensitive** issue or subject is one about which there is much strong feeling or difference of opinion. [*same as* **controversial**] **4** **Sensitive** information concerns matters that may cause embarrassment or threaten security if it is known publicly. **5** A **sensitive** instrument or measuring device is capable of reacting to or recording very small changes. **6** Something that is **sensitive** in a stated way responds to the action of a particular force or stimulus: *photo-sensitive* [=responding to light] □ *pressure-sensitive.* — *adverb* **sensitively:** *The matter will be dealt with sensitively, without undue embarrassment being caused to anybody concerned.*

sensitivity /sɛnsɪ'tɪvɪtɪ/ *noun* (*uncount*)
Sensitivity is the quality or condition of being sensitive: *sensitivity to light* □ *He dealt with the matter with tact and sensitivity.*

sensory /'sɛnsərɪ/ *adjective*
Sensory means of or relating to the physical senses or to sensation: *the sensory organs.*

sensual /'sɛnʃʊəl/ *adjective*
1 **Sensual** means of the senses and the body, as opposed to the mind or the spirit: *sensual experiences.* **2** **Sensual** also has the more specific meaning 'suggesting, enjoying or providing physical, especially sexual, pleasure': *She had a wide, sensual mouth.*

sensuous /'sɛnʃʊəs/ *adjective*
1 **Sensuous** means appealing to, stimulating or giving pleasure to the senses: *the sensuous feeling of warm sand against the skin.* □ *sensuous music.* **2** **Sensuous** also has the same meaning as sensual (sense 2).

sent /sɛnt/ *verb*
Sent is the past tense and past participle of **send**.

sentence /'sɛntəns/ *noun*; *verb*
▻ ***noun***: **sentences**
1 (*grammar*) A **sentence** is a sequence of words, normally containing a subject and a verb, which expresses a complete statement, question or command. When a sentence is written down it begins with a capital letter and ends with a full stop, question mark, or exclamation mark. **2** A **sentence** is also the punishment, decided on by a court and announced by a judge, that a person found guilty of a crime receives: *He received a ten-year prison sentence for armed robbery.* □ *a death sentence.*
▻ ***verb***: **sentences, sentencing, sentenced**
When a convicted criminal **is sentenced**, he or she is told by the judge what the punishment for their crime will be: *The judge sentenced him to life imprisonment.*

sentence adverb /'sɛntəns advɜːb/ *noun*: **sentence adverbs** (*grammar*)
A **sentence adverb** is an adverb such as *unfortunately*, *hopefully*, *frankly*, *honestly*, that you use outside the grammatical structure of a sentence to express your own attitude to what you are saying: *It was apparently a mistake.* □ *Obviously, we cannot guarantee that the operation will be a complete success.* □ Adverbs like this are labelled (*sentence adverb*) in this dictionary.

sentiment /'sɛntɪmənt/ *noun*: **sentiments**
1 (*uncount*) **Sentiment** is tender feelings generally, such as love, sadness, sympathy or pity, especially when the expression of such feelings is considered to be excessive or self-indulgent: *There's little room for sentiment in modern business.* **2** Your **sentiments** on a subject are your views or opinions on that subject, especially when they are influenced by emotion: *'I think we need a change of government sooner rather than later.' 'My sentiments exactly.'* [=I agree wholeheartedly]

sentimental /sɛntɪ'mɛntəl/ *adjective* (*often derogatory*)
1 A **sentimental** person is someone who easily feels and expresses tender emotions, especially love, friendship and pity: *He's a sentimental old fool.* [*same as* **romantic**] **2** **Sentimental** stories or poetry contain or are intended to provoke such emotions. **3** An object that is of **sentimental** value is valuable because of its close association with fond memories of the past. — *adverb* **sentimentally:** *She was sentimentally attached to the old house.*

sentry /'sɛntrɪ/ *noun*: **sentries**
A **sentry** is a soldier whose job is to guard a building or entrance and stop anyone entering or leaving who does not have the right do so. [*same as* **guard**]

separate *verb*; *adjective*
▻ ***verb*** /'sɛpəreɪt/: **separates, separating, separated**
1 If you **separate** two or more people or things, you take, keep, force or place them apart from each other: *The calves are separated from their mothers when they are only a few days old.* □ *The two boys had to be separated in class because they were making so much noise.* [*same as* **split up**] **2** When things that have been joined in some way **separate** they move apart or become

detached from each other: *The space capsule separated from the rocket* **3** If a married couple **separate** they stop living together and live in different places: *They have agreed to separate.* **4** Something **separates** or **is separated** when it divides or is divided into parts: *The crowd separated, allowing him to pass.* □ *Separate the eggs and beat the whites until they form stiff peaks.*

▷ ***adjective*** /ˈsɛpərət/

1 Separate things are distinctly different or individual or unrelated to others: *That's a separate issue.* [*same as* **unconnected**] **2** Something that is **separate** from something else is not attached to it or does not form part of it: *The farm is separate from the rest of the estate.* [*same as* **detached**]

separation /sɛpəˈreɪʃən/ *noun*: **separations**

1 A **separation** between two or more people is a period of time or an interval when they are apart from each other; a married couple have a **separation** when they decide that they will no longer live together in the same house: *They were overjoyed to see each other again after such a long separation.* □ *a legal separation.* **2** A **separation** is also a place or line marking a division: *There was no separation between her home and working life.* **3** (*uncount*) **Separation** is the act of separating or the fact of being separated.

September /sɛpˈtɛmbə(r)/ *noun* (*uncount*)

September is the ninth month of the year, coming after August and before October: *They plan to marry next September.* □ *His birthday is on the thirtieth of September* (written *30 September*). □ *September the fifth* (written *September 5*) □ *I plan to have a week's holiday in September.* □ *a misty September morning.* [see also note at **date**]

septet /sɛpˈtɛt/ *noun*: **septets**

1 A **septet** is a group of seven musicians who perform together. **2** A piece of music composed for a group of seven musicians is also a **septet**.

septic /ˈsɛptɪk/ *adjective*

If a cut or other wound becomes **septic**, it becomes infected with poisonous bacteria: *a septic finger* □ *You must keep the wound clean or it may go septic.* [see also **antiseptic**]

septuplet /ˈsɛptjʊplət/ *noun*: **septuplets**

A **septuplet** is any of seven children born at the same time to the same mother.

sequel /ˈsiːkwəl/ *noun*: **sequels**

1 A book, film or play that continues an earlier story is a **sequel**: *'Kidnapped', a novel by Robert Louis Stevenson, and its sequel, 'Catriona'.* **2** A **sequel** to an event or incident is something that happens after and as a result of it.

sequence /ˈsiːkwəns/ *noun*: **sequences**

1 (*count or uncount*) A **sequence** is a series of things following each other in a particular order or happening one after the other; the **sequence** of a group of things or events is the order in which they follow each other: *a remarkable sequence of events* □ *The numbers follow each other in sequence.* **2** In a film, a **sequence** is a series of short pieces of action that make up a scene: *In the next sequence, she hits him over the head with a bottle.*

sequin /ˈsiːkwɪn/ *noun*: **sequins**

Sequins are small shiny discs made of metal or plastic that are sewn on clothes for decoration.

serenade /sɛrəˈneɪd/ *noun*: **serenades**

1 A **serenade** is a song or other piece of music performed at night under a woman's window by her lover. **2** A **serenade** is also any piece of gentle, romantic music.

serene /səˈriːn/ *adjective*

You can describe someone or something as **serene** if they are calm and peaceful: *a serene smile* □ *She is serene and dignified.* □ *a serene rural landscape.* [*opposite* **troubled**] — *adverb* **serenely:** *She smiled serenely at the children as they played around her.* □ *The cattle grazed serenely.* — *noun* (*uncount*) **serenity** /səˈrɛnɪti/: *the quietness and serenity of the cloisters.*

sergeant /ˈsɑːdʒənt/ *noun*: **sergeants**

A **sergeant** is **1** a non-commissioned officer of the rank next above corporal in the armed forces. **2** a police officer of the rank between constable and inspector.

sergeant-major /sɑːdʒəntˈmeɪdʒə(r)/ *noun*: **sergeant-majors**

A **sergeant-major** is a non-commissioned officer of the highest rank in the armed forces.

serial /ˈsɪərɪəl/ *noun*: **serials**

A **serial** is a story that is published in a newspaper or magazine, or broadcast on radio or television, in several parts: *a serial in six parts* □ *a radio serial* □ *a drama serial.*

serialize or **serialise** /ˈsɪərɪəlaɪz/ *verb*: **serializes, serializing, serialized**

A book or story **is serialized** when it is published or broadcast in several parts.

serial number /ˈsɪərɪəl nʌmbə(r)/ *noun*: **serial numbers**

Something that has a **serial number** has a set of numbers marked or printed on it which identify it and distinguish it from others of the same type or of the same series.

series /ˈsɪərɪz/ *noun*: **series**

1 A **series** is a number of similar, related or identical things arranged or produced one after the other: *a series of brutal murders* □ *He suffered a series of unfortunate accidents.* **2** A television or radio **series** consists of a number of broadcast shows in which the same characters appear or a similar subject is dealt with: *a natural history series* □ *a series of programmes on personal finance* □ *a new series of 'Fawlty Towers'.* [compare **serial**] **3** A group of books, magazine or newspaper articles on a similar subject often with a single title and produced by the same author is also known as a **series**: *the first in our series, 'British Prime Ministers of the 20th Century'.* **4** (*uncount*) A set of electrical devices arranged so that a current passes through each in turn are in **series**.

serious /ˈsɪərɪəs/ *adjective*

1 A **serious** person is solemn, not light-hearted or flippant: *Don't look so serious; it's not as bad as all that.* **2** A **serious** book or newspaper deals with important issues. **3** A **serious** illness is a severe one; a **serious** accident is one which causes or may result in severe injury or death to the people involved or affected by it. **4 Serious** problems are not easy to deal with or solve; someone gets into **serious** trouble when they get themselves into an extremely difficult or dangerous situation, or do something for which they will be punished or dealt with severely: *The business is in serious financial difficulties.* [*same as* **deep**] **5** A **serious** crime is one regarded as being especially bad. **6 Serious** arguments or differences of opinion are important or significant. **7** If you say that you are **serious** or are **serious** about something, you mean you are in earnest and are not joking: *I was being quite serious when I suggested it.* □ *'I'm going hang-gliding tomorrow.' 'You're not serious, surely?'* □ *'Let's go for a walk.' 'You can't be serious! It's pouring with rain.'* — *noun* (*uncount*) **seriousness:** *He doesn't seem to appreciate the serious-*

ness of his situation. □ *She told me, in all seriousness, that she wanted to be an astronaut.*

seriously /ˈsɪərɪəslɪ/ *adverb*
1 **Seriously** means in a serious way or to a serious extent: *Stop laughing; we have to discuss this seriously.* □ (*intensifying*) *He's seriously worried.* **2** (*sentence adverb*) You use **seriously** **a** to emphasize that you mean what you are saying and are not joking: *Seriously though, I couldn't have done it without you.* **b** as a way of commmenting that you are surprised by what someone has just said and asking whether it is really true: *'I'm going to resign.' 'Seriously? I thought you were happy in the job.'*
▷ ***phrase*** If you **take** someone or something **seriously**, you treat them as important.

sermon /ˈsɛːmən/ *noun*: **sermons**
A **sermon** is a talk on a religious or moral subject, often based on a text from the Bible, that a clergyman gives as part of a church service.

serpent /ˈsɛːpənt/ *noun* (*old or literary*): **serpents**
A **serpent** is a snake.

serrated /səˈreɪtɪd/ *adjective*
Something that is **serrated** or that has a **serrated** edge has V-shaped notches along its edge like the teeth on a saw blade: *a plant with oval serrated leaves.*

servant /ˈsɜːvənt/ *noun*: **servants**
1 A **servant** is a person employed in someone else's house to do their household work: *domestic servants.* **2** People also refer to a person who acts or works for the benefit of others in any capacity as a **servant**: *a public servant.* [see also **civil servant**]

serve /sɜːv/ *verb; noun*
▷ ***verb***: **serves, serving, served**
1 a You **serve** a person, community or organization when you work for them: *Margaret has served the firm for 45 years.* □ *people who serve the community as health workers* □ *He served his country* [= was a member of the armed forces] *in two world wars.* □ *She had served her mistress loyally.* **b** You **serve** on a committee or other body if you are a member of it; you **serve** in one of the armed forces, or with a section of them, if you are a member of that force or section; you **serve** under someone if you are a member of *eg* an army or a government led by them: *She was invited to serve on the advisory board.* □ *Serving on a jury can be an upsetting experience.* □ *He served with the Second Parachute Regiment.* □ *During World War 1 she served in the nursing corps.* □ *cabinet members who also served under the former prime minister.*
2 a You **serve** food or drink, or **serve** people, when you give people food or drink, especially at a mealtime: *Shall I serve the soup now?* □ *Simmer the fish for 20 minutes and serve with rice.* □ *Go ahead and serve dinner; don't wait for me.* □ *Has anyone not been served?* □ *Could you serve the wine for me?* □ *The waiter returned and served us with vegetables.* □ *We had to wait almost an hour to be served.* □ *The barman refused to serve us.* **b** Shop assistants **serve** customers when they ask them what they want and fetch it: *Are you being served?*
3 a Something **serves** you well if it works well and lasts a long time: *I'll be sorry to sell that car; it's served me well.* **b** Something **serves** as a certain thing, or **serves** a need, purpose or function, if it is used as a certain thing, or has a certain function: *the piece of waste ground that served as a play area for the local children* □ *This incident may serve as a demonstration of what can go wrong.* □ *It's not a very beautiful bath, but it's comfortable and it serves its purpose.* **c** Something that **serves** to do a certain thing has that effect: *The sight of the crib only served to remind her of her loss.* □ *All this publicity may at least serve to put other women on their guard.* **d** Something that **serves** a particular area or community, or **serves** its needs, provides the people who live there with a necessary service: *a recently built medical centre that serves the needs of the scattered rural community* □ *A single electricity generator served the whole village.*
4 a A person **serves** an apprenticeship when they have a certain period of training and work experience in order to qualify for a particular job or trade. **b** Criminals **serve** a prison sentence when they spend a period of time in prison. **c** (*tennis*) A player **serves**, or **serves** the ball, when he or she starts play by hitting the ball over the net to the opposing player. **d** You **are served** with a court order when you are sent a letter legally requiring you to do something: *She was served with a summons to appear in court on a charge of careless driving.*
▷ ***noun*** (*tennis*): **serves**
A **serve** is the action of hitting the ball over the net to your opponent to start play: *Her second serve went in.* □ *She has a fast and powerful serve.*
▷ ***phrase*** (*informal*) If you say, in reference to someone's misfortune, that it **serves them right**, you mean that they deserve it: *It serves you right for eating too much.*

> ***phrasal verbs***
> You **serve** food **out** or **serve** it **up** when you deal it out to people, especially at a mealtime.

service /ˈsɜːvɪs/ *noun; verb*
▷ ***noun***: **services**
1 a (*uncount*) **Service** is the activity of working for other people or for a community or organization: *countries where military service, or some form of community service, is compulsory for young people* □ *He resigned from the Navy after 25 years' service.* □ *She was warmly thanked for her years of dedicated service to the Guide Movement.* □ *In those days lots of young girls went straight into domestic service.* [= became domestic servants] **b** (*used in the plural*) Your **services** are the work you do, or the tasks you perform, as part of your employment: *He was told that his services would no longer be required.* □ *You will need the services of a good lawyer.* □ *The photocopying agency gave its services free.* **c** (*used in the plural*) Someone's **services** to something are the ways in which they have improved or benefited it: *He was awarded a knighthood for services to broadcasting.* **d** (*used in the singular; formal*) You do someone a **service** when you help them by doing a job for them: *I wonder if you could do me a small service?*
2 a A department of government regarded as working for the benefit of the country or its citizens may be called a **service**: *the civil service* □ *the diplomatic service* □ *the health service.* **b** (*used in the plural*) The armed **services** are the armed forces, or the army, navy and air force. **c** An industry or organization that provides a **service** is one that does jobs for people as distinct from producing goods: *service industries such as catering and hairdressing* □ *Postal services have greatly improved.* **d** A bus or train **service** provides regular public transport: *There's a regular bus service out to the airport.* □ *They run extra services over the holiday period.* **e** (*used in the plural, usually with a plural verb*) The **services** on a motorway are any of the places where you can get petrol, which usually also have toilets, a restaurant and a shop: *The next services aren't for another 30 miles.*
3 a (*uncount*) **Service** in a restaurant or shop is the

process of being attended to or served: *The meal was OK but the service was very slow.* ▫ *The supermarket and the concept of self-service were introduced in the '50s.* **b** (*uncount*) **Service** is an extra charge made, *eg* in a restaurant, for the work the staff do in attending to you: *Is service included in the bill?* [see also **service charge**, **tip**] **c** Your car or some other piece of equipment is given a **service** when it is given a periodic check to see that it is working properly, and is fitted with new parts to replace worn or damaged ones: *The boiler is due for its two-yearly service.* ▫ *Some of these firms provide a free after-sales service.* **d** A vehicle or other kind of machine is in **service** if it is in regular use: *Some of the electric trams have been in service since about 1900.* ▫ *The new-style carriages will come into service next month.* ▫ *All aircraft of this design have been temporarily withdrawn from service.*
4 a (*count or uncount*) A religious **service** is a religious ceremony, especially in a church, usually including hymns and prayers, held for regular worship or for some special occasion: *She attends morning service every Sunday.* ▫ *the words of marriage service* ▫ *a funeral service.* **b** A dinner **service** or tea **service** is a complete set of dishes and other crockery required for serving dinner or tea as a formal meal. **c** (*tennis; uncount or used in the singular*) A player's **service** is his or her action in serving the ball to the opposing player to start play; it is someone's **service** when it is their turn to do this: *She's obviously been working on her service.* ▫ *He lost two service games.*
▻ ***verb***: **services, servicing, serviced**
A vehicle or machine **is serviced** when a garage, mechanic or engineer gives it a periodic check to see that it is working properly: *Have you had your car serviced recently?*
▻ ***phrases*** **1** (*formal*) Someone is **at your service** when they are ready and willing to do things for you: *I'm at your service if you require me.* **2** (*formal*) Someone or something is **of service** to you if they help you or are useful to you: *I'm happy to have been of service to you.*

serviceable /'sɛːvɪsəbəl/ *adjective*
Something that is **serviceable** can be used or is useful, usually for a particular purpose: *These walking boots are still quite serviceable.*

service charge /'sɜːvɪs tʃɑːdʒ/ *noun* (*used in the singular*)
An extra charge added to a restaurant or hotel bill for the work that waiters and other staff do in attending to you is a **service charge**: *a service charge of 10%.*

service industry /'sɜːvɪs ɪndəstrɪ/ *noun*: **service industries**
A **service industry** is any industry that provides a service rather than making goods for sale.

serviceman /'sɛːvɪsmən/ *noun*: **servicemen**
A **serviceman** is a person who is a member of any of the armed forces: *a home for retired servicemen.*

service station /'sɜːvɪs steɪʃən/ *noun*: **service stations**
A **service station** is a petrol station that provides extra services such as car-washing, snacks and toilet facilities.

serviette /sɜːvɪ'ɛt/ *noun*: **serviettes**
A **serviette** is a table napkin.

servile /'sɜːvaɪl/ *adjective*
Someone who is **servile** is excessively obedient and respectful, like a slave. [*same as* **subservient**]

serving /'sɛːvɪŋ/ *noun*: **servings**
A **serving** is an amount of food served at one time: *a small serving of roast potatoes.* [*same as* **helping**]

serving dish /'sɜːvɪŋ dɪʃ/ *noun*: **serving dishes**
A **serving dish** is a dish from which food is served. [see picture at **tableware**]

session /'sɛʃən/ *noun*: **sessions**
1 A **session** is a meeting or series of meetings of a court, council or parliament or a period during which such meetings are regularly held: *legislation to be brought forward in the next parliamentary session.* **2** A **session** of a particular activity is a period of time spent engaged in that activity: *He will need several sessions of physiotherapy before he is able to return to competitive sport.* **3** A **session** is also an academic term or year.
▻ ***phrase*** Parliament, a council, a committee or a court is **in session** when it meets to conduct its business.

set /sɛt/ *verb; noun; adjective*
▻ ***verb***: **sets, setting, set**
1 a You **set** something somewhere when you put or place it there, usually rather carefully: *She lifted the fallen chair and set it upright again.* ▫ *A large plate of food was set in front of me.* ▫ *He brought her a glass of wine and set it beside her on a low table.* [compare **put, place, lay**] **b** Something **is set** somewhere, or in some position, if it is in those surroundings or in that position: *a castle set deep in wooded Perthshire* ▫ *The bank was set back a little from the street, so that you could park in front of it.* ▫ *She had wide-set brown eyes.* **c** To **set** something into a surface is to fix it into it, so that it does not project a lot; an object or surface **is set** with things such as precious stones if they are fixed into its surface: *A number of human skulls had been set into the pillar.* ▫ *a gold ring set with diamonds and pearls.* **d** You **set** the table when you put on it whatever people need for having a meal, such as mats, cutlery and glasses. [*same as* **lay**]
2 The sun **sets** when it sinks below the horizon. [*same as* **go down**; *opposite* **rise**]
3 a You **set** people or things doing something or being in some state when you cause them to be affected in that way: *The sight of him set her heart beating.* ▫ *I'll set the ball rolling by asking the first question.* ▫ *We should be grateful if you could set our minds at rest* [= reassure us] *on this question.* ▫ *Some boys had set the garden shed on fire.* ▫ *The hostages were to be set free immediately.* ▫ *Your question set me wondering.* ▫ *Investigations have been set in motion.* **b** You **set** to work when you start working at something; you **set** people to work doing something when you order them to start working at it: *We set to work immediately to clear up the mess.*
4 a You **set** something such as an instrument, alarm or control when you adjust it to a certain point or level, or to a certain time, so that it works when you want it to: *She paused to set her stopwatch.* ▫ *What time shall I set the alarm for?* ▫ *Set the thermostat to low.* ▫ *I forgot to set the video.* [compare **adjust**] **b** You **set** a trap when you get it ready to work: *How do you set these mousetraps?*
5 a You **set** something such as a date, time, price or limit when you arrange or settle it: *Always set a time limit for jobs; it makes people work more efficiently.* ▫ *We think it will be appropriate to set the minimum contribution at £10.* ▫ *Has a date been set for the wedding?* **b** You **set** someone something such as a task, exercise, test or target when you give it to them to do or achieve: *He was threatening to set us an irregular-verb test.* ▫ *We haven't been set an essay this week.* ▫ *She'd set herself the object of completing her thesis by June.* [compare **assign**] **c** You **set** yourself to do something when you aim at achieving it. **d** You **set** something such as a standard or example when you do something that provides a lead for people to copy or follow: *You should be setting a good example to the*

younger children, not leading them astray. □ *The leading runners were setting an incredible pace.* □ *He'll be trying to beat the new record set by Grey.* □ *trend-setting designers* □ *She gave a friendly and informal speech of welcome, which set the tone for the evening.* □ *This is an exception, not to be regarded as setting a precedent.*

6 a Something such as jelly, jam, cement or concrete **sets** when it becomes firm: *25 minutes' fast boiling should bring the marmalade to setting point.* **b** A woman has her hair **set** by a hairdresser when it is shampooed and shaped while wet into curls or waves, so that it dries in that style. **c** A doctor **sets** a broken bone when he or she adjusts it so that the separated sections fit together again properly. **d** People **set** their faces or jaws when they fix them into a particular expression, especially one of determination: *Her jaw was set and she looked grimly determined.*

7 a To **set** words to music is to compose music to which the words can be sung: *Britten had a particular genius for setting poetry to music.* **b** A story or play **is set** in a certain place or period if that is where and when the action takes place: *This is a play set in the US during the Civil War.* **c** A book or piece of printing **is set** in type of a certain design or size if that is the kind or size of type used for it: *books set in large type for elderly readers.*

▻ ***noun*: sets**

1 A **set** of things is a group or collection of things that belong together, or are used for a particular activity: *The government has issued a new set of guidelines for the teaching of religious studies.* □ *a set of chairs* □ *We had a set of plastic dishes for camping.* □ *My parents had a complete set of George Eliot in brown leather bindings.* □ *My own chess set was incomplete.* □ *a set of golf clubs.* **2** A group of people that behave in a certain way, or have a common interest, are sometimes referred to as a **set** of some kind: *She's got involved with a fast set.* □ *the way the jet set lives* □ *The young set won't tolerate that pointless old-style discipline.* □ *The academic set treated her as one of them.*

Notice that a **set** of things or people can take a singular or plural verb, depending on whether you are referring to them as a unit or as a number of individuals.

3 Pupils in a class are sometimes divided into **sets** for certain activities, usually according to ability: *I'm in the 'A' set for reading.* **4** An apparatus such as a television or radio is often called a **set**: *They'd stolen the television set and the video.* **5** (*tennis*) A **set** is a series of six games: *a five-set match.* **6** A **set** for a film or play is the scenery and furniture used for it, arranged in the film studio or on stage: *We visited the set used for 'Neighbours'.* **7** (*used in the singular*) You ask the hairdresser for a shampoo and **set** when you want your hair curled or waved while wet, so that it dries in that style.

▻ ***adjective***

1 Set describes things that are fixed and do not vary: *There's a set luncheon menu.* □ *an old-fashioned family hotel with set mealtimes* □ *Is there a set procedure for ordering books?* □ *The results revealed a set pattern.* □ *His parents have rather set* [= conservative] *ideas about clothes and that sort of thing.* **2** A **set** phrase is one whose form is always the same: *a set phrase such as 'of no fixed abode'.* **3** A **set** book or **set** text is one that has to be studied for a particular course or exam. **4** A **set** smile is one that does not alter, and so gives an insincere impression. **5** People are **set** or 'all **set**' to do something when they ready to do it or about to do it: *We're all set to put the new networking system into use on Monday.* □ *Are you set? Let's go then.* □ *She looks set for victory in the 400 metres.* □ *They were all set to go on holiday when she was taken ill.* **6** You are **set** on some action if you are determined on it: *He seems set on resigning.*

▻ ***phrases*** **1** For **all set** see **set,** *adjective*, sense **5**, above. **2** Competitors in some races are told to **get set** as a warning to be ready to start, just before the starting signal is given. **3** Someone who is **set in their ways** is unwilling to alter their way of life or their attitudes.

phrasal verbs

set about You **set about** doing something when you start or begin it: *She set about tidying her room.*

set against 1 One thing **is set against** another when it is compared with the other, or considered in relation to it: *Set against the current shortage of skilled labour, the question of improved training is a vital one.* **2** To **set** one person **against** another is to make the one hate or dislike the other: *I was accused of trying to set him against his own family.* **3** Expenses or allowances **are set against** a bill or tax when they are deducted from it.

set apart 1 Something **is set apart** when it is situated some distance away: *The chapel was set a little apart from the other buildings.* **2** A quality or characteristic **sets** someone or something **apart** if it makes them noticeably different or better than others: *It is her daring that sets her apart from other designers.*

set aside 1 Something **is set aside** when it is disregarded or rejected: *The judge's verdict was set aside by the higher court.* **2** If you **set** something **aside**, you put it away for later use: *I have a little money set aside for emergencies.*

set back 1 A process **is set back** when it is delayed or has to be partly repeated: *We regret to inform you that the printing process has been set back at least a fortnight owing to a fault in the machinery.* [see also **setback**] **2** (*informal*) Something **sets** you **back** a certain sum if it costs you that amount: *A new car will set you back at least £8000.*

set down 1 You **set** something **down** when you put it down carefully: *He set the cage gently down on the floor.* **2** A bus, train or other vehicle **sets down** passengers when it stops and allows them to get off: *We asked the driver to set us down about 20 miles beyond Hjerkinn.* **3** You **set down** your views or experiences when you write them down: *He sets down his opinions and his plans for Germany's future in a work entitled 'Mein Kampf'.*

set in Something **sets in** when it becomes firmly established: *It was only November but winter seemed already to have set in.* □ *Depression set in amongst us as the supply of food dwindled.*

set off 1 You **set off** when you start a journey: *They set off early so as to avoid the rush hour.* □ *Early in 1770 they set off on a tour of the European capitals.* **2** A circumstance **sets off** a happening when it starts or causes it: *Her remarks set off a fierce row in the Commons today.* □ *I'd stopped laughing but a look at her face set me off again.* [compare **spark**, **trigger**] **3** An explosive device **is set off** when it is detonated; an alarm **is set off** when it begins to sound: *I somehow managed to set off the burglar alarm when I unlocked the door.* **4** One thing **sets off** another when it emphasizes its good qualities: *You need a red silk scarf or something to set off the outfit.*

set on Someone **sets** an assailant or a dog **on** you when they get them to attack you: *I was set on in the dark by three masked men.*

set out 1 You **set** things **out** when you arrange

them for display, or ready for use: *The traders were setting out their stalls in the market square.* □ *I set out my painting things.* **2** You **set** facts or arguments **out** when you present and explain them: *You'll get a letter from us setting out the conditions of the contract.* **3** You **set out** when you begin a journey: *They set out to walk the West Highland Way.* □ *young folk setting out on life's journey.* **4** You **set out** to do something when it is your intention to do it from the start: *He deliberately set out to make me look foolish.*
set to You **set to** when you begin working or begin to apply yourself to a task: *She set to to finish the work as quickly as she could.* [see also **set-to**]
set up **1** You **set up** a business, or **set up** in business, when you establish a business operation: *He set up a small engineering business making parts for computers.* □ *We set up together in 1989 producing children's clothes.* **2** You **set** something **up** when you arrange it: *Could you set up a meeting between the heads of department?* **3** You **set** something **up** when you erect it: *They set up camp just outside the city limits.* □ *A monument was set up in the glen to the men who were killed in the crash.* **4** Someone **is set up** when they are put into a position of guaranteed security: *That money will set him up for life.* **5** Something **sets** you **up** when it restores your health and spirits or makes you feel good: *A long vigorous walk always sets me up.* **6** (*informal*) A person **sets** you **up** when they trick you. [see also **set-up**]

setback /'sɛtbak/ *noun*: **setbacks**
If you suffer a **setback**, the progress that you have made is reversed for a time so that you take longer to reach your final goal: *Despite numerous setbacks, they eventually succeeded in restoring the house to its former glory.* [*same as* **delay**]

settee /sɛ'tiː/ *noun*: **settees**
A **settee** is a piece of furniture with arms, a back and cushioned or padded seats for two or three people. [*same as* **sofa**, **couch**; see picture at **living room**]

setting /'sɛtɪŋ/ *noun*: **settings**
1 The position in which an instrument's controls are set is a **setting**: *The photographs didn't come out because the camera was on the wrong setting.* **2** A **setting** is also a situation or background within or against which action takes place, such as the scenery and furniture used in filming a scene. **3** The landscape or surroundings in which a building or place is can be referred to as a particular **setting**: *a campsite in a dramatic mountain setting.* **4** A table or place **setting** is a set of cutlery, crockery and glassware laid out on the table for use by one diner: *How many settings should I lay?* **5** A **setting** for a jewel or jewels is the mounting, usually made of gold, silver or platinum, in which it is set: *a diamond cluster in a platinum setting.*

settle /'sɛtəl/ *verb*: **settles, settling, settled**
1 You **settle** in a place when you go there and make your home there: *They settled in New South Wales.* **2** You **settle** something that has not yet been decided or agreed upon when you come to a decision or agreement: *Have they settled the date for the wedding yet?* □ *Could you settle this point for us?* □ *We'll have to find some way of settling our differences.* [*same as* **agree** on, **reconcile**] **3** Something **settles**, or **settles** on a surface, when it comes lightly to rest there: *The butterfly flitted from bush to bush settling briefly on each flower.* □ *A thin film of coal dust had settled on everything.* **4** If land or the foundations of a building **settle**, they sink to a lower level; if something **settles** on the bottom of a container or liquid it sinks to the bottom; something **settles** on the seabed or a river-bed when it sinks and comes to rest there.

phrasal verbs
settle down **1** When someone **settles down** they begin to live a quieter life because they have got married, or they stop moving from place to place because they have found somewhere that they want to live permanently. **2** When you **settle down** to something, or **settle down** to do it, you stop doing other things or make yourself comfortable so that you can give it your full attention: *I had just settled down to do some reading when the telephone rang.*
settle for When you **settle for** something you accept it as a compromise or less-than-ideal option: *Ideally, I would like a job in banking or insurance, but jobs are so scarce at the moment I would settle for anything.*
settle in or **into** If you **have settled in**, or **have settled into** something, you have got used to living in a new place or doing something new: *Are you settling in well in your new home?* □ *He soon settled into his new job.* □ *The rowers settled into a steady rhythm.*
settle on If you **settle on** something, you choose or decide on it from the various options or choices available: *After much discussion, we've settled on a plan of action that everyone is reasonably happy with.*
settle up You **settle up**, or **settle up** with someone, when you pay a bill or a sum of money that you owe them: *I'll just settle up the bill and then we can leave.*

settlement /'sɛtəlmənt/ *noun*: **settlements**
1 (*uncount or count*) **Settlement** is the act or circumstance of settling or being settled; a **settlement** is an agreement, especially one that ends an official dispute: *Neither of the unions involved is likely to vote for settlement of the dispute.* □ *Have the unions and management reached a settlement yet?* □ *modest wage settlements.* **2** A **settlement** is a community or colony of people who have settled in a place: *an Indian settlement by the lake.* **3** (*uncount*) When used of land or buildings, **settlement** is subsidence: *Because of the old mine workings, the area is prone to settlement.* **4** (*uncount*; *legal*) An act which legally transfers ownership of property, or a document enforcing this, is an act or deed of **settlement**.

settler /'sɛtlə(r)/ *noun*: **settlers**
A **settler** is a person who goes to live in a new country or area that has few or no people living in it: *French settlers in Canada.*

set-up /'sɛtʌp/ *noun* (*usually in the singular*; *informal*): **set-ups**
You can refer to the way that a system or organization is arranged or run as a particular kind of **set-up**: *No-one seems to be in charge; it's a strange set-up.*

seven /'sɛvən/ *noun*; *adjective*; *determiner*; *pronoun*
▻ ***noun***: **sevens**
1 (*uncount or count*) **Seven** is **a** the number or figure 7: *One and six are seven.* □ *Three plus four makes seven.* □ *Ten sevens are seventy.* □ *If you look carefully, you'll see it's a seven, not a two.* **b** a pair of shoes or other footwear whose size is represented by the number 7, or a person who wears shoes of this size: *These boots are sevens.* □ *She takes a seven in shoes.* **2** (*uncount*) **Seven** is **a** the age of 7: *He was sent away to school at seven.* **b** the time of 7 o'clock: *He gets up at seven every morning.* **3** (*count*) A **seven** is **a** a set of seven people or things, *eg* a rugby team with seven players: *the Melrose Sevens.* **b** a playing card with seven symbols: *the seven of spades.*
▻ ***adjective***
Someone who is **seven** is seven years old: *a football team for boys aged seven to eleven.*

▻ ***determiner:*** *The fare is seven dollars.* □ *The first seven runners go through to the next round.* □ *Seven days make a week.* □ *It took seven men to lift the car out of the ditch.* □ *a seven-hour flight* □ *He has a seven-year-old daughter.* □ *a class of seven-year-olds.*
▻ ***pronoun:*** *Of the thirty children in the class only seven were girls.* □ *There were seven of us and our parents found it hard to make ends meet.*

seventeen /sɛvən'tiːn/ *noun; adjective; determiner; pronoun*
▻ ***noun***: **seventeens**
1 (*uncount or count*) **Seventeen** is the number or figure 17: *Eight and nine are seventeen.* □ *Two seventeens are thirty-four.* **2** (*uncount*) **Seventeen** is the age of 17: *He learned to drive at seventeen.* **3** (*uncount or count*) In Britain and the USA, a **seventeen** is a shirt size for men represented by the number 17, or a man who wears shirts of this size: *He's a seventeen, not a sixteen and a half.*
▻ ***adjective***
Someone who is **seventeen** is seventeen years old: *He went to college when he was seventeen.*
▻ ***determiner:*** *He was off work for seventeen months.* □ *She has a seventeen-year-old son.*
▻ ***pronoun:*** *I asked for twenty copies of this document, but there are only seventeen here.*

seventeenth /sɛvən'tiːnθ/ *determiner; pronoun; adjective or adverb; noun*: **seventeenths**
1 (often written **17th**) The **seventeenth** person or thing is the one numbered seventeen in a series. **2** (often written $\frac{1}{17}$) A **seventeenth** of something is one of seventeen equal parts of it.

seventh (often written **7th**) /'sɛvənθ/ *determiner; pronoun; adjective or adverb; noun*
▻ ***determiner***
The **seventh** person or thing is the one numbered seven in a series: *He was the seventh son of a seventh son.* □ *Our seats were in the seventh row from the front.*
▻ ***pronoun:*** *His birthday is on the seventh of July.* [see note at **date**] □ *He's the seventh in line to the throne.* □ *Edmund Tudor, father of Henry the Seventh* (written *Henry VII*).
▻ ***adjective or adverb:*** *He was* (or *came*) *seventh in the line of succession.* □ *He came in seventh.*
▻ ***noun*** (often written $\frac{1}{7}$): **sevenths**
A **seventh** of something is one of seven equal parts of it: $\frac{3}{21}$ *is the same as* $\frac{1}{7}$. □ *How do we go about dividing the cake into sevenths?*

seventieth /'sɛvəntɪɪθ/ *determiner; pronoun; adjective or adverb; noun*: **seventieths**
1 (often written **70th**) The **seventieth** person or thing is the one numbered seventy in a series. **2** (often written $\frac{1}{70}$) A **seventieth** of something is one of seventy equal parts of it.

seventy /'sɛvəntɪ/ *noun; adjective; determiner; pronoun*
▻ ***noun***: **seventies**
1 (*uncount or count*) **Seventy** is the number or figure 70. **2** (*uncount*) **Seventy** is the age of 70. **3** (*used in the plural*) Someone who is in their **seventies** is aged between 70 and 79. **4** (*used in the plural*) When the temperature is in the **seventies** it is between 70° and 79° Fahrenheit. **5** (*used in the plural*) The **seventies** are the period between the seventieth and eightieth years of a century.
▻ ***adjective***
Someone who is **seventy** is 70 years old.
▻ ***determiner:*** *A septuagenarian is a seventy-year old.*
▻ ***pronoun:*** *Of the hundred men who set out on the mission, seventy were either killed or wounded.*

sever /'sɛvə(r)/ *verb*: **severs, severing, severed**
1 You **sever** a part of something, or it **is severed**, when you cut right through it so that it is no longer attached: *His head was severed from his body.* **2** You **sever** a connection or relationship you have with someone or something when you put an end to it: *He has severed all links with his family and lives alone on a remote island.*
[*opposite* **join, unite**]

several /'sɛvərəl/ or /'sɛvrəl/ *determiner; pronoun*
▻ ***determiner***
Several people or things are more than two, but not a lot: *Several people have asked where he is.* □ *I've had to remind him several times about locking the door.* [*same as* **a number of**]
▻ ***pronoun:*** *I've read several of her books.* □ *Several of us objected strongly.* □ *'Do you have any brothers and sisters?' 'Several, but they all live abroad.'*

severe /sə'vɪə(r)/ *adjective*
1 Severe weather or other conditions are extreme and difficult to endure; **severe** pain is so extreme that it is difficult to endure: *The cold was so severe several members of the expedition got frostbite.* □ *If the pain gets too severe, take two of these tablets.* [*same as* **harsh**] **2** Someone who is **severe** is very strict towards others: *The headmaster was too severe with him.* **3** Someone who has a **severe** expression looks very serious and stern; **severe** clothes or hairstyles are very plain, usually unattractively so. **4 Severe** consequences or punishments are extremely serious. [*same as* **grave**] — *adverb* **severely:** *She scolded him severely.* □ *(intensifying) He was severely disabled in the accident.* — *noun* (*uncount*) **severity** /sə'vɛrɪtɪ/: *They were shocked by the severity of the sentence.*

sew /soʊ/ *verb*: **sews, sewing, sewed, sewn**
1 You **sew** when you use a needle and thread to stitch or repair fabric: *Would you sew this button back onto my shirt, please?* **2** You **sew** something, such as a piece of clothing, when you make it by stitching pieces of fabric together: *It takes many months to sew a quilt by hand.* **3** You can **sew** if you have learnt the skills or techniques necessary to make or repair things using a thread and needle: *Can he sew?*

phrasal verb
sew up 1 You **sew up** the edges of a gap or hole when you join the edges together using a thread and needle: *She sewed up the split in the skirt.* □ *The surgeon finished the operation and left his assistant to sew up the wound.* **2** (*informal*) If you say that something **is sewn up**, you mean that it has been arranged so that it is certain to be done or completed successfully: *When do you think they will have the deal sewn up?* [*same as* **settled**]

sewage /'suːɪdʒ/ *noun* (*uncount*)
Sewage is waste matter, especially the waste from people's bodies, that is carried away from homes and other buildings in sewers.

sewer /sʊə(r)/ *noun*: **sewers**
A **sewer** is a large pipe or channel for carrying away sewage from drains and water from road surfaces. Sewers are usually underground.

sewerage /'suːərɪdʒ/ *noun* (*uncount*)
Sewerage is the system of sewers in a town or city.

sewing /'soʊɪŋ/ *noun* (*uncount*)
Sewing is **1** the skill or activity of making or repairing things using a needle and thread: *The little girls were*

taught sewing and embroidery. **2** something that is being, or has to be, sewn: *She put down her sewing and looked at him over her glasses.*

sewing-machine /ˈsoʊɪŋməʃiːn/ *noun*: **sewing-machines**
A **sewing-machine** is a machine that stitches fabric: *an electric sewing-machine.*

sex /sɛks/ *noun*: **sexes**
1 The **sexes** are either of two groups into which humans are divided: male, which includes all boys and men; and female, which includes all girls and women. **2** (*uncount*) The **sex** of a person or animal is the physical characteristics which make them either male or female. **3** (*uncount, often adjectival*) **Sex** is sexual intercourse: *have sex* □ *sex education in schools.*

sexism /ˈsɛksɪzm/ *noun* (*uncount*)
Sexism is unfair treatment of one sex by the other or the belief that one sex, especially your own, is superior to the other.

sexist /ˈsɛksɪst/ *noun*: **sexists**
A **sexist** is someone who treats the opposite sex unfairly or thinks that they are inferior.
▷ ***adjective:*** *a sexist attitude* □ *He's sexist.*

sextet /sɛkˈstɛt/ *noun*: **sextets**
1 A **sextet** is a group of six musicians that perform together. **2** A piece of music composed for a group of six musicians is also called a **sextet**.

sextuplet /ˈsɛkstjʊplət/ *noun*: **sextuplets**
A **sextuplet** is any of six children born at the same time to the same mother.

sexual /ˈsɛkʃʊəl/ *adjective*
1 Sexual means concerned with or suggestive of sex or relating to reproduction: *a sexual relationship.* **2** The **sexual** characteristics of a person or animal are those which show whether they belong to the male or female sex. [compare **asexual**]

sexual intercourse /sɛkʃʊəl ˈɪntəkɔːs/ *noun* (*uncount*)
Sexual intercourse is the insertion of a man's penis into a woman's vagina, usually with the release of semen into the vagina. [*same as* **sex**]

sexuality /sɛkʃʊˈalɪtɪ/ *noun* (*uncount*)
A person's **sexuality** is the way in which they express, or their ability to experience, sexual feelings.

sexy /ˈsɛksɪ/ *adjective* (*informal*): **sexier, sexiest**
If you say that someone or something is **sexy**, you mean that they are sexually attractive or sexually exciting: *a sexy blonde* □ *a sexy film.* [*same as* **seductive, sensual**]

sh /ʃ/ *interjection*
You say **'sh!'** when you want other people to stop talking or be quiet: *Sh! I'm trying to listen to the radio.*

shabby /ˈʃabɪ/ *adjective*: **shabbier, shabbiest**
1 Shabby clothes or furnishings are old and worn. [*same as* **tatty**] **2** A person can be described as **shabby** when they are wearing clothes that are old and worn. **3 Shabby** conduct is mean and nasty: *That was a pretty shabby thing to do.* [*same as* **rotten**]

shack /ʃak/ *noun*: **shacks**
A **shack** is a small roughly-built hut or shed.

shackle /ˈʃakəl/ *noun; verb*
▷ ***noun*: shackles**
1 (*usually in the plural*) **Shackles** are either of a pair of metal bands, joined by a chain, locked round a prisoner's wrists or ankles to prevent them moving around freely; you can also refer to the aspects of a system that restrict people's freedom as the **shackles** of that particular system: *throw off the shackles of communism.* **2** A **shackle** is a U-shaped metal loop closed over by a bolt, used for fastening ropes or chains together.
▷ ***verb*: shackles, shackling, shackled**
A person **is shackled** or they **are shackled** to someone or something when they cannot move freely because they have shackles fitted to their wrists or ankles or are tied to that person or thing by shackles.

shade /ʃeɪd/ *noun; verb*
▷ ***noun*: shades**
1 (*uncount*) **Shade** is dimness or coolness caused by the blocking or partial blocking out of sunlight: *Choose plants that will grow in shade.* **2** (*uncount*) **Shade** or the **shade** is an area from which sunlight has been blocked or partially blocked that is darker or cooler as a result: *She sat in the shade of a large oak tree.* **3** (*uncount*) **Shade** is such an area or areas represented in a drawing or painting: *Notice the artist's subtle use of light and shade.* **4** When a person or thing is in **the shade** of, or put in the **shade** by, another person or thing, they are made to appear less good or less impressive because that other person or thing is so much better: *He has lived constantly in the shade of his more talented brother.* □ *His painting puts mine in the shade.* **5** A **shade** is any device used as a shield from direct light: *a lampshade* □ *a sunshade.* **6** A **shade** is a colour that is similar to but slightly different from a primary or secondary colour: *I think I'll buy a darker shade of lipstick.* □ *His face had turned an unpleasant shade of green.* [*same as* **tone**] **7** (*used in the singular*) A **shade** is a small amount: *His attitude is just a shade too flippant for my liking.* □ *'Is the soup too salty?' 'Just a shade, perhaps.'* [*same as* **touch**]
▷ ***verb*: shades, shading, shaded**
1 A building or other object **shades** an area when it blocks or partially blocks sunlight from it; an area **is shaded** when sunlight is prevented or partially prevented from reaching it: *a row of tall trees shading the path* □ *This corner of the garden is shaded for most of the day.* **2** In drawing or painting, you **shade** areas when you draw or paint them so as to give the impression of shade.

shadow /ˈʃadoʊ/ *noun; verb*
▷ ***noun*: shadows**
1 A **shadow** is a dark shape on a surface produced when an object is positioned between the surface and a source of light: *She thought she saw the shadow of a man in the doorway.* □ *The clouds made moving shadows on the lawn.* □ *'I was crying because I can't get my shadow to stick on,' said Peter Pan.* **2** (*uncount*) **Shadow** is an area darkened by the blocking out of light: *She couldn't see what he looked like because his face was in shadow.* **3** If there is a **shadow** cast over something a feeling of gloom or foreboding fills or comes over it: *The news of his death cast a shadow over the proceedings.* **4** If someone becomes a **shadow**, or a **shadow** of their former selves, they become a greatly weakened or otherwise reduced version of the way they have been: *She's a shadow of her former self.* **5** You can refer to a person who is your constant companion or who is following you closely as your **shadow**.
▷ ***verb*: shadows, shadowing, shadowed**
If one person **is shadowing** another, they are following that person closely and often secretly.
▷ ***adjective*** (*BrE*)
In the British Parliament, the **Shadow** Cabinet is a group of leading politicians from the main opposition party who would form the Cabinet if they were elected to government; a **Shadow** spokesman on a

particular issue is one of these politicians whose responsibility is to be concerned with and state his party's policies on that issue: *the Shadow Chancellor.*

shadowy /ˈʃadoʊɪ/ *adjective*
Shadowy is used to describe **1** a place or area that is full of shadows: *He stood in a shadowy alcove.* **2** a shape or figure that is dark and difficult to see: *shadowy figures appeared out of the mist.* [*same as* **indistinct**] **3** people or things that are mysterious and difficult to find out much about: *the shadowy world of international espionage.*

shady /ˈʃeɪdɪ/ *adjective*: **shadier, shadiest**
1 A **shady** place is sheltered from, or gives shelter from, bright sunlight: *We found a shady spot under a tall oak tree.* □ *This part of the garden is too shady for some plants to grow well.* **2** (*informal*) If you describe someone's behaviour or activities as **shady**, you mean they are very likely to be dishonest or illegal: *Some of his business dealings have been a bit shady.* [*same as* **dubious, suspect**]

shaft /ʃɑːft/ *noun*: **shafts**
1 A **shaft** is a vertical passage large enough for people or things to move up and down, *eg* in a mine: *a mine shaft* □ *a lift shaft.* **2** The long straight part or handle of some tools or weapons is also called a **shaft**. **3** A **shaft** is a long bar or rod in a machine that turns round and round making other parts of the machine move: *a crankshaft* □ *a drive shaft.* **4** A **shaft** of light is a ray or beam of light.

shaggy /ˈʃagɪ/ *adjective*: **shaggier, shaggiest**
Shaggy hair or **shaggy** fur is thick and of several different lengths making it look untidy: *a pony with a shaggy mane.*

shake /ʃeɪk/ *verb*; *noun*
▻ ***verb***: **shakes, shaking, shook, shaken**
1 You **shake** something when you move it from side to side or up and down with quick, often violent, movements: *He shook the bottle of tomato sauce.* □ *He grabbed her by the shoulders and shook her.* □ *The wind shook the trees and rattled the windows.* **2** Something **shakes** when it moves from side to side and up and down with quick, often violent, movements: *The earth shook when the bomb landed.* [*same as* **shudder**] **3** If you **shake** your fist or **shake** it at someone or something, you wave it in the air violently and threateningly: *The old man raised his stick and shook it at the boys.* **4** You **shake**, or a part of your body **shakes**, when it trembles, often as a result of shock or severe anxiety: *She was shaking all over.* □ *His hands shook as he reached for the telegram.* **5** You can say that something **has shaken** you, or has **shaken** you up, when it has caused your feelings to be greatly disturbed or upset: *I must say that his aggressive behaviour really shook me.* □ *revelations that shook the nation.* **6** Something that **shakes** your confidence causes it to waver or weaken. **7** (*informal*) To **shake** means to shake hands: *Are we agreed? Let's shake on it then.*
▻ ***noun***: **shakes**
1 A **shake** is an act or the action of shaking. **2** (*informal*) A **shake** is also a very short while or a brief moment: *I'll get this done in two shakes.* [*same as* **tick**] **3** (*plural*; *informal*) The **shakes** are a fit of uncontrollable trembling, especially one that is sometimes experienced by people who drink a lot of alcohol regularly. **4** A **shake** is a drink made with milk and some sort of flavouring: *a chocolate shake.*
▻ ***phrases*** **1** (*informal*) If you say someone is **no great shakes** at something, you mean that they are not very good at it. **2** For **shake a leg** see **leg**. **3** You **shake hands** with another person when you clasp their right hand with your right hand in greeting or as a sign that you have reached an agreement. **4** You **shake your head** when you move it from side to side as a sign that you do not agree or that you do not approve: *'I can't understand why he did it,' he said, shaking his head sadly.*

phrasal verbs
shake off 1 You **shake** something **off** when you get rid of it: *I can't seem to shake off this cold.* **2** If you **shake off** someone or something that has been following you, you get away from or escape from them: *The thieves managed to shake off the police by dodging down an alley.*
shake up (*informal*) **1** If a system or organization **is shaken up**, it is reorganized thoroughly, especially with the intention of making it more efficient. [see also **shake-up**] **2** If something **shakes** you **up**, it makes you more alert or active.

shake-up /ˈʃeɪkʌp/ *noun*: **shake-ups**
When there is a **shake-up** in a system or organization, it is thoroughly re-organized, especially in order to make it work more efficiently. [*same as* **reorganization**]

shaky /ˈʃeɪkɪ/ *adjective*: **shakier, shakiest**
1 If your voice is **shaky**, or your body feels **shaky**, it trembles because you are weak, ill or frightened: *After being in bed for so long my legs feel a bit shaky.* [*same as* **unsteady, wobbly**] **2** (*informal*) You can describe something as **shaky** if you think it is not very strong or very good: *I've heard that his business is a bit shaky.* — *adverb* **shakily:** *The old man pointed shakily to the bookshelf.*

shall /ʃal/ *modal verb*
(negative forms **shall not** or **shan't**; short form **'ll**)
Shall is used with the infinitives of other verbs to express future action, *eg*
1 you say **'I shall'** do something if you intend to do it: *I shall insist that you're included.* □ *We certainly shan't employ him if that's his attitude.* □ *I shan't* (or *I'll not*) *bother next time.*

The old grammar rule that **shall** must be used with *I* and *we* to express the simple future is rarely obeyed in practice; **will** is probably more frequently used: *We will* (or *we shall* or *we'll*) *probably get there about six. I shall* (or *I will* or *I'll*) *be 40 on Friday.* □ *'You'll enjoy that.' 'Yes, I probably shall* (or *will*).

2 you ask **'shall** I' or **'shall** we' do something **a** when you are wondering what to do, or wondering whether or not to do something, or asking someone's advice about what to do: *I'll order those two books, shall I?* □ *What on earth shall I do if he doesn't turn up?* □ *Shall I buy it or shan't I?* □ *What shall I wear tonight?* □ *What shall we do this evening?* **b** to ask if someone would like you to do something: *It's cold in here. Shall I switch on the heating?* **c** to suggest to someone that you should do something together: *Shall we go for a walk?* □ *We'll take the bus, shall we?* **d** in question tags after *let's*: *Let's go on to the next question, shall we?* □ *Let's not get personal, shall we?*
3 (*formal*) you say that something **shall** happen **a** to stress that it is definitely going to happen: *It shall be arranged exactly as you suggest.* □ *You shall have what you want.* **b** to express an order or rule: *Members shall have the right to object.* □ *You are at university to work, and work you shall.*
4 you use **'shall** have' to form a future perfect tense:

We shall have set sail by this time tomorrow.
See also **will, should**.

shallow /ˈʃaloʊ/ *adjective; noun*
▻ ***adjective***
1 Shallow water has very little distance between the surface and the bottom. **2** A **shallow** container has short sides. **3** If you describe a person as **shallow**, you mean that they do not think very deeply or profoundly about things.
[*opposite* **deep**]
▻ ***noun*** (*used in the plural*): **shallows**
The **shallows** are a shallow place or part in a river, lake or the sea: *They hunted for crabs and minnows in the shallows.* [*opposite* **depths**]

sham /ʃam/ *noun; adjective*
▻ ***noun***: **shams**
If someone or something is a **sham**, they are not real or not what they pretend or seem to be: *The trial was a sham.* □ *His opulent lifestyle is a complete sham; he owes thousands of pounds.*
▻ ***adjective:*** *a sham fight.* [*same as* **pretence**]

shamble /ˈʃambəl/ *verb*: **shambles, shambling, shambled**
If someone **shambles** somewhere, or **shambles** along, they walk slowly and awkwardly dragging their feet: *The old man shambled along, bumping into people as he went.* [*same as* **lumber, shuffle**]

shambles /ˈʃambəlz/ *noun* (*singular; informal*)
If you say that something is a **shambles**, you mean it is completely disorganized or in a mess: *Sports day was a shambles; no-one knew who was supposed to do what.* □ *Tidy your room; it's a complete shambles.* [*same as* **chaos, wreck**]

shame /ʃeɪm/ *noun; verb*
▻ ***noun***
1 (*uncount*) **Shame** is an embarrassing or degrading feeling of guilt, foolishness or failure as a result of your own actions or those of another person associated with you; you feel **shame** when you have this feeling. [*same as* **humiliation**; *opposite* **pride**] **2** (*uncount*) If someone brings **shame** on you or your family, they have done something bad or morally wrong which causes people to respect you less because of your association with them. [*same as* **disgrace**; *opposite* **honour**] **3** (*used in the singular*) If you say that something is a **shame** you think it is a regrettable or disappointing event or situation: *'She broke her leg and couldn't take part in the final.' 'What a shame (* or *what a shame for her).* [*same as* **pity**]
▻ ***verb***: **shames, shaming, shamed**
1 If you **are shamed** by someone or something, they make you feel embarrassed. [*same as* **humiliated**] **2** When someone **is shamed** into some action, they are provoked into doing it because they have been made to feel guilty or embarrassed by other people: *He was shamed into telling the truth by his mother.* [*same as* **humble**] **3** If someone **shames** you, they bring disgrace on you or your family.

shamefaced /ʃeɪmˈfeɪst/ *adjective*
You are **shamefaced** if you look ashamed because you know you have done something wrong.

shameful /ˈʃeɪmfəl/ *adjective*
Shameful behaviour or actions are so bad or wrong that they ought to make you feel ashamed: *the latest shameful incident in a life of wickedness and debauchery.* [*same as* **disgraceful**] — *adverb* **shamefully:** *He treated her shamefully.* [*same as* **disgracefully**]

shameless /ˈʃeɪmləs/ *adjective*
A **shameless** person behaves in a way that other people find shocking, but shows or feels no shame: *She's a shameless liar.* — *adverb* **shamelessly**

shampoo /ʃamˈpuː/ *noun; verb*
▻ ***noun***: **shampoos**
1 (*uncount or count*) **Shampoo** is a soapy liquid for washing the hair and scalp: *a bottle of shampoo* □ *I like to try new shampoos.* [see picture at **bathroom**] **2** (*uncount or count*) **Shampoo** is a similar liquid for cleaning carpets or upholstery: *carpet shampoo.* **3** You can refer to an act of washing the hair or a carpet with this liquid as a **shampoo**: *She's going to the hairdresser for a shampoo and set.* □ *Give the carpet a thorough shampoo.*
▻ ***verb***: **shampoos, shampooing, shampooed**
You **shampoo** your hair or a carpet when you wash or clean it using shampoo.

shandy /ˈʃandɪ/ *noun* (*uncount or count*): **shandies**
Shandy or a **shandy** is a drink consisting of a mixture of beer and lemonade: *a pint of shandy* □ *Two shandies, please.*

shan't /ʃɑːnt/ *verb*
Shan't is the spoken, and informal written, form of **shall not**.

shanty town /ˈʃantɪ taʊn/ *noun*: **shanty towns**
A **shanty town** is an area, often close to a large city, where poor people live in rough huts made from pieces of wood, metal or any other material they have been able to gather.

shape /ʃeɪp/ *noun; verb*
▻ ***noun***: **shapes**
1 The **shape** of something is its outline or form: *Is Hawaii kidney-shaped?* □ *He could just distinguish the shape of the ship through the fog.* □ *These changes will affect the shape of the company for years to come.* **2** A **shape** is a figure such as a square, triangle or circle: *geometric shapes.* **3** Your **shape** is your particular figure: *She's an odd shape; thin on top and fat on the bottom.* **4** A **shape** is also any figure or person that you can't see properly: *She thought she could see shapes lurking behind the bushes.*
▻ ***verb***: **shapes, shaping, shaped**
1 You **shape** a material if you give it a particular form; you **shape** an object when you fashion it using your hands or a tool or tools. [*same as* **model, construct, create, form, mould**] **2** If an event or experience **shapes** someone's life or people's lives in general, it has an important influence on them: *Events that shaped history.* **3** You **shape** something to suit a particular purpose when you devise or develop it for that purpose: *He tried to shape his arguments so that they were difficult to contradict.* [*same as* **construct**]
▻ ***phrases*** **1** If you are **in shape** or keep **in shape** you are physically fit and healthy or do exercise to stay fit and healthy, especially for a particular purpose: *You'll have to get in shape if you're going to run the marathon.* □ *She exercises everyday to keep in shape.* [*same as* **fit**] **2 a** You are **out of shape** when you are not as fit and healthy as you can be. [*same as* **unfit**] **b** If something such as a piece of clothing is **out of shape**, it has been stretched or pulled so that it is no longer the shape it should be. **3** Something **takes shape** when it takes on a definite or recognizable form: *Their plans are beginning to take shape.* [*same as* **jell**]

phrasal verb
shape up (*informal*) **1** Something begins to **shape up** in a particular way when it begins to appear or develop in that way: *This is shaping up to be one of the most exciting elections in recent years.* **2** You

shape up when you begin to work or behave in the way that is expected of you: *You had better shape up if you want to keep your job.*

shapeless /ˈʃeɪpləs/ *adjective*
Shapeless things have no definite or attractive shape: *a shapeless old jumper.*

shapely /ˈʃeɪplɪ/ *adjective*
If you describe a person's body or part of their body as **shapely**, you think it is well-formed and attractively shaped: *She has long shapely legs.*

share /ʃɛə(r)/ *verb; noun*
▻ ***verb***: **shares, sharing, shared**
1 You **share** something with another person, or let them **share** it, when you let them have some of it; two or more people **share** something between them when they divide it between them: *I shared my bar of chocolate with her.* □ *Do share my sandwiches; I've got far too many.* □ *They bought a bottle of wine and shared it over dinner.* □ *We'll share the profits between us.* □ *I persuaded him to let me share the bill.* □ *Let's share the cost of the petrol.* □ *We shared the driving.* **2** You **share** something that you use with someone else when they use it too: *He shares a flat with two other students.* □ *The two of you will have to share a room, I'm afraid.* □ *There aren't enough copies for everyone, so some of you will have to share.* □ *Do share my programme.* **3** You **share** something, or **share** in it, when you participate in it, or experience it, with others: *Thank you for letting us share your happy day.* □ *You are invited to share in this exclusive offer.* □ *The whole community shared in welcoming them and making them feel wanted.* □ *We all share the blame.* **4** You **share** something such as a piece of information with someone when you tell them it: *She wanted to share the good news with someone.* □ *He is pictured above sharing a joke with his hostess.* **5** You **share** something such as a feeling, preference, quality or characteristic with someone when you both have it: *I share your anxiety.* □ *We shared many of the same interests.* □ *I shared his appreciation for good music.* □ *We shared a similar sense of humour.* □ *They shared a common background.*
▻ ***noun***: **shares**
1 A **share** of something is an amount or proportion of the total that is given to you to have or do; your **share** is the amount that is fair for you: *We've all earned a share of the profits.* □ *Everyone must have a share in planning the future.* □ *A large share of the repair cost will be borne by the manufacturers.* □ *No doubt every single one of these factors had a share in causing the disaster.* □ *He should acknowledge his share of the responsibility.* □ *I hope you took your full share of the food.* □ *I'll do my share of the housework as long as you do yours.* □ *His share of the winnings was £5000.* □ *She's had her fair share of life's sorrows.* **2** (*usually in the plural*) **Shares** are any of the units into which the total wealth of a business company is divided; if you invest in shares you are entitled to a portion of the company's profits: *Did you buy shares in British Telecom?* □ *stocks and shares* □ *a share issue.*

shapes and diagrams

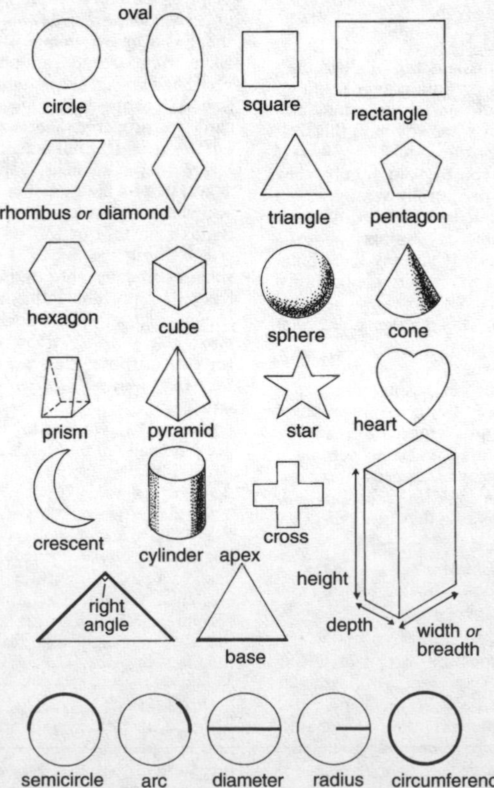

> ***phrasal verb***
> Something **is shared out** amongst two or more people when it is divided so that everyone gets a fair or equal portion of it: *We'll share out the work and it'll be finished before we know it.*

shareholder /ˈʃɛəhoʊldə(r)/ *noun*: **shareholders**
A company's **shareholders** are the people who own shares in it.

shark /ʃɑːk/ *noun*: **sharks**
A **shark** is a large fierce sea fish with many sharp teeth. Sharks eat other fish and have been known to attack people.

sharp /ʃɑːp/ *adjective*; *noun*; *adverb*
▻ ***adjective***: **sharper, sharpest**
1 Sharp objects have a thin edge that can cut or a point that can pierce: *Be careful with that knife; it's very sharp.* □ *A porcupine has sharp spines on its back.* [*opposite* **blunt**] **2** Something tastes **sharp** when it has a bitter pungent taste, like the taste of lemons or limes: *I like the sharp taste of unsweetened lemon juice.* **3** A **sharp** pain is one that feels like you are being suddenly cut or pierced by something sharp: *She felt a sharp pain in her side.* [*same as* **stabbing**] **4** A **sharp** fall or increase is a sudden steep fall or increase; a **sharp** bend or turn is one that goes in another direction very suddenly. **5** If you describe someone as **sharp**, you mean that they are very quick to understand or react: *Be careful what you say in front of him; children can be pretty sharp, you know.* **6** If you are **sharp** with someone, you speak abruptly or harshly to them. **7** If one thing is in **sharp** contrast to another, it is very clearly or easily seen that it is different from that other thing: *His perfect manners were in sharp contrast to his ragged clothes.* **8** If someone has a **sharp** tongue or **sharp** wit, they tend to say hurtful things or use sarcasm. **9** (*informal*) If you refer to someone, especially a man, as a **sharp** dresser, you mean that they wear stylish clothes. [*same as* **snappy**] **10** (*music*) A **sharp** note is higher in pitch by half a note than the normal note; if your singing voice tends to be **sharp** you tend to sing out of tune by being slightly too high in pitch. [*opposite* **flat**]
▻ ***noun*** (*music*): **sharps**
A **sharp** is a sharp note, indicated by the sign (#). [*opposite* **flat**]
▻ ***adverb***
1 If you arrive **sharp** at a stated time, you arrive punctually at exactly that time: *You must be at your desk at 8 o'clock sharp.* [*same as* **on the dot**] **2** If you pull up **sharp**, you stop or are caused to stop suddenly: *The horses were pulled up sharp.* **3** (*music*) If you sing **sharp**, you sing out of tune by being too high in pitch. [*opposite* **flat**]
▻ ***phrase*** (*informal*) If you tell someone to **look sharp**, you tell them to hurry up: *Look sharp now, or we'll miss our train.* — *adverb* **sharply:** *Prices rose sharply.* □ *'What do you think you're doing?' she asked sharply.* □ *The road turns sharply to the left before straightening out again.*

sharpen /ˈʃɑːpən/ *verb*: **sharpens, sharpening, sharpened**
You **sharpen** something when you make it sharp: *The cat was sharpening its claws on the tree.* □ *Make sure your pencil is sharpened.*

sharpener /ˈʃɑːpənə(r)/ *noun*: **sharpeners**
A **sharpener** is a device for sharpening things, especially one for sharpening pencils. [see picture at **office**]

shatter /ˈʃatə(r)/ *verb*: **shatters, shattering, shattered**
1 If something **shatters**, it breaks into tiny pieces or fragments: *The bowl fell off the table and shattered on the concrete floor.* **2** If a person's hopes **are shattered** their hopes are destroyed completely.

shattered /ˈʃatəd/ *adjective*
You can use **shattered 1** to describe someone who is extremely upset or shocked by something that has happened: *He was completely shattered when his brother died.* [*same as* **devastated**] **2** (*informal*) to describe someone who is very tired: *I must get some sleep; I'm shattered.* [*same as* **exhausted**]

shattering /ˈʃatərɪŋ/ *adjective*
1 A **shattering** experience is one that upsets or shocks you very much. **2** A **shattering** blow to your confidence or your plans is one that destroys them completely.
[*same as* **devastating**]

shave /ʃeɪv/ *verb*; *noun*
▻ ***verb***: **shaves, shaving, shaved**
1 When you **shave** part of your body, or a part of your body **is shaved**, you cut the hair from it using a razor or shaver: *She shaves her legs.* □ *The prisoners had their heads shaved.* **2** A man **shaves** when he cuts off the hair that grows on his face using a razor or shaver: *He cut himself shaving.* □ *He looks much younger now that he has shaved off his beard.* **3** If you **shave** off part of the surface of a piece of wood or metal, you cut thin slices off it using a tool with a sharp blade, such as a knife or a plane.
▻ ***noun***: **shaves**
A **shave** is the act or process of cutting the hair that grows on your face with a razor or shaver: *You need a shave.*

shaven /ˈʃeɪvən/ *adjective*
When a part of someone's body is **shaven**, it has been shaved: *monks with saffron robes and shaven heads.* [compare **unshaven**]

shaver /ˈʃeɪvə(r)/ *noun*: **shavers**
A **shaver** is an electrical device with a moving blade or set of blades for shaving hair. [see picture at **bathroom**]

shaving /ˈʃeɪvɪŋ/ *noun*; *adjective*
▻ ***noun*** (*usually used in the plural*): **shavings**
Shavings are thin slices that have been cut off the surface of a piece of wood or metal: *metal shavings.*
▻ ***adjective***
Shaving things are the various items used by men when they shave: *a shaving brush* □ *shaving cream.*

shawl /ʃɔːl/ *noun*: **shawls**
A **shawl** is a large usually square or rectangular piece of cloth that is worn over the head or shoulders, or used to wrap a baby in.

she /ʃiː/ *pronoun*; *noun*
▻ ***pronoun*** (*used as the subject of a verb*)
You use **she** to refer to **1** a woman, girl or female animal that has already been mentioned: *Jane said that she would phone again tomorrow.* □ *'Have you heard from Liz lately?' 'Yes, she rang yesterday.'* □ *I took the dog to the vet and he said she needed an urgent operation.* [see also **her, hers, herself**]

> Notice that you can also use *it* to refer to an animal or baby (of either sex), especially one that you do not know.

2 countries, ships and motor vehicles, thought of by some people as being feminine: *Wherever Britain planted her flag she imposed British standards and prejudices.* □ *When we reached the 'Queen Gertrude' she was already sinking.* □ *She's a good car.*

Notice the following uses: *I was slightly taller than she was* (or *than her*). *I'm not as optimistic as she is* (or *as her*). *It was she who had to break the bad news to his parents.* But: *That's probably her at the door now.*

▻ ***noun*** (*often used as a prefix*): **shes** or **she's**
A **she** is a female: *Is the calf a he or a she?* □ *a she-wolf.*

sheaf /ʃiːf/ *noun*: **sheaves**
A **sheaf** is a bundle, especially of ripe corn, that has been tied together: *He handed her a sheaf of official-looking papers.*

shear /ʃɪə(r)/ *verb*: **shears, shearing, sheared, shorn**
1 You **shear** a hedge or someone's hair when you trim or cut it using clippers. **2** You **shear** sheep when you cut their wool off using a pair of shears.

phrasal verb
If a piece of metal **shears off**, it breaks, usually under pressure: *One of the bolts which secured the panel had sheared off.*

shears /ʃɪərz/ *noun* (*plural*)
A pair of **shears** is a tool with heavy blades that operate like scissors, used for shearing sheep or for trimming plants in the garden. [see picture at **tool**]

sheath /ʃiːθ/ *noun*: **sheaths**
1 A **sheath** is a long close-fitting covering for the blade of a sword or knife. **2** A **sheath** is anything which forms a close-fitting covering, such as a close-fitting style of dress worn by women: *She wore a gold lamé sheath (dress).* **3** (*old*) A **sheath** is also another name for a condom.

sheathe /ʃiːð/ *verb*: **sheathes, sheathing, sheathed**
1 You **sheathe** a sword or knife when you put it into a sheath: *He sheathed his sword.* **2** Something **is sheathed** in a protective or close-fitting covering when it is in it: *fuel rods sheathed in a protective casing of concrete and lead.*

shed[1] /ʃɛd/ *noun*: **sheds**
A **shed** is a wooden or metal outbuilding of any size, for working in or for storage or shelter: *a shearing shed* □ *a garden shed.*

shed[2] /ʃɛd/ *verb*: **sheds, shedding, shed**
1 You **shed** tears when they pour out and fall from your eyes. **2** You **shed** someone's blood when you wound them so that blood flows out of the wound. **3 a** People **shed** their clothes, reptiles **shed** their skins, and birds **shed** their feathers when they cast them off and get rid of them. [*same as* **discard**] **b** A tree or plant **sheds** its leaves when they fall off, especially in the autumn. **c** Business firms or industries **shed** jobs or employees when they reduce the number of jobs or employees in that business or industry. **4** A material **sheds** water when it causes it to flow off its surface.
▻ ***phrase*** For **shed light on** see **light**.

she'd /ʃiːd/
She'd is the spoken, and informal written form of **she would** and **she had**, especially where *had* is an auxiliary verb: *She'd gone for a walk.* □ *She'd be well advised to see a doctor as soon as possible.*

sheen /ʃiːn/ *noun* (*used in the singular or uncount*)
If something has a **sheen**, it has a shine or glossiness on its surface: *hair so black and shiny it appeared to have a bluish sheen.*

sheep /ʃiːp/ *noun*: **sheep**
1 A **sheep** is an animal with a thick coat of wool. Sheep are commonly kept as farm animals for their wool, which is used to make clothing, and for their meat. **2** If you refer to a person as a **sheep**, or you say that people behave like **sheep**, you mean they are meek like a sheep or tend to follow others without thinking, like a flock of sheep.

sheepdog /ˈʃiːpdɒg/ *noun*: **sheepdog**
A **sheepdog** is any of various types of dog used to herd sheep or originally bred to herd sheep.

sheepish /ˈʃiːpɪʃ/ *adjective*
When someone looks **sheepish** they look embarrassed because they feel they have done something silly: *The boys, with sheepish expressions, presented her with a bunch of flowers.* — *adverb* **sheepishly:** *He grinned sheepishly and twisted his cap in his hands.*

sheepskin /ˈʃiːpskɪn/ *noun* (*uncount, often adjectival*)
Sheepskin is leather made from the skin of a sheep, usually with the wool left on it: *a sheepskin rug* □ *a coat made from sheepskin.*

sheer[1] /ʃɪə(r)/ *adjective; adverb*
▻ ***adjective***
1 A **sheer** cliff is vertical or nearly vertical. **2** You use **sheer** for emphasis when you want to describe something that is an absolute or extreme example of a particular state or condition: *It was sheer folly on his part.* □ *He ate every single chocolate, not because he was hungry, but out of sheer greed.* [*same as* **pure**] **3 Sheer** fabric is so fine as to be almost transparent.
▻ ***adverb*** (*formal*): *a massive cliff of ice rose sheer out of the sea.*

sheer[2] /ʃɪə(r)/ *verb*: **sheers, sheering, sheered**

phrasal verb
If something that is moving in a particular direction **sheers off** or **sheers away** it turns aside or changes course suddenly, often in order to avoid hitting something else: *The plane seemed to be heading straight for the tower but sheered off to the right at the last moment.*

sheet /ʃiːt/ *noun*: **sheets**
1 Sheets are large broad pieces of fabric, especially for covering the mattress of a bed: *cotton sheets.* **2** A **sheet** of paper is a single piece of paper, especially of a size that is suitable for writing on. **3** A **sheet** of ice is a broad expanse of it.

sheikh or **sheik** /ʃeɪk/ *noun*: **sheikhs**
A **sheikh** is an Arab ruler or chief.

shelf /ʃɛlf/ *noun*: **shelves**
1 A **shelf** is a horizontal board for laying things on, fixed to a wall or as part of a cupboard. **2** A **shelf** is also any natural feature resembling this, *eg* a narrow projecting piece of rock or ice, or part of the seabed next to a land mass that is shallower than the surrounding ocean. [*same as* **ledge**]
▻ ***phrase*** If you say that someone has been left **on the shelf**, you mean that they no longer have the opportunity to marry, especially because they are now too old.

shell /ʃɛl/ *noun; verb*
▻ ***noun***: **shells**
1 A **shell** is the hard protective outer covering of **a** an egg. **b** a nut. **c** certain creatures such as molluscs, tortoises and turtles. **2** The **shells** that you find on the seashore are the empty coverings of molluscs. **3** A **shell** is also any hard outer case or an empty framework or outer structure: *The interior of the building was completely destroyed in the fire, leaving only a*

charred shell of twisted metal and concrete. **4** A **shell** is a cartridge or round of ammunition for a large-bore gun, such as a shotgun or mortar: *Shells rained down on the city from the enemy positions in the surrounding hills.* **5** If you say that someone comes out of their **shell**, or retreats into their **shell**, you mean that they become more or less outgoing in their relationships with other people.

▻ ***verb***: **shells, shelling, shelled**

1 You **shell** peas, beans, nuts or shellfish when you take them out of their pods or shells. **2** If an army or other military unit **shells** a target, they fire explosive shells at it in order to damage or destroy it: *The rebel militia surrounded the city and began to shell it.*

phrasal verb

(*informal*) You **shell out** for something when you pay for it or spend money on it, often reluctantly: *How much will I have to shell out if I want the latest computer equipment?* [*same as* **fork out**]

she'll /ʃiːl/

She'll is the spoken, and informal written, form of **she will** or **she shall**: *She'll be here tomorrow.*

shellfish /ˈʃɛlfɪʃ/ *noun*: **shellfish**

1 A **shellfish** is any of various sea creatures that have a hard outer shell: *Prawns and mussels are shellfish.* **2** (*uncount*) **Shellfish** is these creatures eaten as food: *Some people are allergic to shellfish.*

shelter /ˈʃɛltə(r)/ *noun*; *verb*

▻ ***noun***: **shelters**

1 (*uncount*) **Shelter** is protection against weather or danger such as is provided by a house or other structure: *They asked if she could give them shelter for the night.* **2** A **shelter** is a place or structure which provides this protection: *The soldiers built a rough shelter of branches covered with tarpaulins.* □ *an air-raid shelter* □ *a bomb shelter.* [*same as* **refuge**]

▻ ***verb***: **shelters, sheltering, sheltered**

1 You **shelter** someone when you protect them from danger or the effects of weather: *The female eagle sheltered her chicks with her wings.* □ *She was accused of sheltering a known criminal.* [*same as* **harbour**] **2** You **shelter** somewhere when you take cover from bad weather or danger: *They sheltered from the storm in an old barn.* □ *'You can't catch me!' he yelled, sheltering behind his mother's skirts.*

sheltered /ˈʃɛltəd/ *adjective*

1 Sheltered places are protected from the wind and rain: *They anchored in a sheltered bay.* [*same as* **secluded**] **2** If you have had a **sheltered** life or a **sheltered** upbringing, you have been protected from, and therefore do not know about, many of the unpleasant things that go on in the world. **3 Sheltered** housing is housing for old or disabled people where they can live independently but with help or supervision available if they need it.

shelve /ʃɛlv/ *verb*: **shelves, shelving, shelved**

1 You **shelve** an area or a cupboard when you fit it with shelves: *I want to shelve that cupboard so that I can keep books in it.* **2** If the land **shelves**, it slopes downwards: *The seabed shelves steeply at this point.* **3** If you **shelve** a proposal or plan, you postpone it or put it aside for a time: *We'll have to shelve our holiday plans meantime.* [*same as* **postpone, suspend**]

shelves /ʃɛlvz/ *noun*

Shelves is the plural of **shelf**.

shelving /ˈʃɛlvɪŋ/ *noun* (*uncount*)

Shelving is **1** any material used for shelves: *He bought some pine shelving.* **2** a set or arrangement of shelves: *The supermarket shelving has been rearranged.*

shepherd /ˈʃɛpəd/ *noun*; *verb*

▻ ***noun***: **shepherds**

A **shepherd** is a person who looks after sheep.

▻ ***verb***: **shepherds, shepherding, shepherded**

You **shepherd** a group of people when you keep them in a group and direct them to or into a place: *Parties of tourists were shepherded from room to room by the guides.*

shepherdess /ˈʃɛpədɛs/ *noun* (*old*): **shepherdesses**

A **shepherdess** is a female shepherd.

shepherd's pie /ʃɛpədz ˈpaɪ/ *noun* (*uncount or count*): **shepherd's pies**

Shepherd's pie is a baked dish of minced meat with mashed potatoes on the top.

sherbet /ˈʃɜːbət/ *noun* (*uncount or count*): **sherbets**

Sherbet is a sharp-tasting fruit-flavoured powder eaten as a sweet; a **sherbet** is a fizzy drink or a sweet made from or containing this powder.

sheriff /ˈʃɛrɪf/ *noun*: **sheriffs**

In the USA, a **sheriff** is a police officer who is responsible for law enforcement in a particular county.

sherry /ˈʃɛrɪ/ *noun* (*uncount or count*): **sherries**

Sherry is a type of strong wine made in Spain, often drunk before a meal; a **sherry** is a glass of this wine: *sweet/dry sherry* □ *Would you like a small sherry?* □ *Two dry sherries, please.*

she's /ʃiːz/

She's is the spoken, and informal written, form of **she is** and **she has**, especially where *has* is an auxiliary verb: *She's my sister.* □ *She's got two children.*

shield /ʃiːld/ *noun*; *verb*

▻ ***noun***: **shields**

1 A **shield** is a piece of armour carried to block an attack with a weapon. **2** A **shield** is a representation of this, usually a vertical rectangle with a rounded bottom, used as an emblem. **3** A **shield** is also a medal or trophy shaped, sometimes only vaguely, like this: *They won the charity shield.* **4** A **shield** is any protective plate or screen: *The beetle has a pair of hard shields on its head.* □ *a windshield.*

▻ ***verb***: **shields, shielding, shielded**

If you **shield** someone, you protect them from harm or danger: *The police believe the murderer is being shielded by a friend or family member.*

shift /ʃɪft/ *verb*; *noun*

▻ ***verb***: **shifts, shifting, shifted**

1 Something **shifts** when it changes its position or direction; you **shift** something when you change its position or direction: *The wind is shifting to the north.* □ *Will you help me shift this wardrobe?* [*same as* **move**] **2** If you **shift** blame or responsibility for something on to someone else, you transfer or re-direct it to them: *It's your fault; don't try to shift the blame on to someone else.* **3** You **shift** the gears in a vehicle when you change them. **4** If you manage to **shift** something that is very heavy or has become stuck, you manage to move, remove or dislodge it: *Nothing will shift this greasy dirt.* □ *Could you give me hand? I can't shift this bookcase.* [*same as* **budge**] **5** (*informal*) If you say that someone or something can **shift**, you mean they are capable of moving very quickly: *It may be a small car, but it can certainly shift.*

▻ ***noun***: **shifts**

1 A **shift** is one of a set of consecutive periods into which a 24-hour working day is divided; the group of workers on duty during any one of these periods is also known as a **shift**. [see also **back shift**, **day shift**,

night shift] **2** A **shift** is also a change of position or direction: *There has been a shift in the wind direction from north to northeasterly.*
▻ ***phrase*** If someone **shifts their ground**, they adopt a new opinion or a new position in an argument: *We managed to get them to shift their ground a little.*

shiftless /ˈʃɪftləs/ *adjective* (*derogatory*)
A **shiftless** person is lazy and has no desire or ambition to do anything or succeed in doing anything: *He is totally shiftless and without any spark of ambition.* [*same as* **aimless**, **idle**; *opposite* **ambitious**]

shifty /ˈʃɪftɪ/ *adjective*: **shiftier**, **shiftiest**
A **shifty** person is sly, untrustworthy or dishonest; if someone's appearance or behaviour is **shifty**, it suggests that they are sly, untrustworthy or dishonest: *I don't trust him; he has a shifty look about him.* [*same as* **furtive**, **devious**]

shilling /ˈʃɪlɪŋ/ *noun*: **shillings**
A **shilling** was an old British coin worth 5 new pence.

shimmer /ˈʃɪmə(r)/ *verb*; *noun*
▻ ***verb***: **shimmers**, **shimmering**, **shimmered**
To **shimmer** means to shine quiveringly with reflected light: *Her dress shimmered as she moved.* ▫ *Moonlight shimmered on the surface of the lake.*
▻ ***noun*** (*usually in the singular*): *a faint shimmer on the surface of the pond.*

shin /ʃɪn/ *noun*; *verb*
▻ ***noun***: **shins**
1 Your **shins** are the bony front parts of your legs below the knee: *The ball hit him on the shin.* [see picture at **body**] **2** A **shin** of beef is the lower part of a leg of beef.
▻ ***verb***: **shins**, **shinning**, **shinned**

> ***phrasal verb***
> If someone **shins up** a tree or an upright pole, they climb it quickly using their hands and feet to grip it: *He shinned up the telegraph pole.*

shine /ʃaɪn/ *verb*; *noun*
▻ ***verb***: **shines**, **shining**, **shone**, **shined** for sense 3 only
1 To **shine** means to give out or reflect light: *The stars shone in the night sky.* ▫ *The sun was shining and the birds were singing.* ▫ *He could see a faint light shining in the distance.* **2** You **shine** a torch or some other source of light at something when you direct the light from it at that thing: *He shone the torch right in my face.* ▫ *Can you shine the light into that corner?* **3** If you **shine** something, you make it bright and gleaming by polishing it: *A small boy shined my shoes for 50p.* **4** If you **shine** at something, you are outstandingly good at it: *In her schooldays, she shone at maths and science.* [*same as* **excel**]
▻ ***noun*** (*used in the singular*)
The **shine** on something is its shining quality or polish: *Don't put a hot cup on that table; you'll take the shine off.* ▫ *This polish will leave your car with a deep lasting shine.* [*same as* **gleam**]
▻ ***phrase*** (*informal*) If someone **takes a shine to you**, they quickly and immediately decide that they like you: *He's quite happy in his new job; his boss seems to have taken a shine to him.*

shingle /ˈʃɪŋgəl/ *noun*: **shingles**
1 (*uncount*) **Shingle** is small pebbles on a seashore or river bank. **2** A **shingle** is a thin rectangular, often wooden, roof tile.

shingles /ˈʃɪŋgəlz/ *noun* (*uncount*)
Shingles is an infectious illness in which a group of nerve ends become inflamed, producing a row of painful spots on the skin, *eg* round the head or waist.

shiny /ˈʃaɪnɪ/ *adjective*: **shinier**, **shiniest**
1 Shiny things reflect light or are polished so that they reflect light: *His shoes are always shiny.* ▫ *I could see a shiny object on the river-bed.* [*same as* **polished**, **gleaming**] **2** If a fabric or part of a piece of clothing is **shiny**, it has become worn leaving a glossy finish.

ship /ʃɪp/ *noun*; *verb*
▻ ***noun***: **ships**
A **ship** is any large boat designed to carry passengers or cargo, especially on sea journeys.
▻ ***verb***: **ships**, **shipping**, **shipped**
1 When something **is shipped** somewhere, it is sent there by ship or by some other means of transport. **2** If a boat **is shipping** water, water is coming on board over the side.

-ship /-ʃɪp/ *suffix*
-ship is added to nouns to make words that refer to
1 a particular rank, position or status: *Your Lordship.* **2** a period of office or rule: *during his chairmanship.* **3** a particular state or condition: *friendship.* **4** a particular type of skill, as in *craftmanship* and *seamanship*. **5** a particular group of individuals: *The club has a large membership.*

shipment /ˈʃɪpmənt/ *noun*: **shipments**
A **shipment** of something is a cargo or consignment of that thing, though not necessarily sent by ship: *The shipment is being sent by train to New York, and from there by air to Moscow.* ▫ *a shipment of spare parts.*

shipping /ˈʃɪpɪŋ/ *noun* (*uncount*)
1 Shipping is ships as traffic: *a gale warning to shipping in the Bay of Biscay.* **2 Shipping** is also the business of transporting goods and freight, especially by ship: *You'll be able to get details of container ships bound for the Far East at the shipping office.*

shipshape /ˈʃɪpʃeɪp/ *adjective*
If something is **shipshape** it is neat and tidy or in good order: *I expect to see your room shipshape when I come to inspect it.*

shipwreck /ˈʃɪprɛk/ *noun*; *verb*
▻ ***noun***: **shipwrecks**
1 (*uncount*) **Shipwreck** is the accidental sinking or destruction of a ship: *After enduring shipwreck and starvation they were eventually rescued by a Chinese junk.* **2** A **shipwreck** or **wreck** is the remains of a sunken or destroyed ship. **3** (*literary*) **Shipwreck** is also used to mean ruin or destruction generally: *some remnants of history that have casually escaped the shipwreck of time.*
▻ ***verb*** (*in the passive*): **shipwrecked**
When people **are shipwrecked** their ship is sunk or destroyed at sea but they manage to reach land: *They were shipwrecked off a small Pacific island.*

shipyard /ˈʃɪpjɑːd/ *noun*: **shipyards**
A **shipyard** is a place where ships are built and repaired: *There are now very few shipyards on the Clyde.*

shirk /ʃɜːk/ *verb*: **shirks**, **shirking**, **shirked**
To **shirk** work or a duty means to avoid doing it or carrying it out: *You shouldn't shirk your responsibilities.*

shirt /ʃɜːt/ *noun*: **shirts**
A **shirt** is any of various styles of long- or short-sleeved pieces of clothing for the upper body, usually with a collar and buttons at the front. [see picture at **clothing**]
▻ ***phrases*** **1** If a man is **in his shirtsleeves**, he is not

wearing a jacket or coat. **2** (*informal*) If you are very angry and someone tells you to **keep your shirt on**, they want you to control your temper. [*same as* **keep your hair on**] **3** (*informal*) If you **put your shirt on** a horse to win a race, you bet all the money you have on it.

shit /ʃɪt/ *noun*; *interjection*
(*vulgar*, *swearword*)
▻ ***noun***: **shits**
1 (*uncount*) **Shit** is faeces. **2** A **shit** is an act of defecating: *do (*or *have) a shit.* **3** (*uncount*; *derogatory*) **Shit** is also rubbish or nonsense: *Don't talk shit!* **4** (*derogatory*) If you refer to someone as a **shit**, you mean they are despicable or very bad.
▻ ***interjection***
Some people say **shit!** when they want to show that they are very annoyed or disappointed about something.

shiver /ˈʃɪvə(r)/ *verb*; *noun*
▻ ***verb***: **shivers, shivering, shivered**
You **shiver** when you tremble or quiver with cold or fear: *She stood shivering in the rain.* [*same as* **shake**]
▻ ***noun***: **shivers**
A **shiver** is an act of shivering or a shivering sensation: *'Let's get in out of this cold wind,' she said with a shiver.* □ *When she looked at the photograph a shiver of disgust went down her spine.* [*same as* **shudder**]
▻ ***phrase*** If something gives you the **shivers**, it makes you feel frightened or gives you a feeling of horror: *Let's get out of here, this place gives me the shivers.*

shivery /ˈʃɪvərɪ/ *adjective*
If you feel **shivery**, you cannot stop trembling or shivering, usually because you are cold.

shoal /ʃoʊl/ *noun*: **shoals**
A **shoal** is a large number of fish swimming and feeding together: *shoals of herring.*

shock /ʃɒk/ *noun*; *verb*
▻ ***noun***: **shocks**
1 (*uncount or count*) If you are suffering from **shock** or something gives you a **shock**, you have, or it causes you to have, a strong emotional reaction because it is very unpleasant or surprising: *What a shock you gave me jumping out like that!* □ *There was general feeling of shock and horror at the news.* **2** (*uncount*) **Shock** is the medical term for a temporary breakdown of all physical functions, *eg* as a result of extreme pain or sudden extreme emotional disturbance: *She's in shock.* **3** If you get an electric **shock**, electricity passes through your body causing an extremely unpleasant sensation with uncontrollable twitching or stiffening of your muscles and limbs: *I got a shock from the cooker.* **4** A **shock** is also a violent blow or shaking effect caused by something such as an explosion, an earthquake or a crash: *There were a series of minor shocks following the earthquake.* **5** A **shock** of corn is a number of sheaves of corn tied or gathered together. **6** If you refer to a person's hair as a **shock**, you mean it is thick and bushy like a shock of corn: *a shock of red hair.*
▻ ***verb***: **shocks, shocking, shocked**
Something **shocks** you if it causes you an unpleasant feeling of surprise, or extreme anger and disgust: *His attitude shocked her.* □ *He seems to enjoy shocking his parents.* [*same as* **appal**]

shocking /ˈʃɒkɪŋ/ *adjective*
1 Shocking is used to describe things that people find extremely surprising, outrageous or disgusting: *shocking behaviour* □ *a shocking story.* **2** (*informal*) Some people use **shocking** to mean very bad: *'What shocking weather we've been having!'*
[*same as* **appalling**]

shod /ʃɒd/ *verb*
Shod is the past tense and past participle of the verb to **shoe**.

shoddy /ˈʃɒdɪ/ *adjective*: **shoddier, shoddiest**
1 Shoddy workmanship or goods are of poor quality having been made or done carelessly, or made using inferior materials. [*same as* **poor**] **2** If you get **shoddy** treatment from someone, they treat you badly. — *adverb* **shoddily:** *shoddily-made furniture.*

shoe /ʃuː/ *noun*; *verb*
▻ ***noun***: **shoes**
1 Shoes are shaped outer coverings for the feet, made of leather or other stiff material, usually covering the feet from the ends of the toes to just below the ankle: *a pair of walking shoes* □ *dancing shoes* □ *sailing shoes* □ *Have you polished your shoes?* [see picture at **clothing**] **2** A horseshoe is also referred to as a **shoe**.
▻ ***verb***: **shoes, shoeing, shod** or **shoed**
A blacksmith **shoes** a horse when he or she fits metal horseshoes on its hooves.

shoelace /ˈʃuːleɪs/ *noun*: **shoelaces**
Shoelaces are long narrow pieces of cord, made *eg* from cotton or leather, that you use to fasten your shoes: *Tie your shoelaces.* □ *Your shoelaces are undone.*

shoestring /ˈʃuːstrɪŋ/ *noun*; *adjective*
▻ ***noun*** (*AmE*): **shoestrings**
Shoestrings are shoelaces.
▻ ***adjective***
A **shoestring** budget or a **shoestring** operation is one which has very little money to spend.
▻ ***phrase*** (*informal*) If you do something **on a shoestring**, or it is done **on a shoestring**, you do it using a very small amount of money: *They furnished their house on a shoestring.* □ *The film was made on a shoestring.*

shone /ʃɒn/ *verb*
Shone is the past tense and past participle of **shine**.

shoo /ʃuː/ *interjection*; *verb*
▻ ***interjection***
You say **'Shoo!'** to a bird or an animal, and sometimes to a person, when you want to chase them away.
▻ ***verb***: **shoos, shooing, shooed**
You **shoo** a bird, animal or person when you chase them off, out or away from somewhere by shouting 'Shoo' and waving your hands in the air.

shook /ʃʊk/ *verb*
Shook is the past tense of **shake**.

shoot /ʃuːt/ *verb*; *noun*
▻ ***verb***: **shoots, shooting, shot**
1 You **shoot** when you fire a gun or other weapon or when you fire a missile, such as a bullet or an arrow at something: *Robin shot the arrow high into the air.* □ *Don't shoot; we're not armed!* **2** People who **shoot** hunt and kill animals or birds with a gun for sport: *Do you shoot?* □ *He shoots pheasants when they are in season, and clay pigeons at other times of the year.* **3** If you **shoot** a person or an animal, you hit and wound or kill them with a missile fired from a gun or a bow: *He shot a red deer stag.* □ *The soldiers shot twelve unarmed civilians.* □ *She shot him dead.* □ *He had been shot in the leg.* **4** You **shoot** questions at someone when you ask them a series of questions forcefully and rapidly like bullets being fired from a gun. [*same as* **fire**] **5** If something **shoots** somewhere or **is shot** somewhere, it moves or progresses there very rapidly as if it had been fired from a gun: *He shot past me pedalling furiously.* □ *Their last win shot them to the top of the league table.* [*same as* **bolt, hurtle**] **6** (*sport*) A player in games such as football or hockey **shoots**

when they strike the ball at the goal. **7** Filmmakers **shoot** a scene when they film it. **8** If a pain **shoots** through part of your body, it travels very quickly through it with a stabbing sensation: *The pain was shooting up his arm and across his chest.* **9** (*informal*) To **shoot** also means to pass quickly through: *shoot the rapids* □ *He caused a serious road accident when he shot the traffic lights.* [=drove through a traffic light when it was red] **10 a** A plant **shoots** when it produces new growth. **b** A vegetable **shoots** when it produces unwanted flowers or seeds. **11 a** (*informal*) You **shoot** pool when you play a game of pool. **b** You **shoot** a particular score in golf when you take that number of strokes to complete a hole or a round: *He shot a birdie at the eighteenth.*
12 (*slang*) If someone **shoots** illegal drugs, they inject themselves with them.

▻ ***noun***: **shoots**

1 A **shoot** is a new or young plant growth: *Deer had nibbled off the new young shoots.* **2** A **shoot** is an outing to hunt birds or animals with guns, or the area of land within which birds or animals are hunted in this way: *He always holds a grouse shoot on the 12th of August.*

▻ ***phrase*** (*informal*) If someone **shoots their mouth off**, they boast, or talk about things that they are not supposed to.

> ***phrasal verbs***
> **shoot down** **1** If an aircraft **is shot down**, it is caused to crash by enemy gunfire. **2** If someone **is shot down** they are killed by gunfire. [*same as* **gun down**] **3** (*informal*) If you **shoot** someone **down**, you dismiss or crush them with savage criticism or ridicule.
> **shoot up** You can say that a child or young person **is shooting up** if you mean that they are growing very rapidly, like the young shoot of a plant.

shop /ʃɒp/ *noun*; *verb*

▻ ***noun***: **shops**

1 A **shop** is a place where goods or services are sold: *a grocer's shop* □ *a shoe shop* □ *a hairdresser's shop* □ *Are the shops open today?* □ *Take faulty goods back to the shop where you bought them.* **2** A **shop** is also a place in which work, especially manual work, of a particular kind is carried out: *a printing shop* □ *a joiner's shop* □ *a blacksmith's shop* □ *Does the garage have a body shop?* [=an area where the bodywork of cars is repaired]

▻ ***verb***: **shops, shopping, shopped**

1 You **shop** when you visit a shop or shops in order to buy goods: *She loves to shop.* [*same as* **go shopping**] **2** (*informal*) If someone **shops** someone else *eg* to the police or someone else in authority, they tell them that that person has committed a crime or done something wrong. [*same as* **grass on**]

▻ ***phrases*** **1** (*informal*) If things are **all over the shop**, they are scattered everywhere or in many places: *His office is a mess; there are books and files all over the shop.* **2** (*informal*) If a business **shuts up shop** it stops trading, either at the end of each working day or permanently: *Many small traders have had to shut up shop since the new supermarket opened.* □ *I'm going to shut up shop early tonight.* **3** People **talk shop** when they discuss their professional concerns away from their work place.

> ***phrasal verb***
> **shop around** **1** You **shop around** when you compare the price and quality of goods in various shops before deciding to buy: *It's worthwhile shopping around; you may get a bargain.* **2** (*informal*) You **shop around** when you explore the full range of options available before committing yourself to any one: *I'm going to shop around to see what courses are on offer, before I decide whether to go to college or take a job.*

shop assistant /ˈʃɒp əsɪstənt/ *noun*: **shop assistants**
A **shop assistant** is a person whose job it is to serve or attend to customers in a shop.

shop floor /ʃɒp ˈflɔː(r)/ *noun* (*uncount*)
1 The **shop floor** is the part of a factory with machines and other equipment where manual work is carried out. **2** The **shop floor** is also used to refer to the workers in a factory as opposed to the management.

shopkeeper /ˈʃɒpkiːpə(r)/ *noun*: **shopkeepers**
A **shopkeeper** is a person who owns and manages a shop: *Napoleon described Britain as a nation of shopkeepers.*

shoplifting /ˈʃɒplɪftɪŋ/ *noun* (*uncount*)
Shoplifting is the crime of taking goods from shops without paying for them.

shopper /ˈʃɒpə(r)/ *noun*: **shoppers**
A person who is shopping is a **shopper**: *The High Street was crowded with shoppers.*

shopping /ˈʃɒpɪŋ/ *noun* (*uncount*)
1 **Shopping** is the activity of visiting shops and buying things: *She likes to go shopping with her friends.* **2** Your **shopping** is the goods you have bought in shops, especially groceries and household goods: *a basket of shopping* □ *He helped her carry the shopping.*

shopping bag /ˈʃɒpɪŋ bag/ *noun*: **shopping bags**
A **shopping bag** is a bag with handles used for carrying shopping. [see picture at **street**]

shopping centre /ˈʃɒpɪŋ sɛntə(r)/ *noun*: **shopping centres**
A **shopping centre** is an area containing a large number of shops of different kinds, or a collection of different shops under one roof, often providing other facilities, *eg* restaurants and toilets.

shop sign /ˈʃɒp saɪn/ *noun*: **shop signs**
A **shop sign** is a painted or printed sign displaying the name of a shop and what it sells. [see picture at **street**]

shop steward /ʃɒp ˈstjʊəd/ *noun*: **shop stewards**
A **shop steward** is a worker in a factory elected by others to be an official trade union representative in negotiations with the management.

shop window /ʃɒp ˈwɪndoʊ/ *noun*: **shop windows**
A **shop window** is a large window in a shop behind which goods for sale are displayed. [see picture at **street**]

shore[1] /ʃɔː(r)/ *noun*: **shores**
1 (*used in the singular*) The **shore** is land bordering on the sea or any other large area of water: *large waves breaking on the shore* □ *a shorebird* [=one that lives or feeds on the shore] □ *They swam to the opposite shore.* **2** (*plural*; *literary*) **Shores** are land or countries that border the sea or any other large area of water: *foreign shores* □ *on the shores of Lake Titicaca.*

▻ ***phrase*** If someone or something goes **on shore**, they go on to the land after being at sea: *The crew of the submarine won't be on shore* (or *ashore*) *for another three months.*

shore[2] /ʃɔː(r)/ *verb*: **shores, shoring, shored**

> *phrasal verb*
> **shore up** **1** A building or other structure that is likely to fall down **is shored up** when it is supported with props. **2** You **shore** someone or something **up** when you give them support to sustain or strengthen them.

shoreline /ˈʃɔːlaɪn/ *noun*: **shorelines**
The **shoreline** is the line formed where land meets water.

shorn /ʃɔːn/ *verb*; *adjective*
▻ ***verb***
Shorn is the past participle of **shear**.
▻ ***adjective***
Shorn hair has been cut very short: *He ran his hand over his shorn head.*

short /ʃɔːt/ *adjective*; *noun*; *verb*
▻ ***adjective***: **shorter**, **shortest**
1 Something that is **short** **a** does not measure much from one end to the other: *She wears her hair very short.* □ *He had short thick fingers.* □ *Which is shorter, a mile or a kilometre?* □ *She regularly walked the short distance to work.* [*opposite* **long**] **b** does not last long: *Is 21 December the shortest day?* □ *He'd made a surprising number of friends in the course of his short life.* □ *We had a short break and then began work again.* □ *I'd gone out for a short walk.* □ *It's only a short film.* □ *We were told to keep our speeches as short as possible.* [*same as* **brief**; *opposite* **long**] **2** You use **short** to describe a period of time that seems to pass very quickly, or during which a surprising amount happens: *In one short year she had managed to get the company firmly back on its feet again.* **3** A book or other piece of writing is **short** if it does not contain much text: *The Palace has issued a short statement to the press.* □ *Her novels are all pretty short.* [*same as* **brief**; *opposite* **long**] **4** **Short** people are below average in height: *She was a short plump woman.* □ *He's shorter than I remember him.* □ *It's such a disadvantage being short.* [*same as* **small**; *opposite* **tall**] **5** A **short** skirt comes down to the knee, or to a point above or below it; boys' shorts are sometimes referred to as **short** trousers. [*opposite* **long**; see also **shorts**] **6** People who have a **short** memory forget things quickly or easily. **7** People who have a **short** temper get angry easily. [see also **short-tempered**] **8** You are **short** with someone when you speak to them or answer them impatiently or rudely: *She was rather short with me at breakfast.* [*same as* **curt**, **abrupt**] **9** (*phonetics*) A sound is **short** if it has the lesser of two recognized lengths, like the *i* in *pill*, as opposed to the *i* in *pile*. [*opposite* **long**] **10** You are **short** of something if you do not have it, or do not have enough of it; something is **short** if there isn't enough of it: *He always seems to be short of money.* □ *Books are something we're certainly not short of in our house.* □ *I can't lend you any cash just now; I'm a bit short myself.* □ *Jo's hurt her ankle, so we're a player short for Saturday's match.* □ *Time is getting short; we've got to hurry.* **11** Something is in **short** supply if there is not enough of it, or not very much: *Properly trained teachers of English are in short supply.*
▻ ***noun*** (*informal*): **shorts**
A **short** is **a** a small measure of a strong alcoholic drink, such as whisky or vodka. **b** (*electricity*) a short circuit.
▻ ***verb*** (*informal*): **shorts**, **shorting**, **shorted**
An electrical system **shorts** when it short-circuits: *The ignition system seems to be shorting.*
▻ ***phrases*** **1** Something **is cut short** when it is interrupted and left unfinished: *News came of her grandmother's death and she had to cut her holiday short.* **2** Something that **falls short** of a certain target or standard does not reach it: *Hygiene in some hospitals falls far short of recognized standards.* [see also **shortfall**] **3** A person or thing is called something **for short** if that is a short form of their name: *We've decided to call her Elizabeth, or Beth for short.* **4** You **go short** of something, especially a necessity such as food, when you do not get it or do not get enough of it: *As children we often went short of food.* □ *I don't want anyone to go short simply because they're too shy to ask for something.* **5** (*slightly formal*) You use '**in short**' when making a statement that sums up the facts you have mentioned: *Our hotel was miles from the centre, it was noisy and the food was awful; in short, I wouldn't recommend it.* **6** If you describe something as **nothing short of** a certain thing you are emphasizing that it is that thing: *Her recovery was nothing short of miraculous.* **7** You **run short** of something when your supply is reduced and you do not have enough of it; a supply of something **runs short** when there is not enough left: *We're running rather short of bread.* □ *Stationery was always running short.* [*same as* **run out**] **8** (*informal, usually humorous*) You describe what someone says as **short and sweet** if it is brief but strongly or rudely worded. **9** A word or name that **is short for** another word, term, phrase, or name is a short form of it: *'Noll' was apparently short for 'Oliver'.* □ *'Won't' is short for 'will not'.* □ *What's AIDS short for?* **10** **a** You are **short of** a figure, amount or place if you have not yet reached it: *We were a couple of miles short of our destination.* □ *She must be only a year or so short of ninety.* □ *We're still short of our target figure.* **b** If you try to achieve something by every means **short of** some extreme act, you try everything you can except that, or without going as far as that: *I've tried every means short of blackmail to persuade her.* □ *Short of breaking down the door I don't see how we're going to get in.* **11** You **stop short** or **are stopped short** when you suddenly stop what you are doing or saying, especially from surprise; something **pulls you up short** or **brings you up short** when it surprises you and interrupts you in what you are thinking, saying or doing: *He was coming along the passage and stopped short when he saw me.* □ *His strange use of the word brought me up short.* □ *I was pulled up short by her horrified expression.* **12** You **stop short of** doing something if you almost, but don't actually, do it: *She stopped just short of calling me a liar.*

shortage /ˈʃɔːtɪdʒ/ *noun*: **shortages**
A **shortage** is a lack or deficiency of something: *There's a shortage of jobs for new graduates.* □ *food shortages.* [*opposite* **abundance**]

shortbread /ˈʃɔːtbred/ *noun* (*uncount*)
Shortbread is a rich sweet crumbly biscuit made with flour, butter and sugar.

shortcake /ˈʃɔːtkeɪk/ *noun* (*uncount*)
1 **Shortcake** is another word for shortbread. **2** **Shortcake** is also a dessert cake consisting of a biscuit base topped with fruit and served with cream: *strawberry shortcake.*

short-change /ʃɔːtˈtʃeɪndʒ/ *verb*: **short-changes**, **short-changing**, **short-changed**
1 You **are short-changed** or someone **short-changes** you when you are buying something when they give you less than the correct amount of change, either by accident or on purpose. **2** (*informal*) You can also say that someone **has short-changed** you if they have cheated you or treated you dishonestly in any way.

short circuit /ʃɔːt ˈsɜːkɪt/ *noun*: **short circuits**
A **short circuit** is a usually accidental connection

made between two incompatible points in an electrical circuit, causing the current to be carried away from its normal path and resulting in the breakdown of the circuit.

short-circuit /ʃɔːt'sɜːkɪt/ *verb*: **short-circuits, short-circuiting, short-circuited**
An electrical appliance or apparatus **short-circuits** when it breaks down because the electrical current is not travelling along its proper path.

shortcoming /'ʃɔːtkʌmɪŋ/ *noun*: **shortcomings**
A **shortcoming** is a fault or weakness that a person or thing has: *We all have our shortcomings.* [*same as* **failing**]

short cut /'ʃɔːt kʌt/ *noun*: **short cuts**
1 A **short cut** is a quicker route between two places: *We took the short cut round the back of the houses.* **2** A **short cut** is also a method that saves time or effort: *I'm afraid it must be done this way; there are no short cuts.*

shorten /'ʃɔːtən/ *verb*: **shortens, shortening, shortened**
You **shorten** something or it **shortens** when you make it or it becomes shorter: *I think you should shorten the sleeves a little.* □ *The days are shortening as autumn approaches.* [*opposite* **lengthen**]

shortening /'ʃɔːtənɪŋ/ *noun* (*uncount*)
In cookery, **shortening** is butter, lard or other fat used for making pastry more crumbly.

shortfall /'ʃɔːtfɔːl/ *noun*: **shortfalls**
1 If there is a **shortfall** in something, there has been a failure to reach a desired or expected level or amount: *There's a shortfall in the grain harvest which will cause prices to rise.* **2** A **shortfall** is the amount or margin by which a desired or expected level has not been reached: *There's a shortfall of £3 million which can't be accounted for.*

shorthand /'ʃɔːthand/ *noun* (*uncount*)
1 **Shorthand** is any of various systems of strokes and dots representing speech sounds and groups of sounds, used as a fast way of recording speech in writing: *We need a secretary who knows shorthand.* □ *He took down all his notes in shorthand.* **2** **Shorthand** is any method of abbreviated writing or any description given in an abbreviated or concise form: *Can you give me a shorthand version of what was said at the meeting?*

short-handed /ʃɔːt'handɪd/ *adjective*
If a business, or any task that requires a number of workers or helpers, is **short-handed**, it is understaffed or does not have enough workers or helpers: *You can help in the kitchen; we're a bit short-handed in there.*

shortlist /'ʃɔːtlɪst/ *noun*; *verb*
▷ ***noun***: **shortlists**
A **shortlist** is a list of the best candidates for a job or post, selected from the total number who have applied or been nominated, from which the successful candidate will be chosen: *Why do so few women get on the shortlist when constituency parties are selecting their parliamentary candidate?* □ *'According to Cocker' was on Dickens's shortlist of possible titles for 'Hard Times'.*
▷ ***verb***: **shortlists, shortlisting, shortlisted**
If an applicant or candidate **is shortlisted** for a job or post, they are placed on a shortlist: *He has been shortlisted for the post of chief executive.*

short-lived /ʃɔːt'lɪvd/ *adjective*
Short-lived things last only for a short time: *Their romance was short-lived.* [*same as* **fleeting**, **brief**; *opposite* **long-lived**]

shortly /'ʃɔːtlɪ/ *adverb*
1 If you say that you will do something **shortly**, or something will happen **shortly**, you mean that you will do it or it will happen soon: *I'll be home shortly.* **2** If something happens **shortly** before or after something else, it happens just before or soon after that other thing: *Shortly after he sat down, he began to feel ill.* **3** If you speak to someone **shortly**, you speak to them in an abrupt and bad-tempered way: *'I don't want any,' he said shortly.* [*same as* **curtly**]

shorts /ʃɔːts/ *noun* (*plural*)
Shorts are trousers with short or very short legs extending from the waist to anywhere between the upper thigh and the knee: *I was wearing a pair of Dad's old army shorts.* [see picture at **clothing**]

short shrift /ʃɔːt 'ʃrɪft/ *noun* (*uncount*)
If someone gives you **short shrift** they dismiss you quickly and rudely without giving you the opportunity to do or say what you want to do or say: *His suggestions were given short shrift.*

short-sighted /ʃɔːt'saɪtɪd/ *adjective*
1 If you are **short-sighted** you can see things clearly only when they are close to you. [*same as* **near-sighted**; *opposite* **long-sighted**] **2** If you say that a person or decision is **short-sighted**, you mean that they do not foresee or anticipate what is likely to happen in the future: *It was a bit short-sighted of you to have invested all your money in an account which requires three month's notice of withdrawal.* [*same as* **hasty**, **imprudent**] — *noun* (*uncount*) **short-sightedness:** *His short-sightedness resulted in a financial crisis.*

short-tempered /ʃɔːt'tɛmpəd/ *adjective*
If a person is **short-tempered**, they are easily made angry or annoyed: *He can be very short-tempered at times.*

short-term /ʃɔːt'tɜːm/ *adjective*
1 **Short-term** plans are concerned only with the near future. **2** **Short-term** also means only for a short time: *He's only here short-term.* [*opposite* **long-term**]

short wave /ʃɔːt'weɪv/ *noun* (*uncount*)
Short wave is a radio frequency with a wavelength of between 10 and 100 metres. [compare **long wave**, **medium wave**]

shot /ʃɒt/ *verb*; *noun*
▷ ***verb***
Shot is the past tense and past participle of **shoot**.
▷ ***noun***: **shots**
1 A **shot** is an act of firing a gun or the sound a gun makes when it is fired: *He took a shot at the deer.* □ *They heard shots coming from the house.* **2** (*uncount*) **Shot** is small metal pellets fired in clusters from a shotgun: *lead shot.* **3** If someone is a good **shot** or a crack **shot**, they can fire a gun accurately so that they always, or nearly always, hit the target. **4** In sport and games, a **shot** is a stroke played, as in golf, or a kick or strike aimed at the goal or another player, as in football or hockey: *What a shot!* **5** A **shot** is a photograph: *That's a good shot of the children on the beach.* **6** A **shot** is also a single piece of filmed action recorded without a break by a single camera: *We see her in close-up in the next shot.* **7** (*used in the singular*) **a** The **shot** is the heavy metal ball, originally a cannonball, which is thrown in the athletics event of putting the shot: *The shot crashed into the side of the cage.* **b** The **shot** is also this event: *Today, the shot and the discus competitions will be decided.* [see also **shot put**] **8** (*informal*) A **shot** is an attempt made: *You'll never learn to do it if you don't have a shot at it.* **9** (*informal*) A **shot** is also a turn or go, *eg* in a game: *Hey, it's my shot now.* □ *Can I have a shot on your bike?* **10** (*informal*) If you are given a **shot** you are given an injection: *You'll have to have a tetanus shot.* **11** (*especially AmE*;

informal) A **shot** of an alcoholic spirit is a drink of it: *Give me a shot of bourbon.* **12** (*old*) Formerly, especially in the nineteen sixties and seventies, the launch by rocket of a spacecraft was referred to as a **shot**: *There were several successful moon shots.*

▻ ***phrases*** **1** (*informal*) If a particular individual **calls the shots**, they are the person who gives the orders or is in charge: *His wife is in charge of the day-to-day running of the business, but he calls the shots.* **2** If you do something **like a shot** you do it extremely quickly without hesitating: *If I was offered a job abroad, I'd take it like a shot.* **3** If something that is failing or faltering is given **a shot in the arm**, it is given something which has the effect of reviving or boosting its performance: *The new development was a real shot in the arm for the local economy.* **4** A **shot in the dark** is a wild guess which may or may not prove to be right.

shotgun /ˈʃɒtgʌn/ *noun*: **shotguns**

A **shotgun** is a gun with a long wide smooth barrel for firing clusters of pellets packed into cylindrical cartridges: *a double-barrelled shotgun.* [=one with two barrels that are loaded separately and can be fired independently]

shot put /ˈʃɒt pʌt/ *noun* (*used in the singular*)

The **shot put** is an athletics event in which contestants throw a heavy metal ball as far as possible.

Note that the action of throwing the metal ball is **putting the shot**.

shot-putter /ʃɒtˈpʌtə(r)/ *noun*: **shot-putters**

A **shot-putter** is an athlete who puts the shot.

should /ʃʊd/ *modal verb*

(negative forms **should not** or **shouldn't**)

Should is used with the infinitive of other verbs **1** as the past tense of **shall a** in reported speech: *He suggested that we should all go to the pub.* □ *I wondered whether or not I should buy it.* **b** instead of **would** in expressing purpose after *so that* and *in order that*: *She took them away for the weekend so that they should feel fresh for Monday's exam.*

2 You say someone **should** do something if **a** it is the right thing to do: *I don't want to give it back, but I suppose I should.* □ *Irresponsible people like that should be punished.* □ *You should be grateful to him.* □ *They really shouldn't leave that child all alone in the house, should they?* [*same as* **ought** to] **b** it is correct, or consistent with the rules: *Shouldn't there be an apostrophe in 'its'?* [*same as* **ought** to] **c** it is sensible, or a good idea, to do it; you use **should** when asking for advice or instructions: *You should get that cut on your head seen to.* □ *Shouldn't we buy one while they're going cheap?* □ *It's an opportunity you shouldn't miss.* □ *You should prepare yourself for the worst.* □ *Perhaps we should ask an expert.* □ *Should I telephone the police?* [*same as* **ought** to] **d** it is an enjoyable thing to do: *You should try the new Chinese restaurant.* [*same as* **ought** to] **e** you are giving instructions: *Bright colours should be washed separately.* □ *The form should be signed and dated.* □ *Your application should reach us no later than 20 January.*

3 You say that something **should** be so, or **should** happen **a** if you think it is probably so, or you expect it to happen: *They should be in Bristol by now.* □ *The bank should have copies of the leaflet.* □ *She should make an excellent head teacher.* □ *You shouldn't have any difficulty getting seats.* [*same as* **ought** to] **b** if there is no reason for it not to be so or happen, according to the available facts: *According to the map we should be near Crieff.* [*same as* **ought** to]

4 You use **should** in the *if*-clause of a conditional sentence that refers to a future possibility, and also after *in case*: *If I should die, think only this of me.* □ *Should you need help, do get in touch with me.* □ *I'll leave the answerphone on in case Evelyn should ring.*

5 You can use **should** after *I* and *we* instead of **would a** in the main clause of a conditional sentence, or a sentence implying a condition: *I should never be able to live with myself if I failed again.* □ *I shouldn't be satisfied myself with a vague arrangement like that.* **b** to express wishes and preferences and to accept invitations: *First of all I should like to thank the organizers.* □ *I should be so grateful if you could book the tickets.* □ *We should much prefer to stay with you.* □ *'Would you care to join us?' 'We should love to.'* **c** to make suggestions, give advice and express opinions: *I should book early if I were you.* □ *In your place I should make an official complaint.* □ *I should imagine Jack will make a little speech.* □ *I shouldn't think there'll be any difficulty.* □ *I should say there were about 70 people there.* □ *'He's very sorry about the mistake.' 'I should hope so.'* [= so he ought to be] □ *'Are they likely to refuse?' 'I should hope not.'* **d** in questions expressing an annoyed or surprised response, *eg* after *how* or *why*: *'Where's Catherine?' 'How should I know?'* □ *Why should anyone want to hurt you?*

6 You also use **should a** to express your attitude to circumstances such as people's reactions: *It's sad that he should feel so bitter.* □ *I wasn't surprised that she should disapprove so strongly.* **b** (*as an alternative to the subjunctive*) in reporting or expressing suggestions, requests and requirements: *His family requested that his invention should be* (or *that his invention be*) *named after him.* □ *It's important that she should keep* (or *that she keep*, or *that she keeps*) *right away from politics for a while.* □ *I suggest that you should read* (or *that you read*) *chapters 4 and 5.*

7 You use '**should** have' when you are referring to the past, *eg* **a** you say someone '**should** have' done something, if it would have been the right, correct or sensible thing to do, or if it would have been enjoyable: *I know I should have apologized.* □ *The titles should have been printed in italics.* □ *He should have gone to the doctor earlier.* □ *You should have seen her expression when he walked in!* [*same as* **ought** to have] **b** you say something '**should** have' happened if you think it has probably happened, or that there is no reason for it not to have happened: *They should have received news by now.* □ *The process should only have taken a couple of minutes and it still hasn't finished.* [*same as* **ought** to have] **c** you can use '**should** have' with *I* and *we* instead of '**would** have' (i) in a conditional sentence or a sentence implying a condition, (ii) in expressing wishes and preferences, and (iii) to express an opinion in an unemphatic way without particular reference to the past: *I should have accepted if I'd been asked.* □ *I should have jumped at the chance myself.* □ *We should have preferred to have had a choice.* □ *I should have thought he'd be satisfied with that.* □ *I shouldn't have said that you could do the journey in under two hours.* **d** you say it's *eg* surprising or sad that something '**should** have' happened if you think it's surprising or sad that it did: *I'm amazed that we should both have had exactly the same idea.* □ *It's most unfortunate that she should have died while he was abroad.*

shoulder /ˈʃoʊldə(r)/ *noun*; *verb*

▻ ***noun***: **shoulders**

1 Your **shoulders** are the parts of your body on either side of your head between your neck and the tops of your arms, or the upper part of your body that stretches across your back from the top of one arm to the other: *She dislocated her left shoulder.* □ *He has broad shoulders.* [see picture at **body**] **2** The **shoulders** of a jacket, dress or other garment are the parts that cover your shoulders: *a jacket with padded shoulders.* **3** A **shoulder** of meat is a cut of meat consisting of an animal's upper foreleg: *a shoulder of lamb.* **4** (*uncount*) The slightly sloping narrow strip at either side of a motorway that vehicles do not normally travel on but may use in an emergency is known as the **shoulder** or the **hard shoulder**. **5** A **shoulder** is anything that has the shape or appearance of a person's shoulder, such as a rounded part of a hill or mountain below the summit.

▻ ***verb*: shoulders, shouldering, shouldered**

1 You **shoulder** a duty or responsibility when you accept it or bear it. **2** You **shoulder** someone or something when you push them using your shoulder or shoulders: *His bodyguard shouldered the journalists aside.*

▻ ***phrases*** **1** (*informal*) If you speak **straight from the shoulder**, you speak frankly and forcefully. **2** You **put your shoulder to the wheel** when you begin to make a great effort or work hard. **3** (*informal*) You **rub shoulders with** other types of people when you meet or associate with them: *In his job he rubs shoulders with the rich and famous.* **4** A soldier **shoulders arms** when he brings his rifle or other weapon to a vertical position tight in to his right side with the barrel against his shoulder. **5** If someone provides you with **a shoulder to cry on**, they are someone that you are able to tell your troubles to. **6** If people do something **shoulder to shoulder**, they do it side by side, or in friendship and agreement.

shoulder bag /ˈʃoʊldə bag/ *noun*: **shoulder bags**
A **shoulder bag** is a bag supported on a person's shoulder by a long strap worn over the shoulder.

shoulder blade /ˈʃoʊldə bleɪd/ *noun*: **shoulder blades**
Your **shoulder blades** are the broad flat triangular bones on your back behind either shoulder.

shoulder strap /ˈʃoʊldə strap/ *noun*: **shoulder straps**
A **shoulder strap** is a strap worn over the shoulder to support a garment or bag: *a dress with thin shoulder straps.*

shouldn't /ˈʃʊdənt/
Shouldn't is the spoken, and informal written, form of **should not**: *I shouldn't have done it.* □ *'Should that dog be on the sofa?' 'No, it shouldn't.'*

should've /ˈʃʊdəv/
Should've is the spoken, and informal written, form of **should have**: *You should've seen him!*

shout /ʃaʊt/ *noun*; *verb*

▻ ***noun*: shouts**

A **shout** is a loud cry or call: *the shouts of the protestors* □ *He gave a warning shout.*

▻ ***verb*: shouts, shouting, shouted**

You **shout** when you say words in a very loud voice: *'Can you hear me now?' he shouted.* □ *There's no need to shout; I'm not deaf.* □ *He listened to his parents shouting angrily at each other.*

> ***phrasal verbs***
> **shout down** If you are trying to speak and someone **shouts** you **down**, they shout continuously so that it is impossible for you to be heard.
> **shout out** You **shout** something **out** when you say it loudly so that it will be heard: *The audience shouted out the answers to the contestants.*

shove /ʃʌv/ *verb*; *noun*

▻ ***verb*: shoves, shoving, shoved**

1 You **shove** something when you push it or thrust it roughly and forcefully: *He shoved past me.* □ *He shoved the paper into my face, jeering loudly as he did so.* **2** (*informal*) If you **shove** something somewhere you put it there roughly or carelessly: *Shove your jacket into my bag.* □ *He just shoved everything into a bag without folding anything.*

▻ ***noun*: shoves**

A **shove** is a forceful push: *He gave me a shove in the ribs.*

> ***phrasal verb***
> **shove off** **1** When you are in a boat and you **shove off**, you start it moving by pushing against the shore or a jetty. **2** (*informal*) When you tell someone to **shove off**, you are telling them rudely to go away.

shovel /ˈʃʌvəl/ *noun*; *verb*

▻ ***noun*: shovels**

1 A **shovel** is a tool with a deep-sided spade-like blade and a handle, for lifting and carrying loose material. **2** A **shovel** is also a machine or part of a machine with a scooping action.

▻ ***verb*: shovels, shovelling (*AmE* shoveling), shovelled (*AmE* shoveled)**

1 You **shovel** something when you lift or carry it with a shovel or with a scooping action as you would with a shovel: *He shovelled the earth into the hole.* **2** If you **shovel** food into your mouth, you put it there quickly and in large quantities.

show /ʃoʊ/ *verb*; *noun*

▻ ***verb*: shows, showing, showed, shown**

1 a You **show** someone something when you let them see it, or point it out to them: *They showed us their holiday photographs.* □ *She insisted on showing me her scar.* □ *I showed him where his great-grandfather was buried.* **b** You **show** someone how to do something when you instruct them how to do it: *Could you show me how to start the washing machine?* □ *I've been shown before how to merge files but I've forgotten.* [compare **instruct**, **demonstrate**] **c** You **show** something when you prove it or make it clear: *This was an unintentional error rather than a deliberate lie, as I hope to show.* □ *Experiments had shown that identical twins shared the same personality to a large extent.* □ *The X-ray showed a fracture of the pelvis.* □ *Incidents like this show you just how careful you have to be.* [compare **prove**, **demonstrate**, **reveal**] **d** You **show** something when you explain it or give information about it: *Table 2 shows how many women died in childbirth between 1930 and 1950, and Table 3 shows the statistics for 1950 to 1970.* **e** A picture or photograph **shows** something if that is what can be seen in it: *The National Gallery painting shows an elderly woman stirring eggs.* □ *The photo showed him as a young man of 20 with a cigarette in his mouth.* [*same as* **depict**, **portray**] **f** Something **shows** a certain result or trend if it indicates it or makes it clear; something **shows** *eg* an improvement, increase or decline if it can be seen to have improved, increased or declined: *Latest government statistics show a worrying increase in armed robberies.* □ *A-level results show a marked improvement over last year's.* □ *Figures for women dying in childbirth show a decline after 1950.* □ *His condition is showing signs of improvement at last.* **g** You **show** someone to a room or a seat when you take them there: *The porter will show you to your room.* [*same as* **take**, **lead**, **guide**, **escort**] **h** To **show** a film, video or transparencies is to project them for people to see; a film that **is showing** at a certain cinema is part of the current programme at that cinema: *I see they're showing 'No Limit' yet again.* ▫ *'Pulp Fiction' is currently showing at the Film House.* **i** Someone who **shows** animals, produce or plants enters them for competitions, in which they are judged on appearance and other qualities. [*same as* **exhibit**]

2 a Something **shows**, or you **show** it, if it is visible or noticeable: *In a few months the scars will hardly show.* ▫ *Your underskirt is showing.* ▫ *The horse was showing the whites of its eyes somewhat alarmingly.* **b** A fabric or garment that doesn't **show** the dirt looks clean even when it is dirty. **c** You **show** an emotion, quality or characteristic, or it **shows**, if it is apparent to other people: *He felt horribly nervous and hoped it didn't show.* ▫ *She showed no distress at his death.* ▫ *I was determined not to show how disappointed I was.* ▫ *Some children show a tendency to lie their way out of difficulties.* [compare **betray**] **d** You **show** a feeling or attitude when you openly express it or indicate it in your behaviour: *She rarely showed her children any affection.* ▫ *They were at last showing an interest in reaching a compromise.* ▫ *You might show some gratitude after all I did for you.* **e** Something such as a piece of work or an action **shows** a quality if it indicates that quality in the person who did it: *Your work shows promise.* ▫ *To take charge of the situation like that shows a certain degree of initiative.* [*same as* **indicate**] **f** You **show** yourself when you position yourself where people can see you, *eg* after you have been hiding: *Stand up and show yourself.* [*same as* **reveal**]

▻ ***noun***: **shows**

1 A **show** is an entertainment in the theatre or on radio or television, including *eg* comic acts, singing and dancing: *watching the Lenny Henry show.* **2** A **show** is also an event at which such things as garden and farm produce, livestock and pets are judged, and prizes awarded for the best of them: *the Annual Rose Show* ▫ *an agricultural show* ▫ *a motor show* ▫ *He won a first prize at the dog show.* **3** A **show** of something is either a sign or indication of it, or a public and deliberate demonstration of it: *She listened to the judge's sentence with no outward show of emotion.* ▫ *The two leaders embraced each other in front of the cameras in a show of friendship.* ▫ *His military manoeuvres near the border were evidently intended more as a show of strength than as a serious threat.* **4** (*uncount*) **Show** is behaviour intended to impress people: *That noisy talking he goes in for on his mobile phone: it's all show.* **5** (*informal*, *derogatory*) You can refer to any organization or operation as a **show**: *Who runs this show?*

▻ ***phrases*** **1** You do something **for show** if you do it just to impress people, or to make the right impression: *The owner had installed a chapel, mainly for show.* **2** If you say in reference to some circumstance '**it just goes to show**' that something is so, you mean that the circumstance proves it: *It just goes to show that you can't trust anyone these days.* **3** Something that is **on show** is placed where the public can look at it: *The new models will be on show from 1 August.* **4** You **have** something **to show for** your efforts or expenditure if you have achieved something useful and visible by them: *He has no qualifications to show for all his years at school.*

phrasal verbs

show off 1 You **show off** when you deliberately behave in a way that draws people's attention to your talents, abilities or anything else about yourself that you are pleased with: *She chose to play a rather difficult piece, largely to show off.* [see also **show-off**] **2** You **show** something **off** when you let other people see it, so that they can admire it: *I was longing to show off my new skiing outfit.* **3** One thing **shows off** another if it emphasizes it or makes it more striking: *You've got a great figure; you should wear clothes that show it off better.*

show up 1 Something **shows up** or **is shown up** when it is clearly visible or obvious: *Her dark-clad figure showed up clearly against the snow.* ▫ *The sun was shining on the window, showing up the children's fingermarks.* ▫ *It took a single searching question to show up the flaw in their argument.* **2** You **are shown up** by someone you are with **a** when they behave so badly that you are ashamed to be associated with them. **b** when they do something much better than you, and make you look stupid. **3** (*informal*; *often with a negative*) Someone **shows up** when they arrive somewhere as arranged: *I arranged to meet him at six, but he didn't show up.* [*same as* **turn up**]

showbiz /ˈʃoʊbɪz/ *noun* (*uncount*, *often adjectival*; *informal*)
Showbiz is show business: *a showbiz magazine.*

show business /ˈʃoʊ bɪznɪs/ *noun* (*uncount*)
Show business is the entertainment industry: *He's in show business.*

showcase /ˈʃoʊkeɪs/ *noun*: **showcases**
1 A **showcase** is a glass case for displaying objects, *eg* in a museum or shop. **2** You can refer to any setting in which a person or thing is displayed to good advantage as a **showcase** for that person or thing: *The fair is a showcase for local arts and crafts.*

showdown /ˈʃoʊdaʊn/ *noun* (*informal*): **showdowns**
A **showdown** is a fight or other contest intended to, or likely to, settle a long-running dispute or quarrel: *The two sides seem to be heading for a showdown.*

shower /ˈʃaʊə(r)/ *noun*; *verb*
▻ ***noun***: **showers**
1 A **shower** of rain, hail or snow is a sudden brief fall of it; a **shower** is any sudden heavy burst or fall of something: *April showers* ▫ *There will be sunshine and showers in the afternoon.* ▫ *A shower of missiles fell on the policemen's heads.* ▫ *a meteor shower.* **2** A **shower** is a device that produces a stream of water for bathing under, usually while standing: *All the rooms have their own toilet and shower.* [see picture at **bathroom**] **3 Showers** are rooms or cubicles fitted with such a device or devices: *Are there showers at the camp site?* **4** If you have a **shower**, you bathe under such a device: *I'm going for a quick shower.* **5** (*informal*) If you refer to a group of people as a **shower**, you think they are all bad or worthless in the same way: *What a shower you are!*
▻ ***verb***: **showers, showering, showered**
1 You **shower** someone with things or you **are showered** with things when you give or receive many things of the same kind all at the same time: *He showered her with gifts.* ▫ *He was showered with compliments.* **2** You **shower** when you bathe under a shower: *He showered and shaved.* **3** It **showers** when rain, hail or snow falls in showers.

shower curtain /ˈʃaʊə kɜːtən/ *noun*: **shower curtains**
A **shower curtain** is a curtain made of waterproof material that you can pull around you while you are in the shower. [see picture at **bathroom**]

showery /ˈʃaʊərɪ/ *adjective*
The weather is **showery** when rain falls in sudden bursts between periods when it is dry.

showing /ˈʃoʊɪŋ/ *noun*: **showings**
1 A **showing** is an act of exhibiting or displaying: *a showing of his recent paintings.* **2** A **showing** is a screening of a cinema film or a performance of some kind: *When is the next showing?* **3** A **showing** is also a display of behaviour as evidence of a fact or someone's ability: *On this showing, he certainly won't get the job.*

showjumper /ˈʃoʊdʒʌmpə(r)/ *noun*: **showjumpers**
A **showjumper** is a rider or a horse that competes in the sport of showjumping.

showjumping /ˈʃoʊdʒʌmpɪŋ/ *noun* (*uncount*)
Showjumping is a competitive sport in which riders on horseback take turns to jump a variety of obstacles, often trying to complete the course within a given time.

showman /ˈʃoʊmən/ *noun*: **showmen**
1 A **showman** is a person who owns or manages some form of public entertainment such as a circus or a stall at a fairground. **2** A **showman** is a person skilled in displaying things, often his or her own abilities, so as to attract maximum attention: *He's a bit of a showman.* — *noun* (*uncount*) **showmanship:** *He's renowned for his showmanship.*

shown /ʃoʊn/ *verb*
Shown is the past participle of **show**.

show-off /ˈʃoʊɒf/ *noun* (*informal*, *usually derogatory*): **show-offs**
A **show-off** is someone who behaves in such a way as to deliberately attract attention or admiration: *What a show-off you are!* [see also **show off** at **show**]

showpiece /ˈʃoʊpiːs/ *noun*: **showpieces**
1 A **showpiece** is an item in an exhibition. **2** A **showpiece** is also a thing that is presented or displayed as an excellent example of its type, to be copied or admired: *a showpiece development.*

showroom /ˈʃoʊruːm/ *noun*: **showrooms**
A **showroom** is a room or building where goods for sale are displayed: *a car showroom.*

showy /ˈʃoʊɪ/ *adjective*: **showier**, **showiest**
Showy things attract attention because they are impressively bright or colourful, though they may not be beautiful or tasteful: *ladies in showy hats* □ *He's a showy dresser.* [*same as* **ostentatious**, **gaudy**, **flashy**] — *noun* (*uncount*) **showiness:** *the showiness of their costumes.*

shrank /ʃraŋk/ *verb*
Shrank is the past tense of **shrink**.

shrapnel /ˈʃrapnəl/ *noun* (*uncount*)
Shrapnel is fragments of metal from the casing of an exploding bomb or shell that fly out in all directions: *He was wounded by shrapnel.*

shred /ʃrɛd/ *noun*; *verb*
▻ ***noun***: **shreds**
1 A **shred** of something is a thin strip cut or ripped off the main part: *His shirt was ripped to shreds by screaming fans.* **2** (*often used in negative statements*) A **shred** is also the smallest piece or amount of something: *The police don't have a shred of evidence against him.*
▻ ***verb***: **shreds, shredding, shredded**
You **shred** something when you rip or cut it into shreds: *All the documents had been shredded.*

shrew /ʃruː/ *noun*: **shrews**
A **shrew** is a small mouse-like animal with a long pointed nose.

shrewd /ʃruːd/ *adjective*: **shrewder**, **shrewdest**
1 A **shrewd** person or a **shrewd** decision has or shows good practical judgement, especially of things that will bring them some advantage: *a shrewd businessman.* **2** A **shrewd** guess is one based on practical experience or logical thinking and is therefore likely to be correct: *I don't know exactly what he's up to, but I can make a shrewd guess.* — *adverb* **shrewdly:** *He invested his money shrewdly.* — *noun* (*uncount*) **shrewdness:** *I was impressed by his shrewdness in financial matters.*

shriek /ʃriːk/ *verb*; *noun*
▻ ***verb***: **shrieks, shrieking, shrieked**
If someone **shrieks**, they utter a piercing scream or speak in a loud shrill voice, *eg* because they are very frightened or angry: *Girls shrieked as the rollercoaster careered down the slope.* □ *'Don't let me fall,' she shrieked.* □ *She shrieked abuse at him.*
▻ ***noun***: **shrieks**
A **shriek** is such a scream: *'There's a mouse under the table,' she said with a shriek.*

shrift see **short shrift**.

shrill /ʃrɪl/ *adjective*: **shriller**, **shrillest**
A **shrill** sound or voice is high-pitched and piercing: *the shrill cry of a hawk.* — *adverb* **shrilly:** *birds whistling shrilly.* — *noun* (*uncount*) **shrillness:** *There was a touch of shrillness in her voice.*

shrimp /ʃrɪmp/ *noun*: **shrimps**
1 A **shrimp** is a small edible long-tailed shellfish, smaller than a prawn: *They fished for freshwater shrimps.* **2** (*informal*) A **shrimp** is a small and slightly-built person.

shrine /ʃraɪn/ *noun*: **shrines**
1 A **shrine** is a sacred place where people go to worship, *eg* the tomb of a saint or other holy person, or a monument erected near it: *a Buddist shrine.* **2** A **shrine** is also any place or thing greatly respected because of its associations with a special person or thing: *a shrine to the spirit of free enterprise.*

shrink /ʃrɪŋk/ *verb*: **shrinks, shrinking, shrank, shrunk**
1 Something **shrinks** when it becomes smaller, *eg* because of exposure to heat, cold or moisture: *That sweater will shrink if you put it in the washing machine.* □ *The lake shrank until it was just a series of muddy pools.* **2** If you **shrink** away from something, you move away from it in horror or disgust: *He tried to touch her, but she shrank away.* **3** If you **shrink** from a task or a duty, you are reluctant to do it or carry it out: *She knew she would have to tell him sooner or later, but she shrank from the prospect of causing him distress.*

shrinkage /ˈʃrɪŋkɪdʒ/ *noun* (*uncount*)
Shrinkage is the act or amount of shrinking: *shrinkage of the market* □ *The cloth is cut slightly too big to allow for shrinkage.*

shrivel /ˈʃrɪvəl/ *verb*: **shrivels**, **shrivelling** (*AmE* **shriveling**), **shrivelled** (*AmE* **shriveled**)
Something **shrivels**, or **shrivels** up, when it shrinks and becomes wrinkled *eg* because it has been dried out or has lost its moisture through exposure to hot air: *Plants shrivelled and died in the hot sun.* □ *When he introduced me as his little guardian angel, I shrivelled up with embarrassment.*

shroud /ʃraʊd/ *noun*; *verb*
▻ ***noun***: **shrouds**
1 A **shroud** is a cloth in which a dead body is wrapped. **2** A **shroud** is also anything that has the effect of covering, wrapping or hiding something completely: *shrouds of mist.*
▻ ***verb***: **shrouds, shrouding, shrouded**
If something **is shrouded** in something, it is covered,

wrapped or hidden in it: *The valley was shrouded in fog.* □ *Their goings-on were shrouded in secrecy.*

Shrove Tuesday /ʃrouv 'tju:zdɪ/ *noun*
Shrove Tuesday is the day in the Christian calendar before Ash Wednesday, on which it was customary to confess your sins. [see also **Pancake Day**]

shrub /ʃrʌb/ *noun*: **shrubs**
A **shrub** is a bushy plant with a woody stem or stems: *trees and shrubs* □ *an ornamental shrub.*

shrubbery /'ʃrʌbərɪ/ *noun* (*uncount or count*): **shrubberies**
Shrubbery is shrubs or small trees forming a thick mass or group; a **shubbery** is a place, especially a part of a garden, where shrubs are grown: *They found him lurking in the shrubbery.* □ *I'm going to create a shrubbery in this part of the garden.*

shrubby /'ʃrʌbɪ/ *adjective*: **shrubbier, shrubbiest**
A **shrubby** plant has many thick or woody stems forming a dense mass like a shrub.

shrug /ʃrʌg/ *verb; noun*
▻ ***verb***: **shrugs, shrugging, shrugged**
You **shrug** when you raise your shoulders briefly as a sign of doubt or indifference.
▻ ***noun***: **shrugs**
A **shrug** is an act of shrugging: *'I have no idea where he is,' she said with a shrug.*

phrasal verb
shrug off **1** You **shrug** *eg* an illness **off** when you get rid of it quickly and easily. **2** You **shrug** *eg* criticism **off** when you dismiss it with calm confidence.

shrunk /ʃrʌŋk/ *verb*
Shrunk is the past participle of **shrink**.

shrunken /'ʃrʌŋkən/ *adjective*
Shrunken means having been shrunk: *a shrunken head* □ *Britain's shrunken manufacturing base.*

shudder /'ʃʌdə(r)/ *verb; noun*
▻ ***verb***: **shudders, shuddering, shuddered**
You **shudder** when your body shakes uncontrollably for a brief moment, especially because of fear, cold or disgust: *She shuddered as she brushed the caterpillar off her sleeve.*
▻ ***noun***: **shudders**
1 A **shudder** is such a momentary shaking movement or feeling: *'It was a ghastly sight!' she said with a shudder.* **2** A **shudder** is also a heavy vibration or shaking movement: *The bus came to a halt with a shudder.*
▻ ***phrase*** You say **'I shudder to think'** something, when it makes you alarmed, embarrassed or disgusted to think of it: *'What horrible plot will he come up with next?' 'I shudder to think!'*

shuffle /'ʃʌfəl/ *verb; noun*
▻ ***verb***: **shuffles, shuffling, shuffled**
1 You **shuffle** when you slide your feet backwards and forwards on the ground without lifting them up; you **shuffle** somewhere when you move forwards sliding your feet along the ground: *Stop shuffling your feet and stand still!* □ *The old man came shuffling along the corridor.* **2 a** You **shuffle** things when you mix them up or rearrange them carelessly: *He shuffled the papers on the desk to give himself something to do with his hands.* **b** You **shuffle** playing cards when you mix them up so they are in a random order.
▻ ***noun***: **shuffles**
1 A **shuffle** is an act or a sound of shuffling: *She could hear the shuffle of feet in the hall.* **2** A **shuffle** is also a short quick sliding movement of the feet in dancing.

shun /ʃʌn/ *verb*: **shuns, shunning, shunned**
You **shun** someone or something when you avoid or keep away from it: *She shunned publicity throughout her career in films.* □ *He was shunned by his workmates for working during the strike.*

shunt /ʃʌnt/ *verb*: **shunts, shunting, shunted**
1 A train or railway carriage **is shunted** when it is moved from one track to another: *The goods train was shunted into a siding.* **2** You **shunt** people or things around when you move or send them from place to place, often without any satisfactory result: *I've been shunted around from one department to the other without getting a straight answer to my enquiry.*

shush /ʃʊʃ/ *interjection*
You say **'Shush'** when you want to tell someone to be quiet: *'Shush! There's someone coming!'*

shut /ʃʌt/ *verb; adjective*
▻ ***verb***: **shuts, shutting, shut**
1 You **shut** something when you close it or move it into a position where it covers an opening, or where its opening is covered; it **shuts** when it closes or moves so as to cover an opening: *He shut the door behind him.* □ *Please shut the gate.* □ *Would you mind if I shut the window?* □ *He shut his eyes as he jumped.* □ *She hastily shoved the papers back into the drawer and shut it.* □ *He shut and locked the cupboard.* □ *My case was so full it wouldn't shut.* [*same as* **close**; *opposite* **open**]
2 A shop or place of business **shuts** or **is shut** when it stops being open to the public, or when the staff in it stop working and go home: *What time do the shops shut on Saturdays?* □ *They shut the library early on Wednesdays.* [*same as* **close**; *opposite* **open**]
▻ ***adjective:*** *The window blew shut with a bang.* □ *She lay there with her eyes shut.* □ *He snores horribly even with his mouth shut.* □ *Most of the pubs will be shut today.* [*same as* **closed**; *opposite* **open**]

phrasal verbs
shut away Someone or something **is shut away** somewhere if they are kept hidden or locked up in a place where no-one sees them: *Her family shut her away in an institution for the insane.* □ *Some of their wedding presents were still shut away in a cupboard unused.*
shut down A business firm or industrial concern **shuts down** or **is shut down** when it stops operating, temporarily or permanently: *Another nuclear power station is to be shut down.* [see also **shutdown**]
shut in **1** You **shut** someone or something **in** a place when you close the exit so that they cannot get out; you **shut** yourself **in** a room when you close or lock the door so that no-one can get in; someone or something **is shut in** somewhere if they are enclosed, surrounded or confined there: *We always shut the hens in at night.* □ *He would shut himself in his bedroom and not emerge for hours.* □ *The house feels a bit shut in with all those tall trees round it.* **2** You **shut** something **in** a door if it gets caught in the door when you shut it: *I somehow managed to shut the poor dog's tail in the car door.*
shut off You **shut** machinery **off** when you switch it off; you **shut off** a supply of gas, water or electricity when you stop it flowing. [*same as* **switch off**]
shut out **1** You **shut** someone **out** of somewhere when you close or lock the entrance so that they cannot get in: *We'd been shut out of the factory by the management.* **2** You **shut out** something such as light when you prevent it from getting in or through somewhere: *They pulled the blinds down to shut out the sun.* **3** You **shut out** thoughts when you stop

yourself having them: *She tried to shut out the memory.*
shut up 1 You **shut** someone or something **up** when you lock them into a place, or confine them there: *Criminals like that should be shut up for good.* □ *I spent eight weeks shut up in my room finishing my thesis.* **2** (*informal*) When you tell someone to **shut up** you are telling them rudely to stop speaking or be quiet; someone **shuts up**, or something **shuts** them **up**, when they stop speaking: *Oh, do shut up!* □ *She shut up eventually and I managed to get some sleep.* □ *I turned round and glared at her, which shut her up for a bit.* **3** You **shut up** a house or shop when you lock the doors and close the windows securely: *They had shut up the house and gone abroad.*

shutdown /'ʃʌtdaʊn/ *noun*: **shutdowns**
A **shutdown** is a complete stoppage of work and the operation of machinery in a factory because of a strike, holiday, damage or lack of demand for its products: *a partial shutdown of the nuclear reactor* □ *The strike resulted in the total shutdown of the plant.*

shutter /'ʃʌtə(r)/ *noun*; *verb*
▻ ***noun***: **shutters**
1 A **shutter** is a panel fixed to the outside of a window. It swings on hinges or slides up and down to open or close: *a house with green shutters* □ *The shop front was protected by heavy metal shutters.* **2** The **shutter** in a camera is a device that opens and closes at different speeds, exposing the film to light.
▻ ***verb***: **shutters, shuttering, shuttered** (*usually in the passive*)
If a window **is shuttered**, it is covered with a shutter or shutters.

shuttle /'ʃʌtəl/ *noun*: **shuttles**
1 In weaving, the **shuttle** is the device carrying the horizontal thread (the **weft**) backwards and forwards between the vertical threads (the **warp**). **2** In a sewing machine, the **shuttle** is the device carrying the lower thread through the loop formed by the upper thread. **3** A **shuttle** is an aircraft, train or bus running a frequent service between two places, often two places that are relatively near each other: *'How will you get from Glasgow to London and back again the same day?' 'I'll take the shuttle.'*

shuttlecock /'ʃʌtəlkɒk/ *noun*: **shuttlecocks**
A **shuttlecock** is an object consisting of a cone-shaped piece of cork or plastic with feathers or imitation feathers attached, hit back and forth in the game of badminton.

shy[1] /ʃaɪ/ *adjective*: **shyer** or **shier, shyest** or **shiest**
1 A **shy** person is someone who feels embarrassed and nervous in the company of others, especially strangers: *She was too shy to meet the visitors.* □ *She's the shyest of the three sisters.* **2 Shy** also means easily frightened or timid: *She gave him a shy smile.* **3** If you are **shy** of something, you are wary or distrustful of it or reluctant to do it: *workshy.* — *adverb* **shyly:** *She smiled shyly.*
▻ ***phrase*** If you **fight shy of** something, you avoid it: *He fought shy of making an outright denial.*

shy[2] /ʃaɪ/ *verb*: **shies, shying, shied**
If a horse **shies**, it jumps suddenly sideways and backwards, usually because it has been startled: *Her horse shied when a rabbit ran across the road.*

phrasal verb
If you **shy away from** something, or **shy away from** doing something, you move away from it suddenly or are very reluctant to do it because it makes you feel anxious or afraid: *She shied away from any direct criticism of her boss.*

Siamese cat /saɪəmiːz 'kat/ *noun*: **Siamese cats**
A **Siamese cat** or **Siamese** is a breed of domestic cat with blue eyes and light brown or pale grey fur.

Siamese twins /saɪəmiːz 'twɪnz/ *noun* (*plural*)
Siamese twins are twins joined together at some part of their body at birth.

sibling /'sɪblɪŋ/ *noun* (*formal*): **siblings**
Your **siblings** are your brothers and sisters: *He has no siblings.* □ *sibling rivalry.*

sick /sɪk/ *adjective*; *noun*
▻ ***adjective***: **sicker, sickest**
1 (*especially old or literary or AmE*) Someone who is **sick** is ill or unwell, physically or mentally: *He's in the Hospital for Sick Children.* □ *as he lay sick in bed* □ *Cindy's very sick.* □ *I'm afraid your wife's a pretty sick woman.* [*same as* **ill**] **2** (*BrE*) You are **sick** when you vomit; you feel **sick** when you feel as if you are going to vomit: *I think I'm going to be sick.* □ *He was sick all over the bedclothes.* □ *I've just been sick again.* □ *She was sick several times in the night.* □ *He complained of feeling sick and hurried out of the room.* □ *The mere sight of a boat makes her feel seasick.* □ *The children get carsick if we drive too long without stopping.* □ *Do you get airsick?* [compare **vomit, throw up**] **3** You are on **sick** leave when you are away from work because you are ill. **4** You get **sick** pay if you are paid a certain amount by your employer or the government while you are ill. **5** (*informal*) You say you are **sick** when you are disappointed or disgusted: *I was pretty sick about it at the time.* [*same as* **fed up**] **6** (*informal*) You say you are **sick** of something if it has been annoying you for a long time and you can't bear it any more: *I'm sick of his complaints.* □ *I'm sick of hearing about her kids.* [*same as* **tired, fed up**] **7 Sick** describes jokes or humour that treat such things as illness and disability in a cruel or uncaring way: *He told a sick joke about a man with one leg.*
▻ ***noun***
1 (*with a plural verb*) The **sick** are people who are ill: *The whole point of the welfare state was to care for the old and sick.* **2** (*uncount*) **Sick** is vomit: *The bedclothes smelt of sick.*
▻ ***phrases*** **1** Something that **makes you sick** disgusts you or makes you angry: *The way he treats his wife makes me sick.* **2** (*informal*) You are **worried sick** about something when you are very worried: *Where on earth have you been? I've been worried sick about you.*

sickbay /'sɪkbeɪ/ *noun*: **sickbays**
A **sickbay** is a room where ill or injured people are treated, *eg* in a boarding school, an army camp, a ship or a place of work.

sicken /'sɪkən/ *verb*: **sickens, sickening, sickened**
1 (*old*) If you **sicken**, you become ill: *She sickened and died.* **2** If you say you **are sickening** for an illness, you are showing symptoms of that illness: *I feel terrible; I think I'm sickening for the flu.* **3** Something **sickens** you when it makes you feel sick with disgust: *He was sickened by the violence.*

sickening /'sɪkənɪŋ/ *adjective*
Something is **sickening** when it makes you feel angry, disgusted or envious: *The camp filled with dead and dying people was a sickening sight.* □ *'He's just bought himself a new Ferrari.' 'I know, it's sickening, isn't it?'* — *adverb* **sickeningly:** *The film was sicken-*

ingly violent. □ (*intensifying*) *He's sickeningly handsome.*

sickle /'sɪkəl/ *noun*: **sickles**
A **sickle** is a tool with a short handle and a curved blade used for cutting grass and grain crops.

sick leave /'sɪk liːv/ *noun* (*uncount*)
When you are on **sick leave**, you are taking time off work because of sickness.

sickly /'sɪklɪ/ *adjective*; *adverb*
▻ ***adjective***: **sicklier**, **sickliest**
1 Someone who is **sickly** is often ill or is susceptible to illness: *He was a sickly child.* **2** Something that is **sickly** is unhealthy: *The soil was so poor only a few sickly plants grew.* **3** Something that is **sickly** makes you feel like you want to vomit: *the sickly smell of decaying flesh* □ *a sickly shade of green.* **4** If someone gives you a **sickly** grin, they smile at you in a weak and silly way.
▻ ***adverb***
Sickly means to an extent that suggests illness: *sickly pale children.*

sickness /'sɪknɪs/ *noun*: **sicknesses**
1 A **sickness** is an illness: *a mysterious sickness.* **2** (*uncount*) **Sickness** is vomiting or nausea: *Have you been having any sickness or diarrhoea?*

side /saɪd/ *noun*; *adjective*; *verb*
▻ ***noun***: **sides**
1 The **side** of something is the position to the left or the right of it, as distinct from the position in front of it or behind it: *She was sitting in an armchair with a low table at her side.* □ *He arrived in court with a policeman on either side of him.* □ *I was aware of someone approaching me from the side.* □ *She moved the pile of books to one side.*
2 a The **sides** of an object are any of the flat surfaces that form its shape, or any surfaces other than its top, bottom, front, back or ends: *How many sides does a cube have?* □ *We'd better tip the wardrobe on to its side.* □ *The tin had a price label on the side.* □ *There was a lot of damage to the passenger side of the vehicle.* □ *I must say I like bedclothes that tuck in at the sides.* **b** The **sides** of an area are the edges of it: *He pulled in to the side of the road.* □ *broad walks with trees planted along both sides* □ *on the other side of the Atlantic* □ *She moved across to the opposite side of the room.* □ *The odd numbers go down the righthand side.* □ *A rectangle has four sides.* **c** The two **sides** of an object or area are its two halves: *the lefthand side of the brain.* □ *Do they drive on the right or left side of the road?* **d** The two **sides** of a thin flat object are its two surfaces: *Write on both sides of the paper.* □ *the other side of the coin.* **e** Something that is on one **side** of a dividing line is in one of the two areas that it separates: *on the far side of the wall.*
3 a Your **sides** are the parts of your body between your armpits and your hips: *The pain in her side was getting worse.* □ *He was lying curled up on his side.* □ *Stand straight with your arms by your sides.* **b** The **sides** of a hill are its slopes: *the steep sides of the Matterhorn.* **c** A **side** of a town is an area or district of it: *We live on the north side of the city.* □ *the Lower East Side.* **d** A **side** of something such as a situation, concern, problem or someone's character is a part or aspect of it: *It's a side of the business that had never interested me before.* □ *He took trouble not to reveal his other, less sociable, side to people who mattered.* **e** The two **sides** of your family are your father's and mother's families: *He's descended from Scott on his mother's side.*
4 a The two **sides** in something such as a game, battle, quarrel or other conflict are the two opposing teams, armies or groups: *For once I was on the winning side.* □ *By now both sides were exhausted.* □ *It was impossible to tell which side had won.* **b** The two **sides** in a discussion are the two parties involved: *The treaty was concluded with expressions of satisfaction on both sides.*
▻ ***adjective***
Side describes things that are **1** located or placed at the side: *I noticed a van parked at the side entrance.* □ *The meal was served from a side table.* **2** less important, secondary or subordinate: *We drove down a side road.* □ *Let's concentrate on the main problem and leave the side issues till later.*
▻ ***phrases*** **1** Someone who remains **at**, or **by**, **your side**, remains near you to give you help, support, comfort and advice: *Her place at a time like this is by her husband's side.* **2** You **err on the side of** some kind of behaviour, such as caution or generosity, when you are over-cautious, or over-generous. **3** Something moves **from side to side** when it moves from left to right and back again repeatedly: *The pendulum of a clock swings from side to side.* **4** You try to **keep on the right side** of someone by doing whatever pleases them, and avoiding annoying them; you **get on the wrong side of** someone when you do something that makes them displeased with you. **5** You **let the side down** when you fall below the standards set by the other members of the group to which you belong, and so endanger its chances of success, or its reputation. **6** Something that is **on all sides**, or **on every side**, of you, surrounds you: *Sheer precipices rose on every side.* **7** You put something **on**, or **to**, **one side** when you leave it to be dealt with separately, or at a later time: *We tend to push important issues to one side and give the trivial ones priority.* **8** Someone who does a job or makes money **on the side** has a job or a source of income, especially one that is slightly illegal, in addition to their main one. **9** (*informal*) Something that is *eg* **on the large side** or **on the narrow side** is slightly too large or narrow: *The meat was on the raw side, so the waiter took it back to the kitchen.* **10 a** Someone who is **on your side** supports you against your opponents: *Whose side are you on?* **b** You have something **on your side** if it gives you an advantage: *She has height on her side.* □ *We had luck on our side.* **11 a** People or things are **side by side** when they are next to each other: *We walked along side by side.* □ *The bodies were laid side by side.* [compare **abreast**, **alongside**, **beside**] **b** People do something **side by side** when they do it together, or when they co-operate: *These were people they'd lived happily side by side with for decades.* **12** You **take sides** or **take** someone's **side** when you support one person or group against another in a conflict or argument: *His mother always took his side.* □ *I refuse to take sides.* **13** You do something **to be on the safe side** if you do it as a precaution: *We'd better book early, to be on the safe side.*
▻ ***verb***: **sides**, **siding**, **sided**

phrasal verb
You **side with** one person against another when you support the one against the other in a quarrel or argument: *I could always count on my brother to side with me against my sister.* □ *Italy immediately sided with Germany.*

sideboard /'saɪdbɔːd/ *noun*: **sideboards**
1 A **sideboard** is a large piece of furniture consisting of shelves or cabinets mounted above drawers or cupboards. [see picture at **living room**] **2 Sideboards** are sideburns.

sideburn /ˈsaɪdbɜːn/ *noun* (*usually in the plural*): **sideburns**
Sideburns are the lines of short hair growing down in front of each of a man's ears: *Long sideburns were fashionable in the 1970s.*

-sided /ˈsaɪdɪd/ *adjective*
You use **-sided** to describe something in terms of the number or kind of sides it has: *A pentagon is a five-sided figure.* □ *A lantern is a glass-sided holder for a light.*

side-effect /ˈsaɪdɪfɛkt/ *noun*: **side-effects**
A **side-effect** is an additional and usually undesirable effect, especially of a drug: *The drug can have serious side-effects.*

sidekick /ˈsaɪdkɪk/ *noun* (*informal*): **sidekicks**
Your **sidekick** is your close friend, partner or deputy: *I wasn't able to speak to the leader of the rebels directly, but I spoke to one of his sidekicks.*

sidelight /ˈsaɪdlaɪt/ *noun*: **sidelights**
A vehicle's **sidelights** are the small lights fitted on each outside edge of the front and rear of the vehicle, often part of a unit containing the headlights and indicator lights. Sidelights are used in fading daylight so that the vehicle can be seen.

sideline /ˈsaɪdlaɪn/ *noun*: **sidelines**
1 The **sidelines** are the lines marking either side or the boundaries at the side of a sports pitch, or the area just outside these boundaries: *He was sent off and had to watch the rest of the match from the sidelines.* **2** A **sideline** is a business or other work carried out in addition to your regular work: *He's really a teacher; repairing people's clocks and watches is just a sideline.*

sidelong /ˈsaɪdlɒŋ/ *adjective*; *adverb*
▷ ***adjective***
Sidelong means from or to the side, not direct or directly: *She gave him a sidelong glance.*
▷ ***adverb:*** *She looked sidelong at him.*

side-saddle /ˈsaɪdsadəl/ *noun*; *adverb*
▷ ***noun***: **side-saddles**
A **side-saddle** is a saddle for a horse specially constructed so that a woman in a skirt can sit with both legs on the same side of the horse's body.
▷ ***adverb***
A woman rides **side-saddle** when she rides a horse sitting in this way.

sideshow /ˈsaɪdʃoʊ/ *noun*: **sideshows**
1 Sideshows are stalls with some form of amusement or game at a fair or beside the main part of a circus. **2** If you say that something is a **sideshow**, you mean that it is not part of the main event or activity: *The unrest in the north of the country is only a sideshow compared to what is happening in the capital city.*

side-step /ˈsaɪdstɛp/ *verb*; *noun*
▷ ***verb***: **side-steps, side-stepping, side-stepped**
You **side-step** something when you avoid it by stepping to one side or by not meeting it directly: *Don't try to side-step the issue.*
▷ ***noun***: **side-steps**
A **side-step** is a step taken to one side.

sidetrack /ˈsaɪdtrak/ *verb*: **sidetracks, sidetracking, sidetracked**
If something **sidetracks** you, or you **are sidetracked** by it, it takes your attention away from what you are doing at the time: *I'm sorry I didn't return your call as promised; I got sidetracked by a problem with the computer system.*

sidewalk /ˈsaɪdwɔːk/ *noun* (*AmE*): **sidewalks**
A **sidewalk** is a pavement. [see pictures at **house** and **street**]

sideways /ˈsaɪdweɪz/ *adverb*; *adjective*
▷ ***adverb***
1 If something goes **sideways** it moves from, to, or towards one side: *He stepped sideways to avoid the hole in the road.* □ *He wasn't promoted; he was just moved sideways.* [=given a post or job of the same rank as the one he held before] **2** If something faces **sideways**, it has one of its sides facing the front or the top: *Turn the wardrobe sideways and it may go in the door.*
▷ ***adjective:*** *He gave her a sideways look.*

siding /ˈsaɪdɪŋ/ *noun*: **sidings**
A **siding** is a short railway line on to which trains, carriages or wagons can be moved temporarily from the main line.

sidle /ˈsaɪdəl/ *verb*: **sidles, sidling, sidled**
You **sidle** somewhere when you go or move there slowly and cautiously, especially when you do not want to attract too much attention: *He sidled up to me and asked me if I wanted to buy a watch.*

siege /siːdʒ/ *noun*: **sieges**
1 A **siege** is the situation when an army surrounds a town or fort and prevents anyone from entering or leaving it, in an attempt to force its surrender: *the siege of Leningrad.* **2** A **siege** is also a police operation using similar tactics used to force a criminal out of a building.
▷ ***phrases*** **1** If an army **has laid siege to** a town, it has begun a siege of that town: *The English troops laid seige to Edinburgh Castle.* **2** If a place is **under seige**, it is surrounded so that no-one can enter or leave.

siesta /sɪˈɛstə/ *noun*: **siestas**
A **siesta** is a short sleep or rest taken in hot countries after the midday meal or in the afternoon.

sieve /sɪv/ *noun*; *verb*
▷ ***noun***: **sieves**
A **sieve** is a utensil with a meshed or perforated bottom, used to separate solids from liquids or large particles from smaller ones. [see picture at **kitchen**]
▷ ***verb***: **sieves, sieving, sieved**
You **sieve** something when you strain or separate it with a sieve: *Sieve the fruit to remove the pips.*
▷ ***phrase*** (*informal*) If you say you **have a head** or **a memory like a sieve**, you mean you are very forgetful.

sift /sɪft/ *verb*: **sifts, sifting, sifted**
1 You **sift** something when you pass it through a sieve so as to separate out lumps or larger particles: *Sift the flour into a bowl.* **2** You **sift** things or **sift** through things when you separate them out or examine them carefully so as to find the things that you want or need: *We will have to sift out all the irrelevant data.* □ *I had to sift through hundreds of pieces of information before I found what I needed.*

sigh /saɪ/ *verb*; *noun*
▷ ***verb***: **sighs, sighing, sighed**
1 You **sigh** when you release a long deep breath, especially as a sign of sadness, longing or relief: *He sighed as he thought of his family far away.* **2** You **sigh** something when you express it by making such a sound: *He sighed his relief.*
▷ ***noun***: **sighs**
A **sigh** is an act or the sound of sighing: *a sigh of relief* □ *She gave a deep sigh.*

sight /saɪt/ *noun*; *verb*
▷ ***noun***: **sights**
1 (*uncount*) **Sight** is the power of seeing or the ability

to see: *His sight is very poor.* □ *She lost her sight in an accident at work.* [*same as* **vision**] **2** (*uncount*) If something is in a place or position where you can see it, it is within your **sight**: *Go away! Get out of my sight!* □ *He disappeared out of sight down a deep hole.* **3** A **sight** is something that is or can be seen: *They lined the deck craning their necks for a last sight of their home town.* □ *What a magnificent sight!* **4** (*usually in the plural*) The **sights** in a place are the things that are particularly interesting to look at: *He took us on a tour of the sights.* **5 Sights** or a **sight** is a device on a weapon through or along which you look to take aim: *a rifle with a telescopic sight.* □ *He had the tiger in his sights but it moved before he could fire.* **6** (*informal*) If you say that someone or something is a **sight**, you mean that they are very untidy or they have a peculiar appearance, especially one that makes you laugh: *He has had his head shaved and wears a ring in his nose. What a sight he is!* **7** (*used in the singular*; *informal*) If someone says that something is a **sight** better or a **sight** more than something else they go on to mention, they are emphasizing that the first thing is a lot better or more than the second thing: *It's a darn sight more expensive to travel by train than by bus.*

▻ ***verb***: **sights, sighting, sighted**

1 You **sight** something, or something **is sighted**, when it is seen or you get a look at or glimpse of it: *After weeks at sea, at last they sighted land.* □ *The mysterious animal has been sighted on open ground on one or two occasions.* **2** You **sight** a weapon when you adjust the sight so that you can take accurate aim, or you take aim using the **sight**.

▻ ***phrases*** **1** If something appears in a particular way **at first sight**, that is the way it appears to begin with before it has been studied or looked at more closely. **2** (*informal*) A **sight for sore eyes** is a very welcome sight: *What a sight for sore eyes you are! We thought you were gone forever.* **3** If soldiers or policemen are ordered to shoot someone or something **at** or **on sight**, they shoot at them as soon as they see them. **4** You **catch sight of** something when you begin to see it or you get a brief view of it: *tourists hoping to catch sight of the Loch Ness monster.* **5** If you say that something **is in sight**, you mean that that it will come or happen soon: *There seemed to be no end in sight.* **6** If you are **in sight of** something, you are near enough to it to be able to see it: *The ship sank when they were in sight of land.* **7** If you **know** somebody **by sight**, you are able to recognize them but do not know them personally. **8** You **lose sight of** someone or something when you can no longer see them; you **lose sight of** some aim or target when you are diverted from it. **9** If you say that something is **out of sight, out of mind**, you mean that because you do not see it, you do not think about it.

10 If you **set your sights on** something, you decide that you will try to achieve it.

sighted /ˈsaɪtɪd/ *adjective*

Sighted people have the power of sight, that is they are not blind. [see also **long-sighted, near-sighted, short-sighted**]

sighting /ˈsaɪtɪŋ/ *noun*: **sightings**

A **sighting** is an occasion when something is seen, especially when it is something that is rarely seen or tries to avoid being seen: *There have been several reported sightings of the man police want to interview.*

sightless /ˈsaɪtlɪs/ *adjective*

A **sightless** person or animal is blind: *a sightless lizard.*

sight-read /ˈsaɪtriːd/ *verb*: **sight-reads, sight-reading, sight-read** /ˈsaɪtrɛd/

You can **sight-read** music when you can read or play music from a printed sheet that you have never seen or played before.

sightseeing /ˈsaɪtsiːɪŋ/ *noun* (*uncount*)

You go **sightseeing** when you visit places of interest: *I think we'll do some sightseeing today.*

sightseer /ˈsaɪtsiːə(r)/ *noun*: **sightseers**

A **sightseer** is a person who visits places of interest.

sign /saɪn/ *noun*; *verb*

▻ ***noun***: **signs**

1 A **sign** is a mark or symbol with a certain meaning: *a minus sign* □ *a multiplication sign* □ *the equals sign* □ *the signs of the zodiac.* **2** A **sign** is a board or panel with words, symbols or pictures on it, giving information or directions: *the illuminated exit signs* □ *neon signs* □ *shop signs* □ *Follow the signs for the A38.* □ *Didn't you see the 'No Smoking' sign?* □ *The sign on the door said very firmly 'No Entry'.* **3** You make **signs** when you try to communicate information to someone by means of movements or gestures with your hands, arms or head: *She made a sign to me to stay out of sight.* □ *He gave a thumbs-up sign to tell me it was OK.* [*same as* **signal**] **4** There is a **sign** of something when some circumstance associated with it is present and shows that it exists or is happening: *At last we see signs of improvement in the nation's economy.* □ *the first signs of spring* □ *The room bore signs of recent occupation.* □ *That particular tone of voice was a sure sign that he was pleased.* □ *She showed no signs of leaving and I wondered if she was going to stay all evening.* □ *He betrayed no sign of having heard me.* **5** There is no **sign** of someone or something if they have not arrived, or if they have disappeared and you cannot find them: *There's still no sign of Audrey.* □ *I seem to have lost that letter; there's no sign of it anywhere.*

▻ ***verb***: **signs, signing, signed**

1 You **sign** a document when you write your signature on it, often as an official indication of agreement: *Sign your name on your new card as soon as you receive it.* □ *Her secretary handed her a pile of letters to sign.* □ *You are required to sign the form in both places.* □ *Sign here, please.* □ *Each page of the contract should be signed by all three parties.* **2** A football club **signs** new players, or a player **signs** with a new club, when they write their signatures on a contract of employment. **3** Deaf people **sign** when they communicate in a language consisting of signs made with the hands.

> The usual verb for communicating with people by signs is **signal** rather than **sign**.

phrasal verbs

sign away You **sign** something **away** when you sign a document legally transferring your ownership of it to someone else.

sign in **1** You **sign in** at *eg* a club or hotel when you officially record your arrival there by signing your name in a book. **2** You **sign** someone **in** as a guest at a club you belong to when you write their name in the book and sign your name alongside theirs.

sign off **1** (*informal*) You say you are **signing off** when you are bringing a letter or a broadcast to an end. **2** A doctor **signs** you **off** work when he or she signs a form saying you are not fit to work: *She was signed off for three weeks.*

sign on **1** You **sign on** for a job or a course when you officially agree to do it by signing a contract or form: *He signed on as mate on a merchant ship.* **2** Unemployed people **sign on** when they sign an

official form stating that they are unemployed, so that they will be entitled to receive money from the government to live on.
sign up 1 You **sign up** with an organization or **sign up** for a job or course when you sign a contract or form stating that you will work for the organization or that you accept the job or place on the course: *He has signed up for a further five years in the army.* □ *She signed up for a French language course.* **2** An employer or organization **signs** you **up** when they engage you to work for them by getting you to sign a contract.

signal /'sɪgnəl/ *noun*; *verb*; *adjective*
▻ ***noun***: **signals**
1 A **signal** is a gesture, light, sound, or action that conveys information or a particular message: *a distress signal* □ *He gave me the signal to start rowing.* □ *The train driver had ignored the stop signal, causing the train to crash.* **2** A **signal** or **signals** are the apparatus used to send messages, *eg* coloured lights or movable arms or metal poles, on a railway network. **3** A **signal** for something is an event or set of circumstances marking the moment for action to be taken: *The steep rise in the rate of inflation was a signal for an increase in interest rates.* **4** A **signal** is also any set of transmitted electrical impulses received as a sound or image, *eg* in television, or the message conveyed by them: *a radar signal.*
▻ ***verb***: **signals, signalling** (*AmE* **signaling**), **signalled** (*AmE* **signaled**)
1 To **signal** is to transmit a message or convey a meaning using signals: *The policeman signalled me to go left.* **2** If something **signals** something it indicates it: *The Chancellor's speech signalled a rise in interest rates.*
▻ ***adjective*** (*formal*)
Signal means notable, conspicuous or remarkable: *a signal triumph.*

signal box /'sɪgnəl bɒks/ *noun*: **signal boxes**
A **signal box** is a building from which signals on a railway line are controlled.

signatory /'sɪgnətərɪ/ *noun* (*formal*): **signatories**
A **signatory** is a person, organization or state that signs a contract, treaty or other document: *Some hundred and fifty nations were signatories to the GATT agreement.*

signature /'sɪgnətʃə(r)/ *noun*: **signatures**
1 Your **signature** is your name, written in your own handwriting and usually always in the same way, as a formal mark of authorization, acceptance or acknowledgement: *Write your signature on the back of the cheque.* □ *I can't read the signature at the end of this letter.* □ *He forged my signature.* **2** (*music*) A **signature** is an indication of key (**key signature**) or time (**time signature**) at the beginning of a line of music.

signature tune /'sɪgnətʃə tjuːn/ *noun*: **signature tunes**
A **signature tune** is a tune used to identify or introduce a particular radio or television programme or performer.

signet ring /'sɪgnɪt rɪŋ/ *noun*: **signet rings**
A **signet ring** is a finger ring with a small flat seal with the owner's initials or some other pattern by which he or she can be identified, used, especially formerly, to stamp documents.

significance /sɪg'nɪfɪkəns/ *noun* (*uncount*)
Something's **significance** is its meaning or importance: *What's the significance of these carvings?* □ *a discovery of great significance to mankind.*

significant /sɪg'nɪfɪkənt/ *adjective*
1 Significant things are important or worth noting: *A significant number of people didn't bother to vote.* □ *a significant discovery.* [*same as* **appreciable**; *opposite* **insignificant**] **2** Something that is **significant** has some meaning or indicates or implies something: *It's very significant that he made no mention of her in his letter.* □ *a significant look.* [*same as* **meaningful, expressive**] — *adverb* **significantly:** *The amount of money that is available to spend on research has been significantly reduced.* □ *He smiled significantly.*

signify /'sɪgnɪfaɪ/ *verb*: **signifies, signifying, signified**
1 If a gesture, symbol or sign **signifies** something, it has that meaning: *What does a skull and crossbones on a yellow background signify?* [*same as* **indicate, denote, represent, stand for**] **2** If you say that something does or does not **signify**, you mean it is or is not important or significant. [*same as* **matter**]

sign language /'saɪn laŋgwɪdʒ/ *noun* (*uncount or count*): **sign languages**
Sign language is any form of communication using gestures to represent words and ideas, especially a formal system of hand gestures used by deaf people; a **sign language** is one of these systems: *The boys couldn't speak any French so they had to use sign language to ask for directions.* □ *American Sign Language.*

signpost /'saɪnpoʊst/ *noun*: **signposts**
A **signpost** is a post or pole put up beside a road or at a junction of two or more roads that carries a sign giving information to motorists or pedestrians: *That signpost said 'Fort William, 3 miles'.*

Sikh /siːk/ *noun*; *adjective*
▻ ***noun***: **Sikhs**
A **Sikh** is a member or follower of an Indian religion, founded in the sixteenth century and developed from Hinduism, but worshipping only one god. — *noun* (*uncount*) **Sikhism**: *the origins of Sikhism.*
▻ ***adjective:*** *a Sikh temple.*

silage /'saɪlɪdʒ/ *noun* (*uncount*)
Silage is plants such as grass cut while it is still green, stored in silos or plastic-covered bales, and fed to farm animals, especially in the winter.

silence /'saɪləns/ *noun*; *verb*; *interjection*
▻ ***noun***: **silences**
1 (*uncount or count*) **Silence** is complete quietness when no sound can be heard; a **silence** is a period when there is no sound or when no-one speaks: *the silence of the forest at night* □ *After a long silence, he asked what the time was.* □ *At the service of remembrance, there was a minute's silence.* □ *Their conversation was punctuated by awkward silences.* **2** (*uncount*) Someone's **silence** is their failure or unwillingness to disclose information or comment on something: *Your silence will be taken as evidence of your guilt.*
▻ ***verb***: **silences, silencing, silenced**
You **silence** someone when you stop them speaking or stop them giving away information; you **silence** something when you cause it to become quiet or stop it making a noise: *She was silenced by a stern look from her father.*
▻ ***interjection***
You say '**Silence**' to people who are talking or making a noise when you want them to be quiet.
▻ ***phrase*** If you do something **in silence**, you do it without speaking: *They stood in silence.*

silencer /'saɪlənsə(r)/ *noun*: **silencers**
A **silencer** is a device fitted to a gun barrel or to an engine exhaust to muffle noise.

silent /'saɪlənt/ *adjective*
1 Silent means very quiet: *The forest was completely silent.* **2** If someone is **silent**, they do not speak; if they are **silent** or remain **silent** they do not give away information, *eg* when they are interrogated by someone. **3 Silent** emotion is expressed in some other way rather than by speech or sound: *She smiled in silent joy.* **4** A letter is **silent** when it is not pronounced: *The 'p' in 'pneumonia' is silent.* **5** A **silent** film has no soundtrack. — *adverb* **silently:** *The leopard moved silently through the jungle.*

silhouette /sɪlu:'ɛt/ *noun; verb*
▻ ***noun***: **silhouettes**
1 A **silhouette** is a dark shape seen against a light background. **2** A **silhouette** is also an outline drawing of a person, especially a portrait in profile, usually filled in in black.
▻ ***verb***: **silhouettes, silhouetting, silhouetted**
An object **is silhouetted** when it appears or is caused to appear as a dark shape against a light background: *A stag appeared on the high ridge, silhouetted against the sky.*

silicon /'sɪlɪkən/ *noun (uncount)*
Silicon is a non-metallic chemical element much used in electronics.

silicon chip /'sɪlɪkən tʃɪp/ *noun*: **silicon chips**
A **silicon chip** is a tiny piece of silicon on which very small electronic circuits, *eg* for use in computers, are formed.

silicone /'sɪlɪkoʊn/ *noun (uncount)*
Silicone is any of various compounds of silicon used in lubricants, paints and rubbers for their resistance to heat, water and electricity.

silk /sɪlk/ *noun*: **silks**
1 (*uncount*) **Silk** is the fine soft fibre produced by the larvae of the silkworm moth. **2** (*count or uncount, often adjectival*) **Silk** is thread or fabric made from these fibres: *embroidery silks* □ *a silk scarf.*

silken /'sɪlkən/ *adjective (literary)*
Silken means made of, or as soft or smooth as, silk: *a silken shawl* □ *He stroked her silken hair.*

silkworm /'sɪlkwɜ:m/ *noun*: **silkworms**
Silkworms are the caterpillars of a type of Chinese moth, that spin silk to form their cocoons.

silky /'sɪlkɪ/ *adjective*: **silkier, silkiest**
Silky things are smooth, soft and shiny like silk: *silky hair.*

sill /sɪl/ *noun*: **sills**
A **sill** is a horizontal piece of wood or stone forming the bottom part of a framework around an opening such as a window or door.

silly /'sɪlɪ/ *adjective; noun*
▻ ***adjective***: **sillier, silliest**
1 Someone is **silly**, or is being **silly**, if they are foolish or stupid, or are behaving in a foolish or stupid manner: *Don't be silly.* □ *You silly fool, why did you do that?* □ *That's the silliest thing I've ever heard.* [*same as* **idiotic**] **2** A **silly** thing, or something that looks **silly**, is ridiculous or has a ridiculous appearance: *Why are you wearing that silly hat?* [*same as* **ludicrous**]
▻ ***noun***: **sillies:** *That's not what I meant, you silly!*

silt /sɪlt/ *noun; verb*
▻ ***noun*** (*uncount or count*): **silts**
Silt is fine sand and mud that is carried and deposited by flowing water: *creatures that feed in the silt at the bottom of the lake* □ *rocks made up of shales and silts.*
▻ ***verb***: **silts, silting, silted**

phrasal verb
If a river or stream **silts up**, it becomes blocked by silt.

silver /'sɪlvə(r)/ *noun; adjective*
▻ ***noun***: **silvers**
1 (*uncount*) **Silver** is a shiny grey precious metal used for making coins, jewellery, plates, cutlery and decorative objects: *The teapot was made of solid silver.* **2** (*uncount*) **Silver** also means objects made of silver: *They have a lot of very valuable silver.* **3** (*uncount*) **Silver** is also used to refer to coins made of or containing some silver or made of other shiny grey metals that look like silver: *Do you have any silver?* **4** (*count*) A **silver** is a silver medal: *He won a gold and two silvers at the Olympics.* **5** (*uncount*) **Silver** is also the whitish-grey or shining colour of the metal: *shades of grey and silver.*
▻ ***adjective***
Something that is **silver** is **1** made of silver: *a silver teapot* □ *The bracelet is silver.* **2** of the colour of silver: *a silver car* □ *silver hair.*

silver birch /sɪlvə 'bɜ:tʃ/ *noun*: **silver birches**
A **silver birch** is a type of tree with greyish-white bark.

silver lining /sɪlvə 'laɪnɪŋ/ *noun (used in the singular)*
A **silver lining** is a positive or good aspect of an otherwise unpleasant or unfortunate situation.

silver medal /sɪlvə 'mɛdəl/ *noun*: **silver medals**
A **silver medal** is a medal made of silver awarded to the person who comes in second place in a race or competition: *He won a silver medal at the Olympics.* — *noun* **silver-medallist** (*AmE* **silver-medalist**): *one of Britain's Olympic silver-medallists.*

silver-plated /sɪlvə'pleɪtɪd/ *adjective*
If a metal object is **silver-plated** it has a thin layer of silver applied to its surface: *The bowl isn't solid silver; it's silver-plated.*

silversmith /'sɪlvəsmɪθ/ *noun*: **silversmiths**
A **silversmith** is a craftsman who makes articles in silver or repairs articles made of silver.

silvery /'sɪlvərɪ/ *adjective*
1 You can use **silvery** to describe things that are the colour of silver or shine like silver: *The moon shed a silvery light on the water's surface.* □ *a fish with silvery scales.* **2** A **silvery** sound is a pleasant light ringing sound, like the sound made by small bells: *a silvery voice.*

similar /'sɪmɪlə(r)/ *adjective*
Two things are **similar**, or one thing is **similar** to another, if they are alike but not exactly the same: *I like the style of this blouse; have you anything similar in green?* □ *Our children happened to be at a similar stage in their education.* □ *She was similar to me in height and build.* □ *His interests were similar to mine, and we got on well.* [*opposite* **different**; compare **same, identical**]

similarity /sɪmɪ'larɪtɪ/ *noun*: **similarities**
When there is a **similarity** between two things they are like each other in some way: *These are two distinct diseases although there are some close similarities in the symptoms.*

similarly /'sɪmɪləlɪ/ *adverb*
1 Similarly means in the same or a similar way: *The whole country has been similarly affected.* **2** (*sentence adverb*) You use **similarly** when you want to say that the thing you are about to mention is the same as or similar to the thing you have mentioned previously: *I*

am very pleased to welcome you and the rest of the staff are similarly delighted that you could join us.

simile /ˈsɪmɪlɪ/ *noun*: **similes**
A **simile** is any phrase in which one thing is described by being compared with another, usually using 'as' or 'like', as in '*eyes sparkling like diamonds*' and '*smooth as silk*'.

simmer /ˈsɪmə(r)/ *verb*; *noun*
▻ ***verb***: **simmers, simmering, simmered**
1 You **simmer** food, or it **simmers**, when you cook it, or it cooks gently in liquid that is at or just below boiling point: *Bring the water up to the boil and simmer the freshly made ravioli for ten minutes or until they float to the top.* ▫ *A huge pot of soup was simmering on the stove.* **2** If a person has strong feelings that **simmer** under the surface, they go on feeling that way for some time without showing it, or before they show it: *Her anger and frustration had been simmering for weeks, until she could contain it no longer.*
▻ ***noun*** (*used in the singular*): *Keep the water at a slow simmer.*

> ***phrasal verb***
> You **simmer down**, or someone tells you to **simmer down**, when you calm down or they tell you to calm down, especially after an angry outburst: *We'll discuss this when you have simmered down a bit.* ▫ *Simmer down; there's no point in shouting.*

simper /ˈsɪmpə(r)/ *verb*; *noun*
▻ ***verb***: **simpers, simpering, simpered**
When a person **simpers** they smile in a silly unnatural way or smile in this way while they are speaking: *When he asked the girls if they were enjoying themselves, they giggled and simpered.* ▫ *'Can I get you anything, sir,' the maid simpered.*
▻ ***noun***: **simpers:** *'Welcome home, sir,' she said with a simper.*

simple /ˈsɪmpəl/ *adjective*: **simpler, simplest**
1 Simple tasks are very easy to do: *The test was simple.* ▫ *'What's two and two.' 'That's simple; four.'* ▫ *It couldn't be simpler.* [*opposite* **difficult, hard**] **2 Simple** things are straightforward, not complex or complicated: *It's a simple matter of putting the plug into the socket and switching on.* ▫ *He explained it in the simplest terms possible.* **3 Simple** designs or styles are plain or basic, not elaborate or luxurious: *She wore a simple black dress and no jewellery.* ▫ *They prefer the simpler lifestyle that travelling can offer them.* [*opposite* **fancy**] **4 Simple** is also used to emphasize that the thing you are discussing is the only important one or the most basic one: *The simple fact is, you're wrong.* **5** (*derogatory*) If you say that someone is **simple**, you mean that they are foolish, gullible or lacking in intelligence: *He's a bit simple when it comes to money matters.* [*same as* **simple-minded**]

simple-minded /sɪmpəlˈmaɪndɪd/ *adjective*
Some people use **simple-minded** to describe someone who has very low intelligence and does not understand things as people of normal intelligence would: *He won't understand; he's a bit simple-minded.* ▫ *He's a simple-minded soul.*

simplicity /sɪmˈplɪsɪtɪ/ *noun* (*uncount*)
Simplicity is the state of being simple, in the sense of being easy to do or understand, or plain: *The recipe is simplicity itself.* ▫ *I like the simplicity of her designs.*

simplification /sɪmplɪfɪˈkeɪʃən/ *noun* (*uncount or count*): **simplifications**
Simplification is the process of making something less complicated or detailed and therefore easier to understand; a **simplification** is an act of making something less complicated or detailed: *simplification of the regulations.*

simplify /ˈsɪmplɪfaɪ/ *verb*: **simplifies, simplifying, simplified**
If something **is simplified**, or you **simplify** it, it is made less complicated or easier to understand: *a campaign to simplify the language used in official forms* ▫ *Can you simplify the design so that it will be easier to follow?*

simplistic /sɪmˈplɪstɪk/ *adjective*
A **simplistic** view or analysis of something makes it seem unrealistically simple and straightforward: *They take a simplistic view of what is, in reality, an extremely complicated problem.* — *adverb* **simplistically:** *I think that the director has interpreted the play too simplistically.*

simply /ˈsɪmplɪ/ *adverb*
1 If something is done **simply** it is done in a straightforward, uncomplicated way: *She was dressed very simply in a plain navy coat.* **2 Simply** means 'just': *It simply isn't true.* **3** (*intensifying*) You can use **simply** for emphasis with adjectives that describe how good or bad something is: *His singing was simply marvellous.* ▫ *Your spelling is simply appalling.* **4 Simply** also has the same meaning as 'merely' or 'only': *I didn't mean to interfere; I simply wanted to find out whether she needed any help.*

simulate /ˈsɪmjʊleɪt/ *verb*: **simulates, simulating, simulated**
1 You **simulate** something when you create or produce something so like it that it looks or seems like the real thing: *The machine simulates the conditions that astronauts will experience in space.* **2** You **simulate** illness or some feeling when you pretend to have or feel it.

simulated /ˈsɪmjʊleɪtɪd/ *adjective*
Simulated materials are artificial materials that have been made to look like natural materials: *simulated pearls* ▫ *simulated leather.*

simulation /sɪmjʊˈleɪʃən/ *noun* (*uncount or count*)
Simulation is the act of simulating something or the methods used to simulate something; a **simulation** is something that has been created artificially to mimic or reproduce a real event or real set of conditions: *by computer simulation* ▫ *a computer simulation.*

simulator /ˈsɪmjʊleɪtə(r)/ *noun*: **simulators**
A **simulator** is a machine that creates artificially the conditions or sensations of a real situation: *a flight simulator.*

simultaneous /sɪməlˈteɪnɪəs/ *adjective*
Two or more events that are **simultaneous** happen or are done at exactly the same time: *simultaneous explosions* ▫ *The concert will be televised with a simultaneous broadcast on radio.* — *adverb* **simultaneously:** *The submarine is capable of firing two missiles simultaneously.*

sin /sɪn/ *noun*; *verb*
▻ ***noun***: **sins**
1 (*uncount or count*) **Sin** is behaviour that is considered to be very bad or immoral, especially disobedience to God or something that breaks religious law; a **sin** is an act that offends against God or breaks a specific religious law: *Let he who is without sin cast the first stone.* ▫ *Lust and avarice are two of the Seven Deadly Sins.* ▫ *Forgive us our sins.* **2** (*uncount*) **Sin** is the condition of being set apart

from God through having broken religious law, or (**original sin**) being born with an inherited sinful nature.

▻ ***verb***: **sins, sinning, sinned**

If someone **sins**, they do something bad or immoral, especially something that is forbidden by religious law or teaching: *I have sinned against heaven.*

▻ ***phrase*** (*informal, old*) If a man and a woman **live in sin**, they live together as husband and wife without being married.

since /sɪns/ *preposition, conjunction or adverb*; *preposition or conjunction*; *adverb*; *conjunction*

▻ ***preposition, conjunction*** or ***adverb***

1 Something that has been so **since** a certain time or event in the past has been so from that time until the present: *I've only been living here since January.* □ *We've been scared to go out in the dark ever since that murder.* □ *Since having her children she has never worked outside the home.* □ *They'd met two years previously, since when they'd never been out of each other's sight.* □ *I've been learning English since 1981, since I was seven, in fact.* □ *We settled our quarrel and have been firm friends ever since.*

> Notice that you say *She's lived here* **since** *1990* but *She's lived here* **for** *four years.*

2 Something that has happened **since** a certain time or event in the past has happened at some time between then and now: *We were good friends at university but have rather lost touch since then.* □ *He's lost a lot of weight since her death.* □ *She had changed a good deal since I'd last seen her.* □ *I haven't heard from him since he left for the States.* □ *We had lunch together on her birthday and I've seen her only once since.* □ *She was reluctant when I first asked her but has since changed her mind.*

▻ ***preposition*** or ***conjunction***

1 It is a certain length of time **since** an event if it happened that length of time ago: *It must be four years since the accident.* □ *It's a long time since I was last here.* □ *It's ages since we met.* **2** If something is *eg* the greatest or best **since** a certain time or event, there has been nothing as great or good from then until now: *This will be the most important state occasion since the Queen ascended the throne.* □ *It's the greatest invention since the wheel.* □ *Unemployment figures are the highest since 1974.*

▻ ***adverb***

You can use **since** like *ago*: *I've long since given up trying to influence him.* □ *There was some trouble many years since.* [*same as* **ago**]

▻ ***conjunction***

You use **since** rather like *as* or *because*, to give the reason for something: *Since you're obviously against it there's no point in pursuing the possibility.* □ *I'd decided to stay in town, since it was Thursday and the shops were open late.* [*same as* **seeing**]

sincere /sɪn'sɪə(r)/ *adjective*

1 Someone who is **sincere** is honest and genuine and means what they say: *Do you think he was sincere when he said he loved me?* **2 Sincere** feeling or behaviour is real, honest and without deceit: *a sincere apology.* [*opposite* **insincere**]

sincerely /sɪn'sɪəlɪ/ *adverb*

Sincerely means truly or genuinely: *I think you're wonderful and I mean that most sincerely.*

▻ ***phrase*** People write **'yours sincerely'** before their signature at the end of formal or business letters. [compare **yours faithfully**, see appendix on **Letter-writing**]

sincerity /sɪn'serɪtɪ/ *noun* (*uncount*)

Sincerity is the state or quality of being truthful and genuine in what you believe and say: *He said it in all sincerity.* □ *He said I was the most important person in his life but I really doubt his sincerity.*

sinew /'sɪnjuː/ *noun* (*uncount or count*): **sinews**

Sinew or a **sinew** is strong cordlike tissue that joins the muscles to the bones in your body. [*same as* **tendon**]

sinewy /'sɪnjuːɪ/ *adjective*

If someone has a **sinewy** body, their body is slim and strong with the muscles well defined: *his sinewy arms.*

sinful /'sɪnfʊl/ *adjective*

1 Sinful behaviour is considered to be wicked according to religious or moral codes: *sinful thoughts.* **2** A **sinful** person has committed a sin or sins or tends to commit sins.

sing /sɪŋ/ *verb*: **sings, singing, sang, sung**

1 You **sing** when you produce sounds or words with your voice in a musical or tuneful way; you **sing** someone to sleep when you do this so that they will relax and go to sleep: *She was singing as she worked.* □ *Will you sing me a song?* □ *He sings in the choir.* □ *She sang 'Rule Britannia'.* □ *She sang the baby a lullaby.* □ *The baby was restless and I tried singing her to sleep.* **2** Birds, animals or insects **sing** when they make musical sounds that are pleasant to listen to: *When she awoke, the sun was up and the birds were singing.* □ *The whales seemed to be singing to each other.* **3** You can also say that something **sings** when it makes a humming, ringing or whistling sound like a musical voice: *The kitchen was warm and cosy, and the kettle was singing on the stove.* □ *Bullets came singing past his ears.*

▻ ***phrase*** You **sing** someone's or something's **praises** when you talk very enthusiatically about their good points or their abilities: *She's always singing the praises of the little fishing village she visits every year on holiday.*

singe /sɪndʒ/ *verb*: **singes, singeing, singed**

If you **singe** something, or it **singes**, you burn it or it burns slightly on the surface or edge: *If the iron is too hot you will singe that delicate fabric.* □ *The cat singed its whiskers lying too close to the fire.*

singer /'sɪŋə(r)/ *noun*: **singers**

A **singer** is someone who sings or whose voice has been specially trained for singing: *Are you a good singer?* □ *He's the singer in a pop group.* □ *an opera singer.*

singing /'sɪŋɪŋ/ *noun* (*uncount, often adjectival*)

Singing is the art or activity of making musical sounds with your voice: *I enjoy singing.* □ *the singing of the birds* □ *the mysterious singing of the humpbacked whale* □ *He has a marvellous singing voice.* □ *She's having singing lessons.*

single /'sɪŋgəl/ *adjective*; *noun*; *verb*

▻ ***adjective***

1 A **single** thing is only one and no more: *A single tear trickled down her cheek.* □ *The room was lit by a single bulb hanging from the middle of the ceiling.* □ *He wrote the whole symphony in a single week.* **2 Single** is used for emphasis **a** with *every*: 'every **single**' person or thing is absolutely every one: *This applies to every single pupil in the school.* □ *I'm afraid I'm booked up every single evening this week.* **b** with *not*: 'not a **single**' thing or person is absolutely none: *There wasn't a single person in sight.* □ *Not a single volunteer came forward.* □ *He didn't borrow a single penny when he started his business.* □ *I can't think of any single invention that has had a greater impact on the way we live.* **c** with a superlative and a count noun: *It was the single most important experience in my life.* □ *the greatest single discovery since Newton and gravity.* **3** Someone who is **single** is not married: *There are plenty of single girls around.* [*opposite* **married**] **4** A **single** room or a **single** bed is for the use of one person only. [compare **double**] **5** A **single** ticket is valid for an outward journey only and cannot be used for the journey back. [compare **return**] **6** **Single** figures are the numerals from 0 to 9: *Attendance at his lectures had dropped to single figures.* **7** People are in **single** file when they are moving forward one behind the other.

▻ ***noun***: **singles**

1 A **single** is **a** a ticket for an outward journey only: *A single to Edinburgh, please.* **b** a record with only one track on each side: *His latest single has reached number three in the charts.* **c** one run in cricket. **2** (*used in the plural*) **Singles** are unmarried people: *She joined a singles club.* **3** (*used in the plural, with a singular or plural verb*) You play **singles** when you play a game of tennis or badminton against one opponent only.

▻ ***verb***: **singles, singling, singled**

phrasal verb

You **single** someone or something **out** from a group when you mention them in particular, or choose them for some kind of special treatment or attention: *The headmaster singled him out for special praise.* □ *No one circumstance can be singled out as the actual cause.*

single bed /sɪŋgəl 'bɛd/ *noun*: **single beds**

A **single bed** is a bed for one person. [see picture at **bedroom**]

single file /sɪŋgəl 'faɪl/ *noun*; *adverb*

▻ ***noun*** (*uncount*)

If people or vehicles stand or move in **single file**, they stand or move one behind the other: *The soldiers marched in single file.*

▻ ***adverb:*** *They walked single file along the narrow ridge.*

single-handed /sɪŋgəl'handɪd/ *adjective or adverb*

A **single-handed** person, or a person who does something **single-handed**, is one who does something alone, without help from other people: *a single-handed yachtsman* □ *He sailed the Atlantic single-handed.*

single-minded /sɪŋgəl'maɪndɪd/ *adjective*

When a person is **single-minded**, they have one clear aim or purpose only: *You have to be absolutely single-minded if you want to succeed in business nowadays.*

single parent /sɪŋgəl 'pɛərənt/ *noun*: **single parents**

A **single parent** is a mother or father bringing up a child or children alone: *an organization for single parents.*

singly /'sɪŋglɪ/ *adverb*

Singly means one at a time or individually: *The animals came to the waterhole singly or in small groups.* □ *The headmaster told the boys he would see them singly, at five minute intervals.* [*same as* **one by one**]

singsong /'sɪŋsɒŋ/ *noun*; *adjective*

▻ ***noun***: **singsongs**

A **singsong** is an informal occasion when people sings songs together for pleasure: *We had a singsong on the bus.*

▻ ***adjective***

If someone speaks with a **singsong** voice, their voice goes up and down in tone or pitch repeatedly as they speak: *a Welshman with a singsong voice.*

singular /'sɪŋgjʊlə(r)/ *adjective*; *noun*

▻ ***adjective***

1 In grammar, a word or form of a word is **singular** when it refers to one person, thing or group, as opposed to two or more: *The noun 'radius' is singular.* □ *'Hoof' is the singular form of 'hooves'.* [see also **plural**] **2** (*formal*) **Singular** is used to refer to things that are extraordinary or very noticeable: *The decision showed a singular lack of judgement on his part.* [*same as* **remarkable**] **3** (*formal, rather old*) **Singular** is also used to refer to things that are very strange or out of the ordinary: *A singular thing happened while I was digging the garden; a magpie dropped a blackbird's egg on my head!* [*same as* **extraordinary**]

▻ ***noun*** (*used in the singular; grammar*)

A word or form of a word in the **singular** expresses the idea of one person or one thing, as opposed to two or more than two: *What is the singular of 'cattle'?*

singularly /'sɪŋgjʊləlɪ/ *adverb* (*intensifying*)

Singularly means 'remarkably' or 'to an extraordinary degree': *I found him to be a singularly unpleasant character.* □ *He proved to be singularly ill-equipped for the job he was required to do.*

sinister /'sɪnɪstə(r)/ *adjective*

Someone who has a **sinister** appearance looks as if they might have evil or dangerous intentions; something **sinister** suggests or threatens that something bad might happen and therefore makes you feel afraid: *a sinister-looking stranger* □ *There's nothing sinister about the review; its primary purpose is to establish if resources are being put to the best possible use.*

sink /sɪŋk/ *verb*; *noun*

▻ ***verb***: **sinks, sinking, sank, sunk**

1 a Something **sinks** when it drops below the surface of a liquid, especially water, and goes on moving downwards through it till it reaches the bottom: *The punt was filling with water and sinking rapidly.* □ *We managed to get the lifeboats launched just before the ship sank.* □ *The body was thrown into the river, where it sank like a stone.* **b** To **sink** a ship is deliberately to make it go to the bottom of the sea, *eg* by attacking it with bombs or torpedoes, or driving holes into its hull: *German U-boats were attacking Allied shipping in the Atlantic and sank a significant number of naval vessels.* □ *That was the week that the battleship 'Hood' was sunk by a torpedo.* **c** Something **sinks** into a surface or substance when it moves down into it: *Our feet sank into the deep snow.* □ *The buildings were sinking as a result of the damage to their foundations.* □ *Venice is slowly sinking into the mud.* **d** The sun **sinks** when it moves down towards the horizon in the evening and disappears below it. **e** A person or animal **sinks** their teeth into something when they bite deeply into it: *The dog leapt at him and sank its teeth into his arm.* **f** Foundations or supports **are sunk** into the ground when they are fixed firmly and deeply in it: *The bridge was supported on concrete blocks sunk into the river bed.* **g** A shaft **is sunk** into the ground when it is dug. **h** (*informal*) You **sink** a ball in games such as snooker or golf when you hit it into a hole. **i** You **sink** money into something such as a business or scheme when you invest money in it, especially a large amount: *They'd sunk all they had into that hotel chain.*

2 a You **sink** somewhere when you go down with a collapsing movement: *I sank gratefully into an armchair.* □ *He sank to his knees.* **b** Your heart **sinks** when something suddenly depresses you: *My heart sank at the thought of keying the work all over again.* **c** Someone who is ill **is sinking** when they are getting steadily worse and are likely to die soon: *Come* *straight away; he's sinking fast.* **d** You wonder, in reference to someone's immoral or dishonest behaviour, how they could **sink** so low, if you are surprised that they could be so wicked. **e** Someone's voice **sinks** when they lower it: *The noise in the auditorium sank to a murmur.* □ *Her voice sank to a whisper.* **f** Amounts **sink** when they decrease or fall to a lower level: *The water level in the reservoir was sinking alarmingly.* □ *The pound has sunk to its lowest level against the Deutschmark for three years.* □ *Morale had sunk to an all-time low.* **g** (*informal*) You **are sunk** when there is no way of avoiding failure or ruin: *If we can't get a loan from the bank, we're sunk.*

▻ ***noun*: sinks**

1 A **sink** is a rectangular metal or stone basin fixed to the kitchen wall with its own taps and drainage system, in which to wash dishes or vegetables. [see picture at **kitchen**] **2** A washbasin in a bathroom is sometimes called a **sink**. [see picture at **bathroom**]

phrasal verb

sink in 1 A liquid **sinks in**, or **sinks into** something, when it becomes absorbed: *We'd better get that wine off the carpet before it sinks in.* **2** (*informal*) News or information that you have received **sinks in** when you fully realize and understand it, or realize what it implies: *They rang me to tell me I'd won, and for a minute it didn't sink in.* [compare **take it in** at **take**]

sinner /ˈsɪnə(r)/ *noun*: **sinners**

A **sinner** is a person who has committed a sin or sins.

sinuous /ˈsɪnjʊəs/ *adjective* (*formal or literary*)

Something that has many curves or bends or that moves with smooth or graceful twists and bends, like a snake, can be described as **sinuous**: *The river flowed in a sinuous path to the sea.* □ *the sinuous movements of the dancers' arms.*

sinus /ˈsaɪnəs/ *noun*: **sinuses**

Your **sinuses** are any of several air-filled hollows in the bones of your skull that connect with your nose.

sip /sɪp/ *verb*; *noun*

▻ ***verb*: sips, sipping, sipped**

You **sip** a drink when you drink it in very small mouthfuls: *She was sitting on a long elegant couch sipping a cocktail.*

▻ ***noun*: sips:** *He managed to take a few sips of water.*

siphon or **syphon** /ˈsaɪfən/ *noun*; *verb*

▻ ***noun*: siphons**

1 A **siphon** is a bent pipe or tube through which, by atmospheric pressure, a liquid is drawn from one container into a second container placed at a lower level. **2** A **siphon** is a bottle from which a liquid, especially soda water, is forced by pressure of gas: *a soda siphon.*

▻ ***verb*: siphons, siphoning, siphoned**

1 You **siphon** a liquid, or **siphon** it **off** when you draw it from one container to another using a siphon. **2** Things **are siphoned** or **siphoned off** when they are taken, often dishonestly, from a store or fund: *He had been siphoning off large sums of money into his personal bank account.*

sir /sɜː(r)/ *noun*: **sirs**

1 Sir is a title used before the Christian name of a knight or baronet: *Sir Galahad.* **2 Sir** is used as a polite or respectful way of addressing a man: *'Can I take your order now, sir?'* □ *Begin the letter 'Dear Sirs'.* □ *Would sir like a newspaper delivered with his morning tea?*

siren /ˈsaɪərən/ *noun*: **sirens**

A **siren** is a warning device that gives out a loud hooting or wailing sound: *an air-raid siren* □ *A fleet of ambulances and fire engines sped to the scene with sirens wailing.*

sissy or **cissy** /ˈsɪsɪ/ *noun* (*derogatory*): **sissies**

If you call a boy or man a **sissy** you mean they are weak and cowardly: *Don't be such a sissy!*

sister /ˈsɪstə(r)/ *noun*; *adjective*

▻ ***noun*: sisters**

1 Your **sister** is a girl or woman who has the same parents as you. **2** Nuns are often given the title **Sister**: *the Little Sisters of Charity* □ *Sister Bernadette.* **3 Sister** is also the title given to a senior female nurse, especially one in charge of a hospital ward: *a theatre sister* [=a senior nurse in charge of an operating theatre] □ *He was given an injection by the sister.* □ *Sister Matheson* □ *I don't know when you will be able to go home; I'll just ask Sister.* **4** Some women refer to other women as their **sisters**, especially when they want to imply that there is a close bond between them because, as women, they share the same experiences.

▻ ***adjective***

Sister is used to describe things that have the same origin or design or are owned by the same organization: *The battle cruiser's sister ship was sunk in the Atlantic.* □ *'The Independent' and its sister paper, 'The Independent on Sunday'.*

sister-in-law /ˈsɪstər ɪnlɔː/ *noun*: **sisters-in-law**

Your **sister-in-law** is your husband's or wife's sister or your brother's wife.

sisterly /ˈsɪstəlɪ/ *adjective*

Sisterly is used to describe a woman's behaviour towards, or her affection for, someone, when it is warm and loving as it would be towards her brother or sister: *Her feelings for him were more sisterly than romantic.*

sit /sɪt/ *verb*: **sits, sitting, sat**

1 a You **are sitting** when your weight is supported on your bottom rather than your feet, your back is upright, and the upper parts of your legs are at right angles to your body: *Are you sitting comfortably?* □ *I sat on the edge of my bed.* □ *She was sitting in an armchair by the fire.* □ *They all sat in a row on one long bench.* □ *Three women were sitting at the table.* □ *We children had to sit cross-legged on the floor.* **b** You **sit** when you lower yourself so that you rest your bottom on some surface: *She brought a chair forward and sat on it.* □ *Somebody sat on my sunglasses.* **c** You **sit** someone somewhere when you ask them to sit there: *I sat Jack at the head of the table.* **d** Something **sits** somewhere if that is where it is; you **sit** something somewhere when you place it there: *The magazine rack usually sat on the floor beside her armchair.* □ *I wound the clock and sat it back on the mantelpiece.* □ *The village sits in a sheltered hollow of the Pennines.* □ *I noticed a large parcel sitting on the table.* □ *I must have left my ticket sitting on the dressing table.* □ *Do use the car; it'll just be sitting doing nothing otherwise.* **e** Clothes **sit** in a certain way if they fit in that way: *I liked the way the skirt sat so neatly on my hips.*

2 a Parliament or a law court **sits** when it meets for official business: *Is the House of Lords sitting today?* **b** You **sit** on a committee if you are a member of it and take part in its meetings: *She sits on the school board as a parents' representative.* **c** You **sit** an examination when you take it: *He's sitting his A-levels next week.* □ *I don't think you're quite ready to sit your driving test.* **d** You **sit** for a photographer or painter when you have your portrait done by them, or are employed as a model by them: *She's been sitting for her portrait.*

▻ ***phrases* 1** For **be sitting pretty** see **pretty**. **2** For **sit on the fence** see **fence**.

phrasal verbs

sit about or **sit around** People **sit about** or **sit around** when they do nothing except sit, usually because there's nothing else to do: *I hate sitting around doing nothing.*

sit back **1** You **sit back** in your chair when you sit comfortably with your back supported. **2** You **sit back** while something is happening if you relax and watch what is going on without taking part: *I'm just going to sit back and see what happens next.* □ *Don't think you can just sit back while the rest of us do all the work.*

sit down **1** You **sit down** when you lower your weight on to your bottom: *He sat down next to me.* □ *Come in and sit yourself down.* □ *Sit down and take out your history books.* **2** You **sit** someone **down** when you make them sit somewhere: *He sat me down and poured a cup of tea for me.* [see also **sit-down**]

sit in on You **sit in on** a meeting, class or discussion when you attend it without taking part in it, in order to watch what happens during it: *School inspectors will be sitting in on all the classes and will be assessing the ability of both teachers and pupils.*

sit on (*informal*) Someone **sits on** something when they fail to deal with it, and so delay progress on it: *He's been sitting on my report for at least a month.*

sit out **1** You **sit out** something when you endure it patiently till it finishes: *Some families sat out the hostilities in the comparative safety of their cellars.* **2** You **sit out** something such as a game or a dance when you don't take part in it: *I'll sit out the next dance, thanks, and get my breath back.*

sit up **1** You **sit up** when you raise yourself into an upright sitting position after you have been lying down or leaning back: *Are you well enough to sit up in bed and have some tea?* **2** You **sit up** late when you don't go to bed: *We sat up all night discussing the situation.* □ *He sits up working till three in the morning.* **3** Something makes you **sit up** when it forces you suddenly to notice what is happening: *Threaten them with redundancy; that'll make them sit up.*

sitcom /ˈsɪtkɒm/ *noun*(*informal*): **sitcoms**
A **sitcom** is a situation comedy: *television sitcoms.*

sit-down /ˈsɪtdaʊn/ *adjective; noun*
▻ ***adjective***
1 (*BrE*) A **sit-down** meal is one which people eat while sitting at a table: *We have sandwiches at lunchtime and a proper sit-down meal in the evenings.* **2** A **sit-down** strike is a strike in which workers occupy a factory or office and refuse to work or leave the premises until an agreement is reached.
▻ ***noun*: sit-downs**
1 (*informal*) If you have a **sit-down**, you rest sitting down for a time: *My feet are aching; I think I'll have a little sit-down.* **2** A **sit-down** is also a sit-down strike. [see also **sit down at sit**]

site /saɪt/ *noun*: **sites**
A **site** is a place where something was, is, or is to be situated, or a place used for a specific activity: *A memorial was built on the site of the massacre.* □ *Your room looks like a bomb site!* □ *an important archaeological site* □ *a building site* □ *a caravan site.*

sit-in /ˈsɪtɪn/ *noun*: **sit-ins**
If workers or students stage a **sit-in**, they occupy a factory, office or other building as a protest.

sitter /ˈsɪtə(r)/ *noun*: **sitters**
1 A **sitter** is someone who poses as a model for an artist or photographer. **2** A **sitter** is also a baby-sitter.

sitting /ˈsɪtɪŋ/ *noun*: **sittings**
A **sitting** is **1** a period of continuous action: *He wrote the whole story at one sitting.* **2** one of the times at which two or more groups eat a particular meal in the same place when there is not enough space for everyone to eat at the same time: *There are two sittings for dinner; the first at seven thirty and the second at nine.* **3** one of the periods during which a model poses for an artist, especially for a portrait. **4** a session or meeting of an official body, such as a court of law.

sitting room /ˈsɪtɪŋruːm/ *noun*: **sitting rooms**
A **sitting room** is a room, *eg* in a private house, for sitting and relaxing in: *a hotel suite with a private sitting room.* [see also **living room, lounge**]

situate /ˈsɪtʃʊeɪt/ *verb*: **situates, situating, situated**
Something **is situated** in a certain place, position or set of circumstances when it is put or placed there: *The house is situated on a particularly exposed stretch of the coastline.* □ *The company's new headquarters will be situated near major road and rail links.* □ *'I don't know how he's situated financially.'* [=what his financial circumstances are]

situation /sɪtʃʊˈeɪʃən/ *noun*: **situations**
1 A **situation** is a set of circumstances or a state of affairs: *What's the situation as far as sales are concerned?* □ *He's always getting himself involved in complicated situations.* **2** A **situation** is also a position or location: *Plant the shrubs in a sunny situation that is protected from the wind.* **3** (*slightly old or formal*) A **situation** is also a job: *Has he found himself a suitable situation yet?* □ *I saw the job advertisement in the 'Situations Vacant' column of the local newspaper.*

situation comedy /sɪtʃʊeɪʃən ˈkɒmədɪ/ *noun*: **situation comedies**
A **situation comedy** is a type of radio or television comedy series with the same set of characters featured in a more or less fixed set of surroundings each week.

six /sɪks/ *noun; adjective; determiner; pronoun*
▻ ***noun*: sixes**
1 (*uncount or count*) **Six** or **a** the number or figure 6: *Six and six are twelve.* □ *Four plus six makes ten.* □ *Three sixes are eighteen.* □ *Is that a six or a zero?* **b** a piece of clothing whose size is represented by the number 6, or a person who wears clothes of this size: *These shoes will be too big for you; they're sixes.* □ *She takes six in shoes.* □ *For women's clothes, six in the USA is equivalent to eight in the UK.* **2** (*uncount*) **Six** is **a** the age of 6: *He could speak French fluently at six.* **b** the time of 6 o'clock: *If he leaves work at six he always gets caught in the rush-hour traffic.* **3** A **six** is **a** a set of six people or things: *The cans of beer are sold in sixes.* **b** a playing card with six symbols: *the six of hearts.* **c** a score of six points: *He shook the dice and threw a six.* **d** a hit in cricket scoring six runs, especially one that goes over the boundary without touching the ground beforehand: *hit the ball for six.*
▻ ***adjective***
Someone who is **six** is six years old: *His mother died when he was six.* □ *a play group for children aged six and under.*
▻ ***determiner:*** *For this recipe you will need the whites of six large eggs.* □ *Six people turned up for the interview.* □ *a six-day journey.*
▻ ***pronoun:*** *Six of the passengers in the coach were badly injured.* □ *There were ten cottages on the estate, six of which were derelict.* □ *The children were divided into two groups; six in one and five in the other.*
▻ ***phrases*** **1** If someone is **at sixes and sevens**, they are in a state of total disorder or confusion: *I can't find my diary; I'm all at sixes and sevens today.* **2** (*BrE; infor-*

mal) If you describe a situation as **six of one and half a dozen of the other**, you mean that it has good and bad points in equal degree.

sixpence /ˈsɪkspəns/ *noun*: **sixpences**
A **sixpence** was an old British coin worth 2½ new pence.

sixteen /sɪkˈstiːn/ *noun*; *adjective*; *determiner*; *pronoun*
▻ ***noun***: **sixteens**
1 (*uncount or count*) **Sixteen** is the number or figure 16: *Eighteen take away two is sixteen.* ▫ *Four sixteens are sixty-four.* **2** (*uncount*) **Sixteen** is the age of 16: *He ran away to sea at sixteen.* **3** (*count or uncount*) A **sixteen** is a piece of clothing whose size is represented by the number 16, or a person who wears clothes of this size: *I used to be an eighteen before I dieted; now I'm a sixteen.*
▻ ***adjective***
Someone who is **sixteen** is sixteen years old: *I'm sixteen on my next birthday.*
▻ ***determiner:*** *He has two dogs and sixteen cats.* ▫ *a sixteen-year old boy.*
▻ ***pronoun:*** *The firm sacked twenty people, leaving only sixteen to run the office.*

sixteenth /sɪkˈstiːnθ/ *determiner*; *pronoun*; *adjective or adverb*; *noun*: **sixteenths**
1 (often written **16th**) The **sixteenth** person or thing is the one numbered sixteen in a series. **2** (often written $\frac{1}{16}$) A **sixteenth** of something is one of sixteen equal parts of it.

sixth (often written **6th**) /sɪksθ/ *determiner*; *pronoun*; *adjective or adverb*; *noun*
▻ ***determiner***
The **sixth** person or thing is the one numbered six in a series: *He is in the sixth year of his medical training.* ▫ *the sixth manned moon flight.*
▻ ***pronoun:*** *Their wedding anniversary is on the 6th of October.* [see also note at **date**] ▫ *Our present queen's father was George the Sixth* (written *George VI*).
▻ ***adjective or adverb:*** *He was sixth in the egg and spoon race.* ▫ *He came in sixth.*
▻ ***noun*** (often written $\frac{1}{6}$): **sixths**
A **sixth** of something is one of six equal parts of it: *Three sixths is the same as one half.* ▫ *Only around one sixth of the children under five received free nursery education.*

sixth form /ˈsɪksθ fɔːm/ *noun*: **sixth forms**
In British secondary schools, the **sixth form** is the classes in which subjects are studied by pupils aged from around sixteen upwards who are taking examinations for entrance into higher education.

sixth-former /ˈsɪksθfɔːmə(r)/ *noun*: **sixth-formers**
A **sixth-former** is a pupil in the sixth form, *ie* in the sixth or seventh year of their secondary education.

sixth sense /sɪksθ ˈsɛns/ *noun* (*used in the singular*)
If someone appears to have a **sixth sense** about something, they seem to be aware of things that cannot be seen, heard, touched, smelled or tasted: *She always knows when there is going to be a storm; she seems to have a sixth sense about it.*

sixtieth /ˈsɪkstɪəθ/ *determiner*; *pronoun*; *adjective or adverb*; *noun*: **sixtieths**
1 (often written **60th**) The **sixtieth** person or thing is the one numbered sixty in a series. **2** (often written $\frac{1}{60}$) A **sixtieth** of something is one of sixty equal parts of it.

sixty /ˈsɪkstɪ/ *noun*; *adjective*; *determiner*; *pronoun*
▻ ***noun***: **sixties**
1 (*uncount or count*) **Sixty** is the number or figure 60. **2** (*uncount*) **Sixty** is the age of 60. **3** (*used in the plural*) Someone who is in their **sixties** is aged between 60 and 69. **4** (*plural*) When the temperature is in the **sixties** it is between 60° and 69° Fahrenheit. **5** (*plural*) The **sixties** are the period between the fiftieth and seventieth years in a century.
▻ ***adjective***
Someone who is **sixty** is 60 years old.
▻ ***determiner:*** *Fitness classes for sixty-year olds and upwards.*
▻ ***pronoun:*** *Bills that should have been paid in thirty days were often unpaid after sixty.*

size /saɪz/ *noun*; *verb*
▻ ***noun***: **sizes**
1 (*uncount*) Something's **size** is its length, breadth, height, volume or extent, or a combination of all or any of these: *What size is his farm?* ▫ *The carpet is the wrong size for this room.* ▫ *icebergs the size of skyscrapers.* ▫ *We won't know how many people will be needed until we can assess the size of the problem.* **2** (*uncount*) Something's **size** is also its largeness, especially when compared with others of the same type: *Have you seen the size of these cabbages?* ▫ *They were completely overwhelmed by the sheer size of the problem.* **3** A **size** is any of a range of graded measurements, *eg* for clothing or shoes: *What size shoe (*or *size of shoe) do you take?* ▫ *His trousers were several sizes too big and were held up with a piece of string.*
▻ ***verb***: **sizes, sizing, sized**
You **size** things when you measure them in order to find their size, or sort them according to size: *The eggs had been sized into small, medium and large.*
▻ ***phrase*** You **cut** someone **down to size** when you do something that will make them realize that they are not as important as they think they are: *He's becoming very conceited and needs to be cut down to size.*

> ***phrasal verb***
> You **size** a person or situation **up** when you study it carefully so as to decide how you can best deal with it.

sizeable or **sizable** /ˈsaɪzəbəl/ *adjective*
Something that is **sizeable** is fairly large: *a sizeable deficit* ▫ *He made a sizeable income from renting his land.*

sizzle /ˈsɪzəl/ *verb*: **sizzles, sizzling, sizzled**
If something **sizzles**, it makes a hissing sound like the sound of food frying in hot oil or the sound of water falling on hot metal: *sausages sizzling on the barbecue.*

skate /skeɪt/ *noun*; *verb*
▻ ***noun***: **skates**
1 Skates are boots with a device fitted to each of their soles for gliding smoothly over surfaces, either a steel blade for use on ice (**ice-skate**) or a set of small wheels for use on wooden and other surfaces (**roller-skate**). **2** A **skate** is also a type of flat fish that lives in the sea.
▻ ***verb***: **skates, skating, skated**
You **skate** when you move around on skates: *We often skate on the river when it is frozen in winter time.*
▻ ***phrases*** **1** (*informal*) If someone tells you to **get your skates on** they are telling you to hurry up: *We'll miss the train if we don't get our skates on.* **2** If someone **is skating on thin ice**, they are doing something very risky.

> ***phrasal verb***
> If you **skate over** or **skate round** something that you find difficult or problematic, you avoid dealing with it or considering it in any detail: *He talked about how prestigious the project was, but skated over the question of where the money would come from to pay for it.*

skateboard /ˈskeɪtbɔːd/ *noun*: **skateboards**
A **skateboard** is a narrow shaped board mounted on sets of small wheels, for riding on in a standing or crouching position.

skater /ˈskeɪtə(r)/ *noun*: **skaters**
A **skater** is a person who skates using ice-skates or roller-skates.

skating /ˈskeɪtɪŋ/ *noun* (*uncount*)
Skating is the sport or activity of moving around on ice wearing skates.

skein /skeɪn/ *noun*: **skeins**
A **skein** is a loose coil of wool or thread.

skeletal /ˈskɛlɪtəl/ *adjective*
1 Skeletal means of or concerned with a skeleton or skeletons. **2** If you describe a person or part of their body as **skeletal**, you mean that they are so thin that they seem to have no flesh on their bones.

skeleton /ˈskɛlɪtən/ *noun*: **skeletons**
1 A animal's **skeleton** is the framework of bones that support its body: *a human skeleton.* **2** You can also refer to a basic structure or idea upon or around which anything is built as its **skeleton**: *The novelist began with the skeleton of an idea in his head which he fleshed out as he began to write.* **3** (*informal*) If you say that someone is a **skeleton**, you mean that they are extremely thin.
▻ ***phrase*** If someone has a **skeleton in their cupboard**, there is some fact or event from their or their family's past that is so unpleasant or shocking that they keep it hidden.

sketch /skɛtʃ/ *noun*; *verb*
▻ ***noun***: **sketches**
1 A **sketch** is a drawing that is done quickly, often used as a guide for a more detailed picture or plan: *This is only a rough sketch of the floor plan, showing where the main rooms will be.* □ *The artist made several sketches before beginning the portrait.* **2** A **sketch** is also a brief outline or short description which includes the main or most important details of a situation or event: *a sketch of daily life in an eighteenth century English village.* **3** A **sketch** is a short piece of acting, usually on a comic subject, that is presented with others in a show on stage or television.
▻ ***verb***: **sketches, sketching, sketched**
If you draw, paint, describe or plan something without including all the details, you **sketch** it, or **sketch** it **out**: *The class were sketching the fishing boats in the harbour.* □ *He sketched out his plan of action in a short written report.*

sketchy /ˈskɛtʃɪ/ *adjective*: **sketchier, sketchiest**
When something, such as information, is **sketchy**, it is incomplete, lacking many details: *Because the area is so remote, details of the incident are sketchy.* □ *He only has the sketchiest idea of how it should be done.*

skewer /ˈskjuːə(r)/ *noun*; *verb*
▻ ***noun***: **skewers**
A **skewer** is a long piece of wood or metal with a sharp point that is pushed through chunks of meat or vegetables that are to be roasted or grilled.
▻ ***verb***: **skewers, skewering, skewered**
You **skewer** something when you push a skewer or some other sharp implement through it so that it is fastened or held: *They stood up in the boats and skewered the fish with bamboo spears.*

ski /skiː/ *noun*; *verb*; *adjective*
▻ ***noun***: **skis**
1 Skis are long narrow strips of wood, metal or plastic that are used for gliding over snow. They are attached to special boots or to the underside of vehicles in place of wheels. **2 Skis** or **water-skis** are similar objects that people wear on each foot and use for moving over the surface of water while being pulled by a fast motor boat.
▻ ***verb***: **skis, skiing, skied** or **ski'd**
You **ski** when you move over snow or water on skis, especially as a sport or leisure activity: *He learnt to ski when he was five years old.* □ *They climbed up the mountain and skied back down.*
▻ ***adjective***
Ski is used to describe things used for or connected with skiing: *a ski instructor* □ *ski boots.*

skid /skɪd/ *verb*; *noun*
▻ ***verb***: **skids, skidding, skidded**
A vehicle **skids** when it slides forwards or sideways out of control and without its wheels turning: *The driver braked on the icy road causing the lorry to skid into a wall.*
▻ ***noun***: **skids:** *He braked too hard and the car went into a skid.*

skier /ˈskiːə(r)/ *noun*: **skiers**
A **skier** is a person who skis on snow.

skiing /ˈskiːɪŋ/ *noun* (*uncount, often adjectival*)
Skiing is the sport or activity of moving over snow using skis: *They go skiing in Austria every winter.* □ *a skiing holiday.*

skilful (*AmE* **skillful**) /ˈskɪlfəl/ *adjective*
Someone who is **skilful** has a lot of skill: *a skilful negotiator* □ *her skilful fingers* □ *In the hands of a skilful surgeon, the operation is nearly always a complete success.* — *adverb* **skilfully:** *He argued skilfully and convincingly.* □ *She skilfully removed the bullet and bandaged the wound.*

skill /skɪl/ *noun*: **skills**
1 Skill is cleverness or expertness at doing something that comes from a lot of practise or from natural ability: *His negotiating technique shows great skill and judgement.* □ *Fly-fishing requires a certain amount of skill and a great deal of patience.* **2** A **skill** is a job or activity which requires training or practise, or a talent or accomplishment which you develop through training or practise: *He is going to night classes to learn basic computer skills.*

skilled /skɪld/ *adjective*
1 Someone who is **skilled** at something is very good at it, usually because they have had a lot of experience or practice: *She's a skilled horsewoman.* [*same as* **expert**] **2** A **skilled** worker is someone who requires a high level of training in order to do his or her job: *Many skilled workers have been made redundant as heavy industries are lost.* [see also **semi-skilled, unskilled**]

skim /skɪm/ *verb*: **skims, skimming, skimmed**
1 If something **skims** a surface, it moves or glides just above it or brushes it lightly as it passes: *The birds flew low over the sea, skimming the surface with their wings.* **2** If you **skim** something floating on the top of a liquid, you remove it with shallow scooping movements: *Boil the meat in lightly salted water, skimming any fat off the cooking liquid.* **3** If, when you read something, you **skim** through it, you read it superficially, often only to take in the main points: *Just give me five minutes to skim through the report.*

skimmed milk /skɪmd ˈmɪlk/ or **skim milk** *noun* (*uncount*)
Skimmed milk is milk from which the cream has been removed by skimming.

skimp /skɪmp/ *verb*: **skimps, skimping, skimped**
If you **skimp** on something, or you **skimp** it, you provide or use only just enough or too little of it, or spend only just enough or too little money or time on it: *Buy the best meat you can afford; it isn't worth skimping on the ingredients if you want a good result.*

skimpy /'skɪmpɪ/ *adjective*: **skimpier, skimpiest**
Something that is **skimpy** is inadequate or too small; **skimpy** clothes barely cover the body or do not cover enough of the body: *How are you able to revise for your exams using only these few skimpy notes?* □ *girls in skimpy bikinis.*

skin /skɪn/ *noun*; *verb*
▻ ***noun***: **skins**
1 (*uncount*) **Skin** is the tissue forming the outer covering on the bodies of humans and animals: *dark skin* □ *You sweat through little pores in your skin.* □ *Do not use this cream on broken or irritated skin.* □ *a skin disease.* **2** (*uncount or count*) You also refer to the outer covering of some types of fruit and vegetable as their **skin**: *potato skins* □ *a banana skin.* [see picture at **fruit**] **3** (*uncount or count*) You can also refer to someone's complexion as their **skin**: *She has beautiful skin.* □ *Do you have a dry or greasy skin?* **4** An animal **skin** is an animal hide, with or without fur or hair attached: *Astrakhan is made from the skins of very young Karakul lambs.* **5** If a **skin** has formed on the surface of a liquid, a semi-solid layer has formed, usually because the surface is exposed to the air.
▻ ***verb***: **skins, skinning, skinned**
1 You **skin** an animal when you strip the skin from its body: *Skin the chicken and cut it into pieces.* **2** You **skin** part of your body when you injure it by scraping the skin from it: *He skinned his knuckles on the concrete wall.*
▻ ***phrases*** **1** You do or complete something **by the skin of your teeth** when you only just manage to do or complete it: *We managed to get through to the next round by the skin of our teeth.* **2** (*informal*) When someone or something **gets under your skin** **a** they annoy and upset you very much: *His remarks really got under my skin.* **b** they cause you to feel a strong passion or attraction for them. **3** If you say that someone or something made you **jump out of your skin**, you mean that they startled or surprised you very much: *When his face appeared at the window, I nearly jumped out of my skin.* **4** (*informal*) If you say that something is **no skin off your nose**, you mean that it does not cause you the slightest concern or nuisance: *He can do what he likes; it's no skin off my nose.* **5** (*informal, often derogatory*) Someone does something to **save their own skin** if they do it to protect themselves from harm or danger, often without being concerned for others that may be affected.

skin-deep /skɪn'diːp/ *adjective*
If you say that something, such as beauty, is **skin-deep**, you mean it is only superficial.

skinflint /'skɪnflɪnt/ *noun* (*informal, rather old*): **skinflints**
If you call someone a **skinflint** you mean that they are very mean, especially with money: *You miserable old skinflint!*

skinhead /'skɪnhɛd/ *noun*: **skinheads**
A **skinhead** is a person, usually a white youth, who has cut their hair very short or shaved their head. Skinheads wear jeans and heavy boots, have anti-establishment attitudes, and are frequently aggressive, especially towards minority groups.

skinny /'skɪnɪ/ *adjective*: **skinnier, skinniest**
Skinny means very thin: *All there was to eat was a couple of skinny chickens.* □ *skinny legs* □ *a skinny youth.*

skint /skɪnt/ *adjective* (*slang*)
If you say you are **skint**, you mean that you have no money: *'Will you lend me £5?' 'No, sorry; I'm skint.'*

skin-tight /skɪn'taɪt/ *adjective*
Skin-tight clothing is very tight-fitting: *skin-tight jeans.*

skip /skɪp/ *verb*; *noun*
▻ ***verb***: **skips, skipping, skipped**
1 You **skip** when you move forward with light springing or hopping steps: *lambs skipping around their mothers.* **2** You **skip** when you make a series of jumps over a skipping-rope: *He skips for five minutes every morning to keep fit.* □ *girls skipping and playing ball games in the school playground.* **3** If you **skip** something, you leave it out or pass over it to the next thing: *I usually skip lunch on weekdays.* □ *I skipped the introduction and began reading Chapter 1.* **4** (*informal*) If a pupil or student **skips** a class or school, they do not attend it: *He's been skipping school for weeks.*
▻ ***noun***: **skips**
1 A **skip** is a skipping movement: *a hop, skip and a jump.* **2** A **skip** is also a large metal container that is filled with unwanted or waste material, *eg* on a building site, and is carried away by a special lorry for disposal elsewhere.
▻ ***phrase*** (*informal*) If someone says **'skip it!'** they mean 'forget it', 'ignore it' or 'it is not important': *'I don't know what you mean by that.' 'Oh, just skip it; it would take too long to explain.'*

skipper /'skɪpə(r)/ *noun*; *verb*
▻ ***noun***: **skippers**
The captain of a ship, aeroplane or sporting team, especially a cricket team is often referred to as the **skipper**: *the skipper of a trawler.*
▻ ***verb***: **skippers, skippering, skippered**
Someone who **skippers** a boat, ship or aeroplane is the person in command of it; someone who **skippers** a sporting team acts as its captain: *Atherton will skipper the English cricket team for the next test.*

skipping-rope /'skɪpɪŋroʊp/ *noun*: **skipping-ropes**
A **skipping-rope** is a rope, often with handles attached to either end, used for jumping over as exercise or as a children's game. It is swung backwards and forwards or twirled in a circular motion by the person skipping or by two other people each holding an end.

skirmish /'skɜːmɪʃ/ *noun*; *verb*
▻ ***noun***: **skirmishes**
1 A **skirmish** is a brief battle during a war, especially away from the main fighting and usually involving small groups of soldiers or fighters: *The Civil War was made up of a series of relatively minor skirmishes and only a few set-piece battles.* **2** A **skirmish** is also any minor fight or dispute: *He was involved in a skirmish with his opposite number in the House of Commons.*
▻ ***verb***: **skirmishes, skirmishing, skirmished:** *Small groups of partisans skirmished with enemy troops in the mountainous country.*

skirt /skɜːt/ *noun*; *verb*
▻ ***noun***: **skirts**
1 A **skirt** is a piece of clothing that hangs from the waist and is worn by women and girls. [see picture at **clothing**] **2** The **skirt** of a woman's dress or coat is the part that hangs down below the waist. **3** A **skirt** is also anything that hangs down loosely as this piece of clothing does, especially the flexible base of a hovercraft.
▻ ***verb***: **skirts, skirting, skirted**
1 Something that **skirts** an area borders it or is situated around the edge of it: *The path skirted the edge of the cliffs before it led inland.* □ *fields skirting the motorway.* **2** You **skirt** something when you move along or around the edge of it: *They skirted round any villages*

or towns as they marched south. **3** If you **skirt** round a problem or difficulty, you avoid facing it.

skittish /ˈskɪtɪʃ/ *adjective*
If someone is being **skittish**, they are behaving in a lively or playful way; if a horse is **skittish**, it is lively or nervous and difficult to control. [*same as* **frisky**]

skittle /ˈskɪtəl/ *noun*: **skittles**
1 A **skittle** is any of the bottle-shaped objects that are placed standing upright and used as targets in the game of skittles. **2** (*uncount*) **Skittles** is a game in which players try to knock down a number of these objects with a ball rolled along the floor or the ground.

skive /skaɪv/ *verb* (*informal*): **skives, skiving, skived**
If you **skive**, or **skive** off, you avoid work or a duty, especially because you are lazy: *He always skiving.* ▫ *They skived off school this afternoon.*

skulk /skʌlk/ *verb*: **skulks, skulking, skulked**
1 If someone **skulks** somewhere, they wait there keeping themselves hidden from view, often because they plan to do something bad or want to avoid meeting people: *He was discovered skulking in the bushes.* **2** If you **skulk** off somewhere, you sneak away often because you have done something wrong or do not want to be noticed.

skull /skʌl/ *noun*: **skulls**
Your **skull** is the framework of bones in your head that surrounds and encloses your brain.

skunk /skʌŋk/ *noun*: **skunks**
1 A **skunk** is a North American animal with black and white fur and a long tail. It defends itself by squirting out an extremely unpleasant-smelling liquid. **2** (*derogatory*) If you call someone a **skunk**, you think they are an extremely unpleasant person.

sky /skaɪ/ *noun*: **skies**
1 (*used in the singular or uncount*) The **sky** is the vast area of space that you can see above the earth and in which clouds, the sun, the moon and stars can be seen. **2** A **sky** or **skies** are the appearance of this area, especially as affected by certain weather conditions or pollution: *a calm cloudless sky* ▫ *the smog-filled skies over London.*
▻ ***phrases*** **1** For **pie in the sky** see **pie**. **2** If you say **the sky's the limit**, you mean that there is no upper limit to the amount of money that may be spent or the things that may be achieved.

sky-blue /skaɪˈbluː/ *noun* (*uncount*)
Sky-blue is a bright light blue, the colour of a cloudless sky.

sky-high /skaɪˈhaɪ/ *adjective or adverb*
Something that is or goes **sky-high** is or goes very high: *sky-high prices* ▫ *The price of coffee rose sky-high.* ▫ *The force of the explosion blew the car sky-high.*

skylight /ˈskaɪlaɪt/ *noun*: **skylights**
A **skylight** is a window in the roof or ceiling of a building.

skyline /ˈskaɪlaɪn/ *noun* (*usually in the singular*): **skylines**
The **skyline** is the outline of buildings, hills and trees seen against the sky.

skyscraper /ˈskaɪskreɪpə(r)/ *noun*: **skyscrapers**
A **skyscraper** is an extremely tall building.

skyward /ˈskaɪwəd/ or **skywards** /ˈskaɪwədz/ *adverb*
If something points or is directed **skyward** or **skywards**, it points or is directed upwards towards the sky: *The missiles were launched skywards.*

slab /slab/ *noun*; *verb*
▻ ***noun***: **slabs**
A **slab** is a thick flat piece or slice of something, or a thick flat object: *The grave was covered with a polished granite slab.* ▫ *Great slabs of ice broke off the glacier into the sea.* ▫ *They paved the area with concrete slabs.*
▻ ***verb***: **slabs, slabbing, slabbed**
You **slab** an area of ground when you pave it with concrete or stone slabs.

slack /slak/ *adjective*; *noun*
▻ ***adjective***: **slacker, slackest**
1 Something is **slack** if it is loose or it is not pulled or stretched tight: *One of my teeth is slack.* ▫ *Pull the rope tight; it's too slack to support the tent.* **2** If someone is lazy or does not do their work carefully or properly, they are **slack** about it. **3** A **slack** period or time is a period or time when there is not much work or activity: *There's usually a slack period in the restaurant between lunchtime and early evening.* **4** **Slack** is also used to describe *eg* discipline or supervision that is not firm or tightly controlled enough.
▻ ***noun*** (*uncount*)
The part of a length of rope or wire that is not pulled tight is the **slack**: *When you have hooked a fish, reel the line in quickly to take up the slack.*

slacken /ˈslakən/ *verb*: **slackens, slackening, slackened**
1 If the pace or intensity of something **slackens** it slows down or becomes less intense: *The wind slackened and veered to the south.* **2** You **slacken** your hold or grip on something when you make it looser or less firm. **3** You **slacken** something that is too tight or that has been tightly fastened when you loosen it: *When you are changing a wheel first slacken the wheel nuts.*

slacks /slaks/ *noun* (*plural*; *old*)
Slacks are loose casual trousers: *She wore cotton slacks and open sandals.*

slag /slag/ *verb* (*slang*): **slags, slagging, slagged**
You **slag** someone, or **slag** them **off**, when you criticize them harshly or say unpleasant things about them.

slain /sleɪn/ *verb*
Slain is the past participle of **slay**.

slam /slam/ *verb*; *noun*
▻ ***verb***: **slams, slamming, slammed**
1 You **slam** a door or a window, or it **slams**, when you shut it or it shuts with great force making a loud banging or crashing sound: *He stormed out, slamming the door behind him.* **2** If something **slams** or **is slammed** into or against something else, it hits it or crashes into it with great force: *He slammed his fist down on the table.* ▫ *The lorry skidded and slammed into the car in front.* **3** (*informal*) If someone **is slammed** *eg* in the press, they are criticized cruelly or severely.
▻ ***noun***: **slams**
A **slam** is an act or the sound of slamming: *The door closed with a slam.*

slander /ˈslɑːndə(r)/ *noun*; *verb*
▻ ***noun*** (*uncount or count*): **slanders**
Slander is the act of making, in speech as distinct from in writing, an untrue statement about a person intended to damage his or her reputation; a **slander** is such a statement: *What he said is completely untrue. Do you think I should sue for slander?* ▫ *That is a deliberate slander.*
▻ ***verb***: **slanders, slandering, slandered**
You **slander** someone when to talk about them in this way.
[compare **libel**]

slanderous /ˈslɑːndərəs/ *adjective*
A statement is **slanderous** when it is untrue and thus unfairly damages someone's reputation.

slang /slaŋ/ *noun* (*uncount*)
Slang is words and phrases used only very informally,

not usually in writing or polite speech, and often only by members of a particular social group or profession: *street slang* □ *RAF slang* □ *a slang expression.*

slanging match /ˈslaŋɪŋ matʃ/ *noun* (*informal*): **slanging matches**
If two people have a **slanging match**, they insult each other angrily, and often loudly.

slangy /ˈslaŋɪ/ *adjective*: **slangier, slangiest**
Slangy speech has a lot of slang in it; a **slangy** expression is very informal and is not used in correct speech or writing.

slant /slɑːnt/ *verb*; *noun*
▻ *verb*: **slants, slanting, slanted**
1 If something **slants** it lies or slopes at an angle and is not horizontal or vertical: *His handwriting slants to the left.* □ *sunlight slanting through the half-open blinds.* **2** If information **is slanted** in a particular way or towards a particular audience or group of people, it is presented in a biased way or is aimed at that audience or group.
▻ *noun* (*used in the singular*)
1 A **slant** is a sloping position, surface or line: *The floor has a definite slant.* **2** If news or information is given a particular **slant**, it is presented so that certain aspects or details are given more emphasis or importance than others, or it is aimed at a particular audience. — *adjective* **slanting:** *She has slanting almond-shaped eyes.*

slap /slap/ *noun*; *verb*; *adverb*
▻ *noun*: **slaps**
1 A **slap** is a blow made with the palm of the hand or anything flat: *He gave the horse a slap on the rump.* **2** A **slap** is also the sound made by such a blow, or by something hitting a flat surface: *the gentle slap of the waves against the side of the boat.*
▻ *verb*: **slaps, slapping, slapped**
1 You **slap** someone or something when you hit them with your hand held flat and your fingers extended, or with something flat: *Mum, David slapped me!* □ *He slapped the other officer across the face with a glove.* **2** You **slap** something down on a flat surface when you bring it down forcefully with a slapping sound: *He slapped a ten pound note down on the table.* **3** (*informal*) If you **slap** something on, you apply it thickly and carelessly: *Don't slap the paint on the wall like that!* □ *I'm just going to slap on some make-up.*
▻ *adverb* (*informal*)
1 You can use **slap** to mean 'exactly' or 'precisely': *His first shot landed slap in the middle of the target.* **2** **Slap** also means heavily, with a slapping sound: *He fell slap in a muddy puddle.*
▻ *phrases* (*informal*) **1** A **slap in the face** is a rude or insulting rejection or refusal. **2** If someone gives you a **slap on the back**, they give you their congratulations by hitting you with the flat of their hand in the middle of your back. **3** A **slap on the wrist** is a gentle punishment or mild warning.

> ***phrasal verb***
> **slap down** (*informal*) If you **slap** someone **down**, you dismiss their suggestions abruptly or make them feel unimportant.

slap-bang /slapˈbaŋ/ *adverb* (*informal*)
1 If something is or lands **slap-bang** in the middle of something, it is or lands right in the middle of it: *We found ourselves slap-bang in the middle of a civil war.* **2** **Slap-bang** also means directly and with force: *He drove slap-bang into the wall.*

slapdash /ˈslapdaʃ/ *adjective*
If work is described as **slapdash**, it is carelessly and hurriedly done: *His work tends to be rather slapdash.*

slapstick /ˈslapstɪk/ *noun* (*uncount*)
Slapstick is a type of comedy based on simple jokes in which actors hit each other, fall over, break things, and generally behave in a rough or boisterous way.

slap-up /ˈslapʌp/ *adjective* (*BrE*; *informal*)
A **slap-up** meal is one in which there is a lot of food of a high quality.

slash /slaʃ/ *verb*; *noun*
▻ *verb*: **slashes, slashing, slashed**
1 If you **slash** something, or **slash** at it, you cut it with violent sweeping strokes using a sharp tool or weapon, or you aim violent sweeping blows at it so as to cut it or break it off: *He slashed his way through the jungle with a machete.* □ *He stamped off in a rage, slashing at the bushes with his stick as he went.* □ *His face had been slashed from the cheek to the chin.* **2** (*informal*) If prices or wages **are slashed**, they are reduced suddenly and drastically.
▻ *noun*: **slashes**
1 A **slash** is a long, especially deep, cut. **2** A **slash** is also a sweeping cutting stroke. **3** A **slash**, or a **slash mark**, is an oblique line in writing or printing.

slat /slat/ *noun*: **slats**
A **slat** is a thin strip, especially of wood or metal, often fixed horizontally with others to form a blind or vent.

slate /sleɪt/ *noun*; *verb*
▻ *noun*: **slates**
1 (*uncount*) **Slate** is a type of rock which splits easily into thin layers, used *eg* to make roofing tiles. **2** A **slate** is a roofing tile made of this. [see picture at **house**] **3** In schools in former times, a **slate** was a piece of this used by pupils for writing on. **4** If a customer in a public house or shop has the cost of the items they buy put on the **slate** or on their **slate**, they do not pay for them at the time and the cost is recorded so that when they pay later the total is known. **5** (*uncount*) **Slate** or **slate-grey** is a dull grey colour.
▻ *verb*: **slates, slating, slated**
You **slate** a roof when you cover it with slates.

slatted /ˈslatɪd/ *adjective*
Slatted items are made using slats: *a slatted blind.*

slaughter /ˈslɔːtə(r)/ *noun*; *verb*
▻ *noun* (*uncount*)
1 **Slaughter** is the killing of animals for their meat: *lambs being fattened for slaughter.* **2** **Slaughter** is also the killing of many people or animals, especially cruelly or violently: *the slaughter of so many young men on the battlefields of France* □ *He was sickened by the slaughter.*
▻ *verb*: **slaughters, slaughtering, slaughtered**
1 An animal **is slaughtered** when it is killed for its meat; people or animals **are slaughtered** when they are killed cruelly or violently, usually in large numbers: *They slaughtered the fatted calf.* □ *They slaughtered everyone who didn't belong to their tribe.* [*same as* **massacre**] **2** (*informal*) You can say that your opponent in a game **slaughtered** you if they defeated you completely and in a humiliating way: *Their team was slaughtered in the final.* [*same as* **massacre**]

slaughterhouse /ˈslɔːtəhaʊs/ *noun*: **slaughterhouses**
A **slaughterhouse** is a place where animals are killed to be sold for food. [*same as* **abattoir**]

slave /sleɪv/ *noun*; *verb*
▻ *noun*: **slaves**
1 In former times, a **slave** was a person with no personal freedom or rights who was owned by and worked as a servant for another person. Slaves were

frequently captured in, and transported from, their own country or region to the place where they were to work. **2** You can also refer to someone who works extremely hard for another person and is badly treated by them as a **slave**: *He treats her like a slave.* **3** A person who submissively obeys someone else's commands in order to please them can also be referred to as a **slave**: *He was her devoted slave.* **4** If you say that you are a **slave** to something, you mean that a great part of your life is taken up by that thing: *She's a slave to her work.*

▻ ***verb***: **slaves, slaving, slaved**

You **slave**, or **slave** at something, when you work very hard and continuously: *She is slaving in the kitchen to get the food ready for the party.* □ *He's slaving away in his study at some report.*

slave driver /ˈsleɪv draɪvə(r)/ *noun* (*informal*): **slave drivers**

If you say that someone is a **slave driver**, you mean that they demand very hard work from others: *Their boss is a bit of a slave driver.*

slaver /ˈslavə(r)/ *verb*: **slavers, slavering, slavered**

An animal **slavers** when spittle or saliva runs from its mouth: *The dog slavered as it was offered a bone.*

slavery /ˈsleɪvərɪ/ *noun* (*uncount*)

1 Slavery is the state of being a slave or the practice of owning slaves: *He was sold into slavery.* □ *William Wilberforce campaigned to abolish slavery.* **2 Slavery** is also very hard work, often for little or no pay.

slavish /ˈsleɪvɪʃ/ *adjective* (*derogatory*)

1 You can use **slavish** to describe things that copy or imitate other things exactly with no attempt being made to introduce any original features or elements, or that follow rules or instructions rigidly without questioning or criticizing them: *slavish copies of classical sculpture.* **2** A person who is **slavish** behaves like a slave in that they obey other people's commands without question or work very hard to please others. — *adverb* **slavishly:** *He had followed her instructions slavishly.*

slay /sleɪ/ *verb* (*old or literary*): **slays, slaying, slew, slain**

To **slay** someone means to kill them: *He was slain in battle.*

sleazy /ˈsliːzɪ/ *adjective* (*informal*): **sleazier, sleaziest**

A **sleazy** place is dirty, neglected-looking and tends to attract people who are not respectable: *She tracked him down in a sleazy little hotel in a Paris slum.*

sled /slɛd/ *noun*: **sleds**

A **sled** is a sledge: *a dog sled.*

sledge /slɛdʒ/ *noun*; *verb*

▻ ***noun***: **sledges**

1 A **sledge** is a vehicle pulled by horses or dogs and has ski-like runners for travelling over snow. **2** A **sledge** is also a small vehicle of similar design on which people, especially children, sit or lie to slide on snow, pushing themselves forward with their hands and feet. [same as **toboggan**]

▻ ***verb***: **sledges, sledging, sledges**

You **sledge** when you travel by sledge or play on a sledge.

sledgehammer /ˈslɛdʒhamə(r)/ *noun*: **sledgehammers**

A **sledgehammer** is a large heavy hammer swung with both arms.

sleek /sliːk/ *adjective*

1 Sleek hair or fur is smooth, soft and glossy. **2** You can also use **sleek** to describe a person who looks well-fed and well-groomed.

sleep /sliːp/ *noun*; *verb*

▻ ***noun***: **sleeps**

1 (*uncount or used in the singular*) **Sleep** is the condition of rest you are in when your eyes are closed and you are in a natural state of unconsciousness: *He looks as if he needs a good night's sleep.* □ *I only had three hours' sleep last night.* □ *He was in such a deep sleep it took several minutes to rouse him.* □ *She talks in her sleep.* **2** (*usually in the singular*) You have a **sleep** when you rest for a time in a condition of natural unconsciousness: *Did you have a good sleep?* □ *She likes to have a little sleep in the afternoons.*

▻ ***verb***: **sleeps, sleeping, slept**

1 You **sleep** when you close your eyes and pass into a natural state of unconsciousness: *Did you sleep well?* □ *Macbeth shall sleep no more.* □ *The children slept for most of the journey.* □ *homeless people sleeping in shop doorways.* **2** A place **sleeps** a certain number of people if it has beds for that number of people: *The apartment sleeps six.* □ *The caravan will sleep two adults and two children pretty comfortably.*

▻ ***phrases*** **1 a** You **go to sleep** when you pass into a sleeping state; you **get to sleep** when you manage to pass into this state: *Go back to sleep.* □ *She lies awake worrying and can't get to sleep.* □ *I didn't get to sleep till four in the morning.* **b** (*informal*) Part of your body **goes to sleep** when it becomes numb, usually because you have been sitting or lying on it preventing the blood from flowing into it: *Your legs go to sleep when you kneel for a long time.* **2** (*with a negative*; *informal*) If you tell someone not to **lose any sleep** over something you mean that it is not worth worrying about. **3 a** A patient who is due for a surgical operation **is put to sleep** when they are given an anaesthetic to make them unconscious during the operation. **b** (*euphemistic*) Vets **put** animals **to sleep** when they kill them painlessly by injecting them with a lethal dose of a drug.

phrasal verbs

sleep around (*informal*) Someone who **sleeps around** is in the habit of having sex casually with different people.

sleep in You **sleep in** when you fail to wake up at the proper time or you sleep for longer than you normally do: *Sorry to be late; I slept in.* [*same as* **oversleep**]

sleep off If you have eaten or drunk too much and you **sleep** it **off**, you recover from the effects by sleeping: *We thought he was just drunk and left him on the floor to sleep it off.*

sleep on You **sleep on** something when you delay making a decision about it until the following morning: *I'm a bit uncertain; could you let me sleep on it?*

sleep together (*euphemistic*) Two people, especially two people who are not married to each other, **are sleeping together** if they are having a sexual relationship.

sleep with (*euphemistic*) One person **sleeps with** another when they have sex with them.

sleeper /ˈsliːpə(r)/ *noun*: **sleepers**

1 You refer to someone who sleeps as a **sleeper**, especially when you are talking about how deeply they normally sleep: *He's always been a light sleeper.* [=is wakened easily] **2** A **sleeper** is a train with carriages that provide sleeping accommodation for passengers: *He's taking the sleeper to London.* **3** (*BrE*) The heavy metal or wooden beams on which a railway track is laid are known as **sleepers**.

sleeping bag /ˈsliːpɪŋ bag/ *noun*: **sleeping bags**
A **sleeping bag** is a large quilted sack for sleeping in, used especially by a person when he or she is camping.

sleeping pill /ˈsliːpɪŋ pɪl/ *noun*: **sleeping pills**
A **sleeping pill** is a pill containing a drug that makes you sleep.

sleepless /ˈsliːpləs/ *adjective*
1 A **sleepness** night is one in which you are unable to sleep, often because you are worried about something. **2** If someone is **sleepless**, they are unable to sleep.

sleepwalk /ˈsliːpwɔːk/ *verb*: **sleepwalks, sleepwalking, sleepwalking**
When a person **sleepwalks** they walk about while they are still asleep: *You shouldn't try to wake someone who is sleepwalking.* — *noun* (*uncount*) **sleepwalking:** *Heidi's sleepwalking was a sign that she was very unhappy.*

sleepy /ˈsliːpɪ/ *adjective*: **sleepier, sleepiest**
1 You feel **sleepy** when you feel tired and want to sleep: *You will know that the drug is working when you begin to feel sleepy.* □ *The children looked very sleepy so she sent them to bed.* [*same as* **drowsy**] **2** A **sleepy** place is very quiet and does not have much going on in it: *a sleepy little village in the Cotswolds.* — *adverb* **sleepily:** *'Is it time for bed yet?' he asked sleepily.*

sleet /sliːt/ *noun*; *verb*
▻ ***noun*** (*uncount*)
Sleet is rain mixed with snow or hailstones: *Sleet and snow showers are forecast.*
▻ ***verb***: **sleets, sleeting, sleeted**
You say it **is sleeting** when sleet is falling: *The temperature dropped sharply and it began to sleet.*

sleeve /sliːv/ *noun*: **sleeves**
1 The **sleeves** of a piece of clothing are the parts that cover, or partly cover, your arms: *a dress with three-quarter length sleeves.* **2** A **sleeve** is also the cardboard or paper envelope in which a record is stored.
▻ ***phrase*** If you **have something up your sleeve**, you have an idea or plan that you are keeping secret from other people meantime, but which you may use at some later time: *I'm certain he has some cunning plan up his sleeve.*

sleeveless /ˈsliːvləs/ *adjective*
A **sleeveless** piece of clothing is one that has no sleeves: *a sleeveless cotton dress* □ *a sleeveless jerkin.*

sleigh /sleɪ/ *noun*: **sleighs**
A **sleigh** is a large sledge drawn by a horse or horses.

sleight of hand /slaɪt əv ˈhand/ *noun* (*uncount*)
1 Sleight of hand is the skill of moving your hands quickly and skilfully so that other people cannot see what you are doing, as a conjuror does when he performs magic tricks. **2** If something is done by **sleight of hand** it is done using skilful deception: *The clause was introduced into the bill now before parliament by sleight of hand.*

slender /ˈslɛndə(r)/ *adjective*
1 A **slender** person is attractively slim: *She is tall and slender.* **2** Something that is **slender** is smaller in size or amount than you would like it to be: *This tax will hit pensioners of slender means hardest.* □ *The government avoided defeat by a margin so slender that they will have to rethink many of their policies.*

slept /slɛpt/ *verb*
Slept is the past tense and past participle of **sleep**.

sleuth /sluːθ/ *noun* (*old or humorous*)
A **sleuth** is a detective: *that famous sleuth, Sherlock Holmes.*

slew /sluː/ *verb*
Slew is the past tense of **slay**.

slice /slaɪs/ *noun*; *verb*
▻ ***noun***: **slices**
1 A **slice** is a thin broad piece cut off something larger: *two slices of toast* □ *thin slices of cold roast beef.* **2** (*informal*) You can also refer to a share or part of something as a **slice**: *He owns a large slice of the business.* **3** (*count or uncount*) In sports such as golf, a **slice** is a stroke which causes the ball to spin sideways and curve away in a particular direction; a player puts **slice** on a ball when he or she causes it to spin and curve away in this way.
▻ ***verb***: **slices, slicing, sliced**
1 You **slice** something when you cut it up into broad thin pieces using a knife or other sharp instrument: *Slice up the cooked fillet into fairly thick steaks.* **2** When something **is sliced**, or **sliced** off, it is cut off a larger piece with a knife or other sharp instrument: *The executioner's axe fell, slicing off her head with a single blow.* **3** If something **slices** through or into something else, it cuts or moves easily through or into it, as a sharp knife would: *The bow of the boat sliced through the waves.*

slick /slɪk/ *adjective*; *noun*
▻ ***adjective***: **slicker, slickest**
1 If you describe a person or their methods of persuasion as **slick** you think they are clever at persuading people to do things but are not necessarily completely honest: *a slick salesman.* **2 Slick** is also used to describe something that is done impressively well or efficiently without seeming to involve much effort: *a slick and well-run operation* □ *a slick performance.* **3 Slick** hair is smooth and glossy.
▻ ***noun***: **slicks**
A **slick**, or an **oil slick**, is a wide layer of spilled oil floating on the surface of water: *The slick has been carried on to the beaches by the wind.* □ *environmental damage caused by a large oil slick in the Persian Gulf.*

slide /slaɪd/ *verb*; *noun*
▻ ***verb***: **slides, sliding, slid**
1 Something **slides** over a surface when it moves or runs smoothly over it: *Slide the key under the door.* □ *The logs came sliding down the chute into the river.* □ *They slid down the muddy bank on their bottoms.* **2** You **slide** something somewhere when you place or move it there with a quick smooth movement: *'Read this when you are alone,' he whispered, sliding a piece of paper into her jacket pocket.* **3** You **slide** when your feet slip on a smooth, wet or icy surface or object: *He slid on a banana skin.* **4** A standard or the level of something **slides** when it gradually moves downwards or gets worse, *eg* through neglect or laziness: *He slid back into his old bad habits.*
▻ ***noun***: **slides**
1 A **slide** is any part that glides smoothly, *eg* the moving part of a trombone. **2** A **slide** is a structure for children to play on, usually with a ladder to climb up and a narrow sloping part to slide down. **3** The small glass plates on which specimens are placed to be viewed through a microscope are called **slides**. **4** A small transparent photograph viewed through and magnified by a projector is a **slide**. [see also **transparency**] **5** A large decorative hair-clip which is pushed into the hair and fastened in position is also called a **slide**.
▻ ***phrase*** If you **let things slide** you allow them to get worse, *eg* through neglect or laziness.

slight /slaɪt/ *adjective*; *verb*; *noun*
▻ ***adjective***: **slighter, slightest**
1 Something that is **slight** is small in amount or

degree: *The weather was warm with a slight breeze.* □ *There's been a slight improvement in his condition.* □ *The difference is very slight.* □ *There was a slight pause before she spoke again.* □ *We've got a slight problem here.* □ *We must go on trying as long as there is the slightest* [= least] *hope of a solution.* [= any hope at all] □ *I'm not the slightest bit worried.* □ *She spoke English without the slightest trace of an accent.* [compare **faint**] **2** A person who is **slight** is slim and not usually very tall: *I caught a glimpse of her slight figure in the crowd.* — *adverb* **slightly:** *'Do you know them?' 'Only slightly.'* □ *We'd slightly underestimated the numbers.* □ *She weighed slightly under five stone.* □ (*moderating*) *I think he's slightly mad.* □ *This is all slightly awkward.* [*same as* **a little, a bit**]

▻ ***verb*** (*formal*): **slights, slighting, slighted**

Someone **slights** you when they insult you by treating you as unimportant, *eg* by ignoring you: *She felt hurt and slighted.*

▻ ***noun***: **slights**

A **slight** is an insult: *Obviously, as he saw it, the appointment of another person was a serious slight on his own abilities.*

▻ ***phrase*** **In the slightest** emphasizes a negative statement: *'Weren't you worried?' 'Not in the slightest.'* □ *It doesn't matter in the slightest.*

slim /slɪm/ *adjective*; *verb*

▻ ***adjective***: **slimmer, slimmest**

1 A **slim** person is attractively thin: *long, slim legs* □ *He's tall and slim.* □ *You are much slimmer than you were the last time I saw you.* **2** You can also use **slim** to describe things that are not thick or wide: *a slim volume of poetry.* **3** A **slim** chance is one that is not very great: *His chances of recovery are pretty slim.* — *noun* (*uncount*) **slimness**: *trying to preserve one's youthful slimness.*

▻ ***verb***: **slims, slimming, slimmed**

You **slim** when you try to make yourself slim or slimmer, especially by dieting or taking exercise: *'I won't have any cake, thank you; I'm slimming.'*

> **phrasal verb**
> If something **is slimmed down,** it is reduced in size: *plans to slim down the workforce (*or *slim the workforce down) to around a hundred people.*

slime /slaɪm/ *noun* (*uncount*)

Slime is a thick unpleasantly slippery or sticky substance that covers the surface of something or that creatures such as slugs and snails produce from their bodies to help them move along: *The garden pond was covered with green slime.* □ *The snail left a trail of slime.*

slimming /'slɪmɪŋ/ *noun*; *adjective*

▻ ***noun*** (*uncount*)

Slimming is the process of trying to get slimmer, usually by dieting: *a slimming diet.*

▻ ***adjective***

Something that is **slimming** has the effect of making someone slimmer or appear slimmer: *a slimming style* □ *That skirt is very slimming.*

slimy /'slaɪmɪ/ *adjective*: **slimier, slimiest**

1 Something **slimy** is like slime, or is covered with or consists of slime: *A snake's skin is actually dry though it may look slimy.* □ *a slimy film on the water's surface* □ *a slimy mess.* **2** (*informal, derogatory*) If you say that a person or their behaviour is **slimy**, you mean that they are too friendly or too humble to be sincere: *a horrid slimy little man.*

sling /slɪŋ/ *noun*; *verb*

▻ ***noun***: **slings**

1 A **sling** is a loop of cloth used to support an injured arm, worn around the neck. **2** A **sling** is a primitive weapon for firing stones, consisting of a strap or pouch in which the stone is placed and swung round fast. **3** A **sling** is also a strap or loop for hoisting, lowering or carrying a weight: *The cow was lifted off the boat in a sling.*

▻ ***verb***: **slings, slinging, slung**

1 (*informal*) You **sling** something somewhere when you throw it or fling it carelessly or using force: *He slung the bags into the back of the lorry.* **2** Something **is slung** somewhere when it is placed there so that it hangs loosely: *a soldier with a rifle slung over his shoulder.* **3** You **sling** something when you launch or fire it from a sling or a catapult: *slinging stones at the cats.*

slink /slɪŋk/ *verb*: **slinks, slinking, slunk**

A person or animal **slinks** somewhere when they go or move there slowly and quietly trying to avoid being noticed, *eg* because they are afraid, ashamed or embarrassed: *The dog slunk away into a corner.*

slinky /'slɪŋkɪ/ *adjective* (*informal*): **slinkier, slinkiest**

1 A **slinky** dress or other piece of clothing clings so that the body's curves are attractively emphasized. **2** Someone's, especially a woman's, walk can be described as **slinky** when they walk or move with slow rolling movements which emphasize their body's curves.

slip /slɪp/ *verb*; *noun*

▻ ***verb***: **slips, slipping, slipped**

1 a You **slip** when you slide accidentally and lose your balance: *She slipped and fell on the wet floor.* **b** Something **slips** when it shifts out of position: *The load had slipped to one side and had to be adjusted before the lorry could continue.* □ *A large amount of snow had slipped off the roof.* □ *Apparently parts of the coast are gradually slipping into the sea.* □ *I could feel my tights slipping down.* **c** Something **slips** from your fingers when you drop it: *The glass slipped from my grasp and shattered on the floor.* **d** Something that you don't intend to say **slips** out if you have said it before you can stop yourself. **e** Something **slips** your mind when you forget it: *I'm afraid I forgot to fetch the laundry; it just slipped my mind.* **f** A level or standard **slips** when it falls or gets lower: *The pound has slipped a little on the foreign exchanges.* □ *Discipline is bad enough in this school; we mustn't let things slip any further.* **g** You say you **are slipping** if you are making mistakes that you wouldn't have made at some earlier stage. **h** A dog **slips** its lead or collar when it gets its head free and escapes. **i** Someone **slips** a disc when one of the discs of cartilage between the vertebrae in their spine is squeezed out of position, causing severe pain. **2 a** You **slip** something somewhere when you pass it there with a smooth sliding action, often deliberately avoiding drawing people's attention to what you are doing: *She slipped the envelope into her pocket.* □ *He slipped her a note under the table.* □ *If we slip the porter a fiver he'll make sure we aren't disturbed.* **b** You **slip** somewhere when you go there quickly and quietly, usually to escape notice: *I'm just slipping out for a moment.* □ *She slipped out through the back door.* □ *The speeches had already started so he slipped quietly in at the back.* □ *She managed to slip past the guards under cover of darkness.* **c** You **slip** into or out of a piece of clothing, or your clothes, when you put them on or take them off quickly: *Just slip out of your clothes, slip into this gown, and the doctor will be along in a moment to examine you.* □ *She slipped the dress on over her head.* □ *He slipped off his shoes and socks.*

▻ ***noun*: slips**
1 A **slip** is an act of sliding accidentally or making a wrong move: *One slip and you could find yourself at the bottom of the cliff.* **2** A **slip** is any slight mistake: *There must be a slip somewhere in the calculations.* □ *She could play really difficult music from sight without a single slip.* □ *Sorry I called you by the wrong name when I introduced you; it was just a slip of the tongue.* **3** A **slip**, or a **slip** of paper, is a small piece of paper: *Please fill in and detach the acceptance slip below.* □ *There was a slip of paper between two pages, acting as a bookmark.* **4** A **slip** is also a woman's loose undergarment for wearing under a dress or skirt. [*same as* **petticoat**]
▻ ***phrases*** **1** (*informal*) You **give** your pursuers **the slip** when you succeed in escaping from them: *He's given us the slip; he must have escaped up a side street.* **2 a** You **let** information **slip** when you say something that reveals it, without intending to: *He let slip that he had had an interview with another company.* **b** You **let** an opportunity **slip** when you fail to take advantage of it: *She never let slip any opportunity of advancing her career.*

> ***phrasal verb***
> You **slip up** when you make a mistake: *There wasn't nearly enough food; someone had evidently slipped up somewhere in the planning.* [see also **slip-up**]

slip-on /ˈslɪpɒn/ *adjective or noun*: **slip-ons**
Slip-on shoes are easily put on and have no laces, buttons or other fastenings: *I prefer slip-ons to shoes with laces.*

slipped disc /slɪpt ˈdɪsk/ *noun*: **slipped discs**
A **slipped disc** is a painful condition in which the layers of tissue (**cartilage**) between any of the joints (**vertebrae**) in the spine move out of place, causing pressure on a spinal nerve.

slipper /ˈslɪpə(r)/ *noun*: **slippers**
Slippers are comfortable indoor shoes made of cloth or some other soft material: *She came to the door in her dressing gown and slippers.* □ *a pair of fur-lined slippers*. [see picture at **clothing**]

slippery /ˈslɪpərɪ/ *adjective*
1 A surface that is **slippery** is wet, greasy or so smooth that it can cause you to slip: *Be careful; the floor is slippery.* **2** A **slippery** object is so smooth, wet or greasy that it is difficult to catch or keep hold of: *Liver is slippery to handle.* **3** If you describe a person as **slippery**, you mean that they are unreliable and not to be trusted: *He's a slippery customer.* **4** A **slippery** problem, situation or subject is difficult to deal with: *The solution to the troubles in Northern Ireland has proved to be a slippery problem for successive governments.*

slipshod /ˈslɪpʃɒd/ *adjective*
If a person or work is **shipshod**, they are untidy or careless or it is carelessly done: *He tends to be careless and shipshod.* □ *a slipshod piece of work.*

slip-up /ˈslɪpʌp/ *noun* (*informal*): **slip-ups**
A **slip-up** is a mistake, often a small and relatively unimportant one: *I made an embarrassing slip-up when I addressed him as 'Madam Chairman'.*

slit /slɪt/ *noun; verb*
▻ ***noun*: slits**
A **slit** is a long narrow cut or opening: *She watched him through a slit in the curtains.* □ *eyes like slits* □ *a skirt with a slit up the back.*
▻ ***verb*: slits, slitting, slit**
You **slit** something, or you **slit** it open, when you make a long narrow cut in it or open it by making such a cut: *Slit open the envelope using a sharp knife.* □ *He slit the fish down the belly and removed the entrails.* □ *She tried to slit her wrists.* [=commit suicide by cutting into the veins in her wrists]

slither /ˈslɪðə(r)/ *verb*: **slithers, slithering, slithered**
1 A snake **slithers** when it moves with smooth sliding movements over the ground. **2** If you **slither** somewhere, you slide or slip smoothly: *They slithered down the muddy bank.*

sliver /ˈslɪvə(r)/ *noun*: **slivers**
A **sliver** of something is a long very thin piece that has been cut or broken off a larger piece: *slivers of glass* □ *delicate slivers of smoked salmon.*

slob /slɒb/ *noun* (*informal, derogatory*): **slobs**
If you call someone a **slob**, you think they are a lazy, untidy or ill-mannered person: *Look at all those dirty clothes scattered about his room. What a slob he is!*

slobber /ˈslɒbə(r)/ *verb*: **slobbers, slobbering, slobbered**
A person or animal **slobbers** when they let saliva run from their mouth. [*same* **drool, slaver**]

> ***phrasal verb***
> (*informal, derogatory*) If someone **slobbers over** another person, they show their admiration or affection too publicly so that it causes that person and other people embarrassment.

slog /slɒg/ *verb; noun*
▻ ***verb*** (*informal*): **slogs, slogging, slogged**
1 To **slog** means to labour or work hard and long at something: *You've been slogging away at that report for hours.* □ *The runners came slogging up the hill, sweating and panting.* **2** If you **slog** something, or one person **slogs** at another, they hit that thing or person hard: *He slogged the ball right over the boundary.* □ *boxers slogging away at each other.*
▻ ***noun*** (*used in the singular; informal*)
1 A **slog** is a hard blow or stroke. **2** If you describe a task or journey as a **slog**, you mean it is long and tiring: *They had walked for miles and still had the long slog to the top of the hill.*

slogan /ˈsloʊgən/ *noun*: **slogans**
A **slogan** is a phrase that is easy to remember used to identify a group or organization, or to advertise a product: *political slogans* □ *The company slogan is 'Stack 'em high and sell 'em cheap'.*

slop /slɒp/ *verb; noun*
▻ ***verb*: slops, slopping, slopped**
1 Liquid **slops** when it splashes or spills, especially over the edge of a container: *There was water slopping around in the bottom of the boat.* □ *Water slopped over the edge of the bucket.* **2** You **slop** a liquid on or over an area when you cause it to spill: *Try not to slop paint all over the carpet.*
▻ ***noun*: slops**
1 (*plural*) **Slops** are waste food or a mixture of liquid and solid waste food fed to pigs. **2** (*plural*) **Slops** are also liquid foods fed to babies or people that are ill. **3** (*uncount or used in the plural*) **Slop** or **slops** are a mixture of urine, faeces and waste water contained in a bucket in a prison cell or a bedpan when there is no sink or toilet available: *a slop bucket*

slope /sloʊp/ *noun; verb*
▻ ***noun*: slopes**
1 A **slope** is a line or surface that is at an angle, being neither horizontal or vertical: *They dragged the cart up the slope.* **2** (*used in the singular*) The **slope** of something is the angle at which it slopes from the vertical or horizontal: *a roof with a slope of 45°.* **3** A **slope** or **ski slope** is a specially prepared track for skiing on the side of a hill or mountain: *He's out on the slopes every day.*

▻ ***verb*: slopes, sloping, sloped**
Something **slopes** when it lies at an angle so that one end is higher than the other: *The land sloped steeply down to the water's edge.*

> ***phrasal verb***
> (*informal*) If someone **slopes off**, they leave, especially trying not to be noticed as they do so: *He tried to slope off while we weren't looking.*

sloppy /ˈslɒpɪ/ *adjective*: **sloppier, sloppiest**
1 Sloppy work or workmanship is done in a careless and untidy way. **2** A **sloppy** person is messy or does things in a careless and untidy way: *He's a very sloppy dresser.* — *adverb* **sloppily:** *This repair has been very sloppily done.*

slosh /slɒʃ/ *verb* (*informal*): **sloshes, sloshing, sloshed**
You **slosh** liquid about when you splash or spill it noisily or carelessly; liquid **sloshes** about *eg* in a container when it splashes about or spills over the edge: *He sloshed cold water on his face.* □ *Seawater sloshed over the side of the boat.*

sloshed /slɒʃt/ *adjective* (*informal*)
Someone who is **sloshed** is drunk: *He was so sloshed he couldn't stand up.*

slot /slɒt/ *noun*; *verb*
▻ ***noun*: slots**
1 A **slot** is a small narrow rectangular opening into which something is fitted or inserted: *Put the money in the slot and take your ticket.* **2** You can also refer to a time, place or position within a schedule as a **slot**: *The party political broadcast was given the nine o'clock slot.*
▻ ***verb*: slots, slotting, slotted**
You **slot** something in, or it **slots** in, when you put it in the space where it fits, or in a schedule: *The shelf should slot easily into the brackets.* □ *The chairman has a very busy schedule but we could probably slot you in between lunch and the board meeting this afternoon.*

sloth /sloʊθ/ *noun* (*uncount*; *formal*)
Sloth is laziness or idleness.

slot machine /ˈslɒt məʃiːn/ *noun*: **slot machines**
A **slot machine** is a machine operated by putting a coin into a slot.

slouch /slaʊtʃ/ *verb*: **slouches, slouching, slouched**
You **slouch** when your body leans or droops in a lazy or relaxed position when you are sitting, standing or walking: *youths slouching against the wall on the street corner* □ *She was slouched on the sofa.*

slough /slʌf/ *verb*: **sloughs, sloughing, sloughed**

> ***phrasal verb***
> **1** A creature such as a snake **sloughs off** its skin when it sheds it, having grown a new one. **2** You **slough** something **off** when you get rid of it or abandon it: *He sloughed off his responsibilities to his family as easily as if they had never existed.*

slovenly /ˈslʌvənlɪ/ *adjective*
A **slovenly** person is careless, untidy or dirty in appearance, in their habits or in the way that they work.

slow /sloʊ/ *adjective*; *adverb*; *verb*
▻ ***adjective*: slower, slowest**
1 Someone or something that is **slow** moves, acts or happens without speed, or takes an unusually long time: *The band was playing a slow waltz.* □ *He has an unusually slow pulse.* □ *I got stuck on the A68 behind a lot of slow lorries.* □ *He's making a slow recovery.* □ *It's bound to be a slow process.* □ *He's a slow worker, but accurate.* □ *You must be patient with the slow learners.* □ *The food was poor and the service slow.* □ *We caught the slow train back to Prague.* □ *Your reactions get much slower as you get older.* [*opposite* **fast, quick, rapid**] **2** People are **slow** to react if they take a long time to do so, or do not do so readily: *She was slow to react to the news.* □ *He was normally slow to take offence.* [*opposite* **quick**] **3** A clock or watch is **slow** if it shows a time that is earlier than the correct time: *The clock in the hall is ten minutes slow.* [*opposite* **fast**] **4** Someone who is **slow** is not very clever and finds learning and understanding difficult: *I was very slow at most school subjects.* [*opposite* **quick, bright**] **5** You can describe a social event or performance as **slow** if it lacks interest and excitement: *The evening was a bit slow to start with, but things livened up later.* [*opposite* **lively**] **6** Business or trade is **slow** when few goods are sold. [*same as* **slack**; *opposite* **brisk**] **7** A **slow** photographic film needs to be exposed to light for a fairly long time. [*opposite* **fast**] — *adverb* **slowly:** *Slowly the sun disappeared below the horizon.* □ *She slowly began to realize that he was not the man she'd thought.* □ *We're progressing slowly but surely.* — *noun* (*uncount*) **slowness:** *The slowness of their progress had begun to irritate her.*
▻ ***adverb*: slower, slowest:** *Drive a bit slower* (or *more slowly*) *so that we don't miss the turn-off.* □ *Do walk a little slower; we can't keep up.* □ *Caution. Slow-moving traffic ahead.* □ *the slowest-growing types of skin tumour* □ *We can use one of the slower-acting drugs.* □ *My watch is going slow again.*

> The adverb **slow** is uncommon except in compounds (*eg slow-moving*), but the comparative **slower** is often used instead of **more slowly**.

▻ ***verb*: slows, slowed, slowed**
Something or someone **slows** to a lower rate of movement or progress when they reduce their speed: *The train slowed to a halt.* □ *He slowed to walking pace.* □ *Her pulse gradually slowed to its normal rate.*

> ***phrasal verbs***
> **slow down 1** Something **slows down** or **is slowed down** when its speed is reduced: *Slow down as you approach a corner.* □ *The driver slowed the bus down and drew in to the side.* □ *Progress has slowed down a good deal.* **2** You **slow down** when you become less busy or active: *You'll be ill if you don't slow down.* □ *She's slowed down a lot in these last few years.*
> **slow up** Something **slows up** or **is slowed up** when its speed is reduced: *She slowed up as she approached the pedestrian crossing.* □ *It'll slow us up if we have to check everything twice.*

slow motion /sloʊ ˈmoʊʃən/ *noun* (*uncount*)
In film or television, **slow motion** is a speed of movement that is much slower than movement in real life, created by increasing the speed at which the camera records the action.

slow-witted /ˈsloʊwɪtɪd/ *adjective*
A **slow-witted** person is not clever and is not able to think as quickly as people of normal intelligence. [*opposite* **quick-witted**]

sludge /slʌdʒ/ *noun* (*uncount*)
Sludge is thick soft mud or a thick greasy substance resembling this: *Clean the sludge from the bottom of the water tank.*

slug /slʌg/ *noun*; *verb*

▻ ***noun*: slugs**
1 A **slug** is a creature similar to a snail but without a shell. **2** (*informal, especially AmE*) A **slug** is a bullet. **3** (*AmE; informal*) A **slug** is also large mouthful or measure of a strong alcoholic spirit: *Give me a slug of that whisky.*
▻ ***verb*** (*informal*): **slugs, slugging, slugged**
If you **slug** someone you strike them with a heavy blow.

sluggish /'slʌgɪʃ/ *adjective*
Something that is **sluggish** is slow-moving or less lively, active or alert than usual: *a sluggish stream* ▫ *The heat has made me feel tired and sluggish.*

sluice /slu:s/ *noun; verb*
▻ ***noun*: sluices**
1 A **sluice** is an artificial channel or drain for water. **2** A **sluice**, or a **sluice-gate**, is a valve or sliding gate for controlling the flow of water in a canal, lock, dam or lake.
▻ ***verb*: sluices, sluicing, sluiced**
1 Water **sluices** away when it drains through such a channel. **2** You **sluice** something, or **sluice** it **down**, when you wash or rinse it by throwing or directing a stream of water over it: *stablelads sluicing down the horseboxes and the cobbled yard.*

slum /slʌm/ *noun*: **slums**
1 A **slum** is a dirty, often overcrowded, building in a bad state of repair, or a street of these buildings. **2** The areas of a city where there is bad housing and poor living conditions are referred to as that city's **slums**: *He was brought up in the slums of Naples.*

slumber /'slʌmbə(r)/ *noun; verb*
▻ ***noun*** (*uncount or count; literary*): **slumbers**
Slumber is sleep: *She fell into a deep slumber.* ▫ *He was awakened from his slumbers by a terrific crash.*
▻ ***verb*** (*literary*): **slumbers, slumbering, slumbered**
To **slumber** means to sleep: *He was slumbering peacefully in a chair by the fire.*

slump /slʌmp/ *verb; noun*
▻ ***verb*: slumps, slumping, slumped**
1 You **slump** somewhere when you fall or sink there heavily: *She slumped down on the settee, completely exhausted.* ▫ *They found him slumped over his desk.* **2** Trade, business activity or prices **slump** when they fall suddenly and sharply.
▻ ***noun*: slumps**
1 A **slump** is a period, especially a long period, when a country's economy is in decline, business activity is depressed, and there is a lot of unemployment: *the post-war slump.* **2** A **slump** in prices is a sharp fall in them: *a slump in house prices.*

slung /slʌŋ/ *verb*
Slung is the past tense and past participle of **sling**.

slunk /slʌŋk/ *verb*
Slunk is the past tense and past participle of **slink**.

slur /slɜ:(r)/ *verb; noun*
▻ ***verb*: slurs, slurring, slurred**
1 You **slur** your speech when you pronounce words unclearly, running them together, *eg* because you are drunk: *His speech was slurred and he was unsteady on his feet.* **2** You **slur** someone's good name or reputation when you say or write bad, often untrue, things about them. **3** (*music*) A musician **slurs** when he or she sings or plays a sequence of notes so that each one flows smoothly into the next without any pauses between them.
▻ ***noun*: slurs**
1 A **slur** is a statement or piece of writing intended to harm someone's good name or reputation. **2** A **slur** is also a slurred speech sound. **3** (*music*) A **slur** is two or more musical notes played or sung so that they flow together smoothly without any pauses, or an instruction or mark in written music indicating the notes that should be played or sung in this way.

slurp /slɜ:p/ *verb*: **slurps, slurping, slurped**
You **slurp** liquid food or drink when you eat or drink making a loud sucking noise with your lips as you take the food or drink into your mouth: *He slurped the soup down.*

slush /slʌʃ/ *noun* (*uncount*)
1 Slush is partly melted snow on the ground. **2** (*informal, derogatory*) Some people call speech or writing **slush** when it is so sentimental that it is silly.

slut /slʌt/ *noun* (*derogatory*): **sluts**
1 If someone calls a woman a **slut** they mean that she is a prostitute or has sexual intercourse with many partners. **2** A dirty or untidy woman is also sometimes called a **slut**.

sly /slaɪ/ *adjective*: **slyer** or **slier, slyest** or **sliest**
1 A **sly** person is cunning and good at deceiving others: *He's a sly old bird!* **2** A **sly** look or smile suggests that the person making it knows something secret. **3 Sly** also means mischievous in a playful manner: *That was a sly trick to play on your best friend!*

smack /smak/ *verb; noun; adverb*
▻ ***verb*: smacks, smacking, smacked**
1 You **smack** someone when you hit them, especially with your open hand, making a slapping sound: *She smacked the little boy on the back of the legs.* **2** (*informal*) Something **is smacked** against something else when it hits it heavily making a loud sound: *He was thrown forward and smacked his forehead on the steering wheel.*
▻ ***noun*: smacks**
1 A **smack** is a blow, or the sound of a blow, made with the open hand: *She gave him a smack on the bottom.* **2** A **smack** is a loud enthusiastic kiss: *He gave his mother a big smack on the cheek.*
▻ ***adverb*** (*informal*)
1 You use **smack** to emphasize that something has hit something else directly and with force: *He drove smack into the tree.* **2** You also use **smack** to indicate that something ends up precisely in the place mentioned: *He landed smack in the middle of the village pond.*
▻ ***phrase*** If someone **smacks their lips**, they bring their lips together and then part them with a loud sound, especially as a way of indicating that they are enjoying what they are eating or drinking.

> ***phrasal verb***
> (*derogatory*) If you say that someone's attitude or behaviour **smacks of** a particular quality, you mean that their attitude or behaviour strongly suggests it: *His sudden concern for their welfare smacks of hypocrisy.*

small /smɔ:l/ *adjective; noun; adverb*
▻ ***adjective*: smaller, smallest** [see note at **little**]
1 Something that is **small** is little in size: *a small jar of coffee* ▫ *We'd like to find a smaller house to move into now that the children have left home.* ▫ *They run a small farm.* ▫ *The smallest size we have in this dress is a 12.* ▫ *The vegetables should be cut up very small.* [= into very small pieces] ▫ *You should have drawn his head smaller.* [*opposite* **big, large**] **2** A **small** amount is not very much of something; a **small** group contains only a few things or people: *Use only a small quantity of bleach.* ▫ *a small sum of money* ▫ *a small group of sup-*

porters. [*opposite* **large**] **3** Someone who is **small** is below average in height: *Small people are at such a disadvantage.* [*same as* **short**; *opposite* **tall**, **big**; compare **large**] **4** A **small** child is a young one: *She's far too small to go to school on her own.* □ *Some of the smaller children were obviously frightened.* [*opposite* **big**] **5 Small** describes things that are not very large, important or serious: *We'd like to present you with this small gift as a token of our appreciation.* □ *Would you do me a small favour?* □ *There's been a small problem with the computer.* □ *We've made a few small alterations.* □ *We went into production on a very small scale in 1989.* □ *small-scale businesses* □ *She never had the smallest* [= least] *intention of doing what she said.* □ *They've come a long way from such small* [= humble] *beginnings.* [compare **slight**] **6** A **small** farmer, shopkeeper or businessman is a person who runs a small farm, shop or business. **7** Someone makes you feel **small** when they say or do something that suggests that you are silly, incompetent or unimportant. **8** The **small** hours are the period after midnight: *I was woken in the small hours by the dog barking.*

▻ ***noun*** (*used in the singular*)

The **small** of your back is the narrow part near the waist: *She felt a sudden twinge of pain in the small of her back.*

small ad /ˈsmɔːl ad/ *noun* (*usually in the plural*; *informal*): **small ads**

The **smalls ads** in a newspaper or magazine are short notices advertising, *eg* items for sale.

small change /smɔːl ˈtʃeɪndʒ/ *noun* (*uncount*)

Small change is coins of low value: *Can you lend me 10 pence, I don't have any small change.*

small fry /ˈsmɔːl fraɪ/ *noun* (*plural*)

1 If you refer to people or things as **small fry**, you think they are unimportant: *They can't compete with a company of this size*; *they're just small fry.* **2** Some people also refer to children as **small fry**.

smallholding /ˈsmɔːlhoʊldɪŋ/ *noun* (*BrE*): **smallholdings**

A **small holding** is a piece of cultivated land smaller than a farm, usually one that is under fifty acres.

small-minded /ˈsmɔːlmaɪndɪd/ *adjective*

Small-minded people lack tolerance and imagination. [*same as* **narrow-minded**]

smallpox /ˈsmɔːlpɒks/ *noun* (*uncount*)

Smallpox is a serious infectious disease which causes a high fever and a severe rash of large blisters that usually leave permanent scars on the skin. Smallpox caused many deaths across the world before a vaccine became widely available.

small print /smɔːl ˈprɪnt/ *noun* (*uncount*)

The **small print** on a contract usually contains the extra information or conditions which the writer of the contract wants to include but does not necessarily want to be read too closely.

small talk /ˈsmɔːl tɔːk/ *noun* (*uncount*)

Small talk is polite conversation about trivial matters such as the weather.

small-time /ˈsmɔːltaɪm/ *adjective* (*informal*)

Small-time means operating on a small scale: *a small-time crook* □ *He doesn't take on big contracts*; *he's strictly small-time.*

smarmy /ˈsmɑːmɪ/ *adjective* (*informal*): **smarmier**, **smarmiest**

If you describe someone or their manner as **smarmy** you mean that they are too attentive and try to charm you with excessive flattery: *a smarmy head waiter.* [*same as* **obsequious**]

smart /smɑːt/ *adjective*; *verb*

▻ ***adjective***: **smarter**, **smartest**

1 A **smart** person is neat and well-dressed; **smart** clothes are neat or fashionable in a fairly formal way: *He's always very smart.* □ *She wore a smart navy suit.* **2** (*sometimes derogatory*) If you say that someone is **smart**, you mean that they are clever or shrewd: *He's smarter than I am.* □ *He's the smartest in the class.* □ *Don't get smart with me!* [=Don't think you are being clever by being cheeky to me!] **3** A **smart** hotel is sophisticated and usually expensive; a **smart** area has fashionable and expensive houses or shops in it: *They live in one of the smarter suburbs.* **4** A **smart** blow is done quickly and forcefully: *You may be able to release the wheel nuts if you give them a smart tap with a hammer.* **5** A **smart** pace is quick or brisk: *They set off at a smart trot.* **6** When people describe man-made objects or machines as **smart**, they are referring to their ability to operate independently or hold and update information, using computer technology: *a smart bomb* □ *a smart card.*

▻ ***verb***: **smarts**, **smarting**, **smarted**

1 If something **smarts**, it causes you to feel a sharp stinging pain in part of your body; if a part of your body **is smarting**, you feel a sharp stinging pain in it: *Don't put too much of that antiseptic on*; *it smarts dreadfully.* □ *Her eyes were smarting from the smoke.* **2** You can also say that you **are smarting** from *eg* an insult or criticism when it causes you to feel acute irritation or distress.

▻ ***phrase*** If someone tells you to **look smart**, they want you to hurry up: *Look smart now, or you'll be late for school.* — *adverb* **smartly:** *a smartly-dressed man* □ *She always dresses smartly.* — *noun* (*uncount*) **smartness:** *I was impressed by the smartness* [=smart appearance] *of their employees.*

smarten /ˈsmɑːtən/ *verb*: **smartens**, **smartening**, **smartened**

> ***phrasal verb***
> You **smarten** someone or something **up** when you make them neater or tidier: *You'd better smarten yourself up for the interview.* □ *The old cottages have recently been smartened up with a new coat of paint.*

smash /smaʃ/ *verb*; *noun*

▻ ***verb***: **smashes**, **smashing**, **smashed**

1 You **smash** something when you break it violently into pieces; something **smashes** or **is smashed** when it is destroyed or broken into pieces in this way: *The hooligans rampaged through the town centre smashing car windscreens and overturning litter bins.* □ *The glass slipped from my hand and smashed on the stone floor.* **2** Something **smashes** into or through something when it hits it or bursts through it violently causing damage: *The firemen smashed through the door.* □ *He smashed his fist down on the table.* □ *The lorry smashed into a wall, killing the driver.* **3** (*informal*) Something **is smashed** when it is broken up or ruined completely: *The police have succeeding in smashing an international drugs ring.* **4** A player in a racquet sport such as tennis **smashes** the ball when they hit it with a powerful overhead stroke.

▻ ***noun***: **smashes**

1 A **smash** is an act, or the sound, of smashing: *He brought his fist down on the table with a smash.* □ *There was a smash of breaking dishes.* **2** In racket sports such as tennis, a **smash** is a powerful overhead stroke.

3 (*informal*) A **smash** is a road traffic accident: *There was a bad smash on the motorway this morning.* **4** (*informal*) A **smash** is a smash hit: *This song is guaranteed to be a smash.*

smashed /'smaʃt/ *adjective* (*informal*)
When someone is or gets **smashed**, they are or get extremely drunk.

smasher /'smaʃə(r)/ *noun* (*informal*): **smashers**
If you say that a person or thing is a **smasher** you like or admire them very much.

smash hit /smaʃ 'hɪt/ *noun* (*informal*)
If a song, play or film is a **smash hit** it is a great success.

smashing /'smaʃɪŋ/ *adjective* (*informal*)
If you say that something is **smashing** you mean that it is excellent or splendid: *That was a smashing party.* □ *You look smashing in that dress.*

smattering /'smatərɪŋ/ *noun* (*used in the singular*)
1 A **smattering** of something is a small amount of it scattered around: *a light smattering of snow.* **2** You have a **smattering** of something, especially a foreign language, when you have a little knowledge of it: *He has* [=can speak] *German, Italian and a smattering of French.*

smear /smɪə(r)/ *verb*; *noun*
▻ ***verb***: **smears, smearing, smeared**
1 You **smear** a sticky or oily substance on a surface when you spread it thickly over that surface: *She smeared suntan lotion all over his back.* **2** Something **smears** or **is smeared** when it becomes or is made to become blurred or smudged: *Her mascara was smeared all over her cheeks.* □ *Be careful not to smear the ink.* **3** If one person **smears** another, they say or write abusively damaging things about them: *His opponents tried to smear the president with allegations of infidelity.*
▻ ***noun***: **smears**
1 A **smear** is a greasy mark or patch: *You didn't do a very good job when you washed the windows; there are smears all over them.* **2** A **smear** is a damaging criticism or accusation: *There's absolutely no truth in the allegation; it's a smear.* **3** A **smear** is a small amount of a substance, *eg* of tissue taken from a woman's cervix, that is placed on a slide for examination under a microscope.

smell /smɛl/ *noun*; *verb*
▻ ***noun***: **smells**
1 (*uncount*) **Smell** is one of your five physical senses; it is the sense by which you receive impressions through your nose: *Compared with other animals human beings have a relatively poor sense of smell.* **2** (*uncount or count*) The **smell** of something is the quality it has that makes you aware of it when you use your nose: *I'm sure there's a smell of burning.* □ *What's that peculiar smell?* □ *Ugh! What a smell!* □ *Some roses have hardly any smell.* □ *A mixture of delicious smells was coming out of the kitchen.* □ *That dog's made an awful smell.* □ *the smell of sweaty bodies* □ *I opened the window to get rid of the cigarette smell.* [*same as* **scent**, **odour**, **aroma**, **perfume**, **stench**]

> A **smell** can be pleasant or unpleasant, but is often unpleasant; an **odour** is generally unpleasant and a **stench** is very unpleasant; an **aroma** is most usually a pleasant smell of savoury food; **fragrance**, a **scent** or a **perfume** are all pleasant smells.

3 You have a **smell** when you sniff something so as to get an impression of it through your nose: *Is this milk all right? Have a smell.*
▻ ***verb***: **smells, smelling, smelled** or **smelt**
1 If you say that something **smells** you usually mean that it has an unpleasant smell: *When did you buy that fish? It's beginning to smell.* □ *Your breath smells; what have you been eating?* □ *His feet smell.* □ *This T-shirt is smelling a bit.* **2** Things **smell** a certain way, or **smell** of something, if that is the impression that you get of them through your nose: *Mmm. Breakfast smells good.* □ *That cream smells sour.* □ *You smell gorgeous tonight.* □ *The living room smelt of cigarettes.* □ *The place smelt as if someone had spilt a bottle of disinfectant all over the floor.* □ *This smells like whisky.* □ *'What's in this bowl?' 'I don't know; what does it smell like?'* **3** You **smell** something, or you can **smell** it, if you become aware of it through your nose: *I smell* (or *can smell*) *gas.* □ *Do you* (or *can you*) *smell a peculiar smell?* □ *We could smell the meal cooking in the basement.* □ *I can smell something burning.* □ *You can almost smell the seaweed when you look at that picture.* □ *I had a bad cold and couldn't smell a thing.* **4** You **smell** something when you deliberately sniff it, so as to get an impression of it through your nose: *Smell this meat. Is it OK?* □ *I'm just smelling these socks to see if I can wear them another day.* **5** You say you **smell** something if you suspect it or think it is likely or possible: *I smell a conspiracy.* □ *He immediately smelt trouble.* □ *She could always smell a bargain.*

smelly /'smɛlɪ/ *adjective* (*informal*): **smellier, smelliest**
Something is **smelly** when it has an unpleasant smell: *smelly socks* □ *a smelly old man.*

smelt¹ /smɛlt/ *verb*
Smelt is the past tense and past participle of **smell**.

smelt² /smɛlt/ *verb*: **smelts, smelting, smelted**
Rock, earth or a mineral containing a metal **is smelted** when it is heated so that the metal is separated out.

smile /smaɪl/ *verb*; *noun*
▻ ***verb***: **smiles, smiling, smiled**
1 You **smile** when you turn the corners of your mouth upwards, with your lips apart or together, showing that you feel pleasure, happiness or amusement: *He rarely smiles.* □ *Why are you smiling?* □ *The bride and bridegroom smiled happily for the camera.* **2** You **smile** at someone or something when you react to them with such an expression: *She smiled at his antics.* □ *He kissed her forehead and she smiled weakly.* **3** To **smile** also means to show with a smile what you think or feel about something: *He couldn't speak, but smiled his thanks.*
▻ ***noun***: **smiles**
A **smile** is an act or way of smiling: *She has a nice smile.* □ *a wry smile* □ *the happy smiles of the children.*

> **phrasal verb**
> (*formal*) If good luck or fortune **smiles on** you, you are lucky or fortunate.

smirk /smɜːk/ *verb*; *noun*
▻ ***verb***: **smirks, smirking, smirked**
People **smirk** when they smile in a self-satisfied or silly way: *He smirked when the headmaster called him up to receive the prize.*
▻ ***noun***: **smirks**
A **smirk** is a self-satisfied or silly smile: *'My school report was much better than yours,' he said with a smirk.* □ *Wipe that silly smirk off your face this minute!*

smithereens /smɪðə'riːnz/ *noun* (*plural*; *informal*)
If something is in **smithereens** or has been smashed to **smithereens**, it is in, or has been broken into, many tiny fragments: *The building had been blown to smithereens by the force of the blast.*

smock /smɒk/ *noun*: **smocks**
1 A **smock** is a loose shirt-like piece of clothing that is slipped over the head and worn over other clothes, *eg* by artists, so that they do not get dirty. **2** A **smock** is also a long loose-fitting blouse worn by women, especially when they are pregnant.

smog /smɒg/ *noun* (*uncount*)
Smog is a mixture of fog and smoke or vehicle exhaust gases that hangs in the air, especially over cities: *smog over the city of Los Angeles.*

smoke /smoʊk/ *noun*; *verb*
▷ ***noun***: **smokes**
1 (*uncount*) **Smoke** is the gases and fine particles that is given off when something is burning: *The chimney was belching black smoke.* □ *I hate the smell of cigarette smoke.* **2** (*informal*) If someone is having a **smoke** they are smoking tobacco: *He's gone outside for a smoke.* **3** (*informal*) A **smoke** is also a cigarette or cigar: *Have you got any smokes?*
▷ ***verb***: **smokes, smoking, smoked**
1 Something **smokes** when it gives off smoke: *The fire is smoking badly.* **2** You **smoke** when you draw the smoke from burning tobacco, in a cigarette, cigar or pipe, into your lungs; people who **smoke** do this as a habit: *I would be grateful if you wouldn't smoke in here.* □ *He has smoked since he was fifteen.* **3** You **smoke** food when you preserve or flavour it by passing smoke over or through it.
▷ ***phrase*** If something such as a building **goes up in smoke**, it is completely destroyed by fire; you can also say that something such as a plan **went up in smoke** when it has been completely ruined or has come to nothing.

smoked /smoʊkt/ *adjective*
Smoked meat, fish, cheese or other foods have been preserved or given a special flavour by the smoke from burning wood of various kinds: *smoked haddock* □ *smoked sausage.*

smokeless /ˈsmoʊkləs/ *adjective*
1 Smokeless fuel produces little or no smoke when it burns. **2** A **smokeless** zone is an area, especially in a town or city, where the use of smoke-producing fuel is not allowed.

smoker /ˈsmoʊkə(r)/ *noun*: **smokers**
If you are a **smoker**, you are in the habit of smoking tobacco, especially cigarettes. [*opposite* **non-smoker**]

smokescreen /ˈsmoʊkskriːn/ *noun*: **smokescreens**
1 A **smokescreen** is a cloud of smoke used to conceal the movements of troops. **2** Anything said or done in order to conceal or hide what is really happening can be referred to as a **smokescreen**.

smoking /ˈsmoʊkɪŋ/ *noun*; *adjective*
▷ ***noun*** (*uncount*)
Smoking is the habit or activity of smoking tobacco: *You should try to give up smoking if you want to avoid heart disease and lung cancer.*
▷ ***adjective***
A **smoking** area in a restaurant, cinema, or other public place, or a **smoking** compartment in a train, is one in which tobacco-smoking is allowed.

smoky /ˈsmoʊkɪ/ *adjective*: **smokier, smokiest**
1 If a fire is **smoky** it is giving off too much smoke, often because the fuel being used is damp. **2** If a room, or the atmosphere in a room, is **smoky**, the air in it is filled with, especially tobacco, smoke: *The bar was hot and smoky.* **3 Smoky** is also used to describe foods or drinks that have a smoked flavour: *smoky bacon crisps* □ *whisky with a smoky flavour.* **4 Smoky** also means hazy or slightly grey in colour: *smoky blue.*

smolder see **smoulder**.

smooth /smuːð/ *adjective*; *verb*
▷ ***adjective***: **smoother, smoothest**
1 A **smooth** surface is even and is not rough, coarse, bumpy or wavy: *a smooth skin* □ *Sand the wood until it is smooth.* **2** A **smooth** sauce or other liquid mixture has an even texture with no lumps in it: *Blend the butter and sugar until it is smooth and creamy.* **3 Smooth** progress is free from problems or difficulties: *a smooth transition to democratic government.* **4** A **smooth** journey is one that is steady and even in movement without jolts or breaks: *a smooth flight* □ *The new top-of-the-range model gives a wonderfully smooth ride.* **5** When a wine or other alcoholic drink feels pleasant in the mouth and is not sharp or bitter you can describe it as **smooth**. **6** If you describe a person, especially a man, as **smooth** you mean that they are too pleasant, polite or charming to be sincere: *a smooth talker.* —*adverb* **smoothly:** *The system was running smoothly.*
▷ ***verb***: **smoothes, smoothing, smoothed**
1 You **smooth** a surface when you make it smooth or smoother: *He sat by her bedside smoothing her hair and talking to her in a whisper.* □ *She smoothed the bedclothes.* **2** You **smooth** roughness or unevenness away when you remove it. **3** You **smooth** things out or over when you make problems or disagreements seem less serious or important: *Neither side is prepared to talk to the other, and unless we can smooth things over between them we will never get a satisfactory agreement.* **4** To **smooth** something means to make it easier: *The proposal is intended to smooth the way to peace.*

smother /ˈsmʌðə(r)/ *verb*: **smothers, smothering, smothered**
1 You **smother** someone, or they **smother**, when you kill them or they die from lack of air, because something has been placed over their mouth so that they are unable to breathe: *He tried to smother her with a pillow.* [*same as* **suffocate**] **2** You **smother** flames when you cover them with something that cuts off the supply of air and stops them burning. **3** Something **is smothered** with a substance when it is completely covered with a thick layer or a large quantity of that substance: *He smothers his food in tomato ketchup.* □ *She smothered his face with kisses.* **4** If you **smother** someone *eg* with love, you give them so much of it that they feel suffocated by it. **5** You **smother** something such as laughter or a yawn when you suppress it or try to hide it: *She smothered a giggle.*

smoulder (*AmE* **smolder**) /ˈsmoʊldə(r)/ *verb*: **smoulders, smouldering, smouldered**
1 Something **smoulders** when it burns slowly or without flames: *Two days after the fire parts of the building were still smouldering.* **2** A feeling, especially anger, **smoulders** when it goes on for a long time without being expressed openly. **3** Someone's eyes **smoulder** when they seem to burn with a bright light, because of anger or passion.

smudge /smʌdʒ/ *noun*; *verb*
▷ ***noun***: **smudges**
1 A **smudge** is a mark or blot spread by rubbing: *She had a smudge of soot on her nose.* **2** A **smudge** is also a faint or blurred shape, *eg* an object seen from a very long distance away: *The boat was just a smudge on the horizon.*
▷ ***verb***: **smudges, smudging, smudged**
1 You **smudge** something when you make a smudge on or of it: *You can create a softer outline if you smudge the charcoal a little.* **2** Something **smudges** when it becomes a smudge: *Your eye make-up is all smudged.*

smug /smʌg/ *adjective* (*derogatory*): **smugger, smuggest**
A **smug** person shows that they are very pleased with themselves and what they have done, especially in a way that is irritating to others: *a smug smile* □ *She's so smug she drives me wild.* [*same as* **complacent, self-satisfied**] — *adverb* **smugly:** *She finished the exam paper before anyone else and sat back smugly.* — *noun* (*uncount*) **smugness:** *I find his smugness unbearable.*

smuggle /ˈsmʌgəl/ *verb*: **smuggles, smuggling, smuggled**
You **smuggle** things in or out of a country when you take them in or out secretly and illegally, *eg* to avoid paying excise duty: *They kept him hidden until he could be smuggled out of the country.* □ *He was sentenced to death for smuggling heroin.*

smuggler /ˈsmʌgələ(r)/ *noun*: **smugglers**
A **smuggler** is a person who carries or brings things into a country secretly and illegally: *a drugs smuggler.*

smuggling /ˈsmʌgəlɪŋ/ *noun* (*uncount*)
Smuggling is the practice of bringing things into a country secretly and illegally: *The captain of the ship was accused of arms smuggling.*

smut /smʌt/ *noun*: **smuts**
1 (*uncount*) **Smut** is dirt or soot: *After the chimney was swept, all the furniture was covered in a layer of smut.* **2** A **smut** is a speck of dirt or soot: *You've got a smut on that clean shirt.* **3** (*uncount*) **Smut** is mildly obscene language, pictures or images: *This so-called newspaper is full of tasteless smut.*

smutty /ˈsmʌtɪ/ *adjective*: **smuttier, smuttiest**
1 Smutty language is mildly obscene. **2** If a surface is **smutty** it has specks of soot or dirt on it: *The windows are all smutty.*

snack /snak/ *noun*: **snacks**
A **snack** is a light meal eaten quickly, or a small item of food eaten between meals: *If we have a big breakfast, we'll only need a snack at lunchtime.* □ *She always has a snack, usually a chocolate bar or a piece of fruit, in the middle of the afternoon.*

snack bar /ˈsnak bɑː(r)/ *noun*: **snack bars**
A **snack bar** is a café or counter serving light meals or sandwiches.

snag /snag/ *noun*; *verb*
▻ ***noun*: snags**
A **snag** is a small problem or drawback: *I'd love to come with you; the only snag is I promised to visit my mother on that day.* □ *It seems too good to be true; are you sure there isn't some hidden snag.*
▻ ***verb*: snags, snagging, snagged**
You **snag** your clothing when you catch it and tear it on a sharp or rough object: *Be careful you don't snag your jumper on that rose bush.*

snail /sneɪl/ *noun*: **snails**
A **snail** is a small slow-moving creature with a soft body partly enclosed in a spiral shell.
▻ ***phrase*** If you do something **at a snail's pace** you do it extremely slowly.

snake /sneɪk/ *noun*; *verb*
▻ ***noun*: snakes**
1 A **snake** is a legless reptile with a long narrow body and a forked tongue. Many types of snake have a poisonous bite: *The adder or viper is the only poisonous snake found in Britain.* □ *The bite of a rattlesnake can be fatal.* **2** (*informal*) If you call someone a **snake**, you mean that they are a treacherous or deceitful person: *What a snake he turned out to be!*
▻ ***verb*: snakes, snaking, snaked**
If something **snakes** somewhere it moves in a twisting way like a snake or follows a winding course: *He cast expertly and the fishing line snaked across the river.* □ *The road snakes through the mountains.*

snap /snap/ *verb*; *noun*; *adjective*
▻ ***verb*: snaps, snapped, snapped**
1 Something **snaps** when it breaks suddenly and cleanly with a sharp cracking noise: *The fish fought so hard that the line snapped.* **2** Something **snaps** shut when it closes quickly and forcefully with a sharp sound. **3** An animal **snaps** when it tries to bite somebody or something: *The dogs were snapping at the cows' heels.* **4** You **snap** at someone when you speak to them in an abrupt, angry or impatient way: *I only asked you what the time was; you don't have to snap at me.* **5** (*informal*) You **snap** something when you take a photograph of it quickly: *I snapped her as she was getting out of the swimming pool.* **6** (*informal*) You **snap** when you suddenly lose your self-control: *She had listened to him snoring for hours when she suddenly snapped and hit him with a pillow.*
▻ ***noun*: snaps**
1 A **snap** is the act or sound of snapping. **2** (*informal*) **Snaps** are photographs, especially when taken without a lot of preparation and using simple equipment: *Would you like to see our holiday snaps?* [see also **snapshot**] **3** A cold **snap** is a sudden short period of cold or frosty weather: *Quite a few of the plants died in that cold snap we had last week.* **4** (*uncount*) **Snap** is a simple card game in which two or more players each lay one card face down in turn until two matching cards, *eg* with the same number, are laid down one on top of the other. The first player to shout 'snap' wins all the cards that have been laid down and the game continues until one player has all the cards.
▻ ***adjective***
A **snap** decision or judgement is made spontaneously without thinking about it for a long time.
▻ ***phrases*** **1** You **snap your fingers** when you make a short loud snapping sound by quickly pressing your thumb across your middle finger, usually to attract someone's attention: *He snapped his fingers to summon the waiter.* **2** (*informal*) If someone is depressed or sulking and you tell them to **snap out of it**, you are telling them to bring themselves out of their depressed state or sulk immediately.

phrasal verb
You **snap up** *eg* a bargain when you buy it without hesitation: *The goods in the sale were all snapped up within an hour of the store opening.*

snappy /ˈsnapɪ/ *adjective*: **snappier, snappiest**
1 If someone is **snappy** they are irritable and inclined to speak to people in a sharp angry way: *He always gets a bit snappy just before an exam.* **2** (*informal*) If you say that someone is a **snappy** dresser, you mean that they dress in very smart fashionable clothes.

snapshot /ˈsnapʃɒt/ *noun*: **snapshots**
A **snapshot** is a photograph, especially one taken without a lot of preparation beforehand, and using simple equipment: *We got some snapshots of the lions feeding.*

snare /snɛə(r)/ *noun*; *verb*
▻ ***noun*: snares**
A **snare** is a device used to trap small animals and consists of a loop of wire or string which catches the animal or bird's foot and tightens as it struggles to get free.
▻ ***verb*: snares, snaring, snared**
You **snare** animals or birds when you trap them using a snare.

snarl /snɑːl/ *verb*; *noun*
▻ ***verb***: **snarls, snarling, snarled**
1 An animal such as dog or a tiger **snarls** when it growls angrily, showing its teeth: *The dog snarled when he tried to open the gate.* **2** A person **snarls** when they say something in an angry or aggressive tone of voice, often twisting their face and drawing their lips back as they do so.
▻ ***noun***: **snarls**
1 A **snarl** is an act of snarling: *the snarls of the caged tiger.* **2** If you say something with a **snarl** you say it in a snarling voice or with a snarling expression.

snatch /snatʃ/ *verb*; *noun*
▻ ***verb***: **snatches, snatching, snatched**
1 You **snatch** something when you grab it suddenly: *The youth snatched her bag and ran off.* **2** You **snatch** at something when you try to get hold of it with a grabbing movement: *He snatched at the fly as it buzzed round his head.* **3** You **snatch** something away when you pull it away suddenly and forcefully: *She snatched her hand away.* **4** (*informal*) If you **snatch** a meal or a few hours sleep, you take it as soon as the opportunity arises or time permits: *We've got ten minutes before the train leaves; just enough time to snatch a cup of coffee and a bun.*
▻ ***noun***: **snatches**
1 A **snatch** is an act of snatching: *She made a snatch at the rope as it swung past her.* **2** (*usually in the plural*) **Snatches** of something, *eg* of a song or conversation, are short parts of it that you overhear or remember: *I could only hear snatches of their conversation, but from what I could gather they were planning some sort of robbery.* **3** (*usually in the plural*) **Snatches** of something, such as sleep or rest are brief periods of it: *They were only able to sleep in snatches while there were no bombs falling.*

sneak /sniːk/ *verb*; *noun*
▻ ***verb***: **sneaks, sneaking, sneaked**
1 You **sneak** somewhere when you go there quietly trying to avoid being noticed: *Robbie sneaked into his parents' bedroom looking for Christmas presents.* **2** You **sneak** something in or out of a place when you bring it in or take it out secretly, especially breaking a rule as a result: *He sneaked his girlfriend into the barracks at night.* **3** You **sneak** a look at something when you look at it quickly without being noticed: *He sneaked a look at the baby as it lay sleeping.*
▻ ***noun***: **sneaks**
A **sneak** is someone who sneaks, especially someone who tells tales: *Why are you listening at the door, you little sneak!*

> ***phrasal verb***
> If you **sneak up on** someone, you creep quietly up behind them, especially so as to take them by surprise: *The cat slowly sneaked up on the pigeon and then suddenly pounced.*

sneaker /ˈsniːkə(r)/ *noun* (*usually in the plural*; *AmE*): **sneakers**
Sneakers are lightweight canvas sports shoes.

sneaking /ˈsniːkɪŋ/ *adjective*
If you have a **sneaking** feeling or a **sneaking** suspicion that something is so, you have a slight feeling or suspicion that is difficult to put out of your mind: *I have a sneaking suspicion that he doesn't want me to be there when he makes the announcement.*

sneaky /ˈsniːkɪ/ *adjective*: **sneakier, sneakiest**
If someone is **sneaky** or they do something **sneaky**, they act in a secret or deceitful way, especially in order to gain an advantage for themselves: *It was really sneaky of you to have gone off and done that without telling anyone.* — *adverb* **sneakily:** *He sneakily read the letter and put it back exactly where he had found it.*

sneer /snɪə(r)/ *verb*; *noun*
▻ ***verb***: **sneers, sneering, sneered**
You **sneer** at someone or something when you show your contempt or scorn for them, especially by drawing your top lip up at one side: *He sneered at my attempts to write poetry.*
▻ ***noun***: **sneers:** *'Have you all seen Wilkins' pathetic little drawing?' he said with a contemptuous sneer.*

sneeze /sniːz/ *verb*; *noun*
▻ ***verb***: **sneezes, sneezing, sneezed**
You **sneeze** when you suddenly, violently and uncontrollably blow air out through your nose making a loud noise as you do so, *eg* because you have the cold or because something has irritated the delicate lining on the inside of your nose.
▻ ***noun***: **sneezes**
A **sneeze** is an act or the sound of sneezing.
▻ ***phrase*** (*informal*) If you say that an offer or opportunity is **not to be sneezed at**, you mean that it should not be regarded or dismissed as being of little value. [*same as* **not to be sniffed at**]

snide /snaɪd/ *adjective*
A **snide** remark or comment expresses criticism or disapproval in an indirect way intended to offend the person to whom it is addressed.

sniff /snɪf/ *verb*; *noun*
▻ ***verb***: **sniffs, sniffing, sniffed**
1 You **sniff** when you draw air through your nose in short sharp bursts making a sound as you do so, especially when you are crying or to show disapproval: *'I don't know what I'm going to do,' she sniffed.* **2** You **sniff** something when you smell it by drawing air into your nose in this way: *The lioness paused, sniffing the air.* □ *She sniffed at the cheese to see if it was ripe.* **3** Some people **sniff** a dangerous or addictive substance when they draw it up into their nose or inhale its fumes: *sniffing cocaine* □ *The youths had been sniffing glue.*
▻ ***noun***: **sniffs**
A **sniff** is an act or the sound of sniffing: *'How dare you speak to me like that?' she said with a sniff.* □ *Have a sniff at this aftershave; it smells horrible, doesn't it?*
▻ ***phrase*** If you say that an offer or opportunity is **not to be sniffed at**, you mean that it should not be regarded or considered as being of little value. [*same as* **not to be sneezed at**]

> ***phrasal verb***
> If an animal **sniffs** something **out**, it finds it or detects it by the sense of smell; if a person **sniffs** something **out**, they discover or detect it by careful tracking like a dog following a scent.

sniffle /ˈsnɪfəl/ *verb*; *noun*
▻ ***verb***: **sniffles, sniffling, sniffled**
You **sniffle** when you sniff repeatedly, *eg* because you have a cold.
▻ ***noun***: **sniffles**
1 A **sniffle** is an act or the sound of sniffling. **2** (*often used in the plural*; *informal*) If you have a **sniffle** or the **sniffles** you have a slight cold which is making your nose run with mucus: *I woke up with a bit of a sniffle.*

snigger /ˈsnɪgə(r)/ *verb*; *noun*
▻ ***verb***: **sniggers, sniggering, sniggered**
You **snigger** when you laugh softly in a foolish or mocking way: *The boys sniggered when she dropped*

her books. □ *If you don't stop sniggering, you will be sent out of the room!*
▻ ***noun***: **sniggers**
A **snigger** is such a laugh: *'Is that what you call a trendy jacket?' he asked with a snigger.*

snip /snɪp/ *verb*; *noun*
▻ ***verb***: **snips, snipping, snipped**
You **snip** something when you cut it, especially with a single quick action or actions with scissors: *Tie a knot in the thread and snip off the loose end.* □ *She snipped off some parsley to put in the soup.* □ *The hairdresser snipped at her hair until it was as short as a boy's.*
▻ ***noun***: **snips**
1 A **snip** is a short quick cut with scissors. **2** (*BrE*; *informal*) A **snip** is something that is for sale at a surprisingly cheap price: *Buy your kids the latest video game; it's a snip at £19.99.* [*same as* **bargain**]

snipe /snaɪp/ *verb*: **snipes, sniping, sniped**
1 If a soldier or gunman **snipes** at someone, he shoots at them from a hidden position. **2** One person **snipes** at another when they attack them verbally, saying nasty or critical things about them.

sniper /'snaɪpə(r)/ *noun*: **snipers**
A **sniper** is a soldier or gunman who shoots at people from a hidden position: *He was killed by an enemy sniper.*

snippet /'snɪpɪt/ *noun*: **snippets**
A **snippet** of something, such as information or news, is a small piece of it.

snivel /'snɪvəl/ *verb*: **snivels, snivelling** (*AmE* **sniveling**), **snivelled** (*AmE* **sniveled**)
1 Someone **snivels** when they speak or act tearfully in a whining or complaining manner: *If it all goes wrong, don't come snivelling to me about it.* **2** You **snivel** when you sniff because you have a runny nose.

snob /snɒb/ *noun*: **snobs**
1 A **snob** is a person who places too high a value on social status, admiring people higher up the social ladder and despising people lower down. **2** A **snob** of a stated kind is a person who prefers things that are exclusive or only available to the best people: *a wine snob.*

snobbery /'snɒbərɪ/ *noun* (*uncount*)
Snobbery is the behaviour that is typical of a snob or snobs.

snobbish /'snɒbɪʃ/ *adjective*
Snobbish people admire things associated with the higher social classes and despise things associated with the lower classes: *She's become unbearably snobbish since they moved to the suburbs.*

snog /snɒg/ *verb* (*informal*): **snogs, snogging, snogged**
People **snog** when they kiss and cuddle each other.

snooker /'snu:kə(r)/ *noun*: **snookers**
1 (*uncount*) **Snooker** is a game in which long leather-tipped sticks (**cues**) are used to hit a white ball (**cue ball**) against coloured balls so as to knock them into holes on the corners and sides of a large cloth-covered table. **2** A **snooker** is a position in this game in which the path between the white ball and the target ball is blocked by another ball.

snoop /snu:p/ *verb* (*informal*): **snoops, snooping, snooped**
Someone **snoops** when they go about looking into other people's affairs or business without permission: *I caught him snooping about in my office.* [*same as* **pry**]

snooty /'snu:tɪ/ *adjective* (*informal*): **snootier, snootiest**
If you describe someone as **snooty** you mean that they think they are better than, and behave rudely towards, other people.

snooze /snu:z/ *verb*; *noun*
▻ ***verb*** (*informal*): **snoozes, snoozing, snoozed**
You **snooze** when you doze or sleep lightly: *He was snoozing in a big armchair by the fire.*
▻ ***noun*** (*informal*): **snoozes**
A **snooze** is a period of light sleeping, especially when it does not last for a long time: *Don't disturb him; he's gone for a little snooze.* [*same as* **nap**]

snore /snɔ:(r)/ *verb*; *noun*
▻ ***verb***: **snores, snoring, snored**
You **snore** when you breathe heavily making snorting sounds while you are sleeping: *Did you know that you snore?* □ *He lay snoring on the couch.*
▻ ***noun***: **snores**
A **snore** is an act or the sound of snoring: *She could hear loud snores coming from his bedroom.*

snorkel /'snɔ:kəl/ *noun*; *verb*
▻ ***noun***: **snorkels**
A **snorkel** is a stiff tube of plastic through which air from above the surface of water can be drawn into the mouth while you are swimming just below the surface.
▻ ***verb***: **snorkels, snorkelling** (*AmE* **snorkeling**), **snorkelled** (*AmE* **snorkeled**)
To **snorkel** means to swim with a snorkel: *The boys are snorkelling over by the reef.*

snort /snɔ:t/ *verb*; *noun*
▻ ***verb***: **snorts, snorting, snorted**
1 An animal **snorts** when it forces air violently and noisily out of its nostrils; a person **snorts** when they make a similar noise by drawing air in through their nostrils: *The rhinoceros thundered towards them snorting angrily.* **2** You **snort** when you say something angrily or contemptuously drawing air in through your nostrils as you speak: *'You know what I think of you!' he snorted angrily.*
▻ ***noun***: **snorts**
A **snort** is an act or the sound of snorting: *the snorts of buffaloes.*

snot /snɒt/ *noun* (*uncount*; *informal*)
Snot is mucus produced inside the nose.

snotty /'snɒtɪ/ *adjective* (*informal*): **snottier, snottiest**
1 If someone has a **snotty** nose it is covered with or dripping with nasal mucus. **2** (*derogatory*) Someone who is **snotty** is self-important and rude to others: *Don't get snotty with me!* □ *Some snotty little man tried to tell me I wasn't allowed to go into that part of the museum.*

snout /snaʊt/ *noun*: **snouts**
The long nose of an animal such as a pig is its **snout**.

snow /snoʊ/ *noun*; *verb*
▻ ***noun*** (*uncount*)
Snow is frozen drops of water that fall from the sky as soft white flakes that cover the ground: *About six inches of snow fell in the night.*
▻ ***verb***: **snows, snowing, snowed**
You say it **is snowing** when snow is falling: *It had been snowing all morning.* □ *Do you think it will snow?*

phrasal verbs
snow in (*used in the passive*) If you **are snowed in**, you cannot leave the place you are in because of heavy snow.
snow under (*used in the passive*) If you **are snowed under** with work, you have a large amount of work, especially paperwork, to deal with.

snowball /'snoʊbɔ:l/ *noun*; *verb*

▻ *noun*: **snowballs**
A **snowball** is a small mass of snow pressed together in the shape of a ball and used by children to throw at each other.
▻ *verb*: **snowballs, snowballing, snowballed**
Something **snowballs** when it develops or increases rapidly and uncontrollably: *They started delivering door-to-door and the business just snowballed from there.*

snowbound /ˈsnoʊbaʊnd/ *adjective*
If you are **snowbound** you are shut in or prevented from travelling because of heavy falls of snow.

snow-capped /ˈsnoʊkapt/ *adjective*
Snow-capped mountains have a covering of snow on their peaks.

snowdrift /ˈsnoʊdrɪft/ *noun*: **snowdrifts**
A **snowdrift** is snow that has been blown together by the wind to form a bank or deep pile.

snowdrop /ˈsnoʊdrɒp/ *noun*: **snowdrops**
A **snowdrop** is a small white flower that appears in early spring.

snowfall /ˈsnoʊfɔːl/ *noun*: **snowfalls**
1 A **snowfall** is the snow that falls on one occasion: *There was a heavy snowfall overnight.* **2** (*uncount or used in the singular*) The **snowfall** in a particular place is the total amount of snow that falls there: *the annual snowfall in the French Alps.*

snowflake /ˈsnoʊfleɪk/ *noun*: **snowflakes**
A **snowflake** is one of the small feathery clumps of frozen water that fall together as snow.

snowline /ˈsnoʊlaɪn/ *noun* (*used in the singular*)
The **snowline** is the level or height on a mountain above which there is a permanent layer of snow.

snowman /ˈsnoʊman/ *noun*: **snowmen**
A **snowman** is a figure made of packed snow that vaguely resembles a person.

snowplough (*AmE* **snowplow**) /ˈsnoʊplaʊ/ *noun*: **snowploughs**
A **snowplough** is a vehicle that is used to clear snow from roads and railway tracks.

snowy /ˈsnoʊɪ/ *adjective*: **snowier, snowiest**
Something that is **snowy** has a lot of snow or is covered with snow: *a snowy day in January* □ *snowy peaks* □ *the Snowy Mountains.*

snub /snʌb/ *verb*; *noun*; *adjective*
▻ *verb*: **snubs, snubbing, snubbed**
You **snub** someone when you insult them by openly ignoring them or otherwise showing your contempt of them: *I tried to speak to her at the party, but she snubbed me.*
▻ *noun*: **snubs**
A **snub** is an act of snubbing: *a brutal snub.*
▻ *adjective*
A **snub** nose is one that is short and flat.

snuff /snʌf/ *noun*; *verb*
▻ *noun* (*uncount*)
Snuff is powdered tobacco that some people take by sniffing it up into their nose.
▻ *verb*: **snuffs, snuffing, snuffed**

> ***phrasal verb***
> **snuff out 1** If you **snuff out** a candle, you stop it burning by placing something over the flame. **2** Something **is snuffed out** when it is put to an end suddenly: *All her hopes and ambitions were snuffed out when she was crippled in the accident.*

snuffle /ˈsnʌfəl/ *verb*: **snuffles, snuffling, snuffled**
You **snuffle** when you breathe, especially breathe in, through a partially blocked nose; an animal **snuffles** when it sniffs or smells with its nose close to the ground: *pigs snuffling in the dried leaves.* [*same as* **sniffle**]

snug /snʌg/ *adjective*: **snugger, snuggest**
1 A **snug** place is sheltered, warm and comfortable. [*same as* **cosy**] **2** If something is a **snug** fit it fits closely and comfortably. — *adverb* **snugly:** *The cat was curled up snugly in front of the fire.*

snuggle /ˈsnʌgəl/ *verb*: **snuggles, snuggling, snuggled**
You **snuggle** somewhere when you settle into a position that is warm and comfortable: *He snuggled down in his sleeping bag.* □ *The kittens snuggled in close to their mother.*

so /soʊ/ *adverb*; *conjunction*
▻ ***adverb***
1 a If something is **so** much the case *that* something else happens, the degree to which the first circumstance is true is the cause of the second; after *if* or a negative, *as to* is sometimes used instead of *that*: *I was so tired that I fell asleep standing up.* □ *So little food was provided that most of us got none.* □ *He'd done so well that she decided to reward him.* □ *The news so upset me that I had to go home.* □ *I'm not so stupid as to believe that.* □ *We couldn't all get into the room, there were so many of us.* **b So** can mean 'in such a way' when used with *that* or *as to*: *He had so arranged things that he could take a holiday whenever he wanted.* □ *Their beaks are so formed as to enable them to crush seeds with ease.* **c So** is used with negatives, in questions and after *if* to mean 'to this extent' or 'to that extent': *Do you have to work so hard?* [= as hard as this?] □ *There was no need for her to be so rude.* □ *I didn't realize it was so late.* □ *What are you so angry about?* □ *Let him try himself if he's so sure he can do it.* □ *How can they afford so enormous a* [= such an enormous] *sum?* **d** (*intensifying*) You use **so** for emphasis, like *very*: *You've been so kind.* [= you really have been kind] □ *We've so enjoyed ourselves. Thank you so much.* □ *I've behaved so stupidly.* □ *So much food goes to waste.* **e** 'Not **so**' can be used like 'not very' and 'not particularly' as a less emphatic version of 'not': *'How is he?' 'Not so well, I'm afraid.'* □ *I'm not so very keen on the idea.* □ *She's not so brilliant after all, it seems.* **f So** is sometimes used instead of *as* in negative comparisons: *It wasn't quite so difficult the second time.* □ *There weren't nearly so many errors as I was expecting.* □ *I like the green, but the blue isn't so pretty.* □ *I don't go out so much nowadays.*
2 You can use **so** as a substitute for a clause or part of one, as a way of avoiding repetition, *eg*: **a** (*subject+verb+so*) **so** often occurs, especially in response to a question, after verbs of thinking and reporting such as *assume, expect, fear, gather, guess, hope, imagine, presume, reckon, suppose, think, understand*, after *I'm afraid, it seems, it appears*, and after the sentence adverbs *apparently* and *evidently*: *'Are you going home at the weekend?' 'I expect so.'* □ *'Has she resigned?' 'It appears so.'* □ *'Is it still raining?' 'I'm afraid so.'* □ *'They're raising my salary.' 'I should hope so.'* □ *She thinks it's cheek and I think so too.* □ *I've told you so already.* □ *'Do they know about it?' 'Apparently so.'*

> Notice that the negative in most cases is *I hope not, I'm afraid not*, and so on, but with the verbs *believe, expect, imagine, suppose* and *think* you can use the form *I don't imagine so, I don't suppose so*.

b (*so+subject+verb*) you use **so** with verbs such as *hear, see, gather* and *understand* to indicate that you are already aware of something you are told: *'Simon's working for us again.' 'So I gather.'* □ *'There's been a bit of bother.' 'So I hear.'* □ *'They're digging up the road.' 'So I see.'* **c** (*so+subject+verb*) you use **so** with *or* and a verb of thinking or reporting to indicate that you have some doubt about the information: *He's got plenty of support, or so he claims.* □ *She had a headache, or so she said.* **d** you use **so** after *if, even, maybe* and *perhaps*: *Are you leaving now? Because if so* [= if you are leaving] *I'd like to come with you.* □ *I know it didn't matter; even so I ought to have apologized.* □ *'She takes so long!' 'Maybe* (or *perhaps*) *so, but she's very thorough.'* **e** 'do **so**' takes the place of a verb and whatever follows it: *I asked him to check the oil but he failed to do so.* □ *'Have you made up a bed for her?' 'I was just doing so when you telephoned.'* □ *I picked up the book and, as I did so, out dropped a slip of paper.* □ *If you haven't read the notice, please do so now.* **f so** can refer back to words describing a state or condition: *She was angry, and quite rightly so.* [= she was right to be angry] □ *The stock market is in a state of confusion and likely to remain so for a few days.* **g** (*so+subject+verb*) you use **so** with *be, have* and the other auxiliary and modal verbs to express agreement, and often surprise: *'There's George now.' 'Oh, so it is.'* □ *'The telephone's ringing.' 'So it is.'* □ *'You've dropped your glove.' 'So I have.'* □ *'You didn't lock the gate.' 'Oh dear, so I didn't.'* □ *'But I thought you agreed?' 'So I did, but I've changed my mind.'* □ *'We're getting off the subject.' 'So we are.'* □ *'You'll enjoy the experience.' 'So I shall.'* □ *'He ought to lose weight.' 'So he ought.'* □ *'Peter would help.' 'So he would.'* □ *'They must have gone.' 'So they must.'* **h** (*so+verb+subject*) you use **so** with *be, have* and the other auxiliary and modal verbs to say that what has been said applies in another case; if one person does something and **so** does another, they both do it: *'I'm exhausted.' 'So am I.'* □ *Melissa worked for us then, and so did her husband.* □ *She's got blonde hair and so has* (or *does*) *her sister.* □ *'I'd love to get out in that sunshine.' 'So would I.'* □ *'I hope we meet again.' 'So do I.'* □ *Well I must rush, and so must you.*

3 Something is **so** if it is true, or is the case: *'You are a teacher by profession, Mr Simpson?' 'That is so.'* □ *'She's nearly fifty.' 'Goodness, is that so?'* □ *I don't know why this should be so, but I'm going to find out.* □ *That just isn't so.*

4 a People use **so** in demonstrating something: *'This snake was about so long,' she said, holding her hands about a metre apart.* □ *Sit with your legs to one side, like so.* **b** You use **so** to introduce a clause after a previous one starting with *as*, to mention a similar or matching circumstance: *Just as people don't like admitting their faults, so they feel hurt if you agree with them when they do admit them.*

▻ ***conjunction***

1 You use **so** in conversation, or in relating events, to draw the facts together, to check that you have understood, and to introduce what follows or comes next, or happens as a result: *So we were wrong after all?* □ *So did you find a replacement?* □ *So what is the purpose, then?* □ *So this is what you've been working on all this time!* □ *Her baby's ill so she can't come to work.* □ *And so then we tried her other number.* **2** You use **so** like **so that**, to introduce a purpose: *I'll put it in my diary straight away so I won't forget.*

▻ ***phrases*** **1 And so on** and **and so forth** are used at the end of a list to indicate that there are more things of the same kind that could be mentioned: *There's not much room left once you've packed the nappies, changing mat, baby food and so on.* **2** You add **or so** after a period or amount to make it sound vaguer or more approximate: *It'll take a day or so to get things sorted out.* □ *ten inches or so of snow.* **3 a** You do one thing **so that** another happens, or **so as to** achieve another, if that is your purpose: *We'd packed the evening before, so that we could leave early.* □ *We'll take turns so that everyone gets a chance.* □ *I removed my shoes so as not to make any noise.* □ *You have to take two short steps, so as to finish on your left foot.* [*same as* **in order that, in order to**] **b So that** and **so as to** can also express result: *The fog was thickening, so that now they could barely see the path.* □ *A thin haze hung in the air, so as to give the countryside a veiled look.*

soak /soʊk/ *verb*: **soaks, soaking, soaked**

1 You **soak** something, or it **soaks**, when you leave it to stand or it is left to stand in liquid for a time: *Soak the dried beans in cold water overnight.* □ *You'll have to soak that shirt in detergent if you want to get the stain out.* **2** You **soak** something, or it **is soaked**, when you make it or it becomes wet through: *The bus drove through a puddle soaking the pedestrians on the pavement.* □ *He fell headfirst into the stream and his clothes were soaked.* **3** If liquid **soaks** in or through something, it penetrates or passes through it: *Water had soaked through the ceiling and was dripping on the carpet.*

phrasal verb

soak up 1 If something **soaks up** a liquid, it draws the liquid through its surface: *The dry earth soaked up the rain.* **2** You **soak up** the sun when you expose your skin to bright sunlight, especially in order to get a tan. **3** Someone **soaks up** information when they take it in, especially easily or eagerly.

soaking /ˈsoʊkɪŋ/ *adjective or adverb*

If something is **soaking** or **soaking** wet, it is wet through: *Come in out of the rain; your clothes are soaking.* □ *He removed his soaking-wet shirt.*

so-and-so /ˈsoʊ ən soʊ/ *noun* (*informal*): **so-and-sos**

1 You use **so-and-so** to refer to a person whose name you do not know or cannot remember: *We always get complaints about this; so-and-so will write in saying it is disgraceful, and so-and-so will say it is the end of civilization as we know it, etc, etc.* **2** You can also use **so-and-so** in place of a vulgar word when you are addressing or talking about someone you think is annoying or unpleasant in some way: *You crafty little so-and-so!*

soap /soʊp/ *noun*; *verb*

▻ ***noun***: **soaps**

1 (*uncount*) **Soap** is a mixture of oils or fats, in the form of a liquid, powder or solid block, used with water to remove dirt. [see picture at **bathroom**] **2** A **soap** is a block of such a substance: *a box of scented soaps.* **3** (*informal*) A **soap** is also a soap opera: *a TV soap.*

▻ ***verb***: **soaps, soaping, soaped**

You **soap** something when you apply soap to it: *He was soaping himself in the shower.*

soapbox /ˈsoʊpbɒks/ *noun*: **soapboxes**

A **soapbox** is an improvized platform for public speech-making, originally an upturned crate for carrying soap used by campaigning politicians so that they could be seen above a crowd: *He's on his soapbox again* [=making his opinions known loudly and forcefully] *about public transport in rural areas.*

soap opera /ˈsoʊp ɒpərə/ *noun*: **soap operas**

A **soap opera** is a radio or television series dealing with the daily life and troubles of a regular group of characters.

soapy /ˈsoʊpɪ/ *adjective*: **soapier, soapiest**
Soapy water has soap added to it: *Wash the sweater in warm soapy water.*

soar /sɔː(r)/ *verb*: **soars, soaring, soared**
1 A bird **soars** when it flies high in the air without flapping its wings; something such as a glider **soars** when it moves smoothly through the air carried on rising currents of warm air. **2** Something **soars** when it rises sharply to a great height or level: *Temperatures soared into the nineties.* □ *soaring prices.*

sob /sɒb/ *verb; noun*
▻ ***verb*: sobs, sobbing, sobbed**
1 You **sob** when you cry while making short bursts of sound as you gulp for breath: *She was sobbing her heart out.* [=crying in this way loudly or for a long time] **2** You **sob** when you speak or try to speak while crying in this way: *'I've lost my doll,' she sobbed.*
▻ ***noun*: sobs**
A **sob** is a gulp for breath made while crying.

sober /ˈsoʊbə(r)/ *adjective; verb*
▻ ***adjective***
1 Sober means not drunk: *He had been drinking all evening but still looked quite sober.* **2 Sober** people are serious or solemn, not frivolous or silly. **3** You can also describe things such as clothes as **sober** when they are plain and suggest seriousness and quiet respectability: *He always wore a sober dark suit and a plain tie.*
▻ ***verb*: sobers, sobering, sobered**

phrasal verb
Someone who is drunk **sobers up** when they recover from the effects of alcohol: *You had better go home to sober up.*

sobering /ˈsoʊbərɪŋ/ *adjective*
A **sobering** thought is one that makes you think about things more seriously.

sobriety /səˈbraɪətɪ/ *noun* (*uncount*)
Sobriety is the state or condition of being sober, especially in the sense of not being drunk.

so-called /soʊˈkɔːld/ *adjective*
You use **so-called** before a noun to indicate that the thing named is known or presented as such though you do not think that it is good enough to merit the title: *a panel of so-called experts.*

soccer /ˈsɒkə(r)/ *noun* (*uncount*)
Soccer is a form of football played with a round ball between two teams of eleven players who attempt to put the ball into the opposing team's goal using their feet or their head.

In most countries of the world, **soccer** is simply called **football.** In the United States, it is known as **soccer** to distinguish it from American football.

sociable /ˈsoʊʃəbəl/ *adjective*
A **sociable** person is friendly and enjoys the company of other people: *He's very sociable.* [*opposite* **unsociable**]

social /ˈsoʊʃəl/ *adjective; noun*
▻ ***adjective***
1 Social is used to describe things that concern people or society as a whole and the quality of human life: *social policies* □ *social issues such as employment and housing* □ *the Social Chapter of the Maastricht Treaty.* [=concerned with such things as the rights of workers in the European Union] **2 Social** also means concerned with the organization and behaviour of people in societies or communities: *social studies including history, politics and economics.* **3 Social** animals are animals that tend to or need to live with others in a group: *bees and other social insects.* **4 Social** is also sometimes used **a** to describe people and means the same as sociable. [*opposite* **antisocial**] **b** to describe things that relate to normal human patterns of behaviour and their need or ability to form social relationships with others: *He doesn't work very social hours.* [*opposite* **unsocial**] **5 Social** events or activities are those in which people meet in friendly gatherings; a **social** club is one where people can meet socially, rather than through business or work.
▻ ***noun*: socials**
A **social** is a social gathering, especially one that is organized by a club or other group. — *adverb* **socially**

socialism /ˈsoʊʃəlɪzm/ *noun* (*uncount*)
Socialism is a political theory or system according to which a nation's wealth and industries belong to the people as a whole rather than being owned by private individuals.

socialist /ˈsoʊʃəlɪst/ *adjective; noun*
▻ ***adjective***
1 Socialist theories or policies advocate or involve socialism. **2 Socialist** political parties or **socialist** states support socialism or are run according to the principles of socialism.
▻ ***noun*: socialists**
A **socialist** is someone who believes in socialism.

socialize or **socialise** /ˈsoʊʃəlaɪz/ *verb*: **socializes, socializing, socialized**
1 You **socialize** when you meet and spend time with other people on an informal friendly basis: *He doesn't socialize much.* □ *The people I socialize with are not the same people that I work with.* **2** (*technical*) People or animals **are socialized** when they are taught or learn how to live in a society, especially by mixing with and co-operating with others.

social life /ˈsoʊʃəl laɪf/ *noun*: **social lives**
Your **social life** is the part of your life or the time that you spend going out with or enjoying the company of other people, as opposed to your working life or your private life: *She has a hectic social life.*

social science /soʊʃəl ˈsaɪəns/ *noun* (*uncount or count*): **social sciences**
The **social sciences** are those subjects that deal with the organization and behaviour of people in societies and communities, including sociology, anthropology, economics and history; a **social science** is one of those subjects.

social scientist /soʊʃəl ˈsaɪəntɪst/ *noun*: **social scientists**
A **social scientist** is a person who studies social science or one of the social sciences.

social security /soʊʃəl sɪˈkjʊərɪtɪ/ *noun* (*uncount*)
1 Social security is a system by which members of a society pay money into a common fund, from which payments are made to individuals by the government in times of unemployment, illness and old age. **2 Social security** is a payment or scheme of payments from such a fund.

social services /soʊʃəl ˈsɜːvɪsɪz/ *noun* (*plural*)
The **social services** are services provided by local or national government for the general welfare of people in society, *eg* housing, education and health.

social work /ˈsoʊʃəl wɜːk/ *noun* (*uncount*)
Social work is work in any of the services provided by government or private organizations for the care of people in need.

social worker /'souʃəl wɜːkə(r)/ *noun*: **social workers**
A **social worker** is a person working for a private or government organization whose job it is to provide help for people in need.

society /sə'saɪətɪ/ *noun*: **societies**
1 (*uncount*) **Society** is people in general, considered as a single community, especially with regard to the customs, laws and institutions that enable them to live together: *the breakdown of society as we know it.* **2** (*count or uncount*) A **society** is a particular group of people who have certain customs, institutions and organizations in common: *an Islamic society* □ *one of the pillars of British society* □ *He studied several primitive societies.* **3** A **society** is an organized club or association of people with similar interests or aims: *a university debating society* □ *a member of the Royal Horticultural Society.* **4** (*uncount, often adjectival*) **Society** or **high society** is the rich fashionable section of the upper class: *He was accepted in high society despite being the son of a miner.* □ *a society hostess.* **5** (*uncount; formal*) **Society** is also the company of other people: *He prefers the society of women.*

sociologist /sousɪ'ɒlədʒɪst/ *noun*: **sociologists**
A **sociologist** is someone who studies the structure and organization of human societies and human behaviour in those societies.

sociology /sousɪ'ɒlədʒɪ/ *noun* (*uncount*)
Sociology is the scientific study of the nature, structure and organization of human society and human behaviour in society.

sock /sɒk/ *noun*: **socks**
A **sock** is a piece of clothing that covers the foot and ankle, sometimes reaching to the knee, and worn inside a shoe or boot: *a pair of woolly socks.* [see picture at **clothing**]
▻ ***phrase*** (*informal*) If someone says you should **pull your socks up**, they mean that you should make an effort to do better than you have been doing recently: *If he doesn't pull his socks up, he'll fail all his exams.*

socket /'sɒkɪt/ *noun*: **sockets**
1 A **socket** is a specially-shaped hole or set of holes into which something is fitted: *an electrical socket.* **2** A **socket** is also a hollow structure in the body into which another part fits: *a ball-and-socket joint* □ *eye sockets.*

soda /'soudə/ *noun*: **sodas**
1 (*uncount or count*) **Soda**, or **soda water**, is fizzy water used for mixing with alcoholic drinks and fruit juices: *whisky and soda* □ *a soda water with lime.* **2** (*especially AmE*) A **soda** is a fizzy soft drink of any kind: *I don't want a beer, I'll just have a soda.* **3** (*uncount; not technical*) **Soda** is a common name given to any of various compounds of sodium in everyday use, *eg* sodium carbonate (**washing soda**) or sodium bicarbonate (**baking soda**).

soda water see **soda**.

sodden /'sɒdən/ *adjective*
If something is **sodden** it is completely soaked with water or other liquid: *The roof had been leaking and the carpets in the bedrooms were sodden.*

sodium /'soudɪəm/ *noun* (*uncount*)
Sodium is a chemical element, a bluish-white metal found naturally only in combination with other substances.

sofa /'soufə/ *noun*: **sofas**
A **sofa** is a piece of furniture for two or more people to sit on, having a back and arms and a comfortable upholstered seat. [*same as* **settee**; see picture at **living room**]

soft /sɒft/ *adjective*: **softer, softest**
1 Something that is **soft a** bends easily or changes shape when you press it: *a soft mattress* □ *soft cushions* □ *There was a line of footprints in the soft deep snow.* □ *The clay was still soft.* [*opposite* **hard, firm**] **b** is smooth and pleasant to feel or touch: *dressed in soft silk* □ *the animal's long soft fur* □ *Her skin was soft and smooth, like a baby's.* □ *those ludicrous TV ads about loo paper that's even softer.* [*opposite* **hard, rough**] **c** gentle, or without force or strength: *soft gentle breezes* □ *a soft little kiss on the cheek.* [*opposite* **strong, violent**] **2 Soft** sounds are quiet: *Her voice was soft and low.* □ *the sound of soft sweet singing* □ *They spoke in soft whispers.* □ *All we heard was a soft thud.* [*opposite* **loud, harsh**] **3 Soft** colours or light are pleasantly pale or dim, so as to have a restful effect: *the soft evening light* □ *soft candlelight* □ *The effect of the light brown panelling is soft and warm.* [*opposite* **bright, harsh**] **4** Someone who has a **soft** heart is kind to other people. [*opposite* **hard**] **5** You are **soft** in your treatment of other people if you are not severe or strict enough: *They shouldn't be so soft on criminals.* [*opposite* **hard**] **6 Soft** water has little calcium or magnesium and so lathers easily. [*opposite* **hard**] **7 Soft** drugs are the kind like cannabis that are believed to be only mildly addictive. [*opposite* **hard**] — *adverb* **softly:** *He stroked her hair softly.* □ *They stood in little groups, conversing softly.* □ *softly lit restaurants.* — *noun* (*uncount*) **softness:** *because of the extreme softness of the water.*
▻ ***phrases*** **1** (*informal*) Someone who is described as **a soft touch** is easily persuaded to do things for you, especially lend or give you money. **2** If you **have a soft spot** for someone, you have an affection for them and are kind to them. **3** Someone who is **soft in the head** is silly or a bit crazy.

soft drink /sɒft 'drɪŋk/ *noun*: **soft drinks**
Soft drinks are cold drinks, such as fruit juices or lemonade, that have no alcohol in them.

soften /'sɒfən/ *verb*: **softens, softening, softened**
1 You **soften** something, or it **softens**, when you make it softer or less stiff: *This lotion cleanses and softens the skin.* □ *Mix two tablespoons of caster sugar into the softened butter.* **2** Someone **softens** when they adopt a less severe or rigid attitude to something: *Ask him one more time; I think there are signs that he is softening a little.* **3** You **soften** something or it **softens** when you make it gentler or less severe: *She added a few frills to soften the plain neckline.*

> ***phrasal verb***
> You **soften** someone **up** when you do something to weaken or break down their opposition so that you can more easily persuade them to agree to something: *She was especially nice to him, softening him up before she asked the favour.*

soft furnishings /sɒft 'fɜːnɪʃɪŋz/ *noun* (*plural*)
Soft furnishings are articles made of fabric that are used to furnish or decorate a room. Soft furnishings include curtains, rugs and cushions.

soft-hearted /sɒft'hɑːtɪd/ *adjective*
Someone who is **soft-hearted** has a kind and sympathetic nature and is generous towards others. [*opposite* **hard-hearted**]

soft-spoken /sɒft'spoukən/ *adjective*
Someone who is **soft-spoken** has a quiet, gentle-sounding voice.

software /'sɒftwɛə(r)/ *noun* (*uncount, often adjectival*)
Software is the programs that are used to operate a

computer as opposed to the machines themselves (**hardware**): *write new software* □ *a software package* □ *a software house.* [=a company that produces and sells computer software]

soggy /ˈsɒgɪ/ *adjective*: **soggier, soggiest**
Something that is **soggy** is thoroughly wet or is unpleasant because of its dampness or wetness: *The pitch was soggy after the heavy rain.* □ *He gave her a soggy kiss.* □ *There was only an apple and a soggy cheese and tomato sandwich in his lunch box.*

soil /sɔɪl/ *noun*: **soils**
1 (*uncount or count*) **Soil** is the loose substance made up of small particles of rock, minerals and decayed plant and animal material that forms the top covering on the land and in which plants grow; a **soil** is a stated kind of this: *The wind had carried away the soil, leaving only bare rock.* □ *a peaty soil* □ *a sandy soil* □ *a fertile soil* □ *plants that grow on poor soil.* **2** (*uncount*) **Soil** is also used to refer to a particular land or country: *military bases on foreign soil* □ *It would years before he was to set foot again on his native soil.* [=he returned to his own country]
▻ ***verb***: **soils, soiling, soiled**
You **soil** something, or it **is soiled**, when you make it dirty or stain it with something, especially slightly or with urine or faeces: *a soiled napkin* □ *He soiled his bedclothes.*

solace /ˈsɒləs/ *noun*
1 (*uncount*) **Solace** is comfort from grief, anxiety or disappointment: *She found some solace from her grief in writing poetry.* **2** (*used in the singular*) A **solace** is something that is a source of comfort in time of grief, anxiety or disappointment: *Her belief in God was a great solace to her.*

solar /ˈsoʊlə(r)/ *adjective*
Solar means **1** of or concerning the sun: *a solar eclipse.* **2** of, by or using energy from the sun's rays: *a solar panel* [=a panel that stores heat from the sun's rays] □ *solar-powered.*

solar system /ˈsoʊlə sɪstəm/ *noun* (*used in the singular*)
Our **solar system** is the sun and all the planets, asteroids and comets that move around it.

sold /soʊld/ *verb*
Sold is the past tense and past participle of **sell**.
▻ ***phrase*** (*informal*) If you are **sold on** a particular idea you are extremely enthusiastic about it or convinced by it: *He was sold on the notion of free medical care for all.*

solder /ˈsoʊldə(r)/ *noun*; *verb*
▻ ***noun*** (*uncount or count*): **solders**
Solder is an alloy melted over the join between two metals, hardening quickly to form a seal.
▻ ***verb***: **solders, soldering, soldered**
You **solder** a joint when you melt solder over it to form a seal.

soldier /ˈsoʊldʒə(r)/ *noun*: **soldiers**
1 A **soldier** is a member of a fighting force, especially a national army. **2** A **soldier** is a member of an army below the rank of officer: *an ordinary soldier.*

sole[1] /soʊl/ *noun*; *adjective*
▻ ***noun***: **soles**
1 The **soles** of your feet are the undersides of your feet that are next to the ground when you walk. [see picture at **body**] **2** The **soles** of shoes or boots are the parts that are next to the ground when you walk, including or not including the heels: *walking shoes with rubber soles* □ *There's something stuck to the sole of your shoe.*[see picture at **clothing**]

sole[2] /soʊl/ *noun*: **sole, soles**
A **sole** is a small flat-bodied sea fish eaten as food: *grey sole* □ *lemon sole.*

sole[3] /soʊl/ *adjective*
Sole means being the only one or belonging to only one person or group of people: *Of the crew of twelve, he was the sole survivor.* □ *The newspaper has sole rights to the story.* □ *He has sole responsibility for an area that stretches from Inverness to Birmingham.*

solely /ˈsoʊllɪ/ *adverb*
1 Solely means 'alone' or 'without others': *He was solely to blame.* **2 Solely** also means 'only' or 'excluding all else': *The deal was done solely for profit.* □ *I'm solely concerned with the administrative side of the business.*

solemn /ˈsɒləm/ *adjective*
1 A **solemn** vow or promise is made in earnest: *He made a solemn vow to avenge her death.* □ *I give you my solemn promise that I will do every thing I can to help you.* **2** A **solemn** occasion is very serious and formal in nature; **solemn** music suggests seriousness and is not light or humorous: *a solemn procession of ex-servicemen and politicians.* **3** You look **solemn** when you look very serious or grave: *the solemn faces of the mourners.* — *adverb* **solemnly:** *The boys stood solemnly while each was asked to repeat the Scout promise.*

solicit /səˈlɪsɪt/ *verb*: **solicits, soliciting, solicited**
1 (*formal*) You **solicit** advice, help or money from someone when you ask them for it: *The government is trying to solicit aid from other countries.* □ *May I solicit your advice on a matter of vital importance to the security of the nation?* **2** (*legal*) A prostitute **solicits** when she or he offers someone sex in return for money: *She was arrested for soliciting.*

solicitor /səˈlɪsɪtə(r)/ *noun*: **solicitors**
A **solicitor** is a lawyer who prepares legal documents, gives legal advice, and speaks on behalf of clients in certain courts of law.

solicitous /səˈlɪsɪtəs/ *adjective* (*formal*)
Someone who is **solicitous** shows anxious interest in and kind concern for someone else and is eager to see that their needs are being properly met: *She talked about you constantly and seemed most solicitous for your welfare.* □ *They were extremely solicitous about attending to our needs.*

solicitude /səˈlɪsɪtjuːd/ *noun* (*uncount; formal*)
Solicitude is anxious interest in and kind concern for another person.

solid /ˈsɒlɪd/ *adjective*; *noun*
▻ ***adjective***
1 Solid substances or objects are firm or hard, and keep their shape, which distinguishes them from liquids and gases: *The water in the pipes was frozen solid.* □ *Her toe came in contact with something solid.* **2 Solid** fuel is wood or coal as distinct from oil or gas. **3 Solid** food is non-liquid food: *He hasn't been able to eat any solid food since his operation.* **4** Something that is made of *eg* **solid** gold or **solid** silver is made of gold or silver right through, as distinct from just having a thin covering of gold or silver: *statues made of solid gold* □ *a solid brass paperweight* □ *a solid oak door.* **5** Something that is **solid** is not hollow: *a solid sphere* □ *The earliest tyres were solid.* **6** (*mathematics*) **Solid** geometry is concerned with three-dimensional figures such as spheres, cubes and pyramids. **7** Something that has no gaps, holes or spaces in it is **solid**: *What's the significance of the solid yellow line?* □ *a solid queue of cars stretching back for five miles* □ *The street was packed solid with spectators.* **8** Things described as

solid are firmly constructed, and unlikely to collapse: *These houses are pretty solid.* □ *nice solid furniture.* [*same as* **sturdy**] **9 Solid** people are sensible and reliable: *Why can't she marry a good solid Englishman?* **10 Solid** describes things such as facts that are firmly established and reliable: *a mass of speculation without any solid proof.* □ *Solid evidence is noticeably lacking.* □ *This is a solid achievement, of which we can all be proud.* **11** People's support for something is **solid** if everyone supports it without exception: *The union spokesman said that the strike remained solid.* **12** Something happens for *eg* two **solid** hours when it continues to happen for two hours without a break: *I waited for three solid hours to be seen by a doctor.* □ *You can't work more than five hours solid.* □ *She puts in four hours' solid practice a day.* — *noun* (*uncount*) **solidity** /sə'lɪdɪtɪ/: *the reassuring solidity of 19th-century buildings.* — *adverb* **solidly:** *solidly constructed buildings* □ *a solidly reliable character* □ *We're solidly behind you.* □ *when you've been working solidly for 16 hours.*

▻ ***noun*: solids**

1 Solids are objects or substances that are hard or firm, and keep their shape, which distinguishes them from liquids and gases: *Steam is a gas, water is a liquid, and ice is a solid.* **2** (*mathematics*) A **solid** is a three-dimensional figure such as a cube or sphere. **3** (*used in the plural*) **Solids** are solid foods: *When should I start the baby on solids?* **4** (*used in the plural*) **Solids** are particles of solid matter in a liquid.

solidarity /sɒlɪ'dærɪtɪ/ *noun* (*uncount*)

Solidarity is loyal mutual support and agreement of interests and actions among members of a group: *worker's solidarity.*

solidify /sə'lɪdɪfaɪ/ *verb*: **solidifies, solidifying, solidified**

When a liquid **solidifies** it changes to a solid: *cool the mixture in the fridge until it solidifies.*

solitary /'sɒlɪtərɪ/ *adjective*

1 A **solitary** object or person is alone and has no others nearby; a **solitary** building is in a remote or secluded place: *A solitary oak stood in the centre of the field.* □ *a solitary cabin high in the mountains.* **2 Solitary** animals spend a lot of time alone and do not form part of a social group: *Cats are solitary animals.* **3** A **solitary** person spends a lot of time alone, especially by choice; a **solitary** activity is one which you do alone. **4** You can use **solitary** in questions and negative statements as an emphatic way of saying 'single': *There isn't one solitary piece of evidence to link him with the crime.*

solitary confinement /sɒlɪtərɪ kən'faɪnmənt/ *noun* (*uncount*)

If someone in prison is in **solitary confinement**, they are kept in a cell by themselves and are not allowed to communicate with other prisoners.

solitude /'sɒlɪtju:d/ *noun* (*uncount*)

Solitude is the state of being alone or remote: *It was the solitude of life in the mountains that attracted him.* □ *You need to be a special type of person to endure long periods of solitude.*

solo /'soʊloʊ/ *noun*; *adjective*; *adverb*

▻ ***noun*: solos**

A **solo** is a piece of music, or a passage within it, for a single voice or instrument, with or without accompaniment.

▻ ***adjective***

Solo is used to describe things that are done or performed alone, without assistance or accompaniment from others: *When was the first solo flight across the Atlantic?*

▻ ***adverb***

When you do something **solo**, you do it alone: *He sailed solo around the world.*

soloist /'soʊloʊɪst/ *noun*: **soloists**

A **soloist** is a singer or musician who performs a solo: *Who are the soloists in this production of Handel's 'Messiah'?*

soluble /'sɒljʊbəl/ *adjective*

1 Soluble substances are capable of being dissolved in liquid: *Are these tablets the sort that are soluble in water?* □ *soluble aspirin.* **2** (*formal*) A **soluble** problem or difficulty is capable of being solved or resolved: *They still believe that the situation is Bosnia is soluble.* [*opposite* **insoluble**]

solution /sə'lu:ʃən/ *noun*: **solutions**

1 (*uncount or count*) **Solution** of a problem or puzzle is the act or process of finding an answer to it; a **solution** is an answer to a problem or puzzle: *The solution of this problem will require all their negotiating skills.* □ *There is no easy solution to the problems in Northern Ireland.* **2** A **solution** is a liquid in which a solid or gas has been dissolved: *a sugar solution.* **3** (*uncount*) The **solution** of a solid or gas is the act or process of dissolving it in a liquid; a solid or gas is in **solution** when it has been dissolved in a liquid.

solve /sɒlv/ *verb*: **solves, solving, solved**

You **solve** a puzzle when you find an answer to it; you **solve** a problem or difficulty when you find a way out of it: *He can usually solve the whole crossword in thirty minutes.* □ *How much would it take to solve your financial problems?*

solvent /'sɒlvənt/ *adjective*; *noun*

▻ ***adjective***

A person or business is **solvent** when they have enough money to pay their debts: *When I'm paid I'll be solvent again!* [*opposite* **insolvent**]

▻ ***noun*: solvents**

A **solvent** is a substance that can turn a solid substance into liquid: *Use paint stripper or some other solvent to remove any paint that has been splashed on the windows.*

sombre /'sɒmbə/ *adjective*

1 If a person or their attitude is **sombre** they are sad, serious or pessimistic; a **sombre** occasion is sad and serious. **2** A **sombre** place is dark and gloomy; **sombre** colours are dark and dull: *The castle was surrounded on all sides by a dark and sombre wood.* □ *He wore a sombre dark grey suit.* — *adverb* **sombrely:** *They were dressed sombrely.*

some /sʌm/ *determiner*; *pronoun*; *adverb*

▻ ***determiner***

1 (*used with uncount nouns and plural nouns*) **Some** represents **a** an indefinite amount, quantity or number; it is used in positive sentences, but can also be used after *if* and in questions, especially when they expect the answer 'yes': *He puts some money in the building society every month.* □ *There's still some tea in the pot.* □ *Wasn't there some cake left from yesterday?* □ *Won't you stay and have some lunch?* □ *If you'd like some coffee it's no problem to make it.* □ *There are some more letters for you to sign.* □ *The square was empty except for some kids who were kicking a football about.* □ *I thought I'd take her some flowers and chocolates.* □ *There are some other matters to attend to.* **b** a large or considerable amount or number: *We drove around for some time before we found a hotel.* □ *He talked at some length.* □ *I may be gone some time.* □ *He's likely to be in hospital for some weeks yet.* □ *She's got some cheek suggesting that!* **c** (*said with emphasis*) at least a little, or at least a few: *Try to show some enthusiasm.* □ *It's all I can afford, but it'll go* *some way towards paying for your trip.* □ *It's nice to know we've got some supporters.* **2** (*used with count, uncount or plural nouns*) You use **some** to refer to unspecified people or things, or to refer to certain people or things without identifying them: *I hope to see you some day soon.* □ *They were arranging to meet at some place in Italy.* □ *Some child had been caught stealing.* □ *Was there some problem with the engine?* □ *There must be some reason for it.* □ *Perhaps it'll come in handy at some later stage.* □ *That's true to some extent.* □ *Some paint can cause allergies.* □ *There are some people who never know when to give up.* □ *Naturally some children learn more quickly than others.* **3 Some** is used before a number or amount to make it more approximate: *holding a dinner for some forty guests* □ *some 30 metres below ground level.* **4** (*informal*) **Some** can be used to suggest either that something is an excellent or impressive example of its type, or that it is quite the opposite: *That was some shot!* □ *That was quite some* [= quite a] *journey.* □ *Some friend she turned out to be!*

▻ ***pronoun:*** *If you want a biscuit there are some in that tin.* □ *There's still some of that ice cream left; would you like some?* □ *Some of the new boys were homesick and some were quite excited about being away from home.* □ *Could you get me some of those little carrots?* □ *Some of us thought he should have resigned.* □ *Most of the wine was drinkable but some had gone off.*

▻ ***adverb*** (*AmE*)

Some means 'a little': *I guess I've improved some.*

[compare **any**, **no**]

somebody /ˈsʌmbədɪ/ *pronoun*

1 Somebody or **someone** is an indefinite person, or a certain, but unidentified, person; **somebody** and **someone** are used in positive sentences, but can also be used after *if* and in questions, especially when they expect the answer 'yes': *Could somebody turn the light off?* □ *Someone must have left the door open.* □ *There's somebody at the door.* □ *Isn't that someone knocking?* □ *She's going out with somebody new, someone called Andrew.* □ *I don't know; ask someone else.* □ *If someone would lay the table, I'll serve the meal.* □ *We need someone with computer experience.* □ *Only someone really incompetent would make that mistake.* □ *There must be somebody who knows where he is.* □ *She wished there was someone to talk to.*

> Notice that though **somebody** and **someone** are singular, both are often followed by the pronoun *they*, which takes a plural verb: *Someone's got to do the work, haven't they? Somebody in the office would lend you their key. When someone is addressing you, you should look at them* (or in formal English, *him or her*).

2 If you think you are **somebody** or **someone**, you think you are important: *He thinks he's someone now that he's been promoted.* **3** People sometimes use **somebody** or **someone** in place of a part of a name they don't remember or don't know: *Edna somebody was on the phone for you.*

[compare **anybody** and **anyone**, **nobody** and **no-one**]

some day or **someday** /ˈsʌmdeɪ/ *adverb*

You can refer to an unknown or unspecified time in the future as **some day**: *Prince William will be king some day.* □ *We'll go and visit them someday soon.*

somehow /ˈsʌmhaʊ/ *adverb*

1 Somehow means in some way that is not yet known, or has not been discovered: *I'll find the money to pay you back somehow.* □ *The thieves had somehow managed to put the alarm out of action.* **2** (*often sentence adverb*) **Somehow** also means 'for a reason that is not easy to explain': *Somehow, I've never been able to talk to her properly about it.* □ *We drifted apart somehow.* □ *It was somehow distasteful to hear him criticizing his mother like that.*

someone /ˈsʌmwʌn/ *pronoun*

The uses of **someone** are shown in the entry for **somebody**.

someplace /ˈsʌmpleɪs/ *adverb* (*AmE informal*)

Someplace means the same as somewhere: *Are you going someplace?* □ *I left my glasses someplace around here.*

somersault /ˈsʌməsɔːlt/ *noun; verb*

▻ ***noun*:** **somersaults**

A **somersault** is a leap or roll in which your body turns a complete circle forwards or backwards, leading with the head.

▻ ***verb*:** **somersaults, somersaulting, somersaulted**

1 You **somersault** when you perform such a leap or roll. **2** Something **somersaults** when it turns over completely, usually several times, as it is travelling along: *The car hit the barrier and somersaulted into a ditch.*

something /ˈsʌmθɪŋ/ *pronoun*

1 Something is any indefinite or unidentified thing, and can refer to an object, topic, quality, action, event or circumstance; it is used in positive sentences, but can also be used after *if* and in questions, especially when the person asking the questions expects the answer 'yes': *She's obviously worrying about something.* □ *You must have something to eat before you go.* □ *If you've got something important to say, say it.* □ *There's something floating in my soup.* □ *Is something wrong?* □ *Something awful must have happened.* □ *There's something odd about that man.* □ *Wasn't there something about it in today's paper?* □ *There's something I ought to tell you.* □ *They mentioned hypnosis, which is something that has always intrigued me.* **2** People sometimes use **something** in place of part of a name or number they don't remember or don't know: *She'd be forty-something, I guess.* □ *The author was Patricia something.* **3** You can use **something** with words such as *over*, *under* and *close to* to indicate an approximate amount or level: *with taxation standing at something close to 50%.* **4** You say that a circumstance or achievement is **something** if you think it is useful: *It's something if you can remember the name of the shop.* □ *'The electricity seems to be on again.' 'Well, that's something.'*

▻ ***phrases*** **1 a** You **make something of** yourself when you have a successful career. **b** You **make something of** or **out of** a circumstance or remark when you see it as something significant: *You're trying to make something out of a perfectly innocent comment.* **2** You add **or something** to indicate your uncertainty about what you have just said: *He's a civil servant or something.* □ *She's called Jenny or Janet or something.* **3** If you say that a thing or person is **quite something** or **really something**, you mean that you are impressed by them: *These sun-dried tomatoes are quite something.* □ *On the tennis court she's really something.* **4 a** If one thing is **something like** another, it is rather like it: *It was a bird something like a starling.* **b** You can use **something like** before an amount to make it more approximate: *Something like 20 cars were involved.* □ *We're something like halfway.* **5** A person or thing that is **something of** a particular thing is that thing to some extent: *She's becoming something of a local celebrity.* □ *It's something of a disadvantage nowadays if you can't use a computer.* **6** You say that **there is something in** a suggestion or idea if you think it is

worth serious consideration: *There's something in what you say.*
[compare **anything, nothing, everything**]

sometime /'sʌmtaɪm/ *adverb; adjective*
▻ ***adverb***
Sometime means at an unknown or unspecified time in the future or the past: *Come up and see me sometime.* ▫ *I'll talk to you about it sometime when you aren't so busy.* ▫ *They should arrive sometime soon.* ▫ *They left this neighbourhood sometime last year.*

> Distinguish between **sometime** and **some time**: *I'll see you sometime this afternoon.* But: *After some time they found their way back on to the right road.*

▻ ***adjective***
Someone who is described as the **sometime** president or chairman of something was formerly its president or chairman.

sometimes /'sʌmtaɪmz/ *adverb*
Sometimes means occasionally: *'Do you ever get headaches?' 'Sometimes.'* ▫ *The word is sometimes used merely for emphasis.* ▫ *Women have sometimes* [= there have been some women who have] *made important discoveries.* ▫ *Sometimes she seems quite clear in her mind, but most of the time she's very confused.* ▫ *I sometimes wish I were back there and at other times I'm glad I'm not.* ▫ *Sometimes they all come, sometimes only my daughter.* [*same as* **from time to time, now and then, on some occasions**]

somewhat /'sʌmwɒt/ *adverb* (*moderating*)
Somewhat means 'rather', 'a little' or 'by some amount or degree': *I was somewhat perturbed by what he told me.* ▫ *'Are you concerned about your exam results?' 'Somewhat.'* ▫ *His fees were somewhat higher than I had expected.*
▻ ***phrase*** **Somewhat of** means 'to some extent' or 'a kind of': *The meeting turned out to be somewhat of a farce.*

somewhere /'sʌmweə(r)/ *adverb*
1 Somewhere refers to an indefinite or unspecified place; you use it in positive sentences, but it can also be used after *if* and in questions, especially if the person asking the questions expects the answer 'yes': *He must be somewhere in the house.* ▫ *Their flat is somewhere near Marble Arch.* ▫ *If you're going somewhere hot, don't forget the sun cream.* ▫ *There's a funny smell coming from somewhere.* ▫ *Do you have somewhere to stay in London?* ▫ *Let's find somewhere where we can talk quietly.* ▫ *Madrid or Barcelona or somewhere like that.* **2** You use **somewhere** when giving an approximate amount or time: *aged somewhere between 45 and 50.* ▫ *There were somewhere in the region of 200 applicants.* ▫ *We should arrive somewhere between 5.00 and 6.00.* ▫ *It was erected somewhere around 1640.*
▻ ***phrases*** **1** You say you **are getting somewhere** if you think you are making progress: *We seem to be getting somewhere at last.* **2** You add **or somewhere** after a place to indicate your vagueness about it: *They met in Nice or somewhere.*
[compare **anywhere, nowhere**]

son /sʌn/ *noun*: **sons**
1 Someone's **son** is their male child: *They have two sons, one aged eight and one aged four.* ▫ *Your son looks very like you.* **2 a** (*often plural*) The **sons** of a particular person or group of people are their male descendants: *the sons of the Spanish invaders.* **b** You can also refer to male persons that are closely associated with a particular activity or event as its **sons**: *a son of the soil* [=a farmer or agricultural labourer] ▫ *sons of the revolution.* **3 a** Some people use **son** as a familiar way of addressing a boy or man: *Are you alright, son?* **b** Roman Catholic priests address men and boys as 'my **son**', especially when they are giving them a blessing or hearing their confession: *God go with you, my son.* **4** In the Christian religion, the **Son** is Jesus Christ considered as the second person in the Holy Trinity, that is the Father, the Son and the Holy Ghost.

sonar /'səʊnɑː(r)/ *noun* (*uncount*)
1 Sonar is an apparatus that uses sound waves to detect underwater objects such as submarines. **2 Sonar** is also the technique used by bats and some marine creatures for navigation and detecting their prey in which they make continuous high-pitched sounds which bounce back off obstacles in their path.

sonata /sə'nɑːtə/ *noun*: **sonatas**
A **sonata** is a piece of classical music, in three or more movements, for a solo instrument, often the piano.

song /sɒŋ/ *noun*: **songs**
1 A **song** is a set of words to be sung, often including accompanying music: *a pop song* ▫ *a folk song* ▫ *the poems and songs of Robert Burns* ▫ *Sing me a song.* ▫ *Do you know the song that starts 'I love to go a-wandering...'?* ▫ *songs of praise.* **2** (*uncount or count*) A **song** is the musical call that is typical of certain types of bird: *the blackbird's early morning song* ▫ *the song of the nightingale* ▫ *birdsong.* **3** (*uncount*) **Song** is the act or art of singing: *poetry and song* ▫ *He suddenly burst into song.*
▻ ***phrases*** (*informal*)
1 If something is going **for a song**, it is being sold at a bargain price; if you get something **for a song**, you buy it for a very cheap price: *These chairs are going for a song.* ▫ *They bought the cottage for a song in 1965.* **2** (*informal*) If someone **makes a song and dance about** something, they make an unnecessary fuss about it: *It's only a minor detail; don't make such a song and dance about it.*

songbird /'sɒŋbɜːd/ *noun*: **songbirds**
Songbirds are birds with musical calls.

sonic /'sɒnɪk/ *adjective*
1 (*only used before a noun*) **Sonic** means relating to or using sound or sound waves. **2** (*technical*) **Sonic** also means travelling at or around the speed of sound in air, approximately 0.34 kilometres per second: *a sonic boom.* [=made by an aircraft as it crosses the sound barrier]

son-in-law /'sʌn ɪn lɔː/ *noun*: **sons-in-law**
Someone's **son-in-law** is the husband of their daughter.

sonnet /'sɒnɪt/ *noun*: **sonnets**
A **sonnet** is a poem with fourteen lines and a regular rhyming pattern: *Shakespeare's sonnets.*

soon /suːn/ *adverb*: **sooner, soonest**
1 Something that happens **soon** happens a short time after the present time, or the time mentioned: *I'll be seeing you very soon.* ▫ *She'll be eighteen soon.* ▫ *Please write soon.* ▫ *I hope you'll be feeling better soon.* ▫ *Her baby's due soon after Christmas.* ▫ *Soon more guests arrived.* ▫ *Let me know as soon as you can.* ▫ *How soon will you know?* ▫ *I had an urgent request for leaflets from Richard, who is soon to depart for Singapore.* ▫ *The ambulance arrived even sooner than we expected it to.* ▫ *Can't we make the meeting any sooner?* ▫ *The soonest I could manage would be the 14th.* [compare **early**] **2** Something that **soon** happens, happens quickly: *The day began dull but it soon brightened up.* ▫ *There were plenty of volunteers, so we soon got the work done.* ▫ *You'll soon get used to the new system.* [*same as* **quickly**]
▻ ***phrases*** **1** Something that happens **as soon as** something else does, happens quickly after it, or at the same time: *As soon as I'd said it I realized my mistake.* ▫ *We'll ring you as soon as we get there.* ▫ *I'll give you*

the money back as soon as I get my pay cheque. [compare **immediately**] **2** Something that will not happen until a certain time **at the soonest** will not happen before then, and may happen later: *We won't know before Friday at the soonest.* [*same as* **at the earliest**] **3** You say that **no sooner** did one thing happen **than** another did to emphasize how quickly the second event followed the first: *No sooner had I settled down to read my book than the telephone rang.* □ *She no sooner accepted the job than she announced she was off to Australia and couldn't take it after all.* **4** If you say that something will happen **sooner or later** you mean that it will happen eventually: *Sooner or later we shall need more staff.* **5** If you say in reference to something you want to happen '**the sooner the better**' you mean you want it to happen soon: *The sooner you realize that you're here to work, the better.* □ *'When's he leaving?' 'The sooner the better, as far as I'm concerned.'* **6** If you say you **would just as soon** do one thing **as** another, you mean that the first thing is as acceptable as the second, and that you would slightly prefer it: *I'd just as soon get to bed early tonight as go out for a drink.* **7 a** If you say that you **would sooner** do one thing, or that you **would sooner** one thing happened, **than** another, you mean you would prefer the first alternative: *I think I'd sooner drive on than stop and waste time.* □ *I'd sooner you kept this a secret for the time being.* **b** If you say that you **would sooner** do something desperate **than** something else, you mean that the second thing is too awful ever to do: *Some of them would die sooner than admit the shameful truth.* [compare **rather**]

soot /sʊt/ *noun* (*uncount*)
Soot is a black powdery substance produced when coal or wood is burned: *The buildings were covered with a layer of soot.*

soothe /suːð/ *verb*: **soothes, soothing, soothed**
1 Something **soothes** when it brings relief *eg* from pain or irritation: *an antiseptic cream that soothes and heals* □ *The medicine soothed her sore throat.* [*opposite* **aggravate**] **2** You **soothe** someone when you calm or comfort them: *She soothed the crying baby by rocking him in her arms and singing to him softly.* — *adjective* **soothing:** *a soothing ointment* □ *a soothing voice.*

sooty /sʊtɪ/ *adjective*: **sootier, sootiest**
Sooty means covered in soot: *After cleaning the chimney his clothes were all sooty.* □ *I can't understand where that sooty mark on the carpet came from.*

sophisticated /sə'fɪstɪkeɪtɪd/ *adjective*
1 A **sophisticated** person has or displays a wide knowledge and experience of the world, especially of culture, fashion and good taste: *a sophisticated audience* □ *She's very sophisticated.* **2 Sophisticated** things are advanced, complex or subtle: *a sophisticated computer-guidance system* □ *a sophisticated argument.*

sophistication /səfɪstɪ'keɪʃən/ *noun* (*uncount*)
Sophistication is the quality of being sophisticated: *the sophistication of modern weapons systems.*

sopping /'sɒpɪŋ/ *adjective or adverb*
If something is **sopping**, or **sopping** wet, it is wet through or full of water: *You better get out of those sopping wet shoes before you catch cold.*

soppy /'sɒpɪ/ *adjective* (*informal*): **soppier, soppiest**
If you describe a person or thing as **soppy**, you mean they are silly or weakly sentimental: *a soppy poem* □ *Don't be so soppy!*

soprano /sə'prɑːnoʊ/ *noun*: **sopranos**
1 A **soprano** is a girl, young boy or woman who has a high singing voice. **2** (*uncount*) People who have this singing voice sing **soprano.** [see also **treble**]

sorcery /'sɔːsərɪ/ *noun* (*uncount*)
Sorcery is the performing of magic using the power of supernatural forces, especially of black magic using the power of evil spirits.

sordid /'sɔːdɪd/ *adjective*
Sordid describes something that involves dishonesty or immorality: *The whole sordid affair was brought to light after a newspaper received an anonymous tip-off.*

sore /sɔː(r)/ *adjective; noun*
▻ ***adjective***
1 Something that is **sore** is painful or tender: *I've got a sore back.* □ *Is your throat sore?* **2** (*AmE*) You are **sore** when you are angry or resentful: *Don't get sore just because I didn't notice your new outfit.*
▻ ***noun*: sores**
A **sore** is a diseased spot or area on the skin, especially an ulcer or boil: *His legs were covered with weeping sores.*
▻ ***phrases*** **1** For **a sore point** see **point**. **2** (*informal*) If something **sticks out like a sore thumb**, it is very noticeable; if someone **sticks out like a sore thumb**, they are out of place or so different from the people they are with that they are immediately noticed.

sorely /'sɔːlɪ/ *adverb* (*intensifying*)
You use **sorely** to mean 'very much' or 'acutely': *He was a good friend to us all and he'll be sorely missed.*

sorrow /'sɒroʊ/ *noun* (*uncount or count; especially literary*): **sorrows**
Sorrow is grief or deep sadness because of your own or someone else's loss or disappointment; a **sorrow** is a cause of this: *She tried to comfort him in his sorrow.* □ *Good night, good night; parting is such sweet sorrow, that I shall say good night, till it be morrow.* □ *Life, with all its joys and sorrows.*

sorrowful /'sɒroʊfəl/ *adjective*
Sorrowful means full of sadness: *a dog with large sorrowful eyes.* — *adverb* **sorrowfully:** *'I wish she was still here,' he said sorrowfully.*

sorry /'sɒrɪ/ *interjection or adjective; adjective*
▻ ***interjection** or **adjective***
You say **'Sorry'** or **'I'm sorry' a** when you are apologizing to someone for something you have done that has upset them, or for being unable to help them: *'I think you're sitting on my jacket.' 'Oh, sorry.'* □ *I'm so sorry to be late.* □ *Sorry I couldn't get to your lecture.* □ *I'm sorry about the mess in here.* □ *Sorry for causing so much confusion.* □ *I hope you said sorry.* □ *I'm sorry, but I shall have to cancel my appointment.* □ *I'm sorry, Mrs Peters is not available at the moment.* □ *No, sorry, that book isn't in stock at present.* **b** when you are announcing something sad or upsetting, or expressing regret or sympathy about it: *I'm sorry to tell you that your application has been unsuccessful.* □ *'She died last night.' 'Oh, I'm so sorry.'* □ *I was very sorry to hear about your grandmother's death.* **c** when you haven't heard what someone has said to you, and you want them to repeat it: *'A cheese and chutney sandwich, please.' 'Sorry?'* □ *I'm sorry, I didn't quite catch your name.* **d** when you have said something wrong and want to correct it: *in Nebraska, sorry, I mean Nevada.* **e** as a polite introduction to saying you disagree: *I'm sorry but I think you're quite wrong.*
▻ ***adjective*: sorrier, sorriest**
1 You are **sorry** for someone when you feel pity or sympathy for them: *I've never felt sorrier for anyone in my life than I did for that announcer.* **2** You are **sorry** for yourself when you have been hurt or upset and are feeling miserable about it: *She was sitting on the bottom step rubbing her ankle and looking sorry for herself.* **3** You are **sorry** for something bad you have done

if you are ashamed of it, or regret it: *I hope you're sorry.* **4** You are **sorry** about a situation if it makes you feel sad or regretful: *No-one was sorry when she decided to leave.* □ *I wasn't sorry when my contract ended.* **5** **Sorry** describes things so bad or inadequate that they should be a cause of shame and regret to those responsible for them: *a sorry tale of neglect* □ *The building is now in a sorry state.* □ *That's a pretty sorry excuse.*

sort /sɔːt/ *noun; verb*

▻ ***noun***: **sorts**

1 You refer to a certain **sort** of thing when you mean one of the types or classes of that thing, or when you are thinking of the thing in terms of its qualities: *What sort of accommodation are you looking for?* □ *She asked me to get her some fruit juice but she didn't say which sort.* □ *the sort of breakfast cereal that consists of grain and dried fruit* □ *There are all sorts of entertainments for the kids.* □ *They stock several different sorts of drawing paper.* □ *Bring a waterproof garment of some sort.* □ *You mustn't use language of that sort in front of the children.* □ *She's studying architecture or design or something of the sort.* □ *I always distrust this sort of claim.* □ *This isn't the sort of world we want our children to grow up in.* □ *'What sort of flat have they got?' 'Oh, pretty comfortable.'* [compare '**like** that', '**like** this', 'what is it **like?**' at **like**]

People often use the form *those* (or *these*) *sort of* with a plural noun, but it sounds slightly better, and still means the same, if you use *that* (or *this*) *sort of*, with a singular noun: *You should ignore that sort of remark* (rather than *those sort of remarks*). With nouns that are always used in the plural, *eg* 'trousers', if you want to avoid *these sort of trousers* you can say *trousers of this sort* or *trousers like these.* [see also **kind, type**]

2 Sometimes '**sort** of' is used without much meaning: *That's a useful sort of gadget.* [= that's a useful gadget] □ *She's an odd sort of person.* [= she's an odd person] **3** You can describe a thing as a **sort** of something to make your description sound vaguer: *He's a sort of general handyman.* □ *A punt is a sort of flat-bottomed boat that you push along with a long pole.* **4** '**Sort** of' can refer to largeness of amount, especially of time or money: *If you earned the sort of money she earns* [= as much money as she earns] *you could afford weekends in Paris too.* □ *We can't check everything twice; we don't have that sort of time.* **5** (*informal*) You can refer to a person as a particular **sort** when describing their personality: *He's not a bad sort.* [= he's quite nice] □ *She's never been the complaining sort.*

▻ ***verb***: **sorts, sorting, sorted**

You **sort** things when you arrange them in order, or put them into groups according to type, class or kind: *Could you sort these cards into alphabetical order for me?* □ *He sorted the applications into 'possibles' and 'rejections'.* □ *I began sorting through the mail.*

▻ ***phrases*** **1** For **nothing of the sort** see **nothing**. **2** Something that is described as a thing **of a sort** or **of sorts** is not a very good one, or not a typical one: *She's a beauty therapist of a sort.* □ *We constructed a tent of sorts from branches and polythene bags.* **3** (*informal*) You feel **out of sorts** when you feel ill or depressed. **4** (*informal*) **Sort of** is used to mean 'rather', 'slightly' or 'more or less': *I've been feeling sort of unsettled lately.* □ *I'd sort of made up my mind to go.* □ *He looked at me sort of suspiciously.*

phrasal verb

sort out **1** You **sort** things **out** when you separate them into groups, organize them, or tidy them: *I should spend an evening sometime sorting out these loose papers.* **2** You **sort** a problem or difficulty **out** when you solve it: *Don't worry about the money; I'm sure we can sort something out.* **3** (*informal*) One person **sorts** another **out** when they punish them or deal with them in such a way as to make them behave properly.

SOS /ɛsoʊ'ɛs/ *noun* (*used in the singular*)

1 An **SOS** is a ship's or aircraft's call for help, consisting of those letters repeated in Morse code: *The captain of the trawler sent an SOS.* **2** (*informal*) An **SOS** is also any urgent call for help: *I got an SOS from my sister asking me to come at once.*

so-so /'soʊsoʊ/ *adjective or adverb* (*informal*)

If you describe something as **so-so**, you mean it is neither very good nor very bad: *'How was your holiday?' 'So-so.'* [*same as* **passable**]

soufflé /'suːfleɪ/ *noun* (*uncount or count*): **soufflés**

Soufflé or a **soufflé** is a light sweet or savoury baked dish consisting of a frothy mass of whipped egg-whites with other ingredients mixed in: *cheese soufflé.*

sought /sɔːt/ *verb*

Sought is the past tense and past participle of **seek**.

sought-after /'sɔːtɑːftə(r)/ *adjective*

Sought-after things are things that many people want to have and try hard to get: *His watercolours are now much sought-after.*

soul /soʊl/ *noun*: **souls**

1 A person's **soul** is the non-physical part of them, with personality, emotions and intellect, widely believed to survive in some form after the death of the body: *Do you believe our souls never die?* **2** (*uncount or count*) If you say that a person has no **soul**, you mean that they do not understand or appreciate things that appeal to the finer human emotions or they do not have ordinary human feelings of sympathy: *A singer with no soul.* □ *Acts of indecency committed by brutes with no soul.* **3** Something's **soul** is its essential nature or the force that motivates it: *the soul of the nation.* **4** (*used in the singular*) If you refer to someone as the **soul** of some virtue or quality, you mean they are a perfect example or model of that virtue or quality: *He's the soul of discretion.* **5** (*informal*) A **soul** is a person, or a person that you think of in a particular way: *The beach was empty; there wasn't a soul to be seen.* □ *I won't tell a soul, I promise.* □ *She's a poor soul.* □ *He's feeling really ill, poor soul.* □ *a village of two hundred souls.* **6** (*uncount*) **Soul** is soul music.

soul-destroying /'soʊldɪstrɔɪɪŋ/ *adjective*

Something **soul-destroying** is very depressing, usually because it is extremely dull, boring or repetitive: *The work is absolutely soul-destroying.*

soulful /'soʊlfəl/ *adjective*

Soulful means having or expressing deep feelings, especially of sadness: *The dog has large soulful eyes.* — *adverb* **soulfully:** *He sang soulfully of the lost days of his youth.*

soulless /'soʊlləs/ *adjective*

1 You describe people as **soulless** when they do not have the finer or deeper human emotions. **2** You describe a job or a task as **soulless** when it is monotonous or mechanical. **3** A **soulless** place is bleak and lifeless.

soul music /'soʊl mjuːzɪk/ *noun* (*uncount*)

Soul music or **soul** is a type of popular Black American music, combining elements from gospel, blues and jazz and typically expressing or dealing with strong emotions, especially love.

sound[1] /saʊnd/ *noun*; *verb*

▻ ***noun***: **sounds**

1 (*uncount*) **Sound** is what you hear, or the impressions you receive through your ears: *Light travels faster than sound.* **2** A **sound** is particular noise: *What's that sound?* ▫ *It was a most peculiar sound.* ▫ *We could hear a tapping sound coming from below.* ▫ *faint sounds of breathing.* ▫ *There were distant sounds of children shouting and laughing.* ▫ *The sound of approaching footsteps broke the silence.* ▫ *She entered without a sound.* [compare **noise**] **3** (*usually in the singular*) The **sound** of something such as a voice or instrument is its particular quality or tone: *This fiddle certainly produces a finer sound.* ▫ *the untrained sound of a child's voice* ▫ *He likes the sound of his own voice.* [= he enjoys talking more than listening] **4** (*used in the singular*) The **sound** of something is the impression it makes on you when you hear about it: *'She wants to see you in her office.' 'Oh dear, I don't like the sound of that.'* ▫ *Let's go and look at the flat; I like the sound of it.* ▫ *He's recovering well by* (or *from*) *the sound of it.* [= according to what I've heard] **5** (*uncount*) **Sound** in a film or a television broadcast is what you hear, *eg* the speech or dialogue, as distinct from what you see on the screen: *the sound engineers* ▫ *a sound editor.* **6** (*used in the singular*) The **sound** on a television set or radio is the volume or volume control: *They had the television on with the sound turned down.*

▻ ***verb***: **sounds, sounding, sounded**

1 Something such as a car horn **sounds** or **is sounded** when it produces its usual noise, or is made to produce it: *A foghorn sounded in the distance.* ▫ *He sounded his horn as he turned into the drive.* ▫ *The fire alarm was sounded at two minutes past three.* [see also **alarm**] **2** Something **sounds** a certain way if that is the impression you get when you hear it or hear about it: *The accompaniment sounds a bit unbalanced.* ▫ *She sounded so friendly on the telephone.* ▫ *You sound upset; are you all right?* ▫ *You sounded just like your father talking.* ▫ *That sounds like* [= that is probably] *Peter at the door now.* ▫ *That sounds like an excellent idea.* ▫ *The party sounds as if it was great fun.* ▫ *It doesn't sound as though there's much hope of a grant.* ▫ *I haven't been there, but it sounds a pleasant enough place for a holiday.* **3** You **sound** a letter in a word if you pronounce it: *You don't sound the h in 'honour'.* **4** A doctor **sounds** a part of you when he or she examines it by tapping it and listening to it: *He sounded my back and chest to make sure there was no lung damage.*

> ***phrasal verb***
> **sound off** (*informal*) Someone **sounds off** when they express their opinion, or complain, angrily or noisily.
> **sound out** You **sound** somebody **out** about something when you ask them what they think about it: *Sound her out to see if she'd like to be secretary.*

sound[2] /saʊnd/ *adjective*; *adverb*

▻ ***adjective***

1 Something that is **sound** is healthy or in good condition, not damaged, injured or weakened: *Fortunately her health is still pretty sound.* ▫ *I don't think those balconies are very sound.* [*opposite* **unsound**] **2** A **sound** investment is one that provides a good profit or return, especially over a long period. [*opposite* **unsound**] **3 Sound** judgement or advice is sensible and reliable. [*opposite* **unsound**] **4** To give someone a **sound** beating is to beat them hard and thoroughly, *eg* as a punishment. **5 Sound** sleep is deep and undisturbed: *I enjoyed six hours' sound unbroken sleep and felt better.*

▻ ***adverb***

You are **sound** asleep when you are sleeping deeply. [*same as* **fast**] — *adverb* **soundly:** *The children were sleeping soundly.* ▫ *They were soundly beaten in the finals.*

sound[3] /saʊnd/ *noun*: **sounds**

A **sound** is a narrow passage of water connecting two seas or separating an island and the mainland: *the Sound of Jura.*

sound effect /'saʊnd ɪfɛkt/ *noun*: **sound effects**

Sound effects are artificially-produced sounds that are used in films and plays to make them seem more realistic.

soundtrack /'saʊndtrak/ *noun*: **soundtracks**

1 A film's **soundtrack** is its music, speech or sound recorded on magnetic tape along the edge of the film and synchronized with the pictures. **2** A **soundtrack** is also a recording of the music from a film.

soup /suːp/ *noun* (*uncount or count*): **soups**

Soup is a liquid food made by boiling meat, vegetables or grains in water: *fish soup* ▫ *carrot soup* ▫ *What's the soup of the day?* ▫ *I never eat soup.*

▻ ***phrase*** (*informal*) If you are **in the soup**, you are in trouble or difficulty: *If Dad catches you, you'll be in the soup.*

> ***phrasal verb***
> (*informal*) A vehicle **is souped up** when its engine is altered so that its speed or power is increased.

soup plate /'suːp pleɪt/ *noun*: **soup plates**

A **soup plate** is a deep plate with a rim, used for eating soup out of. [see picture at **tableware**]

soup spoon /'suːp spuːn/ *noun*: **soup spoons**

A **soup spoon** is a spoon with a round bowl used for eating soup. [see picture at **tableware**]

sour /saʊə(r)/ *adjective*; *verb*

▻ ***adjective***

1 Sour foods or drinks have an acid taste or smell, similar to lemon juice or vinegar: *These grapes are a little sour.* **2 Sour** milk is milk that has begun to ferment and is therefore bad. **3** If someone has a **sour** look on their face, their expression is bad-tempered and unfriendly. **4** If something goes or turns **sour**, it goes bad or wrong: *Their marriage turned sour and they agreed to separate.*

▻ ***verb***: **sours, souring, soured**

Something that **sours** relations or friendships makes them less friendly or harmonious. — *adverb* **sourly:** *'I'm not to blame for my brother's mistakes,' he said sourly.*

source /sɔːs/ *noun*: **sources**

1 A **source** of something is its origin or cause, or the place, thing, person or circumstance from which it begins or develops: *Do you have any other sources of income?* ▫ *The source of the contamination was traced to a tin of meat.* ▫ *He couldn't find the source of the leak.* **2** A river or stream's **source** is the point where it begins: *the search for the source of the Nile.* **3** A **source** is a person, or a book or other document, that provides you with information or evidence: *The journalist refused to disclose his sources.* ▫ *The library will provide you with source material for your essay.* ▫ *We heard it from a reliable source.*

south /saʊθ/ *noun*; *adverb*; *adjective*

▻ ***noun*** (*used in the singular*)

1 The **South** is the direction to your right when you face the sunrise (east): *The army was camped to the south of the river.* ▫ *They crossed the desert from north* *to south.* **2** The **south** is the part of a country or other area that lies towards the south: *the American South* □ *voters in the prosperous south.*

▻ ***adverb***

South means to the south: *swallows flying south for the winter.*

▻ ***adjective***

1 A part of a place with the name or description **south** is a part towards the south: *The surgical wards are in the south wing of the hospital.* □ *He lives in South London.* **2** A **south** wind blows from the south.

southbound /ˈsaʊθbaʊnd/ *adjective*

1 Southbound traffic is travelling south. **2** The **southbound** carriageway of a motorway is the one used by traffic travelling south.

southeast /saʊθˈiːst/ *noun; adverb; adjective*

▻ ***noun*** *(used in the singular)*

1 The **Southeast** is the direction between south and east: *a warm wind blowing from the southeast.* **2** The **southeast** is the part of a country or area that lies towards the southeast: *unemployment in London and the Southeast.*

▻ ***adverb***

Southeast means to the southeast: *If you walk southeast for two miles you will reach the village.*

▻ ***adjective***

1 A part or place with the description **southeast** is the part towards the southeast: *The wall extends along the southeast boundary of the estate.* **2** A **southeast** wind blows from the southeast.

southeasterly /saʊθˈiːstəlɪ/ *adjective; noun*

▻ ***adjective***

1 A **southeasterly** direction or region lies towards the southeast. **2** A **southeasterly** wind blows from the southeast.

▻ ***noun*: southeasterlies**

A **southeasterly** is a wind blowing from the southeast.

southeastern /saʊθˈiːstən/ *adjective*

Southeastern means in or belonging to the southeast of a country or other area: *the southeastern counties of England* □ *a southeastern dialect.*

southerly /ˈsʌðəlɪ/ *adjective; noun*

▻ ***adjective***

1 A **southerly** direction or region lies to the south: *the most southerly point of the British mainland* □ *The wind was coming from a southerly direction.* **2** A **southerly** wind blows from the south.

▻ ***noun*: southerlies**

A **southerly** is wind that blows from the south.

southern /ˈsʌðən/ *adjective*

Southern means in or belonging to the south of a country or other area: *a southern accent* □ *There will be occasional showers in southern districts.* □ *Southern Africa.*

southerner /ˈsʌðənə(r)/ *noun*: **southerners**

A **southerner** is a person who was born in or lives in a southern region or country.

southernmost /ˈsʌðənmoʊst/ *adjective*

The **southernmost** place on a piece of land or other area is the place that is furthest south: *the southernmost island of the archipelago.*

southward /ˈsaʊθwəd/ *adverb; adjective*

▻ ***adverb***

Southward or **southwards** means towards the south: *They travelled southwards towards the plains.*

▻ ***adjective:*** *the southward journey.*

southwest /saʊθˈwɛst/ or /saʊˈwɛst/ *noun; adverb; adjective*

▻ ***noun*** *(uncount)*

1 Southwest, or the **southwest**, is the direction between south and west: *They noticed heavy black clouds to the southwest.* **2** The **Southwest** or the **southwest** is the part of a country or other area that lies towards the southwest: *Cornwall and the Southwest.*

▻ ***adverb***

Southwest means to the southwest: *They were sailing southwest.*

▻ ***adjective***

1 A part or place with the description **southwest** is the part towards the southwest: *the southwest corner of the garden.* **2** A **southwest** wind blows from the southwest.

southwestern /saʊθˈwɛstən/ *adjective*

Southwestern means in or belonging to the southwest of a country or area: *the Southwestern district* □ *southwestern tribes.*

souvenir /suːvəˈnɪə(r)/ *noun*: **souvenirs**

A **souvenir** is something that you keep to remind you of a place or occasion: *a souvenir shop* □ *Did you buy any souvenirs when you were in Japan?* □ *He gave us a copy of the photograph as a souvenir of our visit.* [*same as* **memento**]

sovereign /ˈsɒvrɪn/ *noun; adjective*

▻ ***noun*: sovereigns**

1 A **sovereign** is a king, queen or other supreme ruler or head of a country: *The armed forces owe their allegiance to the sovereign as head of state.* **2** A **sovereign** was an old British gold coin worth £1.

▻ ***adjective***

1 A **sovereign** ruler has supreme power or authority. **2** A **sovereign** state or nation is politically independent.

sovereignty /ˈsɒvrəntɪ/ *noun (uncount)*

Sovereignty is the complete and independent political power that a country has to govern itself: *The government will never sign a treaty which undermines the sovereignty of Parliament.*

sow[1] /soʊ/ *verb*: **sows, sowing, sowed, sown**

Seed **is sown** when it is scattered on or planted in the earth; land or fields **are sown** with crops of a particular kind when their seeds are planted there: *Sow the seed in drills twelve inches apart.* □ *Sow an ounce of grass seed per square yard.* □ *fields sown with winter barley.*

sow[2] /saʊ/ *noun*: **sows**

A **sow** is an adult female pig. [see also **boar**]

soya bean /ˈsɔɪə biːn/ or **soy bean** /ˈsɔ biːn/ *noun*: **soya beans**

Soya beans are a type of Asian bean eaten as a vegetable and used to make oil, flour and soy sauce.

soy sauce /sɔɪ ˈsɔːs/ *noun (uncount)*

Soy sauce is a salty brown sauce made from soya beans, widely used as a flavouring in Eastern (especially Chinese and Japanese) cooking.

spa /spɑː/ *noun*: **spas**

A **spa** is a place where water containing minerals comes out of the ground and where people go to bathe in and drink it because they believe it is good for their health.

space /speɪs/ *noun; verb*

▻ ***noun*: spaces**

1 *(uncount)* **Space** is the three-dimensional medium in which all physical things exist: *time and space* □ *He was staring into space.* [= looking straight ahead at nothing in particular] **2** *(uncount)* **Space** or **outer space** is the region beyond the earth's atmosphere, containing the other planets and the stars: *space exploration.* **3** *(uncount)* There is **space** for something

a *eg* in a place, room or building, if there is a big enough area for it to fit into or take place in: *We don't have the space for all this furniture.* ▫ *We moved to a house in the country to give the children more space to play.* ▫ *He's left all his belongings in our apartment, where they're occupying valuable space.* [*same as* **room**] **b** in a book or other piece of writing, if it can be included within the length allowed: *Unfortunately we're so short of space in the dictionary that we can't include all the words we'd like to.* ▫ *A good deal of space is given to grammatical analysis.* ▫ *I've left space for your signature.* [*same as* **room**] **4** A **space** is **a** a gap or empty area between or among things: *There should be a space of at least half a metre between vehicles.* ▫ *a chance to get out into the countryside and enjoy the wide-open spaces.* **b** a place or position available for filling or using: *I've left a space at the bottom for you to add a message.* ▫ *Please sign in the space below.* ▫ *Find a space and sit down.* ▫ *There are plenty of parking spaces free in the other carpark.* **5** (*used in the singular*) A **space** of time is a period of time: *He got up, showered, shaved and had his breakfast all within the space of twenty-five minutes.* ▫ *After a brief space of time she was back.* [*same as* **interval**]

▻ ***verb***: **spaces, spacing, spaced**

You **space** things when you arrange them with gaps between them: *With such a narrow column of print the words are bound to be unevenly spaced.*

> ***phrasal verb***
> You **space** things **out** when you arrange them with gaps between them: *Use the whole floor and keep yourselves well spaced out.*

space age /ˈspeɪs eɪdʒ/ (when used as an adjective **space-age**) *noun; adjective*

▻ ***noun*** (*used in the singular*)

The **space age** is the present period in history, in which travel in space has become possible.

▻ ***adjective***

1 Space-age technology is very advanced or very sophisticated. **2 Space-age** designs have a futuristic appearance.

spacecraft /ˈspeɪskrɑːft/ *noun*: **spacecraft**

A **spacecraft** is a vehicle that can travel in space: *rockets and other spacecraft.*

spaceship /ˈspeɪsʃɪp/ *noun*: **spaceships**

A **spaceship** is a vehicle that can carry passengers and cargo through space: *the spaceship 'Endeavour'.*

space shuttle /ˈspeɪs ʃʌtəl/ *noun*: **space shuttles**

A **space shuttle** is a type of spacecraft that is designed to make repeated journeys into space.

spacious /ˈspeɪʃəs/ *adjective*

1 A **spacious** interior is large and has plenty of space in it: *a spacious dining room* ▫ *a car with a spacious boot* [*same as* **roomy**] **2 Spacious** places cover a wide area and have a lot of empty space in them: *Herds of antelope inhabit the spacious landscape of the Serengeti.*

spade /speɪd/ *noun*: **spades**

1 A **spade** is a long-handled digging tool with a broad metal blade that you push into the ground with your foot. [see picture at **tool**] **2 a** (*used in the plural*) **Spades** are one of the four suits (♠) in a pack of playing cards: *the ace of spades* ▫ *Spades are trumps.* **b** A **spade** is one of the cards in this suit: *She only had one spade in her hand.*

▻ ***phrase*** If you **call a spade a spade** you speak plainly without trying to make things sound better than they really are.

spaghetti /spəˈɡɛtɪ/ *noun* (*uncount*)

Spaghetti is a type of pasta made in the form of long thin string-like strands: *a plate of spaghetti.*

span /span/ *noun; verb*

▻ ***noun***: **spans**

1 A **span** is the length between the supports of a bridge or arch. **2 Span** is also added to nouns to form compound words which refer to a particular length from end to end in distance or time: *The albatross has a wingspan of more than 2 metres.* ▫ *the lifespan of the average man.* **3** A **span** is also a measure of length equal to the distance between the tips of thumb and little finger on an extended hand.

▻ ***verb***: **spans, spanning, spanned**

To **span** means to extend across or over: *a wooden bridge spanning the gorge* ▫ *an empire that spanned two centuries.*

spangle /ˈspaŋɡəl/ *noun*: **spangles**

A **spangle** is a small piece of glittering material sewn on to clothing for decoration, especially a sequin. — *adjective* **spangled:** *circus performers in spangled tights.*

Spaniard /ˈspanjəd/ *noun*: **Spaniards**

A **Spaniard** is a native or citizen of Spain: *He's a Spaniard, from Barcelona.* [see also **Spanish**]

spaniel /ˈspanjəl/ *noun*: **spaniels**

A **spaniel** is any of several breeds of dog with long drooping ears and a silky coat.

Spanish /ˈspanɪʃ/ *adjective; noun*

▻ ***adjective***

Spanish means concerned with or belonging to Spain, its people or their language: *Christopher Columbus was Italian, not Spanish.* ▫ *the Spanish Armada* ▫ *a Spanish dance.*

▻ ***noun***

1 (*uncount*) **Spanish** is the language spoken in Spain and the Canary Islands, in parts of Central and South America, and in certain Caribbean islands: *When he first went to Spain he couldn't speak a word of Spanish.* **2** (*with a plural verb*) The **Spanish** are the people of Spain.

spank /spaŋk/ *verb*: **spanks, spanking, spanked**

If someone **spanks** a child, they hit it on the bottom with the flat of their hand as a punishment.

spanking /ˈspaŋkɪŋ/ *noun; adverb; adjective*

▻ ***noun*** (*used in the singular*)

A **spanking** is a series of slaps on the bottom with the flat of the hand.

▻ ***adverb*** (*informal*)

You say that something is **spanking** new when it is completely and strikingly new: *He drove up in a spanking new Rolls Royce.*

▻ ***adjective*** (*informal*)

A **spanking** pace is a brisk one.

spanner /ˈspanə(r)/ *noun*: **spanners**

A **spanner** is a tool with one or two specially shaped ends which fit around a nut or bolt which can then be turned by making levering movements with the handle of the spanner. [see picture at **tool**]

spar /spɑː(r)/ *noun; verb*

▻ ***noun***: **spars**

A **spar** is a strong thick pole of wood or metal, especially one used as a mast or beam on a ship.

▻ ***verb***: **spars, sparring, sparred**

> ***phrasal verb***
> **spar with 1** Boxers **spar with** each other when they practise their punches and defensive skills on

each other. **2** You **spar with** another person in an argument when you exchange, often friendly, insults or alternately score points in the argument.

spare /spɛə(r)/ *adjective*; *noun*; *verb*

▻ ***adjective***

1 A thing or a supply that is **spare** is not being used, but is ready for use, or ready to replace the one that is being used, if it becomes necessary: *The spare wheel is located under the floor of the boot.* □ *They stock spare parts for most types of vehicle.* □ *Always take a spare pair of socks in case you get your feet wet.* □ *We can put him in the spare room if he comes to us.* **2** Something that is **spare** is not being used by anyone else, or for anything else: *There were no spare seats on the bus, so we had to stand.* □ *Unfortunately we have no rooms spare just at present.* □ *Has anyone got a spare copy they could lend me?* □ *I don't have any spare cash at the moment.* **3** **Spare** time is any period when you are not working and are therefore free for other activities: *She never has a spare moment.* □ *He spends every spare minute with the children.* □ *What do you do in your spare time?* [*same as* **free**] **4** (*literary*) Someone who is described as **spare** is rather thin: *his spare frame* [*same as* **lean, thin**]

▻ ***noun***: **spares**: *The bulbs wear out rather quickly, but we keep plenty of spares in a box in the attic.*

▻ ***verb***: **spares, sparing, spared**

1 You can **spare** something when you can afford to part with it, or make it available, for some purpose: *Could you spare a moment? I'd like a quick word with you.* □ *Thank you for sparing the time to talk to me.* □ *It's a good investment, if you can spare the cash.* □ *The more space we give to important vocabulary, the less we can spare for infrequently used words.* **2** You have something such as time, money or food to **spare** if you have an extra amount that is not needed: *There's plenty of fruit to spare, so please help yourselves.* □ *Most universities haven't a penny to spare.* □ *I caught the train without a minute to spare.* [= I only just caught it] **3** A person or thing **is spared** when they are not harmed, in spite of being under threat or in great danger: *They had been sentenced to death, but at the last minute he agreed to spare them.* □ *His life was spared but he remained a prisoner for the remainder of it.* □ *Fortunately amidst all the bombing the cathedral had been spared.* **4** You **spare** someone's feelings when you avoid hurting or upsetting them: *We kept well away from the subject of redundancy, in order to spare her feelings.* **5** You **are spared** something unpleasant when you are not forced to suffer it: *At least he was spared the misery of a long and painful illness.* □ *'I had to have ten stitches in the cut, and then it went septic.' 'Oh, spare me the details, please!'* **6** (*with a negative*) If you say no trouble or expense **was spared** in doing something, you mean that a lot of effort was made, or a lot of money was spent, in doing it.

spare part /spɛə 'pɑːt/ *noun*: **spare parts**

A **spare part** is a part for a machine that is used to replace an existing identical part that has become faulty.

sparing /'spɛərɪŋ/ *adjective*

If you are **sparing** with something, you use it economically or in small, often too small, amounts: *be sparing with the salt when cooking.* — *adverb* **sparingly:** *Use the cream sparingly, avoiding the eyes.*

spark /spɑːk/ *noun*; *verb*

▻ ***noun***: **sparks**

1 A **spark** is a tiny red-hot glowing particle thrown off by burning material, or by the friction between two hard surfaces: *The sparks from their campfire started a forest fire.* □ *The flint in a lighter creates the spark which ignites the fuel.* **2** A **spark** is an electrical charge flashing across a gap between two conductors. **3** A trace, hint or glimmer of something can also be called a **spark**: *a spark of intelligence.* **4** (*rather old*) If you refer to someone as a bright **spark**, you mean they are a lively, witty or intelligent person.

▻ ***verb***: **sparks, sparking, sparked**

When burning material or a spark plug **sparks**, it throws off sparks or creates a spark.

phrasal verb

If something **sparks off** an argument or conflict, it causes it to begin: *The police arrested a group of youths, sparking off a riot which took several hours to bring under control.*

sparkle /'spɑːkəl/ *verb*; *noun*

▻ ***verb***: **sparkles, sparkling, sparkled**

1 Something **sparkles** when it gives off small flashes of bright light: *Her eyes sparkled as she laughed.* □ *The sunlight sparkled on the surface of the water.* **2** When a wine or some other drink **sparkles** it gives off small bubbles of carbon dioxide. **3** If a person or their conversation **sparkles** they are very lively and witty.

▻ ***noun***: **sparkles**

1 (*uncount or count*) **Sparkle** or a **sparkle** is an act of sparkling or a sparkling appearance: *the sparkle of diamonds and emeralds.* **2** (*uncount*) **Sparkle** is liveliness or wit: *She seems to have lost her sparkle.* — *adjective* **sparkling:** *sparkling wine* □ *sparkling wit.*

spark plug /'spɑːk plʌg/ or **sparking plug** *noun*: **spark plugs** or **sparking plugs**

A **spark plug** is a small electrical device in a motor vehicle engine that makes the spark to ignite the fuel and air mixture.

sparrow /'sparoʊ/ *noun*: **sparrows**

A **sparrow** is a type of small brown bird that is very common in the countryside and in gardens.

sparse /spɑːs/ *adjective*

Something that is **sparse** is thinly scattered over a wide area or does not exist in large quantities or amounts: *As they climbed higher the vegetation became more and more sparse.* — *adverb* **sparsely:** *a sparsely populated area.*

spartan /'spɑːtən/ *adjective*

Spartan living conditions are harshly basic with no luxuries whatsoever.

spasm /'spazm/ *noun*: **spasms**

1 A **spasm** is a sudden uncontrollable jerk of the body or part of the body caused by a contraction of the muscles. **2** If you do something in **spasms**, you do it intensively for short periods only.

spasmodic /spaz'mɒdɪk/ *adjective*

Something that is **spasmodic** happens or occurs for short periods and at irregular intervals: *spasmodic bursts of activity.* — *adverb* **spasmodically:** *He works spasmodically.*

spastic /'spastɪk/ *adjective*; *noun*

▻ ***adjective***

Spastic is sometimes used to describe people who are affected by spastic paralysis or cerebral palsy, a condition characterized by uncontrollable jerky muscle movements resulting from damage, often caused at birth, to the muscle-controlling area of the brain.

▻ ***noun***: **spastics**

A **spastic** is a person suffering from spastic paralysis or cerebral palsy.

spat /spat/ *verb*
Spat is the past tense and past participle of **spit**.

spate /speɪt/ *noun* (*used in the singular*)
In a river or stream, a **spate** is a sudden rush or increased volume of water; a **spate** of complaints, robberies, or other incidents is a sudden rush of them or increase in their number.
▷ ***phrase*** A river **in spate** flows very fast with a greatly increased volume of water from heavy rain or melting snow.

spatial /ˈspeɪʃəl/ *adjective*
Spatial means of or relating to space (sense 1): *spatial awareness.*

spatter /ˈspatə(r)/ *verb*: **spatters, spattering, spattered**
Something **spatters**, or **is spattered**, on a surface when it splashes over it in scattered drops or patches: *He dropped the tin of paint, spattering it all over the carpet.*

spatula /ˈspatjʊlə/ *noun*: **spatulas**
A **spatula** is a tool with a broad, blunt flexible blade, used, especially in cooking and baking, for mixing or spreading.

spawn /spɔːn/ *noun; verb*
▷ ***noun*** (*uncount*)
Spawn is the eggs of frogs, fish and molluscs, laid in water in a soft transparent jelly-like mass: *frog's spawn.*
▷ ***verb***: **spawns, spawning, spawned**
1 Creatures such as frogs and fish **spawn** when they lay eggs. **2** If one thing **spawns** another, it gives rise to it: *The film's success spawned several sequels.*

speak /spiːk/ *verb*: **speaks, speaking, spoke, spoken**
1 You **speak** when you use your voice to produce words: *He opened his mouth as if he were about to speak.* □ *I was so astonished I could scarcely speak.* □ *Could you speak more slowly?* □ *She hasn't spoken a word since the accident.* □ *His job moved to Glasgow and the children grew up speaking with strong Scottish accents.* □ *After her stroke she had to learn to speak all over again.* **2** You **speak** to people when you say things to them: *She turned to speak to me.* □ *Could I speak to Peter, please?* □ *Don't interrupt when I'm speaking on the telephone.* □ *It was several months before he could bring himself to speak about* (or *of*) *her death.*

> The meanings of **speak** and **talk** are very close, though **speak** is rather more formal than **talk**. It is natural to refer to a single person **speaking**, but to two or more people **talking** to each other: *Some people didn't realize the chairman had begun to speak and went on talking.* You often **speak** to someone to mention a serious matter, or to complain about something: *I've already spoken to the caretaker about the mess in the yard.*

3 You **speak** a language **a** if you are able to communicate with people in it: *Do you speak English?* □ *She speaks several languages fluently.* **b** when you use it to communicate with people: *It sounded to me as if they might be speaking Finnish.* □ *He spoke to her in Czech.* □ *We spoke Welsh at home, but we had to speak English at school.* **4** You **speak** to a group of people when you give a lecture or make a speech: *They invited her to speak to them about her work with deaf children.* □ *He spoke for an hour, entirely without notes.* **5** You **speak** the truth when you are honest, or when what you say represents the facts. [*same as* **tell**] **6** You **speak** your mind when you say what you really think.
▷ ***phrases*** **1** People who **are not speaking**, or **are not on speaking terms**, have quarrelled with each other or become unfriendly, and refuse to communicate: *Apparently Margaret and Agnes aren't speaking.* □ *She hasn't spoken to us since we complained about her dog.* **2** You use **so to speak** to indicate that you are using a colourful or metaphorical expression, not intended to be understood literally: *We must be careful not to kill the goose that lays the golden eggs, so to speak.* [*same as* **as it were**] **3** Something **speaks for itself** if it has an obvious meaning or significance and does not need to be explained: *I hardly need to tell you what has happened; the circumstances speak for themselves.* **4** If you say '**speak for yourself**' to someone who has just included you in a statement, you mean that though it may be true in their case, it is not true in yours: *'We're so careless about remembering to turn off lights.' 'Speak for yourself; I'm pretty careful.'* **5** You **speak highly**, or **speak well, of** a person or thing when you praise them, express approval of them or recommend them: *His commanding officer speaks very well of him.* □ *Her teaching methods are quite highly spoken of.* **6** You **speak ill of** someone when you criticize them, express disapproval of them or condemn them: *We're told we mustn't speak ill of the dead.* **7** (*with a negative*) Nothing or no-one **to speak of** means nothing or no-one important, interesting or worth mentioning: *'Been anywhere exciting this summer?' 'Nowhere to speak of.'*

> ***phrasal verbs***
> **speak for** You **speak for** other people when you express their opinion for them: *Personally I'm quite happy with that suggestion but I can't speak for anyone else, of course.*
> **speak out** You **speak out** *eg* for or against something when you openly or publicly express your approval or disapproval: *Thanks for speaking out in my support.* □ *They had been imprisoned for speaking out against the government.*
> **speak up** **1** You **speak up** when you express your opinion publicly or openly: *Don't be afraid to speak up if you have a criticism to make.* **2** If people ask you to **speak up**, *eg* at a meeting, they want you to speak louder because they can't hear what you're saying.

speaker /ˈspiːkə(r)/ *noun*: **speakers**
1 A **speaker** is a person who speaks, especially someone making a formal speech: *Please welcome our guest speaker, Professor Chalmers.* **2** A **speaker** is a loudspeaker: *a radio cassette with twin* [=two] *speakers.* [see picture at **living room**] **3** The **Speaker** in the British House of Commons and in the law-making assemblies of certain other countries is the person appointed to preside over debates.

speaking /ˈspiːkɪŋ/ *verb; noun*
▷ ***verb***
1 You use **speaking** in expressions such as 'generally **speaking**' or 'strictly **speaking**' to indicate how your statement is intended to apply: *They disapprove of parents helping with homework, generally speaking.* □ *Strictly speaking a spider is an animal.* □ *It could be called a successful coup, politically speaking at least.* **2** You can say '**speaking** as *eg* a commuter', when you are stating something that is based on your experience as a commuter: *Speaking as a former pupil of the school I don't remember bullying being a serious problem.* **3** Sometimes people say '**Speaking**' when answering the telephone to confirm that they are the person you want: *'Is that Felicity Hill?' 'Speaking.'* □ *'Could I speak to Felicity Hill?' 'Speaking.'* **4** You say '**speaking**

of' something that has just been mentioned to introduce another thing related to it: *Speaking of Christmas, has anyone remembered to order a turkey?* [*same as* **talking**]

▷ ***noun*** (*uncount*)

Speaking is the art or activity of giving speeches or talks: *the art of public speaking.*

spear /spɪə(r)/ *noun*; *verb*

▷ ***noun***: **spears**

A **spear** is a weapon that is thrown from the shoulder, consisting of a long pole with a sharp, usually metal, point: *Masai warriors carry spears to mark their status.* □ *They were forced to retreat from the hail of spears.*

▷ ***verb***: **spears, spearing, speared**

You **spear** something when you pierce it with a spear or some other sharp-pointed instrument: *He was idly spearing the peas on his plate with his fork.* □ *The kingfisher speared the fish with its sharp beak, and swallowed it headfirst.*

spearhead /'spɪəhɛd/ *verb*; *noun*

▷ ***verb***: **spearheads, spearheading, spearheaded**

A group of people **spearhead** a movement, campaign or attack when they lead it: *They spearheaded the anti-nuclear movement in the '60s and early '70s.*

▷ ***noun***: **spearheads**

The **spearhead** of an attacking force is the leading part of it: *The spearhead of the invasion was concentrated on the beaches of Normandy.*

spearmint /'spɪəmɪnt/ *noun* (*uncount*)

1 Spearmint is a common variety of mint plant from which a fresh-tasting flavouring is made. **2 Spearmint** is this flavouring, used *eg* in sweets and toothpaste.

special /'spɛʃəl/ *adjective*; *noun*

▷ ***adjective***

Special describes a thing or person that is **1** different from, better than, or more important than, other things of its class: *She'd made him a special meal for his birthday.* □ *when you're buying a gift for someone special* □ *We only drink champagne on special occasions.* □ *You can get special offers from some travel agents.* □ *It was an area of the country that occupied a special place in her affections.* □ *I don't see what's so special about him.* **2** (*especially with negatives, in questions, or after 'if'*) definite or specific: *I had nothing special to do that day.* □ *There was no special reason for mentioning it; I just suddenly remembered it.* □ *Had you someone special in mind?* □ *I'll ring if there's anything special to report.* [*same as* **particular**] **3** appointed, designed, intended or required for a specific purpose: *What we need is a special computer officer.* □ *Special machinery had to be designed to deal with the process.* □ *special schools catering for children with behaviour problems* □ *You need special permission to stay away from college overnight.* **4** exceptional or unusual: *Hers is a special case.* □ *children with special needs* □ *There were special circumstances in this instance.* [*same as* **exceptional, unusual**] **5** greater than usual: *I'd made a special effort to look nice.* □ *make-up that takes special care of sensitive skins.* [*same as* **particular, especial**] **6** individual: *The patients have to have their own special cutlery.* [*same as* **personal, particular**]

▷ ***noun***: **specials**

A **special** is something that is produced or organized for a special purpose, or that is exceptional as distinct from regular or normal, *eg* an extra edition of a newspaper or an extra train service.

specialise see **specialize**.

specialism /'spɛʃəlɪzm/ *noun*: **specialisms**

1 A **specialism** is a subject of study or an activity that you specialize in: *His specialism is the study of animal behaviour.* [*same as* **speciality** (sense 1)] **2** (*uncount*) **Specialism** is the act of limiting oneself to one subject or activity.

specialist /'spɛʃəlɪst/ *noun* (*often adjectival*): **specialists**

If a person is a **specialist** in a particular area of knowledge or expertise, they have made a special study of it: *He's a specialist in diseases of the digestive system.* □ *specialist knowledge.*

speciality /spɛʃɪ'alɪtɪ/ or (*especially in AmE*) **specialty** /'spɛʃəltɪ/ *noun*: **specialities** or **specialties**

1 A **speciality** is a field of study or work that is specialized in: *His speciality is English china and ceramics.* **2** A **speciality** is also something that someone does particularly well or is known for: *Seafood is one of the specialities of the region.*

specialize or **specialise** /'spɛʃəlaɪz/ *verb*: **specializes, specializing, specialized**

You **specialize** when you limit or devote your activities, study or business to a particular activity or subject: *The children have plenty of time to decide which subjects they want to specialize in.* □ *an engineering firm specializing in drilling equipment for the oil industry.* — *noun* (*uncount*) **specialization** /spɛʃəlaɪ'zeɪʃən/: *There is more and more need for specialization in the fields of science and engineering.*

specialized or **specialised** /'spɛʃəlaɪzd/ *adjective*

Things that are **specialized** have a specific purpose or deal with a particular subject or activity: *specialized equipment* □ *specialized knowledge.*

specially /'spɛʃəlɪ/ *adverb*

1 Specially means in a special way or for a special purpose: *a shampoo specially formulated for dry hair* □ *disabled athletes with specially adapted wheelchairs.* **2 Specially** is also a less formal use of 'especially': *We came specially to see you.*

species /'spiːʃiːz/ *noun*: **species**

1 (*technical*) A **species** is a group of closely related animals or plants that are able to breed together and which form a sub-division of a genus. **2** (*formal or humorous*) A **species** is also a kind or type: *What species of machine is this?*

specific /spɪ'sɪfɪk/ *adjective*; *noun*

▷ ***adjective***

1 Specific means of a particular nature or precisely identified: *He doesn't have a specific role.* **2 Specific** also means clear or precise in meaning, not vague: *He gave me specific instructions.* □ *I'm not sure who you mean; can you be more specific?*

▷ ***noun***: **specifics**

1 (*used in the plural*) If you refer to the **specifics** of a general thing, you mean its details, especially details that have still to be discussed or decided: *We discussed the general strategy, but didn't have time to get down to specifics.* **2** (*technical*) A **specific** is a drug used to treat a particular disease.

specifically /spɪ'sɪfɪklɪ/ *adverb*

1 Specifically means particularly or for the purpose stated and no other: *The house was designed specifically for the elderly and disabled.* **2 Specifically** also means exactly and clearly: *I specifically told you not to leave the gate open.* **3** You also use **specifically** when you are giving more precise details of a general statement you have made: *In the next class, we will be looking at the work of the surrealist painters, specifically Max Ernst and Salvador Dali.*

specification /spɛsɪfɪ'keɪʃən/ *noun*: **specifications**
1 **Specifications** are a set of descriptions or directions that are to be followed when something is built or constructed: *The architect drew up specifications for the materials that were to be used in the building's construction.* **2** (*used in the singular*) Something's **specification** is the nature and quality of the parts or materials that it is made up of: *cars made to a high specification.* [= made with high quality materials or including sophisticated technology] **3** (*uncount*) **Specification** is also the act of specifying.

specify /'spɛsɪfaɪ/ *verb*: **specifies, specifying, specified**
You **specify** something when you refer to it or identify it precisely or by name: *The architect has specified concrete roofing tiles, rather than slates, for the roof.* ▫ *The rules clearly specify that a player who commits a professional foul will be sent off.*

specimen /'spɛsɪmɪn/ *noun*: **specimens**
1 A **specimen** is a sample or example of something, especially an object studied or put in a collection: *He brought some interesting specimens back from his field trip to China.* **2** A **specimen** is also a sample of blood, urine or tissue on which medical tests are carried out: *You should take a specimen of urine with you when you come for your appointment at the clinic.*

specious /'spiːʃəs/ *adjective* (*formal, derogatory*)
A **specious** argument or **specious** logic seems to be right or correct, but is really false or flawed.

speck /spɛk/ *noun*: **specks**
A **speck** is a small spot, stain or tiny particle of something: *She got a speck of dust in her eye.* ▫ *The car sped away until it was just a speck in the distance.*

speckled /'spɛkəld/ *adjective*
Speckled means covered with many small marks or spots that are a different colour from the background: *a speckled hen* ▫ *speckled eggs.*

specs /spɛks/ *noun* (*plural; informal*)
Someone's **specs** are their spectacles or glasses: *I've lost my specs.*

spectacle /'spɛktəkəl/ *noun*: **spectacles**
1 A **spectacle** is an unusual thing that may be seen: *In some European countries, you can witness the curious spectacle of a reigning monarch travelling around on a bicycle.* **2** A **spectacle** is also a grand or impressive public display or exhibition: *The massed pipes and drums with the castle in the background made a magnificent spectacle.* **3** If someone makes a **spectacle** of themselves, they do something foolish or ridiculous that makes them the focus of attention. **4** (*used in the plural*) **Spectacles** are a pair of lenses held in a frame over the eyes, used to correct faulty eyesight: *I keep a spare pair of spectacles at the office.*

> **Spectacles** is rather formal. It is more ususal to talk about your **glasses** or **specs**.

spectacular /spɛk'takjʊlə(r)/ *adjective; noun*
▻ ***adjective***
1 Something that is **spectacular** is very impressive to see or watch: *spectacular scenery.* **2** You also use **spectacular** to describe something that is very remarkable or dramatic: *a spectacular success* ▫ *a spectacular rise in profits.* — *adverb* **spectacularly:** *The value of the shares has increased spectacularly.* ▫ *He can be spectacularly stupid at times.*
▻ ***noun*: spectaculars**
A **spectacular** is a spectacular show or entertainment: *a spectacular on ice.*

spectator /spɛk'teɪtə(r)/ *noun*: **spectators**
A **spectator** is a person who watches an event or incident but does not take part in it: *The athletics competition attracted 50 000 spectators.* ▫ *a spectator sport.*

spectra /'spɛktrə/ *noun*
Spectra is the plural of **spectrum**.

spectre (*AmE* **specter**) /'spɛktə(r)/ *noun*: **spectres**
1 A **spectre** is a ghost that can be seen. [*same as* **apparition**] **2** You can also refer to something that causes fear and apprehension as a **spectre**: *the spectre of war.*

spectrum /'spɛktrəm/ *noun*: **spectra** or **spectrums**
1 (*used in the singular*) The **spectrum** is the range of colours that make up white light that are separately visible when the light is passed through a prism. The colours of the spectrum are red, orange, yellow, green, blue, indigo and violet. **2** A **spectrum** is a range of waves, such as light or radio waves, within a particular frequency. **3** A **spectrum** is any broad range in which either end of the range is considered as the opposite of the other: *His writing deals with the whole spectrum of human emotions.*

speculate /'spɛkjʊleɪt/ *verb*: **speculates, speculating, speculated**
1 You **speculate** on or about a matter when you make guesses about it because you do not know all the circumstances or do not have all the necessary facts: *Until we know more, it would be foolish to speculate on the eventual outcome.* **2** You **speculate** in things such as property or stocks and shares when you buy them not knowing what their future price will be, in the hope of quickly making profitable sales.

speculation /spɛkjʊ'leɪʃən/ *noun*: **speculations**
Speculation is the act or process of speculating: *The conclusion he has arrived at is pure speculation.* ▫ *He made all his money in property speculation.*

speculative /'spɛkjʊlətɪv/ *adjective*
Speculative means based on speculation: *a speculative assumption* ▫ *a speculative investment.*

speculator /'spɛkjʊleɪtə(r)/ *noun*: **speculators**
A **speculator** is a person who buys things in the hope of making a profit when they sell them without knowing for sure what the future selling price will be: *a property speculator.*

sped /spɛd/ *verb*
Sped is the past tense and past participle of **speed**.

speech /spiːtʃ/ *noun*: **speeches**
1 (*uncount*) **Speech** is **a** (*often adjectival*) the ability to speak or the activity of speaking: *The stroke deprived him temporarily of the power of speech.* ▫ *Speech is unique to human beings.* ▫ *Phonetics is the study of speech sounds.* ▫ *speech development in young children* ▫ *speech patterns.* **b** spoken language: *words that are used in speech but not in writing* ▫ *In everyday informal speech you reduce both 'we had' and 'we would' to 'we'd'.* **c** the activity of expressing yourself: *There must be no interference with our freedom of speech.* **2** (*used in the singular*) Your **speech** is the way you speak: *Her eyes were unfocused and her speech was slurred.* ▫ *A certain amount of Canadian influence was noticeable in his speech.* **3** (*used in the singular*) The **speech** of a region or country is the dialect or language that is spoken there: *the frequent omission of final consonants in South German speech.* **4** You make, give or deliver a **speech** when you speak formally to a group of people: *We were told to keep our speeches short.* ▫ *the text of the Prime Minister's speech.* **5** A **speech** from a play is a set of lines that are spoken by a particular character: *We were made to learn several*

speeches from 'The Merchant of Venice' and took turns to recite them in class.

speechless /ˈspiːtʃləs/ *adjective*
If you are **speechless**, you are temporarily unable to speak, *eg* because of surprise or shock: *She was speechless with admiration.* □ *When I announced that I was leaving she was speechless.*

speed /spiːd/ *noun*; *verb*
▻ ***noun***: **speeds**
1 (*uncount or count*) **Speed** is the rate at which something travels, is done, or happens: *He came down the hill at top speed.* [= very fast] □ *What is the speed of sound?* □ *Police have videoed drivers on the motorway travelling at speeds well in excess of 100 mph.* □ *You're bound to make mistakes if you work at that speed.* □ *Children grow and develop at different speeds.* [compare **rate**] **2** (*uncount*) **Speed** is also a fast rate of movement or activity: *He took the corner at speed.* □ *The train gathered speed.* □ *Speed is essential in all kinds of rescue work.* **3** If a vehicle has, *eg*, five gear settings, its gearbox is a five-**speed** gearbox. **4** The **speed** of a photographic film is the rate, according to its particular sensitivity, at which it reacts to light.
▻ ***verb***: **speeds, speeding, sped**
1 You **speed** somewhere when you move or travel there quickly: *The cyclists sped down the hill.* □ *She sped out of the room and up the stairs.* **2** (*only used in the continuous tenses*) A driver **is speeding** when he or she is driving faster than the legal limit: *Slow down; you're speeding.* — *noun* (*uncount*) **speeding:** *He was fined for speeding.*

> ***phrasal verb***
> **speed up** (*past tense* **speeded up**) Something **speeds up** or **is speeded up** when it travels or progresses at a faster rate, or is made to do so: *The train speeded up and recovered some of the time lost by the delay.* □ *We'll speed up once we get used to the software.* □ *Can you speed up delivery? These materials are urgently needed.* □ *They're trying out a new roundabout system in order to speed up the flow of traffic.* [*same as* **accelerate**]

speedboat /ˈspiːdbout/ *noun*: **speedboats**
A **speedboat** is a small boat with a powerful engine that can travel at high speeds.

speed limit /ˈspiːd lɪmɪt/ *noun* (*usually in the singular*): **speed limits**
The **speed limit** is the maximum speed at which you are legally allowed to drive a vehicle on a particular road or stretch of road: *The speed limit in built-up areas is 30 miles per hour.* □ *There are no speed limits on the German autobahns.*

speedometer /spɪˈdɒmɪtə(r)/ *noun*: **speedometers**
A **speedometer** is an instrument in a vehicle that shows how fast the vehicle is travelling. [see picture at **car**]

speedy /ˈspiːdɪ/ *adjective*: **speedier, speediest**
Speedy means fast, prompt or without delay: *I was sorry to hear that you had been ill; I hope you make a speedy recovery.* □ *a speedy delivery.*

spell /spɛl/ *verb*; *noun*
▻ ***verb***: **spells, spelling, spelt, spelled**
1 You **spell** a word when you write or say the letters that make it up, in their correct order: *How do you spell your last name?* **2** Letters said or written in a stated order **spell** a particular word: *B, A, D spells 'bad'.* **3** If something **spells** trouble, it is an indication that trouble is about to come: *His expression spelt trouble.*
▻ ***noun***: **spells**
1 A **spell** is a period of time during which something lasts: *We've had a long spell of sunny weather this summer.* □ *He had one or two spells in prison when he was younger.* **2** A **spell** is also a set of words which when spoken are supposed to have magic power; if someone casts a **spell** on someone else they cause that other person to be under the influence of this magic power: *a witch's spell.*

> ***phrasal verb***
> **spell out 1** If you **spell** something **out** to someone, you explain it clearly and in detail: *This is your last warning; I hope I don't have to spell it out!* **2** You **spell** a word **out** when you read, write or speak the letters that form it one by one.

spellbinding /ˈspɛlbaɪndɪŋ/ *adjective*
If something is **spellbinding** it is so impressive or fascinating that you feel as if you are under a magic spell: *a spellbinding performance.*

spellbound /ˈspɛlbaʊnd/ *adjective*
You are **spellbound** when you are so completely charmed or fascinated by someone or something that you seem to be under a magic spell: *The children sat spellbound as Peter Pan appeared to fly around the stage.*

spelling /ˈspɛlɪŋ/ *noun*: **spellings**
1 (*uncount*) **Spelling** is the ability to spell: *Your spelling is dreadful!* **2** A **spelling** is a way a word is spelt: *There are several different spellings of the name including Neil, Neal and Niall.*

spelt /spɛlt/ *verb*
Spelt is the past tense and past participle of **spell**.

spend /spɛnd/ *verb*: **spends, spending, spent**
1 You **spend** money when you use it up by buying or paying for things: *I've spent all my pocket money.* □ *How much did you spend on that dress?* □ *She doesn't like spending money.* □ *He spends his wages as soon as he gets them.* **2** You **spend** time somewhere or on something when you stay there for a time or when you use up time doing it: *He resigned to spend more time with his family.* □ *I spent my holidays painting the flat.*
▻ ***phrase*** (*euphemistic*) You **spend a penny** when you urinate.

spent /spɛnt/ *verb*; *adjective*
▻ ***verb***
Spent is the past tense and past participle of **spend**.
▻ ***adjective***
1 If someone or something is **spent** they are completely exhausted or used up: *She flopped down on the bed, absolutely spent.* **2 Spent** is used to describe certain things that have been used and cannot be used again: *spent matches* □ *The ground was littered with spent cartridges.*

sperm /spɜːm/ *noun*: **sperms** or **sperm**
1 A **sperm** is one of the millions of sex cells produced by male animals and contained in semen. Only a single sperm is needed to fertilize each egg produced by the female. **2** (*uncount*) **Sperm** is the liquid containing these cells that is forced out of the penis during sexual intercourse.

spew /spjuː/ *verb*: **spews, spewing, spewed**
1 Something **spews** out of something when it pours out in a continuous rush or flood; if something **spews** something out it causes it to pour out in a continuous rush or flood: *Great clouds of dust and smoke spewed out of the volcano.* □ *The printer was spewing out thousands of sheets every minute.* **2** (*vulgar*) To **spew** also means to vomit: *He spent most of the journey spewing over the side of the ship.*

sphere /sfɪə(r)/ *noun*: **spheres**
1 A **sphere** is a round solid figure like a ball with a surface on which all points are an equal distance from the centre. [see picture at **shape**] **2** A **sphere** is also a particular field of activity or interest: *His main interest is in the sphere of preventive medicine.* **3** Something that comes within someone's **sphere** is within their range of influence: *Cuba came into the former USSR's sphere of influence.* **4** A class or circle within society is also referred to as a **sphere**: *She moves in an altogether more exalted sphere.*

spherical /'sfɛrɪkəl/ *adjective*
A **spherical** object has the shape of a sphere.

spice /spaɪs/ *noun*; *verb*
▻ ***noun***: **spices**
1 A **spice** is any of various strong-smelling and -tasting substances obtained from plants, and used to flavour food: *Pepper, cloves, nutmeg, ginger, cumin, and cardamom are all spices.* **2** (*uncount*) **Spice** is such substances collectively. **3** (*uncount*) **Spice** is something that adds interest or enjoyment to life: *What you need is a little spice in your life!*
▻ ***verb***: **spices, spicing, spiced**
1 Food or drink **is spiced** when it is flavoured with spice or spices. **2** If something **spices** up your life it adds interest or enjoyment to it.

spick and span /spɪk ən 'span/ *adjective*
A place that is **spick and span** is neat, clean and tidy.

spicy /'spaɪsɪ/ *adjective*: **spicier, spiciest**
1 Spicy foods are flavoured with or smell of spices: *spicy sausage.* **2** (*informal*) A **spicy** story is exciting, especially if it deals with sexual scandal or something that is slightly shocking: *She told me a spicy bit of gossip.*

spider /'spaɪdə(r)/ *noun*: **spiders**
A **spider** is a small creature with eight legs. Many types of spider spin webs to catch the insects on which they feed.

spidery /'spaɪdərɪ/ *adjective*
If someone's handwriting is described as **spidery**, the letters are formed using long thin lines like a spider's legs.

spike /spaɪk/ *noun*: **spikes**
1 A **spike** is a long thin object with a sharp point, especially a pointed piece of metal: *A primitive weapon consisting of a metal ball with vicious spikes.* **2 a** A **spike** is also one of the pointed pieces of metal attached to the soles of running-shoes or to other types of footwear where the wearer needs to grip the surface on which they are walking or running. **b** (*plural*) A pair of running-shoes with these pointed pieces of metal on their soles are referred to as **spikes**. **3** Any long thin pointed part or object such as a head of corn or the cluster of flowers on certain types of plants is also known as a **spike**.

spiky /'spaɪkɪ/ *adjective*: **spikier, spikiest**
Spiky things have spikes or pointed ends: *a plant with spiky leaves* ▫ *spiky hair.*

spill /spɪl/ *verb*: **spills, spilling, spilt, spilled**
1 You **spill** something, or it **spills**, when you cause it to flow, or it flows, out of a container, especially accidentally: *He spilt orange juice down the front of his tie.* ▫ *The water spilled over the edge of the sink.* **2** You can say that large crowds coming out or going into a place in a sudden flow **are spilling** in or out of that place: *The spectators came spilling out of the stadium and soon filled the streets with their chants.* **3** You **spill** someone's blood when you shed it by violent means, *eg* in battle. **4** (*informal*) A rider on a bicycle, motorbike or horse **is spilt** when they are thrown from the saddle.
▻ ***phrase*** (*informal*) If someone **spills the beans** they give away information which was supposed to remain secret.

spillage /'spɪlɪdʒ/ *noun*: **spillages**
1 (*uncount*) **Spillage** is the act of spilling: *the spillage of the lorry's load.* **2 Spillages** are amounts that have been spilled: *Put a tray under the bowl to catch any spillages.*

spilt /spɪlt/ *verb*
Spilt is the past tense and past participle of **spill**.

spin /spɪn/ *verb*; *noun*
▻ ***verb***: **spins, spinning, spun**
1 You **spin** something, or it **spins**, when you turn it, or it turns, round and round a central point, especially quickly: *the Earth spinning on its axis* ▫ *He spun the globe.* **2** You **spin** round when you turn round quickly to face in the opposite direction. **3** When people or machines **spin** they draw out and twist fibres into thread: *She sat by the window spinning.* **4** A **spider** spins its web when it makes it out of threads produced in special glands in its body. **5** If your head **is spinning**, you feel dizzy or very confused. **6** Wet laundry **is spun** when the water is forced out of it in a washing machine or spin drier.
▻ ***noun***: **spins**
1 A **spin** is an act of spinning or a spinning motion: *The car went into a spin.* **2** (*informal*) If you go for a **spin**, you go on a short trip in a car or on a motorbike, for pleasure.

phrasal verb
You **spin** something **out** when you make it last longer that it normally would.

spinach /'spɪnɪtʃ/ *noun* (*uncount*)
Spinach is a plant with large dark green leaves that are eaten as a vegetable: *boiled spinach* ▫ *chopped spinach* ▫ *I'm not very fond of spinach.*

spinal /'spaɪnəl/ *adjective*
Spinal means of or relating to the spine: *spinal injuries.*

spinal column /spaɪnəl 'kɒləm/ *noun*: **spinal columns**
Your **spinal column** is the bones and nerves that form your spine.

spinal cord /spaɪnəl 'kɔːd/ *noun*: **spinal cords**
In people and animals, the **spinal cord** is a long mass of nerve tissue running along the back connecting the brain with nerves in other parts of the body.

spindle /'spɪndəl/ *noun*: **spindles**
1 A **spindle** is a rod with a notched or tapered end, for twisting the thread in spinning. **2** A **spindle** is also a pin or axis on which anything turns.

spindly /'spɪndlɪ/ *adjective* (*informal*): **spindlier, spindliest**
If someone has **spindly** legs or arms their legs or arms are long, thin and frail-looking.

spin drier or **spin dryer** /spɪn 'draɪə(r)/ *noun*: **spin driers** or **spin dryers**
A **spin drier** is a machine that forces the water out of wet laundry by spinning it at high speed in a revolving drum.

spin-dry /spɪn'draɪ/ *verb*: **spin-dries, spin-drying, spin-dried**
You **spin-dry** wet clothes or washing when you remove most of the water from them in a spin drier or washing machine.

spine /spaɪn/ *noun*: **spines**
1 The **spine** is the series of small interlinking bones forming a flexible column along the backs of many animals. [*same as* **backbone**] **2** The **spine** of a book is the narrow middle section of its cover, where the edges of the pages are fastened in. **3** If a plant or animal has **spines** it has long projecting thorn-like growths that it uses as a defence against predators: *a porcupine's spines* □ *a cactus with vicious spines.* **4** (*informal*; *usually in negative statements*) If you say that someone has no **spine** you mean that they lack courage or strength of character: *He's got no spine.* [*same as* **spineless**]

spine-chilling /ˈspaɪntʃɪlɪŋ/ *adjective* (*informal*)
Something **spine-chilling** is very frightening: *a spine-chilling vampire movie.*

spineless /ˈspaɪnləs/ *adjective*
1 Spineless animals have no backbone. [*same as* **invertebrate**] **2** (*informal, derogatory*) If you describe someone as **spineless** you mean that they lack courage or strength of character: *He's too spineless to stand up for himself.* □ *You spineless little creep!*

spin-off /ˈspɪnɒf/ *noun*: **spin-offs**
A **spin-off** is something, especially something valuable, that is developed from an earlier product or idea: *The rapid commercial development of computers was one of the spin-offs of the space programme in the 1960s.*

spinster /ˈspɪnstə(r)/ *noun* (*old, rather derogatory*): **spinsters**
A **spinster** is a woman, especially an elderly woman, who has never been married.

spiny /ˈspaɪnɪ/ *adjective*: **spinier, spiniest**
1 Spiny plants or animals are covered with spines: *the spiny bodies of sea urchins.* **2** A **spiny** problem is difficult to deal with. [*same as* **prickly**]

spiral /ˈspaɪərəl/ *noun*; *adjective*; *verb*
▻ ***noun***: **spirals**
1 A **spiral** is a long curve that winds outwards from a central point in a series of circles that get larger and larger as it moves away from the central point. **2** A **spiral** is also a long curve that winds upwards round and round a central line. **3** A **spiral** in *eg* prices or the value of money is a rise or fall, becoming more and more rapid.
▻ ***adjective:*** *A snail has a spiral shell.* □ *a spiral staircase.*
▻ ***verb***: **spirals, spiralling** (*AmE* **spiraling**), **spiralled** (*AmE* **spiraled**)
To **spiral** means to follow a spiral course or pattern: *prices are spiralling downwards.*

spire /spaɪə(r)/ *noun*: **spires**
A **spire** is a tall thin structure tapering upwards to a point, especially a tower on a church roof.

spirit /ˈspɪrɪt/ *noun*; *verb*
▻ ***noun***: **spirits**
1 A person's **spirit** is their mind, feelings and will as distinct from their physical body, thought of by many as surviving after their death: *I'll be with you in spirit, if not in body.* □ *His spirit lives on in his work.* **2** A **spirit** is this part of a person separated from their body after death and believed to be present as a ghost; a **spirit** is also any supernatural influence or being without a physical body: *try to contact the spirits of the dead* □ *an evil spirit* □ *the Holy Spirit.* **3** (*uncount or count*) The **spirit** of something is the general atmosphere or feeling created by several people at once: *team spirit* □ *It was done in a spirit of goodwill.* **4** (*uncount*) If someone shows **spirit**, they show courage or liveliness, especially in difficult or challenging circumstances: *She has a lot of spirit for someone so young.* **5** (*plural*) Your **spirits** are your emotional state or mood: *She found him in low spirits.* [=depressed] [see also **high spirits**] **6** The **spirit** of something such as a law or agreement is its real meaning or intention as distinct from its literal interpretation: *in accordance with the spirit, not the letter, of the law.* **7 Spirits** are strong alcoholic drinks, *eg* whisky, brandy or gin: *He never drinks spirits.*
▻ ***verb***: **spirits, spiriting, spirited**

phrasal verb
If someone or something **is spirited away** or **spirited off**, they are taken away or carried off secretly and suddenly, as if by magic: *He was spirited away from under the noses of the waiting press.*

spirited /ˈspɪrɪtɪd/ *adjective*
1 A **spirited** person or animal is full of courage or liveliness: *a spirited horse.* **2 Spirited** is also used in compound adjectives to indicate a particular kind of spirit, mood or attitude: *high-spirited* □ *That was very public-spirited of you.*

spiritual /ˈspɪrɪtʃʊəl/ *adjective*
1 Spiritual is used to describe things that concern the spirit or soul, rather than the body or physical things: *Though they live in Canada, Scotland is their spiritual home.* □ *one's spiritual life.* **2** A **spiritual** guide or leader is a person who provides others with guidance or leadership in religious matters. — *adverb* **spiritually:** *spiritually uplifted.*

spiritualism /ˈspɪrɪtʃʊəlɪzm/ *noun* (*uncount*)
Spiritualism is belief in, or the practice of, communication with the spirits of dead people, especially through a person who claims to be specially sensitive (a **medium**). — *noun* (*uncount or count*) **spiritualist:** *a spiritualist meeting* □ *She's one of several spiritualists living in the area.*

spit /spɪt/ *verb*; *noun*
▻ ***verb***: **spits, spitting, spat** or *AmE* **spit**

In British English the past tense and past participle of **spit** is **spat**, whereas in American English **spit** is also sometimes used as the past tense and past participle.

1 Someone **spits** when they force a mass of saliva or mucus from their mouth, often as a gesture of contempt. **2** You **spit** something that you have in your mouth out when you force it out, *eg* because it has an unpleasant taste: *She tried to give him the medicine but he kept spitting it out.* **3** Hot oil or fat **spits** when it is forced into the air in short explosive bursts, usually because it has come into contact with water or something that contains water. **4** You **spit** when you make spluttering noises while you speak, usually because you are very angry. **5** If it **is spitting**, occasional drops of rain are falling.
▻ ***noun***: **spits**
1 (*uncount*) **Spit** is saliva spat from the mouth. [*same as* **spittle**] **2** A **spit** is a long thin metal rod on which meat is roasted over a fire or in an oven. **3** A **spit** is also a long narrow strip of land jutting out into the sea: *a sand spit.*
▻ ***phrase*** (*informal*) If you hesitate in saying something, *eg* because you are afraid of someone's reaction to what you are about to say, and they tell you to **spit it out**, they mean that you should say it immediately.

spite /spaɪt/ *noun*; *verb*

▻ ***noun*** (*uncount*)

Spite is the mean or malicious desire to hurt, upset or annoy someone: *Purely out of spite she went and told him I'd been criticizing him.*

▻ ***verb*** (*only used in the infinitive*)

You do something to **spite** someone when you do it with the intention of hurting, upsetting or annoying them: *To spite me, she accepted an invitation from one of my former boyfriends.*

▻ ***phrase*** **1** You use **in spite of** like *despite*, to introduce a circumstance that makes a surprising contrast with the rest of your statement: *We decided to go to the play in spite of its poor reviews.* □ *In spite of the fact that she was too ill to see anyone, he insisted on visiting her.* **2** You do something **in spite of** yourself when you do it although you don't want to, intend to, or expect to: *I enjoyed the party in spite of myself.* □ *He began shouting and cheering in spite of himself.* [*same as* **despite**; compare **although**]

spiteful /ˈspaɪtfəl/ *adjective*

A **spiteful** person purposely says or does nasty things so as to hurt, upset or annoy other people: *a spiteful remark* □ *That was a horrible spiteful thing to do.* [*same as* **malicious**] — *adverb* **spitefully:** *'You'll never find anyone to marry you,' she said spitefully.* [*same as* **maliciously**]

spitting image /spɪtɪŋ ˈɪmɪdʒ/ *noun* (*singular*; *informal*)

When you say that someone is the **spitting image** of another person you mean they look very like them: *He's the spitting image of his father.*

spittle /ˈspɪtəl/ *noun* (*uncount*)

Spittle is saliva, especially when it spat from the mouth: *His chin was covered in spittle.*

splash /splaʃ/ *verb*; *noun*

▻ ***verb***: **splashes, splashing, splashed**

1 A liquid or semi-liquid substance **splashes** or **is splashed** when it is thrown about in large drops: *The water splashed over the edge of the bucket.* **2** If you **splash** a liquid on to a surface, or a surface **is splashed** with a liquid, you throw liquid over it so that it hits the surface in large drops wetting or staining it: *He splashed his face with cold water.* □ *His coat was splashed with mud.* **3** If a story **is splashed** across the pages of a newspaper it is printed or displayed there boldly: *The story was splashed across the front pages of all the tabloids.*

▻ ***noun***: **splashes**

1 A **splash** is the sound of splashing: *He dived into the water with a loud splash.* **2** A **splash** is a large irregular spot or stain, *eg* of colour: *His coat was covered with splashes of mud.* □ *a black background with splashes of red and orange.* **3** (*informal*) A **splash** is also a small amount or dash, especially of water or some other liquid that is added to something: *Could I have a whisky with just a splash of soda, please.* **4** A **splash** is the display made when a story or information is printed boldly in the pages of a newspaper.

phrasal verb

(*informal*) You **splash out** when you spend money on something that you would not normally spend money on: *I'm going to splash out and buy a new winter coat.*

splatter /ˈsplatə(r)/ *verb*: **splatters, splattering, splattered**

A liquid **splatters** over a surface or a surface **is splattered** with a liquid when it is splashed with it in small scattered drops: *When he was filling his fountain pen he accidentally splattered ink all over his essay.* □ *His clothes were splattered with mud.*

splay /spleɪ/ *verb*: **splays, splaying, splayed**

When you **splay** your fingers or your limbs you spread them outwards so that they are wide apart; you **splay** something out, or it **splays** out, when you cause it to open out, or it opens out, so that it is wider at one end: *large sea birds splaying their wings to dry them in the sun.*

splendid /ˈsplɛndɪd/ *adjective*

1 Something that is **splendid** causes admiration because it is very beautiful or grand: *a splendid banquet* □ *the splendid Georgian terraces of Bath.* [*same as* **impressive**] **2 Splendid** also means very good or excellent: *It's splendid to see you looking so well.* □ *'My company has offered me promotion.' 'Well, isn't that splendid!'* — *adverb* **splendidly:** *The walls of the castle were splendidly adorned with rich tapestries and hangings.* □ *They seem to be getting along splendidly.*

splendour (*AmE* **splendor**) /ˈsplɛndə(r)/ *noun* (*uncount or count*): **splendours**

Splendour is the state or quality of being very grand and beautiful in appearance or style; if you talk about the **splendours** of something you are referring to its most impressive or beautiful aspects: *the splendour of the mountain scenery* □ *one of the splendours of ancient Eygpt.*

splice /splaɪs/ *verb*: **splices, splicing, spliced**

1 You **splice** two pieces of rope when you weave the strands from the end of one piece into the end of the other and so form a secure join. **2** You **splice** two pieces of film or magnetic tape when you join the end of one to the end of the other with adhesive to form a continuous strip.

splint /splɪnt/ *noun*: **splints**

A **splint** is a length of wood or other material that is strapped to a broken limb to fix it in position while the bone heals.

splinter /ˈsplɪntə(r)/ *noun*; *verb*

▻ ***noun***: **splinters**

A **splinter** is a small thin sharp piece broken off a hard material, such as wood or glass.

▻ ***verb***: **splinters, splintering, splinters**

If a hard material, such as wood or glass, **splinters** or **is splintered**, it breaks or is broken into small thin sharp pieces.

split /splɪt/ *verb*; *noun*

▻ ***verb***: **splits, splitting, split**

1 Something **splits** or **is split** when it breaks or is broken into two or more pieces, especially from end to end: *His trousers had split down the back seam.* □ *He used an axe to split the logs into firewood.* **2** You **split** things up or they **split** up when you divide them up or they divide up into separate parts, amounts or groups: *split the atom* □ *The electricity industry was split up into regional companies when it was privatized.* □ *The children were split up into groups of four or five.* [*same as* **separate**] **3** You **split** something between two or more people when you divide it so that each has or takes a share: *If we travel together we can split the cost of the petrol.* [*same as* **share**] **4** Something **splits** open or **is split** open when it bursts or is broken along a line, exposing its contents: *She used a hammer to split open the coconut.* □ *He fell against a rock, splitting his head open.* **5** (*informal*) When someone **splits** they leave a place: *This party's boring; let's split.*

▻ ***noun***: **splits**

1 A **split** is a lengthways break or crack: *There's a split in the trunk of the tree where it was struck by lightning.* **2** A **split** is also a separation or division through disagreement: *a split in the Labour Party over unilateral nuclear disarmament.* **3** A dessert made with a banana sliced lengthways and filled or topped with cream or ice-cream is called a **split**: *a banana split.* **4** (*plural*) If you do the **splits** you spread your legs on the floor so that your body is upright and each leg is at right angles to your body.

▻ ***phrase***

1 If, when you are making a bargain, you **split the difference**, you settle on an amount half-way between the amount you have suggested and that suggested by the other person. **2** If you say that someone **is splitting hairs**, you mean that they are making or arguing about extremely fine and trivial distinctions. **3** (*informal*) You can say that people who are laughing uncontrollably **are splitting their sides**.

> ***phrasal verbs***
> **split off** If something **has split off** or **away**, it has broken away from or become separated from a larger thing or group: *Disease had entered the tree where one of its branches had split off.* □ *Two of the warships had split away from the main convoy.*
> **split up** Married couples or people who have had some sort of close relationship **split up** when they separate from each other or from a group, because of a disagreement: *It looks as if they are going to split up.* □ *They split up six months ago.* [*same as* **break up, part, separate**]

split infinitive /splɪt ɪn'fɪnɪtɪv/ *noun*: **split infinitives** (*grammar*)
In grammar, a **split infinitive** is the construction in which 'to' is separated from the infinitive by an adverb, as in *to boldly go*. Split infinitives are common in speech and writing but are considered by many to be undesirable, if not actually strictly incorrect. Occasionally, the use of a split infinitive is useful in making clear that an adverb refers to a particular verb and not to another verb or adjective in the same sentence.

split-level /splɪt'lɛvəl/ *adjective*
Split-level is used to refer to things that are composed of, or exist on more, than one level: *a split-level sitting room-cum-dining room.*

split second /splɪt 'sɛkənd/ *noun* (*used in the singular*)
A **split second** is a very short period of time: *It all happened in a split second. — adjective* **split-second:** *Racing drivers have to make split-second decisions.*

splitting /'splɪtɪŋ/ *adjective*
If someone says they have a **splitting** headache, they mean that they have a very severe headache.

splutter /'splʌtə(r)/ *verb*; *noun*
▻ ***verb***: **splutters, spluttering, spluttered**
1 If something **splutters** it makes a series of spitting sounds and throws out small drops of liquid or sparks; if someone **splutters** they make spitting sounds because they are choking or because they are trying to clear water or liquid from their air passages: *The hot oil spluttered as she put in the vegetables.* □ *They dragged him on board, coughing and spluttering.* **2** You **splutter** when you speak quickly or incoherently, *eg* because you are angry or embarrassed; you **splutter** words when you say them quickly or indistinctly: *He was spluttering with rage and frustration.* □ *She spluttered an apology.*
▻ ***noun***: **splutters** (*often used in the singular*)
A **splutter** is a sound of spluttering.

spoil /spɔɪl/ *verb*; *noun*
▻ ***verb***: **spoils, spoiling, spoiled** or **spoilt**

> Both **spoiled** and **spoilt** can be used as the past tense or past participle of **spoil**.

1 You **spoil** something when you make it unsatisfactory, useless or valueless: *He spoiled my painting by scribbling all over it.* □ *Eating too much chocolate will spoil your figure.* □ *The countryside will be completely spoiled if they go ahead with the new road.* □ *I won't let anything spoil my chances of getting a university degree.* [*same as* **ruin**] **2** You **spoil** someone, especially a child, when you cause them to become selfish or unable to accept hardship or disappointment because you indulge all their demands and wishes and do not punish them when they do something wrong: *His grandparents spoil him dreadfully.* **3** Food **is spoiled** when it becomes unfit to eat; a ballot paper **is spoiled** when it is made invalid because the voter has not marked it correctly.
▻ ***noun*** (*uncount or plural; formal or literary*)
Spoils are things that have been taken by a victorious army or that are gained by being successful in something: *the spoils of war* □ *After raiding the orchard, the boys went home to divide the spoils.*
▻ ***phrases*** **1** If you **are spoilt for choice**, you have so many things to choose from that you find it difficult to choose one. **2** If someone **is spoiling for a fight**, they are very eager for it and try to bring it about.

spoilsport /'spɔɪlspɔːt/ *noun*: **spoilsports** (*informal*)
A **spoilsport** is someone who spoils, or refuses to join in, the fun of others: *'Don't be such a spoilsport!'*

spoke /spoʊk/ *verb*; *noun*
▻ ***verb***
Spoke is the past tense of **speak**.
▻ ***noun***: **spokes**
The **spokes** of a wheel are any of the ribs or bars that connect the rim to the centre. [see picture at **bicycle**]

spoken /'spoʊkən/ *verb*; *adjective*
▻ ***verb***
Spoken is the past participle of **speak**.
▻ ***adjective***
1 Spoken language is uttered or expressed in speech. **2 Spoken** is also used in compounds to indicate that someone speaks in a particular way: *a soft-spoken Irishman.*
▻ ***phrase***
1 Something that is **spoken for** is reserved for or taken by someone else: *Is this seat spoken for?* **2** You can say that a man or woman is **spoken for** if they are already married, engaged, or in a steady relationship.

spokesman /'spoʊksmən/ *noun*: **spokesmen**
A **spokesman** is a man chosen to speak on behalf of other people, both men and women: *a government spokesman.*

spokesperson /'spoʊkspɜːsən/ *noun*: **spokespeople**
A **spokesperson** is a man or a woman chosen to speak on behalf of others.

spokeswoman /'spoʊkswʊmən/ *noun*: **spokeswomen**
A **spokeswoman** is a woman chosen to speak on behalf of others.

sponge /spʌndʒ/ *noun*; *verb*
▻ ***noun***: **sponges**
1 Sponges are any of various simple sea creatures with soft porous bodies that attach themselves permanently to rocks on the seabed. **2** A **sponge** is the springy skeleton of any of these creatures used for washing your body because it can absorb a lot of water; a **sponge** is also a man-made substitute for this, used for washing or cleaning. [see picture at **bathroom**] **3** A **sponge** is also a a sponge cake or pudding.

▻ ***verb*: sponges, sponging, sponged**
You **sponge** something when you wash or clean it with a sponge: *She sponged the stain off the carpet.*

> ***phrasal verb***
> If someone **sponges off** another person, or **sponges on** them, they get money from them or allow that other person to pay for their living expenses, without doing anything in return. [*same as* **scrounge off**]

sponge bag /'spʌndʒ bag/ *noun*: **sponges bags**
A **sponge bag** is a small waterproof bag for carrying toiletries in when travelling.

sponge cake /'spʌndʒ keɪk/ *noun*: **sponge cakes**
A **sponge** cake is a very light cake made with flour, butter (or margarine), eggs and sugar.

sponge pudding /spʌndʒ 'pʊdɪŋ/ *noun*: **sponge puddings**
Sponge pudding or a **sponge pudding** is a sponge mixture cooked by steaming and eaten as as dessert.

sponge roll /spʌndʒ 'roʊl/ *noun*: **sponge rolls**
A **sponge roll** is a small roll of sponge cake, often with a sweet filling.

spongy /'spʌndʒɪ/ *adjective*: **spongier**, **spongiest**
Spongy things are soft and springy, and sometimes also absorb water, like a sponge: *His gums were spongy and inflamed.* ▫ *The ground was spongy after the rain.*

sponsor /'spɒnsə(r)/ *noun*; *verb*
▻ ***noun*: sponsors**
1 A **sponsor** is **2** a person or organization that finances an event or broadcast in return for advertising: *Now, a word from our sponsor.* ▫ *The amateur football team is having difficulty finding a sponsor.* **3** a person who promises a sum of money to a participant in a fund-raising event provided they complete it or part of it: *Will you be one of my sponsors for the charity walk?* **4** a person who offers to be responsible for another, especially a godparent, or a person who submits a proposal, *eg* for new legislation.
▻ ***verb*: sponsors, sponsoring, sponsored**
You **sponsor** someone or something when you act as sponsor for them or it: *I've got lots of people to sponsor me at 50 pence a mile in the marathon.* ▫ *a sponsored walk.*

sponsorship /'spɒnsəʃɪp/ *noun* (*uncount*)
Sponsorship is the act or an instance of helping someone or something by giving them money, or the money given to help them: *The team wouldn't be able to afford football equipment without sponsorship.*

spontaneity /spɒntə'neɪɪtɪ/ *noun* (*uncount*)
Spontaneity is the quality of being spontaneous: *His painting style gives an impression of movement and spontaneity.*

spontaneous /spɒn'teɪnɪəs/ *adjective*
1 Something that is **spontaneous** happens without being planned or rehearsed, or, as a result of involuntary or instinctive feelings, without outside influence: *a spontaneous round of applause* ▫ *No-one told him to come; his desire to see her had been quite spontaneous.* [*opposite* **planned**] **2 Spontaneous** combustion is fire or burning that occurs by itself because of a chemical reaction, rather than being caused or influenced from outside.

spoof /spu:f/ *noun*: **spoofs** (*informal*)
A **spoof** of something is a copy or imitation of it that ridicules the original in a light-hearted way. [*same as* **parody**]

spooky /'spu:kɪ/ *adjective*: **spookier**, **spookiest** (*informal*)
If you describe something, especially a place, as **spooky** you mean it gives you a vague feeling of fear, often because you believe there may be ghosts there: *I'm not walking through the woods; they're spooky at night.* [*same as* **eerie**]

spool /spu:l/ *noun*: **spools**
A **spool** is a small cylinder on which things such as thread or photographic film are wound: *Make sure the spool is firmly fixed inside the camera before continuing.*

spoon /spu:n/ *noun*: **spoons**
1 A **spoon** is a tool of various sizes with a handle and a round or oval shallow bowl-like part, used for eating, serving or stirring food: *a silver spoon* ▫ *a wooden spoon.* [see picture at **tableware**] **2** A **spoon** is also a spoonful: *I take two spoons of sugar in my coffee.*
▻ ***verb*: spoons, spooning, spooned**
You **spoon** food when you lift it with a spoon from one place to another: *She spooned sauce over the chicken.*

spoonful /'spu:nfʊl/ *noun*: **spoonsful** or **spoonfuls**
A **spoonful** is the amount that a spoon will hold: *I'd like another spoonful of sugar, please.* ▫ *Add a heaped spoonful of cornflour.*

sporadic /spə'radɪk/ *adjective*
Sporadic means occurring from time to time, at irregular intervals: *sporadic gunfire* ▫ *He suffered from sporadic bouts of fever.* [*same as* **intermittent**] — *adverb* **sporadically:** *fighting broke out sporadically.* [*same as* **intermittently**]

spore /spɔ:(r)/ *noun*: **spores**
A **spore** is a tiny cell produced by many plants and other organisms such as bacteria, by which they reproduce.

sport /spɔ:t/ *noun*; *verb*
▻ ***noun*: sports**
1 A **sport** is any activity or competition designed to test physical skills: *Which sports do you enjoy most?* ▫ *He was never very good at sports.* ▫ *the sports reporter of the local newspaper.* **2** (*uncount*) **Sport** is such activities considered collectively: *Some people complain that there is too much sport on television.* **3** (*uncount*) **Sport** is also used to refer to any activity that is done for pleasure or amusement rather than any serious purpose: *They shoot small songbirds for sport.* [*same as* **recreation**] **4** (*informal*) If you say that someone is a **sport** you mean that they are a person who cheerfully accepts defeat, inconvenience or being the butt of jokes: *Paul won't mind if we play a practical joke on him; he's a good sport.* [compare **spoilsport**]
▻ ***verb*: sports, sporting, sported** (*formal or humorous*)
You **sport** something when you wear or display it, especially proudly: *He arrived sporting his new golfing gear.*

sporting /'spɔ:tɪŋ/ *adjective*
1 Sporting means of, taking part in, or for sports: *sporting achievements.* **2** A **sporting** chance is an even chance of success or failure, as you would have in a competitive sport: *He wasn't given a sporting chance.* **3** A **sporting** person is someone who is fairminded and generous, especially in competitive sports: *It was very sporting of you to allow me to take the shot again.* [*same as* **sportsmanlike**]

sports car /'spɔ:ts kɑ:(r)/ *noun*: **sports cars**
A **sports car** is a type of low fast car, often with only two seats and a roof that you can open.

sports jacket /'spɔ:ts dʒakɪt/ *noun*: **sports jackets**

A **sports jacket** is a type of jacket for men, designed for casual wear and often made of tweed.

sportsman /'spɔːtsmən/ *noun*: **sportsmen**
1 A **sportsman** is a man taking part in sport: *The panel is usually made up of famous sportsmen and other celebrities.* **2** A **sportsman** is also a person who plays fair and accepts defeat cheerfully: *You're not much of a sportsman if you go off in the huff every time you lose.*

sportsmanlike /'spɔːtsmənlaɪk/ *adjective*
Sportsmanlike is used to describe someone's behaviour in a competition or contest when they play honestly and fairly, *eg* by generously accepting defeat or celebrating their victory in a way that will not humiliate their defeated opponent. [*same as* **sporting**; *opposite* **unsportsmanlike**]

sportsmanship /'spɔːtsmənʃɪp/ *noun* (*uncount*)
Sportmanship is a sportsmanlike attitude.

sportswoman /'spɔːtswʊmən/ *noun*: **sportswomen**
A **sportwoman** is a woman who takes part in sport.

sporty /'spɔːtɪ/ *adjective*: **sportier, sportiest**
1 A **sporty** person is someone who often takes part in sport: *She's very sporty.* **2** A **sporty** car is one that looks or handles like a sports car: *a sporty-looking family saloon.*

spot /spɒt/ *noun*; *verb*
▻ ***noun*: spots**
1 A **spot** is a small, usually round, mark or stain: *The leopard's coat is covered with spots.* □ *There's a greasy spot on your skirt.* **2** A **spot** is a drop of liquid: *There were a few spots of rain.* **3** A **spot** is also a small amount, especially of liquid: *'Would you like milk in your tea?' 'Yes, just a spot.'* [*same as* **drop**] **4 Spots** are small red marks or blisters that appear on your skin when you have an illness such as measles or chickenpox; you have **spots** when you have pimples on your skin: *How long does it normally take for chickenpox spots to disappear?* □ *He has a big spot on his chin.* **5** You also refer to a particular place or area as a **spot**: *a beauty spot* □ *See if you can find a nice spot for a picnic.* □ *A plaque set into the pavement marks the spot.* □ *This is the very spot where Bonnie Prince Charlie landed in Scotland.* □ *He stood rooted to the spot.* [=not moving at all or unable to move] **6** (*informal*) **a** You can refer to a place of entertainment as a **spot**: *a popular night spot.* **b** You can also refer to a particular place or short period within a television schedule or programme or in a theatre show as a **spot**: *a regular five-minute comedy spot.* **7** (*used in the singular*; *informal*) A **spot** of something is a small amount or brief period of it: *I think I'll do a spot of gardening.* □ *Would you like a spot of lunch before you go?* □ *She's been having a spot of bother with her neighbours.* [*same as* **bit**] **8** A **spot** on someone's character or reputation is a blemish, usually as a result of immoral behaviour. **9** (*informal*) A **spot** is also a spotlight, *ie* the lamp itself rather than the light it casts.
▻ ***verb*: spots, spotting, spotted**
1 (*usually in the passive*) If something **is spotted** with something it is marked with a spot or spots of it: *His clothes were spotted with blood.* **2** You **spot** something when you catch sight of or discover it: *I spotted him coming out of the baker's.* □ *Thank you for pointing out the error; I hadn't spotted it.* **3** You **spot** things, *eg* trains, when you watch for them and record any sightings of them; you **spot** talent when you see it and recognize it: *He spends all his spare time spotting trains (*or *train spotting).* **4** If it **is spotting** with rain, rain is falling lightly in small drops.
▻ ***phrases*** **1** (*informal*) You are **in a tight spot** when you are in a difficult situation. **2** (*informal*) If one person or thing **knocks spots off** another, they are very much better than that other person or thing: *The sound from compact discs knocks spots off old-fashioned cassettes.* **3 a** If you do something **on the spot**, you do it immediately, often without warning: *If you're caught drinking on duty, you will be sacked on the spot.* **b** If you are **on the spot** when something happens, you are at the scene: *He was on the spot when the accident happened, so was able to give the injured passengers first aid.* **c** If someone puts you **on the spot**, they put you in a difficult position, especially one that forces you to take action or make a response when you would rather not: *His question put the Prime Minister on the spot.*

spot check /spɒt 'tʃɛk/ *noun*: **spot checks**
If someone does a **spot check** on something they pick things at random and without previous warning so as to inspect them: *The police are doing a spot check to see whether vehicles have an up-to-date road licence.*

spotless /'spɒtləs/ *adjective*
1 A place that is **spotless** is absolutely clean: *Her house is always spotless.* [*same as* **immaculate**] **2** If someone's character or reputation is **spotless**, they have never done anything wrong. [*same as* **flawless**] — *adverb* **spotlessly:** *The kitchens were kept spotlessly clean.* [*same as* **immaculately**]

spotlight /'spɒtlaɪt/ *noun*; *verb*
▻ ***noun*: spotlights**
1 A **spotlight** is a moveable lamp with a narrow beam that casts a circle of light on a small area, especially of a theatre stage; a **spotlight** is also the circle of light cast by such a lamp: *The background was in shadow with a single spotlight directed on the centre of the stage.* **2** (*used in the singular*) If you are in the **spotlight**, you are the centre of public attention.
▻ ***verb*: spotlights, spotlighting, spotlighted, spotlit**

> Note that the past tense and past participle can be either **spotlighted** or **spotlit**. However, for sense 2 only the form **spotlighted** is used.

1 An area, especially of a stage, **is spotlit** when it is lit up with a spotlight or spotlights. **2** If you **spotlight** something you highlight it or draw particular attention to it: *The survey report spotlights the structural problems in the building.* [*same as* **focus on, highlight**]

spot-on /spɒt'ɒn/ *adjective* (*informal*)
1 If you say that someone or something is **spot-on** you mean that they are exactly right or absolutely accurate: *His returns of serve are always spot-on.* □ *His judgement has always been spot-on.* **2** If you say that something is **spot-on** you mean it is excellent in the sense that it was exactly what was required: *The committee's recommendations were spot-on.*

spotted /'spɒtɪd/ *adjective*
Something that is **spotted** is marked with or has a pattern of spots on it: *a spotted handkerchief* □ *a spotted dog.*

spotty /'spɒtɪ/ *adjective*: **spottier, spottiest**
1 If someone has a **spotty** skin, their skin has many pimples or spots on it: *He has almost recovered from the chickpox though he is still a bit spotty.* □ *a spotty youth.* **2 Spotty** also means the same as spotted.

spouse /spaʊs/ *noun*: **spouses** (*formal or legal*)
Your **spouse** is your husband or wife: *This policy provides insurance cover for the named driver and spouse.*

spout /spaʊt/ *noun*; *verb*
▻ ***noun*: spouts**
1 A **spout** is a projecting tube or pipe through which liquid pours or is poured, as on a teapot or kettle. **2** A

spout is also a jet or stream of liquid, *eg* from a fountain or the blowhole of a whale.
▷ ***verb***: **spouts, spouting, spouted**
1 Liquid **spouts** when it flows or is caused to flow with great force in a jet or stream: *The wound in his chest was spouting blood.* □ *Water was spouting out of the severed water main.* [*same as* **spurt, squirt**] **2** If someone **spouts** something such as poetry, they recite it or speak it lengthily or boringly: *The teacher is always spouting poetry at the children.*

sprain /spreɪn/ *verb; noun*
▷ ***verb***: **sprains, spraining, sprained**
You **sprain** part of your body such as your wrist or ankle when you injure the muscles surrounding it by a sudden twisting or wrenching movement: *He slipped off the pavement spraining his wrist as he fell.* [same as **twist**]
▷ ***noun***: **sprains**
A **sprain** is such an injury, causing pain and swelling: *I don't think her ankle is broken; it's just a sprain.*

sprang /spraŋ/ *verb*
Sprang is the past tense of **spring**.

sprawl /sprɔːl/ *verb; noun*
▷ ***verb***: **sprawls, sprawling, sprawled**
1 You **sprawl** when you sit, lie or fall with your arms and legs spread out wide: *He was sprawled on the couch, snoring his head off.* □ *A hard tackle from one of the opposing players sent him sprawling.* **2** If something **sprawls** over a wide area, it spreads over it in an irregular, straggling, untidy way: *The city sprawled out below them.* [*same as* **straggle**]
▷ ***noun*** (*uncount*)
You refer to an area where a city has spread out in an untidy or irregular way as **sprawl**: *urban sprawl.*

spray /spreɪ/ *noun; verb*
▷ ***noun***: **sprays**
1 (*uncount*) **Spray** is a fine mist of small flying drops of liquid: *The waves crashed against the rocks covering them with spray.* **2** A **spray** is a liquid designed to be applied as a fine mist: *hairspray.* **3** A **spray** is a device for sending out a liquid in a fine mist: *a perfume spray.* [*same as* **aerosol**] **4** A **spray** is a small branch or branching stem cut off a plant or tree with a number of flowers or leaves on it, used as decoration: *a spray of mimosa.*
▷ ***verb***: **sprays, spraying, sprayed**
1 You **spray** something when you cover it with a liquid in the form of a fine mist; a liquid **sprays** when it is comes out of, *eg* an aerosol, in a fine spray: *I'll have to spray the roses (with insecticide) to get rid of the greenfly.* **2** If something **is sprayed** with things it is hit or bombarded with a heavy continuous stream of those things: *The president's car had been sprayed with bullets.*

spread /spred/ *verb; noun*
▷ ***verb***: **spreads, spreading, spread**
1 You **spread** something when you apply it in a smooth coating over a surface; something **spreads** well or easily when it can be spread on a surface: *She spread butter on her toast.* □ *bread spread with jam.* □ *margarine that spreads easily.* **2 a** You **spread** something out, when you open or unfold it, *eg* so that you can see all of it: *He spread the map out on a rock.* **b** A bird **spreads** its wings when it unfolds them so that they are fully extended. **3** Something such as a disease **spreads** when it affects a wider area or a larger number of people: *The rumour spread until the whole town was talking about it.* **4** If something **is spread** out or **spreads** over a wide area, it covers a wide area: *The whole valley was spread out in front of them.* □ *The forest spreads right across Russia from West to East.*
▷ ***noun***: **spreads**
1 (*uncount*) The act of spreading something or the degree to which it spreads is its **spread**: *measures to halt the spread of AIDS.* **2** A **spread** is a food in paste form, for spreading on bread: *a jar of chocolate spread* □ *salmon spread.* **3** A **spread** in a newspaper or magazine is a pair of pages facing each other. **4** (*informal*) A **spread** is a lavish meal: *What a spread!*

spree /spriː/ *noun*: **sprees**
If you go on a **spree**, you spend an extravagant amount of money or drink a lot of alcohol in a relatively short time: *a shopping spree* □ *The police became suspicious when he went on a spending spree.*

sprig /sprɪg/ *noun*: **sprigs**
A **sprig** is a small shoot or twig with leaves on it that someone has picked from a plant: *a sprig of heather.*

sprightly /ˈspraɪtlɪ/ *adjective*
1 If someone, especially someone elderly, is described as **sprightly**, they are lively and full of energy: *She's 92, but still remarkably sprightly.* **2** A **sprightly** dance is one that is performed at a brisk pace.

spring /sprɪŋ/ *noun; verb*
▷ ***noun***: **springs**
1 (*uncount or count*) **Spring** is the season of the year coming between winter and summer. In cool northern regions it lasts from February or March to April or May and is the time when most plants begin to grow and wild birds and animals breed: *It was very wet last spring* □ *They got married on a beautiful spring morning in April.* □ *spring sunshine* □ *spring fashions* □ *a series of cold, damp springs* □ *in the spring of 1994.* **2** A **spring** is a coil of metal wire that can be pressed down or stretched and returns to its original shape when released: *Don't bounce on the bed! You'll break the springs.* **3** A **spring** is a sudden forward or upward leap: *The springbok is so named because it moves forwards in a series of bouncing steps or springs.* **4** (*uncount*) Something that has **spring** has the capacity to return to its original shape after it has been pressed down or stretched: *The mattress has lost its spring.* **5** (*used in the singular*) Someone who has a **spring** in their step, walks with a lively bouncing action. **6** A **spring** is also a place in the ground from which water flows naturally: *cool clear water from a mountain spring.*
▷ ***verb***: **springs, springing, sprang, sprung**
1 An animal **springs** when it leaps forwards or upwards suddenly and quickly, especially from a crouching or standing position; a person **springs**, or **springs** up when they jump up suddenly and quickly from a sitting or lying position: *The lioness was crouching in the long grass ready to spring.* □ *He sprang smartly to his feet and offered her his chair.* □ *The alarm clock went off and he sprang out of bed.* **2** Something **springs** when it moves very quickly and suddenly in a particular direction: *He touched a hidden lever and the secret drawer sprang open.* **3** A person **springs** from somewhere when they appear suddenly and unexpectedly from that place or direction: *Where did you spring from?* **4** Something **springs** into life when it begins to move or operate all of a sudden: *He gave the starting handle a couple of sharp turns and the engine sprang into life.* **5** Something that **springs** from another thing develops or originates from that other thing: *The protest movement sprang from widespread public disquiet about the rapid development of nuclear arms.* [*same as* **originate**] **6** A trap is **sprung**, or a person or animal **springs** it, when they make it close suddenly and violently, especially so that nothing is caught in it. **7** (*informal*) Prisoners **are sprung** from jail when they are helped to escape by friends or accomplices.

▻ ***phrase*** A boat or watertight container **springs a leak** when it develops a gap or hole through which water can flow in or out: *The car radiator has sprung a leak.*

> ***phrasal verbs***
> **spring back** Something **springs back** when it returns with a sudden rapid movement to its original shape or position after being pressed, bent or stretched in the opposite direction: *The branch sprang back hitting him on the face.*
> **spring on** When you **spring** something **on** someone you suddenly do or say something to them that they were not expecting and which therefore surprises them, often unpleasantly: *He's called an emergency meeting this afternoon; I hope he's not going to spring any nasty surprises on us.*
> **spring up** Things **spring up** when they come into existence suddenly: *New factories were springing up all over the country.*

springboard /ˈsprɪŋbɔːd/ *noun*: **springboards**
1 A **springboard** is a board that springs up after being jumped on, used by divers and gymnasts as a launching device. **2** A **springboard** to something is anything that helps you to progress to a higher or more successful position: *He used the band as a springboard to launch him in the music industry.*

spring-clean /sprɪŋˈkliːn/ *verb*: **spring-cleans, spring-cleaning, spring-cleaned**
You **spring-clean** when you thoroughly clean your house, often, but not necessarily, in the spring.

spring cleaning /sprɪŋˈkliːnɪŋ/ *noun* (*uncount*)
Spring cleaning is the thorough cleaning of a house, traditionally carried out in spring.

spring onion /sprɪŋ ʌŋjən/ *noun*: **spring onions**
A **spring onion** is an onion picked when it is young, *ie* while just a tiny white bulb with long thin green shoots, and usually eaten raw in salads.

springtime /ˈsprɪŋtaɪm/ *noun* (*uncount*)
Springtime is the season of spring: *The bulbs flower in springtime.*

springy /ˈsprɪŋɪ/ *adjective*: **springier, springiest**
Something that is **springy** returns to its original shape or position easily after being pushed down, stretched or pulled: *a springy mattress* [*same as* **elastic**]

sprinkle /ˈsprɪŋkəl/ *verb*: **sprinkles, sprinkling, sprinkled**
Something **is sprinkled** on something when it is scattered on it in small drips or particles; something **is sprinkled** with small drops or particles when there is a scattering of them on its surface: *She sprinkled water on the dry fabric to make it easier to iron.* □ *a cake sprinkled with pieces of grated chocolate.*

sprinkler /ˈsprɪŋklə(r)/ *noun*: **sprinklers**
A **sprinkler** is a device that sprinkles, especially one that is used for sprinkling water over a lawn or on a fire to put it out: *The supermarket burned down because it had no sprinkler system.*

sprinkling /ˈsprɪŋklɪŋ/ *noun* (*used in the singular*)
A **sprinkling** of something is a small amount of it thinly scattered over a relatively wide area: *We had a sprinkling of snow in the night.*

sprint /sprɪnt/ *noun*; *verb*
▻ ***noun***: **sprints**
1 A **sprint** is a race at high speed over a short distance. **2** A **sprint** is also a sudden burst of speed *eg* at the end of a long race.
▻ ***verb***: **sprints, sprinting, sprinted**
You **sprint** when you run at full speed: *He sprinted along the platform trying to catch the train as it began to pull out of the station.* [*same as* **race**]

sprinter /ˈsprɪntə(r)/ *noun*: **sprinters**
A **sprinter** is someone who is good at running fast over short distances.

sprite /spraɪt/ *noun*: **sprites**
A **sprite** is a playful fairy.

sprout /spraʊt/ *verb*; *noun*
▻ ***verb***: **sprouts, sprouting, sprouted**
1 A seed **sprouts** when it develops roots and shoots; a plant **sprouts** when it develops new shoots and leaves. **2** When hairs, feathers or horns **sprout** they begin to grow: *When the deer were a few months old they began to sprout horns.* **3** If things **sprout** or **sprout** up somewhere they appear suddenly: *New housing estates were sprouting up all around the city.* [*same as* **shoot up**]
▻ ***noun***: **sprouts**
1 A **sprout** is a new shoot or leaf on a plant. **2 Sprouts** or **brussels sprouts** are green vegetables that look like very small cabbages: *'Yuk! I hate sprouts even more than cabbage!' said Charlotte.*

spruce /spruːs/ *noun*; *adjective*; *verb*
▻ ***noun***: **spruce**
1 A **spruce** or a **spruce tree** is a type of evergreen tree with needles. [=long, very thin leaves]. **2** (*uncount*) **Spruce** is the soft wood of this tree.
▻ ***adjective***
If someone looks **spruce**, they are smartly dressed and well-groomed. [*same as* **smart, neat**]
▻ ***verb***: **spruces, sprucing, spruced**

> ***phrasal verb***
> You **spruce** someone or something **up** when you improve their appearance by making them smarter: *You'll have to spruce yourself up a bit for the interview.* [*same as* **smarten up, tidy up**]

sprung /sprʌŋ/ *verb*
Sprung is the past participle of **spring**. It is also used as a past tense, especially in American English.

spry /spraɪ/ *adjective*: **spryer, spryest**
Someone who is **spry** is lively and active: *a spry old woman.* [*same as* **sprightly**]

spud /spʌd/ *noun*: **spuds** (*informal*)
Some people refer to potatoes as **spuds**.

spun /spʌn/ *verb*
Spun is the past tense and past participle of **spin**.

spur /spɜː(r)/ *noun*; *verb*
▻ ***noun***: **spurs**
1 A **spur** is one of a pair of U-shaped devices with a spike or spiked wheel worn on the heel of a horse-rider's boot, and driven into the horse's sides to make it go faster. **2** A **spur** is also anything that urges or encourages greater effort or progress: *fame is the spur.* **3** A **spur** is a spike or pointed part, *eg* on a cock's leg, or a metal imitation of this fitted to the legs of fighting cocks. **4** A **spur** is also a ridge sticking out from a range of hills or mountains.
▻ ***verb***: **spurs, spurring, spurred**
You **are spurred** into action by something, or **are spurred** on by someone or something, when you are urged or encouraged to act or are urged on to greater effort by that person or thing.
▻ ***phrase*** If you do something **on the spur of the moment**, you suddenly decide to do it on an impulse: *I just decided to visit you on the spur of the moment.*

spurious /ˈspjʊərɪəs/ *adjective* (*formal*)
1 Something is **spurious** when it is not what it pretends to be or is not genuine: *Maintaining profits in line with inflation gives a spurious impression of growth.* **2** **Spurious** logic or a **spurious** argument is based on false or mistaken reasoning.

spurn /spɜːn/ *verb*: **spurns, spurning, spurned** (*formal or literary*)
You **spurn** someone's love or their advances when you reject them scornfully: *He had been spurned by every marriageable girl in the village.* [*same as* **snub, turn down**]

spurt /spɜːt/ *verb*; *noun*
▻ ***verb***: **spurts, spurting, spurted**
If liquid **spurts** or **spurts** from somewhere, it flows or is forced out of that place in a sudden jet: *Oil spurted from the uncapped wells.* □ *Blood was spurting from the wound in his chest.* [*same as* **spout, squirt**]
▻ ***noun***: **spurts**
1 A **spurt** is a jet of liquid suddenly flowing or forced out. [*same as* **spout**] **2** A **spurt** is a sudden increase in speed or activity that last for a short time: *He tends to work in spurts.* □ *As she approached the finishing line, she put on a sudden spurt (of speed).* [*same as* **burst**]

sputter /ˈspʌtə(r)/ *verb*: **sputters, sputtering, sputtered**
If something **sputters**, it makes spitting or popping noises: *The engine sputtered and died.* [*same as* **splutter**]

spy /spaɪ/ *noun*; *verb*
▻ ***noun***: **spies**
1 A **spy** is a person employed by a government or business organization to secretly gather information about political enemies or competitors. **2** A **spy** is also someone who watches others in secret or from a hiding place: *I've had my spies out to see what he does when he's not at home.*
▻ ***verb***: **spies, spying, spied**
1 Someone **spies** for their country or the organization that employs them when they secretly gather information about their enemies or competitors. **2** If someone **spies** on someone they watch them secretly or from a hiding place: *The old woman from across the road has been spying on us from behind her net curtains.* **3** You **spy** something when you catch sight of it: *I spied him as he came round the corner.*

squabble /ˈskwɒbəl/ *verb*; *noun*
▻ ***verb***: **squabbles, squabbling, squabbled**
People **squabble** when they quarrel noisily, especially about something trivial: *The boys were squabbling over who should be first to play the new computer game.*
▻ ***noun***: **squabbles:** *The children had to be supervised to prevent squabbles over toys.*

squad /skwɒd/ *noun*: **squads**
1 A **squad** is a small group of soldiers, often twelve, that drill and work together; a **squad** is also a group of policemen, especially detectives, who work together: *Squad, attention!* □ *a regional crime squad.* **2** A **squad** is any group of people working together: *a bricklaying squad* □ *a squad of brickies.* **3** A **squad** is a set of players from which a sporting team is selected: *a member of the Scottish rugby squad.*

squad car /ˈskwɒd kɑː(r)/ *noun*: **squad cars**
Police cars are sometimes referred to as **squad cars**.

squadron /ˈskwɒdrən/ *noun*: **squadrons**
A **squadron** is **1** a group of between 10 and 18 military aircraft, the main unit of an air force: *a fighter squadron.* **2** a group of warships sent together on a particular mission: *a squadron of frigates and destroyers.* **3** a division of an armoured regiment of soldiers: *Rommel's Panzer squadrons.*

squalid /ˈskwɒlɪd/ *adjective*
1 A **squalid** place is very dirty and neglected: *He lives all alone in a squalid little flat in New York.* **2** You can also describe something concerned with or having low moral standards as **squalid**: *Why should I be concerned about what is written about me in that squalid little newspaper?*
[*same as* **sordid**]

squall /skwɔːl/ *noun*; *verb*
▻ ***noun***: **squalls**
A **squall** is a sudden violent wind or storm that lasts only for a short time and often brings rain or snow: *Atlantic squalls.*
▻ ***verb***: **squalls, squalling, squalled**
If someone **squalls**, they cry or cry out noisily: *a room filled with squalling babies.*

squally /ˈskwɔːlɪ/ *adjective*
When the weather is **squally** there are frequent squalls. [*same as* **stormy, blustery**]

squalor /ˈskwɒlə(r)/ *noun* (*uncount*)
Squalor is the state of being squalid: *They live in squalor in a run-down shack.*

squander /ˈskwɒndə(r)/ *verb*: **squanders, squandering, squandered**
If you **squander** money or resources, you use it up wastefully: *She squandered all the money her parents left her.* □ *squandering the earth's precious resources.* [*opposite* **save**]

square /skwɛə(r)/ *noun*; *adjective*; *verb*; *adverb*
▻ ***noun***: **squares**
1 A **square** is a two-dimensional figure with four sides of equal length and four right angles. [see picture at **shape**] **2** A **square** is any thing shaped like this: *Can I have a square of your chocolate?* **3** A **square** is also an open space in a town, which may or may not be square in shape, often including the surrounding buildings: *He lives in one of the elegant Georgian squares in the West End.* □ *Charlotte Square* □ *Trafalgar Square.* **4** A **square** is an L- or T-shaped instrument with which angles can be measured or straight lines drawn: *a T-square.* **5** The **square** of a number is the number produced when the number is multiplied by itself, hence the square of 8 is 16. **6** (*informal, rather old*) A **square** is someone whose values and tastes you regard as old-fashioned: *What an old square you are, Dad!*
▻ ***adjective***
1 Something that is **square** is square-shaped: *a square sheet of card* □ *The room isn't exactly square so the carpet won't fit.* **2** If something measures so much **square**, it measures that amount along each of its sides; a **square** measurement is one that is obtained by multiplying the length of something by its breadth: *The carpet is three metres square.* □ *an area of three square miles.* **3** If someone has a **square** jaw, their jaw has a strong squarish shape and is less rounded than normal; if someone has **square** shoulders, their shoulders are not rounded, especially because they hold themselves very straight; if someone has a **square** frame, their body is nearly as broad as it is long. **4** A **square** deal is fair and honest. **5** If two people are **square** with each other, they are equal, with neither person owing anything to the other: *Here's the ten pounds I owe you; that makes us square (*or *all square), doesn't it?* [*same as* **quits**] **6** **Square** also means complete or outright: *Number Ten issued a square denial of the allegation.* **7** (*informal, rather old*) People who are **square** are old-fashioned in their tastes or values: *My parents are so square they will never allow me to go to the concert.*
▻ ***verb***: **squares, squaring, squared**

1 If you **square** something, you make it square in shape, with straight lines and right angles: *Square off any uneven ends by cutting straight across the wood.* **2** You **square** a number when you multiply it by itself. **3** If you **square** your shoulders, you push them back and stand very straight, especially as an indication that you are determined or defiant. **4** You **square** a debt, or you **square** up with someone that you owe money to, when you pay the debt off or pay them the money that you owe them. **5** If a point gained in a match **squares** the match, it makes the scores of each team equal: *Robson squared the match with a brilliant header into the back of the goal.* **6** If one thing **squares** with another, they match or correspond; if you **square** one thing with another, you make the first thing match or fit with the second: *His vehement protest that he is completely innocent doesn't square with the facts.* **7** If you **square** something with someone, you get their approval or consent: *You'd better not go ahead with this until you've squared it with the boss.* □ *You eat meat, but how can you square with your conscience the fact that animals have to die as a consequence?* **8** Something such as paper **is squared** when it is marked with a pattern of squares.

▻ ***adverb***

Square means **1** directly: *The blow landed square on his jaw and knocked him out cold.* **2** fairly and honestly: *They beat us fair and square.* [*same as* **squarely**]

▻ ***phrases*** (*informal*) **1** If you have to go **back to square one**, you have to go back to the place or position that you started from originally, with no progress being made. **2** If you try to **square the circle**, you try to do the impossible.

> ***phrasal verb***
> If you **square up to** an opponent or a difficult situation, you face them with determination and prepare to tackle them: *boxers squaring up for the fight.*

squarely /ˈskwɛəlɪ/ *adverb*

Squarely means **1** directly: *Look me squarely in the eye and I'll be able to tell whether you have been lying or not.* **2** in a fair and honest way: *He won the championship fairly and squarely.*

square meal /skwɛə(r) ˈmiːl/ *noun*: **square meals**

A **square meal** is a good nourishing or satisfying meal: *At least when he is at home he can be sure of a comfortable bed and three square meals a day.*

square root /skwɛə(r) ˈruːt/ *noun*: **square roots**

The **square root** of a number is the number which, when multiplied by itself, gives the number in question: *The square root of nine is three.*

squash /skwɒʃ/ *verb*; *noun*

▻ ***verb***: **squashes, squashing, squashed**

1 Something **is squashed** when it is crushed or flattened by pressing or squeezing: *He squashed the beetle under his heel.* □ *What happened to your hat? It's a bit squashed.* □ *My sandwiches got squashed at the bottom of my rucksack.* **2** You **squash** into a confined space when you force your body into it: *Hundreds of commuters were squashed into the trains.* □ *He squashed himself into the only available space.* □ *The little girl was squashed between two enormously fat women.* [*same as* **squeeze**, **crush**] **3** An uprising or rebellion **is squashed** when it is suppressed or put down, usually using force or violence. [*same as* **suppress**] **4** You **squash** someone when you force them into silence with a cutting reply.

▻ ***noun***: **squashes**

1 (*uncount or count*) **Squash** or a **squash** is a drink made from fruit syrup diluted with water: *A bottle of orange squash.* □ *I don't really want wine; I'll just have a squash.* **2** (*usually used in the singular*) If there is a **squash** in a room or other place, it is crowded with people. **3** (*uncount*) **Squash** is a game for two players on a walled indoor court, played with small-headed long-handled rackets and a small rubber ball. **4** (*count or uncount*; *AmE*) A **squash** is any of various marrow-like vegetables of the cucumber family. [see picture at **vegetable**]

squashy /ˈskwɒʃɪ/ *adjective*: **squashier**, **squashiest** (*informal*)

Something **squashy** is soft and easily squashed: *a squashy foam-rubber ball.* [*opposite* **firm**]

squat /skwɒt/ *verb*; *noun*; *adjective*

▻ ***verb***: **squats, squatting, squatted**

1 You **squat** when you crouch down in a low position with your knees fully bent, taking your weight on the soles of your feet or sitting on your heels: *grubby children squatting in the dust.* **2** People **squat** when they occupy land or a building without the legal right to do so.

▻ ***noun***: **squats**

1 A **squat** is a squatting position. **2** A **squat** is a building that has been unlawfully occupied by squatters.

▻ ***adjective***

Squat means short and broad or fat: *a figurine of a squat, pot-bellied man.*

squatter /ˈskwɒtə(r)/ *noun*: **squatters**

A **squatter** is a person who illegally occupies land or an empty building: *The owner of the house had to get a court order to evict the squatters.*

squawk /skwɔːk/ *verb*; *noun*

▻ ***verb***: **squawks, squawking, squawked**

1 A bird or a human baby **squawks** when they make a loud harsh cry or a series of these cries: *The cockatoo squawked as he lifted it from its perch.* □ *Can't you do something to stop that baby squawking?* **2** People **squawk** when they complain loudly.

▻ ***noun***: **squawks:** *the squawks of protest from local inhabitants.* □ *the squawk of a parrot.*

squeak /skwiːk/ *noun*; *verb*

▻ ***noun***: **squeaks**

A **squeak** is a short high-pitched cry or sound, like the sound that a mouse makes or the sound made by a loose or rusty hinge: *She heard the squeak of floorboards as he walked about in the room above.*

▻ ***verb***: **squeaks, squeaking, squeaked**

Someone or something **squeaks** when they make a short high-pitched sound: *The loose floorboard squeaked when he stood on it.*

▻ ***phrase*** If you have **a narrow squeak**, you just avoid disaster or serious injury by the narrowest of margins: *They had a bit of a narrow squeak when they had to make an emergency landing in a field.* [*same as* **narrow escape**]

> ***phrasal verb***
> If you manage to **squeak through**, you succeed, pass or win by the very narrowest of margins: *He just squeaked through to the next round by gaining one point more than his nearest rival.*

squeaky /ˈskwiːkɪ/ *adjective*: **squeakier**, **squeakiest**

A **squeaky** voice is a high-pitched voice; something that is **squeaky** makes a squeaking sound: *a squeaky floorboard.*

squeal /skwiːl/ *noun*; *verb*

▷ ***noun*: squeals**
A **squeal** is a long high-pitched cry: *the children's squeals of delight as the clown poured water over his own head* □ *The pig gave a squeal.* □ *She gave a squeal of pain when he tried to move her.*
▷ ***verb*: squeals, squealing, squealed**
1 A person or animal **squeals** when they give a loud high-pitched cry; someone **squeals** words when they say them with a squeal, especially when they are protesting about something: *'Stop tickling me!' she squealed.* **2** (*informal*) You can say that someone **has squealed** when they have given information to someone that they should have kept secret, especially when the information concerns their friends or associates who will get into trouble as a result.

squeamish /ˈskwiːmɪʃ/ *adjective*
If someone is **squeamish** they are easily disgusted, shocked or offended: *He's too squeamish to be a surgeon.*

squeeze /skwiːz/ *verb*; *noun*
▷ ***verb*: squeezes, squeezing, squeezed**
1 You **squeeze** something when you grasp it or embrace it tightly: *He squeezed my hand to show his sympathy.* □ *He took her in his arms and squeezed her affectionately.* **2** If something **is squeezed** it is pressed forcefully, especially from opposite sides: *You shouldn't squeeze your spots.* **3** You **squeeze** something or squeeze it out when you force it out by squeezing: *Don't hold the baby so tightly, you're squeezing the breath out of him.* □ *freshly-squeezed orange juice* □ *He squeezed some toothpaste on to the brush.* **4** You **squeeze** into or through a narrow space when you force your body into or through it; if you **squeeze** in somewhere you make enough space to fit yourself in; if someone **squeezes** you in, they find space or time for you: *Is there enough space for me to squeeze in beside you?* □ *She squeezed herself into the tight skirt.* □ *The cat squeezed through a narrow gap in the fence.* □ *Since it's an emergency, the dentist might be able to squeeze you in between his other appointments.* **5** You **squeeze** something out of someone when you force them or persuade them to give you or tell you it, often using threats: *The head teacher managed to squeeze a confession out of the boys responsible.* **6** If a person or business **is squeezed** out, they are forced out of the position they previously held by the actions of others: *They are being squeezed out of the market by cheap imports.* **7** If something, such as a business or an organization's budget **is being squeezed**, it is suffering from financial difficulties or it has less money available, usually because of increased costs on one side and reduction of income on the other: *Many small businesses were being squeezed by the high cost of borrowing and reductions in sales during the recession.*
▷ ***noun*: squeezes**
1 A **squeeze** is an act of squeezing: *She gave his hand an affectionate squeeze.* **2** A **squeeze** is also a crowded or crushed state: *It was a tight squeeze getting five people into his small car.* **3** A **squeeze** of something, especially the juice of a citrus fruit, is an amount got by squeezing: *a squeeze of lime juice.* **4** (*usually in the singular*) A **squeeze** is a restriction, especially on spending or borrowing money: *a credit squeeze.* [=when the cost of borrowing is so high that people or businesses can no longer afford it]

squelch /skwɛltʃ/ *noun*; *verb*
▷ ***noun*: squelches**
A **squelch** is a loud gurgling or sucking sound made when something is pressed into or drawn out of a thick sticky substance, *eg* wet mud, or when liquid is suddenly forced out from under something: *She could hear the squelch of his boots as he came across the muddy yard.*
▷ ***verb*: squelches, squelching, squelched**
To **squelch** is to make this sound: *The water inside his boots squelched as he walked.*

squid /skwɪd/ *noun*: **squid** or **squids**
A **squid** is a sea creature with a long rounded soft body and ten trailing arms at one end. [compare **octopus**]

squiggle /ˈskwɪgəl/ *noun*: **squiggles** (*informal*)
A **squiggle** is a short irregular wavy or twisting line, especially one that has been written: *His signature was a series of illegible squiggles.*

squint /skwɪnt/ *noun*; *verb*; *adjective*
▷ ***noun*: squints**
1 If someone has a **squint**, they have an eye disorder in which one of their eyes looks slightly to the side as the other looks forward. **2** (*informal*) If you have or take a **squint** at something you have or take a quick look at it: *Can I take a quick squint at your newspaper?* [*same as* **peek**]
▷ ***verb*: squints, squinting, squinted**
1 If someone **squints** they are affected by a squint: *He squints horribly.* **2** If you **squint** or **squint** at something, you look or look at it through half-closed eyes: *The sudden bright light made him squint.* □ *She shaded her eyes and squinted at the sky.*
▷ ***adjective***
If something is **squint** it is not properly straight or centred: *The parting in your hair is squint.* □ *The side seam of this dress is slightly squint.* [*same as* **askew, crooked**; *opposite* **straight**]

squire /skwɜːm/ *noun*: **squires**
1 (*old*) A **squire** is an owner of a large area of rural land, especially the most important landowner in a district. **2** (*informal*) **Squire** is also a form of address used by one man to another, especially when the name of the man being addressed is not known and he is considered, by the man speaking, to be of a higher status: *What can I get you, squire?*

squirm /skwɜːm/ *verb*: **squirms, squirming, squirmed**
1 Something **squirms** when it wriggles: *a mass of maggots squirming in the bottom of the tin.* **2** You **squirm** when you feel or show embarrassment or discomfort, often with slight twisting movements of your body: *She was squirming with embarrassment.*
[*same as* **writhe**]

squirrel /ˈskwɪrəl/ *noun*: **squirrels**
A **squirrel** is a small animal with a long bushy tail and grey or reddish-brown fur. Squirrels live in trees and eat nuts.

squirt /skwɜːt/ *verb*: **squirts, squirting, squirted**
You **squirt** a liquid or it **squirts**, when you make it shoot out of something in a narrow jet: *He squirted me with his water pistol.* □ *The octopus squirts black ink when it is alarmed.* □ *Water was squirting out of the hose.* [*same as* **spurt**]

stab /stab/ *verb*; *noun*
▷ ***verb*: stabs, stabbing, stabbed**
1 You **stab** someone or something when you wound or pierce them with a pointed instrument or weapon: *He was set upon and stabbed by an unknown assailant.* □ *He was stabbed through the heart.* **2** If you **stab** at something, you make quick thrusting movements at it with something sharp: *He shouted and raged, stabbing at her with his finger.* **3** If pain **stabs**, it produces a sharp piercing sensation in the body: *He had a stabbing pain in his side.*
▷ ***noun*: stabs**
1 A **stab** is an act of stabbing or a stabbing sensation:

a stab wound ▫ *a stab of pain.* **2** (*informal*) If you have a **stab** at something, you try to do it: *Even if you don't know the answer, have a stab at it.* [*same as* **crack, go**]

▻ ***phrase*** Someone who is supposed to be your friend or ally **stabs you in the back** when they betray you.

stability /stəˈbɪlɪtɪ/ *noun* (*uncount*)
Stability is the state or quality of being stable: *What we need most is a period of economic stability.* [*opposite* **instability**]

stabilize or **stabilise** /ˈsteɪbɪlaɪz/ *verb*: **stabilizes, stabilizing, stabilized**
You **stabilize** something or something **stabilizes** when you make it or it becomes stable or more stable: *Share prices have stabilized after a period of sharp increases and dramatic falls.* ▫ *His condition has stabilized and the doctors now believe that he is out of danger.* [*same as* **level out**] — *noun* (*uncount*) **stabilization** /steɪbɪlaɪˈzeɪʃən/ : *the Chamcellor's plans to ensure economic stabilization.*

stable /ˈsteɪbəl/ *adjective*; *noun*
▻ ***adjective***
Something is **stable** **1** when it is firmly balanced or fixed and is not likely to wobble or fall: *That chimney doesn't look very stable.* ▫ *a stable dollar.* [=that stays at around the same value against other currencies without large fluctuations] **2** when it is firmly established, and not likely to be abolished, overthrown or destroyed: *a stable government.* **3** regular or constant: *a stable relationship* ▫ *The patient's condition is stable.* [*same as* **steady**; *opposite* **unstable**]
▻ ***noun***: **stables**
A **stable** is **1** a building in which horses are kept. **2** a place where horses are bred or trained: *a racing stable.*

stack /stak/ *noun*; *verb*
▻ ***noun***: **stacks**
1 A **stack** is a large neat pile, or a pile of things laid one on top of the other: *a haystack* ▫ *a stack of books.* **2** (*often used in the plural*; *informal*) If you talk about there being **stacks** of a particular thing, you mean that there is a large amount of it: *Do come for dinner; we've got stacks of food.* [*same as* **loads**] **3** A **stack** is a large chimney, *eg* on a factory: *a smokestack.*
▻ ***verb***: **stacks, stacking, stacked**
1 You **stack** things when you form them into a neat pile or piles, by laying them one on top of the other. **2** If a place **is stacked** with things it has large numbers of things arranged in piles: *The shed was stacked with logs for the winter.* **3** If circumstances **are stacked** against you, you are at a disadvantage and therefore have very little chance of succeeding.

stadium /ˈsteɪdɪəm/ *noun*: **stadiums** or **stadia**
A **stadium** is a large sports ground with rows of seats for spectators all round it.

staff /stɑːf/ *noun*; *verb*
▻ ***noun***
1 (*with singular or plural verb*) The total number of people who work in an establishment or organization are known as that establishment's or organization's **staff**: *a staff of 50.* ▫ *Mr Noble will be joining the teaching staff as head of the science department after the summer holidays.* **2** (*plural*) **Staff** are the members of such a group: *a meeting of senior staff* ▫ *requests from staff for better canteen arrangements.* **3** In the armed forces, a senior commander's **staff** are the officers that assist him. **4** (**staffs** or **staves**) A **staff** is any stick or rod carried in the hand: *He carried the gold staff of office.* **5** (**staves**) In music, a **staff** is the set of lines and spaces on which music is written.
▻ ***verb***: **staffs, staffing, staffed**
An organization or establishment **is staffed** when it is provided with staff: *There may be some delay in processing your application; we're short-staffed at the moment.* ▫ *a community centre staffed by volunteers.*

stag /stag/ *noun*: **stags**
A **stag** is an adult male deer, especially a red deer.

stage /steɪdʒ/ *noun*; *verb*
▻ ***noun***: **stages**
1 A **stage** is a raised platform on which a performance takes place in a theatre; the **stage** is the theatre as a profession or art form: *The curtains opened to reveal an empty stage.* ▫ *She went on the stage when she was only five years old.* ▫ *a star of stage and screen.* **2** A **stage** is **a** a particular period or distinct part in a process or set of events or the state reached at a particular point in a process: *We will have to finish this part before we can move on to the next stage.* ▫ *What stage are you at now?* ▫ *The submarine is still at the design stage.* ▫ *at an early stage in human evolution.* **b** a part of a journey or route: *The mountain stage of the Tour de France will be held in the French Alps.* ▫ *The first stage of the round-the-world yacht race is from Southampton to Cape Town.* [*same as* **leg**] **3** (*informal*) A **stage** is also a stagecoach.
▻ ***verb***: **stages, staging, staged**
A play or other performance **is staged** when it is organized and presented on the stage; an event **is staged** when it is held or organized.

stagecoach /ˈsteɪdʒkoʊtʃ/ *noun*: **stagecoachs**
A **stagecoach** was a large horse-drawn coach formerly carrying passengers and mail on a regular fixed route.

stage fright /ˈsteɪdʒ fraɪt/ *noun* (*uncount*)
If an actor or other performer has **stage fright**, they have strong feelings of fear or nervousness about appearing in front of an audience.

stage-manage /ˈsteɪdʒ manɪdʒ/ *verb*: **stage-manages, stage-managing, stage-managed**
1 Someone who **stage-manages** a theatre production acts as a stage manager for it. **2** If you **stage-manage** an event, you arrange beforehand what will happen so as to produce a particular effect: *The Prime Minister's stroll through the crowd had been stage-managed so that he would appear to be in touch with the ordinary people.*

stage manager /steɪdʒ ˈmanɪdʒə(r)/ *noun*: **stage managers**
A **stage manager** is a person who works in a theatre supervising the arrangement of scenery and props for a play.

stagger /ˈstagə(r)/ *verb*: **staggers, staggering, staggered**
1 You **stagger** when you walk or move unsteadily, *eg* because you are ill, exhausted or drunk: *He just managed to stagger to his feet.* ▫ *He staggered and fell against the wall.* **2** If something **staggers** you, it causes you to feel extreme shock or surprise: *I was staggered by the price of the tickets for the new production of 'Tristan and Isolde'* **3** You **stagger** two or more things when you arrange them so that they take place or begin and end at different times: *Staff holidays are staggered so that the office can stay open throughout the year.*

staggered /ˈstagəd/ *adjective*
A **staggered** start to a race is one in which competitors begin at different times, *eg* because it is not possible to have more than one competitor on the course at any one time or there are too many entrants for a race to allow them all to begin together.

staggering /ˈstagərɪŋ/ *adjective*

If you describe something as **staggering**, you mean it is almost unbelieveable or it causes you great surprise or shock: *He earns a staggering £1.5 million a year.* [*same as* **astounding, stunning**]

stagnant /'stagnənt/ *adjective*
1 Stagnant water does not flow and is often dirty and foul-smelling because of this: *a stagnant pool.* **2** You can also describe business or an economy as **stagnant** when it is not active or growing: *The government's own figures show that manufacturing output has remained stagnant throughout the period.*

stagnate /stag'neɪt/ *verb*: **stagnates, stagnating, stagnated**
Something **stagnates** when it is or becomes stagnant: *a stagnating economy* □ *I have no intention of stagnating in the same boring job for forty years.*

stag party /'stag pɑːtɪ/ or **stag night** /'stag naɪt/ *noun*: **stag parties** or **stag nights**
A **stag party** or **stag night** is a party for men only, especially one in honour of a man about to be married.

staid /steɪd/ *adjective*
Someone or something is **staid** when they are serious and dull in nature or character: *She's so staid she will never try anything new and exciting.* [*opposite* **frivolous**]

stain /steɪn/ *verb*; *noun*
▷ ***verb***: **stains, staining, stained**
1 If something **stains** easily it is easily marked or discoloured; if a substance **stains** something else it marks or discolours it, often in a way that is difficult to remove: *Be careful not to spill your wine; this carpet stains easily.* □ *Coffee and tea can stain your teeth.* □ *The murderer's clothes will have been stained with blood.* □ *The cutlery was dirty and the tablecloth stained.* [=covered with stains] **2** You **stain** something such as wood when you change or darken its colour by applying a liquid chemical: *Are you going to stain the floorboards after you sand them?*
▷ ***noun***: **stains**
1 A **stain** is a mark or discoloration, often one that is difficult to remove: *bloodstains* □ *There's a stain on your tie.* **2** (*uncount or count*) **Stain** or a **stain** is a liquid chemical applied especially to wood to change or darken its colour; a **stain** is also something that is added to something so that it is easier to see under a microscope: *wood stain* □ *The bacteria react with the stain and turn red.* **3** When there is a **stain** on someone's character or reputation they have done something shameful or dishonourable.

stained glass /steɪnd 'glɑːs/ *noun* (*uncount, often adjectival*)
Stained glass is glass coloured by a special process. Pieces of stained glass are fixed together to make decorative windows, especially in churches: *stained glass windows.*

stainless steel /steɪnləs 'stiːl/ *noun* (*uncount, often adjectival*)
Stainless steel is a metal alloy of steel and chromium that does not rust: *a sink made of stainless steel* □ *stainless steel knives and forks.*

stair /stɛə(r)/ *noun*: **stairs**
1 A **stair** is any of a set of indoor steps connecting the floors of a building. **2** (*used in the plural*) **Stairs** are a set of these: *Halfway down the stairs is a stair where I sit.*

staircase /'stɛəkeɪs/ *noun*: **staircases**
A **staircase** is a set of stairs with its supports and often with a handrail on one or both sides: *a wooden staircase.*

stairway /'stɛəweɪ/ *noun*: **stairways**
A **stairway** is a set of stairs inside or outside a building: *a stone stairway on the outside of the house.*

stairwell /'stɛəwɛl/ *noun*: **stairwells**
A **stairwell** is the vertical opening from the ground floor running upwards through a building, that contains a staircase.

stake /steɪk/ *noun*; *verb*
▷ ***noun***: **stakes**
1 A **stake** is a stick or post, usually pointed at one end, knocked into the ground as a support, *eg* for a young tree or a fence, or used as a marker or for tying a rope to. **2** (*used in the singular*) In former times, the **stake** was a post to which a person was tied before being burned to death as a punishment: *Joan of Arc was burnt at the stake.* **3** A **stake** is also a sum of money risked in betting: *the minimum stake is 50 pence.* **4** If you have a **stake** in something, you have a share, especially a financial share in it which gives you an interest in whether it succeeds or fails: *How can they feel that they have a stake in the country's future if they can't get a job or a decent house to live in?* **5** (*used in the plural*) The **stakes** are the prize or rewards that can be attained if you win something or succeed at something, especially in a horse race. Some horse races have **Stakes** in their titles: *the stakes are high* [=the rewards are great] □ *the Windsor Castle Stakes.*
▷ ***verb***: **stakes, staking, staked**
1 You **stake** a plant or a tree when you support it with a stake driven into the ground: *Stake the peony so that the flowers are supported when they appear.* **2** You **stake** a certain amount of money when you risk it as a bet. **3** If you **stake** your reputation on something, you risk your good name by supporting or promoting it, because you are so confident that it will succeed: *The president has staked his political reputation on getting the legislation through Congress.* **4** If you **stake** someone you risk some of your money by giving them financial support, especially when you believe that you have a good chance of being repaid or getting a good return at some time in the future.
▷ ***phrases*** **1** If you have something **at stake**, it is at risk and may be lost if something does not have a successful outcome: *The business must succeed; our livelihoods are at stake.* **2** If you **stake a claim**, you state or establish your right to have or own something.

phrasal verb
stake out 1 If you **stake** an area of ground **out**, you mark the boundary of it with stakes driven into the ground at regular intervals: *First stake out the area where you want the pond to be, then dig out the earth to a depth of four or five feet at the centre.* **2** (*informal*) If the police **stake out** a building or other place, they watch it continuously so that they can see if any illegal activities are taking place there.

stale /steɪl/ *adjective*
1 Stale food, especially bread or biscuits, is not fresh and is therefore dry and tasteless. **2 Stale** air is not fresh. **3** Something that is **stale** is overused and no longer interesting or original: *You've told that joke so often it's gone a bit stale.* **4** If you describe someone as **stale**, you mean that they are out-of-condition or no longer have any new ideas because they have been doing the same thing for too long: *He's been writing that column for so long he's beginning to get a bit stale.*

stalemate /'steɪlmeɪt/ *noun* (*uncount*)
1 In chess, **stalemate** is a position from which a player cannot move without leaving his or her king in check, so that neither player can win. **2 Stalemate** is a posi-

tion, in any contest or dispute, from which no progress can be made nor winner emerge: *The talks between the unions and management have reached stalemate.* [*same as* **deadlock**]

stalk /stɔːk/ *noun*; *verb*

▻ ***noun***: **stalks**

1 A **stalk** is the main stem of a plant, or the stem by which a leaf, flower or fruit is attached to the main plant. [see picture at **fruit**] **2** A **stalk** is any slender connecting part such as a lever attached to the steering wheel of a car which controls things such as the headlights or horn.

▻ ***verb***: **stalks, stalking, stalked**

1 When an animal **stalks** its prey, it hunts it by following it closely and quietly. **2** If someone **stalks** somewhere, they move there with their body held stiffly and proudly, walking with long strides: *He stalked past them, ignoring their insults.* **3** (*literary*) If something such as death or disease **stalks** an area, it moves silently through it like a threatening spirit.

stall /stɔːl/ *noun*; *verb*

▻ ***noun***: **stalls**

1 A **stall** in a stable, cowshed or other farm building is a compartment for housing a single animal. **2** A **stall** is a table or small open-fronted structure used for displaying goods to be sold in a market or other public place: *She was in charge of the cake stall at the village fête.* **3** A **stall** is a seat, often with a roof-like structure, found in the choir or chancel of some large churches: *the choir stalls.* **4** (*used in the plural*) The **stalls** are the seats on the ground floor of a theatre or cinema: *Are there any seats still available in the front stalls?*

▻ ***verb***: **stalls, stalling, stalled**

1 A vehicle engine **stalls** when it stops running because there is not enough power to keep it going; you **stall** a vehicle engine when you cause it to stop, *eg* because you have not operated the clutch properly and there is not enough power or speed to keep it going. **2** You **stall** when you delay or avoid taking some action; you **stall** someone or something when you put them or it off for a time, especially so that you have time to complete something or be fully prepared for something: *I can't get a definite answer from him; he's been stalling for weeks now.* □ *Do you think we'll be able to stall him for a few more days to give us time to get things in order?*

stallion /ˈstaljən/ *noun*: **stallions**

A **stallion** is an adult male horse, especially one that is kept for breeding.

stalwart /ˈstɔːlwət/ *adjective*; *noun*

▻ ***adjective***

1 A **stalwart** person is strong and sturdy: *half a dozen stalwart farm labourers.* **2** A **stalwart** supporter or fighter for a cause is strong, determined and reliable: *He's always been one of our most stalwart supporters.*

▻ ***noun***: **stalwarts:** *a meeting of the party stalwarts.*

stamina /ˈstamınə/ *noun* (*uncount*)

Stamina is the energy needed to withstand the effects of continued physical or mental effort over a long period: *She's trying to build up her stamina so that she can compete in the marathon.* □ *He didn't have the mental stamina to sustain him through the long months of imprisonment.* [*same as* **resistance, staying power**]

stammer /ˈstamə(r)/ *noun*; *verb*

▻ ***noun*** (*usually used in the singular*)

If someone has a **stammer**, they find it difficult to talk without hesitating before, or repeating, certain speech sounds, especially when these sounds occur at the beginning of words. [see also **stutter**]

▻ ***verb***: **stammers, stammering, stammered**

To **stammer** means to speak or say with a stammer: *'Wh.. Wh.. What do you mean?' he stammered.*

stamp /stamp/ *verb*; *noun*

▻ ***verb***: **stamps, stamping, stamped**

1 You **stamp** your foot when you lift it and bring it down again heavily on the ground, usually as a sign of anger or frustration: *'No, no, no, I will not do it!' she said, stamping her little foot.* **2** If you **stamp** around or **stamp** somewhere, you walk bringing your feet down heavily with every step: *He stamped off in a rage.* □ *I could hear them stamping around upstairs.* **3** If you **stamp** words, letters, a pattern or a design on something, you mark it by pressing with a stamp: *You'll have to have your passport stamped before you can cross the border.* □ *All incoming mail should have the date stamped on it.* **4** A parcel or letter **is stamped** when it has a postage stamp or stamps stuck on it. **5** If something **is stamped** on your mind or your memory, it has made a permanent or deep impression on your mind or is fixed firmly in your memory: *The pathetic faces of the refugees were stamped on his memory for ever.* [*same as* **imprint**] **6** If someone or something **is stamped** as being a particular type or class, they are characterized as being or are put into that class or type: *Because of one small indiscretion, he has been stamped as a cheat and a liar by the media.*

▻ ***noun***: **stamps**

1 (also **postage stamp**) A **stamp** is a small piece of gummed paper showing the official mark of a country's postal system, stuck to mail to show that postage has been paid: *Two first class stamps, please.* **2** A **stamp** is also a block of wood or rubber with which a mark or design is pressed onto a surface, or the mark or design made by pressing this block onto a surface: *a date stamp* □ *Have you had an exit stamp on your passport?* **3** (*used in the singular*) You can refer to any mark or sign that is characteristic of a particular activity or person as the **stamp** of that activity or person: *The crime bears the stamp of a professional.* **4** A **stamp** is an act of stamping the foot: *'No!' she said with a petulant stamp of her foot.*

phrasal verb

If something **is stamped out**, it is ended or destroyed, usually using force: *emergency measures to stamp out crime.* [*same as* **eradicate**]

stampede /stamˈpiːd/ *noun*; *verb*

▻ ***noun***: **stampedes**

1 A **stampede** is a sudden wild rush by a large number of frightened animals. **2** You can also refer to a wild or disorganized rush by a large crowd of frightened or excited people as a **stampede**: *As soon as the doors opened, there was a stampede of excited shoppers all trying to get the best bargains.*

▻ ***verb***: **stampedes, stampeding, stampeded**

To **stampede** is to rush suddenly and wildly in a herd or crowd, or to cause a herd of animals or crowd of people to rush in this way: *The shots stampeded the cattle.* [*same as* **charge**]

stance /stɑːns/ or /stans/ *noun*: **stances**

1 Your **stance** is the way in which you stand, *eg* when you are preparing to play a stroke in a sport such as golf. **2** Your **stance** on a particular issue is your point of view or attitude: *The government has adopted a tough stance on the question of immigration.* [*same as* **standpoint**]

stand /stand/ *verb*; *noun*

▻ ***verb***: **stands, standing, stood**

1 a You **are standing** when you are in an upright position supported on your feet: *Why stand when you can* *sit?* □ *We had to stand all the way from London to Dover.* □ *She was standing by the fire.* □ *Do stand still while I brush your hair.* □ *You're now standing on the very spot where she was beheaded.* **b** You **stand** when you rise into an upright position with your weight supported on your feet: *Now would everyone please stand for the National Anthem.* □ *Haven't you been taught to stand when your teacher comes into the room?* **c** You **stand** *eg* back or aside when you step back or to one side: *She would add a brush stroke here and there and stand back to assess the effect.* □ *We stood to one side to let the ambulance through.* □ *Stand well clear of the automatic doors.* **d** Something **stands** somewhere when it is placed or situated there: *At Najac the village climbs one hill and the castle stands on top of another.* □ *A war memorial stood in the middle of the square.* □ *Various bottles of medicine were standing on the bedside table.* □ *We had a grandfather clock; it stood at the turn in the stair.* □ *The church was one of the few buildings left standing after the bombing.* □ *The tower stood outlined against the sky.* **e** You **stand** something somewhere when you place it there in an upright position: *Stand the roses in a bucket of water for an hour before planting them.* □ *I stood the broom in a corner.* □ *She came in with a candle in a holder and stood it on the mantelpiece.* **2 a** You can use **stand** with a meaning like 'stay' or 'remain' with various words describing states or relationships: *The house had been standing empty for four years.* □ *All this machinery is meanwhile standing idle.* □ *A soldier stood guard over the body.* □ *Macaulay tells how the three men stood alone against the army of Lars Porsena.* □ *For sheer inventiveness, Shakespeare stands alone.* □ *Thank you for updating my information; I stand corrected.* □ *We must stand firm on the question of equal pay.* □ *People tended to stand in awe of his prodigious talent.* **b** Something such as an arrangement or agreement still **stands** if it remains valid or is still in force: *If the offer still stands we should like to accept it.* **c** Things as they **stand** are things in their present state: *As the law stands, he is likely to be refused a work permit.* □ *With the situation as it stands we are unable to put any effective pressure on him.* **d** You **stand** to lose or gain something if you are in circumstances where you are likely to do so: *We stand to make several thousand if the deal goes through.* **e** If someone asks you where you **stand** on a certain issue, they want to know what your opinion is about it, or which side you support. **f** A score or a variable amount **stands** at a certain proportion or level if that is its present state: *The score stands at 3–1.* □ *The betting stood at 10 to 1 against.* □ *The current share price stands at $2.50.* **3 a** (*often with a negative*) Something **stands** circumstances that test its strength or worth if it withstands or survives them: *I don't know how much rough treatment this furniture will stand.* □ *It's an argument that won't stand close examination.* □ *The design has stood the test of time and could even be described as classical.* **b** (*usually with a negative*) You say you cannot **stand** someone or something if you cannot bear them, or if you hate or dislike them: *She can't stand her son's wife.* □ *I can't stand that noise a minute longer.* □ *I don't think I could stand a husband who snored.* □ *I can't stand having to queue for anything.* □ *He couldn't stand anyone even touching him.* [*same as* **bear**, **abide**] **c** A person **stands** trial when they are tried in a court of law: *She will be required to stand trial in the high court.* **d** Someone **stands** for election when they offer themselves as a candidate for people to vote for: *He stood for Colinton in the last local elections.* **4** (*informal*) You **stand** someone something such as a drink or a meal when you buy it for them: *Come on, I'll stand you lunch.*

▻ ***noun*: stands**

1 A **stand** is **a** a base or holder for supporting or holding something: *a cake stand* □ *an umbrella stand* □ *a hat-and-coat stand.* □ *Please bring your own music stand.* **b** A stall, enclosure or enclosed platform for a particular purpose, *eg* one for advertising goods and services at a large indoor exhibition: *They always have a stand at the Modern Homes Exhibition.* □ *There was a bandstand near the park entrance, from which brass bands occasionally entertained the public.* **c** a structure for accommodating spectators at a sports ground: *We had seats in the North Stand.* **2** (*AmE*) A witness takes the **stand** in a law court when he or she goes into the witness box. **3** You make a **stand** against something, or take a **stand** on something when you state your position on some issue and prepare to defend it: *You must take a firm stand on working hours.* □ *You can't help admiring the stand he takes on correct word use, even if it is a losing battle.*

▻ ***phrases*** **1** For **stand a chance** see **chance**. **2** For **stand on your own feet** see **foot**. **3** For **stand to reason** see **reason**. **4** For **stand your ground** see **ground**.

phrasal verbs

stand by **1** You **stand by** when you keep yourself in a state of readiness to act if required to do so: *Two navy helicopters are standing by.* [see also **standby**] **2** You **stand by** someone when you stay close to them and support them through a difficult experience, *eg* when they have been accused of doing something wrong: *I owe so much to my family for standing by me through all this.* **3** You **stand by** your principles or your decision when you do not alter them, in spite of pressure to do so. **4** People **stand by** when they watch and do nothing while something bad is happening: *You feel you can't just stand by and let these kids be ill-treated.*

stand down You **stand down** from an elected position when you resign from it: *He announced that he would be standing down at the next election.* □ *I'd decided to stand down from the committee.*

stand for **1** An abbreviation or symbol **stands for** something if that is what it represents or is short for: *What does AIDS stand for?* **2** (*with a negative*) You refuse to **stand for** something when you refuse to allow it to happen: *If were you I wouldn't stand for that kind of impudence from my subordinates.* **3** Something such as an organization **stands for** something if it is naturally associated with it in people's minds, or has a reputation for it: *Oxford dictionaries stood for accuracy throughout the world.*

stand in You **stand in** for someone when you take their place in some situation, or perform their duties for them: *Couldn't you stand in for me at the meeting?* □ *Many thanks to Marsha for standing in as chairman.* [see also **stand-in**]

stand out **1** Someone or something **stands out** if they are noticeable or conspicuous and attract people's attention: *She had extraordinary flame-coloured hair which made her stand out in a crowd.* **2** Something **stands out** when it strikes you as important: *One particular issue stands out.* **3** You **stand out** for something when you refuse to accept anything less than that: *They're standing out for their 5% pay rise.* **4** You **stand out** against something when you continue to oppose it after most people have accepted it: *One or two linguists still stood out against Ventris's solution.*

stand up **1** You **stand up** when you rise from a sitting or lying position and stand upright: *The men all stood up when she came into the room.* **2** Evidence, an argument or a claim **stands up** under examination if it remains convincing in spite of it: *That argument won't stand up in court.* **3** (*informal*) A person with whom you have a date **stands** you **up** if they deliberately fail to arrive for it. **4** You **stand up** for someone or something that is under attack when you defend or support them: *His mother always stood up for him.* □ *If you don't stand up for your rights, no-one else will.* □ *They'll have to learn to stand up for themselves.* **5** You **stand up** to an attacker when you try to resist them: *If you stand up to him, he's less likely to bully you.* **6** Something **stands up** to hard wear or constant use if it survives it: *The Morris Minor stood up pretty well to the ill treatment it received from her learner-driver daughters.*

standard /'standəd/ *noun*; *adjective*
▻ ***noun***: **standards**
1 A **standard** is a level or degree of quality or value that is established as proper or acceptable and against which things may be compared so as to be measured or judged: *His work is of a very high standard.* □ *They are poor by British standards.* □ *The new hospital offers a high standard of patient care.* □ *The novel was a great success though he felt it was not, according to his own standards, his best work.* **2** (*often in the plural*) **Standards** are principles of behaviour or morality that people adhere to or aim for: *a worrying decline in moral standards* □ *ethical standards.* **3** A **standard** is a flag or other emblem, especially one carried on a pole: *the royal standard of the House of Stuart.*
▻ ***adjective***
1 Standard describes things that are normal or typical, or are most frequently used: *It's standard procedure for the bank to make certain inquiries when you are applying for such a big loan.* □ *He gave the standard excuse that the train had been delayed.* □ *The wood is available in standard lengths.* **2** A **standard** work or text is one that is generally accepted as the one that is most authoritative on a particular subject. **3 Standard** is also used to describe grammar, pronunciation and spelling that are generally accepted as being correct by educated native speakers of a language: *Standard English.*

Standard Grade /standəd 'greɪd/ *noun*: **Standard Grades**
In Scotland, **Standard Grades** are examinations in any of the various subjects studied by pupils in secondary schools, usually taken after four years of study. Standard Grades replaced the former 'O' or 'Ordinary' Grade examinations; a **Standard Grade** is also a pass gained in any of these examinations.

standardize or **standardise** /'standədaɪz/ *verb*: **standardizes, standardizing, standardized**
You **standardize** all the examples of a particular thing when you make them the same or uniform in kind, shape, size or in some other way: *The rules have been standardized across Europe.* — *noun* (*uncount*) **standardization:** *standardization of the regulations affecting the fishing industry.*

standard lamp /'standəd lamp/ *noun*: **standard lamps**
A **standard lamp** is an electric lamp on a tall support whose base sits on the floor. [see picture at **living room**]

standby /'standbaɪ/ *noun*: **standbys**
1 A **standby** is something that is kept ready for use, especially in an emergency: *Though we get fresh milk delivered every day, we always have a tin of dried milk in the cupboard as a standby.* **2** A **standby** or a **standby** ticket is a ticket for a journey by air that is offered at a reduced price because you must wait until just before the flight takes off to see if there is a seat available for you.
▻ ***phrases*** **1** If people are **on standby**, they are ready to be called into action at any time: *The emergency services are on standby in case the river floods.* **2** You travel **on standby** when you travel only if there is a seat available for you.

stand-in /'stand ɪn/ *noun*: **stand-ins**
If someone acts as a **stand-in** for someone else, they take their place or do their job for a time: *The stand-in played so well that he was taken on as a striker with the first team.*

standing /'standɪŋ/ *noun*; *adjective*
▻ ***noun*** (*uncount*)
1 Your **standing** in a group or society is your position, status or reputation relative to others in the group or society. [*same as* **status**] **2** Something of a specific length of time's **standing** has remained in existence or continued for that length of time: *a relationship of several years standing* □ *The quarrel is of long standing.* [*same as* **duration**]
▻ ***adjective***
1 Standing is used to describe actions that are done in or from a standing position: *a standing ovation* □ *From a standing start, he covers the ground faster than any of his team mates.* **2 Standing** also means permanent, regularly used, or continuing in use or force: *It's a standing joke around the office.* □ *a standing committee* □ *a standing army.*

standing order /standɪŋ 'ɔːdə(r)/ *noun*: **standing orders**
A **standing order** is an instruction from an account-holder to their bank to make regular payments of a fixed amount from their account to a third party. [compare **direct debit**]

standoffish /stand'ɒfɪʃ/ *adjective*
Someone who is **standoffish** does not get too closely involved with other people and can seem unfriendly: *I've always found her a bit standoffish.*

standpoint /'standpɔɪnt/ *noun*: **standpoints**
Your **standpoint** is your point of view: *Let's consider this from the standpoint of the ordinary man in the street.* [*same as* **perspective**]

standstill /'standstɪl/ *noun* (*used in the singular*)
If things come to a **standstill**, they come to a complete stop with no progress being made at all: *The money ran out and work came to a standstill.* □ *Traffic is at a standstill because of the heavy snow.*

stank /staŋk/ *verb*
Stank is the past tense of **stink**.

staple /'steɪpəl/ *noun*; *verb*; *adjective*
▻ ***noun***: **staples**
1 A **staple** is a thin U-shaped wire fastener for paper, forced through the paper from a special device into which it is first loaded. [see picture at **office**] **2** A **staple** is also a U-shaped piece of strong wire with pointed ends which is hammered in to hold *eg* wire netting in place. **3 a** A **staple** is a food that forms a basic and important part of your diet: *staples like flour and sugar.* **b** A **staple** is also a main product of a country on which a large part of their economy depends.
▻ ***verb***: **staples, stapling, stapled**
You **staple** two pieces of paper together when you fasten them together with a staple or staples; you **staple** something when you fix it to something else using staples: *The poster was stapled to the telegraph pole.*
▻ ***adjective***
1 Your **staple** diet is the food or foods that you eat reg-

ularly or which form a basic part of your diet: *They lived on a staple diet of rice and beans supplemented by the occasional chicken or fish.* **2** A country's **staple** product or export is their main or most important one.

stapler /ˈsteɪplə(r)/ *noun*: **staplers**
A **stapler** is a special device for driving staples through paper. [see picture at **office**]

star /stɑː(r)/ *noun*; *verb*
▻ ***noun***: **stars**
1 A **star** is a very large mass of burning gas in space, especially one that can be seen as a small bright point of light in the night sky: *Venus is a planet, not a star.* □ *the Milky Way and other star systems.* **2** A **star** is a shape with five or more radiating points, often used as a symbol of rank or excellence: *The teacher gave her a gold star for her essay on the environment.* [see picture at **shape**] **3 a** Astrologers call the planets that they believe have an influence on people's lives the **stars**. **b** An astrologer's prediction of what will happen to you in the future based on the sign of the zodiac under which you were born is referred to as your **stars**. [*same as* **horoscope**] **4** A **star** is a celebrity, especially from the world of entertainment or sport: *a film star* □ *stars of stage and screen* □ *one of the greatest stars of British athletics.* **5** The **star** or **stars** of a play, film or other performance are the people who are the principal performers or who perform in the main role or roles.
▻ ***verb***: **stars, starring, starred**
If an actor or actress **stars** in a play or film they appear in it as the principal performer or one of the principal performers.

starboard /ˈstɑːbəd/ *noun* (*uncount*, *often adjectival*; *technical*)
Starboard is the side of a ship or aircraft that is on your right when you are facing forwards. [*opposite* **port**]

starch /stɑːtʃ/ *noun* (*uncount*)
1 Starch is a white tasteless food substance found in *eg* potatoes, rice and bread. **2 Starch** is also a powder prepared from this used for stiffening clothes.

starched /ˈstɑːtʃt/ *adjective*
Starched clothes are stiffened with starch: *starched collars.*

starchy /ˈstɑːtʃɪ/ *adjective*: **starchier, starchiest**
Starchy foods contain a lot of starch.

stardom /ˈstɑːdəm/ *noun* (*uncount*)
If someone achieves **stardom**, they become very famous, especially in the fields of acting, music or sport.

stare /stɛə(r)/ *verb*; *noun*
▻ ***verb***: **stares, staring, stared**
Someone **stares** at something when they look at it for a long time without looking away: *He stared out of the window.* □ *They stared at him in surprise.* □ *It's rude to stare.* □ *What are you staring at?* □ *He sat staring at the television for hours on end.*
▻ ***noun***: **stares**
A **stare** is **1** an act of staring: *He fixed me with a malevolent stare.* **2** a fixed gaze: *a blank stare.*
▻ ***phrases*** **1** If something **is staring you in the face**, it is very easy for you to see or is too clear to miss: *The answer is staring you in the face if only you would take the trouble to look.* **2** If something unpleasant **is staring you in the face**, it is just about to happen to you: *Financial ruin was staring him the face.*

starfish /ˈstɑːfɪʃ/ *noun*: **starfish**
A **starfish** is a flat sea creature with five arms that stick out around its body to form a star shape.

stark /stɑːk/ *adjective*; *adverb*
▻ ***adjective***
1 Stark means very bare or plain in a harsh or severe way: *a stark landscape unrelieved by any form of vegetation* □ *They found themselves in the stark surroundings of a prisoner-of-war camp.* □ *He had to face up to the stark reality that he was no longer able to do his job properly.* [*same as* **bleak**] **2 Stark** also means complete, utter or downright: *It was stark lunacy.*
▻ ***adverb***
Stark means utterly or completely: *They were all stark naked.* □ (*informal*) *He's gone stark staring mad.*

starlight /ˈstɑːlaɪt/ *noun* (*uncount*)
Starlight is the light from the stars that can be seen at night.

starling /ˈstɑːlɪŋ/ *noun*: **starlings**
A **starling** is a small common songbird with dark glossy speckled feathers and a short tail.

starry /ˈstɑːrɪ/ *adjective*: **starrier, starriest**
Starry means filled with stars or lit with stars: *a starry sky* □ *a starry night.*

starry-eyed /stɑːrɪˈaɪd/ *adjective*
1 Someone is **starry-eyed** about something when they are full of romantic but unrealistic dreams and hopes about it: *She is starry-eyed about her future.* **2** Someone who is **starry-eyed** is so radiantly happy that their eyes shine like stars.

start /stɑːt/ *verb*; *noun*
▻ ***verb***: **starts, starting, started**
1 You **start** doing something when you do something that you were not doing before, and continue to do it: *You may start as soon as you have been handed your question paper.* □ *She started crying.* □ *It started to rain heavily.* □ *I'm going to start dieting tomorrow.* □ *I started nursing terminally ill patients in 1990.* □ *How old were you when you started dancing?* □ *When do you start your training programme?* □ *We used to start work at 7.00 am.* [*same as* **begin**; *opposite* **stop, finish**] **2** You **start a** when you leave on a journey: *I'd like to start at 6.30 so as to be in good time for the ferry.* [*same as* **set off**; *opposite* **arrive**; see also **start off**] **b** when you put any proceeding in motion: *May I start by welcoming tonight's speaker?* □ *Start without me if I'm late.* **3** Something **starts** when it happens or takes place from a certain time onwards: *The meeting should have started half an hour ago.* □ *That noise has started again.* □ *What year did the Peloponnesian War start?* □ *That's how rumours start.* □ *Do the police know how the fire started?* [*same as* **begin**; *opposite* **stop**] **4** You **start** something when you make it happen or set it going: *We ought to start the proceedings straight away.* □ *Apparently the fire was started deliberately.* □ *A gun was fired to start the race.* □ *'Stop shouting at me!' 'Well, you started it!'* □ *Couples are waiting longer and longer to start a family.* □ *I'll ask the first question to start things moving.* □ *What started you going in for newspaper competitions?* **5** Someone **starts** as something if that is their first job: *She started in the theatre as a sound and lighting technician.* [*opposite* **finish** as, **end up** as; see also **start off**] **6** You **start** something such as a business when you establish or create it: *She borrowed money and started a dress shop.* [*same as* **set up**; see also **start up**] **7** You **start** a machine or an engine when you make it operate or set it going; it **starts** when it operates or is set going: *How does the washing machine strat?* □ *The car won't start.* [*opposite* **stop**; see also **start up**] **8** You **start** when you get a surprise or a fright and your body makes a jerking or twitching movement: *She suddenly noticed me*

and started. □ *We all started at the noise.* [*same as* **jump**]

▻ ***noun***: **starts** (*usually in the singular, or uncount*)

1 A **start** is the act, process or point of starting: *We'd better make a start on these letters.* □ *I think we've made a promising start.* □ *After a number of false starts the race eventually got going.* □ *We should have been keeping a record from the start.* □ *The idea looked unworkable from the start.* □ *We've got a very early start tomorrow morning.* □ *That was just the start of my adventures.* □ *It was a disaster from start to finish.* [*same as* **beginning**; *opposite* **end, finish**] **2** You are given a **start** in a race if you are allowed to start a little ahead of the other competitors: *The youngest runners were given a start.* **3** You get a **start** in life or in your career when you get help in the early stages: *He inherited some money, which gave him a bit of a start in life.* **4** You give a **start** when you get a surprise or fright and your body gives a little jerk or twitch: *What a start you gave me!* □ *I woke up with a start.*

▻ ***phrases*** **1** You use **at the start** to refer to the early stages of a situation: *We were warned about this at the start.* [*same as* **at the beginning**] **2** For **fits and starts** see **fit**. **3** You use **for a start** to introduce the first or most important of several things you could mention: *You can't possibly know what he's like; you've never met him, for a start.* **4** You **get off to a good start**, or **to a flying start**, if you do well, or very well, in the early stages of an activity; you **get off to a bad start** when you do badly in the early stages. **5 a** Something that is so **to start with**, is so in the early stages of a situation or series of events: *To start with we thought her headaches were just an excuse to stay off work* [same as **at first**]. **b** You use **to start with** to introduce the first or most important of several things you could mention: *To start with you could get rid of that enormous car and get a smaller one.*

phrasal verbs

start off 1 You **start off** when you leave or set off, *eg* on a journey: *Some of the runners started off at a great rate, only to give up from exhaustion later on.* □ *I started off for the airport at about 6.00.* **2** Someone **starts off** as something if that is their first job: *He started off as a tea boy.* **3** A thing **starts off** as something if that is what it is before it changes: *What started off as a silly joke turned into a major incident.* **4** You **start off** with something, or by doing something, if that is the first thing you do: *Most of our meetings start off with a hymn.* □ *Let's start off by introducing ourselves.* **5** You **start** something or someone **off** when you make them start: *What started this discussion off?* □ *It was those weekly articles on interesting words that started him off wanting to write dictionaries.*

start on 1 You **start on** a task when you tackle it or start dealing with it: *I'm going to start on the garden in the morning.* **2** (*informal*) One person **starts on** another when they start criticizing them: *Don't you start on me, please.* **3** You **start on** a topic when you start talking about it: *Don't get him started on religion again.*

start out 1 You **start out** when you leave on a journey: *What time did you start out from Inverness?* [*same as* **start off**] **2** A person or thing **starts out** as something if that is what they are before they change or develop into something else: *His stamp-collecting started out as a minor interest and became an obsession.* [*same as* **start off**]

start over (*AmE*) You **start over** when you make a second, or fresh, start: *Maybe we can forget what has happened and start over.*

start up 1 You **start** something such as an organization **up** when you set it up or establish it: *She started up several support groups for rape victims.* [*same as* **set up**] **2** You **start up** machinery or a vehicle engine when you make it operate or set it going.

start with Something **starts with** a certain thing, or you **start** it **with**, or **start with**, that thing **a** if it acts as an introduction: *It's best to start with a joke.* □ *Most meetings start with a prayer.* □ *Start your essay with some statement of its subject.* **b** if it is the first item to be dealt with: *What are you reactions? Let's start with you, Pat.* **c** if it forms its first element: *'Wrong' starts with 'W'.* □ *It's bad style to start a sentence with a numeral.*

starter /ˈstɑːtə(r)/ *noun*: **starters**

1 (*singular*) The **starter** is the person who gives the signal for a race to begin. **2** The **starters** are any of the competitors, horses or dogs that assemble for the start of a race, but do not necessarily complete it. **3** The **starter** in a machine or engine is the device that sets it in motion. **4** (*informal*) A **starter** is a dish that is eaten as the first course of a meal: *I'll have the melon as a starter, followed by the ham salad.* [*same as* **hors d'oeuvre**]

startle /ˈstɑːtəl/ *verb*: **startles, startling, startled**

Someone or something **startles** you when it gives you a sudden fright or surprise: *The deer were startled by the shots.* □ *Goodness, how you startled me appearing out of nowhere like that!* □ *I was startled to learn that he had never driven before.* [*same as* **astonish**]

startling /ˈstɑːtlɪŋ/ *adjective*

Something **startling** is so unusual or unexpected that it surprises or shocks people: *The report includes some startling statistics on the the incidence of violent crime in the area.* [*same as* **astonishing**]

starvation /stɑːˈveɪʃən/ *noun* (*uncount*)

If someone is suffering from, or dies from **starvation**, they are made very weak and ill, or die, because they do not have enough food to eat: *With the failure of the crops, there is a real risk that people will begin to die of starvation.*

starve /stɑːv/ *verb*: **starves, starving, starved**

1 People or animals **starve** when they become weak and ill and eventually die because they do not have enough food to eat: *starving refugees.* **2** If you **starve** someone, you do not give them any food: *She starved herself for a week so that she would lose weight.* **3** (*informal*) People often say that they **are starving** when they actually mean that they feel very hungry but are not literally starving: *What's for dinner? I'm starving!* [*same as* **ravenous, famished**] **4** If someone or something **is starved** of something that they need they do not get enough of it: *The project has been starved of funds.* □ *As a child, he had been starved of love.* [*same as* **deprive**]

stash /staʃ/ *verb*: **stashes, stashing, stashed** (*informal*)

If you **stash** something, or **stash** it away, you put it in a secret hiding-place: *He had thousands of pounds stashed away under the floorboards.*

state /steɪt/ *noun*; *verb*

▻ ***noun***: **states**

1 The **state** that someone or something is in is the way they are at any particular time: *He was brought home in a semi-conscious state.* □ *She's still in a state of shock.* □ *She's not in any fit state to stand trial.* □ *You're in no state to drive.* □ *My parents are both in a reasonable state of health.* □ *His mental state is giving cause for concern.* □ *mercury in its liquid state* □ *The company's finances are in a poor state.* □ *a report on the* *state of the nation's health* □ *What a state your clothes are in!* □ *Things are in a pretty awful state here.* □ *That's a nasty state of things.* [= a nasty situation] □ *buildings in various states of preservation.* [compare **condition**] **2** The government announces or declares a **state** of war or a **state** of emergency when the country formally enters a war, or when there is a national emergency: *The drought continued, and a state of emergency was declared.* **3** A **state** is **a** a country regarded as a political unit: *a nation state* □ *the city states of ancient Greece* □ *the member states of the European Union* □ *the state of Israel.* **b** (*often adjectival*) one of the regions into which a country is divided, or that compose a federation, each with its own local government but under the overall political control of a national or federal government, as in *eg* America, Australia or India: *The State of Utah.* □ *Victoria is the smallest state.* □ *the state legislature of Illinois.* **4** (sometimes **State**) (*uncount or used in the singular, often adjectival*) The **state** is the government, or the country as a political organization: *the distribution of authority between Church and State* □ *state officials* □ *They discuss matters of state at their regular weekly meetings.* □ *crimes against the state* □ *accused of betraying state secrets* □ *state-owned institutions* □ *He attended a state school.* **5** (*adjectival*) **State** describes ceremonies and activities that involve the head or ruler of a country: *on state occasions such as the Opening of Parliament* □ *a state visit by the President of France.* **6** (**States**) (*with a singular or plural verb; informal*) The **States** is the United States of America.

▻ ***verb***: **states, stating, stated**

You **state** something when you announce it or make it known, especially formally, in speech or writing: *He stated in his evidence that he had seen the accused leave the nightclub at or around midnight.* □ *State your name, rank and serial number.* □ *You should present yourself at the courthouse at the stated time* (*or at the time stated*). □ *It would help us if you would state your preferences.* □ *Perhaps she can be persuaded to state her intentions.* □ *You will get a chance to state your case later.* □ *I was merely stating my opinion.* □ *as he states in his final chapter* □ *'There's no point in continuing,' she stated flatly.*

▻ ***phrases*** **1** You are **in a state** when you are nervous, anxious or upset: *I always get into a state before exams.* □ *She couldn't find her son anywhere, and she was in quite a state.* **2** When someone such as a monarch or a distinguished statesman dies, and **lies in state**, their body is displayed in public, so that people can come and pay their respects to it.

stateless /'steɪtləs/ *adjective*

A **stateless** person has no nationality or citizenship.

stately /'steɪtlɪ/ *adjective*: **statelier, stateliest**

Stately means noble, dignified and impressive in appearance or manner: *a stately waltz* □ *She was tall and stately.* □ *a stately old sailing ship.* [*same as* **majestic**]

stately home /steɪtlɪ 'hoʊm/ (*BrE*) *noun*: **stately homes**

A **stately home** is a large old house which is open to the public. Stately homes are often the homes or former homes of aristocratic families.

statement /'steɪtmənt/ *noun*: **statements**

1 A **statement** is a thing stated, especially a formal written or spoken declaration: *The Prime Minister will be making a statement in the House this afternoon.* □ *He said he had no knowledge of the incident and made a sworn statement to that effect.* **2** A **statement** is a detailed list of financial transactions, especially one sent by a bank to an account-holder detailing the sums of money they have deposited and withdrawn within a particular period, and their totals. **3** (*uncount; formal*) **Statement** is the act of expressing something in words.

state of affairs /steɪt əv ə'fɛəz/ *noun* (*used in the singular*)

A **state of affairs** is a situation or set of circumstances, especially one that is bad: *This is a sorry state of affairs.* □ *What's the state of affairs as regards the takeover of the company?*

state-of-the-art /steɪt əv ðiː'ɑːt/ *adjective*

State-of-the-art is used to describes things that include the most modern, up-to-date technology available at a particular time in a particular field: *a state-of-the-art music centre.* □ *The new building is state-of-the-art, with heating, lighting and air-conditioning all controlled by a central computer.*

stateroom /'steɪtruːm/ *noun*: **staterooms**

1 A **stateroom** is a large room in a palace occupied by a reigning monarch or president, used for important ceremonial occasions. **2** A **stateroom** is also a large, luxurious private cabin on a ship.

statesman /'steɪtsmən/ *noun*: **statemen**

A **statesman** is an important politician whose experience has earned public respect both in his or her own country and abroad.

static /'statɪk/ *adjective; noun*

▻ ***adjective***

1 Something that is **static** does not move, change or develop: *Wages in the industry have remained static for some years now.* **2** A **static** object is fixed in position and cannot be carried around: *a static camera.*

▻ ***noun*** (*uncount*)

1 **Static** or **static electricity** is electricity produced by friction which collects on a surface, such as hair or nylon fabric, which cannot conduct it. **2** **Static** is disturbance to radio and television signals caused by electricity in the atmosphere.

station /'steɪʃən/ *noun; verb*

▻ ***noun***: **stations**

1 A **station** is a place where passenger trains and buses stop and where passengers can get on or off: *a bus station* □ *a railway station* □ *a map showing all the stations on the London underground* □ *the station at the end of the line* □ *Waverley Station* □ *Please take my seat; I'm getting off at the next station.* □ *Will you drive me to the station tomorrow?* □ *The train was just pulling out of the station.* **2** A **station** is also the local headquarters of a police force: *Where's the nearest police station?* □ *The officers asked him to accompany them to the station.* **3** A building equipped for a particular purpose, such as the generation of electricity, is also called a **station**: *a pumping station* □ *a nuclear power station.* **4** A radio or television channel, or the buildings from which it is broadcast is also referred to as a **station**: *a local radio station* □ *The concert is being broadcast on the other station.* □ *The rebels occupied the national television station.* **5** In some countries, *eg* Australia and New Zealand, a large farm on which cattle or sheep are grazed is a cattle or sheep **station**. **6** Your **station** or your **station** in life is your particular position within the society in which you live, especially your place in its class structure. **7** Someone's **station** is their official post or place of duty: *The security guard was accused of deserting his station.* □ *He was expected to be at his station at the Ministry from seven in the morning until nine in the evening.*

▻ ***verb***: **stations, stationing, stationed**

1 Someone **is stationed** somewhere when they are appointed to a post there: *He was stationed in Germany for much of his army career.* [*same as* **posted**]

2 You **station** yourself somewhere when you stand or sit there, usually so that you can watch what is going on around you: *She stationed herself by the window so that she could watch the people in the street below.*

stationary /'steɪʃənərɪ/ *adjective*
Stationary means **a** standing still or not moving: *Please wait until the train is stationary before you try to open the door.* □ *The bus crashed into the back of a stationary vehicle.* **b** that cannot, or is not intended to be moved: *a stationary caravan.*

stationer /'steɪʃənə(r)/ *noun*: **stationers**
A **stationer** is a person who runs a shop that sells stationery: *The sign said 'Newsagent and Stationer's'.* □ *I bought some typing paper at the stationer's.*

stationery /'steɪʃənərɪ/ *noun* (*uncount*)
Stationery is a collective term for writing materials, such as paper, envelopes, pencils and pens: *The company supplies office stationery.* □ *'Where do you keep the stationery?' 'In the stationery cupboard, over there.'*

stationmaster /'steɪʃənmɑːstə(r)/ *noun*: **stationmasters**
A **stationmaster** is a person who is in charge of a railway station.

station wagon /'steɪʃən wagən/ (*AmE*) *noun*: **station wagons**
A **station wagon** is an estate car.

statistical /stə'tɪstɪkəl/ *adjective*
Statistical means of or shown by statistics: *a statistical analysis of how frequently certain words are used in speech and writing* □ *The report includes a lot of statistical information.* □ *From the statistical evidence it is apparent that men are fifty times more likely to suffer from the disease than women.* — *adverb* **statistically:** *Statistically, a man is unlikely to live as long as a woman.*

statistician /statɪ'stɪʃən/ *noun*: **statisticians**
A **statistician** is a person who gathers and analyses statistics: *figures produced by Treasury statisticians.*

statistics /stə'tɪstɪks/ *noun*
1 (*uncount*) **Statistics** is the science of collecting, presenting and interpreting numerical information. **2 Statistics** are items of information collected and presented in numerical form. One of these items of information expressed as a number is a **statistic**: *The latest crime statistics show that there has been an increase in violent assaults.* □ *government statistics* □ *No-one seems to really care about the victim; they simply become another statistic.*

statue /'statʃuː/ *noun*: **statues**
A **statue** is a figure of a person or animal, usually life-size or larger and made out of stone, wood, or metal, often put up in a public place: *Michelangelo's statue of David* □ *a marble statue.*

statuesque /statʃʊ'ɛsk/ *adjective*
If you describe someone, especially a woman, as **statuesque** you mean that they are tall and graceful: *He arrived at the premiere accompanied by a statuesque blonde.* [*same as* **dignified, imposing**]

statuette /statʃʊ'ɛt/ *noun*: **statuettes**
A **statuette** is a small statue, especially one that is small enough to stand on a shelf: *a statuette of the Eygptian god Osiris.*

stature /'statʃə(r)/ *noun* (*uncount; formal*)
1 Your **stature** is your height: *Because of his small stature, he wasn't often cast as the romantic lead.* **2** Someone's **stature** is the importance that they have gained through their achievements or skill: *His handling of the crisis has increased his stature as an international statesman.* □ *a composer of considerable stature.*

status /'steɪtəs/ *noun* (*uncount or singular*)
1 Your social or professional **status** is your position in relation to others in a society or organization: *a low-status job* □ *Teachers should be given the status they deserve.* **2** Your **status** is your legal position or condition, *eg* with regard to adulthood, marriage or citizenship: *Please indicate your marital status by ticking one of the following: single, married, widowed, divorced.* **3** Something's **status** is its state or condition at a particular time: *What's the patient's status?*

status quo /steɪtəs 'kwoʊ/ *noun* (*singular*)
If you talk about the **status quo** you are referring to the situation as it is now, especially when you are discussing changes that should or should not be made: *maintain the status quo.*

status symbol /'steɪtəs sɪmbəl/ *noun*: **status symbols**
A **status symbol** is something that you have or have bought that shows that you are wealthy or have a high social status: *expensive cars, yachts and other status symbols* □ *A personal coat of arms is regarded as a status symbol.*

statute /'statjuːt/ *noun*: **statutes**
A **statute** is a law or rule, passed by a parliament or other law-making body and recorded in a formal document: *the statute of limitations* □ *According to statute, someone who is once acquitted of a crime cannot be retried for the same crime.* [*same as* **regulation**]

statutory /'statʃʊtərɪ/ *adjective*
Statutory means required or fixed by law or a formal rule: *This condition will not affect your statutory rights.* □ *a statutory incomes policy.*

staunch /stɔːntʃ/ *adjective*; *verb*
▻ ***adjective***: **staunchest**

> Note that the comparative form of **staunch** is 'more staunch' not 'stauncher'.

A **staunch** supporter or ally is a very loyal one: *The United States is one of Britain's staunchest allies.* [*same as* **steadfast**]

▻ ***verb***: **staunches, staunching, staunched**
You **staunch** blood when you stop it flowing or control its flow, usually using something such as a thick piece of cloth held against a wound.

stave /steɪv/ *verb*: **staves, staving, staved**

> ***phrasal verb***
> You **stave off** something such as hunger or disaster if you delay it or stop it happening, especially temporarily: *They had a couple of dry biscuits each to stave off the pangs of hunger.* □ *an attempt to stave off a backbench rebellion.* [*same as* **avert**]

stay /steɪ/ *verb*; *noun*
▻ ***verb***: **stays, staying, stayed**
1 You **stay** somewhere when you continue to be there and do not go away: *He stays at home while his wife goes out to work.* □ *Stay where you are and don't move till I come.* □ *You should stay in bed for a day or two.* □ *He came round earlier but he only stayed for a few minutes.* □ *I'm afraid I can't stay long.* □ *Do stay for supper.* □ *He never stayed more than a few months in any job.* [*same as* **remain**] **2** You **stay** somewhere when you live there temporarily as a visitor or guest: *You're welcome to stay the night here.* □ *Where will you be staying in Singapore?* □ *I'm staying at the Sheraton*

Hotel in Orchard Road. □ *How long are you planning to stay, madam?* □ *I've got some friends in Manchester I can stay with.* □ *He stays with his aunt during the term.* **3** You **stay** in a certain condition, state, situation or position when you continue to be in it and do not change or move: *the secret of staying young* □ *I tried my best to stay awake.* □ *people who can stay calm in a crisis* □ *I'd better stay sober; I'm due to give a lecture.* □ *The place has stayed the same all these years.* □ *Stay like that while I take your photograph.* □ *You'd better stay off work till that leg heals.* [*same as* **remain, keep**]
▻ ***noun*** (*usually in the singular*): **stays**
You have a **stay** somewhere when you spend a period of time there as a visitor or guest: *We had a brief stay in Norwich on our way home.* □ *You evidently managed to see quite a lot during your stay.* □ *Did you enjoy your stay?*
▻ ***phrases*** (*informal*) You **stay put** when you don't move from where you are: *It'll be nice to stay put somewhere after four days' solid travelling.*

phrasal verbs
stay away You **stay away** from a place when you do not go there: *We stayed away from that particular pub till we judged it safe to go back again.*
stay in You **stay in** when you remain at home and do not go out: *I stayed in all morning waiting for the plumber.* □ *I'm staying in tonight; I've got work to do.* □ *We'll just stay in and watch the football.*
stay off You **stay off** something such as a topic or a food if you avoid it: *Mind you stay off the subject of holidays.* □ *Stay off fatty foods for the time being.* [*same as* **keep off**]
stay on You **stay on** somewhere when you remain there after others have left, or after the normal time for leaving: *We had to stay on at school an extra term to sit the Oxford and Cambridge entrance exams.* □ *Some of us stayed on to help clear up.*
stay out **1** You **stay out** of something when you avoid getting involved in it: *I did my best to stay out of their quarrels.* **2** You **stay out** when you remain away from home, especially at night: *I'm only allowed to stay out until midnight.* □ *The cat sometimes stays out all night.* **3** Workers **stay out** when they remain on strike.
stay up You **stay up** when you don't go to bed at your normal bedtime: *I'm going to stay up and get this essay finished.* □ *We stayed up to watch the late film.* □ *Don't stay up too late.*

staying power /ˈsteɪɪŋ paʊə(r)/ *noun* (*uncount*)
If someone has **staying power**, they have the ability to continue doing something for a long period of time without getting tired or giving up: *She has proved that she has the staying power to compete in the marathon.* [*same as* **stamina, endurance**]

stead /stɛd/ *noun*
▻ ***phrase*** If something will **stand you in good stead** it will be useful to you in the future: *The experience you have gained will stand you in good stead when you begin to look for a job.*

steadfast /ˈstɛdfɑːst/ *adjective*
A **steadfast** person is determinedly loyal and firm in their support of someone or something; a **steadfast** gaze is steady and unwavering: *a steadfast supporter* □ *He was steadfast in his belief that they would eventually triumph over their enemies.* [*opposite* **unreliable, weak**] — *adverb* **steadfastly:** *He steadfastly refused to answer the police's questions.* [*same as* **firmly**] — *noun* (*uncount*) **steadfastness:** *the steadfastness of his support for the Prime Minister.*

steady /ˈstɛdɪ/ *adjective; verb*
▻ ***adjective***: **steadier, steadiest**
1 a An object or structure that is **steady** is firmly fixed or balanced and does not move about: *Be careful that pile of books doesn't fall over; it doesn't look very steady.* □ *'That ladder doesn't look very safe.' 'No, it's okay; steady as a rock.'* [*same as* **stable**] **b** If you are **steady** on your feet you are able to walk normally without stumbling or falling; if your hands are **steady** they do not shake; if someone's gaze is **steady** they look at something continuously without looking away. [*opposite* **unsteady**] **2** If something makes **steady** progress it continues to progress in an even continuous way without interruption or sudden changes: *The government's policies have brought a period of steady economic growth with low inflation and falling unemployment.* □ *There has been a steady improvement in her condition.* □ *maintain a steady speed.* **3** A **steady** job is one that can be relied upon to go on for a long time; you have a **steady** relationship with someone when you have a long romantic relationship with them and do not have relationships with other people: *How can you think of getting married when neither of you has a steady income?* □ *Does she have a steady boyfriend?* [*same as* **stable**] **4** If prices are **steady** they are stable and do not go up or down suddenly: *the pound remained steady against the Deutschmark.* [*same as* **stable**] **5** If you describe a person as **steady** you mean that they are sensible and reliable: *He's a very steady young man.*
▻ ***verb***: **steadies, steadying, steadied**
You **steady** something when you make it or it becomes steady or steadier: *She had a large glass of brandy to steady her nerves.* — *adverb* **steadily:** *He worked steadily for six hours without a break.* □ *Her condition got steadily worse.* — *noun* (*uncount*) **steadiness**

steak /steɪk/ *noun*: **steaks**
1 (*uncount or count*) **Steak** is high quality beef used for frying or grilling; a **steak** is a slice of this: *sirloin steak* □ *porterhouse steak* □ *a T-bone steak* □ *My wife is going to have the salmon, and I'll have the steak.* **2 Steak** is also beef cut into chunks and used for stewing or braising. **3** A **steak** is a thick slice of any meat or fish: *a salmon steak.*

steal /stiːl/ *verb*: **steals, stealing, stole, stolen**
1 You **steal** when you take someone else's property without permission and without intending to return it: *His car was stolen during the night.* □ *He stole from the rich to give to the poor.* □ *You had better fasten your handbag properly or someone will steal your purse.*

Note that you **steal** things, but that the people from whom you steal them **are robbed**. If a thief secretly enters someone's house or premises to steal things, you say that the place **has been burgled**. A person who steals is a **thief**, a **robber** or a **burglar**.

2 You **steal** something from someone when you take or get it quickly, without permission or secretly: *steal a kiss* □ *She stole a glance at the handsome visitor.* [*same as* **sneak**] **3** If you **steal** someone's ideas or work, you pretend that they are your own. **4** If someone **steals** somewhere, they move quietly and stealthily so as not to be noticed: *She stole back in through the back door, so that her parents wouldn't know she had been out.* [*same as* **sneak**] — *noun* (*uncount*) **stealing:** *He was accused of stealing.* [*same as* **theft**]

stealth /stɛlθ/ *noun* (*uncount*)
You do something with or by **stealth** when you do it slowly and quietly so that you are not noticed: *You*

can only approach the animals by stealth, keeping down wind of them at all times.

stealthy /ˈstɛlθɪ/ *adjective*: **stealthier, stealthiest**
Stealthy movements are done slowly, quietly and secretively so as to avoid notice: *They watched the lioness making stealthy progress towards the unsuspecting antelope.* — *adverb* **steathily:** *He tiptoed stealthily past her bedroom door.*

steam /stiːm/ *noun*; *verb*; *adjective*
▻ ***noun*** (*uncount*)
1 Steam is the gas formed when water boils. When the surrounding air is colder than the boiling point of water you can see steam rising into the air in the form of a white mist of water droplets. **2 Steam** is the power produced by steam under pressure, used for making machinery work or move.
▻ ***verb***: **steams, steaming, steamed**
1 To **steam** is to give off steam: *a steaming bowl of soup.* **2** You **steam** food when you cook it over boiling water: *Steam the fish for ten minutes.* **3** To **steam** also means to move under the power of steam: *The great liner steamed out of Southampton Water.*
▻ ***adjective***
Steam vehicles or machines are powered by steam: *a steam locomotive* □ *a steamroller* □ *a steam pump.*
▻ ***phrases*** (*informal*) **1** If you **are** or **get steamed up** about something, you get angry or agitated about it. **2** People **let off steam** when they do something which has the effect of releasing the anger or energy that has built up inside them. **3** If something **runs out of steam**, it loses its energy or momentum. **4** If you get somewhere **under your own steam**, you get there by your own efforts.

> ***phrasal verb***
> If something such as a window **steams up**, it becomes covered or clouded with tiny droplets of condensed steam.

steamer /ˈstiːmə(r)/ *noun*: **steamers**
1 A **steamer** is a ship whose engines are powered by steam. **2** A **steamer** is also a type of cooking pot with two sections. Food placed in the upper section is cooked by the steam produced by boiling water in the lower section.

steamroller /ˈstiːmroʊlə(r)/ *noun*: **steamrollers**
A **steamroller** is a large vehicle with wheels consisting of large solid metal cylinders that is driven over newly made roads to flatten the surface.

steamy /ˈstiːmɪ/ *adjective*: **steamier, steamiest**
1 A **steamy** place is full of, or made cloudy by, steam: *The jungle was hot and steamy* □ *The windows were all steamy.* **2** (*informal*) A **steamy** novel or love scene is erotic or full of sexual passion.

steel /stiːl/ *noun*; *verb*
▻ ***noun*** (*uncount*)
Steel is a strong hard metal made from iron mixed with carbon, used to make things such as vehicle bodies and engines, machines and tools: *a steel mill* □ *iron and steel* □ *The soldiers wore steel helmets.* [see also **stainless steel**]
▻ ***verb***: **steels, steeling, steeled**
You **steel** yourself when you make yourself hard or unfeeling so that you are able to deal with something unpleasant: *He steeled himself for the coming battle.* [*same as* **brace**]

steel band /stiːl ˈband/ *noun*: **steel bands**
A **steel band** is a group of musicians that play drums made out of steel petrol drums. Steel bands originated in the West Indies.

steel wool /stiːl ˈwʊl/ *noun* (*uncount*)
Steel wool is thin strands of steel gathered together in a woolly mass, used for polishing and scouring metal.

steelworks /ˈstiːlwɜːks/ *noun* (*used with a singular or plural verb*)
A **steelworks** is a factory where steel is made.

steely /ˈstiːlɪ/ *adjective*: **steelier, steeliest**
Steely mean hard and cold, like steel: *He fixed her with a steely gaze.*

steep /stiːp/ *adjective*; *verb*
▻ ***adjective***: **steeper, steepest**
1 A **steep** slope rises or falls sharply or at a sharp angle: *a steep hill* □ *a steep roof.* [*opposite* **gentle**] **2** (*informal*) If you say that the price of something is **steep** you mean that it is unreasonably high: *£50? That's a bit steep!*
▻ ***verb***: **steeps, steeping, steeped**
You **steep** clothes when you leave them standing in liquid for a time in order to remove stains.
▻ ***phrase*** You say that something **is steeped in** a particular quality or characteristic when it is thoroughly filled with it or deeply influenced by it: *a ceremony steeped in tradition.*

steeple /ˈstiːpəl/ *noun*: **steeples**
A **steeple** is a tall tower with a spire that rises above the roof of a church.

steeplechase /ˈstiːpəltʃeɪs/ *noun*: **steeplechases**
1 A **steeplechase** is a horse race round a course with various hedges and ditches to be jumped: *The Grand National is England's best known steeplechase.* **2** In athletics, the **steeplechase** is a middle-distance track race in which the runners jump various high hurdles and a water jump placed around the course.

steer /stɪə(r)/ *verb*: **steers, steering, steered**
1 You **steer** a vehicle or boat when you guide or control its course or direction: *You'll have to steer carefully if you want to avoid hitting that gatepost.* □ *The pilot steered the plane on to the runway.* **2** You **steer** someone or something in a particular direction when you guide them in that direction *eg* using persuasion: *steer the bill through Congress* □ *He steered the conversation away from the subject of money.* **3** You **steer** a particular course, especially on a ship, when you follow that course: *steer a course north by northwest* □ *steer an easterly course.*
▻ ***phrase*** You **steer clear of** someone or something if you avoid them: *try to steer clear of troublemakers.* [*opposite* **seek**]

steering wheel /ˈstɪərɪŋ wiːl/ *noun*: **steering wheels**
A **steering wheel** is a wheel that controls the steering in a vehicle or ship. [see picture at **car**]

stem /stɛm/ *noun*; *verb*
▻ ***noun***: **stems**
1 A plant's **stem** is the slender central part that grows upward from the root; the **stems** of a plant are also the slender parts by which a leaf, flower or fruit is attached to a branch. **2** The **stem** of a wine glass is the long thin part between the bowl and the base; the **stem** of a pipe is the long thin tube between the bowl and the mouthpiece. **3** (*linguistics*) The part of the word that stays the same when different endings or inflections are added to it is the **stem** of that word. [see also **root**]
▻ ***verb***: **stems, stemming, stemmed**
You **stem** something when you stop or slow it down: *She used a piece of torn sheet to stem the flow of blood.* □ *measures to stem the tide of immigration from Cuba.* [*same as* **check, curb**]

> ***phrasal verb***
> If something **stems from** something else, it has that thing as its origin or cause: *The problems all stem from the government's refusal to provide sufficient money for the health service.* [*same as* **originate in**]

stench /stɛntʃ/ *noun*: **stenches**
A **stench** is a very strong bad smell: *the stench of rotting flesh.*

stencil /'stɛnsɪl/ *noun*; *verb*
▻ ***noun***: **stencils**
1 A **stencil** is a piece of wood, metal or paper with a design or lettering cut out of it. You transfer the design or lettering to a surface by holding the stencil against the surface and forcing ink or paint through the cut-out parts on to the surface to be printed or decorated. **2** A **stencil** is the lettering or design produced in this way.
▻ ***verb***: **stencils, stencilling** (*AmE* **stenciling**), **stencilled** (*AmE* **stenciled**)
You **stencil** a design when you print or produce it using a stencil.

step /stɛp/ *noun*; *verb*
▻ ***noun***: **steps**
1 A **step** is **a** the movement made when you raise your foot off the ground and bring it down again a little further away when you are walking or running: *She walked with quick little steps.* □ *Take one step forward.* **b** the distance covered by this: *It was only a few short steps from the front door to the garden gate.* [*same as* **pace**] **c** the sound of a foot being laid on the ground in walking: *She heard his heavy step on the stairs.* [*same as* **footstep**] **2** A **step** is also a movement of the foot, usually one of several that form a pattern in dancing: *learn the steps of a dance.* **3** A **step** is a raised flat narrow surface on which you step to go from one level to another; a number of **steps** are a series of these flat surfaces one above the other forming a stair or ladder: *She found him sitting on the front step.* □ *There were three steps leading up to the front door.* □ *He was standing on the bottom step of the ladder.* [see also **doorstep**] **4** A **step** is a single action or measure, usually one of a series, taken in order to achieve a particular result: *Now that we have reached this crucial stage, we should discuss what the next step should be.* □ *It's a major step forward in the search for a cure for cancer.* **5** A **step** is a degree or stage in a scale or series. **6** (*used in the plural*) **Steps** are a stepladder.
▻ ***verb***: **steps, stepping, stepped**
1 You **step** somewhere when you move in any direction by taking a step or steps, especially slowly and deliberately, quietly or carefully: *She stepped out of the bath.* □ *He stepped out from behind the door.* □ *Be careful you don't step in that puddle.* **2** You **step** on something when you bring your foot down on top of it, often heavily: *I think you've stepped on some dog dirt.* □ *He stepped on the beetle.* **3** You **step** into a job or role, you become involved in that situation or take on that role, especially easily, casually or carelessly: *He had only been out of university two months when he stepped into a highly paid job in the city.* [*same as* **walk**] **4** You **step** somewhere when you come or go there: *Would you step into my office for a moment, Miss Burns.* □ *I'll show you to your rooms now, if you'd care to step this way.*
▻ ***phrases*** **1** Two or more people walk **in step** when they walk or march putting their feet down at exactly the same time and the same distance apart as each other; if one thing is **in step** with another, they are in harmony with each other. **2** Someone who is walking or marching with others is **out of step** if they are not putting their feet down at the same time as the others; if something is **out of step**, *eg* with current developments, it is not in harmony with them. **3** If something is done **step by step**, it is done gradually. **4** If you **take steps**, you take the necessary action to ensure that something is done. [*same as* **measures**] **5** If you **watch your step**, you proceed with caution, taking care not to anger or offend others.

> ***phrasal verbs***
> **step aside** If someone in a particular post or position **steps aside**, they give up that post or position so that another person can take it: *He stepped aside so that his eldest son could take over the business.*
> **step down** If someone in a position of authority **steps down**, they resign.
> **step in** **1** You **step in** when you take up a position or role as a substitute or replacement for someone else: *One of the speakers suddenly fell ill, so I had to step in at the last minute.* **2** You **step in** when you intervene in an argument: *The United Nations stepped in to try to resolve the conflict.*
> **step up** If the rate or intensity of something **is stepped up**, it is increased: *The union announced it was going to step up its campaign of one-day strikes.*

step- /'stɛp-/ *prefix*
Step- is used before nouns to indicate a person who is related to you not by blood but through a second or later marriage or partnership.

stepbrother /'stɛpbrʌðə(r)/ *noun*: **stepbrothers**
Someone's **stepbrother** is the son of their stepfather or stepmother.

stepchild /'stɛptʃaɪld/ *noun*: **stepchildren**
A **stepchild** is a stepson or stepdaughter.

stepdaughter /'stɛpdɔːtə(r)/ *noun*: **stepdaughters**
Someone's **stepdaughter** is the daughter of their husband or wife by a previous marriage.

stepfather /'stɛpfɑːðə(r)/ *noun*: **stepfathers**
Someone's **stepfather** is the second or later husband of their mother.

stepladder /'stɛpladə(r)/ *noun*: **stepladders**
A **stepladder** is a short ladder with two parts hinged at the top so that it can stand on its own or be folded and carried around. Stepladders have flat steps rather than rungs.

stepmother /'stɛpmʌðə(r)/ *noun*: **stepmothers**
Someone's **stepmother** is the second or later wife of their father.

stepping stone /'stɛpɪŋ stoʊn/ *noun*: **stepping stones**
1 A **stepping stone** is a large stone in a stream or river with its surface above the water level, that is stepped on by people crossing the stream or river. **2** If you refer to something as a **stepping stone** to something else, you mean that it is something that helps you to make progress towards that other thing: *Think of the job as a stepping stone to greater things.*

stepsister /'stɛpsɪstə(r)/ *noun*: **stepsisters**
Someone's **stepsister** is the daughter of their stepfather or stepmother from an earlier marriage.

stepson /'stɛpsʌn/ *noun*: **stepsons**
If your husband or wife has a son from an earlier marriage, he is your **stepson**.

stereo /'stɛrɪoʊ/ *noun*; *adjective*
▻ ***noun***: **stereos**
1 (*uncount*) **Stereo** is sound reproduction directed

through two different speakers simultaneously: *The concert will be broadcast in stereo.* **2** (*informal*) A **stereo** is a record or cassette player with two speakers. [see picture at **living room**]

▻ ***adjective***

Stereo sound is sound reproduction using two speakers.

stereotype /stɛrɪətaɪp/ *noun*; *verb*

▻ ***noun***: **stereotypes**

A **stereotype** is a fixed general impression or set of ideas about what a particular type of person or thing is like which is believed to apply to all the individuals of that type and takes no account of the variations which actually exist.

▻ ***verb***: **stereotypes, stereotyping, stereotyped**

You **stereotype** a person or thing when you think of or characterize them in this over-generalised way.

sterile /'stɛraɪl/ *adjective*

1 A **sterile** animal or plant is incapable of producing young or seeds. [*opposite* **fertile**; *same as* **infertile**] **2** If a place or area is made **sterile** it is made completely clean and free from harmful bacteria. [*same as* **sterilized**] **3** You can also describe a situation as **sterile** when it produces no results or lacks imagination and new ideas: *a sterile argument.*

sterility /stə'rɪlɪtɪ/ *noun* (*uncount*)

Sterility is the state of being sterile.

sterilize or **sterilise** /'stɛrɪlaɪz/ *verb*: **sterilizes, sterilizing, sterilized**

1 You **sterilize** things like medical instruments when you make them absolutely clean and free of germs, *eg* by boiling or heating them: *sterilize the baby's bottle* □ *a machine for sterilizing dentists' instruments.* [*opposite* **contaminate, infect**] **2** A person or animal **is sterilized** when they are made incapable of producing young, especially by means of a surgical operation. — *noun* (*uncount*) **sterilization** /stɛrɪlaɪ'zeɪʃən/

sterling /'stɜːlɪŋ/ *noun* (*uncount, often adjectival*)

Sterling is the system of money used in Britain, based on the pound: *change French francs to sterling* □ *sterling travellers cheques* □ *2.5 million pounds sterling.*

stern /stɜːn/ *adjective*; *noun*

▻ ***adjective***: **sterner, sternest**

1 A **stern** person is extremely strict and severe: *a stern disciplinarian* □ *He looked stern and disapproving.* **2** You can also describe something such as a punishment as **stern** when it is harsh and severe.

▻ ***noun***: **sterns**

The **stern** of a boat or ship is the back end of it: *He sat in the stern.* [compare **bow**]

stethoscope /'stɛθəskoʊp/ *noun*: **stethoscopes**

A **stethoscope** is an instrument used by doctors for listening to the sounds made inside the body, *eg* the heartbeat or sounds of breathing.

stew /stjuː/ *verb*; *noun*

▻ ***verb***: **stews, stewing, stewed**

1 You **stew** food when you cook it slowly and gently in liquid: *Stew the meat and vegetables over low heat for three hours.* **2** You say that tea **is stewed** when it has become very strong and bitter-tasting because it has been allowed to brew for too long. **3** (*informal*) If you let someone **stew**, you leave them for a long time to think about a situation without reassuring them or forgiving their bad behaviour. [*same as* **sweat**]

▻ ***noun***: **stews**

1 A **stew** is a mixture of foods, especially meat and vegetables, cooked slowly in liquid: *beef stew with dumplings.* **2** (*informal*) If you are in a **stew** you are in a very worried or anxious state about something.

steward /'stjuːəd/ *noun*: **stewards**

1 A **steward** is a man who works on a ship, aircraft or train whose job is to look after the passengers. **2** The **stewards** at a sporting event or public march are the people that help to organize it and supervise crowd movements. **3** A **steward** is one of several officials whose role is to ensure that a horse race is run according to the rules.

stewardess /stjuːə'dɛs/ *noun*: **stewardesses**

A **stewardess** is a woman who works on a ship, aircraft or train whose job is to look after the passengers: *an air stewardess.* [*same as* **air hostess**]

stewed /stjuːd/ *adjective*

1 **Stewed** food has been cooked by heating it slowly in liquid: *stewed prunes.* **2** (*informal*) If you say that someone is **stewed**, you mean they are drunk.

stick /stɪk/ *noun*; *verb*

▻ ***noun***: **sticks**

1 A **stick** is a thin branch from a tree, or a thin piece of dead wood: *We gathered dry sticks for the fire.* □ *He threatened us with a big stick.* □ *a crowd armed with sticks and stones* **2** A **stick** or **walking stick** is a long straight piece of wood, typically with a handle, that *eg* an elderly or lame person uses to support them when they walk: *She can still walk without a stick.* □ *He was leaning on his stick.* **3** A **stick** can be any of various narrow pieces of wood shaped for particular purposes: *hockey sticks* □ *a drumstick.* **4** A **stick** of something is a narrow piece of it: *a stick of chalk* □ *a stick of celery* □ *a stick of dynamite* □ *sticks of chewing gum.*

▻ ***verb***: **sticks, sticking, stuck**

1 You **stick** something, especially something narrow or pointed, into or through something else when you push or poke it there: *I stuck the pins back into the notice board.* □ *Pieces of glass were still sticking into his back.* □ *She stuck her head round the door and said 'Hi.'* □ *a ball of wool with a pair of knitting needles stuck through it.* **2** (*informal*) You **stick** something somewhere when you put it there: *Stick your case on top of the wardrobe when you've unpacked.* **3** You **stick** one thing to another when you attach the one to the other with glue or adhesive tape; one thing **sticks** to another when it becomes attached to it: *We managed to stick the two halves together so that the join didn't show.* □ *He stuck a 'For Sale' notice in the window.* □ *I stuck a label on the box.* □ *She licked the flap and stuck it down firmly* □ *These stamps don't stick very well.* □ *The mud stuck to their boots.* **4** (*informal*) You **stick** something when you manage to bear it: *I can't stick people who shout.* □ *It must be an awful job; I don't know how you've stuck it so long.* [see also **stuck**]

▻ ***phrases*** You **get hold of**, or **get, the wrong end of the stick** when you misunderstand something completely.

phrasal verbs

stick around You **stick around** when you stay where you are, or wait there for something: *I stuck around for another month or so, but no jobs cropped up.*

stick at **1** (*informal*) You **stick at** something such as a difficult job when you go on doing it, or persevere with it: *He never sticks at anything for long.* □ *Stick at it!* **2** People who **stick at** nothing are ready to do anything, no matter how dishonest or wicked, to get what they want.

stick by You **stick by** someone when you support them or remain loyal to them, *eg* when they are in trouble: *I'm so grateful to my family for sticking by me.*

stick out **1** Something that **sticks out** extends outwards from an object or surface, or projects from it:

His ears stick out. □ *There was a big nail sticking out of the wall.* [*same as* **project**] **2** You **stick** something **out** when you make it extend outwards or project: *She stuck her tongue out at him.* □ *He stuck his head out of the window.* **3** A person or thing **sticks out** if they are noticeably different or unusual: *She stuck out at university because of her exotic appearance and extraordinary clothes.* **4** Something such as an answer or solution **sticks out** if it is obvious: *The answer was sticking out a mile.* **5** (*informal*) You **stick** it **out** when you manage to endure a difficult period: *I hate it here but I'm going to have to stick it out for at least another two months.*

stick out for You **stick out for** something you want when you continue to insist on it and refuse to accept anything less: *The company has offered us a 5% pay rise but we've agreed to stick out for our original demand of 7%.*

stick to 1 You **stick to** someone or something when you stay with them or follow them closely: *Stick to the path and you won't get lost.* □ *Stick to him and don't let him out of your sight.* **2** You **stick to** an idea if you do not alter it; you **stick to** an activity if you do not change to something else: *She ought to stick to review-writing.* □ *Are you going to stick to your plan?* □ *I stuck to my opinion.* **3** You **stick to** a promise when you do what you promised to: *Don't you worry; we'll stick to the agreement.*

stick together Two or more people **stick together** when they remain together and support one another: *We'll be all right if we stick together.*

stick up 1 Something **sticks up** if it extends or projects upwards from a surface or object: *How do you get your hair to stick up like that?* **2** (*informal*) You **stick** your hand **up** when you raise it, *eg* in a class, to get the teacher's attention. **3** You **stick** something such as a poster or notice **up** when you attach it to a wall for people to look at.

stick up for (*informal*) You **stick up for** a person, principle or ideal when you defend or support them strongly: *You'll have to learn to stick up for yourself when you go to school.* □ *Old-style socialism has so few people to stick up for it.*

stick with 1 You **stick with** a person when you keep with them: *You'll be fine if you stick with Jo.* **2** You **stick with** a thing if you do not change to something else: *I decided to stick with journalism.*

sticker /ˈstɪkə(r)/ *noun*: **stickers**
A **sticker** is a sticky label with a message or picture on it displayed *eg* in the window of a shop or on a car: *a bumper sticker saying 'I love California'.*

sticking plaster /ˈstɪkɪŋ plɑːstə(r)/ *noun* (*uncount or count*): **sticking plasters**
Sticking plaster is sticky fabric or plastic that can be stuck on the skin to cover a wound: *He put a piece of sticking plaster on the cut.*

stick-in-the-mud /ˈstɪk ɪn ðə mʌd/ *noun*: **stick-in-the muds** (*informal, derogatory*)
If you call someone a **stick-in-the-mud** you mean that they are opposed to or resist anything new or adventurous: *Come on, join in the fun; don't be such a stick-in-the-mud!* [*opposite* **adventurous**]

stickler /ˈstɪklə(r)/ *noun*: **sticklers**
If someone is a **stickler** for something, such as accuracy or good manners, they think it is very important and insist that others aim for the same standard as they do: *The headmaster was a stickler for discipline.*

sticky /ˈstɪkɪ/ *adjective*: **stickier, stickiest**
1 A **sticky** substance is able or likely to stick to other surfaces: *His fingers were all sticky.* □ *a sheet of sticky labels.* **2** You can describe the weather as **sticky** when it is uncomfortably warm and humid. [*same as* **muggy**] **3** (*informal*) A **sticky** situation is awkward or unpleasant. [*same as* **embarrassing**]
▻ ***phrase*** If you predict that someone will **come to a sticky end**, you mean that their reckless or criminal behaviour will lead to disaster eventually.

stiff /stɪf/ *adjective*; *adverb*
▻ ***adjective***: **stiffer, stiffest**
1 Something that is **stiff** is rigid and not easily bent or folded: *Clean the shoes with a stiff brush.* □ *The sheets were stiff with starch.* **2** If your joints or muscles are **stiff**, they do not bend or move easily, *eg* because of age, cold or too much exertion: *She's getting a bit stiff now but otherwise for an eighty year old she is very healthy.* □ *He got a stiff neck sitting in a draught.* [*opposite* **supple**] **3** If a door or the top on a container is **stiff** it does not open easily. **4** A **stiff** punishment is harsh and severe: *Anyone involved in violent crime will get a stiff sentence if found guilty.* [*opposite* **lenient**] **5** A **stiff** wind blows strongly. [*opposite* **lenient**] **6** If someone's manner or behaviour is **stiff**, it is not relaxed and is rather formal. **7** If you beat a liquid such as egg white or cream until it is **stiff**, you beat it until it is thick and nearly solid. **8** When there is **stiff** competition, it is very difficult to win or succeed. [*same as* **tough**] **9** (*informal*) A **stiff** drink is a strong alcoholic drink.
▻ ***adverb*** (*informal*)
You use **stiff** to describe an extreme effect or feeling: *Their conversation bored me stiff.* □ *worried stiff* □ *scared stiff.*
— *adverb* **stiffly:** *He bowed stiffly.* □ *'How do you do?' he said stiffly.* — *noun* (*uncount*) **stiffness:** *The symptoms are slight fever and pain and stiffness in the joints.*
▻ ***phrase*** For **have** or **keep a stiff upper lip** see **lip**.

stiffen /ˈstɪfən/ *verb*: **stiffens, stiffening, stiffened**
You **stiffen** something, or it **stiffens**, when you make it, or it becomes, stiff or stiffer: *She stiffened his shirt collars with starch.* □ *The lioness stiffened* [= she tensed her muscles and her body became stiff] *as she scented the antelope.* □ *My knees have stiffened up after that long walk.*

stiff-necked /stɪfˈnɛkt/ *adjective*
If you describe someone as **stiff-necked** you mean that they are arrogantly obstinate: *He's being very stiff-necked about the whole thing.* [*same as* **stubborn**; *opposite* **flexible**]

stifle /ˈstaɪfəl/ *verb*: **stifles, stifling, stifled**
1 If you **are stifling**, you find it difficult to breath, especially because of heat or lack of air. **2** If something **is stifled**, it is killed by stopping its breathing. [*same as* **suffocate**] **3** If you **stifle** a sob or a giggle you stop it from being heard; if you **stifle** opposition or development, you suppress it.

stifling /ˈstaɪflɪŋ/ *adjective*
If a room or other place is **stifling** it is unpleasantly hot or airless: *It was stifling in the crowded railway carriage.*

stigma /ˈstɪgmə/ *noun* (*uncount or count*): **stigmas**
If there is a **stigma** attached to something, people regard it as being shameful or disgraceful in some way; if you suffer from the **stigma** of something you have a shameful feeling or a bad reputation because of it: *There is a stigma attached to AIDS that is very difficult to combat.* □ *The stigma of his father's bankruptcy influenced Dickens throughout his life.*

stile /staɪl/ *noun*: **stiles**
A **stile** is a structure built over a wall or fence consist-

ing of a step or steps that you use to cross over the fence or wall.

still[1] /stɪl/ *adverb*
1 Something that used to be so is **still** so if it continues to be so now: *My parents still live on the Island.* □ *They're still very much in love.* □ *He asked if I was still teaching.* □ *You're not still jogging five miles a day, are you?* [see note at **already**] **2** Someone or something is **still** at a certain stage if they have not progressed beyond it: *Go back to bed; it's still dark.* □ *His mother died when he was still a baby.* □ *He can't still be at university, surely?* **3** (*with a negative*) Something that **still** has not happened has not happened up to the present time, but is expected to happen: *I still haven't sent in my application form.* [*same as* **yet**] **4** Something that has not yet happened may **still** happen if it could happen in the future: *Do you think there's still a chance that they may get back together again?* □ *It's not that late; he may still ring.* **5** There is **still** a certain amount of something left if that amount remains: *There were still two weeks to go before the deadline.* □ *We've still got a few copies left.* **6** Something is **still** so if it remains a fact in spite of what has happened or been said: *I don't care what he's done; he's still my son.* □ *It should still be possible to copy the data from another source.* **7** You **still** do something, although there are good reasons not to, and people tell you not to, if you do it in spite of them: *She still insists that she can manage on her own.* □ *He's still determined to take part.* □ *I still don't agree.* □ *I told him to apologize, but he still wouldn't.* **8** (*sentence adverb*) You use **'Still'** to introduce a circumstance that reduces a problem or difficulty: *It's getting very dark. Still, we've got a torch, haven't we?* **9** You use **still** to emphasize comparative adjectives and adverbs; something that is, *eg* **still** better, is even better: *Let's go out for a meal one evening, or, nicer still, get away for a weekend.* □ *We had moved still further away from a solution.* □ *I didn't want to help with the show, still less take part in it.* [*same as* **even**]

still[2] /stɪl/ *adjective or adverb; adjective; noun*
▻ ***adjective*** or ***adverb***: **stiller, stillest**
You stay **still** when you stay in the same position without moving: *We were told to keep quite still.* □ *Who can stay still the longest?* □ *Do stand still.* □ *The animal remained quite still for several seconds, staring at her.*
▻ ***adjective***
1 Still water is flat and calm; **still** air is without movement; **still** weather is calm and settled, without any wind: *The sea was as still as a pond.* □ *the still air of the morning* □ *It was one of those very still days.* [*same as* **calm**; *opposite* **rough, stormy**] **2 Still** drinks are drinks that are not fizzy. [*opposite* **fizzy, effervescent**] — *noun* (*uncount*) **stillness:** *in the stillness of a hot summer afternoon.*
▻ ***noun***: **stills**
A **still** is a photograph of a scene from a film, used *eg* for publicity.

stillborn /ˈstɪlbɔːn/ *adjective*
A **stillborn** baby or young animal is born dead: *The calf was stillborn.*

still life /stɪl ˈlaɪf/ *noun*: **still lifes**
1 A **still life** is a painting, drawing or photograph of an object or objects, such as fruit, cut flowers, or dead fish or birds, rather than of living things: *She's painting a still life of a basket of fruit.* **2** (*uncount*) **Still life** is this kind of art or photography: *one of the greatest Dutch painters of still life.*

stilt /stɪlt/ *noun*: **stilts**
1 Stilts are either of a pair of long poles with footrests part way up, on which a person can walk around supported high above the ground. **2 Stilts** are any of a set of wooden or metal props on which *eg* a building or jetty is supported above ground or water level.

stilted /ˈstɪltɪd/ *adjective*
If someone's speech or behaviour is **stilted** it is stiff, formal and unnatural: *He made a few stilted attempts at conversation and then lapsed into embarrassed silence.*

stimulant /ˈstɪmjʊlənt/ *noun*: **stimulants**
A **stimulant** is a drug, alcoholic drink or other substance that has the effect of making the body or mind more alert or energetic.

stimulate /ˈstɪmjʊleɪt/ *verb*: **stimulates, stimulating, stimulated**
1 If something **stimulates** some activity or reaction in your body it causes that activity or reaction: *Chewing stimulates the production of saliva.* **2** One thing **stimulates** another when it causes it to become more active or grow or develop faster: *a reduction in interest rates intended to stimulate the economy* □ *The longer days and stronger light of spring and summer stimulates growth in plants.* **3** If something **stimulates** you it fills you with interest and enthusiasm; something **stimulates** interest or enthusiasm when it creates or encourages it: *methods of teaching that stimulate children's creative imagination.* — *adjective* **stimulating:** *a stimulating experience.* — *noun* (*uncount*) **stimulation** /stɪmjʊˈleɪʃən/: *the stimulation of a nerve ending.*

stimulus /ˈstɪmjʊləs/ *noun*: **stimuli**
A **stimulus** is something that causes a reaction, activity or development, or encourages greater effort: *tax reductions intended to provide a stimulus to the property market* □ *an organism that responses to the stimulus of light.*

sting /stɪŋ/ *noun; verb*
▻ ***noun***: **stings**
1 An insect's or other creature's **sting** is a sharp part that can pierce skin and inject poison; a plant's **sting** is a substance that irritates the skin, usually contained on hairs or sharp projecting parts on its surface; a **sting** is also the act of injecting poison in this way, or the poison injected: *a bee sting* □ *Some types of jellyfish can give you a painful sting.* **2** A **sting** is also any sharp tingling pain or any sharply wounding quality or effect, such as is felt by a vicious insult: *the sting of the salt air on his face* □ *He realized that the memory of her had lost its sting at last.*
▻ ***verb***: **stings, stinging, stung**
1 To **sting** means to pierce, poison or wound with a sting: *She was stung by a wasp.* □ *stinging nettles.* **2** To **sting** also means to produce a sharp tingling pain, either physically or emotionally: *He was stung by the criticism.* **3** (*in the passive*) If you **are stung** into action of some sort, you are goaded or incited by *eg* an insult into taking that action. [*same as* **provoked**]
▻ ***phrases*** **1** If something such as a set of circumstances or a piece of news has a **sting in the tail**, it has a part or consequence that it is unexpectedly unpleasant or harmful. **2** If something **takes the sting out** of an unpleasant event or situation, it makes it slightly less painful or difficult to accept.

stingy /ˈstɪndʒɪ/ *adjective*: **stingier, stingiest** (*informal*)
A **stingy** person is mean and will not give or spend money willingly; a **stingy** amount is a very small, ungenerous amount: *The food was alright but the portions were a bit stingy.* [*same as* **mean**; *opposite* **generous**]

stink /stɪŋk/ *verb; noun*
▻ ***verb***: **stinks, stinking, stank, stunk**
1 Something **stinks** when it gives off a strong very

unpleasant smell: *The meat was stinking to high heaven.* [*same as* **reek**, **stench**] **2** If something **stinks** a place out, it fills it with a strong, usually very unpleasant, smell: *He stank the place out with his cheap aftershave.* **3** (*informal*) If you say that a situation or set of circumstances **stink**, you mean that it is offensive, contemptibly bad or immoral: *I think they're up to no good; the whole set up stinks.*

▻ ***noun***: **stinks** (*usually used in the singular*)
A **stink** is a strong and very unpleasant smell: *the stink of rotting fish.* [*same as* **stench**]

▻ ***phrase*** (*informal*) If someone **kicks up a stink**, they make a fuss by complaining loudly.

stinking /ˈstɪŋkɪŋ/ *adjective*; *adverb*

▻ ***adjective***
1 Something that is **stinking** has a very strong unpleasant smell: *Do you have to smoke those stinking cigars?* **2** (*informal*) You can describe something that you think is very unpleasant or bad as **stinking**: *I had a stinking cold.*

▻ ***adverb*** (*informal*; *intensifying*)
Stinking means 'extremely': *He's stinking rich.*

stint /stɪnt/ *noun*: **stints**
A **stint** is a fixed period or amount of work, especially work that is shared with others: *He did a five-year stint as party chairman.* [*same as* **term**, **spell**]

stipulate /ˈstɪpjʊleɪt/ *verb*: **stipulates**, **stipulating**, **stipulated** (*formal*)
You **stipulate** something when you state it as a necessary condition, *eg* of an agreement or contract: *He has told us what sort of material to use but he hasn't stipulated the colour.* ▫ *The government stipulated that peace negotiations could not go ahead until there was a permanent ceasefire.* [*same as* **specify**] — *noun* (*count or uncount*) **stipulation** /stɪpjʊˈleɪʃən/: *He was given a temporary visa with the stipulation that he leave the country as soon as it ran out.* [*same as* **specification**]

stir /stɜː(r)/ *verb*; *noun*

▻ ***verb***: **stirs**, **stirring**, **stirred**
1 You **stir** something when you mix it or move it around by making repeated circular movements with an implement such as a spoon: *The children were allowed to stir the mixture for the Christmas pudding.* ▫ *'Did you put any sugar in my tea?' 'Yes I did, but I think I may have forgotten to stir it.'* **2** You **stir** something into a mixture when you put or mix it in by stirring: *Stir a little cream into the soup before serving.* **3** Something **stirs** you or **stirs** you into action when it has the effect of arousing strong feelings or feelings sufficently strong that you act: *His pathetic appeal to her stirred feelings of sympathy and regret.* ▫ *The union was stirred into action by the announcement of a further round of redundancies.* **4** Something **stirs** when it makes or is caused to make a slight or single movement: *A gentle breeze was stirring the tops of the pine trees.* **5** You **stir** when you wake up and begin to move; you **stir** from a resting, sitting or lying position when you get up or move: *She stirred in her sleep and moaned slightly.* ▫ *The doorbell rang but she didn't stir from her chair.*

▻ ***noun***: **stirs**
1 A **stir** is a circular movement made with a spoon or other implement: *Give the stew a stir occasionally.* **2** If something creates or causes a **stir**, it creates or causes an excited reaction: *The news of his resignation created quite a stir.* [*same as* **commotion**]

> ***phrasal verb***
> (*derogatory*) Someone **stirs up** trouble, or **stirs** things **up**, when they cause trouble: *He's been stirring things up between the workers and the management.*

stir-fry /ˈstɜːfraɪ/ *verb*: **stir-fries**, **stir-frying**, **stir-fried**
You **stir-fry** food when you fry it very quickly over a high heat, and, at the same time, stir or toss the pieces of meat or vegetables in the frying-pan so that they cook evenly.

stirring /ˈstɜːrɪŋ/ *adjective*
A **stirring** speech or story is one that makes people feel excited or enthusiastic. [*same as* **rousing**, **inspiring**]

stirrup /ˈstɪrəp/ *noun*: **stirrups**
A **stirrup** is one of the two metal loops hanging from straps on either side of a horse's saddle, used by the rider to support his or her feet.

stitch /stɪtʃ/ *noun*; *verb*

▻ ***noun***: **stitches**
1 In sewing, a **stitch** is a single fixed length of thread on the surface of fabric or joining two pieces of fabric together, made by pushing the point of the needle in at one place and out at another, pulling the thread through as you do so; in knitting, a **stitch** is a loop linked to others below and on either side, made by twisting the yarn around the needles. **2** A **stitch** is any of the various ways that these are made: *back stitch* ▫ *She demonstrated French knots and other embroidery stitches.* ▫ *Slip a stitch, knit two (stitches) together and pass the slip stitch over ....* **3** A **stitch** is also a length of thread or other similar material used to join the edges of a wound: *When he cut his hand he needed twelve stitches.* ▫ *How soon after the operation will I get the stitches out?* **4** If you get a **stitch**, you feel a sharp ache in the side of your body especially while you are running. **5** (*informal*) When you do not have a **stitch** on, you are naked without even the smallest piece of clothing on your body.

▻ ***verb***: **stitches**, **stitching**, **stitched**
You **stitch** something when you join two pieces or edges together, close up a gap, or decorate the surface of something, with stitches.

▻ ***phrase*** (*informal*) If someone is **in stitches** they are helpless with laughter.

stoat /stoʊt/ *noun*: **stoats**
A **stoat** is a small brown flesh-eating animal similar to a weasel.

stock /stɒk/ *noun*; *adjective*; *verb*

▻ ***noun***: **stocks**
1 (*uncount*) The total amount of goods for sale stored or displayed in a shop is its **stock**. **2** A **stock** of something is a supply kept for future use: *We always keep a good stock of magazines in the waiting-room.* **3** (*uncount or count*) **Stock** is also used to refer to equipment or raw material in use: *British Rail has ordered new rolling stock.* [= engines and carriages] ▫ *current stocks of coal.* **4** (*uncount or count*) **Stock** is liquid in which meat or vegetables have been cooked, used as a base for soups and sauces; a **stock** is a particular kind of this: *chicken stock* ▫ *Boil the beef with an onion, carrot and some herbs to make a clear stock.* ▫ *a stock pot.* [=a large pan used for making stock] **5** The **stock** of a rifle or similar gun is the shaped wooden or plastic part that is held against the user's shoulder. **6** (*uncount*) **Stock** is farm animals collectively. [*same as* **livestock**] **7** (*uncount or count*) **Stock** is the money raised by a company through the selling of shares; **stocks** are the total shares issued by a company or the government or held by an individual shareholder; **stocks** are also a group of shares bought or sold as a unit. **8** (*uncount*) When you talk about people being of a particular **stock** you mean they are descended from people of that type: *He's of good peasant stock.* **9** Someone or something's **stock** is the degree to which people regard them or it in a favourable way:

measures that were intended to raise the government's stock with the public.
▻ ***adjective***
1 Stock means of a standard type or size constantly in demand and always kept in stock: *It is not one of our stock items.* **2** A **stock** phrase is one that is used a lot, especially so over-used as to be meaningless: *The minister responded with the usual stock phrases about the upturn in the economy.*
▻ ***verb***: **stocks, stocking, stocked**
A shop or wholesale supplier **stocks** a particular item when they keep a supply of them for sale: *Do you stock children's books?* [*same as* **keep**]
▻ ***phrases*** **1** If a shop or supplier has something **in stock**, they have it on the premises available for sale immediately: *Do you have the latest* Rolling Stones *album in stock?* **2** For **lock, stock and barrel** see **lock**. **3** If an item normally for sale in a shop is **out of** or **not in stock**, it is not available for sale because it has all been sold or has not yet reached the shop. **4** You **take stock**, or **take stock** of a situation, when you think carefully about every aspect of a situation, usually in order to make a decision about what to do next: *She says she will work for another five years and then take stock.*

> ***phrasal verb***
> You **stock up** on a particular item when you buy a large amount or number of it so that you have a good supply for future use: *stock up on tinned foods.*

stockbroker /ˈstɒkbroʊkə(r)/ *noun*: **stockbrokers**
A **stockbroker** is a person who buys and sells stocks and shares for customers in return for a fee.

stock exchange /ˈstɒk ɪkstʃeɪndʒ/ *noun*: **stock exchanges**
A **stock exchange** is a place where stocks and shares are bought and sold by professional dealers on behalf of customers: *the London Stock Exchange.*

stocking /ˈstɒkɪŋ/ *noun*: **stockings**
A **stocking** is either of a pair of close-fitting coverings for women's legs, made of fine often transparent fabric such as nylon or silk. [see picture at **clothing**]

stockinged /ˈstɒkɪŋd/ *adjective*
If you are in your **stockinged** feet, you have socks, stockings or tights on, but no shoes.

stock-in-trade /stɒk ɪn ˈtreɪd/ *noun* (*singular*)
Someone's **stock-in-trade** is the basic equipment, skills and personal qualities needed for their particular trade or activity: *an urbane manner is the politician's stock-in-trade.*

stockist /ˈstɒkɪst/ *noun*: **stockists**
A **stockist** is a person or shop that stocks a particular item: *The new software should be available from your local stockist from March.*

stock market /ˈstɒk mɑːkɪt/ *noun*: **stock markets**
A **stock market** is a stock exchange, or the trading carried on there: *Dealing on the stock market was brisk.*

stockpile /ˈstɒkpaɪl/ *noun*; *verb*
▻ ***noun***: **stockpiles**
A **stockpile** of a particular commodity is a large store of it kept for future use, especially in times when it is in short supply: *a stockpile of weapons and military equipment.*
▻ ***verb***: **stockpiles, stockpiling, stockpiled**
You **stockpile** something when you obtain quantities of it over a period of time so that you have a large store for future use: *Power stations have been stockpiling coal in preparation for the threatened miners' strike.*

stockroom /ˈstɒkruːm/ *noun*: **stockrooms**
A **stockroom** is a room where goods are stored, especially in a shop or factory.

stock-still /stɒkˈstɪl/ *adjective or, adverb*
Someone is **stock-still**, or is standing **stock-still**, when they are, or are standing, absolutely still without moving at all: *He was standing stock-still, staring vacantly into space.*

stocktaking /ˈstɒkteɪkɪŋ/ *noun* (*uncount*)
1 Stocktaking is the process of making a detailed inventory of all the goods held on the premises of a shop or factory at a particular time, usually for accounting purposes. **2 Stocktaking** is also the process of taking stock of *eg* a situation, especially so as to make a decision about what your next course of action will be.

stocky /ˈstɒkɪ/ *adjective*: **stockier, stockiest**
A **stocky** person is broad and strong-looking, and usually not very tall: *a stocky little man.* [*same as* **thickset**]

stodgy /ˈstɒdʒɪ/ *adjective*: **stodgier, stodgiest**
1 Stodgy food is heavy, sticky and very filling, and often rather tasteless: *It reminded him of the stodgy puddings he used to get in school.* **2** A **stodgy** person is dull and serious; a **stodgy** book or other piece of writing is uninteresting and difficult to read.

stoic /ˈstoʊɪk/ or **stoical** /ˈstoʊɪkəl/ *adjective*
You describe a person as **stoic** or **stoical** when they endure pain, misfortune or difficulties without complaint: *He sat listening with an expression of stoic resignation on his face.* □ *He doesn't make a fuss when he is in pain; he's very stoical.* — *adverb* **stoically:** *She goes on stoically accepting his abuse, year after year.*

stoicism /ˈstoʊɪsɪzm/ *noun* (*uncount*)
Stoicism is the quality of enduring, or the tendency to endure, pain, misfortune or suffering without complaint: *I admire her stoicism.*

stoke /stoʊk/ *verb*: **stokes, stoking, stoked**
You **stoke** a fire or boiler when you add more fuel to it so that it burns with greater heat.

> ***phrasal verb***
> **stoke up** Something **stokes up** trouble or enthusiasm when it has the effect of intensifying it or making it greater.

stole /stoʊl/ *verb*
Stole is the past tense of **steal**.

stolen /ˈstoʊlən/ *verb*; *adjective*
▻ ***verb***
Stolen is the past participle of **steal**.
▻ ***adjective:*** *stolen goods.*

stolid /ˈstɒlɪd/ *adjective*
Stolid means showing little or no interest or emotion, especially in situations where some show of interest or emotion would be usual or normal. [*same as* **impassive**; *opposite* **interested**, **lively**] — *adverb* **stolidly:** *He walked past, stolidly ignoring their whispers and sideways glances.*

stomach /ˈstʌmək/ *noun*; *verb*
▻ ***noun***: **stomachs**
1 The **stomach** is the bag-like organ inside the body into which food passes when swallowed, and where the first stage of digestion takes place: *A cow has two stomaches.* □ *cancer of the stomach.* **2** The area around the abdomen is also loosely referred to as the **stomach**: *I used to have a nice flat stomach.* □ *You'll have to pull your stomach in if you want to tie those trousers.* □ *The doctor prodded her stomach.* □ *They left*

the restaurant with stomachs bulging. [*same as* **belly**; see picture at **body**] **3** (*uncount, often with a negative; informal*) If you say you have the **stomach** for something unpleasant, you mean you have enough courage or determination to do it or face it; if you have the **stomach** for a particular food or meal, you have the desire to eat it: *He dropped out at the last minute; he doesn't have the stomach for the fight.*

▷ ***verb***: **stomachs, stomaching, stomached**
(*often in negative statements or questions; informal*) You can **stomach** someone or something when you can bear them or put up with them: *I can't stomach him; he's the most arrogant man I have ever met.* [*same as* **tolerate**]

stomach-ache /ˈstʌmək eɪk/ *noun* (*uncount or count*): **stomach-aches**
If you have **stomach-ache** or a **stomach-ache**, you have a pain in your stomach.

stomp /stɒmp/ *verb*: **stomps, stomping, stomped**
You **stomp** about when you stamp your feet or tread heavily as you walk: *He went stomping out of the house in a rage.*

stone /stoun/ *noun; verb*
▷ ***noun***: **stones**
1 (*uncount, often adjectival*) **Stone** is the hard solid mineral substance of which rocks are made: *hard as stone* □ *a stone wall* □ *a stone fireplace.* **2** A **stone** is a piece of this, especially one that is fairly small: *He raked the stones off the soil.* **3** A **stone** is any piece of this shaped and used for a particular purpose: *a millstone.* **4** A **stone** is also a shaped and polished piece of a precious or semi-precious mineral: *The largest stone in the crown was a massive diamond.* [*same as* **jewel**] **5** The hard seed in the centre of certain fruits is also called a **stone**: *a cherry stone.* **6** A **stone** is also any small hard, especially rounded, mass, *eg* of hail, or of minerals and salts produced in a diseased organ such as the gall bladder or the kidneys. **7** A **stone** is a standard unit of weight equal to 14 pounds or 6.35 kilograms: *He lost six stone.*

▷ ***verb***: **stones, stoning, stoned**
1 To **stone** someone means to throw stones at them, especially as a punishment: *He was stoned to death by the mob.* **2** You **stone** fruit, such as cherries, olives or peaches, when you remove the single large seeds inside them.

▷ ***phrases*** **1** You **leave no stone unturned** when you try all possibilities or make every possible effort: *The police inspector assured her that he would leave no stone unturned in the hunt for her husband's murderer.* **2** (*informal*) A place that is **a stone's throw away** from another place is a short distance away: *The lake was just a stone's throw away from their back door.*

stone-cold /stounˈkould/ *adjective*
Something that is **stone-cold** is completely cold: *You're late and your meal is stone-cold.* □ *stone-cold soup.*

stoned /stound/ *adjective* (*slang*)
If a person is **stoned**, they are either very drunk or are under the influence of drugs.

stone-dead /stounˈdɛd/ *adjective*
Stone-dead means completely dead.

stone-deaf /stounˈdɛf/ *adjective*
Stone-deaf means completely deaf: *He can't hear a word you say; he's stone-deaf.*

stonemason /ˈstounmeɪsən/ *noun*: **stonemasons**
A **stonemason** is a person skilled in shaping stone for building work.

stony /ˈstɒnɪ/ *adjective*: **stonier, stoniest**
1 Stony ground is covered with or contains a lot of stones. **2 Stony** also means having a hard unfriendly or unfeeling appearance or quality: *his stony gaze* □ *stony-hearted.* [*same as* **hostile, cold**]

stony-broke /stounɪˈbrouk/ *adjective* (*informal*)
If you say you are **stony-broke**, you mean you have absolutely no money. [*same as* **penniless**]

stood /stʊd/ *verb*
Stood is the past tense and past participle of **stand**.

stooge /stuːdʒ/ *noun*: **stooges**
1 A **stooge** is a performer whose role is to provide a comedian with opportunities for making jokes, often also the butt of the jokes. **2** You can also refer to a person who acts as someone's assistant as that person's **stooge**, especially when they are given unpleasant tasks to do or are otherwise exploited by that person.

stool /stuːl/ *noun*: **stools**
A **stool** is a seat with no back and no arms. [see picture at **bedroom**]

stoop /stuːp/ *verb; noun*
▷ ***verb***: **stoops, stooping, stooped**
1 You **stoop** when you carry the upper part of your body bent forwards and downwards. **2** If someone condescends or lowers themselves to do something you can say that they **stoop** to do it: *How could she stoop so low as to marry him?*

▷ ***noun*** (*used in the singular*) *The old woman walked with a pronounced stoop.*

stop /stɒp/ *verb; noun*
▷ ***verb***: **stops, stopping, stopped**
1 a You **stop** something when you don't let it happen, or you prevent it from continuing: *We tried to stop her from rushing off.* □ *A first-aider must know how to stop bleeding.* □ *The important thing is to get the fighting stopped at once.* □ *She had decided what she wanted to do, and no-one was going to stop her.* □ *It's too late to stop the spread of the cancer.* **b** You **stop** doing something that you have been doing for some time when you no longer do it: *Everyone stopped what they were doing and listened.* □ *I've tried to stop smoking lots of times.* □ *Stop behaving like an idiot.* □ *It's stopped raining at last.* □ *At least the cut seems to have stopped bleeding.* □ *Make a practice of stopping to read over what you've written every so often.* □ *now that women don't have to stop work at 60.* □ *After a lot of stopping and starting we got the project launched at last.* □ *'Ouch! Stop it! That's sore!'* **c** Things that are moving, such as people or vehicles, **stop** or **are stopped** when they come to a halt, or do not continue to move: *Does this train stop at Kingussie?* □ *The driver managed to stop the train just in time.* □ *We asked him to stop and let us out at the top of Hanover Street.* □ *We could try and stop a taxi.* □ *A man stopped her and asked if she had change for the meter.* □ *We stopped to get some aspirin from the chemist.*

> Notice the difference between **stop** *doing something* and **stop** *to do something*: if you **stop** *to do* something you stop doing what you are doing, or going where you are going, in order to do something else: *He stopped speaking. The lecturer stopped occasionally to check a date in her notes. I stopped to get petrol. Some people just never stop to think* (or *never stop and think*) [= give themselves time to think before they do something].

d You **stop** somewhere on a journey when you stay there for some time before continuing: *We stopped for the night at St Michel-sur-Odon.* **e** Something that has been happening **stops** when it doesn't continue any more: *Wait for the bleeps to stop before recording your message.* □ *I think the rain's stopped.* □ *Their correspondence stopped abruptly in 1878 for some reason, and never resumed.* **f** A machine or instrument **stops** or **is stopped** when it is switched off, or does not work any longer: *She stopped the tape and set it to rewind.* □ *The clock's stopped again.* **2 a** You **stop** someone's pay when you prevent them from being paid; you **stop** money from someone's wages when you deduct it. *They threatened to stop his grant.* **b** You **stop** a cheque or other form of payment made through a bank when you instruct your bank not to pay it. **3 a** You **stop** a gap when you block it with something: *They'd used some crumpled newspaper to stop the hole.* **b** (*music*) Instrumental players **stop** a string or a hole when they place a finger over it.

▻ ***noun*: stops**

1 (*used in the singular*) Something that is moving comes to a **stop** or is brought to a **stop** when it gets slower and stops moving: *The driver brought the bus to a stop.* □ *We skidded and came to a stop on the grass verge.* [*same as* **halt**] **2** A **stop** is a place where buses or trains stop regularly for passengers to get on or off: *I'm getting off at the next stop.* □ *They've temporarily shifted the bus stop.* **3** Things also come to a **stop** when they do not progress any further: *The fitters' strike had brought production to a complete stop* [*same as* **halt, standstill**] **4** A wedge or other device that holds a door open is called a door **stop**. **5** A full **stop** is the punctuation mark (.).

▻ ***phrases*** **1** You **put a stop to** something when you prevent it from continuing to happen: *I'll soon put a stop to his nonsense.* **2** Someone who will **stop at nothing** is ready to do anything, no matter how wicked or dishonest, to get what they want. **3** For **stop dead** see **dead**.

phrasal verbs

stop off You **stop off** somewhere during a journey when you spend some time there: *I usually stop off at my mother's on the way north.* [*same as* **break your journey**]

stop over You **stop over** somewhere during a journey when you stay one or more nights there: *We'll be stopping over in Singapore for a night on the way to Australia.* [see also **stopover**]

stop up You **stop up** a hole or a gap when you block it with something: *They'd pushed crumpled newspaper up the chimney to stop it up.*

stopgap /ˈstɒpgap/ *noun* (*used in the singular*)

A **stopgap** is something that acts as a temporary substitute for something until that thing can be brought into use or is available: *stopgap measures.*

stopover /ˈstɒpoʊvə(r)/ *noun*: **stopovers**

A **stopover** is a short stay somewhere between two parts of a journey: *They are flying from London to Sydney with a stopover in Singapore.*

stoppage /ˈstɒpɪdʒ/ *noun*: **stoppages**

1 A **stoppage** is an act of blocking or a blockage: *The drain is overflowing because of a stoppage somewhere.* **2** (*especially BrE; usually in the plural*) **Stoppages** are amounts of money, *eg* for income tax or national insurance contributions, that are officially deducted from wages before they are paid to an employee: *He earns £250 a week, before stoppages.* [*same as* **deductions**] **3** A **stoppage** is a stopping of work, as in a strike: *Brirtish Rail lost millions of pounds as a result of the stoppage.*

stopper /ˈstɒpə(r)/ *noun*: **stoppers**

A **stopper** is an object, such as a cork or plug, that is used to close an opening in a container, especially a bottle or jar for holding liquids.

stopwatch /ˈstɒpwɒtʃ/ *noun*: **stopwatches**

A **stopwatch** is a watch fitted with a device that can instantly stop and start the hands so that the time taken by something, *eg* a race, can be measured accurately.

storage /stɔːrɪdʒ/ *noun* (*uncount*)

1 Storage is the act of storing or the state of being stored: *Methods such as freezing and drying are solutions to the problems of storage for goods such as meat.* □ *They put their furniture in storage while they were abroad.* **2** (*often adjectival*) **Storage** is also space used for storing things: *a freezer with a large storage capacity.* **3 Storage** is also the process of storing information in a computer's memory.

store /stɔː(r)/ *noun*; *verb*

▻ ***noun*: stores**

1 A **store** of something is a supply kept for future use: *Squirrels have a store of nuts for the winter.* [*same as* **stock**] **2 a** A **store** is a shop, especially a large one with several departments each selling a particular category of goods (**department store**), or one that is part of a chain (**chain store**): *The company is opening new stores in several major cities.* □ *She wandered round the store looking for the food department.* **b** (*AmE*) A **store** is also a shop, especially one selling a particular type of goods: *a general store* [=selling a variety of goods, especially household goods] □ *a grocery store* □ *a liquor store.* **3** A **store** is a place where stocks or supplies are kept, *eg* a warehouse: *a grain store.* **4** A **store** is also a computer's memory.

▻ ***verb*: stores, storing, stored**

1 You **store** something or **store** it away when you put it aside so that it may be used later: *The coal was stored in the cellar.* **2** You **store** furniture or other belongings when you put them into a warehouse for temporary safekeeping. **3** Information **is stored** on a computer when it is held in the computer's memory.

▻ ***phrases*** **1** You talk about something that is **in store** for you when you are discussing something that is about to happen or which is destined to happen: *She had no idea what was in store for her when she first got married.* **2** If you **set** or **lay great store by** something, you value that thing highly: *She sets great store by his advice.*

phrasal verb

store up **1** You **store** something **up** when you build up a supply of it for future use: *The bears store up fat for the long winter months.* **2** If you **store up** trouble or difficulties for yourself, you do, or do not do, something which brings you trouble or difficulties at some later time: *By not disciplining the children now, they are storing up trouble for the future.* [*same as* **reserve**]

storehouse /ˈstɔːhaʊs/ *noun*: **storehouses**

1 A **storehouse** is a place where things are stored. **2** You can also refer to a person as a **storehouse** of knowledge or ideas, when they have a large fund of useful knowledge or ideas. [*same as* **treasury**]

storey /ˈstɔːrɪ/ (*AmE* **story**) *noun*: **storeys** (*AmE* **stories**)

A **storey** in a building is a level, floor or tier: *a multi-storey car park.*

stork /stɔːk/ *noun*: **storks**

A **stork** is any of various kinds of large wading bird with a long beak, neck and legs.

storm /stɔːm/ *noun*; *verb*

▻ ***noun***: **storms**

1 (*often adjectival*) A **storm** is an outbreak of violent weather, with severe winds and heavy falls of rain, hail or snow, often with thunder and lightning: *storm damage* ▫ *The shipping forecast is for gales and heavy storms in the North Sea.* ▫ *a thunderstorm* ▫ *storm-force winds.* **2** You can also refer to a violent reaction, outburst or show of feeling as a **storm**: *The government's decision created a storm of protest.* ▫ *His remarks caused quite a storm in literary circles.* [*same as* **uproar**] **3** A **storm** of something, such as abuse, is a furious burst of it.

▻ ***verb***: **storms, storming, stormed**

1 Someone **storms** somewhere when they go or leave in a violently angry manner: *He stormed out, slamming the door behind him.* ▫ *She went storming out of the meeting.* [*same as* **charge**] **2** Someone **storms** when they shout angrily: *He stormed and raged, but still she would not change her mind.* **3** Soldiers **storm** an enemy position when they make a sudden violent attack on it so as to capture it: *The army stormed the citadel and captured the king.*

▻ ***phrases*** **1** (*informal*) If you describe an event as a **storm in a teacup**, you mean that you think that a lot of fuss is being made over something relatively unimportant. **2 a** If an army **takes** a place **by storm**, they capture it in a sudden violent attack. [*same as* **seize**] **b** A performer or performance **takes** a place **by storm** when they gain rapid and widespread popularity or approval for their performance: *The film took America by storm.*

stormy /ˈstɔːmɪ/ *adjective*: **stormier, stormiest**

1 The weather is **stormy** when there are strong winds, often with rain, hail or snow, and thunder and lightning. [*opposite* **calm**] **2** If you have a **stormy** relationship with someone you fight or argue with them a lot.

story[1] /ˈstɔːrɪ/ *noun*: **stories**

1 A **story** is a written or spoken description of an event or series of events, real or imaginary: *Tell us a bedtime story.* ▫ *a love story* ▫ *Have you heard the story of the three little pigs?* ▫ *She writes short stories.* [=pieces of fiction that are much shorter than a novel and are often published as part of a collection] **2** A **story** or **storyline** is the plot of a novel, play or film: *The film is full of action, but it doesn't have much of a story.* **3** A **story** is also an article printed in a newspaper or magazine: *He has applied for a court order to prevent the newspaper from printing the story.* ▫ *He was abroad when the story broke.* [=when it first appeared in the newspapers] **4** (*informal*) If someone tells **stories**, they tell lies.

▻ ***phrases*** **1** If you say that available information or facts are **not the whole story** or are **only part of the story**, you mean that there are further facts or additional information which must also be considered in order to get an accurate or complete picture of something. **2** If you are discussing something that is the case in one situation and you go on to discuss another situation where it is also the case, you can say that it is **the same story** in the second situation: *The number of full-time jobs is falling in Britain, and in many other European countries, it's the same story.* **3** You use **the same old story** to refer to an unpleasant or undesirable situation that happens again and again: *It's the same old story; he came from a broken home and got involved in crime as a young teenager.* **4** You use the phrase '**the story goes**' when you are about to tell someone something that is said or believed by many people: *The story goes that he was the son of an Indian prince.*

story[2] see **storey**.

stout /staʊt/ *adjective*

1 If you describe a person, especially an older man, as **stout**, you mean that they are rather fat: *He's getting a bit stout.* **2 Stout** things are thick, strongly constructed and unlikely to break or burst: *You'll need a pair of stout shoes if you want to go hill-walking.* [*same as* **sturdy**] **3** You can describe people or their behaviour as **stout** when they are courageous or determined: *a stout-hearted gentleman* ▫ *He has always been a stout supporter of the party.* ▫ *He made a stout defence of the government.*

stove /stoʊv/ *noun*: **stoves**

A **stove** is a cooker. [see picture at **kitchen**]

stow /stoʊ/ *verb*: **stows, stowing, stowed**

You **stow** something, or **stow** it away, when you put or pack it away, so that it is stored out of sight or where it will not be in the way: *The packing cases were stowed in the ship's hold.* ▫ *You can stow your clothes away in this locker.* [*same as* **store**]

phrasal verb

If someone **stows away** on a ship, aircraft or other vehicle, they hide somewhere on it in the hope of travelling free.

stowaway /ˈstoʊəweɪ/ *noun*: **stowaways**

A **stowaway** is a person who secretly boards a ship or aircraft and hides somewhere on it so as to travel free.

straddle /ˈstradəl/ *verb*: **straddles, straddling, straddled**

1 You **straddle** something when you stand or sit with your legs on either side of it: *He sat on the roof, straddling the ridge.* **2** Something **straddles** a place or period of time when it crosses it from one side to the other: *an aqueduct straddling the valley.*

straggle /ˈstragəl/ *verb*: **straggles, straggling, straggled**

1 Something **straggles** when it grows, moves or spreads loosely and untidily over an area: *weeds straggling over the path.* **2** People or animals **straggle** when they move or stray away from a main group singly or in small numbers: *She called to the children who were straggling behind.*

[*same as* **stray**]

straggler /ˈstraglə(r)/ *noun*: **stragglers**

A **straggler** is a person or animal that has fallen behind or otherwise become detached from a main group.

straggly /ˈstraglɪ/ *adjective*: **stragglier, straggliest**

Straggly things grow or spread out in an untidy way: *straggly unwashed hair* ▫ *Her hair was long and straggly.*

straight /streɪt/ *adjective or adverb*; *adverb*; *noun*

▻ ***adjective or adverb***; **straighter, straightest**

1 Something that is **straight** does not bend or curve: *a straight line* ▫ *You should overtake only on a straight stretch of road.* ▫ *tall and straight, like the trunk of a fir tree.* **2** Something is **straight** when it is absolutely level or upright, not sloping or leaning backwards, forwards or sideways: *When picking up something heavy, bend your knees but keep your back straight.* ▫ *Sit straight.* ▫ *That picture isn't hanging straight.* **3 Straight** hair has no waves or curls in it: *She wore her hair short and straight with a fringe.* **4** Things are **straight** when they are tidy and well organized: *I'm going to spend next week getting the house straight.* [*same as* **tidy**; see also *phrases* below] **5** You are **straight** with someone when you answer them honestly and give your own opinion frankly; **straight** talking is frank discussion and the honest, sometimes cruelly honest, expression of opinion. [*same as* **honest, frank**] **6** You have a **straight** choice when there are only two people or things to choose between; a **straight** fight is a contest between two people only; you make a **straight** swap at a shop when you exchange one item for another of the same value, so that there is no need for a further cash transaction. **7** You have a number of **straight** wins or successes when you have a continuous series of them: *She got straight As in her English assignments.* ▫ *The Scottish had seven straight wins before losing to the Welsh.* ▫ *I won my tennis match in straight sets.* [= I won both the first two sets, so that there was no need for a third] [*same as* **consecutive, successive**] **8** You take whisky **straight** if you don't add water to it. [*same as* **neat**] **9** (*informal*) Two people are **straight** when they have paid what they owe each other, and neither owes the other anything more. [*same as* **quits**] **10** A **straight** actor is someone who performs in serious drama as distinct from musicals or comedy shows. [*same as* **serious**] **11** (*informal*) A **straight** person is a heterosexual as distinct from a homosexual.

▻ ***adverb***

Straight means

1 directly or in a direct line, without changing direction: *The bathroom's straight ahead of you as you go up the stairs.* ▫ *She was staring straight in front of her.* ▫ *That's their house, straight opposite.* ▫ *He walked straight into a lamp post.* ▫ *This road leads straight into the centre of town.* ▫ *The smoke was rising straight up into the sky.* ▫ *Go straight on till you get to the crossroads.* ▫ *It sank straight to the bottom.* [compare **right**] **2** directly or immediately, without doing anything else first: *I'm going straight to the police.* ▫ *Now go straight back to bed.* ▫ *We're leaving straight after lunch.* [compare **right**]

▻ ***noun*: straights**

1 A **straight** is a straight section, *eg* of a road or race track: *As they enter the final straight it's difficult to see who's leading.* **2** (*informal*) A **straight** is a heterosexual person, as opposed to a homosexual.

▻ ***phrases*** **1** If you say you can't **see straight** or can't **think straight** you mean that you can't see or think clearly, *eg* because you are very tired. **2** You **get** something **straight** when you make sure you know and understand the facts of a situation: *Look, let's get this straight. You mean there are two students with the same name?* [see also **straight**, *adjective* sense 4] **3** (*informal*) Criminals **go straight** when they commit no further crimes and lead an honest life. **4** You **keep a straight face** when you prevent yourself smiling or laughing, especially with difficulty: *The statement was so ridiculous that I could hardly keep a straight face.* **5** You do something **straight away** when you do it immediately. **6** For **straight from the shoulder** see **shoulder**. **7** (*informal*) You say something **straight out** when you express your opinion frankly: *I told her straight out that she was wrong.*

straighten /'streɪtən/ *verb*: **straightens, straightening, straightened**

You **straighten** something when you make it straight or level; something **straightens** when it no longer curves or bends and becomes straight: *Women used to use a hot iron to straighten their hair.* ▫ *She straightened his pillows and tidied his bed.* ▫ *He found he couldn't straighten his back.* ▫ *The engineers had to blast through rock to straighten the bends in the road.* ▫ *The road straightens for a ten mile stretch.*

phrasal verbs

straighten out **1** If you **straighten** problems or difficulties **out**, you resolve them or put them right: *He's been trying to straighten out some of the firm's financial problems.* ▫ *I have no idea how to straighten out the mess we've got ourselves into.* **2** If someone who has been behaving badly or doing things in the wrong way **is straightened out**, they stop behaving badly or doing things in the wrong way and begin to behave properly or correctly.

straighten up **1** You **straighten up** when you return to an upright position after having been bent over. **2** You **straighten** a place **up** when you make it neat and tidy.

straightforward /streɪt'fɔːwəd/ *adjective*

1 Straightforward things are simple and without difficulties or complications: *The instructions are quite straightforward.* [*opposite* **complicated**] **2** A **straightforward** person is honest and frank, and does not try to deceive or mislead others: *You can trust him; he's very straightforward.* [*same as* **sincere**; *opposite* **insincere**]

strain /streɪn/ *verb*; *noun*

▻ ***verb*: strains, straining, strained**

1 You **strain** yourself when you injure or weaken yourself or part of your body because of a sudden awkward movement or over-exertion: *He strained his back lifting bags of cement.* ▫ *You'll strain yourself lifting that heavy suitcase.* **2** You **strain** to do something when you make a great effort to do it: *The horses were straining to pull the heavy cart up the hill.* **3** To **strain** something means to make heavy demands on it beyond the acceptable limit: *the quality of mercy is not strained* ▫ *I won't take any more of this; my patience has been strained to the absolute limit.* **4** You **strain** a solid and a liquid when you separate them by pouring them into a sieve or colander; you **strain** the liquid off something when you remove it by pouring it through a sieve or colander.

▻ ***noun*: strains**

1 A **strain** is an injury to a muscle caused by a sudden awkward movement or over-exertion. [*same as* **sprain**] **2** (*uncount or count*) **Strain** is tension or anxiety caused by too many demands being made on you or the feeling of tiredness that results from this: *She's been under terrible strain since her husband became ill.* ▫ *She found looking after her mother a great strain.* [compare **stress**] [*same as* **pressure**] **3** (*uncount*) **Strain** is also the feeling of tension and distrust between groups of people who have different or incompatible aims and objectives: *the strain in relations between the unions and the management.* [*same as* **tension**] **4** (*uncount*) **Strain** is the condition of being tightly stretched or the force that produces this: *The metal buckled under the strain.* **5** (*usually plural*) The **strains** of a musical instrument or tune are its notes. **6** (*used in the singular*) You can refer to the particular manner in which someone expresses something in speech or writing or the meaning conveyed as a **strain**: *He writes about women in a much less sympathetic strain.* **7** A **strain** is a breed or race of animals or plants. **8** A **strain** of a bacterium or virus is a type which has developed new or different characteristics.

phrasal verb

To **strain at** something means to stretch or pull it tightly: *The fish was straining at the line.*

strained /streɪnd/ *adjective*

1 Someone's manner or actions are **strained** when they are not relaxed and natural. [*same as* **forced**] **2** Relations between people are **strained** or an atmosphere is **strained** when it is not friendly or relaxed. [*same as* **tense**]

strait /streɪt/ *noun*: **straits**
1 (*often used in the plural*) A **strait** is a narrow strip of sea between two land masses: *the Straits of Hormuz.* **2** (*used in the plural*) If you say that someone is in desperate or dire **straits** you mean they are experiencing difficulties or hardship, especially financially: *Since he lost all his money, they have been in dire straits.*

straitened /ˈstreɪtənd/ *adjective*
▻ ***phrase*** If you are **in straitened circumstances** you have very little money.

straitjacket /ˈstreɪtdʒakɪt/ *noun*: **straitjackets**
1 A **straitjacket** is a jacket with long sleeves that is put on a dangerous violent person to prevent them injuring themselves or anyone else. The sleeves are crossed at the chest and the loose ends tied behind the person's back so that they are unable to move their arms. **2** You can also call something that prevents freedom of development or expression a **straitjacket**: *the straitjacket of political correctness.*

strait-laced /streɪtˈleɪst/ *adjective*
Someone described as **strait-laced** has strict, often old-fashioned, ideas about morals: *She was shy and strait-laced so it's perhaps surprising she chose a career in films.* [*same as* **prudish**, **puritanical**]

strand /strand/ *noun*; *verb*
▻ ***noun***: **strands**
1 A **strand** is a single thread, hair, wire or fibre that is separate from or may be separated from others: *Use a single strand of embroidery silk to sew the outlines.* ▫ *Twist the strands of wire together to form the rope.* **2** A **strand** is a single or separate element, aspect or part in a story, argument or situation: *In the last chapter, the various strands of the plot are brought together.* [*same as* **thread**]
▻ ***verb***: **strands, stranding, stranded**
1 When a ship **is stranded** it has run aground in shallow water and cannot get free: *The whale had become stranded on the beach.* **2** If you **are stranded** in a place you cannot get away from it *eg* because you have no transport or money: *Her jeep broke down and she was left stranded in a remote village.*

strange /streɪndʒ/ *adjective*
1 A **strange** person or place is one that you do not know or are unfamiliar with: *She phoned the police when she saw a strange man hanging about outside her house.* ▫ *He's never able to sleep in a strange bed.* ▫ *We should remember that the refugees are in a strange country with unfamiliar customs.* [*opposite* **familiar**] **2** Something that is **strange** is odd, out of the ordinary or unpredictable or is difficult to explain or understand: *A strange light appeared in the sky.* ▫ *He's a strange character.* ▫ *Isn't it strange that we haven't heard from him?* ▫ *This soup has a strange taste; what did you put in it?* [*same as* **curious**] **3** If you feel **strange** you feel vaguely ill or ill at ease. [*same as* **funny**, **odd**] — *adverb* **strangely:** *His face was strangely familiar.* ▫ *He looked at me strangely.* — *noun* (*uncount*) **strangeness:** *the strangeness of his behaviour.* [*same as* **oddness**]

stranger /ˈstreɪndʒə(r)/ *noun*: **strangers**
1 A **stranger** is a person whom you do not know: *Don't talk to strangers!* **2** You can refer to someone who is visiting or has just arrived in a place and therefore does not know it well as a **stranger** in that place: *He's a stranger in the town.* [*opposite* **local**] **3** If you are a **stranger** to something you are unfamiliar with it or do not have any experience in it: *He's a stranger to soap and water.* [= he doesn't wash himself]

strangle /ˈstraŋgəl/ *verb*: **strangles, strangling, strangled**
1 To **strangle** someone is to kill them by squeezing their neck, with the hands, or by pulling a cord tight round it. **2** You **strangle** a cry or scream when you suppress it so as to stop the sound being heard. [*same as* **stifle**] **3** Something **is strangled** when its development or expression is forcefully hindered or stopped.

stranglehold /ˈstraŋgəlhoʊld/ *noun*: **strangleholds**
One thing has a **stranglehold** on something else when it has total control of that other thing preventing it from moving freely or developing: *an attempt to free the country from the stranglehold of an increasing brutal and repressive regime.*

strap /strap/ *noun*; *verb*
▻ ***noun***: **straps**
1 A **strap** is a narrow strip of leather or fabric by which a thing is hung, carried or fastened. [see also **shoulder strap**] **2** Especially formerly, a **strap** was a leather belt used to give a beating as punishment. **3** A **strap** is also a loop which standing passengers use to steady themselves on a moving bus or train.
▻ ***verb***: **straps, strapping, strapped**

> ***phrasal verbs***
> **strap in** *or* **into** If you **are strapped in** or **strapped into** a seat in a vehicle or aeroplane, you are wearing a seat belt or safety belt to prevent you from being thrown forward.
> **strap up** If *eg* a doctor **straps up** an injured limb, they wrap it in firm bandages to give it support.

strapping /ˈstrapɪŋ/ *adjective*
If you describe someone as **strapping**, you mean they are tall and strong-looking: *a strapping lad of sixteen.* [*same as* **powerful**]

strata /ˈstrɑːtə/ *noun*
Strata is the plural of **stratum.**

stratagem /ˈstratədʒəm/ *noun*: **stratagems**
A **strategem** is a plan or clever trick, especially one that is used to gain an advantage over an opponent or to achieve something: *a military stratagem* ▫ *You could see what the team's stratagem was, but that didn't stop it from being effective.*

strategic /strəˈtiːdʒɪk/ *adjective*
1 **Strategic** means of or relating to strategy, especially military strategy: *a town of strategic importance to the Bosnian Serbs.* **2** **Strategic** weapons are designed to be fired over long distances directly at an enemy's territory, rather than at close range on a battlefield. — *adverb* **strategically:** *Policemen were strategically placed in areas where violence was most likely to break out.*

strategist /ˈstratədʒɪst/ *noun*: **strategists**
A **stategist** is someone who plans large complex operations, especially military campaigns: *He's a skilful political strategist.* ▫ *the military strategists of the Pentagon.*

strategy /ˈstratədʒɪ/ *noun*: **strategies**
1 (*uncount*) **Strategy** is the process of, or skill in, planning and conducting a military campaign. **2** (*uncount or count*) **Strategy**, or a **strategy**, is a long-term plan for future success or development: *the Chancellor's economic strategy.*

stratum /ˈstrɑːtəm/ *noun*: **strata** (*technical*)
A **stratum** is **1** a horizontal layer of rock. **2** a layer of cells in living tissue. **3** a layer of the atmosphere or the ocean. **4** a level, grade or social class.

straw /strɔː/ *noun*: **straws**
1 (*uncount*) **Straw** is the dried cut stalks of corn and similar crops, used as food and bedding for cattle, or

for weaving into hats and baskets. **2** A **straw** is a thin hollow tube of paper or plastic used for sucking up a drink.

▻ ***phrases*** **1** You **clutch at straws** when you try, in desperation, to get out of a difficult situation by means that are very unlikely to succeed. **2** You say that something is **the last** or **final straw** when it is the last in a whole series of disagreeable events and is the one that makes you feel that you cannot tolerate any more.

strawberry /'strɔːbərɪ/ *noun* (*count or uncount, often adjectival*): **strawberries**
1 A **strawberry** is a small juicy pinkish-red fruit with many small brownish-yellow seeds: *a bowl of strawberries and cream* ▫ *a strawberry tart* ▫ *strawberry ice cream.* [see picture at **fruit**] **2 Strawberry** or **strawberry pink** is the pinkish-red colour of a strawberry.

stray /streɪ/ *verb*; *noun*; *adjective*
▻ ***verb***: **strays, straying, strayed**
1 When people or animals wander away from the place where they should be, they **stray**: *Some of his cattle had strayed on to his neighbour's land.* ▫ *Don't let any of the smaller children stray away from the park.* **2** If you **have strayed** from the subject or main issue in a discussion, you have moved away from it; if you let your thoughts **stray**, you stop concentrating on the thing you should be concentrating on. [*same as* **digress**] **3** (*literary*) If people **stray** from the right path, they behave in an immoral or wicked manner.
▻ ***noun***: **strays**
A **stray** is a lost or homeless pet.
▻ ***adjective***
Stray describes things that are random or occasional and do not happen as part of a regular sequence: *He was killed by a stray bullet.*

streak /striːk/ *noun*; *verb*
▻ ***noun***: **streaks**
1 A **streak** is a long irregular stripe or mark that is different in colour from the rest of the surrounding area: *She has blonde streaks in her hair.* **2** A **streak** of lightning is a flash of lightning. **3** You can also refer to a negative quality or tendency that is evident in a person's character on certain occasions as a **streak** of that quality: *He has a streak of cruelty.* **4** A lucky **streak** is a short period or spell of luck; if someone is on a winning **streak** they win consistently for a time while they are gambling.
▻ ***verb***: **streaks, streaking, streaked**
1 If something **is streaked**, it is marked with a streak or streaks: *His face was streaked with blood.* **2** (*informal*) If someone or something **streaks** somewhere, they move there at great speed: *He streaked down the home straight.* [*same as* **dart**]

streaky /'striːkɪ/ *adjective*: **streakier, streakiest**
1 A **streaky** surface is marked with streaks. **2 Streaky** bacon is a type of bacon that has alternate layers of fat and meat.

stream /striːm/ *noun*; *verb*
▻ ***noun***: **streams**
1 A **stream** is a small narrow river: *a stream ran through the garden.* **2** You can also refer to a continuous flow of people or things as a **stream**: *a steady stream of traffic* ▫ *a stream of insults and abuse.* **3** In schools, children are divided into **streams** when they are grouped together in classes according to age or ability.
▻ ***verb***: **streams, streaming, streamed**
1 When large quantities or numbers of people or things move in a certain direction in a continuous flow, they **stream** from or into that place: *The shipyard workers came streaming out of the gates, all heading for home at the end of their shift.* [*same as* **pour**] **2** Sunlight **streams** into a room when it shines into it strongly: *He opened the curtains and sunlight streamed into the bedroom.* [*same as* **pour**, **flood**] **3** School pupils **are streamed** when they are divided into classes according to age or ability.

streamer /'striːmə(r)/ *noun*: **streamers**
A **streamer** is **1** a long paper ribbon used to decorate a room. **2** a roll of coloured paper that uncoils when thrown.

streamline /'striːmlaɪn/ *verb*: **streamlines, streamlining, streamlined**
1 You **streamline** the shape of a vehicle or aircraft when you make it streamlined. **2** You **streamline** an organization, process or system when you make it simpler and more efficient.

streamlined /'striːmlaɪnd/ *adjective*
1 A **streamlined** shape is one that will slip smoothly through air or water with minimum resistance. **2** A **streamlined** organization, process or system is very efficient with little or no waste of resources. [*opposite* **inefficient**]

street /striːt/ *noun*: **streets**
1 A **street** is a public road, especially one in a town with pavements and buildings at the side or sides: *The streets radiated out from a central square.* **2** The road and the buildings together are also called a **street**: *a street of terraced houses.* **3** The road, the buildings and all the people in the buildings or on the pavements are also sometimes referred to collectively as the **street**: *Stop shouting! The whole street can hear you!* [see picture on next page]
▻ ***phrases*** **1** (*informal*) **a** People who are **on the streets** are homeless: *He couldn't pay the rent and found himself out on the street.* **b** You say that someone is **on the streets** when they are working as a prostitute, especially when they approach people and offer them sex in the streets. **2** (*informal*) You say that something is **streets ahead of** of others when it is much more advanced or much better than they are: *The new product is streets ahead of the competition.* **3 The man in the street** is any average or ordinary person of either sex. **4** (*informal*) If you say that something is **up your street** you mean it is suited to your tastes or abilities: *He'll enjoy this outward bound course; it's right up his street.*

streetcar /'striːtkɑː(r)/ (*AmE*) *noun*: **streetcars**
A **streetcar** is a tram.

street lamp /'striːt lamp/ *noun*: **street lamps**
A **street lamp** or **street light** is a light fixed to a lamp post or the side of a building, for lighting the street. [see picture at **house**]

street sign /'striːt saɪn/ *noun*: **street signs**
A **street sign** or **street name** is a board fixed to a wall especially at a corner, with the name of the street on it. [see picture at **street**]

streetwise /'striːtwaɪz/ *adjective* (*informal*)
Someone who is **streetwise** is experienced in, and able to survive, in the hard and ruthless world of the city streets: *streetwise kids.*

strength /streŋθ/ *noun* (*usually uncount*): **strengths**
1 Your **strength** is **a** the power you have in your muscles: *Some people don't know their own strength.* ▫ *It has amazing strength in its hind legs.* **b** your health and physical energy: *He never really regained his strength.* ▫ *With her remaining strength she just managed to crawl away and hide.* **c** your moral courage or will power: *He lacked strength to resist the lure of money.* ▫ *the remarkable integrity and strength of character*

a street scene

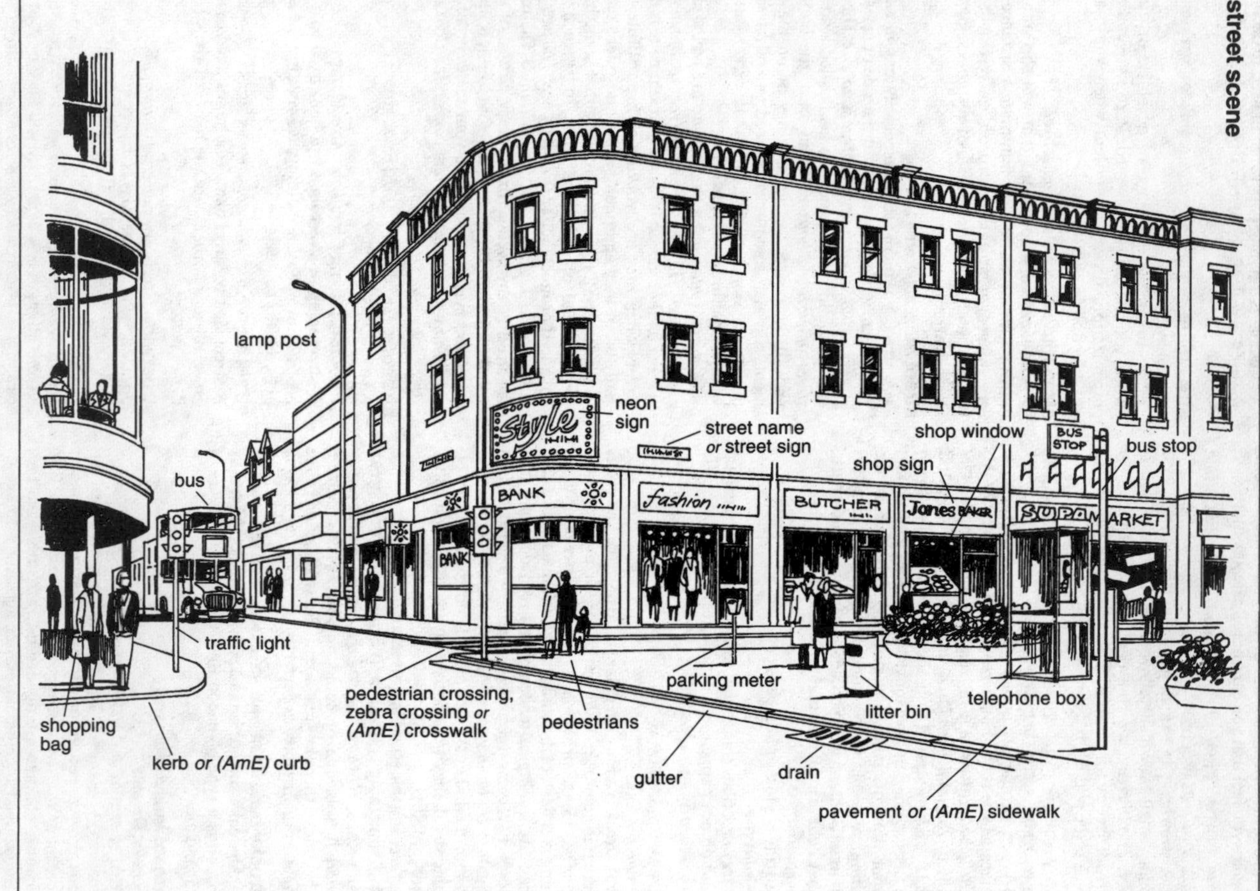

displayed by these teenagers. **d** your power or influence: *the strength of the trade unions* □ *Nato's military strength* □ *Japan's economic strength* □ *The very people from whom she had drawn her strength eventually betrayed her.* □ *strength founded on fear.* **2** The **strength** of an object, structure or material is its ability to withstand pressure, force, rough treatment or prolonged use without breaking, collapsing or wearing out: *steel beams of sufficient strength to take the weight of the roof.* □ *Denim was used because of its strength and durability.* □ *They treat rubber with sulphur to increase its strength.* **3** The **strength** of something is its intensity, or the degree to which it exists: *A show of hands revealed the strength of feeling against the proposal.* □ *the strength of her love for him* □ *the variable strength of the signal according to the wavelength selected.* **4** The **strength** of an argument or case is its effectiveness, or its abililty to persuade people: *the mounting strength of the prosecution's case* □ *evidence that added strength to her claim.* **5** The **strength** of a link or relationship is its degree of firmness or closeness: *the strength of old ties and loyalties.* **6** A group grows in **strength** when it gains more members; it can be described as being at full **strength**, or below **strength**, or at half **strength**, when all its members, or not enough of them, or only half of them, are present or available. **7** (*uncount or count*) The **strength** of a solution or of a drug or alcoholic drink is the amount it contains of the effective ingredient or of alcohol: *solutions of different strengths.* **8** (*count*) The **strengths** of a person or thing are their good points, or the good things about them: *There are various methods and they all have their strengths and weaknesses.* □ *One of her great strengths was her ability to adjust to circumstances.* [*opposite* **weakness**]

▻ ***phrases*** **1** Something **gathers strength** when it gets stronger, larger or more numerous: *Meanwhile the anti-war lobby was gathering strength.* **2** People or things **go from strength to strength** when they keep improving or becoming more successful: *The company went from strength to strength and became one of the biggest employers in the land.* **3** You do something **on the strength of** some circumstance or experience when the circumstance or experience persuades you to do it: *On the strength of this morning's preview we shall be happy to go ahead and offer you the contract.*

strengthen /ˈstrɛŋθən/ *verb*: **strengthens, strengthening, strengthened**

To **strengthen** means to make or become stronger: *social events intended to strengthen the links between the two communities.*

strenuous /ˈstrɛnjʊəs/ *adjective*

Strenuous work or exercise requires great effort or energy: *Digging is very strenuous work.* [*same as* **tough**; *opposite* **effortless**] — *adverb* **strenuously:** *He strenuously denied the charge.* [*same as* **resolutely**]

stress /strɛs/ *noun*; *verb*

▻ ***noun***: **stresses**

1 (*uncount or count*) **Stress** is the state of anxiety or mental strain caused by life's problems or by too much work; a **stress** is anything that causes this state of anxiety or mental strain: *She's suffering from stress.* □ *the stresses of modern living.* **2** (*uncount or count*) **Stress** is strong physical pressure that is applied to an object; a **stress** is something that exerts such pressure: *metal that bends and buckles under stress* □ *The machine measures the stresses exerted on athletes' bones as they train.* □ *a stress fracture.* **3** (*uncount*) If you lay or put **stress** on something, you attach particular importance, emphasis or weight to it: *Their commander laid particular stress on the need for secrecy.* **4** (*uncount*) In speech, **stress** is emphasis placed on a particular syllable or word so that its sound seems stronger than other parts of the word or sentence.

▻ ***verb***: **stresses, stressing, stressed**

1 You **stress** something when you emphasize or attach particular importance to it: *I must stress that your essays must be in on time, otherwise they won't be marked.* [*same as* **underline**] **2** You **stress** a particular word or syllable when you are speaking when you pronounce it with emphasis: *You must go, and I stress 'must'.* **3** You **are stressed** when you feel mental strain or anxiety; something **is stressed** when it is subjected to strong physical pressure.

stressful /ˈstrɛsfəl/ *adjective*

A **stressful** job or activity is one that causes you to feel mental stress: *Being a hospital doctor can be a very stressful job.*

stress mark /ˈstrɛs mɑːk/ *noun*: **stress marks**

A **stress mark** is a written or printed mark used to indicate stress in speech, in this dictionary the mark (/ˈ/) placed before the syllable or word that is stressed.

stretch /strɛtʃ/ *verb*; *noun*

▻ ***verb***: **stretches, stretching, stretched**

1 Tissue or material that is elastic **stretches** or **is stretched** when it is pulled till it becomes tight: *tights that stretch to fit any leg size.* □ *The drums consist of hollowed-out gourds with animal skins stretched over the top.* [*same as* **extend**] **2** Knitted clothing **stretches** when it gets longer or wider, *eg* during washing, and does not return to its original size: *Some woollens shrink and some stretch.* **3** You **stretch** when you extend your body and limbs to their full length and tighten your muscles: *She got out of bed and stretched.* □ *stretching exercises.* □ *Stretch your arms out to the sides.* **4** You **stretch** to reach or get hold of something when you lean or extend your body or an arm in that direction: *I can probably reach it if I stretch.* □ *He stretched up and lifted a book off the shelf.* □ *She stretched over the back of the seat to fasten the children's belts.* **5** Something **stretches** from one point to another if it extends over or covers that distance or area: *The empire stretched from coast to coast of the Mediterranean and as far north as Britain.* □ *The plain stretched endlessly before them.* [*same as* **extend**] **6** A job **stretches** you when it makes you use all your skills and abilities and keeps you working hard: *She felt she wasn't being stretched.* [*same as* **extend**] **7** Your finances or resources **are stretched** when you have scarcely enough for your needs: *Funds are being stretched to the limit.* [*same as* **extend**]

▻ ***noun***: **stretches**

1 (*usually in the singular*) You have a **stretch** when you extend your body and limbs to their full length and tighten your muscles: *It's good to get off your office chair from time to time and have a good stretch.* **2** (*uncount, often adjectival*) A material has a certain amount of **stretch** if it is elastic to some degree: *stretch jeans.* [*same as* **elasticity**] **3** A **stretch** of water or land is an area of water or land: *one of the finest stretches of coastline in Britain.* □ *a stretch of calm water.* [*same as* **extent**] **4** A **stretch** is a period of time: *For long stretches he found himself with nothing to do.* [see also **at a stretch** below] **5** The final straight section of a race course is sometimes referred to as the 'home **stretch**'. [*same as* **straight**] **6** (*informal*) Someone does a **stretch** in prison when they serve a prison sentence: *doing a three-year stretch at Peterhead.*

▻ ***phrases*** **1** You do something for a certain length of time **at a stretch** when you do it continuously throughout that period without a pause: *She would sometimes work for ten hours at a stretch.* **2** Something that cannot **by any stretch of the imagination** be described in some way cannot possibly be described in that way: *You couldn't call it a pretty house by any stretch of the imagination, but it's convenient.* **3** For **stretch a point** see **point**. **4** For **stretch your legs** see **leg**.

> ***phrasal verbs***
> **stretch out 1** You **stretch out** or **stretch** yourself **out** somewhere when you lie there with your legs fully extended: *He was lying stretched out on the bed.* **2** You **stretch out** your hand when you extend it or hold it out straight: *There were beggars everywhere, pathetically stretching their hands out to passers-by.*
> **stretch to** You **stretch to** something when you decide you can afford it: *I think we could stretch to a computer for you.*

stretcher /ˈstretʃə(r)/ *noun*: **stretchers**
A **stretcher** is a length of canvas or other sheeting with poles attached along either side used for carrying a sick or injured person in a lying position.

stretchy /ˈstretʃɪ/ *adjective*: **stretchier, stretchiest**
Stretchy materials are able to, or tend to, stretch. [*same as* **elastic**]

strew /struː/ *verb*: **strews, strewing, strewed, strewn**
You **strew** things about when you scatter them untidily over an area; an area **is strewn** with things when it is covered with an untidy scattering of those things: *The wedding guests strewed the path with rose petals as the bride and bridegroom left the church.* □ *The floor of his office was strewn with books and papers.*

stricken /ˈstrɪkən/ *adjective*
Stricken means showing the effects of, deeply affected by, or disabled by *eg* trouble, grief, illness, or other unpleasant conditions. It is often used in combination with nouns to mean affected by that particular condition: *The helicopter made several attempts to reach the stricken tanker.* □ *famine-stricken Ethiopia* □ *She was grief stricken.* □ *a man well stricken in years.* [= an old man] [see also **panic-stricken**]

strict /strɪkt/ *adjective*: **stricter, strictest**
1 Someone who is **strict** is severe and demands that others, especially children, obey rules, especially rules of polite or good behaviour: *Their father was a strict disciplinarian.* □ *He had a strict upbringing.* [=his parents were strict] [*opposite* **lenient, easy-going**] **2 Strict** instructions or rules must be obeyed: *He was given strict instructions not to open the letter before he reached his destination.* □ *The club has a strict dress code.* [*same as* **rigorous**] **3 Strict** is also used to describe someone who never does anything against their beliefs or the rules of their religion: *a strict vegetarian* □ *a strict Catholic.* **4** You can use **strict** to describe a meaning or interpretation that is exact or precise. **5 Strict** also means complete: *She told me in the strictest confidence that she intended to apply for the post.* [*same as* **total**]

strictly /ˈstrɪktlɪ/ *adverb*
1 Strictly means in a strict way: *He was brought up very strictly.* **2** If something is **strictly** forbidden it is completely forbidden: *Smoking is strictly forbidden.* **3** If something is **strictly** for a particular person or group of people, it is intended for that person or group of people and no-one else: *The bar is strictly for the use of members.*
▷ ***phrase*** When you say that something is, or is not, true or the case **strictly speaking** you mean that it is, or is not, precisely or exactly true or the case: *He's not strictly speaking an artist, more of a performer.*

stride /straɪd/ *noun*; *verb*
▷ ***noun***: **strides**
1 A **stride** is a single long step in walking or running, or a way of walking or running with long steps. **2** If you make great **strides** in something, you make great progress or advances in it.
▷ ***verb***: **strides, striding, strode, stridden**
You **stride** when you walk with long steps or take one long step in crossing something: *He came striding along the path, with his gun over his shoulder.* □ *He strode across the stream.*
▷ ***phrases*** You **get into your stride** when you begin to work or do something well or effectively: *I don't want to stop now; I'm just getting into my stride.*

strident /ˈstraɪdənt/ *adjective*
1 A **strident** voice or sound is loud, harsh and unpleasant to listen to. **2** If someone is **strident** they make their feelings or opinions known loudly and forcefully so as not to be ignored: *Their demands for reform became more and more strident.*

strife /straɪf/ *noun* (*uncount*; *rather formal*)
Strife is a state of bitter conflict or fighting between people or groups of people: *political strife* □ *strife-torn Bosnia.*

strike /straɪk/ *verb*; *noun*
▷ ***verb***: **strikes, striking, struck**
1 a (*formal*) You **strike** someone when you hit them: *He lifted his hand as if to strike her.* □ *She struck the child a vicious blow behind the ear.* □ *She had been struck several times on the head with something blunt and heavy.* [*same as* **hit**] **b** One thing **strikes** another when it hits it or collides with it: *He was struck by a car as he was trying to cross the road.* □ *The bus struck a lamp post and swerved back across the road.* □ *The ball struck him on the side of the head.* □ *She struck her head against the edge of the table as she fell.* [*same as* **hit**] **c** You **strike** the ball in a game such as golf or cricket when you hit it with your club or bat. [*same as* **hit**]
2 a Something such as disaster **strikes** when it happens suddenly: *Cholera struck within days of the refugee camps being set up.* □ *Corinth was struck by earthquakes in 1858 and in 1928.* **b** Lightning **strikes** something when it comes into contact with it: *The tower had been struck by lightning in 1754.* **c** An animal, person or force **strikes** when they make an attack: *The cobra reared its head, preparing to strike.* □ *The killer could strike again.* □ *He kept his troops well out of sight, waiting for the moment to strike.* [*same as* **attack**] **d** Something **strikes** fear or terror into you if it frightens or terrifies you: *Rumours about the gas chambers circulated and struck terror into their hearts.* **e** Workers **strike** when they stop working as a protest against their employer: *We are prepared to strike for fairer wages.*
3 a A thought or idea **strikes** you when it suddenly enters your mind: *A horrible thought struck William; would he miss tea?* □ *It struck me that there had not been time for the news to reach her.* **b** Something **strikes** you as being a certain thing if it give you the impression of being that thing: *He didn't strike me as the type who would beat his wife.* □ *His attitude struck me as very odd.* □ *Well, it didn't strike me as very funny.* **c** You **are struck** by or with something when you are impressed by it: *I can't say I was terribly struck with his designs.* □ *I was immediately by struck the elegant way they expressed themselves even in informal conversation.* [*same as* **impress**]
4 a A clock **strikes** when its bells or chimes sound to announce the time: *The church clock struck six.* **b** You **strike** a note on the piano when you play it; you **strike** a key on a keyboard when you press it.

c Something **strikes** a certain kind of note if it gives you that kind of impression: *Her exotic colouring and bright turban struck a bizarre note in the quiet grey highland village.* **d** Something that is said **strikes** a chord if it appeals to you because it corresponds to what you think or feel yourself: *She was talking about the problems of being a twin, which immediately struck a chord with me.* **e** You **strike** the right balance when you achieve a satisfactory balance or compromise between opposites or extremes: *It's a problem striking a balance between authoritarianism and permissiveness.* **f** You **strike** a bargain with someone when you make a deal or agreement with them. **g** Someone **strikes** a pose or attitude when they adopt a deliberately dramatic position or extreme point of view in order to draw people's attention to themselves. **5 a** You **strike** a match by dragging it against a rough surface, so that it bursts into flame. [*same as* **light**] **b** A coin **is struck** when it is shaped by machinery and a design stamped on either side of it. [*same as* **mint**] **c** You **strike** oil or gold when you find a source of it by digging or drilling in the earth or under water. [*same as* **discover, find**]

▻ ***noun***: **strikes**

1 A **strike** is the refusal to work by a number of workers, as a protest against an employer. **2** Someone goes on a hunger **strike** when they refuse to eat, as a form of protest. **3** A military **strike** is an attack, especially one from the air.

▻ ***phrases*** **1** Workers are **on strike** when they are refusing to work because of a disagreement with their employer. **2** For **strike lucky** see **lucky**. **3** A person **is struck dumb** or **blind** when they are suddenly unable to speak or to see: *I was struck dumb with amazement.* **4** If you are **within striking distance** of someone, or it is **within striking distance**, it is quite near: *we were within striking distance of our destination when we ran into trouble.*

phrasal verbs

strike down Something **strikes** a person **down** if it kills or disables them: *She was in a wheelchair at the age of 25, struck down by multiple sclerosis.* □ *He was struck down by a sniper's bullet.*

strike off Doctors or lawyers **are struck off** when their names are is removed from the professional register for serious misconduct during the practice of their profession, so that they are no longer allowed to practise.

strike out **1** You **strike** words **out** of a piece of writing when you remove them by drawing a line through them: *The word 'not' had been struck out.* [*same as* **cross out, delete**] **2** You **strike out** in a particular direction, when you walk or swim strongly in that direction: *I surfaced and immediately struck out for the shore.* **3** You **strike out** on your own when you start doing independent and original work.

strike up **1** A band **strikes up** when it begins to play: *The band struck up the national anthem.* □ *They struck up with 'Land of Hope and Glory'.* **2** You **strike up** a conversation with someone when you begin it; you **strike up** a friendship with someone when you make friends with someone: *She struck up a number of friendships with fellow commuters.*

striker /'straɪkə(r)/ *noun*: **strikers**

1 A **striker** is a worker taking part in a strike. **2** In football, a **striker** is a player with an attacking role.

striking /'straɪkɪŋ/ *adjective*

1 You describe something as **striking** when it draws your attention because its appearance is beautiful or unusual in some way: *She's a very striking girl.* [*same as* **arresting**; *opposite* **unimpressive**] **2** **Striking** is also used to describe things that are very noticeable or marked: *There are some striking differences between this and the original version.* **3** **Striking** workers are on strike. — *adverb* (*intensifying*) **strikingly:** *a strikingly beautiful woman.*

string /strɪŋ/ *noun*; *verb*

▻ ***noun***: **strings**

1 (*uncount, often adjectival*) **String** is thin cord used *eg* for tying parcels: *The parcel was tied up with string.* □ *a string bag.* **2** The **strings** on a musical instrument such as a violin or guitar are any of a set of pieces of stretched wire, catgut or other material which are vibrated to produce sound: *He stopped playing because he had broken a string.* [see picture at **orchestra**] **3** (*used in the plural*) The **strings** are, or the **string section** is, the musical instruments in an orchestra (and the musicians who play them) from which sound is produced in this way, including the violins, violas, cellos and double basses. [see picture at **orchestra**] **4** A **string** of *eg* pearls is a number of them threaded together to form a necklace. **5** A **string** of things is a series or succession of things of the same type: *a string of complaints.* **6** (*used in the plural*) If a situation or proposal has **strings** attached, it has a number of undesirable conditions or limitations.

▻ ***verb***: **strings, stringing, strung**

1 You **string** an instrument such as a violin or guitar when you fit a string or strings to it. **2** You **string** *eg* beads when you thread them in a row on a string.

▻ ***phrases*** **1** (*informal*) If you **pull strings** you use your influence or your friendly relationships with influential people, in order to get something done: *If you want to get into television, I might be able to pull a few strings to help you on.* **2** If a situation or proposal comes **with no strings attached** or **without strings**, it has no undesirable conditions or limitations: *She said she would be quite happy to go on seeing him, provided there were no strings attached.*

phrasal verbs

string along If you **string** someone **along**, you keep them in a state of false hope by telling them lies or not telling them the true situation.

string out If things **are strung out** they are spread out in a line with spaces between them: *The tanks were strung out across the desert.*

string up (*informal*) If someone **is strung up** they are killed by hanging.

stringent /'strɪndʒənt/ *adjective*

1 **Stringent** rules, laws or limits are very severe or strictly enforced. [*same as* **tough**, **rigorous**; *opposite* **lenient, flexible**] **2** **Stringent** economic conditions are characterized by a lack of money or strict controls on the supply of money. — *adverb* **stringently:** *The limits on spending were stringently enforced.* [*same as* **rigorously**]

stringy /'strɪŋɪ/ *adjective*: **stringier, stringiest**

1 Hair that is **stringy** is thin and rough, like string. **2** **Stringy** meat is full of tough chewy fibres.

strip /strɪp/ *noun*; *verb*

▻ ***noun***: **strips**

A **strip** is **1** a long narrow piece: *a narrow strip of land.* **2** a lightweight uniform worn by members of a sports team: *a football strip.* **3** a striptease performance: *She did a strip.*

▷ *verb*: **strips, stripping, stripped**
1 You **strip** something when you remove it by peeling or pulling it off: *He used a knife to strip the paint.* □ *He stripped the bark off the hazel twig.* **2** Someone **is stripped** of their rank, title or property when it is taken away from them, often because they are in disgrace. **3** You **strip** a bed when you take all the blankets and sheets off it. **4 a** You **strip** someone when you take their clothes off: *She stripped the baby and put him in his bath.* **b** You **strip** when you take your clothes off. [*same as* **undress**]

phrasal verbs
strip off (*informal*) When you **strip off** you take your clothes off.
strip down 1 If someone **strips down** a piece of machinery, such as an engine, they dismantle it or take it to pieces. **2** If you **strip down** to your underwear, you take all your clothes off except your underwear.

strip club /'strɪp klʌb/ *noun*: **strip clubs**
A **strip club** is a club where women, and sometimes also men, take off their clothes for the customers' entertainment.

stripe /straɪp/ *noun*: **stripes**
1 A **stripe** is a band of colour on a different coloured background: *a white material with broad red and blue stripes.* **2** A V-shaped or coloured band worn on the sleeve and indicating a rank in the armed forces is also called a **stripe**: *He got his sergeant's stripes.* [=he was promoted to the rank of sergeant]

striped /straɪpt/ *adjective*
Striped things have a pattern of stripes: *a striped suit* □ *She wore a navy and white striped blouse.*

strip lighting /strɪp 'laɪtɪŋ/ *noun* (*uncount*)
Strip lighting is lighting by tube-shaped fluorescent lamps, not bulbs.

stripper /'strɪpə(r)/ *noun*: **strippers**
1 A **stripper** is someone who performs a striptease. **2** (*uncount*) **Stripper** is a substance for removing paint and varnish: *paint stripper.*

striptease /'strɪpti:z/ *noun* (*uncount or used in the singular, often adjectival*)
Striptease is a form of entertainment in which a person undresses to music in a slow and sexually exciting way: *a striptease artiste* □ *She did a striptease.*

strive /straɪv/ *verb* (*formal*): **strives, striving, strove, striven**
If you **strive** to do something, or **strive** for something, you try very hard to do it, or struggle to gain it: *He strives continuously to be a good husband and father.* □ *We must strive for perfection.*

strode /stroʊd/ *verb*
Strode is the past tense of **stride**.

stroke /stroʊk/ *noun*; *verb*
▷ *noun*: **strokes**
1 A **stroke** is **a** an act of hitting: *He was sentenced to ten strokes of the birch.* **b** the way something is hit, especially the technique or action used in hitting a ball in sport: *a ground stroke.* **2** A single movement in one direction made with a pen, pencil or paintbrush, or the line or mark produced by this, is a **stroke**: *He had signed away their inheritance with a single stroke of the pen.* □ *Apply the paint in long even strokes.* □ *a brush stroke.* **3** A **stroke** is a single pull of the oar in rowing or a single co-ordinated movement with the arms and legs in swimming. **4** (*uncount*) **Stroke** is also used in compounds to refer to a particular style in swimming: *backstroke* □ *breaststroke.* **5** The sound a clock makes when it is striking the hour is a **stroke**: *At the first stroke it will be one o'clock precisely.* **6** A **stroke** is a stroking movement made with the hand as a caress: *She gave the rabbit a stroke.* **7** A **stroke** is a sudden loss of consciousness caused by a blood vessel bursting in the brain, often resulting in death or permanent paralysis down one side of the body. **8** (*informal*; *used in negative statements*) If you say that you haven't done a **stroke**, you mean that you haven't done even the smallest amount of work: *'Haven't you done any work this morning?' 'Not a stroke.'*
▷ *verb*: **strokes, stroking, stroked**
If you **stroke** someone or something, you move your hand over them gently and often repeatedly in one direction, especially as a sign of affection: *The cat loves to be stroked.* □ *He stroked her cheek.*
▷ *phrases* **1** A **stroke of genius** is a very clever or imaginative idea. **2** A **stroke of luck** is a sudden piece of good luck. **3** If something is done or happens **at a stroke** it is done or happens with a single, often sudden, action: *All their jobs were axed at a single stroke.* **4** If something happens **on the stroke of** a stated hour, it happens precisely at that time: *On the stroke of twelve, her golden coach turned back into a pumpkin.*

stroll /stroʊl/ *verb*; *noun*
▷ *verb*: **strolls, strolling, strolled**
To **stroll** means to walk in a slow relaxed way: *He came strolling along the promenade.*
▷ *noun*: **strolls:** *They went for a stroll round the garden.*

strong /strɒŋ/ *adjective*: **stronger, strongest**
1 People who are **strong a** are muscular and physically powerful: *He lifted her up in his strong arms.* □ *I need someone strong to help shift these boulders.* **b** are healthy: *She has a strong consitution.* □ *His heart isn't too strong.* □ *As a child he wasn't very strong.* [*same as* **healthy, robust**; *opposite* **sickly, weak, unhealthy**] **c** have a determined personality and are good at getting what they want: *She was one of those strong women who become dominant in the marriage relationship.* □ *people with a strong personality* □ *We need stronger leadership.* [*same as* **forceful, confident**; *opposite* **weak**] **d** have power or influence: *Her allies were deserting her; she was no longer as strong as she had been.* □ *We're in a much stronger position now.* □ *in the '50s and '60s, when the unions were much stronger.* □ *the militarily strong nations of the world* □ *the formation of strong pressure groups.* [*same as* **powerful, influential**]
2 Something that is **strong a** exerts, or is capable of exerting, a lot of force: *The wind became stronger and stronger.* □ *a strong electrical current* □ *strong magnetic forces* □ *caught in the strong grip of the tide* □ *Carnivores typically have strong jaws and teeth for tearing flesh and crushing bone.* [*opposite* **weak, gentle, mild**] **b** can stand a lot of strain, rough treatment or prolonged use without breaking, collapsing or wearing out: *built on strong foundations.* □ *strong nylon webbing* □ *Those chairs don't look very strong.* □ *mountain equipment that is light but strong.* [*same as* **sturdy, stout, tough, firm**; *opposite* **weak, insubstantial**]
3 a Strong describes anything that is great in degree or intensity: *There was a strong smell of disinfectant.* □ *She likes dishes with a strong flavour.* □ *She had a strong Irish accent.* □ *I had a strong impression that he was hiding something.* □ *There are still strong feelings of resentment amongst the local population.* □ *She had been a strong influence on me.* [*same as* **intense, powerful**; *opposite* **faint, mild**] **b** People who have **strong** views, or express them in **strong** terms, have firm and definite views about something and express them firmly: *He had strong opinions about mixing religion

with politics. □ *We're likely to meet with strong opposition.* □ *There was strong criticism from some quarters.* □ *She expressed strong disapproval.* □ *His strongest supporters were the farmers and country folk.* □ *We should condemn the practice in the strongest possible terms.*

Notice (sense 4d below) that **'strong** language' is offensive language.

c You take **strong** action when you act firmly and with authority: *Strong measures must be taken to prevent the infection spreading.* [*same as* **firm**] **d** A **strong** candidate, competitor, opponent or rival has the ability or qualities needed for winning, or for beating you. **e** A **strong** argument or case is one that is likely to persuade people; **strong** evidence is likely to convince people; **strong** reasons or motives are likely to make you act in a certain way: *She put forward a strong case for reforming the system.* □ *Who had the strongest motive for murder?* □ *There were strong indications that she intended to resign.* □ *We had strong reason to doubt their claim.* [*same as* **powerful**] **f Strong** relationships or links are well established and close: *the strong link of friendship between our two nations.* [*same as* **close**] **g** There is a **strong** chance or possibility of something happening if it is likely to happen: *You've quite a strong chance of being awarded a grant.* [*opposite* **slight**]

4 a Strong describes such things as tea or coffee that contain a lot of the substance that gives them their flavour: *a strong cup of black coffee.* [*opposite* **weak**] **b** A **strong** drug or painkiller contains a large amount of the substance that produces the intended effect. [*same as* **powerful**; *opposite* **mild**] **c Strong** alcoholic drinks contain a large amount of alcohol; some people refer to alcohol generally as **'strong** drink'. [*opposite* **mild**] **d Strong** language is rude or offensive speech, which usually contains swearwords.

5 a Your **strong** subjects are the ones you are good at or know a lot about: *English was always her strongest subject.* □ *I was fairly strong on anatomy and physiology.* [*opposite* **weak**] **b** Your **strong** points are the good things about you, or your good qualities: *Tact isn't one of her strong points.* [*opposite* **weak**] **c** You have **strong** nerves or a **strong** stomach if you do not get frightened or upset easily. [*opposite* **weak**] **d** (*commerce*) Currencies are **strong** when their value is steady or rising; a **strong** economy is a financially successful one: *The pound is falling against a strong dollar.* [*opposite* **weak**]

6 A group is a certain number of people **strong** if it contains that number: *our 50-strong male-voice choir* □ *a crowd of protesters 500 strong.* — *adverb* **strongly:** *strongly constructed apparatus.* □ *a strongly built young man* □ *He was strongly opposed to the idea.* □ *I'm strongly in support of the ban.* □ *I cannot emphasize too strongly the importance of careful planning.* □ *in a strongly worded statement released to the press today* □ *His breath smelt strongly of garlic.* □ *I was strongly influenced by her writings.* □ *strongly anti-Nazi views.*

▻ ***phrase*** (*informal*) Someone or something is still **going strong** if they are are still alive or in existence, and in a lively or healthy condition: *He's 95 and still going strong.* □ *A hundred years on and the charity is still going strong.*
[see also **strength**].

stronghold /'strɒŋhoʊld/ *noun*: **strongholds**
1 A **stronghold** is a place that is strongly defended against attack, *eg* a castle. **2** You also refer to an area or place where there is strong support for *eg* a political party as a **stronghold** of that party: *a Labour stronghold.*

strong verb /strɒŋ 'vɜːb/ *noun*: **strong verbs**
In English and certain other languages, a **strong verb** is a verb with an irregular past tense formed by changing a vowel rather than adding *-d*, as in *sing sang sung* and *write wrote.* [see also **weak verb**]

stroppy /'strɒpɪ/ *adjective*: **stroppier**, **stroppiest** (*informal, derogatory*)
A **stroppy** person is someone who is quarrelsome, bad-tempered and awkward to deal with: *He got a bit stroppy when I asked him to leave.* [*opposite* **cooperative**]

strove /stroʊv/ *verb*
Strove is the past tense of **strive**.

struck /strʌk/ *verb*
Struck is the past tense and past participle of **strike**.

structural /'strʌktʃərəl/ *adjective*
Structural means of or relating to structure, or a basic structure or framework: *The crash was caused by a structural fault in the aircraft's wing.* □ *a structural analysis of moon rock.*

structure /'strʌktʃə(r)/ *noun*; *verb*
▻ ***noun***: **structures**
1 (*uncount*) The **structure** of a thing is the way its parts are arranged or organized into a whole: *the structure of society* □ *a diagram showing the structure of the human heart* □ *the structure of language.* **2** A **structure** is a thing that is built or constructed from smaller parts: *a wooden structure.*
▻ ***verb***: **structures, structuring, structured**
You **structure** something when you organize or arrange it: *You should structure your arguments so that they can be easily followed.*

struggle /'strʌgəl/ *verb*; *noun*
▻ ***verb***: **struggles, struggling, struggled**
1 You **struggle** when you make violent twisting or wriggling movements with your body, especially in order to get free from someone who is restraining you or holding you down: *She kicked and struggled to get free of the two policemen who were trying to arrest her.* □ *He struggled out of the tight diving suit.* **2** You **struggle** when you make a great effort under difficult conditions: *She struggled against her feelings of resentment and bitterness.* [*same as* **fight**] **3** You **struggle** along or through something when you make your way and progress with great difficulty: *'How have you been?' 'Oh, I've been struggling along much as usual.'* □ *He struggled through the French exam.* [*same as* **battle**]
4 You **struggle** with someone or something when you fight against them: *He was struggling with his conscience.*
▻ ***noun***: **struggles**
1 A **struggle** is an act of struggling: *After a brief struggle, the man was finally handcuffed and taken away.* **2** A **struggle** is also a task that requires great effort: *It's a bit of a struggle trying to feed a family of four on only £90 a week.* **3** A fight or contest can also be called a **struggle**: *The struggle between good and evil.*

phrasal verb
You **struggle on** when you manage to survive or progress with great difficulty: *They struggled on through the bleak Antarctic landscape.* □ *Though disabled with arthritis she still manages to struggle on.* [*same as* **battle**]

strum /strʌm/ *verb*: **strums, strumming, strummed**
You **strum** a stringed musical instrument, such as a

guitar, or you **strum** a tune on it, when you play it by making quick movements with your hand across the strings, rather than plucking each string.

strung /strʌŋ/ *verb*
Strung is the past tense and past participle of **string**.

strut /strʌt/ *verb*; *noun*
▻ ***verb***: **struts, strutting, strutted**
A person or animal **struts** when they walk in a proud or self-important way: *peacocks strutting on the lawn* □ *She went strutting past with her nose in the air.*
▻ ***noun***: **struts** (*technical*)
A **strut** is a piece of wood or metal that bears weight or pressure along its length.

stub /stʌb/ *noun*; *verb*
▻ ***noun***: **stubs**
A **stub** is **1** a short piece, *eg* of a cigarette or a pencil, left after the rest has been used up. **2** the part of a cheque or ticket that you keep as a record.
▻ ***verb***: **stubs, stubbing, stubbed**
If you **stub** your toe, you hurt it by accidentally kicking something hard.

> ***phrasal verb***
> When someone **stubs out** a cigarette or cigar, they stop it burning by pressing it against something hard.

stubble /ˈstʌbəl/ *noun* (*uncount*)
1 Stubble is the mass of short stiff stalks left standing in the ground after a crop such as corn or barley has been harvested. **2 Stubble** is also the short stiff hairs that appear as a dark shadow on a man's face and which will eventually grow into a beard if they are not shaved off.

stubborn /ˈstʌbən/ *adjective*
1 A **stubborn** person refuses to change their opinions or decisions even when they are being unreasonable by not doing so. [*same as* **obstinate**] **2** You can also describe a person as **stubborn** when they are very determined and refuse to give up. **3 Stubborn** also describes things that are very difficult to treat, remove or deal with: *a stubborn stain.* — *adverb* **stubbornly:** *He stubbornly refused to listen to reason.* [*same as* **obstinately**] — *noun* (*uncount*) **stubbornness:** *She was exasperated by his stubbornness.* [*same as* **obstinacy**]

stubby /ˈstʌbɪ/ *adjective*: **stubbier, stubbiest**
Stubby things are short and thick: *stubby fingers.*

stuck /stʌk/ *verb*; *adjective*
▻ ***verb***
Stuck is the past tense and past participle of **stick**.
▻ ***adjective***
1 If you get **stuck** when you are trying to do something, you cannot continue with it because you do not know what to do next: *Do the next ten sums in your maths book. If you get stuck, let me know and I will help you.* **2** If something is **stuck** in a particular place or position, it cannot be moved or is unable to move: *The door is stuck.* □ *He got his head stuck between the railings.* **3** You are **stuck** somewhere when you can't leave, although you want to: *We could be stuck on the island for days if this fog doesn't lift.*

stuck-up /stʌkˈʌp/ *adjective* (*informal*)
If you say that someone is **stuck-up**, you think they are snobbish.

stud /stʌd/ *noun*
1 A **stud** is a metal nail or rivet with a large head, used to decorate a surface. **2** The **studs** on a football or rugby boot are any of the small rounded metal or plastic projections on its sole that give added grip on soft or slippery surfaces. **3** A **stud** is a fastener, *eg* fixing a collar to a shirt, consisting of two small discs on either end of a short bar: *a collar stud.* **4** A **stud** is a press stud. **5** A **stud** is a male animal, especially a horse, kept for breeding. **6** A **stud** or a **stud farm** is a place where horses are kept for breeding.

student /ˈstjuːdənt/ *noun*: **students**
1 A **student** is **a** a person following a formal course of study at a college or university. **b** a senior pupil at a secondary school or high school. **2** If you say that someone is a **student** of a particular subject, you mean that they are especially interested in that subject and are trying to learn more about it: *a student of human behaviour.*

studied /ˈstʌdɪd/ *adjective*
Studied is used to describe attitudes or expressions that are carefully practised or whose effect is carefully considered beforehand, and are therefore not spontaneous or sincere: *She showed a studied indifference to everything that was going on around her.*

studio /ˈstjuːdɪoʊ/ *noun*: **studios**
1 An artist's or photographer's **studio** is the place where they work. **2** A **studio** is also a room or building where music recordings, cinema films, or television or radio programmes are made. **3** (*usually in the plural*) The premises of a company making any of these are referred to as that company's **studios**: *Pinewood Studios.*

studious /ˈstjuːdɪəs/ *adjective*
1 Someone who is **studious** has a serious, hard-working approach to study. [*same as* **academic**] **2 Studious** is also used to describe things that are done deliberately or with the great care: *He made a studious inspection of the food they had prepared for the party.* — *adverb* **studiously:** *He studiously avoided any discussion of his past life.*

study /ˈstʌdɪ/ *verb*; *noun*
▻ ***verb***: **studies, studying, studied**
1 You **study** when you spend time gaining knowledge by *eg* reading or attending a college or university; you **study** a particular subject when you spend time learning about it: *Don't disturb him; he's studying for his exams.* □ *She's at university studying law.* **2** You **study** something when you look at it or examine it closely: *She studied the map.* □ *He studied her face for any sign of emotion.*
▻ ***noun***: **studies**
1 (*uncount*) **Study** is the act or process of learning or gaining knowledge *eg* by reading: *Pupils taking A-levels will have two periods set aside each day for study.* □ *a study period.* **2** Your **studies** are work done in the process of gaining knowledge: *She had to interrupt her studies to look after her sick mother.* **3** If you make a **study** of a particular thing, you research it or make a close examination of it: *He has made a study of football hooliganism and its causes.* **4** A **study** is also a work of art done for the sake of practice, or in preparation for a larger or more detailed picture. **5** A **study** is also a piece of music intended to exercise and develop a player's technique: *violin studies.* **6** A **study** is a private room where quiet work or study is carried out: *He's working in his study.*

stuff /stʌf/ *noun*; *verb*
▻ ***noun*** (*uncount*)
1 (*informal*) You can refer to any material or substance as **stuff**, especially when you are not sure exactly what it is: *Is this the right stuff for painting exterior wood?* □ *What's the name of the stuff that you use to put on burns?* □ *She made the cushions out of some sort of silky stuff.* **2** (*informal*) You can also use

stuff to refer to someone's belongings, or to a number of unnamed things collectively: *I want all your stuff out of the house by tomorrow evening.* □ *Have you got all your stuff ready for the trip?* [*same as* **things**] **3** (*literary*) If you refer to something being the **stuff** of something else, you mean that it is its essence or subject matter: *Human frailty is the stuff of many a successful novel.*

▻ ***verb***: **stuffs, stuffing, stuffed**

1 You **stuff** something somewhere when you thrust or push it there hurriedly and roughly: *He stuffed a few things into a bag and took the next train to Birmingham.* **2** In cookery, you **stuff** a bird, such as a chicken, or a vegetable, such as a pepper or large mushroom, when you fill it with a mixture of chopped-up ingredients before you cook it. **3** (*informal*) You **stuff** yourself when you eat a lot of food at one time: *He's always stuffing his face with sweets.* [*same as* **gorge**] **4** (*informal*) If a place **is stuffed** with things, it is crammed or completely filled up with a great many things: *The fridge was stuffed with food.* **5** If a dead animal or bird **is stuffed**, its empty carcass is filled with material to return it to its original shape so that it can be displayed *eg* in a museum.

▻ ***phrases*** **1** (*informal*) If someone **does their stuff** they display their talents or perform the job or task required: *He was out on the dance floor doing his stuff.* □ *You should feel a lot better when the surgeon has done his stuff.* **2** (*offensive slang*) Some people say **get stuffed!** when they are dismissing another person or what they have said rudely and contemptuously. **3** (*informal*) Someone who **knows their stuff** has a thorough knowledge of their subject. **4** If you feel **stuffed up** or your nose is **stuffed up**, you feel that you cannot breathe properly because mucus is blocking your nose and the passages leading to your nose. [*same as* **congested**]

stuffing /ˈstʌfɪŋ/ *noun* (*uncount*)

1 **Stuffing** is padding used to stuff such things as children's toys or cushions. **2** **Stuffing** is also a chopped and seasoned mixture of foods, such as sausagemeat, onion, herbs, and breadcrumbs, with which a bird or roll of meat is stuffed before cooking.

▻ ***phrase*** If someone or something **knocks the stuffing out of** a person or thing, it takes away their strength or power and makes them weak or feeble: *The long illness has knocked the stuffing out of him.*

stuffy /ˈstʌfɪ/ *adjective*: **stuffier, stuffiest**

1 A **stuffy** room or a **stuffy** atmosphere is unpleasant because it lacks fresh, cool air: *The small windowless room was hot and stuffy.* [*same as* **airless**] **2** (*informal*) If you describe a person or their attitudes as **stuffy** you mean that they are formal and boringly conventional or old-fashioned. [*same as* **prim, staid**; *opposite* **interesting, modern**]

stultify /ˈstʌltɪfaɪ/ *verb*: **stultifies, stultifying, stultified** (*formal*)

Something that **stultifies** has the effect of making something appear useless or foolish or is so boring that it makes you lose interest: *Too much television can stultify children's creative development.* [*same as* **stifle**] — *adjective* **stultifying:** *the stultifying effect of repetitive tasks.*

stumble /ˈstʌmbəl/ *verb*: **stumbles, stumbling, stumbled**

1 You **stumble** when you lose your balance and nearly fall because you have caught your foot against something or put it down on an uneven surface: *His horse stumbled on the rocky ground, throwing him out of the saddle.* □ *He stumbled over a hidden branch and fell on his face.* **2** You **stumble** somewhere when you move or walk unsteadily in that direction, often knocking into things as you go: *She stumbled into the room, clutching her chest.* □ *He was stumbling around trying to find the light switch.* [*same as* **stagger**] **3** You **stumble** over words or **stumble** through a speech when you hesitate over a word or words or make frequent mistakes when you are reading aloud.

> ***phrasal verb***
> You **stumble across** or **on** something when you find it or come across it unexpectedly or by chance: *The detective has stumbled on a vital clue.*

stumbling-block /ˈstʌmblɪŋ blɑk/ *noun*: **stumbling-blocks**

A **stumbling-block** is a problem or difficulty that prevents you, or is likely to prevent you, from progressing or achieving what you want to achieve: *The refusal of the Bosnian Serbs to accept the latest UN proposals is likely to prove a major stumbling-block to lasting peace in the region.* [*same as* **obstacle, hindrance**]

stump /stʌmp/ *noun*; *verb*

▻ ***noun***: **stumps**

1 When you cut down a tree the part that is left in the ground is a **stump**. **2** Any short part that is left after a larger part has been removed can also be called a **stump**, *eg* the part of a leg or arm that is left when the remainder has been amputated. **3** In cricket, a **stump** is any of the three thin upright wooden posts which support the horizontal parts of the wicket. **4** (*plural*) In cricket, the whole wicket is frequently referred to as the **stumps**.

▻ ***verb***: **stumps, stumping, stumped**

1 If you **are stumped** by a question or problem, you are not able to answer it or solve it: *When he asked me to solve the next part of the equation, I was completely stumped.* [*same as* **baffled**] **2** If you **stump** somewhere, you walk slowly and heavily with stamping or unsteady steps: *I could hear him stumping around in the attic.*

> ***phrasal verb***
> (*informal*) If someone **stumps up** for something, or **stumps up** the money for it, they pay for it, usually reluctantly: *Her father eventually stumped up the money to pay her fare.* [*same as* **fork out**]

stumpy /ˈstʌmpɪ/ *adjective*: **stumpier, stumpiest**

Something that is **stumpy** is short and thick, like the stump of a tree: *a dog with a stumpy little tail.* [*opposite* **long, tall, thin**]

stun /stʌn/ *verb*: **stuns, stunning, stunned**

1 If something, especially a blow to the head, **stuns** you, it causes you to become unconscious, especially for a short period: *The boxer reeled back against the ropes, momentarily stunned.* **2** If you **are stunned** by something it shocks or astonishes you so much that you are unable to speak or think clearly: *He was stunned into silence.* [*same as* **dumbfounded**]

stung /stʌŋ/ *verb*

Stung is the past tense and past participle of **sting**.

stunk /stʌŋk/ *verb*

Stunk is the past participle of **stink**.

stunning /ˈstʌnɪŋ/ *adjective*

1 (*informal*) If you describe a person as **stunning**, you mean that they are extremely beautiful or handsome: *a stunning blonde.* [*same as* **gorgeous**] **2** (*informal*) Something **stunning** is very impressive: *They had a stunning view of the Matterhorn from their bedroom window.* [*same as* **spectacular**] — *adverb* (*intensifying*)

stunningly: *She had grown into a stunningly beautiful woman.*

stunt /stʌnt/ *verb; noun*
▻ ***verb*: stunts, stunting, stunted**
If something **stunts** the growth or development of another thing, it prevents that other thing from growing or developing fully: *She tried to put him off smoking by telling him it would stunt his growth.* □ *The constant wind had stunted the growth of the few remaining trees.* [*opposite* **encourage**]
▻ ***noun*: stunts**
A **stunt** is **1** a daring act or spectacular event intended to show off talent or attract publicity: *The Conservative's poster campaign is just another publicity stunt.* **2** a dangerous or acrobatic feat performed as part of the action of a film or television programme: *The actor does all his own stunts.* [=does not use a stuntman for difficult or dangerous action shots]

stunted /'stʌntɪd/ *adjective*
Stunted things have not grown or developed fully: *a desolate landscape with only a few stunted trees.*

stuntman /'stʌntman/ or **stuntwoman** /'stʌntwʊmən/ *noun*: **stuntmen** or **stuntwomen**
A **stuntman** or **stuntwoman** is a person employed to take the place of an actor when stunts are being filmed.

stupefy /'stju:pɪfaɪ/ *verb*: **stupefies, stupefying, stupefied** (*usually in the passive*)
1 If you **are stupefied** by *eg* drugs or alcohol, your senses are so dulled by them that you are unable to think clearly or react normally: *He was mumbling incoherently, stupefied with drink.* **2** If you **are stupefied** by something it causes you to be overcome with amazement or astonishment: *I was stupefied by his audacity.* [*same as* **astounded**]

stupendous /stjʊ'pɛndəs/ *adjective*
If you describe something as **stupendous** you think it is amazingly large or impressive: *His winning of the gold medal was a stupendous achievement.* □ *Their duet received stupendous applause.* [*same as* **tremendous**] — *adverb* **stupendously:** *The tour had been stupendously successful.* [*same as* **tremendously**]

stupid /'stju:pɪd/ *adjective*: **stupider, stupidest**
1 A **stupid** person is not intelligent or sensible: *How could you have been so stupid!* □ *He's too stupid for words.* □ *It was a bit stupid of you to have left your keys at home.* □ *I'm sorry; that was a stupid thing to have said.* □ *I made a stupid mistake.* [*same as* **foolish**; *opposite* **wise**] **2** If someone is **stupid** with drugs or as a result of a blow, they are stupefied or senseless: *He got a thump on the head that knocked him stupid.* — *adverb* **stupidly:** *I stupidly thought that it was the right thing to do.* [*same as* **foolishly**; *opposite* **wisely**]

stupidity /stju:'pɪdɪtɪ/ *noun* (*uncount*)
Stupidity is the quality or condition of being stupid: *I was astonished at his stupidity.*

stupor /'stju:pə(r)/ *noun* (*used in the singular*)
If someone is in a **stupor** they are in a semi-conscious condition, *eg* from taking drugs or alcohol: *He lay on the floor in a drunken stupor.*

sturdy /'stɜ:dɪ/ *adjective*: **sturdier, sturdiest**
1 If you are **sturdy** you are strong and healthy; if your body or limbs are **sturdy** they are thick and strong-looking: *The baby is growing up strong and sturdy.* □ *He is small and sturdy.* [*same as* **robust**] **2** Something that is **sturdy** is strongly built or made: *a sturdy pair of walking shoes.* — *adverb* **sturdily:** *sturdily-built* — *noun* **sturdiness:** *the sturdiness of his arms.*

stutter /'stʌtə(r)/ *noun; verb*
▻ ***noun*: stutters**
A **stutter** is a condition in which the person affected is unable to say certain speech sounds without hesitating or repeating the sounds, especially at the beginning of words: *He speaks with a stutter.* [*same as* **stammer**]
▻ ***verb*: stutters, stuttering, stuttered**
Someone **stutters** when they have a stutter or when they say something with a stutter: *He finds it impossible to read aloud because he stutters so badly.* □ *'Wh..wh..what do you mean?' he stuttered.* [*same as* **stammer**]

sty[1] /staɪ/ *noun*: **sties**
A **sty** is a pigsty.

sty[2] or **stye** /staɪ/ *noun*: **sties** or **styes**
A **sty** or **stye** is a painful swelling on the eyelid caused by infection at the base of an eyelash.

style /staɪl/ *noun; verb*
▻ ***noun*: styles**
1 The **style** of something is the way or manner in which it is designed, arranged, presented or done, especially a way that is typical of a certain period, person or group: *From the early 18th century the classical style began to dominate architecture.* □ *a poem in the style of Auden* □ *He could imitate any painter's style with a little practice.* □ *His written style differed remarkably from his manner of talking.* □ *clothing styles through the ages* □ *She had begun to wear her hair in a new, more youthful style.* □ *old-style socialism* □ *Her particular style of leadership was not greatly liked.* **2** (*count or uncount*) Your **style** is your typical way of behaving and your personal attitude to things: *Living in a tent wasn't exactly Rae's style.* □ *In typical style he bought drinks for everyone within shouting range.* **3** (*count or uncount*) The **style** of a product is its fashion or design: *This year's pinafore dress comes in a variety of attractive styles.* □ *minor variations in style.* [*same as* **design**] **4** (*uncount*) Someone or something that has **style** is smart and elegant, especially in an assured or confident way: *She was never dressed in the height of fashion but somehow she had style.*
▻ ***verb*: styles, styling, styled**
1 To **style** something is to shape it in a particular way: *jackets styled to flatter your figure* □ *She was going off to get her hair cut and styled.* [*same as* **shape**] **2** (*literary*) Someone **styles** themselves something when they call themselves by that name: *a lady styling herself Madame Augustine.* □ *these narrow little dwellings, styled maisonettes by the builders.* [*same as* **call**]
▻ ***phrases*** **1** Something that **cramps your style** stops you behaving as freely as you would like: *Taking your little brothers and sisters everywhere with you must cramp your style a bit.* **2** You do something **in style** when you do it the most expensive or elegant way: *There they found they could live in style at no great cost.* □ *Let's have a big wedding; we'll do the thing in style.*

stylish /'staɪlɪʃ/ *adjective*
Stylish things are elegant and fashionable: *She wore a stylish hat.* □ *Their furniture is very stylish.* — *adverb* **stylishly:** *stylishly dressed.*

stylistic /staɪ'lɪstɪk/ *adjective*
Stylistic means relating to style, especially a literary or artistic style: *a stylistic comparison between the two poets.* — *adverb* **stylistically:** *Stylistically, his painting is closer to the Impressionists than the Cubists.*

suave /swɑ:v/ *adjective*
You describe a man as **suave** when he has extremely polite and charming manners: *a suave and sophisticated young man.* [*same as* **smooth**]

sub /sʌb/ *noun*: **subs** (*informal*)
1 A **sub** is a submarine. **2** A **sub** in a team game such as football is a substitute player. **3** Someone who pays **subs** to an organization or club pays their subscription fees to that organization or club.

sub- /sʌb-/ or /səb-/ *prefix*
Sub- is used to form nouns and adjectives with the meaning **1** under or below: *submarine* □ *subterranean.* **2** secondary or lower in rank or importance: *sublieutenant.* □ *subordinate* **3** less than: *subhuman.* **4** a part or division of: *subatomic* □ *subcommittee.*

subconscious /sʌb'kɒnʃəs/ *noun*; *adjective*
▻ ***noun*** (*used in the singular*)
Your **subconscious** is the part of your mind that has thoughts and feelings that you are not fully aware of but which can nevertheless influence your actions or behaviour.
▻ ***adjective***
Something that is **subconscious** exists or happens in your subconscious: *a subconscious urge.* [*opposite* **conscious**]

subcontract *noun*; *verb*
▻ ***noun*** /sʌb'kɒntrakt/: **subcontracts**
A **subcontract** is a secondary contract, by which the hired person or company hires another person or company to carry out the work.
▻ ***verb*** /sʌbkən'trakt/: **subcontracts, subcontracting, subcontracted**
An individual or company **subcontracts** work when they employ another individual or company under a subcontract to do the work that the first individual or company is contracted to do.

subcontractor /sʌbkən'traktə(r)/ *noun*: **subcontractors**
A **subcontractor** is a person or company employed under the terms of a subcontract.

subculture /'sʌbkʌltʃə(r)/ *noun*: **subcultures**
A **subculture** is a group within society that has its own particular customs, beliefs and behaviour, especially a group that is regarded with disapproval by the rest of society.

subdivide /sʌbdɪ'vaɪd/ *verb*: **subdivides, subdividing, subdivided**
If a part or section of something **is subdivided**, it is divided into even smaller parts or sections.

subdivision /'sʌbdɪvɪʒən/ *noun*: **subdivisions**
1 (*uncount*) **Subdivision** is the action or process of subdividing. **2** A **subdivision** is a part or section formed by subdividing a larger part or section.

subdue /səb'dju:/ *verb*: **subdues, subduing, subdued**
If you **subdue** an emotion or urge, you suppress it and bring it under control; a rebellious group of people **are subdued** by someone or something when they are defeated or brought under control by force: *He managed to subdue his feelings of rage.* □ *At any moment troops might be needed to subdue an uprising.* [*same as* **suppress**; *opposite* **arouse**]

subdued /səb'dju:d/ *adjective*
1 Subdued lighting or **subdued** colours are not bright. [*same as* **soft**; *opposite* **bright**] **2** Someone is **subdued** when they are quieter or in lower spirits than usual.

subject *noun*; *adjective*; *verb*
▻ ***noun*** /'sʌbdʒɛkt/: **subjects**
1 The **subject** of something such as a discussion, conversation, speech, book or other piece of writing is the thing, idea or person that is being talked about or written about: *This is boring. Can't we change the subject?* □ *While we're on the subject of pay, is there any chance of a rise?* □ *It's a matter that has been the subject of much debate.* □ *What subject would they like me to talk to them about?* □ *Has anyone any ideas on the subject?* [compare **topic, matter**] **2** The **subject** of a painting is the thing or theme represented by it. **3** A **subject** is one of the things you study at school, college or university, such as English, mathematics, Latin or physics: *Art was my best subject when I was at school.* □ *How many subjects will you be studying next year?* □ *I'm taking four subjects at A-level.* **4** The **subject** of an experiment or an operation is the person on whom the experiment or operation is performed: *Bromsgrove has recently been the subject of a Health Service experiment.* □ *Whilst hypnotized the subject performed a number of actions in obedience to his commands.* **5** The **subjects** of a country are its citizens; the monarch of a country can refer to the citizens of it as his or her **subjects**: *if your parents are both British subjects* □ *when the Queen addresses her subjects.* **6** (*grammar*) The **subject** of a verb, clause or sentence is the person or thing that performs the action of an active verb (*eg* 'he' in *He dropped it*) or is affected by the action of a passive verb (*eg* 'it' in *It was dropped by him*). [see also **object**]
▻ ***adjective***
1 A person or thing is **subject** to something if they are occasionally affected by it, or may be: *He's been subject to bouts of malaria since he returned from the expedition.* □ *Please note that arrival and departure times are subject to alteration at short notice.* □ *The area is subject to flooding.* **2** People are **subject** to something such as a law if they have to obey it: *They are subject to the immigration laws like anyone else.* **3 Subject** states are under the rule of a more powerful state, and are not politically independent.
▻ ***verb*** /səb'dʒɛkt/: **subjects, subjecting, subjected**
You **are subjected** to something unpleasant when you are made to experience or suffer it: *Prisoners were frequently subjected to torture and beatings.* □ *The airport officials subjected each of us to a rigorous body search.*
▻ ***phrase*** Something that will happen **subject to** a stated condition will happen only if that condition is met: *The property is being sold subject to the condition that it will continue to be used as a private dwelling.* □ *The project will go ahead subject to the board's approval.*

subjective /səb'dʒɛktɪv/ *adjective*
Subjective opinions or arguments are based on, or strongly influenced by, personal thoughts and feelings: *analyse the problem, trying not to be too subjective.* [*opposite* **objective**]

subjugate /'sʌbdʒəgeɪt/ *verb*: **subjugates, subjugating, subjugated**
If someone **subjugates** a nation or group of people, they bring them under their control, usually by conquering them in war: *The Romans never succeeding in subjugating the tribes north of the Rhine.* [*same as* **overpower**] — *noun* (*uncount*) **subjugation:** *the subjugation of the Saxons by the Normans after the Conquest.*

subjunctive /səb'dʒʌŋktɪv/ *noun* (*grammar*)
The **subjunctive** is a verb form or mood used in certain languages to express doubt, wish or uncertainty. It can be identified in English by the use of *be* instead of *is*, as in '*Heaven be praised*', the use of *were* instead of *was*, as in '*if I were you*', and the omission of *'s'* from the third person singular form of the verb, as in *'he suggested she put off going'*. The use of the subjunctive is commoner in formal English and spoken American English than in spoken British English.

sublet /sʌb'lɛt/ *verb*: **sublets, subletting, sublet**
You **sublet** land or property that you rent from someone when you allow another person to use it or live in it in return for rent which they pay to you, while you pay rent in turn to the person from whom you are renting.

sublime /sə'blaɪm/ *adjective*
1 Something that is **sublime** is of the highest, most admirable kind and has the effect of lifting your spirits or filling you with awe: *Her singing was sublime.* □ (*informal*) *That meal was sublime!* [*same as* **glorious**] **2** (*only before a noun*; *informal*) You show **sublime** ignorance of something that is going wrong when you are quite unaware of what is happening, and carry on as usual: *She drove down the motorway the wrong way with sublime indifference to the chaos that she was causing.*

subliminal /sʌb'lɪmɪnəl/ *adjective* (*formal or technical*)
Subliminal means existing or occurring below the level of ordinary awareness; therefore, a **subliminal** message is one that you take in without being aware of it.

submachine-gun /sʌbmə'ʃi:ngʌn/ *noun*: **submachine-guns**
A **submachine-gun** is a lightweight portable machine-gun that can be fired from the shoulder or the hip.

submarine /sʌbmə'ri:n/ *noun*: **submarines**
A **submarine** is a type of boat that can travel under the sea as well as on the surface: *a naval submarine.*

submerge /səb'mɜ:dʒ/ *verb*: **submerges, submerging, submerged**
1 Something **submerges** or **is submerged** if it goes or is under the surface of water or other liquid: *Nuclear submarines can stay submerged for weeks on end if necessary.* □ *Environmentalists warned that the rise in water levels would submerge forests for miles around.* **2** If you **are submerged** by something, *eg* work, you have so much of it that you have no time to do anything else. [*same as* **overwhelm, inundate**]

submission /səb'mɪʃən/ *noun*: **submissions**
1 (*uncount*) **Submission** is **a** the state of yielding to the control or demands of someone else: *She behaved with complete submission.* [*same as* **compliance**] **b** the act of sending something to someone for their consideration: *the submission of proposals to the planning committee.* **2** A **submission** is a suggestion or proposal that is offered to, *eg* a court of law, for consideration or approval: *legal submissions.*

submissive /səb'mɪsɪv/ *adjective*
A **submissive** person is willing to or tends to submit to other people's will or demands. [*same as* **meek, passive**]

submit /səb'mɪt/ *verb*: **submits, submitting, submitted**
1 You **submit** when you give in to another person because you are not strong enough to resist them: *They refused to submit to the tyrannical barons.* □ *She was eventually persuaded to submit to his wishes.* [*same as* **yield**] **2** You **submit** to something when you allow yourself to be subjected to it: *They would have to submit to a series of tests.* □ *They agreed to submit themselves to the judgement of the court.* **3** You **submit** a proposal or application when you offer or present it for consideration by others: *He submitted his proposals to the committee.* □ *'My lord, I submit that there is insufficient evidence to convict my client.'*

subnormal /sʌb'nɔ:məl/ *adjective*
Someone who is **subnormal** has a very low level of intelligence or ability compared with other people of their age: *He is mentally subnormal.* [*same as* **retarded**]

subordinate /sə'bɔ:dɪnət/ *adjective*; *noun*; *verb*
▻ ***adjective***
If one person is **subordinate** to another, they are of a lower rank or importance than that other person and take orders from them; something that is **subordinate** to something else is secondary to or of less importance than that other thing: *He assigned the task to one of his subordinate officers.* □ *This matter is subordinate to the main issue.* [*opposite* **superior**]
▻ ***noun***: **subordinates**
A **subordinate** is a subordinate person or thing: *The chief inspector asked one of his subordinates to interview the suspect.* [*opposite* **superior**]
▻ ***verb*** (*formal*): **subordinates, subordinating, subordinated**
If you **subordinate** something to something else you treat it as being less important than that other thing: *She had to subordinate her personal ambition to the more pressing needs of her family.*

subordinate clause /səbɔ:dɪnət 'klɔ:z/ *noun* (*grammar*): **subordinate clauses**
A **subordinate clause** is a clause that adds more information to the main part of a sentence, acting like a noun, adjective or adverb. Subordinate clauses are introduced in a sentence by a conjunction, as in 'The book *that you gave me for Christmas* was fascinating'. [see also **main clause**]

subpoena /sə'pi:nə/ *noun*; *verb (legal)*
▻ ***noun***: **subpoenas**
A **subpoena** is a written order legally obliging a person to appear in a court of law at a specified time. [*same as* **summons**]
▻ ***verb***: **subpoenas, subpoenaing, subpoenaed** or **subpoena'd**
A court **subpoenas** someone when it issues an order that they appear at a specified time, *eg* to give evidence: *The count can subpoena a witness.* [*same as* **summon**]

subscribe /səb'skraɪb/ *verb*: **subscribes, subscribing, subscribed**
1 You **subscribe** to a publication when you pay a sum of money so that you will receive regular issues of it for the period that the payment covers. **2** You **subscribe** to an idea or theory when you agree with or believe in it: *I don't subscribe to the notion that the individual is wholly in control of his own destiny.* [*same as* **support**]

subscriber /səb'skraɪbə(r)/ *noun*: **subscribers**
1 A **subscriber** is someone who pays a sum of money to receive a newspaper or magazine regularly over the period paid for. **2** A **subscriber** is also a person who pays to receive a service: *telephone subscribers.*

subscription /səb'skrɪpʃən/ *noun*: **subscriptions**
A **subscription** is a payment for *eg* a club membership fee or a number of issues of a magazine for a given period: *Members wishing to resign should do so at least a month before their annual subscription is due.* [*same as* **fee**]

subsequent /'sʌbsɪkwənt/ *adjective*
1 (*only before a noun*) **Subsequent** means happening after or following something else: *Last year we had planned to move house, but subsequent events made this impossible.* □ *Their separation and subsequent divorce was the subject of intense media interest.* [*same as* **ensuing**] **2** (*formal*) If one thing is **subsequent** to another it happens after that other thing: *Subsequent to his arrest he made a full confession.* — *adverb* **subsequently:** *He was subsequently found to be completely innocent.* [*same as* **later**]

subservient /səb'sɜ:vɪənt/ *adjective*

1 (*derogatory*) Someone is **subservient** when they are too ready or eager to do what others want: *Her senior ministers were passive and subservient.* **2** If one thing is **subservient** to another it is regarded as being less important than that other thing: *The needs of the individual must necessarily be subservient to those of the wider good.* [*same as* **subordinate**]

subside /səb'saɪd/ *verb*: **subsides, subsiding, subsided**
1 If the surface of land **subsides**, it sinks suddenly to a lower level; if a building **subsides** it sinks lower into the ground: *The building's foundations had to be reinforced to stop it subsiding any further.* **2** A storm or high wind **subsides** when it dies down; a fever **subsides** when the patient's temperature gradually returns to normal; a violent or intense emotion **subsides** when it becomes less and less and disappears. [*same as* **lessen**]

subsidence /'sʌbsɪdəns/ or /səb'saidəns/ *noun* (*uncount*)
If **subsidence** occurs in a place, the ground sinks to a lower level: *The whole area is prone to subsidence because of old mine workings.*

subsidiary /səb'sɪdɪərɪ/ *adjective*; *noun*
▻ ***adjective***
If something is **subsidiary** it is smaller or of less importance than the main thing to which is it connected: *They found a number of subsidiary passages leading away from the burial chamber.* □ *a subsidiary company.*
▻ ***noun***: **subsidiaries**
A **subsidiary** is a company that is owned or controlled by another, usually larger, company: *a subsidiary of News International.*

subsidize or **subsidise** /'sʌbsɪdaɪz/ *verb*: **subsidizes, subsidizing, subsidized**
1 Government **subsidizes** industry or the arts when it pays part of its costs with a subsidy. **2** You **subsidize** someone when you pay part of their living expenses: *His parents had to subsidize him throughout his time at university.* [*same as* **finance, support, sponsor**]

subsidy /'sʌbsɪdɪ/ *noun*: **subsidies**
1 A **subsidy** is a sum of money given, *eg* by a government to an industry or the arts, to help with running costs or to keep product prices low: *If subsidies to hill farmers are withdrawn many of them will go out of business.* [*same as* **grant, support**] **2** (*uncount*) **Subsidy** is financial assistance of this kind.

subsist /səb'sɪst/ *verb*: **subsists, subsisting, subsisted** (*formal*)
If people **subsist** on especially a small amount of food, or if they **subsist** on a particular type of food, it keeps them alive or is just enough to keep them alive: *They subsisted for a great part of the year on roots and berries.* [*same as* **survive**]

subsistence /səb'sɪstəns/ *noun* (*uncount, often adjectival; formal*)
Subsistence is the means of living, or the condition of living with just enough food or income to stay alive: *Nearly three million families in Britain are living at subsistence level.* □ *subsistence farming.* [=in which the food produced is just enough to feed the farmer and his family with none left over to sell]

substance /'sʌbstəns/ *noun* (*uncount or count*): **substances**
1 A **substance** is a particular type of matter, usually with a definite quality: *a sticky substance* □ *The police discovered cocaine and other illegal substances in his flat.* **2** (*uncount*) The **substance** of something spoken or written is its essence or basic meaning: *The substance of her argument was that women were in all ways superior to men.* [*same as* **basis**] **3** (*uncount*) If something has **substance** it is real and can be touched: *Ghosts have no substance.* **4** (*uncount*) **Substance** is the quality of being important or significant, especially in relation to real life: *The President and the Prime Minister were able to discuss several matters of substance in talks that were relaxed and cordial.* **5** (*uncount; formal*) **Substance** is truth: *The rumours of his resignation are completely without substance.* [*same as* **foundation**] **6** (*uncount; literary*) A person of **substance** has wealth and influence: *a woman of substance.*

substantial /səb'stanʃəl/ *adjective*
1 Substantial means a very large amount: *He was awarded a substantial sum in damages.* □ *There has been a substantial improvement in his work this term.* [*opposite* **insignificant**] **2** A **substantial** meal is large and nourishing: *a substantial breakfast of porridge followed by bacon and eggs.* **3 Substantial** describes something that is solidly built: *The garden was surrounded by a substantial stone wall.* **4** Something that is **substantial** is real, not imaginary, and can be seen and touched. [*same as* **concrete**; *opposite* **insubstantial**] **5 Substantial** also means relating to a thing's basic nature or most important part: *I think we can say that we are in substantial agreement.* [*same as* **essential**] **6** You also describe a person or business as **substantial** when they are wealthy and influential: *a substantial land-owning family.*

substantiate /səb'stanʃɪeɪt/ *verb*: **substantiates, substantiating, substantiated**
If you can **substantiate** a statement or claim, you are able to supply evidence confirming that it is true. [*same as* **validate**; *opposite* **disprove**]

substitute /'sʌbstɪtjuːt/ *noun*; *verb*; *adjective*
▻ ***noun***: **substitutes**
A **substitute** is a person or thing that takes the place of, or is used instead of, another: *We have not yet devised an effective substitute.*
▻ ***verb***: **substitutes, substituting, substituted**
If one person or thing **is substituted** for another, they are used instead of, or take the place of, that other person or thing: *If you prefer, you can substitute a low-fat margarine for the butter.* — *noun* (*uncount or count*) **substitution** /sʌbstɪ'tjuːʃən/: *Each team is allowed to make two substitutions in the course of the match.* □ *The substitution of the title 'Ms' for 'Miss' or 'Mrs' is commonly accepted these days.*
▻ ***adjective:*** *a substitute goalkeeper.* [*same as* **reserve**]

subterfuge /'sʌbtəfjuːdʒ/ *noun* (*uncount or count*): **subterfuges**
The use of **subterfuge**, or a **subterfuge**, is the use of a trick or deception for avoiding a difficulty.

subterranean /sʌbtə'reɪnɪən/ *adjective*
Subterranean means situated or operating underground: *subterranean passages.*

subtitle /'sʌbtaɪtəl/ *noun*: **subtitles**
1 A film or television programme with **subtitles** has a printed translation or version of the dialogue at the bottom of the screen. **2** A book or play with a **subtitle** has a second title, usually expanding on or explaining the main title: *George Eliot's 'Silas Marner' has the subtitle 'The Weaver of Raveloe'.*

subtle /'sʌtəl/ *adjective*: **subtler, subtlest**
1 a Something that is **subtle** is not immediately obvious or is difficult to detect or appreciate: *Note the subtle difference in meaning achieved by simply reordering the words in the sentence.* □ *a subtle distinction.* [*opposite* **unsubtle**] **b** A **subtle** flavour, aroma or shade is extremely faint or delicate: *a subtle shade of greenish white.* **2** If someone is **subtle** they are cleverly and

cunningly discreet: *That wasn't a very subtle remark.* □ *You'll have to be very subtle if you want to change his mind without him being aware of it.*

subtlety /ˈsʌtəltɪ/ *noun* (*uncount or count*): **subtleties**
Subtlety is the quality of being subtle; a **subtlety** is a subtle distinction: *He's not known for his subtlety.*

subtract /səbˈtrakt/ *verb*: **subtracts, subtracting, subtracted**
When you **subtract** one number or quantity from another, you take away or deduct the first number or quantity from the second: *If you subtract 7 from 10, you are left with 3.* □ *The children are learning to add and subtract.*

subtraction /səbˈtrakʃən/ *noun* (*uncount or count*): **subtractions**
You do **subtraction** or a **subtraction** when you take one number or quantity away from another.

subtropical /sʌbˈtrɒpɪkəl/ *adjective*
Subtropical is used to describe things that belong to or are typical of the regions of the world close to the tropics: *a subtropical climate.*

suburb /ˈsʌbɜːb/ *noun*: **suburbs**
A **suburb** is a residential district on the edge of a town or city.

suburban /səˈbɜːbən/ *adjective*
1 Suburban means of, for, or in a suburb or the suburbs: *the surprising number of birds and animals that can be found in a suburban garden* □ *a suburban railway.* **2 Suburban** can also be used in a derogatory sense to describe an attitude or way of living typical of people who live in the suburbs and which is regarded as being unimaginative and narrowly middle-class.

suburbia /səˈbɜːbɪə/ *noun* (*uncount; often derogatory*)
Suburbia is used to refer to suburbs collectively and the lifestyle typical of people that live in the suburbs.

subversion /səbˈvɜːʃən/ *noun* (*uncount; formal*)
Subversion is the act or practice of undermining *eg* a political system: *He was accused of religious subversion.*

subversive /səbˈvɜːsɪv/ *adjective; noun*
▻ ***adjective***
Subversive activities are likely to or intended to undermine a political system or some other authority: *The band has a subversive influence on the youth of today.* □ *subversive propaganda.*
▻ ***noun***: **subversives**
A **subversive** is a subversive person. [*same as* **dissident**]

subvert /səbˈvɜːt/ *verb*: **subverts, subverting, subverted**
1 If an organization or individual **subverts** a government or some other legally established authority, they destroy or overthrow it. **2** If someone or something **subverts** a person or group of people, they corrupt their morals or loyalty. [*opposite* **uphold**]

subway /ˈsʌbweɪ/ *noun*: **subways**
1 A **subway** is a passage under a busy road or railway line, especially for pedestrians. **2** (*especially AmE*) A **subway** is an underground railway.

succeed /səkˈsiːd/ *verb*: **succeeds, succeed, succeeded**
1 You **succeed** in doing something when you manage to do it: *He never quite succeeded in getting rid of his Yorkshire accent.* □ *He tried to persuade her but didn't succeed.* □ *She succeeded in passing her driving test first time.* □ *We heard that the British team had succeeded in its attempt to climb the north face.* [*opposite* **fail**; compare **manage**] **2** Something **succeeds** if it has the intended result: *If the plot had succeeded the Houses of Parliament would have been destroyed.* □ *The coup succeeded, much even to the surprise of the people masterminding it.* [*opposite* **fail**] **3** Something such as a partnership or relationship **succeeds** if it works satisfactorily. [*same as* **work**] **4** You **succeed** if you rise to a high position in the career you have chosen: *young recruits all anxious to succeed* □ *You have to be ruthless to succeed in business.* [*same as* **do well**; *opposite* **fail**] **5** You **succeed** someone in a job or position when you are the next person after them to have it: *Henry was invited to succeed Deirdre as secretary.* [*same as* **take over** from] **6** You **succeed** to a title or property when you inherit it, usually on the death of the previous holder or owner: *He succeeded to the title on the death of his father.* □ *in 1837, when Queen Victoria succeeded to the throne.* **7** One thing **succeeds** another when it follows it in time: *They lived through months of anxiety as one crisis succeeded another.* [*same as* **follow**] — *adjective* **succeeding:** *During the succeeding months he began to wonder if he had made a mistake.* [*same as* **following**]

success /səkˈsɛs/ *noun* (*uncount or count*): **successes**
Success is the circumstance of succeeding or the condition of having succeeded; a **success** is something that has turned out well: *Success in life is often measured by the amount of money you have.* □ *Success or failure depends entirely on your own efforts.* □ *The party was quite a success.* [*opposite* **failure**]

successful /səkˈsɛsfəl/ *adjective*
Someone who is **successful** has achieved fame, wealth or power, or all of these; something that is **successful** has turned out well: *a successful businessman* □ *a successful writer* □ *I'm glad to hear that your trip was successful.* [*opposite* **unsuccessful**] — *adverb* **successfully:** *They have successfully identified the gene responsible for the condition.* [*opposite* **unsuccessfully**]

succession /səkˈsɛʃən/ *noun*
1 (*used in the singular*) A **succession** of people or things is a series of them coming one after the other: *We've had a succession of managers, none of whom stayed more than six months.* **2** (*uncount*) The **succession** is the order or right by which one person follows another in an office or post: *With the birth of her son, Jane Seymour had secured the Tudor succession.* □ *the succession of John Major to the Tory leadership.*
▻ ***phrases*** **In succession** means one after the other: *They married and had four children in quick succession over the following five years.*

successive /səkˈsɛsɪv/ *adjective*
Successive means immediately following another or each other: *policies adopted by successive governments.*

successor /səkˈsɛsə(r)/ *noun*: **successors**
Your **successor** is, or your **successors** are, the person or people that follow you or take your place: *His innovative methods were adopted by his successors in the post.*

succinct /səkˈsɪŋkt/ *adjective*
A written or spoken statement that is **succinct** expresses meaning clearly using very few words: *His remarks were succinct and to the point.* [*same as* **concise**; *opposite* **wordy**] — *adverb* **succinctly:** *You put that very succinctly.*

succour (*AmE* **succor**) /ˈsʌkə(r)/ *noun* (*uncount; formal or literary*)
Succour is help or relief given to someone in time of distress or need: *By his thoughtless act he has given succour to the enemy.*

succulent /ˈsʌkjʊlənt/ *adjective*
Succulent is used to describe food that is juicy and delicious: *a succulent peach.*

succumb /səˈkʌm/ *verb*: **succumbs, succumbing, succumbed** (*formal*)
1 If you **succumb** to temptation, persuasion or some

other force that you have been resisting, you give in or surrender to it: *She kept offering me fattening biscuits and cakes, but I refused to succumb to temptation.* □ *At first he was adamant, but she begged and begged him to let her go until he finally succumbed.* [*same as* **yield**] **2** (*literary*) If someone **succumbs** to an illness, they catch it or die of it: *Cholera spread rapidly though the camp and thousands succumbed within a very short time.* [*opposite* **overcome**]

such /sʌtʃ/ *determiner; pronoun*

▷ ***determiner*** (*used with count, uncount and plural nouns*)

1 a '**Such** a thing' means the item just mentioned; '**such** a thing *as*' a certain item is that item: *I'm looking for a device for removing staples, if such a thing exists.* □ *Do you happen to have such a thing as a penknife?* □ *There are no such things as ghosts.* □ *I don't believe there's any such place.* □ *I meant no such thing.* [= I didn't mean that at all] **b** '**Such** a person or thing' means the kind represented by the one just mentioned: *You can't reason with such a person.* □ *There's no excuse for such behaviour.* □ *I don't know how people can say such things.* □ *Where do you find the time for such activities?* □ *We were paid £10 a time, and such a sum seemed a fortune then.* □ *a crow or rook or some such bird.* □ *the Tower of London and other such buildings* □ *All such incidents should be reported to me.* □ *One doesn't get many such opportunities.* □ *There are few such organizations left.*

Notice that **such** is commonly used with negatives, in questions and after *if*, but without another determiner it is less common in positive sentences, where *like that* and *that sort* or *kind of* are more frequently used: *People like that* (rather than *such people*) *should be ignored. I find that kind of discussion* (rather than *such discussions*) *quite useful.*

2 (*often used with adjectives or adjectival phrases*) **a** If something is **such** a thing, or **such** an extreme thing, *that* something else happens, the degree to which the first circumstance is true is the cause of the second; after *if* or a negative, *as to* is sometimes used instead of *that*: *He was running such a high temperature that we had to call the doctor in the middle of the night.* □ *It's such ages since I was here that I can't remember where anything is.* □ *It was such badly made furniture that it fell apart within a few weeks.* □ *We couldn't all sit down, there were such a lot of us.* □ *We're not such idiots as to think that.* **b** **Such** emphasizes how great or extreme something is: *It's such a pleasure to see the sun at last.* □ *We've been having such terrible sales figures recently.* □ *They talk such rubbish.* □ *This has been such an efficiently planned conference.* **c** With negatives, in questions and after *if*, **such** means 'of this or that sort, size or degree': *How did you manage to accumulate such a backlog?* □ *Try it yourself if you're such an expert.* □ *Have you ever heard such stupid nonsense?* □ *How can you believe such obvious lies?* □ *No-one'll help you if you make such a fuss.*

Notice the similar use of '**like** that': *No-one'll help if you make a fuss like that.*

d 'Not **such**' can be used like 'not very' and 'not particularly' as a less emphatic version of 'not': *Perhaps it wasn't such a brilliant idea after all.* **e** **Such** can be used in negative comparisons: *It isn't quite such a problem as I thought it'd be.* □ *We didn't have nearly such good weather this year.*

3 Something that happens or is planned in **such** a way *that* a certain thing results, or in **such** a way *as to* produce a certain result, has that result because of the way it happens or is planned: *She fell in such a way as to crush both ankles.* □ *The seating is arranged in such a way that every member of the audience gets a good view.* □ *The software has been designed in such a way as to be absolutely user-friendly.*

▷ ***pronoun:*** *The incident is not such as to warrant a full enquiry.*

▷ ***phrases*** **1** (*often with a negative*) When you talk about a thing **as such** you mean that thing in its true sense, or that thing without anything else associated with it: *We haven't been promoted as such, but our jobs have been upgraded.* □ *He wasn't keen on gardening as such, but he enjoyed being out in the fresh air.* **2** You use **such and such** to refer to an unidentified or unspecified person or thing: *when you suspect that such and such a person is to blame* □ *and the doctor says you must be injected against such and such or such and such.* **3 a** **Such as** is used to introduce one or more examples of the thing just mentioned: *a profession such as architecture or engineering.* □ *such problems as homesickness, bedwetting and bullying* □ *a drought such as we experienced in the summer of 1976.* **b** **Such** things **as** are possible are all that are possible, even if they are very few: *Such supplies as we can get are used up straight away.* **c** You add, *eg*, '**such as** it is' after mentioning something to indicate that is not very much, or not of a high standard: *the facilities, such as they are* □ *archaeological remains, such as there are.* [compare **so**].

suchlike /ˈsʌtʃlaɪk/ *determiner or pronoun*

You can use **suchlike** to refer to things that are of the same kind as those you have already mentioned: *In a chemist's shop you can buy buy soap, shampoo and suchlike items.* □ *We are cutting down on butter, margarine and suchlike.*

suck /sʌk/ *verb*: **sucks, sucking, sucked**

1 You **suck** liquid into your mouth when you draw it in by squeezing your lips together to form a small hole and pressing in the sides of your mouth: *He was sucking lemonade through a straw.* □ *She was sucking a piece of orange.* **2** You **suck** your thumb or the end of *eg* a pencil when you hold it in your mouth and make movements of your mouth and lips similar to those for sucking in liquids. **3** You **suck** a sweet when you hold it in your mouth, drawing its flavour out with squeezing and rolling movements inside the mouth. **4** A baby or young animal **sucks** when it draws milk into its mouth from its mother's breast or udder.

phrasal verb

(*informal*) You **suck up to** someone when you try to please them by flattering them or being especially helpful or obedient.

sucker /ˈsʌkə(r)/ *noun*: **suckers**

1 A **sucker** is **a** a cup-shaped organ that an animal uses to attach itself to a surface by suction. **b** a small cup-shaped piece of plastic or rubber that is used to stick things to a surface by suction. **2** (*informal*) If you call someone a **sucker** you mean that they are easily deceived or taken advantage of. [*same as* **mug**]

suckle /ˈsʌkəl/ *verb*: **suckles, suckling, suckled**

A mother **suckles** her baby when she feeds it with milk from her breast or, in some animals, her udder; a baby or young animal **suckles** when it sucks milk from its mother's breast or udder.

suction /ˈsʌkʃən/ *noun* (*uncount*)

Suction is the drawing away of air or liquid to create a vacuum which then draws in another gas or liquid, or the force which causes two surfaces to stick together when the air between them is removed.

sudden /'sʌdən/ *adjective*
Something that is **sudden** happens quickly: *His death was very sudden.* □ *a sudden inspiration* □ *a sudden impact* □ *a sudden increase in deaths from food poisoning.*
▻ ***phrase*** If something happens **all of a sudden** it happens suddenly: *All of a sudden, the door slammed shut.* — *adverb* **suddenly:** *It happened quite suddenly.* □ *I suddenly remembered who he was.* □ (*sentence adverb*) *Suddenly, there were crowds of people all around him.* — *noun* (*uncount*) **suddenness:** *The suddenness of his death shocked everyone.* [*same as* **abruptness**]

suds /sʌdz/ *noun* (*plural*)
Suds are a mass of bubbles produced on water when soap or other detergent is dissolved in the water: *soap suds.*

sue /suː/ *verb*: **sues, sueing, sued**
You **sue** a person or organization when you take legal proceedings against them to claim money that they owe you or to compensate for some wrong that they have done you: *He is sueing his former employer for wrongful dismissal.* [*same as* **prosecute**]

suede or **suède** /sweɪd/ *noun* (*uncount, often adjectival*)
Suede is soft leather with a raised velvet-like surface: *a handbag made of suede* □ *a suede jacket.*

suet /'suːɪt/ *noun* (*uncount, often adjectival*)
Suet is a hard fat taken from around the kidneys of sheep or cattle and used to make pastry and puddings: *beef suet* □ *suet pastry.*

suffer /'sʌfə(r)/ *verb*: **suffers, suffering, suffered**
1 You **suffer** when you feel or endure pain, sorrow or some other extremely unpleasant physical or mental sensation: *He was killed instantly so he can't have suffered much.* **2** If you **suffer** from a disease or illness, it causes you pain, discomfort or distress: *She suffers from arthritis.* □ *She suffers from depression.* **3** If something **suffers** as a result of some circumstance or action, it deteriorates as a result of that circumstance or action: *When his parents were divorcing his schoolwork suffered badly.* **4** (*usually with a negative*) You **suffer** someone or something when you tolerate them: *She doesn't suffer fools gladly.* [*same as* **bear**]

sufferance /'sʌfərəns/ *noun* (*uncount*)
▻ ***phrase*** If something is done **on sufferance** it is tolerated, but not welcomed or encouraged: *If he comes to stay, I warn you now that he will only be here on sufferance.*

sufferer /'sʌfərə(r)/ *noun*: **sufferers**
Sufferers from a particular disease or illness are people who suffer from it: *He's an asthma sufferer.*

suffering /'sʌfərɪŋ/ *noun* (*uncount or count*): **sufferings**
Suffering is the fact or condition of feeling or enduring pain, sorrow or some other extremely unpleasant physical or mental sensation; **sufferings** are unpleasant mental or physical sensations that are felt or endured: *She had to endure years of pain and suffering.* □ *He seemed indifferent to the sufferings of his victims.* [*same as* **discomfort, misery**]

suffice /sə'faɪs/ *verb* (*formal*): **suffices, sufficing, sufficed**
If something **suffices** it is enough or good enough for a particular purpose: *The income from his weaving sufficed for his modest needs.*

sufficiency /sə'fɪʃənsɪ/ *noun* (*used in the singular*)
A **sufficiency** is a large enough amount of something: *There's an ample sufficiency of fresh water on the island.* [*opposite* **insufficiency**]

sufficient /sə'fɪʃənt/ *adjective*
If something is **sufficient** it is enough or adequate: *'Can you lend me some money for the journey?' 'Yes, will £50 be sufficient?'* [*opposite* **insufficient**] — *adverb* **sufficiently:** *He was sufficiently disillusioned to consider resignation.*

suffix /'sʌfɪks/ *noun*: **suffixes**
A **suffix** is a group of letters that is added to the end of a word or word stem to create a new word or word class, eg the *-s* in *monkeys* and the *-tude* in *certitude*.

suffocate /'sʌfəkeɪt/ *verb*: **suffocates, suffocating, suffocated**
If someone **suffocates**, they die because they are prevented from breathing, usually because there is something over their nose or mouth which prevents air getting to their lungs: *The piglet suffocated when its mother accidentally lay on it.* □ *She felt as if she was suffocating in the hot and airless room.* — *noun* (*uncount*) **suffocation** /sʌfə'keɪʃən/: *The baby died of suffocation.*

suffrage /'sʌfrɪdʒ/ *noun* (*uncount*)
Suffrage is the right to vote in political elections: *universal adult suffrage.* [=the right to vote for all adults, male and female]

suffuse /sə'fjuːz/ *verb* (*usually in the passive*): **suffuses, suffusing, suffused**
An area **is suffused** with light or colour when light or colour covers it or is spread throughout it: *clouds suffused with pink and orange hues.* [*same as* **bathe**]

sugar /'ʃʊgə(r)/ *noun*; *verb*
▻ ***noun***: **sugars**
1 (*uncount, often adjectival*) **Sugar** is a sweet-tasting substance obtained from sugar cane and other plants and used in the form of white or brown crystals or powder to sweeten food and drinks: *granulated sugar* □ *icing sugar* □ *Do you take sugar in your tea?* □ *sugar syrup* [=made from sugar and water] □ *a sugar refinery.* **2** A number of cubes or teaspoonfuls of this substance added to tea or coffee are referred to as one **sugar**, two **sugars**, and so on: *'What do you take in your tea?' 'Milk and two sugars, please.'* **3** (*informal*) **Sugar** is sometimes used as an affectionate or familiar form of address: *Come along sugar, you'll be late for school.*
▻ ***verb***: **sugars, sugars, sugared**
1 You **sugar** *eg* tea or coffee when you sweeten it by adding sugar: *Have you sugared this tea?* **2** Something **is sugared** when it is coated with sugar: *sugared almonds.*

sugar beet /'ʃʊgə biːt/ *noun* (*uncount*)
Sugar beet is a variety of plant grown for its white roots from which sugar is obtained.

sugar cane /'ʃʊgə keɪn/ *noun* (*uncount*)
Sugar cane is a tall tropical grass with thick woody stems from which sugar (**cane sugar**) is obtained.

sugary /'ʃʊgərɪ/ *adjective*
1 A **sugary** substance is like sugar in taste or appearance. **2 Sugary** foods or drinks contain sugar or too much sugar: *For healthy teeth, drink plenty of milk and avoid sugary drinks.* **3** (*informal*) A **sugary** sentiment is exaggeratedly or insincerely pleasant or affectionate.

suggest /sə'dʒɛst/ *verb*: **suggests, suggesting, suggested**
1 You **suggest** something when you offer it as an idea, possibility, recommendation or proposal: *We were asked to suggest ways of raising money.* □ *Someone suggested a jumble sale.* □ *If you like fish, let me suggest the salmon.* □ *Can you suggest a better alternative?* □ *Can anyone suggest someone who might take on the*

job of secretary? □ *Get the travel agents to suggest somewhere.* □ *He suggested waiting till the morning.* □ *I suggest that she finishes her degree first.* □ *They suggested that we should set up* (or *that we set up*) *an independent group.* [*same as* **propose**] **2** (*with a negative, or in questions*) You are **suggesting** something when you are implying that it is so: *Are you suggesting that I'm lying?* □ *I'm not suggesting for a minute that she doesn't do her job adequately.* □ *It would be wrong to suggest that the word is always used in a bad sense.* [*same as* **hint, imply**] **3** One thing **suggests** another if it implies it or makes it seem likely: *His initial response suggested that he would be difficult to persuade.* [*same as* **indicate**] **4** A circumstance **suggests** an idea to you if it makes the idea come into your head: *It was the sight of children playing with empty cardboard boxes that first suggested the Loxbox climbing frame to him.*

suggestible /sə'dʒɛstɪbəl/ *adjective*
A **suggestible** person is easily influenced by suggestions made by others: *Children can be highly suggestible and you should be very careful about what they watch on television.*

suggestion /sə'dʒɛstʃən/ *noun*: **suggestions**
1 A **suggestion** is a proposal or recommendation: *You don't have to agree with me; it was just a suggestion.* □ *We want to try a new restaurant; do you have any suggestions?* **2** A **suggestion** is a hint or trace of something: *She looked at him with just a suggestion of a smile.* **3** (*uncount*) **Suggestion** is the process by which a hypnotist creates a belief or impulse in the mind of a hypnotised person. **4** (*uncount*) **Suggestion** is the act of suggesting: *a suggestion box.*

suggestive /sə'dʒɛstɪv/ *adjective*
1 If one thing is **suggestive** of another it leads you to think of that other thing: *The colours the artist has used in the painting are suggestive of violent emotion.* **2** **Suggestive** comments or remarks are intended to make you think about sex.

suicidal /su:ɪ'saɪdəl/ *adjective*
1 Someone is **suicidal** if they feel that they want to kill themselves: *Sometimes he gets so depressed he is suicidal.* **2** You can also describe someone's actions or behaviour as **suicidal** when they are so reckless that they put their lives at risk: *He was driving at a suicidal speed.* □ *It would be suicidal for the company* [=it would ruin it] *if it took on the contract without adequate finance.*

suicide /su:ɪsaɪd/ *noun* (*uncount or count*)
Suicide is the act of deliberately killing yourself; a **suicide** is an instance of this, or a person that deliberately kills himself or herself: *He committed suicide.* □ *The suicide rate amongst young men is higher than that amongst young women.* □ *an alarming number of suicides.*

suit /su:t/ *noun*; *verb*
▻ ***noun***: **suits**
1 A **suit** is a usually fairly formal set of clothes made from the same material and consisting of a jacket with trousers for men and a jacket and skirt, or trousers, for women. [see picture at **clothing**] **2** A **suit** is also an outfit worn on specific occasions or for a specific activity: *a ski suit* □ *a dinner suit* □ *a tracksuit* □ *a diving suit.* **3** A **suit** is any of the four groups into which a pack of playing-cards is divided, *ie* hearts, clubs, diamonds and spades. **4** A **suit** is a lawsuit.
▻ ***verb***: **suits, suiting, suited**
1 Something **suits** you when it is convenient or acceptable and satisfies your needs or requirements: *We should meet to discuss this as soon as possible. Would Friday suit you?* □ *We can change the appointment if you find that it doesn't suit you.* □ *She came home because she found the climate in India didn't suit her.* □ *He can be very charming when it suits him.* **2** If something **suits** you, it looks attractive on you or makes you look attractive: *Green doesn't suit you.* □ *That hat suits you.* **3** If you **suit** yourself you do what you want to do, not what others want you to do: *'I don't really want to come with you.' 'Suit yourself.'*
▻ ***phrase*** If someone does something and you **follow suit**, you do the same thing as they have done: *James went for a swim, and after finishing my drink, I followed suit.*

suitable /'su:təbəl/ *adjective*
If something is **suitable** it is of the right type or quality for a particular purpose: *I don't have any clothes that would be suitable for the funeral.* □ *She plans to remarry after a suitable period of mourning.* □ *Make sure you take a waterproof jacket and boots suitable for hiking.* □ *Is he a suitable person to hold public office?* □ *This is not a suitable environment in which to bring up young children.* □ *The film is not suitable for children under 12.* [*opposite* **unsuitable**] — *adverb* **suitably:** *Parents should make sure that pupils come to school suitably dressed.* — *noun* (*uncount*) **suitability:** *I'm doubtful about his suitability for the post.*

suitcase /'su:tkeɪs/ *noun*: **suitcases**
A **suitcase** is a large container with flat stiffened sides and a handle that you use for carrying your clothes and other belongings when you are travelling.

suite /swi:t/ *noun*: **suites**
1 A **suite** is a set of rooms, *eg* in a hotel, that are used for a particular purpose: *a function suite* □ *the honeymoon suite.* **2** A **suite** is also a matching set of furniture for a particular room: *a three-piece suite* [=a settee and two armchairs for a living or sitting room] □ *We bought a new bathroom suite* [=a matching bath, WC and wash basin] □ *a dining-room suite.* **3** (*music*) A **suite** is a set of instrumental pieces *eg* in related keys or in the same musical form: *an orchestral suite.*

suitor /'sju:tə(r)/ *noun*: **suitors** (*old*)
If a woman has a **suitor** she is being courted by a man who wants to marry her.

sulk /sʌlk/ *verb*; *noun*
▻ ***verb***: **sulks, sulking, sulked**
Someone **sulks** when they show their anger and resentment, usually over something unimportant, by being silent and bad-tempered: *He's sulking in his bedroom because I refused to buy him the latest video game.* [*same as* **brood**]
▻ ***noun*** (*often plural*): **sulks:** *She's having a fit of the sulks because she didn't get her own way.*

sulky /'sʌlkɪ/ *adjective*: **sulkier, sulkiest**
If someone is **sulky**, they are sulking or have a tendency to sulk: *'You can't make me eat my porridge if I don't want to,' he said with a sulky frown.* □ *She's the sulkiest, most unpleasant child I have ever come across.* [*same as* **sullen**]

sullen /'sʌlən/ *adjective*
1 You describe someone or their expression as **sullen** when they are silently and stubbornly bad-tempered or they show their dislike or resentment in this way: *He listened with an expression of sullen resentment to the teacher's criticism of his work.* [*same as* **sulky**] **2** (*literary*) A **sullen** sky or **sullen** weather is dark and dismal.

sulphur (*AmE* **sulfer**) /'sʌlfə(r)/ *noun* (*uncount*)
Sulphur is a yellow mineral found in the earth that burns with a blue flame and gives off an unpleasant smell. Sulphur is used to make matches.

sultan /'sʌltən/ *noun*: **sultans**
A **sultan** is the ruler of certain Muslim countries: *the Sultan of Oman.*

sultana /sʌl'tɑ:nə/ *noun*: **sultanas**
1 The wife, mother, sister or daughter of a sultan is known as a **sultana**. **2 Sultanas** are dried seedless grapes used in cooking.

sultry /'sʌltrɪ/ *adjective*: **sultrier, sultriest**
1 If the weather is **sultry**, it is unpleasantly hot and humid. [*same as* **sweltering**] **2** A woman whose appearance or expression suggests that she is sexually passionate can also be described as **sultry**: *a sultry blonde.*

sum /sʌm/ *noun*; *verb*
▻ ***noun***: **sums**
1 The **sum** of two or more numbers or quantities is the figure which results when they are added together. **2** You refer to an amount of money as a **sum**, or a **sum** of money: *He was paid a large sum for his services.* ▫ *It was discovered that he has been stealing small sums over a long period of time.* **3** A **sum** is also a simple arithmetical calculation: *I can't do this sum.* ▫ *He always gets all his sums right.*
▻ ***verb***: **sums, summing, summed**

> ***phrasal verb***
> **sum up 1** You **sum up** what has been said or discussed previously when you summarize the main points: *We discussed the proposed changes for most of the meeting, with the chairman taking a few moments at the end to sum up.* **2** You **sum** something **up** when you describe its character or nature in a few brief words: *The holiday can be summed up in one word: disastrous.* **3** You **sum** a situation **up** when you make an accurate assessment of it, often very quickly: *She can usually sum a situation up in a couple of minutes.* **4** A judge in a court of law **sums up** when he or she restates the main points of the case before the jury retires to consider its verdict. [see also **summing-up**]

summarize or **summarise** /'sʌməraɪz/ *verb*: **summarizes, summarizing, summarized**
You **summarize** something when you make or present a summary of it: *The union's demands can be summarized as follows: shorter hours and more pay.* [*same as* **sum up**]

summary /'sʌmərɪ/ *noun*; *adjective*
▻ ***noun***: **summaries**
A **summary** is a short account which gives the main points of something: *Can you give me a brief summary of what was discussed at the meeting?* ▫ *a summary of the main events at this year's festival.* [*same as* **resumé**]
▻ ***adjective***
Summary actions are done or performed quickly or take effect immediately, often without the usual formalities: *The court has issued a summary warrant for his arrest.* ▫ *the summary execution of several high-ranking officers.* — *adverb* **summarily** (*formal*): *He was summarily dismissed.*

summer /'sʌmə(r)/ *noun* (*uncount or count*)
Summer is the warmest season of the year, coming between spring and autumn and lasting from around late May until the beginning of September in cool northern regions: *It was very hot last summer.* ▫ *He plays tennis in summer and rugby in winter.* ▫ *on a hot summer's day in July* ▫ *summer clothes* ▫ *summer holidays* ▫ *We always seemed to have hot dry summers when I was a child.* ▫ *in the summer of 1969.*

summer school /'sʌmə sku:l/ *noun*: **summer schools**
A **summer school** is a course of study held during the summer, *eg* at a university, while the students taking full-time courses are on holiday.

summertime /'sʌmətaɪm/ *noun* (*uncount*)
Summertime is the season of summer: *The garden looks its best in summertime.*

summing-up /sʌmɪŋ'ʌp/ *noun*: **summings-up**
In a court of law the judge's **summing-up** is the statement he or she makes before the jury retires which summarizes or restates the main points of the case.

summit /'sʌmɪt/ *noun*: **summits**
1 The **summit** of a mountain or hill is its highest point: *Edmund Hillary and Tenzing Norgay reached the summit of Everest in 1953.* **2** (*used in the singular*) The **summit** of your career or profession is the highest possible level of achievement or the highest position it is possible to attain. **3** A **summit**, or **summit conference**, is a conference between heads of government or other senior officials: *the Toyko summit between the heads of the leading industrialized nations.*

summon /'sʌmən/ *verb*: **summons, summoning, summoned**
1 If you **are summoned** by someone, you are ordered to come or appear before them: *He was summoned to the headmaster's office.* ▫ *The rebel members of the party were summoned to the Chief Whip's office.* **2** If someone **summons** you to do something, they order or call upon you to do it: *He said he had been summoned by God to spread the good news.*

> ***phrasal verb***
> If you **summon up** your courage, your strength or the energy to do something, you make a great effort to be courageous or have enough strength or energy to do it: *I couldn't summon up the courage to tell him.* ▫ *He's so lazy he can't even summon up the energy to get up and switch off the television.* [*same as* **muster**]

summons /'sʌmənz/ *noun*; *verb*
▻ ***noun***: **summonses**
1 A **summons** is a written order legally obliging a person to attend a court of law at a specified time: *a summons to the High Court.* **2** A **summons** is any order made by someone in authority which instructs another person to come or to do something: *He was almost sure he would be promoted, and waited impatiently for the summons from Number Ten.*
▻ ***verb***: **summonses, summonsing, summonsed**
You **are summonsed** when you are served with a court summons.

sumptuous /'sʌmptʃʊəs/ *adjective*
Sumptuous means superbly rich and luxurious in appearance: *a room with sumptuous decoration.* [*same as* **lavish**] — *adverb* **sumptuously:** *The king's apartments were sumptuously decorated.* [*same as* **lavishly**]

sum total /sʌm 'toʊtəl/ *noun* (*used in the singular*)
The **sum total** of something is the complete or final total: *The sum total of my wealth at the moment is £75.* ▫ *What is the sum total of your achievements since you left school?*

sun /sʌn/ *noun*; *verb*
▻ ***noun***: **suns**
1 (*singular*) The **sun** is the star that is the source of light, heat and gravity for the Earth and all the planets in our solar system: *the sun, the moon and the stars* ▫ *The sun rises in the east and sets in the west.* **2** (*uncount or used in the singular*) You also refer to the

heat or light from this star as the **sun**: *lizards basking in the hot midday sun.* □ *The back of the house faces south and gets a lot of sun.* **3** A **sun** is also any star with a system of planets revolving around it.
▷ ***verb***: **suns, sunning, sunned**
You **sun** yourself when you expose yourself to the sun's rays: *The cat lay sunning itself on the patio.*

sunbathe /ˈsʌnbeɪð/ *verb*: **sunbathes, sunbathing, sunbathed**
You **sunbathe** when you expose your body to the sun in order to get a suntan: *It can be dangerous to sunbathe for too long.*

sunbeam /ˈsʌnbiːm/ *noun*: **sunbeams**
A **sunbeam** is a ray of light from the sun.

sunbed /ˈsʌnbed/ *noun*: **sunbeds**
A **sunbed** is a bed-like device with electrically powered sun-lamps fitted above, and often also beneath, a transparent screen on which you lie, for artificially tanning the whole body.

sunburn /ˈsʌnbɜːn/ *noun* (*uncount*)
If you have **sunburn** your skin is red and sore because you have remained in strong sunlight for too long.

sunburnt /ˈsʌnbɜːnt/ *adjective*
A person or part of their body is **sunburnt** when their skin has been burned by the sun making it red, and often sore.

sundae /ˈsʌndeɪ/ *noun*: **sundaes**
A **sundae** is a sweet dish of ice-cream, topped with fruit, nuts, syrup or other ingredients.

Sunday /ˈsʌndɪ/ *noun* (*uncount or count*): **Sundays**
Sunday is the first day of the week, coming after Saturday and before Monday. Many Christians go to church on Sunday: *We arrived on Sunday.* □ *We don't work on Sunday* (or *on Sundays*). □ (*AmE*) *Is the store open Sundays?* □ *This Sunday's and next Sunday's matches will be televised.* □ *He's always at home on Sunday mornings.*

Sunday school /ˈsʌndɪ skuːl/ *noun* (*uncount or count*): **Sunday schools**
Sunday school, or a **Sunday school**, is a class for children held on Sundays in which they are given religious instruction, often in church buildings and before a regular church service: *go to Sunday school* □ (*often adjectival*) *a Sunday-school teacher.*

sundial /ˈsʌndaɪəl/ *noun*: **sundials**
A **sundial** is an instrument that uses sunlight to tell the time by the changing position of the shadow that a vertical arm casts on a horizontal surface marked with the hours.

sundown /ˈsʌndaʊn/ *noun* (*especially AmE*: *uncount*)
Sundown is the same as sunset.

sundry /ˈsʌndrɪ/ *adjective*
Sundry means various, assorted or miscellaneous: *The stall was selling cakes, biscuits and sundry items of home-baking.* □ *David, Charles and Rebecca were there, along with sundry others.*
▷ ***phrases*** If you refer to **all and sundry**, you mean everybody: *The invitation is open to all and sundry.*

sunflower /ˈsʌnflaʊə(r)/ *noun*: **sunflowers**
A **sunflower** is a tall plant with large yellow flowers. The seeds from sunflowers produce a light oil (**sunflower oil**) widely used in cooking.

sung /sʌŋ/ *verb*
Sung is the past participle of **sing**.

sunglasses /ˈsʌŋglɑːsɪz/ *noun* (*plural*)
Sunglasses are glasses with dark-coloured lenses, worn to protect the eyes from bright sunlight.

sunk /sʌŋk/ *verb*
Sunk is the past participle of **sink**.

sunken /ˈsʌŋkən/ *adjective*
1 A **sunken** ship is one that has sunk to the bottom of the sea. **2** If someone has **sunken** cheeks or eyes, deep hollows have formed in their cheeks or around their eyes, often because they have been ill. **3** A **sunken** area of land is at a lower level than the ground which surrounds it: *a sunken garden with a pond and potted shrubs.*

sunlamp /ˈsʌnlamp/ *noun*: **sunlamps**
A **sunlamp** is a electric lamp which gives out light similar to the rays of the sun, used to relieve certain muscular and joint pains and for artificially tanning the skin.

sunlight /ˈsʌnlaɪt/ *noun* (*uncount*)
Sunlight is light from the sun: *Very little sunlight penetrates the forest's dense canopy.*

sunlit /ˈsʌnlɪt/ *adjective*
A place that is **sunlit** is filled with sunlight or brightly lit by the sun: *She was portrayed sitting in a sunlit room with a book on her lap.*

sunny /ˈsʌnɪ/ *adjective*: **sunnier, sunniest**
1 A **sunny** day is one on which the suns shines and it is not cloudy or wet: *I think it's going to be a sunny afternoon.* **2** A **sunny** room or other place is filled with sunshine or brightly lit by sunlight: *in a sunny corner of the garden.* **3** Someone who has a **sunny** personality or disposition is always cheerful and pleasant to be with. [*opposite* **gloomy**]

sunrise /ˈsʌnraɪz/ *noun*: **sunrises**
1 (*uncount*) **Sunrise** is the time when the sun appears above the eastern horizon in the morning and it begins to get light: *He got up at sunrise and worked until it got dark in the evening.* [*same as* **dawn**] **2** (*count or uncount*) A **sunrise** is the light and colours that you see in the sky as the sun begins to rise above the horizon in the morning.
[*opposite* **sunset**; *same as* **daybreak**]

sunroof /ˈsʌnruːf/ *noun*: **sunroofs**
A **sunroof** is a transparent panel in a car roof, for letting in sunlight, often also opening for ventilation. [see picture at **car**]

sunset /ˈsʌnset/ *noun*: **sunsets**
1 (*uncount*) **Sunset** is the time when the sun disappears below the western horizon in the evening and it begins to get dark: *They worked in the fields from sunrise to sunset.* [*same as* **dusk, nightfall**] **2** (*count or uncount*) A **sunset** is the light and colours, ranging from pale yellow to dark orange and purple, that you see in the sky when the sun begins to disappear below the horizon: *a glorious summer sunset* □ *They sat on the balcony watching the sunset.*
[*opposite* **sunrise**]

sunshine /ˈsʌnʃaɪn/ *noun* (*uncount*)
1 Sunshine is good weather with the sun shining brightly: *Aberdeen had ten hours of continuous sunshine yesterday.* □ *The weather forecast is for sunshine and showers.* **2 Sunshine** is also the light or heat of the sun: *She sat in the garden enjoying the sunshine.* □ *The wolf cubs were playing happily in the sunshine.*

sunstroke /ˈsʌnstroʊk/ *noun* (*uncount*)
Sunstroke is an illness caused by being in the hot sun for too long, in which your body temperature rises, you stop sweating and eventually lose consciousness: *He was taken to hospital suffering from sunstroke.*

suntan /'sʌntan/ *noun*: **suntans**
If someone has a **suntan** their skin has been turned light brown through exposure to the sun. [see also **tan**]

sun-tanned /'sʌntand/ *adjective*
Someone who is **sun-tanned** has a suntan: *He came back from holiday sun-tanned and healthy-looking.*

sun visor /'sʌn vaɪzə(r)/ *noun*: **sun visors**
A **sun visor** is a moveable flap fixed to the interior of a car which is used to shield the eyes from strong sunlight. [see picture at **car**]

super /su:pə(r)/ or /sju:pə(r)/ *adjective*
1 (*informal*) If you say that someone or something is **super** you mean they are extremely good or excellent: *That was a super meal.* ▫ *I like her very much; she's a super person.* [*same as* **terrific**, **great**] **2** (*only before a noun*) **Super** is also used to describe things that are larger, more powerful or better in some way than other things of the same type: *a new generation of super computers.*

super- /su:pə(r)/ *prefix*
Super- is combined with other words to mean **1** great or extreme in size or degree: *supertanker.* **2** above or beyond: *the supernatural.* **3** outstanding: *a superhero.*

superb /sʊ'pɜ:b/ *adjective*
If you describe something as **superb**, you think it is outstandingly excellent: *a superb performance* ▫ *The facilities in the new sports centre are superb.* ▫ *a holiday destination offering plenty of outdoor activities in the superb setting of the Canadian Rockies.* [*same as* **marvellous**] — *adverb* **superbly:** *She plays superbly.* ▫ *superbly equipped laboratories.*

supercilious /su:pə'sɪlɪəs/ *adjective*
Someone who is **supercilious** treats others as if they are of little importance: *a supercilious smile.* [*same as* **haughty**]

superficial /su:pə'fɪʃəl/ *adjective*
1 Something that is **superficial** is on or near the surface: *He suffered superficial burns to his hands and face.* **2 Superficial** also means not thorough or detailed: *He appears only to have a superficial knowledge of the subject.* **3** Something **superficial** is that which is apparent when looked at quickly, but may not be real or genuine: *There are superficial similarities between the two plants, but they are actually completely different species.* **4** If you describe a person as **superficial**, you mean that they lack the capacity for serious thought or sincere emotion: *I found her a trifle superficial.* [*same as* **shallow**] — *adverb* (*sentence adverb*) **superficially:** *Superficially, there is little difference between them.*

superfluous /sʊ'pɜ:flʊəs/ *adjective*
Something that is **superfluous** is unnecessary or unwanted, often because there is sufficient already: *These items are being auctioned because they are superfluous to requirements.*

superhuman /su:pə'hju:mən/ *adjective*
Superhuman strength or ability is much greater than ordinary human strength or ability: *You will have to make a superhuman effort if you want to break the world record.*

superimpose /su:pərɪm'poʊz/ *verb*: **superimposes, superimposing, superimposed**
If you **superimpose** one thing on another, you put the one thing on top of the other, usually so that the thing that is underneath can still be partly seen: *In the film, the images of the moving spacecraft have been superimposed on the background using sophisticated techniques.*

superintendent /su:pərɪn'tɛndənt/ *noun*: **superintendents**
1 A **superintendent** is a senior police officer above the rank of chief inspector: *Superintendent Peters.* **2** A **superintendent** is also a person who is responsible for supervising a particular building, project or department: *the superintendent of works.*

superior /sʊ'pɪərɪə(r)/ *adjective*; *noun*
▷ ***adjective***
1 If one person is **superior** to another, they are higher in rank or position than that other person: *You should report this to your superior officer.* [*opposite* **subordinate**] **2** If one thing is **superior** to another, it is better in quality than that other thing: *This wine is far superior to the one we had last week.* [*opposite* **inferior**] **3** You can describe something as **superior** when it is of high quality: *superior-quality wines.* [*opposite* **inferior**] **4** If someone has a **superior** attitude, they think they are better than other people: *'So you think you can do it as well as I can, do you?' he asked with a superior smile.* **5** (*used after a noun*) The head of certain religious communities is given the title **Superior**: *the Mother Superior.* [=the head of a community of nuns] **6** In printing, a **superior** letter, number or other character is one that is printed above the line. — *noun* (*uncount*) **superiority** /sʊpɪərɪ'ɒrɪtɪ/: *military superiority* ▫ *'Of course, someone from your background wouldn't know anything about French literature.' she said with effortless superiority.*
▷ ***noun*: superiors**
Your **superior** or **superiors** are people who are higher in rank or position than you are, especially in work: *I'll have to refer the matter to my superiors.* [*opposite* **subordinate**]

superlative /sʊ'pɜ:lətɪv/ *adjective*; *noun*
▷ ***adjective***
1 Superlative means 'the best' or 'of the highest quality': *a superlative example of the genre.* **2** In grammar, the **superlative** form of an adjective or adverb ends in '-est', or is preceded by the word 'most', to express the highest degree of the quality in question: *'Richest', 'best' and 'most comfortable' are all superlative forms.*
▷ ***noun*** (*grammar*)
A **superlative** is a superlative form of an adjective or adverb: *Her description of him was peppered with superlatives.*

supermarket /'su:pəmɑ:kɪt/ *noun*: **supermarkets**
A **supermarket** is a large shop selling food and other, mainly household, goods in which customers serve themselves. [see picture at **street**]

supernatural /su:pə natʃərəl/ *adjective*; *noun*
▷ ***adjective***
Supernatural is used to describe forces or experiences that are impossible to explain by the laws of nature or science: *She was believed to have supernatural powers and was burned as a witch.*
▷ ***noun*** (*used in the singular*)
The powers or experiences believed to come from or be connected with unknown forces or spirits are referred to as the **supernatural**.

superpower /'su:pəpaʊə(r)/ *noun*: **superpowers**
A **superpower** is a nation with great political, economic or military power and influence; the word refers particularly to the United States or the former Soviet Union.

supersede /su:pə'si:d/ *verb*: **supersedes, superseding, superseded** (*often in the passive*)
If something **is superseded** by something else, its place is taken by that other, usually more up-to-date or efficient, thing: *Will the private car ever be superseded by*

alternative forms of transport? □ *The airship was soon superseded by the less cumbersome passenger aeroplane.*

supersonic /suːpəˈsɒnɪk/ *adjective*
Supersonic aircraft are capable of travelling faster than the speed of sound (approximately 331.5 metres per second).

superstar /ˈsuːpəstɑː(r)/ *noun*: **superstars**
A **superstar** is a very famous person, especially an actor, entertainer, sportsman or sportswoman: *the footballing superstar, Diego Maradona.*

superstition /suːpəˈstɪʃən/ *noun*: **superstitions**
1 (*uncount*) **Superstition** is belief in things that are not real or possible, especially the belief that certain objects or actions have the power to influence events or people's lives, bringing good or bad luck. **2** A **superstition** is a belief in something that is not real or possible.

superstitious /suːpəˈstɪʃəs/ *adjective*
If you are **superstitious**, you believe that certain objects or actions have the power to influence people's lives or future events: *Many cultures are superstitious about having their photograph taken, believing that the camera can steal their soul.*

supervise /ˈsuːpəvaɪz/ *verb*: **supervises, supervising, supervised**
If someone **supervises** you, they watch you to make sure that you are doing something correctly or are behaving as you should: *The senior pupils are going on a field expedition where they will be supervised by Mr Phillips, the assistant head teacher.* □ *Trainees should be supervised at all times.* — *noun* (*uncount*) **supervision:** *Homework should be done under parental supervision when necessary.*

supervisor /ˈsuːpəvaɪzə(r)/ *noun*: **supervisors**
A **supervisor** is a person who is responsible for making sure that other people's work is done correctly.

supervisory /ˈsuːpəvaɪzərɪ/ *adjective*
Someone whose role or job is **supervisory** checks on or watches others to make sure they do things correctly: *He's a qualified engineer working, in a supervisory capacity, on a North Sea oil rig.*

supper /ˈsʌpə(r)/ *noun* (*uncount or count*): **suppers**
Supper is a light evening meal or snack eaten after your main evening meal: *We had a light supper of poached eggs on toast.* □ *What would you like for supper?* □ *They normally have supper around nine o'clock.*

supplant /səˈplɑːnt/ *verb* (*formal*): **supplants, supplanting, supplanted**
If one person or thing **supplants** another, they take the place of or replace that other person or thing, sometimes using force or unfair means: *When the dominant male in the pride gets too old to defend his position, he will be supplanted by a younger, fitter lion.* □ *He had been supplanted in her affections by a man ten years his junior.* [*same as* **replace**, **oust**]

supple /ˈsʌpəl/ *adjective*
1 Your joints are **supple** when they bend easily and have a wide range of movement. [*same as* **flexible**; *opposite* **stiff**] **2** A **supple** person has joints that bend easily and are not stiff. — *noun* (*uncount*) **suppleness:** *Gymnasts have to maintain the suppleness of their joints by rigorous and frequent training.* [*opposite* **stiffness**]

supplement /ˈsʌpləmənt/ *noun*; *verb*
▷ ***noun***: **supplements**
1 A **supplement** is something added to make something complete or to make up a deficiency: *vitamin supplements.* **2** A **supplement** is also an extra section added to a book to give additional information or to correct previous errors. [*same as* **appendix**] **3** A **supplement** is also a separate part, often a glossy magazine printed in colour, that is added to a newspaper or magazine on certain occasions, *eg* on Sundays.
▷ ***verb***: **supplements, supplementing, supplemented**
You **supplement** something when you add to it, especially in order to make up for some lack or deficiency: *She does occasional freelance work to supplement her income.* □ *They supplemented their diet by eating grubs and insects.*

supplementary /sʌplɪˈmɛntərɪ/ *adjective*
You use **supplementary** to describe something that is added to another thing: *The Prime Minister has dealt with the point in his written answer and will not be taking supplementary questions in the House.* [*same as* **additional**]

supplementary benefit /sʌplɪmɛntərɪ ˈbɛnɪfɪt/ *noun* (*BrE*; *uncount*)
Supplementary benefit is the former name for **income support** money supplied regularly to people with no income, or with a very low one.

supplier /səˈplaɪə(r)/ *noun*: **suppliers**
A **supplier** is a business company or individual who supplies other businesses with goods or equipment: *invoices from suppliers* □ *the supermarket's local suppliers.*

supply /səˈplaɪ/ *verb*; *noun*
▷ ***verb***: **supplies, supplying, supplied**
1 You **supply** someone with something when you provide them with it: *Teams are working to supply the refugees with food and medicines.* **2** When something **supplies** a need or requirement it provides enough of something to satisfy that need or fulfil that requirement: *The North Sea will supply a large proportion of Britain's energy needs in the form of gas and oil until well into the next century.* [*same as* **provide**]
▷ ***noun***: **supplies**
1 A **supply** of something is the amount supplied, especially regularly: *The cheese factory needs a reliable supply of milk.* **2** A **supply** is also an amount than can be drawn on or used: *They have a good supply of wood for the winter.* □ *They have a generator which gives them their own electricity supply.* □ *The water supply had been cut off.* **3** (*plural*) **Supplies** are food and other necessary equipment gathered together or taken on a journey: *They had to turn back because their supplies were running low.* **4** (*uncount*) **Supply** is a degree of availability of something or the fact of its being produced and made available: *Fruit was in very short supply.* □ *the law of supply and demand.*

support /səˈpɔːt/ *verb*; *noun*
▷ ***verb***: **supports, supporting, supported**
1 If something **supports** an object or structure it keeps it upright or holds it in place: *The arches were supported by heavy stone pillars.* **2** You **support** *eg* a person or organization when you give active encouragement and try to help them succeed: *Support the Liberal Democrats.* **3** If you **support** someone you provide them with the means to live or exist: *His parents will have to support him until he gets a job.* **4** You **support** a sporting team when you follow their fortunes loyally, especially by going to their matches regularly: *'Who do you support?' 'Real Madrid.'* **5** If a theory or claim **is supported** by a fact or evidence, that fact or evidence helps to show that it is true or accurate. [*same as* **corroborated**]
▷ ***noun***: **supports**
1 (*uncount*) Financial **support** is money given to

enable someone to live or to enable a business to continue: *The business folded when the banks withdrew their support.* **2** A **support** is something that supports an object or structure: *The massive wooden supports were knocked away and the ship slipped slowly into the water.*

supporter /sə'pɔːtə(r)/ *noun*: **supporters**
A **supporter** is a person who supports a particular sporting team, a political party, a cause or a proposal: *He is one of the president's strongest supporters.* □ *a life-long supporter of nuclear disarmament* □ *The train was full of Arsenal supporters.* □ *a supporter of various charities.* [*same as* **ally**]

supporting /sə'pɔːtɪŋ/ *adjective*
The **supporting** cast in a film or play are the actors who play the minor roles, rather than the leading actors and actresses.

supportive /sə'pɔːtɪv/ *adjective*
A **supportive** person is someone who gives help and support to another person who is going through a difficult time: *She was very supportive when I was going through my divorce.*

suppose /sə'poʊz/ *verb*; *conjunction*
▻ ***verb***: **supposes, supposing, supposed**
1 You **suppose** that something is so if you think it is likely to be so: *He was evidently iller than we had supposed.* □ *What do you suppose has happened to him?* □ *I can only suppose he's been delayed.* □ *You don't suppose he's had an accident, do you?* □ *'Will they have got home yet?' 'I don't suppose so.'* □ *I don't suppose they've encountered the problem before.* [see note at **think**] **2 Suppose** is used in expressing and seeking opinion, *eg* about what to do; 'I **suppose**' can indicate uncertainty or lack of enthusiasm: *'Was it a useful conference?' 'I suppose so.'* □ *You don't suppose we should report the error?* □ *I suppose we ought to wait till she arrives.* □ *'You can't ring them at this late hour.' 'I suppose not.'* □ *'We could leave a note.' 'I suppose we could.'* **3** You can use 'I don't **suppose**' rather like 'I wonder' to make polite or indirect requests: *I don't suppose anyone's got a spare copy, have they?* □ *I don't suppose you could give me a lift?*
▻ ***conjunction***
1 You say **suppose** or **supposing** something happened or happens when you are wondering what effect it would have: *Supposing you forgot to set the alarm and somebody broke in, you'd be to blame, wouldn't you?* □ *Suppose you fall and hurt yourself when you're out alone in the mountains?* **2** 'Always **supposing**' means 'as long as' or 'on the assumption that' something is so: *We'll have to hire the hall for two days, always supposing it's available.* **3** You can use **suppose** or **supposing** to make suggestions or give advice about what to do: *Suppose we just forget the whole thing?* □ *Supposing you have another try?*

supposed /sə'poʊzd/ *adjective*
1 Someone or something that is **supposed** to be or do something is **a** intended to be or do that thing: *What kind of remark is that supposed to be?* □ *'They don't match.' 'They're not supposed to.'* □ *You're not supposed to take it seriously.* □ *What's this dot supposed to represent?* **b** expected to be or do that thing, *eg* according to some rule or arrangement: *We're not supposed to know about this.* □ *You're not supposed to talk in the library.* □ *I thought you were supposed to be taking things easily.* □ *The opening ceremony was supposed to take place today.* **c** believed or reported to be or do that thing: *Exercise is supposed to cure everything.* □ *I haven't read it but it's supposed to be very amusing.*
2 You use **supposed** before a noun or noun phrase to express your doubt about its description: *the supposed advantages of private pensions* □ *her supposed intimate friendship with the princess.*
See also **meant** at **mean**.

supposedly /sə'poʊzɪdlɪ/ *adverb*
You use **supposedly** when you want to show that you have some doubts about the truth of the fact or circumstance you are discussing: *He's supposedly one of the greatest experts in the field.* [*same as* **allegedly**]

supposition /sʌpə'zɪʃən/ *noun* (*uncount or count*): **suppositions**
Supposition is the act of supposing; a **supposition** is something that is thought or assumed to be true, though it may not be: *That's pure supposition with no basis in fact.* □ *The supposition was that the princess had gone into hiding.* [*same as* **speculation**]

suppress /sə'prɛs/ *verb*: **suppresses, suppressing, suppressed**
1 You **suppress** feelings when you hold them in and do not express them: *She suppressed a strong desire to scream.* [*same as* **stifle**] **2** If an uprising or rebellion **is suppressed** by *eg* an government, they put a stop to it or crush it: *The rebellion was ruthlessly suppressed by the army.* **3** If information **is suppressed** it is prevented from being broadcast, printed or otherwise made publicly known: *The report on the government's links with the arms trade was suppressed.* [*same as* **withhold**] — *noun* (*uncount*): **suppression**: *suppression of the emotions.*

supremacy /sʊ'prɛməsɪ/ *noun* (*uncount*)
Supremacy is the state of being supreme; **supremacy** is also absolute power or authority over others: *air supremacy.* [=control of the skies by the airforce of one country] □ *The new breed of absolute monarchs had won the battle for supremacy over the church.*

supreme /sʊ'priːm/ *adjective*
1 Something that is **supreme** is the greatest, being of the highest rank, power or importance: *Eisenhower was supreme commander of the Allied forces in Europe.* □ *God, the Supreme Being* □ *the United States' Supreme Court.* **2 Supreme** is also used to emphasize that the quality or condition mentioned is of the greatest degree: *It's of supreme importance that only he should be given this information.* □ *They fought with supreme courage.* **3** People, especially soldiers, make the **supreme** sacrifice when they die fighting for a cause. [*same as* **utmost**] — *adverb* (*intensifying*) **supremely:** *a supremely confident young man.*

sure /ʃʊə(r)/ *adjective*; *adverb*
▻ ***adjective***: **surer, surest**
1 a You are **sure** about something, or **sure** it is so, when you have no doubts about it: *I feel sure I wrote the number down correctly.* □ *'You think we can achieve these targets?' 'I'm sure of it.'* □ *I could never be sure that she wasn't joking.* □ *He didn't seem very sure of his facts.* □ *'We should get tickets OK.' 'I wouldn't be too sure about that.'* [*same as* **certain**; *opposite* **unsure, uncertain**] **b** You say you are not **sure** about something if you do not know about it: *I wasn't sure if you were intending to go too.* □ *We're not sure how to make this work.* □ *I'm not sure whether I've done it right or not.* □ *'Does this train stop at York?' 'I'm not sure.'* [*same as* **certain**] **c** Something is **sure** to happen if it is probably or definitely going to happen: *If you don't take your umbrella it's sure to rain.* □ *There's sure to be another bus soon.* □ *You're sure to hear from us tomorrow or Friday.* [*same as* **certain**] **d** You are **sure** of achieving something if there is no risk of your failing to do so: *He's sure of getting a place at Oxford.* □ *We'd*

better set off early to be sure of getting there before dark. [*same as* **certain**]
2 a Sure describes something that can be relied on to have a certain effect: *There's no surer way to alienate people than to give them unnecessary instructions.* □ *This is the surest means I know of keeping away the mosquitoes.* **b** Someone who has *eg* a **sure** manner or step behaves or walks confidently. **c** Someone who has a **sure** knowledge or understanding of something knows or understands it thoroughly.
▻ ***adverb*** (*informal*)
1 People sometimes use '**Sure**' like 'certainly' or 'of course' to express agreement or give permission: *'We'll talk about this sometime.' 'Sure.'* □ *'May I borrow your pen?' 'Sure.'* **2** (*especially AmE*) **Sure** is also used for emphasis: *'You like it here then?' 'We sure do.'*
▻ ***phrases*** **1** (*rather old*) When you tell someone to **be sure to** do something, you are telling them not to forget to do it: *Be sure to visit the cathedral.* **2** You know something **for sure** when you have no doubts about it: *I knew for sure that he was lying.* □ *We don't yet know for sure whether she's agreed.* **3** You **make sure** that things happen the way you want them to when you check the situation, or take action, so that there is no risk of them not happening that way: *I made sure that there was nobody else in the room.* □ *Make sure the backup has worked.* □ *Make sure they give you their consent in writing.* **4** You use **sure enough** to confirm that what was thought to be so is actually so: *'It looks like rain,' she said, and sure enough the first drops began to fall there and then.*

sure-footed /ʃʊəˈfʊtɪd/ *adjective*
A **sure-footed** person or animal is not likely to slip or stumble when they are moving about on *eg* steep mountain sides.

surely /ˈʃʊəlɪ/ *adverb* (*sentence adverb*)
1 You use **surely** in questions and exclamations to express disbelief, or to appeal to people to agree with you: *Surely it's not four o'clock already!* □ *Surely you're not serious?* □ *Surely someone has his address?* □ *Surely you remember that incident?* □ *This is surely one of the most shameful episodes in parliamentary history.* □ *I don't need to repeat all that, surely?* □ *'I don't suppose she'll remember.' 'Oh, surely she will.'* □ *'The banks won't be closed today, will they?' 'Oh, surely not.'* **2** (*Scottish or AmE*) People use '**Surely**' like 'Certainly' or 'Of course', to give permission or agree to something: *'You couldn't lend me ten pence, could you?' 'Surely.'*
▻ ***phrase*** Something that is happening **slowly but surely** may be happening very gradually but it is definitely happening: *A new management style was slowly but surely taking over.*

surf /sɜːf/ *noun* (*uncount*)
Surf is the mass of white foam produced when waves break on rocks or on the shore.

surface /ˈsɜːfɪs/ *noun*; *adjective*; *verb*
▻ ***noun***: **surfaces**
1 The **surface** of something is its upper or outer side, often with regard to texture or appearance: *a smooth surface* □ *Lay the material down on a flat surface.* □ *full of craters like the surface of the moon* □ *a cleaner for all kitchen and bathroom surfaces.* **2** The **surface** of a body or container of liquid is its top or upper level: *The ship sank slowly beneath the surface.* □ *insects that can travel across the water's surface.* **3** Something that seems a certain way on the **surface** appears that way from the outside, though it may be different in ways that are hidden or are under the surface: *On the surface he has always seemed like a nice chap, but I suspect there are things we don't know about him.*
▻ ***adjective***
1 Surface means at, on or relating to a surface: *surface mail* □ *a surface wound* □ *surface vessels.* [=as opposed to submarines] **2 Surface** describes things that have no importance or depth: *surface charm.* [*same as* **superficial**]
▻ ***verb***: **surfaces, surfacing, surfaced**
1 Something **surfaces** when it comes up to the surface of water: *The submarine surfaced nearby.* [*opposite* **submerge, sink**] **2** A road **is surfaced** when it is covered with a hard smooth material. **3** If something **surfaces**, it becomes apparent: *A rift has surfaced in the Cabinet between the ministers in favour of tax cuts and those favouring a small rise.* [*same as* **disappear**] **4** (*informal*) You **surface** when you get out of bed: *He didn't surface until well after midday.*

surfboard /ˈsɜːfbɔːd/ *noun*: **surfboards**
A **surfboard** is a special long narrow board that you stand or lie on while surfing.

surfeit /ˈsɜːfɪt/ *noun* (*used in the singular; formal*)
If you say that there is a **surfeit** of something, you mean that there is too much of it: *They were suffering the effects of a surfeit of wine.*

surfer /ˈsɜːfə(r)/ *noun*: **surfers**
A **surfer** is a person who goes surfing.

surfing /ˈsɜːfɪŋ/ *noun* (*uncount*)
Surfing is the sport of riding towards the shore on the crests of large breaking waves, using a surfboard.

surge /sɜːdʒ/ *noun*; *verb*
▻ ***noun***: **surges**
A **surge** is a sudden powerful rush, a sudden powerful forward movement or a sudden sharp increase in something: *He felt a surge of bitter anger.* □ *The crowd burst through the doors in a great surge.* □ *The news prompted a surge of activity on the world's stock markets.* □ *There was a surge in sales of 'Middlemarch' after it was televised.*
▻ ***verb***: **surges, surging, surged**
1 If a crowd **surges** forward it goes forward with a powerful rushing movement. **2** If an engine **surges** its power increases suddenly, and usually dies away again. **3** If a feeling or emotion **surges** up inside you it appears in a sudden powerful wave or rush.

surgeon /ˈsɜːdʒən/ *noun*: **surgeons**
A **surgeon** is a doctor who specializes in performing surgery: *a general surgeon.*

surgery /ˈsɜːdʒərɪ/ *noun*: **surgeries**
1 (*uncount*) **Surgery** is the treatment of disease or injury by cutting into the patient's body to remove or repair the affected part: *He had to have major heart surgery.* **2** A **surgery** is the place where a doctor or dentist sees his or her patients and carries out treatment: *The doctor will visit you at home if you can't come to the surgery.* **3** A **surgery** is also a set period during which a local MP or councillor is available to be consulted by his or her constituents, or the place where this happens: *He has a weekly surgery in the local school.*

surgical /ˈsɜːdʒɪkəl/ *adjective*
1 Surgical means of, for use in, or by means of surgery: *a surgical operation* □ *a surgical mask* □ *surgical equipment.* **2 Surgical** is also used to describe things that are used to treat a particular illness or physical condition: *He will have to wear a surgical stocking until his leg is completely healed.* — *adverb* **surgically:** *The lump will have to be surgically removed.*

surly /ˈsɜːlɪ/ *adjective*: **surlier, surliest**
You can describe someone whose manner or speech is

bad-tempered and rude as **surly**: *The youth gave him a surly look when he asked him to turn down the music.* □ *He made a surly remark under his breath.*

surmise /sə'maɪz/ *verb*: **surmises, surmising, surmised** (*formal*)
You **surmise** that something is the case if you guess or suppose that it is the case based on what information is available but without clear proof: *The intruder, we surmised, must have been a child.* [*same as* **infer**]

surmount /sə'maʊnt/ *verb*: **surmounts, surmounting, surmounted** (*formal*)
1 If you **surmount** problems or obstacles, you overcome them or manage to deal with them successfully: *At this stage, I'm not sure if we will be able to surmount all the obstacles that have been placed in our way.* **2** (*usually in the passive*) One thing **is surmounted** by another when the second thing is on top of the first thing: *The walls were surmounted by vicious-looking barbed wire.*

surmountable /sə'maʊntɪbəl/ *adjective*
Problems or obstacles that are **surmountable** can be overcome or dealt with successfully. [*opposite* **insurmountable**]

surname /'sɜːneɪm/ *noun*: **surnames**
Your **surname** is your family name or last name, rather than your forename or Christian name: *Jones is a common British surname.*

surpass /sə'pɑːs/ *verb*: **surpasses, surpassing, surpassed**
If you say that something **surpasses** something else, you mean that it goes beyond it in amount or extent or is of much better quality: *The profits surpassed all our expectations.* □ *That was a wonderful meal. You really surpassed yourself!*

surplus /'sɜːpləs/ *noun*; *adjective*
▷ ***noun***: **surpluses**
1 A **surplus** of something is an amount that exceeds the amount required or used: *In the European Union there are massive surpluses of meat and milk.* [*opposite* **lack**] **2** (*commerce*) The amount by which income is greater than expenditure is a **surplus**: *a surplus on the current account.* [*opposite* **deficit**]
▷ ***adjective***
Surplus goods are those that are left over or extra after needs have been met: *surplus grain.*

surprise /sə'praɪz/ *noun*; *verb*
▷ ***noun***: **surprises**
1 A **surprise** is a sudden unexpected event, or a feeling of slight shock that such an event gives you: *It was a bit of a surprise to find him there.* □ *What a surprise you gave me!* □ *I hope he doesn't come up with any nasty surprises.* **2** (*uncount*) **Surprise** is the act of catching someone unawares or the feeling that you get when something unexpected happens: *She turned with a look of surprise.* □ *If we use torches we might lose the element of surprise.* □ *We arranged a surprise party for him.*
▷ ***verb***: **surprises, surprising, surprised**
1 If something **surprises** you it causes you surprise or shock because it is unexpected: *His answer really surprised me.* □ *It wouldn't surprise me if he was late again.* **2** If you **surprise** someone, you catch them doing something they shouldn't be doing or attack them when they are not expecting it: *I surprised him trying to sneak in by the back door.*
▷ ***phrase*** You **take** someone **by surprise** when you catch them unawares or surprise them.

surprised /sə'praɪzd/ *adjective*
If you are **surprised** by something it gives you a feeling of surprise; if you have a **surprised** expression you show surprise: *I was very surprised when he announced that he was resigning.* □ *He had a surprised look on his face.* [*same as* **astonished**]

surprising /sə'praɪzɪŋ/ *adjective*
If you find something **surprising** it is so unusual or unexpected that it makes you feel surprised: *It's surprising how many people believe in ghosts.* □ *a surprising number of people voted for him.* [*same as* **extraordinary**; *opposite* **unsurprising**]

surreal /sə'rɪəl/ or **surrealistic** /sərɪə'lɪstɪk/ *adjective*
You might describe something as **surreal** or **surrealistic** when it has a strange unreal quality like things that occur in dreams: *Unexpectedly finding myself in a room full of people dressed in eighteenth-century costumes was a surreal experience.*

surrealism /sə'rɪəlɪzm/ *noun* (*uncount*)
Surrealism is a 20th-century movement in art, literature and cinema which tries to represent often unrelated objects or events in a strange dreamlike way. — *noun or adjective* **surrealist:** *an exhibition of paintings and sculpture by Salvador Dali and other surrealists* □ *a surrealist painting.*

surrender /sə'rɛndə(r)/ *verb*; *noun*
▷ ***verb***: **surrenders, surrendering, surrendered**
1 You **surrender** when you stop fighting or resisting an enemy and give yourself up to them to show that you admit defeat: *After the bombs fell on Hiroshima and Nagasaki, the Japanese surrendered.* □ *After a two-day siege, the gunmen surrendered to the police.* [*same as* **give in**] **2** You **surrender** to a temptation or emotion when you allow yourself to be overcome by it, after a period of trying to resist it: *She surrendered herself to utter despair, and wept bitterly.* [*same as* **give in, yield**] **3** You **surrender** something to someone when you hand it over to them, either voluntarily or under pressure from them: *After a long struggle, they gave up trying to keep their home, and surrendered the keys to the building society.*
▷ ***noun*** (*count or uncount*)
Surrender is the act of surrendering; a **surrender** is an act of surrendering: *May 1945 saw the final surrender of the German troops.*

surreptitious /sʌrəp'tɪʃəs/ *adjective*
A **surreptitious** action is done secretly or so as not to be seen by others, usually because they will disapprove of it: *His friend gave him a surreptitious wink from behind the teacher's back.* □ *He's been making surreptitious phone calls to his old girlfriend.* [*same as* **secret, furtive**] — *adverb* **surreptitiously:** *He passed her a note surreptitiously.*

surrogate /'sʌrəgət/ *adjective*; *noun*
▷ ***adjective***
Surrogate means used or acting as a substitute for another person or thing: *a surrogate mother.*[=a woman who has a baby for a another woman who is not able to give birth to a child herself]
▷ ***noun***: **surrogates**
A **surrogate** is a person or thing that is used or acts as a substitute for another person or thing.

surround /sə'raʊnd/ *verb*: **surrounds, surrounding, surrounds**
1 If one thing **surrounds** another it is all round it: *The town was surrounded by desert.* □ *He was surrounded by reporters.* □ *We seem to be surrounded by problems on every side.* **2** If soldiers or policemen **surround** a place, they position themselves all round it so that no-one can escape: *Come out with your hands up! We have the building surrounded.* **3** If you **surround** yourself with people or things, you make sure that you have a lot of them around you: *He surrounded himself with people*

that he could trust. □ *She likes to surround herself with beautiful things.*

surrounding /sə'raʊndɪŋ/ *adjective*
Surrounding is used to describe things that are all round a stated place or position: *He had climbed Everest and several of the surrounding mountains.* □ *Cholera spread quickly through the refugee camp and the surrounding villages.* [*same as* **neighbouring**]

surroundings /sə'raʊndɪŋz/ *noun (plural)*
Your **surroundings** are the places and things around you: *a house in pleasant surroundings.*

surveillance /sə'veɪləns/ *noun (uncount)*
Surveillance is a close watch kept on a person, especially someone suspected of criminal activities: *The FBI had been keeping him under surveillance for several months.*

survey /sə'veɪ/ *verb; noun*
▻ ***verb*: surveys, surveying, surveyed**
1 You **survey** something when you look at it or examine it at length or in detail, in order to get a general view: *The general could survey the whole battlefield from his vantage point on the hill.* □ *He surveyed the horizon looking for any sign of land.* [*same as* **scan**] **2** A building **is surveyed** when a surveyor examines it in order to assess its condition or value. **3** Someone **surveys** an area of land when they measure heights and distances in order to draw a detailed map or establish the position of a proposed building or excavation.
▻ ***noun*** /'sɜːveɪ/: **surveys**
1 If someone carries out a **survey** they ask people questions so that they can make an assessment of public opinion or customer preference. **2** A **survey** is also an inspection of a building to assess its condition or value or the collecting of land measurements for map-making.

surveyor /sə'veɪə(r)/ *noun*: **surveyors**
A **surveyor** is a person whose job is to survey land and buildings.

survival /sə'vaɪvəl/ *noun (uncount)*
Survival is the fact of continuing to live or the likelihood of continuing to live in certain, especially difficult or dangerous, circumstances: *If they have had the sense to dig themselves into the snow, they will have increased their chances of survival significantly.* □ *the struggle for survival* □ *In today's business world, survival of the fittest means survival of the fastest.*

survive /sə'vaɪv/ *verb*: **survives, surviving, survived**
1 You **survive** when you remain alive after having come close to death: *It's a miracle that anyone survived the crash.* □ *He survived for four years on a diet of berries and coconuts.* **2** If someone **survives** someone else, especially a relative, they live on after their death: *He is survived by his wife, Mary, and two sons.* [*same as* **outlive**] **3** Something such as a tradition or custom **survives** when it remains in existence and does not die out.

surviving /sə'vaɪvɪŋ/ *adjective*
Your **surviving** relatives are the members of your family who are still alive: *She is my oldest surviving relative.*

survivor /sə'vaɪvə(r)/ *noun*: **survivors**
1 A **survivor** is someone who has survived *eg* a shipwreck or aircrash: *The helicopter picked up all the survivors.* **2** If you call someone a **survivor** you mean that they are always able to continue even in the most difficult times: *He'll be back in the centre of things in no time; he's a great survivor.*

susceptibility /səsɛptə'bɪlɪtɪ/ *noun (uncount or count)*: **susceptibilities**
Susceptibility to something is the state or degree of being susceptible to it; **susceptibilities** are strong feelings or sensibilities.

susceptible /sə'sɛptɪbəl/ *adjective*
1 If you are **susceptible** to something you are likely to suffer from it: *susceptible to colds.* **2** A **susceptible** person tends to feel things deeply. [*same as* **sensitive**] **3** If someone is **susceptible** to persuasion, they are likely to be persuaded. [*same as* **open**; *opposite* **resistant**]

suspect *verb; noun*
▻ ***verb*** /sə'spɛkt/: **suspects, suspecting, suspected**
1 You **suspect** something when you consider that it is likely: *I suspect that he may be allergic to cats.* **2** You **suspect** a person when you think they may possibly be or probably are guilty of a crime or other wrongdoing: *The police suspect that he was a member of the gang that carried out a series of violent robberies.* □ *Surely you don't suspect me?* **3** You **suspect** someone's motives when you distrust them.
▻ ***noun*** /'sʌspɛkt/: **suspects**
A **suspect** is a person suspected of committing a crime: *a murder suspect.*

suspend /sə'spɛnd/ *verb*: **suspends, suspending, suspended**
1 Something **is suspended** when it is hanging from a point above or is held up by the air or a liquid: *The lamp was suspended from a hook in the ceiling.* □ *A cloud of dust was suspended above the city* □ *particles suspended in liquid.* **2** You **suspend** something when you bring it to a stop or postpone it for a time: *Work was suspended until safety inspectors had made a series of checks.* [*same as* **delay**] **3** If someone **is suspended** from their job, school or team, they are removed or excluded temporarily as a punishment or during an investigation of a possible wrongdoing: *He was automatically suspended for three matches.*

suspenders /sə'spɛndəz/ *noun (plural)*
1 Suspenders are a set of elastic straps attached to a belt that are used for holding up women's stockings. **2** (*AmE*) **Suspenders** are braces for holding up trousers.

suspense /sə'spɛns/ *noun (uncount)*
Suspense is a state of nervous or excited uncertainty: *I wish they would announce the winner; the suspense is killing me!* □ *He wouldn't tell anyone what the result was and kept them in suspense right up until the last moment.* [*same as* **anticipation**]

suspension /sə'spɛnʃən/ *noun*: **suspensions**
1 (*uncount*) **Suspension** is the act of suspending or the state of being suspended: *We won't be asking for your resignation, but you will be under suspension until further notice.* **2** The **suspension** in a motor vehicle is the system of springs and shock absorbers that supports its body on its axles. **3** (*technical*) A **suspension** is a mixture of solid particles suspended in a liquid or gas: *Antibiotics are usually administered to babies and young children in a liquid suspension.*

suspension bridge /sə'spɛnʃən brɪdʒ/ *noun*: **suspension bridges**
A **suspension bridge** is a bridge with the road or railway hanging from cables supported between towers.

suspicion /sə'spɪʃən/ *noun*: **suspicions**
1 (*uncount or count*) **Suspicion** is the process of suspecting or the feeling that causes you to believe that something is wrong or that someone may be guilty of wrongdoing; a **suspicion** is an instance of this feeling: *His odd behaviour aroused suspicion.* □ *The two men*

regarded each other with suspicion. □ *He was arrested on suspicion of burglary.* □ *I don't know who broke my window, but I have my suspicions.* □ *I get the suspicion that he wants to get rid of me.* **2** A **suspicion** of something is a trace of it or a very small amount: *There's just a suspicion of cayenne pepper in the sauce.* □ *There was a suspicion of malice in her tone.* [*same as* **hint**]

▻ ***phrases*** **1** If someone is **above suspicion**, they are too highly regarded or respected to be suspected of a crime or wrongdoing. **2** When someone is **under suspicion** they are suspected of a crime or wrongdoing: *Until we find the true culprit, everyone is under suspicion.*

suspicious /sə'spɪʃəs/ *adjective*

1 If you are **suspicious** of someone, you do not trust them; if you are **suspicious** about something you suspect that something is wrong or that you are not being told the truth: *I've always been very suspicious of his motives.* □ *She became suspicious when he started coming home late from work.* **2 Suspicious** behaviour arouses suspicion. — *adverb* **suspiciously:** *He was behaving very suspiciously.*

sustain /sə'steɪn/ *verb*: **sustains, sustaining, sustained**

1 You **sustain** something when you continue to do it, or you maintain it or keep it in existence, over a period of time: *I doubt whether he will be able to sustain that level of effort over a long period of time.* [*same as* **keep up**] **2** Food **sustains** you when it gives you the strength and energy you need; something other than food **sustains** you when it gives you the help, support or strength you need to continue: *He was sustained by an unshakeable belief in his own abilities.* [*same as* **keep going**] **3** You **sustain** an injury when you receive or suffer it: *The injuries he sustained in the fall were so severe he may never walk again.* **4** In a court of law, an objection made by the lawyer representing one side to a question or comment made by the lawyer representing the other side **is sustained** when the judge declares that the objection is valid and the question or comment is to be withdrawn: *'I object, my lord!' 'Objection sustained.'*

sustaining /sə'steɪnɪŋ/ *adjective* (*formal*)

Sustaining food or drink gives you strength and nourishment: *They all stopped work for half an hour and had a sustaining bowl of broth.*

sustenance /'sʌstənəns/ *noun* (*uncount; formal*)

Sustenance is anything that provides nourishment for your body or spirits: *spiritual sustenance.*

swab /swɒb/ *noun*: **swabs**

A **swab** is a piece of cotton wool or gauze used to clean wounds, apply antiseptics, or take a sample of fluid from the body for examination.

swagger /'swagə(r)/ *verb*; *noun*

▻ ***verb***: **swaggers, swaggering, swaggered**

If someone **swaggers**, they walk swinging their body from side to side in an exaggerated self-important way: *One of the youths swaggered up to the policeman with an insolent smile on his face.*

▻ ***noun*** (*used in the singular*): *She walks with a swagger.*

swallow /'swɒloʊ/ *verb*; *noun*

▻ ***verb***: **swallows, swallowing, swallowed**

1 You **swallow** something when you move the muscles in your throat so that it passes from your mouth down the tube to your stomach: *Help! I've swallowed a fly!* □ *He swallowed the drink in one gulp.* **2** You **swallow** when you make this movement with your throat, often because you suddenly feel nervous: *He swallowed hard before replying.* [*same as* **gulp**] **3** You **swallow** your pride when you repress it; you **swallow** your tears when you hold them back: *I had to swallow my pride and apologise to her.* **4** You **swallow** something when you accept it meekly or without questioning it: *No matter how badly he treats her, she just has to swallow it because her job is so important to her.* □ *You don't really expect the British public to swallow that story, do you?*

▻ ***noun***: **swallows**

1 A **swallow** is an act of swallowing or the amount swallowed at one time: *The kingfisher downed the fish in one quick swallow.* **2** A **swallow** is a small bird with long wings and a divided tail. Swallows eat insects that they catch while they are flying.

swam /swam/ *verb*

Swam is the past tense of **swim**.

swamp /swɒmp/ *noun*; *verb*

▻ ***noun*** (*uncount or count*): **swamps**

Swamp or a **swamp** is very wet ground or an area of this, especially when it is densely covered with plants or trees: *a mangrove swamp.*

▻ ***verb***: **swamps, swamping, swamped**

1 If you **are swamped** with things you have great number or amount to deal with at one time: *The switchboard was swamped with phone calls after his broadcast.* [*same as* **inundate**] **2** If something **is swamped** it is flooded or filled with water. [*same as* **inundate, saturate**]

swampy /'swɒmpɪ/ *adjective*: **swampier, swampiest**

Swampy land is covered with swamp or swamps.

swan /swɒn/ *noun*: **swans**

A **swan** is a large white bird with a long neck that lives on rivers and lakes.

swan song /'swɒn sɒŋ/ *noun*: **swan songs**

A musician, poet or other artist's **swan song** is their last performance or piece of work before they die or retire: *Shelley's poem 'The Triumph of Life' turned out to be his swan song.*

swap or **swop** /swɒp/ *verb*; *noun*

▻ ***verb***: **swaps, swapping, swapped**

You **swap** one thing for another when you exchange it for that other thing; you **swap** with another person when you give them something you have in exchange for something they have: *I've swapped the lampshades round; do you think they look better this way?* □ *I'll swap you two of my sweets for one of your chocolates.* □ *They met for tea on Fridays to swap gossip.*

▻ ***noun***: **swaps**

1 A **swap** is an exchange: *do a swap.* **2** A **swap** is also a thing that is exchanged or offered in exchange for something else: *Do you have any swaps?*

swarm /swɔːm/ *noun*; *verb*

▻ ***noun***: **swarms**

1 A **swarm** of bees is a large group of them that gather around a queen bee and fly off with her in search of a new home. **2** A **swarm** is also any large group of insects or other small creatures flying or moving along together: *swarms of mosquitoes* □ *a swarm of locusts.* **3** A **swarm** of people is a large group of them moving along together: *He was pursued by a swarm of photographers and journalists.* [*same as* **horde**]

▻ ***verb***: **swarms, swarming, swarmed**

1 Bees and other insects **swarm** when they gather or move along together in a swarm. **2** If you say that somewhere **is swarming** with insects or people, you mean that there are crowds or large numbers of them in that place: *The airport was swarming with police and security men.* [*same as* **teem**]

swarthy /'swɔːðɪ/ *adjective*: **swarthier, swarthiest**

A **swarthy** person has dark-coloured skin: *Their*

swarthy features were more Mediterranean than North European.

swat /swɒt/ *verb*: **swats, swatting, swatted**
You **swat** something such as a fly when you crush it by hitting it suddenly, often using a flat implement: *He spent the whole evening swatting mosquitoes with a rolled-up newspaper.*

swathe /sweɪð/ *verb*; *noun*
▻ ***verb***: **swathes, swathing, swathed** (*usually in the passive*)
Someone **is swathed** in a wrapping of some sort, *eg* bandages, when they or part of their body is covered by it: *His head was swathed in bandages.* ▫ *In the early morning, the hills were swathed in mist.*
▻ ***noun***: **swathes**
Swathes of a fabric, bandages or other material are lengths or pieces of it used as a wrapping or binding.

sway /sweɪ/ *verb*; *noun*
▻ ***verb***: **sways, swaying, swayed**
1 Something **sways** when it moves from side to side, especially slowly and smoothly: *The band began to play and soon the whole audience was swaying to the rhythm.* ▫ *The branches swayed in the breeze.* ▫ *The flimsy bridge rocked and swayed as they crossed.* **2** If you influence or persuade people so that they change their opinions or actions, they **are swayed** by your arguments or views: *You can try putting the argument to him, but he's unlikely to be swayed.*
▻ ***noun*** (*uncount*)
1 Something's **sway** is the swaying motion it has: *The sway of the wooden bridge under her feet made her dizzy.* **2** The **sway** of one person or group of people over another or others is the control or influence they exert over that other person or group.
▻ ***phrase*** If one person **holds sway** over another person or group of people, they have great power or influence over them: *countries where the Church still holds great sway.*

swear /swɛə(r)/ *verb*: **swears, swearing, swore, sworn**
1 If you **swear** you use language that is rude, obscene or offensive, particularly to people's religious beliefs: *He burnt his hand on the cooker and swore loudly.* ▫ *He's always swearing.* ▫ *He was expelled for swearing at the headmaster.* [*same as* **curse**] **2** To **swear** also means to take a solemn oath or make a solemn promise to do something: *The witness swore on the Bible to tell the whole truth and nothing but the truth.* ▫ *swear allegiance to the Crown.* **3** If you **swear** that something is true, or can **swear** to it, you say solemnly and very firmly that it is true: *It's true, I swear.* ▫ *Can you swear to it that you have never seen this man before today?*

> ***phrasal verbs***
> **swear by 1** You **swear by** someone, especially God or a god, when you ask them to guarantee your solemn promise or statement: *'Do you swear by Almighty God to tell the truth, the whole truth, and nothing but the truth.'* **2** (*informal*) If someone **swears by** something, such as a remedy, they have complete faith in its value or usefulness: *He has been taking vitamin tablets for years, and swears by them.*
> **swear in** When a public official **is sworn in** they take the oath of their new office; a witness or a jury **is sworn in** when they take the formal oath in a court of law before giving or hearing evidence.

swearword /ˈswɛəwɜːd/ *noun*: **swearwords**
A **swearword** is a word that is considered rude or offensive.

sweat /swɛt/ *noun*; *verb*
▻ ***noun***
1 (*uncount*) **Sweat** is the salty moisture that comes out of the pores in your skin, especially when you are hot, nervous or frightened: *His brow was dripping with sweat.* [see also **perspiration**] **2** If you are in a **sweat** or break out in a **sweat**, you are sweating or begin to sweat heavily because you are hot, afraid or anxious about something: *She broke out in a cold sweat when she thought about the interview the next day,* ▫ *He suffers from fatigue and night sweats.*
▻ ***verb***: **sweats, sweating, sweated**
1 a You **sweat** when moisture comes out of the pores in your skin because you are hot, nervous or afraid: *He was sweating heavily when he returned from his run.* [see also **perspire**] **b** You can say that someone **is sweating** if they are nervous or anxious about something, even if they are not actually sweating: *I'm not going to tell him yet; let him sweat for a bit.* **2** If cheese **sweats** it releases a sweat-like moisture, because it is being kept in a place that is too warm.
▻ ***phrases*** (*informal*) **1** If you **sweat blood** you work very hard; if you **are sweating blood** over something you are very anxious and worried about it: *She sweated blood trying to get the essay finished in time.* ▫ *I am sweating blood over this exam.* **2** You **sweat it out** when you wait in a nervous or anxious state for a difficult or uncomfortable situation to come to an end: *There's nothing more we can do; we'll just have to sweat it out until help arrives.*

sweater /ˈswɛtə(r)/ *noun*: **sweaters**
A **sweater** is a piece of warm clothing that you wear on the upper part of your body. It has long sleeves and is usually made from a knitted material such as wool. [*same as* **jersey**, **jumper**, **pullover**; compare **cardigan**, **sweatshirt**; see picture at **clothing**]

sweatshirt /ˈswɛtʃɜːt/ *noun*: **sweatshirts**
A **sweatshirt** is a long-sleeved casual piece of clothing that you wear on the upper part of your body. Sweatshirts are usually made of a thick soft cotton fabric with a fleecy lining and were originally worn for sports.

sweaty /ˈswɛtɪ/ *adjective*: **sweatier, sweatiest**
1 When people's bodies or clothes are **sweaty** they are wet with sweat or are stained with, or smell of, sweat: *His palms were sweaty.* ▫ *sweaty socks.* **2 Sweaty** work causes you to sweat because it makes you very warm.

swede /swiːd/ *noun* (*count or uncount*): **swedes**
A **swede** is a type of large turnip with flesh that turns pale orange when it is boiled: *a field of swedes* (or *swede*) ▫ *boiled swede.* [see picture at **vegetable**]

sweep /swiːp/ *verb*; *noun*
▻ ***verb***: **sweeps, sweeping, swept**
1 You **sweep** a floor or other surface when you brush it in order to remove dirt, dust or rubbish: *She was sweeping the yard with a big broom.* ▫ *This floor looks as if it hasn't been swept for weeks.* [see also **sweep up**] **2** If something **is swept** away or aside, it is pushed aside quickly or removed quickly and completely: *He swept all their objections aside.* ▫ *The bridge was swept away in the flood.* **3** If something **is swept** in a particular direction, it is lifted with a sudden scooping or brushing movement: *He grabbed her in both arms, sweeping her off her feet.* ▫ *The boy was swept overboard by a huge wave breaking over the bows.* **4** If you **are swept** along by something, you are carried along by it with little or no control over the direction it is forcing you to take: *Barnaby, without any clear understanding of what he was doing, was swept along by the wild enthusiasm of the mob.* **5** If something **sweeps**

through an area or in a particular direction, it moves, passes or spreads smoothly and quickly through that area or in that direction: *Fire swept through the city's flimsy wooden buildings destroying everything in its path.* [*same as* **tear**] **6** If someone or something **sweeps** past or in a particular direction, they walk or move smoothly and quickly in a proud, impressive or determined manner: *The cars carrying the president and his entourage swept into the driveway.* □ *She swept past the waiting fans and jumped into a taxi without once looking in their direction.* **7** If a road or geographical feature **sweeps** in a particular direction it lies or stretches in a long curve across the land: *a long line of rolling hills sweeping down to the sea.* **8** Someone's eyes **sweep**, or an instument **sweeps** across a wide area when they move across it so as to obtain a view of it: *a radio telescope constantly sweeping the night sky.*

▻ ***noun***: **sweeps**

1 If you give a floor or other surface a **sweep**, you brush it so as to remove loose dirt and rubbish: *Will you give the front step a quick sweep?* **2** A **sweep** is also a long swinging movement made with the arm: *He indicated the room with a sweep of his arm.* **3** (*usually in the singular*) The **sweep** *eg* of a road or a feature of the landscape is the long curved line that it makes on the land: *The long sweep of the Cheviot Hills rose up from the rolling Border landscape.* **4** (*usually in the singular*) If something deals with the broad **sweep** of a particular subject it covers or includes all the parts of that subject: *His book deals with the broad sweep of European history from the Romans to the present day.* [*same as* **range**] **5** A **sweep** is also an act of moving over a wide area in order to search for something: *The helicopters made several sweeps of the area trying to locate the missing yacht.* **6** (*informal*) A **sweep** is a chimneysweep.

▻ ***phrases*** **1** You **make a clean sweep** a series of contests when you win them all. **2** If an unpleasant fact or circumstance is **swept under the carpet**, it is deliberately hidden or ignored.

> ***phrasal verb***
> You **sweep up** when you gather things together using a brush or broom, and remove them: *Sweep up the fallen leaves and put them on the compost heap.* □ *When you've finished cutting the bread remember to sweep up any crumbs and put them in the bin.*

sweeper /'swi:pə(r)/ *noun*: **sweepers**

1 Sweeper is used in compound words to mean a person or machine that sweeps: *a street-sweeper* □ *a carpet-sweeper.* **2** A **sweeper** is a football player who normally plays behind the line of defenders but can also move forward suddenly to an attacking position.

sweeping /'swi:pɪŋ/ *adjective*

1 A **sweeping** change is thorough and has a wide-ranging effect: *The government introduced sweeping changes in the social security system.* [*same as* **extensive**] **2** A **sweeping** statement is too general and does not make allowance for any possible exceptions. **3** If you describe a victory as **sweeping** you mean it is complete and decisive.

sweet /swi:t/ *adjective*; *noun*

▻ ***adjective***: **sweeter, sweetest**

1 Sweet things taste like sugar and are not sour, salty or bitter: *a hot sweet drink* □ *These oranges are deliciously sweet.* **2** A **sweet** smell is fragrant and pleasant; a **sweet** song or **sweet** music is very pleasant to listen to: *the sweet scent of violets* □ *the sweet song of the nightingale.* **3 Sweet** wine tastes of the sugar in the fruit: *I prefer a slightly sweeter wine.* [*opposite* **dry**] **4 Sweet** air or water is fresh and pure and is free from pollution: *The mountain air smelt sweet and clean.* **5** A **sweet** person is charming or has a likeable or pleasant nature: *It was sweet of you to do that for me.* □ *She has such a sweet nature.* □ *She gave him her sweetest smile.* **6** (*informal*) If you describe a child or small animal as **sweet**, you think they are very charming or lovable: *Oh, look at the sweet little kittens!* □ *Janey looked ever so sweet in her party dress.* [*same as* **cute**]

▻ ***noun***: **sweets**

1 Sweets are small pieces of a sugar-based mixture, in various shapes and with various flavourings, that are sucked or chewed: *Children nowadays eat far too many sweets.* **2** A **sweet** is a dessert: *We had chocolate mousse for sweet.*

▻ ***phrases*** (*slightly old*) Someone is **sweet on** another person when they like that other person very much or are in love with them: *He's been sweet on Muriel since they were students.* — *adverb* **sweetly:** *She smiled sweetly.* — *noun* (*uncount*) **sweetness:** *the sweetness of her smile* □ *oranges specially selected for their sweetness.*

sweetcorn /'swi:tkɔ:n/ *noun* (*uncount*)

Sweetcorn is the small yellow grains that grow in tightly-packed rows on the hard tapering stalks (**cobs**) of a type of maize. The grains are eaten as a vegetable while they are still young and sweet. [see picture at **vegetable**]

sweeten /'swi:tən/ *verb*: **sweetens, sweetening, sweetened**

You **sweeten** food or drink by adding something, such as sugar or honey, to make it sweet or sweeter.

> ***phrasal verb***
> You **sweeten** someone **up** when you are especially nice to them for a time, with the aim of making them more likely to agree to something that you need their permission or approval for.

sweetener /'swi:tənə(r)/ *noun*: **sweeteners**

A **sweetener** is a substance used to sweeten food or drink, especially one that is used as a substitute for sugar: *artificial sweeteners.*

sweetheart /'swi:thɑ:t/ *noun*: **sweethearts**

1 (*old*) Your **sweetheart** is your boyfriend or girlfriend: *They were childhood sweethearts.* **2** Some people use **sweetheart** when they are talking to someone they are very fond of: *'What's the matter, sweetheart?'*

sweet tooth /swi:t 'tu:θ/ *noun* (*singular*)

Someone has a **sweet tooth** when they are fond of sweet-tasting foods.

swell /swɛl/ *verb*; *noun*

▻ ***verb***: **swells, swelling, swelled, swollen**

1 Something **swells** when it gradually increases in size so that it becomes more rounded or bigger than it was originally: *Her feet and ankles began to swell and she had to take off her boots.* **2** To **swell** also means to increase in number, size or intensity: *Lowland militiamen were recruited to swell the ranks of Cumberland's army of occupation.* [*same as* **expand**] **3** If you say that your chest or heart **swelled** with emotion, especially pride, you mean that it expanded or felt as if it was expanding because of the intensity of the emotion: *His mother's heart swelled with pride as she listened to him playing.* **4** A sound **swells** when it becomes gradually louder, often then dying away again: *The music swelled as the aria reached its climax.* **5** If something **swells**, something else fills it so that it forms a rounded shape: *The wind swelled the sails and the great ship moved slowly out of the bay.*

▻ ***noun*** *(used in the singular)*
1 If there is a **swell** on the sea there is a rolling or heaving movement without any waves breaking: *a heavy swell in the Minch.* **2** In music, a **swell** is a gradual increase in sound.

swelling /ˈswɛlɪŋ/ *noun*: **swellings**
1 A **swelling** is an area on the surface of your body that has become raised up or enlarged, *eg* because of injury or disease: *The boxer had a large swelling over one eye.* [*same as* **bump**] **2** (*uncount*) **Swelling** is the state or condition of being swollen: *pain and swelling around the joints.* [*same as* **inflammation**]

sweltering /ˈswɛltərɪŋ/ *adjective*
If you say it is **sweltering** you mean the weather or a place is uncomfortably hot; if you are **sweltering** you are uncomfortably hot: *a sweltering day in August* □ *It's sweltering outside.* □ *I'm sweltering in this heavy jacket.* [*same as* **stifling, scorching**]

swept /swɛpt/ *verb*
Swept is the past tense and past participle of **sweep**.

swerve /swɜːv/ *verb*: **swerves, swerving, swerved**
If a vehicle or other moving object **swerves**, it turns or moves aside suddenly or sharply, often so as to avoid a collision: *Motorists had to swerve to avoid the boy as he dashed headlong across the road.* □ *The car swerved into a lamppost.*

swift /swɪft/ *adjective*; *noun*
▻ ***adjective***: **swifter, swiftest**
1 Swift means fast-moving or able to move fast: *a swift runner* □ *The cheetah is the swiftest land animal.* **2 Swift** also means quick or prompt: *The police response was swift and effective.* □ *Do we have time for a swift drink?* — *adverb* **swiftly:** *They moved swiftly and silently through the jungle.* — *noun* (*uncount*) **swiftness:** *The fire moved with terrifying swiftness, destroying everything in its path.* [*same as* **speed**]
▻ ***noun***: **swifts**
A **swift** is a type of small insect-eating bird similar to the swallow but with longer wings and a shorter tail.

swig /swɪg/ *verb*; *noun*
▻ ***verb*** (*informal*): **swigs, swigging, swigged**
If you **swig** a drink, you drink it in large gulps, especially from a bottle: *He was slumped in a corner, swigging whisky straight from the bottle.*
▻ ***noun*** (*informal*): **swigs:** *He took two or three large swigs from the water bottle.*

swill /swɪl/ *verb*; *noun*
▻ ***verb***: **swills, swilling, swilled**
If liquid **swills** around or **is swilled** around inside something, it moves or is caused to move back and forth inside it: *There was almost a foot of filthy water swilling around in the bottom of the boat.*

swim /swɪm/ *verb*; *noun*
▻ ***verb***: **swims, swimming, swam, sum**
1 You **swim** when you push your body through water by moving your arms and legs; you **swim** or can **swim** when you have learnt how to do this: *They swam in the river every morning.* □ *Do you swim?* □ *I can't swim.* □ *The water's too deep to wade through; we'll have to swim.* □ *Newborn babies seem to be able to swim naturally.* **2** You **swim** a specified distance or a stretch of water when you cover that distance or cross that stretch of water in this way: *Who was the first person to swim the English Channel?* □ *She swims thirty lengths of the pool every morning.* □ *The herd had to swim the river where crocodiles lay in wait.* **3** If something **is swimming** in something or **swimming** with something, it is floating in it or flooded with it: *a few pieces of fatty meat swimming in greasy gravy.* **4** If your head **is swimming**, you are dizzy.

▻ ***noun*** *(used in the singular)*
A **swim** is a period of time spent swimming: *Did you have a nice swim?* □ *I'm going for a swim.*

swimmer /ˈswɪmə(r)/ *noun*: **swimmers**
A **swimmer** is someone or something that swims: *The pool was full of swimmers.* □ *He's not a very strong swimmer.* □ *Penguins are excellent swimmers.*

swimming bath /ˈswɪmɪŋ bɑːθ/ *noun* (*often used in the plural*): **swimming baths**
A **swimming bath** is a public, usually indoor, swimming pool: *He did most of his training for the Olympics in the local swimming baths.*

swimming costume /ˈswɪmɪŋ kɒstjuːm/ *noun*: **swimming costumes**
A **swimming costume** is the same as a swimsuit.

swimming pool /ˈswɪmɪŋ puːl/ *noun*: **swimming pools**
A **swimming pool** is an artificial pool specially built, either indoors or outdoors, for people to swim in: *He has a heated swimming pool in his garden.*

swimming trunks /ˈswɪmɪŋ trʌŋks/ *noun* (*plural*)
Swimming trunks are short pants worn by men and boys for swimming.

swimsuit /ˈswɪmsuːt/ *noun*: **swimsuits**
A **swimsuit** is a piece of clothing worn by women when they go swimming. Swimsuits usually cover the body but not the legs or arms.

swindle /ˈswɪndəl/ *verb*; *noun*
▻ ***verb***: **swindles, swindling, swindled**
If someone **swindles** you, they cheat you or trick you; if you **are swindled** out of something, someone gets it from you dishonestly by cheating or tricking you: *The old lady was swindled out of her life savings by a very plausible salesman.* [*same as* **con**]
▻ ***noun***: **swindles**
A **swindle** is an act or instance of cheating or dishonest trickery: *He and his accomplices were involved in an elaborate swindle.* [*same as* **racket**]

swindler /ˈswɪndlə(r)/ *noun*: **swindlers**
A **swindler** is a person who swindles others: *He's a cheat and a swindler.* [*same as* **trickster**]

swine /swaɪn/ *noun*: **swines**
1 (*plural*; *old*) **Swine** are pigs. **2** If you call someone a **swine**, you mean they behave towards others in a cruel or very unpleasant way: *He's an absolute swine!*

swing /swɪŋ/ *verb*; *noun*
▻ ***verb***: **swings, swinging, swung**
1 Something **swings** when it moves backwards or forwards or from side to side, pivoting from a fixed point above or at the side; you **swing** something when you move it in this way: *They marched along to the sound of the pipes, arms and kilts swinging.* □ *The children were swinging from a rope tied to the branch of a tree.* □ *a body swinging from a gibbet.* **2** Something **swings** when it moves or turns with a long curving or sweeping movement; you **swing** something from one position to another when you cause it to move in this way: *The car swung into the path of a lorry.* □ *She sat up and swung her legs over the edge of the bed.* **3** You **swing** round when you turn round suddenly to face in the opposite direction; public opinion or someone's mood **swings** or **is swung** when it changes or turns or is caused to change or turn suddenly: *She swung round to face him.* □ *The terrorist outrage had the effect of swinging public opinion in favour of the death penalty.* **4** (*informal*) If you manage to **swing** something, you manage to arrange or fix it successfully: *I'll see if I can swing it for you to join me in Paris.* **5** If you **swing** at someone or something,

you try to hit them: *He swung at me with a baseball bat.*

▻ ***noun***: **swings**

1 A **swing** is a seat hanging from ropes or chains attached above to a frame or branch, on which you sit or stand to swing backwards and forwards; a **swing** is also an instance of swinging on such a seat. **2** A **swing** is a swinging movement: *He took a swing at the ball with his racket, but missed.* **3** A **swing** is also a sudden change, *eg* in mood or in the pattern of voting: *a large swing in the opinion polls in favour of Labour* ▫ *She is prone to dramatic mood swings.* **4** A golfer's **swing** is his or her technique or stance when swinging the club back to hit the ball. **5** (*uncount*) **Swing** is jazz or jazzy dance music with a strong regular rhythm, popularized by bands in the 1930s.

▻ ***phrases*** **1** If you **get into the swing** of something you become very involved in it or sufficiently involved in it so that you begin to enjoy it. **2** If something such as a party is **in full swing**, it is at its liveliest stage.

swingeing /ˈswɪndʒɪŋ/ *adjective* (*formal*)

Swingeing is used to describe things that are very severe and therefore difficult to bear: *swingeing cuts in public expenditure.* [*same as* **harsh, excessive**]

swipe /swaɪp/ *verb*; *noun*

▻ ***verb***: **swipes, swiping, swiped**

1 If you **swipe** at something, you try to hit it hard with a swinging movement of your arm: *He swiped at the wasp that was buzzing around his head.* **2** (*informal*) If someone **swipes** something, they steal it: *Someone's swiped my ruler.*

▻ ***noun***: **swipes:** *He took a swipe at the ball, but missed.*

swirl /swɜːl/ *verb*; *noun*

▻ ***verb***: **swirls, swirling, swirled**

Something **swirls** when it moves round and round quickly: *the swirling skirts of the dancers* ▫ *They trudged on through the storm with snow swirling around them and the wind tugging at their clothes.*

▻ ***noun***: **swirls:** *The helicopter took off, raising great swirls of dust.*

swish /swɪʃ/ *verb*; *noun*

▻ ***verb***: **swishes, swishing, swished**

If something **swishes** or **is swished**, it moves or is caused to move through the air with a soft rustling or brushing sound: *The horses were grazing quietly, swishing their tails to get rid of the flies.*

▻ ***noun***: **swishes:** *The pigeons landed with a swish of wings.*

Swiss /swɪs/ *adjective*; *noun*

▻ ***adjective***

Swiss means concerned with or belonging to Switzerland, its people, or the dialects of German and French spoken by them: *He goes climbing in the Swiss Alps.* ▫ *a Swiss watch* ▫ *a Swiss canton.*

▻ ***noun***: **Swiss**

1 A **Swiss** is a native or citizen of Switzerland. **2** (*uncount*) **Swiss** is either of the dialects of German and French spoken in Switzerland.

switch /swɪtʃ/ *noun*; *verb*

▻ ***noun***: **switches**

1 A **switch** is a device that makes or breaks an electrical circuit. A switch is usually operated by moving a knob or lever to turn an appliance or a light on or off. **2** A **switch** is also a complete change or change-over: *There's been a switch in policy from one in favour of tax cuts to tax increases.* [*same as* **shift**]

▻ ***verb***: **switches, switching, switched**

1 You **switch** two people or things or two people or things **are switched** when one is exchanged or substituted for the other, especially quickly and without other people noticing: *The police believe that two members of the gang switched bags at the airport.* [*same as* **swap**] **2** If you **switch** to or **switch** over to a different system or way of doing things, you transfer or change to that other system or way of doing things: *They switched over to North Sea gas.*

phrasal verbs

switch off **1** You **switch off** a light or other electrical appliance, or you **switch** it **off**, when you cut off its supply of electricity by operating a switch: *Be sure to switch off all the lights when you come to bed.* ▫ *Switch the lights off when you leave.* [*same as* **turn off, put off**; *opposite* **switch on**] **2** You **switch off** when you stop thinking or worrying about something that you usually think or worry about a lot: *Even when he's at home, supposed to be relaxing, he doesn't seem to be able to switch off.* ▫ *As soon as she starts talking about how wonderful her children are, I just switch off.* [= stop listening or lose interest in what she is saying]

switch on You **switch on** a light or other electrical appliance, or you **switch** it **on**, when you operate a switch so that the light comes on or the appliance begins to work: *I'm freezing; I'm going to switch on the heating.* [*same as* **turn on, put on**; *opposite* **switch off**]

switchboard /ˈswɪtʃbɔːd/ *noun*: **switchboards**

A **switchboard** is **1** a board on which incoming telephone calls are connected manually or electronically, or the person who operates this equipment: *I'll ask the switchboard to connect you with the chairman's office.* **2** a board from which various pieces of electrical equipment are controlled.

swivel /ˈswɪvəl/ *verb*: **swivels, swivelling** (*AmE* **swiveling**), **swivelled** (*AmE* **swiveled**)

When something **swivels**, or **is swivelled**, it turns, or is caused to turn around a fixed central point to face in a different direction: *She swivelled round to face him.* ▫ *He swivelled his chair round to face the screen.* [*same as* **swing**]

swollen /ˈswoʊlən/ *verb*; *adjective*

▻ ***verb***

Swollen is the past participle of **swell**.

▻ ***adjective***

Something that has gradually grown so that it is fatter or bigger than usual is **swollen**: *a swollen ankle* ▫ *undernourished children with swollen bellies* ▫ *fields submerged by the swollen river.*

swoon /swuːn/ *verb*: **swoons, swooning, swooned** (*old or literary*)

If someone **swoons** they faint, especially as a result of strong emotions: *She swooned into his arms.* ▫ *young girls swooning over their pop idols.*

swoop /swuːp/ *verb*; *noun*

▻ ***verb***: **swoops, swooping, swooped**

1 A bird, aeroplane or hang-glider **swoops** when it flies downwards with a smooth fast sweeping movement: *swallows swooping and gliding over the rooftops* ▫ *The hawk swooped down and caught the mouse in its talons.* **2** A group of police, customs officers or soldiers swoop on a place when they all move towards it together quickly and suddenly so as to surprise the people they are trying to catch or attack: *The raiding party swooped down from the hills and carried off horses and cattle.* [*same as* **descend**]

▻ ***noun***: **swoops:** *A large force of police made a swoop on the street market looking for stolen goods.* [*same as* **onslaught**]

▻ ***phrase*** A number of things are dealt with or done **at one fell swoop** when they are all dealt with or done at one time rather than gradually or in stages: *The legacy meant that they could pay off their mortgage and all their other debts at one fell swoop.*

swop see **swap**.

sword /sɔːd/ *noun*: **swords**
A **sword** is a weapon with a long blade sharpened on one or both edges.
▷ ***phrase*** When two people with different or opposite opinions argue, you can say that they **have crossed swords**, or **have crossed swords with** each other.

swore /swɔː(r)/ *verb*
Swore is the past tense of **swear**.

sworn /swɔːn/ *verb*; *adjective*
▷ ***verb***
Sworn is the past participle of **swear**.
▷ ***adjective***
1 If someone makes a **sworn** statement, they swear that everything contained in the statement is the truth. **2** If two people are **sworn** enemies, they make it known that they hate each other.

swot /swɒt/ *verb*; *noun*
▷ ***verb*** (*informal*): **swots, swotting, swotted**
If you **swot**, you study hard, especially for school examinations. [*same as* **revise**]
▷ ***noun***: **swots** (*derogatory*)
If you call someone a **swot**, you mean that they work hard, or are clever, at school work.

> ***phrasal verb***
> If you **swot up**, or **swot up** on a particular subject, you read a lot and try to learn as much as possible about it.

swum /swʌm/ *verb*
Swum is the past participle of **swim**.

swung /swʌŋ/ *verb*
Swung is the past tense and past participle of **swing**.

sycamore /ˈsɪkəmɔː(r)/ *noun*: **sycamores**
1 A **sycamore** or **sycamore tree** is a tree that grows in Europe and Asia and has large five-pointed leaves which fall off in the autumn. [see picture at **tree**] **2** (*uncount*, *often adjectival*) **Sycamore** is the hard wood of the sycamore tree.

syllabic /sɪˈlabɪk/ *adjective*
Syllabic means of or relating to syllables, or the division of words into syllables.

syllable /ˈsɪləbəl/ *noun*: **syllables**
A **syllable** is any of the parts, consisting of one or more sounds and usually including a vowel or a consonant acting like a vowel, that a spoken word can be divided into: *The word 'telephone' has three syllables, 'te', 'le', and 'phone', and 'tiger' has two, 'ti' and 'ger'.*

syllabus /ˈsɪləbəs/ *noun*: **syllabuses** or **syllabi** /ˈsɪləbaɪ/
A **syllabus** is a list or programme of subjects that are included in a course of study, especially a course of study that leads to an examination: *Are there any modern British playwrights included in the A-level English Literature syllabus?*

symbol /ˈsɪmbəl/ *noun*: **symbols**
1 A **symbol** of something such as an idea or emotion is a thing that represents or suggests that thing: *The cross is a symbol of Christianity.* □ *In the painting, the skull is a symbol of the inevitability of death.* □ *In Europe, the swastika is now regarded as a symbol of fascism and persecution.* **2** A **symbol** for such things as a quantity, idea, object or mathematical operation is a letter, number or shape used to represent it, *eg* the *x* used in mathematics to represent the multiplication process, % for per cent, or $ for the US dollar.

symbolic /sɪmˈbɒlɪk/ *adjective*
1 **Symbolic** means used or regarded as a symbol, or using symbols: *The objects surrounding the figure in the portrait are symbolic.* □ *symbolic writing.* **2** If something is **symbolic** of another thing, it represents that other thing: *The closure of the plant is symbolic of the general decline in Britain's industry.* — *adverb* **symbolically:** *The physical presence of Christ is represented symbolically in the distribution of bread and wine at the Eucharist.*

symbolism /ˈsɪmbəlɪzəm/ *noun* (*uncount*)
Symbolism is the use of symbols to represent things, such as ideas or emotions, especially in art or literature.

symbolize or **symbolise** /ˈsɪmbəlaɪz/ *verb*: **symbolizes, symbolizing, symbolized**
Something that **symbolizes** another thing is used to represent that other thing: *He was dressed in purple robes to symbolize his royal blood.* [*same as* **signify**]

symmetric /sɪˈmɛtrɪk/ or **symmetrical** /sɪˈmɛtrɪkəl/ *adjective*
Symmetric or **symmetrical** means having two halves that are exact copies of each other, with each half a mirror image of the other: *a symmetrical pattern.* [*opposite* **asymmetric, asymmetrical**] — *adverb* **symmetrically:** *coloured squares arranged symmetrically on the canvas.*

symmetry /ˈsɪmətrɪ/ *noun* (*uncount*)
1 Something that has **symmetry** has two parts or halves that are exactly the same, with one part or half the mirror image of the other. **2** You can also say that a building or work of art has **symmetry** when the parts from which it is formed are arranged in a way that is pleasing to look at. [*opposite* **asymmetry**]

sympathetic /sɪmpəˈθɛtɪk/ *adjective*
1 You are **sympathetic** to someone when you show that you understand their feelings of sadness or distress and try to help them by doing or saying kind or comforting things: *The hospital staff were all very sympathetic when her husband died.* [*same as* **understanding, concerned**] **2** You can describe a person or their character as **sympathetic** when they are kind-hearted or can understand easily how others think or feel about things. **3** If you are **sympathetic** to *eg* a cause, you agree with it and support it. — *adverb* **sympathetically:** *She patted his hand sympathetically.*

sympathize or **sympathise** /ˈsɪmpəθaɪz/ *verb*: **sympathizes, sympathizing, sympathized**
You **sympathize** with someone when you feel or show sympathy for them or approval of their ideas and opinions: *I know you must be feeling very upset, and I do sympathize.* □ *It's difficult to sympathize with such an extreme point of view.*

sympathizer or **sympathiser** /ˈsɪmpəθaɪzə(r)/ *noun*: **sympathizers**
You can refer to a person who supports or approves of the policies of a political party or other organization without necessarily being directly involved with it as a **sympathizer** of that party or organization: *a Nazi sympathizer.*

sympathy /ˈsɪmpəθɪ/ *noun*: **sympathies**
1 (*uncount*) **Sympathy** is understanding of and sensitivity to the sadness or suffering of others, often shown in expressions of sadness or pity: *I was so sorry to hear of the death of your husband; you have my deepest sympathy.* □ *She deserves all she gets; I don't have any sympathy for her.* [*same as* **commiseration, compas-**

sion] **2** (*uncount or count*) If you have **sympathy** with someone's ideas or actions you support or approve of them; your **sympathies** lie with a particular person or thing when you agree with or support them, rather than someone or something else. **3** (*uncount*) If you do something in **sympathy** with another person or group of people, you do it in order to demonstrate your support for them: *When the miners came out on strike several other unions came out in sympathy.*

symphony /ˈsɪmfənɪ/ *noun*: **symphonies**
A **symphony** is a long musical work in usually three or four parts, or movements, to be played by a large orchestra.

symptom /ˈsɪmptəm/ *noun*: **symptoms**
1 A **symptom** of an illness is something wrong with your body or part of your body that shows that you have that illness: *He has all the symptoms of flu; fever, headache and aching limbs.* **2** You can also refer to something that is a sign or indication that a certain, usually bad, state or condition exists as a **symptom** of that state or condition: *They regard the increase in crime as a symptom of a more general decline in moral standards.* [*same as* **indication**]

symptomatic /sɪmptəˈmatɪk/ *adjective*
Something that is **symptomatic** of a particular state or condition is a sign that that state or condition exists: *Their lack of respect for older people is symptomatic of a more uncaring attitude generally.* [*same as* **suggestive**, **indicative**]

synagogue /ˈsɪnəgɒg/ *noun*: **synagogues**
A **synagogue** is a building where Jews gather to worship or study their religion.

synchronize or **synchronise** /ˈsɪŋkrənaɪz/ *verb*: **synchronizes, synchronizing, synchronized**
1 You **synchronize** one action or operation with another when you make them happen, move or operate together at the same speed and in exact time with each other: *The swimmers' movements were synchronized with each other and with the music.* □ *We should synchronize our watches before we begin.* **2** In a film or television broadcast the soundtrack **is synchronized** with the pictures when the sound heard precisely matches the action seen.

syndicate /ˈsɪndɪkət/ *noun*: **syndicates**
1 A **syndicate** is a group of business people or organizations that come together to work on or manage a single project: *Local industrialists have formed a syndicate to bid for the mining contracts.* **2** A crime **syndicate** is an association of criminals that organize illegal activities over a wide area: *a drugs syndicate.* [*same as* **ring**] **3** A news **syndicate** is an association of journalists that sell stories to a variety of newspapers.

syndrome /ˈsɪndroʊm/ *noun*: **syndromes**
1 A **syndrome** is a set of symptoms that are typical of a particular physical or mental illness: *Down's syndrome* □ *Asherman syndrome.* **2** You can also refer to a pattern of events or qualities that are characteristic of a particular problem or condition as a **syndrome**: *His behaviour is typical of male mid-life crisis syndrome.*

synonym /ˈsɪnənɪm/ *noun*: **synonyms**
A **synonym** for a word is one which has the same, or very nearly the same, meaning: *The words 'bright', 'intelligent', 'quick-witted', and 'smart' are all synonyms for 'clever'.*

> In this dictionary synonyms are shown in bold type preceded by the words 'same as', and are placed at the end of the definitions or entries to which they apply. [see also **antonym**]

synonymous /sɪˈnɒnəməs/ *adjective*
1 If a word or expression is **synonymous** with another word or expression they have the same meaning: *'Being economical with the truth' is synonymous with 'lying'.* **2** If you say that one thing is **synonymous** with another you mean it is so closely associated with that other thing that when thinking of one thing you automatically think of the other: *'Britain' is often mistakenly seen as being synonymous with 'England'.*

synopsis /sɪˈnɒpsɪs/ *noun*: **synopses**
A **synopsis** is a short version of something longer, *eg* of the plot of a book, play or film. [*same as* **summary**]

syntax /ˈsɪntaks/ *noun* (*uncount; grammar*)
Syntax is the set of grammatical rules that are used to position and connect words correctly to form phrases and sentences in a language.

synthesis /ˈsɪnθəsɪs/ *noun*: **syntheses** /ˈsɪnθəsiːz/
1 (*uncount*) The **synthesis** of a substance is its production by a process of combining or blending different parts to form a complex whole. **2** A **synthesis** is something, such as a chemical substance or a style, that is produced by combining or blending different parts or elements: *This architectural style is a complex synthesis of classical and modern elements.* [*same as* **blend**]

synthesize or **synthesise** /ˈsɪnθɪsaɪz/ *verb*
Something **is synthezised** when it is produced by combining simpler parts to make a complex whole; a drug or other chemical **is synthesized** when it is produced by combining various chemicals to create something that is very similar to a natural product. [*same as* **blend**]

synthetic /sɪnˈθɛtɪk/ *adjective*
1 Synthetic materials or substances have been created artificially by combining various chemicals or by combining artifical rather than natural substances: *synthetic fibres* □ *The cake was filled with synthetic cream.* [*same as* **man-made**, **imitation**; *opposite* **genuine**] **2** If you say that someone's behaviour is **synthetic** you mean that they are not sincere or genuine: *Her caring attitude was completely synthetic and adopted simply to enhance her media image.* [*same as* **fake**, **artificial**; *opposite* **genuine**]

syphilis /ˈsɪfɪlɪs/ *noun* (*uncount*)
Syphilis is a very serious disease that is passed from one person to another during sexual activity, or from an infected mother to her child.

syphon see **siphon**.

syringe /sɪˈrɪndʒ/ *noun*: **syringes**
A **syringe** is a medical instrument consisting of a hollow cylinder with a thin hollow needle attached. Liquid can be drawn into or pushed out of the cylinder by means of a plunger inside the cylinder. [see also **hypodermic**]

syrup /ˈsɪrəp/ *noun* (*uncount or count*)
1 Syrup is the thick sweet sticky concentrated sugary liquid made from the juice of plants, *eg* the maple, or by melting sugar in water, used in cooking and as a sauce: *maple syrup* □ *Make a sugar syrup by dissolving two cups of sugar in a cup of water.* **2 Syrup** or a **syrup** is also any medicine in the form of a thick sugar-flavoured liquid: *cough syrup.*

syrupy /ˈsɪrəpɪ/ *adjective*
1 A **syrupy** liquid is thick like syrup. **2** If you describe something or someone's behaviour as **syrupy**, you think it is too sweetly sentimental or too nice: *She writes syrupy romantic novels.*

system /ˈsɪstəm/ *noun*: **systems**

1 A particular **system** is **a** a set of connected or related parts that together form a complex whole: *Britain's system of government* □ *the education system* □ *a modern transport system* □ *the human digestive system.* **b** an arrangement of mechanical, electrical or electronic parts that function as a single unit: *a computer system* □ *the railway signalling system* □ *a stereo system* **2** A **system** is an organized method of working or way of doing a particular task, or a set of rules that are used to do something: *the parliamentary system of government* □ *She doesn't seem to use any sort of logical system for keeping her accounts.* □ *The firm is introducing a new system of invoicing in the new year.* □ *a numbering system based on numerals and letters.* **3** (*used in the singular*) When people refer to the **system** they mean the institutions that administer and control various aspects of life in society regarded as being difficult or impossible to influence or change, especially by the ordinary person: *It's impossible to make any real changes when you are always up against the system.*

▻ ***phrase*** When you have been feeling *eg* anger, sorrow or frustration and you manage to **get it out of your system** you succeed in getting rid of that feeling by expressing it openly: *Have a good cry and get it all out of your system.*

systematic /sɪstəˈmatɪk/ *adjective*
Systematic is used to describe a way of working or behaving that is done according to a clearly-worked out plan or method: *a systematic check to make sure that no name has been omitted from the register.* □ *The Nazis undertook a systematic extermination of the Jews.* [*same as* **methodical**] — *adverb* **systematically**: *You will have to check all the records systematically.* [*same as* **methodically**]

T

T or **t** /tiː/ *noun*: **Ts** or **t's**
T is the twentieth letter of the English alphabet: *Americans tend not to use 't' spelling for the past participles of verbs like burn and learn.*

ta /tɑː/ (*BrE*) *interjection*
Ta is an informal or child's word for 'thank you'.

tab¹ /tab/ *noun*: **tabs**
1 A **tab** is a small piece or strip of fabric, metal or paper attached to an article, for hanging it up, opening it, holding it or for identification: *You open the can by pulling the metal tab.* **2** (*AmE*) In a restaurant, the **tab** is the bill: *He offered to pick up the tab.* [= pay the bill]
▻ ***phrase*** (*informal*) You **keep tabs on** someone or something when you watch them closely so that you know exactly what they are doing and where they are: *Investors are advised to keep close tabs on the development of share prices.*

tab² /tab/ *noun*: **tabs**
A **tab** is a key on a typewriter or computer keyboard which sets and finds the position of the margins and columns.

tabby /ˈtabɪ/ *noun*: **tabbies**
A **tabby**, or **tabby cat**, is a cat with grey or brown fur marked with dark stripes.

table /ˈteɪbəl/ *noun*; *verb*
▻ ***noun***: **tables**
1 (*count or uncount*) A **table** is a piece of furniture with a flat surface that you use for putting things on, typically with four legs to support it: *a coffee table* ▫ *a small side table* ▫ *They sat round the kithen table discussing politics.* ▫ *Children must be taught to behave properly at table.* **2** A **table** is a group of *eg* words or numbers arranged in columns and rows: *He consulted the table of contents to see if there was a chapter on statistics.* ▫ *Last year's results are shown in Table 1.* ▫ *Nowadays children scarcely need to learn their multiplication tables.* [= sets of statements such as 'five fives are twenty-five, five sixes are thirty ...]
▻ ***verb***: **tables, tabling, tabled**
You **table** a subject when you suggest that it should be discussed by *eg* a committee or in parliament: *Labour has tabled a motion of no confidence in the government.*
▻ ***phrases*** **1** A subject or proposal is **on the table** when it has been presented for discussion. **2** You **turn the tables on** someone when you reverse a situation completely and put them in a totally different, and usually worse, position. **3** Something that is done **under the table** is done secretly, rather than publicly or officially: *I suspect he has changed his stance as a result of some under-the-table bribery.*

tableau /ˈtabloʊ/ *noun*: **tableaux** /ˈtabloʊ/ or **tableaus** /ˈtabloʊz/
A **tableau** is a scene, especially from history or literature, that people dressed in costume recreate on stage, usually without speaking or moving from their positions throughout: *Lucia was stringing pearls for the tableau of Mary Queen of Scots.*

tablecloth /ˈteɪbəlklɒθ/ *noun*: **tablecloths**
A **tablecloth** is a cloth for covering a table, especially for use during meals.

table manners /ˈteɪbəl manəz/ *noun* (*plural*)
Your **table manners** are the way you behave when you are eating a meal at table: *You can be sure that people will notice your table manners, and to some extent judge you by them.*

tablespoon /ˈteɪbəlspuːn/ *noun*: **tablespoons**
1 A **tablespoon** is a large spoon which is used for serving food. **2** A **tablespoon** or **tablespoonful** of something is the amount that a tablespoon holds, used as a measurement in cookery: *two tablespoonfuls of sugar.* [see picture at **tableware**]

tablet /ˈtablət/ *noun*: **tablets**
1 A **tablet** is a dose of medicine in the form of a small disc or ball: *Take two tablets four times daily.* [*same as* **pill**] **2** A **tablet** of something such as soap is a flat solid piece of it: *There was a large new tablet of scented pink soap beside the washbasin.* **3** A **tablet** is also a flat piece of stone or wood, with words carved in its surface: *I read the words on the memorial tablet fixed to the wall.*

table tennis /ˈteɪbəl tenɪs/ *noun* (*uncount*)
Table tennis is an indoor game based on tennis that is played by hitting a light hollow ball with small bats across a net fitted to a table.

tableware /ˈteɪbəlweə(r)/ *noun* (*uncount*)
The cutlery and dishes that you put on the table for meals can be referred to as **tableware**.

tabloid /ˈtablɔɪd/ *noun*: **tabloids**
A **tabloid** is a newspaper with relatively small pages and usually written in an informal style with a lot of photographs. [compare **broadsheet**]

taboo /təˈbuː/ *noun*; *adjective*
▻ ***noun***: **taboos**
A **taboo** is anything which people are not allowed to do, and that is forbidden for religious reasons or by custom: *the old taboos against cousins marrying* ▫ *There used to be more of a taboo against people kissing in public.*
▻ ***adjective:*** *The subject of sex is still more or less taboo in most cultures* ▫ *Young people come out with these taboo words quite happily.*

tabulate /ˈtabjʊleɪt/ *verb*: **tabulates, tabulating, tabulated**
You **tabulate** information when you arrange it in columns or in the form of a table.

tacit /ˈtasɪt/ *adjective* (*formal*)
Something that is **tacit** is understood but not actually stated clearly: *The no-smoking rule in the office is maintained by tacit agreement of the staff.* [*same as* **implied**] — *adverb* **tacitly:** *In giving the man such a short sentence, many women felt that the judge was tacitly condoning male violence.*

taciturn /ˈtasɪtɜːn/ *adjective*
A **taciturn** person says very little: *We didn't like him*

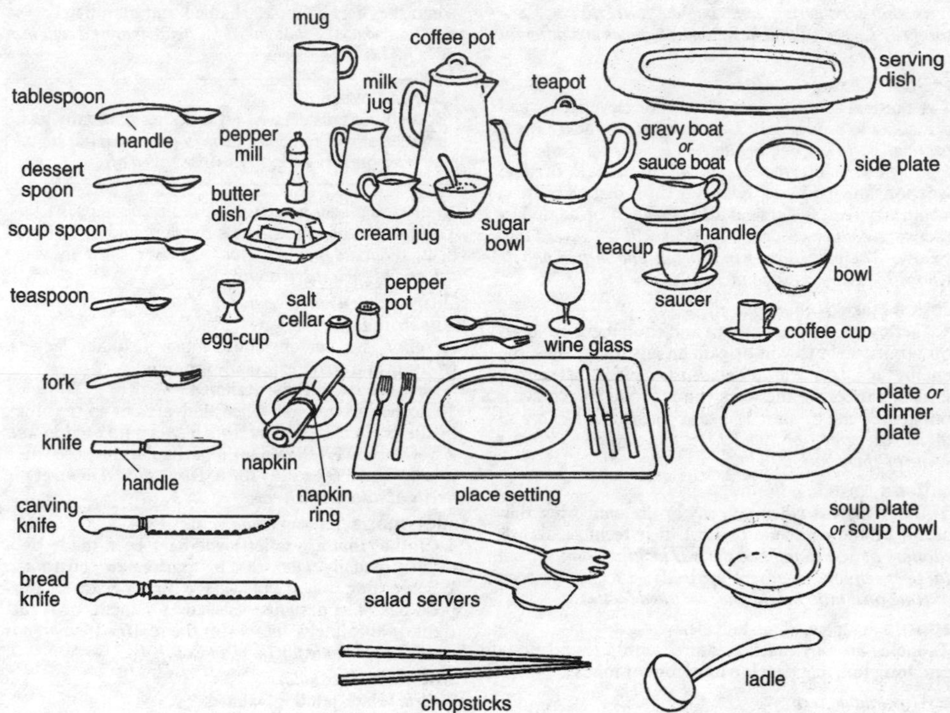

much; he was distant and taciturn. [*same as* **silent, morose**]

tack /tak/ *noun; verb*

▻ ***noun*: tacks**

1 A **tack** is a short nail with a sharp point and a broad flat head: *We hammered in tacks all round the edge of the carpet.* **2** (*count or uncount*) A **tack** is also **a** (*sailing*) a direction taken by someone sailing a ship: *We were on a north-westerly tack.* **b** a course or direction in thought or action: *If this approach doesn't work we can try a different tack.* □ *You seem to have changed tack halfway through your essay and started discussing something not quite relevant to the topic.*

▻ ***verb*: tacks, tacking, tacked**

1 You **tack** something to a surface when you fasten or attach it with tacks: *Make sure the stair carpet is properly tacked down.* **2** People sailing a ship **tack** when they change direction to take best advantage of the wind.

> ***phrasal verb***
> You **tack** one thing **on** to another when you attach or add it as as an extra part, especially hastily and with too little consideration: *Many Scots felt that the government treated them as an afterthought, and something to be tacked on at the end when the serious business had been dealt with.*

tackle /ˈtakəl/ *verb; noun*

▻ ***verb*: tackles, tackling, tackled**

1 You **tackle** a a task or problem when you try to deal with it: *I'd better tackle the ironing.* □ *It's a problem that the government hasn't begun to tackle yet.* **2** You **tackle** someone when you speak to them directly about something they have done wrong, or about a problem that you think they should be dealing with: *Have you tackled Susan yet about the issue of keys to members of staff?* **3** You **tackle** a player from the opposing team in games such as football or rugby when you try to get the ball from them: *He was injured when another player tackled him.*

▻ ***noun*: tackles**

1 A **tackle** is an act of trying to get the ball away from a player on the opposing team in games such as football or rugby. **2** (*uncount*) **Tackle** is the equipment needed for a particular sport or activity: *a shop selling fishing tackle* □ *shaving tackle.*

tacky /ˈtakɪ/ *adjective*: **tackier, tackiest**

1 Something that is **tacky** feels slightly sticky: *Watch out; the paint is still tacky.* **2** (*informal*) **Tacky** things are also **a** cheap, badly made and in poor taste: *street women dressed in their cheap tacky finery*. **b** unpleasant or nasty: *I wanted nothing to do with her tacky private life.* [*same as* **sordid, squalid**]

tact /takt/ *noun* (*uncount*)

You treat people with **tact** when you are careful not to say or do anything that might upset or offend them: *The situation needs to be handled with tact and diplomacy.*

tactful /ˈtaktfəl/ *adjective*

You are **tactful** when you are careful not to say or do

anything that might upset or offend people: *She's always very tactful when she deals with students and their problems.* □ *It would be tactful not to to ask her about her divorce.* — *adverb* **tactfully:** *Try to find out what it is that's bothering him; but do it tactfully!* □ *She tactfully suggested that he might be happier in a different job.*

tactical /'taktɪkəl/ *adjective*
1 A **tactical** action is well planned or cleverly worked out so as to produce the best possible result: *He ran a tactical race, keeping behind the leaders until the last lap, when he overtook them all to win.* **2** **Tactical** weapons are used over relatively short distances from a military base. **3** **Tactical** also means of or related to tactics: *a soldier with great tactical skill.* — *adverb* **tactically:** *The poll showed that about one in five people who voted Labour did so tactically.*

tactics /'taktɪks/ *noun* (*plural*)
1 **Tactics** are the ways troops and equipment are used on a battlefield to win or gain an advantage over the enemy: *a soldier with a detailed knowledge of tactics.* **2** Your **tactics** are the ways you act so as to achieve a particular end or aim: *The government's tactics are to divide the group of rebel MPs and so bring at least some of them back into line.*

tactless /'taktləs/ *adjective*
You are **tactless** when you say or do something that could offend someone or hurt their feelings: *It was tactless of you to tell her she was looking plumper.* □ *a tactless remark.* — *adverb* **tactlessly:** *'I see you've been putting on a little weight,' he remarked tactlessly.*

tadpole /'tadpoʊl/ *noun*: **tadpoles**
Tadpoles are tiny black creatures with a round body and long tail, that develop into frogs or toads.

tag[1] /tag/ *noun*; *verb*
▻ ***noun***: **tags**
A **tag** is a piece of fabric or paper attached *eg* to a garment or to an item for sale, that gives information such as washing instructions or the price: *a price tag.* [*same as* **label**]
▻ ***verb***: **tags, tagging, tagged**

> ***phrasal verb***
> You **tag along** when you follow or accompany someone, especially without being invited: *I'm going round to Jerry's tonight and I don't want you tagging along.*

tag[2] /tag/ *noun* (*uncount*)
Tag is a children's game in which one child chases others and tries to catch or touch one of them, who then chases the others.

tagliatelle /tagljə'tɛlɪ/ or /taljə'tɛlɪ/ *noun* (*uncount*)
Tagliatelle is pasta made in the form of long narrow ribbons.

tail /teɪl/ *noun*; *verb*
▻ ***noun***: **tails**
1 An animal's, bird's or fish's **tail** is the part, often long and thin, at the back or end of its body: *Dogs wag their tails when they are happy.* **2** Any part of an object that hangs down at, or projects from, its back or rear can be referred to as a **tail**: *the tail of a shirt* □ *an aircraft's tail.* **3** (*used in the plural, with a singular or plural verb*) **Tails** is the side of a coin that does not have the ruler's or president's head on it: *She tossed the penny and it came down tails.* **4** (*used in the plural*) A man is wearing **tails** when he is wearing a formal jacket with two long parts hanging down at the back.
▻ ***verb*** (*informal*): **tails, tailing, tailed**
You **tail** someone when you follow them closely: *The police tailed him to the airport.*
▻ ***phrase*** Someone has their **tail between their legs** when they feel or look ashamed and humiliated: *She told him what she thought of his behaviour and sent him off with his tail between his legs.*

> ***phrasal verb***
> Something **tails off** when it becomes gradually less, smaller or weaker: *The rise in house prices has tailed off over the last year.* □ *His voice tailed off.*

tail end /teɪl 'ɛnd/ *noun* (*usually in the singular*)
The **tail end** of something is the very end or last part of it: *What did they say about pay rises? I just heard the tail end of their discussions.*

tailor /'teɪlə(r)/ *noun*; *verb*
▻ ***noun***: **tailors**
A **tailor** is a person whose job is to make jackets, trousers and coats, especially for men.
▻ ***verb***: **tailors, tailoring, tailored**
1 Clothes **are tailored** when they are cut so that they fit the body closely: *She wore a smart tailored jacket.* **2** Something **is tailored** for a particular purpose when it is designed especially for it: *cars tailored to meet the needs of disabled drivers.*

tailor-made /teɪlə'meɪd/ *adjective*
1 Clothes that are **tailor-made** have been made by a tailor, usually to fit a particular customer. **2** Something that is **tailor-made** for a person or purpose has been designed specially for them, or is just right or absolutely suitable for them: *Mrs Malaprop is a part tailor-made for Patricia Routledge.*

taint /teɪnt/ *verb*; *noun*
▻ ***verb***: **taints, tainting, tainted**
To **taint** something is to spoil it by adding something undesirable to it: *Cover the onions properly or they'll taint everything else* [= make everything else taste of onions] *in the fridge.* □ *politicians whose reputations have been tainted by the breath of scandal.*
▻ ***noun*** (*used in the singular; formal*): *a career spoilt by the taint of corruption and bribery.* — *adjective* **tainted:** *Rebecca thought about her own youth, and the dark secrets of those early tainted days.*

take /teɪk/ *verb*; *noun*
▻ ***verb***: **takes, taking, taken, took**
1 a You **take** something or someone with you if you have them with you when you go: *Please take me shopping with you.* □ *Don't forget to take your key with you.* □ *We give everybody a little present so that they have something to take home with them.* **b** You **take** something or someone from one place to another when you carry or lead them there: *We'd better take these chairs in out of the rain.* □ *Should I take her some grapes or something?* □ *I'm just taking the dog for a walk.* □ *Sometimes she took her class to places like the museum or zoo.* □ *The A40 takes you towards Oxford.* □ *The 23 bus takes you into the centre of town.* □ *Your talents should take you far.* [compare **carry**, **convey**]

> Notice that you **take** something to a place where neither you nor your listener are: *Do we need to take sandwiches with us on the trip?* Someone **brings** something to the place where you are, and you **bring** something to the place where your listener is: *Do bring the children with you when you come next time. Shall I bring my photos round later?* You **fetch** something when you go and get it, and return with it: *I'm just going to fetch Peter from his dancing class.*

c You **take** someone somewhere when you drive them there: *I'll take you to the station.*
2 a You **take** something from somewhere or someone when you remove it: *We took the sheets off the bed.* □ *Do take your feet off the table.* □ *No-one's going to take my baby from me.* [*same as* **remove**; see also **take away** below] **b** You **take** one number from another when you subtract the first from the second: *Take 65 from 92; that leaves 27.* [see also **take away** below] **c** You **take** something when you reach and get it, or help yourself to it, or get it from somewhere: *She took a book down from the shelf.* □ *Take a leaflet from the pile here.* □ *He took a second piece of cake.* □ *The title 'Present Laughter' is taken from a song in 'Twelfth Night'.* **d** You **take** something when you put out a hand to receive it or get hold of it: *He took the credit card that I handed to him.* □ *She took him by the hand and led him away.* □ *Take my hand and you won't get lost.* □ *Let me take your coat and I'll hang it up.* **e** When choosing something, *eg* in a shop, you say you'll **take** a certain thing if that is what you want: *I'll take two kilos of potatoes, please.* □ *I'll take this one; I prefer the colour.* [*same as* **have**] **f** Someone **takes** something of yours if they remove it without permission, or steal it: *Someone's taken my bike.* □ *The thieves didn't take much: just some money and jewellery.*
3 a People **take** things such as food, drink or medicine when they swallow them: *He's unable to take any solid food.* □ *Take one pill night and morning.* **b** You **take** certain foods, or **take** them a certain way, if it is your habit to eat them, or eat them that way: *I think she takes tea rather than coffee.* □ *Do you take your porridge with sugar or salt?* □ *Does anyone take sugar in their coffee?* **c** You **take** a certain size in clothes or shoes if that is the size you need: *I usually take a size 14 in dresses.* □ *I'd like to buy a pair of trainers; I take sixes.* **d** (*grammar*) A verb **takes** an object if it normally has one: *'Buy' can take an indirect object as well as a direct one.*
4 a You **take** something such as responsibility, command, or control when you are given, or assume, authority to act in some situation: *The police arrived and took control.* □ *Someone has to take charge of things.* □ *Would you like to take responsibility for the project?* □ *The Conservatives took office again in 1970.* □ *as long as you can take the initiative when you are required to.* **b** You **take** an opportunity of doing something when you judge the moment to be appropriate for it, and do it: *I'd like to take this opportunity of thanking the organizers.* **c** You **take** a job when you start earning your living at something: *She took a job as a waitress.* **d** You **take** a job that you are being offered when you agree to do it: *I've decided to take the post.* **e** You **take** a holiday or a break when you have one: *Let's take five minutes' rest.* □ *She usually takes two weeks' leave in July.* **f** People **take** their places when they go to the position they should be in: *Please take your places for the next dance.* **g** If someone invites you to **take** a seat they are asking you to sit down. **h** You **take** a house or apartment when you rent it: *We took a cottage in the Highlands for the Easter holidays.* **i** You **take** a certain form of transport when you travel by it: *I took the train to Perth.* **j** You **take** a certain route when you follow it: *Take the M90 as far as Milnathort.* □ *Take the second turning on the left after the war memorial.* □ *I don't recognize this place; I think we've taken a wrong turning.* **k** You **take** things in a certain order when you deal with them in that order: *Let's take first things first.* **l** If someone says to you '**Take** a certain person or thing' they are pointing them out as an example: *Not all classical music is serious; take some of Beethoven, for example.*
5 a You **take** pupils for a particular subject when you teach it to them: *She went round from school to school taking the children for gym sessions.* □ *I take the sixth form for history on a Tuesday.* **b** You **take** a subject at school or university when you study it, *eg* for an exam: *If they take Latin they have to drop French.* □ *You used to be able to take up to 10 O-Grade subjects.* □ *I took maritime law in my third year.* **c** You **take** an exam or test when you do it: *I shall be taking my finals this June.* □ *They all take an arithmetic test at the end of the first term.* □ *I'm taking two A levels this summer and three next year.* □ *He refused to take a urine test.* [compare **sit** sense 2c]
6 a You **take** something if you are willing to accept it: *Never take the blame for anything.* □ *We regret that we cannot take cheques without a banker's card.* □ *I'm afraid it will mean taking a reduction in pay.* **b** You **take** someone's advice or assurance when you accept it, believe it or follow it: *If you'd taken my advice we'd be home by now.* □ *It's true; you can take my word for it.* □ *Take it from me* [= believe me], *he'll have sold it by now.* **c** (*often with a negative*) You **take** orders from someone if you are willing to obey them: *I refuse to take instructions from someone who knows nothing about the job.*
7 a You **take** someone's side in a quarrel, fight or argument when you support them: *His mother always took his side.* **b** You **take** a certain attitude to something if that is the way you regard it: *The board may take a rather more serious view of the incident.* **c** You **take** a liking or dislike to someone or something when you start liking or disliking them: *We've recently taken a liking to a restaurant on South Street.* □ *For some reason I took an immediate dislike to him.* **d** You **take** something such as pleasure or comfort from some circumstance if it gives you pleasure or comfort: *She took some comfort from the fact that he'd died painlessly.* □ *They take enormous pleasure in their grandchildren's doings.*
8 a Something **takes** a certain number of people or things if it has room for them: *The class isn't quite full; we can take one or two more people.* □ *I don't think the car will take any more luggage.* **b** (*often with a negative*) If you can **take** something unpleasant you can bear it: *He couldn't take the pain any more.* □ *I won't take that kind of rudeness from anyone.* □ *Her new super-efficient image was rather hard to take.* □ *nursery furniture that can take any amount of rough treatment.* **c** You **take** news or an event in a particular way if you react to it in that way: *She took the news well.* □ *He took his wife's death badly.* [= he was very upset by it] □ *The police didn't take his complaint seriously.* □ *Tell me the worst; I can take it.* **d** You **take** something as a certain thing if you think that it is that thing: *He smiled briefly, which I took as a hopeful sign.* □ *When I first met my tutor I took her for a student.* □ *I took this gesture of hers to be a form of apology.*
9 a Military forces **take** a place when they capture it: *He led his troops across Asia, taking one city after another* □ *On 26 January 1885 Khartoum was taken and General Gordon killed.* [*same as* **capture**, **occupy**] **b** You **take** a prize when you win it: *She took first prize in the chess competition.* □ *He took a first in his finals at Cambridge.* **c** People **are taken** ill, or **taken** in some other way, when they become ill suddenly, or when some other condition suddenly affects them: *The news took me completely by surprise.* □ *His abruptness can take you aback sometimes.* □ *the dance troupe that has taken Paris by storm.* **d** Something that you insert or inject into living tissue **takes** when it produces the

right reaction or grows and develops in the right way: *The first skin graft didn't take.*

10 a A task or process **takes** you a certain amount of time, or you **take** a certain amount of time to complete it, if that is the amount of time it lasts for, needs or requires: *This job is going to take us all day.* □ *She took an hour getting ready.* □ *My letter took three weeks to get to Australia.* □ *It can take ages to get across London if the traffic is bad.* □ *The repairs shouldn't take long.* □ *How long did the journey take you?* □ *It may take months for the scars to disappear.* **b** A task or procedure **takes** a certain quantity of *eg* people, things or attempts if they are needed in achieving or performing it: *It took three people to hold him down.* □ *It took five pints of blood to restore the amount he'd lost.* □ *It took us several tries to connect the printer successfully.* □ *Persuading her is going to take some doing.* [= is going to be difficult] **c** An action, move or activity **takes** some quality or characteristic if that is what the person performing it needs for it: *It takes courage to admit you're wrong.* □ *Dieting takes willpower and determination.*

11 a You **take** someone's temperature when you measure it using a thermometer: *Have you taken her temperature this morning?* **b** You **take** measurements when you measure the dimensions of something, such as its length, width or height: *They take your measurements and the suit is ready for you within a week.* **c** You **take** notes *eg* at a meeting or lecture when you write down points to remind you what was said: *As secretary she was required to take the minutes.* □ *rows of students eagerly taking notes* □ *I'll just take a quick note of your telephone number if I may.* **d** You **take** a message when you write it down or memorize it, so that you can pass it on to the person it is intended for. [see also **take down**] **e** You **take** a photograph of something when you photograph it or record it with your camera: *That was a lovely photo that Pam took of you.* □ *Why don't you take the church with that tree in the foreground?*

12 a Take is used with a lot of nouns formed from verbs, with the same meaning as the verb; *eg* 'take a look' means to look: *She took a step forward.* □ *Someone's already taken a bite out of this apple.* □ *She finds it difficult to take decisions.* □ *Take a look at these results.* □ *He was in the habit of taking an afternoon walk in the botanic gardens.* □ *Action must be taken to ensure that this sort of thing does not recur.* **b** You **take** notice of something, or **take** an interest in it, when you pay attention to it, or are interested in it: *Take no notice of the numbers on the left.* □ *He took an interest in her academic progress.* **c** You **take** care or trouble with something when you do it carefully: *Take great care to stabilize the patient's neck before lifting her.* □ *She'd taken a lot of trouble over the drawing.*

▻ ***noun*** (*cinema*): **takes**

A **take** is a single attempt at filming any of the individual shots that the final film is made up of: *It took six takes before the director was happy with the shot.*

▻ ***phrases*** **1** You **are taken with** someone or something when you find that you like them: *I've been trying this new form of exercise and I'm quite taken with it.* **2** If you say to someone **'I take it that'** something is so, you mean you assume it is, and expect them to confirm that it is: *I take it that you'll be at this evening's lecture?* □ *I took it that you two would like to be put next to each other in the seating plan.* **3** (*informal*) Something that **takes it out of** you, or that **takes a lot out of** you, tires, exhausts or weakens you: *Radiotherapy tends to take it out of you, but it's worth it.* □ *All this worry and anxiety has taken a lot out of her.*

phrasal verbs

For **take aback** see **aback**.

take after You **take after** your parents or some other relation if you are like them in appearance, character or abilities: *Phil is the musical one; he takes after his mother.*

take against You **take against** someone or something when you begin to dislike them: *She's taken against her sister for some reason, and won't have her in the house.*

take apart 1 You **take** something **apart** when you separate it into the different pieces that form it: *We'll probably have to take the bookcase apart to get it up the stairs.* **2** (*informal*) You **take** someone **apart** when you criticize them: *I suppose he must be used to being taken apart by the press.*

take away 1 You **take** something **away** when you remove it: *The nurse came in and took away my empty plate.* [see also **takeaway**] **2** You **take** something **away** from someone or something when you deprive them of it, or remove it permanently from them: *They may take your driving licence away from you.* □ *No-one can take your memories away.* **3** You **take** one amount **away** from another when you subtract the first from the second; '**take away**' is sometimes used like 'minus': *From three little maids take one away.* □ *Let's see, he's 76; 1994 take away 76; so he was born in 1918.*

take back 1 Something **takes** you **back** when it reminds you of the past: *Seeing that film again took me right back to my chldhood.* **2** You **take** something **back** when you return it to the place it came from: *I've got some books to take back to the library.* [*same as* **return**] **3** You **take** goods **back** to a shop when you return them there because they are unsuitable, and either exchange them or get your money back; a shop or business **takes** goods **back** if it is willing to accept goods rejected by customers: *We can only take goods back if it can be shown that they were faulty before they left the factory.* **4** You **take** something you have said **back** when you admit that you shouldn't have said it, *eg* because it was rude or inaccurate: *I take back all those things I said about him; he's really quite human.* [*same as* **withdraw**]

take down 1 You **take** something **down** when you remove it from a high position where it has been placed or fixed: *She reached up and took down a book.* □ *It's time we took down the decorations.* □ *All the pictures and posters had been taken down and the walls looked awfully bare.* **2** You **take down** your trousers when you pull them down, *eg* so that you can sit on the toilet. **3** You **take down** something that someone tells you when you write it down: *She took down the message as he gave it to her over the telephone.* □ *Have you got that reference? I forgot to take it down.* **4** To **take** a building or other structure **down** is to remove it bit by bit or reduce it to ground level: *The old Customs House was taken down in 1883.* □ *We took the tent down as soon as it was daylight.* [*same as* **demolish, dismantle, pull down**; *opposite* **erect, put up**]

take in 1 One thing **takes in** another when it includes it: *The report should be expanded to take in working conditions.* □ *The boundary had been changed to take in parts of Somerset.* **2** You **take in** something that you see or are told when you understand what it means: *She's been told he's dead but I don't think she's taken it in.* [*same as* **grasp**] **3** You **take in** clothes when you adjust the seams to make them fit more closely. **4** Someone **takes** you **in** when they manage to cheat or deceive you: *They were taken in completely by the trick.* **5** You **take** a homeless person **in** when you let them stay in your house: *He'd been taken in by neighbours one night when his stepfather threw him out.*

take off **1** You **take off** things you are wearing when you remove them from your body: *Do take your coat off.* □ *He took off his glasses and polished them with his hanky.* □ *They like you to take your walking boots off outside.* **2** An aircraft **takes off** when it leaves the ground at the beginning of a flight: *The plane was on the tarmac at Dar-es-Salaam, waiting to take off for Lilongwe.* [see also **takeoff**] **3** (*informal*) You **take off** for somewhere, or **take** yourself **off** there when you leave to go there, especially suddenly: *I called round only to find that he'd taken off for Bangkok that very morning.* □ *I decided to take myself off to the country for a few days' peace.* **4** Something **takes off** when it becomes very popular or successful: *The bottle-bank scheme took off, was a marvellous success, and was copied everywhere.* **5** You **take** time **off** when you have a holiday or break and do not go to work: *I'm taking all next week off.* □ *Take the day off tomorrow and come with me.*

take on **1** You **take** a task or job **on** when you agree to do it: *He agreed to take on the responsibility for the project.* [*same as* **undertake**] **2** You **take** someone **on** when you give them a job: *We take on extra staff at Christmas.* [*same as* **employ**] **3** You **take on** a more powerful person or organization if you compete against them, challenge them or fight them: *I'd think twice before taking on the union.* **4** Something **takes on** a quality, meaning or appearance when it begins to have it: *The garden was rapidly taking on the appearance of a bomb site.* □ *His words have taken on a new significance in the light of recent events.* [*same as* **assume**]

take out **1** You **take** something **out** when you get it from the place it is in: *She opened her purse and took out a pound coin.* □ *I took my jacket out of the cupboard.* **2** You **take** money **out** when you withdraw it from your bank account for your own use: *I took £30 out only this morning and I seem to have spent it all.* **3** You **take out** an insurance policy when you arrange for something to be insured: *Remember to take out travel insurance.* **4** You have some part of you **taken out** when it is extracted, cut away or surgically removed: *He'd had his appendix taken out at the age of 11.* □ *If you don't want me to take the tooth out I can try and save it.* [*same as* **extract**, **remove**] **5** You **take** someone **out** when you invite them to go somewhere with you, *eg* to the theatre, and pay for them: *I'd like to take you out for a meal sometime.* □ *Sometimes his niece called at the home and took him out for a drive.*

take out on (*informal*) You **take** *eg* your anger **out on** someone when you behave badly towards them because you are angry, even though they are not responsible for the way you feel: *She found herself taking her frustration out on the children.*

take over **1** To **take over** a company or organization is to gain control of it: *In 1989 the firm was taken over by a Paris-based consortium.* [see also **takeover**] **2** You **take over** a job from another person when you start doing it after they have stopped doing it: *When did she take over as manager?* □ *Meet Janet, who will be taking over Catherine's job next week.* **3** You **takes over** the controls of a vehicle from someone who has been driving when you take their place and drive it: *I took over at the wheel when we reached Lincoln.*

take to **1** You **take to** someone or something when you begin to like them or be fond of them: *Alan brought the German couple round and I took to them straight away.* □ *I hope the children will take to skiing.* **2** You **take to** doing something if you begin to do it regularly: *She's taken to wearing black tights and very short skirts.* **3** (*rather literary*) You **take to** a place when you go there: *The rebels took to the hills.* □ *He took to his bed and died.*

take up **1** Something **takes up** a certain amount of time or space if it needs or uses that amount: *The task took up most of the morning.* □ *His belongings are all in our flat, where they're taking up a lot of room.* **2** You **take up** something such as a pastime, interest or activity when you begin to involve yourself in it: *Maybe I'll take up the violin when I retire.* □ *He's recently taken up golf.* **3** You **take up** a job, post or appointment when you begin your duties: *She will be taking up her position as Warden in October '94.* **4** You **take up** something that has been interrupted when you continue from where you stopped: *Robert took up the narrative from where he'd left off before dinner.* **5** You **take up** something that is worrying you with someone whose responsibility it is when you discuss it with them or ask them to deal with it: *I shall take the matter up with my MP.*

take up on **1** You **take** someone **up on** an offer, proposal or challenge when you accept it: *Thanks for the invitation; I'll take you up on that sometime.* **2** You **take** someone **up on** a point they have made when you challenge them about it, because you disagree with it or want it better explained.

take upon You **take** it **upon** yourself to do something when you do it although it is unnecessary, or not your duty: *She took it upon herself to make sure that everybody got a drink.*

take up with You **take up with** a person, especially someone that other people disapprove of, when you become friends with them.

takeaway /'teɪkəweɪ/ *noun*: **takeaways**
A **takeaway** is **1** a cooked meal that you buy in a restaurant but take home to eat. **2** a restaurant which sells cooked meals that you take home to eat.

taken /'teɪkən/ *verb*
▻ *verb*
Taken is the past participle of **take**.

takeoff /'teɪkɒf/ *noun* (*count or uncount*): **takeoffs**
Takeoff is the act of an aircraft leaving the ground at the beginning of a flight: *Takeoff will be delayed by one hour.* [see also **take off** at take, compare **landing**]

takeover /'teɪkoʊvə(r)/ *noun*: **takeovers**
There is a **takeover** when someone buys enough shares in a company to take control of it. [see also **take over** at **take**]

taker /'teɪkə(r)/ *noun* (*usually in the plural*; *informal*): **takers**
You can say there are no **takers** for something such as a drink, a challenge or a bet when no-one wants it, or is prepared to accept it: *I offered them some of my homemade beer but there weren't any takers.*

takings /'teɪkɪŋz/ *noun* (*plural*)
The **takings** are the amount of money taken *eg* at a concert or in a shop: *The shop's takings are down on last year's.*

talc /talk/ *noun* (*uncount*)
Talc is talcum powder.

talcum powder /'talkəm paʊdə(r)/ *noun* (*uncount*)
Talcum powder is a fine, often perfumed, powder which people put on their bodies after washing.

tale /teɪl/ *noun*: **tales**
1 A **tale** is a story, especially one involving imaginary events or magic: *tales of King Arthur and his knights.* **2** A **tale** is also an account of an interesting or exciting event that really happened: *climbers with exciting tales to tell about climbing in the Himalayas.*

talent /'talənt/ *noun* (*count or uncount*): **talents**
Talent is the special or natural skill or ability that means that you do something well: *She has a talent for acting.* □ *He has absolutely no talent at all.* □ *musical talents.* — *adjective* **talented:** *a talented young singer.*

talk /tɔːk/ *verb*; *noun*
▷ ***verb***: **talks, talking, talked**
1 a People **talk** when they say things to one another, or have a conversation: *Jason's one and a half and just beginning to talk.* □ *It's noisy here; can't we find somewhere quieter to talk?* □ *I could hear people talking next door.* □ *I can't hear you if you all talk at once.* □ *She was shy and rather difficult to talk to.* □ *What were you two talking about?* □ *I'd rather not talk about that if you don't mind.* □ *We talked ourselves almost hoarse that first evening.* □ *The kids are so excited about Christmas, they're talking of nothing else.* □ *It's good to hear people talking Welsh in the street.* □ *Groups of delegates stood around, talking in various languages.* [see note at **speak**] **b** You **talk** to someone when you discuss something with them: *Could I talk to you for a moment?* □ *I'm not the person to ask; you ought to talk to a doctor.* □ *I'd like to talk to you about future plans.* □ *You're the only person I can talk to.* **c** You say that people **are talking** if there is a lot of casual or careless discussion about something, *eg* someone's private life: *You ought to be more careful; people are beginning to talk.* [*same as* **gossip**] **d** (*informal*) Someone **talks** when they give secret information to other people, *eg* to the police: *If he doesn't talk soon we'll have to find a way of making him.* □ *Someone must have talked.* **e** You **talk** to people about something when you give a lecture or an informal speech: *He'd been invited to talk to the mothers' group about childhood illnesses.*
2 a People **talk** something such as sport or business when they discuss it: *Let's not talk politics all night.* □ *men who meet in the pub to talk football.* **b** Someone who **is talking** sense is saying something wise or sensible; someone who **is talking** nonsense or rubbish is saying something stupid or ignorant. **c** (*informal*) You say you **are talking** something such as a lot of money if that is what you are referring to or meaning: *It won't be cheap; we're talking thousands of pounds here.* □ *I take it you're talking genuine diamonds?*
▷ ***noun***: **talks**
1 You have a **talk** with someone when you have a discussion or conversation with them: *I enjoyed our little talk; it was useful.* **2** You give a **talk** when you give a lecture or make an informal speech: *It just remains for me to thank our speaker for her excellent talk on mosaics.* □ *I'm off to a talk on fungi.* **3** (*used in the plural*) **Talks** are negotiations or formal discussions between the representatives of opposing parties in a dispute, or of different countries: *The peace talks continue tomorrow.* □ *trade talks.* **4** (*uncount*) **Talk** is careless or casual discussion between people, *eg* about things that don't concern them, such as someone's private life: *There's been a lot of silly talk about her relations with a certain friend of her husband.* [*same as* **rumour, gossip**] **5** (*uncount*) **Talk** also means ineffective words as opposed to effective action: *Take no notice of his threats; that's just idle talk.* □ *There's been talk of reforming the system, but nothing's happened yet.* **6** (*uncount*) The way someone is talking is **talk** of a certain kind: *Challenge the management? That's fighting talk.*
▷ ***phrases*** **1** (*informal*) If you say '**you can talk**', '**you can't talk**', or '**Look who's talking!**' to someone who has been criticizing someone else for some fault, you mean that they have the same fault themselves: *'You're such a careless driver.' 'You can talk, after last week's near-collision.'* **2** Someone who **knows what they're talking about** has expert knowledge or reliable information about something: *I'd recommend buying shares in it, and I know what I'm talking about.* **3** (*informal*) You say '**now you're talking**' to someone who is at last making a proposal that interests you. **4** You say '**talking of**' a certain thing when you want to mention another thing connected with it: *Talking of grants, have you remembered to post that application form?* [*same as* **speaking**]

phrasal verbs
talk down to Someone who **talks down to** you speaks to you as though you were not very intelligent: *We felt we were being talked down to by the folk from headquarters.* [*same as* **patronize**]
talk into or **talk out of** You **talk** someone **into** doing something if you persuade them to do it; you **talk** them **out of** it when you persuade them not to do it: *Don't try to talk me into selling.* □ *I think we've talked him out of resigning.*
talk of Someone who **is talking of** doing something has mentioned it as a vague intention or possible plan: *He's talking of going abroad for a year.*
talk over You **talk** something, especially a problem, **over** with someone when you discuss it with them: *Let's just talk it over quietly.*
talk round You **talk** someone **round** when you persuade them to do what you want them to: *She's refusing to co-operate but I think we can probably talk her round.*

talkative /'tɔːkətɪv/ *adjective*
A **talkative** person talks a lot: *She got more and more talkative as the evening went on.* □ *Some of the children in the class are not very talkative.* [*same as* **garrulous, loquacious**]

tall /tɔːl/ *adjective*: **taller, tallest**
1 Tall people are above average in height: *The boy was tall for his age.* □ *a tall dark girl.* [*opposite* **short, small**] **2 Tall** also describes narrow objects, *eg* trees, that are above average in height: *these enormously tall conifers* □ *huge tall skyscrapers.* [*opposite* **small, low**; see note at **high**] **3** You use **tall** to state someone's height, or to refer to people's height in a relative way: *He's already six feet tall.* □ *One twin was slightly taller than the other.* □ *How tall are you?* [see also **high**] **4** (*slightly humorous*) **Tall** describes things that are unreasonable in some way, *eg* 'a **tall** story' is impossible to believe, and 'a **tall** order' is an unreasonable request or an impossible task.

tally /'talɪ/ *verb*; *noun*
▷ ***verb***: **tallies, tallying, tallied**
Two or more things or numbers **tally** if they are the same, give the same results, or match each other: *The accounts of the accident do not tally.* □ *The numbers in the first column should tally with those in the third, but they don't.*
▷ ***noun***: **tallies**
A **tally** is a note or record kept, *eg* of points scored or money spent: *We need someone to keep a tally of everyone's marks.*

talon /'talən/ *noun*: **talons**
The **talons** of a bird of prey are its hooked claws.

tambourine /tambə'ri:n/ *noun*: **tambourines**
A **tambourine** is a small round drum with skin stretched tight on one side only, and with small round pieces of metal round the edge. You play a **tambourine** by shaking it or hitting it with your hand.

tame /teɪm/ *adjective*; *verb*
▻ ***adjective***: **tamer, tamest**
1 Animals that are **tame** are used to living or working with people: *She keeps a tame sheep as a pet.* [*same as* **domesticated**; *opposite* **wild**] **2** (*derogatory*) If you describe someone as **tame** you mean they do what they are told too obediently, or that they are rather feeble, and lack spirit: *I'll never get my colleagues to go on this march; they're all too tame.* [*same as* **docile, meek, submissive**; *opposite* **aggressive, pushy**] **3** Something that is **tame** is dull and unexciting: *It was a tame ending to an otherwise exciting story.* [*same as* **boring**; *opposite* **exciting**]
▻ ***verb***: **tames, taming, tamed**
1 You **tame** an animal when you train it to be obedient, and accustom it to living or working with people, so that it is no longer afraid of them: *You shouldn't try to tame foxes and hedgehogs.* [*same as* **train**] **2** You **tame** dangerous people or things when you find ways of controlling them, sometimes so as to be able to use them for a particular purpose: *taming the power of the ocean*

tamper /'tampə(r)/ *verb*: **tampers, tampering, tampered**

> ***phrasal verb***
> You **tamper with** something when you interfere or meddle with it, especially in such a way as to cause damage, or when you have no right to do so: *The papers on my desk had been tampered with while I was away.*

tampon /'tampɒn/ *noun*: **tampons**
A **tampon** is a cylinder-shaped piece of compressed cottonwool that a woman puts inside her vagina to absorb blood during menstruation.

tan /tan/ *noun*; *adjective*; *verb*
▻ ***noun***: **tans**
1 (*usually in the singular*) A **tan** is a suntan: *She came back from Italy with a deep tan.* **2** (*uncount*) **Tan** is a yellowish-brown colour.
▻ ***adjective:*** *She was wearing a tan waistcoat.*
▻ ***verb***: **tans, tanning, tanned**
You **tan** when your skin becomes brown in the sun: *My skin doesn't tan easily.*

tandem /'tandəm/ *noun*: **tandems**
A **tandem** is a long bicycle for two people, with two seats and two sets of pedals placed one behind the other.
▻ ***phrase*** Two people, groups, or pieces of equipment work **in tandem** with each other when they work in co-operation: *Ecologists must work in tandem with politicians if anything is to be done about the problem of the environment.*

tandoori /tan'dʊərɪ/ *adjective*
Tandoori food is food cooked in an Indian style in a clay oven: *tandoori chicken.*

tang /taŋ/ *noun*: **tangs**
A **tang** is a strong or sharp taste, flavour or smell: *We could smell the salty tang of the sea air less than a mile away*

tangent /'tandʒənt/ *noun*: **tangents**
(*geometry*) A **tangent** is a straight line that touches a curve but does not cut through it.
▻ ***phrase*** You **go off at a tangent** when you begin to think or talk about something completely different.

tangerine /tandʒə'ri:n/ *noun*: **tangerines**
A **tangerine** is a type of small orange with a loose, reddish-orange skin.

tangible /'tandʒɪbəl/ *adjective*
Something that is **tangible** is real or definite enough to be observed or felt: *The reforms were beginning to yield tangible results at last.* □ *Companies increasingly want to see tangible benefits from their investment in technology.* [*same as* **actual, concrete, evident**; *opposite* **abstract, intangible**] — *adverb* **tangibly:** *The evil in the place was something you were immediately, almost tangibly, aware of.*

tangle /'taŋgəl/ *noun*; *verb*
▻ ***noun***: **tangles**
1 A **tangle** of something such as wire, rope, or hair is an untidy twisted mass of it: *Let me comb your hair; it's all in a tangle* □ *All that was left of the vehicle was tangle of blackened metal.* □ *an impenetrable tangle of brambles.* **2** A **tangle** is also a confused or complicated state or situation: *He has got himself into a bit of tangle financially.* [*same as* **mess, muddle**]
▻ ***verb***: **tangles, tangling, tangled**
1 Something such as hair or wool **tangles**, or gets **tangled**, or **tangled** up, when it gets twisted or knotted: *She had long curly hair that tangled easily.* □ *a tangled heap of metal* □ *The wool was all tangled up at the bottom of her bag.* **2** You get **tangled** up in something such as rope when it gets wound round you and traps you; something such as rope or hair gets **tangled** round something, or **tangled** up in it when it gets wound round it: *Her hair got tangled up in the grating at the bottom of the swimming pool, and she nearly drowned.* **3** You get yourself **tangled** up in something undesirable when you get involved in it: *I wouldn't get tangled up with those people if I were you.* — *adjective* **tangled:** *He smoothed the matted, tangled hair away from her bruised face.*

> ***phrasal verb***
> (*informal*) You **tangle with** someone when you become involved in a fight or argument with them: *It's foolish to tangle with the police.*

tank /taŋk/ *noun*: **tanks**
A **tank** is **1** a large container for holding, storing or transporting liquids or gas: *There's no water left in the hot tank.* □ *The petrol tank's full.* **2** a heavy steel-covered military vehicle armed with guns: *He was a tank commander during the war.*

tankard /'taŋkəd/ *noun*: **tankards**
A **tankard** is a large metal mug usually with a handle and sometimes with a lid, used especially for drinking beer.

tanker /'taŋkə(r)/ *noun*: **tankers**
A **tanker** is a ship or large lorry which transports large amounts of liquid: *a milk tanker.*

tanned /'tand/ *adjective*
You are **tanned** when the sun has made your skin darker in colour: *She came back from Spain looking fit and tanned.*

tannery /'tanərɪ/ *noun*: **tanneries**
A **tannery** is a place where animal skins are made into leather.

tantalizing or **tantalising** /'tantəlaɪzɪŋ/ *adjective*
Something that is **tantalizing** is attractive, exciting or tempting but may be something that you cannot have or enjoy: *Tantalizing smells were coming from the*

kitchen. □ *a tantalizing glimpse of freedom.* — *adverb* **tantalizingly:** *We were tantalizingly close to the summit, but did the sensible thing and turned back as the snow began to fall.*

tantamount /'tantəmaʊnt/ *adjective*
▻ *phrase* One thing is **tantamount to** another when it has the same effect, value or result as the other thing does: *The statement he gave the police is tantamount to an admission of guilt.* [*same as* **equivalent to**]

tantrum /'tantrəm/ *noun*: **tantrums**
Someone, especially a child, throws a **tantrum** when they have a fit of bad temper, usually with a lot of kicking and screaming.

tap[1] /tap/ *verb*; *noun*
▻ *verb*: **taps, tapping, tapped**
You **tap** something when you strike it lightly with your fingers or with something you are holding: *She tapped the lid gently with a hammer.* □ *He tapped on the door with his walking stick.* □ *Someone tapped me on the shoulder.* □ *He tapped his fingers on the table in time to the music.* □ *I could hear him tapping out a message on his radio.*
▻ *noun*: **taps**
A **tap** is an act of tapping , or the feeling of being tapped: *I felt a light tap on my shoulder.* □ *He gave his pipe a tap against the chimney.*

tap[2] /tap/ *noun*; *verb*
▻ *noun*: **taps**
A **tap** is a device attached to a pipe, with a handle that you turn to allow liquid or gas to flow from the pipe: *I turned the cold tap on.* □ *Did you turn the tap off?* □ *Just leave the tap running.* □ *Let the tap run for a few minutes.* □ *I can hear a tap dripping somewhere.* [*same as* **faucet**; see pictures at **bathroom, kitchen**]
▻ *verb*: **taps, tapping, tapped**
1 You **tap** a supply or source when you start using it: *The course he took made him tap sources of knowledge he didn't know he had.* □ *In some areas, wind power has been successfully tapped, creating an alternative method of producing energy.* **2** To **tap** someone's telephone is to attach a device to their line, which allows you to listen secretly to their telephone conversations: *They knew now they were being watched, and they had reason to believe that their telephone was being tapped.*

tape /teɪp/ *noun*; *verb*
▻ *noun*: **tapes**
1 (*uncount*) **Tape**, or **magnetic tape**, is thin, narrow plastic ribbon with a magnetic coating used for recording sounds or images: *I've got the soundtrack recorded on tape.* □ *video tape.* **2** A **tape** is a length of magnetic ribbon wound on a cassette, used to record sound or images: *She sent us a tape of 'Jesus Christ Superstar'.* □ *Have you got a spare blank tape?* □ *I looked through her collection of tapes.* □ *Is there a tape in the video recorder?* **3** (*count or uncount*) **Tape** is fabric in the form of a narrow strip, used *eg* in dressmaking; a **tape** is a short piece of this sewn into clothes, *eg* for tying or fastening them, or for labelling them: *I laboriously sewed name tapes into all the childrens' school clothes.* **4** (*uncount*) **Tape** or **adhesive tape** is thin plastic ribbon with a sticky surface used *eg* for securing parcels, or sticking one thing to another: *sticky tape* □ *I gave the children some tape so that they could stick their paintings to the wall.* **5** The **tape** at the end of a race track is a string or paper ribbon stretched above the finishing line.
[see also **red tape**]
▻ *verb*: **tapes, taping, taped**
1 You **tape** a programme or music when you record it on magnetic tape: *Don't forget to tape the next episode.* **2** You **tape** things when you secure them or stick them somewhere with sticky tape: *The boxes were taped up ready to send to Cambridge.* □ *I taped the envelope to the top of the parcel.*

tape deck /'teɪp dɛk/ *noun*: **tape decks**
A **tape deck** is a machine that you play and record tapes on, usually part of a hi-fi.

tape measure /'teɪp mɛʒə(r)/ *noun*: **tape measures**
A **tape measure** is a length of plastic, cloth or thin metal tape, marked with inches, feet and yards or centimetres and metres, used for measuring.

taper /'teɪpə(r)/ *noun*; *verb*
▻ *noun*: **tapers**
A **taper** is a long thin candle.
▻ *verb*: **tapers, tapering, tapered**
Something that **tapers** becomes gradually narrower towards one end: *The road tapered gradually and became a narrow farm track.* — *adjective* **tapered:** *She wore a satin wedding dress with tapered sleeves.* — *adjective* **tapering:** *long delicate tapering fingers.*

phrasal verb
An amount **tapers off** when it decreases: *There's a boom in sales over Christmas, which tapers off in January.*

tape recorder /'teɪp rɪkɔːdə(r)/ *noun*: **tape recorders**
A **tape recorder** is a machine which records sounds on magnetic tape and reproduces them.

tape recording /'teɪp rɪkɔːdɪŋ/ *noun*: **tape recordings**
A **tape recording** is a recording of something on tape: *I made a tape recording of last night's concert.*

tapestry /'tapɪstrɪ/ *noun*: **tapestries**
1 (*count or uncount*) A **tapestry** is a piece of cloth with a design, often a picture, sewn on it in wool or thick thread: *the Bayeux tapestry* □ *She made tapestry covers for the cushions.* **2** (*used in the singular*; *literary*) You can refer to something that is colourful and interesting as a **tapestry**: *It's all part of life's rich tapestry.*

tar /tɑː(r)/ *noun* (*uncount*)
Tar is **1** a thick dark sticky liquid that goes hard when it gets cold and is used *eg* in making roads. **2** a similar substance produced when tobacco burns: *These cigarettes are low-tar.*

target /'tɑːgɪt/ *noun*; *adjective*; *verb*
▻ *noun*: **targets**
1 A **target** is **a** a place, person or thing that an attack is aimed at: *The army's target was the disused mine.* □ *high-ranking ministers who have become a target for terrorists.* **b** an object that you aim at in shooting practice or competitions, typically a flat round board marked with coloured concentric circles. **2** You are the **target** of something, *eg* criticism or blame, when you are being criticized or blamed for something: *With her hen-like walk and bossy tone she was an easy target for parody.* [compare **butt**] **3** Your **target** is a result that you are trying to achieve: *My target is to have saved £300 by the end of the year.* [*same as* **aim, goal**]
▻ *adjective*
A programme's **target** audience, and a publication's **target** readers, are the people that the programme or publication is primarily intended for or aimed at: *We see the target user as a young person in the 16-20 age group.*
▻ *verb*: **targets, targeting, targeted**
1 A product or publication **is targeted** at a particular group if it is aimed at them: *journals such as the New Scientist that are targeted at the interested amateur* □ *A lot of thought goes into the placing of TV ads, so*

that they can target specific social groups. **2** Guns or missiles **are targeted on** particular places when they are aimed at them, ready to be fired if the need arises.
▻ ***phrase*** You are **on target** when you are working at the correct rate and will finish or achieve something on time: *The builders are on target to finish the new bridge by the end of the summer.*

tariff /ˈtarɪf/ *noun*: **tariffs**
1 A **tariff** is a tax paid on a particular type of goods brought in to the country. **2** A **tariff** is also a list of prices or charges: *a hotel tariff.*

tarmac /ˈtɑːmak/ *noun*
1 (*uncount*) **Tarmac** is a mixture of small stones mixed with tar, used *eg* to make road surfaces. **2** (*used in the singular*) The **tarmac** is an area covered with tarmac, especially an airport runway: *They walked out on to the tarmac towards the plane.*

tarnish /ˈtɑːnɪʃ/ *verb*: **tarnishes, tarnishing, tarnished**
1 Metal **tarnishes** when it becomes dull and stained: *Silver tarnishes easily.* **2** Something **tarnishes** *eg* your reputation when it spoils or damages it: *She tarnished her record last year by being beaten in the second round of the French championships.* — *adjective* **tarnished:** *a tarnished silver bracelet* ▫ *his tarnished reputation.*

tarpaulin /tɑːˈpɔːlɪn/ *noun*: **tarpaulins**
A **tarpaulin** is a sheet of heavy canvas which has been made waterproof.

tart¹ /tɑːt/ *noun*: **tarts**
1 A **tart** is a pastry case, especially one without a top, with a sweet filling such as fruit or jam: *jam tarts.* **2** (*derogatory, informal*) A **tart** is a female prostitute.

tart² /tɑːt/ *adjective*: **tarter, tartest**
1 Food, especially fruit, is **tart** when it tastes bitter: *Are you sure this rhubarb was ready to pick? It tastes a bit tart.* **2** A **tart** remark is sarcastic and cruel. [*same as* **caustic, cutting**; *opposite* **kind**] — *adverb* **tartly:** *He spoke rather tartly to me.*

tartan /ˈtɑːtən/ *noun* (*uncount or count*): **tartans**
Tartan is woollen cloth of a type associated particularly with Scotland, with a check pattern made up of vertical and horizontal stripes of different colours; individual **tartans** are the various check patterns used by individual Scottish families: *chair covers made of tartan* ▫ *a tartan skirt* ▫ *I purchased a book about the tartans of Scotland.*

task /tɑːsk/ *noun*: **tasks**
A **task** is a piece of work that you have to do: *The company uses computers for a wide range of different tasks.* ▫ *I still had the task of checking all the entries for errors.* [*same as* **job**; compare **chore**]

tassel /ˈtasəl/ *noun*: **tassels**
A **tassel** is a bunch of threads tied firmly at one end, hung on *eg* curtains, cushions or lampshades for decoration: *ceremonial robes decorated with golden tassels.*

taste /teɪst/ *noun*; *verb*
▻ ***noun***: **tastes**
1 (*uncount*) **Taste** is one of your five physical senses; it is the sense by which you recognize what you are eating or drinking, or what food or drink are like, when you touch them with your tongue: *Your sense of taste loses its sharpness as you get older.* **2** (*count or uncount*) The **taste** of something is its particular flavour, or the impression you get of it when you touch it with your tongue, *eg* whether it is sweet, salty or sour: *One of the dishes had a slight taste of curry.* ▫ *people who can distinguish easily between the tastes of different wines* ▫ *I'd never liked the taste of boiled carrots.* ▫ *coffee with a distinctly odd taste* ▫ *soup with hardly any taste* ▫ *I woke up with a horrible taste in my mouth.* **3** (*used in the singular*) You have a **taste** of something when you take a small amount of it into your mouth to find out what it is, or what it is like: *What do you think this is? Here, have a taste.* ▫ *I had a little taste of the soup to make sure it had enough salt in it.* **4** (*used in the singular*) You have a **taste** of something when you experience it briefly, usually for the first time: *She'd already had a taste of boarding-school life, and had hated it.* **5** (*used in the singular*) You have a **taste** for something if you like or enjoy it: *I was getting quite a taste for adventurous holidays.* ▫ *He never lost his taste for fast expensive cars.* **6** (*uncount or count*) Your **taste** is the type of choice you make when buying or selecting things, or the kinds of things that you like; people say you have good **taste** if they approve of your choices, or bad or poor **taste** if they disapprove: *I've always admired your taste in ties.* ▫ *The décor showed excellent taste.* ▫ *The house was furnished in rather poor taste.* ▫ *She had somewhat expensive tastes in clothes and jewellery.*
▻ ***verb***: **tastes, tasting, tasted**
1 Food or drink **tastes** a certain way, or **tastes** of something, if that is its flavour, or the impression it gives you when you touch it with your tongue: *The cream tasted sour.* ▫ *Doesn't this porridge taste a bit burnt to you?* ▫ *'Is this salt or sugar?' 'I don't know; what does it taste like?'* ▫ *I took a mouthful of the wine; it tasted like vinegar.* ▫ *coffee that tasted as if it had been boiled* ▫ *a creamy sauce tasting slightly of asparagus.* **2** You **taste** something, or you can **taste** it, when you become aware of its flavour: *You can't taste things properly when you have a cold.* ▫ *I thought I could taste cinnamon in the cake.* **3** You **taste** food or drink when you try a little of it to find out what it is, or what it is like: *She cut a little piece of cheese for me to taste.* **4** You **taste** something when you experience it briefly, usually for the first time: *Having tasted the luxury of hotel accommodation she was reluctant to go back to living in a tent.*
▻ ***phrases*** **1** Something that someone says or does is **in bad taste** or **in poor taste** if it is offensive and is likely to upset people; things people say or do are **in good taste** if they are not offensive to others: *a joke in very poor taste.* ▫ *His humour isn't always in the best of taste.* [compare **tasteless**] **2** Something that is **to your taste** is something you like or enjoy: *War films weren't really to his taste.*

tasteful /ˈteɪstfʊl/ *adjective*
Something is **tasteful** if it is attractive and shows good judgement or taste: *The internal decor was simple but tasteful.* [*same as* **elegant**; *opposite* **tasteless**] — *adverb* **tastefully:** *The room is tastefully decorated in blue and gold.*

tasteless /ˈteɪstləs/ *adjective*
1 Food that is **tasteless** has too little flavour. [*same as* **bland, insipid**; *opposite* **tasty**] **2** Something that is **tasteless** is unattractive, lacks quality, and does not show good judgement or taste: *the tasteless decor of the 1960s.* [*opposite* **elegant, tasteful**] **3** Stories, remarks or jokes that are **tasteless** are offensive or vulgar. [*same as* **in bad taste, in poor taste**]

tasting /ˈteɪstɪŋ/ *noun*: **tastings**
A **tasting** is a usually social event at which people can try a particular food or drink: *a wine tasting.*

tasty /ˈteɪstɪ/ *adjective*: **tastier, tastiest**
Food is that is **tasty** has a good, pleasant and usually savoury flavour. [*opposite* **bland, insipid, tasteless**]

tatters /ˈtatəz/ *noun* (*plural*)
▻ ***phrase*** **1** Clothes that are **in tatters** are badly torn. **2** Something that is **in tatters** has been ruined: *His life was in tatters after his divorce.*

tattoo[1] /təˈtuː/ *verb*; *noun*
▻ ***verb***: **tattoos, tattooing, tattooed**
To **tattoo** a person, or to **tattoo** a picture or pattern on them, is to mark a picture or pattern on their skin by making tiny holes in their skin that coloured dye is put into: *He had a picture of an eagle tattooed on his chest.*
▻ ***noun***: **tattoos**
A **tattoo** is a picture or pattern tattooed on a person's skin: *I suddenly spotted the tattoo of a butterfly on the sole of her right foot.*

tattoo[2] /təˈtuː/ *noun*: **tattoos**
A **tattoo** is a public outdoor display of military exercises and music presented by the army, navy or air force.

tatty /ˈtatɪ/ *adjective* (*informal, derogatory*): **tattier, tattiest**
Something **tatty** is untidy, old and worn: *I keep some tatty old clothes for when I'm working in the garden.* [*same as* **shabby**]

taught /tɔːt/ *verb*
Taught is the past tense and past participle of **teach**.

taunt /tɔːnt/ *verb*; *noun*
▻ ***verb***: **taunts, taunting, taunted**
You **taunt** someone when you say unpleasant, cruel or hurtful things to them: *The other girls taunted her and called her 'little Miss Know-all'.*
▻ ***noun***: **taunts**
A **taunt** is a cruel, unpleasant and often hurtful remark: *She got used to their taunts and stopped being upset by them.*

taut /tɔːt/ *adjective*
Something **taut** is pulled or stretched tight: *a taut rope.* [*opposite* **slack**]

tavern /ˈtavən/ *noun* (*old*): **taverns**
A **tavern** is a public house.

tawny /ˈtɔːnɪ/ *adjective*: **tawnier, tawniest**
Something **tawny** is yellowish-brown in colour: *She has tawny hair and green eyes.*

tax /taks/ *noun*; *verb*
▻ ***noun*** (*uncount or count*): **taxes**
A **tax** is an amount of money that people and businesses must pay towards a country's expenses that is taken by the government from people's salaries or income, from the profits of businesses, and from the sale of goods and services: *He pays more tax because he earns more.* □ *a tax on savings* □ *tax cuts* □ *a rise in taxes.*
▻ ***verb***: **taxes, taxing, taxed**
1 A government **taxes** people or businesses when it makes them give part of the money they earn to the government as tax: *The government plans to tax high earners more heavily.* □ *Married women can be taxed separately from their husbands.* **2** A government **taxes** goods when a sum of money, often a percentage, is added to the price charged to customers, and this sum is then paid to the government. **3** A sum of money **is taxed** when part of it must be paid to the government: *All personal savings are taxed.*

taxation /takˈseɪʃən/ *noun* (*uncount*)
1 Taxation is the system or procedure, by a government, of taking money from the citizens of a country to pay for the expense of running it. **2 Taxation** is also the amount of money people have to pay to the government as tax: *high taxation rates.*

tax disc /ˈtaks dɪsk/ *noun*: **task disks**
A **tax disk** is a small round certificate attached to the windscreen of a motor vehicle, as proof that its owner has paid road tax. [see picture at **car**]

taxi /ˈtaksɪ/ *noun*; *verb*
▻ ***noun***: **taxis**
A **taxi** is a car with a driver that you can hire to take you from one place to another, in return for a fare that increases the further you travel.
▻ ***verb***: **taxis, taxiing, taxied**
An aircraft **taxis** when it moves slowly along the runway before takeoff or after landing.

taxing /ˈtaksɪŋ/ *adjective*
A task or job is **taxing** if it needs or takes a lot of mental or physical effort. [*same as* **demanding**]

taxi rank /ˈtaksɪ raŋk/ *noun*: **taxi ranks**
A **taxi rank** is a place where taxis wait until people hire them.

taxpayer /ˈtakspeɪə(r)/ *noun*: **taxpayers**
A **taxpayer** is a person who pays tax.

tea /tiː/ *noun*: **teas**
1 (*uncount*) **a Tea** is the dried leaves of an evergreen shrub or tree grown in Asia: *a packet of tea.* **b Tea** is also a drink made by pouring boiling water on these leaves. Many people serve tea with added sugar, milk or lemon, and it can be drunk hot or cold: *He poured himself another cup of tea.* □ *a pot of tea.* **2** A **tea** is a cup of tea: *Three teas and one coffee, please.* **3** (*uncount*) **Tea** is also any similar drink made using boiling water, especially one made with the leaves or flowers of other plants: *mint tea* □ *beef tea.* **4** (*uncount or count*) **Tea** is a light afternoon meal at which tea, sandwiches and cakes are served. **5** (*BrE*; *uncount or count*) For many people, **tea** is the main meal, served in the early evening: *Tea is ready when he gets home from work.* [compare **dinner, lunch**]
▻ ***phrase*** (*informal*) You can say that something is **not your cup of tea** when you don't like it: *French films are not really my cup of tea.*

teabag /ˈtiːbag/ *noun*: **teabags**
A **teabag** is a small bag of thin paper containing tea leaves, that you put in a pot or cup and pour boiling water over.

teach /tiːtʃ/ *verb*: **teaches, teaching, taught**
1 You **teach** someone something when you pass on your knowledge about it to them or give them lessons or instructions, *eg* by showing them how to do it, or telling them about it: *She'd been taught to read before she started school.* □ *Will you teach me to swim?* □ *Dad taught me how to drive.* □ *We teach them the basic essentials of first aid.* [compare **instruct**] **2** You **teach** a subject, or **teach**, when you give lessons to students or others, *eg* at a school or university, and help them learn about something: *My wife teaches in the local primary school.* □ *She teaches German at a private school.* □ *He teaches at Glasgow University.* □ *He found himself a job in Prague, teaching English to adults.* □ *She goes round prisons and teaches the prisoners art.* □ *I used to teach an evening class in vegetarian cookery.* □ *She taught herself Czech from an old dictionary and grammar book.* **3** You **teach** someone to think something or behave in a particular way when you tell or persuade them that it is right to do so: *Haven't you been taught to stand up when your teacher enters the room?* □ *We'd been taught never to tell lies.* □ *I wish she'd teach her kids how to behave.* □ *Jesus teaches us patient endurance.* □ *The church had always taught that the sun went round the earth.* □ *They used to teach us that boys never cry.* **4** Your experiences **teach** you something when you learn from them what to expect or how to react in certain circumstances: *Life in*

Britain had taught her never to rely on the trains being on time. □ *My experience with children had taught me how unwise it was to keep criticizing them.*
▷ ***phrase*** If you say **'that'll teach you to do** something' to someone you mean that he or she will have learnt from the unpleasant effects of some experience not to do it again: *That'll teach me to go out without an umbrella.*

teacher /'tiːtʃə(r)/ *noun*: **teachers**
A **teacher** is a person whose job is to teach, especially in a school. [compare **lecturer**]

teaching /'tiːtʃɪŋ/ *noun*: **teachings**
1 (*uncount*) **Teaching** is the work or profession of a teacher: *I'm going into teaching when I graduate.* **2** (*usually in the plural*) The **teachings** of a particular person, especially someone with original or influential ideas, are the principles and beliefs that they teach to other people: *the teachings of Gandhi.*

tea cosy /'tiː koʊzɪ/ *noun*: **tea cosies**
A **tea cosy** is a thick cover for a teapot, for keeping the tea hot. [see picture at **kitchen**]

teacup /'tiːkʌp/ *noun*: **teacups**
A **teacup** is a medium-sized cup used especially for drinking tea. [see picture at **tableware**]

teak /tiːk/ *noun* (*uncount*)
Teak is a hard yellow-brown wood used for making furniture and in boat-building: *The table and chairs are teak.*

tea leaf /'tiː liːf/ *noun* (*usually in the plural*): **tea leaves**
Tea leaves are the dried leaves of the tea plant, which you use to make tea by pouring boiling water over them.

team /tiːm/ *noun*; *verb*
▷ ***noun***: **teams**
1 A **team** is a group of people forming one side in a game: *He was now in the school's first football team.* **2** A **team** of people is a group of them working together on something: *She joined a research team investigating the causes of schizophrenia.*
▷ ***verb***: **teams, teaming, teamed**

> ***phrasal verb***
> You **team up** with someone if you join with them to do something together: *In 1988 the SDP teamed up with the Liberal Party, forming the LIberal Democratic party.*

teamwork /'tiːmwɜːk/ *noun* (*uncount*)
Teamwork is co-operation between people who are working together on a job or task: *The aim of the project is to encourage teamwork, which is now being recognized as the essential element in an organization's success.*

teapot /'tiːpɒt/ *noun*: **teapots**
A **teapot** is a pot with a spout and handle used for making and pouring tea. [see pictures at **kitchen** and **tableware**]

tear[1] /tɪə(r)/ *noun*: **tears**
Tears are the drops of clear salty liquid that come out of your eyes when you cry.
▷ ***phrase*** You are **in tears** when you are crying: *She burst into tears.*

tear[2] /teə(r)/ *verb*; *noun*
▷ ***verb***: **tears, tearing, tore, torn**
1 You **tear** something such as paper or cloth when you pull it till it separates into two or more pieces, or gets a hole in it: *I tore the letter into little pieces and dropped it in the bin.* □ *He tore a huge hole in his shorts climbing over the fence.* □ *I've gone and torn my skirt.* □ *The stitching tore as I tried to wrench my jacket free.* □ *She's apparently torn a ligament in her knee.* [*same as* **rip**] **2** You **tear** something from somewhere you remove it from there by pulling it till it separates or comes away: *I tore out a page from my notebook.* □ *Why can't you use scissors to cut out all those newspaper articles instead of tearing them out?* □ *He tore the poster off the wall.* □ *The animal's claws had torn the flesh away at his shoulder.* **3** You **are torn** between two possibilities or sides when you cannot decide which to choose or be loyal to: *He was torn between his longing for Helen and not wanting to upset his parents.* □ *People who had relations both in East and West Germany felt very torn.* **4** (*informal*) You **tear** somewhere when you run or travel very fast: *She tore down the road on her bicycle.* □ *We tore off home as soon as the bell rang.* □ *She was tearing along, hair and clothes flying.* [*same as* **dash, rush**]
▷ ***noun***: **tears**
A **tear** is a hole in something made by pulling or tearing: *There was a large right-angled tear in the seat of his shorts.* □ *Childbirth often resulted in a tear in the mother's tissues, which went unrepaired.* [see also **wear and tear**]
▷ ***phrases*** You **tear** something **open** by opening it with a tearing action, especially hastily: *She tore the letter open.* □ *I found a fresh carton of fruit juice and started to tear it open.*

> ***phrasal verb***
> **tear apart** **1** To **tear** something **apart** is to pull or tear it into pieces: *A hunk of meat was thrown to the bear, which it proceeded to tear apart.* **2** Something **tears** a country or other community **apart** if it causes quarrels, fighting or ill feeling within it: *the ancient feud that had torn the family apart.* **3** Something **tears** you **apart** if it upsets or distresses you: *The sight of these crippled children begging everywhere is enough to tear you apart.*
> **tear at** You **tear at** a surface when you remove parts of it with a violent scraping action: *She had torn at his cheeks with her fingernails.*
> **tear away** You **tear** someone **away** from a place, or from something they are watching or doing when you force them to leave it: *if you can tear him away from his computer for a few minutes* □ *Once back in the island community she couldn't bear to tear herself away.*
> **tear down** **1** You **tear down** something such as a picture or poster when you pull it violently off a wall. **2** People **tear** a building **down** when they hastily or violently reduce it to ground level by pulling parts of it away. [*same as* **pull down**]
> **tear off** You **tear off** your clothes when you remove them hastily: *She tore off her jacket and skirt and leapt into the river.*
> **tear up** You **tear** something **up** by tearing it into lots of small pieces: *I immediately tore up the bill.*

tearaway /'teərəweɪ/ (*BrE*) *noun* (*informal*): **tearaways**
A **tearaway** is a young person who does not consider other people and acts in a careless, selfish way.

teardrop /'tɪədrɒp/ *noun*: **teardrops**
A **teardrop** is a single tear.

tearful /'tɪəfəl/ *adjective*
You are **tearful** if you feel like crying, or are crying slightly. — *adverb* **tearfully:** *She smiled tearfully.*

tear gas /'tɪə gas/ *noun* (*uncount*)
Tear gas is a gas which makes your eyes sting and fill with tears: *The police used tear gas to control the riot.*

tear-stained /ˈtɪəsteɪnd/ *adjective*
Your face or cheeks are **tear-stained** if there are traces of tears on them.

tease /tiːz/ *verb; noun*
▻ ***verb***: **teases, teasing, teased**
1 You **tease** someone when you make fun of them, often in a slightly cruel or unkind way: *It isn't fair to tease her about her spots.* **2** You **tease** a person or animal if you annoy them deliberately or unkindly: *Don't tease the kitten like that.*
▻ ***noun*** (*used in the singular*)
A **tease** is a person who makes fun of people, often in a slightly cruel or unkind way: *Her older brother is a terrible tease.*

teaspoon /ˈtiːspuːn/ *noun*: **teaspoons**
1 A **teaspoon** is a small spoon used for putting sugar into tea or coffee. [see picture at **tableware**] **2** A **teaspoon** or **teaspoonful** is the amount that a teaspoon holds, sometimes used as a measurement: *She put two teaspoonfuls of sugar in her coffee.* □ *Add a level teaspoonful of baking powder.* □ *Give him a teaspoonful of the medicine night and morning.*

teat /tiːt/ *noun*: **teats**
1 A **teat** is a piece of shaped rubber with a small hole, attached to a bottle for a baby to drink milk through. **2** An animal's **teat** is the pointed piece of flesh that young animals suck to obtain milk. [compare **nipple**]

teatime /ˈtiːtaɪm/ (*BrE*) *noun* (*uncount*)
Teatime is the time in the afternoon when people have tea.

tea towel /ˈtiː taʊəl/ *noun*: **tea towels**
A **tea towel** is a cloth for drying dishes after they have been washed. [see picture at **kitchen**]

tech /tɛk/ (*BrE*) *noun* (*informal*): **techs**
A **tech** is a technical college.

technical /ˈtɛknɪkəl/ *adjective*
1 Technical means relating to practical skills or applied sciences, especially those sciences used in industry: *You'll have to ask the technical experts.* **2 Technical** language is the special vocabulary used in a particular subject; certain words of this kind are labelled (*technical*) in this dictionary: *I enjoyed reading the New Scientist, even though some of the articles were too technical for me.* □ *a list of the technical terms used in computing.* **3 Technical** is also used with reference to skill in the execution or performance of an art or craft: *piano-playing of great technical brilliance.*

technical college /ˈtɛknɪkəl kɒlɪdʒ/ (*BrE*) *noun*: **technical colleges**
A **technical college** is a college that teaches practical skills and applied sciences that are useful to industry and business.

technicality /tɛknɪˈkalɪtɪ/ *noun*: **technicalities**
1 The **technicalities** of a process are the technical details that it involves: *I'm really not interested in the technicalities of book publishing.* **2** A **technicality** is a usually minor or unimportant detail associated with the strict interpretation of the law or rules: *The judge dismissed the case on a technicality.*

technically /ˈtɛknɪklɪ/ *adverb*
1 (*sentence adverb*) Something is **technically** true if it is true but is actually not very important or relevant: *A policeman told me that technically I was breaking the law by parking on the pavement, but that it would be OK just for a few minutes.* **2 Technically** is used with reference to practical skills and applied sciences used in industry: *France Telecom boasts one of the most technically advanced communication systems in the world.* **3 Technically** also relates to skill in the execution or performance of an art or craft: *a technically brilliant performance of this concerto.*

technician /tɛkˈnɪʃən/ *noun*: **technicians**
A **technician** is a person who specializes or is skilled in a practical art or science, especially one employed to do practical work *eg* in a laboratory.

technique /tɛkˈniːk/ *noun*: **techniques**
1 (*uncount*) **Technique** is ability or skill in the practical aspects of an art or subject, such as painting, music or sport: *I heard him play the viola at about the age of ten, and he demonstrated remarkable technique even then.* **2** A **technique** is a practical skill or method: *He is studying the techniques of film-making.*

technology /tɛkˈnɒlədʒɪ/ *noun*: **technologies**
1 Technology is the study, or the use, of science for practical purposes, *eg* in industry, business, agriculture and medicine. **2** (*count or uncount*) A **technology** is a particular subject or area of work requiring a range of technical skills: *modern computer technology.* — *adjective* **technological** /tɛknəˈlɒdʒɪkəl/: *technological developments that will allow computers to be even more powerful.* — *adverb* **technologically:** *a technologically advanced country.* — *noun* **technologist** /tɛkˈnɒlədʒɪst/: *technologists working in computing.*

teddy /ˈtɛdɪ/ *noun*: **teddies**
A **teddy**, or **teddy bear**, is a child's stuffed toy bear: *She now had quite a collection of teddy bears, which sat in a row at the end of her bed.*

tedious /ˈtiːdɪəs/ *adjective*
Something that is **tedious** is boring because it is too long or is dull: *The job is tedious and badly paid.* □ *a rather tedious meeting.* [*same as* **monotonous**; *opposite* **exciting**]

tedium /ˈtiːdɪəm/ *noun* (*uncount*)
Tedium is the state of being bored: *the endless tedium of dinner with his boring relations.* [*same as* **boredom**]

teem /tiːm/ *verb*: **teems, teeming, teemed**
A place **is teeming** with people or things when it is full of them: *The shops were teeming with people.* — *adjective* **teeming:** *the teeming streets of Bombay.*

teenage /ˈtiːneɪdʒ/ *adjective*
1 Teenage people are aged between thirteen and nineteen: *They have three teenage children.* **2 Teenage** things belong to or are suitable for people aged between thirteen and nineteen: *the latest teenage fashions.*

teenager /ˈtiːneɪdʒə(r)/ *noun*: **teenagers**
A **teenager** is a person aged between thirteen and nineteen.

teens /tiːnz/ *noun* (*plural*)
1 Your **teens** are the years of your life when you are aged between thirteen and nineteen. **2** The **teens** are the numbers from thirteen to nineteen.

teeter /ˈtiːtə(r)/ *verb*: **teeters, teetering, teetered**
You **teeter** when you stand or move unsteadily: *She teetered along the road on her high heels.* [*same as* **wobble**]
▻ ***phrase*** Something **is teetering on the brink** of *eg* defeat or disaster if it is very close to defeat or disaster.

teeth /tiːθ/ *noun*
Teeth is the plural of **tooth**. [see picture at **body**]

teethe /tiːð/ *verb*: **teethes, teething, teethed**
A baby **is teething** when its first teeth are growing.

teething troubles /ˈtiːθɪŋ trʌbəlz/ *noun* (*plural*)
Teething troubles are the problems or difficulties that

occur at the beginning of a project, or with a new piece of machinery: *We're having teething troubles with the new computer system.*

teetotal /tiːˈtoʊtəl/ *adjective*
A person who is **teetotal** never drinks alcohol.

teetotaller /tiːˈtoʊtələ(r)/ *noun*: **teetotallers**
A **teetotaller** is a person who never drinks alcohol.

TEFL /ˈtɛfəl/ *noun* (*uncount*)
TEFL is the teaching of English as a foreign language.

telecommunications /tɛlɪkəmjuːnɪˈkeɪʃənz/ *noun* (*uncount*)
Telecommunications is the science or technology of sending information and messages over a distance by *eg* telephone, television or telegraph.

telegram /ˈtɛlɪgram/ *noun*: **telegrams**
A **telegram** is a message sent by telegraph and delivered in printed form, in Britain now only used for messages sent abroad.

telegraph /tɛlɪgrɑːf/ *noun*; *verb*
▻ ***noun*** (*used in the singular*; *old*)
The **telegraph** is a system of sending messages or information over a long distance by sending electrical or radio signals that can be printed out at the other end.
▻ ***verb*** (*old*): **telegraphs, telegraphing, telegraphed**
You **telegraph** someone when you send them a message using the telegraph system; you **telegraph** a message if you send it using the telegraph system.

telepathy /tɪˈlɛpəθɪ/ *noun* (*uncount*)
Telepathy is the communication of thoughts directly from your mind to another person's mind without using words or signs. — *adjective* **telepathic** /tɛlɪˈpaθɪk/: *Some people believe telepathic communication is possible.* — *adverb* **telepathically**: *Can twins communicate telepathically?*

telephone /ˈtɛlɪfoʊn/ *noun*; *verb*
▻ ***noun*** (*count or uncount*): **telephones**
A **telephone** is an instrument, usually consisting of a microphone and receiver mounted in a handset, which allows you to speak to someone at a distance by transmitting sound in the form of electrical signals: *Could you answer the telephone for me?* □ *The telephone stopped ringing just as she picked it up.* □ *I spoke to her on the telephone last night.* □ *I'm using the portable telephone.* □ *Where's the nearest public telephone?* □ *He can't be contacted by telephone.* □ *What's your telephone number?* □ *Could I make a telephone call?* [see picture at **office**]
▻ ***verb***: **telephones, telephoning, telephoned**
You **telephone** someone when you use a telephone to speak to them: *I'll telephone you as soon as I get home tonight.* □ *I tried to telephone him but he wasn't at home.* □ *Don't forget to telephone if you're going to be late.* [*same as* **ring**]
▻ ***phrase***
1 You are **on the telephone** if you have a telephone that is connected to the public telephone system: *She isn't on the telephone so you'll have to write her a letter.* **2** You are **on the telephone** when you are talking to someone using a telephone: *Dr Shepherd is on the telephone to another caller just now; can I get him to call you back?* [see also **phone**]

telephone box /ˈtɛlɪfoʊn bɒks/ or **phone box** *noun*: **telephone boxes**
A **telephone box** is a small covered area in a public place containing a telephone that anyone can use. [see picture at **street**]

telephone directory /ˈtɛlɪfoʊn daɪrɛktərɪ/ or **phone book** *noun*: **telephone directories**
A **telephone directory** is a book containing a list of the names, addresses and telephone numbers of all or most of the telephone owners in a particular area.

telephone exchange /ˈtɛlɪfoʊn ɪkstʃeɪndʒ/ *noun*: **telephone exchanges**
A **telephone exchange** is a building where telephone lines are connected when you make telephone calls.

telephone number /ˈtɛlɪfoʊn nʌmbə(r)/ *noun*: **telephone numbers**
A **telephone number** is the series of numbers that you dial to speak to a particular person on the telephone: *Give me your telephone number, and I'll ring you tonight.*

telephonist /tɪˈlɛfənɪst/ *noun*: **telephonists**
A **telephonist** is someone who operates a telephone system in a large building or telephone exchange, receiving calls and connecting callers to the people they want to speak to.

telephoto lens /tɛlɪfoʊtoʊ ˈlɛnz/ *noun*: **telephoto lenses**
A **telephoto lens** is a camera lens which produces large images of distant or small objects.

telescope /ˈtɛlɪskoʊp/ *noun*: **telescopes**
A **telescope** is an instrument in the form of a tube with a combination of lenses and mirrors inside, which makes distant objects seem closer and larger, used *eg* for looking at stars and planets. [compare **microscope**]

teletext /ˈtɛlɪtɛkst/ *noun* (*uncount*)
Teletext is a service which provides news and information that is regularly updated and can be seen in written form on a television screen.

televise /ˈtɛlɪvaɪz/ *verb*: **televises, televising, televised**
An event **is televised** when it is filmed and shown on television: *The Winter Olympics are going to be televised.*

television /ˈtɛlɪvɪʒən/ *noun*: **televisions**
1 (*count or uncount*) A **television**, or **television set**, is an apparatus with a screen and speakers which is able to receive radio waves and reproduce them in the form of images and sounds: *We've bought a new colour television set.* □ *Remember to turn the television off.* □ *I'll just turn the television on and get the news.* □ *I saw an amazing film on television the other day.* □ *What's on television tonight?* □ *Alastair was on television last night; did you see him?* □ *Do you watch a lot of television?* [see picture at **living room**] **2** (*uncount*) **Television** is the sending of images and sound in the form of radio waves that can be reproduced on a screen in your home: *cable television* □ *satellite television* □ *She works in television.* □ *television and radio* □ *the television industry.*

telex /ˈtɛlɛks/ *noun*; *verb*
▻ ***noun***: **telexes**
1 A **telex**, or **telex machine**, is a machine that sends messages that are typed on it, and that types the messages it receives. **2** A **telex** is also a message sent or received using a telex machine. **3** (*uncount*) **Telex** is an international service which allows customers to send messages to other customers using a telex machine.
▻ ***verb***: **telexes, telexing, telexed**
You **telex** when you send a message using a telex machine: *She telexed the order to the Paris shop.*

tell /tɛl/ *verb*: **tells, telling, told**
1 You **tell** someone something when you give them information: *Could you tell me your name?* □ *I'm looking forward to telling you my news.* □ *She wrote and told me all about the wedding.* □ *I'm just writing to tell you how grateful I am.* □ *I thought I told you I'd be late tonight.* □ *We weren't told what the result was.* □ *Tell me why you disagree.* □ *'I'm to blame,' she told them.* **2** You

tell a story or tale when you say what happens in it, point by point: *Dad used to keep us amused on long car journeys by telling us stories.* □ *It wasn't long before she began telling me the story of her life.* [*same as* **relate, narrate, repeat**] **3** You **tell** the truth when you give people the real facts about something, or say what actually happened; you **tell** a lie when you make a false statement, intending to deceive people: *I don't think she's telling us the whole truth.* □ *If the truth were told, I don't think he behaved all that heroically.* □ *He admitted that he'd told several lies.* **4** You can **tell** what is so, or what is happening, if you can see or judge accurately: *'Who's leading?' 'Difficult to tell at the moment.'* □ *I couldn't tell whether he was pleased or not.* □ *He could tell from her face that he'd said the wrong thing.* □ *You can tell by the smell that it's made from goats' milk.* □ *As far as I can tell, the structure is pretty sound.* **5** You can **tell** the difference between things if you can distinguish between them: *By the age of ten a child ought to be able to tell the difference between right and wrong.* □ *I'd never been able to tell one twin from the other.* [see also **tell apart** below] **6** A child learns to **tell** the time when he or she learns how to work out what time a clock or watch is showing. **7** You **tell** someone to do something when you order, ask or instruct them to do it: *The doctor told me not to worry.* □ *I was told to wait in the corridor.* □ *Tell me what to do next.* □ *Can you tell me how to start the washing machine?* □ *Stop making difficulties and do as you're told.* □ *The children wouldn't do as they were told.* [= were being disobedient] **8** A circumstance **tells** you something when it indicates what is the case, or what you should do: *Their expressions told me immediately that something had gone terribly wrong.* □ *when your climbing experience tells you to get off the mountain as quickly as possible* **9** A book or piece of writing **tells** you something if it informs or instructs you about it: *This report tells me nothing new.* □ *His diary tells us how close to starvation they were.* □ *The instructions tell you to wash the blades before you use the machine.* **10** A difficult or unpleasant experience that you are having begins to **tell** when it starts having a noticeably bad effect on you: *The nights without sleep were beginning to tell; he looked haggard and exhausted.* [see also **tell on** below]

▻ ***phrases*** **1** For **all told** see **all**. **2** (*informal*) You use **'I can tell you'** and **'I can't tell you'** to emphasize what you are saying: *There's something odd going on here, I can tell you.* □ *I can't tell you what a relief it is to see you.* **3** (*informal*) You say **'I told you so'** rather cruelly to someone who has ignored your advice or warning, and has since found out that you were right. **4** You say **there's no telling** what will happen, or what is the case, if it is impossible to judge: *There's no telling how things may develop in the next twelve months.* **5** (*informal*) You say **'you're telling me'** to express emphatic agreement: *'He was a bit rude about it.' 'You're telling me!'*

phrasal verbs

tell apart You can **tell** things **apart** when you can see the difference between them: *He has identical twin daughters and can hardly tell them apart himself.*

tell off You **tell** someone **off** when you scold them about something: *He told me off for leaving the light on.* □ *I got told off for not passing on the message.* [*same as* **scold, reprimand, rebuke**; see also **telling-off**]

tell on **1** An unpleasant or tiring experience begins to **tell on** you if it has a noticeably bad effect on you: *The strain was beginning to tell on her.* **2** (*informal*) If you have done something wrong, and someone **tells on** you, they go and inform someone in authority what you have done: *She was probably the kind of child who enjoyed telling on her schoolmates.*

telling /'tɛlɪŋ/ *adjective*
You describe something as **telling** if it is effective or significant: *a telling remark.* [*same as* **significant**]

telling-off /tɛlɪŋ'ɒf/ *noun* (*usually in the singular*)
You give someone a **telling-off** if you speak to them angrily or seriously because they have done something wrong: *His teacher gave him a telling-off for being late again.* [see also **tell off** at **tell**]

telltale /'tɛlteɪl/ *adjective*
Telltale signs or comments show or suggest something that is secret or hidden: *I could see that she had been crying from the telltale signs of tears on her cheeks.*

telly /'tɛlɪ/ *noun* (*count or uncount*; *informal*): **tellies**
A **telly** is a television: *watch the telly* □ *turn the telly on or off* □ *There's a good film on the telly tonight.* □ *My sister is going to be on telly.*

temp /tɛmp/ *noun* (*informal*): **temps**
A **temp** is an employee, especially an office worker, who is employed for a short or limited period of time only. [see also **temporary**]

temper /'tɛmpə(r)/ *noun*; *verb*

▻ ***noun*** (*uncount or count, usually in the singular*): **tempers**
1 Your **temper** is the degree of control you have over your emotions, with particular reference to whether or not you get angry easily: *She's got a bad temper.* [= she gets angry easily] □ *He has an even temper.* [= he doesn't get angry easily] □ *She rarely betrayed any signs of temper, even when pushed to the limit by her colleagues.* **2** Your **temper** is the way you are feeling at a particular moment, with reference to how cheerful or angry you are: *I hope you'll be in a better temper when I get home.* □ *I was in a perfectly good temper till you said that.* □ *People's tempers were beginning to fray.* [= people were beginning to get angry] [compare **mood, humour**]

▻ ***verb***: **tempers, tempering, tempered**
One thing **tempers** another when it reduces its impact, whether pleasant or unpleasant: *Her delight that the operation had gone well was slightly tempered by the realization that she now had one leg shorter than the other.*

▻ ***phrases*** **1** You are **in a temper** when you are angry: *The argument had put him in a temper.* **2** You **lose your temper** when you suddenly get angry and start shouting.

temperament /'tɛmpərəmənt/ *noun* (*count or uncount*): **temperaments**
Your **temperament** is the natural character which governs the way you behave and think: *She has a very calm temperament.* □ *The difference in temperament between her and her brother is quite surprising.*

temperamental /tɛmpərə'mɛntəl/ *adjective*
1 A **temperamental** person has unpredictable and often violent changes of mood, especially used to describe someone who loses their temper easily and often. **2** A machine is **temperamental** when it does not work reliably or consistently: *This car is a bit temperamental and doesn't always start immediately in the morning.*

temperate /'tɛmpərət/ *adjective*
A **temperate** climate has mild temperatures that are neither very hot or very cold: *Britain lies in the earth's northern temperate zone.* [compare **tropical**]

temperature /'tɛmpərətʃə(r)/ *noun*: **temperatures**
1 Your **temperature** is the heat of your body: *He has no fever; his temperature's only 37°.* **2** The **temperature** of a place is how hot or cold it is there: *Heat the oven to a temperature of 150°.*

▻ *phrases* **1** You **have a temperature** when you have a fever. **2** You **take** someone's **temperature** when you use a thermometer to measure it: *I took her temperature and it was normal.*

tempest /'tɛmpɪst/ *noun* (*literary*): **tempests**
A **tempest** is a violent storm with very strong winds.

tempestuous /tɛm'pɛstʃʊəs/ *adjective*
A person who is **tempestuous** displays violent or intense emotion: *I suppose you'd describe her personality as tempestuous.* □ *They'd had a shortlived and tempestuous relationship.* [*same as* **volatile**] — *adverb* **tempestuously:** *There she was, a girl of about twenty, in jeans and a leather jacket, sitting on the edge of the pavement and weeping tempestuously.*

tempi /'tɛmpiː/ *noun*
Tempi is a plural form of **tempo**.

temple[1] /'tɛmpəl/ *noun*: **temples**
A **temple** is a building in which the members of some religions worship: *a Sikh temple.*

temple[2] /'tɛmpəl/ *noun*: **temples**
Your **temples** are the two flat parts at the side of your head in front of your ears. [see picture at **body**]

tempo /'tɛmpoʊ/ *noun*: **tempos** or **tempi**
The **tempo** of a piece of music is the speed at which it should be or is played.

temporary /'tɛmpərərɪ/ or /'tɛmpərɪ/ *adjective*
Something that is **temporary** lasts for a short or limited period of time only: *a temporary failure in power* □ *her temporary absence from the office* □ *a student with a temporary job for the summer.* [see also **temp**] — *adverb* **temporarily** /'tɛmpərərɪlɪ/: *I only worked for the company temporarily.*

tempt /tɛmpt/ *verb*: **tempts, tempting, tempted**
1 Someone **tempts** you to do something, either something wrong, or something that they want you to do, when they try to persuade you to do it by making it seem a desirable thing to do: *He realized she was trying to tempt him into bed, but he was not interested.* □ *Building societies were thinking up a variety of new incentives to tempt people into opening accounts.* **2** You **are tempted** to do something if you would very much like to do it but are worried that it would be wrong or too risky: *I was tempted to go climbing but was deterred by a possible avalanche risk.* **3** People sometimes say 'can I **tempt** you to something' when they are offering it to you: *Can I tempt you to another piece of cake?*

temptation /tɛmp'teɪʃən/ *noun* (*uncount or count*): **temptations**
Temptation is the feeling of being tempted to do something that you know might be wrong or harmful: *I could resist temptation no longer.* □ *The temptation to slap her was becoming irresistible.* □ *A young man alone in a big city for the first time is exposed to a variety of temptations.* □ *If you leave the biscuits within reach they'll be too much of a temptation.*

tempting /'tɛmptɪŋ/ *adjective*
Something that is **tempting** attracts you and makes you want to have it: *That's a very tempting offer.* □ *the tempting smell of freshly baked bread.*

ten /tɛn/ *noun*; *adjective*; *determiner*; *pronoun*
▻ *noun*: **tens**
1 (*uncount or count*) **Ten** is **a** the number or figure 10: *Eight and two make ten.* □ *Two fives are ten.* **b** a piece of clothing whose size is represented by the number 10, or a person who wears clothes of that size: *She was a ten before she had her baby.* □ *These shoes are tens.* □ *My son takes a ten in shoes.* □ *Do you have this dress in a ten?* **2** (*uncount*) **Ten** is **a** the age of 10: *My son started learning German at ten.* **b** the time of 10 o'clock: *I'll be here by ten tomorrow morning.* **3** (*count*) A **ten** is **a** a set of ten people or things: *The children were divided into tens.* [= groups containing ten children] **b** a playing card with ten symbols: *My highest card is the ten of clubs.*
▻ *adjective*
Someone who is **ten** is ten years old: *She'll be ten in December.* □ *children aged ten and under.*
▻ *determiner: The train journey cost ten pounds.* □ *She was off work for ten weeks when she had her baby.* □ *The first ten people to arrive will be let in free.* □ *It took ten days' work to finish the job.* □ *a ten-year-old child* □ *clothes for ten-year-olds.*
▻ *pronoun: Ten of the children were chosen to meet the Queen.* □ *All ten were taken to London in the school minibus.* □ *We don't have many copies of the magazine left, perhaps as few as ten.*

tenacious /tɪ'neɪʃəs/ *adjective*
You are **tenacious** if you are determined not to give up or stop doing something: *If they think you are interested, motivated and tenacious enough to make a success of the project, they will support you.* [*same as* **persistent, determined**] — *adverb* **tenaciously:** *She kept to her point tenaciously and would not give way.* — *noun* (*uncount*) **tenacity** /tɪ'nasɪtɪ/: *Everyone admires her tenacity.*

tenancy /'tɛnənsɪ/ *noun*: **tenancies**
1 (*uncount*) **Tenancy** is the temporary renting of property or land that belongs to someone else: *I'm hoping to renew my tenancy agreement.* **2** A **tenancy** is the period during which property or land is rented from the person who owns it: *a five-year tenancy.*

tenant /'tɛnənt/ *noun*: **tenants**
A **tenant** is a person who pays rent to another person in return for the use of their property or land.

tend[1] /tɛnd/ *verb*: **tends, tending, tended**
Something **tends** to happen if it often happens, usually happens or is likely to happen: *She tends to get up later at the weekends.* □ *The bus tends to be early on Monday mornings.*
▻ *phrase* You use **'I tend to** *eg* think' as a polite way of introducing your opinion: *He says this will cause ill feeling and I tend to agree with him.*

tend[2] /tɛnd/ *verb* (*formal*): **tends, tending, tended**
You **tend** a sick person if you care for them while they are ill; you **tend** something if you look after it: *They offered their services to tend sick children and to visit the homes of the poor.* □ *We should tend the garden more often.*

tendency /'tɛndənsɪ/ *noun*: **tendencies**
1 You have a **tendency** to act in a certain way when there is something in your character that makes you act in that way: *She has a tendency to think she can do everything without trying.* **2** There is a **tendency** for something if it starts happening more generally or more often: *There is a tendency for people to move from the countryside into the cities.* **3** A **tendency** is a group within a group of people, political party or movement: *the criminal tendency in society.*

tender[1] /'tɛndə(r)/ *adjective*: **tenderer, tenderest**
1 A **tender** person is loving and gentle; something is **tender** when it shows love and kindness: *She is kind and tender to all her patients.* □ *She spoke a few tender words to him.* □ *a tender smile.* **2** You are **tender**, or have a **tender** heart, if you are easily hurt or upset. **3** Part of your body is **tender** if it is easily hurt when touched, usually because it has been hurt before: *Her arm is still bruised and tender.* **4** Meat is **tender** when it

is easily chewed or cut. **5** A person is at a **tender** age if they are young and likely to be easily harmed: *a young girl of tender years.* — *adverb* **tenderly:** *She spoke to him tenderly.* □ *He smiled tenderly at his baby daughter.* — *noun* (*uncount*) **tenderness:** *feelings of great tenderness.*

tender² /'tɛndə(r)/ *verb*; *noun*
▻ ***verb*** (*formal*): **tenders, tendering, tendered**
You **tender** *eg* an apology, a suggestion or your resignation when you offer or present it.
▻ ***noun***: **tenders**
A **tender** is a formal offer, usually in writing, to do a job or supply goods in return for a stated amount of money and by a stated date.

tenderize or **tenderise** /'tɛndəraɪz/ *verb*: **tenderizes, tenderizing, tenderized**
You **tenderize** meat when you soften it or make it tenderer, *eg* by marinating it.

tendon /'tɛndən/ *noun*: **tendons**
A **tendon** is a length of strong tissue that joins a muscle to a bone.

tendril /'tɛndrɪl/ *noun*: **tendrils**
A **tendril** is a thin, curling stem which some plants use to attach themselves to *eg* trees, other plants or walls.

tenner /'tɛnə(r)/ (*BrE*) *noun* (*informal*): **tenners**
A **tenner** is a ten-pound note or ten pounds: *It only cost me a tenner.* □ *Do you have change for a tenner?*

tennis /'tɛnɪs/ *noun* (*uncount*)
Tennis is a game in which two players or two pairs of players use rackets to hit a light ball across a net on a grass-covered or hard rectangular court: *The children are playing tennis.* □ *a tennis match* □ *a tennis court.*

tenor /'tɛnə(r)/ *noun*; *adjective*
▻ ***noun*** (*often adjectival*): **tenors**
1 A **tenor** is a male singer whose voice has the highest normal range for an adult man: *a famous Italian tenor.* **2** (*uncount*) Men who have this voice sing **tenor**: *He had a fine tenor voice.* □ *I practised the tenor part.* **3** (*used in the singular*) The **tenor** of something is its general character or meaning: *I didn't read the whole article; just enough to grasp its general tenor.* □ *when something happens to disturb the calm tenor of your life.*
▻ ***adjective***
A **tenor** wind instrument has a relatively low range of notes: *He plays the tenor saxophone.*

tenpin bowling /tɛnpɪn 'boʊlɪŋ/ *noun* (*uncount*)
Tenpin bowling is an indoor game in which you roll a large heavy ball down a polished wooden track at ten objects (called **skittles** or **tenpins**) with the aim of knocking as many down as possible.

tense¹ /tɛns/ *noun* (*uncount or count; grammar*): **tenses**
A verb's **tense** is the form of the verb that shows whether the action is being done at the moment (the **present tense**), was done some time ago (the **past tense**) or will be done in the future (the **future tense**), and whether it has been completed or not.

tense² /tɛns/ *adjective*; *verb*
▻ ***adjective***: **tenser, tensest**
1 You are **tense** when you are feeling upset and tired and are nervous and unable to relax: *The flight had been delayed five hours and all of the passengers were getting tense.* **2** Something is **tense** if it is tightly stretched: *The muscles in her neck were tense.* [*same as* **taut**] **3** A situation is **tense** if it makes people worried or nervous.
▻ ***verb***: **tenses, tensing, tensed**

phrasal verb
You **tense up** if you become nervous and worried: *He always comes home tensed up after a busy day at work.*

tension /'tɛnʃən/ *noun*: **tensions**
1 (*uncount or used in the plural*) **Tension** is the worry or nervousness that you feel when something unpleasant, difficult or dangerous is happening: *the usual tensions between relations at the family party* □ *I could hear the tension in her voice.* **2** (*uncount*) The **tension** of a length of *eg* rope, wire or string is how tightly it is being stretched.

tent /tɛnt/ *noun*: **tents**
A **tent** is a shelter made of canvas or other material supported by poles or a frame and fastened to the ground with ropes and pegs, that can be taken down and carried from place to place.

tentacle /'tɛntɪkəl/ *noun*: **tentacles**
Tentacles are the long, thin parts that grow on the head or near the mouth of certain animals such as the octopus, used for grasping things and for feeding with.

tentative /'tɛntətɪv/ *adjective*
1 You behave in a **tentative** way when you are not certain how to act: *She took a few tentative steps towards him.* [*same as* **hesitant, cautious**] **2** A conclusion is **tentative** if it is not finally agreed on or decided. [*same as* **provisional**] — *adverb* **tentatively:** *She moved tentatively towards the door.*

tenterhooks /'tɛntəhʊks/ *noun* (*plural*)
▻ ***phrase*** You are **on tenterhooks** if you are impatient, nervous and excited about something that is due to happen soon: *Don't keep me on tenterhooks; tell me if you passed the exam or not.*

tenth (often written **10th**) /tɛnθ/ *determiner*; *pronoun*; *adjective or adverb*; *noun*
▻ ***determiner***
The **tenth** person or thing is the one that is numbered ten in a series: *The meeting will take place at the end of the tenth week after Christmas.* □ *the 10th Duke of Northumberland.*
▻ ***pronoun:*** *This is the tenth of her books on the history of Scotland.* □ *She's tenth from the right in the front row.* □ *I'll be arriving on the 10th of November.* [see note at **date**]
▻ ***adjective or adverb:*** *I was* (or *came*) *tenth in the history exam.* □ *She came in tenth in the marathon.*
▻ ***noun*** (often written $\frac{1}{10}$): **tenths**
A **tenth** of something is one of ten equal parts of it: *One tenth of the population has been to university.* □ *One tenth of voters didn't vote in the election.*

tenuous /'tɛnjʊəs/ *adjective*
Something is **tenuous** if it is slight and has little strength, and may not really exist: *He had some, albeit tenuous, links with the Royal Family, which he made much of.*

tenure /'tɛnjə(r)/ or /'tɛnjʊə(r)/ *noun* (*uncount; formal*)
1 Tenure is the legal right of holding of an office, position or property. **2 Tenure** is also the length of time a person holds an office, position or property: *The Labour Party has long fought for security of tenure for council tenants.* □ *He made several important changes during his brief tenure of office.*

tepid /'tɛpɪd/ *adjective*
1 Tepid liquid is slightly or only just warm: *The water in the bath was only tepid.* [*same as* **lukewarm**; compare **hot, cold**] **2** A reaction is **tepid** when it is not very enthusiastic: *Her performance was met with tepid applause.*

term /tɜːm/ *noun; verb*

▷ ***noun*: terms**

1 A **term** is a word or expression, often one with a particular meaning in a specialized field: *everyday words such as 'memory' that have become specialized computing terms* □ *You used the term 'totalitarian' several times; what did you mean by it?* □ *a phenomenon we could call 'settling' for want of a better term.* **2** (*used in the plural*) You express or describe something in certain **terms** when you use a certain kind of language: *It is the duty of the government to condemn this practice in the strongest possible terms.* □ *Perhaps you could reword that in simple terms that we can all understand?* **3** (*used in the plural*) You discuss something in certain **terms**, or in **terms** of a certain thing, when you are thinking of it from that point of view: *The house would be ideal in terms of getting to work quickly.* □ *They thought of the heavens in terms of a sphere with the earth at its centre.* □ *The venture was a disaster in financial terms.* **4** (*used in the plural*) You think or talk in **terms** of doing something if you are intending or planning to do it: *We should be thinking in terms of saving for our retirement.* □ *They're talking in terms of publishing next February.* **5** (*used in the plural*) The **terms** of something such as an agreement or contract are the individual points, rules and conditions that it contains: *according to the terms of her will* □ *Read the terms and conditions carefully before signing.* **6 a** (*count or uncount*) A **term** is one of the divisions into which the school and university year is divided, normally three in the UK, generally called *the autumn term* (or *the winter term* or *the Christmas term*), *the spring term* (or *the Easter term*) and *the summer term*: *We spend three terms on Greek history and three on Roman.* □ *the last week of term.* **b** A **term** is a period of time during which a certain party or official is entitled to be in power or hold office: *during her second term of office as prime minister* □ *as I approach the end of my three-year term as chairman.* **c** A convicted criminal serves a prison **term** when he or she is kept in prison for a certain length of time: *Conviction for fraud could lead to a long term of imprisonment.*

▷ ***verb*: terms, terming, termed**

You **term** something a certain thing when you describe it as that thing: *The meeting could hardly be termed a success.* □ *children termed 'educationally subnormal'.*

▷ ***phrases*** **1** You **come to terms** with a personal problem or difficulty when you learn to live with it and accept it: *Children are usually better at coming to terms with their disabilities than their parents are.* **2** You give your opinion, usually a disapproving one, **in no uncertain terms** when you express it strongly: *He denounced the policy in no uncertain terms.* **3** You refer to **the short term** and **the long term** in discussions about plans or results in the immediate future, or over a period extending further into the future: *We can expect economic improvement in the long term, but the short-term prospect is one of cutbacks and cancellations.* **4** People are dealt with **on equal terms** or **on the same terms** if they are all treated alike: *Female candidates are selected on equal terms with male ones for places at these once exclusively male colleges.* **5** You are **on** good **terms** with someone if you have a friendly relationship with them: *We parted on fairly amicable terms for once.*

terminal /ˈtɜːmɪnəl/ *noun; adjective*

▷ ***noun*: terminals**

1 A **terminal** is building from which passengers leave and where they arrive, *eg* at an airport: *a bus terminal* □ *Your flight to Paris goes from terminal one at Heathrow.* **2** A computer **terminal** is a keyboard attached to a visual display unit, which allows a user to use a central computer: *All of the secretaries have terminals attached to the company's main computer.*

▷ ***adjective***

1 A **terminal** illness is one that will cause death. [*same as* **fatal**, **incurable**] **2** A **terminal** patient is one who is dying. — *adverb* **terminally:** *He is terminally ill with cancer.*

terminate /ˈtɜːmɪneɪt/ *verb* (*formal*): **terminates, terminating, terminated**

1 You **terminate** something if you make it finish; something **terminates** when it finishes: *The bank is going to terminate their agreement with you.* □ *The contract will terminate next year.* □ *The football match terminated in a draw.* □ *Her pregnancy had to be terminated in the sixth month.* **2** A bus or train **terminates** in a particular place when it finishes its journey there: *The train terminates at Dundee.* — *noun* (*uncount*) **termination** /tɜːmɪˈneɪʃən/: *the termination of the contract.*

terminology /tɜːmɪˈnɒlədʒɪ/ *noun* (*count or uncount*): **terminologies**

The **terminology** of a subject or area is the words and phrases used in it: *Christian terminology.*

terminus /ˈtɜːmɪnəs/ *noun*: **termini** or **terminuses**

A **terminus** is a large building at the end of a railway line or bus route.

termite /ˈtɜːmaɪt/ *noun*: **termites**

A **termite** is a small, pale-coloured insect that lives with others in large colonies and eats wood.

terrace /ˈterɪs/ *noun*: **terraces**

1 (*BrE*) A **terrace** is a row of identical houses joined together. **2** A **terrace** is also a raised, level, paved area by the side of a house: *Let's have lunch on the terrace.* **3** (*used in the plural*) The **terraces** are the open areas where spectators stand at *eg* football and rugby matches: *They watched the match from the terraces.* **4** (*usually in the plural*) **Terraces** are a series of raised level banks of earth, like large steps on the side of a hill, where *eg* vines are grown.

terraced house /terɪst ˈhaʊs/ (*BrE*) *noun*: **terraced houses**

A **terraced house** is one that is joined to others on either side to form a terrace. [see picture at **house**]

terrain /təˈreɪn/ *noun* (*uncount*)

The **terrain** in an area is the type of land there, especially the particular physical features found there: *The trucks have been specially designed for use in rough terrain.*

terrapin /ˈterəpɪn/ *noun*: **terrapins** or **terrapin**

A **terrapin** is a small turtle that lives in fresh water.

terrible /ˈterɪbəl/ *adjective*

1 Someone or something is **terrible** when they are very bad: *She's a terrible singer.* □ *The food was absolutely terrible.* □ *terrible weather.* **2** You can use **terrible** to emphasize how great or large something is: *He's a terrible gossip.* □ *It's a terrible waste of money.* **3** A **terrible** experience causes suffering or hardship: *a terrible accident.* **4 a** You feel or look **terrible** if you feel or look ill: *You look terrible this morning!* **b** You feel **terrible** about something wrong or harmful that you have done if you are sorry about it: *I feel terrible that you had to spend so much; you must let me pay you back.*

terribly /ˈterɪblɪ/ *adverb* (*intensifying; informal*)

You can use **terribly** to emphasize how great or large something is: *She's terribly happy.* □ *I feel terribly guilty about it.* □ *I'm terribly sorry I'm so late.* [*same as* **very**]

terrier /ˈtɛrɪə(r)/ *noun*: **terriers**
A **terrier** is any of several types of small dog originally used for hunting.

terrific /təˈrɪfɪk/ *adjective*
1 Something is **terrific** if you are very pleased with it or think it is excellent: *This book is terrific.* □ *a terrific holiday.* [*same as* **fantastic**, **marvellous**] **2** Something can be described as **terrific** if it is very great or powerful: *a terrific storm* □ *She won a terrific amount of money at the casino.*

terrifically /təˈrɪfɪklɪ/ *adverb* (*intensifying; informal*)
You use **terrifically** for emphasis: *I was terrifically impressed by his calm handling of the crisis.*

terrify /ˈtɛrɪfaɪ/ *verb*: **terrifies, terrifying, terrified**
Something **terrifies** you if it makes you very frightened: *Flying terrifies me.* — *adjective* **terrified:** *I'm terrified of the dark.* □ *She looked absolutely terrified.* [*same as* **terror-stricken**] — *adjective* **terrifying:** *It was a terrifying experience.* □ *He thinks flying is terrifying.*

territorial /tɛrɪˈtɔːrɪəl/ *adjective*
Territorial means of or relating to the land a country controls or owns: *territorial borders.*

territory /ˈtɛrɪtərɪ/ *noun*: **territories**
1 (*count or uncount*) A country's **territory** is the land it controls or owns: *This is British territory.* □ *a meeting of the two presidents on neutral territory* □ *one of Spain's territories on the coast of Africa.* **2** (*uncount*) **Territory** is an area of land: *the mountainous territory in the north of the country.* **3** (*uncount*) **Territory** is also an area of knowledge, interest or activity: *This is familiar territory to the fans of his films.*

terror /ˈtɛrə(r)/ *noun*: **terrors**
1 (*uncount*) **Terror** is very great fear: *Feelings of terror gripped her as she boarded the plane.* □ *She screamed in terror as the car came speeding towards her.* [*same as* **dread, horror**] **2** A **terror** is something or someone which makes you feel very frightened: *ghosts and witches and other terrors.*

terrorism /ˈtɛrərɪzm/ *noun* (*uncount*)
Terrorism is the organized use of violence by small or illegal political organizations to force a government or community to act in a certain way or accept certain demands: *The government is committed to putting a stop to terrorism.* — *noun* **terrorist** /ˈtɛrərɪst/: *Several of the terrorists were killed in a battle with the army and police.* □ *terrorist activities.*

terrorize or **terrorise** /ˈtɛrəraɪz/ *verb*: **terrorizes, terrorizing, terrorized**
Someone **terrorizes** you if they frighten you and threaten to use violence against you: *She was terrorized by bullies while she was at school.*

terror-stricken /ˈtɛrərstrɪkən/ or **terror-struck** /ˈtɛrə strʌk/ *adjective*
You are **terror-stricken** or **terror-struck** if you are very frightened. [*same as* **terrified**]

terse /tɜːs/ *adjective*: **terser, tersest**
Language is **terse** when it is brief and to the point, and often rather rude: *She wrote a terse reply to his letter.* [*same as* **succinct**; *opposite* **wordy**]

test /tɛst/ *noun*; *verb*
▻ ***noun***: **tests**
1 A **test** is **a** a usually short and relatively informal examination of a person's knowledge or abilities: *She didn't pass the French test.* □ *All of the students must sit a test at the end of the year.* □ *a spelling test.* **b** a trial or experiment which assesses how well something works: *The doctors will carry out tests to see if the drug cures cancer or not.* □ *The new aircraft will undergo extensive tests before it is brought into service.* **2** (*usually in the plural*) You undergo **tests** when doctors check various parts of your body, such as your blood, to try to discover what, if anything, is wrong with you: *He was taken to hospital for tests.* **3** (*cricket or rugby*) A **test** is a test match: *the second test against Australia.*
▻ ***verb***: **tests, testing, tested**
1 You **test** someone if you examine and assess their knowledge or abilities, especially by a short, relatively informal trial: *She tested her pupils on their spelling.* **2** You **test** something when you examine it to see what it is like or how well it works: *Scientists will have to test the drug before it can be given to patients.* □ *She tested the water with her elbow to see if it was too hot for the baby.* **3** Someone **tests** positive or negative for something when it is shown by a test that they have it, or do not have it, in their body: *He tested positive for the virus.*

testament /ˈtɛstəmənt/ *noun* (*formal*): **testaments**
One thing is a **testament** to another when it proves that it is true or exists: *The quality of her work is a testament to her talents.* [see also **New Testament, Old Testament**]

test case /ˈtɛst keɪs/ *noun* (*legal*): **test cases**
A **test case** is a case whose result will be used as a model for future, similar cases.

testicle /ˈtɛstɪkəl/ *noun*: **testicles**
A man's **testicles** are the two glands beneath his penis which produce sperm.

testify /ˈtɛstɪfaɪ/ *verb* (*formal*): **testifies, testifying, testified**
1 You **testify** in court if you give evidence during a court case: *She testified against him in the case.* □ *Several witness can testify to her lying and cheating.* **2** One thing **testifies** to another if it proves that it is true or exists: *Many people believe things in nature testify to the existence of God.*

testimony /ˈtɛstɪmənɪ/ *noun*: **testimonies**
1 A **testimony** is a formal statement made under oath, especially in a law court: *The police have the testimonies of several witnesses.* **2** One thing is a **testimony** to another if it proves that it is true or exists: *This book is a testimony to her courage.*

test match /ˈtɛst matʃ/ *noun* (*cricket or rugby*): **test matches**
A **test match** is a match that is one of a series played by the same two international teams: *the second test match between Australia and Pakistan.*

test tube /ˈtɛst tjuːb/ *noun*: **test tubes**
A **test tube** is a thin glass tube that is closed at one end, and that is used in chemical experiments.

test-tube baby /ˈtɛsttjuːb ˈbeɪbɪ/ *noun*: **test-tube babies**
A **test-tube baby** is a baby that develops from an egg that has been removed from the mother's body, fertilized in a laboratory, and replaced in her womb.

tetanus /ˈtɛtəˈnəs/ *noun* (*uncount*)
Tetanus is a serious infectious disease that causes your muscles, especially those in your jaw, to go stiff.

tether /ˈtɛðə(r)/ *verb*: **tethers, tethering, tethered**
You **tether** an animal to a post if you tie it to it.
▻ ***phrase*** You are **at the end of your tether** if you are very tired and do not have the patience or strength to cope with problems or difficulties.

text /tɛkst/ *noun*: **texts**
1 (*used in the singular*) The **text** of *eg* a book is the main part of it that consists of printed words, as opposed to *eg* any illustrations: *The book needs some pictures to complement the text.* **2** The **text** is the actual words used by an author or speaker: *the printed text of his speech.* **3** (*uncount*) **Text** is any printed or

written words. **4** A **text** is any book that is used for a course of study: *a list of texts needed for the French literature course.*

textbook /ˈtɛkstbʊk/ *noun*: **textbooks**
A **textbook** is a book containing information on a particular subject, used by students at school, college or university: *a biology textbook used in secondary schools.*

textile /ˈtɛkstaɪl/ *noun*: **textiles**
A **textile** is any cloth or fabric made by weaving or knitting: *a new textile made from artificial fibre* □ *the textile industry.*

texture /ˈtɛkstʃə(r)/ *noun; verb*
▷ ***noun*** (*uncount or count*): **textures**
Something's **texture** is the way it feels when you touch it: *This paper has a rather rough texture.* □ *the fine texture of silk* □ *cheese with a crumbly texture.*

-th /θ/ *suffix*
You add **-th** to numbers written in figures that are greater than three, or that end in a number greater than three, to form ordinal numbers: *10th* □ *24th.*

> These numbers are pronounced as if they were written words. For example, **8th** is pronounced in the same way as **eighth** and **10th** is pronounced in the same way as **tenth**.

than /ðən/ or /ðan/ *conjunction or preposition*
1 Than is used after the comparative forms of adjectives and adverbs to introduce the second part of a comparison: *My sister's bigger than me* (or *than I am*, or, more formally, *than I*). □ *She married a man considerably older than herself.* □ *We had less than a week to finish the work.* □ *The sorting process was more difficult than we thought it would be.* □ *I'd spoken louder than I meant to.* □ *There were fewer applicants than we had expected; in fact far fewer than usual* (or *than there usually are*). □ *Social workers are dealing with more drug-related cases than ever before.* □ *Don't spend longer than necessary on that job.* □ *It's a lot warmer than when we last met* (or *than it was the last time we met*). **2 Than** is also used after *rather* and *sooner* to introduce the second, and usually unwanted or less desirable, of two options or possibilities: *I'd rather leave now than wait and risk getting caught in the rush hour.* □ *I'd much rather go by train than by car.* □ *Why don't we take sandwiches rather than waste time looking for a cafe?* □ *I'd sooner watch a play than a chat show.*
[see also **different than** at **different**, **less than** at **less**, **more than** at **more**, **other than** at **other**, **rather than** at **rather**, **(would) sooner than** at **soon**]

thank /θaŋk/ *verb; noun*
▷ ***verb***: **thanks, thanking, thanked**
You **thank** someone when you express your gratitude for something they have given you, or done, or said: *Did you remember to thank Granny for your birthday present?* □ *We wish to thank all our customers for their support over the past year.* □ *I want personally to thank you all for coming.* □ *Their leader thanked the mayor for his words of welcome.* □ *Don't thank me; just take it.* □ *I can never thank you enough.*
▷ ***noun*** (*used in the plural*): **thanks**
You express your **thanks** to someone when you express your gratitude to them for something: *Philip received a letter of thanks from the headmaster.* □ *Generally you get little thanks for the efforts you make.* □ *Our grateful thanks go to all who participated.*
▷ ***phrases* 1** You **have** someone or something **to thank for** something if they are responsible for its existence: *We have the Czechs to thank for the contact lens and the helicopter.* □ *We've got the Government to thank for this mess.* **2** People sometimes use **'thank God'**, **'thank goodness'** or **'thank heavens'** to express their relief about something: *She has no other injuries, thank God!* □ *Thank goodness for people prepared to stand up to authority.* □ *Thank heavens she escaped in time.* **3** You say **'thank you'**, or more informally, **'thanks'**, to someone when you express your gratitude for something they have given you, done, or said: *Thank you very much, Sally.* □ *Thank you for listening so sympathetically.* □ *Thank you for your last letter.* □ *Thank you very much indeed for the lovely present.* □ *Thank you so much for your kind words.* □ *'Help yourself to sugar.' 'Thank you.'* □ *'What was your journey like?' 'Fairly straightforward, thank you.'* □ *'How are you?' 'I'm fine, thanks.'* □ *Well, thanks a lot for your help.* □ *Many thanks for the information.* □ *Very many thanks for the complimentary tickets.* □ *Goodnight, and thanks again for the lovely meal.* □ *They never say thank you.* □ *He was nearly out of the door when she managed a belated 'thank you'.* □ *He read us out a thank-you letter from the Red Cross.* [compare **please**]

> Notice that although **'thanks'** is more informal than **'thank you'**, **'many thanks'** is fairly formal.
> You use **'thanks'** or **'thank you'** to accept something that someone has offered you, and **'no, thanks'** or **'no, thank you'** to refuse it politely: *'Would you like to join us?' 'Yes, thank you* (or *yes, please*)*, we'd love to.' 'Have some more tea?' 'Oh, no, thanks, I've had plenty already.' 'I don't want any breakfast, thank you,' said Alice.*

4 Something happens **thanks to** someone or something if they are responsible for it happening: *Thanks to her efforts, four major hospitals are now providing this important treatment.* □ *We missed our chance of beating them, thanks to bad weather.* **5** (*informal*) You say that someone **will not thank you for** doing something if it is likely to upset or annoy them: *They wouldn't thank me for disturbing them at two in the morning.*

thankful /ˈθaŋkfəl/ *adjective*
You are **thankful** when you are very happy, relieved or grateful: *I was just thankful that no-one was hurt.* — *adverb* **thankfully:** *Thankfully, no-one was badly injured in the crash.*

thankless /ˈθaŋkləs/ *adjective*
A **thankless** task is one that means a lot of hard work for you, but which no-one will be pleased or grateful for: *Cleaning up after the children is always a thankless task.*

Thanksgiving /ˈθaŋksgɪvɪŋ/ *noun* (*uncount*)
Thanksgiving, or **Thanksgiving Day**, is a public holiday at which people give thanks to God for the harvest. **Thanksgiving** is held on the fourth Thursday in November in the United States and the second Monday in October in Canada.

that /ðat/ or /ðət/ *determiner; pronoun; conjunction; adverb*
(The pronunciation /ðət/ is used only when **that** is a conjunction or relative pronoun.)
▷ ***determiner*** (*demonstrative, used with singular count nouns, and uncount nouns*; the plural is **those**; see separate entry)
That person or thing is **1** the one you are indicating, usually some distance from you: *Who's that lady with the dark hair, standing by the window?* □ *Do you see that church tower over there?* □ *This skirt's too tight; I'd better try that one on again.* [*opposite* **this**] **2** the one already mentioned or known about: *Dictionaries are*

primarily intended for finding out the meanings of words, but in practice people seldom use them for that purpose. □ *What's that funny noise?* □ *Where's that letter from Rosemary?* □ *You don't believe all that nonsense about her unhappy childhood, do you?* □ *during that last evening in Vienna.*

▻ ***pronoun*** (*demonstrative*; the plural is **those**; see separate entry)

1 You use **that** to mean a thing or place you are indicating, identifying, or referring to: *That's a very pretty dress you're wearing.* □ *Abbeyhill Primary? That's the school Flora goes to, isn't it?* □ *No washing-up liquid. I must add that to my list.* □ *I don't think the rope will reach as far as that.* **2 That** can refer to a point in time: *Before that we had always gone to the Mediterranean for our holidays.* □ *After that we'll be free to start planning a new project.* **3** You use **that** when identifying a person, *eg* someone on the telephone: *Who was that telephoning just now?* □ *Is that you, Jack?* □ *Hallo? Is that Mrs Brotherstone?* □ *Was that Peter going out of the door?* □ *Isn't that the lady from the post office?* [see also **this**] **4** You use **that** to refer to any fact, event, situation, circumstance, idea or opinion just mentioned, or known to your hearer: *'I won!' 'That's great!'* □ *'We can't get a train direct to Nottingham.' 'That's a nuisance.'* □ *'Could I drive you home?' 'That would be very kind of you.'* □ *He's been ill, apparently; that's why we haven't heard from him for so long.* □ *Well, that's the story so far.* □ *If that's true, we ought to warn them.* □ *Is that really a possibility?* □ *A lot of the reviewers have mentioned that.* □ *You mustn't talk like that.* □ *It isn't as simple as that.*

▻ ***pronoun*** (*relative*)

1 You can use **that** in the same way as *which*, *who* or *whom* to introduce a clause describing, defining or specifying the person, people, thing or things you have just mentioned: *We had an anxious telephone call from the lady that* (or *who*) *lives across the road.* □ *I must find someone that* (or *whom*) *I can rely on.* □ *Here's the application that* (or *which*) *arrived yesterday.* □ *I love the cakes that* (or *which*) *my aunt makes.* □ *Everything that could have been done has been done.* □ *This is the best method that I know of.* □ *I went to live abroad the year that I graduated.* □ *Is there anywhere that you'd prefer to go?* [see also **which, who, whom**]

> You cannot use **that** after a preposition: *the matter with which* (not *with that*) *we are presently concerned.*
> You can omit **that** where it is the object of the verb or of a preposition: *I've made a list of things that we need* (or *things we need*). *I've never read the book that you're* (or *the book you're*) *referring to. I've done all that I* (or *all I*) *can to help her.*

2 That introduces a relative clause after *it is* or *it was*, when used for emphasizing something: *It's the waste that horrifies me.*

▻ ***conjunction***

1 That is used after verbs and expressions of saying, thinking and feeling to introduce what is said, thought or felt; it may follow a verb, adjective or noun; **that** can be omitted in many cases, as shown in the examples below: *She told me that she didn't* (or *told me she didn't*) *want a baby just yet.* □ *I've warned them that I'll* (or *warned them I'll*) *be late.* □ *Neighbours reported that he was missing.* □ *He suggested that I should contact you.* □ *I know that there's* (or *I know there's*) *something seriously wrong with him.* □ *I do hope that I* (or *hope I*) *can help you.* □ *I'm disappointed that you can't* (or *disappointed you can't*) *join us.* □ *I'm afraid that our* (or *afraid our*) *decision is final.* □ *I'm amazed that it* (or *amazed it*) *works.* □ *I'm sorry that you're* (or *I'm sorry you're*) *still ill.* □ *It's absolutely true that the weather affects your mood.* □ *It's vital that help reaches them immediately.* □ *It's a pity that you don't* (or *a pity you don't*) *agree.* □ *There's no doubt that she's losing her memory.* □ *What gave you the idea that I* (or *the idea I*) *was a feminist?* □ *The claim that stress during pregnancy affects the baby is well-founded.* **2 That** is used after *so* **a** to express result: *She spoke so fast that I couldn't understand her.* □ *The door was standing open, so that I could hardly help overhearing their conversation.* **b** to express purpose: *We should get there early so that we can welcome people as they arrive.* [see also **so**] **3** You use **that** to introduce a clause after *it is* or *it was*, when emphasizing some point: *It wasn't till after he retired that he took up golf.*

▻ ***adverb***

1 That means to the extent or degree you are indicating or meaning: *The bookcase is about that high.* □ *I don't think the rope will reach that far.* **2** (*intensifying, often with a negative*; *informal*) Something that is 'not **that** good' or 'not all **that** good' is not as good as people say, or as might be expected: *'Did you enjoy the film?' 'Not that much.'* □ *I don't find his jokes that funny.* □ *It's not all that difficult to learn.* [*same as* **very**]

▻ ***phrases*** **1** You use **at that** to add a point in an emphatic way to what has been said: *He had an old violin, and a fine one at that.* [*same as* **too**] **2** You use **that is** and **that is to say** to explain more clearly something you have just said: *I once painted this house, that is, painted a picture of it.* **3** For **that's it** see **it**. **4** You use **'that's that'** to say there is no more to be said or done about a certain thing: *I'm not going and that's that.* □ *They'd decided to sell the business, so that was that.* **5** For **this and that** see **this**.

thatched /ˈθatʃt/ *adjective*

A **thatched** roof is a roof made of straw or reeds; a **thatched** house or cottage is one with a thatched roof.

that'll /ðatəl/

That'll is the spoken, and informal written, form of **that will**.

that's /ðats/

That's is the spoken, and informal written, form of **that is**.

thaw /θɔː/ *verb*; *noun*

▻ ***verb***: **thaws, thawing, thawed**

1 Snow or ice **thaws** when it melts. **2** You **thaw** anything frozen, especially frozen food, when you put it in a place where it can become warmer and so is fit to cook or eat: *You should thaw the meat before you cook it.* □ *She left the frozen pastry on the table to thaw.* [*same as* **defrost**] **3** It **thaws** when the weather becomes warm enough to begin to melt snow and ice: *It's beginning to thaw.* **4** You **thaw**, or **thaw** out, when you become less stiff and numb with cold: *His fingers gradually began to thaw out.* **5** People **thaw**, or **thaw** out, if they become more friendly or relaxed.

▻ ***noun*** (*usually in the singular*)

1 There is a **thaw** when there is a period of warm weather after snow or frost, and ice and snow begin to melt. **2** There is a **thaw** in a relationship if the two sides become more friendly or relaxed towards each other: *a thaw in the relationship between east and west.*

the /ðə/, /ðɪ or ðiː/ *determiner* (*the definite article*)

(The pronunciation /ðə/ is used before words beginning with a consonant, /ðɪ/ is used before words beginning with a vowel, and /ðiː/ is the stressed form, used for emphasis.)

1 a The is used before singular and plural count nouns, and before uncount nouns to refer to particu-

lar people or things, either being indicated or specified, or already mentioned or known about: *You see the tall girl over there in the green jacket?* □ *The train for Coventry is running ten minutes late.* □ *You ought to see the dentist about that toothache.* □ *We sent all the children home because of the snow.* □ *Only half the cake was eaten.* □ *They've recaptured both the escaped prisoners.* □ *The happiness of my own children is my main concern.* □ *I found the missing cheque.* □ *The candidates we interviewed yesterday were a more promising lot.* □ *'Have you still got those leaflets?' 'Which ones?' 'The ones about pay and conditions.'* □ *The twins met Geoff at Harvard and the three became good friends.* [compare **a**] **b The** refers to a particular person, thing or group where there is only one that exists, or that your hearer knows about, so it is frequent in titles and is used in some geographical names, *eg* of rivers, seas and mountains: *the sun, the moon and the stars* □ *His Holiness the Pope* □ *the Prime Minister* □ *the Thames* □ *the Pacific* □ *the Alps* □ *the United States* □ *the Holocaust* □ *I spent Christmas with the Nelson family.* **c** You put **the** before the plural form of a surname to mean a couple or a family with that name: *He knows the Morrisons.*
2 The is used **a** before a singular count noun to refer to a thing in general rather than to a particular thing of that type: *The computer has revolutionized the way we live.* □ *When was the microscope invented?* □ *Can you play the piano?* □ *The alligator is native to America.* **b** before an adjective or past participle to refer to a class of people or things described by it, and more rarely, to refer to one person or thing: *a school for the blind* □ *The homeless increase in number every day.* □ *the unemployed* □ *The French are on our side.* □ *when the accused was led into court* □ *The deceased was a popular member of the community.* □ *We're expected to achieve the unachievable.*
3 You use **the** with the stressed pronunciation /ðiː/ to show that you mean **a** the most famous one, or the one that everyone knows about: *'I got introduced to Barbara Castle yesterday.' 'What, the Barbara Castle?'* **b** the best or most fashionable one: *It's the restaurant to go to.*
4 The is used **a** before ordinal numbers, *eg*, especially in BrE, in dates: *That's the fifth time she's rung today.* □ *Tuesday November the seventh* or *Tuesday the seventh of November* (usually written *Tuesday 7 November*). **b** to refer to decades and temperature ranges: *London during the 60s* □ *a warm day, with temperatures in the 20s.* **c** before units of measurement, when talking about rates: *Our Mini does fifty miles to the gallon.* □ *Freelance editors are paid by the hour.*
5 The is used **a** before superlative adjectives, and before words such as *only*, *same*, *first*, *last*, because only one person or thing is meant; **the** can also precede superlative adverbs: *the only survivor of the crash* □ *I keep getting the same error message.* □ *the last house in the road* □ *the finest example of this style* □ *I like this one the best* (or *like this one best*). **b** before comparative adjectives and before words such as *other*, *former* and *latter*, where you are thinking of, or comparing, only two people or things: *The older child may be jealous of the new baby.* □ *They were both handsome, Angus perhaps the better-looking of the two.* □ *I've found one slipper, but where's the other?* **c** before each of a pair of comparatives to express a situation where one thing changes in relation to another: *The harder I tried the less successful I became.* □ *The sooner he leaves, the better.* [= I hope he leaves soon]

theatre (*AmE* **theater**) /ˈθɪətə(r)/ *noun*: **theatres**
1 A **theatre** is a building with a stage, where *eg* plays and operas are performed: *We were at the theatre on Friday night; we saw 'Love's Labour's Lost'.* □ *I don't go to the theatre much now.* **2** (*used in the singular*) The **theatre** is the writing and production of plays in general and the world and profession of actors and theatre companies: *She's looking for a job in the theatre.* **3** A **theatre** is an operating theatre: *The surgeon has been in theatre all day.*

theatrical /θɪˈatrɪkəl/ *adjective*
1 Theatrical means of theatres, plays or acting. **2 Theatrical** behaviour or gestures are artificial and exaggerated and done only for effect. [*same as* **histrionic**]

theft /θɛft/ *noun*: **thefts**
1 (*uncount*) **Theft** is the crime of stealing: *He was arrested and charged with theft.* **2** A **theft** is an act of taking someone else's property illegally: *There have been several thefts from houses in the area recently.*

their /ðɛə(r)/ *determiner* (*possessive*)
1 Their refers to something that belongs to the people or things just mentioned, or known about: *My parents have just sold their house.* □ *People began shouting and waving their arms.* □ *Most of the books had lost their covers.* □ *I objected to their* (or *them*) *using my sitting room for rehearsing in.* **2 Their** is often used in referring to singular words such as *anyone*, *no-one*, *someone* and *person*, where the sex is not specified, as a way of avoiding 'his', 'her' or the very formal expression 'his or her': *Has anyone not got their textbook?* □ *Nobody was willing to give up their free time to help.* **3 Their** is used in referring to certain people with titles: *Their Royal Highnesses the Prince and Princess of Wales.*
[see also **theirs**]

theirs /ðɛəz/ *pronoun* (*possessive*)
1 You use **theirs** to refer to something that belongs to the people you have mentioned: *The Brooks have the flat above, so our bedroom is right underneath theirs.* □ *What about the Japanese students? Theirs is a special case in many ways.* □ *Our interests and theirs usually coincide.* □ *When it comes to manners, they don't like ours and we don't like theirs.* □ *His basic salary was the same as theirs.* □ *The fault was definitely theirs.* □ *Those letters are not theirs to sell.* □ *The battle was won, and the prize, at last and forever, was theirs.* □ *He told the social workers it was a family matter and no business of theirs.* □ *I met a friend of theirs at the drama club.* **2 Theirs** is also used in reference to singular words such as *someone*, *anyone*, *no-one*, *person*, where the sex is not specified, as a way of avoiding 'his', 'hers', or the very formal expression 'his or hers': *We need to have access to a word-processor, so if anyone isn't using theirs, could they let me know?*

them /ðɛm/ or /ðəm/ *pronoun* (*used as the object of a verb or preposition, and in other positions*)
1 You use **them** to refer to people or things that have already been mentioned, or are known about: *My cousins have invited me to visit them.* □ *She unpacked her purchases and put them away.* □ *I've given them permission to leave early.* □ *They'd brought their dog with them.* □ *You can't buy presents for all of them.* □ *The kids disappeared, but luckily someone spotted them playing in a field.* □ *They're divorced now, but I'm still friends with them both.* □ *I've no objections to them* (or *their*) *using the hall, provided they leave it tidy.* □ *'The Johnsons said they'd collect you.' 'Oh, that's kind of them; was that them on the telephone just now?'* □ *They're off to China on Monday, lucky them.* □ *I can't walk nearly as fast as them* (or, more formally,

as fast as they do). □ *You're a lot younger than them* (or, more formally, *than they are*). **2 Them** is often used to refer to singular words such as *anyone*, *someone*, *no-one* and *person*, where the sex is not specified, as a way of avoiding 'him', 'her', or the very formal expression 'him or her': *Has anyone got a penknife on them?* □ *If there's someone you'd like to bring, do invite them.*

theme /θiːm/ *noun*: **themes**
1 The **theme** of a piece of writing, discussion or speech is its subject: *She had taken the works of Jane Austen as the theme of her essay.* **2** A **theme** in art, a book or play is a repeated or recurring image or idea in it: *Friendship is one of the major themes of the book.* **3** (*music*) **a** A **theme** is a melody that is repeated and developed in a number of ways within a particular work or composition. **b** A **theme**, or **theme** song, is a short piece of music used at the beginning and end of a radio or television programme.

themselves /ðɛm'sɛlvz/ or /ðəm'sɛlvz/ *pronoun* (*reflexive*)
1 You use **themselves** as the object of a verb or preposition **a** to refer to people or things where the action of the verb is performed by the same people or things: *They'd built themselves a house on the edge of the village.* □ *Various problems immediately present themselves.* □ *It's up to the householders to discuss the matter between themselves.* **b** in referring to singular words such as *anyone*, *someone*, *no-one* and *person*, as a way of avoiding 'himself', 'herself' or the very formal 'himself or herself': *I admire anyone who can express themselves so fluently in public.* **2** You also use **themselves** for emphasis and for clarity, and as an emphatic form of 'them': *Within the forests themselves a number of features should be looked for.* □ *Women were classified not by the work they did themselves, but by the work done by their husbands.* □ *Men generally marry women younger than themselves.* **3** People are being **themselves** when they are behaving as they normally do: *They were being themselves, and it was I who was playing a game.* **4** People do something **themselves** when they do it without help from others: *Most users were happy to employ a bureau rather than do it all themselves.*
For **by themselves** see **by**.

then /ðɛn/ *adverb*
1 a Then means at that time in the past or future: *There wasn't as much traffic then as there is now.* □ *There have been been a few developments since then.* □ *I've got one more chapter to read and then you can have the book.* □ *Phone about ten; I should be home by then.* □ *Is the party really likely to go on till then?* **b Then** also introduces what happens or comes next, after the event or thing you have just mentioned: *He looked at her, then turned away.* □ *She studied medicine at Cambridge and then trained at Guy's Hospital in London.* □ *Carry on as far as the traffic lights, then turn right.* □ *I've got to wash a few things; then there's the shopping to do and the lunch to cook.*
2 (*sentence adverb*) **Then** is used, often in conversation, to mean **a** 'in that case', in expressing what follows, or results from, something just mentioned: *They'll probably refuse; then what do we do?* □ *'The Brown Jug Cafe isn't terribly good.' 'Let's go somewhere else, then.'* □ *'I started studying law but I gave it up.' 'So what subject are you doing now, then?'* □ *If you weren't satisfied, then you should have made that clear at the time.* □ *When a woman loses weight over a man, then you know she's in love.* **b** to continue a story after a pause: *She was just walking home, then, and it had begun to snow.* **c** to comment on, make a connection with, or form a conclusion from, something that has just been said or done: *Your mind is made up, then?* □ *That must have been a bit of a shock, then?* □ *I think we're all ready to leave, then.* **d** after words such as *now*, *well*, *right*, *okay*, to get people's attention: *Now then, who'd like an ice cream?* □ *Well then, I think we'd better hurry up.* □ *Right then, let's go.* **e** after *and* and *but* to make a comment that adds to, or modifies, the impression just given: *And then there are the children to consider.* □ *St Abbs would be a nicer place to go; but then it's further away.* **f** at the end of conversations: *Goodbye, then.* □ *See you later, then.*
▻ ***phrase*** **Then and there** and **there and then** mean immediately, at once and in that very place: *I sat down and wrote a reply then and there.*

thence /ðɛns/ *adverb* (*old, formal*)
Thence means from the place or time that has just been mentioned: *We travelled to Dover, and thence to Calais by boat train.*

theologian /θɪə'loʊdʒən/ *noun*: **theologians**
A **theologian** is a person who studies God, religion and religious belief: *an eminent Catholic theologian.*

theology /θɪ'ɒlədʒɪ/ *noun* (*uncount*)
Theology is the study of God, religion and religious belief: *Catholic theology.* — *adjective* **theological** /θɪə'lɒdʒɪkəl/: *a Protestant theological college.*

theorem /'θɪərəm/ *noun* (*mathematics*): **theorems**
A **theorem** is a statement that can be proved to be true by applying generally accepted ideas or theories.

theoretical /θɪə'rɛtɪkəl/ *adjective*
Something is **theoretical** if it is based on theory and ideas rather than practical knowledge or experience: *the field of theoretical physics.*

theoretically /θɪə'rɛtɪklɪ/ *adverb*
You can use **theoretically** to indicate that even though something should happen or be true in theory, it may not really happen or be true: *It is theoretically possible to travel from Glasgow to Edinburgh in one hour.*

theorize or **theorise** /'θɪəraɪz/ *verb*: **theorizes, theorizing, theorized**
You **theorize** about something if you develop theories and ideas about it in your mind: *We can only theorize as to the reasons for the accident.* [*same as* **speculate**]

theory /'θɪərɪ/ *noun*: **theories**
1 A **theory** is a series of ideas and general principles which explain something: *the theory of relativity.* **2** A **theory** is also an idea or explanation which has not yet been proved: *I've got several theories about his illness.* [*same as* **conjecture**] **3 Theory** is the set of general principles or rules of a particular subject or skill: *political and economic theory* □ *music theory.*
▻ ***phrase*** You can use **in theory** to indicate that although something should happen or be true it may not really happen or be true: *This is a good idea in theory but one which probably wouldn't work in practice.*

therapeutic /θɛrə'pjuːtɪk/ *adjective*
Something is **therapeutic** if it makes you feel well or better and more relaxed: *I've always found having tea in the garden very therapeutic.*

therapist /'θɛrəpɪst/ *noun*: **therapists**
1 A **therapist** is a person who is trained in a particular type of therapy: *a speech therapist.* **2** (*especially AmE*) A **therapist** is a psychotherapist: *My therapist told me I worry too much.*

therapy /'θɛrəpɪ/ *noun* (*uncount or count*): **therapies**
Therapy is the treatment of physical or mental diseases and problems without the use of operations, and often without drugs: *different therapies that help treat stress.*

there /ðɛə(r)/ *adverb*
1 (*demonstrative*) You use **there a** to indicate or refer to a place usually some distance away from where you are; you often use **there** for emphasis at the beginning of a sentence, *eg* when you see someone or something, or sometimes to accompany the action of handing something to someone: *'Where's my notepad?' 'You left it over there on the windowsill.'* □ *Do you see that doorway there with the carving over it?* □ *'Here I am, on the roof.' 'Goodness, how did you get up there?'* □ *Now where did the ball go? Oh, there it is.* □ *There's Dad, look, talking to Mr Jeffries.* □ *There goes Dr Peters, off on his rounds.* □ *There* (or *here*) *are the leaflets you wanted.* [*opposite* **here**] **b** to refer to any place, other than where you are, that has just been mentioned; you also use **there** when asking for someone on the telephone: *'Is Philip in his office?' 'He was there a minute ago.'* □ *Just go to Reception and the lady there will direct you.* □ *'Why were you in Llandudno?' 'I'd gone there for a conference.'* □ *'Hallo, Jean speaking.' 'Hi, Jean, it's Susan here. Is Roger there?'* **c** to refer to a point, stage or position, *eg* in a story, activity or sequence of events: *Well, don't stop there; what happened next?* □ *Let's see, yesterday's rehearsal finished in the middle of Act Four; let's just carry on from there.* □ *Well, it took you a while to get there, but it's the right answer.* **d** in conversation, to mean 'on that point', or 'on that subject': *Sorry, I can't agree with you there.* □ *You're certainly right there, Pete.* **e** to talk about things existing; something is **there** if it exists, is real, or is available: *'Has your headache gone?' 'No, it's still there.'* □ *Macbeth is reaching out to grasp a dagger that isn't really there.* □ *Libraries are there for the use of the public.*
2 (also /ðə(r)/) **There** is used like a pronoun, as the subject of a verb, to talk about things that arrive, appear, happen, exist or are available **a** with the verb *be*, often combined with modal or auxiliary verbs: *There's someone at the door.* □ *There've only been a few visitors this morning.* □ *Were there any messages for me?* □ *I don't expect there to be any phone calls.* □ *There being no further questions, we shall proceed.* □ *Has there been an accident?* □ *I'm afraid there are no vacancies at present.* □ *There weren't many copies left.* □ *'Where shall we eat?' 'There's always the station buffet.'* □ *There seemed to be nowhere to sleep.* □ *There needs to be some sort of checking process.* □ *Let me know if there's anything you want.* □ *Is there going to be a celebration?* □ *There's to be a drinks party, isn't there?* □ *There'd be trouble if she found out.* □ *There won't be any difficulty, will there?* □ *What on earth is there to worry about?* □ *I think there must be something wrong with the printer.* □ *There appears to be some mistake here.* □ *There can be no excuse for such stupidity.* **b** (*formal or literary*) with other verbs: *There comes a moment when you can no longer pretend.* □ *There remains the matter of the will.* □ *There follows a long section about her childhood.* □ *There stood a church on this spot at one time.*
▻ ***phrases*** **1** (*informal*) If you describe someone as **not all there** you mean that they are not quite normal mentally: *Since the accident she hasn't been quite all there.* **2** (*informal*) People say rudely '**so there**' to someone after telling them something, to mean that that is the situation, whether they like it or not: *I absolutely refuse to lend it to you, so there.* **3** '**There, there**' and **there now**' are used for comforting or reassuring people: *There now, don't cry.* **4** For **there and then** see **then**. **5** '**There it is**' sums up a situation: *So there it is; nothing more we can do at the moment.* **6** You say '**there you are**', or, informally, **there you go a** when handing something to someone: *'Have you got that list of addresses?' 'There you are.'* **b** to sum up a situation, especially an unsatisfactory one that has to be accepted: *Things could be better, but there you are.* **c** You say '**there you are**' to point out that you were right about something: *There you are, I knew it would work in the end.*

thereabouts /ðɛərə'baʊts/ *adverb*
▻ ***phrase*** You can use **or thereabouts** after a number, amount, degree or time to mean near that number, amount, degree or time: *I met him in 1967, or thereabouts.* □ *She's 85, or thereabouts.*

thereafter /ðɛər'ɑːftə(r)/ *adverb* (*formal*)
Thereafter means after or from the time mentioned: *I first went to America in 1978 and went every year thereafter.*

thereby /ðɛə'baɪ/ *adverb* (*formal*)
Thereby means as a result or in consequence: *Smaller companies were merged into the parent company, thereby creating a single organization.*

therefore /'ðɛəfɔː(r)/ *adverb*
You use **therefore** in reference to some circumstance you have just mentioned to mean 'so', 'for that reason' or 'because of that': *Unexpected difficulties have arisen and we are therefore behind schedule.* □ *A simpler, and therefore faster, method has been devised.* □ *The treatment is evidently causing unwanted side effects and should therefore be discontinued.* □ *Her personal integrity, and therefore her reliability as a witness, were under attack.*

thereupon /ðɛərə'pɒn/ *adverb* (*formal*)
Thereupon means immediately after an event and often as a result of it: *I showed my passport to an official, who thereupon asked me to step aside for questioning.*

thermal /'θɜːməl/ *adjective*; *noun*
▻ ***adjective***
1 Thermal means of, caused by or producing heat: *thermal energy.* **2 Thermal** clothing is designed to keep you warm in cold weather.
▻ ***noun*: thermals**
A **thermal** is a rising current of warm air, used by *eg* birds in flight to move upwards.

thermometer /θə'mɒmɪtə(r)/ *noun*: **thermometers**
A **thermometer** is an instrument for measuring your temperature, usually made of a thin glass tube with degrees marked along the side, filled with mercury which rises and falls in response to heat: *The thermometer shows a reading of 103°.*

Thermos /'θɜːməs/ *noun* (*trademark*): **Thermoses**
A **Thermos**, or **Thermos flask**, is a container which keeps hot liquid hot and cold liquid cold: *The children take hot drinks to school in their Thermos flasks.*

thermostat /'θɜːməstat/ *noun*: **thermostats**
A **thermostat** is an apparatus which controls the temperature of *eg* a room, water or oven automatically, by switching the heating system off or on.

thesaurus /θɪ'sɔːrəs/ *noun*: **thesauruses**
A **thesaurus** is a book which lists words and their synonyms according to their meanings: *a dictionary and thesaurus combined.*

these /ðiːz/ *determiner*; *pronoun*
▻ ***determiner*** (*demonstrative*, *plural* of **this**)
1 These things or people are the ones being indicated, usually close to you, being held by you, or on your body, or the ones just mentioned, or the ones about to be specified: *Compare these two graphs.* □ *We shall examine some of these points in more detail.* □ *Both these beautiful fish have smooth tapering bodies.* □ *And*

so, for these and other reasons the plan was rejected. □ *There was a sheet of notepaper on the desk, and on it were these words.* [*opposite* **those**] **2 These** times, or **these** days, are the present time: *Nobody knows how to waltz these days.* [= nowadays] □ *These last few weeks* [= the ones just past, up to the present] *have been dreadful.* [compare **those**] **3** (*informal*) **These** sometimes introduces people or things into a story: *But later these two guys showed up.*

▻ ***pronoun*** (*demonstrative, plural* of **this**): *Look, these are my fitted cupboards.* □ *All these are approximate figures.* □ *Of these, the higher proportion were black.* □ *These are all reasons for his enormous popularity.* □ *For men like these, a university education was never thought of as a possibility.* □ *No-one has the right to criticize in cases such as these.* □ *These are difficult times for everyone.* [compare **those**]

thesis /ˈθiːsɪs/ *noun*: **theses**
1 A **thesis** is a long written essay or report, based on your research and presented for an advanced university degree such as an MSc, MLitt or PhD: *I finished my thesis in 1992.* **2** A **thesis** is also an idea or theory expressed in a logical way and presented as a basis for argument or discussion.

they /ðeɪ/ *pronoun* (*used as the subject of a plural verb*)
1 You use **they** to refer to people, animals or things already mentioned or known about: *These flowers smell lovely, don't they?* □ *When we made the dogs sleep in the kennel they barked all night.* □ *I asked my parents, but they both refused to tell me.* □ *They all came to see her off at the station.* **2 They** can also be used with the vague meanings 'people', 'those in authority', 'the experts', or 'those involved': *And now they say that jogging's bad for you.* □ *They're putting up the price of stamps in January.* □ *Apparently they've found the stolen painting.* **3** You can use **they** in referring to singular words such as *anyone*, *someone*, *no-one* or *person*, where the sex is not specified, as a way of avoiding 'he', 'she', or the very formal 'he or she': *Anyone can join in, can't they?* □ *No-one admits that they're* (or, very formally, *he or she is*) *prejudiced.*

they'd /ðeɪd/
They'd is the spoken, and informal written, form of
1 they had: *They'd better hurry up.* **2 they would**: *They say they'd rather wait.*

they'll /ðeɪl/
They'll is the spoken, and informal written, form of **they will**: *They'll be here tomorrow.*

they're /ðɛə(r)/ or /ðeɪə(r)/
They're is the spoken, and informal written, form of **they are**: *They're going to be late again.*

they've /ðeɪv/
They've is the spoken, and informal written, form of **they have**: *They've forgotten all about me.*

thick /θɪk/ *adjective*: **thicker, thickest**
1 Something that is **thick** has a relatively large distance between its opposite sides: *a thick slice of bread* □ *Old cottages had these very thick walls to keep the heat in.* □ *These telephone directories seem to get thicker every year.* [*opposite* **thin**] **2** You use **thick** when referring to the width or depth of something: *a slice of bread at least an inch thick.* **3 Thick** string or rope has a wide diameter. [*same as* **stout**] **4** Something such as hair, or a forest, or a crowd, that consists of a large number of things, is described as **thick** if the things it consists of are plentiful, and close together. [*same as* **dense**; *opposite* **thin, sparse**] **5** A **thick** liquid contains a lot of solid matter: *thick vegetable soup* □ *a thick creamy cheese sauce.* **6** Fog, mist or smoke are **thick** when you can hardly see anything throught them: *The fog is getting thicker.* □ *Thick cloud hid the summits from view.* **7** A person's voice or speech is **thick** if it is not clear, *eg* because they are upset. **8** (*informal; derogatory*) If you describe someone as **thick**, you mean they are stupid, or slow at understanding things: *He's always been a bit thick.* [*same as* **stupid**] — *adverb* **thickly:** *She spread the jam thickly on the bread.* □ *Fallen leaves lay thickly on the ground.* □ *Trees grew thickly on either side of the road.*

▻ ***phrases*** **1** (*informal*) You say that something is **a bit thick** if you think it is unfair: *That's a bit thick, asking you to work for less money.* **2** You are **in the thick of** something if you are very busy with it: *We're in the thick of decorating at the moment.* **3** Things happen, or come, **thick and fast** if they happen or come quickly and in great numbers: *The insults were flying thick and fast.* **4** Someone who supports you **through thick and thin** remains loyal to you through all your difficulties. **5** Something is **thick with** something else if it is covered with it or full of it: *The room was thick with smoke.* □ *The streets were thick with people.* **6** You do something **through thick and thin** if you continue to do it no matter what happens and in spite of any difficulties: *He has been my friend through thick and thin.*

thicken /ˈθɪkən/ *verb*: **thickens, thickening, thickened**
1 Fog or smoke **thickens** when it becomes harder to see through: *The cloud began to thicken as we climbed towards the summit.* **2** You **thicken** a liquid when you make it thicker and more solid: *She thickened the sauce by boiling it rapidly.*

thicket /ˈθɪkɪt/ *noun*: **thickets**
A **thicket** is a mass of bushes and trees growing very close together.

thickness /ˈθɪknəs/ *noun*: **thicknesses**
1 (*uncount*) The **thickness** of something is its diameter, width or depth: *Each layer of pastry should be the same thickness.* **2** A **thickness** of something is a layer of it: *Iron the garment through several thicknesses of blotting paper, and you'll find that the greasy stain will disappear.*

thickset /θɪkˈsɛt/ *adjective*
A person is **thickset** if they have a broad, heavy, short body.

thick-skinned /θɪkˈskɪnd/ *adjective*
You are **thick-skinned** if you are not easily hurt by unpleasant things other people say to you or about you: *You need to be thick-skinned to be a policeman.* [*opposite* **thin-skinned**]

thief /θiːf/ *noun*: **thieves**
A **thief** is a person who steals things from someone else, especially secretly and often without using violence: *Thieves had broken into the shop and got away with thousands of pounds' worth of jewellery.* [compare **burglar, robber**]

thigh /θaɪ/ *noun*: **thighs**
Your **thighs** are the fleshy parts at the top of your legs, between your knees and your hips. [see picture at **body**]

thimble /ˈθɪmbəl/ *noun*: **thimbles**
A **thimble** is a small metal or plastic cap that you wear on the end of your finger to protect it from the point of the needle while sewing.

thin /θɪn/ *adjective*; *verb*
▻ ***adjective***: **thinner, thinnest**
1 Something that is **thin** has a relatively short distance between its opposite sides: *a thin slice of bread* □ *This house has very thin walls.* □ *A thin layer of snow covered the ground.* [*opposite* **thick**] **2** A **thin** person or

animal is not fat: *She is far too thin.* □ *He's a lot thinner now.* [*same as* **lean**, **skinny**; *opposite* **fat**; compare **slim**] **3 Thin** liquids contain very little solid matter: *She served me some thin watery soup.* [*opposite* **thick**] **4 Thin** is used to describe something that consists of a number of different things, such as hair or a crowd, if the things it consists of are not numerous, and are scattered: *thin hair* □ *The crowd in the gallery was getting thinner.* [*same as* **sparse**; *opposite* **thick**] **5** A **thin** excuse is one that no-one believes; a **thin** disguise fails to conceal the person or thing underneath it. [*same as* **unconvincing**] — *adverb* **thinly:** *She spread the butter thinly on the bread.*

▻ ***verb***: **thins, thinning, thinned**

1 Your hair **is thinning** if you are beginning to go bald. **2** Fog or mist **thins** when it becomes easier to see through.

▻ ***phrases*** **1** For **into thin air** see **air**. **2** For **thin on the ground** see **ground**. **3 a** Your temper **is wearing thin** if you are beginning to get angry; your patience **is wearing thin** if you are getting impatient. **b** A joke that **is wearing thin** has been told so often that it is no longer funny.

> ***phrasal verbs***
> **thin down** You **thin** a liquid **down** when you add more water to it.
> **thin out 1** You **thin** things **out** when you remove some so that there is more space between the rest: *The lettuce seedlings will need thinning out in about a month's time.* **2** Something such as a crowd **thins out** when there are fewer people and they are more scattered: *The trees began to thin out as we climbed higher.*

thing /θɪŋ/ *noun*: **things**

1 a You can refer to any physical object, even a creature, as a **thing**, to avoid specifying it by a more exact word: *Bullets are funny things: they rarely do what is expected of them.* □ *I hate throwing things away.* □ *Now where do I sign this thing?* □ *She had a craving for salty things.* □ *What's that black marble thing on the mantelpiece?* □ *all living things.* **b** (*used in the plural*) Your **things** are your possessions: *her jewellery and other personal things* □ *I needed somewhere to keep my things.* □ *Most of our patients have individual rooms, so that they can have their own things around them.* **c** (*used in the plural*) Your **things** are also your clothes: *Right, you can put on your things again.* **d** You refer to the equipment or clothing you use for any activity as *eg* the cleaning **things** or your swimming **things**: *She set out her painting things.* □ *after we'd washed and put away the dinner things.*

2 a You can refer to any matter, fact, concept, action, task, arrangement, event or circumstance as a **thing**: *I daresay he'll want to change a few things.* □ *such things as access, choice, information and safety* □ *Don't meddle in things you don't understand.* □ *The same word can mean different things.* □ *I've a few things to do first.* □ *Why do bad things always happen to people who don't deserve them?* □ *Women don't mind that sort of thing in men.* □ *He says things he doesn't really mean.* □ *Don't say things like that.* □ *Oh, and another thing, don't forget to turn on the electric blanket.* □ *The best thing about being a lone parent is the independence.* □ *The important thing is to know what you are dying for.* **b** (*with a negative*) You use 'a **thing**' to mean 'anything': *I don't know a thing about it.* □ *I couldn't see a thing.* □ *Don't worry if he barks at you; it doesn't mean a thing.* **c** (*used in the plural*) You can refer to life or circumstances in general as **things**: *Things are not so simple.* □ *Things are changing rapidly.* □ *Are you satisfied with things as they are?* □ *Things are becoming intolerable at the club.* □ *Things were different then.* □ *How are things with you?* □ *Things aren't going very well for us at present.* **d** (*informal*) Something that is referred to as your **thing** is something you are especially interested in or good at: *Better ask Alan; computers are his thing.* **e** Something that is said to be 'the **thing**' is fashionable or important: *Red braces are the thing at present.* □ *Cars are the thing with the teenagers round here.*

3 (*usually informal*) You can refer to, or address, people as **things** of a certain kind, in expressions that show your attitude or feelings towards them: *His daughter was a pretty little thing.* □ *Sorry if I upset you, old thing.* □ *'I've had flu.' 'You poor thing!'* □ *They've still got a week's holiday, lucky things.*

▻ ***phrases*** **1** You refer to something **among** or **amongst other things** if it is one of several that you could mention: *Amongst other things, he opposed the City Elections of 1725.* **2** You **do the right thing** when you act wisely or honourably; you **do the wrong thing** when you make a mistake or act stupidly: *I suppose it's what she wanted and she's done the right thing.* **3** (*informal*) You **do your own thing** when you do what you want to do yourself: *At weekends I need to be free to do my own thing.* **4** You use **'for one thing'** to give one particular reason for your opinion and imply that there are several others: *You'll never get the choir to sing that; it's too difficult, for one thing.* **5** If you say that something is **a good thing**, or **no bad thing**, you mean it is beneficial or lucky: *It's no bad thing, in fact, to write a short essay about each of your main characters.* □ *It's a good thing she was away when the news broke.* **6** (*informal*) You **have a thing about** something if it makes you nervous, or if you like it or dislike it to an unusual degree: *He's got a thing about graveyards.* □ *Like a lot of teenage girls, she had a thing about horses.* **7** If you say a certain event or circumstance is **just one of those things** you mean it is difficult to explain, or couldn't have been prevented: *Nobody was to blame; it was just one of those things.* **8** You describe something as **just the thing** if it is exactly what you need: *Thanks for the wire-cutters; they're just the thing.* **9** (*informal*) People **make a big thing of** something if they treat it as important: *Some people make such a big thing of birthdays.* **10** (*informal*) You are **on to a good thing** when you have discovered a way of benefiting yourself. **11 The real thing** is something genuine, as opposed to an imitation of it, or something that might be mistaken for it: *This tastes quite like butter, but I prefer the real thing.* □ *If you've never been in love, how can you be sure this is the real thing?* **12** You use **'the thing is'** to introduce an explanation, or to emphasize an important point: *You see, the thing is, she's started stealing again.* □ *The thing is that you have to grab people's attention.* **13** You use **with one thing and another** to indicate that there are several reasons for something, without saying what they are: *And so, with one thing and other, he felt better about life than he had done for a long time.*

thingummy /'θɪŋəmɪ/ *noun* (*informal*): **thingummies**

You can use **thingummy**, **thingumajig** and **thingumabob** to refer vaguely to a person or thing, *eg* one whose name you do not know or can't remember: *I need a thingummy for cleaning the windscreen.*

think /θɪŋk/ *verb*; *noun*

▻ ***verb***: **thinks, thinking, thought**

1 a You **think** when you use your intelligence and your powers of reasoning to make decisions and form opinions and conclusions: *Come on, think!* □ *People never stop and think.* □ *'Wait a minute. I'm thinking.'*

□ *Would you like a day or two to think about it?* □ *You can't think properly when you're tired.* □ *I've been trying to think how best to help.* **b** You **think** something if that is your opinion, and you very often use 'I **think**' as a polite way of introducing your opinion: *Candidates are asked to circle whichever answers they think appropriate.* □ *He thinks drugs are evil.* □ *What does the doctor think is the cause?* □ *People think that being a crime writer makes you a detective.* □ *He takes no interest in what anyone else thinks.* □ *I thought it odd that she'd left no message.* □ *'Is this the right way to deal with it?' 'No, I don't think so.'* □ *I think it's OK, but Alan thinks differently.* □ *I think there could be trouble.* □ *I didn't think any harm would come of it.* [compare **believe, suppose, imagine**]

Notice that with verbs of thinking and supposing, if the idea or opinion is negative, you usually make the verb of thinking negative, rather than the clause following it: *I don't think we should tell him yet* (rather than *I think we shouldn't tell him yet*). *'Does she need any help?' 'She doesn't think so'* (or *'She thinks not'*).

c You **think** something is so when you have the impression, especially the wrong impression, that it is: *He used to admire himself in the mirror when he thought no-one was looking.* □ *He evidently thinks I'm joking.* □ *Hallo! I thought you were in Italy!* **d** You say you **think** something is so when you are not certain that it is, as distinct from knowing that it is: *'What time's the train?' 'One-forty, I think, but we'd better check.'* □ *The couple are thought to be on a motoring holiday in France.* [compare **believe**] **e** You **are thinking** something when you are having thoughts or ideas that you don't announce out loud: *She lay awake thinking how miserable she was.* □ *'Shouldn't we be leaving?' 'I was just thinking that.'* □ *I couldn't help thinking we were making a big mistake, but didn't like to say so.* □ *He left as soon as possible, thinking to himself that he'd had a lucky escape.* **f** You say it is *eg* sad or pleasant to **think** that something is so if the reflection makes you sad or pleased: *It pleased me to think that I had made a small contribution to the success of the book.* [same as **reflect**] **g** You **think** you will do something if you intend to do it, and you often use **'I think'** or even **'I thought'** before stating your intention or idea: *I think I'll take the dog out.* □ *He had an hour to spare, and thought he'd take a taxi ride round London.* □ *'What are you doing tonight?' 'I thought I might go round to Janet's.'* □ *'Coming for lunch?' 'I don't think so, not just yet.'* □ *'Are you going to the lecture?' 'I think probably not.'*

2 a You **think** about, or of, things when they occupy your mind: *Who thinks of death at twenty-eight?* □ *Nowadays she thinks about nothing but dancing.* **b** You **think** of, or about, something when you take it into consideration, or remember to deal with it: *You're marvellous; you've thought of everything.* □ *'Suppose there are no planes because of the fog?' 'I hadn't thought of that.'* □ *Is there anything else we should be thinking about?* □ *Did anyone think of warning* (also *think to warn*) *the cleaner that the office would be closed?* [compare **remember, consider**] **c** You **think** of something when you invent it, using your brains and imagination: *So far no-one had thought of a really good slogan.* [*same as* **think up**; compare **invent**] **d** If you can **think** of a certain thing you can recall or remember it: *I can think of at least two Shakespeare characters who openly announce themselves as villains.* □ *Yes, but I can't think which plays they come into.* [compare **remember**] **e** You **think** of other people when you show concern for their welfare: *You never think of anyone but yourself, do you?* [compare **consider**] **f** What you **think** of something or someone is your opinion of their qualities or character: *What do you think of the idea?* □ *We didn't think much of that suggestion.* □ *Her books are quite well thought of by the critics.* □ *He's highly thought of in the medical world.* □ *I don't know who the girl is, but he obviously thinks a lot of her.* [= likes her a lot] □ *Please don't think badly of me, but I feel I must refuse.* **g** You **think** of one thing as another if you regard it as that thing: *You should think of your labour as a commodity.* □ *He thinks of Polonius as a tedious old fool.* **h** You are **thinking** of, or about, doing something if you are planning or intending to do it: *I was thinking of giving up teaching.* [compare **consider**] **i** You often use **think** in expressions of surprise, horror, worry and frustration: *Look here! Just whom do you think you're talking to?* □ *Whatever were you thinking of, leaving the children alone like that?* □ *I can't think where I've left my glasses.* [compare **imagine**, see also **to think** below]

▻ ***noun*** (*used in the singular; informal*)

You have a **think** about something when you consider what to do about it: *Let me know about the proposal when you've had a think about it.*

▻ ***phrases*** **1** You use **'anybody would think'** and **'you'd have thought'** to express surprise at people's inappropriate behaviour: *The way you're behaving, anyone would think you didn't want the job.* □ *You'd have thought she'd failed, she looked so depressed.* **2** You deal with something **as you think best** or **as you think fit** when you deal with it as sensibly as you can. **3** For **come to think of it** see **come**. **4** You use **'just think!'** to introduce an idea that is making you feel worried or excited: *Just think of the expense!* □ *Just think! This time tomorrow I'll be in Hong Kong.* **5** You **say what you think** about something or someone if you state your frank, usually critical, opinion of them. **6** You **think better of** doing something you had intended to do when you change your mind and decide not to do it: *Several times they've threatened to sue us, and then thought better of it.* **7** You **think nothing of** something, or of doing something, if you consider it quite normal or usual: *Nobody thinks anything these days of a man and woman sharing a flat.* □ *She thought nothing of running ten or so miles a day.* **8** Someone advises you to **think twice** or **think again** about doing something if they think you would be wrong to do it: *I'd think twice about selling the house if I were you.* **9** For **think the world of** see **world**. **10** You use **'to think'** to recall some circumstance with surprise or horror: *To think we believed her!*

phrasal verbs

think back You **think back** when you remember things that happened to you in the past: *Think back to your own childhood.* □ *When I thought back over the interview I wondered how I could have been so cheeky.*

think out You **think** something **out** when you consider it or plan it in detail: *I've thought it all out, and I know exactly what I'm going to say.* □ *The whole thing was badly thought out and badly organized.*

think over You **think** something **over** when you consider it carefully: *He may change his mind when he's had time to think it over.* □ *Think over what I've told you.*

think through You **think** something **through** when you consider each point or aspect in turn: *One cannot, if one really thinks it through, accept their argument.*

think up You **think** something **up** if you invent it: *Who on earth thinks up these brand names?* [*same as* **devise**]

thinker /ˈθɪŋkə(r)/ *noun*: **thinkers**
A **thinker** is a person who thinks, especially in a particular way, or a person who is famous for their ideas: *an original thinker* □ *Rousseau, Voltaire and other 18th-century thinkers.*

thinking /ˈθɪŋkɪŋ/ *noun*; *adjective*
▻ ***noun*** (*uncount*)
1 **Thinking** is the act of using your mind or brain to produce thoughts: *You must do some serious thinking before you decide on a career.* **2** Your **thinking** on a subject is what you think about it, your opinion or judgement: *What's your thinking on this?*
▻ ***adjective***
A **thinking** person is an intelligent person who is interested in important events and serious issues: *a magazine for the thinking woman.*
▻ ***phrases*** **1** (*informal*) You **put your thinking-cap on** if you think carefully about something, especially to try to solve a problem or come up with an idea. **2** You can add **to my way of thinking** to a statement to emphasize that it is your opinion: *This whole plan is, to my way of thinking, a serious mistake.*

thin-skinned /θɪnˈskɪnd/ *adjective*
You are **thin-skinned** if you are easily hurt or upset by unpleasant things that other people say to you or about you: *I'm trying to be less thin-skinned about criticism.* [*same as* **sensitive**; *opposite* **thick-skinned**]

third (often written **3rd**) /θɜːd/ *determiner*; *pronoun*; *adjective or adverb*; *noun*
▻ ***determiner***
1 The **third** person or thing is the one that is numbered three in a series: *during the third week of term* □ *the 3rd Duke of Atholl.* **2** **Third** gear is the gear above second gear and below fourth gear in a motor vehicle: *Are you still in third gear?*
▻ ***pronoun:*** *He will give the third of his talks tonight.* □ *She's third from the end in the back row.* □ *We're leaving on the 3rd of May.* □ *in the reign of George the Third* (written *George III*). [see note at **date**]
▻ ***adjective or adverb:*** *She came* (or *was*) *third in the music exam.* □ *He came in third in the race.*
▻ ***noun*** (often written $\frac{1}{3}$): **thirds**
1 A **third** of something is one of three equal parts of it: *A third of the class failed the exam.* **2** (*BrE*) A **third** is an honours degree of the third, and usually lowest, class: *She got a third in French.* **3** (*uncount*) **Third** is the gear in a motor vehicle that is faster than second and slower than fourth.

thirdly /ˈθɜːdlɪ/ *adverb*
You use **thirdly** to introduce the third point that you want to make, or the third reason that you want to give: *And thirdly, I can't afford it.*

third party /θɜːd ˈpɑːtɪ/ *noun*: **third parties**
A **third party** is a person who is not directly involved in an agreement, contract or legal agreement between two people, but who is involved by chance: *There is a third party who saw the fight and can act as witness.*

third-party /ˈθɜːdpɑːtɪ/ *adjective*
You have **third-party** insurance if your insurance will cover the cost of any damage you cause to other people or their property but will not cover the cost of damage to your own property. [compare **comprehensive**]

third person /θɜːd ˈpɜːsən/ (*used in the singular: grammar*)
In speech analysis, the **third person** is the term used to refer to the person, thing, people or things being spoken about, represented by the pronouns *he*, *she*, *it* and *they*. [see also **first person**, **second person**]

third-rate /θɜːdˈreɪt/ *adjective*
Something is **third-rate** if it of a very bad quality or standard: *a third-rate spy film.*

Third World /θɜːd ˈwɜːld/ *noun* (*uncount*)
The **Third World** is the poorer or developing countries in Africa, Asia and Latin America.

thirst /θɜːst/ *noun*
1 (*used in the singular*) A **thirst** is the need to drink: *The singing left her with a great thirst.* **2** (*uncount*) **Thirst** is the feeling of dryness caused by needing to drink, or the state of not having enough to drink: *people dying of thirst.* **3** (*used in the singular*) A **thirst** for something is a strong desire or longing for it: *a thirst for success.*

thirsty /ˈθɜːstɪ/ *adjective*: **thirstier**, **thirstiest**
1 You are **thirsty** if you need or want to drink: *She was tired, thirsty and hungry after the climb.* **2** You describe an activity as **thirsty** work if it is strenuous or energetic and makes you feel thirsty: *I must have a drink; all this dancing is thirsty work.* — *adverb* **thirstily:** *He drank thirstily.*

thirteen /θɜːˈtiːn/ *noun*; *adjective*; *determiner*; *pronoun*
▻ ***noun***: **thirteens**
1 (*uncount or count*) **Thirteen** is the number or figure 13: *Ten and three are thirteen.* **2** (*uncount*) **Thirteen** is the age of 13: *You'll become a teenager at thirteen.* **3** (*count or uncount*) A **thirteen** is something represented by the number 13, especially a piece of clothing or footwear whose size is represented by this number, or a person who wears clothes or footwear of this size: *This shop doesn't stock thirteens.* □ *Robbie takes thirteens and his little sister takes tens.*
▻ ***adjective***
Someone who is **thirteen** is thirteen years old.
▻ ***determiner:*** *I lived in Paris for thirteen months.* □ *thirteen-year-old pupils.*
▻ ***pronoun:*** *There were originally twenty students taking the course, but now there are only thirteen.*

thirteenth /θɜːˈtiːnθ/ *determiner*; *pronoun*; *adjective or adverb*; *noun*: **thirteenths**
1 (often written **13th**) The **thirteenth** person or thing is the one numbered thirteen in a series. **2** (often written $\frac{1}{13}$) A **thirteenth** of something is one of thirteen equal parts of it.

thirtieth /ˈθɜːtɪθ/ *determiner*; *pronoun*; *adjective or adverb*; *noun*: **thirtieths**
1 (often written **30th**) The **thirtieth** person or thing is the one numbered thirty in a series. **2** (often written $\frac{1}{30}$) A **thirtieth** of something is one of thirty equal parts of it.

thirty /ˈθɜːtɪ/ *noun*; *adjective*; *determiner*; *pronoun*
▻ ***noun***: **thirties**
1 (*uncount or count*) **Thirty** is the number or figure 30. **2** (*uncount*) **Thirty** is the age of 30: *Many women have children by thirty.* **3** (*used in the plural*) Someone who is in their **thirties** is aged between 30 and 39. **4** (*used in the plural*) The temperature is in the **thirties** when it is between 30° and 39°. **5** (*used in the plural*) The **thirties** are the period between the thirtieth and fortieth years of a century: *a book about Britain in the thirties* □ *the nineteen-thirties.*
▻ ***adjective***
Someone who is **thirty** is thirty years old.
▻ ***determiner:*** *a magazine for thirty-year-olds.*
▻ ***pronoun:*** *Twenty applications for the job arrived yesterday and another thirty arrived this morning.*

this /ðɪs/ *determiner*; *pronoun*; *adverb*
▻ ***determiner*** (*demonstrative, used with singular count nouns, and uncount nouns*; the plural is **these**; see separate entry)

1 This person or thing is **a** the one being indicated, usually close to you, or being held by you, or on your body: *I don't often wear this brooch.* □ *Have a look at this horrible spot on my nose.* □ *This calendar's for you.* □ *Who made all this mess?* □ *Excuse me, can you help this lady? She wants to know about bus times.* [*opposite* **that**] **b** the one just mentioned or about to be specified: *It's inadequate, and for this* (or *for that*) *reason, I'd rather wait till we have more material.* □ *OK, I agree, but on this one condition, that we invite Margaret to propose the vote of thanks.* [compare **that**] **2 This** place is the one you are in: *the rocks that form this planet.* **3 This** week, month or year is the present one; **this** Friday is the one coming, in the present week; **this** evening is the evening of today: *I'm busy this morning but I can see you this afternoon.* □ *Last Thursday was a holiday; this Thursday we're interviewing all day; next Thursday is the Board meeting.* □ *We're going away this weekend.* □ *at this point in time* □ *I've been waiting this past hour for you.* **4** (*informal*) In spoken English, people use **this** to introduce a person or thing into a story: *The car stopped, and this chap got out.* □ *Then somebody made this brilliant suggestion.*

▻ ***pronoun*** (*demonstrative*; the plural is **these**; see separate entry)

You use **this 1 a** to refer to something you are indicating or identifying, usually close to you, or being held by you, or on your body, or to refer to a point close to you: *This is the blouse I bought last week.* □ *Will the carpet stretch as far as this?* **b** to mean the present moment: *I expected to be finished before this.* □ *Where are you going after this?* **c** to introduce one person to another, or to identify yourself, *eg* on the telephone: *Have you met Marion, Deirdre? Marion, this is Deirdre.* □ *Is that you, Neil? Hallo, this is Anne.*

> Notice that when asking who is at the other end of the telephone line BrE speakers usually say 'Who is that?', and AmE speakers 'Who is this?'

2 to refer to the present situation, or to something about to be specified, or, instead of **that**, to refer to any fact, event, situation, circumstance or idea just mentioned: *This is terrible; I just can't get them to understand.* □ *Is it going to go on being as complicated as this?* □ *It's great having everyone together like this.* □ *There's something you're all forgetting, and it's this.* □ *Thanks for your comment, Jan; this is* (or *that's*) *an important point.* □ *There's no backup procedure; this* (or *that*) *may become a problem later on.*

▻ ***adverb***

You can use **this 1** with hand movements, to show the size of something: *The creature was about this long.* **2** (*intensifying, often with a negative; informal*) to refer to the degree to which something is so: *I didn't think the job would be this easy.* □ *You didn't tell me it would be this far away.*

▻ ***phrases*** **1** You can refer to unimportant events, activities or topics, which you do not want to specify, as **this and that**: *'What were you talking about?' 'Oh, just this and that.'* **2 This or that** person or thing is any unspecified person or thing: *when I ask students to consider this or that point* □ *This or that person may disagree.* □ *and they get talking and find they have this or that in common.*

thistle /ˈθɪsəl/ *noun*: **thistles**

A **thistle** is a plant with prickly leaves and usually purple flowers.

thorn /θɔːn/ *noun*: **thorns**

1 A **thorn** is a hard, sharp point sticking out from the stem or branch of certain plants. **2** (*count or uncount*) A **thorn** is a bush with thorns on its branches: *a thorn hedge.*

▻ ***phrase*** Someone is **a thorn in your side**, or **a thorn in your flesh**, if they continually annoy or bother you: *He's a thorn in the government's side.*

thorny /ˈθɔːnɪ/ *adjective*: **thornier**, **thorniest**

1 A **thorny** bush or tree is covered with thorns. **2** A **thorny** problem, question or subject is one that it is difficult to discuss or deal with: *The unions need to discuss the thorny matter of the annual pay rise.* [*same as* **tricky**]

thorough /ˈθʌrə/ or /ˈθʌroʊ/ *adjective*

1 A person is **thorough** if they are extremely careful and pay attention to every detail: *He's an extremely thorough and accomplished lawyer.* **2** A **thorough** piece of work has been done carefully, with every detail fully considered: *The report has been based on thorough research.* □ *The company runs a thorough testing programme for all new products.* **3 Thorough** can be used for emphasis, with the meaning 'complete' or 'absolute': *The whole thing was a thorough waste of time.* — *adverb* **thoroughly:** *He always works thoroughly and efficiently.* □ *The product has been tested thoroughly.* □ *I thoroughly agree.* □ *a thoroughly happy and confident child.* — *noun* (*uncount*) **thoroughness:** *the thoroughness of the programme to test new products* □ *work done with her characteristic thoroughness.*

thoroughbred /ˈθʌrəbrɛd/ or /ˈθʌroʊbrɛd/ *noun*: **thoroughbreds**

A **thoroughbred** is an animal, especially a horse, bred from the best animals, carefully developed over many years.

thoroughfare /ˈθʌrəfɛə(r)/ or /ˈθʌroʊfɛə(r)/ *noun* (*formal*): **thoroughfares**

A **thoroughfare** is a public road or street: *the town's main thoroughfare.*

those /ðoʊz/ *determiner; pronoun*

▻ ***determiner*** (*demonstrative*, *plural* of **that**)

1 Those people or things are the ones being indicated, usually at some distance from you, or the ones just mentioned or known about: *You see those two men sitting on the bench?* □ *What a smell those cats make!* □ *Half those onions have gone bad.* □ *We can discuss some of those points later.* [*opposite* **these**] **2 Those** times, or **those** days, are the past times just mentioned: *In those days young girls couldn't just dress as they liked.* [compare **these**] **3** You use **those**, often followed by a relative clause, to identify a group: *Will those students who have not yet registered please do so immediately?* □ *He could only investigate those cases referred to him by members of parliament.*

▻ ***pronoun*** (*demonstrative*, *plural* of **that**): *I want some shoes like those.* □ *Surely you've got smarter clothes than those to put on?* □ *Those were just some of the questions that arose.* □ *There are several thousand murders each year, and of those a large proportion remain unsolved.* □ *Those were great times.* □ *May I remind those of you who are staying to check the lecture list, and wish those about to depart a pleasant journey?* [compare **these**]

though /ðoʊ/ *conjunction; adverb*

▻ ***conjunction***

1 Though is used, often with *even*, to mean 'in spite of the fact that' or 'in spite of being', and you use it when mentioning circumstances that contrast surprisingly with your main statement: *He insisted on taking his test, even though he hadn't a hope of passing.* □ *Though evidently surprised to see us, they gave us a warm welcome.* [compare **although**] **2** You also use **though** to modify the impression you have given in your main statement: *I enjoyed her new play, though not as much* *as her previous one.* ▫ *He was an enthusiastic though rather unreliable member of the committee.* ▫ *'You don't like her much, do you?' 'No. Though I do admire her energy.'* [*same as* **although**]

▻ ***adverb*** (*sentence adverb*)

Though comes at the end of a statement that contrasts with something already said: *I'm rather busy today; I would like to see you, though.* ▫ *'They're nice children.' 'Yes. Noisy, though.'* [*same as* **however**]

▻ ***phrase*** For **as though** see **as**.

thought /θɔːt/ *verb; noun*

▻ ***verb***

Thought is the past tense and past participle of **think**.

▻ ***noun***: **thoughts**

1 A **thought** is an idea or opinion that you have: *I can't bear the thought of getting old.* ▫ *I've had thoughts of leaving for years.* ▫ *She looked lost in her private thoughts.* ▫ *He's written a book containing his thoughts on modern Britain.* **2** (*uncount*) **Thought** is **a** the act of thinking: *She looks lost in thought.* **b** serious and careful consideration: *A lot of careful thought has gone into this proposal.* ▫ *I promise to give some thought to the problem.* **3** (*uncount*) The **thought** of a particular group of people, place or time are the ideas which are typical of them or common then: *recent scientific thought* ▫ *different schools of religious thought.*

thoughtful /ˈθɔːtfəl/ *adjective*

1 A **thoughtful** person is quiet and serious and thinks deeply: *a thoughtful child.* [*same as* **reflective**] **2** A **thoughtful** person considers the needs and wants of other people; a **thoughtful** act is done by a thoughtful person: *It was very thoughtful of you to offer to help.* ▫ *a thoughtful gesture.* [*same as* **considerate**; *opposite* **thoughtless, inconsiderate**] **3** A **thoughtful** piece of work has been done carefully and seriously: *She has written a thoughtful review of the book.* — *adverb* **thoughtfully:** *She thoughtfully asked if there was anything she could do.* ▫ *It was very thoughtfully done.*

thoughtless /ˈθɔːtləs/ *adjective*

A **thoughtless** person does not consider the needs and wants of others; a **thoughtless** act is done by a thoughtless person: *How could you be so thoughtless towards Miss Bates?* [*same as* **inconsiderate**; *opposite* **thoughtful**] — *adverb* **thoughtlessly:** *He thoughtlessly destroyed all the computer files without checking if they were needed first.*

thousand /ˈθaʊzənd/ *noun; determiner; pronoun*

▻ ***noun***: **thousand** or **thousands**

A **thousand** or one **thousand** is the number or figure 1000: *Ten times one hundred is one thousand.* ▫ *Five hundred plus five hundred make one thousand.* ▫ *How many thousands are there in a million?* ▫ *The total came to six thousand, eight hundred and twenty-four* (written *6824*).

▻ ***determiner:*** *There were nearly a thousand applicants for fifty college places.* ▫ *We're getting fifty thousand dollars for the movie rights.* ▫ *We'd driven over two thousand kilometers.*

▻ ***pronoun***: **thousand** or **thousands:** *Five thousand of his employees attended his funeral.* ▫ *Thousands have been made homeless.* ▫ *Tourists pass through here in their thousands.* ▫ *I've received literally thousands of letters from readers.*

> Notice that the determiner and pronoun are often used informally just to mean a lot: *I've told him a thousand times* (or *thousands of times*) *not to leave his bike on the stairs.*

▻ ***phrases*** **1** (*informal*) **A thousand and one** things is a very large number of them: *I've a thousand and one things to see to before we leave.* **2 Tens of thousands** and **hundreds of thousands** are used in rough estimates of very large numbers of people or things: *Tens of thousands of Serbs took part in the anti-war demonstration on 31 May.*

thousandth /ˈθaʊzəndθ/ *determiner; pronoun; adjective or adverb*: **thousandths**

1 (often written **1000th**) The **thousandth** person or thing is the one numbered one thousand in a series. **2** (often written $\frac{1}{1000}$) A **thousandth** of something is one of a thousand equal parts of it: *several thousandths of a second.*

thrash /θraʃ/ *verb*: **thrashes, thrashing, thrashed**

1 To **thrash** someone is to hit them repeatedly or several times, especially with a whip or similar weapon: *He threatened to thrash him.* **2** You **thrash** someone if you beat them thoroughly or by a lot of points in a game or match: *The Australian rugby team thrashed the English team.* ▫ *She always thrashes me at tennis.* **3** You **thrash** about or around if you move around violently or wildly: *He lay thrashing on the bed.* ▫ *The dog thrashed around, trying to break free.* — *noun* (*used in the singular*) **thrashing** /ˈθraʃɪŋ/: *He got a thrashing from his father.* ▫ *The team got a thrashing.*

> ***phrasal verb***
> You **thrash** a matter or problem **out** if you discuss it thoroughly so as to solve it, decide what it is best to do about it, or reach an agreement about it: *The countries are working together to thrash out a trade agreement.*

thread /θrɛd/ *noun; verb*

▻ ***noun***: **threads**

1 a (*uncount*) **Thread** is long lengths of very thin silk, cotton or wool, twisted together for sewing with: *I have run out of blue thread.* ▫ *a length of thread.* **b** A **thread** is a length of very thin silk, cotton or wool: *There are some loose threads on your skirt.* **2** The **thread** on a screw, nut or bolt is the raised spiral ridge round it. **3** (*usually in the singular*) The **thread** of *eg* an argument or story is the theme that connects all its different parts or elements: *I soon lost the thread of what he was saying.* ▫ *Jim lost the thread of his speech several times.*

▻ ***verb***: **threads, threading, threaded**

1 a You **thread** a needle when you pass a length of thread through the hole in the top of it. **b** You **thread** *eg* beads on a string when you pass a length of string through the holes in the beads. **2** You **thread** your way through people, things or a busy place when you pass carefully through them: *They threaded their way through the crowds towards the exit.*

threadbare /ˈθrɛdbɛə(r)/ *adjective*

Threadbare clothes or fabric have been used a lot and have become thin and untidy as a result: *He wears a threadbare old suit when doing the gardening.*

threat /θrɛt/ *noun*: **threats**

1 A **threat** is a warning that someone is going to hurt you or might hurt you, especially if you do not do what they tell you to do: *Several threats have been made against her life.* ▫ *death threats.* **2** A person or thing is a **threat** if they are likely to harm or hurt you: *His attitude is a threat to the whole project.* **3** There is a **threat** of something dangerous or unpleasant if there is a sign that it is or may be about to happen: *There's a threat of rain today.* ▫ *War brings the threat of disease and famine.* [*same as* **risk**]

threaten /ˈθrɛtən/ *verb*: **threatens, threatening, threatened**

1 You **threaten** to do something that will harm or upset someone, or **threaten** them with something, when you say you will do it or carry it out: *She threatened to leave him if he didn't agree to her going out to work.* □ *I threatened to call the police.* □ *They threatened me with the sack if I didn't stop making trouble among the workforce.* □ *Don't you try and threaten me.* **2** Someone **threatens** you with a weapon when they hold it ready to use against you, in order to make you do something: *He threatened me with a revolver, and made me sit on the sofa while he searched the drawers.* **3** Something undesirable **threatens**, or **threatens** you, if it seems likely to happen, and be harmful: *Famine threatens ten million people in Somalia.* □ *A storm was threatening.* □ *The march threatened to get out of control.* **4** Something undesirable **threatens** something when it endangers it: *flare-ups in the Middle East that threaten world peace* □ *He knew that this affair could threaten his political career.*

threatening /ˈθrɛtənɪŋ/ *adjective*
A person or thing that is **threatening** is likely to cause harm: *He became aggressive and threatening when the police arrived.* □ *She's been receiving threatening phone calls.* — *adverb* **threateningly:** *He moved threateningly towards her.*

three /θriː/ *noun; adjective; determiner; pronoun*
▻ ***noun***: **threes**
1 (*uncount or count*) **Three** is **a** the number or figure 3: *One and two make three.* □ *Four threes are twelve.* **b** a piece of clothing whose size is represented by the number 3, or a person who wears clothes of this size: *The shoes are threes.* □ *She takes a three in shoes.* **2** (*uncount*) **Three** is **a** the age of 3: *He started going to nursery school when he was three.* **b** the time of 3 o'clock: *Their flight arrives at three this afternoon.* **3** A **three** is **a** a set of 3 things or people. **b** a playing card with three symbols: *the three of hearts.*
▻ ***adjective***
Someone who is **three** is three years old: *His daughter will be three next week.*
▻ ***determiner:*** *a three-year-old child* □ *books for three-year-olds* □ *This sandwich cost three pounds.* □ *Three pounds is a lot for a box of chocolates.* □ *She got the job finished in three hours.*
▻ ***pronoun:*** *Three of the children were chosen to be angels in the play.* □ *We did have six copies of the book but there are only three left now.*

three-dimensional /θriːdaɪˈmɛnʃənəl/ *adjective*
A **three-dimensional** object has height, width and depth: *three-dimensional objects* □ *a three-dimensional image.*

three-quarters /θriːˈkwɔːtəz/ *adjective*
Three-quarters of something is half plus one quarter of it: *The test will last three-quarters of an hour.*

thresh /θrɛʃ/ *verb*: **threshes, threshing, threshed**
A person or machine **threshes** *eg* wheat or corn when they beat it in order to remove the grain.

threshold /ˈθrɛʃhoʊld/ *noun* (*formal*): **thresholds**
1 (*usually in the singular*) A **threshold** is the doorway or entrance to a room or building: *She stood on the threshold, uncertain whether to go in or not.* □ *I hope you never cross the threshold of my house again!* **2** The **threshold** is the point, level or limit at which something starts to happen or changes, *eg* at which you begin to feel pain: *The Chancellor has promised new tax thresholds.*
▻ ***phrase*** You are **on the threshold of** something when you are about to start it: *She's on the threshold of an exciting new career.*

threw /θruː/ *verb*
Threw is the past tense of **throw**.

thrift /θrɪft/ *noun* (*uncount*)
Thrift is the careful spending or use of money, and often other things, without unnecessary waste.

thrifty /ˈθrɪftɪ/ *adjective*: **thriftier, thriftiest**
A **thrifty** person spends money carefully, or uses other resources carefully, so that there is no unnecessary waste: *a thrifty housekeeper.* [*same as* **economical**, **frugal**; *opposite* **extravagant**]

thrill /θrɪl/ *verb; noun*
▻ ***verb***: **thrills, thrilling, thrilled**
Someone or something **thrills** you if they make you feel suddenly excited or pleased: *The sight of snow on the mountain tops always thrills me.*
▻ ***noun***: **thrills**
A **thrill** is **1** a sudden glowing feeling of excitement or pleasure: *She felt a thrill of excitement when she saw him.* **2** something such as an event which makes you feel suddenly excited or pleased: *The visit to Rome was a real thrill.*

thrilled /θrɪld/ *adjective*
You are **thrilled** if you are very pleased and excited about something: *I was thrilled to be able to meet the Queen.*

thriller /ˈθrɪlə(r)/ *noun*: **thrillers**
A **thriller** is an exciting story, play or film, usually about frightening or dangerous events.

thrilling /ˈθrɪlɪŋ/ *adjective*
Something is **thrilling** when it is exciting: *a thrilling performance of the music.*

thrive /θraɪv/ *verb*: **thrives, thriving, thrived, throve**

> **Thrived** and **throve** are both used as the past tense, although **thrived** is now the usual form.

People **thrive** when they grow strong and healthy; a business **thrives** when it is successful, especially financially. — *adjective* **thriving:** *a thriving new shopping area.*

throat /θroʊt/ *noun*: **throats**
Your **throat** is **1** the top part of the passage which leads from your mouth and nose to your stomach: *She's got a sore throat.* □ *A small fish bone got stuck in his throat.* **2** the front part of your neck: *He grabbed me by the throat.* [see picture at **body**]
▻ ***phrases*** **1** Two people are **at each other's throats** if they are arguing bitterly or violently: *They've been at each other's throats over this matter for the past couple of days.* **2** Someone **rams** something **down your throat** if they keeping talking about it, especially continually or aggressively, to try to make you believe or accept it: *People don't want religious beliefs rammed down their throats.* **3** Something **sticks in your throat** if you cannot accept, believe or say it: *He wanted me to apologize but the words stuck in my throat.*

throb /θrɒb/ *verb; noun*
▻ ***verb***: **throbs, throbbing, throbbed**
1 Part of your body **throbs** if it beats *eg* with emotion or pain: *My head is throbbing.* **2** Something **throbs** if it beats or vibrates with a strong, regular rhythm: *The music throbbed in her ears.*
▻ ***noun*** (*usually in the singular*): *She felt a throb of pain in her left arm.* □ *He could hear the throb of the music.*

throes /θroʊz/ *noun* (*plural*)
▻ ***phrase*** (*formal*) You are **in the throes of** something if you are involved in a difficult or painful struggle with it: *Larry was in the throes of a particularly severe attack of malaria.*

thrombosis /θrɒmˈboʊsɪs/ *noun* (*medicine*): **thromboses**
A **thrombosis** is a clot that forms in a blood vessel.

throne /θroʊn/ *noun*: **thrones**
1 A **throne** is a special, usually highly decorated, chair that a monarch or bishop uses on official occasions. **2** (*used in the singular*) The **throne** is the office of the king or queen: *when she came to the throne* □ *while he was on the throne* □ *the heir to the throne.*

throng /θrɒŋ/ *noun*; *verb*
▻ ***noun***: **throngs**
A **throng** is a crowd of people or things: *A throng of people rushed out ot the room.* [*same as* **multitude**]
▻ ***verb***: **throngs, thronging, thronged**
People **throng** somewhere when a lot of them gather or move there: *People thronged the streets to see the Queen pass.* □ *the audience thronging into the theatre.*

throttle /ˈθrɒtəl/ *noun*; *verb*
▻ ***noun***: **throttles**
A vehicle's **throttle** is a pedal or lever which controls the amount of fuel supplied to the engine and thus the engine's speed.
▻ ***verb***: **throttles, throttling, throttled**
To **throttle** someone means to injure or kill them by holding them tightly by the throat: *She was so angry she wanted to throttle him.*

through (*AmE* **thru**) /θruː/ *preposition*; *adverb*; *adjective*
▻ ***preposition***
1 a To move **through** a hole or gap is to enter it at one side and come out at the other; to move **through** a tunnel or tube is to pass along it, or to go in at one end and come out at the other: *Go down the street and through the arch.* □ *the blood flowing through our veins.* **b** One thing goes **through** another if it is positioned so that it enters it at one side and comes out at the other: *The tunnel goes right through the Alps.* □ *On the chair lay a ball of wool with a pair of knitting needles stuck through it.* **c** To cut **through** something is to cut it into two pieces: *A steel sheet had slipped off the trailer in front and sliced straight through the roof of his car.* □ *Rabbits had nibbled through the wire fence.* **d** To move **through** a place, area or medium is to move across it or pass from one point to another in it: *The other route takes you through prettier countryside.* □ *I once drove through Paris during the rush hour.* □ *He ducked as a brick came flying through the air.* □ *A feeling of despair swept through her.* □ *The infection spread quickly through the school.* **e** You get **through** a barrier when you pass from one side of it to the other: *It took us an hour to get through customs.* **f** Something passes **through** a surface or layer when it passes from one side to the other: *Water was dripping through the ceiling.* □ *Sunlight streamed through the curtains.* **g** You see, hear or feel something **through** a surface or a layer when it is between you and the thing you can see, hear or feel: *Through the window of the space ship they saw the moon.* □ *We sometimes heard them quarrelling through the wall.* □ *She could feel him shivering through the thick tweed of his jacket.* **h** You look at something **through** an instrument such as a lens when you use it to give you a clearer image: *observing the stars through a telescope.*
2 You look, read, work or go **through** things when you examine them or deal with them bit by bit: *Would you glance through this pile of applications?* □ *She'd got stuck halfway through the book.* □ *We'd already searched through the boxes in the attic.* □ *You should read through the evidence at least twice.* □ *I went through my pockets again: no key.* **a** (*AmE*) Something happens *eg* Friday **through** Monday if it happens from Friday up till, and including, Monday: *The parking restrictions are in force Monday through Friday.*

> Notice that BrE speakers would say 'in force from Monday to Friday'.

b Something happens or exists **through** a period of time if it happens or exists from the beginning of it till the end: *You can't go through life trusting no-one.* □ *The food they had would probably last them through the winter.* **c** You live **through** a period or event if it occurs during your lifetime: *people of fifty and over, who lived through the Second World War.* **d** You go **through** an experience when you have it: *A court trial wasn't an experience he wanted to go through again.* □ *No wonder she's depressed, after all she's been through.* **e** To go **through** a process is to undergo it: *The instruments are then put through a series of tests.* □ *They were now two-thirds of the way through their training course.* **f** You get **through** a test or exam when you pass it: *She got through her driving test first time.*
3 a One thing happens **through** another if it happens because of it: *The monastery may have been attacked by the Vikings or fallen down through neglect.* □ *We were falling behind schedule through no fault of our own.* **b** You achieve something **through** some action if that is the means you use to achieve it: *People forgot the acts of violence through which the state had come into being.* **c** You organize something **through** someone when you get them to deal with it: *We'd booked the theatre seats through a ticket agency.*
▻ ***adverb***
1 The adverb **through** reflects the uses of the preposition: *He opened the door and went through into the kitchen.* □ *Much of the traffic is just passing through and could be diverted.* □ *The bridge lifts up its two halves to let ships through.* □ *There's a covering of cloud but with luck the sun may break through.* □ *Loads of students sit the exam but fewer than half get through.* □ *She gave up her training halfway through.* **2** You read or look something **through** when you read it from beginning to end, not necessarily thoroughly: *He looked the document through quickly and signed it.* □ *I'd never read the text right through.* **3** Something happens all day, or the whole day, **through**, if it happens from the beginning to the end of the day: *The wind howled all night through.* **4** Something that is cooked or warmed **through** is thoroughly cooked or warmed: *Make sure that frozen food is properly heated through before you eat it.* **5** You are wet **through** or soaked **through** when all the layers of clothing you are wearing are wet. **6** You get **through**, or are put **through**, to someone when you are connected with them by telephone: *Could you put me through to headquarters?* □ *I was in the office when the call came through.*
▻ ***adjective***
1 A **through** train, journey or ticket takes you all the way to your destination, so that you do not have to change vehicles, or buy another ticket.
2 Through traffic passes straight through a place without stopping. **3** You are **through** with something when you are no longer going to do it, *eg* because you have finished dealing with it, or because you are tired of it: *I'll be glad when I'm through with marking these papers.* □ *I decided I was through with teaching.* **4** (*informal*) You are **through** with a person when you don't want to see them any longer or have anything more to do with them: *As far as I'm concerned, you and I are through.*
▻ ***phrase*** **Through and through** means completely or thoroughly: *Those people are evil through and through.* □ *I thought I knew her through and through.*

throughout /θruːˈaʊt/ *preposition or adverb*
1 Something happens **throughout** a period of time or an event if it happens frequently during it, or is the case during the whole of it: *Throughout 1912 he flew test planes.* □ *Mathematics is studied throughout the*

first two years. □ *They will need medical care throughout their lives.* □ *Christmas Day was a great success and the children behaved excellently throughout.* **2** Something happens **throughout** a place or area if it happens or is the case in all parts of it: *He has performed throughout the world.* □ *Teaching throughout the school is highly traditional.* □ *The houses are fully modernized and have double glazing and central heating throughout.* **3** Something happens **throughout** something such as a book or play if it happens frequently during it or is the case from the beginning to the end of it: *I shall refer constantly to her theory throughout the next two chapters.* □ *He is on stage throughout the whole of Act IV.* □ *The magazine is now printed in full colour throughout.*

throve /θroʊv/ *verb*
Throve is the past tense of **thrive**.

throw /θroʊ/ *verb; noun*
verb: **throws, throwing, threw, thrown**
1 a You **throw** something that you are holding somewhere when you let go of it with a strong forward movement, so that it moves or flies through the air: *She threw a cushion at him.* □ *Throw me that book, will you?* □ *The ball is thrown from player to player till someone drops it.* □ *Someone had thrown a brick through the window.* □ *I threw another log on the fire.* **b** To **throw** something or someone into some place or position is to put or force them there suddenly, violently, casually or carelessly: *She hastily threw some clothes into a suitcase.* □ *He came in and threw his jacket over a chair.* □ *Passengers were thrown violently forward in their seats by the impact.* □ *He'd thrown his coat round her shoulders.* [*same as* **fling**] **c** You **throw** clothes on or off when you put them on or take them off in a hurry: *She threw off her tracksuit and pulled on a clean T-shirt.* □ *I threw on a coat and dashed out into the rain.* **d** You **throw** your arm or some other part of you somewhere when you move it there suddenly: *She wanted to throw her arms round him and comfort him.* □ *He threw his head back and roared with laughter.* □ *Respectable people will throw up their hands in horror* [= will be shocked] *at such behaviour.* **e** You **throw** yourself somewhere if you move there suddenly: *He threw himself wearily into an armchair.* □ *She had a sudden desire to throw herself into his arms.* □ *She threw herself at him, punching him with her small closed fists.* □ *They threw themselves against the door.* [*same as* **fling**] **f** When using a dice, you **throw** a certain number if that is the number the dice shows when it lands: *Next time I threw a six.*
2 a You **throw** yourself or your energy into some activity when you involve yourself in it energetically: *She threw her energy into developing the business.* □ *In an effort to forget his disappointment he'd thrown himself into his work.* **b** Something **throws** you into a particular state or situation when it causes you to be in that state or situation: *The blow threw her off balance.* □ *These additional expenses have thrown the budget into confusion.* □ *She suddenly realized how little time she had left, and was immediately thrown into a panic.*
3 a Something **throws** light or shadow somewhere if it causes it to fall there: *His tall figure threw a long shadow across the lawn.* □ *The moon threw a strange white light over the bed.* **b** Something **throws** light on a question or issue if it makes it clearer; it **throws** doubt on it if it makes it uncertain: *Police investigations had so far failed to throw any light on her baffling death.* □ *Recent incidents have thrown some doubt on her ability to cope.* **c** You **throw** a look or glance at something when you look quickly at it: *She kept throwing furtive glances at the report lying on his desk.* □ *She threw him a wide smile.*
4 a (*informal*) Something **throws** you if it confuses you, usually because you don't expect it: *It really throws you when another actor forgets his move.* □ *Her remark threw me for a minute.* **b** A horse **throws** its rider if it makes him or her fall off: *The donkey threw its rider to the ground.* □ *He was thrown from his horse and killed.*
5 a You **throw** a party when you give it: *The local chief threw a grand party in our honour.* **b** Someone **throws** a fit or tantrum when they get very angry and upset and lose control of their behaviour: *He didn't shout or throw a tantrum; he just stood looking at Dad.* □ *She might throw a fit of jealousy.*
▻ ***noun***: **throws**
A **throw** is an act of throwing, or someone's turn to throw, *eg* in a game or competition: *He achieved a throw of 60.84 metres, to win the silver medal.* □ *It's your throw again.* [see also **stone's throw**]
▻ ***phrase***
1 You **throw** a door or window **open** when you open it wide; you **throw** your doors **open** to people when you welcome them in. **2** To **throw** a discussion **open** to people is to invite them to take part: *It was decided to throw the debate open to a wider audience.*

phrasal verbs
throw about or **throw around** People **throw** money **about** or **around** when they spend it fast or extravagantly.
throw away 1 You **throw** something **away** when you get rid of it: *Just throw away what you don't need.* □ *150 tonnes of unwanted medicine are thrown away every year.* [*same as* **throw out**] **2** You **throw away** something such as money, or a chance, opportunity or advantage, when you waste it or fail to make proper use of it: *It was disappointing to have thrown away valuable points through silly errors.* □ *We throw away thousands of pounds a year on things we don't need.* □ *You've got potential; don't throw away your chances of a good career.* [*same as* **waste**]
[see also **throwaway**]
throw in A person who is selling you something **throws in** something else if they give you the second thing free: *Buy this elegant decanter from us and we'll throw in a set of wine glasses.*
throw off You **throw off** something such as an illness when you get rid of it or recover from it: *He's hoping to throw off the virus in time for Saturday's match.*
throw out 1 You **throw** something **out** when you get rid of it, *eg* by putting it in a dustbin: *They used every scrap of food; nothing was ever thrown out.* □ *I can't find yesterday's newspaper; perhaps someone threw it out.* [*same as* **throw away**] **2** To **throw** someone **out** of a place or a job is to force them to leave it: *She paid the rent regularly, so I couldn't very well throw her out of the cottage.* □ *He'd gone to a nightclub but had been thrown out.* **3** Something such as a proposal **is thrown out** when it is rejected: *He'd produced several designs, but they'd all been thrown out.* □ *I urge the House to throw out this amendment.* **4** You **throw out** something such as a challenge, hint or suggestion when you make it rather casually. **5** Something **throws out** your plans or calculations when it spoils or upsets them: *These computer breakdowns all throw the schedule out.*
throw together You **throw** something **together** when you make it in a hurry: *I used to be able to throw a dress together in an evening and wear it next day.* □ *If you care to stay and eat with us I'm sure we can throw a meal of some sort together.*

throw up **1** (*informal; especially AmE*) You **throw up** when you feel ill and food comes up from your stomach and out through your mouth: *Be sick in the toilet if you must; I don't want you throwing up all over this carpet.* [*same as* **vomit**, **be sick**] **2** Something **throws up** questions, problems or facts when it brings them to your notice: *Our latest computer search has thrown up some interesting data.* **3** Something moving **throws up** *eg* dust if it disturbs it and makes it rise: *the cloud of dust thrown up by the tramping of heavy feet* □ *The motor boat threw up a lot of spray.* **4** You **throw up** your job or career when you leave it or give it up.

throwaway /'θroʊəweɪ/ *adjective*
1 A **throwaway** object is meant to be thrown away after you have used it: *a throwaway lighter.* [compare **disposable**] **2** A **throwaway** remark or act is said or done without thinking carefully or without taking care: *His criticism of the government was limited to a throwaway line at the end of his speech.* [see also **throw away** at **throw**]

throwback /'θroʊbak/ *noun* (*usually in the singular*)
A person, animal, plant or idea is a **throwback** when it belongs to an earlier period in time, or is characteristic of an earlier period in time: *His ideas are a throwback to the late 19th-century.* □ *It's a throwback from the period between the wars.*

thru see **through**.

thrush /θrʌʃ/ *noun*: **thrushes**
A **thrush** is a common small or medium-sized bird with brown feathers and a spotted chest.

thrust /θrʌst/ *verb; noun*
▷ ***verb***: **thrusts, thrusting, thrust**
1 You **thrust** someone or something somewhere when you push them suddenly and violently there: *She thrust him through the door and then locked it.* **2** You **thrust** somewhere, or **thrust** your way somewhere, when you push your way there: *She thrust her way through the crowds.* □ *He thrust past them all to get to the front of the queue.*
▷ ***noun***: **thrusts**
1 A **thrust** is a sudden or violent movement forward: *He made several thrusts with his sword.* **2** (*uncount*) **Thrust** is the force that is produced by a rocket or jet engine which propels an aircraft or spacecraft forwards and upwards. **3** (*used in the singular*) The **thrust** of an argument or idea is the most important theme, message or part of it: *The main thrust of his research is the forces which cause language to develop and change.*

phrasal verb
You **thrust** something **on** someone, or you **thrust** it **upon** them, when you force them to have it.

thud /θʌd/ *noun*: **thuds**
A **thud** is a dull sound like that of something heavy falling to the ground: *He could hear the thud of avalanches even though the mountain was nearly a mile away.* □ *The book fell to the floor with a thud.*

thug /θʌg/ *noun*: **thugs**
A **thug** is a violent and brutal man or criminal: *a gang of thugs.*

thumb /θʌm/ *noun; verb*
▷ ***noun***: **thumbs**
Your **thumb** is the short thick finger, set lower than and at a different angle from the other four fingers on your hand: *She held it gently between her thumb and forefinger.*
▷ ***verb***: **thumbs, thumbing, thumbed**
1 You **thumb** *eg* a book or magazine, or **thumb** through it, if you turn its pages over and glance at the words and pictures on them: *She thumbed through the guidebook, looking for a chapter on the churches in the town.* □ *a grimy, much-thumbed copy.* **2 a** You **thumb** a lift when you stand next to a road and signal with your thumb to passing drivers to show that you would like a free lift in the vehicle they are driving. **b** You **thumb** your way somewhere when you travel there by getting free lifts from drivers: *She managed to thumb her way right across France to Spain.* [*same as* **hitch-hike**]
▷ ***phrase***
1 If you say someone is **all thumbs**, you mean they are awkward and clumsy in performing manual tasks: *My hands were freezing and I was all thumbs as I tried to unlock the door.* **2** Someone **gives** you **the thumbs-up** when they express approval of your proposal and indicate that you may proceed with it; they **give** you **the thumbs-down** when they reject your proposal. **3** You are **under** someone's **thumb** if you are completely controlled or dominated by them.

thumbnail /'θʌmneɪl/ *noun; adjective*
▷ ***noun***: **thumbnails**
Your **thumbnails** are the nails on your thumbs.
▷ ***adjective***
A **thumbnail** sketch is one that is brief and concise.

thumbs-up /θʌmz'ʌp/ *noun* (*used in the singular*)
Someone gives you the **thumbs-up** when they express approval.

thump /θʌmp/ *verb; noun*
▷ ***verb***: **thumps, thumping, thumped**
1 One person **thumps** another if they hit them with heavy blows, *eg* with their hand: *He thumped me on the back.* **2** You **thump** something somewhere if you put it there with a heavy dull sound; something **thumps** somewhere if it moves there with a heavy dull sound: *She thumped the book down on the table.* □ *He thumped up the stairs.* □ *The shutters thumped backwards and forwards in the wind.* **3** You can say that your heart **is thumping** if it is beating strongly: *Her heart was thumping with terror.*
▷ ***noun***: **thumps**
1 A **thump** is a heavy blow, *eg* with the hand: *A good thump on the back should help him stop choking.* **2** A **thump** is also a dull sound, *eg* one caused by a heavy blow: *She could hear the thump of boots on the stairs.*

thunder /'θʌndə(r)/ *noun; verb*
▷ ***noun*** (*uncount*)
1 Thunder is a deep rumbling or loud cracking sound heard after a flash of lightning: *My children are afraid of thunder.* □ *a clap of thunder* □ *a storm with thunder and lightning.* **2** The **thunder** of something is the loud, deep, rumbling noise that it makes: *the thunder of hooves as the cavalry charged.*
▷ ***verb***: **thunders, thundering, thundered**
1 It is **thundering** when you can hear the deep rumbling or loud cracking sound that occurs just after a flash of lightning: *I don't like going out when it's thundering.* **2** Something **thunders** when it makes a loud rumbling noise while moving: *The tanks thundered over the bridge.* **3** Someone **thunders** when they say something in a loud, angry voice: *'How dare you speak to me like that!' he thundered.*

thunderbolt /'θʌndəboʊlt/ *noun*: **thunderbolts**
A **thunderbolt** is a flash of lightning immediately followed by thunder.

thundering /ˈθʌndərɪŋ/ *adjective* (*informal*)
Thundering means very great: *He's nothing but a thundering idiot.*

thunderous /ˈθʌndərəs/ *adjective*
A **thunderous** noise is loud and rumbling: *The audience broke into thunderous applause at the end of her song.*

thunderstorm /ˈθʌndəstɔːm/ *noun*: **thunderstorms**
A **thunderstorm** is a storm with thunder and lightning and usually heavy rain.

Thursday /ˈθɜːzdɪ/ *noun* (*count or uncount*): **Thursdays**
Thursday is the fourth day of the week, coming after Wednesday and before Friday: *I'll be leaving on Thursday.* □ *She usually goes shopping on a Thursday* (or *on Thursdays*). □ (*AmE*) *She doesn't work Thursdays.* □ *The meeting will be held this Thursday instead of next Thursday.* □ *Let's go on Thursday evening.*

thus /ðʌs/ *adverb* (*rather formal*)
You use **thus 1** (*sentence adverb*) in reference to something you have mentioned to mean 'as a result of that': *The research is incomplete; thus there are few conclusions we can draw at this stage.* □ *The viability of the schedule, and thus the likely completion date, still have to be determined.* □ *companies that are financially sound and thus good credit risks* □ *Alcoholic drink provides calories, giving energy and thus reducing the appetite.* [*same as* **therefore**] **2** in reference to something you have just described to mean 'in that manner': *Thus ended Mary's wedding day.* □ *The building remained thus, virtually unaltered, for about two centuries.* [compare **like** that] **3** to mean 'in the following way': *My problems may be explained thus.* [compare **like** this]

thwart /θwɔːt/ *verb*: **thwarts, thwarting, thwarted**
Someone or something **thwarts** you or your plans if they stop you from doing what you want to do: *Scotland's hopes of winning the match were thwarted by a goal scored in the closing minutes.* [*same as* **frustrate, hinder**; *opposite* **encourage**]

thyme /taɪm/ *noun* (*uncount*)
Thyme is a herb with tiny pale blue flowers and sweet-smelling leaves which are used to flavour food.

thyroid /ˈθaɪrɔɪd/ *noun*: **thyroids**
Your **thyroid**, or **thyroid gland**, is a large gland in your neck that produces hormones and helps regulate the body's energy levels.

tiara /tɪˈɑːrə/ *noun*: **tiaras**
A **tiara** is a piece of jewellery like a small crown that a woman may wear on formal occasions.

tick /tɪk/ *noun*; *verb*
▻ ***noun***: **ticks**
1 A **tick** is a small mark, usually a line with an acute angle at the bottom, used *eg* to show that something is correct or to mark off items on a list which have been dealt with: *There was a big red tick at the bottom of his essay.* [see also **check**] **2** A **tick** is a usually soft regular tapping or clicking sound, such as that made by a watch or clock: *a clock with a loud tick.* **3** (*BrE*; *informal*) A **tick** is a short time or a moment: *I'll be finished in two ticks.*
▻ ***verb***: **ticks, ticking, ticked**
1 You **tick** something if you put a mark on it to show that it is correct or that you dealt with it: *She ticked the items on her list as she bought them.* [see also **check**] **2** A clock or watch or mechanical instrument **ticks** when it makes a regular clicking or tapping sound: *A lot of modern watches don't actually tick.* □ *She could hear the safe mechanism ticking.*
▻ ***phrase*** (*informal*) You think about **what makes** someone **tick** if you think about their reasons for behaving, speaking and thinking in the way that they do: *I've never been able to work out what makes her tick.*

phrasal verbs
tick away or **tick by** Time **ticks away** or **ticks by** when it passes: *The hours ticked by and he still hadn't arrived.*
tick off **1** You **tick** items **off** when you put a written tick beside them to show they have been dealt with: *She ticked off each job as she finished it.* **2** (*informal*) You **tick** someone **off** if you speak angrily to them because they have done something wrong. [*same as* **scold**]
tick over A business, system, or engine **is ticking over** if it is operating, or continuing to operate, at a low level of activity or at the lowest possible speed: *We've got just enough work to keep us ticking over till Christmas.*

ticket /ˈtɪkɪt/ *noun*: **tickets**
1 A **ticket** is a printed piece of paper or card which shows that you have paid a fare, *eg* for travel on a bus or train or for admission to a theatre or cinema, or that you are allowed to use certain services, such as a library: *a return ticket to London* □ *a single ticket to Madrid* □ *a bus ticket* □ *a cinema ticket* □ *My season ticket expired at the end of last week.* □ *She renewed her annual library ticket.* [see also **season ticket**] **2** A **ticket** is also a label, especially one attached to an item of clothing, that shows its price and size: *What does it say on the ticket?*

tickle /ˈtɪkəl/ *verb*; *noun*
▻ ***verb***: **tickles, tickling, tickled**
1 You **tickle** someone if you touch part of their body lightly and so that they experience a tingling or light prickling feeling that makes them laugh: *I don't like people tickling my feet.* □ *Her hair was tickling her shoulder.* **2** Part of your body **tickles** if you feel a tingling or light prickling sensation there: *Something was making her nose tickle.* **3** (*informal*) Something such as a situation **tickles** you if you find it amusing: *The thought of them turning up for what they believed was a free meal really tickled him.*
▻ ***noun*** (*used in the singular*): *He gave my feet a tickle to wake me up.*

ticklish /ˈtɪklɪʃ/ *adjective*
1 You are **ticklish** if people can make you laugh by lightly touching part of your body; part of your body is **ticklish** if people can make you laugh by touching it lightly: *Don't touch my feet! They're ticklish.* **2** A **ticklish** problem is one that is difficult to deal with, or one that needs to be dealt with carefully: *The supervisor was landed with the ticklish task of asking him to take a shower before coming to work.*

tidal /ˈtaɪdəl/ *adjective*
Tidal refers to things that are affected by or depend on the tides: *The river is tidal for a mile before it reaches the sea.*

tidal wave /ˈtaɪdəl weɪv/ *noun*: **tidal waves**
A **tidal wave** is an enormous wave caused by the sea floor moving, that travels very quickly and causes a lot of destruction if it touches land.

tide /taɪd/ *noun*; *verb*
▻ ***noun***: **tides**
1 a (*count, often in the singular*) The **tide** is the regular rise and fall in the level of the sea caused by the pull of

the sun and moon: *The tide is going out.* □ *A sign on the beach saying 'No swimming. Dangerous tides.'* **b** (*uncount*) **Tide** refers to the particular level of the sea at a particular moment in time: *High tide is at 2 o'clock.* □ *low tide.* **2** (*usually in the singular*) The **tide** of *eg* opinion is the movement or change in people in general's view of something: *The tide of public opinion has turned against the monarchy recently.* **3** A **tide** of things is a large amount of them: *the rising tide of complaints against the press.*
▻ ***verb***: **tides, tiding, tided**

> ***phrasal verb***
> (*informal*) Something **tides** you **over** if it helps you to get through a difficult period: *I borrowed some money from my brother to tide me over till I can get to the bank.*

tidings /'taɪdɪŋz/ *noun* (*plural*; *old*)
You are given **tidings** of someone or something if someone gives you news of them.

tidy /'taɪdɪ/ *adjective*; *verb*
▻ ***adjective***: **tidier, tidiest**
1 Something is **tidy** when it is neat and every part of it is arranged in good or proper order: *a tidy desk.* [*opposite* **untidy**] **2** A **tidy** person arranges things in good or proper order and does not make a mess: *I wish my children were a bit tidier.* □ *She has a tidy mind.* [*opposite* **untidy**] **3** (*informal*) A **tidy** sum of money is a fairly large one: *He made a tidy profit on the sale of his house.* — *adverb* **tidily:** *She put the books away tidily on the shelves.*
▻ ***verb***: **tidies, tidying, tidied**
You **tidy** a place if you make it neat, or arrange the things in it neatly: *There'll be no television until you've tidied your room.*

> ***phrasal verbs***
> **tidy away** You **tidy** something **away** if you put it away neatly: *She tidied the clothes away in the cupboard.*
> **tidy up** You **tidy up** if you make a place neat, *eg* by putting things away in their proper place: *It took him a couple of hours to tidy up after the party.*

tie /taɪ/ *verb*; *noun*
▻ ***verb***: **ties, tying, tied**
1 You **tie** two things together, or **tie** one thing to another, when you attach or fasten the one to the other using something such as string or rope: *He left his dog tied to a drainpipe by the kitchen door.* □ *On the bank one of the men was tying the rope to a tree.* □ *She tied her boots together by the laces to make them easier to carry.* [*opposite* **untie**] **2** You **tie** something such as string round something, or **tie** something with *eg* string, when you put string round it and fasten the ends together in a knot or bow: *We were taught how to tie and address a parcel.* □ *She drew on her robe, tying it firmly at the waist.* □ *She had tied her hair back in a pony tail.* □ *The old remedy for a sore throat was to tie an old sock round your neck.* [*opposite* **untie**] **3** You **tie** something such as string or ribbon in a bow or knot, or **tie** a bow or knot in it, when you tie the ends together in a bow or knot: *We wore sashes tied in a bow at the back.* [*opposite* **untie**] **4** You **tie** something such as shoelaces or a tie when you form them into the proper kind of bow or knot: *She finished tying the bandage.* □ *skills such as riding a bicycle and tying your laces.* [*opposite* **untie**] **5** One person or thing **is tied** to another when they are linked, bound, or committed, to them in some way: *the emotional and mental link that ties the child to its mother* □ *In that way, you're tying the supplier to a legal contract.* **6** One competitor **ties** with another when they finish with an equal score or result: *Sandy Lyle and he tied for eighth place.* □ *He tied with Reg Coleman in the final.*
▻ ***noun***: **ties**
1 A **tie** is a narrow strip of material that is worn, especially by men as part of neat or formal dress, round the neck under a shirt collar, and tied in a knot or bow at the front: *Most of the candidates turned up in shirts and ties.* [see picture at **clothing**, see also **bow tie**] **2** A **tie** is a relationship that unites people, or a connection that links a person to a place: *We were bound together by close ties of friendship.* □ *The new boarding schools for girls had the effect of loosening family ties.* □ *Now that her parents had died, she had fewer ties with her native country.* [*same as* **bond**, **link**] **3** You regard something as a **tie** if you think it restricts you and limits your activities: *Pet animals are such a tie.* [*same as* **restriction**] **4** A **tie** in a competition is a result where two or more competitors achieve the same score, or are equally successful: *In the event of a tie for first place, the two winning teams will each perform their item again before the judges.* [compare **draw**]

> ***phrasal verbs***
> **tie down 1** Something **ties** you **down** if it restricts your freedom: *He didn't want to be tied down by family responsibilities.* **2** You **tie** someone **down** when you make them commit themselves to some engagement: *I'll try and tie her down for 8 March.*
> **tie in with** One thing **ties in with** another if it is connected with it or fits in with it: *The lecture will tie in with an exhibition of paintings to be shown at the same time.*
> **tie up 1** You **tie** something **up** when you tie string or rope round it: *I keep your letters tied up with a ribbon.* [*opposite* **untie**] **2** You **tie up** somewhere, or **tie** a boat **up** somewhere, when you fasten it with a rope to a fixed object on land: *We tied up at the quay.* □ *There was a barge tied up at the jetty.* **3** You **tie up** an animal such as a horse, goat or dog when you fasten it with a rope to a fixed object. [*opposite* **untie**] **4** Someone **ties** you **up** when they tie rope round you to stop you moving or escaping: *She was tied up to the bed.* [*opposite* **untie**] **5** You **tie up** your shoes or laces when you pull the laces tight and tie them: *He bent down and tied up his trainers.* [*opposite* **untie**] **6** (*often in the passive*) Money **is tied up** when it is reserved for a particular use and is not available for other purposes: *It's no good tying up money for years unless you're certain you won't need it.* **7** You **are tied up** when you are busy: *I'm going to be pretty tied up for the rest of the day.* **8** One thing **ties up** with, or **is tied up** with, another if it is connected with it, or fits in with it: *His interest in David Hume was tied up with his own atheism.* **9** Someone **is tied up** with something if they are involved in it: *The police obviously believe he's tied up with the murder.* **10** To **tie up** a matter is to settle it, solve it, or deal with it satisfactorily: *a few unsolved crimes that need tying up.*

tier /tɪə(r)/ *noun*: **tiers**
A **tier** is one of a series of layers or rows placed one above the other: *a theatre with several tiers of seats* □ *the first tier of the wedding cake.*

tiger /'taɪgə(r)/ *noun*: **tigers**
1 A **tiger** is **a** a very large wild cat with a striped, dark yellow coat, found in Asia. **b** the male of this species.

2 If you refer to a person as a **tiger** you mean that they are fierce and courageous.

tight /taɪt/ *adjective*; *adverb*

▻ ***adjective***: **tighter**, **tightest**

1 Tight clothing fits you closely; something that is **tight**, or too **tight**, fits too closely, and is uncomfortable: *teenagers in tight jeans* □ *The skirt's a bit on the tight side; I'll try on a larger size.* [*opposite* **loose**] **2** Something such as string or fabric is stretched **tight** when it has been stretched or pulled so that it is smooth or straight: *Their faces were gaunt, with the skin stretched tight over their cheekbones.* [*same as* **taut**] **3** A **tight** knot is so firmly tied that it is difficult to undo; something such as a lid or screw is **tight** if it is difficult to turn, unscrew, or undo. **4** Things or people are in a **tight** group when they are close together: *The children stood in a tight little circle round her.* **5 Tight** is used to describe things that are controlled firmly and carefully: *The company needs to keep a tight control on spending.* □ *She keeps a tight rein on her emotions.* **6** Money is **tight** if there isn't much of it and you have to take care how you spend it. **7** A **tight** match or contest is one which is closely fought by opponents who are evenly matched. **8** A **tight** schedule or plan does not allow for any time to be lost, or for any relaxation. **9** If you are in a **tight** spot, you are in a difficult situation: *She's always getting herself into tight spots; she just doesn't know when to keep quiet.* **10** If you have a **tight** feeling in part of your body, you feel stiff, sore or uncomfortable there, *eg* because you are nervous or worried or because you have strained a muscle: *She had a tight feeling in her chest that made breathing difficult.* **11** (*informal*) Someone who is **tight** is drunk. — *adverb* **tightly:** *She tied the parcel tightly.* □ *People were packed tightly together in cattle trucks.* □ *The skin was stretched tightly over his bones.* □ *a tightly controlled accounts system* □ *She clutched the letter tightly to her chest.* □ *He held the baby tightly.* □ *She kept her eyes tightly closed.* — *noun* (*uncount*) **tightness:** *She always gets a feeling of tightness in her stomach before exams.*

▻ ***adverb***

1 You hold someone or something **tight** when you hold them firmly, sometimes close to your body: *She put her arms around him and held him tight.* □ *He had the keys clutched tight in his hand.* [*same as* **tightly**] **2** Things that are shut **tight** are firmly closed: *She shut her eyes tight and tried to go to sleep.* [*same as* **tightly**] [see also **tights**, **airtight**, **watertight**]

tighten /ˈtaɪtən/ *verb*: **tightens**, **tightening**, **tightened**

1 You **tighten** your hold on something if you hold it more tightly or firmly: *She tightened her grip on the wheel.* **2** You **tighten** *eg* a rope, chain or piece of string if you pull it so that it is tight and not loose. **3** You **tighten** something that fastens something if you make it hold something more firmly: *He bent down and tightened his shoelaces.* □ *The string on this parcel needs tightening.* □ *This bolt is coming loose; it needs tightening up.* **4** You **tighten** a system if you make it stricter or more closely controlled: *The rules governing who qualifies for this benefit have been tightened up.*

tight-fisted /taɪtˈfɪstɪd/ *adjective*

Someone is **tight-fisted** if they are not prepared to spend or share their money. [*same as* **mean**, **miserly**, **stingy**]

tight-lipped /taɪtˈlɪpt/ *adjective*

You are **tight-lipped** about something if you are determined to say nothing about it.

tightrope /ˈtaɪtroʊp/ *noun*: **tightropes**

A **tightrope** is a length of rope or wire that is stretched tightly between two supports, on which an acrobat balances and performs tricks.

▻ ***phrase*** You can say that someone **is walking a tightrope** between two opposite extremes when they are trying to maintain a balance between the two but there is a high risk that they will fail: *market traders constantly walking a tightrope between substantial gains and massive losses.*

tights /taɪts/ *noun* (*plural*)

Tights are, or a pair of **tights** is, a close-fitting nylon or woollen garment that covers the feet, legs and body to the waist, worn by women and dancers: *She's got a ladder in her tights.* [see picture at **clothing**]

tigress /ˈtaɪgrɪs/ *noun*: **tigresses**

1 A **tigress** is a female tiger. **2** If a woman is referred to as a **tigress** she is fierce and courageous, especially in fighting to protect her family or her principles.

tile /taɪl/ *noun*: **tiles**

A **tile** is a thin, flat, usually square piece of *eg* clay or cork, used to cover *eg* roofs, floors or walls: *a house with red tiles on the roof* □ *carpet tiles.*

tiled /ˈtaɪld/ *adjective*

Something such as a roof, floor or wall is **tiled** if it is covered with tiles.

till[1] /tɪl/ *preposition or conjunction*

1 Something that happens **till** a certain time, or **till** a certain thing happens, goes on happening up to that point, then stops: *They've got a summer sale on till the end of June.* □ *I'll work from morning till night if necessary.* □ *He kept the smile on his face till she had closed the door.* □ *The building was in use till fairly recently.* [*same as* **until**] **2** (*often with a negative*) Something that does not happen **till** a certain time, or **till** a certain thing happens, happens at that time or point, but not before; you wait **till** a certain time for something to happen if it does not happen before then: *The baby's not due till next month.* □ *It wasn't till he was safely installed in his seat in the aircraft that he began to relax.* □ *I could hardly wait till Friday, when I'd be seeing him again.* [*same as* **until**]

till[2] /tɪl/ *noun*: **tills**

A **till** is a drawer or container where money taken from customers in a shop, restaurant or bar is put.

tilt /tɪlt/ *verb*: **tilts**, **tilting**, **tilted**

You **tilt** an object if you put it into a position so that one side or end is higher than the other: *She tilted the bottle and a few drops of water trickled out.* □ *He was sitting slumped in his chair, with his head tilting forwards.* [*same as* **slope**]

timber /ˈtɪmbə(r)/ *noun*: **timbers**

1 (*uncount*) **Timber** is wood, especially wood that has been prepared for building or carpentry. **2** The **timbers** in *eg* a building or ship are the heavy wooden beams that form its frame.

time /taɪm/ *noun*; *verb*

▻ ***noun***: **times**

1 (*uncount*) **Time** is the medium that continually passes, and that we measure in *eg* minutes, hours, days, months and years: *Conditions improved as time passed.* □ *When you have a high fever you seem to lose all sense of time.* □ *It happened twice in a short period of time.*

2 Time is used to refer to **a** a particular point in time that can be expressed in hours and minutes, and read from a clock: *It was difficult to tell what time of day it was.* □ *What time does your train arrive?* □ *We'd better check the times of the buses.* □ *the starting and finishing times of the exams* □ *It was daylight by the time we reached the summit.* □ *What time is it?* □ *The time is now eleven forty-five.* □ *What time does your watch say?*

□ *What time did he leave?* □ *I'll stay here till it's time for the evening performance.*

> You can express and write the time in a variety of ways: *12.00 am* (or *twelve, twelve o'clock, twelve in the morning, twelve noon, midday*); *12.00 pm* (or *twelve, twelve o'clock, twelve at night, midnight*); *10.15* (or *a quarter past ten, quarter past ten, ten fifteen,* (*AmE*) *a quarter after ten*); *3.20* (or *twenty past three, twenty minutes past three, three twenty,* (*AmE*) *twenty after three*); *9.30* (or *half past nine, nine thirty, half nine,* (*AmE*) *half after nine*); *12.45* (or *a quarter to one, quarter to one, twelve forty-five,* (*AmE*) *a quarter of one*); *2.55* (or *five to three, five minutes to three, two fifty-five,* (*AmE*) *five of three*).

b (*uncount*) the official system for calculating time in any particular part of the world: *Greenwich Mean Time* □ *You will arrive in Prague at 10.30 local time.* **c** (*uncount or used in the singular*) the period or length of time that is spent doing something, or that is available for some activity: *In tutorials we spend a lot of time just talking.* □ *They spent a lot of time together.* [= they met often] □ *During a lecture you have no time to decide on the relative importance of the things you are being told.* □ *all the things I wish I could find time to do* □ *He now has time for his garden, and time to play with his grand-daughter.* □ *Set aside time for preparing the meal.* □ *Certain checking procedures had to be abandoned because of lack of time.* □ *It may take a long time to win their confidence.* □ *Surely it's a waste of time discussing this?* □ *We're running out of time.* □ *I need some time to myself.* □ *So you were by yourself in the house all that time?*

3 You use **times** and **time** to refer to **a** (*often in the plural*) a period characterized by particular experiences or events: *It was a reminder of less happy times.* □ *We talked about old times.* □ *There were good times and bad times.* □ *in times of crisis* □ *He's been through an unhappy time recently.* □ *Have a good time!* [= enjoy yourself] **b** (*often in the plural*) a period of history: *during medieval times* □ *since pre-industrial times* □ *traditions that have lasted down to modern times* □ *in the time of King James I.* **c** (*used in the plural*) the present period, or present circumstances or conditions: *We live in dangerous times.* □ *Times are changing.* □ *You should try to keep up with the times more.* □ *It had been a tough year, and times were tight.*

4 a A **time** when something happens is an occasion, or point in time, when it does: *at the time of her marriage* □ *They tried to contact us when they were over, but unfortunately we were away at the time.* □ *We might need his help some time.* □ *There were times when he regretted not having a wife and family.* □ *Disaster could strike at any time.* □ *Call me next time you need a lift anywhere.* □ *I'd have been pleased to see him at any other time.* □ *The last time I saw him he was drunk.* □ *It was the only time I ever saw Anderson close to tears.* □ *You take a risk every time you cross the road.* □ *This time you'll have to go on your own.* **b** (*uncount or used in the singular*) It is **time**, or the right **time**, to do something when it would be the suitable or right thing to do: *Isn't it time you were getting married?* □ *It's time we went home.* □ *This is not the time for quarrelling amongst ourselves.* □ *I think it's time for a party.* □ *It was time to confess the truth.* **c** You often use **-time** to indicate the period around a particular event, festival or time of year: *He'll be home at Christmastime.* □ *visit Greece in the springtime* □ (*informal*) *We'll expect you back about marchtime, then.*

5 (*used in the plural*) **a** The number of **times** you do something is the number of occasions on which you do it; something happens a certain number of **times** a day or year if it happens on that number of occasions each day or year: *She had phoned a dozen times, without success.* □ *He married three times.* □ *He wrote several times a week.* □ *Take one tablespoonful three times a day.* **b** One thing is a certain number of **times** greater than, or as great as, another if it is equal to the other multiplied by that number: *Sound travels nearly five times as fast in water as in air.* □ *The incidence of the disease here is many times higher than the national average.* □ *I earn four times what I did when I started in this job.* **c** You can use **times** to mean 'multiplied by': *Three times eight is twenty-four.* [$= 3 \times 8 = 24$]

> Notice that you usually say *twice* rather than *two times*: *If you get a garage to do the repairs you'll pay three times what I'd charge you.* But: *It'll be twice as expensive to go to a garage. She tried his number twice. Twice* (or *two times*) *six is twelve.*

6 (*uncount; music*) A piece of music is in *eg* four **time** if it has four beats to the bar; it is in *eg* waltz **time** if it is in waltz rhythm. **7** (*uncount*) 'Half **time**', and '**time**', or 'full **time**', are the middle and the end of *eg* a football match or similar event.

▻ ***verb*: times, timing, timed**

1 You **time** an event when you measure the amount of time it takes: *I taped my speech and timed it.* □ *Could you time me running once round the track?* **2** You **time** an event for a particular time when you plan that it will happen at that time: *A number of cultural events had been timed to coincide with the opening celebrations.* **3** Something said or done is well **timed** if it occurs when it can be most effective; it is badly **timed** if it occurs when it can cause most difficulty or damage: *The controversy could not have been worse timed for the Prime Minister.* □ *You've timed your request well.* [see also **well-timed**]

▻ ***phrases*** **1** If you say it's **about time** something was done, you mean that it ought to be done; people say '**and about time**' or '**about time, too**' when something that ought to have been done earlier has at last been done: *It's about time they mended this pavement.* **2 a** Something happens **ahead of time** if it happens before it is scheduled to happen: *The plane had landed five minutes ahead of time.* **b** Someone such as an artist or sociologist who is **ahead of their time** has ideas that other people don't understand the importance of until much later. **3** If you say that something will be dealt with **all in good time** you mean that it will certainly be dealt with, though not immediately. **4 a** (*informal*) Something that happens **all the time** or **the whole time** happens frequently: *You're so busy the whole time.* □ *Why do you have to criticize me all the time?* [compare **always**] **b** Something that was so **all the time** was so even though no-one realized it: *So you were right all the time.* **5** Something that is expected **any time now** is likely to arrive or happen very soon. **6** Something that involves one, or a certain number of, people or things **at a time** involves them one after the other, or in groups of that number: *Only one editor at a time may work on the networked text.* □ *He leapt up the stairs three at a time.* □ *She was often abroad for weeks at a time.* **7** Something that may be the case **at any one time** is a possibility at any particular unspecified time: *At any one time there may be up to forty patients in the waiting room.* **8** Something that was so **at one time** was so in the past: *You kept hens at one time, didn't you?* **9** Something that is not good **at the best of times** is normally bad: *He was not an easy man to deal with at the best of times.* **10 a** You do two or more things **at the same time** if you do them both together, or all together: *It's difficult to whistle and sing at the same time.* [compare **at once**] **b** You use '**at the same time**' to mean 'however', when making a point that contrasts with something that has just been said: *At the same time, he ought not to have taken the risk.* [*same as* **however**] **11** Something that happens **at times** happens occasionally: *You must have been lonely at times?* [*same as* **sometimes**] **12** Something or someone that was **before your time** existed or happened before you were born: *Clark Gable was a bit before my time.* **13** Someone who is **behind the times** has old-fashioned attitudes. **14** Something happens **for the first time** if it has never happened before; something happens **for the last time** if it never happens again afterwards: *when you're in love for the first time* □ *I realized I was probably seeing him for the last time.* **15 For the time being** refers to present circumstances, with the suggestion that a change will be needed soon: *Continue taking these pills for the time being.* [*same as* **for the moment**] **16** Something that happens **from time to time** happens occasionally: *He would send us a postcard from time to time.* [*same as* **occasionally, now and again, now and then**] **17** You **have no time for** someone or something if you dislike them or disapprove of them: *I've little time for people who won't try.* **18** You say it is **high time** a certain thing was done if you think it ought to be done now: *It's high time they put a pedestrian crossing on this road.* **19** Something that is going to happen **in** *eg* **a month's time** is going to happen after one month: *I'm meeting her for lunch in five days' time.* **20** You arrive **in good time** for an event if you arrive well before it is due to start. **21** You are **in time** for something if you arrive early enough to have it or take part in it: *You've arrived just in time for lunch.* [*opposite* **too late**] **22** A clock or watch that **keeps good time** is accurate: *My watch was keeping perfect time till recently.* **23** You **make good time** on a journey if you reach places more quickly than you expect to: *We made good time as far as Oxford, and then got held up by roadworks.* **24** Something that takes **no time**, or **no time at all**, is done very quickly: *Could you wait a second? I'll be finished in no time.* **25** You do something for **old times' sake** when do it because of its associations with happy times in the past. **26 'Once upon a time'** means 'at a time in the past', and is the traditional way of beginning a children's story. **27** Something happens **on time** if it happens at the scheduled time: *The lecture began on time.* [*opposite* **late**] **28** You do something to **pass the time** if you do it while waiting for something else to happen, or because you are bored and have nothing else to do: *She went into the National Gallery to pass the time till her lecture.* **29** Something that **takes time** happens slowly or gradually: *It will take time for the scars to heal.* **30** You **take time out** to do something when you take a break, *eg* from your work, to do it: *Even when I was working for my PhD I would take time out to go to the cinema occasionally.* **31** You **take your time** doing something if you do it slowly, or only eventually: *You took your time coming to see me.* **32** Children learn to **tell the time** when they learn how to work out what time a clock or watch is showing. **33** Something that happens **time after time**, or **time and again**, or **time and time again** happens often or repeatedly: *Time after time ministers have tried to shift the blame for unemployment on to the downturn in the the economy.* **34** If someone says to you **'time's up'**, or **'your time's up'**, they mean that the time allowed for something, *eg* answering a question in a quiz, is finished. **35** If you say **'time will tell'** you mean that it will not be known for some time whether things are working out as you expect or want.

time-honoured /'taɪm ɒnərd/ *adjective*
A **time-honoured** tradition or practice is one that has been used or followed for a long time and is therefore respected.

timeless /'taɪmləs/ *adjective*
Something is **timeless** if its beauty, quality or value is not affected or lessened by the passage of time: *His novels are timeless.*

time limit /'taɪm lɪmɪt/ *noun*: **time limits**
A **time limit** is a fixed length of time during which something must be done and finished: *No time limit has been set for this project.*

timely /'taɪmlɪ/ *adjective*
Something is **timely** if it happens or arrives at the right time or at a suitable moment: *the timely arrival of reinforcements.*

time out /taɪm 'aʊt/ *noun*
▻ ***phrase*** You **take time out** to do something if you take a break from something else such as work to do it: *She took time out from her studies to go to the cinema once a week.*

timer /'taɪmə(r)/ *noun*: **timers**
A **timer** is an instrument like a clock that switches a machine on or off at set times: *The timer turns the heating on at 5 o'clock.*

time scale /'taɪm skeɪl/ *noun*: **time scales**
The **time scale** for an event or process is the period of time over which it happens or its various stages happen: *The creation of the universe took place over a much longer timescale than the six days recorded in the Old Testament.*

timetable /'taɪmteɪbəl/ *noun*: **timetables**
A **timetable** is **1** a list of the departure and arrival times of *eg* trains, coaches, buses and aircraft. **2** a plan that shows when certain things should be done, especially the order of classes in a school.

time zone /'taɪm zoʊn/ *noun*: **time zones**
A **time zone** is any one of the 24 sections that the world is divided into and in each of which one standard time is used.

timid /'tɪmɪd/ *adjective*
A **timid** person or animal is shy and easily frightened or alarmed: *a timid little boy* □ *a timid smile.* [*same as* **nervous**; *opposite* **confident**] — *adverb* **timidly:** *She smiled timidly.*

timing /'taɪmɪŋ/ *noun* (*uncount*)
1 A person's **timing** is their ability to know when to do or say something so as to achieve the best possible effect, or get the most advantage: *The performers on the whole display excellent comic timing.* □ *Your timing is perfect; I was just going to serve lunch; I trust you'd like some?* **2** The **timing** of an event is the act of deciding how long it should last and when it should take place: *The timing of the election is crucial to the government.*

tin /tɪn/ *noun*: **tins**
1 (*uncount*) **Tin** is a soft, silver-white metal, used to coat other metals, and in alloys: *This kettle is made out of stainless steel, not tin.* □ *tin cans.* **2** A **tin** is a metal container with a lid for storing food such as biscuits and cakes: *a cake tin* □ *a tin of chocolate biscuits.* **3** A **tin** of food is a metal container in which food is sealed to keep it fresh for long periods: *I'll open a tin of baked beans.* [*same as* **can**]

tincture /'tɪŋktʃə(r)/ *noun*: **tinctures**
A **tincture** of something is a slight flavour or trace of it. [*same as* **tinge**]

tinder /'tɪndə(r)/ *noun* (*uncount*)

Tinder is dry material, especially wood, which is used to light fires.

tinge /tɪndʒ/ *noun* (*usually in the singular*): **tinges**
A **tinge** of *eg* colour or of a quality or feeling is a slight amount of it: *a slight pink tinge in the evening sky* ▫ *There was a tinge of sadness in her voice.* [*same as* **hint**]

tinged /ˈtɪndʒd/ *adjective*
Something is **tinged** with *eg* a colour or feeling when there is a slight amount of it in it: *Her eyes were tinged with red where she had been crying.*

tingle /ˈtɪŋgəl/ *verb*: **tingles, tingling, tingled**
1 Part of your body **tingles** when you can feel a prickling or slightly stinging sensation there: *The cold salty air made the skin on her face tingle.* **2** You **tingle** with *eg* excitement when you seem to feel it in every nerve of your body.

tinker /ˈtɪŋkə(r)/ *verb* (*informal*): **tinkers, tinkering, tinkered**
You **tinker** with *eg* a machine if you make a lot of small or unimportant changes to it, usually to try to improve it: *He spent the whole morning tinkering with the engine of his motorbike.*

tinkle /ˈtɪŋkəl/ *verb*; *noun*
▻ ***verb***: **tinkles, tinkling, tinkled**
Something **tinkles** if it makes a sound like small bells ringing: *Ice cubes tinkled in the jugs of lemonade as she carried them into the garden.*
▻ ***noun***: **tinkles**
A **tinkle** is a ringing sound: *The doorbell gave a tinkle.*
▻ ***phrase*** (*informal*) You **give** someone **a tinkle** if you contact them by telephone.

tinned /ˈtɪnd/ *adjective*
Tinned food is preserved in tins: *tinned soup.*

tinny /ˈtɪnɪ/ *adjective*: **tinnier, tinniest**
1 A **tinny** sound is high-pitched and unpleasant as if it was passing through thin metal: *a tinny computer-generated voice.* **2** Something is **tinny** if it is made of thin or poor quality metal: *his tinny old car.* [*same as* **flimsy**]

tin-opener /ˈtɪnoupənə(r)/ *noun*: **tin-openers**
A **tin-opener** is a small tool for opening tins of food. [see picture at **kitchen**]

tinsel /ˈtɪnsəl/ *noun* (*uncount*)
Tinsel is long strips of shiny coloured metal or plastic threads used as a decoration especially at Christmas.

tint /tɪnt/ *noun*; *verb*
▻ ***noun***: **tints**
1 A **tint** is colour, especially one that is a slightly different shade of another, or one that has been made softer by adding white: *She has a bluish tint in the white part of her eyes.* **2** A **tint** is also a hair dye that eventually washes out.
▻ ***verb***: **tints, tinting, tinted**
You **tint** something if you colour it slightly; you **tint** your hair if you colour it with a tint.

tiny /ˈtaɪnɪ/ *adjective*: **tinier, tiniest**
Something is **tiny** when it is very small: *a baby's tiny hands and feet* ▫ *Her handwriting is so tiny, you can barely read it.* ▫ *The Conservatives won the election by the tiniest margin.* [*same as* **minute**[2]; *opposite* **big, large**]

tip[1] /tɪp/ *noun*: **tips**
The **tip** of something long and narrow is its end, or a small cover fitted over the end: *arrows with poison tips* ▫ *He drew out a cigar, bit off its tip, and lit it.* ▫ *She kissed him on the tip of his nose.* ▫ *He traced the line of the scar with the tip of his index finger.* ▫ *The dog was covered in mud from its nose to the tip of its tail.* [see also **fingertip**, compare **point**]
▻ ***phrase***
1 a Something is **on the tip of your tongue** when you are about to say it but decide not to: *It was on the tip of her tongue to say she'd rather have dinner with a snake, but she stopped herself.* **b** Something such as a name is **on the tip of your tongue** when although you know it you can't quite remember it. **2** For **tip of the iceberg** see **iceberg**.

tip[2] /tɪp/ *verb*; *noun*
▻ ***verb***: **tips, tipping, tipped**
1 You **tip** an object in some direction, or **tip** it up, when you make it lean away from the upright or level position: *He tipped back his stool.* ▫ *The chairs were tipped forward against the tables.* ▫ *I grasped the heavy jug and tipped it up carefully.* ▫ *He tipped his hat over his eyes.* **2** You **tip** things somewhere when you make them slide from a container so that they fall there: *She tipped some chocolate raisins into my hand.* ▫ *They just tip the rubbish over the side of the ship.* ▫ *She tipped the contents of her toy box on to the floor.* [*same as* **pour**]
▻ ***noun***: **tips**
1 A **tip** is **a** a place where rubbish is dumped: *The beach had been used by the locals as a rubbish tip.* [*same as* **dump**] **b** a heap of something such as coal or mining waste. **2** (*used in the singular*; *informal*) Any very untidy place can also be described as a **tip**: *His bedroom was always a tip.*

> ***phrasal verb***
> **tip out** You **tip out** a container, or **tip out** its contents, when you turn it over so that its contents slide or fall out: *Our travel bags were tipped out by the customs officer.* ▫ *The sergeant tipped the contents of her handbag out on to the counter.*
> **tip over** You **tip** something **over** when you make it fall over or turn over; something **tips** over when it leans over or falls over: *The rowing boat tipped over.* [*same as* **overturn, upset**]

tip[3] /tɪp/ *noun*; *verb*
▻ ***noun***: **tips**
1 You give people such as waiters, taxi-drivers or hairdressers a **tip** when you give them a small sum of money to thank them for the service they have performed: *The service was excellent and I left a large tip.* **2** You also give someone a **tip** when you give them a useful piece of advice: *Another useful tip is to cut up parsley or mint with scissors, in a cup.*
▻ ***verb***: **tips, tipping, tipped:** *We'd better tip the waiter a couple of pounds.* ▫ *Don't tip unless for some unusual or special service.* ▫ *The French always tip very generously.*

> ***phrasal verb***
> **tip off** (*informal*) Someone **tips** you **off** about something that has happened or is going to happen when they tell you privately or secretly about it: *George, they aren't going to find out a thing if we don't tip them off.* ▫ *A man was brought in for questioning after a neighbour became suspicious and tipped off the police.* [see also **tip-off**]

tip-off /ˈtɪpɒf/ *noun* (*informal*): **tip-offs**
Someone gives you a **tip-off** about something that has happened or is going to happen when they tell you or warn you about it secretly: *The police had had an anonymous tip-off that the gang were planning to rob the bank.* [see also **tip off** at **tip**[3]]

tipple /ˈtɪpəl/ *noun* (*informal*): **tipples**
A person's **tipple** is their favourite alcoholic drink: *Whisky and soda is his favourite tipple.*

tipsy /ˈtɪpsɪ/ *adjective* (*informal*): **tipsier, tipsiest**
A person is **tipsy** if they are slightly drunk: *The sherry in the trifle had made her tipsy.*

tiptoe /ˈtɪptoʊ/ *verb*: **tiptoes, tiptoeing, tiptoed**
You **tiptoe** somewhere if you walk there very quietly on the tips of your toes: *She tiptoed out of the room so as not to wake the baby.*
▻ ***phrase*** You walk somewhere **on tiptoe** when you walk on the tips of your toes so as not to make any noise; you stand **on tiptoe** when you stand on the tips of your toes to make yourself as tall as possible: *I can only reach the top shelf if I stand on tiptoe.*

tirade /taɪˈreɪd/ *noun* (*formal*): **tirades**
A **tirade** is a long angry speech that criticizes a person or thing: *a long tirade against government policy.*

tire[1] /taɪə(r)/ *verb*: **tires, tiring, tired**
1 Something **tires** you, or **tires** you out, if it makes you tired and in need of rest. **2** You **tire** of something when you begin to lose patience with it or become bored with it: *I'm beginning to tire of his constant criticism and complaints.*

tire[2] see **tyre**.

tired /taɪəd/ *adjective*
1 You are **tired** when you have been very busy with something and need to rest or sleep: *Come and sit down by the fire; you must be tired after your long journey.* ▫ *I don't want to go for a walk; I'm too tired.* [compare **exhausted**] **2** Something such as your eyes or voice is **tired** when it shows that you need to rest or sleep: *'Please come and help me,' she said in a tired voice.* **3** You are **tired** of something when you aren't interested in it any more or are bored with it: *I'm tired of wearing the same old clothes every day.* — *adverb* **tiredly:** *She smiled tiredly.* — *noun* (*uncount*) **tiredness:** *A good night's sleep will help me get over my tiredness.* [*same as* **exhaustion**]

tireless /ˈtaɪələs/ *adjective*
A **tireless** person works hard and never seems to get tired or to need rest: *She's been a tireless worker for the charity.*

tiresome /ˈtaɪəsəm/ *adjective*
A **tiresome** person or thing makes you feel annoyed or bored. [*same as* **irritating, tedious**]

tiring /ˈtaɪərɪŋ/ *adjective*
Something is **tiring** if it makes you feel tired and need rest or sleep: *a tiring journey from Madrid to Paris* ▫ *a tiring day at work.*

tissue /ˈtɪʃuː/ or /ˈtɪsjuː/ *noun*: **tissues**
1 (*uncount*) **Tissue** is a group of cells with a similar structure that have a particular function in an animal or plant: *muscle tissue.* **2** A **tissue** is a piece of thin, soft paper used as a handkerchief, that you throw away after use: *a box of tissues.* **3** (*uncount*) **Tissue**, or **tissue paper**, is fine, thin, soft paper, used *eg* for protecting fragile objects: *She wrapped the china cups in tissue paper before packing them in the box.*
▻ ***phrase*** A story that someone tells, especially an elaborate or complicated one, is **a tissue of lies** if it is completely false.

titbit /ˈtɪtbɪt/ *noun*: **titbits**
1 A **titbit** is a small tasty piece of food: *Avoid giving your dog too many titbits; he will get fat.* **2** A **titbit** is also a small but interesting piece of gossip: *Her column always includes some fascinating titbits about the stars.*

titillate /ˈtɪtɪleɪt/ *verb*: **titillates, titillating, titillated**
Something **titillates** someone if it excites them, especially in a sexual way: *newspaper pictures that titillate the reader.*

title /ˈtaɪtəl/ *noun*: **titles**
1 The **title** of *eg* a book, play, piece of music or work of art is its name: *What's the title of her new novel?* **2** A **title** is also an often descriptive heading, *eg* of a chapter in a book or a legal document. **3** A person's **title** is **a** a word used before their name, such as 'Doctor', 'Lord' or 'Lady'. **b** a word that describes the job they do or their position in an organization: *Her title is 'Personnel Director'.* **4** (*sport*) A **title** is the position of champion: *Agassi beat Sampras to take the title.* [*same as* **championship**]

titled /ˈtaɪtəld/ *adjective*
A **titled** person has a title that shows they have a high social rank, such as 'Lord', 'Lady', 'Duke' and 'Duchess'.

title role /ˈtaɪtəl roʊl/ *noun*: **title roles**
The **title role** in a play or film is the character that gives the play or film its name, *eg* 'King Lear'.

titter /ˈtɪtə(r)/ *verb*: **titters, tittering, tittered**
A person **titters** when they laugh in a silly, nervous or embarrassed way. [*same as* **giggle, snigger**]

titular /ˈtɪtʃʊlə(r)/ *adjective*
Titular means having the title of an office without its authority or duties: *The Queen is Australia's titular head of state.*

to /tuː/ or /tə/ *preposition*; *adverb*
▻ ***preposition***
1 You use **to** for expressing **a** movement in the direction of something: *Which is the quickest way to Dundee from here?* ▫ *We got to the summit late in the afternoon.* ▫ *Just let me move these books to one side.* ▫ *I'm off to bed now.* ▫ *She's gone round to Sarah's.* ▫ *Are you going to her party?* ▫ *We're invited to the wedding.* **b** the action or circumstance of facing or pointing in some direction: *'That's him,' she said, pointing to a bearded man in the corner.* ▫ *She was sitting on the floor with her back to the fire.* **c** the position of something from where you are: *To the east the sky was already getting lighter.* ▫ *Havelock Road is the first turning to the right.* ▫ *To your left is a modern sculpture of Poseidon.* [compare **on**] **d** contact or close connection: *He tied the dog to a lamp post.* ▫ *Pin the pattern pieces to the fabric.* ▫ *The glue stuck to my fingers.* ▫ *She put the whistle to her lips.*
2 You use **to** in expressing **a** progress in the direction of some state or situation: *Disorganization can only lead to disaster.* ▫ *her sudden rise to fame.* **b** the result of some action or process: *He rocked the baby to sleep.* ▫ *The man had been battered to death with a club.* **c** change into another state: *The water turned to ice.* **d** the reaction or response that something produces in you: *To my embarrassment he began to cry.* ▫ *We hope the arrangements are to your satisfaction.* **e** the effect that doing something has on you: *Selling now would not be to your advantage.*
3 You use **to a** in telling the time, or specifying a time: *It's twenty minutes to six.* ▫ *He's coming at quarter to eight.* **b** in specifying an extent or range in terms of where it begins and ends: *We serve breakfast from eight to ten.* ▫ *The deadline has been extended to the end of March.* ▫ *There's only a fortnight to the exam.* ▫ *He bears the scars to this day.* ▫ *The road is under repair all the way from Soutra to Carfraemill.* ▫ *The job will take from eight to twelve weeks.* ▫ *people aged from 40 to 60* ▫ *We'll undertake any work, from cleaning your car to painting your house.* [compare **till**] **c** for

expressing proportion, *eg* in scores: *At half time we were winning by two goals to one.* **d** for expressing rate: *How many Singapore dollars are there to a pound?* □ *Our calculations were based on five glasses of wine to the bottle.*
4 You can use **to a** in expressions of giving, informing and communicating, often where an indirect object is also possible: *Could you give this envelope to Jack?* (or *give Jack this envelope*) □ *I'll send the photos back to you.* (or *send you back the photos*) □ *I still haven't written to Shirley.* □ *Did you get any response to your query?* □ *I saw her talking to George in the lobby.* □ *lecturing to an audience of students.* **b** with many verbs, adjectives and nouns expressing relationships of various kinds: *Add 25 to 36.* □ *How did he react to the news?* □ *I object to that.* □ *I've agreed to the proposal.* □ *He listened to the tape again.* □ *I'd better attend to those letters.* □ *Who were you referring to?* □ *Does this belong to you?* □ *I'm glad I'm not married to him.* □ *Where's the key to the cellar?* □ *There's apparently no solution to the problem.* □ *They've made some alterations to the timetable.* □ *She was secretary to five successive managing directors.* □ *Can't you be a bit nicer to Gerry?*
5 You do something **to** music or **to** a particular noise when that music or noise accompanies what you do: *The owl sang to a small guitar.* □ *They came out on the balcony to the cheers of the waiting crowd.*
▻ ***adverb***
1 You pull a door **to** when you close it but do not shut it completely. **2** You come **to** when you regain consciousness: *He came to a few minutes later.*
▻ ***phrases*** **1** You **have** somewhere **to yourself** when you are the only person there: *I've got the house to myself this weekend.* **2** You say, about some situation or process, **there's nothing to it**, or **that's all there is to it**, to emphasize how simple or easy it is. **3** For **to and fro** see **fro**. **4** For **up to** see **up**.
▻ ***to + infinitive***
To is used before the infinitive form of a verb
1 after certain verbs, adjectives and nouns: *We used to go every weekend.* □ *We promised to join them later.* □ *I was invited to address them.* □ *I ought to have been prepared.* □ *I pretended not to hear.* □ *I expect to finish soon.* □ *I hope to have completed it by June.* □ *I'll be happy to entertain them.* □ *He's coming to stay soon.* □ *It's time to go to bed.* **2** in place of the infinitive and what follows it, as a way of avoiding repetition: *I asked him to come for a walk but he didn't want to.* □ *'You couldn't give me lift, could you?' 'I'd be delighted to.'* **3** for expressing purpose or intention: *I got the bus into town to do some shopping.* [see also **in order to** at **order**, **so as to** at **so**] **4** for saying how you want your comment to be understood: *To put it simply, the bill will mean more respect for women.* □ *To be fair to her, she did try to warn us.* **5** instead of a 'report' clause, after certain verbs: *the evening on which the attack is asserted to have taken place* □ *I estimate the distance to be about 35 kilometres.* □ *He was discovered to be allergic to wheat.* **6** after words such as *enough* and *too*: *They're too stupid to know the difference.* □ *I'm hungry enough to eat a camel.* **7** after question words in indirect speech: *I've no idea what to pack.* □ *Can you tell me how to do it?* **8** with the verb *be* in referring to intentions, chance or fate: *Bill's to be in Singapore next week.* □ *As it happened, I was to meet her again the very next day.* □ *You'll have to speak a bit louder if the people at the back are to hear.* [= if you want them to hear] **9** in certain other kinds of constructions: *Give the kids plenty to keep them occupied.* □ *It'll take me a year to pay the money back.* □ *The creatures were delightful to watch.* □ *Jim was the first to break the silence.* □ *I'm sorry to cause extra work.* □ *The effect of her remark was to make everyone feel awkward.* □ *I woke up to find myself in unfamiliar surroundings.*

toad /toʊd/ *noun*: **toads**
A **toad** is a frog-like creature with a dry skin, that lives on land and breeds in water.

toadstool /'toʊdstuːl/ *noun*: **toadstools**
A **toadstool** is one of several kinds of fungi that look like mushrooms but are often poisonous.

toast /toʊst/ *verb*; *noun*
▻ ***verb***: **toasts, toasting, toasted**
1 You **toast** bread when you make it brown and crisp by exposing it to direct heat, *eg* under a grill or in a toaster. **2** You **toast** part of your body when you make it warm by exposing it to heat, *eg* by sitting in front of a fire: *She toasted her toes by the fire.* **3** You **toast** someone when you wish them good luck, good health or success in the future and take a sip of a usually alcoholic drink: *Everyone raised their glasses to toast the bride and groom.* □ *They toasted her in orange juice and lemonade.*
▻ ***noun***: **toasts**
1 (*uncount*) **Toast** is bread which has been made brown and crisp by being exposed to direct heat, *eg* under a grill or in a toaster: *She had toast and marmalade for breakfast.* **2** You drink a **toast** to someone when you wish them good luck, good health or success in the future and then take a sip of a usually alcoholic drink: *I'd like you all to join me in drinking a toast to the bride and groom.* **3** (*usually in the singular*) A person or thing is the **toast** of a place when they are very admired there: *Her singing is the toast of the festival.*

toaster /'toʊstə(r)/ *noun*: **toasters**
A **toaster** is an electric, box-shaped machine with slots in the top for holding slices of bread, used for turning bread into toast. [see picture at **kitchen**]

tobacco /tə'bakoʊ/ *noun* (*uncount*)
Tobacco is **1** the leaves from a plant that are dried and rubbed, and that can be smoked in a pipe, made into cigarettes, or made into blocks to chew: *pipe tobacco* □ *He bought some more tobacco.* **2** the plant that these leaves come from.

tobacconist /tə'bakənɪst/ *noun*: **tobacconists**
A **tobacconist** or **tobacconist's** is a shop that sells tobacco, cigarettes, cigars and pipes, and sometimes sweets and newspapers.

toboggan /tə'bɒgən/ *noun*: **toboggans**
A **toboggan** is a long, light sledge which curves up at the front, used for riding over snow and ice. — *noun* (*uncount*) **tobogganing**: *Let's go tobogganing.*

today /tə'deɪ/ *noun* (*uncount*) *or adverb*
1 Today is the present day: *Today is Friday.* □ *I'm going shopping today.* □ *He'll be arriving later today.* □ *I'll do it today.* **2 Today** is also the present time: *the young people of today.*
[compare **tomorrow**, **yesterday**]

toddle /'tɒdəl/ *verb*: **toddles, toddling, toddled**
A small child **toddles** when it walks with unsteady steps: *My baby daughter is just learning to toddle.*

toddler /'tɒdlə(r)/ *noun*: **toddlers**
A **toddler** is a very young child who is just beginning or has just learnt to walk.

to-do /tə'duː/ *noun* (*informal*): **to-dos**
There is a **to-do** about something if a lot of people get angry, concerned or excited about it: *What a to-do! It would have been quicker to walk.*

toe /toʊ/ *noun*: **toes**
1 Your **toes** are the five jointed parts at the end of each of your feet: *She has to stand on her toes to reach the top shelf.* [see picture at **body**] **2** The **toe** of a shoe or sock is the front part of it that covers the toes: *He's got holes in the toes of his socks.*
▻ *phrases* **1** You **toe the line** when you behave in the way that is expected or demanded of you by others. **2** You **tread on someone's toes** if you offend or upset them.

toenail /'toʊneɪl/ *noun*: **toenails**
Your **toenails** are the nails at the ends of your toes: *a broken toenail* □ *I need to cut my toenails.* [see picture at **body**, compare **fingernail**]

toffee /'tɒfɪ/ *noun* (*uncount or count*): **toffees**
Toffee or a **toffee** is a sticky sweet which is usually either chewy or hard, made by boiling sugar and butter: *a box of toffees* □ *Have another toffee.* □ *Which do you prefer, toffee or chocolate?*

toffee apple /'tɒfɪ apəl/ *noun*: **toffee apples**
A **toffee apple** is an apple, covered with a thin layer of toffee, on a stick.

together /tə'gɛðə(r)/ *adverb*
1 People are **together** when they are with each other: *At last we were together.* □ *We wanted to be alone together.* □ *We wish you a happy and prosperous future together.* **2** People do something **together** when they do it with each other: *They'd been living together for many years.* □ *We decided to travel together to the conference.* □ *We sometimes dined together.* □ *The police and army could work together more effectively.* **3** People or things are grouped **together** when they gather, or are put, in one place, or close to one another: *We like to keep the young and the adults together.* □ *We huddled together for warmth.* □ *He gathered his papers together.* **4** You join things **together** when you join them to each other: *Join the widths together.* □ *Knit the next two stitches together.* □ *Multiply the three numbers together.* □ *He rubbed his hands together in anticipation.* □ *His brows were drawn together in a frown.* **5** Things happen **together** when they happen at the same time: *Then we'll all die together!* **6** You deal with things **together** when you deal with them at the same time, or in the same operation: *Where the actions brought against various defendants are related, they should be heard and determined together.* **7** Items **together** produce a total if that is the amount they represent when they are combined: *Taken together the files provide data on more than 62000 patients.* □ *The two lists together included 205 democrats.* **8** Things that go **together** suit each other, so that they are able to exist in harmony with each other: *Liberal democracy and capitalism go together.* □ *If you think purple and yellow go together, OK.* **9** One thing excels, or is worth, several other things put **together** if even in combination they can't beat it: *My classical dictionary was worth all my other reference books put together.*
▻ *phrase* **Together with** is used like *along with*, *in addition to*, *as well as*, and *including*, as an emphatic form of *with*: *Jill arrived on Saturday, together with the children.* □ *She handed me his curriculum vitae, together with the most recent correspondence.* □ *Accommodation, together with an evening meal and a tip, came to £55.*

togetherness /tə'gɛðənəs/ *noun* (*uncount*)
Togetherness is a feeling of closeness, sympathy and understanding between two or more people.

toggle /'tɒgəl/ *noun*: **toggles**
A **toggle** is a fastening, *eg* for garments, consisting of a small bar of wood or plastic that is passed through a loop of material.

toil /tɔɪl/ *verb*; *noun*
▻ ***verb*** (*formal*): **toils, toiling, toiled**
People **toil**, or **toil** away, when they work for a long time doing a hard, difficult or unpleasant job: *He toiled away at the garden until he'd cleared all the dead bushes and trees.* [*same as* **labour**]
▻ ***noun*** (*uncount*; *formal*)
Toil is hard, difficult or unpleasant work that takes a long time.

toilet /'tɔɪlət/ *noun*: **toilets**
A **toilet** is **1** a bowl-like container with a seat that you use when you want to get rid of urine or faeces from your body, and that has a water supply for washing this into a drain. [see picture at **bathroom**] **2** a room containing a toilet. [*same as* **lavatory**]
▻ *phrase* Someone **goes to the toilet** when they use a toilet to get rid of urine or faeces from their body.

toilet paper /'tɔɪlət peɪpə(r)/ *noun* (*uncount*)
Toilet paper is thin paper used for cleaning the body after getting rid of urine or faeces.

toiletries /'tɔɪlətrɪz/ *noun* (*plural*)
Toiletries are the things that you use when you wash yourself, arrange your hair or apply make-up, including *eg* soap, shampoo, deodorant, toothpaste, aftershave and perfume.

toilet roll /'tɔɪlət roʊl/ *noun*: **toilet rolls**
A **toilet roll** is a roll of toilet paper. [see picture at **bathroom**]

token /'toʊkən/ *noun*; *adjective*
▻ ***noun***: **tokens**
1 A **token** is a piece of paper that is worth a stated amount of money, and that can be used to buy goods: *a book token worth five pounds.* [compare **voucher**] **2** A **token** is something given as a souvenir, or as a sign of *eg* affection: *I gave her a small brooch as a token of my affection.* [*same as* **keepsake**] **3** A **token** is also a small round piece of metal or plastic that can be used instead of money, *eg* in some machines.
▻ ***adjective***
Token describes something that is a symbol or sign of something but that has no real value or effect: *Workers were offered an extremely small pay rise as a token gesture of the management's good intentions.* □ *She was the token woman on the committee.*

told /toʊld/ *verb*
Told is the past tense and past participle of **tell**.
▻ *phrase* For **all told** see **all**.

tolerable /'tɒlərəbəl/ *adjective*
1 Something is **tolerable** when it is unpleasant but you are able to bear or accept it: *The pain is just tolerable.* [*same as* **bearable**; *opposite* **intolerable**, **unbearable**] **2** (*rather old*) A **tolerable** amount or number is a reasonable fairly large amount or number: *There are a tolerable number of decent paintings in the local gallery.*

tolerant /'tɒlərənt/ *adjective*
A **tolerant** person is fair towards other people and accepts their right to have different religious and political beliefs: *Most Muslims have a very tolerant attitude towards Christians.* □ *He's become more tolerant of others as he's got older.* [*opposite* **intolerant**]
— *noun* (*uncount*) **tolerance:** *All children need to learn tolerance.* □ *society's tolerance of people of different faiths.*

tolerate /'tɒləreɪt/ *verb*: **tolerates, tolerating, tolerated**
1 You **tolerate** people with different religious or political beliefs and opinions when you treat them fairly

and with respect: *He'll have to learn to tolerate other people's views.* **2** You **tolerate** *eg* something painful or unpleasant when you are able to bear it or accept it: *I don't think I can tolerate all this noise for much longer.* [*same as* **endure**] — *noun* (*uncount*) **toleration:** *her toleration of people with opposing political views* □ *religious toleration.*

toll[1] /toʊl/ *noun*: **tolls**

1 (*usually in the singular*) The death **toll** in an accident, military attack or natural disaster is the number of people killed in or by it: *The death toll from Monday's earthquake has risen to more than 3000.* **2** A **toll** is the fee or tax that you have to pay to use some bridges and roads: *There are tolls on most French motorways.*

▻ *phrase* An event **takes its toll** when it begins to have an effect and begins to cause *eg* hardship or suffering: *The hard work was beginning to take its toll on all of us.*

toll[2] /toʊl/ *verb*: **tolls, tolling, tolled**

A large bell **tolls** when it rings with slow, regular strokes.

tomato /tə'mɑːtoʊ/ (*AmE*/tə'meɪtoʊ/) *noun*: **tomatoes**

A **tomato** is a round or oval fleshy, juicy red fruit, eaten as a vegetable *eg* in salads: *cheese and tomato sandwiches.* [see picture at **vegetable**]

tomb /tuːm/ *noun*: **tombs**

A **tomb** is a room-like structure either above or below ground, where a dead body is buried: *Lenin's tomb in Moscow.*

tomboy /'tɒmbɔɪ/ *noun*: **tomboys**

A **tomboy** is a girl who likes rough and adventurous games and activities.

tombstone /'tuːmstoʊn/ *noun*: **tombstones**

A **tombstone** is a piece of stone with a dead person's name written on it, placed over that person's grave. [*same as* **gravestone**]

tome /toʊm/ *noun* (*literary*): **tomes**

A **tome** is a large, heavy book: *He always has his head in some musty old tome.*

tomorrow /tə'mɒroʊ/ *noun* (*uncount*) *or adverb*

1 Tomorrow is the day after today: *Today is Monday and tomorrow is Tuesday.* □ *I'll do it tomorrow.* □ *He'll be arriving by plane tomorrow morning.* **2 Tomorrow** is also the future: *the children of tomorrow.* [compare **today, yesterday**]

ton /tʌn/ *noun*: **tons**

1 A **ton** is **a** in Britain, a unit of weight equal to 2240 lb or approximately 1016.05 kg. **b** in America, a unit of weight equal to 2000 lbs or approximately 907.2 kg. **2** A **ton** or **metric ton** is a tonne. **3** (*used in the plural*; *informal*) You have **tons** of things if you have a lot of them: *She's got tons of clothes.*

▻ *phrases* **1** (*informal*) You **come down on** someone **like a ton of bricks** if you speak to them angrily or punish them severely: *Your father will come down on you like a ton of bricks if he discovers you've been stealing again.* **2** (*informal*) If you say that something **weighs a ton** you mean it is very heavy: *This suitcase weighs a ton.* □ *Get off my knee; you weigh a ton!*

tone /toʊn/ *noun*; *verb*

▻ ***noun***: **tones**

1 The **tone** of a person's voice is the quality it has that shows or expresses what they are feeling, or their mood: *I could tell she was angry from the tone of her voice.* □ *She spoke to him in an encouraging tone.* □ *I didn't like the tone of his voice.* **2** A **tone** is one of several sounds that you hear when you use the telephone: *a dialling tone* □ *I keep getting the engaged tone.* **3** The **tone** of a musical instrument or singing voice is the quality and pitch of the sound it produces: *a cello with a mellow tone.* **4** The **tone** of a piece of writing or speech is its general character, contents or style: *A lot of people will be offended by the tone of your article.* **5** A **tone** is a brighter or darker version of a particular colour: *The room is painted in several tones of blue.*

▻ ***verb***: **tones, toning, toned**

phrasal verbs

tone down You **tone down** something you have written or said if you make it less critical, less forceful or less offensive: *You should tone down the language in your speech.*

tone in One thing **tones in** with another if it matches it or if they look attractive together: *The pink curtains toned in with the deep red walls.*

tone up You **tone up** muscles or part of your body if you do exercises to make it stronger or healthier: *She's been swimming to try to tone up her stomach muscles.*

tone-deaf /toʊn'dɛf/ *adjective*

A person who is **tone-deaf** is not able to distinguish notes of different pitch, and so cannot sing in tune.

tongs /tɒŋz/ *noun* (*plural*)

Tongs are, or a pair of **tongs** is, a tool consisting of two movable arms joined in the middle or at one end, used for holding and lifting objects: *garden tongs.*

tongue /tʌŋ/ *noun*: **tongues**

1 Your **tongue** is the fleshy organ attached to the floor of your mouth, that you use for eating, licking, tasting and speaking: *She ran her tongue over her lips.* □ *Don't you dare stick your tongue out at me!* **2** You can use **tongue** to refer to a person's particular manner of speaking: *She has a sharp tongue.* **3** A **tongue** is a particular language: *speaking in some foreign tongue* □ *I answered in my own tongue.* **4** (*uncount*) **Tongue** is the cooked tongue of *eg* oxen and sheep, used as food. **5** The **tongue** in a shoe or boot is the leather flap underneath the opening.

▻ *phrases* **1** A word that is difficult to **get your tongue round** is difficult to pronounce. **2** You **hold your tongue** when you say nothing or keep quiet. **3** If you ask someone, especially a shy child, if they've **lost their tongue**, you are asking why they are so quiet, or why they are not responding: *What's the matter? Lost your tongue?* **4** For **on the tip of your tongue** see **tip**. **5** A piece of news or gossip **sets tongues wagging** when everybody starts discussing it. **6** A **slip of the tongue** is a mistake you make when speaking: *Sorry I got your name wrong; it was just a slip of the tongue.* **7** You do or say something **with your tongue in your cheek** if you do or say it without being serious about it, or without really meaning it: *She obviously had her tongue in her cheek when she wrote this letter.* □ *a tongue-in-cheek remark.*

tongue-tied /'tʌŋtaɪd/ *adjective*

People are **tongue-tied** when they are too shy, embarrassed or nervous to speak: *The children stood in tongue-tied silence.*

tongue twister /'tʌŋ twɪstə(r)/ *noun*: **tongue twisters**

A **tongue twister** is a phrase or sentence that is difficult to say quickly, usually because it contains a series of similar consonant sounds, *eg* 'She sells sea shells on the sea shore'.

tonic /'tɒnɪk/ *noun*: **tonics**

1 (*uncount*) **Tonic**, or **tonic water**, is a clear, bitter-tasting fizzy drink: *gin and tonic.* **2 a** A **tonic** is a medicine that makes you feel stronger or gives you energy. **b** A **tonic** is also any person or thing that makes you feel more lively or cheerful: *He's so full of enthusiasm he's a real tonic.* **c** (*uncount*) **Tonic** is a lotion that you put on *eg* your skin or hair to improve its quality and appearance.

tonight /tə'naɪt/ *noun* (*uncount*) *or adverb*
Tonight is the night or evening of the present day: *I won't get to bed until late tonight.* □ *I'm going to see her tomorrow night.* □ *Are you going to watch tonight's television programme on French cooking?* [compare **evening**]

tonnage /'tʌnɪdʒ/ *noun* (*usually in the singular*)
A ship's **tonnage** is the amount of space it has for carrying cargo.

tonne /tʌn/ *noun*: **tonnes**
A **tonne** is a metric unit of weight equal to 1000 kg or approximately 2204.6 lb. [compare **ton**]

tonsil /'tɒnsəl/ *noun*: **tonsils**
Your **tonsils** are the two oval lumps of tissue on either side of your tongue at the back of your throat.

tonsillitis /tɒnsɪ'laɪtɪs/ *noun* (*uncount*)
Tonsillitis is a painful swelling of the tonsils, caused by an infection.

too /tu:/ *adverb*
1 You use **too a** when adding someone or something that what has been said also applies to: *Bridget too had that experience.* □ *His father used to hit his mother, and sometimes the children too.* □ *Democracy and discipline are inseparable; so too are citizens' rights and obligations.* □ *'I'm fed up.' 'Me, too.'* [= so am I] [*same as* **also**, **as well**] **b** (*sentence adverb*) when adding another aspect or point to what has been said: *Then, too, there are the physical injuries to be attended to.* □ *'She's nice. Clever, too.'* [*same as* **in addition, as well**] **c** (*sentence adverb*) after an additional comment that emphasizes some striking aspect of a situation: *I was astonished that such things could happen, and in our village, too.* □ *'Here's the waiter.' 'And about time, too.'* [compare **at that; see that**]
2 (*intensifying*) You use **too** before adjectives, adverbs and *many* and *much* **a** to mean 'more than necessary or desirable', often followed by an infinitive, or by *for* and an infinitive, to indicate that as a result something is impossible: *He's a little too pleased with himself.* □ *They give us far too much work to do.* □ *You read too many dieting articles.* □ *Don't go too far ahead.* □ *Some young people are too embarrassed to talk about it.* □ *It isn't too late to refuse.* □ *a fate too awful to contemplate* □ *Some of the tasks are too difficult for children to do.* □ *She was walking too fast for me to catch up.* □ *It's too early for the post to have arrived yet.*

Notice that where **too** is used with an adjective followed by a singular noun, you need *a* or *an* before the noun: *Victory was achieved at too great a cost.*

b (*old*) to mean 'very': *You're too kind.* [compare **so**]
▻ ***phrases*** **1** For **too** *eg* clever **by half** see **half**. **2** For **none too** see **none**. **3** You use **not too** like *not very*, as a weak form of 'not', usually as an alternative to using an opposite expression: *They certainly don't look too cheerful.* □ *I didn't feel too good myself.* □ *It isn't too hard to guess.* **4 Only too** and **all too** emphasize that something is so to a particularly great, even unwelcome, extent: *Boys and girls never shared flats then; now it's all too commonplace.* □ *They're only too aware of the disadvantages.*

took /tʊk/ *verb*
Took is the past tense of **take**.

tool /tu:l/ *noun*: **tools**
A **tool** is any piece of equipment that you hold in your hand, including a spade, hammer or saw.
▻ ***phrases*** **1** Workers **down tools** when they stop working as a protest, or when they go on strike. **2** The **tools of your trade** are the things that you use in your particular trade or profession: *Books are the tools of a librarian's trade.*

toot /tu:t/ *verb*; *noun*
▻ ***verb***: **toots, tooting, tooted**
You **toot** *eg* your car horn when you make it produce a quick, short sound, or a series of quick, short sounds: *She tooted the other car when it pulled out in front of her.*
▻ ***noun***: **toots:** *He gave a toot on his horn to let her know he'd arrived.*

tooth /tu:θ/ *noun*: **teeth**
1 Your **teeth** are the hard, bone-like objects set in your jaws, that you use for biting and chewing: *He needs a filling in one of his back teeth.* □ *You'll have to have this tooth out.* □ *false teeth.* [see also **wisdom tooth**] **2** The **teeth** of *eg* a comb or saw are its row of small points. **3** (*used in the plural*) An organization, law or group has **teeth** if it has enough power to be effective.
▻ ***phrases*** **1** You **fight** someone or something **tooth and nail** if you fight them as hard as you can or with all your strength: *She has vowed to fight the government's proposals tooth and nail.* **2** You **grit your teeth** if you press them together tightly, *eg* so that you can bear pain. **3** You can say that someone **is lying in** or **through their teeth** if they are deliberately lying. **4** (*informal*) You can describe someone as **long in the tooth** when they are old: *Now he's nearly 90 he's getting a bit long in the tooth to stay out dancing all night.* [see also **sweet tooth**]

toothache /'tu:θeɪk/ *noun* (*uncount*)
You have **toothache** when you have a pain in or near a tooth: *You'd better go to the dentist if you've got toothache.*

toothbrush /'tu:θbrʌʃ/ *noun*: **toothbrushes**
A **toothbrush** is a small brush that you use for cleaning your teeth. [see picture at **bathroom**]

toothless /'tu:θləs/ *adjective*
A person or thing is **toothless** if they have no teeth: *the baby's toothless smile.*

toothpaste /'tu:θpeɪst/ *noun* (*uncount*)
Toothpaste is paste that you use to clean your teeth. [see picture at **bathroom**]

toothpick /'tu:θpɪk/ *noun*: **toothpicks**
A **toothpick** is a small sharp piece of *eg* wood or plastic that you can use for removing food from between your teeth.

top[1] /tɒp/ *noun*; *adjective*; *adjective or adverb*; *verb*
▻ ***noun***: **tops**
1 The **top** of something is **a** its highest part, point or level: *She climbed to the top of the tower.* □ *I waited for him at the top of the steps.* □ *distant mountain tops* □ *The chair lift took us right to the top.* □ *Don't fill my mug to the top.* □ *Begin reading at the top of the page.* □ *Take a card from the top of the pile.* □ *The neediest people should be at the top of the list.* [*opposite* **bottom**] **b** its upper surface: *a chest of drawers with a metal top* □ *He drummed his fingers on the table top.* **2** The **top** of a container or of something such as a pen is its lid or cap: *I took the top off a ginger ale.* □ *She screwed the top back on.* □ *a silver-coloured pen top.* **3** The **top** of the road or garden is the end of it: *Go to the top of the road and turn left.* [compare **bottom**] **4** A **top** is a piece of clothing such as a sweater, T-shirt or blouse, for the upper part of the body, or the upper part of an outfit

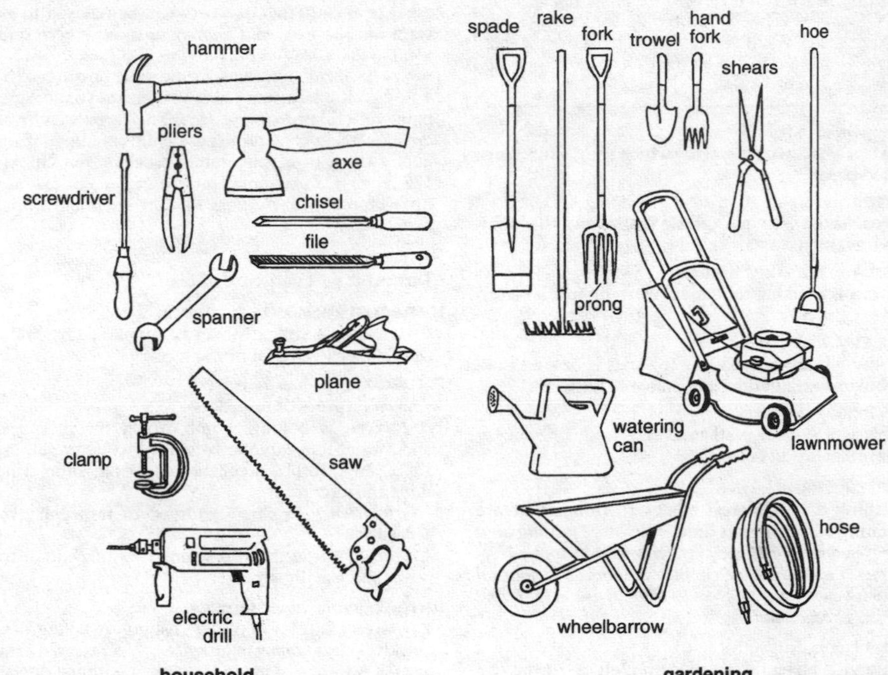

consisting of a lower and upper part: *She put on shorts and a sleeveless top.* ◻ *Where's my pyjama top?* [compare **bottom**] **5** (*used in the singular*) The **top** of an organization or group is the highest or most important level in it: *Planning involves those at the top of the organization.* ◻ *She's already at the top of her profession.* ◻ *Life is tough at the top.* ◻ *He was near the top of the class in most subjects.* [*opposite* **bottom**] **6** The **top** of a scale is its highest point: *people at the top of the income range.*

▻ ***adjective:*** *Write your name in the top right-hand corner of the page.* ◻ *reading clockwise from top left* ◻ *exercises for the top half of the body.* ◻ *Take the top card.* ◻ *My office is on the top floor.* ◻ *the top level of management* ◻ *a small number of top officials* ◻ *winners of the top three awards* ◻ *He wanted to get to one of the top universities.* ◻ *I was in top gear, but still moving quite slowly.* [*opposite* **bottom**]

▻ ***adjective or adverb***: To be or come **top** of a class or a group of competitors is to get the highest marks or score: *teams that regularly come top of the league table* ◻ *You're still top of the class, aren't you?*

▻ ***verb***: **tops, topping, topped**

1 You **top** *eg* a cake with something when you cover its upper surface with it: *Top the pudding with some whipped cream.* **2** Someone or something **tops** *eg* a poll or list when they come first in it: *The album is being released next week and is expected to top the charts.* **3** A total **tops** a certain figure if it is greater than it: *Donations to our charity topped nine million pounds last year.* **4** One thing **tops** another if it is even better or more extraordinary than the other: *The news shocked him, but nothing could top the revelations of the previous day.* [*same as* **better, surpass**]

▻ ***phrases*** **1** For **at the top of your voice** see **voice**. **2** Someone **blows their top** when they get very angry and lose their temper or start shouting. **3 From top to bottom** means from the highest to the lowest point, or completely: *The building shook from top to bottom.* ◻ *The Cabinet is split from top to bottom.* **4** You are covered in something, or dressed in it, **from top to toe** if you are covered, or dressed, completely in it: *He was dressed from top to toe in gold.* [*same as* **from head to foot**] **5** For **off the top of your head** see **head**. **6 a** One thing is **on top of** another if it is covering the other, or covering its upper surface: *He fell over and several people collapsed on top of him.* ◻ *Spread the tomato and cheese on top.* ◻ *Custard grows a skin on top as it cools.* **b** You use **on top of** rather than **on** in referring to something on a tall or high object: *My case was still on top of the wardrobe.* ◻ *We were approaching a hill with a castle on top.* **c** Things forming a pile are described as being piled **one on top of the other**: *reference books sitting one on top of another in untidy heaps.* **d** One thing happens **on top of** another if it happens as well, increasing the effect of the other: *She was suffering from depression, and then, on top of that, she got flu.* **e** Someone who is, keeps, or gets, **on top of** something such as their work has it well organized or under control. **f** You let something get **on top of you** when you allow yourself to be overwhelmed or upset by it: *Don't let all that paperwork get on top of you.* **6** For **on top of the world** see **world**. **7 a** One thing is **over the top of** another if it is covering it, or covering its upper surface: *She stuck a fresh label over the top of the old one.* ◻ *Sprinkle the grated chocolate evenly over the top.* **b** (*informal*) You describe something as **over the top** if it is so extreme as to be unacceptable.

> ***phrasal verb***
> **top up** (*informal*) **1** You **top up** a partly empty container when you fill it again: *Let me top up your glass.* [*same as* **refill**] **2** You **top up** something such as your salary when you add to it by some means: *Doctors continue to top up their incomes by private work.* [see also **top-up**]

top² /tɒp/ *noun*: **tops**
A **top** is a wooden or metal toy which spins round on a pointed base.

top gear /tɒp ˈgɪə(r)/ *noun* (*used in the singular*)
Top gear is the gear in a vehicle that allows that vehicle to travel at its fastest speeds.

top hat /tɒp ˈhat/ *noun*: **top hats**
A **top hat** is a tall hat for a man, worn on formal occasions.

top-heavy /tɒpˈhɛvɪ/ *adjective*
Something is **top-heavy** if the top part is heavier than the bottom part, making it unstable or unsteady.

topic /ˈtɒpɪk/ *noun*: **topics**
A **topic** is a subject or theme: *His favourite topic of conversation is Italian food.*

topical /ˈtɒpɪkəl/ *adjective*
Something that is **topical** relates to things that are happening at the present time: *They were putting on a new, revised version of the play, with a lot of topical references.* □ *Published every two months, the journal deals with such topical issues as drug abuse, AIDS, and the crisis in education*

topless /ˈtɒpləs/ *adjective*
A woman is **topless** if she has no clothes on the top part of her body.

topmost /ˈtɒpmoʊst/ *adjective*
The **topmost** thing in a group or series is the one right at the top: *in the topmost branches of the tree.*

topping /ˈtɒpɪŋ/ *noun* (*count or uncount*): **toppings**
A **topping** is food that covers or decorates the top of a dish of food: *vegetable pie with cheese topping.*

topple /ˈtɒpəl/ *verb*: **topples, toppling, toppled**
1 Something that has been standing upright **topples** if it becomes less steady or stable and falls over: *She caught the vase as it toppled from the shelf.* □ *The pile of books began to topple over.* **2** (*often in the passive*) A leader or government **is toppled** if another person or group of people take or win power from them. [*same as* **overthrow**]

top-secret /tɒpˈsiːkrət/ *adjective*
Something is **top-secret** if it is very secret or officially classed as a secret: *The plans for the invasion were marked 'top-secret'.*

top-up /ˈtɒp ʌp/ *noun* (*informal*): **top-ups**
If someone has drunk most or all of a drink, and you give them a **top-up**, you refill their glass: *Let me give you a top-up.* [see also **top up**]

torch /tɔːtʃ/ *noun*: **torches**
A **torch** is a small electric light that you carry in one hand and that uses batteries for power.

torchlight /ˈtɔːtʃlaɪt/ *noun* (*uncount*)
Torchlight is the light from a torch or torches: *It was nearly midnight and he had to try and repair the car by torchlight.*

tore /tɔː(r)/ *verb*
Tore is the past tense of **tear²**.

torment *noun*; *verb*
▻ ***noun*** /ˈtɔːmɛnt/: **torments**
1 (*uncount*) **Torment** is very great pain, suffering or worry: *Waiting for my exam results was sheer torment.* □ *He spent the next few days in torment, not knowing if his family were alive or dead.* **2** Something that causes great pain, suffering or worry can be referred to as a **torment**: *The long cold journey must have been a torment to them.*
▻ ***verb*** /tɔːˈmɛnt/: **torments, tormenting, tormented**
1 Something **torments** you if you makes you feel great pain, suffering or worry: *He is still tormented by bad dreams.* **2** Someone **torments** a child or animal if they annoy them in a deliberately cruel or spiteful way: *She caught some boys tormenting a cat.* — *noun* **tormentor:** *His tormentors were arrested and charged with assault.*

torn /tɔːn/ *verb*
Torn is the past participle of **tear²**.

tornado /tɔːˈneɪdoʊ/ *noun*: **tornadoes**
A **tornado** is a violent storm accompanied by circling wind, that causes a lot of damage.

torpedo /tɔːˈpiːdoʊ/ *noun*; *verb*
▻ ***noun***: **torpedos** or **torpedoes**
A **torpedo** is a long, bomb which moves quickly underwater and explodes when it hits its target, usually a ship. **Torpedos** can be fired from submarines, ships and aircraft.
▻ ***verb*** (*often in the passive*): **torpedoes, torpedoing, torpedoed**
A ship **is torpedoed** if it is struck by a torpedo or torpedos and usually sunk.

torrent /ˈtɒrənt/ *noun*: **torrents**
1 A **torrent** is a lot of water rushing or falling down quickly: *It was raining in torrents.* □ *Her tears fell in torrents.* **2** A **torrent** of abuse is a violent outburst directed towards someone: *He was met by a torrent of insults.*

torrential /təˈrɛnʃəl/ *adjective*
Rain is **torrential** if it is falling very heavily.

torso /ˈtɔːsoʊ/ *noun*: **torsos**
Your **torso** is the main part of your body, not including your arms, legs and head.

tortoise /ˈtɔːtəs/ *noun*: **tortoises**
A **tortoise** is a slow-moving animal with a hard shell covering its body. **Tortoises** can draw their heads and legs into their shells to protect them.

tortoiseshell /ˈtɔːtəsʃɛl/ *noun* (*uncount*)
Tortoiseshell is the brown and yellow shell of a sea turtle that is used to make *eg* combs and jewellery.

tortuous /ˈtɔːtjʊəs/ *adjective*
1 A **tortuous** road is full of twists and turns: *a tortuous mountain road.* **2 Tortuous** is also used to describe something that is complicated and difficult to follow: *a novel with a tortuous plot.* — *adverb* **tortuously:** *The road wound tortuously through the mountains.*

torture /ˈtɔːtʃə(r)/ *noun*; *verb*
▻ ***noun***: **tortures**
1 (*uncount*) **Torture** is the act of deliberately causing someone severe pain or mental suffering, usually as a punishment or to get information from them: *the threat of torture and imprisonment.* **2** Something that causes severe pain or mental suffering can be referred to as a **torture**: *Waiting for them to come back was a torture for the soldiers' wives.*
▻ ***verb***: **tortures, torturing, tortured**
One person **tortures** another if they make them suffer severe pain or mental distress to punish them or to get information from them: *He'd been tortured by the enemy during the war.*

Tory /ˈtɔːrɪ/ *noun*: **Tories**
A **Tory** is a member or supporter of the British

Conservative Party: *the Tory Prime Minister* □ *The election was a victory for the Tories.*

toss /tɒs/ *verb; noun*

▻ ***verb*: tosses, tossing, tossed**

1 You **toss** something somewhere if you throw it there lightly and carelessly: *He tossed the keys over to me.* □ *She tossed the clothes into the suitcase without folding them.* **2** You **toss** about when you move from side to side repeatedly or continually: *She tossed and turned in her bed all night.* □ *a ship tossed around by the storm.* **3** You **toss** your head when you move it upwards suddenly, usually as a sign of impatience or anger: *He tossed his head angrily.* **4** You **toss** a coin when you throw it into the air and guess which side will land facing up, usually as a way of making a decision or settling a disagreement: *'I want the top bunk.' 'So do I.' 'OK, we'll toss for it.'* **5** You **toss** food if you mix it gently to make sure all of it is covered with the liquid it is to be served in: *You should toss the salad just before you serve it.* **6** A horse **tosses** its rider when it throws him or her to the ground.

▻ ***noun*** (*usually in the singular*): *She gave a toss of her head.* □ *This is too important a decision to decide by the toss of a coin.*

phrasal verb

You **toss up** for something when you throw a spinning coin into the air and guess which side will land facing upwards, as a way of making a decision or settling a disagreement. [see also **toss-up**]

toss-up /'tɒsʌp/ *noun* (*used in the singular; informal*)

A situation is a **toss-up** if it is impossible to decide which of two possible results is the one which will occur: *The match is a toss-up; either team could win if they played well enough.* [see also **toss up**]

tot[1] /tɒt/ *noun*: **tots**

1 A **tot** is a small child. [*same as* **toddler**] **2** A **tot** of an alcoholic drink is a small amount of it: *a tot of whisky*

tot[2] /tɒt/ *verb*: **tots, totting, totted**

phrasal verb

tot up (*informal*) **1** You **tot** numbers **up** when you add them together: *Can you give me just a moment while I tot up your bill?* **2** A sum of money **tots up** when it increases: *The interest on your investment account has been totting up nicely meanwhile.*

total /'toʊtəl/ *noun; adjective; verb*

▻ ***noun*** (*count or uncount, often adjectival*): **totals**

A **total** is a number or amount that you get when you add everything together: *I've got a total of six hundred books.* □ *the total number of employees working for the company* □ *There were thirty people at the meeting in total.* [*same as* **sum total**]

▻ ***adjective***

1 Total means 'complete' or absolute': *The procedure must be carried out in total secrecy.* □ *On Friday there was a total eclipse of the sun, which we watched from the dyke.* □ *There ought to be a total ban on smoking in public places.* **2** (*informal*) **Total** is used for emphasis, with the meaning 'utter' or 'absolute': *The journey was a total nightmare.* □ *I felt a total idiot.* — *adverb* **totally:** *I agree with you totally.* □ *He is totally deaf.* □ *Next day the rash had totally disappeared.* □ *I may be totally stupid, but I still don't see the point.* [*same as* **completely, utterly**]

▻ ***verb*: totals, totalling, totalled**

1 A series of numbers **total** an amount when that is the amount they make when added together: *His income totals £19000 a year.* □ *Donations to the charity received in the last couple of days total up to £456.* **2** You **total** a series of numbers or items when you add them together: *The figures in the last column can be totalled to get the final result.*

totalitarian /toʊtalɪ'tɛərɪən/ *adjective*

A **totalitarian** system of government is one in which a single party controls everything and no other parties are allowed to exist: *a totalitarian regime.*

totality /toʊ'talɪtɪ/ *noun* (*uncount; formal*)

The **totality** of something is the complete amount of it or the whole of it: *Make sure you take into account the totality of the costs involved.*

totter /'tɒtə(r)/ *verb*: **totters, tottering, tottered**

1 You **totter** if you move in a weak, unsteady way as if you are about to fall, *eg* because you are old or ill: *He tottered down the road, leaning heavily on his walking stick.* **2** Something **totters** if it moves in an unsteady way as if it is going to fall over: *The pile of cups tottered dangerously on the tray as she carried it upstairs.* **3** A system *eg* of government **totters** if it becomes very unstable and is just about to collapse: *The whole banking system was tottering on the brink of collapse.*

touch /tʌtʃ/ *verb; noun*

▻ ***verb*: touches, touching, touched**

1 You **touch** something when you lightly put your fingers or hand, or some other part of you, on it, *eg* to feel it: *Please do not touch the exhibits.* □ *'Don't touch,' she said again.* □ *I could reach up and touch the ceiling.* □ *See if you can touch your left knee with your right elbow.* □ *They touched fingertips briefly.* □ *He touched a button on the control panel.* **2** Two things **touch** when they come into contact: *They stood together, heads almost touching.* □ *She ran off, feet barely touching the ground.* □ *He felt a trickle of blood touch his lip.* **3** (*often with a negative*) To **touch** someone or something is also to interfere with them or harm them: *Has someone been touching my papers?* □ *I never touched your tape recorder.* □ *I won't touch you, I promise.* **4** (*usually with a negative*) Someone who never **touches** a certain thing avoids it or refuses to have anything to do with it: *Graham rarely touched alcohol.* □ *I've never touched a chocolate since.* □ *I haven't touched a cent of the money.* □ *Normally he wouldn't touch a job as trivial as this.* **5** You **are touched** by something when it affects you emotionally, making you feel *eg* sad, sympathetic, or grateful: *The parson was deeply touched by her story.* □ *He was so touched by her gesture that he burst into tears.* □ *Henry's loyalty touched her.* [*same as* **move**] **6** An amount **touches** a certain figure or level if it gets as high as that: *Temperatures touched 40°C yesterday.* □ *When Amstrad's profits touched £160 million, the shares rose to 230 pence.* **7** (*used with a negative*) You say that no-one can **touch** a particular person at doing something if they are so good at it that they have no rivals: *No-one can touch him as a presenter.*

▻ ***noun*: touches**

1 (*usually in the singular*) A **touch** is an act of touching: *You can also, at the touch of a button, double the width of the pattern on the screen.* □ *She stiffened at the touch of his fingers.* □ *His touch was firm yet gentle.* **2** (*uncount*) Your sense of **touch** is the sense that tells you about the quality of a surface, *eg* when you feel it with your fingers: *Its fur felt dry and coarse to the touch.* □ *Whiskers react to taste as well as to touch.* **3** A **touch** is a detail that you add to improve something; you put the finishing **touches** to something when you make the last few adjustments to it: *She was putting the final touches to the display.* □ *The mistletoe placed just over the front door was a cunning touch.* **4** (*usually* *in the singular*) A **touch** of something is a small quantity, trace or degree of it: *The woodwork could do with a touch of paint.* □ *He noted the touch of sarcasm in her voice.* □ *The narrative includes some enjoyable comic touches.* □ *There could be a touch of frost tonight.* [*same as* **hint, trace**] **5** (*used in the singular*) Someone's **touch** in doing something is their manner of doing it, especially if it is skilful: *He had a true musician's touch.* □ *Professor Uitsmijter has a deft touch in translation.* □ *Sadat was already losing his popular touch.* □ *The feminine touch was everywhere evident.*

▻ ***phrases*** **1** (*informal*) You use **a touch** to mean 'slightly': *He was more than a touch bruised by her dismissal.* **2 a** You get **in touch** with someone when you contact them by writing or telephoning; you are, keep, or stay, **in touch** with them if you meet, telephone, or write to each other regularly; you **lose touch** with someone when you meet and contact each other less and less often: *Here's my number in case you need to get in touch.* □ *I haven't seen her for a while, though of course we've been in touch by phone.* □ *Our regular newsletter keeps everyone in touch.* □ *We are in close touch with our allies on this matter.* □ *I'm afraid I've completely lost touch with her.* **b** You are **in touch** with a subject or situation if you have all the latest information about it, and you are **out of touch** with it if you haven't; you **lose touch** with it when you fail to keep your knowledge of it up to date: *He's reckoned to be in closer touch with the mood of the far left than the others are.* □ *They're out of touch with reality.* □ *You attend conferences so as not to lose touch with developments.* **3** Something is **touch and go** when it is just as likely to turn out badly as it is to turn out well: *It was touch and go whether he'd survive the operation.* □ *I didn't think I'd make it; it was touch and go till the last minute.* **4** For **touch wood** see **wood**.

phrasal verbs

touch down An aircraft **touches down** somewhere when it lands there. [see also **touchdown**]

touch on or **touch upon** You **touch on** or **upon** something when you mention it briefly, *eg* while dealing with another subject: *We shall merely touch on some of these questions, without attempting an answer.*

touch up You **touch** something **up** when you improve its appearance with slight alterations or additions: *You can see that the photograph has been touched up.* □ *I touch up the paintwork from time to time.*

touchdown /ˈtʌtʃdaʊn/ *noun* (*count or uncount*): **touchdowns**
Touchdown, or a **touchdown**, is the landing of an aircraft or spacecraft: *the spacecraft's successful touchdown in the Arizona desert.* [see also **touch down**]

touching /ˈtʌtʃɪŋ/ *adjective*
Something is **touching** if it makes you feel pity or sympathy: *I found the film very touching.*

touchline /ˈtʌtʃlaɪn/ *noun*: **touchlines**
The **touchlines** are the two lines that mark the side boundaries of a football or rugby pitch.

touchy /ˈtʌtʃɪ/ *adjective* (*informal*): **touchier, touchiest**
1 A person is **touchy** if they are easily annoyed or offended. **2** A **touchy** subject is one that you need to handle or deal with with care and tact, *eg* because it might offend someone: *The whole question of salaries is a touchy one in this company.*

tough /tʌf/ *adjective*: **tougher, toughest**
1 Something is **tough** if it is strong and is not easily cut, broken, torn or worn out: *You'll need a tough pair of shoes for climbing.* □ *These toys are tough and suitable for use in the garden.* **2** People or animals that are **tough** are strong and fit and can tolerate pain or hardship: *a tough police officer* □ *You'll need to be tough to do well as a doctor.* **3** Meat that is **tough** is difficult to chew. **4** A **tough** problem or issue is difficult to deal with: *'How can we make sure the children are getting a healthy diet when their families are too poor to afford decent food?' 'Yes, that's tough one.'* **5 Tough** laws or decisions are strict and severe, and may cause hardship: *We have to make some tough decisions if the company is to be restored to profitability.* **6** (*informal*) You can say that something is **tough** if it is unlucky or unpleasant: *tough luck* □ *I'm afraid it's just tough if you don't like it.*

▻ ***phrase*** (*informal*) You **get tough** with someone if you begin to deal more forcefully, strictly or severely with them: *Crime is on the increase and it's time the police got tough.*

toughen /ˈtʌfən/ *verb*: **toughens, toughening, toughened**
1 Someone **is toughened**, or **is toughened** up, when they become stronger and more able to deal with hardship: *He'll be toughened up by a career in the army.* **2** To **toughen** something is to make it stronger: *toughen the laws on violent crime.* — *adjective* **toughened:** *toughened glass.*

toupee /ˈtu:peɪ/ *noun*: **toupees**
A **toupee** is a small wig worn usually by a man to cover a bald patch on his head.

tour /tʊə(r)/ *noun*; *verb*

▻ ***noun***: **tours**
A **tour** is **1** a long journey round a place stopping at various places along the way: *a coach tour of Italy.* **2** a short visit round a particular place: *a tour of the cathedral.*

▻ ***verb***: **tours, touring, toured**
You **tour** a place **1** if you travel round it: *He spent the summer touring round Germany.* **2** if you visit it: *You can tour the castle with or without a guide.*

tourism /ˈtʊərɪzm/ *noun* (*uncount*)
1 Tourism is travelling to and visiting places for pleasure and relaxation: *He gave the reason for his visit as tourism.* **2 Tourism** is also the industry that provides services, such as accommodation and catering, for tourists: *She's hoping to work in tourism when she leaves college.*

tourist /ˈtʊərɪst/ *noun*: **tourists**
A **tourist** is a person who travels for pleasure and relaxation: *French tourists in Italy* □ *famous tourist attractions.*

tournament /ˈtʊənəmənt/ *noun*: **tournaments**
A **tournament** is a competition in which only players who win matches can progress to the next round of the competition: *a golf tournament.*

tousled /ˈtaʊzəld/ *adjective*
Tousled hair is untidy and tangled.

tout /taʊt/ *verb*: **touts, touting, touted**
1 A person **touts** for *eg* trade or business when they try to persuade people to give it to them: *guides touting for trade at the station.* **2** You **tout** something if you try to sell it to people: *He touted the books all round the college but no-one would buy them.*

tow /toʊ/ *verb*; *noun*

▻ ***verb***: **tows, towing, towed**
A vehicle, or a driver driving a vehicle, **tows** another vehicle if he or she pulls it behind them with a rope or chain: *My car broke down and my brother had to tow me to the garage.*

▻ ***noun*** (*usually in the singular*)

Someone gives you a **tow** if they pull the vehicle you are driving behind their own: *My van has broken down and I'll have to get a tow.*
▻ ***phrases*** **1** You take someone **in tow** when you take them along with you, *eg* because you are looking after them: *He was taken in tow by a more experienced employee.* ▫ *She arrived at the party with her children in tow.* **2** A vehicle is **on tow** when it is being towed.

towards /tə'wɔːdz/ or **toward** /tə'wɔːd/ *preposition*
1 You move, face, look or point **towards** a place, person or thing when you move, face, look or point in their direction: *A man was coming along the path towards him.* ▫ *He leant towards Bill and whispered something.* ▫ *The boy turned toward her and smiled.* ▫ *All eyes were directed toward the President.* ▫ *Her back was towards him.* **2** A trend or shift **towards** some situation or state is change or progress in the direction of it: *the trend towards greater weight and height among children* ▫ *The shift towards formal politics gave the working class a chance to engage in the struggle to remodel society.* **3** You work **towards** something when you takes steps to achieve it: *Bush's moves toward energy conservation* ▫ *Nothing had so far been done towards making the refugees more comfortable.* **4** A sum of money goes **towards** something if it helps to pay for it: *Their donations will be put towards the cost of the project.* ▫ *Grants are available toward the cost of house improvements.* **5** Something is adjusted **towards** a certain thing if it is organized so as to take special account of it: *The curriculum is weighted towards practical subjects.* ▫ *the bias towards managerial and commercial interests.* **6** Your attitude or policy **towards** a person or thing is the way you regard them or deal with them: *the current US policy toward Cambodia* ▫ *people with a deferential attitude toward authority* ▫ *She's been behaving oddly towards me.* ▫ *Portia promptly forgets to show mercy towards Shylock.* **7** Something happens **towards** a particular time if it happens just before that time: *One afternoon towards the end of 1973 Bernard was driving through Oxford.* ▫ *Towards dawn he managed to get an hour or so's sleep.* **8** Something that is positioned **towards** a certain area is near it: *The toilets are located towards the rear of the aircraft.*

towel /'taʊəl/ *noun*: **towels**
1 A **towel** is a piece of thick, soft cotton cloth that you use for drying yourself after washing: *a bath towel.* [see picture at **bathroom**] **2** A **towel** is also a sanitary towel. [see also **tea towel**]

towelling (*AmE* **toweling**) /'taʊəlɪŋ/ *noun* (*uncount*)
Towelling is thick, soft cotton cloth that can absorb water and is used for making towels.

tower /'taʊə(r)/ *noun*; *verb*
▻ ***noun***: **towers**
A **tower** is a tall, narrow building, or a tall, narrow part of a larger building: *the church's clock tower* ▫ *the Tower of London.*
▻ ***verb***: **towers, towering, towered**
People or things **tower** over or above you when they are a lot taller than you are or reach up high: *He is very tall and towers above the other children.*
▻ ***phrase*** Someone is **a tower of strength** if they give you a lot of help, support or encouragement: *She was a tower of strength during my long illness.*

tower block /'taʊə blɒk/ *noun*: **tower blocks**
A **tower block** is a very tall building where people live or work.

towering /'taʊərɪŋ/ *adjective*
1 Towering things are very tall or high: *the city centre, with its towering office blocks* ▫ *towering grey cliffs.* **2** Someone who is in a **towering** rage is very angry: *George arrived home in a towering rage.*

town /taʊn/ *noun*: **towns**
1 A **town** is a place where people live and work, with streets and buildings and a name. A **town** is usually smaller than a city but larger than a village: *the town of Rye in Kent.* **2** (*uncount*) **Town** is the centre of a town or city where there are shops and offices: *We had lunch in town.* **3** (*uncount*) **Town** is also the town that you live in: *He's left town for the holidays.*
▻ ***phrases*** **1** You go **down town** when you head for the city centre. **2** (*informal*) You **go to town** over something if you do it very thoroughly or with great enthusiasm, or spend a lot of money on it: *She really went to town over her wedding, with bridesmaids, and expensive cake, flowers, the lot!* **3** (*informal*) You go **out on the town** if you visit the places of entertainment in a town or city, especially its restaurants and bars. **4** You go **up to town** when you travel to the chief town or city in your area, or to the city centre, from somewhere outside it: *I thought I'd go up to town and do some shopping.*

town hall /taʊn 'hɔːl/ *noun*: **town halls**
A **town hall** is a building where the official business of a town is carried out by local-government employees.

township /'taʊnʃɪp/ *noun*: **townships**
In South Africa, a **township** is a town, or the area just outside a town, where black and coloured citizens live.

towpath /'toʊpɑːθ/ *noun*: **towpaths**
A **towpath** is a path beside a canal or river.

toxic /'tɒksɪk/ *adjective*
A **toxic** chemical or substance is poisonous: *This medicine is toxic in very high doses.*

toxin /'tɒksɪn/ *noun*: **toxins**
A **toxin** is a poison.

toy *noun*; *adjective*; *verb*
▻ ***noun***: **toys**
A **toy** is an object such as a doll made for a child to play with.
▻ ***adjective***
A **toy** object is a model of a real one made for a child to play with: *a toy oven* ▫ *toy soldiers.*
▻ ***verb***: **toys, toying, toyed**

phrasal verb
toy with 1 You **toy with** an object if you move it about but are not really interested in it or do not really want it: *She wasn't very hungry and only toyed with her food.* **2** You **toy with** an idea if you think about it in a casual way, but without deciding definitely what to do: *She toyed with the possibility of moving house but couldn't really be bothered with all the work involved.*

trace /treɪs/ *noun*; *verb*
▻ ***noun***: **traces**
1 A **trace** is a mark or sign somewhere that shows that some person, animal or thing has been there: *There were traces of footsteps in the sand.* ▫ *I could see the traces of tears on her cheeks.* **2** There is a **trace** of something if there is a very small amount of it: *There was a trace of pink in the sky.* ▫ *The victim had traces of blood under her fingernails.* **3** (*used in the singular, usually with a negative*) Something that there is no **trace** of does not exist or has disappeared completely: *She never showed a trace of respect for anyone else's abilities.* ▫ *Next morning there wasn't a trace of him; he had vanished in the night.*

▻ *verb*: **traces, tracing, traced**

1 You **trace** someone or something if you follow signs or clues and eventually find them: *The police managed to trace him as far as Dover, where he was arrested.* ▫ *He was trying to trace his relatives.* **2** You **trace** the development of something if you follow or describe its progress carefully: *a detailed account tracing the growth in the use of computers during the 1980s* ▫ *She has been able to trace her family back to the 16th century.* **3** You **trace** a drawing, diagram or map if you make a copy of it by covering it with a sheet of very thin paper and drawing over the lines underneath.

▻ *phrase* Someone or something that disappears **without trace** disappears completely: *She vanished without trace and was never heard of again.*

tracing /'treɪsɪŋ/ *noun*: **tracings**

A **tracing** is a copy of a drawing made on very thin paper.

tracing paper /'treɪsɪŋ peɪpə(r)/ *noun* (*uncount*)

Tracing paper is thin, transparent paper that you use when you want to trace *eg* drawings, diagrams or maps.

track /trak/ *noun*; *verb*

▻ ***noun***: **tracks**

1 A **track** is a mark on the ground left by a person, animal or thing that has passed, especially a footprint: *He followed the bear's tracks through the forest.* ▫ *tyre tracks.* **2** A **track** is also a rough path or road: *They were able to drive up a narrow track leading up to the foot of the mountain.* **3** A **track** is also an area of ground with a circular or semi-circular course on it, that is used for racing: *an athletics track* ▫ *a race track.* **4** (*uncount or count*) **Track** or **railway track** is a length of ground with rails laid on it, that trains are driven along: *Passengers are not allowed to walk across the tracks.* **5** A **track** on a CD, tape or record is one of several songs or pieces of music recorded on it: *I like the last track best of all.* **6** (*used in the singular*) The **track** of something is the course that it follows while travelling or moving: *She followed the track of the comet with her telescope.*

▻ *verb*: **tracks, tracking, tracked**

You **track** an animal or person if you follow the marks or footprints they make as they travel or move, usually with the intention of catching them: *The police tracked the thief to his home.*

▻ *phrases* **1** You **keep track of** someone or something if you make sure you know where they are, what they are doing, or what is happening to them. You **lose track of** them if you don't know where they are, what they are doing or what is happening to them any more: *You should try and keep track of the money you spend.* ▫ *I somehow lost track of my suitcase between the airport and the station.* **2** (*informal*) You **make tracks** if you leave a place: *It's time I started making tracks.* **3** You are **on the right track** if you are thinking or acting in a way that means you will be successful or will arrive at the correct conclusion. You are **on the wrong track** if you are thinking or acting in a way that means you will not be successful or will arrive at the wrong conclusion. **4** When you have been walking or moving forwards and you **stop dead in your tracks** you stop suddenly and remain standing in the same position: *She heard a noise behind her and stopped dead in her tracks.*

> ***phrasal verb***
> You **track** someone or something **down** if you find them after a thorough search or by following a track they have left: *I never did manage to track down my luggage.*

track record /trak 'rɛkɔːd/ *noun*: **track records**

Your **track record** is all the things you have done well or successfully together with all your failures: *He has an excellent track record as an administrator.*

tracksuit /'traksuːt/ *noun*: **tracksuits**

A **tracksuit** is a warm suit consisting of a loose top and trousers, that you wear *eg* when exercising, or to keep your body warm before and after exercise: *I go jogging in a tracksuit.*

tract /trakt/ *noun*: **tracts**

1 A **tract** of land is an area of land: *The company have applied to build houses on the tract of open land to the south of the town.* **2** A **tract** is a short essay or book, especially one on a religious subject.

tractable /'traktəbəl/ *adjective* (*informal*)

A **tractable** person is easily managed, controlled or persuaded: *a tractable child.* [*same as* **docile, obedient, pliant**; *opposite* **intractable**]

traction engine /'trakʃən ɛndʒɪn/ *noun*: **traction engines**

A **traction engine** is a large engine used for pulling heavy loads over rough ground.

tractor /'traktə(r)/ *noun*: **tractors**

A **tractor** is a heavy, slow-moving vehicle with two large rear wheels, that is used for pulling *eg* farm machinery or heavy loads.

trade /treɪd/ *noun*; *verb*

▻ ***noun***: **trades**

1 (*uncount*) **Trade** is the buying and selling of goods or services: *He made his money through trade.* ▫ *foreign trade* ▫ *the arms trade.* **2** A person's **trade** is their job, especially when it requires special skills and training: *a young man who is still learning his trade* ▫ *My father is a carpenter by trade.* **3** A particular **trade** is the business done at a particular time, or for a particular market: *the tourist trade* ▫ *a seasonal trade in woolly hats.*

▻ *verb*: **trades, trading, traded**

People, companies or countries **trade** when they buy and sell goods and services: *The company trades in French produce only.* ▫ *The government is encouraging firms to trade with China.*

> ***phrasal verb***
> You **trade** an old item **in** for a new one when the old one is accepted towards the cost of the new one: *I'm going to trade in my car for a newer model.*

trademark /'treɪdmɑːk/ *noun*: **trademarks**

1 A **trademark** is a name, word or symbol that is used to represent a company, is shown on the goods it produces, and that can't be used by another company. Words in this dictionary that are trademarks are labelled (**trademark**). **2** A person's **trademark** is a characteristic or feature that is typical of them or is associated with them in other people's minds: *the elegance and sophistication that was Coco Chanel's trademark.*

trader /'treɪdə(r)/ *noun*: **traders**

A **trader** is a person who buys and sells goods, often in a market: *a tea trader* ▫ *traders with stalls at the local market.*

tradesman /'treɪdzmən/ *noun*: **tradesmen**

A **tradesman** is **1** a person who buys and sells goods, especially a shopkeeper, and especially one who will deliver to your house. **2** a person who has been trained in a particular skill or trade.

tradespeople /'treɪdzpiːpəl/ *noun* (*plural*)

Tradespeople are people whose work involves the buying and selling of goods.

trade union /treɪd 'ju:njən/ *noun*: **trade unions**
A **trade union** or **trades union** is an organization of workers formed to protect the workers and generally try to improve working conditions and pay: *trade union leaders.*

tradition /trə'dɪʃən/ *noun*: **traditions**
1 A **tradition** is a belief, custom or story that has been passed on from one generation to the next without changing: *Going for a swim in the sea on 1 May is a family tradition.* □ *keep up the tradition and give your son his father's Christian name.* **2** (*uncount*) **Tradition** is the passing of beliefs and customs from one generation to the next: *respect for tradition.* □ *break with tradition.*

traditional /trə'dɪʃənəl/ *adjective*
Traditional customs have existed for a long time without changing: *the traditional English breakfast* □ *traditional peasant costumes.* — *adverb* **traditionally:** *In Britain, women traditionally get married in white dresses.*

traffic /'trafɪk/ *noun*; *verb*
▻ ***noun*** (*uncount*)
1 Traffic is all the vehicles moving along a road: *Traffic is always heaviest early in the morning.* □ *recent increases in the amount of air traffic over southern England.* **2 Traffic** is also illegal trade: *international traffic in heroin* □ *the traffic in endangered species.*
▻ ***verb***: **traffics, trafficking, trafficked**
A person **traffics** in goods when they buy and sell them even though it is illegal to do so: *He was convicted of trafficking in heroin.* — *noun* **trafficker:** *drugs traffickers.*

traffic jam /'trafɪk dʒam/ *noun*: **traffic jams**
A **traffic jam** is a long line of vehicles that cannot move because the road is blocked: *We were stuck in a traffic jam for two hours.*

traffic light /'trafɪk laɪt/ *noun* (*usually in the plural*)
Traffic lights are a system of red, amber and green lights that control traffic at road junctions: *The traffic lights are about to change.* [see picture at **street**]

traffic warden /'trafɪk wɔ:dən/ (*BrE*) *noun*: **traffic wardens**
A **traffic warden** is a person whose job is to check cars are parked in the proper places and that drivers have paid parking fees.

tragedy /'tradʒədɪ/ *noun*: **tragedies**
1 a A **tragedy** is a serious play, film, opera or novel with a sad ending, especially one in which the main character is eventually destroyed or killed: *Shakespeare's tragedy 'King Lear'.* **b** (*uncount*) **Tragedy** is such plays as a group: *an actress famous for her performances in tragedy.* [compare **comedy**] **2** (*count or uncount*) A **tragedy** is a sad, serious or terrible event: *The trip to the sea ended in tragedy when one of the boys was drowned.* □ *A fuel leak in the engine was the cause of the tragedy.* [*same as* **catastrophe, disaster**]

tragic /'tradʒɪk/ *adjective*
1 Something that is **tragic** is sad and upsetting: *a tragic accident.* **2 Tragic** novels, films and plays have sad endings, or are in the style of tragedy: *a tragic hero.* — *adverb* **tragically:** *be tragically killed in an accident.*

trail /treɪl/ *verb*; *noun*
▻ ***verb***: **trails, trailing, trailed**
1 You **trail** something, or something **trails**, when you drag it, or it drags, loosely along the ground behind you: *Her dress trailed on the floor.* □ *He trailed the toy boat through the water.* **2** You **trail** along when you walk or move slowly, usually because you are tired: *The children trailed along behind their father.* □ *He's always trailing round after me.* □ *She trailed back home.* **3** You **are trailing** in a race or competition when you are behind or have a lower score than the other competitors: *She's trailing by 1 game to 4.* □ *The Conservatives are trailing Labour by 10 points in this opinion poll.* **4** You **trail** a person or animal when you follow or hunt them: *The police are trailing the suspects.* **5** A plant **trails** when it grows so long it hangs over a surface towards the ground: *roses trailing over the wall.*
▻ ***noun***: **trails**
1 A **trail** is a series of marks left by a person, animal or thing, especially one that you are following: *The thieves left a clear trail behind them.* □ *lose the trail.* **2** A **trail** is also a path or track through wild or rough country: *follow the trail up the mountain.*

phrasal verbs
trail away or **trail off** A sound **trails away** or **trails off** when it becomes fainter: *His voice trailed away until she couldn't hear what he was saying at all.*

trailer /'treɪlə(r)/ *noun*: **trailers**
1 A **trailer** is a type of wheeled vehicle pulled behind another vehicle, used *eg* for transporting heavy loads. [see picture at **vehicle**] **2** (*AmE*) A **trailer** is a caravan. **3** A **trailer** for a film or television programme is a series of short pieces from it that give audiences an impression of what it is like, and that is used to advertise it.

train /treɪn/ *noun*; *verb*
▻ ***noun***: **trains**
1 A **train** is a string of railway carriages or trucks pulled by an engine: *catch a train* □ *take a train* □ *miss the train* □ *travel by train* □ *get on the train* □ *the train to Boston* □ *change trains in Paris.* **2** The **train** of a long dress is the back part that drags on the floor: *a wedding dress with a long train.*
▻ ***verb***: **trains, training, trained**
1 You **train** a person or animal to do something when you teach them how to do it: *She trained her dog to fetch sticks.* **2** You **train** as something when you are taught how to do it or learn how to do it: *I'm training as a teacher.* □ *He wants to train to be a dentist.* □ *They trained together at medical school.* **3** You **train** for a competition or performance when you prepare for it by doing exercises and eating the right food: *My sister is training for the marathon.* **4** You **train** *eg* a gun or camera on something when you point it in that direction. **5** You **train** a plant somewhere when you make it grow in a certain direction, *eg* by pruning or cutting off parts of it, or by providing supports on which it will grow: *a pretty yellow-flowered climbing plant that had been trained up the back wall of the house.* — *adjective* **trained:** *She's a trained teacher.*
▻ ***phrase*** Your **train of thought** is a connected series of thoughts: *Don't interrupt my train of thought.*

trainee /treɪ'ni:/ *noun*: **trainees**
A **trainee** is a person who is in the process of being trained for a job: *a trainee manager.*

trainer /'treɪnə(r)/ *noun*: **trainers**
1 A **trainer** is a person who trains animals or sportsmen and sportswomen. **2** (*BrE*; *usually in the plural*) **Trainers** are soft shoes worn for running: *buy a pair of trainers* □ *buy some trainers* □ *I don't have any trainers.*

training /'treɪnɪŋ/ *noun* (*uncount*)
1 Training is instruction in how to do a particular job: *staff training* □ *You'll need training before you can start work as a postman.* □ *be given training in the company's*

computer systems. **2** You are in **training** when you are preparing for a sports competition by doing exercises and eating the right food: *go into training for the marathon.*

traipse /treɪps/ *verb*: **traipses, traipsing, traipsed**
You **traipse** somewhere when you walk there slowly because you are tired or because it is a long journey: *She traipsed up the hill carrying three bags of heavy shopping.*

trait /treɪt/ *noun*: **traits**
A **trait** is a particular characteristic or quality someone or something has: *The test is supposed to reveal major character traits; whether a person is generally pessimistic or optimistic, introvert or extrovert, etc.*

traitor /'treɪtə(r)/ *noun*: **traitors**
A **traitor** is a person who is not loyal to their country or friends and betrays them to their enemies: *He was a traitor to his country.*

trajectory /trə'dʒɛktərɪ/ *noun*: **trajectories**
The **trajectory** of a moving object, such as a bullet, is the course that it follows through the air: *work out the trajectory of the bullet.*

tram /tram/ *noun*: **trams**
A **tram** is an electric passenger vehicle which runs on rails laid in the streets. [*same as* **street car**]

tramp /tramp/ *noun*; *verb*
▻ ***noun***: **tramps**
A **tramp** is a person with no fixed home or job, who travels from place to place on foot and who lives by begging and doing odd jobs.
▻ ***verb***: **tramps, tramping, tramped**
You **tramp** when you walk with slow, firm, heavy footsteps: *tramp wearily home* □ *tramp from shop to shop* □ *tramp the streets.*

trample /'trampəl/ *verb*: **tramples, trampling, trampled**
1 You **trample** on something when you tread heavily or roughly on it, and usually harm or damage it: *The sheep trampled the wheat.* □ *The children trampled all over the flowers.* □ *He was trampled to death.* □ *If you stand there you'll get trampled on.* □ *cigarette ash trampled into the carpet.* **2** You **trample** on someone if you treat them roughly or carelessly, and hurt or upset them: *trample all over her feelings.*

trampoline /'trampəli:n/ *noun*: **trampolines**
A **trampoline** is a piece of tough canvas stretched across a frame for acrobats, gymnasts and children to jump on.

trance /trɑ:ns/ *noun*: **trances**
You are in a **trance** when you are in a sleep-like or half-conscious state in which you are unaware of what is going on around you: *The hypnotist put several people in the audience in a trance.*

tranquil /'traŋkwɪl/ *adjective*
A **tranquil** place or person is quiet, calm and peaceful: *a tranquil village nestling in the hills* □ *a tranquil sleep.* [*same as* **serene**; *opposite* **agitated, disturbed, noisy**]

tranquillity (*AmE* **tranquility**) /traŋ'kwɪlɪtɪ/ *noun* (*uncount*)
Tranquillity is the state of being quiet, calm and peaceful: *She loved the tranquillity of the valley.*

tranquillize or **tranquillise** (*AmE* **tranquilize**) /'traŋkwɪlaɪz/ *verb*: **tranquillizes, tranquillizing, tranquillized**
People or animals **are tranquillized** when they are given drugs that make them become calmer or more relaxed, or that help them to sleep.

tranquillizer or **tranquilliser** (*AmE* **tranquilizer**) /'traŋkwɪlaɪzə(r)/ *noun*: **tranquillizers**
A **tranquillizer** is a drug that makes people feel calmer and more relaxed, and helps them sleep: *She was prescribed tranquillizers for anxiety.*

trans- /tranz/ or /trans/ *prefix*
Trans- is used to form adjectives, and means 'across', 'beyond' or 'on the other side of': *transatlantic.*

transact /tran'zakt/ *verb*: **transacts, transacting, transacted**
To **transact** business is to do the various things involved in it, *eg* arrange deals or contracts, or buy and sell things: *The purchase had been transacted without the consent of the whole committee being obtained.*

transaction /tran'zakʃən/ *noun*: **transactions**
A **transaction** is a business deal: *Bank customers whose accounts go into overdraft will be charged for each transaction.*

transatlantic /tranzət'lantɪk/ *adjective*
1 Transatlantic travel or journeys involve crossing the Atlantic, usually between North America and Europe: *a transatlantic flight.* **2 Transatlantic** things belong, are from, or happen on the other side of the Atlantic.

transcend /tran'sɛnd/ *verb*: **transcends, transcending, transcended**
One thing **transcends** another when it is better, greater or more important than it is, or goes beyond it: *a problem that transcends political differences* □ *The desire for world peace transcends national boundaries.*

transcribe /tran'skraɪb/ *verb*: **transcribes, transcribing, transcribed**
1 You **transcribe** a text when you write it out in full from notes, or copy it from one place to another: *She took notes at the lecture and transcribed them later.* □ *He transcribed the poem into his diary.* **2** You **transcribe** spoken words when you make a written copy of them: *She transcribed the children's songs.*

transcript /'transkrɪpt/ *noun*: **transcripts**
A **transcript** is a written copy of something spoken: *a transcript of the trial.*

transfer /trans'fɜ:(r)/ *verb*; *noun*
▻ ***verb***: **transfers, transferring, transferred**
1 You **transfer** something when you move it from one place or person to another: *He transferred his keys and money from his jacket to his trouser pocket.* □ *transfer computer files on to floppy disk* □ *The money will be transferred to your savings account.* □ *She has been transferred to our London offices.* □ *Power has been transferred from the President to the Prime Minister.* **2** You **transfer** when you change *eg* to a different job or place: *He's transferring to our Washington office.* **3** You **transfer** when you change from one vehicle, line or passenger system to another: *You can go by train from London to Aberdeen but you'll probably have to transfer at Edinburgh.*
▻ ***noun***: **transfers**
1 (*count or uncount*) A **transfer** is an act of moving something or someone from one place to another: *He isn't happy working in London and has asked for a transfer to Paris.* □ *the transfer of money to his account.* **2** A **transfer** is a piece of paper with a design or picture on one side, that can be ironed or rubbed on to another surface. **3** (*AmE*) A **transfer** is a ticket that allows a passenger to continue a journey on another route.

transferable /trans'fɜ:rəbəl/ *adjective*
A ticket is **transferable** when you can give it to someone else to use: *Tickets that have your name on, such as plane tickets, are usually not transferable.*

transference /transfərəns/ *noun* (*uncount*; *formal*)
Transference is the act of moving or transferring something from one person, place or group to another: *the transference of power from central to local government.*

transfixed /trans'fɪkst/ *adjective* (*literary*)
You are **transfixed** if you are so frightened, shocked or surprised by something that you cannot move: *She stood there transfixed with terror as the figure drew closer.*

transform /trans'fɔːm/ *verb*: **transforms, transforming, transformed**
You **transform** something when you change its appearance, nature or function completely: *A fresh coat of paint will transform this room.* □ *The wasteland behind the house was transformed into a beautiful garden.* — *noun* (*count or uncount*) **transformation** /transfə'meɪʃən/: *the transformation of the wasteland into a garden* □ *There have been several transformations in his appearance over the past ten years.* □ *a country undergoing political transformation.*

transfusion /trans'fjuːʒən/ *noun*: **transfusions**
A patient is given a **transfusion** when they are given blood taken from someone else: *a blood transfusion.*

transient /'tranzɪənt/ *adjective*
Something that is **transient** lasts or stays for a short time only: *Some birds are only transient visitors to Britain.* [*same as* **fleeting, temporary, transitory**; *opposite* **permanent**]

transistor /tran'zɪstə(r)/ *noun*: **transistors**
1 A **transistor** is a small piece of electronic equipment used in *eg* radios and televisions to make sound louder. **2** A **transistor**, or **transistor radio**, is a small radio that can be carried easily.

transit /'tranzɪt/ *noun* (*uncount*)
▻ ***phrase*** Goods or passengers are **in transit** when they are being taken or are travelling from one place to another: *Her luggage got lost in transit.*

transition /tran'zɪʃən/ *noun* (*count or uncount*): **transitions**
A **transition** is a change from one place, state or form to another: *the transition from adolescence to adulthood* □ *The country is in transition.*

transitional /tran'zɪʃənəl/ *adjective*
A **transitional** stage is a stage during which the form of something changes or develops: *The country will pass through a transitional period between constitutions.*

transitive /'tranzɪtɪv/ *adjective* (*grammar*)
A **transitive** verb is a verb that has a direct object, such as the verb *hit* in the phrase *hit the ball.* [compare **intransitive**]

transitory /'tranzɪtərɪ/ *adjective*
Something that is **transitory** lasts only for a short time: *the transitory nature of human life.* [*same as* **transient**; *opposite* **lasting**]

translate /trans'leɪt/ *verb*: **translates, translating, translated**
1 You **translate** writing or speech when you put it into another language: *I'm translating this book into English.* □ *a novel translated from German.* [compare **interpret**] **2** (*formal*) You **translate** one thing into another when you change it into that other thing: *She finds it difficult to translate her ideas into practise.*

translation /trans'leɪʃən/ *noun*: **translations**
1 A **translation** is writing or speech that has been put into one language from another: *This novel is a translation from French.* □ *a new translation of the book.* **2** (*uncount*) **Translation** is the process of putting writing or speech into another language: *Language students need to be good at translation.*

translator /trans'leɪtə(r)/ *noun*: **translators**
A **translator** is someone who translates writing or speech from one language to another. [compare **interpreter**]

translucent /tranz'luːsənt/ *adjective* (*formal*)
Something that is **translucent** allows light to pass through it, but does not allow objects to be seen clearly through it: *dazzling white beaches and gentle translucent seas.* [*same as* **clear, transparent**; *opposite* **opaque**]

transmission /tranz'mɪʃən/ *noun*: **transmissions**
1 A **transmission** is a radio or television broadcast: *The transmission was heard by millions of people all over the world.* **2** (*uncount*) **Transmission** is the broadcasting of television and radio programmes: *the transmission of radio signals by satellite* □ *The television company received complaints about the programme after its transmission.* **3** (*uncount*) **Transmission** is also the passing of something from one person or place to another: *the transmission of disease.*

transmit /tranz'mɪt/ *verb*: **transmits, transmitting, transmitted**
1 Television or radio programmes and electronic signals **are transmitted** when they are sent out using radio waves: *The Olympic Games were transmitted by satellite all over the world.* [*same as* **broadcast**] **2** Something **is transmitted** when it is passed from one place or person to another: *The disease can be transmitted from cows to humans.* □ *a sexually transmitted disease.*

transmitter /tranz'mɪtə(r)/ *noun*: **transmitters**
A **transmitter** is a piece of equipment that sends and receives signals for television and radio programmes.

transparency /tran'sparənsɪ/ *noun*: **transparencies**
1 (*technical*) A **transparency** is a small photograph on glass or plastic in a frame, that you look at by putting in a projector that shines light behind it: *The students were shown transparencies of different parts of the heart.* [*same as* **slide**] **2** (*uncount*; *formal*) **Transparency** is the quality something has when you can see through it.

transparent /tran'sparənt/ *adjective*
1 You can see through a **transparent** object: *transparent glass.* [*same as* **clear, see-through**; *opposite* **opaque**] **2** Something is **transparent** when it is easily understood or recognized: *His motives were transparent.* [*same as* **obvious, evident**] — *adverb* **transparently:** *It was transparently clear that he was lying.*

transpire /tran'spaɪə(r)/ *verb* (*formal*): **transpires, transpiring, transpired**
1 Something secret or not previously known about **transpires** when people find out about it: *It later transpired that he had been in Paris all the time.* **2** Something **transpires** when it happens: *wait and see what transpires.*

transplant /'transplɑːnt/ *noun*; *verb*
▻ ***noun***: **transplants**
A **transplant** is a surgical operation in which a damaged organ is replaced by an organ from another person's body, or a damaged area of skin or bone is replaced by a piece of skin or bone from another part of the patient's body: *a kidney transplant.*
▻ ***verb*** /trans'plɑːnt/: **transplants, transplanting, transplanted**
1 A bodily organ **is transplanted** when it is taken from

a donor and put into the body of a patient by means of a surgical operation. **2** Things **are transplanted** when they are moved from one place to another: *The seedlings can be transplanted when they are about four inches tall.*

transport *noun; verb*
▻ ***noun*** /'transpɔ:t/ (*uncount*)
1 Transport is the vehicles that you travel in, such as cars, trains, aircraft and boats: *Do you have your own transport?* ▫ *My car has broken down so I've got no transport at the moment* ▫ *travel by public transport.* **2 Transport** is also the moving of people or things from one place to another: *the transport of goods by road and rail.*
▻ ***verb*** /tran'spɔ:t/: **transports, transporting, transported**
You **transport** people or things when you move them from one place to another: *He runs a business that transports chemicals by road.*

transportation /transpɔ:'teɪʃən/ (*AmE*) *noun* (*uncount*)
Transportation means transport.

transpose /tran'spoʊz/ *verb*: **transposes, transposing, transposed**
You **transpose** two things when you make them change places: *If you transpose the 'i' and 'a' in 'dairy' you get 'diary'.*

transvestite /tranz'vɛstaɪt/ *noun*: **transvestites**
A **transvestite** is a person who likes wearing the clothes of the opposite sex.

trap /trap/ *noun; verb*
▻ ***noun*: traps**
1 A **trap** is a piece of equipment, or a hole, usually with food attached, for catching animals: *a mouse trap.* **2** A **trap** is also a device for tricking someone into doing or saying something, or a system for catching people who are doing something wrong: *Police have set up a speed trap to catch motorists driving too quickly.* **3** A **trap** can also be an unpleasant or dangerous situation that you cannot escape easily: *families caught in the poverty trap.*
▻ ***verb*: traps, trapping, trapped**
1 You **trap** *eg* an animal when you catch it in a trap. **2** You **trap** someone when you trick them into doing or saying something. **3** You **are trapped** when you cannot escape from an unpleasant or dangerous place or situation: *Many passengers were trapped when the train ran off the lines.* ▫ *Thousands of families in Britain are trapped in a life of poverty and hardship.*

trapdoor /'trapdɔ:(r)/ *noun*: **trapdoors**
A **trapdoor** is a small door or opening in a floor or ceiling.

trapeze /trə'pi:z/ *noun*: **trapezes**
A **trapeze** is a short bar hanging between two ropes high up from the ground, that gymnasts or acrobats perform tricks on.

trappings /'trapɪŋz/ *noun* (*plural*)
The **trappings** of a particular occasion, ceremony or position are the items, *eg* clothes, money or power, that go with it: *possess all the trappings of success.*

trash /traʃ/ *noun* (*uncount*)
1 (*AmE*) **Trash** is rubbish: *One of his chores is to take out the trash.* **2** (*informal, derogatory*) **Trash** is anything that is of poor quality: *Don't waste your money on trash.* ▫ *Children shouldn't be encouraged to read trash.*

trashcan /'traʃkan/ (*AmE*) *noun*: **trashcans**
A **trashcan** is a dustbin.

trashy /'traʃɪ/ *adjective* (*informal, derogatory*): **trashier, trashiest**
Something that is **trashy** is of very poor quality: *trashy novels.*

trauma /'trɔ:mə/ *noun*: **traumas**
1 (*uncount*) **Trauma** is a state of shock caused by a physical wound or injury, or by a very upsetting experience: *Many passengers suffered long-lasting mental trauma as a result of the crash.* **2** A **trauma** is a very upsetting, unpleasant or frightening experience: *the trauma of getting divorced.*

traumatic /trɔ:'matɪk/ *adjective*
A **traumatic** event or experience is very upsetting, unpleasant or frightening: *Moving to a new house can be traumatic.* [*same as* **distressing, shocking**]

travel /'travəl/ *verb; noun*
▻ ***verb*: travels, travelling** (*AmE* **traveling**), **travelled** (*AmE* **traveled**)
1 You **travel** when you go to a place or from place to place, especially abroad or far from home: *She spent the summer travelling around Europe.* ▫ *He travels to work by train.* ▫ *How fast does sound travel?* **2** You **travel** a particular distance when you make a journey of that distance: *I travelled forty miles to see him.*
▻ ***noun*: travels**
1 (*uncount*) **Travel** is the act of travelling: *air travel.* **2** (*used in the plural*) Your **travels** are the journeys you make, especially abroad: *He won't get back from his travels until next month.*

travel agency /'travəl eɪdʒənsɪ/ *noun*: **travel agencies**
A **travel agency** is a shop where you can make arrangements and buy tickets for holidays and journeys.

travel agent /'travəl eɪdʒənt/ *noun*: **travel agents**
1 A **travel agent** is a person who owns or works in a travel agency. **2** A **travel agent**, or **travel agent's**, is a travel agency: *I've got to call at the travel agent's to collect the tickets.*

traveller (*AmE* **traveler**) /'travələ(r)/ *noun*: **travellers**
A **traveller** is a person who travels a lot or who is making a journey.

traveller's cheque (*AmE* **traveler's check**) /'travələrz tʃɛk/ *noun*: **traveller's cheques**
A **traveller's cheque** is a cheque bought at a bank, that can be exchanged for the local currency when you are abroad.

traverse /trə'vɜ:rs/ *verb* (*formal*): **traverses, traversing, traversed**
You **traverse** a place when you go across, over or through it: *He traversed the room slowly.*

travesty /'travəstɪ/ *noun*: **travesties**
A **travesty** is an example or copy of something that gives a false or bad impression of the real thing: *His trial was a travesty of justice.* [*same as* **distortion**]

trawler /'trɔ:lə(r)/ *noun*: **trawlers**
A **trawler** is a fishing boat which catches fish in the large net it drags behind it.

tray /treɪ/ *noun*: **trays**
A **tray** is a flat piece of *eg* wood, metal or plastic with raised edges, for carrying food and drink: *She piled the plates and saucers on the tray.* ▫ *a tray of cakes and sandwiches.* [see picture at **kitchen**]

treacherous /'trɛtʃərəs/ *adjective*
1 A **treacherous** person is someone who betrays you or is disloyal to you: *Treacherous Ian had seen me entering the office late in the evening and reported me to one of the directors.* [*same as* **disloyal**; *opposite* **loyal**] **2** Things such as weather conditions, or conditions *eg*

at sea or in the mountains, can be described as **treacherous** if they make sailing, driving, or climbing very dangerous or risky: *Motorists are warned of treacherous driving conditions on Scotland's roads tonight.* □ *There are treacherous currents in this stretch of the river, so it is unsafe to swim.* [*same as* **dangerous, hazardous**]

treachery /'trɛtʃən/ *noun* (*uncount*)
Treachery is the act of doing something that could lead to your country, or someone who trusts you, being harmed. [*same as* **betrayal, disloyalty**]

treacle /'tri:kəl/ *noun* (*uncount*)
Treacle is a sweet, thick, dark, sticky liquid made from sugar and used *eg* in cakes: *treacle tart.*

tread /trɛd/ *verb*; *noun*
▻ ***verb***: **treads, trod, trodden** or **trod**
1 You **tread** on something when you walk or step on it: *Don't tread on the flowers.* □ *I accidentally trod on the dog's tail.* **2** You **tread** in a particular way when you walk in that way: *She trod carefully over the broken glass.* **3** You **tread** something *eg* into the ground when you crush it with your foot or feet: *Don't tread the ash into the carpet!* □ *He put the plant in the hole and trod the soil down firmly round it.* □ *There are crumbs on the carpet; mind you don't tread them in.* □ *Everybody took part in treading the grapes.* [*same as* **trample**]
▻ ***noun***: **treads**
1 (*used in the singular*) Your **tread** is the sound you make while walking: *the heavy tread of their boots on the bridge.* **2** (*count or uncount*) The **tread** on a tyre is the raised pattern on the surface, that grips the road.
▻ ***phrase*** You **tread carefully** when you are careful about how you act and behave: *Tread carefully or you'll upset her.*

treason /'tri:zən/ *noun* (*uncount*)
Treason is the crime of doing anything that might lead to your country being harmed, such as giving national secrets to an enemy: *commit treason* □ *be executed for treason.*

treasure /'trɛʒə(r)/ *noun*; *verb*
▻ ***noun***: **treasures**
1 Treasure is wealth and riches, especially in the form of gold, silver, precious stones and jewels, collected over a period of time and often kept hidden: *buried treasure.* **2** (*used in the plural*) **Treasures** are things of great value, especially works of art. **3** (*informal*) You can call someone a **treasure** if they are a good friend and help you a lot.
▻ ***verb***: **treasures, treasuring, treasured**
You **treasure** something that is valuable and precious to you: *She treasures the photographs of her grandchildren.*

treasurer /'trɛʒərə(r)/ *noun*: **treasurers**
A club's **treasurer** is the person responsible for its money and accounts.

treasury /'trɛʒəri/ *noun*: **treasuries**
The **treasury** is the government department responsible for a country's finances, including the collection of taxes.

treat /tri:t/ *verb*; *noun*
▻ ***verb***: **treats, treating, treated**
1 You **treat** someone or something in a particular way when you deal with them or behave towards them in that way: *She treated him badly.* □ *Don't treat the accident as a joke.* □ *Mountains are dangerous, especially in winter, and must be treated with respect.* **2** A doctor or nurse **treats** a patient or illness when they give the patient medical care to make them better: *one of several ways to treat patients suffering from depression.* **3** You **treat** *eg* wood when you coat it with a substance that will protect it, *eg* from the effects of bad weather. **4** You **treat** someone when you pay for something special, such as a meal, for them: *I'll treat you to lunch seeing it's your birthday.* □ *I decided to treat myself to some new clothes.*
▻ ***noun***: **treats**
A **treat** is something such as an outing, meal or present given as a gift by one person to another.

treatise /'tri:tɪs/ *noun*: **treatises**
A **treatise** is a formal piece of writing that discusses a subject in detail: *Darwin's treatise 'The Origin of Species'.*

treatment /'tri:tmənt/ *noun*: **treatments**
1 (*count or uncount*) **Treatment**, or a **treatment**, is the medical or surgical care given to a patient, or to cure an illness: *need dental treatment* □ *He's developing a new treatment for flu.* **2** (*uncount*) Your **treatment** of something or someone is the way you deal with them or behave towards them: *His treatment of women is terrible.* □ *Monet's characteristic treatment of light and shadow* □ *rough treatment.*

treaty /'tri:tɪ/ *noun*: **treaties**
A **treaty** is a formal agreement between countries or governments: *a peace treaty* □ *the Treaty of Paris.*

treble[1] /'trɛbəl/ *determiner*; *adjective*; *verb*
▻ ***determiner***
One thing is **treble** the size or amount of something else when it is three times as large or there are three times as much of it: *House prices are treble what they were ten years ago.*
▻ ***adjective***
You use **treble** before a number when that number occurs three times in a row: *Her phone number is nine, five, six, treble eight, two* [= 956 8882]
▻ ***verb***: **trebles, trebling, trebled**
Something **trebles** when it becomes three times as large: *House prices have trebled in the last ten years.* [see also **triple**]

treble[2] /'trɛbəl/ *noun*: **trebles**
1 (*uncount*) The **treble** in a piece of written music is the upper range of notes in it, especially those played with the right hand on a piano. [see also **clef**] **2** A **treble** is a young boy with a high singing voice. **3** (*uncount*) A boy who has this singing voice sings **treble**. [compare **alto**]

treble clef /trɛbəl 'klɛf/ *noun*: **treble clefs**
A **treble clef** is a sign at the beginning of a piece of written music that shows that the music is written in a high pitch.

tree /tri:/ *noun*: **trees**
A **tree** is a tall plant with a hard trunk and branches on its upper part: *a clump of trees* □ *an oak tree* □ *cut down several trees.* [see also **Christmas tree, family tree**]
▻ ***phrase*** (*informal*) You are **barking up the wrong tree** if you have the wrong idea about something, or the wrong approach to it: *I can't help thinking they are on the right track, and that it's we who are barking up the wrong tree.*

trek /trɛk/ *verb*; *noun*
▻ ***verb***: **treks, trekking, trekked**
You **trek** somewhere when you go on a long, difficult journey there, usually on foot: *He trekked up to the source of the Ganges.*
▻ ***noun***: **treks**
A **trek** is a long, hard journey, usually on foot: *a two-month trek across Africa.*

trellis /ˈtrɛlɪs/ *noun*: **trellises**
A **trellis** is a frame made of narrow wooden strips, used to support climbing plants.

tremble /ˈtrɛmbəl/ *verb*: **trembles, trembling, trembled**
1 You **tremble** when you shake, *eg* because you are cold or frightened: *She was trembling with cold.* □ *His hands were trembling as he rang the bell.* **2** Your voice **trembles** when it sounds unsteady: *Her voice trembled with excitement.* [*same as* **vibrate**]

tremendous /trɪˈmɛndəs/ *adjective*
1 Something that is **tremendous** is great in size or amount: *This car can travel at tremendous speeds.* □ *I've got a tremendous amount of work still to do.* [*same as* **enormous**, **huge**; *opposite* **tiny**] **2** (*informal*) Something that is **tremendous** is very good: *a tremendous performance of the opera.* □ *That's tremendous news! I'm so pleased.* [*opposite* **bad**] — *adverb* **tremendously:** *The film is tremendously exciting.* □ *I admire him tremendously.*

tremor /ˈtrɛmə(r)/ *noun*: **tremors**
1 A **tremor** is a shaking or trembling movement that you cannot control or stop: *He spoke with a slight tremor in his voice.* **2** A **tremor** is also a small earthquake: *There have been tremors in the Los Angeles region recently.*

tremulous /ˈtrɛmjʊləs/ *adjective* (*formal*)
Someone who is **tremulous** is shaking, *eg* with fear, nervousness or excitement: *'Who are you people?' she ventured in a tremulous voice.*

trench /trɛntʃ/ *noun*: **trenches**
A **trench** is a long narrow hole dug in the ground, *eg* for soldiers to hide in.

trend /trɛnd/ *noun*: **trends**
A **trend** is a general movement or direction, especially the direction something follows as it changes or develops: *the latest fashion trends* □ *the trend towards healthier eating* □ *There is a trend away from large cars.*
▻ ***phrase*** You **set the trend** if you start a new fashion.

trendy /ˈtrɛndɪ/ (*BrE*) *adjective* (*informal*): **trendier, trendiest**
Trendy people or things are fashionable: *a trendy club* □ *trendy clothes.*

trepidation /trɛpɪˈdeɪʃən/ *noun* (*uncount; formal*)
Trepidation is fear or nervousness: *I awaited my turn to jump with some considerable trepidation.*

trespass /ˈtrɛspəs/ *verb*: **trespasses, trespassing, trespassed**
You **trespass** when you enter someone else's land without permission: *The children were caught trespassing on the king's land.* — *noun* **trespasser:** *Trespassers will be prosecuted.*

trial /ˈtraɪəl/ *noun*: **trials**
1 (*count or uncount*) A **trial** is a legal process by which a jury listens to evidence and decides whether a person accused of a crime is guilty or innocent: *He will stand trial for murder* □ *They are still awaiting trial* □ *There are doubts about his chances of getting a fair trial.* **2** A **trial** is a test done to make sure that something works properly or that someone can do something properly before being permanently accepted or approved: *The new model will have to undergo several trials before it can be sold to members of the public.* □ *She's got the job for a trial period of three months.* **3** A **trial** is a person or thing that you worry about or that causes you problems: *Her son is a great trial to her.* **4** (*usually in the plural*) The **trials** of something are the worry, trouble and problems that it causes you: *the trials of raising a family.*
▻ ***phrases*** **1 a** A person charged with a crime is **on trial** when they are being tried in a court of law: *She is on trial for burglary.* **b** A piece of machinery, drug or person is **on trial** when they are being tested to check that they work properly before being permanently accepted or approved. **2** You do something by **trial and error** when you keep trying different ways or different things until you find the correct, proper or best one: *He learnt to cook by trial and error.*

trial run /traɪəl ˈrʌn/ *noun*: **trial runs**
A **trial run** is a test to make sure you can do something properly, or that something works properly, before it is actually needed: *take the new car for a trial run before the race.*

triangle /ˈtraɪaŋgəl/ *noun*: **triangles**
1 A **triangle** is a flat shape with three sides and three angles. [see picture at **shapes**] **2** A **triangle** is a musical instrument consisting of a metal bar shaped into a triangle that you hit with a metal stick to play. [see picture at **orchestra**]

triangular /traɪˈaŋgjʊlə(r)/ *adjective*
A **triangular** object has the shape of a triangle: *a triangular scarf.*

tribal /ˈtraɪbəl/ *adjective*
Tribal describes things that belong to or are done by a tribe or tribes: *tribal dances* □ *tribal warfare.*

tribe /traɪb/ *noun*: **tribes**
A **tribe** is a group of families or communities who are linked by social, economic and political ties, and who usually have a common culture, language and leader: *She's a member of the Zulu tribe.*

tribesman /ˈtraɪbzmən/ or **tribeswoman** /ˈtraɪbzwʊmən/ *noun*: **tribesmen, tribeswomen**
A **tribesman** is a man, and a **tribeswoman** is a woman, who belongs to a particular tribe.

tribulation /trɪbjʊˈleɪʃən/ *noun* (*count or uncount; formal*): **tribulations**
Tribulation is suffering, great sorrow or trouble: *a life filled with tribulation* □ *a book describing her trials and tribulations during the war.*

tribunal /traɪˈbjuːnəl/ *noun*: **tribunals**
A **tribunal** is a group of people appointed to investigate particular problems and disputes: *an industrial tribunal*

tributary /ˈtrɪbjʊtərɪ/ *noun*: **tributaries**
A **tributary** is a stream or river that flows into a larger river or lake.

tribute /ˈtrɪbjuːt/ *noun*: **tributes**
1 (*count or uncount*) A **tribute** is something that you give or say to express praise, thanks, admiration or affection: *A programme about his life and work was shown on the television as a tribute when he died.* □ *Everybody paid tribute to her courage.* **2** (*usually in the singular*) One thing is a **tribute** to another when it is a sign of how good it is: *Her success was a tribute to all her hard work.*

trick /trɪk/ *noun*; *adjective*; *verb*
▻ ***noun***: **tricks**
1 To play a **trick** on someone is to do or say something to deceive or fool them: *That was a mean trick to play.* □ *He wondered if the sound was real, or if his imagination was playing tricks on him.* **2** A **trick** is also a clever or skilful act which surprises, puzzles or amuses people: *a card trick.* **3** A **trick** is a special, usually clever, way of doing something: *The cupboard door sticks and there's a trick to opening it.* □ *the tricks of the trade.*
▻ ***adjective***
1 Trick photography uses a clever arrangement of images to produce photgraphs showing things that

are physically impossible. **2 Trick** questions are cleverly phrased to prevent you understanding some significant point, so that you are easily trapped into giving a wrong answer.
▻ ***verb***: **tricks, tricking, tricked**
Someone **tricks** you when they deceive or cheat you, especially to make you do something you don't want to do: *He realized he had been tricked.* ▫ *She was tricked into agreeing to help.* ▫ *She tricked him out of his money.*
▻ ***phrases*** **1** (*informal*) Something **does the trick** when it does what you want or need it to do: *She had a nasty cold but the medicine did the trick.* [= made her better] **2** (*AmE*) **Trick or treat** is the children's practice of dressing up on Hallowe'en to call at people's houses to threaten to play a trick unless they are given sweets.

trickery /'trɪkərɪ/ *noun* (*uncount*)
Trickery is the use of tricks to deceive or cheat: *She used trickery to discover what his plans are.*

trickle /'trɪkəl/ *verb*; *noun*
▻ ***verb***: **trickles, trickling, trickled**
1 Liquid **trickles** when it flows in a thin or slow stream: *tears trickling down his face.* **2** Things or people **trickle** when they move slowly and gradually: *People began to trickle into the hall for the talk.* ▫ *Donations were trickling in.*
▻ ***noun***: **trickles**
1 (*usually in the singular*) A **trickle** of liquid is a thin slow stream: *The waterfall was reduced to a trickle.* ▫ *A trickle of blood is running down his leg.* **2** A **trickle** of people or things is a slow or gradual flow or movement of them: *The children ran into the sea in trickles.* ▫ *The flow of refugees was down to a trickle.* ▫ *A trickle of people were still entering the hall.*

tricky /'trɪkɪ/ *adjective*: **trickier, trickiest**
A **tricky** problem or situation is one that must be dealt with or handled with skill and care: *The US government's decision to welcome Gerry Adams has put John Major in a tricky position.*

tricycle /'traɪsɪkəl/ *noun*: **tricycles**
A **tricycle** is a vehicle with two wheels at the back and one at the front, driven by pedals.

tried /traɪd/ *verb*
Tried is the past participle and past tense of **try**.
▻ ***phrase*** Something is **tried and tested** when it has been tested and has been proved to be good or to work properly.

trifle /'traɪfəl/ *noun*; *verb*
▻ ***noun***: **trifles**
1 (*usually in the plural*) **Trifles** are things that are not very important or valuable: *Don't waste your money on trifles.* **2** (*count or uncount*) **Trifle** or a **trifle** is a dessert made from plain cake spread with jam or jelly and fruit and topped with custard and cream.
▻ ***verb***: **trifles, trifling, trifled**

> ***phrasal verb***
> You **trifle with** a person or their feelings when you treat them without respect.

▻ ***phrase*** You use **a trifle** to describe something that exists or is true to a small extent: *I'm a trifle surprised that he didn't come with you.* ▫ *She was a trifle breathless after the run.*

trifling /'traɪflɪŋ/ *adjective*
A **trifling** matter is not important. [*same as* **insignificant, trivial**; *opposite* **important**]

trigger /'trɪgə(r)/ *noun*; *verb*
▻ ***noun***: **triggers**
The **trigger** of a gun is the small lever that you squeeze to make it fire.
▻ ***verb***: **triggers, triggering, triggered**
One event **triggers** another, or **triggers** it **off**, when it causes it to start or happen: *The smoke triggered off the fire alarm.* ▫ *Their quarrel was triggered by a silly disagreement over money.*

trike /traɪk/ *noun* (*informal*): **trikes**
A **trike** is a tricycle.

trillion /'trɪljən/ *noun*: **trillions**
1 a In Britain and Europe, a **trillion** is a million million millions. **b** In the US and Canada, a **trillion** is a million millions. **2** (*used in the plural*; *informal*) There are **trillions** of something if there are a very large number of them: *There are trillions of things we could do.* [compare **billion**]

trilogy /'trɪlədʒɪ/ *noun*: **trilogies**
A **trilogy** is a group of three plays, novels, poems or operas which have the same subject but are each complete in themselves.

trim /trɪm/ *verb*; *noun*; *adjective*
▻ ***verb***: **trims, trimming, trimmed**
1 You **trim** something when you cut a little from it to make it neat and tidy: *My hair needs trimming.* **2** You **trim** something when you make it smaller by removing part of it: *trim hundreds of pounds off the cost.* **3** You **trim** *eg* clothes when you decorate them: *She trimmed her dress with lace.* ▫ *a fur-trimmed coat.*
▻ ***noun*** (*usually in the singular*): **trims**
You have a **trim** when a hairdresser cuts your hair to make it neater without changing your hairstyle.
▻ ***adjective***: **trimmer, trimmest**
1 Something that is **trim** is neat and tidy: *a house with a trim garden front and back.* **2** A person who is **trim** has a neat, slim figure.

trimming /'trɪmɪŋ/ *noun*: **trimmings**
1 (*uncount*) **Trimming** is ribbon, lace or some other decoration added *eg* to a garment. **2** (*used in the plural*) The **trimmings** are the vegetables and sauces usually served with a particular dish: *roast beef with all the trimmings.*

trinket /'trɪŋkɪt/ *noun*: **trinkets**
A **trinket** is a small cheap ornament or piece of jewellery.

trio /'tri:oʊ/ *noun* (*with a singular or plural verb*): **trios**
A **trio** is a group of three people or things, especially three singers, musicians or instruments: *a piece of music arranged for guitar trio.*

trip /trɪp/ *verb*; *noun*
▻ ***verb***: **trips, tripping, tripped**
1 You **trip** if you catch your foot on something and fall, or nearly fall, over: *She tripped over the edge of the carpet.* ▫ *He tripped up the stairs.* ▫ *Mind you don't trip on the step.* [*same as* **stumble**] **2** You **trip** someone if you put something such as your own foot in front of them so that they fall, or nearly fall, over it: *One of the boys tripped her up.*
▻ ***noun***: **trips**
1 A **trip** is a short journey to a place and back again: *a shopping trip* ▫ *a trip to the zoo.* **2** (*usually in the singular*) A **trip** is an act of catching your foot in something and falling, or nearly falling, over: *She had a nasty trip on the steps.* [*same as* **stumble**] **3** (*slang*) A **trip** is also a strange, dream-like experience caused by taking a drug.

tripartite /traɪ'pɑ:taɪt/ *adjective*
A **tripartite** thing is divided into, or is made up of, three parts: *a tripartite legal system.*

tripe /traɪp/ *noun* (*uncount*)

1 Tripe is parts of the stomach of a cow or sheep, used as food. **2** (*informal*) What someone says or writes is **tripe** if it is nonsense. [*same as* **rubbish**]

triple /'trɪpəl/ *adjective*; *determiner*; *verb*
▻ ***adjective***
A **triple** thing is made up of three parts or things: *a triple bypass* □ *a triple somersault.*
▻ ***determiner***
One thing is **triple** the size or quantity of another if it is three times as large, or there are three times as much of it: *We've had triple the number of applications we had last year.*
▻ ***verb***: **triples, tripling, tripled**
You **triple** something if you make it three times as great, much or many; something **triples** if it becomes three times as great, much or many: *The number of students taking English has tripled this year.*

triplet /'trɪplət/ *noun*: **triplets**
Triplets are three children born to the same mother at the same time. [compare **twin**]

triplicate /'trɪplɪkət/ *noun*
▻ ***phrase*** You write something **in triplicate** when you make three copies of it or write it three times: *Please fill out this form in triplicate.*

tripod /'traɪpɒd/ *noun*: **tripods**
A **tripod** is a stand with three legs for supporting *eg* a camera.

trite /traɪt/ *adjective*
A **trite** remark is one that has no meaning, usually because it has been repeated or used so often. [*same as* **hackneyed**]

triumph /'traɪəmf/ *noun*; *verb*
▻ ***noun***: **triumphs**
1 A **triumph** is a great victory, success or achievement: *It was a personal triumph for her.* **2** (*uncount*) **Triumph** is the feeling of joy or happiness that you feel when you win a great victory or are successful: *a shout of triumph.*
▻ ***verb*** (*formal*): **triumphs, triumphing, triumphed**
You **triumph** if you win a victory or are successful: *She has managed to triumph over hardship and poverty.*

triumphant /traɪ'ʌmfənt/ *adjective*
Someone who is **triumphant** is very happy because they have won a victory or been successful: *the triumphant medal-winners.* — *adverb* **triumphantly:** *She ran triumphantly across the finishing line.*

trivia /'trɪvɪə/ *noun* (*plural*)
Trivia are unimportant or minor matters or details: *He gets too involved in trivia to be able to recognize the really important issues.*

trivial /'trɪvɪəl/ *adjective*
Something **trivial** is not very important: *This are only one or two trivial errors in your essay.* [*same as* **insignificant**]

triviality /trɪvɪ'alɪtɪ/ *noun*: **trivialities**
1 Trivialitities are unimportant things: *Don't waste your time worrying about trivialities.* **2** (*uncount*) The **triviality** of something is the fact it is unimportant: *the triviality of his novels.* [*same as* **importance**]

trivialize or **trivialise** /'trɪvɪəlaɪz/ *verb*: **trivializes, trivializing, trivialized**
You **trivialize** something if you make it seem unimportant, or less important than it really is: *She feels her position in the company is trivialized.*

trod /trɒd/ *verb*
Trod is the past tense of **tread.**

trodden /'trɒdən/ *verb*; *adjective*
▻ ***verb***
Trodden is the past participle of **tread.**
▻ ***adjective***
Ground is **trodden** when it has been flattened by a lot of people walking over it.

trolley /'trɒlɪ/ *noun*: **trolleys**
1 A **trolley** is a small cart or basket on wheels used for carrying *eg* luggage or shopping: *Most supermarket trolleys have a seat where small children can sit.* **2** A **trolley** is also a small table on wheels, usually with a shelf underneath, used for carrying *eg* food and plates from the kitchen to the dining room. **3** (*AmE*) A **trolley** is a tram.

trombone /trɒm'boʊn/ *noun*: **trombones**
A **trombone** is a brass musical wind instrument, which has a sliding tube for changing the pitch of notes. [see picture at **orchestra**]

troop /truːp/ *noun*; *verb*
▻ ***noun***: **troops**
1 (*usually in the plural*) **Troops** are soldiers: *British troops in Northern Ireland* □ *troop movements.* **2** A **troop** of people or animals is a group of them: *a troop of children.*
▻ ***verb***: **troops, trooping, trooped**
People **troop** somewhere when they go there in a group: *The children trooped off the bus.*

trophy /'troʊfɪ/ *noun*: **trophies**
A **trophy** is something such as a cup, medal or plate given as a prize for winning a race or competition: *She won the school's tennis trophy two years running.*

tropical /'trɒpɪkəl/ *adjective*
Tropical places or things relate to, are in or are from the tropics: *tropical rainforests* □ *a tropical island.*

tropics /'trɒpɪks/ *noun* (*plural*)
The **tropics** are the hot, dry parts of the earth near the equator.

trot /trɒt/ *verb*; *noun*
▻ ***verb***: **trots, trotting, trotted**
1 A horse **trots** when it runs at a moderate pace, taking small steps: *She made the horse trot along the path.* [compare **canter, gallop**] **2** You **trot** somewhere if you move quite quickly, taking small steps: *The little boy trotted along behind his father.*
▻ ***noun*** (*usually in the singular*): *She made the horse slow down so that it was moving at a trot.* □ *He headed off at a trot.*
▻ ***phrase*** You do a series of things **on the trot** when you do them one after the other: *He missed three meetings on the trot.*

trouble /'trʌbəl/ *noun*; *verb*
▻ ***noun***: **troubles**
1 (*uncount*) You have **trouble** doing something if you find it difficult to do or if it gives you a lot of problems or a lot of work: *A washing machine will save you a lot of time and trouble.* □ *I didn't have any trouble finding a new job.* **2** (*used in the singular*) The **trouble** in a particular situation or with a particular person is the thing about them that will cause problems: *The trouble with this plan is that it's too expensive.* □ *It's a beautiful house but it needs a new roof, that's the trouble.* □ *Your trouble is that you're too generous.* **3** (*uncount*) **a** You have *eg* heart **trouble** or kidney **trouble** when there is something wrong with your heart or kidneys: *She's had back trouble for several years now.* **b** A car has engine **trouble** when its engine doesn't work properly. **4** (*uncount*) There is **trouble** if people are fighting or arguing: *I knew there was going to be trouble.* □ *He's always making trouble.* **5** (*used in the plural*) Your **troubles** are your worries and problems: *I hope that all my troubles are over now.*

▻ ***verb***: **troubles, troubling, troubled**
Something **troubles** you if you are worried about it: *I wish you'd tell me what's troubling you.* ▫ *She's troubled by the idea that her husband might lose his job.* — *adjective* **troubling:** *There are several aspects of this problem that I find troubling.*

▻ ***phrases*** **1** (*informal*) You can say that someone **is asking for trouble** if they are acting in a way that is likely to give them problems later on. **2** You can use phrases such as '**Could I trouble you ...**' and '**Might I trouble you ...**' when you want to ask someone to do something for you, especially when you want to be particularly polite, or when you want to apologize for disturbing them: *Might I trouble you to open the window a little?* ▫ *Could I trouble you for the salt?* **3** You **go to a lot of trouble** to do something if it gives you a lot of work, or requires effort: *I went to a lot of trouble to get this copied for you.* **4 a** Someone is **in trouble** if they have serious problems: *The company is in financial trouble.* ▫ *He's in trouble with the law.* **b** A child is **in trouble** when he or she has done something wrong and will be punished for it: *She's in trouble for not doing her homework.* **5** Something that is **no trouble** doesn't take much effort to do or deal with: '*Thanks for looking after Amy.*' '*That's OK, she was no trouble*'. **6** You **save yourself the trouble** of doing something that requires effort when you avoid doing it. **7** You **take the trouble** to do something, or **go to the trouble** of doing it, when you make the effort to do it: *He didn't even take the trouble to answer the letter.* **8** You **take trouble with** or **over** something if you spend a lot of time doing it carefully or correctly: *She took a lot of trouble over the meal.*

troubled /ˈtrʌbəld/ *adjective*
1 A **troubled** person has a lot of worries or problems: *he was tired, upset and troubled by a vague feeling of guilt.* **2** A **troubled** time or organization has a lot of problems to resolve: *Britain's troubled rail services.*

troublemaker /ˈtrʌbəlmeɪkə(r)/ *noun*: **troublemakers**
A **troublemaker** is a person who continually and usually deliberately causes trouble, fights or arguments.

troublesome /ˈtrʌbəlsəm/ *adjective*
A **troublesome** person or thing is one that causes worry or problems.

trough /trɒf/ *noun*: **troughs**
1 A **trough** is a long, low, narrow open container that holds water or feed for animals. **2** A **trough** is a low point: *There is a trough in the demand for electricity after midnight.* [*opposite* **peak**]

troupe /tru:p/ *noun*: **troupes**
A **troupe** is a group of *eg* actors or singers who work together.

trousers /ˈtraʊzəz/ *noun* (*plural*)
Trousers are a garment for the lower part of the body, that reaches from the waist and that covers each leg separately down to the ankle: *He's wearing blue trousers.* ▫ *Girls aren't allowed to wear trousers to school.* ▫ *a pair of velvet trousers.* [see picture at **clothing**]

> **Trouser** is the adjectival form used before another noun: *She put the ticket in her trouser pocket.* ▫ *trouser buttons.*

trout /traʊt/ *noun* (*uncount or count*): **trout**
A **trout** is a kind of fish that lives in rivers and lakes: *She bought a couple of trout for supper.*

trowel /ˈtraʊəl/ *noun*: **trowels**
A **trowel** is **a** a small, hand-held tool with a flat blade that you use for applying and spreading *eg* plaster. **b** a small, hand-held tool with a slightly curved blade, used in gardening. [see picture at **tool**]

truancy /ˈtru:ənsɪ/ *noun* (*uncount*)
Truancy is the practice of being absent from school without permission: *He was expelled for truancy.*

truant /ˈtru:ənt/ *noun*: **truants**
A **truant** is a pupil who is absent from school without permission.

▻ ***phrase*** Children **play truant** if they are absent from school without permission.

truce /tru:s/ *noun*: **truces**
A **truce** is an agreement to stop fighting for a usually short period of time: *The French called a truce.* ▫ *The other side didn't agree to the truce.*

truck /trʌk/ *noun*: **trucks**
1 (*AmE*) A **truck** is a lorry. [see picture at **vehicle**] **2** (*BrE*) A **truck** is a large vehicle that is open at the back and that is used for transporting *eg* animals. [compare **lorry**] **3** (*BrE*) A **truck** is also an open railway wagon for carrying goods.

trudge /trʌdʒ/ *verb*; *noun*

▻ ***verb***: **trudges, trudging, trudged**
You **trudge** somewhere if you walk with slow, heavy, tired steps: *The children trudged along in the snow.* ▫ *He trudged up the stairs.*

▻ ***noun*** (*usually in the singular*): *a long trudge up the hill* ▫ *the weary trudge home from school.*

true /tru:/ *adjective*; *adverb*

▻ ***adjective***: **truer, truest**
1 A **true** story or statement is one that is based on facts or real happenings, as distinct from being invented: *a movie based on the true story of a gypsy girl* ▫ *The public want to be given true facts and figures.* ▫ *Is it true about the bank collapsing?* ▫ *It's incredible, but true, that the sun's dying.* [*same as* **correct**; *opposite* **untrue, false**] **2** Something is **true** if it happens, or is the case: *People avoid you if you have a handicap, and this is all the more true if the handicap is a mental one.* ▫ *That may have been true before the war.* **3** Your **true** feelings are your real ones; the **true** cause of something is the thing that really caused it: *We're learning more about the true nature of the disease.* ▫ *We hide our true selves from others.* ▫ *I wonder what their true intentions are?* ▫ *You're getting the shares at far less than their true value.* [*same as* **real**] **4** A person or thing that is a **true** example of something has the right characteristics to be called that thing: *He was a true mercenary; he just wanted money.* ▫ *The superpowers are the only states with true independence.* ▫ *Steve showed true brotherly love.* ▫ *We're seeing the end of true socialism.* [*same as* **genuine**] **5** A structure, or part of one, is **true** if it is straight and in the right position: *I haven't managed to get the cupboard door quite true.*

▻ ***adverb*** (*sentence adverb, sometimes used as an answer*)
You can use '**true**' like '**it's true**' or '**that's true**' to admit that something is the case: *True, we can't go back to those times.* ▫ *'But she's usually a bit late.' 'True.'*

▻ ***phrases*** **1** Something such as a dream, wish or prediction **comes true** when it actually happens; **a dream come true** is one that has come true: *She now had her own house and garden; it was like a dream come true.* **2** You use '**it's true**' and '**that's true**' to admit that something is the case: *There are problems, it's true, but none we can't solve.* ▫ *'But she's got the right background.' 'That's true.'* **3 a** You are **true to** your word or promise if you do what you have promised to do: *True to his word, Nichols phoned back that evening.* [*same as* **faithful**] **b** You are **true to** your principles when you do what you believe is right. [*same as* **loyal, faithful**]

c You are **true to** yourself if you behave in a natural and genuine way, without pretence or deceit.

truffle /'trʌfəl/ *noun*: **truffles**
1 A **truffle** is a usually round sweet made typically with cream, butter, chocolate and rum, and coated in cocoa. **2** A **truffle** is also a type of dark round fungus which grows underground and is good to eat.

truly /'tru:lɪ/ *adverb*
1 What **truly** happens, or what you **truly** think, is what really happens, or what you really think: *Is that truly what he said?* □ *What's truly happening?* □ *Tell me what you truly want to do.* [*same as* **really**] **2** You say you are *eg* **truly** amazed or **truly** grateful if you genuinely feel that way: *We were truly shocked by the levels of racism.* □ *I'm truly sorry.* [*same as* **genuinely**] **3** Someone or something that is **truly** a certain thing is genuinely or completely that thing: *He's often described as a truly Christian prince.* □ *We may never have a truly classless society.* [*same as* **genuinely**, **completely**, **utterly**] **4** (*intensifying*) **Truly** can also be used for emphasis: *a truly remarkable new novel.* [*same as* **absolutely**, **quite**] **5** (*sentence adverb*) You use '**truly**' to emphasize that you mean or believe what you are saying: *Truly, this is the chance I've been waiting for.*
▻ ***phrases*** **1** For **well and truly** see **well**. **2** At the end of a formal business letter people sometimes write '**Yours truly**,' before signing their name.

trump /trʌmp/ *noun* (*usually in the plural*)
Trumps are the suit of cards which has been declared to have a higher value than any other suit in some card games such as whist.
▻ ***phrase*** Your **trump card** is a secret advantage that you have: *Cheap labour - the trump card always in the hands of our competitors.*

trumpet /'trʌmpɪt/ *noun*; *verb*
▻ ***noun***: **trumpets**
A **trumpet** is a brass musical instrument with a narrow tube and flared bell and a powerful, high, clear tone, that you blow into to play. [see picture at **orchestra**]
▻ ***verb***: **trumpets, trumpeting, trumpeted**
An elephant **trumpets** when it makes its typical loud cry.
▻ ***phrase*** You **blow your own trumpet** when you boast about yourself and your achievements.

truncated /trʌŋ'keɪtɪd/ *adjective*
Something that is **truncated** has been shortened: *He had time only to give a truncated version of the speech he had prepared.*

truncheon /'trʌnʃən/ *noun*: **truncheons**
A **truncheon** is a short, thick heavy stick, carried by police officers. [*same as* **baton**]

trundle /'trʌndəl/ *verb*: **trundles, trundling, trundled**
1 A vehicle **trundles** if it moves heavily, slowly and noisily: *The lorry trundled through the deserted streets.* **2** You **trundle** something somewhere if you push it along slowly and noisily on its wheels: *He trundled the wheelbarrow down to the bottom of the garden.*

trunk /trʌŋk/ *noun*: **trunks**
1 The **trunk** of a tree is its main stem without the branches and roots: *a fallen tree trunk.* **2** A person's **trunk** is the main part of their body, not including the head and limbs. **3** A **trunk** is a large rigid box or chest for storing or transporting clothes and personal items. **4** (*AmE*) The **trunk** of a car is its boot. **5** An elephant's **trunk** is its long, strong nose.

trunks /trʌŋks/ *noun* (*plural*)
Trunks are close-fitting shorts or pants that men and boys wear while swimming: *swimming trunks.*

trust /trʌst/ *verb*; *noun*
▻ ***verb***: **trusts, trusting, trusted**
1 You **trust** someone when you believe they are honest or loyal and have no intention of harming you: *Remember that your children trust you.* □ *I picked out ten men I could trust.* □ *I had to tell my friend that his wife was not to be trusted.* [*same as* **rely on**] **2** You **trust** someone to do something when you believe they will do it properly: *Can I trust you to keep a complete secret?* □ *He'd built a team he could trust to do anything in his absence.* □ *You can trust me to get a fair deal.* □ *She was so moved she couldn't trust herself to speak.* [*same as* **rely on**] **3** You **trust** someone with something when you give it to them expecting them to take care of it: *Now, can I trust you with my car?* □ *Obviously Miles didn't trust her with his camera.* □ *No wonder they didn't want to trust her with their children.* [compare **entrust**] **4** You **trust** something when you believe it is reliable, safe or sound: *I don't trust that machine; it's gone wrong before.* □ *This is above all a boat you can trust.* □ *The details cannot be trusted.* □ *Apparently people trust Yorkshire accents.* **5** You **trust** other people's judgement, or your own, when you think they, or you, are right about something: *He wasn't sure that he dared trust his instincts.* □ *So you don't trust the judgement of art critics?* **6** (*usually with a negative*) You say you don't know if you can **trust** your eyes or ears when you can hardly believe what you are seeing or hearing. **7** (*old or formal*) If you say you **trust** that something is so, you are expressing the hope or expectation that it is: *All is well with you, I trust?* □ *I trust you will correct me if I'm wrong.* □ *I trust that's agreeable to you?*
▻ ***noun***: **trusts**
1 (*uncount*) You have **trust** in someone if you believe that they are honest or loyal and intend you no harm: *Between members of a family there is a high degree of mutual trust.* □ *He had to find a way of gaining their trust.* □ *You took advantage of my trust in you.* **2** (*uncount*) Someone or something is in your **trust** if you are responsible for them; you are in a position of **trust** when you are responsible for looking after something, or for keeping something secret: *The children were placed in my trust.* □ *What was so distasteful was that the Prince's valet had betrayed a position of trust.* **3** A **trust** is an arrangement by which money or property is managed for someone by an organization or a number of named individuals: *They used the money to set up a trust account for their child.*
▻ ***phrases*** **1** Money that is kept **in trust** for you is managed and invested by an organization on your behalf. **2** You **take** something that you are told **on trust** when you accept or believe it without checking it personally: *New and established ideas will be subjected to scrutiny, and not just accepted on trust.* **3** If you say, in reference to something silly that someone has done, '**trust** them **to do** that', you mean it is typical of them to do such a silly thing: *Trust you to fall in love with someone you can't have.*

trustee /trʌ'sti:/ *noun*: **trustees**
A **trustee** is a person who manages money or property for someone else.

trusting /'trʌstɪŋ/ *adjective*
A **trusting** person believes that other people are honest and do not mean to harm or hurt them: *a young boy with a trusting nature.*

trustworthy /'trʌstwɜ:ðɪ/ *adjective*
A **trustworthy** person is able to be trusted or depended on. [*same as* **reliable**]

trusty /'trʌstɪ/ *adjective*: **trustier, trustiest**
A **trusty** person or thing is one that you can trust or rely on: *my trusty old typewriter.*

truth /tru:θ/ *noun*: **truths** /tru:ðz/
1 (*uncount*) **Truth** is the state of being real, true or genuine: *Truth is often stranger than fiction.* □ *There is an element of truth in what he's told you.* **2** (*used in the singular*) The **truth** is all the facts about something: *The truth is, she doesn't love you any more.* □ *He always tries to tell the truth.* □ *She can usually be relied on to speak the truth.* **3** A **truth** is a generally accepted fact about something: *scientific truths.*
▻ ***phrases*** **1** You can say **in truth** or **in all truth** when you really believe something: *In all truth, I expected her to do better than this.* **2** You can say **to tell you the truth** when you want to admit something: *To tell you the truth, I can't remember where I parked the car.*

truthful /tru:θfəl/ *adjective*
1 A **truthful** person tells the truth: *She found it hard being truthful with him.* [*same as* **honest**] **2** A statement is **truthful** when it is true: *a truthful answer.* [*same as* **accurate**] — *adverb* **truthfully:** *She always tries to answer questions truthfully.*

try /traɪ/ *verb*; *noun*
▻ ***verb***: **tries**, **trying**, **tried**
1 You **try** to do something, or **try** and do it, when you make an effort to do it, because you need to, or want to, do it: *Back in the car, I tried to use the mobile phone.* □ *Oh, Aunt Louise, try to understand.* □ *Try and calm down.* □ *I came here to try and find him.* □ *He was trying not to laugh.* □ *I know you're nervous, but try not to be.* □ *You can't close your ears, no matter how hard you try.* □ *Sorry I didn't contact you; I did try to.* [*same as* **attempt**]

Notice that the form '**try** *and* do something' is used only with **try**, and never with **tries**, **tried** or **trying**: *Did you try and contact her?* But: *Were you trying to contact her?*

2 You **try** something when you use it or do it, *eg* to see if you like it, or if it is useful or effective: *people who are prepared to try new products* □ *Try the following exercise.* □ *You could try working for a nursing agency.* [see also **try out**] **3** You **try** a place or person when you go there to see if they can provide you with something you want, or want to know: *Try the village shop.* □ *Try the Hatchett Inn.* □ *I was recommended to try the local library.* **4** You **try** a door or window when you attempt to open it; you **try** *eg* a doorbell when you attempt to get some response from it; you **try** a person when you call their telephone number: *I tried the handle.* □ *He tried the starter button.* □ *Did you try her pulse?* □ *I'll try him again this evening.* **5** You **try** for something such as a job, or a place at university, when you make an effort to get it: *I was going to try for Oxford.* □ *He thought he might try for a part in the play.* **6** (*often in the passive*) A person who is accused of a crime **is tried** when they appear in a court of law before a judge and jury, who decide whether or not they are guilty: *He was to be tried by the Bavarian people's court.* □ *A court was set up to try the King for treason against the People of England.*
▻ ***noun***: **tries**
1 You have a **try** at something if you attempt to do it: *It was a ludicrous idea for avoiding paying for a licence, but he evidently thought it was worth a try.* □ *I was tempted to give curtain-making another try.* □ *Why don't you at least have a try at it?* **2** (*rugby*) A **try** is a score of three or four points gained by a player who succeeds in placing the ball over the opponent's goal line: *He scored two tries in the match against Scotland.*

phrasal verbs
try on You **try** clothes **on** when you put them on to see if they fit you and look nice: *I want to try on my costume.*
try out You **try** something **out** when you use it or do it, to see if you like it, or if it is useful or effective: *Try out our quick and tasty recipe.* □ *Harrison's watch was first tried out at sea by Captain Cooke.*

trying /'traɪɪŋ/ *adjective*
A person or thing is **trying** if it causes you a lot of worry or problems and makes you impatient or angry: *It's been a very trying day.*

T-shirt or **tee-shirt** /'ti:ʃɜ:t/ *noun*: **T-shirts**
A **T-shirt** is a light, casual shirt, often with no collar and usually with short sleeves: *You ought to wear a shirt and tie to work, not a T-shirt.* [see picture at **clothing**]

tub /tʌb/ *noun*: **tubs**
1 A **tub** is a round container of any size: *a tub that will hold several gallons of water* □ *a tub of ice cream.* **2** (*informal*) A **tub** is also a bath.

tuba /'tju:bə/ *noun*: **tubas**
A **tuba** is a large brass musical instrument with a low pitch. [see picture at **orchestra**]

tubby /'tʌbɪ/ *adjective* (*informal*): **tubbier**, **tubbiest**
A **tubby** person is rather fat. [*same as* **plump**]

tube /tju:b/ *noun*: **tubes**
1 A **tube** is a long, round hollow pipe used for *eg* conveying liquids or as a container: *She attached one end of the tube to the tap.* □ *a cardboard tube for carrying posters.* **2** A **tube** is a long, hollow container made from soft metal or plastic with a cap at one end, used for holding paste which is got out by squeezing: *a tube of toothpaste.* **3** **Tubes** in the body are long hollow structures: *bronchial tubes.* **4** (*BrE*; *used in the singular*) The **tube** is an underground railway, especially in London: *Did you come by tube or by bus?*

tuberculosis /tju:bɜ:kjʊ'loʊsɪs/ *noun* (*uncount*)
Tuberculosis is a serious infectious disease that can affect any part of the body but especially the lungs.

tubing /'tju:bɪŋ/ *noun* (*uncount*)
Tubing is a length of tube or series of tubes: *several feet of rubber tubing.*

tuck /tʌk/ *verb*: **tucks**, **tucking**, **tucked**
1 You **tuck** one garment, or one part of a garment, into another when you put any loose ends inside so that it is firm or tidy; you **tuck** a garment in when you put any loose ends inside *eg* your trousers or skirt to make it firm or neat: *He tucked his shirt in.* □ *She tucked her blouse into her skirt.* **2** You **tuck** *eg* your legs up when you put them into a folded position underneath your body: *She sat on the sofa with her legs tucked up.* **3** You **tuck** *eg* a child up or in when you fold the edges of the bedclothes tightly round them: *She tucked the child in.* **4** You **tuck** something somewhere if you put it into a small, hidden place: *He tucked the letter away out of sight.* **5** Something **is tucked** away when it is hidden or out of sight: *a tiny village tucked away in the bottom of the valley.*

phrasal verb
(*informal*) People **tuck in**, or **tuck into** food, when they willingly or happily eat a lot of food: *The children tucked into supper.*

Tuesday /'tju:zdɪ/ *noun* (*count or uncount*): **Tuesdays**
Tuesday is the second day of the week, coming after

Monday and before Wednesday: *She left on Tuesday.* □ *I usually work at home on Tuesdays* (or *on a Tuesday*). □ (*AmE*) *She doesn't work Tuesdays.* □ *Tuesday's meeting has been cancelled.* □ *Tuesday morning.*

tuft /tʌft/ *noun*: **tufts**
A **tuft** of something such as hair, feathers, wool or grass is a small bunch of it growing together.

tug /tʌg/ *verb*; *noun*
▻ ***verb***: **tugs, tugging, tugged**
You **tug** something, or **tug** at it, when you pull it sharply or strongly towards you: *She tugged at the rope.*
▻ ***noun***: **tugs**
1 (*usually in the singular*) You give something a **tug** when you pull it sharply or strongly towards you. **2** A **tug** or **tugboat** is a small boat with a very powerful engine, for towing larger ships: *Several tugboats were moored in the harbour.*

tuition /tjuːˈɪʃən/ *noun* (*uncount*)
Tuition is teaching or instruction, especially in a college or university, in how to play a musical instrument, or in small groups: *piano tuition* □ *private maths tuition* □ *tuition fees.*

tulip /ˈtjuːlɪp/ *noun*: **tulips**
A **tulip** is a brightly-coloured cup-shaped flower that appears in the spring.

tumble /ˈtʌmbəl/ *verb*; *noun*
▻ ***verb***: **tumbles, tumbling, tumbled**
1 People or things **tumble** when they fall suddenly and uncontrollably: *He tumbled down the stairs.* □ *Thomas was just at the stage of learning to walk, and kept tumbling over.* □ *The bike skidded and tumbled into a ditch, throwing him over the handlebars.* **2** People or things **tumble** somewhere when they move in disorganized, disorderly way: *The car stopped and a lot of childen tumbled out.* □ *Thoughts tumbled about in her brain.*
▻ ***noun*** (*usually in the singular*)
You have, or take, a **tumble** when you fall over.

> ***phrasal verb***
> (*informal*) You **tumble to** a fact when you realize it: *I finally tumbled to the fact he'd been lying all along.*

tumble drier or **tumble dryer** /ˈtʌmbəl draɪə(r)/ *noun*: **tumble driers**
A **tumble drier** is a machine that dries wet clothes or washing by turning them round and blowing hot air into them. — *verb* **tumble-dry:** *Do want these sheets tumble-dried?* □ *Don't tumble-dry anything made of silk.*

tumbler /ˈtʌmblə(r)/ *noun*: **tumblers**
A **tumbler** is a large drinking glass without a handle or stem.

tummy /ˈtʌmɪ/ *noun* (*informal*): **tummies**
Your **tummy** is your stomach. It is usually used by or to young children: *She lay the baby down on her tummy.* □ *He's got an upset tummy.*

tumour (*AmE* **tumor**) /ˈtjuːmə(r)/ *noun*: **tumours**
A **tumour** is a mass of diseased tissue or cells in the body: *a tumour on a lung* □ *a brain tumour* □ *This tumour isn't malignant.*

tumult /ˈtjuːmʌlt/ *noun* (*count or uncount*; *formal*)
A **tumult** is a loud or confused noise, especially one made by a crowd: *He waited for the tumult to die down before beginning his speech.*

tumultuous /tjuːˈmʌltʃʊəs/ *adjective* (*formal*)
A **tumultuous** event is noisy because people are happy and excited: *The crowd gave him a tumultuous welcome.* □ *tumultuous applause.*

tuna /ˈtjuːnə/ *noun* (*count or uncount*): **tuna** or **tunas**
Tuna, or **tuna fish**, are large sea fish that are used as food: *tuna sandwiches.*

tune /tjuːn/ *noun*; *verb*
▻ ***noun***: **tunes**
A **tune** is series of musical notes making an arrangement that is pleasing to listen to. [*same as* **melody**]
▻ ***verb***: **tunes, tuning, tuned**
1 You **tune** a musical instrument when you make sure its strings or keys produce the right notes: *This guitar needs tuning.* **2** (*often in the passive*) A radio or television **is tuned** to a particular station or programme when you can listen to or watch that station or programme: *The radio is tuned to the BBC.* **3** Someone **tunes** an engine or machine when they adjust it to make it run properly.
▻ ***phrases*** **1** Someone **changes** their **tune** if they change their opinions of or attitude towards someone or something: *He always used to be rude to me but he's changed his tune recently and been much nicer.* **2** A musical instrument is **in tune** when it produces the right notes; a person sings **in tune** when they sing the right notes; a musical instrument is **out of tune** when it produces the wrong notes; a person sings **out of tune** when they sing the wrong notes: *Your guitar isn't properly in tune.* **3** You are **in tune with** other people if you agree with them or are sympathetic towards them; you are **out of tune** with them if you do not agree with them or are not sympathetic towards them: *His ideas are out of tune with modern political thinking.* **4** (*informal*) **To the tune of** a particular amount means having that amount as a total: *She's in debt to the tune of several thousand pounds.*

tuneful /ˈtjuːnfəl/ *adjective*
A piece of music is **tuneful** if has a clear, pleasant tune.

tunic /ˈtjuːnɪk/ *noun*: **tunics**
A **tunic** is **1** a loose garment with no sleeves, that usually reaches to your hips or knees. **2** a close-fitting jacket with a high collar and belt that is worn as part of a soldier's or policeman's uniform.

tunnel /ˈtʌnəl/ *noun*; *verb*
▻ ***noun***: **tunnels**
A **tunnel** is a long underground passage, usually through or under something such as a mountain, river or sea: *the Channel tunnel.*
▻ ***verb***: **tunnels, tunnelling** (*AmE* **tunneling**), **tunnelled** (*AmE* **tunneled**)
A person or animal **tunnels** somewhere if they make a tunnel under or through something: *We'll have to tunnel under the mountain.*
▻ ***phrase*** You can say that **there is light at the end of the tunnel** if you can see that your current problems, difficulties or hard work are going to be followed by a more relaxing, pleasant period: *She's been working very hard for the past few months but there is light at the end of the tunnel now.*

turban /ˈtɜːbən/ *noun*: **turbans**
A **turban** is a man's head covering consisting of a length of cloth wound round his head, worn especially by Muslims and Sikhs.

turbine /ˈtɜːbaɪn/ *noun*: **turbines**
A **turbine** is a motor or engine in which a wheel or drum with blades is driven round by a flow of *eg* water, steam or gas to produce electricity.

turbulent /ˈtɜːbjʊlənt/ *adjective*
1 A **turbulent** period of time is one in which there is a lot of violence, social unrest and confusion: *the turbulent period between the wars.* **2 Turbulent** water or air currents change direction suddenly and violently, making ships and aircraft shake: *the choppy, turbulent*

sea. [*same as* **stormy**; *opposite* **calm**] — *noun* (*uncount or used in the singular*) **turbulence** /ˈtɜːbjʊləns/: *This aircraft has been designed to withstand turbulence.* □ *The turbulence made many of the aircraft's passengers feel sick.*

turf /tɜːf/ *noun*; *verb*

▻ ***noun*** (*uncount*)

Turf is short, thick grass and the soil it is growing in.

▻ ***verb***: **turfs, turfing, turfed**

1 Someone **turfs** an area of ground when they cover it with turf. **2** (*BrE*; *informal*) You **turf** something somewhere if you throw it there: *She turfed him out of the house.* □ *Could you turf that book over to me, please?*

turgid /ˈtɜːdʒɪd/ *adjective*

Turgid language or words sound important and solemn but do not mean very much. [*same as* **pompous**]

turkey /ˈtɜːkɪ/ *noun*: **turkeys**

1 Turkeys are large farmyard birds that are bred for their flesh. **2** (*uncount*) **Turkey** is the flesh of this bird, used as food: *We had roast turkey for dinner.*

turmoil /ˈtɜːmɔɪl/ *noun* (*uncount*)

Turmoil is a state of confusion, worry or disorder: *a mind in turmoil* □ *The whole airport was in turmoil after the bomb threat.*

turn /tɜːn/ *verb*; *noun*

▻ ***verb***: **turns, turning, turned**

1 a You **turn** when you move to face in another direction; you **turn** *eg* your head or eyes when you move them to look in another direction: *He turned and walked away.* □ *They turned to face each other.* □ *Charlotte turned towards her husband.* □ *She turned her head and smiled.* □ *Laura turned her eyes on me.* [see also **turn away**, **turn round**] **b** You **turn** right or left, or in a particular direction, when you change the direction you are moving in: *Turn left here, and at the next junction turn right into Chevisham Road.* □ *The car turned down a narrow street.* □ *Eventually you turn a corner and the leisure centre is straight ahead of you.* **c** Something **turns**, or **is turned**, in a certain direction if it faces or points that way: *Her toes turn inwards when she walks.* **d** You **turn** something when you change its position so that a different part is on top or facing forward: *How often do you turn your mattress?* □ *Turn the garment inside out to iron.* □ *I realized I was turning the pages without actually reading.* **e** You **turn** something from a container on to or into something when you transfer it there: *Turn the mixture into an ovenproof dish.* **f** A wheel or similar structure **turns** or **is turned** when it spins or rotates: *We looked up at the windmill and watched the sails turning.* □ *Turn the wheel slightly towards you.* [*same as* **circle**, **spin**, **revolve**, **rotate**] **g** You **turn** *eg* a knob, handle, key, tap or switch when you hold it and twist it, in order to open, close, stop or start something: *Turn the knob clockwise.* □ *I didn't dare turn the key in the lock.* □ *He was horrified to see the door knob slowly turning.* [see also **turn off**, **turn on**, **turn down**, **turn up**]

2 a You **turn** to a certain page when you find that page: *Turn to page 52 for details.* **b** You **turn** to someone or something when you seek help or advice from them: *She turned to him in her despair.* □ *I had nowhere to turn for advice.* □ *To understand how our modern Cabinet developed, we must turn again to history.* **c** You **turn** to something, or **turn** your thoughts or attention to it, when you start thinking or talking about it: *It's a subject we often turn to on this show.* □ *He turned his attention once again to the French educational system.* **d** You **turn** to a certain activity when you start it, or start taking part in it: *Czechs and Slovaks were turning to organic farming.* □ *He encouraged her to turn to novel-writing as a means of support.*

3 a One thing **turns**, or **is turned**, into or to another thing when it changes into it: *We'll help you turn your dream into reality.* □ *They bought a disused police station and turned it into a hotel.* □ *stories in which people turn into animals* □ *The puddles had turned to ice.* **b** A person or thing **turns** something, *eg* a certain colour, when they become that colour or begin to have a certain quality; leaves **turn** when they become brown or yellow in autumn; milk **turns** when it goes sour: *Her face turned scarlet.* □ *The way he drives would turn your hair white.* □ *Most young girls of 25 would turn pale at the idea.* □ *He can turn a bit nasty sometimes.* □ *The leaves were already beginning to turn.* **c** You **turn** a certain age when you become that age: *I'll be turning sixty next year.*

▻ ***noun***: **turns**

1 A **turn** is **a** an act of turning: *You perform the jump and turn as a single movement.* □ *A supply of clean water is available at the turn of a tap.* □ *The earth takes 24 hours to make one complete turn on its axis.* **b** a curve, bend or change of direction: *He was waiting for her at the turn of the stairs.* □ *Here a right turn took him off the coastal road.* **2** (*used in the singular*) A **turn** is an alteration or development in a situation: *Unfortunately the Japanese shares took a downward turn.* □ *The weather had taken a turn for the better.* □ *People were bewildered by this new turn of events.* [compare **twist**] **3** (*used in the singular*) The **turn** of the century, decade or year is the period that includes the end of one and the beginning of the next: *The scheme had lost momentum by the turn of the decade.* □ *They reckon the product could be ready at the turn of the year.* □ *By the turn of the century some two million men and women were employed in mines and factories.* **4** It is your **turn** to do something when you have a duty, right or chance to do it: *You've had two turns already.* □ *It was my turn to fetch water.* □ *Lydia judged it her turn to speak.* □ *It was Caroline's turn to laugh.* [= This time, it was Caroline who laughed] **5** You do a **turn**, *eg* in a show or at a party, when you do a short act or performance: *Le Tissier was the star turn.* **6** A **turn** of phrase or expression is a particular way of expressing yourself, or of wording something: *Marie had an elegant turn of phrase.* **7** A person or vehicle that is capable of a fair **turn** of speed can move fast.

▻ ***phrases*** **1** You are *eg* happy and sad **by turns** when you alternate between the two moods. **2** You **do** someone **a good turn** when you do something that benefits them. **3** If you describe things as happening or being dealt with **in turn**, you mean that they happen or are dealt with in a sequence, one after the other: *Katharine looked at each face in turn.* □ *He passed the diary to the clerk of court, who in turn passed it to Sir Humphrey.* **4** Something that happens **at every turn** happens whenever it can: *He was evidently determined to humiliate her at every turn.* **5** You speak or act **out of turn** when you do or say something clumsy, unsuitable or ill-mannered. **6** People **take turns** or **take it in turns** to do something when they do it one after the other: *We took turns looking after him.* □ *The students take it in turns to open the discussion.*

phrasal verbs

turn against Someone **turns against** you, or **is turned against** you, when they start disliking or distrusting you: *The allies thought that eight years of war would have turned the people against Saddam.* □ *Students turned against their universities.*

turn around is used in the same way as **turn round**.

turn away **1** You **turn away**, or **turn** *eg* your head **away**, when you move so as not to face something: *She was just about to turn away from the window* *when she saw something move.* □ *He turned his face away.* **2** You **turn** someone or something **away** when you send them away, reject them or exclude them: *We had to turn volunteers away in their hundreds.* □ *To refuse to give credit could turn away valuable business.*

turn back **1** You **turn back** when you return in the direction you have come from: *The pilot tried to turn back to Schiphol airport.* **2** You **turn** people **back** when you stop them coming any further, and make them return in the direction they have come from: *People crossing from the other side were turned back by the border guards.*

turn down **1** You **turn down** *eg* a proposal, offer or request when you reject it or refuse it: *I thought Luke was going to turn down the idea.* □ *Apparently she turned him down.* [*same as* **refuse**, **reject**; *opposite* **accept**] **2** You **turn down** something such as a radio or heating apparatus when you adjust its controls so as to reduce the sound or heat it is producing: *She decided to go downstairs and ask them to turn down their music.* [*opposite* **turn up**]

turn in (*informal*) **1** You **turn in** when you go to bed: *How about a drink before we turn in?* **2** You **turn** a person **in** when you hand them over to the police.

turn off **1** You **turn off** the road you are going along when you take one that leads away from it: *You turn off the high street just before the bridge.* □ *The car turned off down a side street.* [see also **turn-off**] **2** You **turn off** *eg* the water, the electricity, or a device, when you operate a tap, switch or knob to stop it flowing or working: *Turn off the water at the mains.* □ *She turned off the tap.* □ *Could you turn the light off?* **3** To **turn** someone **off** is to make them lose interest in something: *Advertising brochures can actually turn people off.* [*same as* **put off**; *opposite* **turn on**]

turn on **1** You **turn** *eg* the water, the electricity, or a device **on**, when you operate a tap, switch or knob to start it flowing or working: *She stretched out a hand to turn on the bedside light.* □ *He turned the cold tap on.* [*opposite* **turn off**] **2** (*informal*) Someone or something **turns** you **on** if they interest you, attract you, or excite you sexually. **3** A person or animal **turns on** you when they attack you; someone **turns** their anger **on** you when they start being angry with you or attacking you: *Suddenly he turned on me and started criticizing me.*

turn out **1** You **turn out** a light or a gas fire when you operate a switch to stop it shining or giving out heat. [*same as* **turn off**; *opposite* **turn on**] **2 a** Things **turn out** a certain way when they happen that way: *You shouldn't encourage your readers to think their lives will turn out like your novels.* □ *When things turned out well, he usually claimed the credit.* **b** Something **turns out** to be a certain thing when it is discovered to be that thing: *Mail-order plants can turn out not to be the ones you ordered.* □ *The driver, as it turned out, was a retired admiral.* **3** Something such as a factory or a place of education **turns out** a certain type of thing or person if they produce them: *The industry is turning out cheaper and cheaper PCs.* □ *centres of higher education that turn out highly skilled software engineers.* **4** You **turn out** a container when you take everything out of it; you **turn out** the contents of a container when you tip them out: *We all turned out our pockets.* □ *She turned out the ash trays.* □ *You can turn the pudding out on to a plate, like a jelly.* **5** You **turn** someone **out**, or **turn** them **out** of a place, when you make them leave it: *She wept and begged him not to turn her out.* □ *They'd been turned out of their council flat.* [*same as* **expel**] **6** People **turn out** *eg* for an event or an election when they come and participate, or come and vote: *Voters turned out in large numbers in the safe seats.* [see also **turnout**] **7** Someone who **is** well **turned out** is smartly dressed.

turn over **1** Something **turns over**, or **is turned over**, when its position is changed so that its downward-facing side faces upward: *Turn the leaf over and look at the underside.* □ *He was turning over the pages of a magazine.* **2** You **turn over** *eg* in bed when you roll over so that you are lying on your other side. **3** You **turn** something **over** in your mind when you think about it: *I sat quietly, turning over the day's events.* **4** You **turn** something **over** to someone when you give it to them, *eg* because it is their rightly theirs; you **turn** a person **over** *eg* to the police when you hand them over: *Why shouldn't we turn you over to the police?* [*same as* **surrender**]

turn round or **turn around** **1** To **turn round** is to move so as to face in the opposite direction, or to spin or revolve; you **turn** something **round** when you move it to face in the opposite direction: *She ordered him to turn round and face her.* □ *We just turned the car round and drove home.* **2** You **turn** something that is said **round** when you alter the way it is expressed. **3** A failing business company **is turned round** when it is reorganized so as to become successful.

turn up **1** Someone **turns up** somewhere when they arrive or appear there: *She turned up at my flat last night.* □ *He always turned up late for meals.* □ *He doesn't turn up very often these days.* **2** Something **turns up** when it is found: *That lost cheque turned up, by the way.* □ *Sorry you lost your job; I hope something else turns up soon.* **3** You **turn up** *eg* facts or evidence when you discover them. **4** You **turn up** something such as a radio or a heater when you adjust its controls so as to increase the sound or heat it is producing: *Could you turn the television up a bit?* [*opposite* **turn down**]

turning /'tɜːnɪŋ/ *noun*: **turnings**
A **turning** is a place where one road leads away from another: *Take the second turning on the right.*

turning point /'tɜːnɪŋ pɔɪnt/ *noun*: **turning points**
A **turning point** is a time at which an important or significant change occurs that will alter someone's life: *He's reached a turning point in his career.*

turnip /'tɜːnɪp/ *noun*: **turnips**
Turnips are round, white vegetables that grow under the ground: *turnip soup.* [see picture at **vegetable**]

turn-off /'tɜːnɒf/ *noun*: **turn-offs**
A **turn-off** is a road that leads away from a main road: *Her farm is at the end of this turnoff.* [see also **turn off** at **turn**]

turnout /'tɜːnaʊt/ *noun* (*used in the singular*)
The **turnout** at a meeting or event is the number of people who attend it: *The turnout was poor because of the bad weather.* [see also **turn out** at **turn**]

turnover /'tɜːnoʊvə(r)/ *noun* (*uncount*)
1 A company's **turnover** is the total value of goods it sells during a certain period of time: *The company has an annual turnover of around two millions pounds.* **2** The **turnover** of workers in a company is the rate at which workers leave and are replaced by new workers.

turntable /'tɜːnteɪbəl/ *noun*: **turntables**
A **turntable** is the flat round part of a record player that you put the records on.

turn-up /'tɜːnʌp/ *noun* (*usually in the plural*): **turn-ups**
Turn-ups are **a** the pieces of material at the bottom of each trouser leg that are folded up. **b** trousers with bottoms that have been folded up.
▻ ***phrase*** (*informal*) An event can be described as **a turn-up for the book** if it is a surprise.

turpentine /'tɜːpəntaɪn/ *noun* (*uncount*)
Turpentine is a thick, oily liquid used *eg* to make paint thinner.

turps /'tɜːps/ *noun* (*uncount*; *informal*)
Turps is turpentine.

turquoise /'tɜːkwɔɪz/ *noun*; *adjective*
▻ ***noun***: **turquoises**
1 (*count or uncount*; *often adjectival*) **Turquoise** is a light blue-green precious stone used in jewellery: *a gold necklace studded with pearls, amethysts and turquoises* □ *turquoise earrings.* **2** (*uncount*) **Turquoise** is a light blue-green colour.
▻ ***adjective:*** *a turquoise sea.*

turret /'tʌrɪt/ *noun*: **turrets**
A **turret** is a small tower on a castle or other building.

turtle /'tɜːtəl/ *noun*: **turtles**
A **turtle** is a large reptile with a hard shell and flippers for swimming, that usually lives in the sea.

tusk /tʌsk/ *noun*: **tusks**
Tusks are the long, curved, pointed teeth that project from the mouth of some animals including the elephant, walrus and wild boar.

tussle /'tʌsəl/ *noun*; *verb*
▻ ***noun***: **tussles**
A **tussle** is an energetic or sharp struggle or fight, especially between two people who both want something: *The dog was bitten during the tussle over the bone.*
▻ ***verb***: **tussles**, **tussling**, **tussled:** *The two boys tussled over whose turn it was to ride the bicycle.*

tut /tʌt/ or **tut-tut** /tʌt'tʌt/ *interjection* (*often humorous*)
People say '**tut**' or '**tut-tut**' to express slight annoyance or disapproval.
The written words **tut** and **tut-tut** in origin represent a clicking noise that people make with their tongue against their teeth, to express disapproval or annoyance.

tutor /'tjuːtə(r)/ *noun*; *verb*
▻ ***noun***: **tutors**
A **tutor** is **1** a university or college teacher who teaches students individually or in small groups, or who gives them general advice and checks their progress. **2** a private teacher who teaches at the pupil's home: *my French tutor.*
▻ ***verb***: **tutors**, **tutoring**, **tutored**
Someone **tutors** a person when they teach them a subject; he or she **tutors** a subject when they teach it: *I've been tutoring Spanish at night school.*

tutorial /tjuː'tɔːrɪəl/ *noun* (*often adjectival*): **tutorials**
A **tutorial** is a lesson given by a university or college tutor to an individual student or small group of students: *a history tutorial* □ *a tutorial group.*

TV /tiː 'viː/ *noun*: **TVs**
1 (*uncount*) **TV** is television: *I've been watching TV all afternoon.* **2** A **TV** is a television set.

twaddle /'twɒdəl/ *noun* (*uncount*; *informal*)
Twaddle is silly or meaningless writing or talk: *'What's your star sign?' 'I'm a Leo; but you don't believe all that twaddle, do you?*

twang /twaŋ/ *noun*: **twangs**
A **twang** is a sharp ringing sound like that produced by plucking a tightly-stretched string.

tweed /twiːd/ *noun* (*uncount*, *often adjectival*)
Tweed is a thick, rough woollen cloth with coloured threads in it: *a suit made of green tweed* □ *a tweed jacket.*

tweet /twiːt/ *verb*: **tweets**, **tweeting**, **tweeted**
A bird **tweets** when it makes a series of short, high-pitched, tuneful sounds.

tweezers /'twiːzəz/ *noun* (*plural*)
Tweezers, or a pair of **tweezers**, are a small tool consisting of two lengths of metal joined at one end, that you can use for *eg* pulling out individual hairs or holding small objects. [see picture at **bathroom**]

twelfth /twɛlfθ/ (often written **12th**) *determiner*; *pronoun*; *adjective or adverb*; *noun*
▻ ***determiner***
The **twelfth** person or thing is the one that is numbered twelve in a series: *the twelfth king of Scotland.*
▻ ***pronoun:*** *This is the twelfth of his books on French history.* □ *She's the twelfth from the right in the front row.* □ *The letter was posted on the 12th of December.* [see note at **date**]
▻ ***adjective or adverb:*** *She came* (or *was*) *twelfth in the test.* □ *He came in twelfth.*
▻ ***noun*** (often written $\frac{1}{12}$): **twelfths**
A **twelfth** of something is one of twelve equal parts of it: *One twelfth of the students failed the exam.*

twelve /twɛlv/ *noun*; *adjective*; *determiner*; *pronoun*
▻ ***noun***: **twelves**
1 (*count or uncount*) **Twelve** is **a** the number or figure 12: *Eight and four are twelve.* □ *Three twelves are thirty-six.* **b** a piece of clothing whose size is represented by the number 12, or a person who wears clothes of this size: *These shoes are twelves.* □ *He takes a twelve in shoes.* □ *She's been on a diet and is a twelve now.* **2** (*uncount*) **Twelve** is **a** the age of 12: *She started learning German at 12.* **b** the time of 12 o'clock, either noon or midnight: *Her train gets in at 12 tomorrow.* [see also **dozen**]
▻ ***adjective***
Someone who is **twelve** is twelve years old: *She'll be twelve next week.* □ *children aged twelve and under.*
▻ ***determiner:*** *The train fare was twelve pounds.* □ *She was off school for twelve weeks.* □ *It took him twelve days to finish the job.* □ *a twelve-year-old child* □ *books for twelve-year-olds.*
▻ ***pronoun:*** *Twelve of them were chosen to be in the choir.* □ *'How many apples do you want?' 'Twelve will be enough.'*

twentieth /'twɛntɪəθ/ *determiner*; *pronoun*; *adjective or adverb*; *noun*: **twentieths**
1 (often written **20th**) The **twentieth** person or thing is the one that is numbered twenty in a series. **2** (often written $\frac{1}{20}$) A **twentieth** of something is one of twenty equal parts of it.

twenty /'twɛntɪ/ *noun*; *adjective*; *determiner*; *pronoun*
▻ ***noun***: **twenties**
1 (*count or uncount*) **Twenty** is the number or figure 20: *Two tens are twenty.* □ *Three twenties are sixty.* **2** (*uncount*) **Twenty** is the age of 20: *She took her driving test at twenty.* **3** (*used in the plural*) Someone who is in their **twenties** is aged between 20 and 29. **4** (*used in the plural*) The temperature is in the **twenties** when it is between 20° and 29°. **5** (*used in the plural*) The **twenties** are the period between the nineteenth and twenty-ninth years of a century: *the nineteen-twenties.*

▻ ***adjective***
Someone who is **twenty** is 20 years old: *I'm leaving home as soon as I'm twenty.*
▻ ***determiner:*** *twenty-year-old students.*
▻ ***pronoun:*** *Three people were killed and a further twenty were injured.*

twice /twaɪs/ *adverb; adverb or determiner*
▻ ***adverb***
1 Something that happens **twice** happens two times: *I've already tried to contact her twice this morning.* **2** Something that happens *eg* **twice** a year, or **twice** yearly, happens on two occasions every year: *The dose should be administered twice a day* (or *twice daily*).
▻ ***adverb or determiner*** Something that is *eg* **twice** as big as, or **twice** the size of, something else, is two times as big as, or double the size of, the second thing: *He's twice her age.* □ *It could cost twice that amount.* □ *Cut a piece of cord about twice the width of the picture.* □ *Women are twice as likely as men to get skin cancer.* □ *Unemployment in the area was twice as high as the national average.*
▻ ***phrases*** **1** (*usually with a negative*) Something that you don't **look twice at** is something that hardly attracts your attention: *Lovely Antoinette won't look twice at you, Alan.* **2** For **once or twice** see **once**. **3 a** (*usually with a negative*) Something that you don't **think twice** about is something that doesn't worry or concern you: *The average consumer doesn't think twice about which factory produces the goods.* **b** If you tell someone to **think twice** before, or about, doing something that you consider unwise, you are warning them not to do it: *If I were you I'd think twice before giving up the course.* [*same as* **reconsider**]

twiddle /ˈtwɪdəl/ *verb*: **twiddles, twiddling, twiddled**
1 You **twiddle** *eg* a knob or button when you twist it round and round: *He twiddled the knob on the radio until he found a station.* **2** You **twiddle** with something when you twist it round without thinking in your fingers: *She sat twiddling with her hair.*
▻ ***phrase*** You **twiddle your thumbs** when you move them round and round each other, usually as a sign that you're bored or have nothing to do.

twig /twɪg/ *noun*: **twigs**
A **twig** is a small, thin piece that grows from the branch of *eg* a tree or bush: *She collected dried twigs to put on the bonfire.*

twilight /ˈtwaɪlaɪt/ *noun* (*uncount*)
Twilight is the time of day when the sun is just below the horizon and there isn't much light, especially immediately after sunset: *Some birds only sing at twilight.* [compare **dawn**]

twin /twɪn/ *noun; adjective*
▻ ***noun*: twins**
Twins are two people or animals born to the same mother at the same time: *Anne and Jean are twins.* □ *her twin sister.*
▻ ***adjective***
Twin things are a pair of things that are very similar and are close together: *a room with twin beds.* [see picture at **bedroom**]

twine /twaɪn/ *noun; verb*
▻ ***noun*** (*uncount*)
Twine is strong string or cord: *a ball of twine for use in the garden.*
▻ ***verb*: twines, twining, twined**
You **twine** one thing around another when you twist it around it: *She twined the scarf round her neck.*

twinge /twɪndʒ/ *noun*: **twinges**
1 A **twinge** is a sudden sharp stabbing pain: *He still gets a twinge in his back from time to time.* **2** You feel a **twinge** of *eg* an unpleasant emotion or guilt when you suddenly experience that emotion or feel guilty: *a twinge of fear* □ *a twinge of doubt.*

twinkle /ˈtwɪŋkəl/ *verb; noun*
▻ ***verb*: twinkles, twinkling, twinkled**
1 A star or light **twinkles** when it shines with a bright, glittering light: *She could see the lights twinkling through the trees.* **2** Your eyes **twinkle** if they shine or sparkle with amusement, excitement or humour.
▻ ***noun*** (*usually in the singular*): *the twinkle of lights through the trees* □ *When he smiled, there was a twinkle in his eye.*

twirl /twɜːl/ *verb*: **twirls, twirling, twirled**
You **twirl** round if you turn or spin round quickly; you **twirl** something round if you turn or spin it round quickly: *She twirled the umbrella above her head.*

twist /twɪst/ *verb; noun*
▻ ***verb*: twists, twisting, twisted**
1 You **twist** something when you wind or turn it round, especially when you hold one part of it still while turning another part, or when you turn different parts in opposite directions: *She twisted the scarf round in her hands.* □ *He twisted the knob on the radio.* □ *Don't twist the button off!* **2 a** You **twist**, or **twist** round, when you turn the top part of your body round: *He twisted round in his seat.* **b** You **twist** part of your body if you injure it by turning it too sharply: *He's twisted his ankle badly.* [same as **sprain**] **3** A road **twists** when it follows a winding course: *The road twisted up through the mountains.* **4** You **twist** two things together if you wind one around the other or wind them together: *He twisted the pieces of wire together.* □ *A piece of wire was twisted round his leg.* **5 a** Something **is twisted** when its shape or form is changed in an unpleasant or extreme way: *He twisted his face into an ugly sneer.* **b** You **twist** someone's words when you give them a different meaning: *The media twist everything you say.*
▻ ***noun*: twists**
1 You give something a **twist** when you turn it round sharply: *You'll have to give the lid a good hard twist to get it off.* **2** A **twist** is a sharp turning movement which injures something: *She gave her ankle a nasty twist when she fell.* **3** A **twist** is an unexpected event, development or change, *eg* at the end of a story: *Events took a rather bizarre twist towards the end.*
▻ ***phrases*** **1** (*informal*) You can say that someone is **round the twist** if you think they are mad or crazy. **2** For **twist** someone's **arm** see **arm**[1]. **3** For **twist** someone **round your little finger** see **finger**.

twisted /ˈtwɪstɪd/ *adjective*
A person's mind or behaviour is **twisted** if it is unpleasantly abnormal: *She's become bitter and twisted as she's got older.*

twit /twɪt/ *noun* (*informal*): **twits**
If someone calls another person a **twit** they think that the other person is a fool or idiot: *Don't be such a twit!*

twitch /twɪtʃ/ *verb; noun*
▻ ***verb*: twitches, twitching, twitched**
1 You **twitch** if you move with jerky movements: *She could feel her eye twitching.* □ *He could see the curtains twitching.* **2** You **twitch** something if you pull it sharply or jerkily: *She twitched her skirt down below her knees.*
▻ ***noun*: twitches**
A **twitch** is a sharp or jerky movement: *His eye has developed a nervous twitch.*

twitter /ˈtwɪtə(r)/ *verb*: **twitters, twittering, twittered**
1 Birds **twitter** when they make a series of light, high-

pitched sounds. **2** A person **twitters** if they say something or speak with a high-pitched voice, often making small nervous or excited movements at the same time.

two /tuː/ *noun; adjective; determiner; pronoun*

▻ ***noun*: twos**

1 (*count or uncount*) **Two** is **a** the number or figure 2: *One plus one make two.* ▫ *Three twos are six.* **b** a piece of clothing whose size is represented by the number 2, or a person who wears this size: *My daughter takes size two in shoes.* ▫ *These shoes are twos, not threes.* **2** (*uncount*) **Two** is **a** the age of 2: *She began going to a nursery at two.* **b** the time of two o'clock: *My flight leaves at two this afternoon.* **3** (*count*) A **two** is a playing card with two symbols: *the two of diamonds.*

A set of two things is called a **pair**.

▻ ***adjective***

Someone who is **two** is two years old: *Amy was two at Christmas.*

▻ ***determiner:*** *The fare only cost two pounds.* ▫ *I was on holiday for two weeks.* ▫ *It only took me two hours to read this book.* ▫ *a two-year-old girl* ▫ *toys for two-year-olds.*

▻ ***pronoun:*** *Two of us were chosen to represent the school.* ▫ *I did have six oranges but I've only got two left now.*

▻ ***phrases***

1 You cut, break or divide something **in two** if you cut, break or divide it into two separate pieces: *The ship broke in two in the storm.* ▫ *She cut the apple in two and gave a piece to each child.* **2** 'A thing **or two**' means the same as 'one or two things', or a few things: *The workmen still have a job or two to do.* **3** You **put two and two together** if you realize what the obvious conclusion or result of something will be: *It was only when they both disappeared together that I started putting two and two together.* **4** (*informal*) If you say '**that makes two of us**' you mean that you are in the same situation as the person who is speaking to you: *'I don't like him at all.' 'That makes too of us,' she replied.*

two-faced /tuːˈfeɪst/ *adjective*

A **two-faced** person behaves in a dishonest way: *a two-faced liar and cheat.* [*same as* **deceitful, hypocritical**]

twopence or **tuppence** /ˈtʌpəns/ (*BrE*) *noun* (*uncount; old*)

Twopence is the sum of two pence.

two-way /tuːˈweɪ/ *adjective*

1 Two-way means able to move, moving or allowing movement in two opposite directions: *a two-way street* ▫ *two-way traffic.* **2** A **two-way** radio or communication system is able to both send and receive messages.

tycoon /taɪˈkuːn/ *noun*: **tycoons**

A **tycoon** is a rich and powerful businessman or businesswoman.

type /taɪp/ *noun; verb*

▻ ***noun*: types**

1 You refer to a **type** of something **a** when you mean a particular class or variety of it: *I've noticed three types of worm in my garden.* ▫ *Choose a conditioner to suit your hair type.* ▫ *What type of bed do you sleep on?* ▫ *Parental participation will depend on the type and size of the school.* ▫ *We can't afford facilities of the type you get in leisure centres.* ▫ *the non-reflecting type of screen* ▫ *The reactors are of the Chernobyl type.* ▫ *a nice, light, magazine-type article* ▫ *type-D hepatitis.* [*same as* **kind, sort, variety**] **b** when you are thinking of it in terms of its qualities: *'What type of girl is she?' 'Studious, very serious.'* **c** when you are thinking of it in relation to things that have some of the same qualities as it has: *This type of health problem increases with age.* ▫ *Behaviour of that type must be firmly dealt with.* ▫ *It's more efficient than most gadgets of its type.*

People often use the form *these* (or *those*) *type of* with a plural noun, but it sounds slightly better, and still means the same, if you use *this* (or *that*) *type of*, with a singular noun: *A government bill is needed to deal with this type of matter* (rather than *these type of matters*). With nouns that are always used in the plural, *eg* 'pants', you can avoid *these type of pants* by saying *pants of this type*, or *pants like these*. [see also **kind, sort**]

2 (*informal*) You can refer to a person as a certain **type** when you are classifying them in terms of their appearance or qualities: *Harriet wasn't the nervy type.* ▫ *This suit was popular with city types last year.* ▫ *I've met his type before.* **3** (*uncount*) **Type** is the style and size of printing used *eg* in books, newspapers or computer output: *The words were printed in heavy type.*

▻ ***verb*: types, typing, typed**

1 You **type** words when use a typewriter or word-processor to write them: *Authors are advised to type their own scripts on a word-processor.* **2** Things **are typed** when they are classified: *A blood sample was sent to the laboratory for typing.*

▻ ***phrase*** (*informal*) Someone that you say is **not your type** is not the kind of person you find attractive or interesting.

phrasal verbs

type in You **type in** data or commands, or **type** them **into** a computer, when you enter them by pressing keys on a keyboard: *If you want to run a program, simply type in its name.*

type up You **type up** *eg* handwritten notes when you produce a typed, usually fuller and more formal, version of them: *He hadn't yet typed up the minutes of the previous meeting.*

typecast /ˈtaɪpkɑːst/ *verb* (*usually in the passive*): **typecast, typecasting, typecast**

The form **typecast** is used as the present tense, the past tense and the past participle.

An actor or actress **is typecast** if they are always given the same type of parts to play: *He's frightened of being typecast as a villain.*

typewriter /ˈtaɪpraɪtə(r)/ *noun*: **typewriters**

A **typewriter** is a machine with a series of keys that are pressed to produce letters in print: *She prepared the report using a typewriter.* [see picture at **office**]

typewritten /ˈtaɪprɪtən/ *adjective*

A **typewritten** document is one that has been written using a typewriter or word-processor: *The bank sent me a typewritten statement of my account.*

typhoid /ˈtaɪfɔɪd/ *noun* (*uncount*)

Typhoid is an infectious disease that causes a fever, serious stomach problems, and sometimes death.

typhoon /taɪˈfuːn/ *noun*: **typhoons**

A **typhoon** is a violent storm in the China Sea and western Pacific area.

typical /ˈtɪpɪkəl/ *adjective*

1 Something is **typical** when it has all the usual characteristics of the group or class it belongs to: *typical Scottish weather* ▫ *It's just another typical horror film.* ▫ *What would your typical day be like?* ▫ *She's typical of all the women who both work and have a family.*

[*same as* **characteristic**] **2** Behaviour is **typical** of a person or thing if they behave exactly as you expect them to behave and as they always behave: *A hostile reaction is typical of him* □ *That's typical of her!*

typically /'tɪpɪklɪ/ *adverb*
1 Something is **typically** the case if it is so in most cases: *An insect is a small invertebrate, typically with six legs and two pairs of wings.* **2** People or things that are **typically** something have all the characteristics you associate with that thing: *He had a typically British approach to embarrassing problems; he pretended they didn't exist.*

typify /'tɪpɪfaɪ/ *verb*: **typifies, typifying, typified**
1 A person or thing **typifies** *eg* a class of people, group of things or a situation when they have all the characteristics of those people or things or that situation: *His behaviour typifies the attitude of the older generation towards young people.* **2** (*usually in the passive*) A person or thing **is typified** by something that shows what it is like or that is typical of it: *Modern western society is typified by a gulf between people with money and people with none.*

typing /'taɪpɪŋ/ *noun* (*uncount*)
Typing is the activity of producing written words using a typewriter or word-processor: *She took a course in shorthand and typing.*

typist /'taɪpɪst/ *noun*: **typists**
A **typist** is a person whose job involves typing, usually in an office. [compare **secretary**; see picture at **office**]

tyrannical /tɪ'ranɪkəl/ *adjective*
A **tyrannical** government or ruler is cruel, unjust and ruthless towards the people they rule. [*same as* **despotic**]

tyranny /'tɪrənɪ/ *noun* (*uncount*)
Tyranny is cruel, unjust and ruthless use of authority or power by a person or group of people who have absolute power over their country or state: *His book is a study of tyranny in Europe in the nineteeth century.*

tyrant /'taɪərənt/ *noun*: **tyrants**
A **tyrant** is a cruel, unjust and ruthless ruler with absolute power: *The president was accused of being a tyrant by some of his political opponents.*

tyre (*AmE* **tire**) /taɪə(r)/ *noun*: **tyres**
A **tyre** is a thick rubber ring usually filled with air, that is placed over a wheel: *My car has got a flat tyre.* □ *The tyre burst when she cycled over a broken bottle.* [see pictures at **bicycle, car**]

U

U /juː/ or **u** *noun*: **Us** or **u's**
U is the twenty-first letter of the English alphabet.

ubiquitous /juːˈbɪkwɪtəs/ *adjective* (*formal*)
Something that is **ubiquitous** seems to be everywhere: *The personal computer will become a ubiquitous part of the home environment.*

udder /ˈʌdə(r)/ *noun*: **udders**
An **udder** is the bag-like part of a cow's, or female sheep's or goat's body that produces milk.

UFO /juːɛfˈoʊ/ *noun* (*informal*): **UFOs**
A **UFO** is an unidentified flying object.

ugh /ʌg/ *interjection*
Ugh is the written form of a sound people make in their throats to express disgust: *'Ugh! It tastes horrible.'*

ugly /ˈʌglɪ/ *adjective*: **uglier, ugliest**
1 An **ugly** person or thing is unpleasant to look at: *I was feeling really overweight and ugly.* □ *They've got a bull terrier called Fred, and he's quite the ugliest dog I've ever seen.* □ *What an ugly vase!* **2** An **ugly** situation is one that dangerous or violent, or threatening to become so: *There were a few ugly incidents before the match started.* □ *There was an ugly scene between them at the dinner table.* □ *Things were turning ugly.* □ *An ugly mood was developing.*

ulcer /ˈʌlsə(r)/ *noun*: **ulcers**
An **ulcer** is a sore area on the skin, or a damaged area on the surface of an internal organ, which takes a long time to heal: *She developed a stomach ulcer.* □ *He suffers from mouth ulcers.*

ulterior /ʌlˈtɪərɪə(r)/ *adjective*
Someone has **ulterior** motives if there are hidden or secret reasons for them acting in a particular way: *He's suddenly become keen to spend time with me; I'm sure he must have an ulterior motive.*

ultimate /ˈʌltɪmət/ *adjective*
1 Ultimate describes something that comes at the end of a series of stages or events: *Constant encouragement and daily physiotherapy will contribute to her ultimate recovery.* □ *What's your ultimate destination?* □ *The ultimate responsibility for mistakes lies with the manager.* **2 Ultimate** also describes something regarded as supreme in a particular situation: *Some people would still like to see capital punishment retained as the ultimate deterrent.* □ *Then she asked me to babysit for her, which was the ultimate insult.*
▷ ***phrase*** You describe something as **the ultimate in** a certain quality if it constitutes the supreme demonstration of that quality: *Furniture that is the ultimate in elegance and sophistication.*

ultimately /ˈʌltɪmətlɪ/ *adverb*
1 (*sentence adverb*) You use **ultimately** when you are talking about the circumstance that will prove the most important in the end: *Ultimately, everything will depend on how much money we have to spend.* **2** Something happens **ultimately** when it happens at the end of a long period of time or series of events: *The elections were ultimately a victory for Nelson Mandela.* [*same as* **finally**]

ultimatum /ʌltɪˈmeɪtəm/ *noun* (*formal*): **ultimatums** or **ultimata** /ʌltɪˈmeɪtə/
You give someone an **ultimatum** when you warn them officially that you will act in a certain way towards them unless they do what you tell them to do: *Hitler ignored the British ultimatum.*

ultra- /ʌltrə/ *prefix*
Ultra- means 'extreme' or 'extremely' and is used to form adjectives: *ultra-Conservative politicians* □ *an ultra-modern computing system.*

ultrasound /ˈʌltrəsaʊnd/ *noun* (*uncount*)
Ultrasound is sound waves that human ears cannot hear.

ultraviolet /ʌltrəˈvaɪələt/ *adjective*
Ultraviolet light is an invisible type of light that turns the skin darker.

umbilical cord /ʌmbɪlɪkəl ˈkɔːd/ *noun*: **umbilical cords**
The **umbilical cord** is the long tube that connects a baby to its mother inside her womb, and that transfers oxygen and food from the mother to her baby.

umbrella /ʌmˈbrɛlə/ *noun*: **umbrellas**
1 a An **umbrella** is an object that protects people from rain, consisting of a round piece of fabric on a light folding frame: *It started to rain heavily so she put her umbrella up.* **b** An **umbrella** is also a similar but larger object that protects people from the sun: *They all sat out in the garden under umbrellas.* **2** (*usually in the singular*) An organization or group acts as an **umbrella** for several smaller ones when it brings them together, provides them with protection, and co-ordinates their activities: *an umbrella organization* □ *countries that come under the NATO umbrella.*

umpire /ˈʌmpaɪə(r)/ *noun*; *verb*
▷ ***noun***: **umpires**
In certain games, *eg* tennis and cricket, the **umpire** is the person who makes sure players follow the rules and play fairly.
▷ ***verb***: **umpires, umpiring, umpired**
You **umpire** a game when you supervise it and make sure players follow the rules and play fairly: *In all his years of umpiring at Wimbledon, he had never been sworn at and abused like this.*

umpteen /ʌmpˈtiːn/ *determiner* (*informal*)
Umpteen means a great many: *There are umpteen reasons why you shouldn't leave school yet.* □ *I've had to remind him umpteen times about closing that window.* [*same as* **innumerable**]

umpteenth /ʌmpˈtiːnθ/ *determiner* (*informal*)
The **umpteenth** person or thing is the latest in a long series: *You're the umpteenth person to ask me that.* □ *For the umpteenth time, don't put banana skins in the wastepaper basket!*

un- /ʌn/ *prefix*
1 Un- is added to the front of nouns, adjectives and

adverbs to form words with the opposite meaning: *unkindness* □ *unpopular* □ *unhappily.* **2 Un-** is added **a** to the front of verbs to indicate the reversing of a process: *undo* □ *unbutton.* **b** to the front of the past participles of verbs to show that an action or process has not taken place: *unwashed garments* □ *unmarried mothers* □ *The question remains unanswered.*

unable /ʌn'eɪbəl/ *adjective*
You are **unable** to do something if you cannot do it, *eg* because you don't have the strength, skill, power, time, opportunity or resources to do it: *He learnt to speak again but is unable to walk.* □ *The children are unable at times to concentrate, or even keep their eyes open.* □ *She nodded, unable for a moment to speak.* □ *The computer is unable to carry out your command until you give your document a name.* □ *I regret that I shall be unable to be present.* □ *people who are unable to afford the fees* □ *The hospital quickly became unable to cope with the casualties as more and more arrived.* [*opposite* **able**; see also **inability**]

unacceptable /ʌnək'sɛptəbəl/ *adjective*
Something is **unacceptable** if it cannot be allowed to happen, continue or exist because it is wrong: *His behaviour is unacceptable.* — *adverb* **unacceptably:** *There is an unacceptably high level of pollution in the river.*

unaccountable /ʌnə'kaʊntəbəl/ *adjective*
1 Something is **unaccountable** if it is impossible to explain why or how it happened: *The sudden disappearance of the ship in what was a calm sea is unaccountable.* **2** Someone who is **unaccountable** does not have to explain their reasons for acting as they do: *Many of Scotland's services are run by people who are unaccountable to the public.* — *adverb* (*sometimes sentence adverb*) **unaccountably:** *She was feeling unaccountably depressed.* □ *Unaccountably, a different message from usual was coming up on the screen.*

unaccounted /ʌnə'kaʊntɪd/ *adjective*
▻ ***phrase*** Something is **unaccounted for** if you do not know what has happened to it or how it has been used: *There are several thousand pounds unaccounted for in these account books.*

unaccustomed /ʌnə'kʌstəmd/ *adjective*
1 You are **unaccustomed** to something if you are not used to doing it: *I'm unaccustomed to speaking in public.* **2** Something such as behaviour is **unaccustomed** if it is not usual or not expected: *They were enjoying the unaccustomed fine weather.*

unadulterated /ʌnə'dʌltəreɪtɪd/ *adjective*
1 Something that is **unadulterated** is pure, and has no impurities or harmful substances added to it or mixed with it: *unadulterated drinking water.* **2** (*informal*) You can also use **unadulterated** for emphasis: *Lying in the sun with nothing to do is unadulterated bliss.* [*same as* **absolute, sheer, utter**]

unaffected /ʌnə'fɛktɪd/ *adjective*
1 You are **unaffected** by something if it does not affect you or make you act differently: *Most people working here have been unaffected by the changes in company policy.* **2** An **unaffected** person behaves in a natural, sincere or genuine way: *an unaffected young woman.*

unaided /ʌn'eɪdɪd/ *adjective*
You do something **unaided** if you do it on your own and without help: *My baby daughter can't yet feed herself unaided.*

unambiguous /ʌnam'bɪgjʊəs/ *adjective*
Written or spoken words are **unambiguous** if they have one meaning and that meaning is clear: *The law is quite unambiguous on this point.* □ *Blair is being called upon for a clear and unambiguous statement of Labour principles and policy.* [*same as* **unequivocal**]

unanimous /juː'nanɪməs/ *adjective*
A decision or agreement is **unanimous** when everyone involved agrees: *The decision to strike was unanimous.* — *adverb* **unanimously:** *He was elected unanimously.*

unannounced /ʌnə'naʊnst/ *adjective*
Someone does something **unannounced** if they do it without telling you about it beforehand: *The Queen arrived unannounced.*

unanswered /ʌn'ɑːnsəd/ *adjective*
Unanswered questions are ones that have not yet been answered: *There was a pile of unanswered letters on his desk.* □ *There are a lot of unanswered questions about the Big Bang.*

unapproachable /ʌnə'proʊtʃəbəl/ *adjective*
A person is **unapproachable** if they behave in a formal and unfriendly way so that people find them difficult or impossible to talk to: *Many politicians complained that the Prime Minister was unapproachable.*

unarmed /ʌn'ɑːmd/ *adjective*
You are **unarmed** if you are carrying no weapons: *soldiers trained in unarmed combat.*

unashamed /ʌnə'ʃeɪmd/ *adjective*
You are **unashamed** of your behaviour if you are not ashamed of it and do not regret doing it: *She stood before her accusers, proud and unashamed.* — *adverb* **unashamedly:** *She is unashamedly traditional in her attitude towards marriage.*

unassuming /ʌnə'sjuːmɪŋ/ or /ʌnə'suːmɪŋ/ *adjective*
A person or thing is **unassuming** if they are modest and quiet: *a shy and unassuming young man.*

unattached /ʌnə'tatʃt/ *adjective*
1 A person is **unattached** if they are not having a steady romantic or sexual relationship with another person: *Do you know any unattached men who might be interested in Annabel?* **2** Something that is **unattached** is not attached, associated or connected with anything: *The nursery is unattached to any primary school.*

unattended /ʌnə'tɛndɪd/ *adjective*
People or things are **unattended** when no-one is with them or looking after them: *Passengers are asked not to leave their luggage unattended.*

unattractive /ʌnə'traktɪv/ *adjective*
An **unattractive** person or thing is not pleasant to look at: *a rather unattractive modern house.* □ *Conceitedness is one of her more unattractive qualities.*

unauthorized or **unauthorised** /ʌn'ɔːθəraɪzd/ *adjective*
Something is **unauthorized** if it is done or produced without official permission: *an unauthorized biography.*

unavoidable /ʌnə'vɔɪdəbəl/ *adjective*
Something is **unavoidable** if it cannot be avoided: *I'm sorry to give you extra work, but I'm afraid it's unavoidable.* — *adverb* **unavoidably:** *I was unavoidably delayed.*

unaware /ʌnə'wɛə(r)/ *adjective*
You are **unaware** of something if you know nothing about it or are not aware of it: *How could I have helped him when I was completely unaware of his drug-taking?* □ *She was unaware that her son was having problems at school.*

unawares /ʌnə'wɛərz/ *adverb*
▻ ***phrase*** Something **catches** or **takes you unawares** if you are surprised by it and did not expect it: *The food shortages have caught most of us unawares.*

unbalanced /ʌnˈbalənst/ *adjective*
1 A person is **unbalanced** if they are slightly mad and are not thinking or behaving sensibly: *The experiences of the past few weeks have left him mentally unbalanced.* **2** A story or report is **unbalanced** if it unfairly emphasizes some things and ignores others: *The journalist gave an unbalanced version of the events in his article.* [*same as* **biased**; *opposite* **impartial**]

unbearable /ʌnˈbɛərəbəl/ *adjective*
Something is **unbearable** if it is too unpleasant, painful or difficult to cope with or bear: *The pain was unbearable.* [*same as* **intolerable**] — *adverb* **unbearably:** *It's unbearably hot here in summer.*

unbeatable /ʌnˈbiːtəbəl/ *adjective*
Something that is **unbeatable** is very good or is the best: *A catalogue that offers unbeatable value for money.*

unbelievable /ʌnbɪˈliːvəbəl/ *adjective*
1 (*informal*) You can say that something is **unbelievable** when it is very good or surprising: *'This new machine is incredibly fast.' 'I know, it's unbelievable, isn't it?'* [*same as* **incredible**, **remarkable**, **astonishing**] **2** A theory is **unbelievable** if it is very unusual or unexpected and you cannot believe it: *I have to say that I find his story completely unbelievable.* [*same as* **incredible**, **unconvincing**, **implausible**] — *adverb* (*sometimes intensifying*) **unbelievably:** *She's unbelievably thin for someone who eats so many sweet things.* □ *He's unbelievably rich.*

unbending /ʌnˈbɛndɪŋ/ *adjective*
Someone who is **unbending** is **1** rather severe and unfriendly, and finds it hard to relax. **2** strict in their attitude to something, and unwilling to alter their ideas: *The headmistress was a stern and unbending disciplinarian.*

unborn /ʌnˈbɔːn/ *adjective*
An **unborn** child is a baby that is still developing inside its mother's womb.

unbroken /ʌnˈbroʊkən/ *adjective*
A line or series that is **unbroken** has no gaps or breaks in it: *He can trace his ancestry in an unbroken line back to the fifteenth century.*

unbutton /ʌnˈbʌtən/ *verb*: **unbuttons, unbuttoning, unbuttoned**
You **unbutton** your clothes when you undo the buttons: *He unbuttoned his shirt.*

uncalled-for /ʌnˈkɔːld fɔː(r)/ *adjective*
Unpleasant behaviour that is described as **uncalled-for** is unnecessary and unjustifiable: *Your insulting comments were quite uncalled-for, and I think you should apologize.*

uncanny /ʌnˈkanɪ/ *adjective*: **uncannier, uncanniest**
Something is **uncanny** when it is strange or mysterious: *She had the uncanny talent for knowing exactly what I was thinking.*

unceasing /ʌnˈsiːsɪŋ/ *adjective*
Something is **unceasing** if it never stops: *We had a fortnight of unceasing rain.*

unceremonious /ʌnsɛrɪˈmoʊnɪəs/ *adjective*
You act in an **unceremonious** way towards someone if you make no attempt to be polite: *He went over to the door, opened it, took hold of her arm, and with a curt and unceremonious 'Out you go!' pushed her through it.* — *adverb* **unceremoniously:** *He was marched to the door and unceremoniously dumped in the street.*

uncertain /ʌnˈsɜːtən/ *adjective*
1 Something that is **uncertain** is not definitely known, or is not decided: *Several top executives have resigned, for reasons which remain uncertain.* □ *The relevance of these results is uncertain.* □ *It is uncertain whether a ballot would obtain the necessary support.* □ *His future career seemed uncertain.* [*same as* **unsure**, **doubtful**, **in doubt**; *opposite* **certain**, **definite**] **2** You are **uncertain** about something when you do not know definitely about it, or cannot decide about it: *I was uncertain how much he knew.* □ *He looked up, uncertain where he was.* □ *There were cases where employees were left uncertain about their objectives and responsibilities.* □ *He seemed uncertain of his facts.* □ *Melissa stopped short, uncertain what to do.* □ *She was uncertain how to proceed.* □ *He sounded nervous and uncertain.* [*same as* **unsure**, **doubtful**, **in doubt**; *opposite* **certain**, **sure**] **3** Something that proceeds in an **uncertain** manner does not proceed fast and smoothly: *Progress was uncertain and slow.* — *adverb* **uncertainly:** *She smiled at him uncertainly.* [*same as* **hesitantly**]

uncertainty /ʌnˈsɜːtəntɪ/ *noun*: **uncertainties**
1 (*uncount*) You are in a state of **uncertainty** about something, or there is **uncertainty** about it, when you you don't know what is happening or what to do: *She had no idea where her son was, and all the uncertainty was upsetting her badly.* **2** (*usually in the plural*) **Uncertainties** are things that may or may not happen: *Life is full of uncertainties.* [*opposite* **certainty**]

unchallenged /ʌnˈtʃaləndʒd/ *adjective*
Something is or goes **unchallenged** when people accept it without questioning or criticizing it: *His views have gone unchallenged for many years, and it's time we took a fresh look at them.*

uncharted /ʌnˈtʃɑːtɪd/ *adjective*
You can describe something as **uncharted** territory when it is completely new to you and you know nothing about it: *I've studied chemistry before but nuclear physics is uncharted territory for me.*

unchecked /ʌnˈtʃɛkt/ *adjective*
Something harmful or unwanted continues **unchecked** when it is allowed to go on or increase without being stopped or controlled: *The death toll from heart disease in Scotland continues to rise unchecked.*

uncivilized or **uncivilised** /ʌnˈsɪvəlaɪzd/ *adjective*
1 a Uncivilized behaviour is rude and sometimes cruel or violent: *Do you think it's uncivilized to eat with your fingers?* □ *She thinks her husband's friends are boorish and uncivilized.* **b Uncivilized** conditions are poor or primitive: *Conditions in the villages are pretty uncivilized.* **2** (*informal*) You do something at an **uncivilized** time if you do it at a time that most people would consider inconvenient, *eg* very early in the morning: *I'm sorry to ring you at such an uncivilized hour, but I wanted to catch you before you left for work.*

uncle /ˈʌŋkəl/ *noun*: **uncles**
Your **uncle** is the brother of your mother or father, or the husband of your aunt: *Uncle Tim works in a bank.*

unclean /ʌŋˈkliːn/ *adjective*
1 Something that is **unclean** is dirty or impure: *Unclean drinking water can be a source of cholera.* **2** (*religion*) In some religions certain animals are considered **unclean**, and people avoid eating meat from them: *Muslims and Jews regard pigs as unclean.*

unclear /ʌŋˈklɪə(r)/ *adjective*
1 Something that is **unclear** has not been well explained or is not obvious: *It's unclear why she left her job.* □ *His argument is unclear and difficult to follow.* **2** You are **unclear** about something when you do not understand it: *I'm sorry; I'm still unclear on that point; could you explain again?*

uncomfortable /ʌŋˈkʌmftəbəl/ *adjective*
1 a Something such as shoes or clothes are **uncomfortable** if they are not comfortable to wear: *These*

new shoes are still really uncomfortable. **b** Something such as a chair is **uncomfortable** if it is not comfortable to sit in. **2** You are **uncomfortable** when you are not in a relaxed, comfortable position: *I had a very uncomfortable ride in the back of his van.* **3** You feel **uncomfortable** when you feel upset, nervous, embarrassed or worried: *She is uncomfortable with people she doesn't know.* — *adverb* **uncomfortably:** *She was sitting uncomfortably on a hard chair.* □ *He smiled uncomfortably, and wouldn't look her in the eye.*

uncommon /ʌŋ'kɒmən/ *adjective*
1 Something is **uncommon** when it is rare or unusual: *'Is there much bullying?' 'No, fortunately it's very uncommon.'* □ *This bird is an uncommon visitor to Britain.* **2** (*formal, old*) **Uncommon** also means very great or extreme: *a young girl of uncommon musical talent.* — *adverb* **uncommonly:** *She is uncommonly talented.*

uncommunicative /ʌŋkə'mju:nɪkətɪv/ *adjective*
Someone who is **uncommunicative** refuses to talk, or to tell you what they think or feel: *He's turning into a typical teenager: moody and uncommunicative.*

uncompromising /ʌŋ'kɒmprəmaɪzɪŋ/ *adjective*
An **uncompromising** person refuses to change or alter their beliefs: *He has been uncompromising in his opposition to the government's plans.*

unconcerned /ʌŋkən'sɜ:nd/ *adjective*
You are **unconcerned** about something when you are not worried about it or interested in it, especially when you should be: *You seem extraordinarily unconcerned, in the circumstances.* □ *She was unconcerned about the prospect of months of unemployment.*

unconditional /ʌŋkən'dɪʃənəl/ *adjective*
Something that is **unconditional** is not qualified or limited: *an unconditional surrender* □ *an unconditional agreement.* — *adverb* **unconditionally:** *It is required that you agree to these terms unconditionally.*

unconfirmed /ʌŋkən'fɜ:md/ *adjective*
An **unconfirmed** report is one that has not yet been officially confirmed as true: *There were unconfirmed rumours that the queen was going to visit the school.*

unconnected /ʌŋkə'nektɪd/ *adjective*
Two things are said to be **unconnected** if there is no connection or link between them: *His wife told reporters that he was abroad on business unconnected with recent developments in the company.*

unconscious /ʌŋ'kɒnʃəs/ *adjective; noun*
▻ ***adjective***
1 An **unconscious** person is in a sleep-like state, *eg* as a result of severe illness, or a head injury: *He was unconscious for four days after the accident.* [*same as* **senseless**; *opposite* **conscious**] **2** You are **unconscious** of something when you are not aware of it: *She was quite unconscious of how unpopular she was.* **3** Your behaviour is **unconscious** if you are not aware of what you are doing; a desire is **unconscious** if you are not aware that you have it: *She had a genuine and I'm sure quite unconscious eagerness to make sure everyone around her was happy.* □ *Perhaps it's an expression of an unconscious need for affection.*
▻ ***noun*** (*used in the singular*)
Your **unconscious** is the deepest part of your mind, which contains thoughts and desires that you are not aware of: *Many people believes dreams are full of fears and desires from the unconscious.* — *adverb* **unconsciously:** *The cover of my notepad was covered with the doodles I had unconsciously made whilst deep in thought.* □ *Unconsciously she probably resents her sister's success.*

unconstitutional /ʌŋkɒnstɪ'tju:ʃənəl/ *adjective*
Something that is **unconstitutional** is not allowed by the laws of a country or the rules of an organization: *The Supreme Court ruled that the measures were unconstitutional.* [*opposite* **constitutional**]

uncontrollable /ʌŋkən'troʊləbəl/ *adjective*
Something such as an emotion or desire is **uncontrollable** if you can't do anything to control it or get rid of it: *She suddenly had an uncontrollable urge to kick something.* — *adverb* **uncontrollably:** *She cried uncontrollably at Alice's funeral.*

unconventional /ʌŋkən'venʃənəl/ *adjective*
Your behaviour is **unconventional** if it is unusual or different from most other people's behaviour: *Their lifestyle was unconventional to the point of eccentricity.* □ *unconventional clothes.* — *adverb* **unconventionally:** *She likes to dress unconventionally.*

unconvincing /ʌŋkən'vɪnʃɪŋ/ *adjective*
You describe something as **unconvincing**
1 if you do not believe it, or if you think it is unlikely to be true: *He produced a somewhat unconvincing excuse for being late* [*same as* **lame, unlikely**] **2** if you think it is improbable, or does not reflect reality: *The plot and the characters are unconvincing.* [*same as* **improbable**]

uncooperative /ʌŋkoʊ'ɒpərətɪv/ *adjective*
Someone who is being **uncooperative** is refusing to help you or do what you ask: *He was being deliberately uncooperative.*

uncoordinated /ʌŋkoʊ'ɔ:dɪneɪtɪd/ *adjective*
A person or thing is **uncoordinated** if their various parts do not work together smoothly or well: *The publicity campaign had been run in a hasty, disorganized, uncoordinated fashion, and nothing was achieved by it.* □ *I'm too uncoordinated to be good at games.*

uncork /ʌŋ'kɔ:k/ *verb*: **uncorks, uncorking, uncorked**
You **uncork** a bottle when you remove the cork from it.

uncount /ʌŋ'kaʊnt/ *adjective*
In this dictionary, **uncount** describes nouns (also called **uncountable** nouns) that have only one form, such as *happiness* and *courage,* as distinct from nouns that have both a singular and a plural form such as *dog* and *nose*, which are referred to as **count** nouns; uncount nouns are normally used without the determiners *a* or *the*.

uncouth /ʌŋ'ku:θ/ *adjective*
An **uncouth** person behaves in a rude and unpleasant way: *He is aggressive and uncouth.*

uncover /ʌŋ'kʌvə(r)/ *verb*: **uncovers, uncovering, uncovered**
1 You **uncover** something secret or hidden when you discover it and make it known to other people: *The police had uncovered a plot to kidnap a leading politician.* **2** You **uncover** something when you remove what is covering it: *You can uncover your eyes now.*

uncritical /ʌŋ'krɪtɪkəl/ *adjective*
Someone who is **uncritical** accepts things without questioning them or criticizing them: *his uncritical acceptance of everything she tells him.*

undaunted /ʌn'dɔ:ntɪd/ *adjective*
You are **undaunted** if you are still enthusiastic or hopeful in spite of problems or disappointments: *People turned up in large numbers for the fête, undaunted by the weather.* □ *So far her experiments had failed to yield the results she wanted, but she continued her research undaunted.*

undecided /ʌndɪ'saɪdɪd/ *adjective*

You are **undecided** about something if you haven't made a decision about it yet: *I'm still undecided about whether to take that job or wait for something better to turn up.* □ *Ten people voted in favour of the proposal, six were against, and three were undecided.* □ *That matter remains undecided for the present.*

undeniable /ʌndɪ'naɪəbəl/ *adjective*
Something that is **undeniable** is clearly the case: *There's been an undeniable improvement in traffic flow since these roundabouts were installed.* □ *They're not the most brilliant children, certainly, but their enthusiasm and willingness to learn are undeniable.* — *adverb* **undeniably:** *Emma was a clever, assured, and undeniably pretty girl.*

under /'ʌndə(r)/ *preposition; adverb; adjective*
▻ ***preposition***
1 One thing is **under** another **a** if it is lower than it, or directly below it: *He had a great purple bruise under his right eye.* □ *I read the caption under the photograph.* □ *She regarded me from under her fringe.* □ *He kept a toy revolver under the bed.* □ *working in the fields under a midday sun* □ *The grains are examined under a microscope.* □ *Brown the pizza under the grill.* [*opposite* **over**, **above**; see note at **below**] **b** if it is covered or hidden by it: *The key was kept under a flowerpot.* □ *A cat scuttled from under a bush towards the door.* □ *Under her cardigan she wore a blue woollen dress.* □ *Her hair was out of sight under a floppy straw hat.* □ *He hid his concern under a calm exterior.* [*same as* **beneath**] **c** if it is below its surface: *They held his face under the water.* □ *We found a shoe buried under the sand.* [*same as* **beneath**] **d** if it supports it: *The floor shook under them.* □ *The bed groaned under his weight.* [*same as* **beneath**]
2 One thing goes **under** another **a** if it goes beneath it at one side and comes out at the other: *the old superstition about not walking under a ladder* □ *The tunnel goes under the river.* **b** if it moves to a position below or beneath it: *He crept under the table and wouldn't come out.* □ *Throwing yourself under a bus won't solve anything.* □ *She slipped deeper under the bedclothes.*
3 Something is **under** a certain number, amount or age if it is less than it: *His fine was set at just under £5000.* □ *children under the age of 5* □ *if you are over 16 but under 19* □ *He'd have been dead in under a minute if she hadn't known what to do.* [*opposite* **over**]
4 a The people **under** you at your place of work are the people you are supervising or in charge of: *I'm Clementine Fry and you'll be working under me.* □ *Except for the butler, the staff are under my command.* [*opposite* **over**; see note at **below**] **b** Something happens **under** a particular king, queen, government or leader if it happens while they are reigning or in power: *Under a Labour government the situation might not be very different.* □ *Under the leadership of Hugh Gaitskell the party was dominated by a trend away from socialism.* **c** You are studying **under** someone when that person is guiding your work: *At Cambridge he studied under the scholar Walter Headlam.* □ *The research continues under Professor John Howie.*
5 a Something happens **under** certain circumstances or conditions if it happens while they exist, or as a result of them: *There are men drilling in the road outside, so we're working under very difficult conditions.* □ *He was adamant that under no circumstances would he* [= however great the pressure he would not] *sell the property.* **b** Something that happens **under** a law or agreement, happens because the law or agreement says it must: *We are entitled to free speech under the laws of this state.* □ *The manager of the shop was charged under the Indecent Advertisements Act.* □ *The annual rent payable under the lease was £9800.* **c** Something that is *eg* being constructed, or being discussed, is **under** construction, or **under** discussion: *More prisons were under construction.* □ *Proposals are under consideration to transfer disputes like these to industrial tribunals.* **d** You are **under** strain or pressure when you are being affected by it: *Sales staff find themselves under pressure to work on Sundays.* □ *Her face still showed the strain she had been under.* **e** You are **under** the influence of someone or something when they control your behaviour or judgement: *He was under the influence of his Communist friend Murphy.* □ *He was still under her spell.* □ *driving under the influence of alcohol.* **f** You are **under** the impression that something is so if you have some reason to believe it is: *He's obviously under the impression that women are pathetic, helpless creatures.* □ *She wore green a lot, under the misapprehension that her husband liked her in it.* **g** An operation is performed **under** an anaesthetic if the patient is anaesthetized before it is performed.
6 a Things can be found **under** *eg* a certain name or heading if that is the section into which they have been put according to some system of classification: *Leisure activities are grouped under a number of different headings.* □ *File this letter under Complaints.* **b** You write or publish something **under** a particular name if that name appears on your work as the name of the author: *She had published a poem in 'The Listener' under a pseudonym.* **c** Products are sold or marketed **under** a certain name or label if that is their trade name or brand name.
▻ ***adverb***
Under as an adverb reflects some of the senses of the preposition: *He blow-dried her hair, turning the ends neatly under with a brush.* □ *He lifted up the barbed wire and I squeezed under.* □ *She went under again, her lungs filling with salty water.* □ *Only 6% of the population are ten or under.*
▻ ***adjective***
Under describes the lower, downward-facing part of something: *The bird has a blackish patch on the under surface of its wing.*
▻ ***phrase*** For **under way** see **way**.

under- /ʌndə(r)/ *prefix*
1 Under- is added to words to mean beneath or below: *rubbish trampled underfoot.* □ *the undersurface of its wing* **2 Under-** is also added to words to indicate that something is not properly or sufficiently done, or that there is not enough of it: *underfed children* □ *a potentially valuable resource which remains seriously underdeveloped.*

under-age /ʌndər'eɪdʒ/ *adjective*
A person who is **under-age** is not old enough, according to a law, to do a certain thing: *You can't go into the casino; you're under-age.* □ *the problem of under-age drinking.*

undercarriage /'ʌndəkarɪdʒ/ *noun*: **undercarriages**
An aircraft's **undercarriage** is the structure into which the wheels are fitted, that supports it as it lands and takes off, and is folded up into its fuselage while it is in flight.

underclothes /'ʌndəkloʊðz/ *noun* (*plural*)
Your **underclothes** are the clothes you wear next to your skin, such as a bra, vest or pants. [*same as* **underwear**]

undercover /ʌndə'kʌvə(r)/ *adjective or adverb*
Undercover work is done or carried out in secret: *an undercover agent* □ *evidence gathered by members of the police force working undercover.*

undercurrent /'ʌndəkʌrənt/ *noun*: **undercurrents**
1 In a river or the sea, an **undercurrent** is a strong flow of water in a particular direction under the surface.

2 An **undercurrent** is also a hidden tendency or characteristic that is different from what appears on the surface: *There was a growing undercurrent of disquiet about the way the company's projects were being planned and run.*

undercut /ʌndəˈkʌt/ *verb*: **undercuts, undercutting, undercut**
Someone **undercuts** you if they sell the same thing as you are selling but at a lower price: *He's undercutting my prices by several pounds.*

underdeveloped /ˈʌndədɪvɛləpt/ *adjective*
An **underdeveloped** country is one that does not have modern industries and can provide its citizens only with a limited health or education system: *The European parliament gives grants to help underdeveloped countries in Africa.*

underdog /ˈʌndədɒg/ *noun*: **underdogs**
An **underdog** is **1** the weaker of the two contestants or sides taking part in a match, whom no-one expects to win: *I always stick up for the underdog.* **2** any member of society who is in a situation in which it is difficult to do well and be successful, and who is therefore regarded as unfairly treated by society: *Children like these grow up to be society's underdogs.*

underdone /ʌndəˈdʌn/ *adjective*
Food that is **underdone** has not been cooked long enough or properly.

underestimate /ʌndərˈɛstɪmeɪt/ *verb*: **underestimates, underestimating, underestimated**
1 You **underestimate** the value of something, or an amount, when your estimate is too low: *The builder underestimated the number of bricks needed and has ordered more.* **2** You **underestimate** someone if you do not realize how good, talented, clever or successful they are, or how strong their feelings are: *People shouldn't underestimate him; he'll probably be a very good Prime Minister.*

underfoot /ʌndəˈfʊt/ *adverb*
1 The condition of the ground **underfoot** is how it feels to you as you walk on it: *The grass was damp underfoot.* **2** You tread something **underfoot** when you walk on it so that it gets squashed or pushed into the ground: *The field was covered with plastic cups and paper plates, trampled underfoot by yesterday's huge crowds.*

undergarment /ˈʌndəgɑːmənt/ *noun* (*formal*): **undergarments**
An **undergarment** is a piece of underwear: *the drawer containing my bras, pants and other undergarments.*

undergo /ʌndəˈgoʊ/ *verb*: **undergoes, undergoing, underwent, undergone**
1 You **undergo** some unpleasant or necessary procedure when it is carried out on you, or happens to you: *He underwent major heart surgery several years ago.* **2** Someone or something **undergoes** *eg* a change when it happens to them: *The city centre had undergone a transformation.*

undergraduate /ʌndəˈgradjʊət/ *noun*: **undergraduates**
An **undergraduate** is a person studying for their first degree at college or university: *when I was an undergraduate at St Andrews* □ *undergraduate courses.* [compare **graduate, postgraduate**]

underground *noun*; *adjective*; *adverb*
▻ ***noun*** /ˈʌndəgraʊnd/
1 (*uncount or used in the singular*) The **Underground** in a city is a system of electric trains running in tunnels below the ground: *the London Underground* □ *commuters travelling across London by underground.* □ *Take the Underground to Charing Cross.* □ *Where's the nearest underground station?* [*same as* **subway, tube**] **2** (*used in the singular*) People organized into a group working secretly against the government or establishment are referred to as the **underground**.
▻ ***adjective*** /ˈʌndəgraʊnd/
1 Underground things exist or happen below the surface of the ground: *an underground cave* □ *an underground car park* □ *the underground railway* □ *underground exploration.* **2 Underground** also describes unofficial or illegal activities carried on in secret against the government or establishment: *underground newspapers and magazines.*
▻ ***adverb*** /ʌndəˈgraʊnd/
1 Things that happen or exist **underground** happen or exist below the surface of the ground: *animals that live in burrows underground* □ *He had spent a large part of his working life underground.* □ *The little creature paused briefly at the entrance to its hole, then disappeared underground.* **2** People go **underground** when they hide from the police or from those in authority, because their activities are illegal and they are afraid of getting caught: *It became virtually a one-party state, and opposition parties were driven underground.*

undergrowth /ˈʌndəgroʊθ/ *noun* (*uncount or used in the singular*)
The **undergrowth** in a wood, forest or jungle is a thick growth of bushes and plants under the trees: *He struggled through the undergrowth.* □ *Their progress was hindered by thick undergrowth.*

underhand /ʌndəˈhand/ *adjective or adverb*
Underhand behaviour is dishonest or deceitful, and usually directed towards harming someone else or gaining an advantage for yourself: *That was a mean, underhand thing to do.* □ *She had managed to get herself promoted by somewhat underhand means.* [*same as* **deceitful, sly**]

underline /ʌndəˈlaɪn/ *verb*: **underlines, underlining, underlined**
1 You **underline** words when you draw a line under them, *eg* to indicate emphasis, or to indicate to a printer that they are to be printed in italics. **2** You **underline** something you are saying when you emphasize it or draw special attention to it: *And I'd like to underline that last point.*

underlying /ʌndəˈlaɪɪŋ/ *adjective*
Underlying describes aspects or features of objects or situations that are not easily noticed when you first look at them: *the underlying factors responsible for the rise in the crime rate* □ *There are plenty of underlying similarities between languages, even between those that look very different from each other.*

undermine /ʌndəˈmaɪn/ *verb*: **undermines, undermining, undermined**
To **undermine** a person or system is to reduce or weaken their support and make them less strong and secure: *I feel she's trying to undermine my position in the company.* □ *the influences that are undermining the structure of society.* □ *Try not to criticize children; it undermines their confidence and self respect.*

underneath /ʌndəˈniːθ/ *preposition*; *adverb*; *noun*; *adjective*
▻ ***preposition***
1 One thing is **underneath** another **a** if it is under it or beneath it: *The bomb exploded underneath his car as he was preparing to leave home.* □ *He felt something hard underneath his foot.* □ *We sheltered underneath the arch.* [*same as* **under, beneath**] **b** if it is directly below it: *Many people were actually smoking underneath the*

'no smoking' signs. □ *She signed her own name underneath Melanie's signature.* [*same as* **below**, **beneath**] **c** if it is covered by it: *There was dirt underneath my fingernails.* □ *She was wearing a linen jacket, and underneath that a blouse and blue jeans.* □ *She tucked her legs up underneath her.* [*same as* **under**, **beneath**] **d** if it is hidden or concealed by it: *She's a tough lady underneath that quiet exterior.* [*same as* **beneath**]
2 One thing goes **underneath** another when it goes under it at one side and comes out at the other: *The boat glided underneath a bridge.* □ *You can run the hot and cold water pipes underneath the floorboards.* [*same as* **under**, **beneath**]
▻ ***adverb:*** *The poster bore a picture of a calf, with the words 'Stop This Cruelty' underneath.* □ *We stripped away the plaster to expose the bare brick underneath.* □ *He was wearing a jacket with a cashmere sweater underneath.* □ *He wasn't a bad person underneath.*
▻ ***noun*** (*used in the singular*)
The **underneath** of something is its downward-facing part or surface: *Braque has twisted the neck of the violin so that the top and underneath of it are visible simultaneously.*
▻ ***adjective:*** *He had achieved the look by cutting the underneath layers of her hair shorter than the outer layers.*

underpants /'ʌndəpants/ *noun* (*plural*)
A man's or boy's **underpants** are the garment that covers his body from his waist or hips to his thighs, and that he wears under his trousers: *All my luggage was stolen and I was left without even a clean pair of underpants.*

underpass /'ʌndəpɑːs/ *noun*: **underpasses**
An **underpass** is a tunnel that people can use to walk under a road or railway. [*same as* **subway**]

underprivileged /ʌndə'prɪvɪlɪdʒd/ *adjective*
Underprivileged people have less money, fewer possessions and opportunities, and poorer living conditions than most people in society.

underrate /ʌndə'reɪt/ *verb*: **underrates**, **underrating**, **underrated**
You **underrate** a person or thing when you fail to recognize or appreciate how clever or able they are: *Don't underrate him; he's an extremely shrewd and able politician.* [*same as* **underestimate**] — *adjective* **underrated:** *He's a very underrated composer.*

underside /'ʌndəsaɪd/ *noun*: **undersides**
The **underside** of an object is its side or surface that faces downwards: *Take a look at the underside of the leaf.*

undersized /ʌndə'saɪzd/ *adjective*
Undersized people, animals or things are smaller than normal.

understand /ʌndə'stand/ *verb*: **understands**, **understanding**, **understood**
1 You **understand** someone, or **understand** what they are saying, when you know what they mean, or what they are referring to: *He pretended not to understand me.* □ *Sorry, I don't understand.* □ *I began to understand what she meant.* □ *I never understand a word Finn writes.* □ *I want it back tomorrow, though; is that understood?* □ *I understood him to say he wouldn't be back till Wednesday.* **2** You **understand** a language if you know what people are saying when they are speaking it: *She's a good girl but she doesn't understand English too well.* □ *They didn't understand a word of French.* **3** You **understand** a person if you know why they behave the way they do: *He often complained that she didn't understand him; in fact she understood him only too well.* □ *I had never really understood Alice.* □ *We help boys and girls to understand each other.* **4** You **understand** something such as a machine or system if you know how it works: *Peter will help you; he understands computers better than I do.* **5** You **understand** a situation, or **understand** why something is happening, if you know the reasons for it: *I cannot understand why anyone would want to hurt him.* □ *I don't understand what's causing the error.* □ *I can understand you being bitter.* □ *I understand her point of view.* □ *Women get anxious because they do not understand the physical changes they are experiencing.* **6** You **understand** that something is the case when you realize or appreciate that it is: *Does he understand that planning permission is required?* □ *We do understand that reforms are needed.* **7** You say you **understand** that something is so if you have been told that it is: *The publication date has been postponed; or so I understand.* □ *Bush was understood to have welcomed the change of government in Israel.* □ *I understand that about three years have passed since you left?* [*same as* **gather**]
▻ ***phrase*** You **make yourself understood** when you get people to understand what you are trying to tell them: *He had to remove his oxygen mask to make himself understood.*

understandable /ʌndə'standəbəl/ *adjective*
1 You say that someone's behaviour is **understandable** if you think they have reacted to something in a reasonable, natural or normal way: *He reacted with understandable fury to the implied insult.* □ *Her reaction was understandable in the circumstances.* [*same as* **comprehensible**] **2** Something that is **understandable** can be understood: *He had such a strong accent that his speech was barely understandable.* □ *data that is readily understandable by a computer.* [*same as* **comprehensible**] — *adverb* **understandably:** *She was understandably upset.*

understanding /ʌndə'standɪŋ/ *noun*; *adjective*
▻ ***noun***: **understandings**
1 (*uncount or used in the singular*) You have an **understanding** of something if you have some knowledge of it or familiarity with it: *I had no more than a basic understanding of Polish* □ *An understanding of computing is essential for this job.* **2** (*uncount or used in the singular*) Your **understanding** of a situation is the way you interpret the information you have about it: *It was my understanding that the documents would be sent by first-class post.* **3** People come to an **understanding** about something when they reach an informal agreement about it: *They have arrived at an understanding that will allow both of them a certain amount of freedom.* **4** (*uncount*) There is **understanding** between people when they are sympathetic towards, and trust, each other: *the need for greater international understanding.*
▻ ***adjective***
An **understanding** person is kind and sympathetic: *My boss was very understanding about my problems at home, and gave me some extra leave to sort things out.*
▻ ***phrase*** You agree to one thing **on the understanding that** another thing will happen when you make it a condition of the agreement that the second thing will happen: *He was offered the job on the understanding that he would stay for at least six months.* □ *I accepted this post on the understanding that I would be allowed to organize and staff my own department.*

understate /ʌndə'steɪt/ *verb*: **understates**, **understating**, **understated**
You **understate** something when you represent it as being less important or smaller than it really is: *I think you have understated the size of the problem.*

understatement /ʌndə'steɪtmənt/ *noun*: **understatements**
If you describe what someone has said about something as an **understatement** you mean it does not accurately represent the extent to which what they say is true: *To say that his work is inadequate is an understatement; it's atrocious.*

understood /ʌndə'stʊd/ *verb*; *adjective*
▻ ***verb***
Understood is the past tense and past participle of **understand**.
▻ ***adjective***
Something that is **understood** is implied but not actually expressed or stated, or is realized without people having to talk about it: *It is understood that staff will be prepared to supervise games periods from time to time.* □ *The reasons for her leaving were generally understood although no-one discussed them.*

understudy /ʌndə'stʌdɪ/ *noun*: **understudies**
The **understudy** of someone such as an actor, actress or opera singer is a person who has learnt their part, so as to be able to take their place on stage if necessary: *The star of the show was ill and her understudy had to go on instead.*

undertake /ʌndə'teɪk/ *verb* (*informal*): **undertakes, undertaking, undertook, undertaken**
1 You **undertake** a duty or task when you accept responsibility for it, and start on it: *You should think very carefully before you undertake the responsibilities of an adoptive parent* **2** You **undertake** to do something when you promise to do it: *The police have undertaken to review airport security.* □ *She undertook to be responsible for turning the lights off at night.*

undertaker /'ʌndəteɪkə(r)/ *noun*: **undertakers**
An **undertaker** is a person whose job is organizing funerals and preparing dead bodies for burial or cremation.

undertaking /'ʌndəteɪkɪŋ/ *noun* (*formal*): **undertakings**
1 An **undertaking** is a duty, responsibility or task that you agree or promise to do: *It will be an enormous undertaking to equip every member of staff with their own terminal.* **2** You give an **undertaking** that you will do something when you promise to do it: *The government is failing in its undertaking to protect the poorest members of the community from the effects of inflation.*

undertone /'ʌndətoʊn/ *noun*: **undertones**
1 You say something in an **undertone** when you say it in a quiet voice that others can barely hear. **2** (*usually in the plural*) Something has **undertones** of a particular quality or feeling when that quality or feeling is there but is not very obvious or clearly expressed: *Some Christian ceremonies have pagan undertones.* [*same as* **overtones**]

undertook /ʌndə'tʊk/ *verb*
Undertook is the past tense of **undertake**.

undervalue /ʌndə'valju:/ *verb*: **undervalues, undervaluing, undervalued**
You **undervalue** someone or something when you regard them or treat them, as less important or valuable than they really are: *The nurses are a much-undervalued section of the community.*

underwater /ʌndə'wɔ:tə(r)/ *adjective or adverb*
Something that happens, exists, works or is carried out **underwater** happens, exists, works or is carried out below the surface of water: *an underwater camera* □ *underwater filming* □ *I can't swim underwater.*

underway /ʌndə'weɪ/ *adjective*
Something is **underway** when it has started: *Work on the new motorway got underway last week.* [*same as* **under way**]

underwear /'ʌndəweə(r)/ *noun* (*uncount*)
Your **underwear** is the clothing that you wear under your outer clothing, *eg* pants, vests and bras.

underwent /ʌndə'wɛnt/ *verb*
Underwent is the past tense of **undergo**.

underworld /'ʌndəwɜ:ld/ *noun* (*used in the singular*)
The **underworld** is the world of organized crime and criminals.

undesirable /ʌndɪ'zaɪərəbəl/ *adjective*
Undesirable people or things are unpleasant or harmful in some way: *Cuts in public spending are bound to have an undesirable effect on the health of the community.* □ *Some of these drugs have undesirable side effects.*

undetected /ʌndɪ'tɛktɪd/ *adjective*
Something remains **undetected** when people do not realize it is happening, or fail to find out about it: *The illicit withdrawals of large sums from the bank went undetected for several months.*

undid /ʌn'dɪd/ *verb*
Undid is the past tense of **undo**.

undies /'ʌndi:z/ *noun* (*plural*; *informal*)
A woman's **undies** are her underwear.

undignified /ʌn'dɪgnɪfaɪd/ *adjective*
Undignified behaviour is embarrassing and makes you look foolish: *She landed in an undignified heap at the bottom of the steps.*

undiscovered /ʌndɪs'kʌvəd/ *adjective*
Something remains **undiscovered** when no-one finds out about it: *His body lay undiscovered in the flat for several weeks.* □ *a previously undiscovered work by Pergolesi.*

undisguised /ʌndɪs'gaɪzd/ *adjective*
An **undisguised** feeling is one that you display openly and do not try to hide: *She watched her son receive his certificate with undisguised pride.*

undisputed /ʌndɪ'spju:tɪd/ *adjective*
Something that is **undisputed** is not questioned or doubted by anyone: *her talent is undisputed.* □ *Professor Gebbie is the undisputed leader in this area of research.*

undistinguished /ʌndɪ'stɪŋgwɪʃt/ *adjective*
Someone or something is **undistinguished** if there is nothing particularly good about them: *an undistinguished career as a journalist.*

undivided /ʌndɪ'vaɪdɪd/ *adjective*
You give someone or something your **undivided** attention when you concentrate on them completely: *If you come to see me tomorrow I'll be able to give you my undivided attention.*

undo /ʌn'du:/ *verb*: **undoes, undoing, undid, undone**
1 You **undo** something when you unfasten it or loosen it: *She undid her shoelaces.* □ *He undid his coat and took it off.* □ *Can you undo this knot for me?* □ *He undid the string and unwrapped the parcel.* **2** You **undo** something that has been done if you reverse the effect or result it has had: *One silly error undid weeks of hard work.*

undoing /ʌn'du:ɪŋ/ *noun* (*uncount*; *formal*)
Something that is described as your **undoing** is the reason why you fail or are unsuccessful: *He's clever enough but laziness is his undoing.*

undone /ʌn'dʌn/ *adjective*

1 Work is **undone** when it hasn't been done: *The kitchen was filthy and the washing had been left undone.* **2** Clothes and shoes are **undone** when they are not fastened: *One of your shoelaces has come undone.*

undoubted /ʌn'daʊtɪd/ *adjective*
Undoubted is used to describe something that definitely exists or is true: *Credit cards are an undoubted convenience.* □ *her undoubted talent for drawing.* [*same as* **evident**] — *adverb* **undoubtedly:** *That was undoubtedly the high point of his career.*

undreamed-of /ʌn'dri:md ɒv/ or **undreamt-of** /ʌn'drɛmt ɒv/ *adjective*
Things that are **undreamed-of** are much better or worse than you thought possible: *He was now the possessor of undreamed-of wealth.* □ *The book was an undreamt-of success.*

undress /ʌn'drɛs/ *verb*: **undresses, undressing, undressed**
You **undress** when you take your clothes off; you **undress** someone when you take their clothes off: *We had to undress in a draughty room with no heating.* □ *She undressed her baby and put her in the bath.*

undressed /ʌn'drɛst/ *adjective*
You are **undressed** when you have taken your clothes off.
▷ ***phrase*** You **get undressed** when you take your clothes off; you **get** someone else **undressed** when you take their clothes off them: *It takes him ages to get dressed or undressed.* □ *He got the children undressed and ready for bed.*

undue /ʌn'dju:/ *adjective* (*formal*)
Undue means too much, or excessive: *He drives with undue caution.* — *adverb* **unduly** /ʌn'dju:lɪ/: *No-one seemed unduly* [= particularly] *worried when she failed to turn up.* [*same as* **excessively, greatly**]

undulate /'ʌndjʊleɪt/ *verb*: **undulates, undulating, undulated**
Something that **undulates** moves up and down gently like waves: *the gently undulating hills.*

undying /ʌn'daɪɪŋ/ *adjective* (*literary*)
Undying love or affection lasts forever: *her undying love for her husband.* [*same as* **everlasting, eternal**]

unearth /ʌn'ɜ:θ/ *verb*: **unearths, unearthing, unearthed**
You **unearth** something **1** when you uncover it or excavate it: *The ruins of a Roman fort have been unearthed near the town centre.* **2** you discover it: *I managed to unearth that article on idioms I was telling you about.*

unearthly /ʌn'ɜ:θlɪ/ *adjective*
1 (*informal*) You do something at an **unearthly** time when you do it very early: *I had to get up at the unearthly hour of 4.30.* **2 Unearthly** happenings, sights or noises are strange, mysterious and usually frightening: *Suddenly there was an unearthly shriek.* [*same as* **weird**]

uneasy /ʌn'i:zɪ/ *adjective*: **uneasier, uneasiest**
1 You feel **uneasy** about something if you are worried, nervous or anxious about it: *She felt increasingly uneasy as time went on and still her husband did not return.* [*same as* **ill at ease**] **2** An **uneasy** situation is one in which there is tension, or in which people feel anxious and uncertain: *Relations between him and his father had been strained and uneasy of late.* □ *There was an uneasy silence at the end of his speech.* — *adverb* **uneasily:** *She wriggled uneasily in her seat.* — *noun* (*uncount*) **uneasiness:** *She tried to hide her feelings of uneasiness from the children.*

uneconomic /ʌni:kə'nɒmɪk/ or **uneconomical** /ʌni:kə'nɒmɪkəl/ *adjective*
Things that are **uneconomic** either waste money, or fail to make a profit: *The plan proved to be uneconomic.* □ *Some forms of fuel are uneconomical.* [compare **unprofitable, wasteful**]

unemployed /ʌnɪm'plɔɪd/ *adjective; noun*
▷ ***adjective***
Someone who is **unemployed** does not have a job: *He's been unemployed for over a year now.* [*same as* **jobless**]
▷ ***noun*** (*plural*)
The **unemployed** are people who do not have jobs: *The government runs several schemes to help the unemployed find work.* [*same as* **jobless**]

unemployment /ʌnɪm'plɔɪmənt/ *noun* (*uncount*)
1 Unemployment is the state of being unemployed: *government measures to deal with the unemployment problem.* **2 Unemployment** is also used to refer to the number of unemployed people: *Unemployment has risen again for the fourth month running.*

unemployment benefit /ʌnɪmplɔɪmənt 'bɛnɪfɪt/ *noun* (*uncount*)
Unemployment benefit is a sum of money paid regularly by the state to people who do not have jobs.

unending /ʌn'ɛndɪŋ/ *adjective*
Something that is **unending**, especially something boring or annoying, seems as if it is never going to stop: *Today was just an unending succession of interruptions.*

unenviable /ʌn'ɛnvɪəbəl/ *adjective*
You are in an **unenviable** position when you are in a situation where you have an unpleasant job or task that you would rather not do: *I had the unenviable task of telling her that her work did not meet the required standard.*

unequal /ʌn'i:kwəl/ *adjective*
1 A social or political system that is **unequal** does not treat people equally or fairly: *the unequal treatment of men and women.* [*opposite* **equitable, fair**] **2** You are **unequal** to a job or task if you do not have the ability, skill, willpower, strength or courage to do it: *I felt unequal to the task of clearing up the mess, and left it till the morning.* **3** Two things are **unequal** when they are not the same size or value: *a mixture made up of unequal amounts of sand and cement.*

unequivocal /ʌnɪ'kwɪvəkəl/ *adjective* (*formal*)
Something that is **unequivocal** is clearly stated or expressed, so that there can be no doubt about it: *He has the party's unequivocal support.* □ *What we want from the party leader is an unequivocal statement of policy.* [*same as* **unambiguous**] — *adverb* **unequivocally:** *He has unequivocally stated that he continues to support for the Prime Minister.*

unerring /ʌn'ɜ:rɪŋ/ *adjective*
You have an **unerring** ability to do something if you always do it accurately or well: *She had an unerring talent for spotting promising youngsters.* □ *His aim was unerring.*

unethical /ʌn'ɛθɪkəl/ *adjective*
Behaviour that is **unethical** is morally wrong, or is wrong according to the rules operating within a particular profession: *He has acted in a most unethical manner.* □ *Desirable as it may be, euthanasia is strictly unethical.* [*same as* **immoral**; *opposite* **ethical**]

uneven /ʌn'i:vən/ *adjective*
1 An **uneven** surface is not smooth or flat: *She tripped on the uneven pavement.* [*same as* **bumpy**] **2** An **uneven** edge is not smooth and straight: *He grinned, revealing broken, uneven teeth.* [*same as* **ragged**] **3** Work or progress that is **uneven** is not consistent: *Her work has been very uneven this term.* [*same as* **inconsistent, erratic**] **4** An **uneven** contest or competition is one in

which one side or competitor is much better than the other, and is bound to win.

uneventful /ʌnɪˈventfʊl/ *adjective*
You describe a period of time as **uneventful** if nothing interesting, surprising, exciting or important happens during it: *The holidays were pretty uneventful.*

unexpected /ʌnɪkˈspɛktɪd/ *adjective*
Something that is **unexpected** occurs when you are not expecting it, and surprises you: *Well, this is an unexpected pleasure; I hadn't expected to see you here.* □ *His second heart attack wasn't altogether unexpected.* — *adverb* **unexpectedly:** *Sorry to be late; I was unexpectedly delayed; someone rang me at the office just as I was leaving.*

unfailing /ʌnˈfeɪlɪŋ/ *adjective*
A quality that is **unfailing** is always present and remains strong and reliable: *Thanks to her unfailing good humour and encouragement we managed to get the crisis sorted out.* [*same as* **constant**]

unfair /ʌnˈfɛə(r)/ *adjective*
1 Something that is **unfair** is not right or just: *It's unfair to criticize her in her absence.* □ *You're being very unfair to me.* [*same as* **unjust**] **2** A system that is **unfair** does not treat people equally or fairly: *The tax system is unfair.* — *adverb* **unfairly:** *The Prime Minister has been unfairly criticized for his alleged lack of decisiveness.*

unfaithful /ʌnˈfeɪθfʊl/ *adjective*
Someone who is **unfaithful** to their husband, wife or lover has a sexual relationship with someone else: *He promised he would never be unfaithful again.*

unfamiliar /ʌnfəˈmɪlɪə(r)/ *adjective*
1 A person is **unfamiliar** to you if you don't know them, or have never met them before: *The lady on my right was unfamiliar to me, and we introduced ourselves.* □ *when you're surrounded by unfamiliar faces.* **2** Things are **unfamiliar** to you if you have never seen them or heard them before: *He found himself in unfamiliar surroundings.* □ *I'm afraid the term is unfamiliar to me.* **3** You are **unfamiliar** with something if you haven't seen it or heard of it before, or if you are not acquainted with it: *There will be guides on duty everywhere to help those of you who are unfamiliar with the layout of the building.* [*opposite* **familiar**]

unfashionable /ʌnˈfaʃənəbəl/ *adjective*
Things that are **unfashionable** are not fashionable or popular: *Wide ties were becoming unfashionable.* □ *It's unfashionable to smoke nowadays.* — *adverb* **unfashionably:** *She was wearing unfashionably flared trousers.*

unfasten /ʌnˈfɑːsən/ *verb*: **unfastens, unfastening, unfastened**
You **unfasten** something when you undo the buttons, zip, fastening or catch that keeps it closed: *Could you unfasten my necklace for me?* □ *I couldn't unfasten the catch on my bracelet.* □ *The children's safety belts unfasten in the middle, not at the side.* □ *Passengers are reminded not to unfasten their seat belts until all the engines have been switched off.* □ *The dog has learnt how to unfasten the gate.* [*same as* **undo**; *opposite* **fasten, do up**]

unfavourable (*AmE* **unfavorable**) /ʌnˈfeɪvərəbəl/ *adjective*
1 **Unfavourable** conditions are likely to stop you being successful in what you are trying to do, or to give you problems: *The weather is unfavourable for an attempt on the summit.* [*same as* **adverse**; *opposite* **favourable**] **2** You have an **unfavourable** opinion of something if you don't like it, don't agree with it or don't approve of it: *an unfavourable review of the film.* — *adverb* **unfavourably:** *Our education system compares unfavourably with those of France and Germany.*

unfeeling /ʌnˈfiːlɪŋ/ *adjective*
An **unfeeling** person does not feel sympathy for other people: *unfeeling reporters.* □ *I'm sorry to seem unfeeling, but I can't solve your problems for you.* [*same as* **hard-hearted**]

unfinished /ʌnˈfɪnɪʃt/ *adjective*
Work that is **unfinished** hasn't been finished or completed: *The builders left the house unfinished when the money ran out.* [*same as* **incomplete**]

unfit /ʌnˈfɪt/ *adjective*
1 A person or thing is **unfit** for a particular purpose if they are not good enough, or not in a good enough condition, for it: *She is unfit for such a responsible position.* □ *This food is unfit to eat.* □ *You're obviously unfit to go to work today.* **2** You are **unfit** when you have not been taking regular exercise: *I'm so unfit these days; I can't run upstairs without getting breathless.*
[*opposite* **fit, healthy**]

unflinching /ʌnˈflɪntʃɪŋ/ *adjective*
Unflinching actions or behaviour confront danger and unpleasantness instead of trying to avoid them: *an unflinching account of the horrors of life in a concentration camp.*

unfold /ʌnˈfoʊld/ *verb*: **unfolds, unfolding, unfolded**
1 You **unfold** something when you open it or spread it out: *He unfolded the newspaper and began to read.* **2** A situation **unfolds** when it develops or becomes clear to people: *Everyone has been watching the events on television as they unfold.*

unforeseen /ʌnfɔːˈsiːn/ *adjective*
An **unforeseen** event is one that no-one expected or predicted would happen: *The flight has been cancelled due to unforeseen circumstances.*

unforgettable /ʌnfəˈgɛtəbəl/ *adjective*
An experience that is **unforgettable** is so good or so bad that it has made a lasting impression on you: *The trip to Africa was an unforgettable experience.*

unforgivable /ʌnfəˈgɪvəbəl/ *adjective*
Something you do is **unforgivable** if it is very bad or cruel and so cannot be forgiven: *It's an unforgivable way to treat a child.*

unfortunate /ʌnˈfɔːtʃənət/ *adjective*
1 You are **unfortunate** if you are unlucky: *She was unfortunate to only win second prize.* **2** Something is **unfortunate** **a** if it is not suitable or proper: *It was a rather unfortunate comment in the circumstances.* **b** if it is a shame that it happened: *It's unfortunate you didn't get here earlier.* □ *an unfortunate injury.* [*same as* **regrettable**]

unfortunately /ʌnˈfɔːtʃənətlɪ/ *adverb* (*sentence adverb*)
You can use **unfortunately** to show that you are sorry about something or regret it: *I won't be able to come, unfortunately.* □ *Unfortunately, by the time the doctor arrived he was already dead.*

unfounded /ʌnˈfaʊndɪd/ *adjective*
Something that is **unfounded** is not based on facts: *The accusations against him have been proved to be unfounded.* [*same as* **groundless**]

unfriendly /ʌnˈfrɛndlɪ/ *adjective*
An **unfriendly** person does not behave in pleasant, friendly or sympathetic way: *I hope you didn't think I was being unfriendly when I didn't shake your hand.*

unfurnished /ʌnˈfɜːnɪʃt/ *adjective*

You rent an **unfurnished** flat or house when you rent one that doesn't have any furniture in it.

ungainly /ʌnˈgeɪnlɪ/ *adjective*: **ungainlier, ungainliest**
An **ungainly** person moves in a way that is awkward and clumsy: *She was thought to be too tall and ungainly for classical ballet.*

ungrateful /ʌnˈgreɪtfʊl/ *adjective*
An **ungrateful** person does not appreciate, or is not grateful for, something that has been done for them or given to them: *You must write and say thank you, otherwise you'll seem ungrateful.*

unguarded /ʌnˈgɑːdɪd/ *adjective*
A person or place is **unguarded** if they are not guarded or protected: *She wandered off leaving her handbag unguarded.*
▻ ***phrase*** You do or say something in **an unguarded moment** if you do or say it without being as careful as you normally would be: *The photographer caught the Prime Minister in an unguarded moment, with his head in his hands.*

unhappy /ʌnˈhapɪ/ *adjective*: **unhappier, unhappiest**
1 You are **unhappy** when you are feeling sad and depressed: *I was so unhappy at that school.* □ *He had an unhappy childhood.* □ *That was the unhappiest day of my life.* □ *a very unhappy occasion* □ *He looks unhappy.* **2** A situation is **unhappy** if it is caused by, or brings, problems or unpleasantness: *an unhappy state of affairs.* □ *It was an unhappy marriage.* [*same as* **unfortunate**] **3** You are **unhappy** about something if you are not satisfied with it: *I'm unhappy about the arrangements made for his education.* [*opposite* **happy**] — *adverb* **unhappily:** *She walked unhappily towards the house.* □ (*sentence adverb*) *Unhappily, the treatment was unsuccessful.* — *noun* (*uncount*) **unhappiness:** *signs of her unhappiness.*

unhealthy /ʌnˈhɛlθɪ/ *adjective*: **unhealthier, unhealthiest**
1 Someone who is **unhealthy** does not have good health and is often ill. **2** Something that is described as **unhealthy** may be physically, mentally or emotionally harmful: *an unhealthy environment for a child* □ *They eat a lot of unhealthy food.* □ *He has an unhealthy interest in violent crimes.*

unheard-of /ʌnˈhɜːd ɒv/ *adjective*
Something that is **unheard-of** is surprising or shocking because it has never happened before: *Divorce was almost unheard-of in 19th-century England.* [*same as* **unprecedented**]

unheeded /ʌnˈhiːdɪd/ *adjective*
Something such as a warning goes **unheeded** if it is ignored: *Her cries for help went unheeded.*

unhurried /ʌnˈhʌrɪd/ *adjective*
You do something in an **unhurried** way if you do it without hurrying or rushing: *He spoke in a calm, unhurried voice.*

unicorn /ˈjuːnɪkɔːn/ *noun*: **unicorns**
In fairy tales, a **unicorn** is an animal like a horse with a long straight horn on its forehead.

unidentified /ʌnaɪˈdɛntɪfaɪd/ *adjective*
A person or thing is **unidentified** if no-one knows who or what they are: *The police are trying to trace a so-far unidentified caller who rang Mrs Phipps at about nine o'clock.*

unidentified flying object /ʌnaɪˈdɛntɪfaɪd flaɪɪŋ ɒbdʒɪkt/ *noun*: **unidentified flying objects**
An **unidentified flying object** is any flying vehicle that can't be identified or isn't recognized, and that some people think comes from another planet.

unification /juːnɪfɪˈkeɪʃən/ *noun* (*uncount*)
The **unification** of a state or country is the act or process of unifying it: *the re-unification of Germany.*

uniform /ˈjuːnɪfɔːm/ *noun*; *adjective*
▻ ***noun*: uniforms**
A **uniform** is a special set of clothing worn by members of a particular organization or profession, or by the pupils at a particular school: *school uniform* □ *The policeman wasn't in uniform.*
▻ ***adjective***
Things that are **uniform** are all the same, or do not change or vary: *She ruled lines of uniform length.* □ *The room must be kept at a uniform temperature.* [*same as* **regular**]

uniformed /ˈjuːnɪfɔːmd/ *adjective*
A **uniformed** person is someone wearing a uniform: *He was accompanied by two uniformed policemen.*

uniformity /juːnɪˈfɔːmɪtɪ/ *noun* (*uncount*)
Uniformity is the state in which every person or thing is exactly the same, or behaves in exactly the same way: *the uniformity of modern architecture.*

unify /ˈjuːnɪfaɪ/ *verb*: **unifies, unifying, unified**
To **unify** people or things is to bring them together into a single united or harmonious group: *He is desperately doing what he can to unify the party and humour the dissidents before next week's conference.* — *adjective* **unified:** *The party has managed to present a unified face on most issues during the conference.*

unilateral /juːnɪˈlatərəl/ *adjective*
A **unilateral** decision is one taken by only one of the people or groups involved: *Britain must act in conjunction with its European neighbours, and shouldn't take unilateral action.* [compare **bilateral**, **multilateral**] — *adverb* **unilaterally:** *Canada has acted unilaterally in banning fishing in this part of the Atlantic.*

unimaginable /ʌnɪˈmadʒɪnəbəl/ *adjective*
Something is **unimaginable** if it is impossible to imagine or understand what it is like, *eg* because you have no experience of it: *the unimaginable horror of waking up in the middle of an operation.*

unimaginative /ʌnɪˈmadʒɪnətɪv/ *adjective*
An **unimaginative** person does not use their imagination, and has no new or original ideas: *unimaginative and outdated teaching methods.*

unimpeachable /ʌnɪmˈpiːtʃəbəl/ *adjective*
A person or thing that is **unimpeachable** cannot be criticized: *her unimpeachable good taste.*

uninhabitable /ʌnɪnˈhabɪtəbəl/ *adjective*
A place is **uninhabitable** if the conditions there are so poor it is impossible for people to live in it: *Pollution is making parts of the planet uninhabitable.* [*opposite* **habitable**]

uninhabited /ʌnɪnˈhabɪtɪd/ *adjective*
An **uninhabited** place is a place where no-one lives: *an uninhabited desert island.*

uninhibited /ʌnɪnˈhɪbɪtɪd/ *adjective*
You are **uninhibited** if you behave in an open and relaxed way that shows you are not embarrassed: *There was a lot of very uninhibited dancing at the party.*

uninspired /ʌnɪnˈspaɪəd/ *adjective*
A performance that is **uninspired** is dull: *his uninspired reading of the poem.*

uninspiring /ʌnɪnˈspaɪərɪŋ/ *adjective*
Something that is **uninspiring** fails to make you feel excited, enthusiastic or interested: *Despite being one of London's most expensive restaurants, the food was pretty uninspiring.* [*same as* **disappointing**]

unintelligible /ʌnɪn'telɪdʒəbəl/ *adjective*
Something that is said or written is **unintelligible** if it is impossible to understand. [*opposite* **intelligible**]

unintentional /ʌnɪn'tenʃənəl/ *adjective*
Something is **unintentional** if it is not done on purpose: *I'm sorry I upset you; it was unintentional.* [*same as* **accidental**; *opposite* **deliberate**] — *adverb* **unintentionally:** *I offended her unintentionally.*

uninterested /ʌn'ɪntrɪstɪd/ *adjective*
You are **uninterested** in something if you are not interested in it: *I was uninterested in the programme and turned it off.* [compare **disinterested**]

uninvited /ʌnɪn'vaɪtɪd/ *adjective*
Someone who is **uninvited** is someone you have not invited to go with you or to take part in something: *uninvited guests* □ *He came along uninvited.*

union /'juːnjən/ *noun*: **unions**
1 A **union** is an organization of people or groups that share a common purpose, desire or need, especially a **trade union**, a workers' organization that tries to improve pay and working conditions: *She is leader of one of the big teaching unions.* □ *union members* □ *the university students' union.* **2** (*uncount*) The **union** of two or more people or groups is the act of bringing them together to form a single, united whole: *the union of left and right in the political party.*

unique /juː'niːk/ *adjective*
1 Something that is **unique** is the only one of its kind: *Christians are not unique in believing that there is life after death.* **2** Something that is **unique** to a person or thing belongs to, or concerns, them alone: *These orchids are unique to the desert.* **3** (*informal*) **Unique** can also mean unusual, outstanding, or special in some way: *His singing is unique.*

unisex /'juːnɪseks/ *adjective*
Something that is **unisex** is suitable for both men and women: *a unisex hairstyle.*

unison /'juːnɪsən/ *noun* (*uncount*)
▻ ***phrase*** People act **in unison** when they all act in the same way at the same time: *The children find it difficult to play their instruments in unison.*

unit /'juːnɪt/ *noun*: **units**
A **unit** is **1** a single item or part that is the smallest item or part in a larger whole: *The history course is divided into six units, covering six different periods.* **2** a group of people who live or work together: *the family unit* □ *Doctors, nurses and social workers co-operate as a unit to provide care in the community* **3** a part of a machine that performs a particular function: *the computer's visual display unit.* □ *the school's language unit.* **4** a hospital department: *She's a doctor in the burns unit.* **5** a fixed or standard measurement of *eg* time or length: *A gram is a unit of weight.*

unite /juː'naɪt/ *verb*: **unites, uniting, united**
People or things **unite** or **are united** when they join together and behave as a group: *It is our duty to unite and oppose the plans.* □ *Their troubles had the effect of uniting them even more strongly.*

united /juː'naɪtɪd/ *adjective*
1 People are **united** about something if they agree about it: *They are united in their opposition to the proposals.* **2** A country is **united** when the different areas, counties or provinces have been joined together to form a single country: *Shall we see a united Ireland one day?*

United Kingdom /juːnaɪtɪd 'kɪŋdəm/ *noun* (*uncount*)
The **United Kingdom** is the official name of the kingdom consisting of England, Scotland, Wales and Northern Ireland.

United Nations /juːnaɪtɪd 'neɪʃənz/ *noun* (*uncount*)
The **United Nations** is an organization consisting of representatives from most countries of the world, that works to promote international peace and co-operation.

unity /'juːnɪtɪ/ *noun* (*uncount*)
There is **unity** between people when they agree to act together: *the goal of European political and financial unity.*

universal /juːnɪ'vɜːsəl/ *adjective*
1 Something that is **universal** relates to or affects the whole world or all the people in it: *the universal desire to have children* □ *the universal threat of pollution.* **2** **Universal** also means widespread or general: *This book will be of universal interest.* — *adverb* **universally:** *The discovery is being universally acclaimed as a major breakthrough.*

universe /'juːnɪvɜːs/ *noun* (*usually in the singular*)
The **universe** is everything that exists everywhere, on earth and in space: *The universe is thought to be expanding.* □ *Scientists keep trying to pinpoint the moment when the universe was created.*

university /juːnɪ'vɜːsɪtɪ/ *noun*: **universities**
A **university** is a place of education where students go to study when they finish school, and where they study for degrees: *She is hoping to go to university when she leaves school.* □ *a university student* □ *Glasgow University.*

unjust /ʌn'dʒʌst/ *adjective*
A decision, law or system that is **unjust** does not treat people fairly: *Black members of the community think the proposals are unjust.*

unjustified /ʌn'dʒʌstɪfaɪd/ *adjective*
An action or belief is **unjustified** if there is no good reason for it: *He felt the punishment was unjustified.* [*opposite* **justified, justifiable**]

unkempt /ʌŋ'kempt/ *adjective*
Something such as hair is **unkempt** when it isn't tidy, especially when it hasn't been combed. [*same as* **untidy, scruffy**]

unkind /ʌŋ'kaɪnd/ *adjective*: **unkinder, unkindest**
Someone is **unkind** if they are unpleasant, unsympathetic, and rather cruel: *How could you be so unkind to her?* □ *It was unkind of you to speak to her so rudely.* — *noun* (*uncount*) **unkindness:** *I found her unkindness very upsetting.*

unknown /ʌn'noʊn/ *adjective*; *adverb*; *noun*
▻ ***adjective***
Someone or something is **unknown** if people do not know them or do not know who or what they are: *The number of people infected with the virus is unknown.* □ *the tomb of the unknown soldier.* [*same as* **unfamiliar**]
▻ ***adverb***
Someone does something **unknown** to you, if they do it without telling you about it: *Unknown to me, she'd already resigned her job.*
▻ ***noun*** (*used in the singular*)
The **unknown** is anything that people do not know about or are not familiar with: *fear of the unknown.*

unlawful /ʌn'lɔːfʊl/ *adjective*
An activity is **unlawful** when it is illegal.

unleaded petrol /ʌnledɪd 'petrəl/ *noun* (*uncount*)
Unleaded petrol is petrol with very little lead in it: *Most hired cars take unleaded petrol.*

unless /ʌn'lɛs/ *conjunction*
Unless means 'except if' or 'if not' and introduces the only circumstances in which the statement you are making is not true, or the only circumstances in which the thing you are talking about will not happen: *No student should be penalized for misspellings, unless* [= except when] *the word is so badly spelt as to be unrecognizable.* □ *Unless* [= except where] *otherwise stated, the price includes delivery.* □ *Unless* [= except in the unlikely event that] *there's a downpour overnight, the race will go ahead.* □ *Don't try this yourself unless* [= except if] *you are expert with a computer.* □ *Unless food reaches* [= if food does not reach] *the drought-stricken areas soon, many more will die.* □ *They threatened to kill me unless I backed out* [= if I did not back out] *of the deal.* □ *Unless you talk* [= if you do not talk] *to people regularly, you can't claim to know what they're thinking.* □ *Unless you're connected with the show, could you please leave?* [= all those not connected with it should leave] □ *Can you be ready to start in about ten minutes? Unless you've changed your mind about coming?* [= as long as you haven't changed your mind] □ *'Would you like a drink?' 'Not unless* [= only if] *you're having one yourself.'*

unlike /ʌn'laɪk/ *preposition*
1 One person or thing is **unlike** another if they are different from them: *He's unlike his brother in that he's much more enthusiastic about his school work.* □ *She's quite unlike her mother to look at.* □ *Unlike her sister, she got married very young.* **2** An action or behaviour is **unlike** someone when you do not expect that person to act or behave in that way: *It was unlike her to get so upset.*

unlikely /ʌn'laɪklɪ/ *adjective*
1 Something that is **unlikely** to be so is probably not so: *We'll do the usual tests, but it's unlikely that the lump is malignant.* □ *She's unlikely to have wandered very far.* [*opposite* **likely**] **2** Something that is **unlikely**, or **unlikely** to happen, probably will not happen: *In these democratic times a military coup seems unlikely.* □ *It's unlikely that we'll get a grant towards the repairs.* □ *In these circumstances clients are unlikely to complain.* □ *It's a mystery that's unlikely ever to be solved.* □ *There are unlikely to be any developments before tomorrow.* □ *In the unlikely event of sabotage, there would be copies of everything.* [*opposite* **likely**] **3** You can use **unlikely** to describe surprising or unexpected things that actually occur: *Theirs was as unlikely a marriage as you could find.* □ *Nino Cerruti may seem an unlikely fashion king.* [*same as* **improbable**] **4** You describe something such as an explanation as **unlikely** if you don't think it can be right: *This interpretation is unlikely, for three reasons.* [*opposite* **likely**]

unlimited /ʌn'lɪmɪtɪd/ *adjective*
Something is **unlimited** if you can have as much of it as you want or can use: *This ticket allows unlimited travel on all train services for two months.* □ *The country does not have an unlimited amount of money to spend on health care.* [*opposite* **limited, restricted**]

unload /ʌn'loʊd/ *verb*: **unloads, unloading, unloaded**
1 You **unload** *eg* cargo or goods from a vehicle when you remove them: *He helped me unload the shopping from the car.* □ *ships unloading at the docks.* **2** You **unload** a gun when you take the bullets out of it; you **unload** a camera when you take the film out of it. **3** (*informal*) You **unload** something unpleasant, or something you do not want, on to someone else when you get rid of it by giving it to them: *She unloads all the difficult jobs on to me.*

unlock /ʌn'lɒk/ *verb*: **unlocks, unlocking, unlocked**
You **unlock** *eg* a door or window when you undo the lock on it: *She unlocked her suitcase and took her pyjamas out.* □ *an unlocked door.*

unlucky /ʌn'lʌkɪ/ *adjective*: **unluckier, unluckiest**
1 Something is **unlucky** if it brings or causes bad luck: *Some people believe 13 is an unlucky number.* **2** An **unlucky** person has bad luck: *It was unlucky that you failed.*
[*opposite* **lucky**]

unmade /ʌn'meɪd/ *adjective*
An **unmade** bed has not had its blankets and sheets arranged neatly after being slept in.

unmanageable /ʌn'manɪdʒəbəl/ *adjective*
An **unmanageable** person or thing is difficult to use or control: *Her son has become completely unmanageable since he was arrested for theft.*

unmanned /ʌn'mand/ *adjective*
Unmanned spacecraft are controlled automatically, *eg* by computer, and do not have pilots.

unmarried /ʌn'marɪd/ *adjective*
An **unmarried** person is not married: *an unmarried mother.*

unmentionable /ʌn'mɛnʃənəbəl/ *adjective*
Something is **unmentionable** if it is not talked about because it is embarrassing or indecent: *Sex is an unmentionable subject in some societies.*

unmistakable or **unmistakeable** /ʌnmɪ'steɪkəbəl/ *adjective*
A person or thing is **unmistakable** if they are easily recognized and won't be mistaken for anyone or anything else: *the unmistakable voice of Maria Callas.*

unmitigated /ʌn'mɪtɪgeɪtɪd/ *adjective* (*formal*)
Unmitigated is used for emphasis in referring to something bad, and has the meaning 'total' or 'utter': *The performance was an unmitigated disaster.*

unmoved /ʌn'mu:vd/ *adjective*
Someone is **unmoved** by something if they are not affected by it emotionally: *He appeared unmoved as the judge read out the sentence.*

unnatural /ʌn'natʃərəl/ *adjective*
1 Something is **unnatural** if it is different to the way things usually happen in nature: *The colour of the flowers in the painting looks completely natural.* **2** A person's behaviour is **unnatural** if it does not seem to be honest or sincere: *Her laughter seemed unnatural and contrived.* [*opposite* **affected, insincere**] — *adverb* **unnaturally:** *an unnaturally high temperature.*

unnecessary /ʌn'nɛsəsərɪ/ *adjective*
Something is **unnecessary** if it is not necessary, or is more than is needed or wanted: *We must try to avoid all unnecessary expense for the next few months.* — *adverb* **unnecessarily:** *I think you're worrying unnecessarily.*

unnerve /ʌn'nɜ:v/ *verb*: **unnerves, unnerving, unnerved**
Something **unnerves** you if it makes you feel less confident and slightly worried or afraid: *His silence unnerved me.* — *adjective* **unnerving:** *I found the whole experience unnerving.* □ *an unnerving silence.*

unnoticed /ʌn'noʊtɪst/ *adjective*
Someone or something is **unnoticed** if they are not seen by anyone: *He managed to slip into the room unnoticed.*

unobtrusive /ʌnəb'tru:sɪv/ *adjective*
Something is **unobtrusive** if it is not noticeable: *He tried to be as unobtrusive as possible.* [*opposite* **prominent**] — *adverb* **unobtrusively:** *She slipped unobtrusively into the room.*

unoccupied /ʌn'ɒkjʊpaɪd/ *adjective*
A building is **unoccupied** if no-one is living or working in it: *The house has been unoccupied for years.*

unofficial /ʌnə'fɪʃəl/ *adjective*
Something is **unofficial** if it has not yet received official approval: *Unofficial estimates suggest unemployment is still rising.* — *adverb* **unofficially:** *Unofficially, I can tell you that you've passed your exams.*

unorthodox /ʌn'ɔːθədɒks/ *adjective*
Unorthodox behaviour, ideas or beliefs are not generally accepted or used: *her unorthodox ways of treating arthritis.*

unpack /ʌn'pak/ *verb*: **unpacks, unpacking, unpacked**
You **unpack** *eg* a suitcase when you take things out of it: *Do you mind if I unpack first?*

unpaid /ʌn'peɪd/ *adjective*
1 A person is **unpaid** if they are not paid for the work they do. **2** A job is **unpaid** if the people doing it are not paid: *unpaid overtime.* **3 Unpaid** bills have not yet been settled: *Among the pile of unanswered letters were several unpaid bills.*

unparalleled /ʌn'parəlɛld/ *adjective*
Something is **unparalleled** when there is no other example that is as good as it is: *The play was an unparalleled success.*

unpleasant /ʌn'plɛzənt/ *adjective*
1 Something is **unpleasant** when you do not like it: *an extremely unpleasant smell* □ *an unpleasant surprise.* **2** An **unpleasant** person is rude: *an unpleasant, bad-tempered person.* [*same as* **disagreeable**] — *adverb* **unpleasantly:** *He sneered unpleasantly.*

unpopular /ʌn'pɒpjʊlə(r)/ *adjective*
An **unpopular** person or thing is generally disliked: *the government's unpopular decision to increase tax.*

unprecedented /ʌn'prɛsɪdɛntɪd/ *adjective*
Something is **unprecedented** if it has never happened before: *Her refusal to curtsey to the Queen is unprecedented.* [*same as* **unheard-of**]

unpredictable /ʌnprɪ'dɪktəbəl/ *adjective*
A person or thing is **unpredictable** if you never know how they are going to act or behave: *The weather can be pretty unpredictable.*

unprofessional /ʌnprə'fɛʃənəl/ *adjective*
Behaviour is **unprofessional** if it does not follow the rules that govern a particular profession, or is not of the standard expected in that profession: *He was accused of unprofessional conduct and forbidden from working as a doctor again.*

unprofitable /ʌn'prɒfɪtəbəl/ *adjective*
Business is **unprofitable** if it does not make any money: *Farming has often been unprofitable.*

unprovoked /ʌnprə'voʊkt/ *adjective*
You are the victim of an **unprovoked** attack if someone attacks you without having a reason for attacking you.

unqualified /ʌn'kwɒlɪfaɪd/ *adjective*
1 You are **unqualified** if you do not have any formal qualifications, especially if you don't have the qualifications needed for a particular job: *I'm unqualified to advise you, I'm afraid.* □ *Concern was expressed about the increasing number of unqualified people offering medical treatment.* **2 Unqualified** means absolute or complete, or not limited in any way: *The performance was an unqualified success.*

unquestionable /ʌn'kwɛstʃənəbəl/ *adjective*
Something is **unquestionable** if it is clearly true or clearly exists: *Her ability is unquestionable, but I'm not so sure about her experience.* — *adverb* **unquestionably:** *She is an unquestionably fine actress.*

unquestioning /ʌn'kwɛstʃənɪŋ/ *adjective*
You are **unquestioning** if you do not argue or protest about something; your beliefs are **unquestioning** if you do not consider them fully: *her unquestioning trust in him* □ *an unquestioning belief in God.*

unravel /ʌn'ravəl/ *verb*: **unravels, unravelling** (*AmE* **unraveling**), **unravelled** (*AmE* **unraveled**)
1 You **unravel** something *eg* knitted or knotted when you loosen and undo the stitches or knots so that you are left with lengths of wool or thread. **2** Something *eg* knitted or knotted **unravels** if it becomes loose and undone: *The jumper started to unravel at the end of the sleeves.* **3** You **unravel** *eg* a complicated puzzle or mystery if you solve or explain it.

unreal /ʌn'rɪəl/ *adjective*
An experience is **unreal** if it is so strange it seems not to be real or really happening: *The whole event seemed unreal, somehow.* [*opposite* **real**]

unrealistic /ʌnrɪə'lɪstɪk/ *adjective*
Someone is **unrealistic**, or has **unrealistic** ideas, when they hope or believe that things are possible when they are not: *She was hoping to be able to give up work when she reached 50 but this proved to be unrealistic.*

unrelenting /ʌnrɪ'lɛntɪŋ/ *adjective*
1 Someone's behaviour is **unrelenting** if they refuse to change their opinions or behaviour: *her unrelenting opposition to divorce.* **2** Something is **unrelenting** when it goes on and on without stopping or without losing power or strength: *The rain was unrelenting.*

unreliable /ʌnrɪ'laɪəbəl/ *adjective*
People or machines are **unreliable** if they cannot be trusted or relied on: *He's totally unreliable.* □ *an unreliable old car.* [*opposite* **reliable**]

unremitting /ʌnrɪ'mɪtɪŋ/ *adjective*
Something is **unremitting** if it continues without stopping: *an unremitting flow of questions.* [*same as* **constant**]

unrepentant /ʌnrɪ'pɛntənt/ *adjective*
You are **unrepentant** if you are not ashamed of your beliefs or behaviour.

unrest /ʌn'rɛst/ *noun* (*uncount*)
Unrest is a state of conflict or confusion resulting from dissatisfaction with or opposition to those in authority: *The proposed changes in the local taxation system led to a lot of public unrest.*

unrivalled (*AmE* **unrivaled**) /ʌn'raɪvəld/ *adjective*
Something is **unrivalled** if it is far better than anything else: *The museum contains an unrivalled collection of manuscripts.*

unroll /ʌn'roʊl/ *verb*: **unrolls, unrolling, unrolled**
You **unroll** something that has been rolled up when you open it out so that it is flat: *He unrolled the map and put it on the ground.*

unruly /ʌn'ruːlɪ/ *adjective*: **unrulier, unruliest**
1 Unruly people are difficult to control. **2 Unruly** hair is not easily kept in place and quickly becomes untidy.

unsafe /ʌn'seɪf/ *adjective*
Something is **unsafe** if it is dangerous: *The ruins are unsafe and are going to be demolished.*

unsatisfactory /ʌnsatɪs'faktərɪ/ *adjective*
Something is **unsatisfactory** if it is not good enough: *His work is unsatisfactory; he'll have to do it again.* [*opposite* **satisfactory**]

unsatisfied /ʌn'satɪsfaɪd/ *adjective*

You are **unsatisfied** with something if you are not happy with it: *She was unsatisfied with the reason he gave for being late.*

unsavoury (*AmE* **unsavory**) /ʌn'seɪvərɪ/ *adjective*
Something is **unsavoury** if it is unpleasant or unacceptable, especially if it is immoral: *Sam was rather an unsavoury character.* □ *an unsavoury part of town.*

unscathed /ʌn'skeɪðd/ *adjective*
You are **unscathed** if you escape an unpleasant or dangerous situation without being harmed or injured: *They escaped from the burning building unscathed.*

unscheduled /ʌn'ʃɛdju:ld/ or /ʌn'skɛdju:ld/ *adjective*
An **unscheduled** event is one that is not planned: *The train will make an extra, unscheduled stop at Birmingham.*

unscrew /ʌn'skru:/ *verb*: **unscrews, unscrewing, unscrewed**
You **unscrew** something if you remove its lid or top by twisting it; you **unscrew** something if you remove or loosen the screws in it: *She unscrewed the plug to change the fuse.*

unscrupulous /ʌn'skru:pjʊləs/ *adjective*
An **unscrupulous** person has no moral principles and is prepared to act dishonestly.

unseemly /ʌn'si:mlɪ/ *adjective* (*formal*)
Someone's behaviour is **unseemly** if it is not suitable, polite or decent: *an unseemly public argument over the money the Prime Minister earns.*

unseen /ʌn'si:n/ *adjective*
Something is **unseen** if it cannot be seen: *She slipped into the meeting unseen by the people already there.*

unselfish /ʌn'sɛlfɪʃ/ *adjective*
An **unselfish** person considers the feelings and needs of other people: *a caring and unselfish attitude towards the poor.* [*opposite* **selfish**; compare **generous**]

unsettle /ʌn'sɛtəl/ *verb*: **unsettles, unsettling, unsettled**
Something **unsettles** you if it makes you less calm, and more nervous or uncertain: *There are fears that a rise in the price of oil will unsettle the market.*

unsettled /ʌn'sɛtəld/ *adjective*
1 A situation is **unsettled** if it is likely to change: *unsettled weather.* **2** You are **unsettled** if you cannot relax, and are excited or worried about something.

unsettling /ʌn'sɛtəlɪŋ/ *adjective*
Something is **unsettling** if it makes you anxious and upset: *It's very unsettling to not know what is happening.*

unshakable or **unshakeable** /ʌn'ʃeɪkəbəl/ *adjective*
Your beliefs are **unshakable** if they cannot be changed: *her unshakable faith in her father.* [*same as* **firm**]

unsightly /ʌn'saɪtlɪ/ *adjective*: **unsightlier, unsightliest**
Something is **unsightly** if it is not pleasant to look at: *an unsightly pile of rubbish on the pavement.* [*same as* **ugly**]

unskilled /ʌn'skɪld/ *adjective*
Unskilled workers do not have any special skills or training; **unskilled** work does not require workers with any special skill or training. [compare **semi-skilled, skilled**]

unsociable /ʌn'soʊʃəbəl/ *adjective*
An **unsociable** person dislikes or avoids the company of other people. [*opposite* **sociable**; compare **antisocial**]

unsocial /ʌn'soʊʃəl/ *adjective*
Unsocial hours of work occur outside the normal working day: *Junior doctors often have to work unsocial hours at night and at the weekend.*

unsolicited /ʌnsə'lɪsɪtɪd/ *adjective*
Something is **unsolicited** if it is given to you or happens without being asked for: *unsolicited advice.*

unsolved /ʌn'sɒlvd/ *adjective*
A mystery remains **unsolved** if no-one has been able to solve it: *an unsolved murder.*

unsophisticated /ʌnsə'fɪstɪkeɪtɪd/ *adjective*
1 An **unsophisticated** person does not have wide experience of the world, especially of culture and the arts: *an unsophisticated schoolboy.* **2** An **unsophisticated** system or machine is simple: *an unsophisticated adding machine.*

unsound /ʌn'saʊnd/ *adjective*
1 A conclusion, argument or method is **unsound** if the ideas behind it are wrong and it is therefore not reliable: *He claims the evidence in the case is unsound.* **2** A building is **unsound** if it is likely to collapse.

unspeakable /ʌn'spi:kəbəl/ *adjective*
Something is **unspeakable** if it is too bad or unpleasant to be spoken about: *an unspeakable crime.*

unspoiled /ʌn'spɔɪld/ or **unspoilt** /ʌn'spɔɪlt/ *adjective*
A place or thing is **unspoiled** if it has not been spoiled or damaged in any way: *the unspoiled beauty of the countryside around Rome.*

unspoken /ʌn'spoʊkən/ *adjective*
Your thoughts or feelings are **unspoken** if you do not tell them to other people: *an unspoken desire for reconciliation.*

unstable /ʌn'steɪbəl/ *adjective*
1 When an object or situation is **unstable** it is likely to move, fall over or change suddenly because it is not firmly fixed or established. **2** An **unstable** person has a tendency to become emotionally or mentally disturbed.

unsteady /ʌn'stɛdɪ/ *adjective*: **unsteadier, unsteadiest**
1 You are **unsteady** when you cannot walk with firmness and might fall over; your hands are **unsteady** when they shake as you do something: *She's still unsteady on her feet after her bout of pneumonia.* **2** A pile of things is **unsteady** when it is likely to collapse. — *adverb* **unsteadily:** *He got unsteadily to his feet.*

unstuck /ʌn'stʌk/ *adjective*
▻ ***phrases*** **a** Something **comes unstuck** if it comes away from the thing it was attached to: *Some of the photos in my album have come unstuck.* **b** A plan **comes unstuck** if it goes wrong; people **come unstuck** if they fail to achieve the result they are aiming for: *If you don't tell the truth on your application form, you're likely to come badly unstuck at your interview.*

unsuccessful /ʌnsək'sɛsfʊl/ *adjective*
A person or plan is **unsuccessful** if they are not successful: *She was unsuccessful in her attempt to climb K2.* □ *an unsuccessful business venture.* [*opposite* **successful**] — *adverb* **unsuccessfully:** *She tried, unsuccessfully, to pass her driving test.*

unsuitable /ʌn'su:təbəl/ *adjective*
Something is **unsuitable** for a particular purpose if it is not suitable for it: *This computer system is unsuitable for our purposes.*

unsuited /ʌn'su:tɪd/ *adjective*
1 A person or thing is **unsuited** to a particular task if they are not suitable for it: *He's unsuited for any type of physical work.* **2** Two people are **unsuited** if they are not likely to get on well: *They're so unsuited I never though they'd get married.*

unsung /ʌn'sʌŋ/ *adjective*
Unsung is used to describe people whose efforts or

achievements have not been noticed by people in general: *He's one of the unsung heroes of the trade union movement.*

unsure /ʌn'ʃʊə(r)/ *adjective*
1 You are **unsure** about something when you do not know definitely about it, or cannot decide about it: *Some parents are unsure about how to start toilet training.* □ *I was unsure about the correct postal address.* □ *When people are unsure of a spelling they usually spell the word as it sounds.* □ *He was unsure how to handle the problem.* □ *He stopped, unsure how much to say.* □ *'Tree homes?' asked Fenella, unsure whether she'd heard correctly.* □ *If unsure, seek qualified advice.* □ *Anne bit her lip and looked unsure.* [*same as* **uncertain**, **doubtful**; *opposite* **sure**, **certain**] **2** You are **unsure** of yourself if you lack confidence: *She was still a little unsure of herself in American society.* □ *Like many men, deep down he was unsure of himself.* **3** You are **unsure** of someone or something when you do not know if you can rely on them: *He held on to the railings, unsure of his footing.* □ *I was unsure of their support.* **4** Something that is **unsure** is **a** not definitely known, or not decided: *The date of the vase is unsure, probably mid sixth century.* **b** not confidently and smoothly carried out: *The baby's movements are conscious, but unsure and imprecise.*

unsuspecting /ʌnsə'spɛktɪŋ/ *adjective*
An **unsuspecting** person is not aware of something that is about to happen to them, or is not aware of danger: *if the attacker approaches his unsuspecting victim from behind.*

unsympathetic /ʌnsɪmpə'θɛtɪk/ *adjective*
A person is **unsympathetic** if they are unfriendly and are not prepared to help: *an unsympathetic reply to her appeal for help.* [*opposite* **sympathetic**]

untangle /ʌn'taŋgəl/ *verb*: **untangles**, **untangling**, **untangled**
You **untangle** something with knots in it when you undo them: *He spent hours trying to untangle the string.*

untenable /ʌn'tɛnəbəl/ *adjective*
1 An argument or theory that is **untenable** cannot be supported or defended against criticism. **2** Your position, *eg* in a political situation, is **untenable** when opposition towards you reaches such a level that you are forced to abandon it.

unthinkable /ʌn'θɪŋkəbəl/ *adjective*
Something is **unthinkable** if it is too unpleasant to think about: *I couldn't bear to imagine what life would be like without him; it was unthinkable.*

unthinking /ʌn'θɪŋkɪŋ/ *adjective*
An **unthinking** person does not think carefully enough before acting about the probable effects of their action or behaviour, and therefore behaves insensitively or foolishly: *the unthinking attitude of the media towards private suffering.*

untidy /ʌn'taɪdɪ/ *adjective*: **untidier**, **untidiest**
1 Something is **untidy** when the things in it are not arranged neatly: *I don't mind the house being untidy as long as it is reasonably clean.* **2** An **untidy** person does not keep their things tidy or arranged neatly or in order: *He's the untidiest and most disorganized person I have ever met.*

untie /ʌn'taɪ/ *verb*: **unties**, **untying**, **untied**
You **untie** something when you undo the knots or bows in it; you **untie** *eg* a parcel when you undo the string around it by undoing the knots in it: *She untied the laces and took her shoes off.*

until /ʌn'tɪl/ *preposition or conjunction*
1 Something that happens **until** a certain time, or **until** a certain thing happens, goes on happening up to that point, and then stops: *The Peel programme is on the air from 11 pm until 2 am.* □ *I was here until after ten last night.* □ *Roxburgh Castle was held by the English from 1346 until 1460.* □ *From then until 1882 he worked with Armstrong's son.* □ *His interest in chemistry continued until the end of his life.* □ *The arrangement worked fine until a year ago.* □ *Follow this track until you see a wall ahead of you.* □ *He carried on working until Debbie brought him a cup of tea.* □ *Whisk two egg whites until firm, and fold into the mixture.* [*same as* **till**] **2** (*often with a negative*) Something that does not happen **until** a certain time, or **until** a certain thing happens, happens at that time or point, but not before; you wait **until** a certain time for something to happen if it does not happen before then: *Baker was not promoted until 15 June 1858.* □ *Why wait until after a general election to propose the reforms?* □ *It took the Venetians until 1420 to win control over the whole territory.* □ *The ceremony had to be postponed until 2 September, because of a typhoon.* □ *It wasn't until after she had spoken that she realized how violently she had reacted.* □ *The casualty should not be moved until medical help arrives.* [*same as* **till**]

unto /'ʌntuː/ *preposition* (*old or literary*)
Unto means 'to': *Unto us a child is born; unto us a son is given.* □ *The secret things belong unto the Lord.*

untold /ʌn'toʊld/ *adjective*
You can use **untold** to say that something unpleasant is very severe: *The storm caused untold damage to the crops.*

untouched /ʌn'tʌtʃəd/ *adjective*
1 Something that is **untouched** has not been touched, moved, changed or harmed in any way: *These manuscripts have lain untouched in the library for years.* **2** A meal is **untouched** if it has not been eaten: *He sent the sandwiches back untouched.*

untoward /ʌntə'wɔːd/ *adjective*
An **untoward** event is one that is not expected, that happens at an inconvenient time, and that causes problems: *Nothing untoward happened during the flight.* [*same as* **troublesome**, **unexpected**]

untrained /ʌn'treɪnəd/ *adjective*
An **untrained** person does not have the skills or knowledge required for a particular job or task: *The hospital doesn't let untrained nurses give injections.* [*opposite* **trained**]

untried /ʌn'traɪd/ *adjective*
A system or plan is **untried** when it hasn't been used or tested yet; an **untried** person or animal has been trained but hasn't been tested yet: *Some of the horses lined up for the race are untried over such a long distance.* □ *The new company, largely composed of untried journalists, was bound to make a few mistakes.*

untroubled /ʌn'trʌbləd/ *adjective*
You are **untroubled** by something when you do not worry about it or are not affected by it: *Few people are untroubled by the presence of armed police on the streets.* [*same as* **unconcerned**; *opposite* **anxious**, **troubled**]

untrue /ʌn'truː/ *adjective*
1 Something is **untrue** when it is not true. [*same as* **false**] **2** Someone is **untrue** to you if they are unfaithful to you: *He was untrue to his wife.* [*opposite* **faithful**]

untrustworthy /ʌn'trʌstwɜːðɪ/ *adjective*
Someone is **untrustworthy** if you cannot rely on them and you cannot trust them: *She has proved herself untrustworthy in the past.* [*opposite* **trustworthy**, **reliable**]

untruth /ʌn'truːθ/ *noun (formal)*: **untruths** /ʌn'truːðz/
An **untruth** is a lie.

untruthful /ʌn'truːθfʊl/ *adjective*
A person is **untruthful** if they lie and are dishonest: *She was being untruthful when she told you she didn't love you.* [*same as* **deceitful**; *opposite* **honest**]

untutored /ʌn'tjuːtəd/ *adjective*
An **untutored** person has no knowledge of a particular subject: *To my untutored eye that vase looks modern, whereas an expert will tell you it was made in the 18th century.* [*same as* **untrained**; *opposite* **trained**, **expert**]

unused *adjective*
1 /ʌn'juːsəd/ You are **unused** to something if you are not familiar with it, *eg* because you haven't done it very much: *He was unused to having to cook his own meals.* [*same as* **unaccustomed**; *opposite* **used**, **accustomed**] **2** /ʌn'juːzəd/ Something that is **unused** has never been used.

unusual /ʌn'juːʒʊəl/ *adjective*
Something is **unusual** if it does not happen very much, or if you don't see it or do it very much: *It's unusual for him to be late.* □ *It's unusual to see daffodils out this early.* [*same as* **rare**, **uncommon**; *opposite* **usual**]

unusually /ʌn'juːʒʊəlɪ/ *adverb*
1 You can use **unusually** to describe something that is *eg* greater or larger than usual: *He was unusually polite.* [= He isn't usually as polite as this] □ *It was unusually cold for the time of year.* □ *an unusually large cat.* **2** (*sentence adverb*) **Unusually** is used to indicate that what you describing is not typical: *Unusually for him, he actually managed to arrive early.*

unveil /ʌn'veɪl/ *verb*: **unveils**, **unveiling**, **unveiled**
1 You **unveil** *eg* a new painting or statue when you remove the cloth covering it, usually as part of a formal opening ceremony: *The Prime Minister agreed to unveil the new portrait of himself.* **2** You **unveil** *eg* your plans or ideas when you tell people about them for the first time: *The government has yet to unveil its plans for education reform.*

unwanted /ʌu'wɒntəd/ *adjective*
Something is **unwanted** when no-one wants it: *an unwanted gift.*

unwarranted /ʌn'wɒrəntəd/ *adjective (formal)*
Something is **unwarranted** when it isn't justified, deserved or reasonable: *She felt the newspaper article was an unwarranted attack on her position.*

unwelcome /ʌn'wɛlkəm/ *adjective*
Something is **unwelcome** when you don't want it; a guest or visitor is **unwelcome** when you do not want them to come: *an unwelcome experience* □ *He's unwelcome here.* [*opposite* **welcome**]

unwell /ʌn'wɛl/ *adjective*
You are **unwell** if you are ill: *He's been feeling unwell for a while now.* [*opposite* **well**]

unwieldy /ʌn'wiːldɪ/ *adjective*
1 An **unwieldy** object is large and awkward to carry, move or manage: *Prams are often too unwieldy to be taken on buses and trains.* **2** An **unwieldy** system is too big or badly organized to be efficient: *Many people find the country's legal system unwieldy and expensive.* [*same as* **cumbersome**]

unwilling /ʌn'wɪlɪŋ/ *adjective*
You are **unwilling** to do something if you are not happy about doing it: *She was unwilling to discuss her problems with her doctor.* [*same as* **reluctant**; *opposite* **willing**] — *adverb* **unwillingly:** *She unwillingly agreed to go and see her doctor.* — *noun (uncount)* **unwillingness:** *his typical unwillingness to help.*

unwind /ʌn'waɪnd/ *verb*: **unwinds**, **unwinding**, **unwound**
1 (*informal*) You **unwind** when you relax: *I always try to unwind at the weekends.* □ *What better way to unwind at the end of a busy day than by treating yourself to a long hot bath?* [*same as* **wind down**] **2** You **unwind** something when you make it straight; something **unwinds** when it becomes straight: *The ball of string was beginning to unwind.* [*same as* **unravel**]

unwise /ʌn'waɪz/ *adjective*
Something that is **unwise** is not sensible: *It would be unwise of you to lend him money without first asking if he's got a job.* [*same as* **ill-advised**, **foolish**; *opposite* **prudent**] — *adverb* **unwisely:** *He agreed, rather unwisely in my opinion, to let them use his flat for a party.*

unwitting /ʌn'wɪtɪŋ/ *adjective*
People or their actions are **unwitting** if they do not realize what they are doing, or are not aware of what is really happening: *the unwitting victims who had been conned out of their savings.* [*same as* **unsuspecting**] — *adverb* **unwittingly:** *You have unwittingly caused a lot of trouble.*

unwonted /ʌn'wɒntəd/ *adjective (formal)*
Something is **unwonted** if it not usual or habitual: *He put an arm round her in an unwonted show of affection.* [*same as:* **unaccustomed**, **unusual**; *opposite* **frequent**]

unworthy /ʌn'wɜːðɪ/ *adjective*
Someone is **unworthy** of something if they do not deserve it: *I'm unworthy of the honour bestowed on me.* [*same as* **undeserving**; *opposite* **worthy**, **deserving**]

unwound /ʌn'waʊnd/ *verb*
Unwound is the past tense and past participle of **unwind**.

unwrap /ʌn'rap/ *verb*: **unwraps**, **unwrapping**, **unwrapped**
You **unwrap** something if you take off the paper that is covering it: *She unwrapped the parcel.* [*opposite* **wrap**]

unwritten /ʌn'rɪtən/ *adjective*
1 Things that are **unwritten** have not been written, or have not been recorded in writing: *It's a good thing that most of the books people intend to write remain unwritten.* □ *an unwritten agreement.* **2** An **unwritten** rule or law is one that does not formally exist but which people traditionally accept and follow: *Are there any unwritten rules that I ought to know about?*

unzip /ʌn'zɪp/ *verb*: **unzips**, **unzipping**, **unzipped**
You **unzip** *eg* a piece of clothing when you unfasten or open it by undoing a zip: *He unzipped his anorak and took it off.* [*opposite* **zip up**]

up /ʌp/ *preposition*; *adverb*; *adjective or adverb*; *verb*

▻ ***preposition***

1 Up something means towards, or at, a high, or higher, level or position on it, or to the top of it: *The porter carried our luggage up the steps.* □ *She was already halfway up the hill.* □ *He was pointing up the slope.* □ *The cat got stuck up a tree.* **2 Up** something such as a road means towards a position, or in a position, further along it; **up** a river means along it in the direction of its source: *They were off, weaving at speed up the road.* □ *There's a hardware shop further up the street on your left.* □ *Shipping came up the Danube as far as Ulm.*

▻ ***adverb***

1 a To move **up** is to move to a higher level or position; to be **up** somewhere is to be at a high level or position: *The dog jumped up on to her lap.* □ *He put his feet up on the couch.* □ *He picked up the three sheets of paper.* □ *She pulled up the hood of her waterproof.* □ *Next thing you know, women's hemlines have gone up by about three feet.* □ *The doctor looked up from his* *notebook.* ▫ *The church was rebuilt from the foundations up.* ▫ *He's up in the bedroom.* ▫ *We had to spend the night up on the mountain.* ▫ *We stood and looked back from 200 feet up.* **b** You sit **up** when you get into a sitting position after lying down or leaning back; you stand **up** when you get into a standing position after lying down or sitting; you hang or stand objects **up** somewhere when you position them vertically, or above the ground: *He got up from his knees.* ▫ *I picked myself up off the floor.* ▫ *Stephen jumped up.* ▫ *She sat up straight.* ▫ *He hung his coat up in the wardrobe.* ▫ *We framed the picture and stuck it up on the wall.* **c** To come **up** to a person or place is to approach them and stop in front of them: *People come up to you in the street and ask for your autograph.* ▫ *A car drew up at one of the houses opposite.*

2 People also use **up** to mean **a** further on, *eg* along a road: *The hotel is five miles further up, past the castle grounds.* **b** further north: *The Newcastle travel-to-work area extends up into Northumberland.* **c** towards the senior levels of an organization: *Everyone counts in this place, from the bottom up.*

3 Up is used in certain expressions with the meaning 'at an end' or 'finished': *Your time's up.* ▫ *The game's up!*

4 Up is used with various verbs to indicate **a** total consumption or removal: *Someone's used up the last of the milk.* ▫ *Drink up your coffee.* ▫ *We'd better clear up this mess.* **b** secure fastening or closing: *They've sealed up the cave.* ▫ *He'd been gagged and tied up.* **c** separation or dispersal: *The party didn't break up till 2 am.* ▫ *She tore the letter up into little bits.* **d** violent treatment or destruction: *I was the girl who used to beat up the boys.* ▫ *The pub was blown up by a terrorist bomb.* **e** increase in level, *eg* of heat or sound: *Heat up the oven first.* ▫ *Could you turn the television up a bit?* **f** squeezing together or compression: *There's room for another person if we all move up.*

▻ ***adjective or adverb***

1 You are **up** when you are not in bed: *He's not up yet.* ▫ *I usually got up at six.* ▫ *He'd been up most of the night attending to a sick child.* ▫ *They sat up late talking.* **2** A figure or amount is **up** when it has increased: *Profits are up by 10%.* ▫ *The pound moved up against the dollar.* **3** A team is a certain number of points **up** when they are winning by that amount; you are a certain sum **up** after some transaction if you have profited by that amount: *Rangers were two goals up after the first half.* ▫ *I found myself £5 up after the first race.*

▻ ***verb*** (*informal*): **ups, upping, upped**

1 You **up** an amount if you raise or increase it: *We upped the price to £40 000.* **2** You **up** and do something if you do it unexpectedly: *Suddenly he upped and left his wife.*

▻ ***phrases*** **1 a** You say that something **is up** when there is something wrong: *What's up? You look upset.* ▫ *Something's up with this machine.* **b It is all up** with someone when they are facing something such as death or complete ruin. **2** (*informal*) Something that is **on the up and up** is improving all the time, or becoming increasingly successful: *Business is on the up and up this year.* **3 a** One thing is **up against** another when it is touching it, pressing on it, or very close to it: *She was watching the fish with her nose up against the tank.* **b** You are **up against** a difficulty or challenge, or **up against it**, when you have a difficulty or challenge to face: *We're up against serious competition in our field.* **4** You are **up and about** when you are out of bed and able to get on with your tasks: *Most women are up and about a few days after having their babies.* **5** To be **up for** *eg* sale, review or election is to be available for it, due for it, or due to be considered for it: *Do you want to put the baby up for adoption?* ▫ *He'll come up for parole in six months' time.* **6** For **up front** see **front**. **7 a** Something extends **up to** a certain point if it extends as far as that: *She drew the blankets up to her chin.* **b** Something lasts **up to** or **up till** a certain time if it extends or lasts until that point or time: *Up to* (or *up till*) *now, I've always resigned myself to rented accommodation.* **c** You are **up to** a task, or **up to** doing something, if you are able to do it, or are well enough to do it: *Is he up to the job?* ▫ *I'm not quite up to returning to work yet.* **d** (*informal*) What you are **up to** is what you are busy with: *What have you been up to recently?* **e** (*informal*) You say that someone is **up to** something, or **up to** no good, if you think they are doing something secret or dishonest. **f** (*informal*) Something that is not **up to** much is not very interesting: *We didn't think the town centre was up to much.* **g** Something that is **up to** you is a matter that you have to decide or deal with yourself: *'Shall I tell her now or later?' 'That's up to you.'* ▫ *It isn't up to me to organize the schedule.* **8** For **up to date** see **date**[1]. **9** You are **up with** a subject when you know the latest news or facts about it. **10** Something is the right **way up** if it is in the right position, with the top at the top: *He was holding his book the wrong way up.* ▫ *Which way up does this picture go?* **11** For **well up in** or **on** see **well**.

up-and-coming /ʌpənd'kʌmɪŋ/ *adjective*
An **up-and-coming** person is beginning to become successful or well known: *an up-and-coming young actress.*

upbeat /ʌp'biːt/ *adjective* (*informal*)
You are **upbeat** about something if your cheerful or hopeful about it: *I feel very upbeat about my job.* [*same as* **optimistic**; *opposite* **gloomy**]

upbringing /'ʌpbrɪŋɪŋ/ *noun* (*uncount*)
Your **upbringing** is the general instruction and education you received as a child, and that forms your character and values: *her upbringing in a religious household.*

update /ʌp'deɪt/ *verb*: **updates, updating, updated**
You **update** something if you add new information or new features to it to make sure it remains accurate and modern: *The software will need to be updated regularly.* [*same as* **revise**]

up-end /ʌp'ɛnd/ *verb*: **up-ends, up-ending, up-ended**
You **up-end** something if you turn it upside down: *He up-ended the box and all the toys fell out.*

upfront /ʌp'frʌnt/ *adjective* (*informal*)
You are **upfront** about something if you are honest or open about it: *She was quite upfront about why she'd decided not to give me the job.* [*same as* **candid**; *opposite* **secretive**]

upgrade /ʌp'greɪd/ *verb*: **upgrades, upgrading, upgraded**
1 You **upgrade** a person when you promote them; you **upgrade** their job when you make it more important: *Her job has been upgraded from 'assistant manager' to 'manager'.* **2** You **upgrade** a machine or piece of equipment when you improve its quality or replace it with a better model: *This car will need upgrading in a couple of years.*
[*opposite* **downgrade**]

upheaval /ʌp'hiːvəl/ *noun* (*count or uncount*): **upheavals**
Something is an **upheaval** if it is a change that causes a lot of disturbance or trouble: *Moving offices will be quite an upheaval.* ▫ *a period of social upheaval after the war.* [*same as* **shake-up**]

upheld /ʌp'hɛld/ *verb*
Upheld is the past tense and past participle of **uphold**.

uphill /ʌp'hɪl/ *adjective or adverb*
You go **uphill** when you move up a slope: *He ran uphill.*
▻ *phrase* You can describe something as **an uphill struggle** or **an uphill task** if it requires a lot of work or effort: *It was an uphill struggle getting the children ready for school in the morning.*

uphold /ʌp'hoʊld/ *verb*: **upholds, upholding, upheld**
You **uphold** *eg* a law or principle when you support it or maintain it; you **uphold** a decision when you state that it is correct: *Police officers are expected to uphold the law.* □ *His conviction was upheld when he appealed against it.* [*same as* **defend, stand by**]

upholstered /ʌp'hoʊlstəd/ *adjective*
Upholstered furniture has springs and a cover that make it comfortable to sit on: *an upholstered sofa.*

upholstery /ʌp'hoʊlstərɪ/ *noun* (*uncount*)
Upholstery is the springs and covers for a chair or sofa.

upkeep /'ʌpkiːp/ *noun* (*uncount*)
The **upkeep** of something such as a building is the task of keeping it in good condition, or the cost of keeping it in good condition: *Local residents have been asked to pay for the upkeep of the public gardens.* [*same as* **maintenance**]

upland /'ʌpland/ *noun*: **uplands**
The **uplands** are the high or hilly areas of *eg* a country. [*opposite* **lowlands**]

uplifted /ʌp'lɪftəd/ *adjective* (*formal*)
Uplifted faces or arms are pointing upwards: *He fixed his dark eyes on her uplifted face.* □ *A sea of uplifted faces swam before her.* [*same as* **raised**]

uplifting /ʌp'lɪftɪŋ/ *adjective*
An experience is **uplifting** if it makes you feel happier or more hopeful: *an uplifting speech from the Prime Minister.* [*same as* **inspiring, elevating**]

upmarket /ʌp'mɑːkɪt/ *adjective*
Upmarket goods and places are expensive and are bought or visited by people with sophisticated tastes: *an upmarket skiing resort.* [*same as* **exclusive**]

upon /ə'pɒn/ *preposition*
1 Upon has a similar range of uses to those of *on*, but is more formal and literary; it may be used to give clarity or emphasis: *a city built upon a hill* □ *He rose upon his elbows.* □ *A copy of the Radio Times lay open upon the table.* □ *All eyes were upon her.* □ *She wiped her hands upon her apron.* □ *There was no concern upon her face, only curiosity.* □ *It was the first time the operation had been performed upon a young child.* **2** Many verbs, adjectives and nouns that are followed by *on* can also use **upon**: *May I call upon the secretary to read the minutes?* □ *people dependent upon state assistance* □ *our reliance upon electronic equipment.* **3** One thing happens **upon** another happening if it happens immediately after, or as a result of, the other: *Please register at reception upon arrival.* □ *Women's careers usually ended upon marriage.* □ *The certificates will be issued upon payment of a fee.* **4** An object or event is **upon** you when it is approaching very close: *The Land Rover was almost upon her before she heard its engine.* □ *Winter is upon us again.* **5** You use the construction, *eg* 'mile **upon** mile of something' to emphasize the extent of something: *We drove through mile upon mile of tea plantations.* □ *The main area comprises row upon row of microcomputers.*

upper /'ʌpə(r)/ *adjective*; *noun*
▻ ***adjective***
The **upper** part of something is the part of it that is above the rest, or the top part of it: *the upper part of her arm* □ *the upper floors of the building* [*same as* **higher**; *opposite* **lower**]
▻ ***noun***: **uppers**
A shoe's **upper** is the top part of it above the sole.
▻ *phrase* You have **the upper hand** in a situation when you have more power than anyone else and are in control.

upper class /ʌpə'klɑːs/ *noun*: **upper classes**
The **upper classes** are the people who belong to the highest social class above the middle class: *The upper classes usually send their children to private schools.* □ *upper-class attitudes.* [compare **middle class, working class**]

uppermost /'ʌpəmoʊst/ *adjective or adverb*
Something is **uppermost** when **1** it is in the highest position: *the uppermost floors of the building* □ *She stacked the containers with their lids uppermost.* **2** it is the most important: *Concerns for his safety were uppermost in my mind.*

upright /'ʌpraɪt/ *adjective*; *adverb*
▻ ***adjective***
1 You are **upright** when your back is straight: *The bicycle was upright against the wall.* **2 Upright** also refers to machines or equipment that are vertical, or taller than they are wide: *an upright freezer* □ *an upright piano* □ *an upright vacuum cleaner.* **3** People are **upright** when they have behave in an honest, responsible and moral way. [*opposite* **dishonest**]
▻ ***adverb***: *She sat upright.* □ *He stood the bicycle upright against the wall.*

uprising /'ʌpraɪzɪŋ/ *noun*: **uprisings**
An **uprising** is a rebellion. [*same as* **revolt**]

uproar /'ʌprɔː(r)/ *noun* (*uncount or used in the singular*)
There is **uproar** when a lot of people make a lot of noise, or people complain loudly or angrily about something: *There was uproar when the government announced it was putting taxes up.*

uproarious /ʌp'rɔːrɪəs/ *adjective*
Something is **uproarious** if it is very funny and makes you laugh: *an uproarious film.* [*same as* **amusing**] — *adverb* **uproariously:** *an uproariously funny play.*

uproot /ʌp'ruːt/ *verb*: **uproots, uprooting, uprooted**
1 You **uproot** a plant when you pull it and its roots out of the ground. **2** You **uproot** someone if you take them away from the surroundings they are used to: *During the Revolution, whole families were uprooted and sent to work on distant farms, or in factories or mines.*

ups and downs /ʌpzən'daʊnz/ *noun* (*plural*)
Something goes through a series of **ups and downs** when it goes through alternating periods of success and failure: *Their relationship went through several ups and downs before they finally decided to get married.*

upset *adjective*; *verb*; *noun*
▻ ***adjective***
1 /ʌp'sɛt/ You are **upset** when you are unhappy or distressed: *She was upset when her father died.* □ *He was upset by the argument with his wife.* **2** Your stomach is **upset** if you feel sick *eg* because of something you have eaten or an infection: *an upset stomach.*

> Notice that the pronunciation of the adjective where it precedes the noun is /'ʌpsɛt/.

▻ ***verb*** /ʌp'sɛt/: **upsets, upsetting, upset**
1 A person or thing **upsets** you if they make you feel unhappy or distressed: *Something's upsetting her.* □ *I didn't mean to upset him.* **2** You **upset** *eg* plans or a system if you ruin or spoil it: *You must try not to upset the baby's routine.* **3** Something you eat or an

infection **upsets** you if it makes you feel sick. **4** (*formal*) You **upset** something if you accidentally knock it over: *She upset the bowl and the soup ran all over the floor.* — *adjective* **upsetting:** *This is a very upsetting film.* □ *She found the whole affair most upsetting.*

▻ ***noun*** /ˈʌpsɛt/: **upsets**

You have a stomach **upset** if something you have eaten or an infection has made you feel sick.

upshot /ˈʌpʃɒt/ *noun* (*in the singular*)

The **upshot** of *eg* a discussion is the final outcome or result: *The upshot of it all was that the plans were abandoned.*

upside down /ʌpsaɪdˈdaʊn/ *adjective or adverb*

1 Something is **upside down** if the part that is usually at the top is at the bottom: *He was holding the book upside down.* □ *She turned the cup upside down and examined the base.* □ *Haven't you got the lampshade upside down?* [*same as* **inverted, upturned**] **2** A place is turned **upside down** when it is reduced to a state of confusion or disorder: *I turned my bedroom upside down looking for my purse, but I couldn't find it anywhere.*

upstage /ʌpˈsteɪdʒ/ *verb*: **upstages, upstaging, upstaged**

One person or thing **upstages** another when they attract more attention: *The President's speech today was upstaged by student demonstrations in the streets outside.*

upstairs /ʌpˈstɛəz/ *adverb*; *adjective*; *noun*

▻ ***adverb***

You go **upstairs** if you go to an upper floor; something is **upstairs** if it is on an upper floor: *She ran upstairs to her bedroom.* □ *His study is upstairs.* [*opposite* **downstairs**]

▻ ***adjective***: *an upstairs bathroom* □ *an upstairs window.*

▻ ***noun*** (*singular*)

The **upstairs** of a building is an upper floor, especially the part of a house above the ground floor: *They've shut off the upstairs and live in the downstairs rooms only.*

upstanding /ʌpˈstandɪŋ/ *adjective* (*formal*)

A person is **upstanding** if they are honest: *He's a fine, upstanding member of the community.* [*same as* **trustworthy**]

upstart /ˈʌpstɑːt/ *noun*

An **upstart** is an arrogant, usually young, person who has quickly acquired power or wealth: *I refuse to allow some young upstart to come in here and start telling me what to do!*

upstream /ʌpˈstriːm/ *adverb*

Something moves **upstream** if it moves towards the source of a river or stream and against the current: *She found it hard to row upstream.* [*opposite* **downstream**]

upsurge /ʌpˈsɜːdʒ/ *noun* (*used in the singular*)

There is an **upsurge** in something when there is a sudden sharp rise or increased amount of it: *The upsurge in violence was attributed to the introduction of the government's new Criminal Justice Bill.*

uptake /ˈʌpteɪk/

▻ ***phrases*** (*informal*) Someone who is **quick on the uptake** is quick to understand or realize something; they are **slow on the uptake** if they are slow to understand or realize it: *He isn't very quick on the uptake but he works well once he's sure what to do.*

uptight /ˈʌptaɪt/ *adjective* (*informal*)

Someone is **uptight** if they are **1** nervous or worried about something: *He always gets uptight about exams.* [*same as* **anxious, tense**; *opposite* **calm, relaxed**] **2** angry about something: *She always gets uptight when I ask her about it.* [*same as* **irritated**]

up-to-date /ʌptəˈdeɪt/ *adjective*

1 Something is **up-to-date** if it is brand-new: *up-to-date computing equipment.* **2** You are **up-to-date** about something when you have all the latest information about it: *Doctors have to keep themselves up-to-date with developments in medicine.*

▻ ***phrase*** You **bring** *eg* equipment **up-to-date** when you replace your existing equipment with more modern equipment: *It'll cost the company thousands of pounds to bring its computing systems up-to-date.*

upturn /ˈʌptɜːn/ *noun*: **upturns**

There is an **upturn** in *eg* economic activity if there is an increase in it. [*same as* **upsurge, recovery**]

upward /ˈʌpwəd/ *adverb*; *adjective*

▻ ***adverb*** (also **upwards**)

1 To move or look **upward** or **upwards** is to move or look towards a higher position or level: *The 'up' arrow moves the cursor upwards.* □ *The road climbed upwards.* □ *The policeman glanced upwards.* □ *She eased the lid upward and off.* □ *Her lips turned upwards at the corners.* □ *Children are trained in computer use from the lowest classes upwards.* [*opposite* **downward, downwards**] **2** Someone or something faces **upward** or **upwards** when they face the sky or ceiling, as distinct from the floor or ground: *He held his hands out, palms upward.* □ *He turned the body face upwards.* [*opposite* **downward, downwards**] **3** A movement **upward** or **upwards** in *eg* prices or salaries is an increase: *Prices are forced upwards.* □ *The upward-spiralling cost of health care.* [*opposite* **downward, downwards**]

▻ ***adjective:*** *a steady upward climb* □ *She followed his upward gaze.* □ *the steep upward price curve.* [*opposite* **downward**]

▻ ***phrase***

1 Children **from** the age of five **upwards**, or aged five **and upwards**, are five-year-old children and older children. **2** An amount **upwards of** a certain number is greater than that number: *We had upwards of 200 replies.*

uranium /jʊˈreɪnɪəm/ *noun* (*uncount*)

Uranium is a heavy silver-white radioactive metal used as a nuclear fuel.

urban /ˈɜːbən/ *adjective*

Urban means of, relating to, or situated in a town or city: *a modern, urban lifestyle.* [*opposite* **rural**]

urbanize or **urbanise** /ˈɜːbənaɪz/ *verb*: **urbanizes, urbanizing, urbanized**

People **urbanize** a district if they make it more like a town or city.

urchin /ˈɜːtʃɪn/ *noun* (*old*): **urchins**

An **urchin** is a poor child who does not usually have a home or family.

urge /ɜːdʒ/ *verb*; *noun*

▻ ***verb***: **urges, urging, urged**

1 You **urge** someone to do something if you try to persuade them to do it, usually with some force: *I urge you to reconsider your position.* □ *I urged him to stay at school until he was 18.* **2** You **urge** a particular course of action when you strongly advise or recommend it: *The ministers had urged a referendum on the Maastricht treaty.*

▻ ***noun***: **urges**

You have an **urge** to do something if you have a strong impulse or desire to do it, but cannot explain it: *I have absolutely no urge to visit America.* □ *She's got the urge to visit Nepal.* [*same as* **desire, compulsion**]

urgent /ˈɜːdʒənt/ *adjective*
1 Something is **urgent** if you need to do something about it at once or as soon as possible: *He needs urgent medical attention.* □ *Is this work urgent?* □ *an urgent message.* **2** You speak in an **urgent** way when you are worried or anxious about something: *her urgent pleas for money to help starving children.* — *noun* (*uncount*) **urgency:** *affairs of great urgency* □ *a sense of urgency in her voice.* — *adverb* **urgently:** *These medical supplies are needed urgently.* □ *We urgently need more help.*

urinal /jʊˈraɪnəl/ *noun*: **urinals**
A **urinal** is any receptacle, usually fitted to a wall, that men and boys can urinate into.

urinate /ˈjʊərɪneɪt/ *verb*: **urinates, urinating, urinated**
To **urinate** means to pass urine from the body.

urine /ˈjʊərɪn/ *noun* (*uncount*)
Urine is the pale yellowish liquid that is produced by the kidneys and discharged from the body via the bladder.

urn /ɜːn/ *noun*: **urns**
1 An **urn** is a vase with a lid and two handles, used to contain a dead person's ashes. **2** An **urn** is a large metal cylinder used for making large amounts of tea or coffee: *a coffee urn.*

us /ʌs/ *pronoun* (*used as the object of a verb or preposition, and in other positions*)
You use **us 1** to refer to yourself and one or more other people, sometimes including the person you are addressing: *The success of the day surprised us both.* □ *Her death has deeply upset us all.* □ *Ahead of us a headland loomed.* □ *Why didn't we wait? That was silly of us.* □ *It was left to us three to decide on a date.* □ *The big girls bullied us little girls.* □ *I'll make us a cup of tea.* □ *That date gives us a clue.* □ *It would take us an hour to get there.* □ *Let us briefly consider some aspects of spelling.* □ *Far too hospitable, that's us.* □ *She's got more important people than us to consider.* □ *They're better armed than us* (or, formally, *than we are*). □ *When you're as old as us* (or, formally, *as we are*) *you'll think differently.* □ *Do you think they saw us waving?* □ *I hope you don't mind us* (or *our*) *borrowing it.* **2** to refer to people in general, yourself included: *The environment is the responsibility of all of us.* **3** (*informal*) to refer to yourself: *Give us a kiss.* [compare **we**]

usable /ˈjuːzəbəl/ *adjective*
Something is **usable** if it can be used in some way or for some purpose: *Some of this software will be usable in other ways.*

usage /ˈjuːzɪdʒ/ *noun*: **usages**
1 (*uncount*) **Usage** is the act of using something or the way it is used: *There is usually a surge in energy usage around 9pm.* **2** (*uncount*) **Usage** is also the way words are used: *a book on English usage.* **3** A **usage** is a particular way a word or expression is used: *a typical French Canadian usage of a French word.*

use[1] *verb*; *noun*
▻ ***verb*** /juːz/: **uses, using, used**
1 You **use** something when you do something with it, for some purpose, or as the means of carrying out some task: *Could I use your telephone?* □ *I've got a spare anorak you can use.* □ *A baby elephant has to discover how to use its trunk.* □ *Why don't they use their brains?* □ *It seemed undesirable to use force against the Yugoslavs.* □ *Cut round the edge using a pair of sharp scissors.* □ *Routine office tasks can be efficiently handled using a microcomputer.* □ *From early times, amber was widely used in jewellery.* □ *There are definite skills to be used in interviewing.* □ *I use a small plastic bucket to keep the worms in.* □ *She let them use her garden as a short cut to the common.* □ *English is used as the medium of instruction.* □ *If you were allowed extra time, what would you use it for?* □ *Drivers going to and from the docks are being advised not to use Newhaven Road.* [see also **used**[3]] **2** You **use** a particular word or phrase when you say it or write it: *I suggest you shouldn't use words you don't understand.* □ *We use the word 'family' in so many different ways.* □ *There is no crisis of identity, to use a psychological term.* **3** A room or building **is being used** when people are occupying it: *I never use that room; it's kept locked.* **4** You **use** something when you consume it and reduce its quantity: *Who's been using my shampoo?* **5** You **use** particular products if you obtain and consume them in your daily life: *Don't you use a moisturizer?* □ *What kind of soap do you normally use?* □ *Have you ever used drugs?* **6** A machine or apparatus **uses** a certain type of fuel if that is what it requires to work: *I think you'll find that most hired cars use unleaded petrol.* [*same as* **run on**] **7** You **use** something such as your skills or qualifications when you do work that requires them: *You can't really use a history degree unless you're going to be a historian or a teacher.* [*same as* **apply**] **8** You **use** people when you selfishly get them to do things for you, or take advantage of their willingness or their abilities in order to benefit yourself: *I'm using you like a nursemaid.* □ *She used people for her own ends.* [compare **exploit**] **9** (*informal*) If you say you could **use** *eg* a drink you mean you need one: *I could probably use a walk anyway.* □ *I can always use five grand.* [*same as* **could do with**]
▻ ***noun*** /juːs/: **uses**
1 The **use** of something is **a** (*uncount*) the act, process or activity of using it: *I'm not against the use of antibiotics.* □ *the increasing use of computers in research* □ *the efficient use of resources within an organization* □ *materials specifically designed for use in the training of teachers* □ *Is the car available for use during the daytime?* **b** (*uncount or count*) the purpose you use it for; something has a **use** if it can be used for a purpose: *Where the acquisition of premises involves a change of use, planning permission is required.* □ *Dogs once had their uses in agriculture.* □ *Cotton wool is an essential in babycare; its uses include cleaning parts of the body and applying talcum powder.* □ *Can you find a use for this bag of tools?* **c** (*uncount*) the extent to which it is used: *Cocaine use has overtaken heroin use.* **2** (*uncount*) You get a lot of **use** out of something when it meets your needs satisfactorily and you use it a lot: *We've had plenty of use out of this car.* **3** (*uncount*) You have the **use** of *eg* your legs or arms if they function properly: *He lost the use of both his legs in an accident.* **4** (*uncount or count*) The **use** of a word is the act of using it; a **use** of a word is a particular meaning that it has: *the indiscriminate and ill-informed use of the term 'fundamentalism'* □ *This modern use of the word 'ideology' can be traced back to Marx.*
▻ ***phrases*** **1** You **have no use for** something if you don't need it: *These creatures live their lives in darkness, so they have no use for eyes.* **2** Something comes **into use** when people begin to use it; it is **in use** when it is being used; something goes **out of use** when people stop using it: *When the light shows, the lift is in use.* □ *The old road was still in use until comparatively recently.* □ *words and expressions that have fallen out of use.* **3** You **make use of** something when you use it, or use it for a purpose: *Try to make use of different types of history books.* □ *What use can be made of this evidence?* □ *You're not making the best use of your talents.* **4 a** If you say it's **no use** doing something, or ask **what use** it is, you mean that it is not worth doing it,

because nothing will be achieved by it: *It's no use trying to escape.* □ *What's the use of worrying?* □ *Oh, what use is it to explain all that to you?* [compare **pointless**] **b** A person or thing that is **no use** cannot perform the task they're required to perform: *I want advice, and my parents are absolutely no use.* □ *'I need something with a sharp point.' 'Is this any use to you?'* □ *I'll never be any use with a keyboard.* [compare **useless**, **hopeless**] **5** Something that is **of use** is useful or helpful: *Doctors can only be of use where the patients want to be cured.* □ *This book will be of use both as an explanation of legal principles and as a reference for specific legal points.* **6** Something is **put to use** when it is used: *Everything was put to good use; nothing was wasted.* [*same as* **utilize**]

phrasal verb
use up You **use** something **up** **1** when you consume it bit by bit, and leave none: *We're rapidly using up the mineral resources of our planet.* □ *Has the milk all been used up?* **2** when you make sure that none of it is wasted or has to be thrown away: *Our leaflet provides lots of ideas for using up leftover scraps of Christmas food.*

use² /juːs/ see note at **used²**.

used¹ /juːst/ *adjective*
You are **used** to something if you have always or often experienced it or done it, and so are accustomed to it; you get, or become, **used** to something when you become accustomed to it, and it no longer surprises you: *I'm used to being on my own.* □ *They're not used to walking very long distances.* □ *To Katherine, a New-Yorker, used to apartment blocks, London houses were especially impressive.* □ *He wasn't used to women having jobs and being financially independent.* □ *Mrs Hardman had grown used to her independence.* □ *I'm still getting used to the new car.* □ *You soon get used to having a little baby in the family again.* □ *I'll never get used to how light it is here in the evenings.* [*same as* **accustomed** to, **familiar** with]

used² /juːst/ *modal verb* (*followed by* **to** *and an infinitive*)
Something that **used** to be so, or **used** to happen, was so, or happened regularly, in the past: *The manor house used to belong to Miss Pritchett.* □ *I'm not as strong as I used to be.* □ *My memory isn't what it used to be.* [= is not as good as it was] □ *There used to be a rubbish dump here.* □ *There used not to be all this pressure.* □ *Lesotho, or Basutoland, as it used to be called.* □ *I used to cycle to work.* □ *What good times we used to have.* □ *That's the sort of question Father used to ask me.* □ *Do you remember how he used to talk to himself all the time?* □ *'Do you get the 'Radio Times'? 'I used to, but I don't any more.'*

The negative form of *used to* is *used not to*, or more informally, *didn't use* /juːs/ *to*; questions are also frequently expressed with *did* and *use*: *There used not to be* (or *there didn't use to be*) *a roundabout here. Didn't she use to have* (or *used she not to have*) *long hair? Did you use to be* (or *used you to be*) *a friend of Alice's? What did we use to do?* (or *what used we to do?*)

used³ /juːzd/ *adjective*
1 A **used** car has already had at least one owner. [*opposite* **new**, **brand-new**] **2** A **used** glass, **used** handkerchief or **used** towel has been used by someone, and is therefore dirty and needs a wash: *The chambermaid had to collect the used towels and replace them with fresh ones.* [*opposite* **clean**, **fresh**]

useful /ˈjuːsfʊl/ *adjective*
1 Something is **useful** if you can use it in different ways or for a particular purpose: *I find this sort of tool really useful in the garden.* □ *useful information.* [*same as* **helpful**, **practical**; *opposite* **useless**] **2** A person is **useful** if they try to help other people: *She made herself useful tidying the kitchen.*
▻ ***phrase*** Something **comes in useful** if you can use it for a particular purpose or in a particular situation: *Your teaching experience will come in useful when you are working on dictionaries for foreign learners.*
— *adverb* **usefully:** *You could spend your time more usefully.* — *noun* (*uncount*) **usefulness:** *the usefulness of modern drugs that fight disease.*

useless /ˈjuːsləs/ *adjective*
1 Something is **useless** if you cannot use it for anything: *This computer is useless without a printer.* [*opposite* **useful**] **2** (*informal*) You are **useless** at something if you are bad at it: *He's absolutely useless at dancing.* [*same as* **hopeless**; *opposite* **good**]
▻ ***phrase*** You can say **it's useless** if doing something will not achieve the result you need: *It's useless asking her to help you when she's in such a bad mood.* □ *I tried to save his life but it was useless.* [*same as* **hopeless**]

user /ˈjuːzə(r)/ *noun*: **users**
A **user** is a person who uses a particular product or machine: *computer users* □ *the local public transport users committee.*

user-friendly /juːzəˈfrɛndlɪ/ *adjective*
A product or machine is **user-friendly** if it is designed to be easy or pleasant to use, or easy to follow or understand: *Computers are much more user-friendly nowadays.*

usher /ˈʌʃə(r)/ *noun*; *verb*
▻ ***noun***: **ushers**
An **usher** is a person who shows people to their seats, *eg* in a church or theatre.
▻ ***verb***: **ushers, ushering, ushered**
You **usher** someone *eg* in or out of a place when you politely show them the way: *He ushered me into his office.* [*same as* **escort**]

usherette /ʌʃəˈrɛt/ *noun*: **usherettes**
An **usherette** is a woman who shows people to their seats in a theatre or cinema, and who sells sweets, soft drinks and programmes.

usual /ˈjuːʒʊəl/ *adjective*; *noun*
▻ ***adjective***
Usual describes the things that most frequently happen, are done, or are the case: *There were the usual grumbles when I suggested a walk.* □ *The usual procedure is as follows.* □ *He completed his exams in four months, instead of the usual six.* □ *She answered with her usual honesty.* □ *You don't sound your usual happy self.* □ *It's quite usual to hold an inquest in these circumstances.* □ *As is usual on these occasions, the important guests left first.* □ *The food wasn't as good as usual.* □ *He was more subdued than usual.* □ *This is an ideal indoor plant, adapting well to the higher-than-usual temperatures.* □ *Does the awareness that an experiment is taking place make people behave differently from usual?* [*same as* **customary**]
▻ ***noun or pronoun*** (*used in the singular*)
1 You can refer to the things that happen, or are done, most frequently, as the **usual**: *Any special jobs this*

morning, or just the usual? **2** (*informal*) If you ask for your **usual** in a public bar, you want the drink that people know you choose most frequently: *'My usual, Vince, please,' she said.*
▻ ***phrase*** Something that happens **as usual** happens as it always, or regularly, or often, does: *I went to bed about midnight, as usual.* ◻ *The crisis was resolved, and everything went on as usual.* ◻ *As usual, the lift was out of order.*

usually /ˈjuːzʊəlɪ/ *adverb*
Something that **usually** happens or is so is the thing that most frequently happens, or is so in most cases: *He had a beard but no moustache, which is usually a bad sign.* ◻ *On Fridays there's usually a disco at the youth club.* ◻ *I don't usually cry in front of strangers.* ◻ *People usually don't know that girls' voices break too.* ◻ *The verb is usually in the passive.* ◻ *Jasper, usually so calm, was speechless with rage.* [*same as* **generally, normally**]
▻ ***phrase*** Something that is **more than usually** *eg* pleasant or nasty is even pleasanter or even nastier than it usually is, or is unusually pleasant or nasty: *Her appetite was more than usually healthy.*

usurp /jʊˈzɜːp/ *verb* (*formal*): **usurps, usurping, usurped**
You **usurp** something such as power or authority when you to take it by force and without having any right to it.

utensil /jʊˈtɛnsɪl/ *noun*: **utensils**
A **utensil** is any object used in the home, especially the kitchen: *knives, saucepans and other kitchen utensils.*

uterus /ˈjuːtərəs/ *noun* (*medicine*): **uteruses**
A woman's **uterus** is her womb.

utilitarian /jʊtɪlɪˈtɛərɪən/ *adjective*
Something is **utilitarian** when it is intended to be useful rather than beautiful: *the small, utilitarian staff bedrooms.* [*same as* **functional**]

utility /jʊˈtɪlɪtɪ/ *noun*: **utilities**
1 (*uncount*) The **utility** of something is how useful it is: *We still need to assess the utility of the equipment.* [*same as* **usefulness**] **2** A **utility** or a **public utility** is an important public service, such as water, gas and electricity.

utilize or **utilise** /ˈjuːtɪlaɪz/ *verb*: **utilizes, utilizing, utilized**
You **utilize** something when you use it, especially in some practical way: *Engineers are working on ways to utilize the power of the wind.* [*same as* **exploit, make use of**] — *noun* (*uncount*) **utilization** /juːtɪlaɪˈzeɪʃən/: *careful utilization of resources.*

utmost /ˈʌtmoʊst/ *adjective; noun*
▻ ***adjective***
You can use **utmost** to emphasize that something is the greatest possible of its kind: *I have the utmost respect for her judgement.* ◻ *It's of the utmost importance.*
▻ ***noun*** (*used in the singular*)
You do your **utmost** to achieve something when you try as hard as you can: *He tried his utmost to win.* ◻ *I promised to do my utmost to help him.*

utopian /jʊˈtoʊpɪən/ *adjective*
Utopian describes any social system or situation in which everyone is satisfied and as happy as possible: *utopian dreams of world peace.* [*same as* **idealistic**]

utter[1] /ˈʌtə(r)/ *verb*: **utters, uttering, uttered**
You **utter** something when you say it: *She had not uttered a word during the hour-long meeting.*

utter[2] /ˈʌtə(r)/ *adjective*
Utter is used for emphasis, and means complete, total or absolute: *To my utter amazement, he agreed to help out.* ◻ *What an utter fool I've been!* — *adverb* (*usually intensifying*) **utterly:** *That was an utterly stupid thing to say.* ◻ *I was utterly convinced he was lying.* ◻ *We spent an utterly delightful evening round at his house.*

utterance /ˈʌtərəns/ *noun* (*formal*): **utterances**
An **utterance** is something that you say: *The meaning of every utterance is dependent on context.* ◻ *The prime Minister's last utterance before the general election was 'We shall win.'* [*same as* **declaration, statement**]

U-turn /ˈjuːtɜːn/ *noun*: **U-turns**
1 A vehicle or its driver does a **U-turn** when the driver makes it turn round to face in the other direction. **2** Someone such as a government does a **U-turn** if they change their minds completely about something: *The government has been forced to do a U-turn on its plans for the health service.* [*same as* **reversal**]

V

V or **v** /viː/ *noun*: **Vs, v's**
V is the twenty-second letter of the English alphabet.

vac /vak/ *noun* (*BrE*; *informal*): **vacs**
A **vac** is a university vacation: *Where are you going in the summer vac?*

vacancy /ˈveɪkənsɪ/ *noun*: **vacancies**
1 A **vacancy** is a job that is not being done by anyone: *The company has a vacancy in the accounts department.* □ *The vacancy has now been filled.* [= Someone has been appointed to do the job] [*same as* **opening**] **2** A hotel or guesthouse has **vacancies** when it has rooms that are not being used: *There was a sign in the window saying 'No Vacancies'.*

vacant /ˈveɪkənt/ *adjective*
1 Something such as a seat or room is **vacant** when no-one is using it: *Is that seat vacant?* □ *None of the hotels had a vacant room.* □ *The toilet is vacant now.* [*same as* **empty, free, unoccupied**; *opposite* **occupied, engaged**] **2** A job is **vacant** when no-one is doing it and people can apply for it: *The newspaper publishes details of all the vacant positions in the town.* [*same as* **unfilled**] **3** Someone who has a **vacant** expression looks as if they are not noticing what is happening round them, or not understanding things that are being said to them: *He looked up from his book with a vacant expression.* [*same as* **blank**] — *adverb* **vacantly:** *She appeared to be staring vacantly into space.*

vacate /vəˈkeɪt/ *verb*: **vacates, vacating, vacated**
You **vacate** a place or position when you leave it or stop occupying it: *He was ordered to vacate the premises.* □ *Hotel guests must vacate their rooms by 10.00am.* □ *I applied for his job when he vacated it.* [*same as* **leave, quit**]

vacation /vəˈkeɪʃən/ *noun*: **vacations**
1 (*AmE*; *count or uncount*) A **vacation** is a holiday: *I always take my annual vacation in July.* □ *He's going on vacation in November.* **2** A **vacation** is a holiday between terms at a university, college, or court of law: *I had a lot of reading to do during the summer vacation.* □ *What are you going to do over the vacation?*

vaccinate /ˈvaksɪneɪt/ *verb*: **vaccinates, vaccinating, vaccinated**
A doctor or nurse **vaccinates** someone against a disease when he or she gives them a vaccine, usually in the form of an injection, that prevents them catching the disease: *She has been vaccinated against polio.* [compare **innoculate**]

vaccination /vaksɪˈneɪʃən/ *noun* (*count or uncount*): **vaccinations**
You have a **vaccination** when you are given a vaccine, usually in the form of an injection, that prevents you catching a particular disease: *a polio vaccination* □ *the country's programme of vaccination against measles.* [compare **innoculation**]

vaccine /ˈvaksiːn/ *noun* (*count or uncount*): **vaccines**
A **vaccine** is a substance containing bacteria or viruses given to people, usually by injection, to prevent them catching a particular disease: *develop a new vaccine against flu* □ *the polio vaccine* □ *a batch of measles vaccine.*

vacillate /ˈvasɪleɪt/ *verb* (*formal*): **vacillates, vacillating, vacillated**
Someone **vacillates** when they keep changing their opinions, feelings and decisions: *Governments have frequently vacillated uncertainly in the face of pressures and problems.* [*same as* **waver**]

vacuum /ˈvakjʊəm/ *noun*; *verb*
▻ ***noun***: **vacuums**
1 (*informal*) A **vacuum** is a vacuum cleaner: *I had the vacuum on, so I probably wouldn't have heard the telephone.* **2** A **vacuum** is a space that contains no air, gas or matter: *Scientists must do some experiments in a vacuum.* **3** A **vacuum** is also a feeling of emptiness or loss: *Her departure has left a vacuum in the company.* [*same as* **void**]
▻ ***verb*** (*informal*): **vacuums, vacuuming, vacuumed**
You **vacuum** something when you clean it with a vacuum cleaner: *I haven't vacuumed the living room yet.*

vacuum cleaner /ˈvakjʊəm kliːnə(r)/ *noun*: **vacuum cleaners**
A **vacuum cleaner** is an electrically powered machine that cleans by sucking up dust and dirt.

vacuum flask /ˈvakjʊəm flɑːsk/ *noun*: **vacuum flasks**
A **vacuum flask** is a container that keeps drinks hot or cold. [*same as* **Thermos flask**]

vacuum-packed /vakjʊəm ˈpakt/ *adjective*
Something that is **vacuum-packed** is packed in a container from which all the air has been removed: *These nuts are vacuum-packed for freshness.*

vagina /vəˈdʒaɪnə/ *noun*: **vaginas**
A woman's **vagina** is the passage connecting her external sex organs to her womb.

vagrant /ˈveɪgrənt/ *noun*: **vagrants**
A **vagrant** is a person who has no permanent home or job: *He had lived as a vagrant for many months before being taken in by a group of monks.* [compare **tramp, hobo**] — *noun* (*uncount*) **vagrancy:** *He was arrested for vagrancy.*

vague /veɪg/ *adjective*: **vaguer, vaguest**
1 Something that is **vague** is not clearly expressed or explained: *He only left vague instructions.* □ *The invitation was so vague as to be non-existent.* [*same as* **imprecise**; *opposite* **clear**] **2** You are **vague** if you do not express yourself clearly. **3** Something is **vague** if you cannot see it clearly: *She could see the vague outline of the castle through the fog.* [*same as* **indistinct, dim, hazy**] **4** Someone who is being **vague** is deliberately not giving you very much information about something: *She gets very vague when people ask about her parents.* □ *I've left that point deliberately vague in my report.* [*same as* **evasive, unspecific**] **5** You describe a person as **vague** when they look as if they do not understand what is being said to them or are not thinking clearly: *He looked up with a vague expression*

at the sound of his name. [*same as* **absent-minded, abstracted**] **6** You have a **vague** memory or recollection of something if you do not remember it very clearly: *I had a vague notion that I'd seen him somewhere before.* [*same as* **dim**] **7** A **vague** feeling of something is a slight feeling of it: *I had a vague sense of guilt about the whole incident.* [*same as* **slight, obscure**] — *adverb* **vaguely:** *I can only vaguely remember my grandparents.* □ *felt vaguely surprised to see him there.* □ *Miriam nodded vaguely, obviously not attending to what I'd just said.*

vain /veɪn/ *adjective*: **vainer, vainest**
1 (*derogatory*) A **vain** person pays too much attention to their appearance, or is too pleased with their looks or their abilities: *She's the vainest woman I've ever met.* □ *He was one of those habitually vain people who keep glancing at themselves in the mirror when they think no-one's looking.* [*same as* **conceited**; *opposite* **modest**] **2** A **vain** attempt has no useful or successful effect or result: *a vain plea for help.* [*same as* **futile**]
▻ ***phrases*** You do something **in vain** if you do it without getting the result you want: *I tried in vain to make her change her mind.* □ *It was important for the war effort to convince people that the young men dying in their thousands on the battlefield were patriotic heroes who had not died in vain.*

vale /veɪl/ *noun* (*literary*): **vales**
A **vale** is a valley.

valentine /ˈvaləntaɪn/ *noun*: **valentines**
1 A **valentine** is a greetings card that you send to someone, usually anonymously, as a token of love or affection on St Valentine's Day (14 February). **2** Your **valentine** is the person you send a valentine to.

valet /ˈvaleɪ/ (*BrE* /ˈvalɪt/) *noun*: **valets**
A man's **valet** is the male servant who looks after his clothes and helps him to dress.

valiant /ˈvalɪənt/ *adjective* (*formal*)
Someone who is **valiant** is brave or determined in a difficult situation: *Fellow-miners made a valiant effort to reach the trapped men.* □ *She will be remembered for her valiant one-woman stand against the power of the unions.* [*same as* **courageous, heroic**; *opposite* **cowardly**] — *adverb* **valiantly:** *She struggled valiantly to keep awake.*

valid /ˈvalɪd/ *adjective*
1 A **valid** reason, argument or proposition is based on the truth or on sound reasoning: *have a valid excuse for arriving late* □ *a valid complaint.* [*same as* **authentic, legitimate, justifiable**; *opposite* **invalid**] **2** A ticket or official document is **valid** when it is legally acceptable for use: *This passport is valid for ten years.* □ *This ticket is valid only for travel at the weekends.* □ *Your visa isn't valid any more.* □ *Your visa is no longer valid.* [*opposite* **invalid**] — *noun* (*uncount*) **validity** /vəˈlɪdətɪ/: *No-one is questioning the validity of your statement.*

validate /ˈvalɪdeɪt/ *verb*: **validates, validating, validated**
One thing **validates** another when it proves it to be correct or makes it legal: *His arrest for murder validates her claim that he is dangerous.* □ *The visa must be validated by the embassy before you can use it.* [*same as* **verify, authenticate**]

Valium /ˈvalɪəm/ (*trademark*) *noun* (*uncount*)
Valium is a drug that people take to make them feel less tense and nervous.

valley /ˈvalɪ/ *noun*: **valleys**
A **valley** is an area of low flat land between hills or mountains, often with a river running through: *the Thames valley.*

valour (*AmE* **valor**) /ˈvalə(r)/ *noun* (*uncount*)
Valour is courage or bravery, especially in battle. [*same as* **heroism**; *opposite* **cowardice**]

valuable /ˈvaljʊəbəl/ *adjective*
1 Something **valuable** is worth a lot of money: *a valuable diamond bracelet.* **2 Valuable** help or advice is very useful: *With her qualifications and experience she should make a truly valuable contribution to the team.* [*opposite* **valueless, worthless**; compare **invaluable**]

valuables /ˈvaljʊəbəlz/ *noun* (*plural*)
Your **valuables** are things that are valuable or important to you, especially things such as your jewellery, money and passport: *She keeps all her valuables in a safe.*

valuation /valjʊˈeɪʃən/ *noun*: **valuations**
A **valuation** is a judgement or assessment of how much money something is worth, especially one given by an expert: *The current valuation of the collection, made by a team of Spanish experts over the past six years, is considered to be well below the market value of the works.*

value /ˈvaljuː/ *noun*; *verb*
▻ ***noun*: values**
1 (*uncount or count*) The **value** of something such as property, or a work of art, is the amount of money it is worth: *The goods had a retail value of £12000* □ *the falling value of the dollar* □ *The value of the furnishings will be taken into account.* □ *the present range of property values* □ *Gold and silver jewellery can be expected to rise in value.* [compare **worth**] **2** (*usually uncount*) The degree to which something is important or useful is its **value**: *buildings of historical and architectural value* □ *The pen had been used by her grandmother, so had some sentimental value.* □ *He realized the value of education for his career.* □ *Such discussions have a limited value.* □ *These awards recognize the value of good coaching.* [compare **worth**] **3** (*usually in the plural*) Your **values** are the things in life that you consider important, or the principles and beliefs that influence your behaviour: *the gap between people's moral values and their actual day-to-day behaviour.* [*same as* **principles, standards**] **4** (*used after a noun*) Something has *eg* rarity **value**, or novelty **value**, if it is important or useful because it is rare or unusual: *He may have thought there was propaganda value in defending the Catholic Church.* □ *Entries for the competition will be judged purely on their entertainment value.* **5** (*mathematics*) The **value** of a symbol or letter is the quantity it represents: *Find the value of x in the equation 2x + y = 9.*
▻ ***verb*: values, valuing, valued**
1 An expert **values** something such as a house or work of art when he or she decides how much money it is worth: *An agent valued the cottage at £20000* □ *three million tonnes of agricultural products, valued at 33 million dollars.* **2** You **value** something if you consider it important: *People should value their health more.* □ *We value tolerance here and we respect one another's liberties.* □ *Two of the things women said they valued most in their jobs were the social contact, and the companionship of their workmates.* □ *I too value her friendship.* □ *We'd greatly value your advice.* [*same as* **appreciate, prize**] — *adjective* **valued:** *We are offering you, as one of our valued customers, special discounts this winter.*
▻ ***phrases*** **1 Value for money** is what you get when the things you buy are worth what you pay for them; something is **good value**, or **value for money**, if it is worth the money you pay for it: *The other restaurant offers much better value for money.* □ *Ask yourself if it's reasonable value for money.* □ *These electrical goods are all good value.* **2** Something is **of value** if it is

worth a certain amount of money, or if it is important or useful: *The letters are of no value to me, but may be of interest to historians.* □ *This material is likely to be of substantial value to the investigator.* □ *An inner-city nature reserve will be of immense value to the community.* **3** You **put a value on** something when you decide what it is worth; you **put** or **place a high value on** something if you think it is important or useful: *The Sioux Indians placed a high value on generosity.* □ *a society that places a high value on being clever and articulate* □ *It's hard to put a value on elaborate workmanship like this.* **4** You **take** what someone says **at face value** when you understand them to mean what they say, without wondering what else might be implied: *Are the Prime Minister's words about not increasing taxation to be accepted at face value?* □ *Taken at face value, the argument seems justified.*

value-added tax /valju:'adɪd taks/ *noun* (*uncount*)
Value-added tax or **VAT** is a tax added to the price of goods and services sold.

value judgement /'valju: dʒʌdʒmənt/ *noun*: **value judgements**
A **value judgement** is a judgement of how important, useful or valuable something is based on your own personal opinions and not on facts.

valuer /'valjʊə(r)/ *noun*: **valuers**
A **valuer** is a person whose job is to decide how much money things are worth.

valve /valv/ *noun*: **valves**
A **valve** is a device that opens and closes to control the one-way flow of liquid or gas in a pipe or tube: *the valve in a bicycle tyre* □ *a heart valve.* [see also **safety valve**]

vampire /'vampaɪə(r)/ *noun*: **vampires**
In horror stories, **vampires** are people who have died, but who leave their graves at night to suck the blood of living people, so as to keep themselves alive.

van /van/ *noun*: **vans**
A **van** is a vehicle that is larger than a car but smaller and lighter than a lorry, that is used for transporting goods or people. [see picture at **vehicle**]

vandal /'vandəl/ *noun*: **vandals**
A **vandal** is a person who deliberately damages or destroys things, especially public property: *these vandals who are allowed to roam free and cover every wall within reach with vulgar graffiti.*

vandalism /'vandəlɪzm/ *noun* (*uncount*)
Vandalism is the deliberate damaging of things, especially public property: *widespread vandalism in inner-city areas.*

vandalize or **vandalise** /'vandəlaɪz/ *verb*: **vandalizes, vandalizing, vandalized**
Property **is vandalized** if it is deliberately damaged or destroyed by someone: *The local station was vandalized over the weekend.*

vanguard /'vaŋgɑ:d/ or /'vangɑ:d/ *noun* (*singular*)
▻ ***phrase*** Someone is **in the vanguard of** *eg* a movement or research when they are playing an important and leading role in it: *The scientists' work is in the vanguard of cancer research.*

vanilla /və'nɪlə/ *noun* (*uncount, often adjectival*)
Vanilla is a flavouring that comes from a tropical plant, used in ice cream, chocolate, and other sweet foods: *'Which flavour would you like?' 'Vanilla, please.'* □ *vanilla ice cream.*

vanish /'vanɪʃ/ *verb*: **vanishes, vanishing, vanished**
Something **vanishes** when **1** it disappears suddenly: *She vanished into the mist.* □ *vanish without trace.* **2** it ceases to exist: *Dinosaurs vanished millions of years ago.* [*same as* **die out**]

vanity /'vanɪtɪ/ *noun* (*uncount*)
Vanity is the feeling you have when you are very proud of your appearance or abilities: *She refused to wear her glasses out of sheer vanity.* [*same as* **conceit**; *opposite* **modesty**]

vanquish /'vaŋkwɪʃ/ *verb* (*literary*): **vanguishes, vanguishing, vanguished**
You **vanguish** an enemy, or an undesirable feeling in yourself, when you defeat or overcome them: *She remained tense, trying to vanquish that anxiety which she always felt on long flights.*

vantage point /'vɑ:ntɪdʒ pɔɪnt/ *noun*: **vantage points**
A **vantage point** is a position that gives you a clear view of something: *He could see everyone walking along the road from his vantage point on the hill.*

vapour (*AmE* **vapor**) /'veɪpə(r)/ *noun* (*uncount*)
Vapour is a mass of tiny drops of moisture forming a cloud or mist: *water vapour.*

variability /veərɪə'bɪlɪtɪ/ *noun* (*uncount*)
The **variability** of something is the state or condition of being variable: *the variability and unpredictability of her moods.*

variable /'veərɪəbəl/ *adjective*; *noun*
▻ ***adjective***
Something that is **variable** is **1** likely to change at any time: *The weather forecast says that wind direction will be variable today.* [*same as* **changeable**] **2** can be varied or changed as you want: *This washing machine has variable water temperature.*
▻ ***noun***: **variables**
1 A **variable** is a thing that can change in size or quantity at any time: *The time your journey will take will depend on a number of variables, such as the weather conditions and the amount of traffic on the motorway.* **2** (*mathematics*) A **variable** is a symbol that can represent any of a range of quantities or values.

variance /'veərɪəns/ *noun* (*uncount*)
▻ ***phrase*** One thing is **at variance with** another when it seems to disagree with it, conflict with it or contradict it: *His account of the incident was at variance, in a number of respects, with the report submitted by the police.* [*same as* **at odds with**]

variant /'veərɪənt/ *noun*; *adjective*
▻ ***noun***: **variants**
A **variant** is a form of something that is different to another form of the same thing: *There are several variants to the end of this story.* □ *American spelling variants.*
▻ ***adjective***: *variant forms* □ *a variant spelling.*

variation /veərɪ'eɪʃən/ *noun*: **variations**
1 Something that is a **variation** on a certain thing is the same thing presented in another form: *The fashionable thing to say about Shakespeare nowadays is that his plays are all variations on a basic four or five themes.* **2** (*count or uncount*) A **variation** in something is a change or alteration in its size, quantity, level, rate or character: *areas such as holiday accommodation, which are subject to a seasonal variation in demand.* □ *Day followed day, with little variation in routine.* □ *We now have a good idea of the temperature variations that have affected Britain throughout her geological and ecological history.*

varicose veins /varɪkəs 'veɪnz/ *noun* (*plural*)
Varicose veins are veins, usually in the leg, that have become twisted and swollen, causing pain and often requiring surgery.

varied /ˈvɛərɪd/ *verb; adjective*
▻ ***verb***
Varied is the past tense and past participle of **vary**.
▻ ***adjective***
Something is **varied** when it is made up of a lot of different things: *She had had a very varied career.*

variegated /ˈvɛərɪgeɪtɪd/ *adjective*
A plant is **variegated** when its leaves have patches of different colours or shades on them.

variety /vəˈraɪətɪ/ *noun*: **varieties**
1 (*uncount*) **Variety** is the quality of consisting of things that are different from one another: *The key to a healthy, nourishing diet is variety.* ▫ *The landscape is full of variety and beauty.* ▫ *Customers might like more variety in the menu.* ▫ *ways of bringing variety and interest into lessons* ▫ *There were complaints about the lack of variety in the Art curriculum.* ▫ *the rich variety of flora and fauna.* [*same as* **diversity**] **2** (*used in the singular, with a singular or plural verb*) A **variety** of things is a number or range of them, of different kinds: *badgers, foxes and a rich variety of birds* ▫ *We're testing out a variety of different methods.* ▫ *They're responsible for a wide variety of building and maintenance work.* ▫ *A variety of reasons were* (or *was*) *offered for the long delay.* ▫ *There are* (or *there is*) *a variety of excellent schools in the area.* [*same as* **range**, **assortment**] **3** A **variety** of something is a type or kind of it: *Take two potatoes of the same variety and place one in the fridge.* ▫ *Grapes come in many different varieties and qualities.* ▫ *dictionaries of regional and overseas varieties of English* ▫ *They let you sample different varieties of cheese.* ▫ *There are several varieties of dried beans* (or *dried bean*). **4** (*uncount, often adjectival*; *theatre, television*) **Variety** shows consist of performances of different kinds, *eg* dancing, singing, acrobatics and comedy acts: *The 9 o'clock news regularly held the attention of 50 per cent of the population, and comedy and variety 40 per cent.* ▫ *a variety act.*

various /ˈvɛərɪəs/ *adjective*
1 Various means 'several different': *I've worked for various companies.* **2 Various** is also used to describe things that are very different to each other: *Their interests are many and various.* [*same as* **different**, **disparate**, **diverse**; *opposite* **same**]

variously /ˈvɛərɪəslɪ/ *adverb*
Variously means 'in different ways' or 'at different times': *This book has been variously described as fascinating and dull*

varnish /ˈvɑːnɪʃ/ *noun; verb*
▻ ***noun*** (*uncount*)
Varnish is a liquid containing oil that is painted on *eg* wood and dries forming a hard clear shiny surface. [see also **nail varnish**]
▻ ***verb***: **varnishes, varnishing, varnished**
You **varnish** *eg* furniture when you coat it with varnish.

vary /ˈvɛərɪ/ *verb*: **varies, varying, varied**
1 Things that **vary** differ, *eg* in amount, size, degree, quality or content: *Rates may vary a lot around these averages.* ▫ *Mistakes vary considerably in kind.* ▫ *Libraries vary in design and arrangement.* ▫ *Courses vary a good deal both in their length and the number of people attending them.* ▫ *The answers of course varied.* [*same as* **differ**] **2** Things may **vary a** within a particular range: *The fur colour may vary from pale to dark.* ▫ *Estimates vary between £100 and £2000.* **b** according to some changing factor or circumstance: *The risk of contracting the disease varies with age.* ▫ *The texture of seaweed varies according to the humidity of the air.* ▫ *The amount payable varies according to a number of different factors.* **c** depending on the individual person or place concerned: *The ease or difficulty with which people find jobs varies from place to place.* ▫ *Reactions varied enormously from person to person.* ▫ *Growth varies with the individual.* **3** Something **varies** if it is different at different times: *The evening ritual never varied.* ▫ *The number of staff required varies from time to time.* ▫ *Your duties may vary from week to week.* ▫ *Relationships vary over time.* ▫ *Body temperature may vary slightly over a 24-hour period.* [*same as* **change**] **4** You **vary** something when you change it, or introduce differences into it, *eg* in amount, quality or content: *Museums may have to vary their hours of opening from time to time.* ▫ *Accents vary the way words are pronounced.* ▫ *We tend not to vary our diet enough.* ▫ *Customers may vary their orders and their delivery instructions.* [*same as* **alter**, **modify**] — *adjective* **varying:** *computer-users of varying ability* ▫ *Most candidates attempted the question, with varying degrees of success.*

vase /vɑːz/ (*AmE* /veɪs/) *noun*: **vases**
A **vase** is a glass or pottery container, used for holding cut flowers or as an ornament. [see picture at **living room**]

vasectomy /vəˈsɛktəmɪ/ *noun*: **vasectomies**
A **vasectomy** is a surgical operation performed on a man to sterilize him, in which the tube that carries sperm to his penis is cut.

vast /vɑːst/ *adjective*
Something is **vast** when it is extremely large in size, extent, or amount: *vast wheat-growing plains.* ▫ *The problems facing the countries of the former USSR are vast and extremely complex.* [*same as* **immense, huge**]

vastly /ˈvɑːstlɪ/ *adverb*
Vastly means 'greatly' or 'very much': *Technology has vastly improved in recent years.* [*same as* **immensely**, **enormously**]

VAT see **value-added tax**

vat /vat/ *noun*: **vats**
A **vat** is a large barrel or tank for storing or holding liquids.

vault[1] /vɔːlt/ *noun*: **vaults**
1 A bank **vault** is a room with strong walls and doors where things such as money and jewellery are kept. **2** A **vault** in a church is an underground room where people are buried. **3** A **vault** is an arched roof or ceiling, especially in a church.

vault[2] /vɔːlt/ *verb*: **vaults, vaulting, vaulted**
You **vault** something, or **vault** over something, when you leap over it, usually by placing your hands on it and swinging your legs over: *vault over the wall.*

've /əv/ *verb*
've is a short form of **have**, used after pronouns: *we've* ▫ *they've.*

veal /viːl/ *noun* (*uncount*)
Veal is the flesh of a calf, used as food.

veer /vɪə(r)/ *verb*: **veers, veering, veered**
Something such as a moving object or the wind **veers** in a particular direction when it moves round or turns suddenly in that direction: *The wind veered round to the west.* ▫ *The road veers to the left just beyond the church.*

vegetable /ˈvɛdʒɪtəbəl/ *noun* (*often adjectival*): **vegetables**
Vegetables are plants such as potatoes, carrots and onions, used for food and often eaten with *eg* meat and fish: *vegetable curry.* [see picture on next page]

vegetarian /vɛdʒɪˈtɛərɪən/ *noun* (*often adjectival*): **vegetarians**

vegetables

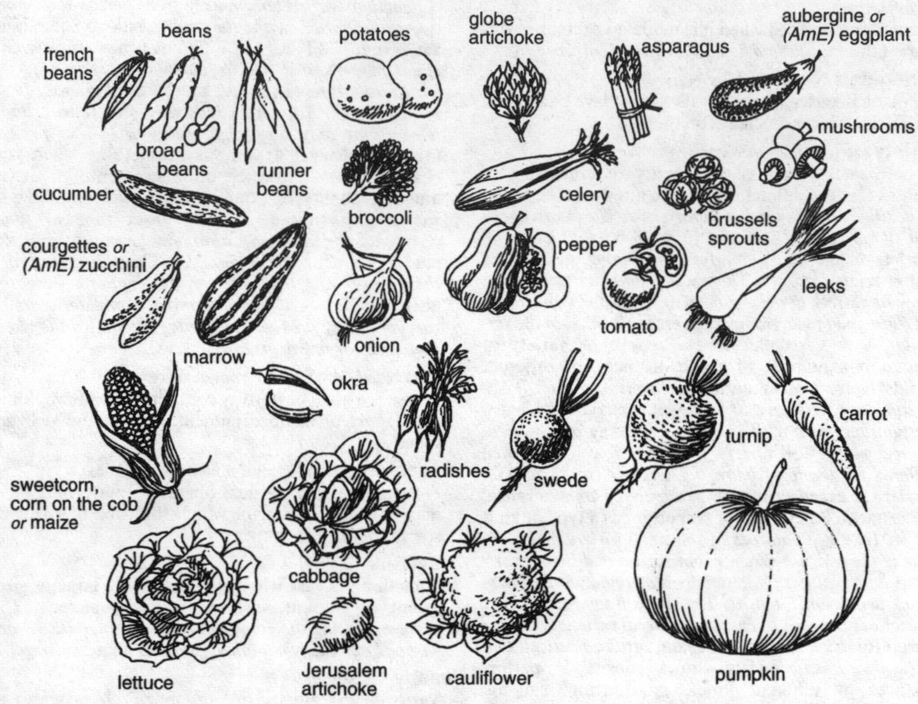

A **vegetarian** is a person who does not eat meat or fish: *vegetarian cookery books.*

vegetate /ˈvɛdʒɪteɪt/ *verb*: **vegetates, vegetating, vegetated**
You **vegetate** when you live a dull, boring life with little activity or excitement: *She seems happy to spend her time vegetating in front of the television.*

vegetation /vɛdʒɪˈteɪʃən/ *noun* (*uncount*)
Vegetation is plants in general or growing in a mass: *dense forest vegetation.*

vehement /ˈviːəmənt/ *adjective*
You are **vehement** about something when you express your opinion about it forcefully: *She was vehement in her condemnation of the level of government support given to carers.* [*same as* **eager**, **fervent**, **passionate**] — *adverb* **vehemently:** *She argued vehemently in support of the government.* — *noun* (*uncount*) **vehemence:** *She spoke to him with such icy vehemence that he was shocked and deeply hurt.* [*same as* **passion**]

vehicle /ˈviːɪkəl/ *noun*: **vehicles**
1 A **vehicle** is a machine such as a bus, lorry or car, used for transporting people or things. **2** A **vehicle** is also a person or thing that is used to communicate or express ideas or opinions: *Newspapers can be vehicles for political propaganda.*

veil /veɪl/ *noun*: **veils**
1 A **veil** is **a** a piece of fabric covering a woman's head or face, forming part of traditional dress in some societies. **b** a piece of net attached to a woman's hat or worn on her head by *eg* a bride. **2** A **veil** of *eg* mist is fine mist that partly hides or covers something: *a veil of cloud covering the summit.* **3** (*literary*) A **veil** is also anything that hides or conceals something: *a veil of secrecy.*

veiled /veɪld/ *adjective*
1 A woman is **veiled** when she is wearing a veil, especially as part of a traditional costume. **2** You make a **veiled** comment when you do not say clearly what you mean, and only hint at your real meaning or intention: *make veiled threats* □ *veiled criticism.*

vein /veɪn/ *noun*: **veins**
1 The **veins** are the blood vessels that carry blood back to the heart. [compare **artery**] **2** A **vein** in rock is a layer of metal or mineral running through it. [*same as* **seam**] **3** The **veins** on a leaf or an insect's wing are the fine tubes running through it. **4** You write or speak in a particular **vein** when you express yourself in that manner or mood: *We began to talk about our days at college together in the 60s, and the conversation continued in this nostalgic vein for half an hour or more.* □ *Confusions of this kind are amusing, of course, but, in a more serious vein, they highlight the areas where greater clarification is necessary.*

velocity /vəˈlɒsɪtɪ/ *noun* (*count or uncount*; *technical*): **velocities**
The **velocity** of something is the speed with which it moves in a particular direction: *the velocity of light.*

velvet /ˈvɛlvɪt/ *noun, adj.*
▻ ***noun*** (*uncount, often adjectival*)
Velvet is a fabric, originally manufactured from silk, with the threads cut short one side, so as to give a smooth soft surface that is pleasant to stroke: *velvet cushions.* — *adverb* **velvety:** *She stroked the animal's velvety coat.*

types of vehicles

vendetta /vɛn'dɛtə/ *noun*: **vendettas**
A **vendetta** is long-standing bitter quarrel between people or families. [*same as* **feud**]

vending machine /'vɛŋdɪŋ mə'ʃi:n/ *noun*: **vending machines**
A **vending machine** is a machine that sells *eg* sweets, drinks and cigarettes, that you operate by putting money in and pressing buttons.

vendor /'vɛndə(r)/ *noun*: **vendors**
1 A **vendor** is a person selling goods from a stall in the street: *a news vendor.* **2** (*legal*) The **vendor** of property is the person who is selling it.

veneer /və'nɪə(r)/ *noun*
1 (*used in the singular*) A **veneer** is an appearance or way of behaving that misleads people and hides what someone is really like: *a veneer of respectability.* [*same as* **façade**] **2** (*uncount or count*) **Veneer**, or a **veneer**, is a thin layer of a fine material, especially wood, fixed to the surface of a lower quality material to make it look more attractive.

venerable /'vɛnərəbəl/ *adjective* (*formal*)
A **venerable** person deserves to be greatly respected, usually because they are old or wise.

venerate /'vɛnəreɪt/ *verb*: **venerates, venerating, venerated**
You **venerate** a person or thing when you respect or value them highly: *The herb known as sweet bay was venerated by the Greeks and Romans.* [*same as* **esteem, revere**] — *noun* (*uncount*) **veneration** /vɛnə'reɪʃən/: *They were taught to treat holy men and women with veneration.*

venereal disease /vənɪərɪəl dɪ'zi:z/ *noun* (*count or uncount*): **venereal diseases**
A **venereal disease** is any of several diseases passed on by sexual intercourse.

Venetian blind /və'ni:ʃən blaɪnd/ *noun*: **Venetian blinds**
A **Venetian blind** is a window blind made of thin, horizontal layers of *eg* plastic or metal, strung together one beneath the other, that can be adjusted to let in or shut out light.

vengeance /'vɛndʒəns/ *noun* (*uncount*)
Vengeance is revenge, or the deliberate harming of someone in return for harm they have done, *eg* to you or your family: *The sorrow of bereavement was replaced in her by an ever-growing desire for vengeance.* [*same as* **revenge, retribution**]
▷ ***phrase*** Something that happens, or is done, **with a vengeance**, happens, or is done, in an intensive manner: *It had begun to snow with a vengeance, and they would be lucky to get safely off the mountain without losing their way.* □ *She was on her knees in the kitchen, scrubbing the floor with a vengeance.*

vengeful /'vɛndʒfʊl/ *adjective* (*literary*)
A person feels **vengeful** when they are eager for revenge.

venison /'vɛnɪsən/ *noun* (*uncount*)
Venison is the flesh of a deer, used as food.

venom /'vɛnəm/ *noun* (*uncount*)
1 Venom is a poisonous liquid that some snakes and spiders inject into the animal they bite or sting. **2 Venom** is also bitterness, anger or hatred expressed especially in language or your tone of voice: *He made the remark in a voice filled with venom.*

venomous /'vɛnəməs/ *adjective*
1 A **venomous** snake or spider can inject poison into any animal that it bites or stings. [*same as* **poisonous**] **2 Venomous** behaviour expresses feelings of bitterness, anger and hatred: *a venomous look in her eyes.*

vent /vɛnt/ *noun*; *verb*
▷ ***noun***: **vents**
A **vent** is an hole or opening that allows air, gas, or liquid into or out of a confined space: *an air vent in the tunnel.*

▻ *verb* (*formal*): **vents, venting, vented**
You **vent** your feelings, or **give vent to** them, when you express them openly: *Don't vent your anger on me.* □ *He gave vent to his frustration by punching the wall.*

ventilate /'vɛntɪleɪt/ *verb*: **ventilates, ventilating, ventilated**
You **ventilate** a room when you allow fresh air to circulate through it. — *adjective* **ventilated:** *a badly ventilated office.* — *noun* (*uncount*) **ventilation** /vɛntɪ'leɪʃən/: *This room has poor ventilation.*

ventilator /'vɛntɪleɪtə(r)/ *noun*: **ventilators**
A **ventilator** is **1** a device by means of which fresh air is brought into a room or building, and stale air is removed. **2** a machine that fills and empties the lungs of people who are having difficulty breathing: *They've had to put him on a ventilator.*

ventriloquist /vɛn'trɪləkwɪst/ *noun*: **ventriloquists**
A **ventriloquist** is an entertainer who can speak without moving their lips, so that they can make it seem as if the sound is coming from somewhere else; ventriloquists usually use a large doll as part of their act, and pretend to hold a conversation with it.

venture /'vɛntʃə(r)/ *noun*; *verb*
▻ ***noun***: **ventures**
1 A **venture** is something exciting, difficult or dangerous that you do: *Learning to climb was a whole new venture for me.* **2** A business **venture** is a business project, especially one that involves some risk. [*same as* **enterprise**]
▻ *verb* (*formal*): **ventures, venturing, ventured**
You **venture** to do something or **venture** into something if you do it even though you expect opposition or failure: *She ventured to criticize the chairman.* □ *I wouldn't venture into a new business unless I had the backing of my bank manager.*
1 You **venture** an *eg* opinion or criticism if you say it cautiously, usually because you expect opposition: *I ventured to suggest that we could save time by doing some of the checks by a computer search.* □ *'Shouldn't you be working?' she ventured.* **2** You **venture** somewhere dangerous or unpleasant if you go there: *I was reluctant to venture out in bad weather.*

venue /'vɛnju:/ *noun*: **venues**
A **venue** is a place where an event takes place: *The venue for the match hasn't been chosen yet.*

veranda or **verandah** /və'randə/ *noun*: **verandas**
A **veranda** is an area at the side of a house or other building that has a roof but no walls: *Shall we have tea on the veranda?*

verb /vɜ:b/ *noun* (*grammar*): **verbs**
1 A **verb** is one of the 'parts of speech' and is used to describe such things as actions (*eg I opened the door*), happenings (*It started to rain*), thought (*I expect you know already*), speech (*'No,' answered Megan*). **2** Verbs may take a direct object (*She turned the handle*), an indirect object (*He told me about it*), or both (*She sent me a postcard*). Verbs that take a direct object are called 'transitive verbs', and can be turned into the passive form (*The road had been widened*). **3** Some verbs do not take an object (*He laughed politely*, *I went over to look*). These are called 'intransitive verbs', and they are not used in the passive form, although in some cases the past participle can be used in a passive way (*the escaped prisoners*, *newly arrived passengers*). **4** A lot of verbs can have both intransitive and transitive uses (*We danced together*, *we danced a waltz together*). **5** Some verbs link people or things with something you want to say about them (*He became very ill*, *She is a psychologist*, *He seemed worried*); the part of the sentence that follows the verb in these cases (*very ill*, *a psychologist*, *worried*) is called the 'complement'. **6** Some verbs, whether transitive or intransitive, are always followed by an additional adverbial word or phrase, called an 'adjunct' (*She put the file on the table*, *You behaved impolitely*).

verbal /'vɜ:bəl/ *adjective*
1 Verbal means relating to words: *when children begin to develop their verbal skills* □ *A picture or diagram is often more use than a verbal explanation.* **2** A **verbal** communication is expressed in spoken words, as distinct from being written down: *verbal abuse* □ *a verbal agreement* **3 Verbal** also means relating to verbs: *the range of possible verbal constructions.* — **verbally:** *Crying is used less and less as a way of getting attention as children learn to communicate their needs verbally.*

verbalize or **verbalise** /'vɜ:bəlaɪz/ *verb*: **verbalizes, verbalizing, verbalized**
You **verbalize** your feelings or thoughts when you express them in words: *when little children begin to verbalize their needs.*

verbatim /vɜ:'beɪtɪm/ *adjective or adverb*
Verbatim means using exactly the same words: *He gave me a verbatim report of the conversation he had had with her.* □ *You will be required to repeat the vow verbatim after me.* [*same as* **word for word**]

verbose /vɜ:'bɒs/ *adjective*
A person, a piece of writing or speech that is **verbose** uses too many words: *Where Neil Kinnock is fiery, verbose and excitable, Mr Smith is calm, believable and dependable.* [*same as* **long-winded**; *opposite* **concise**]

verdict /'vɜ:dɪkt/ *noun*: **verdicts**
1 A **verdict** is a decision taken by a jury in a court of law: *The jury hasn't reached its verdict yet.* **2** Your **verdict** on something is your opinion of it or your decision about it: *So what's your verdict on this new brand of coffee?*

verge /vɜ:dʒ/ *noun*; *verb*
▻ ***noun*** (*usually in the singular*)
The **verge** is the strip of grass that runs along the side of a road.
▻ ***verb***: **verges, verging, verged**
One thing **verges** on another when it is very close to being or becoming that thing: *His enthusiasm verges on obsession.* [*same as* **border**]
▻ ***phrase*** You are **on the verge of** something when you are just about to start doing it: *She was on the verge of tears.* □ *The company is on the verge of making a major decision about its future.*

verifiable /'vɛrɪfaɪəbəl/ *adjective*
Something is **verifiable** if you can check or confirm that it is true: *All scientific results should be verifiable by other scientists.*

verify /'vɛrɪfaɪ/ *verb*: **verifies, verifying, verified**
You **verify** something when you check or confirm that it is true or accurate: *These figures will have to be verified by an accountant.* □ *Could you please verify which plane you'll be travelling on?* — *noun* (*uncount*) **verification** /vɛrɪfɪ'keɪʃən/: *The system will be used in credit-card verification and electronic payment-processing.*

veritable /'vɛrɪtəbəl/ *adjective* (*often humorous*)
Veritable means 'real', 'genuine' or 'accurately described as such': *He's a veritable genius!*

vermilion /və'mɪlɪən/ *noun* (*uncount, often adjectival*)
Vermilion is a bright red colour.

vermin /'vɜ:mɪn/ *noun* (*plural*)
Vermin are all types of wild animal that spread dis-

ease or cause damage, *eg* to crops, especially rats and mice: *The building is overrun with vermin.*

vernacular /və'nakjʊlə(r)/ *noun* (*usually in the singular*)
The **vernacular** of a country or area is the everyday form of language usually spoken there, as opposed to a more formal or literary form of the same language: *I learnt German in Swabia, where I picked up quite a lot of the local vernacular alongside the classical form.*

versatile /'vɜːsətaɪl/ *adjective*
1 A person who is **versatile** has a lot of different skills and is good at adapting to different kinds of work: *She's very versatile, and will be able to perform all the required tasks well.* **2** Something is **versatile** if it can be used in different situations or in different ways: *Cheese is a versatile cooking ingredient.* — *noun* (*uncount*) **versatility** /vɜːsə'tɪlɪtɪ/: *The roles he has played in the last few years display his incredible versatility as an actor.*

verse /vɜːs/ *noun*: **verses**
1 A **verse** is **a** one of several divisions of a poem: *a poem with eight verses.* **b** one of several divisions of a song: *Do you know the words to the second verse of this song?* **2** (*uncount*) **Verse** is poetry: *a story in verse.* [compare **prose**] **3** The **verses** in the Bible are the numbered sections that each chapter is divided into: *John, chapter one, verse one.*

versed /vɜːst/ *adjective* (*formal*)
▷ ***phrase*** You are **versed in** something if you know a lot about it and can use it well: *She's well versed in both Latin and Greek.*

version /'vɜːʃən/ *noun*: **versions**
A **version** of something is any of several types or forms in which it exists, especially one particular form of a piece of writing, or one particular person's account of an incident: *You must give your version of the accident to the police.* □ *the film version of the novel* □ *the first and second versions of this report.*

versus /'vɜːsəs/ *preposition*
1 In sport or a competition, **versus** means 'against'. **2 Versus** is also used to mean 'in comparison to', especially when the two things in question are opposed: *It's a question of expense versus convenience.*

vertebra /'vɜːtɪbrə/ *noun*: **vertebrae** /'vɜːtɪbriː/
Your **vertebrae** are the small bones that together form your spine.

vertebrate /'vɜːtəbrət/ or /'vɜːtəbreɪt/ *noun*: **vertebrates**
A **vertebrate** is any creature that has a spine, including fishes, birds and mammals. [compare **invertebrate**]

vertical /'vɜːtɪkəl/ *adjective*
1 a Something is **vertical** if it is in an upright position: *Very few of the temple columns are still vertical.* **b** A **vertical** line is one that runs from top to bottom. [*opposite* **horizontal**] **2 Vertical** also means 'very steep': *the almost vertical west face of the mountain.* — *adverb* **vertically:** *The numbers should be entered vertically in this column.*

vertigo /'vɜːtɪgoʊ/ *noun* (*uncount*)
Vertigo is a feeling of dizziness and sickness, caused by looking down from a height: *He suffers badly from vertigo.*

very /'verɪ/ *adverb*; *adjective*
▷ ***adverb*** (*intensifying*)
1 Very emphasizes or intensifies, and is itself often intensified by the addition of *indeed*; it is used before **a** adjectives and adverbs: *That's very kind of you indeed.* □ *We very easily forget these things.* □ *They have a very satisfactory working relationship.* □ *Her children are still very young.* □ *You've made some very good points.* **b** past participles that have become adjectives: *We're very excited.*

> Notice that you can intensify other past participles with *much*, and verbs with *very much*: *Her style was much imitated. She obviously wanted the job very much.* [see next sense]

c the words *few*, *little*, *many*, *much*: *Very few people turned up.* □ *There was very little we could do.* □ *In very many of these cases there is no solution.* □ *I very much agree with you.*
2 Very also emphasizes **a** superlative words: *We use the very latest methods.* □ *We'll only have to wait an hour at the very most.*

> Notice that you use *much* and *very much* to intensify comparatives: *This is much more satisfactory. She's walking very much better now.*

b the words *own*, *same*, *first* and *last*: *a room of my very own* □ *I was allowed my very own key.* □ *Strangely enough, he used the very same words as you did.* □ *She was one of the first, if not the very first, to use this technique.* □ *Help arrived at the very last moment.*
▷ ***adjective***
1 Very emphasizes nouns that represent an extreme of some sort: *We were at the very top of the mountain when the mist descended.* □ *I didn't actually stay till the very end.* □ *You can see the marks of burning along the very edge.* □ *the man at the very centre of the affair.* **2** The **very** person or thing is exactly the one, or exactly the kind, that has been mentioned; it can emphasize demonstratives such as **that**: *She seems to be the very person we need for the work.* □ *'Is this the file you wanted?' 'It's the very one; thanks.'* □ *I was going to ask you that very question myself.* [compare **just** the] **3** This **very** moment is the present moment; one thing happens at the **very** time that another does if they happen at the same time: *I've just arrived home this very minute.* □ *She would be ill, at the very time when we need all the help we can get.* □ *I developed flu on the very day of the audition.*
▷ ***phrases*** You use **not very** before adjectives and adverbs as a weak form of 'not', usually to avoid using an opposite expression which you really mean: *That wasn't very nice of you.* [= That was nasty of you] □ *Things aren't going very well.* [= Things are going badly] □ *I can't hear you very well.* [= I can hardly hear you] □ *It shouldn't be very difficult* [= It should be easy] *to find a replacement.* □ *'Do you like it?' 'Not very much.'* [= 'Not at all' or 'No']

vessel /'vɛsəl/ *noun*: **vessels**
1 A **vessel** is a ship or large boat: *a Spanish fishing vessel.* **2** (*formal*) A **vessel** is also a container, especially one for liquid: *the church's communion vessels.*

vest /vɛst/ *noun*: **vests**
1 A **vest** is a thin sleeveless undergarment for the top half of the body: *If you feel the cold so badly, you should wear a vest.* **2** (*AmE*) A **vest** is a waistcoat.

vested /'vɛstid/ *adjective*
Power or authority is **vested** in someone if they have been given it legally or officially: *By the authority vested in me, I now declare you man and wife.*

vested interest /vɛstɪd 'ɪntərəst/ *noun*: **vested interests**
You have a **vested interest** in something if you are directly affected by it or closely associated with it, and so are keen that it should do well: *The directors have a vested interest in the company making as much money as possible.*

vestige /ˈvɛstɪdʒ/ *noun* (*formal*): **vestiges**
A **vestige** of something is a slight amount or trace of it, left after most of it has disappeared: *The British monarchy retains only vestiges of its former power.*

vet /vɛt/ *noun; verb*
▷ ***noun***: **vets**
A **vet** is a veterinary surgeon.
▷ ***verb***: **vets, vetting, vetted**
You **vet** a person or thing when you examine them thoroughly to check they are suitable or acceptable: *Every newspaper article was vetted before it was published.*

veteran /ˈvɛtərən/ *noun*: **veterans**
1 A **veteran** is a person with a lot of experience in a particular activity especially if they have been involved in that activity for a long time: *She's a veteran of the equal rights campaign.* **2** A **veteran** is also someone who served in the armed forces, especially during a war: *a Vietnam veteran.*

veterinarian /vɛtərɪˈneərɪən/ *noun* (*AmE*): **veterinarians**
A **veterinarian** is a veterinary surgeon.

veterinary /ˈvɛtərɪnərɪ/ *adjective*
Veterinary means 'concerned with diseases of animals': *a veterinary practice serving several small villages.*

veterinary surgeon /ˈvɛtərɪnərɪ sɜːdʒən/ *noun*: **veterinary surgeons**
A **veterinary surgeon** is a person qualified to treat diseases of animals.

veto /ˈviːtoʊ/ *noun; verb*
▷ ***noun***: **vetoes**
Someone has a **veto** if they have the right to formally reject a proposal or forbid an action: *the President's power of veto.*
▷ ***verb***: **vetoes, vetoing, vetoed**
You **veto** something if you formally reject or forbid it: *I thought it was a good idea but the company director vetoed it.*

vex /vɛks/ *verb* (*old or formal*): **vexes, vexing, vexed**
Someone or something **vexes** you if they annoy you or if you worry about them: *'What vexes me, my poor Emmy, is not my misfortune, but yours,' George said.* — *adjective* **vexing:** *The whole problem is rather vexing.* [*same as* **annoying**]

vexed /vɛkst/ *adjective*
1 A **vexed** issue, problem or question is talked about a lot because it is difficult to solve or answer. **2** (*rather old*) You are **vexed** if you are annoyed: *He looks pretty vexed.*

via /vɪə/ or /vaɪə/ *preposition*
1 You travel **via** a place if you go through it on your way somewhere: *She travelled from Paris, via Dijon and Avignon, and finally on to Nice.* **2** One thing is achieved **via** another if it is achieved through it: *She sent me a message via my brother.*

viable /ˈvaɪəbəl/ *adjective*
A plan is **viable** if it has a reasonable chance of being successful: *Does my idea sound viable to you?* [*same as* **workable, feasible**] — *noun* (*uncount*) **viability** /vaɪəˈbɪlɪtɪ/: *The viability of the project is now called seriously into question.*

viaduct /ˈvaɪədʌkt/ *noun*: **viaducts**
A **viaduct** is a bridge-like structure of stone arches that supports a road or railway across *eg* a valley.

vibes /vaɪbz/ *noun* (*plural; informal*)
The **vibes** a place gives you are the feelings it gives you: *This old cottage gives me bad vibes.*

vibrant /ˈvaɪbrənt/ *adjective*
1 A **vibrant** person is full of life and energy. [*same as* **vivacious**] **2** A **vibrant** colour is strong and bright: *a vibrant orange dress.* [*same as* **vivid**] — *adverb* **vibrantly:** *The room was vibrantly painted in a series of orange, red and yellow stripes.*

vibrate /vaɪˈbreɪt/ *verb*: **vibrates, vibrating, vibrated**
Something **vibrates** when it shakes or trembles slightly: *Every time a train passed beneath the ground, the whole building seemed to vibrate.* — *noun* **vibration** /vaɪˈbreɪʃən/: *These vibrations must be coming from the car's engine.*

vicar /ˈvɪkə(r)/ *noun*: **vicars**
A **vicar** is the minister of a parish in the Church of England.

vicarage /ˈvɪkərɪdʒ/ *noun*: **vicarages**
A **vicarage** is a house where a vicar lives.

vicarious /vɪˈkɛərɪəs/ *adjective*
A **vicarious** pleasure or feeling is one that you do not experience yourself, but that you experience when you watch other people doing or feeling it: *He took a vicarious pleasure in seeing his children learn.* [*same as* **second-hand**] — *adverb* **vicariously:** *The television audience vicariously senses the terrifying proximity of these enormous gorillas as Attenborough edges closer to them.*

vice[1] /vaɪs/ *noun*: **vices**
1 A **vice** is a bad habit: *Smoking is his only vice.* [*opposite* **virtue**] **2** (*uncount*) **Vice** is the name given to all criminal activities relating to pornography, prostitution, gambling and drugs.

vice[2] (*AmE* **vise**) /vaɪs/ *noun*: **vices**
A **vice** is a tool with heavy movable metal jaws, that can be fixed to a bench or table, and that holds the object you are working on so that it doesn't move.

vice- /vaɪs/ *prefix*
Vice- means 'next in rank to, and acting as deputy for': *the vice-chairman* □ *the last viceroy of India.*

vice-president /vaɪsˈprɛzɪdənt/ *noun*: **vice-presidents**
The **vice-president** is the person who is next in rank after the president, and who may replace the president on some formal occasions: *the vice-president of the United States.*

vice versa /vaɪs ˈvɜːsə/ or /vaɪsə ˈvɜːsə/ *adjective*
Vice versa means 'the other way round' or 'with the order changed round': *Husbands may invite their wives and vice versa.* [= wives may invite their husbands] □ *from me to you and vice versa.* [*same as* **conversely**]

vicinity /vɪˈsɪnɪtɪ/ *noun* (*usually in the singular; formal*)
One thing is in the **vicinity** of another when it is near it or in the same area as it: *He wanted a cheap hotel in the vicinity of the station.* □ *She asked a policeman if there was a post office in the vicinity.* [= nearby]

vicious /ˈvɪʃəs/ *adjective*
1 A **vicious** animal or person is violent, cruel and dangerous: *a vicious criminal.* [*same as* **ferocious, savage**] **2** A **vicious** remark is spiteful or hurtful. [*same as* **malicious**; *same as* **savage**] — *adverb* **viciously:** *The dog viciously attacked the flock of sheep.* □ *She pulled his hair viciously.*

vicious circle /vɪʃəs ˈsɜːkəl/ *noun*: **vicious circles**
A **vicious circle** is a situation in which any attempt to solve one problem creates other problems which in turn cause the original problem to appear again.

victim /ˈvɪktɪm/ *noun*: **victims**
A **victim** is a person or animal that is killed, is made to suffer or is tricked or teased: *He was the victim of a*

violent attack by a gang of youths. □ *the innocent victims of the war* □ *a murder victim.*

victimize or **victimise** /ˈvɪktɪmaɪz/ *verb* (*often in the passive*): **victimizes, victimizing, victimized**
Someone **is victimized** if they are treated unfairly or with hostility: *Members of the Bangladeshi community feel they have been victimized by the council in the past months.* [*same as* **pick on, discriminate against**] — *noun* (*uncount*) **victimization** /vɪktɪmaɪˈzeɪʃən/: *the victimization of foreign workers.*

victor /ˈvɪktə(r)/ *noun* (*formal*): **victors**
The **victor** is the winner or winning side in a war or contest: *the victor of the recent General Election.*

Victorian /vɪkˈtɔːrɪən/ *adjective; noun*
▻ ***adjective***
1 Victorian describes things and events that are from or belong to the reign of Queen Victoria (1837–1901). **2 Victorian** attitudes or values reflect a strict sense of what is proper behaviour: *her rather Victorian attitude towards sex.*
▻ ***noun***: **Victorians**
A **Victorian** is a person who lived during the reign of Queen Victoria.

victorious /vɪkˈtɔːrɪəs/ *adjective*
A person or group of people is **victorious** if they win, especially a war or contest: *the victorious French army.*

victory /ˈvɪktərɪ/ *noun*: **victories**
1 A **victory** is a situation in which you are successful against an opponent, *eg* in a war or contest: *the British victory at the Battle of Trafalgar* □ *the result was an unexpected victory for Scotland.* **2** (*uncount*) **Victory** is success against an opponent, *eg* in a war or contest: *Becker has little chance of victory now he is so many points behind.*

video /ˈvɪdɪoʊ/ *noun; verb*
▻ ***noun***: **videos**
1 A **video** is a copy of a film or television programme, or a filmed recording of an event, on magnetic tape, that you watch using a video recorder and television set: *Shall we watch a video tonight?* □ *We can hire a video of the film at the shop in the village.* □ *She had a video made of her wedding.* **2** A **video** is also a video recorder: *My video's broken; I must get someone in to repair it.* **3** (*uncount*) **a Video** is the recording of sound and images on magnetic tape for watching with a video recorder and television set: *the growing use of video in schools.* **b Video** is also the magnetic tape that sound and images can be recorded on using a video recorder or video camera: *This film is now out on video.* [*same as* **videotape**]
▻ ***verb***: **videos, videoing, videoed**
You **video** a film or television programme when you make a copy of it on magnetic tape using a video recorder; you **video** an event when you make a film of it on magnetic tape using a video camera: *I forgot to video last night's film.* □ *The christening is going to be videoed.*

video camera /ˈvɪdɪoʊ kamərə/ *noun*: **video cameras**
A **video camera** is a camera that is used to make a film of an event on magnetic tape, that you watch using a video recorder and television set.

video game /ˈvɪdɪoʊ geɪm/ *noun*: **video games**
A **video game** is an electronic game that you play using a small computer attached to a television set or visual display unit.

video recorder /ˈvɪdɪoʊ rɪkɔːdə(r)/ *noun*: **video recorders**
A **video recorder** is a machine that records and plays videos, usually connected to a television set.

videotape /ˈvɪdɪoʊteɪp/ *noun* (*uncount*)
Videotape is magnetic tape that images and sound can be recorded on to.

vie /vaɪ/ *verb*: **vies, vying, vied**
You **vie** with someone for something if you compete with them to obtain it: *Children vie with each other, often unconsiously, for their mother's attention.*

view /vjuː/ *noun; verb*
▻ ***noun***: **views**
1 The **view** from a place is everything that can be seen from it, especially the surrounding countryside and buildings: *From the top of the tower there is a fine view over the South Bohemian countryside.* □ *She gazed out of the train window at the passing view.* □ *There are good walks out on to the headlands, with their panoramic views of the Straits.* **2** (*used in the singular*) You have a **view** of something when you can see it: *From the window she had a partial view of the terrace.* □ *You're obscuring my view of the screen.* □ *Did you get a full view of his face?* □ *I could see the lorry in my rear-view mirror.* **3** (*uncount*) Something is in **view** when you can see it, and out of **view** when you cannot: *Only the rear of the house was in view.* □ *His face was healed in full view of all those present.* □ *paintings that have been stored for decades in the basement, out of public view* □ *Liz disappeared from view round the curve.* □ *as the last runners limped into view.* [*same as* **sight**] **4** (*used in the singular*) You get *eg* a general, impartial or biased **view** of facts if that is the way they are presented to you: *I believe we get a full and fair view of the situation from this report.* [*same as* **assessment, review, survey**] **5** Your **view** on any subject is your opinion about it: *He had strong views on just about everything.* □ *He rejects the Marxist view that political power derives from economic power.* □ *Adenauer took the view* [= thought] *that it was pointless to divide the country further by too much emphasis on the Nazi era.* □ *There's no evidence to support this view.* □ *Is this too optimistic a view?* □ *That's certainly the majority view.* □ *Members may have different views about the role of local councillors.* [*same as* **opinion**] **6** (*usually in the singular*) Your **view** of something is your attitude to it, or the way you regard it: *He was a statesman, with a statesman's view of his responsibilities.* □ *She had a satirist's black view of life.* □ *the propagandist view of literature was roundly condemned.* □ *We must take a broader view.* [*same as* **attitude**; compare **point of view**]
▻ ***verb***: **views, viewing, viewed**
1 You **view** something in a particular way if you regard it in that way: *Circumstances naturally affect the way an individual thinks, behaves and views the world.* □ *People tend to view unusual behaviour with suspicion.* □ *Speakers view their voices as an important part of their self-image.* [*same as* **regard**] **2** You **view** something when you look at it, *eg* with some kind of instrument: *There's a facility for viewing the text page by page on the screen.* □ *It's like trying to view something through the wrong end of a telescope.* □ *She stood back and viewed the painting from a distance.* **3** You **view** something such as a house when you inspect it, usually when you are deciding whether to buy it: *Charles took me to view the piano.* — *noun* (*uncount*) **viewing** /ˈvjuːɪŋ/: *Television-viewing dominates their lives.* □ *programmes suitable for broadcasting at peak viewing times.*
▻ ***phrases*** **1** You use **in my view** when giving your own opinion about something: *It's silly in my view to marry someone you don't love.* **2** You do something with a certain purpose **in view** if you do it for that purpose: *She had hired a car for a day or two, with a trip to the clinic in view.* □ *What object have you in view?* **3** You

make a decision **in view of** certain circumstances when those circumstances influence your decision: *In view of the worsening weather perhaps we should wait till tomorrow.* **4** Something is **on view** when it is in a place where the public can see it: *The sculptures will remain on view till 30 November.* □ *I acknowledged their greetings with a dignified wave, rather like a royal personage on view.* **5** You do something **with a view to** a certain purpose when you do it for that purpose: *people who buy cottages with a view to retirement* □ *More power points were being installed, with a view to equipping every member of staff with a PC.*

viewer /'vju:ə(r)/ *noun*: **viewers**
A **viewer** is a person watching television: *Several million viewers watched last night's film.*

viewpoint /'vju:pɔɪnt/ *noun*: **viewpoints**
1 Your **viewpoint** is your opinion of something: *I'd like your viewpoint on this idea.* [*same as* **point of view**] **2** A **viewpoint** is also a place that you get a good view from: *She saw the whole firework display from her viewpoint on the bridge.*

vigil /'vɪdʒɪl/ *noun*: **vigils**
A **vigil** is a period during which you stay awake or stay quietly in one place, usually to take care of a sick person, as part of a religious festival, or to make a protest: *She kept a vigil at his bedside.* □ *the Easter vigil* □ *Protestors held a vigil outside the embassy.*

vigilant /'vɪdʒɪlənt/ *adjective*
You are **vigilant** when you watch what is happening carefully, in order to be ready for possible trouble or danger: *Nurses in intensive care need to be especially vigilant.* [*same as* **alert**, **watchful**] — *noun* (*uncount*) **vigilance** /'vɪdʒɪləns/: *The baby is getting better but there's still a need for considerable vigilance.*

vigilante /vɪdʒɪ'lantɪ/ *noun* (*usually in the plural*): **vigilantes**
Vigilantes are a group of people who join together to protect their community from crime and catch criminals.

vigorous /'vɪgərəs/ *adjective*
1 A **vigorous** action is done with strong, energetic movements: *He gave my hand a vigorous shake.* □ *You should take some form of vigorous daily exercise.* [*same as* **energetic**, **strenuous**] **2** A **vigorous** person is strong and healthy: *He was a still-vigorous man in his late seventies.* **3** You make **vigorous** efforts to do something when you act with energy and enthusiasm: *The committee thanked them warmly for their vigorous support of the day-care scheme.* — *adverb* **vigorously:** *The dog shook itself vigorously, scattering drops of water everywhere.* □ *He argued vigorously in favour of the proposal.*

vigour (*AmE* **vigor**) /'vɪgə(r)/ *noun* (*uncount*)
Vigour is great physical or mental strength and energy: *He was valued for his vigour and inventiveness, and was respected as a reliable man of business.*

vile /vaɪl/ *adjective* (*informal*): **viler**, **vilest**
You can say that something is **vile** when you think it is extremely bad or unpleasant: *this vile weather we've been having lately* □ *This cheese is absolutely vile!* [*same as* **foul**, **nasty**]

villa /'vɪlə/ *noun*: **villas**
A **villa** is a large, attractive house, especially one in a country area or one used for holidays: *She's rented a villa in Spain for the winter.*

village /'vɪlɪdʒ/ *noun*: **villages**
A **village** is a group of houses, shops, and other buildings that is smaller than a town and that is in a country area: *the village of Ivychurch in Kent* □ *a village shop.*

villain /'vɪlən/ *noun*: **villains**
1 A **villain** is a wicked person, or someone who deliberately breaks the law or harms other people: *Several Shakespearean characters, Don John, for instance, face the audience and openly admit to being villains.* [*same as* **scoundrel**, **rogue**] **2** The **villain** in a story is the main wicked or evil character in it. [*opposite* **hero**, **heroine**]

villainy /'vɪlənɪ/ *noun* (*uncount*; *formal*)
Villainy is wicked, evil or criminal behaviour: *He has been well punished for his villainy.*

vindicate /'vɪndɪkeɪt/ *verb*: **vindicates**, **vindicating**, **vindicated**
You **are vindicated** **1** when your behaviour, actions or ideas are proved to have been correct: *It was a glorious victory, and his choice of players had been fully vindicated.* **2** when you are proved not to be to blame for something that has happened: *He had maintained his innocence throughout, and was completely vindicated by the findings of the report.* [*same as* **justify**, **absolve**]

vindictive /vɪn'dɪktɪv/ *adjective*
A **vindictive** person deliberately tries to hurt or harm another person, usually because they think they have themselves been hurt or harmed by that person: *There's no need to be so vindictive. It wasn't my fault you lost your job.* [*same as* **malicious**, **spiteful**; *opposite* **kind**] — *adverb* **vindictively:** *'I think he deserved all he got,' she said vindictively.*

vine /vaɪn/ *noun*: **vines**
A **vine** is any of various climbing plants that produce grapes.

vinegar /'vɪnɪgə(r)/ *noun* (*uncount*)
Vinegar is a sour liquid usually made from beer or wine and served with *eg* salad or chips.

vineyard /'vɪnjəd/ *noun*: **vineyards**
A **vineyard** is an area of land where vines are planted for the production of wine: *a vineyard in the Champagne-producing part of France.*

vintage /'vɪntɪdʒ/ *adjective*
1 **Vintage** wine is good quality wine produced in a particular year: *the 1968 vintage* □ *vintage port.* **2** **Vintage** work or behaviour is exactly the type or quality of work or behaviour that you expect from someone: *The remark was vintage Churchill.* □ *a vintage Beetles record.* [*same as* **classic**]

vinyl /'vaɪnɪl/ *noun* (*uncount*)
Vinyl is a type of strong plastic, used *eg* for making furniture and floor coverings: *We bought some cheap vinyl chairs for the garden.*

viola /vɪ'oʊlə/ *noun*: **violas**
A **viola** is a musical instrument of the violin family that is larger than the violin and lower in pitch. [see picture at **orchestra**; compare **cello**]

violate /'vaɪəleɪt/ *verb*: **violates**, **violating**, **violated**
1 You **violate** a law, agreement or oath if you break it or do not do what it says: *You have violated the terms of your contract.* [*same as* **break**, **contravene**] **2** You **violate** a holy place if you do not behave properly or respectfully there: *The tombs had already been violated before the archaeologists arrived.* [*same as* **desecrate**] **3** You **violate** a person's peace or privacy if you disturb them: *The tranquility of the village was violated by a coach full of noisy tourists.* — *noun* **violation** /vaɪə'leɪʃən/: *a gross violation of basic human rights.*

violence /'vaɪələns/ *noun* (*uncount*)
1 **Violence** is behaviour intended to hurt, injure or kill people, involving *eg* hitting, kicking, or the use of weapons such as knives, guns or bombs: *the effect of screen violence on the minds of young viewers* □ *further*

outbreaks of street violence □ *There is to be yet another inquiry into the causes of football violence.* □ *He had been the victim of a mindless act of violence.* □ *The men of violence must not be allowed to triumph.* **2** You do something with **violence** if you do it with energy or force, usually because you are angry: *She slammed the door with unnecessary violence.* □ *He uttered these last words with unaccustomed violence.* **3 Violence** is the quality of being violent: *We were expecting the storm, but were not prepared for its violence.*

violent /'vaɪələnt/ *adjective*
1 People are **violent** when they use physical force, *eg* hitting, punching or kicking, or weapons, to hurt, injure or kill other people: *He looked as if he might become violent at any moment and I backed away.* □ *the increase in violent crime.* **2** Someone who meets a **violent** death, or a **violent** end, dies unexpectedly in painful way, usually by being murdered: *Her brother had met a violent death in a terrorist bombing outrage.* **3 Violent** describes emotions, or relations between people, in which there is great intensity of feeling or bitterness: *She's got a violent temper.* □ *They had a violent disagreement.* □ *There were several violent exchanges between the Government and Opposition front benches today.* □ *She made a violent attack on the Government's education policy.* □ *She took a violent dislike to me for some reason.* [*opposite* **mild**] **4 Violent** physical happenings involve a lot of force or energy: *There was a violent explosion.* **5 Violent** language contains threats, abuse, and swearwords. **6** You have a **violent** pain or a **violent** headache if it is very severe. **7 Violent** colours are very strong and bright: *She was wearing a cotton suit in a rather violent green.* — *adverb* **violently:** *Prisoners who behave violently are kept in special cells.* □ *I could hear them arguing violently downstairs.* □ *He died violently at the hands of a hired assassin.* □ *I was violently sick.* □ *The driver swore violently at me.*

violet /'vaɪələt/ *noun*: **violets**
1 A **violet** is a small wild plant with purple or white flowers. **2** (*uncount*) **Violet** is the purple colour of this flower. [*same as* **purple**, **lavender**]

violin /vaɪə'lɪn/ *noun*: **violins**
A **violin** is a musical instrument with a shaped body and a neck along which four strings are stretched. It is held with one end under the chin and played with a bow. [see picture at **orchestra**; compare **cello**, **viola**]

violinist /vaɪə'lɪnɪst/ *noun*: **violinists**
A **violinist** is a person who plays the violin.

VIP /viː aɪ 'piː/ *noun* (*often adjectival*): **VIPs**
A **VIP** is a very important person who is given special treatment: *The airport has a private lounge for VIPs.* □ *the VIP lounge* □ *We received VIP treatment.*

viper /'vaɪpə(r)/ *noun*: **vipers**
A **viper** is a poisonous snake found in Britain. [*same as* **adder**]

virgin /'vɜːdʒɪn/ *noun*; *adjective*
▻ ***noun***: **virgins**
A **virgin** is a person, especially a woman, who has never had sexual intercourse.
▻ ***adjective***
Something can be described as **virgin** if it is in its original fresh clean state: *They climbed higher so that they could ski on the virgin snow above the tree line.* [*same as* **untouched**] **Virgin** land has never been explored or cultivated: *The West was still largely virgin and unexplored.* □ *Our electronics specialists are venturing into virgin territory in developing this software.*

virginity /və'dʒɪnɪtɪ/ *noun* (*uncount*)
Your **virginity** is your state before your first experience of sexual intercourse: *In those days respectable girls didn't lose their virginity before marriage.*

virile /'viraɪl/ *adjective*
A man who is described as **virile** has the qualities that people consider to be typically masculine, especially physical strength, a handsome appearance, a forceful personality, and a strong sexual appetite: *She took a fancy to the virile young ski instructor.* — *noun* (*uncount*) **virility** /vɪ'rɪlɪtɪ/: *He isn't a man who feels the need to prove his virility by having lots of girlfriends.*

virtual /'vɜːtʃʊəl/ *adjective*
A **virtual** state of things is a situation so close to it as to be more or less the same thing: *They have virtual monopoly of sales in the Far East.* □ *We are witnessing the virtual collapse of the steel industry.* □ *We were faced with virtual mutiny when we suggested alterations to the working hours.* □ *He is in virtual control of the department.*

virtually /'vɜːtʃʊəlɪ/ *adverb*
You can use **virtually** to refer to something that is almost or nearly true and that can be regarded as true for most purposes: *The war is virtually over.* □ *It's virtually impossible to tell the imitation from the real thing.* □ *You're virtually the only person I trust.* [*same as* **more or less, to all intents and purposes, practically**]

virtual reality /vɜːtʃʊəl rɪ'alɪtɪ/ *noun* (*uncount*)
Virtual reality is a computer-created environment that the person operating the computer is able to be a part of.

virtue /'vɜːtʃuː/ or /'vɜːtjuː/ *noun*: **virtues**
1 A **virtue** is a quality thought of as morally good: *He has many virtues, including honesty.* **2** (*uncount*) **Virtue** is thinking and acting in a way that is thought of as morally good. [*same as* **righteousness**] **3** (*count or uncount*) The **virtue** of something is a good, desirable or admirable quality that it has: *The virtue of this type of battery is its long life.* □ *He believes firmly in the virtues of more open and honest government.* □ *There is no virtue in arriving early as we'll only have to wait when we get there.* [compare **vice**]
▻ ***phrase*** (*formal*) You can use **by virtue of** to explain why something is true or is the case: *She is eligible for British citizenship by virtue of her mother being British.*

virtuoso /vɜːtʃʊ'oʊsoʊ/ *noun*: **virtuosos** or **virtuosi** /vɜːtʃʊ'oʊsɪ/
A **virtuoso** is a person who is exceptionally good at something, especially a brilliant musician: *a virtuoso pianist* □ *a virtuoso performance.*

virtuous /'vɜːtʃʊəs/ or /'vɜːtjʊəs/ *adjective*
A **virtuous** person behaves in a morally good or religious way: *She has always lived a virtuous life.* — *adverb* **virtuously:** *He always tries to behave virtuously.*

virulent /'vɪrʊlənt/ *adjective*
1 A **virulent** disease is extremely dangerous: *a virulent strain of flu.* **2** Words, actions or feelings that are **virulent** are bitterly hostile: *Saturday's centre page had carried a virulent attack on her .* □ *She was frequently virulent about her work colleagues.* [*same as* **acrimonious, vicious**] — *noun* (*uncount*) **virulence:** *an infection of unusual virulence.* — *adverb* **virulently:** *The press went on attacking her as virulently as ever.*

virus /'vaɪərəs/ *noun*: **viruses**
1 A **virus** is any of several types of germ that often cause disease: *a new strain of flu virus* □ *a virus infection.* **2** In computers, a **virus** is a piece of computer

code put into a program to destroy data. It is passed on to computers in which the program is used.

visa /'vi:zə/ *noun*: **visas**
A **visa** is an official permit stamped into your passport to allow you to enter, leave or travel through a country: *European citizens don't need to have a visa for Britain.*

vis-à-vis /vi:z ə 'vi:/ *preposition*
You can use **vis-à-vis** when you are comparing one thing, or the amount of one thing, with another: *The rise in the Japanese interest rates did not slow down the drop in the value of the yen vis-à-vis other currencies.*

viscount /'vaɪkaʊnt/ *noun*: **viscounts**
A **viscount** is a member of the British nobility below an earl and above a baron in rank.

viscountess /'vaɪkaʊntɪs/ *noun*: **viscountesses**
A **viscountess** is **1** the wife or widow of a viscount. **2** a woman with the same rank as a viscount.

vise see **vice**[2]

visibility /vɪzɪ'bɪlɪtɪ/ *noun* (*uncount*)
Visibility is the range in which you can see clearly in particular weather or lighting conditions: *The fog has resulted in poor visibility on all roads in the area.* □ *Visibility is down to 40 metres.*

visible /'vɪzɪbəl/ *adjective*
1 An object is **visible** when you can see it: *These cells are not visible to the naked eye.* □ *The hill is just visible from my bedroon window.* **2** A situation or state, or a change in a situation or state, is **visible** when it can be recognized, noticed or seen: *The improvement in her health is barely visible as yet.* □ *a period of visible growth in company performance.* [*same as* **apparent**] — *adverb* **visibly:** *She was visibly upset.*

vision /'vɪʒən/ *noun*: **visions**
1 (*uncount*) **Vision** is the ability to see: *The vision in her right eye is much better than that in her left.* □ *He has very little vision left in either eye.* [*same as* **sight**] **2** You have a **vision** of something when you can imagine what it is like or what it will be like in the future. **3** (*uncount*) You have **vision** when you are able to imagine what is likely to happen and plan wisely for it: *The company needs to employ managers with vision.* **4** (*uncount*) **Vision** is the picture on a television screen: *This television is so old the vision is very poor.*

visionary /'vɪʒənərɪ/ *noun*; *adjective*
▷ ***noun***: **visionaries**
A **visionary** is **1** a person who has visions or miraculous religious or spiritual experiences. **2** a person who has the imagination and inspiration to see how things are going to develop in the future: *one of the country's political visionaries.*
▷ ***adjective***: *an inspired and visionary leader.*

visit /'vɪzɪt/ *verb*; *noun*
▷ ***verb***: **visits, visiting, visited**
1 You **visit** someone when you go or come to see them, and usually spend time with them: *She's gone to visit her brother for the weekend.* **2** You **visit** a place when you go to look at it, usually because it is interesting: *Millions of foreign tourists visit London each year.* **3** You **visit** *eg* the doctor or dentist when you go to see them about your health or teeth: *How long is it since you last visited the dentist?*
▷ ***noun***: **visits:** *I've arranged to pay him a visit next month.* □ *a brief visit to the Paris office* □ *a visit to the zoo* □ *a visit to the dentist.*

visitor /'vɪzɪtə(r)/ *noun*: **visitors**
A **visitor** is someone who visits a person or place: *Millions of foreign visitors travel to London each year.* □ *Have you had any visitors today?* □ *Buckingham Palace is open to visitors only in the summer.*

visor /'vaɪzə(r)/ *noun*: **visors**
A **visor** is the movable part of a helmet that can be pulled down to cover the face. [see also **sun visor**]

vista /'vɪstə/ *noun*: **vistas**
1 (*literary*) A **vista** is a view into the distance, especially one that is long and narrow, and has *eg* rows of trees on both sides. **2** A **vista** is also a range of ideas, possibilities or problems: *The job has opened up whole new vistas for me.*

visual /'vɪʒʊəl/ *adjective*
Visual means relating to or received through sight or vision: *a visual image* □ *the visuals arts, such as sculpture and photography* □ *visual comedy.* — *adverb* **visually:** *His jokes are usually very funny visually.* □ *The performance of this opera is visually stunning, although the singing is disappointing.*

visual aid /vɪʒʊəl 'eɪd/ *noun*: **visual aids**
Visual aids are things such as pictures, films and slides that help you learn, remember, teach or present information.

visual display unit /vɪʒʊəl dɪs'pleɪ ju:nɪt/ *noun*: **visual display units**
A **visual display unit** is a VDU.

visualize or **visualise** /'vɪʒʊəlaɪz/ *verb*: **visualizes, visualizing, visualized**
You **visualize** something when you form a clear picture of it in your mind: *I can't visualize him at all from your description.*

vital /'vaɪtəl/ *adjective*
1 Something is **vital** when it is essential, especially to the success or failure of a project or plans: *She made a vital error in the program and the whole computer system went wrong.* □ *It is vital to keep a copy of all the relevant papers in the correct file.* **2** People are **vital** when they are lively and have a lot of energy: *a bright, vital child.* — *adverb* **vitally:** *It is vitally important to keep copies of these documents.*

vitality /vaɪ'talɪtɪ/ *noun* (*uncount*)
Vitality is liveliness and energy: *Young children should be full of vitality.*

vital statistics /vaɪtəl stə'tɪstɪks/ *noun* (*plural*)
A woman's **vital statistics** are her bust, waist and hip measurements.

vitamin /'vɪtəmɪn/ *noun*: **vitamins**
Vitamins are any of a group of natural substances that are essential for healthy life, and that are found in various foods: *Strawberries are very high in vitamin C.* □ *Vitamin A is found in milk.* □ *vitamin pills.*

vitriolic /vɪtrɪ'ɒlɪk/ *adjective* (*formal*)
Speech or criticism is **vitriolic** when it is extremely bitter or hateful: *The newspapers launched a viriolic attack on what they referred to as cowards, weaklings and miserable traitors.*

viva /'vaɪvə/ *noun*: **vivas**
A **viva** is an oral examination, especially at a university.

vivacious /vɪ'veɪʃəs/ *adjective*
A **vivacious** person is attractive and lively: *a vivacious young woman.* — *adverb* **vivaciously:** *She smiled at him vivaciously.*

vivacity /vɪ'vasɪtɪ/ *noun* (*uncount*)
Vivacity is the quality of being lively and attractive: *her natural vivacity.*

vivid /'vɪvɪd/ *adjective*
1 A **vivid** colour is strong and bright: *She painted the walls vivid yellow.* **2** Speech, writing or memories are

vivid when they give or create a strong, clear image: *She gave a vivid account of the incident.* □ *Children often have vivid imaginations.* — *adverb* **vividly:** *a vividly coloured portrait* □ *The photographs reminded me vividly of my childhood.* □ *I remember my grandmother vividly.* — *noun* (*uncount*) **vividness:** *She writes with vividness about her travels in Africa.*

vivisection /vɪvɪ'sɛkʃən/ *noun* (*uncount*)
Vivisection is the practice of cutting open live animals to do scientific and medical experiments on them.

vixen /'vɪksən/ *noun*: **vixens**
A **vixen** is a female fox.

V-neck /'viː nɛk/ *noun*: **V-necks**
A **V-neck** is any garment, but especially a pullover, that has a neck opening formed to make a point at the front. [see picture at **clothing**]

vocabulary /və'kabjʊlərɪ/ *noun*: **vocabularies**
1 (*count or uncount*) Your **vocabulary** is all the words you know in a particular language: *She has a very wide vocabulary for a two-year-old.* □ *Foreign learners of English often have problems increasing their vocabulary.* **2** (*used in the singular*) The **vocabulary** of a language is all the words in it: *new words in the English vocabulary.* **3** (*count or uncount*) The **vocabulary** of a particular group or profession is the range of specialist terms they use: *The document was written in legal vocabulary that made it difficult to understand.* [compare **jargon**]

vocal /'voʊkəl/ *adjective*; *noun*
▷ ***adjective***
1 A person or group of people is **vocal** if they express their opinions loudly and forcefully: *Right-wing conservatives are usually vocal members of their local communities.* **2** **Vocal** means relating to or produced by the human voice: *an opera-singer with a wide vocal range* □ *vocal music.*
▷ ***noun*** (*usually in the plural*): **vocals**
A popular song's **vocals** are its words: *She sings lead vocals with the band.*

vocal cords /'voʊkəl kɔːdz/ *noun* (*plural*)
Your **vocal cords** are the folds of tissue in your larynx that are vibrated by the breath to produce sound.

vocalist /'voʊkəlɪst/ *noun*: **vocalists**
A **vocalist** is a singer, especially in a pop group.

vocation /voʊ'keɪʃən/ *noun* (*count or uncount*): **vocations**
If a person has a **vocation** they have a strong feeling that they are especially suitable for a particular job or profession, especially one that involves helping other people: *Many people regard nursing as a vocation.* □ *He's a teacher by vocation.*

vocational /voʊ'keɪʃənəl/ *adjective*
Vocational training or education gives you the skills needed to do a particular job: *The college offers a whole range of vocational courses.*

vociferous /və'sɪfərəs/ *adjective* (*formal*)
A person is **vociferous** if they say what they think in a loud and forceful way: *a vociferous group of protesters.*

vodka /'vɒdkə/ *noun* (*uncount*)
Vodka is a strong, colourless alcoholic drink.

vogue /voʊg/ *noun* (*used in the singular*)
The **vogue** is what is fashionable and popular: *Long, straight skirts are all the vogue at the moment.*
▷ ***phrase*** Something is **in vogue** when it is fashionable and popular: *Bright colours are not in vogue at the moment.*

voice /vɔɪs/ *noun*; *verb*
▷ ***noun***: **voices**
1 a Your **voice** is the way you speak and sing: *I couldn't recognize the voice talking to me on the phone.* □ *I recognized her by her voice.* □ *She has a very soft singing voice.* □ *'Hurry up,' she said in a loud voice.* □ *She spoke in a nervous voice.* **b** (*uncount*) Your **voice** is the ability to speak: *He keeps losing his voice.* **2** (*used in the singular*) You have a **voice** if you have the right to say what you think: *The unions believe they should have a voice in deciding social policy.* **3** (*grammar*) The active **voice** and **passive** voice describe the function of a verb in being either active or passive.
▷ ***verb***: **voices, voicing, voiced**
You **voice** *eg* an opinion when you express it in speech: *She was amongst the first to voice her fears that the plan wouldn't work.*
▷ ***phrases*** **1** You say something **at the top of your voice** when you say it as loud as you can: *You'll have to speak at the top of your voice if the people at the back of the room are to hear.* **2** You **lower your voice** if you begin to speak more quietly; you **raise your voice** if you begin to speak more loudly. **3** You **keep your voice down** if you speak quietly, *eg* so people cannot hear what you are saying: *'Keep your voice down, someone might hear you,' he whispered.*

void /vɔɪd/ *noun*; *adjective*
▷ ***noun*** (*literary*): **voids**
1 A **void** is a large, empty space: *There was a gaping void in the ice just below the tent.* **2** A **void** is also a feeling that someone or something is missing: *It was as if a great void had opened up, and I could not at first believe that we would probably never see each other again.*
▷ ***adjective*** (*formal*)
Something such as a contract or ticket is **void** or **null and void** if it is not valid.

volatile /'vɒlətaɪl/ *adjective*
1 A situation is **volatile** if it is likely to change quickly, especially if it is likely to become more dangerous or violent: *Several people are being held hostage on the plane and the situation remains volatile.* [*same as* **explosive, tense**; *opposite* **calm**] **2** A **volatile** person becomes angry or violent quickly. [*same as* **unstable**; *opposite* **patient, calm**]

volcanic /vɒl'kanɪk/ *adjective*
A **volcanic** area has a lot of volcanoes on it or was formed by volcanoes: *a volcanic island.*

volcano /vɒl'keɪnoʊ/ *noun*: **volcanoes**
A **volcano** is a cone-shaped mountain with an opening at the top, out of which hot melted rock, ash and gases are forced when the volcano erupts.

volition /və'lɪʃən/ *noun* (*uncount*; *legal*)
▷ ***phrase*** You do something **of your own volition** when you do it willingly or choose to do it: *I didn't have to make him do it; he did it of his own volition.*

volley /'vɒlɪ/ *noun*; *verb*
▷ ***noun***: **volleys**
1 A **volley** of gunfire is the firing of several guns at the same time: *A volley of shots rang out across the valley.* **2** In some sports, *eg* tennis and badminton, a **volley** is the shot that you play if you hit the ball back to your opponent before it hits the ground and bounces on your side of the net.
▷ ***verb***: **volleys, volleying, volleyed**
In *eg* tennis and badminton, a player **volleys** if they hit the ball back to their opponent before it touches the ground and bounces.

volleyball /'vɒlɪbɔːl/ *noun* (*uncount*)
Volleyball is a game in which two teams hit a large,

light ball backwards and forwards over a high net with their hands.

volt /voʊlt/ *noun*: **volts**
A **volt** is a measure of the force of an electrical current.

voltage /ˈvoʊltɪdʒ/ *noun*: **voltages**
The **voltage** of an electrical current is a measure of its force expressed as a number of volts.

voluble /ˈvɒljʊbəl/ *adjective (formal)*
A **voluble** person speaks a lot or at great length, with energy or enthusiasm: *He became more voluble as the evening wore on.* — *adverb* **volubly:** *The two Frenchmen at the corner table were arguing volubly about something.*

volume /ˈvɒljuːm/ *noun*: **volumes**
1 (*uncount*) The **volume** on a radio, television or hi-fi system is **a** the amount of sound it produces: *He turned up the volume.* □ *The television was playing at full volume.* **b** the knob that controls the amount of sound coming from it: *The volume has got stuck.* **2 a** A **volume** is **b** a book: *She took a volume off the shelf at random.* **c** a book that is part of a whole series of books: *volume three of the encyclopedia.* **3** (*used in the singular*) The **volume** of an object, gas or liquid is the amount of space that it occupies: *The volume of water expands as it gets hotter.* [compare **capacity**] **4** (*used in the singular*) The **volume** of something is the usually large amount there is of it: *the volume of traffic during the rush hour* □ *the terrific volume of his work.*

voluminous /vəˈljuːmɪnəs/ *adjective*
1 Voluminous clothing is made with a lot of material, which hangs or swings loosely: *in the 50s, when girls wore tight elastic belts and voluminous skirts supported by stiff petticoats.* [*same as* **full**] **2 Voluminous** writings are very full, long and detailed: *Miss Hughes, who edited their voluminous correspondence, does not admit to having been bored by it.*

voluntarily /vɒlənˈtarəlɪ/ *adverb*
You do something **voluntarily** when you do it willingly, or because you choose to, and not because you are forced to: *The judge's ruling was that he had not been forced out of the house as he claimed, but had left it voluntarily.*

voluntary /ˈvɒləntərɪ/ *adjective*
1 Voluntary actions are things you do because you choose to, and not because you are forced to: *Some of them decided to take voluntary redundancy.* □ *Participation in the organized evening activities will be voluntary.* □ *organizations supported by voluntary contributions.* **2 Voluntary** work is done by people who are not paid for it: *She does voluntary work at the local hospital.* **3 Voluntary** workers are people who work but are not paid for it: *The advice office relies on the work of voluntary staff.* **4** A **voluntary** organization has voluntary workers working for it: *The charity is purely a voluntary organization.*

volunteer /vɒlənˈtɪə(r)/ *verb*; *noun*
▻ ***verb***: **volunteers, volunteering, volunteered**
1 You **volunteer** for something if you offer to do or help do it freely, without being persuaded or forced to do it: *She volunteered to stay late to help get the work finished.* □ *Several workers volunteered to retire early.* **2** (*informal*) You **volunteer** someone for something if you promise that they will do a particular job or help another person: *I'm volunteering you for the late shift at work.* **3** You **volunteer** for the army, navy or air force if you offer to join it. [compare **conscript**] **4** You **volunteer** information if you give it without being asked.
▻ ***noun***: **volunteers**
A **volunteer** is **1** a person who willingly offers to do something: *The company needs volunteers for its retirement programme.* **2** a person who does unpaid work: *The charity is looking for volunteers to help in some of its shops.* **3** a person who chooses to join the army, navy or air force. [compare **conscript**]

voluptuous /vəˈlʌptʃʊəs/ *adjective*
A **voluptuous** woman has a shapely, well-developed body that is sexually attractive: *a tall, voluptuous actress.*

vomit /ˈvɒmɪt/ *verb*; *noun*
▻ ***verb***: **vomits, vomited, vomiting**
Someone **vomits** if food and drink comes back up from their stomach and is forced out of their mouth. [compare **throw up**]
▻ ***noun*** (*uncount*)
Vomit is food and drink that has come from a person's stomach and out through their mouth.

voracious /vəˈreɪʃəs/ *adjective*
1 A person or animal is **voracious** if they eat large quantities of food: *that voracious scavenger, the vulture.* **2** You have a **voracious** appetite for something if you want a lot of it or do it often or a lot: *She's a voracious reader.* — *adverb* **voraciously:** *He read voraciously as a child but never looks at a book now.*

vortex /ˈvɔːteks/ *noun* (*formal*): **vortexes** or **vortices** /ˈvɔːtɪsiːz/
1 A **vortex** is a whirlpool or whirlwind. **2** A **vortex** is also a dangerous situation which people cannot stop themselves from being drawn into.

vote /voʊt/ *noun*; *verb*
▻ ***noun***: **votes**
1 There is a **vote** when people formally express their choice or give their opinion, *eg* when they say who should be elected, or which of several ideas they support: *As there are two candidates for this position we'll have to have a vote.* □ *There's going to be a vote on this bill in parliament tomorrow.* **2** (*usually in the singular*) Your **vote** is your opinion or choice, especially in a national election: *The Conservative candidate will get my vote.* **3** (*used in the singular*) People have the **vote** when they have the right to express their choice or opinion in an election: *There are still some countries in the world where women don't have the vote.* **4** (*used in the singular*) The **vote** is the support given by a particular group or number of people, or to a particular candidate or group, in an election: *This candidate will attract the middle-class vote.* □ *She got 43% of the vote.*
▻ ***verb***: **votes, voting, voted**
You **vote** for or against something when you show that you are, or are not, in favour of a proposal or plan; you **vote** for or against someone when you say that you want or do not want them to be elected. You usually vote by making a mark on a piece of paper: *I voted for the Labour candidate at the last election.* □ *He always votes Conservative.* □ *She voted in favour of joining the European Community.*

phrasal verbs
vote in People **vote** a political party **in** if they show in an election that they want that party to govern the country: *Major was voted in with a very slim majority.*
vote out People **vote** a political party **out** if they show in an election that they do not want them to govern the country any more: *Labour were voted out in 1979.*

voter /ˈvoʊtə(r)/ *noun*: **voters**
A **voter** is a person who has the right to vote in an election: *He has lost a lot of the voters' support.*

vouch /vaʊtʃ/ *verb*: **vouches, vouching, vouched**
1 You **vouch** for someone when you can guarantee they will behave properly, and will be responsible for their behaviour: *She offered to vouch for him.* **2** You **vouch** for something if you know and can guarantee that something exists or is reliable: *I can vouch for her honesty.*

voucher /vaʊtʃə(r)/ *noun*: **vouchers**
A **voucher** is a ticket or piece of paper that can be used, instead of money, to buy something: *I bought her a gift voucher for her birthday.*

vouchsafe /vaʊtʃ'seɪf/ *verb* (*literary*): **vouchsafes, vouchsafing, vouchsafed**
You **vouchsafe** *eg* a reply or answer when you give a reply or answer: *I did not vouchsafe to reply.*

vow /vaʊ/ *noun*; *verb*
▷ ***noun***: **vows**
A **vow** is a solemn promise: *I made a vow to never hurt him again.*
▷ ***verb***: **vows, vowing, vowed**
You **vow** something when you promise solemnly to do it: *She vowed to lose weight before the wedding.*

vowel /'vaʊəl/ *noun*: **vowels**
A **vowel** is any speech-sound made with an open mouth and no contact between the mouth, lips, teeth, or tongue. In English, the **vowels** are shown by the letters *a e i o u* and sometimes by *y*. [compare **consonant**]

voyage /'vɔɪɪdʒ/ *noun*: **voyages**
A **voyage** is a long journey, especially one on a ship or in a spacecraft: *She met her husband on the voyage out to India.*

voyager /'vɔɪɪdʒə(r)/ *noun*: **voyagers**
A **voyager** is a person who goes on a usually difficult or dangerous voyage: *the first voyagers across the Atlantic.*

vulgar /'vʌlgə(r)/ *adjective*
1 People describe objects as **vulgar** if they consider them showy and tasteless in style or design: *garish carpets with vulgar designs.* [*same as* **common, tasteless**; *opposite* **tasteful, elegant**] **2** Language or behaviour is described as **vulgar** if it refers in a coarse way to such things as sex, defecation or urination. [*same as* **coarse**; *opposite* **polite**] — *noun* (*uncount*) **vulgarity** /vʌl'garɪti/: *designs of startling vulgarity* ▫ *He had behaved with quite shocking vulgarity.*

vulnerable /'vʌlnərəbəl/ *adjective*
Someone who is **vulnerable** can easily be hurt or harmed physically or emotionally: *It is the children who most vulnerable in situations like this, and they are the ones to suffer.* ▫ *Singapore was imagined to be vulnerable only to attack by sea.* ▫ *You're in a fairly vulnerable position yourself.* ▫ *You feel very vulnerable at a job interview, with all those pairs of coldly critical eyes upon you.* — *noun* (*uncount*) **vulnerability** /vʌlnərə'bɪlɪti/: *her vulnerability to criticism.*

vulture /'vʌltʃə(r)/ *noun*: **vultures**
A **vulture** is a very large bird that feeds mainly on dead animals.

vying /vaɪɪŋ/ *verb*
Vying is the present participle of **vie**.

W or **w** /ˈdʌbəljuː/ *noun*: **Ws** or **w's**
W is the twenty-third letter of the English alphabet: *'Wrap' begins with W.*

wad /wɒd/ *noun*: **wads**
1 A **wad** of something such as paper or cotton wool is a flattened mass of it, used for packing or padding: *She lined the box with wads of newspaper.* **2** A **wad** of banknotes is a thick bundle of them.

waddle /ˈwɒdəl/ *verb* (*derogatory if used about a person*): **waddles, waddling, waddled**
A duck, or a fat person, **waddles** somewhere when they walk along swaying from side to side.

wade /weɪd/ *verb*: **wades, wading, waded**
You **wade** when you walk through deep water: *I waded out deeper and deeper into the lake.* □ *The bridge had collapsed and we had to wade across the river.*

> ***phrasal verb***
> You **wade through** boring or difficult books or papers when you read them slowly and with a lot of effort.

wafer /ˈweɪfə(r)/ *noun*: **wafers**
A **wafer** is a thin light biscuit, eaten especially with ice cream.

waffle¹ /ˈwɒfəl/ *noun*: **waffles**
A **waffle** is a light thick kind of pancake, with a pattern of squares on its surface, usually eaten with jam and cream.

waffle² /ˈwɒfəl/ *verb*; *noun*
▻ ***verb***: **waffles, waffling, waffled**
People **waffle** when they talk or write a lot without saying anything useful.
▻ ***noun*** (*uncount*): *Don't bother to read his article; it's just waffle.*

waft /wɒft/ *verb*: **wafts, wafting, wafted**
Something such as smoke, a smell or a sound **wafts** or **is wafted** somewhere when it is carried through the air: *Children's voices wafted up to us from the valley.* [*same as* **float**]

wag /wag/ *verb*: **wags, wagging, wagged**
1 A dog **wags** its tail when it waves it from side to side as a sign of pleasure; its tail **wags** when it waves from side to side: *The dog ran to greet us, its tail wagging.* **2** You **wag** your finger at someone when you shake it up and down at them, especially while warning or scolding them. **3** (*informal*) Tongues or chins **wag** when people chatter or gossip.

wage¹ /weɪdʒ/ *noun*: **wages**
1 (*used in the singular*) A person's **wage** is the amount of money they are regularly paid, usually per week, for the work they do, especially if this is manual or unskilled work: *In those days a miner's average wage was £5.* **2** (*used in the plural*) A person's **wages** are the actual money they receive for their work: *We had to pay the rent and the household expenses out of my wages.* [see also **salary**, **pay**]

wage² /weɪdʒ/ *verb*: **wages, waging, waged**
People **wage** war or a campaign when they begin it and go on fighting it: *They always seemed to be waging war on neighbouring states.* □ *We have been waging a desperate campaign against the drug-pushers.*

wager /ˈweɪdʒə(r)/ *noun* (*old*): **wagers**
A **wager** is a bet that you make on the possible result of something.

waggle /ˈwagəl/ *verb*: **waggles, waggling, waggled**
You **waggle** something when you move it up and down or from side to side; something **waggles** when it moves up and down or from side to side: *They moved around the dance floor, waggling their arms in the air.* □ *The end of his nose waggled when he talked.*

wagon or **waggon** /ˈwagən/ *noun*: **wagons**
A **wagon** is **1** a four-wheeled vehicle for carrying loads, pulled by a horse. [*same as* **cart**] **2** a railway truck for carrying goods.

waif /weɪf/ *noun*: **waifs**
A **waif** is a child all alone in the world, without a home or family.

wail /weɪl/ *verb*; *noun*
▻ ***verb***: **wails, wailing, wailed**
People **wail** when they cry or complain loudly: *'He keeps pulling my hair,' she wailed.*
▻ ***noun***: **wails:** *There was a wail of indignation from two-year-old Jamie.*

waist /weɪst/ *noun*: **waists**
1 Your **waist** is the narrow middle part of your body between your ribs and your hips: *He put his arm round her waist and led her away.* [see picture at **body**] **2** The **waist** of a piece of clothing is the part shaped to fit your waist: *The waist was getting too tight for me.*

waistband /ˈweɪstband/ *noun*: **waistbands**
The **waistband** on a pair of trousers or a skirt is the strengthened strip of material that fits round your waist.

waistcoat /ˈweɪstkoʊt/ *noun*: **waistcoats**
A **waistcoat** is a close-fitting, sleeveless waist-length garment worn especially by men under their jackets. [see picture at **clothing**]

waistline /ˈweɪstlaɪn/ *noun*: **waistlines**
1 Your **waistline** is the shape or size that you are round the waist: *We tend to lose our waistlines as we get older.* **2** The **waistline** of a dress is the part that is shaped to fit you at, or in the area of, the waist: *a dress with a high waistline.*

wait /weɪt/ *verb*; *noun*
▻ ***verb***: **waits, waiting, waited**
1 You **wait** when you do nothing, or delay doing something, or remain in the same place, until the thing happens that you are expecting to happen: *I had to wait half an hour for a bus.* □ *Wait till you're older.* □ *You go on ahead; don't wait for me.* □ *I waited for her to finish eating.* □ *Children were running about the playground, waiting to be collected.* □ *What are you waiting

for? □ *We were kept waiting for twenty minutes.* **2** You **wait** your turn when you wait till it is your turn to do something. **3** Something **is waiting** for you when it is ready for you to deal with: *A large pile of mail was waiting for him on the hall table.* **4** You say that something can **wait** if you think it can be done or dealt with later: *The washing-up can wait till we get back.* **5** You **wait** at table when you act as a waiter or waitress and serve others with food. — *noun* **waiting:** *The waiting was agony.* □ *There's usually a waiting period of about a week.*

▻ ***noun*** (*usually in the singular*): **waits:** *We've got a wait of 40 minutes till the train goes.*

▻ ***phrases*** **1** Someone who **can't wait** to do something is impatient and eager to do it: *I can't wait to tell the others.* □ *She couldn't wait to leave school.* **2** You say **wait a moment** or **a minute** or **a second** when you are interrupting what someone else is saying, or what you are saying yourself: *Wait a second; that can't be true.* □ *Wait a minute; have I got that right?* **3** You say **wait and see** to people to tell them to be patient about something, and not get anxious unnecessarily: *The treatment may or may not help; we must just wait and see.* **4** You say **'you wait'** to someone when you are giving them a warning or threatening them: *You won't find marriage as easy as you think; just you wait!*

> ***phrasal verbs***
> **wait about** or **wait around** You **wait about** or **around** when you do nothing, or remain in the same place, till something happens that you are expecting to happen: *I don't want to have to wait about at the airport.*
> **wait on** **1** You **wait on** people in a restaurant when you act as a waiter or waitress and serve them with food. **2** You **wait on** people, or **wait on** them hand and foot, when you do everything for them and get them everything they need.
> **wait up** You **wait up** when you stay out of bed at night waiting for someone's arrival or return, or some other event: *I'll be late back; don't wait up for me.*

waiter /ˈweɪtə(r)/ *noun*: **waiters**
A **waiter** is a man or boy who serves people with food and drink at a restaurant.

waiting list /ˈweɪtɪŋ lɪst/ *noun*: **waiting lists**
You are put on the **waiting list** for something that you have asked for but is not yet available or possible when your name is added to list of people also wanting it: *There's a long waiting list for non-urgent surgical operations.*

waiting room /ˈweɪtɪŋ ruːm/ *noun*: **waiting rooms**
A **waiting room** is a room for people to wait in, *eg* at a railway station or doctor's surgery.

waitress /ˈweɪtrəs/ *noun*: **waitresses**
A **waitress** is a woman or girl who serves people with food and drink at a restaurant.

waive /weɪv/ *verb*: **waives, waiving, waived**
1 Someone in authority **waives** a rule in a particular situation when they decide that it need not be obeyed. [*opposite* **maintain**] **2** You **waive** your claim or right to something when you decide not to insist on it.

wake[1] /weɪk/ *verb*: **wakes, waking, woke** (*AmE* **waked**), **woken** (*AmE* **waked**)
You **wake** when you stop sleeping and become conscious; someone or something **wakes** you when they make you stop sleeping: *I woke at about 5.00 am.* □ *The birds woke me.* □ *Could you wake me early?* □ *He was woken by the sound of shouting.* [compare **waken, awake, awaken**]

▻ ***phrase*** Your **waking hours** are the time you spend awake as distinct from sleeping: *He spent all his waking hours working at his computer.*

> ***phrasal verb***
> **wake up** **1** You **wake up** when you stop sleeping and become conscious; someone or something **wakes** you **up** when they make you stop sleeping: *Once I've woken up I like to get up.* **2** Something **wakes** you **up** when it stirs you out of a lazy or inactive state: *I give my students a test from time to time, which usually wakes them up.* **3** You **wake up** to a fact, circumstance or situation when you become aware of it: *It's time they woke up to the fact that young people are not all lazy good-for-nothings.* □ *He suddenly woke up to his danger.*

wake[2] /weɪk/ *noun*: **wakes**
The **wake** of a ship or aircraft is the line of disturbed water or air left by it.

▻ ***phrases*** **1** You leave something **in your wake** if you cause it or leave it behind you wherever you go: *As a girl she left broken hearts in her wake wherever she went.* □ *The fire raged on, leaving blackened trees in its wake.* **2** One thing follows **in the wake of** another if it is caused by the other: *Disease nearly always follows in the wake of floods.*

waken /ˈweɪkən/ *verb*: **wakens, wakening, wakened**
1 You **waken** when you wake up; something **wakens** you when it wakes you up: *He wakened feeling refreshed.* □ *The sun wakened me early.* **2** You **waken** to a fact or situation, especially an unpleasant one, when you become aware of it: *Too late she wakened to the terrible reality.*

walk /wɔːk/ *verb; noun*

▻ ***verb***: **walks, walking, walked**
1 You **walk** when you go in some direction on foot, moving your feet one after the other and always having one or other foot on the ground: *Is your baby walking yet?* □ *They walked along the street stopping to look in shop windows.* □ *We must have walked at least six miles.* □ *He walked the streets looking for work and a place to stay.* **2** You **walk** someone somewhere when you walk there with them, or make them walk somewhere, supporting or dragging them: *He used to walk me home every day after school.* □ *They each grabbed one of her arms and walked her to the car.* **3** You **walk** a dog when you take it out for exercise.

▻ ***noun***: **walks**
1 A **walk** is a journey on foot: *I'm just taking the dog for a walk.* □ *Who wants to come for a long walk with me?* □ *It's a five-minute walk to the school.* **2** (*used in the singular*) A **walk** is the motion, or pace, of walking: *She slowed to a walk.* **3** (*used in the singular*) A person's **walk** is their distinctive manner of walking: *I recognised his walk.* **4** A **walk** is a street or wide formal path: *Her address is 155 Leith Walk.* **5** A **walk** is a route for walking, for pleasure or exercise: *There are some nice walks round this area.*

> ***phrasal verbs***
> **walk away** You **walk away** with a prize when you win it easily.
> **walk in on** You **walk in on** someone when you disturb them unintentionally by entering the place where they are, not knowing they are there.
> **walk into** You **walk into** trouble or a dangerous situation when you involve yourself in it through your own lack of caution.

walk off **1** Someone **walks off** when they go away: *He walked off leaving her with three small children.* **2** You **walk off** with a prize when you win it easily. **3** (*informal*) Someone **walks off** with something that does not belong to them when they steal it, or take it without asking the permission of the owner: *We don't want people getting into the house and walking off with all our valuables.*
walk out **1** Employees **walk out** when they go on strike and leave their workplace in a group. **2** You **walk out** of a meeting, film or other show when you leave it before the end as a sign of your anger or disapproval. **3** You **walk out** on someone when you leave them: *It isn't the first time my husband's walked out on me.*

walker /'wɔːkə(r)/ *noun*: **walkers**
A **walker** is a person who goes for walks, especially in the hills or countryside, for pleasure and exercise: *She'd always been a keen walker.*

walkie-talkie /wɔːkɪ 'tɔːkɪ/ *noun*: **walkie-talkies**
A **walkie-talkie** is a small personal radio that *eg* members of the police force carry round with them and use for communicating with colleagues.

walking /'wɔːkɪŋ/ *noun* (*uncount*)
Walking is the activity of going for walks in the hills or countryside for pleasure and exercise: *a walking holiday* □ *a pair of walking boots* □ *She enjoyed walking and cycling.* [*same as* **hiking**]

walking stick /'wɔːkɪŋ stɪk/ *noun*: **walking sticks**
A **walking stick** is a stick, especially one with a curved handle, that people use for support or balance in walking.

walk of life /wɔːk əv 'laɪf/ *noun*: **walks of life**
Your **walk of life** is your social rank, and the kind of job or profession you have: *We have members from all walks of life, and they all get on well with each other.*

walkout /'wɔːkaʊt/ *noun*: **walkouts**
A **walkout** is a strike: *Employees staged a walkout today at the local factory.*

walkover /'wɔːkoʊvə(r)/ *noun*: **walkovers**
You describe a competition or match that you have won as a **walkover** if you won it easily.

wall /wɔːl/ *noun*; *verb*
▻ ***noun***: **walls**
1 A **wall** is a solid vertical brick or stone structure of narrow width, substantial length, and variable height, that serves, *eg*, as a barrier, a territorial division or a protection: *We sat on the wall and ate our sandwiches.* □ *a high garden wall.* [see picture at **house**] **2** The **walls** of a room or building are its vertical sides: *The place will look better once we've hung some pictures on the walls.* □ *There was only one window in the north wall.* [see picture at **living room**] **3** (*biology*) The sides of a cell or of a hollow organ can be referred to as its **walls**. **4** A mass of something forming a barrier can be called a **wall** of something: *a wall of fire* □ *a wall of water* □ *a wall of rock.*
▻ ***phrase*** (*informal*) Something that is **driving**, or **sending you up the wall** is making you feel very angry and frustrated. [*same as* **drive you mad**]
▻ ***verb***: **walls, walling, walled**

phrasal verbs
wall off You **wall off** an area when you build a wall round it to separate it: *We walled off the vegetable garden.*
wall up A room, window or doorway **is walled up** when a wall is built to close it up.

wallaby /'wɒləbɪ/ *noun*: **wallabies**
A **wallaby** is a plant-eating Australian animal similar to, but smaller than, a kangaroo.

walled /wɔːld/ *adjective*
A **walled** city, town or garden is surrounded by a wall.

wallet /'wɒlɪt/ *noun*: **wallets**
1 A **wallet** is a flat folding case made *eg* of leather, for holding banknotes and credit cards. [*same as* **pocketbook**] **2** A transparent plastic folder or envelope for holding papers is often called a **wallet**.

wallop /'wɒləp/ *verb* (*informal*): **wallops, walloping, walloped**
You **wallop** someone when you hit them hard: *Your father'll wallop you when he finds out.* [*same as* **spank, beat, smack**]

wallow /'wɒloʊ/ *verb*: **wallows, wallowing, wallowed**
1 An animal **wallows** in mud or shallow water when it rolls about in it for pleasure. **2** You **wallow** in circumstances or emotions, whether pleasant or unpleasant, when you let yourself enjoy them in an unreasonable, excessive or selfish way: *He wallowed in her admiration.* □ *wallowing in self-pity.* **3** A ship **wallows** when it rolls from side to side in a rough sea. [*same as* **flounder**]

wallpaper /'wɔːlpeɪpə(r)/ *noun*; *verb*
▻ ***noun*** (*uncount*)
Wallpaper is paper used to decorate the interior walls of buildings: *patterned wallpaper.* [see picture at **living room**]
▻ ***verb***: **wallpapers, wallpapering, wallpapered:** *I've at last finished wallpapering the bedroom.*

wall-to-wall /wɔːl tə 'wɔːl/ *adjective*
A **wall-to-wall** carpet covers the whole floor of a room.

walnut /'wɔːlnʌt/ *noun*: **walnuts**
A **walnut** is an edible nut with a hard round wrinkled light-brown shell, formed in two halves.

walrus /'wɔːlrəs/ *noun*: **walruses** or **walrus**
A **walrus** is a large sea animal similar to a seal, that has whiskers and two long downward-pointing teeth or tusks.

waltz /wɔːlts/ or /wɔːls/ *noun*; *verb*
▻ ***noun***: **waltzes**
A **waltz** is a slow or fast dance that you perform with a partner, with a rhythm of three beats to the bar; a **waltz** is also a piece of music for this dance.
▻ ***verb***: **waltzes, waltzing, waltzed**
1 You **waltz** with someone when you perform a waltz with them. **2** (*informal*) You **waltz** somewhere when you walk there with easy confidence: *She waltzed in here expecting us to stop everything and attend to her.*

wan /wɒn/ *adjective*: **wanner, wannest**
Someone who is **wan** is pale and tired, *eg* from illness, exhaustion or grief.

wand /wɒnd/ *noun*: **wands**
A **wand** is a long thin rod that magicians or fairies wave about in order to perform magic.

wander /'wɒndə(r)/ *verb*: **wanders, wandering, wandered**
1 You **wander** when you walk or travel about, aiming for no particular destination: *We wandered through the old part of the town.* □ *She sometimes wandered the streets alone at night.* **2** Your mind or attention **wanders** when you stop concentrating on what you are doing and think about other things: *Sometimes during lessons her thoughts wandered.* [*same as* **stray**] **3** You say a person **is wandering** when their mind is confused

and they say things that don't make sense, *eg* when they are very old or very ill.

wane /weɪn/ *verb*: **wanes, waning, waned**
1 The moon **wanes** when it gets narrower as the sun lights up less of its surface. [*opposite* **wax**] **2** Something that has been great, strong or powerful, **wanes** when it decreases in size, strength, power or influence: *Support for the party was waning rapidly.* [*same as* **decline**]
▻ ***phrase*** Something that is **on the wane** is getting smaller or weaker: *Britain's influence was already on the wane.*

wangle /ˈwaŋgəl/ *verb* (*informal*): **wangles, wangling, wangled**
You **wangle** something you want when you manage to get it by clever organization or persuasion: *She managed to wangle the occasional trip abroad at the firm's expense.*

want /wɒnt/ *verb*; *noun*
▻ ***verb***: **wants, wanting, wanted**
1 You **want** something when you feel a need or desire for it: *Do you want anything to eat?* ▫ *What do you want for your birthday?* ▫ *I can make more copies if you want.* ▫ *I ought to go, but I don't want to.* ▫ *She wants us to let her know by tonight.* ▫ *I want these essays handed in by Friday.* ▫ *I don't want you wasting your time.* ▫ *The manager wants you* [= wants to see you]. ▫ *The cat wants out* [= wants to go out].

> Note that when the verb is positive, the politer form *would like* may be used instead of *want*: *I'd like these finished by six o'clock. What would you like for tea?*

2 If you tell someone they **want** to do something you are advising them to do it: *You want to take more care.* ▫ *You want to turn left just before you reach the school.* ▫ *You don't want to miss 'The Ladykillers' on television tonight.* **3** (*informal*) Something **wants** doing if it needs to be done: *Do these potatoes want peeling?* ▫ *You want your head examined* [= you must be crazy]. ▫ *These boots want a good clean.* **4** A person who **is wanted** is **a** being asked for by someone: *You're wanted on the telephone.* **b** being sought by the police: *He's wanted for murder.*
▻ ***noun***: **wants**
1 (*used in the plural*) Your **wants** are the things you need or require: *The local shop supplies all our wants.* **2** (*used in the singular*) A **want** of something is a lack of it: *Your remarks showed a want of tact to say the least.* **3** (*uncount*) **Want** is poverty or need: *We must help those in want.*
▻ ***phrases*** **1** You do or use one thing **for want of** another when you do it or use it because the other is not possible or available: *We usually refer to it as the patio, for want of a better term.* **2** You are **in want of** something when you need it: *I was in want of a bit of sympathy and support.*

wanting /ˈwɒntɪŋ/ *adjective* (*literary*)
▻ ***phrase*** If you **find** someone or something **wanting**, or if they are **found wanting**, they are not as good as you expect them to be: *When courage is needed, we shall not be found wanting.*

wanton /ˈwɒntən/ *adjective*
You describe destruction or cruelty as **wanton** if there seems to be no reason or motive for it: *They had been causing wanton damage to park benches and other council property.* [*same as* **gratuitous, reckless**] — *adverb* **wantonly:** *wantonly destroying the environment.* [*same as* **gratuitously, recklessly**]

war /wɔː(r)/ *noun*; *verb*
▻ ***noun*** (*count or uncount*): **wars**
1 A **war** is a period of fighting between countries; **war** is fighting between countries, or an openly acknowledged state of armed conflict: *medieval wars* ▫ *the Iran-Iraq war* ▫ *In 1939 war was declared on Germany.* ▫ *the threat of nuclear war.* **2** Any long-continued struggle, campaign or fierce contest can be called a **war**: *the war against drug-dealing* ▫ *a trade war* ▫ *We must make war on the cigarette-advertisers.*
▻ ***verb***: **wars, warring, warred**
Countries **war** with each other when they fight each other: *when Britain and France were warring over the possession of Malta and Gibraltar.* — *adjective* **warring:** *warring nations.*
▻ ***phrases*** **1** Countries that are **at war** are openly fighting each other. **2** A country **goes to war** when it starts fighting with another country. **3** (*informal*) You say that someone looks as if they **have been in the wars** if they appear to have been injured.

warble /ˈwɔːbəl/ *verb* (*literary*): **warbles, warbling, warbled**
A bird **warbles** when it sings sweetly.

ward /wɔːd/ *noun*; *verb*
▻ ***noun***: **wards**
1 A **ward** in a hospital is a room with beds for patients: *She's been put in Ward 5, the children's ward.* **2** A **ward** is any of the areas into which a town or district is divided for elections. **3** (*legal*) A **ward** is a person, especially a child whose parents are dead, who is in the care of an adult acting as their guardian; a person is made a **ward of court** when they are put under the protection of a court of law for their own safety.
▻ ***verb***: **wards, warding, warded**

> ***phrasal verb***
> **ward off** **1** When someone or something is hitting you, you **ward off** the blows by shielding or protecting yourself from them. [*same as* **fend off**] **2** You **ward off** unpleasant things such as danger, trouble or illness when you do something to prevent them from affecting you: *Some people take vitamin pills to ward off colds and flu.* ▫ *She chanted a spell to ward off the demons.* [*same as* **stave off**]

-ward /wəd/ *suffix*
You can form adverbs of direction by adding **-ward** or **-wards** to nouns for places or directions; you can form adjectives of direction by adding **-ward** to nouns for places or directions: *We were travelling northwards.* ▫ *going homewards* ▫ *She glanced heavenward.* ▫ *an eastward direction* ▫ *the homeward journey.*

warden /ˈwɔːdən/ *noun*: **wardens**
1 The **warden** of a hostel or a student residence is the person in charge of it and of the people staying in it. **2** A **warden** is a public official responsible for ensuring that the law is obeyed: *a traffic warden* ▫ *African game wardens.* **3** (*AmE*) The **warden** of a prison is the officer in charge of it.

warder /ˈwɔːdə(r)/ or **wardress** /ˈwɔːdrəs/ *noun*: **warders** or **wardresses**
A **warder**, or **wardress**, is a male, or female, prison officer in charge of prisoners.

wardrobe /ˈwɔːdroʊb/ *noun*: **wardrobes**
1 A **wardrobe** is a tall cupboard, usually in your bedroom, for you to hang your clothes in. **2** You can refer to your own collection of clothes as your **wardrobe**: *I must go through my wardrobe and see if I've got anything suitable to wear for the wedding.*

-wards see **-ward**.

ware /wɛə(r)/ *noun*: **wares**
1 (*uncount*) **Ware** is used in naming types of manufactured goods that are made of a particular material (*eg glassware*, *silverware*), or have a particular range of use (*eg kitchenware*). **2** (*used in the plural*) A shopkeeper's or trader's **wares** are the goods that they have for sale.

warehouse /ˈwɛəhaʊs/ *noun*: **warehouses**
A **warehouse** is a large building in which goods or materials are stored.

warfare /ˈwɔːfɛə(r)/ *noun* (*uncount*)
Warfare is the activity of fighting wars: *chemical warfare* □ *Minor quarrels would suddenly flare into open warfare.*

warhead /ˈwɔːhɛd/ *noun*: **warheads**
A **warhead** is the front part of a missile, containing the explosive: *nuclear warheads.*

warlike /ˈwɔːlaɪk/ *adjective*
A **warlike** people or nation are well-trained in fighting, and keen to start and fight wars: *Most of the east-coast tribes were gentle rather than warlike.* [*same as* **belligerent**]

warm /wɔːm/ *adjective*; *verb*
▷ ***adjective***: **warmer**, **warmest**
1 Something that is **warm** has a moderately high, comfortable and pleasant temperature; you are **warm** when you feel moderately and comfortably hot, but not too hot: *a nice warm bedroom* □ *Yesterday was lovely and warm.* □ *warm weather* □ *Are you sure you're warm enough? Come nearer the fire.* **2 Warm** clothes are made of thick fabrics, or of wool, to protect you from the cold: *Bring a warm sweater for the evenings.* **3 Warm** people are kind-hearted, friendly, generous and affectionate: *She had a warm and motherly personality.* □ *They gave me such a warm welcome.* □ *The hotel had a warm and friendly atmosphere.* □ *He was rarely warm or affectionate.* □ *Thank you for your warm and enthusiastic support.* [*opposite* **cool**, **cold**, **unfriendly**] **4 Warm** colours are typically deep and strong, and contain a lot of red or yellow. **5** You tell someone they are getting **warm** when they are getting close to the right answer, *eg* in a guessing game. — *adverb* **warmly:** *Make sure the children are warmly dressed.* □ *He shook her hand warmly.*
▷ ***verb***: **warms, warming, warmed**
1 You **warm** something when you increase its temperature, or make it hotter, by applying heat to it: *The milk needs to be warmed slightly.* □ *We haven't enough hot-water bottles to warm all the beds.* **2** You **warm** a part of you, or **warm** yourself, by touching, or getting close to, a source of heat: *She warmed her hands on her coffee cup.* □ *He was warming himself in front of the fire.*

phrasal verbs
warm to 1 You **warm to** a job or an idea when you become more enthusiastic about it or interested in it: *At first he was unwilling to consider moving, but he's gradually warming to the idea.* **2** You **warm** to a person when you begin to like them or approve of them more.
warm up 1 You **warm** something **up** when you increase its temperature or make it hotter; something **warms up** when it increases in temperature or gets hotter: *I'll warm up the soup.* □ *The coffee soon warmed us up.* □ *It warms up very quickly once the sun rises.* [*opposite* **cool down**] **2** A party or other event **warms up** when it gets livelier. **3** An engine or other machine **warms up** when it reaches a condition ready for use a short time after you have switched it on or started it. **4** You **warm up** for some energetic activity such as a race by exercising your body gently in preparation for it. [see also **warm-up**]

warm-blooded /ˈwɔːmblʌdɪd/ *adjective*
Warm-blooded animals, such as human beings, have a blood temperature that is higher than that of the surrounding atmosphere and remains more or less the same all the time. [*opposite* **cold-blooded**]

warmhearted /ˈwɔːmhɑːtɪd/ *adjective*
A **warmhearted** person is kind, affectionate and generous. [*opposite* **cold**]

warmonger /ˈwɔːmʌŋgə(r)/ *noun*: **warmongers**
A **warmonger** is someone in a position of influence who encourages people to prepare for, or start, a war. [*opposite* **pacifist**]

warmth /wɔːmθ/ *noun* (*uncount*)
1 Warmth is pleasant or comfortable heat, or the condition or quality of being warm: *We lay on our backs, enjoying the sun's warmth.* □ *They lay close together for warmth.* □ *The thin blanket provided some warmth.* **2 Warmth** is affection, friendliness or enthusiasm: *We were immediately won over by her warmth and friendliness.* □ *'I suppose we could try,' he said without warmth.*

warm-up /ˈwɔːmʌp/ *noun*: **warm-ups**
A **warm-up** is a series of exercises you do to prepare your body for some energetic activity, such as a race: *warm-up exercises.*

warn /wɔːn/ *verb*: **warns, warning, warned**
1 You **warn** people about a possible or approaching danger or difficulty when you make them aware of it, or inform them in advance about it: *We were warned that there might be delays.* □ *Doctors are not doing enough to warn the public of the dangers of these new pain-killing drugs.* [*same as* **alert**] **2** You **warn** someone to do something when you advise them strongly to do it: *He warned us to book early.* □ *The AA are warning drivers not to travel today unless their journey is absolutely necessary.* [*same as* **advise**] **3** You **warn** someone when you scold them for having done something wrong, and threaten them with punishment if they repeat the offence: *There'll be trouble next time you do that, I'm warning you!*

phrasal verb
You **warn** people **off** when you order them, or force them, with threats of danger or punishment, to go away, or stop their investigations into something: *The sight of a burglar alarm does warn the average intruder off.*

warning /ˈwɔːnɪŋ/ *noun*; *adjective*
▷ ***noun***: **warnings**
1 A **warning** is a statement issued to make people aware of a possible danger or difficulty; a happening that makes you aware of a problem or danger can also be called a **warning**: *The meteorological office have issued the following gale warning.* □ *There's a police warning of icy roads this morning.* □ *You should regard this heart attack as a warning.* **2** A **warning** is also a scolding for an offence, with a threat of punishment if the offence is repeated: *There'll be no second warning; next time you'll be expelled from the school.*
▷ ***adjective***: *One of the warning signs is pain in the left arm.* □ *He quickly changed the subject, in response to a warning glance from his wife.* — *adverb* **warningly**: *She glanced warningly in his direction.*

warp /wɔːp/ *verb*: **warps, warping, warped**
1 Materials such as wood **warp** or **are warped** when they become twisted out of shape through the shrink-

ing and expanding effects of damp and heat: *Doors and window frames will warp if left untreated.* **2** Something **warps** a person's character when it damages it so that it becomes strange or abnormal: *adult personalities warped by the experience of childhood abuse.* — *adjective* **warped:** *a warped sense of humour.*

▻ ***noun*: warps**

1 A **warp** in a continuous dimension such as time or space is a break or an irregularity, such as a displacement forwards or backwards. **2** (*usually in the singular*) In weaving, the **warp** is the set of threads stretched the length of the loom, under and over which the other set of threads are passed. [see also **weft**]

warpath /ˈwɔːpɑːθ/ *noun* (*used in the singular*)

▻ ***phrase*** You say someone is **on the warpath** when they are angry and in a mood for fighting or for scolding someone.

warrant /ˈwɒrənt/ *verb*; *noun*

▻ ***verb*: warrants, warranting, warranted**

Something **warrants** a particular action if it makes it necessary or desirable: *The circumstances are suspicious enough to warrant a full investigation.* [*same as* **justify**]

▻ ***noun*: warrants**

A **warrant** is a legal document giving permission for something, *eg* arresting someone, or searching property: *The police cannot enter these premises without a search warrant.*

warren /ˈwɒrən/ *noun*: **warrens**

A **warren** is an underground system of tunnels linking rabbit burrows and holes.

warrior /ˈwɒrɪə(r)/ *noun*: **warriors**

A **warrior** is a skilled fighting man, especially of earlier times.

warship /ˈwɔːʃɪp/ *noun*: **warships**

A **warship** is a ship equipped with guns, for fighting battles at sea.

wart /wɔːt/ *noun*: **warts**

A **wart** is a little hard lump that grows on your skin, especially on your face or the backs of your hands.

wartime /ˈwɔːtaɪm/ *noun* (*uncount*)

Wartime is a period during which a war is going on: *a wartime recipe book* □ *People have to put up with a lot of hardship in wartime.*

wary /ˈwɛərɪ/ *adjective*: **warier, wariest**

You are **wary** about something if you are cautious about it, usually because it is new, or because it might involve danger or cause problems: *Be wary of accepting a lift from anyone.* — *adverb* **warily**: *'How much will it cost?' she asked warily.*

was /wɒz/ *verb*

Was is the form of the past tense of **be** that is used with *I*, *he*, *she* and *it*.

wash /wɒʃ/ *verb*; *noun*

▻ ***verb*: washes, washing, washed**

1 You **wash** something when you clean it with soap and water: *She usually washed the clothes on a Monday.* □ *I washed and dried the dishes.* □ *This fabric washes very well.* □ *I must wash those dirty marks off the wall.* **2** You **wash**, or **wash** a part of you, when you clean yourself with soap and water; an animal **washes** itself when it licks itself all over; you **wash** an injury when you let water flow over it: *Always wash your hands before eating.* □ *I washed and dressed hastily.* □ *Wash cuts thoroughly before you cover them.* **3** Water **washes** against or over something when it flows against or over it: *The water had risen and was already washing over her shoes.* **4** Flowing water **washes** objects or substances somewhere when it sweeps them along: *Her body was washed ashore some miles up the coast.* □ *Part of the bridge had been washed away.* □ *Dangerous chemicals are being washed downstream.* □ *Some of the sewage washes straight into the sea.* **5** (*informal*) If you say that a particular excuse or theory won't **wash**, you mean that it has obvious things wrong with it, so people are unlikely to believe it: *That explanation won't wash with the committee.*

▻ ***noun*: washes**

1 (*usually in the singular*) You give something a **wash** when you wash it; you have a **wash** when you wash yourself. **2** (*used in the singular*) The **wash** is all the clothes washed together on any occasion, or the process of washing, drying and ironing them them: *Is my blue shirt still in the wash?* □ *the average family wash.* **3** A **wash** is a thin application of water-based paint *eg* on walls or in pictures.

phrasal verbs

wash down 1 You **wash down** a pill by swallowing it with a drink of water; you **wash down** food when you have drink to accompany it. **2** You **wash down** walls or other vertical surfaces when you wash them from top to bottom: *The paintwork needs washing down.*

wash out 1 You **wash out** a dirty mark or stain when you get rid of it by washing with soap and water: *That coffee stain hasn't washed out of my skirt.* **2** You **wash out** a container when you wash the inside of it thoroughly. **3** A match or other sports event **is washed out** when it has to be cancelled because of rain.

wash up 1 You **wash up** when you wash the dishes and cutlery that have been used for a meal. **2** (*AmE*) You **wash up** when you wash your face and hands: *I'll go and get washed up before dinner.* **3** Something **is washed up** somewhere when it is carried there by flowing water or the sea: *A lot of fish had been washed up on the shore during the storm.*

washable /ˈwɒʃəbəl/ *adjective*

Washable clothes or fabrics can be washed without being damaged: *The label will tell you whether it's washable.*

washbasin /ˈwɒʃbeɪsən/ *noun*: **washbasins**

A **washbasin** or **basin** is a bowl-shaped fitting in a bathroom, usually fixed to a wall, with hot and cold taps, a plug and a waste pipe. [see picture at **bathroom**]

washcloth /ˈwɒʃklɒθ/ *noun* (*AmE*): **washcloths**

A **washcloth** is a small square cloth for washing yourself with. [*same as* **flannel**, **facecloth**; see picture at **bathroom**]

washed-out /wɒʃtˈaʊt/ *adjective*

1 Colours that are **washed-out** are pale and faded-looking: *washed-out pink curtains.* **2** Someone who is **washed-out** looks pale and tired.

washer /ˈwɒʃə(r)/ *noun*: **washers**

A **washer** is a flat ring of rubber or metal for keeping a joint tight.

washing /ˈwɒʃɪŋ/ *noun* (*uncount*)

The **washing** is clothes collected together ready for washing, or clothes that are in the process of being washed or dried: *He was in the garden hanging out the washing.*

washing machine /ˈwɒʃɪŋ məʃiːn/ *noun*: **washing machines**

A **washing machine** is a machine for washing clothes. [see picture at **kitchen**]

washing powder /ˈwɒʃɪŋ paʊdə(r)/ *noun* (*uncount*)
Washing powder is soap or detergent in the form of powder, for washing clothes.

washing-up /wɒʃɪŋˈʌp/ *noun* (*uncount*)
You do the **washing-up** when you wash the dishes and cutlery that have been used for a meal: *Is this the washing-up bowl?* □ *a bottle of washing-up liquid.* [see picture at **kitchen**]

washout /ˈwɒʃaʊt/ *noun*: **washouts**
1 (*informal*) An event that is a **washout** is a failure: *The demonstration was a complete washout.* **2** A match or other sports event that is cancelled or stopped because of rain is also a **washout**.

washroom /ˈwɒʃruːm/ *noun* (*AmE*): **washrooms**
A **washroom** is a room containing toilets and washbasins, *eg* in an office building.

wasn't /ˈwɒzənt/
Wasn't is the spoken, and the informal written, form of **was not**: *She wasn't pleased.* □ *It was a great evening, wasn't it?*

wasp /wɒsp/ *noun*: **wasps**
A **wasp** is a stinging insect similar to a bee, with a thin waist and a black-and-yellow-striped body.

wastage /ˈweɪstɪdʒ/ *noun* (*uncount*)
Wastage of something is the circumstance of wasting it: *the appalling wastage of human lives.*

waste /weɪst/ *verb*; *noun*; *adjective*
▻ ***verb***: **wastes, wasting, wasted**
1 You **waste** time, money or energy when you use or spend too much of them on unimportant or unnecessary things: *Don't waste time checking the figures just now.* □ *It's the job of advertisers to help us waste our money.* □ *You're wasting your energy on something that isn't worthwhile.* [*same as* **squander**] **2** You **waste** things when you throw them away unused: *You're not going to waste all that food, are you?* **3** You **waste** an opportunity when you don't take advantage of it; you **waste** your talents when you fail to make the best use of them. **4** Something **is wasted** on someone if they do not deserve it or appreciate it: *I'm not going to waste any more sympathy on her.* □ *A beautiful house like that is wasted on Jack; he knows nothing about architecture.* **5** You **waste** no time in doing something if you do it as soon as possible: *He certainly wasted no time in ingratiating himself with the management and getting himself promoted.*
▻ ***noun***: **wastes**
1 (*used in the singular*) You say that something is a **waste** of time, money or energy if you think it does not deserve to have time, money or energy spent on it: *Christmas presents are a terrible waste of money.* **2** (*used in the singular*) A **waste** of an opportunity, or of your talents, is the failure to make the best use of them. **3** (*uncount*) **Waste** is the unnecessary using up of resources: *The waste of paper in most offices is quite shocking.* **4** (*uncount*) **Waste** from a manufacturing process is the materials and substances that are thrown away after use: *industrial waste.* **5** (*uncount*; *formal*) The body's **waste** is the substances excreted from it in the urine or faeces. **6** (*often in the plural*; *literary*) A **waste** is large expanse of empty and infertile land: *the Arctic wastes.*
▻ ***adjective***
1 Waste material is material that is rejected because it is not needed: *waste paper.* **2 Waste** ground or land is ground that is lying unused, uninhabited or uncultivated. **3** (*formal*) The body's **waste** products are substances excreted in the urine or faeces.
▻ ***phrase*** Something **goes to waste** if it is thrown away unused or allowed to rot or go bad so that it cannot be used.

phrasal verb
People **waste away** when they become thin and weak through illness.

wastebasket /ˈweɪstbaskɪt/ *noun*: **wastebaskets**
A **wastebasket** is a wastepaper basket.

wastebin /ˈweɪstbɪn/ *noun*: **wastebins**
A **wastebin** is a bin for rubbish. [see picture at **kitchen**]

wasted /ˈweɪstɪd/ *adjective*
A **wasted** action is one that is unnecessary or that achieves nothing: *It was a wasted visit; she was busy and couldn't see us.*

wasteful /ˈweɪstfəl/ *adjective*
An activity that is **wasteful** uses too much of a particular resource, or uses it up carelessly: *It's wasteful to leave the tap running.*

wasteland /ˈweɪstland/ *noun*
A **wasteland** is an area of empty and infertile land.

wastepaper basket /ˈweɪstpeɪpə bɑːskɪt/ *noun*: **wastepaper baskets**
A **wastepaper basket** or **wastepaper bin** is a basket or bin for waste paper and other household or office waste. [see picture at **living room**]

waste pipe /ˈweɪst paɪp/ *noun*: **waste pipes**
A **waste pipe** is a pipe carrying waste water from a sink, washbasin or bath.

watch /wɒtʃ/ *verb*; *noun*
▻ ***verb***: **watches, watching, watched**
1 You **watch** someone or something when you look at them moving or doing something: *He stood watching the children playing in the park.* □ *We watched the procession go past.* □ *I'm just bathing the baby; stay and watch if you like.* □ *I don't like being watched.* □ *Watch how a horse's legs move when it runs.* **2** You **watch** television, a programme, a match, or other performance or entertainment when you spend time looking at it and seeing how it develops or turns out: *We usually watch 'Question Time' on a Thursday.* **3** You **watch** someone or something when you guard them, look after them, attend to them or keep checking them: *Could you watch the children for me while I go to the chemist's?* □ *She asked us to watch her handbag.* □ *Watch the milk; make sure it doesn't boil over.* **4** You **watch** a situation when you follow what happens and see how it develops: *We have all been watching developments in the Middle East.* **5** The police **watch** a person when they follow them and spy on them; they **watch** a building when they keep it under observation. **6** You **watch** what you're doing when you pay proper attention and take care to avoid accidents: *Do watch where you're going! You nearly knocked me over!* □ *Careful! Watch you don't slip!*
▻ ***noun***: **watches**
1 A **watch** is a small clock that you wear usually on a strap round your wrist for telling the time: *I glanced at my watch and found it had stopped.* **2** (*count or uncount*) A **watch** is a period of duty during which you look after something, *eg* a ship, so that you can warn people of danger; you keep **watch**, or are on **watch**, when you are performing the duty of looking out for danger: *The night was divided into two four-hour watches.*
▻ ***phrases*** **1** You **keep a watch on** a situation when you observe it closely and see how it develops, so that you can take the right action when necessary. **2** You are **on the watch for** a particular thing when you are waiting for it to appear or happen: *They'll be on the watch for mistakes.* **3** (*informal*) You say **'watch it!'** to someone to warn them to be careful. **4** For **watch your step** see **step**.

phrasal verbs

watch out **1** You **watch out** when you take care and pay attention to what you are doing: *You can easily take the wrong road if you don't watch out.* **2** You **watch out** for something when you wait for it to appear or happen, so that you can take the right action: *Watch out for sheep on the road.* □ *Watch out for any signs of illness.*

watch over You **watch over** someone or something when you guard them or look after them: *God watches over us while we sleep.*

watchband /ˈwɒtʃband/ *noun* (*AmE*): **watchbands**
A **watchband** is a watchstrap.

watchdog /ˈwɒtʃdɒg/ *noun*: **watchdogs**
1 A **watchdog** is a dog that is kept to guard property. **2** A person or group appointed to protect something, such as people's rights or the environment, can be referred to as as a **watchdog**.

watcher /ˈwɒtʃə(r)/ *noun*: **watchers**
A **watcher** is someone who is looking carefully at something to see what happens: *At last, to the delight of the hidden watchers, the animal emerged from its hole.*

watchful /ˈwɒtʃfəl/ *adjective*
Someone who is **watchful** notices everything that happens: *The cubs played about in the grass under the watchful eye of their mother* [*opposite* **inattentive**]

watchman /ˈwɒtʃmən/ *noun*: **watchmen**
A **watchman** is a man employed to guard property or premises at night.

watchstrap /ˈwɒtʃstrap/ *noun*: **watchstraps**
A **watchstrap** is a strap attached to a watch, for you to wear round your wrist.

watchtower /ˈwɒtʃtaʊə(r)/ *noun*: **watchtowers**
A **watchtower** is a high tower from which a sentry keeps watch.

watchword /ˈwatʃwɔːd/ *noun*: **watchwords**
A group's or party's **watchword** is a short phrase that is easily remembered and repeated and reminds them of their most important principle: *Remember our watchword: strength through unity!* [*same as* **motto, slogan**]

water /ˈwɔːtə(r)/ *noun*; *verb*

▻ ***noun***: **waters**

1 (*uncount*) **Water** is the liquid that falls from the sky as rain and forms seas, lakes and rivers, that has no colour, taste or smell, and that all animals need to drink in order to stay alive; **water** forms steam when it boils, and ice when it freezes: *Shall I get you a glass of water?* □ *All bedrooms have hot and cold running water.* □ *The water supply will be cut off for two hours this morning.* □ *How far can you swim under water?* **2** (*uncount or used in the plural*) Any area of water, such as a lake, river or the sea, can be referred to as the **water**; you can also refer to the **waters** of a particular river, sea or ocean: *Don't go too near the water.* □ *the freezing waters of the North Atlantic.* **3** (*used in the plural*) A country's **waters** are the area of sea round its coast, considered part of its territory: *They were caught fishing in Icelandic waters.*

▻ ***verb***: **waters, watering, watered**

1 You **water** plants when you pour water into the soil they are in, to make them grow. **2** Your mouth **waters** when it produces a large amount of the liquid called saliva, usually when you see or smell food, or are about to eat. **3** Your eyes **water** when they hurt and fill with tears: *The smoke made our eyes water.*

▻ ***phrases*** **1** Goods that are transported **by water** are carried by ships. **2** A theory or argument that **holds water** is one that you can find no mistakes in, or that you can prove. **3** You are **in deep water** when you are in trouble, danger or difficulty. **4** (*formal*) People **pass water** when they urinate. **5** (*informal*) You **pour** or **throw cold water on** someone's suggestion or proposal when you criticize it or express a lack of enthusiasm for it. **6** You **tread water** when you keep yourself afloat and upright in deep water by moving your legs gently. **7** An area that is **under water** is flooded: *The entire country of Bangladesh was under water.*

phrasal verb

water down **1** You **water down** a liquid such as wine when you make it thinner or weaker by adding water. [*same as* **dilute**] **2** You **water down** such things as comments, criticisms or proposals when you alter them so as to make them less offensive, or easier to accept: *The newspapers had all printed a somewhat watered-down version of his speech.* [*same as* **tone down**]

waterborne /ˈwɔːtəbɔːn/ *adjective*
Things that are **waterborne** are carried by water: *waterborne germs.*

water closet see **WC**.

watercolour (*AmE* **watercolor**) /ˈwɔːtəkʌlə(r)/ *noun*: **watercolours**
1 (*uncount or used in the plural*) **Watercolour** is paint for painting pictures with, that you mix with water rather than oil; **watercolours** are the coloured paints you use: *a watercolour landscape.* **2** A painting done with watercolours is a **watercolour**: *a watercolour of Tower Bridge, London.*

watercress /ˈwɔːtəkrɛs/ *noun* (*uncount*)
Watercress is a plant that grows in water, whose hot-tasting leaves are used in salads. [see also **cress**]

waterfall /ˈwɔːtəfɔːl/ *noun*: **waterfalls**
A **waterfall** is a part of a river where the water drops suddenly down steep rocks or over a cliff.

waterfront /ˈwɔːtəfrʌnt/ *noun* (*used in the singular*)
A **waterfront** is the part of a town built along the edge of a river, lake, or the sea.

waterhole /ˈwɔːtəhoʊl/ *noun*: **waterholes**
A **waterhole** is a pond, pool or spring in a desert area, where animals can drink.

watering can /ˈwɔːtərɪŋ kan/ *noun*: **watering cans**
A **watering can** is a water-container with a handle and a spout, for watering plants. [see picture at **tool**]

waterlogged /ˈwɔːtəlɒgd/ *adjective*
1 Ground that is **waterlogged** is so wet that the soil cannot hold any more water: *waterlogged playing fields.* **2** A **waterlogged** boat is so full of water that it can no longer float, and is likely to sink.

water main /ˈwɔːtə meɪn/ *noun*: **water mains**
A **water main** is a large underground pipe carrying a public water supply.

watermelon /ˈwɔːtəmɛlən/ *noun*: **watermelons**
A **watermelon** is a large melon with dark green skin, red juicy flesh and black seeds. [see picture at **fruit**]

waterproof /ˈwɔːtəpruːf/ *adjective*; *noun*; *verb*

▻ ***adjective***

Clothing or material that is **waterproof** will not let water pass through it: *waterproof jackets and trousers.*

▻ ***noun***: **waterproofs**

A **waterproof** is a waterproof coat. [*same as* **raincoat**]

▻ ***verb***: **waterproofs, waterproofing, waterproofed**

To **waterproof** a material or surface is to make it waterproof.

watershed /ˈwɔːtəʃɛd/ *noun*: **watersheds**
1 A **watershed** is the high land from which two rivers rise and flow in opposite directions. **2** A **watershed** in history, or in someone's life, is an important point or happening that marks the beginning of a new stage or development: *After playing Shylock I began to be regarded as a serious actor; that was the watershed in my career.*

waterside /ˈwɔːtəsaɪd/ *noun* (*used in the singular*)
The **waterside** is the edge of a river, lake or sea, or a street along the edge of it.

water-ski /ˈwɔːtəskiː/ *verb*: **waterskis, waterskiing, waterskied**
To **waterski** is to travel over water on special skis, pulled by a motor boat. —*noun* (*uncount*) **waterskiing**: *windsurfing and waterskiing equipment for hire.*

watertight /ˈwɔːtətaɪt/ *adjective*
1 Something that is **watertight** is so well sealed that water cannot get into it or through it: *a watertight compartment.* **2** A **watertight** plan, argument, excuse or explanation is one that you can find nothing wrong with: *Only one of the suspects appeared to have a watertight alibi for the evening of the murder.*

waterway /ˈwɔːtəweɪ/ *noun*: **waterways**
A **waterway** is a channel, *eg* a canal or river, used by ships or smaller boats.

waterworks /ˈwɔːtəwɜːks/ *noun*: **waterworks**
A **waterworks** is a building where water is purified and stored for distribution to the public.

watery /ˈwɔːtərɪ/ *adjective*
1 Watery food or drink contains too much water or does not taste strong enough: *watery tea.* **2 Watery** sunlight is weak pale sunlight that appears between showers. **3 Watery** eyes water easily. **4** A **watery** smile is a weak unenthusiastic one.

watt /wɒt/ *noun*: **watts**
A **watt** is a unit of measurement of electrical power: *a 100-watt light bulb.*

wave /weɪv/ *verb*; *noun*
▻ ***verb***: **waves, waving, waved**
1 You **wave**, or **wave** your hand, when you raise your hand and move it from side to side to say hello or goodbye to someone, or to signal to them: *She waved to me from the window.* □ *He turned and waved goodbye as he reached the corner.* □ *Look, there's Granny; wave your hand to her.* **2** You **wave** something when you hold it up and move it from side to side: *We were all given flags to wave at the Queen's car as it passed.* **3** Things **wave** when they move about in the wind: *The branches waved to and fro gently in the breeze.* **4** You **wave** someone in a certain direction when you make a hand movement to indicate that they should go in that direction: *They shifted the barrier to one side and waved us through.* □ *A waiter approached but she waved him away.* □ *We were waved on by a policeman.* **5** You **wave** hair when you curl it loosely; hair that **waves** curls loosely and naturally.
▻ ***noun***: **waves**
1 A **wave** is the action of waving your hand: *She gave me a wave as soon she spotted me.* **2** A **wave** is a long raised mass of water moving across the sea or other water surface, that breaks into foam as it reaches the shore: *The waves pounded against the rocks.* **3** (*physics*) A **wave** is a narrow area of disturbance passing through particles and producing energy by which such things as sound, light and heat are transmitted: *sound waves* □ *radio waves.* **4** (*uncount*) 'Long **wave**', 'short **wave**' and 'medium **wave**' refer to wavelengths used for broadcasting: *Can you only get Radio Three on medium wave?* **5** A **wave** is also any of the circles of disturbance moving outwards from the central point of a shock such as an earthquake: *shock waves caused by the explosion.* **6** (*count or used in the singular*) A **wave** in hair is a soft loose curl; hair that has a **wave** curls loosely and naturally. **7** You experience a **wave** of a particular feeling when it spreads through you: *She felt a wave of nausea coming over her.* □ *There was a mounting wave of panic and hysteria anongst the audience as the fire spread.* **8** A **wave** of some kind of occurrence is a sudden increase in instances of it: *the recent wave of car thefts.* **9** A heat **wave** is a period of very hot weather.

phrasal verbs
wave aside You **wave aside** a difficulty or objection when you decide that it is not important enough to consider.
wave off You **wave** someone **off** when you accompany them to their place of departure and wave goodbye to them as they leave: *We all went to wave her off at the station.*

waveband /ˈweɪvband/ *noun*: **wavebands**
A **waveband** is a range of wavelengths used for radio transmissions of a particular type.

wavelength /ˈweɪvlɛŋθ/ *noun*: **wavelengths**
A **wavelength** is **1** (*physics*) the distance from a point on one wave to the same point on the next wave. **2** (*radio*) the length of the radio wave used by a particular broadcasting station.
▻ ***phrase*** People who are **on the same wavelength** understand each other well and tend to have similar opinions about things.

waver /ˈweɪvə(r)/ *verb*: **wavers, wavering, wavered**
1 You **waver** when you become less decisive or confident about something, or can't decide what to do: *Customers who wavering between the two models may find this information booklet useful.* □ *Her belief in her own ability never wavered.* [*same as* **faltered**] **2** Something such as a person's eyes **waver** when their focus becomes unsteady, or moves slightly.

wavy /ˈweɪvɪ/ *adjective*: **wavier, waviest**
1 Wavy hair curls loosely: *She had dark hair, wavy rather than curly.* **2** A **wavy** line or outline curves upwards and downwards in a series of regular curves.

wax[1] /waks/ *noun*; *verb*
▻ ***noun*** (*uncount*)
1 Wax is a solid shiny fatty substance, that softens when heated, is easily formed into different shapes, and is used to make candles and polish: *piles of Dutch cheeses with their distinctive coating of red wax.* **2** The sticky, yellowish stuff that forms in your ears is also called **wax**.
▻ ***verb***: **waxes, waxing, waxed**
1 You **wax** something such as furniture or a vehicle when you polish it with wax. **2** To **wax** a fabric is to treat it with wax to make it waterproof: *waxed jackets.* **3** Women **wax** their legs when they pull the hairs off them by applying a layer of hot wax to the skin and then peeling it off.

wax[2] /waks/ *verb*: **waxes, waxing, waxed**
1 The moon **waxes** when it gets larger as the sun lights up more of its surface. [*opposite* **wane**] **2** Something **waxes** when it increases in strength or power: *Any writer's reputation tends to wax and wane over the years.* [*same as* **grow**; *opposite* **shrink**] **3** (*literary*) Someone **waxes** *eg* enthusiastic about something

when they start getting enthusiastic in the way they describe it. [*same as* **become**]

waxwork /ˈwakswɜːk/ *noun*: **waxworks**
1 A **waxwork** is a lifelike model, usually of somebody famous, made of wax. **2** (*used in the plural, with a singular or plural verb*) You go to the **waxworks** when you visit a museum of wax models of famous people: *The waxworks are* (or *is*) *closed on Mondays.*

waxy /ˈwaksɪ/ *adjective*: **waxier, waxiest**
Something that is **waxy** looks or feels like wax: *the white waxy face of a corpse.*

way /weɪ/ *noun*; *verb*
▻ ***noun***: **ways**
1 a The **way** somewhere is the route or direction you take to get there: *Could you tell me the way to the town centre?* □ *I know the way. Follow me.* □ *Which is the best way to Chichester from here?* □ *We decided to go a different way home.* **b** The **way** somewhere is also the journey there, used in expressions such as 'all the way': *They argued all the way back.* □ *I can come with you some of the way.* **c** 'The **way** in' is the entrance, or the door through which you go into a place, and 'the **way** out' is the exit, or the door through which you go out of it. **d** You go or look a certain **way** when you go or look in a certain direction: *Look both ways before crossing.* □ *a one-way street* □ *I'm going your way* [= in the direction you want to go] *if you'd like a lift.* **e** Someone is round your **way** when they are in the area where you live or work: *Give us a ring next time you're round our way.* **f** Something is the right **way** round, or the right **way** up, if it is in the right position, or is facing the right direction: *You're holding your chopsticks the wrong way round.* □ *Surely that lampshade should be the other way up?* **g** A little **way** or a long **way** is a short or long distance in space or time: *They could see a road sign a little way ahead.* □ *The date of the wedding still seemed a long way off.*
2 Someone or something that is in the **way**, or in your **way**, is blocking your progress, or stopping you from moving freely or from seeing clearly: *It was difficult cleaning the house, with the children constantly getting in her way.* □ *She moved the baby's pram out of my way.* □ *A police vehicle was blocking the way.*
3 a The **way** to do something is how to do it, or the means or method of doing it: *What's the quickest way of getting fit?* □ *This isn't the only way to do it.* □ *You can cook rice in a variety of ways.* □ *You must deal with the problem your own way.* □ *Is there no way of shortening the process?* □ *Make a list of the points you want to raise; that way we'll save time.* **b** The **way** someone does something is the manner or style in which they do it, or the quality their action or behaviour has: *She's done her hair a new way.* □ *I approved of the way she dressed.* □ *I was horrified at the way he treated his wife.* □ *She died in some rather mysterious way.* □ *That's no way to speak to* [= don't be rude to] *your father.* □ *You'd think her husband was a monster, the way* [= considering how] *she speaks about him.* □ *I can't cook the way* [= as expertly as] *my mother did.* **c** Someone has a **way** of doing something if their behaviour has that effect, or if they tend to do it as a habit: *He had a way of making you feel uneasy.* □ *The way he ignored women used to infuriate me.* □ *I didn't like her way of treating other people as fools.* □ *Disasters have a way of happening in threes.* **d** 'The **way**' something happens can refer to the fact that it happens, or the extent to which it happens: *We were amazed at the way Prague had changed in two years.* **e** (*used in the plural*) People's **ways** are their habits, customs and typical behaviour: *I'll never understand the ways of this community.* **f** You get into the **way** of doing something when you start doing it regularly: *Try and get into the way of relaxing in the evenings.* [*same as* **habit**] **g** You get or have your **way**, or your own **way**, when you manage to arrange things to suit yourself: *The fees will be doubled if the committee get their way.* **h** A **way** of regarding something is a particular attitude to it: *There are different ways of looking at the issue.* **i** Something that is so in a **way** or in some **ways** is partly so; something that is so in many **ways** is so to a large extent: *I pitied her in a way.* □ *In many ways the situation is the same as it was.* **j** The **way** you feel is how or what you feel: *If that's the way you feel about it, you'd better not join in.* □ *I didn't know you felt that way.* **k** The **way** someone or something looks is their appearance: *He could remember the way she looked as a young girl.*
4 You can use **way** with a lot of verbs to express progress: *He pushed his way to the front of the crowd.* □ *We soon ate our way through the contents of the fridge.*
▻ ***adverb*** (*informal*)
Way is used to mean 'very far', in emphasizing distance or extent beyond, behind, above or below something: *It's way past my bedtime.* □ *She was already way ahead of us.* □ *We're way below target for sales this year.*
▻ ***phrases*** **1** Something that is **across**, or **over, the way**, is on the opposite side, *eg* of the street: *She lives just over the way.* **2** You say something is **always the way** if it happens frequently: *It's often the way that the second child has more confidence.* **3** You use **by the way** to introduce a point that you want to mention while you remember it, though it may not be relevant to the present subject: *By the way, where did you put the tickets?* **4 a** You go to a place **by way of** another place when you take a route that passes through the other place: *Why don't you travel to Prague by way of Vienna?* [*same as* **via**] **b** You do one thing **by way of** another when the second thing is implied or intended by the first: *He nodded in our direction by way of a greeting.* **5** Something such as a chance or opportunity **comes your way** when it becomes available to you. **6** You **find your way** somewhere when you get there, *eg* by using a map or asking people: *Will you find your way home OK?* □ *Athens is an easy city to find your way round.* **7 a** Something **gives way** when it collapses: *The bridge may give way at any time.* **b** Something **gives way** when it fails or breaks down under pressure: *His nerve gave way when he was halfway up the cliff.* **c** You **give way** when you agree to something as a result of persuasion or pressure: *She finally gave way to the children's pleas.* **8** One thing **goes a long way towards** achieving another if it helps considerably to achieve it: *Your contributions tonight will go a long way towards setting up the hospital.* **9** Someone who **has a way with** a certain kind of thing or person is good at dealing with them: *He has a way with difficult customers.* **10** Someone who **has a way with them** has an attractive manner and is good at impressing people. **11** You **have** things **your own way** when you manage to arrange things to suit yourself: *She wants everything her own way.* **12** If you tell someone they can't **have it both ways**, you mean that they must choose between two alternatives. **13** Someone or something that is **in a bad way** is in a poor condition. **14 In a big**, or **small**, **way**, describes the scale or importance of an activity: *They're planning to go into ELT publishing in a big way.* **15** Something that is good **in its way** has qualities that make it acceptable up to a limited standard.
16 In no way is an emphatic way of saying 'not': *I'm in no way suggesting that you're to blame.* [*same as* **not at all, not in the least**] **17** You use **in the way of** to specify

a particular kind of resource, usually in questions or with negatives: *How much have we got left in the way of cash?* □ *There's nothing in the way of facilities for young people here.* **18** You **lead the way** somewhere when you guide someone there. **19** You **learn your way around** when you accustom yourself to your new surroundings or duties. **20** You **look the other way** when you pretend not to notice something. **21** You **lose your way** when you leave your intended route by mistake and don't know where you are. **22** You **make your way** somewhere when you go there: *We made our way back to the hotel.* **23** You **make way for** someone or something when you move aside to give them space or room: *The crowd parted to make way for the ambulance.* **24** (*informal*) You say 'there's **no two ways about it**' to emphasize that something is certain. **25** (*informal*) You answer '**no way**' to a proposal or suggestion if you consider it unacceptable or impossible. **26** Something that is **on the way out** is becoming unfashionable. **27 a** You are **on the way**, or **on your way**, somewhere when you are going there: *I met him on my way to the lecture.* **b** Someone is **on their way** towards doing something when they are progressing towards achieving it: *She's well on the way to becoming a millionaire.* **28 a** A job that is **out of the way** is finished: *Just let me get my thesis out of the way and I'll start thinking about the wedding.* **b** A place that is **out of the way** is a long distance from main routes: *an out-of-the-way village.* **c** A place is **out of your way** if you will not be passing through it on your journey: *Could you give me a lift to the station if it's not out of your way?* **d** You go **out of your way** to help someone when you make a special effort to do so. **e** You keep **out of** someone's **way** when you try to avoid meeting them. **29** You **pay your way** when you pay your own debts and living expenses as distinct from being dependent on someone else. **30** You say **'that's the way!'** to show encouragement and approval when someone responds or behaves as you want them to. **31** A project is **under way** when it has begun; you are **under way** when you have started on a journey somewhere.

waylay /weɪˈleɪ/ *verb*: **waylays, waylaying, waylaid**
Someone **waylays** you when they wait for you to pass and delay you by talking to you: *Chisholm waylaid me in the corridor and talked for twenty minutes about some obscure point.*

way of life /weɪ əv ˈlaɪf/ *noun* (*usually in the singular*): **ways of life**
Your **way of life** is your normal routine and your typical activities and behaviour: *Getting married would mean completely changing his way of life.*

-ways /weɪz/ *suffix*
You add **-ways** to nouns like *length* and *width* to form adverbs of direction: *Lengthways, the room measured 22 feet.* [= it was 22 feet long] [see also **-wise**]

wayside /ˈweɪsaɪd/ *noun* (*used in the singular*)
The **wayside** is the edge of a road: *wayside flowers.*
▻ ***phrase*** Someone or something **falls by the wayside** when they fail in what they are trying to do, or get neglected and forgotten about: *Dyslexic children used to fall by the wayside because no-one understood what was wrong with them.*

wayward /ˈweɪwəd/ *adjective*
A **wayward** person has a rebellious personality and is inclined to be disobedient and difficult to control. [*opposite* **obedient**]

WC /dʌbəljuːˈsiː/ *noun*: **WCs**
A **WC** is a water closet or toilet, especially one in which the bowl is mechanically flushed with water.

we /wiː/ or /wɪ/ *pronoun* (*used as the subject of a verb*)
You use **we** to refer to **1** yourself and one or more other people, sometimes including the person you are addressing: *Robert was just behind me as we reached the summit.* □ *We were both very impressed.* □ *If you're free we could go out this evening.* □ *We three should meet more often.* □ *We taxmen know what people think of us.* □ *Are we all agreed about this?* **2** people or human beings in general, yourself included: *the times we live in.* [see also **us, our, ours, ourselves**]

weak /wiːk/ *adjective*: **weaker, weakest**
1 Someone who is **weak** lacks physical strength and energy: *The illness left her almost too weak to stand.* □ *weak ankles.* **2** Something that is **weak** is not functioning effectively, or is likely to fail or break: *a weak heart* □ *a weak link in the chain.* **3** A person or group is **weak** if they lack power or influence: *Militarily weak as they were, they could put up no resistance.* **4** (*commerce*) A **weak** currency is one that is dropping in value: *a weak dollar.* **5 Weak** people are too easily influenced by others, or yield too easily to temptation: *the kind of weak person who would rather agree than cause a fuss* □ *a man of weak character.* **6 Weak** tea or coffee has too much water in it, so does not have the strong flavour it should have. **7** A **weak** argument is a silly unconvincing one: *He offered some weak excuse and left early.* **8** A **weak** smile is an unenthusiastic one. **9** Someone or something that is **weak** on a particular type of skill or material has too little of it: *They're strong on computing skills, weak on grammar and punctuation.* — *adverb* **weakly:** *She sank weakly into an armchair.* □ *Weakly, I obeyed instead of resisting.*

weaken /ˈwiːkən/ *verb*: **weakens, weakening, weakened**
1 A person or thing **is weakened** when their strength, power or effectiveness is reduced: *Weakened by hunger, they were an easy prey to infection.* □ *Constant use had weakened the hinge and it gave way.* □ *Recent political defeats had weakened her authority.* [*opposite* **strengthen**] **2** You **weaken** when you yield to pressure, persuasion or temptation.

weakling /ˈwiːklɪŋ/ *noun*: **weaklings**
1 A **weakling** is a physically weak person or animal. **2** Someone who is weak in a certain way can be called a **weakling**: *a political weakling* □ *a moral weakling.*

weakness /ˈwiːknəs/ *noun*: **weaknesses**
1 (*uncount*) **Weakness** is the condition of being weak: *weakness brought on by hunger and exhaustion.* [*opposite* **strength**] **2** A **weakness** is a fault or failing: *Her weaknesses somehow made her the more lovable.* [*opposite* **virtue**] **3** (*usually in the plural*) The **weaknesses** of a system, or of a person performing some kind of work, are the areas in which they do not function or perform well: *The test is designed to show up students' major strengths and weaknesses.* [*opposite* **strength**]. **4** (*used in the singular*) You have a **weakness** for something if you like it: *her well-known weakness for fine jewels.*

weak verb /wiːk ˈvɜːb/ *noun*: **weak verbs**
The **weak verbs** in English are the regular kind, which form their past tense and past participle with *-d*

weal /wiːl/ *noun*: **weals**
A **weal** is a raised red mark made on your skin by something such as a whip.

wealth /wɛlθ/ *noun*
1 (*uncount*) **Wealth** is money and property, or the possession of plenty of these: *There was a lot of wealth around in those days; people could afford things.* □ *One day he would be a man of wealth.* [*opposite* **poverty**] **2** (*uncount*) A country's **wealth** is its resources: *There is still considerable mineral wealth waiting to be exploited.* **3** (*used in the singular*) A **wealth** of some-

thing is a large quantity of it: *I can provide a wealth of examples.*

wealthy /'wɛlθɪ/ *adjective; noun*
▷ ***adjective***: **wealthier, wealthiest**
1 A **wealthy** person possesses a lot of money and property and other valuable things: *His family was comfortably off rather than wealthy.* [*same as* **rich**; *opposite* **poor**] **2** A **wealthy** country is one that is financially strong because of its industry or its valuable natural resources: *the wealthy Gulf states.* [*same as* **rich**] **3** A **wealthy** area has a lot of rich people living in it: *in London's wealthy Belgravia.* [*same as* **affluent**; *opposite* **poor**]
▷ ***noun*** (*plural*)
The **wealthy** are people who are rich.

wean /wiːn/ *verb*: **weans, weaning, weaned**
1 A mother **weans** her baby when she gradually stops feeding it with milk from her breast and gives it increasing amounts of other kinds of food: *I had him completely weaned on to solid foods at six months.* **2** You **wean** someone off, or from, something such as a drug or dangerous habit by helping them gradually to give it up: *new devices for weaning people off cigarettes.*

weapon /'wɛpən/ *noun*: **weapons**
1 A **weapon** is an instrument or device used to kill and injure people in a war or fight: *a hoard of rifles, grenades and other weapons* ▫ *nuclear weapons.* [*same as* **arm**] **2** (*usually in the singular*) Any means of defeating an opponent can be called a **weapon**: *Surprise is our best weapon.*

wear /wɛə(r)/ *verb; noun*
▷ ***verb***: **wears, wearing, wore, worn**
1 You **are wearing** something when you are dressed in it, or have it on your body; a man **wears** a beard if he has one: *When last seen he was wearing blue shorts and a red anorak.* ▫ *What did you wear for the wedding?* ▫ *I never wear yellow.* ▫ *Do you usually wear spectacles?* ▫ *He wore an earring in one ear.* ▫ *How long have you been wearing that moustache?* ▫ *She rarely wore perfume.* ▫ *He wears his hair rather long.*

> Notice that **put on,** not **wear**, is used to refer to the process of dressing yourself in something: *He's becoming an expert at putting on his turban.*

2 You **wear** your hair or beard a certain length or in a certain style if you have it cut that length or in that style: *A lot of men with long hair are wearing it in a pony tail.* ▫ *She wore her hair very short.* **3** You say that a person or their face **is wearing** a certain expression if they have that expression: *His face wore a defeated look.* **4** Clothing and carpets **wear**, or **wear** thin, when they become thin and develop holes through use. **5** Clothing and fabrics that **wear** well, last well and can bear a lot of use: *This dress has worn well.* **6** A hole **is worn** in something when it develops through heavy use: *The constant passage of feet had worn a deep hollow in the step.* ▫ *A bare patch had been worn in the carpet.* — *noun* **wearer:** *wearers of contact lenses.*
▷ ***noun*** (*uncount*)
1 Clothes suitable for certain purposes or occasions are referred to, especially in shops, as **wear** for those purposes or occasions: *leisure wear* ▫ *a new range of sportswear* ▫ *menswear.* **2 Wear** is the amount or type of use that things such as clothing, fabrics or carpets get: *Is the carpeting likely to be subjected to heavy wear?* **3 Wear** is also damage caused through frequent use: *The machinery is already showing signs of wear.*
▷ ***phrases*** **1 a** You say that something such as a joke or excuse **is wearing thin** if it has been said or used too often, and so sounds silly, ineffective or unconvincing. **b** Your patience **is wearing thin** when you are getting impatient and annoyed. **2** Someone or something that is **the worse for wear** is in a poor state through too much activity, too much alcohol, or too much use.

> ***phrasal verbs***
> **wear away** Something **wears away** or **is worn away** when it becomes thin or disappears completely through frequent use or rubbing: *The pattern on the handle had completely worn away.*
> **wear down 1** Something **wears down** or **is worn down** when it gets shorter or thinner through frequent use or rubbing: *The stone steps were all worn down in the middle.* **2** You **wear** a person **down** when you get them to agree to something by asking them repeatedly.
> **wear off** A feeling or pain **wears off** when it becomes less strong or severe and gradually disappears: *By lunchtime her headache had worn off.*
> **wear on** Time **wears on** when it passes: *As the year wore on he began to realize she'd gone for good this time.*
> **wear out 1** Something **wears out** or **is worn out** when it gets so weakened or rubbed through frequent use that it can no longer be worn or used: *The children can wear out a pair of new shoes in a couple of months.* ▫ *A swimming costume soon wears out.* **2** You **wear** someone **out** when you tire them or exhaust them: *The kids wear me out.* [see also **worn out** at **worn**]
> **wear through** Something **wears through** when it develops a hole through heavy or frequent use or rubbing: *He wore the jersey constantly and both elbows had worn through.*

wearable /'wɛərəbəl/ *adjective*
Clothes that are **wearable** are in good enough condition to be worn.

wear and tear /wɛər ən 'tɛə(r)/ *noun* (*uncount*)
Wear and tear is damage caused in the course of normal use: *Your joints suffer a lot of wear and tear over the years.*

wearing /'wɛərɪŋ/ *adjective*
A job or activity is **wearing** when it uses up your energy, patience and concentration and makes you tired: *There's no more wearing job than teaching.*

wearisome /'wɪərɪsəm/ *adjective*
Things that are **wearisome** make you feel tired, bored and frustrated: *We spent many wearisome hours waiting for news.* [*same as* **tedious**]

weary /'wɪərɪ/ *adjective; verb*
▷ ***adjective*** (*literary*): **wearier, weariest**
1 You are **weary** when you are tired or exhausted: *We were all weary from overwork.* ▫ *She managed a weary smile.* **2** You are **weary** of something when you have lost the patience needed for it: *I was thoroughly weary of trying to please him.* — *adverb* **wearily:** *She struggled wearily to her feet.* — *noun* (*uncount*) **weariness**: *He passed his hand across his forehead in a gesture of weariness.*
▷ ***verb*** (*literary*): **wearies, wearying, wearied**
1 Something **wearies** you when it tires or bores you. **2** You **weary** of something when you get tired of it or lose interest in it: *The children soon wearied of waiting.* [*same as* **tire**]

weather /'wɛðə(r)/ *noun; verb*
▷ ***noun*** (*uncount or used in the singular*)

The **weather** is the condition of the atmosphere in any area at any time, with regard to sun, cloud, temperature, wind and rain: *a spell of dry sunny weather* □ *It rained once; otherwise the weather was fine.* □ *icy weather conditions.*

▻ ***verb***: **weathers, weathering, weathered**

1 Wood and rock **weather** when they are altered in colour, texture and shape through exposure to wind, sun and rain. **2** You **weather** a difficult situation when you manage to survive it and go on living normally when it is over.

▻ ***phrases*** **1** You say someone **is making heavy weather of** something if you think they are making unnecessarily slow and difficult progress with it. **2** You are **under the weather** when you are not as healthy as you usually are: *I've been feeling a bit under the weather recently.* [*same as* **off-colour**]

weatherbeaten /ˈwɛðəbiːtən/ *adjective*

The skin of your face is **weatherbeaten** if it has become brown, shiny and deeply lined through exposure to sun, wind and rain: *sailors with weatherbeaten faces.*

weathercock /ˈwɛðəkɒk/ *noun*: **weathercocks**

A **weathercock** is a weathervane in the form of a farmyard cock.

weather forecast /ˈwɛðə fɔːkɑːst/ *noun*: **weather forecasts**

The **weather forecast** is a regular report in the newspaper or on radio or television, on the weather conditions that are expected to develop during the coming hours or days.

weatherman /ˈwɛðəman/ or **weathergirl** /ˈwɛðəgɜːl/ *noun*: **weathermen** or **weathergirls**

The **weathermen** and **weathergirls** are the people who present and explain the weather forecast on radio or television.

weathervane /ˈwɛðəveɪn/ *noun*: **weathervanes**

A **weathervane** is a revolving metal arrow that turns to point in the direction of the wind, with arms for each of the four compass points, fixed *eg* to the top of a church spire.

weave /wiːv/ *verb*; *noun*

▻ ***verb***: **weaves, weaving, wove** or **weaved, woven**

Weaved is used as the past tense and past participle in sense 4. **1** You **weave** cloth in a machine called a loom, passing fine threads under and over a set of thicker fixed threads called the warp: *She taught herself to spin and weave.* □ *In some factories children of six were employed weaving carpets.* **2** You **weave** such things as baskets by passing strips of material in and out between fixed rods. **3** You **weave** garlands by twisting the stems of plants and flowers together. **4** You **weave**, or **weave** your way through things, when you progress by passing left and right between them: *We weaved our way through the Saturday-morning shoppers.* — *adjective* **woven:** *a selection of woven and knitted fabrics.*

▻ ***noun*** (*usually in the singular*)

The **weave** of a fabric is the pattern or texture the threads make, depending on how they are arranged, and how loosely or tightly they have been woven together: *a loose open weave.*

weaver /ˈwiːvə(r)/ *noun*: **weavers**

A **weaver** is a person who weaves cloth.

web /wɛb/ *noun*: **webs**

1 A **web** is a network of fine, sticky threads constructed by a spider to trap insects. **2** A **web** of things such as lies or reasons is a complicated series of them, in which one develops from, or depends on, another. **3** The piece of skin connecting the toes of a swimming bird or animal is a **web**. — *adjective* **webbed:** *The bird has a long neck, pointed wings and webbed feet.*

webbing /ˈwɛbɪŋ/ *noun* (*uncount*)

Webbing is strong fabric woven into strips for making into belts and straps.

wed /wɛd/ *verb*: **weds, wedding, wed** or **wedded**

1 (*old or literary*) Two people **wed** when they get married; you **wed** someone when you marry them. **2** You **are wedded** to an idea if you support it strongly and consistently: *He was a man wedded to his principles.*

we'd /wiːd/

We'd is the spoken, or informal written, form of **1 we would** or **we should**: *We'd have accepted if they'd invited us.* □ *We'd prefer seats at the front.* **2 we had** usually where *had* is the auxiliary verb: *She was pleased with the work we'd done.*

wedding /ˈwɛdɪŋ/ *noun*: **weddings**

A **wedding** is a marriage ceremony: *We've been invited to a wedding next weekend.* □ *a bride's wedding dress.*

wedge /wɛdʒ/ *noun*; *verb*

▻ ***noun***: **wedges**

1 A **wedge** is a piece of solid wood, rubber or other material, thick at one end and thin at the other, that you push into a narrow gap between things to fix them in position. **2** A triangular section of something such as a cake can be called a **wedge**: *a thick wedge of pie.*

▻ ***verb***: **wedges, wedging, wedged**

1 You **wedge** something in position when you fix it with a wedge or any object that works like one: *She used a piece of folded cardboard to wedge the door open.* **2** Something **is wedged** into a place when it is firmly pushed or fixed in there: *She manage to wedge herself into a corner from which she could watch everything.*

▻ ***phrases*** **1** You **drive a wedge** between people who were formerly friendly or united by causing quarrels and ill feeling between them, in order to spoil their relationship. **2** You call a development that seems harmless or unimportant **the thin end of the wedge** if it looks to you like the beginning of something much larger that will have a harmful effect.

Wednesday /ˈwɛdənzdeɪ/ or /ˈwɛnzdeɪ/ *noun* (*count or uncount*): **Wednesdays**

Wednesday is the fourth day of the week, coming after Tuesday and before Thursday: *We arrive in Amsterdam on Wednesday.* □ *We have the afternoon off on Wednesdays* (or *on a Wednesday*). □ (*AmE*) *I go shopping Wednesdays.* □ *I'll keep Wednesday morning free.* □ *Where's last Wednesday's Times?* □ *We can come this Wednesday or next Wednesday.*

wee /wiː/ *adjective*: **weer, weest** (*informal*; *especially Scottish*)

Wee things are little or small: *You'll probably be left with a wee scar.* □ *It's a wee bit difficult to explain.*

weed /wiːd/ *noun*; *verb*

▻ ***noun***: **weeds**

1 A **weed** is a wild plant growing among cultivated plants or anywhere where it is not wanted: *flowerbeds full of weeds.* **2** (*informal, derogatory*) If you describe a man as a **weed** you mean he is thin and weak-looking, or that he has a feeble personality.

▻ ***verb***: **weeds, weeding, weeded**

You **weed** a garden, flowerbed or field when you pull the weeds out of it.

phrasal verb

You **weed out** people or things that you don't want in a group when you identify them and get rid of them: *We weeded out all the applicants who had no English-teaching experience.*

weedy /ˈwiːdɪ/ *adjective*: **weedier, weediest**
1 A **weedy** garden or flowerbed is full of weeds: *The drive was weedy and neglected.* **2** (*informal, derogatory*) If you describe a man as **weedy** you mean he is thin and weak-looking.

week /wiːk/ *noun*: **weeks**
1 A **week** is a period of seven days, beginning on Sunday or Monday, or any period of seven days: *We'll meet early next week to discuss this.* □ *I was away all last week.* □ *The deadline is in five weeks' time.* □ *They eat out at least three evenings a week.* □ *The rent is £30 per week.* **2** The **week** is the five days from Monday to Friday, as distinct from the weekend: *She works so hard during the week that she sleeps most of Saturday and Sunday.* **3** You say you work a **week** of a certain number of hours if that is the number of hours you work every week: *She works a 45-hour week.*
▻ ***phrases*** **1 A week last** Friday is the Friday before the last one. **2 A week on** Friday, or **a week next** Friday, or Friday **week**, is the Friday after the next one. **3 A week today** or **today week** is exactly one week from today, on the same day of the week; **a week tomorrow** or **tomorrow week** is exactly one week from tomorrow. **4 A week ago today** is exactly one week before today, on the same day of the week; **a week ago yesterday** is exactly one week before yesterday.

weekday /ˈwiːkdeɪ/ *noun*: **weekdays**
A **weekday** is any day of the week except Saturday and Sunday: *No parking was allowed during weekday rush hours.*

weekend /wiːkˈɛnd/ *noun*: **weekends**
The **weekend** is Saturday and Sunday: *The banks are all closed at weekends.* □ *Are you going home for the weekend?* □ *I'm free this weekend and next weekend.* □ *Only the weekend staff are on duty.* □ *How about spending a weekend in Paris?*

weekly /ˈwiːklɪ/ *adjective*; *adverb*; *noun*
▻ ***adjective***
Weekly describes things that happen or are done, produced or issued every week or once a week: *his weekly wage packet* □ *her weekly visit to the hospital* □ *a weekly magazine.*
▻ ***adverb***
Something that happens **weekly** happens every week, or once a week: *They met twice weekly in termtime.* □ *their twice-weekly game of squash* □ *He was paid weekly.*
▻ ***noun*: weeklies**
A **weekly** is a magazine or newspaper that is published once a week. [compare **daily**]

weep /wiːp/ *verb*; *noun*
▻ ***verb*: weeps, weeping, wept**
You **weep** when you cry, as an expression of grief or other emotion: *She lay on her bed, weeping bitterly.*
▻ ***noun*** (*used in the singular*): *She couldn't help having the occasional weep.*

weepy /ˈwiːpɪ/ *adjective*: **weepier, weepiest**
You are **weepy** when you are feeling upset and keep crying. [*same as* **tearful**]

weft /wɛft/ *noun* (*usually in the singular*): **wefts**
In weaving, the **weft** is the set of threads that are passed over and under the fixed threads in a loom. [see also **warp**]

weigh /weɪ/ *verb*: **weighs, weighing, weighed**
1 You **weigh** something when you measure how heavy it is, using scales: *He used to weigh himself every morning.* **2** Somebody or something **weighs** a certain amount if that is how heavy they are: *The fish must have weighed at least 6 kilos.* □ *What do you weigh?* **3** You **weigh** something in your hand when you hold it loosely to feel how heavy it is.
▻ ***phrases*** **1** A ship **weighs anchor** when it raises its anchor before sailing. **2** You **weigh your words** when you choose them carefully before you speak.

phrasal verbs
weigh down 1 You **are weighed down** by a load or burden if it stops you moving or progressing easily: *It will take longer to reach the summit if you're weighed down by a rucksack.* **2** Worries **weigh** you **down** when they occupy your mind and depress you.
weigh in A wrestler or boxer **weighs in** before a fight, and a jockey before and after a race, when they are weighed officially.
weigh out You **weigh** something **out** when you measure the quantity you need by weight, using scales: *She weighed out a pound of flour.*
weigh up You **weigh up** such things as facts, possibilities or alternatives when you consider them in relation to one another so as to be able to make the right choice or decision. [*same as* **assess**]
weigh on A problem **weighs on** or **upon** you when it occupies your mind and depresses you.
weigh with Something **weighs with** people if it impresses them: *Your previous experience should weigh with the appointments board.*

weight /weɪt/ *noun*; *verb*
▻ ***noun*: weights**
1 (*uncount or used in the singular*) The **weight** of a person or thing is their heaviness, or the amount they weigh: *Your luggage must not exceed the permitted weight.* □ *Some dinosaurs reached a body weight of over 30 tons.* **2** (*uncount*) You gain **weight** or put on **weight** when you get heavier or fatter; you lose **weight** or take off **weight** when you get lighter or slimmer: *He's been putting on a lot of weight recently.* □ *Do you think I've lost weight?* **3** A **weight** is one of a set of pieces of metal that weigh a standard amount, for using with scales, against which you balance other objects in order to find out how heavy they are: *a set of brass weights.* **4** A **weight** is any heavy load or object, *eg* one designed for pressing or holding something down; specially designed **weights** are used in activities such as weightlifting and weight training: *a paperweight* □ *The baby was becoming quite a weight to carry round.* **5** (*used in the singular*) You bear the **weight** of responsibility for something when it is your duty to attend to it. [*same as* **burden**] **6** You have a **weight** on your mind when you are worried about something: *It took a weight off my mind to know they'd got home safely.* **7** (*uncount*) The **weight** of something such as evidence or support is the major part of it: *The weight of the evidence points to the 'big bang' theory being correct.* **8** (*uncount*) An opinion that carries **weight** is one that people trust or believe.
▻ ***verb*: weights, weighting, weighted**
1 You **weight** something, or **weight** it down, when you put heavy objects into it or on to it, *eg* to make it sink, or to stop it from being blown away: *We weighted the tent down with stones.* **2** A system that **is weighted** in favour of particular people gives them an advantage: *a tax system weighted in favour of the wealthy.*
▻ ***phrases*** **1** You **pull your weight** when you do your full share of work, *eg* in a team or group. **2** You **put your weight on** your leg or foot when you stand on it: *His ankle's improving but he can't put any weight on it yet.* **3** You **take the weight off** your feet when you sit down for a rest. **4** (*informal*) **a** Someone **throws their weight about** when they give orders to other people in

an unnecessarily rude way. **b** You **throw your weight behind** someone or something when you enthusiastically support them. **5** Someone or something that is **worth their weight in gold** is very useful or helpful.

weightless /ˈweɪtləs/ *adjective*
1 Something that is **weightless** is so light as to weigh almost nothing. **2** Astronauts are **weightless** when they are in space and not affected by gravity, and so they can float about. — *noun* (*uncount*) **weightlessness:** *experiencing weightlessness for the first time.*

weightlifting /ˈweɪtlɪftɪŋ/ *noun* (*uncount*)
Weightlifting is the sport in which people compete to see who can lift the heaviest weight. — *noun* **weightlifter:** *Britain's team of weightlifters for the Olympics.*

weight training /ˈweɪt treɪnɪŋ/ *noun* (*uncount*)
Weight training is a kind of physical training in which you use pieces of apparatus fitted with weights to build up your muscles.

weighty /ˈweɪtɪ/ *adjective*: **weightier, weightiest**
Weighty matters are important, grave or serious: *Another weighty consideration must be taken into account.* [*opposite* **trivial, unimportant**]

weir /wɪə(r)/ *noun*: **weirs**
A **weir** is a shallow barrier or dam constructed across a river to control its flow.

weird /wɪəd/ *adjective*: **weirder, weirdest**
Weird people or things are strange or queer: *a weird sense of humour* ▫ *Since he went away to college he's gone a bit weird; you know, long hair, beard, open-toed sandals, that kind of thing.* — *adverb* **weirdly:** *weirdly dressed women.*

welcome /ˈwɛlkəm/ *verb*; *interjection*; *noun*; *adjective*
▻ *verb*: **welcomes, welcoming, welcomed**
1 You **welcome** a guest or visitor when you receive them with a warm and friendly greeting: *I must go and welcome the new arrivals.* **2** A place **welcomes** people if they are encouraged to visit it: *The museum welcomes children.* **3** You **welcome** suggestions when you encourage people to make them. **4** You **welcome** an action or development if you approve of it: *The taxation adjustments have been generally welcomed.* — *adjective* **welcoming:** *He gave us a welcoming smile.*
▻ *interjection*
You say '**Welcome!**' to someone to express pleasure at their arrival: *Welcome home!* ▫ *Welcome to Singapore!*
▻ *noun*: **welcomes**
A **welcome** is the act of receiving and greeting someone who has arrived, in a warm and friendly way: *Our hosts gave us a tremendous welcome.*
▻ *adjective*
1 You are **welcome** somewhere if people receive you there gladly: *Visitors are welcome at all hours.* ▫ *You're always a welcome guest here.* **2** You say that someone is **welcome** to do something when you are giving them permission, or encouraging them, to do it: *You're welcome to borrow the car.* **3** You say that someone is **welcome** to something if you would like them to take it or have it: *She's welcome to my old bicycle if she'd like it.* **4** Something that is **welcome** is appreciated by the person to whom it is offered or given: *We were given a most welcome cup of tea.* ▫ *A glass of sherry would be very welcome, thank you.*
▻ *phrase* You say '**You're welcome!**' as a polite response to someone who has thanked you. [*same as* **not at all, it's a pleasure**]

weld /wɛld/ *verb*; *noun*
▻ *verb*: **welds, welding, welded**
1 You **weld** pieces of metal or plastic together by pressing them together, first heating their edges to soften them; pieces of metal can also **be welded** by fusing or melting them together using electricity. **2** (*formal*) You **weld** people into a group when you unite them so that they fit together or work together in a satisfactory way: *It took six months to weld them into a competent team.* — *noun* **welder:** *They were both employed as welders at the shipyard.*
▻ *noun*: **welds**
A **weld** is a joint between two pieces of metal or plastic made by welding.

welfare /ˈwɛlfɛə(r)/ *noun* (*uncount*)
1 The **welfare** of a person or group is their health, comfort and contentment: *The Social Services Department were primarily responsible for the child's welfare.* **2** (*often adjectival*) **Welfare** describes work concerned with the health, education, housing, and financial difficulties of the members of a community: *the welfare services* ▫ *welfare workers.* **3** (*AmE*) Financial support given to those in need is referred to as **welfare**: *reduced to living off welfare.* [compare **benefit**]

welfare state /wɛlfɛə ˈsteɪt/ *noun* (*used in the singular*)
The **welfare state** is a system in which the government uses income from taxes to look after citizens' welfare, with the provision of free health care, old-age pensions, and financial support for the disabled or unemployed.

well[1] /wɛl/ *adverb*; *adjective*; *interjection*
▻ *adverb*: **better, best**
1 You do something **well** when you do it skilfully or efficiently, or at a high standard: *She already speaks and writes Czech quite well.* ▫ *He didn't perform as well as he normally does.* ▫ *She coped well under difficult circumstances.* **2 Well** also means **a** satisfactorily: *I'm glad everything has turned out well for you.* ▫ *Did the children behave well?* **b** thoroughly, properly or fully: *Did you know the dead girl well?* ▫ *The baby was so well wrapped up against the cold that he could hardly be seen.* ▫ *The phenomenon has already been well researched.* **3** Someone who is doing **well** is having success in their career, or making plenty of money. **4** People who live **well** live a comfortable or luxurious life. **5 Well** is used to emphasize certain adverbial and adjectival expressions: *It's well past my bedtime.* ▫ *We were well ahead of the others.* ▫ *Stand well clear of the lift doors.* ▫ *Keep well back.* ▫ *She's well over fifty.* ▫ *The castle is well worth a visit.* ▫ *I'm well aware of the difficulties.* **6 Well** is used with *may*, *might* and *could* to emphasize the likelihood or probability of something: *You may well be right.* ▫ *Errors may well be frequent.* **7** (*often informal*) **Well** is combined with words such as *quite*, *perfectly*, *jolly*, and with swearwords such as *damn* and *bloody*, to express impatience or annoyance: *You can quite well telephone yourself.* ▫ *He jolly well ought to apologize.* ▫ *I'm damn well going to report him.* ▫ *You know perfectly well I don't take milk.*
▻ *adjective*: **better**
You are **well** when you are healthy: *I do hope your family are all well.* ▫ *He hasn't been well lately.* ▫ *I'm not feeling very well.* [*opposite* **ill**]
▻ *interjection*
You use **well** for various purposes in conversation, *eg*
1 when asking for a response or explanation: *Well, what do you think?* **2** to introduce a reply: *Well, I think we should wait and see.* **3** to continue telling something after an interruption: *Well now, where were we?* ▫ *Well, when at last we got to the youth hostel ...* **4** to express reactions such as surprise or annoyance: *Well, of all the cheek!* **5** to introduce a correction to what you have said: *He's got two children, well, five if you count*

his second wife's. **6** when hesitating, or expressing doubt: *She's, well, not exactly his wife.*
▷ ***phrases*** **1** If you say **all is well** you mean that the situation is satisfactory: *I hope all is well with you?* **2** For **all very well** see **all**. **3** You use **as well** in several ways, *eg* **a** like *too* or *also*, when mentioning another person or thing that what you have said applies to: *He inherits all the money, and the house as well.* □ *When my husband retires I'll retire as well.* □ *We'll be visiting our other daughter as well.* **b** You say that it would be **as well** or just **as well** to do something if you think it would be sensible to do it: *It would be just as well to book the tickets now.* **c** If you say you may or might **as well** do something you mean that you will do it although you are not eager to: *I may as well admit it before you ask.* **d** If you say it is **just as well** that something is so you mean it is lucky or satisfactory that it is so: *It was just as well you arrived when you did.* □ *The weather turned out wet, which was just as well, because I was too busy to go anyway.* **4** You refer to one thing **as well as** another when you mean the first in addition to the second: *She has all her school work to do, as well as looking after her sick mother.* □ *I've still got the shopping to do, as well as the washing and ironing.* **5** You say you **can't very well** do something if you think it would not be wise to do it: *I couldn't very well tell her the truth.* **6** You **leave**, or **let, well alone** when you decide not to interfere with things that are satisfactory. **7** People **mean well** if they have helpful or kindly intentions, even if they make mistakes or upset others. **8** You say **'Oh well'** to express your acceptance of a disappointment: *Oh well, I suppose we can't always win.* **9** Something that is **pretty well** so is nearly so: *We've pretty well finished.* **10** People **think well of** you if they approve of you. **11** (*old or formal*) You use **very well** in accepting an order or agreeing to a request: *Very well; you may come with us tomorrow.* **12** You use **well and good** to express satisfaction with a situation: *If they really want to leave, well and good.* **13** Something that is **well and truly** done is thoroughly or completely done: *We were well and truly beaten this time.* **14** You say **'well done!'** to someone to praise them for having done something successfully: *You've achieved excellent results; well done!* **15 a** Someone who is **well off** has plenty of money: *He came from a well-off family.* **b** You are **well off** for something when you have plenty of it: *The citizens of Prague are well off for opera houses.* **c** You are **well off** when you are in circumstances that you ought to be contented with: *Some people don't know when they're well off.* **16** (*informal*) If you say you are **well out of** a difficult situation you mean you are lucky to have escaped from it. **17** (*informal*) You are **well up in**, or **on**, a subject if you know a lot about it. *I don't know the answer. I'm not very well up on the history of China.*

well[2] /wɛl/ *noun*; *verb*
▷ ***noun***: **wells**
A **well** is a hole dug deep into the ground to give access to a supply of water, oil or gas.
▷ ***verb***: **wells, welling, welled**

> ***phrasal verb***
> Tears **well up** in your eyes when they start filling your eyes: *He felt the tears welling up and turned his head away.*

we'll /wiːl/
We'll is the spoken, or informal written, form of **we will** or **we shall**: *We'll have lunch in town, shall we?*

well-advised /wɛləd'vaɪzd/ *adjective*
You tell someone they would be **well-advised** to do something if you think it would be sensible for them to do it: *You'd be well-advised to apply for that job.*

well-balanced /wɛl'balənst/ *adjective*
1 A **well-balanced** person is someone who is sane and sensible, and is not troubled by emotional difficulties: *I was surprised to find that this well-balanced and fulfilled woman had had such a disturbed childhood.* **2** A **well-balanced** diet contains a good variety of healthy foods.

well-behaved /wɛlbɪ'heɪvd/ *adjective*
A **well-behaved** child is polite and obedient: *Her new class of seven-year-olds seemed quiet and well-behaved.*

wellbeing /wɛl'biːɪŋ/ *noun* (*uncount*)
Your **wellbeing** is your state of health and happiness; you have a sense of **wellbeing** when you feel well, happy and contented: *I'm thinking only of your wellbeing.*

well-bred /wɛl'brɛd/ *adjective*
A **well-bred** person is polite and has good manners: *It wasn't considered well-bred to talk with your mouth full.* [*opposite* **ill-bred**]

well-built /wɛl'bɪlt/ *adjective*
A **well-built** person, especially a man, has a strong, muscular appearance: *He was tall and well-built.* [*opposite* **slight, puny**]

well-dressed /wɛl'drɛst/ *adjective*
Well-dressed people wear smart clothes: *She always looked neat and well-dressed.* [*same as* **elegant, smart**; *opposite* **scruffy**]

well-earned /wɛl'ɜːnd/ *adjective*
Something is **well-earned** if the person who gets it deserves it: *She was enjoying a well-earned rest in Cyprus after several months' intensive work.*

well-fed /wɛl'fɛd/ *adjective*
People who are **well-fed** get plenty to eat regularly: *The children looked well-fed and contented.*

well-founded /wɛl'faʊndɪd/ *adjective*
A fear or suspicion that is **well-founded** is based on knowledge of the the facts and probabilities: *Her suspicions proved well-founded.* [*same as* **justified**; *opposite* **baseless**]

well-groomed /wɛl'gruːmd/ *adjective*
Someone who is **well-groomed** takes care of their appearance and looks clean, neat and smart: *well-groomed hair.*

well-heeled /wɛl'hiːld/ *adjective* (*informal*)
People who are **well-heeled** are rich: *her well-heeled relatives.*

well-informed /wɛlɪn'fɔːmd/ *adjective*
1 People who are **well-informed** about something have a thorough and reliable knowledge of it. **2** A **well-informed** person has a lot of varied knowledge.

wellington /'wɛlɪŋtən/ *noun*: **wellingtons**
Wellingtons or **wellington boots** are waterproof rubber or plastic boots that loosely cover your foot and the lower part of your leg: *a pair of red wellingtons.*

well-intentioned /wɛlɪn'tɛnʃənd/ *adjective*
A **well-intentioned** person wants to be kind or helpful but their efforts sometimes have unfortunate effects: *My well-intentioned attempt to comfort her just made her worse.* [*same as* **well-meaning**]

well-kept /wɛl'kɛpt/ *adjective*
Things that are **well-kept** are carefully looked after: *a well-kept garden* □ *well-kept hands and nails.* [*opposite* **neglected**]

well-known /wɛl'noun/ *adjective*
Someone or something that is **well-known** is famous, or is familiar to, or known by, a lot of people: *well-known television personalities.* □ *It's well known that violence breeds violence.*

well-mannered /wɛl'mɑnəd/ *adverb*
A **well-mannered** person is polite and has good manners: *Her son was charming and well-mannered.* [*opposite* **rude, ill-mannered**]

well-meaning /wɛl'mi:nɪŋ/ *adjective*
A **well-meaning** person wants to be helpful and kind, but their efforts sometimes have unfortunate results: *well-meaning but disastrous interference.* [*same as* **well-intentioned**]

well-meant /wɛl'mɛnt/ *adjective*
Something that is **well-meant** is intended to be helpful, but may have unfortunate results: *well-meant but foolish advice.*

well-nigh /wɛl'naɪ/ *adverb*
Something that is **well-nigh** so is almost so: *The place must be well-nigh unrecognizable after all these years.* [*same as* **all but**]

well-preserved /wɛlprɪ'zɜ:vd/ *adjective*
A **well-preserved** person looks younger than they are: *She must have been in her sixties, but was well preserved and still very elegant.*

well-read /wɛl'rɛd/ *adjective*
A **well-read** person has read a lot of books and learnt a lot from them: *He seemed intelligent and well-read.*

well-spoken /wɛl'spoukən/ *adjective*
Someone who is **well-spoken** has a polite, clear and correct way of speaking: *She was received and looked after by a well-spoken young man.*

well-thought-of /wɛl 'θɔ:t ɒv/ *adjective*
Someone or something that is **well thought of** has a good reputation and is respected and admired: *He's a well-thought-of composer here, but unknown abroad.* [*same as* **respected, highly regarded**]

well-thought-out /wɛl θɔ:t 'ɑut/ *adjective*
Something that is **well thought out** is planned in a careful and thorough manner: *The play had a well-thought-out and original plot.*

well-timed /wɛl'taɪmd/ *adjective*
Well-timed remarks or actions are made or performed at a good or suitable moment: *her well-timed intervention* □ *Your arrival was well timed; I'm just pouring out drinks.*

well-to-do /wɛl tə 'du:/ *adjective*
Someone who is **well-to-do** has plenty of money: *Her parents were well-to-do professionals.* [*same as* **wealthy, rich, well off**]

well-tried /wɛl'traɪd/ *adjective*
Something that is **well tried** has been found to be reliable from frequent testing: *back to the old well-tried education methods.* [*opposite* **untried**]

wellwisher /'wɛlwɪʃə(r)/ *noun*: **wellwishers**
A **wellwisher** is someone who is concerned for your welfare and happiness and wants you to be successful: *Her dressing room was filled with flowers from admirers and wellwishers.*

well-worn /wɛl'wɔ:n/ *adjective*
1 A **well-worn** object or garment has been used or worn a lot, and looks old: *a well-worn dictionary.* **2** A **well-worn** expression or joke is one that everyone knows and is tired of hearing.

welly /'wɛlɪ/ *noun* (*informal*): **wellies**
Wellies are wellingtons: *Is there a spare pair of wellies for me?*

welt /wɛlt/ *noun*: **welts**
The **welt** of a sweater is the band of stronger, tighter knitting round the waist.

welter /'wɛltə(r)/ *noun* (*used in the singular*)
A **welter** of things is a confused mass of them: *We had difficulty finding our way through the welter of instructions.* [*same as* **jumble, muddle**]

wend /wɛnd/ *verb* (*literary*): **wends, wending, wended**
▷ ***phrase*** You **wend your way** somewhere when you go there, especially slowly.

went /wɛnt/ *verb*
Went is the past tense of **go**.

wept /wɛpt/ *verb*
Wept is the past tense and past participle of **weep**.

were /wɜ:(r)/ *verb*
1 Were is the form of the past tense of **be** used with *we* and *they*, and with *you* (plural or singular). **2** (*especially formal*) In wishes and conditional sentences **were** is often used instead of **was**: *I wish I were dead.* □ *If I were a rich man I wouldn't have to work hard.* □ *Were he to resign now, he would forfeit a proportion of his pension.* □ *She found herself treated as if she were royalty.*
▷ ***phrases*** **1** For **as it were** see **as**. **2** You say **'If I were you'** when you are giving someone advice: *I'd book early if I were you.* [*same as* **in your place**]

we're /wɪə(r)/
We're is the spoken, and informal written, form of **we are**: *I'm afraid we're a bit late.* □ *We're hoping to see you here in July.*

weren't /wɜ:nt/
Weren't is the spoken, and informal written, form of **were not**: *You weren't in when I rang before.* □ *Weren't we going to visit your mother today?*

west /wɛst/ *noun; adverb; adjective*
▷ ***noun*** (*used in the singular*)
1 The **west** is the direction in which the sun sets: *Rain clouds appeared to the west of us.* □ *The wind moved round from north to west.* **2** The **west** is the part of a country or other area that lies towards the west: *The West of Scotland was largely colonized by Irish invaders.* □ *The west tends to get more rain.* **3** The **West** is the term given to **a** the countries of Europe and North America, as distinct from those of Asia. **b** (*history*) the non-communist countries as distinct from the communist countries of the East. **c** (*history*) the part of the United States to the west of the Mississippi.
▷ ***adverb***
West means to the west: *The train was heading west.* □ *Glasgow lies west of Edinburgh.* □ *The west-facing windows get the late sun.*
▷ ***adjective***
1 A part of a place with the name or description **west** is a part towards the west: *the famous west window of the cathedral* □ *West Yorkshire.* **2** A **west** wind blows from the west.
▷ ***phrase*** (*informal*) Something that **has gone west** has disappeared.

westbound /'wɛstbɑund/ *adjective*
1 Westbound traffic is travelling west. **2** The **westbound** carriageway of a motorway is the one used by traffic travelling west.

westerly /'wɛstəlɪ/ *adjective*
1 A **westerly** direction or region lies towards the west: *the most westerly island of the group.* □ *We were driving*

in a westerly direction. **2** A **westerly** wind blows from the west.

western /ˈwɛstən/ *adjective; noun*

▻ ***adjective***

Western means in or belonging to the west of a country or other area: *The snow will turn to rain in milder western areas.*

▻ ***noun*: westerns**

A **western** is a film or story about 19th-century cowboys in the west of the US.

westernize or **westernise** /ˈwɛstənaɪz/ *verb*: **westernizes, westernizing, westernized**

A country **is westernized** when products, clothing, ideas and behaviour that are typical of Europe and North America are introduced into it.

westward /ˈwɛstwəd/ *adverb; adjective*

▻ ***adverb***

Westward or **westwards** means towards the west: *We turned westwards.*

▻ ***adjective***: *the westward trail.*

wet /wɛt/ *adjective; noun; verb*

▻ ***adjective*: wetter, wettest**

1 Something that is **wet** is covered or soaked in water, rain, sweat or other liquid: *His face was wet with perspiration.* □ *a pile of wet clothes.* [*opposite* **dry**]

> Compare **moist** and **damp**, which both mean slightly wet: *a moist atmosphere; The grass feels damp.*

2 Wet weather is rainy weather; you say it is **wet** when it is raining. [*opposite* **dry, fine**] **3** Things such as paint, ink or cement are **wet** when they have not yet dried or hardened: *The signature was still wet.* [*opposite* **dry**] **4** People's eyes are **wet** when they have been crying; faces are **wet** when they are covered with tears: *wet cheeks.* [*opposite* **dry**] **5** A baby is **wet** when its nappy is soaked with urine. [*opposite* **dry**] **6** (*informal, derogatory*) If you describe a person as **wet** you mean they have no strength of personality, enthusiasm or confidence. [*same as* **feeble, ineffectual**]

▻ ***noun*** (*uncount*)

The **wet** is the rain: *These cushions were left out in the wet all night.*

▻ ***verb*: wets, wetting, wet** or **wetted**

1 (**wet** or **wetted**) You **wet** something when you get water or another liquid over it: *Wet your hair thoroughly before applying shampoo.* □ *The rain had got in and wet a corner of the carpet.* □ *She wetted a corner of her apron and used it to wipe the baby's face.* [*same as* **soak, splash**] **2** (**wet**) A person, especially a child, **wets** the bed, their clothes or themselves when they urinate in their bed or clothes: *He's wet his pants again.*

▻ ***phrase*** You are **wet through** when your clothing is soaked, *eg* with rain: *They came home wet through.*

wet blanket /wɛt ˈblaŋkɪt/ *noun* (*derogatory*): **wet blankets**

If you call someone a **wet blanket** you mean that they lack the ability to enjoy things themselves, and tend to spoil other people's enjoyment.

wet suit /ˈwɛt suːt/ *noun*: **wet suits**

A **wet suit** is a tight-fitting thick rubber suit worn by divers, canoeists and underwater swimmers to keep themselves warm.

we've /wiːv/

We've is the spoken, and informal written, form of **we have**: *We've plenty of cash for today.* □ *We'll do that when we've finished this.*

whack /wak/ *verb; noun* (*informal*)

▻ ***verb*: whacks, whacking, whacked**

You **whack** someone or something when you hit them hard: *He used to whack us with a hairbrush.* [*same as* **hit, beat, spank**] — *noun* **whacking:** *I lost count of the number of whackings I got at school.*

▻ ***noun*: whacks**

1 A **whack** is a hard blow, or the sound it makes: *His mother gave him a whack on the behind.* **2** (*used in the singular*) Your **whack** of something is your share of it; the full **whack** is the maximum contribution or charge: *Don't worry; we'll all get our whack of the profits.* □ *If you're not a student, or under 26, you have to pay the full whack.*

whacked /wakt/ *adjective* (*informal*)

You say you are **whacked** when you are tired or exhausted.

whale /weɪl/ *noun*: **whales**

A **whale** is a huge sea animal shaped like a fish, that breathes air through an opening on top of its head.

▻ ***phrase*** (*informal*) You **have a whale of a time** when you enjoy yourself thoroughly.

whaling /ˈweɪlɪŋ/ *noun* (*uncount*)

Whaling is the hunting and killing of whales.

wharf /wɔːf/ *noun*: **wharfs** or **wharves**

A **wharf** is a stone or wooden platform built beside the sea or a river, for loading and unloading ships.

what /wɒt/ *pronoun; determiner; interjection; adverb*

▻ ***pronoun*** (*interrogative*)

You use **what** in asking for something to be identified or specified, or in talking about knowing things and finding things out: *What's the time?* □ *What's the matter?* □ *What else do you remember?* □ *What do you want to be when you grow up? A doctor?* □ *'Try hammering it down.' 'What with?'* □ *What's it got to do with you?* [= it isn't your business] □ *What does it matter anyway?* [= it doesn't matter] □ *What are you so worried about?* [= why are you so worried?] □ *Do you remember what his surname is?* □ *I'd no idea what to do.* □ *It's a quotation, but I don't know what from.*

▻ ***determiner*** (*interrogative*): *What time is it?* □ *What sort of clothes would be suitable for the tropics?* □ *I wasn't sure what temperature to set the oven at.* □ *He works in health care, but in what capacity I can't remember.* [see note at **which**]

▻ ***pronoun*** (*relative*)

You introduce a clause with **what 1** in describing or defining something: *Thanks for the information; it's just what I wanted.* □ *He usually says what he means.* □ *Is that what you're trying to say?* □ *Make sure you get what you want out of life.* □ *What you need is a good long sleep.* □ *He made what I thought was a rather silly joke.* **2** to refer to the whole of an amount or supply, usually implying that it is small: *I've eaten what was left of the food.* **3** to mean 'anything or everything that': *I'll do what I can to help.* [*same as* **whatever**]

▻ ***determiner*** (*relative*): *We'll share what food we have.* □ *I've spent what little there was.* □ *They provided what hospitality they could.*

▻ ***determiner***

What is used in exclamations and questions that express delight, admiration, disgust or annoyance: *What a lie!* □ *What nonsense!* □ *What a stupid suggestion!* □ *What beautiful flowers!* □ *What awful clothes he wears!* □ *What a pleasure it is to see the sun!* □ *What business is it of theirs?* □ *They don't realize what fun reading can be.*

▻ ***interjection***

You use **what** in conversation in various ways, *eg* **1** to respond to someone who addresses you, wanting to ask you something: *'Granny?' 'What?' 'How do you* *spell 'gauge'?* **2** (*informal*) to ask someone to repeat something, because you didn't hear it properly: *'Have you seen my dictionary?' 'What?' 'Have you seen my dictionary?'* □ *'It's a thesaurus.' 'A what?'* **3** to express surprise: *'I've finished.' 'What, already?'*

▻ ***adverb*** (*sentence adverb*)

You use **what** to introduce a guess or rough estimate: *We've known each other for, what, 25 years.*

▻ ***phrases*** **1** You say **'I know what'** or **'I tell you what'** when you have had an idea: *I know what; we'll have curried eggs.* **2** (*informal*) People say **'so what?'** or **'what of it?'** to express impatience or annoyance at someone's comment or observation: *'I see you've bought a new raincoat.' 'So what?'* **3** For **what about** see **about**. **4** You use **what have you** like 'etc', *eg* at the end of a list, to mean 'and other things of the same kind': *newspapers, magazines and what have you.* [*same as* **and so on**] **5** You use **what if** to mean 'what shall we do if' when mentioning something that might go wrong: *What if she objects?* **6** People sometimes say impatiently **'what is it?'** in response to someone who addresses them, wanting to ask them something: *'Mum.' 'Yes, what is it now? I'm busy.'* **7** If you ask **what** someone or something **is like** you are asking for a description or account of them: *What's she like?* □ *What does it look like?* [see also **like**] **8** For **what's more** see **more**. **9** (*informal*) Someone who knows **what's what** knows all the important things, either about a situation, or life generally. **10** (*informal*; *especially AmE*) If you ask **what's with** a person or thing you mean what is the matter with them: *What's with Rosie today? She's so bad-tempered.* **11** You use **what with** to introduce an explanation for something that has gone wrong: *What with the bomb scare and panic I quite forgot to pay the bill.*

whatever /wɒt'ɛvə(r)/ *pronoun*; *determiner*; *adverb*

▻ ***pronoun*** (*relative*)

You use **whatever** to mean 'anything or everything that': *They're loyal and will vote for whatever he advises.* □ *I'll do whatever I can to stop her worrying.*

▻ ***determiner*** (*relative*): *We'll help in whatever way you need.* □ *They'll pocket whatever valuables you leave behind.*

▻ ***pronoun***

Whatever is also used **1** (also **what ever**) for emphasis in questions that express surprise or concern: *Whatever can he be doing all this time?* **2** to express vagueness or lack of certainty about the identity or nature of something: *He wanted us each to write a limerick, whatever that may be.* **3** to say that something is so, or must be done, in any circumstances: *Whatever happens, you can rely on me.* □ *Whatever else you do, don't panic.* □ *If you have any worries, whatever they are, please contact me.* □ *Whatever his faults, I'm still fond of him.*

▻ ***determiner:*** *If, for whatever reason* [= for some or any reason, whatever it is], *you decide to withdraw a large sum, please give us a month's warning.* □ *She should not have left the baby alone, whatever excuse she had.*

▻ ***adverb***

You use **whatever** for emphasis after a negative noun expression, to mean the same as 'at all': *I remember nothing whatever about the match.* □ *There's no reason whatever to be anxious.* [*same as* **whatsoever**]

▻ ***phrases*** **1** (*informal*) You add **'or whatever'** after mentioning something particular, to mean 'or anything else of that kind': *when you're ironing or whatever.* **2** (*informal*) You say **'whatever you say'** in response to someone's suggestion, to show you are willing to accept it.

what'll /'wɒtəl/

What'll is the spoken, and the informal written, form of **what will**: *What'll happen to him?*

what's /wɒts/

What's is the spoken, or informal written, form of **1 what is**: *What's that noise?* □ *What's she doing?* **2 what has**, where *has* is an auxiliary verb: *What's been happening?*

whatsoever /wɒtsoʊ'ɛvə(r)/ *adverb*

Whatsoever is used for emphasis after negative noun expressions to mean the same as 'at all': *I gave him no encouragement whatsoever.* □ *'Have you any doubt?' 'None whatsoever.'*

wheat /wi:t/ *noun* (*uncount*)

Wheat is a crop of the grass family, or its grain, which is used for making bread: *fields of wheat.*

wheedle /'wi:dəl/ *verb*: **wheedles, wheedling, wheedled**

You **wheedle** something out of someone when you use a mixture of cunning and charm to persuade them to give it to you; you **wheedle** someone into doing something when you persuade them to do it: *I'll see if I can wheedle some money out of Dad for the trip.* □ *The children would wheedle her into letting them stay up late.*

wheel /wi:l/ *noun*; *verb*

▻ ***noun*****: wheels**

1 A **wheel** is one of the circular objects on which a vehicle moves along the ground, fitted on to a rod or axle, round which it turns or rotates; bicycles have two wheels, and cars four. **2** A **wheel** is any circular turning device with a mechanical function: *a water wheel* □ *a spinning wheel.* **3** The steering wheel of a vehicle is referred to as the **wheel**: *There was a uniformed police officer at* (or *behind*) *the wheel.* — *adjective* **wheeled:** *lorries, cars, bicycles and other wheeled vehicles.*

▻ ***verb*****: wheels, wheeling, wheeled**

1 You **wheel** a wheeled conveyance such as a bicycle, pram or wheelchair, or someone or something in it or on it, somewhere, when you push them there: *The patient was wheeled back to the ward.* □ *We wheeled our trolleys round to the carpark.* **2** Troops, birds, aircraft and other vehicles **wheel** when they move in a curve: *The marching column wheeled left.* **3** You **wheel** round when you turn round suddenly: *He wheeled round when he heard my voice behind him.*

wheelbarrow /'wi:lbaroʊ/ *noun*: **wheelbarrows**

A **wheelbarrow** is a small cart with a wheel in front and two legs at the back, and two handles for lifting and pushing it with, that you use for carrying things in, especially in the garden. [see picture at **tool**]

wheelchair /'wi:ltʃɛə(r)/ *noun*: **wheelchairs**

A **wheelchair** is a chair with wheels in which people who are ill or cannot walk can be pushed, or can push themselves, around.

wheeze /wi:z/ *verb*; *noun*

▻ ***verb*****: wheezes, wheezing, wheezed**

People **wheeze** when they breathe noisily and with difficulty, *eg* when they have asthma or lung trouble: *His face was blue and he was wheezing heavily.*

▻ ***noun*****: wheezes**: *I could hardly understand what he was saying through the coughs and wheezes.*

when /wɛn/ *adverb*; *conjunction*; *pronoun*

▻ ***adverb*** (*interrogative*)

You use **when** to ask about the time that something is happening, during what period it happened, or how soon it is going to happen; you also use **when** in talking about knowing or finding out the time of something: *'When does the plane arrive?' 'It's due at 10.40.'* □ *'She's off to Budapest.' 'Oh, when?' 'Next week.'* □ *'When did mini skirts first come into fashion?' 'In the late '60s.'* □ *Have you any idea when you'll be finished?* □ *People don't necessarily know when to seek expert advice.*

▻ ***conjunction***

When means **1** 'at the time, or during the period,

that': *She always locks the door when she goes to bed.* □ *It happened when I was abroad.* **2** 'as soon as': *I'll come when I've done the washing-up.* **3** 'at any time that' or 'whenever': *Come when you can.* □ *When possible, we take patients to the theatre.* **4** 'but just then': *I was about to leave when the telephone rang.* **5** 'because then': *Ring tomorrow, when I'll have more information.* **6** 'in spite of the fact that' or 'considering that': *Why stand when you can sit?* **7** 'though': *People have this fear of computers, when in fact their whole purpose is to make life easier.*

▻ ***pronoun*** (*interrogative*): *They stayed talking, until when I can't say.*

▻ ***pronoun*** (*relative*): *I got angry with her last Thursday, since when she hasn't spoken to me.* □ *It'd be nice to go back to when people went round in carriages.* □ *That was an era when life was harder.*

whence /wɛns/ *adverb; conjunction*

▻ ***adverb*** (*interrogative; formal or literary*)

You ask **whence** something comes if you want to know **1** the place it has come from: *They enquired whence I had come.* **2** the cause of it, or the reason for it: *I cannot explain whence this misunderstanding arose.*

▻ ***conjunction***: *Missed appointments will be charged for, whence the importance of arriving on time.*

whenever /wɛn'ɛvə(r)/ *conjunction; adverb*

▻ ***conjunction***

Whenever means **1** 'any or every time that': *She gets furious whenever she fails to get her way.* □ *We visit her whenever possible.* **2** 'if ever, at any time': *I'll be here whenever you need me.*

▻ ***adverb***

You use **whenever** to express uncertainty about the time or date of something: *He was killed at the battle of Flodden, whenever that was.*

▻ ***phrase*** (*informal*) You add **or whenever** after mentioning a particular time, to mean 'or some other time': *We could meet for a drink next week, or whenever.*

where /wɛə(r)/ *adverb; pronoun; conjunction*

▻ ***adverb*** (*interrogative*)

1 You use **where** to ask about the place something or someone is in or at, or is going to, or was obtained from; you also use **where** in talking about knowing or finding out places: *Where's my wallet?* □ *Where does this road takes us?* □ *'There's a shooting star!' 'Where?'* □ *He could remember roughly where the cave was.* □ *Shakespeare says it, but I can't think where.* □ *Could you advise me where to buy a good map?* **2 Where** can also refer to a point or stage in a series of events, or in a situation: *Where did our marriage go wrong?*

▻ ***pronoun*** (*interrogative*): *Where have you come from?* □ *Who can tell us where we got up to in Chapter 3?*

▻ ***conjunction or pronoun*** (*relative*)

You use **where 1** in identifying, specifying, or giving information about a place: *We went to see the village where I was born.* □ *I've read up to where the children discover the secret cave.* □ *I wanted to visit Pontefract, where the cakes come from.* □ *We stopped at Bradford, where* [= and there] *we collected Jane.* **2** to mean 'any place that': *I must be nice to have enough money to travel where you like.* □ *Just sit where you want.* [*same as* **wherever**] **3** in identifying a case, situation or point, or an aspect of something: *It was one of those situations where you had to be very tactful.* □ *This is a good example of where you use 'might', not 'may'.* □ *That's where you're wrong.* **4** to mean 'in any situation in which': *We try to keep families together where we can.* □ *Where possible, names have been disguised.* [*same as* **wherever**] **5** to mean 'in certain situations in which', when you are presenting a contrast: *It's sometimes easier to talk to a stranger, where you wouldn't want to confide in a friend or relation.*

whereabouts *adverb; noun*

▻ ***adverb*** /wɛərə'baʊts/ (*interrogative*)

If you ask **whereabouts** something or someone is, or is going, you want to know approximately where they are, or are going: *Whereabouts does this friend of yours live?* □ *Whereabouts will you be going in Zambia?* □ *But didn't he say whereabouts he hid it?*

▻ ***noun*** /'wɛərəbaʊts/ (*plural*)

The place that a person or thing is in is their **whereabouts**: *Anyone who has seen them or knows their whereabouts is asked to contact the police.*

whereas /wɛər'az/ *conjunction*

Whereas introduces a clause that presents a contrast and means 'but' or 'though actually': *Stanley was a big man, whereas he wife was small and thin.* □ *If I got a flat tyre tomorrow I could cope, whereas I couldn't have before.*

whereby /wɛə'baɪ/ *pronoun* (*relative; formal*)

A system, plan or procedure **whereby** something happens or is achieved is the cause of it, or the means of achieving it; **whereby** means 'by which': *We thought up a plan whereby we could force the council to pay the bulk of the repair cost.*

wherein /wɛər'ɪn/ *adverb; pronoun*

▻ ***adverb*** (*interrogative; literary*)

If you ask **wherein** something exists, you want to have its existence explained: *Wherein lies the justification for the extermination of whole peoples?*

▻ ***pronoun*** (*relative; old or legal*)

Wherein means 'in which': *God's power, wherein we place our trust.*

where's /wɛəz/

Where's is the spoken, and informal written, form of **1 where is**: *Where's Bill?* □ *Where's he going to sleep tonight?* **2 where has**, when *has* is an auxiliary verb: *Where's she been?*

whereupon /wɛərə'pɒn/ *conjunction*

Whereupon means 'immediately after which', or 'as a result of which': *Her manager asked her to work overtime without pay, whereupon she resigned.*

wherever /wɛər'ɛvə(r)/ *conjunction; adverb*

▻ ***conjunction***

You use **wherever 1** to mean 'in, at or to any or every place that': *Her diary accompanied her wherever she went.* □ *Wherever he found himself, he would head for the nearest bookshop.* **2** to mean 'in any situation or case in which': *Wherever possible, students are placed with native-speaking families.* **3** to mean 'the place where' in referring to an unknown or unspecified place: *Could you post it on to wherever Alison's living now?* **4** to say that something is so, or must be done, no matter where someone or something is, or goes: *Wherever else you go, you must see Rome.* □ *I'll never forget you, wherever I am.*

▻ ***adverb***

You use **wherever 1** to express uncertainty about the place where something is: *St Adamnan's Church, wherever that is.* **2** (also **where ever**) as an emphatic form of **where**: *Wherever did you get that idea?*

▻ ***phrase*** (*informal*) You add **or wherever** after mentioning a particular place, to mean 'or some other place': *I could meet you at Brown's Restaurant, or wherever.*

wherewithal /'wɛəwɪðɔːl/ *noun* (*used in the singular*)

You have the **wherewithal** to do something if you have the means, resources, necessary equipment or cash to do it with: *Where does she find the wherewithal to do all that travelling?*

whet /wɛt/ *verb*: **whets, whetting, whetted**
Something **whets** your appetite for something when it increases your desire for it: *The photographs had whetted their appetite for a Himalayan holiday.*

whether /ˈwɛðə(r)/ *conjunction*
You use **whether** **1** to introduce an indirect question: *I must find out whether the trains are still running.* □ *I doubt whether she realizes.* □ *His release will depend on whether he is thought to pose a danger.* □ *I felt some uncertainty as to whether she was really suitable.* [*same as* **if**] **2** to introduce an indirect question with alternative possibilities: *I didn't know whether to laugh or cry.* □ *Let me know whether or not you're interested.* **3** to state that something is so, or applies, or must be done, in either of two possible circumstances, or in any of several: *You must tell them it was your fault, whether or not anyone suspects it.* □ *The rules, whether fair or unfair, are not our concern.* □ *whatever form of transport you use, whether car, bus, train, bicycle, or your own feet.*

whew see **phew**.

which /wɪtʃ/ *determiner; pronoun*
▷ ***determiner*** (*interrogative*)
You use **which** in asking for a particular person or thing to be selected or identified from a group of possible ones, or in referring to a choice between possible people or things: *Which colour do you prefer?* □ *Which restaurant shall we eat at today?* □ *In which city is the Statue of Liberty?* □ *Which three things do you treasure most?* □ *Let me know which train you'll be arriving on.* □ *She has a job in local government, but in which department I couldn't tell you.*

> **What** is used rather than **which** where the possible people or things are not limited to a known group: *What clothes would be suitable for a holiday in Iceland?*

▷ ***pronoun*** (*interrogative*): *Which of the twins is studying medicine?* □ *Which is your room?* □ *I didn't know which to choose.* □ *He's going to be sent to Vienna or Prague, but he hasn't heard which yet.*
▷ ***pronoun*** (*relative*)
1 You use **which** in specifying or describing things: *This is the kind of thing which inevitably increases costs.* □ *He was genuinely keen to meet his constituents and visit the areas in which they lived.*

> You can use **that** instead of **which** except after a preposition, and can leave out **which** except after a preposition or where it is the subject of a verb: *Here's the booklet which* (or *that*) *tells you about university grants. Here's the booklet which* (or *that*) *you wanted,* or *Here's the booklet you wanted. This is the very chair she used to sit in.*

2 You can use **which**, after a comma, to add a comment on something: *I visited their new premises, which I'm very impressed by.* □ *This interesting idea, which is being tried out in one or two districts, is not strictly a new one.* □ *I'm sorry about the error, for which I'm afraid I have no excuse.* □ *The annual report, copies of which have been circulated, will be discussed later.* □ *He said he could speak Russian, which was untrue.*
▷ ***phrases*** **1** You use **in which case** to say what results from the possible circumstances you have mentioned: *My father may have to go into hospital, in which case I won't be going on holiday.* **2** You say you can't tell **which is which** if you cannot distinguish between two people or things that are very alike.

whichever /wɪtʃˈɛvə(r)/ *determiner; pronoun*
▷ ***determiner***
You use **whichever** **1** (*relative*) in specifying or identifying things or people from a group to mean 'the one that', or 'any that', or 'all that': *You're welcome to borrow whichever swimming costume fits you better.* □ *I'd be grateful for help from whichever teachers are free this afternoon.* **2** to mean 'depending on which', in referring to a number of possibilities: *I could give you an appointment at 10.00 or 10.30, whichever time is more convenient for you.* **3** to say that something is so, or must be done, in any of several possible choices or circumstances: *We're going to be late, whichever way we go.* □ *Whichever work shift you're on, please remember to clock in and out.*
▷ ***pronoun***: *The girls walked along laughing, their heads turning to whichever of them took up the conversation.* □ *No-one needs these magazines, so take whichever you want.* □ *I could ring you at home or at work, whichever you prefer.* □ *There are several choices of software, but whichever we select, we can't change it later.*

whiff /wɪf/ *noun*: **whiffs**
1 A **whiff** of something is a slight smell of it, or a little rush of it: *He caught a whiff of new paint as he opened the door.* □ *a whiff of smoke* □ *a whiff of fresh air.* **2** A **whiff** of something such as scandal or danger is a slight sign or suggestion of it.

while /waɪl/ *conjunction; noun; verb*
▷ ***conjunction***
1 Something that happens **while** something else is happening **a** happens at the same time as something else: *She drove the guests home while I did the washing-up.* **b** happens for as long as something else is happening: *God guards us while we sleep.* **c** happens during the time that something else is happening: *We were burgled while we were abroad.* **2** You also use **while** **a** to introduce a clause that presents a contrast to the main clause: *In 1961 just over 2 persons divorced per 1000, while in 1981 it was 12.* [*same as* **whereas**] **b** to mean 'although': *While I see your point, I still don't agree.* [*same as* **though, although**]
▷ ***noun*** (*used in the singular*)
A **while** is a length of time, of no particular extent: *After a while, I began to make friends amongst the undergraduates.* □ *It's been quite a while since I last saw him, two months at least.* □ *You'll feel better in a little while.*
▷ ***phrases*** **1** Something that happens **in between whiles** happens in the gaps between periods of some other activity. **2** (*informal*) If you say you will **make it worth** someone's **while** you mean that you will pay or reward them well for doing some special service for you. **3** Something that happens **once in a while** does not happen often: *It doesn't matter if the children go to bed late once in a while.* **4** Something that is **worth your while** is worth doing, and is a good use of your time: *It wouldn't be worth your while to go on trying.* [see also **worthwhile**]
▷ ***verb***: **whiles, whiling, whiled**

> ***phrasal verb***
> You **while away** the time doing something if you spend it in that way: *We whiled away the hour till dinner reminiscing about the past.*

whilst /waɪlst/ *conjunction*
You use **whilst** like **while**: *He watched her closely, whilst appearing to consult his notes.* □ *Whilst his book is quite informative, it isn't the important contribution we were expecting from him.*

whim /wɪm/ *noun*: **whims**
A **whim** is a sudden idea, fancy, or desire for something, that you get for no particular reason: *The child was full of odd whims.* □ *I might visit Spain or Italy, as the whim takes me.*
▻ ***phrase*** People act **at whim** when they do things from a passing desire rather than for any strong reason. [*same as* **on impulse**]

whimper /'wɪmpə(r)/ *verb*; *noun*
▻ ***verb***: **whimper, whimpering, whimpered**
Babies, children and animals **whimper** when they make feeble little cries of pain or discontent: *I was just getting back into bed when the baby started whimpering again.* □ *'Walk slower,' she whimpered.*
▻ ***noun***: **whimpers:** *She was kept awake by the baby's tearful whimpers.*

whimsical /'wɪmzɪkəl/ *adjective*
A person, remark or action that is **whimsical** is playfully humorous, and usually slightly odd: *He will be remembered for his whimsical humour and his eccentricities.* [*same as* **quaint**] — *noun* (*uncount*) **whimsicality** /wɪmzɪ'kalɪtɪ/: *There is a certain charm and whimsicality in his poems, which is what makes them so popular.* — *adverb* **whimsically:** *'We could try cycling backwards,' he suggested whimsically.*

whine /waɪn/ *verb*; *noun*
▻ ***verb***: **whines, whining, whined**
1 Animals **whine** when they give long high thin cries of pain or distress: *The dog was whining to be let in.* **2** (*informal*) People, especially children, **whine** when they complain, or say something in a complaining tone: *Oh, stop whining!* □ *He's always whining about something.* □ *'It's not fair,' she whined.* **3** A machine or other apparatus **whines** when it makes a thin, high-pitched noise: *Machinery above whined, and the lift jolted to a halt.*
▻ ***noun***: **whines**: *We could hear the whine of the lift as it ascended.* □ *I get nothing but whines and complaints from her.*

whinge /wɪndʒ/ *verb*: **whinges, whinging, whinged**
People **whinge** when they complain, especially unnecessarily and annoyingly. [*same as* **grumble**]

whip /wɪp/ *noun*; *verb*
▻ ***noun***: **whips**
1 A **whip** is a long narrow strip of leather, or a narrow rope, attached to a handle, for striking people or animals with: *There was a noise like the crack of a whip.* **2** (*politics*) A Party **Whip** is a member of a parliamentary party who is responsible for other members' discipline, and for making them attend to vote on important issues. **3** A dessert made with beaten egg whites or cream is sometimes called a **whip**: *raspberry whip.*
▻ ***verb***: **whips, whipping, whipped**
1 You **whip** a person or animal when you strike them with a whip: *Children were whipped for disobedience.* **2** The wind **whips** your face when it strikes it with the action or force of a whip. [*same as* **lash**] **3** You **whip** something somewhere when you move it there with a sharp, sudden action; someone or something **whips** somewhere when they move sharply and suddenly like a whip: *The branch whipped back.* □ *He whipped out a revolver.* □ *He whipped round at the sound.* **4** (*informal*) Someone **whips** something if they steal it. **5** You **whip** egg whites or cream by stirring them fast till they are thick, stiff and light. [*same as* **beat, whisk**] — *noun* **whipping:** *His persistent misbehaviour had resulted in numerous whippings.*

phrasal verb
whip up 1 You **whip up** something such as support, enthusiasm or anger among people when you do or say things that encourage it: *Political activists had been whipping up discontent amongst the workers.* **2** (*informal*) You **whip up** a meal when you prepare it in a hurry.

whip-round /'wɪp raʊnd/ *noun*: **whip-rounds**
A group of people have a **whip-round** when they all contribute money quickly, *eg* to buy a present for someone, or to pay for something for themselves.

whir see **whirr.**

whirl /wɜːl/ *verb*; *noun*
▻ ***verb***: **whirls, whirling, whirled**
1 Things or people **whirl** when they go round and round rapidly; you **whirl** something when you make it go round and round with a rapid circling action: *whirling autumn leaves* □ *whirling dancers* □ *He whirled the sword round his head.* **2** You say your head **is whirling** when you feel excited and confused. [same as **spin**]
▻ ***noun***: **whirls**
1 A **whirl** of something is a circling movement or pattern: *whirls of smoke* □ *a whirl of colour.* **2** (*used in the singular*) A **whirl** of some activity is a period that is full of it: *Life then was just a whirl of parties.*
▻ ***phrases*** **1** (*informal*) You say your head is **in a whirl** when you are confused and excited. **2** (*informal*) If something new or experimental is suggested to you, and you say you will **give it a whirl**, you mean you intend to try it. [*same as* **give it a try**]

whirlpool /'wɜːlpuːl/ *noun*: **whirlpools**
A **whirlpool** is a fast-circling current in the sea or a river, that pulls anything sailing or floating near it down into its centre.

whirlwind /'wɜːlwɪnd/ *noun*; *adjective*
▻ ***noun***: **whirlwinds**
A **whirlwind** is wind with a violent circling motion, moving across land or sea.
▻ ***adjective***
Whirlwind describes an event such as a romance or wedding that develops or takes place unusually quickly or soon: *a whirlwind marriage.*

whirr or **whir** /wɜː(r)/ *verb*; *noun*
▻ ***verb***: **whirrs** or **whirs, whirring, whirred**
Something that **whirrs** moves or spins rapidly with a humming noise: *She put the switch down and the fans whirred into life.*
▻ ***noun*** (*used in the singular*): *the whirr of helicopter blades.*

whisk /wɪsk/ *verb*; *noun*
▻ ***verb***: **whisks, whisking, whisked**
1 You **whisk** things off a surface when you brush or sweep them lightly away: *He whisked the crumbs off the table.* **2** You **whisk** something about when you wave it sharply about: *The creature whisked its tail from side to side.* **3** You **whisk** someone somewhere when you take them there, or have them taken there, rapidly: *The doctor immediately whisked her into hospital.* **4** You **whisk** egg whites or cream when you stir them rapidly till they are stiff, thick and light. [*same as* **whip, beat**]
▻ ***noun***: **whisks**
A **whisk** is a kitchen tool, usually made of wire, for whisking egg whites and cream. [see picture at **kitchen**]

whisker /'wɪskə(r)/ *noun*: **whiskers**
1 (*usually in the plural*) The **whiskers** of an animal

such as a cat or mouse are the long coarse hairs growing round its mouth. **2** (*used in the plural*) A man's **whiskers** are the parts of his beard growing on his cheeks, or all the hair on his face and chin, including his moustache.

whisky (*AmE, Irish* **whiskey**) /ˈwɪskɪ/ *noun*: **whiskies** or **whiskeys**

1 (*uncount*) **Whisky** is an alcoholic spirit made from the grain of barley or rye: *a glass of whisky.* **2** A **whisky** is a type of whisky or a glass of it: *After two large whiskies you're certainly not fit to drive.*

whisper /ˈwɪspə(r)/ *verb; noun*

▻ ***verb***: **whispers, whispering, whispered**

You **whisper** something when you say it very quietly, breathing the words rather than sounding or voicing them: *I whispered the message to her.* ▫ *What are you girls whispering about?* ▫ *'Keep very still,' she whispered.*

▻ ***noun***: **whispers**

You speak in a **whisper** or in **whispers** when you breathe your words rather than sounding or voicing them: *She dropped her voice to a whisper.*

whistle /ˈwɪsəl/ *verb; noun*

▻ ***verb***: **whistles, whistling, whistled**

1 You **whistle** by forcing air out through your lips or teeth, so as to produce a musical sound: *He was whistling a familiar tune.* ▫ *I could hear her whistling happily to herself in the kitchen.* ▫ *He whistled to his dog to come back.* **2** Something such as a bullet **whistles** somewhere when it makes a high sound as it moves through the air: *A bullet whistled past my ear.* **3** The wind **whistles** when it makes a loud high rushing sound. **4** A steam train or kettle **whistles** when it makes a long high loud sound as steam is forced out through a narrow opening. **5** A bird **whistles** when it sings.

▻ ***noun***: **whistles**

1 A **whistle** is the sound you make when you whistle: *He gave a soft whistle of astonishment.* **2** A **whistle** is a device that produces a whistling sound, *eg* one operated by steam on a railway train or kettle, or one blown by a referee to control play on the pitch, or a simple musical pipe: *The referee blew the whistle for half time.*

white /waɪt/ *adjective; noun*

▻ ***adjective***: **whiter, whitest**

1 Something that is **white** is the colour of snow or milk: *small white fluffy clouds.* ▫ *Are you getting your sheets really white?* ▫ (*with the noun omitted*) *The purple heather is pretty, but the white is more unusual.* **2** Someone who is **white** belongs to one of the pale-skinned European races: *the arrival of the white man in Africa.* **3** People go **white a** when they become abnormally pale, from shock or illness: *Her face was white with fear.* ▫ *He turned as white as a sheet.* **b** when their hair becomes white, usually in old age: *My mother had gone quite white in the few years I'd been away.* **4 White** is used to describe pale varieties of things, as distinct from dark ones: *white grapes.* **5 White** wine is pale-coloured wine made from white grapes or from peeled black ones. [*opposite* **red**] **6 White** bread is made with **white** flour, that has had the dark coarse part of the grain removed. [*opposite* **brown, wholemeal**] **7 White** coffee or tea has milk or cream added to it: *I usually take my coffee white.* [*opposite* **black**]

▻ ***noun***: **whites**

1 (*uncount*) **White** is the colour of snow or milk: *It's nice to wear a lot of white in the summer.* **2** A **white** or **White** is a white person, of European race: *the longed-for truce between blacks and whites.* **3** (*count or uncount*) The **white** of an egg, **egg white**, or **white of egg** is the clear liquid surrounding the yolk: *two egg whites* ▫ *You can get the stain out with egg white* (or *white of egg*). **4** The **whites** of your eyes are the white parts surrounding the round coloured parts. **5** (*used in the plural*) **Whites** are sheets and pillowslips and other white items of household linen.

white-collar /ˈwaɪt kɒlə(r)/ *adjective*

White-collar workers have office jobs, as distinct from manual jobs in industry.

white elephant /waɪt ˈɛlɪfənt/ *noun*: **white elephants**

A **white elephant** is an expensive but useless and unwanted possession, usually an inconveniently large one.

white-hot /waɪt ˈhɒt/ *adjective*

Something metal that is **white-hot** is extremely hot, hotter than red-hot.

white lie /waɪt ˈlaɪ/ *noun*: **white lies**

A **white lie** is a forgivable lie, especially one that you tell to avoid hurting someone's feelings.

white meat /ˈwaɪt miːt/ *noun* (*uncount*)

White meat is pale-coloured meat, *eg* veal, chicken and turkey, as distinct from red meat such as beef.

whiten /ˈwaɪtən/ *verb*: **whitens, whitening, whitened**

Something **whitens** when it becomes paler in colour, or goes white; you **whiten** things when you make them whiter: *We soaked the dishcloth in bleach to whiten it.* [*same as* **bleach**]

white spirit /waɪt ˈspɪrɪt/ *noun* (*uncount*)

White spirit is a colourless liquid produced from petroleum, used for thinning paint.

whitewash /ˈwaɪtwɒʃ/ *noun; verb*

▻ ***noun***

1 (*uncount*) **Whitewash** is a mixture of lime and water, for giving a white coating to walls, especially on the outsides of buildings. **2** (*uncount or used in the singular*) **Whitewash** is the activity or effect of presenting facts in a way that hides their unpleasantness: *propaganda and whitewash* ▫ *The police report was an obvious whitewash.* [*same as* **cover-up**] **3** (*used in the singular; informal; sport*) A **whitewash** is a decisive defeat inflicted on an opponent.

▻ ***verb***: **whitewashes, whitewashing, whitewashed**

1 You **whitewash** a building when you paint it with whitewash: *freshly whitewashed cottages.* **2** You **whitewash** an affair, or someone's reputation, when you conceal some facts about them, and present others in a way that hides their unpleasantness. [*same as* **cover up**] **3** You **whitewash** your opponents in a game when you defeat them completely, especially so that they fail to score at all: *It was thanks to Wright that Ireland whitewashed France in this weekend's rugby match.* [*same as* **trounce**]

whiting /ˈwaɪtɪŋ/ *noun*: **whiting**

A **whiting** is a small edible fish related to the cod.

whittle /ˈwɪtəl/ *verb*: **whittles, whittling, whittled**

> ***phrasal verbs***
>
> **whittle away** An amount, *eg* of money, **is whittled away** when it is gradually used up till there is none left.
>
> **whittle down** You **whittle** something such as a list **down**, when you reduce its size or length: *We managed to whittle down the guest list to 150.*

whizz or **whiz** /wɪz/ *verb; noun*

▻ ***verb*** (*informal*): **whizzes, whizzing, whizzed**

Something **whizzes** somewhere when it moves there very fast: *A bullet whizzed past his head.* □ *We whizzed along in her sports car.*
▻ ***noun*** (*informal*): **whizzes**
Someone who is a **whizz** at something is an expert at it: *She's a whizz at computing.*

whizz kid /ˈwɪz kɪd/ *noun* (*informal*): **whizz kids**
A **whizz kid** is someone who achieves success early, through ability and ambition.

who /huː/ *pronoun*
1 (*interrogative, used as the subject of a sentence or clause*) You use **who** in asking the name or identity of a person or people, and in talking about knowing or finding out their name or identity: *Who told you that?* □ *Who's the girl in the blue sweater?* □ *There are men digging up the street; I've no idea who they are.* □ *Someone has been selected but we haven't been told who yet.* [see also **whom**]
2 (*relative, used as the subject of a clause*) You use **who** **a** to identify, specify or describe a person or people: *Where's the waitress who served us?* □ *It was Gran who answered the telephone.* □ *We must also consider those who are unemployed.* □ *A glazier is a person who mends windows.* □ *Anyone who thinks that is crazy.* [see also **whom**]

> You can use **that** instead of **who**: *There's the waitress that served us.*

b after a comma, to add a clause making a comment about a person or people: *The music is by Bellini, who was born 190 years ago today.* [see also **whom**]
▻ ***phrase*** You know **who's who** if you know who everyone is, especially everyone important, and what their job or rank is.

who'd /huːd/
Who'd is the spoken, and informal written, form of **1 who would**: *I wonder who'd be willing to help us?* □ *He's a man who'd do anything to advance his career.* **2 who had**: *I wish I knew who'd done this.* □ *I recognized the voice of the woman who'd called earlier.*

whodunit or **whodunnit** /huːˈdʌnɪt/ *noun* (*informal*)
A **whodunit** is a book, play or film about a murder, in which you are not told the identity of the murderer till the end.

whoever /huːˈɛvə(r)/ *pronoun*
You use **whoever 1** (*relative*) 'to mean any person or people that', or 'the person that': *Whoever gets all the answers right wins a case of champagne.* □ *Whoever made this cake is a terrific cook.* □ *I want you to find whoever murdered my son.* □ *The job will go to whoever has the best qualifications.* **2** to say that something is so, or must be done, in the case of any or every possible person: *Whoever calls, tell them I'm not available* □ *Whoever we select as headteacher, we can hardly expect standards to rise immediately.* **3** (also **who ever**) as an emphatic form of **who**: *Who ever told you such nonsense?* **4** to express vagueness or lack of certainty about the identity of a person or people: *It was built by the Albigensians, whoever they were.*

whole /hoʊl/ *noun; adjective*
▻ ***noun*** (*used in the singular*)
1 The **whole** of something is all of it; this use is often emphatic: *It didn't rain for the whole of July.* □ *We wasted the whole of one morning searching for the file.* □ *The power cut had affected the whole of Manchester.* **2** A **whole** is something that is complete in itself, especially if it consists of elements that fit satisfactorily together: *The sections seem unconnected, but in fact they form a satisfactory whole.* □ *Two halves make a whole.*
▻ ***adjective***
1 A **whole** thing is all of it; this use is often emphatic: *She sat down and ate a whole loaf of bread.* □ *I've never been so insulted in my whole life.* □ *The building took a whole year to complete.* □ *We had to wait three whole hours at the hospital.*

> With proper names, **the whole of** is used, rather than the adjective **whole**: *The whole of Europe* (or *All Europe*, or *All of Europe*) *was being drawn into the war*.

2 Something that is **whole** is not divided or broken into pieces: *You have to swallow these pills whole.* □ *There are only two cups left whole.* [*same as* **in one piece**] **3 Whole** food has been altered as little as possible from its natural state by processing or manufacturing. **4** You use **whole** emphatically with words like *point, purpose* and *reason* to mean 'main, or one and only': *But our whole reason for coming to Krumlov was to see the palace.* **5 Whole** is used for emphasis to mean 'things as large as' or 'entire': *Whole cities were wiped out by the plague.* **6** (*informal*) **Whole** is used to emphasize certain nouns that express quantity or degree, and also the adjective *new*: *I've got a whole pile of work to do.* □ *Things are a whole lot better than they might have been.* □ *We're suggesting a whole new approach to the problem.* [compare **altogether, completely, entirely, wholly**]
▻ ***phrases* 1** If you refer to something **as a whole**, you are referring to it as a complete unit or group, rather than to individual parts or members of it: *Of course there are outstandingly good teachers and students, but in the university as a whole the academic standard is sinking.* **2** You use **on the whole** to sum up a situation, or your opinion of something, after you have taken everything into consideration: *What sort of book is it on the whole?* [*same as* **generally, generally speaking, all things considered, all in all, as a rule, by and large, in the main, for the most part**]

wholehearted /hoʊlˈhɑːtɪd/ *adjective*
Wholehearted describes support or agreement that is sincere and enthusiastic: *You have my wholehearted approval.* — *adverb* **wholeheartedly:** *I wholeheartedly support what you say.*

wholemeal /ˈhoʊlmiːl/ *adjective*
Wholemeal flour is made from the wheat grain complete with its husk; **wholemeal** bread is made with wholemeal flour.

wholesale /ˈhoʊlseɪl/ *adjective or adverb*
Wholesale describes **1** the selling of goods in large quantities and at cheap rates, *eg* to shopkeepers for sale to the public: *best-quality carpets available at wholesale prices* □ *I could get your groceries wholesale for you.* [compare **retail**] **2** an activity carried out on a huge scale, especially one involving uncontrolled destruction: *the wholesale slaughter of innocent civilians* □ *Church treasures were removed wholesale and disappeared into private collections.* [compare **indiscriminate**]

wholesaler /ˈhoʊlseɪlə(r)/ *noun*: **wholesalers**
A **wholesaler** is a person who buys goods on a large scale and sells them in smaller quantities to shopkeepers for sale to the public. [*opposite* **retailer**]

wholesome /ˈhoʊlsəm/ *adjective*
Wholesome describes **1** an attractively healthy personal appearance: *He preferred wholesome-looking young girls.* **2** food and activities that make you healthy: *wholesome exercise.* □ *The meals were plain but wholesome.* **3** attitudes that are wise and sensible: *a more wholesome approach to sex education.*

who'll /huːl/
Who'll is the spoken, and informal written, form of **who will** and **who shall**: *Who'll take responsibility?* □ *I know someone who'll be able to help.*

wholly /'hoʊlɪ/ *adverb* (*sometimes intensifying*)
Wholly means completely: *I'm not wholly convinced.* □ *It's wholly different from anything we've tried before.* □ *The situation is wholly unsatisfactory.*

whom /huːm/ *pronoun*
1 (*interrogative, used as the object of a verb or preposition, but often replaced by* **who** *in informal English*) You use **whom** in asking the name or identity of a person or people, and in talking about knowing or finding out their name or identity: *Whom* (or *who*) *would you consider suitable?* □ *Whom* (or *who*) *did you want to speak to?* □ *To whom are you referring?* □ *I wondered whom* (or *who*) *to ask.* □ *I suspect a certain person, I won't say whom* (or *who*). □ *He enquired who* (rather than *whom*) *else I'd met.*
2 (*relative, used as the object of a verb or preposition, but often replaced by* **who** *in informal English*) You use **whom a** in identifying, specifying or describing a person or people: *I need to find workers whom* (or *who*) *I can trust.* □ *Isn't that the lady whom* (or *who*) *you were dancing with?* □ *Bill was a man to whom we could all turn in a crisis.*

> You can use **that** instead of **whom**, and you can omit **whom** altogether, except following a preposition: *I must find someone whom* (or *that*) *I can rely on*, or *someone I can rely on*; but: *It was interesting to meet the man about whom the press have had so much to say.*

b (*often replaced by* **who** *in informal English*) after a comma, to add a comment about a person or people: *She lived with her sister, whom* (or *who*) *she secretly hated.* □ *I rang the Jessops, from whom I'd just had a postcard.*

whoop /wuːp/ *verb*; *noun*
▻ ***verb***: **whoops, whooping, whooped**
You **whoop** when you give a shout of triumph, excitement or delight.
▻ ***noun***: *The news was received by the children with whoops of glee.*

whoopee /wuː'piː/ *interjection*
You shout **'whoopee!'** to express excitement and delight: *We've won! Whoopee!*

whooping cough /'huːpɪŋ kɒf/ *noun* (*uncount*)
Whooping cough is an infectious disease of children, with violent coughing followed by a noisy gasp for breath, and sometimes vomiting.

whoops /wʊps/ *interjection*
You say **'whoops!'** to express surprise or concern when you have a slight accident or make a mistake, or see someone else do so. [*same as* **oops**]

whore /hɔː(r)/ *noun* (*offensive*): **whores**
A **whore** is a prostitute.

who're /'huːə(r)/
Who're is the spoken form of **who are**: *workers who're underpaid.*

who's /huːz/
Who's is the spoken, and informal written, form of **1 who is**: *Would you see who's at the door?* **2 who has**: *anyone who's got money to spare.*

whose /huːz/ *pronoun or determiner*
1 (*interrogative*) You use **whose** in asking the identity of the person or people that something belongs to, and in talking about knowing or finding out their identity: *Whose boots are these?* □ *Whose turn is it to wash up?* □ *Goodness knows whose all these cars are.* □ *We couldn't decide whose suggestion to adopt.* **2** (*relative*) You use **whose a** to specify, identify or describe a person, people, thing or things in terms of someone or something associated with, or belonging to, them: *Children whose parents are paying for their education generally achieve higher marks.* □ *He found mosses whose greens were bright with life.* □ *I was joined by a lady whose face looked familiar.* **b** after a comma, to add a comment about a person, people, thing or things in terms of someone or something associated with, or belonging to, them: *shy nocturnal creatures, whose burrows were somewhere along the river bank* □ *I must particularly thank my parents, without whose help I couldn't have succeeded.*

who've /huːv/
Who've is the spoken form of **who have**: *members who've already paid their subscriptions.*

why /waɪ/ *adverb*; *pronoun*; *interjection*
▻ ***adverb*** (*interrogative*)
You use **why** in asking the reason for something, and in talking about knowing or finding out the reason for something: *Why aren't you in bed?* □ *Why do you want to know that?* □ *Why can't people be reasonable?* □ *'I must call Phil.' 'Why bother? He'll have left by now.'* □ *The contest has been cancelled but we haven't heard why.* □ *So that's why I ended up doing science.*
▻ ***pronoun*** (*relative*)
You can use **why** after *reason*: *Is there any good reason why I should get involved?*
▻ ***interjection***
1 (*especially AmE*) **Why** expresses such things as surprise, recognition and annoyance: *Why, it's Geoff! Good to see you again!* **2** People also use **why** to challenge a comment or question, especially if it is an implied criticism: *'Are you leaving already?' 'Why, have you any objection?'*
▻ ***phrase*** You use **why not** to make, or agree to, a suggestion: *Why don't you ask her?* □ *'Like a drink?' 'Why not?'* [= yes, OK]

wick /wɪk/ *noun*: **wicks**
1 The **wick** of a candle is the string in it that projects at the top, which you light. **2** The **wick** of a paraffin lamp or cigarette-lighter is a strip of material by which fuel is supplied to the flame.

wicked /'wɪkɪd/ *adjective*
1 Wicked people and **wicked** behaviour cause deliberate harm, especially to other people: *Wicked rulers quickly surround themselves with natural bullies.* [*same as* **evil**] **2** A **wicked** sense of humour is slightly unkind but enjoyable and attractive: *a wicked joke* □ *a wicked grin.* [*same as* **sly**, **roguish**] — *adverb* **wickedly**: *Someone wickedly suggested painting the statue.* — *noun* (*uncount*) **wickedness:** *the wickedness of the present regime.*

wicker /'wɪkə(r)/ *adjective*
Wicker chairs, fences and baskets are made of wickerwork.

wickerwork /'wɪkəwɜːk/ *noun* (*uncount, often adjectival*)
Wickerwork is material consisting of woven twigs or canes, made into furniture, baskets and fences: *wickerwork garden furniture.*

wicket /'wɪkɪt/ *noun* (*cricket*): **wickets**
A **wicket** is a row of three small wooden posts stuck upright in the ground at either end of the pitch, at which the bowler aims the ball, so as to try and get the batsman out; the playing area between the wickets is also called the **wicket**.

wide /waɪd/ *adjective*; *adverb*: **wider, widest**

▻ ***adjective***

1 Something that is **wide** extends a long way from side to side: *a wide expanse of water* □ *The baby gave a wide, happy grin.* □ *a narrow waist and wide hips.* [*same as* **broad**] **2** You use **wide** in referring to the measurement of something from side to side, or its width: *The doorway isn't wide enough.* □ *How wide is the swimming pool?* □ *the point where the river is at its widest* □ *We need a table roughly three metres long and two metres wide.* [see note at **broad**, see also **width**] **3** Someone's eyes are **wide** when they are open to their greatest extent: *Their eyes were wide with alarm.* **4** A **wide** variety, selection or range includes lots of different things: *Our menu offers a wide choice of local dishes.* □ *Her experience in adult education was impressively wide.* [compare **broad**] **5** Something gets **wide** support, or **wide** publicity if a lot of people approve of it, or hear about it: *Her lecture tour achieved wide publicity.* [*same as* **widespread**] **6** A **wide** gap or difference is a big one: *The gap between rich and poor gets wider all the time.* **7** A shot or blow that is **wide**, or **wide** of its target, or the mark, misses the thing it is aimed at: *His aim was wide.* — *adverb* **widely:** *He grinned widely.* □ *He was widely travelled and spoke several languages.* □ *Opinions about the treatment differed widely.* □ *Her books are widely read on the continent.*

▻ ***adverb***

1 You open something **wide** when you open it to its greatest extent: *The door was left wide open.* □ *She was asleep but her eyes were wide open.* □ *Could you open your mouth wider?* □ *Stand with your legs wide apart.* □ *She had wide-set brown eyes.* **2** A shot or blow that goes **wide** misses its target: *The ball went wide.*

▻ ***phrases*** **1** For **far and wide** see **far**. **2** You are **wide awake** when you are fully awake or aware of things happening round you.

-wide /waɪd/ *suffix*

-wide is added to a word for a place or area to form adjectives and adverbs that mean throughout its extent: *The campaign had nationwide support.* □ *She travelled worldwide.*

widen /ˈwaɪdən/ *verb*: **widens, widening, widened**

Something **widens** or **is widened** when it becomes, or is made, wider: *The road narrows and widens again.* □ *We had to widen the doorway to accommodate her wheelchair.* □ *Her eyes widened in astonishment.* □ *the widening difference in incomes* □ *We shall be widening the range of our goods and services over this coming year.* [*opposite* **narrow**; compare **broaden**]

wide-ranging /waɪdˈreɪndʒɪŋ/ *adjective*

Something **wide-ranging** covers a large variety of subjects or topics: *a woman of many talents and wide-ranging interests* □ *Our discussions were wide-ranging and productive.*

widespread /ˈwaɪdspred/ *adjective*

Something that is **widespread** extends over a wide area, or involves large numbers of people: *Recent heavy rain has caused widespread flooding.* □ *There has been widespread discontent over the new local tax.*

widow /ˈwɪdoʊ/ *noun*: **widows**

A **widow** is a woman whose husband is dead and who has not remarried: *She was left a widow at 35.*

widowed /ˈwɪdoʊd/ *adjective*

A person is **widowed** if their husband or wife has died: *She has a widowed sister in London.*

widower /ˈwɪdoʊə(r)/ *noun*: **widowers**

A **widower** is a man whose wife is dead, and who has not remarried.

widowhood /ˈwɪdoʊhʊd/ *noun* (*uncount*)

Widowhood is the condition of being, or process of becoming, a widow, or the period during which a woman is a widow: *Widowhood comes tragically early to many soldiers' wives.* □ *throughout her 25-year widowhood.*

width /wɪdθ/ *noun* (*uncount or count*): **widths**

1 The **width** of something is its measurement from side to side: *I need a piece of glass 35 centimetres in length and 24 in width.* □ *The cloth comes in two different widths.* □ *What width is the bed?* □ *Its body was about the width of my little finger.* [see picture at **shape**] **2 Width** is also the quality of being wide: *a river of considerable width* □ *her width of experience.* [*same as* **breadth**] **3** You swim a **width** when you swim from one side to the other of a swimming-pool: *They have to swim five widths non-stop before they're allowed in the deep end.* [*opposite* **length**; *same as* **breadth**]

wield /wiːld/ *verb*: **wields, wielding, wielded**

1 You **wield** a tool or weapon when you lift it ready to use it: *The dog shrank away as the man wielded his walking stick.* [*same as* **brandish**] **2** You **wield** power, authority or influence when you have it or use it: *Headteachers used to wield too much authority for the good of the school.* [*same as* **exert**]

wife /waɪf/ *noun*: **wives**

A man's **wife** is the woman to whom he is married: *He introduced me to his wife.* □ *She thought she'd enjoy being a wife and mother.* □ *a special lunch for the diplomats' wives* □ *She's the wife of a Paris financier.*

wig /wɪg/ *noun*: **wigs**

A **wig** is a covering of false hair, worn *eg* by actors, or by people who are bald: *She used a number of different wigs and disguises.*

wiggle /ˈwɪgəl/ *verb*; *noun*

▻ ***verb*** (*informal*): **wiggles, wiggling, wiggled**

Something **wiggles** when it moves from side to side or up and down in little curves; you **wiggle** something when you move it from side to side or up and down with a slight jerking action: *His hips wiggled as he walked.* □ *The rabbit wiggled its nose.* [compare **waggle, jiggle**]

▻ ***noun***: **wiggles**: *You have to give the key a little wiggle to make it work.* — *adjective* **wiggly:** *She drew a wiggly line for the horizon.*

wild /waɪld/ *adjective*; *noun*

▻ ***adjective***: **wilder, wildest**

1 Wild animals live in their natural environment and are not dependent on man: *a herd of wild cattle.* [*opposite* **tame, domestic, domesticated**] **2 Wild** plants, or plants that grow **wild**, are plants that grow in a natural, uncultivated state: *wild flowers.* [*opposite* **cultivated, garden**] **3 Wild** land or a **wild** region is uncultivated and often uninhabited: *The garden was left wild.* □ *a wild, mountainous landscape.* **4 Wild** behaviour is excited or uncontrolled behaviour: *The spectators went wild.* □ *A wild fury seized her.* □ *He was wild with grief.* [*same as* **frantic**] **5** (*AmE*) Someone who is **wild** is angry: *He gets wild if I interrupt.* [*same as* **furious**] **6** Someone's eyes are **wild** if they are staring and full of fear or madness. **7 Wild** weather is stormy: *a wild night.* [*opposite* **calm**] **8 Wild** ideas and plans are a bit crazy and unlikely to work. [*same as* **impractical**] **9** A **wild** guess is a rough or approximate one that you make without much thought. **10** (*informal*) You are **wild** about something if you are very enthusiastic about it: *I'm not wild about* [= I don't like] *the carpet.* [*same as* **mad** about] — *adverb* **wildly**: *They were jumping up and down, yelling wildly.* □ *I found myself guessing wildly.* □ *The whole scheme was wildly impractical.*

▻ ***noun*: wilds**
1 (*used in the singular*) The **wild** is a wild animal's or plant's natural environment or their life in it: *They eventually returned the cub to the wild.* **2** (*used in the plural*) The **wilds** are areas remote from towns, where hardly anyone lives: *They live out in the wilds.* ▫ *somewhere in the wilds of Scotland.*
▻ ***phrases*** **1 a** A garden **runs wild** when the grass and plants in it grow in an uncontrolled way, because no-one is looking after it. **b** Children **run wild** when they live a life of freedom, with no discipline or control. **2** For **beyond your wildest dreams** see **dream**.

wild card /ˈwaɪld kɑːd/ *noun* (*computers*): **wild cards**
A **wild card** is a character that can be substituted for any other character, *eg* in a file name.

wilderness /ˈwɪldənəs/ *noun* (*usually in the singular*): **wildernesses**
1 A **wilderness** is an uncultivated or uninhabited region, such as a desert or a mountainous area: *Visit the Rockies, the last remains of the North American wilderness.* **2** You describe a garden as a **wilderness** if it full of weeds and overgrown plants, because no-one is looking after it.
▻ ***phrase*** A politician is **in the wilderness** when he or she is in the state of being without office or influence after playing a leading role.

wildfire /ˈwaɪldfaɪə(r)/ *noun* (*uncount*)
▻ ***phrase*** Something such as news or an infectious disease **spreads like wildfire** if it spreads very fast.

wild-goose chase /waɪld ˈguːs tʃeɪs/ *noun*: **wild-goose chases**
A **wild-goose chase** is a search that cannot succeed, usually for reasons unknown to the searcher.

wildlife /ˈwaɪldlaɪf/ *noun* (*uncount*)
Wildlife is wild animals, birds and plants in general: *We are damaging and gradually destroying the world's wildlife.*

wiles /waɪlz/ *noun* (*plural*)
Someone's **wiles** are the cunning behaviour they use to get something they want: *I knew all his little wiles and was no longer taken in by them.* [*same as* **tricks**]

wilful /ˈwɪlfʊl/ *adjective*
1 Someone who causes **wilful** damage or destruction causes it deliberately or intentionally. **2** A **wilful** person is determined to do what they want in the way that they want to. [*same as* **headstrong**] — *adverb* **wilfully**: *Iago wilfully sets about destroying the marriage.*

will[1] /wɪl/ *modal verb* (short form **'ll**, negative form **won't**)
1 Will is used with the infinitives of other verbs to form a future tense; you say something **will** happen if it is going to happen: *Lunch will be ready in five minutes.* ▫ *Maybe they won't notice.* ▫ *When will I be told if I've got a place?* ▫ *What will you be doing this time tomorrow?* [see note at **shall**]
2 (*BrE*) **Will** is used with *have to* to mean 'must': *You'll have to hurry.*
3 You say you **will** do something if you intend to do it, or are willing or determined to do it: *OK, I'll ring you tomorrow.* ▫ *We will never give in.* ▫ *'You may forget.' 'No, I won't.'* ▫ *Promise you'll write to me.* ▫ *He won't do his homework.* ▫ *The car won't start.* ▫ *It'll start if you treat it gently.*
4 You use **will a** to ask someone to do something: *Please will you shut the door?* ▫ *Will you be quiet!* ▫ *Watch the milk for me, will you?* **b** to express commands: *You will apologize to your mother immediately!* **c** to indicate capacity or ability, or lack of objection to doing something: *The table will seat ten.* ▫ *Any of our branches will exchange the goods.* ▫ *Some folk will do anything for money.* **d** to invite someone to do something: *Will you have a coffee?* **e** to say that something is to be expected: *Accidents will happen.* ▫ *A good teacher will know when a child is unhappy.* **f** to state what applies in certain circumstances: *An unemployed young person living at home will not receive housing benefit.* **g** to state what you think is probable: *That will be Ted at the door.* ▫ *They'll know by now.* **h** to express criticism of the way someone keeps behaving, emphasizing the word **will**: *She will leave her clothes all over the floor.*
5 You use **'will** have' **a** to form a future perfect tense: *He'll have got used to the idea by the morning.* ▫ *How much will you have completed by the end of next week?* **b** to say what you think has probably happened: *You'll have realized that we're soap-opera fans.* ▫ *He'll have forgotten to turn on the answering machine.* ▫ *Won't she have had time to read the report by now?*
see also **shall, would.**

will[2] /wɪl/ *noun*; *verb*
▻ ***noun*: wills**
1 (*uncount or used in the singular*) Your **will** is your power of consciously deciding, or deliberately choosing, what to do: *How much free will do we really have?* [*same as* **choice**] **2** Your **will** is what you want to do yourself or your determination to do it: *I did it against my will.* ▫ *a clash of wills.* **3** (*used in the singular*) The **will** to do something is the desire or determination to do it: *She's lost the will to live.* **4** A person's **will** is a document containing their instructions for sharing out their property after their death: *Have you made your will?*
▻ ***verb*: wills, willing, willed**
You **will** something to happen when you try to make it happen by, or as if by, using mental force or willpower: *She willed herself to keep on running.*
▻ ***phrases*** **1** You can do something **at will** if you can do it whenever, and however, you want to: *Some visitors prefer a guided tour, others like to wander round the castle at will.* **2** If you say that **with the best will in the world** you cannot manage something, you mean that however much you would like to be able to do it, it is impossible.

willing /ˈwɪlɪŋ/ *adjective*
1 You are **willing** to do something if you are happy to do it, or do not object to doing it when someone asks you to: *She was only too willing to give up her job and get married.* ▫ *Would you be willing to sponsor me?* [*same as* **ready**, **prepared**; *opposite* **unwilling**, **reluctant**] **2 Willing** people are eager to do something, or enthusiastic about doing it: *She had assembled a little gang of willing helpers.* ▫ *The job is now complete, thanks to all the willing assistance we received.* ▫ *They're willing enough, but not very efficient.* [*opposite* **reluctant**] — *adverb* **willingly**: *They willingly gave up their weekends to help build the hostel.* [*same as* **freely**; *opposite* **reluctantly**] — *noun* (*uncount*) **willingness:** *She found amongst the Malawian students a real willingness to work.* [*opposite* **reluctance**]

willow /ˈwɪloʊ/ *noun*: **willows**
A **willow** is a tree with narrow pointed leaves, especially the variety with hanging branches that grows beside rivers.

willpower /ˈwɪlpɑʊə(r)/ *noun* (*uncount*)
Willpower is the determination, perseverence and self-

discipline needed to achieve something: *She learnt to walk again through sheer willpower and determination.* □ *I ought to diet, but I haven't the willpower to do it effectively.*

willy-nilly /wɪlɪˈnɪlɪ/ *adverb*
Something that happens to you **willy-nilly** happens whether you want it to or not, and you cannot stop it happening: *You have to remember to tell these people you don't want the book they're offering, otherwise it'll be sent to you willy-nilly.*

wilt /wɪlt/ *verb*: **wilts, wilting, wilted**
Plants **wilt** when they bend over from lack of water, or because they are dying. [*same as* **droop**]

wily /ˈwaɪlɪ/ *adjective*: **wilier, wiliest**
Someone who is **wily** thinks of clever ways of getting what they want, especially using tricks, deception or subtle persuasion: *wily politicians.* [*same as* **cunning, crafty, artful**]

win /wɪn/ *verb*; *noun*
▻ ***verb***: **wins, winning, won**
1 You **win** something such as a war, competition, race, game, election or bet when you defeat your opponents in it, or finish in first place: *In 1801 Nelson fought and won the battle of Copenhagen.* □ *You couldn't tell which side was winning.* □ *You've won! Well done!* **2** You **win** something such as a prize, victory or contract when you obtain it after competing or fighting for it against other people: *An American firm has won the contract for the reconstruction job.* □ *It must have been your smile that won you the part.* **3** You **win** something you want, such as someone's love, respect or approval, when you earn it through your behaviour or achievements, or succeed in getting it: *Always a brilliant and flamboyant performer, he won the hearts of audiences everywhere.*
▻ ***noun***: **wins**: *The Socialists had two surprise wins in this week's by-elections*
▻ ***phrase*** (*informal*) If you say '**you can't win**' in some situation, you mean that circumstances are so arranged that anything you try is bound to fail: *If I don't wash the dishes he calls me lazy; if I do he says I'm doing it all wrong; you can't win with someone like that.*

> ***phrasal verbs***
> **win over** or **win round** You **win** someone **over**, or you **win** them **round**, when you manage to gain their support, or persuade them to do what you want.
> **win through** You **win through** when you manage to survive or get through a difficult or dangerous situation with an effort or struggle.

wince /wɪns/ *verb*; *noun*
▻ ***verb***: **winces, wincing, winced**
You **wince** when you jump or start slightly, or screw up your face, in pain or in expectation of it: *The drill touched a nerve in her tooth, and she winced.* [*same as* **flinch**]
▻ ***noun***: **winces**: *She saw my involuntary wince as I looked at the price tag.*

winch /wɪntʃ/ *noun*; *verb*
▻ ***noun***: **winches**
A **winch** is a cylinder round which a rope or chain is wound, for lifting, lowering or pulling heavy loads.
▻ ***verb***: **winches, winching, winched**
You **winch** something somewhere when you lift, lower or pull it using a winch.

wind¹ /wɪnd/ *noun*; *verb*
▻ ***noun***: **winds**
1 (*count or uncount*) A **wind** is a current of air moving or blowing from any direction across the earth's surface: *The gale-force winds had brought hundreds of trees down.* □ *Their long hair blew about in the wind.* □ *gusts of wind* □ *It was intensely hot, with hardly a breath of wind.* **2** (*uncount*) Your **wind** is your breath or your breath supply: *He quickly gets short of wind and has to rest.* **3** The gas that collects in your stomach and causes pain or discomfort is also called **wind**: *People say beans give you wind, but I haven't noticed it.* **4** (*uncount, often adjectival*) **Wind** describes the section of an orchestra that includes instruments such as the oboe, clarinet, flute and trumpet, that you play by blowing: *wind instruments* □ *wind players* □ *the wind section.* [see also **woodwind**]
▻ ***verb***: **winds, winding, winded**
You **are winded** when the air is suddenly squeezed out of your lungs and you cannot breathe for a moment: *She was winded by her fall, but otherwise unhurt.*
▻ ***phrases*** **1** (*informal*) You **get the wind up** when you get anxious or alarmed; you **put the wind up** someone when you make them anxious or alarmed. **2** You **get wind of** something when you hear about it: *They had somehow got wind of our financial difficulties.* **3** Something that is **in the wind** is being planned or considered: *A proposal was in the wind to close the school.*

wind² /wɪnd/ *verb*: **winds, winding, wound**
1 You **wind** one thing round another when you wrap it round the other several times: *She wound a long woollen scarf round her neck.* □ *The snake had wound itself round the table leg.* **2** A road or river **winds** somewhere if it has a lot of bends on its way there; you **wind** your way somewhere when you follow a twisting path or route: *winding lanes* □ *The funeral procession wound its way through the village.* **3** You **wind** a clock, watch or other clockwork device when you tighten its spring by turning a knob or key, so that it continues to go.

> ***phrasal verbs***
> **wind down** **1** You **wind down** the window of a vehicle when you lower it by turning a handle. **2** A clock, clockwork device, or machine **winds down** when it is about to stop and works more and more slowly. **3** A business **is wound down** when its activities and the number of its employees are gradually reduced.
> **wind forward** or **wind back** You **wind** a cassette tape **forward** or **back** when you make it move on to a position nearer its end, or back to a position nearer its beginning. [*same as* **wind on, rewind**]
> **wind up** **1** You **wind up** a clock, watch or clockwork device when you tighten its spring by turning a key or knob, so that it continues to go. **2** You **wind up** the window of a vehicle when you close it by turning a handle. **3** To **wind up** a business is to close it. **4** You **wind up** an activity when you bring it to a conclusion and stop it: *We wound up the seminar with a final discussion.* **5** (*informal*) Someone **winds** you **up** when they tease you. **6** (*informal*) You **wind up** somewhere if that is where you are at the end of a series of happenings: *He'll wind up in jail if he isn't careful.* [*same as* **end up, finish up**]

windfall /ˈwɪndfɔːl/ *noun*: **windfalls**
A **windfall** is a substantial sum of money that you receive unexpectedly or get by luck.

wind instrument /ˈwɪnd ɪnstrəmənt/ *noun*: **wind instruments**

A **wind instrument** is a musical instrument such as a clarinet, flute or trumpet that you play by blowing. [see picture at **orchestra**]

windmill /'wɪndmɪl/ *noun*: **windmills**
A **windmill** is a mill for grinding grain, or a machine for pumping water or generating electricity, whose energy comes from its huge arms, called sails, that are turned round by the wind.

window /'wɪndoʊ/ *noun*: **windows**
1 A **window** is a glass-covered opening in a wall or vehicle to look out through and to let in light: *He liked to sleep with the window wide open.* □ *The ball hit the window and broke it.* □ *I saw the dictionary I wanted in the bookshop window.* [see picture at **house**] **2** (*computers*) A **window** is a rectangular section containing certain information, that can be displayed on part of the screen and used independently. **3** A **window** is also a gap in a schedule that is available for some purpose.

window box /'wɪndoʊ bɒks/ *noun*: **window boxes**
A **window box** is a box fitted outside a window for growing plants in.

window frame /'wɪndoʊ freɪm/ *noun*: **window frames**
A **window frame** is the wooden or metal frame that is fixed into a window opening and fitted with glass.

window pane /'wɪndoʊ peɪn/ *noun*: **window panes**
The **window panes** of a building are the pieces of glass in the windows.

window shopping /'wɪndoʊ ʃɒpɪŋ/ *noun* (*uncount*)
Window shopping is the activity of looking at goods in shop windows, as a substitute for buying something.

windowsill /'wɪndoʊsɪl/ *noun*: **windowsills**
A **windowsill** or **window ledge** is the narrow shelf or ledge along the bottom of a window, on the outside or the inside.

windpipe /'wɪndpaɪp/ *noun*: **windpipes**
Your **windpipe** is the tube that joins the back of your throat to your lungs, through which you breathe air in and out.

windscreen /'wɪndskriːn/ *noun*: **windscreens**
The **windscreen** of a motor vehicle is the front window, through which the driver looks. [*same as* **windshield**; see picture at **car**]

windscreen-wiper /'wɪndskriːnwaɪpə(r)/ *noun* (*usually in the plural*): **windscreen-wipers**
Windscreen-wipers are the narrow metal arms with a rubber edge that swing from side to side across a vehicle's windscreen to clear it of rain. [see picture at **car**]

windshield /'wɪndʃiːld/ *noun*: **windshields**
A **windshield** is **1** (*AmE*) a windscreen. [see picture at **car**] **2** the protective transparent plastic screen on the front of a motorbike.

windsurfing /'wɪndsɜːfɪŋ/ *noun* (*uncount*)
Windsurfing is the sport of riding over the waves on a board with a sail, called a **windsurfer** or **sailboard**. [*same as* **sailboarding**]

windswept /'wɪndswɛpt/ *adjective*
1 (*literary*) A **windswept** area is exposed to strong winds: *a bleak and windswept mountainside.* **2** People look **windswept** when their hair is untidy from being blown about by the wind.

windy /'wɪndɪ/ *adjective*: **windier**, **windiest**
It is **windy** when there are strong winds blowing: *a windy day* □ *The weather was cold and windy.* □ *a windy hillside.*

wine /waɪn/ *noun* (*uncount or count*): **wines**
Wine is an alcoholic drink made from black grapes (**red wine**) or white grapes (**white wine**); you can also make it from other fruits, vegetables or plants: *a bottle of ginger wine* □ *Australian wines* □ *a wine-coloured dress.*

wine bar /'waɪn bɑː(r)/ *noun*: **wine bars**
A **wine bar** is a place people go to to buy or drink wine.

wine glass /'waɪn glɑːs/ *noun*: **wine glasses**
Wine glasses are drinking glasses with long stems, used for serving wine in. [see picture at **tableware**]

wing /wɪŋ/ *noun*: **wings**
1 A bird's or insect's **wings** are the two limbs or organs that it flies with. **2** An aircraft's **wings** are the two long flat structures that project from either side of its body. **3** A vehicle's **wings** are the four corner sections of its body, forming covers for the wheels. [see picture at **car**] **4** A **wing** of a building is a part projecting from the central or main section: *The east wing was destroyed by fire in 1783.* **5** (*football, hockey, netball*) The left and right **wings** are the two long sides of a pitch, or the position of the players at each end of the line of forwards. **6** (*used in the plural*; *theatre*) The **wings** are the areas at each side of a stage, where performers wait to enter, hidden from the audience: *I always got nervous waiting in the wings.* **7** A **wing** of a political party or other organization is a group within it that has its own distinct views and character: *These proposals will please the Labour left wing.* □ *right-wing attitudes* □ *the political wing of the IRA.*
▻ ***phrase*** A bird is **on the wing** when it is flying.

winger /'wɪŋə(r)/ *noun*: **wingers**
1 (*football*) The **wingers** are the players on the right and left wings. **2** (*politics*) Left-**wingers** and right-**wingers** are people with left-wing or right-wing views.

wingspan /'wɪŋspan/ *noun*: **wingspans**
The **wingspan** of a bird, insect or aircraft is the distance from the tip of one wing to the tip of the other.

wink /wɪŋk/ *verb*; *noun*
▻ ***verb***: **winks**, **winking**, **winked**
You **wink** at someone when you shut one eye briefly as a informal signal to them, *eg* that you are joking, or that you are referring to something that is a secret between you.
▻ ***noun***: **winks:** *I looked up to see him giving her a big wink.*
▻ ***phrase*** You **don't sleep a wink** when you don't go to sleep at all: *I was so worried I didn't sleep a wink all night.*

winner /'wɪnə(r)/ *noun*: **winners**
The **winner** of a competition or prize is the person who wins it: *the winner of the 400-metres hurdles.*

winning /'wɪnɪŋ/ *adjective*; *noun*
▻ ***adjective***
1 The **winning** entry or competitor in a competition is the one that has won: *the winning shot* □ *the winning team* □ *The winning entries will be published in tomorrow's newspaper.* **2** **Winning** also describes things such as behaviour or a smile that are attractive and make people like you: *They obviously can't resist your winning smile.* [*same as* **charming**]
▻ ***noun*** (*used in the plural*): **winnings**
Your **winnings** are the money you win from bets and gambling: *Her winnings that night amounted to several hundred.*

winter /'wɪntə(r)/ *noun* (*uncount or count*): **winters**
Winter is the coldest season of the year, coming between autumn and spring, and lasting from late November till March in cool northern regions: *It didn't snow all last winter.* □ *He doesn't go out much in winter.*

□ *This is just the drink for a cold winter's evening.* □ *winter sports* □ *a series of wet winters* □ *in the winter of 1981.*

wintertime /ˈwɪntətaɪm/ *noun* (*uncount*)
Wintertime is the winter period or season: *In wintertime these cottages get no sun at all.*

wintry /ˈwɪntrɪ/ *adjective*: **wintrier, wintriest**
Wintry weather is cold, snowy weather, typical of winter: *The showers are expected to turn wintry later.*

wipe /waɪp/ *verb*: **wipes, wiping, wiped**
1 You **wipe** something when you clean or dry its surface by rubbing it lightly, *eg* with a damp cloth: *We cleared and wiped the table.* **2** You **wipe** your feet when you rub the soles of your shoes on the doormat to clean them before entering a house; you **wipe** your hands on a towel or cloth when you dry them by rubbing them on it: *She hastily wiped her hands on her apron.* **3** You **wipe** the dishes when you dry them with a cloth after they have been washed. **4** You **wipe** dirt or liquid off something when you remove it, *eg* with a cloth: *She wiped her tears away with the back of her hand.* **5** (*electronics*) You **wipe** material from an audio or video tape, or a computer disk, when you remove it; you **wipe** a tape or disk when you remove material from it. [compare **erase**]

> ***phrasal verbs***
> **wipe out** Things **are wiped out** when they are destroyed or completely got rid of: *The plague wiped out whole villages.* □ *Smallpox has been almost completely wiped out.* [*same as* **eradicate**]
> **wipe up** You **wipe up** liquid when you remove it from a surface with a cloth: *What can I use to wipe up this mess with?*

wiper /ˈwaɪpə(r)/ *noun*: **wipers**
A vehicle's **wipers** are its windscreen-wipers.

wire /waɪə(r)/ *noun*; *verb*
▻ ***noun***: **wires**
1 (*uncount or count*) **Wire** is metal that has been pulled into a narrow strip that bends easily and is used *eg* for fastening things, or making things such as fences; a **wire** is a length or piece of this, or lots of pieces twisted into a cable, used *eg* for carrying an electric current, or in telecommunications for connecting one place with another: *I found some strong wire to mend the gate with.* □ *a wire fence* □ *telephone wires* □ *You connect the brown wire to the terminal marked L.* **2** (*AmE*) A **wire** is a telegram: *Send me a wire to say when you're arriving.*
▻ ***verb***: **wires, wiring, wired**
(*AmE*) You **wire** someone when you send them a telegram: *She wired me that she'd be arriving Saturday.*

> ***phrasal verb***
> You **wire up** an electrical or electronic apparatus when you fit it with electrical wires for connecting it to the power supply: *You can use the computer as soon as I get it wired up.*

wireless /ˈwaɪələs/ *noun* (*old*): **wirelesses**
A **wireless** is a radio: *I turned on the wireless to get the news.*

wire netting /waɪəˈnetɪŋ/ *noun* (*uncount*)
Wire netting is wire twisted into the form of network for use as fencing.

wire wool /waɪəˈwʊl/ *noun* (*uncount*)
Wire wool is a mass of fine wire used for cleaning metal objects such as saucepans.

wiring /ˈwaɪərɪŋ/ *noun* (*uncount*)
The **wiring** in a building is the wires that make up its electrical system: *The wiring is unsafe and must be renewed.*

wiry /ˈwaɪərɪ/ *adjective*: **wirier, wiriest**
1 A **wiry** person is slim but strong and athletic. **2 Wiry** hair is coarse and wavy.

wisdom /ˈwɪzdəm/ *noun*
1 (*uncount*) **Wisdom** is the ability to make sensible judgements and decisions, especially on the basis of your knowledge and experience: *She lacks wisdom and maturity.* □ *He was able, with the wisdom of his years, to take a detached view.* [*same as* **prudence, common sense**; *opposite* **foolishness**] **2** (*used in the singular*) You say you doubt or question the **wisdom** of doing something if you don't think it is sensible to do it: *I've never seen the wisdom of punishing children physically.*

wisdom tooth /ˈwɪzdəm tuːθ/ *noun*: **wisdom teeth**
Your **wisdom teeth** are the last four double teeth to develop, at the back of each side of your upper and lower jaw.

wise /waɪz/ *adjective*; *verb*
▻ ***adjective***: **wiser, wisest**
1 A **wise** person makes sensible decisions and judgements on the basis of their knowledge and experience: *He proved a wise and tolerant ruler.* □ *You were wise to refuse.* □ *It would be a wise move to sell the house while the market's good.* □ *Are you really resigning? Do you think that's wise?* [*same as* **prudent, sensible**; *opposite* **foolish**] **2** (*informal*) You are **wise** to something if you know about it; you get **wise** to something when you find out about it; someone puts you **wise** to something when they tell you about it: *I soon got wise to her underhand methods.* — *adverb* **wisely:** *She wisely decided to stay indoors.* □ *They've chosen very wisely.*
▻ ***phrases*** You are **none the wiser** or **no wiser** about something that has been explained, or that has happened, if you do not understand the explanation, or do not realize what has happened: *The instruction book left us none the wiser.* □ *I usually serve instant coffee, and no-one's ever any the wiser.*
▻ ***verb***: **wises, wising, wised**

> ***phrasal verb***
> (*informal*) You **wise up** when you find out the facts about something: *It's time you wised up about those people; they're just taking advantage of you.*

-wise /waɪz/ *suffix*
You add **-wise** to nouns **1** to form adverbs of direction or manner: *Let me just measure the carpet lengthwise.* □ *He is shown lying with his arms folded crosswise.* [see also **-ways**] **2** (*informal*) to form adverbs meaning with regard to a certain thing: *How are we getting on time-wise?*

wisecrack /ˈwaɪzkrak/ *noun*: **wisecracks**
A **wisecrack** is a joke or a smart remark: *wisecracks about mothers-in-law.* [*same as* **quip**]

wish /wɪʃ/ *verb*; *noun*
▻ ***verb***: **wishes, wishing, wished**
1 (*formal*) You **wish** to do something if you want to do it, or intend to do it: *I wish to hand in my resignation.* □ *I do not wish to discuss the matter further.* □ *Do you wish to make an official complaint?* [*same as* **want, would like**] **2** You **wish** that something were so when you long for it to be so, especially vainly: *I wish I'd realized earlier how ill she was.* □ *He wished he were cleverer.* [*same as* **if only**] **3** You **wish** someone would do something if you would like them to do it, or you think they ought to do it: *I do wish you'd sit still.* □ *I wish he'd knock before coming in.* □ *I stood there wish-*

ing he'd go away. **4** You **wish** for something when you long for it, especially vainly: *She often wished for a quieter life.* **5** You **wish** for something when you silently express a desire for it, which you are supposed to believe will be magically fulfilled: *As she dug the knife into her birthday cake she wished for a puppy.* **6** If you **wish** someone something such as luck, success or happiness, you are expressing the hope that they will have it: *I wish you all the best for the future.* **7** You **wish** someone a happy birthday, or a happy new year when you say 'Happy Birthday!' or 'Happy New Year!' to them, to show you hope they'll have a good time. **8** (*literary*) You **wish** someone good day when you say 'good day' to them as you leave them: *He wished them good afternoon and left.*

▻ ***noun***: **wishes**

1 A **wish** is a desire: *I knew of his wish to marry and have children.* **2** (*used in the plural*; *literary*) Your **wishes** are what you want to be done: *She had disobeyed her parents' wishes.* **3** (*used in the plural*) You send someone your best **wishes** when you express a hope for their health and happiness: *Do give my good wishes to your parents.* **4** People make a **wish**, *eg* in fairy tales, or as a custom on special occasions, when they express a desire, often silently, which they are supposed to believe will be magically fulfilled: *You will all get a wish if you help to stir the Christmas pudding.*

▻ ***phrase*** If you say that you **would not wish** some bad experience **on anyone**, you mean it is so unpleasant that no-one should have to suffer it: *I wouldn't wish migraines on my worst enemy.*

wishful thinking /wɪʃfəl 'θɪŋkɪŋ/ *noun* (*uncount*)

If you describe someone's expectations as **wishful thinking** you mean that they are basing them more on what they want to happen than on what is likely to happen.

wisp /wɪsp/ *noun*: **wisps**

A **wisp** of something is a thin little piece of it: *Wisps of hair escaped from under her hat.* □ *There was a tiny wisp of smoke on the horizon.*

wispy /'wɪspɪ/ *adjective*: **wispier, wispiest**

Something that is **wispy** is in separate thin little pieces: *His hair was grey and wispy.* □ *There were one or two wispy white clouds.*

wistful /'wɪstfʊl/ *adjective*

People are **wistful** when they are longing sadly for something that they realize they cannot have: *'We can't afford a holiday,' he said with a wistful smile.* — *adverb* **wistfully:** *We gazed wistfully at the tables laden with food.*

wit /wɪt/ *noun*: **wits**

1 (*uncount or used in the singular*) **Wit** is the ability to express yourself amusingly: *She had a ready wit and found it easy to make people laugh.* □ *The lecture was entitled 'Wit and wordplay in Shakespeare'.* [*same as* **humour**] **2** Someone who is described as a **wit**, or as quite a **wit**, has the ability to talk amusingly. **3** (*used in the singular*) You have the **wit** to do something if you have enough common sense or intelligence to do it: *Fortunately he had the wit to keep quiet when the dangerous subject was mentioned.* **4** (*used in the plural*) Your **wits** are your ability to think fast in a difficult situation: *He had had to use his wits to escape arrest on many occasions.*

▻ ***phrases*** **1** (*informal*) You are **at your wits' end** when you cannot think how to deal with a problem and are in despair about it. **2** You **have**, or **are keeping, your wits about you** when you are constantly prepared to deal with dangers and difficulties. **3** Something scares or frightens you **out of your wits** when it terrifies you: *I was scared out of my wits when I heard the footsteps coming nearer.* **4** You **pit your wits against** someone when you compete with them in a trial of intelligence: *Now's your chance to pit your wits against our computer.*

witch /wɪtʃ/ *noun*: **witches**

A **witch** is a person, especially a woman, who is supposed to have magic powers and to use them *eg* to harm people: *They say a witch cast a spell on him and made him dumb.*

witchcraft /'wɪtʃkrɑːft/ *noun* (*uncount*)

Witchcraft is the use of magic powers, especially to harm people.

witch hunt /'wɪtʃ hʌnt/ *noun*: **witch hunts**

People conduct a **witch hunt** when they search out those whom they are unjustly blaming for something that has gone wrong, in order to punish them.

with /wɪð/ or /wɪθ/ *preposition*

1 a One person or thing is **with** another when they are together in one place: *I walked with her as far as the corner.* □ *The bill had been filed with my private correspondence.* **b** You do something **with** another person or other people when you both, or all, do it together: *I enjoyed dancing with him.* □ *He's been playing with the Arsenal team for six years now.* □ *I'll have a word with Dad about it tomorrow.* **c With** is used after verbs of mixing: *Mix the flour with the oil.* □ *She mingled with the crowd.* **d** To move **with** a current or trend is to follow it or go in the same direction: *Their boat was drifting with the tide.* **e** One quality comes **with** another if it develops at the same time or rate as the other: *Discretion comes with age.* **f** You leave something **with** someone when you leave it in their care: *Leave your case with the hall porter.* □ *Leave the matter with me.* **g** Some verbs of separating or getting rid of are followed by **with**: *I parted with her at the station.* □ *We can dispense with formality.* □ *Have you finished with those books?* **h** (*informal*) You say you are **with** someone when you understand what they are telling you: *Are you with me?* **i** You say you are **with** someone if you support them: *We're with you all the way.*

2 a You do something **with** a tool, object or other thing when you do it using that tool, object or thing: *I managed to hammer the nail in with my shoe.* □ *Use a wooden spoon to stir the batter with.* □ *With the help of a couple of volunteers we soon got the place clean.* **b With** is used after verbs of covering and filling: *Our shoes got plastered with mud.* □ *It's television that fills their heads with these silly ideas.* **c With** follows verbs of providing: *We can supply you with the necessary textbooks.* □ *We were all equipped with pencils and notepads.* **d** You are in some state **with** a feeling or condition if the feeling or condition causes it: *He was white with fear.* □ *They'll be green with jealousy.* □ *She was shaking with fury.* **e With** is also used in giving the reason or purpose for an action: *My brother-in-law telephoned with bad news about my sister.* □ *She was admitted to hospital with chest pains.*

3 a One person fights **with** another when the one opposes the other: *She's quarrelled with her brother.* □ *I've tried arguing with her, but she won't be persuaded.* **b With** is used after verbs of agreeing, disagreeing and comparing: *I disagree with you totally.* □ *His statement doesn't correspond with what the others say.* □ *The curtains clash with the carpet.* □ *Sales have improved compared with last year.*

4 a With is used in describing or identifying people or things, or in specifying their state, in terms of features, characteristics or clothing: *that house with the blue door* □ *a woman with black hair and a fringe* □ *the man over there with the tweed jacket* □ *a dog with a limp*

□ *Don't come back with your clothes all dirty.* **b** You use **with** to specify the qualities of an action or the gestures that accompany it: *They won with ease.* □ *He answered with a nod.*
5 a You use **with** to specify circumstances that affect a situation: *With your qualifications, you're bound to get the job.* □ *I can't go abroad with my mother being so ill.* **b With** is used to specify the person or thing that a circumstance or action concerns: *What's wrong with you?* □ *What shall we do with these old newspapers?* □ *I can't do a thing with my hair.* □ *Who deals with correspondence?* □ *She takes a lot of trouble with her work.* □ *The trouble with you is you're too soft-hearted.* **c** People sometimes use **with** after adverbs and adverbial phrases in exclamations expressing a wish or order: *Down with* [= get rid of] *management!* □ *Come on, kids, into bed with you!*
▷ ***phrases*** **1 a** You are **with it** when you are concentrating on, or paying attention to, what is happening round you: *Sorry, I'm not with it this morning.* **b** (*old informal*) Someone or something that is **with it** is fashionable: *Those are very with-it earrings you're wearing.* **2** (*literary*) **With that** and **with this** are used in telling a story to mean 'at that point', or 'after doing or saying that': *'Ten o'clock tomorrow,' she said, and with that she rang off.*

withdraw /wɪð'drɔː/ *verb*: **withdraws, withdrawing, withdrew, withdrawn**
1 (*formal*) You **withdraw** somewhere quieter or more private when you move there: *She withdrew to her bedroom to think things over.* **2** Troops **withdraw** or **are withdrawn** from a base or from a conflict when they are removed from it. **3** You **withdraw** something from somewhere when you remove it or pull it back from there: *He was talking to someone out of the window, then he suddenly withdrew his head.* □ *She withdrew her hand from his.* **4** You **withdraw** money from a bank account when you take it out for your use: *He had withdrawn £2000 on 8 October.* **5** You **withdraw** from an activity when you announce that you will no longer be taking part in it: *She was forced by a leg injury to withdraw from the finals.* [*same as* **drop out**] **6** You **withdraw** something such as a statement or comment when you say you did not mean it: *I'm sorry, I withdraw that remark.* □ *He later withdrew his confession.* [*same as* **take back**] **7** You **withdraw** something such as an offer or service when you cancel it or stop providing it: *She threatened to withdraw her financial support.* **8** (*psychology*) People **withdraw** when they become silent and refuse to communicate with or respond to others.

withdrawal /wɪð'drɔːl/ *noun* (*usually uncount*): **withdrawals**
1 The **withdrawal** of something is the act or process of removing it or cancelling it: *Withdrawal of government funding would mean the cancellation of important projects.* □ *the withdrawal of troops from the disputed territory* □ *They insisted on an official withdrawal of the allegation.* **2** Someone's **withdrawal** from an activity or organization is their decision not to take part in it, or belong to it any longer: *owing to her last-minute withdrawal from the contest.* **3 Withdrawal** from a drug is the process of stopping using it after you have become addicted to it; **withdrawal** symptoms are the pain and discomfort people suffer when they try to give up a drug they have become addicted to. **4** (*psychology*) **Withdrawal** is behaviour in which a person becomes silent and refuses to communicate with other people or respond to them. **5** (*count*) You make a **withdrawal** from your bank account when you take out a sum of money for your use: *You should check the withdrawals listed on your bank statement.*

withdrawn /wɪð'drɔːn/ *verb*; *adjective*
▷ ***verb***
Withdrawn is the past participle of **withdraw**.
▷ ***adjective***
A person who is **withdrawn** is silent and shy, and finds it hard to communicate with other people or respond to them: *a quiet, withdrawn little girl.* [*same as* **detached, distant**; *opposite* **outgoing**]

withdrew /wɪð'druː/ *verb*
Withdrew is the past tense of **withdraw**.

wither /'wɪðə(r)/ *verb*: **withers, withering, withers**
1 Plants **wither** when they fade, dry up and die; something **withers** them when it makes them fade, dry up and die: *The drought had withered the new green shoots.* □ *a vase of wild flowers, looking a bit withered.* **2** Something **withers** or **withers** away when it fades and disappears: *love that never withers.* [*same as* **die**]

withered /'wɪðəd/ *adjective*
A person's body is described as **withered** if the skin is old and wrinkled: *his withered old hand.*

withering /'wɪðərɪŋ/ *adjective*
A **withering** glance or remark is a scornful one: *'You have no taste,' said she in withering tones.*

withhold /wɪð'hoʊld/ *verb*: **withholds, withholding, withheld**
You **withhold** something from someone who wants it when you refuse to give it to them: *Withhold your consent till you've had a chance to examine the documents in person.* □ *He had withheld vital information from the police.* □ *Your grant is being withheld till we have evidence that your project is a worthwhile one.* [*same as* **keep back**]

within /wɪ'ðɪn/ or /wɪ'θɪn/ *preposition*; *adverb*
▷ ***preposition***
1 Something that is **within** something else is inside it: *Within the school grounds uniform must be worn.* □ *There have been a lot of staff changes within the organization.* **2** Something stays **within** a particular limit if it does not go beyond it: *She was within her rights in insisting on compensation.* □ *You must try to live within your income.* **3** You are **within** a certain distance of somewhere when you are less than that distance from it: *They were within 12 miles of the South Pole.* **4** You are **within** sight, **within** reach or **within** earshot of something if you can see it, reach it or hear it: *We were within sight of land at last.* □ *Could you check something for me in the dictionary if it's within reach?* □ *The children were playing within earshot a little way along the beach.* **5** Something takes place **within** a certain time if it takes place in less than that time: *The network has failed three times within just a few weeks.* □ *Death can follow within seconds.*
▷ ***adverb*** (*old*): *They entered the cave and gazed at the wonders within.* □ *The garden was deserted, but voices were coming from within.* □ *She spoke cheerfully, trying not to betray the anxiety she felt within.*

without /wɪ'ðaʊt/ or /wɪ'θaʊt/ *preposition*
1 You are **without** someone else, or you do something **without** someone else, when you and they are not together: *Can't you go home without me?* □ *I couldn't bear life without you.* □ *She was without her husband that night.* **2** A person or thing that is **without** something does not have it: *We were without electricity for two days.* □ *houses without running water* □ *I went out without my key.* □ *windows without any glass in them* □ *He's better-looking without his beard.* □ *She's quite without conscience when it comes to promoting her own interests.* **3** You manage to do something **without** a particular thing if you do it not having or using that

thing: *How did you open the door without the key?* □ *Without more evidence the police cannot make an arrest.* □ *They entered without permission.* **4** You do something **without** behaving or reacting in a particular way, or doing a particular thing, if you do not behave or react in that way, or do that thing: *She replied without smiling.* □ *He glanced at me without recognition.* □ *She agreed without a moment's hesitation.* □ *He went away without leaving any forwarding address.* **5** One thing happens **without** another thing happening if the other thing does not happen: *They made their own beds without being told.* □ *We were relieved that we'd got up and down the mountain without anyone getting hurt.* □ *We achieved our targets without difficulty.* □ *People are being imprisoned without trial.* □ *I made several inquiries, without result.* **6** If you say that something would have happened **without** a particular circumstance, you mean that it was because of that particular circumstance that it didn't happen: *I would have died without their help.*

withstand /wɪð'stand/ *verb*: **withstands, withstanding, withstood**
A person or thing **withstands** something harmful when they are strong enough to survive it: *Her health will never withstand another winter like the last.* □ *Singapore could have withstood bombardment from the sea but was not prepared for a land attack.* [*same as* **resist, cope with, survive**]

witness /'wɪtnəs/ *noun*; *verb*
▻ ***noun***: **witnesses**
1 A **witness** to an event is someone who sees it, and can therefore tell other people about it: *We have accounts of the eruption from several contemporary witnesses.* **2** A **witness** is a person who gives evidence about the facts of a case in a court of law: *She appeared as a witness for the prosecution.* **3** A **witness** is also a person who signs their own name on a document that another person has just signed, to confirm that the other person's signature is genuine.
▻ ***verb***: **witnesses, witnessing, witnessed**
1 You **witness** something if you see it happen: *The incident in the restaurant was witnessed by at least fifty diners.* **2** You **witness** someone's signature when you sign your own name to confirm that their signature is genuine.
▻ ***phrases*** **1** A circumstance **bears witness** to something if it is evidence of it: *The chaos in the room bore witness to the struggle which had taken place earlier.* **2** You **are witness to** something if you observe it taking place: *I have never before been witness to such cruelty.*

witness box /'wɪtnəs bɒks/ *noun*: **witness boxes**
A **witness box** or **witness stand** is the wooden enclosure from which a witness gives evidence in a court of law.

witticism /'wɪtɪsɪzm/ *noun*: **witticisms**
A **witticism** is a joke or a witty remark. [*same as* **quip**]

witty /'wɪtɪ/ *adjective*: **wittier, wittiest**
Someone or something that is **witty** is cleverly amusing: *I enjoyed reading your witty letter in the Times.*

wives /waɪvz/
Wives is the plural of **wife**.

wizard /'wɪzəd/ *noun*: **wizards**
1 A **wizard** is a man, especially in fairy stories, who has magic powers. [*same as* **magician, sorcerer**] **2** (*informal*) Someone is a **wizard** at something if they are very good at it: *She's a financial wizard.*

wizened /'wɪzənd/ *adjective*
A person, fruit or vegetable that is **wizened** is wrinkled with age: *a few wizened apples* □ *His face was lean and wizened.*

wobble /'wɒbəl/ *verb*
▻ ***verb***: **wobbles, wobbling, wobbled**
1 Something **wobbles** when it shakes unsteadily: *The cyclist wobbled and then regained his balance.* □ *His flesh wobbled as he walked.* **2** Someone's voice **wobbles** when they speak unsteadily, *eg* when they are about to cry. — *adjective* **wobbly:** *a wobbly ladder* □ *I felt wobbly when I got out of bed for the first time.* [*same as* **unsteady**]

wodge /wɒdʒ/ *noun* (*informal*): **wodges**
A **wodge** is a thick piece of something: *a wodge of fruit cake* □ *Someone had used a wodge of newspaper to stop up the hole.*

woe /woʊ/ *noun* (*literary or humorous*): **woes**
1 (*uncount*) **Woe** is misery or sorrow; someone tells you a tale of **woe** when they tell you their troubles. **2** (*used in the plural*) A person's **woes** are their troubles and misfortunes: *We had a coffee together and she told me all her woes.*

woebegone /'woʊbɪgɒn/ *adjective*
People are **woebegone** when they are miserable or unhappy: *She gave a little wave as we drove away, a woebegone expression on her face.* [*same as* **crestfallen, dejected**]

woeful /'woʊfʊl/ *adjective* (*literary*)
1 People are **woeful** when they are sad: *She turned a woeful, tearstained face towards me.* [*opposite* **joyful**] **2 Woeful** is often used to emphasize, and express concern or disgust at, the lack of something: *their woeful ignorance of grammar.* — *adverb* **woefully:** *He woefully recounted how his money had been stolen.* □ *Medical supplies are woefully inadequate.*

wok /wɒk/ *noun*: **woks**
A **wok** is a large, bowl-shaped pan used for cooking dishes in the Chinese style.

woke /woʊk/ *verb*
Woke is the past tense of **wake**.

woken /'woʊkən/ *verb*
Woken is the past participle of **wake**.

wolf /wʊlf/ *noun*; *verb*
▻ ***noun***: **wolves**
A **wolf** is a wild animal of the dog family that hunts and eats other animals.
▻ ***verb*** (*informal*): **wolfs, wolfing, wolfed**
You **wolf** food, or **wolf** it down, when you eat it quickly or greedily, because you are hungry. [*same as* **bolt down, gobble**; *opposite* **nibble**]

woman /'wʊmən/ *noun*: **women**
1 A **woman** is an adult human female: *The children she had taught would all be grown men and women by now.* □ *The arrangement will apply to married and single women alike.* □ *a woman judge* □ *Men are so rude about women drivers.* **2** (*uncount*; *literary*) **Woman** refers to women in general: *Woman is a more subtle creature than man.*

-woman /'wʊmən/
-woman is used to form nouns for **1** women performing specific jobs, as in *policewoman*. **2** women of a specific nationality, as in *Frenchwomen*.

womanhood /'wʊmənhʊd/ *noun* (*uncount*)
Womanhood is the state of being a woman, especially an adult woman as distinct from a girl: *His daughters were in their teens and rapidly approaching womanhood.*

womankind /wʊmən'kaɪnd/ *noun* (*uncount*)
Womankind is women as a group or class: *As a writer she speaks for all womankind.*

womanly /'wʊmənlɪ/ *adjective*
Womanly behaviour and qualities are those that peo-

ple consider suitable in a woman: *His need to be looked after roused her womanly instincts.* [compare **feminine, manly**]

womb /wuːm/ *noun*: **wombs**
A woman's **womb** is the hollow organ in her body inside which babies develop before they are born: *the child growing in the womb.* [*same as* **uterus**]

women /ˈwɪmɪn/
Women is the plural of **woman**.

womenfolk /ˈwɪmɪnfoʊk/ *noun* (*old; plural*)
The **womenfolk** of a community or family are the female members of it.

Women's Liberation /wɪmɪnz lɪbəˈreɪʃən/ or **Women's Lib** *noun* (*uncount*)
Women's Liberation is a movement, started by women, whose aim is to change society so that women have the same rights and opportunities as men.

won /wʌn/ *verb*
Won is the past tense and past participle of **win**.

wonder /ˈwʌndə(r)/ *verb; noun; adjective*
▻ ***verb***: **wonders, wondering, wondered**
1 You **wonder** about things when you are uncertain about them or can't decide about them, or are curious about them: *I wonder if I ought to call her and remind her?* ▫ *As he walked home he was wondering what to make for the evening meal.* ▫ *We were just beginning to wonder whether you'd forgotten about the meeting.* ▫ *That police car's been parked outside their house all day; I wonder why.* ▫ *'I wonder where he'll have got to?' 'I've been wondering that too.'* ▫ *I've often wondered about her background.* **2** You can begin polite requests with 'I **wonder** if' or 'whether': *'Excuse me; I wonder if you could help me? I'm looking for the Botanic Gardens.'* ▫ *I was wondering whether you might have an evening free this week?* **3** (*usually with a negative*) You **wonder** at things when you are surprised at them: *In the circumstances her reluctance is hardly to be wondered at.* ▫ *I shouldn't wonder if he has* [= he probably has] *high blood pressure.* ▫ *I don't wonder that customers are dissatisfied; the standard of service is appalling.*
▻ ***noun***: **wonders**
1 (*uncount*) **Wonder** is surprise or amazement: *We all gasped in wonder as we rounded the corner and saw the view.* **2** A **wonder** is something that produces amazement or astonishment: *the wonders of modern surgery.* **3** (*used in the singular*) You say it is a **wonder** that something is so if it is extraordinary that it is: *It's a wonder she survived at all in those arctic conditions.* ▫ *It's a wonder he didn't go straight to the police and report you.*
▻ ***adjective***
Wonder describes things that are notable for achieving marvels: *a wonder drug.*
▻ ***phrases*** **1** Someone or something **does wonders** or **works wonders** if they achieve marvellous results: *That treatment you gave me has worked wonders with my back.* ▫ *Her speech today did wonders for party morale.* **2** If you say it is **no wonder, small wonder** or **little wonder** that something is so you mean it is not surprising that it is: *'She didn't get the job.' 'No wonder, if she behaved as rudely as she normally does.'*

wonderful /ˈwʌndəfʊl/ *adjective*
You call something **wonderful** **1** if it is enjoyable or makes you happy: *It's just wonderful being reunited with my family at last.* **2** if you are impressed by it: *They get wonderful results with plastic surgery nowadays.* — *adverb* **wonderfully:** *He has responded wonderfully to the treatment.* ▫ *It was one of those wonderfully mild autumn days.*

wonderment /ˈwʌndəmənt/ *noun* (*uncount*)
Wonderment is surprise or astonishment: *We gazed about us in wonderment.*

wondrous /ˈwʌndrəs/ *adjective* (*literary*)
Something **wondrous** is astonishing or impressive: *wondrous achievements such as walking on the moon.*

wonky /ˈwɒŋkɪ/ *adjective* (*informal*): **wonkier, wonkiest**
Things that are **wonky** are unsteady, badly made, or not straight: *Is that table safe? It looks a bit wonky.*

wont /woʊnt/ or /wɒnt/ *adjective* (*literary*)
You are **wont** to do something if you do it regularly, habitually or often: *She had herself many of the failings she was wont to criticize in other people.* [*same as* **inclined**]

won't /woʊnt/
Won't is the spoken, and informal written, form of **will not**: *This pen won't write.*

woo /wuː/ *verb*: **woos, wooing, wooed**
1 (*old*) A man **woos** a woman when he tries to gain her love, especially in the hope of marrying her. **2** To **woo** people is to try to gain their support: *Election time comes and they start wooing the voters with unrealistic promises of tax cuts.*

wood /wʊd/ *noun*: **woods**
1 (*often adjectival*) **Wood** is the material of which the trunks and branches of trees are formed, used for constructing buildings and furniture, and as a fuel: *planks of wood* ▫ *In the old days golf-club shafts were made of wood, not metal.* ▫ *There was a smell of wood smoke from a nearby cottage chimney.* ▫ *The elegant wall panels were wood, not plastic.* [*same as* **timber**; see also **wooden**] **2** A **wood** is an area of growing trees; a large area of trees can be referred to as the **woods**: *A path led through the woods.* ▫ *Behind the house was a small birch wood.*
▻ ***phrases*** **1** If you say that someone **can't see the wood for the trees** you mean that they are so concerned with detail that they cannot see the obvious or general point. **2** You superstitiously say **'touch wood!'**, sometimes touching something wooden at the same time, when things are all right and you do not want them to go wrong: *There haven't been any problems with the computer so far, touch wood!*

wooded /ˈwʊdɪd/ *adjective*
Land that is **wooded** is covered with trees: *a wooded landscape.*

wooden /ˈwʊdən/ *adjective*
1 Wooden things are made of wood: *a small wooden gate.* **2** If you describe actors or their performance as **wooden** you mean that they perform in a stiff, unnatural way, without much expression or liveliness.

woodland /ˈwʊdlənd/ *noun* (*uncount or count*)
Woodland is land largely covered with trees: *acres of natural woodland* ▫ *the ancient woodlands of northern Britain.* [*same as* **forest**]

woodwind /ˈwʊdwɪnd/ *noun* (*uncount, with a singular or plural verb, often adjectival*)
The **woodwind** are the wind instruments of an orchestra that are made, or were formerly made, of wood, including the flute, oboe, clarinet and bassoon: *players in the woodwind section* ▫ *woodwind instruments.* [see picture at **orchestra**]

woodwork /ˈwʊdwɜːk/ *noun* (*uncount*)
1 Woodwork is the art or activity of making things out of wood. [*same as* **carpentry**] **2** You refer to the wooden parts of a building, such as the doors and window frames, as the **woodwork**: *The woodwork needs a coat of paint.*

woodworm /ˈwʊdwɜːm/ *noun*: **woodworm** or **woodworms**
1 Woodworm are the larvae of a type of beetle, which make small circular holes in wood as they eat through it. **2** (*uncount*) **Woodworm** is also the damage caused to wood by woodworm eating holes in it: *There's a lot of woodworm in this chair.*

woody /ˈwʊdɪ/ *adjective*: **woodier, woodiest**
1 A **woody** landscape has lots of trees in it. [*same as* **wooded**] **2** (*botany*) A **woody** stem is thick and hard, like wood; **woody** plants have woody stems.

woof /wʊf/ *noun*; *verb* (*informal*)
▻ ***noun***: **woofs**
'**Woof!**' is the sound of a dog's bark: *The puppy gave a little woof.*
▻ ***verb***: **woofs, woofing, woofed**
A dog **woofs** when it barks.

wool /wʊl/ *noun*; (*uncount*)
1 Wool is the soft hair of sheep and certain other animals. **2** (*often adjectival*) **Wool** is the material produced from animals' wool, which is spun into thread for knitting or weaving fabric, and used for making clothes, carpets and blankets: *balls of knitting wool* □ *shawls made of the finest wool* □ *Some people can't wear wool next to their skin.* □ *pure wool blankets* □ *Are these sweaters wool or cotton?* [see also **cotton wool, steel wool, wire wool**]
▻ ***phrase*** (*informal*) You **pull the wool over** someone's **eyes** when you deliberately deceive or trick them.

woollen /ˈwʊlən/ *adjective*; *noun*
▻ ***adjective***
Woollen fabrics and articles are made of wool: *woollen sweaters.*
▻ ***noun*** (*used in the plural*): **woollens**
Woollens are clothes made of wool, especially knitted ones, or fabrics made of wool: *winter woollens* □ *specialists in tweeds and woollens.*

woolly /ˈwʊlɪ/ *adjective*; *noun*
▻ ***adjective***: **woollier, woolliest**
1 Woolly things are made of wool, or look like wool: *thick woolly socks* □ *animals with woolly coats* □ *The surface of the leaves is white and woolly.* **2** (*derogatory*) If you describe someone's ideas as **woolly**, you mean that they are vague and muddled: *woolly thinking* □ *one of those woolly-minded newspaper articles.* [*opposite* **clear**]
▻ ***noun*** (*informal*): **woollies**
A **woolly** is a woollen garment, especially a knitted one: *She opened the drawer she kept her winter woollies in.*

word /wɜːd/ *noun*; *verb*
▻ ***noun***: **words**
1 A **word** is a single unit of spoken or written language, and is written or printed with a space on either side of it: *What's another word for 'replace'?* □ *Could you supply us with a brief article of roughly 500 words?* □ *Brevity is, in Shakespeare's words, the soul of wit.* □ *It's impossible to convey the scene in words.* □ *I want you describe, in your own words, what sort of person King Lear is.* **2** (*used in the singular, with a negative*) You say you cannot hear or understand, or do not believe, a **word** of what someone is saying, if you cannot hear or understand, or do not believe, any of it: *It's an amusing story, though I must say I don't believe a word of it.* **3** You have a **word** or a few **words** with someone when you have a short conversation with them about something: *I'd like a word with you about that report you wrote.* **4** You offer a **word** of *eg* advice or caution to people when you give them a short warning or piece of advice: *One last word of warning to the walking group: please keep within sight of each other.* □ *Before we close tonight's programme, a word to all pet-owners ...* **5** (*uncount or used in the singular*) People send or bring **word** about something when they send or bring you news or a message about it; you can refer to news or a rumour as the **word**: *She left word with her secretary that she'd be late.* □ *Is there any word of the planned royal visit in today's paper?* □ *The latest word on the injured child is that he's progressing satisfactorily.* □ *The word got about that she was writing her memoirs.* **6** (*used in the singular*) You give someone your **word** when you promise them something solemnly: *I give you my word of honour I won't forget.* □ *I never doubted your word for a minute.* **7** (*used in the singular*) You give people the **word** to do something when you ask them or order them to do it, or give them a signal for action: *Our troops were waiting for the word to advance.* □ *If you want more copies, just say the word.* □ *My father was the kind of man who expected his word to be obeyed.* **8** (*used in the plural*) **Words** also means discussion as distinct from action: *It's deeds we want, not words.* **9** (*used in the plural*) The **words** of a song are its text or lyrics: *She played the hymn tune through and asked if I knew the words.* **10** Actors learn their **words** when they learn the speeches they have to recite.
▻ ***verb***: **words, wording, worded**
You **word** something you want to say in a particular way when you select words that express your meaning accurately or acceptably: *She worded her refusal as firmly as she dared.* □ *I'm sorry, I worded that tactlessly.*
▻ ***phrases*** **1** You receive information **by word of mouth** when you hear it from people rather than read it or hear it on radio or television. **2** You use *too* with **for words** to emphasize an adjective or adverb: *The situation is too idiotic for words.* **3** You complain that you **cannot get a word in edgeways** if someone else is talking so much that you get no opportunity to say anything yourself. **4** (*informal*) You **have words** with someone when you have an angry argument with them. **5** You use **in a word** to introduce a word or phrase that sums up what you have been saying: *Our prospects are, in a word, gloomy.* **6** You use **in other words** when you are about to express what you have said in a clearer, easier way: *people who are 'vertically challenged', in other words, small.* **7** (*often with a negative*) Something that is stated **in so many words** is stated directly, in clear, precise terms; **not in so many words** means not in exact, precise terms, but indirectly: *'Did they offer you the job?' 'Not in so many words, but they made it pretty obvious they wanted me.'* **8** You are **lost for words** when you are so surprised or confused that you cannot think what to say. **9** Someone who **does not mince their words** does not try to avoid offending people when telling them something unpleasant. **10** You **put in a word**, or **a good word, for** someone when you speak about them to someone important in a way that gives a good impression of them: *I'll try and put in a good word for you with the manager.* **11** You **take** someone **at their word** when you act on the assumption that they really mean what they say or promise: *Thank you for the offer; I may take you at your word.* **12** You **take** someone's **word for it** when you accept what someone says as true, because you have no opportunity of checking personally. **13** You get **the last word** in an argument if you bring it to an end by making a point that your opponent cannot answer. **14 a** You repeat something **word for word** when you reproduce it in exactly the same words: *They published the statement I gave them absolutely word for word.* **b** Something is translated

word for word when it is translated into words that correspond exactly with those in the original language: *a word-for-word translation.* **15 Words fail you** when you are so surprised, overwhelmed or annoyed that you cannot express yourself.

wording /ˈwɜːdɪŋ/ *noun* (*uncount*)
The **wording** of anything you say or write is the words you choose to express your meaning: *It was several hours before the wording of the trade agreement was adjusted to everyone's satisfaction.*

word-perfect /wɜːdˈpɜːfɪkt/ *adjective*
You are **word-perfect** if you can repeat from memory something you have learnt, such as your part in a play, without any mistakes.

wordplay /ˈwɜːdpleɪ/ *noun* (*uncount*)
Wordplay is the activity of making puns, or jokes based on words that have a similar sound, but different meaning.

word-processor /wɜːdˈprousɛsə(r)/ *noun*: **word-processors**
A **word-processor** is an electronic machine with a screen and keyboard, on which text can be composed for printing out, storing or future editing. — *noun* (*uncount*) **word-processing**: *Applicants must have experience in typing and word-processing.*

wordy /ˈwɜːdɪ/ *adjective*: **wordier, wordiest**
Someone or something that is **wordy** uses too many words, especially unnecessarily long words: *His style was wordy and imprecise.* □ *those wordy novelists of the nineteenth century.* [*opposite* **concise, succinct**]

wore /wɔː(r)/ *verb*
Wore is the past tense of **wear**.

work /wɜːk/ *noun*; *verb*
▻ ***noun***: **works**
1 a (*uncount*) **Work** is employment or a job: *Thousands of graduates are still looking for work.* □ *She had been in work for only two months when she was made redundant, and she has now been out of work for two years.* **b** (*uncount*) You refer to your place of employment as **work**: *She usually leaves work at 4.30.* □ *He came to work drunk on several occasions.* □ *He changed out of his work clothes and went home.* **c** (*uncount*) **Work** is the tasks that are involved in a job, or the tasks you do because they have to be done in order to achieve something: *Some days we don't finish work till 7.00 pm.* □ *She often brings work home with her.* □ *Housework bored her.* □ *We've still got some work to do on the roof.* □ *He's involved in social work.* **d** (*uncount*) **Work** on a particular subject is research or investigation into it: *the recent work on genes carried out by French scientists.*
2 a (*uncount*) **Work** is what you produce as a result of carrying out the tasks connected with your job or with achieving something: *She would spend ages every evening marking her pupils' work.* □ *Your essay was an excellent piece of work.* □ *Couldn't you present your work more neatly?* **b** (*used in the singular*) Something that is the **work** of a certain person has been done by them: *The model village was entirely the children's own work.* □ *Deliberate destruction on this scale is the work of madmen.* **c** (*count*) Something such as a painting, book, play, poem or musical composition is a **work**: *the complete works of Milton* □ *Mozart was at this time engaged on at least three major works.*
3 a (*uncount*) **Work** is used in the names of particular crafts and their products: *our range of basketwork furniture* □ *an exhibition of needlework and embroidery.* **b** (*uncount*) **Work** specifies parts of a building made in a certain material, or the material itself: *The stonework and woodwork are being restored.* □ *We scraped off the old peeling paintwork.* **c** (*used in the plural*) **Works** are building or repair operations: *roadworks* □ *the Ministry of Works.* **d** (*used in the plural, informal*) The **works** of a watch or any larger machine are its operating parts. **e** (*with a singular or plural verb*) A **works** is the place where a particular product is manufactured: *the gasworks* □ *The works are closing this autumn.*
▻ ***verb***: **works, working, worked**
1 a Someone who **is working** is employed or has a paid job: *Will you stop working at 60?* □ *He works freelance for a publishing firm.* □ *I worked as a waitress for several months.* **b** You **work** when you do the tasks you are employed to do, or tasks that need to be done in order to achieve something: *They work a forty-hour week.* □ *You work far too hard.* □ *students working for their final exams* □ *He's still working on his thesis.* □ *You must work at your backhand.* **c** You **work** people hard if you make them work hard. **d** An exercise that **works** a part of your body makes it move energetically.
2 a You **work** a machine when you operate it; a machine or device **works** a certain way if that is the way it operates or is operated: *She had to learn how to work a road drill.* □ *I'd no idea how the video worked.* **b** Things **work** a certain way if they operate or develop according to a certain pattern: *Most relationships don't work like that.* **c** A machine, device or apparatus **works** if it operates properly: *Does this television set work?* □ *Your right indicator light isn't working.* **d** A plan, idea, or system **works** if it successful or effective: *To her surprise the trick worked.* □ *The new arrangements are obviously not working.* □ *If alternative medicine works, why condemn it?* **e** A circumstance that **works** against you gives you a disadvantage; something that **works** for you or in your favour gives you an advantage: *The new tax system will actually work in your favour.* **f** You **work** on the basis that something is so when you accept it as correct in order to act or take decisions: *I'm working on the assumption that all committee members can help with the fête.*
3 a Craftsmen **work** in certain materials if they use them: *Recently he has been working in bronze.* **b** Craftsmen **work** objects when they make them or shape them: *earrings worked in silver.* **c** You **work** land when you cultivate it.
4 a You **work** yourself into a state such as a rage or panic when you let yourself get into that state: *It's no good working yourself into a fury.* [see also **work up**] **b** You **work** your way somewhere when you get there with an effort: *She worked her way along the rock ledge.* **c** You **work** something somewhere when you manage to get it into that position; something **works** somewhere when it gets into that position: *He worked the nail out of his sole.* □ *One of the screws had worked loose.*
▻ ***phrases*** **1** You are **at work a** when you are at your place of employment: *She wasn't at work today.* **b** when you are working: *She's hard at work on another novel.* **2** (*informal*) You **have your work cut out** when you are faced with a challenging task: *You'll have your work cut out controlling that class.* **3** (*informal*) You **make short work of** something **a** when you do it or complete it quickly. **b** when you eat it quickly. **4** People **put a lot of work into** a task when they spend a lot of time and energy on it. **5** You **set to work** on a task when you start doing it: *We'll set to work on the stocktaking next week.* □ *We set to work clearing up.*

phrasal verbs

work off You **work off** something such as anger or excess energy when you get rid of it by energetic activity.

work on 1 If you say you **are working on** something you mean you are trying to finish or improve it. **2** You **work on** someone when you use various means of persuasion to get them to do what you want.

work out 1 You **work out** the answer or solution to a question or problem when you find it after some thinking, reasoning or calculating: *Could you work out the distance to Solihull for me?* □ *I worked out that he must be 52.* □ *I couldn't work out what her motives might be.* **2** Something **works out** at a certain amount if it is calculated to be that amount: *With the discount, the tickets work out at £5 per person.* **3** Things **work out** when they come to a satisfactory conclusion: *If things work out we'll be able to go on holiday together this year.* **4** (*sport*) You **work out** by performing a set of energetic physical exercises: *Giles was working out in the gym.*

work up 1 You **work** yourself or others **up** into a state, *eg* of anger or excitement, when you make yourself or them get into that state: *I can't discuss the matter with you when you're so worked up.* □ *Mark Antony's speech works the crowd up into a fury.* **2** You **work up** something such as enthusiasm, energy or an appetite for something when you do something that makes you have it: *Go for a run and you'll soon work up an appetite for dinner.* **3** You **work up** to something difficult when you approach it in easy stages: *Start with a short run and work up gradually to the full marathon distance.*

workable /ˈwɜːkəbəl/ *adjective*
A system or scheme that is **workable** is capable of operating efficiently and effectively: *We'll have to find a workable solution somehow.* [same as **practicable**]

workbench /ˈwɜːkbentʃ/ *noun*: **workbenches**
A **workbench** is the table at which a mechanic or craftsman works.

workbook /ˈwɜːkbʊk/ *noun*: **workbooks**
A **workbook** is a student's exercise book containing text for studying, and questions, with spaces for the answers.

worker /ˈwɜːkə(r)/ *noun*: **workers**
1 A **worker** is a person who has a job in industry or business, especially an employee as distinct from an employer or manager: *There was the usual management-worker tension.* **2 Worker** is used in the names of certain jobs: *research workers in the pharmaceutical industry* □ *social workers.* **3** You describe someone as a **worker** of a certain quality if that is the way they work: *He's always been a slow worker.* □ *She's a very inaccurate worker.*

workforce /ˈwɜːkfɔːs/ *noun* (*used in the singular*)
The **workforce** of a company, an industry, or the whole country, is all the people working in it: *Japan's workforce* □ *The workforce has halved over the last three years.*

working /ˈwɜːkɪŋ/ *noun*; *adjective*
▻ ***noun*** (*used in the plural*): **workings**
The **workings** of an organization or system are the processes by means of which it operates: *She tried to explain to me the mysterious workings of the stock market.*
▻ ***adjective***
1 Working hours are the period of the day when offices and businesses are open; your **working** hours, **working** day or **working** week are the number of hours you work each day or week; your **working** life is the part of your life during which you have a job or are of a suitable age to be employed in one: *Please call the emergency number if you need help outside working hours.* □ *Their working week has effectively been reduced from 34 to 32 hours.* □ *He'd spent his whole working life in the same job.* **2** People's **working** conditions are those they experience at their place of employment: *The children labour from dawn to dusk in appalling working conditions.* **3** You have a **working** knowledge of something such as a language if you know enough to use for your particular purposes: *She had acquired a working knowledge of most European languages.* **4** A machine or apparatus that is in **working** order is operating properly.

working class /wɜːkɪŋ ˈklɑːs/ *noun* (*with a singular or plural verb*): **working classes**
The **working class** or **working classes** are the section of the population who do mainly manual, as distinct from skilled, jobs, are paid wages rather than salaries, and own little property: *He was proud of his working-class background.*

workload /ˈwɜːkloʊd/ *noun* (*usually in the singular*): **workloads**
Your **workload** is the amount of work you are given to do: *With all this extra paperwork the workload of most teachers has doubled.*

workman /ˈwɜːkmən/ *noun*: **workmen**
A **workman** is a man employed to do manual work, *eg* repairs to buildings or construction work: *The workmen had already begun to dismantle the scaffolding.* [compare **labourer**, **worker**]

workmanlike /ˈwɜːkmənlaɪk/ *adjective*
You describe a piece of work that someone has done as **workmanlike** if you think it has been done skilfully: *a well-thought-out and workmanlike report.* [*opposite* **amateurish**]

workmanship /ˈwɜːkmənʃɪp/ *noun* (*uncount*)
Workmanship is the skill of a craftsman, especially where it is evident in the appearance of a finished product: *Barnsley's furniture was remarkable for its consistently high standard of workmanship.* [*same as* **craftsmanship**]

workmate /ˈwɜːkmeɪt/ *noun* (*informal*): **workmates**
Your **workmates** are the people you work with at your place of employment, especially in industry: *He had been humiliated in front of his workmates.* [*same as* **fellow-worker**, **co-worker**; compare **colleague**]

work of art /wɜːk əv ˈɑːt/ *noun*: **works of art**
1 Works of art are such things as paintings and sculptures, especially those of high quality: *The gallery houses the country's best-known works of art.* **2** (*humorous*) You can describe something, especially something with a lot of complex detail, as a **work of art** if it has been skilfully done: *Her timetables were works of art.*

workplace /ˈwɜːkpleɪs/ *noun* (*usually in the singular*): **workplaces**
Your **workplace** is the building or room where you perform your job: *the importance of safety in the workplace.*

workshop /ˈwɜːkʃɒp/ *noun*: **workshops**
1 A **workshop** is a room, building or business where the work of construction, repair, design or production goes on: *The faulty machines had all been returned to the workshop.* □ *Wallpaper of this kind is a typical product of Morris's workshop.* **2** When people attend a

workshop on a particular subject they take part together in discussions and practical work in order to learn more about it. [*same as* **seminar**]

workshy /ˈwɜːkʃaɪ/ *adjective* (*derogatory*)
If you call someone **workshy** you mean that they are too lazy to take a job, or that they try to avoid doing any hard work in the job that they have.

workstation /ˈwɜːksteɪʃən/ *noun*: **workstations**
A person's **workstation** in an office is their computer terminal with its screen and keyboard.

work surface /ˈwɜːk sɜːfɪs/ *noun*: **work surfaces**
A **work surface** or **worktop** is a flat surface fitted over the top of pieces of kitchen equipment such as the fridge, washing machine and cupboards, on which you can prepare food: *easy-to-clean worktops.* [see picture at **kitchen**]

worktop /ˈwɜːktɒp/ see **work surface**.

work-to-rule /wɜːktəˈruːl/ *noun* (*used in the singular*)
A **work-to-rule** is a form of protest by workers, in which they slow work down deliberately by strictly following every rule of procedure, and doing no additional work.

world /wɜːld/ *noun*: **worlds**
1 a (*used in the singular*) The **world** is the earth, or the planet we inhabit: *Nowadays you can fly halfway round the world in a matter of hours.* □ *the highest mountain in the world* □ *destruction of the world's wildlife* □ *His name is familiar all over the world.* **b** A **world** is any planet: *creatures from other worlds.* **c** (*used in the singular*) The **world** refers to human affairs throughout our planet: *the present state of the world* □ *world history* □ *discoveries that changed the world.* **d** 'All the **world**' or 'the whole **world**' means everybody: *The whole world must have heard the story by now.* **e World** experts on a subject and the **world** champion in a sport are the best in the world; **world** championships and **world** tournaments are those in which the best players or athletes compete to decide the world champion: *She's the world authority on tropical skin diseases.* □ *In the post-war years Britain declined from her position as a world power.*
2 You use **world** to classify **a** particular groups of countries: *the Third-World countries* □ *Naturalists still commonly refer to North and South America as the New World.* **b** periods of history or civilization: *famous cities of the ancient world* □ *the modern world* □ *the prehistoric world.* **c** Your **world** is your individual way of life and your range of daily experiences: *We all live in our own narrow worlds.* □ *For a few days I was privileged to enter the world of the Royals.* **d** A **world** can be an environment characterized by a certain quality: *the world of the imagination* □ *Alice passes through the looking glass into a world that is all the wrong way round.* **e** A particular area of activity is a **world** of that activity: *the world of sport* □ *the financial world.* **f** Living things are divided into **worlds**: *the insect world* □ *the plant world.*
3 a 'This **world**' and 'the next **world**' or 'the **world** to come' are used to refer to our present life, and the life after death: *Perhaps she'll be happier in the next world.* **b** (*used in the singular*) The **world** is the busy crowded life of most people, in which money and possessions are important, seen from the point of view of someone who has not experienced it, or who rejects it: *Soon her children would go out into the world.* □ *She wanted to escape from the world.* □ *He tried to ignore the outside world.*
▻ *phrases* **1** Someone who wants **the best of both worlds** wants the benefits of both alternatives with the disadvantages of neither. **2** A baby **comes** or **is brought into the world** when it is born. **3** People who have **come up** or **down in the world** have been successful and risen, or done badly and fallen, in social status. **4** Someone who is **dead to the world** is fast asleep. **5** You use **in the world** for emphasis with negatives and question words such as *how* and *why*: *She seemed to be without a care in the world.* □ *What in the world did you say to him?* **6** You say you would **not** do something **for the world** if you want never to do it: *I wouldn't hurt her for the world.* **7** You are **on top of the world** when you are feeling very cheerful. **8** Something that is **out of this world** is exceptionally fine or splendid. **9** You **think the world of** someone if you love or admire them greatly. **10** There is **a world of difference** between things if they are entirely different. **11** Something that does you **a world of good** makes you feel much better. **12** Something that happens **the world over** happens throughout the whole world: *Pollution is affecting people's health the world over.* [*same as* **worldwide**] **13** Things that are **worlds apart** are entirely different.

world-class /wɜːldˈklɑːs/ *adjective* (*sport*)
Competitors and competitions that are **world-class** are of the highest standard in the world: *world-class tennis-players.*

world-famous /ˈwɜːldfeɪməs/ *adjective*
Someone or something **world-famous** is well known throughout the world: *playing under the baton of a world-famous conductor.*

worldly /ˈwɜːldlɪ/ *adjective* (*literary*): **worldlier, worldliest**
1 Worldly things are things that belong to our life on earth, as distinct from spiritual or eternal things: *worldly pleasures.* **2** Your **worldly** goods or possessions are your money and property and the other things you own: *She had no near relatives to leave her worldy goods to.* **3** A **worldly** person is **a** too concerned with possessions, money and luxuries. [*same as* **materialistic**] **b** experienced, capable and confident in dealing with life's practical matters.

world war /ˈwɜːldˈwɔː(r)/ *noun* (*history*): **world wars**
A **world war** is a war in which many countries all over the world become involved, especially the Great War (*World War I*) of 1914–18 or the war of 1939–45 (*World War II*).

worldwide /wɜːldˈwaɪd/ *adjective or adverb*
Something that is happening **worldwide** is happening throughout the world: *The effects of the recession are being felt worldwide.* □ *There could be a worldwide famine.*

worm /wɜːm/ *noun*; *verb*
▻ ***noun***: **worms**
1 A **worm** is a long narrow cylindrical animal without a backbone or legs, especially one that lives in the soil. **2** (*used in the plural*) People and animals who have **worms** have worm-like parasites living in their intestines.
▻ ***verb***: **worms, worming, wormed**
1 You **worm** your way somewhere when you get there gradually, *eg* by crawling: *He wormed his way along the tunnel.* **2** You **worm** your way into someone's favour, affections or confidence when you do things to make them like you or trust you, so that you can get something you want from them.

phrasal verb
You **worm** information **out** of someone who is trying to keep it secret by questioning them cleverly till you manage to get them to tell you it: *We managed to worm out the secret at last.* [*same as* **coax**]

worn /wɔːn/ *verb*; *adjective*
▷ ***verb***
Worn is the past participle of **wear**.
▷ ***adjective***
1 People look **worn** when they look tired: *She had a thin face with a worn expression.* **2** A **worn** piece of clothing or furniture looks old, thin or faded, because of long use: *an old worn cardigan* □ *The curtains were worn and shabby.*
▷ ***phrases*** **1** You are **worn out** when you are exhausted: *I felt too worn out to contribute to the conversation.* **2** A piece of clothing or furniture that is **worn out** is too old, faded or badly damaged by long use to be used any longer. [*same as* **shabby**, **tatty**]

worry /ˈwʌrɪ/ *verb*; *noun*
▷ ***verb***: **worries, worrying, worried**
1 You **worry** when there is a problem in your mind that you keep thinking about, *eg* something you are uncertain about, or something that might go wrong: *I used to worry when he was out and I had no idea where he was.* □ *I sometimes worry that he'll never find a job.* □ *You're always worrying about something.* □ *Don't worry; we've got just enough petrol to get home.* **2** Something **worries** you if you are upset or concerned about it, or keep wondering what to do about it: *Do you know if anything in particular was worrying her?* □ *It worries me to think that she can get out of the gate by herself.* □ *It doesn't worry me* [= I don't mind] *if you go on smoking and kill yourself.* □ *He worries me with his dangerous driving.* **3** You **worry** someone with a problem when you disturb them by telling them about it or asking their opinion: *There's no point in worrying her about it; she wouldn't understand.* [*same as* **bother**] — *adjective* **worried:** *I got worried when he still hadn't come home by midnight.* □ *Are you worried about the exam?* □ *I'm worried in case I forget everything.* □ *He was worried that she'd refuse.* □ *She turned a worried face towards me.* — *noun* **worrier:** *My parents have always been terrible worriers.* — *adjective* **worrying:** *the worrying increase in crime.* [*same as* **disturbing**]
▷ ***noun***: **worries**
1 (*uncount or used in the singular*) **Worry** is what you feel when you have a problem that you keep thinking about, *eg* something you are uncertain about, or something that might go wrong: *There's no cause for worry.* □ *The worry of bringing up three children on her own became too much for her.* [*same as* **anxiety**] **2** A **worry** is a problem you keep thinking about, or something you are uncertain about: *financial worries* □ *Feel free to come to me with your worries.* □ *Her main worry was that her colleagues might find out.*
▷ ***phrase*** (*informal*) You say '**Not to worry**' to people as an expression of reassurance when something has gone wrong: *'Not to worry; it was a very cheap glass.'* [*same as* **never mind**]

worse /wɜːs/ *adjective*; *adverb*
▷ ***adjective***
1 Worse is the comparative of **bad**: *The situation is getting worse by the hour.* □ *'How was the interview?' 'All right, I suppose. It could have been worse.'* □ *I'd hate to drown. I can hardly imagine a worse death.* **2** Someone who is ill gets **worse** when they become more seriously ill: *I'm afraid she's getting worse.*
▷ ***adverb***
Worse is the comparative of **badly**: *The bomb damaged some property on the east side, but the shops on the west side fared much worse.*
▷ ***phrases*** **1** Something that happens **for the worse** makes the situation more difficult than it was: *Overnight things took a turn for the worse.* **2** For **from bad to worse** and **for better or worse** see **bad**, **better**. **3** You say that someone **might do worse than** do a particular thing if you think they should do it: *They might do worse than chose a poet as president.* **4** People are **none the worse** for a bad experience if they have not been harmed by it: *She had a few bruises but otherwise appeared none the worse for her fall.* **5** For **worse for wear** see **wear**. **6** You are **worse off** if you have less money than you had, or than someone else has, or if your circumstances are more difficult than they were, or more difficult than someone else's: *The new community tax is going to leave most of us worse off* [= with less money]. □ *Educationally, our children are worse off than children elsewhere in Europe.* **7** If you say '**Worse was to follow**', or '**Worse was to come**', you mean that the situation became more difficult or unpleasant than you have so far described.

worsen /ˈwɜːsən/ *verb*: **worsens, worsening, worsened**
Things **worsen** when they get more difficult, unpleasant or grave; something **worsens** a situation if it makes it more difficult: *The patient's condition worsened in the night.* □ *With the situation worsening by the minute she found herself beginning to panic.* □ *I think it might only worsen things if you tried to apologize.*

worship /ˈwɜːʃɪp/ *verb*; *noun*
▷ ***verb***: **worships, worshipping, worshipped**
1 You **worship** gods, or God, when you honour them with praise, prayer and hymns: *Let us worship the Lord.* □ *We must have freedom to worship in our own way.* **2** You **worship** someone or something if you love or admire them, especially so much that you cannot see their faults or dangers: *She was an inspired teacher; the kids worshipped her.* [*same as* **idolize**] — *noun* **worshipper:** *The bomb came straight through the church roof and landed on the floor, but to the relief of the assembled worshippers, failed to explode.* □ *Former sun-worshippers can find themselves developing skin cancer.*
▷ ***noun***
1 (*uncount*) **Worship** is the activity of worshipping: *A church is a place of worship; please behave respectfully.* □ *To the '60s generation the Beatles were objects of worship.* **2** (*BrE*) 'Your **Worship**' and 'His **Worship**' are respectful titles used for addressing or referring to a mayor or magistrate.

worst /wɜːst/ *adjective*; *adverb*; *pronoun*; *noun*
▷ ***adjective***
Worst is the superlative of **bad**: *That was one of the worst plays I've ever seen.* □ *He was forced to get up and attend a meeting when his illness was at its worst.* □ *Of all my experiences, that was the worst.* □ *That's a worst-case estimate* [= an estimate based on things going as wrong as they can go].
▷ ***adverb***
Worst is the superlative of **badly**: *Widows on a fixed pension fare worst.* □ *These are the worst-affected areas.*
▷ ***pronoun:*** *There's a human soul even in the worst of these criminals.*
▷ ***noun*** (*used in the singular*)
The **worst** refers to a possibility or a stage in a situation that is the most difficult or grave: *We're hoping the worst is over.* □ *If the worst happens, and she dies, he'll be facing a charge of homicide.*
▷ ***phrases*** **1** Something that is so **at the worst** or **at worst** is so from the most unfavourable or pessimistic point of view: *At the worst, all we have to do is find a telephone and get help.* □ *At best he's ambitious, at worst a power-seeker without conscience or qualifications.* **2** You say that something may happen **if the worst comes to the worst** if you think it may happen if things develop in the most unfavourable way: *If the*

worst comes to the worst I may have to stop running altogether.

worth /wɜːθ/ *preposition*; *noun*

▷ ***preposition***

1 Something is **worth** a certain amount of money if it has that value, or can be sold for that amount: *The house must be worth at least £100 000.* ▫ *I've no idea what these pictures are worth.* ▫ *I gave the jug to a jumble sale; I didn't think it was worth more than a couple of pounds.* **2** (*informal*) A person who is **worth** a certain amount of money owns money or property of that value: *She must be worth two million.* **3** Something is **worth** doing if it is a good thing to do: *They may have special reductions for children; it's worth asking.* ▫ *He didn't think the television was worth repairing.* ▫ *I did go to the exhibition, but there was nothing worth seeing.* ▫ *The Tower is certainly worth a visit.* **4** Something that is **worth** it, or **worth** the trouble or bother, is a good thing to do: *He thought he might drive across to Glasgow, but decided it wasn't worth the trouble.* ▫ *I hated having to learn Latin, but it was worth it to get into university.*

▷ ***noun*** (*uncount*)

1 An amount of money's **worth** of something is the quantity that can be bought for that amount; a certain period's **worth** of work or supplies is the amount that takes, or lasts for, that amount of time: *Three thousand pounds' worth of equipment was destroyed in the fire.* ▫ *They had only three days' worth of food left.* ▫ *We've lost two weeks' worth of work.* **2** A person's **worth** is the value, importance or usefulness that they are thought to have: *Most people underestimate their own worth.*

▷ ***phrases*** **1** You do something **for all you are worth** when you do it as energetically as you can: *She pedalled for all she was worth.* **2** You add **'for what it's worth'** after making an offer or suggestion, to indicate that you doubt whether what you are saying is useful: *I've made a list of possible improvements, for what it's worth.* **3** Something that is **worth your while** is a good thing to do: *It would be well worth your while to enquire if they have grants available.*

worthless /ˈwɜːθləs/ *adjective*

Something or someone that is **worthless** has no use or value: *He's got himself involved in some worthless scheme.* ▫ *I felt worthless and degraded.*

worthwhile /wɜːθˈwaɪl/ *adjective*

Something that is **worthwhile** is worth the time, money or energy that is spent on it, or is useful, interesting and enjoyable: *It's good to feel you're doing a thoroughly worthwhile job.* ▫ *A trip to the museum is always worthwhile.* [*same as* **constructive, useful**]

worthy /ˈwɜːðɪ/ *adjective*: **worthier, worthiest**

1 (*literary*) A **worthy** person or thing deserves people's admiration and respect: *a worthy member of the community* **2** (*formal*) Someone or something is **worthy** of something if they deserve it: *an achievement worthy of recognition* ▫ *It's a worthy cause; I suppose we should support it.* [*same as* **deserving opposite, unworthy**] **3** (*formal*) Behaviour or a performance that is **worthy** of someone is of the standard you would expect from them: *It was a spectacular effort, and worthy of a champion.*

would *modal verb* (short form **'d**, negative form **wouldn't**)

1 Would is used with the infinitive of other verbs as the past tense of **will a** in reported speech: *She said she'd be leaving at 10.00 am.* ▫ *I hoped they wouldn't notice.* ▫ *I asked him to write every week, and he promised he would.* **b** in indicating willingness: *He wanted money, but I wouldn't lend him any.* ▫ *The television wouldn't work when I turned it on this morning.* **c** in indicating habitual behaviour: *Wherever she happened to be, she would always telephone me at six.* **d** in indicating resistance to advice: *I told him she wasn't well enough to receive visitors, but he would insist on going to see her.*

2 Would is used **a** to express willingness or readiness to do something: *He'd do anything for her.* ▫ *I'd die rather than admit the truth.* **b** in expressing wishes and longings: *I wish she would telephone.* ▫ *If only they'd give us another chance.* **c** to suggest that something is probable: *You'd remember Great-Uncle Bob, I imagine.* **d** in conditional sentences, and in discussing probabilities: *If I gave up now I'd never forgive myself.* ▫ *You wouldn't get there any faster if you went by car.* ▫ *It wouldn't be safe to let the children come home on their own, would it?*

> Notice that you usually use the past tense of the verb in the *if*-clause: *If you took* (not *would take*) *the bus, you'd get there just as fast.*

3 You use **would**, with emphasis, **a** to comment that someone's behaviour was to be expected: *'She refused.' 'She would.'* ▫ *That's the sort of generous thing he would do.* **b** to express annoyance or frustration at some development: *It would rain just as we're setting out.*

4 Would is used politely to express **a** requests: *Would you mind turning the radio down?* ▫ *I wonder if you would close the window a little?* ▫ *Please would you look after my bag for me?* **b** proposals: *Would you care to accompany me?* ▫ *Would you like to join in?* **c** preferences and desires: *I'd love to see your drawing when you've finished.* ▫ *I'd rather have coffee.* ▫ *I would be so grateful if you could send me a copy.* **d** suggestions, advice and opinions: *I'd set off early if I were you.* ▫ *In your place I think I would get a cat.* ▫ *I would think red is a better choice.*

5 You use **'would** have' **a** to talk about probability in the past: *He wouldn't have seen your note; it was too dark.* **b** in conditional sentences referring to the past and in discussing past probabilities: *I would have called you if I had known you were in town.* ▫ *We weren't late, but it wouldn't have mattered anyway.*

> Notice that you usually use *had* with the past participle of the verb in the *if*-clause: *She wouldn't have caught the train if she had waited* (not *would have waited*) *any longer.*

c in expressing preferences referring to the past: *Would you have preferred to stay another day?* **d** to express your opinion: *I would have thought he could afford to pay.* [see also **should**]

would-be /ˈwʊdbiː/ *adjective*

Would-be describes what people would like to become: *a gathering of poets and would-be poets.*

wouldn't /ˈwʊdənt/

Wouldn't is the spoken, and informal written, form of **would not**: *He'd enjoy that, wouldn't he?* ▫ *If only he wouldn't snore.*

would've /ˈwʊdəv/

Would've is the spoken, and informal written, form of **would have**: *It would've been kinder to warn me.*

wound[1] /waʊnd/ *verb*

Wound is the past tense and past participle of **wind**.

wound[2] /wuːnd/ *noun*; *verb*

▷ ***noun*: wounds**
A **wound** is an injury to the body of a person or animal caused *eg* by a cut or blow, in which the flesh is usually broken open; the cut that a surgeon makes in your flesh when operating on you is also called a **wound**: *She was taken to hospital, where her wounds were cleaned and dressed.* □ *He almost died of his wounds.* [*same as* **injury**]
▷ ***verb*: wounds, wounding, wounded**
1 You **wound** a person or animal if you injure them with a weapon that breaks open their flesh, such as a knife or gun: *wounded soldiers.* **2** You, or your feelings, **are wounded** by something that someone says or does if you feel hurt and upset about it: *I had evidently wounded her deeply by criticizing her work.*

wove /woʊv/ *verb*
Wove is the past tense of **weave**.

woven /ˈwoʊvən/ *verb*
Woven is the past participle of **weave**.

wow /waʊ/ *interjection* (*informal*)
You say '**Wow!**' to express astonishment or admiration: *Wow! That's great!*

wrack see **rack**.

wrangle /ˈraŋgəl/ *verb; noun*
▷ ***verb*: wrangles, wrangling, wrangled**
People **wrangle** with each other when they quarrel or argue noisily or bitterly: *My brother and sister-in-law seemed to spend most of their time wrangling about one thing or another.*
▷ ***noun*: wrangles:** *We were very poor, so there were constant wrangles over money.*

wrap /rap/ *verb*: **wraps, wrapping, wrapped**
You **wrap** something in a material such as paper or cloth when you fold the material round it so as to cover it: *He hastily wrapped the knife in some newspaper.* □ *Some of the chocolates were wrapped in silver paper.* □ *We will wrap and post your gifts free.*

phrasal verbs
wrap round 1 You **wrap** something such as paper or cloth **round** something when you put it round it so as to cover it: *She found a paper hankie to wrap round the bleeding finger.* **2** You **wrap** your arms, fingers or hands **round** something when you put them round it tightly: *She wrapped her arms round his neck.* □ *I wrapped my fingers round the hot mug.* **3** (*computers*) The text on a screen **wraps round** if it starts a new line as soon as the last character space on the previous line is filled.
wrap up 1 You **wrap** something **up** when you fold paper or cloth round it: *She arrived with her swimming things wrapped up in a towel.* **2** People **wrap up** when they put on warm clothes: *Do wrap up well if you're going out into the snow.* **3** You say that someone **is wrapped up** in something such as their work if they think about it all the time. **4** (*informal*) You **wrap up** a particular matter or task when you bring it to a satisfactory conclusion.

wrapper /ˈrapə(r)/ *noun*: **wrappers**
A **wrapper** is any of the paper or transparent covers that manufacturers put round such things as packets of food to protect them: *Ice-cream wrappers littered the pavement outside the shop.* □ *sweet wrappers.*

wrapping /ˈrapɪŋ/ *noun*: **wrappings**
A **wrapping** is a covering of paper or other material put round something to protect it: *The children were sitting amidst a pile of Christmas wrappings, playing with their new toys.*

wrapping paper /ˈrapɪŋ peɪpə(r)/ *noun* (*uncount*)
Wrapping paper is special decorated or fine paper used for putting round presents.

wrath /rɒθ/ *noun* (*literary; uncount*)
Wrath is anger: *the wrath of God.*

wreak /riːk/ *verb*: **wreaks, wreaking, wreaked**
1 (*informal*) Something **wreaks** havoc or damage when it causes it on a large scale: *The constant rainstorms were wreaking havoc on the harvest.* **2** (*literary*) You **wreak** revenge or vengeance on someone when you deliberately do something terrible to them, in return for the harm they have done you.

wreath /riːθ/ *noun*: **wreaths**
A **wreath** is a ring-shaped arrangement of flowers and leaves, epecially one that is placed on a grave or coffin as a symbol of love and remembrance for the person who has died.

wreathed /riːðd/ *adjective* (*literary*)
One thing is **wreathed** in another when it is covered or surrounded with it: *mountain tops wreathed in clouds.*

wreck /rɛk/ *verb; noun*
▷ ***verb*: wrecks, wrecking, wrecked**
1 A ship **is wrecked** when it is badly damaged and sinks, *eg* after hitting rocks. **2** You **wreck** something **a** when you break it or destroy it: *Don't let the children use my computer; they'll wreck it.* **b** when you upset it or spoil it: *The car broke down on the first day, which completely wrecked our holiday.* [*same as* **ruin**]
▷ ***noun*: wrecks**
1 (*used in the singular*) The **wreck** of a ship is its destruction at sea, usually by stormy weather or rocks. **2** A **wreck** is **a** a badly damaged ship lying on rocks or at the bottom of the sea: *The bay is full of wrecks.* **b** a crashed aircraft or ruined vehicle. **3** (*informal*) If you call a person a **wreck**, you mean that they are in a bad or exhausted state of physical and mental health: *I realized I'd end up a wreck if I went on drinking.*

wreckage /ˈrɛkɪdʒ/ *noun* (*uncount*)
Wreckage is what remains of a ship, aircraft or vehicle after it has been badly damaged or destroyed: *Pieces of wreckage lay widely scattered around the crash site.*

wren /rɛn/ *noun*: **wrens**
A **wren** is a small brown bird with short rounded wings and an upright tail.

wrench /rɛntʃ/ *verb; noun*
▷ ***verb*: wrenches, wrenching, wrenched**
1 You **wrench** something somewhere when you pull or twist it violently out of position: *The handle had been wrenched off the door.* □ *He grabbed my arm and wrenched it behind my back.* **2** You **wrench** yourself away from something that is holding your attention or fascinating you when you force yourself to leave it: *If you children can wrench your eyes from the screen for a few minutes, we'll have tea.* [*same as* **drag away**] **3** You **wrench** a part of your body such as an ankle or shoulder when you hurt it by twisting it. [*same as* **strain**]
▷ ***noun*: wrenches**
1 (*usually in the singular*) You give something a **wrench** when you pull or twist it violently. **2** (*used in the singular*) You can describe something such as a painful parting or separation from someone as a **wrench**: *Leaving home was always a wrench.* **3** A **wrench** is also a spanner-like tool for gripping and turning fittings used with screws, called nuts and bolts.

wrestle /ˈrɛsəl/ *verb*: **wrestles, wrestling, wrestled**
1 You **wrestle** with someone, especially as a sport, when you fight with them by trying to grip and throw them, or hold them down against the ground. **2** You

wrestle with a piece of equipment when you try to make it work: *She wrestled helplessly with the gears.* [*same as* **struggle**, **grapple**] **3** You **wrestle** with a problem when you try to solve it. — *noun* **wrestler:** *He had huge muscles, like a wrestler's.* — *noun* (*uncount*) **wrestling:** *The old ladies seemed most of all to enjoy the boxing and wrestling on TV.* ▫ *a wrestling match.*

wretch /rɛtʃ/ *noun*: **wretches**
People refer to someone who is either very wicked or very miserable as a **wretch**: *I'll have my revenge on the wretch who stole my instruction book.* ▫ *A poor ragged little wretch was crouching in the corner.*

wretched /'rɛtʃɪd/ *adjective*
1 Wretched describes someone or something that is in a very bad or miserable condition: *I'd had a headache all day and felt wretched.* ▫ *There were five of them living in a wretched little caravan.* ▫ *living in wretched poverty*. **2** (*informal*) People call things that are annoying them **wretched**: *That wretched car broke down again today.*

wriggle /'rɪgəl/ *verb*: **wriggles**, **wriggling**, **wriggled**
1 You **wriggle** when you twist your body about; you **wriggle** something, especially a part of your body, when you twist it about: *Do stop wriggling and sit still!* ▫ *If you can still wriggle your fingers, I don't think you've broken your arm.* **2** You **wriggle** somewhere when you get there by crawling or by twisting and turning: *They wriggled through the pipe.*

> ***phrasal verb***
> (*informal*) You **wriggle out of** a duty, responsibility, or trouble, when you cleverly manage to avoid it. [*same as* **get out of**]

wring /rɪŋ/ *verb*: **wrings**, **wringing**, **wrung**
1 You **wring** something wet, such as a cloth, or **wring** it out, when you squeeze the liquid out of it by twisting it; you **wring** liquid from something such as a wet cloth when you twist it to squeeze out the liquid: *He wrung out his shirt and hung it up to dry.* ▫ *She stood on the bank wringing the water from her hair.* **2** You **wring** something such as information or a confession from or out of someone when you force them to give it to you: *The police had somehow wrung an admission of guilt from him.* [*same as* **coerce**, **extract**] **3** To **wring** a bird's neck is to kill it by twisting its neck. **4** People **wring** their hands when they keep gripping them together and twisting them about in anxiety or distress.
▻ ***phrase*** Hair or clothing that is **wringing wet** is very wet.

wrinkle /'rɪŋkəl/ *noun*; *verb*
▻ ***noun***: **wrinkles**
1 (*usually in the plural*) **Wrinkles** are the lines or creases that form in your skin, especially on your face, as you get older: *Look, I'm getting wrinkles.* **2** A **wrinkle** is a slight crease in any surface: *She smoothed the wrinkles out of the tablecloth.*
▻ ***verb***: **wrinkles**, **wrinkling**, **wrinkled**
You **wrinkle** your forehead when you frown; you **wrinkle** your nose when you screw it up, *eg* when there is a bad smell. — *adjective* **wrinkled:** *She laid her wrinkled old hand over mine.* ▫ *Her clothes were all wrinkled, as though she had slept in them.*

wrist /rɪst/ *noun*: **wrists**
Your **wrist** is the joint between your hand and your arm: *She wore long sleeves, with a frill at the wrist.* [see picture at **body**]

wristwatch /'rɪstwɒtʃ/ *noun*: **wristwatches**
A **wristwatch** is a watch fitted to a strap, that you wear round your wrist.

writ /rɪt/ *noun*: **writs**
A **writ** is a legal document that is sent to you to order you to do something or not to do something.

write /raɪt/ *verb*: **writes**, **writing**, **wrote**, **written**
1 You **write** something when you produce words, letters or numbers using a pen or pencil on paper: *Some children leave school barely able to read or write.* ▫ *I wrote her telephone number on the back of a receipt.* ▫ *She used to try and write at least ten pages a day.* **2** You **write** something such as a book, poem or piece of music when you compose or create it, in manuscript, typescript or on a computer; the person who **writes** something is its author or composer: *Who wrote the 'Enigma Variations'?* ▫ *She had written and published two novels before she was twenty.* **3** People who **write** create books or contribute articles to newspapers and magazines, especially as a living: *She'd always wanted to write.* ▫ *He writes for one of the literary journals.* **4** You **write** someone a letter, or **write** to them, when you communicate with them by means of a letter: *He wrote asking us for information about grants.* ▫ *Write Granny a note to say thank you, won't you?* ▫ *I feel like writing and complaining.* ▫ *Didn't I write to you from Prague?* ▫ *He writes that it's very hot in Budapest.* ▫ *'Dearest Nancie,' she wrote, 'it's ages since you heard from me.'*

> Notice that in AmE you say, *eg*, *She wrote me from Paris*, and in BrE, *She wrote to me from Paris*.

5 You **write** something such as a cheque when you fill in the necessary information on it and sign it: *The doctor wrote me a prescription for antibiotics.* ▫ *She wrote a cheque for £55 and handed it to me.*

> ***phrasal verbs***
> **write back** You **write back** to someone who has sent you a letter when you reply to them by letter: *I wrote to her several times, but she never wrote back.*
> **write down** You **write** something **down** when you put it down or record it on paper with a pen or pencil: *I can give you her address; have you got something to write it down with?*
> **write in** You **write in** to a radio or television programme, or an organization, when you send them a letter: *Please write in to us with your suggestions.*
> **write into** Something such as a condition or arrangement **is written into** a contract or agreement if it is included in it.
> **write off 1** You **write off** to an organization or company for something when you send them a letter asking for it: *We wrote off to the travel company for a holiday brochure.* **2** You **write off** money that someone owes you, or that you have lost, when you accept that you are not going to get it back: *Last year we had to write off debts amounting to £60000.* **3** You **write off** something if you decide that it is not going to succeed and that you will not spend any more time, effort or money on it: *The doctors had just about written me off when, miraculously, I recovered.* [see also **write-off**]
> **write out 1** You **write** something **out** when you write it on paper: *I'll write out the recipe for you, if you like.* **2** You **write out** something such as a cheque when you fill it in and sign it: *If you wait a minute I'll write you out a receipt.*
> **write up 1** You **write up** something such as a report or notes when you write or rewrite them in a full, neat, easily readable form. **2** You **write up** your diary when you record your activities in it up to the present time. [see also **write-up**]

write-off /ˈraɪtɒf/ *noun*: **write-offs**
A vehicle that is a **write-off** has been so badly damaged in an accident that it is not worth repairing.

writer /ˈraɪtə(r)/ *noun*: **writers**
1 A **writer** is a person who writes things such as books and articles, especially for a living: *In tonight's programme we shall be talking to the writer John Mortimer.* [*same as* **author**] **2** The **writer** of something such as a letter, poem or article is the person who wrote it: *We shall track down the writer of the anonymous letter.*

write-up /ˈraɪtʌp/ *noun*: **write-ups**
A **write-up** is an article about something such as a new theatre production, or some new activity or product, written for a newspaper or magazine: *The Evening Herald gave the new centre an enthusiastic write-up.*

writhe /raɪð/ *verb*: **writhes, writhing, writhed**
You **writhe** when you twist yourself about violently, *eg* when you are in severe pain: *She lay writhing in agony.* [*same as* **squirm**]

writing /ˈraɪtɪŋ/ *noun*: **writings**
1 (*uncount*) **Writing** is written or printed words: *I could see the letter on the table but it was too far away for me to read the writing.* □ *Make sure you get their consent in writing.* **2** (*uncount*) Your **writing** is your handwriting: *I recognized her big untidy writing on the envelope.* **3** (*uncount*) **Writing** is the art or activity of writing books or articles, especially as a living: *Have you ever considered writing as a career?* **4** (*uncount*) **Writing** is also the material written: *This is an excellent piece of writing.* □ *Her writing shows promise.* **5** (*used in the plural*) An author's **writings** are the works that he or she has written: *I've read all Hume's philosophical writings.* [*same as* **work**]

writing paper /ˈraɪtɪŋ peɪpə(r)/ *noun* (*uncount*)
Writing paper is fine smooth paper for writing letters on. [see picture at **office**]

written /ˈrɪtən/ *verb*; *adjective*
▻ ***verb***
Written is the past participle of **write**: *Her written works include novels and plays.*
▻ ***adjective***
1 A **written** agreement or rule is one that has been made official by being recorded in print or writing: *He made a written undertaking to pay me a regular monthly sum.* [*opposite* **unwritten**] **2** A **written** exam is one in which candidates have to write something, as distinct from carrying out practical work or giving spoken, or oral, answers.

wrong /rɒŋ/ *adjective*; *adverb*; *noun*; *verb*
▻ ***adjective***
1 There is something **wrong** when things are unsatisfactory in some way: *You look worried; is anything wrong?* □ *The doctors can't find out what's wrong with him.* □ *There's obviously nothing wrong with your hearing.* □ *What's wrong with being ambitious, anyway?* **2** Things that are **wrong** are incorrect or unsuitable: *Our calculations were wrong.* □ *I'm always saying the wrong thing.* □ *He's the wrong person for this post.* □ *Surely that photo's the wrong way round?* □ *Miss, why have you marked this sum wrong?* [*opposite* **right**] **3** You are **wrong** about something if your opinion about it is incorrect: *I was quite wrong about her motives.* □ *It's possible we might be wrong.* □ *If you think it's going to be easy, you're wrong.* [*same as* **mistaken**; *opposite* **right**] **4** Something that you do is **wrong** if it is bad or immoral: *It's wrong to cheat.* □ *Jail is where you go when you do something wrong.* □ *What am I supposed to have done wrong?* □ *You're wrong to waste your talents.* [*opposite* **right**] **5** The **wrong** side of a piece of cloth or clothing is the side that faces inwards and is not intended to be seen. [*opposite* **right**] — *adverb* **wrongly:** *I thought, wrongly, that the plane left at 10.00.* □ *They'd estimated the required quantities wrongly.*
▻ ***adverb:*** *You've spelt his name wrong.* □ *I shouldn't have told her just then; I timed it all wrong.* [*opposite* **right**]
▻ ***noun***: **wrongs**
1 (*uncount*) **Wrong** is used to refer to behaviour and actions that are bad, immoral or unjust: *By the age of ten children ought to know the difference between right and wrong.* □ *They have done wrong and must be punished.* **2** A **wrong** is an unjust act, circumstance, or piece of behaviour: *You've done her a great wrong in spreading this malicious story about her.* □ *We have a duty to right the wrongs of an unjust society.*
▻ ***verb***: **wrongs, wronging, wronged**
You **wrong** someone when you treat them unjustly, or judge them unfairly: *I'm afraid I wronged you in distrusting your opinion.*
▻ ***phrases*** **1** You **get** something **wrong** when you make a mistake: *They've got the date wrong on the programme.* **2** You **get** a person or situation **wrong** when you misunderstand them: *Don't get me wrong; I approve of what you're doing.* □ *You've got it all wrong; nobody hates you.* **3** For **get on the wrong side of** someone see **side**. **4** Something **goes wrong** if it stops working properly or progressing satisfactorily: *Our marriage started going wrong almost from the start.* □ *Something's gone wrong with the backup system.* **5** You **go wrong** when you make a mistake: *I wonder where I went wrong?* **6** You are **in the wrong** when you do something immoral, unjust or illegal: *However just their cause, if protesters break the law they are in the wrong.*

wrongdoer /ˈrɒŋduːə(r)/ *noun*: **wrongdoers**
A **wrongdoer** is a person guilty of an immoral or illegal act: *The wrongdoers will be caught and fined.* [*same as* **culprit**]

wrongdoing /ˈrɒŋduːɪŋ/ *noun* (*uncount*)
Wrongdoing is immoral or illegal behaviour or actions: *They maintained that there had been no wrongdoing on their part.*

wrongful /ˈrɒŋfʊl/ *adjective*
A **wrongful** act is an unjust or illegal one: *One of the sacked men was suing the company for wrongful dismissal.* — *adverb* **wrongfully:** *She had been wrongfully arrested and detained, and was seeking compensation.*

wrote /roʊt/ *verb*
Wrote is the past tense of **write**.

wrought /rɔːt/ *verb*; *adjective*
▻ ***verb*** (*literary*)
Wrought is a past tense and past participle meaning 'made' or 'produced': *The illness had wrought a terrible change in her appearance.*
▻ ***adjective***
Wrought metal has been hammered and bent into a particular shape, as distinct from being cast: *wrought-iron gates.*

wrung /rʌŋ/ *verb*
Wrung is the past tense and past participle of **wring**.

wry /raɪ/ *adjective*
1 A **wry** smile or a **wry** sense of humour expresses a mixture of bitterness and amusement: *'It might be worse,' he said with a wry laugh.* [*same as* **ironic**] **2** You make a **wry** face when you screw up your features as a reaction to the bitter taste of something. — *adverb* **wryly:** *She smiled wryly.* [*same as* **ironically**]

X or **x** /ɛks/ *noun*: **Xs** or **x's**
1 X is the twenty-fourth letter of the English alphabet: *'Xylophone' begins with an 'x'.* **2 X** is used when you don't know or don't want to use the name of a person or place: *interviews with Miss X, the politician's mistress.* **3** (*mathematics*) You use **x** when a number or quantity is unknown: $x = a+b$. **4** (*informal*) People sometimes write a row of **Xs** at the end of a letter, to represent kisses.

xenophobia /zɛnə'foʊbɪə/ *noun* (*uncount*)
Xenophobia is an unreasoning dislike or suspicion of foreigners and their ways: *In conversation she revealed a hostility towards the inhabitants that amounted to xenophobia.*

Xerox /'zɛrɒks/ or /'zɪərɒks/ *noun*; *verb* (*trademark*)
▻ ***noun***: **Xeroxes**
1 A **Xerox** is a photocopy of a document. **2** A **Xerox**, or **Xerox machine**, is a machine for photocopying documents. [*same as* **photocopier**]
▻ ***verb***: **Xeroxes, Xeroxing, Xeroxed**
You **Xerox** a document when you make a photocopy of it: *I cut out the article and xeroxed it for the files.*

Xmas /'krɪsməs/ *noun* (*uncount*)
Xmas is a written form of 'Christmas', in which 'X' is the Greek letter representing 'Ch', traditionally used as a short form of 'Christ'.

X-ray /'ɛks reɪ/ *noun*; *verb*
▻ ***noun***: **X-rays**
1 X-rays are a form of radiation that can pass through certain substances that light cannot pass through, and can produce an image on film of objects that they pass through. **2** (*count or uncount*) An **X-ray** is a photograph taken using X-rays, or the process of taking it: *He pinned the X-ray of her lungs up on a lighted screen in front of us.* □ *The doctor sent me to the hospital for an X-ray on my neck.* □ *Mrs Peterson is to go for X-ray at 11.45.*
▻ ***verb***: **X-rays, X-rayed, X-raying**
You **are X-rayed** when a photograph is taken of part of your body using X-rays: *Her wrist was X-rayed and found to be broken.*

xylophone /'zaɪləfoʊn/ *noun*: **xylophones**
A **xylophone** is a musical instrument consisting of a series of wooden or metal bars of different lengths, played by being struck with wooden hammers. [see picture at **orchestra**]

Y or **y** /waɪ/ *noun*: **Ys** or **y's**
1 Y is the twenty-fifth letter of the English alphabet: *Should 'shyer' be spelt with an i or a y?* **2** (*mathematics*) You use **y** to show the second of two unknown numbers or quantities: $y = x^2$. [see also **X**]

-y /ɪ/ *suffix*
1 -y is added to nouns to form adjectives with the sense 'full of', 'characterized by' and 'having the quality of': *spotty* □ *icy* □ *shiny.* **2 -y** is also added to nouns as a way of expressing affection or fondness: *There's a good doggy.* □ *children without any mummy or daddy.* **3 -y** is a noun-forming ending used with adjectives to indicate the quality or state associated with the adjective: *jealousy* □ *modesty.*

yacht /jɒt/ *noun*: **yachts**
A **yacht** is a boat or small ship with sails, and often with an engine, used for racing or sailing for pleasure.

yachting /ˈjɒtɪŋ/ *noun* (*uncount*)
Yachting is the activity or sport of sailing yachts: *I don't think I'd enjoy the discipline of a yachting holiday.*

yam /jam/ *noun*: **yams**
1 A **yam** is a large potato-like root vegetable. **2** (*AmE*) A **yam** is a sweet potato.

Yank /jaŋk/ (*BrE*) *noun* (*informal, offensive*): **Yanks**
A **Yank** is someone from the United States.

yank /jaŋk/ *verb*; *noun*
▷ ***verb*** (*informal*): **yanks, yanking, yanked**
You **yank** something when you pull it suddenly and sharply: *I tried yanking the plant up by its roots.*
▷ ***noun*** (*usually in the singular*; *informal*): **yanks:** *He came up behind me and gave my hair a yank.*

Yankee /ˈjaŋkɪ/ (*BrE*) *noun* (*informal, offensive*): **Yankees**
A **Yankee** is a Yank.

yap /jap/ *verb*: **yaps, yapping, yapped**
1 A puppy or small dog **yaps** when it produces a series of high-pitched barks. **2** (*informal, derogatory*) A person who **yaps**, or **yaps** on, talks continuously, especially in a loud high annoying voice, about unimportant things: *The dinner was very enjoyable until everyone started yapping on about how I should taken my studies more seriously.*

yard¹ /jɑːd/ *noun*: **yards**
A **yard** is a unit of length equal to 3 feet or 0.9144 metres: *The garden's almost 80 yards long, but only 10 yards wide.*

yard² /jɑːd/ *noun*: **yards**
1 A **yard** is an area of ground belonging to a building, and usually surrounded by a wall: *We had the gate widened so that people could drive in and park in the old stable yard.* **2** (*AmE*) Your back **yard** is your back garden, the garden behind your house. **3 Yard** is used in terms for enclosed outdoor working areas, or areas used for certain purposes: *the Merseyside shipyards.* □ *another dockyard strike* □ *We found some useful bits and pieces at the scrapyard.*

yardstick /ˈjɑːdstɪk/ *noun*: **yardsticks**
You use something as a **yardstick** when you use it as a standard by which you can judge things: *In our society, money is the crucial yardstick of success.*

yarn /jɑːn/ *noun*: **yarns**
1 (*uncount*) **Yarn** is thread spun from *eg* wool or cotton, for use in knitting, weaving, or mending: *Remember to take some mending yarn and a needle.* **2** A **yarn** is a story, usually told with a degree of exaggeration: *It sounded like one of those sailors' yarns.* □ *She spun me some yarn about her husband belonging to the KGB.* □ *adventure yarns.*

yawn /jɔːn/ *verb*; *noun*
▷ ***verb***: **yawns, yawning, yawned**
1 You **yawn** when you open your mouth wide and take a deep breath, often as an involuntary action and usually when you are tired or bored. **2** You can say that a big hole or gap **yawns** before you as you approach it: *The mouth of the cave yawned in front of us.* □ *Where yesterday there had been solid ground there now yawned an immense crater.* — *adjective* **yawning:** *They gazed down in horror through the yawning gap in the floorboards.*
▷ ***noun*** (*usually in the singular*): **yawns**
1 A **yawn** is an act of yawning: *She tried to stifle a yawn.* **2** (*informal*) People also refer to a boring event or activity as a **yawn**: *University lectures were a yawn on the whole.*

yeah /jɛ/ or /jɛə/ *interjection* (*informal*)
Yeah means 'yes'.

year /jɪə(r)/ *noun*: **years**
1 A **year** is the period of 365 days or twelve months from 1 January to 31 December, during which the earth goes once round the sun: *during 1948 and the following year* □ *Was 1969 the year men first landed on the moon?* □ *I didn't get away for a holiday at all last year.* □ *Is it your silver wedding anniversary this year or next year?* [see also **leap year**]
2 A **year** can be any period of twelve months: *It's two years today since she died.* □ *He worked abroad for several years.* □ *millions of years ago.* □ *These carvings are thousands of years old.* □ *a two-year-old child.* **3** The academic **year**, school **year** or university **year** is the period of time (usually from autumn to the following summer in the UK) during which schools and universities provide courses of study at a range of levels: *He's in his last year at school.* □ *during my third year at Cambridge* □ *the fifth-year pupils.* **4** The financial **year** is the period of time (from the beginning of April to the end of the following March in the UK) that is used by businesses as a basis for working out their finances: *the report issued at the end of the financial year.* **5** (*used in the plural*; *informal*) You use **years** to mean a long time: *It's years since I last saw her.* □ *We've known each other for years and years.*
▷ ***phrases*** **1** Something that is the case **all year round** or **all the year round** does not alter from season to season: *I wanted to live somewhere where it was warm all*

the year round. □ *The hotel stays open all year round.* **2** Something that goes on happening **year in, year out** happens regularly every year: *Some people seem quite happy to go to the same place for their summer holidays, year in, year out.*

yearly /ˈjɪəlɪ/ *adjective; adverb*

▻ ***adjective***

1 Yearly events happen once every year: *I go for a yearly check-up at the hospital.* [*same as* **annual**] **2** A **yearly** amount is an amount relating to any year: *if your yearly income exceeds £18000* □ *the yearly death rate from smoking-related diseases.* [*same as* **annual**]

▻ ***adverb***: *your bus pass must be renewed yearly.*

yearn /jɜːn/ *verb*: **yearns, yearning, yearned**

You **yearn** for something if you want it very much: *The golden age which he yearns for is merely his lost youth.* □ *He found himself yearning for the cool overcast highlands* □ *She yearned to be free of the constant pressure.* [*same as* **long**]

▻ ***noun*** (*count or uncount*): **yearnings**: *As old age approached she felt a yearning to return to her native Vancouver.*

-year-old /jɪərˈoʊld/ *suffix*

-year-old follows numbers to form adjectives and nouns that specify age: *a ten-year-old child* □ *a group of six-year-olds* □ *the physical changes that occur in the eleven-to fourteen-year-old age group.* □ *year-old calves.*

yeast /jiːst/ *noun* (*uncount*)

Yeast is a kind of fungus that is used in bread-making to make the dough rise, and also in the production of alcoholic drinks.

yell /jɛl/ *verb; noun*

▻ ***verb*** (*rather informal*): **yells, yelling, yelled**

1 You **yell** when you shout loudly: *There he was, holding desperately on to a branch, yelling at me to help him.* **2** People, especially children, **yell** when they cry loudly: *Jonathon fell over on the pavement and started yelling his head off.*

▻ ***noun*** (*rather informal*): **yells:** *He hit his thumb with the hammer and gave a yell of pain.* □ *She'll feel better once she's had a good yell.* □ *Just give me a yell when you're ready.*

yellow /ˈjɛloʊ/ *noun; adjective; verb*

▻ ***noun*** (*count or uncount*): **yellows**

Yellow is the colour of the sun, butter, egg yolk or lemons, or is any shade of this colour: *an unpleasant yellow* □ *the browns and yellows of autumn* □ *We painted the ceiling a pale yellow.*

▻ ***adjective***: **yellower, yellowest**

1 Yellow things are the same colour as the sun, butter, egg yolk or lemons: *yellow roses* □ *They're yellow, not orange.* □ (*with the noun omitted*) *The red tiles are nice, but the yellow are prettier.* **2** (*informal, derogatory*) **Yellow** means cowardly: *He has a yellow streak.* □ *You'd fight back if you weren't so yellow!*

▻ ***verb***: **yellows, yellowing, yellowed**

Something **yellows** or **is yellowed** if it turns or is turned yellow: *yellowing leaves* □ *an old newspaper, torn and yellowed.*

yellow fever /jɛloʊ ˈfiːvə(r)/ *noun* (*uncount*)

Yellow fever is a serious disease caused by a virus transmitted by the bite of a mosquito.

yellowish /ˈjɛloʊɪʃ/ *adjective*

Something that is **yellowish** is slightly yellow in colour: *Her skin had a yellowish tinge, as though she had lived in the tropics.*

yelp /jɛlp/ *verb; noun*

▻ ***verb***: **yelps, yelping, yelped**

A dog **yelps** when it gives a sharp high-pitched bark, *eg* when it has been hurt or is frightened; a person **yelps** when they give a sharp cry, especially of pain: *The puppy was sitting holding up its front paw, yelping pitifully.* □ *I yelped in agony.*

▻ ***noun***: **yelps:** *She gave a yelp of pain.*

yen[1] /jɛn/ *noun* (*used in the singular; informal*)

You have a **yen** for something when you have a strong desire to have it or do it: *He'd always had a yen to be a writer.* [*same as* **hankering, longing**]

yen[2] /jɛn/ *noun*: **yen**

The **yen** is the standard unit of Japanese currency.

yep /jɛp/ *interjection* (*informal*)

Yep means yes.

yes /jɛs/ *interjection*

You use **yes 1** as a positive or affirmative reply **a** to confirm something: *'Are they leaving before lunch?' 'Yes, they're hoping to.'* □ *'I gather you've had experience of this work?' 'Yes, a little.'* □ *'Isn't Susan coming?' 'Yes, later.'* **b** to accept an offer: *'Shall I call a taxi?' 'Oh yes, please, if you would.'* □ *'Coffee?' 'Yes, please.'* **c** to give permission: *'May I take this chair?' 'Yes, of course, do.'* **d** to agree with something: *'It's too late to call them now.' 'Yes, I suppose so.'* **e** to agree to do something or express willingness: *'Take this note to the headmaster, would you?' 'Yes, sir.'* [*opposite* **no**] **2** to disagree with a negative statement or a question expecting a negative answer, usually adding a positive statement: *'You didn't warn me about this.' 'Yes, I did, yesterday.'* □ *'You two haven't met before, have you?' 'Yes we have; we met at Leeds last year.'* [*opposite* **no**] **3** to respond or show you are listening when someone calls you or addresses you by name; shop assistants sometimes say **'yes**?' to a customer to enquire what he or she wants: *'Dad?' 'Yes?' 'What's an affidavit?'* **4** to encourage someone to continue with what they are telling you, or to respond to what they have said: *Yes? What did she say then?* □ *'It's not round; it's more like an egg.' 'Yes, I see.'* **5** to say you have remembered something you were trying to remember: *Now what was her name? Oh yes, Amanda.*

yesterday /ˈjɛstədɪ/ *adverb; noun*

▻ ***adverb***

Yesterday is the day before today: *I didn't go to work yesterday.* □ *Where were you yesterday morning?* □ *Have you still got yesterday's paper?* □ *I found the door unlocked when I came home yesterday evening.*

> Notice that although you usually say '*yesterday* evening' (rather than '*last* evening'), you always say '*last* night'.

▻ ***noun*** (*uncount; literary*)

You can use **yesterday** to refer the recent past: *the fashions of yesterday.*

yet /jɛt/ *adverb; conjunction*

▻ ***adverb***

1 (*used with a negative or in questions*) Something that has not happened **yet** has not happened up to the present time, but is expected to happen, will probably happen, or may happen: *Your parcel hasn't arrived yet.* □ *We haven't decided what to call her yet.* □ *'Have you phoned Irene?' 'No, not yet.'* □ *Hasn't she finished those letters yet?* □ *There haven't been any major difficulties yet.* □ *'Did you pass?' 'I don't know yet.'* □ *I hadn't yet received confirmation of my appointment.*

> Notice that with **yet** you use the perfect tense of verbs that represent action, and the present tense of verbs that represent a state: *I haven't heard yet*, but *I don't know yet*. But in AmE the past tense of action verbs is often used rather than the perfect: *I didn't see my tutor yet.*
> The position of **yet** changes when you are referring

to the past: *It wasn't yet five o'clock. I didn't yet know. I hadn't yet heard.*
Compare **yet** and **already**: **yet** is used with a negative or in questions and often expresses surprise at a delay; **already** can be used in positive statements or in positive and negative questions, and expresses surprise that something has happened so soon: *Has the mail been collected yet? Hasn't it been collected yet? It's already been collected. Has it been collected already? Oh, not already, surely?* [see note at **already**]

2 (*with a negative*) Something that is not to be done **yet** should not be done now, although it will be done later: *You can't go to bed yet; it's far too early.* □ *I'd rather you didn't tell anyone else yet.* □ *Don't tighten the lids yet; wait for the jam to cool.* □ *You're not leaving yet* (or *already*), *are you?* [= as early as this] **3** Something may **yet** happen if there is still a possibility of it happening: *She may yet make a success of it.* [*same as* **still**] **4** (*literary*) **Yet** is used like **still** in other ways: *Enjoy yourself while there's yet time.* □ *There's life in me yet, you know.* □ *You're young yet; there's plenty of time to decide.* □ *He left us 30 years ago, but I can hear his laugh yet.* [*same as* **still**] **5 Yet** adds emphasis to a period of time during which something will continue to be the case: *The shops won't be shutting for an hour yet.* □ *He'll be in hospital for a while yet.* **6** Something that is **yet** to happen, or that you have **yet** to do, is something that has not happened, or that you have not done, that may now be rather unlikely: *I've yet to discover a more efficient method than this.* □ *A genuine cure for baldness has yet to be invented.* **7 Yet** emphasizes *again*, *another* and *more*, and can be used like *still*, rather formally, to emphasize comparatives: *Someone's altered the clock yet again.* □ *She's got yet another cold.* □ *There was yet more trouble piling up.* □ *We wish him yet greater success in the future.* [compare **still, even**] **8 Yet** is used after a superlative to mean 'up to the present time': *It's my best effort yet.* [*same as* **so far**]
▻ ***conjunction*** (*formal*)
Yet is used like *but* to introduce a circumstance that contrasts with the one you have mentioned: *She knew what danger she was in, yet she remained at her position.* □ *A simple yet elegant solution to the problem.* □ *I've never tried skiing, and yet there's no reason why I shouldn't.*
▻ ***phrase*** (*with a negative*) Something that has not happened **as yet** has not happened up to the present, and may not happen: *No-one has complained as yet.* □ *a picturesque and as yet unspoilt seaside village.* [compare **so far**]

yew /juː/ *noun*: **yews**
A **yew**, or **yew tree**, is an evergreen tree with dark needle-like leaves and red berries.

yield /jiːld/ *verb*; *noun*
▻ ***verb***: **yields, yielding, yielded**
1 (*formal*) You **yield** to someone or something when you stop resisting them: *Again the Prime Minister has had to yield to pressure and back down over a key point in his policy.* □ *Tell yourself that you are not going to yield to temptation.* □ *I suppose I shall have to yield to your superior wisdom.* [*same as* **give way, back down**] **2** You **yield** to traffic coming from a certain direction when you let it go first: *Yield to vehicles coming from the right.* **3** You **yield** something that you have control of to someone when you let them take control of it: *They refuse to yield up any of the territory they have recently occupied.* □ *In the end she was forced to yield control of the company to her son.* [*same as* **surrender**] **4** (*formal*) Something **yields** when it gives way, bends or breaks under pressure: *The door was shut, but yielded to a gentle push.* □ *The bed yielded under his weight.* □ *The roof had yielded under the enormous weight of snow.* [*same as* **give way**] **5** To **yield** a crop, a profit, or results, is to produce them: *They're ancient, these apple trees, but they yield an enormous crop every year.* □ *Discussions are OK only if they yield useful ideas.* □ *Eva's investments yielded a satisfactory income, so she saw no point in getting a job.*
▻ ***noun***: **yields**
The **yield** that something has is the amount it produces: *I think you're getting a poor yield for your investment.* □ *Farmers are under continual pressure to increase their yield.*

yippee /jɪˈpiː/ *interjection* (*informal*)
People, especially children, shout **'yippee!'** when they are pleased or excited about something.

yob /jɒb/ or **yobbo** /ˈjɒboʊ/ (*BrE*) *noun* (*informal*): **yobs** or **yobbos**
Boys who behave rudely or roughly are sometimes referred to as **yobs** or **yobbos**: *In the worst incident, 300 yobs showered police with broken bottles in the centre of Coventry.* [*same as* **lout, hooligan**]

yodel /ˈjoʊdəl/ *verb*: **yodels, yodelling** (*AmE* **yodeling**), **yodelled** (*AmE* **yodeled**)
People **yodel** when they sing in a style that alternates rapidly between a normal voice level and a much higher level.

yoga /ˈjoʊgə/ *noun* (*uncount*)
Yoga is a system of exercise in which you move your body into various difficult positions; yoga aims at increasing your fitness and suppleness, and relaxing your mind.

yoghurt, **yoghourt** or **yogurt** /ˈjɒgət/ *noun*: **yoghurts**
1 (*uncount*) **Yoghurt** is a semi-liquid food made from fermented milk, often flavoured with fruit: *Try eating your muesli mixed with natural yoghurt.* **2** A **yoghurt** is a carton or tub of yoghurt: *I bought two yoghurts, in case you wanted one.*

yoke /joʊk/ *noun*: **yokes**
1 A **yoke** is a wooden frame placed over the necks of oxen to keep them moving side by side when they are pulling a plough or cart. **2** You suffer under a **yoke** when you are in a situation in which your freedom is restricted, or unwelcome burdens are imposed on you: *countries that have lately thrown off the yoke of communism.*

yolk /joʊk/ *noun* (*count or uncount*): **yolks**
The **yolk** is the yellow part in the middle of an egg.

yonder /ˈjɒndə(r)/ *adjective or adverb* (*old*)
Yonder means 'over there': *in the field yonder* □ *over on yonder hill.* □ *The nearest village was often referred to as 'yonder' by the locals.*

you /juː/ *pronoun* (*used as the subject of a plural verb, or as the object of a verb or preposition*)
1 A speaker or writer uses **you** to refer to the person, or the people, that he or she is addressing: *'Who's first?' 'You are.'* □ *I've got news for you.* □ *Hi, Emmy; I haven't seen you for ages; how are you?* □ *She's slightly older than you.* □ *Was that you calling just now?* □ *I heard you complaining to him.* □ *Thanks; that was really nice of you.* □ *I don't want you getting the wrong idea.* □ *'I've hurt my back.' 'Oh, poor you.'* □ *You realize, all of you, that tonight is a special occasion?* □ *I want to thank you both for your hospitality.* **2 You** can be followed by a plural noun or number: *It's time you kids got some sleep.* □ *I'd like you three to collect the supplies.* **3 You** is used, followed by a noun, for calling a person or people something nice or nasty: *You angel!* □ *You clever creature!* □ *You silly idiot!* □ *You lying hypocrites!* □ *'I've just had flu.' 'You poor thing!'*

4 **You** is used like the more formal *one* to refer to people in general, including yourself, or even to refer to yourself in an indirect way: *You see very few cases of the disease nowadays.* □ *They ought to warn you when they're going to cut the water supply off.* □ *You had to be tough to survive those training courses.*

you'd /juːd/ *verb*
You'd is the spoken, and informal written, form of **1** **you would**: *You didn't tell me you'd be late home tonight.* **2** **you had**, especially where *had* is an auxiliary verb: *You'd better buy some more bread while you're out.*

you'll /juːl/
You'll is the spoken, and informal written, form of **you will**: *You'll be late if you don't hurry.*

young /jʌŋ/ *adjective*; *noun*
▻ ***adjective***: **younger**, **youngest**
1 A **young** person, animal or thing has not lived very long, or is in the early stages of development or existence: *families with young children* □ *Maureen was the youngest in the class* □ *He's two years younger than me.* □ *She looks quite young for her age still.* □ *Your mother's very young-looking, isn't she?* □ *The rocks in this region are comparatively young.* □ *How can I help you today, young lady?* □ *We'll have to think of something to keep the young ones* [= the children] *amused.* □ *The younger generation have a language entirely of their own.* [*opposite* **old**] **2** **Young** styles and clothes are designed for young people: *I think this dress is a bit young for me.* [*opposite* **old**] **3** As an older person, you can refer to your youth as your **young** days, or your **younger** days: *I was a lot fitter in my younger days.* **4** (*literary*) You can say that the evening or night is still **young** if it is not very late.
▻ ***noun*** (*plural*)
1 The **young** of animals and birds are their babies: *Some birds feed their young on insects.* [*same as* **offspring**] **2** The **young** are young people in general: *music and fashion for the young.*

youngish /ˈjʌŋɪʃ/ *adjective*
A **youngish** person is quite young in age or appearance: *The clerk was a youngish man with an earnest expression and red hair.* □ *Moores is young, well, youngish at 45.*

youngster /ˈjʊŋstə(r)/ *noun* (*informal*): **youngsters**
A **youngster** is a young person, especially a child: *Do bring the youngsters with you; they'd enjoy it.*

your /jɔː(r)/ *determiner* (*possessive*)
1 A speaker or writer uses **your** to refer to things that belong or relate to the person or people he or she is addressing: *May I see your driving licence?* □ *What are your names?* □ *How are your parents?* □ *At your age I was already earning my living.* □ *I'm sure she won't mind your* (or *you*) *borrowing it.* **2** When *you* is being used to refer to people in general instead of the more formal *one*, **your** is used in place of *one's*: *when you can't bear your relations a minute longer.* **3** (*rather old*) **Your** is used like *the* to refer to a typical member of a class: *while your average wage-earner is struggling to make a little go a long way.* **4** **Your** is used in addressing people who have royal or noble titles: *if Your Majesty is sufficiently rested* □ *We hope that Your Royal Highnesses have enjoyed the visit.* □ *Thank you, Your Grace.*

you're /jɔː(r)/
You're is the spoken, and informal written, form of **you are**: *You're going to be late.* □ *'I'm ten stone.' 'You're not!' 'I am.'*

yours /jɔːz/ *pronoun* (*possessive*)
1 A speaker or writer uses **yours** to refer to something belonging to the person or people he or she is addressing: *Disciplining children is not the teacher's job; it's yours.* □ *That's my sherry; yours is on the sideboard.* □ *I've packed my boots; where are yours?* □ *I met a friend of yours the other day.* **2** People write **'Yours** sincerely' or **'Yours** faithfully', or less formally **'Yours'**, before signing their name at the end of a letter: *All the best to Janet. Yours, Hamish.* □ *With many thanks for your help, Yours sincerely, M Robinson.* [see also **Letter-writing** in Appendices]

yourself /jɔːˈself/ *pronoun* (*reflexive*): **yourselves** /jɔːˈselvz/
1 A speaker or writer uses **yourself** (when addressing one person) and **yourselves** (when addressing more than one) **a** as the object of a verb or preposition where the subject of the verb is 'you' or the person or people addressed: *Have you hurt yourself?* □ *Make yourselves comfortable.* □ *Give yourself a break.* □ *You should look after yourself better.* **b** to emphasize 'you', or as an emphatic form of 'you': *'Who told you?' 'You told me yourself.'* □ *You may not approve of it yourself, but it doesn't worry me.* □ *Remember there are people far worse off than yourself.* **2** You do something **yourself** when you do it without help or participation by anyone else: *You'll be able to finish the rest yourselves.* **3** If you are not **yourself** you are not feeling well: *I don't think you've been yourself lately.* □ *I do hope you're feeling yourself again.*
▻ ***phrase*** For **by yourself** see **by**.

youth /juːθ/ *noun*: **youths** /juːðz/
1 (*uncount*) Your **youth** is the early part of your life, especially the period between childhood and mature adulthood: *I was a reasonable dancer in my youth.* □ *I felt I was wasting my youth and wanted to break away and go abroad.* [compare **adolescence**] **2** (*uncount*) **Youth** is also the condition of being young: *the energy and vitality of youth.* □ *I had youth on my side, and my opponent was beginning to tire.* □ *She was perhaps thirty, but had not lost the bloom of youth.* **3** A **youth** is **a** (*BrE*; *slightly derogatory*) a young boy or man: *A group of youths were standing outside the chip shop.* **b** a young person of either sex. **4** (*plural*) The **youth** are young people in general: *the youth of today.* □ *The youth of this country face an impossible task when it comes to finding jobs.*

youth club /ˈjuːθ klʌb/ *noun*: **youth clubs**
A **youth club** is a place or organization that provides leisure activities for young people.

youthful /ˈjuːθfʊl/ *adjective*
1 Someone who is **youthful** is **a** young: *He had the role of adviser to the youthful king.* **b** young-looking, in view of their age: *Her father was a youthful fifty-year-old.* □ *Even at the age of 65 she had a marvellously youthful complexion.* **2** **Youthful** qualities, characteristics and activities are those associated with, or belonging to, young people: *youthful pleasures* □ *youthful pursuits* □ *They were full of youthful enthusiasm.*

youth hostel /ˈjuːθ hɒstəl/ *noun*: **youth hostels**
A **youth hostel** is a place that provides cheap and simple accommodation for people, especially young people, who are on holiday.

you've /juːv/
You've is the spoken, and informal written, form of **you have**, especially where *have* is an auxiliary verb: *I hope you've remembered your driving licence.*

yo-yo /ˈjoʊjoʊ/ *noun*: **yo-yos**
A **yo-yo** is a toy consisting of a circular, grooved piece of wood or other material, attached to a piece of string that is wound through the groove; you play with a yo-yo by making it rise and fall on the string.

yuppie or **yuppy** /ˈjʌpɪ/ *noun* (*informal, usually derogatory*): **yuppies**
A **yuppie** is an ambitious young professional person who earns a lot of money: *Then came the yuppies with their designer ski wear and new fast cars.*

Z

Z or **z** /zɛd/ *noun*: **Zs** or **z's**
Z is the last letter of the English alphabet.

zany /ˈzeɪnɪ/ *adjective*: **zanier, zaniest**
Zany people or things are amusing in a crazy or mad way: *the zany humour of the now legendary Monty Python team.*

zap /zap/ *verb* (*informal*): **zaps, zapping, zapped**
1 To **zap** someone is to kill them, usually by shooting them. **2** You **zap** while you are watching television if you change channels frequently using a remote-control device: *She was sitting in front of the television, aimlessly zapping between channels.*

zeal /ziːl/ *noun* (*uncount*; *formal*)
Zeal is great enthusiasm or keenness: *religious zeal.* [*same as* **ardour, fervour**; *opposite* **apathy**]

zealot /ˈzɛlət/ *noun* (*often derogatory*): **zealots**
A **zealot** is a very keen, determined, often fanatical, supporter of a political or religious cause. [*same as* **fanatic**]

zealous /ˈzɛləs/ *adjective*
Someone who is **zealous** about something is very keen and enthusiastic about it: *From her childhood she had been a zealous supporter of environmental causes.* □ *the over-zealous pursuit of consistency.* — *adverb* **zealously**: *He was a dedicated politician, serving zealously on several committees.*

zebra /ˈzɛbrə/ or /ˈziːbrə/ *noun*: **zebras** or **zebra**
A **zebra** is a black-and-white-striped animal related to the horse, found living wild in Africa.

zebra crossing /zɛbrə ˈkrɒsɪŋ/ (*BrE*) *noun*: **zebra crossings**
A **zebra crossing** is a place on a road where pedestrians may cross, marked by black and white stripes painted on the ground, at which drivers must stop to allow people to walk across. [*same as* **pedestrian crossing**; see picture at **street**]

zenith /ˈzɛnɪθ/ *noun* (*used in the singular*)
The **zenith** of something is its highest or most successful point: *in the days when Britain's imperial might was at its zenith* □ *He was at the zenith of his political career when a heart attack struck him down.* [*same as* **climax, high point**]

zero /ˈzɪəroʊ/ *noun*; *adjective or determiner*; *verb*
▻ ***noun***: **zeros** or **zeroes**
1 (*count or uncount*) **Zero** is the number or figure 0: *Fifteen, minus six, minus nine, is zero.* □ *You write one hundred thousand with a one followed by five zeros.* □ *It accelerates from zero to 100 kph in under five seconds.* □ *I've got that telephone number for you: it's six two zero* (or *O*) *eight five seven.* [= 620857] [*same as* **nought**; compare **O, nil, love**] **2** (*uncount*) **Zero** is 0° centigrade, or freezing point: *Temperatures overnight will drop to 5 degrees below zero.* **3 Zero** means nothing, or the point where there is none of something: *Motorists are warned that thick fog in the area has reduced visibility virtually to zero.*
▻ ***adjective or determiner***
Zero means 'not any' or 'no': *The anti-smoking lobby want a zero-tolerance policy with regard to smoking in public places.* □ *To achieve zero inflation would be an impossibiliity.* □ *We'll try to restore the program, but I think our chances are zero.*
▻ ***verb***: **zeroes, zeroing, zeroed**

> ***phrasal verb***
> **zero in on 1** To **zero in on** a target is to move towards it and aim at it: *Saddam's missiles were zeroing in all too successfully on Israeli targets.* **2** You **zero in on** something such as a problem when you identify it and concentrate your attention on it: *He zeroed in on the company's major problem.* □ *Your enemies lose no time in zeroing in on your failings.*

zest /zɛst/ *noun*
1 (*uncount or used in the singular*) **Zest** is liveliness and enthusiasm: *She had a great zest for life.* □ *He was full of zest as usual.* [*same as* **enthusiasm**] **2** (*used in the singular*) The enjoyment you get out of your life or out of some activity is referred to as its **zest**: *When the children grew up and left home, some of the zest went out of her life.* [*same as* **enjoyment**] **3** (*uncount*; *cookery*) **Zest** is lemon or orange skin.

zigzag /ˈzɪgzag/ *noun*; *verb*
▻ ***noun***: **zigzags**
A **zigzag** is a line with a series of sharp bends to the left and right in it: *The path wound in a zigzag up the mountain.*
▻ ***verb***: **zigzags, zigzagging, zigzagged**
Someone or something **zigzags** when they follow a zigzag course as they move: *The path zigzagged up the mountain.*

zinc /zɪŋk/ *noun* (*uncount*)
Zinc is a bluish-white metal used *eg* to make brass.

zip /zɪp/ *noun*; *verb*
▻ ***noun***: **zips**
A **zip**, or **zip fastener**, is a device for fastening *eg* clothes and bags, consisting of two rows of metal or nylon teeth with a sliding tab which you pull to make the two rows of teeth fit into each other: *She slipped on her anorak and did up the zip.*
▻ ***verb***: **zips, zipping, zipped**
You **zip** something when you fasten it with a zip: *You have to zip the two flaps together.* [*opposite* **unzip**]

> ***phrasal verb***
> You **zip up** a piece of clothing when you fasten it with a zip; a garment that **zips up** has a zip to fasten it: *I put on my boots and zipped them up.* □ *Elderly people may have difficulty putting on garments that zip up at the back.*

zip code /ˈzɪp koʊd/ (*AmE*) *noun*: **zip codes**
A **zip code** is a post code.

zipper /ˈzɪpə(r)/ *noun*: **zippers**
A **zipper** is a zip.

zodiac /ˈzoʊdɪak/ *noun* (*used in the singular*)
The **zodiac** is a representation of the night sky, usually in the form of a circular diagram, showing the position of the planets and stars. It is divided into twelve sections which each have a name and special symbol (the **signs of the zodiac**).

zombie /ˈzɒmbɪ/ *noun* (*informal, derogatory*): **zombies**
Someone who is referred to as a **zombie** seems not to be aware of what is going on round them, lacks energy, and acts in a slow, automatic-looking manner.

zone /zoʊn/ *noun*: **zones**
A **zone** is an area or region characterized by a particular feature or quality, or by some activity that goes on there: *hordes of refugees fleeing from the war zone.* □ *They were moving residents out of the danger zone.* □ *vegetation that is found only in the temperate zones of the earth.*

zoo /zuː/ *noun*: **zoos**
A **zoo** is a place where wild animals are kept for the public to see, and for study and breeding.

zoology /zoʊˈɒlədʒɪ/ *noun* (*uncount*)
Zoology is the scientific study of animals. [compare **biology, botany**] — *adjective* **zoological** /zoʊəˈlɒdʒɪkəl/: *the zoological section of the library.* — *noun* **zoologist:** *He was a member of a team of zoologists studying the behaviour of wolves.*

zoom /zuːm/ *verb*: **zooms, zooming, zoomed**
1 You **zoom** somewhere when you move quickly: *The car zoomed off up the road.* **2** Prices **zoom** upwards when they increase very quickly.

phrasal verb
A camera **zooms in** on someone or something when it is operated so as to give a close-up image of them.

zoom lens /ˈzuːm lɛnz/ *noun*: **zoom lenses**
A **zoom lens** is a camera lens that can bring the thing being photographed into close-up view.

zucchini /zʊˈkiːnɪ/ *noun* (*AmE*): **zucchini**
A **zucchini** is a courgette. [see picture at **vegetable**]

Appendices

Letter-Writing

The letters we write as private individuals fall into two broad categories: those to people who are personal friends or members of our family; and those to officials, institutions, businesses and other organizations.

Letters in the first category are informal in style and are often a means of sharing our thoughts and feelings with the person to whom we are writing, as well as giving them news and information.

In the second category, letters are usually more formal in style since their main function is to provide or ask for information. The intended reader of the letter is often not known to us personally.

For formal letters it is often helpful to make a rough draft so that you are sure that you have covered all the points you want to make, and they are arranged in a logical sequence. Avoid using complicated sentence constructions. While it is a good idea to vary the length of sentences for the sake of interest and variety, in general sentences should be kept short. It is very likely that the reader of your letter has a lot of other letters to deal with, and will not be able to spend more than a few minutes reading each one.

Any letter, whether formal or informal, should be written clearly or typed accurately. Guidance on the way letters should be set out is given in the examples which follow.

Informal letter

25 Laburnum Road
ABERDEEN
AB6 6FW

In letters to personal friends you usually give your own address, but do not include theirs, as you would in a more formal letter.

Friday 20th March

Dear Anne,

Notice the use of contractions in this informal letter.

I was delighted to get your long letter yesterday. I hadn't expected to hear from you so soon after your removal, as I'd been thinking you'd be much too busy arranging your new home and settling the children into their new school.

I'm so glad all your lovely furniture survived the move intact, and that nothing is missing. I hope you have nice neighbours and that Tom and Jane make friends quickly. Of course they will miss their old school friends for a while but they have so many hobbies and interests I'm sure they will soon belong to as many clubs as they did here, and that all their spare time will be occupied with interesting activities.

We all miss you, and I especially miss our daily chats. Peter is lost without someone to talk to over the garden fence about golf and gardening! We must arrange to visit each other later in the year, perhaps during the school holidays. I'm sure you will want to come back to Scotland for New Year, and of course you must stay with us.

I was sorry to hear that your mother isn't very well, but at least you are closer to her now and can keep an eye on her. She must be delighted that the children can visit her every week.

The weather here has been very cold but there has been plenty of sunshine, so we mustn't complain too much. I'm looking forward to the first signs of spring in the garden.

I'm sending you some interesting cuttings from the Press and Journal to keep you up to date with local news, including the list of graduates from the university, with David's name at the top of the second column. He has a job offer from a company in France, and I think he is going to take it. It's all very exciting.

I don't have any more news at the moment, but will write again soon. Let me know how your mother is in your next letter.

Love

Marion

Because the person being written to is a close personal friend of the writer, the ending 'Love' or 'Lots of love' is used.

Other closing expressions in an informal letter are 'Best wishes', 'All the best', 'Kind regards' and 'Yours'.

Formal letter

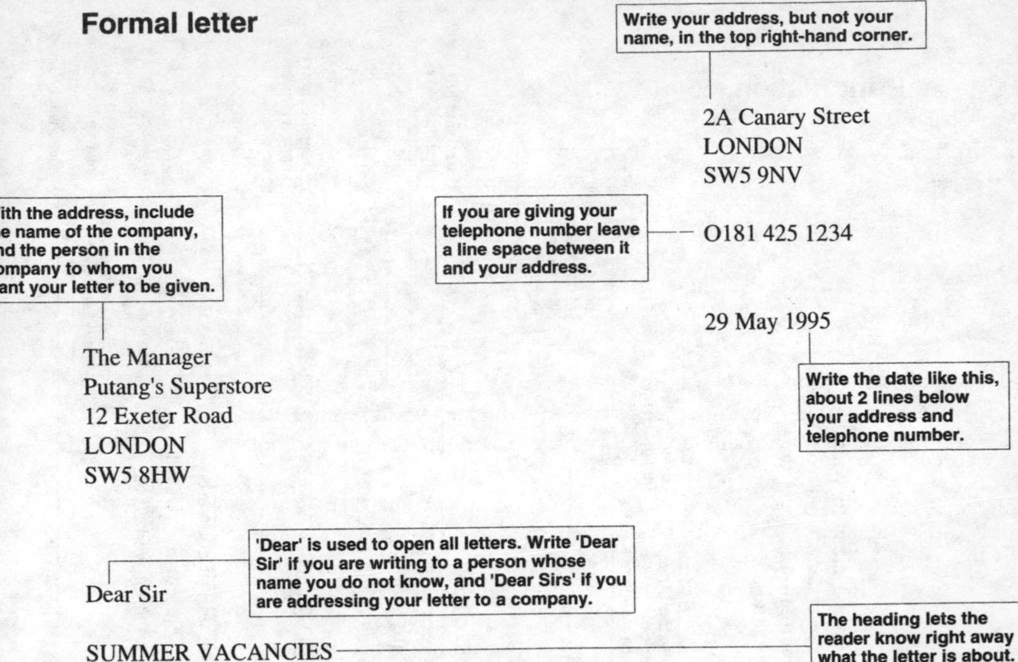

Write your address, but not your name, in the top right-hand corner.

2A Canary Street
LONDON
SW5 9NV

If you are giving your telephone number leave a line space between it and your address.

O181 425 1234

29 May 1995

Write the date like this, about 2 lines below your address and telephone number.

Vith the address, include he name of the company, nd the person in the ompany to whom you vant your letter to be given.

The Manager
Putang's Superstore
12 Exeter Road
LONDON
SW5 8HW

Dear Sir

'Dear' is used to open all letters. Write 'Dear Sir' if you are writing to a person whose name you do not know, and 'Dear Sirs' if you are addressing your letter to a company.

SUMMER VACANCIES

The heading lets the reader know right away what the letter is about.

I should be very grateful if you could let me know if any vacancies for temporary work arise over the next six or eight weeks.

You will see from the enclosed CV that I am a student of English and have recent experience of work as a shop assistant where I was responsible for handling cash. I am fit, quick to learn new skills, and would be available for either day or night duties.

As a regular customer of Putang's I know that a high standard of personal hygiene and a smart appearance are of great importance. If you require a reference as to my honesty and reliability, this may be obtained from my landlady, Mrs D Blaine, at the address given above, or from the manager of the the company named in my CV.

I look forward to hearing from you.

This is a useful expression. It can be used when you are asking for something in a formal letter. The words *'look foward to'* are always followed by a verb ending in *-ing*.

Yours faithfully

If you are addressing the person by name (*eg* 'Dear Mrs Bennet'), use 'Yours sincerely' instead

Pauline Hill
enc

Print your name below the signature, especially if your signature is difficult to read.

You write *enc* below your name to show you are sending another document with the letter.

Punctuation

You use punctuation to make what you are writing clear to your readers, so that they can read it fluently, and understand what you mean with as little difficulty as possible. Punctuation reflects the pauses and changes in tone that you use when speaking.

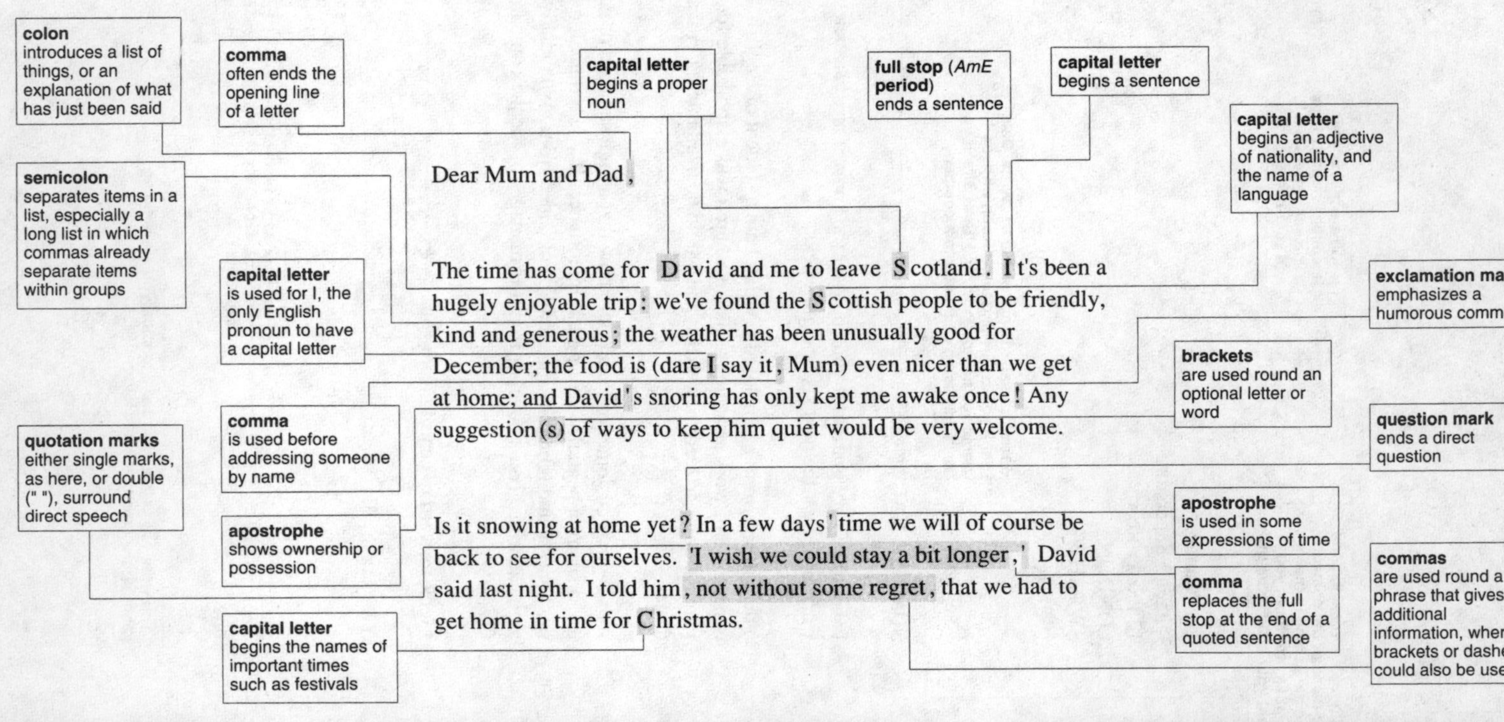

Dear Mum and Dad,
The time has come for David and me to leave Scotland. It's been a hugely enjoyable trip: we've found the Scottish people to be friendly, kind and generous; the weather has been unusually good for December; the food is (dare I say it, Mum) even nicer than we get at home; and David's snoring has only kept me awake once! Any suggestion(s) of ways to keep him quiet would be very welcome.
Is it snowing at home yet? In a few days' time we will of course be back to see for ourselves. 'I wish we could stay a bit longer,' David said last night. I told him, not without some regret, that we had to get home in time for Christmas.
colon introduces a list of things, or an explanation of what has just been said
comma often ends the opening line of a letter
capital letter begins a proper noun
full stop (*AmE* **period**) ends a sentence
capital letter begins a sentence
capital letter begins an adjective of nationality, and the name of a language
semicolon separates items in a list, especially a long list in which commas already separate items within groups
capital letter is used for I, the only English pronoun to have a capital letter
exclamation mark emphasizes a humorous comment
brackets are used round an optional letter or word
comma is used before addressing someone by name
quotation marks either single marks, as here, or double (" "), surround direct speech
question mark ends a direct question
apostrophe shows ownership or possession
apostrophe is used in some expressions of time
comma replaces the full stop at the end of a quoted sentence
commas are used round a phrase that gives additional information, where brackets or dashes could also be used
capital letter begins the names of important times such as festivals

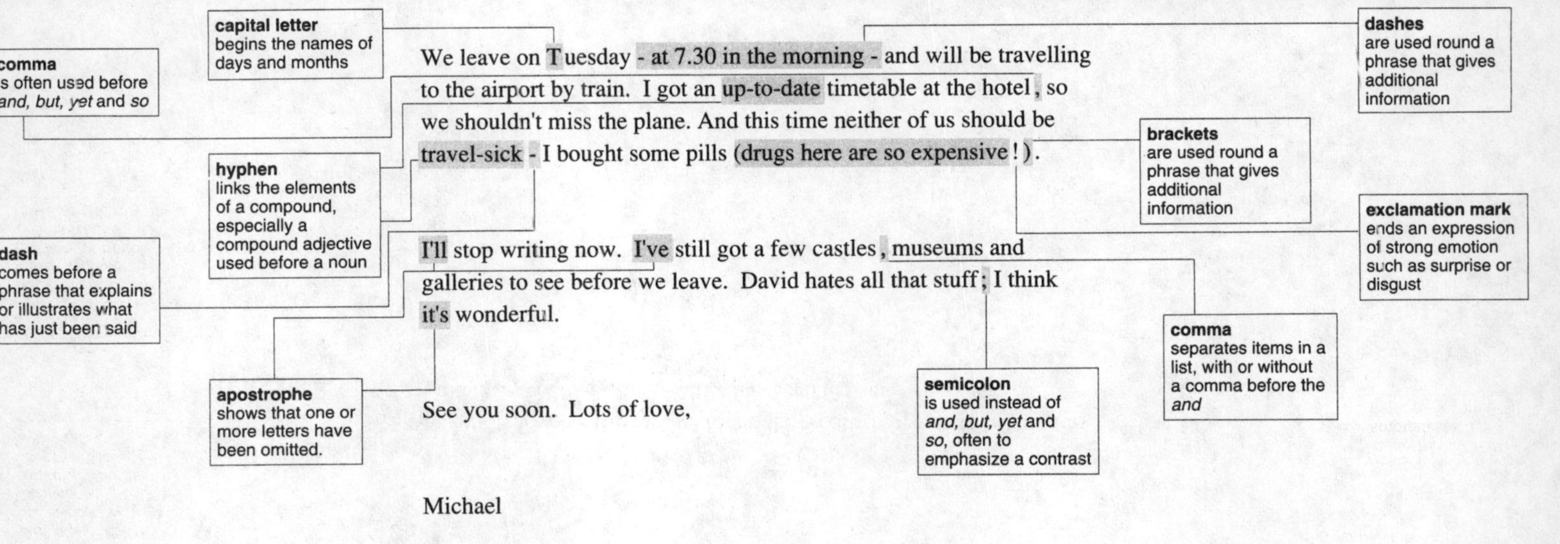

capital letter
begins the names of days and months
comma
is often used before *and, but, yet* and *so*
hyphen
links the elements of a compound, especially a compound adjective used before a noun
dash
comes before a phrase that explains or illustrates what has just been said
apostrophe
shows that one or more letters have been omitted.

We leave on Tuesday - at 7.30 in the morning - and will be travelling to the airport by train. I got an up-to-date timetable at the hotel, so we shouldn't miss the plane. And this time neither of us should be travel-sick - I bought some pills (drugs here are so expensive!).

I'll stop writing now. I've still got a few castles, museums and galleries to see before we leave. David hates all that stuff; I think it's wonderful.

See you soon. Lots of love,

Michael

dashes are used round a phrase that gives additional information

brackets are used round a phrase that gives additional information

exclamation mark ends an expression of strong emotion such as surprise or disgust

comma separates items in a list, with or without a comma before the *and*

semicolon is used instead of *and, but, yet* and *so*, often to emphasize a contrast

Abbreviations

AA Automobile Association; an organization for car-owners, which helps them in emergencies.
a/c account
AD (*Latin*) *anno domini*, meaning 'in the year of our lord'; used in dates since the birth of Jesus Christ: *AD 43.*
adj (*grammar*) adjective
adv (*grammar*) adverb
AGM Annual General Meeting
AIDS Acquired Immune Deficiency Syndrome
A Level Advanced Level
am or **AM** (*Latin*) *ante meridiem*, meaning 'before midday'; used in stating times: *The meeting will start at 10.30 am.*
anon anonymous; used in reference to written works, especially poems, whose author is unknown.
APEX or **apex** advance purchase excursion; a reduced fare for journeys booked in advance.
approx approximate or approximately
Apr April
arr arrives or arrival; used in transport timetables
ASA 1 Advertising Standards Authority. 2 American Standards Association; written after photographic film speeds: *100 ASA.*
asap (*informal*) as soon as possible
assoc association
asst assistant
Aug August
Ave Avenue; used in addresses: *8 Elm Ave.*

b born: *b 1564.*
BA Bachelor of Arts; a first university degree in an arts subject.
B and B bed and breakfast
BBC British Broadcasting Corporation
BC before Christ; used in dates before the birth of Jesus Christ: *104 BC.*
BR British Rail
Bros brothers; used in company names: *Moss Bros Ltd.*
BSc Bachelor of Science; a first university degree in a science subject.
BST British Summer Time; a system of time one hour ahead of GMT, used in Britain during the summer.
BT British Telecom
BTEC Business and Technology Education Council; an organization that awards qualifications in business and technical subjects.

C Celsius or Centigrade: *Water boils at 100°C.*
c 1 (*Latin*) *circa*, meaning 'about' or 'approximately'; used before dates: *c 1830.* 2 century: *19c literature.*
CALL computer-assisted language learning
CBE Commander of the British Empire; an award for professional excellence or for outstanding services to the country, superior to the OBE.
CBI Confederation of British Industry; an organization representing employers in British industry.
cc 1 cubic centimetre. 2 cubic capacity.
CD compact disk
CD-ROM (*computers*) compact disk read-only memory; a disk that stores large amounts of information that cannot be altered or deleted.
cf compare
CFC chlorofluorocarbon; a gas believed to damage the ozone layer.
ch or **chap** chapter
CIA Central Intelligence Agency; the US government agency responsible for security.
CID Criminal Investigation Department; the detective branch of the police.
cl centilitre or centilitres
cm centimetre or centimetres
Co 1 Company. 2 County.
c/o care of; used in the address of someone who is staying with someone else: *D Lloyd, c/o Mrs Jones, 4 Brynmawr Lane.*
COBOL Common Business-Oriented Language; a computer language.
C of E Church of England
Col Colonel; a military rank: *Col F Peters.*
conj (*grammar*) conjunction
contd continued: *contd overleaf.*
Corp Corporation; used in company names in the US.
Cresc Crescent; used in addresses: *Mornington Cresc.*
cu cubic
CV or **cv** (*Latin*) *curriculum vitae*, meaning 'course of life'; a written summary of your experience and qualifications.
cwt hundredweight

d died: *d 1977.*
3-D three-dimensional
dB decibel
Dec December
dep departs or departure; used in transport timetables.
dept department
Dip Diploma

DIY do-it-yourself
DJ disc jockey
DOS (*computers*) disk-operating system
doz dozen
Dr 1 Doctor: *Dr Allen.* **2** Drive; used in addresses: *11 Morningside Dr.*
DSS Department of Social Security

E east or eastern: *E Africa.*
ea each
EAP English for Academic Purposes
ECU European Currency Unit
ed edited by, or editor, or edition
EFL English as a Foreign Language
ELT English Language Teaching
eg for example: *computing abbreviations, eg DOS, CD-ROM, e-mail.*
e-mail (*computers*) electronic mail
EMU 1 Economic and Monetary Union. 2 European Monetary Union.
enc or **encl** enclosed or enclosure; written at the end of a business letter when you are enclosing something else in the envelope.
ESL English as a Second Language
ESP 1 English for Special Purposes, or English for Specific Purposes; the teaching of English for a particular profession or course of study: *ESP for nurses.* **2** extrasensory perception; the ability to know or to feel things without the use of the five ordinary senses.
esp especially
Esq (*rather old*) Esquire; written in addresses after a man's name, instead of 'Mr' before it: *E. Pitt Esq.*
et al (*Latin*) *et alii*, meaning 'and others', or *et alia*, meaning 'and other things'.
etc (*Latin*) *et cetera*, meaning 'and the rest', 'and so on', or 'and other things of a similar kind': *music, drama, the arts, etc.*
ext extension number (of a telephone): *Call me on 0541 6326, ext 252.*

F Fahrenheit: 32°F.
f female, or (*grammar*) feminine
FBI Federal Bureau of Investigation; the US police department particularly concerned with national security.
FC Football Club
FE Further Education
Feb February
fem (*grammar*) feminine
ff and the pages following the page mentioned: *See page 19 ff.*
FIFA International Association Football Federation
fig 1 figure or illustration. **2** figurative or figuratively; used to indicate the metaphorical use of a word.
fl oz fluid ounce or fluid ounces
FM (*radio*) frequency modulation; a transmission system using a varying wave frequency.
Fr Father; a title used for Christian priests.
Fri Friday
FT the Financial Times; quoted in financial reports.
ft foot or feet

g gram or grams
gall gallon or gallons
GB Great Britain (England, Wales and Scotland).
GCSE General Certificate of Secondary Education; an examination schoolchildren take when they are about 16.
Gen General; a senior military rank: *Gen Westmorland.*
GMT Greenwich Mean Time; the system of time in the UK that is used to calculate time in other parts of the world.
GNP Gross National Product; the total value of all goods and services a country produces in a year.
Govt Government
GP general practitioner; a family doctor who is not a specialist.
Gt Great; used in addresses: *Gt Smith Street.*

HGV heavy goods vehicle
HM His Majesty or Her Majesty; used in the title of a king or queen.
HMS His or Her Majesty's Ship
Hon Honourable; a title used *eg* to refer to Members of Parliament, and used by some members of the nobility.
Hons Honours; used in referring to first university degrees of a high standard: *Mary Duncan BA (Hons).*
hp horse power
HQ headquarters
hr or **hrs** hour or hours: *2 hrs 5 min.*
Hz (*radio*) hertz; a unit of frequency.

ID (*informal*) identification or identity
ie (*Latin*) *id est*, meaning 'that is', or ' in other words'; used to make the meaning clearer: *consonants, ie sounds that are not vowel sounds.*
IMF International Monetary Fund
in inch or inches
Inc or **inc** incorporated; used in company names in the US.
incl including or inclusive
IOU (*informal*) I owe you; a signed piece of paper showing that you owe someone some money.
IPA International Phonetic Alphabet; the pronunciation system used in most dictionaries.
IQ intelligence quotient; a system for measuring people's intelligence.
ISBN International Standard Book Number; a code number for identifying a published work.
IT Information Technology
ITV Independent Television; British television companies that are paid for by advertising.

Jan January
Jnr, Jr or **Jun** Junior; used in names to refer to a son if his name is the same as his father's.

K (*informal*) one thousand; used in job advertisements: *salary rising to £30K.*

kg kilogram or kilograms
km kilometre or kilometres

L **1** Lake; used on maps: *L Victoria*. **2** large; used on clothing. **3** learner; a sign attached to a vehicle driven by someone who has not yet passed their driving test.
l **1** left. **2** line. **3** litre or litres.
lb pound or pounds
Lieut or **Lt** Lieutenant; a military rank, and a US police rank.
lit literary or literature
LP long-playing record
Lt see **Lieut**
Ltd Limited; used after the names of private companies.
LV luncheon voucher
LW (*radio*) long wave

M **1** medium; used on clothing. **2** motorway: *a traffic jam on the M25*.
m **1** male. **2** (*grammar*) masculine. **3** mile or miles. **4** metre or metres. **5** million. **6** married.
MA Master of Arts; in Scotland a first university degree in an arts subject, in England a second degree in an arts subject.
mag (*informal*) magazine
Mar March
masc (*grammar*) masculine
max maximum
MBA Master of Business Administration; an advanced university degree.
MBE Member of the British Empire; an award for professional excellence or for outstanding services to the country.
med medium
MD **1** Doctor of Medicine. **2** (*informal*) managing director.
MEP Member of the European Parliament
Messrs (*French*) *messieurs*; used as the plural of *Mr* in the names of businesses.
Met (*informal*) the Metropolitan Police (London).
mg milligram or milligrams
MHz megahertz
micro microcomputer
min **1** minute or minutes. **2** minimum.
misc miscellaneous
Mk mark or model; used in identifying car types.
ml millilitre or millilitres
MoD Ministry of Defence
Mon Monday
MOT test Ministry of Transport test; a compulsory annual check made on vehicles of more than a certain age.
MP Member of Parliament
mph miles per hour
Mr mister; the usual title before a man's surname if he has no other title: *Mr A Berowne*.
Mrs the usual title before a woman's surname if she is married and has no other title: *Mrs E Scott*.
MS multiple sclerosis
Ms used as a title before a woman's surname to avoid any reference to her marital status: *Ms A Thomson*.
MSc Master of Science; an advanced university degree.
Mt Mount; used on maps: *Mt Etna*.
mth month
MW **1** (*radio*) medium wave. **2** megawatt.

N north or northern: *N Dakota*.
n (*grammar*) noun
n/a **1** not applicable. **2** not available.
Nat national
NATO North Atlantic Treaty Organization; a group of countries that give military help to each other.
NB (*Latin*) *nota bene*, meaning 'note well'; used before important notes and reminders.
NE northeast
neg (*grammar*) negative
NHS National Health Service; the British system of free medical treatment.
NI National Insurance
no or **No** number: *nos 10-25*.
Nov November
nr or **Nr** near; used before place names in addresses.
NSPCC National Society for the the Prevention of Cruelty to Children
NT **1** National Trust; an organization concerned with the preservation of historic buildings and areas of natural beauty. **2** National Theatre.
NW northwest or northwestern

OAP old-age pensioner
OBE Order of the British Empire; an award for professional excellence or for outstanding services to the country, superior to the MBE.
Oct October
OED Oxford English Dictionary
o n o (*informal*) or nearest offer; used in notices and advertisements about goods for sale.
OPEC Organization of Petroleum-Exporting Countries
opp opposite
OS Ordnance Survey; a range of maps of standard design and presentation.
OU Open University
oz, ozs ounce, ounces

P parking; used on road signs.
p **1** page: *p 8*. **2** pence or penny: *50p*.
p and p or **p & p** postage and packing; used in stating mail-order prices: *price £25 + £2.50 p & p*.
PA **1** personal assistant. **2** public address system; the system of microphones enabling a speaker to be heard by the audience.
p a (*Latin*) *per annum*, meaning 'per year' or 'yearly'.
par or **para** paragraph
PAYE pay-as-you-earn; a method of collecting tax.
PC **1** personal computer. **2** police constable. **3** politically correct; used in reference to

language that avoids giving offence, especially to minority groups.
pc 1 per cent. 2 postcard.
pd paid
PE physical education
PG parental guidance; used of a film which may be unsuitable for children under 15.
PhD Doctor of Philosophy; an advanced university degree awarded for a thesis based on personal research work
PIN or **PIN number** personal identification number; the secret number you key when using a cash card in a cash machine.
pkt packet
pl 1 Place; used in adresses: *2 Picardy Pl.* 2 (*grammar*) plural.
PLC public limited company: *Marks and Spencer PLC.*
PM (*informal*) Prime Minister
pm or **PM** (*Latin*) *post meridiem*, meaning 'after midday'; between midday and midnight: *Dinner will be served at 7.30 pm.*
PO post office
pop 1 popular. 2 population.
pos (*grammar*) positive
pp 1 pages: *see pp 21-27.* 2 (*Latin*) *per pro*, meaning 'for and on behalf of'; used before the name of another person when you are signing for them: *pp C Turner.*
p & p see **p and p**
PR 1 proportional representation; a system of election. 2 public relations: *He's a PR officer in the firm.*
pr 1 pair. 2 price.
prep (*grammar*) preposition
Pres President
Prof Professor
PS postscript; used before a note added at the end of a letter.
pt 1 part. 2 pint. 4 point. 5 part time.
PT physical training
Pt Port: *Pt Jervis.*
PTO please turn over; used at the bottom of a page.
pw per week

Q question
QED (*Latin*) *quod erat demonstrandum*, meaning 'which was to be demonstrated'; used in presenting a proof, *eg* in geometry.
qv (*Latin*) *quod vide*, meaning 'which see'; used in reference books to tell readers to look for something in another place.

R river; used on maps: *R Exe.*
r right
RAC Royal Automobile Club; an organization for car-owners, which helps them in emergencies.
RAF Royal Air Force
RC Roman Catholic
Rd Road; used in addresses: *7 Morningside Rd.*
RE religious education
Ref or **ref** 1 referee. 2 reference.
Rep 1 Representative; used in reference to members in the US Congress. 2 Republican; a US political party.
Rev or **Revd** Reverend; the title of a member of the Christian clergy.
RI religious instruction
RIP (*Latin*) *requiescat in pace*, meaning 'may he or she rest in peace'; words written on a gravestone.
RN 1 Royal Navy. 2 Registered Nurse.
RP Received Pronunciation; an English accent typical, especially formerly, of educated people.
rpm revolutions per minute
RSA Royal Society of Arts; a British association that promotes education for the arts and trades and which sets EFL examinations together with the University of Cambridge Local Examinations Syndicate.
RSPCA Royal Society for the Protection of Animals
RSVP (*French*) *répondez s'il vous plaît*, meaning 'please reply'; used on formal invitations.
Rt Hon Right Honourable; used as a title for prime ministers, Cabinet ministers, and certain members of the nobility.

S 1 south or southern. 2 small; of sizes.
sae stamped addressed envelope
SAS Special Air Service; a specially trained branch of the British Army.
Sat Saturday
SCE Scottish Certificate of Education; an examination taken in Scotland by 16- to 18-year-olds.
sci-fi science fiction
SE south-east or south-eastern
Sen 1 Senator. 2 see **Snr**.
Sept September
Sgt Sergeant; a military and police rank.
SIS Secret Intelligence Service (in the US).
Snr, Sr or **Sen** Senior; used in names to refer to a father if his name is the same as his son's.
Soc society: *Ramsey Drama Soc.*
Sq Square; used in addresses: *5 Raeburn Sq.*
St 1 Saint; used in place names: *St Andrews.* 2 Street: *18 Princes St.*
Sta or **Stn** station
STD 1 subscriber trunk dialling; the telephone system of making long-distance calls direct. 2 sexually transmitted disease.
Sun Sunday
SW 1 southwest or southwestern. 2 (*radio*) short wave.

t or **tn** ton or tons, tonne or tonnes
TA Territorial Army; in the UK a military force of people who train in their free time.
TB tuberculosis
tbs or **tbsp** tablespoonful or tablespoonfuls; used in recipes: *2 tbs sugar.*
TEFL Teaching English as a Foreign Language
tel telephone number
temp 1 temperature. 2 temporary (employee).
TESL Teaching English as a Second Language
TESOL Teaching English to Speakers of Other Languages
Thur or **Thurs** Thursday
TUC Trades Union Congress; an association of British trade unions.

Tue or **Tues** Tuesday
TV television

U universal; used of films officially declared suitable for people of all ages.
UCCA Universities' Central Council on Admissions
UEFA Union of European Football Associations
UFO unidentified flying object
UHT ultra-heat-treated; used with reference to milk that has been heated to a high temperature so that it lasts longer.
UK United Kingdom (Great Britain and Northern Ireland).
UN United Nations; a world peace-keeping organization.
US United States
USA United States of America
Utd united: *Manchester Utd.*

V volt or volts: *a 1.5 V battery.*
v 1 (*Latin*; also **vs**) *versus*, meaning 'against': *a Scotland v England match.* 2 verse. 3 (*informal*) very: *v good.* 4 (*grammar*; also **vb**) verb.
VAT value-added tax; a tax on goods and services
vb see **v**
VCR video cassette recorder
VD venereal disease (see also **STD**)
VDU visual display unit
vg very good
VHF (*radio*) very high frequency
VIP (*informal*) very important person: *A number of VIPs were at the reception.*
vol 1 volume; used to refer to set of books: *see vol 2, chapter 3.* 2 volume; the three-dimensional measurement of an object or an area.
VP Vice President
vs see **v**
VSO Voluntary Service Overseas; an organization that sends people to developing countries to use their skills and knowledge to help the local population.

W 1 west or western. 2 watt or watts: *a 100-watt lightbulb.*
WC water closet; an old-fashioned word for toilet.
Wed or **Weds** Wednesday
WHO World Health Organization
wk week
WP word-processing
wt weight

X the category of films declared suitable only for adults
XL extra-large; used on clothing.

yd yard or yards
YHA Youth Hostels Association
YMCA Young Men's Christian Association; an organization that provides accommodation for young people.
yr year